Accounting Standards

2007/2008

Extant at 30 April 2007

General Editor

David Chopping

Moore Stephens LLP

a Wolters Kluwer business

Wolters Kluwer (UK) Limited
145 London Road
Kingston upon Thames
Surrey KT2 6SR
Tel: 0870 777 2906
Fax: 020 8247 1184
E-mail: customerservices@cch.co.uk
www.cch.co.uk

Typeset by YHT Ltd, London
Printed and bound in Italy by Legoprint–Lavis (TN)

Contents

iv   *Contents*

Preface

This book presents, in one convenient bound volume, all UK accounting standards and UITF abstracts extant at 30 April 2007. These have been updated for amendments made since the documents were originally issued. This volume also includes current UK exposure drafts and discussion papers.

Significant revisions for 2007/2008 include the following:

- FRSSE – Effective January 2007
- Amendments to FRS 17
- UITF 41 Scope of FRS 20 (IFRS 2)
- UITF 42 Reassessment of embedded derivatives
- UITF 43 The interpretation of equivalence for the purposes of section 228A of the Companies Act 1985
- UITF 44 FRS 20 (IFRS 2) Group and treasury share transactions
- UITF 45 Liabilities arising from Participating in a Specific Market – Waste Electrical and Electronic Equipment
- Reporting Statement: Retirement Benefits - Disclosures
- FRED 40 Accounting for Heritage Assets
- ED of Amendments to FRS 25
- ED of Amendments to FRS 3
- ED of Statement – Half-Yearly Financial Reports
- Consultation Paper on IFRS for Small and Medium Sized Entities

As noted above, the text of standards and abstracts has been changed where later guidance amends the original documents. However, in the case of some of the changes made by FRSs 23 to 26 the changes apply to only some entities. In these cases, the original text has been left unaltered, but a footnote includes the text to be used in relevant cases.

FRSs 21 to 26 and 29 are all UK versions of international standards. The format in which they were originally published included all original text of the relevant IFRS or IAS, with deletions and additions made by the ASB clearly marked. In this volume, such changes have been made, and are not marked. The text as presented therefore represents the requirements applicable in the UK, without reference to how this differs from the IFRS or IAS on which those requirements are based.

As in previous years, footnotes have been added to refer to any major changes to legal or other references included in standards. However, these are not intended to provide a comprehensive summary. No attempt has been made to update any references to legislation in Northern Ireland or the Republic of Ireland.

One of the major forthcoming changes in UK practice is the introduction of the Companies Act 2006. When the accounting sections of that Act come into force then virtually all statutory references given in Accounting Standards will require revision.

Part One

Introduction

Introduction

HISTORY OF THE ACCOUNTING STANDARDS COMMITTEE

The Accounting Standards Committee ('ASC'), originally known as the Accounting Standards Steering Committee, was set up in January 1970 by the Council of The Institute of Chartered Accountants in England and Wales with the object of developing definitive standards for financial reporting.

The Institute of Chartered Accountants of Scotland and the Institute of Chartered Accountants in Ireland became members of the Committee in 1970, the Chartered Association of Certified Accountants and the Chartered Institute of Management Accountants joined in 1971 and the Chartered Institute of Public Finance and Accountancy in 1976.

From 1 February 1976 the ASC was reconstituted as a joint committee of the six member bodies who then acted collectively through the Consultative Committee of Accountancy Bodies ('CCAB'). On 1 January 1986, the CCAB was incorporated and the ASC became a Committee of CCAB Limited.

The Councils of the six major accountancy bodies in the United Kingdom and Ireland approved and issued accounting standards following proposals developed by the ASC.

On 1 August 1990 the ASC was replaced by the Accounting Standards Board ('ASB').

During its existence the ASC issued 55 EDs, 2 SORPs, 28 discussion papers and other documents and 65 technical releases. It also franked 14 industry SORPs. Thirty-four SSAPS or revised SSAPS were recommended to and approved by the Councils of the six member-bodies of CCAB.

The CCAB agreed that 'all statements (Exposure Drafts, Discussion Papers, Technical Releases and similar documents) issued by ASC and extant at 1 August 1990 will remain documents of record under the aegis of the CCAB. SORPs issued or franked by ASC will continue in force under the aegis of CCAB until formally withdrawn or superseded'.

REPORT OF THE REVIEW COMMITTEE ON THE MAKING OF ACCOUNTING STANDARDS

The Review Committee, under the Chairmanship of Sir Ron Dearing (now Lord Dearing) was appointed in November 1987 by the CCAB to review and make recommendations on the standard-setting process.

In September 1988 the Review Committee presented its report to the CCAB. The Report's recommendations included:

- Accounting standards should remain, as far as possible, the responsibility of auditors, preparers and users of accounts and there should not be a general move towards incorporating them into law.
- A Financial Reporting Council should be created covering at high level a wide constituency of interests, whose Chairman would be appointed jointly by the Secretary of State for Trade and Industry and the Governor of the Bank of England, to guide the standard-setting body on work programmes and issues of public concern; to see that the work on accounting standards is properly

financed; and to act as a powerful proactive public influence for securing good accounting practice.

- The task of devising accounting standards should be discharged by a newly constituted, expert Accounting Standards Board, with a full-time Chairman and Technical Director. Its total membership would not exceed nine. The Board would issue standards on its own authority. In the interests of clearly drawn standards avoiding compromise decisions, a majority of two thirds of the Board would suffice for approval of a standard. Government would have observer status.
- The Accounting Standards Board should establish a capability of high standing to publish authoritative, though non-mandatory, guidance on emerging issues.
- A Review Panel should be established to examine contentious departures from accounting standards by large companies.

THE PRESENT STANDARD-SETTING REGIME

General

In 1990 the Government announced the establishment of the Financial Reporting Council under the Chairmanship of Sir Ron Dearing. Sir Sydney Lipworth was appointed Chairman with effect from 1 January 1994. The present arrangements for setting accounting standards and enforcing compliance follow closely the recommendations of the Review Committee. The organisation is as shown in the diagram on page 5.

The ASB replaced the ASC on 1 August 1990. The funding for the present organisation is drawn from three broad sectors: the accountancy profession; the financial community; and the Government.

Accounting Standards

The Companies Act 1989 introduced into the Companies Act 1985 a definition of 'accounting standards' along with the requirement for directors of companies, other than most small or medium sized companies, to disclose whether the accounts have been prepared in accordance with applicable accounting standards, particulars of any material departure from those standards and the reasons for the departure. Under section 245B of the Companies Act 1985, where the accounts of a company do not comply with the requirements of the Act, the court may order the preparation of revised accounts, and that all or part of the costs be borne by such of the directors as were party to the approval of the defective accounts.

At its first meeting the ASB unanimously agreed to adopt the 22 extant SSAPs issued by the ASC. Adoption by the ASB gives the SSAPs the status of accounting standards within the meaning of the Companies Act 1985. In adopting the SSAPs the ASB noted that with the passage of time certain legal references in the SSAPs have become outdated. The preface to this volume explains the updating that has been carried out to the documents that have been included herein.

The ASB announced that accounting standards that it develops and issues are to be known as Financial Reporting Standards (FRSs) and exposure drafts of FRSs are to be known as Financial Reporting Exposure Drafts (FREDs).

```
┌─────────────────────────────────────────────────┐
│            Financial Reporting Council          │
│                                                 │
│     The Financial Reporting Council guides the ASB. │
└─────────────────────────────────────────────────┘
```

```
┌────────────────────────────┐        ┌────────────────────────────┐
│ Financial Reporting Review │        │ Accounting Standards Board │
│ Panel                      │        │ (ASB)                      │
│                            │        │                            │
│ The Review Panel enquires  │        │ The ASB develops, issues   │
│ into annual accounts       │        │ and withdraws accounting   │
│ where it appears that the  │        │ standards.                 │
│ requirements of the        │        │                            │
│ Companies Act, including the│       │                            │
│ requirement that annual    │        │                            │
│ accounts shall show a true and │    │                            │
│ fair view, might have      │        │                            │
│ been breached.             │        │                            │
└────────────────────────────┘        └────────────────────────────┘
```

```
                              ┌────────────────────────────┐
                              │ Urgent Issues Task Force   │
                              │ (UITF)                     │
                              │                            │
                              │ The UITF's main role is to │
                              │ assist the ASB in areas where │
                              │ an accounting standard     │
                              │ or Companies Act provision │
                              │ exists, but where          │
                              │ unsatisfactory or conflicting │
                              │ interpretations have       │
                              │ developed or seem likely to │
                              │ develop.                   │
                              └────────────────────────────┘
```

The ASB has so far issued twenty-nine Financial Reporting Standards (together with one for smaller entities updated as the need arises), certain amendments to earlier Standards and a number of Exposure Drafts and Discussion Documents.

Statement of Principles

The ASB has developed a Statement of Principles for Financial Reporting. This is not itself an accounting standard. It sets out the principles that the ASB believes should underlie the preparation and presentation of company accounts. Its primary purpose is to assist the ASB in the development and review of accounting standards and to provide those interested in its work with an understanding of the ASB's approach to the formulation of accounting standards.

The Statement was first published in December 1999 and is reproduced in Part Two.

Statement of Aims

The ASB has published its 'Statement of Aims'. The Statement sets out the ASB's general approach to its task and lists a number of fundamental guidelines which it follows in conducting its affairs. The 'Statement of Aims' is reproduced at the end of this chapter.

Consultation

The ASB has stated that it is anxious to operate the maximum possible consultation and be as open as possible in its dealings. In addition to issuing exposure drafts of FRSs and of Statements the ASB also publishes discussion papers on individual topics as they reach appropriate stages of development.

Urgent Issues Task Force abstracts

The UITF's main role is to assist the ASB in areas where an accounting standard or a Companies Act provision exists, but where unsatisfactory or conflicting interpretations have developed or seem likely to develop. In such circumstances it operates by seeking a consensus as to the accounting treatment that should be adopted. Such a consensus is reached against the background of the ASB's declared aim of relying on principles rather than detailed prescription.

The ASB makes the UITF abstracts publicly available for the guidance of users, preparers and auditors of financial information.

Extant abstracts should be considered to be part of the corpus of practices forming the basis for determining what constitutes a true and fair view. Such abstracts consequently may be taken into consideration by the Financial Reporting Review Panel in deciding whether financial statements call for review.

The ASB's Foreword to UITF abstracts is reproduced in Part Five. This explains the authority, scope and application of the UITF abstracts issued by the ASB. These abstracts set out the consensus reached by its Urgent Issues Task Force on particular issues.

Statements of Recommended Practice

The ASC developed and issued two SORPs together with an Explanatory foreword to SORPs. In addition the ASC 'franked' SORPs developed by bodies representative of the industry/sector to which the SORP would apply. The ASB has announced that it will not issue its own SORPs. However, SORPs will be developed by bodies recognised by the ASB to provide guidance on the application of accounting standards to specific industries. The ASB will not 'frank' such SORPs. Instead, where it is satisfied about certain particulars it will require to be appended to the SORP a 'negative assurance statement'. Further details are contained in Part Seven.

International Financial Reporting Standards

Listed groups, and in future companies on AIM, are now required to comply with International Financial Reporting Standards (IFRS) rather than UK accounting standards. This option is also available to all UK companies, other than charities. IFRS are issued by the International Accounting Standards Board (IASB).

Financial Reporting Standards (and UITFs) continue to apply for those companies using UK GAAP, although the ASB and UITF both now take into account international practice prior to issuing any guidance, and some standards are effectively UK versions of international standards.

Aims & Objectives
(Issued July 2003)

AIMS

The Accounting Standards Board contributes to the achievement of the Financial Re-porting Council's fundamental aim of supporting investor, market and public confidence in the financial and governance stewardship of listed and other entities by pursuing its own aims of establishing and improving standards of financial accounting and reporting, for the benefit of users, preparers, and auditors of financial information.

OBJECTIVES

The Board intends to achieve its aims by:

Developing principles to guide it in establishing standards and to provide a frame-work within which others can exercise judgement in resolving accounting issues.   1

Issuing new accounting standards, or amending existing ones, in response to evolving business practices, new economic developments and deficiencies being identified in current practice.   2

Addressing urgent issues promptly.   3

Working with the International Accounting Standards Board (IASB), with national standards-setters and relevant European Union (EU) institutions to encourage high quality in the IASB's standards and their adoption in the EU.   4

OPERATING GUIDELINES

In carrying out its work the Board will

Be objective and ensure that the information resulting from the application of accounting standards faithfully represents the underlying commercial activity. Such information should be neutral in the sense that it is free from any form of bias intended to influence users in a particular direction and should not be designed to favour any group of users or preparers.   1

Ensure that accounting standards are clearly expressed and supported by a reasoned analysis of the issues.   2

Determine what should be incorporated in accounting standards based on research, public consultation and careful deliberation about the usefulness of the resulting information.   3

Ensure that there is consistency both from one accounting standard to another and between accounting standards and company law.   4

Issue accounting standards only when the expected benefits exceed the perceived costs. The Board recognises that reliable cost/benefit calculations are seldom possible. However, it will always assess the need for standards in terms of the significance and extent of the problem being addressed and will choose the standard which appears to be most effective in cost/benefit terms.   5

Take account of the desire of the financial community for evolutionary rather than revolutionary change in the reporting process where this is consistent with the objectives outlined above.   6

Follow best practice in its own governance and processes, deploy resources effectively and liaise with the Council's other Boards to promote and benefit from operating synergies wherever possible.   7

WITHDRAWN STANDARDS

Accounting Standards		Date issued	Date withdrawn
SSAP 1	Accounting for associated companies (revised April 1982) Superseded by FRS 9	January 1971	November 1997
SSAP 2	Disclosure of accounting policies Superseded by FRS 18	November 1971	December 2000
SSAP 3	Earnings per share Superseded by FRS 14	February 1972	October 1998
SSAP 6	Extraordinary items and prior year adjustments (revised August 1986) Superseded by FRS 3	April 1974	October 1992
SSAP 7	Accounting for changes in the purchasing power of money (Provisional)	May 1974	January 1978
SSAP 8	The treatment of taxation under the imputation system in the accounts of companies Superseded by FRS 16	August 1974	December 1999
SSAP 10	Statements of source and application of funds Superseded by FRS 1	July 1975	September 1991
SSAP 11	Accounting for deferred tax Superseded by SSAP 15	August 1975	October 1978
SSAP 12	Accounting for depreciation Superseded by FRS 15	December 1977	February 1999
SSAP 14	Group accounts Superseded by FRS 2	September 1978	July 1992
SSAP 15	Accounting for deferred tax Superseded by FRS 19	October 1978	December 2000
SSAP 16	Current cost accounting	March 1980	July 1988
SSAP 17	Accounting for post balance sheet events Superseded by FRS 21	August 1980	May 2004
SSAP 18	Accounting for contingencies Superseded by FRS 12	August 1980	September 1998
SSAP 20	Foreign currency translation Superseded by FRS 23, for entities applying that standard Remains in force for other companies	April 1983	December 2004
SSAP 22	Accounting for goodwill (revised July 1989) Superseded by FRS 10	December 1984	December 1997

SSAP 23	Accounting for acquisitions and mergers Superseded by FRS 6	April 1985	September 1994
SSAP 24	Accounting for pension costs Superseded by FRS 17	May 1988	November 2000
FRS 1	Cash flow statements Superseded by FRS 1 (revised 1996)	September 1991	October 1996
FRS 4	Capital instruments Partly superseded by FRS 25 Fully superseded where FRS 26 is applied	December 1993	December 2004
FRS 13	Derivatives and other financial instruments: disclosures Superseded by FRS 25, where entities are complying with the disclosure requirements of that standard	September 1998	December 2004
FRS 14	Earnings per share Superseded by FRS 22	October 1998	December 2004

UITF Abstracts		*Date issued*	*Date withdrawn*
UITF 1	Convertible bonds-supplemental interest/premium Superseded by FRS 4	July 1991	December 1993
UITF 2	Restructuring costs Superseded by FRS 3	October 1991	October 1992
UITF 3	Treatment of goodwill on disposal of a business Superseded by FRS 10	December 1991	December 1997
UITF 6	Accounting for post-retirement benefits other than pensions Superseded by FRS 17	November 1992	November 2000
UITF 7	True and fair override disclosures Superseded by FRS 18	December 1992	December 2000
UITF 8	Repurchase of own debt Superseded by FRS 4	March 1993	December 1993
UITF 9	Accounting for operations in hyper-inflationary economies Superseded by FRS 24, for companies complying with that standard	June 1993	December 2004
UITF 10	Disclosure of directors' share options. Withdrawn	September 1994	December 2002
UITF 11	Capital instruments: issuer call options Superseded by FRS 26, for companies complying with that standard	September 1994	December 2004

UITF 12	Lessee accounting for reverse lease premiums and similar incentives Superseded by UITF 28	December 1994	February 2001
UITF 13	Accounting for ESOP trusts Superseded by UITF 38	June 1995	June 2004
UITF 14	Disclosure of changes in accounting policy Superseded by FRS 18	November 1995	December 2000
UITF 15	Disclosure of substantial acquisitions Superseded by UITF 15 (revised 1999)	January 1996	February 1999
UITF 16	Income and expenses subject to non-standard rates of tax Superseded by FRS 16	February 1997	December 1999
UITF 17	Employee share schemes Superseded by FRS 20	October 2000, revised December 2003	April 2004
UITF 18	Pension costs following the 1997 tax changes in respect of dividend income Superseded by FRS 17	December 1997	November 2000
UITF 20	Year 2000 issue: accounting and disclosures Withdrawn	March 1998	July 2000
UITF 30	Date of award to employees of shares or rights to shares Superseded by FRS 20	March 2001	April 2004
UITF 33	Obligations in capital instruments Superseded by FRS 25	February 2002	December 2004
UITF 37	Purchases and sales of own shares Superseded by FRS 25	October 2003	December 2004

Part Two

Statement of Principles

The Statement of Principles for Financial Reporting was agreed on by the Accounting Standards Board in October 1999. At that time, the Board comprised:

Sir David Tweedie	(Chairman)
Allan Cook CBE	(Technical Director)
David Allvey	
Ian Brindle	
Dr John Buchanan	
John Coombe	
Raymond Hinton	
Huw Jones	
Professor Geoffrey Whittington	
Ken Wild	

Statement of principles for financial reporting

(Issued December 1999)

Contents

Detailed list of contents

Chapter 2: The reporting entity

Principles

Explanation

Chapter 3: The qualitative characteristics of financial information

Principles

Explanation

Chapter 4: The elements of financial statements

Principles

Explanation

Statement of principles for financial reporting

Introduction

PURPOSE

This Statement of Principles for Financial Reporting sets out the principles that the **1**
Accounting Standards Board believes should underlie the preparation and presentation of general purpose financial statements.*

The primary purpose of articulating such principles is to provide a coherent frame of **2**
reference to be used by the Board in the development and review of accounting
standards and by others who interact with the Board during the standard-setting
process.

Such a frame of reference should clarify the conceptual underpinnings of proposed **3**
accounting standards and should enable standards to be developed on a consistent
basis by reducing the need to debate fundamental issues each time a standard is
developed or revised. As such, it will play an important role in the development of
accounting standards. It is expected that it will play a similar role in the development
of Statements of Recommended Practice.

The Statement is being published because knowledge of the principles should assist **4**
preparers and users of financial statements, as well as auditors and others, to
understand the Board's approach to formulating accounting standards and the
nature and function of information reported in general purpose financial statements.
The principles will also help preparers and auditors faced with new or emerging
issues to carry out an initial analysis of the issues involved in the absence of
applicable accounting standards.

STATUS

The Statement of Principles is not an accounting standard, nor does it have a status **5**
that is equivalent to an accounting standard. It therefore does not contain requirements on how financial statements should be prepared or presented.

SCOPE

Types of financial report

Financial information takes many different forms. For the purposes of the State- **6**
ment, it has been categorised:

(a) *special purpose financial reports*—Financial information prepared by the entity
     itself at the behest of, and in the form specified by, persons who have the
     authority to obtain the information they require to meet their needs. Reg-
     ulatory returns, tax returns and financial reports prepared for bankers are
     examples of such reports.
(b) *general purpose financial reports*—Financial information that, although pre-
     pared by the entity itself, is not in the form of a special purpose financial report.
     Such reports comprise:

**The meaning of the term 'general purpose financial statements' is explained in paragraph 6(b)(i).*

(i)   *general purpose financial statements*—for example, annual financial statements and the financial statements contained in interim reports, preliminary announcements and summary financial statements. General purpose financial statements are generally referred to in the Statement hereafter simply as 'financial statements'.

(ii) *other types of general purpose financial report*—for example, directors' reports, statements by the chairman, operating and financial reviews, historical summaries and trend information (such as five-year summaries), letters to shareholders and similar items.

(c)   *other financial information*—Financial information that has not been prepared by the reporting entity itself, such as news articles and analysts' reports.

A diagram summarising and providing examples of the various categories of financial information is on the following page.

7   The primary focus of the Statement of Principles is on those financial statements that are required to give a true and fair view of the reporting entity's financial performance and financial position. For most entities, those statements will be their full annual financial statements. The Statement's principles will also be applicable to financial statements that are intended to be consistent with financial statements required to give a true and fair view (such as financial statements contained in interim reports, preliminary announcements and summary financial statements), although additional considerations are relevant in the context of such statements.

8   Whilst the Statement does not address to any significant extent other types of general purpose financial report, it will be relevant to such reports insofar as they provide financial information that is intended to be consistent with the financial statements.

Types of entity

9   The principles in the Statement are intended to be relevant to the financial statements of profit-oriented reporting entities, regardless of their size and whether they are private or public sector entities.* The Statement is, broadly speaking, also relevant to the financial statements of not-for-profit entities, although some of the principles need to be re-expressed and others need changes of emphasis before they can be applied to that sector.

TRUE AND FAIR

10   The concept of a true and fair view lies at the heart of financial reporting in the UK and the Republic of Ireland. It is the ultimate test for financial statements and, as such, has a powerful, direct effect on accounting practice. No matter how skilled the standard-setters and law-makers are, it is the need to show a true and fair view that puts their requirements in perspective.

11   The true and fair view is, furthermore, a dynamic concept because its content evolves in response to changes in, inter alia, accounting and business practice. This dynamism pervades the whole system of financial reporting, affecting the interpretation of every requirement and instigating and providing direction to the development of accounting practice.

The application of accounting standards to the public sector is discussed more fully in the Foreword to Accounting Standards.

CATEGORIES OF FINANCIAL INFORMATION

Information useful for economic decisions

General purpose financial reports

Annual reports (and similar periodic reports)

General purpose financial statements (including annual financial statements, interim financial statements, preliminary announcements and summary financial statements)

Primary financial statements	Notes to financial statements	Accompanying information	Other general purpose financial reports	Other information
Examples:	Examples:	Examples:	Examples:	Examples:
• Statement(s) of financial performance (for example, profit and loss account and statement of total recognised gains and losses)	• Accounting policies	• Operating and financial review	• Letters to shareholders	• Special purpose financial reports
• Statement of financial position (for example, balance sheet)	• Analyses of figures in the primary financial statements	• Chairman's statement	• Press releases and similar media announcements	• Analysts reports
• Cash flow statement	• Information about uncertainties affecting recognised assets and liabilities	• Directors' report		• General economic statistics
		• Historical summaries and trend information		• News articles about company
		• Non-accounting and non-financial information		

12   It is inherent in the nature of the true and fair view concept that financial statements will not give a true and fair view unless the information they contain is sufficient in quantity and quality to satisfy the reasonable expectations of the readers to whom they are addressed. Such expectations change over time and the Board seeks, through its accounting standards and other authoritative pronouncements, both to respond to those expectations and to influence them. The Statement of Principles may therefore be expected to contribute to the development of the concept.

13   The Statement of Principles does not, however, define the meaning of true and fair— it is detailed legal requirements, accounting standards and, in their absence, other evidence of generally accepted accounting practice, rather than the Statement itself, that normally determine the content of financial statements. Nevertheless, as the Statement is a set of high-level principles designed to help in setting standards, it has the true and fair view concept at its foundation. Its insistence on relevance and reliability as prime indicators of the quality of financial information is just one example of this.

THE STANDARD-SETTING PROCESS

14   As already explained, the main role of the Statement of Principles is in the standard-setting process. The principles are, however, only one of the factors that are considered when setting standards. Other factors include:

   (a)   legal requirements,
   (b)   cost/benefit considerations,
   (c)   industry-specific issues,
   (d)   the desirability of evolutionary change, and
   (e)   implementation issues.

15   The relative importance of each of these factors in the formulation of an accounting standard will vary from case to case. As a result, a standard may adopt an approach that is different from that suggested by the principles. For example:

   (a)   In order not to deny the Statement the opportunity to assist in the law's development, it has not been developed within the constraints imposed by legislation. However, accounting practice develops within the legal frameworks that regulate financial reporting; therefore, if there is an inconsistency between the law and the principles on a particular issue, any accounting standard on that issue will usually need to adopt an approach that is different from that suggested by the principles.*
   (b)   In setting standards the Board weighs the costs and benefits of its proposals to ensure that they are justified on cost/benefit grounds, and this may also result in an accounting standard adopting an approach that is different from that suggested by the principles. The benefits of new accounting practices will come from improvements in economic decision-making by users. The costs will include the costs of preparation and might also include, for example, the possible loss or diminution of competitive position.

16   As legal requirements, accounting techniques and markets evolve, the Board believes that it will be possible to reduce the number of conflicts between the Statement and accounting standards and that fewer new conflicts will emerge.

The relationship between the accounting requirements imposed by legislation and the Statement of Principles and the inconsistencies between the two are explained in Appendix I.

It will be made clear in each accounting standard how the standard relates to the Statement of Principles.   **17**

REVISIONS TO THE STATEMENT

The Statement may be revised from time to time in the light of the Board's experience of working with it and in response to developments in accounting thought.   **18**

Chapter 1: The objective of financial statements

Put simply, the objective of financial statements is to provide information that is useful to those for whom they are prepared. However, the objective needs to be expressed more precisely if it is to be of any use in determining the form and content of financial statements. This chapter does that by considering the persons for whom financial statements are prepared, the information needs of such persons and the role that financial statements play in meeting those needs.

PRINCIPLES

- The objective of financial statements is to provide information about the reporting entity's financial performance and financial position that is useful to a wide range of users for assessing the stewardship of the entity's management and for making economic decisions.
- That objective can usually be met by focusing exclusively on the information needs of present and potential investors, the defining class of user.
- Present and potential investors need information about the reporting entity's financial performance and financial position that is useful to them in evaluating the entity's ability to generate cash (including the timing and certainty of its generation) and in assessing the entity's financial adaptability.

EXPLANATION

The objective of financial statements

Useful to a wide range of users

1.1   Financial information about the activities and resources of an entity is typically of interest to many people. Although some of these people are able to command the preparation of special purpose financial reports in order to obtain the information they need, the rest—usually the vast majority—rely on general purpose financial reports, such as financial statements and other financial information. Many people are therefore potentially interested in an entity's financial statements.

1.2   It does not follow that financial statements are prepared specifically for all those interested persons. However, although there continues to be debate about for whom precisely they are prepared, there is no doubt that they are prepared for a range of persons that extends far beyond existing investors. These persons are referred to in the Statement as the 'users'.

Useful for making economic decisions

1.3   The persons potentially interested in an entity's financial statements need information on that entity for a variety of purposes.

  (a)   *Present and potential investors (hereafter generally referred to simply as 'investors')*. In its stewardship role, management is accountable for the safekeeping of the entity's resources and for their proper, efficient and profitable use. Providers of risk capital are interested in information that helps them to assess how effectively management has fulfilled this role. They are also interested in information that is useful in taking decisions about their investment or potential investment in the entity. They are, as a result, concerned with the risk inherent in, and return provided by, their investments, and need information on the entity's financial performance and financial position that helps them to assess its cash-generation abilities and its financial adaptability.

(b) *Lenders.* Lenders are interested in information that helps them to assess whether their loans will be repaid, and related interest will be paid, when due. Similarly, potential lenders are interested in information that helps them to decide whether to lend to the entity and on what terms.

(c) *Suppliers and other trade creditors.* Suppliers and other trade creditors are interested in information that helps them to decide whether to sell to the entity and to assess the likelihood that amounts owing to them will be paid when due.

(d) *Employees.* Employees are interested in information on their employer's stability and profitability, with particular reference to that part (for example, the subsidiary or branch) of the entity in which they work. They are also interested in information that enables them to assess their employer's ability to provide remuneration, employment opportunities and retirement and other benefits.

(e) *Customers.* Customers are interested in information about the entity's continued existence. That is especially so when they have a long-term involvement with, or are dependent on, the entity, as will generally be the case if product warranties are involved or if specialised replacement parts may be needed.

(f) *Governments and their agencies.* Governments and their agencies are interested in the allocation of resources and, therefore, the activities of entities. They also require information that assists them in regulating the activities of entities, assessing taxation and providing a basis for national statistics. Although much of this information is obtained through special purpose financial reports, its consistency with published general purpose financial reports such as financial statements often needs to be demonstrated.

(g) *The public.* Entities affect members of the public in a variety of ways. For example, they may make a substantial contribution to a local economy by providing employment and using local suppliers. The public, including the local community, may therefore be interested in information that is useful in assessing the trends and recent developments in the entity's prosperity and the range of its activities.

This analysis illustrates that, although those potentially interested in an entity's 1.4 financial statements need that information for a variety of purposes, all the purposes involve taking informed economic decisions. Even present investors assessing the stewardship of the entity's management do so in order to decide whether, amongst other things, to hold or sell their investment in the entity and to reappoint or replace the management.

Information on financial performance and financial position

The economic decisions for which users need financial statements will not all be the 1.5 same. Although different decisions usually require different information, there is, as can be seen from paragraph 1.3, some overlap in the information required: all potential users are interested, to varying degrees, in the financial performance and financial position of the entity as a whole.

General purpose financial reports focus on this common interest of users. Their 1.6 objective is therefore to provide information about the financial performance and financial position of an entity that is useful to a wide range of users for assessing the stewardship of management and for making economic decisions (including those based on assessments of the stewardship of management).

As financial statements are the principal means of communicating accounting 1.7 information on an entity to interested parties and are a central feature of general purpose financial reporting, they carry much of the burden that is placed on general purpose financial reporting to meet this objective.

The limitations of financial statements

1.8   Financial statements do not seek to meet all the information needs of users: users will usually have to supplement the information they obtain from financial statements with information from other sources. Furthermore, financial statements have various inherent limitations that make them an imperfect vehicle for reflecting the full effects of transactions and other events on a reporting entity's financial performance and financial position. For example:

(a)   they are a conventionalised representation of transactions and other events that involves a substantial degree of classification and aggregation and the allocation of the effects of continuous operations to discrete reporting periods.

(b)   they focus on the financial effects of transactions and other events and do not focus to any significant extent on their non-financial effects or on non-financial information in general.

(c)   they provide information that is largely historical and therefore do not reflect future events or transactions that may enhance or impair the entity's operations, nor do they anticipate the impact of potential changes in the economic environment.

1.9   These inherent limitations mean that some information on the financial performance and financial position of the reporting entity can be provided only by general purpose financial reports other than financial statements—or in some cases is better provided by such reports. For example, although a description of the business environment and markets in which a reporting entity operates and the strategies it has adopted is usually needed to put into context the numerical information provided by the financial statements, it is generally better to provide such information in the material accompanying the financial statements than in the financial statements themselves.*

Investors as the defining class of user

1.10   As explained in paragraph 1.3, the perspective from which investors view financial performance and financial position is one that focuses on the entity's cash-generation ability and financial adaptability. This perspective is also of fundamental importance to other users, because an entity's ability to generate cash and to respond to unexpected needs and opportunities ultimately determines its capacity over the medium to long term to repay loans, meet interest payments, pay employees and suppliers, and undertake investment. For example, although in origin the perspective of lenders and other creditors differs from that of investors, they require similar information to investors when their interests are long-term or the risk of loss is significant. That is because they will want to use that information as a frame of reference against which to evaluate the more specific information they obtain.

1.11   Therefore, in preparing financial statements, the rebuttable assumption is made that financial statements that focus on the interest that investors have in the reporting entity's financial performance and financial position will, in effect, also be focusing on the common interest that all users have in that entity's financial performance and financial position.

*Accompanying information is discussed in Chapter 7.

It follows that, in determining which information to include in the financial state- 1.12
ments and how to present that information, it can usually be presumed that:

(a) information that is needed by investors will be given in either the financial
     statements or some other general purpose financial report; and
(b) information that is not needed by investors need not be given in the financial
     statements.

The information required by investors

Financial performance

The financial performance of an entity comprises the return it obtains on the 1.13
resources it controls, the components of that return and the characteristics of those
components.

Investors require information on financial performance because such information: 1.14

(a) provides an account of the stewardship of management and is useful in
     assessing the past and anticipated performance of the entity;
(b) is useful in assessing the entity's capacity to generate cash flows from its existing
     resource base and in forming judgements about the effectiveness with which the
     entity has employed its resources and might employ additional resources; and
(c) provides feedback on previous assessments of financial performance and can
     therefore assist users in modifying their assessments for, or in developing
     expectations about, future periods.

Financial position

An entity's financial position encompasses the economic resources it controls, its 1.15
financial structure, its liquidity and solvency, its risk profile and risk management
approach, and its capacity to adapt to changes in the environment in which it
operates.

Investors require information on financial position because: 1.16

(a) information about the economic resources controlled and the use made of them
     in the past helps in assessing the stewardship of management and the entity's
     ability to generate cash in the future;
(b) information about financial structure is useful in assessing how future cash
     flows will be distributed among those with an interest in or claims on the entity.
     It is also useful in assessing how successful the entity has been in managing its
     resources, its requirements for future finance and its ability to raise that finance;
(c) information about liquidity and solvency helps in assessing the ability of the
     entity to meet its financial commitments as they fall due;
(d) information on an entity's risk profile and risk management approach is useful
     in evaluating its current performance and financial adaptability, and in asses-
     sing its ability to generate cash in the future; and
(e) information on an entity's capacity to adapt to changing circumstances (in
     other words, its financial adaptability) is useful in assessing the extent to which
     the entity is at risk, or able to benefit, from unexpected changes.

Generation and use of cash

Information about the ways in which an entity generates and uses cash in its 1.17
operations, its investment activities and its financing activities provides an additional

perspective on its financial performance—one that is largely free from allocation and valuation issues.

1.18   Investors need such information because it is useful in assessing and reviewing previous assessments of:

(a)   liquidity and solvency;
(b)   the relationship between profits and cash flows;
(c)   the implications that financial performance has for future cash flows; and
(d)   other aspects of financial adaptability.

Financial adaptability

1.19   An entity's financial adaptability is its ability to take effective action to alter the amount and timing of its cash flows so that it can respond to unexpected needs or opportunities.

1.20   Financial adaptability is desirable for an entity because it helps it to mitigate the risks associated with operations, which in turn helps it to survive during a time of low (or possibly negative) cash flows from operations. It may also enable an entity to take advantage of unexpected investment opportunities. On the other hand, it also generally involves making sacrifices. For example, although holding assets that are readily marketable provides some financial adaptability, the rate of return involved may be lower than could be earned from holding less liquid assets.

1.21   The extent to which—and the ways in which—it is desirable for an entity to be financially adaptable will depend on the risks the entity faces and on the appetite for risk of its investors.

1.22   Financial adaptability comes from several sources, including the ability to:

(a)   raise new capital, perhaps by issuing debt securities, at short notice;
(b)   repay capital or debt at short notice;
(c)   obtain cash by selling assets without disrupting continuing operations; and
(d)   achieve a rapid improvement in the net cash inflows generated by operations.

Chapter 2: The reporting entity

It is important that entities that ought to prepare and publish financial statements do, in fact, do so and that those financial statements report on all relevant activities and resources. This chapter focuses on these issues—in other words, on identifying and circumscribing the reporting entity.

PRINCIPLES

- An entity should prepare and publish financial statements if there is a legitimate demand for the information that its financial statements would provide and it is a cohesive economic unit.
- The boundary of the reporting entity is determined by the scope of its control. For this purpose, first direct control and, secondly, direct plus indirect control are taken into account.

EXPLANATION

Entities that should prepare and publish financial statements

It is essential that entities that ought to prepare and publish financial statements do, in fact, do so. For similar reasons, if there is no justification for an entity to prepare and publish financial statements, it should not be required to do so.   **2.1**

For the preparation of financial statements to be justified in any particular case, there needs to be a legitimate demand for the information that the financial statements would provide. This means, inter alia, that the information provided by the financial statements will need to be useful and that the benefits to be derived by providing the financial statements will need to exceed the costs of doing so.   **2.2**

The financial statements of an entity will report on the entity's transactions and on other events that affect its financial performance and financial position. However, if the information provided by the financial statements is to be useful, the entity that is the subject of the financial statements (the reporting entity) needs to be a cohesive economic unit. This ensures accountability—the reporting entity is held to account for all the things it can control—and it gives the reporting entity a determinable boundary—because activities and resources are either within its control or outside its control.   **2.3**

The boundary of a reporting entity

The control an entity exerts can be direct or indirect.   **2.4**

(a) An entity has direct control of an asset if it has the ability in its own right to obtain the future economic benefits embodied in that asset and to restrict others' access to those benefits. An entity has direct control of its own activities and resources but does not have direct control of any other activities and resources.

(b)   An entity indirectly controls an asset if it has control of an entity that has direct control of the asset.* A parent company therefore has indirect control of the activities and resources of its subsidiary.

2.5   If the boundary of the reporting entity is determined by reference to direct control only, when one entity controls another, there will be two reporting entities: the controlling entity and its activities and resources; and the controlled entity and its activities and resources. On the other hand, if the boundary is determined by reference to direct plus indirect control, there will in the same circumstances be a reporting entity that comprises the controlling entity, the controlled entity and all their activities and resources. This reporting entity is often referred to as 'the group'.

2.6   Both these approaches result in useful information being provided, and both are therefore used in the model described in the Statement.

(a)   Direct control is used to determine the boundary of the reporting entity that prepares single entity financial statements. Those financial statements will therefore deal with the gains, losses, assets and liabilities directly controlled or borne by the entity but no other gains, losses, assets or liabilities.

(b)   Direct plus indirect control is used to determine the boundary of the reporting entity that prepares consolidated financial statements. Those financial statements will deal with the gains, losses, assets and liabilities directly controlled or borne by the entity as well as those that are indirectly controlled or borne by that entity through its control of other entities.

2.7   It may be that, although an entity can influence another entity, it does not control it. Such entities do not comprise a single reporting entity.†

What is control?

2.8   Control has two aspects: the ability to deploy the economic resources involved and the ability to benefit (or to suffer) from their deployment. To have control, an entity must have both these abilities.

2.9   This can be contrasted with the position in a trusteeship or agency arrangement, where the abilities are held by different parties. For example, in a trusteeship, the trustee—unless required to act in a predetermined way—has the power to deploy the trust's resources whilst the beneficiaries benefit from their deployment.

2.10   Control in the context of assets and liabilities is considered in more detail in Chapter 4; indirect control—through control over other entities—is considered in the paragraphs below.

---

*For simplicity, the discussion in this chapter assumes that one entity (the parent) directly controls the other (the subsidiary). However, the discussion applies equally if the parent controls the subsidiary by controlling one or more other entities that themselves control the subsidiary. It also applies when a parent's control of its subsidiary is achieved through the combined influence of itself and other entities that it controls.

†The accounting treatment of such relationships is addressed in Chapter 8.

Controlling an entity

When does one entity control another?

An entity will have control of a second entity if it has the ability to direct that entity's operating and financial policies with a view to gaining economic benefit from its activities.   **2.11**

Control may be evidenced in a variety of ways depending on its basis (for example ownership or other rights) and the way in which it is exercised (interventionist or not). Although control of another entity has traditionally involved share ownership and voting rights, that need not be the case. Indeed, some forms of control do not involve an investment of any kind.*   **2.12**

There is no single piece of evidence that is proof of an investor's control in all circumstances, although evidence that will help to determine whether control exists can be obtained by considering: **2.13**

(a)   the respective rights held;
(b)   the inflows and outflows of benefit; and
(c)   exposure to risk—how and to what extent the investor suffers or gains from variability in outcome.

These sources of evidence are interrelated because the rights an investor holds in the investee usually determine its entitlement to benefits generated by the investee and therefore usually its exposure to risk from variations in the benefits that the investee generates.   **2.14**

When determining whether the investor controls the investee, it is the relationship between the entities in practice, rather than the theoretical level of influence, that is important. The paragraphs below explain some of the factors that may need to be taken into account in determining whether control exists.   **2.15**

Powers of veto and reserve powers

Control implies the ability to restrict others from directing the financial and operating policies of the controlled entity. Powers of veto and reserve powers may therefore form part of the rights by which an investor exercises control. However, such powers are unlikely to form the sole basis of control because they do not provide a basis for deploying the resources of the investee nor do they ensure the corresponding flows of benefit.   **2.16**

Predetermined operating and financial policies

An investee whose operating and financial policies are predetermined will be controlled by the investor if the investor gains the benefits arising from the investee's net assets and is exposed to the risks inherent in them (ie the variability of outcome).   **2.17**

Latent control

If an investor has the ability to control an investee, it is usually presumed to be exercising control, even if such control is not apparent. Generally speaking, the only   **2.18**

Although control need not involve an investment, for simplicity this chapter uses the term 'investor' to mean 'entity with the interest in the other entity' and 'investee' to mean 'entity in which the investor has an interest'.

evidence that could rebut this presumption is evidence that a third entity is actually deploying the investee's resources on its own behalf and benefiting from them. It is, for example, not enough to show that the investee appears to be independent—it may be implementing the operating and financial policies desired by its investor without being given explicit instructions to do so.

Management but not control

2.19   Control needs to be distinguished from management. If an entity manages a second entity on its own behalf (ie it expects to benefit from the net assets of the second entity other than merely receiving a management fee) then it controls the second entity because it has the two abilities referred to in paragraph 2.8. A fee structure that in substance amounts to an interest in the net assets of an entity is treated as an ability to benefit (or to suffer) from the deployment of those net assets (sometimes referred to as an equity interest), whatever it is called.

2.20   On the other hand, if an entity manages the second entity on behalf of another party, it is not exposed to the benefits arising from, or risks inherent in, the activities of the second entity because the manager's interest in the managed entity is normally limited to its fee. As such, it does not have the second ability referred to in paragraph 2.8 and therefore does not have control of the second entity.

Chapter 3: The qualitative characteristics of financial information

In deciding which information to include in financial statements, when to include it and how to present it, the aim is to ensure that financial statements yield information that is useful. This chapter considers the qualities of financial information that make it useful.

PRINCIPLES

- Information provided by financial statements needs to be relevant and reliable and, if a choice exists between relevant and reliable approaches that are mutually exclusive, the approach chosen needs to be the one that results in the relevance of the information provided being maximised.
- Information is relevant if it has the ability to influence the economic decisions of users and is provided in time to influence those decisions.
- Information is reliable if:
  (a) it can be depended upon by users to represent faithfully what it either purports to represent or could reasonably be expected to represent, and therefore reflects the substance of the transactions and other events that have taken place;
  (b) it is free from deliberate or systematic bias and material error and is complete; and
  (c) in its preparation under conditions of uncertainty, a degree of caution has been applied in exercising the necessary judgements.
- Information in financial statements needs to be comparable.
- As an aid to comparability, information in financial statements needs to be prepared and presented in a way that enables users to discern and evaluate similarities in, and differences between, the nature and effects of transactions and other events over time and across different reporting entities.
- Information provided by financial statements needs to be understandable, although information should not be excluded from the financial statements simply because it would not be understood by some users.
- Information is understandable if its significance can be perceived by users that have a reasonable knowledge of business and economic activities and accounting and a willingness to study with reasonable diligence the information provided.
- Information that is material needs to be given in the financial statements and information that is not material need not be given.
- Information is material to the financial statements if its misstatement or omission might reasonably be expected to influence the economic decisions of users.

The relationship between these characteristics is portrayed in the diagram on the following page.

EXPLANATION

Relevance

Relevance is a general quality that is used as a selection criterion at all stages of the financial reporting process. Information provided by financial statements needs to be relevant. Furthermore, where choices have to be made between options that are relevant and reliable but mutually exclusive, the option selected should be the one that results in the relevance of the information package as a whole being maximised—in other words, the one that is reliable and would be of most use in taking economic decisions.   **3.1**

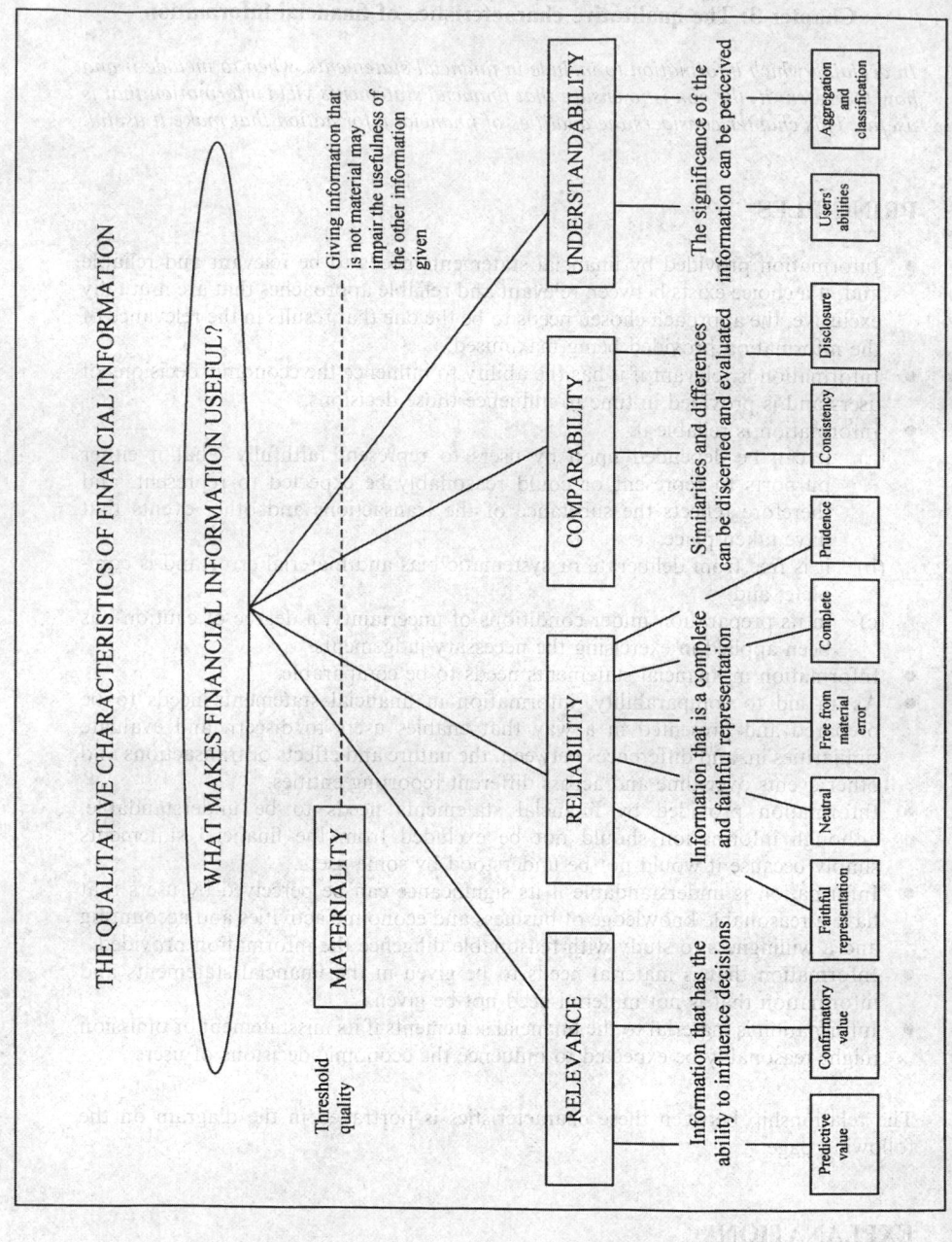

THE QUALITATIVE CHARACTERISTICS OF FINANCIAL INFORMATION

WHAT MAKES FINANCIAL INFORMATION USEFUL?

MATERIALITY

Threshold quality

Giving information that is not material may impair the usefulness of the other information given

RELEVANCE

Information that has the ability to influence decisions

Predictive value

Confirmatory value

RELIABILITY

Information that is a complete and faithful representation

Faithful representation

Neutral

Free from material error

Complete

Prudence

COMPARABILITY

Similarities and differences can be discerned and evaluated

Consistency

Disclosure

UNDERSTANDABILITY

The significance of the information can be perceived

Users' abilities

Aggregation and classification

Information is relevant if it has the ability to influence the economic decisions of users and is provided in time to influence those decisions. **3.2**

Relevant information has predictive value or confirmatory value. It has predictive value if it helps users to evaluate or assess past, present or future events, and it does not need to be in the form of an explicit forecast to have predictive value. Information has confirmatory value if it helps users to confirm or correct their past evaluations and assessments. Information may have both predictive value and confirmatory value. For example, information about the current level and structure of asset holdings helps users to assess the entity's ability to exploit opportunities and react to adverse situations. The same information helps to confirm past assessments about the structure of the entity and the outcome of operations. **3.3**

The ability to use information in financial statements to make assessments is enhanced by the way in which it is presented. For example, the predictive value of information provided by the financial performance statement is enhanced if unusual or infrequent items of gains or losses are disclosed and if information is provided that helps users to assess the likely incidence of similarly unusual or infrequent gains or losses in the future. In the same way, presentations that help users to understand the recurring/non-recurring nature of the various gains and losses also improve the predictive value of the performance statement. **3.4**

Maximising the relevance of financial information involves maximising its predictive and confirmatory value. **3.5**

There are a number of different perspectives from which an entity's financial performance and financial position could be viewed and the perspective adopted could have a significant effect on the assets and liabilities recognised and on their carrying amounts. In view of the objective of financial statements, the perspective that is usually most relevant is based on the assumption that the entity is to continue in operational existence for the foreseeable future. This perspective is commonly referred to as the going concern assumption. **3.6**

Reliability

Information provided by financial statements needs to be reliable. **3.7**

Information is reliable if: **3.8**

(a) it can be depended upon by users to represent faithfully what it either purports to represent or could reasonably be expected to represent;
(b) it is free from deliberate or systematic bias (ie it is neutral);
(c) it is free from material error;
(d) it is complete within the bounds of materiality; and
(e) in its preparation under conditions of uncertainty, a degree of caution (ie prudence) has been applied in exercising judgement and making the necessary estimates.

Faithful representation

The portrayal of a transaction or other event in the financial statements depends, inter alia, on: **3.9**

(a) the rights and obligations arising and the weight attached to each;
(b) how the rights and obligations to which most weight has been attached are characterised;

(c)   which measurement basis (or bases) and presentation techniques are used to depict the rights and obligations; and

(d)   the way in which the elements arising from the transaction or other event are presented in the financial statements.

3.10   A transaction or other event is faithfully represented in the financial statements if the way in which it is recognised, measured and presented in those statements corresponds closely to the effect of that transaction or event.

3.11   It needs to be borne in mind that most financial information is subject to some risk of being less than a faithful representation of what it purports to portray. This is partly due to inherent difficulties in identifying the transactions and other events to be dealt with and in identifying the consequences of such transactions and events that need to be measured. It reflects the difficulties in devising and applying measurement and presentation techniques that can convey messages that reflect those transactions and events. Furthermore, references to faithful representation need to be understood in the context of the Statement as a whole, which limits the kind of information that may properly be included in financial statements.

3.12   Faithful representation involves identifying *all* the rights and obligations arising from the transaction or event, giving greater weight to those that are likely to have a commercial effect in practice, then accounting for and presenting the transaction or other event in a way that reflects that commercial effect—in other words, in a way that reflects its substance.

3.13   The substance of a transaction or other event is not always consistent with that suggested by its legal form: although the effects of the legal characteristics of a transaction or other event are themselves a part of its substance and commercial effect, they have to be construed in the context of the transaction as a whole, including any related transactions. For example, an entity may pass legal ownership of an item of property to another party, yet, when the circumstances are looked at as a whole, it may be found that arrangements exist that ensure that the entity continues to have access to the future economic benefits embodied in that item of property. In such circumstances, the accounting needs to reflect this continuing interest.

3.14   A group or series of transactions that achieves an overall commercial effect will often need to be viewed as a whole in order to be accounted for in accordance with its substance.

Neutrality

3.15   The information provided by financial statements needs to be neutral—in other words, free from deliberate or systematic bias. Financial information is not neutral if it has been selected or presented in such a way as to influence the making of a decision or judgement in order to achieve a predetermined result or outcome.

Complete and free from material error

3.16   In requiring information provided by financial statements to represent faithfully what it purports to represent and to be neutral, there is an implication that the information is complete and free from error—at least within the bounds of materiality. Information that contains a material error or has been omitted for reasons other than materiality can cause the financial statements to be false or misleading and thus unreliable and deficient in terms of their relevance.

This reference to being complete within the bounds of materiality is important because completeness is relative: financial statements are a highly aggregated portrayal of an entity's financial performance and financial position and therefore cannot show everything.

3.17

Prudence

Uncertainty surrounds many of the events and circumstances that are reported on in the financial statements and it is dealt with in those statements by disclosing the nature and extent of the uncertainty involved and by exercising prudence.

3.18

Prudence is the inclusion of a degree of caution in the exercise of the judgements needed in making the estimates required under conditions of uncertainty, such that gains and assets are not overstated and losses and liabilities are not understated. In particular, under such conditions it requires more confirmatory evidence about the existence of, and a greater reliability of measurement for, assets and gains than is required for liabilities and losses.

3.19

However, it is not necessary to exercise prudence where there is no uncertainty. Nor is it appropriate to use prudence as a reason for, for example, creating hidden reserves or excessive provisions, deliberately understating assets or gains, or deliberately overstating liabilities or losses, because that would mean that the financial statements are not neutral and, therefore, are not reliable.

3.20

Comparability

Information in an entity's financial statements gains greatly in usefulness if it can be compared with similar information about the entity for some other period or point in time in order to identify trends in financial performance and financial position. Information about an entity is also much more useful if it can be compared with similar information about other entities in order to evaluate their relative financial performance and financial position.

3.21

Information in financial statements therefore needs to be comparable—at least as far as is possible. Furthermore, to help users to make comparisons, such information needs to be prepared and presented in a way that enables users to discern and evaluate similarities in, and differences between, the nature and effects of transactions and other events taking place over time and across different reporting entities. This can usually be achieved through a combination of consistency and disclosure of accounting policies.

3.22

Consistency

Comparability generally implies consistency throughout the reporting entity within each accounting period and from one period to the next. However, consistency is not an end in itself nor should it be allowed to become an impediment to the introduction of improved accounting practices. Consistency can also be useful in enhancing comparability between entities, although it should not be confused with a need for absolute uniformity.

3.23

Disclosure of accounting policies

In order to determine whether consistency exists or to assist in the making of comparisons despite inconsistencies, users need to be able to identify any differences between:

3.24

   (a)   the accounting policies adopted by an entity to account for like transactions and other events;

   (b)   the accounting policies adopted from period to period by an entity; and

   (c)   the accounting policies adopted by different entities.

3.25   Disclosure of the accounting policies employed in the preparation of the financial statements, of any changes in those policies and of the effects of such changes therefore enhances the usefulness of financial statements.

Understandability

3.26   Information provided by financial statements needs to be understandable—in other words, users need to be able to perceive its significance.

3.27   Whether financial information is understandable will depend on:

   (a)   the way in which the effects of transactions and other events are characterised, aggregated and classified. For example, information that does not properly reflect and communicate the substance of transactions and other events will not help users to understand the entity's financial performance or financial position.

   (b)   the way in which the information is presented. (This is considered further in Chapter 7.)

   (c)   the capabilities of users. Those preparing financial statements are entitled to assume that users have a reasonable knowledge of business and economic activities and accounting and a willingness to study with reasonable diligence the information provided.

Materiality

3.28   Materiality is the final test of what information should be given in a particular set of financial statements. While the paragraphs above describe the characteristics that, if present, will mean that the usefulness of the financial information has been maximised, the materiality test asks whether the resulting information content is of such significance as to require its inclusion in the financial statements.

3.29   Materiality is therefore a threshold quality that is demanded of all information given in the financial statements. Furthermore, when immaterial information is given in the financial statements, the resulting clutter can impair the understandability of the other information provided. In such circumstances, the immaterial information will need to be excluded.

3.30   An item of information is material to the financial statements if its misstatement or omission might reasonably be expected to influence the economic decisions of users of those financial statements, including their assessments of management's stewardship.

3.31   Whether information is material will depend on the size and nature of the item in question judged in the particular circumstances of the case. The principal factors to be taken into account are set out below. It will usually be a combination of these factors, rather than any one in particular, that will determine materiality.

   (a)   The item's size is judged in the context both of the financial statements as a whole and of the other information available to users that would affect their evaluation of the financial statements. This includes, for example, considering how the item affects the evaluation of trends and similar considerations.

(b)   Consideration is given to the item's nature in relation to:

    (i)   the transactions or other events giving rise to it;

    (ii)   the legality, sensitivity, normality and potential consequences of the event or transaction;

    (iii) the identity of the parties involved; and

    (iv) the particular headings and disclosures that are affected.

If there are two or more similar items, the materiality of the items in aggregate as well as of the items individually needs to be considered.   **3.32**

Constraints on the qualitative characteristics

On occasion, a conflict will arise between the characteristics of relevance, reliability, comparability and understandability. In such circumstances, a trade-off needs to be found that still enables the objective of financial statements to be met.   **3.33**

Relevance and reliability

Sometimes the information that is the most relevant is not the most reliable and vice versa. Choosing the amount at which to measure an asset or liability will sometimes involve just such a conflict. In such circumstances, it will usually be appropriate to use the information that is the most relevant of whichever information is reliable.*   **3.34**

Conflict between relevance and reliability can also arise over the timeliness of information. That is because a delay in providing information can make it out-of-date, which will affect its relevance, yet reporting on transactions and other events before all the uncertainties involved are resolved may affect the information's reliability. On the other hand, leaving information out of the financial statements because of reliability concerns may affect the completeness, and therefore reliability, of the information that *is* provided. Although financial information should generally be made available as soon as it is reliable and entities should do all that they reasonably can to speed up the process necessary to make information reliable, financial information should not be provided until it is reliable.   **3.35**

Neutrality and prudence

There can also be tension between two aspects of reliability—neutrality and prudence—because, whilst neutrality involves freedom from deliberate or systematic bias, prudence is a potentially biased concept that seeks to ensure that, under conditions of uncertainty, gains and assets are not overstated and losses and liabilities are not understated. This tension exists only where there is uncertainty, because it is only then that prudence needs to be exercised. When there is uncertainty, the competing demands of neutrality and prudence are reconciled by finding a balance that ensures that the deliberate and systematic understatement of gains and assets and overstatement of losses and liabilities do not occur.   **3.36**

Understandability

It may not always be possible to present a piece of relevant, reliable and comparable information in a way that can be understood by all the users with the capabilities   **3.37**

---

*Choosing between alternative measurement bases is considered in Chapter 6.

described in paragraph 3.27(c). However, information that is relevant and reliable should not be excluded from the financial statements simply because it is too difficult for some users to understand.

Chapter 4: The elements of financial statements

Elements of financial statements are the building blocks with which financial statements are constructed—the classes of items that financial statements comprise. This chapter identifies those elements and explains their attributes.

PRINCIPLES

- The elements of the financial statements are:

    (a)   assets
    (b)   liabilities
    (c)   ownership interest*
    (d)   gains†
    (e)   losses‡
    (f)   contributions from owners
    (g)   distributions to owners.

- Assets are rights or other access to future economic benefits controlled by an entity as a result of past transactions or events.
- Liabilities are obligations of an entity to transfer economic benefits as a result of past transactions or events.
- Ownership interest is the residual amount found by deducting all of the entity's liabilities from all of the entity's assets.
- Gains are increases in ownership interest not resulting from contributions from owners.
- Losses are decreases in ownership interest not resulting from distributions to owners.
- Contributions from owners are increases in ownership interest resulting from transfers from owners in their capacity as owners.
- Distributions to owners are decreases in ownership interest resulting from transfers to owners in their capacity as owners.

EXPLANATION

The elements of financial statements

Depicting the effects of transactions and other events

Financial statements need to reflect, in an appropriate manner and as far as is practicable, the effects of transactions and other events on the reporting entity's financial performance and financial position. This involves a high degree of classification and aggregation. Order is imposed on this process by specifying and defining the classes of items—the elements of financial statements—that encapsulate the key aspects of the effects of those transactions and other events.   **4.1**

The elements of financial statements are: **4.2**

---

*This element is given various descriptions in financial statements including, for example, equity, owners' equity, shareholders' equity, equity capital, capital, capital and reserves, partners' capital, shareholders' funds, proprietorship and ownership.

†This term incorporates all forms of income and revenue as well as all recognised gains (realised and unrealised) on non-revenue items.

‡This term incorporates all forms of expenses, sometimes referred to as revenue expenditure, and all recognised losses (realised and unrealised) on non-revenue items.

(a) in the case of the balance sheet (or statement of financial position)—assets, liabilities and ownership interest;
(b) in the case of the profit and loss account and any other statement of financial performance—gains and losses;
(c) contributions from owners; and
(d) distributions to owners.

4.3 Contributions from owners and distributions to owners are not the same as, and need to be distinguished from, other increases or decreases in ownership interest (in other words, gains and losses), which is why they are elements even though they are not identified with any particular primary financial statement.

4.4 Elements have been specified and defined to analyse comprehensively the way in which the financial effects of transactions and other events are represented in financial statements. However, as the cash flow statement represents only one type of financial effect—cash flows—analysis into elements is not relevant to that statement.

Recognition

4.5 Simply because a transaction or other event results, say, in a new asset being created, it does not follow that that new asset will be recognised. The criteria that need to be met before the effects of a transaction or other event on the elements will be recognised are considered in Chapter 5.

Assets

Definition

4.6 Assets are defined as follows:

Assets are rights or other access to future economic benefits controlled by an entity as a result of past transactions or events.

4.7 Although assets commonly have other features that help identify them—for example, they may be acquired at a cost and they may be tangible, exchangeable or legally enforceable—those features are not essential characteristics of an asset and their absence is not sufficient in itself to preclude an item from qualifying as an asset.

Rights or other access

4.8 An asset is not the item of property itself, but rather the rights or other access to some or all of the future economic benefits derived from the item of property.*

4.9 These rights or other access can be obtained in various ways. Often they are obtained by legal ownership of the underlying item of property. Such ownership usually gives the owner access to a number of future economic benefits, including the ability to use the item of property, to sell or exchange it or to exploit its value by, for example, pledging it as security for borrowing.

The term 'item of property' has been used in this chapter to differentiate between the control of rights or other access to future economic benefits (the asset) and the thing from which those future economic benefits are derived (the item of property). It is recognised however that, in other contexts, the term may have a different meaning and could, for example, refer to the subdivided property rights.

However, legal rights to future economic benefits derived from an item of property can be obtained without having legal ownership of the property itself, as is the case, for example, where property is leased. **4.10**

Other legal rights that give rise to assets include the right to require other parties to make payments or render services and the right to use a patent or trade mark. **4.11**

Access to future economic benefits—and therefore an asset—can also exist in the absence of legal rights. An example might be an unpatented invention. **4.12**

Future economic benefits

Capacity to obtain future economic benefits is the essence of an asset and is common to all assets irrespective of their form. Therefore, to be an asset, the right or other access must be capable, singly or in combination with other assets, of yielding economic benefits. **4.13**

This future economic benefit need not, however, be certain. Indeed, there is always some uncertainty whether expected future economic benefits will be obtained either to the extent expected or at all. In some cases, that uncertainty is so great that the asset is not recognised.* **4.14**

Future economic benefits eventually result in net cash inflows to the entity. Assets are not, however, always direct representations of cash flows: they are rights and other access to the future economic benefits that can generate or be used to generate future cash flows. In particular: **4.15**

(a) cash (including bank deposits) can be exchanged for virtually any good or service that is available or it can be saved and exchanged for them in the future. The command that cash gives over resources is the basis of its future economic benefits.

(b) debtors, investments and similar assets represent future economic benefits because they are direct claims to cash inflows that are expected to occur when customers pay their accounts, when investees pay interest or dividends, or when an investment is repaid or sold.

(c) payments made to external parties for services to be received from them in the future (such as prepayments) result in access to future economic benefits because they represent rights to receive services or to return of the payment.

(d) other assets provide access to future economic benefits through their ability to be:

    (i) exchanged for cash, claims to cash or other goods and services;

    (ii) used to provide goods or services; or

    (iii) used to settle liabilities.

As there does not need to be certainty that the economic benefits will arise, items that represent the right to exchange property on terms that will or may be favourable are also assets. For example, an option to acquire an asset will, subject to the other criteria being met, be an asset even if the price payable under the option is currently more than the market price of the asset. **4.16**

Controlled by the entity

The definition of an asset requires that the rights or other access to future economic benefits are controlled by the reporting entity. An entity will control the rights or other access if it has the ability both to obtain for itself any economic benefits that will arise and to prevent or limit the access of others to those benefits. **4.17**

*The recognition process is discussed in Chapter 5.

4.18   This control does not need to be legally enforceable, which means that weight can be given to economic and social sanctions when these are effective in inducing entities to fulfil promises or to comply with widely accepted business practices or customs.

4.19   The requirement that the rights or other access should be controlled by the entity treating them as its asset means that a particular right or other access to future economic benefits will appear in only one set of single entity financial statements, because such rights or access can be directly controlled by only one entity. (As indirect control is important in determining the boundaries of reporting entities, a right that is directly controlled by one entity and indirectly controlled by a second— through its control of the first entity—will be an asset both of the first entity and of the reporting entity that comprises both entities, ie the group.*)

4.20   On the other hand, a single item of property may give rise to assets of more than one entity. If two entities control the rights to different future economic benefits from the same item of property, both entities will have an asset (subject to the other aspects of the definition being met). However, although the item of property underlying the asset will be the same, the assets will be different because the future economic benefits are different. For example, if an entity leases an item of property to another entity, both entities will recognise an asset based on rights relating to the leased item of property although, as the lessor's rights will not be identical to the lessee's, the assets will not be the same.

4.21   An item of property will be an asset of an entity even though that entity cannot dispose of it without fundamentally changing the nature of its business, as would be the case if, for example, a hotel company with one hotel sold its hotel or a television franchise company sold its franchise. In such cases, although the rights to future economic benefits derived from the hotel or television franchise are the essence of the entity's business, it controls those rights and is therefore still in a position to choose if and when to realise the economic benefits involved. On the other hand, it is generally not possible for an entity to choose if and when to realise the economic benefits derivable from factors such as its market share, superior management or good labour relations because the rights or other access to such benefits cannot be controlled independently of the business as a whole. The entity therefore does not have the control of these benefits envisaged by the Statement, which means that such factors are not assets of the entity.

Past transactions or events

4.22   If the reporting entity's control of the rights or other access to the future economic benefits involved is to represent an asset, it needs to be the result of *past* transactions or events. A reporting entity that has access to future economic benefits but did not, until after the balance sheet date, have the ability to restrict the access of others to those benefits, did not have an asset at the balance sheet date.

Liabilities

Definition

4.23   Liabilities are defined as follows:

> Liabilities are obligations of an entity to transfer economic benefits as a result of past transactions or events.

*Determining the boundaries of reporting entities is considered in Chapter 2.

Obligations

For there to be a liability there must be an obligation that might result in the transfer of economic benefits. **4.24**

The notion of an obligation implies that the entity is not free to avoid the outflow of resources. If an obligation exists, although an entity may offer inducements to its creditors to cancel or postpone settlement, it will not be able to insist that they accept such an offer. **4.25**

Although many liabilities are based on legal obligations, a legal obligation is not a *necessary* condition: a liability can exist in the absence of legal obligations if commercial considerations create a constructive obligation. **4.26**

A decision to transfer economic benefits does not, in itself, create a constructive obligation because the transfer can be avoided by changing the decision. On the other hand, a constructive obligation would be created if such a decision was coupled with an event that both created a valid expectation that the entity involved would implement that decision and meant that the entity could not realistically withdraw from it. For example, a constructive obligation may be created by communicating a decision to follow a particular course of action to another party. Such an obligation may also be created by an established pattern of past practice. **4.27**

When preparing financial statements, it is usually most relevant to assume that the reporting entity is to continue in operational existence for the foreseeable future. It does not follow from this assumption, however, that, in preparing financial statements, the entity should be treated as being obliged to adopt a course of action that will enable it to continue in operational existence. Even if an obligation needs to be incurred to enable the entity to continue existing operations, until the entity ceases to be able to avoid the outflow of resources involved, there will be no obligation and, therefore, no liability. **4.28**

Transfer of economic benefits

Certainty that the obligation *will* result in a transfer of future economic benefits is not necessary. Obligations that are not likely to result in a transfer of economic benefits—such as the guarantee of another entity's debt where that entity is expected to remain solvent—are liabilities, even though they may not be recognised in financial statements (or may be recognised with a carrying amount of nil). **4.29**

Similarly, although many liabilities involve transfers of known amounts of cash, that need not be the case: a liability could involve an obligation to transfer an uncertain amount, and it could involve an obligation to transfer economic benefits other than cash—for example, by providing services or by undertaking to repair goods that are the subject of warranties. The recognition criteria described in Chapter 5 will filter out those liabilities that involve too much uncertainty to be recognised in the primary financial statements. **4.30**

Past transactions or events

For a liability to exist at the balance sheet date, the obligation to transfer economic benefits must have resulted from a *past* transaction or event. For example, in the circumstances described in paragraph 4.27—where the event that gave rise to the obligation was the communication of the decision to transfer economic benefits—the **4.31** liability will have existed at the balance sheet date only if the communication took place on or before that date.

4.32   Sometimes a series of events must take place before the entity will have an obligation to transfer economic benefits. In such circumstances, whether the obligation exists depends on whether any of the events that have still to take place are under the entity's control. If they are, the entity retains discretion to avoid the transfer, so no obligation exists. For example, as long as it is possible to avoid a penalty clause in a contract by performing, a liability in respect of the penalty will not arise. In contrast, an obligation to repair goods subject to warranty cannot be avoided once the goods have been sold on terms that include the warranty, so the sale marks the inception of the liability.

Offsetting rights and obligations

4.33   When a transaction or other event gives rise to a number of rights and obligations, it is necessary to consider whether some or all of those rights and obligations need to be offset either with each other or with rights and obligations that arise from other transactions or events. This raises issues of:

(a)   definition—when do rights and obligations represent separate assets and liabilities and when should some or all of them be aggregated or offset? This issue is considered in paragraphs 4.34-4.36.

(b)   recognition—when should rights that represent an asset and obligations that represent a liability be combined and recognised as a single asset or liability? This Statement envisages no circumstances in which assets and liabilities will be treated in this way.

(c)   presentation—when is it appropriate to present assets offset against liabilities (or vice versa) in the balance sheet? This issue is considered in Chapter 7.

4.34   If a right to receive future economic benefits and an obligation to transfer future economic benefits exist and the reporting entity has the ability—which is assured—to insist on net settlement of the balances, the right and obligation together form a single asset or liability regardless of how the parties intend to settle the balances.

4.35   When an entity enters into an agreement with another, it usually obtains certain rights and, in exchange, accepts certain obligations. Before any act of performance under the agreement has taken place, the entity does not have control of the future economic benefits arising from performance, nor does it have an obligation to transfer economic benefits that arise on performance. What it *does* have, however, is a contract that represents a net position comprising a combined right and obligation either to participate in the exchange or alternatively to be compensated (or to compensate) for the consequences of the exchange not taking place. Initially, the rights and obligations are likely to be exactly offsetting, although that will often not remain the case. The rights and obligations arising under such unperformed executory contracts together represent a single asset or liability.

4.36   It may be that the contract has been performed partially but is equally proportionately unperformed—in other words, that both parties to the contract have still to perform to an equal degree the actions promised by and required of them under the contract. In such a case, although the rights and obligations relating to the performed part of the contract may represent separate assets and liabilities, the rights and obligations relating to the unperformed part will together represent a single asset or liability.

Ownership interest

Ownership interest is defined as follows: **4.37**

> Ownership interest is the residual amount found by deducting all of the entity's liabilities from all of the entity's assets.

Since ownership interest is defined as a residual interest, the distinction between   **4.38** liabilities and ownership interest is highly significant. Owners invest in an entity in the hope of a return, at least part of which will usually be provided by the transfer to them from the entity of economic benefits (for example the payment of dividends). However, owners, unlike creditors, do not have the ability to insist that a transfer is made to them regardless of the circumstances: theirs is a residual interest in the assets of the entity after all the liabilities have been deducted.

Gains and losses

Definitions

Financial statements draw a distinction between changes in ownership interest   **4.39** arising from transactions with owners in their capacity as owners and other changes. These latter changes are gains and losses and are defined as follows:

> Gains are increases in ownership interest not resulting from contributions from owners.

> Losses are decreases in ownership interest not resulting from distributions to owners.

The terms 'gains' and 'losses' therefore include items that are often referred to as   **4.40** 'revenue' and 'expenses', as well as gains and losses arising from, for example, the disposal of fixed assets and the remeasurement of assets and liabilities.

Offsetting gains and losses

Some transactions give rise to a gain (or a loss) that is the net of two amounts: the   **4.41** revenue or income arising from the transaction and the expenses or costs incurred in generating that revenue. For example, the profit that arises on selling an item of stock is the difference between the sale proceeds and the cost of the item sold. For the purpose of the Statement, the sale proceeds and cost of the item sold are separate items—the former being a gain and the latter a loss. Whether such gains and losses are shown separately in the financial statements is a presentation issue and is considered in Chapter 7.

Contributions from owners and distributions to owners

Definitions

The remaining elements of financial statements relate to transactions with the owners   **4.42** in their capacity as owners and are defined as follows:

> Contributions from owners are increases in ownership interest resulting from transfers from owners in their capacity as owners.

> Distributions to owners are decreases in ownership interest resulting from transfers to owners in their capacity as owners.

In their capacity as owners

4.43   Contributions from, and distributions to, owners include only those transactions to which owners are a party *in their capacity as owners.* Increases or decreases in ownership interest that result from transactions entered into with owners in other capacities (for example, as customers or suppliers) are gains or losses. In some cases a single transaction combines a transaction with owners in their capacity as owners and a transaction with them in some other capacity.

Contributions from owners

4.44   Contributions from owners involve the owners making a contribution to the entity by transferring assets, performing services, or accepting ownership interest in satisfaction of liabilities. Rights in the ownership interest are usually granted in return for a contribution from owners.

Distributions to owners

4.45   Distributions to owners include the payment of dividends and the return of capital. A purchase by a company of its own shares is an example of a return of capital and is therefore reflected in financial statements by reducing the amount of ownership interest.

Chapter 5: Recognition in financial statements

When the reporting entity undertakes a transaction or when some other relevant event occurs, the effect of that transaction or event on the elements of financial statements will need to be recognised in the financial statements if certain criteria are met. This chapter considers that recognition process.

PRINCIPLES

- If a transaction or other event has created a new asset or liability or added to an existing asset or liability, that effect will be recognised* if:

    (a) sufficient evidence exists that the new asset or liability has been created or that there has been an addition to an existing asset or liability; and

    (b) the new asset or liability or the addition to the existing asset or liability can be measured at a monetary amount with sufficient reliability.

- In a transaction involving the provision of services or goods for a net gain, the recognition criteria described above will be met on the occurrence of the critical event in the operating cycle involved.

- An asset or liability will be wholly or partly derecognised† if:

    (a) sufficient evidence exists that a transaction or other past event has eliminated‡ all or part of a previously recognised asset or liability; or

    (b) although the item continues to be an asset or a liability, the criteria for recognition are no longer met.

EXPLANATION

The recognition process

The stages of the recognition process

The objective of financial statements is achieved to a large extent through the recognition of elements in the primary financial statements—in other words, the depiction of elements both in words and by monetary amounts and the inclusion of those amounts in the primary financial statement totals. This recognition process has the following stages:

5.1

(a) initial recognition, which is where an item is depicted in the primary financial statements for the first time;

(b) subsequent remeasurement, which involves changing the amount at which an already recognised asset or liability is stated in the primary financial statements; and

(c) derecognition, which is where an item that was until then recognised ceases to be recognised.

---

*The term 'recognised' is used in the Statement to mean depicting an item both in words and by a monetary amount and including that amount in the primary financial statement totals.

†The term 'derecognised' is used in the Statement to mean that an item ceases to be recognised.

‡To simplify the text, the word 'eliminated' is used in this chapter in place of the phrase 'consumed, transferred, disposed of, expired, settled or extinguished'.

Transactions and events other than transactions

5.2   The recognition process requires that all events that may have an effect on elements of the financial statements are, as far as is possible, identified and reflected in an appropriate manner in the financial statements.

5.3   Transactions are the most common form of such events and are therefore the most common reason for recognising and derecognising items. Events other than transactions may nevertheless also result in the recognition or derecognition of items. For example:

(a)   events such as discovery, growth, extraction, processing or innovation may result in the creation of new assets that may meet the recognition criteria. Similarly, the imposition of a penalty by a court may create a new liability that meets the recognition criteria.

(b)   events (such as a fire) that cause damage to an asset and events (such as the elapse of time) that result in an obligation expiring may result in a need to derecognise the asset or liability involved.

The effect of transactions and other events

5.4   No matter what element or change in element is being considered, the starting point for the recognition process is the effect that the transaction or other event involved has had on the reporting entity's assets and liabilities, because it is the assets and liabilities that demonstrate the lasting effect of changes in other elements. The interrelationship between the elements means that the recognition of one item as an element (or the recognition of a change in an element, including its derecognition) will inevitably result in the recognition of, or change in, another element. Thus, if a new asset is recognised, there will also be recognised a decrease in another asset, a new or increased liability, a gain, or a contribution from owners (or a combination of these).

5.5   A transaction or other event could have one of several effects on a reporting entity's assets and liabilities.

(a)   It might create a new asset or liability or add to an existing asset or liability. When this is the case, it will be necessary to determine whether the new asset or liability (or the addition thereto) should be recognised, because not all assets and liabilities are recognised. Paragraphs 5.12-5.21 consider initial recognition in detail.

(b)   It might provide additional evidence about an existing but unrecognised asset or liability and, as a result, enable that item to be recognised. This is also considered in paragraphs 5.12-5.21.

(c)   It might change some aspect of an already recognised asset or liability. This change may involve:

(i)   the nature of the item. For example, an item of raw material may be converted through the production process into finished goods. Similarly, convertible debt may be converted into equity shares. A change in the nature of an item will usually require a change in description, possibly by reclassification from one balance sheet caption to another or by renaming within a balance sheet caption. The amount at which the item is stated in the financial statements may also need to be changed.

(ii)   a change to the flow of benefits associated with an already recognised asset or liability. For example, the market value of a property may change as a result of changes in its development or income potential. Doubts about the creditworthiness of a debtor may alter perceptions of the collectability of the amount due from that debtor. Similarly, new information may cause the reporting entity to alter its estimate of the amount to be paid out to settle a liability of uncertain amount. A change in the flow of benefits associated with an item may require a change in the amount at which the item is stated. Changes in the amount at which an item is stated (in other words, subsequent remeasurements) are considered in Chapter 6.

(d)   It might involve transferring, using up or consuming an asset or settling, extinguishing or transferring a liability. On the other hand, it might leave intact certain of the rights to future economic benefits inherent in an asset whilst transferring, using up or consuming others, or it might leave intact certain obligations inherent in a liability whilst settling, extinguishing or transferring others. In all such circumstances it will be necessary to consider whether the existing asset or liability that has been affected should be derecognised in whole or in part. Paragraphs 5.22-5.25 consider derecognition further.

The references in the definitions of assets and liabilities to past transactions or events   **5.6**
ensure that the non-cash effects of transactions and other events will, as far as is possible, be reflected in the financial statements in the accounting period in which they occur and not, for example, in the period in which any cash involved is received or paid. This is commonly referred to as the 'accruals concept'.

Whether the reporting entity is a going concern can play a significant role in the   **5.7**
recognition process. For example, some contracts stipulate that the rights they give one party to the contract will lapse if that party discontinues its operations. Similarly, the reliability of measures—an important factor in the recognition process—may be affected if the reporting entity is not able to continue its operations. As explained in Chapter 3, the qualitative characteristic of relevance usually requires the going concern assumption to be applied.

Uncertainty and the recognition process

Ideally, all assets, liabilities, gains, losses and other elements would be recognised   **5.8**
immediately they arise. Similarly, in an ideal world an asset or liability would be derecognised as soon as it had ceased to exist or would be remeasured as soon as the need for remeasurement arose. In practice, however, entities operate in an uncertain environment and this uncertainty may sometimes make it necessary to delay the recognition process.

If uncertainty exists, totally reliable information will become available only when the   **5.9**
uncertainty has resolved itself. However, to defer a stage of the recognition process until the uncertainty has resolved itself will often reduce the relevance of the financial statements. It may also reduce their reliability because they will not represent faithfully the transactions and other events of the reporting period. Financial statements achieve a balance between these competing demands by seeking to provide information that has no more than an acceptable degree of uncertainty but not seeking to provide information that is totally free from uncertainty.

In the business environment, uncertainty usually exists in a continuum, so the   **5.10**
recognition process involves selecting the point on the continuum at which uncertainty becomes acceptable. The exact location of this point on the continuum will vary, depending on circumstances. For example, if additional information about the possible outcomes of an obligation is disclosed, it will usually be possible to recognise a liability despite this uncertainty. Furthermore, if a number of similar uncertain items are involved, it may be practicable to determine a sufficiently reliable measure

for the items taken as a whole despite the impracticality of determining a sufficiently reliable measure for each item individually.

5.11   There will nevertheless be circumstances in which it is not possible to reduce the uncertainty to an acceptable level. If that is the case, the recognition process will be deferred until such time as the uncertainty has been reduced to an acceptable level (and the effect of the transaction or other event will instead usually be reported in the notes to the financial statements).

Initial recognition

Categories of uncertainty

5.12   In the initial recognition process, there are two broad categories of uncertainty that could arise:

(a)   element uncertainty, which involves uncertainty whether an item exists and meets the definitions of the elements of financial statements; and

(b)   measurement uncertainty, which concerns the appropriate monetary amount at which to recognise the item.

Element uncertainty

5.13   Whether the rights or other access that underlie a potential asset exist, whether they are controlled by the reporting entity and whether they may yield future economic benefits may all be subject to uncertainty. Similarly, in the case of a potential liability there could be uncertainty whether the obligation exists and whether that obligation might require the reporting entity to transfer economic benefits.

5.14   Uncertainty of this kind (element uncertainty) is countered by evidence—the more evidence there is about an item and the better the quality of that evidence, the less uncertainty there will be over the item's existence and nature. To recognise an item it is necessary to have sufficient evidence, both in amount and quality, that the item exists and is an asset or liability of the reporting entity. This is reflected in the first of the two criteria for initial recognition, which requires that sufficient evidence must exist that a new asset or liability has been created or that there has been an addition to an existing asset or liability.

5.15   What constitutes sufficient evidence is a matter of judgement in the particular circumstances of each case although, while the evidence needs to be adequate, it need not be (and often cannot be) conclusive. The main source of evidence will be past or present experience with the item itself or with similar items, including:

(a)   evidence provided by the event that has given rise to the possible asset or liability;

(b)   past experience with similar items (for example, successful research and development in the past);

(c)   current information directly relating to the possible asset or liability; and

(d)   evidence provided by transactions of other entities in similar assets and liabilities.

Measurement uncertainty

5.16   To recognise an item, it is necessary to attribute a monetary amount to it. This involves two steps: selecting a suitable measurement basis (ie historical cost or current value) for the item and determining an appropriate monetary amount for the basis chosen.*

Uncertainty about the appropriate monetary amount at which to recognise the item (in other words, measurement uncertainty) is reflected in the second of the criteria for initial recognition, which requires that the new asset or liability or addition to an existing asset or liability can be measured at a monetary amount with sufficient reliability.

5.17

Prudence

As explained earlier, in order to recognise a loss (or gain), it is necessary to consider whether there is sufficient evidence that a decrease (or increase) in ownership interest has occurred and whether the amount of the loss (or gain) can be measured with sufficient reliability. As explained in Chapter 3, if there is uncertainty prudence requires:

5.18

(a)　more confirmatory evidence about the existence of an asset or gain than about the existence of a liability or loss; and

(b)　a greater reliability of measurement for assets and gains than for liabilities and losses.

However, the exercise of prudence does not justify the omission of assets or gains when there is sufficient evidence of occurrence and reliability of measurement or the inclusion of liabilities or losses when there is not. Nor does it justify any other deliberate and systematic overstatement of liabilities or losses or deliberate and systematic understatement of assets or gains.

5.19

Unperformed contracts

As explained in Chapter 4, when an entity enters into an agreement with another party, it obtains certain rights and, in exchange, accepts certain obligations. Before any act of performance under the agreement has taken place, the entity will have only a net position comprising a combined right and obligation either to participate in the exchange or alternatively to be compensated (or to compensate) for the consequences of the exchange not taking place. Although this right and the obligation will usually be in balance initially, changing circumstances may cause an imbalance to arise, in which case the net position will be either an asset or a liability.

5.20

This asset or liability will be recognised if the recognition criteria described in paragraphs 5.14 and 5.17 are met (and if the amount at which the asset or liability is to be measured is not nil). In particular:

5.21

(a)　the criterion that sufficient evidence must exist that the new asset or liability has been created will generally be met if it can be shown that the agreement is enforceable and, as a result, that a party to the agreement cannot cancel it (or otherwise fail to perform in accordance with it) without being obliged to compensate for such non-performance.

(b)　the criterion that the new asset or liability must be capable of being measured at a monetary amount with sufficient reliability is dealt with in Chapter 6.

(c)　if the historical cost basis of measurement is being used, the carrying amount will be the cost of entering into the agreement, which is usually nil. In effect, therefore, the contract is recognised at nil. An unperformed non-derivative

*The measurement process is described in Chapter 6.

contract with no initial cost will nevertheless be recognised if it has become an onerous contract.

Derecognition

Derecognition because the asset or liability has been eliminated

5.22   Assets tend, in due course, to be consumed, transferred or otherwise disposed of, or they expire. For example, cash may be spent, debtors may be collected, raw materials may be consumed or processed, finished goods may be sold and the service potential of a machine may be fully used up. Similarly, liabilities tend to be settled, extinguished, transferred, or they expire. For example, creditors may be paid, a warranty attaching to goods sold may expire, long-term debt may be exchanged for other debt and obligations to perform in accordance with agreed contractual terms may be met. In all such circumstances, it may be necessary to derecognise some or all of the asset or liability involved.

5.23   It is usually relatively simple to determine whether and when a previously recognised asset or liability needs to be derecognised. For example, using the examples given in the previous paragraph, the cash will be derecognised when it is paid out, the raw materials as they are being used and so on (in other words, when the asset is eliminated). However, some transactions leave intact certain of the rights to future benefits inherent in an asset (or obligations inherent in a liability) while eliminating others. In such circumstances, analysis is required to ascertain whether the effect of the transaction should be reflected by derecognising some or all of the assets and liabilities involved. For example, if the reporting entity no longer has control of some of the rights that previously constituted an asset while retaining control of some of the other rights, the asset may need to be partially derecognised (or the existing asset completely derecognised and a new asset recognised instead).

5.24   Ideally, an asset or liability would be derecognised as soon as it has been eliminated. However, there will sometimes be uncertainty about an item's continued existence. In such circumstances, derecognition will not take place until sufficient evidence exists that the transaction or other event has resulted in the elimination of the item. When there is uncertainty, prudence usually requires more confirmatory evidence about the existence of, and a greater reliability of measurement for, assets than is required for liabilities. This tends to mean that, if there is any significant uncertainty about an asset's continued existence, it will be derecognised. However, in the case of a liability, more evidence of its elimination will be needed before it will be derecognised.

Derecognition because the criteria for recognition are no longer met

5.25   After initial recognition, an asset or liability will usually continue to be recognised until it has been eliminated, at which point it will be derecognised. It is possible, however, that, although there has been no significant change in the inherent nature of an already recognised asset or liability—in other words, although the asset or liability has not been eliminated—the criteria for recognition described in paragraphs 5.14 and 5.17 are no longer met. For example, an event may have occurred since initial recognition that has resulted in there no longer being sufficient evidence that the asset or liability concerned exists. Similarly, an event may have created additional uncertainty and, as a result, a previously recognised asset or liability can no longer be measured with sufficient reliability. On the rare occasions when this is the case, that asset or liability will be derecognised even though it has not been eliminated.

Revenue recognition

It was explained earlier in the chapter that, because of the interrelationship between the elements, the starting point for the recognition process is always the effect that the transaction or other event involved has had on the reporting entity's assets and liabilities. For example, assuming that no contribution from owners or transfer to owners is involved: **5.26**

(a) if the effect of the transaction or other event is to increase the entity's recognised net assets, a gain will be recognised.
(b) a loss will be recognised if, and to the extent that, previously recognised assets have been reduced or eliminated or cease to qualify for recognition as assets without a commensurate increase in other assets or reduction in liabilities. Similarly, a loss will be recognised when and to the extent that a liability is incurred or increased without a commensurate increase in recognised assets or a reduction in other liabilities.

However, although the starting point for the recognition process may be the effect on assets and liabilities, the notions of matching and the critical event in the operating cycle will often help in identifying these effects. **5.27**

Matching

Matching has two forms. **5.28**

(a) Time matching involves the recognition of receipts (and payments) directly associated with the passage of time as gains (and losses) on a systematic basis over the course of the period involved. For example, rent paid at the beginning of a rental period is recognised as a loss over the course of the rental period, with amounts paid in advance of such recognition being recognised as an asset.
(b) Revenue/expenditure matching involves the recognition of expenditure directly associated with the generation of specific gains as a loss in the same period as the gains are recognised, rather than in the period in which the expenditure is incurred. For example, the cost incurred in obtaining or producing an item of stock is recognised in the performance statement as a loss in the same reporting period as the gain on selling that item, and in the meantime is recognised as an asset.

Almost all expenditure is undertaken with a view to acquiring some form of benefit in exchange. Consequently, if matching were used in an unrestricted way, it would be possible to delay the recognition in the performance statement of most items of expenditure insofar as the hoped-for benefits still lay in the future. The Statement imposes a degree of discipline on this process because only items that meet the definitions of, and relevant recognition criteria for, assets, liabilities or ownership interest are recognised in the balance sheet. **5.29**

This means that the Statement does not use the notion of matching as the main driver of the recognition process. Nevertheless, the Statement envisages that: **5.30**

(a) if the future economic benefits embodied in the asset are eliminated at a single point in time, it is at that point that the asset will be derecognised and a loss recognised; and
(b) if the future economic benefits are eliminated over several accounting periods— typically because they are being consumed over a period of time—the cost of the asset that comprises the future economic benefits will be recognised as a loss in the performance statement over those accounting periods.

5.31   When expenditure is being allocated to more than one accounting period, the amount allocated to each accounting period will depend on the circumstances involved, although the aim is always to recognise the expenditure as a loss on a systematic basis over the periods in which the asset delivers up its benefits. For example, if the association of the expenditure with the generation of specific gains can be only broadly or indirectly determined, it will often be necessary to assume that the asset declines in a systematic manner over its expected life.

5.32   Two implications of adopting the approach in the Statement, rather than using matching as a main driver of recognition, are that:

(a)   expenditure or some other form of loss that cannot justifiably be shown to be associated with control of rights or other access to future economic benefits will be recognised in the performance statement as a loss in the period in which it is incurred; and

(b)   expenditure incurred with a view to future economic benefits but whose relationship to such benefits is too uncertain to warrant recognition of an asset will be recognised immediately as a loss.

Critical event in the operating cycle

5.33   Sometimes it is easier to identify the appropriate point at which to recognise gains arising from the provision of services or goods—and therefore changes to the entity's assets and liabilities—by focusing on the operating cycle of the reporting entity and, in particular, on the critical event in that cycle.*

5.34   The critical event is the point in an operating cycle at which there will usually be sufficient evidence that the gain exists and it will usually be possible to measure that gain with sufficient reliability. In other words, it is the point at which the recognition criteria described earlier in the chapter will be met and the gain and related change to assets and liabilities will be recognised.

5.35   For many types of transaction, the critical event in the operating cycle is synonymous with full performance. In such cases a gain will be recognised when the entity providing the service or goods has fully performed. That need not, however, be the case: the critical event could occur at other times in the cycle and there could be more than one critical event in the cycle.

5.36   The identity of the critical event or events of an operating cycle will depend on the particular circumstances involved. For example:

(a)   if the reporting entity has carried out all its obligations under an agreement except for a few minor acts of performance, the critical event will have occurred.

(b)   if a sale is contingent upon acceptance by the buyer, the critical event will usually occur before acceptance unless the act of acceptance creates substantial uncertainty whether the contractual obligations will be met. The critical event will not usually have occurred if the likelihood of the goods or services not being accepted is significant.

(c)   the operating cycle might involve a contract that is performed in stages, for each of which there is a critical event. (Contracts to build large buildings are

---

In order to keep the explanation simple, it has been assumed in paragraphs 5.33-5.36 that the transaction being discussed is expected to generate a net profit and that the issue is therefore when to recognise that profit when using the historical cost basis of measurement. If the contract is expected to generate a loss the historical cost carrying amount will be adjusted immediately to reflect that expected loss.

usually an example of such an operating cycle.) In such circumstances, the gain that is expected to be earned on the contract as a whole will need to be allocated among the critical events.

Chapter 6: Measurement in financial statements

Measuring an asset or liability entails deciding on the measurement basis to be used and determining the monetary amount that is appropriate for that basis. It may also involve revising the monetary amount when certain events occur. This chapter describes the measurement process and explains how a choice is made between the measurement bases available.

PRINCIPLES

- In drawing up financial statements, a measurement basis—either historical cost or current value*—needs to be selected for each category of assets or liabilities. The basis selected will be the one that best meets the objective of financial statements and the demands of the qualitative characteristics of financial information, bearing in mind the nature of the assets or liabilities concerned and the circumstances involved.
- An asset or liability being measured using the historical cost basis is recognised initially at transaction cost. An asset or liability being measured using the current value basis is recognised initially at its current value at the time it was acquired or assumed.
- Subsequent remeasurement will occur if it is necessary to ensure that:
  - (a) assets measured at historical cost are carried at the lower of cost and recoverable amount;
  - (b) monetary items denominated in foreign currency are carried at amounts based on up-to-date exchange rates; and
  - (c) assets and liabilities measured on the current value basis are carried at up-to-date current values.
- Such remeasurements, however, will be recognised only if:
  - (a) there is sufficient evidence that the monetary amount of the asset or liability has changed; and
  - (b) the new amount of the asset or liability can be measured with sufficient reliability.

EXPLANATION

Alternative bases of measurement

6.1   Assets and liabilities have several different monetary attributes that could be represented in financial statements. Assets could, for example, be stated at historical cost, replacement cost or net realisable value and liabilities could, for example, be stated at historical cost, the cost of discharging the liability by the most economical means available or (in some cases) the amount that the entity could currently raise by issuing a similar debt security. The single most important characteristic that distinguishes these monetary attributes (which are known as measurement bases) is whether they are based on historical cost or current value. This chapter concentrates on that distinction.

6.2   These measurement bases could be used in financial statements in one of several ways. In particular:

- (a) a single measurement basis could be used for all assets and liabilities. For example, all assets and liabilities could be measured using historical cost. This is

The term 'historical cost' is, unless stated otherwise, used in the Statement to refer to the particular version of the historical cost basis described in paragraph 6.18. Similarly, the term 'current value' is used to refer to the value determined in accordance with paragraphs 6.7-6.9.

known as the historical cost system. Alternatively, all assets and liabilities could be measured at current value. This is known as the current value system.

(b) some categories of assets or liabilities could be measured on a historical cost basis and some on a current value basis. This is known as the mixed measurement system. In reality there is not one mixed measurement system but many, each involving a different mix of historical cost and current value.

The mixed measurement system permits the measurement basis to be selected   6.3
separately for each category of assets or liabilities. It also permits the use of historical cost (or current value) for all assets and liabilities if historical cost (or current value) is the most appropriate measure for each of those categories. Thus it can be adapted to fit the particular circumstances involved.

The Statement therefore envisages that the mixed measurement system will be used   6.4
and it focuses on the mix of historical cost and current value to be adopted. In doing so, it describes a framework that would guide the choice of basis for each category of assets or liabilities.

One approach that is not appropriate is to remeasure a category of assets or liabilities   6.5
at current value, then retain those assets or liabilities at that same amount indefinitely or for a long period of time. Such measures will usually soon cease to be up-to-date current values and will then be neither a historical cost nor a current value. As such, they disturb the comparability and consistency of accounting measurement and are not consistent with the principles contained in the Statement.

Alternative measures of current value

The current value of an asset could be determined by reference to entry value   6.6
(replacement cost), exit value (net realisable value) or value in use (discounted present value of the cash flows expected from continuing use and ultimate sale by the present owner). For some assets (for example investments in actively traded securities), these three alternative measures of current value produce very similar amounts, with only small differences due to transaction costs. However, for other assets (for example fixed assets specific to the business), differences between the alternative measures can be material.

It is therefore necessary to select from these alternative measures of current value the   6.7
measure that maximises the relevance of the current value basis. Current value is at its most relevant when it reflects the loss that the entity would suffer if it were deprived of the asset involved. That measure, which is often referred to as the 'deprival value' or the 'value to the business', will depend on the circumstances involved.

(a) In most cases, as the entity will be putting the asset to profitable use, the asset's value in its most profitable use (in other words, its recoverable amount) will exceed its replacement cost. In such circumstances, the entity will, if deprived of the asset, replace it, and the current value of the asset will be its current replacement cost.

(b) An asset will not be replaced if the cost of replacing it exceeds its recoverable amount. In such circumstances, the asset's current value is that recoverable amount.

   (i) When the most profitable use of an asset is to sell it, the asset's recoverable amount will be the amount that can be obtained by selling it, net of selling expenses; in other words, its net realisable value.

      (ii)   When the most profitable use of an asset is to consume it—for example by continuing to operate it—its recoverable amount will be the present value of the future cash flows obtainable and cash flows obviated as a result of the asset's continued use and ultimate disposal, net of any expenses that would need to be incurred; in other words, its value in use.

6.8   This can be portrayed diagrammatically as follows:

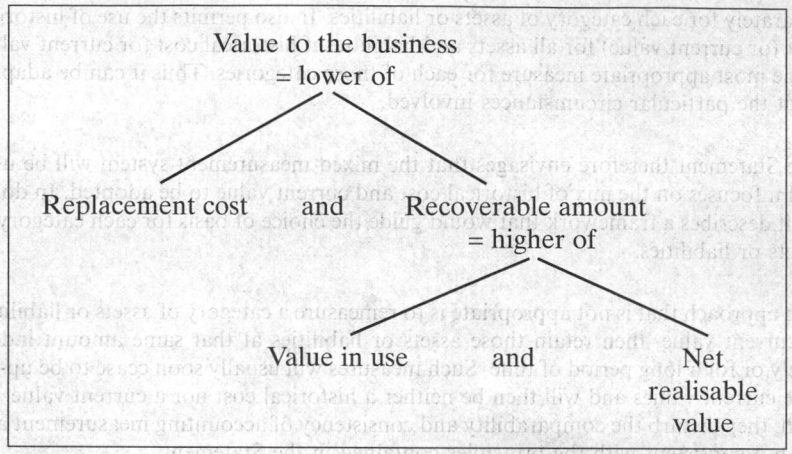

6.9   It is possible to select a current value for a liability in a similar manner (using the concept of 'relief value'). The relief value of a liability is the lowest amount at which the entity could divest itself of the obligation involved—in other words, the lowest amount at which the liability could, hypothetically, be settled.

The measurement process

6.10   It is not the function of financial statements to represent directly the total value that the reporting entity would fetch in an exchange transaction. Instead, the financial statements provide information designed to assist users to make judgements about the entity's financial performance and financial position and it is these judgements, in combination with other information, that enable, inter alia, a value for the entity to be assessed. The purpose of the measurement process is therefore to measure the effects of the transactions and events of the period on the financial performance and financial position of the entity.

Initial recognition

6.11   An asset or liability that is being measured using the historical cost basis will be recognised initially at transaction cost or, if an event other than a transaction is involved, at its fair value at the time it was acquired or assumed. The transaction cost of an asset acquired or liability assumed is the fair value of the consideration given or received in exchange for that asset or liability.

6.12   An asset or liability that is being measured using the current value basis will be recognised initially at its current value at the time it was acquired or assumed.

6.13   This means that, regardless of the measurement basis used, assets and liabilities that arise from transactions carried out at fair value—which is the vast majority of assets and liabilities—will be measured on initial recognition at their transaction cost. That is because, in the case of such a transaction, the fair value of the consideration paid or received (ie the transaction cost) is equal to the current value of the asset or liability at the time of acquisition.

It can generally be assumed that, in the absence of evidence to the contrary, a **6.14** transaction has been carried out at fair value. In such circumstances, the transaction cost involved can be determined by reference to the fair value of either the asset (or liability) acquired or the consideration paid (or received); whichever fair value is easiest to measure will usually be used. For example (and assuming in both cases that there is no evidence suggesting that the transaction was not carried out at fair value):

(a) if the reporting entity purchases mining rights in exchange for an immediate cash payment, those rights would usually be measured on initial recognition at the cash amount because that amount is easier to measure than the fair value of the rights.

(b) if the entity purchases an asset from an employee for an immediate cash payment, it may not be clear whether it also involves a payment for services provided by the employee. Where such uncertainty exists, it may be easier to measure the fair value of the asset purchased than the fair value of the services provided. If the former amount is, for example, less than the amount of the payment, the difference will be remuneration.

If an asset or liability arises from a transaction that was not carried out at fair value, **6.15** it will often be more appropriate to measure the asset or liability at current value rather than historical cost. Choosing a measurement basis is considered in paragraphs 6.23-6.29.

The initial recognition criteria described in Chapter 5 stipulate that, to be recognised, **6.16** the asset or liability involved needs to be capable of being measured at a monetary amount with sufficient reliability. Whether a measure is sufficiently reliable for inclusion in primary financial statements depends on the quantity and quality of the evidence available to confirm that the measure has the attributes of reliability described in Chapter 3. A measure derived from a generally accepted valuation methodology and supported by a reasonable amount of confirmatory evidence will usually be a sufficiently reliable measure.

Subsequent remeasurement

If a *pure* historical cost measurement basis is being used, the carrying amount of an **6.17** asset or liability will always be the amount at which it was initially recognised; in other words, there is no subsequent remeasurement stage. The carrying amount of an asset or liability measured at historical cost may nevertheless need to be changed so that the item remains at cost. For example, as work is carried out on work-in-progress, so the carrying amount is changed to reflect the additional costs incurred. Similarly, in the case of assets that are consumed over more than one accounting period (such as fixed assets), the amount at which the asset was recognised initially will be reduced over the expected life of the asset so as to allocate the asset's cost over its expected life. Adjustments may also need to be made to the carrying amount of other assets and liabilities to reflect cost and income allocations. These adjustments are not remeasurements; they are adjustments to maintain the carrying amount at an amount based on historical cost.

In practice, however, this 'pure historical cost basis' is rarely used. Instead, to make **6.18** historical cost more relevant to the needs of users, a variation is used that involves a limited amount of remeasurement. The purpose of this remeasurement is to ensure that:

(a)   assets are not reported at amounts greater than their recoverable amount; and
(b)   monetary assets and liabilities denominated in currencies other than the reporting currency are stated at an amount that is based on up-to-date exchange rates.

All references in the Statement to the historical cost basis are, unless stated otherwise, references to this version of the historical cost basis.

6.19   When the current value basis of measurement is being used, remeasurement takes place to ensure that the assets or liabilities involved are measured at an up-to-date current value. Such remeasurements will, however, be recognised in the financial statements only if:

(a)   there is sufficient evidence that the amount of the asset or liability has changed. For example, if consideration is being given to writing down the carrying amount of an asset to its recoverable amount, there will need to be sufficient evidence that the asset's recoverable amount *is* lower than its carrying amount; and
(b)   the new amount of the asset or liability is capable of being measured with sufficient reliability.

6.20   What constitutes sufficient evidence is a matter of judgement in the particular circumstances of each case although, whilst the evidence will need to be adequate, it need not (and often cannot) be conclusive. Relevant considerations as to whether the evidence is sufficient will include its persuasiveness and whether the change implies that a gain or a loss has occurred.*

6.21   Although the nature of the evidence will vary from item to item, its primary source will be past or present experience with the item itself or with similar items. This will include evidence provided by:

(a)   current information directly relating to the item (eg the current physical condition of items of stock, their current selling price, and current levels of orders for them).
(b)   other entities' transactions in similar assets and liabilities. If such transactions are frequent and the items traded are very similar to the item held by the reporting entity (ie there is an efficient market in homogeneous items), such evidence will often be sufficient. However, as the frequency of transactions decreases or differences between the items traded and the item held by the reporting entity increase, the evidence will become less persuasive and is less likely to be sufficient on its own.
(c)   past experience with a group of similar items (eg the levels of losses arising in the past on stock of different ages).

6.22   The issues to be considered in deciding whether the new amount of the asset or liability is capable of being measured with sufficient reliability are identical to the reliability of measurement issues considered in the context of initial recognition (see paragraph 6.16).

---

*These factors, and the sources of evidence referred to in paragraph 6.21, are broadly similar to those that need to be taken into account when considering, in the initial recognition stage, whether there is sufficient evidence that an asset or liability itself has been changed (see paragraph 5.15).

Choosing a measurement basis and deciding whether to change it

In choosing the measurement basis to be used for a particular category of assets or **6.23** liabilities, the aim is to select the basis that is most appropriate bearing in mind:

(a) the objective of financial statements and the qualitative characteristics of financial information, in particular relevance and reliability;
(b) the nature of the assets or liabilities concerned; and
(c) the particular circumstances involved.

Although these factors may not change, the measurement basis that best meets them **6.24** may. For example, to the extent that markets develop, measurement bases that were once thought unreliable may become reliable. Similarly, to the extent that access to markets develops, so a measurement basis that was once thought insufficiently relevant may become the most relevant measure available.

Although it is often difficult to make general statements about the appropriate **6.25** measurement basis for any particular category of assets or liabilities, the observations set out in paragraphs 6.26-6.29 can be made.

The need for financial information to be relevant means that, in selecting a mea- **6.26** surement basis, the focus will be on providing information about financial performance and financial position that is useful in evaluating the reporting entity's cash-generation abilities and in assessing its financial adaptability.

The carrying amounts of assets and liabilities need to be sufficiently reliable.* If only **6.27** one of the measures available is reliable, it will be the one used provided that it is also relevant. On the other hand, if both the historical cost measure and the current value measure are reliable, the better measure to use will be the one that is the most relevant.

Current value measures are sometimes characterised as less reliable than historical **6.28** cost measures. Such a characterisation tends to assume, however, that all historical cost measures are transaction-based and involve little estimation, which is not the case. For example, adjustments made to the historical cost carrying value of debtors to make allowance for bad and doubtful debts involve a degree of estimation that is not dissimilar to that involved in estimating current values not derived from an active market—and the results are often of broadly similar reliability. There is a similar level of estimation involved in determining the cost of self-generated assets and by-products, and generally in all circumstances involving allocations of substantial amounts of indirect costs. The hurdle that a measure must clear to be deemed reliable is set at the same height for current value measures as for historical cost measures.

Assessments of relevance and reliability need to take into account what the asset or **6.29** liability represents. For example, if an entity 'stores' its spare cash by making an investment, that investment's relevance to the entity will be derived from the specific future cash flows that it represents rights to. The measure that will most faithfully represent those rights will generally be current value. Similarly, if an entity has a liability of uncertain amount, that liability's relevance to the entity will be derived from the most up-to-date information about those uncertainties. The measure that most faithfully represents those uncertainties will again generally be current value.

---

*What the characteristic of reliability entails is considered in detail in Chapter 3 and is also dealt with in paragraphs 6.16 and 6.35-6.38.

Measurement issues

Going concern

6.30   Financial statements are usually prepared—and measures are usually arrived at—on the basis that the reporting entity is a going concern because measures based on break-up values tend not to be relevant to users seeking to assess the entity's cash-generation ability and financial adaptability.

Discounting

6.31   Most transactions take place at fair value. Rational buyers and sellers will ensure that this fair value reflects the time value of money and the risk associated with the future expected cash flows, which means that market prices generally will reflect such factors.

6.32   This chapter has explained that assets will, depending on the circumstances, be carried in the financial statements at historical cost, replacement cost, net realisable value or value in use and that liabilities will, again depending on the circumstances, be carried at historical cost or the lowest amount at which the liability could be settled. Historical cost and replacement cost are both market prices and will there-fore, for the reason set out in paragraph 6.31, take into account the time value of money and the risk associated with the future expected cash flows.

6.33   To be consistent, these factors need also to be reflected in the other measures that can be used to determine the carrying amount of assets (in other words, value in use and net realisable value) and the carrying amount of any liabilities measured by reference to expected future cash flows. It follows that, when basing carrying amounts on future cash flows, those cash flows will need to be discounted.

6.34   The discount rate used will reflect the risks associated with the future expected cash flows involved (unless those future expected cash flows are already risk-adjusted) and the time value of money. As such, it will reflect the risks specific to the item being measured but not the more general risks of the entity as a whole.*

Arriving at a measure in the face of uncertainty

6.35   It is quite common for there to be uncertainty about the appropriate monetary amount at which to measure an asset or liability. The existence of this uncertainty (measurement uncertainty) is acknowledged in the initial recognition and subsequent remeasurement criteria, both of which insist that the monetary amount at which an asset or liability is to be recognised is capable of being measured with sufficient reliability.

6.36   If uncertainty exists, the only way to determine an appropriate monetary amount for the asset or liability is through the use of estimates. As long as a generally accepted estimation method is used and the measure is supported by a reasonable amount of confirmatory evidence—prudence requires a greater reliability of measurement for assets (and gains) than for liabilities (and losses)—the use of estimates is acceptable and will not prevent the measure from being sufficiently reliable to be used in the financial statements.

*Discounting is discussed in greater detail in a Working Paper 'Discounting in Financial Reporting' published by the Board in April 1997.

Estimating an appropriate carrying amount will often involve adopting one of the following approaches.   **6.37**

(a) If there is a reasonably efficient market for the item or for very similar items, a market-based measure such as a market price could be used as the carrying amount because the market consensus over the amount of the benefits inherent in the item is likely to mean that the measure will be reliable.

(b) If the entity has a group of homogeneous but not identical items, the expected value of the entire group could be used, provided the group is of a sufficient size and there is sufficient evidence of the various possible outcomes and their probabilities to permit an explicit calculation of expected value.*

(c) If neither of these approaches is practicable, a best estimate will need to be used. If there is a minimum amount that is reasonably assured, the item will be stated at no less than that minimum amount, and a higher amount will be used if that is a better estimate.

If the monetary amount at which an asset or liability is recognised is subject to significant uncertainty, the degree of uncertainty surrounding the estimate will usually be disclosed in order to avoid the impression that the outcome is certain. Such a disclosure might provide details of the significant assumptions and measurement basis used, the range of possible outcomes, and the principal factors that affect the outcome.   **6.38**

Capital maintenance adjustments and changing prices

Put simply, accounting profit is the return the reporting entity has earned on its capital. Therefore, in order to account properly for accounting profit, it is necessary to differentiate between return *on* capital and return *of* capital. This involves defining and measuring the capital of the entity.   **6.39**

Under the accounting model described by the Statement and adopted by almost all profit-making entities, the capital of the entity is defined as the monetary amount of ownership interest (the financial capital maintenance concept) and is measured in nominal amounts.   **6.40**

With this approach, the capital of the entity will be maintained if the amount of gains during a period is at least equal to the amount of losses in that period. This means that any surplus of gains over losses during a period represents a return *on* capital for that period.   **6.41**

Whilst this approach is satisfactory under conditions of stable prices, it is open to criticism when general or specific price changes are significant.   **6.42**

(a) General price changes can affect the significance of reported profits and of ownership interest. If this problem is acute, an approach will need to be adopted that involves recognising profit only after adjustments have been made to maintain the purchasing power of the entity's financial capital.

Expected value is a weighted average of all possible outcomes, calculated using the probability of occurrence of an outcome as its weight. For a group of similar items, individual items will have different outcomes, and the number of items having a particular outcome will be related to the probability of that outcome. Hence, the expected value will represent a reasonable estimate of the monetary amount of the benefits associated with the entire group. For instance, in considering a large portfolio of non-interest bearing debts, it may be unlikely that any individual debt will prove to be bad, but some degree of non-payment is normally expected; hence a loss representing this expected reduction in economic benefits is recognised. If each debt were to be considered individually and measured at its most likely outcome, each debtor might be judged more likely than not to pay, and hence no bad debt provision would be made. However, this would not represent a reasonable measure of future economic benefits for the entire group.

(b)   Specific price changes can affect the significance of reported profits and financial position. If the problem is acute, it will be necessary to adopt a system of accounting that informs the user of the significance of specific price changes for the entity's financial performance and financial position.

Chapter 7: Presentation of financial information

Good presentation ensures that the essential messages of the financial statements are communicated clearly and effectively and in as simple and straightforward a manner as possible. This chapter explains what good presentation entails. It also considers the information that often accompanies financial statements and explains some of the roles fulfilled by such information.

PRINCIPLES

- Financial statements comprise primary financial statements and supporting notes that amplify and explain the primary financial statements. The primary financial statements themselves comprise the statement of financial performance,* the statement of financial position or balance sheet, and the cash flow statement.
- The presentation of information on financial performance focuses on the components of that performance and on the characteristics of those components.
- The presentation of information on financial position focuses on the types and functions of assets and liabilities held and on the relationships between them.
- The presentation of cash flow information will show the extent to which the entity's various activities generate and use cash, and will distinguish in particular between those cash flows that result from operations and those that result from other activities.
- Disclosure of information in the notes to the financial statements is not a substitute for recognition and does not correct or justify any misrepresentation or omission in the primary financial statements.

EXPLANATION

Presentation of information in financial statements

Clear, effective and simple communication

As financial statements are a means of communication, the objective of the presentation adopted is to communicate clearly and effectively and in as simple and straightforward a manner as is possible without loss of relevance or reliability and without unnecessarily increasing the length of the financial statements. **7.1**

Highly structured and aggregated

Even if it were practicable it would not be appropriate for financial statements to report every single aspect of every relevant transaction and event: the mass of detail would obscure the message. The presentation of information in financial statements therefore involves a high degree of interpretation, simplification, abstraction and aggregation—in other words, a loss of detailed information. Nevertheless, if this process is carried out in an orderly manner, greater knowledge will result because such a presentation will: **7.2**

(a) convey information that would otherwise have been obscured;
(b) highlight those items, and relationships between items, that are generally of most significance;

*Although many entities in the UK and the Republic of Ireland at present prepare two statements of financial performance, the number of statements prepared is a matter of convention and legal requirement; no significant financial reporting principle is involved. For simplicity, however, the Statement generally refers to 'the statement of financial performance'.

(c)   facilitate comparability between different entities' financial statements; and
(d)   be more understandable to users.

7.3   The primary focus of financial statements is on the entity's cash generation and financial adaptability. This focus is met through a set of interrelated reports (known as the primary financial statements) on:

(a)   financial performance (the profit and loss account and the statement of total recognised gains and losses are examples of financial performance statements);
(b)   financial position (the balance sheet); and
(c)   cash inflows and outflows (the cash flow statement),

and a series of supporting disclosures (the notes to the financial statements).

7.4   The notes and primary financial statements form an integrated whole, with the notes amplifying and explaining the statements by, for example, providing:

(a)   more detailed information on items recognised in the primary financial statements. Good presentation strikes a balance between the detail provided on the face of the primary financial statements and that provided in the notes, thus avoiding cluttering up the former and obscuring their message.
(b)   context for, or an alternative view of, items recognised in the primary financial statements. For instance, if a balance sheet includes a liability that is in dispute, the related note might disclose the range of possible outcomes. Similarly, the notes usually provide segmental information to supplement the primary financial statements, which focus on the reporting entity in aggregate.
(c)   relevant information that it is not practicable to incorporate in the primary financial statements, for example because of pervasive uncertainty.

7.5   The notes to the financial statements therefore represent a very important part of the overall information package. Nevertheless, disclosure of information in the notes is not a substitute for recognition and does not correct or justify any misrepresentation in or omission from the primary financial statements.

Classification

7.6   In order to facilitate the analysis of the information provided, items that are similar are presented together in the financial statements and distinguished from dissimilar items.

7.7   The classifications used to achieve this also have regard to the additional insights that can be obtained by considering the relationships between different classes of items, for example the relative sizes of profits and capital employed or debtors and sales.

7.8   Classifications that are similar or related are presented in financial statements in a manner that highlights that similarity or relationship. For example, different kinds of current assets are shown adjacent to each other, and current liabilities are usually shown in a manner that highlights their relationship to current assets.

Good presentation

Statement of financial performance

7.9   The financial performance of a reporting entity is made up of components that exhibit differing characteristics in terms of, for example, nature, cause, function, relative continuity or recurrence, stability, risk, predictability and reliability. All these components are relevant to an assessment of financial performance and therefore need to be reported on in the statement of financial performance, although their individual characteristics mean that some will carry more weight in some assessments of financial performance than others.

Information on financial performance needs to be presented in a way that focuses attention on these components and on their key characteristics. Therefore, although it is not of fundamental importance whether one or more than one performance statement is provided, the presentation—including the headings used and the items that appear under each heading—is important. Good presentation of financial performance information typically involves: **7.10**

(a)   recognising only gains and losses in the statement of financial performance.
(b)   classifying components by reference to a combination of function (such as production, selling and administrative) and of the nature of the item (such as employment costs, interest payable and amounts written off investments).
(c)   distinguishing amounts that are affected in different ways by changes in economic conditions or business activity (for example, by providing segmental information or by presenting income from continuing and discontinued operations as separate components).
(d)   identifying separately:

   (i)   items that are unusual in amount or incidence judged by the experience of previous periods or expectations of the future.
   (ii)   items that have special characteristics, such as financing costs and taxation.
   (iii) items that are related primarily to the profits of future, rather than current, accounting periods, such as some research and development expenditure.

Gains and losses are generally not offset in presenting information on financial performance. For example, as explained in Chapter 4, if a transaction involves both a receipt and a cost (as is the case, for example, when an item of stock is sold), the transaction will usually be best presented by showing the gain (the receipt) separately from the loss (the cost). However, gains and losses will be offset if: **7.11**

(a)   they relate to the same event or circumstance; and
(b)   disclosing the gross components is not likely to be useful for an assessment of either future results or the effects of past transactions and events.

For example, if a profit is made on the disposal of a fixed asset, that profit is usually best presented by showing it as a gain rather than by showing the sales proceeds as a gain separately from the depreciated cost of the asset.

Balance sheet

In assessing the financial position of an entity, users are most interested in the types and amounts of assets and liabilities held and the relationship between them, and in the function of the various assets. Information on the reporting entity's financial position therefore needs to be presented in a way that focuses attention on these aspects. Good presentation typically involves: **7.12**

(a)   recognising only assets, liabilities and ownership interest in the balance sheet;
(b)   delineating the entity's resource structure (major classes and amounts of assets) and its financial structure (major classes and amounts of liabilities and ownership interest). The main basis for deciding the number of classes and the content of each is that the result will help users to assess the nature, amounts

and liquidity of available resources and the nature, amounts and timing of obligations that require or may require liquid resources for settlement.

(c)   distinguishing assets by function. For example, assets held for sale will be reported separately from assets held on a continuing basis for use in the entity's activities.

7.13   In presenting information on the reporting entity's financial position, assets will not be offset against liabilities.*

Cash flow statement

7.14   Cash flow information will be of most use if it shows the extent to which the entity's activities generate and use cash, distinguishing in particular cash flows that are the result of operations from cash flows that result from other activities. This might include, for example, showing separately cash received from trading activities, cash used to repay debt, cash used to distribute dividends and cash reinvested.

Accompanying information

7.15   Financial statements are often accompanied and complemented by information that does not form part of the financial statements. Examples of such information include five-year trend information, operating and financial reviews, directors' reports and statements by the chairman. The Statement refers to such information as accompanying information.†

7.16   Although accompanying information generally has the same objective as financial statements, it usually comprises a different kind of information. For example, it often includes:

(a)   narrative disclosures describing and explaining the entity's activities;
(b)   historical summaries and trend information;
(c)   non-accounting, and non-financial, information; and
(d)   evolutionary or experimental disclosures that are not considered suitable for inclusion in the financial statements.

7.17   Some of the accompanying information therefore deals with matters that are not in the financial statements and some deals with matters that are in the financial statements, but from a different perspective. However, none of the accompanying information will be inconsistent with the information in the financial statements.

7.18   The more complex entities and their transactions become, the more users need an objective and comprehensive analysis and explanation of the main features underlying their financial performance and financial position. Such disclosures, which are typically included in the reporting entity's operating and financial review, are best presented in the context of a discussion of the entity's business as a whole and will be most useful if they discuss:

The offsetting of rights and obligations to produce a single asset or liability is considered in paragraphs 4.33-4.36.

†*Such information is sometimes referred to as 'supplementary information'. However, the Statement avoids that term because it is also sometimes used to refer to certain information that is included within the financial statements.*

(a)   the main factors underlying the entity's financial performance, including the principal risks, uncertainties and trends involved in each of the main business areas and how the entity is responding to them;

(b)   the dynamics of the entity's financial position, including the strategies being adopted on capital structure and treasury policy; and

(c)   the activities and expenditure of the period that can be regarded as a form of investment in the future.

Highlights and summary indicators

Financial statements and accompanying information sometimes include amounts, ratios, and other computations that attempt to distil key information about the reporting entity's financial performance and financial position. Such highlights and summary indicators cannot, on their own, provide a basis for meaningful analysis or prudent decision-making. It is therefore essential that they are not presented in a way that exaggerates their importance.   **7.19**

That having been said, well-presented highlights and summary indicators are useful to users who: **7.20**

(a)   require only very basic information, such as the amount of sales or dividends; or

(b)   will proceed to a detailed appraisal of all the financial information, since highlights and summary indicators may suggest particular aspects of the information that need to be analysed further.

As already mentioned, financial statements are a means of communication. Therefore, notwithstanding the limited usefulness of highlights and summary indicators, if such information is provided it needs to be presented in a manner and context that enable its meaning to be communicated to users. This will often entail explaining the reasons for changes in the relative or absolute size of the figures from one period to the next.   **7.21**

Chapter 8: Accounting for interests in other entities

Financial statements need to reflect the effect on the reporting entity's financial performance and financial position of its interests in other entities. This involves various measurement and presentation issues. Rather than being dealt with in the relevant chapters and therefore in isolation from each other, they are dealt with together in this chapter. For similar reasons, various consolidation issues are dealt with in this chapter.

PRINCIPLES

- Single entity financial statements and consolidated financial statements present the interests the reporting entity may have in other entities from different perspectives.
- In single entity financial statements, interests in other entities are dealt with by focusing on the income and (depending on the measurement basis adopted) capital growth arising from those interests.
- In consolidated financial statements, the way in which interests in other entities are dealt with depends on the degree of influence involved.
  - (a)   An interest that involves control of another entity's operating and financial policies is dealt with by incorporating the controlled entity as part of the reporting entity.
  - (b)   An interest that involves joint control of, or significant influence over, another entity's operating and financial policies is dealt with by recognising the reporting entity's share of that other entity's results and resources in a way that does not involve showing those results and resources in the performance statement and balance sheet as if they were controlled by the reporting entity.
  - (c)   Other interests are dealt with in the same way as any other asset.
- Although consolidated financial statements are the financial statements of the group as a whole, they are prepared from the perspective of the parent's shareholders and, as a result, ultimately focus on the parent's ownership interest in its subsidiaries. The effect on benefit flows of any outside equity interest in the subsidiaries will therefore be separately identified.
- Consolidated financial statements reflect the whole of the parent's investment in its subsidiaries, including purchased goodwill.
- A transaction involving the amalgamation of two or more reporting entities is reflected in the consolidated financial statements in accordance with its character. Therefore, a transaction that is of the character of:
  - (a)   an acquisition is reflected in the consolidated financial statements as if the acquirer purchased the acquiree's assets and liabilities as a bundle of assets and liabilities on the open market.
  - (b)   a merger is reflected in the consolidated financial statements as if the new reporting entity, comprising all the parties to the transaction, had always existed.

EXPLANATION

Degree of influence

8.1   Although an entity's interest in a second entity may take many different forms, the key factor in determining its effect on the first entity's financial performance and financial position is the degree of influence it exerts over the operating and financial policies of the second entity involved.

The degree of influence exerted will depend on the facts of each particular case. **8.2** Ownership of shares is usually the main basis of influence because owning voting rights confers influence. However, while the level of ownership of shares and voting rights is indicative of an entity's relationship with its investee,* it is not by itself sufficient to define the relationship because of the possible effect of other agreements, arrangements or working practices. Indeed, any mixture of share ownership, voting rights or agreements, formal or informal, can provide a means of influencing or controlling another entity.

The highest degree of influence that an entity can have over an investee is control. As **8.3** Chapter 2 explains, control comprises the ability to deploy the economic resources involved and to benefit (or to suffer) by their deployment. Other degrees of influence have these same aspects; in effect, the ability to influence the activities of the investee with a view to gaining economic benefits from that influence.

Although it is possible to classify the degree of influence that an entity has over its **8.4** investee in an almost infinite number of ways, it is sufficient for the purposes of the Statement to classify it as follows:

(a) *Control*—where the entity controls the investee.
(b) *Joint control*—where the entity does not itself control the investee, but shares control through some form of arrangement jointly with others.
(c) *Significant influence*—where the entity has neither control nor joint control, but exerts a degree of influence over the investee's operating and financial policies that is at the least a significant influence and at the most just short of control.
(d) *Lesser or no influence*—where any influence that the entity has over the investee's operating and financial policies is less than a significant influence.

Reflecting the effects of interests in other entities

Consolidated financial statements and single entity financial statements

The effect on the entity's financial performance and financial position of an interest **8.5** in an investee is reflected in the first entity's financial statements in different ways depending on the type of financial statements being prepared.

(a) Financial statements of a reporting entity whose boundary has been drawn by reference to the scope of its direct control—in other words, single entity financial statements—take a narrow view of the reporting entity's interests in other entities and, as a result, reflect only the income and (depending on the measurement basis adopted) capital growth arising from those interests.
(b) Financial statements of a reporting entity whose boundary has been drawn by reference to the scope of the entity's control (both direct and indirect)—in other words, consolidated financial statements—present an expanded view of the reporting entity's interests in other entities that reflects the reporting entity's influence over, and its accountability for, the activities and resources of its investees.

Because of the narrow view taken in single entity financial statements, interests in **8.6** other entities are treated like any other asset in those financial statements. On the other hand, the treatment of such interests in the consolidated financial statements will depend on the degree of influence involved, as explained more fully in paragraphs 8.7-8.10.

Although it is not necessary for an interest in another entity to involve an investment, that is the most common form. For simplicity, therefore, this chapter uses the term 'investee' to mean 'entity in which the first entity has an interest'.

Interests involving control

8.7   As already explained in Chapter 2, if an entity controls* one or more other entities, the controlling entity (the parent) and the controlled entities (the subsidiaries) will be a reporting entity (the group). The group's financial statements (consolidated financial statements) are prepared by aggregating the gains, losses, assets, liabilities and cash flows of the parent and its subsidiaries. This ensures that the effects on the parent's financial performance and financial position of its interests in its subsidiaries are fully reflected in the financial statements.

8.8   Paragraphs 8.11-8.13 consider various issues relating to the preparation of consolidated financial statements.

Interests involving joint control or significant influence

8.9   If the reporting entity shares joint control of, or exercises significant influence over, another entity, it will be directly involved in and affected by that other entity's activities. Its interest in its investee is therefore reflected in the consolidated financial statements in a way that:

(a)   recognises the reporting entity's share of the results and net assets of the investee; and

(b)   does not misrepresent the extent of its influence over the investee—in other words, it does not treat activities and resources that are not controlled by the reporting entity as if they are controlled by the reporting entity. At present, the only commonly recognised method of accounting for investments that achieves this end is the equity method of accounting. This is where the reporting entity's share of the results and net assets of the investee are brought into its financial statements on a single line in the performance statement and balance sheet respectively. There are different types of equity method, usually involving the presentation of a greater or lesser degree of information than that just described, but in each case the reporting entity's share of the net results and of the position of the investee are not combined in the primary financial statements on a line-by-line basis with the reporting entity's own activities and resources.

Interests involving lesser or no influence

8.10   If the reporting entity's influence over its investee does not involve control, joint control or significant influence, the reporting entity will not be accountable for the investee's activities. In such circumstances, the only amounts recognised in the consolidated financial statements will be the investment (if any) and any income derived therefrom.

Consolidated financial statements

8.11   The gains, losses, assets, liabilities and cash flows of all subsidiaries are reflected in full in the consolidated financial statements, even if a subsidiary is not wholly-owned. This reflects the parent's ability, through its control, to deploy both its own economic resources and those of its subsidiaries even where it does not wholly own the subsidiaries.

For simplicity, the discussion in the chapter assumes that the ultimate parent has 'direct' control of all its subsidiaries. However, it applies equally to situations in which the parent controls its subsidiary through its control of that subsidiary's parent. It also applies when the parent's control of its subsidiary is achieved through the combined influence of itself and other entities that it controls.

However, the extent of outside ownership interests is an important factor in con- **8.12**
sidering the parent's access and exposure to the results of its subsidiaries. Therefore,
although consolidated financial statements are the financial statements of the group
as a whole, they ultimately focus on the parent's ownership interest in the entities
within its control. The effect of any outside equity interest (the minority interest) on
benefit flows will therefore be separately identified in the financial statements.

Purchased goodwill (sometimes referred to as goodwill arising on acquisition) is the **8.13**
part of a parent's investment in its subsidiary that has not been attributed to the
separately identified assets and liabilities of the subsidiary. Although it is not an asset
in itself, it is part of a larger asset (the investment). Furthermore, it does not
represent a decrease in that larger asset's value and therefore a loss: it represents *part*
of the asset's value. Therefore, if the parent's investment is to be fully reflected in the
group's financial statements and the parent is to be held accountable for its investment in full, purchased goodwill needs to be recognised as if it were an asset.

Accounting for business combinations

An amalgamation of two or more reporting entities—sometimes referred to as a **8.14**
business combination—can take a number of different forms. All these forms can be
characterised as either:

(a) a purchase—such transactions are commonly referred to as acquisitions; or
(b) a uniting of interests—such transactions are commonly referred to as mergers.

An acquisition is a business combination that is in the nature of an acquisition by **8.15**
one entity of another entity. The transaction therefore results in an existing reporting
entity being enlarged and is reflected in the consolidated financial statements by
treating the assets and liabilities of the entity acquired and the purchased goodwill as
if the transaction was the purchase of a bundle of assets and liabilities on the open
market.

On the other hand, a merger is in the nature of a coming together of two entities to **8.16**
form a new reporting entity. This is reflected in the financial statements of the new
reporting entity comprising all the parties to the transaction as if that entity had
always existed. As a result, the assets and liabilities of each party to the transaction
are treated as if they were acquired by the new reporting entity at the time that they
were acquired by the party concerned: none of the assets or liabilities is treated as
being purchased at the time of the business combination as part of a bundle of assets
and liabilities on the open market.

Contents of Appendices

Appendix I
The Statement and the legal requirements concerning the form and content of financial statements

INTRODUCTION

1   The Statement was not developed within the constraints imposed by the law. As a result, there was a risk that inconsistencies could arise between the Statement and the law that would invalidate the Statement as a frame of reference for standard-setting. The purpose of this appendix is to:

(a)   explain why the approach was nevertheless adopted;

(b)   describe the main respects in which legislation is inconsistent with the Statement; and

(c)   explain why these inconsistencies do not prevent the Statement from being an acceptable framework to be used by standard-setters.

WHY THE STATEMENT WAS NOT DEVELOPED WITHIN LEGAL CONSTRAINTS

2   There are two main reasons why the Statement was developed without taking into account the legal frameworks that regulate financial reporting. First, on a practical level, the Statement is intended to be relevant to the financial statements of *all* profit-oriented organisations, and it would have been difficult to develop a set of principles that was both consistent in all respects with all the legal requirements relating to such financial statements and also sufficiently detailed for the Board's purposes. Secondly, there was a concern that, if the Statement of Principles was developed within the constraints imposed by the law, it would be denied the opportunity to assist in the development of that law. This would have been a pity because it is framework documents such as the Statement that provide direction to the development of such legal frameworks and help to ensure that such development takes place in a coherent way.

3   It is nevertheless recognised that the approach would not have been appropriate, despite these reasons, if there had been many significant differences between the Statement and the various legal frameworks involved. Paragraphs 4-13 describe briefly the main inconsistencies that exist at present between the principles in the Statement and the legal requirements that apply in Great Britain to the form and content of individual and group accounts prepared by companies that are not banks or insurance companies. Paragraph 14 concludes that these inconsistencies do not invalidate the Statement as a frame of reference to be used in the development of accounting standards for such entities. Although the paragraphs below deal with one type of entity only, the inconsistencies identified are believed to be typical of those that exist in the case of other entities. As a result, it is believed that the conclusion reached in paragraph 14 can be applied to all entities.

MAIN INCONSISTENCIES BETWEEN THE STATEMENT AND THE LAW

The reporting entity

4   Section 258 of the Companies Act 1985 identifies subsidiary undertakings by a list of tests. Although these tests are founded mainly on the concept of control, they may in

some cases either fail to identify as a subsidiary undertaking an entity that is controlled by another or they may identify as a subsidiary undertaking an entity that is not controlled. Hence those companies that are identified as subsidiary undertakings by applying the Companies Act tests may not always correspond to those the Statement would identify as subsidiaries.*

In practice, this difference tends not to be a problem because of other factors. For example, the Act's requirements concerning the treatment of subsidiaries that involve severe long-term restrictions on the rights of the parent reduce the practical effect of this difference in approach, as do the treatments of quasi-subsidiaries and jointly controlled entities required by FRS 5 'Reporting the Substance of Transactions' and FRS 9 'Associates and Joint Ventures'.   **5**

The elements of financial statements

One implication of the Act is that proposed dividends are required to be recognised as liabilities, although they would not usually fall within the Statement's definition of a liability.†   **6**

Recognition

The Act states that only profits realised at the balance sheet date can be included in the profit and loss account (Schedule 4, paragraph 12). The Act defines realised profits, but does so in a way that allows the precise meaning of the term to be capable of development. The Statement adopts a different approach in which, rather than restrict the recognition of gains in the statement or statements of financial performance to those that are realised, it restricts their recognition to those that can be measured with sufficient reliability and for which sufficient evidence exists that they have actually arisen.   **7**

Although the Statement and the Act clearly adopt different approaches, the way in which the Act defines a realised profit means that the exact effect of this difference is not clear. The potential inconsistency described in paragraph 12—concerning the number and format of the statement or statements of financial performance—makes the effect of the difference in approach even less clear.   **8**

Measurement

The Statement envisages that, if the current value basis of measurement is regarded as the most appropriate measurement basis for a particular category of assets, all assets within that category will be recognised at their current value. That current value will, furthermore, be determined by reference to the value to the business rule. However, although the Act (Schedule 4, paragraph 31) permits: **9**

(a)   intangible fixed assets other than goodwill to be included at current cost;
(b)   tangible fixed assets to be included at market value or current cost;

Editor's note: While there have been changes to the details of this section of CA 1985 since the Statement of Principles was published, the point made in this paragraph remains broadly valid.

†*Editor's note: This is no longer the case, as the Companies Act was amended with effect for accounting periods beginning on or after 1 January 2005. Therefore proposed dividends no longer fall to be treated as a liability under the Companies Act 1985.*

(c)   fixed asset investments to be included at market value or directors' valuation; and

(d)   current asset investments and stocks to be included at current cost,

current assets other than investments and stocks are required to be included in the balance sheet at the lower of cost and net realisable value (Schedule 4, paragraphs 22 and 23). Thus, for some assets the Act requires the use of measurement bases that may differ from those suggested by the Statement. It also means that the Act does not permit the use of the range of current value measures that are envisaged by the Statement's value to the business rule.*†

10   The Statement also envisages that some categories of liabilities could be measured at current value, whereas the Act does not specifically refer to this possibility.

Presentation

11   The balance sheet and profit and loss account of a company must be prepared in accordance with one of the statutory formats (although these formats may, subject to certain constraints, be adapted to suit the particular circumstances). Some specific items are also required to be shown in every profit and loss account (Schedule 4, paragraphs 1-3). These requirements may necessitate a presentation that differs in certain respects from what would be suggested by following the presentation principles set out in the Statement. These inconsistencies can, however, generally be overcome by providing additional disclosures.

12   The Act requires in most cases the preparation of, inter alia, a profit and loss account in one of the statutory formats and it makes no reference to any other performance statement. The Statement, on the other hand, is less specific about the format of any profit and loss account provided, and it acknowledges that entities may prepare more than one performance statement or may alternatively prepare a single statement that is more comprehensive than the profit and loss account the Act requires. As such, although the preparation of a profit and loss account in one of the statutory formats would meet the requirements of the Act *and* (subject to the point made in the preceding paragraph) be consistent with the Statement, other presentations possible under the Statement may not comply with the Act's requirements.

13   The Act requires the profit and loss account to show separately the aggregate amount of any dividends paid and proposed (Schedule 4, paragraph 3(7)).‡ The Statement envisages that, as dividends are a distribution to owners and not a gain or loss, they will *not* be reported in a performance statement but will instead be reported in the reconciliation of movements in shareholders' funds.

THE STATEMENT AS A SATISFACTORY FRAME OF REFERENCE FOR STANDARD-SETTERS

14   Of the inconsistencies identified above, probably the most significant is the one relating to the recognition of gains: the Act requires that only profits realised at the

---

Legislative proposals are being prepared by the European Commission to permit a wider use of current values in the measurement of financial instruments. This demonstrates both that the constraints of law are not immutable and that desirable change can be motivated by accounting developments guided by the framework described in the Statement.

†*Editor's note: Changes to Schedule 4 (and Schedule 8) since the Statement of Principles was published now allow the use of fair values in more circumstances than are assumed in the Statement.*

‡*Editor's note: This has now changed, and dividends proposed are no longer shown in a profit and loss account. This is as a result of FRS 21 coming into force, with equivalent changes to the FRSSE, as well as the revision of CA 1985.*

balance sheet date are to be recognised in the profit and loss account, whilst the Statement adopts an approach that is not based on the notion of realisation. Although, as already mentioned, the precise effect of this difference in approach is not clear, the Board does not believe that this difference in approach invalidates the statement as a satisfactory frame of reference for standard-setting. It notes, for example, that realised profits are defined in the Act in a way that is intended to enable its meaning to develop. It also notes that EU legislative proposals are being prepared which, if implemented, would permit the recognition in the profit and loss account of certain gains that might not be regarded by some as realised profits. This suggests that the legal requirements in this area are capable of evolving in response to the reasonable demands of accounting practice. In such circumstances, it seems appropriate that the Statement of Principles should try to give direction to, rather than merely follow, such changes.

As the Statement is expected to provide direction to the development of the legal   **15**
requirements concerning the form and content of financial statements, the Board's expectation is that inconsistencies between the Statement and legal requirements will tend to be temporary and that the law will not be a permanent impediment to the adoption of approaches consistent with the Statement.

NORTHERN IRELAND AND THE REPUBLIC OF IRELAND

The following table gives the references to legislation in Northern Ireland and in the   **16**
Republic of Ireland corresponding to the legislation in Great Britain referred to in this appendix.

Paragraph	Great Britain Companies Act 1985	Northern Ireland Companies (Northern Ireland) Order 1986	Republic of Ireland*
4	Section 258	Article 266	GAR 1992, Regulation 4
7	Schedule 4, paragraph 12	Schedule 4, paragraph 12	CAA 1986, section 5
9	Schedule 4, paragraphs 22 and 23	Schedule 4, paragraphs 22 and 23	CAA 1986, Schedule, paragraphs 10 and 11
9	Schedule 4, paragraph 31	Schedule 4, paragraph 31	CAA 1986, Schedule, paragraph 19
11	Schedule 4, paragraphs 1-3	Schedule 4, paragraphs 1-3	CAA 1986, section 4
13	Schedule 4, paragraph 3(7)	Schedule 4, paragraph 3(7)	CAA 1986, section 4(15)

* CAA 1986 = Companies (Amendment) Act 1986
  GAR 1992 = European Communities (Companies: Group Accounts) Regulations 1992

Appendix II
The Statement and IASC's 'Framework for the preparation and presentation of financial statements'

1   It is the Board's view that a common set of principles is necessary to achieve further harmonisation in international accounting practice. For that reason, the Statement of Principles is based on the International Accounting Standards Committee's 'Framework for the Preparation and Presentation of Financial Statements' (the IASC Framework), which was itself derived from the Statements of Financial Accounting Concepts issued in the USA by the Financial Accounting Standards Board.*

2   This appendix compares the Statement with the IASC Framework and highlights and explains the main differences. The appendix does not deal in detail with any other conceptual documents, although the principles and explanations in the Statement are similar to those set out in the conceptual statements issued by other leading accounting standard-setters, including those in Australia, Canada, New Zealand and the USA.

3   The Statement is much more detailed than the IASC Framework, which means that it deals with many issues on which the IASC Framework is silent. These differences in detail have not been treated as differences for the purposes of this appendix.

4   The commentary below follows the structure and order of the Statement and it uses the headings of that document.

INTRODUCTION

5   There are no significant differences between the two documents.

CHAPTER 1: THE OBJECTIVE OF FINANCIAL STATEMENTS

6   The objective of financial statements set out in the Statement is almost identical to that set out in the IASC Framework, although there are two minor differences.

    (a)   The Statement's description of the objective refers specifically to information that is useful for 'assessing the stewardship of management', while the IASC Framework's description does not. However, as both documents refer to providing information that is useful for making economic decisions and agree that the reason why the stewardship of management is assessed is to take economic decisions, this difference is of no practical effect.

    (b)   Although the objective in the IASC Framework refers to providing information about changes in financial position while the Statement's objective does not, it is clear from both documents that it is expected that such information will be provided.

7   Only the Statement refers to the notion of a defining class of user (the investor). This notion is used in the Statement to give a focus that would otherwise be lacking for the selection and presentation of financial information.

---

*Editor's note: The IASC framework was adopted by the International Accounting Standards Board (IASB) in April 2001.

CHAPTER 2: THE REPORTING ENTITY

This chapter deals with two separate reporting entity issues: identifying a reporting **8** entity and determining the boundary of a reporting entity. The two documents adopt a similar approach to the first issue, although neither deals with it in any detail. Only the Statement deals with the second issue. It was thought that the Statement would not be complete if it did not explain which activities and resources should be reported on in financial statements.

CHAPTER 3: THE QUALITATIVE CHARACTERISTICS OF FINANCIAL INFORMATION

In most respects the two documents adopt the same approach to the desirable **9** characteristics of financial information. For example, they both identify relevance, reliability, understandability and comparability as qualitative characteristics, and they describe those characteristics in very similar terms. There are however some differences:

(a)   Materiality is not treated in the same way in that, while the IASC Framework treats it as a subcategory of relevance and describes it as a *quantitative* characteristic, the Statement treats it as a separate characteristic and describes it as relating to both the nature and size of the item. However, the overall effect of the two documents will be the same because they agree that information should be included in the financial statements if it might reasonably be expected to influence the economic decisions of users and it can be excluded if it is not expected to have that effect.
(b)   The IASC Framework describes the accruals basis and the going concern assumption as underlying assumptions. Although the Statement does not give them such a title, their role and the way in which they are described are, to all intents and purposes, the same.

These differences are minor and will have little effect in practice.

CHAPTER 4: THE ELEMENTS OF FINANCIAL STATEMENTS

The two documents adopt the same approach to this subject, although: **10**

(a)   the elements that the Statement refers to as ownership interest, gains and losses are referred to by the IASC Framework as equity, income and expenses;
(b)   the Statement defines as elements contributions by owners and distributions to owners while, in the IASC Framework, these are merely movements within owners' equity.

These differences are essentially concerned with nomenclature rather than principle.

CHAPTER 5: RECOGNITION IN FINANCIAL STATEMENTS

Both the IASC Framework and the Statement approach the initial recognition **11** process by asking whether a new asset or liability has been created (or an existing one has been added to), then applying recognition criteria to that new (or increased) asset or liability to determine whether it should be recognised. Both documents also adopt similar recognition criteria, although they are described in slightly different terms in that, while the Statement's criteria require, inter alia, that sufficient evidence should exist that the new asset or liability has been created or that there has been an addition to an existing asset or liability, the IASC Framework refers to it needing to be probable that any future economic benefit associated with the item will flow to or from the enterprise. The Board believes that this difference reflects a development in accounting thought since the publication of the IASC Framework.

12   The Statement deals with derecognition, a topic not covered in the IASC Framework. The Board believes that this reflects the fact that, as transactions and the instruments transacted have become more complex since the IASC Framework was published, greater emphasis than hitherto needs to be placed on the principles that underlie the derecognition process.

CHAPTER 6: MEASUREMENT IN FINANCIAL STATEMENTS

13   The Statement and the IASC Framework adopt different approaches to the subject of measurement. For example, while the IASC Framework briefly describes the measurement bases that might be used, the Statement goes on to develop a framework to guide the choice of measurement basis. It also discusses the measurement bases much more extensively than the IASC Framework and it uses the value to the business model to decide between alternative measures of current value. This material has been included in the Statement in order to help introduce a degree of consistency into the measurement process. For similar reasons, the Statement, unlike the IASC Framework, discusses subsequent remeasurement in detail.

CHAPTER 7: PRESENTATION OF FINANCIAL INFORMATION

14   The IASC Framework contains very little on this subject. The Statement nevertheless deals with it because the Board believes that good presentation is an essential element in effective financial reporting.

CHAPTER 8: ACCOUNTING FOR INTERESTS IN OTHER ENTITIES

15   Although the IASC Framework contains no material on this subject, the Statement deals with it because the Board believes it is an important issue.

Appendix III
Background to issues dealt with in the Statement

BACKGROUND TO THE STATEMENT OF PRINCIPLES

When the Board was formed in 1990, it recognised that, if it was to develop **1**
accounting standards that were consistent with each other, it needed to develop a
coherent frame of reference to guide it in its work. Indeed, one of the recommendations of the committee that recommended that the Accounting Standards Board
should be established was that further work on a conceptual framework should be
undertaken.*

The frame of reference that the Board subsequently developed became the basis for a **2**
series of discussion drafts of individual chapters that were published in the early
1990s. Those drafts were revised and reissued together, in 1995, as an exposure draft
of the complete Statement of Principles for Financial Reporting. A second exposure
draft was published in March 1999.

The Board started to develop its frame of reference by looking to the accounting **3**
principles that, at that time, underpinned accounting practice in the UK. However,
those principles were found wanting because:

(a) they were developed piecemeal at different times in response to particular
     problems and were not consistent with one another.
(b) some of them had not kept up with modern developments. For example, many
     had their origins in accounting solutions devised for manufacturing companies
     with an emphasis on accounting for stocks and fixed assets. Some of those
     principles are not as effective in coping with the more complex financial
     reporting issues of today, such as those arising from intangibles and complex
     contractual arrangements.
(c) some of them were out of line with developments internationally.

The Board therefore concluded that, although many of those principles continued to
be relevant and appropriate, some would have to be modified and some additional
principles were needed to produce a framework that was consistent, up-to-date and
reasonably complete.

The main principles in this Statement are derived from that informal frame of **4**
reference. Many of them have been examined closely over the last nine years during
the development of new accounting standards (and the revision of existing ones) and
have benefited from that examination, with some of the principles being refined and
some developed further as a result. Furthermore, a number of the principles now
play significant roles in accounting standards and have found general acceptance.
For example:

(a) FRS 2 'Accounting for Subsidiary Undertakings' uses the reporting entity con-
     cept described in Chapter 2 of the Statement;
(b) FRS 4 'Capital Instruments', FRS 5 'Reporting the Substance of Transactions',
     FRS 7 'Fair Values in Acquisition Accounting' and FRS 12 'Provisions, Con-
     tingent Liabilities and Contingent Assets' are based on the definitions of assets
     and liabilities set out in Chapter 4; and

*See 'The Making of Accounting Standards': Report of the Review Committee under the Chairmanship of Sir
Ron Dearing CB (1988).

(c)   FRS 11 'Impairment of Fixed Assets and Goodwill' uses the recoverable amount notion described in Chapter 6.

Therefore, although in places the Statement may sound unfamiliar, it actually bears a close resemblance to much of existing practice.

5   The Board has in its work programme a number of projects that are exploring further some of the issues covered in the Statement. Although it is possible that this work may result in changes needing to be made to what is said in the Statement, that does not create a difficulty because the Board does not regard the Statement as its final word on the principles that underlie financial reporting. Accounting thought is continually evolving and it is only to be expected that the Statement will need to be revised from time to time.*

6   The remainder of this appendix discusses, and sets out the rationale behind, aspects of the Statement that would benefit from a fuller explanation. The discussion is organised by reference to the sections in the Statement (ie Introduction, Chapter 1 etc) to which they relate.

INTRODUCTION

General purpose financial statements

7   The Statement classifies financial information into special purpose financial reports, general purpose financial reports and other financial information, and explains that annual financial statements prepared to comply with companies legislation are examples of a general purpose financial report. Describing annual financial statements in this way is not intended to imply that such statements are all-purpose financial statements, because they are not. The term 'general purpose financial reports' has been used because it highlights the difference between special purpose financial reports and other financial reports.

Smaller entities and not-for-profit entities

8   Although the principles set out in the Statement are intended to be relevant to the financial statements of all profit-oriented entities, it has been prepared with large entities uppermost in mind: accounting issues are generally at their most complex where large entities are involved and it is only right that the Board should seek to prepare a Statement that will help it to address these issues. That does not mean, however, that the Statement would have been fundamentally different had it been prepared with smaller entities in mind. The principles in Chapters 2-8, for example, would have remained unchanged. As the financial statements of small entities probably have a narrower range of users and tend to be used for a narrower range of purposes, the objective of those financial statements might have needed to be expressed differently. This difference would, however, be one of application rather than principle.

9   The Statement explains that, although it is relevant to the financial statements of not-for-profit entities, some of the principles need to be re-expressed and others need

---

*Editor's note: The most obvious subsequent product of the Statement is FRS 18 'Accounting Policies' which is based on a number of the principles covered in the Statement.

changes of emphasis before they can be applied to that sector. The Board has requested its Public Sector and Not-for-profit Committee to study the issue and make recommendations in due course.*

CHAPTER 1: THE OBJECTIVE OF FINANCIAL STATEMENTS

A wide range of users

Although it is sometimes suggested that the legal position is that a company's annual   **10** financial statements are prepared for its shareholders only, neither companies legislation nor, so far as the Board is aware, case law suggests that the courts should or would take such a view. Indeed, since companies legislation requires companies to put a copy of their annual financial statements on the public record, it is clear that the law envisages that those financial statements will be used by the public at large— a much wider range of people than existing shareholders. This position is reflected in the Statement.

It is not reasonable to expect financial statements to meet the information needs of   **11** everyone who chooses to use them. They focus on the common interest that users have in the financial performance and financial position of the reporting entity as a whole. That means that they do not address the special interests that many users will have and they do not satisfy all users equally well. Users will therefore usually need to supplement the information they obtain from financial statements with information from other sources.

Investors as the defining class of user

The Statement explains that investors are to be treated as the defining class of user.   **12** Investors are interested in financial information on the reporting entity as a whole. Other users require exactly the same information as a frame of reference against which to judge the more specialised information they obtain from other sources. For example, although potential lenders will gather specialised information from a range of sources to help them decide whether, and at what price, to lend to the reporting entity, they will also use information derived from the financial statements of the entity as a whole.Economic decisions and stewardship

The Statement explains that the financial statements provide information that is   **13** useful in assessing stewardship and for making economic decisions. At first sight these objectives—assessing stewardship and making economic decisions—seem mutually exclusive because stewardship reports are often thought to be limited to the use of historical cost whereas decision-useful reports are thought to require the comprehensive use of current values. The Board does not, however, believe that they are mutually exclusive.

(a) Stewardship reports are limited to using historical cost only if a very narrow view is taken of what a stewardship report entails. However, the Statement takes a broad view in that it regards stewardship as being not merely about the safekeeping and proper use of an entity's resources but also about their efficient and profitable use.

(b) The need for financial statements to provide information that is relevant for making economic decisions seems to suggest that more assets and liabilities than hitherto should be measured at current value. However, it does not

*Editor's note: This issue has now led the ASB to issue a proposed interpretation of the Statement of Principles for Public Benefit Entities.

necessarily follow that there needs to be comprehensive use of current values: experience shows that much historical cost information can also have predictive value.

CHAPTER 2: THE REPORTING ENTITY

Identifying a reporting entity

14   Although those who are entrusted with resources by others are accountable to them for those resources and should therefore probably provide them with a set of accounts, when the Statement considers which entities should prepare financial statements it is considering a much wider issue: which entities should prepare financial statements and make them available to a wide range of users? This is a complex issue and, as it has been the practice in the UK and the Republic of Ireland for legislators to determine which profit-oriented entities should prepare financial statements, is an issue that the Statement discusses in general terms only.

The boundary of the reporting entity

15   There are two main approaches that can be used to determine the boundary of a reporting entity: one approach concentrates wholly on ownership (the proprietary view) and the other concentrates on the group as an entity, unified and encompassed by the parent's control (the entity view).

(a)   The proprietary view regards ownership and the resulting access to benefits as of paramount interest to users. As a result, ownership is used to provide the basis of consolidated financial statements. On a strict proprietary view, the investor's ability to influence or even control its investee is irrelevant: consolidated financial statements will aggregate the parent's direct and indirect ownership interests in a proportional consolidation (the line-by-line consolidation of the investor's share of each item) as this shows the parent's access to benefit from all of its investments.

(b)   On the entity view, the parent's ability to control its subsidiaries is all-important, regardless of the size of its ownership interest in the activities of the entity that it directs. The consolidated financial statements therefore consolidate in full the assets and liabilities of any entity that the parent controls—even if the entity is not a wholly-owned subsidiary—and the parent's ownership interest and any outside equity interest in a subsidiary are treated merely as part of an overall ownership interest.

16   The appropriate perspective to use depends on the relative usefulness of the information each provides. The Statement regards the entity view as providing the most useful information, and therefore uses control to determine the boundary of a reporting entity.

Single entity financial statements of parent companies

17   The Statement explains that, once a reporting entity has been identified, two boundaries will be drawn—one based on direct control and one based on direct plus indirect control. This means that, where a company is controlled by another company, both companies will be reporting entities as will the group of companies that they constitute.

18   Some commentators suggest that, because the activities and resources of a parent and its subsidiary are difficult to separate economically, it is inappropriate for an

entity to report on the activities it carries out and the resources it holds in isolation from the activities and resources of its subsidiaries. This view suggests that companies preparing consolidated financial statements should not also be expected to prepare single entity financial statements. Some might argue that the present legal position—in which parent companies are not required to prepare profit and loss accounts—could be used to support this view. However, if it is inappropriate for a parent to report on the activities it carries out and the resources it holds in isolation from the activities and resources of its subsidiaries, it would seem to follow that it is also inappropriate for those subsidiaries to report in isolation from their parent; in other words, subsidiaries whose activities and resources are reported on in consolidated financial statements should not be required to prepare single entity financial statements. That is not the present legal position.

The Board's view is that, although the usefulness of single entity financial statements   **19** has decreased as the structure of business organisations has become more complex, single entity financial statements—whether for parent companies or subsidiaries— still have a role to play, albeit a much narrower role than that of the financial statements of the group as a whole. Drawing a boundary by reference to direct control reflects this view.

CHAPTER 3: THE QUALITATIVE CHARACTERISTICS OF FINANCIAL INFORMATION

Materiality and relevance

Although the Statement of Principles expects the financial information given in   **20** financial statements to be both material and relevant, it describes these two characteristics in similar ways. In particular, the tests of whether information is material and whether it is relevant are both based on influencing the economic decisions of users—although relevance involves *the ability* to influence decisions while materiality involves the reasonable expectation that decisions *will* be influenced. Similarly, both characteristics involve a consideration of the size and nature of the items or information involved. There are, however, important differences between the characteristics.

(a)   Materiality is a threshold characteristic—a discrete test—used to decide whether to include information in the financial statements. If an item of information is material, it will need to be included and if it is not, it need not be included. Relevance, on the other hand, is a 'continuous' quality; one item of information will be more relevant than another and the information given will (subject to other constraints) be that which is the most relevant.

(b)   Put simply, characteristics such as relevance, reliability, comparability and understandability provide direction to the financial reporting selection process, thus enabling the usefulness of the information to be maximised. The materiality test, which recognises that some information has to be left out of financial statements, then asks whether the information is useful enough to be given.

Prudence

Accounting practice has evolved significantly over the last thirty years and, as a   **21** result, has become much more sophisticated in the way that it seeks to reflect the nuances of business activity. This is acknowledged in the Statement through its emphasis on specific principles rather than general notions and assumptions. In the case of prudence, for example, the smoothing of reported profits has become as great a concern as their overstatement and, as a result, the deliberate understatement of assets and gains and the deliberate overstatement of liabilities and losses are no longer seen as a virtue. Indeed, it is now widely accepted that the use of prudence in this way can seriously affect the quality of the information provided.

22   This has been reflected in international practice for some time now. For example, the framework documents published by the International Accounting Standards Committee (IASC) and the accounting standard-setters in Canada and the USA describe prudence (sometimes referred to as conservatism) as involving a degree of caution in the exercise of the judgements needed in making the estimates required under conditions of uncertainty. The standard-setters in Australia and New Zealand have adopted a similar approach, although they have subsumed prudence within the notion of reliability.

23   The Statement's approach to prudence is consistent with the way in which accounting practice has evolved and with the approaches adopted internationally. It:

(a)   treats prudence as one of the attributes that need to be present if financial information prepared under conditions of uncertainty is to be reliable;

(b)   describes prudence as the inclusion of a degree of caution in the exercise of the judgements needed in making the estimates required under conditions of uncertainty; and

(c)   makes it clear that prudence is a potentially biased concept and that care should therefore be taken to ensure that it does not result in the deliberate and systematic understatement of assets and gains and the overstatement of liabilities and losses.

Understandability

24   In an ideal world, financial statements would be prepared in a way that makes them intelligible to all users, regardless of their level of expertise or experience. However, as entities are increasingly complex and many of them enter into increasingly complex transactions, it can be difficult to represent their financial performance and financial position both faithfully and in a way that can be understood by all users. The Statement recognises this by explaining that the basis on which financial statements are to be prepared is that users have a reasonable knowledge of business and economic activities and accounting.

25   This means that financial statements will not always be capable of being understood by all users. Although this sounds an unsatisfactory state of affairs, it is, in fact, the present position. Users who do not have a reasonable knowledge of business and economic activities and accounting use the services of those who have that knowledge to help them derive information from the financial statements.

Relevance versus reliability

26   Although it is sometimes argued that the characteristics of relevance and reliability are often in conflict, such conflicts are exaggerated. As the Statement makes clear, reliability is a hurdle to be cleared (ie is the information sufficiently reliable?), not a competition that has to be won (ie is this information the most reliable?). This means that the approach to be adopted in preparing the financial statements will be the one that is the most relevant of those that are reliable. A conflict will therefore arise between the characteristics only in the rare circumstances in which the reliable approaches are not relevant and the relevant approaches are not reliable.

CHAPTER 4: THE ELEMENTS OF FINANCIAL STATEMENTS

Identifying the elements

In essence, the preparation of financial statements involves finding the best way to **27** categorise financial information about the transactions and other events that affect a reporting entity's financial performance and financial position. It is generally accepted that the best way to report this information is to focus on what has happened to the entity over the reporting period (for example, revenues and expenses, gains and losses, cash flows, and capital transactions) and what is its position as a result (assets and liabilities). These effects will inevitably have to be reflected in the financial statements in a highly aggregated form, and the Statement envisages that order will be imposed on this process by specifying and defining the classes of items (elements) that encapsulate the key aspects of those effects.

Should the definitions of the elements be interrelated and, if so, which definitions should be based on which?

The performance statement elements and the balance sheet elements could, in theory, **28** be defined independently of each other. However, such an approach risks leaving gaps or creating areas of overlap. It would also have been inconsistent with the notion that primary financial statements should articulate, a fundamental and long-accepted characteristic of such statements. The Statement therefore uses definitions that are interrelated.

It follows that either the balance sheet elements should be based on the definitions of **29** the performance statement elements or vice versa. As the accounting process is essentially about allocating the effects of transactions and other events to reporting periods, it might seem more logical to define the performance statement elements and then base the balance sheet elements on those definitions. This approach requires the use of robust definitions of the performance statement elements in order to provide the unity, order and discipline needed for an effective framework. Those definitions need therefore to be precise and comprehensive, and they need to avoid placing reliance on management intent or referring to generally accepted accounting principles. However, accounting standard-setters around the world have carried out an exhaustive search for robust definitions of performance statement elements and have concluded that such definitions do not exist. On the other hand, robust definitions of balance sheet elements do exist. The Statement, like all the conceptual documents developed by all the leading accounting standard-setters around the world, therefore defines the balance sheet elements and bases the definitions of the performance statement elements on those definitions.

How many elements should there be and how should they be defined?

It is obviously both important and necessary to distinguish cash flows and capital **30** transactions from other things that happen to an entity. It is, however, not immediately clear whether it is important or realistic to treat, say, all the credits in the performance statement as a single type of element and expect them to meet a single definition (and all the debits as a separate single element and expect them to meet a single definition). A similar question arises concerning the debits and credits in the balance sheet.

Reporting on the financial performance and financial position of an entity involves **31** providing an account of the reporting entity's use of, and command over, economic resources. The Statement therefore bases its definitions on flows and prospective flows of future economic benefits embodied in economic resources. Thus, assets are defined as 'rights or other access to future economic benefits controlled by an entity as a result of past transactions or events', liabilities as 'obligations of an entity to transfer economic benefits as a result of past transactions or events', and, apart from ownership interest, no other balance sheet elements are identified.

32   As the items in the profit and loss account are typically referred to as revenue, expenses, gains and losses, it would seem natural to use similar terminology in the Statement. Indeed, that is the approach adopted in the USA by the Financial Accounting Standards Board. However, as it has been decided that the definitions of the performance statement elements should be based on the definitions of the balance sheet elements, it is possible to define the credits in the performance statement in terms of increases in net assets not resulting from capital contributions and the debits in the performance statement as decreases in net assets not resulting from capital distributions. The issue the Board therefore had to consider was whether more comprehensive definitions should be used in order to differentiate between types of performance statement debits and credits.

33   At the moment, the Board is carrying out a review of FRS 3 'Reporting Financial Performance'. As part of this work, it is considering possible ways of restructuring the performance statements that are provided at present. It may be that, as a result of this work, it will conclude that gains and revenue should be differentiated from each other. Similarly, it may be concluded that losses and expenses should be differentiated from each other. However, until then, there does not appear to be sufficient reason for the Statement of Principles to distinguish revenue from gains and expenses from losses. It therefore identifies one credit performance statement element (gains) and one debit performance statement element (losses). IASC's 'Framework for the Preparation and Presentation of Financial Statements' adopts the same approach, except that it calls the two elements 'income' and 'expenses'.

34   It is recognised that, by not differentiating gains from revenue (and losses from expenses), items that are commonly referred to as 'revenue' (and 'expenses') have had to be referred to in the Statement as 'gains' (and 'losses') or vice versa. That is not ideal but is not regarded as sufficient reason to justify differentiation.

Implications of the approach adopted to specifying and defining the elements

35   Under the approach adopted in the Statement, if costs are to be carried forward (ie deferred) to a subsequent period to match income being earned in that period, they will need to meet the definition of an asset (and meet the relevant recognition criteria). This will mean, inter alia, asking whether the costs to be deferred constitute future economic benefits. It is recognised that the application of this approach in practice will result in some of the costs that are at present deferred and shown as assets being recognised as losses because they do not represent future economic benefits. Similarly, some of the credit items that are deferred at present in the balance sheet might, under the principles, need instead to be recognised as income because they do not qualify as liabilities. Nevertheless, the Board believes that the approach provides what is needed for an effective framework.

36   It is worth noting that the Statement's approach is almost identical to the approach adopted in the conceptual documents of IASC and the other leading accounting standard-setters around the world, including the standard-setters in Australia, Canada, New Zealand and the USA. It is also worth noting that the definitions of assets and liabilities set out in the Statement already provide the foundation for several UK accounting standards, including FRS 5 'Reporting the Substance of Transactions'. Indeed, through the Board's own work, the work of UK bodies preparing Statements of Recommended Practice, and the work of the

aforementioned standard-setters, the elements and their definitions have for many years now been playing an important role in the standard-setting process throughout the world.

It has nevertheless been suggested by some that the approach means that the balance sheet will become the main accounting statement and the performance statement will be relegated to a statement of residual amounts. It means nothing of the kind. First, the Board accepts that the primary focus of users is on the performance statement and that this is likely to remain the case for the foreseeable future. Secondly, using definitions of assets and liabilities to define gains and losses is merely a means to an end—that end being to improve the quality of financial statements in general and, through the discipline that the definitions will impose on the recognition of gains and losses, performance statements in particular.   **37**

It has also been suggested in the past that the approach means that the profit or loss for the period will be the difference between the opening and closing balance sheets, adjusted for capital contributions and distributions. Although it is correct to say that the amount of the difference is equal to the total of all the components of financial performance, it is an oversimplification to suggest that this means that the difference is regarded as the profit or loss for the period. The Board has spent much time and energy since its inception on improving the way in which financial performance is reported, and the focus of this work has been the need to move away from placing so much significance on any one line of the performance statement. FRS 3 —which was issued in 1992—makes it clear that the focus of performance reporting should be on the components of financial performance and on the characteristics of those components. This is also the approach adopted in the Statement.   **38**

Finally, some commentators have suggested that, by defining the performance statement elements by reference to movements in assets and liabilities, the Statement will shift the focus of accounting away from transactions. The Board does not agree with this suggestion. Accounting is a process that is primarily concerned with allocating the effects of transactions to reporting periods, and the approach set out in the Statement will achieve exactly that.   **39**

CHAPTER 5: RECOGNITION IN FINANCIAL STATEMENTS

The role of realisation in the Statement

The Statement envisages that all gains and losses will be recognised in a performance statement. Furthermore, as the Statement does not specify different recognition criteria for different performance statements (or for different parts of the same, single performance statement), realised profits may conceivably be shown alongside unrealised profits.   **40**

An alternative approach might have been to base recognition on the notions of realisation and realised profit. For example, the Statement could have assumed that only realised gains would be recognised in the performance statements. It could, alternatively, have assumed that realised gains would be recognised in one performance statement (or in one part of a single performance statement) while unrealised gains would be recognised in a second performance statement (such as the statement of total recognised gains and losses) or in a separate part of the single performance statement. The main reasons that are usually put forward in support of this approach, and the counter-arguments, are set out below.   **41**

Companies legislation

42   Companies legislation specifies that companies should include only profits realised at the balance sheet date in their profit and loss account. It could be argued that, for this reason alone, realisation should be acknowledged as a recognition criterion.

43   However, the development of the Statement has not been constrained by legal requirements because the Board believes that accounting practice evolves best if regard is had in documents such as the Statement of Principles to what is deemed to be right rather than what is required by law. The implications of this for the Statement of Principles are considered in Appendix I.

Distributable profits

44   Companies making distributions of income to their shareholders must make them from distributable profits. It is therefore sometimes argued that, if users are to have a proper understanding of the level of sustainable dividends and of the prospects of dividend growth, it is important that the level of distributable profits is reported and that dividends paid and payable are reported in the context of those distributable profits.

45   However, in practice—and particularly for a group—the potential for distributions, whether from profits or return of capital, is dependent on many factors, including companies legislation in the countries in which the operations are carried out, corporate structure, currency and dividend controls, and the entity's financial adaptability. In these circumstances it is unrealistic to suppose that distributability per se can serve as a primary focus of the presentation of financial performance.

Realisation as a criterion for determining what should be recognised

46   Regardless of the legal requirements, it is a desirable attribute of items included in the profit and loss account, particularly gains, that their existence should be reasonably certain. The realisation notion is one means of determining whether the existence of a gain is reasonably certain. However, in the Board's view, it is not necessarily the best way.

47   The realisation notion originally came into use in order to protect creditors from the uncertainties that arise in accruals accounting, and its purpose was to try to ensure that profits were not overstated and that there was sufficient cash available to distribute those profits without the company becoming insolvent. In this guise the notion was understood to involve the conversion into cash of non-cash resources and rights to cash.

48   As business practice developed, so the purpose of the notion changed and it came to be used to ensure that only gains that were reasonably certain and unlikely to reverse were included in the profit and loss account. Similarly, its meaning evolved to include conversion into claims to cash.

49   Developments since then have, however, made even this version of the notion irrelevant in some areas. For example, it is now often possible to be reasonably certain that a gain exists and to measure that gain reliably even if no disposal has occurred. Furthermore, the introduction of cash flow statements means that cash-based profit and loss accounts have largely been outgrown. A number of attempts have been made to update the notion to take account of these developments. For example, it has been suggested that changes in the market value of securities for which an active

market exists are also realised, even though no claim to cash is involved. Similarly, some have suggested that the test should be extended to include gains that are realisable, in other words capable of being converted into cash or claims for cash.

However, in general it is not a good idea to bend a term so that it has a meaning **50** other than its natural meaning. A better approach in this case would seem to be to focus on the underlying objective and then encapsulate that objective in the recognition criteria. It is the Board's view that the objective is to recognise a gain only if there is reasonable certainty that it exists and if it can be measured reliably. The initial recognition and subsequent remeasurement criteria set out in the Statement are designed to achieve that end.

CHAPTER 6: MEASUREMENT IN FINANCIAL STATEMENTS

The mixed measurement system

For many years entities carried all their assets and liabilities in their balance sheet at **51** historical cost. However, the relevance of such measures in periods when prices have moved markedly has often been questioned and, to counteract this perceived fading relevance, the majority of larger UK listed companies now measure some of their assets at current values and some at cost. (According to Company Reporting No 80 (February 1997), more than 65 per cent of the companies in that journal's database had adopted this approach.)

Although this approach is commonly referred to as the modified historical cost basis, **52** that term is something of a misnomer because it is a mixed measurement system. The Statement therefore uses this latter term.

The Statement explains that assets and liabilities have a number of different **53** monetary attributes that could be represented in financial statements. It also explains that the single most important characteristic that distinguishes these monetary attributes is whether they are based on historical cost or current value. The remainder of its discussion is expressed in terms of this distinction.

In theory, the Statement could have adopted one of three broad approaches to **54** measurement.

(a) It could have assumed strict adherence to historical cost in all circumstances. In view of existing practice, this would have been a revolutionary step. For example, when respondents to the Accounting Standards Committee's ED 51 'Accounting for fixed assets and revaluations' (1990) were asked whether it would be practicable to prohibit the carrying of selected fixed assets at revalued amounts, 96 per cent of those who answered the question believed it was not practicable.

(b) It could have assumed the adoption of a comprehensive current value system under which all assets and all liabilities, or at least the great majority of them, would be carried at current values. This too would have been a revolutionary step and it is not an approach that the Board has considered in the past nor is it one that it expects to consider in the foreseeable future.

(c) It could have assumed the continuance of the present, mixed measurement system. Previous consultations have shown that the majority of respondents favour this approach. For example, just over 70 per cent of those who responded to the Board's Discussion Paper 'The Role of Valuation in Financial Reporting' (1993) favoured continued use of the mixed measurement system.

55   In preparing the Statement, the Board has assumed the continued use of the mixed measurement system. This system has the advantage of requiring reporting entities to match the measurement basis used for a particular category of assets or liabilities to the circumstances relating to that category and, in so doing, acknowledges the different trade-offs between relevance and reliability in the measurement of different types of balance sheet item. The system is also flexible in that the mix of historical cost and current value can be changed as accounting thought develops and markets evolve.

Choosing a measurement basis

56   The main focus of the Statement's chapter on measurement is the measurement debate that is of most relevance today—what mix of historical cost and current value should be used. The Statement provides a framework to guide the choice of an appropriate measurement basis for each balance sheet category and thereby helps to apply some discipline and logic to the selection process. This should result in an improvement in the relevance and comparability of the information being provided.

57   The characteristic of relevance plays a major role in the framework described in the Statement. Current value information can be relevant in two rather different ways.

(a)   For assets that generate cash flows indirectly through use—such as property, plant and equipment—a current value gives an up-to-date measure of the total resources invested and provides a basis for calculating the current cost of using the asset within the period.

(b)   For assets and liabilities that represent rights to specific future cash flows— financial assets and financial liabilities—the market price gives the value of those cash flows at that time.

58   Whereas for the first type of balance sheet item some degree of choice may be appropriate for each entity in determining whether market values should be used as the basis of measure, the same flexibility may be less appropriate if extended to the second type because of their more direct relationship to future cash flows.

59   As the Statement explains, although the factors that should be used to determine the most appropriate measurement basis are unlikely to change, the measurement basis that best meets those factors may. Indeed, the Board expects that, if markets develop, greater use will probably be made of current value because measures that were once thought not relevant or unreliable may become both the most relevant measure and reliable. That having been said, it is unlikely that the framework set out in the Statement will suggest the use of current values other than for certain types of investments, commodity stocks and financial instruments. Under the framework, the practice of measuring some fixed assets at current value is also likely to continue.

CHAPTER 7: PRESENTATION OF FINANCIAL INFORMATION

Presentation of gains and losses

60   The way in which information on financial performance is presented is of fundamental importance to the quality of financial reporting. The Statement does not, however, deal with this matter in any detail, primarily because it is an issue that is being actively considered in the Board's review of FRS 3. If that review identifies principles about the presentation of gains and losses that could usefully be incorporated in the Statement, the Statement will be amended.

Dividends paid and payable

The Statement makes it clear that, regardless of the number of performance state- **61**
ments prepared, they will deal with gains and losses only and no items that are not
gains and losses will be recognised in them. As dividends paid and payable are not
gains and losses, the Statement envisages that they will not be included in the profit
and loss account or other performance statement. Although that seems logical—
dividends are not a component of financial performance—it is not consistent with
how such dividends are dealt with at present. This issue is being considered as part of
the review of FRS 3*.

Recycling

The Statement explains that items that are not gains or losses are not included in the **62**
performance statement, which means that the notion of recycling† is not consistent
with the principles. This is another matter that is being considered in the review of
FRS 3.

CHAPTER 8: ACCOUNTING FOR INTERESTS IN OTHER ENTITIES

Accounting for minority interests

As explained in paragraph 15, there are, in theory, two opposing perspectives from **63**
which minority interests could be viewed when preparing consolidated financial
statements: one perspective concentrates wholly on ownership (the proprietary view)
and the other on the group as an entity, unified and encompassed by the parent's
control (the entity view). The Statement considers that the entity view provides the
most useful information and therefore uses control to determine the boundary of a
reporting entity.

One implication of adopting the entity view is that all subsidiaries, even those that **64**
are not wholly-owned, will be fully consolidated. However, it is useful to show the
extent of outside ownership interests since this is an important factor in determining
the interest of investors in the reporting entity as a whole. This important feature—
ownership—would be ignored if the focus was exclusively on the entity view. The
Statement therefore envisages that any outside equity interests in entities within the
parent's control will be identified in the primary financial statements. In this way the
financial statements will reflect the parent's ownership interests in the entities within
its control.

Editor's note: See FRED 22 'Revision of FRS 3 "Reporting Financial Performance".'

†By 'recycling' the Statement means recognising a gain or loss in the performance statement in one period then,
in a later period, recognising some or all of that gain or loss under a different heading in either the same or a
different performance statement because the nature of the item is deemed to have changed in some way.

Part Three

Accounting Standards

Foreword to accounting standards

(Issued June 1993)

Contents

Foreword to accounting standards

INTRODUCTION

1   This foreword explains the authority, scope and application of accounting standards issued or adopted by the Accounting Standards Board (the Board).* The foreword also considers the procedure by which the Board issues accounting standards and their relationship to International Accounting Standards, issued by the International Accounting Standards Committee.

2   The Board at its meeting on 24 August 1990 agreed to adopt the 22 extant Statements of Standard Accounting Practice (ssaps) issued by the Councils of the six major accountancy bodies following proposals developed by the Accounting Standards Committee (ASC).† Adoption by the Board gave these ssaps the status of accounting standards within Part VII of the Companies Act 1985,‡ (the Act) and within Part VIII of the Companies (Northern Ireland) Order 1986§ (the Order). This status will apply until each ssap is amended, rescinded or replaced by new accounting standards.

3   Accounting standards developed by the Board are designated Financial Reporting Standards (frss). Accounting standards developed by the ASC and adopted by the Board continue to be known as ssaps.

4   frss are based on the Statement of Principles for Financial Reporting currently in issue, which addresses the concepts underlying the information presented in financial statements. The objective of this Statement of Principles is to provide a framework for the consistent and logical formulation of individual accounting standards. The framework also provides a basis on which others can exercise judgement in resolving accounting issues.

5   The Board may issue pronouncements other than frss, including the Urgent Issues Task Force 'Abstracts'. The Board will indicate the authority, scope and application of pronouncements other than frss as they are issued. UITF Abstracts are the subject of a separate foreword.

---

*The Accounting Standards Board is a committee of The Accounting Standards Board Limited. The Accounting Standards Board Limited is prescribed as a standard setting body for the purposes of Section 256(1) of the Companies Act 1985 with effect from 20 August 1990 by The Accounting Standards (Prescribed Body) Regulations 1990 (S.I. 1990 No. 1667). The Accounting Standards Board Limited is prescribed as a standard setting body for Northern Ireland for the purposes of Article 264(1) of the Companies (Northern Ireland) Order 1986 with effect from 15 October 1990, by the Accounting Standards (Prescribed Body) Regulations (Northern Ireland) 1990 (S.R. 1990 No. 338).

†Prior to 1 August 1990 accounting standards in the United Kingdom and Republic of Ireland were issued by the Councils of the six major accountancy bodies following proposals developed by the ASC. Since 1 August 1990 the Board has taken over the role of issuing accounting standards applicable in the United Kingdom. The Institute of Chartered Accountants in Ireland issues accounting standards applicable in the Republic of Ireland.

‡References to the Companies Act 1985 are to that Act as amended by, inter alia, the Companies Act 1989 and the Companies Act 1985 (Bank Accounts) Regulations 1991 (S.I. 1991 No. 2705).

§References to the Companies (Northern Ireland) Order 1986 (S.I. 1986 No. 1032 (N.I. 6)) are to that Order as amended by, inter alia, the Companies (Northern Ireland) Order 1990 (S.I. 1990 No. 593 (N.I. 5)), the Companies (No. 2) (Northern Ireland) Order 1990 (S.I. 1990 No. 1504 (N.I. 10)) and the Companies (1986 Order) (Bank Accounts) Regulations (Northern Ireland) Order (S.R. 1992 No. 258).

AIMS OF THE ACCOUNTING STANDARDS BOARD

The aims of the Board are set out in the document 'The Accounting Standards **6**
Board – Statement of Aims'.

AUTHORITY OF ACCOUNTING STANDARDS

FRSs issued and SSAPs adopted by the Board are 'accounting standards' for the pur- **7**
poses of the Act, which requires accounts, other than those prepared by small or
medium-sized companies (as defined by the Act), to state whether they have been
prepared in accordance with applicable accounting standards and to give particulars
of any material departure from those standards and the reasons for it. References to
accounting standards in the Act are contained in paragraph 36A of Schedule 4,
paragraph 49 of Part I of Schedule 9 and paragraph 18B of Part I of Schedule 9A.*
The equivalent references in the Order are in paragraph 36A of Schedule 4, paragraph 49 of Part I of Schedule 9 and paragraph 18B of Part I of Schedule 9A.

Directors of companies incorporated under the Companies Acts are required by the **8**
Act to prepare accounts that give a true and fair view of the state of affairs of the
company, and where applicable the group, at the end of the financial year and of the
profit or loss of the company or the group for the financial year.

The Consultative Committee of Accountancy Bodies (CCAB) is committed to pro- **9**
moting and supporting compliance with accounting standards by its member bodies
and by their members, whether as preparers or auditors of financial information.

The Councils of the CCAB bodies therefore expect their members who assume **10**
responsibilities in respect of financial statements to observe accounting standards.
The Councils have agreed that:

(a) where this responsibility is evidenced by the association of members' names
     with such financial statements in the capacity of directors or other officers,
     other than auditors, the onus will be on them to ensure that the existence and
     purpose of accounting standards are fully understood by fellow directors and
     other officers. Members should also use their best endeavours to ensure that
     accounting standards are observed and that significant departures found to be
     necessary are adequately disclosed and explained in the financial statements.
(b) where members act as auditors or reporting accountants, they should be in a
     position to justify significant departures to the extent that their concurrence
     with the departures is stated or implied. They are not, however, required to
     refer in their report to departures with which they concur, provided that ade-
     quate disclosure has been made in the notes to the financial statements.

The CCAB bodies, through appropriate committees, may enquire into apparent **11**
failures by their members to observe accounting standards or to ensure adequate
disclosure of significant departures.

The Board notes the continuing application of previously adopted SSAPs in the **12**
Republic of Ireland through their on-going promulgation by the Institute of Chartered Accountants in Ireland (ICAI). It further notes ICAI's intention of maintaining
close liaison with the Board on promulgating, with appropriate modifications for
legal differences, FRSs for application in the Republic of Ireland. The objective of the
Board and ICAI is a regime of accounting standards common to both the United
Kingdom and the Republic of Ireland.

**Editor's note: Also paragraph 56 of the new Schedule 9A inserted by the Companies Act 1985 (Insurance
Companies Accounts) Regulations 1993 (S.I. 1993 No. 3246).*

SCOPE AND APPLICATION OF ACCOUNTING STANDARDS

13   Accounting standards are applicable to financial statements of a reporting entity that are intended to give a true and fair view of its state of affairs at the balance sheet date and of its profit or loss (or income and expenditure) for the financial period ending on that date. Accounting standards need not be applied to immaterial items.

14   Accounting standards should be applied to United Kingdom and Republic of Ireland group financial statements (including any amounts relating to overseas entities that are included in those financial statements). Accounting standards are not intended to apply to financial statements of overseas entities prepared for local purposes.

15   Where accounting standards prescribe information to be contained in financial statements, such requirements do not override exemptions from disclosure given by law to, and utilised by, certain types of entity.

COMPLIANCE WITH ACCOUNTING STANDARDS

16   Accounting standards are authoritative statements of how particular types of transaction and other events should be reflected in financial statements and accordingly compliance with accounting standards will normally be necessary for financial statements to give a true and fair view.

17   In applying accounting standards it is important to be guided by the spirit and reasoning behind them. The spirit and reasoning are set out in the individual FRSs and are based on the Board's Statement of Principles for Financial Reporting.

18   The requirement to give a true and fair view may in special circumstances require a departure from accounting standards. However, because accounting standards are formulated with the objective of ensuring that the information resulting from their application faithfully represents the underlying commercial activity, the Board envisages that only in exceptional circumstances will departure from the requirements of an accounting standard be necessary in order for financial statements to give a true and fair view.

19   If in exceptional circumstances compliance with the requirements of an accounting standard is inconsistent with the requirement to give a true and fair view, the requirements of the accounting standard should be departed from to the extent necessary to give a true and fair view. In such cases informed and unbiased judgement should be used to devise an appropriate alternative treatment, which should be consistent with the economic and commercial characteristics of the circumstances concerned. Particulars of any material departure from an accounting standard, the reasons for it and its financial effects should be disclosed in the financial statements. The disclosure made should be equivalent to that given in respect of departures from specific accounting provisions of companies legislation.

20   The Financial Reporting Review Panel (the Review Panel) and the Department of Trade and Industry have procedures for receiving and investigating complaints regarding the annual accounts of companies in respect of apparent departures from the accounting requirements of the Act, including the requirement to give a true and fair view.* The Review Panel will be concerned with material departures from accounting standards, where as a result the accounts in question do not give a true

---

Similar provisions exist for receiving and investigating complaints regarding the annual accounts of companies in respect of apparent departure from the accounting requirements of the Order.

and fair view, but it will also cover other departures from the accounting provisions of the Act. The Review Panel is empowered by regulations made under the Act to apply to the court for a declaration or declarator that the annual accounts of a company do not comply with the requirements of the Act and an order requiring the directors of the company to prepare revised accounts.* The Department of Trade and Industry has similar powers.

THE PUBLIC SECTOR

The prescription of accounting requirements for the public sector in the United   **21** Kingdom is a matter for the Government. Where public sector bodies prepare annual reports and accounts on commercial lines, the Government's requirements may or may not refer specifically either to accounting standards or to the need for the financial statements concerned to give a true and fair view. However, it can be expected that the Government's requirements in such cases will normally accord with the principles underlying the Board's pronouncements, except where in the particular circumstances of the public sector bodies concerned the Government considers these principles to be inappropriate or considers others to be more appropriate.

In the Republic of Ireland accounting standards will normally be applicable to   **22** reporting entities in the public sector as such entities are either established under companies legislation or are established under special legislation which requires them to produce financial statements which give a true and fair view.

THE ISSUE OF A FINANCIAL REPORTING STANDARD

Topics that become the subject of FRSs are identified by the Board either from its own   **23** research or from external sources, including submissions from interested parties.

When a topic is identified by the Board as requiring the issue of an FRS the Board   **24** commissions its staff to undertake a programme of research and consultation. This programme involves consideration of and consultation on the relevant conceptual issues, existing pronouncements and practice in the United Kingdom, the Republic of Ireland and overseas and the economic, legal and practical implications of the introduction of particular accounting requirements.

When the issues have been identified and debated by the Board a discussion draft is   **25** normally produced and circulated to parties who have registered their interest with the Board. When the issues require a more discursive treatment a discussion paper may be published instead. The purpose of either of these documents is to form a basis for discussion with parties particularly affected by, or having knowledge of, the issues raised in the proposals. An exposure draft of an accounting standard (a Financial Reporting Exposure Draft or FRED) is then published to allow an opportunity for all interested parties to comment on the proposals and for the Board to gauge the appropriateness and level of acceptance of those proposals.

The exposure draft is refined in the light of feedback resulting from the period of   **26** public exposure. There may follow another period of public or selective exposure prior to the issue of an FRS. Although the Board weighs carefully the views of interested parties, the ultimate content of an FRS must be determined by the Board's own judgement based on research, public consultation and careful deliberation about the benefits and costs of providing the resulting information.

The Review Panel does not operate in the Republic of Ireland.

APPLICABILITY OF AN ACCOUNTING STANDARD TO TRANSACTIONS ENTERED INTO BEFORE THE STANDARD WAS ISSUED

27   When a new accounting standard is issued the question arises whether its provisions should be applied to transactions which took place prior to the promulgation of the standard. The general policy of the Board is that the provisions of accounting standards should be applied to all material transactions irrespective of the date at which they are entered into. This is because exemption of certain transactions leads to similar transactions being accounted for differently in the same set of accounts, and can also hinder the comparison of the accounts of one entity with another.

28   In a few instances, application of the provisions of accounting standards to past transactions will entail a considerable amount of work and may result in information which is difficult for the user of accounts to interpret. In such a case, in drafting the standard, the Board will consider incorporating an exclusion for transactions which took place prior to the promulgation of the standard.

29   In some instances, a new standard may have unforeseen consequences where financial statements are used to monitor compliance with contracts and agreements. The most widespread example is the covenants contained in banking and loan agreements, which may impose limits on measures such as net worth or gearing as shown in the borrower's financial statements.

30   The Board considers that the developing nature of accounting requirements is a long-established fact that would be known to the parties when they entered into the agreement. It is up to the parties to determine whether the agreement should be insulated from the effects of a future accounting standard or, if not, the manner in which it might be renegotiated to reflect changes in reporting rather than changes in the underlying financial position.*† The Board, therefore, has no general policy of exempting transactions occurring before a specific date from the requirements of new accounting standards.

EARLY ADOPTION OF FINANCIAL REPORTING EXPOSURE DRAFTS‡

31   An exposure draft is issued for comment and is subject to revision. Until it is converted into an accounting standard the requirements of any existing accounting standards that would be affected by proposals in the exposure draft remain in force.

32   Some companies or other reporting entities may wish to provide additional information reflecting proposals in an exposure draft. In the Board's view there are two ways that this can be achieved:

(a)   insofar as the information does not conflict with existing accounting standards, it could be incorporated in the financial statements. It should be remembered, however, that the proposals may change before forming part of an accounting standard and the consequences of a change to the proposals should be considered.

The British Bankers' Association has indicated that it does not believe that problems arising from breaches in covenants consequent upon changes in accounting policies will occur frequently in practice.

†*Editor's note: It remains to be seen whether the view of the British Bankers' Association is altered by the introduction of FRS 17.*

‡*Similar conventions apply to discussion documents issued by the Board.*

(b)   the information could be provided in supplementary form.

REVIEWS OF ACCOUNTING STANDARDS

Accounting standards are issued against the background of a business environment that evolves over time. The Board is, therefore, receptive to comments on accounting standards, recognising that, for some, a substantial period may be needed before their effectiveness can be judged, while in other cases there may be special reasons why an earlier review is necessary. However, the Board believes that it will normally be appropriate to allow new accounting standards a period in which to become established before commencing a process of formal post-issue review.   **33**

ACCOUNTING STANDARDS AND THE LEGAL FRAMEWORK

In its debates on any accounting topic the Board initially develops its views by considering how its principles of accounting apply to the possible accounting options available for that topic. However, in deciding what is the most appropriate treatment the Board must also consider the environment in which its standards are to be applied. The legislation with which reporting entities must comply forms an important part of that environment. Accordingly, FRSs are drafted in the context of current United Kingdom and Republic of Ireland legislation and European Community Directives with the aim of ensuring consistency between accounting standards and the law.   **34**

The status of accounting standards under United Kingdom legislation is addressed in the Opinion by Miss Mary Arden QC* 'The true and fair requirement', which is published as an appendix to this Foreword.   **35**

INTERNATIONAL ACCOUNTING STANDARDS†

FRSs are formulated with due regard to international developments. The Board supports the International Accounting Standards Committee in its aim to harmonise international financial reporting. As part of this support an FRS contains a section explaining how it relates to the International Accounting Standard (IAS) dealing with the same topic. In most cases, compliance with an FRS automatically ensures compliance with the relevant IAS. Where the requirements of an accounting standard and an IAS differ, the accounting standard should be followed by entities reporting within the area of application of the Board's accounting standards.   **36**

WITHDRAWAL OF EXPLANATORY FOREWORD TO STATEMENTS OF STANDARD ACCOUNTING PRACTICE

The 'Explanatory Foreword' to SSAPs, issued by the ASC in May 1975 and revised in May 1986, is superseded by this Foreword and is accordingly withdrawn.   **37**

Now the Honourable Mrs Justice Arden.

†Editor's note: Now International Financial Reporting Standards.

Appendix
Accounting Standards Board– The true and fair requirement

OPINION

1   This Opinion is concerned with the effect of recent changes in the law on the relationship between accounting standards and the requirement in Sections 226 and 227 of the Companies Act 1985 (as amended) that accounts drawn up in accordance with the Companies Act 1985 give a true and fair view of the state of affairs of the company, and where applicable the group, at the end of the financial year in question and of the profit or loss of the Company or group for that financial year. (I shall call this requirement 'the true and fair requirement'). As is well known, the true and fair requirement is overriding. Thus both sections provide that where in special circumstances compliance with the requirements of the Act as to the matters to be included in the accounts would be inconsistent with the true and fair requirement there must be a departure from those requirements to the extent necessary to give a true and fair view (sections 226(5) and 227(6)). The meaning of the true and fair requirement, as it appeared in earlier legislation, was discussed in detail in the Joint Opinions which I wrote in 1983 and 1984 with Leonard Hoffmann Q.C. (now the Right Hon. Lord Justice Hoffmann).

2   As stated in those Opinions, the question whether accounts satisfy the true and fair requirement is a question of law for the Court. However, while the true and fair view which the law requires to be given is not qualified in any way, the task of interpreting the true and fair requirement cannot be performed by the Court without evidence as to the practices and views of accountants. The more authoritative those practices and views, the more ready the Court will be to follow them. Those practices and views do not of course stand still. They respond to such matters as advances in accounting and changes in the economic climate and business practice. The law will not prevent the proper development of the practices and views of accountants but rather, through the process of interpretation, will reflect such development.

3   Up to August 1990 the responsibility for developing accounting standards was discharged by the Accounting Standards Committee ('the ASC'). Since August 1990 that responsibility has been discharged by the Accounting Standards Board ('the Board'). The Foreword to Accounting Standards approved by the Board describes in particular the circumstances in which accounts are expected to comply with accounting standards. For this purpose the key paragraph is paragraph 16, which provides

> 'Accounting standards are authoritative statements of how particular types of transaction and other events should be reflected in financial statements and accordingly compliance with accounting standards will normally be necessary for financial statements to give a true and fair view.'

The Foreword also describes the extensive process of investigation and consultation which precedes the issue of a standard and explains that the major accountancy bodies expect their members to observe accounting standards and may enquire into apparent failures by their members to observe standards or ensure adequate disclosure of departures from them.

4   What is the role of an accounting standard? The initial purpose is to identify proper accounting practice for the benefit of preparers and auditors of accounts. However, because accounts commonly comply with accounting standards, the effect of the

issue of standards has also been to create a common understanding between users and preparers of accounts as to how particular items should be treated in accounts and accordingly an expectation that save where good reason exists accounts will comply with applicable accounting standards.

The Companies Act 1989 now gives statutory recognition to the existence of accounting standards and by implication to their beneficial role in financial reporting. This recognition is achieved principally through the insertion of a new section (Section 256) into the Companies Act 1985 and of a new disclosure requirement into Schedule 4 to that Act. Section 256 provides:

> '256. (1) In this Part 'accounting standards' means statements of standard accounting practice issued by such body or bodies as may be prescribed by regulations.
> (2) References in this Part to accounting standards applicable to a company's annual accounts are to such standards as are, in accordance with their terms, relevant to the company's circumstances and to the accounts.
> (3) The Secretary of State may make grants to or for the purposes of bodies concerned with –
> (a) issuing accounting standards,
> (b) overseeing and directing the issuing of such standards, or
> (c) investigating departures from such standards or from the accounting requirements of this Act and taking steps to secure compliance with them.
> (4) Regulations under this section may contain such transitional and other supplementary and incidental provisions as appear to the Secretary of State to be appropriate.'

In addition the notes to financial statements prepared under Schedule 4 must now comply with the following new requirement:*

> '36A. It shall be stated whether the accounts have been prepared in accordance with applicable accounting standards and particulars of any material departure from those standards and the reasons for it shall be given.'

Another significant change brought about by the 1989 Act is the introduction of a procedure whereby the Secretary of State or a person authorised by him may ask the Court to determine whether annual accounts comply with inter alia the true and fair requirement (Section 245B of the Companies Act 1985). The Financial Reporting Review Panel ('the Review Panel') has been authorised by the Secretary of State for this purpose. By agreement with the Department of Trade and Industry the ambit of the Review Panel is normally public and large private companies, with the Department exercising its powers in other cases.

The changes brought about by the Companies Act 1989 will in my view affect the way in which the Court approaches the question whether compliance with an accounting standard is necessary to satisfy the true and fair view requirement. The Court will infer from Section 256 that statutory policy favours both the issue of accounting standards (by a body prescribed by regulation) and compliance with them: indeed Section 256(3)(c) additionally contemplates the investigation of departures from them and confers power to provide public funding for such purpose. The Court will also in my view infer from paragraph 36A of Schedule 4 that (since

5

6

7

*This requirement also applies to group accounts drawn up under Schedule 4A. In addition the accounts of banking and insurance companies and groups drawn up under Schedules 9 and 9A must make the same disclosure. There is an exemption for small and medium-sized companies and for certain small and medium-sized groups.

the requirement is to disclose particulars of non-compliance rather than of compliance) accounts which meet the true and fair requirement will in general follow rather than depart from standards and that departure is sufficiently abnormal to require to be justified. These factors increase the likelihood, to which the earlier Joint Opinions referred, that the Courts will hold that in general compliance with accounting standards is necessary to meet the true and fair requirement.

8   The status of accounting standards in legal proceedings has also in my view been enhanced by the changes in the standard-setting process since 1989. Prior to the Companies Act 1989 accounting standards were developed by the ASC, which was a committee established by the six professional accountancy bodies who form the Consultative Committee of Accountancy Bodies ('the CCAB') and funded by them. The standard-setting process was reviewed by a committee established by the CCAB under the chairmanship of Sir Ron Dearing CB. The report of that Committee (the Dearing Report), which was published in 1988 and is entitled The Making of Accounting Standards, contained a number of recommendations, including recommendations leading to what are now paragraph 36A and Section 245B and the further recommendation that the standard-setting body should be funded on a wider basis. As a result of the implementation of these recommendations the standard-setting body no longer represents simply the views of the accountancy profession. Its members are appointed by a committee drawn from the Council of the Financial Reporting Council Limited ('the FRC'). The Council includes representatives of the Government, representatives of the business and financial community and members of the accountancy profession. Moreover, the Board is now funded, via the FRC, jointly by the Government, the financial community and the accountancy profession.

9   The statements referred to in Section 256 are of standard accounting practice. Parliament has thus recognised the desirability of standardisation in the accountancy field. The discretion to determine the measure of standardisation is one of the matters left to the Board. By definition, standardisation may restrict the availability of particular accounting treatments. Moreover the Act does not require that the practices required by a standard should necessarily be those prevailing or generally accepted at the time.

10   As explained in the earlier Joint Opinions in relation to statements of standard accounting practice, the immediate effect of the issue of an accounting standard is to create a likelihood that the court will hold that compliance with that standard is necessary to meet the true and fair requirement. That likelihood is strengthened by the degree to which a standard is subsequently accepted in practice. Thus if a particular standard is generally followed, the court is very likely to find that accounts must comply with it in order to show a true and fair view. The converse of that proposition, that non-acceptance of a standard in practice would almost inevitably lead a court to the conclusion that compliance with it was not necessary to meet the true and fair requirement, is not however the case. Whenever a standard is issued by the Board, then, irrespective of the lack in some quarters of support for it, the court would be bound to give special weight to the opinion of the Board in view of its status as the standard-setting body, the process of investigation, discussion and consultation that it will have undertaken before adopting the standard and the evolving nature of accounting standards.

11   The fact that paragraph 36A envisages the possibility of a departure from an 'applicable accounting standard' (in essence, any relevant standard: see section 256(2), above) does not mean that the Companies Act permits a departure in any case where the disclosure is given. The departure must have been appropriate in the particular case. If the Court is satisfied that compliance with a standard is necessary

to show a true and fair view in that case, a departure will result in a breach of the true and fair requirement even if the paragraph 36A disclosure is given.

Experience shows that from time to time and for varying reasons deficiencies in accounting standards appear. Following a recommendation in the Dearing Report, the Board has established a sub-committee called the Urgent Issues Task Force ('the UITF') to resolve such issues on an urgent basis in appropriate cases. The members of the UITF include leading members of the accountancy profession and of the business community. The agenda of the UITF is published in advance to allow for public debate. The UITF's consensus pronouncements (contained in abstracts) represent the considered views of a large majority of its members. When the UITF reaches its view, it is considered by the Board for compliance with the law and accounting standards and with the Board's future plans. If an abstract meets these criteria the Board expects to adopt it without further consideration. It will then be published by the Board. The expectation of the CCAB, the Board and the profession is that abstracts of the UITF will be observed. This expectation has been borne out in practice. Accordingly in my view, the Court is likely to treat UITF abstracts as of considerable standing even though they are not envisaged by the Companies Acts. This will lead to a readiness on the part of the Court to accept that compliance with abstracts of the UITF is also necessary to meet the true and fair requirement.

12

The Joint Opinions were particularly concerned with the effect of standards on the concept of true and fair. The approach to standards taken in the Joint Opinions is consistent with the approach of the Court in Lloyd Cheyham v. Littlejohn [1987] BCLC 303 at 313. In that case Woolf J. (as he then was) held that standards of the ASC were 'very strong evidence as to what is the proper standard which should be adopted'.

13

As regards the concept of true and fair, I would emphasise the point made in the Joint Opinions that the true and fair view is a dynamic concept. Thus what is required to show a true and fair view is subject to continuous rebirth and in determining whether the true and fair requirement is satisfied the Court will not in my view seek to find synonyms for the words 'true' and 'fair' but will seek to apply the concepts which those words imply.

14

It is nearly a decade since the Joint Opinions were written. Experience and legislative history since then have both illustrated the subtlety and evolving nature of the relationship between law and accounting practice. Accounting standards are now assured as an authoritative source of the latter. In consequence it is now the norm for accounts to comply with accounting standards. I would add this. Just as a custom which is upheld by the courts may properly be regarded as a source of law, so too, in my view, does an accounting standard which the court holds must be complied with to meet the true and fair requirement become, in cases where it is applicable, a source of law in itself in the widest sense of that term.

15

Mary Arden

Erskine Chambers
Lincoln's Inn
21st April 1993

[SSAP 4]
Accounting for government grants

(Issued April 1974; revised July 1990; amended October 1992 and December 2000)

Contents

Accounting for government grants

The provisions of this statement of standard accounting practice should be read in conjunction with the (Explanatory) Foreword to accounting standards *and need not be applied to immaterial items.*

Part 1 – Explanatory note

INTRODUCTION

Government assistance takes many forms, including grants, equity finance, sub- 1
sidised loans and advisory assistance. This statement deals with the accounting treatment and disclosure of government grants and other forms of government assistance. It is also indicative of best practice for accounting for grants and assistance from other sources.

Government grants are made in order to persuade or assist enterprises to pursue 2
courses of action which are deemed to be socially or economically desirable. The range of grants available is very wide and changes regularly, reflecting changes in government policy. More significantly different grants tend to be given on different terms as to the eligibility, manner of determination, manner of payment and conditions to be fulfilled. While this statement has been written in the context of grants available at the time of its preparation, it is intended that it will be equally applicable to other grants that may be created in the future.

For the purposes of this statement, the term 'government' is defined widely. Thus, it 3
includes not only the national government and all of the various tiers of local and regional government of any country, but also government agencies and 'non-departmental public bodies' (or quangos). It also includes the Commission of the European Communities and other EC bodies, together with other international bodies and agencies.

BASIC CONCEPTS

The 'accruals' concept requires that revenue and costs are accrued, matched with one 4
another so far as their relationship can be established or justifiably assumed, and dealt with in the profit and loss account of the period to which they relate. Government grants should therefore be recognised in the profit and loss account so as to match them with the expenditure towards which they are intended to contribute.

The 'prudence' concept requires that revenue and profits are not anticipated, but are 5
recognised by inclusion in the profit and loss account only when realised in the form either of cash or of other assets the ultimate cash realisation of which can be established with reasonable certainty. Accordingly, government grants should not be recognised in the profit and loss account until the conditions for their receipt have been complied with and there is reasonable assurance that the grant will be received.

In many cases, the grant-making body has the right to recover all or part of a grant 6
paid if the enterprise has not complied with the conditions under which the grant was made. On the assumption that the enterprise is a going concern, the application of the prudence concept does not normally require postponement of the recognition of the grant in the profit and loss account solely because there is a possibility that it might have to be repaid in the future. The enterprise should consider regularly whether there is a likelihood of a breach of the conditions on which the grant was

made. If such a breach has occurred, or appears likely to occur, and it is probable that some grant will have to be repaid, provision should be made for the liability.

7   The treatment for taxation purposes of government grants varies according to the terms of the grant and the particular statute or regulation under which it is made. At one extreme, some grants are free of all tax; at the other, some are taxed as income on receipt. It is sometimes suggested that because grants are taxed as income on receipt they are intended to be regarded as income and should be credited to the profit and loss account as they are received. However, the treatment of an item for tax purposes does not necessarily determine its treatment for accounting purposes, and immediate recognition in the profit and loss account may result in an unacceptable departure from the principle that government grants should be matched with the expenditure towards which they are intended to contribute. Any timing differences that may arise between a tax charge and the recognition of the corresponding credit in the profit and loss account should be dealt with in accordance with FRS 19 'Deferred tax'.*

ESTABLISHING THE RELATIONSHIP BETWEEN GRANTS RECEIVED AND EXPENDITURE

8   The matching of grants received and expenditure is straightforward if the grant is made as a contribution towards specified items of expenditure (whether capital, revenue or a particular combination) and is described as such.

9   Difficulties arise where the terms of the grant do not specify precisely the expenditure it is intended to meet, but use such phrases as 'to assist with a project' or 'to encourage job creation', or where the basis of calculation is related to two or more criteria (for example the capital expenditure incurred and the number of jobs created). In these circumstances, it is usually appropriate to consider the circumstances which give rise to the payment of instalments of the grant. If the grant is paid when evidence is produced that certain expenditure has been incurred, the grant should be matched with that expenditure. If the grant is paid on a different basis, it will usually be paid on the achievement of a non-financial objective, such as the creation of a specified number of new jobs; in these circumstances, the grant should be matched with the identifiable costs of achieving that objective, for example the cost of creating and, if applicable, maintaining for the required period the specified new jobs.

10   In some cases, there may be persuasive evidence that the actual expenditure towards which the grant is intended to contribute differs from the expenditure that forms the basis of payment. Such evidence may be contained in the formal application for the grant and subsequent correspondence and negotiation with the grant-making body. Where such evidence exists and is sufficiently persuasive, it is appropriate to match the grant received with the identified expenditure and this approach should be preferred to that outlined in the previous paragraph. For example, a discretionary grant might be given 'to assist with a project', with instalments of the grant being payable on the production of evidence that specific capital expenditure had been incurred; but it might be clear from correspondence that the grant had been made as a contribution to other costs as well, such as the provision of working capital or the meeting of initial training costs.

*Editor's note: References to FRS 19 added with effect for accounting periods ending on or after 23 January 2002. Previously, the reference was to SSAP 15.

Where a grant is paid on the achievement of a non-financial objective, the costs of   **11**
achieving that objective must be identified or estimated on a reasonable basis. For
example, if a grant is given on condition that jobs are created and maintained for a
minimum period, the grant should be matched with the cost of providing jobs for
that period, taking due account of the incidence of the costs incurred. As the costs of
job creation will often be higher in the early stages of a project, because of start-up
costs and the fact that a significant element of wage costs will initially be non-
productive, the matching principle may require that an equivalent, higher proportion
of the grant should be recognised in the earlier periods.

RECOGNITION OF GRANTS IN THE PROFIT AND LOSS ACCOUNT

Once the relationship between the grant and the related expenditure has been   **12**
established, the recognition of the grant in the profit and loss account will follow.
The grant should be recognised in the same period as the related expenditure.

In certain circumstances, government grants may be given for the immediate   **13**
financial support or assistance of an enterprise or for the reimbursement of costs
previously incurred, without conditions regarding the enterprise's future actions or a
requirement to incur further costs. Government grants may also be given to finance
the general activities of an enterprise over a specified period or to compensate for a
loss of income; in some instances, the extent of these grants may be such as to
constitute a major source of income for the enterprise. Grants that are payable on
this basis should be recognised in the profit and loss account of the period in respect
of which they are paid or, if they are not stated to be paid in respect of a specified
period, in the profit and loss account of the period in which they become receivable.

Where an enterprise is required to repay a government grant, either in whole or in   **14**
part, the full amount to be repaid, after taking into account any unamortised
deferred income relating to the grant, should be charged to the profit and loss
account immediately it becomes repayable. Where appropriate, the repayment
should be dealt with in accordance with FRS 3 'Reporting Financial Performance' as
an exceptional item.

BALANCE SHEET TREATMENT OF GRANTS

The application of this statement may result in part or all of a grant that has been   **15**
received not being recognised immediately in the profit and loss account. Any
unrecognised amounts should normally be included in the balance sheet as deferred
income. Where a grant is made as a contribution towards expenditure on fixed assets,
there are two possible balance sheet treatments, both of which result in the grant
being matched with the related expenditure in the profit and loss account. These are:

(a)   to treat the amount of the grant as deferred income which is credited to the
      profit and loss account by instalments over the expected useful economic life of
      the related asset on a basis consistent with the depreciation policy; or
(b)   to deduct the amount of the grant from the purchase price or production cost
      of the related asset, with a consequent reduction in the annual charge for
      depreciation.

It is considered that both treatments are acceptable and are capable of giving a true
and fair view. However, the CCAB has received Counsel's opinion that paragraphs
17 and 26 of Schedule 4 to the Companies Act 1985 have the effect of prohibiting
enterprises to which the legislation applies from accounting for grants made as a

contribution towards expenditure on fixed assets by deducting the amount of the grant from the purchase price or production cost of the related asset.

16   Where a government grant takes the form of a transfer of non-monetary assets, the amount of the grant is the fair value of the assets transferred.

DISCLOSURE

17   The financial statements should disclose the accounting policy adopted in respect of government grants in terms which make clear the method or methods adopted. The period or periods over which grants are credited to the profit and loss account should be disclosed insofar as this is practicable given the number and variety of grants that are being received. Normally, it will be sufficient to give a broad indication of the future periods in which grants already received will be recognised in the profit and loss account.

18   Where the results for the period have been affected materially by amounts credited in respect of government grants, and/or where the results of future periods are expected to be affected materially by the recognition in the profit and loss account of grants already received, it is important for an understanding of the financial statements that the effects on the results or the financial position of the enterprise should be disclosed.

19   Government assistance to an enterprise may also be given in a form other than grants, for example consultancy and advisory services, subsidised loans and credit guarantees. Where such assistance has had a material effect on the results for the period, the nature and, where measurable, the effects of the assistance should be disclosed.

20   Under SSAP 18 'Accounting for contingencies'* potential liabilities to repay grants should only be provided for to the extent that repayment is probable. A material contingent loss not so provided for should be disclosed, except where the possibility of repayment is remote.

Part 2 – Definition of terms

21   *Government* includes government and inter-governmental agencies and similar bodies whether local, national or international.

22   *Government grants* are assistance by government in the form of cash or transfers of assets to an enterprise in return for past or future compliance with certain conditions relating to the operating activities of the enterprise.

Part 3 – Standard accounting practice

23   Subject to paragraph 24 of this statement, government grants should be recognised in the profit and loss account so as to match them with the expenditure towards which they are intended to contribute. In the absence of persuasive evidence to the contrary, government grants should be assumed to contribute towards the expenditure

---

Editor's note: SSAP 18 has been superseded by FRS 12 'Provisions, contingent liabilities and contingent assets'. However, the introduction of FRS 12 has not materially altered the accounting requirements in respect of potential liabilities to repay grants, and accordingly the point made in this paragraph remains valid.

that is the basis for their payment. To the extent that grants are made as a contribution towards specific expenditure on fixed assets, they should be recognised over the expected useful economic lives of the related assets. Grants made to give immediate financial support or assistance to an enterprise or to reimburse costs previously incurred should be recognised in the profit and loss account of the period in which they become receivable. Grants made to finance the general activities of an enterprise over a specific period or to compensate for a loss of current or future income should be recognised in the profit and loss account of the period in respect of which they are paid.

The foregoing requirements are subject to the proviso that a government grant **24** should not be recognised in the profit and loss account until the conditions for its receipt have been complied with and there is reasonable assurance that the grant will be received.

Where the recognition in the profit and loss account of part or all of a grant that has **25** been received is deferred, the amount so deferred should be treated as deferred income. To the extent that the grant is made as a contribution towards expenditure on a fixed asset, in principle it may be deducted from the purchase price or production cost of that asset. The CCAB has received Counsel's opinion, however, that the option to deduct government grants from the purchase price or production cost of fixed assets is not available to companies governed by the accounting and reporting requirements of the Companies Act 1985, as outlined in paragraph 34.

Grants relating to leased assets in the accounts of lessors should be accounted for in **26** accordance with the requirements of SSAP 21 'Accounting for leases and hire purchase contracts'.

Potential liabilities to repay grants either in whole or in part in specified circum- **27** stances should only be provided for to the extent that repayment is probable. The repayment of a government grant should be accounted for by setting off the repayment against any unamortised deferred income relating to the grant. Any excess should be charged immediately to the profit and loss account.

DISCLOSURE

The following information should be disclosed in the financial statements: **28**

(a) the accounting policy adopted for government grants;
(b) the effects of government grants on the results for the period and/or the financial position of the enterprise;
(c) where the results of the period are affected materially by the receipt of forms of government assistance other than grants, the nature of that assistance and, to the extent that the effects on the financial statements can be measured, an estimate of those effects.

Potential liabilities to repay grants in specified circumstances should, if necessary, be **29** disclosed in accordance with paragraph 16 of SSAP 18 'Accounting for contingencies'.*

*__*Editor's note__: SSAP 18 was superseded by FRS 12 'Provisions, contingent liabilities and contingent assets' September 1998. The reference should be read as paragraph 91 of FRS 12.*

TRANSITIONAL PROVISIONS

30   Any adjustments arising as a result of a change in accounting policy to comply with the requirements of this statement should be accounted for as a prior year adjustment in accordance with FRS 3 'Reporting Financial Performance'.

APPLICATION TO SMALLER ENTITIES

30A   Reporting entities applying the Financial Reporting Standard for Smaller Entities currently applicable are exempt from this accounting standard.

DATE FROM WHICH EFFECTIVE

31   The accounting practices set out in this statement should be adopted as soon as possible. They should be regarded as standard accounting practice in respect of financial statements relating to accounting periods beginning on or after 1 July 1990.

Part 4 – Legal requirements in Great Britain and Northern Ireland

References are to the Companies Act 1985 and the Companies (Northern Ireland) Order 1986.

32   The balance sheet formats in Schedule 4 require that accruals and deferred income should be shown either under the heading 'Creditors' or separately as 'Accruals and deferred income'. This is relevant to the disclosure of deferred income in relation to government grants. (Standard paragraph 25).*

33   Paragraph 12 of Schedule 4 requires that the amount of any item shall be determined on a prudent basis and, in particular, that only profits realised at the balance sheet date shall be included in the profit and loss account. (Paragraph 91 of the Schedule defines realised profits in relation to a company's accounts as 'such profits of the company as fall to be treated as realised profits for the purposes of those accounts in accordance with principles generally accepted with respect to the determination for accounting purposes of realised profits at the time when those accounts are prepared'.) (Standard paragraph 24)†

34   Paragraph 17 of Schedule 4 requires that, subject to any provision for depreciation or diminution in value, the amount to be included in the balance sheet in respect of any fixed asset shall be its purchase price or production cost. Paragraph 26(1) states that the purchase price of an asset shall be determined by adding to the actual price paid any expenses incidental to its acquisition. The CCAB has received Counsel's opinion that these paragraphs have the effect of prohibiting enterprises to which the legislation applies from accounting for grants made as a contribution towards

---

*Editor's note: The same applies to small companies, adopting the special provisions available to them, under Schedule 8 to the Companies Act 1985.

†Editor's note: Paragraph 12 of Schedule 8 contains an identical requirement. Paragraph 91 of Schedule 4 is no longer in force. Instead, the definition of realised profits is contained in section 262(3) of the Companies Act 1985. The definition, while not identical, is similar to that quoted in the standard.

expenditure on fixed assets by deducting the amount of the grant from the purchase price or production cost of the related asset. (Standard paragraph 25)*

Paragraph 50 (2) of Schedule 4 provides that 'The following information shall be **35** given with respect to any other contingent liability not provided for:

(a)   the amount or estimated amount of that liability;
(b)   its legal nature; and
(c)   whether any valuable security has been provided by the company in connection with that liability and if so, what'. (Standard paragraph 29)†

Part 5 – Legal requirements in the Republic of Ireland

References are to the Companies (Amendment) Act 1986 and the Schedule to that Act unless otherwise stated.

Note 8 to the balance sheet formats in the Schedule provides that government grants **36** included in the item 'Accruals and deferred income' must be shown separately in a note to the accounts if not shown separately in the balance sheet. However, Note 8 does not impose an obligation to include government grants under 'Accruals and deferred income' and such grants may, therefore, be placed under a separate heading. This separate heading is often placed between liabilities and share capital/reserves. If a new heading is adopted (using Section 4(12)), the requirement under Note 8 to have a separate mention of the amount is not applicable. (Standard paragraph 25)

Section 5(c) of the Act requires that the amount of any item shall be determined on a **37** prudent basis and, in particular, that only profits realised at the balance sheet date shall be included in the profit and loss account. (Paragraph 72 of the Schedule defines realised profits in relation to a company's accounts as 'such profits of the company as fall to be treated as realised profits for the purposes of those accounts in accordance with principles generally accepted with respect to the determination for accounting purposes of realised profits at the time when those accounts are prepared'.) (Standard paragraph 24)

Paragraph 5 of the Schedule requires that, subject to any provision for depreciation **38** or diminution in value, the amount to be included in respect of any fixed asset shall be its purchase price or production cost. Paragraph 14(1) states that the purchase price of an asset shall be determined by adding to the actual price paid any expenses incidental to its acquisition. The CCAB has received legal opinion that the equivalent paragraphs in UK legislation have the effect of prohibiting enterprises to which the legislation applies from accounting for grants made as a contribution towards expenditure on fixed assets by deducting the amount of the grant from the purchase price or production cost of the related asset. (Standard paragraph 25)

Paragraph 36(2) of the Schedule provides that 'The following information shall be **39** given with respect to any other contingent liability not provided for:ff(a)the amount or estimated amount of that liability;

(b)   its legal nature; and

Editor's note: The same paragraph numbers apply to small companies under Schedule 8 to the Companies Act 1985.

†*Editor's note: In the case of small companies the reference should be to paragraph 46(2) of Schedule 8 to the Companies Act 1985. The wording is identical.*

(c)   whether any valuable security has been provided by the company in connection with that liability and if so, what'. (Standard paragraph 29)

40   The Companies (Amendment) Act 1983, Section 40 requires the convening of an extraordinary general meeting not later than 28 days from the earliest day on which it is known to a director of the company that its net assets have fallen to half or less of the company's called-up share capital (that a 'financial situation' exists). The 1983 Act also extends the reporting duties of auditors by requiring auditors to state whether in their opinion there existed at the balance sheet date a 'financial situation' in the context of Section 40 which would require the convening of an extraordinary general meeting. For the purpose of calculating the net assets of the company, the term 'liability' should be taken to include not only creditors, but also provisions for liabilities and charges, accruals and deferred income. Government grants treated as deferred income should, therefore, be regarded as a liability for the purposes of calculating net assets under Section 40.

Part 6 – Compliance with International Accounting Standard No.20 'Accounting for Government Grants and Disclosure of Government Assistance'

41   The requirements of International Accounting Standard No.20 'Accounting for Government Grants and Disclosure of Government Assistance' accord very closely with the content of the United Kingdom and Irish Accounting Standard No.4 (Revised) 'Accounting for government grants' and accordingly compliance with SSAP 4 (Revised) will ensure compliance with IAS 20 in all material respects.*

---

*Editor's note: Subsequent to the latest revision of SSAP 4, IAS 20 has been reformatted (in 1994) and an SIC has been issued, 'SIC 10 Government assistance — No specific relation to operating activities'. IAS 20 was also amended by IAS 10 'Events after the balance sheet date' and by IAS 41 'Agriculture'.

The comment made in SSAP 4 remains basically true, but there are some differences between the standards. In particular, IAS 20 always allows capital grants to be treated as deferred income or deducted from the cost of the asset. While SSAP 4 also supports this treatment in principle, it is not allowed for UK companies as explained in paragraphs 15, 25 and 34 of SSAP 4.

[SSAP 5]
Accounting for value added tax

(Issued April 1974)

This statement seeks, by presenting a standard accounting practice, to achieve uniformity of accounting treatment of VAT in financial statements.

Part 1 – Explanatory note

GENERAL

VAT is a tax on the supply of goods and services which is eventually borne by the **1** final consumer but collected at each stage of the production and distribution chain. As a general principle, therefore, the treatment of VAT in the accounts of a trader should reflect his role as a collector of the tax and VAT should not be included in income or in expenditure whether of a capital or of a revenue nature. There will however be circumstances, as noted below, in which a trader will himself bear VAT and in such circumstances the accounting treatment should reflect that fact.

PERSONS NOT ACCOUNTABLE FOR VAT

Persons not accountable for VAT will suffer VAT on inputs. For them VAT will **2** increase the cost of all goods and services to which it applies and should be included in such costs. In particular, the VAT on fixed assets should be added to the cost of the fixed assets concerned.

ACCOUNTABLE PERSONS WHO ALSO CARRY ON EXEMPTED ACTIVITIES

In the case of persons who also carry on exempted activities there will be a residue of **3** VAT, which will fall directly on the trader and which will normally be arrived at by division of his activities as between taxable outputs (including zero-rated) and those which are exempt. In such cases, the principle that such VAT will increase the costs to which it applies and should be included in such costs will be equally applicable. Hence the appropriate portion of the VAT allocable to fixed assets should, if irrecoverable, be added to the cost of the fixed assets concerned and the proportion allocable to other items should, if practicable and material, be included in such other items. In some cases, for example where financial and VAT accounting periods do not coincide, an estimate may be necessary.

NON-DEDUCTIBLE INPUTS

All traders will bear tax in so far as it relates to non-deductible inputs (for example, **4** motor-cars, other than for resale, and certain business entertaining expenses). Such tax should therefore be included as part of the cost of those items. A similar situation exists in the Republic of Ireland where traders dealing in products such as motor-cars, radios and television sets will bear some non-deductible VAT on the input cost of these items.

AMOUNTS DUE TO OR FROM THE REVENUE AUTHORITIES

5   The net amount due to or from the revenue authorities in respect of VAT should be included as part of debtors or creditors and will not normally require separate disclosure.

CAPITAL COMMITMENTS

6   The estimated amount of capital commitments should include the appropriate amount, if any, of irrecoverable VAT.

COMPARISONS

7   Where it has been customary for purchase tax (or sales taxes in the Republic of Ireland) to be included in turnover, it may be desirable in the initial years of VAT to disclose the turnover of periods in which such tax applied both gross and net of tax so as to assist in comparisons. In some cases, for example retailers, it may not be possible to ascertain the amount of purchase tax (or sales taxes) included in turnover; in those cases an explanatory note will be desirable. Where customs or excise duties are included in turnover and such duties are reduced to take account of VAT, an explanatory note may be necessary.

Part 2 – Standard accounting practice

TURNOVER

8   Turnover shown in the profit and loss account should exclude VAT on taxable outputs*. If it is desired to show also the gross turnover, the VAT relevant to that turnover should be shown as a deduction in arriving at the turnover exclusive of VAT.

IRRECOVERABLE VAT

9   Irrecoverable VAT allocable to fixed assets and to other items disclosed separately in published accounts should be included in their cost where practicable and material.

APPLICATION TO SMALLER ENTITIES

9A   Reporting entities applying the Financial Reporting Standard for Smaller Entities currently applicable are exempt from this accounting standard.

DATE FROM WHICH EFFECTIVE

10   The accounting practices set out in this statement should be adopted as soon as possible and regarded as standard in respect of accounting periods starting on or after 1st January 1974.

---

*Editor's note: Section 262(1) of the Companies Act 1985 defines 'turnover' in relation to a company.

[SSAP 9]
Stocks and long-term contracts

(Issued May 1975; Part 6 added August 1980; revised September 1988)

Contents

Stocks and long-term contracts

The provisions of this statement of standard accounting practice should be read in conjunction with the (Explanatory) Foreword to accounting standards *and need not be applied to immaterial items.*

Part 1 – Explanatory note

STOCKS

1   The determination of profit for an accounting year requires the matching of costs with related revenues. The cost of unsold or unconsumed stocks will have been incurred in the expectation of future revenue, and when this will not arise until a later year it is appropriate to carry forward this cost to be matched with the revenue when it arises; the applicable concept is the matching of cost and revenue in the year in which the revenue arises rather than in the year in which the cost is incurred. If there is no reasonable expectation of sufficient future revenue to cover cost incurred (e.g., as a result of deterioration, obsolescence or a change in demand) the irrecoverable cost should be charged to revenue in the year under review. Thus, stocks normally need to be stated at cost, or, if lower, at net realisable value.*

2   The comparison of cost and net realisable value needs to be made in respect of each item of stock separately. Where this is impracticable, groups or categories of stock items which are similar will need to be taken together. To compare the total realisable value of stocks with the total cost could result in an unacceptable setting off of foreseeable losses against unrealised profits.

3   In order to match costs and revenue, 'costs' of stocks should comprise that expenditure which has been incurred in the normal course of business in bringing the product or service to its present location and condition. Such costs will include all related production overheads, even though these may accrue on a time basis.

4   The methods used in allocating costs to stocks need to be selected with a view to providing the fairest possible approximation to the expenditure actually incurred in bringing the product to its present location and condition. For example, in the case of retail stores holding a large number of rapidly changing individual items, stock on the shelves has often been stated at current selling prices less the normal gross profit margin. In these particular circumstances this may be acceptable as being the only practical method of arriving at a figure which approximates to cost.

Editor's note: The introductory paragraph of SSAP 9 bases the accounting treatment for stock on the matching concept. Given the changes introduced by FRS 18 'Accounting policies' this is somewhat at odds with the most fundamental current accounting requirements. FRS 18 stresses, however, that it has not eliminated the concept of matching, simply amended it. As paragraph 9 of Appendix IV to FRS 18 makes clear, the intention is that the definition of assets and liabilities of FRS 5, and the requirement that the non-cash effects of transactions be recorded when they occur, provide a discipline within which matching can operate. The practical import of this is limited, as the accounting treatment dictated by SSAP 9 can be as easily supported under FRS 18 as under SSAP 2. SSAP 9 has not been amended as a result of the issue of Application Note G Revenue Recognition to FRS 5. However, the guidance on the recognition of revenue on long-term contracts now needs to be read in the light of that Application Note.

NET REALISABLE VALUE

Net realisable value is the estimated proceeds from the sale of items of stock less all   5
further costs to completion and less all costs to be incurred in marketing, selling and
distributing directly related to the items in question.

REPLACEMENT COST

Items of stock have sometimes been stated in financial statements at estimated   6
replacement cost where this is lower than net realisable value. Where the effect is to
take account of a loss greater than that which is expected to be incurred, the use of
replacement cost is not regarded as acceptable. However, in some circumstances
(e.g., in the case of materials, the price of which has fluctuated considerably and
which have not become the subject of firm sales contracts by the time the financial
statements are prepared) replacement cost may be the best measure of net realisable
value. Also, where a company adopts the alternative accounting rules of the Companies Act 1985, items of stock may be stated at the lower of current replacement
cost and net realisable value.

LONG-TERM CONTRACTS

Separate consideration needs to be given to long-term contracts. Owing to the length   7
of time taken to complete such contracts, to defer recording turnover and taking
profit into account until completion may result in the profit and loss account
reflecting not so much a fair view of the results of the activity of the company during
the year but rather the results relating to contracts that have been completed in the
year. It is therefore appropriate to take credit for ascertainable turnover and profit
while contracts are in progress in accordance with paragraphs 8 to 11 below.

Companies should ascertain turnover in a manner appropriate to the stage of   8
completion of the contracts, the businesses and the industries in which they operate.

Where the business carries out long-term contracts and it is considered that their   9
outcome can be assessed with reasonable certainty before their conclusion, the
attributable profit should be calculated on a prudent basis and included in the
accounts for the period under review. The profit taken up needs to reflect the proportion of the work carried out at the accounting date and to take into account any
known inequalities of profitability in the various stages of a contract. The procedure
to recognise profit is to include an appropriate proportion of total contract value as
turnover in the profit and loss account as the contract activity progresses. The costs
incurred in reaching that stage of completion are matched with this turnover,
resulting in the reporting of results that can be attributed to the proportion of work
completed.

Where the outcome of long-term contracts cannot be assessed with reasonable cer-   10
tainty before the conclusion of the contract, no profit should be reflected in the profit
and loss account in respect of those contracts, although, in such circumstances, if no
loss is expected it may be appropriate to show as turnover a proportion of the total
contract value using a zero estimate of profit.

If it is expected that there will be a loss on a contract as a whole, all of the loss should   11
be recognised as soon as it is foreseen (in accordance with the prudence concept).
Examples of how this can be achieved are given in Appendix 3. Initially, the foreseeable loss will be deducted from the work in progress figure of the particular
contract, thus reducing it to net realisable value. Any loss in excess of the work in

progress figure should be classified as an accrual within 'Creditors' or under 'Provisions for liabilities and charges' depending upon the circumstances. Where unprofitable contracts are if such magnitude that they can be expected to utilise a considerable part of the company's capacity for a substantial period, related administration overheads to be incurred during the period to the completion of those contracts should also be included in the calculation of the provision for losses.

DISCLOSURE IN FINANCIAL STATEMENTS

12   A suitable description of the amount at which stocks (excluding long-term contract balances) are stated in financial statements would be 'at lower of cost and net realisable value.'

13   In the case of long-term contracts:

(a)   long-term contract balances classified under the balance sheet heading of 'Stocks' are stated at total costs incurred, net of amounts transferred to the profit and loss account in respect of work carried out to date, less foreseeable losses and applicable payments on account. A suitable description in the financial statements would be 'at net cost, less foreseeable losses and payments on account.'

(b)   cumulative turnover (i.e., the total turnover recorded in respect of the contract in the profit and loss accounts of all accounting periods since inception of the contract) is compared with total payments on account. If turnover exceeds payments on account an 'amount recoverable on contracts' is established and separately disclosed within debtors. If payments on account are greater than turnover to date, the excess is classified as a deduction from any balance on that contract in stocks, with any residual balance in excess of cost being classified with creditors.

14   In order to give an adequate explanation of the affairs of the company, the accounting policies followed in arriving at the amount at which stocks and long-term contracts are stated in the financial statements should be set out in a note. Where differing bases have been adopted for different types of stocks and long-term contracts, the amount included in the financial statements in respect of each type will need to be stated.

FURTHER PRACTICAL CONSIDERATIONS

15   The basic considerations which must be taken into account in determining cost and net realisable value in relation to stocks and long-term contracts are set out in Parts 2 and 3 of this statement. The majority of problems which arise in practice in determining these amounts result from considerations which are relevant to particular businesses and are not of such universal application that they can be the subject of a statement of standard accounting practice. Accordingly, Appendix 1 sets out in more detail some general guidelines which may be of assistance in determining cost and net realisable value and in identifying those situations in which net realisable value is likely to be less than cost. Appendix 1 also sets out considerations which need to be borne in mind in calculating the amount of profit to be taken into account in respect of long-term contracts.

Part 2 – Definition of terms

16   Stocks comprise the following categories:

(a)   goods or other assets purchased for resale;
(b)   consumable stores;
(c)   raw materials and components purchased for incorporation into products for sale;
(d)   products and services in intermediate stages of completion
(e)   long-term contract balances; and
(f)   finished goods.

Cost is defined in relation to the different categories of stocks as being that expen-   **17**
diture which has been incurred in the normal course of business in bringing the
product or service to its present location and condition. This expenditure should
include, in addition to cost of purchase (as defined in paragraph 18), such costs of
conversion (as defined in paragraph 19) as are appropriate to that location and
condition.

Cost of purchase comprises purchase price including import duties, transport and   **18**
handling costs and any other directly attributable costs, less trade discounts, rebates
and subsidies.

Cost of conversion comprises: **19**

(a)   costs which are specifically attributable to units of production, eg direct labour,
      direct expenses and sub-contracted work;
(b)   production overheads (as defined in paragraph 20);
(c)   other overheads, if any, attributable in the particular circumstances of the
      business to bringing the product or service to its present location and condition.

Production overheads: Overheads incurred in respect of materials, labour or services   **20**
for production, based on the normal level of activity, taking one year with another.
For this purpose each overhead should be classified according to function (eg production, selling or administration) so as to ensure the inclusion, in cost of conversion,
of those overheads (including depreciation) which relate to production, notwithstanding that these may accrue wholly or partly on a time basis.

Net realisable value: The actual or estimated selling price (net of trade but before   **21**
settlement discounts) less:

(a)   all further costs to completion; and
(b)   all costs to be incurred in marketing, selling and distributing.

Long-term contract: A contract entered into for the design, manufacture or con-   **22**
struction of a single substantial asset or the provision of a service (or of a
combination of assets or services which together constitute a single project) where
the time taken substantially to complete the contract is such that the contract activity
falls into different accounting periods. A contract that is required to be accounted for
as long-term by this accounting standard will usually extend for a period exceeding
one year. However, a duration exceeding one year is not an essential feature of a
long-term contract. Some contracts with a shorter duration than one year should be
accounted for as long-term contracts if they are sufficiently material to the activity of
the period that not to record turnover and attributable profit would lead to distortion of the period's turnover and results such that the financial statements would not
give a true and fair view, provided that the policy is applied consistently within the
reporting entity and from year to year.

Attributable profit: That part of the total profit currently estimated to arise over the   **23**
duration of the contract, after allowing for estimated remedial and maintenance
costs and increases in costs so far as not recoverable under the terms of the contract,

that fairly reflects the profit attributable to that part of the work performed at the accounting date. (There can be no attributable profit until the profitable outcome of the contract can be assessed with reasonable certainty.)

24   *Foreseeable losses:* Losses which are currently estimated to arise over the duration of the contract (after allowing for estimated remedial and maintenance costs and increases in costs so far as not recoverable under the terms of the contract). This estimate is required irrespective of:

   (a)   whether or not work has yet commenced on such contracts;
   (b)   the proportion of work carried out at the accounting date;
   (c)   the amount of profits expected to arise on other contracts.

25   *Payments on account:* All amounts received and receivable at the accounting date in respect of contracts in progress.

Part 3 – Standard accounting practice

STOCKS

26   The amount at which stocks are stated in periodic financial statements should be the total of the lower of cost and net realisable value of the separate items of stock or of groups of similar items.

27   Stocks should be sub-classified in the balance sheet or in the notes to the financial statements so as to indicate the amounts held in each of the main categories in the standard balance sheet formats (as adapted where appropriate) of Schedule 4 to the Companies Act 1985, Schedule 4 to the Companies (Northern Ireland) Order 1986 and, in the Republic of Ireland, the Schedule to the Companies (Amendment) Act 1986.*

LONG-TERM CONTRACTS

28   Long-term contracts should be assessed on a contract by contract basis and reflected in the profit and loss account by recording turnover and related costs as contract activity progresses. Turnover is ascertained in a manner appropriate to the stage of completion of the contract, the business and the industry in which it operates.

29   Where it is considered that the outcome of a long-term contract can be assessed with reasonable certainty before its conclusion, the prudently calculated attributable profit should be recognised in the profit and loss account as the difference between the reported turnover and related costs for that contract.

30   Long-term contracts should be disclosed in the balance sheet as follows:

   (a)   the amount by which recorded turnover is in excess of payments on account should be classified as 'amounts recoverable on contracts' and separately disclosed within debtors;
   (b)   the balance of payments on account (in excess of amounts (i) matched with turnover; and (ii) offset against long-term contract balances) should be classified as payments on account and separately disclosed within creditors;

Editor's note: In the case of small companies adopting the special exemptions available to them, the reference is to Schedule 8 to the Companies Act 1985. Small companies would not be required to provide any sub-analysis of stocks (other than distinguishing between stocks and payments on account) in order to comply with this paragraph of the standard.

(c) the amount of long-term contracts, at costs incurred, net of amounts transferred to costs of sales, after deducting foreseeable losses and payments on account not matched with turnover, should be classified as 'long-term contract balances' and separately disclosed within the balance sheet heading 'Stocks.' The balance sheet note should disclose separately the balances of:

    (i)   net cost less foreseeable losses; and
    (ii) applicable payments on account;

(d) the amount by which the provision or accrual for foreseeable losses exceeds the costs incurred (after transfers to cost of sales) should be included within either provisions for liabilities and charges or creditors as appropriate.

Consequent upon the application of this revised standard, the corresponding amounts in the financial statements will need to be restated on a comparable basis.   **31**

STATEMENT OF ACCOUNTING POLICIES

The accounting policies that have been applied to stocks and long-term contracts, in particular the method of ascertaining turnover and attributable profit, should be stated and applied consistently within the business and from year to year.   **32**

APPLICATION TO SMALLER ENTITIES

Reporting entities applying the Financial Reporting Standard for Smaller Entities currently applicable are exempt from this accounting standard.   **32A**

DATE FROM WHICH EFFECTIVE

The accounting practices set out in this statement should be adopted as soon as possible and regarded as standard in respect of financial statements relating to accounting periods beginning on or after 1 July 1988.   **33**

Part 4 – Note on legal requirements in Great Britain and Northern Ireland

All paragraph references unless otherwise indicated are to Schedule 4 to the Companies Act 1985 and Schedule 4 to the Companies (Northern Ireland) Order 1986.

Paragraph 22 requires that, under the historical cost accounting rules, 'the amount to be included in respect of any current asset shall be its purchase price or production cost.' Paragraph 23(1) provides for the inclusion of the asset at net realisable value if lower than purchase price or production cost.*   **34**

Paragraph 90 [paragraph 89 of Schedule 4 to the Companies (Northern Ireland) Order 1986] provides that 'the purchase price of any asset . . . includes any consideration (whether in cash or otherwise) given by the company in respect of that asset.' Counsel's opinion, obtained by the ASC, has indicated that one purpose of   **35**

---

*Editor's note: In the case of small companies, this reference should be read as to paragraph 22 of Schedule 8 to the Companies Act 1985.

this paragraph is to enable debtors to be stated at face value, that is, at amounts which include a profit element, and that this does not conflict with paragraph 22.*

36   Paragraph 26 requires expenses incidental to the acquisition of an asset to be included in the purchase price. It also requires the inclusion of directly attributable production overheads in the production cost of an asset and permits the inclusion of overheads which are only indirectly attributable to the production of an asset and interest on borrowed capital. In cases where interest is included the fact must be stated and the amount of interest included must be disclosed in a note to the financial statements. Paragraph 26 also prohibits the inclusion of distribution costs.†

37   Paragraph 27 allows the following methods for valuation of stocks (but requires that the method chosen must be one which appears to the directors to be appropriate in the circumstances of the company):

(a)   the method known as 'first in, first out' (FIFO);
(b)   the method known as 'last in, first out' (LIFO);
(c)   a weighted average price; and
(d)   any other method similar to any of the methods mentioned above.‡

38   This standard requires the use of a method which provides a fair approximation to the expenditure actually incurred. The use of some of the methods allowed by paragraph 27 of the Schedule will not meet this requirement.

39   In particular, the use of the LIFO method can result in the reporting of current assets at amounts that bear little relationship to recent costs. This may result in not only a significant misstatement of balance sheet amounts but also a potential distortion of current and future results. This places a special responsibility on the directors to be assured that the circumstances of the company require the adoption of such a valuation method in order for the accounts to give a true and fair view.

40   Paragraph 27(3) requires a company to state in a note to the accounts the difference between the replacement cost of stocks and their book amount – as determined by 37(a) to (d) above – where this difference is material.§

41   It is further provided in paragraph 27(5) that if the most recent actual purchase price or production cost before the balance sheet date appears to the directors of the company to constitute a more appropriate standard of comparison, then that amount may be used as a surrogate for replacement cost.*

42   Paragraph 31(5) provides that, where a company adopts the alternative accounting rules, 'stocks may be included at their current cost.'¶¶

43   Paragraph 89 [paragraph 88 of Schedule 4 to the Companies (Northern Ireland) Order 1986] provides that provisions are amounts 'retained as reasonably necessary

---

Editor's note: Paragraph 90 of Schedule 4 has been removed. This reference is now to section 262(1) of the Companies Act 1985.

†Editor's note: In the case of small companies, the reference is to paragraph 26 of Schedule 8 to the Companies Act 1985.*

‡Editor's note: Paragraph 27 of Schedule 8 to the Companies Act 1985 contains identical requirements.*

§Editor's note: There are no equivalents of these provisions in Schedule 8.*

¶¶Editor's note: Paragraph 31 of Schedule 8 to the Companies Act 1985 contains identical requirements.*

for the purpose of providing for any liability or loss which is either likely to be incurred, or certain to be incurred but uncertain as to amount or as to the date on which it will arise.'*

Paragraph 91† [paragraph 90 of Schedule 4 to the Companies (Northern Ireland) Order 1986] declares that realised profits are 'such profits of a company as fall to be treated as realised profits for the purposes of those accounts in accordance with principles generally accepted with respect to the determination for accounting purposes of realised profits.' It is a 'generally accepted principle' that it is appropriate to recognise profit on long-term contracts when the outcome can be assessed with 'reasonable certainty.' The principle of recognising profit on long-term contracts under this standard, therefore, does not contravene this paragraph.   **44**

Part 5 – Note on legal requirements in the Republic of Ireland

The legal requirements in Great Britain and Northern Ireland are mirrored, in respect of the Republic of Ireland, in the Schedule to the Companies (Amendment) Act 1986. The following table indicates the corresponding paragraphs in respect of all the references contained in Part 4 of this statement.   **45**

Schedule 4 to the Companies Act 1985	*Schedule 4 to the Companies (Northern Ireland) Order 1986*	*The Schedule to the Companies (Amendment) Act 1986*
Paragraph 22	Paragraph 22	Paragraph 10
Paragraph 23(1)	Paragraph 23(1)	Paragraph 11(1)
Paragraph 26	Paragraph 26	Paragraph 14
Paragraph 27	Paragraph 27	Paragraph 15‡
Paragraph 27(4)	Paragraph 27(4)	Paragraph 15(4)
Paragraph 27(5)	Paragraph 27(5)	Paragraph 15(5)
Paragraph 31(5)	Paragraph 31(5)	Paragraph 19(5)
Paragraph 89	Paragraph 88	Paragraph 70
Paragraph 90	Paragraph 89	Paragraph 71
Paragraph 91	Paragraph 90	Paragraph 72

*Editor's note: The equivalent provision in Schedule 8 is paragraph 58.

†Editor's note: Now section 262(3).

‡There is no provision for the LIFO method of stock valuation in paragraph 15 of the Schedule to the Companies (Amendment) Act 1986.

Part 6 – Compliance with International Accounting Standard No. 2 'Valuation and presentation of inventories in the context of the historical cost system' and No. 11 'Accounting for construction contracts'

46   The requirements of International Accounting Standard No. 2 'Valuation and presentation of inventories in the context of the historical cost system' and International Accounting Standard No. 11 'Accounting for construction contracts'* accord very closely with the content of the United Kingdom and Irish Accounting Standard No. 9 (Revised) 'Stocks and long-term contracts' and accordingly compliance with SSAP 9 will ensure compliance with both IAS 2 and IAS 11 in all material respects.

Editor's note: Revised versions of IAS 2 'Inventories' and IAS 11 'Construction contracts' were issued in November 1993. IAS 2 has subsequently been further revised, with the changes effective for periods beginning on or after 1 January 2005. As a result of the changes to IAS 2, there are no significant differences between the standards. There are no significant differences between IAS 11 and SSAP 9 in principle, but IAS 11 is far less prescriptive in terms of the precise accounting treatment to be adopted once attributable profits have been determined.

Appendix 1

This appendix is for general guidance and does not form part of the statement of standard accounting practice.

Further practical considerations

Many of the problems involved in arriving at the amount at which stocks and long-term contracts are stated in financial statements are of a practical nature rather than resulting from matters of principle. This appendix discusses some particular areas in which difficulty may be encountered.

THE ALLOCATION OF OVERHEADS

Production overheads are included in cost of conversion (as defined in Part 2) 1 together with direct labour, direct expenses and sub-contracted work. This inclusion is a necessary corollary of the principle that expenditure should be included to the extent to which it has been incurred in bringing the product 'to its present location and condition' (paragraph 17 of part 2). However, all abnormal conversion costs (such as exceptional spoilage, idle capacity and other losses) which are avoidable under normal operating conditions need for the same reason, to be excluded.

Where firm sales contracts have been entered into for the provision of goods or 2 services to customer's specification, overheads relating to design, and marketing and selling costs incurred before manufacture, may be included in arriving at cost.

The costing methods adopted by a business are usually designed to ensure that all 3 direct material, direct labour, direct expenses and sub-contracted work are identified and charged on a reasonable and consistent basis but problems arise on the allocation of overheads which must usually involve the exercise of personal judgement in the selection of an appropriate convention.

The classification of overheads necessary to achieve this allocation takes the function 4 of the overhead as its distinguishing characteristic (e.g., whether it is a function of production, marketing, selling or administration), rather than whether the overhead tends to vary with time or with volume.

The costs of general management, as distinct from functional management, are not 5 directly related to current production and are, therefore, excluded from cost of conversion and, hence, from the cost of stocks and long-term contracts.

In the case of smaller organisations whose management may be involved in the daily 6 administration of each of the various functions, particular problems may arise in practice in distinguishing these general management overheads. In such organisations the cost of management may fairly be allocated on suitable bases to the functions of production, marketing, selling and administration.

Problems may also arise in allocating the costs of central service departments, the 7 allocation of which should depend on the function or functions that the department is serving. For example the accounts department will normally support the following functions:

(a) production – by paying direct and indirect production wages and salaries, by controlling purchases and by preparing periodic financial statements for the production units;

(b) marketing and distribution – by analysing sales and by controlling the sales ledger;

(c) general administration – by preparing management accounts and annual financial statements and budgets, by controlling cash resources and by planning investments.

Only those costs of the accounts department that can reasonably be allocated to the production function fall to be included in the cost of conversion.

8   The allocation of overheads included in the valuation of stocks and long-term contracts needs to be based on the company's normal level of activity, taking one year with another. The governing factor is that the cost of unused capacity should be written off in the current year. In determining what constitutes 'normal' the following factors need to be considered:

(a) the volume of production which the production facilities are intended by their designers and by management to produce under the working conditions (eg single or double shift) prevailing during the year;

(b) the budgeted level of activity for the year under review and for the ensuing year;

(c) the level of activity achieved both in the year under review and in previous years.

Although temporary changes in the load of activity may be ignored, persistent variation should lead to revision of the previous norm.

9   Where management accounts are prepared on a marginal cost basis, it will be necessary to add to the figure of stocks so arrived at, the appropriate proportion of those production overheads not already included in the marginal cost.

10   The adoption of a conservative approach to the valuation of stocks and long-term contracts has sometimes been used as one of the reasons for omitting selected production overheads. In so far as the circumstances of the business require an element of prudence in determining the amount at which stocks and long-term contracts are stated, this needs to be taken into account in the determination of net realisable value and not by the exclusion from cost of selected overheads.

METHODS OF COSTING

11   It is frequently not practicable to relate expenditure to specific units of stocks and long-term contracts. The ascertainment of the nearest approximation to cost gives rise to two problems:

(a) the selection of an appropriate method for relating costs to stocks and long-term contracts (eg job costing, batch costing, process costing, standard costing);

(b) the selection of an appropriate method for calculating the related costs where a number of identical items have been purchased or made at different times (eg unit cost, average cost or FIFO).

12   In selecting the methods referred to in paragraphs 11(a) and (b) above, management must exercise judgement to ensure that the methods chosen provide the fairest practicable approximation to cost. Furthermore, where standard costs are used they need to be reviewed frequently to ensure that they bear a reasonable relationship to

actual costs obtaining during the period. Methods such as base stock and LIFO are not usually appropriate methods of stock valuation because they often result in stocks being stated in the balance sheet at amounts that bear little relationship to recent cost levels. When this happens, not only is the presentation of current assets misleading, but there is potential distortion of subsequent results if stock levels reduce and out of date costs are drawn into the profit and loss account.

The method of arriving at cost by applying the latest purchase price to the total **13** number of units in stock is unacceptable in principle because it is not necessarily the same as actual cost and, in times of rising prices, will result in the taking of a profit which has not been realised.

One method of arriving at cost, in the absence of a satisfactory costing system, is the **14** use of selling price less an estimated profit margin. This is acceptable only if it can be demonstrated that the method gives a reasonable approximation of the actual cost.

In industries where the cost of minor by-products is not separable from the cost of **15** the principal products, stocks of such by-products may be stated in accounts at their net realisable value. In this case the costs of the main products are calculated after deducting the net realisable value of the by-products.

THE DETERMINATION OF NET REALISABLE VALUE

The initial calculation of provisions to reduce stocks from cost to net realisable value **16** may often be made by the use of formulae based on predetermined criteria. The formulae normally take account of the age, movements in the past, expected future movements and estimated scrap values of the stock, as appropriate. Whilst the use of such formulae establishes a basis for making a provision which can be consistently applied, it is still necessary for the results to be reviewed in the light of any special circumstances which cannot be anticipated in the formulae, such as changes in the state of the order book.

Where a provision is required to reduce the value of finished goods below cost, the **17** stocks of the parts and sub-assemblies held for the purpose of the manufacture of such products, together with stocks on order, need to be reviewed to determine if provision is also required against such items.

Where stocks of spares are held for sale, special consideration of the factors in **18** paragraph 16 of this appendix will be required in the context of:

(a)   the number of units sold to which they are applicable;
(b)   the estimated frequency with which a replacement spare is required;
(c)   the expected useful life of the unit to which they are applicable.

Events occurring between the balance sheet date and the date of completion of the **19** financial statements need to be considered in arriving at the net realisable value at the balance sheet date (eg a subsequent reduction in selling prices). However, no reduction falls to be made when the realisable value of material stocks is less than the purchase price, provided that the goods into which the materials are to be incorporated can still be sold at a profit after incorporating the materials at cost price.

THE APPLICATION OF NET REALISABLE VALUE

The principal situations in which net realisable value is likely to be less than cost are **20** where there has been:

(a) an increase in costs or a fall in selling price;
(b) physical deterioration of stocks;
(c) obsolescence of products;
(d) a decision as part of a company's marketing strategy to manufacture and sell products at a loss;
(e) errors in production or purchasing.

Furthermore, when stocks are held which are unlikely to be sold within the turnover period normal in that company (ie excess stocks), the impending delay in realisation increases the risk that the situations outlined in (a) to (c) above may occur before the stocks are sold and needs to be taken into account in assessing net realisable value.

LONG-TERM CONTRACTS

21 In ascertaining costs of long-term contracts it is not normally appropriate to include interest payable on borrowed money. However, in circumstances where sums borrowed can be identified as financing specific long-term contracts, it may be appropriate to include such related interest in cost, in which circumstances the inclusion of interest and the amount of interest so included should be disclosed in a note to the financial statements.

22 In some businesses, long-term contracts for the supply of services or manufacture and supply of goods exist where the prices are determined and invoiced according to separate parts of the contract. In these businesses the most appropriate method of reflecting profits on each contract is usually to match costs against performance of the separable parts of the contract, treating each such separable part as a separate contract. In such instances, however, future revenues from the contract need to be compared with future estimated costs and provision made for any foreseen loss.

23 Turnover (ascertained in a manner appropriate to the industry, the nature of the contracts concerned and the contractual relationship with the customer) and related costs should be recorded in the profit and loss account as contract activity progresses. Turnover may sometimes be ascertained by reference to valuation of the work carried out to date. In other cases, there may be specific points during a contract at which individual elements of work done with separately ascertainable sales values and costs can be identified and appropriately recorded as turnover (eg because delivery or customer acceptance has taken place). This accounting standard does not provide a definition of turnover in view of the different methods of ascertaining it as outlined above. However, it does require disclosure of the means by which turnover is ascertained.

24 In determining whether the stage has been reached at which it is appropriate to recognise profit, account should be taken of the nature of the business concerned. It is necessary to define the earliest point for each particular contract before which no profit is taken up, the overriding principle being that there can be no attributable profit until the outcome of a contract can reasonably be foreseen. Of the profit which in the light of all the circumstances can be foreseen with a reasonable degree of certainty to arise on completion of the contract, there should be regarded as earned to date only that part which prudently reflects the amount of work performed to date. The method used for taking up such profit needs to be consistently applied.

25 In calculating the total estimated profit on the contract, it is necessary to take into account not only the total costs to date and the total estimated further costs to completion (calculated by reference to the same principles as were applied to cost to date) but also the estimated future costs of rectification and guarantee work, and any

other future work to be undertaken under the terms of the contract. These are then compared with the total sales value of the contract. In considering future costs, it is necessary to have regard to likely increases in wages and salaries, to likely increases in the price of raw materials and to rises in general overheads, so far as these items are not recoverable from the customer under the terms of the contract.

Where approved variations have been made to a contract in the course of it and the **26** amount to be received in respect of these variations has not yet been settled and is likely to be a material factor in the outcome, it is necessary to make a conservative estimate of the amount likely to be received and this is then treated as part of the total sales value. On the other hand, allowance needs to be made for foreseen claims or penalties payable arising out of delays in completion or from other causes.

The settlement of claims arising from circumstances not envisaged in the contract or **27** arising as an indirect consequence of approved variations is subject to a high level of uncertainty relating to the outcome of future negotiations. In view of this, it is generally prudent to recognise receipts in respect of such claims only when nego- tiations have reached an advanced stage and there is sufficient evidence of the acceptability of the claim in principle to the purchaser, with an indication of the amount involved also being available.

The amounts to be included in the year's profit and loss account will be both the **28** appropriate amount of turnover and the associated costs of achieving that turnover, to the extent that these amounts exceed corresponding amounts recognised in pre- vious years. The estimated outcome of a contract which extends over several accounting years will nearly always vary in the light of changes in circumstances and for this reason the result of the year will not necessarily represent the proportion of the total profit on the contract which is appropriate to the amount of work carried out in the period; it may also reflect the effect of changes in circumstances during the year which affect the total profit estimated to accrue on completion.

Appendix 2

This appendix is for general guidance and does not form part of the statement of standard accounting practice.

Glossary of terms

The use of the following terms in describing the accounting policies adopted in arriving at the amount at which stocks and long-term contracts are stated in financial statements should be restricted in conformity with the definitions given to each. Where these definitions are inapplicable, alternative expressions should be used and explained.

1   *Average cost:* The calculation of the cost of stocks on the basis of the application to the unit of stocks on hand of an average price computed by dividing the total cost of units by the total number of such units. This average price may be arrived at by means of a continuous calculation, a periodic calculation or a moving periodic calculation.

2   *Base stock:* The calculation of the cost of stocks on the basis that a fixed unit value is ascribed to a predetermined number of units of stock, any excess over this number being valued on the basis of some other method. If the number of units in stock is less than the predetermined minimum, the fixed unit value is applied to the number in stock.

3   *Completed long-term contract:* A long-term contract on which no further work, apart from maintenance work, is expected to take place.

4   *Current cost* of stock is the lower of:

(a)   its net current replacement cost; and
(b)   its net realisable value.

5   *FIFO (first in, first out):* The calculation of the cost of stocks on the basis that the quantities in hand represent the latest purchases or production.

6   *LIFO (last in, first out):* The calculation of the cost of stocks on the basis that the quantities in hand represent the earliest purchases or production.

7   *Replacement cost:* The cost at which an identical asset could be purchased or manufactured.

8   *Standard cost:* The calculation of the cost of stocks on the basis of periodically predetermined costs calculated from management's estimates of expected levels of costs and of operations and operational efficiency and the related expenditure.

9   *Unit cost:* The cost of purchasing or manufacturing identifiable units of stocks.

Appendix 3

This appendix is for general guidance and does not form part of the statement of standard accounting practice.

Long-term contracts: further consideration of financial statement presentation

The classification of an 'amount recoverable on contracts' within debtors is a somewhat unfamiliar concept which needs careful consideration. **1**

The determination of the point at which ownership of completed work passes from the contractor to the customer is a complex matter of legal form and industry practice. **2**

An 'amount recoverable on contracts' may not have the contractual status of a debtor in strict legal form. However, it is well established under the accruals concept of revenue and cost recognition that this should not preclude debtors and creditors from being recorded, where this is necessary to reflect the substance of a transaction. **3**

An essential test for an 'amount recoverable on contracts' to be recorded as an asset is that it should be realisable. This applies equally whether the balance is classified as a debtor or as an element of work in progress. **4**

An 'amount recoverable on contracts' represents an excess of the value of work carried out to date (which has been recorded as turnover) over cumulative payments on account. The amount and realisability of the balance therefore depend on the value of work carried out being ascertained appropriately. The balance arises as a derivative of this process of contract revenue recognition and is directly linked to turnover. In substance, it represents accrued revenue receivable and has the attributes of a debtor. **5**

Accordingly, the standard concludes that 'amounts recoverable on contracts' should be classified as debtors, although separate disclosure is prescribed. Counsel's opinion obtained by the ASC confirms that 'amounts recoverable on contracts' should be classified under 'Debtors' and cannot be classified under 'Stocks.' **6**

In determining the amounts at which long-term contracts should be included in the financial statements, contracting activity should be reviewed on an individual contract by contract basis. The following example illustrates the process of applying the principles set out in the standard to long-term contracts. **7**

Project Number

	1	2	3	4	5	Balance Sheet Total	Profit & Loss Account
Recorded as turnover – being value of work done	145	520	380	200	55		1,300
Cumulative payments on account	(100)	(600)	(400)	(150)	(80)		
Classified as amounts recoverable on contracts	45			50		95DR	
Balance (excess) of payments on account		(80)	(20)		(25)		
Applied as an offset against long-term contract balances – see below		60	20		15		
Residue classified as payments on account		(20)	–		(10)	(30)CR	
Total costs incurred	110	510	450	250	100		
Transferred to cost of sales	(110)	(450)	(350)	(250)	(55)		(1,215)
	–	60	100	–	45		
Provision/accrual for foreseeable losses charged to cost of sales				(40)	(30)		(70)
		60	100		15		
Classified as provision/accrual for losses				(40)		(40)CR	
Balance (excess) of payments on account applied as offset against long-term contract balances		(60)	20		(15)		
Classified as long-term contract balances		–	80			80DR	
Gross profit or loss on long-term contracts	35	70	30	(90)	(30)		15

PROJECT 1
Profit and Loss Account – cumulative

Included in turnover	145
Included in cost of sales	(110)
Gross profit	35

Balance Sheet
The amount to be included in debtors under 'amounts recoverable on contracts' is calculated as follows:

Cumulative turnover	145
LESS: Cumulative payments on account	(100)
Included in debtors	45

In this case, all the costs incurred to date relate to the contract activity recorded as turnover and are transferred to cost of sales, leaving a zero balance in stocks. NB If the outcome of the contract could not be assessed with reasonable certainty, no profit would be recognised. If no loss is expected, it may be appropriate to show as turnover a proportion of the total contract value using a zero estimate of profit.

PROJECT 2
Profit and Loss Account – cumulative

Included in turnover	520
Included in cost of sales	(450)
Gross profit	70

Balance sheet
As cumulative payments on account are greater than turnover there is a credit balance, calculated as follows:

Cumulative turnover	520
LESS: Cumulative payments on account	(600)
Excess payments on account	(80)

This credit balance should firstly be offset against any debit balance on this contract included in stocks and then any residual amount should be classified under creditors as a payment received on account as follows:

Total cost incurred to date	510
LESS: Cumulative amounts recorded as cost of sales	(450)
	60
LESS: Excess payments on account (above)	(80)
Included in creditors	(20)

The amount to be included in stocks is zero and the credit balance of 20 is classified as a payment received on account and included in creditors.

The balance sheet note on stocks should disclose separately the net cost of 60 and the applicable payments on account of 60.

PROJECT 3
Profit and Loss Account – cumulative

Included in turnover	380
Included in the cost of sales	(350)
Gross profit	30

Balance sheet

As with Project 2, cumulative payments on account are greater than turnover and there is a credit balance calculated as follows:

Cumulative turnover	380
LESS: Cumulative payments on account	(400)
Excess payments on account	(20)

This credit balance should firstly be offset against any debit balance on this contract included in stocks and the residual amount, if any, should be classified under creditors as a payment received on account.

The amount to be included in stocks under long-term contract balances is calculated as follows:

Total costs incurred to date	450
LESS: Cumulative amounts recorded as costs of sales	(350)
	100
LESS: Excess payments on account (above)	(20)
Included in long-term contract balances	80

The balance sheet note on stocks should disclose separately the net cost of 100 and the applicable payments on account of 20.

PROJECT 4
Profit and Loss Account – cumulative

Included in turnover	200
Included in cost of sales	(290)
Gross loss	(90)

Balance sheet

The amount to be included in debtors under 'amounts recoverable on contracts' is calculated as follows:

Cumulative turnover	200
LESS: Cumulative payments on account	(150)
Included in debtors	50

The amount to be included as a provision/accrual for foreseeable losses is calculated as follows:

Total costs incurred to date		250
LESS: Transferred to cost of sales	(250)	
Foreseeable losses on contract as a whole	(40)	
		(290)
Classified as provision/accrual for foreseeable losses		(40)

Note that the credit balance of 40 is not offset against the debit balance of 50 included in debtors.

PROJECT 5

Profit and Loss Account – cumulative

Included in turnover	55
Included in cost of sales	(85)
Gross loss	(30)

Balance Sheet

As cumulative payments on account are greater than turnover there is a credit balance, calculated as follows:

Cumulative turnover	55
LESS: Cumulative payments on account	(80)
Excess payments on account	(25)

The credit balance should firstly be deducted from long-term contract balances (after having deducted foreseeable losses) and the residual balance included in creditors under payments received on account as follows:

Total costs incurred to date		100
LESS: Transferred to cost of sales	(55)	
Foreseeable losses on contract as a whole	(30)	
		(85)
		15
LESS: Excess payments on account (above)		(25)
Included in creditors		(10)

The balance sheet note on stocks should disclose separately the net cost of 15 and the applicable payments on account of 15.

[SSAP 13]
Accounting for research and development

(Issued December 1977; revised January 1989)

Contents

Accounting for research and development

The provisions of this statement of standard accounting practice should be read in conjunction with the (Explanatory) Foreword to accounting standards *and need not be applied to immaterial items.*

Part 1 – Explanatory note

BASIC CONCEPTS

The accounting policies to be followed in respect of research and development   1
expenditure must have regard to the fundamental accounting concepts including the 'accruals' concept by which revenue and costs are accrued, matched and dealt with in the period to which they relate and the 'prudence' concept by which revenue and profits are not anticipated but are recognised only when realised in the form either of cash or of other assets the ultimate cash realisation of which can be established with reasonable certainty. It is a corollary of the prudence concept that expenditure should be written off in the period in which it arises unless its relationship to the revenue of a future period can be established with reasonable certainty.*

THE DIFFERENT TYPES OF RESEARCH AND DEVELOPMENT EXPENDITURE

The term 'research and development' is currently used to cover a wide range of   2
activities, including those in the services sector. The definitions of the different types of research and development used in this statement are based on those used by the Organisation for Economic Co-operation and Development for the purposes of collecting data world-wide.

Classification of expenditure is often dependent on the type of business and its   3
organisation. However, it is generally possible to recognise three broad categories of activity, namely pure research, applied research and development. The definitions of the individual categories are set out in Part 2.

The dividing line between these categories of expenditure is often indistinct and   4
particular expenditure may have characteristics of more than one category. This is especially so when new products or services are developed through research and development to production, when the activities may have characteristics of both development and production.

Research and development activity is distinguished from non-research activity by the   5
presence or absence of an appreciable element of innovation. If the activity departs from routine and breaks new ground it should normally be included; if it follows an established pattern it should normally be excluded.

Examples of activities that would normally be included in research and development   6
are:

(a)   experimental, theoretical or other work aimed at the discovery of new knowledge, or the advancement of existing knowledge;
(b)   searching for applications of that knowledge;

*Editor's note: The glosses of the prudence and accruals concepts provided in this paragraph are no longer quite consistent with the terms as used in FRS 18 'Accounting policies.' This does not affect the accounting practices to be adopted.

(c)   formulation and design of possible applications for such work;

(d)   testing in search for, or evaluation of, product, service or process alternatives;

(e)   design, construction and testing of pre-production prototypes and models and development batches;

(f)   design of products, services, processes or systems involving new technology or substantially improving those already produced or installed;

(g)   construction and operation of pilot plants.

7   Examples of activities that would normally be excluded from research and development would include:

(a)   testing analysis either of equipment or product for purposes of quality or quantity control;

(b)   periodic alterations to existing products, services or processes even though these may represent some improvement;

(c)   operational research not tied to a specific research and development activity;

(d)   cost of corrective action in connection with break-downs during commercial production;

(e)   legal and administrative work in connection with patent applications, records and litigation and the sale or licensing of patents;

(f)   activity, including design and construction engineering, relating to the construction, relocation, rearrangement or start-up of facilities or equipment other than facilities or equipment whose sole use is for a particular research and development project;

(g)   market research.

THE ACCOUNTING TREATMENT OF RESEARCH AND DEVELOPMENT

8   Expenditure incurred on pure and applied research can be regarded as part of a continuing operation required to maintain a company's business and its competitive position. In general, no one particular period rather than any other will be expected to benefit and therefore it is appropriate that these costs should be written off as they are incurred. Expenditure on pure or applied research may not be treated as an asset (Companies Act 1985, Schedule 4, paragraph 3(2)(c)).*

9   The development of new products or services is, however, distinguishable from pure and applied research. Expenditure on such development is normally undertaken with a reasonable expectation of specific commercial success and of future benefits arising from the work, either from increased revenue and related profits or from reduced costs. On these grounds it may be argued that such expenditure, to the extent that it is recoverable, should be deferred to be matched against the future revenue.

10   It will only be practicable to evaluate the potential future benefits of development expenditure if:

(a)   there is a clearly defined project; and

(b)   the related expenditure is separately identifiable.

11   The outcome of such a project would then need to be examined for:

(a)   its technical feasibility; and

(b)   its ultimate commercial viability considered in the light of factors such as:

(i)   likely market conditions (including competing products or services);

Editor's note: An identical provision is included in paragraph 3(2)(c) of Schedule 8 to the Companies Act 1985.

(ii)   public opinion;

(iii)   consumer and environmental legislation.

Furthermore a project will be of value: **12**

(a)   only if further development costs to be incurred on the same project, together with related production, selling and administrative costs, will be more than covered by related revenues; and

(b)   adequate resources exist, or are reasonably expected to be available, to enable the project to be completed and to provide any consequential increases in working capital.

The elements of uncertainty inherent in the considerations set out in paragraphs 11   **13** and 12 are considerable. There will be a need for different persons with different types of judgement to be involved in assessing the technical, commercial and financial viability of the project. Combinations of the possible differing assessments which they might validly make can produce different assessments of the existence and amounts of future benefits.

If these uncertainties are viewed in the context of the concept of prudence, the future   **14** benefits of most development projects would be too uncertain to justify carrying the expenditure forward. Nevertheless, in certain industries it is considered that there are a number of major development projects that satisfy the stringent criteria set out in paragraphs 10 to 12. Accordingly, when the expenditure on development projects is judged on a prudent view of available evidence to satisfy these criteria, it may be carried forward and amortised over the period expected to benefit.

At each accounting date the unamortised balance of development expenditure should   **15** be examined project by project to ensure that it still fulfils the criteria in paragraphs 10 to 12. Where any doubt exists as to the continuation of those circumstances the balance should be written off.

Fixed assets may be acquired or constructed in order to provide facilities for research   **16** and/or development activities. The use of such fixed assets usually extends over a number of accounting periods and accordingly they should be capitalised and written off over their useful life. The depreciation so written off should be included as part of the expenditure on research and development and disclosed in accordance with SSAP 12.*

EXCEPTIONS

Where companies enter into a firm contract: **17**

(a)   to carry out development work on behalf of third parties on such terms that the related expenditure is to be fully reimbursed, or

(b)   to develop and manufacture at an agreed price calculated to reimburse expenditure on development as well as on manufacture,

any such expenditure which has not been reimbursed at the balance sheet date should be dealt with as contract work-in-progress.

Expenditure incurred in locating and exploiting oil, gas and mineral deposits in the   **18** extractive industries does not fall within the definition of research and development used in this accounting standard. Development of new surveying methods and techniques as an integral part of research on geological phenomena should, however, be included in research and development.

---

*Editor's note: SSAP 12 has been superseded by FRS 15 'Tangible fixed assets'.

DISCLOSURE

19   While there are uncertainties inherent in research and development projects, such activities are important in forming a view of a company's future prospects. Detailed disclosure raises considerable problems of definition and the disclosure requirements of this standard are therefore limited to:

(a)   accounting policy as required by FRS 18 'Accounting policies';
(b)   disclosure of the total amount of research and development expenditure charged in the profit and loss account, distinguishing between the current year's expenditure and amounts amortised from deferred expenditure;
(c)   the movements on deferred development expenditure during the year.

20   Having regard to the problems of definition and disclosure referred to above, the scope of disclosure required under paragraph 19(b) is (except in the case of Republic of Ireland companies) restricted in effect to companies which are public limited companies, or special category companies*, or subsidiaries of such companies, or which exceed by a multiple of 10 the criteria for defining a medium-sized company under the Companies Act 1985.

Part 2 – Definition of terms

The following definition is used for the purpose of this statement:

21   Research and development expenditure means expenditure falling into one or more of the following broad categories (except to the extent that it relates to locating or exploiting oil, gas or mineral deposits or is reimbursable by third parties either directly or under the terms of a firm contract to develop and manufacture at an agreed price calculated to reimburse both elements of expenditure):

(a)   *pure (or basic) research:* Experimental or theoretical work undertaken primarily to acquire new scientific or technical knowledge for its own sake rather than directed towards any specific aim or application;
(b)   *applied research:* Original or critical investigation undertaken in order to gain new scientific or technical knowledge and directed towards a specific practical aim or objective;
(c)   *development:* Use of scientific or technical knowledge in order to produce new or substantially improved materials, devices, products or services, to install new processes or systems prior to the commencement of commercial production or commercial applications, or to improving substantially those already produced or installed.

Part 3 – Standard accounting practice

SCOPE

22   This standard applies to all financial statements intended to give a true and fair view of the financial position of profit or loss, but, except in the case of Republic of Ireland companies (see paragraphs 45 and 46), the provisions set out in paragraph 31 regarding the disclosure of the total amounts of research and development charged in the profit and loss account need not be applied by an entity that:

*Editor's note: Now banking and insurance companies.

(a) is not a public limited company or a special category company* (as defined by Section 257 of the Companies Act 1985)† or a holding company that has a public limited company or a special category company as a subsidiary; and

(b) satisfies the criteria, multiplied in each case by 10, for defining a medium-sized company under Section 248‡ of the Companies Act 1985, as amended from time to time by statutory instrument and applied in accordance with the provisions of Section 249‡ of the Act.§

APPLICATION TO SMALLER ENTITIES

Reporting entities applying the Financial Reporting Standard for Smaller Entities currently applicable are exempt from this accounting standard. **22A**

ACCOUNTING TREATMENT

The cost of fixed assets acquired or constructed in order to provide facilities for research and development activities over a number of accounting periods should be capitalised and written off over their useful lives through the profit and loss account. **23**

Expenditure on pure and applied research (other than that referred to in paragraph 23) should be written off in the year of expenditure through the profit and loss account. **24**

Development expenditure should be written off in the year of expenditure except in the following circumstances when it may be deferred to future periods: **25**

(a) there is a clearly defined project, and
(b) the related expenditure is separately identifiable, and
(c) the outcome of such a project has been assessed with reasonable certainty as to:
  (i) its technical feasibility, and
  (ii) its ultimate commercial viability considered in the light of factors such as likely market conditions (including competing products), public opinion, consumer and environmental legislation, and

(d) the aggregate of the deferred development costs, any further development costs, and related production, selling and administration costs is reasonably expected to be exceeded by related future sales or other revenues, and

Editor's note: Now banking and insurance companies as defined in section 744 of the Companies Act 1985.

†*There is no exact equivalent of 'special category companies' in the Republic of Ireland. The Sixth Schedule to the 1963 Act refers to 'special classes of company' which include banking, discount and assurance companies but not shipping companies.*

‡*Editor's note: Now section 247.*

§**Equivalent legal references.**

Great Britain	Northern Ireland	Republic of Ireland
Companies Act 1985	*Companies (Northern Ireland) Order 1986*	*Companies (Amendment) Act 1986*
Section 248 (Now section 247)	Article 256 (as amended)	Section 8
Section 249 (Now section 247)	Article 257	Section 9
Section 257 (Now section 744)	Article 265	*Companies Act 1963* Sixth Schedule, paragraph 23

(e)   adequate resources exist, or are reasonably expected to be available, to enable the project to be completed and to provide any consequential increases in working capital.

26   In the foregoing circumstances development expenditure may be deferred to the extent that its recovery can reasonably be regarded as assured.

27   If an accounting policy of deferral of development expenditure is adopted, it should be applied to all developmental projects that meet the criteria in paragraph 25.

28   If development costs are deferred to future periods, they should be amortised. The amortisation should commence with the commercial production or application of the product, service, process or system and should be allocated on a systematic basis to each accounting period, by reference to either the sale or use of the product, service, process or system or the period over which these are expected to be sold or used.

29   Deferred development expenditure for each project should be reviewed at the end of each accounting period and where the circumstances which have justified the deferral of the expenditure (paragraph 25) no longer apply, or are considered doubtful, the expenditure, to the extent to which it is considered to be irrecoverable, should be written off immediately project by project.

DISCLOSURE

30   The accounting policy on research and development expenditure should be stated and explained.

31   The total amount of research and development expenditure charged in the profit and loss account should be disclosed, analysed between the current year's expenditure and amounts amortised from deferred expenditure.

32   Movements on deferred development expenditure and the amount carried forward at the beginning and the end of the period should be disclosed under intangible fixed assets in the balance sheet.

DATE FROM WHICH EFFECTIVE

33   The accounting and disclosure requirements set out in this statement should be adopted as soon as possible and regarded as standard in respect of financial statements relating to accounting periods beginning on or after 1 January 1989.

Part 4 – Note on legal requirements in Great Britain and Northern Ireland

*All paragraph references unless otherwise indicated are to the Companies Act 1985 and the Companies (Northern Ireland) Order 1986.**

34   Paragraph 3(1) of Schedule 4 enables any items required to be shown in a company's balance sheet or profit and loss account to be shown in greater detail than required by the format adopted.

Editor's note: *All of the references to Schedule 4 also apply to Schedule 8.*

Paragraph 3(2)(c) of Schedule 4 provides that a company's balance sheet or profit   **35**
and loss account may include an item representing or covering the amount of any
asset or liability, income or expenditure not otherwise covered by any of the items
listed in the accounts format adopted. Cost of research shall not be treated as an
asset in any company's balance sheet.

Paragraph 19(1) of Schedule 4 does not allow provision to be made for a temporary   **36**
diminution in value other than for a fixed asset investment.

Paragraph 19(2) of Schedule 4 requires provision for diminution in value to be made   **37**
in respect of any fixed asset which has diminished in value if the reduction is expected
to be permanent (whether its useful economic life is limited or not) and the amount
to be included in respect of it to be reduced accordingly. Any such provisions not
shown in the profit and loss account shall be disclosed (either separately or in
aggregate) in a note to the accounts.

Paragraph 19(3) requires that where the reasons for which any provision was made   **38**
have ceased to apply to any extent, then the provision shall be written back to the
extent that it is no longer necessary. Any amounts written back in accordance with
this subparagraph which are not shown in the profit and loss account shall be
disclosed (either separately or in aggregate) in a note to the accounts.

Paragraph 20(1) of Schedule 4 requires that notwithstanding that an item in respect   **39**
of development costs is included under fixed assets in the balance sheet formats set
out in Part 1 of Schedule 4, an amount may only be included in a company's balance
sheet in respect of development costs in special circumstances.

Paragraph 20(2) of Schedule 4 requires that if any amount is included in a company's   **40**
balance sheet in respect of development costs the following information shall be
given in a note to the accounts:

(a)   the period over which the amount of those costs originally capitalised is being
      or is to be written off; and
(b)   the reasons for capitalising the development costs in question.

Paragraph 6(c) of Schedule 7 requires the Directors' Report to contain an indication   **41**
of the activities (if any) of the company and its subsidiaries in the field of research
and development.

Section 269(2)(b) of the Companies Act 1985 on the treatment of development costs   **42**
requires that where the unamortised development expenditure carried forward is not
treated as a realised loss when determining distributable reserves, the notes to the
financial statements shall disclose:

(a)   the fact that the amount of the unamortised development expenditure is not to
      be treated as a realised loss for the purposes of calculating distributable profits;
      and
(b)   the circumstances that the directors relied upon to justify their decision not to
      treat the unamortised development expenditure as a realised loss.

Part 5 – Note on legal requirements in the Republic of Ireland

*References are to the Companies (Amendment) Act 1986 and to the Schedule to that
Act unless otherwise stated.*

43   Section 4(5) of the Act enables any items required to be shown in a company's balance sheet or profit and loss account to be shown in greater detail than required by the format adopted.

44   Section 4(12) of the Act provides that the balance sheet, or profit and loss account, of a company may include an item representing or covering the amount of any asset or liability or income or expenditure not otherwise covered by any of the items listed in the format adopted but that costs of research shall not be treated as assets in the balance sheet of a company.

45   Paragraph 43(4) of the Schedule requires the amount expended on research and development in the financial year, and any amount committed in respect of research and development in subsequent years, to be stated.

46   Paragraph 43(5) of the Schedule provides that where, in the opinion of the directors, the disclosure of any information required by Paragraph 43(4) would be prejudicial to the interests of the company, that information need not be disclosed, but the fact that any such information has not been disclosed shall be stated.

47   Paragraph 7(1) of the Schedule does not allow provision to be made for a temporary diminution in value other than for a fixed asset investment.

48   Paragraph 7(2) of the Schedule requires provision for diminution in value to be made in respect of any fixed asset which has diminished in value if the reduction is expected to be permanent (whether its useful economic life is limited or not) and the amount to be included in respect of it shall be reduced accordingly. Any such provisions which are not shown in the profit and loss account shall be disclosed (either separately or in aggregate) in a note to the accounts.

49   Paragraph 7(3) of the Schedule requires that where the reasons for which any provision was made have ceased to apply to any extent, then the provision should be written back to the extent that it is no longer necessary. Any amounts written back in accordance with this sub-paragraph which are not shown in the profit and loss account shall be disclosed (either separately or in aggregate) in a note to the accounts.

50   Paragraph 8(1) of the Schedule requires that notwithstanding that an item in respect of development costs is included under fixed assets in the balance sheet formats set out in Part 1 of the Schedule, an amount may only be included in a company's balance sheet in respect of development costs in special circumstances.

51   Paragraph 8(2) of the Schedule requires that if any amount is included in a company's balance sheet in respect of development costs, the following information shall be given in a note to the accounts:

(a)   the period over which the amount of those costs originally capitalised is being or is to be written off, and

(b)   the reasons for capitalising the development costs in question.

52   Section 13(c) of the Act requires the Directors' Report to contain an indication of the activity, if any, of the company and its subsidiaries, if any, in the field of research and development.

53   Section 45A of the Companies (Amendment) Act 1983 on the treatment of development costs, provides that where development costs are shown in a company's accounts any amount shown as an asset in respect of those costs shall be treated as a realised loss for the purpose of determining profits available for distribution. This provision does not apply to any part of that amount representing an unrealised profit made on revaluation of these costs; nor does it apply if:

(a) there are special circumstances justifying the directors of the company concerned in deciding that the amount mentioned in respect thereof in the company's accounts shall not be treated as a realised loss, and

(b) the note to the accounts required by paragraph 8(2) of the Schedule states that the amount is not to be so treated and explains the circumstances relied upon to justify the decision of the directors to that effect.

Part 6 – Compliance with International Accounting Standard No. 9 'Accounting for research and development activities'

The requirements of International Accounting Standard No. 9 'Accounting for research and development activities'* accord very closely with the content of the United Kingdom and Irish Accounting Standard No. 13 (Revised) 'Accounting for research and development' and accordingly compliance with SSAP 13 (Revised) will ensure compliance with IAS 9 in all material aspects.

54

Editor's note: IAS 9 was superseded by IAS 38 'Intangible Assets' issued September 1998. There are two main differences between SSAP 13 and IAS 38:

- *IAS 38 requires development costs to be capitalised where the recognition criteria are met. SSAP 13 allows, but does not require, this treatment;*
- *there is no equivalent in the IAS of paragraph 25(d) of SSAP 13. This paragraph requires that the aggregate costs are expected to be exceeded by aggregate revenues. This means that where any development project is likely to lead to a loss, however small, no asset may be recognised. Under the IAS, an asset could be recognised, although it would need to be written down to reflect any impairment.*

IAS 38 has subsequently been revised again, and a new version of the standard applies from 2005. It does not alter the main differences identified.

[SSAP 19]
Accounting for investment properties*

(Issued November 1981; amended October 1992 and July 1994)

Contents

*Editor's note: The equivalent international accounting standard is IAS 40 'Investment Property'. There are some differences between the standards. In particular, IAS 40 allows companies to adopt either the fair value model (similar to the treatment under SSAP 19) or the cost model. The cost model is not allowed under SSAP 19. Under IAS 40, where a company adopts the fair value model then any changes in value are dealt with in the income statement.

Accounting for investment properties

The provisions of this Statement of Standard Accounting Practice should be read in conjunction with the (Explanatory) Foreword to Accounting Standards. *The provisions apply equally to financial statements prepared under the historical cost convention and to financial statements prepared under the current cost convention. They need not be applied to immaterial items.*

Part 1 – Explanatory note

Under the accounting requirements of SSAP 12 'Accounting for depreciation',* fixed assets are generally subject to annual depreciation charges to reflect on a systematic basis the wearing out, consumption or other loss of value whether arising from use, effluxion of time or obsolescence through technology and market changes. Under those requirements it is also accepted that an increase in the value of such a fixed asset does not generally remove the necessity to charge depreciation to reflect on a systematic basis the consumption of the asset.   **1**

A different treatment is, however, required where a significant proportion of the fixed assets of an enterprise is held not for consumption in the business operations but as investments, the disposal of which would not materially affect any manufacturing or trading operations of the enterprise. In such a case the current value of these investments, and changes in that current value, are of prime importance rather than a calculation of systematic annual depreciation. Consequently, for the proper appreciation of financial position, a different accounting treatment is considered appropriate for fixed assets held as investments (called in this standard 'investment properties').   **2**

Investment properties may be held by a company which holds investments as part of its business such as an investment trust or a property investment company.   **3**

Investment properties may be held by a company whose main business is not the holding of investments.   **4**

Where an investment property is held on a lease with a relatively short unexpired term, it is necessary to recognise the annual depreciation in the financial statements to avoid the situation whereby a short lease is amortised against the investment revaluation reserve whilst the rentals are taken to the profit and loss account.   **5**

This statement requires investment properties to be included in the balance sheet at open market value. The statement does not require the valuation to be made by qualified or independent valuers; but (in paragraph 12) calls for disclosure of the names or qualifications of the valuers, the bases used by them and whether the person making the valuation is an employee or officer of the company. However, where investment properties represent a substantial proportion of the total assets of a major enterprise (e.g., a listed company) the valuation thereof would normally be carried out: **6**

(a)   annually by persons holding a recognised professional qualification and having recent post-qualification experience in the location and category of the properties concerned; and

(b)   at least every five years by an external valuer.

**Editor's note: SSAP 12 has been superseded by FRS 15 'Tangible fixed assets'. There has been no material change to the accounting requirement mentioned in this paragraph.*

Part 2 – Definition of terms

7   For the purposes of this statement, but subject to the exceptions in paragraph 8 below, an *investment property* is an interest in land and/or buildings:

(a)   in respect of which construction work and development have been completed; and

(b)   which is held for its investment potential, any rental income being negotiated at arm's length.

8   The following are exceptions from the definition:

(a)   A property which is owned and occupied by a company for its own purposes is not an investment property.

(b)   A property let to and occupied by another group company is not an investment property for the purposes of its own accounts or the group accounts.

Part 3 – Standard accounting practice

9   [*Withdrawn by FRS 15*]

10   Investment properties should not be subject to periodic charges for depreciation on the basis set out in SSAP 12* except for properties held on lease which should be depreciated on the basis set out in SSAP 12* at least over the period when the unexpired term is 20 years or less.

11   Investment properties should be included in the balance sheet at their open market value.†

12   The names of the persons making the valuation, or particulars of their qualifications, should be disclosed together with the bases of valuation used by them. If a person making a valuation is an employee or officer of the company or group which owns the property this fact should be disclosed.

13   Subject to paragraph 14 below, changes in the market value of investment properties should not be taken to the profit and loss account but should be taken to the statement of total recognised gains and losses (being a movement on an investment revaluation reserve), unless a deficit (or its reversal) on an individual investment property is expected to be permanent, in which case it should be charged (or credited) in the profit and loss account of the period. In the special circumstances of investment companies as defined in companies legislation (as mentioned in paragraphs 31 and 66 of FRS 3 'Reporting Financial Performance') and of property unit trusts it may not be appropriate to deal with such deficits in the profit and loss account. In such cases they should be shown only in the statement of total recognised gains and losses.

14   Paragraph 13 does not apply to the financial statements of:

(a)   insurance companies and groups (and consolidated financial statements incorporating such entities) where changes in the market value of investment properties (including those comprising assets of the long-term business) are included in the profit and loss account.

(b)   pension funds where changes in the market value of investment properties are dealt with in the relevant fund account.

*Editor's note: SSAP 12 has been superseded by FRS 15 'Tangible fixed assets'.

†*Editor's note: See also UITF Abstract 28 'Operating lease incentives'.

The carrying value of investment properties and the investment revaluation reserve **15** should be displayed prominently in the financial statements.

APPLICATION TO SMALLER ENTITIES

Reporting entities applying the Financial Reporting Standard for Smaller Entities **15A** currently applicable are exempt from this accounting standard.

DATE FROM WHICH EFFECTIVE

The accounting and disclosure requirements in this statement should be adopted as **16** soon as possible and regarded as standard in respect of financial statements relating to accounting periods starting on or after 1 July 1981.*

Part 4 – Legal requirements in UK and Ireland

The application of this standard will usually be a departure, for the overriding **17** purpose of giving a true and fair view, from the otherwise specific requirement of the law to provide depreciation on any fixed asset which has a limited useful economic life. In this circumstance there will need to be given in the notes to the accounts 'particulars of that departure, the reasons for it, and its effect'. Paragraphs 62–65 of FRS 18 'Accounting policies' specify disclosures that should be made in connection with this statutory requirement.†

In Great Britain paragraphs 19 and 32 of Schedule 4 (for banking companies and **18** groups paragraphs 26 and 42 of Schedule 9) to the Companies Act 1985 set out the legal requirements relating to provisions for diminution in value that are expected to be permanent. In the case of insurance companies and groups reported under the amended Schedule 9A to the Companies Act 1985 (introduced by SI 1993/3246) note 9 on the profit and loss account format and paragraph 29(7) of the Schedule set out the relevant statutory requirements.‡

There are legal requirements similar to Schedule 4§ in Northern Ireland (the Com- **19** panies (Northern Ireland) Order 1986 Schedule 4 paragraphs 19 and 32 and Schedule 9 paragraphs 26 and 42) and in the Republic of Ireland (the Companies (Amendment) Act 1986 (the Schedule paragraphs 7 and 20) and the European Communities (Credit Institutions: Accounts) Regulations 1992 (the Schedule paragraphs 26 and 42)). Requirements similar to the amended Schedule 9A are expected to be enacted in Northern Ireland and the Republic of Ireland.

*Editor's note: The amendment in July 1994 (revised paragraphs 13 and 14) became standard in respect of financial statements relating to accounting periods ending on or after 22 September 1994. Earlier adoption was encouraged but not required. The amendment noted that 'if an enterprise changes its presentation of revaluation deficits as a result of this amendment, the classification of reserves and comparative figures should be restated in accordance with FRS 3 'Reporting financial performance'.

†Editor's note: This matter has now been complicated by revisions to both Schedule 4 and Schedule 8 to the CA 1985. Under the fair value rules included in those schedules, investment properties may be stated at fair value if this would be allowed under IFRS, but in this case the changes in fair value are taken to the profit and loss account. There is therefore, still a discrepancy between the statutory provisions and SSAP 19, even if the fair value rules are adopted.

‡Editor's note: For small companies, the references are to paragraphs 19 and 32 of Schedule 8 to the Companies Act 1985.

§Editor's note: Also similar to Schedule 9.

[SSAP 20]
Foreign currency translation*

(*Issued April 1983*)

Contents

__Editor's note:__ SSAP 20 has been superseded by FRS 23, but only for entities which comply with that standard. In order to comply with FRS 23, entities must also comply with FRS 26. For other entities, SSAP 20 remains in force.

Foreign currency translation

The provisions of this statement of standard accounting practice should be read in conjunction with the (Explanatory) Foreword to accounting standards and need not be applied to immaterial items. The provisions apply to financial statements prepared under either the historical cost convention or the current cost convention.

This statement sets out the standard accounting practice for foreign currency translation, but does not deal with the method of calculating profits or losses arising from a company's normal currency dealing operations; neither does it deal specifically with the determination of distributable profits.

Part 1 – Explanatory note

BACKGROUND

A company may engage in foreign currency operations in two main ways: 1

(a)   Firstly, it may enter directly into business transactions which are denominated in foreign currencies; the results of these transactions will need to be translated into the currency in which the company reports.

(b)   Secondly, foreign operations may be conducted through a foreign enterprise which maintains its accounting records in a currency other than that of the investing company; in order to prepare consolidated financial statements it will be necessary to translate the complete financial statements of the foreign enterprise into the currency used for reporting purposes by the investing company.

OBJECTIVES OF TRANSLATION

The translation of foreign currency transactions and financial statements should   2
produce results which are generally compatible with the effects of rate changes on a company's cash flows and its equity and should ensure that the financial statements present a true and fair view of the results of management actions. Consolidated statements should reflect the financial results of and relationships as measured in the foreign currency financial statements prior to translation.

PROCEDURES

In this statement the procedures which should be adopted when accounting for   3
foreign operations are considered in two stages, namely:

(a)   the preparation of the financial statements of an individual company; and
(b)   the preparation of consolidated financial statements.

THE INDIVIDUAL COMPANY STAGE

During an accounting period, a company may enter into transactions which are   4
denominated in a foreign currency. The result of each transaction should normally be translated into the company's local currency using the exchange rate in operation on the date on which the transaction occurred; however, if the rates do not fluctuate significantly, an average rate for a period may be used as an approximation. Where the transaction is to be settled at a contracted rate, that rate should be used; where a trading transaction is covered by a related or matching forward contract, the rate of exchange specified in that contract may be used.

5   Once non-monetary assets, e.g., plant, machinery and equity investments, have been translated and recorded they should be carried in the company's local currency. Subject to the provisions of paragraph 30 concerning the treatment of foreign equity investments financed by foreign currency borrowings, no subsequent translations of these assets will normally need to be made.

6   At the balance sheet date monetary assets and liabilities denominated in a foreign currency, e.g., cash and bank balances, loans and amounts receivable and payable, should be translated by using the rate of exchange ruling at that date, or, where appropriate, the rates of exchange fixed under the terms of the relevant transactions. Where there are related or matching forward contracts in respect of trading transactions, the rates of exchange specified in those contracts may be used.

7   An exchange gain or loss will result during an accounting period if a business transaction is settled at an exchange rate which differs from that used when the transaction was initially recorded, or, where appropriate, that used at the last balance sheet date. An exchange gain or loss will also arise on unsettled transactions if the rate of exchange used at the balance sheet date differs from that used previously.

8   Exchange gains or losses arising on settled transactions in the context of an individual company's operations have already been reflected in cash flows, since a change in the exchange rate increases or decreases the local currency equivalent of amounts paid or received in cash settlement. Similarly, it is reasonably certain that exchange gains or losses on unsettled short-term monetary items will soon be reflected in cash flows. Therefore, it is normally appropriate, because of the cash flow effects, to recognise such gains and losses as part of the profit or loss for the year; they should be included in profit or loss from ordinary activities unless they arise from events which themselves would fall to be treated as extraordinary items, in which case they would be included as part of such items.

9   When dealing with long-term monetary items, additional considerations apply. Although it is not easy to predict what the exchange rate will be when a long-term liability or asset matures, it is necessary, when stating the liability or the asset in terms of the reporting currency, to make the best estimate possible in the light of the information available at the time; generally speaking translation at the year-end rate will provide the best estimate, particularly when the currency concerned is freely dealt in on the spot and forward exchange markets.

10   In order to give a true and fair view of results, exchange gains and losses on long-term monetary items should normally be reported as part of the profit or loss for the period in accordance with the accruals concept of accounting; treatment of these items on a simple cash movements basis would be inconsistent with that concept. Exchange gains on unsettled transactions can be determined at the balance sheet date no less objectively than exchange losses; deferring the gains whilst recognising the losses would not only be illogical by denying in effect that any favourable movement in exchange rates had occurred but would also inhibit fair measurement of the performance of the enterprise in the year. In particular, this symmetry of treatment recognises that there will probably be some interaction between currency movements and interest rates and reflects more accurately in the profit and loss account the true results of currency involvement.

11   For the special reasons outlined above, both exchange gains and losses on long-term monetary items should be recognised in the profit and loss account. However, it is necessary to consider on the grounds of prudence whether the amount of the gain, or the amount by which exchange gains exceed past exchange losses on the same items, to be recognised in the profit and loss account should be restricted in the exceptional

cases where there are doubts as to the convertibility or marketability of the currency in question.

Gains or losses on exchange arising from transactions between a holding company   **12**
and its subsidiaries, or from transactions between fellow subsidiaries, should normally be reported in the individual company's financial statements as part of the profit or loss for the year in the same way as gains or losses arising from transactions with third parties.

THE CONSOLIDATED FINANCIAL STATEMENTS STAGE

The method used to translate financial statements for consolidation purposes should   **13**
reflect the financial and other operational relationships which exist between an investing company and its foreign enterprises.

In most circumstances the closing rate/net investment method, described in para-   **14**
graphs 15 to 20, should be used and exchange differences accounted for on a net investment basis. However, in certain specified circumstances (see paragraphs 21 to 24) the temporal method should be used.

THE CLOSING RATE/NET INVESTMENT METHOD

This method recognises that the investment of a company is in the net worth of its   **15**
foreign enterprise rather than a direct investment in the individual assets and liabilities of that enterprise. The foreign enterprise will normally have net current assets and fixed assets which may be financed partly by local currency borrowings. In its day-to-day operations the foreign enterprise is not normally dependent on the reporting currency of the investing company. The investing company may look forward to a stream of dividends but the net investment will remain until the business is liquidated or the investment disposed of.

Under this method the amounts in the balance sheet of a foreign enterprise should be   **16**
translated into the reporting currency of the investing company using the rate of exchange ruling at the balance sheet date. Exchange differences will arise if this rate differs from that ruling at the previous balance sheet date or at the date of any subsequent capital injection (or reduction).

Amounts in the profit and loss account of a foreign enterprise should be translated at   **17**
the closing rate or at an average rate for the accounting period. The use of the closing rate is more likely to achieve the objective of translation, stated in paragraph 2, of reflecting the financial results and relationships as measured in the foreign currency financial statements prior to translation. However, it can be argued that an average rate reflects more fairly the profits or losses and cash flows as they arise to the group throughout an accounting period. The use of either method is therefore permitted, provided that the one selected is applied consistently from period to period.

No definitive method of calculating the average rate had been prescribed, since the   **18**
appropriate method may justifiably vary as between individual companies. Factors that will need to be considered include the company's internal accounting procedures and the extent of seasonal trade variations; the use of a weighting procedure will in most cases be desirable. Where the average rate used differs from the closing rate, a difference will arise which should be dealt with in reserves.

The results of the operations of a foreign enterprise are best reflected in the group   **19**
profit and loss account by consolidating the net profit or loss shown in its local

currency financial statements without adjustment (other than for normal consolidation adjustments). If exchange differences arising from the retranslation of a company's net investment in its foreign enterprise were introduced into the profit and loss account, the results from trading operations, as shown in the local currency financial statements, would be distorted. Such differences may result from many factors unrelated to the trading performance or financial operations of the foreign enterprise; in particular, they do not represent or measure changes in actual or prospective cash flows. It is therefore inappropriate to regard them as profits or losses and they should be dealt with as adjustments to reserves.

20   Although equity investments in foreign enterprises will normally be made by the purchase of shares, investments may also be made by means of long-term loans and inter-company deferred trading balances. Where financing by such means is intended to be, for all practical purposes, as permanent as equity, such loans and inter-company balances should be treated as part of the investing company's net investment in the foreign enterprise; hence exchange differences arising on such loans and inter-company balances should be dealt with as adjustments to reserves.

THE TEMPORAL METHOD

21   For most investing companies in the UK and Ireland foreign operations are normally carried out through foreign enterprises which operate as separate or quasi-independent entities rather than as direct extensions of the trade of the investing company.

22   However, there are some cases in which the affairs of a foreign enterprise are so closely interlinked with those of the investing company that its results may be regarded as being more dependent on the economic environment of the investing company's currency than on that of its own reporting currency. In such a case the financial statements of the foreign enterprise should be included in the consolidated financial statements as if all its transactions had been entered into by the investing company itself in its own currency. For this purpose the temporal method of translation should be used; the mechanics of this method are identical with those used in preparing the accounts of an individual company, as stated in paragraphs 4 to 12.

23   It is not possible to select one factor which of itself will lead a company to conclude that the temporal method should be adopted. All the available evidence should be considered in determining whether the currency of the investing company is the dominant currency in the economic environment in which the foreign enterprise operates. Amongst the factors to be taken into account will be:

(a)   the extent to which the cash flows of the enterprise have a direct impact upon those of the investing company;
(b)   the extent to which the functioning of the enterprise is dependent directly upon the investing company;
(c)   the currency in which the majority of the trading transactions are denominated;
(d)   the major currency to which the operation is exposed in its financing structure.

24   Examples of situations where the temporal method may be appropriate are where the foreign enterprise:

(a)   acts as a selling agency receiving stocks of goods from the investing company and remitting the proceeds back to the company;
(b)   produces a raw material or manufactures parts or sub-assemblies which are then shipped to the investing company for inclusion in its own products;

(c)   is located overseas for tax, exchange control or similar reasons to act as a means of raising finance for other companies in the group.

THE TREATMENT OF FOREIGN BRANCHES

For the purpose of this statement, foreign operations which are conducted through a foreign branch should be accounted for in accordance with the nature of the business operations concerned. Where such a branch operates as a separate business with local finance, it should be accounted for using the closing rate/net investment method. Where the foreign branch operates as an extension of the company's trade and its cash flows have a direct impact upon those of the company, the temporal method should be used.   **25**

AREAS OF HYPER-INFLATION*

Where a foreign enterprise operates in a country in which a very high rate of inflation exists it may not be possible to present fairly in historical cost accounts the financial position of a foreign enterprise simply by a translation process. In such circumstances the local currency financial statements should be adjusted where possible to reflect current price levels before the translation process is undertaken.   **26**

THE SPECIAL CASE OF EQUITY INVESTMENTS FINANCED BY FOREIGN BORROWINGS

Under the procedures set out in this statement, exchange gains or losses on foreign currency borrowings taken up by an investing company or foreign enterprise would normally be reported as part of that company's profit or loss from ordinary activities and would flow through into the consolidated profit and loss account.   **27**

Where an individual company has used borrowings in currencies other than its own to finance foreign equity investments, or where the purpose of such borrowings is to provide a hedge against the exchange risk associated with existing equity investments, the company may be covered in economic terms against any movement in exchange rates. It would be inappropriate in such cases to record an accounting profit or loss when exchange rates change.   **28**

Therefore, provided the conditions set out in this paragraph apply, the company may denominate its foreign equity investments in the appropriate foreign currencies and translate the carrying amounts at the end of each accounting period at the closing rates of exchange. Where investments are treated in this way, any resulting exchange differences should be taken direct to reserves and the exchange gains or losses on the borrowings should then be offset, as a reserve movement, against these exchange differences. The conditions which must apply are as follows: **29**

(a)   in any accounting period, exchange gains or losses arising on the borrowings may be offset only to the extent of exchange differences arising on the equity investments;

(b)   the foreign currency borrowings, whose exchange gains or losses are used in the offset process, should not exceed, in the aggregate, the total amount of cash that the investments are expected to be able to generate, whether from profits or otherwise; and

Editor's note: See UITF Abstract 9 'Accounting for operations in hyper-inflationary economies'. This is also now covered by FRS 24. However, FRS 24 is applicable to the same entities as FRS 23, and therefore cannot apply to any entity applying SSAP 20.

(c)   the accounting treatment adopted should be applied consistently from period to period.

30   Similarly, within a group, foreign borrowings may have been used to finance group investments in foreign enterprises or to provide a hedge against the exchange risk associated with similar existing investments. Any increase or decrease in the amount outstanding on the borrowings arising from exchange movements will probably be covered by corresponding changes in the carrying amount of the net assets under-lying the net investments (which would be reflected in reserves). Since in this case the group will be covered in economic terms against any movement in exchange rates, it would be inappropriate to record an accounting profit or loss when exchange rates change.

31   In the consolidated financial statements, therefore, subject to certain conditions, the exchange gains or losses on such foreign currency borrowings, which would other-wise have been taken to the group profit and loss account, may be offset as reserve movements against exchange differences on the retranslation of the net investments. The conditions which must apply are as follows:

(a)   the relationship between the investing company and the foreign enterprises concerned should be such as to justify the use of the closing rate method for consolidation purposes;

(b)   in any accounting period, exchange gains or losses arising on foreign currency borrowings may be offset only to the extent of the exchange differences arising on the net investments in foreign enterprises;

(c)   the foreign currency borrowings, whose exchange gains or losses are used in the offset process, should not exceed, in the aggregate, the total amount of cash that the net investments are expected to be able to generate, whether from profits or otherwise; and

(d)   the accounting treatment adopted should be applied consistently from period to period.

32   Where the provisions of paragraph 29 have been applied in the investing company's financial statements to a foreign equity investment which is neither a subsidiary nor an associated company, the same offset procedure may be applied in the con-solidated financial statements.

Part 2 – Definition of terms

33   *Financial statements* are balance sheets, profit and loss accounts, statements of source and application of funds, notes and other statements, which collectively are intended to give a true and fair view of the financial position and profit or loss.*

34   *Company* includes any enterprise which comes within the scope of statements of standard accounting practice.

35   *An exempt company* is one which:

(a)   is registered in Great Britain and does not prepare its accounts in accordance with either Sections 149 and 152 of the Companies Act 1948;† or

*****Editor's note:** The reference to statements of source and application of funds should be read as a reference to cash flow statements for those companies required to prepare such a statement under FRS 1. The reference to other statements should be taken to include the statement of total recognised gains and losses.*

†***Editor's note:** Now sections 226 and 227 of the Companies Act 1985.*

(b)   is registered in Northern Ireland and is exempted from full disclosure by Part 3 of Schedule 6A to the Companies Act (Northern Ireland) 1960 as amended by the Companies (Northern Ireland) Order 1982; or

(c)   is registered in the Republic of Ireland and is exempted from full disclosure by Part 3 of Schedule 6 to the Companies Act 1963.

A foreign enterprise is a subsidiary, associated company or branch whose operations are based in a country other than that of the investing company or whose assets and liabilities are denominated mainly in a foreign currency.   **36**

A foreign branch is either a legally constituted enterprise located overseas or a group of assets and liabilities which are accounted for in foreign currencies.   **37**

Translation is the process whereby financial data denominated in one currency are expressed in terms of another currency. It includes both the expression of individual transactions in terms of another currency and the expression of a complete set of financial statements prepared in one currency in terms of another currency.   **38**

A company's *local currency* is the currency of the primary economic environment in which it operates and generates net cash flows.   **39**

An *exchange rate* is a rate at which two currencies may be exchanged for each other at a particular point in time; different rates apply for spot and forward transactions.   **40**

The *closing rate* is the exchange rate for spot transactions ruling at the balance sheet date and is the mean of the buying and selling rates at the close of business on the day for which the rate is to be ascertained.   **41**

A *forward contract* is an agreement to exchange different currencies at a specified future date and at a specified rate. The difference between the specified rate and the spot rate ruling on the date the contract was entered into is the discount or premium on the forward contract.   **42**

The *net investment* which a company has in a foreign enterprise is its effective equity stake and comprises its proportion of such foreign enterprise's net assets; in appropriate circumstances, intra-group loans and other deferred balances may be regarded as part of the effective equity stake.   **43**

Monetary items are money held and amounts to be received or paid in money and, where a company is not an exempt company, should be categorised as either short-term or long-term. Short-term monetary items are those which fall due within one year of the balance sheet date.   **44**

Part 3 – Standard accounting practice

When preparing the financial statements of an individual company the procedures set out in paragraphs 46 to 51 should be followed. When preparing consolidated financial statements, the procedures set out in paragraphs 52 to 58 should be followed.   **45**

INDIVIDUAL COMPANIES

Subject to the provisions of paragraphs 48 and 51 each asset, liability, revenue or cost arising from a transaction denominated in a foreign currency should be translated into the local currency at the exchange rate in operation on the date on which   **46** the transaction occurred; if the rates do not fluctuate significantly, an average rate for a period may be used as an approximation. Where the transaction is to be settled at a contracted rate, that rate should be used. Where a trading transaction is covered by a related or matching forward contract, the rate of exchange specified in that contract may be used.

47   Subject to the special provisions of paragraph 51, which relate to the treatment of foreign equity investments financed by foreign currency borrowings, no subsequent translations should normally be made once non-monetary assets have been translated and recorded.

48   At each balance sheet date, monetary assets and liabilities denominated in a foreign currency should be translated by using the closing rate or, where appropriate, the rates of exchange fixed under the terms of the relevant transactions. Where there are related or matching forward contracts in respect of trading transactions, the rates of exchange specified in those contracts may be used.

49   All exchange gains or losses on settled transactions and unsettled short-term monetary items should be reported as part of the profit or loss for the year from ordinary activities (unless they result from transactions which themselves would fall to be treated as extraordinary items, in which case the exchange gains or losses should be included as part of such items).*

50   Exchange gains and losses on long-term monetary items should also be recognised in the profit and loss account; however, it is necessary to consider on the grounds of prudence whether, in the exceptional cases outlined in paragraph 11, the amount of the gain, or the amount by which exchange gains exceed past exchange losses on the same items to be recognised in the profit and loss account, should be restricted.

51   Where a company has used foreign currency borrowings to finance, or provide a hedge against, its foreign equity investments and the conditions set out in this paragraph apply, the equity investments may be denominated in the appropriate foreign currencies and the carrying amounts translated at the end of each accounting period at closing rates for inclusion in the investing company's financial statements. Where investments are treated in this way, any exchange differences arising should be taken to reserves and the exchange gains or losses on the foreign currency borrowings should then be offset, as a reserve movement, against these exchange differences. The conditions which must apply are as follows:

(a)   in any accounting period, exchange gains or losses arising on the borrowings may be offset only to the extent of exchange differences arising on the equity investments;†

(b)   the foreign currency borrowings, whose exchange gains or losses are used in the offset process, should not exceed, in the aggregate, the total amount of cash that the investments are expected to be able to generate, whether from profits or otherwise;* and

(c)   the accounting treatment adopted should be applied consistently from period to period.

*Editor's note: This is of no practical relevance given the de facto abolition of extraordinary items by FRS 3.

†Editor's note: See also UITF Abstract 19 'Tax on gains and losses on foreign currency borrowings that hedge an investment in a foreign enterprise'.

CONSOLIDATED FINANCIAL STATEMENTS

When preparing group accounts for a company and its foreign enterprises, which **52** includes the incorporation of the results of associated companies or foreign branches into those of an investing company, the closing rate/net investment method of translating the local currency financial statements should normally be used.

Exchange differences arising from the retranslation of the opening net investment in **53** a foreign enterprise at the closing rate should be recorded as a movement on reserves.

The profit and loss account of a foreign enterprise accounted for under the closing **54** rate/net investment method should be translated at the closing rate or at an average rate for the period. Where an average rate is used, the difference between the profit and loss account translated at an average rate and at the closing rate should be recorded as a movement on reserves. The average rate used should be calculated by the method considered most appropriate for the circumstances of the foreign enterprise.

In those circumstances where the trade of the foreign enterprise is more dependent **55** on the economic environment of the investing company's currency than that of its own reporting currency, the temporal method should be used.

The method used for translating the financial statements of each foreign enterprise **56** should be applied consistently from period to period unless its financial and other operational relationships with the investing company change.

Where foreign currency borrowings have been used to finance, or provide a hedge **57** against, group equity investments in foreign enterprises, exchange gains or losses on the borrowings, which would otherwise have been taken to the profit and loss account, may be offset as reserve movements against exchange differences arising on the retranslation of the net investments provided that:

(a) the relationships between the investing company and the foreign enterprises concerned justify the use of the closing rate method for consolidation purposes;
(b) in any accounting period, the exchange gains and losses arising on foreign currency borrowings are offset only to the extent of the exchange differences arising on the net investments in foreign enterprises;*
(c) the foreign currency borrowings, whose exchange gains or losses are used in the offset process, should not exceed, in the aggregate, the total amount of cash that the net investments are expected to be able to generate, whether from profits or otherwise;* and
(d) the accounting treatment is applied consistently from period to period.

Where the provisions of paragraph 51 have been applied in the investing company's **58** financial statements to a foreign equity investment which is neither a subsidiary nor an associated company, the same offset procedure may be applied in the consolidated financial statements.

DISCLOSURE

The methods used in the translation of the financial statements of foreign enterprises **59** and the treatment accorded to exchange differences should be disclosed in the financial statements.

Editor's note: See also UITF Abstract 19 'Tax on gains and losses on foreign currency borrowings that hedge an investment in a foreign enterprise'.

60   The following information should also be disclosed in the financial statements:

(a)   for all companies, or groups of companies, which are not exempt companies, the net amount of exchange gains and losses on foreign currency borrowings less deposits, identifying separately:

(i)   the amount offset in reserves under the provisions of paragraphs 51, 57 and 58; and

(ii)   the net amount charged/credited to the profit and loss account;

(b)   for all companies, or groups of companies, the net movement on reserves arising from exchange differences.*

APPLICATION TO SMALLER ENTITIES

60A   Reporting entities applying the Financial Reporting Standard for Smaller Entities currently applicable are exempt from this accounting standard.

DATE FROM WHICH EFFECTIVE

61   The accounting and disclosure requirements set out in this statement should be adopted as soon as possible. They should be regarded as standard in respect of financial statements relating to accounting periods beginning on or after 1 April 1983.

Part 4 – Legal requirements in UK and Ireland

62   Paragraphs 63 to 69 below apply to companies preparing accounts in compliance with Sections 149 and 152* of the Companies Act 1948 or with Sections 143 and 146 of the Companies Act (Northern Ireland) 1960. The references to the Schedule which follow are to Schedule 8† to the Companies Act 1948 (as inserted by Section 1 of the Companies Act 1981). References to the Schedule will also be to Schedule 6 to the Companies Act (Northern Ireland) 1960, as inserted by Article 3 of the Companies (Northern Ireland) Order 1982, when this is brought into operation on 1 July 1983.

63   Paragraph 12 of the Schedule requires that the amount of any item shall be determined on a prudent basis and, in particular, that only profits realised at the balance sheet date shall be included in the profit and loss account. (Paragraph 90 of the Schedule‡ defines realised profits in relation to a company's accounts as 'such profits of the company as fall to be treated as realised profits for the purposes of those accounts in accordance with principles generally accepted with respect to the determination for accounting purposes of realised profits at the time when those accounts are prepared').

64   Paragraph 15 of the Schedule permits a departure from paragraph 12 of the Schedule if it appears to the directors that there are special reasons for such a departure. Particulars of any departure, the reasons for it and its effect must be given in a note to the accounts.

*Editor's note: Now sections 226 and 227 of the Companies Act 1985.

†Editor's note: Now Schedule 4, and for small companies, Schedule 8, to the Companies Act 1985.

‡Editor's note: Now section 262(3) of the Companies Act 1985.

For companies other than exempt companies, all exchange gains taken through the **65** profit and loss account, other than those arising on unsettled long-term monetary items, are realised. For such companies the application of paragraph 50 of this statement may result in unrealised exchange gains on unsettled long-term monetary items being taken to the profit and loss account. In this statement the need to show a true and fair view of results, referred to in paragraph 10 above, is considered to constitute a special reason for departure from the principle under paragraph 15 of the Schedule.

This statement is based on the assumption that the process of translation at closing **66** rates for the purposes of this statement does not constitute a departure from the historical cost rules under Section C of the Schedule nor does it give rise to a diminution in value of an asset under Section B of the Schedule.

Paragraph 58 (1) of the Schedule requires that, where sums originally denominated in **67** foreign currencies are brought into the balance sheet or profit and loss account, the basis on which those sums have been translated into sterling shall be stated.*

Part I of the Schedule lays down the choice of formats permitted for the presentation **68** of accounts. Distinction is drawn between operating and other income and expense. For this reason it is necessary to consider the nature of each foreign exchange gain or loss and to allocate each accordingly. Gains or losses arising from trading transactions should normally be included under 'Other operating income or expense' while those arising from arrangements which may be considered as financing should be disclosed separately as part of 'Other interest receivable/payable and similar income/expense'. Exchange gains or losses which arise from events which themselves fall to be treated as extraordinary items should be included as part of such items.

Paragraph 46 of the Schedule requires the following information to be disclosed **69** about movements on any reserve:

(a) the amount of the reserve at the date of the beginning of the financial year and as at the balance sheet date respectively;
(b) any amounts transferred to or from the reserve during that year; and
(c) the source and application respectively of any amounts so transferred.†

Paragraphs 1 and 2 of Schedule 2 to the Companies Act 1981 permit certain com- **70** panies to prepare accounts in compliance with Sections 149A and 152A of and Schedule 8A to the Companies Act 1948 instead of Sections 149 and 152 and Schedule 8.‡ Paragraph 11 (9) of Schedule 8A requires disclosure of the basis on which foreign currencies have been converted into sterling. Schedule 2 to the Companies (Northern Ireland) Order 1982 will permit similar companies registered in Northern Ireland to prepare accounts in accordance with Sections 143A and 146A of and Schedule 6A to the Companies Act (Northern Ireland) 1960 which require the same disclosure.

Similar legal requirements are expected to be enacted in the Republic of Ireland. **71**

Editor's note: For small companies, the reference is to paragraph 51(1) of Schedule 8 to the Companies Act 1985.

†Editor's note: For small companies, the reference is to paragraph 43 of Schedule 8 to the Companies Act 1985.*

‡Editor's note: These requirements have been replaced by the special provisions for banking companies and groups in Schedule 9 to the Companies Act 1985 and for insurance companies and groups in Schedule 9A.*

Part 5 – Compliance with International Accounting Standard No. 21 'Accounting for the effects of changes in foreign exchange rates'

72　Compliance with the requirements of Statement of Standard Accounting Practice No. 20 'Foreign currency translation' will automatically ensure compliance with International Accounting Standard No. 21 'Accounting for the effects of changes in foreign exchange rates.'*

---

*__*Editor's note:__ A revised version of IAS 21 was issued in November 1993. A further revision was issued in December 2003, which came into force in 2005. There are few differences between SSAP 20 and IAS 21 when dealing with the recording of transactions in company financial statements. In terms of consolidated financial statements, the major current difference is that IAS 21 prohibits the use of the closing rate for the translation of transactions during the year. SIC 19 and 30 also affect the currency in which transactions should be measured and presented, whilst SIC 11 affects capitalisation of losses resulting from severe currency devaluations. The revised version of IAS 21 differs materially from SSAP 20. It deals with the functional and therefore measurement currency of entities and with the presentation currency, the currency in which amounts are actually reported. Given that functional currency is crucial under IAS 21, the revised version draws no distinction between entities which are integral and entities which are not. In addition, IAS 32 requires certain currency disclosures not included in SSAP 20, whilst IAS 39 affects the treatment of foreign currency derivatives, and foreign currency items against which the reporting entity has hedged. IAS 21 has now been implemented in the UK as FRS 23. However, SSAP 20 continues to apply to those companies that have not adopted FRS 26.*

[SSAP 21]
Accounting for leases and hire purchase contracts

(Issued August 1984; amended February 1997)

Foreword

Over the past few years, leasing has grown in importance such that it is now a major source of finance for industry in the UK. In consequence, the question of how to account for various types of lease has itself become important. ssap 21 distinguishes finance leases from operating leases and sets out standard practice for each. It codifies accepted practice for some aspects of lease accounting and introduces a requirement for lessees to capitalise material finance leases – which a significant number of companies are doing already.

Why is a capitalisation requirement necessary? When a company is leasing a substantial amount of assets instead of buying them, the effect is that, unless the leased assets and obligations are capitalised, potentially large liabilities build up off balance sheet; equally, the leased assets employed are not reflected on the balance sheet. These omissions may mislead users of a company's accounts – both external users and the company's own management. ssap 21 therefore requires assets held under finance leases and the related leasing obligations to be capitalised on a company's balance sheet.

Capitalisation of finance leases will be helpful in at least two respects: to external users of companies' accounts and for internal management purposes. External users may use a company's accounts when making investment or credit decisions. Capitalisation of assets held under finance leases results in a company's assets and obligations being more readily apparent than if leased assets and obligations are not recognised. The information provided by ssap 21 should in this way enhance the usefulness of the accounts for decision-making purposes.

In the latter context, divisional managers may in some cases not be aware of or involved in the choice of finance for the assets which they use. Without capitalisation, the choice to lease instead of buy could result in a divisional manager's performance being assessed by reference to a misleading figure of capital employed, whilst at the group level assets (and obligations, and thus gearing) would be similarly understated. ssap 21 removes these anomalies by requiring recognition on a balance sheet of the leased assets and related obligations.

It is sometimes argued that leased assets should not be recognised on a company's balance sheet as the company does not have legal title to the asset. Whilst it is true that a lessee does not have legal ownership of the leased asset, however, he has the right to use the asset for substantially the whole of its useful economic life. These rights are for most practical purposes equivalent to legal ownership. It has long been accepted that assets held under hire purchase contracts should be recognised on the balance sheet of the hirer of the asset. ssap 21 extends this treatment to finance leasing; it recognises that whether an asset is owned, leased or held under a hire purchase contract, it represents an economic resource which is needed in the business and which the accounts ought to reflect in a consistent manner.

Detailed guidance notes are published separately from the attached standard. They are non-mandatory and their primary purpose is to recommend practical methods which will assist companies to comply with the standard.

Finally I would stress that the standard, like all accounting standards, need not be applied to immaterial items. Hence, it is only of relevance to companies engaged in a significant amount of leasing.

Ian Hay Davison, *Chairman*

Accounting Standards Committee

[SSAP 21]
Accounting for leases and hire purchase contracts

Contents

Accounting for leases and hire purchase contracts

The provisions of this Statement of Standard Accounting Practice should be read in conjunction with the (Explanatory) Foreword to Accounting Standards *and need not be applied to immaterial items. The provisions apply equally to financial statements prepared under the historical cost convention and to financial statements prepared under the current cost convention.This statement does not apply to lease contracts concerning the rights to explore for or to exploit natural resources such as oil, gas, timber, metals and other minerals. Nor does it apply to licensing agreements for items such as motion picture films, video recordings, plays, manuscripts, patents and copyrights.*

Part 1 – Explanatory note

BACKGROUND

1   Leases and hire purchase contracts are means by which companies obtain the right to use or purchase assets. In the UK there is normally no provision in a lease contract for legal title to the leased asset to pass to the lessee.

2   A hire purchase contract has similar features to a lease except that under a hire purchase contract the hirer may acquire legal title by exercising an option to purchase the asset upon fulfilment of certain conditions (normally the payment of an agreed number of instalments).

3   Current tax legislation provides that in the normal situation capital allowances can be claimed by the lessor under a lease contract but by the hirer under a hire purchase contract.

4   Lessors fall into three broad categories. They may be companies, including banks and finance houses, which provide finance under lease contracts to enable a single customer to acquire the use of an asset for the greater part of its useful life; they may operate a business which involves the renting out of assets for varying periods of time probably to more than one customer; or they may be manufacturer or dealer lessors who use leasing as a means of marketing their products, which may involve leasing a product to one customer or to several customers.

5   As a lessor and lessee are both parties to the same transaction it is appropriate that the same definitions should be used and the accounting treatment recommended should ideally be complementary. However, this will not mean that the recorded balances in both financial statements will be the same because the taxation consequences and hence the pattern of cash flows will be different.

FORMS OF LEASE

6   Leases can appropriately be classified into finance leases and operating leases. The distinction between a finance lease and an operating lease will usually be evident from the terms of the contract between the lessor and the lessee.

7   An operating lease involves the lessee paying a rental for the hire of an asset for a period of time which is normally substantially less than its useful economic life. The lessor retains most of the risks and rewards of ownership of an asset in the case of an operating lease.

A finance lease usually involves payment by a lessee to a lessor of the full cost of the   **8**
asset together with a return on the finance provided by the lessor. The lessee has
substantially all the risks and rewards associated with the ownership of the asset,
other than the legal title. In practice all leases transfer some of the risks and rewards
of ownership to the lessee, and the distinction between a finance lease and an
operating lease is essentially one of degree.

Sometimes, the lessor may receive part of his return in the form of a guarantee from   **9**
an independent third party, in which case the lease may be a finance lease as far as
the lessor is concerned, but not from the lessee's point of view.

Briefly, this standard requires that a finance lease should be capitalised by the lessee,   **10**
that is, accounted for as the purchase of rights to the use and enjoyment of the asset
with simultaneous recognition of the obligation to make future payments. A hire
purchase is normally accounted for in a similar way. Under an operating lease, only
the rental will be taken into account by a lessee.

The effect of a lease is to create a set of rights and obligations related to the use and   **11**
enjoyment by the lessee of a leased asset for the term of the lease. Such rights
constitute the rewards of ownership transferred under the lease to the lessee whilst
the obligations, including in particular the obligation to continue paying rent for the
period specified in the lease, constitute the risks of ownership so transferred. Where
the rights and obligations of the lessee are such that his corresponding rewards and
risks are, despite the absence of the ability to obtain legal title, substantially similar
to those of an outright purchaser of the asset in question, the lease will be a finance
lease.

Conceptually, what is capitalised in the lessee's accounts is not the asset itself but his   **12**
rights in the asset (together with his obligation to pay rentals). However, the definition of a finance lease is such that a lessee's rights are for the practical purposes
little different from those of an outright purchaser. Hence, it is appropriate that
lessees should include these assets in their financial statements, but they should
describe them as 'leased assets' to distinguish them from owned assets.

Part 2 – Definition of terms

Company includes any enterprise which comes within the scope of statements of   **13**
standard accounting practice.

A *lease* is a contract between a lessor and a lessee for the hire of a specific asset. The   **14**
lessor retains ownership of the asset but conveys the right to the use of the asset to
the lessee for an agreed period of time in return for the payment of specified rentals.
The term 'lease' as used in this statement also applies to other arrangements in which
one party retains ownership of an asset but conveys the right to the use of the asset to
another party for an agreed period of time in return for specified payments.

A *finance lease* is a lease that transfers substantially all the risks and rewards of   **15**
ownership of an asset to the lessee. It should be presumed that such a transfer of risks
and rewards occurs if at the inception of a lease the present value of the minimum
lease payments including any initial payment, amounts to substantially all (normally
90 per cent or more) of the fair value of the leased asset. The present value should be
calculated by using the interest rate implicit in the lease (as defined in paragraph 24).
If the fair value of the asset is not determinable, an estimate thereof should be used.

16   Notwithstanding the fact that a lease meets the conditions in paragraph 15, the presumption that it should be classified as a finance lease may in exceptional circumstances be rebutted if it can be clearly demonstrated that the lease in question does not transfer substantially all the risks and rewards of ownership (other than legal title) to the lessee. Correspondingly, the presumption that a lease which fails to meet the conditions in paragraph 15 is not a finance lease may in exceptional circumstances be rebutted.

17   An *operating lease* is a lease other than a finance lease.

18   A *hire purchase contract* is a contract for the hire of an asset which contains a provision giving the hirer an option to acquire legal title to the asset upon the fulfilment of certain conditions stated in the contract.

19   The *lease term* is the period for which the lessee has contracted to lease the asset and any further terms for which the lessee has the option to continue to lease the asset, with or without further payment, which option it is reasonably certain at the inception of the lease that the lessee will exercise.

20   The *minimum lease payments* are the minimum payments over the remaining part of the lease term (excluding charges for services and taxes to be paid by the lessor) and:

(a)   in the case of the lessee, any residual amounts guaranteed by him or by a party related to him; or

(b)   in the case of the lessor, any residual amounts guaranteed by the lessee or by an independent third party.

21   The *gross investment* in a lease at a point in time is the total of the minimum lease payments and any unguaranteed residual value accruing to the lessor.

22   The *net investment* in a lease at a point in time comprises:

(a)   the gross investment in a lease (as defined in paragraph 21): *less*

(b)   gross earnings allocated to future periods.

23   The *net cash investment* in a lease at a point in time is the amount of funds invested in a lease by a lessor, and comprises the cost of the asset plus or minus the following related payments or receipts:

(a)   government or other grants receivable towards the purchase or use of the asset;

(b)   rentals received;

(c)   taxation payments and receipts, including the effect of capital allowances;

(d)   residual values, if any, at the end of the lease term;

(e)   interest payments (where applicable);

(f)   interest received on cash surplus;

(g)   profit taken out of the lease.

24   The *interest rate implicit in a lease* is the discount rate that at the inception of a lease, when applied to the amounts which the lessor expects to receive and retain produces an amount (the present value) equal to the fair value of the leased asset. The amounts which the lessor expects to receive and retain comprise (a) the minimum lease payments to the lessor (as defined in paragraph 20), plus (b) any unguaranteed residual value, less (c) any part of (a) and (b) for which the lessor will be accountable to the lessee. If the interest rate implicit in the lease is not determinable, it should be estimated by reference to the rate which a lessee would be expected to pay on a similar lease.

Fair value is the price at which an asset could be exchanged in an arm's length 25 transaction less, where applicable, any grants receivable towards the purchase or use of the asset.

Unguaranteed residual value is that portion of the residual value of the leased asset 26 (estimated at the inception of the lease), the realisation of which by the lessor is not assured or is guaranteed solely by a party related to the lessor.

Finance charge is the amount borne by the lessee over the lease term, representing the 27 difference between the total of the minimum lease payments (including any residual amounts guaranteed by him) and the amount at which he records the leased asset at the inception of the lease.

Gross earnings comprise the lessor's gross finance income over the lease term, 28 representing the difference between his gross investment in the lease (as defined in paragraph 21) and the cost of the leased asset less any grants receivable towards the purchase or use of the asset.

The *inception of a lease* is the earlier of the time the asset is brought into use and the 29 date from which rentals first accrue.

Initial direct costs are those costs incurred by the lessor that are directly associated 30 with negotiating and consummating leasing transactions, such as commissions, legal fees, costs of credit investigations and costs of preparing and processing documents for new leases acquired.

Part 3 – Standard accounting practice

HIRE PURCHASE AND LEASING

Those hire purchase contracts which are of a financing nature should be accounted 31 for on a basis similar to that set out below for finance leases. Conversely, other hire purchase contracts should be accounted for on a basis similar to that set out below for operating leases.

ACCOUNTING BY LESSEES

A finance lease should be recorded in the balance sheet of a lessee as an asset and as 32 an obligation to pay future rentals. At the inception of the lease the sum to be recorded both as an asset and as a liability should be the present value of the minimum lease payments, derived by discounting them at the interest rate implicit in the lease.

In practice in the case of a finance lease the fair value of the asset will often be a 33 sufficiently close approximation to the present value of the minimum lease payments and may in these circumstances be substituted for it.

The combined benefit to a lessor of regional development and other grants together 34 with capital allowances, which reduce tax liabilities, may enable the minimum lease payments under a finance lease to be reduced to a total which is less than the fair value of the asset. In these circumstances, the amount to be capitalised and depreciated should be restricted to the minimum lease payments. A negative finance charge should not be shown.

35   Rentals payable should be apportioned between the finance charge and a reduction of the outstanding obligation for future amounts payable. The total finance charge under a finance lease should be allocated to accounting periods during the lease term so as to produce a constant periodic rate of charge on the remaining balance of the obligation for each accounting period, or a reasonable approximation thereto.

36   An asset leased under a finance lease should be depreciated over the shorter of the lease term (as defined in paragraph 19) and its useful life. However, in the case of a hire purchase contract which has the characteristics of a finance lease, the asset should be depreciated over its useful life.

37   The rental under an operating lease should be charged on a straight-line basis over the lease term, even if the payments are not made on such a basis, unless another systematic and rational basis is more appropriate.*

ACCOUNTING BY LESSORS

38   The amount due from the lessee under a finance lease should be recorded in the balance sheet of a lessor as a debtor at the amount of the net investment in the lease after making provisions for items such as bad and doubtful rentals receivable.

39   The total gross earnings under a finance lease should normally be allocated to accounting periods to give a constant periodic rate of return to the lessor's **net cash investment** in the lease in each period. In the case of a hire purchase contract which has characteristics similar to a finance lease, allocation of gross earnings so as to give a constant periodic rate of return on the finance company's **net investment** will in most cases be a suitable approximation to allocation based on the net cash investment. In arriving at the constant periodic rate of return, a reasonable approximation may be made.

40   As an alternative to paragraph 39, an allocation may first be made out of gross earnings of an amount equal to the lessor's estimated cost of finance included in the net cash investment calculation, with the balance being recognised on a systematic basis.

41   Tax free grants that are available to the lessor against the purchase price of assets acquired for leasing should be spread over the period of the lease and dealt with by treating the grant as non-taxable income.

42   An asset held for use in operating leases by a lessor should be recorded as a fixed asset and depreciated over its useful life.

43   Rental income from an operating lease, excluding charges for services such as insurance and maintenance, should be recognised on a straight-line basis over the period of the lease, even if the payments are not made on such a basis, unless another systematic and rational basis is more representative of the time pattern in which the benefit from the leased asset is receivable.†

44   Initial direct costs incurred by a lessor in arranging a lease may be apportioned over the period of the lease on a systematic and rational basis.

Editor's note: See also UITF Abstract 28 'Operating lease incentives'.

†*Editor's note: See also UITF Abstract 28 'Operating lease incentives'.*

MANUFACTURER/DEALER LESSOR

A manufacturer or dealer lessor should not recognise a selling profit under an   **45**
operating lease. The selling profit under a finance lease should be restricted to the
excess of the fair value of the asset over the manufacturer's or dealer's cost less any
grants receivable by the manufacturer or dealer towards the purchase, construction
or use of the asset.

SALE AND LEASEBACK TRANSACTIONS Accounting by the seller/lessee

In a sale and leaseback transaction which results in a finance lease any apparent   **46**
profit or loss (that is, the difference between the sale price and the previous carrying
value) should be deferred and amortised in the financial statements of the seller/lessee
over the shorter of the lease term and the useful life of the asset.

If the leaseback is an operating lease: **47**

(a)   any profit or loss should be recognised immediately, provided it is clear that the
transaction is established at fair value;
(b)   if the sale price is below fair value, any profit or loss should be recognised
immediately except that if the apparent loss is compensated by future rentals at
below market price it should to that extent be deferred and amortised over the
remainder of the lease term (or, if shorter, the period during which the reduced
rentals are chargeable);
(c)   if the sale price is above fair value, the excess over fair value should be deferred
and amortised over the shorter of the remainder of the lease term and the
period to the next rent review (if any).

Accounting by the buyer/lessor

A buyer/lessor should account for a sale and leaseback in the same way as he   **48**
accounts for other leases, that is, using methods set out in paragraphs 38 to 45 above.

DISCLOSURE BY LESSEES

The gross amounts of assets which are held under finance leases* together with the   **49**
related accumulated depreciation should be disclosed by each major class of asset.
The total depreciation allocated for the period in respect of assets held under finance
leases should be disclosed by each major class of asset.

The information required by paragraph 49 may, as an alternative to being shown   **50**
separately from that in respect of owned fixed assets, be integrated with it such that
the totals of gross amount, accumulated depreciation, net amount and depreciation
allocated for the period for each major class of asset are included with similar
amounts in respect of owned fixed assets. Where this alternative treatment is
adopted, the net amount of assets held under finance leases* included in the overall
total should be disclosed. The amount of depreciation allocated for the period in
respect of assets held under finance leases* included in the overall total should also
be disclosed.

*Including the equivalent information in respect of hire purchase contracts which have characteristics similar to
that type of lease (see paragraph 31).

51   The amounts of obligations related to finance leases* (net of finance charges allocated to future periods) should be disclosed separately from other obligations and liabilities, either on the face of the balance sheet or in the notes to the accounts.

52   These net obligations under finance leases* should be analysed between amounts payable in the next year, amounts payable in the second to fifth years inclusive from the balance sheet date, and the aggregate amounts payable thereafter. This analysis may be presented either (a) separately for obligations under finance leases* or (b) where the total of these items is combined on the balance sheet with other obligations and liabilities, by giving the equivalent analysis of the total in which it is included. If the analysis is presented according to (a) above, a lessee may, as an alternative to analysing the net obligations, analyse the gross obligations, with future finance charges being separately deducted from the total.

53   The aggregate finance charges allocated for the period in respect of finance leases* should be disclosed.

54   Disclosure should be made of the amount of any commitments existing at the balance sheet date in respect of finance leases* which have been entered into but whose inception occurs after the year end.

55   The total of operating lease rentals* charged as an expense in the profit and loss account should be disclosed, analysed between amounts payable in respect of hire of plant and machinery and in respect of other operating leases.*

56   In respect of operating leases,* the lessee should disclose the payments which he is committed to make during the next year, analysed between those in which the commitment expires within that year, in the second to fifth years inclusive and over five years from the balance sheet date, showing separately the commitments in respect of leases of land and buildings and other operating leases.*

57   Disclosure should be made of the policies adopted for accounting for operating leases* and finance leases.*

DISCLOSURE BY LESSORS

58   The net investment in (i) finance leases and (ii) hire purchase contracts at each balance sheet date should be disclosed.

59   The gross amounts of assets held for use in operating leases,* and the related accumulated depreciation charges, should be disclosed.

60   Disclosure should be made of:
   (a)   the policy adopted for accounting for operating leases* and finance leases* and, in detail, the policy for accounting for finance lease income;*
   (b)   the aggregate rentals receivable in respect of an accounting period in relation to (i) finance leases* and (ii) operating leases;* and
   (c)   the cost of assets acquired, whether by purchase or finance lease,* for the purpose of letting under finance leases.*

Including the equivalent information in respect of hire purchase contracts which have characteristics similar to that type of lease (see paragraph 31).

APPLICATION TO SMALLER ENTITIES

Reporting entities applying the Financial Reporting Standard for Smaller Entities **60A**
currently applicable are exempt from this accounting standard.

DATE FROM WHICH EFFECTIVE FOR LESSORS AND FINANCE COMPANIES

The accounting practices set out in this statement should be adopted as soon as **61**
possible and regarded as standard for financial statements relating to accounting
periods beginning on or after 1 July 1984 in respect of leases and hire purchase
contracts (a) entered into on or after 1 July 1984 or (b) which have five years or more
to run on 1 July 1984. If the provisions of this statement are not applied retroactively
to all leases and hire purchase contracts existing at 1 July 1984, lessors and finance
companies should disclose the amounts of gross earnings from finance leases and hire
purchase contracts for the current year and the comparative period which have
arisen under each of the principal bases used.*

DATE FROM WHICH EFFECTIVE FOR LESSEES AND HIRERS

The accounting practices set out in this statement should be adopted by lessees and **62**
hirers as soon as possible and regarded as standard in respect of financial statements
relating to accounting periods beginning on or after 1 July 1987. However, the
disclosure requirements in paragraphs 52 and 54 to 57 should be regarded as standard in respect of financial statements relating to accounting periods beginning on or
after 1 July 1984.

Part 4 – Legal requirements in Great Britain

Paragraph 50 (5) of Schedule 8† provides that 'Particulars shall also be given of any **63**
other financial commitments which:

(a)   have not been provided for; and
(b)   are relevant to assessing the company's state of affairs.'

Insofar as finance leases are capitalised by lessees, the obligations under finance
leases are provided for in the accounts. This will not be the case to the extent that
lessees take advantage of the delayed implementation of capitalisation as set out in
paragraph 62.

Paragraph 53(6)‡ of Schedule 8† requires disclosure of the 'amount charged to **64**
revenue in respect of sums payable in respect of the hire of plant and machinery'
(Standard, paragraphs 49, 50, 53 and 55 and guidance notes).

---

*Editor's note: The amendment in February 1997 (the removal of the option in paragraph 41 to gross up tax free
grants) became standard in respect of financial statements relating to accounting periods ending on or after 22
June 1997. Earlier adoption was encouraged but not required.*

†*Editor's note: Now Schedule 4 to the Companies Act 1985, and Schedule 8 in the case of small companies. In
the case of small companies the reference to paragraph 50(5) is to paragraph 46(5).*

‡*Editor's note: Paragraph 53(6) was repealed by S.I. 1996 No.189.*

65   The balance sheet formats in Schedule 8* require that creditors falling due within one year should be shown separately from creditors falling due after more than one year (Standard, paragraph 52 and guidance notes).

66   The balance sheet formats in Schedule 8* provide that the 'amount falling due after more than one year shall be shown separately for each item included under debtors'. This is relevant to the disclosure of amounts receivable by a lessor (Standard, paragraph 58 and guidance notes).

Part 5 – Legal requirements in Ireland

NORTHERN IRELAND

67   The Schedule references in Part 4 (paragraphs 63 to 66) apply equally to Schedule 6 of the Companies Act (Northern Ireland) 1960, as inserted by Article 3 of the Companies (Northern Ireland) Order 1982.

REPUBLIC OF IRELAND

68   General provisions as to accounts are set out in the Sixth Schedule to the Companies Act 1963. There are no legal requirements in the Republic of Ireland similar to those outlined in Part 4.

Part 6 – Compliance with International Accounting Standard No. 17 'Accounting for leases'

69   The requirements of International Accounting Standard No. 17 'Accounting for leases'† accord very closely with the content of the United Kingdom and Irish Accounting Standard No. 21 'Accounting for leases and hire purchase contracts' and accordingly compliance with SSAP 21 will ensure compliance with IAS 17 in all material respects.

---

*Editor's note: Now Schedule 4 to the Companies Act 1985, and Schedule 8 in the case of small companies. In the case of small companies the reference to paragraph 50(5) is to paragraph 46(5).

†Editor's note: A revised version of IAS 17 was issued in December 1997. This eliminated the previous option of using the net cash investment method required by SSAP 21 for allocating finance lease payments received by the lessor. In addition, there are some differences between the tests for the classification of a lease between the two standards, and IAS 17 now requires rather more disclosure than is required by SSAP 21. SIC 27 has also been issued 'Evaluating the substance of transactions in the legal form of a lease,' as well as SIC 15 'Operating leases – incentives'. A further revised version of IAS 17 was issued in December 2003. This draws a distinction between inception and commencement of a lease, and makes some changes to the treatment of initial costs. However, the main aim of the change was to deal with operating leases over properties held as investment properties.

Guidance Notes on SSAP 21:
Accounting for leases and hire purchase contracts

(Issued August 1984)

These notes are for guidance only and do not form part of the statement of standard accounting practice.

Contents

INTRODUCTION

General

1   The statement of Standard Accounting Practice on Accounting for Leases and Hire Purchase Contracts sets out objectives and disclosure requirements. The primary purpose of the guidance notes is to recommend practical methods which will assist companies to comply with the standard. The guidance notes are not mandatory.

2   The aim in writing the guidance notes has been to cover the most common situations which will be met in practice. It is not possible to lay down methods which will cover all situations.

3   The guidance notes do not recognise the effect of the transitional provisions set out in paragraphs 61 and 62 of the standard. In the periods affected by these provisions different methods and disclosures may be required.

4   All references in the guidance notes to legal requirements are to the UK Companies Acts; the examples assume that companies are subject to Schedule 8, Companies Act 1948.*

5   The definitions of terms in the standard apply also to the guidance notes.

6   The effects of value added tax have been ignored in the guidance notes.

Materiality

7   The standard, in common with all standards, need not be applied to immaterial items. In this context, the relevant criterion is the size of the lease (or leases in aggregate, if more than one) in the context of the size of the lessee or lessor.

8   In deciding whether or not a lease is material, regard should be had to the effect which treating the lease according to the main requirements of the standard (e.g., capitalising it) would have on the financial statements as a whole. Thus, it may be necessary to consider the effect of (in this example) capitalisation on (a) total fixed assets, (b) total borrowings and obligations, (c) the gearing ratio and (d) the profit or loss for the year (as a result of the difference between charging the lease payment and charging the total of depreciation plus finance charge). If capitalisation of the lease would not have a material effect on any of these items, the lease need not be capitalised.

The simplified approach to accounting for small leases

9   Where a lease is material, the main provisions of the standard will need to be applied. Thus, a finance lease will need to be capitalised by a lessee. Similarly, a finance lease should be shown as a receivable by a lessor.

10 However, Part I of these guidance notes describes the use of simplified methods for leases and suggests when they may be used. In particular, paragraphs 32 to 36 describe the simplified approach to lessee accounting whereby a lessee may use the straight-line method to write off finance charges under a finance lease. Part II discusses a number of methods of lessors' income recognition, including simplified methods (see, for example paragraphs 81, 95, 119 and 122).

*Editor's note: Now Schedule 4 to the Companies Act 1985.

Hire purchase and leasing

It is not intended that this standard should change the existing best practice for accounting for hire purchase contracts by either finance companies or hirers.   **11**

Most hire purchase contracts are of a financing nature. Generally, the option to purchase the asset is exercisable at below market value – often at a nominal amount – such that the hirer can be expected from the outset to take up the option. The standard therefore provides that such hire purchase contracts should be accounted for on a basis similar to that set out for finance leases.   **12**

Less commonly, there are found hire purchase contracts which are not of a financing nature. For example, the option to purchase may be exercisable at a relatively high price such that the hirer may not take it up. The standard therefore provides that such hire purchase contracts should be accounted for on a similar basis to that set out for operating leases.   **13**

Part I – Lessee accounting

INTRODUCTION

Part I explains the accounting requirements for lessees in the following sections: **14**

A – GENERAL PRINCIPLES

A lessee should classify his leases in (a) operating leases and (b) finance leases, according to the definitions in paragraphs 15 to 17 of the standard. Additional guidance on lease classification may be found in paragraphs 133 to 138.   **15**

Operating leases

The right to use an asset or the obligation to pay rentals under an operating lease should not be recorded in the balance sheet but a lessee should disclose certain information by way of note to the financial statements (see paragraphs 57 to 63). The rentals under an operating lease should be charged on a straight-line basis over the lease term, even if the payments are not made on such a basis, unless another systematic and rational basis is more appropriate. Thus, in situations such as rental holidays in which a lease has been arranged so that, for example, no payment is made in the first year (although the asset is in use during that year), the total rentals should be charged over the period in which the asset is in use.*   **16**

*Editor's note: The last sentence was superseded by UITF Abstract 12 'Lessee accounting for reverse premiums and similar incentives' which has itself now been superseded by UITF Abstract 28 'Operating lease incentives'.

Finance leases

17   Under a finance lease the lessee acquires substantially all the benefits of the use of an asset for the greater part of its useful economic life and takes on substantially all of the risks associated with ownership. In economic substance it is similar to the purchase of an asset even though legal title to the asset remains with the lessor.

18   The risks of ownership of an asset include unsatisfactory performance, obsolescence and idle capacity. The benefits include the right to the unencumbered use of the asset over most of its useful economic life.

19   The two aspects of a finance lease should be recorded in the lessee's balance sheet. The right to use the asset should be capitalised and shown as a fixed asset. The obligation to pay rentals should be shown as a liability.

B – THE ARITHMETIC OF CAPITALISING FINANCE LEASES

20   The capitalisation of finance leases is now illustrated by means of numerical examples. Three methods of writing off finance charges are shown:

(a)   the actuarial method;
(b)   the 'Rule of 78' (or 'Sum of the Digits') method; and
(c)   the straight-line method.

The standard (paragraph 35) provides that the 'total finance charge under a finance lease should be allocated to accounting periods during the lease term so as to produce a constant periodic rate of charge on the remaining balance of the obligation for each accounting period, or a reasonable approximation thereto'. Of the above three methods, the actuarial method gives the most accurate result.

Terms of the lease

21   The examples illustrated are based on the following lease:

> A lessee leases an asset on a non-cancellable lease contract with a primary term of five years from 1 January 1987. The rental is £650 per quarter payable in advance. The lessee has the right to continue to lease the asset after the end of the primary period for as long as he wishes at a peppercorn rent. In addition the lessee is required to pay all maintenance and insurance costs as they arise. The leased asset could have been purchased for cash at the start of the lease for £10,000.

22   A lessee should, strictly, record a finance lease at the present value of the minimum lease payments (Standard, paragraph 32). However, for most practical purposes, it will be acceptable to record the leased asset at its fair value (Standard, paragraph 33). (The present value of the minimum lease payments in a finance lease will normally be at least 90% of the fair value of the leased asset.) The two approaches would produce different results where the lessor expects to benefit from a residual value which is not guaranteed by the lessee. In this example it is assumed for simplicity that the asset has no residual value at the end of the lease term. At the start of the lease, therefore, the lessee should capitalise the asset in his balance sheet at a cost of £10,000 and also record the obligation under the finance lease of £10,000 as a liability. Guidance on a more rigorous determination of the amount to be capitalised in respect of a leased asset is given in paragraphs 64 to 68.

The minimum lease payments amount to 20 × £650 = £13,000. The total finance **23**
charges under the lease are therefore £3,000.

The total finance charges should be allocated to accounting periods during the lease **24**
so as to produce a constant periodic rate of charge on the remaining balance of the
obligation for each accounting period. This calculation is shown in Table 1.

The actuarial method

TABLE 1 **25**

CALCULATION OF THE PERIODIC FINANCE CHARGE IN THE LEASE

Period	Capital sum at start of period	Rental paid	Capital sum during period	Finance charge (2.95% per quarter)*	Capital sum at end of period
	£	£	£	£	£
1/87	10,000	650	9,350	276	9,626
2/87	9,626	650	8,976	265	9,241
3/87	9,241	650	8,591	254	8,845
4/87	8,845	650	8,195	242	8,437
				1,037	
1/88	8,437	650	7,787	230	8,017
2/88	8,017	650	7,367	217	7,584
3/88	7,584	650	6,934	205	7,139
4/88	7,139	650	6,489	191	6,680
				843	
1/89	6,680	650	6,030	178	6,208
2/89	6,208	650	5,558	164	5,722
3/89	5,722	650	5,072	150	5,222
4/89	5,222	650	4,572	135	4,707
				627	
1/90	4,707	650	4,057	120	4,177
2/90	4,177	650	3,527	104	3,631
3/90	3,631	650	2,981	88	3,069
4/90	3,069	650	2,419	71	2,490
				383	
1/91	2,490	650	1,840	54	1,894
2/91	1,894	650	1,244	37	1,281
3/91	1,281	650	631	19	650
4/91	650	650	–	–	–
				110	
		£13,000		£3,000	

*The quarterly finance charge of 2.95% may be calculated in a number of ways: (a) by trial and error, (b) by
financial pocket calculator or computer program, (c) by a mathematical formula, or (d) by reference to present
value tables.*

26   The annual rental may therefore be apportioned between a finance charge and a capital repayment based on the figures in Table 1:

TABLE 2

APPORTIONMENT OF ANNUAL RENTALS – ACTUARIAL METHOD

	Finance charge £	Capital Repayment £	Total rental £
1987	1,037	1,563	2,600
1988	843	1,757	2,600
1989	627	1,973	2,600
1990	383	2,217	2,600
1991	110	2,490	2,600
	£3,000	£10,000	£13,000

27   The allocation of the finance charge to accounting periods by the actuarial method in Table 1 is not easy to calculate manually and it may be appropriate to use the rule of 78 or the straight-line method as an approximation. These are discussed in turn.

Rule of 78

28   The rule of 78 may normally be regarded as an acceptable approximation to the actuarial method; it works well provided that the lease term is not very long (say, not more than seven years) and interest rates are not very high. The calculations using the rule of 78 are as follows:

TABLE 3

'RULE OF 78' CALCULATIONS

Period	Number of rentals not yet due		Finance charge per annum	
			£	£
1/87	19		= 300	
2/87	18		= 284	
3/87	17		= 268	
4/87	16		= 253	
				1,105
1/88	15		= 237	
2/88	14		= 221	
3/88	13		= 205	
4/88	12		= 190	
				853
1/89	11		= 174	
2/89	10	÷ 190 × 3000	= 158	
3/89	9		= 142	
4/89	8		= 126	
				600
1/90	7		= 110	
2/90	6		= 95	
3/90	5		= 79	
4/90	4		= 63	
				347
1/91	3		= 47	
2/91	2		= 32	
3/91	1		= 16	
4/91	–		= –	
				95
	190*		£3,000	£3,000

*This total may be calculated using the formula

$\dfrac{n(n+1)}{2}$ where n is the number of periods in question.

Hence in this case n = 19 and $\dfrac{19 \times 20}{2}$ = 190.

The term 'Rule of 78' arose because, if finance charges are allocated over a one year period, months 1 to 12 when added together add up to 78. Here, the weights add up to 190.   **29**

In this example rentals are payable in advance. Hence the final payment is made on the first day of period 4/91, and no interest should be allocated to that period. If the rentals had been payable in arrears, then one unit of interest would have been chargeable to that period, and 20 units to period 1/87, with corresponding changes to the other periods.   **30**

Having calculated the finance charge as in paragraph 28 using the rule of 78, all the other calculations are continued in the same way as for the actuarial method.   **31**

The straight-line method

32   As noted above, and as can be seen in Table 5 below, the use of the rule of 78 results in a close approximation to the actuarial method. However, it may be appropriate in certain cases to use the straight-line method. This is the simplest of the methods illustrated. It does not attempt to produce a constant periodic rate of change, but if used in connection with a relatively small lease it may produce figures which in any year are not significantly different from those which would be produced by one of the other methods. What is a small lease will depend on the size of the company.

33   The calculations using the straight-line method are as follows. The finance charges under the lease should be apportioned on a straight-line basis over the period of the lease in which rentals are being paid:

£3,000 ÷ 5 = £600 per annum

34   The annual rental may be apportioned between the finance charge and the capital repayment as follows:

TABLE 4

APPORTIONMENT OF ANNUAL RENTALS – STRAIGHT-LINE METHOD

	Finance charge £	Capital repayment £	Total rental £
1987	600	2,000	2,600
1988	600	2,000	2,600
1989	600	2,000	2,600
1990	600	2,000	2,600
1991	600	2,000	2,600
	£3,000	£10,000	£13,000

35   The finance charges as calculated under the actuarial method, the rule of 78 and the straight-line method are compared below:

TABLE 5

COMPARISON OF FINANCE CHARGES

	Actuarial £	%	Rule of 78 £	%	Straight-line £	%
1987	1,037	34	1,105	37	600	20
1988	843	28	853	28	600	20
1989	627	21	600	20	600	20
1990	383	13	347	12	600	20
1991	110	4	95	3	600	20
	£3,000	100	£3,000	100	£3,000	100

Whether the straight-line method (or the rule of 78) provides a reasonable approximation to an accurate method depends on the facts of each case. Where a lease is small in relation to the size of the lessee, the difference between the methods may not be material.

36   It is sometimes argued that, in order to establish whether the straight-line method provides a reasonable approximation, it is necessary to calculate the finance charge allocation on two or more bases. This is not necessarily so. In some cases the *total* finance charges may not be material in which case the straight-line method may be used: there will be no need to compare the allocation under the straight-line method with that under any other method.

Variation clauses

Where a lease contains an interest variation clause which adjusts the rental by reference to movements in Finance House base rate, or some other indicator, no adjustment need normally be made to the calculations, such as those in Table 1, which are carried out at the start of the lease. Any increase or reduction in rentals should be accounted for as an increase or reduction in finance charges in the period in which it arises. **37**

Where a lease contains a tax variation clause which adjusts the rental in order to protect the parties from the effects of tax changes, any increase or reduction in rentals should be accounted for as an increase or reduction in finance charges. Where the reduction in rentals exceeds the future finance charges, the excess should be applied to reduce future depreciation charges. **38**

Depreciation

The leased asset should be depreciated on a basis compatible with that adopted for assets which are owned. SSAP 12 'Accounting for depreciation'* requires an asset to be depreciated by allocating the cost less estimated residual value of the asset as fairly as possible to the periods expected to benefit from its use. **39**

The period over which a leased asset should be depreciated is the shorter of (a) the lease term and (b) the asset's useful life. The lease term is the primary period of the lease (i.e., the non-cancellable part) together with any secondary periods during which the lessee has the contractual right to continue to use the asset and which right, at the start of the lease, it is reasonable to expect him to exercise. **40**

In this example the lessee estimates that the lease will be continued for a further two years after the end of the primary period so that he should depreciate the leased asset over seven years. This is the period over which he depreciates similar assets which he owns. **41**

In most cases the residual value of leased assets at the end of the lease is likely to be small so that even where the lessee has the right to share in the ultimate residual value it is usual to assume for the purposes of establishing an appropriate depreciation charge that it will be nil. This will be the case whether the residual value takes the form of sale proceeds or a rebate of rentals. **42**

In this example the lessee estimates that the asset will have a useful life of seven years and that the residual value will be nil. The annual depreciation charge on a straight-line basis is therefore: **43**

$$£10,000 \div 7 = £1,429$$

In the case of a hire purchase contract which has the characteristics of a finance lease, it is expected from the outset that the hirer will take up the option to purchase. **44**

Editor's note: Superseded by FRS 15 'Tangible fixed assets' published February 1999.

Hence, the asset should be depreciated over its useful life, regardless of the term of the hire contract.

Calculation of balance sheet values

45   The leased asset should be described in the balance sheet as 'Assets held under finance leases'. The liability should be described as 'Obligations under finance leases'. The net book value of the asset at the end of each year, if straight-line depreciation is used, will be:

TABLE 6

BALANCE SHEET VALUES – LEASED ASSETS

	Cost	Accumulated depreciation	Net book value of assets held under finance lease
	£	£	£
31.12.87	10,000 –	1,429 =	8,571
31.12.88	10,000 –	2,858 =	7,142
31.12.89	10,000 –	4,287 =	5,713
31.12.90	10,000 –	5,716 =	4,284
31.12.91	10,000 –	7,145 =	2,855
31.12.92	10,000 –	8,574 =	1,426
31.12.93	10,000 –	10,000 =	–

46   The obligations under finance leases (i.e., the capital element of future rentals payable) will be calculated as follows:

TABLE 7

BALANCE SHEET VALUES – LEASING OBLIGATIONS

	Obligations under finance leases outstanding at start of year	Capital repayment	Obligations under finance leases outstanding at year end
	£	£	£
31.12.87	10,000 –	1,563 =	8,437
31.12.88	8,437 –	1,757 =	6,680
31.12.89	6,680 –	1,973 =	4,707
31.12.90	4,707 –	2,217 =	2,490
31.12.91	2,490 –	2,490 =	–
31.12.92			
31.12.93			

(These figures assume that the actuarial method is being used. The capital repayments are taken from Table 2.)

Comparison of the balance sheet amounts of the capitalised leased asset

47   The figures in Tables 6 and 7 are compared below:

TABLE 8

LEASED ASSETS AND OBLIGATIONS

	NBV of assets held under finance leases	Obligations under finance leases outstanding at year end		Difference
	£	£		£
31.12.87	8,571 –	8,437	=	134
31.12.88	7,142 –	6,680	=	462
31.12.89	5,713 –	4,707	=	1,006
31.12.90	4,284 –	2,490	=	1,794
31.12.91	2,855 –	–	=	2,855
31.12.92	1,426 –	–	=	1,426
31.12.93	– –	–	=	–

The differences shown in the third column do not appear separately on a balance sheet. They are timing differences which result from capitalising a lease, and are needed for the calculation of deferred tax (see paragraphs 171 to 173*). Charging the total of depreciation and interest to the profit and loss account is likely to result in recognition of the total costs of a finance lease in a different pattern from that in which the rentals are paid and the tax allowances are received. In this example, the costs are recognised later because the asset is depreciated over seven years whereas the instalments are paid over five years. Hence the timing differences cause a temporary, reversing, increase in equity, which is reflected in the above table by asset values being temporarily higher than the obligations.

C – BALANCE SHEET PRESENTATION, NOTE DISCLOSURE AND LEGAL REQUIREMENTS FOR LESSEES

A finance lease will be shown in a lessee's balance sheet both as an asset and as an **48** obligation. At the start of the lease the amount of the asset and the obligation will be the same but they are unlikely to be so in subsequent years. The obligation under the lease may be paid off before the asset is fully depreciated.

Schedule 8 to the Companies Act 1948† contains, inter alia, formats which must be **49** followed by companies (except those subject to Schedule 8A‡) in the presentation of their accounts. Leased assets and leasing obligations are not specifically mentioned in the formats, but paragraphs 3(1) and (2) of the 8th Schedule* provide that items may be shown in greater detail than required by the formats and that new items may be inserted for items not covered by the formats.

Assets held under finance leases are not legally owned by the lessee. (The same **50** applies to assets subject to hire purchase contracts, until the purchase option is exercised.) The lessee's right is to use the asset, not to own it. Similarly, a lessee's obligations under a finance lease are not, from a legal point of view, debt but rather obligations under a bailment to hire. Therefore, in order to reflect this legal difference, assets held under finance leases and the related obligations should be described in such a way as to be distinguishable from owned assets and debt respectively.

*Editor's note: The ASB noted in FRS 19 'Deferred tax' that it would be consistent with that FRS if paragraphs 170 and 173–175 of these Guidance Notes, and the references to them, were deemed to be deleted.

†Editor's note: Now Schedule 4 to the Companies Act 1985.

‡Editor's note: Now Schedules 9 and 9A to the Companies Act 1985.

51   The standard permits a company to aggregate the amounts which are required to be presented on a balance sheet or disclosed in notes in respect of (i) finance leases and (ii) hire purchase contracts which have characteristics similar to finance leases. It is expected that most companies will choose to combine the amounts.

52   Assets held under finance leases and hire purchase contracts should generally be integrated with owned fixed assets on a balance sheet. The analysis of fixed assets may be in one of two forms: either

(a)   the notes to the accounts should contain details of the assets held under finance leases and hire purchase contracts, by class of asset; or

(b)   the fixed assets note should analyse, by class of asset, the combined total of owned assets and assets held under finance leases and hire purchase contracts. In order to distinguish owned assets from non-owned assets, a note similar to the following should be shown:

'The net book value of fixed assets of £x includes an amount of £8,571 in respect of assets held under finance leases and hire purchase contracts'.

53   Obligations under finance leases and hire purchase contracts should be analysed between those amounts payable within one year and those amounts payable in more than one year. These two amounts should be described, either on the face of the balance sheet or in the notes to the accounts, as 'Obligations under finance leases and hire purchase contracts' under the headings of 'Creditors: amounts falling due within one year' and 'Creditors: amounts falling due after more than one year' respectively.

54   Alternatively, obligations under finance leases and hire purchase contracts may be combined with other items (for example, bank loans and overdrafts) under each of the 'Creditors' headings referred to in the preceding paragraph.

55   The standard requires the amount of obligations under finance leases and hire purchase contracts falling due after more than one year, or the total in which it is included, to be further analysed as to amounts due in the second to fifth years inclusive from the balance sheet date and the aggregate amounts payable thereafter.

56   Where the treatment in paragraph 54 is adopted, a note such as the following will comply with the disclosure requirements and with company law:

Bank loans, overdrafts, obligations under finance leases and hire purchase contracts

These comprise:

Bank loans and overdrafts	20,000
Obligations under finance leases and hire purchase contracts (see paragraph 47)	8,437
	£28,437

The maturity of the above amounts is as follows:

Under one year		10,000
Over one year		
In the second to fifth years inclusive	12,500	
Over five years	5,937	
		18,437
		£28,437

The £10,000 should be included under the heading 'Creditors: amounts falling due within one year'; the £18,437 should be included under the heading 'Creditors: amounts falling due after more than one year'. (The Stock Exchange additionally requires listed companies to disclose the amount payable in the second year after the balance sheet date.)

Note disclosure – profit and loss account

Paragraph 53(6) of Schedule 8* to the Companies Act 1948 requires disclosure of the amount, if material, charged to revenue in respect of sums payable in respect of the hire of plant and machinery. To comply with this requirement it is necessary to disclose the amounts charged to revenue for operating leases and finance leases and hire purchase contracts. In the latter cases this would consist of depreciation and finance charges.   **57**

The following is an example of an appropriate note which combines these legal requirements with those of the standard (assuming that the company has a charge for each item):

	£
Profit is stated after charging:	
Depreciation of owned assets	a
Depreciation of assets held under finance leases and hire purchase contracts	b
Interest payable – bank loans and overdrafts and other loans repayable within five years	c
Finance charges payable – finance leases and hire purchase contracts	d
Hire of plant and machinery – operating leases	e
Hire of other assets – operating leases	f

(Note: amounts charged to revenue in respect of finance leases and hire purchase contracts are shown separately under the headings of depreciation (£b) and finance charges (£d) (total, £g.))

Notes:

1. This amount is required to be disclosed by paragraphs 49 and 50 of the standard as well as in compliance with paragraph 53(6) of Schedule 8.*
2. This amount is required to be disclosed by paragraph 53 of the standard as well as in compliance with paragraph 53(6) of Schedule 8.*
3. This amount is required to be disclosed by paragraph 55 of the standard as well as in compliance with paragraph 53(6) of Schedule 8.*
4. This is required to be disclosed by paragraph 55 of the standard. When added to the amount in the above line for hire of plant and machinery, it gives the total charge in respect of operating leases.

Disclosure of commitments under operating leases

In the case of operating leases, the standard requires a lessee to disclose, in addition to the amount charged in the year, the yearly amount of the payments to which he is committed at the year end (the annual commitment). This will not necessarily be the same as the amount paid in the year then ending as it will include a full year's rental for leases which have been taken out during the year and it will exclude rentals in respect of leases which terminated during the year. The annual payments to which he   **58**

*Editor's note: Became para 53(6) of Schedule 4 to the Companies Act 1985, but repealed by S.I. 1996 No. 89.

is committed should be analysed between those in which the commitment expires within that year, in the second to fifth years inclusive and over five years from the balance sheet date. Leases of land and buildings are to be shown separately from other operating leases.

59   In the case of these disclosure requirements, materiality should be borne in mind. Thus if either the amounts for leases of land and buildings or for other leases are not material, the two categories may be aggregated. If the total is immaterial, no disclosure needs to be made.

60   A suggested note is set out below:

At 31 December 1987 the company had annual commitments under non-cancellable operating leases as set out below.

£000's	1987		1986	
	Land and Buildings	Other	Land and Buildings	Other
Operating leases which expire:				
within one year	30	100	25	90
in the second to fifth years inclusive	80	50	75	40
over five years	120	20	110	10
	230	170	210	140

The majority of leases of land and buildings are subject to rent reviews.

Other disclosures

61   SSAP 2 'Disclosure of accounting policies'* already requires disclosure of the accounting policies followed for dealing with items which are judged material or critical in determining profit or loss for the year and in stating the financial position. The present standard does not change the need to give such information and therefore disclosure should be made of the policies adopted for capitalisation and depreciation of leased assets and for the recognition of finance charges, where material.

62   It may also be necessary, in order to show a true and fair view, to disclose information relevant to lease contracts or hire purchase contracts which is of particular significance to users of financial statements. This may include such items as:

(a)   the nature of any contingent rentals such as those based on usage or sales;
(b)   the nature of any contingent liability, for example costs which may arise at the end of the lease term.

Further, as with any other form of financing, it may be appropriate to disclose financial restrictions imposed by the lease or hire purchase agreement such as limitations on additional borrowing or further leasing.

63   The standard (paragraph 54) requires disclosure of the amount of any material commitments in respect of finance leases which have been entered into but whose inception occurs after the year end. This is analogous to the legal requirement in

*Editor's note: SSAP 2 has now been superseded by FRS 18 'Accounting policies'.

respect of capital commitments in paragraph 50(3)(a) of Schedule 8* to the Companies Act 1948.

D – INITIAL RECORDING OF THE LEASED ASSET

As noted in paragraph 22 above, strictly, a lessee should record a finance lease at the **64** present value of the minimum lease payments. (The minimum lease payments comprise all payments guaranteed by the lessee including rentals and any residual value guaranteed by him.) However, the present value of the minimum lease payments in a finance lease will normally be at least 90% of the fair value of the leased asset. For most practical purposes therefore it will be acceptable to record the leased asset at its fair value.

There are two occasions on which the leased asset would not be recorded at fair **65** value. The first is where both the fair value and the present value of the minimum lease payments are known and the fair value is found to be not a sufficiently close approximation to the present value. Such cases are likely to be rare, as, by definition, the two figures are likely to be within 10% of each other.

The second possibility would be where the fair value of the asset is not known. Whilst **66** this would be unusual in the UK, it may occur, for example where the asset can be obtained from only one manufacturer and he will make it available only by way of a finance lease. In such a case, a lessee should follow the rule in paragraph 32 of the standard and record the finance lease at the present value of the minimum lease payments. The present value should be determined by reference to the interest rate implicit in a lease. This is defined in paragraph 24 of the standard; it should be noted in particular that if the interest rate implicit in a lease is not determinable, it should be estimated by reference to the rate which a lessee would be expected to pay on a lease of similar term and in respect of the same class of asset.

Set out below is an example of the procedure to be followed in the circumstances **67** described in paragraph 66. Assume that a lessee has entered into a finance lease for an asset whose fair value he does not know. The minimum lease payments are five annual instalments of £2,500 each, payable in advance.

The lessee establishes that a typical implicit rate of interest for leases of this type is 11%. He therefore discounts the payments as follows:

TABLE 9

PRESENT VALUE CALCULATION

Year	Discount factor	Payment	Present value
0	1.000	2,500	2,500
1	0.901	2,500	2,252
2	0.812	2,500	2,030
3	0.731	2,500	1,828
4	0.659	2,500	1,647
	4.103		10,257

The asset should be recorded at £10,257, the balance of £2,243 (12,500 − 10,257) representing finance charges.

Editor's note: Now Schedule 4 to the Companies Act 1985.

68   In some cases, there may be difficulties in deciding whether or not a lease is a finance lease, for example where the fair value of the asset is not known. Additional guidance on this and similar problems is given in paragraphs 133 to 138 and 180 to 181.

Part II – Lessor accounting

INTRODUCTION

69   Part II explains the accounting requirements for lessors in the following sections:

	Paragraphs
A – General principles	70–73
B – Finance leases – background considerations	74–87
C – The arithmetic of lessor accounting for finance leases	88–122
D – Balance sheet presentation, note disclosure and legal requirements for lessors	123–131

A – GENERAL PRINCIPLES

70   A lessor should classify his leases into (a) finance leases, and (b) operating leases.

71   Under a finance lease a lessor retains legal title to an asset but passes substantially all the risks and rewards of ownership to the lessee in return for a stream of rentals. In substance, under a finance lease, the lessor provides finance and expects a return thereon.

72   In the case of an operating lease the lessor retains both the legal title and the risks and rewards of ownership of the asset. It may not be possible to predict with certainty the future rentals and expenses, as they may be received and incurred under successive lease agreements with one or more parties; furthermore, the equipment may become obsolete, and changes in the level of economic activity may affect demand. In substance, under an operating lease the lessor is trading with the assets he leases.

73   The lessor should account for leases in accordance with their economic substance. Hence, a finance lease should be accounted for on a basis similar to that for a loan, rather than as a fixed asset subject to depreciation. Conversely, an operating lease should be accounted for by capitalising and depreciating the leased asset.

B – FINANCE LEASES – BACKGROUND CONSIDERATIONS

74   The standard deals, inter alia, with calculation of the carrying value of the finance lease receivables and with lessors' profit recognition. It requires the receivables to be carried on a balance sheet at an amount based on the net investment in the lease. Conversely, it requires that profit recognition should normally be based on the lessor's net *cash* investment.

75   The net investment in a lease is initially the cost of the asset to the lessor, less any government or other grants receivable (i.e., the fair value).

76   The rentals paid by the lessee should be apportioned by the lessor between (a) gross earnings (i.e., the lessor's interest earned) and (b) a repayment of capital.

Over the period of the lease the net investment in the lease (i.e., the carrying value of **77** the receivables) will therefore be the fair value of the asset less those portions of the rentals which are apportioned as a repayment of capital.

For the purposes of profit recognition, however, the total gross earnings should **78** normally be allocated to accounting periods to give a constant periodic rate of return on the lessor's net *cash* investment (NCI) in the lease in each period. (Paragraph 40 of the standard allows an alternative method, which is also partly based on NCI. This is described in paragraph 94 below.) The NCI is based on the funds which the lessor has invested in the lease. The amount of funds invested in a lease by a lessor is different from the net investment in the lease because there are a number of other cash flows which affect the lessor, in addition to those which affect net investment. In particular, tax cash flows are an important component of the NCI. The components of the NCI are listed in paragraph 23 of the standard.

Sometimes a lessor receives an amount which takes the form of a deposit or of non- **79** recourse indebtedness. This amount may be received from the lessee and may in economic substance have the nature of an advance rental. It may be appropriate for the lessor to include such receipts and any repayments thereof in computing the net cash investment for the purpose of allocating gross earnings to accounting periods.

In the case of hire purchase, profit recognition should also, in principle, be based on **80** net cash investment. However, since the capital allowances under a hire purchase contract accrue to the lessee, the finance company's net cash investment is often not significantly different from its net investment; hence allocation of gross earnings (i.e., finance charges) based on net investment will in most cases be a suitable approx- imation to allocation based on net cash investment.

The standard permits a reasonable approximation to be made in arriving at the **81** constant periodic rate of return. Hence there are a number of different methods of profit recognition which may comply with the standard. Some of these methods are illustrated in the next section. However, other methods may be appropriate for use by lessors of any size where they provide a reasonable approximation to the methods described below. It may be appropriate for a lessor to use one of the methods specifically described for its large leases and a simplified method for other leases. What is a large lease will depend on the size of the company.

Initial direct costs are costs such as commissions and legal fees which are often **82** incurred by lessors in negotiating and arranging a lease. The definition (standard, paragraph 30) is not intended to exclude salesperson's costs. Initial direct costs may be apportioned over the lease term on a systematic basis (or may be written off immediately). The same effect as apportioning the costs over the lease term may be achieved by either (a) treating the costs as a deduction from the total gross earnings before the latter are allocated to accounting periods or (b) recognising sufficient gross earnings in the first year to cover the costs. In the case of an operating lease initial direct costs may also either be written off immediately or be deferred and amortised over the lease term.

In most finance leases the estimated residual values of leased assets will be small. **83** They are usually left out of calculations to apportion income from the lease and are accounted for as they arise. Where estimated residual values are used in assessing the lessor's investment in a lease, the estimate should be reviewed regularly and any permanent reduction in the estimated residual value (net of any profits to be recognised later in the lease) should be recognised immediately by an appropriate charge in the profit and loss account.

84   Where individual finance leases are for relatively small amounts, the administration costs in collecting the rentals may be significant. It may therefore be necessary to take them into account when determining an appropriate method of allocating the gross earnings. Failure to take administration costs into account in that manner could result in the recognition in a particular period of costs relating to a lease which exceed the gross earnings recognised in respect of the lease in that period.

85   There will always be a degree of uncertainty about cash flows which are predicted for a number of years ahead. Factors about which there may be uncertainties include:

(a)   doubts about the ability of the lessee to fulfil his obligations under the lease;

(b)   any term in the lease which suggests that the lease is cancellable without appropriate compensation for the lessor;

(c)   doubts about the ability of the lessor to utilise capital allowances at the time he anticipated being able to do so at the start of the lease;

(d)   material uncertainty about interest rates where the lessor is dependent on borrowed funds and the lease rentals are fixed;

(e)   uncertainty concerning future tax changes in the territory where the lease is operative.

86   The treatment to be followed by the lessor will depend on the degree of uncertainty relating to cash flows. If the degree of uncertainty is not great, such that (a) collectibility of the minimum lease payments is reasonably assured and (b) there are no important uncertainties surrounding the amount of unreimbursable costs yet to be incurred by the lessor under the lease, then it will normally be appropriate to classify the lease as a finance lease. The necessity to make a provision for bad debts based on experience of similar finance lease receivables would not preclude a lessor from classifying a lease as a finance lease. In such circumstances the lessor should in general not change the way in which he recognises gross earnings, but should make specific provisions for those cash flows about which the uncertainty exists, such as a provision for bad debts.

87   The degree of uncertainty of cash flows may however be such as to indicate that the lease does not have the characteristics of a finance lease and should more appropriately be accounted for as an operating lease.

C – THE ARITHMETIC OF LESSOR ACCOUNTING FOR FINANCE LEASES

88   There will in most cases be a close relationship between the initial evaluation of a lease and the way in which it is subsequently accounted for. Many lessors evaluate leases by using a method similar to that shown in Table 13 (see paragraph 109). In such an evaluation, the pricing of the rental determines the rate of return in each period. Hence, the manner in which the income is recognised is related to the original lease evaluation.

89   The general approach in the standard is to regard each rental receivable as partly gross earnings and partly a return of capital. A method has to be determined for making this allocation of each rental between the gross earnings and the capital repayment.

90   The total rentals receivable will be known in advance from the terms of the contract and the fair value of the asset will generally be known so that the gross earnings may be calculated.

The numerical examples are based on rates of tax and allowances which, according   **91**
to indications at the time of writing (August 1984), will be in force from April 1986
onwards, that is, a 35% rate of corporation tax and 25% writing down allowances.

As already noted, the standard requires that gross earnings should normally be   **92**
allocated to accounting periods so as to give a constant periodic rate of return (or a
reasonable approximation thereto) on the lessor's net cash investment (NCI) in the
lease in each period. This implies the use of a so-called 'after-tax' method such as:

(a)   the actuarial method after tax; or
(b)   the investment period method (IPM).

These methods are illustrated below. However, as shown in paragraphs 120 to 122
below, other methods may yield acceptable results.

The fact that these methods are known as 'after-tax' methods does not mean that   **93**
they seek to allocate the profit after tax to accounting periods. Rather, the term
means that the gross earnings are being allocated on a basis which takes into account
the tax effect on cash flows – that is, the allocation is based on the NCI.

The standard (paragraph 40) also allows a lessor to adopt a method which involves   **94**
making an allocation out of gross earnings of an amount equal to the lessor's estimated cost of finance included in the net cash investment calculation; the balance
remaining after this allocation is then recognised on a systematic basis. For example,
allocation of the profit after estimated finance costs on the rule of 78 basis has the
merit, in the case of a lease providing for equal rentals at equal intervals, of relating
profit recognition to the amount of outstanding future rentals, non-payment of
which is one of the principal risks for the lessor. Since the cost of finance allocation is
taken from the NCI calculation, it reflects the tax effects of cash flows, hence this
method is also an 'after-tax' method.

The concept of earning a constant periodic rate of return on the net cash investment   **95**
is commonly known as the investment period principle (IPP), of which the actuarial
method after tax and the IPM are two of the most common methods. The actuarial
method after tax is the most accurate method. The IPM is based on similar principles. Other methods have also been developed which attempt to produce the same
constant periodic rate of return. They are not all illustrated here. If they come close
to producing the constant periodic rate of return, then they can be used.

The examples are based on a lease as follows: **96**

> The terms of the lease used in this example are the same as those set out in
> paragraph 21 and used in the lessee examples in Part 1. A lessor leases an asset
> to a lessee on a non-cancellable finance lease for five years from 1 January 1987.
> The rental is £650 per quarter payable in advance. The lessee pays all the
> maintenance and insurance costs as they arise. The cost of the asset is £10,000.

The lessor obtains writing down allowances on the leased asset at the rate of 25%.
The rate of corporation tax is 35%. The lessor's year end is 31 December and he pays
or recovers tax nine months after the year end.

In the examples which follow, the lessor always needs funds to support the lease, that   **97**
is, the lease does not generate a cash surplus. In other cases, a cash surplus may arise
in certain periods, for example if the lessor buys the asset later in his accounting year,
or where for other reasons tax allowances are receivable earlier in the lease. In these
circumstances the lessor would use the surplus cash to invest and earn a return which
would be attributed to the lease. Competition may force the lessor to take any

interest earnings on surplus cash into account when fixing the rental. Any cash surplus would tend to arise late in the lease and so the estimate of interest earnings should be made on a conservative basis. It should be treated in the lease evaluations as set out in Tables 10 and 13 as the converse of interest paid.

The actuarial method after tax

98   The actuarial method after tax is a method which recognises all significant cash flows which affect a lease. It apportions the gross earnings over the period of the lease to give a constant periodic rate of return on the net cash investment. The net cash investment in a lease at a point in time is the amount of funds invested in a lease by the lessor, and comprises the cost of the asset plus or minus the following related payments or receipts:

(a)   government or other grants receivable towards the purchase or use of the asset;
(b)   rentals received;
(c)   taxation payments and receipts including the effect of capital allowances;
(d)   residual values, if any, at the end of the lease term less any estimated rebate of rental arising therefrom;
(e)   interest payments (where applicable);
(f)   interest received on cash surplus (if any);
(g)   profit taken out of the lease.

It is sometimes argued that the net cash investment need not be adjusted for profit taken out of the lease, but this assumes that all cash received is used to reduce the investment and ignores the fact that some of the cash will be used, for example, to meet indirect costs and pay dividends. Even if the surplus is not distributed or used to pay indirect costs, it should be regarded as unconnected with the lease. If the profit is not taken out of the lease, the level of cash needed to finance the lease and the interest charges are understated.

99   The calculations are illustrated in Tables 10 and 13. In Table 10, it is assumed for simplicity of illustration that the lessor has no interest cost. A more realistic way of making the allocation, where interest payable is introduced into the calculation, is illustrated in Table 13 (paragraph 109).

TABLE 10

ACTUARIAL METHOD AFTER TAX – NO INTEREST PAYMENTS

Period (3 months)	Net cash investment at start of period	Cash flows in period (Note 1)	(Note 2)	Average net cash investment in period	Profit taken out of lease (2.06% Note 3)	Net cash investment at end of period
	£	£	£	£	£	£
1/87	–	(10,000)	650	(9,350)	(193)	(9,543)
2/87	(9,543)		650	(8,893)	(183)	(9,076)
3/87	(9,076)		650	(8,426)	(174)	(8,600)
4/87	(8,600)		650	(7,950)	(164)	(8,114)
			2,600		(714)	
1/88	(8,114)		650	(7,464)	(154)	(7,618)
2/88	(7,618)		650	(6,968)	(143)	(7,111)
3/88	(7,111)		650	(6,461)	(133)	(6,594)
4/88	(6,594)	(35)	650	(5,979)	(123)	(6,102)
			2,600		(553)	

Period (3 months)	Net cash investment at start of period	Cash flows in period (Note 1)	(Note 2)	Average net cash investment in period	Profit taken out of lease (2.06% Note 3)	Net cash investment at end of period
	£	£	£	£	£	£
1/89	(6,102)		650	(5,452)	(112)	(5,564)
2/89	(5,564)		650	(4,914)	(101)	(5,015)
3/89	(5,015)		650	(4,365)	(90)	(4,455)
4/89	(4,455)	(254)	650	(4,059)	(84)	(4,143)
			2,600		(387)	
1/90	(4,143)		650	(3,493)	(72)	(3,565)
2/90	(3,565)		650	(2,915)	(60)	(2,975)
3/90	(2,975)		650	(2,325)	(48)	(2,373)
4/90	(2,373	(418)	650	(2,141)	(44)	(2,185)
			2,600		(224)	
1/91	(2,185)		650	(1,535)	(31)	(1,566)
2/91	(1,566)		650	(916)	(19)	(935)
3/91	(935)		650	(285)	(6)	(291)
4/91	(291)	(541)	650	(182)	(4)	(186)
			2,600		(60)	
1/92	(186)			(186)	(4)	(190)
2/92	(190)			(190)	(4)	(194)
3/92	(194)			(194)	(4)	(198)
4/92	(198)	198		–	–	–
					(12)	
		(10,000)	13,000		(1,950)	
		(1,050)				

Notes*:

100

1. (a) The fair value of the asset is £10,000.

   (b) Tax at the rate of 35% is payable at the beginning of period 4 in each year. It is calculated on rentals less capital allowances. (Interest received which arises on any cash surplus would also be taxable.) The figure of £(1,050) is the total of tax payments less recoveries.

   (c) In arriving at the figure of £198 of tax recoverable in period 4/92, it has been assumed that the lessor receives an allowance of the amount of expenditure – £2,372 – which is unrelieved after five years' writing down allowances have been claimed. This will be the case where the lessor sells the asset for its tax written down value and passes the proceeds to the lessee as a rebate of rentals; in this instance the allowance of £2,372 will take the form of tax relief on the rebate of rentals rather than a balancing allowance. (The sales proceeds and the rebate of rentals are not shown in the Table, as their net cash flow effect is nil.) In other circumstances, such as where the lessor continues to hold the asset, the tax written down value of £2,372 will remain part of a pool and will continue to attract a stream of allowances totalling £2,372 on a reducing balance basis into the indefinite future. In such circumstances, it may be appropriate for the lessor to make an adjustment in respect of the delay in receiving the allowances.

2. Rentals of £650 are payable in advance.

3. The profit taken out of the lease is calculated at 2.06% on the average net cash invested in each period until period 3/92, after which point the lessor no longer

Editor's note: to table 10.

has funds invested in the lease. The calculations made to arrive at 2.06% will normally be carried out by financial institutions by computer program, but it can be attained by trial and error. The calculation is, initially, carried out ignoring the profit taken out of the lease and this will then leave a balance of surplus cash left over at the end which represents the approximate profit on the transaction.

By dividing the total profit by the total average net cash investment in the period, an approximate percentage is obtained. As the profit taken out of the lease each quarter affects the average net cash investment in the following quarter, the net cash investment at the end of the whole transaction will not be zero until the percentage used is refined as in the above example to 2.06%.

101   The profit and loss accounts resulting from the cash flows in paragraph 100 are:

TABLE 11

PROFIT AND LOSS ACCOUNTS – NO INTEREST PAYMENTS

	1987 £	1988 £	1989 £	1990 £	1991 £	1992 £	Total £
Rental	2,600	2,600	2,600	2,600	2,600	–	13,000
Less capital repayment	(1,502)	(1,749)	(2,005)	(2,255)	(2,508)	19	(10,000)
Profit before tax (= gross earnings)	1,098	851	595	345	92	19	3,000
	£	£	£	£	£	£	£
Taxation	(35)	(254)	(418)	(541)	198	–	(1,050)
	1,063	597	177	(196)	290	19	1,950
Deferred tax (see para. 174‡)	(349)	(44)	210	420	(230)	(7)	–
Net profit	£714	£553	£387	£224	£60	£12	£1,950
Average net cash investment in the period:*	8,655	6,718	4,697	2,718	729	142	
Gross earnings expressed as a % return on the average net cash investment in the period:	12.7%	12.7%	12.7%	12.7%	12.6%†	13.4%†	

102   Table 11 is constructed from the bottom line upwards. The net profit for each year is taken from Table 10. The rentals and tax payments and recoveries are also found in Table 10. The net profit figures should then be grossed up by the rate of tax of 35%, giving the profit before tax (e.g., £714 ÷ 0.65 = £1,098). The figures for deferred tax and capital repayments may then be found.

*These amounts may be derived from the column 'Average net cash investment in period' in Table 10, for example £(9,350 + 8,893 + 8,426 + 7,950) ÷ 4 = £8,655.

† Rounding error.

*‡**Editor's note:** the ASB noted in FRS 19 'Deferred tax' that it would be consistent with that FRS if paragraphs 170 and 173–175 of these Guidance Notes, and the references to them, were deemed to be deleted.*

Table 11 is used to arrive at one figure only, namely the capital repayment in each   **103**
year. In practice none of the other figures in the table will be used, as when financial
statements are being drawn up actual figures will be used, i.e., it is not necessary to
accumulate individual figures lease by lease for interest and tax; these will be calculated in total for a company.

In Table 11 the effects of the five year lease contract spread over into six financial   **104**
years. In fact the capital repayments for 1991 and 1992 may be added together for all
practical purposes.

The capital repayments may be expressed in percentage terms: **105**

1987	1988	1989	1990	1991/92	Total
£1,502	£1,749	£2,005	£2,255	£2,489	£10,000
15%	17%	20%	23%	25%	100%

Using the method set out above, the percentages of the capital repayment by year   **106**
may be calculated for any lease and, as long as tax and interest rates remain
unchanged, the percentages so calculated may be applied to any other lease which
possesses the same ratio of capital to rental payments and whose inception date is the
same. Thus it is not always necessary to undertake a separate calculation for each
individual lease.

The lessor's balance sheets would include the amounts shown below. The relevant   **107**
disclosure requirements are described in paragraphs 123 to 131.

TABLE 12

BALANCE SHEETS – EXTRACTS

	1987 £	1988 £	1989 £	1990 £	1991 £	1992 £
Assets: Net Investment in finance leases	8,498	6,749	4,744	2,489	(19)	–
Tax recoverable	–	–	–		198	–
Deferred tax	–	–	–	237	7	–
	£8,498	£6,749	£4,744	£2,726	£186	–
Liabilities:						
Deferred tax	349	393	183	–	–	–
Current tax	35	254	418	541	–	–
Cash deficit*	8,114	6,102	4,143	2,185	186	–
	£8,498	£6,749	£4,744	£2,726	£186	–

The actuarial method after tax – building in interest payments

Where a lessor borrows funds to finance his leases a more realistic reflection of his   **108**
cash flows may be obtained by building into the cash flows in Table 10 payments of
interest on his borrowings. The tax charges will of course alter as will the amount
required to finance the lease in each period.

Table 10 may thus be re-stated as follows: **109**

*These amounts represent the net cash investment (as referred to in paragraph 98 above). The cash deficits will
not in practice appear as separate items on a balance sheet, but they represent the amount of funds invested in a
lease by the lessor; this may be equity or debt or a mixture of the two.*

TABLE 13

ACTUARIAL METHOD AFTER TAX – BUILDING IN INTEREST
PAYMENTS

Period (3 months)	Net cash investment at start of period	Cash flows in period (Note 1)	(Note 2)	Average cash investment in period	Interest paid (Note 3)	Profit taken out of lease (Note 4)	Net cash investment at end of period
	£	£	£	£	£	£	£
1/87	–	(10,000)	650	(9,350)	(234)	(33)	(9,617)
2/87	(9,617)		650	(8,967)	(224)	(32)	(9,223)
3/87	(9,223)		650	(8,573)	(214)	(30)	(8,817)
4/87	(8,817)		650	(8,167)	(204)	(29)	(8,400)
			2,600		(876)	(124)	
1/88	(8,400)		650	(7,750)	(194)	(28)	(7,972)
2/88	(7,972)		650	(7,322)	(183)	(26)	(7,531)
3/88	(7,531)		650	(6,881)	(172)	(25)	(7,078)
4/88	(7,078)	272	650	(6,156)	(154)	(22)	(6,332)
			2,600		(703)	(101)	
1/89	(6,332)		650	(5,682)	(142)	(20)	(5,844)
2/89	(5,844)		650	(5,194)	(130)	(18)	(5,342)
3/89	(5,342)		650	(4,692)	(117)	(17)	(4,826)
4/89	(4,826)	(8)	650	(4,184)	(105)	(15)	(4,304)
			2,600		(494)	(70)	
1/90	(4,304)		650	(3,654)	(91)	(13)	(3,758)
2/90	(3,758)		650	(3,108)	(78)	(11)	(3,197)
3/90	(3,197)		650	(2,547)	(64)	(9)	(2,620)
4/90	(2,620)	(245)	650	(2,215)	(55)	(8)	(2,278)
			2,600		(288)	(41)	
1/91	(2,278)		650	(1,628)	(41)	(6)	(1,675)
2/91	(1,675)		650	(1,025)	(26)	(4)	(1,055)
3/91	(1,055)		650	(405)	(10)	(1)	(416)
4/91	(416)	(440)	650	(206)	(5)	(1)	(212)
			2,600		(82)	(12)	
1/92	(212)			(212)	(5)	(1)	(218)
2/92	(218)			(218)	(5)	(1)	(224)
3/92	(224)			(224)	(6)	(1)	(231)
4/92	(231)	226		1	(1)	–	–
		6			(17)	(3)	
		(10,000)	13,000		(2,460)	(351)	
		(189)					

Notes:

1.

    (a)   The fair value of the asset is £10,000.

    (b)   Tax is payable at the beginning of period 4 in each year. It is calculated on rentals, interest paid and capital allowances. (Interest received which arises on any cash surplus would also be taxable.) In period 4/92 the £6 is tax recoverable in 1993. The figure of £(189) is the total of tax payments less recoveries.

    (c)   See note 1(c) to Table 10.

2.   Rentals of £650 are payable in advance.

3.   Interest paid is calculated at 2.5% per quarter on the average net cash investment in each period.

4.   The profit taken out of the lease is calculated at 0.36% on the average net cash invested in each period until period 3/92. (For an explanation of how this is calculated, see note 3 to Table 10.)

Similarly, profit and loss accounts resulting from the cash flows in Table 13 are: **110**

TABLE 14
PROFIT AND LOSS ACCOUNTS – BUILDING IN INTEREST PAYMENTS

	1987 £	*1988* £	*1989* £	*1990* £	*1991* £	*1992* £	*Total* £
Rental	2,600	2,600	2,600	2,600	2,600	–	13,000
Less capital repayment	(1,533)	(1,742)	(1,998)	(2,249)	(2,500)	22	(10,000)
Gross earnings	1,067	858	602	351	100	22	3,000
Interest	(876)	(703)	(494)	(288)	(82)	(17)	(2,460)
Profit before tax	191	155	108	63	18	5	540
Taxation	272	(8)	(245)	(440)	226	6	(189)
	463	147	(137)	(377)	244	11	351
Deferred tax (see para. 174*)	(339)	(46)	207	418	(232)	(8)	–
Net profit	£124	£101	£70	£41	£12	£3	£351

This table is constructed in a manner similar to Table 11, as described in paragraph 102.

Where a lease contains interest variation clauses which adjust the rental by reference **111**
to movements in Finance House base rate, or some other indicator, no adjustment
need normally be made to the calculations in paragraphs 109 and 110. Any increase
or reduction in rentals should be accounted for as an increase or reduction in gross
earnings in the period in which it arises; this treatment will compensate for the
additional finance cost incurred in the same period.

The investment period method

As referred to above, the investment period method is used by some leasing com- **112**
panies as an alternative to the actuarial method after tax.

The investment period method of accounting for finance leases allocates the gross **113**
earnings over that part of the lease in which the lessor has a net cash investment in
proportion to the net cash investment at each interval.

Using the cash flows set out in paragraph 109 the allocation of gross earnings **114**
becomes:

** Editor's note: the ASB noted in FRS 19 'Deferred tax' that it would be consistent with that FRS if paragraphs
170 and 173–175 of these Guidance Notes, and the references to them, were deemed to be deleted.*

TABLE 15

ALLOCATION OF GROSS EARNINGS UNDER IPM

Period	Net cash investment at end of period* £	Gross earnings allocation £	Total gross earnings for year £
1/87	9,617	285	
2/87	9,223	274	1,070
3/87	8,817	262	
4/87	8,400	249	
1/88	7,972	236	
2/88	7,531	223	
3/88	7,078	210	857
4/88	6,332	188	
1/89	5,844	173	
2/89	5,342	158	
3/89	4,826	143	602
4/89	4,304	128	
1/90	3,758	111	
2/90	3,197	95	
3/90	2,620	78	352
4/90	2,278	68	
1/91	1,675	50	
2/91	1,055	31	
3/91	416	12	99
4/91	212	6	
1/92	218	6	
2/92	224	7	
3/92	231	7	20
4/92	–	–	
	£101,170	£3,000	£3,000

The allocation of gross earnings is calculated as follows:

$$1/87 \; £9,617 \times \frac{3,000}{101,170} = £285$$

The same calculation is repeated for each period.

115   The profit and loss accounts resulting from Table 15 are as follows:

Use of the average net cash investment figures from Table 13 would yield the same result as use of the end-of-period figures. The reason for this is that the interest paid and the profit taken out of the lease are both proportional to the average NCI; hence the closing NCI figures are also proportional to the average NCI.

TABLE 16

PROFIT AND LOSS ACCOUNTS – INVESTMENT PERIOD METHOD

	1987 £	1988 £	1989 £	1990 £	1991 £	1992 £	Total £
Rental	2,600	2,600	2,600	2,600	2,600	–	13,000
Less capital repayment	(1,530)	(1,743)	(1,998)	(2,248)	(2,501)	20	(10,000)
Gross earnings	1,070	857	602	352	99	20	3,000
Interest	(876)	(703)	(494)	(288)	(82)	(17)	(2,460)
Profit before tax	194	154	108	64	17	3	540
Taxation	272	(8)	(245)	(440)	226	6	(189)
	466	146	(137)	(376)	243	9	351
Deferred tax	(340)	(46)	207	418	(232)	(7)	–
Net profit	£126	£100	£70	£41	£11	£2	£351

This table is constructed differently from Tables 11 and 14. Under the IPM, the allocation of the gross earnings is calculated as shown in Table 15. The capital repayment may therefore be found by subtraction. The figures for interest are the same as those in Tables 13 and 14. The profit before tax may be found by subtraction; note that the total is the same as in Table 14 but the allocation among the years is slightly different. The tax payable figures are the same as in Tables 13 and 14. The net profit is calculated as 65% of the profit before tax, and the deferred tax line is calculated as a balancing figure.

Hire purchase

As noted in paragraph 80, for hire purchase contracts, allocation of finance charges   **116**
to accounting periods based on the net investment will in most cases be a suitable alternative to allocation based on net cash investment. The following two methods are therefore illustrated, using the rentals and other details set out in paragraph 21:

(a)   the actuarial method before tax;
(b)   the rule of 78.

The actuarial method before tax

In this example the finance charges of £3,000 on the hire purchase contract (i.e., total   **117**
rentals receivable minus the cost of the asset) are apportioned over the period of the contract to give a constant periodic rate of return on the net investment. In this method, the effects of taxation are ignored in apportioning the finance charges (hence the description 'before tax'). Interest on borrowed funds is usually ignored in this method but may be taken into account.

The calculations are the same as in Tables 1 and 2 in paragraphs 25 and 26. The   **118**
results are as follows:

TABLE 17

ACTUARIAL METHOD BEFORE TAX

	1987 £	1988 £	1989 £	1990 £	1991 £	Total £
Rentals receiveable	2,600	2,600	2,600	2,600	2,600	13,000
Less capital repayments	1,563	1,757	1,973	2,217	2,490	10,000
Finance charges	£1,037	£843	£627	£383	£110	£3,000
Average sum outstanding in the period	8,778	7,144	5,308	3,246	929	
Finance charges expressed as a % return on the average net investment in the period:	11.8%	11.8%	11.8%	11.8%	11.8%	

The rule of 78

119   The calculations for apportioning the finance charge on the basis of the rule of 78 are the same as those shown in Table 3 in paragraph 28. For a hire purchase company it is particularly important to be aware that the rule of 78 has a tendency to front-load income, which tendency becomes more pronounced the higher finance charges are relative to the amount financed. Therefore, in the case of longer contracts (say, over seven years) the actuarial method before tax is preferred.

Comparison of methods

120   The allocation of gross earnings (or finance charges) under the methods described above may be compared as follows:

TABLE 18

COMPARISON OF GROSS EARNINGS ALLOCATION

	1987 £	1988 £	1989 £	1990 £	1991 £	1992 £	Total £
Actuarial method after tax (para. 110)	1,067	858	602	351	100	22	3,000
IPM (para. 115)	1,070	857	602	352	99	20	3,000
Actuarial method before tax (para. 118)	1,037	843	627	383	110	–	3,000
Rule of 78 (paras. 119 and 28)	1,105	853	600	347	95	–	3,000

121   A number of points may be noted from the above table. Under the assumption of 35% tax and 25% writing down allowances, the two after-tax methods give very similar results. The reason for this is that the lease never goes into surplus (see paragraph 109). If different assumptions are made about rates of tax and allowances, cash surpluses may arise in certain periods and in these circumstances the actuarial method after tax and the IPM yield different results. In the former method, the interest received on the cash surplus (the re-investment income) is brought back and recognised in the periods when the lessor has funds invested in the lease, rather than taken to income when it arises. Thus no profit is recognised in the periods when the lease is in surplus. Because of this effect, the lessor may be in an exposed position in this period in the event, for example, of early termination of the lease by the lessee. If

this method is used, it may therefore be necessary to make an appropriate provision for early termination losses so that the net investment in the lease does not exceed the termination value at any time. Under the IPM, any re-investment income is recognised when it arises, that is, it is not brought back and recognised in the periods in which the lessor has funds invested in the lease. Thus, where cash surpluses arise, the IPM is more conservative than the actuarial method after tax.

Depending on the materiality of the amounts involved, it may be appropriate under **122** assumptions such as those used in the above numerical examples to use the actuarial method before tax and the rule of 78 to allocate gross earnings from finance leases, although these methods are primarily intended for use in allocating finance charges from hire purchase contracts.

D – BALANCE SHEET PRESENTATION, NOTE DISCLOSURE AND LEGAL REQUIREMENTS FOR LESSORS

The standard requires disclosure of the net investment in (a) finance leases and (b) **123** hire purchase contracts at each balance sheet date. The amounts should be described as receivables. Whereas in lessee accounting the figures in respect of leases and hire purchase contracts may be aggregated, in the case of lessors and finance companies the amounts in respect of each should be shown separately.

For companies subject to Schedule 8* of the Companies Act 1948, the net investment **124** in finance leases and hire purchase contracts should be included in current assets under the heading 'Debtors' and described as 'finance lease receivables' and/or 'hire purchase receivables' as appropriate. It should be analysed in the notes to the accounts between those amounts receivable within one year and those amounts receivable thereafter.

A suitable form of disclosure would be: **125**

BALANCE SHEET AS AT 31 DECEMBER 1987

		1986
Current assets		
Finance lease and hire purchase receivables	£1200	£1100

Note to the accounts:
1. The amounts receivable under finance leases and hire purchase contracts comprise:

Finance leases	900	820
Hire purchase contracts	300	280
	£1200	£1100

Included in the totals receivable is £900 (1986 £850) which falls due after more than one year.

The standard requires that the gross amounts (i.e., original cost or revaluation) and **126** accumulated depreciation of assets held for use in operating leases should be disclosed. This information could be incorporated into tables showing the amounts for other fixed assets or could be shown as a separate table. It is recognised that, for banks, assets held for use in operating leases are different in nature from a bank's

Editor's note: Now Schedule 4 to the Companies Act 1985.

infrastructure (e.g., its own premises). Hence it may not be appropriate to combine assets held for use in operating leases with a bank's infrastructure for capital adequacy purposes.

127   Details of the accounting policies followed by lessors in respect of both operating leases and finance leases are required by the standard, as well as by SSAP 2, 'Disclosure of accounting policies'. This would include information on the depreciation policy for assets leased on operating leases. The standard places particular emphasis on detailed disclosure of the policy adopted for recognition of finance lease income by lessors. This might include items such as the basic method of income recognition (e.g., investment period method); the policies followed in respect of initial direct costs; and assumptions about tax rates and payment dates.

128   It may also be necessary in order to show a true and fair view to disclose information relating to leases and hire purchase contracts which is of particular significance to users of accounts. This may include: contingent liabilities; contingent rentals payable or receivable (e.g., rentals receivable on a hotel may be related to its profits and therefore the income in future years may fluctuate); or new-for-old guarantees given (e.g. on computer leases).

Lessors' turnover

129   In the case of operating leases, a lessor's turnover should be the aggregate rentals receivable in respect of the accounting period.

130   In the case of finance leases, a lessor should disclose gross earnings as turnover. (This is analogous to 'interest receivable' in the case of a bank.) However, as this provides an incomplete measure of a lessor's activity, disclosure should also be made in the notes of the aggregate rentals receivable under finance leases and of the cost of assets acquired for letting under finance leases.

131   The term 'turnover', although used in the Companies Act formats, is not normally used in the leasing industry. Paragraph 3(3) of Schedule 8* to the Companies Act 1948 requires directors to adapt the headings used in the formats in any case where the special nature of a company's business requires such adaptation. It may therefore be appropriate to use a term such as 'gross earnings under finance leases'.

Part III – Problem areas

INTRODUCTION

132   Part III gives guidance on problem areas in accounting for leases as follows:

Editor's note: Now Schedule 4 to the Companies Act 1985.

A – LEASE DEFINITION AND CLASSIFICATION

The definition of a lease is contained in paragraph 14 of the standard. However, in practice there are a number of arrangements which may in substance be leases even though different terms are used to describe them. Whether such an arrangement falls within the definition of a lease is a question to be decided in the light of the facts of each case. For example, a bare-boat charter (a charter of a boat without a crew) will generally have the characteristics of a lease, and the terms of the charter will enable the parties to determine whether it is a finance lease or an operating lease. There are also other arrangements which would not normally be lease contracts (although in exceptional cases they could in substance be leases). An example of these other arrangements is where company A builds a plant on the basis that company B is obliged to buy sufficient of the output of the plant (whether or not B requires it) in order to give a full payout on the cost of the assets involved, together with a normal profit margin: such arrangements are sometimes called take-or-pay contracts or through-put agreements. In many cases such arrangements will in substance be more in the nature of long-term purchase/supply contracts than contracts 'for the hire of a specific asset . . . (under which) the lessor retains ownership of the asset but conveys the right to the use of the asset to the lessee for an agreed period of time in return for the payment of specified rentals' (standard, paragraph 14). **133**

A finance lease is defined in paragraphs 15 and 16 of the standard. The definition in paragraph 15 involves considering whether substantially all the risks and rewards of ownership are transferred to the lessee; the presumption is that this transfer occurs if at the inception of the lease the present value of the minimum lease payments amounts to (normally) 90% or more of the fair value of the leased asset. An alternative way of considering whether substantially all the risks and rewards are transferred to the lessee and whether therefore the lease is a finance lease is to consider whether the present value of any amounts excluded from the minimum lease payments exceeds 10% of the fair value. The amounts excluded from the minimum lease payments are (a) in the case of a lessee, amounts (usually residual amounts) which are unguaranteed or which are guaranteed by a third party, and (b) in the case of a lessor, any unguaranteed residual value. Hence, if these amounts are (or are anticipated to be) insignificant, a finance lease may be indicated. **134**

Exceptionally, it may not be practicable to determine the lease classification based on consideration of whether the present value of the minimum lease payments amounts to (normally) 90% or more of the fair value of the leased asset; equally, it may not be practicable to use the '10% approach' suggested above. In such a case, there may be other means of determining whether or not substantially all the risks and rewards of ownership of an asset are transferred to the lessee. For example, if a lessee has the use of an asset for the period in which substantially all the economic benefits can be derived from the asset, then a finance lease is indicated. **135**

In considering the classification of leases, especially in difficult and marginal cases, the role of residual values is particularly important. Of the residual value of a leased asset (i.e., its value at the end of the lease term), some or the whole (a) may be guaranteed by the lessee to the lessor or (b) may be guaranteed to the lessor by a third party or (c) may be unguaranteed. That part of the residual value which is guaranteed by the lessee (or by a party related to him) is included in the lessee's minimum lease payments. As far as the lessor is concerned his minimum lease payments include any residual amounts guaranteed by the lessee or by an independent third party. Thus the amounts which a lessor expects to receive in relation to the lease may exceed the minimum lease payments which a lessee expects to make to the extent of (a) residual amounts guaranteed by a third party and/or (b) unguaranteed residual amounts. (Insuring residual values is equivalent to obtaining a third party **136** guarantee.) Two examples may illustrate the effect of residual values on lease classification.

137   Consider first a lease of an asset which has a fair value of £3,900. The lessee is required to make three annual payments of £1,000 in advance. The lessor estimates that the asset will have a residual value of £1,500 at the end of the three years; the manufacturer guarantees to buy it back for £1,200.

The minimum lease payments as far as the lessee is concerned are £3,000; from the lessor's point of view they are £4,200. The unguaranteed residual value (URV) is £300 (£1,500–£1,200). The interest rate implicit in the lease is that rate which equates the lessor's minimum lease payments (£4,200) and the URV (£300) to the fair value of £3,900. The expected cash flows are therefore:

	Lessee	Lessor
T = 0	1,000	1,000
T = 1	1,000	1,000
T = 2	1,000	1,000
T = 3	–	1,500
	£3,000	£4,500

In this instance it is clear even without performing any calculations that the lease is an operating lease for the lessee, because, even with a zero rate of interest, the minimum lease payments are less than 90% of the fair value. Similarly, the lease is a finance lease from the lessor's point of view because the URV is less than 10% of the fair value of the asset before discounting; when discounted the URV would be even smaller. The presence of a third party guarantee means that the two parties to the lease classify it in different ways. (This is recognised in paragraph 9 of the standard.) If there had been no third party guarantee the lease would have been an operating lease for both lessor and lessee.

Where the figures are different and the classification is not as obvious as in the above example, the implicit rate of interest should be calculated using one of the methods suggested in paragraph 24 of the standard.

138   A slightly different problem relating to residual values may be illustrated by means of a further example.

    A lessee takes out a lease under which the total of his minimum lease payments approximately equals the fair value of the asset. The present value of the minimum lease payments will therefore be a smaller amount and the classification of the lease may appear borderline. In such a case the lessee should consider the substance of the transaction rather than the precise arithmetic of the 90% test. For example, the minimum lease payments may include a residual value which is guaranteed by the lessee. If this guaranteed value is in fact considerably less than the probable residual value of the leased asset, then it is likely that the lessor will sell the asset in the open market and the lessee will not be called on to pay the amount which he guaranteed. This would suggest that the lessor is trading in the asset rather than providing finance, and that the lease is an operating lease.

B – LAND AND BUILDINGS

Land and buildings which are subject to lease agreements should be accounted for using the same criteria as other assets. **139**

Many leases of land and buildings are for only a small part of the useful life of the building and the lessee does not obtain the economic benefits of ownership arising, for example, from any increase in value. Moreover, since the leases usually provide for regular rent reviews, the rent payable is regularly brought up to current market rates and the lease thereby has the characteristics not of a financing arrangement but of the provision of a service. Most leases involving land and buildings would therefore be classified as operating leases. **140**

There may, however, be instances when a lease of land and buildings has the characteristics of a financing arrangement and in such cases the lease would normally be classified as a finance lease. Examples might be: (a) a lease of a building with a relatively short useful life, for example a warehouse built to a customer's specification or a building with a specific use such as a battery house; or (b) certain leasebacks of office buildings in a sale and leaseback arrangement (see paragraphs 150 to 160). **141**

As with all types of lease, it is important in deciding whether a lease of land and buildings is a finance lease or an operating lease to consider its characteristics, in particular to consider whether or not substantially all the risks and rewards of ownership of the land and buildings in question are transferred to the lessee. It should be noted that under the definition of a finance lease set out in paragraphs 15 and 16 of the standard, the classification which results from the application of the '90% formula' to the lease may be rebutted if the lease in question does not transfer substantially all the risks and rewards of ownership to the lessee; this may occur for example because of rent reviews which revert the principal rewards of ownership to the lessor. **142**

In the context of land and buildings the term 'open market value' is commonly used for what is described elsewhere in this standard as 'fair value'. **143**

Nothing in the standard precludes the recognition as a fixed asset of an amount paid in the form of a premium as consideration for a leasehold interest. **144**

C – LEASING BY MANUFACTURERS OR DEALERS

Manufacturers or dealers may offer customers the choice of either buying or leasing an asset. The leases offered may be either finance leases or operating leases, and may be described by a variety of terms, including hire or rental agreements. **145**

Where a manufacturer or dealer enters into an operating lease, no sale has been made and it is therefore not appropriate to recognise a selling profit when the asset is first leased. A manufacturer or dealer lessor should account for an operating lease in the same way as any other lessor. **146**

When a manufacturer or dealer enters into a finance lease such transactions give rise to two types of income: (a) the initial profit or loss at the start of the lease which is equivalent to the profit or loss resulting from an outright sale of the asset being leased, and (b) the finance charges (or gross earnings) over the period of the lease. **147**

As the offer of a lease agreement is often influenced by a manufacturer's or dealer's marketing considerations, the pricing of the lease may not necessarily be based on **148** the normal outright sale price. Hence the initial selling profit on a lease should be restricted to an amount which will enable the finance charges under the lease to be based on the rate of interest which, in the absence of such marketing considerations, the lessor would expect to charge the lessee. The rate of interest should take into account any tax benefits accruing to the lessor.

149   Consider the following example. A manufacturer makes a machine which costs him £10,000. He normally sells the machine for £12,500 giving him a profit on the sale of £2,500.

The manufacturer offers the machine on a five year finance lease with a rental of £687.50 payable quarterly in advance. Using the figures in Table 1, paragraph 25, this rental would justify a capital cost of £10,577 for the cost of the asset. (Using the implicit rate in Table 1 of 2.95% per quarter, a quarterly rental of £650 is equivalent to a capital cost of £10,000. Therefore a quarterly rental of £687.50 is equivalent to a capital cost of:

$$£10,000 \times \frac{687.50}{650.00} = £10,577).$$

That is, where the implicit rate is not known, an estimate thereof has to be used in order to calculate the capital cost. The manufacturer should therefore restrict his selling profit to £577 at the start of the lease. The balance of the profit arises as gross earnings over the period of the lease.

D – SALE AND LEASEBACK TRANSACTIONS

150   A sale and leaseback transaction takes place when an owner sells an asset and immediately re-acquires the right to use the asset by entering into a lease with the purchaser.

151   Before dealing with the accounting for the sale and leaseback transaction itself, the carrying value of the asset in question should be reviewed. If the asset has suffered an impairment it should be written down to its recoverable amount. This is nothing to do with sale and leaseback specifically, but it is a step which should be taken so that the sale and leaseback accounting is not distorted.

152   Once that first step has been taken, the asset will be carried at fair value, or less. It is then necessary to determine whether the leaseback is an operating lease or a finance lease. This should be decided according to the criteria for all leases as set out in paragraphs 15 to 17 of the standard.

Finance leaseback

153   If the leaseback is a finance lease, the seller-lessee is in effect re-acquiring substantially all the risks and rewards of ownership of the asset. In other words, he never disposes of his ownership interest in the asset, and so it would not be correct to recognise a profit or loss in relation to an asset which (in substance) never was disposed of.

154   However, it is possible that a sale and leaseback resulting in a finance lease may be arranged on terms reflecting a higher or lower capital value than the book value of the asset (i.e., so as to reflect an *apparent* profit or loss). For example, an asset which has a carrying value of £70 may be sold at £120 and leased back on a finance lease. In such a case, the lease payments would (other things being equal) be higher than if the sale and leaseback had been arranged at carrying value. The standard therefore provides that the £50 apparent profit should be deferred and amortised (i.e., credited to income) over the lease term: this will have the effect of reducing the rentals – which are shown as interest and depreciation of the leased-back asset – to a level consistent with the previous carrying value of the asset. Where the asset is carried at below fair value, it may be appropriate to revalue it. If, in the same example, the fair value of the asset were £100, the asset could be revalued to that amount, and there would remain only £20 of apparent profit to be deferred and amortised over the lease term. The effect would then be to reduce the rentals to a level consistent with the fair value of the asset.

As an alternative to calculating the apparent profit and deferring and amortising that amount, the same result can be achieved by leaving the previous carrying value unchanged, setting up the amount received on sale as a creditor, and treating the lease payments partly as principal and partly as a finance charge. This treatment will reflect the substance of the transaction, namely that it represents the raising of finance secured on an asset which is held and not disposed of. **155**

Operating leaseback

Conversely, if the leaseback is an operating lease, the seller-lessee has disposed of substantially all the risks and rewards of ownership of the asset, and so has realised a profit or loss on the disposal. Provided that the transaction is established at fair value, the profit or loss should be recognised. However, it is possible that a sale and leaseback transaction can be arranged at other than fair value. If the sale price is above fair value (paragraph 47(c) of the standard), the excess will not be genuine profit, but will arise solely because the operating lease rentals payable in the ensuing years will also be at above fair value. The standard therefore provides that the excess of sale price over fair value should not be recognised as profit in the year but should be credited to income, over the shorter of the remainder of the lease term and the period to the next rent review (if any), so as to reduce the rentals payable to a level consistent with the fair value of the asset. **156**

This may be illustrated as follows: **157**

Carrying value of asset	£70	
Fair value of asset	£100	Recognise profit
Sale price	£120	on sale of £30
Annual rental (for 5 years)	£28	

The excess of the sale price over fair value should be deferred and amortised (credited to income) over the non-cancellable period, i.e.:

$$\frac{120-100}{5} = £4 \text{ p.a.}$$

This credit will in effect reduce the rentals from £28 p.a. to £24 p.a.

The converse situation may also arise, namely that the sale price is below fair value (standard, paragraph 47(b)). This could arise for two reasons. First, the sale could simply be a bad bargain, for example because the seller-lessee needed to raise cash quickly. In that case any profit or loss should be recognised immediately. Second, the price may be artificially low so as to compensate for future rentals at below market price. Depending on the previous carrying value, either a profit or loss may arise. These cases are considered in turn. **158**

159   The following figures illustrate the case where a profit arises, even though the price is artificially low so as to compensate for future rentals at below market price:

Carrying value	£70	
Sale price	£80	Profit £10
Fair value	£100	
Annual rental (5 years)	£20	

The profit of £10 should be recognised immediately, but the difference between £80 and £100 should not be recognised.

160   Conversely, an apparent loss may arise if the sale price is below the carrying value as well as being below fair value. This is illustrated as follows:

Carrying value	£95	
Sale price	£80	Apparent loss £15
Fair value	£100	
Annual rental (5 years)	£20	

In such a case, provided the apparent loss is compensated by below market rentals, the loss should not be recognised but should be deferred and amortised so as to give the effect of increasing the rentals to a level consistent with a selling price of £95. The loss should be deferred and amortised (i.e., debited to income) over the remainder of the lease term (or, if shorter, the period during which the reduced rentals are chargeable).

E – SUB-LEASES AND BACK-TO-BACK LEASES

161   The main provisions of the standard and the other sections of these guidance notes deal principally with leases in which only two parties, the lessor and the lessee, are involved. However, some lease arrangements are more complex and involve three (or more) parties. There are many different types of arrangement and it is not possible to give guidance on all of them. In addition, there are variations in the terms used to describe the leases and the parties to the lease. The notes in this section are intended therefore to give guidance on the general principles of three-party lease arrangements.

162   The three parties may be termed (a) the original lessor, (b) the intermediate party and (c) the ultimate lessee. In effect, the intermediate party may be both a lessee in the original lease and a lessor as regards the sub-lease.

163   Unless the original lease agreement is replaced by a new agreement, the accounting by the original lessor should not be affected by the fact that the intermediate party enters into a sub-lease.

164   The accounting by the intermediate party will depend on the structure of his arrangements with the original lessor and the ultimate lessee.

165   If the intermediate party's role is in substance that of a broker or an agent for transactions between the original lessor and the ultimate lessee such that there is no recourse to the intermediate party in the event of default, then the intermediate party should not include the asset or obligation in his balance sheet and should account for any income due to him on a systematic and rational basis. For example, a pure commission might be recognised immediately, whilst a guarantee fee might be spread over the period of risk. For both operating and finance leases, he should treat any contingent loss as required by SSAP 18.*

Conversely, the intermediate party may enter into a lease with the original lessor, the **166** terms of which require him to make payments to the lessor regardless of whether the ultimate lessee completes his payments. That is, the asset would be sub-leased by the intermediate party to the ultimate lessee, but the lease agreement between the original lessor and the intermediate party would remain in effect. If the original lease is a finance lease, the intermediate party should record his obligation thereunder. If the sub-lease is also a finance lease, the intermediate party should account for it as such; this will result in his showing an obligation under the original lease and a receivable under the sub-lease. If the sub-lease is an operating lease, the leased asset remains as a fixed asset. The principal differences which arise if the sub-lease is a finance lease as opposed to an operating lease are that the intermediate party (a) treats the asset as a receivable instead of a fixed asset and (b) recognises income according to finance lease principles.

The ultimate lessee should classify the sub-lease according to paragraphs 15 to 17 of **167** the standard and account for it accordingly.

In the context of complex multi-party leases, paragraph 16 of the standard is par- **168** ticularly important. This paragraph permits the presumption that a lease should be classified as a finance lease to be rebutted if it can be clearly demonstrated that in the circumstances in question the lease does not transfer substantially all the risks and rewards of ownership to the lessee. This rebuttal can be relevant, for example, where there is a series of sub-leases which results in a series of partial interests in an asset with each party carrying a percentage of the total risks in return for a percentage of the total rewards.

Where the intermediate party is not relieved of his primary obligation under the **169** original lease and where the sub-lease is a finance lease, it is sometimes thought that this results in the leased asset's being capitalised in the accounts of two companies. This is not the case. The asset is capitalised only in the books of the ultimate lessee. The remaining balances are in the nature of indebtedness between the parties.

F – DEFERRED TAXATION

The accounting requirements for dealing with deferred tax are set out in SSAP 15 **170** 'Accounting for deferred taxation'. The present standard in no way changes these requirements. It should be noted, however, that at the time of writing SSAP 15 is under review.†

Lessee's deferred taxation

Where a lessee charges the full rental he pays as a tax expense in the year of payment, **171** timing differences may arise. These differences may be either (a) to the extent that the depreciation and finance charge exceed or fall short of the rental on a finance lease or (b) to the extent of any deferral or accrual of the rental on an operating lease. The lessee should consider whether deferred tax needs to be provided on these timing differences.

Editor's note: SSAP 18 has been superseded by FRS 12.

†*Editor's note: See note to paragraph 173.*

172   The amounts in question in the example in Part 1 are those shown in column three of Table 8 in paragraph 47.

173*   The timing difference described above will need to be considered together with all other timing differences which a lessee may experience and, unless the conditions set out in paragraphs 27 to 30 of SSAP 15 are met, a provision for deferred tax will be required.

Lessor's deferred taxation

174*   It will be seen from paragraph 101 that capital allowances have a material impact on a lessor's position. If deferred tax were not provided by a lessor he would report profits in some periods and losses in others.

175*   SSAP 15 requires that the total position of a company must be looked at and not just one contract. A lessor therefore needs to consider the likely pattern of future timing differences. For example, he may be able to decide not to provide for deferred tax because any reduction in leasing may be offset by increases of tax allowances in other areas.

G – REGIONAL DEVELOPMENT GRANTS

Lessors and RDGs

176   Leases which involve equipment on which a regional development grant (RDG) may be claimed need special consideration. The lessor may claim a grant (currently of 15% or 22%) towards the cost of purchasing an asset. The grant is not taxable and the lessor may also claim capital allowances on the full purchase price of the asset. The rentals charged to the lessee will reflect the benefit the lessor has obtained from both the RDG and the capital allowances. Unless any adjustments are made, the lessor's profit and loss account may show a loss before tax and a profit after tax from such a lease.

177   Some consider that presentation of a loss before tax and a profit after tax leads to difficulties in interpreting the accounts, and therefore prefer to adjust the profit and loss account by 'grossing up' the RDG by the rate of taxation to show it as a gross amount as if tax were payable on the grant.

178   The difference between the two approaches is illustrated in the following example. The figure shown represent the aggregate profit and loss accounts for all the years affected by the lease and, for simplicity, ignore interest.

---

*Editor's note: The ASB noted in FRS 19 'Deferred tax' that it would be consistent with that FRS if paragraphs 170 and 173–175 of these Guidance Notes, and the references to them, were deemed to be deleted.

†Editor's note: The ASB noted in FRS 19 'Deferred tax' that it would be consistent with that FRS if paragraphs 170 and 173–175 of these Guidance Notes, and the references to them, were deemed to be deleted.

TABLE 19
REGIONAL DEVELOPMENT GRANT PRESENTATION

	Actual transaction		Adjusted presentation	
	£	£	£	£
Rentals receivable over the lease term		750		750
Cost of asset	1,000		1,000	
Less RDG	220		338	
		780		662
Profit/(Loss) before tax		(30)		88
Taxation recoverable (payable)		87		(31)
Profit after tax		£57		£57

The standard permits either approach to be followed.* If a company grosses up its **179** RDGs, it should disclose the amount by which the profit before tax and the tax charge have been increased as a result of grossing up such grants.

Lessees and RDGs

In cases where the asset which is leased qualifies for an RDG the position of the **180** lessee also calls for attention. In the example in paragraph 178 the net cost of the asset after allowing for the RDG is £780. The total rentals payable amount to £750 which is less than the net cost of the asset.

In these circumstances an appropriate way of dealing with the situation is to capi- **181** talise the asset at £750 and to assume that no finance charge is payable. The £750 would then be depreciated over the shorter of the lease term or the useful life of the asset. It is not considered appropriate to show a negative finance charge.

H – BAD DEBTS

Since a lessor's profit on a finance lease is assessed on the basis of the whole of the **182** lease period, it is essential that bad debts resulting from the failure of the lessee to pay rentals throughout the period are taken into consideration.

The level of bad debts will depend upon the type of business the lessor writes. In **183** many instances bad debts will not be significant; in other instances they may be.

As noted in paragraph 86, where a pattern of bad debt experience can be established, **184** a lessor should make a provision for bad debts but this should not in general change the way in which he recognises gross earnings.

Where there is a significant risk of bad debts, the carrying value of the leasing **185** receivable should be determined having regard to the amount expected to be realised from the leased asset. For example, if it is likely that the asset will be re-possessed, the lessor may need to consider the amount which he will be able to recover through that route. As explained in paragraph 87 the bad debt risk may be sufficient to render classification as a finance lease inappropriate.

---

*Editor's note: The amendment to SSAP 21 in February 1997 removed the option to gross up tax free grants.

Part IV – Leased assets and current cost accounting

INTRODUCTION

186   Part IV gives guidance on the procedures to be used for accounting for leased assets under SSAP 16 'Current cost accounting'. At the time of writing these guidance notes, SSAP 16 is under review*. However it remains in force until replaced.

ACCOUNTING BY LESSEES

187   A lessee should record a finance lease in his balance sheet as an asset and as an obligation to pay future rentals. For CCA purposes the asset and the obligation should be considered separately. The lessee's asset forms part of his operating capability which should be maintained.

188   The asset, which will be included amongst fixed assets in the lessee's balance sheet, should be restated at its value to the business on the basis suggested in the Guidance Notes on SSAP 16 'Current cost accounting'. The depreciation charge in each period should be based on current costs.

189   The obligation to pay future rentals is equivalent to a borrowing and should be included in the calculation of the gearing adjustment for CCA purposes.

190   In the example of lessee accounting given in Part I the amounts which have to be restated for CCA purposes in respect of the asset are shown in paragraph 45 and the obligations under finance leases which are to be taken into account in calculating the gearing adjustment are listed in paragraph 46.

191   The part of the rental under a lease which is apportioned as a finance charge should be included as part of the interest costs in the CCA profit and loss account. These amounts are given in paragraphs 26, 28, 34 and 35.

192   Rentals under an operating lease are charged to the profit and loss account and would not normally require adjustment for CCA purposes.

ACCOUNTING BY LESSORS

193   Assets held by lessors for use in operating leases should be restated for CCA purposes on the same basis as any other fixed asset. The lessor is trading in assets and it is appropriate that he maintains his operating capability in terms of the particular fixed assets he is using.

194   Where a lessor is engaged in finance leasing, the rentals he will receive will be fixed in money terms and he therefore has a monetary asset rather than a physical asset in his balance sheet. A monetary working capital adjustment relating to the finance lease receivables should therefore be made for CCA purposes.

**Editor's note: SSAP 16 was suspended in June 1985 and withdrawn in July 1988.*

[SSAP 25]
Segmental reporting*

(Issued June 1990)

Contents

Editor's note: IFRS 8 Operating Segments has been issued by the IASB. This standard takes effect for accounting periods beginning on or after 1 January 2009. When the IFRS was at the exposure stage the ASB indicated that it would consider whether or not to update the UK requirements.

Segmental reporting

The provisions of this statement of accounting practice should be read in conjunction with the (Explanatory) Foreword to accounting standards *and need not be applied to immaterial items.*

Part 1 – Explanatory note

PURPOSE OF SEGMENTAL INFORMATION

1   Many entities carry on several classes of business or operate in several geographical areas, with different rates of profitability, different opportunities for growth and different degrees of risk. It is not usually possible for the user of the financial statements of such an entity to make judgements about either the nature of the entity's different activities or their contribution to the entity's overall financial results unless the financial statements provide some segmental analysis of the information they contain. The purpose of segmental information is, therefore, to provide information to assist the users of financial statements:

(a)   to appreciate more thoroughly the results and financial position of the entity by permitting a better understanding of the entity's past performance and thus a better assessment of its future prospects; and

(b)   to be aware of the impact that changes in significant components of a business may have on the business as a whole.

2   This accounting standard should ensure as far as possible that the segmental information reported by an entity is disclosed on a consistent basis, year by year. However, caution should be exercised if comparing similar segments in different entities, because, in addition to any differences in accounting policies adopted, the basis of accounting for inter-segment sales or the treatment of common costs may not be consistent between entities.

SCOPE AND APPLICABILITY

3   This accounting standard contains provisions relating to the statutory segmental disclosure requirements contained in companies legislation in the United Kingdom and the Republic of Ireland. All companies are required to comply with these provisions.

4   This accounting standard also contains provisions relating to the disclosure of inter-segment turnover, geographical segment result, segment net assets, origin of turnover, and segmental information about associated undertakings, which are not required by companies legislation. These provisions apply to any entity that:

(a)   is a public limited company or has a public limited company as a subsidiary; or

(b)   is a banking or insurance company or group (as defined for the purposes of Part VII of the Companies Act 1985); or

(c)   exceeds the criteria, multiplied in each case by 10, for defining a medium-sized company under Section 248* of the Companies Act 1985, as amended from time to time by statutory instrument.

Editor's note: Now section 247.

However, a subsidiary that is not a public limited company or a banking or insurance company need not comply with these provisions if its parent provides segmental information in compliance with this accounting standard.

All entities are encouraged to apply the provisions of this accounting standard in all financial statements intended to give a true and fair view of the financial position and profit or loss. **5**

Where, in the opinion of the directors, the disclosure of any information required by this accounting standard would be seriously prejudicial to the interests of the reporting entity, that information need not be disclosed; but the fact that any such information has not been disclosed must be stated. This repeats the exemption contained in paragraph 55(5) of Schedule 4 to the Companies Act 1985* in the wider context of this accounting standard. **6**

DETERMINING REPORTABLE SEGMENTS

Information contained in financial statements can be segmented in two principal ways – by class of business and geographically. The Companies Act 1985 recognises both of these bases in paragraph 55 of Schedule 4, referring to the geographical areas as 'markets'. Paragraph 55 states that in analysing the source (in terms of either business or market) of turnover or profit or loss the directors should have regard to the manner in which the company's activities are organised. Paragraph 55 also states that it is for the directors to determine whether the company has carried on business of two or more classes or has supplied markets that differ substantially from each other and that where, in the opinion of the directors, the classes of business or the markets do not differ substantially from each other they may be treated as one. **7**

In identifying separate reportable segments, the directors should have regard to the overall purpose of presenting segmental information (as set out in paragraph 1) and the need of the user of the financial statements to be informed where an entity carries on operations in different classes of business or in different geographical areas that: **8**

(a) earn a return on investment that is out of line with the remainder of the business; or
(b) are subject to different degrees of risk; or
(c) have experienced different rates of growth; or
(d) have different potentials for future development.

Each class of business or geographical segment that is significant to an entity as a whole should be identified as a reportable segment. For the purposes of this accounting standard a segment should normally be regarded as significant if: **9**

(a) its third party turnover is ten per cent or more of the total third party turnover of the entity; or
(b) its segment result, whether profit or loss, is ten per cent or more of the combined result of all segments in profit or of all segments in loss, whichever combined result is the greater; or
(c) its net assets are ten per cent or more of the total net assets of the entity.

The directors should review the definitions of the segments annually and re-define them when appropriate. In doing so the directors should have regard to the **10**

Throughout this statement of standard accounting practice, references to paragraph 55 of Schedule 4 to the Companies Act 1985 should be read in the Republic of Ireland as references to paragraph 41 of the Schedule to the Companies (Amendment) Act 1986.

fundamental objective of this accounting standard, which is to achieve, as far as possible, consistency and comparability between years.

CLASSES OF BUSINESS

11 A separate class of business is a distinguishable component of an entity that provides a separate product or service or a separate group of related products or services.

12 When deciding whether or not an entity operates in different classes of business, the directors should take into account the following factors:

(a) the nature of the products or services;
(b) the nature of the production processes;
(c) the markets in which the products or services are sold;
(d) the distribution channels for the products;
(e) the manner in which the entity's activities are organised;
(f) any separate legislative framework relating to part of the business, for example, a bank or an insurance company.

13 Although it is possible to identify certain characteristics that differentiate between classes of business, no single set of characteristics is universally applicable nor is any single characteristic determinative in all cases. Consequently, determination of an entity's classes of business must depend on the judgement of the directors.

GEOGRAPHICAL SEGMENTS

14 A geographical segment is a geographical area comprising an individual country or a group of countries in which an entity operates, or to which it supplies products or services.

15 A geographical analysis should help the user of the financial statements to assess the extent to which an entity's operations are subject to factors such as the following:

(a) expansionist or restrictive economic climates;
(b) stable or unstable political regimes;
(c) exchange control regulations;
(d) exchange rate fluctuations.

16 It is not practicable to define a method of grouping that will reflect all the differences between international business environments and that would apply to all entities. The selected grouping should reflect the purpose of presenting segmental information (as set out in paragraph 1) and the factors noted in paragraphs 8 and 15. Although geographical proximity may indicate similar economic trends and risks, this will not necessarily be the case.

INFORMATION TO BE DISCLOSED

General

17 The entity should define in its financial statements each reported class of business and geographical segment.

Turnover

The factors listed in paragraph 15 apply both to the geographical locations of the **18** entity's operations and to the geographical locations of its markets. The user of the financial statements gains a fuller understanding of the entity's exposure to these factors, if turnover is disclosed according to both location of operations and location of markets. For the purposes of this accounting standard, origin of turnover is the geographical area *from* which products or services are supplied to a third party or another segment. Destination of turnover is the geographical area *to* which goods or services are supplied. Because disclosure relating to segment results and net assets will generally be based on location of operations, an analysis of turnover on the same basis will enable the user to match turnover, result and net assets on a consistent basis, and to relate all three to the perceived risks and opportunities of the segments. For these reasons this accounting standard requires the disclosure of sales by origin, but reporting entities should also disclose turnover by destination unless there is no material difference between the two. If there is no material difference, a statement to that effect is required.

Inter-segment sales and transfers are often a material part of the total turnover of the **19** reportable segments and in such cases they should be analysed segmentally and shown separately. The geographical analysis of inter-segment turnover should be disclosed by origin. Analysis by destination usually has little or no value and would not normally be provided.

The Companies Act 1985 and the Companies (Northern Ireland) Order 1986 contain **20** provisions exempting banking and insurance companies and groups from the requirement to disclose turnover in certain circumstances. In the Republic of Ireland, similar exemptions are extended to special classes of companies (banking, discount and insurance companies) under the Companies Act 1963. Certain other entities – for example, building societies – are subject to different statutory rules from those applied to companies. Where turnover is not required by statute to be disclosed, it is not required by this accounting standard to be disclosed segmentally. The fact that such turnover has not been disclosed segmentally should be stated.

Segment result

The entity should disclose the result of each reportable segment before accounting **21** for taxation, minority interests and extraordinary items. The geographical analysis of segment result should normally be based on the areas from which products or services are supplied.

In the majority of entities, different classes of business or geographical segments are **22** financed by different proportions of interest-bearing debt and equity. The interest earned or incurred by individual segments is therefore a result of the entity's overall financial policy rather than a proper reflection of the results of the various segments. Consequently, comparisons of profit between segments or between different years for the same segment are likely to be meaningless if interest is included in arriving at the result. For these reasons, it will normally be appropriate for segment results to be disclosed before taking account of interest. However, where all or part of the entity's business is to earn and/or incur interest (as in the financial sector, for example), or where interest income or expense is central to the business (as in the contracting or travel businesses, for example), interest should normally be included in arriving at the segment result.

Common costs

23   Common costs are costs relating to more than one segment. They should be treated in the way that the directors deem most appropriate in pursuance of the objectives of segmental reporting. Entities may apportion some common costs for the purpose of internal reporting and, in such cases, it may be reasonable for such costs to be similarly apportioned for external reporting purposes. If the apportionment would be misleading, common costs should not be apportioned in the segmental disclosures but should be deducted from the total of the segment results. Costs that are directly attributable to individual reportable segments are not common costs for the purposes of this accounting standard and therefore should be allocated to those segments, irrespective of the fact that they may have been borne by a different segment or by the Head Office.

Segment net assets

24   The net assets of each reportable segment should be disclosed. In most cases these will be the non-interest bearing operating assets less the non-interest bearing operating liabilities. However, to the extent that the segment result is disclosed after accounting for interest as described in paragraph 22, the corresponding interest-bearing operating assets and liabilities should also be included.

25   Segment operating assets and liabilities may include assets and liabilities relating exclusively to one segment and also an allocated portion of assets and liabilities that relate jointly to more than one segment. Assets and liabilities used jointly by more than one segment should be allocated to the segments on a reasonable basis. Assets and liabilities that are not used in the operations of any segment should not be allocated to segments. Operating assets of a segment should not normally include loans or advances to, or investments in, another segment unless interest therefrom has been included in arriving at the segment result on the basis set out in paragraph 22.

Associated undertakings

26   Sometimes associated undertakings form a significant part of a reporting entity's results or assets. In such circumstances the following information should be analysed segmentally and shown separately in the segmental report:

(a)   the reporting entity's share of the profits or losses of associated undertakings before accounting for taxation, minority interests and extraordinary items; and

(b)   the reporting entity's share of the net assets of associated undertakings (including goodwill to the extent that it has not been written off) stated, where possible, after attributing fair values to the net assets at the date of acquisition of the interest in each associated undertaking.

However, it is recognised that this information might be unobtainable or publication might be prejudicial to the business of the associate. In such circumstances the disclosure is not required but the reason for non-disclosure should be stated by way of note, together with a brief description of the omitted business or businesses.

27   For the purposes of this accounting standard, associated companies form a significant part of the reporting entity's results or assets if, in total, they account for at least 20% of the total result or 20% of the total net assets of the reporting entity.

General

The total of the amounts disclosed by segment should agree with the related total in the financial statements. If it does not, the reporting entity should provide a reconciliation between the two figures. Reconciling items should be properly identified and explained. **28**

Comparative figures for the previous accounting period should be provided. If a change is made to the definitions of the segments or to the accounting policies that are adopted for reporting segmental information, the nature of the change should be disclosed. The reason for the change and the effect of the change should be stated. The previous year's figures should be restated to reflect the change. **29**

Part 2 – Definition of terms

A *class of business* is a distinguishable component of an entity that provides a separate product or service or a separate group of related products or services. **30**

A *geographical segment* is a geographical area comprising an individual country or group of countries in which an entity operates, or to which it supplies products or services. **31**

Origin of turnover is the geographical segment from which products or services are supplied to a third party or to another segment. **32**

Destination of turnover is the geographical segment to which products or services are supplied. **33**

Part 3 – Standard accounting practice

If an entity has two or more classes of business, or operates in two or more geographical segments which differ substantially from each other, it should define its classes of business and geographical segments in its financial statements, and it should report with respect to each class of business and geographical segment the following financial information: **34**

(a)   turnover, distinguishing between (i) turnover derived from external customers and (ii) turnover derived from other segments;
(b)   result, before accounting for taxation, minority interests and extraordinary items; and
(c)   net assets.

The reporting entity should disclose the geographical segmentation of turnover by origin. It should also disclose turnover to third parties by destination or state where appropriate that this amount is not materially different from turnover to third parties by origin. Segment result will normally be disclosed before taking account of interest. However, where all or part of the entity's business is to earn and/or incur interest, or where interest income or expense is central to the business, interest should normally be included in arriving at the segment result. Net assets will normally be non-interest bearing operating assets less the non-interest bearing operating liabilities, but to the extent that the segment result is disclosed after accounting for interest the corresponding interest-bearing assets or liabilities should also be included.

35   When both parent and consolidated financial statements are presented, segmental information should be presented on the basis of the consolidated financial statements.

36   The reporting entity should disclose the following information segmentally in relation to its associated undertakings if these account for at least 20% of its total result or 20% of its total net assets:

(a)   the entity's share of the results of associated undertakings before accounting for taxation, minority interests and extraordinary items; and

(b)   the entity's share of the net assets of associated undertakings (including goodwill to the extent it has not been written off) stated, where possible, after attributing fair values to the net assets at the date of acquisition of the interest in each undertaking.

The segmental disclosure should be of the aggregate amounts of all associated undertakings for which the information is available and should be shown separately in the segmental report. However, this information need not be disclosed if it is unobtainable or publication would be prejudicial to the business of the associate. In such circumstances, the reason for non-disclosure should be stated by way of note, together with a brief description of the omitted business or businesses.

37   The total of the amounts disclosed by segment should agree with the related total in the financial statements. If it does not, the reporting entity should provide a reconciliation between the two amounts. Reconciling items should be properly identified and explained.

38   Comparative figures for the previous accounting period should be provided. If, however, on the first occasion on which an entity provides a segmental report the necessary information is not readily available, comparative figures need not be provided.

39   The directors should re-define the segments when appropriate. If a change is made to the definitions of the segments or to the accounting policies that are adopted for reporting segmental information, the nature of the change should be disclosed. The reason for the change and its effect should be stated. The previous year's figures should be re-stated to reflect the change.

40   This accounting standard contains provisions relating to the statutory segmental disclosure requirements contained in companies legislation in the United Kingdom and the Republic of Ireland. All companies are required to comply with these provisions.

41   This accounting standard also contains provisions relating to segmental disclosures which are not required by companies legislation.* These provisions apply to any entity that:

---

*Disclosures not required by the Companies Act 1985 are those set out in paragraphs 34(a)ii, 34(b) insofar as it relates to geographical segment result, 34(c), 34 insofar as it relates to origin of turnover, and 36. (**Editor's note:** Also, as from February 1996, paragraph 34(b) insofar as it relates to business segment result.)

(a)   is a public limited company or that has a public limited company as a sub-
      sidiary; or
(b)   is a banking or insurance company or group (as defined for the purposes of
      Part VII of the Companies Act 1985); or
(c)   exceeds the criteria, multiplied in each case by 10, for defining a medium-sized
      company under section 247* of the Companies Act 1985, as amended from
      time to time by statutory instrument.

However, a subsidiary that is not a public limited company or a banking or insurance
company need not comply with these provisions if its parent provides segmental
disclosures in compliance with this accounting standard.

All other entities are encouraged to apply the provisions of this accounting standard   **42**
in all financial statements intended to give a true and fair view of the financial
position and profit or loss.

Where, in the opinion of the directors, the disclosure of any information required by   **43**
this accounting standard would be seriously prejudicial to the interests of the
reporting entity, that information need not be disclosed. The fact that any such
information has not been disclosed must be stated.

Entities that are not required by statute to disclose turnover in their financial   **44**
statements are not required by this accounting standard to disclose turnover segmentally. The fact that turnover has not been disclosed segmentally should be stated
in the financial statements.

APPLICATION TO SMALLER ENTITIES

Reporting entities applying the Financial Reporting Standard for Smaller Entities   **44A**
currently applicable are exempt from this accounting standard.

DATE FROM WHICH EFFECTIVE

The provisions of this statement of standard accounting practice should be adopted   **45**
as soon as possible and regarded as standard in respect of financial statements
relating to accounting periods beginning on or after 1 July 1990.

Part 4 – Legal and International Stock Exchange requirements in Great Britain and Northern Ireland

COMPANY LAW

*All paragraph references, unless otherwise indicated, are to the Schedules to the
Companies Act 1985 and the Companies (Northern Ireland) Order 1986.*

Paragraph 55(1) of Schedule 4 requires all companies that, in the course of the   **46**
financial year, have carried on business of two or more classes that (in the opinion of
the directors) differ substantially from each other to state:

---

*Equivalent legal references:

Great Britain	Northern Ireland	Republic of Ireland
Companies Act 1985	*Companies (Northern Ireland) Order 1986*	*Companies (Amendment) Act*
Section 247	Article 256 (as amended)	Section 8

(a)   a description of each class of business;

(b)   the amount of turnover attributable to each class of business; and

(c)   the amount of the profit or loss of the company before taxation that is, in the opinion of the directors, attributable to each class of business.*

47   Paragraph 55(2) of Schedule 4 requires all companies that, in the course of the financial year, have supplied geographical markets that (in the opinion of the directors) differ substantially from each other to state the amount of the turnover attributable to each market.

48   Paragraph 55(3) of Schedule 4 provides that, in analysing the source (in terms of either classes of business or markets) of turnover or profit or loss for the purposes of paragraph 55, the directors of the company shall have regard to the manner in which the company's activities are organised.

49   Paragraph 55(4) of Schedule 4 provides that, for the purposes of paragraph 55:

(a)   classes of business which, in the opinion of the directors, do not differ substantially from each other shall be treated as one class;

(b)   markets which, in the opinion of the directors, do not differ substantially from each other shall be treated as one market; and

(c)   any amounts properly attributable to one class of business or to one market which are not material may be included in the amount stated in respect of another.

50   Paragraph 55(5) of Schedule 4 states that where, in the opinion of the directors, the disclosure of any information required by paragraph 55 would be seriously prejudicial to the interests of the company, that information need not be disclosed but the fact that any such information has not been disclosed must be stated.

51   Schedule 9 deals with the special provisions for banking and insurance companies and groups.† Paragraph 17 of Schedule 9 requires the following matters to be stated by way of note, if not otherwise shown:

(a)   the turnover for the financial year, except in so far as it is attributable to the business of banking or discounting;

(b)   if some or all of the turnover is omitted by reason of its being attributable to the business of banking or discounting, the fact that it is so omitted; and

(c)   the method by which turnover stated is arrived at.

52   Paragraph 17(5) of Schedule 9‡ provides that a company should not be subject to the requirements of paragraph 17 if it is neither a parent company nor a subsidiary undertaking and the turnover which, apart from sub-paragraph 17(5), would be required to be stated does not exceed £1 million.

53   Schedule 10 deals with the directors' report where accounts are prepared in accordance with the special provisions for banking or insurance companies or groups.§ Paragraph 2 provides that where a company prepares group accounts in accordance

---

Editor's note: The parts of paragraph 55(1) and (3) relating to profit or loss were repealed in February 1996 (S.I. 1996 No. 189). In the case of small companies, paragraph 49 of Schedule 8 to the Companies Act 1985 requires that companies disclose only the percentage of turnover attributable to markets outside the United Kingdom.

†*Editor's note: Schedule 9 as amended deals with banking companies and groups; paragraph 76 requires analysis of specified income items by geographical market. Schedule 9A deals with insurance companies and groups; paragraph 75 requires certain analysis by class of business.*

‡*Editor's note: Superseded by the present Schedules 9 and 9A.*

§*Editor's note: Now repealed.*

with the special provisions and, in the course of the financial year to which the accounts relate, the group has carried on business of two or more classes (other than banking or discounting of a class prescribed for the purpose of paragraph 17(2) of that Schedule) that in the opinion of the directors differ substantially from each other, there shall be contained in the directors' report a statement of:

(a) the proportions in which the turnover for the financial year (so far as stated in the consolidated accounts) is divided amongst those classes (describing them); and

(b) as regards business of each class, the extent or approximate extent (expressed in money terms) to which, in the opinion of the directors, the carrying on of business of that class contributed to, or restricted, the profit or loss of the company for that year (before taxation).

Classes of business which, in the opinion of the directors, do not differ substantially from each other, are to be treated as one class.

INTERNATIONAL STOCK EXCHANGE

The International Stock Exchange of the United Kingdom and the Republic of Ireland Ltd* sets out its requirements for segmental information in the 'Admission of Securities to Listing'.† Section 5, Chapter 2, paragraph 21(c) of that publication requires: **54**

'a geographical analysis of both net turnover and contribution to trading results of those trading operations carried on by the company (or group) outside the United Kingdom and the Republic of Ireland'.

No analysis of the contribution to trading results is required unless the contribution to profit or loss from a specific area is 'abnormal' in nature. 'Abnormal' is defined as substantially out of line with the normal ratio of profit to turnover. **55**

Part 5 – Legal and International Stock Exchange requirements in the Republic of Ireland

COMPANY LAW

All paragraph references, unless otherwise indicated, are to the Schedule to the Companies (Amendment) Act 1986.

Paragraph 41(1) requires all companies that, in the course of the financial year, have carried on business of two or more classes that (in the opinion of the directors) differ substantially from each other to state: **56**

(a) a description of each class of business; and
(b) the amount of turnover attributable to each class of business.

Paragraph 41(2) requires all companies that, in the course of the financial year, have supplied geographical markets that (in the opinion of the directors) differ substantially from each other, to state the amount of the turnover attributable to each market. **57**

*Editor's note: The London and Republic of Ireland stock exchanges are now separate. In the UK, listing rules are now issued by the Financial Services Authority.

†Editor's note: These requirements have been deleted as they are covered by SSAP 25.

58   Paragraph 41(3) provides that, in analysing the source (in terms of either classes of business or markets) of turnover, the directors of the company shall have regard to the manner in which the company's activities are organised.

59   Paragraph 41(4) provides that, for the purposes of paragraph 41:

(a)   classes of business which, in the opinion of the directors, do not differ substantially from each other shall be treated as one class;

(b)   markets which, in the opinion of the directors, do not differ substantially from each other shall be treated as one market; and

(c)   any amounts properly attributable to one class of business or to one market which are not material may be included in the amount stated in respect of another.

60   Paragraph 41(5) states that where, in the opinion of the directors, the disclosure of any information required by paragraph 41 would be seriously prejudicial to the interests of the company, that information need not be disclosed but the fact that any such information has not been disclosed must be stated.

61   Banking, discount and insurance companies are regarded as special classes of companies and as such come within Part III of the Sixth Schedule to the Companies Act 1963 which exempts them from the disclosure requirements of the Schedule to the Companies (Amendment) Act 1986.

62   The International Stock Exchange of the United Kingdom and the Republic of Ireland Ltd* sets out its requirements for segmental information in the 'Admission of Securities to Listing'. Section 5, Chapter 2, paragraph 21(c) of that publication requires:

'a geographical analysis of both net turnover and contribution to trading results of those trading operations carried on by the company (or group) outside the United Kingdom and the Republic of Ireland'.

63   No analysis of the contribution to trading results is required unless the contribution to profit or loss from a specific area is 'abnormal' in nature. 'Abnormal' is defined as substantially out of line with the normal ratio of profit to turnover.

Editor's note: The London and Republic of Ireland stock exchanges are now separate. In the UK, the listing rules are now issued by the Financial Services Authority.

Part 6 – Compliance with International Accounting Standard No.14 'Reporting Financial Information by Segment'*

Compliance with the requirements of this accounting standard will ensure com- **64** pliance with IAS 14 in all material respects, except in the following circumstances.

(a) This accounting standard does not require the basis of inter-segment pricing to be disclosed. This information must be disclosed in order to comply with IAS 14.

(b) This accounting standard requires the disclosure of segment 'net assets', whereas IAS 14 refers to 'assets employed'. However, as stated in paragraph 34, net assets will normally be the non-interest bearing operating assets less the non-interest bearing operating liabilities, and in those cases net assets will not be materially different from assets employed.

(c) This accounting standard gives the following exemptions which do not appear in IAS 14.

   (i) An entity need not disclose segmental information if disclosure would be seriously prejudicial to its interests.

   (ii) An entity that is not required by statute to disclose turnover is not required to disclose turnover segmentally.

   (iii) A subsidiary that is not a public limited company or a banking or insurance company need not make the segmental disclosures required by this accounting standard if its parent does so.

Editor's note: A revised version of IAS 14 'Segment reporting' was issued in September 1997. This differs appreciably from SSAP 25. IAS 14 is applicable to enterprises whose equity or debt securities are publicly traded, including those in the process of issuing equity or debt securities which will be publicly traded. IAS 14 requires disclosure to be provided in respect of both the primary and secondary basis of segmentation, with different disclosures in each case. IAS 14 provides guidance on how to determine whether the primary basis of segmentation is geographical or by class of business, and states that management's approach to the organisation of the business is relevant in determining the segments to be used. There are a number of disclosures required by IAS 14 for the primary basis of segmentation which have no equivalent in SSAP 25, including the cost of property, plant and equipment (tangible fixed assets) and intangible assets acquired for each segment during the period, the deprecation and amortisation charges for each segment, the amount of non-cash expenses and the basis of inter-segment pricing.

With effect for accounting periods beginning on or after 1 January 2009, IAS 14 is replaced by IFRS 8 Operating Segments. This standard takes a very different approach to that which underpins both IAS 14 and SSAP 25. In particular the segmentation required is based primarily on the internal reporting structure used within the entity, and the basis on which information is presented to the chief operating decision maker. Given the emphasis on internal reporting, the specific disclosures required (for example, the measure of profit to be analysed) are also based on the nature of the information that is used internally. IFRS 8 applies to companies and groups with traded securities, or in the process of a public listing, although the IASB has stated that it will reconsider this in the near future.

Appendix: Illustrative segmental report

This Appendix is for general guidance only and does not form part of the Statement of Standard Accounting Practice

| | CLASSES OF BUSINESS | | | | | | | |
| | Industry A | | Industry B | | Other industries | | Group | |
	1990 £000	1989 £000	1990 £000	1989 £000	1990 £000	1989 £000	1990 £000	1989 £000
TURNOVER								
Total sales:	33,000	30,000	42,000	38,000	26,000	23,000	101,000	91,000
Inter-segment sales	(4,000)	–	–	–	(12,000)	(14,000)	(16,000)	(14,000)
Sales to third parties	29,000	30,000	42,000	38,000	14,000	9,000	85,000	77,000
PROFIT BEFORE TAXATION								
Segment profit	3,000	2,500	4,500	4,000	1,800	1,500	9,300	8,000
Common costs							300	300
Operating profit							9,000	7,700
Net interest							(400)	(500)
							8,600	7,200
Group share of the profits before taxation of associated undertakings	1,000	1,000	1,400	1,200	–	–	2,400	2,200
Group profit before taxation							11,000	9,400
NET ASSETS								
Segment net assets	17,600	15,000	24,000	25,000	19,400	19,000	61,000	59,000
Unallocated assets							3,000	3,000
							64,000	62,000
Group share of the net assets of associated undertakings	10,200	8,000	8,800	9,000	–	–	19,000	17,000
Total net assets							83,000	79,000

GEOGRAPHICAL SEGMENTS

	United Kingdom 1990 £000	United Kingdom 1989 £000	North America 1990 £000	North America 1989 £000	Far East 1990 £000	Far East 1989 £000	Other 1990 £000	Other 1989 £000	Group 1990 £000	Group 1989 £000
TURNOVER										
Turnover by destination										
Sales to third parties	34,000	31,000	16,000	14,500	25,000	23,000	10,000	8,500	85,000	77,000
Turnover by origin										
Total sales	38,000	34,000	29,000	27,500	23,000	23,000	12,000	10,500	102,000	95,000
Inter-segment sales	–	–	(8,000)	(9,000)	(9,000)	(9,000)	–	–	(17,000)	(18,000)
Sale to third parties	38,000	34,000	21,000	18,500	14,000	14,000	12,000	10,500	85,000	77,000
PROFIT BEFORE TAXATION										
Segment profit	4,400	2,900	2,500	2,300	1,800	1,900	1,000	900	9,300	8,000
Common costs									300	300
Operating profit									9,000	7,700
Net interest									(400)	(500)
									8,600	7,200
Group share of the profit before taxation of associated undertakings	950	1,000	1,450	1,200	–	–	–	–	2,400	2,200
Group profit before taxation									11,000	9,400
NET ASSETS										
Segment net assets	16,000	15,000	25,000	26,000	16,000	15,000	4,000	3,000	61,000	59,000
Unallocated assets									3,000	3,000
									64,000	62,000
Group share of the net assets of associated undertakings	8,500	7,000	10,500	10,000	–	–	–	–	19,000	17,000
Total net assets									83,000	79,000

Unallocated assets consist of assets at the Group's head office in London amounting to £2.4 million (1989 £2.5 million) and at the Group's regional office in Hong Kong amounting to £0.6 million (1989 £0.5 million).

Financial Reporting Standard 1 (Revised 1996) is set out in paragraphs 1–50.

The Statement of Standard Accounting Practice set out in paragraphs 4–50 should be read in the context of the Objective as stated in paragraph 1 and the definitions set out in paragraphs 2 and 3 and also of the Foreword to Accounting Standards and the Statement of Principles for Financial Reporting currently in issue.

The Explanation set out in paragraphs 51–68 shall be regarded as part of the Statement of Standard Accounting Practice insofar as it assists in interpreting that statement.

Appendix III 'The development of the FRS' reviews considerations and arguments that were thought significant by members of the Board in reaching the conclusions on FRS 1 (Revised 1996).

[FRS 1]
Cash flow statements (revised 1996)*

(Issued October 1996)

Contents

*****Editor's note:** FRS 1 has been revised by FRS 25. The various changes to FRS 1 have been included in the text, with footnotes showing where the changes have been made. The changes are effective for accounting periods beginning on or after 1 January 2005.*

Adoption of FRS 1 (Revised 1996) by the Board

Appendices

Cash flow statements (revised 1996)

Summary

GENERAL

Financial Reporting Standard 1 (Revised 1996) 'Cash Flow Statements' requires **a**
reporting entities within its scope to prepare a cash flow statement in the manner set
out in the FRS. Cash flows are increases or decreases in amounts of cash, and cash is
cash in hand and deposits repayable on demand at any qualifying institution less
overdrafts from any qualifying institution repayable on demand.

SCOPE

The FRS applies to all financial statements intended to give a true and fair view of the **b**
financial position and profit or loss (or income and expenditure) except those of:

(i)   subsidiary undertakings where 90 per cent or more of the voting rights are
      controlled within the group, provided that consolidated financial statements in
      which those subsidiary undertakings are included are publicly available;
(ii) mutual life assurance companies;
(iii) pension funds;
(iv) open-ended investment funds, subject to certain further conditions;
(v)   for two years from the effective date of the FRS, building societies that, as
      required by law, prepare a statement of source and application of funds in a
      prescribed format; and
(vi) small entities (based on the small companies exemption in companies
      legislation).

FORMAT FOR THE CASH FLOW STATEMENT

An entity's cash flow statement should list its cash flows for the period classified **c**
under the following standard headings:

- operating activities (using either the direct or indirect method)
- returns on investments and servicing of finance
- taxation
- capital expenditure and financial investment
- acquisitions and disposals
- equity dividends paid
- management of liquid resources
- financing.

The last two headings can be shown in a single section provided a subtotal is given
for each heading.

Individual categories of inflows and outflows under the standard headings should be **d**
disclosed separately either in the cash flow statement or in a note to it unless they are
allowed to be shown net. Cash inflows and outflows may be shown net if they relate
to the management of liquid resources or financing and the inflows and outflows
either:

(i)   relate in substance to a single financing transaction (which is one that fulfils the conditions in paragraph 35 of FRS 4 'Capital Instruments'*); or†

(ii) are due to short maturities and high turnover occurring from rollover or reissue (for example, short-term deposits or a commercial paper programme).

The requirement to show cash inflows and outflows separately does not apply to cash flows relating to operating activities.

LINKS TO OTHER PRIMARY STATEMENTS

e   Because the information given by a cash flow statement is best appreciated in the context of the information given by the other primary statements, the FRS requires two reconciliations, between:

(i)   operating profit and the net cash flow from operating activities; and
(ii) the movement in cash in the period and the movement in net debt.

Neither reconciliation forms part of the cash flow statement but each may be given either adjoining the statement or in a separate note.

f   The movement in net debt should identify the following components and reconcile these to the opening and closing balance sheet amounts:

- the cash flows of the entity
- the acquisition or disposal of subsidiary undertakings (excluding cash balances)
- other non-cash changes
- the recognition of changes in market value and exchange rate movements.

INSURANCE COMPANIES AND GROUPS

g   Insurance companies and groups should include the cash flows of their long-term business only to the extent of cash transferred to, and available to meet the obligations of, the company or group as a whole. The cash flow statement of an insurance company or group should include a section for cash flows relating to portfolio investments rather than a section for cash flows relating to the management of liquid resources.

BANKS

h   The cash flow statement of an entity qualifying as a bank should include under operating activities cash flows relating to investments held for trading. A bank need not include a section on the management of liquid resources or the reconciliation of cash flows to the movement in net debt.

*The conditions set out in paragraph 35 of FRS 4 are:
(a)   the debt and the facility are under a single agreement or course of dealing with the same lender or group of lenders;
(b)   the finance costs for the new debt are on a basis that is not significantly higher than that of the existing debt;
(c)   the obligations of the lender (or group of lenders) are firm: the lender is not able legally to refrain from providing funds except in circumstances the possibility of which can be demonstrated to be remote; and
(d)   the lender (or group of lenders) is expected to be able to fulfil its obligations under the facility.

†*Editor's note:* The section of FRS 1 included in this summary has itself been amended by FRS 25. The reference to FRS 4 no longer holds, as the paragraph of FRS 4 has been removed with effect for accounting periods beginning on or after 1 January 2005. The section of FRS 1 of which this summary is a direct copy, has itself been amended by the removal of the section in parentheses and of the footnote.

OTHER DISCLOSURES

Material transactions not resulting in movements of cash should be disclosed in the   i
notes to the cash flow statement, if the disclosure is necessary for an understanding of
the underlying transactions. A consolidated cash flow statement should identify and
explain the circumstances and effect of restrictions preventing the transfer of cash
from one part of the group to meet obligations of another.

Financial Reporting Standard 1 (Revised 1996)

Objective

The objective of this FRS is to ensure that reporting entities falling within its scope: 1

(a) report their cash generation and cash absorption for a period by highlighting
     the significant components of cash flow in a way that facilitates comparison of
     the cash flow performance of different businesses; and
(b) provide information that assists in the assessment of their liquidity, solvency
     and financial adaptability.

Definitions

The following definitions shall apply in this FRS and in particular in the Statement of   2
Standard Accounting Practice set out in paragraphs 4–50.

Active market:-
A market of sufficient depth to absorb the investment held without a significant
effect on the price.

Bank:-
An entity whose business is to receive deposits or other repayable funds from the
public and to grant credits for its own account.*

Cash:-
Cash in hand and deposits repayable on demand with any qualifying financial
institution, less overdrafts from any qualifying financial institution repayable on
demand. Deposits are repayable on demand if they can be withdrawn at any time
without notice and without penalty or if a maturity or period of notice of not more
than 24 hours or one working day has been agreed. Cash includes cash in hand and
deposits denominated in foreign currencies.

Cash flow:-
An increase or decrease in an amount of cash.

---

*This definition is based on:
(a) in Great Britain, section 262 of the Companies Act 1985, itself based on the definition in the Banking Act
     1987;
(b) in Northern Ireland, Article 270 of the Companies (Northern Ireland) Order 1986;
(c) in the Republic of Ireland, section (2)(2) (other than paragraph (b)) of the Companies (Amendment)
     Act 1986.

Equity dividends:-
Dividends relating to instruments classified as equity in accordance with FRS 25 '(IAS 32) Financial Instruments: Disclosure and Presentation'.*

Insurance company or group:-
A company that carries on an insurance business and is regulated accordingly or an insurance group as defined in the relevant legislation.†

Investment fund:-‡
An entity:
(a)   whose business consists of investing its funds mainly in securities, with the aim of spreading investment risk and giving members the benefit of the results of the management of its funds;
(b)   none of whose holdings in other entities (except those in other investment funds) represents more than 15 per cent by value of the investing entity's investments; and
(c)   that has not retained more than 15 per cent of the income it derives from securities.

Liquid resources:-
Current asset investments held as readily disposable stores of value. A readily disposable investment is one that:
(a)   is disposable by the reporting entity without curtailing or disrupting its business;
and is either:
(b)(i)   readily convertible into known amounts of cash at or close to its carrying amount, or
(b)(ii)   traded in an active market.

Net debt:-
The borrowings of the reporting entity (comprising capital instruments classified as liabilities in accordance with FRS 25 '(IAS 32) Financial Instruments: Disclosure and Presentation', together with related derivatives, and obligations under finance leases) less cash and liquid resources. Where cash and liquid resources exceed the borrowings of the entity reference should be to 'net funds' rather than to 'net debt'.§

Editor's note: The definition of equity dividends has been changed by FRS 25 with effect for accounting periods beginning on or after 1 January 2005.

†In the UK an insurance company is one to which Part II of the Insurance Companies Act 1982 applies. The equivalent reference in the Republic of Ireland is the Companies (Amendment) Act 1986 section 2(3). In the UK an insurance group is defined in section 255A of the Companies Act 1985. In the Republic of Ireland an insurance company or group is one to which Regulation 3 of the European Community (Insurance Undertakings: Accounts) Regulations 1996 applies.

‡This definition is based on three of the four conditions defining an investment company in companies legislation– in Great Britain section 266 of the Companies Act 1985; in Northern Ireland, Article 274 of the Companies (Northern Ireland) Order 1986; and in the Republic of Ireland, section 47 of the Companies (Amendment) Act 1983. Under the definition above, investment companies as defined in companies legislation will qualify as investment funds but so should certain investment entities that are not companies or do not qualify under companies legislation because they distribute capital.

§*Editor's note:* The definition of net debt has been changed by FRS 25 with effect for accounting periods beginning on or after 1 January 2005.

Non-equity dividends:-
Dividends relating to instruments classified as liabilities in accordance with FRS 25 '(IAS 32) Financial Instruments: Disclosure and Presentation'.*

Overdraft:-
A borrowing facility repayable on demand that is used by drawing on a current account with a qualifying financial institution.

Qualifying financial institution:-
An entity that as part of its business receives deposits or other repayable funds and grants credits for its own account.

References to companies legislation mean: **3**

(a)   in Great Britain, the Companies Act 1985;
(b)   in Northern Ireland, the Companies (Northern Ireland) Order 1986; and
(c)   in the Republic of Ireland, the Companies Acts 1963-90 and the European Communities (Companies: Group Accounts) Regulations 1992.

Statement of Standard Accounting Practice

Reporting entities falling within the scope of paragraph 5 of Financial Reporting **4** Standard 1 (Revised 1996) are required to provide as a primary statement within the reporting entity's financial statements a cash flow statement drawn up in accordance with the standard accounting principles set out in paragraphs 6-48 of the FRS.

SCOPE

The FRS applies to all financial statements intended to give a true and fair view of the **5** financial position and profit or loss (or income and expenditure) except those of:

(a)   subsidiary undertakings where 90 per cent or more of the voting rights are controlled within the group, provided that consolidated financial statements in which the subsidiary undertakings are included are publicly available.
(b)   mutual life assurance companies.
(c)   pension funds.
(d)   open-ended investment funds that meet all the following conditions:

     (i)   substantially all of the entity's investments are highly liquid;
     (ii)   substantially all of the entity's investments are carried at market value; and
     (iii)   the entity provides a statement of changes in net assets.

(e)   for two years from the effective date of the FRS, building societies, as defined by the Building Societies Act 1986 in the UK and by the Building Societies Act 1989 in the Republic of Ireland, that prepare, as required by law, a statement of source and application of funds in a prescribed format.
(f)   companies incorporated under companies legislation and entitled to the exemptions available in the legislation for small companies when filing accounts with the Registrar of Companies.
(g)   entities that would have been in category (f) above if they were companies incorporated under companies legislation.

**Editor's note: The definition of non-equity dividends has been changed by FRS 25 with effect for accounting periods beginning on or after 1 January 2005.*

PREPARATION OF CASH FLOW STATEMENTS

6   The cash flow statement should include all the reporting entity's inflows and outflows of cash. Transactions that do not result in cash flows of the reporting entity should not be reported in the cash flow statement.

Format for cash flow statements

7   An entity's cash flow statement should list its cash flows for the period classified under the following standard headings:

- operating activities
- dividends from joint ventures and associates
- returns on investments and servicing of finance
- taxation
- capital expenditure and financial investment
- acquisitions and disposals
- equity dividends paid
- management of liquid resources
- financing.

The first seven headings should be in the sequence set out above. Operating cash flows can be presented by either the direct method (showing the relevant constituent cash flows) or the indirect method (calculating operating cash flows by adjustment to the operating profit reported in the profit and loss account). The cash flows relating to the management of liquid resources and financing can be combined under a single heading provided that the cash flows relating to each are shown separately and separate subtotals are given. Appendix I of the FRS contains examples of cash flow statements for an individual company, a group, a bank and an insurance group.

CLASSIFICATION OF CASH FLOWS

8   Except for cash inflows and outflows that are shown net (as permitted by paragraph 9), the individual categories of inflows and outflows under the standard headings set out in paragraphs 11-32 should be disclosed separately, where material, in the cash flow statement or in a note. The cash flow classifications may be subdivided further to give a fuller description of the activities of the reporting entity or to provide segmental information.

9   The requirement to show cash inflows and outflows separately does not apply to cash flows relating to operating activities. Cash inflows and outflows within the management of liquid resources or financing may also be netted against each other if they either:

(a)   relate in substance to a single financing transaction, or*
(b)   are due to short maturities and high turnover occurring from rollover or reissue (for example, short-term deposits or a commercial paper programme).

10 Each cash flow should be classified according to the substance of the transaction giving rise to it. That substance should be used to determine the most appropriate standard heading under which to report any cash flows that are not specified in the categories set out in paragraphs 11-32 below. However, cash flows relating to interest

*Editor's note: This paragraph has been amended by FRS 25. For accounting periods beginning on or after 1 January 2005 it no longer makes reference to FRS 4.

paid should always be classified under 'returns on investments and servicing of finance' even if the interest has been capitalised in the other primary statements.

CLASSIFICATION OF CASH FLOWS BY STANDARD HEADING

Operating activities

Cash flows from operating activities are in general the cash effects of transactions and other events relating to operating or trading activities, normally shown in the profit and loss account in arriving at operating profit. They include cash flows in respect of operating items relating to provisions, whether or not the provision was included in operating profit. **11**

A reconciliation between the operating profit reported in the profit and loss account and the net cash flow from operating activities should be given either adjoining the cash flow statement or as a note. The reconciliation is not part of the cash flow statement: if adjoining the cash flow statement, it should be clearly labelled and kept separate. The reconciliation should disclose separately the movements in stocks, debtors and creditors related to operating activities and other differences between cash flows and profits. **12**

Dividends received from joint ventures and associates should be included as separate items between operating activities and returns on investment and servicing of finance. **12A**

Returns on investments and servicing of finance

'Returns on investments and servicing of finance' are receipts resulting from the ownership of an investment and payments to providers of finance, non-equity shareholders (eg the holders of preference shares) and minority interests, excluding those items required by paragraphs 11-32 to be classified under another heading. **13**

Cash inflows from returns on investments and servicing of finance include: **14**

(a) interest received, including any related tax recovered; and
(b) dividends received, net of any tax credits (except dividends from equity accounted entities).

Cash outflows from returns on investments and servicing of finance include: **15**

(a) interest paid (even if capitalised), including any tax deducted and paid to the relevant tax authority;
(b) cash flows that are treated as finance costs (this will include issue costs on debt and non-equity share capital);*
(c) the interest element of finance lease rental payments;
(d) dividends paid on non-equity shares of the entity; and
(e) dividends paid to minority interests.

Taxation

The cash flows included under the heading 'taxation' are cash flows to or from taxation authorities in respect of the reporting entity's revenue and capital profits. For a subsidiary undertaking, cash flows relating to group relief should be included **16**

---

*Editor's note: This paragraph has been amended by FRS 25. For accounting periods beginning on or after 1 January 2005 it no longer makes reference to FRS 4.

in this section. Cash flows in respect of other taxation, including payments and receipts in respect of Value Added Tax, other sales taxes, property taxes and other taxes not assessed on the profits of the reporting entity, should be dealt with as set out in paragraphs 39-40 of the FRS.

17　Taxation cash inflows include cash receipts from the relevant tax authority of tax rebates, claims or returns of overpayments. For a subsidiary undertaking, payments received from other members of the group for group relief should be included as cash inflows.

18　Taxation cash outflows include cash payments to the relevant tax authority of tax, including payments of advance corporation tax. For a subsidiary undertaking, payments made to other members of the group for group relief should be included as cash outflows.

Capital expenditure and financial investment

19　The cash flows included in 'capital expenditure and financial investment' are those related to the acquisition or disposal of any fixed asset other than one required to be classified under 'acquisitions and disposals' as specified in paragraphs 22-24 of the FRS and any current asset investment not included in liquid resources dealt with in paragraphs 26-28. If no cash flows relating to financial investment fall to be included under this heading the caption may be reduced to 'capital expenditure'.

20　Cash inflows from 'capital expenditure and financial investment' include:

(a)　receipts from sales or disposals of property, plant or equipment; and
(b)　receipts from the repayment of the reporting entity's loans to other entities or sales of debt instruments of other entities other than receipts forming part of an acquisition or disposal or a movement in liquid resources, as specified respectively in paragraphs 22-24 and 26-28 of the FRS.

21　Cash outflows from 'capital expenditure and financial investment' include:

(a)　payments to acquire property, plant or equipment; and
(b)　loans made by the reporting entity and payments to acquire debt instruments of other entities other than payments forming part of an acquisition or disposal or a movement in liquid resources, as specified respectively in paragraphs 22-24 and 26-28 of the FRS.

Acquisitions and disposals

22　The cash flows included in 'acquisitions and disposals' are those related to the acquisition or disposal of any trade or business, or of an investment in an entity that is or, as a result of the transaction, becomes or ceases to be either an associate, a joint venture, or a subsidiary undertaking.

23　Cash inflows from 'acquisitions and disposals' include:

(a)　receipts from sales of investments in subsidiary undertakings, showing separately any balances of cash and overdrafts transferred as part of the sale;
(b)　receipts from sales of investments in associates or joint ventures; and
(c)　receipts from sales of trades or businesses.

24　Cash outflows from 'acquisitions and disposals' include:

(a)   payments to acquire investments in subsidiary undertakings, showing separately any balances of cash and overdrafts acquired;
(b)   payments to acquire investments in associates and joint ventures; and
(c)   payments to acquire trades or businesses.

Equity dividends paid

The cash outflows included in 'equity dividends paid' are dividends paid on the   **25**
reporting entity's, or, in a group, the parent's, equity shares, excluding any advance
corporation tax.

Management of liquid resources

The 'management of liquid resources' section should include cash flows in respect of   **26**
liquid resources as defined in paragraph 2. Each entity should explain what it
includes as liquid resources and any changes in its policy. The cash flows in this
section can be shown in a single section with those under 'financing' provided that
separate subtotals for each are given.

Cash inflows in management of liquid resources include: **27**

(a)   withdrawals from short-term deposits not qualifying as cash in so far as not
netted under paragraph 9(b); and
(b)   inflows from disposal or redemption of any other investments held as liquid
resources.

Cash outflows in management of liquid resources include :   **28**

(a)   payments into short-term deposits not qualifying as cash in so far as not netted
under paragraph 9(b); and
(b)   outflows to acquire any other investments held as liquid resources.

Financing

Financing cash flows comprise receipts or repayments of principal from or to   **29**
external providers of finance. The cash flows in this section can be shown in a single
section with those under 'management of liquid resources' provided that separate
subtotals for each are given.

Financing cash inflows include: **30**

(a)   receipts from issuing shares or other equity instruments; and
(b)   receipts from issuing debentures, loans, notes, and bonds and from other long-
term and short-term borrowings (other than overdrafts).

Financing cash outflows include: **31**

(a)   repayments of amounts borrowed (other than overdrafts);
(b)   the capital element of finance lease rental payments;
(c)   payments to reacquire or redeem the entity's shares; and
(d)   payments of expenses or commissions on any issue of equity shares.

The amounts of any financing cash flows received from or paid to equity accounted   **32**
entities should be disclosed separately.

RECONCILIATION TO NET DEBT

33   A note reconciling the movement of cash in the period with the movement in net debt should be given either adjoining the cash flow statement or in a note. The reconciliation is not part of the cash flow statement: if adjoining the cash flow statement, it should be clearly labelled and kept separate. The changes in net debt should be analysed from the opening to the closing component amounts showing separately, where material, changes resulting from:

(a)   the cash flows of the entity;
(b)   the acquisition or disposal of subsidiary undertakings;
(c)   other non-cash changes; and
(d)   the recognition of changes in market value and exchange rate movements.

Where several balance sheet amounts or parts thereof have to be combined to form the components of opening and closing net debt, sufficient detail should be shown to enable the cash and other components of net debt to be respectively traced back to the amounts shown under the equivalent captions in the balance sheet. A possible format for the analysis of net debt is provided in the examples in Appendix I.

BANKS

34   Banks should include as cash only cash and balances at central banks and loans and advances to banks repayable on demand. The cash flow statement of a bank should include under operating activities receipts and payments relating to loans made to other entities and cash flows relating to investments held for trading. A bank need not include a section on the management of liquid resources nor the reconciliation of cash flows to the movement in net debt. Appendix I contains an example of a cash flow statement for a bank.

INSURANCE COMPANIES AND GROUPS

35   The cash flow statement of an entity qualifying as an insurance company or group should include a section for cash flows relating to 'portfolio investments' rather than a section for cash flows relating to the 'management of liquid resources'. Instead of the analysis of the movement in net debt that is generally required, insurance companies and groups should provide an analysis of the movement in portfolio investments less financing, either adjoining the cash flow statement or in a note. The reconciliation is not part of the cash flow statement: if adjoining the cash flow statement, it should be clearly labelled and kept separate. The reconciliation of operating profit to net cash flow from operating activities should normally take profit or loss on ordinary activities before tax as its starting point. Appendix I contains an example of a cash flow statement for an insurance group.

36   Insurance companies and groups, other than mutual life assurance companies to which the FRS does not apply, should include the cash flows of their long-term business—long-term life, pensions and annuity businesses or their equivalents in relation to overseas operations—only to the extent of cash transferred and available to meet the obligations of the company or group as a whole. The note analysing the movements in the balance sheet amounts of portfolio investments and financing during the period should distinguish movements relating to the long-term business to the extent that these are included in the balance sheet amounts.

EXCEPTIONAL AND EXTRAORDINARY ITEMS AND CASH FLOWS*

Where cash flows relate to items that are classified as exceptional or extraordinary in the profit and loss account they should be shown under the appropriate standard headings, according to the nature of each item. The cash flows relating to exceptional or extraordinary items should be identified in the cash flow statement or a note to it and the relationship between the cash flows and the originating exceptional or extraordinary item should be explained.   **37**

Where cash flows are exceptional because of their size or incidence but are not related to items that are treated as exceptional or extraordinary in the profit and loss account, sufficient disclosure should be given to explain their cause and nature.   **38**

VALUE ADDED TAX AND OTHER TAXES

Cash flows should be shown net of any attributable Value Added Tax or other sales tax unless the tax is irrecoverable by the reporting entity. The net movement on the amount payable to, or receivable from, the taxing authority should be allocated to cash flows from operating activities unless a different treatment is more appropriate in the particular circumstances concerned. Where restrictions apply to the recoverability of such taxes, the irrecoverable amount should be allocated to those expenditures affected by the restrictions. If this is impracticable, the irrecoverable tax should be included under the most appropriate standard heading.   **39**

Taxation cash flows other than those in respect of the reporting entity's revenue and capital profits and Value Added Tax, or other sales tax, should be included within the cash flow statement under the same standard heading as the cash flow that gave rise to the taxation cash flow, unless a different treatment is more appropriate in the particular circumstances concerned.   **40**

FOREIGN CURRENCIES

Where a portion of a reporting entity's business is undertaken by a foreign entity, the cash flows of that entity are to be included in the cash flow statement on the basis used for translating the results of those activities in the profit and loss account of the reporting entity. The same basis should be used in presenting the movements in stocks, debtors and creditors in the reconciliation between operating profit and cash from operating activities. Where intragroup cash flows are separately identifiable and the actual rate of exchange at which they took place is known, that rate, or an approximation thereto, may be used to translate the cash flows in order to ensure that they cancel on consolidation. If the rate used to translate intragroup cash flows is not the actual rate, any exchange rate differences arising should be included in the effect of exchange rate movements shown as part of the reconciliation to net debt.   **41**

HEDGING TRANSACTIONS

When a futures contract, forward contract, option contract or swap contract is accounted for as a hedge, the cash flows of the contract should be reported under the same standard heading as the transaction that is the subject of the hedge.   **42**

Editor's note: Notwithstanding the comments in this section, there are no extraordinary items in the UK since the introduction of FRS 3.

GROUPS

43 Cash flows that are internal to the group should be eliminated in the preparation of a consolidated cash flow statement. Where a subsidiary undertaking joins or leaves a group during a financial year the cash flows of the group should include the cash flows of the subsidiary undertaking concerned for the same period as that for which the group's profit and loss account includes the results of the subsidiary undertaking.

44 The cash flows of any equity accounted entity should be included in the group cash flow statement only to the extent of the actual cash flows between the group and the entity concerned, for example dividends received in cash and loans made or repaid.

ACQUISITIONS AND DISPOSALS OF SUBSIDIARY UNDERTAKINGS

45 A note to the cash flow statement should show a summary of the effects of acquisitions and disposals of subsidiary undertakings indicating how much of the consideration comprised cash. Material effects on amounts reported under each of the standard headings reflecting the cash flows of a subsidiary undertaking acquired or disposed of in the period should be disclosed, as far as practicable. This information could be given by dividing cash flows between continuing and discontinued operations and acquisitions.

MATERIAL NON-CASH TRANSACTIONS

46 Material transactions not resulting in movements of cash of the reporting entity should be disclosed in the notes to the cash flow statement if disclosure is necessary for an understanding of the underlying transactions.

RESTRICTIONS ON REMITTABILITY

47 A note to the cash flow statement should identify the amounts and explain the circumstances where restrictions prevent the transfer of cash from one part of the business or group to another.

COMPARATIVE FIGURES

48 Comparative figures should be given for all items in the cash flow statement and such notes thereto as are required by the FRS with the exception of the note to the statement that analyses changes in the balance sheet amounts making up net debt (or the equivalent note for insurance companies and groups) and the note of the material effects of acquisitions and disposals of subsidiary undertakings on each of the standard headings.

DATE FROM WHICH EFFECTIVE

49 The accounting practices set out in the FRS should be regarded as standard in respect of financial statements relating to accounting periods ending on or after 23 March 1997. Earlier adoption is encouraged but not required.*

*Editor's note: The changes introduced by FRS 25 are effective for accounting periods beginning on or after 1 January 2005.

WITHDRAWAL OF FRS 1 (ISSUED SEPTEMBER 1991)

The FRS supersedes FRS 1 issued in September 1991. **50**

Explanation

DEFINITIONS

Cash flows

Cash flows are defined as increases or decreases in cash. Cash includes cash in hand, **51**
deposits repayable on demand and overdrafts. Deposits are repayable on demand if
they are in practice available within 24 hours without penalty. No investments,
however liquid or near maturity, are included as cash. Overdrafts are included as
cash because of their role as negative cash balances—a cheque drawn on an account
can either reduce the cash balance or increase the overdraft. Although banks take
large volumes of short-term and demand deposits, they do not usually have borrowings with the characteristics of an overdraft.

Liquid resources

The definition of liquid resources is expressed in general terms, emphasising the **52**
liquidity of the investment and its function as a readily disposable store of value
rather than setting out a narrow range of investment instruments. Depending on the
entity's policy (which should be disclosed), term deposits, government securities, loan
stock, equities and derivatives may each form part of that entity's liquid resources,
provided they meet the definition. Short-term deposits would also fall within the
definition, though the requirement that they should be readily convertible into
known amounts of cash at or close to their carrying amounts would tend to exclude
any that are more than one year from maturity on acquisition.

Net debt

The objective of the reconciliation of cash flows to the movement in net debt is to **53**
provide information that assists in the assessment of liquidity, solvency and financial
adaptability. Net debt is defined to include borrowings less liquid resources because
movements in net debt so defined are widely used as indicating changes in liquidity,
and therefore assist in assessing the financial strength of the entity. The definition
excludes non-equity shares of the entity because, although these have features that
may be similar to those of borrowings, they are not actually liabilities of the entity.
The definition also excludes debtors and creditors because, while these are short-term
claims on and sources of finance to the entity, their main role is as part of the entity's
trading activities.

SCOPE

Most small reporting entities are exempt from the requirement to include a cash flow **54**
statement as part of their financial statements. This exemption does not extend to
public companies or to banking companies, insurance companies, authorised persons
under the Financial Services Act 1986,* or members of a group containing one or
more of the above-mentioned entities. The scope of this exemption is currently being

*In the UK. The equivalent reference in the Republic of Ireland is the Investment Intermediaries Act 1995.

re-examined as part of a wider examination of the reporting requirements for small entities. However, the Board encourages small reporting entities to include a cash flow statement as part of their financial statements, if it would provide useful information to users of those financial statements and the benefits of the exercise outweigh the costs.*

CLASSIFICATION OF CASH FLOWS

55   In setting the conditions for netting cash flows, paragraph 9 permits the cash flows over the period of a single financing transaction to be reported net.†

56   In order to improve the comparability of cash flow statements of different entities, paragraphs 11-31 give examples of certain standard subdivisions that should be separately disclosed, if material. Reporting entities are encouraged, however, to disclose additional information relevant to their particular circumstances. One form of segmentation that may often be useful is a division of cash flows from operating activities into those relating to continuing and to discontinued operations (as defined in FRS 3 'Reporting Financial Performance'). In some circumstances it may also be useful to divide cash flows in a way that reflects different degrees of access to the underlying cash balances—this may be of especial relevance in regulated industries such as the insurance industry.

57   Certain accounting standards, such as SSAP 13 'Accounting for research and development', SSAP 21 'Accounting for leases and hire purchase contracts' and FRS 5 'Reporting the Substance of Transactions', specify how certain transactions are to be recognised and classified for financial reporting on the basis of the substance of the transaction. In order to achieve consistent treatment in the cash flow statement this FRS requires cash flows, too, to be classified according to the substance of the transaction giving rise to them. For example, cash flows relating to development costs that are capitalised would be included under 'capital expenditure'. Cash flows relating to finance leases are to be divided into the part relating to interest, to be classified under 'servicing of finance', and the part making up repayment of the capital amount, to be classified under 'financing'. Similarly, the cash flows relating to finance costs are to be classified under 'returns on investments and servicing of finance'. However, the Board believes that it is important to show the total of cash flows relating to interest paid in the cash flow statement. The FRS therefore requires interest paid to be included as servicing of finance, regardless of whether it is capitalised.‡

CLASSIFICATION OF CASH FLOWS BY STANDARD HEADING

Operating activities

58   The FRS allows operating cash flows to be presented using either the direct or the indirect method. A cash flow statement presented under the direct method shows operating cash receipts and payments (including, in particular, cash receipts from customers, cash payments to suppliers and cash payments to and on behalf of employees), aggregating to the net cash flow from operating activities. Rather than reporting the individual component cash flows to arrive at the net cash inflow or

---

*Editor's note: See also section D of the Financial Reporting Standard for Smaller Entities.

†Editor's note: The original final sentence of this paragraph, which referred to FRS 4, has been removed by FRS 25.

‡Editor's note: Two references to FRS 4 in this paragraph have been removed by FRS 25.

outflow from operating activities, the cash flow statement under the indirect method derives the net cash inflow or outflow by means of a reconciliation from operating profit. The FRS requires the reconciliation even if the direct method is used. The reconciliation adjusts operating profit for non-cash charges and credits and brings in operating item cash flows relating to provisions, whether or not the provision was deducted in arriving at operating profit. Examples of such cash flows are redundancy payments falling under a provision for the termination of an operation or for a fundamental reorganisation or restructuring (paragraph 20a and b of FRS 3 'Reporting Financial Performance'), also operating item cash flows provided for on an acquisition.

In some businesses material debtors and creditors may arise in relation to the pur-   **59** chase and sale of investments, including investments forming part of liquid resources. The changes in such debtors and creditors should be included in the reconciliation of operating profit to the net cash flow from operating activities only to the extent that the purchase and sale of the investments giving rise to them form part of the operating activities of the entity.

Returns on investments and servicing of finance

Interest paid and received and dividends received may result from investing activities,   **60** the management of liquid resources, financing or in some cases operating activities. To the extent that entities such as banks, insurance companies or investment companies show interest received or paid and dividends received in their profit and loss accounts as part of their operating profit they should include related cash flows as part of their operating cash flows, unless the interest paid clearly relates to financing –for example, relating to a bank's subordinated loans—in which case it should be included under 'returns on investments and servicing of finance'.

Taxation

The taxation cash flows of a reporting entity in relation to revenue and capital profits   **61** may result from complex computations that are affected by the operating, investing and financing activities of an entity. The Board believes that it is not useful to divide taxation cash flows into constituent parts relating to the activities that gave rise to them because the apportionment will, in many cases, have to be made on an arbitrary basis. As taxation cash flows generally arise from activities in an earlier period, apportioning the taxation cash flows would in any event not necessarily report the taxation cash flows along with the transactions that gave rise to them. Accordingly, the Board believes that taxation cash flows in relation to revenue and capital profits should be disclosed in a separate section within the cash flow statement entitled 'taxation'.

INSURANCE COMPANIES AND GROUPS

One purpose of a cash flow statement is to provide information that assists in the   **62** assessment of the liquidity, solvency and financial adaptability of an entity. This objective, however, is of only limited application to an insurance company or group. In interpreting the information given by the cash flow statement of an insurance company or group, users should bear in mind that cash inflows of premiums to insurance companies may not increase their liquidity in the same way as cash received for interest or dividends because the receipt of premiums engenders provision requirements for future claims and reserve requirements for solvency.

EXCEPTIONAL AND EXTRAORDINARY ITEMS AND CASH FLOWS*

63   The FRS requires cash flows relating to exceptional or extraordinary items to be identified and explained, to allow a user to gain an understanding of the effect of the underlying transactions on the cash flows. This requirement means that cash flows relating to reorganisation charges that are exceptional must be disclosed separately and explained. The FRS also requires identification of cash flows that are exceptional because of their size or incidence but are not related to items that are treated as exceptional or extraordinary in the profit and loss account. For a cash flow to be exceptional on the grounds of its size alone, it must be exceptional in relation to cash flows of a similar nature. A large prepayment against a pension liability is an example of a possible exceptional cash flow unrelated to an exceptional or extraordinary item in the profit and loss account.

VALUE ADDED TAX

64   The cash flows of an entity include Value Added Tax (VAT) where appropriate and thus strictly the various elements of the cash flow statement should include VAT. However, this treatment does not take into account the fact that normally VAT is a short-term timing difference as far as the entity's overall cash flows are concerned and the inclusion of VAT in the cash flows may distort the allocation of cash flows to standard headings. The Board believes that, in order to avoid this distortion and to show cash flows attributable to the reporting entity's activities, cash flows should be shown net of sales taxes and the net movement on the amount payable to, or receivable from, the taxing authority should be allocated to cash flows from operating activities unless a different treatment is more appropriate in the particular circumstances concerned.

FOREIGN CURRENCIES

65   Because of the complementary nature of the profit and loss account and the cash flow statement in reflecting different but related aspects of an entity's performance in the period, the standard requires the cash flow statement to be translated using the same rate as the profit and loss account, unless the actual rate at the date of the transaction is used. Cash flows between members of a group should not be included in the consolidated cash flow statement. However, these cash flows may not cancel unless the actual rate at the date of transfer is used for translation. The FRS allows the actual rate to be used where intragroup cash flows are separately identifiable and the actual rate is known.

HEDGING TRANSACTIONS

66   Entities may undertake hedging transactions that result in cash flows. The Board is considering as part of its project on derivatives and other financial instruments the way in which such transactions should be reflected in financial statements. As an interim measure it has decided to confine the recognition of hedges in cash flow statements. An example of the presentation of a hedging transaction in accordance with the FRS would be the inclusion under 'returns on investments and servicing of

---

*****Editor's note**: *Notwithstanding the comments in this paragraph, there are no extraordinary items in the UK since the introduction of FRS 3.*

finance' of the cash flows of interest rate swaps held as a hedge of an entity's own debt.*

MATERIAL NON-CASH TRANSACTIONS

Consideration for transactions may be in a form other than cash. Since the purpose of a cash flow statement is to report cash flows, non-cash transactions should not be reported in a cash flow statement. However, to obtain a full picture of the alterations in financial position caused by the transactions for the period, separate disclosure of material non-cash transactions (such as shares issued for the acquisition of a subsidiary, the exchange of major assets or the inception of a finance lease contract) is also necessary.   **67**

RESTRICTIONS ON REMITTABILITY

The note identifying the amounts and explaining the circumstances where restrictions prevent the transfer of cash from one part of the business or group to another should refer only to circumstances where access is severely restricted by external factors such as strict exchange control rather than where the sole constraint is a special purpose designated by the reporting entity itself. Depending on the regulatory environment, cash balances in escrow, deposited with a regulator or held within an employee share ownership trust may be subject to restrictions on remittability that should be disclosed.   **68**

Editor's note: The project on derivatives and other financial instruments gave rise to FRS 25 and FRS 26.

Adoption of FRS 1 (revised 1996) by the Board

Financial Reporting Standard 1 (Revised 1996) – 'Cash Flow Statements' was approved for issue by the nine members of the Accounting Standards Board.

Sir David Tweedie (Chairman)
Allan Cook (Technical Director)
David Allvey
Ian Brindle
John Coombe
Raymond Hinton
Huw Jones
Professor Geoffrey Whittington
Ken Wild

Appendix I – Examples of cash flow statements

EXAMPLE 1 A CASH FLOW STATEMENT FOR AN INDIVIDUAL COMPANY – XYZ LIMITED
CASH FLOW STATEMENT FOR THE YEAR ENDED 31 DECEMBER 1996

Reconciliation of operating profit to net cash inflow from operating activities

	£000	£000
Operating profit		6,022
Depreciation charges		899
Increase in stocks		(194)
Increase in debtors		(72)
Increase in creditors		234
Net cash inflow from operating activities		6,889

CASH FLOW STATEMENT

	£000
Net cash inflow from operating activities	6,889
Returns on investments and servicing of finance (note 1)	2,999
Taxation	(2,922)
Capital Expenditure	(1,525)
	5,441
Equity dividends paid	(2,417)
	3,024
Management of liquid resources (note 1)	(450)
Financing (note 1)	57
Increase in cash	**2,631**

Reconciliation of net cash flow to movement in net debt (note 2)

Increase in cash in the period	**2,631**	
Cash to repurchase debenture	149	
Cash used to increase liquid resources	450	
Change in net debt*		**3,230**
Net debt at 1.1.96		**(2,903)**
Net funds at 31.12.96		**327**

*In this example all changes in net debt are cash flows.

NOTES TO THE CASH FLOW STATEMENT

Note 1 – GROSS CASH FLOWS

	£000	£000
Returns on investments and servicing of finance		
Interest received	3,011	
Interest paid	(12)	
		2,999
Capital expenditure		
Payments to acquire intangible fixed assets	(71)	
Payments to acquire tangible fixed assets	(1,496)	
Receipts from sales of tangible fixed assets	42	
		(1,525)
Management of liquid resources		
Purchase of treasury bills	(650)	
Sale of treasury bills	200	
		(450)
Financing		
Issuing of ordinary share capital	211	
Repurchase of debenture loan	(149)	
Expenses paid in connection with share issues	(5)	
		57

Note 2 – ANALYSIS OF CHANGES IN NET DEBT

	At 1 Jan 1996 £000	Cash flows £000	Other changes £000	At 31 Dec 1996 £000
Cash in hand, at bank	42	847		889
Overdrafts	(1,784)	1,784		
		2,631		
Debt due within 1 year	(149)	149	(230)	(230)
Debt due after 1 year	(1,262)		230	(1,032)
Current asset investments	250	450		700
TOTAL	(2,903)	3,230	–	327

EXAMPLE 2 A CASH FLOW STATEMENT FOR A GROUP – XYZ GROUP PLC
CASH FLOW STATEMENT FOR THE YEAR ENDED 31 DECEMBER 1996

	£000	£000
Cash flow from operating activities (note 1)		15,672
Dividends received from associates		350
Returns on investments and servicing of finance*(note 2)		(2,239)
Taxation		(2,887)
Capital expenditure and financial investment (note 2)		(865)
Acquisitions and disposals (note 2)		(17,824)
Equity dividends paid		(2,606)
Cash outflow before use of liquid resources and financing		**(10,399)**
Management of liquid resources (note 2)		700
Financing (note 2) - Issue of shares	600	
Increase in debt	2,347	
		2,947
Decrease in cash in the period		**(6,752)**

Reconciliation of net cash flow to movement in net debt (note 3)

	£000	£000
Decrease in cash in the period		**(6,752)**
Cash inflow from increase in debt and lease financing		(2,347)
Cash inflow from decrease in liquid resources		(700)
Change in net debt resulting from cash flows		(9,799)
Loans and finance leases acquired with subsidiary		(3,817)
New finance leases		(2,845)
Translation difference		643
Movement in net debt in the period		**(15,818)**
Net debt at 1.1.96		**(15,215)**
Net debt at 31.12.96		**(31,033)**

**This heading would include any dividends received other than those from equity accounted entities included in operating activities.*

NOTES TO THE CASH FLOW STATEMENT

Note 1 – RECONCILIATION OF OPERATING PROFIT TO OPERATING CASH FLOWS

	Continuing £000	Discontinued £000	Total £000
Operating Profit	18,829	(1,616)	17,213
Depreciation charges	3,108	380	3,488
Cash flow relating to previous year restructuring provision (note 4)		(560)	(560)
Increase in stocks	(11,193)	(87)	(11,280)
Increase in debtors	(3,754)	(20)	(3,774)
Increase in creditors	9,672	913	10,585
Net cash inflow from continuing operating activities	16,662		
Net cash outflow in respect of discontinued activities		(990)	
Net cash inflow from operating activities			15,672

Note 2 – ANALYSIS OF CASH FLOWS FOR HEADINGS NETTED IN THE CASH FLOW STATEMENT

	£000	£000
Returns on investments and servicing of finance		
Interest received	508	
Interest paid	(1,939)	
Preference dividend paid	(450)	
Interest element of finance lease rental payments	(358)	
Net cash outflow for returns on investments and servicing of finance		(2,239)
Capital Expenditure and financial investment		
Purchase of tangible fixed assets	(3,512)	
Sale of trade investment	1,595	
Sale of plant and machinery	1,052	
Net cash outflow for capital expenditure and financial investment		(865)
Acquisitions and disposals		
Purchase of subsidiary undertaking	(12,705)	
Net overdrafts acquired with subsidiary	(5,516)	
Sale of business	4,208	
Purchase of interest in a joint venture	(3,811)	
Net cash outflow for acquisitions and disposals		(17,824)

Management of liquid resources*

Cash withdrawn from 7 day deposit	200
Purchase of government securities	(5,000)
Sale of government securities	4,300
Sale of corporate bonds	1,200

Net cash outflow from management of liquid resources — 700

Financing

Issue of ordinary share capital	600
Debt due with a year:	
increase in short-term borrowings	2,006
repayment of secured loan	(850)
Debt due beyond a year:	
new secured loan repayable in 2000	1,091
new unsecured loan repayable in 1998	1,442
Capital element of finance lease rental payments	(1,342)
	2,347

Net cash inflow from financing — 2,947

Note 3 – ANALYSIS OF NET DEBT

	At 1 Jan 1996	Cash Flow	Acquisition† (excl. cash and overdrafts)	Other non-cash changes	Exchange movement	At 31 Dec 1996
	£000	£000	£000	£000	£000	£000
Cash in hand, at bank	235	(1,250)			1,392	377
Overdrafts	(2,528)	(5,502)			(1,422)	(9,452)
		(6,752)				
Debt due after 1 year	(9,640)	(2,533)	(1,749)	2,560	(792)	(12,154)
Debt due within 1 yr	(352)	(1,156)	(837)	(2,560)	1,465	(3,440)
Finance leases	(4,170)	1,342	(1,231)	(2,845)		(6,904)
		(2,347)				
Current asset investments	1,240	(700)				540
TOTAL	(15,215)	(9,799)	(3,817)	(2,845)	643	(31,033)

XYZ Group PLC includes resources term deposits of less than a year, government securities and AA rated corporate bonds.

†*This column would include any net debt (excluding cash and overdrafts) disposed of with a subsidiary undertaking.*

Note 4 – CASH FLOW RELATING TO EXCEPTIONAL ITEMS

The operating cash outflows include under discontinued activities an outflow of £560,000, which relates to the £1,600,000 exceptional provision for a fundamental restructuring made in the 1995 accounts.

Note 5 - MAJOR NON-CASH TRANSACTIONS

a. During the year the group entered into finance lease arrangements in respect of assets with a total capital value at the inception of the leases of £2,845,000.

b. Part of the consideration for the purchases of subsidiary undertakings and the sale of a business that occurred during the year comprised shares and loan notes respectively. Further details of the acquisitions and the disposal are set out below.

Note 6 – PURCHASE OF SUBSIDIARY UNDERTAKINGS

	£000
Net assets acquired	
Tangible fixed assets	12,194
Investments	1
Stocks	9,384
Debtors	13,856
Taxation recoverable	1,309
Cash at bank and in hand	1,439
Creditors	(21,715)
Bank overdrafts	(6,955)
Loans and finance leases	(3,817)
Deferred taxation	(165)
Minority shareholders' interests	(9)
	5,522
Goodwill	16,702
	22,224
Satisfied by	
Shares allotted	9,519
Cash	12,705
	22,224

The subsidiary undertakings acquired during the year contributed £1,502,000 to the group's net operating cash flows, paid £1,308,000 in respect of net returns on investments and servicing of finance, paid £522,000 in respect of taxation and utilised £2,208,000 for capital expenditure.

Note 7 – SALE OF BUSINESS

	£000
Net assets disposed of	
Fixed assets	775
Stocks	5,386
Debtors	474
	6,635
Loss on disposal	(1,227)
	5,408

Satisfied by	
Loan notes	1,200
Cash	4,208
	5,408

The business sold during the year contributed £200,000 to the group's net operating cash flows, paid £252,000 in respect of net returns on investments and servicing of finance, paid £145,000 in respect of taxation and utilised £209,000 for capital expenditure.

EXAMPLE 3 **A CASH FLOW STATEMENT FOR A BANK – XYZ INTERNATIONAL BANK PLC**
CASH FLOW STATEMENT FOR THE YEAR ENDED 31 DECEMBER 1996

Reconciliation of operating profit to net operating cash flows

	£m	£m
Operating profits		223.6
Increase in accrued income and prepayments		(161.2)
Increase in accruals and deferred income		118.1
Provision for bad and doubtful debts		20.8
Loans and advances written off net of recoveries		(50.7)
Depreciation and amortisation		42.4
Interest on subordinated loan added back		9.9
Profits on sale of investment debt and equity securities		(1.1)
Provisions for liabilities and charges		3.4
Other non-cash movements		6.3
Net cash flow from trading activities		211.5
Net increase in collections/transmissions	(81.1)	
Net increase in loans and advances to banks and customers	(1,419.1)	
Net increase in deposits by banks and customer accounts	2,542.8	
Net increase in debt securities in issue	39.9	
Net increase in non-investment debt and equity securities	(197.3)	
Net increase in other assets	(18.7)	
Net increase in other liabilities	18.6	
		885.1
Net cash inflow from operating activities		1,096.6

CASH FLOW STATEMENT

Net cash inflow from operating activities	**1,096.6**
Dividends from associates	10.3
Returns on investments and servicing of finance (note 1)	(20.5)
Taxation	(88.0)
Capital expenditure and financial investment (note 1)	(90.3)
	908.1
Acquisitions and disposals (note 1)	15.1
Equity dividends paid	(57.2)
	866.0
Financing (note 1)	6.0
Increase in cash	**872.0**

NOTES TO THE CASH FLOW STATEMENT

Note 1 – GROSS CASH FLOWS

Returns on investments and servicing of finance	£m	£m
Interest paid on loan capital	(9.9)	
Preference dividends paid	(10.4)	
Dividends paid to minority shareholders in subsidiary undertaking	(0.2)	
		(20.5)
Capital expenditure of financial investment		
Purchase of investment securities	(14.7)	
Sale and maturity of investment securities	5.7	
Purchase of tangible fixed assets	(121.4)	
Sales of tangible fixed assets	40.1	
		(90.3)
Acquisitions and disposals		
Investment in associated undertaking	(56.1)	
Sale of investment in associated undertaking	71.2	
		15.1
Financing		
Issue of ordinary share capital	18.3	
Repayments of loan capital	(12.3)	
		6.0

Note 2 – ANALYSIS OF THE BALANCES OF CASH AS SHOWN IN THE BALANCE SHEET

	At 1.1.96 £m	Cash flow £m	At 31.12.96 £m
Cash and balances at central banks	1,342.9	148.5	1491.4
Loans and advances to other banks repayable on demand	23,743.6	723.5	24,467.1
	25,086.5	872.0	25,958.5

The group is required to maintain balances with the Bank of England which, at 31 December 1996, amounted to £54.0 million (1995 - £43.3 million).

Certain subsidiary undertakings of the group are required by law to maintain reserve balances with the Federal Reserve Bank in the United States of America. Such reserve balances amounted to $30.4 million at 31 December 1996 (1995 - $28.6 million).

Note 3 – ANALYSIS OF CHANGES IN FINANCING DURING THE YEAR

	Share capital £m	Loan capital £m
Balance at 1 January 1996	435.3	1,248.1
Effect of foreign exchange differences		(115.7)
Cash inflow/(outflow) from financing	18.3	(12.3)
Other movements	(0.1)	
Balances at 31 December 1996	453.5	1,120.1

EXAMPLE 4 **A CASH FLOW STATEMENT FOR AN INSURANCE GROUP – XYZ INSURANCE GROUP PLC**
CASH FLOW STATEMENT FOR THE YEAR ENDED 31 DECEMBER 1996

Profit on ordinary activities before tax

	£m	£m
Operating profit before taxation after interest		300.2
Depreciation of tangible fixed assets	31.6	
Increase in general insurance technical provisions	198.5	
Decrease in amounts owed by agents	18.1	
Profits relating to long-term business	(135.3)	
Cash received from long-term business (note 1)	74.0	
Loan interest expense	38.7	
		225.6
Net cash inflow from operating activities		525.8

CASH FLOW STATEMENT

Net cash inflow from general business	484.4
Shareholders' net cash inflow from long-term business	74.0
Other operating cash flows attributable to shareholders	(32.6)
Net cash inflow from operating activities	**525.8**
Dividends from associates	22.1
Interest paid (note 2)	(41.9)
Taxation paid	(54.2)
Capital expenditure	(52.1)
Acquisitions and disposals (note 2)	(313.5)
Equity dividends paid	(135.3)
Financing (note 2)	424.6
	375.5

CASH FLOWS WERE INVESTED AS FOLLOWS:

Increase in cash holdings		**22.8**
Net portfolio investment		
(not including long-term business) (note 2)		
Ordinary shares (note 2)	127.2	
Fixed income securities (note 2)	27.9	
Investment properties (note 2)	197.6	
		352.7
Net investment of cash flows		**375.5**

Movement in opening and closing portfolio investments net of financing (note 3)

	£m	£m	£m
Net cash inflow for the period		**22.8**	
Cash flow			
Portfolio investments		352.7	
Increase in loans		(213.9)	
Movement arising from cash flows			161.6
Movement in long-term business			82.8
Acquired with subsidiary			145.1
Changes in market values and exchange rate effects			142.6
Total movement in portfolio investments net of financing			532.1
Portfolio investments net of financing at 1.1.96			**2,692.3**
Portfolio investments net of financing at 31.12.96			**3,224.4**

NOTES TO THE CASH FLOW STATEMENT

Note 1 – CASH FLOWS OF THE LONG-TERM BUSINESS (OPTIONAL)

	£m
Premiums received	497.3
Claims paid	(326.1)
Net portfolio investments	(66.9)
Other net cash flows	(14.4)
Net cash inflow before retention and transfers	89.9
Transferred to general fund	(74.0)
Cash retained in long-term business	15.9

Note 2 – ANALYSIS OF CASH FLOWS FOR HEADINGS NETTED IN THE CASH FLOW STATEMENT

	£m	£m
Interest paid		
Interest paid	(35.2)	
Interest element of finance lease rental payments	(6.7)	
		(41.9)
Acquisitions and disposals		
Acquisition of subsidiary	(330.4)	
Net cash acquired with subsidiary	16.9	
		(313.5)
Financing		
Issue of ordinary share capital	210.7	
Repayment of long-term loan	(232.7)	
New fixed rate loan repayable 2000	446.6	
Net cash inflow from financing		424.6
Portfolio investments		
Purchase of ordinary shares	(869.5)	
Purchase of fixed income securities	(1,325.3)	
Purchase of investment property	(197.6)	
Sale of ordinary shares	742.3	
Sale of fixed income securities	1,297.4	
Net cash outflow on portfolio investments		(352.7)

Note 3 – MOVEMENT IN CASH, PORTFOLIO INVESTMENTS AND FINANCING

	At 1 Jan 1996*	Cash Flow	Changes in long-term business	Acquired with subsidiary (excl. cash)	Changes to market value and currencies	Other changes	At 31 Dec 1996*
	£m	£m	£m	£m	£m	£m	£m
Cash in hand, at bank	15.3	22.8	15.9		(2.3)		51.7
Ordinary shares	1,258.1	127.2	25.1	128.4	77.2		1,616.0
Fixed income securities	2,246.7	27.9	41.8	122.8	36.4		2,475.6
Investment properties	390.5	197.6			(12.4)		575.7
		352.7					
Loans due within 1 year	(325.7)	232.7		(19.7)	16.1	(31.2)	(127.8)
Loans due after 1 year	(892.6)	(446.6)		(86.4)	27.6	31.2	(1,366.8)
		(213.9)					
TOTAL	2,692.3	161.6	82.8	145.1	142.6	–	3,224.4

Note 4 - PURCHASE OF SUBSIDIARY UNDERTAKING

	£m	£m
Net cash acquired with subsidiary undertaking		16.9
Portfolio investments less financing acquired with subsidiary undertaking		145.1
Other net assets		108.1
		270.1
Goodwill		60.3
		330.4
Settled by:		
Payment of cash		330.4

The subsidiary undertakings acquired during the year contributed £57.4m to the group's net operating cash flows, paid £6.2m in respect of interest, paid £4.9m in respect of taxation and utilised £13.2m for capital expenditure.

These amounts are the same as the balance sheet amounts reported by the insurance group and include amounts relating to long-term business which are required by the EC Insurance Accounts Directive to be consolidated.

Appendix II – Compliance With International Accounting Standards

The International Accounting Standard on cash flows is IAS 7 'Cash Flow State-   **1**
ments'. IAS 7 requires an entity to present its cash flows from operating, investing
and financing activities. The cash flows to be reported are inflows and outflows of
cash and cash equivalents leading to the reporting of the change in cash and cash
equivalents for the period. For the reasons set out in Appendix III the FRS has
modified the original FRS 1, which required a cash flow statement similar to that
prepared under IAS 7.

The main difference between the standards

The FRS defines cash flows to include only movements in cash (cash in hand and   **2**
deposits repayable on demand, less overdrafts). IAS 7 defines cash flows as movements in both cash and cash equivalents. Cash equivalents are defined as short-term,
highly liquid investments that are readily convertible to known amounts of cash and
subject to insignificant risk of changes in value. In the FRS cash flows relating to cash
equivalents are to be included in the new 'management of liquid resources' section.
The narrower definition of cash in the FRS is consistent with the definition of 'cash' in
IAS 7.

Minor differences between the standards

The requirements of the FRS also differ from IAS 7 in the following ways: **3**

- IAS 7 does not have any exemptions from its scope. The FRS gives exemption to
  small entities, subsidiary undertakings 90 per cent of whose voting rights are
  controlled within the group, mutual life assurance companies, pension funds and
  certain open-ended investment funds. Building societies that prepare a statement
  of source and application of funds in the prescribed format are permitted two
  years' exemption from the effective date of the FRS.
- IAS 7 (paragraph 22) allows the following cash flows to be reported net:

    (a) cash receipts and payments on behalf of customers when the cash flows
         reflect the activities of the customer rather than those of the entity; and
    (b) cash receipts and payments for items in which the turnover is quick, the
         amounts are large, and the maturities are short.

Cash flows fulfilling the conditions for net reporting in paragraph 9 of the FRS would
also fulfil the conditions in paragraph 22(b) of IAS 7. The FRS has no equivalent
permission for cash flows relating to customers to be shown net, since for some
businesses the cash flows relating to customers can be an important source of finance.

- IAS 7 classifies cash flows under three headings: 'cash flows from operating
  activities', 'cash flows from investing activities', and 'cash flows from financing
  activities'. The FRS specifies a fuller analysis using eight headings.
- Unlike the FRS, IAS 7 does not require a reconciliation of the movement in cash
  flows to the movement in net debt.
- IAS 7 requires cash flows of a foreign subsidiary to be translated at the exchange
  rates prevailing at the dates of the cash flows. A weighted average exchange rate
  may be used that approximates to the actual rate. The FRS states that cash flows
  should be translated at the same rate as the profit and loss account but allows the
  use of actual rates or an approximation thereto for intragroup transactions.

Appendix III The development of the FRS

HISTORY

1   In September 1991 the Board issued FRS 1 'Cash Flow Statements' to replace SSAP 10 'Statements of source and application of funds'. The requirement for a cash flow statement instead of a statement of source and application of funds represented a radical change in financial reporting. In March 1994, when companies had had two years' practical experience with FRS 1, the Board called for comment on the functioning of the standard. The revised FRS is based on the subsequent proposals in FRED 10 'Revision of FRS 1 "Cash Flow Statements"' and the comments received on them.

THE FUNCTION OF A CASH FLOW STATEMENT

2   A cash flow statement has increasingly come to be recognised as a useful addition to the balance sheet and profit and loss account in their portrayal of financial position, performance and financial adaptability. Historical cash flow information gives an indication of the relationship between profitability and cash-generating ability, and thus of the quality of the profit earned. In addition, analysts and other users of financial information often, formally or informally, develop models to assess and compare the present value of the future cash flows of entities. Historical cash flow information could be useful to check the accuracy of past assessments and indicate the relationship between the entity's activities and its receipts and payments.

3   Assessing the opportunities and risks of an entity's business and the stewardship of its management requires an understanding of the nature of its business, which includes the way it generates and uses cash. A cash flow statement in conjunction with a profit and loss account and balance sheet provides information on financial position and performance as well as liquidity, solvency and financial adaptability. It is, therefore, important that the cash flow statement should cross-refer to the information given in the other primary statements. For this reason FRS 1 required a reconciliation of operating profit to cash flow from operating activities and some reconciliation with balance sheet figures. The revised FRS clarifies the link between cash flows and balance sheet movements by requiring a reconciliation between the cash flow statement and components of 'net debt', a widely used tool of financial analysis.

4   Although a cash flow statement shows information about the reporting entity's cash flows in the reporting period, it provides incomplete information for assessing future cash flows. Some cash flows result from transactions that took place in an earlier period and some cash flows are expected to result in further cash flows in a future period. Accordingly, cash flow statements should normally be used in conjunction with profit and loss accounts and balance sheets when making an assessment of future cash flows.

5   The Board specified a cash flow statement in FRS 1 rather than continue with a funds flow statement, which was usually based on changes in working capital, for the reasons given below.

   (a)   Funds flow data based on movements in working capital can obscure movements relevant to the liquidity and solvency of an entity. For example, a significant decrease in cash available may be masked by an increase in stock or debtors. Entities may, therefore, run out of cash while reporting increases in working capital. Similarly, a decrease in working capital does not necessarily indicate a cash shortage and a danger of failure.

(b) As cash flow monitoring is a normal feature of business life and not a specialised accounting technique, cash flow is a concept that is more widely understood than are changes in working capital.

(c) Cash flows can be a direct input into a business valuation model and, therefore, historical cash flows may be relevant in a way not possible for funds flow data.

(d) A funds flow statement is based largely on the difference between two balance sheets. It reorganises such data, but does not provide new data. The cash flow statement and associated notes required by the FRS may include data not disclosed in a funds flow statement.

CHANGES IMPLEMENTED BY THE REVISED FRS

General comments

The comments received on the functioning of FRS 1 indicated widespread support for   **6**
a cash flow statement but also a belief that the statements produced by applying FRS 1 fell short in a number of respects from what could be achieved. The Board concluded that FRS 1 could be improved to make the cash flow statement a better means of communication between preparers and users of financial statements. FRED 10's proposals for amending the cash flow standard were generally well received by the commentators and have largely been taken up in the revised FRS.

Definition of cash flows and introduction of 'management of liquid resources' section

The issue most often raised in the comments on FRS 1 was its definition of cash   **7**
equivalents, although there was no consensus on an alternative. The definition was criticised as not reflecting the way in which businesses were managed: in particular, the requirement that to be a cash equivalent an investment had to be within three months of maturity when acquired was considered unrealistic. The definition of cash equivalents had also been a controversial issue in the comments on ED 54, the exposure draft preceding FRS 1. As a result of these comments the Board proposed to omit cash equivalents from cash flows and use only cash (cash in hand and deposits repayable on demand, less overdrafts) as the basis of the cash flows reported in a cash flow statement. The proposal received widespread support and the revised FRS is based on a similar definition of cash.

To reflect better the way that entities manage their cash and similar assets and to   **8**
distinguish cash flows in relation to this activity from other investment decisions, the revised FRS has a section dealing separately with the cash flows arising from the management of liquid resources. Liquid resources are to be identified by each reporting entity according to its policy (which should be disclosed) with the proviso that they include only current asset investments. Cash flows relating to items such as short-term deposits and other cash equivalents under the original standard are to be reported as cash flows under 'management of liquid resources'. The comments supported the FRED's proposal to introduce a section for cash flows relating to the management of liquid resources.

The adoption of a strict cash approach and introduction of the section for cash flows   **9**
relating to the management of liquid resources have the following advantages. The approach:

(a) avoids an arbitrary cut-off point in the definition of cash equivalents;

(b) distinguishes cash flows arising from accumulating or using liquid resources from those for other investing activities; and

(c) provides information about an entity's treasury activities that was not previously available to the extent that the instruments dealt in fell within the definition of cash equivalents.

INFORMATION ABOUT LIQUIDITY

10 The FRS sets out in its objective the twin purposes of a cash flow statement: to report the cash generation and cash absorption of an entity; and to provide information to assist users to assess its liquidity, solvency and financial adaptability. The majority of those commenting on FRED 10 accepted this objective but a minority believed that a cash flow statement cannot reflect appropriately changes in an entity's liquidity because it focuses only on changes in an entity's cash. Those expressing this concern usually supported a change in focus to the movement in an entity's net debt or net funds.

11 The FRS retains the focus on cash rather than using a broader measure such as net debt because the focus on cash:

- highlights the significant components of cash that make up a cash flow statement;
- shows as cash flow movements transactions that would not be captured by a broader measure such as net debt in any case where the transaction involved an exchange of items that both fell within that broader measure;
- facilitates comparison of the cash flow performances of different entities; and
- is in line with the international focus on cash.

Recognising that movements in net debt can also provide information on an entity's liquidity, solvency and financial adaptability and are often used in discussions of performance, the revised FRS requires an analysis of the movement in net debt or net funds in the period to be given adjoining the cash flow statement or as a note to it.

SCOPE

12 In developing the FRS the Board has considered the comments on the scope of FRS 1 and FRED 10. Almost one-third of those commenting on FRS 1 mentioned aspects of its scope.

(a) Small entities

At the date of issuing the revised FRS the Board has in hand a separate project reviewing the application of accounting standards to small entities. It will decide in the course of that project whether to continue the exemption of small companies from the requirement to provide a cash flow statement.*

(b) Subsidiary undertakings

The FRS exempts wholly-owned subsidiary undertakings and those where 90 per cent of the voting rights in the subsidiary undertaking are controlled within its group. Where the parent group holds 90 per cent of the voting rights in a subsidiary undertaking it is likely that the liquidity, solvency and financial adaptability of the subsidiary undertaking will essentially depend on the group rather than its own cash flows. The exemption is conditional on consolidated financial statements in which the subsidiary undertaking is included being publicly available. The original standard exempted wholly-owned subsidiary undertakings from the requirement to provide a

*Editor's note: See now section D of the Financial Reporting Standard for Smaller Entities.

cash flow statement subject to a number of further conditions and the extension and simplification of the exemption was generally supported when proposed by the FRED.

(c) Pension funds

The FRS makes it clear that pension funds are exempt from preparing a cash flow statement because such a statement would add little to the information already available from the fund account and net assets statement.

(d) Investment funds

The FRS exempts open-ended investment funds from preparing a cash flow statement if three conditions are fulfilled, relating to the liquidity of investments held, whether they are held at market value and whether a statement of changes in net assets is provided. Where these conditions are met a cash flow statement for an open-ended investment fund would be of very limited additional use. Investment funds are defined in paragraph 2 of the FRS using three of the conditions for qualifying as an investment company in companies legislation. A fourth condition in the legislation requires that capital profits should not be distributed. The Board agreed with those who commented that this condition was not relevant to the exemption and that its inclusion in the standard would have unreasonably excluded unauthorised investment companies that complied with all the relevant conditions.

FORMAT OF CASH FLOW STATEMENT

The Board believes that, to achieve the objectives of cash flow reporting by presenting the information in a way that is useful and easy to understand, individual cash flows should be classified according to the activity that gave rise to them. To promote comparability amongst different entities, the FRS prescribes the following standard headings: 'operating activities', 'returns on investments and servicing of finance', 'taxation', 'capital expenditure and financial investment', 'acquisitions and disposals', 'equity dividends paid', 'management of liquid resources' and 'financing'. In general the commentators supported proposals in FRED 10 to split 'investing activities' into 'capital expenditure' and 'acquisitions and disposals' and reporting dividends paid after these (in the FRS only equity dividends are included below acquisitions and disposals because the Board accepted the arguments of some commentators that non-equity dividends should be reported alongside interest paid). Except for insurance companies, the examples use a format that results in a residual amount of the increase or decrease in cash during the period. This format was preferred by those consulted on this issue, although they did not want the presentation to be mandatory. The FRS therefore follows FRED 10 in allowing reporting entities to choose the format of their cash flow statements, provided these comply with the requirements for classification and order.

Both in the consultation on the original cash flow standard and in that on the proposals in FRED 10 some commentators requested that the format of the cash flow statement should be changed to highlight the free cash flows of an entity. There were several interpretations of the exact composition of 'free cash flows'—indeed the commentators themselves suggested several different definitions—but a key issue was to distinguish cash flows for investing to maintain the business from cash flows for investing to expand the business. The Board believes that it is not feasible for an accounting standard to set out how to distinguish expenditure for expansion from expenditure for maintenance. As proposed in FRED 10, the FRS requires cash flows to be analysed into those relating to capital expenditure and those relating to

13

14

acquisitions and disposals. This distinction should not be interpreted as reflecting on the one hand maintenance expenditure and on the other expenditure for expansion because, depending on the circumstances, these may be included under either heading.

GROSS OR NET CASH FLOWS

15   To allow preparers flexibility to emphasise the relevant information for their entities as they wish, the FRS allows the gross cash flows to be shown either in the cash flow statement or in a note. The FRS also allows net reporting for cash flows relating to the management of liquid resources and financing:

(a)   where there is in substance a single financing transaction that fulfils the conditions in paragraph 35 of FRS 4 'Capital Instruments' (determining when committed facilities can be taken into account in determining the maturity of debt); or

(b)   where the inflows and outflows are due to short maturities and high turnover occurring from rollover or reissue.

Condition (b) would allow the netting of inflows and outflows relating to a constantly renewed short-term facility or a commercial paper programme.

16   Several commentators on the original cash flow standard were concerned about whether gross presentation was appropriate for all cash flows because the volume of some investing or financing transactions was so large that their disproportionate size tended to swamp the other cash flows reported. Other commentators noted that the costs of collecting information on gross cash flows could be high while they doubted the value of that information. FRED 10 proposed that the gross amounts should be shown, in a note if preferred, for all cash flows (other than operating cash flows under the indirect method). A minority of those commenting on FRED 10 also raised concerns with the requirement for gross cash flows even in the notes. However, the Board consulted users, who confirmed that they valued the disclosure of gross amounts. The requirement for gross cash flows therefore is retained in the FRS, except that only net amounts need be shown in relation to rollover and reissue transactions. The international standard allows cash flows to be shown net where turnover is quick, amounts large and maturities short.

CLASSIFICATION OF CASH FLOWS

17   The FRS requires that a cash flow should be classified according to the substance of the transaction or event that gave rise to it. The substance of a transaction may be determined by applying an accounting standard (for example, SSAP 21 'Accounting for leases and hire purchase contracts', FRS 4 'Capital Instruments' or FRS 5 'Reporting the Substance of Transactions'). The approach based on substance should result in transactions and events being treated on the same basis in cash flow statements as in the other primary statements where treatment is also determined by substance. However, to give a complete picture of interest cash flows in a period, the FRS requires all interest cash flows to be reported under servicing of finance, even if some interest is capitalised in the other financial statements.

DIRECT OR INDIRECT CASH FLOWS

18   In developing FRS 1 the Board considered the respective merits of the so-called 'direct' and 'indirect' methods for reporting net cash flow from operating activities. The principal advantage of the direct method is that it shows operating cash receipts

and payments. Knowledge of the specific sources of cash receipts and the purposes for which cash payments were made in past periods may be useful in assessing future cash flows. However, the Board noted that it did not believe that in all cases the benefits to users of this information outweighed the costs to the reporting entity of providing it and, therefore, did not require the information to be given. The Board remains of this view, and the FRS continues to encourage the direct method only where the potential benefits to users outweigh the costs of providing it.

RECONCILIATION OF OPERATING PROFIT TO OPERATING CASH FLOWS

The FRS permits the reconciliation of operating profit to operating cash flows to be **19** shown either adjoining the cash flow statement, if it is separately identified and clearly labelled, or as a note. Although many commentators welcomed the proposal in FRED 10 to allow the reconciliation to appear above the cash flow statement, others believed the effect would be to detract from the emphasis on cash flows by wedging the statement itself between two reconciliations—one to operating profit, the other to net debt—neither of which represented cash flows. While not prohibiting such a presentation, the wording in the FRS would also permit both reconciliations to follow the primary statement. Some commentators were concerned about how cash flows in relation to provisions should be classified in cash flow statements. The FRS makes it clear that cash flows from operating activities should include cash flows in respect of operating items in relation to any provision, whether on acquisitions, or on termination or for a fundamental reorganisation or restructuring (under paragraph 20a and b of FRS 3).

BANKS

The Board has discussed the application of the requirement for a cash flow statement **20** with representatives of the banking industry. The banks had argued for exemption during the development of FRS 1 on the basis that a bank's cash is its stock-in-trade and that more useful information would be given by a statement dealing with the capital resources available to the bank. The Board agreed that capital resources were an important indicator of the solvency and financial adaptability of financial institutions, but also believed that a cash flow statement could provide users of financial statements published by banks with useful information on the sources of cash and how it had been utilised. The Board remains of the view that cash flow statements for banks contain information on their generation and use of cash that may be useful to the users of their financial statements, and the FRS contains no exemption for banks.

Example 3 in Appendix I shows a cash flow statement for a bank. The special nature **21** of banking and its regulation is recognised in the format headings and by splitting the cash flows from operating activities to show separately the cash flows from trading. A bank may hold a wide range of investments of different maturities for trading or investment and manage its liquidity in relation to all its assets and liabilities. It is therefore difficult to make a meaningful distinction by attempting to identify cash flows that relate to the management of a bank's liquid resources. Banking entities are not required to provide a reconciliation to net debt because, given the nature of their business, changes in net debt have limited meaning. Other measures, such as regulatory capital ratios, may give a better appreciation of a bank's solvency and financial adaptability.

BUILDING SOCIETIES

22   FRED 10 proposed that building societies should prepare cash flow statements on the same basis as banks and that their existing exemption should be ended. The proposal depended on changes in the legislation on financial reporting by building societies to make it effective. The Board still believes that the proposals in FRED 10 were correct, given the similarity and competition between the banks and building societies. However, the FRS has extended the existing exemption for building societies for a further two years to develop a consensus on cash flow statements and related aspects of financial reporting for banks and building societies.

INSURANCE COMPANIES AND GROUPS

23   In developing the FRS the Board considered the application of FRS 1 to insurance companies and groups. Comments from the insurance industry had raised several issues that were believed to arise because of the special nature of the business. A general issue raised was the meaning of a cash flow statement for an insurance company. The special implications of cash flow statements for insurance companies are discussed in paragraph 62 of the Explanation. The FRS encourages segmentation of the cash flows to assist users to understand the nature of the reporting entity's cash flows and the relationship between them. One suggestion is to use segmentation to reflect different degrees of access to cash balances. This would allow insurance companies to divide their businesses into segments to reflect the degree of access that shareholders had to cash balances.

24   The Board believes that cash flows arising from the long-term business of an insurance company or group should be dealt with in the cash flow statement only to the extent of cash transferred to, and available to meet the obligations of, the company or group as a whole. The internal cash flows of the long-term business may be shown in a note to the cash flow statement. The Board takes this approach because the shareholders of an insurance company generally have restricted rights to any profits, and associated cash surpluses, made by the long-term business. Because insurance companies and groups are now required by companies legislation to consolidate the long-term business, these funds need to be included in the note to the cash flow statement analysing the changes in the balance sheet amounts for portfolio investments net of financing.

25   Appendix I contains an example of a cash flow statement for an insurance group. By including a section showing the cash flows relating to portfolio investments, this format recognises the special nature of an insurance business, in particular the importance of generating resources for investment to meet provision requirements for future claims and reserve requirements for solvency. The example for insurance companies contains an analysis of the movement in portfolio investments less financing rather than an analysis of net debt as generally required. Presenting information on portfolio investments less financing recognises that the required balance sheet format for insurance companies does not distinguish between fixed and current financial assets.

EXCEPTIONAL AND EXTRAORDINARY ITEMS AND CASH FLOWS

26   To reflect the changes introduced by FRS 3 'Reporting Financial Performance', the text now acknowledges the extreme rarity of extraordinary items post-FRS 3. The FRS also explicitly recognises the possibility that cash flows can be exceptional of themselves because of their size or incidence without relating to an exceptional item

in the profit and loss account. Sufficient disclosure should be made to explain their cause and nature.

VALUE ADDED TAX AND OTHER TAXES

The existence of Value Added Tax (VAT), and other sales taxes, raises the question **27** whether the relevant cash flows should be reported gross or net of the tax element and how the balance of tax paid to, or repaid by, the taxing authorities should be reported. Generally, sales taxes, including VAT, are payable by the ultimate consumer of the goods or services concerned. A business providing goods or services on which VAT is payable (even if at a zero rate) is generally able to reclaim the VAT incurred by it in providing those goods or services. However, businesses that make exempt supplies are unable to reclaim VAT. Between these two categories are partially exempt businesses that can reclaim part of the VAT incurred by them.

The cash flows of an entity include VAT where appropriate and thus strictly the **28** various elements of the cash flow statement should include VAT. However, this treatment does not take into account the fact that normally VAT is a short-term timing difference as far as the entity's overall cash flows are concerned and the inclusion of VAT in the cash flows may distort the allocation of cash flows to standard headings. In order to avoid this distortion and to show cash flows attributable to the reporting entity's activities, the Board believes that cash flows should be shown net of sales taxes and the net movement on the amount payable to, or receivable from, the taxing authority should be allocated to cash flows from operating activities unless a different treatment is more appropriate in the particular circumstances concerned.

FOREIGN EXCHANGE

To meet the concern that intragroup cash inflows and outflows might not cancel each **29** other out if average or closing rates are used to translate them for preparing consolidated cash flow statements, the FRS permits entities to use actual rates for intragroup cash flows envisaging that these will be applied where there are large single cash flows at rates significantly different from the average or closing rate used for the other cash flows. Several commentators had raised the treatment of foreign currency in cash flow statements. Because of the various approximations that may be required in particular cases, the Board has not sought to specify in detail the methods to be used to deal with foreign exchange differences. It has, however, set out the principle that in translating the cash flows of foreign entities the same basis should be used as for the translation of the profit and loss account. The FRS now clarifies that this principle applies also to the presentation of stocks, debtors and creditors in the reconciliation from operating profits and cash flow from operating activities.

HEDGING

FRS 1 required cash flows that result from transactions undertaken to hedge another **30** transaction to be reported under the same standard heading as the transaction that is the subject of the hedge. Several commentators expressed concern that the FRS 1 requirement relating to hedging was too broad, for example it could justify cash flows relating to loans taken out to finance overseas investment being classified under 'investing' rather than 'financing'. To meet these concerns the FRS requires that the effect of hedging should be reflected in the cash flow statement only where hedging is by futures contracts, forward contracts, option contracts or swap contracts. This is a pragmatic position that follows the US cash flow standard while awaiting the outcome of the Board's project on derivatives and other financial instruments, which will consider all aspects of hedging and its recognition.

FRS 3 'REPORTING FINANCIAL PERFORMANCE'

31   The FRS encourages entities to analyse cash flows on the same basis as that required by FRS 3 in the profit and loss account and to show separately cash flows relating to continuing and discontinued operations. There was widespread support for such analyses when proposed by FRED 10 but commentators did not support a requirement for them.

RESTRICTIONS ON REMITTABILITY

32   Several of the comments received on FRS 1 had indicated that disclosures of restricted cash balances would be useful. FRED 10 proposed the disclosure of cash not available for use elsewhere in the group. The FRS requires disclosure for both businesses and groups of the circumstances and effect of restrictions preventing the transfer of cash from one part to another. Paragraph 68 of the Explanation gives examples of items that, depending on the regulatory environment, might be required to be disclosed.

[FRS 2]
Accounting for subsidiary undertakings*

(Issued July 1992)

Contents

Editor's note: FRS 2 has been amended by 'Amendment to FRS 2 Accounting for subsidiary undertakings – legal changes' with effect for accounting periods beginning on or after 1 January 2005. The changes made by that amendment have been reflected in the text of the standard. The text of the amendment has therefore not been included.

Accounting for subsidiary undertakings

Summary

Financial Reporting Standard No. 2 – 'Accounting for Subsidiary Undertakings'   **a**
(the FRS) sets out the conditions under which an undertaking that is the parent
undertaking of other undertakings (its subsidiary undertakings) should prepare
consolidated financial statements. The FRS also sets out the manner in which consolidated financial statements are to be prepared. The purpose of consolidated
financial statements is to provide financial information about the economic activities
of a group. The Companies Act 1985, as amended by the Companies Act 1989 (the
amended Act is referred to as 'the Act') defines a parent undertaking and its subsidiary undertakings that together make up a group. The FRS adopts these definitions.

The FRS supersedes Statement of Standard Accounting Practice No. 14 – 'Group   **b**
accounts' and the Board's 'Interim Statement: Consolidated Accounts', except for
the following paragraphs of the Interim Statement: paragraphs 32 and 33, A9 and
A10, on joint ventures and paragraphs 38, A13 – A18 and A23 dealing with the
amendments to SSAP 1 'Accounting for Associated Companies'.*

The FRS applies to all parent undertakings. A parent undertaking that does not report   **c**
under the Act should comply with the requirements of the FRS except to the extent
that these are not permitted by any statutory framework under which the undertaking reports.

A parent undertaking should prepare consolidated financial statements for its group   **d**
in accordance with the standard accounting practice set out in the FRS unless it uses
one of the exemptions permitted by the Act and set out in paragraph 21 of the FRS.

The Act and the FRS exempt a parent undertaking from preparing consolidated   **e**
financial statements if:

(i)   its group is small or medium-sized and not an ineligible group as defined in
section 248; or
(ii)   it is a wholly-owned or majority-owned subsidiary undertaking and its
immediate parent undertaking is established under the law of a member state of
the European Community. Exemption is conditional on compliance with certain further conditions in section 228; or
(iii) it is a wholly-owned or majority-owned subsidiary undertaking and its parent
undertaking is not established under the law of an EEA state. Exemption is
conditional on compliance with certain further conditions in section 228A; or†
(iv) all of its subsidiary undertakings are permitted or required to be excluded from
consolidation by section 229.

The consolidated financial statements should be prepared by consolidating financial   **f**
information for the parent undertaking and all its subsidiary undertakings, except
for any subsidiary undertakings that are to be excluded from consolidation by virtue
of the requirements of the Act and the FRS.

A subsidiary undertaking is to be excluded from consolidation if: **g**

(i)   severe long-term restrictions substantially hinder the exercise of the parent
undertaking's rights over the subsidiary undertaking's assets or management; or

---

*Editor's note: Superseded by FRS 9 'Associates and Joint Ventures'.

*†Editor's note: (iii) added by 'Amendment to FRS 2 Accounting for subsidiary undertakings – legal changes'.
Original (iii) renumbered (iv) by the same amendment.*

(ii) the group's interest in the subsidiary undertaking is held exclusively with a view to subsequent resale and the subsidiary undertaking has not previously been consolidated.*

The Act permits rather than requires exclusion in cases (i) and (ii) above. The FRS requires exclusion in these circumstances because the same conditions that justify permitting exclusion also make consolidation inappropriate. In addition, the FRS requires the circumstances in which subsidiary undertakings are to be excluded from consolidation to be interpreted strictly. It is important that only those subsidiary undertakings whose consolidation would be inappropriate are excluded from consolidation so that consolidated financial statements reflect in full the resources, obligations and results of the group.

h   The FRS requires additional disclosures for subsidiary undertakings excluded from consolidation and requires them to be accounted for as follows:

(i)   Subsidiary undertakings excluded from consolidation because of severe long-term restrictions are to be treated as fixed asset investments. They are to be included at their carrying amount when the restrictions came into force, subject to any write down for impairment, and no further accruals are to be made for profits or losses of those subsidiary undertakings, unless the parent undertaking still exercises significant influence. In the latter case they are to be treated as associated undertakings.

(ii) Subsidiary undertakings excluded from consolidation because they are held exclusively for resale and have not previously been consolidated are to be included as current assets at the lower of cost and net realisable value.†

i   Minority interests in total should be reported separately in the consolidated balance sheet and profit and loss account. When an entity becomes a subsidiary undertaking the assets and liabilities attributable to its minority interest should be included on the same basis as those attributable to the interest held by the parent and other subsidiary undertakings. The effect of this for an acquisition is that all the subsidiary undertaking's identifiable assets and liabilities are included at fair value as required by the Act. No goodwill should be attributed to the minority interest.

j   Intra-group transactions may result in profits or losses being included in the book value of assets to be included in the consolidation; the FRS requires the elimination in full of any such profits or losses because, for the group as a whole, no profits or losses have arisen.

k   Uniform group accounting policies should generally be used in preparing the consolidated financial statements; in exceptional cases different policies may be used with disclosure.

l   The financial statements of all subsidiary undertakings to be used in preparing consolidated financial statements should have the same financial year end and be for the same accounting period as those of the parent undertaking of the group. Where the financial year of a subsidiary undertaking differs from that of the parent undertaking of the group, interim financial statements for that subsidiary undertaking prepared to the parent undertaking's accounting date should be used. If this is impracticable, earlier financial statements of the subsidiary undertaking may be used, provided they are prepared for a financial year that ended not more than three months earlier.

*****Editors note:** *Reference to required exclusion on grounds of dissimilar activities removed by 'Amendment to FRS 2 Accounting for subsidiary undertakings – legal changes'.*

†**Editors note:** *Reference to treatment of subsidiary undertakings excluded on grounds of dissimilar activities removed by 'Amendment to FRS 2 Accounting for subsidiary undertakings – legal changes'.*

Changes in membership of a group occur on the date control passes, whether by a   **m**
transaction or other event. Changes in the membership of the group during the
period should be disclosed.

When a subsidiary undertaking is acquired the FRS requires its identifiable assets and   **n**
liabilities to be brought into the consolidation at their fair values at the date that
undertaking becomes a subsidiary undertaking, even if the acquisition has been made
in stages. When a group increases its interest in an undertaking that is already its
subsidiary undertaking, the identifiable assets and liabilities of that subsidiary
undertaking should be revalued to fair value and goodwill arising on the increase in
interest should be calculated by reference to that fair value. This revaluation is not
required if the difference between fair values and carrying amounts of the identifiable
assets and liabilities attributable to the increase in stake is not material.

The effect of consolidating the parent and its subsidiary undertakings may be that   **o**
aggregation obscures useful information about the different undertakings and
activities included in the consolidated financial statements. Parent undertakings are
encouraged to give segmental analysis to provide readers of consolidated financial
statements with useful information on the different risks and rewards, growth and
prospects of the different parts of the group. The specification of such analysis,
however, falls outside the scope of the FRS.

The accounting practices set out in the FRS should be adopted as soon as possible and   **p**
regarded as standard for periods ending on or after 23 December 1992, except for
Republic of Ireland companies, who should regard it as standard after the date of
application of the Irish legislation implementing the European Community Seventh
Directive.* Such Irish companies should adopt the accounting practices in the FRS as
soon as possible after the enactment of the implementing legislation.

Objective

The objective of this FRS is to require parent undertakings to provide financial   **1**
information about the economic activities of their groups by preparing consolidated
financial statements.† These statements are intended to present financial information
about a parent undertaking and its subsidiary undertakings as a single economic
entity to show the economic resources controlled by the group, the obligations of the
group and the results the group achieves with its resources.‡

**Editor's note: Enacted in 1992. See paragraph 98 of this FRS.*

†*'Financial statements' is the term used in the FRS to mean the same as the term 'accounts' used in the*
Companies Acts.

‡*The Companies Act 1985, as amended by the 1989 Act, contains detailed provisions relating to consolidated*
financial statements. The FRS considers the application of the Act and adds to its provisions where necessary.

Definitions

The following definitions apply for the purposes of the FRS and in particular the statement of standard accounting practice set out in paragraphs 18 to 56.

The terms defined below which are also defined in the Act have the same meaning in the FRS as in the Act, notwithstanding that in some cases the FRS definition is a summary or explanation rather than a repetition of the definition in the Act. The definitions should therefore be interpreted by reference to the full provisions of the Act. The marginal notes give the main references in the Act. References to sections and schedules are to those of the Act unless otherwise stated.

2   *The Act:-*
Companies Act 1985 as amended by the Companies Act 1989.

3   *Companies (Northern Ireland) Order 1986:-*
Companies (Northern Ireland) Order 1986 as amended by the Companies (Northern Ireland) Order 1990 and the Companies (No 2) (Northern Ireland) Order 1990.

4   *Consolidated financial statements:-*
The financial statements of a group prepared by consolidation.

5   *Consolidation:-*
The process of adjusting and combining financial information from the individual financial statements of a parent undertaking and its subsidiary undertaking to prepare consolidated financial statements that present financial information for the group as a single economic entity.

6   *Control:-*
The ability of an undertaking to direct the financial and operating policies of another undertaking with a view to gaining economic benefits from its activities.

[FRS defining phrase used in s258(4)(a)]*

7   *Dominant influence:-*
Influence that can be exercised to achieve the operating and financial policies desired by the holder of the influence, notwithstanding the rights or influence of any other party.

(a)   In the context of paragraph 14(c) and section 258(2)(c) *the right to exercise a dominant influence* means that the holder has a right to give directions with respect to the operating and financial policies of another undertaking with which its directors are obliged to comply, whether or not they are for the benefit of that undertaking.

[From 10A Sch 4(1)]

(b)   *The actual exercise of dominant influence* is the exercise of an influence that achieves the result that the operating and financial policies of the undertaking influenced are set in accordance with the wishes of the holder of the influence and for the holder's benefit whether or not those wishes are explicit. The actual exercise of dominant influence is identified by its effect in practice rather than by the way in which it is exercised.

[FRS defining phrase used in s258(4)(a)]

---

*Editor's note: Reference to legislation added by 'Amendment to FRS 2 Accounting for subsidiary undertakings – legal changes'.

(c) *The power to exercise dominant influence* is a power that, if exercised, would give rise to the actual exercise of dominant influence as defined in paragraph 7b.*

Equity method:-   8

A method of accounting for an investment that brings into the consolidated profit and loss account the investor's share of the investment undertaking's results and that records the investment in the consolidated balance sheet at the investor's share of the investment undertaking's net assets including any goodwill arising to the extent that it has not previously been written off.

[*From s262*]   *Group:-*   9

A parent undertaking and its subsidiary undertakings.

[FRS *defining*   *Interest held on a long-term basis:-*   10
phrase used in   An interest which is held other than *exclusively with a view to sub-*
s260]   *sequent resale.*

[FRS *defining*   *Interest held exclusively with a view to subsequent resale:-*   11
phrase used in
s299(3)(c)]   (a)   An interest for which a purchaser has been identified or is being sought, and which is reasonably expected to be disposed of within approximately one year of its date of acquisition; or

(b)   an interest that was acquired as a result of the enforcement of a security, unless the interest has become part of the continuing activities of the group or the holder acts as if it intends the interest to become so.

[FRS *defining*   *Managed on a unified basis:-*   12
phrase used in   Two or more undertakings are managed on a unified basis if the
s258(4)(b)]   whole of the operations of the undertakings are integrated and they are managed as a single unit. Unified management does not arise solely because one undertaking manages another.

[*From*   *Minority interest in a subsidiary undertaking:-*   13
4A Sch 17]   The interest in a subsidiary undertaking included in the consolidation that is attributable to the shares held by or on behalf of persons other than the parent undertaking and its subsidiary undertakings.

[*From s258*   *Parent undertaking and subsidiary undertaking:-*   14
and 10A Sch]   An undertaking is the parent undertaking of another undertaking (a subsidiary undertaking) if any of the following apply.

[*From*   (a)   It holds a majority of the voting rights in the undertaking.
s258(2)(a)]   (b)   It is a member of the undertaking and has the right to appoint
[*From*   or remove directors holding a majority of the voting rights at
s258(2)(b)   meetings of the board on all, or substantially all, matters.
and 10A Sch 3]   (c)   It has the right to exercise a dominant influence over the undertaking:

[*From*   (i)   by virtue of provisions contained in the undertaking's
s258(2)(c)   memorandum or articles; or
and 10A Sch 4]   (ii)   by virtue of a control contract. The control contract must
[*From*   be in writing and be of a kind authorised by the memor-
s258(2)(c)   andum or articles of the controlled undertaking. It must
and 10A Sch 4]   also be permitted by the law under which that undertaking is established.

Editor's note: (c) added by 'Amendment to FRS 2 Accounting for subsidiary undertakings - legal changes'.

(d) It is a member of the undertaking and controls alone, pursuant to an agreement with other shareholders or members, a majority of the voting rights in the undertaking. *[From s258(2)(d)]*

(e) (i) it has the power to exercise, or actually exercises, dominant influence or control over the undertaking; or *[From s258(4)]*

(ii) it and the undertaking are managed on a unified basis.*

(f) A parent undertaking is also treated as the parent undertaking of the subsidiary undertakings of its subsidiary undertakings. *[From s258(5)]*

For the purpose of section 258 [parent and subsidiary undertakings] an undertaking shall be treated as a member of another undertaking: *[From s258(3)]*

(i) if any of its subsidiary undertakings is a member of that undertaking; or

(ii) if any shares in that other undertaking are held by a person acting on behalf of the parent undertaking or any of its subsidiary undertakings.

Any shares held, or powers exercisable, by a subsidiary undertaking should be treated as held or exercisable by its parent undertaking. *[From 10A Sch 9]*

15 [Withdrawn]†

16 *Undertaking:-* *[From s259]*
A body corporate, a partnership or an unincorporated association carrying on a trade or business with or without a view to profit.

17 *Voting rights in an undertaking:-* *[From 10A Sch 2(1)]*
Rights conferred on shareholders in respect of their shares or, in the case of an undertaking not having a share capital, on members, to vote at general meetings of the undertaking on all, or substantially all, matters. Schedule 10A deals with the attribution of voting rights in certain circumstances.

---

*Editor's note: (e) amended by 'Amendment to FRS 2 Accounting for subsidiary undertakings – legal changes'.

†Editor's note: Definition of participating interests withdrawn by 'Amendment to FRS 2 Accounting for subsidiary undertakings – legal changes'.

Statement of standard accounting practice

The statement of standard accounting practice set out in paragraphs 18 to 56 of the FRS should be read in the context of the Objective of the FRS as stated in paragraph 1, the definitions set out in paragraphs 2 to 17 and also of the Foreword to Accounting Standards and the Statement of Principles for Financial Reporting currently in issue.

In the statement of standard accounting practice marginal notes give the main references to the Act. If no marginal reference is given the requirement is that of the FRS alone. The statement of standard accounting practice should be interpreted by reference to the full provisions of the Act notwithstanding that the statement summarises certain provisions of the Act. References to sections and schedules are to those of the Act unless otherwise stated.

The Explanation section of the FRS, set out in paragraphs 59 to 94, shall be regarded as part of the statement of standard accounting practice in so far as it assists in interpreting that statement.

SCOPE

This standard applies to all parent undertakings that prepare the financial statements described below, whether or not they report under the Act. Parent undertakings that prepare consolidated financial statements intended to give a true and fair view of the financial position and profit or loss (or income and expenditure) of their group should prepare such statements in accordance with the requirements of the FRS. A parent undertaking that uses one of the exemptions from preparing consolidated financial statements (described in paragraph 21) but prepares individual financial statements intended to give a true and fair view of its own financial position and profit or loss (or income and expenditure) should include the statement required by paragraph 22. The FRS does not otherwise deal with the individual financial statements of a parent undertaking. **18**

Parent undertakings that do not report under the Act should comply with the requirements of the FRS, and of the Act where referred to in the FRS, except to the extent that these requirements are not permitted by any statutory framework under which such undertakings report. **19**

This Standard does not apply to retirement benefit schemes, which are within the scope of FRS 17 ' Retirement benefits'.* **19A**

APPLICATION TO SMALLER ENTITIES

Reporting entities applying the Financial Reporting Standard for Smaller Entities (FRSSE) currently applicable are exempt from the FRS unless preparing consolidated financial statements, in which case they should apply the FRS to such statements as required by the FRSSE. **19B**

*Editor's note: Paragraph 19A added by 'Amendment to FRS 2 Accounting for subsidiary undertakings – legal changes' and paragraph 19B consequently renumbered.

CONSOLIDATED FINANCIAL STATEMENTS

Preparation of consolidated financial statements

20   A parent undertaking should prepare consolidated financial state-   [s227, s228
ments for its group unless it uses one of the exemptions set out in   *and s248*]
paragraph 21.

Exempt parent undertakings

21   A parent undertaking is exempt from preparing consolidated financial statements for its group on any one of the following grounds.

(a)   The group is small or medium-sized and is not an ineligible   [s248]
group as defined in section 248. A group is ineligible if any of its
members is a public company, a person who carries on an
insurance market activity or a person who has permission
under Part 4 of the Financial Services and Markets Act 2000 to
carry on a regulated activity.

(b)   The parent undertaking is a wholly-owned subsidiary under-   [s228]
taking and its immediate parent is established under the law of
an EEA state. Exemption is conditional on compliance with
certain further conditions set out in section 228 (2). A parent
undertaking is not exempt if any of its securities are admitted to
trading on a regulated market of any EEA state within the
meaning of Council Directive 93/22/EEC.

(c)   The parent undertaking is a majority-owned subsidiary   [s228]
undertaking and meets all the conditions for exemption as a
wholly-owned subsidiary undertaking set out in section 228(2)
as well as the additional conditions set out in section 228(1)(b).

(d)   The parent undertaking is a wholly owned subsidiary of   [s228A]
another undertaking and that parent undertaking is not
established under the law of an EEA state. Exemption is conditional on compliance with certain further conditions set out in
section 228A(2). The exemption does not apply to a parent
undertaking if any of its securities are admitted to trading on a
regulated market of any EEA State within the meaning of
Council Directive 93/22/EEC.

(e)   The parent undertaking is a majority-owned subsidiary
undertaking and meets all of the conditions for exemption as a
wholly owned subsidiary undertaking set out in section 228A(2)
as well as the additional conditions set out in section
228A(1)(b).

(f)   All of the parent undertaking's subsidiary undertakings are   [s229(5)]
permitted or required to be excluded from consolidation by
section 229. (The conditions of section 229 are more fully
described in paragraph 25 and are elaborated on in paragraphs
76 to 78.)*

---

*__Editor's note:__ 21(a) to (e) amended by 'Amendment to FRS 2 Accounting for subsidiary undertakings – legal
changes' to take account of changes in the legal exemption for intermediate parent undertakings.*

[*s231 and 5 Sch Part 1*]	The Act sets out disclosure requirements for parent companies not required to prepare consolidated financial statements. In addition to providing this information, a parent undertaking making use of an exemption from preparing consolidated financial statements should state that its financial statements present information about it as an individual undertaking and not about its group. This statement should include or refer to a note giving the grounds on which the parent undertaking is exempt from preparing consolidated financial statements, as required by Schedule 5 paragraph 1(4). **22**

Undertakings to be included in the consolidation

[*s229(1)*]	As required by the Act, the consolidated financial statements should include the parent undertaking and all its subsidiary undertakings, except those that are required to be excluded under the conditions set out in paragraph 25 below. **23**

Disproportionate expense and undue delay

[*FRS allows s229(3)(b) exclusion only where the undertaking is not material*]	Neither disproportionate expense nor undue delay in obtaining the information necessary for the preparation of consolidated financial statements can justify excluding from consolidation subsidiary undertakings that are individually or collectively material in the context of the group. **24**

Subsidiary undertakings to be excluded from consolidation

[*s229(3)*]	The exclusions required by this paragraph are based on the exclusions permitted or required by section 229(3).* A subsidiary undertaking should be excluded from consolidation where: **25**
[*FRS requires exclusion permitted by s229(3)(a)*]	(a) severe long-term restrictions substantially hinder the exercise of the rights of the parent undertaking over the assets or management of the subsidiary undertaking. The rights referred to are those by reason of which the parent undertaking is defined as such under section 258 and in the absence of which it would not be the parent undertaking; or
[*FRS restricts exclusion permitted by s229(3)(c)*]†	(b) the interest in the subsidiary undertaking is held exclusively with a view to subsequent resale (as defined in paragraph 11) and the subsidiary undertaking has not previously been consolidated in group accounts prepared by the parent undertaking.
[*s231 and5 Sch 15(4)*]	As required by the Act, subject to the conditions and exemptions of section 231, the names of any subsidiary undertakings excluded from the consolidation and the reasons why they have been excluded should be given. **26**

Editor's note: Reference to s229(4) removed by 'Amendment to FRS 2 Accounting for subsidiary undertakings – legal changes'.

†Editor's note: Restricted by 'Amendment to FRS 2 Accounting for subsidiary undertakings – legal changes'.

ACCOUNTING FOR EXCLUDED SUBSIDIARY UNDERTAKINGS

Severe long-term restrictions

27 A subsidiary undertaking excluded on the grounds set out in paragraph 25(a) [severe long-term restrictions] should be treated as a fixed asset investment. If restrictions were in force at its acquisition date, the subsidiary undertaking should be carried initially at cost; if restrictions came into force at a later date, the subsidiary undertaking should be carried at a fixed amount calculated using the equity method at that date. While the restrictions are in force, no further accruals should be made for the profits or losses of that subsidiary undertaking, unless the parent undertaking still exercises a significant influence over it. If this is the case, it should treat the subsidiary undertaking as an associated undertaking using the equity method. The carrying amount of subsidiary undertakings subject to severe long-term restrictions should be reviewed and written down for any impairment in value. When impairment is assessed, each subsidiary undertaking should be considered individually. Any intra-group amounts due from subsidiary undertakings excluded on the grounds of severe long-term restrictions should also be reviewed and written down, if necessary.

28 When the severe restrictions cease and the parent undertaking's rights are restored, the amount of the unrecognised profit or loss that accrued during the period of restriction for that subsidiary undertaking should be separately disclosed in the consolidated profit and loss account of the period in which control is resumed. Similarly, any amount previously charged for impairment that needs to be written back as a result of restrictions ceasing should be separately disclosed.

Held exclusively with a view to subsequent resale

29 A subsidiary undertaking that is excluded from consolidation on the grounds set out in paragraph 25(b) [held exclusively with a view to subsequent resale] should be recorded in the consolidated financial statements as a current asset at the lower of cost and net realisable value.

Different activities   [4A Sch 18]

30 [Withdrawn]*

Disclosures for subsidiary undertakings excluded from consolidation

31 In addition to the disclosures required by Schedule 5, subject to   [s231 and
    section 231, the following information should be given in the con-   5 Sch 15–20]
    solidated financial statements for subsidiary undertakings not
    included in the consolidation:
    (a) particulars of the balances between the excluded subsidiary
         undertakings and the rest of the group;
    (b) the nature and extent of transactions of the excluded subsidiary
         undertakings with the rest of the group;

*Editor's note: Withdrawn by 'Amendment to FRS 2 Accounting for subsidiary undertakings – legal changes'.

(c) for an excluded subsidiary undertaking carried other than by the equity method, any amounts included in the consolidated financial statements in respect of:

    (i) dividends received and receivable from that undertaking; and

    (ii) any write-down in the period in respect of the investment in that undertaking or amounts due from that undertaking.

Disclosures for excluded subsidiary undertakings in general apply to individual excluded subsidiary undertakings. However, if the information about excluded subsidiary undertakings is more appropriately presented for a sub-unit of the group comprising more than one excluded subsidiary undertaking, the disclosures may be made on an aggregate basis. Any individual sub-unit for these disclosures is to include only subsidiary undertakings excluded under the same sub-section of section 229. Individual disclosures should be made for any excluded subsidiary undertaking, including its sub-group where relevant, that alone accounts for more than 20% of any one or more of operating profits, turnover or net assets of the group. The group amounts should be measured by including all excluded subsidiary undertakings.   **32**

Disclosures for principal subsidiary undertakings

[s231 and 5 Sch Part II] In addition to the disclosures required by Schedule 5, and, like those, subject to the exemptions and conditions of section 231, the following should be shown for each subsidiary undertaking whose results or financial position principally affects the figures in the consolidated financial statements: **33**

(a) the proportion of voting rights held by the parent and its subsidiary undertakings; and

(b) an indication of the nature of its business.

Disclosure of the basis of dominant influence

[s231 and 5 Sch 15(5)] Where an undertaking is a subsidiary undertaking only because its parent undertaking has the power to exercise, or actually exercises, dominant influence or control over it, the consolidated financial statements should disclose the basis of the parent undertaking's dominant influence or control in addition to the disclosures required, subject to section 231, by Schedule 5 paragraph 15(5).*   **34**

Minority interests

[4A Sch 17(2)] The consolidated balance sheet should show separately the aggregate of the capital and reserves attributable to minority interests at the end of the period under 'Minority interests' in accordance with Schedule 4A paragraph 17(2). This amount represents the aggregate share of net assets or liabilities of subsidiary undertakings included in the consolidation that are attributable to the minority interests.   **35**

---

*Editor's note: Replaced by 'Amendment to FRS 2 Accounting for subsidiary undertakings – legal changes'.

36   The consolidated profit and loss account should show separately the aggregate of profit or loss on ordinary activities for the period attributable to the minority interests under 'Minority interests' in accordance with Schedule 4A paragraph 17(3). Any extraordinary profit or loss attributable to minority interests should be shown separately in accordance with Schedule 4A paragraph 17(4).

37   Profits or losses arising in a subsidiary undertaking should be apportioned between the controlling and minority interests in proportion to their respective interests held over the period in which the profits or losses arose. Where the losses in a subsidiary undertaking attributable to the minority interest result in its interest being one in net liabilities rather than net assets, the group should make provision to the extent that it has any commercial or legal obligation (whether formal or implied) to provide finance that may not be recoverable in respect of the accumulated losses attributable to the minority interest.

38   Whether the assets and liabilities of a subsidiary undertaking are included at fair values or adjusted carrying amounts,* those attributable to the minority interest should be included on the same basis as those attributable to the interests held by the parent and its other subsidiary undertakings. However, goodwill arising on acquisition should only be recognised with respect to the part of the subsidiary undertaking that is attributable to the interest held by the parent and its other subsidiary undertakings. No goodwill should be attributed to the minority interest.

CONSOLIDATION ADJUSTMENTS

Intra-group transactions

39   To the extent that they are reflected in the book value of assets to be included in the consolidation, profits or losses on any intra-group transactions should be eliminated in full. Amounts in relation to debts and claims between undertakings included in the consolidation should also be eliminated. The elimination of profits or losses relating to intra-group transactions should be set against the interests held by the group and the minority interest in respective proportion to their holdings in the undertaking whose individual financial statements recorded the eliminated profits or losses.†   *[FRS requirement in relation to 4A Sch 6. The Act allows partial elimination but the FRS requires elimination in full]*

Accounting policies

40   Subject to paragraph 41 below, uniform group accounting policies should be used for determining the amounts to be included in the consolidated financial statements, if necessary by adjusting for consolidation the amounts which have been reported by subsidiary undertakings in their individual financial statements.   *[4A Sch 3(1)]*

Where the acquisition method of accounting is to be used in consolidating a subsidiary undertaking, Schedule 4A paragraph 9 requires the identifiable assets and liabilities of the undertaking acquired to be included in the consolidation at their fair values as at the date of acquisition

Where the merger method of accounting is to be used, Schedule 4A paragraph 11 requires the assets and liabilities of the subsidiary undertaking to be consolidated at the amounts at which they stand in that undertaking's financial statements, subject to any adjustments authorised or required by the Act.

†**Editor's note:** *Reference to elimination of profits on transactions with group undertakings excluded as a result of dissimilar activities removed by 'Amendment to FRS 2 Accounting for subsidiary undertakings – legal changes'.*

[*4A Sch 3(2)*] In exceptional cases, different accounting policies may be used. **41** Where the directors of the parent undertaking depart from the Act's general requirement to use the same group accounting rules to value or otherwise determine the assets and liabilities to be included in the consolidated financial statements, Schedule 4A paragraph 3(2) requires disclosure of the particulars, which should include the different accounting policies used.

Accounting periods and dates

The financial statements of all subsidiary undertakings to be used in **42** preparing the consolidated financial statements should, wherever practicable, be prepared to the same financial year end and for the same accounting period as those of the parent undertaking of the group.

[*FRS preference of alternatives permitted by 4A Sch 2(2)*] Where the financial year of a subsidiary undertaking differs from **43** that of the parent undertaking of the group, interim financial statements should be prepared to the same date as those of the parent undertaking of the group for use in the preparation of the consolidated financial statements. If it is not practicable to use such interim financial statements, the financial statements of the subsidiary undertaking for its last financial year should be used, providing that year ended not more than three months before the relevant year end of the parent undertaking of the group. In this case any changes that have taken place in the intervening period that materially affect the view given by the group's financial statements should be taken into account by adjustments in the preparation of the consolidated financial statements.

The following information should be given for each subsidiary **44** undertaking which is included in the consolidated financial statements on the basis of information prepared to a different date or for a different accounting period from that of the parent undertaking of the group:

(a) the name of the subsidiary undertaking;

(b) the accounting date or period of the subsidiary undertaking; and

(c) the reason for using a different accounting date or period for the subsidiary undertaking.

CHANGES IN COMPOSITION OF A GROUP

Date of changes in group membership

The date for accounting for an undertaking becoming a subsidiary **45** undertaking is the date on which control of that undertaking passes to its new parent undertaking. This date is the date of acquisition for Schedule 4A paragraph 9 or the date of merger. The date for accounting for an undertaking ceasing to be a subsidiary undertaking is the date on which its former parent undertaking relinquishes its control over that undertaking.

Ceasing to be a subsidiary undertaking

46　When an undertaking ceases to be a subsidiary undertaking during a period, the consolidated financial statements for that period should include the results of that subsidiary undertaking up to the date that it ceases to be a subsidiary undertaking and any gain or loss arising on that cessation, to the extent that these have not been already provided for in the consolidated financial statements.

47　The gain or loss directly arising for the group on an undertaking ceasing to be its subsidiary undertaking is calculated by comparing the carrying amount of the net assets of that subsidiary undertaking attributable to the group's interest before the cessation with any remaining carrying amount attributable to the group's interest after the cessation together with any proceeds received. The net assets compared should include any related goodwill that has not previously been either written off through the profit and loss account or attributed to prior period amortisation or impairment on applying paragraph 70 of FRS 10 'Goodwill and Intangible Assets'. This calculation of gain or loss applies whether the cause of the undertaking ceasing to be a subsidiary undertaking is a direct disposal, a deemed disposal or other event.

48　In addition to the disclosures required by Schedule 4A paragraph 15, the consolidated financial statements should give the name of any material undertaking that has ceased to be a subsidiary undertaking in the period, showing any ownership interest retained. Where any material undertaking has ceased to be a subsidiary undertaking other than by the disposal of at least part of the interest held by the group, the circumstances should be explained. [4A Sch 15]

Becoming or ceasing to be a subsidiary undertaking other than by a purchase or exchange of shares

49　Where an undertaking has become or ceased to be a subsidiary undertaking other than as a result of a purchase or exchange of shares, the circumstances should be explained in a note to the consolidated financial statements.

CHANGES IN STAKE

Acquiring a subsidiary undertaking in stages

50　Schedule 4A paragraph 9 requires that the identifiable assets and liabilities of a subsidiary undertaking be included in the consolidation at fair value at the date of its acquisition, that is, the date it becomes a subsidiary undertaking. This requirement is also applicable where the group's interest in the undertaking that becomes a subsidiary undertaking is acquired in stages. [4A Sch 9]

Increasing an interest held in a subsidiary undertaking

51　When a group increases its interest in an undertaking that is already its subsidiary undertaking, the identifiable assets and liabilities of that subsidiary undertaking should be revalued to fair value and goodwill arising on the increase in interest should be calculated by reference to those fair values. This revaluation is not required if the difference between net fair values and carrying amounts of the assets and liabilities attributable to the increase in stake is not material.

Reducing an interest held in a subsidiary undertaking

Where a group reduces its interest in a subsidiary undertaking, it should record any profit or loss arising calculated as the difference between the carrying amount of the net assets of that subsidiary undertaking attributable to the group's interest before the reduction and the carrying amount attributable to the group's interest after the reduction together with any proceeds received. The net assets compared should include any related goodwill not previously written off through the profit and loss account. Where the undertaking remains a subsidiary undertaking after the disposal, the minority interest in that subsidiary undertaking should be increased by the carrying amount of the net identifiable assets that are now attributable to the minority interest because of the decrease in the group's interest. No amount for goodwill that arose on acquisition of the group's interest in that subsidiary undertaking should be attributed to the minority interest.
52

DISTRIBUTIONS

Restrictions on distribution

Where significant statutory, contractual or exchange control restrictions on distributions by subsidiary undertakings materially limit the parent undertaking's access to distributable profits, the nature and extent of the restrictions should be disclosed.
53

Tax on the accumulated reserves of overseas subsidiary undertakings

[*Deleted.*]
54

DATE FROM WHICH EFFECTIVE

The accounting practices set out in this statement should be adopted as soon as possible and regarded as standard in respect of consolidated financial statements relating to periods ending on or after 23 December 1992 except for those companies considered below. The accounting practices in this statement should be adopted by Republic of Ireland companies as soon as possible after the enactment of the Irish legislation implementing the European Community Seventh Directive and regarded as standard in respect of consolidated financial statements for periods specified in the date of application of that legislation.*
55

---

*Editor's note: See paragraph 98 of this FRS. The date of application is accounting periods beginning on or after 1 September 1992. The changes made by 'Amendment to FRS 2 Accounting for subsidiary undertakings – legal changes' are effective for accounting periods beginning on or after 1 January 2005.

WITHDRAWAL OF SSAP 14 'GROUP ACCOUNTS' AND 'INTERIM STATEMENT: CONSOLIDATED ACCOUNTS'

56   [*Not reproduced as all changes have been reflected in the material reproduced in this volume.*]

Financial Reporting Standard No. 2 'Accounting for Subsidiary Undertakings' was adopted by the unanimous vote of the nine members of the Accounting Standards Board

Members of the Accounting Standards Board

David Tweedie	(Chairman)
Allan Cook	(Technical Director)
Robert Bradfield	
Sir Bryan Carsberg	
Elwyn Eilledge	
Michael Garner	
Donald Main	
Roger Munson	
Graham Stacy	

'Amendment to Financial Reporting Standard 2 'Accounting for Subsidiary Undertakings': Legal Changes' was approved for issue by the ten members of the Accounting Standards Board.

Ian Mackintosh	(Chairman)
Andrew Lennard	(Technical Director)
Michael Ashley	
Douglas Flint	
Anthony Good	
Roger Marshall	
Isobel Sharp	
John Smith	
Jonathan Symonds	
Peter Westlake	

Compliance with international accounting standards

57   Compliance with the amended FRS ensures substantial compliance with the relevant provisions of International Accounting Standard 27 'Consolidated and Separate Financial Statements' (IAS 27), as amended by IFRS 5 'Non-current Assets Held for Sale and Discontinued Operations'. However, IAS 27: (a) does not include an exemption from consolidation for subsidiaries where severe long-term restrictions exist and (b) does not exempt subsidiaries that are held exclusively with a view to resale. IFRS 5 requires newly acquired subsidiaries held for sale to be measured at the lower of carrying value and fair value less costs to sell; the assets and liabilities of the subsidiary may not be offset and should be presented separately from other assets and liabilities in the balance sheet.*†

58   [Deleted]

---

*The assets and liabilities of the newly acquired subsidiary held for sale may be presented together with the assets and liabilities of any other assets or disposal groups held for sale by the entity.

†**Editor's note:** Paragraphs 57 and 58 replaced by 'Amendment to FRS 2 Accounting for subsidiary undertakings – legal changes', taking account of changes to relevant IFRSs.

Explanation

The purpose of consolidated financial statements

For a variety of legal, tax and other reasons undertakings generally choose to con- **59**
duct their activities not through a single legal entity but through several undertakings
under the ultimate control of the parent undertaking of that group. For this reason
the financial statements of a parent undertaking by itself do not present a full picture
of its economic activities or financial position. Consolidated financial statements are
required in order to reflect the extended business unit that conducts activities under
the control of the parent undertaking.

The legal background to the FRS

In the United Kingdom the preparation of consolidated financial statements for **60**
companies is governed by the Act and the Companies (Northern Ireland) Order
1986. These implement in their respective jurisdictions the provisions of the European Community Seventh Directive. The FRS is drafted to be consistent with the
Act, supplementing it with guidance on its application and additional requirements
where necessary. The definitions and statement of standard accounting practice
contain marginal notes that give references to the Act where these are relevant. Any
differences in the application of the FRS in Northern Ireland are explained in the
sections setting out the legal provisions in that jurisdiction (paragraph 97). The
application of the FRS in the Republic of Ireland is explained in the section on the
legal requirements in the Republic of Ireland (paragraph 98).

Parent undertakings not subject to the Act

The FRS is drafted in terms derived from the Act but applies to all parent under- **61**
takings that prepare financial statements intended to give a true and fair view. A
parent undertaking not subject to the Act should comply with the requirements of
the FRS, and of the Act where referred to in the FRS, except to the extent that these
requirements are not permitted by any statutory framework under which the
undertaking reports. By reference to the Act, which in most cases accords with
requirements the FRS might otherwise introduce itself in respect of such undertakings,
the FRS achieves a single set of requirements relating to the preparation of consolidated financial statements both for companies that report under the Act and for
other undertakings.

The relationship between the legal background and accounting principles

The accounting concept that underlies the presentation of consolidated financial **62**
statements for a group as a single economic entity is summarised in the definition of
control in paragraph 6. Although the definition of parent and subsidiary undertakings in the Act are founded mainly on the accounting concept of control, section
258 uses a list of tests including control to determine which undertakings are parent
and subsidiary undertakings. In the main the effect of applying the tests in the Act is
the same as using a criterion based solely on the accounting concept of control. There
may, however, be cases where section 258 identified more than one undertaking as
the parent undertaking of the same subsidiary undertaking. Where more than one
undertaking is thereby identified as a parent of one subsidiary undertaking, not more
than one of those parents can have control as defined in paragraph 6.*

*Editor's note: Amended by 'Amendment to FRS 2 Accounting for subsidiary undertakings – legal changes'.

63   In practice such apparent differences between the effects of applying the Act and the standard can generally be resolved by taking into account the following factors:

    (a)   the existence of a quasi subsidiary (paragraph 64); or

    (b)   the existence of severe long-term restrictions on the rights of the parent undertaking (paragraph 65); or

    (c)   the existence of a joint venture agreement, whether formal or informal (paragraphs 66 and 67).

64   Undertakings that are directly or indirectly controlled by another undertaking and are sources of benefit to that other, but do not qualify according to the tests in the Act as subsidiary undertakings, are described as 'quasi subsidiaries'. The definition and treatment of quasi subsidiaries are not dealt with in this standard.*

65   The Act allows a subsidiary undertaking to be excluded from consolidation if the parent undertaking suffers severe long-term restrictions that substantially hinder the exercise of its rights over the assets or management of the subsidiary undertaking. Paragraph 78(c) discusses severe long-term restrictions further.

66   The control that identifies undertakings as parent and subsidiary undertakings should be distinguished from shared control, for example, as in a joint venture. It is the parent undertaking's sole control of its subsidiary undertakings that gives it access to its subsidiary undertakings' resources. The parent undertaking extends its economic activities through its subsidiary undertakings using their assets and liabilities in a similar way to its own. The ability of an undertaking that shares control to direct the operating and financial policies of the undertaking in which control is shared is circumscribed by the need to take account of the wishes of the other parties that share control. An undertaking identified as a parent by section 258 that shares control over its subsidiary undertaking may be suffering from severe long-term restrictions, as discussed in paragraph 78(c), in relation to the undertaking in which it shares control.

67   Where the tests of the Act identify more than one undertaking as the parent of one subsidiary undertaking it is likely that they have shared control and, therefore, their interests in the subsidiary undertaking are in effect interests in a joint venture and should be treated accordingly. Alternatively, one or more of the undertakings identified under the Act as a parent undertaking may exercise a non-controlling but significant influence over its subsidiary undertaking, in which case it would be more appropriate to treat that subsidiary undertaking in the same way as an associated undertaking rather than to include it in the consolidation.

Identifying parent and subsidiary undertakings

68   Parent and subsidiary undertakings are defined in the FRS by applying the provisions of section 258, which are repeated in an abbreviated form in paragraph 14 of the FRS. In addition, the FRS defines some of the phrases that are used in the Act to define undertakings that are parent or subsidiary undertakings. Paragraphs 69–74 below consider some of the terms used.

---

*At the time of issue of the FRS, the Board is in the course of developing a separate standard dealing inter alia with quasi subsidiaries. [**Editor's note:** Now FRS 5 'Reporting the Substance of Transactions'.]

Dominant influence

The Act uses 'dominant influence' as a key phrase in two of the conditions of section **69**
258 that identify parent and subsidiary undertakings.

Section 258(2)(c) identifies an undertaking as a parent undertaking if it has the right **70**
to exercise a dominant influence over another undertaking:

(a) by virtue of provisions contained in the undertaking's memorandum or articles;
     or
(b) by virtue of a control contract.

Schedule 10A paragraph 4(1) states that for the purposes of sub-section 258(2)(c) 'an
undertaking shall not be regarded as having the right to exercise a dominant influence over another undertaking unless it has a right to give directions with respect to
the operating and financial policies of that other undertaking which its directors are
obliged to comply with whether or not they are for the benefit of that other
undertaking'. This forms the basis of the definition set out in paragraph 7(a) of the
FRS. In the United Kingdom directors are bound by a common law duty to act in the
best interests of their company. For this reason there may, in some cases, be a risk
that accepting a right to exercise dominant influence, as here defined, would be in
breach of the above duty.

In a second reference to dominant influence, section 258(4)(a) identifies an under- **71**
taking as the subsidiary undertaking of another (its parent undertaking) if that other
has the power to exercise, or actually exercises, dominant influence over it. Schedule
10A paragraph 4(3) provides that the definition of the 'right to exercise a dominant
influence' for the purposes of section 258(2)(c) shall not affect the construction of
'actually exercises a dominant influence' in section 258(4)(a). The FRS defines the
'actual exercise of dominant influence' as the exercise of an influence that achieves
the result that the operating and financial policies of the undertaking influenced are
set in accordance with the wishes of the holder of the influence and for its benefit
(whether or not those wishes are explicit). The FRS defines 'the power to exercise
dominant influence' as a power that, if exercised, would give rise to the actual
exercise of dominant influence.*

As indicated in paragraph 7(b) of the FRS, the actual exercise of dominant influence is **72**
identified by its effect in practice rather than the means by which it is exercised. The
effect of the exercise of dominant influence is that the undertaking under influence
implements the operating and financial policies that the holder of the influence
desires. Thus a power of veto or any other reserve power that has the necessary effect
in practice can form the basis whereby one undertaking actually exercises a dominant
influence over another. However, such powers are likely to lead to the holder actually
exercising a dominant influence over an undertaking only if they are held in conjunction with other rights or powers or if they relate to the day-to-day activities of
that undertaking and no similar veto is held by other parties unconnected to the
holder. The full circumstances of each case should be considered, including the effect
of any formal or informal agreements between the undertakings, to decide whether
or not one undertaking actually exercises a dominant influence over another.
Commercial relationships such as that of supplier, customer or lender do not of
themselves constitute dominant influence.

A parent undertaking may actually exercise its dominant influence in an interven- **73**
tionist or non-interventionist way. For example, a parent undertaking may set

Editor's note: Amended by 'Amendment to FRS 2 Accounting for subsidiary undertakings – legal changes'.

directly and in detail the operating and financial policies of its subsidiary under-taking or it may prefer to influence these by setting out in outline the kind of results it wants achieved without being involved regularly or on a day-to-day basis. Because of the variety of ways that dominant influence may be exercised evidence of continuous intervention is not necessary to support the view that dominant influence is actually exercised. Sufficient evidence might be provided by a rare intervention on a critical matter. Once there has been evidence that one undertaking has exercised a dominant influence over another, then the dominant undertaking should be assumed to con-tinue to exercise its influence until there is evidence to the contrary. However, it is still necessary for the preparation of the consolidated financial statements to examine the relationship between the undertakings each year to assess any evidence of change in status that may have arisen.

Managed on a unified basis

74   Section 258(4)(b) identifies an undertaking as a parent undertaking of another undertaking (its subsidiary undertaking) if it and that other undertaking are man-aged on a unified basis. Undertakings are managed on a unified basis if the whole of the operations of the undertakings are integrated and they are managed as a single unit. Unified management does not arise solely because one undertaking manages another because this may not fulfil the condition that the operations of the under-takings are integrated.*

Preparation of consolidated financial statements

75   The requirements of the FRS apply to all parent undertakings that prepare con-solidated financial statements intended to give a true and fair view of the financial position and profit or loss of the group. In giving such a view the same accounting principles apply in general to consolidated financial statements as would apply to the financial statements of a single entity. Parent undertakings should comply with the requirements of the FRS in preparing consolidated financial statements giving a true and fair view, even if the parent undertaking is not specifically required to prepare consolidated financial statements.

Exclusion of subsidiary undertakings from consolidation

76   The Act requires that all the subsidiary undertakings of a parent undertaking are to be included in the consolidated financial statements for that group, subject to the exceptions permitted by section 229(2) and (3). The circumstances in which the Act permits a subsidiary undertaking to be excluded from consolidation are the following:

Permissive exclusions
(a)   'if its inclusion is not material for the purpose of giving a true and fair view; but two or more undertakings may be excluded only if they are not material taken together'; or
(b)   'where the information necessary for the preparation of group accounts cannot be obtained without disproportionate expense or undue delay'; or
(c)   'where severe long-term restrictions substantially hinder the exercise of the rights of the parent company over the assets or management of that under-taking'; or

*Editor's note: References to participating interests removed by 'Amendment to FRS 2 Accounting for sub-sidiary undertakings – legal changes'.

(d)   'where the interest of the parent company is held exclusively with a view to subsequent resale'.*

Within this statutory framework, the FRS elaborates on the conditions for exclusion **77** set out in the Act so that these identify, as far as possible, only those undertakings, defined as subsidiary undertakings by section 258, that are not controlled by their parent undertaking in a way that would in principle justify consolidation. This gives effect to the Board's view that a parent undertaking should consolidate all those undertakings that are its subsidiary undertakings unless there are circumstances that make consolidation inappropriate. Under the circumstances set out in paragraph 78(c) and (d) below, the FRS requires the parent undertaking to exclude a subsidiary undertaking because the same conditions that justify permitting exclusion of a subsidiary undertaking also make consolidation of that undertaking inappropriate. Exclusion from consolidation is not the only way of clarifying the effect on the group of the circumstances affecting some of its subsidiary undertakings; exclusion should only be used exceptionally. In many cases circumstances, such as restrictions or activities with special risks, are better dealt with by disclosure, for example by giving additional segmental information, rather than by exclusion from consolidation of the subsidiary undertakings concerned.

In order to help preparers identify the exceptional cases where it is inappropriate to **78** consolidate a subsidiary undertaking, the exclusions allowed section 229(2) and (3) are discussed below.†

Materiality
(a)   The FRS deals only with material items. Thus this ground for exclusion requires no special mention in the FRS. The Act only allows exclusion for two or more subsidiary undertakings if they are not material taken together.

Disproportionate expense and undue delay
(b)   In principle neither expense nor delay can justify excluding from consolidation subsidiary undertakings that are individually or collectively material in the context of the group.

Severe long-term restrictions
(c)   Restrictions are only relevant to justify the exclusion of a subsidiary undertaking from consolidation if the restrictions substantially hinder the exercise of the rights of the parent undertaking over the assets or management of the subsidiary undertaking. The rights affected must be those by reason of which the undertaking holding them is the parent undertaking and without which it would not be the parent undertaking. Severe long-term restrictions justify excluding a subsidiary undertaking from consolidation only where the effect of those restrictions is that the parent undertaking does not control its subsidiary undertaking. Severe long-term restrictions are identified by their effect in practice rather than by the way in which the restrictions are imposed. For example, a subsidiary undertaking should not be excluded because restrictions are threatened or because another party has the power to impose them unless such threats or the existence of such a power has a severe and restricting effect in practice in the long term on the rights of the parent undertaking. Generally, restrictions are dealt with better by disclosure than by non-consolidation. However, the loss of the parent undertaking's control over its subsidiary

Editor's note: Reference to required exclusion on grounds of dissimilar activities and reference to interests in subsidiary undertakings previously not having been consolidated removed by 'Amendment to FRS 2 Accounting for subsidiary undertakings – legal changes'.

†Editor's note: Reference to required exclusion on grounds of dissimilar activities removed by 'Amendment to FRS 2 Accounting for subsidiary undertakings – legal changes'.

undertaking resulting from severe long-term restrictions would make it misleading to include that subsidiary undertaking in the consolidation. Where a subsidiary undertaking is subject to an insolvency procedure in the United Kingdom, control over that undertaking may have passed to a designated official (for example, an administrator, administrative receiver or liquidator) with the effect that severe long-term restrictions are in force. A company voluntary arrangement does not necessarily lead to loss of control. In some overseas jurisdictions even formal insolvency procedures may not amount to loss of control.

Interest held exclusively with a view to subsequent resale

(d)   This exclusion applies only to those undertakings that have never formed a continuing part of group activities and have not previously been included in consolidated financial statements prepared by the parent undertaking. Paragraph 11 defines the two sets of circumstances in which an interest in a subsidiary undertaking is considered to be held exclusively with a view to subsequent resale. The first set of circumstances (paragraph 11(a)) depends on an immediate intention to sell and the expectation of a sale within approximately one year. An interest for which a sale is not completed within a year of its acquisition may still fulfil the conditions of paragraph 11(a) if, at the date the accounts are signed, the terms of the sale have been agreed and the process of disposing of that interest is substantially complete. The second set of circumstances (paragraph 11(b)) depends on the way in which the interest was acquired, that is, whether it was acquired as a result of the enforcement of a security. The provisions of Schedule 10A paragraph 8(b) may be relevant in determining whether such an interest has been acquired. This paragraph provides that rights attached to shares held as a security are to be treated as held by the person providing the security, where the shares are held in connection with the granting of loans as part of normal business activities and, apart from the right to exercise them to preserve the value of the security or to realise it, the rights are exercisable only in the interests of the provider of the security.

Treatment of excluded subsidiary undertakings

Severe long-term restrictions

79   (a)   Where severe long-term restrictions are in force so that a subsidiary undertaking is no longer under the control of its parent undertaking, that subsidiary undertaking should not be consolidated. From the date severe long-term restrictions come into force and until they are lifted, the subsidiary undertaking subject to the restrictions should be excluded from consolidation and treated instead as a fixed asset investment. If restrictions are in force when the subsidiary undertaking is acquired, it should be carried initially at cost; if restrictions came into force at a later date, the subsidiary undertaking should be carried at a fixed amount calculated using the equity method as at the date the restrictions came into force. If, in spite of severe long-term restrictions, the parent undertaking retains significant influence over a subsidiary undertaking, the investment should be treated as an associated undertaking using the equity method. Because severe long-term restrictions may give rise to impairment, the FRS requires the value of the excluded subsidiary undertaking to be reviewed to assess whether any impairment has occurred. Any intra-group amounts due from such excluded subsidiary undertakings may also be affected by severe long-term restrictions, particularly if the restrictions extend to remittances. These balances should also be reviewed and provision made as necessary.

Held exclusively for resale

(b) A subsidiary undertaking held exclusively for resale and not previously included in the consolidated financial statements of the parent undertaking does not form part of the continuing activities of the group. Although the parent undertaking (as identified by section 258 and paragraph 14 of the FRS) may control such a subsidiary undertaking, its control is temporary and is not used to deploy the underlying assets and liabilities of that subsidiary undertaking as part of the continuing group's activities for the benefit of the parent undertaking of the group. The subsidiary undertaking is therefore excluded from consolidation and the temporary nature of the parent undertaking's interest is recognised by carrying it as a current asset at the lower of cost and net realisable value.

(c) [Withdrawn]*

Intra-group guarantees re excluded subsidiary undertakings

(d) Liabilities to third parties of one group member guaranteed by another are themselves included in the consolidated financial statements so that intra-group guarantees do not normally require disclosure. Guarantees in respect of subsidiary undertakings excluded from consolidation have to be treated in the same way as guarantees given by members of the group to third parties because, in these cases, the intra-group guarantees relate to liabilities that are not included gross in the consolidated financial statements.

Minority interests

Despite the title 'Minority interests', there is in principle no upper limit to the proportion of shares in a subsidiary undertaking which may be held as a minority interest while the parent undertaking still qualifies as such under section 258 of the Act (described in paragraph 14 of the FRS). The amounts reported in the consolidated balance sheet and profit and loss account for the minority interests indicate the extent to which the assets and liabilities and profits and losses of subsidiary undertakings included in the consolidation are attributable to shareholders other than the parent or its other subsidiary undertakings. The effect of the existence of minority interests on the returns to investors in the parent undertaking is best reflected by presenting the net identifiable assets attributable to minority interests on the same basis as those attributable to group interests. Using the same basis for including group assets and liabilities, irrespective of the extent to which they are attributable to the minority interest, presents the assets and liabilities on a consistent basis for the group as a whole. **80**

The FRS requires that losses be attributed to the minority interest in a loss making subsidiary undertaking, regardless of whether or not this leads to a debit balance for the minority interest; to do otherwise would obscure the comparison between the assets and liabilities and results attributable to the minority interest and those attributable to the group interests both during the periods when the accumulated losses accrue and afterwards, if these are then made good by later profits. Accumulated losses of subsidiary undertakings do not of themselves necessarily require funding by the parent undertaking and a debit balance for minority interests represents net liabilities attributable to the shares held by the minorities in that subsidiary undertaking rather than a debt due from them. The group should provide for any commercial or legal obligation (whether formal or implied) to provide finance that may not be recoverable in respect of the accumulated losses attributable **81**

Editor's note: Reference to different activities withdrawn by 'Amendment to FRS 2 Accounting for subsidiary undertakings – legal changes'.

to the minority interests. Provisions of this sort would include the minorities' share of any liability guaranteed by the group, or any liability that the group itself would be likely to settle for commercial or other reasons, if the subsidiary undertaking could not do so itself. Any provision made with respect to minority debit balances should be set directly against the minority interest amount in the profit and loss account and the balance sheet.

82   The FRS requires that the goodwill arising on acquisition of a subsidiary undertaking that is not wholly owned should be recognised only in relation to the group's interest and that none should be attributed to the minority interest. Although it might be possible to estimate by extrapolation or valuation an amount of goodwill attributable to the minority when a subsidiary undertaking is acquired, this would in effect recognise an amount for goodwill that is hypothetical because the minority is not a party to the transaction by which the subsidiary undertaking is acquired.*

Consolidation adjustments and intra-group transactions

83   Presenting information about the economic activities of the group as a single economic entity in consolidated financial statements requires adjustment for intra-group transactions of the amounts reported in the individual financial statements of the parent and its subsidiary undertakings. Intra-group transactions may result in a profit or loss that is included at least temporarily in the book value of group assets. To the extent that such assets are still held in the undertakings included in the consolidation at the balance sheet date, the related profits or losses recorded in the individual financial statements have not arisen for the group as a whole and must therefore be eliminated from group results and asset values. The elimination should be in full, even where the transactions involve subsidiary undertakings with minority interests. Transactions between undertakings included in the consolidation deal with the assets and liabilities that are wholly within the group's control, even if they are not wholly owned. From the perspective of the group as a single entity no profit or loss arises on intra-group transactions because no increase or decrease in the group's net assets has occurred. Profits or losses arising on transactions with undertakings excluded from consolidation because they are held exclusively with a view to subsequent re-sale or because of severe long-term restrictions need not be eliminated, except to the extent appropriate where significant influence is retained and the subsidiary undertaking is treated as an associated undertaking. However, it is important to consider whether it is prudent to record any profit arising from transactions with subsidiary undertakings excluded on these grounds.†

Changes in composition of a group

84   The date on which an undertaking becomes or ceases to be another undertaking's subsidiary undertaking marks the point at which a new accounting treatment for that undertaking is applied. The relevant date is the date on which control passes and paragraph 45 of the FRS is framed in these terms. This date should also be the one on which an undertaking begins or ceases to qualify as a parent or subsidiary undertaking under section 258. The date on which control passes is a matter of fact and cannot be backdated or otherwise altered.

Editor's note: See also UITF Abstract 31 'Exchanges of businesses or other non-monetary assets for an interest in a subsidiary, joint venture or associate.'

†*Editor's note:* Reference to elimination of profits or losses where a subsidiary undertaking was excluded on grounds of dissimilar activities removed by 'Amendment to FRS 2 Accounting for subsidiary undertakings – legal changes'.

Where control is transferred by a public offer, the date control is transferred is the   **85**
date the offer becomes unconditional, usually as a result of a sufficient number of
acceptances being received. For private treaties, the date control is transferred is
generally the date an unconditional offer is accepted. Where an undertaking becomes
or ceases to be a subsidiary undertaking as a result of the issue or cancellation of
shares, the date control is transferred is the date of issue or cancellation. The date
that control passes may be indicated by the acquiring party commencing its direction
of the operating and financial policies of the acquired undertaking or by changes in
the flow of economic benefits. The date on which the consideration for the transfer of
control is paid is often an important indication of the date on which a subsidiary
undertaking is acquired or disposed of. However, the date the consideration passes is
not conclusive evidence of the date of the transfer of control because this date can be
set to fall on a date other than that on which control is transferred, with compensation for any lead or lag included in the consideration. Consideration may also paid
in instalments.

An undertaking may cease to be a subsidiary undertaking as a result of the parent   **86**
undertaking losing control over it because of changes in the rights it holds or in those
held by another party in that subsidiary undertaking. A parent undertaking may also
lose control of its subsidiary undertaking because of changes in some other
arrangement that gave it control without there being any change in the former parent
undertaking's holding in its former subsidiary undertaking. For example, control
may pass if there is a change in voting rights or in how these are allocated. In these
circumstances neither a gain nor a loss accrues in the consolidated financial statements, unless there is a payment for the transfer of control, because there is no
change in the net assets attributable to the group's holding in the former subsidiary
undertaking. The assets and liabilities of the former subsidiary undertaking should
cease to be consolidated but should be shown instead as an associated undertaking or
investment as appropriate.

An undertaking usually ceases to be a subsidiary undertaking because the group   **87**
reduces its proportional interest in that undertaking. The reduction of the group's
interest may result from its directly disposing of part of the interest it holds or from a
deemed disposal. Any reduction in the group's proportional interest other than by a
direct disposal is a deemed disposal. Disposals and deemed disposals may give rise to
profits or losses for the group, which should be calculated as set out in paragraph 47.
There may be other losses or gains that arise for the group as a result of an
undertaking ceasing to be a subsidiary undertaking. These are not part of the direct
gain or loss described here but may need to be provided for, if they are quantifiable,
or otherwise disclosed to show the full effect of the cessation. Deemed disposals may
arise where the group's interest in a subsidiary undertaking is reduced, inter alia:

(a)   because the parent undertaking and its group do not take up their full allo-
      cation of rights in a rights issue; or
(b)   because the parent undertaking and its group do not take up their full share of
      scrip dividends while other equity holders in that subsidiary undertaking take
      up some, at least, of their share; or
(c)   because another party has exercised its options or warrants; or
(d)   because the subsidiary undertaking has issued shares to parties other than the
      parent undertaking and its group.

Changes in stake

When an undertaking is first consolidated, its identifiable assets and liabilities are   **88**
initially brought into the consolidation at their fair values at the date of its acquisition as a subsidiary undertaking (the acquisition method of accounting as provided

by Schedule 4A paragraph 9). Where a subsidiary undertaking is acquired in stages, its net identifiable assets and liabilities are to be included in the consolidation at their fair values on the date it becomes a subsidiary undertaking, rather than at the date of the earlier purchases. Using other methods to compute the amounts to be included in the consolidation would fail to give a full picture of the assets and liabilities acquired that now comprise part of the group's resources.

89   The effect of the Schedule 4A paragraph 9 method of acquisition accounting is to treat as goodwill, or negative goodwill, the whole of the difference between, on the one hand, the fair value, at the date an undertaking becomes a subsidiary undertaking, of the group's share of its identifiable assets and liabilities and, on the other hand, the total acquisition cost of the interests held by the group in that subsidiary undertaking. This applies even where part of the acquisition cost arises from purchases of interests at earlier dates. In the generality of cases this method provides a practical means of applying acquisition accounting because it does not require retrospective assessments of the fair values of the identifiable assets and liabilities of the acquired undertaking. In special circumstances, however, not using fair values at the dates of earlier purchases, while using an acquisition cost part of which relates to earlier purchases, may result in accounting that is inconsistent with the way the investment has been treated previously and, for that reason, may fail to give a true and fair view. For example, an undertaking that has been treated as an associated undertaking by a group may then be acquired by that group as a subsidiary undertaking. Using the method required by Schedule 4A paragraph 9 to calculate goodwill on such an acquisition has the effect that the group's share of profits or losses and reserve movements of its associated undertaking becomes reclassified as goodwill (usually negative goodwill). A similar problem may arise where the group has substantially restated its investment in an undertaking that subsequently becomes its subsidiary undertaking. For example, where such an investment has been written down because it is impaired, the effect of applying the Schedule 4A paragraph 9 method of acquisition accounting would be to increase reserves and create an asset (goodwill). In the rare cases where the Schedule 4A paragraph 9 calculation of goodwill would be misleading, goodwill should be calculated as the sum of goodwill arising from each purchase of an interest in the relevant undertaking adjusted as necessary for any subsequent impairment. Goodwill arising on each purchase should be calculated as the difference between the cost of that purchase and the fair value at the date of that purchase of the identifiable assets and liabilities attributable to the interest purchased. The difference between the goodwill calculated on this method and that calculated on the method provided by the Act is shown in reserves. Section 227(6) sets out the disclosures required in cases where the statutory requirement is not applied.*

90   Where a group increases its stake in an undertaking that is already its subsidiary undertaking the consideration paid may not be equal to the fair value of the identifiable assets and liabilities previously attributed to the minority and now acquired from the minority. If the assets and liabilities were not revalued to fair values before calculating the goodwill arising on the change in stake, then the difference between the consideration paid and the relevant proportion of the carrying value of net assets acquired would be made up in part of goodwill and in part of changes in value. The FRS requires that the assets and liabilities of the subsidiary undertaking be revalued to fair value at the date of the increase in stake unless the difference between the fair values and the carrying amounts of the share of net assets acquired is not material.

91   Where the group decreases its stake in an undertaking whether or not it continues to be a subsidiary undertaking, a profit or loss generally arises. Consolidated financial

*Editor's note: See also FRS 18 'Accounting Policies'.

statements are prepared from the perspective of investors in the parent undertaking of the group. Where the group disposes of part of its interest in a subsidiary undertaking it transacts directly with third parties and a profit or loss for the group arises and is reported in the consolidated financial statements. This can be contrasted with the treatment of intra-group transactions where no profit or loss arises for the group as a whole because the transaction involves only undertakings included in the consolidation and under common control and does not directly involve any third party.

Distributions

[*Deleted.*]   92

Disclosures

The FRS refers to the disclosure requirements of the Act and, where appropriate, adds   93
further disclosure requirements of its own. By referring to certain of the disclosure requirements in the Act in the text of the statement of standard accounting practice the FRS extends these disclosure requirements to parent undertakings not subject to the Act. Requirements of the Act are identified by section or schedule numbers; reference to the Act itself is necessary to ascertain the full disclosures required.

Segmental information

Segmental information has a particular importance in group financial reporting. The   94
aggregation and adjustments required to consolidate financial information for the parent undertaking and its subsidiary undertakings may obscure information about the different undertakings and activities included in the consolidated financial statements. The information about the separate group activities that may be obscured by consolidation can be restored by giving information about the group on a segmental basis. Parent undertakings should consider how to provide segmental information for their group, indicating the different risks and rewards, growth and prospects of the different parts of the group and treating the requirements of SSAP 25 'Segmental reporting' as a minimum rather than a limit to disclosure. Two examples of how segmental information could supplement consolidated financial statements are given below.

Segmentation rather than exclusion for certain subsidiary undertakings
(a)   Where the FRS discusses excluding subsidiary undertakings from consolidation, it stresses the importance of the completeness of the information presented in the consolidated financial statements. Thus, where subsidiary undertakings engage in different activities or are subject to certain restrictions that are not such as to require exclusion from consolidation under the FRS, the most complete picture is presented by consolidating the subsidiary undertakings concerned and giving additional information or by identifying the assets, liabilities and results attributable to undertakings engaging in those activities or subject to those restrictions.

Minority interests
(b)   Users of consolidated financial statements who are interested in assessing the effect of the existence of minority interests in certain parts of the group on the expected returns to investors in the parent undertaking may find it helpful to have information showing the amounts attributable to the minority interest in different group segments.

NOTE OF LEGAL REQUIREMENTS

Legal requirements in Great Britain

References are to the Companies Act 1985 as amended by the Companies Act 1989.

Readers should refer to the Act itself for an understanding of the relevant points of law. This section lists only the main sections in the Act containing provisions in relation to subsidiary undertakings. The provisions of the Act are not considered further here because they are dealt with in the many references to the Act in the other sections of the FRS.

Main sections of the Companies Act

95   The main sections of the Companies Act containing provisions relating to the preparation of consolidated financial statements are the following.

Section 227	'Duty to prepare group accounts'
Section 228	'Exemption for parent companies included in accounts of larger group'
Section 228A	'Exemption for parent companies included in non-EEA group accounts'*
Section 229	'Subsidiary undertakings included in the consolidation'
Section 230	'Treatment of individual profit and loss account where group accounts prepared'
Section 231	'Disclosure required in notes to accounts: – related undertakings'
Section 248	'Exemption for small and medium-sized groups'
Section 249	'Qualification of group as small or medium-sized'
Section 258	'Parent and subsidiary undertakings'
Section 259	'Meaning of "undertaking" and related expressions'
Section 262	'Minor definitions'
Section 262A	'Index of defined expressions'
Schedule 4A (*All paragraphs*)	'Form and Content of Group Accounts'
Schedule 5 (*All paragraphs*)	'Disclosure of Information: Related Undertakings'
Schedule 10A (*All paragraphs*)	'Parent and Subsidiary Undertakings: supplementary provisions'

Disclosure requirements

96   The following sections and paragraphs give the main disclosure requirements of the Act with respect to consolidated financial statements.

Section 227(4)–(6)
Section 228(2)
Section 231
Schedule 4A – Paragraphs 3, 4, 13, 14, 15, 17
Schedule 5 – 'Disclosure of Information: Related Undertakings'
  Part I – 'Companies not Required to Prepare Group Accounts'
  Part II – 'Companies Required to Prepare Group Accounts'

*Editor's note: Reference inserted by 'Amendment to FRS 2 Accounting for subsidiary undertakings – legal changes'. Reference to participating interests removed.

Legal requirements in Northern Ireland

The legal requirements in Northern Ireland are very similar to those in Great Britain. **97**
The following table shows the Articles and Schedules in the Companies (Northern
Ireland) Order 1986 which correspond to the legal references in paragraphs 95–96
above.

Companies Act 1985 *(as amended)*	*The Companies* *(Northern Ireland) Order 1986* *(as amended)*
Section 227	Article 235
Section 228	Article 236
Section 229	Article 237
Section 230	Article 238
Section 231	Article 239
Section 248	Article 256
Section 249	Article 257
Section 258	Article 266
Section 259	Article 267
Section 260	Article 268
Section 262	Article 270
Section 262A	Article 270A

Schedules	
Sched 4A (*all paragraphs*)	Sched 4A (*all paragraphs*)
Sched 5 (Parts I & II) (*all paragraphs*)	Sched 5 (Parts I & II) (*all paragraphs*)
Sched 10A (*all paragraphs*)	Sched 10A (*all paragraphs*)

Legal Requirements in the Republic of Ireland

The principal legislation is contained in the European Communities (Companies: **98**
Group Accounts) Regulations **1992** ('the Regulations'), SI No 201 of 1992, which
implement the EC Seventh Directive. The Regulations amend certain group accounts
related provisions in the Companies Acts **1963–1990** and also apply provisions in
that legislation to group accounts.

This section is not a summary of all the legal provisions related to group accounts. It
gives a listing of the contents of the Regulations and the Irish equivalent for UK
legal references.

Readers are advised to refer to the Regulations for an understanding of relevant legal
points.

European Communities (Companies: Group Accounts) Regulations – contents:

Regulation 1	Citation, commencement, and construction
Regulation 2	Application
Regulation 3	Interpretation
Regulation 4	Subsidiary undertaking – definition
Regulations 5 & 6	Requirement to present group accounts
Regulations 7–9	Exemptions from requirement to present group accounts
Regulations 10–12	Exclusions from consolidation
Regulations 13 & 14	General provisions in relation to group accounts
Regulation 15	Format of accounts
Regulation 16	Group balance sheet and group profit and loss account

Regulations 17 & 18	Acquisition and merger accounting
Regulations 19 & 20	The acquisition method of accounting
Regulations 21 & 22	The merger method of accounting
Regulation 23	Acquisition of a group
Regulations 24–26	Methods of consolidation
Regulation 27	Changes in composition of a group
Regulations 28–31	Valuation
Regulation 32	Joint ventures
Regulations 33 & 34	Associated undertakings – equity method of accounting
Regulation 35	Participating interest
Regulations 36–40	Publication of information
Regulation 41	Offences
Regulations 42–45	Amendments to the Companies (Amendment) Act 1986

Schedule

Part 1 Paragraphs 1–10   Amendments to the Schedule to the Companies (Amendment) Act 1986

Part 2 paragraphs 11–23   Information required by way of notes to the group accounts

Table of equivalent legal references in the Republic of Ireland:

References in text

FRS 2	GB REFERENCE	ROI REFERENCE
Summary		
para a	Companies Act 1985 as amended by the Companies Act 1989 ('the Act')	The Companies Acts 1963–2003 and the European Communities (Companies: Group Accounts) Regulations 1992 ('the Regulations')
para e	section 228	Regulations 8 & 9
	section 229	Regulations 10–12
	section 248	Regulations 6 & 7
para p	–	The date of application is accounting periods beginning on or after 1st September 1992
Statement of Standard Accounting Practice		
para 7a	section 258(2)(c)	Regulation 4(1)(b)
para 14	section 258	Regulation 4
para 21a	section 248	Regulations 6 & 7
para 21b	section 228(2)	Regulation 8(3)
para 21c	section 228(1)(b)	Regulation 8(1)(b)
para 21d	section 229	Regulations 10–12
para 22	Companies Act Schedule 5 Part 1	Regulation 8(3)(d)
para 25	section 229(3) and (4)	Regulations 11 & 12
para 25a	section 258	Regulation 4
para 26	section 231	Companies (Amendment) Act 1989, section 16
para 31	section 231 and Schedule 5	Companies (Amendment) Act 1986, section 16
para 32	section 229	Regulations 11 & 12
para 33	section 231	Companies (Amendment) Act 1986, section 16
para 34	section 231 Schedule 5, 15(5)	–

para 35	Schedule 4A 17(2)	Regulations, Schedule para 8(2)
para 36	Schedule 4A 17(3)	Regulations, Schedule para 9(1)–(2)
para 36	Schedule 4A 17(4)	Regulations, Schedule para 9(3)–(4)
para 41	Schedule 4A para 3(2)	Regulation 29(3) and 30(3)
para 45	Schedule 4A para 9	Regulation 19 does not mention the date of acquisition
para 48	Schedule 4A para 15	Regulation 27
para 50	Schedule 4A para 9	Regulation 19(2)
para 55	–	The date of application is accounting periods beginning on or after 1st September 1992

Explanation

para 62	section 258	Regulation 4
para 66	section 258	Regulation 4
para 68	section 258	Regulation 4
para 69	section 258	Regulation 4
para 71	section 258(2)(c)	Regulation 4(1)(b)
	Schedule 10A para 4(1)	Regulation 4(5)
para 71	section 258(4)(a)	Regulation 4(1)(c)(i)
	Schedule 10A para 4(3)	Regulation 4(7)
	section 258(2)(c)	Regulation(1)(a)(ii)
para 74	section 258(4)(b)	Regulation 4 (1)(c)(ii)
para 76	section 229(2)–(4)	Regulations 10–12
para 77	section 258	Regulation 4
para 78	section 229(2)–(4)	Regulation 10–12
para 80	section 258	Regulation 4
para 84	section 258	Regulation 4
para 88	Schedule 4A para 9	Regulation 19
para 89	Schedule 4A para 9	Regulations 19–20
	section 227(6)	Regulation 14(3)
	section 258	Regulation 4

References in footnotes:

FRS 2	ROI REFERENCE
para 1**	European Communities (Companies: Group Accounts) Regulations 1992
para 38*	Regulation 19(2) — Acquisitions Regulation 22(2) — Mergers

References in margins:

FRS 2	ROI REFERENCE	FRS 2	ROI REFERENCE
para 7a	Regulation 4(5)	para 14b	Regulation 4(1)(a)(ii) & 4(2)
para 7b	No Irish equivalent		
para 10	Regulation 35(1)	para 14c(i)	Regulation 4(1)(b)(i)
para 25a	Regulation 11(a)	para 14c(ii)	Regulation 4(1)(b)(ii)
para 25b	Regulation 11(c)	para 14d	Regulation 4(1)(a)(iii)
para 25c	Regulation 12(1)	para 14e	Regulation 4(1)(c)
para 11	Regulation 11(c)	para 14f	Regulation 4(1)(d)
Para 12	Regulation 4(1)(c)(ii)	para 15	Regulation 35
para 13	Regulation Schedule 8(2)	para 16	Regulation 3(1)
para 14	Regulation 4	para 17	Regulation 3(4)
para 14a	Regulation 4(1)(a)(i)		

para 20	Regulation 5(1), 7, 8, 9, 10–12	para 34	–
para 21a	Regulations 6 & 7	para 35	Regulation Schedule para 8(2)
para 21b	Regulations 8 & 9	para 36	Regulation Schedule para 9
para 21c	Regulations 8 & 9	para 39	Regulations specify that
para 21d	No Irish equivalent to 229(5)		elimination should only refer to 'undertakings dealt
para 22	Regulation 8(3)(d)		with in the Group
para 23	Regulation 5(2)		Accounts', ie the FRS goes
para 24	Regulation 11(b)		further than the
para 25	Regulations 11 & 12		Regulations
para 26	Companies (Amendment) Act 1986, section 16	para 40	Regulations refer to uniform valuation methods
para 30	Companies (Amendment) Act 1986, section 16	para 41	Regulations 29(3) and 30(3)
		para 43	Regulation 26(2)
para 31	Companies (Amendment) Act 1986, section 16	para 44	No Irish equivalent
		para 48	No Irish equivalent
para 33	Companies (Amendment) Act 1986, section 16		

The development of the standard

This section does not form part of the Financial Reporting Standard

HISTORY OF THE FRS

i   Statement of Standard Accounting Practice No. 14 (SSAP 14) 'Group Accounts', issued September 1978, dealt with the presentation of group accounts for a group of companies. The practice of preparing group accounts for companies and their subsidiaries had been well established in the United Kingdom and Ireland since 1947. However, the issue of International Accounting Standard No. 3 'Consolidated Financial Statements' made it desirable for there to be a domestic standard on the subject.

ii   SSAP 14 was drafted to accord with relevant provisions of the Companies Acts then in force. At that time the Companies Acts did not include detailed rules regarding the preparation of group accounts.

iii   SSAP 14 defined a holding company and a subsidiary company by reference to the legal definitions current at that time. The terms now used are 'parent undertaking' and 'subsidiary undertaking' which are defined in the Companies Act 1985, as amended by the Companies Act 1989 (the Act). The Act now contains new provisions on group accounts to implement the European Community Seventh Company Law Directive with the result that the requirements of SSAP 14 are no longer entirely consistent with current legislation.

iv   The need to revise SSAP 14 for changes in the law has provided an opportunity to conduct a thorough review of the standard. This was undertaken initially by the Accounting Standards Committee whose proposals were issued as ED 50 'Consolidated accounts' in June 1990. The Accounting Standards Board issued the 'Interim Statement: Consolidated Accounts' in December 1990, to give timely guidance on how certain provisions of the Act were to be interpreted in the preparation of consolidated accounts. The Interim Statement also made the changes to SSAP 14 'Group Accounts' that were required as a consequence of the statutory changes. The issue of the FRS by the Accounting Standards Board completes the review process.

SUMMARY OF THE PRINCIPAL CHANGES FROM STATEMENT OF STANDARD ACCOUNTING PRACTICE No. 14 – 'GROUP ACCOUNTS'

SSAP 14 defined a company as a subsidiary of another 'if, but only if,   **v**

(a) that other either:

   (i)   is a member of it and controls the composition of its board of directors; or
   (ii) holds more than half in nominal value of its equity share capital; or

(b) the first mentioned company is a subsidiary of any company which is that other's subsidiary, and it otherwise comes within the terms of section 154 of the Companies Act 1948' (now repealed).

The FRS defines a parent undertaking and a subsidiary undertaking in the same way as the Act using a set of conditions that are based on whether one undertaking controls another. These are set out in paragraph 14 of the FRS.

The FRS requires a parent undertaking not making use of an exemption to prepare   **vi** consolidated financial statements for its group. SSAP 14 exceptionally allowed alternative forms of group reporting if the resulting group accounts were considered to give a fairer view of the financial position of the group as a whole than would consolidated financial statements.

SSAP 14 exempted from the obligation to prepare group accounts only holding   **vii** companies that were wholly owned subsidiaries not otherwise required by law to prepare group accounts. The FRS follows the Act in allowing other exemptions from preparing consolidated financial statements. A parent undertaking is in general exempt from the requirement to prepare consolidated financial statements if its group is a small or medium-sized one; or if it is wholly or majority-owned by an undertaking established under the law of a member state of the European Community; or if all its subsidiary undertakings fall within the exclusions from consolidation.

The circumstances in which subsidiary undertakings are to be excluded from the   **viii** consolidation have changed in certain respects from those in SSAP 14.

(a) SSAP 14 required a subsidiary to be excluded from consolidation if its activities were so dissimilar from those of other companies within the group that its consolidation would be misleading and information would be better provided by presenting financial statements for the excluded subsidiary separate from the financial statements for the rest of the group. The FRS requires a subsidiary undertaking to be excluded from consolidation if, exceptionally, its activities are so different from other subsidiary undertakings included in the consolidation that its inclusion in the consolidation would be incompatible with the obligation to give a true and fair view.

(b) SSAP 14 required a subsidiary to be excluded from consolidation if the holding company held more than half of the subsidiary's equity share capital but either: (a) it did not own share capital carrying more than half the votes; or (b) contractual or other restrictions were imposed on its ability to appoint the majority of the board of directors. Although the FRS does not have the same exclusion, the FRS will in most cases have the same practical effect because (a) an undertaking is a subsidiary undertaking if another undertaking holds a majority of its voting rights and (b) exclusion is required where severe long-term restrictions substantially hinder the rights of the parent undertaking over the assets or management of its subsidiary undertaking.

(c)   SSAP 14 required exclusion from consolidation of a subsidiary where control was intended to be temporary. The FRS requires consolidation where one undertaking controls another and, therefore, has not based exclusion on control being temporary. However, it does require exclusion from consolidation of a subsidiary undertaking held exclusively with a view to resale which has not previously been consolidated. This condition for exclusion is more restrictive than the temporary control test.

ix   SSAP 14 required that the consolidated financial statements should contain sufficient information about material subsidiaries acquired or sold to enable shareholders to appreciate the effect on the consolidated results. There are now specific disclosure requirements in the law, as well as in accounting standards in respect of acquisitions, and the general SSAP 14 requirement is not repeated in the FRS. In addition FRS 1 'Cash Flow Statements' contains a requirement to show the cash flow effects of acquisitions and disposals.

x   SSAP 14 sets out the effective date of acquisition or disposal as the earlier of the date on which consideration passes or the date on which an offer becomes or is declared unconditional. This is replaced in the FRS by a single triggering date which is the date control of the undertaking passes. This date is a matter of fact and cannot be backdated or otherwise altered.

xi   SSAP 14 required that debit balances for the minority interests should only be recognised in the balance sheet if there was a binding obligation on minority shareholders to make good losses incurred which they were able to meet. The FRS requires minority interests to be debited in full with their share of any loss whether or not this results in a debit balance, subject to the need for a provision discussed below. A debit for minority interests does not represent a liability of the minority shareholders and it may be misleading to refer to their being obliged to make good losses. The group should make provision to the extent that it has any commercial or legal obligation (whether formal or implied) to provide finance that may not be recoverable in respect of the accumulated losses attributable to minority interests.

SUMMARY OF THE PRINCIPAL CHANGES FROM THE BOARD'S 'INTERIM STATEMENT: CONSOLIDATED ACCOUNTS'

xii   In December 1990 the Board issued the 'Interim Statement: Consolidated Accounts' to give timely guidance on the application of certain provisions of the new Act to the preparation of consolidated financial statements. The Interim Statement dealt mainly with the interpretation of the new phrases used in the conditions that identified parent and subsidiary undertakings and with the exclusions from consolidation permitted or required by the Act for certain subsidiary undertakings. Although the drafting has changed to fit the format of an accounting standard, the FRS incorporates the guidance given by the Interim Statement except in the following areas.

(a)   Dominant influence is now defined without explicit reference to control although the effect of dominant influence is the same as control.

(b)   The explanation dealing with subsidiary undertakings whose activities are so different that consolidation is incompatible with the obligation to give a true and fair view now states explicitly that the contrast between Schedule 9 and 9A companies and other companies or between profit and not-for-profit undertakings is not sufficient of itself to justify non consolidation.

(c)   The Interim Statement defined a joint venture. The FRS deals only with accounting for subsidiary undertakings leaving joint ventures as a separate project.

SUMMARY OF THE PRINCIPAL CHANGES FROM EXPOSURE DRAFT No. 50 – 'CONSOLIDATED ACCOUNTS'

Exposure Draft No. 50 (ED 50) 'Consolidated accounts' was issued in June 1990 by the Accounting Standards Committee. It proposed standard accounting practice for the preparation of consolidated accounts covering both accounting for subsidiary undertakings and accounting for associated undertakings and joint ventures. The FRS deals only with accounting for subsidiary undertakings in consolidated financial statements. The Board is engaged in another project considering accounting for associated undertakings and joint ventures.   xiii

The Explanatory Note in ED 50 considered the purpose of consolidated accounts, the basis of consolidation and the meaning of control. The FRS deals only briefly in its explanation section with the conceptual background to financial reporting for groups. The conceptual basis of consolidated financial statements and consideration of the group as a reporting entity are to be considered by the Board in the chapter of its Statement of Principles dealing with the boundaries of the reporting entity.   xiv

ED 50 used the terms 'subsidiary', 'parent' and 'enterprise' in line with earlier accounting standards. Commentators on its proposals considered that it would be more appropriate to use the terminology of the Act on which the FRS is based. The FRS now refers to 'subsidiary undertaking', 'parent undertaking' and 'undertaking'. However, in line with the Board's other published work, the FRS uses 'financial statements' instead of 'accounts' as used in the Act.   xv

ED 50 proposed definitions for the phrases used in the Act in the criteria for identifying parent and subsidiary undertakings. The FRS elaborates on these definitions in the light of the comments received on the ED. The general thrust of the definitions remains the same but the following changes are worth noting: xvi

(a) 'Dominant influence' is no longer defined in terms of control but by its ability to achieve the operating and financial policies desired by the holder of the influence, notwithstanding the rights or influence of any other party. The actual exercise of dominant influence is identified by its effect in practice rather than the way in which it is exercised. The effect of dominant influence is the same as the effect of control.
(b) The role of reserve powers and powers of veto in the actual exercise of dominant influence has been clarified.

ED 50 proposed that a parent undertaking using an exemption from preparing consolidated accounts should make additional disclosures if its individual financial statements alone were not sufficient to give a true and fair view of its financial position. ED 50 noted that in some cases such additional information might better be presented by providing consolidated financial statements for the whole group. This proposal attracted adverse comment because, in certain circumstances, its effect would be to take away an exemption given by the Act. The FRS requires a parent undertaking using an exemption to state that its financial statements present information about it as an individual undertaking and not about its group. Parent undertakings using any of the exemptions should also make the disclosures set out in Schedule 5 Part 1 of the Companies Act.   xvii

ED 50 proposed definitions for the phrases used in the Act to set the conditions under which a subsidiary undertaking was permitted or required to be excluded from consolidation. As a result of the comments received the guidance of the FRS on how these conditions are to be interpreted has changed slightly from that given in ED 50   xviii although the emphasis remains on interpreting these conditions restrictively. The main changes are set out below.

(a) *Interests held exclusively with a view to subsequent resale.* A second part has been added bringing acquisitions as a result of the enforcement of a security within the definition of interests held exclusively with a view to subsequent resale unless the subsidiary undertaking has become part of the continuing activities of the group or the holder acts as if it intends the interest to become so.

(b) *Activities so different that consolidation would be incompatible with the obligation to give a true and fair view.* ED 50 proposed that such an incompatibility could arise only from consolidating a Schedule 9 or 9A company with non Schedule 9 or 9A companies. Several commentators considered that a requirement not to consolidate Schedule 9 and 9A companies with others might result in a loss of useful and comparable information on group activities as a whole. Linking incompatibility with the true and fair view to issues relating to the format in which financial statements were presented was considered unsatisfactory. The FRS, therefore, stresses that the key feature of this exclusion is that including a given subsidiary undertaking in the consolidation is incompatible with the obligation to give a true and fair view. The FRS notes that this incompatibility will be so exceptional in practice that it would be misleading to associate it with any particular contrast of activities. For example, the contrasts between Schedule 9 or 9A companies and other companies or between profit and not-for-profit undertakings would not of themselves be sufficient to justify nonconsolidation.

xix ED 50 followed SSAP 14 and proposed that losses should only be debited to minority interests where they resulted in a debit balance if there was a binding and reliable obligation on the minority to make good any such losses. The FRS's treatment for the minority's share of losses is explained in paragraph xi above.

xx ED 50 proposed dropping the requirement of SSAP 14 (paragraph 18) that appropriate adjustments should be made to the consolidated financial statements for any abnormal transactions in the intervening period between the end of the period of a subsidiary and the later one of the group. Commentators considered that some disclosure of this sort would be useful. The FRS requires that, where a subsidiary undertaking's financial year end differs from that of the parent undertaking, the consolidated financial statements should be prepared using interim financial statements or, only if this is impracticable, its financial statements for its last financial year ending not more than three months before that of the group's parent undertaking. In this latter case adjustment is required for changes in the intervening period that materially affect the view given by the consolidated financial statements.

xxi ED 50 proposed that the effective date of acquisition or disposal be the earlier of:

(a) the date on which the consideration passes; or
(b) the date at which an offer becomes or is declared unconditional; or
(c) the date of such other event at which control is gained or ceases to exist.

The FRS now sets the date of changes in membership of the group as the date that control passes. The Explanation (paragraphs 84 and 85) considers the transactions and events that indicate when control passes.

xxii ED 50 proposed that its requirement to include the appropriate proportion of the results of a subsidiary undertaking that has been disposed of should be subject to the requirements of SSAP 6 'Extraordinary items and prior year adjustments' (paragraphs 11–14) dealing with the disposal of a segment. The FRS does not refer to SSAP 6 and requires that the consolidated profit and loss account should include the results of a subsidiary undertaking up to the date of its disposal. The Board is proposing to supersede SSAP 6 with an FRS developed from FRED 1 'The Structure of Financial Statements – Reporting of Financial Performance.'*

The FRS has dropped the proposed requirement of ED 50 in respect of disposals to   **xxiii** disclose the amount of purchased goodwill attributable to business or business segments disposed of and how that goodwill has been treated in determining the profit or loss on disposal. These disclosures are still required by paragraph 52(b) of SSAP 22 'Accounting for goodwill'.† The treatment of goodwill on disposal is set out in paragraph 47, which requires that the net assets disposed of include any related goodwill not previously written off through the profit and loss account.

In response to criticism of the ED 50 proposals, the FRS changes the treatment for   **xxiv** increases in stake in a subsidiary undertaking. ED 50 did not propose to require a revaluation to fair value on an increase in stake, and, consequently, the goodwill balance arising could have consisted of an amount relating to revaluation of net identifiable assets as well as goodwill. The FRS requires that the goodwill should be calculated by revaluing the subsidiary undertaking's assets and liabilities to fair value at the date of the change in stake, unless the difference between fair values and carrying amounts is not material.

In 2004 FRS 2 was amended to reflect changes to the Act that were introduced by the   **xxv** Companies Act 1985 (International Accounting Standards and Other Accounting Amendments) Regulations 2004 (SI 2004 No. 2947).‡

---

*Editor's note: This became FRS 3 'Reporting financial performance'.

†Editor's note: This is now dealt with in FRS 10 'Goodwill and Intangible Assets'.

‡Editor's note: Added by 'Amendment to FRS 2 Accounting for subsidiary undertakings – legal changes'.

[FRS 3]
Reporting financial performance*

(Issued October 1992; amended June 1993 and June 1999)

Contents

Editor's note: FRS 3 has been further amended by FRS 22 and FRS 25, with effect for accounting periods beginning on or after 1 January 2005.

Reporting financial performance

Summary

Financial Reporting Standard No. 3 'Reporting Financial Performance' (the FRS) **a**
introduces: changes to the format of the profit and loss account; a note of historical
cost profits and losses; a statement of total recognised gains and losses; and a
reconciliation of movements in shareholders' funds. The FRS supersedes Statement of
Standard Accounting Practice No. 6 (Revised) 'Extraordinary items and prior year
adjustments' (SSAP 6), amends SSAP 3 'Earnings per share' and makes consequential
changes to a number of other accounting standards.

A layered format is to be used for the profit and loss account to highlight a number **b**
of important components of financial performance:

(i)   results of continuing operations (including the results of acquisitions);
(ii) results of discontinued operations;
(iii) profits or losses on the sale or termination of an operation, costs of a funda-
     mental reorganisation or restructuring and profits or losses on the disposal of
     fixed assets; and
(iv) extraordinary items.

  The thrust of this approach can be illustrated diagrammatically.

Continuing	*Discontinued*
Normal operations	Normal operations
The items listed in b(iii) above	The items listed in b(iii) above

Extraordinary items — being unusual items outside ordinary activies

In presenting the profit and loss account the following requirements should be **c**
observed:

(i)   The analysis between continuing operations, acquisitions (as a component of
       continuing operations) and discontinued operations should be disclosed to the
       level of operating profit (which for non-financial reporting entities is normally
       profit before income from shares in group undertakings). The analysis of
       turnover and operating profit is the minimum disclosure required in this respect
       on the face of the profit and loss account.
(ii)   All exceptional items, other than those in (iii) below, should be included under
       the statutory format headings to which they relate. They should be separately
       disclosed by way of note or, where it is necessary in order that the financial
       statements give a true and fair view, on the face of the profit and loss account.
(iii) The following items, including provisions in respect of such items, should be
       shown separately on the face of the profit and loss account after operating
       profit and before interest:
       – profits or losses on the sale or termination of an operation;
       – costs of a fundamental reorganisation or restructuring; and
       – profits or losses on the disposal of fixed assets.

(iv)　Extraordinary items should be disclosed.

d　[Withdrawn]*

e　The note of historical cost profits and losses is a memorandum item, the primary purpose of which is to present the profits or losses of reporting entities that have revalued assets on a more comparable basis with those of entities that have not. It is an abbreviated restatement of the profit and loss account which adjusts the reported profit or loss, if necessary, so as to show it as if no asset revaluations had been made. Unless the historical cost information is unavailable, the note is required whenever there is a material difference between the result as disclosed in the profit and loss account and the result on an unmodified historical cost basis; it should be presented immediately following the profit and loss account or the statement of total recognised gains and losses.

f　The statement of total recognised gains and losses is a primary financial statement that enables users to consider all recognised gains and losses of a reporting entity in assessing its overall performance. It, therefore, includes the profit or loss for the period together with all other movements on reserves reflecting recognised gains and losses attributable to shareholders. The statement is not intended to reflect the realisation of gains recognised in previous periods nor does it deal with transfers between reserves, which should continue to be shown in the notes to the financial statements.

g　The reconciliation of movements in shareholders' funds brings together the performance of the period, as shown in the statement of total recognised gains and losses, with all the other changes in shareholders' funds in the period, including capital contributed by or repaid to shareholders.

h　Prior period adjustments should be accounted for by restating the comparative figures for the preceding period in the primary statements and notes and adjusting the opening balance of reserves for the cumulative effect. The cumulative effect of the adjustments should also be noted at the foot of the statement of total recognised gains and losses of the current period. The effect of prior period adjustments on the results for the preceding period should be disclosed where practicable.

i　The accounting practices set out in the FRS should be adopted as soon as possible and regarded as standard in respect of financial statements relating to accounting periods ending on or after 22 June 1993.

Objective

1　The objective of the FRS is to require reporting entities falling within its scope to highlight a range of important components of financial performance to aid users in understanding the performance achieved by a reporting entity in a period and to assist them in forming a basis for their assessment of future results and cash flows.

*****Editor's note:** Paragraph withdrawn by FRS 22. The paragraph referred to calculation and disclosure of earnings per share.*

Definitions

The following definitions apply for the purposes of the FRS *and in particular the statement of standard accounting practice set out in paragraphs 12 to 33.*

Ordinary activities:-   **2**
Any activities which are undertaken by a reporting entity as part of its business and such related activities in which the reporting entity engages in furtherance of, incidental to, or arising from, these activities. Ordinary activities include the effects on the reporting entity of any event in the various environments in which it operates, including the political, regulatory, economic and geographical environments, irrespective of the frequency or unusual nature of the events.

Acquisitions:-   **3**
Operations of the reporting entity that are acquired in the period.

Discontinued operations:-   **4**
Operations of the reporting entity that are sold or terminated and that satisfy all of the following conditions.

(a) The sale or termination is completed either in the period or before the earlier of three months after the commencement of the subsequent period and the date on which the financial statements are approved.
(b) If a termination, the former activities have ceased permanently.
(c) The sale or termination has a material effect on the nature and focus of the reporting entity's operations and represents a material reduction in its operating facilities resulting either from its withdrawal from a particular market (whether class of business or geographical) or from a material reduction in turnover in the reporting entity's continuing markets.
(d) The assets, liabilities, results of operations and activities are clearly distinguishable, physically, operationally and for financial reporting purposes.

Operations not satisfying all these conditions are classified as continuing.

Exceptional items:-   **5**
Material items which derive from events or transactions that fall within the ordinary activities of the reporting entity and which individually or, if of a similar type, in aggregate, need to be disclosed by virtue of their size or incidence if the financial statements are to give a true and fair view.

Extraordinary items:-   **6**
Material items possessing a high degree of abnormality which arise from events or transactions that fall outside the ordinary activities of the reporting entity and which are not expected to recur. They do not include exceptional items nor do they include prior period items merely because they relate to a prior period.

Prior period adjustments:-   **7**
Material adjustments applicable to prior periods arising from changes in accounting policies or from the correction of fundamental errors. They do not include normal recurring adjustments or corrections of accounting estimates made in prior periods.

Total recognised gains and losses:-   **8**
The total of all gains and losses of the reporting entity that are recognised in a period and are attributable to shareholders.

9   *Companies Act 1985:-*
The Companies Act 1985 as amended by the Companies Act 1989.

10   *Companies (Northern Ireland) Order 1986:-*
The Companies (Northern Ireland) Order 1986 as amended by the Companies (Northern Ireland) Order 1990 and the Companies (No. 2) (Northern Ireland) Order 1990.

11   *Companies (Amendment) Act 1986:-*
The Republic of Ireland Companies (Amendment) Act 1986 as amended by the Companies Act 1990 and by the European Communities (Companies: Group Accounts) Regulations 1992 (*the* 1992 *Regulations*).

Statement of Standard Accounting Practice

The statement of standard accounting practice set out in paragraphs 12 to 33 of the FRS *should be read in the context of the Objective of the* FRS *as stated in paragraph 1, the definitions set out in paragraphs 2 to 11 and also of the foreword to Accounting Standards and the Statement of Principles for Financial Reporting currently in issue.*

The Explanation section of the FRS, *set out in paragraphs 35 to 66, shall be regarded as part of the statement of standard accounting practice insofar as it assists in interpreting that statement*

SCOPE

12   The FRS applies to all financial statements intended to give a true and fair view of a reporting entity's financial position and profit or loss (or income and expenditure). Every such reporting entity should apply the requirements of the FRS except to the extent that these requirements are not permitted by the statutory framework (if any) under which the entity reports.

APPLICATION TO SMALLER ENTITIES

12A   Reporting entities applying the Financial Reporting Standard for Smaller Entities currently applicable are exempt from this accounting standard.

PROFIT AND LOSS ACCOUNT

13   All gains and losses recognised in the financial statements for the period should be included in the profit and loss account or the statement of total recognised gains and losses. Gains and losses may be excluded from the profit and loss account only if they are specifically permitted or required to be taken directly to reserves by this or other accounting standards or, in the absence of a relevant accounting standard, by law.

Continuing and discontinued operations

14   The aggregate results of each of continuing operations, acquisitions (as a component of continuing operations) and discontinued operations should be disclosed separately. The results of acquisitions included in continuing operations should not include those that are also discontinued in the same period. The minimum disclosure required down to the operating profit level on the face of the profit and loss account in respect of continuing operations, acquisitions and discontinued operations is the analysis of turnover and operating profit (which for non-financial reporting entities is normally profit before income from shares in group undertakings). The analysis

between continuing operations, acquisitions (as a component of continuing operations) and discontinued operations of each of the other statutory profit and loss account format items between turnover and operating profit should be given by way of note where not shown on the face of the profit and loss account. In those circumstances where a reporting entity presents allocations of interest or tax between continuing and discontinued operations, the method and underlying assumptions used in making the allocations should be disclosed.

Where an acquisition, or a sale or a termination, has a material impact on a major   15
business segment this should be disclosed and explained.

Acquisitions

Where it is not practicable to determine the post-acquisition results of an operation   16
to the end of the current period, an indication should be given of the contribution of the acquisition to the turnover and operating profit of the continuing operations in addition to the information required by the Companies Act 1985*. If an indication of the contribution of an acquisition to the results of the period cannot be given, this fact and the reason should be explained.

Discontinued operations

Only income and costs directly related to discontinued operations should appear   17
under the heading of discontinued operations. Reorganisation or restructuring of continuing operations resulting from a sale or termination should be treated as part of continuing operations.

The consequences of a decision to sell or terminate an operation

If a decision has been made to sell or terminate an operation, any consequential   18
provisions should reflect the extent to which obligations have been incurred that are not expected to be covered by the future profits of the operation. This principle requires that the reporting entity should be demonstrably committed to the sale or termination. This should be evidenced, in the former case, by a binding sale agreement and, in the latter, by a detailed formal plan for termination from which the reporting entity cannot realistically withdraw. The provision should cover only (a) the direct costs of the sale or termination and (b) any operating losses of the operation up to the date of sale or termination, in both cases, after taking into account the aggregate profit, if any, to be recognised in the profit and loss account from the future profits of the operation. Unless the operation qualifies as a discontinued operation in the period under review, the write down of assets and any provisions should appear in the continuing operations category. In the subsequent period when the operation does qualify as discontinued, the provisions should be used to offset the results of the operation in the discontinued category. The related disclosure in that subsequent period, however, should be to show the results of the discontinued operation under each of the statutory format headings with the utilisation of the provision analysed as necessary between the operating loss and the loss on sale or termination of the discontinued operation and disclosed on the face of the profit and loss account immediately below the relevant items.

Companies Act 1985 Schedule 4A paragraph 13. The equivalent reference in Northern Ireland legislation is the Companies (Northern Ireland) Order 1986 Schedule 4A paragraph 13.

The nearest equivalent reference in the Republic of Ireland is the 1992 Regulations section 27 which sets out a general requirement for disclosure in the case of changes in the composition of a group.

Exceptional items

19   All exceptional items, other than those included in the items listed in paragraph 20, should be credited or charged in arriving at the profit or loss on ordinary activities by inclusion under the statutory format headings to which they relate. They should be attributed to continuing or discontinued operations as appropriate. The amount of each exceptional item, either individually or as an aggregate of items of a similar type, should be disclosed separately by way of note, or on the face of the profit and loss account if that degree of prominence is necessary in order to give a true and fair view. An adequate description of each exceptional item should be given to enable its nature to be understood.

20   The following items, including provisions in respect of such items, should be shown separately on the face of the profit and loss account after operating profit and before interest, and included under the appropriate heading of continuing or discontinued operations:

(a)   profits or losses on the sale or termination of an operation;
(b)   costs of a fundamental reorganisation or restructuring having a material effect on the nature and focus of the reporting entity's operations; and
(c)   profits or losses on the disposal of fixed assets. In calculating the profit or loss in respect of the above items consideration should only be given to revenue and costs directly related to the items in question.

When the net amount of (a) or (c) above is not material, but the gross profits or losses are material, the relevant heading should still appear on the face of the profit and loss account with a reference to a related note analysing the profits and losses. Relevant information regarding the effect of these items on the taxation charge and, in the case of consolidated financial statements, any minority interests should both be shown in a note to the profit and loss account. As a minimum the related tax and the minority interest should both be shown in aggregate, but if the effect of the tax and minority interests differs for the various categories of items further information should be given, where practicable, to assist users in assessing the impact of the different items on the net profit or loss attributable to shareholders. The taxation effects of these items are also referred to in paragraphs 23 and 24.

Profit or loss on the disposal of an asset

21   The profit or loss on the disposal of an asset should be accounted for in the profit and loss account of the period in which the disposal occurs as the difference between the net sale proceeds and the net carrying amount, whether carried at historical cost (less any provisions made) or at a valuation.

Extraordinary items

22   Any extraordinary profit or loss should be shown separately on the face of the profit and loss account, after the profit or loss on ordinary activities after taxation but before deducting any appropriations such as dividends paid or payable and, in the case of consolidated financial statements, after the figure for minority interests. The amount of each extraordinary item should be shown individually either on the face of the profit and loss account or in a note and an adequate description of each extraordinary item should be given to enable its nature to be understood. The tax on extraordinary profit or loss and, in the case of consolidated financial statements, the extraordinary profit or loss attributable to minority shareholders should be shown separately as a part of the extraordinary item either on the face of the profit and loss

account or in a note. Any subsequent adjustments to the tax on extraordinary profit or loss in future periods should be shown as an extraordinary item.

Taxation

Any special circumstances that affect the overall tax charge or credit for the period, or that may affect those of future periods, should be disclosed by way of note to the profit and loss account and their individual effects quantified. Such disclosures should include any special circumstances affecting the tax attributable to the items specified in paragraph 20. The effects of a fundamental change in the basis of taxation should be included in the tax charge or credit for the period and separately disclosed on the face of the profit and loss account. **23**

The tax on items of the type listed in paragraph 20 or on an extraordinary profit or loss should be determined by computing the tax on the profit or loss on ordinary activities as if the items did not exist, and comparing this notional tax charge with the tax charge on the profit or loss for the period (after extraordinary items). Any additional tax charge or credit (including deferred tax) arising should be attributed to the items. If there are items in both groups in the same period, the tax on the items combined should be calculated then apportioned between the two groups in relation to their respective amounts, unless a more appropriate basis of apportionment is available. If a more appropriate basis is adopted the method of apportionment should be disclosed. **24**

EARNINGS PER SHARE

[Withdrawn]* **25**

NOTE OF HISTORICAL COST PROFITS AND LOSSES

Where there is a material difference between the result as disclosed in the profit and loss account and the result on an unmodified historical cost basis, a note of the historical cost profit or loss for the period should be presented. Where full historical cost information is unavailable or cannot be obtained without unreasonable expense or delay, the earliest available values should be used. The note of the historical cost profit or loss should include a reconciliation of the reported profit on ordinary activities before taxation to the equivalent historical cost amount and should also show the retained profit for the financial year reported on the historical cost basis. The note should be presented immediately following the profit and loss account or the statement of total recognised gains and losses. **26**

STATEMENT OF TOTAL RECOGNISED GAINS AND LOSSES

A primary statement should be presented, with the same prominence as the other primary statements, showing the total of recognised gains and losses and its components. The components should be the gains and losses that are recognised in the period insofar as they are attributable to shareholders.† **27**

*Editor's note: Paragraph withdrawn by FRS 22.

†*As explained in UITF Abstract 3 and paragraphs 6 and 7 of SSAP 22 'Accounting for Goodwill', the immediate write-off to reserves of purchased goodwill is not a recognised loss. (**Editor's note:** UITF 3 and SSAP 22 have been superseded by FRS 10 'Goodwill and Intangible Assets'.)*

RECONCILIATION OF MOVEMENTS IN SHAREHOLDERS' FUNDS

28   A note should be presented reconciling the opening and closing totals of shareholders' funds of the period.

PRIOR PERIOD ADJUSTMENTS

29   Prior period adjustments should be accounted for by restating the comparative figures for the preceding period in the primary statements and notes and adjusting the opening balance of reserves for the cumulative effect. The cumulative effect of the adjustments should also be noted at the foot of the statement of total recognised gains and losses of the current period. Where practicable, the effect of a prior period adjustment on the results for the preceding period should be disclosed. Where it is not practicable to make this disclosure, that fact, together with the reasons, should be stated.

COMPARATIVE FIGURES

30   Comparative figures should be given for all items in the primary statements and such notes thereto as are required by the FRS. The comparative figures in respect of the profit and loss account should include in the continuing category only the results of those operations included in the current period's continuing operations.

INVESTMENT COMPANIES

31   [Withdrawn]*

INSURANCE BUSINESSES

31A   The requirements of paragraphs 21 and 26 do not apply to the financial statements of insurance companies or insurance groups as defined in companies legislation† for the gains or losses arising on the holding or disposal of investments. Additionally, the requirements of paragraphs 21 and 26 do not apply to consolidated financial statements to the extent they include insurance companies or insurance groups. However, for insurance companies and insurance groups both realised and unrealised gains and losses on investments held as part of their investment portfolios should be included as part of the investment return in the profit and loss account.

DATE FROM WHICH EFFECTIVE

32   The accounting practices set out in the FRS should be adopted as soon as possible and regarded as standard in respect of financial statements relating to accounting periods ending on or after 22 June 1993.‡

Editor's note: Paragraph withdrawn by FRS 25.

†*Companies Act 1985 Section 744 and Section 255a(5).*

   The equivalent legislation in Northern Ireland is the Companies (Northern Ireland) Order 1986 Article 2 and Article 263A(5). The equivalent legislation in the Republic of Ireland is the Companies (Amendment) Act 1986 Section 2(3) and the European Communities (Companies: Group Accounts) Regulations 1992 regulation 6(2)(g).

‡*Editor's note: The amendment to paragraph 31A in June 1999 was effective for financial statements relating to accounting periods ending on or after 23 August 1999.*

WITHDRAWAL OF ssap 6 AND AMENDMENT OF OTHER STATEMENTS

[Not reproduced as all changes have been reflected in the material reproduced in this volume.]

Financial Reporting Standard No. 3 'Reporting Financial Performance' was adopted by a vote of eight of the nine members of the Accounting Standards Board. Mr Bradfield dissented. His dissenting view is set out after the illustrative examples.

Members of the Accounting Standards Board

David Tweedie	(Chairman)
Allan Cook	(Technical Director)
Robert Bradfield	
Sir Bryan Carsberg	
Elwyn Eilledge	
Michael Garner	
Donald Main	
Roger Munson	
Graham Stacy	

Compliance with International Accounting Standards

The requirements of the FRS are consistent with International Accounting Standard 5   **34** 'Information to be Disclosed in Financial Statements'* and International Accounting Standard 8 'Unusual and Prior Period Items and Changes in Accounting Policies'. The FRS is also consistent with the exposure draft of a proposed revised International Accounting Standard—'Extraordinary Items, Fundamental Errors and Changes in Accounting Policies' issued by the International Accounting Standards Committee in July 1992.†

*Editor's note: This was replaced in August 1997 by a revised version of IAS 1, now titled 'Presentation of Financial Statements'.

†Editor's note: A revised version of IAS 8, now titled 'Net profit or loss for the period, fundamental errors and changes in accounting policies', was issued in November 1993.

There are a number of differences between FRS 3 and its various international equivalents.
* *IAS 1 requires a second performance statement, which can either be similar to a statement of total recognised gains and losses or closer to a reconciliation of movements in shareholders' funds;*
* *there is no international equivalent of the requirement to disclose amounts in respect of acquisitions separately, although IAS 27 suggests that this might be useful;*
* *FRS 3 is more specific than IAS 8 when dealing with exceptional items (a term not used in IAS) in terms of allocation to a statutory heading and those items which can be shown after operating profit;*
* *IFRS 5 now deals with the treatment of discontinued operations, on a basis very different to that in FRS 3, with less disclosure and a test based on actual disposal or allocation to a disposal group.*
* *IAS 8 has been revised further, with a new version of the standard brought out in December 2003. This abolishes extraordinary items and treating prior period adjustments in the current year. It also requires prior period adjustments for all material errors, not just fundamental ones. IFRS 5 deals with discontinued operations, and replaces IAS 35. The proposals were published in the UK as FRED 32.*

The current version of IAS 8 is that issued in 2003, and effective since 2005, whilst discontinued operations are now covered by IFRS 5.

Explanation

COMPONENTS OF FINANCIAL PERFORMANCE

35   The many parts of a reporting entity's activities exhibit features which differ in stability, risk and predictability, indicating a need for the separate disclosure of components of financial performance in the profit and loss account and in the statement of total recognised gains and losses. The disclosure of these components is designed to facilitate understanding of the performance achieved in a period and to assist users in deciding on the extent to which past results are useful in helping to assess potential future results. A component, of whatever nature, should be shown separately if it has a special significance for the assessment of some aspect of performance.

36   The total of all recognised gains and losses attributable to shareholders of a reporting entity includes the following components:

(a)   profit or loss before the deduction of dividends;
(b)   adjustments to the valuation of assets; and
(c)   differences in the net investment in foreign enterprises arising from changes in foreign currency exchange rates.

37   The profit and loss account and statement of total recognised gains and losses are intended to present all the entity's gains and losses recognised in a particular period. Profit or loss of a period focuses on what a reporting entity earns for its output (revenue) and what it sacrifices to obtain that output (expenses). Gains and losses may be excluded from the profit and loss account only if they are specifically permitted or required to be taken directly to reserves by this or other accounting standards or, in the absence of a relevant accounting standard, by law. For example, a gain on the revaluation of a fixed asset should be reflected directly in the statement of total recognised gains and losses of the period in which the revaluation takes place. The realisation, or part realisation, of such a gain on the sale of the asset in a subsequent period is not itself a gain of that later period but, rather, confirmation of a gain that had already occurred by the time of the revaluation. Consequently, the gain or loss on the disposal of the asset is to be calculated as the difference between the net sale proceeds and the net carrying amount.

PROFIT AND LOSS ACCOUNT

Continuing and discontinued operations

38   The objective of reporting separately the results of continuing operations, acquisitions (as a component of continuing operations) and discontinued operations is to assist users, first, in assessing the financial performance of these aspects of a reporting entity's operations and, secondly, in forming a basis for the assessment of future income. Separate presentation assists analysis of the significance of the part of a reporting entity's operations that has ceased and of new operations that have been acquired. The various aspects of the definition and requirements regarding discontinued operations are explained in paragraphs 41 to 44. In respect of acquisitions, the requirement is to disclose their post-acquisition results for the period in which the acquisition occurs. In some circumstances it may also be useful to users for the results of acquisitions for the first full financial year for which they are a part of the reporting entity to be disclosed in the notes.

39   The FRS requires each of the statutory profit and loss account headings between turnover and operating profit to be analysed between continuing operations,

acquisitions (as a component of continuing operations) and discontinued operations. For non-financial reporting entities operating profit is normally profit before income from shares in group undertakings, although in certain cases income from associated undertakings or from other participating interests may be considered to be part of operating profit. In order to avoid too much data on the face of the profit and loss account, the minimum disclosure required there in respect of continuing operations, acquisitions and discontinued operations is the analysis of turnover and operating profit. A similar analysis is required between continuing and discontinued operations for the items specifically required to be disclosed by paragraph 20; where practicable this analysis should identify, either on the face of the profit and loss account or in the notes, the amounts arising in respect of acquisitions.

The analysis in respect of continuing operations, acquisitions and discontinued **40** operations is required only to the profit before interest level because interest payable is often a reflection of a reporting entity's overall financing policy, involving both equity and debt funding considerations on a group wide basis, rather than an aggregation of the particular types of finance allocated to individual segments of the reporting entity's operations. Any allocation of interest would involve a considerable degree of subjectivity, that could leave the user uncertain as to the relevance and reliability of the information. If a reporting entity wishes to provide such an allo- cation, the FRS requires that the method and underlying assumptions used in making the allocation be disclosed.

Discontinued operations

The FRS requires operations to be classified as discontinued when the sale or termi- **41** nation is completed either in the period or before the earlier of three months after the commencement of the subsequent period and the date on which the financial statements are approved. Only the results of operations up to the balance sheet date should be included; operations in the subsequent period should be included in the results of that period, separately classified as discontinued if material. Any income and costs associated with a sale or termination that has not been completed are to be included in the continuing category. In some cases it may be appropriate to disclose separately in a note to the profit and loss account the results of operations which although not discontinued are in the process of discontinuing, but they should not be classified as discontinued.

To be included in the category of discontinued operations, a sale or termination must **42** have a material effect on the nature and focus of the reporting entity's operations and represent a material reduction in its operating facilities resulting either from its withdrawal from a particular market (whether class of business or geographical) or from a material reduction in turnover in its continuing markets. The nature and focus of a reporting entity's operations refers to the positioning of its products or services in their markets including the aspects of both quality and location. For example, if a hotel company which had traditionally served the lower end of the hotel market sold its existing chain and bought luxury hotels then, while remaining in the business of managing hotels, the group would be changing the nature and focus of its operations. A similar situation would arise if the same company were to sell its hotels in, say, the United States of America and buy hotels in Europe. The regular sales and replacements of material assets which are undertaken by a reporting entity as part of the routine maintenance of its portfolio of assets should not be classified as dis- continuances and acquisitions. In the example, the sale of hotels and the purchase of others within the same market sector and similar locations would be treated as wholly within continuing operations.

43   To be classified as discontinued a sale or termination should have resulted from a strategic decision by the reporting entity either to withdraw from a particular market (whether class of business or geographical) or to curtail materially its presence in a continuing market (i.e. 'downsizing'). The sale or termination of a component of a reporting entity's operations which is undertaken primarily in order to achieve productivity improvements or other cost savings is a part of that entity's continuing operations and the effects of the sale or termination should be included under that heading.

44   To be classified as discontinued, the assets, liabilities, results of operations and activities of an operation must be clearly distinguishable, physically, operationally and for financial reporting purposes. If the financial results of a sold or terminated operation are not identifiable separately from the accounting records or to a material extent can only be derived through making allocations of income or expenses, then the operation cannot be classified as a discontinued operation. For example, a manufacturing facility that is closed down but which lacks an external market price for its output cannot be classified as a discontinued operation.

The consequences of a decision to sell or terminate an operation

45   Paragraph 18 sets out the principle underlying the establishment of provisions as a consequence of a decision to sell or terminate an operation. This principle focuses on the fact that an obligation arises at the point when the reporting entity becomes demonstrably committed to the sale or termination. Evidence of the commitment might be the public announcement of specific plans, the commencement of implementation, or other circumstances effectively obliging the reporting entity to complete the sale or termination. A binding contract entered into after the balance sheet date may provide additional evidence of asset values and commitments at the balance sheet date. In the case of an intended sale for which no legally binding sale agreement exists, no obligation has been entered into by the reporting entity; accordingly, provisions for the direct costs of the decision to sell and for future operating losses should not be made. In accordance with normal practice, however, any impairments in asset values should be recorded.

Exceptional items

46   Exceptional items are defined in paragraph 5. They are an inherent part of the normal activities of a reporting entity and are included in the computation of profit or loss on ordinary activities but, because of their exceptional size or incidence, require separate disclosure to explain the performance of a period. Exceptional items may arise from a variety of sources and for larger or more complex businesses they are likely to occur in one form or another in most periods. They should not be aggregated on the face of the profit and loss account under one heading of exceptional items but, rather, each should be included within its natural statutory format heading or paragraph 20 category and separately disclosed in accordance with the requirements of paragraphs 19 and 20. The nature of exceptional items makes it necessary to distinguish exceptional profits from exceptional losses, in the notes if not on the face of the profit and loss account. The profits or losses on the disposal of fixed assets in paragraph 20 (c) are not intended to include profits and losses that are in effect no more than marginal adjustments to depreciation previously charged. In any references to profit or loss as including or excluding exceptional items, an explanation should be given of the relevance of their inclusion or exclusion (as the case may be) in the context of considering the results of the period or assessing maintainable earnings.

Exceptional items may occur in either continuing or discontinued operations and **47** need to be identified individually as belonging to one or other category. In showing the amount of each exceptional item, individual items or groups of a similar type of item should not be combined if separately they relate to continuing and to discontinued operations.

Extraordinary items

Extraordinary items are defined in paragraph 6. Extraordinary items should be **48** shown on the face of the profit and loss account before deducting any appropriations such as dividends paid or payable and, in the case of consolidated financial statements, after the figure for minority interests. Extraordinary items are extremely rare as they relate to highly abnormal events or transactions that fall outside the ordinary activities of a reporting entity and which are not expected to recur. In view of the extreme rarity of such items no examples are provided. Items falling into the category of exceptional in accordance with the terms of the FRS cannot, by definition, be extraordinary.

The FRS follows companies legislation in requiring the tax on extraordinary profit or **49** loss and, in the case of consolidated financial statements, the minority shareholders' interest in an extraordinary profit or loss, to be shown separately.

Taxation

Companies legislation requires disclosure in the notes of the details of any special **50** circumstances that affect any liability to taxation, whether for the financial year in question or for future years, and whether in respect of profits, income or capital gains. Such special circumstances could include, for example, the effect on the tax charge of losses whether utilised or carried forward. This disclosure can be useful in understanding the period's charge or credit in respect of taxation, particularly when there are items of the type specified in paragraph 20. It is recognised that analysing an entity's total taxation charge between component parts of its result for a period can involve arbitrary allocations that tend to become less meaningful the more components there are. However, in respect of items such as disposal profits or losses the tax can often be identified with the exceptional item concerned and the relationship between the profit or loss and the attributable tax may be significantly different from that in respect of operating profits or losses. In such circumstances it is relevant to identify the tax charge or credit more specifically. Disclosure of special circumstances can also be useful in assessing likely future amounts of taxation. Therefore, the FRS requires that the notes should not only disclose the existence of any special circumstances but should also quantify their individual effects.

The application of the accounting concept of consistency requires that the tax effects **51** of an extraordinary item should themselves be treated as extraordinary. This principle would apply even where an extraordinary item and its tax effects are recognised in different periods, such as where the tax relief in respect of an extraordinary loss is not recognised until it is utilised in a subsequent period.

EARNINGS PER SHARE

[Withdrawn]* **52**

Editor's note: Paragraph withdrawn by FRS 22.

SEGMENTAL REPORTING

53   It is important for a thorough understanding of the results and financial position of a reporting entity that the impact of changes on material components of the business should be highlighted. To assist in this objective, if an acquisition, a sale or a termination has a material impact on a major business segment the FRS requires that this impact should be disclosed and explained.

NOTE OF HISTORICAL COST PROFITS AND LOSSES

54   The note of historical cost profits and losses is a memorandum item that is an abbreviated restatement of the profit and loss account adjusting the reported profit or loss, if necessary, so as to show it as if no asset revaluations had been made. Adjustments are made for such items as:

(a)   gains recognised in prior periods in the statement of total recognised gains and losses and realised in the current period; for example, the difference between the profit on the disposal of an asset calculated on depreciated historical cost and that calculated on a revalued amount; and

(b)   the difference between an historical cost depreciation charge and the depreciation charge calculated on the revalued amount included in the profit and loss account of the period.

55   Two reasons for disclosing the profit or loss for a period on the unmodified historical cost basis of accounting are commonly cited. The first is, that for as long as discretion exists on the timing or scale of revaluations included in financial statements, the unmodified historical cost basis will give the reported profits or losses of different reporting entities on a more comparable basis. The second is the wish of certain users to assess the profit or loss on sale of assets based on their historical cost, rather than, as the FRS requires, on their revalued carrying amount. In acknowledgement of these concerns, the Board has made the provision of a note of historical cost profits and losses a requirement of the FRS in those circumstances where there is a material difference between the result as disclosed in the profit and loss account and the result on an unmodified historical cost basis. Where full historical cost information is unavailable or cannot be obtained without unreasonable expense or delay, the earliest available values should be used. The note of historical cost profits and losses should be presented immediately following the profit and loss account or the statement of total recognised gains and losses. In consolidated financial statements, the profit and loss account figure for minority interests should be amended for the purposes of this note to reflect the adjustments made where they affect subsidiary companies with a minority interest. For the purpose of paragraph 26 the following are not deemed to be departures from the historical cost convention: (a) adjustments necessarily made to cope with the impact of hyper-inflation on foreign operations and (b) the practice of market makers and other dealers in investments of marking to market where this is an established industry practice.

STATEMENT OF TOTAL RECOGNISED GAINS AND LOSSES

56   The range of important components of financial performance which the FRS requires reporting entities to highlight would often be incomplete if it stopped short at the profit and loss account, since certain gains and losses are specifically permitted or required by law or an accounting standard to be taken directly to reserves. An example is an unrealised gain, such as a revaluation surplus on fixed assets. It is necessary to consider all gains and losses recognised in a period when assessing the financial performance of a reporting entity during that period. Accordingly, the FRS requires, as a primary statement, a statement of total recognised gains and losses to

show the extent to which shareholders' funds have increased or decreased from all the various gains and losses recognised in the period. It follows from this perspective that the same gains and losses should not be recognised twice (for example, a holding gain recognised when a fixed asset is revalued should not be recognised a second time when the revalued asset is sold).

Statements of total recognised gains and losses contribute further to the purposes of financial reporting by: **57**

(a) combining information about operating and related performance with other aspects of a reporting entity's financial performance; and

(b) providing information (jointly with the other primary statements) that is useful for assessing the return on investment in a reporting entity.

If a reporting entity has no recognised gains or losses other than the profit or loss for the period a statement to this effect immediately below the profit and loss account will satisfy the requirement of paragraph 27.

Where there is a material recognised movement between the amount attributable to   **58** different classes of shareholders which does not affect total shareholders' funds an explanatory footnote to the statement may be appropriate. An example might be an appropriation of profit to accrue a premium on redemption of preference shares.

RECONCILIATION OF MOVEMENTS IN SHAREHOLDERS' FUNDS

The profit and loss account and the statement of total recognised gains and losses   **59** reflect the performance of a reporting entity in a period. There are, however, other changes in shareholders' funds that can also be important in understanding the change in the financial position of the entity. The purpose of the reconciliation of movements in shareholders' funds is to highlight those other changes. If included as a primary statement, the reconciliation should be shown separately from the statement of total recognised gains and losses.

PRIOR PERIOD ADJUSTMENTS

The majority of items relating to prior periods arise mainly from the corrections and   **60** adjustments which are the natural result of estimates inherent in accounting and more particularly in the periodic preparation of financial statements. They are dealt with in the profit and loss account of the period in which they are identified and their effect is stated where material. They are not exceptional or extraordinary merely because they relate to a prior period; their nature will determine their classification. Prior period adjustments, that is prior period items which should be adjusted against the opening balance of retained profits or reserves, are rare and limited to items arising from changes in accounting policies or from the correction of fundamental errors.

Estimating future events and their effects requires the exercise of judgement and will   **61** require reappraisal as new events occur, as more experience is acquired or as additional information is obtained. Because a change in estimate arises from new information or developments, it should not be given retrospective effect by a restatement of prior periods. Sometimes a change in estimate may have the appearance of a change of accounting policy and care is necessary to avoid confusing the two.

Where possible, the objective of comparability requires, *inter alia*, that there is   **62** consistency of accounting treatment within each accounting period and from one period to the next. FRS 18 'Accounting policies' requires an entity to adopt those accounting policies that are most appropriate to its particular circumstances. Accordingly, a change in accounting policy will be made only where a new policy is judged more appropriate. Where transactions or events that are clearly different in substance from those previously occurring necessitate the introduction of an accounting policy in circumstances where no policy previously existed, that is not a change in accounting policy. Following a change in accounting policy, the amounts for the current and corresponding periods should be restated on the basis of the new policies. The cumulative adjustments should also be noted at the foot of the statement of total recognised gains and losses of the current period and included in the reconciliation of movements in shareholders' funds of the corresponding period in order to highlight for users the effect of the adjustments.

63   In exceptional circumstances it may be found that financial statements of prior periods have been issued containing errors which are of such significance as to destroy the true and fair view and hence the validity of those financial statements. The corrections of such fundamental errors and the cumulative adjustments applicable to prior periods have no bearing on the results of the current period and they are therefore not included in arriving at the profit or loss for the current period. They are accounted for by restating prior periods, with the result that the opening balance of retained profits will be adjusted accordingly, and highlighted in the reconciliation of movements in shareholders' funds. As the cumulative adjustments are recognised in the current period, they should also be noted at the foot of the statement of total recognised gains and losses of the current period.

COMPARATIVE FIGURES

64   Comparative figures should be given for all items in the primary statements and such notes thereto as are required by the FRS. To aid comparison, the comparative figures in respect of the profit and loss account should be based on the status of an operation in the financial statements of the period under review and should, therefore, include in the continuing category only the results of those operations included in the current period's continuing operations. The comparative figures appearing under the heading 'continuing operations' may include figures which were shown under the heading of acquisitions in that previous period; no reference need be made to the results of those acquisitions, since they are not required to be presented separately in the current year. Where, however, information on acquisitions is provided voluntarily in respect of the first full year, it may be helpful to provide comparative figures for those acquisitions. Similarly, the comparative figures for discontinued operations will include both amounts relating to operations discontinued in the previous period and amounts relating to operations discontinued in the period under review, which in the previous period would have been included as part of continuing operations. The analysis of comparative figures between continuing and discontinued operations is not required on the face of the profit and loss account.

INVESTMENT COMPANIES

65   [Withdrawn]*

66   [Withdrawn]*

Editor's note: Paragraphs withdrawn by FRS 25.

Note on legal requirements

GREAT BRITAIN

General

The requirements of Schedules 4 and 4A to the Companies Act 1985* relating to the   **67**
form and content of company and group financial statements set out formats for the
profit and loss account allowing some flexibility in certain circumstances in the
manner in which the information is presented. The provisions of the FRS supplement
those legal requirements, while remaining within their bounds.

Disclosure

Companies Act 1985 Schedule 4 paragraph 54   **68**

'(1) The basis on which the charge for United Kingdom corporation tax and
United Kingdom income tax is computed shall be stated†.
(2) Particulars shall be given of any special circumstances which affect liability
in respect of taxation of profits, income or capital gains for the financial year or
liability in respect of taxation of profits, income or capital gains for succeeding
financial years.'

Companies Act 1985 Schedule 4A paragraph 13   **69**

'(1) The following information with respect to acquisitions taking place in the
financial year shall be given in a note to the accounts.'
'(4) The profit or loss of the undertaking or group acquired shall be stated—
(a)   for the period from the beginning of the financial year of the undertaking
      or, as the case may be, of the parent undertaking of the group, up to the
      date of the acquisition, and
(b)   for the previous financial year of that undertaking or parent undertaking;

and there shall also be stated the date on which the financial year referred to in
paragraph (a) began.'‡

Companies Act 1985 Schedule 4A paragraphs 15 and 16   **70**

'15 Where during the financial year there has been a disposal of an undertaking
or group which significantly affects the figures shown in the group accounts,
there shall be stated in a note to the accounts—
(a)   the name of that undertaking or, as the case may be, of the parent
      undertaking of that group, and
(b)   the extent to which the profit or loss shown in the group accounts is
      attributable to profit or loss of that undertaking or group.
16 The information required by paragraph 13, or . . . 15 above need not be
disclosed with respect to an undertaking which—

*The requirements relating to banking and insurance companies and groups are set out in Schedule 9 to the
Companies Act 1985. [Editor's note: Insurance companies are now Schedule 9A. Small companies are covered by
Schedule 8.]

†Editor's note: Paragraph 54(1) was repealed February 1996.

‡Editor's note: Paragraph 13(4) was repealed February 1996.

(a)   is established under the law of a country outside the United Kingdom, or
(b)   carries on business outside the United Kingdom,

if in the opinion of the directors of the parent company the disclosure would be seriously prejudicial to the business of that undertaking or to the business of the parent company or any of its subsidiary undertakings and the Secretary of State agrees that the information should not be disclosed.'

Definition

71   Companies Act 1985 section 266

'(1) In section 265 "investment company" means a public company which has given notice in the prescribed form (which has not been revoked) to the registrar of companies of its intention to carry on business as an investment company, and has since the date of that notice complied with the requirements specified below.
(2) Those requirements are—
(a)   that the business of the company consists of investing its funds mainly in securities, with the aim of spreading investment risk and giving members of the company the benefit of the results of the management of its funds,
(b)   that none of the company's holdings in companies (other than those which are for the time being in investment companies) represents more than 15 per cent. by value of the investing company's investments,
(c)   that distribution of the company's capital profits is prohibited by its memorandum or articles of association,
(d)   that the company has not retained, otherwise than in compliance with this Part, in respect of any accounting reference period more than 15 per cent. of the income it derives from securities.'

NORTHERN IRELAND

72   Schedules 4 and 4A of the Companies (Northern Ireland) Order 1986 are similar to Schedules 4 and 4A of the Companies Act 1985 as referred to in paragraph 67.

73   Paragraph 54 of Schedule 4 of the Companies (Northern Ireland) Order 1986 is similar to paragraph 54 of Schedule 4 of the Companies Act 1985 as set out in paragraph 68.

74   Paragraphs 13, 15 and 16 of Schedule 4A of the Companies (Northern Ireland) Order 1986 are similar to paragraphs 13, 15 and 16 of Schedule 4A of the Companies Act 1985 as set out in paragraphs 69 and 70.

75   Article 274 of the Companies (Northern Ireland) Order 1986 is similar to section 266 of the Companies Act 1985 as set out in paragraph 71.

REPUBLIC OF IRELAND

76   The Schedule of the Companies (Amendment) Act 1986 is similar to Schedule 4 of the Companies Act 1985 as referred to paragraph 67.

77   Paragraph 40 of the Schedule of the Companies (Amendment) Act 1986 is similar to paragraph 54 of Schedule 4 of the Companies Act 1985 as set out in paragraph 68.

Section 27 of the 1992 Regulations sets out a general requirement for disclosure in **78** the case of changes in the composition of a group. There are no specific equivalents to paragraphs 13(4) 15 and 16 of Schedule 4A of the Companies Act 1985 as set out in paragraphs 69 and 70.

Section 47 of the Companies (Amendment) Act 1983 is similar to section 266 of the **79** Companies Act 1985 as set out in paragraph 71.

Illustrative examples

These illustrative examples are for general guidance and do not form part of the Financial Reporting Standard. The best form of the disclosure will depend on individual circumstances.

The example on pages 400 to 404 includes two profit and loss accounts along with a statement of total recognised gains and losses, a note of historical cost profits and losses, a reconciliation of movements in shareholders' funds and certain related notes. The following matters should also be noted:

The entity is a group of companies.

The group has made acquisitions and disposals of operations during the year under review.

In this example there is no extraordinary item. However, the positioning of such an item on the face of the profit and loss account is shown although in practice the caption would not appear if no extraordinary items existed.

The profit and loss account examples include the disclosure of earnings per share numbers and a pro forma reconciliation statement for adjusted earnings per share numbers is also shown.

The profit and loss account examples have been prepared using Format 1* as contained in Schedule 4 of the Companies Act 1985. Equivalent information should be shown if any of the other statutory formats are used.

The example on page 405 is one of a Companies Act investment company.

---

*The equivalent legislation in Northern Ireland is Format 1 in Schedule 4 of the Companies (Northern Ireland) Order 1986.

The equivalent legislation in the Republic of Ireland is Format 1 in the Schedule to the Companies (Amendment) Act 1983.

Profit and loss account example 1

	1993 £million	1993 £million	1992 as restated £million
Turnover			
Continuing operations	550		500
Acquisitions	50		
	600		
Discontinued operations	175		190
		775	690
Cost of sales		(620)	(555)
Gross profit		155	135
Net operating expenses		(104)	(83)
Operating profit			
Continuing operations	50		40
Acquisitions	6		
	56		
Discontinued operations	(15)		12
Less 1992 provision	10		
		51	52
Profit on sale of properties in continuing operations		9	6
Provision for loss on operations to be discontinued			(30)
Loss on disposal of discontinued operations	(17)		
Less 1992 provision	20		
		3	
Profit on ordinary activities before interest		63	28
Interest payable		(18)	(15)
Profit on ordinary activities before taxation		45	13
Tax on profit on ordinary activities		(14)	(4)
Profit on ordinary activities after taxation		31	9
Minority interests		(2)	(2)
[Profit before extraordinary items]		29	7
[Extraordinary items] (included only to show positioning)		–	–
Profit for the financial year		29	7
Dividends		(8)	(1)
Retained profit for the financial year		21	6*

*Editor's note: Example of disclosure of earnings per share withdrawn by FRS 22.

Profit and loss example 2

	Continuing operations	Acquisitions	Discontinued operations	Total	Total
	1993	1993	1993	1993	1992 as restated
	£million	*£million*	*£million*	*£million*	*£million*
Turnover	550	50	175	775	690
Cost of sales	(415)	(40)	(165)	(620)	(555)
Gross profit	135	10	10	155	135
Net operating expenses	(85)	(4)	(25)	(114)	(83)
Less 1992 provision			10	10	
Operating profit	50	6	(5)	51	52
Profit on sale of properties	9			9	6
Provision for loss on operations to be discontinued					(30)
Loss on disposal of discontinued operations			(17)	(17)	
Less 1992 provision			20	20	
Profit on ordinary activities before interest	59	6	(2)	63	28
Interest payable				(18)	(15)
Profit on ordinary activities before taxation				45	13
Tax on profit on ordinary activities				(14)	(4)
Profit on ordinary activities after taxation				31	9
Minority interests				(2)	(2)
[Profit before extraordinary items]				29	7
[Extraordinary items] (included only to show positioning)				–	–
Profit for the financial year				29	7
Dividends				(8)	(1)
Retained profit for the financial year				21	6*

Editor's note: Example of disclosure of earnings per share withdrawn by FRS 22.

Statement of total recognised gains and losses

	1993 £million	1992 as restated £million
Profit for the financial year	29	7
Unrealised surplus on revaluation of properties	4	6
Unrealised (loss)/gain on trade investment	(3)	7
	30	20
Currency translation differences on foreign currency net investments	(2)	5
Total recognised gains and losses relating to the year	28	25
Prior year adjustment (as explained in note x)	(10)	
Total gains and losses recognised since last annual report	18	

Note of historical cost profits and losses

	1993 £million	1992 as restated £million
Reported profit on ordinary activities before taxation	45	13
Realisation of property revaluation gains of previous years	9	10
Difference between a historical cost depreciation charge and the actual depreciation charge of the year calculated on the revalued amount	5	4
Historical cost profit on ordinary activities before taxation	59	27
Historical cost profit for the year retained after taxation, minority interests, extraordinary items and dividends	35	20

Notes to the financial statements

Note required in respect of profit and loss account example 1

| | 1993 | | | 1992 (as restated) | | |
	Continuing	Discontinued	Total	Continuing	Discontinued	Total
	£million	£million	£million	£million	£million	£million
Cost of sales	455	165	620	385	170	555
Net operating expenses						
Distribution costs	56	13	69	46	5	51
Administrative expenses	41	12	53	34	3	37
Other operating income	(8)	0	(8)	(5)	0	(5)
	89	25	114	75	8	83
Less 1992 provision	0	(10)	(10)			
	89	15	104			

The total figures for continuing operations in 1993 include the following amounts relating to acquisitions: cost of sales £40 million and net operating expenses £4 million (namely distribution costs £3 million, administrative expenses £3 million and other operating income £2 million).

Note required in respect of profit and loss account example 2

| | 1993 | | | 1992 | | |
	Continuing	Discontinued	Total	Continuing	Discontinued	Total
	£million	£million	£million	£million	£million	£million
Turnover				500	190	690
Cost of sales				385	170	555
Net operating expenses						
Distribution costs	56	13	69	46	5	51
Administrative expenses	41	12	53	34	3	37
Other operating income	(8)	0	(8)	(5)	0	(5)
	89	25	114	75	8	83
Operating profit				40	12	52

The total figure of net operating expenses for continuing operations in 1993 includes £4 million in respect of acquisitions (namely distribution costs £3 million, administrative expenses £3 million and other operating income £2 million).

Reconciliation of movements in shareholders' funds

	1993	1992 as restated
	£million	£million
Profit for the financial year	29	7
Dividends	(8)	(1)
	21	6
Other recognised gains and losses relating to the year (net)	(1)	18
New share capital subscribed	20	1
Goodwill written-off*	(25)	
Net addition to shareholders' funds	15	25
Opening shareholders' funds (originally £375 million before deducting prior year adjustment of £10 million)	365	340
Closing shareholders' funds	380	365

Reserves

	Share premium account	Revaluation reserve	Profit and loss account	Total
	£million	£million	£million	£million
At beginning of year as previously stated	44	200	120	364
Prior year adjustment			(10)	(10)
At beginning of year as restated	44	200	110	354
Premium on issue of shares (nominal) value £7 million)	13			13
Goodwill written-off*			(25)	(25)
Transfer from profit and loss account of the year			21	21
Transfer of realised profits		(14)	14	0
Decrease in value of trade investment		(3)		(3)
Currency translation differences on foreign currency net investments			(2)	(2)
Surplus on property revaluations		4		4
At end of year	57	187	118	362

Note: Nominal share capital at end of year £18million (1992 £11 million).

*****Editor's note:** FRS 10 does not now permit goodwill to be written off directly to reserves, but it did not require prior year figures (such as 1993) to be restated.*

Companies Act investment company*

Profit and loss account

	1993 £million	1992 £million
Revenue	35	30
Expenses	(11)	(10)
	24	20
Interest payable	(5)	(7)
Profit on ordinary activities before taxation	19	13
Tax on profit on ordinary activities	(4)	(3)
Profit on ordinary activities after taxation	15	10
Minority interests	(1)	(1)
Profit available for distribution	14	9
Dividends	(13)	(8)
Transfer to revenue reserves	1	1

Statement of total recognised gains and losses

	1993 £million	1992 £million
Capital profit on investments		
Realised gains and losses	52	70
Unrealised gains and losses	138	75
	190	145
Tax	(16)	(22)
Minority interest	(1)	(4)
Unrealised surplus on revaluation of tangible fixed assets	4	2
Capital surplus for the year	177	121
Revenue profit available for distribution	14	9
Total recognised gains and losses for the year	191	130
Distributable profits		
Revenue profit available for distribution	14	9
Dividends	(13)	(8)
Transfer to distributable reserves	1	1
Non-distributable profits		
Transfer to non-distributable reserves	177	121
	178	122

---

*Editor's note: This example was not removed by FRS 25, although all references to investment companies in the main text of FRS 3 were removed by that standard.

Dissenting view

Mr Bradfield dissents from the FRS because he fears that it could frequently produce misleading measures of performance. He notes that it emphasises the components of pre-tax profit, which are now to include the results of business disposals. Shareholders will attach a different level of significance to each of these components – profits from trading being the most important in assessing the underlying performance. However, the FRS ignores, so far as the face of the profit and loss account is concerned, the often material impact in the eyes of shareholders of tax, minority interests and the issue of further shares on each of these components. Here, he believes, the FRS meets neither its own objective nor the intent of many passages in the Board's Statement of Principles.

Under the FRS, the results from trading and business disposals are shown as separate components of profit before tax but are combined thereafter. Information on the tax and minority interests relating to disposals is required, where practicable, to be given in the notes. However, there is no requirement to identify the disposals component of 'profit before tax', 'profit after tax and minorities' or 'earnings per share'. Under SSAP 6, which the FRS replaces, business disposal profits were excluded from all these measures.

Business disposal profits reflect internally generated goodwill often accrued over many years, together with an element of inflation; they are different in kind from the trading results of the year. Pending realisation, they constitute a hidden reserve. They may attract little tax and rarely contain a minority interest. By contrast, Mr Bradfield notes, it is the magnitude and quality of the earnings from trading, after tax and minority interests, that are the focus of attention for the shareholder as he uses the financial statements to assess the continuity of the source of dividends.

Mr Bradfield believes it imperative that users should clearly see the effects of tax and minorities on trading results attributable to shareholders. If, in an international group of companies, the pre-tax trading profits in a low tax regime were to fall and those in a high tax regime were to rise by an identical amount, the shareholder would be materially worse off. SSAP 6 clearly displayed this decline; the FRS serves only to mask it.

Mr Bradfield notes that increasing tax and minority interests can convert an improvement in trading profit, from one year to the next, into a decline in profit attributable to shareholders. Also, where both disposal profits and losses arise, a modest pre-tax result from disposals can be transformed into a substantial after-tax result. Superimposing these elements of profit, as opposed to displaying them separately, may create a reassuring facade which will hide the underlying trend from many users of accounts. If, in addition, there has been a rights issue or an acquisition for shares, users will be left without a single indicator of whether the entity has done well or badly. SSAP 6, when faithfully applied, coped with all these situations.

In Mr Bradfield's view, such outcomes conflict with many of the qualities of financial statements referred to in chapter 2 of the draft Statement of Principles ('The Objective of Financial Statements and Qualitative Characteristics of Financial Information'). These qualities include:

> 'comparability', whereby 'users must be able to compare the financial statements of an enterprise over time to identify trends in its financial . . . performance' (paragraph 34); and 'understandability', whereby information should be 'readily understandable by users' (paragraph 38).

Furthermore, Mr Bradfield believes that the main sub-totals from 'profit before taxation on ordinary activities' downwards impart no useful information to the user. They therefore conflict with the twin primary characteristics of 'relevance' (paragraph 23) and 'reliability' (paragraph 26); in the latter case because of failure to 'represent faithfully the effect of the transactions and other events' (paragraph 28). Mr Bradfield therefore believes that the FRS will fail to meet the reasonable expectations of users of financial statements.

Mr Bradfield has suggested some alternative routes for the FRS. One would require each of the headings 'profit before tax', 'profit after tax and minorities' and 'earnings per share' to be analysed into two parts: one from trading and one from disposals. This remains an option open to preparers. He believes that it would enable individual profit and loss accounts, five year summaries and summary financial statements to present helpful and realistic pictures that accord with users' expectations of financial reporting.

The development of the Standard

GENERAL

i   SSAP 6, which is superseded by FRS 3, was originally issued in 1974 and was based on the 'all-inclusive' concept of profit. It was revised as recently as 1986, but, in spite of a number of improvements that were included, there remained significant problems with its interpretation in practice, particularly in respect of the variety of treatments of apparently similar events as either ordinary or extraordinary items in the profit and loss account. The 1986 revision had not achieved the objective of narrowing the differences and variety of accounting practice in this area and calls for change had been heard from users of financial statements as well as from many preparers and auditors involved with the problem.

ii   The Board responded by proposing a major change to the presentation of financial performance both in the profit and loss account itself and for items passing through reserves. Its initial proposals were issued in a discussion draft in April 1991 and these were developed in Financial Reporting Exposure Draft 1 'The Structure of Financial Statements – Reporting of Financial Performance' (FRED 1) published in December 1991.

iii   The FRS has retained the essential features of FRED 1, in particular the shift of emphasis from a single performance indicator. The Board believes that the performance of complex organisations cannot be summarised in a single number and has therefore adopted an 'information set' approach that highlights a range of important components of performance. This approach inevitably means that financial statements will sometimes appear more complex than under the former standard. However, it is widely accepted that certain totals in the profit and loss account, such as profit before tax and earnings per share, have been used too simplistically and have obscured the significance of relevant underlying components of financial performance. The presentation and disclosure requirements of the FRS should provide a framework which will facilitate the analysis and interpretation of the various aspects of performance.

iv   Under the previous SSAP 6 approach, the inconsistencies underlying earnings per share (calculated before extraordinary items) were not clearly evident to users of financial statements and automatic reliance was often placed on the resultant numbers without there being sufficient awareness of the subjective judgements of the preparers in what was included or excluded. In future earnings per share will be all-inclusive with the result that significant variations from one period to another or the absence of expected variations, whatever the cause, will demand some explanation. Earnings per share will tend to be more volatile than under SSAP 6, because, for example, they will include all business disposal profits and losses, but, as indicated above, there was, in any event, significant inconsistency in how SSAP 6 was applied in practice. Moreover, the FRS permits preparers of financial statements to present additional versions of earnings per share provided that (a) the assumptions on which they are based are explicitly disclosed, (b) the reasons for presenting the additional versions are explained and (c) there is consistency in the approach adopted. It is recognised that users may develop methods to calculate and publish an adjusted earnings per share of individual reporting entities on the basis of an independent assessment of financial statements. The FRS should facilitate such assessments by requiring the provision of a range of relevant information.

v   It will be for users to identify particular components that they consider of significance in varying circumstances. This is a feature of the information set approach. For the reasons stated above, it will not be appropriate under FRS 3 (any more than it was in practice under SSAP 6) for users to pay particular attention to any 'headline' number on the face of the profit and loss account or statement of total recognised gains and losses without considering the number's composition. Using the information required by the FRS either on the face of the financial statements or in the notes, users should adapt any headline number to give the performance measure required. The Board considers that the FRS is an important step forward in providing the requisite information to users in a form designed to assist a more mature understanding and analysis of financial performance. Where summarised or highlighted information is presented, (such as a preliminary announcement) it will be the responsibility of the presenters of such information to emphasise the particular components of performance which are of significance in their specific circumstances.

PRINCIPAL CHANGES FROM FRED 1

The consequences of a decision to sell or terminate an operation

FRED 1 did not address the making of provisions in respect of operations that are to be discontinued in future periods. In response to comments received, this issue has been addressed in the FRS.
     vi

Exceptional items

In the light of the proposed severe restrictions on what should be categorised as extraordinary, FRED 1 proposed that a material profit or loss on the sale or termination of an operation should always be shown on the face of the profit and loss account. The FRS has extended this disclosure to two other items – costs of a fundamental reorganisation or restructuring having a material effect on the nature and focus of the reporting entity's operations and profits or losses on the disposal of fixed assets. FRED 1 also proposed that the tax and minority interest attributable to a profit or loss on sale or termination should be shown in a note. In view of the additional items required to be shown on the face of the profit and loss account by the FRS, the Board has given further thought to the question of attributable tax and minority interests and has added paragraphs requiring as a minimum that the aggregate tax and minority interest related to these three items should be disclosed. Preparers should provide further information, where practicable and relevant, identifying the tax and minority interest related to individual categories of these items, in order to assist users in assessing the impact of individual items on the net profit or loss attributable to shareholders.
     vii

A concern was expressed by respondents to FRED 1 about exceptional items and the prominence they were to be given. In summary, the view was that exceptional items should not be transferred to a single heading of 'exceptional', because profit before exceptional items could then become the focus of financial statement presentations, with the implication that no exceptional items are expected in the future. To meet this concern the FRS requires all exceptional items (other than three specific types of item) to be included in the income or expense heading to which they relate.
     viii

Revenue investment (discretionary expenditure)

The discussion draft introduced the concept of discretionary expenditure. Users of financial statements had encouraged the Board to require disclosure of expenses that are incurred largely for the benefit of future periods and that can therefore be varied by material amounts without affecting current revenues. The draft sought to do this by including a definition along these lines and amplifying it by reference to common
     ix

examples of such expenses, viz., research and development expense, training, advertising and major maintenance.

x   In FRED 1 the concept of discretionary expenditure was developed and in the process the name 'discretionary expenditure' was changed to 'revenue investment'. More detailed guidance was given as to what should be included under this heading and a minimum disclosure requirement was proposed. This was for the disclosure, where material, of the charges to the profit and loss account of the period in respect of research and development, training, advertising and major maintenance and refurbishment. A requirement for an explanation of all material changes between the current and prior period in the level of revenue investment was also proposed.

xi   These revenue investment proposals failed to attract support in the context of the proposed accounting standard, and the Board therefore concluded that they should not be pursued by that means. The Board remains of the view that appropriate disclosures of this kind can be of assistance to users of financial statements but in the light of the responses to FRED 1 concluded that the concept can best be developed within the Board's proposals for an Operating and Financial Review to support a company's annual report – i.e. as part of a wider discussion of a company's performance.* The Board's decision on the FRED 1 proposal on revenue investment does not in any way affect the existing requirements of SSAP 13 – 'Accounting for research and development' and the Companies Act 1985 regarding the disclosure of research and development activities.

Reconciliation of movements in shareholders' funds

xii   Several respondents to FRED 1, in commenting on the statement of total recognised gains and losses, suggested it should be extended to provide a complete reconciliation of the movements in shareholders' funds. The Board agreed that changes in shareholders' funds other than those included in the statement of total recognised gains and losses can also be important in understanding the change in the financial position of a reporting entity and concluded that this additional information should be required in a reconciliation of movements in shareholders' funds. In order not to divert attention from the components of performance of the total of recognised gains and losses for the period, it specified that if included as a primary statement, the reconciliation should be shown separately from the statement of total recognised gains and losses.

Editor's note: See paragraphs 16 to 18 of the ASB Statement 'Operating and financial review'.

Financial Reporting Standard 4 is set out in paragraphs 1–67.

The Statement of Standard Accounting Practice set out in paragraphs 18–67 should be read in the context of the Objective as stated in paragraph 1 and the definitions set out in paragraphs 2–17 and also of the Foreword to Accounting Standards and the Statement of Principles for Financial Reporting currently in issue.

The Application Notes specify how some of the requirements of FRS 4 are to be applied to transactions that have certain features.

The Explanation set out in paragraphs 68–102 and the Application Notes shall be regarded as part of the Statement of Standard Accounting Practice insofar as they assist in interpreting that statement.

Appendix III 'The development of the FRS' reviews considerations and arguments that were thought significant by members of the Board in reaching the conclusions on FRS 4. The Board adopted the FRS on the basis of the overall considerations; individual members gave greater weight to some factors than to others.

[FRS 4]
Capital instruments*

(Issued December 1993)

Contents

Application notes

Adoption of FRS 4 by the Board

---

*Editor's note: FRS 4 has been substantially amended by FRS 25, with effect for accounting periods beginning on or after 1 January 2005. Given the number of changes, specific reference has not been made in the notes to the withdrawal of specific paragraphs of the standard. Reference has been made to paragraphs amended by FRS 25. The contents list has not been amended.

Those parts of FRS 4 which remain are applicable only to companies which are not complying with FRS 26, as explained in paragraph 18 of FRS 4.

Appendix I – Note on legal requirements

Appendix II – Compliance with international accounting standards

Appendix III – The development of the FRS

Capital instruments

Summary

[Withdrawn]

Objective

1   The objective of this FRS is to ensure that costs associated with capital instruments that are classified as liabilities are allocated to accounting periods on a fair basis over the period the instrument is in issue; and that the financial statements provide relevant information concerning the nature and amount of the entity's source of finance.*

Definitions

The following definitions shall apply in this FRS and in particular in the Statement of Standard Accounting Practice set out in paragraphs 18-67.

2   *Capital instruments:-*
All instruments that are issued by reporting entities as a means of raising finance, including shares, debentures, loans and debt instruments, options and warrants that give the holder the right to subscribe for or obtain capital instruments. In the case of consolidated financial statements the term includes capital instruments issued by subsidiaries except those that are held by another member of the group included in the consolidation.

3-5   [Deleted]

6   *Debt:-*
Capital instruments that are classified as liabilities.

7   [Deleted]

8   *Finance costs:-*
The difference between the net proceeds of an instrument and the total amount of the payments (or other transfers of economic benefits) that the issuer may be required to make in respect of the instrument.

9   [Deleted]

10   *Issue costs:-*
The costs that are incurred directly in connection with the issue of a capital instrument, that is, those costs that would not have been incurred had the specific instrument in question not been issued.

11   *Net proceeds:-*
The fair value of the consideration received on the issue of a capital instrument after deduction of issue costs.

Editor's note: Amended by FRS 25.

[Deleted]   **12-15**

Term (of a capital instrument):-   **16**
The period from the date of issue of the capital instrument to the date at which it will
expire, be redeemed, or be cancelled.

If either party has the option to require the instrument to be redeemed or cancelled
and, under the terms of the instrument, it is uncertain whether such an option will be
exercised, the term should be taken to end on the earliest date at which the instrument would be redeemed or cancelled on exercise of such an option.

If either party has the right to extend the period of an instrument, the term should
not include the period of the extension if there is a genuine commercial possibility
that the period will not be extended.

[Deleted]   **17**

Statement of standard accounting practice

SCOPE

Financial Reporting Standard 4 applies to all financial statements intended to give a   **18**
true and fair view of a reporting entity's financial position and profit or loss (or
income and expenditure) for a period, but does not apply to entities applying FRS 26
(IAS 39) 'Financial Instruments: Measurement'. The terminology used in this
statement will be appropriate for those reporting entities that are companies. Entities
other than companies should adapt the terminology as appropriate.*

The FRS applies to accounting for capital instruments by entities that issue them. It   **19**
does not address accounting for investments in capital instruments issued by other
entities.

The scope of the FRS includes capital instruments denominated in a foreign cur-   **20**
rency. However, the FRS does not address the translation of foreign currency
amounts relating to such instruments into the reporting currency or the accounting
for foreign exchange differences arising from such translations.

The requirements of the FRS apply to all capital instruments with the following   **21**
exceptions:

(a)   warrants issued to employees under employee share schemes;
(b)   leases, which should be accounted for in accordance with SSAP 21;
(c)   equity shares issued as part of a business combination that is accounted for as a
      merger.

In applying the requirements of the FRS, capital instruments that are issued at the   **22**
same time in a composite transaction should be considered together. They should be
accounted for as a single instrument unless they are capable of being transferred,
cancelled or redeemed independently of each other.

Editor's note: Amended by FRS 25.

APPLICATION TO SMALLER ENTITIES

22a   Reporting entities applying the Financial Reporting Standard for Smaller Entities currently applicable are exempt from this accounting standard.

23-26   [Deleted]

DEBT

Carrying amount and allocation of finance costs

27   Immediately after issue, debt should be stated at the amount of the net proceeds.

28   The finance costs of debt should be allocated to periods over the term of the debt at a constant rate on the carrying amount. All finance costs should be charged in the profit and loss account, except in the case of investment companies, which are addressed in paragraph 52.

29   The carrying amount of debt should be increased by the finance cost in respect of the reporting period and reduced by payments made in respect of the debt in that period.

30   Accrued finance costs may be included in accruals rather than in the carrying amount of debt to the extent that the finance costs have accrued in one accounting period and will be paid in cash in the next. Any such accrual should be included in the carrying amount of the debt for the purposes of calculating finance costs and gains and losses arising on repurchase or early settlement.

31   Where the amount of payments required by a debt instrument is contingent on uncertain future events such as changes in an index, those events should be taken into account in the calculation of the finance costs and the carrying amount once they have occurred.

Repurchase of debt

32   Gains and losses arising on the repurchase or early settlement of debt should be recognised in the profit and loss account in the period during which the repurchase or early settlement is made.

33-67   [Deleted]

Explanation

CAPITAL INSTRUMENTS

68   The definition of capital instruments, given in paragraph 2, includes all kinds of shares and debt instruments as well as options and warrants to obtain such instruments. It characterises capital instruments as a means of raising finance: an instrument may be within the definition whether or not the consideration given for its issue takes the form of cash. Capital instruments may take the form of contracts between two parties (for example a borrower and its bank) as well as an issue of transferable securities.

IDENTIFICATION OF DISTINCT CAPITAL INSTRUMENTS

In order to apply the requirements of the FRS it is necessary to determine whether **69** instruments issued at the same time should be accounted for individually or not. Accounting for the individual instruments is required by paragraph 22 if (and only if) the instruments are capable of being transferred, cancelled or redeemed independently of each other. For example, if debt and warrants are issued simultaneously and the warrants can be transferred, cancelled or redeemed independently of the debt, the two components should be accounted for separately. It would be necessary in such a case to apportion the proceeds of the issue to each component.

[Deleted]   **70-72**

THE TERM OF DEBT

The FRS requires debt to be accounted for by allocating finance costs over the term **73** of the instrument at a constant rate. The term of the instrument is usually self-evident but where either party has the option to extend the term, or to require the instrument to be redeemed early, such options should be carefully evaluated. If there is an option for early redemption, the term should be taken to end on the earliest date the option could be exercised, unless there is no genuine commercial possibility that the option will be exercised. The term should not include any period for which the instrument might be extended unless such an extension is virtually certain at the time the instrument is issued: that is, there is no genuine commercial possibility that the period will not be extended.*

In evaluating the commercial possibilities of options, it should be assumed that the **74** parties will act in accordance with their economic interests. A severe deterioration in the creditworthiness of the issuer should not be anticipated, but should be taken into account when it occurs. For example, in the case of a zero coupon bond, the return to the lender consists entirely of the amount received at maturity. If the lender under such an instrument had the right to require early redemption, but on exercise of that right he would receive only the original issue price, it would be unrealistic to assume that he would exercise it unless the issuer's creditworthiness deteriorated to a significant extent. The term of such a bond would therefore normally be taken to extend to its final maturity.

FINANCE COSTS

The FRS requires finance costs to be recognised at a constant rate on the carrying **75** amount of debt. In some instances the nominal yield on the debt will not be materially different from the amount required by the FRS to be recognised and in these circumstances calculations will not be necessary in order to derive the information required by the FRS.

The FRS also requires all finance costs to be charged in the profit and loss account. **76** However, the FRS does not prohibit the capitalisation of finance costs as part of the cost of an asset by way of a simultaneous transfer from the profit and loss account that is separately disclosed.

[Deleted]   **77-91**

Editor's note: Reference to non-equity interests removed by FRS 25.

ISSUE COSTS

92   The FRS requires issue costs, as defined, to be accounted for as a reduction in the proceeds of a capital instrument. Such costs are not assets as defined in the Board's draft Statement of Principles because they do not provide access to any future economic benefits.

93   [Deleted]

94   In the case of most debt instruments, the issuer has the use of funds during the life of the instrument, and in return pays interest. The benefit obtained from the issue costs is reflected in the interest expense: indeed, issue costs are in some cases economically indistinguishable from a discount on issue. Issue costs are therefore appropriately accounted for as an adjustment to the amount of the liability, which effectively results in their being charged over the life of the instrument. If it became clear that the instrument would be redeemed early, then the amortisation of the issue costs and any discount on issue would have to be accelerated.

95   Where the life of an instrument is indeterminate, the benefit of the issue costs is reflected in terms of the financing indefinitely. In such a case, the issue costs are therefore not taken to the profit and loss account until such time as the instrument is redeemed or cancelled.

96   Care should be taken in the determination of the amount that falls to be treated as issue costs to avoid the danger of overstating finance costs over the life of the instrument in question. For this reason, the definition of issue costs is deliberately restrictive. The definition does not admit costs of researching and negotiating sources of finance or of ascertaining the suitability or feasibility of particular instruments, nor allocations of internal costs that would have been incurred had the instrument not been issued: for example management remuneration. The costs incurred in connection with a financial restructuring or renegotiation also do not qualify as issue costs; such costs relate to previous sources of finance and not to any instrument that may be issued following the restructuring or renegotiation. Costs that do not qualify as issue costs should be written off to the profit and loss account as incurred.

97   The requirement of the FRS that issue costs are reflected in the amounts charged to the profit and loss account over the term of a capital instrument is not intended to prohibit the subsequent charging of issue costs to the share premium account by means of a transfer between reserves. The amounts that may be charged to the share premium account are determined by the requirements of companies legislation.

98-102   [Deleted]

Application notes

[Deleted]

Appendices I - III

[Deleted]

Financial Reporting Standard 5 is set out in paragraphs 1–39.

The Statement of Standard Accounting Practice set out in paragraphs 11–39 should be read in the context of the Objective as stated in paragraph 1 and the definitions set out in paragraphs 2–10 and also of the Foreword to Accounting Standards and the Statement of Principles for Financial Reporting currently in issue.

The Application Notes specify how some of the requirements of FRS 5 are to be applied to transactions that have certain features.

The Explanation set out in paragraphs 40–103 and the Application Notes shall be regarded as part of the Statement of Standard Accounting Practice insofar as they assist in interpreting that statement.

Appendix III 'The development of the FRS' reviews considerations and arguments that were thought significant by members of the Board in reaching the conclusions on FRS 5.

[FRS 5]
Reporting the substance of transactions

(Issued April 1994, amended December 1994, September 1998 and November 2003)*

Contents

*Editor's note: FRS 5 has been amended by FRS 25 with effect for accounting periods beginning on or after 1 January 2005 and by the amendments to FRS 26 with effect for accounting periods beginning on or after 1 January 2007.

Application notes
  A   CONSIGNMENT STOCK
  B   SALE AND REPURCHASE AGREEMENTS
  C   FACTORING OF DEBTS
  D   SECURITISED ASSETS
  E   LOAN TRANSFERS
  F   PRIVATE FINANCE INITIATIVE AND SIMILAR CONTRACTS
  G   REVENUE RECOGNITION

Adoption of FRS 5 by the Board

Appendices
  I Note on legal requirements
  II Compliance with International Accounting Standards
  III The development of the FRS

Reporting the substance of transactions

Summary

GENERAL

a   Financial Reporting Standard 5 'Reporting the Substance of Transactions' requires an entity's financial statements to report the substance of the transactions into which it has entered. The FRS sets out how to determine the substance of a transaction (including how to identify its effect on the assets and liabilities of the entity), whether any resulting assets and liabilities should be included in the balance sheet, and what disclosures are appropriate. The FRS also contains some provisions in respect of how transactions should be reported in the profit and loss account and the cash flow statement.

b   The FRS will not change the accounting treatment and disclosure of the vast majority of transactions. It will mainly affect those more complex transactions whose substance may not be readily apparent. The true commercial effect of such transactions may not be adequately expressed by their legal form and, where this is the case, it will not be sufficient to account for them merely by recording that form.

c   Transactions requiring particularly careful analysis will often include features such as –

   (i)   the party that gains the principal benefits generated by an item is not the legal owner of the item,
   (ii) a transaction is linked with others in such a way that the commercial effect can be understood only by considering the series as a whole, or
   (iii) an option is included on terms that make its exercise highly likely.

d   The FRS sets out principles that will apply to all transactions. In addition, there are five Application Notes that describe the application of the FRS to transactions with certain features: consignment stock; sale and repurchase agreements; factoring; securitised assets; and loan transfers. The Application Notes need not be referred to in all cases. At the start of each Note there is a 'Features' section that may serve as a quick reference point to determine whether further study is required. In addition, each Note concludes with a table summarising its main provisions.

Identification and recognition of the substance of transactions

e   A key step in determining the substance of any transaction is to identify whether it has given rise to new assets or liabilities for the entity and whether it has increased or decreased the entity's existing assets or liabilities. Assets are, broadly, rights or other access to future economic benefits controlled by an entity; liabilities are, broadly, an entity's obligations to transfer economic benefits.

f   The future economic benefits inherent in an asset are never completely certain in amount; there is always some risk that the benefits will turn out to be greater or less than expected. Whether the entity gains or suffers from such variations in benefits is evidence of whether it has an asset.

g   The definition of a liability requires an obligation to transfer benefits. Evidence that an entity has such an obligation is given if there is some circumstance in which the entity is unable to avoid an outflow of benefits.

Once identified, an asset or liability should be recognised (ie included) in the balance   **h**
sheet, provided that there is sufficient evidence that an asset or liability exists, and the
asset or liability can be measured at a monetary amount with sufficient reliability.

Following its recognition, an asset may be affected by a subsequent transaction.   **i**
Where the transaction does not significantly alter the entity's rights to benefits or its
exposure to risks, the entire asset should continue to be recognised. Conversely,
where the transaction transfers to others all significant rights to benefits and all
significant exposure to risks, the entity should cease to recognise the asset in its
entirety. Finally, in other cases where not all significant benefits and risks have been
transferred, it may be appropriate to amend the description or monetary amount of
an asset and, where necessary, recognise a liability for any obligations it has
assumed.

Linked presentation for certain non-recourse finance arrangements

A special form of presentation, termed a 'linked presentation', should be used for   **j**
certain non-recourse finance arrangements. This presentation shows, on the face of
the balance sheet, the finance deducted from the gross amount of the item it finances.
It should be used where, although the entity has significant rights to benefits and
exposure to risks relating to a specific item, the item is financed in such a way that the
maximum loss the entity can suffer is limited to a fixed monetary amount. For use of
a linked presentation it is necessary that both –

(i)   the finance will be repaid only from proceeds generated by the specific item it
      finances (or by transfer of the item itself) and there is no possibility whatsoever
      of a claim on the entity being established other than against funds generated by
      that item (or the item itself), and
(ii) there is no provision whatsoever whereby the entity may either keep the item on
      repayment of the finance or re-acquire it at any time.

Disclosure of the substance of transactions

Adequate disclosure of a transaction is important to an understanding of its com-   **k**
mercial effect. For most transactions, the disclosures currently required will be
sufficient for this purpose. However, where the nature of any recognised asset or
liability differs from that of items usually found under the relevant balance sheet
heading, the differences should be explained. Furthermore, to the extent that a
transaction has not resulted in the recognition of assets or liabilities, disclosure may
nevertheless be required in order to give an understanding of its commercial effect.

Quasi-subsidiaries*

Sometimes assets and liabilities are placed in an entity (a 'vehicle') that is in effect   **l**
controlled by the reporting entity but does not meet the legal definition of a subsidiary. Where the commercial effect for the reporting entity is no different from that
which would result were the vehicle a subsidiary, the vehicle will be a 'quasi-
subsidiary'.

*Editor's note: While not amended by the changes to FRS 2, it is the ASB's view that the relevance of the section
of FRS 5 dealing with quasi-subsidiaries has declined with the changes to FRS 2 effective from 2005 since some
entities which might previously have been classified as quasi-subsidiaries will now fall within the amended
definition of a subsidiary.*

m The FRS requires the assets, liabilities, profits, losses and cash flows of any quasi-subsidiary to be included in the consolidated financial statements of the group that controls it in the same way as if they were those of a subsidiary. However, where a quasi-subsidiary is used to finance a specific item in such a way that the provisions of paragraph j above are met from the point of view of the group, the assets and liabilities of the quasi-subsidiary should be included in consolidated financial statements using the linked presentation described in paragraph j.

n Disclosure is required, in summary form, of the financial statements of quasi-subsidiaries.

Financial Reporting Standard 5

Objective

1 The objective of this FRS is to ensure that the substance of an entity's transactions is reported in its financial statements. The commercial effect of the entity's transactions, and any resulting assets, liabilities, gains or losses, should be faithfully represented in its financial statements.

Definitions

The following definitions shall apply in this FRS and in particular in the Statement of Standard Accounting Practice set out in paragraphs 11–39.

2 *Assets:-*
Rights or other access to future economic benefits controlled by an entity as a result of past transactions or events.

3 *Control in the context of an asset:-*The ability to obtain the future economic benefits relating to an asset and to restrict the access of others to those benefits.

4 *Liabilities:-*
An entity's obligations to transfer economic benefits as a result of past transactions or events.

5 *Risk:-*
Uncertainty as to the amount of benefits. The term includes both potential for gain and exposure to loss.

6 *Recognition:-*
The process of incorporating an item into the primary financial statements under the appropriate heading. It involves depiction of the item in words and by a monetary amount and inclusion of that amount in the statement totals.

7 *Quasi-subsidiary:-*
A quasi-subsidiary of a reporting entity is a company, trust, partnership or other vehicle that, though not fulfilling the definition of a subsidiary, is directly or indirectly controlled by the reporting entity and gives rise to benefits for that entity that are in substance no different from those that would arise were the vehicle a subsidiary.

Control of another entity:- **8**
The ability to direct the financial and operating policies of that entity with a view to
gaining economic benefit from its activities.

Subsidiary:- **9**
A subsidiary undertaking as defined by companies legislation.

Companies legislation:- **10**

(a)   In Great Britain, the Companies Act 1985;
(b)   in Northern Ireland, the Companies (Northern Ireland) Order 1986; and
(c)   in the Republic of Ireland, the Republic of Ireland Companies Acts 1963–1990
      and the European Communities (Companies: Group Accounts) Regulations
      1992.

Statement of Standard Accounting Practice

SCOPE

Subject to paragraph 12, Financial Reporting Standard 5 applies to all transactions **11**
of a reporting entity whose financial statements are intended to give a true and fair
view of its financial position and profit or loss (or income and expenditure) for a
period. In the FRS, the term 'transaction' includes both a single transaction or
arrangement and also a group or series of transactions that achieves or is designed to
achieve an overall commercial effect.

The following are excluded from the scope of the FRS, unless they are a part of a **12**
transaction that falls within the scope of the FRS:

(a)   forward contracts and futures (such as those for foreign currencies or
      commodities);
(b)   foreign exchange and interest rate swaps;
(c)   contracts where a net amount will be paid or received based on the movement
      in a price or an index (sometimes referred to as 'contracts for differences');
(d)   expenditure commitments (such as purchase commitments) and orders placed,
      until the earlier of delivery or payment; and
(e)   employment contracts.

Where the substance of a transaction or the treatment of any resulting asset or **13**
liability falls not only within the scope of this FRS but also directly within the scope of
another FRS, a Statement of Standard Accounting Practice ('SSAP'), or a specific
statutory requirement governing the recognition of assets or liabilities, the standard
or statute that contains the more specific provision(s) should be applied.

APPLICATION TO SMALLER ENTITIES

Reporting entities applying the Financial Reporting Standard for Smaller Entities **13A**
currently applicable are exempt from this accounting standard unless preparing
consolidated financial statements, in which case they should apply the FRS to such
statements as required by the FRSSE.

13B   Paragraphs 14 to 31 of the FRS do not apply to the recognition and derecognition of financial assets and financial liabilities within the scope of paragraphs 14 to 42 of FRS 26 (IAS 39) 'Financial Instruments: Recognition and Measurement'.*

GENERAL

The substance of transactions

14   A reporting entity's financial statements should report the substance of the transactions into which it has entered. In determining the substance of a transaction, all its aspects and implications should be identified and greater weight given to those more likely to have a commercial effect in practice. A group or series of transactions that achieves or is designed to achieve an overall commercial effect should be viewed as a whole.

Quasi-subsidiaries

15   Where the entity has a quasi-subsidiary, the substance of the transactions entered into by the quasi-subsidiary should be reported in consolidated financial statements.

THE SUBSTANCE OF TRANSACTIONS

Identifying assets and liabilities

16   To determine the substance of a transaction it is necessary to identify whether the transaction has given rise to new assets or liabilities for the reporting entity and whether it has changed the entity's existing assets or liabilities.

17   Evidence that an entity has rights or other access to benefits (and hence has an asset) is given if the entity is exposed to the risks inherent in the benefits, taking into account the likelihood of those risks having a commercial effect in practice.

18   Evidence that an entity has an obligation to transfer benefits (and hence has a liability) is given if there is some circumstance in which the entity is unable to avoid, legally or commercially, an outflow of benefits.

19   Where a transaction incorporates one or more options, guarantees or conditional provisions, their commercial effect should be assessed in the context of all the aspects and implications of the transaction in order to determine what assets and liabilities exist.

Recognition of assets and liabilities

20   Where a transaction results in an item that meets the definition of an asset or liability, that item should be recognised in the balance sheet if –

    (a)   there is sufficient evidence of the existence of the item (including, where appropriate, evidence that a future inflow or outflow of benefit will occur), and

    (b)   the item can be measured at a monetary amount with sufficient reliability.

*Editor's note: Added by amendments to FRS 26, with effect for accounting periods beginning on or after 1 January 2007. While this paragraph has been placed under a heading dealing with smaller entities, it applies to entities that are not small.

Transactions in previously recognised assets

Continued recognition of an asset in its entirety

Where a transaction involving a previously recognised asset results in no significant **21**
change in –

(a)   the entity's rights or other access to benefits relating to that asset, or
(b)   its exposure to the risks inherent in those benefits,

the entire asset should continue to be recognised and a financial liability recognised
for the consideration received*. In particular this will be the case for any transaction
that is in substance a financing of a previously recognised asset, unless the conditions
for a linked presentation given in paragraphs 26 and 27 are met, in which case such a
presentation should be used.

Ceasing to recognise an asset in its entirety

Where a transaction involving a previously recognised asset transfers to others –   **22**

(a)   all significant rights or other access to benefits relating to that asset, and
(b)   all significant exposure to the risks inherent in those benefits,

the entire asset should cease to be recognised.

Special cases

Paragraphs 21 and 22 deal with most transactions affecting items previously   **23**
recognised as assets. In other cases where there is a significant change in the entity's
rights to benefits and exposure to risks but the provisions of paragraph 22 are not
met, the description or monetary amount relating to an asset should, where necessary, be changed and a liability recognised for any obligations to transfer benefits
that are assumed. These cases arise where the transaction takes one or more of the
following forms:

(a)   a transfer of only part of the item in question;
(b)   a transfer of all of the item for only part of its life; and
(c)   a transfer of all of the item for all of its life but where the entity retains some
        significant right to benefits or exposure to risk.

In the special cases referred to in paragraph 23, where the amount of any resulting   **24**
gain or loss is uncertain, full provision should be made for any probable loss but
recognition of any gain, to the extent it is in doubt, should be deferred. In addition,
where the uncertainty could have a material effect on the financial statements, this
fact should be disclosed in the notes to the financial statements.

The meaning of 'significant'

In applying paragraphs 21–23 above and paragraph 26 below, 'significant' should be   **25**
judged in relation to those benefits and risks that are likely to occur in practice, and
not in relation to the total possible benefits and risks.

*__Editor's note:__ Amended by FRS 26, with effect for accounting periods beginning on or after 1 January 2007.

Linked presentation for certain non-recourse finance arrangements

26　Where a transaction involving an item previously recognised as an asset is in substance a financing – and therefore meets the condition of paragraph 21 regarding no significant change in the entity's access to benefits or exposure to risks – but the financing 'ring-fences' the item such that –

(a)　the finance will be repaid only from proceeds generated by the specific item it finances (or by transfer of the item itself) and there is no possibility whatsoever of a claim on the entity being established other than against funds generated by that item (or the item itself),

(b)　there is no provision whatsoever whereby the entity may either keep the item on repayment of the finance or re-acquire it at any time, and

(c)　all of the conditions given in paragraph 27 are met,

the finance should be shown deducted from the gross amount of the item it finances on the face of the balance sheet within a single asset caption (a 'linked presentation'). The gross amounts of the item and the finance should be shown on the face of the balance sheet and not merely disclosed in the notes to the financial statements. A linked presentation should also be used where an item that is financed in such a way that all of the above three conditions are met has not been recognised previously as an asset.

27　A linked presentation should be used only where all of the following are met:

(a)　the finance relates to a specific item (or portfolio of similar items) and, in the case of a loan, is secured on that item but not on any other asset of the entity;

(b)　the provider of the finance has no recourse whatsoever, either explicit or implicit, to the other assets of the entity for losses and the entity has no obligation whatsoever to repay the provider of finance;

(c)　the directors of the entity state explicitly in each set of financial statements where a linked presentation is used that the entity is not obliged to support any losses, nor does it intend to do so;

(d)　the provider of the finance has agreed in writing (in the finance documentation or otherwise) that it will seek repayment of the finance, as to both principal and interest, only to the extent that sufficient funds are generated by the specific item it has financed and that it will not seek recourse in any other form, and such agreement is noted in each set of financial statements where a linked presentation is used;

(e)　if the funds generated by the item are insufficient to pay off the provider of the finance, this does not constitute an event of default for the entity; and

(f)　there is no provision whatsoever, either in the financing arrangement or otherwise, whereby the entity has a right or an obligation either to keep the item upon repayment of the finance or (where title to the item has been transferred) to re-acquire it at any time. Accordingly:

(i)　where the item is one (such as a monetary receivable) that directly generates cash, the provider of the finance will be repaid out of the resulting cash receipts (to the extent these are sufficient); or

(ii)　where the item is one (such as a physical asset) that does not directly generate cash, there is a definite point at which either the item will be sold to a third party and the provider of the finance repaid from the proceeds (to the extent these are sufficient) or the item will be transferred to the provider of the finance in full and final settlement.

Where all of these conditions hold for only part of the finance, a linked presentation should be used for only that part. In such cases, the maximum future payment that the reporting entity could make (other than from funds generated by the specific item being financed) should be excluded from the amount deducted on the face of the balance sheet.

In respect of an arrangement for which a linked presentation is used, profit should be   **28**
recognised on entering into the arrangement only to the extent that the non-returnable proceeds received exceed the previous carrying value of the item. Thereafter, any profit or loss deriving from the item should be recognised in the period in which it arises. The net profit or loss recognised in each period should be included in the profit and loss account and separate disclosure of its gross components should be given in the notes to the financial statements.

Offset

Assets and liabilities should not be offset. Debit and credit balances should be   **29**
aggregated into a single net item where, and only where, they do not constitute separate assets and liabilities. For offset of financial assets and financial liabilities, FRS 25 'Financial Instruments: Disclosure and Presentation' applies.*

Disclosure of the substance of transactions

Disclosure of a transaction in the financial statements, whether or not it has resulted   **30**
in assets or liabilities being recognised or ceasing to be recognised, should be sufficient to enable the user of the financial statements to understand its commercial effect.

Where a transaction has resulted in the recognition of assets or liabilities whose   **31**
nature differs from that of items usually included under the relevant balance sheet heading, the differences should be explained.

QUASI-SUBSIDIARIES†

Identification of quasi-subsidiaries

In determining whether another entity (a 'vehicle') gives rise to benefits for the   **32**
reporting entity that are in substance no different from those that would arise were the vehicle a subsidiary, regard should be had to the benefits arising from the net assets of the vehicle. Evidence of which party gains these benefits is given by which party is exposed to the risks inherent in them.

In determining whether the reporting entity controls a vehicle regard should be had   **33**
to who, in practice, directs the financial and operating policies of the vehicle. The ability to prevent others from directing those policies is evidence of control, as is the ability to prevent others from enjoying the benefits arising from the vehicle's net assets.

Where the financial and operating policies of a vehicle are in substance pre-   **34**
determined, contractually or otherwise, the party possessing control will be the one that gains the benefits arising from the net assets of the vehicle. Evidence of which

Editor's note: Amended by FRS 25.

†*Editor's note: While the amendment to FRS 2 has not strictly changed FRS 5, the preface to the amendment notes that many entities previously considered to be quasi-subsidiaries are likely to be subsidiaries in the future.*

party gains these benefits is given by which party is exposed to the risks inherent in them.

Accounting for quasi-subsidiaries

35   Subject to paragraph 37, the assets, liabilities, profits, losses and cash flows of a quasi-subsidiary should be included in the group financial statements of the group that controls it in the same way as if they were those of a subsidiary. Where an entity has a quasi-subsidiary but no subsidiaries and therefore does not prepare group financial statements, it should provide in its financial statements consolidated financial statements of itself and the quasi-subsidiary, presented with equal prominence to the reporting entity's individual financial statements.*

36   Paragraph 35 should be applied by following the requirements regarding the preparation of consolidated financial statements set out in companies legislation and in FRS 2 'Accounting for Subsidiary Undertakings'. However, quasi-subsidiaries should be excluded from consolidation only where the interest in the quasi-subsidiary is held exclusively with a view to subsequent resale† and the quasi-subsidiary has not previously been included in the reporting entity's consolidated financial statements.

37   Where a quasi-subsidiary holds a single item or a single portfolio of similar items and the effect of the arrangement is to finance the item in such a way that the provisions of paragraphs 26 and 27 are met from the point of view of the group, the quasi-subsidiary should be included in consolidated financial statements using a linked presentation.

Disclosure of quasi-subsidiaries

38   Where one or more quasi-subsidiaries are included in consolidated financial statements, this fact should be disclosed. A summary of the financial statements of each quasi-subsidiary should be provided in the notes to the financial statements, unless the reporting entity has more than one quasi-subsidiary of a similar nature, in which case the summary may be given on a combined basis. These summarised financial statements should show separately each main heading in the balance sheet, profit and loss account, statement of total recognised gains and losses and cash flow statement for which there is a material item, together with comparative figures.

DATE FROM WHICH EFFECTIVE

39   Subject to paragraph 39A, the accounting practices set out in the FRS should be regarded as standard in respect of financial statements relating to accounting periods ending on or after 22 September 1994.‡ Earlier adoption is encouraged but not required.

Editor's note: Since FRS 5 was issued, FRS 2 has been revised. Some investments that would previously have fallen within the definition of a quasi-subsidiary under FRS 5 may now fall within the definition of a subsidiary under FRS 2.

†As defined in FRS 2, paragraph 11.

‡Editor's note: The effective date for Application Note F Private Finance Initiative and Similar Contracts is accounting periods ending on or after 10 September 1998. The effective date for Application Note G Revenue Recognition is accounting periods ending on or after 23 December 2003.

(a) The requirements of paragraph 29 in so far as they relate to balances arising **39A** either from insurance broking transactions or, for insurers (including Lloyd's syndicates), from insurance transactions placed through brokers, and

(b) the accounting practices set out in the FRS, in so far as they relate to financial reinsurance accounted for by Lloyd's syndicates as at 31 December 1993,

should be regarded as standard in respect of financial statements relating to accounting periods ending on or after 22 September 1996. Where, in accordance with the previous sentence, the accounting practices set out in the FRS are not applied for accounting periods ending on or after 22 September 1994, this fact and, where available, a quantification of the effect should be disclosed.'

Explanation

SCOPE

The scope of the FRS, as set out in paragraph 11, extends to all kinds of transactions, **40** subject only to the exclusions given in paragraph 12 and 13B.* Most transactions are straightforward, giving rise to a number of standard rights and obligations with the result that their substance and commercial effect are readily apparent. Applying established accounting practices will be sufficient to ensure that the substance of such transactions is properly reported in the financial statements, without the need to refer to the FRS.

Conversely, applying established accounting practices may not be sufficient to por- **41** tray the substance of more complex transactions whose commercial effect may not be readily apparent. For such transactions it will be necessary to refer to the FRS in order to ensure that their substance is correctly identified and properly reported.

Exclusions from the FRS

Paragraph 12 excludes from the FRS certain contracts for future performance except **42** where they are merely a part of a transaction (or of a group or series of transactions) that falls within the FRS.†

Paragraph 13B excludes from the requirements in paragraphs 14 to 31 of the FRS **42A** those transactions in financial instruments that fall within the scope of the dere-cognition requirements of FRS 26 (IAS 39) 'Financial Instruments: Recognition and Measurement'.‡

Other standards

The FRS sets out general principles relevant to reporting the substance of all trans- **43** actions. Other accounting standards, the Application Notes of the FRS and companies legislation apply general principles to particular transactions or events. It follows that where a transaction falls within the scope of both the FRS and another accounting standard or statute, whichever contains the more specific provisions should be applied. Nevertheless, the specific provisions of any standard or statute

---

*Editor's note: Amended by FRS 26 with effect for accounting periods beginning on or after 1 January 2007.

†Editor's note: Amended by FRS 26 with effect for accounting periods beginning on or after 1 January 2007.

‡Editor's note: Inserted by FRS 26 with effect for accounting periods beginning on or after 1 January 2007.

should be applied to the substance of the transaction and not merely to its legal form and, for this purpose, the general principles set out in FRS 5 will be relevant.

44   Pension obligations are an example of an item falling within the scope of both FRS 5 and another standard, the latter being FRS 17 'Retirement benefits'. As FRS 17 contains the more specific provisions on accounting for pension obligations and does not require consolidation of pension funds, such funds should not be consolidated as quasi-subsidiaries. FRS 5, however, contains the more specific provisions in respect of certain other transactions that may take place between an entity and its pension fund, for example a sale and repurchase agreement relating to one of the entity's properties.

45   The relationship between SSAP 21 'Accounting for lease and hire purchase contracts' and FRS 5 is particularly close. In general, SSAP 21 contains the more specific provisions governing accounting for stand-alone leases that fall wholly within its parameters, although the general principles of the FRS will also be relevant in ensuring that leases are classified as finance or operating leases in accordance with their substance. However, for some lease arrangements, and particularly for those that are merely one element of a larger arrangement, the FRS will contain the more specific provisions. An example is a sale and leaseback arrangement where there is also an option for the seller/lessee to repurchase the asset; in this case the provisions of Application Note B are more specific than those of SSAP 21.

THE SUBSTANCE OF TRANSACTIONS

General principles

46   Paragraph 14 of the FRS sets out general principles for reporting the substance of a transaction. Particularly for more complex transactions, it will not be sufficient merely to record the transaction's legal form, as to do so may not adequately express the commercial effect of the arrangements. Notwithstanding this caveat, the FRS is not intended to affect the legal characterisation of a transaction, or to change the situation at law achieved by the parties to it.

Features of more complex transactions

47   Transactions requiring particularly careful analysis will often include features such as –

(a)   the separation of legal title to an item from rights or other access to the principal future economic benefits associated with it and exposure to the principal risks inherent in those benefits,*

(b)   the linking of a transaction with others in such a way that the commercial effect can be understood only by considering the series as a whole, or

(c)   the inclusion of options or conditions on terms that make it highly likely that the option will be exercised or the condition fulfilled.

(a) Separation of legal title from benefits and risks

48   A familiar example of the separation of legal title from benefits and risks is a finance lease. Another is goods sold under reservation of title. In both cases, the location of legal title will not normally be expected to have a commercial effect in practice. Thus the party having the benefits and risks relating to the underlying property should

---

*For ease of reading, 'rights or other access to future economic benefits' are frequently referred to hereafter as 'rights to benefits' or 'benefits', and 'exposure to the risks inherent in those benefits' is frequently referred to hereafter as 'exposure to risks' or 'risks'.

recognise an asset in its balance sheet even though it does not have legal title. Arrangements involving the separation of legal title from benefits and risks are dealt with in detail in Application Note B.

(b) Linking of transactions

The linking of two or more transactions extends the possibilities for separating legal **49** title from benefits and risks. A sale of goods linked with a commitment to repurchase may leave the original owner with the principal benefits and risks relating to the goods if the repurchase price is set at the costs, including interest, incurred by the other party in holding the goods. In such a case, application of the FRS will result in the transaction being accounted for as a financing rather than a sale, showing the asset and a corresponding liability on the balance sheet of the original owner.

(c) Inclusion of options

Some sale transactions are accompanied by an option, rather than a commitment, **50** for either the original owner to repurchase or the buyer to resell. Often the commercial effect of such an arrangement is that an economic penalty (such as the forgoing of a profit) would be suffered by the party having the option if it failed to exercise it. Some transactions incorporate both a put option for the buyer and a call option for the original owner, in such a way that it will almost certainly be in the commercial interests of one of the parties to exercise its option (as for example where both options have the same exercise price and are exercisable on the same date). In such cases, there will be no genuine commercial possibility that the original owner will fail to repurchase the item and application of the FRS will again result in the transaction being accounted for as a financing rather than a sale.

Assessing commercial effect by considering the position of other parties

Whatever the substance of a transaction, it will normally have commercial logic for **51** each of the parties to it. If a transaction appears to lack such logic from the point of view of one or more parties, this may indicate that not all related parts of the transaction have been identified or that the commercial effect of some element of the transaction has been incorrectly assessed.

It follows that in assessing the commercial effect of a transaction, it will be important **52** to consider the position of all of the parties to it, including their apparent expectations and motives for agreeing to its various terms. In particular, where one party to the transaction receives a lender's return but no more (comprising interest on its investment perhaps together with a relatively small fee), this indicates that the substance of the transaction is that of a financing. This is because the party that receives a lender's return is not compensated for assuming any significant exposure to loss other than that associated with the creditworthiness of the other party, nor is the other party compensated for giving up any significant potential for gain.

Identifying assets and liabilities

In accounting terms, the substance of a transaction is portrayed through the assets **53** and liabilities, including contingent assets and liabilities, resulting from or altered by the transaction. A key step in reporting the substance of any transaction is therefore to identify its effect on the assets and liabilities of the entity.

Assets – control of access to benefits

54   The definition of an asset requires that access to future economic benefits is controlled by the entity. Access to future economic benefits will normally rest on a foundation of legal rights, although legally enforceable rights are not essential to secure access. Control is the means by which the entity ensures that the benefits accrue to itself and not to others. Control can be distinguished from management (ie the ability to direct the use of an item that generates the benefits) and, although the two often go together, this need not be so. For example, the manager of a portfolio of securities does not have control of the securities, as he does not have the ability to obtain the economic benefits associated with them. Such control rests with his appointer who has delegated to the manager the right to take day-to-day decisions about the composition of the portfolio.

Assets – risk

55   The future economic benefits inherent in an asset are never completely certain in amount; there is always the possibility that the actual benefits will be greater or less than those expected, or will arise sooner or later than expected. For instance, the value of stocks may rise or fall as market conditions change; foreign currency balances may become worth more or less because of exchange rate movements; debtors may default or be slow in paying. This uncertainty regarding the eventual benefit is referred to as 'risk', with the term encompassing both an upside element of potential for gain and a downside element of exposure to loss.

56   The entity that has access to the benefits will usually also be the one to suffer or gain if these benefits turn out to be different from those expected. Hence, evidence of whether an entity has access to benefits (and hence has an asset) is given by whether it has the risks inherent in those benefits.

Liabilities – obligations to transfer benefits

57   The definition of liabilities requires an obligation to transfer economic benefits. Whilst most obligations are legally enforceable, a legal obligation is not a necessary condition for a liability. An entity may be commercially obliged to adopt a certain course of action that is in its long-term best interests in the widest sense, even if no third party can legally enforce that course. As illustrated in paragraph 50 above, the prospect of a commercial or economic penalty if a certain action is not taken may negate a legal right to refrain from taking that action.

58   The notion of obligation implies that the entity is not free to avoid an outflow of resources. Where there is some circumstance in which the entity is unable to avoid such an outflow whether for legal or commercial reasons, it will have a liability. However, in accordance with SSAP 18 'Accounting for contingencies'* if the entity's obligation is contingent on the occurrence of one or more uncertain future events (as under a stand-alone guarantee given by the entity) its liability may not be recognised.†

*Editor's note: SSAP 18 has been superseded by FRS 12 'Provisions, contingent liabilities and contingent assets'.

†Editor's note: The accounting treatment mentioned in respect of guarantees may no longer quite apply to an entity which complies with FRS 26. As a result of the changes to FRS 26 (in respect of financial guarantees) such companies will normally have to record financial guarantees initially at their fair value, and thereafter at the higher of the unamortised balance of the initially recorded fair value and the amount that would be recognised under FRS 12.

Options

On its own, an option to acquire an item of property in the future represents a **59** different asset from ownership of the property itself. For example, when an option to purchase shares at a future date is acquired, the only asset is the option itself; the asset 'shares' will be acquired only on exercise of the option. Similarly, an unconditional obligation is not the same as a contingent commitment to assume such an obligation at another party's option. Although both are liabilities, they are different liabilities and if recognised in the balance sheet their descriptions will be different.

Where an option is part of a more complex transaction, it may not necessarily **60** represent a separate asset or liability of the type discussed in paragraph 59. For example, an option may serve, in conjunction with the other aspects of the transaction, to give one party access to the future benefits arising from an item of property without legal ownership. Alternatively the terms of an option, together with other aspects of the overall transaction, may in effect create an unconditional obligation even though the legal obligation is expressed as being conditional on the exercise of the option. Options of this kind should be accounted for by considering the substance of the transaction as a whole.

In determining the substance of a transaction incorporating options, in accordance **61** with paragraph 14, greater weight must be given to those aspects and implications more likely to have a commercial effect in practice. This will involve considering the extent to which there is a genuine commercial possibility that the option will be exercised or, alternatively, that it will not be exercised. In extreme cases, there will be no genuine commercial possibility that the option will be exercised, in which case the existence of that option should be ignored; alternatively, there will be no genuine commercial possibility that an option will fail to be exercised, in which case its future exercise should be assumed. For example, a transaction may be structured in such a way that the cost of exercising an option will almost inevitably be lower (or, alternatively, higher) than the benefits obtained from its exercise. As another example, there may be a combination of put and call options such that it will almost certainly be in the commercial interests of one or other party to exercise its option. In both these cases, the substance of the overall transaction is that the parties have outright, and not optional or conditional, obligations and access to benefits. In less extreme cases, further analysis will be required. It may be necessary to consider the true commercial objectives of the parties and the commercial rationale for the inclusion of such options in the transaction. This may reveal either that the parties in substance have outright obligations and access to benefits, or, alternatively, that the parties' obligations and access to benefits are genuinely optional or conditional.

In assessing the commercial effect of an option, all the terms of the transaction and **62** the circumstances of the parties that are likely to be relevant during the exercise period of the option should be taken into account. It should be assumed that each of the parties will act in accordance with its economic interests. Any actions that the parties would take only in the event of a severe deterioration in liquidity or creditworthiness should not be anticipated but should be taken into account only when such a deterioration occurs (for example, when creditworthiness has declined because of the prospect of imminent cash flow difficulties).

Guarantees and conditional provisions

Paragraphs 59–62 should also be applied to guarantees and other conditional pro- **63** visions. The commercial effect of such provisions should in all cases be determined in the context of the overall transaction.

Recognition of assets and liabilities

64   Once it appears from analysis of a transaction that an asset or liability has been acquired or assumed by an entity, it is necessary to apply various recognition tests to determine whether the asset or liability should be included in the balance sheet.

65   The general criteria set out in paragraph 20* require that an asset or liability should be recognised only where it can be measured with 'sufficient' reliability. The effect of prudence is that less reliability of measurement is acceptable when recognising items that involve decreases in equity (eg increases in liabilities) than when recognising items that do not (eg increases in assets). It follows that, particularly for liabilities, where a reasonable estimate of the amount of an item is available, the item should be recognised.

Transactions in previously recognised assets

66   Following its recognition, an asset may be affected by a subsequent transaction and it will be necessary to consider whether, as a result of the transaction, the description or monetary amount of the asset needs to be changed. In this regard paragraphs 21–28 and 67–88 will apply.

Continued recognition of an asset in its entirety

67   Paragraph 21 requires that where there is no significant change in the entity's rights to benefits, its previously recognised asset should continue to be recognised. In the same way, the entity will continue to have an asset where its exposure to the risks inherent in the benefits of the asset is not significantly altered. Even if the proceeds generated by the asset are directed in the first instance to another party, provided the entity gains or suffers from all significant changes in those proceeds it should be regarded as having the benefits of the asset and should continue to recognise it.†

68   Thus, under paragraph 21, it will not be appropriate to cease to recognise any part of an asset where the transaction entered into is in substance a financing of that asset, even if the financing is without recourse. Such financing transactions leave the entity with those rights to benefits and exposures to risks (including potential for gain) that are likely to have a commercial effect in practice, as well as creating a liability to repay the finance. The only exception to this is non-recourse finance arrangements that meet the conditions for a linked presentation given in paragraphs 26–27. Although such arrangements are in substance financings, their particular features are such that a linked presentation is required to portray all the effects of the arrangement. This is explained further in paragraphs 76–80 below.

Ceasing to recognise an asset in its entirety

69   Conversely, paragraph 22 requires that where a transaction transfers to others all significant rights to benefits and all significant exposure to risks that relate to a previously recognised asset, the entire asset should cease to be recognised.‡

*These criteria are drawn from Chapter 4 of the Board's draft Statement of Principles. (**Editor's note:** Similar in final Statement published December 1999 Chapter 5.)*

†**Editor's note:** *Amended by FRS 26 with effect for accounting periods beginning on or after 1 January 2007.*

‡**Editor's note:** *Amended by FRS 26 with effect for accounting periods beginning on or after 1 January 2007.*

Special Cases

Paragraphs 21 and 22 deal with the great majority of transactions affecting pre-   **70**
viously recognised assets. However, in other cases there may be a significant change
in the entity's rights to benefits and exposure to risks but not a complete transfer of
all significant benefits and risks. In such cases, it will be necessary to consider
whether the description or monetary amount of the asset needs to be changed and
also whether a liability needs to be recognised for any obligations assumed or risks
retained. These special cases arise where the transaction takes one or more of the
following forms:

(a)   a transfer of only part of the item in question;
(b)   a transfer of all of the item for only part of its life; and
(c)   a transfer of all of the item for all of its life but where the entity retains some
      significant right to benefits or exposure to risk.

(a) Transfer of only part of an item

Transfer of part of an item that generates benefits may occur in one of two ways. The   **71**
most straightforward is where a proportionate share of the item is transferred. A
second, less straightforward way of transferring a part of an item arises where the
item comprises rights to two or more separate benefit streams, each with its own
risks. A part of the item will be transferred where all significant rights to one or more
of those benefit streams and associated exposure to risks are transferred whilst all
significant rights to the other(s) are retained. In both these cases, the entity would
cease to recognise the part of the original asset that has been transferred by the
transaction, but would continue to recognise the remainder. A change in the
description of the asset might also be required.*

(b) Transfer of an item for only part of its life

Paragraph 23 also applies to a transaction that transfers all of an item that generates   **72**
benefits for only part of its life. Provided that the entity's access to benefits and
exposure to risks following the transaction are both significantly different from those
it had before the transaction, the description or monetary amount of the asset previously recognised would need to be changed. For example, an entity may sell an
item of property but agree to repurchase it in a substantially depreciated form (as for
example where the item will be used for most of its life by the buyer). In this case the
entity's original asset has changed from being the original item of property to a
residual interest in that item and, in addition, the entity has assumed a liability of its
obligation to pay the repurchase price. Sale and repurchase agreements are dealt with
further in Application Note B.

(c) Transfer of an item for all of its life with some benefit or risk retained

Finally, paragraph 23 applies to a transaction that transfers an item that generates   **73**
benefits for all of its life, but leaves the entity with significant rights to benefits or
exposure to risks relating to that item. Whilst control has passed to the transferee,
the retention of significant rights to benefits or exposure to risks has the result that
the transaction fails to meet the conditions in paragraph 22 for ceasing to recognise
an asset in its entirety. For example, an entity may sell an investment in a subsidiary
with the consideration including an element of deferred performance-related consideration. Provided that significant rights to benefits and exposure to risks

_____
Editor's note: Amended by FRS 26 with effect for accounting periods beginning on or after 1 January 2007.

associated with the subsidiary have passed to the buyer (as will be the case where the deferred consideration is only a portion of the subsidiary's profits arising in only a limited period), both the description and the monetary amount of the asset will need to be changed. This reflects the fact that the asset is no longer an investment in a subsidiary but rather is a debtor for the performance-related consideration (although, under the provisions of SSAP 18*, the debtor may be measured at nil and therefore not recognised but merely disclosed). As another example, an entity may sell equipment subject to a warranty in respect of the condition of the equipment at the time of sale, or subject to a guarantee of its residual value. This would normally transfer all significant rights to benefits and some significant exposure to risks to the buyer (these being those arising from the equipment's future use and resale), but leave the seller with some significant risk in the form of obligations relating to the equipment's future performance or residual value. The seller would therefore cease to recognise the equipment as an asset, but would recognise a liability for its warranty obligation or guarantee (with the liability being accounted for in accordance with the provisions of SSAP 18†).

Measurement and profit recognition

74   In any of the above three classes of transaction, there arises the issue of how to measure the change in the entity's assets or liabilities and any resulting profit or loss. This measurement process requires that the previous carrying value of the asset is apportioned into an amount relating to those benefits and risks disposed of and an amount relating to those retained. In some cases, measurement will be relatively easy; for instance this might be the case where a proportionate share of the original asset is retained as described in paragraph 71 above or where there are similar and frequent transactions in liquid and freely accessible markets. In other cases, measurement may be more difficult with the result that the amount of any gain or loss is uncertain. In such cases, in accordance with the provisions of SSAP 18*, paragraph 24 requires a prudent approach to be adopted, with full provision being made for any probable loss but recognition of any gain, to the extent it is in doubt, being deferred.

The meaning of 'significant'

75   In applying paragraphs 21–23 and 26 it may be necessary to determine whether certain rights to benefits or exposure to risks are 'significant'. When this is done, greater weight should be given to what is likely to have a commercial effect in practice. In particular, whether any retained risk is 'significant' should be judged not against the total possible variation in benefits, but against that variation which is likely to occur in practice.‡

Linked presentation for certain non-recourse finance arrangements

General principles

76   Sometimes an entity finances an item on terms that the provider of the finance has recourse to only the item it has financed and not to the entity's other assets. It is sometimes argued that the effect of such arrangements is that the entity no longer has

Editor's note: SSAP 18 has been superseded by FRS 12 'Provisions, contingent liabilities and contingent assets'.

†Editor's note: SSAP 18 was superseded by FRS 12 'Provisions, contingent liabilities and contingent assets'.

‡Editor's note: Amended by FRS 26 with effect for accounting periods beginning on or after 1 January 2007.

an asset in respect of the item, nor does it have a liability for the finance. For the purpose of determining the appropriate accounting treatment, non-recourse finance arrangements can be classified into two types.

Separate presentation of an asset and liability

The first type of arrangement is where, although in the event of default the provider   **77** of the finance can obtain repayment only by enforcing its rights against the specified item, the entity retains rights to all the benefits generated by the item and can repay the finance from its general resources in order to preserve those rights. In such a case the entity has both an asset (its access to all the benefits generated by the item) and a liability (its obligation to repay the finance) and they should be included in the balance sheet in the normal way.

Linked presentation

The second type of non-recourse finance arrangement is where the finance will be   **78** repaid only from benefits generated by the specified item. Although the entity has rights to any surplus benefits remaining after repayment of the finance, it has no right or obligation to keep the item or to repay the finance from its general resources. In these cases the entity does not have an asset equal to the gross amount of the item (as it does not have access to all the future benefits generated by it), nor a liability for the full amount of the finance (as the financier will be repaid only from benefits generated by the specific item and not from benefits generated by any other assets of the entity). However, the entity does retain rights to those benefits and exposure to those risks that are likely to have a commercial effect in practice – ie the significant benefits and risks. It is retention of the significant benefits and risks that distinguishes this type of non-recourse financing from the transactions described in paragraph 23 that transfer a part of an asset. Where there is no transfer of significant benefits and risks the transaction is in substance a financing arrangement and the other party would usually receive a lender's return and no more. Conversely, the transactions described in paragraph 23 involve a transfer of significant benefits and risks. Indications of such transactions are where the other party has rights to benefits greater than those associated with a lender's return and has corresponding exposure to some significant risk.

[Withdrawn]*   **79-80**

Detailed conditions for use of a linked presentation

A linked presentation is appropriate only where the commercial effect for the entity   **81** is that the item is being sold but the sale process is not yet complete. Thus there must be no doubt whatsoever that the claim of the provider of the finance is limited strictly to funds generated by the specific item it finances. It must be clear that there is no legal, commercial or other obligation under which the entity may fund any losses (from whatever cause) on the items being financed or transfer any economic benefits (apart from those generated by the item). In addition, the entity must have no right or obligation to repay the finance from its general resources, to keep the item on repayment of the finance or to re-acquire it in the future. These principles are reflected in the detailed conditions for use of a linked presentation set out in paragraph 27.

*Editor's note: Paragraphs 79 and 80 deleted by amendments to FRS 26 with effect for accounting periods beginning on or after 1 January 2007.

82   Condition 27(a) requires that the finance relates to a specific item or group of similar items. A linked presentation should not be used where the finance relates to two or more items that are not part of a portfolio, or to a portfolio containing items that would otherwise be shown under different balance sheet captions. Similarly, a linked presentation should not be used where the finance relates to any kind of business unit, or for items that generate the funds required to repay the finance only by being used in conjunction with other assets of the entity. The item must generate the funds required to repay the finance either by unwinding directly into cash or by its sale to a third party.*

83   Conditions 27(b)–(e) require that there is no recourse and no other condition (legal, commercial or other) that could result in the entity supporting losses, from whatever cause, on the items being financed (or, as discussed in the next paragraph, supporting such losses beyond a fixed monetary ceiling). Recourse could take a number of forms, for instance: an agreement to repurchase non-performing items or to substitute good items for bad ones; a guarantee given to the provider of the finance or any other party (of performance, proceeds or other support); a put option under which items can be transferred back to the entity; a swap of some or all of the amounts generated by the item for a separately determined payment; or a penalty on cancelling an ongoing arrangement such that the entity bears the cost of any items that turn out to be bad. Normal warranties given in respect of the condition of the item at the time the non-recourse finance arrangement is entered into would not breach this condition; however, warranties relating to the condition of the item in the future or to its future performance would do so.

84   If there is partial recourse for losses up to a fixed monetary ceiling, a linked presentation may still be appropriate in respect of that part of the finance for which there is no recourse. However, where the entity provides any kind of open-ended guarantee (ie one that does not have a fixed monetary ceiling) a linked presentation should not be used. An example of such an open-ended guarantee would be a guarantee of completion provided by a property developer.

85   [Withdrawn]†

86   Condition 27(f) requires there to be no provision for the entity to repurchase the item being financed. For instance, where legal title to the item has been transferred, a linked presentation should not be used to the extent that one party has a put or a call option to effect repurchase, or where there is an understanding between the parties that the item will be re-acquired in the future.

Profit or loss recognition and presentation

87   Where a linked presentation is used, profits or losses should be recognised in the period in which they arise so as to reflect the fact that the entity continues to gain or suffer from the performance of the underlying gross item. For example, on entering into the arrangement, a gain will arise only to the extent that the non-returnable proceeds received exceed the previous carrying value of the item. In subsequent periods, a gain (or loss) will arise to the extent that the income from the item exceeds (or falls short of) the amounts due to the provider of finance in respect of that period.

*Editor's note: Amended by FRS 26 with effect for accounting periods beginning on or after 1 January 2007.

†*Editor's note: Paragraph deleted by amendments to FRS 26 with effect for accounting periods beginning on or after 1 January 2007.

Finally, any gain resulting from an onward sale of the item to a third party will arise only in the period in which the onward sale occurs.

Where a linked presentation is adopted in the balance sheet, normally it will be sufficient for only the net amount of any income or expense recognised in each period to be included in the profit and loss account, with the gross components being disclosed by way of note. However, the gross components should be shown on the face of the profit and loss account by using a linked presentation where the effect of the arrangement on the performance of the entity is so significant that to include merely the net amount of income or expense within the captions shown on the face of the profit and loss account would not be sufficient to give a true and fair view. **88**

Offset

[Withdrawn]* **89-91**

Disclosure of the substance of transactions

Paragraph 30 requires that disclosure of a transaction should be sufficient to enable the user of the financial statements to understand its commercial effect. For the vast majority of transactions this involves no more than those disclosures currently required. However, this may not be sufficient to portray fully the commercial effect of more complex transactions, in which case further information will need to be disclosed. **92**

Assets and liabilities resulting from more complex transactions will not necessarily be exactly the same as those resulting from more straightforward transactions. The greater the differences the greater the need for disclosure. For example, certain assets may not be available for use as security for liabilities of the entity; or certain liabilities, whilst not qualifying for the linked presentation set out in paragraphs 26–27 may, in the event of default, be repayable only to the extent that the assets on which they are secured yield sufficient benefits. **93**

Even where a transaction does not result in any items being recognised in the balance sheet, the need for disclosure should still be considered. The transaction may give rise to guarantees, commitments or other rights and obligations which, although not sufficient to require recognition of an asset or liability, require disclosure in order that the financial statements give a true and fair view. **94**

QUASI-SUBSIDIARIES

Identification of quasi-subsidiaries

An entity may directly control access to future economic benefits or may control such access through the medium of another entity, normally a subsidiary. Control through the medium of another entity is of such widespread significance that it underlies the statutory definition of a subsidiary undertaking and is reflected in the requirement for the preparation of consolidated accounts. However, such control is not confined to cases where another entity is a subsidiary as defined in statute. 'Quasi-subsidiaries' are sometimes established by arrangements that give as much effective control over another entity as if that entity were a subsidiary. **95**

Editor's note: Deleted by FRS 25.

Benefits

96   In deciding whether or not an entity is a quasi-subsidiary, access to the whole of the benefit inflows arising from its gross assets and responsibility for the whole of the benefit outflows associated with its liabilities are not the key considerations. In practice, many subsidiaries do not give rise to a possible benefit outflow for their parent of an amount equal to their gross liabilities – indeed, the limiting of benefit outflows in the event of losses occurring may have been a factor for the parent in establishing a subsidiary. In addition, as the liabilities of a subsidiary have a prior claim on its assets, the parent will not have access to benefit inflows of an amount equal to those gross assets. For this reason, it is necessary to focus on the benefit flows associated with the net assets of the entity. Often evidence of where these benefits lie is given by which party stands to suffer or gain from the financial performance of the entity – ie which party has the risks inherent in the benefits.

Control

97   Control is the means by which one entity determines how the assets of another entity are employed and by which the controlling entity ensures that the resulting benefits accrue to itself and not to others. Control may be evidenced in a variety of ways depending on its basis (eg ownership or other rights) and the way in which it is exercised (interventionist or not). Control includes the ability to restrict others from directing major policies, but a power of veto will not of itself constitute control unless its effect is that major policy decisions are taken in accordance with the wishes of the party holding that power. One entity will not control another where there is a third party that has the ability to determine all major issues of policy.

98   In some cases, arrangements are made for allocating the benefits arising from the activities of an entity such that active exercise of control is not necessary. The party or parties who will gain the benefits (and bear their inherent risks) are irreversibly specified in advance. No party has direct control in the sense of day-to-day direction of the entity's financial and operating policies, since all such matters are predetermined. In such cases, control will be exercised indirectly via the arrangements for allocating the benefits and it will be necessary to look at the effects of those arrangements to establish which party has control. It follows that, for the reasons set out in paragraph 96 above, the party possessing control will be the one that gains the benefits arising from the net assets of the entity.

Accounting for quasi-subsidiaries

99   In essence, consolidation is founded on the principle that all the entities under the control of the reporting entity should be incorporated into a single set of financial statements. Applying this principle has the result that the assets, liabilities, profits, losses and cash flows of any entity that is a quasi-subsidiary should be included in group financial statements in the same way as if they were those of a member of the statutory group (this is referred to below as 'inclusion of a quasi-subsidiary in group financial statements').

100   The entities that constitute a group are determined by companies legislation. Companies legislation also requires that where compliance with its provisions would not be sufficient to give a true and fair view, the necessary additional information shall be given in the accounts or in a note to them*. Inclusion of a quasi-subsidiary in group

---

*In Great Britain section 227(5) of the Companies Act 1985. Equivalent references for Northern Ireland and the Republic of Ireland are given in paragraphs 5 and 6 respectively of Appendix 1 'Note on legal requirements'.

financial statements is necessary in order to give a true and fair view of the group as legally defined and thus constitutes provision of such additional information.

Companies legislation and FRS 2 'Accounting for Subsidiary Undertakings' permit or require subsidiaries to be excluded from consolidation in certain circumstances. However, as inclusion of a quasi-subsidiary in group financial statements is required in order that those financial statements give a true and fair view of the group, these exclusions are generally not appropriate for a quasi-subsidiary. The following considerations are relevant.

101

(a) An immaterial quasi-subsidiary is outside the scope of this FRS, which need not be applied to immaterial items.

(b) Where severe long-term restrictions substantially hinder the exercise of the rights of the reporting entity over the assets or management of another entity, the reporting entity will not have the control necessary for the definition of a quasi-subsidiary to be met. Where the financial and operating policies of another entity are predetermined, this affects the manner in which control of that entity is exercised, but does not preclude the entity from being a quasi-subsidiary.

(c) Disproportionate expense or undue delay in obtaining information justifies excluding a quasi-subsidiary only if it is immaterial.

(d) Where there are significant differences between the activities of a quasi-subsidiary and those of the group that controls it, these should be disclosed. However, the quasi-subsidiary should nevertheless be included in the consolidation in order that the group financial statements present a true picture of the extent of the group's activities.

It is appropriate to exclude a quasi-subsidiary from consolidation only where the interest in the quasi-subsidiary is held exclusively with a view to subsequent resale and the quasi-subsidiary has not previously been included in the reporting entity's consolidated financial statements. In determining if this exclusion is appropriate in a particular instance, reference should be made to FRS 2.

Some arrangements for financing an item on a non-recourse basis involve placing the item and its finance in a quasi-subsidiary as a means of 'ring-fencing' them. Where, as a result, the conditions of paragraphs 26 and 27 are met from the point of view of the group as legally defined, the item and its finance should be included in the group financial statements by using a linked presentation. As noted above, the inclusion of a quasi-subsidiary in group financial statements forms additional information, necessary in order to give a true and fair view of the group as legally defined – the quasi-subsidiary is not part of that group. Where an item and its finance are effectively ring-fenced in a quasi-subsidiary, a true and fair view of the position of the group is given by presenting them under a linked presentation. In this situation, the group does not have an asset equal to the gross amount of the item, nor a liability for the full amount of the finance. However, where the item and its finance are similarly ring-fenced in a subsidiary, a linked presentation may not be used. This is because the subsidiary is part of the group as legally defined – hence the item and its finance, being an asset and a liability of the subsidiary, are respectively an asset and liability of the group. The subsidiary would be consolidated in the normal way in accordance with companies legislation and a linked presentation would not be used (unless a linked presentation were appropriate in the subsidiary's individual financial statements).

102

Disclosure of quasi-subsidiaries

103   When one or more quasi-subsidiaries are included in the consolidated financial statements of a statutory group, companies legislation requires the fact that such additional information has been included, and the effect of its inclusion, to be clearly disclosed.*

*In Great Britain section 227 of the Companies Act 1985. Equivalent references for Northern Ireland and the Republic of Ireland are given in paragraphs 5 and 6 respectively of Appendix I 'Note on legal requirements'.

Application notes

These Application Notes specify how the requirements of FRS 5 are to be applied to transactions that have certain features. For such transactions, observance of the Notes will normally be sufficient to ensure compliance with the requirements of FRS 5.

The tables, flow chart and illustrations shown in the shaded areas are provided as an aid to understanding and shall not be regarded as part of the Statement of Standard Accounting Practice.

It is not intended that the accounting treatment determined by FRS 5 or the terminology used in the Application Notes should change the situation at law achieved by the parties. Accordingly, it is not intended that the legal effectiveness of any transfer should be affected.

Contents

A   CONSIGNMENT STOCK
B   SALE AND REPURCHASE AGREEMENTS
C   FACTORING OF DEBTS
D   SECURITISED ASSETS
E   LOAN TRANSFERS
F   PRIVATE FINANCE INITIATIVE AND SIMILAR CONTRACTS
G   REVENUE RECOGNITION

APPLICATION NOTE A – CONSIGNMENT STOCK

NB: Although this Application Note is drafted in terms of the motor trade it applies equally to similar arrangements in other industries.

Features

Consignment stock is stock held by one party (the 'dealer') but legally owned by   A1
another (the 'manufacturer'), on terms that give the dealer the right to sell the stock in the normal course of its business or, at its option, to return it unsold to the legal owner. The stock may be physically located on the premises of the dealer, or held at a car compound or other site nearby. The arrangement has a number of commercial advantages for both parties: the dealer is able to hold or have faster access to a wider range of stock than might otherwise be practicable; the manufacturer can avoid a build-up of stock on its premises by moving it closer to the point of sale; and both benefit from the greater sales potential of the arrangement.

The main features of a consignment stock arrangement are as follows: A2

(a)   The manufacturer delivers goods to the dealer, but legal title does not pass until one of a number of events takes place, eg the dealer has held the goods for a specified period, adopts them by using them as demonstration models, or sells them to a third party. Until such a crystallising event, the dealer is entitled to return the goods to the manufacturer or the manufacturer is able to require their return or insist that they are passed to another dealer.

(b)   Once legal title passes, the transfer price becomes payable by the dealer. This price may be fixed at the date goods are delivered to the dealer, it may vary with the period between delivery and transfer of title, or it may be the manufacturer's list price at the date of transfer of title.

(c) The dealer may also be required to pay a deposit to the manufacturer, or to pay the latter a display or financing charge. This deposit or charge may be fixed for a period (eg one year) or may fluctuate. Its amount is usually set with reference to the dealer's past sales of the manufacturer's goods or to average or actual holdings of consignment stock. It may (or may not) bear interest. In some cases, a finance company will pay the deposit or charge to the manufacturer and will charge interest thereon to the dealer.

(d) Other terms of the arrangement will usually cover items such as inspection and access rights of the manufacturer, and responsibility for damage, loss or theft and related insurance. These are usually of minor importance in determining the accounting treatment.

Analysis

A3 The purpose of the analysis below is to determine whether, at any particular time, the dealer has an asset in the stock and a corresponding liability to pay the manufacturer for it. To this end, it is necessary to identify whether the dealer has access to the benefits of the stock and exposure to the risks inherent in those benefits. From the dealer's perspective, the principal benefits and risks of consignment stock are as follows:

Benefits:
(i) the future cash flows from sale to a third party and the right to retain items of stock in order to achieve such a sale;
(ii) insulation from changes to the transfer price charged by the manufacturer for its stock (eg because the manufacturer has increased its list price); and
(iii) the right to use the stock (eg as a demonstration model) by adopting it.

Risks:
(i) the risk of being compelled to retain stock that is not readily saleable or is obsolete, resulting in no sale or a sale at a reduced price; and
(ii) the risk of slow movement, resulting in increased costs of financing and holding the stock and an increased risk of obsolescence.

Paragraphs A5–A10 show how the various features of a consignment stock agreement will determine where the above benefits and risks lie. The stock should be included on the dealer's balance sheet where the dealer has access to its principal benefits and bears the principal risks inherent in those benefits.

A4 In determining the substance of an agreement, it will be necessary to look at all its features and give greater weight to those that are more likely to have a commercial effect in practice. In addition, it will be necessary to consider the interaction between the features and to evaluate the arrangement as a whole.

Manufacturer's right of return (benefit (i))

A5 The dealer's access to the benefits of the stock will be constrained by any right of the manufacturer to require goods to be returned or transferred to another dealer. The likely commercial effect of this constraint should be assessed. For instance, if a high proportion of the consignment stock is returned or transferred without compensation, this indicates that the stock is not an asset of the dealer. Conversely, if the dealer is able to resist requests made by the manufacturer for transfers and in practice actually does so, or in practice the manufacturer compensates the dealer for agreeing to transfer stock in accordance with the manufacturer's wishes, this indicates that the stock is an asset of the dealer.

Dealer's right of return (risk (i))

If the dealer has a right to return stock without payment of a penalty, it will not bear   **A6**
obsolescence risk. This indicates that the dealer has neither the asset 'stock', nor a
liability to pay the manufacturer for it. Again, the likely commercial effect of any
such right of return and the significance of obsolescence risk should be considered. If
the right of return is exercised frequently or the manufacturer regularly provides a
significant incentive (such as a price discount or a free extension to the consignment
period) to persuade the dealer not to return stock where it would otherwise do so,
this indicates that the stock is not an asset of the dealer. Conversely, if the dealer
either has no right to return stock, or in practice does not exercise its right or is
charged a significant penalty for doing so, this indicates that the dealer bears the
principal risks relating to the stock and the stock is an asset for it. In such cases the
dealer will also have a corresponding liability (legal or commercial) to pay for the
stock.

Stock transfer price and deposits (benefit (ii), risk (ii))

Whether the dealer is insulated from changes in the prices charged by the manu-   **A7**
facturer for its stock depends on how the stock transfer price is determined. Where
the price is based on the manufacturer's list price at delivery, then the manufacturer
is unable to pass on any subsequent price changes, which indicates that the stock
became an asset of the dealer at the date of delivery. Conversely, if the price charged
to the dealer is the manufacturer's list price at the date of the transfer of legal title,
this indicates that the stock remains an asset of the manufacturer until legal title is
transferred.

The stock transfer price will also affect the incidence of slow movement risk and who   **A8**
bears the variable cost of financing the stock until sold. In a simple arrangement
where there is no deposit and stock is supplied for a fixed price that is payable by the
dealer only when legal title is transferred it will be clear that the manufacturer bears
the slow movement risk. The manufacturer will bear the slow movement risk
wherever the transfer price is not determined by reference to the length of time for
which stock is held (such as where the transfer price is the manufacturer's list price at
either delivery or transfer of legal title). Conversely, if in the same basic arrangement,
the price to be paid by the dealer increases by a factor that varies with the time the
stock is held and approximates to commercial interest rates, then it will be equally
clear that the dealer bears the slow movement risk. This may be so even where the
financing element of the price charged to the dealer is based on average past
movements of stocks held by that dealer (eg for administrative convenience), or is
levied in another form (eg a display charge).

The existence of a deposit complicates the analysis. The main question to be   **A9**
answered is whether the effect of the deposit is that the dealer, rather than the
manufacturer, bears variations in the stock financing costs that are due to slow
movement. For example, this could be achieved by a substantial, interest-free deposit
whose amount is related to levels of stock held by the dealer. Alternatively, a finance
company might advance the deposit to the manufacturer and charge interest thereon
(in whatever form) to the dealer.

Dealer's right to use the stock (benefit (iii))

Whilst a right for the dealer to use the stock in its business will not, of itself, be   **A10**
sufficient to make the stock an asset of the dealer, the exercise of the right will usually

have this effect. Such exercise will usually cause the transfer of legal title to the dealer and give rise to an unconditional obligation for it to pay the manufacturer.

Required accounting

Substance of the transaction is that the stock is an asset of the dealer

A11   Where it is concluded that the stock is in substance an asset of the dealer, the stock should be recognised as such on the dealer's balance sheet, together with a corresponding liability to the manufacturer. Any deposit should be deducted from the liability and the excess classified as a trade creditor. The notes to the financial statements should explain the nature of the arrangement, the amount of consignment stock included in the balance sheet and the main terms under which it is held, including the terms of any deposit.

Substance of the transaction is that the stock is not an asset of the dealer

A12   Where it is concluded that the stock is not in substance an asset of the dealer, the stock should not be included on the dealer's balance sheet until the transfer of title has crystallised. Any deposit should be included under 'other debtors'. The notes to the financial statements should explain the nature of the arrangement, the amount of consignment stock held at the year-end, and the main terms under which it is held, including the terms of any deposit.

Table

Indications that the stock is not an asset of the dealer at delivery	Indications that the stock is an asset of the dealer at delivery
Manufacturer can require the dealer to return stock (or transfer stock to another dealer) without compensation, or Penalty paid by the dealer to prevent returns/transfers of stock at the manufacturers request.	Manufacturer cannot require dealer to return or transfer stock, or Financial incentives given to persuade dealer to transfer stock at manufacturer's request.
Dealer has unfettered right to return stock to the manufacturer without penalty and actually exercises the right in practice.	Dealer has no right to return stock or is commercially compelled not to exercise its right of return.
Manufacturer bears obsolescence risk, eg: - obsolete stock is returned to the manufacturer without penalty; or - financial incentives given by manufacturers to prevent stock being returned to it (eg on a model change or if it become obsolete).	Dealer bears obsolescence risk, eg: - penalty charged if dealer returns stock to manufacturer; or - obsolete stock cannot be returned to the manufacturer and no compensation is paid by manufacturer for losses due to obsolescence.
Stock transfer price charged by manufacturer is based on manufacturer's list price at date of transfer of legal title.	Stock transfer price charged by manufacturer is based on manufacturer's list price at date of delivery.

| Manufacturer bears slow movement risk, eg;
 - transfer price set independently of time for which dealer holds stock, and there is no deposit. | Dealer bears slow movement risk, eg:
 - dealer is effectively charged interest as transfer price or other payments to manufacturer vary with time for which dealer holds stock; or
 - dealer makes substantial interest-free deposit that varies with the levels of stock held. |

APPLICATION NOTE B – SALE AND REPURCHASE AGREEMENTS

The principles in this Application Note apply only to those transactions falling within the scope of paragraphs 14 to 31 of FRS 5, and not to those falling within the scope of paragraphs 14 to 42 of FRS 26 'Financial Instruments: Recognition and Measurement'.*

NB: For ease of reading the parties to a sale and repurchase agreement are referred to below as 'seller' and 'buyer', notwithstanding that analysis of the transaction in accordance with this Application Note may result in the seller continuing to show an asset on its balance sheet.

Features

Sale and repurchase agreements are arrangements under which assets are sold by one party to another on terms that provide for the seller to repurchase the asset in certain circumstances. A similar commercial effect may be achieved by arrangements under which one party holds an asset on behalf of another: although such arrangements are not sale and repurchase agreements, a similar analysis is appropriate and these are therefore covered by this Application Note.   **B1**

The main features of a sale and repurchase agreement will usually be: **B2**

(a) the sale price – this may be market value or another agreed price (analysed in paragraph B9);

(b) the nature of the repurchase provision – this may be: an unconditional commitment for both parties; an option for the seller to repurchase (a call option); an option for the buyer to resell to the seller (a put option); or a combination of put and call options; (analysed in paragraphs B10–B12);

(c) the repurchase price – this may: be fixed at the outset; vary with the period for which the asset is held by the buyer; or be the market price at the time of repurchase. It may also be designed to permit the buyer to recover incidental holding costs (eg insurance) if these do not in fact continue to be met by the seller; (analysed in paragraphs B13–B14); and

(d) other provisions, including where appropriate: for the seller to use the asset whilst it is owned by the buyer; for determining the time of repurchase; or for remarketing the asset if it is to be sold to a third party; (analysed in paragraphs B15–B18).

*Editor's Note: Paragraph added by amendments to FRS 26 with effect for accounting periods beginning on or after 1 January 2007.

FRS 5 APPLICATION NOTES

Analysis

Overview of basic principles

B3 The purpose of the analysis is to determine both whether the seller has an asset (and what is the nature of that asset), and whether the seller has a liability to repay the buyer some or all of the amounts received from the latter.

B4 In a straightforward case, the substance of a sale and repurchase agreement will be that of a secured loan – ie the seller will retain all significant rights to benefits relating to the original asset and all significant exposure to the risks inherent in those benefits and will have a liability to the buyer for the whole of the proceeds received. For example, this would be the case where the seller has in effect an unconditional commitment to repurchase the original asset from the buyer at the sale price plus interest. The seller should account for this type of arrangement by showing the original asset on its balance sheet together with a liability for the amounts received from the buyer.

B5 In certain more complex cases, it may be determined that a sale and repurchase agreement is not in substance a financing transaction and that the seller retains access to only some of the benefits of the original asset and retains only some of their inherent risks. Where this is so, in accordance with paragraph 23, the description or monetary amount of the original asset should be changed and a liability recognised for any obligation to transfer benefits that is assumed. It will also be necessary to give full disclosure of these more complex arrangements in the notes to the financial statements.

B6 The substance of the arrangement may be more readily apparent if the position of both buyer and seller are considered, together with their apparent expectations and motives for agreeing to its various terms. In particular, where the substance is that of a secured loan, the buyer will require that it is assured of a lender's return on its investment and the seller will require that the buyer earns no more than this return. Thus whether or not the buyer earns such a return is an important indicator of the substance of the transaction.

Benefits and risks

B7 The analysis that follows shows how the features set out in paragraph B2 may result in the seller having a liability to the buyer or in the seller retaining rights to some or all of the benefits of the original asset and exposure to some or all of the risks inherent in those benefits. These benefits and risks will usually include some or all of the following:

Benefits:
(i)   the benefit of any expected increase in the value of the asset; and
(ii) benefits arising from use or development of the asset.

Risks:
(i)   the risk of an unexpected variation (adverse or favourable) in the value of the asset;
(ii) the risk of obsolescence; and
(iii) where repurchase is not at a set date, the risk of a variation in the cost of financing the asset because of the variable period between sale and repurchase.

B8 In analysing any specific agreement in practice, it will be necessary to look at all the features of the agreement and give greater weight to those that are more likely to have a commercial effect in practice. In addition, it will be necessary to consider the interaction between the features in order to determine the substance of the arrangement as a whole.

Feature (a) – Sale price

A sale price of other than the market value of the asset at the time of sale indicates **B9** that some benefit and risk have been retained by the seller, such that the seller has an asset (either the original asset or a new one) or a liability to the buyer. Even where the sale price is the asset's market value, the seller may nevertheless have an asset or a liability since the other terms of the arrangement may result in the seller retaining significant benefits and risks.

Feature (b) – Nature of repurchase provision

1. Commitment

Any type of unconditional commitment for the seller to repurchase will give rise to **B10** both a liability and an asset for the seller: the liability being the seller's commitment to pay the repurchase price; and the asset being continued access to some or all of the benefits of the original asset that forms the subject of the sale and repurchase agreement. The price at which repurchase will occur and the other provisions of the arrangement will determine the exact nature of the seller's asset; these are dealt with in paragraphs B13–B18 below.

There may in effect be a commitment to repurchase even without a strict legal **B11** obligation. In particular, this will be the case where there is an option (or a combination of options) on terms that leave no genuine commercial possibility that the option will fail to be exercised. For example, the exercise price of a call option may be set at a significant discount to expected market value, the seller may need the asset to use on an ongoing basis in its business, or the asset may provide in effect the only source of the seller's future sales. Unwritten understandings between the parties may also result in a commercial commitment for the seller to repurchase even in the absence of a strict legal obligation. Such a commitment is more likely to exist where the buyer's business does not usually involve it in taking on risks of a kind associated with the asset.

2. Put and call options

In some cases the seller may have a call option to repurchase the asset but have no **B12** commitment to do so, or the buyer may have a put option to transfer the asset back to the seller without the seller having an equivalent right to insist on repurchase. It will be important to determine why the parties have agreed to such a one-sided option and to assess the commercial effect of the option with regard to all aspects of the arrangement, including whether the seller has a commercial need to repurchase the asset. This analysis may reveal that, in substance, there is a commitment to repurchase as discussed above. Conversely, such an analysis may reveal that the buyer assumes significant benefits and risks relating to the original asset, indicating that the seller has neither the original asset, nor a liability for the option's exercise price. In such a case, where the seller holds a call option it will have a new asset in the form of the option itself; where the buyer has a put option, the seller will have a contingent liability to the buyer for the exercise price of the option (contingent on the buyer exercising its option). In both cases, the seller's new asset or liability should be recognised or disclosed, on a prudent basis, following the principles set out in SSAP 18 'Accounting for contingencies'.*

---

*Editor's note: SSAP 18 has been superseded by FRS 12 'Provisions, contingent liabilities and contingent assets'.

Feature (c) – Repurchase price and provision for a lender's return

B13   In the most straightforward case, the repurchase price will be the sum of the original sale price, plus any major costs incurred by the buyer and a lender's return (comprising interest on the sale price and costs incurred by the buyer, perhaps with a relatively small fee), but no more. In this case, even if the repurchase provision takes the form of an option, the repurchase price indicates that the substance of the transaction is that of a secured loan, with the benefits and risks of the asset remaining with the seller. This is because the buyer is not compensated for assuming any significant exposure to loss, nor is the seller compensated for giving up any significant potential for gain, thus indicating that the transaction is, in substance, a financing. It will be necessary to look at the arrangement as a whole to establish whether the buyer receives a lender's return since the means of providing it will vary. For example, it may be achieved by lease or other regular payments, licence fees, adjustment to the original sales price or the calculation of the repurchase price.

B14   Conversely, if the buyer is not assured of a lender's return, this indicates that some benefit and risk have been passed to the buyer such that the seller has not retained the original asset. The seller may, nevertheless, have a different asset (and a corresponding liability). For example, if a manufacturer sells equipment but agrees to repurchase it in a substantially different form towards the end of its economic life, the manufacturer has both a liability (to pay the repurchase price) and an asset (the equipment as at the repurchase date).

Feature (d) – Other provisions

1. Ability to use the asset

B15   Whilst the ability of the seller to determine the use of the original asset does not, of itself, result in the substance of the transaction being that of a secured loan, it will usually indicate this is so. Continued use of the asset by the seller may indicate that it has a commercial obligation to repurchase even if it has no legal obligation to do so, for instance if there is a commercial need for the seller to repurchase or an expectation that it will do so.

B16   Where the seller continues to use the asset in its business by entering into a sale and leaseback transaction, the provisions of both SSAP 21 'Accounting for leases and hire purchase contracts' and this Application Note will be relevant. Where, in the terms of this Application Note, the substance of the transaction is that of a secured loan, it will be structured so that no significant benefits or risks are passed to the buyer, with the rentals and other lease payments providing the buyer with a lender's return. Thus, in the terms of SSAP 21, 'substantially all the risks and rewards of ownership' of the asset will remain with the seller, the leaseback will be classified as a finance lease, and the transaction will be accounted for as the raising of finance secured on the asset. If, on the other hand, the leaseback is in substance an operating lease, the transaction will be accounted for as a sale of the original asset.

2. Profits or losses on a sale of the asset to a third party

B17   In some cases, the seller may retain access to any increase in the value of the asset via provisions that pass to it substantially all of any profit arising on a sale by the first buyer to a third party (subject to the buyer receiving a lender's return). In addition the buyer may be protected from risk of loss, for instance by the seller being obliged to reimburse the whole or part of any loss on a sale to a third party, or the original sale price being such that losses are unlikely to occur in practice. The substance of such an arrangement is that of a secured loan.

3. Use of special entities ('vehicles')

Some cases may involve a sale to a special entity (a 'vehicle') that is partly or wholly   **B18**
financed by a party other than the seller (eg a financial institution). In such a case, the
seller will usually retain access to any increase in the value of the asset and, where
relevant, the benefits from its use, via a right either to repurchase the asset or, in the
event that the seller does not repurchase, to receive the majority of any profits from a
future sale to a third party. In addition, the seller may provide protection against loss
to the other investors in the vehicle, eg by providing a subordinated loan to the
vehicle that acts as a cushion to absorb any losses or by guaranteeing the value of the
asset in the event that it is sold on to a third party. Such provisions are clear
indications that the substance of the transaction is that of a secured loan. Where the
terms of the arrangement taken as a whole mean that the investors in the vehicle are
reasonably assured of recovering their original investment and earning a lender's
return (but no more) thereon, the substance of the transaction will be that of a
secured loan.

Required accounting

Substance of the transaction is that of a secured loan

Where the substance of the transaction is that of a secured loan, the seller should   **B19**
continue to recognise the original asset and record the proceeds received from the
buyer as a liability. Interest – however designated – should be accrued. The carrying
amount of the asset should be reviewed and provided against if necessary. The notes
to the financial statements should describe the principal features of the arrangement,
including the status of the asset and the relationship between the asset and liability.

Where the transaction is a sale and leaseback, no profit should be recognised on   **B20**
entering into the arrangement and no adjustment made to the carrying value of the
asset. As stated in the guidance notes to SSAP 21, this represents the substance of the
transaction, "namely the raising of finance secured on an asset that continues to be
held and that is not disposed of".

Substance of the transaction is that the seller has a different asset

Where the seller has a new asset or liability (for example, merely a call option to   **B21**
repurchase the original asset), it should recognise or disclose that new asset or liability on a prudent basis in accordance with the provisions of SSAP 18.* In particular,
the seller should recognise (and not merely disclose) a liability for any kind of
unconditional obligation it has entered into. Where doubts exist regarding the
amount of any gain or loss arising, full provision should be made for any expected
loss but recognition of any gain, to the extent that it is in doubt, should be deferred
until it is realised. The notes to the financial statements should describe the main
features of the arrangement, including: the status of the asset; the relationship
between the asset and the liability; and the terms of any provision for repurchase
(including any options) and of any guarantees.

**Editor's note: SSAP 18 has been superseded by FRS 12 'Provisions, contingent liabilities and contingent
assets'.*

FRS 5 APPLICATION NOTES

Table

Indications of sale of original asset to buyer (nevertheless, the seller may retain a different asset)	Indications of no sale of original asset to buyer (secured loan)
	Sale price does not equal market value at date of sale.
No commitment for seller to repurchase asset, eg: - call option where there is a real possibility the option will fail to be exercised.	Commitment for seller to repurchase asset, eg: - put and call option with the same exercise price; - either a put or a call option with no genuine commercial possibility that the option will fail to be exercised; or - seller requires asset back to use in its business, or asset is in effect the only source of seller's future sales.
Risk of changes in asset value borne by buyer such that buyer does not receive solely a lender's return, eg: - both sale and repurchase price equal market value at date of sale/purchase.	Risk of changes in asset value borne by seller such that buyer receives solely a lender's return, eg: - repurchase price equals sale price plus costs plus interest; - original purchase price adjusted retrospectively to pass variations in the value of the asset to the seller; - seller provides residual value guarantee to buyer or subordinated debt to protect buyer from falls in the value of the asset.
Nature of the asset is such that it will be used over the life of the agreement, and the seller has no rights to determine its use. Seller has no rights to determine asset's development or future sale.	Seller retains right to determine asset's use, development or sale, or rights to profits therefrom.

Illustrations

Illustration 1

A, a house-builder, agrees with B, a bank, to sell to B some of the land within its land bank. The arrangements surrounding the sale are as follows:

(a) the sales price will be open market value as determined by an independent surveyor;

(b) B grants A the right to develop the land at any time during B's ownership, subject to its approval of the development plans, which approval shall not be unreasonably withheld; for this right, A pays all the outgoings on the land plus an annual fee of 5 per cent of the purchase price;

(c) B will maintain a memorandum account in respect of the land for the purpose of determining the price to be paid by A should A ever re-acquire the land or any adjustments necessary to the original purchase price. In this account will be entered the purchase price, any expenses incurred by B in relation to the transaction, a sum added quarterly (or on the sale by B of the land) calculated by reference to B's base lending rate plus 2 per cent applied to the daily balance on the account; and from the account will be deduced any annual fees paid by A to B;

(d) B grants A an option to acquire the land at any time within the next five years; the acquisition price is to be the balance on the memorandum account at the time of exercising the option;

(e) A grants B an option to require it to repurchase the land at any time within the next five years, the price to be the balance on the memorandum account at that time;

(f) on the expiry of five years from the date of acquiring the land, B will offer it for sale generally; and at any time prior to that it may with the consent of A offer the land for sale; and

(g) in the event of B selling the land to a third party, the proceeds of sale shall be deducted from the memorandum account maintained by B and the balance on the account shall be settled between A and B in cash, as a retrospective adjustment of the price at which B originally purchased the land from A.

The commercial effect of the above arrangement is that of a secured loan. A continues to bear all significant benefits and risks relating to the land, retains control of its development, and bears all resulting gains and losses (via either exercise of its call option, or adjust to the purchase price on sale of the land to a third party). This latter feature also gives rise to a liability for A to repay the whole of the sale proceeds received from B. In addition, B is assured of a lender's return (and no more): whilst the regular payments by A to B to secure the right to develop the land are not sufficient to provide this, B's return is guaranteed through the operation of the memorandum account and its role in determining the option price on a resale.

Illustration 2

This illustration is similar to the first but makes use of V, a vehicle company, and a subordinated loan to effect the purchase. A agrees with B (the bank) and V to sell land within its land bank to V. Relevant terms are as follows:

(a) the sale price is open market value;

(b) B grants V a loan of 60 per cent of the market value to effect the purchase, with A providing V with a subordinated loan of the balance of the consideration. B's loan bears interest at the bank's base rate plus 2 per cent: A's loan bears interest at 10 per cent. All payments of interest and capital on A's loan are subordinated to all sums due to B in any period;

(c) V grants A the right to develop the land at any time during V's ownership, subject to its approval. For this right, A pays V a market rental on the land. If this is less than the interest payable on V's loan from B, then A will advance the amount of the shortfall as an addition to its subordinated loan;

(d) V grants A an option to acquire the land at any time within the next five years, at a price equal to the original sales price plus any incidental costs incurred by V;

(e) on the expiry of five years from the date of acquiring the land, V will offer it for sale generally, and at any time before then may with the consent of A offer the land for sale; and

(f) in the event of V selling the land, to the extent that the proceeds of sale and any other cash accumulated in V exceed any sums due to B and A under the terms of their respective loans, an immediate payment shall be made to A as a retrospective adjustment of the price at which V originally purchased the land from A.

In this illustration, the substance of the transaction is that of a secured loan. A continues to bear all significant benefits and risks relating to the land, it continues to have the ability to develop it and access to the whole of any profits from its future sale. In addition, the subordinated loan from A provides a cushion to absorb losses on the disposal of the land by the vehicle; this ensures that all foreseeable losses accrue to A and thus protects the position of the bank. In practice, such subordinated loans are often sufficiently large to make any loss by the bank through a loss in value of the land extremely remote. Where this is not the case or there is no subordinated loan, the necessary protection may be provided through put options – such as are incorporated within Illustration 1 – which enable the buyer to require the seller to repurchase the asset. Where the substance of the transaction is that of a secured loan, the buyer will require that the terms of the arrangement taken as a whole mean it is reasonably assured of receiving return of the purchase price and any costs it incurs plus a lender's return (but no more) on its investment.

APPLICATION NOTE C – FACTORING OF DEBTS*

NB: For ease of reading the parties to a factoring agreement are referred to in this Application Note as 'seller' and 'factor', notwithstanding that analysis of the transaction in accordance with this Application Note may result in the seller continuing to show the factored debts as an asset on its balance sheet.

Features

C1   Factoring of debts is a well established method of obtaining finance, sales ledger administration services, or protection from bad debts. The principal features of a factoring arrangement are as follows:

(a)   Specified debts are transferred to the factor (usually by assignment). The transfer may be of complete debtor balances or of all invoices relating to named debtors (perhaps subject to restrictions on the amount that will be accepted from any one debtor).

(b)   The factor offers a credit facility that permits the seller to draw up to a fixed percentage of the face value of the debts transferred. Normally these advances are repaid as and when the underlying debts are collected, often by paying the money that is collected into a specially nominated bank account for the benefit of the factor.

(c)   The factor may also offer a credit protection facility (or insurance cover). This will limit or eliminate the extent to which the factor has recourse to the seller for debts that are in default.

(d)   The factor may administer the sales ledger of the seller. Where such a service is provided, the factor becomes responsible for collecting money from debtors and pursuing those that are slow in paying. In such cases the fact that debts have been factored is likely to be disclosed to the seller's customers; this may not be necessary in other circumstances.

C2   On the transfer of debts, the factoring charges levied on the seller will be set by the factor with reference to expected collections from the debtors and any credit

*Editor's note: This Application Note is deleted in its entirety by amendments to FRS 26, for those entities complying with that standard, with effect for accounting periods beginning on or after 1 January 2007.

protection services provided (sales ledger administration services are usually invoiced separately). These charges may be fixed at the outset or subject to adjustment at a later date to reflect actual collections; they may be payable immediately or on some future date.

Analysis

Overview of basic principles

The purpose of the analysis below is to determine the appropriate accounting **C3** treatment in the seller's financial statements. There are three possible treatments:

(a)   to remove the factored debts from the balance sheet and show no liability in respect of any proceeds received from the factor ('derecognition');
(b)   to show the proceeds received from the factor deducted from the factored debts on the face of the balance sheet within a single asset caption (a 'linked presentation'); or
(c)   to continue to show the factored debts as an asset, and show a corresponding liability within creditors in respect of the proceeds received from the factor (a 'separate presentation').

In order to determine the appropriate accounting treatment, it is necessary to answer **C4** two questions:

(a)   whether the seller has access to the benefits of the factored debts and exposure to the risks inherent in those benefits (referred to below as 'benefits and risks'); and
(b)   whether the seller has a liability to repay amounts received from the factor.

Where the seller has transferred all significant benefits and all significant risks relating to the debts, and has no obligation to repay the factor, derecognition is appropriate; where the seller has retained significant benefits and risks relating to the debts but there is absolutely no doubt that its downside exposure to loss is limited, a linked presentation should be used; and in all other cases a separate presentation should be adopted.

Benefits and risks

The main benefits and risks relating to debts are as follows: **C5**

Benefits:
(i)   the future cash flows from payment by the debtors.

Risks:
(i)   slow payment risk; and
(ii)   credit risk (the risk of bad debts).

Analysis of benefits

At first glance it may appear that the factor has access to the cash flows from **C6** payments by debtors. This may be particularly so if the money that is collected is to be paid direct to the factor (or into a specially nominated bank account for its benefit). However, it may actually be the seller that benefits from payments by debtors, these payments merely representing the primary source from which the factor will be repaid. In particular, where the seller has an obligation to repay any sums received from the factor on or before a set date regardless of the level of collections from the underlying debts, it is clear that the seller has the benefit of payments by debtors, exposure to their inherent risks and a liability to the factor. Such an arrangement should be accounted for by using a separate presentation. Conversely, where the seller receives a single non-returnable cash payment from the factor and the only future payments to be made are by the seller passing to the factor all and any payments from debtors as and when paid, the seller will both have transferred the benefits and risks of the factored debts and have no obligation to repay amounts received from the factor.

This latter arrangement would qualify for derecognition.

C7   Considering the benefits in isolation will not normally enable a clear decision to be made on the appropriate accounting treatment for a factoring. The cash flows may appear similar in both of the above arrangements – an initial cash inflow for the seller followed by a later cash outflow (or a sacrifice of a cash inflow that would otherwise occur). For this reason, the risks (both upside potential for gain and downside exposure to loss) are more significant than the benefits.

Slow payment risk: credit facility

C8   The first main risk associated with non-interest bearing debts is slow payment risk (including the upside potential from prompt payment by debtors). Where the finance cost charged by the factor is essentially a fixed sum determined at the time the transfer is made, the factor will bear the risk of slow payment; where it varies to reflect the speed of collection of the debts subsequently, the seller will bear that risk. Close attention to the arrangements and to their commercial effect in practice may be necessary to determine whether a variable finance cost falls upon the seller since it may take various forms, including a bonus for early settlement, or a retrospective adjustment to the purchase price.

Credit risk: credit protection facility

C9   Credit risk is the other main risk associated with trade debts. If there is no recourse to the seller for bad debts, the factor will bear this risk; if there is full recourse, the seller will bear it. Furthermore, as non-payment is merely the ultimate form of slow payment, where credit risk is retained by the seller, the latter will normally also bear at least some risk of slow payment. For example, where the arrangement takes the form of the seller repurchasing debts that remain outstanding after a given time, the seller bears the slow payment risk beyond this time as well as bearing the credit risk.

Administration arrangements and service-only factoring

C10   For the purpose of deciding upon the appropriate accounting treatment, the administration arrangements will not be directly significant (provided they are on an arm's length basis, and for a fee that is commensurate with the service provided). In a service-only factoring arrangement, where the factor administers the sales ledger but cash is received no earlier than if the debts had not been factored, the seller retains access to the benefits of the debts and exposure to their inherent risks. Thus such an arrangement should be accounted for by using a separate presentation.

Derecognition

Derecognition (ie ceasing to recognise the factored debts in their entirety) is **C11** appropriate only where the seller retains no significant benefits and no significant risks relating to the factored debts.

Whilst the commercial effect of any particular transaction should be assessed taking **C12** into account all its aspects and implications, the presence of all of the following indicates that the seller has not retained significant benefits and risks, and dere-cognition is appropriate:

(a)   the transaction takes place at an arm's length price for an outright sale;
(b)   the transaction is for a fixed amount of consideration and there is no recourse whatsoever, either implicit or explicit, to the seller for losses from either slow payment or non-payment. Normal warranties given in respect of the condition of the debts at the time of the transfer (eg a warranty that goods have been delivered or that the borrower's credit limit had not been breached at the time of granting him credit) would not breach this condition. However, warranties relating to the condition of the debts in the future or to their future perfor-mance (eg that debtors will not move into arrears in the future) would breach the condition. Other possible forms of recourse are set out in paragraph 83; and
(c)   the seller will not benefit or suffer in any way if the debts perform better or worse than expected. This will not be the case where the seller has a right to further sums from the factor which vary according to the future performance of the debts (ie according to whether or when the debtors pay). Such sums might take the form of deferred consideration, a retrospective adjustment to the purchase price, or rebates of certain charges; they include all forms of variable finance cost.

Where any of the above three features is not present, this indicates that the seller has **C13** retained benefits and risks relating to the factored debts and, unless these are insig-nificant, either a separate presentation or a linked presentation should be adopted.

Whether any benefit and risk retained are 'significant' should be judged in relation to **C14** those benefits and risks that are likely to occur in practice, and not in relation to the total possible benefits and risks. For example, if for a portfolio of factored debts of 100, expected bad debts are 5 and there is recourse to the seller for credit losses of up to 10, significant risk will have been retained (as the seller would bear losses of up to twice those expected to occur). Accordingly, in this example, derecognition would not be appropriate and either a linked presentation or a separate presentation should be used. The terms of any roll-over provisions and their effect in practice require careful consideration since these may result in the seller continuing to bear significant risk where, at first sight, it appears that the arrangements do not have this effect. For example, the pricing of future transfers may be adjusted to reflect recent slow pay-ment or bad debt experience and there may be a significant disincentive (eg a penalty) for the seller to cancel the arrangement. This may result in the seller continuing to bear significant risk, albeit disguised as revised charges for debts factored subsequently.

Linked presentation

A linked presentation will be appropriate where, although the seller has retained **C15** significant benefits and risks relating to the factored debts, there is absolutely no doubt that its downside exposure to loss is limited to a fixed monetary amount. A linked presentation should be used only to the extent that there is both absolutely no doubt that the factor's claim extends solely to collections from the factored debts, and no provision for the seller to re-acquire the debts in the future. The conditions that need to be met in order for this to be the case are set out in paragraph 27 and explained in paragraphs 81–86. When interpreting these conditions in the context of a factoring arrangement the following points apply:

condition (a) (specified assets) –
    a linked presentation should not be used where the debts that have been factored cannot be separately identified.

condition (d) (that the factor agrees in writing there is no recourse, and such agreement is noted in the financial statements) –
    the inclusion of an appropriate statement in the factoring agreement will meet the first part of this condition.

C16   Where debts are factored on an ongoing basis, the arrangements for terminating the agreement must be carefully analysed in order to ensure that the conditions for a linked presentation are met. It will be necessary that, although the factor does not take on any new debts, it continues to bear losses on debts already factored and is not able to transfer them back to the seller. Where this is not the case, there remains the possibility that the factor will return debts that it suspects to be bad by terminating the arrangement. In such a case the seller's exposure to loss is not limited, and a separate presentation should be adopted.

Separate presentation

C17   Where the seller has retained significant benefits and risks relating to the debts and the conditions for a linked presentation are not met, a separate presentation should be adopted.

Required accounting

Derecognition

C18   Where the seller has retained no significant benefits and risks relating to the debts and has no obligation to repay amounts received from the factor, the debts should be removed from its balance sheet and no liability shown in respect of the proceeds received from the factor. A profit or loss should be recognised, calculated as the difference between the carrying amount of the debts and the proceeds received.

Linked presentation

C19   Where the conditions for a linked presentation are met, the proceeds received, to the extent they are non-returnable, should be shown deducted from the gross amount of the factored debts (after providing for bad debts, credit protection charges and any accrued interest) on the face of the balance sheet. An example is given in illustration 2 below. The interest element of the factor's charges should be recognised as it accrues and included in the profit and loss account with other interest charges. The notes to the financial statements should disclose: the main terms of the arrangement; the gross amount of factored debts outstanding at the balance sheet date; the factoring charges recognised in the period, analysed as appropriate (eg between interest and other charges); and the disclosures required by conditions (c) and (d) in paragraph 27.

Separate presentation

Where neither derecognition nor a linked presentation is appropriate, a separate   **C20**
presentation should be adopted, ie a gross asset (equivalent in amount to the gross
amount of the debts) should be shown on the balance sheet of the seller within assets,
and a corresponding liability in respect of the proceeds received from the factor
should be shown within liabilities. The interest element of the factor's charges should
be recognised as it accrues and included in the profit and loss account with other
interest charges. Other factoring costs should be similarly accrued and included in
the profit and loss account within the appropriate caption. The notes to the financial
statements should disclose the amount of factored debts outstanding at the balance
sheet date.

Table

Indications that derecognition is appropriate (debts are not an asset of the seller)	Indications that a linked presentation is appropriate	Indications that a separate presentation is appropriate (debts are an asset of the seller)
Transfer is for a single, non-returnable fixed sum.	Some non-returnable proceeds received, but seller has rights to further sums from the factor (or vice versa) whose amount depends on whether or when debtors pay.	Finance cost varies with speed of collection of debts, eg: - by adjustment to consideration for original transfer; or - subsequent transfers priced to recover costs of earlier transfers
There is no recourse to the seller for losses.	There is either no recourse for losses, or such recourse has a fixed monetary ceiling.	There is full recourse to the seller for losses.
Factor is paid all amounts received from the factored debts (and no more). Seller has no rights to further sums from the factor.	Factor is paid only out of the amounts collected from the factored debts, and sell has no right or obligation to repurchase debts.	Seller is required to repay amounts received from the factor on or before a set date, regardless of timing or amounts of collections from debtors.

Illustrations

Illustration 1 – Factoring with recourse (separate presentation)

Company S enters into a factoring arrangement with F, with the following
principal terms:

(a) S will transfer (by assignment) all its trade debts to F, subject only to credit
approval by F and a limit placed on the proportion of the total that may be
due from any one debtor;

(b) F administers S's sales ledger and handles all aspects of collection of the
debts in return for an administration charge at an annual rate of 1 per cent,
payable monthly, based upon the total debts factored at each month-end;

(c) S may draw up to 70 per cent of the gross amount of debts factored and outstanding at any time, such drawings being debited in the books of F to a factoring account operated by F for S;

(d) weekly, S assigns and sends copy invoices to F as they are raised. F sends statements to debtors, following up all overdue invoices by telephone or letter;

(e) F credits collections from debtors to the factoring account, and debits the account monthly with interest calculated on the basis of the daily balances on the account using a rate of base rate plus 2 per cent. Thus this interest charge varies with the amount of finance drawn by S under the finance facility from F, the speed of payment of the debtors and the base rate;

(f) any debts not recovered after 90 days are reassigned to S for an immediate cash payment, which is credited to the factoring account;

(g) F pays for all other debts, less any advances and interest charges made, 90 days after the date of their assignment to F, and debits the payment to the factoring account; and

(h) on termination of the agreement the balance on the factoring account is settled in cash.

The commercial effect of the above arrangements is that, although the debts have been legally transferred to F, the benefits and risks are retained by S. S continues to bear the slow payment risk as the interest charged by F varies with the speed of payment by the debtors; S continues to bear all of the credit risk as it must pay for any debts not recovered after 90 days, and it therefore has unlimited exposure to loss. In addition, S in effect has an obligation to repay amounts received from F on or before a set date regardless of the levels of collections from the factored debts – either out of collections from debtors on the day they pay, or from its general resources after 90 days, whichever is the earlier. Thus a separate presentation should be adopted.

Illustration 2 – Factoring without recourse (linked presentation)

S enters into an agreement with F with the following principal terms:

(a) S will transfer (by assignment) to F such trade debts as S shall determine, subject only to credit approval by F and a limit placed on the proportion of the total that may be due from any one debtor. F levies a charge of 0.15 per cent of turnover, payable monthly, for this facility;

(b) S continues to administer the sales ledger and handle all aspects of collection of the debts;

(c) S may draw up to 80 per cent of the gross amount of debts assigned at any time, such drawings being debited in the books of F to a factoring account operated by F for S;

(d) weekly, S assigns and sends copy invoices to F as they are raised;

(e) S is required to bank the gross amounts of all payments received from debts assigned to F direct into an account in the name of F. Credit transfers made by debtors direct into S's own bank account must immediately be paid to F;

(f) F credits such collections from debtors to the factoring account, and debits the account monthly with interest calculated on the basis of the daily balances on the account using a rate of base rate plus 2.5 per cent. Thus this interest charge varies with the amount of finance drawn by S under the finance facility from F, the speed of payment of the debtors and base rate;

(g) F provides protection from bad debts. Any debts not recovered after 90 days are credited to the factoring account, and responsibility for their collection is passed to F. A charge of 1 per cent of the gross value of all debts factored is levied by F for this service and debited to the factoring account;

(h) F pays for the debts, less any advances, interest charges and credit protection charges, 90 days after the date of purchase, and debits the payment to the factoring account; and

(i) on either party giving 90 days' notice to the other, the arrangement will be terminated. In such an event, S will transfer no further debts to F, and the balance remaining on the factoring account at the end of the notice period will be settled in cash in the normal way.

The commercial effect of this arrangement is that, although the debts have been legally transferred to F, S continues to bear significant benefits and risks relating to them. S continues to bear slow payment risk as the interest charged by F varies with the speed of collections of the debts. Hence, the gross amount of the debts should continue to be shown on its balance sheet until the earlier of collection and transfer of all risks to F (ie 90 days). However, S's maximum downside loss is limited since any debts not recovered after 90 days are in effect paid for by F, which then assumes all slow payment and credit risk beyond this time. Thus, even for debts that prove to be bad, S receives some proceeds.* Hence, assuming the conditions given in paragraphs 26 and 27 are met, a linked presentation should be adopted. The amount deducted on the face of the balance sheet should be the lower of the proceeds received and the gross amount of the debts less all charges to the factor in respect of them. In the above example, for a debt of 100 this latter amount would be calculated at 100 less the credit protection fee of 1 and the maximum finance charge (calculated for 90 days at base rate plus 2.5 per cent). Assuming the proceeds received of 80 are lower than this, and accrued interest charges at the year-end are 2, the arrangement would be shown as follows:

Current Assets

Stock	x
Debts factored without recourse:	
Gross debts (after providing for credit protection	
fee and accrued interest)	97
less: non-returnable proceeds	(80)
	17
Other debtors	x

In addition, the non-returnable proceeds of 80 would be included within cash and the profit and loss account would include both the credit protection expense of 1 and the accrued interest charges of 2.

APPLICATION NOTE D – SECURITISED ASSETS†

Features

Securitisation is a means by which providers of finance fund a specific block of assets rather than the general business of a company. The assets that have been most commonly securitised in the UK are household mortgages. Other receivables such as

---

*For a debt of 100 that subsequently proves to be bad, the proceeds received would be 100, less the credit protection fee of 1, less an interest charge calculated for 90 days at base rate plus 2.5%.

†*Editor's note: This Application Note is deleted in its entirety by amendments to FRS 26, for entities complying with that standard, with effect for accounting periods beginning on or after 1 January 2007.*

credit card balances, hire purchase loans and trade debts are sometimes securitised, as are non-monetary assets such as property and stocks. This Application Note applies to all kinds of assets.

D2   The main features are generally as follows:

(a)   The assets to be securitised are transferred by a company (the 'originator') to a special purpose vehicle (the 'issuer') in return for an immediate cash payment. Additional deferred consideration may also be payable.

(b)   The issuer finances the transfer by the issue of debt, usually tradeable loan notes or commercial paper (referred to below as 'loan notes'). The issuer is usually thinly capitalised and its shares placed with a party other than the originator – charitable trusts have often been used for this purpose – with the result that the issuer is not classified as a subsidiary of the originator under companies legislation. In addition, the major financial and operating policies of the issuer are usually predetermined by the agreements that constitute the securitisation, such that neither the owner of its share capital nor the originator has any significant continuing discretion over how it is run.

(c)   Arrangements are made to protect the loan noteholders from losses occurring on the assets by a process termed 'credit enhancement'. This may take the form of third party insurance, a third party guarantee of the issuer's obligations or an issue of subordinated debt (perhaps to the originator); all provide a cushion against losses up to a fixed amount.

(d)   The originator is granted rights to surplus income (and, where relevant, capital profits) from the assets – ie to cash remaining after payment of amounts due on the loan notes and other expenses of the issuer. The mechanisms used to achieve this include: servicing or other fees; deferred sale consideration; 'super interest' on amounts owed to the originator (eg subordinated debt); dividend payments; and swap payments.

(e)   In the case of securitised debts, the originator may continue to service the debts (ie to collect amounts due from borrowers, set interest rates etc). In this capacity it is referred to as the 'servicer' and receives a servicing fee.

(f)   Cash accumulations from the assets (eg from mortgage redemptions) are reinvested by the issuer until loan notes are repaid. Any difference between the interest rate obtained on reinvestments and that payable on the loan notes will normally affect the originator's surplus under (d) above. The terms of the loan notes may provide for them to be redeemed as assets are realised, thus minimising this reinvestment period. Alternatively, cash accumulations may be invested in a 'guaranteed investment contract' that pays a guaranteed rate of interest (which may be determined by reference to a variable benchmark rate such as LIBOR) sufficient to meet interest payments on the loan notes. Another alternative, used particularly for short-term debts arising under a facility (eg credit card balances), is a provision for cash receipts (here from card repayments) to be reinvested in similar assets (eg new balances on the same credit card accounts). This reinvestment in similar assets will occur for a specified period only, after which time cash accumulations will either be used to redeem loan notes or be reinvested in other more liquid assets until loan notes are repaid.

(g)   In certain circumstances, for example if tax changes affect the payment of interest to the noteholders or if the principal amount of loan notes outstanding declines to a specified level, the issuer may have an option to buy back the notes. Such repurchase may be funded by the originator, in which case the originator will re-acquire the securitised assets.

D3   From the originator's standpoint, the effect of the arrangement is usually that it continues to obtain the benefit of surplus income (and, where relevant, capital profits) from the securitised assets and bears losses up to a set amount. Usually, however, the originator is protected from losses beyond a limited amount and has transferred catastrophe risk to the issuer.

Analysis

The purpose of the analysis is to determine the following:　　　　　　　**D4**

(a) the appropriate accounting treatment in the originator's individual company financial statements. There are three possible treatments:

  (i) to remove the securitised assets from the balance sheet and show no liability in respect of the note issue, merely retaining the net amount (if any) of the securitised assets less the loan notes as a single item ('derecognition');

  (ii) to show the proceeds of the note issue deducted from the securitised assets on the face of the balance sheet within a single asset caption (a 'linked presentation'); or

  (iii) to show an asset equivalent in amount to the gross securitised assets within assets, and a corresponding liability in respect of the proceeds of the note issue within creditors (a 'separate presentation');

(b) the appropriate accounting treatment in the issuer's financial statements. Again there are three possible treatments: derecognition, a linked presentation or a separate presentation; and

(c) the appropriate accounting treatment in the originator's group accounts. This involves issues of:

  (i) whether the issuer is a subsidiary or (more usually) a quasi-subsidiary of the originator such that it should be included in the originator's group accounts; and

  (ii) where the issuer is a quasi-subsidiary, whether a linked presentation should be adopted in the originator's consolidated accounts.

Each of these is considered in more detail below.

(a) Originator's individual accounts

Overview of basic principles

The principles for determining the appropriate accounting treatment in the origi-　**D5**
nator's individual company financial statements are similar to those applied in both Application Note C – 'Factoring of debts' and in Application Note E – 'Loan transfers'. It is necessary to establish what asset and liability (if any) the originator now has, by answering two questions:

(a) whether the originator has access to the benefits of the securitised assets and exposure to the risks inherent in those benefits (referred to below as 'benefits and risks') and

(b) whether the originator has a liability to repay the proceeds of the note issue.

Where the originator has transferred all significant benefits and risks relating to the securitised assets and has no obligation to repay the proceeds of the note issue, derecognition is appropriate; where the originator has retained significant benefits and risks relating to the securitised assets but there is absolutely no doubt that its downside exposure to loss is limited, a linked presentation should be used; and in all other cases a separate presentation should be adopted.

D6   The benefits and risks relating to securitised assets will depend on the nature of the particular assets involved. In the case of interest bearing loans, the benefits and risks are described in paragraph E6 of Application Note E – 'Loan transfers'.

Derecognition

D7   Derecognition (ie ceasing to recognise the securitised assets in their entirety) is appropriate only where the originator retains no significant benefits and no significant risks relating to the securitised assets.

D8   Whilst the commercial effect of any particular transaction should be assessed taking into account all its aspects and implications, the presence of all of the following indicates that the originator has not retained significant benefits and risks, and derecognition is appropriate:

(a)   the transaction takes place at an arm's length price for an outright sale;

(b)   the transaction is for a fixed amount of consideration and there is no recourse whatsoever, either implicit or explicit, to the originator for losses from whatever cause. Normal warranties given in respect of the condition of the assets at the time of the transfer (eg in a mortgage securitisation, a warranty that no mortgages are in arrears at the time of transfer, or that the income of the borrower at the time of granting the mortgage was above a specified amount) would not breach this condition. However, warranties relating to the condition of the assets in the future or to their future performance (eg that mortgages will not move into arrears in the future) would breach the condition. Other possible forms of recourse are set out in paragraph 83; and

(c)   the originator will not benefit or suffer if the securitised assets perform better or worse than expected. This will not be the case where the originator has a right to further sums from the vehicle that vary according to the eventual value realised for the securitised assets. Such sums could take a number of forms, for instance deferred consideration, a performance-related servicing fee, payments under a swap, dividends from the vehicle, or payments from a reserve fund.

Where any of these three features is not present, this indicates that the originator has retained benefits and risks relating to the securitised assets and, unless these are insignificant, either a separate presentation or a linked presentation should be adopted.

D9   Whether any benefit and risk retained are 'significant' should be judged in relation to those benefits and risks that are likely to occur in practice, and not in relation to the total possible benefits and risks. Where the profits or losses accruing to the originator are material in relation to those likely to occur in practice, significant benefit and risk will be retained. For example, if for a portfolio of securitised assets of 100, expected losses are 0.5 and there is recourse to the originator for losses of up to 5, the originator will have retained all but an insignificant part of the downside risk relating to the assets (as the originator bears losses of up to ten times those expected to occur). Accordingly, in this example, derecognition will not be appropriate and either a linked presentation or a separate presentation should be used.

Linked presentation

D10   A linked presentation will be appropriate where, although the originator has retained significant benefits and risks relating to the securitised assets, there is absolutely no doubt that its downside exposure to loss is limited to a fixed monetary amount. A linked presentation should be used only to the extent that there is both absolutely no doubt that the noteholders' claim extends solely to the proceeds generated by the securitised assets, and there is no provision for the originator to re-acquire the securitised assets in the future. The conditions that need to be met in order for this to be the case are set out in paragraph 27 and explained in paragraphs 81–86. When interpreting these conditions in the context of a securitisation the following points apply:

condition (a) (specified assets) –
a linked presentation should not be used where the assets that have been securitised cannot be separately identified. Nor should a linked presentation be used for assets that generate the funds required to repay the finance only by being used in conjunction with other assets of the originator;

condition (d) (agreement in writing that there is no recourse; such agreement noted in the financial statements) –
where the noteholders have subscribed to a prospectus or offering circular that clearly states that the originator will not support any losses of either the issuer or the noteholders, the first part of this condition will be met. Provisions that give the noteholders recourse to funds generated by both the securitised assets themselves and third party credit enhancement of those assets would also not breach this condition;

condition (f) (no provision for the originator to repurchase assets) –
where there is provision for the originator to repurchase only part of the securitised assets (or otherwise to fund the redemption of loan notes by the issuer), the maximum payment that could result should be excluded from the amount deducted on the face of the balance sheet. Where there is provision for the issuer (but not the originator) to redeem loan notes before an equivalent amount has been realised in cash from the securitised assets, a linked presentation may still be appropriate provided there is no obligation (legal, commercial or other) for the originator to fund the redemption (eg by repurchasing the securitised assets).

These conditions should be regarded as met notwithstanding the existence of an **D11** interest rate swap agreement between the originator and the issuer, provided all the following conditions are met:

(a)   the swap is on arm's length market-related terms and the obligations of the issuer under the swap are not subordinated to any of its obligations under the loan notes;
(b)   the variable interest rate(s) that are swapped are determined by reference to publicly quoted rates that are not under the control of the originator;
(c)   at the time of transfer of the assets to the issuer, the originator had hedged exposures relating to these assets (either individually or as part of a larger portfolio) and entering into the swap effectively restores the hedge position left open by their transfer. Thereafter, where the hedging of the originator's exposure under the swap requires continuing management, any necessary adjustments to the hedging position are made on an ongoing basis. This latter requirement will be particularly relevant where any prepayment risk involved cannot be hedged exactly.

The conditions for a linked presentation should also be regarded as met notwithstanding the existence of an interest rate cap agreement between the originator and the issuer provided that, in addition to all the above conditions being met, the securitisation was entered into before 22 September 1994.

In the case of securitisations of revolving assets that arise under a facility (eg credit **D12** card balances), a careful analysis of the mechanism for repaying the loan notes is

FRS 5 APPLICATION NOTES

required in order to establish whether or not conditions (b) and (f) in paragraph 27 are met. For such assets, the loan notes are usually repaid from proceeds received during a period of time (referred to as the 'repayment period'). The proceeds received in the repayment period will typically comprise both repayments of securitised balances existing at the start of the repayment period and repayments of balances arising subsequently (for example arising from new borrowings in the repayment period on the credit card accounts securitised). In order that the conditions for a linked presentation are met, it is necessary that loan notes are repaid only to the extent that there have been, in total, cash collections from securitised balances existing at the start of the repayment period equal to the amount repaid on the loan notes. This is necessary in order to ensure that the issuer is allocated its proper share of any losses.

D13   It will also be necessary to analyse carefully any provisions that enable the originator to transfer additional assets to the issuer in order to establish whether or not conditions (b) and (f) in paragraph 27 are met. To the extent that the originator is obliged to replace poorly performing assets with good ones, there is recourse to the originator and a linked presentation should not be used. However, where there is merely provision for the originator to add new assets to replace those that have been repaid earlier than expected (and thus to 'top up' the pool in order to extend the life of the securitisation), the conditions for a linked presentation may still be met. For a linked presentation to be used, it is necessary that the addition of new assets does not result in either the originator being exposed to losses on the new or the old assets, or in the originator re-acquiring assets. Provided these features are present, the effect is the same as if the noteholders were repaid in cash and they immediately reinvested that cash in new assets, and a linked presentation may be appropriate.

Separate presentation

D14   Where the originator has retained significant benefits and risks relating to the securitised assets and the conditions for a linked presentation are not met, the originator should adopt a separate presentation.

Multi-originator programmes

D15   There are some arrangements where one issuer serves several originators. The arrangement may be structured such that each originator receives future benefits based on the performance of a defined portfolio of assets (typically those it has transferred to the issuer and continues to service or use). For instance, in a mortgage securitisation, the benefits accruing to any particular originator may be calculated as the interest payments received from a defined portfolio of mortgages, less costs specific to that portfolio (eg insurance premiums, payments for credit facilities), less an appropriate share of the funding costs of the issuer. The effect is that each originator bears significant benefits and risks of a defined pool of mortgages, whilst being insulated from the benefits and risks of other mortgages held by the issuer. Thus each originator should show that pool of mortgages for which it has significant benefits and risks on the face of its balance sheet, using either a linked presentation (if the conditions for its use are met) or a separate presentation.

(b) Issuer's accounts

D16   The principles set out in paragraphs D5–D15 for the originator's individual financial statements also apply to the issuer's financial statements. In a securitisation, the issuer usually has access to all future benefits from the securitised assets (in the case of mortgages, to all cash collected from mortgagors) and is exposed to all their inherent risks. Hence, derecognition will not be appropriate. In addition, the noteholders usually have recourse to all the assets of the issuer (these may include the securitised assets themselves, the benefit of any related insurance policies or credit enhancement, and a small amount of cash). In this situation, the issuer's exposure to loss is not limited, and use of a linked presentation will not be appropriate. Thus the issuer should usually adopt a separate presentation.

(c) Originator's group financial statements

Assuming a separate presentation is used in the issuer's financial statements but not in those of the originator, the question arises whether the relationship between the issuer and the originator is such that the issuer should be included in the originator's group financial statements. The following considerations are relevant: **D17**

(a)   Where the issuer meets the definition of a subsidiary, it should be consolidated in the normal way by applying the relevant provisions of companies legislation and FRS 2. Where the issuer is not a subsidiary, the provisions of this FRS regarding quasi-subsidiaries are relevant.

(b)   In order to meet the definition of a quasi-subsidiary, the issuer must give rise to benefits for the originator that are in substance no different from those that would arise were the entity a subsidiary. This will be the case where the originator receives the future benefits arising from the net assets of the issuer (principally the securitised assets less the loan notes). It is not necessary that the originator could face a possible benefit outflow equal in amount to the issuer's gross liabilities. Strong evidence of whether this part of the definition is met is whether the originator stands to suffer or gain from the financial performance of the issuer.

(c)   The definition of a quasi-subsidiary also requires that the issuer is directly or indirectly controlled by the originator. Usually securitisations exemplify the situation described in paragraphs 34 and 98, in that the issuer's financial and operating policies are in substance predetermined (in this case under the various agreements that constitute the securitisation). Where this is so, the party possessing control will be the one that has the future benefits arising from the issuer's net assets.

It follows that it should be presumed that the issuer is a quasi-subsidiary where either of the following is present: **D18**

(a)   the originator has rights to the benefits arising from the issuer's net assets, ie to those benefits generated by the securitised assets that remain after meeting the claims of noteholders and other expenses of the issuer. These benefits may be transferred to the originator in a number of forms, as described in paragraph D2(d); or

(b)   the originator has the risks inherent in these benefits. This will be the case where, if the benefits are greater or less than expected (eg because of the securitised assets realising more or less than expected), the originator gains or suffers.

In general, where an issuer's activities comprise holding securitised assets and the benefits of its net assets accrue to the originator, the issuer will be a quasi-subsidiary of the originator. Conversely, the issuer will not be a quasi-subsidiary of the originator where the owner of the issuer is an independent third party that has made a substantial capital investment in the issuer, has control of the issuer, and has the benefits and risks of its net assets. **D19**

Where the issuer is a quasi-subsidiary of the originator, the question arises whether a linked presentation should be adopted in the originator's group financial statements. It follows from paragraph 37 that where the issuer holds a single portfolio of similar **D20** assets, and the effect of the arrangement is to ring-fence the assets and their related finance in such a way that the provisions of paragraphs 26 and 27 are met from the point of view of the group, a linked presentation should be used.

Required accounting

Originator's individual financial statements

Derecognition

D21   Where the originator has retained no significant benefits and risks relating to the securitised assets and has no obligation to repay the proceeds of the note issue, the assets should be removed from its balance sheet, and no liability shown in respect of the proceeds of the note issue. A profit or loss should be recognised, calculated as the difference between the carrying amount of the assets and the proceeds received.

Linked presentation

D22   Where the conditions for a linked presentation are met, the proceeds of the note issue (to the extent they are non-returnable) should be shown deducted from the securitised assets on the face of the balance sheet within a single asset caption. Profit should be recognised and presented in the manner set out in paragraphs 28 and 87–88. The following disclosures should be given:

(a)   a description of the assets securitised;
(b)   the amount of any income or expense recognised in the period, analysed as appropriate;
(c)   the terms of any options for the originator to repurchase assets or to transfer additional assets to the issuer;
(d)   the terms of any interest rate swap or interest rate cap agreements between the issuer and the originator that meet the conditions set out in paragraph D11;
(e)   a description of the priority and amount of claims on the proceeds generated by the assets, including any rights of the originator to proceeds from the assets in addition to the non-recourse amounts already received;
(f)   the ownership of the issuer; and
(g)   the disclosures required by conditions (c) and (d) in paragraph 27.

D23   Where an originator uses a linked presentation for several different securitisations that all relate to a single type of asset (ie all the assets, if not securitised, would be shown within the same balance sheet caption), these may be aggregated on the face of the balance sheet. However, securitisations of different types of asset should be shown separately. In addition, details of each material arrangement should be provided in the notes to the financial statements, unless they are on similar terms and relate to a single type of asset, in which case they may be disclosed in aggregate.

Separate presentation

D24   Where neither derecognition nor a linked presentation is appropriate, a separate presentation should be adopted, ie a gross asset (equal in amount to the gross amount of the securitised assets) should be shown on the balance sheet of the originator within assets, and a corresponding liability in respect of the proceeds of the note issue shown within liabilities. No gain or loss should be recognised at the time the securitisation is entered into (unless adjustment to the carrying value of the assets independent of the securitisation is required). Disclosure should be given in the notes to the financial statements of the gross amount of assets securitised at the balance sheet date.

Issuer's financial statements

D25

The requirements set out in paragraphs D21–D24 for the originator's individual financial statements also apply to the issuer's financial statements. For the reasons set out in paragraph D16, in most cases the issuer will be required to adopt a separate presentation, in which case the provisions of paragraph D24 will apply.

Originator's consolidated financial statements

D26

Where the issuer is a quasi-subsidiary of the originator, its assets, liabilities, profits, losses and cash flows should be included in the originating group's consolidated financial statements. Where the provisions of paragraph D20 are met, a linked presentation should be applied in the consolidated financial statements and the disclosures required by paragraphs D22 and D23 should be given; in all other cases a separate presentation should be used and the disclosure required by paragraph D24 should be given.

Indications that derecognition is appropriate (securitised assets are not assets of the originator)	Indications that a linked presentation is appropriate	Indications that a separate presentation is appropriate (securitiesed assets are assets of the originator)
Originator's individual financial statements		
Transaction price is arm's length price for an outright sale.	Transaction price is not arm's length price for an outright sale.	Transaction price is not arm's length for an outright sale.
Transfer is for a single, non-returnable fixed sum.	Some non-returnable proceeds received, but originator has rights to further sums from the issuer, the amount of which depends on the performance of the securitised assets.	Proceeds received are returnable, or there is a provision whereby the originator may keep the securitiesed assets on repayment of the loan notes or re-acquire them.
There is no recourse to the originator for losses.	There is either no recourse for losses, or such recourse has a fixed monetary ceiling.	There is or may be full recourse to the originator for losses, eg: - originator's directors are unable to unwilling to state that it is not obliged to fund any losses; - noteholders have not agreed in writing that they will seek repayment only from funds generated by the securitised assets.

Originator's consolidated financial statements		
Issuer is owned by an independent third party that made a substantial capital investment, has control of the issuer, and has the benefits and risks of its net assets.	Issuer is a quasi-subsidiary of the originator, but the conditions for a linked presentation are met from the point of view of the group.	Issuer is a subsidiary of the originator.

APPLICATION NOTE E – LOAN TRANSFERS*

NB: In this Application Note, the following terminology is used:

(a) the 'lender' is the party that has rights to principal and interest under the original loan agreement, and is purporting to transfer them;

(b) the 'transferee' is the party purporting to acquire the loan, and includes a new lender (in a novation), an assignee and a sub-participant;

(c) the 'borrower' is the party that has obligations to make payments of principal and interest under the original loan agreement; and

(d) references to the transfer of a 'loan' or 'loans' apply equally to the transfer of both a single loan and a portfolio of loans.

Features

E1 This Application Note deals with the transfer of interest-bearing loans to an entity other than a special purpose vehicle. The main features of a loan transfer are as follows:

(a) Specified loans are transferred from a lender to a transferee by one of the methods set out in paragraph E2 below, in return for an immediate cash payment. The transfer may be of the whole of a single loan, part of a loan, or of all or part of a portfolio of similar loans.

(b) Payments of principal and interest collected from borrowers are passed to the transferee (either direct or via the lender). In some cases, there may be a difference between amounts received from borrowers and those passed to the transferee (the lender retaining or making up the difference), or if a borrower fails to make payments when due, the lender may nevertheless make payments to the transferee.

E2 Loans cannot be 'sold' in the same way as tangible assets. However, there are three methods by which the benefits and risks of a loan can be transferred:

Novation: The rights and obligations under the loan agreement are cancelled and replaced by new ones whose main effect is to change the identity of the lender. Although rights can be transferred by other means, novation is the only method of transferring obligations (eg to supply funds under an undrawn loan facility) with the consequent release of the lender.

Assignment: Rights (to principal and interest), but not obligations, are transferred to a third party (the 'assignee'). There are two types of assignment: statutory assignment, which must relate to the whole of the loan and where notice in writing must be given to the borrower and other obligors (eg a guarantor); and equitable assignment, which may relate to only part of a loan and which does not require notice to the borrower. Both types are subject to equitable rights arising before

Editor's note: This Application Note is deleted in its entirety by amendments to FRS 26, for entities complying with that standard, with effect for accounting periods beginning on or after 1 January 2007.

notice is received. For example, a right of set-off held by the borrower against the lender will be good against the assignee for any transactions undertaken before the borrower receives notice of the assignment.

Sub-participation: Rights and obligations are not formally transferred but the lender enters into a non-recourse back-to-back agreement with a third party, the 'sub participant', under which the latter deposits with the lender an amount equal to the whole or part of the loan and in return receives from the lender a share of the cash flows arising on the loan.

The terms of a loan transfer will usually not be identical to those of the original loan, **E3** and a gain or loss will arise for the lender. This gain or loss may occur in one of two ways: first, if all future payments made by the borrower (and only such payments) are to be passed to the transferee, the consideration for the transfer will differ from the carrying amount of the loan and the lender's gain or loss will be realised in cash immediately. Alternatively, the consideration for the transfer may be set equal to the carrying amount of the loan, and the amounts to be paid by the borrower and those to be passed on to the transferee will differ. In this case, the lender's gain or loss will be the net present value of this difference and will be realised in cash over the term of the loan.

Analysis

Overview of basic principles

The purpose of the analysis is to determine the appropriate accounting treatment in **E4** the financial statements of the lender. There are three possible treatments:

(a) to remove the loan (or a part of it) from the balance sheet and show no liability in respect of the amounts received from the transferee ('derecognition');

(b) to show the amounts received from the transferee deducted from the loan on the face of the balance sheet within a single asset caption (a 'linked presentation'); or

(c) to continue to show the loan as an asset, and show a corresponding liability within creditors in respect of the amounts received from the transferee (a 'separate presentation').

The principles to be applied to determine the appropriate accounting treatment are **E5** similar to those applied in both Application Note D – 'Securitised assets' relating to individual (rather than consolidated) financial statements and in Application Note C – 'Factoring of debts'. It is necessary to answer two questions:

(a) whether the lender has access to the benefits of the loans and exposure to the risks inherent in those benefits (referred to below as 'benefits and risks'); and

(b) whether the lender has a liability to repay the transferee.

Where the lender has transferred all significant benefits and risks relating to the loans and has no obligation to repay the transferee, derecognition is appropriate (this would be the case where all future cash flows from borrowers – but only those cash flows – are passed to the transferee as and when received). Where the lender has retained significant benefits and risks relating to the loans but there is absolutely no doubt that its downside exposure to loss is limited, a linked presentation should be used (this is likely to be rare for a loan transfer). In all other cases a separate presentation should be adopted.

Benefits and risks

E6   The main benefits and risks relating to loans are as follows:

Benefits:
(i)   the future cash flows from payments of principal and interest.

Risks:
(i)   credit risk (the risk of bad debts);
(ii)   slow payment risk;
(iii) interest rate risk (the risk of a change in the interest rate paid by the borrower. Included in this risk is a form of basis risk, ie the risk of a change in the interest rate paid by the borrower not being matched by a change in the interest rate paid to the transferee);
(iv)   reinvestment/early redemption risk (the risk that, where payments from the loans are reinvested by the lender before being paid to the transferee, the rate of interest obtained on the reinvested amounts is above or below that payable to the transferee); and
(v)   moral risk (the risk that the lender will feel obliged, because of its continued association with the loans, to fund any losses arising on them).

Analysis of benefits

E7   At first sight it may appear that the transferee has access to the cash collected from borrowers. However, as set out in more detail in paragraphs C6 and C7, the cash flows may appear similar even where different accounting treatments are appropriate and considering the benefits in isolation will not normally enable a clear decision to be made. Rather, it is necessary to determine which party is exposed to the risks relating to the loans (both upside potential for gain and downside exposure to loss).

Analysis of risks

E8   The benefit of cash payments of principal and interest are subject to the five risks outlined in paragraph E6. The first of these, credit risk, will be borne by the lender to the extent there is recourse to it for bad debts; if there is no such recourse, the transferee will bear the credit risk.

E9   The second risk, slow payment, will be borne by the party that suffers (or benefits) if borrowers pay later (or earlier) than expected. If amounts are passed to the transferee only when received from the borrower, the transferee will bear this risk; if the lender pays amounts to the transferee regardless of whether it has received an equivalent payment from the borrower, the lender will bear it.

E10   Interest rate risk will be borne by the lender where the interest it receives from the borrower and payments it makes to the transferee are not directly related*. Where any changes in the interest rate charged to the borrower are passed on to the transferee after a short administrative delay, the lender may not bear significant interest rate risk; however, where any delays are significant the lender will bear significant risk.

E11   The lender will bear reinvestment risk where payments received from the borrower are not immediately passed on to the transferee but are reinvested by the lender for a

---

* *'Directly related' in this context means that either the interest rates paid and received are both fixed, or the two rates are tied to the same external rate eg LIBOR.*

period. An exception would be where the transferee is entitled to all of any interest actually earned (but no more) on the amounts reinvested by the lender.

The final risk is moral risk. For either derecognition or a linked presentation to be appropriate, the lender must have taken all reasonable precautions to eliminate this risk such that it will not feel obliged to fund any losses. This will include ensuring that the arrangements for servicing the loans reflect the standards of commercial behaviour expected of the lender.

E12

Derecognition

Derecognition (ie ceasing to recognise the loans in their entirety) is appropriate only where the lender retains no significant benefits and no significant risks relating to the loans. In determining whether any benefit and risk retained are 'significant', greater weight should be given to what is more likely to have a commercial effect in practice.

E13

The three possible methods of transferring the benefits and risks relating to a loan are described in paragraph E2; each may result in derecognition in appropriate cases:

E14

(a)   A novation (ie the replacement of the original loan by a new one with the consequent release of the lender) will usually transfer all significant benefits and risks, provided that there are no side agreements that leave benefits and risks with the lender.

(b)   An assignment (ie the transfer of the rights to principal and interest that constitute the original loan, whilst not transferring any obligations) may also transfer all significant benefits and risks, provided that, in addition to there being no side agreements that leave benefits and risks with the lender, there are no unfulfilled obligations (eg to supply additional funds in the event of a restructuring of the loan) and any doubts regarding intervening equitable rights are satisfied.

(c)   A sub-participation (ie the entering into an additional non-recourse back-to-back agreement with the sub-participant rather than the transfer of any of the rights or obligations that constitute the original loan itself) may also transfer all significant benefits and risks, provided that the lender's obligation to pay amounts to the transferee eliminates its access to benefits from the loans but extends only to those benefits. Thus the sub-participant must have a claim on all specified payments from the loans but on only those payments, and there must be no possibility that the lender could be required to pay amounts to the sub-participant where it has not received equivalent payments from the borrower.* Where this is the case, the loans no longer constitute an asset of the lender, nor does the deposit placed by the sub-participant represent a liability; it will therefore be appropriate to derecognise the loans. Particular attention should be paid to the effect of the borrower asking for a rescheduling. The lender may, for commercial reasons, wish to agree to a rescheduling plan, whereas the sub participant may simply look to the lender for compensation if it is not repaid. Where the lender has an obligation (legal, commercial or other) to provide such compensation, derecognition will not be appropriate.

Whilst the commercial effect of any particular transaction should be assessed taking into account all its aspects and implications, the presence of all of the following indicates that the lender has not retained significant benefits and risks, and derecognition is appropriate:

E15

Where only part of the payments due under the original loan are eliminated in this way, it may be appropriate to derecognise only part of the original loan. This is addressed in paragraphs E19 and E20 below.

(a)   the transaction takes place at an arm's length price for an outright sale;

(b)   the transaction is for a fixed amount of consideration and there is no recourse whatsoever, either implicit or explicit, to the lender for losses from whatever cause. Normal warranties given in respect of the condition of the loans at the time of the transfer (eg a warranty that no loan was in arrears at the time of transfer) would not breach this condition. However, warranties relating to the condition of the loans in the future or to their future performance (eg that loans will not move into arrears in the future) would breach the condition. Other possible forms of recourse are set out in paragraph 83; and

(c)   the lender will not benefit or suffer in any way if the loans perform better or worse than expected. This will not be the case where the lender has a right to further sums that vary according to the future performance of the loans (ie according to whether or when borrowers pay, or according to the amounts borrowers pay). Such sums might take the form of an interest differential, deferred consideration, a performance-related servicing fee or payments under a swap.

Where any of these three features is not present, this indicates that the lender has retained benefits and risks relating to the loan and, unless these are insignificant, either a separate presentation or a linked presentation should be adopted.

E16   Whether any benefit and risk retained are 'significant' should be judged in relation to those benefits and risks that are likely to occur in practice, and not in relation to the total possible benefits and risks. Where the profits or losses accruing to the lender are material in relation to those likely to occur in practice, significant benefit and risk will be retained, such that derecognition will not be appropriate and either a linked presentation or a separate presentation should be used.

Linked presentation

E17   A linked presentation will be appropriate where, although the lender has retained significant benefits and risks relating to the loans, there is absolutely no doubt that its downside exposure to loss is limited to a fixed monetary amount. A linked presentation should be used only to the extent that there is both absolutely no doubt that the transferee's claim extends solely to cash collected from the loans, and no provision for the lender to keep or re-acquire the loans by repaying the transferee. The conditions that need to be met in order for this to be the case are set out in paragraph 27 and explained in paragraphs 81–86.

Separate presentation

E18   Where the lender retains significant benefits and risks relating to the loans and the conditions for a linked presentation are not met, a separate presentation should be adopted.

Transfers of part of a loan

E19   In some cases the amount received by the lender from the transferee represents only part of the original loan. As explained in paragraph 71, where the effect of the arrangement is that a part of the loan is transferred, derecognition of that part will be appropriate. This will be the case where each party has a proportionate share of all future cash collected from the loan (and of related profits and losses). For example, were the transferee to be entitled to 40 per cent of any cash flows from payments of both principal and interest as and when paid by the borrower (ie it does not receive cash if such payments are not made), the lender should cease to recognise 40 per cent of the loan. Conversely, if the lender bears losses in preference to the transferee and thus retains significant risk relating to the loans, derecognition of any part of them is not appropriate. For example, were the transferee to have first claim on any cash flows arising from a portfolio of loans with the lender's share acting as a cushion to absorb any losses, the lender should continue to show the gross amount of the whole portfolio on the face of its balance sheet (although if the conditions for a linked presentation are met, it should be used).

In other cases, the entire principal amount of a loan may be funded by the transferee, but there may be a difference between the interest payments due from the borrower and those the lender has agreed to pass on to the transferee. In such cases derecognition of a part of the original loan may still be appropriate provided that the lender's interest differential does not result in it bearing significant risks relating to the loan. For instance, if the lender's interest differential is fixed and is in substance no more than a fee for originating or administering the loan, derecognition will be appropriate. Conversely, if the lender's interest differential varies depending on the performance of the loan (as where it acts as a cushion to absorb losses or the lender bears interest rate risk), either a separate presentation or a linked presentation should be used. A linked presentation should be used only where the lender's maximum loss is capped, as might be the case where a variable rate loan is funded by a fixed rate one (if the lender's maximum loss is capped at the fixed interest payments due to the transferee). However, a linked presentation should not be used where the lender's maximum loss is not capped, as will be the case where a fixed rate loan is funded by a variable rate one, or where a loan in one currency is funded by a loan in another. The principles in this paragraph apply equally where the transferee funds only part of the principal amount of the original loan.

E20

Administration arrangements

Whether or not the lender continues to administer the loans is not, of itself, relevant to deciding upon the appropriate accounting treatment. However, the administration arrangements may affect where certain benefits and risks lie. For instance, where the lender's servicing fee is not an arm's length fee for the services provided, this indicates it has retained significant benefits and risks relating to the loans.

E21

Required accounting

Derecognition

Where the lender has retained no significant benefits and risks relating to the loans and has no obligation to repay the transferee, the loans should be removed from its balance sheet and no liability shown in respect of the amounts received from the transferee. A profit or loss may arise for the lender in the two ways set out in paragraph E3. Where the profit or loss is realised in cash it should be recognised, calculated as the difference between the carrying amount of the loans and the cash proceeds received. Where, however, the lender's profit or loss is not realised in cash and there are doubts as to its amount, full provision should be made for any expected loss but recognition of any gain, to the extent it is in doubt, should be deferred until cash has been received.

E22

Linked presentation

Where the conditions for a linked presentation are met, the proceeds received, to the extent they are non-returnable, should be shown deducted from the gross amount of the loans on the face of the balance sheet. Profit should be recognised and presented as set out in paragraphs 28 and 87–88. The notes to the financial statements should

E23

disclose: the main terms of the arrangement; the gross amount of loans transferred and outstanding at the balance sheet date; the profit or loss recognised in the period, analysed as appropriate; and the disclosures required by conditions (c) and (d) in paragraph 27.

Separate presentation

E24   Where neither derecognition nor a linked presentation is appropriate, a separate presentation should be adopted, ie a gross asset (equivalent in amount to the gross amount of the loans) should be shown on the balance sheet of the lender within assets, and a corresponding liability in respect of the amounts received from the transferee should be shown within creditors. No gain or loss should be recognised at the time of the transfer (unless adjustment to the carrying value of the loan independent of the transfer is required). The notes to the financial statements should disclose the amount of loans subject to loan transfer arrangements that are outstanding at the balance sheet date.

Table

Indications that derecognition is appropriate (off lender's balance sheet)	Indications that a linked presentation is appropriate	Indications that a separate presentation is appropriate (on lender's balance sheet)
Transfer is for a single, non-returnable fixed sum.	Some non-returnable proceeds received, but lender has rights to further sums whose amount depends on whether or when the borrowers pay.	The proceeds received are returnable in the event of losses occurring on the loans.
There is no recourse to the lender for losses from any cause.	There is either no recourse for losses, or such recourse has a fixed monetary ceiling.	There is full recourse to the lender for losses.
Transferee is paid all amounts received from the loans (and no more), as and when received. Lender has no rights to further sums from the loans or the transferee.	Transferee is paid only out of amounts received from the loans, and lender has no right or obligation to repurchase them.	Lender is required to repay amounts received from the transferee on or before a set date, regardless of the timing or amounts of payments by the borrowers.

APPLICATION NOTE F – PRIVATE FINANCE INITIATIVE AND SIMILAR CONTRACTS

NB   In this Application Note the following terminology is used:

(a)   the entity (usually a public sector body) that acquires services under the Private Finance Initiative (PFI) contract is referred to as the 'purchaser'.

(b)   the entity (usually a private sector body) that provides services under the PFI contract in return for payments from the purchaser is referred to as the 'operator'.

(c)   the road, hospital, prison etc that is the subject of the PFI contract is referred to as the 'property'. The word 'asset' is reserved for items that are recognised in the balance sheet.

FEATURES

Under a PFI contract, the private sector is responsible for supplying services that traditionally have been provided by the public sector. It is integral to most PFI contracts that the operator designs, builds, finances and operates a property in order to provide the contracted service. Examples of such properties are roads, bridges, hospitals, prisons, offices, information technology systems and educational establishments.   **F1**

The main features of a PFI contract are as follows: **F2**

(a)   A contract to provide services is awarded by the purchaser (a public sector entity) to the operator (a private sector entity). The contract will specify the level of service required over the period of the contract. Usually, the contract also provides for a single ('unitary') payment to be made in each period, linked to factors such as availability, performance and levels of usage.

(b)   A property, which is legally owned by or leased to the operator, will usually be necessary to perform the contracted service. Such properties include buildings (eg a prison or hospital), roads, railways, bridges, vehicles, and computer systems. Under the PFI contract, the operator will typically design, build, finance and operate the property. The contract may specify features or standards required of the property, for example, in order to satisfy statutory obligations of the purchaser. The property may or may not have potential for third-party use during the term of the PFI contract.

(c)   The PFI contract will specify arrangements for the property at the end of the contract term (which may include various options available to one or both parties). Legal title to the property may pass to the purchaser for a fixed, perhaps nominal, price. Alternatively, or in addition, there may be provision to re-tender the PFI contract for a further term and for the property to pass to the successful new operator. In either of these cases the PFI contract may require the property to be maintained to a minimum standard or to have a stated remaining useful economic life at the end of the contract term. Further possibilities are that the operator retains legal title to the asset at the end of the PFI contract or that the purchaser acquires legal title to the property for its market value at the time.

(d)   As a public sector body, the purchaser is required to demonstrate that the involvement of the private sector offers value for money when compared with alternative ways of providing the services. This is generally achieved by a transfer of risk from the public to the private sector.

Contracts of a similar nature to PFI contracts exist between entities in the private sector, for example some contracts for warehousing and distribution services, where a property is necessary to perform the contracted service. This Application Note is relevant to such contracts.   **F3**

ANALYSIS

Overview of basic principles

Present practice is not to capitalise contracts for services. However, where a property is needed to fulfil a contract for services, present practice may require the property to be recognised as the purchaser's asset. (For example, this is the case for some take-   **F4** or-pay contracts where the operator builds a specialist property with little alternative use.) The purpose of the analysis below is to determine:

(a)   whether the purchaser in a PFI contract has an asset of the property used to provide the contracted services together with a corresponding liability to pay the operator for it or, alternatively, has a contract only for services; and

(b)   whether the operator has an asset of the property used to provide the contracted services or, alternatively, a financial asset being a debt due from the purchaser.

F5   Under the general principles of the FRS, a party will have an asset of the property where that party has access to the benefits of the property and exposure to the risks inherent in those benefits. If that party is the purchaser, it will have a corresponding liability to pay the operator for the property where the commercial effect of the PFI contract is to require the purchaser to pay amounts to the operator that cover the cost of the property.

F6   In some cases the contract may be separable, ie the commercial effect will be that elements of the PFI payments operate independently of each other. 'Operate independently' means that the elements behave differently and can therefore be separately identified. Where this is the case, and where some elements relate only to services (such as cleaning, laundry, catering etc) rather than to the property, any such service elements are not relevant to determining whether each party has an asset of the property and should be ignored. A contract may be separable in various circumstances (see paragraph F10).

F7   Once any separable service elements have been excluded, PFI contracts can be classed into:

(a)   those where the only remaining elements are payments for the property. These will be akin to a lease and SSAP 21 'Accounting for leases and hire purchase contracts' (interpreted in the light of the FRS) should be applied.

(b)   other contracts (ie where the remaining elements include some services). These contracts will fall directly within the FRS rather than SSAP 21.

F8   For those contracts that fall directly within the FRS, the question of whether a party has an asset of the property should be determined by looking at the extent to which each party would bear any variations in property profits (or losses). There are three important principles to be considered when undertaking such an analysis:

(a)   A range of factors will be relevant in determining the extent to which each party would bear any variations in property profits (or losses) and it will be necessary to look at the overall effect of these factors when taken together.

(b)   However, any potential variations in profits (or losses) that relate purely to a service should be excluded since it is only the property that may be included on the balance sheet of one of the parties, not the capitalised value of the whole service contract. Consequently, potential variations relating to the provision of services are not relevant to determining whether each party has an asset of the property.

(c)   Paragraph 14 requires that, in determining the appropriate accounting treatment, greater weight should be given to those features that are more likely to have a commercial effect in practice. Where there is no genuine commercial possibility of a particular scenario or cash flow occurring, this scenario/cash flow should be ignored.

F9   The principles outlined above are considered in more detail below, under the following headings:

- Separation of the contract
- Should SSAP 21 or the FRS be applied?
- How to apply SSAP 21
- How to apply the FRS

Subsequently, the required accounting is explained.

Separation of the contract

In some cases the contract may be separable, ie the commercial effect will be that   **F10**
elements of the PFI payments operate independently of each other. 'Operate independently' means that the elements behave differently and can therefore be
separately identified. Any such separable elements that relate solely to services
should be excluded when determining whether each party has an asset of the
property. In establishing whether the contract is separable, regard should be had to
the terms of the contract and how the payments vary under different scenarios: it will
not be relevant that the contract designates the payments as 'unitary' or, indeed,
what labels they are given. In particular, where the PFI contract includes ancillary
services, such as catering and cleaning, the payments for these services may be
separable. A contract may be separable in a variety of circumstances, including but
not limited to the following.

(a)   The contract identifies an element of a payment stream that varies according to
      the availability of the property itself and another element that varies according
      to usage or performance of certain services.
(b)   Different parts of the contract run for different periods or can be terminated
      separately. For example, an individual service element can be terminated
      without affecting the continuation of the rest of the contract.
(c)   Different parts of the contract can be renegotiated separately. For example, a
      service element is market tested and some or all of the cost increases or
      reductions are passed on to the purchaser in such a way that the part of the
      payment by the purchaser that relates specifically to that service can be
      identified.

Should SSAP 21 or the FRS be applied?

Paragraph 13 requires that where a transaction falls within the scope of both this FRS   **F11**
and another FRS or a SSAP, the standard that contains the more specific provision(s)
should be applied. As explained in paragraph 45, for transactions that contain a
stand-alone lease, SSAP 21 will be the relevant standard. Other transactions, in particular those containing a lease as an element of a larger arrangement, will fall within
the FRS.

A PFI contract will contain a stand-alone lease (so that SSAP 21, interpreted in the   **F12**
light of the FRS, should be applied) where the only elements remaining after excluding
any separable service elements are payments for the property.

Other PFI contracts, ie those where there are some non-separable service elements,   **F13**
will fall directly within the FRS.

How to apply SSAP 21

F14   In applying SSAP 21, the key question is whether the lease is a finance lease, ie one that "transfers substantially all the risks and rewards of ownership of an asset to the lessee.* One indication of this is given by comparing the present value of the minimum lease payments with the fair value of the asset (often referred to as the '90 per cent test'). However, in many cases such a numerical test will not be required. The principal risks and rewards of ownership in a leasing context are usually demand and residual value. Where substantially all of the risks and rewards associated with these lie with the purchaser, it will be clear, without performing any calculations, that the lease is a finance lease (ie that the property is an asset of the purchaser). Only where there is a sharing of risk will a 90 per cent test be required.

F15   Even where a 90 per cent test is used, it is important neither to apply this as the only test nor to apply a 90 per cent cut-off in a mechanistic way. The overriding principle is to establish whether the purchaser has substantially all of the risks and rewards of ownership.

F16   Where a 90 per cent test is used, the question arises what rate should be used to discount the minimum lease payments. The principles underlying SSAP 21 require a discount rate that relates only to the property. A rate based in some way on the return from the entire PFI contract may **not** be a suitable rate to use since it will include an allowance for the risk relating to the service element of the contract. Where the service element is perceived as being riskier, relative to the property, this will give rise to a rate that is too high. Since a prerequisite for using SSAP 21 is that the payments for the property have been separated from those for services, it will usually be possible to derive such a property-specific rate from the PFI contract. Where sufficient information is not available, the rate should be estimated by reference to the rate that would be expected on a similar lease (ie a lease of a similar property in a similar location and for a similar term). The estimate of the rate should be reviewed together with (i) the present value of the lease payments, (ii) the assumed fair value of the property, and (iii) the assumed residual value, to ensure that all figures are reasonable and mutually consistent.

F17   In determining what are the minimum lease payments, regard should be had to what is likely to have a commercial effect in practice. It follows that the minimum lease payments will comprise the expected PFI payments for the property, less any amount for which there is genuine possibility of non-payment.

F18   A further factor to be taken into account is residual value risk. Where this risk both is significant and lies with the purchaser, it is normally evidence that the PFI contract in substance contains a finance lease and the property is an asset of the purchaser. An example is where the property has a material remaining useful economic life at the end of the PFI contract and is passed to the purchaser for a nominal or substantially fixed amount.

How to apply the FRS

What variations are relevant?

F19   For those contracts that fall directly within the FRS, whether a party has an asset of the property will depend on whether it has access to the benefits of the property and exposure to the associated risks. This will be reflected in the extent to which each

*SSAP 21, paragraph 15.

party bears the potential variations in property profits (or losses). The principle here is to distinguish potential variations in costs and revenues that flow from features of the property—which are relevant to determining who has an asset of the property (see paragraphs F22-F50) – from those that do not—and which are therefore not relevant to determining who has an asset of the property (see paragraph F20).

There may be features that could lead directly to profit variations for reasons that **F20** relate purely to a service. Such variations may take the form of potential penalties for underperformance, or potential variations in revenues or in operating costs. These should be ignored when assessing who has an asset of the property, irrespective of their size. For example, a penalty may arise in a PFI contract for a prison because the security staff have not been trained satisfactorily, or in a PFI contract involving a catering facility because the food purchased is not up to standard. Similarly, potential variations in operating costs may relate purely to a service, for example the cost of raw materials and consumables in a catering facility. Such potential variations are irrelevant to determining which party has an asset of the property.

There may be a significant number of property factors (for example, those listed in **F21** paragraph F22). It will be important to assess the effect of all relevant factors and the interaction between them, giving greater weight to those that are more likely to have a commercial effect in practice. It will not be appropriate to focus on one feature in isolation. It will be necessary to consider both the probability of any future profit variation arising from a property factor and its likely financial effect. Additional costs may be incurred to correct a problem rather than risking the imposition of a much greater penalty, in which case the relevant variation to consider is the likely increase in costs rather than the possible penalty. Similarly, a possible increase in future costs may be avoided by altering some feature of the property at a lower net cost, in which case the variation to consider is the cost of altering the property.

Factors relevant to the property

As noted in paragraph F19, in applying the FRS the key test is to establish who will **F22** bear any variations in property profits (or losses). Depending on the particular circumstances, a range of factors may be relevant to this assessment of profit variation. The principal factors that, depending on the particular circumstances, may be relevant are:

- graphs F32–F34)
- who determines the nature of the property (see paragraphs F35–F37)
- penalties for underperformance or non-availability (see paragraphs F38 and F39)
- potential changes in relevant costs (see paragraphs F40 and F41)
- obsolescence, including the effects of changes in technology (see paragraphs F42 and F43)
- the arrangements at the end of the contract and residual value risk (see paragraphs F44–F48).

The above list of the factors to be considered should be applied only with reference to **F23** the analysis given in paragraphs F24-F50. The key features of the analysis are summarised and illustrated in the table at the end of this Application Note.

Demand risk

Demand risk is the risk that demand for the property will be greater or less than **F24** predicted or expected. Where demand risk is significant, it will normally give the clearest evidence of who should record an asset of the property. Demand risk is imposed by the economic conditions of the market in which the PFI contract is written. Its existence and significance cannot be altered by the terms of the contract; the contract can only allocate demand risk between the parties to the contract, for example by allowing renegotiation of the contract at certain demand levels.

F25   The first step is to identify whether demand is a significant risk. There may be instances where there is little genuine uncertainty about the level of future demand for the services provided by the property. For example, in a short-term IT contract there may be very little likelihood of demand varying greatly from the levels predicted under the contract. In such a case, demand risk is not significant and little weight should be given to this test. In other cases there may be much genuine uncertainty over the extent to which a property will be used – for example, a new road to be built in a newly developed area. In these cases demand risk will be significant and who bears it will be highly relevant to determining the appropriate accounting treatment.

F26   The length of the contract may influence the significance of demand risk. In general, demand risk will be greater the longer the term of the contract, since it is usually more difficult to forecast for later periods.

F27   It is also important to distinguish where demand risk is insignificant from where the terms of the contract are such that it is passed to one or other party. For example, there may be much uncertainty over the demand for a certain type of property in the long term. However, the terms of a long-term PFI contract for such a property may be such that the purchaser would fill the PFI property in preference to properties not subject to PFI, with the effect that it is very unlikely that the PFI property will not be full. In such a case, the purchaser has retained demand risk.

F28   Where it is established that demand risk is significant, it is necessary to determine who will bear it, ie who will bear the effects of reasonably likely changes in demand. This will depend on the answers to two interrelated questions:

(a)   Will the payments between the operator and the purchaser reflect the usage of the property or does the purchaser have to pay the operator regardless of the level of usage (paragraphs F29 and F30)?

(b)   Who will gain if demand is greater than expected (paragraph F31)?

F29   Where the PFI payments do not vary substantially with demand or usage of the property (although they may vary with other factors), the purchaser will be obliged to pay for the output or capacity of the property (eg prison places, hospital beds) whether or not it is needed (ie whether or not there are sufficient prisoners or patients). This is evidence that the property is the purchaser's asset and the purchaser has a liability to pay for it. In particular, if the purchaser, in substance, is obliged to pay a minimum amount (ie there is no genuine commercial possibility of non-payment) whether or not it will need the property, and the minimum amount more than covers the cost of the property, this is evidence that the property is an asset of the purchaser. In making this assessment of demand risk, any penalties or reductions in payments for non-availability of the property should be ignored: these relate to whether the property is in a state fit for use and do not affect the incidence of demand risk.

F30   Conversely, where the PFI payments will vary proportionately over all reasonably likely levels of demand, the purchaser will not be obliged to pay for the property to the extent it is not needed, which is evidence that the property is the operator's asset.

In addition, the party that bears demand risk will gain if demand is greater than **F31** expected. If the purchaser bears demand risk, it will benefit from additional usage of the property at little or no extra property cost (for example, if payment for a hospital outpatients facility is largely independent of its usage, the purchaser will benefit from additional patients being treated when usage is high at little or no extra cost). This is evidence that the property is an asset of the purchaser. Conversely, if the operator bears demand risk, it will benefit from the increased payments that result from any additional usage of the property (for example, if payment for a hospital outpatients facility is based on throughput, the operator will benefit from additional usage payments when usage is high, although it may bear little or no extra cost). This is evidence that the property is an asset of the operator.

The presence, if any, of third-party revenues

A feature of some PFI contracts is that the property is expected to be used by third **F32** parties. Where the operator relies on revenues from third parties to cover its property costs, this is evidence that the property is an asset of the operator.

Conversely, where third-party usage is minimal or merely a future possibility, it is **F33** more likely that the property is an asset of the purchaser. This would particularly be the case where the purchaser in some way guarantees the operator's income from the property or where there is genuine scope for significant third-party use of the property but the purchaser significantly restricts such use.

The existence of third-party revenues may be linked to the incidence of demand risk. **F34** For example, the purchaser may have the option to reduce its usage of the property, in which case the operator will attempt to find third parties to use the resulting spare capacity. If the purchaser's option is a genuine one with a real possibility of exercise, and if the operator bears a significant risk of a large fall in property income as a result, this is evidence that the property is an asset of the operator.

Who determines the nature of the property

This factor relates to who determines how the PFI contract is to be fulfilled and, in **F35** particular, what kind of property (road, hospital etc) is to be built. Where in essence the purchaser determines the key features of the property and how it is to be operated, bearing the cost implications of any changes to the method of operation, this is evidence that the property is its asset. The purchaser may determine the key features of the property explicitly by agreeing them as terms of the PFI contract or, for example, through a contractual acceptance provision at the end of the con-struction phase. Alternatively, the purchaser may implicitly determine the key features of the property. For example, a contract for a road may specify that the road will revert to the purchaser in a predefined state after a relatively short period: this may have the effect that the operator has little discretion over the standard of road to build in the first instance or how it is maintained subsequently.

Conversely, where the operator has significant and ongoing discretion over how to **F36** fulfil the PFI contract and makes the key decisions on what property is built and how it is operated, bearing the consequent costs and risks, this is an indication that the property is the operator's asset. For example, this would be the case if the operator is free to redesign the property extensively during the term of the contract (perhaps even to scrap the original property and build a replacement), in the hope of reducing its costs. Similarly, in a PFI contract to design, build and operate a road, the operator may have complete discretion over the balance between the quality of the original road built and the consequent level of maintenance costs.

FRS 5 APPLICATION NOTES

F37   Design risk is the risk that the design of the property is such that, even if it is constructed satisfactorily, it will not fully meet the requirements of the contract. This is part of the question of who determines the nature of the property, discussed above. In contrast, construction risk refers to who bears the financial implications of cost and time overruns during the construction period (and related warranty repairs caused by poor building work after the asset has been completed). Construction risk is not generally relevant to determining which party has an asset of the property once construction is completed, because such risk normally has no impact during the property's operational life. However, construction risk may be relevant where it calls into question the other evidence. In particular, if the purchaser is bearing construction risk in a project in which the property is claimed to be that of the operator, it will be necessary to look closely at the other terms of the transaction to determine whether the property really is the operator's asset and is not actually an asset of the purchaser.

Penalties for underperformance or non-availability

F38   Many PFI contracts provide for penalties if the property is below a specified standard or is unavailable because of operator fault. (Penalties relating purely to services, however, are not relevant and should not be brought into the assessment.) These penalties may take the form of either cash payments or reductions in revenue. It will be important to assess both the likelihood of the penalty occurring in practice and whether the likely payments are significant. For example, a penalty may have little impact in practice because the contract gives the operator ample time to rectify the fault or the penalty is invoked only if the property is completely unavailable. Where, as in this example, potential penalties are either not significant or are unlikely to occur, this is evidence that the property is an asset of the purchaser.

F39   Conversely, the penalty mechanism may have the effect that the operator's profits associated with the property are genuinely subject to significant potential variation. For example, a PFI contract for a road may contain penalty clauses if lanes are closed for more than a minimal period for maintenance, with the penalty being significant and having a reasonable possibility of occurring. This would be evidence that the property is an asset of the operator.

Potential changes in relevant costs

F40   Potential changes in relevant costs may be dealt with in different ways under a PFI contract. (Only changes in property costs are relevant; changes in service costs are not relevant and should not be brought into the assessment.) The contract may have the effect that any significant future cost increases can be passed on to the purchaser, which would be evidence that the property is an asset of the purchaser. For example, this would be the case where the PFI payments will vary with specific indices so as to reflect the operator's costs.

F41   Conversely, where the operator's costs are both significant and highly uncertain, and there is no provision for cost variations to be passed on to the purchaser, this is evidence that the property is an asset of the operator. For example, this would be the case where the payments are fixed or vary in relation to a general inflation index such as the Retail Prices Index. Similar considerations apply to any cost savings and how they are shared between the parties.

FRS 5   APPLICATION NOTES

Obsolescence, including the effects of changes in technology

Whether obsolescence or changes in technology are relevant will depend on the nature of the contract. In contracts for the introduction of information technology systems, it will be of great significance who bears the future costs and any benefits associated with obsolescence or changes in technology: in other cases (eg a roads contract) it is likely to be of much less significance.   **F42**

Where the potential for obsolescence or changes in technology are significant, the party that bears the costs and any associated benefits will be the one for whom there is evidence that the property is its asset.   **F43**

The arrangements at the end of the contract and residual value risk

Residual value risk is the risk that the actual residual value of the property at the end of the contract will be different from that expected. This risk is more significant the shorter the PFI contract is in relation to the useful economic life of the property. Where it is significant, residual value risk will normally give clear evidence of who should record an asset of the property. In part, residual value risk stems directly from the economic conditions of the market for the property, ie the rise or fall of prices relevant to the property. The price aspects of residual value risk cannot be reduced or increased by the contract. The contract can only influence those aspects of residual value risk relating to the condition of the property at the end of the contract.   **F44**

Where this risk is significant, who bears it will depend on the arrangements at the end of the contract. For example, the purchaser will bear residual value risk (providing evidence that the property is its asset) where: **F45**

(a) it will purchase the property for a substantially fixed or nominal amount at the end of the contract;
(b) the property will be transferred to a new operator, selected by the purchaser, for a substantially fixed or nominal amount; or
(c) payments over the term of the PFI contract are sufficiently large for the operator not to rely on an uncertain residual value for its return.

Where the purchaser has an option to purchase the property or, alternatively, an option to 'walk' and leave the property with the operator, the practical effect of the option should be carefully analysed. In particular, where there is no genuine possibility that a purchase option will not be exercised (or, alternatively, that a 'walk' option will be exercised), the option will not transfer residual value risk to the operator.   **F46**

The significance of a minimal payment for the residual interest at the end of the contract depends on other features of the contract. If the property has a significant remaining useful economic life, such minimal payment will be evidence, in the absence of evidence to the contrary, that the purchaser paid for the property over the term of the PFI contract. This in turn is evidence that the property was an asset of the purchaser throughout.   **F47**

Conversely, the operator will bear residual value risk (providing evidence that the property is its asset) where: **F48**

(a) it will retain the property at the end of the PFI contract; or
(b) the property will be transferred to the purchaser or another operator at the prevailing market price.

FRS 5 APPLICATION NOTES

Assessment of relevant factors

F49   In determining whether each party has an asset of the property, it will not be appropriate to focus on one feature in isolation. Rather, the combined effect of all relevant factors should be considered for a range of reasonably possible scenarios, with greater weight being given to those outcomes that are more likely to occur in practice.

F50   In addition, it will often be useful in weighing all the evidence to consider the position of the various parties to the transaction, including their apparent expectations and motives for agreeing to its various terms. For example, an assessment of the operator's financing* may indicate a level of debt funding that could be credible only if another party stood behind the operator. In such circumstances the PFI contract would be deemed a financing arrangement and thus indicate that the property is an asset of the purchaser. Similarly, a financing arrangement would be indicated where, in the event that the contract is terminated early, the bank financing will be fully paid out by the purchaser under all events of default, including operator default.

REQUIRED ACCOUNTING

Purchaser has an asset of the property

F51   Where it is concluded that the purchaser has an asset of the property and a liability to pay for it, these should be recorded in its balance sheet. The initial amount recorded for each should be the fair value of the property.† Subsequently, the asset should be depreciated over its useful economic life and the liability should be reduced as payments for the property are made. In addition, an imputed finance charge on the liability should be recorded in subsequent years using a property-specific rate (paragraph F16 discusses how to determine such a rate). The remainder of the PFI payments (ie the full payments, less the capital repayment and the imputed financing charge) should be recorded as an operating cost. If the purchaser has any other obligations in relation to the PFI contract, these should be accounted for in accordance with FRS 12 'Provisions, Contingent Liabilities and Contingent Assets'‡

F52   Generally, the purchaser should recognise each property when it comes into use. An exception is where the purchaser bears significant construction risk, in which case it should recognise the property as it is constructed.

Purchaser does not have an asset of the property

F53   Where it is concluded that the purchaser does not have an asset of the property, there may nevertheless be other assets or liabilities that require recognition. These can arise in respect of contributions, acquisition of the residual and other obligations of the purchaser.

**All aspects of the financing arrangements should be taken into account, eg the use of senior or subordinated debt and the presence of any guarantees.*

†*For a lease the sum to be recorded both as an asset and as a liability is the present value of the minimum lease payments, derived by discounting them at the interest rate implicit in the lease.*

‡*FRS 12 will be issued in September 1998 and it will be effective for accounting periods ending on or after 23 March 1999. (**Editor's note:** FRS 12 has now been issued.)*

Contributions

Contributions to a PFI contract by the purchaser may take a number of forms, **F54** including an up-front cash payment or the contribution of existing assets for development by the operator. The accounting treatment of such contributions depends on whether they give rise to future benefits for the purchaser. For example:

- If the contribution of an existing property results in lower service payments, the carrying amount of the property should be reclassified as a prepayment (current asset) and subsequently charged as an operating cost over the period of reduced PFI payments. If there is in effect a sale of part of the contributed asset (for example, a parcel of surplus land that is not used in the PFI contract), any profit should be recognised in accordance with paragraphs 23 and 24 (as explained in paragraphs 70–74).
- If the contribution does not give rise to a future benefit for the purchaser, it should be charged as an expense when the contribution is made. For example, a capital grant might be given for which the operator would have qualified even if the transaction had not been part of the PFI, or short-life assets might be donated to the contract for no value.

Acquisition of the residual

In some PFI transactions, all or part of the property (eg the land element) will pass to **F55** the purchaser at the end of the contract. Where the contract specifies that this transaction should take place at market value at the date of transfer, no accounting is required until the date of transfer, as this represents future capital expenditure for the purchaser.

Where the contract specifies the amount (including zero) at which the property will **F56** be transferred to the purchaser at the end of the contract, the specified amount will not necessarily correspond with the expected fair value of the residual estimated at the start of the contract. Any difference must be built up over the life of the contract in order to ensure a proper allocation of payments made between the cost of services under the contract and the acquisition of the residual. At the end of the contract the accumulated balance (whether positive or negative), together with any final payment, should exactly match the originally estimated fair value of the residual. For example, if the expected residual value at the end of a 30-year contact is £20 million, but the contract specifies that £30 million should be paid by the purchaser for that residual at that date, then a credit balance of £10 million should be accrued over the life of the contract, with the corresponding charge each year being included in the service expense. The payment of £30 million at the end of the contract will extinguish the balance of £10 million and establish an asset of £20 million, representing the value of the residual.

If, during the life of the contract, expectations change so that the expected value of **F57** the residual falls (but there are no changes to the payments scheduled under the contract), then consideration should be given to whether there has been an impairment. Ultimately, a positive difference may become negative, in which case a provision is required. Using the example in paragraph F56, if the expected residual value fell to zero after five years, then an expense and a liability of £20 million would be recorded immediately. The remaining £10 million is still accrued over the life of the contract, giving a final liability of £30 million which is paid at the end of the contract.

Other obligations of the purchaser

F58   If the purchaser has any other obligations in relation to the PFI contract, these should be accounted for in accordance with FRS 12 'Provisions, Contingent Liabilities and Contingent Assets'.*

Operator has an asset of the property

F59   Where it is concluded that the operator has an asset of the property, it should record this asset in its balance sheet. The asset should initially be recorded at its cost and then depreciated to its expected residual value over its useful economic life (which, unless the property is to be retained by the operator on the expiry of the PFI contract, will be constrained by the term of the PFI contract). Where the contract specifies a sum for which the residual value will be transferred to the purchaser, the difference between the amount payable and the expected residual value should be accounted for in a similar way to the accounting treatment adopted by the purchaser (see paragraph F56), on the assumption that the difference is accounted for by higher or lower PFI payments during the life of the contract. If the operator is obliged to meet any liabilities as a result of the contract (eg environmental clean-up costs), these should be recorded separately, within liabilities.

Operator does not have an asset of the property

F60   Where it is concluded that the operator does not have an asset of the physical property, it will, instead, have a financial asset, being a debt due from the purchaser for the fair value of the property. This asset should be recorded at the outset and reduced in subsequent years as payments are received from the purchaser. In addition, finance income on this financial asset should be recorded in subsequent years using a property-specific rate (paragraph F16 discusses how to determine such a rate). The remainder of the PFI payments (ie the full payments, less the capital repayment and the imputed financing charge) should be recorded within operating profit.

FRS 12 will be issued in September 1998 and it will be effective for accounting periods ending on or after 23 March 1999. (Editor's note:** FRS 12 has now been issued.)*

FLOW CHART

This flow chart summarises the decision route set out in this Application Note.

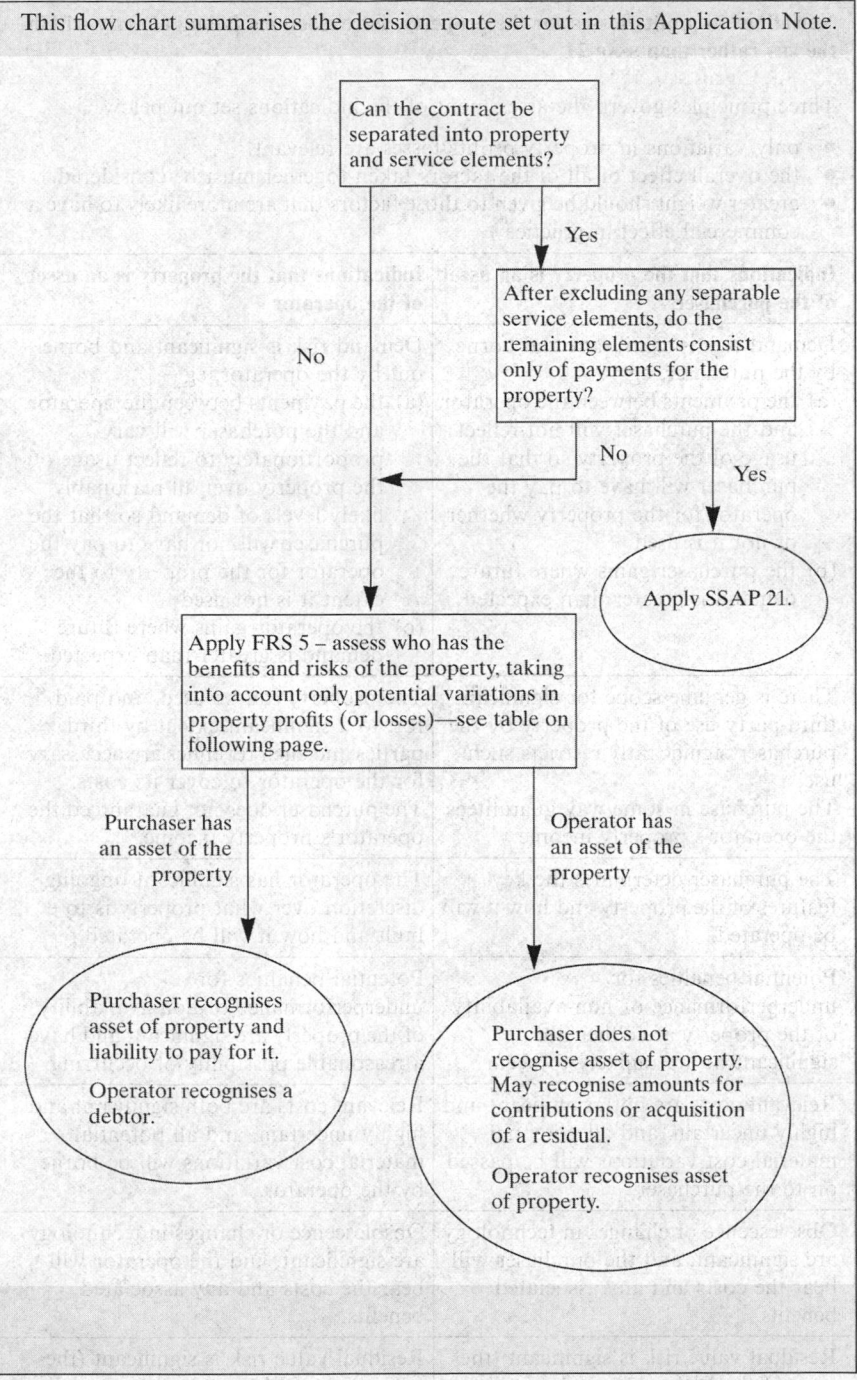

Can the contract be separated into property and service elements?

No ← →

Yes

After excluding any separable service elements, do the remaining elements consist only of payments for the property?

No

Yes

Apply SSAP 21.

Apply FRS 5 – assess who has the benefits and risks of the property, taking into account only potential variations in property profits (or losses)—see table on following page.

Purchaser has an asset of the property

Operator has an asset of the property

Purchaser recognises asset of property and liability to pay for it.

Operator recognises a debtor.

Purchaser does not recognise asset of property. May recognise amounts for contributions or acquisition of a residual.

Operator recognises asset of property.

TABLE

Variations in profits/losses for the property, intransactions falling directly within the FRS rather than SSAP 21

Three principles govern the assessment of the indications set out below:

- only variations in property profits/losses are relevant.
- the overall effect of all of the factors taken together must be considered.
- greater weight should be given to those factors that are more likely to have a commercial effect in practice

Indications that the property is an asset of the purchaser	Indications that the property is an asset of the operator
Demand risk is significant and borne by the purchaser, eg (a) the payments between the operator and the purchaser will not reflect usage of the property so that the purchaser will have to pay the operator for the property whether or not it is used (b) the purchaser gains where future demand is greater than expected.	Demand risk is significant and borne out by the operator, eg (a) the payments between the operator and the purchaser will vary proportionately to reflect usage of the property over all reasonably likely levels of demand so that the purchaser will not have to pay the operator for the property to the extent it is not used (b) the operator gains where future demand is greater than expected.
There is genuine scope for significant third-party use of the property by the purchaser significantly restricts such use. The purchase in some way guarantees the operator's property income.	The property can be used, and paid for, to a significant extent by third parties and such revenues are necessary for the operator to cover its costs. The purchaser does not guaranteed the operator's property income.
The purchaser determines the key features of the property and how it will be operated.	The operator has significant ongoing discretion over what property is to e built and how it will be operated.f
Potential penalties for underperformance or non-availability of the property are either not significant or are unlikely to occur.	Potential penalties for underperformance or non-availability of the property are significant and have a reasonable possibility of occurring.
Relevant costs are both significant and highly uncertain, and all potential material cost variations will be passed on to the purchaser.	Relevant costs are both significant and highly uncertain, and all potential material cost variations will be borne by the operator.
Obsolescence or changes in technology are significant, and the purchaser will bear the costs and any associated benefits.	Obsolescence or changes in technology are significant, and the operator will bear the costs and any associated benefits.
Residual value risk is significant (the term of the PFI contract is materially less than the useful economic life of the property) and borne by the purchaser.	Residual value risk is significant (the term of the PFI contract is materially less than the useful economic life of the property) and borne by the operator.

FRS 5 APPLICATION NOTES

Indications that the property is an asset of the purchaser	Indications that the property is an asset of the operator
The position of the parties to the transaction is consistent with the property being an asset of the purchaser, eg (a) the operator's debt funding is such that it implies the contract is in effect a financing arrangement (b) the bank financing would be fully paid out by the purchaser if the contract is terminated under all events of default including operator default.	The position of the parties to the transaction is consistent with the property being an asset of the operator, eg (a) the operator's funding includes a significant amount of equity (b) the bank financing would be fully paid out by the purchaser only in the event of purchaser default or limited force majeure circumstances.

APPENDIX APPLICATION NOTE G – REVENUE RECOGNITION

Introduction

This Application Note deals with revenue recognition from the supply of goods or services by a seller to its customers. It sets out basic principles of revenue recognition which should be applied in all cases. It also provides specific guidance for: **G1**

- long-term contractual performance;
- separation and linking of contractual arrangements;
- bill and hold arrangements;
- sales with rights of return; and
- presentation of turnover as principal or as agent.

The Application Note does not apply to the following arrangements: **G2**

- those resulting from transactions in financial instruments;
- those arising from insurance contracts; and
- those which are dealt with more specifically elsewhere in this, and other, accounting standards.

Definitions

The following additional definitions apply in the Application Note: **G3**

Fair value

The amount at which goods or services could be exchanged in an arm's length transaction between informed and willing parties, other than in a forced or liquidation sale.

Performance

The fulfilment of the seller's contractual obligations to a customer through the supply of goods and services.

Right to consideration

A seller's right to the amount received or receivable in exchange for its performance. This right does not necessarily correspond to amounts falling due in accordance with a schedule of stage payments which may be specified in a contractual arrangement. Whilst stage payments will often be timed to coincide with performance, they may not correspond exactly. Stage payments reflect only the agreed timing of payment, whereas a right to consideration arises through the seller's performance.

Basic Principles

G4   A seller recognises revenue under an exchange transaction with a customer, when, and to the extent that, it obtains the right to consideration in exchange for its performance. At the same time, it typically recognises a new asset, usually a debtor.

G5   When a seller receives payment from a customer in advance of performance, it recognises a liability equal to the amount received, representing its obligation under the contract. When the seller obtains the right to consideration through its performance, that liability is reduced and the amount of the reduction in the liability is simultaneously reported as revenue.

G6   A seller may obtain a right to consideration when some, but not all, of its contractual obligations have been fulfilled. Where a seller has partially performed its contractual obligations, it recognises revenue to the extent that it has obtained the right to consideration through its performance.

G7   Revenue should be measured at the fair value of the right to consideration. Subject to paragraphs G8 - G9 or other evidence to the contrary, this will normally be the price specified in the contractual arrangement, net of discounts, value added tax and similar sales taxes.

G8   Where the effect of the time value of money is material to reported revenue, the amount of revenue recognised should be the present value of the cash inflows expected to be received from the customer in settlement. The unwinding of the discount should be credited to finance income as this represents a gain from a financing transaction.

G9   Where at the time revenue is recognised on a transaction there is a significant risk that there will be default on the amount of consideration due and the effect is material to reported revenue, an adjustment to the price specified in the contractual arrangement will be necessary to arrive at the amount of revenue to be recognised.

G10   Subsequent adjustments to a debtor as a result of changes in the time value of money and credit risk should not be included within revenue.

Turnover

G11   Turnover (which may be described as 'sales' in a seller's financial statements) is the revenue resulting from exchange transactions under which a seller supplies to customers the goods or services that it is in business to provide.*

*These transactions are often referred to as being part of the seller's 'operating activities'.

FRS 5   APPLICATION NOTES

A seller may enter into other exchange transactions such as the sale of fixed assets. **G12**
Such transactions do not normally give rise to turnover, as they do not normally fall
within the class of transactions set out in paragraph G11.*

Areas of specific guidance

Although revenue recognition is normally straightforward, in a number of areas **G13**
inconsistencies have arisen in practice. In addition to the basic principles outlined
above, which should be applied in all cases, the Application Note addresses a number
of specific types of transaction. These are confined to transactions that are generally
regarded as giving rise to turnover.

Long-term contractual performance

Statement of Standard Accounting Practice 9 'Stocks and long-term contracts' **G14**
(SSAP 9) sets out requirements for accounting and disclosure under a long-term
contract. The Application Note provides additional guidance on the recognition of
turnover derived from such contracts, but does not amend the requirements of that
accounting standard.

Features

A seller's performance under a contractual arrangement with a customer for the **G15**
design, manufacture or construction of a single substantial asset or the provision of a
service may be significant in the context of the seller's overall business activities and
fall into different financial periods.

Recognition of turnover arising from these contractual arrangements on their **G16**
completion, and not at interim stages, would result in the seller's financial statements
reflecting the results relating to contracts that had been completed during the
financial period, rather than its performance during the period. Therefore, in
accordance with SSAP 9, the seller should recognise changes in its assets or liabilities,
and related turnover, that represent the accrual, over the course of the contract, of its
right to consideration.

Analysis

The purpose of the analysis below is to assess how changes in a seller's assets or **G17**
liabilities, and related turnover, that arise from its performance under an incomplete
long-term contract should be recorded in its financial statements.

A seller should recognise turnover in respect of its performance under a long-term **G18**
contract when, and to the extent that, it obtains the right to consideration. This
should be derived from an assessment of the fair value of the goods or services
provided to its reporting date as a proportion of the total fair value of the contract.
In some contracts, this proportion will correspond with the proportion of expenditure incurred in comparison with total expenditure; however, this will not always be
the case. For all contracts, the guiding principle is to consider the stage of completion
of the contractual obligations, which reflects the extent to which the seller has
obtained the right to consideration (as defined in paragraph G3). As a result, different stages of contracts may vary in their relative profitability.

*For example, paragraph 20 of FRS 3 requires material profits or losses on the sale of fixed assets to be shown
after operating profit.*

FRS 5 APPLICATION NOTES

G19   The fair values used should represent those applicable on inception of the contract, unless the contractual terms specify that changes in prices will be passed on to the customer. Paragraphs G22 - G42 may be relevant when attributing fair values to the goods or services which have been provided up to the seller's reporting date.

Required accounting

G20   The application of SSAP 9 to the recording of a seller's long–term contractual performance results in the seller recognising turnover as contract activity progresses, to the extent that the outcome of the contract can be assessed with reasonable certainty.

G21   The seller should recognise changes in its assets or liabilities, and turnover, in accordance with the stage of completion of its contractual obligations, which reflects the extent to which it has obtained the right to consideration. The amount of turnover recognised should be derived from the proportion of costs incurred only where these provide evidence of the seller's performance and hence the extent to which it has obtained the right to consideration.

Separation and linking of contractual arrangements

Features

G22   A single contractual arrangement may require a seller to provide a number of different goods or services (or 'components') to its customers. These components may be unrelated and capable of being sold individually; alternatively, two or more components may be so closely related that their individual sale is not commercially feasible from either the seller's or the customer's perspective.

G23   A seller may provide a number of goods or services to customers as a package, in which the amount payable is set below the price at which these items would be sold individually.

Analysis

G24   The purpose of the analysis below is to determine whether, as a result of its performance:

(a)   the seller should recognise a change in its assets or liabilities, and turnover, in respect of its right to consideration for each component on an individual basis; or

(b)   two or more components should be combined and turnover recognised on that basis.

G25   A contractual arrangement should be accounted for as two or more separate transactions only where the commercial substance is that the individual components operate independently of each other. 'Operate independently' means that each component represents a separable good or service that the seller can provide to customers, either on a stand alone basis or as an optional extra. Alternatively, one or more component(s) may be capable of being provided by another supplier. This separation for accounting purposes is frequently referred to as the 'unbundling' of a contractual arrangement.

Conversely, the commercial substance of two or more separate contracts may require them to be accounted for as a single transaction. This is frequently referred to as the 'bundling' of a contractual arrangement. **G26**

Where various components are to be unbundled, the seller should normally be capable of attributing a reliable fair value to each of them by reference to individual transactions. If various components are combined and sold at a price less than the total fair values of the individual components, the reduction should be allocated to each component pro rata to their fair values. **G27**

Where it is not possible to attribute reliable fair values to every component, the seller may be able to unbundle the arrangement where reliable fair values can be obtained for either the completed or the uncompleted component(s). For example, where reliable fair values can be obtained only for the uncompleted components, the seller may be able to calculate by deduction a value for the completed components. Where a reliable fair value cannot be obtained for the uncompleted component(s), particular care must be taken to ensure that turnover is not overstated for the completed components. That is because the contract price may be set at a discount from the total amount at which the components would be sold individually. **G28**

Required accounting

Components operate independently of each other

Where a contractual arrangement consists of various components that operate independently of each other and a reliable fair value can be attributed to every component, the seller should recognise changes in its assets or liabilities, and related turnover, in respect of its right to consideration for each component as if it were an individual contractual arrangement. **G29**

Where reliable fair values can be attributed only to the uncompleted component(s), the fair value of the uncompleted component(s) should be deducted from the total fair value of the contract to derive the amount of turnover attributable to the completed component(s). Where reliable fair values cannot be attributed to the uncompleted component(s), particular care must be taken to ensure that turnover is not overstated for the completed components. **G30**

Where reliable fair values cannot be attributed to individual completed or uncompleted components, the seller should recognise changes in its assets or liabilities, and turnover, for those components as a single, bundled, contractual arrangement. For example, where a contractual arrangement consists of three components and a reliable fair value can be attributed only to the second and third components combined, and not to any components individually, a fair value should be attributed to the first component in accordance with paragraph G30. The second and third components are then viewed together in accordance with paragraph G32 when determining the point at which changes in its assets or liabilities, and turnover, attributable to those components should be recognised by the seller. **G31**

Components do not operate independently of each other

Where a contractual arrangement consists of various components that do not operate independently of each other, the seller should account for them together to reflect the seller's performance of its obligations as a whole in obtaining the right to consideration. Where the contractual arrangement meets the definition of a long- **G32**

FRS 5 APPLICATION NOTES

term contract in SSAP 9, it should be accounted for in accordance with that standard and paragraphs G14 - G21 of this Application Note.

Illustrations

Sales of software and related maintenance services

G33   A customer may purchase 'off the shelf' packaged software from a seller, which also offers separately a support service that provides helpline assistance and advice about the package's operation. An analysis of the arrangement shows that the customer has no commercial obligation or requirement to purchase the support service; it is not needed for the software package to operate satisfactorily. The seller's performance is made up of two components and it should recognise turnover separately for each.

G34   Conversely, a seller may enter into a contractual arrangement for the supply of bespoke software, together with its maintenance and the customer's right to future upgrades for a period of three years. An analysis of the arrangement shows that the maintenance and upgrades are required in order to ensure that the software continues to operate satisfactorily throughout the three year period and that these services are offered only by the supplier of the software. The commercial substance of the arrangement is therefore that the customer is paying for a three year service agreement. The seller should treat all three components (the software, the upgrades and the maintenance) as linked, and recognise turnover on a long-term contractual basis.

Inception fees

G35   A contractual arrangement may require the payment of a fee at inception which permits the customer to purchase goods or services over a period of time. In determining when the seller should recognise turnover attributable to the fee, it should determine whether or not the fee and the charges for goods or services operate independently of each other.

G36   The fee and the charges for goods or services may often together provide the seller's return on the contract as a whole. This may be the case, for example, where payment of the fee entitles the customer to purchase goods or services at lower prices than would otherwise be payable. In these circumstances the seller should record the fee as turnover on a systematic basis over the average period in which goods or services are expected to be provided to the customer. Before the seller has provided goods or services, it should report a liability for the fee to the extent that this has not been included in turnover.

G37   Where it can be demonstrated that the seller has no further obligations to the customer in respect of the fee, the seller should record the fee as turnover on the date on which it becomes entitled to it. This may be the case, for example, where, notwithstanding payment of the fee, the customer is required to pay for all goods or services supplied under the arrangement at the current commercial rate.

Vouchers

G38   A seller may, in a single transaction, sell goods or services and vouchers, where the vouchers are redeemable against future purchases from the seller. Where the fair value of the voucher is significant in the context of the transaction, revenue should be reported at the amount of consideration received or receivable less the fair value of the voucher issued. The latter represents a liability for future performance, which is extinguished and recognised in revenue when the voucher is tendered as part of the consideration on a future transaction.

The fair value of a voucher will often be less than its face value. In determining the **G39** fair value of a voucher, regard should be paid to the terms of the voucher, including:

(a) the range of the goods or services which the customer can obtain on redemption of the vouchers;
(b) the discount the customer obtains when redeeming the voucher compared with the discount which might be obtained by customers who do not redeem vouchers;
(c) the length of time before which the right to use the voucher expires; and
(d) the extent to which the voucher is similar to other vouchers that are distributed to customers free of charge.

Regard should also be paid to the proportion of vouchers that are expected to be redeemed.

An analysis of the above factors may indicate that the fair value of a voucher is not **G40** significant; in effect the issue of the voucher is an inducement to undertake a future transaction rather than being a separable component of the original transaction. In such circumstances, no adjustment is required to revenue at the time the voucher is issued.

At each reporting date, the seller should review its estimated liability for outstanding **G41** vouchers having regard to experience of the proportion that are redeemed and expire. Adjustments to the estimate should be included within revenue.

Vouchers distributed free of charge, independently of another transaction, do not **G42** give rise to a liability except where redemption of the voucher will result in products being sold at a loss. Where this is the case, the seller has entered into an onerous contract and provision will need to be made in accordance with FRS 12 'Provisions, Contingent Liabilities and Contingent Assets'. When the vouchers are redeemed, the seller should recognise revenue at the amount received for the product, ie after deducting the discount obtained for the vouchers.

Bill and hold arrangements

Features

Under a bill and hold arrangement, a seller enters into a contractual arrangement **G43** with a customer for the supply of goods where there is transfer of title but physical delivery is deferred to a later date.

Analysis

The purpose of the analysis below is to determine whether, in the circumstances **G44** described in paragraph G43, the seller should:

(a) recognise turnover and a right to consideration; or
(b) continue to recognise the goods as stock.

In accordance with the general principles of the FRS the goods cease to be assets of **G45** the seller and become assets of the customer (and in exchange the seller obtains the right to consideration) when the seller transfers to the customer access to the significant benefits relating to the goods and exposure to the risks inherent in those benefits. From the customer's perspective, the principal benefits and risks include:

Benefits

(a) the right to obtain the goods as and when required;
(b) the sole right to the goods for their sale to a third party and the future cash flows from such a sale; and
(c) insulation from changes in prices charged by the seller (eg because the seller has revised its standard price list).

Risks

(a) slow movement, resulting in increased costs of financing and holding of the goods, and an increased risk of obsolescence; and
(b) being compelled to take delivery of goods that have become obsolete or not readily saleable, resulting in no onward sale or a sale at a reduced price.

G46 In order for the seller to have the right to recognise changes in its assets or liabilities, and turnover, arising from its right to consideration in respect of the bill and hold arrangement, the terms of the contractual arrangement between the seller and the customer should include all of the following characteristics:

(a) the goods should be complete and ready for delivery;
(b) the seller should not have retained any significant performance obligations other than the safekeeping of the goods and their shipment when the customer requests this;
(c) subject to any rights of return, the seller should have obtained the right to consideration regardless of whether the goods are shipped, at the customer's request, to its delivery address. Where rights of return are granted, particular consideration is required of the commercial substance of the related sales, especially the transfer of risk. Rights of return are addressed at paragraphs G49-G59 below;
(d) the goods should be identified separately from the seller's other stock and should not be capable of being used to fill other orders that are received between the date of the bill and hold sale and shipment of the goods to the customer; and
(e) the bill and hold terms should be in accordance with the commercial objectives of the customer and not the seller. For example, where the delay in the delivery of the goods is to meet the customer's need for flexibility in the timing and location of delivery, and the conditions set out in paragraphs (a) to (d) above are met, it will be appropriate for the seller to recognise changes in assets or liabilities, and turnover.

Required accounting

Substance of the transaction is that the goods represent an asset of the customer

G47 Where it is concluded that the stock is an asset of the customer, resulting in the seller having a right to consideration, the seller should recognise the related changes in its assets or liabilities, and turnover.

Substance of the transaction is that the goods represent an asset of the seller

Where it is concluded that the stock remains an asset of the seller, it should be retained on the seller's balance sheet. Any amounts received from the customer should be included within creditors in accordance with paragraph G5. **G48**

Sales with rights of return

Features

The terms of contractual arrangements may allow customers to return goods that they have purchased and obtain a refund or release from the obligation to pay. **G49**

Rights of return may be included explicitly or implicitly within contractual arrangements. Alternatively, they may arise through statutory requirements. **G50**

Analysis

The purpose of the analysis below is to determine the effect of rights of return on a seller's recognition of changes in its assets or liabilities, and turnover. **G51**

The inclusion of rights of return in a contractual arrangement may affect both the quantification of the seller's right to consideration, compared to an otherwise identical arrangement which does not have these rights, and the point at which the seller should recognise that right. This is because rights of return give rise to a contractual obligation on the part of the seller to transfer economic benefits to its customer and in some cases oblige the seller to defer recognition of the sales transaction so long as substantially all of the risks associated with the goods are retained. **G52**

The seller's recognition of its right to consideration and contractual obligation to transfer economic benefits to its customer in respect of rights of return are linked transactions. In consequence, changes in the seller's assets or liabilities should reflect the loss expected to arise from the rights of return. Turnover should exclude the sales value of estimated returns. **G53**

A seller will generally be able to estimate reliably the sales value of returns, having regard to risk, which may be less than its maximum potential obligation. It will generally be possible to derive a reliable estimate from historical experience of the amount of comparable goods returned as a proportion of comparable sales. **G54**

If a seller is unable to estimate reliably the expected value of returns, the maximum potential amount should be calculated in accordance with the terms of its contractual arrangement with the customer and excluded from turnover. **G55**

In some cases, the risk of return may be so significant that substantially all of the risks associated with the goods are retained by the seller and accordingly the seller does not have the right to consideration. In such circumstances the seller should not recognise any changes in its assets or liabilities, and turnover, from the transaction. Any amounts received from the customer should be accounted for as a payment in advance, in accordance with paragraph G5. **G56**

FRS 5 APPLICATION NOTES

Required accounting

G57   A seller should record changes in its assets or liabilities, and turnover, to the extent that its performance has earned it the right to consideration, taking account of the expected loss in accordance with paragraphs 23 and 73. The amount recorded as turnover should exclude the sales value of estimated returns from the total sales value of the goods supplied to customers.

G58   At each reporting date, the seller should review its estimate of returns, having regard to changes in expectations and the expiry of contractual rights of return. Subsequent adjustments to the estimate should be recorded within revenue.

G59   Where a seller has been precluded from recognising changes in its assets or liabilities, and turnover, because substantially all of the risks associated with the goods are retained and so has not earned the right to consideration, it should recognise these changes and turnover on the earlier of the dates on which:

(a)   it is capable of estimating the level of returns with reliability; and
(b)   the right of return expires or is surrendered.

Presentation of turnover as principal or as agent

Features

G60   A seller may act on its own account when contracting with its customers for the supply of goods in return for the right to consideration. In such transactions the seller is frequently referred to as a principal.

G61   Alternatively, a seller may act as an intermediary, earning a fee or commission in return for arranging the provision of goods or services on behalf of a principal. In such transactions, the seller is frequently referred to as an agent.

Analysis

G62   The purpose of the analysis below is to determine whether a seller obtains the right to consideration by performing its contractual obligations:

(a)   as principal in an exchange transaction with its customer; or
(b)   as agent in relation to a transaction between its principal and the principal's customer.

G63   The general principles of the standard require that, in order for a seller to account for exchange transactions as principal, it should normally have exposure to all significant benefits and risks associated with at least one of the following:

(a)   Selling price: the ability, within economic constraints, to establish the selling price with the customer, either directly or, where the selling price of an item is fixed, indirectly by providing additional goods or services or adjusting the terms of a linked transaction; or
(b)   Stock: exposure to the risks of damage, slow movement and obsolescence, and changes in suppliers' prices.

G64   Where the seller has not disclosed that it is acting as agent, there is a rebuttable presumption that it is acting as principal.

G65   Additional factors which indicate that a seller may be acting as principal include:

(a)   performance of part of the services, or modification to the goods supplied;
(b)   assumption of credit risk; and
(c)   discretion in supplier selection.

In contrast, where a seller acts as agent it will not normally be exposed to the   **G66**
majority of the benefits and risks associated with the exchange transaction. Agency
arrangements will typically include the following characteristics:

(a)   the seller has disclosed the fact that it is acting as agent;
(b)   once the seller has confirmed its customer's order with a third party, the seller
       will normally have no further involvement in the performance of the ultimate
       supplier's contractual obligations;
(c)   the amount that the seller earns is predetermined, being either a fixed fee per
       transaction or a stated percentage of the amount billed to the customer; and
(d)   the seller bears no stock or credit risk, other than in circumstances where it
       receives additional consideration from the ultimate supplier in return for its
       assumption of this risk.

Required accounting

Seller acts as principal

Where the substance of a transaction is that the seller acts as principal, it should   **G67**
report turnover based on the gross amount received or receivable in return for its
performance under the contractual arrangement.

Seller acts as agent

Where the substance of a transaction is that the seller acts as agent, it should report   **G68**
as turnover the commission or other amounts received or receivable in return for its
performance under the contractual arrangement. Any amounts received or receivable
from the customer that are payable to the principal should not be included in the
agent's turnover.

Illustrations

A seller acts as a building contractor for the construction of a new office block. An   **G69**
analysis of the arrangement shows that the terms of the seller's contract with its
customer include a negotiated selling price, credit risk for amounts due from the
customer, primary responsibility for the construction and quality of the new building
and discretion as to whether it carries out the work itself or employs subcontractors.
The seller is acting as principal and should account for the gross amount of turnover,
regardless of whether it carries out the work itself or employs subcontractors to carry
out part or all of the construction activities.

A seller acts as an online retailer from a website, where it advertises holidays. An   **G70**
analysis of the arrangement shows that it acts as an intermediary between its customers and the ultimate sellers of the holidays and that it does not set the selling
price. Its contractual terms of business include an exclusion of any liability to its
customers once they have been put in touch with the ultimate sellers. The seller is
paid a fee for each customer that purchases a holiday from an ultimate seller and has
no involvement in the transaction after it has put the customer in touch with the
ultimate seller. The seller is acting as agent and its turnover should include only the
fees it receives from the ultimate seller.

FRS 5 APPLICATION NOTES

G71   A department store provides space for concessionaires to sell products and receives a fixed amount of rental income from the concessionaire. An analysis of the factors discussed in paragraphs G63 - G66 shows that the concessionaire is acting as principal in an exchange transaction with its customers and is entitled to the amounts received from the sale of the goods and services. In these circumstances, the concessionaire should include within its turnover the amounts received or receivable in respect of the sale of the goods and services. The department store should not include within its turnover the value of the concessionaire's sales.

Disclosure - seller acts as agent

G72   Where a seller acts as agent, it is encouraged, where practicable, to disclose the gross value of sales throughput as additional, non-statutory information. Where such disclosure is given, a brief explanation of the relationship of recognised turnover to the gross value of sales throughput should be given.

Adoption of FRS 5 by the Board

Financial Reporting Standard 5 – 'Reporting the Substance of Transactions' was approved for issue by the nine members of the Accounting Standards Board.

David Tweedie	(Chairman)
Allan Cook	(Technical Director)
Robert Bradfield	
Ian Brindle	
Sir Bryan Carsberg	
Michael Garner	
Raymond Hinton	
Donald Main	
Graham Stacy	

'Amendment to FRS 5 "Reporting the Substance of Transactions": Private Finance Initiative and Similar Contracts – September 1998' (Application Note F) was approved for issue by the ten members of the Accounting Standards Board.

Sir David Tweedie	Chairman
Allan Cook	Technical Director
David Allvey	
Ian Brindle	
Dr John Buchanan	
John Coombe	
Raymond Hinton	
Huw Jones	
Professor Geoffrey Whittington	
Ken Wild	

'Amendment to FRS 5 "Reporting the Substance of Transactions": Revenue Recognition – November 2003' was approved for issue by a vote of eight of the nine members of the Accounting Standards Board. Mr Wild dissented.

Members of the Accounting Standards Board

Mary Keegan	Chairman
Allan Cook CBE	Technical Director
Douglas Flint	
Huw Jones	
Roger Marshall	
Isobel Sharp	
John Smith	
Jonathan Symonds	
Ken Wild	

Appendix I
Note on legal requirements

GREAT BRITAIN

References are to the Companies Act 1985

Group accounts

1   Definitions of 'parent undertaking' and 'subsidiary undertaking' are set out and explained in section 258 and Schedule 10A.

2   Other provisions of the Companies Act relevant to the preparation of consolidated accounts are given in paragraphs 95 and 96 of FRS 2 'Accounting for Subsidiary Undertakings'.

3   *The requirement to show a true and fair view*

Section 227 provides the following:

"(1)   If at the end of a financial year a company is a parent company the directors shall, as well as preparing individual accounts for the year, prepare group accounts.

(2)   Group accounts shall be consolidated accounts comprising –
(a)   a consolidated balance sheet dealing with the state of affairs of the parent company and its subsidiary undertakings, and
(b)   a consolidated profit and loss account dealing with the profit or loss of the parent undertaking and its subsidiary undertakings.

(3)   The accounts shall give a true and fair view of the state of affairs as at the end of the financial year, and the profit or loss for the financial year, of the undertakings included in the consolidation as a whole, so far as concerns members of the company.

(4)   A company's group accounts shall comply with the provisions of Schedule 4A as to the form and content of the consolidated balance sheet and consolidated profit and loss account and additional information to be provided by way of notes to the accounts.

(5)   Where compliance with the provisions of that Schedule, and the other provisions of this Act, as to the matters to be included in a company's group accounts or in the notes to those accounts, would not be sufficient to give a true and fair view, the necessary additional information shall be given in the accounts or in a note to them.

(6)   If in special circumstances compliance with any of those provisions is inconsistent with the requirement to give a true and fair view, the directors shall depart from that provision to the extent necessary to give a true and fair view.

Particulars of any such departure, the reasons for it and its effect shall be given in a note to the accounts."*

---

*Editor's note: Section 227 has now been substantially redrafted, since it needs to deal with those companies preparing group accounts under IFRS as well as those applying UK GAAP. However, the substance of the requirements, now contained in sections 227 and 227A of the Act has not altered.

Section 255A(6) states that, in the case of a banking or insurance company, the references to the provisions of Schedule 4A in section 227(5) and (6) shall be read as references to those provisions as modified by Part II of Schedule 9.

Offset

The Companies Act contains the following provisions relating to offset: **4**

Schedule 4 paragraph 5 (an identical requirement for banking companies and groups is contained in Schedule 9 paragraph 5)

> 'Amounts in respect of items representing assets or income may not be offset against amounts in respect of items representing liabilities or expenditure (as the case may be), or vice versa.'

Schedule 4 paragraph 14 (an identical requirement for banking companies and groups is contained in Schedule 9 paragraph 21)

> 'In determining the aggregate amount of any item the amount of each individual asset or liability that falls to be taken into account shall be determined separately.'*

NORTHERN IRELAND

The legal requirements in Northern Ireland are identical to those in Great Britain. In   **5**
particular:

Article 266 of and Schedule 10A to the Companies (Northern Ireland) Order 1986 are identical to section 258 of and Schedule 10A to the Companies Act 1985 as referred to in paragraph 1 above.

Other provisions of companies legislation relevant to the preparation of consolidated accounts, as referred to in paragraph 2 above, are given in paragraph 97 of FRS 2 'Accounting for Subsidiary Undertakings'.

Articles 235 and 263A(5) of the Companies (Northern Ireland) Order 1986 are identical to sections 227 and 255A(5) respectively of the Companies Act 1985 as referred to in paragraph 3 above.

Paragraphs 5 and 14 of Schedule 4 to the Companies (Northern Ireland) Order 1986 are identical to paragraphs 5 and 14 of Schedule 4 to the Companies Act 1985 as referred to in paragraph 4 above.

REPUBLIC OF IRELAND

The legal requirements in the Republic of Ireland are similar to those in Great   **6**
Britain. In particular:

Regulation 4 of the European Communities (Companies: Group Accounts) Regulations 1992 is similar to section 258 of and Schedule 10A to the Companies Act 1985 as referred to in paragraph 1 above.

Editor's note: A similar requirement for insurance companies and groups is contained in Schedule 9A paragraph 3(4) 'subject to the provisions of this Schedule', and Schedule 8 for small companies.

Other provisions of companies legislation relevant to the preparation of consolidated accounts, as referred to in paragraph 2 above, are given in the insert replacing paragraph 98 of FRS 2 'Accounting for Subsidiary Undertakings'.

Regulations 5, 13 and 14 of the European Communities (Companies: Group Accounts) Regulations 1992 are similar to section 227 of the Companies Act 1985 as referred to in paragraph 3 above. As regards banks, section 5(1) of the European Communities (Credit Institutions: Accounts) Regulations 1992 is similar to section 255A(5) of the Companies Act 1985 as referred to in paragraph 3 above. Pending implementation of the EC Insurance Accounts Directive (91/674 EC) there is no legislation similar to section 255A(5) for insurance companies.

Sections 4(11) and 5(e) of the Companies (Amendment) Act 1986 are similar to paragraphs 5 and 14 of Schedule 4 to the Companies Act 1985 as referred to in paragraph 4 above.

Appendix II
Compliance with International Accounting Standards

There is no International Accounting Standard on this subject. The International Accounting Standards Committee (IASC) has issued a 'Framework for the Preparation and Presentation of Financial Statements'. The definitions of assets and liabilities set out in the FRS and the principles underlying it are similar in all material respects to those set out in the IASC's Framework. However, neither International Accounting Standards nor the Framework currently envisage use of a linked presentation for certain non-recourse finance as required by paragraphs 26–28 of the FRS.*

*Editor's note: IAS 18 Revenue deals with revenue recognition and is now covered by Application Note G to FRS 5. IFRIC 12 now deals with service concessions, covering similar areas to those included in Application Note F.

Appendix III
The development of the FRS

GENERAL

1   The problems of what is commonly referred to as 'off balance sheet financing' became evident during the 1980s. In that period, a number of complex arrangements were developed that, if accounted for in accordance with their legal form, resulted in accounts that did not report the commercial effect of the arrangement. In particular, concern grew over arrangements for financing a company's operations in such a way that, if the arrangement were accounted for merely by recording its legal form, the finance would not be shown as a liability on the balance sheet.

2   At the same time, there was rapid innovation in financial markets. New arrangements for financing assets were developed, the accounting for which was not immediately obvious. An example of one such arrangement is securitisation, whereby an asset and its non-recourse finance are tightly ring-fenced using a separate vehicle company.

3   These developments raised fundamental questions about the nature of assets and liabilities and when they should be included in the balance sheet. Questions were also raised about the accounting for some transactions that had been used by businesses for many years. For example, some queried whether factoring should be accounted for as a secured loan rather than as a sale of debts.

4   The FRS has been developed to address these issues and to deal with the problems caused by the misleading effects that 'off balance sheet financing' can have on the accounts. As that term indicates, the most widely recognised effect is the omission of liabilities from the balance sheet. However, the assets being financed, as well as the finance itself, are excluded, with the result that both the resources of the entity and its financing are understated. There may also be important effects on the profit and loss account. For instance, a profit may be reported on a 'sale' that is, in substance, a secured loan. As another example, what is in substance a finance charge may be either omitted from the profit and loss account altogether or described as some other kind of expense. All of these effects make it harder for the reader of the accounts to assess the true economic position of the reporting entity because they obscure the true extent and nature of its borrowings, its assets and the results of its activities.

5   The Board believes that financial statements should represent faithfully the commercial effects of the transactions and other events they purport to represent. This requires transactions to be accounted for in accordance with their substance and not merely their legal form, since the latter may not fully indicate the commercial effect of the arrangements entered into.

HISTORY OF DOCUMENTS ISSUED

TR 603

6   The first authoritative document to address this issue was Technical Release 603 (TR 603) – 'Off Balance Sheet Financing and Window Dressing', issued in December 1985 by the Institute of Chartered Accountants in England and Wales. The main provision of this short, preliminary document was that, in determining the accounting treatment of transactions, their economic substance rather than their mere legal form should be considered.

ED 42

TR 603 was followed by ED 42 'Accounting for special purpose transactions', which   7
was issued in March 1988 by the Accounting Standards Committee (ASC). ED 42
took a general approach, providing guidance that could be applied to a variety of
situations, rather than specifying detailed rules for specific transactions. It proposed
that assets and liabilities arising from off balance sheet transactions be included in
the balance sheet rather than merely disclosed in the notes. For this purpose, ED 42
described the essential characteristics of assets and liabilities. It also proposed that
'controlled non-subsidiaries' should be consolidated as if they were subsidiaries as
legally defined. The definition of a controlled non-subsidiary was substantially the
same as that of a quasi-subsidiary given in FRS 5.

ED 49

ED 49 'Reflecting the substance of transactions in assets and liabilities' was issued by   8
the ASC in May 1990. ED 49 responded to the comments received on ED 42 as well
as certain changes in the law. The ED continued to take a general approach, proposing analysis of the substance of transactions by reference to the essential
characteristics of assets and liabilities. It also continued to propose that controlled
non-subsidiaries should be consolidated in group accounts, although these vehicle
entities were renamed 'quasi subsidiaries'. The main changes from ED 42 were: the
inclusion, for the first time, of general recognition tests; the inclusion of Application
Notes specifying how the draft standard was to be applied to five specific transaction
types (including securitisation and factoring) – these were included at the specific
request of commentators to ED 42 and their inclusion was later supported by the
majority of commentators to ED 49; and the addition of guidance on identifying
control.

Bulletin 15

Respondents to ED 49 raised, inter alia, the concern that the treatment it proposed   9
for factoring was inconsistent with that proposed for securitisation. This led the
Accounting Standards Board to review the accounting for securitisation and, in
October 1991, to issue proposals (in Bulletin 15) under which most securitised assets
would be shown on the balance sheet, the arrangement being accounted for as a
secured loan. This was on the grounds that, in most securitisations, the originating
entity retains significantly all of the profits from the securitised assets. Although the
entity has strictly limited its exposure to losses on those assets, the same is true for
other non-recourse finance arrangements and for limited liability subsidiaries, where
it is accepted that assets and liabilities should be reported gross.

The respondents to Bulletin 15 were divided on whether securitisations should be   10
accounted for on balance sheet as a secured loan, or off balance sheet as a sale. Views
on both sides of the argument were strongly held, reflecting different beliefs about
the primary purpose of the balance sheet. Those who favoured securitisations being
accounted for on balance sheet believed that the primary use of the balance sheet is in
assessing the amounts, timing and certainty of future cash flows. In their view, the
total resources that underlie these future cash flows (and on which income will be
earned in the future) should be shown on one side of the balance sheet, and the
means by which they are financed should be shown on the other. They also pointed
out that typically, the originating entity continues to gain significantly all the profits
from the securitised assets and to be exposed to all those losses likely to occur in
practice.

11   Those respondents who favoured securitisations being accounted for as a sale and therefore off balance sheet believed that the primary use of the balance sheet is in assessing the maximum possible loss to which the entity is exposed. They thought that the accounting treatment of securitisations (and perhaps other forms of non-recourse finance) should concentrate on showing that the originating entity has a limited downside exposure to loss, and that only a net asset of the amount to which the entity is exposed should be presented.

12   The Board debated in detail the issues raised by the respondents and also consulted numerous interested parties. It concluded that users of accounts need to know both the entity's gross resources and finance (as these determine the size of its future income) and the net amount of these (as this is the maximum loss the entity can suffer). Hence the Board developed a new kind of presentation – a 'linked presentation' – under which the finance is deducted from the gross securitised assets on the face of the balance sheet. This presentation shows the gross resources that underlie the business (and on which income will be earned in the future), yet highlights that the entity has a strictly limited exposure to loss.

FRED 4

13   Finally, in February 1993, the Board issued FRED 4 'Reporting the Substance of Transactions'. This carried through the general principles set out in ED 49 with only two major changes. The first was the introduction of proposals for a linked presentation for certain forms of non-recourse finance (including securitisations), as described above. These proposals attracted general support and are retained in the FRS with only one minor change which is described in paragraphs 29–32 below.

14   The only other major change from ED 49 was the inclusion of detailed criteria for when items may be offset in accounts. These prohibited offset of amounts denominated in different currencies or bearing interest on different bases, on the grounds that, for two items to be offset, they must exactly eliminate one another. Such elimination would not be present where the items were in different currencies or bore interest on different bases, because of the currency or interest rate risk that was present. It was therefore proposed that the two items should not be offset but should be reported as separate assets and liabilities. This proposal has been modified in the FRS, in the light of comments received, as described below.

15   Other, less significant changes from ED 49 were: the inclusion of definitions of assets and liabilities as opposed to a description of their 'essential characteristics' (these definitions are drawn from the Board's draft Statement of Principles); the provision of more guidance on accounting for transactions with options; the inclusion, for the first time, of criteria for when assets should cease to be recognised; the introduction of a distinction between control of an asset and control of another entity; and changes to some of ED 49's recognition tests, including removing the proposal that recognition be based on a 'reasonable accounting analogy'.

Matters considered in the light of responses to FRED 4

16   Most of the respondents to FRED 4 agreed with its principal proposals and these have been largely retained in the FRS. The following paragraphs describe those points on which respondents expressed concern and, where appropriate, explain, with reasons, the changes the Board has made to the proposals of FRED 4 or the Board's reasons for not adopting a change.

Complexity of the FRS

Several respondents expressed concern that FRED 4 was complex and difficult to **17**
understand. In part, this complexity stemmed from the inclusion of proposals for a
linked presentation as set out above. Another reason for the FRED being difficult to
understand was its general approach of specifying principles applicable to all
transactions rather than detailed rules for specific situations. Whilst this general
approach was supported, there was concern that the resulting principles appeared
somewhat abstract and difficult to comprehend on a first reading.

To meet these concerns, the structure and drafting of the FRED have been reviewed **18**
and, where possible, simplified. In addition, the Explanation section to the FRS gives
examples where appropriate. However, the Board believes this is a complex area that
cannot be reduced to a few simple rules without the danger of over-simplification.
Indeed, simple rules, mechanically applied, would result in accounts that do not
report substance.

Offset

As noted above, FRED 4 proposed prohibiting offset of amounts denominated in **19**
different currencies or bearing interest on different bases but asked for comments on
this prohibition. The majority of those who commented favoured either allowing or
requiring offset of such items. Their reasons included: that the balance sheet does
not, in general, show currency or interest rate exposures, hence grossing up the items
does not necessarily allow a better assessment of these risks; that the currency or
interest rate risk may be hedged such that the risk portrayed by grossing up may, in
fact, no longer exist; that given freely accessible and liquid foreign exchange markets,
monetary items in different currencies can be regarded as being freely convertible,
and essentially a single item; and that the balance sheet should focus on portraying
credit risk since users expect to get information about credit risk from the balance
sheet, but not about currency or interest rate risks. A majority of the Board is
persuaded by these arguments and, accordingly, the FRS requires offset of amounts
denominated in different currencies or bearing interest on different bases provided
that certain criteria are met.

The Board also considered whether it should require disclosure of amounts in dif- **20**
ferent currencies or bearing interest on different bases that have been offset. Such
disclosure would allow the user to draw up a balance sheet incorporating all items
that do not exactly eliminate one another. However, such a balance sheet would give
only part of the information needed to assess the entity's exposure to currency and
interest rate risk. For a full assessment, it would be necessary to disclose the currency
and interest rate profile of all recognised assets and liabilities as well as the effects of
'off balance sheet' instruments such as swaps and options. The Board decided that it
was not yet in a position to specify comprehensive disclosure of such risks and that to
require disclosures that gave only partial information on currency and interest rate
risk would be potentially misleading. Accordingly, the FRS does not require disclosure of amounts that have been offset.

FRED 4 also proposed prohibiting offset where the right to settle net was contingent **21**
(for example on the counterparty going into liquidation). This was on the basis that
as such contingent rights could not have been exercised at the balance sheet date,
they should not be reflected in the assets and liabilities reported at that date. After
reviewing the comments on this issue, the Board decided that provided: (a) the right
to settle net can be invoked in all situations of default; and (b) the entity's debit
balance matures no later than its credit balance, the amounts should be offset. This is

because in such a situation there is no possibility that the entity could be required to pay out its credit balance without first having recovered its debit balance.

22   Finally, FRED 4 did not propose the approach taken in US and certain other overseas accounting standards that require for offset that the reporting entity intends to settle net; FRED 4 required merely that the reporting entity has the ability to do so. The reason FRED 4 did not propose this approach is that the intended manner of settlement is essentially a matter of administrative convenience and does not affect the economic position of the parties. This reasoning was supported by commentators and, accordingly, the conditions given in the FRS for offset are not based on the intent of the reporting entity.

Ceasing to recognise assets

23   FRED 4 contained criteria for when assets should cease to be recognised. These required both that no significant access to benefits was retained and that any risk retained was immaterial. Commentators were particularly concerned over the second of these conditions: for instance that it might require continued recognition of an asset sold with a residual value guarantee or of a subsidiary sold with deferred performance-related consideration.

24   As a result, the FRS distinguishes three types of transactions. The first is transactions that transfer all significant rights to benefits relating to an asset and all significant exposures to the risks inherent in those benefits. For such transactions, the asset should cease to be recognised in its entirety. Conversely, where a transaction transfers no significant rights to benefits relating to an asset or no significant exposures to their inherent risks, the asset should continue to be recognised in its entirety. The third type of transaction comprises those special cases where not all significant benefits and risks have been transferred, but it is necessary to amend the description or monetary amount of the original asset or to recognise a new liability for any obligations assumed. Examples of this third type of transaction are given in paragraphs 71–73.

Contracts for future performance

25   For the avoidance of doubt, the Board decided that contracts for future performance, such as swaps, forward contracts and purchase commitments, should be removed from the scope of the FRS, except where they are merely a part of a transaction (or of a connected series of transactions) that falls within the FRS. The accounting for such contracts is a complex area that requires further research and consultation before an FRS dealing with their accounting could be issued.

Options

26   FRED 4's approach to options and the new guidance it contained were generally supported. However, the comments revealed some uncertainty over the approach to be taken to options for which there is a genuine commercial possibility both that the option will be exercised and that it will not be exercised, but the transaction is structured such that one or other outcome is significantly more likely. The FRS provides that the commercial effect of an option should be assessed in the context of all the aspects and implications of the transaction. It also explains that it may be necessary to consider the true commercial objectives of the parties and the commercial rationale for the inclusion of the option in the transaction in order to

establish whether the parties' rights and obligations are, in substance, optional or conditional or, alternatively, outright.

Finally, for the avoidance of doubt, the FRS emphasises that, in assessing the com-   **27** mercial effect of an option, all the terms of the transaction and the circumstances of the parties that are likely to be relevant during the exercise period of the option should be taken into account – and not just conditions existing at the balance sheet date.

Linked presentation for subsidiaries

The FRS carries through the proposal in FRED 4 that where an item and its non-   **28** recourse finance are 'ring-fenced' in a quasi-subsidiary in such a way that the con- ditions for a linked presentation are met from the point of view of the group, the quasi-subsidiary should be included in consolidated financial statements using a linked presentation. However, if in a similar arrangement the item and its finance are held by a subsidiary, a linked presentation may not be used. In this case, the sub- sidiary is part of the group as legally defined: hence the item and its finance, being an asset and liability of the subsidiary, are respectively an asset and a liability of the group and companies legislation requires them to be shown in consolidated accounts in the normal way. Some respondents argued that the commercial effect is the same regardless of whether the vehicle is a subsidiary or a quasi-subsidiary, and hence the same accounting treatment should be adopted. However, companies legislation does not permit this. In legal terms, the inclusion of a quasi-subsidiary constitutes the provision of *additional* information about the group as legally defined and thus a quasi-subsidiary may be included in any way necessary to give a true and fair view of that group. However, a subsidiary is *part of* the group as legally defined and com- panies legislation requires the subsidiary to be consolidated in the normal way.

The use of swaps in securitisations

The Board was asked to clarify whether, in a securitisation, an interest rate swap or   **29** an interest rate cap between an originator and an issuer would restrict use of a linked presentation. FRED 4 required, as does the FRS, that, for a linked presentation, there must be 'no recourse whatsoever' to the originator and 'no possibility whatsoever of a claim being established on the entity [ie the originator] other than against funds generated by that item [ie the securitised assets]'. These provisions would prohibit use of a linked presentation where there is an interest rate swap or an interest rate cap between the originator and the issuer.

However, the argument was put to the Board that an exception to this principle was   **30** appropriate because the risks are often hedged by the originator as part of its normal hedging activities and thus payments to the issuer under the swap or cap would not represent a net loss to the originator. In many cases, the originator will have hedged any interest rate (and related) risks relating to the securitised assets prior to the securitisation, with the result that the securitisation opens up a gap in the originator's hedging portfolio by removing a hedged asset without removing its hedge. The most natural way to close this gap is for the issuer and the originator to enter into an interest rate swap or cap. Such a swap or cap will also be advantageous to the issuer by providing it with a hedge of the difference in the interest rate received on its newly acquired assets and that paid on its loan notes. It was also stated that, in the case of an interest rate swap (although not in the case of an interest rate cap), the issuer is currently unable to enter into a suitable swap with a third party as there is currently no market for such swaps in the UK (principally because the swap would require an amortising amount of principal to reflect actual repayments of the securitised assets).

31   The Board believes, as a matter of principle, that a linked presentation should be permitted only where there is no recourse whatsoever to the originator and accordingly should not be permitted where there is an interest rate swap or cap between the originator and the issuer. However, it decided with reluctance and as a pragmatic and provisional response to the issue, to permit use of a linked presentation in the originator's accounts notwithstanding the presence of an interest rate swap between the originator and the issuer in a securitisation provided certain strict criteria are met. (These are set out in paragraph D11.) In reaching this decision, the Board took into account the interaction of its decision with the present framework for regulating banks. The Board was also swayed by the fact that there is currently no market for such swaps in the UK and hence the issuer is unable to enter into a suitable swap with anyone other than the originator. For interest rate caps, the Board decided to give a similar concession but to resctrict it to those securitisations in existence prior to 22 September 1994 since the availability of a suitable market for interest rate caps means there is no need for future transactions of this kind to be undertaken with the originator and the issuer where a linked presentation is used.

32   The Board's decision with respect to interest rate swaps represents an interim measure and will be reviewed in the light of developments in securitisations and of progress made in the Board's forthcoming project on derivatives.

Disclosures of derecognised assets

33   Three of the Application Notes to FRED 4 contained specific disclosure requirements in respect of derecognised assets. Commentators generally thought these requirements were excessive, they have not been retained in the FRS.

AMENDMENT TO FRS 5 – INSERTION OF APPLICATION NOTE F 'PRIVATE FINANCE INITIATIVE AND SIMILAR CONTRACTS'

The Preface to this amendment issued September 1998 stated the following:The Application Note has been prepared in response to the need for clarification of how the principles and requirements of FRS 5 should apply to transactions conducted under the UK Government's Private Finance Initiative (PFI). The Note will also be appropriate for other contracts of a similar nature.

The amendment was published as an Exposure Draft in December 1997 for public comment. In finalising this document the Accounting Standards Board has taken into consideration the comments received in response to the Exposure Draft and has consulted interested parties. In particular, in the final version of the Note the Board has clarified the question of separability and which variations in profits (or losses) should be taken into account when determining who has an asset of the property in a PFI contract.

The development of the Application Note

The need for guidance on revenue recognition

1   The absence of a UK standard dealing explicitly with revenue recognition has been a source of muted but continuing criticism for some time. Different entities and industries have followed practices that are in some respects inconsistent with one another. More generally, there are different views of what revenue is or represents, and of how financial statements should portray a business's operating activities.

In practice, those seeking guidance on whether or when to recognise revenue have   2
turned to International Accounting Standards (IAS) or accounting standards
adopted in the United States. The international standard, IAS 18 'Revenue', was
originally issued in 1982 and substantially revised in 1993. US requirements on the
subject are to be found in various standards issued by the Financial Accounting
Standards Board (FASB) and pronouncements of its Emerging Issues Task Force;
the US Securities and Exchange Commission has also issued a relevant Staff
Accounting Bulletin (SAB 101 'Revenue Recognition in Financial Statements' issued
in 1999).

In recent years it has become common for investors in certain industries and start-up   3
businesses to focus on revenue growth as an important indicator of a company's
ability to meet its targets and achieve (or regain) profitability. This has led to, or
highlighted, certain divergences in accounting treatments, some of which have been
eliminated by pronouncements of the Urgent Issues Task Force, addressing specific
issues. The Board therefore took the subject of revenue recognition on to its agenda
and in July 2001 issued a Discussion Paper 'Revenue Recognition'.

A challenge for all standard setters in addressing this subject has been the need to tie   4
in the principles of revenue recognition with other development work in progress. In
September 2002 the International Accounting Standards Board and the FASB
agreed to combine their work on this subject into a joint project that focused on the
recognition of revenue based on the recognition of changes in assets and liabilities.

The Board considered whether it should develop its Discussion Paper into a new   5
Financial Reporting Standard. It decided against this course of action for two reasons. First, in accordance with its convergence policy the Board intends to issue full
standards on major topics of concern only after consultation with the Board's
international partners. Secondly, at this stage the principles underlying the international project on revenue recognition have not yet been determined.

Nevertheless, questions continue to arise on accounting practices in this area. The   6
Board has therefore issued this Application Note to promote the consistent treatment of exchange transactions that are reported as turnover.

The rationale of the application note

The Application Note contains basic principles of revenue recognition which set out   7
the general approach and should be applied in all cases. These are accompanied by
specific guidance for five types of transactions which give rise to turnover and have
been subject to differing interpretations in practice.

The Application Note is based on the principle that a seller generates revenue by   8
performing its contractual obligations and in exchange obtains the right to consideration. This entitles the seller to recognise either:

(a)   an increase in assets (such as a debtor); or
(b)   a decrease in liabilities (normally the release from an obligation arising from
      receipt of a payment in advance of performance).

9   The principle that a seller generates revenue by performing its contractual obligations to the customer is consistent with the idea of performance under the law of contract.*

10   The intention of the Application Note is to codify existing good practice and ensure that entities report turnover in accordance with the substance of their contractual arrangements with customers.

Matters considered in the light of responses to the Exposure Draft

11   This Application Note is based on an Exposure Draft which was published in February 2003. The following paragraphs give further details of the Board's reasoning for the requirements of the Application Note and explain changes made to the Exposure Draft.

The basic principles

The right to consideration

12   The Exposure Draft contained the basic principle that the seller obtains 'the right to be paid' in return for its performance of its obligations under a contractual arrangement. Some respondents were unclear as to what was meant by this right and how the proposals were linked to the seller's performance of its contractual obligations. The Exposure Draft stressed that the right to be paid does not necessarily correspond to the falling due of stage payments. Nevertheless, a number of respondents queried what else this right might represent.

13   In agreeing a contract, the seller and the customer will wish to ensure that they minimise the risk of losses arising from default by the other party. One way in which this is achieved is through the specification of stage payments. Often these stage payments will reflect the seller's performance of its contractual obligations in providing something of value to the customer. However, an exact correspondence is not necessarily obtained with a claim for stage payments; stage payments may fall short of or exceed the right to consideration that the seller has obtained through its performance.

14   The right to consideration does not represent a contractual right to demand stage payments from the customer. Rather, a seller obtains the right to consideration in exchange for the performance of its obligations under a contractual arrangement with a customer. This approach avoids the recognition of revenue being distorted by the timing of payment; to do so would move towards cash accounting. This would lead to a lack of comparability and allow wide discretion in reporting revenue.

15   The Application Note contains a definition of performance to emphasise the importance of the seller's performance. Furthermore, in the interests of clarity, the Application Note uses the term 'the right to consideration' in place of 'the right to be paid' to emphasise that this right does not necessarily correspond to stage payments. The Application Note stresses that a seller recognises revenue when, and to the extent that, it obtains this right as a result of its performance of its contractual obligations.

*Sir Guenter Treitel, in 'The Law of Contract' makes the point as follows: "A party who performs a contract in accordance with its terms is thereby discharged from his obligations under it. Such performance also normally entitles him to enforce the other party's undertakings." (Tenth edition), 1999, (page 697).

The measurement of revenue

The Exposure Draft proposed that revenue should be measured at the fair value of the consideration receivable. It noted that this would normally be the amount specified in the contractual arrangement, with adjustments made, where material, for the time value of money and risk. A number of respondents suggested that this requirement would result in widespread changes to current practice.   16

The difficulty stems from the fact that, while the great majority of transactions are conducted at fair value, the amounts at which these are reported in financial statements depart, to some degree at least, from a strict representation of fair value. If the seller's right to consideration were to be stated at fair value, strictly, it should reflect both a discount in respect of any interest free period and an allowance for possible default by the debtors.   17

The Board is concerned that adjustments should be made to the price specified in the contractual arrangement in those cases where revenue would otherwise be materially overstated. This might be the case where the buyer makes payments on interest free credit over a number of years, or where at the time of the sale, the seller knows that there is a significant risk about the customer's ability to pay. This is made clear in paragraphs G8 and G9.   18

The Board believes that the Application Note achieves a reasonable accommodation between the principle that revenue should be recognised at fair value, which it asserts, and the present state of international practice in this area. It notes that this is consistent with the requirements of IAS 18 (paragraphs 9 - 12).   19

Payment received in advance of performance

A contract may require the customer to make payment in advance of the seller's performance. In such situations the seller recognises a liability equal to the amount of consideration received, representing its obligation under the contract. The seller is released from its obligation when its performance under the contract earns it the right to consideration.   20

The Application Note requires that liabilities relating to payments received in advance are reported at the amount the seller has received, for taking them on, which is their entry value. Some respondents to the Exposure Draft observed that the use of entry value reflected a fundamental assumption in this area which required debate.   21

The Board agrees that the measurement of assets and liabilities is a fundamental issue and is participating in various initiatives which it is hoped will develop thinking in the UK and elsewhere on these issues. The Application Note is not intended to pre-empt the outcome of this work. The Board notes, however, that this requirement of the Application Note reflects the prevailing practice in the UK and the Republic of Ireland.   22

In the Board's view there are also conceptual reasons for reporting liabilities for payments in advance at the amount received. In the normal case of a profitable contract the amount received will be greater than the expected cost of performance. On making a payment in advance, the customer will have a claim on the entity to receive value for the amount paid. If the liability were reported at the cost of performance, the financial statements would not faithfully report the entity's obligation to its customer. Reducing the liability would also give rise to a reported gain, which   23 might suggest that the success of the business in a particular period depended on obtaining orders rather than satisfying customers.*

Partial performance

24   Some respondents requested further clarification as to how the principles in the Exposure Draft should be applied to situations where the seller's contractual performance is incomplete.

25   The final Application Note contains additional guidance on this issue. It states that there will be some arrangements where the seller obtains a right to consideration when some, but not all, of its contractual obligations have been fulfilled. Where a seller has partially performed its contractual obligations, the Application Note stresses that it recognises revenue to the extent that it has obtained the right to consideration through the performance of its contractual obligations in supplying goods and services.

26   Obtaining the right to consideration does not necessarily involve delivery or the transfer of title. For example, if a seller is constructing a building to a customer's design, the customer may gain neither title nor physical custody until construction is complete. Nevertheless, the seller obtains the right to consideration through its performance as construction activity progresses, reflecting the value of the work performed to date.

Sales tax

27   The current treatment of sales tax is well established and is set out in both legal requirements and in other accounting standards.

(a)   Section 262 (1) of the Companies Act 1985† defines turnover in relation to a company as the amounts derived from the provision of goods and services falling within the company's ordinary activities, after deduction of:

(i)   trade discounts,

(ii)   value added tax, and

(iii)   any other taxes based on the amounts so derived.

(b)   SSAP 5 'Accounting for value added tax' requires that turnover should exclude VAT on taxable outputs.

28   The final Application Note contains guidance on the treatment of sales taxes which is consistent with the requirements noted in paragraph 27 above.

Specific guidance

29   As well as setting out basic principles of revenue recognition, the Application Note also provides specific guidance in areas that have given rise to either inconsistency in practice or inappropriate accounting.

This issue is explored in greater depth in 'Liabilities and how to account for them: an exploratory essay', which is available at wwwfiasbfiorgfiuk/public/downloadsficfm.

†*The corresponding provision in Northern Ireland is Article 270(1) The Companies (NI) Order 1986, inserted by The Companies (NI) Order 1990 (SI 1990/593) (NI 5) Article 24; and in the Republic of Ireland, Paragraph 75, Schedule to Companies (Amendment) Act 1986.*

Long-term contractual performance

SSAP 9 contains guidance for the accounting and disclosure by a seller of its per-   **30**
formance under a long–term contract. The Application Note also contains guidance
for the recognition of turnover on such contracts and does not amend the requirements of SSAP 9.

Some respondents to the Exposure Draft commented that SSAP 9 was already   **31**
adequate in prescribing the treatment in this area. It was also suggested that the
guidance in the Exposure Draft could change existing practices as set out in SSAP 9,
on the grounds that the Exposure Draft advocated a move away from measuring
performance as the proportion of costs incurred to date in comparison with total
expenditure.

SSAP 9 does not require costs incurred to date to be used in measuring turnover in a   **32**
long-term contract. Paragraph 9 notes that the profit taken up needs to reflect the
proportion of work carried out at the accounting date. There will be contracts where
costs incurred to date do reflect the work performed and in such circumstances it
would be appropriate to use the proportion of costs incurred in comparison with
total expenditure in measuring revenue; however, this will not always be the case.
The incurrence of costs by a seller, does not, in itself, justify the recognition of
revenue. The Application Note therefore re-emphasises that the key principle in
recognising revenue is the seller's performance of its contractual obligations.

Separation and linking of contractual arrangements

Most respondents were supportive of the proposals in the Exposure Draft which   **33**
provided guidance on when the seller should combine or unbundle any separate
components contained in a single contractual arrangement.

The Exposure Draft noted that one of the requirements for the unbundling of a   **34**
contractual arrangement was whether or not reliable fair values could be attributed
to at least the uncompleted components. Some respondents were unsure as to the
degree of reliability that was required.

The existence of measurement uncertainty is acknowledged in the criteria for the   **35**
recognition of an asset. This requires that the monetary amount at which an asset is
to be measured is capable of being measured with sufficient reliability. As discussed
in the Board's Statement of Principles, if uncertainty exists, the only way to determine an appropriate monetary amount is through the use of estimates.

However, in order for the seller to account for a contractual arrangement as separate   **36**
transactions, the Application Note requires that the individual components operate
independently and represent goods or services that the seller can provide on a stand
alone basis or as an optional extra. Therefore, if the components do operate independently, the seller should be able to arrive at a measure that is sufficiently reliable
to meet the asset recognition criteria.

Separation and linking of contractual arrangements - vouchers

The Board received requests from respondents to clarify the accounting treatment of   **37**
points schemes and money-off coupons. The final Application Note therefore contains additional guidance in respect of revenue recognition in this area. It uses the
term 'vouchers' which is intended to encompass all types of arrangements where the
seller is committed to perform in the future at a reduced price.

38   The Board notes that issues might also arise as to whether the seller might have an onerous contract, for example if the exercise of the vouchers would result in products being sold at a loss. Where this is the case, it will be necessary to consider whether the vouchers give rise to an obligation on the part of the seller. Where an entity is obliged to supply goods or services at a loss, that is an onerous contract and provision will need to be made in accordance with FRS 12 'Provisions, Contingent Liabilities and Contingent Assets'.

Separation and linking of contractual arrangements - inception fees

39   The Exposure Draft contained proposals on when the seller should record turnover in respect of non-refundable fees. In the final Application Note, the term 'inception fees' has been used in place of non-refundable fees. That is because the principle as to when the seller should recognise turnover in respect of a fee does not necessarily depend on whether or not a fee is refundable. Whilst the fact that a fee is stated to be non-refundable may suggest that the seller has no further performance obligations in respect of that fee, in some cases an obligation to provide goods or services may remain.

Bill and hold arrangements

40   Most respondents agreed with the guidance in the Exposure Draft on bill and hold arrangements. Some, however, disagreed with the condition that the goods should be identified separately from the seller's other stock in order for the seller to recognise revenue. It was suggested that the separate identification of the goods should not be necessary where the item is fungible.

41   The Board reconsidered this point when finalising the Application Note. It concluded that the buyer would not have the principal benefits and risks until the goods have been identified separately from the seller's other goods; the seller would continue to bear these benefits and risks until that time. This condition was therefore retained in the final Application Note. The Board also noted that this requirement is consistent with both IAS 18 and SAB 101.

Sales with rights of return

42   Most respondents agreed with the proposals in the Exposure Draft which required the seller to exclude from turnover the sales value of estimated returns. However, some respondents were concerned that the proposals would require extensive changes to 'point of sale' systems in order to capture the required information on returns.

43   The Board's subsequent research has indicated that a seller will generally be able to estimate reliably the level of returns without the need for extensive systems changes. The final Application Note stresses that a seller will generally be able to derive a reliable estimate from historical experience of the proportion of comparable goods returned as a proportion of comparable sales.

44   Some respondents suggested that the proposals on sales with rights of return were inconsistent with the derecognition principles of the FRS. The Board debated this issue during the development of the Exposure Draft and, for the reasons outlined below, believes that the provisions are consistent with the FRS.

The Board noted that the FRS requires that an entire asset should be derecognised **45** when a transaction transfers all significant rights or other access to benefits and all significant exposure to the risks inherent in those benefits. The FRS also contains requirements (paragraph 23) which cover transactions that have resulted in a significant change in the entity's rights to benefits and exposure to risk, but where the provisions for full derecognition are not met. This might be where a transaction involves a transfer of all of the item for all of its life, but where the entity retains some significant right to benefits or exposure to risk. In such circumstances, the FRS requires the description or monetary amount to be changed and a liability recognised for any obligations to transfer benefits that are assumed.

A particular issue raised by some respondents was a perceived inconsistency between **46** the requirements of the FRS in respect of receivables "sold" or securitised with full recourse to the seller (Application Notes C and D) and the treatment proposed in the Exposure Draft for expected returns of goods sold. No sale recognition was given to the former, to the extent that there was any possibility that the receivables could be put back to the transferor; for goods sold, however, the Exposure Draft proposed, and the final Application Note confirms, that revenue should generally be recognised after making an estimate of future returns.

The Board concluded that a different approach was needed to reflect a fundamental **47** difference in the effect of the two transactions. A "sale" of receivables with full recourse does not change in the slightest the exposure of the seller to the benefits and risks attaching to the receivables: the speed of collection and the incidence of defaults are both borne by the seller to the same extent as if no transaction had taken place. The only effect is a cash advance, which should be recognised as a liability. By contrast, a normal sale of goods with rights of return is a significant event for the seller in that it transfers the great majority of the benefits and risks relating to the goods (for example, the purchaser is able to use the goods as it wishes and is exposed to the risk of subsequent damage). For the seller, subject to a provision for the return of some portion, the sale crystallises the profit from the production/sale process.

The objective of the FRS is to ensure that the substance of an entity's transactions **48** are reported in its financial statements and that the commercial effect should be faithfully represented. The Board believes that the requirements on sales with rights of return are consistent with this objective and with the provisions of the FRS.

Presentation of turnover as principal or as agent

Respondents were generally supportive of the proposals in the Exposure Draft which **49** provided guidance as to whether the seller should be regarded as acting as principal or agent in an exchange transaction with a customer.

In determining whether the seller is acting as principal or agent, the final Application **50** Note gives greater prominence to the question of whether the agency relationship is disclosed. It states that where the seller has not disclosed that it is acting as agent, there is a rebuttable presumption that it is acting as principal.

The Board received requests to clarify the application of the principles in the **51** Exposure Draft to trading concessions operated in department stores. The Board recognises that there are a wide variety of potential arrangements between department stores and concessionaires. However, where the department store is not acting as principal in an exchange transaction with the concessionaire's customers, it would be inappropriate for the department store to include within its own revenue the value of the concessionaire's sales. The final Application Note makes this clear.

Disclosure of accounting policies

52   The Board believes that preparers should provide disclosures that will help users understand the entity's adopted accounting policies and how they have been applied. This is one of the objectives of FRS 18 'Accounting Policies', which stresses that sufficient information should be provided in the financial statements to meet this objective. Entities should therefore have regard to the requirements of that standard when considering the disclosures required in respect of accounting policies. The Board's statement on the 'Operating and Financial Review' also contains guidance on accounting policies. It stresses the fact that the Operating and Financial Review should highlight accounting policies that are key to an understanding of the entity's performance and financial position.

Implementation

53   The Board considered whether or not special transitional arrangements should be included in the final Application Note and concluded that they were not required. Accordingly, on implementation an entity should compare its current accounting for revenue with the requirements of this Application Note. If any change is required, it should consider whether this represents a change of accounting policy or of estimation technique in accordance with FRS 18 'Accounting Policies'.

Dissenting view

Mr Wild dissents from the issue of this Amendment to FRS 5 because he believes that the Application Note it inserts, rather than significantly improving the quality of UK financial reporting, could introduce sufficient confusion over the principles to be adopted to have a detrimental effect on such reporting.

Internationally, revenue recognition is the subject of a joint project by the International Accounting Standards Board (IASB) and the Financial Accounting Standards Board (FASB) in the US. Mr Wild agrees that the ASB should not seek to issue a comprehensive revenue standard until the IASB and FASB have completed their review and accepts that the Application Note is intended to be an interim measure. However, he believes the Application Note is an inadequate compromise between a desire to establish principles and a desire to avoid major changes to existing practice for the majority of transactions. As a result, to the extent that current practice is open to abuse, the requirements of the Application Note are not sufficiently precise or clear to prevent it. Moreover, the inconsistent application of underlying principles, in favour of the status quo, may create confusion and, perhaps, extend opportunities for abuse.

Examples of aspects of the Application Note which particularly concern Mr Wild in this way are set out below.

- The requirement to measure revenue at the fair value of the right to consideration means, in principle, that account has to be taken of both the time value of money and the risk of default. While Mr Wild acknowledges that this principle may well be appropriate in the context of a full revenue standard, and is indeed set out in the international standard on revenue, he notes that it is not consistently applied in practice either in the UK or elsewhere. The Application Note attempts to reconcile this theory with practice by suggesting that existing practice is adopted merely on the grounds of materiality. Mr Wild thinks this leaves the position unhelpfully ambiguous for many entities.

- Mr Wild believes the treatment of sales with rights of return contradicts principles set out in other Application Notes to FRS 5. While in his view the treatment of sales with rights of return is appropriate to the current state of development of principles for revenue recognition, it is inconsistent with the existing requirements for the derecognition of items as a result of arrangements carried out other than as part of the normal business operating cycle. Consequently the various Application Notes seem to specify different treatments depending on the intent of the directors on any particular occasion. He thinks the confusion resulting from such an apparently self evident contradiction between the requirements of different Application Notes to the same standard could lead to those Application Notes being undermined, and could be exploited by those seeking to construct complex financial arrangements.

Financial Reporting Standard 6 is set out in paragraphs 1–39

The Statement of Standard Accounting Practice set out in paragraphs 4–39 should be read in the context of the Objective as stated in paragraph 1 and the definitions set out in paragraphs 2–3 and also of the Foreword to Accounting Standards and the Statement of Principles for Financial Reporting currently in issue.

The Explanation set out in paragraphs 40–89 shall be regarded as part of the Statement of Standard Accounting Practice insofar as it assists in interpreting that statement.

Appendix III 'The development of the FRS' reviews considerations and arguments that were thought significant by members of the Board in reaching the conclusions on FRS 6.

[FRS 6]
Acquisitions and mergers*

(Issued September 1994)

Contents

Editor's note: FRS 6 has been amended by FRS 25 with effect for accounting periods beginning on or after 1 January 2005.

Adoption of FRS 6 by the Board

Appendices
   I Note on legal requirements
   II Compliance with international accounting standards
   III The development of the FRS
   IV Illustrative example of disclosure of reorganisation and integration costs

Acquisitions and mergers

Summary

Financial Reporting Standard 6 'Acquisitions and Mergers' sets out the circumstances in which the two methods of accounting for a business combination—acquisition accounting and merger accounting—are to be used. **a**

Acquisition accounting regards the business combination as the acquisition of one company by another; the identifiable assets and liabilities of the company acquired are included in the consolidated balance sheet at their fair value at the date of acquisition, and its results included in the profit and loss account from the date of acquisition. The difference between the fair value of the consideration given and the fair values of the net assets of the entity acquired is accounted for as goodwill. **b**

Merger accounting, on the other hand, treats two or more parties as combining on an equal footing. It is normally applied without any restatement of net assets to fair value, and includes the results of each for the whole of the accounting period. Correspondingly, it does not reflect the issue of shares as an application of resources at fair value. The difference that arises on consolidation does not represent goodwill but is deducted from, or added to, reserves. **c**

The FRS requires acquisition accounting to be used for any business combination where a party can be identified as having the role of an acquirer, since this method of accounting reflects the application of resources by the acquirer and the net assets acquired. **d**

Merger accounting is restricted to, and required for, those business combinations where the use of acquisition accounting would not properly reflect the true nature of the combination. A merger is a business combination in which, rather than one party acquiring control of another, the parties come together to share in the future risks and benefits of the combined entity. It is not the augmentation of one entity by the addition of another, but the creation of what is effectively a new reporting entity from the parties to the combination. **e**

A combination meets the definition of a merger only if it satisfies the five criteria set out in paragraphs 6 – 11 of the FRS. These criteria relate to: **f**

1 the way the roles of each party to the combination are portrayed;
2 the involvement of each party to the combination in the selection of the management of the combined entity;
3 the relative sizes of the parties to the combination;
4 whether shareholders of the combining entities receive any consideration other than equity shares in the combined entity;
5 whether shareholders of the combining entities retain an interest in the performance of only part of the combined entity.

Where a combination meets these criteria, acquisition accounting is not permitted as this method would not fairly present the effect of the combination. **g**

The FRS also contains provisions for applying merger accounting to mergers effected by the creation of a new holding company, and also to certain group reconstructions where acquisition accounting may not be appropriate. **h**

i   The FRS contains disclosure requirements applying to business combinations accounted for by using merger accounting so that the transition from separate entities to the merged entity can be understood; and further disclosure requirements, replacing those in SSAP 22 'Accounting for goodwill', for business combinations accounted for by using acquisition accounting, so that the effect of the acquisition can be understood.*

Financial Reporting Standard 6

Objective

1   The objective of this FRS is: to ensure that merger accounting is used only for those business combinations that are not, in substance, the acquisition of one entity by another but the formation of a new reporting entity as a substantially equal partnership where no party is dominant; to ensure the use of acquisition accounting for all other business combinations; and to ensure that in either case the financial statements provide relevant information concerning the effect of the combination.

Definitions

2   The following definitions shall apply in this FRS and in particular in the Statement of Standard Accounting Practice set out in paragraphs 4 – 39.

Acquisition:-
A business combination that is not a merger.

Business combination:-
The bringing together of separate entities into one economic entity as a result of one entity uniting with, or obtaining control over the net assets and operations of, another.

Equity shares:-
Shares classified as equity in accordance with FRS 25 '(IAS 32) Financial Instruments: Disclosure and Presentation'.†

Group reconstruction:-
Any of the following arrangements:

(a)   the transfer of a shareholding in a subsidiary undertaking from one group company to another;
(b)   the addition of a new parent company to a group;
(c)   the transfer of shares in one or more subsidiary undertakings of a group to a new company that is not a group company but whose shareholders are the same as those of the group's parent;
(d)   the combination into a group of two or more companies that before the combination had the same shareholders.

Merger:-
A business combination that results in the creation of a new reporting entity formed

---

*Editor's note: Subsequent to the issue of FRS 6, SSAP 22 has itself been replaced by FRS 10 'Goodwill and Intangible Assets'.

†Editor's note: Definition amended by FRS 25.

from the combining parties, in which the shareholders of the combining entities come together in a partnership for the mutual sharing of the risks and benefits of the combined entity, and in which no party to the combination in substance obtains control over any other, or is otherwise seen to be dominant, whether by virtue of the proportion of its shareholders' rights in the combined entity, the influence of its directors or otherwise.

Non-equity shares:-
Shares classified as liabilities in accordance with FRS 25 '(IAS 32) Financial Instruments: Disclosure and Presentation.'*

References to companies legislation mean: 3

(a)   in Great Britain, the Companies Act 1985;
(b)   in Northern Ireland, the Companies (Northern Ireland) Order 1986; and
(c)   in the Republic of Ireland, the Companies Acts 1963–90 and the European Communities (Companies: Group Accounts) Regulations 1992.

Statement of Standard Accounting Practice

The marginal notes give the main references to the Companies Act 1985 in Great Britain. For the equivalent references in companies legislation in Northern Ireland and the Republic of Ireland see Appendix I.

SCOPE

Financial Reporting Standard 6 applies to all financial statements that are intended   4 to give a true and fair view of a reporting entity's financial position and profit or loss (or income and expenditure) for a period. Although the FRS is framed in terms of an entity becoming a subsidiary undertaking of a parent company that prepares consolidated financial statements, it also applies where an individual company or other reporting entity combines with a business other than a subsidiary undertaking.

APPLICATION TO SMALLER ENTITIES

Reporting entities applying the Financial Reporting Standard for Smaller Entities   4A currently applicable are exempt from this accounting standard unless preparing consolidated financial statements, in which case they should apply the FRS to such statements as required by the FRSSE.

*Editor's note: Definition amended by FRS 25.

USE OF MERGER ACCOUNTING

5   A business combination should be accounted for by using merger
accounting if:

(a)   the use of merger accounting for the combination is not pro-   *[4A Sch 4(1)]*
hibited by companies legislation; and

(b)   the combination meets all the specific criteria set out in paragraphs 6–11 below and thus falls within the definition of a
merger.

Acquisition accounting should be used for all other business combinations, except as provided in paragraphs 13 and 14

Criteria for determining whether the definition of a merger is met

6   *Criterion 1* – No party to the combination is portrayed as either
acquirer or acquired, either by its own board or management or by
that of another party to the combination.

7   *Criterion 2* – All parties to the combination, as represented by the
boards of directors or their appointees, participate in establishing the
management structure for the combined entity and in selecting the
management personnel, and such decisions are made on the basis of a
consensus between the parties to the combination rather than purely
by exercise of voting rights.

8   *Criterion 3* – The relative sizes of the combining entities are not so
disparate that one party dominates the combined entity by virtue of
its relative size.

9   *Criterion 4* – Under the terms of the combination or related
arrangements, the consideration received by equity shareholders of
each party to the combination, in relation to their equity shareholding, comprises primarily equity shares in the combined entity;
and any non-equity consideration, or equity shares carrying substantially reduced voting or distribution rights, represents an
immaterial proportion of the fair value of the consideration received
by the equity shareholders of that party. Where one of the combining
entities has, within the period of two years before the combination,
acquired equity shares in another of the combining entities, the
consideration for this acquisition should be taken into account in
determining whether this criterion has been met.

10   For the purpose of paragraph 9, the consideration should not be
taken to include the distribution to shareholders of:

(a)   an interest in a peripheral part of the business of the entity in
which they were shareholders and which does not form part of
the combined entity; or

(b)   the proceeds of the sale of such a business, or loan stock
representing such proceeds.

A peripheral part of the business is one that can be disposed of
without having a material effect on the nature and focus of the
entity's operations.

Criterion 5 – No equity shareholders of any of the combining entities　**11**
retain any material interest in the future performance of only part of
the combined entity.

For the purposes of paragraphs 6–11 above any convertible share or　**12**
loan stock should be regarded as equity to the extent that it is converted into equity as a result of the business combination.

Group reconstructions

A group reconstruction may be accounted for by using merger　**13**
accounting, even though there is no business combination meeting
the definition of a merger, provided:

[4A Sch 10]
    (a)　the use of merger accounting is not prohibited by companies
         legislation;
    (b)　the ultimate shareholders remain the same, and the rights of
         each such shareholder, relative to the others, are unchanged;
         and
    (c)　no minority's interest in the net assets of the group is altered by
         the transfer.

Combination effected by using a new parent company

Where a combination is effected by using a newly formed parent　**14**
company to hold the shares of each of the other parties to a combination, the accounting treatment depends on the substance of the
business combination being effected: that is, whether a combination
of the entities other than the new parent company would have been
an acquisition or a merger. If the combination would have been an
acquisition, one entity can be identified as having the role of an
acquirer. This acquirer and the new parent company should first be
combined by using merger accounting; then the other parties to the
business combination should be treated as acquired by this combined
company by using the acquisition method of accounting. On the
other hand, where the substance of the business combination effected
by a new parent company is a merger, the new parent company and
the other parties should all be combined by using merger accounting.

Applicability to various structures of business combination

The provisions of the FRS, which are explained by reference to an　**15**
acquirer or issuing entity that issues shares as consideration for the
transfer to it of shares in the other parties to the combination, should
also be read so as to apply to other arrangements that achieve similar
results.

MERGER ACCOUNTING

[4A Sch 11]
With merger accounting the carrying values of the assets and　**16**
liabilities of the parties to the combination are not required to be
adjusted to fair value on consolidation, although appropriate
adjustments should be made to achieve uniformity of accounting
policies in the combining entities.

17   The results and cash flows of all the combining entities should be brought into the financial statements of the combined entity from the beginning of the financial year in which the combination occurred, adjusted so as to achieve uniformity of accounting policies. The corresponding figures should be restated by including the results for all the combining entities for the previous period and their balance sheets for the previous balance sheet date, adjusted as necessary to achieve uniformity of accounting policies.

18   The difference, if any, between the nominal value of the shares issued plus the fair value of any other consideration given, and the nominal value of the shares received in exchange should be shown as a movement on other reserves in the consolidated financial statements. Any existing balance on the share premium account or capital redemption reserve of the new subsidiary undertaking should be brought in by being shown as a movement on other reserves. These movements should be shown in the reconciliation of movements in shareholders' funds.

19   Merger expenses are not to be included as part of this adjustment, but should be charged to the profit and loss account of the combined entity at the effective date of the merger, as reorganisation or restructuring expenses, in accordance with paragraph 20 of FRS 3 'Reporting Financial Performance'.

ACQUISITION ACCOUNTING

20   Business combinations not accounted for by merger accounting should be accounted for by acquisition accounting. Under acquisition accounting, the identifiable assets and liabilities of the companies acquired should be included in the acquirer's consolidated balance sheet at their fair value at the date of acquisition. The results and cash flows of the acquired companies should be brought into the group accounts only from the date of acquisition. The figures for the previous period for the reporting entity should not be adjusted. The difference between the fair value of the net identifiable assets acquired and the fair value of the purchase consideration is goodwill, positive or negative.*   [4A Sch 9]

DISCLOSURE

Acquisitions and mergers

21   The following information in respect of all business combinations occurring in the financial year, whether accounted for as acquisitions or mergers, should be disclosed in the financial statements of the acquiring entity or, in the case of a merger, the entity issuing shares: [4A Sch 13(2)]

   (a)   the names of the combining entities (other than the reporting entity);
   (b)   whether the combination has been accounted for as an acquisition or a merger;
   (c)   the date of the combination.

*The date of acquisition and the acquisition of a subsidiary undertaking in stages are dealt with in FRS 2, paragraphs 45, 50, 84–85, 88–89.

Mergers

In respect of each business combination accounted for as a merger, **22**
other than group reconstructions falling within paragraph 13, the
following information should be disclosed in the financial statements
of the combined entity for the period in which the merger took place:

[*Extension of* (a) an analysis of the principal components of the current year's
4A Sch 13(4)*]   profit and loss account and statement of total recognised gains
     and losses into
      (i) amounts relating to the merged entity for the period after
        the date of the merger, and
      (ii) for each party to the merger, amounts relating to that
        party for the period up to the date of the merger.

[*Extension of* (b) an analysis between the parties to the merger of the principal
4A Sch 13(4)*   components of the profit and loss account and statement of
     total recognised gains and losses for the previous financial year;

[*4A Sch* (c) the composition and fair value of the consideration given by the
13(3)]   issuing company and its subsidiary undertakings;

     (d) the aggregate book value of the net assets of each party to the
     merger at the date of the merger;

[*4A Sch* (e) the nature and amount of significant accounting adjustments
13(6)]   made to the net assets of any party to the merger to achieve
     consistency of accounting policies, and an explanation of any
     other significant adjustments made to the net assets of any
     party to the merger as a consequence of the merger; and

[*4A Sch* (f) a statement of the adjustments to consolidated reserves result-
13(6)]   ing from the merger.

The analysis of the profit and loss account in (a) and (b) above
should show as a minimum the turnover, operating profit and
exceptional items, split between continuing operations, discontinued
operations and acquisitions; profit before taxation; taxation and
minority interests; and extraordinary items.

Acquisitions

The disclosure requirements for business combinations accounted for **23**
as acquisitions apply as follows:

(a) those in paragraphs 24–35 are required for each material
    acquisition; and, with the exception of those in paragraph 35,
    should also be given for other acquisitions in aggregate;

(b) the additional disclosure requirements in paragraph 36 apply to
    substantial acquisitions as defined in paragraph 37.

[*4A Sch*   The composition and fair value of the consideration given by the **24**
13(3)]   acquiring company and its subsidiary undertakings should be disclosed. The nature of any deferred or contingent purchase
consideration should be stated, including, for contingent consideration, the range of possible outcomes and the principal factors that
affect the outcome.

---

*Editor's note: Paragraph 13(4) was repealed February 1996.

25   A table should be provided showing, for each class of assets and liabilities of the acquired entity: [4A Sch 13(5)]

(a)   the book values, as recorded in the acquired entity's books immediately before the acquisition and before any fair value adjustments;

(b)   the fair value adjustments, analysed into
  (i)   revaluations
  (ii)   adjustments to achieve consistency of accounting policies, and
  (iii)   any other significant adjustments,
  giving the reasons for the adjustments; and

(c)   the fair values at the date of acquisition.

The table should include a statement of the amount of purchased goodwill or negative goodwill arising on the acquisition.

26   In the table required by paragraph 25, provisions for reorganisation and restructuring costs that are included in the liabilities of the acquired entity, and related asset write-downs, made in the twelve months up to the date of acquisition should be identified separately.

27   Where the fair values of the identifiable assets or liabilities, or the purchase consideration, can be determined only on a provisional basis at the end of the accounting period in which the acquisition took place, this should be stated and the reasons given. Any subsequent material adjustments to such provisional fair values, with corresponding adjustments to goodwill, should be disclosed and explained.

28   As required by FRS 3, in the period of acquisition the post-acquisition results of the acquired entity should be shown as a component of continuing operations in the profit and loss account, other than those that are also discontinued in the same period; and where an acquisition has a material impact on a major business segment this should be disclosed and explained.

29   Where it is not practicable to determine the post-acquisition results of an operation to the end of the period of acquisition, an indication should be given of the contribution of the acquired entity to the turnover and operating profit of the continuing operations. If an indication of the contribution of an acquired entity to the results of the period cannot be given, this fact and the reason should be explained.

30   Any exceptional profit or loss in periods following the acquisition that is determined using the fair values recognised on acquisition should be disclosed in accordance with the requirements of FRS 3, and identified as relating to the acquisition.

31   The profit and loss account or notes to the financial statements of periods following the acquisition should show the costs incurred in those periods in reorganising, restructuring and integrating the acquisition. Such costs are those that:

(a)   would not have been incurred had the acquisition not taken place; and

(b)   relate to a project identified and controlled by management as part of a reorganisation or integration programme set up at the time of acquisition or as a direct consequence of an immediate post-acquisition review.

Movements on provisions or accruals for costs related to an acqui-   **32**
sition should be disclosed and analysed between the amounts used for the specific purpose for which they were created and the amounts released unused.

In accordance with FRS 1, the cash flow statement should show the   **33**
amounts of cash and cash equivalents paid in respect of the consideration, net of any cash and cash equivalents balances transferred as part of the acquisition. In addition, a note to the cash flow statement should show a summary of the effects of acquisitions indicating how much of the consideration comprised cash and cash equivalents and the amounts of cash and cash equivalents transferred as a result of the acquisition.

In accordance with FRS 1, material effects on amounts reported under   **34**
each of the standard headings reflecting the cash flows of the acquired entity in the period should be disclosed, as far as is practicable, as a note to the cash flow statement. This information need be given only in the financial statements for the period in which the acquisition occurs.

[4A Sch   For a material acquisition, the profit after taxation and minority   **35**
13(4)*]   interests of the acquired entity should be given for:

(a)   the period from the beginning of the acquired entity's financial year to the date of acquisition, giving the date on which this period began; and

(b)   its previous financial year.

Substantial acquisitions

[Extension of   For acquisitions meeting the conditions set out in the next para-   **36**
4A Sch 13(4)†]   graph, the following information should be disclosed in the financial statements of the combined entity for the period in which the acquisition took place:

(a)   the summarised profit and loss account and statement of total recognised gains and losses of the acquired entity for the period from the beginning of its financial year to the effective date of acquisition, giving the date on which this period began; this summarised profit and loss account should show as a minimum the turnover, operating profit and those exceptional items falling within paragraph 20 of FRS 3; profit before taxation; taxation and minority interests; and extraordinary items;

(b)   the profit after tax and minority interests for the acquired entity's previous financial year.

---

*Editor's note: Paragraph 13(4) was repealed in February 1996.

†Editor's note: Paragraph 13(4) was repealed February 1996.

This information should be shown on the basis of the acquired entity's accounting policies prior to the acquisition.

37   The disclosures in paragraph 36 should be given for each business combination accounted for by using acquisition accounting where:

(a)   for listed companies, the combination is a Class I* or Super Class I transaction under the Stock Exchange Listing Rules†;

(b)   for other entities, either
   (i)   the net assets or operating profits of the acquired entity exceed 15 per cent of those of the acquiring entity, or
   (ii)   the fair value of the consideration given exceeds 15 per cent of the net assets of the acquiring entity;

and should also be made in other exceptional cases where an acquisition is of such significance that the disclosure is necessary in order to give a true and fair view. For the purposes of (b) above, net assets and profits should be those shown in the financial statements

for the last financial year before the date of the acquisition; and the net assets should be augmented by any purchased goodwill eliminated against reserves as a matter of accounting policy and not charged to the profit and loss account.

DATE FROM WHICH EFFECTIVE

38   The accounting practices set out in the FRS should be regarded as standard in respect of business combinations first accounted for in financial statements relating to accounting periods commencing on or after 23 December 1994. Earlier adoption is encouraged but not required.

WITHDRAWAL OF SSAP 23 AND AMENDMENT OF SSAP 22

39   The FRS supersedes SSAP 23 'Accounting for acquisitions and mergers' and paragraphs 48 – 51 of SSAP 22 'Accounting for goodwill'.

Explanation

INTRODUCTION

40   Two different methods have been used to account for business combinations: merger accounting and acquisition accounting.

41   In merger accounting the financial statements of the parties to the combination are aggregated, and presented as though the combining entities had always been part of the same reporting entity. Accordingly, although the merger may have taken place part of the way through the financial year, the results of the combining entities for the full financial year are reflected in the group accounts for the period and

---

Editor's note: See UITF Abstract 15 (revised 1999) 'Disclosure of Substantial Acquisitions'.

†*Editor's Note: The Listing Rules are now issued by the Financial Services Authority in its capacity as the UK Listing Authority.*

corresponding amounts are presented on the same basis. The accounting policies of the combining entities are adjusted to achieve uniformity, but the assets and liabilities need not be adjusted to reflect fair values at the date of the combination. Under merger accounting, a difference may arise on consolidation between the nominal value of the shares issued, taken together with the fair value of any other consideration, and the aggregate of the nominal values of the shares received in exchange. Such difference is not goodwill, as it does not result from the difference between the fair value of the consideration and the fair value of the identifiable net assets. It should be shown as a movement on consolidated reserves. Any share premium accounts and capital redemption reserves of the new subsidiary undertaking are not preserved as such in the consolidated accounts, since they do not relate to the share capital of the reporting entity, but are brought in by being shown as a movement on other reserves.

In acquisition accounting the results of the acquired company are brought into the **42** group accounts only from the date of acquisition. The identifiable assets and liabilities acquired are included at fair value in the consolidated accounts and are therefore stated at their cost to the acquiring group. The fair value of the consideration given is set against the aggregate fair value of the net identifiable assets acquired and any resulting balance is goodwill, if positive, or else a negative consolidation difference called negative goodwill.*

The fact that a particular business combination does not meet the criteria for merger **43** accounting, and is thus accounted for by using acquisition accounting, does not preclude the acquirer from obtaining merger relief in its individual accounts under the provisions of section 131 of the Companies Act 1985 if the requirements of that section are met. In such cases, in the consolidated accounts, acquisition accounting is applied in the normal way: goodwill is still calculated by comparing the fair value of the shares issued, rather than their nominal or recorded value, with the fair value of the net assets acquired; and any resulting excess over the nominal value of the shares issued, taken together with the fair value of any other consideration, is shown, not as share premium, but as a separate reserve.

DEFINITION OF A MERGER AND AN ACQUISITION

A merger is a rare type of business combination in which two or more parties come **44** together for the mutual sharing of benefits and risks arising from the combined businesses, in what is in substance an equal partnership, each sharing influence in the new entity. No party can be regarded as acquiring control over another, or becoming controlled by another; and the reporting entity formed by the combination must be regarded as a new entity rather than the continuation of one of the combining entities, enlarged by its having obtained control over the others.

An acquisition is defined as any business combination that is not a merger. In many **45** acquisitions, the shareholders of the acquired party do not have a continuing interest in the combined entity, but instead sell their shareholdings for cash or other non-equity consideration. Even where all parties in an acquisition retain an interest in the combined entity, the parties do not come together on equal terms; one party has a greater degree of influence than the others, and is seen as acquiring the other entities in exchange for a share in the combined entity. An acquisition is therefore a transaction that is, in substance, the application of resources by the acquiring entity to

---

*The treatment of such balances is dealt with in SSAP 22 'Accounting for Goodwill' and is the subject of a current ASB project see FRED 12. (**Editor's note:** See now FRS 10 'Goodwill and Intangible Assets'.)*

obtain control of one or more other entities, by the payment of cash, transfer of other assets, the incurring of a liability or the issue of shares.

46   The legal form of a business combination will normally be for one company to acquire shares in one or more others. This fact does not make that company an acquirer in the sense discussed above. Similarly, the question of whether the combined entity should be regarded as a new reporting entity is not affected by whether or not a new legal entity has been formed to acquire shares in others.

RATIONALE FOR MERGER ACCOUNTING

47   In a merger, no party to the combination can be properly regarded as obtaining control over the other; rather, the parties to the combination join together on an equal footing to form a combined enterprise for their mutual benefit.

48   For such mergers it is misleading to account for the combination as the application of resources by one party to obtain control over the other, since this assumes a distinction in the roles of the parties that does not reflect reality. Furthermore, it is only the legal structure of the combination that would determine which party would be treated under acquisition accounting as the acquirer, and thus determine the party whose net assets would be treated as being acquired and whose goodwill would be recognised.

49   A merger is a true mutual sharing of the benefits and risks of the combined entity. Therefore the joint history of the entities that have combined will be relevant to the combined group's shareholders. This record will be provided by merger accounting because it treats the separate businesses as though they were continuing as before, only now jointly owned and managed. If acquisition accounting were to be used, it would focus artificially on only one of the parties to the combination, which would lead to a discontinuity in information reported on the combined entity.

50   Thus the concept of a merger is of a partnership or pooling of interests, where all the parties to the combination participate in the combined businesses of the merged entity on substantially equal terms; and where the substance of the arrangement is such that the reporting entity cannot be regarded as merely being enlarged by the acquisition of the other entities, but must be considered as effectively a new reporting entity.

51   In a business combination that qualifies as a merger, expenses of the combination are similar in nature to expenses of a fundamental reorganisation or restructuring, and should be charged to the profit and loss account for the period in which the merger occurred, shown as an exceptional item in accordance with paragraph 20 of FRS 3. This is not intended to prohibit the subsequent charging of issue costs to the share premium account by means of a transfer between reserves.

RATIONALE FOR ACQUISITION ACCOUNTING

52   The acquisition of another entity is a transaction by which an entity seeks to increase the assets under its control. Acquisition accounting is appropriate for most business combinations since it reflects in the financial statements the application of resources by one party to the combination in order to obtain control of the other, represented by the fair value of the net assets over which control is obtained together with goodwill.

The profits of the acquired company are brought into account only from the date of   **53**
the combination and the history of the group is seen as the history of the acquirer
with occasional additions when it acquires other entities.

DECIDING WHETHER A BUSINESS COMBINATION IS A MERGER OR AN ACQUISITION

The FRS requires that to determine whether a business combination meets the defi-   **54**
nition of a merger, it should be assessed against certain specified criteria; failure to
meet any of these criteria indicates that the definition was not met and thus that
merger accounting is not to be used for the combination.

Individually these tests are insufficient to define the intangible quality of a true   **55**
merger, and may appear arbitrary. Nevertheless, taken as a whole, they provide a
reasonable basis for determining whether a particular business combination meets
the definition of a merger and thus should be accounted for by using merger
accounting.

In applying the criteria, it is necessary to consider the substance and not just the form   **56**
of the arrangements, and to take account of all relevant information related to the
combination. It is important to have regard to the transaction as a whole, including
any related arrangements that are connected with the business combination either
because they are entered into in contemplation of that combination or because they
are part of the process by which that combination is effected. The vast majority of
business combinations will be acquisitions and only in rare circumstances will a
combination fulfil all the detailed conditions for it to be treated as a merger.

Parties to the combination

For the purposes of assessing whether a combination is a merger meeting the criteria,   **57**
the parties to the combination are considered as comprising not solely the business of
each entity that is combining but also the management of the entity and the body of
its shareholders.

Merger accounting is not appropriate for a combination where one of the parties   **58**
results from a recent divestment by a larger entity, because the divested business will
not have been independent for a sufficient period to establish itself as being a party
separate from its previous owner. Only once the divested business has established a
track record of its own can it be considered as a party to a merger. However, a party
to a combination may divest itself of a peripheral part of its business before the
combination (or as part of the arrangements for the combination) and still meet the
criteria for merger accounting.

Where a party to the combination is not a company with share capital, the conditions   **59**
applying to equity shares should be interpreted as applying to those elements of its
capital structure that allocate rights to profits and control.

Criterion 1 – role of the parties

An essential feature of a merger is that it represents a genuine combining of the   **60**
interests of the parties; such a genuine combination of interests cannot exist if one
party portrays itself, or another party, as having a dominant role as an acquirer or
the subservient role of being acquired.

61   Where the terms of a share-for-share exchange indicate that one party has paid a premium over the market value of the shares acquired, this is evidence that that party has taken the role of an acquirer unless there is a clear explanation for this apparent premium other than its being a premium paid to acquire control.

62   The circumstances surrounding the transaction may provide evidence to indicate the nature of a business combination. The following, while not individually conclusive, would need to be considered: the form by which the combination was achieved, the plans for the combined entity's future operations (for example, whether any closures or disposals related more to one party than another), and the proposed corporate image (such as the name, logo and the location of the headquarters and principal operations). Where a publicly quoted company is a party to a business combination, the content of communications with its shareholders is likely also to be relevant in determining the substance of the transaction.

Criterion 2 – dominance of management

63   An essential feature of the genuine combination of interests underlying the definition of a merger is that all parties to the combination are involved in determining the management of the combined entity and reach a consensus on the appropriate structure and personnel; if decisions can be reached only by the exercise of majority voting rights against the wishes of one of the parties to the merger, or if one party clearly dominates this process, this indicates that the combination is not a genuine pooling of interests. However, this does not preclude the possibility of all, or most, of the management team of the combined entity coming from only one of the parties, provided that this clearly reflects the wishes of the others.

64   In applying this test, it is necessary to consider not only the formal management structure of the combined entity, but also the identity of all persons involved in the main financial and operating decisions and the way in which the decision-making process operates in practice within the combined entity.

65   Normally the management of the combined entity would contain representatives of each of the combining parties. Where the senior management structure and personnel of the combined entity are essentially those of one of the combining parties, this criterion will not have been met unless it is clear that all the parties to the merger genuinely participated in the decision.

66   In applying this test it is necessary to consider only the decisions made in the period of initial integration and restructuring at the time of the combination; but both the short-term effects and expected long-term consequences of decisions made in this period need to be considered.

Criterion 3 – relative size of the parties

67   Where one party is substantially larger than the other parties it would be presumed that the larger party can or will dominate the combined undertaking. This will not be consistent with treating such a business combination as a merger as the combined entity will not be a substantially equal partnership.

68   A party would be presumed to dominate if it is more than 50 per cent larger than each of the other parties to the combination, judged by reference to the ownership interests; that is, by considering the proportion of the equity of the combined entity attributable to the shareholders of each of the combining parties. However, this presumption may be rebutted if it can be clearly shown that there is no such dominance; other factors, such as voting or share agreements, blocking powers or other arrangements, can mean that a party to the combination has more influence, or conversely less influence, than is indicated by its relative size. Circumstances that rebut the presumption of dominant influence based on relative sizes would need to be disclosed and explained.

Criterion 4 – non-equity consideration

Criterion 4 is concerned with the extent to which equity shareholders of the com-   **69**
bining entities receive any consideration other than equity shares (as defined in paragraph 2 above) in the combined entity. Cash, other assets, loan stock and preference shares are all examples of non-equity consideration.

As stated in the note on legal requirements (Appendix I), companies legislation   **70**
provides that one of the conditions for merger accounting is that the fair value of any consideration other than the issue of equity shares (as defined in companies legislation) did not exceed 10 per cent of the nominal value of the equity shares issued. Criterion 4 requires a further condition to be met, that all but an immaterial proportion of the fair value of the consideration received must be in the form of equity shares (as defined in paragraph 2); this definition of equity, which is that adopted in FRS 25 '(IAS 32) Financial Instruments: Disclosure and Presentation', is narrower than that of companies legislation, and is used to avoid the possibility of criterion 4 being met by the use of shares that, although within the statutory definition of equity, have characteristics that are closer to non-equity.*

The FRS requires that all arrangements made in conjunction with the combination   **71**
must be taken into account. Equity shareholders will be considered to have disposed of their shareholding for cash where any arrangement is made in connection with the combination that enabled them to exchange or redeem the shares they received in the combination for cash (or other non-equity consideration); for example, a vendor placing or similar arrangement should be treated as giving rise to non-equity consideration. However, a normal market selling transaction, or privately arranged sale, entered into by a shareholder is not made in conjunction with the combination and does not prevent the criterion being met.

A business combination may not be accounted for as a merger if a material part of   **72**
the consideration that the issuing entity offers the equity shareholders in the other parties is in the form of shares with substantially reduced rights. Such an offer would be contrary to the concept that a merger is the mutual sharing in risks and rewards of the combined entity. Some adjustment to the rights attaching to the shares held by the non-issuing entities' shareholders may be compatible with the combination being a merger, as business combinations result from a negotiating process where different pre-existing rights have to be reconciled. Whether any change in the rights of one group of shareholders is sufficient to prevent that business combination being treated as a merger will depend on the facts in any individual case, taking into account such matters as what rights shareholders originally had, the total arrangement negotiated, time limits and whether any new restrictions apply equally to all sets of shareholders. In determining whether equity shares with reduced rights have been issued, both rights to vote and rights to distributions attaching to the shares would need to be taken into account. If any of these individual rights were significantly reduced or circumscribed the combination would fail to fulfil this condition.

Editor's note: Reference to FRS 4 removed, and replaced by reference to FRS 25 by FRS 25.

73   If one entity has acquired an interest in another in exchange for non-equity consideration, or equity shares with significantly reduced rights, within the two years before those entities combined, such consideration should be regarded as part of the consideration for the combination for the purpose of determining whether this criterion is met.

74   Sometimes a peripheral part of the business of one of the combining parties will be excluded from the combined entity. The FRS states that shares in the peripheral business, or the proceeds of sale of the business, that are distributed to the shareholders of that party to the combination as part of the arrangements for the combination are not to be counted as part of the consideration for the purposes of this criterion.

Criterion 5 – minorities etc

75   Criterion 5 is concerned with a party retaining an interest in only part of the combined entity. The concept of a merger is that the participants enter into a mutual sharing of the risks and rewards of the whole of the new entity, including the pooled future results of the combined entity. This concept is incompatible with certain participants having a preferential interest in one part of the combined entity. This criterion would not, therefore, be met if the share of the equity in the combined entity allocated to the shareholders of one of the parties to the combination depended to any material extent on the post-combination performance of the business, or any part of it, formerly controlled by that party.

76   This criterion would similarly not be met where earn-outs or similar performance-related schemes are included in the arrangements to effect a merger. The test is also failed if there is any material minority (defined by companies legislation as 10 per cent) of shareholders left in one of the combining parties that have not accepted the terms of the combination offer.

77   However, the criterion would not necessarily be invalidated by an arrangement whereby the allocation of consideration between the shareholders of the combining parties depended on the determination of the eventual value of a specific liability or asset contributed by one of the parties—such as the eventual outcome of a claim against one of the parties, or the eventual sales value of a specific asset owned by one of the parties—as opposed to the future operating performance of that party.

GROUP RECONSTRUCTIONS

78   In addition to mergers as defined above, merger accounting may also be appropriate for a group reconstruction, provided that the relative rights of the ultimate shareholders are not altered. Such reconstructions include not only the transfer of shares in a subsidiary undertaking within a group, but also arrangements such as the introduction of a new holding company, the splitting off of one or more subsidiary undertakings, as in some demergers, where a separate group is formed, and the bringing together into a new group of two or more companies that were previously under common ownership. Acquisition accounting would require the restatement at fair value of the assets and liabilities of the company transferred, and the recognising of goodwill, which is likely to be inappropriate in the case of a transaction that does not alter the relative rights of the ultimate shareholders.

79   Where a minority interest exists, merger accounting is permitted only for those group reconstructions that do not change the interest of the minority in the net assets of the group. Thus the transfer of a subsidiary undertaking within a subgroup that has a

minority shareholder may qualify for merger accounting; but acquisition accounting must be used for the transfer of a subsidiary undertaking out of, or into, such a subgroup. If a minority has effectively acquired, or disposed of, rights to part of the net assets of the group, the FRS requires the transfer to be accounted for by using acquisition accounting rather than merger accounting.

DISCLOSURE

The disclosure requirements in the FRS cover and supplement those in companies legislation. **80**

Mergers

With merger accounting the financial statements of the combined entity are drawn **81**
up by combining the results of the combining entities for the whole of the financial year in which the merger occurred. Users, particularly those who have been assessing the parties to the combination as separate businesses, may require information on the financial performance of the individual parties. The FRS therefore requires an analysis of the profit and loss account and statement of total recognised gains and losses into pre- and post-merger amounts; and a further analysis of the pre-merger amounts between each of the parties to the merger. An analysis between the parties of the preceding financial year is also required. However, it is not necessary, where revaluation gains or losses have been recognised as a result of a valuation at the year-end, to obtain further valuations at the date of the merger in order to apportion the gains or losses between pre- and post-merger periods.

Group reconstructions that are accounted for by using merger accounting are **82**
exempted from the disclosure requirements in the FRS, but must still give the information required by companies legislation.

Acquisitions

The disclosure requirements of the FRS provide information about the resources **83**
applied in acquisitions, the net assets acquired and the effects on the consolidated financial statements of the acquiring group. Separate presentation of the results of acquisitions assists analysis of the significance of new operations that have been acquired. In some circumstances it may also be useful to users for the results of acquisitions for the first full financial year for which they are a part of the reporting entity to be disclosed in the notes.

Paragraph 23 of the FRS requires the disclosures in paragraphs 24–35 to be given for **84**
each material acquisition, and those in paragraphs 24–34 to be given for other acquisitions in aggregate. Materiality must be judged by whether the information relating to the acquisition might reasonably be expected to influence decisions made by the users of general purpose financial statements. Paragraph 36 applies further disclosure requirements to certain substantial acquisitions.

In order to give a true and fair view of post-acquisition financial performance, **85**
paragraph 30 of the FRS requires disclosure of exceptional profits or losses determined using fair values recognised on an acquisition. Examples include profits or losses on the disposal of acquired stocks where the fair values of stocks sold lead to abnormal trading margins after the acquisition; the release of provisions in respect of an acquired loss-making long-term contract that the acquirer makes profitable; and the realisation of contingent assets or liabilities at amounts materially different from

their attributed fair values. In accordance with the requirements of FRS 3, exceptional items would be included in the profit and loss account format headings to which they relate, and would be disclosed by way of note, or on the face of the profit and loss account if necessary to give a true and fair view.

86   FRS 3 requires the profits or losses on the post-acquisition sale or termination of an operation, or on the disposal of fixed assets, to be shown in the profit and loss account below operating profit. Post-acquisition integration, reorganisation and restructuring costs, including provisions in respect of them, would, if material, be reported as exceptional items; but only if the restructuring is fundamental, having a material effect on the nature and focus of the enlarged group's operations, would the costs be shown below operating profit as an item falling under paragraph 20 of FRS 3. Paragraph 31 of FRS 6 requires that costs of reorganising, restructuring and integration that relate to an acquisition, whether relating to a fundamental restructuring or not, should be shown separately from other exceptional items.

87   The costs of reorganising, restructuring and integrating an acquired entity may extend over more than one period. For major acquisitions, therefore, management may wish to state in the notes to the financial statements the nature and amount of such costs expected to be incurred in relation to the acquisition (including asset write-downs), indicating the extent to which they have been charged to the profit and loss account. If part of these costs relate to asset write-downs (beyond any impairments recognised in adjusting to fair values on the acquisition) it may be useful to distinguish these from cash expenditure. An illustrative example of how such information might be shown is included as Appendix IV to the FRS.

Substantial acquisitions

88   Where an acquisition has been made that has a substantial effect on the consolidated results of the acquiring entity, additional disclosures are required to enable the user to assess the effect of the acquisition on the consolidated results. Although control over the acquired entity is obtained only at the date of acquisition, in most cases it is a continuing business that is acquired, and information on the results for the period up to the date of acquisition is relevant to the user. For acquisitions that meet the size tests in paragraph 37, the FRS therefore requires the disclosure of the results of the acquired entity for the part of its financial year up to the date of the acquisition, and for its previous financial year. Since neither of these periods will necessarily be twelve months, their commencing dates should also be indicated.

89   Several components of the pre-acquisition results are required to be shown for the part of the acquired entity's financial year up to the date of acquisition, since this period may be particularly relevant to an understanding of the post-acquisition results and may not otherwise be publicly reported. Equivalent information for the preceding financial year is likely to be of less relevance, and the disclosure requirement is limited to profit after tax and minority interests. The FRS requires this information to be given on the basis of the acquired entity's accounting policies before the acquisition; in some cases, the management of the acquiring entity may consider it helpful in explaining the impact of the acquisition to give, in addition, the same information restated onto the basis of the acquiring entity's accounting policies.

Adoption of FRS 6 by the board

Financial Reporting Standard 6 – 'Acquisitions and Mergers' was approved for issue by the eight members of the Accounting Standards Board.

Sir David Tweedie   (Chairman)
Allan Cook   (Technical Director)
Robert Bradfield
Ian Brindle
Michael Garner
Raymond Hinton
Donald Main
Graham Stacy

Appendix I
Note on legal requirements

GREAT BRITAIN

References are to the Companies Act 1985

Merger accounting

1   The Companies Act describes the acquisition method of accounting (Schedule 4A paragraph 9) and the merger method of accounting (Schedule 4A paragraph 11). Schedule 4A paragraph 10 lays down the conditions that must be met if a business combination is to be accounted for as a merger. The conditions are:

(a)   that at least 90 per cent of the nominal value of the relevant shares (those with unrestricted rights to participate both in distributions and in the assets on liquidation) in the undertaking acquired is held by or on behalf of the parent company and its subsidiary undertakings;

(b)   that the proportion referred to in (a) was attained pursuant to an arrangement providing for the issue of equity shares by the parent company or one or more of its subsidiary undertakings;

(c)   that the fair value of any consideration other than the issue of equity shares given pursuant to the arrangement by the parent company and its subsidiary undertakings did not exceed 10 per cent of the nominal value of the equity shares issued; and

(d)   that adoption of the merger method of accounting accords with generally accepted accounting principles or practice.

2   Where a group is acquired, the Companies Act requirements described in the previous paragraph also apply. References to shares of the undertaking acquired are to be construed as references to the shares of the acquired group's parent and references to the assets and liabilities, income and expenditure, and capital and reserves of the undertaking acquired are to be construed as references to the same elements of the group acquired, after making the necessary set-off and adjustments required for the consolidated accounts (Schedule 4A paragraph 12).

Disclosures

3   The following information shall be given in a note to the accounts for all business combinations taking place in the financial year:

(a)   the names of the entities involved;

(b)   whether the combination has been accounted for by the acquisition or merger method of accounting (Schedule 4A paragraph 13(2)).

4   In addition, for any business combination that significantly affects the figures shown in the group accounts, the following further information shall be given:

(a)   the composition and fair value of the consideration for the acquisition given by the parent and its subsidiary undertakings (Schedule 4A paragraph 13(3));

(b)   the profit or loss of the undertaking or group acquired for the period up to the date of the acquisition from the beginning of the financial year of that undertaking or group, and for the previous financial year of that undertaking or group. The date on which this financial year began should also be stated (Schedule 4A paragraph 13(4)).*

Where the acquisition method of accounting has been adopted, the book values **5** immediately prior to acquisition and fair values at the date of acquisition of each class of assets and liabilities of the acquired entity shall be stated in tabular form, including a statement of the amount of any goodwill or negative consolidation difference arising on the acquisition, together with an explanation of any significant adjustments made (Schedule 4A paragraph 13(5)).

Where the merger method of accounting has been adopted, an explanation shall be **6** given of any significant adjustments made in relation to the amounts of the assets and liabilities of the undertaking or group acquired, together with a statement of any resulting adjustment to the consolidated reserves (including the restatement of opening consolidated reserves) (Schedule 4A paragraph 13(6)).

None of the information required by paragraph 13 of Schedule 4A to the Act need be **7** disclosed for an undertaking which:

(a) is established under the law of a country outside the United Kingdom; or
(b) carries on business outside the United Kingdom if, in the opinion of the directors of the parent company, the disclosure would be seriously prejudicial to the business of that undertaking or to the business of the parent company or any of its subsidiary undertakings and the Secretary of State agrees that the information should not be disclosed (Schedule 4A paragraph 16).

Share premium and merger relief

Section 130(1) of the Companies Act provides that if a company issues shares at a **8** premium, whether for cash or otherwise, a sum equal to the aggregate amount or value of the premiums on those shares should be transferred to an account called the share premium account. The provisions of the Companies Act relating to the reduction of a company's share capital apply, with exceptions, as if the share premium account were part of its paid-up share capital.

Limited relief from the above ('merger relief') is given by sections 131–134. **9**

Section 131 of the Companies Act provides, inter alia, that, subject to specified **10** conditions, where an issuing company has secured at least a 90 per cent equity holding in another company, section 130 does not apply to the premium on shares issued in the transaction which takes the holding in that other company to at least 90 per cent.

Section 133(1) provides that the premium on any shares to which the relief in sections **11** 131 and 132 of the Companies Act applies may also be disregarded in determining the amount at which any shares, or other consideration provided for the shares issued, are to be included in the offeror company's balance sheet.

The Companies Act requires the disclosure of additional information where merger **12** relief is taken. Schedule 5 paragraphs 10 and 29† refer respectively to companies that are not obliged to prepare group accounts and those that are. They apply to arrangements attracting merger relief, that is, where a company allots shares in

*Editor's note: Paragraph 13(4) was repealed February 1996.

†Editor's note: Paragraphs 10 and 29 were repealed February 1996.

consideration for the issue, transfer or cancellation of shares in another body corporate ('the other company') in circumstances such that section 131(2) (merger relief) applies to the premiums on the shares.

13   If the company makes such an arrangement during the financial year, the following information shall be given:

(a)   the name of the other company;

(b)   the number, nominal value and class of shares allotted;

(c)   the number, nominal value and class of shares in the other company issued, transferred or cancelled; and

(d)   particulars of the accounting treatment adopted in the consolidated accounts in respect of the issue, transfer or cancellation.

14   In addition, for companies that are required to prepare group accounts Schedule 5 paragraph 29(2)* requires the disclosure of particulars of the extent to which and manner in which the profit or loss for the financial year shown in the consolidated accounts is affected by any profit or loss of the other company, or any of its subsidiary undertakings, that arose before the time of the arrangement.

Accounts of the parent company

15   The FRS deals only with the method of accounting to be used in group accounts; it does not deal with the form of accounting to be used in the acquiring or issuing company's own accounts and in particular does not restrict the reliefs available under sections 131–133 of the Companies Act.

16   Where a dividend is paid to the acquiring or issuing company out of pre-combination profits, it would appear that it need not necessarily be applied as a reduction in the carrying value of the investment in the subsidiary undertaking. Such a dividend received should be applied to reduce the carrying value of the investment to the extent necessary to provide for a diminution in value of the investment in the subsidiary undertaking as stated in the accounts of the parent company. To the extent that this is not necessary, it appears that the amount received will be a realised profit in the hands of the parent company.

NORTHERN IRELAND

17   The legal requirements in Northern Ireland are similar to those in Great Britain. The following table shows the references to the Companies (Northern Ireland) Order 1986 that correspond to the marginal references in the FRS and the legal references in paragraphs 1–16 above.

Editor's note: *Paragraph 29 was repealed February 1996.*

Great Britain: the Companies Act 1985   **Northern Ireland: the 1986 Order**

Merger accounting

Schedule 4A paragraphs 9–12	Schedule 4A paragraphs 9–12

Disclosures

Schedule 4A paragraph 13	Schedule 4A paragraph 13
Schedule 4A paragraph 16	Schedule 4A paragraph 16

Share premium and merger relief

Sections 130–134	Articles 140–144
Schedule 5 paragraph 10	Schedule 5 paragraph 10
Schedule 5 paragraph 29	Schedule 5 paragraph 29

REPUBLIC OF IRELAND

The following table shows the references to the European Communities (Companies: **18** Group Accounts) Regulations 1992 and the Companies Act 1963 that correspond to the marginal references in the FRS and the legal references in paragraphs 1 – 16 above.

Great Britain: the Companies Act 1985   **Republic of Ireland: the 1992 Regulations**

Merger accounting

Schedule 4A paragraph 9	Paragraph 19
Schedule 4A paragraph 10	Paragraph 21
Schedule 4A paragraph 11	Paragraph 22
Schedule 4A paragraph 12	Paragraph 23

Disclosures

Schedule 4A paragraph 13(2)	The Schedule paragraph 12(2)
Schedule 4A paragraph 13(3)–13(6)	No exact equivalent; paragraph 27 of the 1992 Regulations states that if the composition of the undertakings dealt with in the group accounts has changed significantly in the course of a financial year, the group accounts must include information that makes the comparison of successive sets of group accounts meaningful.
Schedule 4A paragraph 16	No equivalent

Share premium and merger relief

Section 130	Companies Act 1963 section 62
Sections 131–134	No equivalent
Schedule 5 paragraph 10	No equivalent
Schedule 5 paragraph 29	No equivalent

Merger relief in the Republic of Ireland

19   As there is currently no legislation equivalent to merger relief in the Republic of Ireland, no explicit relief from the requirement of section 62(1) of the Companies Act 1963 to establish a share premium account is available.

20   However, section 149(5) of the Companies Act 1963 provides that, whilst, in general, pre-acquisition profits of acquired subsidiaries may not be treated in the holding company's accounts as revenue profit, an exemption from that provision is available in that, where the directors and auditors are satisfied and so certify that it would be fair and reasonable and would not prejudice the rights and interests of any person, the profits or losses attributable to any shares in a subsidiary may be treated in a manner otherwise than in accordance with that subsection.

21   The possible need for legal advice in relation to the application of section 149(5) to merger accounting should be considered before merger accounting is applied to Republic of Ireland companies.

Appendix II
Compliance with International Accounting Standards

The requirements of the FRS are consistent with International Accounting Standard 22 'Business Combinations' (revised 1993),* except for the provision in paragraph 13 of that standard relating to reverse acquisitions, which is incompatible with companies legislation in the UK and the Republic of Ireland.†

Editor's note: IAS 22 has now been replaced by IFRS 3. This eliminates merger accounting and requires acquisition accounting for all business combinations within its scope.

†*Editor's note: UITF Information Sheet No 17 (issued 31 July 1996) noted that there could be some instances where it would be right and proper to invoke the true and fair override and apply reverse acquisition accounting, although each case should be considered on its merits.*

Appendix III
The development of the FRS

HISTORY

Before the Companies Act 1981

1   Although some use was made of merger accounting in the UK before the Companies Act 1981, and indeed an exposure draft of an accounting standard, ED 3, was published (in 1971), there was concern that the share premium provisions of the Companies Act 1948 might be interpreted so as to prohibit the use of merger accounting. This view was confirmed by the decision in *Shearer v Bercain* in 1980.

The Companies Act 1981 and SSAP 23

2   The Companies Act 1981 introduced the concept of merger relief, removing the legal obstacle to merger accounting. Following this, the Accounting Standards Committee (ASC) issued an exposure draft, ED 31, converted into an accounting standard, SSAP 23 'Accounting for acquisitions and mergers', in 1985.

3   SSAP 23 based its concept of a merger on whether or not the arrangements for the combination resulted in material resources leaving the group. This concept was supported by four criteria defining the circumstances in which merger accounting was permitted:

(a)   the business combination results from an offer to the holders of all equity shares and the holders of all voting shares that are not already held by the offeror; and

(b)   the offeror has secured, as a result of the offer, a holding of (i) at least 90 per cent of all equity shares (taking each class of equity separately) and (ii) the shares carrying at least 90 per cent of the votes of the offeree; and

(c)   immediately prior to the offer, the offeror does not hold (i) 20 per cent or more of all equity shares of the offeree (taking each class of equity separately) or (ii) shares carrying 20 per cent or more of the votes of the offeree; and

(d)   not less than 90 per cent of the fair value of the total consideration given for the equity share capital (including that given for shares already held) is in the form of equity share capital; not less than 90 per cent of the fair value of the total consideration given for voting non-equity share capital (including that given for shares already held) is in the form of equity and/or voting non-equity share capital.

4   Note, however, that merger accounting remained optional even if these criteria were met.

The EC Seventh Directive and the Companies Act 1989

5   The EC Seventh Company Law Directive introduced more stringent requirements to be met before merger accounting was permitted. The conditions of the Directive were implemented in Great Britain, with some additional provisions, by the Companies Act 1989, as amendments to the Companies Act 1985. These conditions are:

(a)   that at least 90 per cent of the nominal value of the relevant shares (those with unrestricted rights to participate both in distributions and in the assets on liquidation) in the undertaking acquired is held by or on behalf of the parent company and its subsidiary undertakings;

(b) that the proportion referred to in (a) was attained pursuant to an arrangement providing for the issue of equity shares by the parent company or one or more of its subsidiary undertakings;

(c) that the fair value of any consideration other than the issue of equity shares given pursuant to the arrangement by the parent company and its subsidiary undertakings did not exceed 10 per cent of the nominal value of the equity shares issued; and

(d) that adoption of the merger method of accounting accords with generally accepted accounting principles or practice.

In requiring compliance with generally accepted accounting principles, the Companies Act clearly acknowledged that merger accounting would not be appropriate for all business combinations that met the first three conditions.   **6**

The comparison, in condition (c), with the nominal value of shares issued is also noteworthy. The nominal value is of no economic significance. In contrast, the corresponding condition (d) of SSAP 23 refers to the fair value of the equity shares issued.   **7**

Limiting the use of merger accounting—the ED 48 proposals

ED 48 was issued by the ASC in February 1990 in response to widespread concern that the SSAP 23 conditions were too readily circumvented. It proposed to limit the use of merger accounting to a very restricted class of combinations that could be regarded as 'true' mergers. These were to be defined as a combination that was effectively an equal partnership between the combining parties, where no party saw itself as either an acquirer or an acquiree. In addition, there had to be continuing involvement from the management of each of the parties in the combined entity; and the parties were to be of broadly equal size. Any minority not accepting the merger offer was not to exceed 10 per cent, and no material consideration other than equity shares was permitted.   **8**

ED 48 then proposed that merger accounting would be required, and not merely permitted, for all combinations meeting these conditions (although, as a practical matter, it has been suggested that it would be relatively easy for merging parties to ensure that one of the conditions was not met, without fundamentally altering the commercial substance of the transaction, if they did not wish to use merger accounting—and thus for practical purposes the option to use acquisition accounting might be seen to remain).   **9**

Although respondents to ED 48 were generally in agreement with its proposals, there was criticism of the conditions for merger accounting, in particular of their subjective nature, which, it was expected, would give rise to difficulties in applying them consistently.   **10**

International Accounting Standards

The merger concept underlying ED 48 is similar to that proposed for a 'uniting of interests' in the International Accounting Standard 22, revised in 1993,* although that standard does not develop tests for identifying when a combination is a merger. IAS 22 defines a uniting of interests as: **11**

*Editor's note: IAS 22 was further revised in 1998 and has now been replaced by IFRS 3.

'a business combination in which the shareholders of the combining enterprises combine control over the whole, or effectively the whole, of their net assets and operations to achieve a continuing mutual sharing in the risks and benefits attaching to the combined entity such that neither party can be identified as the acquirer.'

FRED 6

12   In considering the application of merger accounting, the Board was concerned by the apparent choice available in many cases between acquisition and merger accounting, and that two business combinations with very similar economic substance could be accounted for in different ways, with substantial differences in reported results and balance sheets not only for the financial year in which the combination occurred but for several years thereafter. The Board also found it difficult to identify any theoretical basis to justify the use of merger accounting for the wide range of business combinations for which it was then permissible.

13   In issuing FRED 6, the Board therefore adopted the intention of ED 48, of narrowing the use of merger accounting.

14   No major changes were proposed, but the Board sought to remove subjectivity where possible. The approach of the FRED was based on the belief that merger accounting should be applied to only a few rare instances of business combinations that were properly regarded as mergers, and that the vast majority of business combinations were more appropriately accounted for as acquisitions.

15   The definition of a merger was redrafted, but its intent was unchanged. The definition of an acquisition was amended to make it clear that all combinations were either mergers or acquisitions.

16   The six conditions under which merger accounting would have been permitted by ED 48 were redrafted as five criteria, as follows:

> *Criterion 1* – redrafted form of ED 48 condition (a).
>
> *Criterion 2* – amended form of ED 48 condition (b), acknowledging that to require the board of a merged entity to have equal participation from each of the parties to the merger might prevent the parties to the merger from choosing the management they considered most appropriate; and might lead to too much focus on the numerical representation of each party on the new board at the expense of considering where the real decision taking influence lay.
>
> *Criterion 3* – redrafted form of ED 48 condition (e).
>
> *Criterion 4* – redrafted form of ED 48 condition (c).
>
> *Criterion 5* – redrafted form of ED 48 conditions (d) and (f), reducing these to a more general principle.

Disclosure

17   The disclosure requirements proposed by ED 48 were extended to require analysis into pre-combination and post-combination periods of several items in the profit and loss account, and the statement of total recognised gains and losses, rather than focusing solely on profit after tax and extraordinary items.

MATTERS CONSIDERED IN THE LIGHT OF RESPONSES TO FRED 6

A large majority of the respondents to FRED 6 agreed with the proposals it contained, **18** and these are accordingly unchanged. The following paragraphs describe those points on which respondents expressed concern and explain whether or not a change was made and the Board's reasoning for its decision.

Disclosure requirements on an acquisition

The full disclosure requirements proposed in the FRED relating to the pre-combina- **19** tion results of the parties to a merger, and the acquired entity in an acquisition, were supported by a majority of respondents, and particularly by users of accounts. Concern was expressed, however, at the practical difficulties in obtaining this information relating to acquisitions, and many preparers of financial statements questioned whether such disclosures were, in practice, of value to users.

The Board has therefore reconsidered the extent of the disclosures required in respect **20** of the acquired company, and has made three main relaxations in the requirements:

(a) less detailed analysis of the results of the acquired company up to the date of acquisition is now required;

(b) only the profit after tax and minority interests for its previous financial year is now required to be shown; and

(c) fuller disclosure is now required only for substantial acquisitions, defined as being 'Class I'* or 'Super Class I' where the acquirer is a listed company, or in excess of 15 per cent of net assets or profits for others.

The FRS now states that this information is to be given using the accounting policies of the acquired company, instead of being restated using the acquirer's accounting policies.

Some respondents suggested that it would be more helpful for all disclosure **21** requirements relating to acquisitions to be consolidated into one standard. The Board has accordingly included in this FRS the proposed disclosure requirements set out in FRED 7 (which were based on those in SSAP 22), amended to take account of responses made to that FRED. It has also incorporated references to the disclosure requirements relating to acquisitions in FRS 1 and FRS 3, unchanged other than to make it clear that the disclosures should be made separately for each material acquisition, and for other acquisitions in aggregate.

Disclosure requirements on a merger

The Board concluded that, in the case of a merger, no relaxation of the proposed **22** disclosures was appropriate. Because of the continuing involvement of management of both parties to the merger, the practical difficulties would be less, and the likely significance of the merger to the shareholders would make it desirable to provide fuller information. Although it was argued that analysing pre-merger results among the parties was in some sense contrary to the concept of merger accounting, in that the financial statements were drawn up on the basis that the parties had always been merged, the Board took the view that full information on the combining parties separately was important to an understanding of the combined entity.

*Editor's note: See UITF Abstract 15 (revised 1999) 'Disclosure of substantial acquisitions'.

Definitions and criteria for merger accounting

23   The definitions of mergers and acquisitions, and the criteria for merger accounting, were generally agreed as appropriate by respondents, and only minor drafting changes have been made. Criterion 4 has been amended to make clear the effect of an entity disposing of part of its business prior to the combination.

Group reconstructions

24   There was general agreement with the proposed use of merger accounting in group reconstructions, but some respondents requested that this should be more widely available. The Board has therefore agreed to widen the definition of group reconstructions, provided minority rights are unaffected, to include situations where a new holding company is created; where a 'horizontal group' of companies under common ownership become a group under the companies legislation definition; and where a part of a group is transferred to a new company, not part of the group but owned by the same shareholders as the group.

Merger expenses

25   The FRED proposed that merger expenses should be charged to the profit and loss account. Although a majority of respondents supported this proposal, there was significant support for deducting such costs from reserves, in a way similar to the costs of issuing an equity instrument under FRS 4. The Board believes, however, that there is a fundamental difference between the costs of issue of an equity instrument, which raises new capital, from which the costs may sensibly be deducted, and the costs of a merger, which does not raise new capital, but which requires an expenditure of resources that should therefore be charged to the profit and loss account. The Board has clarified that these costs should be shown as an exceptional item in accordance with paragraph 20 of FRS 3.

Demergers

26   Several respondents suggested that the FRS should deal with the accounting issues arising on demergers as well. However, the Board took the view that such issues as arise on a demerger are unrelated to those of business combinations, and should not be dealt with in the same FRS (although the restructuring that takes place on a demerger may fall within the group restructuring provisions of this FRS).

Alternative view – prohibiting the use of merger accounting

27   The Preface to the FRED set out an alternative view, that the use of merger accounting should be prohibited (other than for certain group reconstructions). This alternative view attracted little support; most commentators thought that mergers, although rare, were a separate class of business combination for which merger accounting should be available. The Board has, accordingly, not proceeded with that proposal.

Appendix IV
Illustrative example of disclosure of reorganisation and integration costs

This example is provided as an aid to understanding and does not form part of the Financial Reporting Standard.

Paragraph 87 of the Explanation suggests that, for major acquisitions, management may wish to include in the notes to the financial statements the amount of reorganisation and other costs to be incurred in relation to the acquisition. The following example indicates one way in which this optional information might be presented. The best form of the disclosure will depend on individual circumstances.

COSTS OF REORGANISING AND INTEGRATING ACQUISITIONS

	Acquisition of European business (note (a)) £ million	Other acquisitions £ million	TOTAL £ million
Announced but not charged as at the previous year-end	–	25	25
Announced in relation to acquisitions during the year	170	–	170
Adjustments to previous years' estimates	–	(5)	(5)
	170	20	190
Charged in the year			
– operating profit	55	12	67
– elsewhere	65	–	65
	120	12	132
Announced but still to be charged at 31 December 1995	50	8	58

Note (a): Acquisition of European business

	£ million
Cost of acquisition	400
Reorganisation and integration expenditure announced	
Fundamental restructuring:	
–withdrawal from existing US business and related redundancies	65
Other items (to be charged to operating profit):	
–other redundancy costs	75
– re-branding and redesign costs	30
Announced reorganisation and integration costs as shown in above table	170
Total investment	570

In addition to the £120 million expenditure shown in the above table, reorganisation and integration costs charged during the year include £30 million in respect of write-downs to fixed assets consequent on the closure of the XYZ plant.

Financial Reporting Standard 7 is set out in paragraphs 1–31.

The Statement of Standard Accounting Practice set out in paragraphs 4–31 should be read in the context of the Objective as stated in paragraph 1 and the definitions set out in paragraphs 2–3 and also of the Foreword to Accounting Standards and the Statement of Principles for Financial Reporting currently in issue.

The Explanation set out in paragraphs 32–85 shall be regarded as part of the Statement of Standard Accounting Practice insofar as it assists in interpreting that statement.

Appendix III 'The development of the FRS' *reviews considerations and arguments that were thought significant by members of the Board in reaching the conclusions on* FRS *7. The views of the member who dissented are set out in Appendix IV.*

[FRS 7]
Fair values in acquisition accounting*

(Issued September 1994)

Contents

Editor's note: FRS 7 has been amended by FRS 25 with effect for accounting periods beginning on or after 1 January 2005.

Adoption of FRS 7 by the Board

Appendices

Fair values in acquisition accounting

Summary

GENERAL

a   Financial Reporting Standard 7 'Fair Values in Acquisition Accounting' sets out the principles of accounting for a business combination under the acquisition method of accounting. Companies legislation requires the identifiable assets and liabilities of the acquired entity to be included in the consolidated financial statements of the acquirer at their fair values at the date of acquisition. The difference between these and the cost of acquisition is recognised as goodwill or negative goodwill. The results of the acquired entity are included in the profit and loss account of the acquiring group from the date of acquisition.

FAIR VALUES OF IDENTIFIABLE ASSETS AND LIABILITIES

b   The assets and liabilities recognised in the allocation of fair values should be those of the acquired entity that existed at the date of acquisition. They should be measured at fair values that reflect the conditions at the date of the acquisition.

c   The liabilities of the acquired entity should not include provisions for future operating losses. Changes in the assets and liabilities resulting from the acquirer's intentions or from events after the acquisition should be dealt with as post-acquisition items. Similarly, costs of reorganisation and integrating the business acquired, whether they relate to the acquired entity or the acquiring group, should be dealt with as post-acquisition costs and do not affect the fair values at the date of acquisition.

d   Fair values should be based on the value at which an asset or liability could be exchanged in an arm's length transaction. The fair value of monetary items should take into account the amounts expected to be received or paid and their timing.

e   Unless they can be measured at market value, the fair values of non-monetary assets will normally be based on replacement cost, but should not exceed their recoverable amount as at the date of acquisition. The recoverable amount reflects the condition of the assets on acquisition but not any impairments resulting from subsequent events. The FRS specifies the methods for determining fair values of individual categories of assets and liabilities.

INVESTIGATION PERIOD AND GOODWILL ADJUSTMENTS

f   The identification and valuation of assets and liabilities acquired should be completed, if possible, by the date on which the first post-acquisition financial statements of the acquirer are approved by the directors. If it has not been possible to complete the investigation of fair values by that date, provisional valuations should be made; these should be amended if necessary in the next financial statements with a corresponding adjustment to goodwill.

COST OF ACQUISITION

g   The cost of acquisition is the amount of cash or cash equivalents paid and the fair value of other purchase consideration given by the acquirer, together with the expenses of the acquisition. The FRS explains the methods used to determine the amounts to be ascribed to constituent parts of the purchase consideration.

Where the payment of consideration for an acquisition is to be made after the date of **h** acquisition, reasonable estimates of the amounts expected to be paid should be included in the cost of acquisition at their present values.

Financial Reporting Standard 7

Objective

The objective of this FRS is to ensure that when a business entity is acquired by **1** another, all the assets and liabilities that existed in the acquired entity at the date of acquisition are recorded at fair values reflecting their condition at that date; and that all changes to the acquired assets and liabilities, and the resulting gains and losses, that arise after control of the acquired entity has passed to the acquirer are reported as part of the post-acquisition financial performance of the acquiring group.

Definitions

The following definitions shall apply in this FRS and in particular in the Statement of **2** Standard Accounting Practice set out in paragraphs 4–31.

Acquisition:-
A business combination that is accounted for by using the acquisition method of accounting.

Business combination:-
The bringing together of separate entities into one economic entity as a result of one entity uniting with, or obtaining control over the net assets and operations of, another.

Date of acquisition:-
The date on which control of the acquired entity passes to the acquirer. This is the date from which the acquired entity is accounted for by the acquirer as a subsidiary undertaking under FRS 2 'Accounting for Subsidiary Undertakings'.

Fair value:-
The amount at which an asset or liability could be exchanged in an arm's length transaction between informed and willing parties, other than in a forced or liquidation sale.

Identifiable assets and liabilities:-
The assets and liabilities of the acquired entity that are capable of being disposed of or settled separately, without disposing of a business of the entity.

Recoverable amount:-
The greater of the net realisable value of an asset and, where appropriate, the value in use.

Value in use:-
The present value of the future cash flows obtainable as a result of an asset's continued use, including those resulting from the ultimate disposal of the asset.

3   References to companies legislation mean:

(a)   in Great Britain, the Companies Act 1985;

(b)   in Northern Ireland, the Companies (Northern Ireland) Order 1986; and

(c)   in the Republic of Ireland, the Companies Acts 1963–90 and the European Communities (Companies: Group Accounts) Regulations 1992.

Statement of Standard Accounting Practice

SCOPE

4   Financial Reporting Standard 7 applies to all financial statements that are intended to give a true and fair view of a reporting entity's financial position and profit or loss (or income and expenditure) for a period. Although the FRS is framed in terms of the acquisition of a subsidiary undertaking by a parent company that prepares consolidated financial statements, it also applies where an individual company or other reporting entity acquires a business other than a subsidiary undertaking.

APPLICATION TO SMALLER ENTITIES

4A   Reporting entities applying the Financial Reporting Standard for Smaller Entities currently applicable are exempt from this accounting standard unless preparing consolidated financial statements, in which case they should apply the FRS to such statements as required by the FRSSE.

DETERMINING THE FAIR VALUES OF IDENTIFIABLE ASSETS AND LIABILITIES ACQUIRED

Principles of recognition and measurement on an acquisition

5   The identifiable assets and liabilities to be recognised should be those of the acquired entity that existed at the date of the acquisition.

6   The recognised assets and liabilities should be measured at fair values that reflect the conditions at the date of the acquisition.

Application of the principles

7   As a consequence of the above principles, the following do not affect fair values at the date of acquisition and therefore fall to be treated as post-acquisition items:

(a)   changes resulting from the acquirer's intentions or future actions;

(b)   impairments, or other changes, resulting from events subsequent to the acquisition;

(c)   provisions or accruals for future operating losses or for reorganisation and integration costs expected to be incurred as a result of the acquisition, whether they relate to the acquired entity or to the acquirer.

8   The application of these principles to specific classes of asset and liability is detailed in paragraphs 9–22 below. Subject to those paragraphs, fair values should be determined in accordance with the acquirer's accounting policies for similar assets and liabilities.

Tangible fixed assets

The fair value of a tangible fixed asset should be based on: **9**

(a) market value, if assets similar in type and condition are bought and sold on an open market; or

(b) depreciated replacement cost, reflecting the acquired business's normal buying process and the sources of supply and prices available to it.

The fair value should not exceed the recoverable amount of the asset.

Intangible assets

Where an intangible asset is recognised, its fair value should be based on its repla- **10**
cement cost, which is normally its estimated market value.

Stocks and work-in-progress

Stocks, including commodity stocks, that the acquired entity trades on a market in **11**
which it participates as both a buyer and a seller should be valued at current market
prices.

Other stocks, and work-in-progress, should be valued at the lower of replacement **12**
cost and net realisable value. Replacement cost is for this purpose the cost at which
the stocks would have been replaced by the acquired entity, reflecting its normal
buying process and the sources of supply and prices available to it—that is, the
current cost of bringing the stocks to their present location and condition.

Quoted investments

Quoted investments should be valued at market price, adjusted if necessary for **13**
unusual price fluctuations or for the size of the holding.

Monetary assets and liabilities

The fair value of monetary assets and liabilities, including accruals and provisions, **14**
should take into account the amounts expected to be received or paid and their
timing. Fair value should be determined by reference to market prices, where
available, by reference to the current price at which the business could acquire similar
assets or enter into similar obligations, or by discounting to present value.

Contingencies

Contingent assets and liabilities should be measured at fair values where these can be **15**
determined. For this purpose reasonable estimates of the expected outcome may be
used.

Business sold or held exclusively with a view to subsequent resale

Where an interest in a separate business of the acquired entity is sold as a single unit **16**
within approximately one year of the date of acquisition, the investment in that
business should be treated as a single asset for the purposes of determining fair
values. Its fair value should be based on the net proceeds of the sale, adjusted for the

fair value of any assets or liabilities transferred into or out of the business, unless such adjusted net proceeds are demonstrably different from the fair value at the date of acquisition as a result of a post-acquisition event. This treatment should be applied to any business operation, whether a separate subsidiary undertaking or not, provided that its assets, liabilities, results of operations and activities are clearly distinguishable, physically, operationally and for financial reporting purposes, from the other assets, liabilities, results of operations and activities of the acquired entity.

17   Where the business has not been sold by the time of approval of the first financial statements after the date of acquisition, the fair value of the interest in the business should be based on the estimated net proceeds of the sale, provided:

(a)   a purchaser has been identified or is being sought; and

(b)   the disposal is reasonably expected to occur within approximately one year of the date of the acquisition. The interest in the business or, if it is not a separate subsidiary undertaking, in the assets of the business, should be shown within current assets. When the sale price is subsequently determined, the original estimate of fair value should be adjusted to reflect the actual sale proceeds.

18   If the subsidiary undertaking or business operation is not, in fact, sold within approximately one year of the acquisition, it should be consolidated normally with fair values attributed to the individual assets and liabilities as at the date of acquisition, and corresponding adjustments to goodwill.

Pensions and other post-retirement benefits

19*   The fair value of a deficiency or, to the extent that it can be recovered through reduced contributions or through refunds from the scheme, a surplus in a funded pension or other post-retirement benefits scheme, or accrued obligations in an unfunded scheme, should be recognised as a liability or an asset of the acquiring group.

20   Changes in pension or other post-retirement arrangements following an acquisition should be accounted for as post-acquisition items and should be dealt with in accordance with the requirements of the standard concerned with pension costs.

Deferred taxation

21   Deferred tax on adjustments to record assets and liabilities at their fair values should be recognised in accordance with the requirements of FRS 19 'Deferred tax'.

22   Deferred tax assets that were not regarded as recoverable and hence were not recognised before the acquisition may, as a consequence of the acquisition, satisfy the recognition criteria of FRS 19. Assets of the acquired entity should be recognised in the fair value exercise. Those of the acquirer or other entities within the acquiring group should be recognised as a credit to the tax charge in the post-acquisition period.

Investigation period and goodwill adjustments

23   The recognition and measurement of assets and liabilities acquired should be completed, if possible, by the date on which the first post-acquisition financial statements of the acquirer are approved by the directors.

Editor's note: Amended by FRS 17 'Retirement benefits' with effect from 2005.

If it has not been possible to complete the investigation for determining fair values by the date on which the first post-acquisition financial statements are approved, provisional valuations should be made; these should be amended, if necessary, in the next financial statements with a corresponding adjustment to goodwill. **24**

Any necessary adjustments to those provisional fair values and the corresponding adjustment to purchased goodwill should be incorporated in the financial statements for the first full financial year following the acquisition. Thereafter, any adjustments, except for the correction of fundamental errors, which should be accounted for as prior period adjustments, should be recognised as profits or losses when they are identified. **25**

DETERMINING THE COST OF ACQUISITION

The cost of acquisition is the amount of cash paid and the fair value of other purchase consideration given by the acquirer, together with the expenses of the acquisition as described in paragraph 28. Where a subsidiary undertaking is acquired in stages, the cost of acquisition is the total of the costs of the interests acquired, determined as at the date of each transaction. **26**

Where the amount of purchase consideration is contingent on one or more future events, the cost of acquisition should include a reasonable estimate of the fair value of amounts expected to be payable in the future. The cost of acquisition should be adjusted when revised estimates are made, with consequential corresponding adjustments continuing to be made to goodwill until the ultimate amount is known. **27**

Fees and similar incremental costs incurred directly in making an acquisition should, except for the issue costs of shares or other securities that are required by FRS 25 '(IAS 32) Financial Instruments: Disclosure and Presentation' to be accounted for as a reduction in the proceeds of a capital instrument, be included in the cost of acquisition. Internal costs, and other expenses that cannot be directly attributed to the acquisition, should be charged to the profit and loss account.* **28**

DISCLOSURES

The disclosures that should be made relating to an acquisition are set out in paragraphs 21 and 23–37 of FRS 6 'Acquisitions and Mergers'. **29**

DATE FROM WHICH EFFECTIVE

The accounting practices set out in the FRS should be regarded as standard in respect of business combinations first accounted for in financial statements relating to accounting periods commencing on or after 23 December 1994. Earlier adoption is encouraged but not required. **30**

AMENDMENT OF SSAP 22

[*Not reproduced as* SSAP *22 has now been superseded.*] **31**

__Editor's note:__ Reference to FRS 25 added by that standard, and reference to FRS 4 removed.

Explanation

INTRODUCTION

32   The FRS is consistent with the requirements of companies legislation regarding the acquisition method of accounting. It sets out principles for identifying the assets and liabilities of an acquired entity and determining their fair values, and for determining the cost of acquisition.

33   Under the acquisition method of accounting, the identifiable assets and liabilities acquired are recognised at their fair values as at the date of acquisition, and the difference between these and the cost of acquisition is accounted for as goodwill or negative goodwill.

DETERMINING THE FAIR VALUES OF IDENTIFIABLE ASSETS AND LIABILITIES ACQUIRED

Existing assets and liabilities of the acquired entity

34   The identifiable assets and liabilities over which the acquirer obtains control are those representing rights to future economic benefits and obligations to transfer economic benefits, including contingent rights and obligations, of the acquired entity that were in existence before the date of acquisition.

35   The identifiable assets and liabilities may include items that were not previously recognised in the financial statements of the acquired entity. These include assets and liabilities that are not normally recognised in accounts where no acquisition is involved, because other accounting standards preclude their immediate recognition. Examples are:

(a)   pension surpluses or deficiencies identified on an acquisition that are otherwise recognised over several financial years in an entity's financial statements, in accordance with the requirements of SSAP 24 'Accounting for pension costs'*;

(b)   contingent assets that may be assigned a value on acquisition, but cannot otherwise be recognised in financial statements because SSAP 18 'Accounting for contingencies'† precludes the recognition of a contingent gain until realisation becomes reasonably certain.

36   The examples given above are included in the identifiable assets and liabilities because when an acquisition is made it is necessary to identify and recognise, so far as possible, all assets and liabilities acquired, provided they can be reliably valued. If this is not done, the reporting of post-acquisition performance is distorted by changes in assets and liabilities not being recognised in the correct period. The usual accounting practice, for example, of deferring recognition of contingent assets, does not apply, because the recognition of an acquired asset represents the expectation that the amounts expended on its acquisition will be recovered; it does not anticipate a future gain. It is, however, necessary to review the recoverable amounts of such assets to ensure that provision is made for any probable losses.

37   Certain contingent assets and liabilities that crystallise as a result of the acquisition would also be recognised, provided that the underlying contingency was in existence

---

*Editor's note: SSAP 24 has been superseded by FRS 17 'Retirement benefits'.

†Editor's note: SSAP 18 has been superseded by FRS 12 'Provisions, contingent liabilities and contingent assets'.

before the acquisition. An example is where the acquired entity has previously entered into a contract that contains a clause under which obligations are triggered in the event of a change of ownership.

Identifiable liabilities include items such as onerous contracts and commitments that existed at the time of acquisition, whether or not the corresponding obligations were recognised as liabilities in the financial statements of the acquired entity. When an acquisition is made, provisions for liabilities would be recognised as identifiable liabilities only if such commitments had been made by the acquired entity before the date of acquisition. In the case of business closure decisions made by the acquired entity before the date of acquisition, the principles for recognising consequential provisions are set out in FRS 3 'Reporting Financial Performance', which states that obligations are incurred when there is a detailed formal plan for termination from which the entity cannot realistically withdraw.* **38**

Exclusion of post-acquisition costs

The FRS does not permit provisions for future losses or for reorganisation costs expected to be incurred as a result of the acquisition to be included as liabilities acquired: they are not liabilities of the acquired entity as at the date of acquisition. As an example, if the acquirer decides to close a factory of the acquired entity as a measure to integrate the combined operations, this is a post-acquisition event. Only if the acquired entity was already committed to this course of action, and unable realistically to withdraw from it, would it be regarded as pre-acquisition. Similarly, if the acquirer undertakes a reorganisation to integrate the acquired operation or to improve its efficiency, this is also a post-acquisition event. **39**

Where provisions for future costs were made by an acquired entity shortly before an acquisition took place, for example during the course of negotiations with the acquirer, it would be necessary to pay particular attention to the circumstances in order to determine whether obligations were incurred by the acquired entity before the acquisition. Only if the acquired entity was demonstrably committed to the expenditure whether or not the acquisition was completed would it have a liability at the date of acquisition. If obligations were incurred by the acquired entity as a result of the influence of the acquirer, it would be necessary to consider whether control of the acquired entity had been transferred at an earlier date and, consequently, whether the date of acquisition under the requirements of FRS 2 'Accounting for Subsidiary Undertakings' pre-dated such commitments.† Under paragraph 26 of FRS 6 'Acquisitions and Mergers', disclosure is required of provisions made by the acquired entity within the twelve months preceding the date of acquisition. **40**

Measurement of identifiable assets and liabilities

Most acquisitions are not made on the basis of individual transactions in assets and liabilities. The acquisition transaction does not itself determine the values attributed to each asset and liability acquired and for this reason companies legislation and accounting standards require a fair value exercise to determine initial carrying amounts of assets and liabilities on an acquisition. **41**

*FRS 3, paragraph 18.

†Under paragraph 45 of FRS 2 the date of acquisition may be indicated by the acquiring entity commencing its direction of the operating and financial policies of the acquired undertaking or by changes in flow of economic benefits.

42   Although the FRS contains specific requirements for determining fair values of different classes of assets and liabilities, the concept of fair value underlying the specific rules is the value at which the asset, or liability, could be exchanged in an arm's length transaction between informed and willing parties.

43   Where similar assets are bought and sold on a readily accessible market, the market price will represent the fair value. Where quoted market prices are not available, market prices can often be estimated, either by independent valuations, or valuation techniques such as discounting estimated future cash flows to their present values. In some cases, where quoted market prices are not available, subsequent sales of acquired assets may provide the most reliable evidence of fair value at the time of the acquisition.

44   Where a fair value is based on a market price, it is important to ensure that such price is appropriate to the circumstances of the acquired business. For example, it may be possible to obtain a price for secondhand plant and machinery of the type used in the business, but the secondhand market may deal in very small volumes; or the items may not be identical in terms of the ability to obtain maintenance or technical support from the manufacturer or for the machinery to be customised to the requirements of the business. In general, unless the acquired business is genuinely able to consider the purchase of secondhand equipment as a viable alternative to purchasing direct from the manufacturer, the fair value of plant and machinery is more appropriately determined from the replacement cost of an equivalent new asset, depreciated where appropriate to reflect its age and condition.

45   The fair value attributed to an asset should not exceed the value the business is able to recover from the asset, either from its disposal or, in the case of a fixed asset, by continuing to use the asset. Where the fair value is based on a market price, the net realisable value will be similar to the fair value, differing only by costs of realisation and the dealer's margin. However, where the fair value is based on depreciated replacement cost or cost of manufacture, the net realisable value and, in the case of a fixed asset, the value in use will also need to be considered.

46   Both net realisable value and value in use at the time of the acquisition are unaffected by the acquirer's intentions for the future use of the asset. Net realisable value represents the amount for which the business would be able to sell the asset, whether or not such sale is intended. Similarly, the value in use of a fixed asset at the time of the acquisition depends, not on the intended use, but on the most profitable possible use of the asset.

Impaired assets

47   Where the replacement cost of an acquired asset is not recoverable in full (owing, for example, to lack of profitability, under-utilisation or obsolescence), the fair value is the estimated recoverable amount. The FRS requires that a valuation at recoverable amount should reflect the condition of the asset on acquisition but not any impairments resulting from subsequent events.

48   Where acquired assets that had not been impaired before acquisition are disposed of after acquisition for a reduced price (for example, as part of a post-acquisition reorganisation of the enlarged group), any losses resulting from their disposal would be treated as post-acquisition losses, ie attributed to the reorganisation, and would not reduce the fair values as at the date of acquisition.

In some cases recoverable amount can be determined only by considering as a whole **49**
a group of assets that are used jointly, rather than by attempting to determine the
recoverable amount of each identifiable asset in that group. Aggregation in such
cases serves to facilitate the attribution of cash flows to the assets that help to
generate them.

Tangible fixed assets

Where reliable market values are obtainable—for example, for quoted investments **50**
and certain types of property—fair value would be based on current market values of
similar assets. As explained in paragraph 44 above, for many types of fixed asset—
for example most plant and machinery, and specialised properties specific to the
business—fair value is represented by gross replacement cost reduced by depreciation
to take account of the age and condition of the asset. Depreciation rates need to
reflect estimated asset lives and residual amounts used by the acquirer for similar
types of asset; otherwise, without there being any change in the asset's use or
intended use, the first post-acquisition profit and loss account would reflect the
adjustment from the previous management's depreciation rate to the acquirer's
depreciation rate.

For certain assets it is not easy to determine current replacement cost; neither is it **51**
possible to estimate the value of the future services that an asset can provide through
its continued use, because of the inherent subjectivity of such a valuation. In such
circumstances the historical cost of the asset updated by the use of price indices may
be the most reliable means of estimating replacement cost. Where prices have not
changed materially it would be acceptable to use a carrying value based on historical
cost as a reasonable proxy for fair value.

Stocks and work-in-progress

Where stocks are replaced by purchasing in a ready market—for example, com- **52**
modities and dealing stocks—to which the acquired entity has access, fair value is
represented by market value. Where there is no ready market for a category of
stocks—for example, most manufactured stocks—fair value is represented by the
current cost to the acquired company of reproducing the stocks.

The FRS requires account to be taken of the way the acquired business purchased or **53**
manufactured the stocks. For example, for a business purchasing in wholesale
markets the replacement cost would be the wholesale price; and the replacement cost
of finished goods of a manufacturer will be the current cost of manufacture, not the
cost of buying in finished goods from another manufacturer. Although this replacement cost takes account of the effects of input price changes during the period the
stocks are held, no addition would be made for unrealised profit that would not
normally be recognised in the acquired entity until the stocks are sold.

The current cost of manufacture for finished goods and work-in-progress would be **54**
based on current standard costs where these are employed. In practice, where there is
a short manufacturing cycle, replacement cost may not be materially different from
historical cost.

For long-term, maturing stocks, replacement cost would be based on market values **55**
if stocks at similar stages of completion are regularly traded in the market. In other
cases, where such market transactions do not occur because either there is no market
or the market is very thin, and where it is difficult to find replacement cost because
replacement would be impossible in the short term, a surrogate for replacement cost

may be found in the historical cost of bringing the stocks to their present location and condition, including an amount representing an interest cost in respect of holding the stock.

56   For long-term contracts, SSAP 9 'Stocks and long-term contracts' requires turnover and cost of sales to be recognised as the contract progresses, and attributable profit to be recognised prudently as it is earned. For this reason, no adjustments to book values would be required to such contracts, other than adjustments that would normally result from assessing the outcome of the contract under SSAP 9, or reflecting the changeover to the acquirer's accounting policies.*

57   In estimating the net realisable value of stocks, an acquirer may reach a judgement about the value of slow-moving or redundant stocks that differs from that of the management of the acquired entity. However, any material write-down of the carrying value of stocks in the acquired entity's books before or at the time of the acquisition would need to be justified by the circumstances of the acquired entity before acquisition. If exceptional profits appear to have been earned on the realisation of stocks after the date of the acquisition, it will be necessary to re-examine the fair values determined on acquisition as required by paragraphs 23–25 of the FRS and, if necessary, to make an adjustment to these values and a corresponding adjustment to goodwill. If, alternatively, the profit is attributable to post-acquisition events it should be disclosed as an exceptional item as required by paragraph 30 of FRS 6.

Quoted investments

58   The fair value of quoted investments will normally be their market price. However, it may be necessary to adjust the market price to allow for short-term fluctuations or, in the case of large holdings, to reflect either a lower realisable value representing the difficulties of disposal or a higher value for a holding representing a substantial voting block.

Monetary assets and liabilities

59   Most short-term monetary assets and liabilities, including trade debtors and creditors, would be recognised at amounts expected to be received or paid on settlement or redemption.

60   The fair values of certain long-term monetary items may, however, be materially different from their book values. One example is where an acquired entity is carrying material amounts of long-term debt at fixed rates that do not reflect current borrowing rates. The fair value will be greater or lower than book value depending on the direction of changes in interest rates since the debt was issued. Another example is a material long-term debtor where the delay in settlement is not compensated by an interest charge reflecting current market rates.

61   The FRS requires monetary items to be stated at fair values where these are materially different from book values. Where the monetary item is a quoted security, its fair value is normally its market price. The fair values of other monetary items may be determined by considering the current terms on which a similar monetary asset or liability could be acquired or assumed, or by discounting to their present values the

---

__Editor's note:__ Account may also need to be taken of Application Note G to FRS 5 to the extent that this may affect the valuation of long-term contracts.

total amounts expected to be received or paid. The choice of interest rate to be applied to long-term borrowings would be affected by current lending rates for an equivalent term, the credit standing of the issuer and the nature of any security. For long-term debtors (after any necessary provisions have been made) the interest rate would be based on current lending rates.

The differences between fair values arrived at by discounting and the total amounts **62** receivable or payable in respect of the relevant items represent discounts or premiums on acquisition that would be dealt with in the financial statements of the acquiring group as interest income or expense—that is, by allocation to accounting periods over the term of the monetary items at a constant rate based on their carrying amounts.

Where debt instruments issued by the acquired company are quoted, market values **63** at the date of acquisition would be used instead of present values. However, in cases where a reduced pre-acquisition market value of an acquired entity's debt reflected the market's perception that it was at risk of being unable to fulfil its repayment obligations, the reduction would not be recognised in the fair value allocation if the debt was expected to be repaid at its full amount.

Contingencies

The value attributed to a contingent asset or liability needs to reflect the best estimate **64** of the likely outcome; otherwise the post-acquisition profit and loss account will reflect the change from the previous management's estimate to the acquirer's estimate, without any related event or change in circumstances. In rare cases where a commitment or a contingent asset is of a kind that is normally assumed or acquired in an arm's length transaction (for example, underwriting commitments), its fair value would reflect the market price for such transactions.

Business sold or held exclusively with a view to subsequent resale

Where the acquisition of a group of companies includes a subsidiary undertaking or **65** a discrete business operation that has been sold, or is expected to be sold, as a single unit within approximately a year of the acquisition it is appropriate to treat the investment in this business as a single asset, and to assign a single fair value to the whole investment rather than assign individual fair values to the various assets and liabilities that are included in the operation to be sold. The asset the group acquires is regarded as the investment in the subsidiary undertaking or business operation, rather than the individual items; and the actual net realised value will normally provide the most reliable evidence of fair value at the date of acquisition. One effect of this treatment is that goodwill is effectively apportioned between the part of the acquired group that is to be kept and the part sold, with the result that no further adjustment to write off the goodwill relating to the business disposed of, to comply with UITF Abstract 3 'Treatment of goodwill on disposal of a business',* would be necessary. Where the effect is material, the net proceeds would be discounted to obtain their present value at the date of acquisition (taking into account any distribution of profits from the business). The principle explained in paragraph 85 below for attributing expenses to the cost of an acquisition would also apply to the costs of disposals.

Where the disposal has not been completed at the time of the first financial state- **66** ments after the acquisition, the fair value is based on the estimated sales proceeds.

*Editor's note: UITF 3 has been superseded by FRS 10 'Goodwill and intangible assets'.

Any initial estimate of fair value would normally be adjusted to actual net realised value within the period allowed for completing the investigation of fair values, with the change being adjusted against goodwill.

67   Such intended disposals would neither have been previously consolidated by the acquirer, nor have formed a continuing part of the activities of the acquiring group. In these circumstances, for an interest in a subsidiary undertaking, companies legislation* permits, and FRS 2 requires, the interest to be recognised as a current asset in the acquirer's consolidated accounts. The results of its operations during the holding period are excluded from the profit and loss account of the acquiring group.

68   The FRS requires the same principles of valuation to be applied to disposals of other business operations that are not subsidiary undertakings. Therefore, for example, the assets of a division held for resale would be shown as a single separately described current asset.

69   In the following circumstances it would be appropriate to estimate separately fair values at the acquisition date and to record a post-acquisition profit or loss on disposal:

(a)   the acquirer has made a material change to the acquired business before disposal;

(b)   specific post-acquisition events occur during the holding period that materially change the fair value of the business from the fair value estimated at the date of acquisition; or

(c)   the disposal is completed at a reduced price for a quick sale.

Pensions and other post-retirement benefits

70   The FRS requires that where an acquired entity sponsors a defined-benefit pension scheme, or a defined-benefit post-retirement scheme other than a pension scheme, the allocation of fair values should include an asset in respect of a surplus in a funded scheme and a liability in respect of a deficiency in a funded scheme or accrued obligations relating to an unfunded scheme.†

71‡   The fair value of the deficiency or surplus should be measured in accordance with the requirements of FRS 17 'Retirement Benefits'. The extent to which a surplus can be recovered should also be determined in accordance with the requirements of FRS 17.

72§   [Withdrawn]

73   The valuation of the pension fund surplus or deficit depends on several assumptions: interest rates, inflation and investment returns; the likely turnover of staff; and future salary increases; and the acquirer would apply its own judgement in determining these assumptions. However, the FRS requires changes in pension or other post-retirement arrangements following an acquisition to be accounted for as post-acquisition items. An example is the cost of improvements to benefits granted to

---

*In Great Britain, the Companies Act 1985, section 229(3)(c); in Northern Ireland, the Companies (Northern Ireland) Order 1986, Article 237(3)(c); and in the Republic of Ireland the European Communities (Companies:Group Accounts) Regulations 1992, Regulation 11(c).

†*Editor's note: The final sentence of this paragraph was deleted by FRS 17 'Retirement benefits'.*

‡*Editor's note: The text was amended by FRS 17 'Retirement benefits'.*

§*Editor's note: Deleted by FRS 17 'Retirement benefits'.*

members of an acquired scheme as part of a policy of harmonising remuneration packages in the enlarged group. This treatment is consistent with accounting for any changes stemming from the acquisition that affect the pension arrangements of the acquirer's own workforce, and has the effect of treating changes in pension arrangements on the same basis as the realignment of any other aspects of remuneration. The cost of post-acquisition changes to pension and other post-retirement arrangements would be dealt with in accordance with the requirements of FRS 17 relating to variations in pension cost.

Deferred taxation

Adjustments to record assets and liabilities of the acquired entity at their fair values are treated in the same way as they would be if they were timing differences arising in the entity's own accounts. For example, a non-monetary asset, such as a building, would be valued on acquisition at its market value. Any tax that would become payable if the asset were sold at that value would be provided for only if, before the acquisition, the acquired entity had entered into a binding agreement to sell the asset and rollover relief was not available.   **74**

There might be deferred tax assets, typically unrelieved tax losses, that were not recognised before the acquisition because there was insufficient evidence that they would be recoverable. The acquisition might make the recovery of the losses sufficiently likely to enable them to be recognised as assets in accordance with the criteria set out in FRS 19 'Deferred tax'. If the losses had arisen in the acquired entity, they would be regarded as contingent assets that had crystallised as a result of the acquisition and hence, consistently with paragraph 37, would be recognised as assets in the fair value exercise. If the losses had arisen in the acquiring group, they would not be assets of the acquired entity and hence would not be recognised in the fair value exercise.   **75**

DETERMINING THE COST OF ACQUISITION

Fair values of the components of the purchase consideration

In order to apply the requirements of the FRS, it is necessary to determine the fair values of the constituent parts of the purchase consideration. The purchase consideration may comprise: **76**

(a)   cash or other monetary items, including the assumption of liabilities by the acquirer;
(b)   capital instruments issued by the acquirer, including shares, debentures, loans and debt instruments, share warrants and other options relating to the securities of the acquirer; or
(c)   non-monetary assets, including securities of another entity.

Cash and other monetary consideration

Where the purchase consideration is in the form of cash or other monetary assets given or liabilities assumed, its fair value is normally readily determinable as the amount paid or payable in respect of the item. When settlement of cash consideration is deferred, fair values are obtained by discounting to their present value the amounts expected to be payable in the future. The appropriate discount rate is the rate at which the acquirer could obtain a similar borrowing, taking into account its credit standing and any security given.   **77**

Capital instruments

78   Where shares (and other capital instruments) issued by the acquirer are quoted on a ready market, the market price on the date of acquisition would normally provide the most reliable measure of fair value. Where control is transferred by a public offer, the relevant date is the date on which the offer or, where there is a series of revised offers, the successful offer becomes unconditional, usually as a result of a sufficient number of acceptances being received. Where, owing to unusual fluctuations, the market price on one particular date is an unreliable measure of fair value, market prices for a reasonable period before the date of acquisition, during which acceptances could be made, would need to be considered.

79   Where securities issued by the acquirer are not quoted or, if they are quoted, the market price is unreliable owing, for example, to the lack of an active market in the quantities involved, it would be necessary to make a valuation of those securities. The fair value would be estimated by taking into account items such as:

(a)   the value of similar securities that are quoted;
(b)   the present value of the future cash flows of the instrument issued;
(c)   any cash alternative to the issue of securities; and
(d)   the value of any underlying security into which there is an option to convert.

Where it is not possible to value the consideration given by any of the above methods, the best estimate of its value may be given by valuing the entity acquired.

Non-monetary consideration

80   Where the purchase consideration takes the form of non-monetary assets, fair values would be determined by reference to market prices, estimated realisable values, independent valuations, or other available evidence.

Contingent consideration

81   The terms of an acquisition may provide that the value of the purchase consideration, which may be payable in cash, shares or other securities at a future date, depends on uncertain future events, such as the future performance of the acquired company. An example is an 'earn-out', where consideration payable to the vendor takes the form of an initial payment, together with further payments based on a multiple of future profits of the acquired company. By its nature, the fair value of such contingent consideration cannot be determined precisely at the date of acquisition. The FRS requires that the cost of acquisition should include a reasonable estimate of its fair value. Where it is not possible to estimate the total amounts payable with any degree of certainty, at least those amounts that are reasonably expected to be payable would be recognised. Initial estimates would be revised as further and more certain information becomes available.

82   Where contingent consideration is to be satisfied by the issue of shares, the amount attributed to that consideration will need to be allocated between equity and liabilities in accordance with FRS 25 '(IAS 32) Financial Instruments: Disclosure and Presentation'.*

83   [Withdrawn]†

Editor's note: Paragraph amended by FRS 25.

†*Editor's note: Paragraph deleted by FRS 25.*

Acquisition agreements may require payments to be made in various forms, for **84** example as non-competition payments or as bonuses to the vendors who continue to work for the acquired company. In such circumstances, it is necessary to determine whether the substance of the agreement is payment for the business acquired, or an expense such as compensation for services or profit sharing. In the first case the expected payments would be accounted for as contingent purchase consideration; in the other case the payments would be treated as expenses of the period to which they relate.

Acquisition expenses

Acquisition expenses to be treated as part of the cost of acquisition include incre- **85** mental costs such as professional fees paid to merchant banks, accountants, legal advisers, valuers and other consultants. Such expenses exclude any allocation of costs that would still have been incurred had the acquisition not been entered into— for example, the costs of maintaining an acquisitions department or management remuneration; such costs would be charged to the profit and loss account as incurred. Expenses of issuing shares and other capital instruments that qualify as issue costs are not added to the cost of acquisition.*

Adoption of FRS 7 by the Board

Financial Reporting Standard 7 – 'Fair Values in Acquisition Accounting' was approved for issue by a vote of seven of the eight members of the Accounting Standards Board. Mr Main dissented. His dissenting view is set out in Appendix IV.

Members of the Accounting Standards Board

Sir David Tweedie   (Chairman)
Allan Cook   (Technical Director)
Robert Bradfield
Ian Brindle
Michael Garner
Raymond Hinton
Donald Main
Graham Stacy

*Editor's note: Paragraph amended by FRS 25.

Appendix I
Note on legal requirements

GREAT BRITAIN

References are to the Companies Act 1985

1   The Companies Act describes the acquisition method of accounting in Schedule 4A paragraph 9:

   (a)   The identifiable assets and liabilities of the undertaking acquired shall be included in the consolidated balance sheet at their fair values as at the date of acquisition. The 'identifiable' assets or liabilities of the undertaking acquired mean the assets or liabilities that are capable of being disposed of or discharged separately, without disposing of a business of the undertaking (Schedule 4A paragraph 9(2)).

   (b)   The income and expenditure of the undertaking acquired shall be brought into the group accounts only as from the date of the acquisition (Schedule 4A paragraph 9(3)).

   (c)   There shall be set off against the acquisition cost of the interest in the shares of the undertaking held by the parent company and its subsidiary undertakings the interest of the parent company and its subsidiary undertakings in the adjusted capital and reserves of the undertaking acquired. The resulting amount if positive shall be treated as goodwill, and if negative as a negative consolidation difference (Schedule 4A paragraph 9(4)-(5)).

   (d)   The 'acquisition cost' is defined as the amount of any cash consideration and the fair value of any other consideration, together with such amount (if any) in respect of fees and other expenses of the acquisition as the company may determine; and 'the adjusted capital and reserves' of the undertaking acquired are defined as the capital and reserves at the date of the acquisition after adjusting the identifiable assets and liabilities of the undertaking to fair values as at that date (Schedule 4A paragraph 9(4)).

Share premium and merger relief

2   Section 130(1) of the Act provides that if a company issues shares at a premium, whether for cash or otherwise, a sum equal to the aggregate amount or value of the premiums on those shares should be transferred to an account called the share premium account. The provisions of the Act relating to the reduction of a company's share capital apply, with exceptions, as if the share premium account were part of its paid-up share capital.

3   Limited relief from the above ('merger relief') is given by sections 131-134.

4   Section 131 provides, inter alia, that, subject to specified conditions, where an issuing company has secured at least a 90 per cent equity holding in another company, section 130 does not apply to the premium on shares issued in the transaction that takes the holding in that other company to at least 90 per cent.

5   Section 133(1) provides that the premium on any shares to which the relief in sections 131 and 132 applies may also be disregarded in determining the amount at which any shares or other consideration provided for the shares issued is to be included in the offeror company's balance sheet.

Share premium and fair value

Shares forming part of the consideration are valued at their fair value for the pur- **6**
poses of computing acquisition cost and goodwill under paragraph 9(4) of Schedule
4A. By contrast, the value of the share premiums arising on the shares issued, for the
purposes of section 130, is based on the value to the issuing company of the consideration it has received. Where these values are different, or where (if the merger
relief provisions apply) the premiums are disregarded, the cost of investment in the
parent company's books will be different from the cost of acquisition for the purposes of paragraph 9(4). In such circumstances the difference should form a separate
element of consolidated reserves, and does not form part of goodwill.

NORTHERN IRELAND

The legal requirements in Northern Ireland are very similar to those in Great Britain. **7**
The following table shows the references to the Companies (Northern Ireland) Order
1986 that correspond to the legal references in paragraphs 1-6 above.

Great Britain	Northern Ireland
Schedule 4A paragraph 9	Schedule 4A paragraph 9
Sections 130-134	Articles 140-144

REPUBLIC OF IRELAND

The following table shows the references to the European Communities (Companies: **8**
Group Accounts) Regulations 1992 and the Companies Act 1963 that correspond to
the legal references in paragraphs 1-6 above.

Great Britain	Republic of Ireland
Schedule 4A paragraph 9	Regulation 19
Section 130	Companies Act 1963 section 62
Sections 131–134	No equivalent

Appendix II
Compliance with International Accounting Standards

The International Accounting Standards Committee (IASC) has issued a revised standard IAS 22 'Business Combinations'.* The principal areas where the revised IAS 22 and the FRS are at variance† are as follows. First, the revised IAS 22 requires that fair values of identifiable assets and liabilities acquired in an acquisition should be determined by reference to their intended use by the acquirer. The FRS requires the identifiable assets and liabilities to be recorded at their fair values as at the date of acquisition. Secondly, certain adjustments that would be treated as fair value adjustments under the revised IAS 22, for example those for additional liabilities recognised to reflect an acquirer's different intentions regarding an acquisition, would be accounted for as post-acquisition items under the FRS.

Editor's note: IAS 22 has now been replaced by IFRS 3. This potentially requires the identification of a greater number of intangible assets than FRS 7.

†*The Board's reasons for adopting proposals that differ from those of the IASC's revised IAS 22 are set out in Appendix III, at paragraphs 15-16 and 27-28.*

Appendix III
The development of the FRS

GENERAL AND HISTORY

The principle of attributing fair values in consolidated financial statements to the 1 assets and liabilities of newly acquired subsidiaries has been recognised in UK accounting standards for many years and, since 1989, in companies legislation.

SSAP 14

SSAP 14 'Group accounts', which was published in 1978, required the purchase 2 consideration for the acquisition of a subsidiary to be allocated between the underlying net tangible and intangible assets other than goodwill on the basis of the fair value to the acquiring company. The standard gave no guidance on how to determine fair values.

SSAP 22

SSAP 22 'Accounting for goodwill', issued in 1984, gave limited guidance on how to 3 identify the assets and liabilities of an acquired business that should be regarded as separable from the purchased goodwill arising on the acquisition. It also sanctioned the practice that had evolved of adjusting the fair values ascribed to the separable net assets acquired to include provisions for anticipated future losses or costs of reorganisation. Such provisions were permitted to be recognised in the fair value exercise if the future losses or costs were taken into account in arriving at the purchase price.

Subsequently, however, concern among users began to emerge over the extent to 4 which the use of provisions could potentially be hidden or abused. The Accounting Standards Committee (ASC) took action to address these concerns by amending SSAP 22 to include some specific disclosure requirements relating to the fair value exercise. The revised SSAP 22, published in 1989, required disclosure of adjustments made to the book values of the assets and liabilities of an acquired business, analysed into revaluations and provisions. It also required disclosure of movements on provisions related to acquisitions, analysed into the amounts used and the amounts released unused or applied for another purpose. At the same time as SSAP 22 was being amended, the ASC was developing an accounting standard on fair value accounting (see paragraph 6 below).*

Companies Act 1989

The Companies Act 1989 introduced a new Schedule 4A to the Companies Act 1985, 5 which set out rules regarding the form and content of consolidated financial statements. The Act requires that, in accounting for the acquisition of a subsidiary, the subsidiary's identifiable assets and liabilities must be included in the consolidated balance sheet at their fair values as at the date of acquisition. There is no guidance in the Act on how to determine the fair values of assets and liabilities acquired.

---

*Editor's note: SSAP 22 has been replaced by FRS 10 'Goodwill and Intangible Assets'.

ED 53

6   The ASC issued a discussion paper in 1988, followed in 1990 by an exposure draft, ED 53 'Fair value in the context of acquisition accounting'. ED 53 contained proposals for determining fair values of assets and liabilities identified in an acquisition, for dealing with anticipated reorganisation costs and for valuing the consideration given for an acquisition.

7   ED 53 proposed that fair values should be determined from the perspective of the acquiring company, based on circumstances at the date of acquisition. Its proposals for dealing with acquisition provisions did not permit provision to be made for future trading losses of acquired businesses but did, however, continue to permit provisions for reorganisation costs to be made as fair value adjustments if there was a clearly defined programme of reorganisation that had been costed in reasonable detail and there was evidence that the acquirer took account of the plans and costs in formulating the offer.

ASB Discussion Paper

8   In April 1993, the Board published a Discussion Paper, 'Fair values in acquisition accounting'. The Board adopted much of the work of the ASC in framing its proposals, but concluded that a different approach to the recognition of liabilities was necessary to address a number of issues, including those raised in responses to ED 53. A theme common to several of the commentators' responses had been that the basic principles underlying ED 53's approach had not been properly developed and in particular that the exposure draft had failed to rationalise its conclusions on key issues such as the recognition of reorganisation and future loss provisions.

9   The Discussion Paper contained proposals that attempted to draw a clear distinction of principle between recording the elements of the purchase transaction, including accounting for the pre-acquisition assets and liabilities of the acquired business, and the items that should fall into the post-acquisition period. The proposals would have precluded provisions both for future losses in acquired businesses and, as a departure from ED 53, for reorganisation costs following an acquisition from being included as fair value adjustments. The principal reasons for proposing such a radical change to existing practices were threefold:

(a)   the proposals for dealing with the recognition of anticipated future losses and reorganisation costs were consistent with the Board's draft Statement of Principles regarding the recognition of liabilities;

(b)   the proposals were consistent with the philosophy behind the 'information set' approach in FRS 3 'Reporting Financial Performance' in respect of presenting the financial effects of post-acquisition activities, including reorganisation of acquired businesses;

(c)   to meet users' concerns on perceived scope for abuse; it was doubtful whether an alternative approach of developing a standard founded on enhanced disclosure of acquisition provisions, supplemented by specific and probably arbitrary rules on cut-off between pre- and post- acquisition items would prove as effective in the long term as an approach built on the Board's draft Statement of Principles.

FRED 7 was published in December 1993. It retained the essential features of the **10** proposals in the Discussion Paper, while refining and clarifying them to take account of the comments received.

Views on the proposal in the Discussion Paper that all costs of reorganising acquired **11** businesses should be treated as charges to post-acquisition profits had been divided, with a small majority in favour of the proposed treatment. Support had been strongest among user groups, who generally welcomed the transparency of the proposals in providing a proper basis for analysing the financial consequences of acquisition activities. Opposition had been voiced by many—although by no means all—preparers, who argued that the proposals belied the reality of the way acquisitions are handled because they failed to reflect the fact that the cost of an acquisition and subsequent, directly related expenditure are the product of a single investment decision. As an example, many commentators had argued that the costs incurred in the immediate post-acquisition period to implement a business plan to reorganise an acquisition were probably discrete and significant and were an integral part of the investment appraisal process; such costs, they contended, should not be reported in the group's trading results. The purchase and integration of a subsidiary, in their eyes, was in substance a single capital transaction, despite the fact that some elements might be revenue in form.

The Board set out in FRED 7 the basis for its conclusions on the proposed treatment of **12** post-acquisition reorganisation costs. The main arguments, which are equally applicable to the FRS, are summarised as follows.

(a) The proposals were made in the context of the fundamental changes to the disclosure of financial performance that were introduced by FRS 3. If a company incurs material revenue expenditure to improve future profitability, the costs are normally charged to the profit and loss account. FRS 3 and the Operating and Financial Review both provide the facility for proper disclosure and explanation of the resulting volatility in the reported results. The Board believed that all such expenditure should be treated similarly, whether it related to a reorganisation following an acquisition or to a reorganisation of an ongoing business. It would be left to investment analysis to assess the benefit to an entity of a reorganisation.

(b) The proposals in respect of the recognition of liabilities were consistent with the Board's draft Statement of Principles. The approach rested on whether there was an obligation in the acquired entity at the acquisition date. The Board recognised that, where an acquisition was made, the acquirer might have taken into account additional costs to reorganise the operations of the combining entities and such costs might have been factored into the investment decision and the amount of purchase consideration to be offered. However, it did not follow that these costs should be deemed to increase the liabilities of the acquired entity existing at the acquisition date.

(c) The proposals, which required reorganisations related to acquisitions to be treated on the same footing as any other reorganisations, set out principles that avoided the need to define cutoff points between items to be included in the fair value exercise and items to be recognised in the post-acquisition period, which would have been difficult to achieve. Framing an alternative approach on the basis of the acquirer's intentions at the time of the acquisition would, in the Board's opinion, have led to artificial distinctions being drawn not only between the treatment of reorganisations affecting the acquired business and consequential changes in the existing business of the acquirer, but also between reorganisations that were planned at the time of acquisition and those that occurred later.

13   Many commentators had argued that the 'acquirer's perspective' should be retained as a principle for attributing fair values to the assets and liabilities acquired. They had contended that because the purchase consideration was based on the acquirer's assessment of the fair value of the acquired entity and its underlying assets and liabilities, it followed that the allocation of the purchase consideration should also be based on the acquirer's perspective.

14   The Board is of the view that under its draft Statement of Principles, management intent is not a sufficient basis for recognising changes to an entity's assets and liabilities. It is events, not intentions for future actions, that increase or decrease an entity's assets or liabilities. When intentions are translated into actions that commit the entity to particular courses of action, the accounting should then reflect any obligations or changes in assets that arise from those actions. In relation to acquisition accounting, the Board concluded that events of a post-acquisition period that resulted in the recognition of additional liabilities or the impairment of existing assets of an acquired entity should be reported as events of that period rather than of the pre-acquisition period.

15   Some commentators expressed concern that the proposals for precluding any reorganisation provisions as fair value adjustments were more restrictive than the requirements in the USA or International Accounting Standards. They urged the Board to go no further than to achieve consistency with US GAAP which, although not permitting provisions for future losses of acquired companies to be recognised as fair value adjustments, would allow adjustments to be made to take account of management intentions in the valuation of acquired assets, including, for example, provisions in respect of the intended closure of facilities in the acquired entity that are duplicated in the enlarged group.

16   In developing FRED 7, the Board took into account the fact that US GAAP in this area considerably pre-dates the development of the present framework of general accounting concepts in the USA, as well as the IASC framework and the UK draft Statement of Principles, which are similar. The Board took the view that its proposals were consistent with the conceptual frameworks that had been developed elsewhere and, in particular, noted that the principle of accounting for obligations rather than management intentions was gaining greater acceptance internationally.

MATTERS CONSIDERED IN THE LIGHT OF RESPONSES TO FRED 7

17   The following paragraphs refer to comments made by respondents to FRED 7, and explain with reasons the changes the Board has made to the proposals of the FRED or the Board's reasons for rejecting arguments for changes. Individual Board members gave greater weight to some factors than to others.

Reorganisation provisions

18   FRED 7 proposed that the identifiable assets and liabilities recognised in the fair value exercise should be those of the acquired entity that existed at the date of acquisition, and should include provisions neither for future operating losses nor for reorganisation and integration costs expected to be incurred as a result of the acquisition.

This proposal met with outright support from institutional investors, analysts and   **19**
users of accounts; substantial support from accountancy firms and accountancy
bodies; and strong, though not unanimous, opposition from preparers of accounts.

The main arguments raised by respondents opposed to the proposals in the FRED are   **20**
summarised below, together with the Board's response to the arguments.

Commercial reality

It was argued that the FRED ignored the commercial reality of the transaction, namely   **21**
that the acquirer's management takes the reorganisation and integration costs into
account in its 'project plan' for the acquisition, and regards these costs as part of the
'investment'; they should therefore be treated as akin to additional consideration.
Furthermore, it was argued, under the FRED's proposals the acquisition of a poorly
organised business that is then reorganised by the acquirer gives a different
accounting result from the acquisition of an equivalent but well-organised business
that is not in need of reorganisation.

Of those who preferred the status quo on reorganisation provisions, most agreed that   **22**
the existing situation was unsatisfactory and that tighter definitions and controls
were needed; in particular, there was little support for continuing to allow provisions
to be made for future losses of the acquired business, and most agreed that there
should be rules to restrict the use of reorganisation provisions made as fair value
adjustments.

The Board has carefully reconsidered the arguments against its proposals, which   **23**
reiterated the arguments raised by a majority of preparers against the proposals in
the Discussion Paper. The Board recognises the strength of feeling held in some
quarters against this aspect of its proposals, which changes long-standing accounting
practice. It has also balanced these views with those of user and other groups who
supported the proposals. While not discounting the reasons or rationale underlying
the position of those opposed to its proposals, the Board decided that it should
develop an FRS on the basis of the proposals in FRED 7. It believes that this FRS will
lead to clearer and more consistent reporting than has been the case under existing
practices. Furthermore, the Board remains of the view that the approach adopted in
the FRS is more soundly based on principle than would be an alternative approach
that sought to improve existing standards by addressing disclosure issues and
developing detailed rules that had the principal objective of constraining reorganisation provisions solely in order to prevent abuse.

Without repeating all the arguments underlying the Board's position as set out in   **24**
FRED 7, the Board reaffirms that the principles in the FRS for determining the fair
values of the assets and liabilities of the acquired entity adhere closely to the Board's
draft Statement of Principles in respect of the recognition of assets and liabilities, and
to the philosophy behind FRS 3 (complemented by the Operating and Financial
Review) for reporting financial performance and other gains and losses.

The FRS, therefore, follows the principle (as set out in the draft Statement of Prin-   **25**
ciples) that identifiable liabilities are limited to obligations of the acquired entity that
existed at the date of acquisition and, consequently, other changes should fall into
the post-acquisition period. The Board recognises that rationalisation expenditures,
whether to improve or to integrate part of the business following an acquisition, are
undertaken because they are expected to result in lasting and long-term benefits.
However, in the Board's view this does not justify the effective capitalisation of that

expenditure as goodwill, irrespective of whether it was planned at the time of the acquisition or whether the plans were formulated after the acquisition took place.

26   The Board also takes the view that the acquisition of a well-organised company is a different transaction from the acquisition of a company in need of reorganisation, and there is no reason why the two transactions should result in the same accounting outcome. In one case the acquirer is reporting the acquisition of a business whose previous management ran it efficiently; in the other, the acquirer is reporting the acquisition of a less efficient business and the subsequent expenditure intended to improve it. In the first case, the success of the business was apparent before the acquirer agreed to buy it; in the second, the value of the reorganisation expenditure will be judged subsequently by the increase in profitability of the acquired business that is achieved.

International competitiveness and international GAAP

27   It was suggested by some respondents that the FRED's approach, by being stricter in some respects than the corresponding provisions of accounting standards in other countries (in particular, US GAAP and the International Accounting Standard) would damage the competitiveness of UK companies. Conversely, others have argued that the existing flexible accounting practices in the UK have encouraged UK companies to overpay for acquisitions compared with foreign companies. The Board takes the view that accounting standards should be neutral as to economic effect. Therefore, the FRS seeks to provide greater clarity in the reporting of acquisition activities. The more transparent accounting resulting from the FRS and from other accounting reforms that the Board has undertaken should contribute to sound economic decisions.

28   The Board carefully considered the international harmonisation issue during the development of FRED 7. As noted in paragraph 16 above, the Board believes that the FRS is consistent with the conceptual frameworks that have been adopted by various standard-setting bodies.

'Socio-economic' consequences

29   Some respondents also claimed that acquirers will be less willing to acquire companies in need of reorganisation, thus allowing inefficient management to remain and preventing rationalisation that is beneficial to the economy as a whole. However, the Board notes that the cash flow effect of a transaction is the same whichever accounting treatment is adopted.

Understandability of financial statements

30   Several preparers of accounts suggested that the reporting of acquisitions would be more difficult to understand, because the full cost to the acquirer will not be clear and the post-acquisition results will be distorted by reorganisation and integration costs. However, users who responded were unanimous that the FRED's proposals would provide them with clearer and more informative information on acquisitions.

31   In response to those commentators who argued that the financial statements should be capable of showing the full cost of the investment in an acquisition, including the intended costs of post-acquisition reorganisation, the FRS has introduced a recommendation that the planned reorganisation expenditure relating to the acquisition should be disclosed in the notes to the financial statements (see paragraph 40 below).

Anti-avoidance measures

There was concern that the requirements of the FRS could be circumvented by col- **32** lusion between the vendor and the acquirer, resulting for example in the vendor entering into obligations to restructure the business on the instructions of the acquirer before the formal transfer of control.

The Discussion Paper had proposed that any reorganisation provisions made by the **33** vendor in the six months before the acquisition should be treated as post-acquisition; however, this was generally regarded as unnecessarily draconian and was omitted from the FRED.

The FRS deals with the issue in three ways. First, it emphasises that provisions should **34** be included in the balance sheet of the acquired company at the date of acquisition only if that entity had a commitment from which it could not realistically withdraw whether or not the acquisition had been completed. Secondly, it draws attention to the possibility that the effective transfer of control took place at an earlier date than the formal transfer of shares. Thirdly, there is an additional disclosure requirement (included in FRS 6) for any provisions for reorganisation made by the acquired company within 12 months before the date of acquisition to be shown separately in the 'fair value table'.

Conclusion

The Board gave careful consideration to the arguments of those opposed to the **35** proposals in the FRED, and acknowledged the strength of feeling particularly among many preparers of accounts. However, it concluded that the arguments put forward were essentially those it had already addressed in coming to its initial views expressed in the Discussion Paper and FRED 7. Moreover, where the arguments concern the understandability of financial statements, due regard must be given to the views of the professional users of accounts—in particular, the institutional investors and analysts, who were fully in support of the proposals.

Other issues

'Acquirer's perspective'

Several respondents (including both some of those who supported the FRED's **36** approach to reorganisation provisions as well as some of those who opposed it) argued that the fair values should be determined from the 'acquirer's perspective'. However, the Board took the view that this term had no single clear meaning, and might be interpreted to indicate that fair values should take into account the decisions of the acquirer taken after the acquisition. For this reason, the Board has avoided using the term in the FRS, but has added more specific descriptions of the extent to which the acquirer's estimates and perceptions are taken into account in determining fair values. The concept of fair value underlying these specific rules remains, however, the value at which the asset, or liability, could be exchanged in an arm's length transaction between informed and willing parties. This concept is independent of the particular circumstances of either the acquirer or the acquired business.

Disclosure of provisions for reorganisation costs

37   Several respondents were concerned that, if reorganisation and similar costs relating to an acquisition were reported in the profit and loss account in accordance with the provisions of FRS 3, such costs might be reported as a deduction from the results of acquisitions, or as part of continuing activities; or, if they related to a fundamental reorganisation of the acquiring entity, as an exceptional item outside operating profit. Users might therefore find it difficult to ascertain the total costs relating to acquisitions. Instead, they proposed that a new category of exceptional item should be defined, to include all costs of reorganisation, restructuring and integration relating to an acquisition, that would not form part of operating profit.

38   The Board concluded that this alternative proposal would confuse different kinds of costs relating to acquisitions, some of which might properly be excluded from operating profit but others of which were just as much an operating cost as the costs of routinely reorganising an existing part of the business. Furthermore, the introduction of a new class of exceptional item would lead to considerable difficulties of definition, as in many cases it was difficult to draw a clear distinction between costs relating to the acquisition, and similar costs relating to the acquirer's existing business that might well still have been incurred had the acquisition not taken place.

39   The Board therefore decided against introducing a new class of exceptional item. FRS 6, which now includes all disclosure requirements relating to acquisitions, sets out in paragraph 86 how the requirements of FRS 3 apply to costs relating to acquisitions.

40   In addition, paragraph 87 of FRS 6 suggests that management may wish to show, in a note to the financial statements, the total expenditure announced in relation to reorganisation and integration of acquisitions, together with the expenditures charged in the profit and loss account in the period and the further amount expected to be incurred. This would provide users with a clear statement of the total costs involved with the acquisition, and companies would be able to add what further explanation and discussion of the figures they think appropriate.

Pension surpluses

41   The FRED proposed that an actuarial surplus or deficit on a pension scheme operated by the acquired company should be recognised as an asset or liability on acquisition. Many respondents thought it imprudent to carry such a surplus as an asset, as it was often uncertain whether it could be realised. They therefore proposed that, whilst provision should still be made for a deficit, a surplus should not be recognised as an asset.

42   The Board has reconsidered the issue, and concluded that, although recognition of a surplus is consistent with the principles on which the FRS is based, it is important that the fair value attributed to such a surplus is justified. The FRS therefore requires the fair value of a surplus to be determined taking into account the extent to which, and timescale over which, the surplus is reasonably expected to be realised, normally in the form of reductions in future contributions This requirement was amended by FRS 17 so that a surplus is recognised to the extent that it can be recovered through reduced contributions or through refunds from the scheme.

43   The Board is currently reviewing the existing accounting standard on pension costs, SSAP 24*. However, the Board decided that to omit reference to pension surpluses and

*SSAP 24 was superseded by FRS 17.

deficits in the FRS, or to require fair values to be based on the assets or liabilities recognised by the acquired company in its own accounts under SSAP 24, might result in the omission of significant assets and liabilities and subsequent misstatement of profits of the enlarged group.

Acquisition expenses

The FRED proposed that the amount of incidental expenses that fall to be treated as **44** an addition to the cost of acquisition should be restricted to incremental costs that would not have been incurred had the acquisition not taken place, and did not permit the capitalisation of internal costs even where they might be directly related to the acquisition. This proposal was consistent with the revised IAS 22 and US GAAP, and took a deliberately restrictive view to avoid the danger of overstating the cost of acquisition.

An alternative view is that the incremental cost approach is anomalous where the **45** equivalent services, such as legal advice or acquisition search and investigation services, are provided by in-house departments rather than by external advisers or consultants.

There was substantial support from respondents for each view. The Board concluded **46** that the difficulty of defining 'incremental' for in-house facilities might lead to excessive costs being capitalised, with the resulting overstatement of profits. This outweighed the possible anomalies that might arise. The proposals in the FRED have accordingly been carried through to the FRS.

Discounting

The FRED proposed that monetary assets and liabilities should be discounted to **47** present value where they were materially different from nominal amounts. Although this was supported, a substantial minority of respondents were concerned over the introduction of discounting on a piecemeal basis, applying only to assets and liabilities of an acquisition, rather than as part of a more general application of discounting to all assets and liabilities.

The Board has reaffirmed its view that monetary assets and liabilities acquired in an **48** acquisition should be included at their fair value at the time of the acquisition; this fair value will depend on the estimated amounts and timing of payments, and, in the case of long-term items not bearing interest at current market rates, may be materially different from their face value or nominal value. Significant distortions to reported profits may arise if such items are not included at their fair value. Discounting is an established and widely used valuation technique, and is one method of arriving at an estimate of fair value. The Board notes that this treatment is also consistent with the revised IAS 22 and with US GAAP.

Appendix IV
Dissenting view

1   Mr Main dissents from the FRS because of its treatment of the costs an acquiring company incurs to convert an acquired entity into the business unit it envisaged when making the acquisition. He was content at the exposure draft stage to let the proposal go forward in order to elicit a public response. However, he has found his concern reinforced by comments received and therefore feels unable to vote for the FRS.

2   Mr Main believes that it is very rare for a company to acquire another without intending to make changes to the acquired business to enable it to operate efficiently. Such changes may include, on the one hand, investment in, and reorganisation of, the assets being acquired to enable products or services to be provided efficiently, and, on the other hand, reductions of excessive manpower, buildings or equipment to enable an adequate profit to be earned.

3   Mr Main believes that the need for such changes and the likely cost of executing them are invariably known to the acquirer at the time the acquisition is made, and that the normal practice of management when considering a proposed acquisition for approval is to aggregate the acquisition price with these costs of bringing the acquired entity into a state acceptable to the buyer, in order to arrive at the investment total against which the expected earnings are judged.

4   The requirements of the FRS will prevent a company from recognising in the financial statements at the time of acquisition the costs of the intended changes. It is only when such costs are committed irrevocably that they are to be included in the financial statements, and even then, to the extent that these costs are not capital expenditure, they cannot be included as part of the investment cost of the acquisition.

5   For these reasons the financial statements will, in his view, be misleading and fail to provide accountability for the transactions that have taken place.

6   Mr Main supports the view expressed by many commentators on the Discussion Paper and exposure draft, as set out in paragraphs 11 and 21 of 'The development of the FRS' (Appendix III), that the costs of an acquisition and subsequent directly related expenditure are the product of a single investment decision; and that the purchase and integration of a subsidiary are in substance a single capital transaction. He believes that the opposition to this view by certain commentators reflected less an endorsement of the principles underlying the FRS than a reaction to perceived abuses in previous practice, including the making of excessive acquisition provisions to cover future trading losses and types of expenditure whose relationship to the acquisition was remote. He would summarise the responses to the exposure draft on this point as follows:

(a) from preparers of accounts: overwhelming opposition;

(b) from users: acceptance, because they want to know the amount of post-acquisition provisions (which he considers to be a valid point), but a view that they would ignore the amounts charged against profits (indicating that they do not regard such charges as a proper reduction of profit);

(c) from auditors: acceptance, because it can be very difficult at times to pass judgement on directors' decisions as to the proper capital provision for post-acquisition costs.

Mr Main believes that the concerns over past abuses could be met, without over-turning long-standing practice, by a standard that provided a stricter definition of what costs should be permitted to be included in acquisition provisions, together with more detailed note disclosure of the provisions made. Provisions would be restricted to costs to be incurred within twelve months of the acquisition, and would exclude any costs relating to the acquiring entity's own activities. Provisions for future losses would also be prohibited. Notes to the financial statements would be required to disclose the separate elements of the provisions involved and the actual expenditure subsequently charged against the provisions. Surplus provisions would be required to be adjusted against goodwill rather than be released to the profit and loss account. He believes that the disclosure requirements in the related FRS 6 would provide sufficient information on the effects of an acquisition without the need for the radical change in practice introduced in FRS 7   **7**

Mr Main believes that his alternative would ensure that: **8**

(a)   the total cost of the acquisition investment decision would be reflected clearly in the financial statements;
(b)   accountability could be measured; and
(c)   the potential for abuse would be removed and auditors would have a clear standard against which the contents of the provision could be judged.

Financial Reporting Standard 8 is set out in paragraphs 1–7.

The Statement of Standard Accounting Practice set out in paragraphs 3–7 should be read in the context of the Objective as stated in paragraph 1 and the definitions set out in paragraph 2 and also of the Foreword to Accounting Standards and the Statement of Principles for Financial Reporting currently in issue.

The Explanation set out in paragraphs 8–23 shall be regarded as part of the Statement of Standard Accounting Practice insofar as it assists in interpreting that statement.

Appendix IV 'The development of the FRS' reviews considerations and arguments that were thought significant by members of the Board in reaching the conclusions on FRS 8.

[FRS 8]
Related party disclosures

(Issued October 1995)

Contents

Related party disclosures

Summary

a   Financial Reporting Standard 8 'Related Party Disclosures' requires the disclosure of:

   (i)   information on related party transactions and (ii)the name of the party controlling the reporting entity and, if different, that of the ultimate controlling party whether or not any transactions between the reporting entity and those parties have taken place.

   Aggregated disclosures are allowed subject to certain restrictions.

b   Two or more parties are related parties when at any time during the financial period:(i)one party has direct or indirect control of the other party; or (ii)the parties are subject to common control from the same source; or (iii)one party has influence over the financial and operating policies of the other party to an extent that that other party might be inhibited from pursuing at all times its own separate interests; or (iv)the parties, in entering a transaction, are subject to influence from the same source to such an extent that one of the parties to the transaction has subordinated its own separate interests.

c   No disclosure is required in consolidated financial statements of intragroup transactions and balances eliminated on consolidation. A parent undertaking is not required to provide related party disclosures in its own financial statements when those statements are presented with consolidated financial statements of its group.

d   Disclosure is not required in the financial statements of subsidiary undertakings, 90 per cent or more of whose voting rights are controlled within the group, of transactions with entities that are part of the group or investees of the group qualifying as related parties provided that the consolidated financial statements in which that subsidiary is included are publicly available.

Financial Reporting Standard 8

Objective

1   The objective of this FRS is to ensure that financial statements contain the disclosures necessary to draw attention to the possibility that the reported financial position and results may have been affected by the existence of related parties and by material transactions with them.

Definitions

2   The following definitions shall apply in this FRS and in particular in the Statement of Standard Accounting Practice set out in paragraphs 3-7.

2.1 Close family:-

Close members of the family of an individual are those family members, or members of the same household, who may be expected to influence, or be influenced by, that person in their dealings with the reporting entity.

2.2 Control:-

The ability to direct the financial and operating policies of an entity with a view to gaining economic benefits from its activities.

2.3 Key management:-

Those persons in senior positions having authority or responsibility for directing or controlling the major activities and resources of the reporting entity.

2.4 Persons acting in concert:-

Persons who, pursuant to an agreement or understanding (whether formal or informal), actively co-operate, whether by the ownership by any of them of shares in an undertaking or otherwise, to exercise control or influence* over that undertaking.

2.5 Related parties:-

(a) Two or more parties are related parties when at any time during the financial period:

    (i) one party has direct or indirect control of the other party; or

    (ii) the parties are subject to common control from the same source; or

    (iii) one party has influence over the financial and operating policies of the other party to an extent that that other party might be inhibited from pursuing at all times its own separate interests; or

    (iv) the parties, in entering a transaction, are subject to influence from the same source to such an extent that one of the parties to the transaction has subordinated its own separate interests.

(b) For the avoidance of doubt, the following are related parties of the reporting entity:

    (i) its ultimate and intermediate parent undertakings, subsidiary undertakings, and fellow subsidiary undertakings;

    (ii) its associates and joint ventures;

    (iii) the investor or venturer in respect of which the reporting entity is an associate or a joint venture;

    (iv) directors† of the reporting entity and the directors of its ultimate and intermediate parent undertakings; and

    (v) pension funds for the benefit of employees of the reporting entity or of any entity that is a related party of the reporting entity;

(c) and the following are presumed to be related parties of the reporting entity unless it can be demonstrated that neither party has influenced the financial and

---

**in terms of paragraph 2.5 (a) (iii).*

†*Directors include shadow directors, which are defined in companies legislation (see Appendix I) as persons in accordance with whose directions or instructions the directors of the company are accustomed to act.*

operating policies of the other in such a way as to inhibit the pursuit of separate interests:

    (i)   the key management of the reporting entity and the key management of its parent undertaking or undertakings;

    (ii)   a person owning or able to exercise control over 20 per cent or more of the voting rights of the reporting entity, whether directly or through nominees;

    (iii) each person acting in concert in such a way as to be able to exercise control or influence* over the reporting entity; and

    (iv) an entity managing or managed by the reporting entity under a management contract.

(d)   Additionally, because of their relationship with certain parties that are, or are presumed to be, related parties of the reporting entity, the following are also presumed to be related parties of the reporting entity:

    (i)   members of the close family of any individual falling under parties mentioned in (a)-(c) above; and

    (ii)   partnerships, companies, trusts or other entities in which any individual or member of the close family in (a)-(c) above has a controlling interest.

Sub-paragraphs (b), (c) and (d) are not intended to be an exhaustive list of related parties.

2.6 Related party transaction:-

The transfer of assets or liabilities or the performance of services by, to or for a related party irrespective of whether a price is charged.

Statement of Standard Accounting Practice

SCOPE

3   Financial Reporting Standard 8 applies to all financial statements that are intended to give a true and fair view of a reporting entity's financial position and profit or loss (or income and expenditure) for a period. The FRS does not, however, require disclosure:

(a)   in consolidated financial statements, of any transactions or balances between group entities that have been eliminated on consolidation;

(b)   in a parent's own financial statements when those statements are presented together with its consolidated financial statements;

(c)   in the financial statements of subsidiary undertakings, 90 per cent or more of whose voting rights are controlled within the group, of transactions with entities that are part of the group or investees of the group qualifying as related parties, provided that the consolidated financial statements in which that subsidiary is included are publicly available;

(d)   of pension contributions paid to a pension fund; and

(e)   of emoluments in respect of services as an employee of the reporting entity.

Reporting entities taking advantage of the exemption in (c) above are required to state that fact.

---

in terms of paragraph 2.5 (a) (iii).

The FRS does not require disclosure of the relationship and transactions between the **4** reporting entity and the parties listed in (a)-(d) below simply as a result of their role as:

(a) providers of finance in the course of their business in that regard;
(b) utility companies;
(c) government departments and their sponsored bodies,

even though they may circumscribe the freedom of action of an entity or participate in its decision-making process; and

(d) a customer, supplier, franchiser, distributor or general agent with whom an entity transacts a significant volume of business.

APPLICATION TO SMALLER ENTITIES

Reporting entities applying the Financial Reporting Standard for Smaller Entities **4A** currently applicable are exempt from this accounting standard.

DISCLOSURE OF CONTROL

When the reporting entity is controlled by another party, there should be disclosure **5** of the related party relationship and the name of that party and, if different, that of the ultimate controlling party. If the controlling party or ultimate controlling party of the reporting entity is not known, that fact should be disclosed. This information should be disclosed irrespective of whether any transactions have taken place between the controlling parties and the reporting entity.

DISCLOSURE OF TRANSACTIONS AND BALANCES

Financial statements should disclose material transactions undertaken by the **6** reporting entity with a related party. Disclosure should be made irrespective of whether a price is charged. The disclosure should include:

(a) the names of the transacting related parties;
(b) a description of the relationship between the parties;
(c) a description of the transactions;
(d) the amounts involved;
(e) any other elements of the transactions necessary for an understanding of the financial statements;
(f) the amounts due to or from related parties at the balance sheet date and provisions for doubtful debts due from such parties at that date; and
(g) amounts written off in the period in respect of debts due to or from related parties.

Transactions with related parties may be disclosed on an aggregated basis (aggregation of similar transactions by type of related party) unless disclosure of an individual transaction, or connected transactions, is necessary for an understanding of the impact of the transactions on the financial statements of the reporting entity or is required by law.

DATE FROM WHICH EFFECTIVE

The accounting practices set out in the FRS should be regarded as standard in respect **7** of financial statements relating to accounting periods commencing on or after 23 December 1995. Earlier adoption is encouraged but not required.

Explanation

THE EFFECT OF RELATED PARTIES

8   In the absence of information to the contrary, it is assumed that a reporting entity has independent discretionary power over its resources and transactions and pursues its activities independently of the interests of its individual owners, managers and others. Transactions are presumed to have been undertaken on an arm's length basis, ie on terms such as could have obtained in a transaction with an external party, in which each side bargained knowledgeably and freely, unaffected by any relationship between them.

9   These assumptions may not be justified when related party relationships exist, because the requisite conditions for competitive, free market dealings may not be present. Whilst the parties may endeavour to achieve arm's length bargaining the very nature of the relationship may preclude this occurring. Sometimes the nature of the relationship between the parties is such that the disclosure of the relationship alone will be sufficient to make users aware of the possible implications of related party transactions. For this reason, transactions between a subsidiary undertaking, 90 per cent or more of whose voting rights are controlled within the group, and other members and investees of the same group are not required to be disclosed in the separate financial statements of that subsidiary undertaking.

10   Even when terms are arm's length, the reporting of material related party transactions is useful information, because the terms of future transactions are more susceptible to alteration as a result of the nature of the relationship than they would be in transactions with an unrelated party. Although the existence of a related party relationship sometimes precludes arm's length transactions, non-independent parties can deal with each other at arm's length, as in the situation where a parent undertaking places no restrictions on two subsidiaries, giving them complete freedom in deciding whether to deal with each other and on what terms. However, assertions in financial statements about transactions with related parties should not imply that the related party transactions were effected on terms equivalent to those that prevail in arm's length transactions unless the parties have conducted the transactions in an independent manner.

APPLYING THE DEFINITION OF 'RELATED PARTY'

Party

11   The definition of a related party encompasses both an individual or an entity, such as a company or unincorporated business, and a group of individuals or entities acting in concert. Groups of individuals or entities are included in this definition because, although a single individual or entity (having, for example only a small shareholding) might not be able to divert a particular reporting entity from pursuing its own separate interests, this could be achieved by the individual or entity acting in concert with others.

Relationship

12   The definition is limited to parties having a relationship with a reporting entity that affects the pursuit of separate interests of either the reporting entity or the other party, since transactions with such parties could have a significant effect on the financial position and operating results of the reporting entity. Consequently, subsidiary undertakings and associates are related parties of the investor. The reporting

entity and a major customer or supplier are not related parties by virtue of that connection alone because the reporting entity still retains the freedom to make decisions in its own separate interests.

Common control

Entities subject to common control are included in the definition of a related party   **13** because the controlling entity could cause such entities to transact or not to transact with one another or to transact on particular terms. The relationship could therefore have a material effect on the performance and financial position of the reporting entity. Common control is deemed to exist when both parties are subject to control from boards having a controlling nucleus of directors in common.

Common influence

The difference between control and influence is that control brings with it the ability   **14** to cause the controlled party to subordinate its separate interests whereas the outcome of the exercise of influence is less certain. Two related parties of a third entity are not necessarily related parties of each other. For example:

(a)   entities are not related parties by reason only of their being associated companies of the same investor. The parties are subject only to influence rather than common control, hence the relationship between them is normally too tenuous to justify their being treated as related parties of each other;

(b)   similarly when one party is subject to control and another party is subject to influence from the same source, those two parties are not necessarily related parties of each other. Since one of the parties is subject only to influence rather than control, the relationship between them would not normally justify their being treated as related parties of each other; and

(c)   two entities are not related parties simply because they have a director in common.

In all circumstances, however, it will be appropriate to consider whether one or both transacting parties, subject to control and influence from the same source or common influence, have subordinated their own separate interests in entering into that transaction.

Pension funds

The fact that certain pension funds are related parties of the reporting entity is not   **15** intended to call into question the independence of the trustees with regard to their fiduciary obligations to the members of the pension scheme. Transactions between the reporting entity and the pension fund may be in the interest of members but nevertheless need to be reported in the accounts of the reporting entity.

SCOPE

Related party disclosure provisions do not apply in circumstances where to comply   **16** with them conflicts with the reporting entity's duties of confidentiality arising by operation of law (although operation of law would not include the effects of terms stipulated in a contract). For example, banks are obliged by law to observe a strict duty of confidentiality in respect of their customers' affairs and the FRS would not override the obligation to preserve the confidentiality of customers' dealings.

Exempt subsidiary undertakings

17   The FRS grants certain exemptions to subsidiary undertakings 90 per cent or more of whose voting rights are controlled within the group. These subsidiaries do not have to disclose transactions with other group companies and investees of the group qualifying as related parties. The latter includes associates and joint ventures of other group companies with whom the reporting subsidiary has transacted in circumstances falling under paragraph 2.5(a)(iv). Disclosure would, however, be required of transactions with related parties of the reporting subsidiary other than those that are excluded by the exemption.

DISCLOSURE OF CONTROL

18   If the reporting entity is controlled by another party, that fact is relevant information, irrespective of whether transactions have taken place with that party, because the control relationship prevents the reporting entity from being independent in the sense described in paragraph 8. Indeed, the existence and identity of the controlling party may sometimes be at least as relevant in appraising an entity's prospects as are the performance and financial position presented in its financial statements. The controlling party may establish the entity's credit standing, determine the source and price of its raw materials, determine the products it sells, to whom and at what price, and may affect the source, calibre and even the primary concern and allegiance of its management.

DISCLOSURE OF TRANSACTIONS

Transactions

19   Disclosure is required of all material related party transactions. As transactions include donations to or by the entity, related party transactions are required to be disclosed whether or not a price is charged. The following are examples of related party transactions that require disclosure by a reporting entity in the period in which they occur:

- purchases or sales of goods (finished or unfinished);
- purchases or sales of property and other assets;
- rendering or receiving of services;
- agency arrangements;
- leasing arrangements;
- transfer of research and development;
- licence agreements;
- provision of finance (including loans and equity contributions in cash or in kind);
- guarantees and the provision of collateral security; and
- management contracts.

Materiality

20   Transactions are material when their disclosure might reasonably be expected to influence decisions made by the users of general purpose financial statements. The materiality of related party transactions is to be judged, not only in terms of their significance to the reporting entity, but also in relation to the other related party when that party is:

(a)   a director, key manager or other individual in a position to influence, or accountable for stewardship of, the reporting entity; or

(b)   a member of the close family of any individual mentioned in (a) above; or

(c)   an entity controlled by any individual mentioned in (a) or (b) above.

Aggregation

Disclosure of details of particular transactions with individual related parties would   **21**
frequently be too voluminous to be easily understood. Accordingly, similar transactions may be aggregated by type of related party. For example, in the individual
accounts of a group company, purchases or sales with other group companies can be
aggregated and described as such. However, this should not be done in such a way as
to obscure the importance of significant transactions. Hence purchases or sales of
goods should not be aggregated with purchases or sales of fixed assets. Nor should a
material related party transaction with an individual be concealed in an aggregated
disclosure.

Other elements of the transaction

Paragraph 6(e) requires disclosure of 'any other elements of the [related party]   **22**
transactions necessary for an understanding of the financial statements'. An example
falling within this requirement would be the need to give an indication that the
transfer of a major asset had taken place at an amount materially different from that
obtainable on normal commercial terms.

RELATIONSHIP WITH STATUTORY AND LONDON STOCK EXCHANGE REQUIREMENTS*

There are extensive statutory and London Stock Exchange requirements and reliefs   **23**
regarding disclosure of related party transactions and relationships. In certain
instances, the FRS will extend existing disclosure requirements; in other instances, the
statutory and London Stock Exchange disclosure requirements go beyond those of
the FRS. The location of the principal statutory and London Stock Exchange
requirements is given in Appendices I and II respectively.

Editor's note: Requirements in relation to listed companies are now issued by the Financial Services Authority
in its capacity as UK Listing Authority.

Adoption of FRS 8 by the board

Financial Reporting Standard 8 – 'Related Party Disclosures'was approved for issue by the ten members of the Accounting Standards Board.

Sir David Tweedie	(Chairman)
Allan Cook	(Technical Director)
David Allvey	
Ian Brindle	
Michael Garner	
Richard Goeltz	
Raymond Hinton	
Huw Jones	
Professor Geoffrey Whittington	
Ken Wild	

Appendix I
Note on legal requirements

Great Britain

The following table lists only the main statutory provisions relating to related party   **1**
disclosures.

Companies Act 1985

section 231	Disclosure required in notes to accounts: related undertakings
Schedule 5	Disclosure of information: related undertakings
Part I	Companies not required to prepare group accounts
Part II	Companies required to prepare group accounts
section 232	Disclosure required in notes to accounts: emoluments and other benefits of directors and others
section 741	"Director" and "shadow director"
Schedule 6	Disclosure of information: emoluments and other benefits of directors and others
section 234	Duty to prepare directors' report
Schedule 7	Matters to be dealt with in directors' report
Schedule 4	Form and content of company accounts
Part I	
Section B	*The required formats for accounts*
paragraph 50	*Guarantees and other financial commitments*
paragraph 59*	*Dealings with or interests in group undertakings*
paragraph 59A	*Guarantees and other financial commitments in favour of group undertakings*
Schedule 4A	Form and content of group accounts
paragraph 1(2)	*General rules - application of Schedule 4 paragraph 59 to group accounts*
paragraph 21	*Consolidated balance sheet and profit and loss account formats for associated undertakings and for other participating interests.*

Special provisions relating to banking and insurance companies and groups are
contained in Schedules 9 and 9A respectively.

**Editor's note: paragraph 59 was repealed February 1996.*

NORTHERN IRELAND

2   The statutory requirements in Northern Ireland are identical with those in Great Britain. The following table shows the provisions in the Companies (Northern Ireland) Order 1986 that correspond to the following provisions in the Companies Act 1985 (see paragraph 1 above).

Great Britain	*Northern Ireland*
section 231	Article 239
Schedule 5 *Parts I and II*	Schedule 5 *Parts I and II*
section 232	Article 240
section 741	Article 9
Schedule 6	Schedule 6
section 234	Article 242
Schedule 7	Schedule 7
Schedule 4 *Part 1 Section B* *paragraphs 50, 59 and 59A*	Schedule 4 *Part I Section B* *paragraphs 50, 59 and 59A*
Schedule 4A *paragraphs 1(2) and 21*	Schedule 4A *paragraphs 1(2) and 21*

Banking companies and groups

Schedule 9	Schedule 9

Insurance companies and groups

Schedule 9A	Schedule 9A as amended by the Companies (1986 Order) (Insurance Companies Accounts) Regulations (Northern Ireland) 1994.

REPUBLIC OF IRELAND

3   The following table shows the provisions in the European Communities (Companies: Group Accounts) Regulations 1992, and the Companies Acts 1963-90 that correspond to the provisions in the Companies Act 1985 (see paragraph 1 above).

Great Britain	*Republic of Ireland*	
section 231	regulation 36	1992 Regulations
Schedule 5 *Parts I and II*	section 16	Companies (Amendment) Act 1986
	regulation 44	1992 Regulations
	schedule, paragraphs 4,18-22	1992 Regulations

section 232	section 191	Companies Act 1963
section 741	section 27	Companies Act 1990
Schedule 6	schedule, paragraph 16 sections 41-43 schedule, paragraph 17	1992 Regulations Companies Act 1990 1992 Regulations
section 234	section 158	Companies Act 1963
Schedule 7	sections 13,14 & 16	Companies (Amendment) Act 1986
	regulation 37 section 63	1992 Regulations Companies Act 1990
Schedule 4 *Part I Section B*	schedule, paragraphs 1-3	Companies (Amendment) Act 1986
paragraph 50	schedule, paragraph 36	Companies (Amendment) Act 1986
paragraph 59	schedule, paragraph 45	Companies (Amendment) Act 1986
paragraph 59A	schedule, paragraph 45A	Companies (Amendment) Act 1986
Schedule 4A *paragraph 1(2)*	regulation 15(2)	1992 Regulations
paragraph 21	schedule, paragraph 2	1992 Regulations
	Banking companies and groups	
Schedule 9	European Communities (Credit Institutions: Accounts) Regulations 1992	
	Insurance companies and groups	
Schedule 9A	Part III, Schedule 6 Companies Act 1963	

(NB EC Directive 91/674, Accounts and consolidated accounts of Insurance Undertakings, has not yet been implemented in the Republic of Ireland.)

Appendix II
Note on London Stock Exchange requirements

'The Listing Rules' published by the London Stock Exchange* deal with related party transactions, which are defined somewhat differently from those in the FRS, albeit with a large degree of overlap. Chapter 11 'Transactions with related parties' defines related party transactions and sets out the requirements and exceptions for such transactions. Further disclosure requirements in respect of related parties are contained in Chapter 12 'Financial information'

__Editor's note:__ The Listing Rules are now issued by the Financial Services Authority in its capacity as the UK Listing Authority.

Appendix III
Compliance with International
Accounting Standards

Compliance with the FRS will ensure compliance with International Accounting Standard 24 'Related Party Disclosures' in all material respects except for the exemption in relation to certain subsidiaries. The FRS does not require disclosure in the financial statements of subsidiary undertakings, 90 per cent or more of whose voting rights are controlled within the group, of transactions with entities that are part of the group or investees of the group qualifying as related parties, provided that the consolidated financial statements in which that subsidiary is included are publicly available. IAS 24 does not require disclosure in the financial statements of a wholly-owned subsidiary if its parent is incorporated in the same country and provides consolidated financial statements in that country.*

Editor's note: A revised version of IAS 24 was issued in December 2003. This removes the exemption for subsidiaries entirely.

Appendix IV
The development of the FRS

HISTORY OF DOCUMENTS ISSUED

ED 46

1   ED 46 'Disclosure of related party transactions' was issued by the Accounting Standards Committee in April 1989. The major disclosure proposal was to report abnormal related party transactions. Detail required included the name and relationship of the transacting parties as well as the basis on which the transaction price had been determined. Aggregated disclosures were permitted subject to certain restrictions. Other proposals were: disclosure of the existence and nature of controlling related party relationships, whether or not any transactions had taken place between the parties; and disclosure of economic dependence. Economic dependence was deemed to exist where the transactions between an entity and another party, or other facts arising from a relationship with another party, had a pervasive influence on the entity.

FRED 8

2   FRED 8 'Related Party Disclosures' was published in March 1994. There were two main differences between ED 46 and FRED 8. First, FRED 8 proposed that *all* material related party transactions should be disclosed because reporting control relationships and related party transactions drew attention to the possibility that the financial statements might have been affected by the relationship. The provision in ED 46 allowing aggregated disclosures by aggregating similar transactions by type of related party was retained. The other major change from ED 46 was that FRED 8 did not require the disclosure of economic dependence. The Board believes that disclosure of any such dependence, if required, should not be in a standard dealing with related party transactions since a customer or supplier is not normally regarded as a related party.

International and overseas accounting standards

3   The International Accounting Standard, IAS 24 'Related Party Disclosures', requires the disclosure of all material related party transactions. This approach is also adopted in the US standard FAS 57 'Related Party Disclosures', and the Australian, Canadian and New Zealand related party standards. In all material respects the definition of a related party and the disclosure requirements are the same in those standards as in FRS 8.

Statutory and London Stock Exchange requirements

4   There are extensive statutory and London Stock Exchange requirements regarding disclosure of related party transactions. The requirements principally concern transactions between companies and their directors and principal shareholders and their connected parties. Both sets of requirements are designed to focus on the stewardship aspect of directors' duties, whilst the FRS concentrates on the relevance of the information to users of accounts.

MATTERS CONSIDERED IN THE LIGHT OF RESPONSES TO FRED 8

The following paragraphs refer to comments made by respondents to FRED 8, and   5
explain, with reasons, the changes made by the Board to the proposals of the FRED or
the Board's reasons for rejecting arguments for change.

Definition of a related party

Influence

Several respondents remarked that the phrase in the definition section of the FRED   6
that described influence was too vague and should specify the level of influence that
would trigger related party status. The description of the level of influence has
therefore been strengthened so as to include the notion of the possible restriction on
the ability of one of the parties to pursue at all times its own separate interests.

Common influence

In FRED 8, two or more parties were related parties when, *inter alia*, for all or part of   7
the financial period one of the parties was subject to control and the other to
influence from the same source. It was pointed out to the Board that, for those
subsidiaries that are part of a large group, this could impose a reporting burden in
their individual financial statements. A subsidiary not qualifying for an exemption
from disclosure of transactions with other group companies and investees of the
group qualifying as related parties might be unaware that it had had transactions
with a related party being an associate of the group where the investment in that
associate was held by another group company. In acknowledgement of this difficulty
and that for two parties to be related parties there has to be a relationship between
them, the Board has changed this part of the definition to include only transacting
parties subject to influence from the same source to such an extent that one of the
parties has subordinated its own separate interests.

Deemed/presumed

In the FRED, the definition of a related party was followed by two lists of types of   8
related party:

(a)   those deemed to be related parties; and
(b)   those presumed to be related parties.

A number of respondents commented that, in some cases, the nature of the relationship of some parties classed as 'deemed' in the FRED did not justify this
classification. Hence, in the standard, close families of directors have been moved to
the 'presumed' list. This meets the criticism that those parties may not always have
the requisite level of influence to qualify as a related party.

Immediate family

The immediate family of directors, substantial shareholders and key employees was   9
stated in the FRED to be a possible type of related party. Several commentators asked
for 'immediate family' to be more closely defined, some querying the use of the
phrase 'members of the same household' and some the references to certain relatives
and not others. The Board, in recognition of the fact that the emphasis should be on

influence rather than on the immediacy of the family relationship, decided to substitute 'close family' for 'immediate family', in line with IAS 24. 'Close family' is defined as 'those family members or members of the same household who may be expected to influence, or be influenced by, that person in their dealings with the reporting entity.' The phrase 'members of the same household' has been retained to accommodate the view of the Board that related parties in this context are not necessarily confined to the individual's legal family.

10 per cent shareholding threshold

10   FRED 8 included the presumption that a shareholder owning 10 per cent or more of the voting rights of the reporting entity was a related party. Twenty-eight out of the forty-six respondents addressing this issue wanted the threshold to be raised (the most common figure mentioned being 20 per cent). Subsequent research indicated that the presumption of related party status at 10 per cent would capture many situations where the requisite level of influence was not present but rebuttal of the presumption would be necessary nonetheless. The Board accordingly decided to raise the threshold to 20 per cent.

Scope

Wholly-owned subsidiary exemption

11   Disclosure of transactions with entities that are part of the group or associates or joint ventures of the group was not required by the FRED in the financial statements of wholly-owned subsidiaries. The Board's reasons for granting this exemption were that the ultimate holding company is named in the notes to the financial statements and those wishing to find out more information about the group could do so provided that consolidated financial statements were 'publicly available'.

12   Those who supported the wholly-owned subsidiary exemption in general terms wished to extend its scope by:

(a)   describing the wholly-owned subsidiary as a 'wholly-owned subsidiary undertaking';

(b)   reducing the threshold to 90 per cent owned subsidiaries; and

(c)   widening the definition to take into account preference shares held by a third party and small numbers of shares held by employees, in what would otherwise be a wholly-owned subsidiary, as part of an employee share scheme.

In response to the above comments, the Board decided to widen the exemption with the effect that disclosure is not required in the financial statements of subsidiary undertakings, 90 per cent or more of whose voting rights are controlled within the group, of transactions with entities that are part of the group or investees of the group qualifying as related parties.

13   Several commentators remarked that disclosure of transactions with group companies is not available in the consolidated financial statements as such transactions are eliminated on consolidation and disclosure should therefore be made in the individual financial statements of the subsidiary. The Board, however, believes that in the case of a subsidiary undertaking, 90 per cent or more of whose voting rights are controlled within the group, the nature of the relationship is such that disclosure of the fact that the exemption has been invoked is sufficient to alert the reader of the financial statements to the possible existence of related party transactions.

Small company exemption

A majority of those who responded to the question of whether small companies **14** should be granted an exemption from the disclosure of related party transactions considered that no exemption should be granted. The reason given was that these transactions were likely to be of greater significance in small than in larger companies. The minority who would have preferred the granting of an exemption cited as their main reason the fact that the costs of providing the additional disclosures would outweigh the benefits of reporting them. Subsequent to the receipt of comments on FRED 8, further consultation was undertaken. Representations from those auditing and using the accounts of small companies reinforced the view that appropriate related party disclosure is particularly important and relevant information in their financial statements, since transactions with related parties are more likely to be material in small companies.

The Board noted that Parts II and III of Schedule 6 to the Companies Act 1985, **15** which applies equally to companies of all sizes and is concerned mainly with dealings in favour of directors and connected persons, overlapped in many respects with the disclosure requirements of the FRS; however, the FRS was broader in scope and, in particular, expressed more clearly than the statute the spirit of Schedule 6; it also clarified, to the benefit of both preparers and auditors, the disclosures necessary to meet the fundamental requirement that accounts should give a true and fair view.

In considering this question, the Board was aware of the work, which it had itself **16** commissioned, of a working party of the Consultative Committee of Accountancy Bodies (CCAB) investigating possible bases for exempting small companies from some of the requirements of accounting standards. Concern was expressed that if small companies were to be exempt from the requirements of the FRS in advance of the outcome of this work, some transactions which would normally be disclosed could be hidden using the exemption as justification. Accordingly, the Board decided that the FRS should apply to all financial statements that are intended to give a true and fair view, with no exemption for small companies. For the reasons given above, the Board believes that the FRS essentially clarifies existing requirements applicable to small companies, rather than extends them to a significant degree. Its decision on the FRS should not be taken as an indication of how it might react to the eventual final report of the CCAB working party in relation to this or other accounting standards.*

Banker/client confidentiality

Concern was expressed by banking entities and associations that disclosure of all **17** material related party transactions in the accounts of banks could result in a breach of the confidentiality of the relationship between banker and client. The confidentiality of this relationship is part of the common law and is also a provision of the 'Good Banking' code of practice. Consequently the Board agreed to include a further paragraph in the Explanation section of the FRS to recognise the legal obligation borne by banks in this respect.

Disclosure of all material related party transactions

FRED 8 proposed disclosure of all material related party transactions. This proposal **18** was supported by the majority of respondents. Those who suggested a return to the ED 46 proposal that the disclosure requirement should be confined to abnormal

*Editor's note: Following the final report the Board issued the Financial Reporting Standard for Smaller Entities.

transactions with related parties argued that reporting all related party transactions did not provide useful information. The Board's view is that, when transactions with related parties are material in aggregate, they are of interest whatever their nature.

Materiality

19   A number of commentators noted that the area of materiality was one on which further guidance was required in addition to that given by the FRED. In response to this concern, further explanation has been given to address the perspective that needs to be considered when a related party transaction has been undertaken directly or indirectly with an individual in a position to influence, or accountable for steward-ship of, the reporting entity (for example, a director or a substantial shareholder).

Fair value

20   FRED 8 required 'any other elements of the [related party] transactions necessary for an understanding of the financial statements' to be disclosed and suggested, as an example, a material difference between the fair value and the transacted amount where material transfers of assets, liabilities or services had taken place. Commen-tators addressing this issue were evenly divided in their views. Those in favour of the disclosure endorsed the Board's view that such information is useful because there is more scope for transactions between related parties to be at artificial prices as a result of the relationship. Those who opposed the disclosure argued that ascertaining a fair value for these transactions would be unduly burdensome and impracticable, since in many cases a fair value could not be obtained, particularly within groups. Whilst retaining its original view that this disclosure is relevant for an understanding of the financial statements, the Board acknowledged the observations of commentators. The Explanation has been amended to suggest as an example of 'any other elements of the [related party] transactions necessary for an understanding of the financial statements' an indication that the transfer of a major asset has taken place at an amount materially different from that obtainable on normal commercial terms. The Board believes that the absence of this information could reasonably be expected to influence decisions made by users of general purpose financial statements.

Financial Reporting Standard 9 is set out in paragraphs 1-61.

The Statement of Standard Accounting Practice, which comprises the paragraphs set in bold type, should be read in the context of the Objective as stated in paragraph 1 and the definitions set out in paragraphs 4 and 5 and also of the Foreword to Accounting Standards and the Statement of Principles for Financial Reporting currently in issue.

The explanatory paragraphs contained in the FRS shall be regarded as part of the Statement of Standard Accounting Practice insofar as they assist in interpreting that statement.

Appendix III 'The development of the FRS' reviews considerations and arguments that were thought significant by members of the Board in reaching the conclusions on the FRS.

[FRS 9]
Associates and joint ventures

(Issued November 1997)

Contents

Associates and joint ventures

Summary

a   Financial Reporting Standard 9 'Associates and Joint Ventures' sets out the definitions and accounting treatments for associates and joint ventures, two types of interests that a reporting entity may have in other entities. The FRS also deals with joint arrangements that are not entities. The definitions and treatments prescribed have been developed to be consistent with the Accounting Standards Board's approach to accounting for subsidiaries (dealt with in FRS 2 'Accounting for Subsidiary Undertakings'). The requirements are consistent with companies legislation.*

b   The table below describes the different sorts of interests that a reporting entity may have in other entities or arrangements – the shaded sections indicate those covered by the FRS. The defining relationships described in the table form the basis for the definitions used in the FRS.

* The relationship between companies legislation and the standard is discussed in Appendix I.

Entity/ arrangement	Nature of relationship	Description of the defining relationship – the full definitions are given in paragraph 4 of the FRS
Subsidiary	Investor controls its investee.	Control is the ability of an entity to direct the operating and financial policies of another entity with a view to gaining economic benefits from its activities. To have control an entity must have both: (i) the ability to deploy the economic resources of the investee or to direct it; and (ii) the ability to ensure that any resulting benefits accrue to itself (with corresponding exposure to losses) and to restrict the access of others to those benefits.
Joint arrangement that is not an entity	Entities participate in an arrangement to carry on part of their own trades or businesses.	A joint arrangement, whether or not subject to joint control, does not constitute an entity unless it carries on a trade or business of its own.
Joint venture	Investor holds a long-term interest and shares control under a contractual arrangement.	The joint venture agreement can override the rights normally conferred by ownership interests with the effect that: ● acting together, the venturers can control the venture and there are procedures for such joint action ● each venturer has (implicitly or explicitly) a veto over strategic policy decisions. There is usually a procedure for settling disputes between venturers and, possibly, for terminating the joint venture.
Associate	Investor holds a participating interest and exercises significant influence.	The investor has a long-term interest and is actively involved, and influential, in the direction of its investee through its participation in policy decisions covering the aspects of policy relevant to the investor, including decisions on strategic issues such as: (i) the expansion or contraction of the business, participation in other entities or changes in products, markets and activities of its investee; and (ii) determining the balance between dividend and reinvestment.
Simple investment		The investor's interest does not qualify the investee as an associate, a joint venture or a subsidiary because the investor has limited influence or its interest is not long-term.

The investor's consolidated financial statements

c   The table below sets out the treatments in consolidated financial statements for the different interests that a reporting entity may have in other entities and for joint arrangements that are not entities – the shaded sections indicate the treatments covered by the FRS.

Type of investment	Treatment in consolidated financial statements
Subsidiaries	The investor should consolidate the assets, liabilities, results and cash flows of its subsidiaries.
Joint arrangements that are not entities	Each party should account for its own share of the assets, liabilities and cash flows in the joint arrangement, measured according to the terms of that arrangement, for example pro rata to their respective interests.
Joint ventures	The venturer should use the gross equity method showing in addition to the amounts included under the equity method,* on the face of the balance sheet, the venturer's share of the gross assets and liabilities of its joint ventures, and, in the profit and loss account, the venturer's share of their turnover distinguished from that of the group. Where the venturer conducts a major part of its business through joint ventures, it may show fuller information provided all amounts are distinguished from those of the group. Appendix IV sets out an optional columnar presentation.
Associates	The investor should include its associates in its consolidated financial statements using the equity method. In the investor's consolidated profit and loss account the investor's share of its associates' operating result should be included immediately after group operating result. From the level of profit before tax, the investor's share of the relevant amounts for associates should be included within the amounts for the group. In the consolidated statement of total recognised gains and losses the investor's share of the total recognised gains and losses of its associates should be included, shown separately under each heading, if material. In the balance sheet the investor's share of the net assets of its associates should be included and separately disclosed. The cash flow statement should include the cash flows between the investor and its associates. Goodwill arising on the investor's acquisition of its associates, less any amortisation or write-down, should be included in the carrying amount for the associates but should be disclosed separately. In the profit and loss account the amortisation or write down of such goodwill should be separately disclosed as part of the investor's share of its associates' results.
Simple investments	The investor includes its interests as investments at either cost or valuation.

The treatment under the equity method required by the FRS is set out in paragraph 4 and summarised under Associates in the above table.

The investor's own financial statements

In the investor's own financial statements associates and joint ventures should be   **d**
treated as fixed asset investments, at cost less any amounts written off, or at a
valuation.

Disclosures

The FRS requires the following disclosures separately for associates and joint ventures   **e**
that exceed certain thresholds.

(i)   Where an investor's aggregate share in its associates exceeds 15 per cent of any
      of the gross assets, gross liabilities, turnover or, on a three-year average,
      operating result of the investing group, the investor's aggregate share of each of
      the following should be shown:
      ● turnover (unless it is already included as a memorandum item)
      ● fixed assets, current assets, liabilities due within one year and liabilities due
        after one year or more.
(ii) Where an investor's aggregate share in its joint ventures exceeds 15 per cent of
      any of the gross assets, gross liabilities, turnover or, on a three-year average,
      operating result of the investing group, the investor's aggregate share of each of
      the following should be shown:
      ● fixed assets, current assets, liabilities due within one year and liabilities due
        after one year or more.
(iii) For any associate or joint venture where the investor's share of that individual
      entity exceeds 25 per cent of any of the gross assets, gross liabilities, turnover
      or, on a three-year average, operating result of the investing group, the
      investor's share of the following items for that entity should be shown:
      ● turnover
      ● profit before tax
      ● taxation
      ● profit after tax
      ● fixed assets
      ● current assets
      ● liabilities due within one year
      ● liabilities due after one year or more.

Financial Reporting Standard 9

Objective

1   The objective of this FRS is to reflect the effect on an investor's financial position and performance of its interests in two special kinds of investments – associates and joint ventures – for whose activities it is partly accountable because of the closeness of its involvement:

- in associates, as a result of its participating interest and significant influence
- in joint ventures, as a result of its long-term interest and joint control.ffThe FRS also deals with joint arrangements that do not qualify as associates or joint ventures because they are not entities.

Scope

2   **Subject to the provisions of paragraph 3, the FRS applies to all financial statements that are intended to give a true and fair view of a reporting entity's financial position and profit or loss (or income and expenditure) for a period.**

3   **Reporting entities applying the Financial Reporting Standard for Smaller Entities (FRSSE) currently applicable are exempt from the FRS unless preparing consolidated financial statements, in which case they should apply the FRS to such statements as required by the FRSSE.**

Definitions

4   The following definitions shall apply in the FRS and in particular in the Statement of Standard Accounting Practice set out **in bold type**.

Associate:–*
An entity (other than a subsidiary) in which another entity (the investor) has a PARTICIPATING INTEREST and over whose operating and financial policies the investor EXERCISES A SIGNIFICANT INFLUENCE.

PARTICIPATING INTEREST:–
An interest held in the shares† of another entity on a long-term basis for the purpose of securing a contribution to the investor's activities by the exercise of control or influence arising from or related to that interest. The investor's interest

---

This definition is consistent with the definition of an associated undertaking in companies legislation:

(a)   in Great Britain, paragraph 20 of Schedule 4A to(CA)the Companies Act 1985;

(b)   in Northern Ireland, paragraph 20 of Schedule 4A to the Companies (Northern Ireland) Order 1986; and

(c)   in the Republic of Ireland, Regulation 34 of the European Communities (Companies: Group Accounts) Regulations 1992.

The statutory definitions in Great Britain and Northern Ireland specifically exclude non-corporate joint ventures that are proportionally consolidated. The full definitions are given in Appendix I.

†*The reference to shares is to allotted shares in an entity with a share capital, to rights to share in the capital in an entity with capital but no share capital, and to interests conferring any right to share in the profits, or imposing a liability to contribute to the losses or giving an obligation to contribute to debts or expenses in a winding up for an entity without capital.*

must, therefore, be a beneficial one and the benefits expected to arise* must be linked to the exercise of its significant influence over the investee's operating and financial policies. An interest in the shares of another entity includes an interest convertible into an interest in shares or an option to acquire shares.

Companies legislation provides that a holding of 20 per cent or more of the shares of an entity is to be presumed to be a participating interest unless the contrary is shown.† The presumption is rebutted if the interest is either not long-term or not beneficial.

EXERCISE OF SIGNIFICANT INFLUENCE:–
The investor is actively involved and is influential in the direction of its investee through its participation in policy decisions covering aspects of policy relevant to the investor, including decisions on strategic issues such as:

(a)   the expansion or contraction of the business, participation in other entities or changes in products, markets and activities of its investee; and
(b)   determining the balance between dividend and reinvestment.

Companies legislation provides that an entity holding 20 per cent or more of the voting rights in another entity should be presumed to exercise a significant influence over that other entity unless the contrary is shown.‡ For the purpose of applying this presumption, the shares held by the parent and its subsidiaries in that entity should be aggregated.§ The presumption is rebutted if the investor does not fulfil the criteria for the exercise of significant influence set out above.

Further guidance on how to apply the definition of an 'associate' in practice is given in paragraphs 13–17 with 'participating interest' considered in paragraph 13 and 'exercise of significant influence' in paragraphs 14–17.

Control:–
See definition under *subsidiary*.

Dividends are not the only way a beneficial interest can be enjoyed: there are other ways of extracting benefit, for example, through a management contract with a fee based on performance (making the receiver of the fee more than just a manager).

†*In Great Britain, section 260 of the Companies Act 1985.*
In Northern Ireland, Article 268 of the Companies (Northern Ireland) Order 1986.
In the Republic of Ireland, Regulation 35 of the European Communities (Companies: Group Accounts) Regulations 1992.

‡*In Great Britain, paragraph 20 of Schedule 4A to the Companies Act 1985.*
In Northern Ireland, paragraph 20 of Schedule 4A to the Companies (Northern Ireland) Order 1986.
In the Republic of Ireland, Regulation 34 of the European Communities (Companies: Group Accounts) Regulations 1992.

§*The provisions in companies legislation that deal with the voting rights to be taken into account in applying the rebuttable presumption are:*
(a)   in Great Britain, paragraphs 5-11 of Schedule 10A to the Companies Act 1985;
(b)   in Northern Ireland, paragraphs 5-11 of Schedule 10A to the Companies (Northern Ireland) Order 1986; and
(c)   in the Republic of Ireland, Regulation 4 of the European Communities (Companies: Group Accounts) Regulations 1992.

Entity:—

A body corporate, partnership, or unincorporated association carrying on a trade or business with or without a view to profit. The reference to carrying on a trade or business means a trade or business of its own and not just part of the trades or businesses of entities that have interests in it.

Equity method:—

A method of accounting that brings an investment into its investor's financial statements initially at its cost, identifying any goodwill arising. The carrying amount of the investment is adjusted in each period by the investor's share of the results of its investee less any amortisation or write-off for goodwill, the investor's share of any relevant gains or losses, and any other changes in the investee's net assets including distributions to its owners, for example by dividend. The investor's share of its investee's results is recognised in its profit and loss account. The investor's cash flow statement includes the cash flows between the investor and its investee, for example relating to dividends and loans.

Gross equity method:—

A form of equity method under which the investor's share of the aggregate gross assets and liabilities underlying the net amount included for the investment is shown on the face of the balance sheet and, in the profit and loss account, the investor's share of the investee's turnover is noted.

Interest held on a long-term basis:—

An interest that is held other than exclusively with a view to subsequent resale. An interest held exclusively with a view to subsequent resale is:

(a)   an interest for which a purchaser has been identified or is being sought, and which is reasonably expected to be disposed of within approximately one year of its date of acquisition; or

(b)   an interest that was acquired as a result of the enforcement of a security,†, unless the interest has become part of the continuing activities of the group or the holder acts as if it intends the interest to become so.

Investee:—

An entity in which the investor has invested.

Joint arrangement that is not an entity:—

A contractual arrangement under which the participants engage in joint activities that do not create an entity because it would not be carrying on a trade or business of its own. A contractual arrangement where all significant matters of operating and financial policy are predetermined does not create an entity because the policies are those of its participants not of a separate entity.‡

The first sentence of this definition is the same as the definition of 'undertaking' in companies legislation:

(a)   in Great Britain, section 259 of the Companies Act 1985;

(b)   in Northern Ireland, Article 267 of the Companies (Northern Ireland) Order 1986; and

(c)   in the Republic of Ireland, Regulation 3 of the European Communities (Companies: Group Accounts) Regulations 1992.

†*"Enforcement of a security" should be interpreted to include any other arrangement that has in substance the same effect.*

‡*Under FRS 5 'Reporting the substance of transactions', where all significant matters of operating and financial policy are predetermined in a contractual arrangement, if one party gains the benefits arising from the net assets of that arrangement and is exposed to the risks inherent in them, then that party possesses control and the arrangement is that party's quasi-subsidiary.*

Further guidance on how to apply this definition in practice is given in paragraphs 8 and 9.

Joint venture:
An entity in which the reporting entity holds an interest on a long-term basis and is JOINTLY CONTROLLED by the reporting entity and one or more other venturers under a contractual arrangement.

JOINT CONTROL:–
A reporting entity jointly controls a venture with one or more other entities if none of the entities alone can control that entity but all together can do so and decisions on financial and operating policy essential to the activities, economic performance and financial position of that venture require each venturer's consent.

Further guidance on how to apply this definition in practice is given in paragraphs 10–12 with 'joint control' considered in paragraphs 11 and 12.

Subsidiary:–
A subsidiary undertaking as defined by paragraph 14 of FRS 2 'Accounting for Subsidiary Undertakings', which is consistent with companies legislation.* In principle, a subsidiary is an entity over which another entity (the investor) has CONTROL.

CONTROL:–
The ability of an entity to direct the operating and financial policies of another entity with a view to gaining economic benefits from its activities.

References to companies legislation mean: 5

(a)   in Great Britain, the Companies Act 1985;
(b)   in Northern Ireland, the Companies (Northern Ireland) Order 1986; and
(c)   in the Republic of Ireland, the Companies Acts 1963–90 and the European Communities (Companies: Group Accounts) Regulations 1992.

APPLYING THE KEY DEFINITIONS IN PRACTICE

The definitions set out in paragraph 4 identify five ways in which entities further their   6
economic activities through investments or joint arrangements. Four of those involve interests in other entities – subsidiaries, joint ventures, associates and other investments. The basis for the classification of the interests in other entities is the relationship in practice between the investor and its investee. The fifth way involves joint arrangements that do not amount to entities. Subsidiaries are dealt with in FRS 2 and are not specifically addressed in this FRS. The FRS does not provide any guidance on the treatment of investments that are not associates or joint ventures. The paragraphs below deal with joint arrangements that are not entities, and with joint ventures and associates in that order because it reflects the decreasing degree of the reporting entity's direct involvement.

*Paragraph 14 of FRS 2 is based on the following:
(a)   in Great Britain, section 258 of and Schedule 10A to the Companies Act 1985;
(b)   in Northern Ireland, Article 266 of and Schedule 10A to the Companies (Northern Ireland) Order 1986;
*   and*
(c)   in the Republic of Ireland, Regulation 4 of the European Communities (Companies: Group Accounts)
*   Regulations 1992.*

7   Both associates (through the holding of a participating interest) and joint ventures are defined by reference to long-term interests. Whether any investee qualifies as an associate or joint venture should therefore be judged on long-term factors and, once an investee has qualified as an associate or joint venture, minor or temporary changes in the relationship between investor and investee should not affect its status. In particular, the status of an entity as an associate or joint venture does not change according to whether it is profitable or has net assets or is loss-making or has net liabilities or, once it has been accounted for as an associate or joint venture, whether the investor intends to keep its interest or dispose of it.

A joint arrangement that is not an entity

8   A reporting entity may enter a variety of commercial arrangements but not all of these result in the creation of entities. Even if the participants have a long-term interest and have joint control within an arrangement, that arrangement is not a joint venture as defined in the FRS unless it constitutes an entity. For a joint arrangement to amount to an entity, it must carry on a trade or business, meaning a trade or business of its own and not just part of its participants' trades or businesses. In its activities the joint arrangement must therefore have some independence (within the objectives set by the agreement governing the joint arrangement) to pursue its own commercial strategy in its buying and selling; it must either have access to the market in its own right for its main inputs and outputs or, at least, be able to obtain them from the participants or sell them to the participants on generally the same terms as are available in the market. The following indicate that the joint activities undertaken in a joint arrangement do not amount to its carrying on a trade or business of its own – and therefore that the joint arrangement is not an entity:

(a)   the participants derive their benefit from product or services taken in kind rather than by receiving a share in the results of trading;* or

(b)   each participant's share of the output or result of the joint activity is determined by its supply of key inputs to the process producing that output or result.

9   In practice, a joint arrangement will not be an entity if, rather than its activities amounting to its carrying on a trade or business of its own, it is no more than a cost- or risk-sharing means of carrying out a process in the participants' trades or businesses – for example a joint marketing or distribution network or a shared production facility. Carrying on a trade or business normally denotes a continuing activity with repetition of the buying and selling activities and, therefore, a joint arrangement carrying out a single project (as, for example, occurs in the construction industry) is unlikely to be carrying on a trade or business of its own, being instead a facility or agent in its participants' trades or businesses. The nature of a joint arrangement may change over time – for example, a pipeline operated as a joint arrangement that initially provided a service only directly to the participants may develop into a pipeline business providing services to others, where access to the pipeline is sold in the market. Changes in the nature of a joint arrangement should be reflected in its accounting treatment.

A joint venture

10   An entity is a joint venture only with respect to an investor that shares control in it. An investor may have an interest in an entity that is a joint venture to some of its

---

This condition includes the possibility of a venturer taking in cash its share of the joint venture's product if the commodity is actively traded.

other investors. However, if that investor does not share control of the entity, the entity for that investor is merely an investment and should be accounted for as such.

Joint control

Joint control, like control itself, is a relationship that has a benefit aspect.* The **11** venturers exercise their joint control for their mutual benefit, each conducting its part of the contractual arrangement with a view to its own benefit. Each venturer that shares control should play an active role in setting the operating and financial policies of the joint venture, at least at a general strategy level. This does not preclude one venturer managing the joint venture provided that the venture's principal operating and financial policies are collectively agreed by the venturers and the venturers have the power to ensure that those policies are followed. In some cases an investor may qualify as the parent of an entity under the definition of a subsidiary in FRS 2 (for example by holding a majority of the voting rights in that entity) but contractual arrangements with the other shareholder mean that in practice the shareholders share control over their investee. In such a case the interests of the minority shareholder amount to "severe long-term restrictions" that "substantially hinder the exercise of the rights of the parent undertaking over the assets or management of the subsidiary undertaking".† The subsidiary therefore should not be consolidated but should instead be treated as a joint venture according to the requirements of this FRS.

The effect of the requirement in the definition for consent to high-level strategic **12** decisions of joint control is to give each venturer a veto on such decisions. This veto is what distinguishes a joint venturer from a minority holder of the shares in a joint stock company because the latter, having no veto, is subject to majority rule (except for the limited statutory protection for the minority). The requirement for each venturer's consent to high-level strategic decisions does not have to be set out in the joint venture agreement, provided that the joint venture works in practice on the basis of securing such consent.

An associate

Participating interest

One of the conditions for an investment to qualify as an associate is that its investor **13** should have a participating interest. A participating interest includes an interest convertible into an interest in shares or an option to acquire shares. Start-up situations, or other operations in which an investor holds convertibles or options rather than the shares themselves, may therefore qualify as associates if an entity initially has a close involvement in the strategic operating and financial policies, despite only a limited equity interest (for example, by a management contract rather than a holding of shares), and has an option to purchase shares later.

Exercise of significant influence

For an investment to be an associate, its investor must exercise significant influence **14** over the investee's operating and financial policies. The relationship between an

---

*Control is defined in FRS 2 and FRS 5 to include a benefit aspect, ie the ability to direct is with a view to gaining economic benefits.

†Subsidiary undertakings where there are severe long-term restrictions of this sort are required by paragraph 25 of FRS 2 to be excluded from consolidation.

investor and its associate can be contrasted with an interest in an ordinary fixed asset investment. The investor needs an agreement or understanding, formal or informal, with its associate to provide the basis for its significant influence. An investor exercising significant influence will be directly involved in the operating and financial policies of its associate. Rather than passively awaiting the outcome of its investee's policies, the investor uses its associate as a medium through which it conducts a part of its activities (although the associate need not be in the same business as the investor). Over time, the associate will generally implement policies that are consistent with the strategy of the investor and avoid implementing policies that are contrary to the investor's interests. Therefore, if an investee persistently implements policies that are inconsistent with its investor's strategy, that investor does not exercise significant influence over its investee.

15   The investor's active involvement in the operating and financial policies of its associate requires inter alia that it should have a voice in decisions on strategic issues such as determining the balance between dividend and reinvestment. The investor's long-term interest in the future cash flows of its investee is compatible with a policy of reinvestment by the investee; the investor may not, therefore, always press its investee to follow a strategy of paying high dividends. The investor's participation in policy decisions is with a view to gaining economic benefits from the activities of the investee; its expectation of gain through such participation exposes it to the risks relating to the investee's activities, including the possibility of losses being sustained.

16   The investor's involvement in its associate is usually achieved through nomination to the board of directors (or its equivalent) but may result from any arrangement that allows the investor to participate effectively in policy-making decisions. It is unlikely that an investor can exercise significant influence unless it has a substantial basis of voting power. A holding of 20 per cent or more of the voting rights in another entity suggests, but does not ensure, that the investor exercises significant influence over that entity.

17   The decisive feature in identifying investments that are associates is the actual relationship between investor and investee. The actual relationship usually becomes clear soon after an investment is acquired but arrangements (such as the number of board members the investor may nominate and the proposed decision-taking process) may be used to evaluate the relationship before its record is established. If the actual relationship develops differently from that assumed from the arrangements on acquisition, it may be necessary to modify the treatment originally adopted in the financial statements. Once the actual relationship has been established and the investor has qualified as exercising significant influence over an entity, it should be regarded as continuing to exercise such influence until an event or transaction removes the investor's ability to do so.

TREATMENT OF A JOINT ARRANGEMENT THAT IS NOT AN ENTITY

18   **Participants in a joint arrangement that is not an entity should account for their own assets, liabilities and cash flows, measured according to the terms of the agreement governing the arrangement.**

19   A joint arrangement that is not an entity includes any contractual arrangement between the participants to conduct certain activities jointly where those activities do not amount to the joint arrangement carrying on a trade or business of its own. Paragraphs 8 and 9 give guidance on determining when activities constitute the carrying on of a trade or business by the joint arrangement and when, therefore, a

joint arrangement is an entity. Those paragraphs also describe certain activities that are unlikely to constitute an entity.

ACCOUNTING FOR JOINT VENTURES

In consolidated financial statements an investor should include its joint ventures using   **20**
the gross equity method in all its primary financial statements. In the investor's indi-
vidual financial statements, investments in joint ventures should be treated as fixed asset
investments and shown either at cost, less any amounts written off, or at valuation.

Under the gross equity method the joint ventures should receive the same treatment as   **21**
set out for associates in paragraphs 27–30 except that:

* **in the consolidated profit and loss account the investor's share of its joint ventures'**
  turnover should also be shown – but not as part of group turnover. In the segmental
  analysis too, the investor's share of its joint ventures' turnover should be clearly
  distinguished from the turnover for the group itself.
* **in the consolidated balance sheet the investor's share of the gross assets and**
  liabilities underlying the net equity amount included for joint ventures should be
  shown in amplification of that net amount.

Except for items below profit before tax in the profit and loss account, any supplemental   **22**
information given for joint ventures, either in the balance sheet or in the profit and loss
account, must be shown clearly separate from amounts for the group and must not be
included in the group totals.

Because an investor's joint control of its joint venture is a more direct form of   23
influence than the significant influence exercised over associates, a reporting entity
that conducts a major part of its business through joint ventures may wish to give
more detailed supplementary information about them. One option for including
supplementary information about joint ventures is the columnar presentation based
on the gross equity method included as an example in Appendix IV.

A STRUCTURE WITH THE FORM BUT NOT THE SUBSTANCE OF A JOINT VENTURE

A participant in a structure with the appearance of a joint venture but used only as a   **24**
means for each participant to carry on its own business should account directly for its
part of the assets, liabilities and cash flows held within that structure.

Joint ventures are to be included using the gross equity method. However, sometimes   25
a reporting entity operates through a structure that has the appearance of a joint
venture, being a separate entity in which the participants hold a long-term interest
and exercise joint management, but which confers extremely limited commonality of
interest between the venturers because each venturer, in effect, operates its own
business independently of the other venturers within that structure. The nature of
such a structure means that the framework entity acts merely as an agent for the
venturers, with each venturer able to identify and control its share of the assets,
liabilities and cash flows within that framework. In these cases, to reflect the substance of its operations each venturer should account directly for its share of the
assets, liabilities and cash flows arising within the entity.

ACCOUNTING FOR ASSOCIATES

26   A reporting entity that prepares consolidated financial statements should include its associates in those statements using the equity method in all the primary statements. In the investor's individual financial statements, its interests in associates should be treated as fixed asset investments and shown either at cost, less any amounts written off, or at valuation.

The investor's consolidated profit and loss account

27   In the investor's consolidated profit and loss account the investor's share of its associates' operating results should be included immediately after group operating result (but after the investor's share of the results of its joint ventures, if any). Any amortisation or write-down of goodwill arising on acquiring the associates should be charged at this point and disclosed. The investor's share of any exceptional items included after operating profit (paragraph 20 of FRS 3) or of interest should be shown separately from the amounts for the group. At and below the level of profit before tax, the investor's share of the relevant amounts for associates should be included within the amounts for the group, although for items below this level, such as taxation, the amounts relating to associates should be disclosed. Where it is helpful to give an indication of the size of the business as a whole, a total combining the investor's share of its associates' turnover with group turnover may be shown as a memorandum item in the profit and loss account but the investor's share of its associates' turnover should be clearly distinguished from group turnover. Similarly, the segmental analysis of turnover and operating profit (if given) should clearly distinguish between that of the group and that of associates.

The investor's consolidated statement of total recognised gains and losses

28   In the consolidated statement of total recognised gains and losses the investor's share of the total recognised gains and losses of its associates should be included, shown separately under each heading, if the amounts included are material, either in the statement or in a note that is referred to in the statement.

The investor's consolidated balance sheet

29   The investor's consolidated balance sheet should include as a fixed asset investment the investor's share of the net assets of its associates shown as a separate item. Goodwill arising on the investor's acquisition of its associates, less any amortisation or write-down, should be included in the carrying amount for the associates but should be disclosed separately.

The investor's consolidated cash flow statement

30   The investor's consolidated cash flow statement should include dividends received from associates as a separate item between operating activities and returns on investments and servicing of finance. Any other cash flows between the investor and its associates should be included under the appropriate cash flow heading for the activity giving rise to the cash flow. None of the other cash flows of the associates should be included.

APPLYING THE EQUITY METHOD AND THE GROSS EQUITY METHOD

In calculating the amounts to be included in the investor's consolidated financial **31** statements by the equity method for associates and the gross equity method for joint ventures, the same principles should be applied as are applied in the consolidation of subsidiaries.

(a)   When an entity acquires an associate or joint venture, fair values should be attributed to the investee's underlying assets and liabilities, identified using the investor's accounting policies, and these fair values should provide the basis for subsequent depreciation. Both the consideration paid in the acquisition and the goodwill arising should be calculated in the same way as on the acquisition of a subsidiary. The investee's assets used in calculating the goodwill arising on its acquisition should not include any goodwill carried in the balance sheet of the investee itself. Subject to the presentation requirement in paragraph 29 of the FRS, the goodwill balance should be treated in accordance with the provisions of FRS 10 'Goodwill and Intangible Assets'.

(b)   Where profits and losses resulting from transactions between the investor and its associate or joint venture are included in the carrying amount of assets in either entity, the part relating to the investor's share should be eliminated. Where the transaction provides evidence of the impairment of those assets or any similar assets, this should be taken into account.

(c)   In arriving at the amounts to be included by the equity method, the same accounting policies as those of the investor should be applied.

(d)   Where the period-end of an associate or joint venture differs from that of the investor, the entity should be included on the basis of financial statements prepared to the investor's period-end. Where this is not practicable, the entity should be included on the basis of financial statements prepared for a period ending not more than three months before the investor's period-end. Where using these financial statements would release restricted, price-sensitive information, financial statements prepared for a period that ended not more than six months before the investor's period-end may be used. Any changes after the period-end of the associate or joint venture and before that of its investor that would materially affect the view given by the investor's financial statements should be taken into account by adjustment.

Where the investor is a group, its share of its associate or joint venture is the aggregate **32** of the holdings of the parent and its subsidiaries in that entity. The holdings of any of the group's other associates or joint ventures should be ignored for this purpose. Where an associate or joint venture itself has subsidiaries, associates or joint ventures, the results and net assets to be taken into account by the equity method are those reported in that investee's consolidated financial statements (including the investee's share of the results and net assets of its associates and joint ventures), after any adjustment necessary to give effect to the investor's accounting policies.

The investor may hold options, convertibles or non-equity shares in its associate or joint **33** venture. In certain circumstances, the conditions attaching to such holdings are such that the investor should take them into account in reflecting its interest in its investee under the equity or gross equity method. In such cases, the costs of exercising the options or converting the convertibles, or future payments in relation to the non-equity shares, should also be taken into account. The necessary calculation depends on the relevant circumstances in any particular case but care should be taken not to count any interest twice – for example, by including a greater share of the investee under the equity method than that which would arise on the basis of the investor's existing equity

holding while simultaneously writing up the value of options held in the investee to reflect an increase in market value.

34   To apply either the equity method or the gross equity method, the investor's share in its investee needs to be calculated. Where the investee is corporate, the investor's share is usually calculated at its proportional holding of ordinary shares in that entity because this is the basis of its entitlement to dividends and other distributions. In some cases the arrangements for sharing dividends and other distributions may be more complicated; for example, they may depend on the nature of the distribution to be made or the way that the underlying cash flows arise. In these cases the substance of the respective rights held needs to be assessed to establish the most appropriate measure of the investor's share.

35   Paragraph 31 requires procedures in applying the equity methods for associates and joint ventures that are similar to those used in the consolidation of subsidiaries. However, an investor controls its subsidiaries, thus providing access to the information necessary for these procedures, but it exercises only significant influence over its associates or jointly controls its joint ventures. Where access to information is limited, estimates may be used. However, if the information available to the investor is extremely limited, the investor's relationship with its investee will need to be reassessed because there may be doubt in such instances whether its influence is significant or whether it jointly controls its investment.

36   Among the adjustments required by paragraph 31 is the elimination of the investor's share of any profits or losses from transactions between the investor and its investee that are included in the carrying amount of assets in either entity. This adjustment applies only in the investor's consolidated financial statements. The adjustment required applies to transfers of assets or liabilities to set up a joint venture or to acquire an initial stake in an associate as well as to all other transactions during the life of the associate or joint venture. Because associates and joint ventures are not part of the group, balances between the investor and its associates or joint ventures are not eliminated and therefore unsettled normal trading transactions should be included as current assets or liabilities.

37   Regulations on the dissemination of information may restrict the extent to which the financial statements of an investor may contain information about its associates and joint ventures unless such information is available to other interested parties at the same time. An investor should plan how to satisfy any regulations on the publishing of information about its associates and joint ventures.

IMPAIRMENT

38   **Where there has been an impairment in any goodwill attributable to an associate or joint venture, the goodwill should be written down. The amount written off in the accounting period should be separately disclosed.**

39   Any impairment in the underlying net assets of an associate or joint venture would normally be reflected at the level of the entity itself (ie by writing down the relevant assets) or in the adjustments made to apply the equity or gross equity method; accordingly, no further provision against the investor's share of these net assets should usually be necessary.

COMMENCEMENT OR CESSATION OF AN ASSOCIATE OR JOINT VENTURE RELATIONSHIP

The date on which an investment becomes an associate is the date on which the investor   **40**
begins to fulfil the two essential elements of the definition of an associated undertaking:
the holding of a participating interest and the exercise of significant influence. The date
on which an investment ceases to be an associate is the date on which it ceases to fulfil
either element. The date on which an investment becomes a joint venture is the date on
which the investor begins to control that entity jointly with other venturers, provided it
has a long-term interest. The date on which an investment ceases to be a joint venture is
the date on which the investor ceases to have joint control.* When an interest in an
associate or joint venture is disposed of, the profit or loss arising on disposal should be
calculated after taking into account any related goodwill that has not previously been
either written off through the profit and loss account or attributed to prior period
amortisation or impairment on applying the transitional arrangements of FRS 10
'Goodwill and Intangible Assets'.

Where an investment in an associate or joint venture is acquired or disposed of in stages,   **41**
processes similar to those set out for subsidiaries in FRS 2 (paragraphs 50–52) should be
followed.

When an entity ceases to be either an associate or joint venture, the initial carrying   **42**
amount of any interest retained in the entity is based on the percentage retained of the
final carrying amount for the former associate or joint venture at the date the entity
ceased to qualify as such, including any related goodwill as required by paragraph 40.
The initial carrying amount calculated on this basis should be reviewed and written
down, if necessary, to its recoverable amount.

When an entity ceases to be either an associate or joint venture, the investor may   **43**
retain all or some of its interest in that entity as a simple investment. An interest in
another entity that ceases to be a joint venture may still qualify as an associate. Once
an interest qualifies as long-term it should continue to be treated as long-term,
whether the investor intends to keep its interest or dispose of it. The initial carrying
amount of any interest retained in a former associate or joint venture is a surrogate
cost derived from the former carrying amount rather than any consideration paid. In
applying the requirement to review and write down that initial amount, if necessary,
to its recoverable amount, it should be noted that the recoverable amount may be
affected by the amount that has been paid in dividend or by other distributions to
owners. The treatment required for remaining investments in former associates and
joint ventures is similar to that applied to any remaining interest in an entity that has
ceased to be a subsidiary (paragraph 47 of FRS 2).

THE TREATMENT OF LOSSES AND INTERESTS IN NET LIABILITIES

The investor should continue to record changes in the carrying amount for each   **44**
associate and joint venture even if application of the equity method or gross equity
method results in an interest in net liabilities rather than net assets. The only exception
is where there is sufficient evidence that an event has irrevocably changed the relationship between the investor and its investee, marking its irreversible withdrawal from
its investee as its associate or joint venture.

**Paragraph 7 of the FRS is relevant in determining the date on which an investment ceases to be an associate or
joint venture.*

45 Evidence that the necessary irrevocable change has taken place includes a public statement by the investor that it is withdrawing, with a demonstrable commitment to the process of withdrawal, or evidence that the direction of the operating and financing policies of the investee is to become the responsibility of the investee's creditors, including its bankers, rather than its equity shareholders. Where an interest in net liabilities arises, the amount recorded is shown as a provision or liability.

NON-CORPORATE ASSOCIATES AND JOINT VENTURES

46 **Where an investor has an interest in a non-corporate associate or joint venture, the investor should ensure that all its liabilities with respect to that entity are reflected appropriately in its financial statements.**

47 Where an investor has an interest in an unincorporated entity, a liability could arise – for example as a result of joint and several liability in a partnership – that would exceed the amount resulting from taking into account only the investor's share of net assets. In such circumstances it may be necessary either to include an additional amount for that liability or to report it as a contingent liability.

AN INVESTOR THAT DOES NOT PREPARE CONSOLIDATED FINANCIAL STATEMENTS

48 **Where an investor does not prepare consolidated financial statements, it should present the relevant amounts for associates and joint ventures, as appropriate, by preparing a separate set of financial statements or by showing the relevant amounts, together with the effects of including them, as additional information to its own financial statements. Investing entities that are exempt from preparing consolidated financial statements, or would be exempt if they had subsidiaries, are exempt from this requirement.**

INVESTMENT FUNDS

49 **Investment funds, such as those in the venture capital and investment trust industry, should include all investments that are held as part of their investment portfolio in the same way (ie at cost or market value), even those over which the investor has significant influence or joint control. Investments are held as part of an investment portfolio if their value to the investor is through their marketable value as part of a basket of investments rather than as media through which the investor carries out its business.**

50 In the venture capital and investment trust industry, the business of the investor is to provide capital to other entities, often accompanied by advice and guidance. The stake taken by the investor and the rights attributable to that stake vary according to circumstances but the investor's relationship to its investment tends to be that of a portfolio investor. In these circumstances, for consistency, the stake is properly accounted for as an investment according to the method of accounting applied to other investments within that investment portfolio rather than as an associate or joint venture, even if the investor has significant influence or joint control. Outside their investment portfolio, venture capital funds and investment trusts may hold investments that qualify as associates or joint ventures. Such investments should be included using the equity method or the gross equity method, whatever the nature of their investor's business. For investment funds, investments that are associates or joint ventures often arise in a field of activity that is closely related or complementary to that of the investor.

DISCLOSURES

The following disclosures should be made in addition to the amounts required on the   51
face of the primary financial statements under the equity method or the gross equity
method.

For all associates and joint ventures

The names of the principal associates and joint ventures should be disclosed in the   52
financial statements of the investing group, showing for each associate and joint venture:

(a)   the proportion of the issued shares in each class held by the investing group,
      indicating any special rights or constraints attaching to them;
(b)   the accounting period or date of the financial statements used if they differ from
      those of the investing group; and
(c)   an indication of the nature of its business.

Any notes relating to the financial statements of associates and joint ventures, or   53
matters that should have been noted had the investor's accounting policies been applied,
that are material to understanding the effect on the investor of its investments should be
disclosed, in particular noting the investor's share in contingent liabilities incurred
jointly with other venturers or investors and its share of the capital commitments of the
associates and joint ventures themselves.

If there are significant statutory, contractual or exchange control restrictions on the   54
ability of an associate or joint venture to distribute its reserves (other than those shown
as non-distributable), the extent of the restrictions should be indicated.

The amounts owing and owed between an investor and its associates or its joint ventures   55
should be analysed into amounts relating to loans and amounts relating to trading
balances. This disclosure may be combined with those required by FRS 8 'Related Party
Disclosures'.

A note should explain why the facts of any particular case rebut either the presumption   56
that an investor holding 20 per cent or more of the voting rights of another entity
exercises significant influence over the operating and financial policies of that entity or
the presumption that an investor holding 20 per cent or more of the shares of another
entity has a participating interest.

Additional disclosures at 15 and 25 per cent thresholds

The disclosures required for all associates and joint ventures should be supplemented if   57
certain thresholds are exceeded. The thresholds are applied by comparing the investor's
share for either its associates in aggregate or its joint ventures in aggregate or its
individual associates or joint ventures, as appropriate, of the following:

- gross assets
- gross liabilities
- turnover
- operating results (on a three-year average)

with the corresponding amounts for the investor group (excluding any amount included
by the equity method for associates and the gross equity method for joint ventures). If
any of the relevant amounts for the investor's share exceeds the specified proportion of
the same amounts for the investor group, the threshold has been exceeded and the
additional disclosures in paragraph 58 should be made.

58   The following are the additional disclosures that should be made.

(a)   Where the aggregate of the investor's share in its associates exceeds a 15 per cent threshold with respect to the investor group, a note should give the aggregate of the investor's share in its associates of the following:

- turnover (unless it is already included as a memorandum item)
- fixed assets
- current assets
- liabilities due within one year
- liabilities due after one year or more.

(b)   Where the aggregate of the investor's share in its joint ventures exceeds a 15 per cent threshold with respect to the investor group, a note should give the aggregate of the investor's share in its joint ventures of the following:

- fixed assets
- current assets
- liabilities due within one year
- liabilities due after one year or more.

(c)   Where the investor's share in any individual associate or joint venture exceeds a 25 per cent threshold with respect to the investor group, a note should name that associate or joint venture and give its share of each of the following:

- turnover
- profit before tax
- taxation
- profit after tax
- fixed assets
- current assets
- liabilities due within one year
- liabilities due after one year or more.

If that individual associate or joint venture accounts for nearly all of the amounts included for that class of investment, only the aggregate, not the individual, information need be given, provided that this is explained and the associate or joint venture identified.

In addition to the disclosures in (a)–(c) above, further analysis should be given where this is necessary to understand the nature of the total amounts disclosed. In deciding into which balance sheet headings the amounts should be analysed, regard should be had to the nature of the businesses and, therefore, which are the most relevant and descriptive balance sheet amounts to disclose. It may be important to give an indication of the size and maturity profile of the liabilities held.

DATE FROM WHICH EFFECTIVE

59   The accounting practices set out in the FRS should be regarded as standard in respect of financial statements relating to accounting periods ending on or after 23 June 1998. Earlier adoption is encouraged but not required.

WITHDRAWAL OF SSAP 1 AND INTERIM STATEMENT AND AMENDMENT OF FRS 1 (REVISED 1996)

60   The FRS supersedes SSAP 1 'Accounting for associated companies' and withdraws the remaining paragraphs of the Interim Statement 'Consolidated Accounts'.

61   The FRS makes the following changes to FRS 1 (Revised 1996) 'Cash Flow Statements' in respect of the treatment of dividends received from associates and joint ventures.

[*Not reproduced as all changes have been reflected in the material reproduced in this volume.*]

Adoption of FRS 9 by the Board

Financial Reporting Standard 9 – 'Associates and Joint Ventures' was approved for issue by the ten members of the Accounting Standards Board.

Sir David Tweedie	(Chairman)
Allan Cook	(Technical Director)
David Allvey	
Ian Brindle	
Dr John Buchanan	
John Coombe	
Raymond Hinton	
Huw Jones	
Professor Geoffrey Whittington	
Ken Wild	

Appendix I
Note on legal requirements

1   The general legal background to the requirements of the FRS are considered in paragraphs 2–6. Paragraphs 7–11 set out the relevant legal provisions in Great Britain with the corresponding references for Northern Ireland in paragraph 12 and the Republic of Ireland in paragraph 13.

GREAT BRITAIN

The Companies Act 1985 and the approach taken in the FRS

2   An associate is defined in the FRS as an entity in which the investor holds a participating interest, and over which it exercises significant influence, with the result that an associate will also qualify as an associated undertaking as defined in the Companies Act 1985. The requirement for associates to be included in the investor's consolidated financial statements using the equity method of accounting is also consistent with the requirement for associated undertakings in the Act.

3   A joint venture is defined in the FRS as an entity in which each joint venturer has a long-term interest and has joint control. A joint venturer, therefore, fulfils the conditions for having a participating interest and exercising a significant influence, with the result that all joint ventures meeting the definition in the FRS will also qualify as associated undertakings as defined in the Act. The Act does not define a 'joint venture', although it refers to 'managing jointly' in its description of non-corporate joint ventures that are permitted to be included using proportional consolidation.

4   The FRS requires joint ventures to be included in the investor's consolidated financial statements using the gross equity method. This method provides information in addition to that given by the traditional equity method and its use is therefore consistent with the requirement of the Act for associated undertakings to be included by the equity method.

5   The FRS notes that a reporting entity sometimes carries out some of its operations through entities with the form of a joint venture but where there is limited commonality of interest between the venturers as each, in effect, operates its own business within the structure. Unless these arrangements constitute an undertaking (as defined in section 259 of the Act), the Act is silent on the treatment, and the requirement of the FRS is that each of the participants should account for its share of the assets and liabilities directly as its own. Even in cases where the contractual arrangements are performed through the medium of an undertaking, if the nature of those arrangements means that the undertaking acts merely as an agent for the participants then, in such cases, they should follow the requirements of the FRS by accounting directly for their share of the assets and liabilities.

6   A similar analysis applies to the treatment of joint arrangements that are not entities. The FRS requires participants in such arrangements to account directly for their own assets, liabilities and cash flows. However, a joint arrangement may qualify as an undertaking under the Act even though it does not carry on its own trade or business (eg where the joint arrangement is a body corporate or a partnership). In such cases the nature of those arrangements means that the undertaking acts merely as an agent for the venturers and, therefore, they should account directly for their share of the assets and liabilities.

The provisions of the Companies Act 1985

The Act defines an "associated undertaking" in paragraph 20 of Schedule 4A.   **7**

"(1) An "associated undertaking" means an undertaking in which an undertaking included in the consolidation has a participating interest and over whose operating and financial policy it exercises a significant influence, and which is not–

(a) a subsidiary undertaking of the parent company, or
(b) a joint venture dealt with in accordance with paragraph 19 [of Schedule 4A].

(2) Where an undertaking holds 20 per cent or more of the voting rights in another undertaking, it shall be presumed to exercise such an influence over it unless the contrary is shown.

(3) The voting rights in an undertaking mean the rights conferred on shareholders in respect of their shares or, in the case of an undertaking not having a share capital, on members, to vote at general meetings of the undertaking on all, or substantially all, matters.

(4) The provisions of paragraphs 5 to 11 of Schedule 10A (rights to be taken into account and attribution of rights) apply in determining for the purposes of this paragraph whether an undertaking holds 20 per cent or more of the voting rights in another undertaking."

Section 260 of the Act defines a "participating interest" as follows: **8**

"(1) ... an interest held by an undertaking in the shares of another undertaking which it holds on a long-term basis for the purpose of securing a contribution to its activities by the exercise of control or influence arising from or related to that interest.

(2) A holding of 20 per cent or more of the shares of an undertaking shall be presumed to be a participating interest unless the contrary is shown.

(3) The reference in subsection (1) to an interest in shares includes–

(a) an interest which is convertible into an interest in shares, and
(b) an option to acquire shares or any such interest;

and an interest or option falls within paragraph (a) or (b) notwithstanding that the shares to which it relates are, until the conversion or the exercise of the option, unissued.

(4) For the purposes of this section an interest held on behalf of an undertaking shall be treated as held by it."

Paragraph 22 of Schedule 4A requires that: **9**

"(1) The interest of an undertaking in an associated undertaking, and the amount of profit or loss attributable to such an interest, shall be shown by the equity method of accounting (including dealing with any goodwill arising in accordance with paragraphs 17 to 19 and 21 of Schedule 4).

(2) Where the associated undertaking is itself a parent undertaking, the net assets and profits or losses to be taken into account are those of the parent and its subsidiary undertakings (after making any consolidation adjustments)."

Paragraph 21 of Schedule 4A stipulates the position in the balance sheet and the   **10** profit and loss account formats of interests in associated undertakings and other participating interests and income from such interests.

11   The Act does not define a joint venture. However, paragraph 19 of Schedule 4A provides that:

"(1) Where an undertaking included in the consolidation manages another under-taking jointly with one or more undertakings not included in the consolidation, that other undertaking ("the joint venture") may, if it is not –

(a)   a body corporate, or

(b)   a subsidiary undertaking of the parent company,

be dealt with in the group accounts by the method of proportional consolidation.

(2) The provisions of this Part* relating to the preparation of consolidated accounts apply, with any necessary modifications, to proportional consolidation under this paragraph."

NORTHERN IRELAND

12   The legal requirements in Northern Ireland equivalent to those in Great Britain quoted in paragraphs 7–11 are set out in the following table.

Great Britain: *Companies Act 1985*	*Northern Ireland:* *Companies (Northern Ireland) Order 1986*
paragraph 20 of Schedule 4A	paragraph 20 of Schedule 4A
section 260	Article 268
paragraph 22 of Schedule 4A	paragraph 22 of Schedule 4A
paragraph 21 of Schedule 4A	paragraph 21 of Schedule 4A
paragraph 19 of Schedule 4A	paragraph 19 of Schedule 4A

*The reference to 'Part' appears to mean Schedule 4A.

REPUBLIC OF IRELAND

The legal requirements in the Republic of Ireland equivalent to those in Great   **13**
Britain quoted in paragraphs 7–11 are set out in the following table.

Great Britain:	*Republic of Ireland:*
Companies Act 1985	*European Communities (Companies: Group Accounts) Regulations 1992*
paragraph 20 of Schedule 4A	Regulation 34
section 260	Regulation 35
paragraph 22 of Schedule 4A	Regulation 33
paragraph 21 of Schedule 4A	paragraph 10 of the Schedule
paragraph 19 of Schedule 4A	Regulation 32

Appendix II
Compliance with international accounting standards

1   The International Accounting Standards Committee (IASC) has one standard for associates – IAS 28 'Accounting for Investments in Associates' – and another for joint ventures and other joint arrangements – IAS 31 'Financial Reporting of Interests in Joint Ventures'.*

IAS 28 'Accounting for Investments in Associates'

2   For associates, the requirements of the FRS and IAS 28 are similar, both requiring the use of the equity method in the investor's consolidated financial statements. There are the following minor differences.

- IAS 28 defines an associate as an enterprise in which the investor has significant influence, whereas the FRS is consistent with companies legislation and defines an associate by the investor's holding of a participating interest and exercise of significant influence. Furthermore, the emphasis in the FRS is on the actual exercise of significant influence, whereas IAS 28 defines significant influence as "the power to participate in the financial and operating policy decisions of the investee". The IAS 28 definition would therefore apply to investors that had the ability to exercise significant influence but were not actually exercising it. This difference may have a limited effect in practice because the best evidence of an entity's ability to exercise significant influence is the fact that it is exercising such an influence.
- IAS 28 contains a rebuttable presumption of significant influence where an investor holds, directly or indirectly through subsidiaries, 20 per cent or more of the voting power of the investee. There is a similar presumption of the exercise of significant influence in companies legislation. However, the FRS moves away from using a 20 per cent threshold as the defining threshold, noting that a holding of 20 per cent or more of the voting rights in another entity suggests, but does not ensure, that the investor exercises significant influence over that entity. The presumption of the exercise of significant influence at the 20 per cent threshold is rebutted if the investor does not fulfil the criteria for the exercise of significant influence.
- IAS 28 excludes from equity accounting any associate that is acquired and held exclusively with a view to its subsequent disposal in the near future or which operates under severe long-term restrictions that significantly impair its ability to transfer funds to the investor. The FRS does not have any specific exclusions but the conditions relating to the exercise of significant influence are unlikely to be fulfilled by an investment operating under severe long-term restrictions and the definition of a participating interest specifies an interest that is held on a long-term basis, which excludes one held exclusively with a view to disposal.
- IAS 28 requires an associate to be included in its investor's individual financial statements using the equity method or at cost or revalued amount. The FRS requires an associate to be carried at cost or valuation in its investor's individual financial statements.

Editor's note: Both IAS 28 and IAS 31 were revised in 1998. They have now been revised further with new versions published in December 2003. Among the changes made to IAS 28 are that there is a specific exclusion for venture capital organisations and similar holding interests that would otherwise be associates, potential voting rights are to be taken into account in determining if an entity is an associate, there is some clarification on temporary influence and long-term restrictions, and there are revised rules on recognition of losses. Among the changes to IAS 31 are a similar exemption for venture capital organisations and similar, and similar rules on temporary joint control and long-term restrictions.

- IAS 28 requires that the investor's consolidated income statement should reflect its share of the results of the operations of the investee. The FRS specifies that the investor's share of its associates' operating results should be brought into its consolidated profit and loss account immediately after the line showing group operating profit but after its share of the operating results of its joint ventures, if any.
- The FRS requires additional disclosures to the amounts shown under the equity method for associates that in aggregate exceed 15 per cent of gross assets, gross liabilities, turnover or, on a three-year average, operating result for the investing group and for each individual associate that exceeds 25 per cent of gross assets, gross liabilities, turnover or, on a three-year average, operating result for the investing group. These are not required by IAS 28.

IAS 31 'Financial Reporting of Interests in Joint Ventures'

Although both the FRS and IAS 31 take joint control as the defining relationship **3** between an investor and its joint ventures, IAS 31 defines a joint venture in terms of a contractual arrangement while the FRS defines a joint venture in terms of an entity.* The effect of this difference in definition is that of the three types of joint venture identified in IAS 31 – jointly controlled operations, jointly controlled assets and jointly controlled entities – only the last qualifies as a joint venture as defined in the FRS. IAS 31 does not include an explicit definition of an entity or guidance on how to distinguish jointly controlled operations and jointly controlled assets from jointly controlled entities. The FRS provides guidance on whether an entity exists, which depends on whether the joint activities amount to the carrying on of a trade or business. In the FRS jointly controlled operations and jointly controlled assets are dealt with as joint arrangements that are not entities. However, the treatment required for jointly controlled operations and jointly controlled assets is the same in the FRS and IAS 31 – participants should recognise directly in their own financial statements, and consequently in their consolidated financial statements, their share of the assets and liabilities of jointly controlled operations and of any jointly controlled assets.

The FRS requires joint ventures to be included in their investor's consolidated **4** financial statements using the gross equity method – which expands the traditional equity method with a note of the investor's share of the turnover, gross assets and liabilities of the joint ventures. In IAS 31, the equity method is an 'allowed alternative' for jointly controlled entities but the 'benchmark' treatment is proportional consolidation, with a choice of two reporting formats – including the investor's share of its joint ventures either line-by-line or as separate line items for assets, liabilities, profit and expenses.

IAS 31 requires interests in jointly controlled entities to be treated as ordinary **5** investments if they:

(a) are acquired and held exclusively with a view to subsequent disposal in the near future; or
(b) operate under severe long-term restrictions that significantly impair their ability to transfer funds to the venturer.

The FRS has no need for such exclusions, because the conditions relating to the definition of a joint venture are unlikely to be fulfilled in these circumstances.

*As noted in Appendix I, the definition in the FRS is in line with companies legislation, where only 'associated undertakings' qualify to use the equity method.

6   IAS 31 requires a venturer to disclose the aggregate amounts of each of current assets, long-term assets, current liabilities, long-term liabilities, income and expenses related to its interests in jointly controlled entities.* The FRS requires instead additional levels of disclosure where joint ventures in aggregate exceed a 15 per cent threshold or individual joint ventures exceed a 25 per cent threshold of certain key indicators (paragraphs 57 and 58). The FRS requires amounts included for joint ventures to be analysed into at least fixed assets, current assets, liabilities due within one year and liabilities due after one year or more.

Unless the venturer uses the reporting format for proportional consolidation where separate line items are included for the venturer's share of the assets, liabilities, income and expenses of its joint venture.

Appendix III
The development of the FRS

HISTORY

For a variety of legal, tax, economic and other reasons, business activities are often **1** conducted through a network of connected entities, including subsidiaries, joint ventures and associates. Joint ventures are increasingly popular as a means of gaining access to new markets, new technologies or scarce resources and sometimes as a means of sharing risks.

In March 1996 the Board issued FRED 11 'Associates and Joint Ventures' containing **2** proposals developed in the light of comments on its earlier Discussion Paper (July 1994) to revise the current standard, SSAP 1 'Accounting for associated companies'. SSAP 1 was originally issued in 1971 as a response to the growing practice of entities of conducting parts of their businesses through associates. The standard ensured that the investor's consolidated financial statements reflected the effect of a reporting entity's investments in associates by including such entities using the equity method. SSAP 1 was revised in 1982.

The Board decided to carry out a full review of SSAP 1 because that standard: **3**

- did not cover the identification of, and accounting for, joint ventures.
- encouraged but did not require additional disclosures where significant interests were included by equity accounting. There was little evidence of additional disclosures being made.
- permitted in the Board's view an, at times, too literal interpretation of the definition of an associated company (associate), which was applied to the form of the reporting entity's interest in another entity rather than the substance.

The proposals in FRED 11 were generally well received and the FRS carries forward **4** unchanged the proposals on the following topics:-

- the definitions of associates and joint ventures
- the inclusion of associates in the investor's consolidated financial statements using the equity method
- the measurement principles required by the equity method
- the commencement or cessation of an associate or joint venture relationship
- the treatment of losses and interests in the net liabilities where losses have accumulated.

On three topics some respondents, albeit a minority, did not support the proposals in **5** FRED 11 and put forward some well argued objections. The Board has considered carefully the comments made and has consulted further on these issues. To meet some of the concerns expressed, the proposed treatments in FRED 11 have been modified.

- Joint ventures are now treated as a single class of investment rather than the two classes proposed by FRED 11 and the gross equity method is now required for all joint ventures. The result is to give a better impression of the scale of resources committed to joint ventures in relation to those of the reporting entity than is conveyed by the traditional equity method.
- The investor's share of the results of its equity accounted entities is now included immediately after group operating profit rather than in group operating profit, as proposed in FRED 11.

- The level of detail required for additional disclosures for associates or joint ventures at a 15 per cent threshold has been reduced from that proposed in FRED 11 – but further analysis is required where this is necessary to understand the nature of the amounts shown. The disclosures for individual associates or joint ventures that individually exceed a 25 per cent threshold in relation to the investor have been aligned with the disclosures in aggregate at the 15 per cent threshold.

THE BASIC PRINCIPLES

6   A key issue for the Board in considering associates and joint ventures has been the need to develop proposals for them that would form part of a coherent and consistent policy for the treatment of all of a reporting entity's interests in other entities and other joint arrangements that are not entities. The Board has therefore addressed how to distinguish joint ventures from associates on the one hand and subsidiaries on the other and how to distinguish associates from simple investments. In the FRS these distinctions are based on the nature of the investor's relationship with the investee – which is also what justifies the different accounting treatments proposed to reflect the different interests.

- If the investor controls its investee, the investee is its subsidiary and should be consolidated.
- If the reporting entity participates in a joint arrangement that is not an entity (ie it does not carry on a trade or business of its own), it should account directly for its share of the assets, liabilities and cash flows of the joint arrangement according to the terms of the agreement governing the arrangement.
- If the investor controls the investee not by itself but jointly with other entities, the investee is its joint venture. A special accounting treatment – the gross equity method – is proposed to reflect this relationship.
- If the investor neither controls nor jointly controls its investee but still has significant influence over the investee's operating and financial policies, the investee is its associate. The equity method is traditionally used to reflect this relationship.
- If the investor neither controls nor jointly controls its investee, nor has significant influence over the investee's operating and financial policies, the investee is merely an investment. There is no special relationship to account for and the investor should include the investment in both its individual and consolidated financial statements in the same way.

7   The principles set out above are very similar to those underlying the proposals in FRED 11, but the latter have been modified in two following respects.

(a) Joint arrangements that are not entities

FRED 11 defined joint ventures as entities in a similar way to the FRS, thus also departing from the IASC standard on joint ventures, IAS 31, which includes as joint ventures not only jointly controlled entities but also jointly controlled operations and jointly controlled assets. FRED 11 considered jointly controlled operations and jointly controlled assets only briefly in its 'Explanation' section. The FRS addresses joint arrangements that are not entities much more fully by including a definition with an explanation of how to determine whether a set of activities constitutes an entity. In the FRS the treatment for such joint arrangements is the same as that proposed in FRED 11.

(b) Joint ventures

FRED 11 proposed identifying two classes of joint ventures: those where the venturers shared in common the benefits and risks, which were to be included by the equity method, and those where each venturer had its own separate interest, which were to be included by proportional consolidation. The FRS now emphasises the special nature of joint control by identifying joint ventures as a single class of investments wholly separate from associates, to be included by a special method of accounting – the gross equity method. However, in practice the difference from the proposals in FRED 11 may be limited because the sort of arrangement that, under FRED 11, would have been most clearly identifiable as a joint venture to be proportionally con-solidated will, under the FRS, be accounted for by each participant bringing in directly its share of any assets, liabilities and cash flows to reflect the substance of the arrangement as a structure within which each participant carries on its own business.

A JOINT ARRANGEMENT THAT IS NOT AN ENTITY

Paragraph 6 of the FRS identifies a joint arrangement that is not an entity as the way **8** in which a reporting entity can further its economic activities through investments or joint arrangements that involves the reporting entity most directly. The FRS requires each participant in such a joint arrangement to account directly for its own share of the assets, liabilities and cash flows relating to the joint arrangement, its share being measured by reference to the terms of the joint arrangement. If a joint arrangement is not an entity, accounting treatments whose purpose is to reflect a reporting entity's interests in other entities in its consolidated financial statements – such as con-solidation, proportional consolidation and equity accounting – are irrelevant in deciding how to treat that arrangement. The 'Explanation' section of FRED 11 dealt in a similar way with joint arrangements.

JOINT VENTURES

Definition

The FRS sets out three conditions to be fulfilled for a joint arrangement to meet the **9** definition of a joint venture.

(a)   The business activities undertaken under the joint arrangement must constitute an entity.
(b)   The venturer must jointly control the entity.
(c)   The investor's interest must be held for the long term.

In FRED 11 condition (c) was not stated explicitly.

The definition of an entity in the FRS is built on that of an undertaking in companies **10** legislation as proposed in FRED 11 but, in response to the comments, the FRS gives more guidance on the application of the definition, elaborating on a key aspect – the carrying on of a trade or business. The distinction between joint arrangements that are entities and those that are not is important because the equity method can apply only to interests in entities. For a joint arrangement that does not amount to an entity, the only possible accounting procedure is that each party involved should recognise directly its own share of assets, liabilities and cash flows, measured by reference to the agreement governing the joint arrangement.

Treatment

11   The gross equity method required by the FRS for joint ventures amplifies the net amounts included under the equity method by showing in the consolidated profit and loss account and balance sheet the investor's share of its joint ventures' turnover, gross assets and gross liabilities. The manner in which these additional details are presented expands the information given by the traditional equity method without changing its nature – the investment in joint ventures is still shown as a net amount and joint ventures' turnover is excluded from that of the group. The effect of this is that the gross equity method, like the traditional equity method, is consistent with the use of control as the basis of asset recognition (in that the net investment represents the asset that is controlled by the venturer) while going some way to meet concerns expressed by a minority of respondents that the traditional equity method understated the scale of activity undertaken through joint ventures.

12   In addition to concerns about the adequacy of the equity method for joint ventures, some respondents who opposed the proposals in FRED 11 for joint ventures believed that either:

(a)   all joint ventures should be included by proportional consolidation, particularly because that is the benchmark treatment for joint ventures in IAS 31; or

(b)   the division of joint ventures into two classes proposed in FRED 11 was either not valid in principle or difficult to apply in practice. FRED 11 proposed distinguishing between:

(i)   the majority of joint ventures, where the venturers shared in common the benefits, risks and obligations of their joint venture as a separate business, which were to be included using the equity method; and

(ii)   other joint ventures, where each venturer had a separate interest in the benefits, risks and obligations of the venture, which were to be included by proportional consolidation.

13   The difference of opinion between those supporting an equity method for joint ventures and those supporting proportional consolidation is reflected in an international debate on the treatment of joint ventures. IAS 31 notes that, in a jointly controlled entity (a joint venture under the FRS), a venturer has control over its share of future economic benefits through its share of the assets and liabilities of the venture. IAS 31 does not recommend the use of the equity method, on the grounds that proportional consolidation better reflects the substance and economic reality of a venturer's interest in a jointly controlled entity, ie control over the venturer's share of the future economic benefits. The Board rejects proportional consolidation for joint ventures because it believes that it can be misleading to represent each venturer's joint control of a joint venture – which allows it to direct the operating and financial policies of the joint venture only with the consent of the other venturers – as being in substance equivalent to its having sole control of its share of each of that entity's assets, liabilities and cash flows. The key features of control are that the controlling party has the ability to direct or deploy what it controls without consultation and the ability to take the benefit from what it directs or deploys without question of entitlement. The problems with treating a venturer's joint control as equivalent to its sole control of its share are particularly clear for cash flow reporting where, under proportional consolidation, the venturer would include its share of the cash flows of its joint venture directly as its own cash flows.

14   Another argument on which IAS 31 supports proportional consolidation for jointly controlled entities is that it results in the joint arrangements of the investor being reflected in the same way in its consolidated financial statements, whether its joint activities are carried on through jointly controlled assets, jointly controlled

operations or jointly controlled entities. However, the Board believes there is an essential difference between activities carried on directly by the reporting entity itself through its jointly controlled assets or operations and activities carried out through an entity controlled jointly with other entities. In jointly controlled assets or operations, the benefits, risks and obligations for each entity relate only to the entity's share of the assets and liabilities involved in the joint activity. In contrast, in a jointly controlled entity the investors usually share in common the benefits, risks and obligations of the entity as a whole rather than those of the individual assets and liabilities of that entity.

The Board believes that some flexibility is important to reflect the diversity of joint **15** ventures and to enable reporting entities to reflect the nature of their interests. In some cases, the reporting entity may want to give more information about its joint venture on the face of its financial statements. Provided that any additional information given for joint ventures is in a form that is consistent with the gross equity method, the Board encourages experimentation. Appendix IV sets out an optional columnar presentation that may be used where joint ventures represent a major part of the reporting entity's business. The columnar presentation keeps separate the amounts relating to joint ventures from the amounts for the group itself and remains consistent with the equity method because it is formatted to provide an additional analysis of the net amounts included under the equity method.

A STRUCTURE WITH THE FORM BUT NOT THE SUBSTANCE OF A JOINT VENTURE

The FRS requires that venturers should account directly for their own share of the **16** assets, liabilities and cash flows of a structure with the appearance of a joint venture used only as a means for the each participant to carry on their own business. In spite of its appearance, such a structure is not a joint venture because of the extremely limited commonality of interest between the participants. The proposal in FRED 11 for proportional consolidation where a joint venture acts only as a framework for each venturer carrying on its own activities also recognised that the equity method was not appropriate in such cases.

ASSOCIATES

Identification

As proposed in FRED 11, to be consistent with companies legislation, the FRS defines **17** an associate by reference to its investor having a participating interest and exercising significant influence over it. In the earlier Discussion Paper, both associates and joint ventures were identified as a single class of investments called 'strategic alliances' and the emphasis was on the investor acting as a partner in the business of its investee. Some commentators found this emphasis on a partnership between an investor and its associate unhelpful and contrary to their understanding of a partnership. As a result the Board decided to drop the approach that used 'strategic alliances', and has reverted to the approach underlying SSAP 1, which emphasises participation in the operating and financial policies of the investee.

All investees qualifying as associates under the FRS would have qualified as associates **18** under SSAP 1, which defined an associate as an interest held for the long term where the investor is in a position to exercise significant influence. However, an entity may have qualified as an associate under SSAP 1 yet not qualify as such under the definitions in the FRS because a long-term interest is not always a participating interest, and being in a position to exercise significant influence does not always amount to the actual exercise of such an influence. In practice, these differences may have a limited effect because the best evidence that an entity is in a position to exercise significant influence is that it is actually exercising such influence. Applying the definition in this FRS should ensure that the substance of the relationship between the investor and investee is reflected thus correcting any instances of the too literal application of the SSAP 1 definition – for example, where the investor has a 20 per cent holding but in practice does not actually exercise significant influence.

Treatment

19   The requirement in the FRS for associates to be included in the investor's consolidated financial statements using the equity method of accounting represents no change to the requirements of SSAP 1 or the proposals in the Discussion Paper and FRED 11, the overwhelming majority of commentators agreeing with equity accounting for associates. Using the equity method for associates is in keeping with the principle that the assets and liabilities of a group are delineated by the extent of the parent's control because the equity method represents an investor's interest in an associate as a single asset – an investment – albeit one that is measured in terms of net assets and changes in net assets. An investor controls its interest in an associate but does not control its share of its associate's underlying assets and liabilities. For these reasons proportional consolidation is not appropriate for associates because it misrepresents the extent of the investor's influence over its associate's underlying assets and liabilities (and, in particular, its cash flows).

20   One possible alternative to the equity method would be to include associates at market value. However, providing information on that basis would not be consistent with the information provided by consolidated financial statements about a parent and its subsidiaries. Equity accounting for associates is consistent with consolidation for subsidiaries because it recognises the investor's share of its associates' results and changes in net assets, reflecting that associates are used as media through which the investor carries on its business, sometimes as substitutes for subsidiaries.

APPLYING THE EQUITY METHOD

21   Paragraph 33 of the FRS deals with cases where part of the investor's interest in its associate or joint venture arises from its holding of options, convertibles or non-equity shares. The basis of this paragraph is the requirement in FRS 5 (paragraph 14) that the substance of transactions should be reported. "In determining the substance of a transaction, all its aspects and implications should be identified and greater weight given to those more likely to have a commercial effect in practice." The investor should therefore account for the substance of its interest in its associates or joint ventures in cases where this is affected by its holdings of options, convertibles or non-equity shares. One example where an adjustment to the investor's interest may be necessary is where the price of exercising or converting options or convertibles is so low that there is commercially near-certainty that they will be exercised or converted.

22   Consistently with the exclusion of the results of associates or joint ventures from group operating profit, the FRS amends FRS 1 (Revised 1996) to include the cash flows relating to dividends received from associates and joint ventures as separate items between operating activities and returns on investment and servicing of finance in the investor's consolidated cash flow statement. FRED 11 proposed that the results of equity accounted entities should be included as part of group operating profit and therefore proposed that dividends received from such entities should be included as operating cash flows. The treatment in this FRS reflects the fact that dividends from

associates and joint ventures are not on a comparable basis to the cash flows arising from the group's operating activities and have a different significance from its returns on investments.

DISCLOSURES

One of the Board's objectives in reviewing SSAP 1 was to improve the information given about associates and joint ventures, particularly where they play a significant part in the reporting entity's operations. The equity method, by including only the net assets and results, had been criticised as failing to show the full amount of resources and obligations arising from the venturer's involvement. SSAP 1 required more detailed information to be given where, in the context of the financial statements of the investing group, the results of one or more associated companies were so material, or the interests in them were so material, that more detailed information about them would assist in giving a true and fair view. This requirement resulted in little extra disclosure in practice.   **23**

The FRS follows FRED 11 and the earlier Discussion Paper in requiring a layered approach to disclosures, with additional disclosures of aggregate amounts only when associates or joint ventures represent a significant part of the reporting entity's business at a 15 per cent threshold and with additional disclosures on an individual basis only in the rare cases when an individual associate or joint venture exceeds a 25 per cent threshold. However, there are two changes in the disclosure requirements from those proposed in FRED 11.   **24**

(a)   The FRS requires the 15 per cent threshold for additional aggregate disclosures to be applied separately for associates and joint ventures as these are now classified as two different categories of investment.
(b)   The FRS reduces the disclosures required both in aggregate at the 15 per cent threshold and for individual associates and joint ventures at the 25 per cent threshold.

These changes should reduce the concerns about the level of required disclosures that some respondents noted on FRED 11 – adverse comment was particularly marked in respect of the proposal for the disclosure of condensed financial information for any associate or joint venture that exceeded a 25 per cent threshold. The Board has successively attempted to meet concerns about the level of the disclosures by carefully targeting any disclosures to be required. FRED 11 itself reduced the number of disclosures proposed from those proposed in the Discussion Paper. The disclosures required at the 25 per cent threshold for individual associates and joint ventures are now consistent with those required in aggregate at the 15 per cent threshold, in particular the investor's share of the relevant amounts is to be disclosed rather than the amount relating to the whole associate or joint venture.

However, the FRS still includes a requirement for some additional individual disclosures for any highly significant associate or joint venture. The main objections to the proposal for individual disclosures in FRED 11 were that it would entail greater disclosure for some individual associates and joint ventures than for individual subsidiaries and might lead to the disclosure of commercially sensitive information. The Board has carefully considered these objections and, as a response, stresses the very high threshold level that is set to trigger the disclosures. An individual associate or joint venture rarely breaches this threshold – however, when it does, it plays such a significant role in a reporting entity while, unlike a subsidiary, outside the reporting entity's control, that the Board believes the proposed disclosures are necessary for the reporting entity to discharge its accountability and to give a true and fair view of its financial position and performance.   **25**

Appendix IV
Examples of alternative ways of giving information on joint ventures

The examples set out in this appendix are provided for general guidance only and do not form part of the FRS.

EXAMPLE 1 – the normal presentation using the equity method for associates and the gross equity method for joint ventures.

EXAMPLE 2 – an optional columnar presentation for joint ventures where they constitute a major part of the reporting entity's business.

Examples 1 and 2 use the same underlying information.

EXAMPLE 1 – THE NORMAL PRESENTATION

CONSOLIDATED PROFIT AND LOSS ACCOUNT

This format is illustrative only. The amounts shown for 'Associates' and 'Joint ventures' are subdivisions of the item for which the statutory prescribed heading is 'Income from interests in associated undertakings'. The subdivisions may be shown in a note rather than on the face of the profit and loss account.

	£m	£m
Turnover: group and share of joint ventures	*320*	
Less: share of joint ventures' turnover	*(120)*	
Group turnover		200
Cost of sales		(120)
Gross profit		80
Administrative expenses		(40)
Group operating profit		40
Share of operating profit in		
Joint ventures	30	
Associates	24	
		54
		94
Interest receivable (group)		6
Interest payable		
Group	(26)	
Joint ventures	(10)	
Associates	(12)	
		(48)
Profit on ordinary activities before tax		52
Tax on profit on ordinary activities*		(12)
Profit on ordinary activities after tax		40
Minority interests		(6)
Profit on ordinary activities after taxation and minority interest		34
Equity dividends		(10)
Retained profit for group and its share of associates and joint ventures		24

*Tax relates to the following:	Parent and subsidiaries	(5)
	Joint ventures	(5)
	Associates	(2)

CONSOLIDATED BALANCE SHEET

	£m	£m	£m
Fixed assets			
Tangible assets		480	
Investments			
Investments in joint ventures:			
Share of gross assets	130		
Share of gross liabilities	(80)		
		50	
Investments in associates		20	
			550
Current assets			
Stock		15	
Debtors		75	
Cash at bank and in hand		10	
		100	
Creditors (due within one year)		(50)	
Net current assets			50
Total assets less current liabilities			600
Creditors (due after more than one year)			(250)
Provisions for liabilities and charges			(10)
Equity minority interest			(40)
			300
Capital and reserves			
Called up share capital			50
Share premium account			150
Profit and loss account			100
Shareholders' funds (all equity)			300

NOTES

In the example, there is no individual associate or joint venture that accounts for more than 25 per cent of any of the following for the investor group (excluding any amount for associates and joint ventures):

- gross assets
- gross liabilities
- turnover
- operating results (on a three-year average).

Additional disclosures for joint ventures (which in aggregate exceed the 15 per cent threshold)

	£m	£m
Share of assets		
Share of fixed assets	100	
Share of current assets	30	
		130
Share of liabilities		
Liabilities due within one year or less	(10)	
Liabilities due after more than one year	(70)	
		(80)
Share of net assets		50

Additional disclosures for associates (which in aggregate exceed the 15 per cent threshold)

	£m	£m
Share of turnover of associates		90
Share of assets		
Share of fixed assets	4	
Share of current assets	28	
		32
Share of liabilities		
Liabilities due within one year or less	(3)	
Liabilities due after more than one year	(9)	
		(12)
Share of net assets		20

EXAMPLE 2 – AN OPTIONAL PRESENTATION

CONSOLIDATED PROFIT & LOSS ACCOUNT

This format is illustrative only. The amounts shown for 'Associates' and 'Joint ventures' are subdivisions of the item for which the statutory prescribed heading is 'Income from interests in associated undertakings'. The subdivisions may be shown in a note rather than on the face of the profit and loss account.

	£m Group	£m Interests in joint ventures	£m Total
Turnover	200	120	320
Cost of sales	(120)	(85)	(205)
Gross profit	80	35	115
Administrative expenses	(40)	(5)	(45)
Operating profit	40	30	70

Share of operating profit in		
Joint ventures	30	
Associates	24	
Total operating profit:		
group and share of		
joint ventures and associates	94	
Interest receivable (group)	6	
Interest payable		
Group	(26)	
Joint ventures	(10)	
Associates	(12)	
		(48)
Profit on ordinary activities		
before tax	52	
Tax on profit on		
ordinary activities*		(12)
Profit on ordinary activities		
after tax *(carried forward)*	40	

* Tax relates to the following:	Parent and subsidiaries	(5)
	Joint ventures	(5)
	Associates	(2)

£m

**Profit on ordinary activities
after tax** *(brought forward)*   40

Minority interests   (6)

**Profit on ordinary activities after
taxation and minority interest**   34

Equity dividends   (10)

**Retained profit for group and its
share of associates and joint ventures**   24

CONSOLIDATED BALANCE SHEET

	£m *Group*	£m *Interests in joint ventures**	£m *Total*
Fixed assets			
Tangible assets	480	100	*580*
Investments			
Investments in joint ventures	50	*(50)*	
Investments in associates	20		*20*
	550		*600*
Current assets			
Stock	15	5	*20*
Debtors	75	23	*98*
Cash at bank and in hand	10	2	*12*
	100	30	*130*
Creditors (due within one year)	(50)	(10)	*(60)*
Net current assets	50	20	*70*
Total assets less current liabilities	600	120	*670*
Creditors (due after more than one year)	(250)	(70)	*(320)*
Provision for liabilities and charges	(10)		*(10)*
Net assets	340		340
Equity minority interest	(40)		
	300		
Capital and reserves			
Called up share capital	50		
Share premium account	150		
Profit and loss account	100		
Shareholders' funds (all equity)	300		

Additional disclosures

The same additional disclosures should be made as in Example 1.

---

* *The boxed amounts, totalling 50 without the shaded amount, show the investor's share of the assets and liabilities of its joint ventures – the shaded (50) transfers this amount to the fixed assets of the group as 'investments in joint ventures'.*

Financial Reporting Standard 10 is set out in paragraphs 1–78.

The Statement of Standard Accounting Practice, which comprises the paragraphs set in bold type, should be read in the context of the Objective as stated in paragraph 1 and the definitions set out in paragraphs 2 and 3 and also of the Foreword to Accounting Standards and the Statement of Principles for Financial Reporting currently in issue.

The explanatory paragraphs contained in the FRS shall be regarded as part of the Statement of Standard Accounting Practice insofar as they assist in interpreting that statement.

Appendix III 'The development of the FRS' reviews considerations and arguments that were thought significant by members of the board in reaching the conclusions on the FRS. The views of the member who dissented are set out in Appendix IV.

[FRS 10]
Goodwill and intangible assets

(Issued December 1997)

Contents

Appendices
I Note on legal requirements
II Compliance with International Accounting Standards
III The development of the FRS
IV Dissenting view
V Effect on realised profits of elimination of goodwill against reserves

Goodwill and intangible assets

Summary

GENERAL

a   Financial Reporting Standard 10 'Goodwill and Intangible Assets' sets out the principles of accounting for goodwill and intangible assets. Its objective is to ensure that purchased goodwill and intangible assets are charged in the profit and loss account in the periods in which they are depleted.

THE NATURE OF GOODWILL AND INTANGIBLE ASSETS

b   The accounting requirements for goodwill reflect the view that goodwill arising on an acquisition is neither an asset like other assets nor an immediate loss in value. Rather, it forms the bridge between the cost of an investment shown as an asset in the acquirer's own financial statements and the values attributed to the acquired assets and liabilities in the consolidated financial statements. Although purchased goodwill is not in itself an asset, its inclusion amongst the assets of the reporting entity, rather than as a deduction from shareholders' equity, recognises that goodwill is part of a larger asset, the investment, for which management remains accountable.

c   An intangible item may meet the definition of an asset when access to the future economic benefits that it represents is controlled by the reporting entity, either through custody or legal protection. However, intangible assets fall into a spectrum ranging from those that can readily be identified and measured separately from goodwill to those that are essentially very similar to goodwill. The basic principles set out for initial recognition, amortisation and impairment of intangible assets that are similar in nature to goodwill are therefore closely aligned with those set out for goodwill.

INITIAL RECOGNITION

d   Purchased goodwill and intangible assets should be capitalised as assets. Internally generated goodwill should not be capitalised and internally developed intangible assets should be capitalised only where they have a readily ascertainable market value.

AMORTISATION

e   The required approach seeks to charge goodwill to the profit and loss account only to the extent that the carrying value of the goodwill is not supported by the current value of the goodwill within the acquired business. Systematic amortisation is a practical means of recognising the reduction in value of goodwill that has a limited useful economic life. It is also a means of ensuring that where goodwill is not capable of continued measurement (so that impairment reviews cannot reasonably be performed each year), its depletion is recognised over a prudent, but not unrealistically short, period.

f   Reflecting the view of goodwill as the bridge between the value of an acquired business in the entity's own financial statements and the values of its net identifiable assets shown in the consolidated financial statements, the useful economic life of purchased goodwill is defined as the period over which the value of an acquired business is expected to exceed the values of its identifiable assets and liabilities.

There is a rebuttable presumption that the useful economic lives of purchased **g** goodwill and intangible assets are limited and do not exceed 20 years from the date of acquisition. However, there may be grounds for rebutting that presumption and regarding the useful economic life as greater than 20 years, or even indefinite. This may be done only if the goodwill or intangible asset is expected to be capable of continued measurement (so that annual impairment reviews can be performed).

Where goodwill and intangible assets are regarded as having limited useful economic **h** lives, they should be amortised over those lives. Where goodwill and intangible assets are regarded as having indefinite useful economic lives, they should not be amortised.

Companies legislation requires goodwill to be amortised over a limited period. **i** Hence, where the financial statements of a company include goodwill that is not amortised, they should explain that the departure from this specific requirement is necessary for the overriding purpose of providing a true and fair view, also detailing the reasons for and the effect of the departure.

IMPAIRMENT REVIEWS

An asset is regarded as impaired if its recoverable amount (the higher of net rea- **j** lisable value and value in use) falls below its carrying value. Impairment reviews should be performed to ensure that goodwill and intangible assets are not carried at above their recoverable amounts. Where goodwill and intangible assets are amortised over a period that does not exceed 20 years, impairment reviews need be performed only at the end of the first full financial year following the initial recognition of the goodwill or intangible asset and, in other periods, if events or changes in circumstances indicate that its carrying value may not be recoverable in full. Where goodwill and intangible assets are not amortised, or are amortised over a period exceeding 20 years, impairment reviews should be performed each year.

REVALUATION AND RESTORATION OF PAST LOSSES

Intangible assets with readily ascertainable market values may be revalued by **k** reference to those market values.

The reversal of a past impairment loss may be recognised only if it can clearly and **l** demonstrably be attributed to the unforeseen reversal of the external event that caused the recognition of the original impairment loss. Past impairment losses may not be restored when the restoration in value is generated internally.

NEGATIVE GOODWILL

Negative goodwill should be recognised and separately disclosed on the face of the **m** balance sheet, immediately below the goodwill heading. It should be recognised in the profit and loss account in the periods in which the non-monetary assets acquired are depreciated or sold. Any negative goodwill in excess of the values of the non-monetary assets should be written back in the profit and loss account over the period expected to benefit from that negative goodwill.

DISCLOSURES

There are few disclosure requirements other than those normally required for any **n** type of fixed asset. Significant additional disclosure requirements include requirements to explain:

- the bases of valuation of intangible assets
- the grounds for believing a useful economic life to exceed 20 years or to be indefinite
- the treatment adopted for negative goodwill.

Financial Reporting Standard 10

Objective

The objective of this FRS is to ensure that: **1**

(a) capitalised goodwill and intangible assets are charged in the profit and loss account in the periods in which they are depleted; and

(b) sufficient information is disclosed in the financial statements to enable users to determine the impact of goodwill and intangible assets on the financial position and performance of the reporting entity.

Definitions

The following definitions shall apply in the FRS and in particular in the Statement of   **2**
Standard Accounting Practice set out **in bold type**.

Class of intangible assets:-
A category of intangible assets having a similar nature, function or use in the business of the entity.

Licences, quotas, patents, copyrights, franchises and trade marks are examples of categories that may be treated as separate classes of intangible assets. Further subdivision may be appropriate, for example where different types of licence have different functions within the business. Intangible assets that are used within different business segments may be treated as separate classes of intangible assets.

Identifiable assets and liabilities:-
The assets and liabilities of an entity that are capable of being disposed of or settled separately, without disposing of a business of the entity.

Impairment:-
A reduction in the recoverable amount of a fixed asset or goodwill below its carrying value.

Intangible assets:-
Non-financial fixed assets that do not have physical substance but are identifiable and are controlled by the entity through custody or legal rights.

An identifiable asset is defined by companies legislation as one that can be disposed of separately without disposing of a business of the entity. If an asset can be disposed of only as part of the revenue-earning activity to which it contributes, it is regarded as indistinguishable from the goodwill relating to that activity and is accounted for as such.

In the context of an intangible asset, control is normally secured by legal rights: a franchise or licence grants the entity access to the benefits for a fixed period; a patent or trade mark restricts the access of others. In the absence of legal rights, it is more difficult to demonstrate control. However, control may be obtained through custody. This could be the case where, for example, technical or intellectual knowledge arising from development activity is maintained secretly.

Where it is expected that future benefits will flow to the entity, but those benefits are not controlled through legal rights or custody, the entity does not have sufficient control over the benefits to recognise an intangible asset. For example, an entity may have a portfolio of clients or a team of skilled staff. There may be an expectation that the clients within the portfolio will continue to seek professional services from the entity, or that the team of staff will continue to make their expert skills available to the entity. However, in the absence of custody or legal rights to retain the clients or staff, the entity has insufficient control over the expected future benefits to recognise them as assets.

Software development costs that are directly attributable to bringing a computer system or other computer-operated machinery into working condition for its intended use within the business are treated as part of the cost of the related hardware rather than as a separate intangible asset.

The definition does not encompass assets, such as prepaid expenditure, that are not fixed assets.

Net realisable value:-
The amount at which an asset could be disposed of, less any direct selling costs.

Purchased goodwill:-
The difference between the cost of an acquired entity and the aggregate of the fair values of that entity's identifiable assets and liabilities. Positive goodwill arises when the acquisition cost exceeds the aggregate fair values of the identifiable assets and liabilities. Negative goodwill arises when the aggregate fair values of the identifiable assets and liabilities of the entity exceed the acquisition cost.

Readily ascertainable market value:-
The value of an intangible asset that is established by reference to a market where:

(a)   the asset belongs to a homogeneous population of assets that are equivalent in all material respects; and
(b)   an active market, evidenced by frequent transactions, exists for that population of assets.

Intangible assets that meet those conditions might include certain operating licences, franchises and quotas. Other intangible assets are by their nature unique: although there may be similar assets, they are not equivalent in all material respects and so do not have readily ascertainable market values. Examples of such assets include brands, publishing titles, patented drugs and engineering design patents.

Recoverable amount:-
The higher of net realisable value and value in use.

Residual value:-
The net realisable value of an asset at the end of its useful economic life. Residual values are based on prices prevailing at the date of acquisition (or revaluation) of the asset and do not take account of expected future price changes.

Useful economic life:-
The useful economic life of an intangible asset is the period over which the entity expects to derive economic benefit from that asset. The useful economic life of purchased goodwill is the period over which the value of the underlying business acquired is expected to exceed the values of its identifiable net assets.

If purchased goodwill includes intangible assets that have not been recognised separately because they cannot be measured reliably, the useful economic lives of those intangible assets will have a bearing on that of the goodwill as a whole.

Value in use:-
The present value of the future cash flows obtainable as a result of an asset's continued use, including those resulting from its ultimate disposal.

References to companies legislation mean: **3**

(a)   in Great Britain, the Companies Act 1985;
(b)   in Northern Ireland, the Companies (Northern Ireland) Order 1986; and
(c)   in the Republic of Ireland, the Companies (Amendment) Act 1986 and the European Communities (Companies: Group Accounts) Regulations 1992.

SCOPE

Subject to the provisions of paragraph 5, the FRS applies to all financial statements that   **4** are intended to give a true and fair view of a reporting entity's financial position and profit or loss (or income and expenditure) for a period. Although the requirements of the FRS that relate to business combinations are framed in terms of the acquisition of a subsidiary undertaking by a parent company that prepares consolidated accounts, they also apply whenever any reporting entity acquires a business or an investment accounted for using the equity method.

Reporting entities applying the Financial Reporting Standard for Smaller Entities   **5** (FRSSE) currently applicable are exempt from the FRS unless preparing consolidated financial statements, in which case they should apply the FRS to such statements as required by the FRSSE.

The requirements of the FRS apply to all intangible assets with the exception of: **6**

(a)   oil and gas exploration and development costs;
(b)   research and development costs; and
(c)   any other intangible assets that are specifically addressed by another accounting standard.

Initial recognition of positive goodwill and intangible assets

Goodwill

Positive purchased goodwill should be capitalised and classified as an asset on the   **7** balance sheet.

Internally generated goodwill should not be capitalised.   **8**

Intangible assets

An intangible asset purchased separately from a business should be capitalised at its   **9** cost.

An intangible asset acquired as part of the acquisition of a business should be capitalised separately from goodwill if its value can be measured reliably on initial recognition. It should initially be recorded at its fair value, subject to the constraint that, unless the asset has a readily ascertainable market value, the fair value should be   **10**

limited to an amount that does not create or increase any negative goodwill arising on the acquisition.

11   FRS 7 'Fair Values in Acquisition Accounting' requires that where an intangible asset is recognised, its fair value should be based on its replacement cost. FRS 7 goes on to explain that the replacement cost will normally be the asset's estimated market value but that it may be estimated by other methods.*

12   It is not possible to determine a market value for unique intangible assets such as brands and publishing titles. Replacement cost may be equally difficult to determine directly. However, certain entities that are regularly involved in the purchase and sale of unique intangible assets have developed techniques for estimating their values indirectly and these may be used for initial recognition of such assets at the time of purchase. Techniques used can be based, for example, on 'indicators of value' – such as multiples of turnover – or on estimating the present value of the royalties that would be payable to license the asset from a third party.

13   **If its value cannot be measured reliably, an intangible asset purchased as part of the acquisition of a business should be subsumed within the amount of the purchase price attributed to goodwill.**

14   **An internally developed intangible asset may be capitalised only if it has a readily ascertainable market value.**

AMORTISATION OF POSITIVE GOODWILL AND INTANGIBLE ASSETS

Requirement for amortisation

15   **Where goodwill and intangible assets are regarded as having limited useful economic lives, they should be amortised on a systematic basis over those lives.**

16   The circumstances in which useful economic lives may be regarded as longer than 20 years are set out in paragraph 19.

17   **Where goodwill and intangible assets are regarded as having indefinite useful economic lives, they should not be amortised.**

18   Companies legislation requires goodwill that is treated as an asset to be amortised systematically over a finite period. Where a company's financial statements depart from this requirement, the departure must be justified as being required for the overriding purpose of providing a true and fair view. The circumstances in which useful economic lives may be regarded as indefinite are set out in paragraph 19. The necessary disclosure requirements are set out in paragraph 59.

Determining useful economic lives

19   **There is a rebuttable presumption that the useful economic lives of purchased goodwill and intangible assets are limited to periods of 20 years or less. This presumption may be rebutted and a useful economic life regarded as a longer period or indefinite only if:**

   (a)   the durability of the acquired business or intangible asset can be demonstrated and justifies estimating the useful economic life to exceed 20 years; and

FRS 7 'Fair values in acquisition accounting', paragraph 10.

(b)   the goodwill or intangible asset is capable of continued measurement (so that annual impairment reviews will be feasible).

The transient nature of many business opportunities makes it appropriate for there   **20**
to be a presumption that the 'premium' that an acquired business has over its net
asset value cannot be maintained indefinitely. However, in some circumstances there
may be grounds for regarding the premium as more durable and assigning it a longer
or even indefinite economic life. Durability depends on a number of factors such as:

- the nature of the business
- the stability of the industry in which the acquired business operates
- typical lifespans of the products to which the goodwill attaches
- the extent to which the acquisition overcomes market entry barriers that will continue to exist
- the expected future impact of competition on the business.

The useful economic lives of goodwill and intangible assets will usually be uncertain.   **21**
This uncertainty does not in itself form grounds for treating a useful economic life as
indefinite or for adopting a 20-year period by default. Where, for example, the useful
economic life of goodwill or an intangible asset is expected to be less than 20 years,
the FRS requires an estimate of the useful economic life to be made.

Whilst uncertainty forms grounds for estimating the useful economic life on a pru-   **22**
dent basis, it does not form grounds for choosing a life that is unrealistically short.

Goodwill and intangible assets will not be capable of continued measurement if the   **23**
cost of such measurement is viewed as being unjustifiably high. This will be the case
when, for example:

- acquired businesses are merged with existing businesses to such an extent that the goodwill associated with the acquired businesses cannot readily be tracked thereafter
- the management information systems used by the entity cannot identify and allocate cash flows at a detailed income-generating unit level
- the amounts involved are not sufficiently material to justify undertaking the detailed procedures of annual impairment reviews.

Where access to the economic benefits associated with an intangible asset is achieved   **24**
through legal rights that have been granted for a finite period, the economic life of the
asset may extend beyond that period only if, and to the extent that, the legal rights are
renewable and renewal is assured. The amount of the asset that is treated as having the
longer useful economic life should exclude those costs that will recur each time the legal
right is renewed.

There may be both economic and legal factors influencing the useful economic life of   **25**
an intangible asset: economic factors determine the period over which it is expected
that future economic benefits will arise; legal factors may restrict the period over
which the entity continues to control access to these benefits. The useful economic
life of an asset is the shorter of the period over which it is expected that the future
benefits will arise and that over which it is expected that the entity will control the
benefits.

It follows that where a legal right securing access to an intangible asset has been   **26**
granted for a finite period, as may be the case with a patent or licence, the useful
economic life assigned to the asset cannot in general exceed that finite period. It
would be appropriate to assign a longer useful economic life only if, and to the extent

that, the legal right is renewable and renewal is assured. Renewal may be regarded as being assured if:

(a)   the value of the intangible asset does not reduce as the initial expiry date approaches, or reduces only by an amount reflecting the cost of renewal of the underlying legal right;

(b)   there is evidence, possibly based on past experience, that the legal rights will be renewed; and

(c)   where the entity is required to abide by any conditions under the terms of the legal right and breach of those conditions may prevent renewal, there is no evidence that any of those conditions have been or will be breached.

27   It follows that, where legal rights are essential to the benefits arising from the use of an intangible asset, the asset may be regarded as having an indefinite life only if such legal rights can remain in force indefinitely or are renewable indefinitely with each renewal process being assured.

Residual value

28   **In amortising an intangible asset, a residual value may be assigned to that asset only if such residual value can be measured reliably. No residual value may be assigned to goodwill.**

29   In practice, the residual value of an intangible asset is often insignificant. It is likely that the residual value of an intangible asset will be significant and capable of being measured reliably only when:

(a)   there is a legal or contractual right to receive a certain sum at the end of the period of use of the intangible asset; or

(b)   there is a readily ascertainable market value for the residual asset.

Method of amortisation

30   **The method of amortisation should be chosen to reflect the expected pattern of depletion of the goodwill or intangible asset. A straight-line method should be chosen unless another method can be demonstrated to be more appropriate.**

31   The pattern of depletion of intangible assets will normally be relatively uncertain and occur with the passing of time. A straight-line method of amortisation will normally be the most appropriate. However, there may be circumstances, for instance where a licence entitles the holder to produce a finite quantity of a product, where another method is more appropriate. It is unlikely that there will be circumstances in which there is justification and evidence to support a method of amortisation for goodwill that is less conservative than straight-line.

32   A method of amortisation that aims to produce a constant rate of return on the carrying value of an investment is not one that aims to reflect the pattern of depletion of goodwill. Hence, interest methods, such as the 'reverse sum of digits' method, are not appropriate methods of amortising goodwill.

Review of useful economic lives

33   **The useful economic lives of goodwill and intangible assets should be reviewed at the end of each reporting period and revised if necessary. If a useful economic life is revised, the carrying value of the goodwill or intangible asset at the date of revision should be**

amortised over the revised remaining useful economic life. If the effect of the revision is to increase the useful economic life to more than 20 years from the date of acquisition, the additional requirements of the FRS that apply to goodwill and intangible assets that are amortised over periods of more than 20 years or are not amortised become applicable.*

IMPAIRMENT OF POSITIVE GOODWILL AND INTANGIBLE ASSETS

Requirement for impairment reviews

Goodwill and intangible assets that are amortised over a finite period not exceeding 20 years from the date of acquisition should be reviewed for impairment: **34**

(a) **at the end of the first full financial year following the acquisition ('the first year review'); and**
(b) **in other periods if events or changes in circumstances indicate that the carrying values may not be recoverable.**

If an impairment is identified at the time of the first year review, this impairment reflects: **35**

(a) an overpayment;
(b) an event that occurred between the acquisition and the first year review; or
(c) depletion of the acquired goodwill or intangible asset between the acquisition and the first year review that exceeds the amount recognised through amortisation.

The requirements of the FRS are such that the recognition of an impairment loss must be justified in the same way as the absence of an impairment loss, ie by reference to expected future cash flows. In particular, a belief that the value of goodwill will not be capable of continued measurement in future does not justify writing off the whole balance at the time of the first year impairment review: it should be possible to perform the first year impairment review by updating investment appraisal calculations. The remaining carrying value would then be amortised over a period not exceeding 20 years.   **36**

Goodwill and intangible assets that are amortised over a period exceeding 20 years from the date of acquisition or are not amortised should be reviewed for impairment at the end of each reporting period.   **37**

After the first period the reviews need only be updated. If expectations of future cash flows and discount rates have not changed significantly, the updating procedure will be relatively quick to perform. If there have been no adverse changes in the key assumptions and variables, or if there was previously substantial leeway between the carrying value and estimated value in use, it may even be possible to ascertain immediately that an income-generating unit is not impaired.   **38**

Procedures for performing impairment reviews

Except as permitted in paragraph 40, impairment reviews should be performed in accordance with the requirements of FRS 11 'Impairment of Fixed Assets and Goodwill.'   **39**

*Editor's Note: See also UITF Abstact 27 'Revisions to estimates of the useful economic life of goodwill and intangible assets'.

40   The first year impairment review required by paragraph 34(a) may be performed in two stages:

(a)   initially identifying any possible impairment by comparing post-acquisition performance in the first year with pre-acquisition forecasts used to support the purchase price; and

(b)   performing a full impairment review in accordance with the requirements of FRS 11 only if the initial review indicates that the post-acquisition performance has failed to meet pre-acquisition expectations or if any other previously unforeseen events or changes in circumstances indicate that the carrying values may not be recoverable.

41   If an impairment loss is recognised, the revised carrying value, if being amortised, should be amortised over the current estimate of the remaining useful economic life.

42   If goodwill arising on consolidation is found to be impaired, the carrying amount of the investment held in the accounts of the parent undertaking should also be reviewed for impairment.

REVALUATION AND RESTORATION OF PAST LOSSES

43   Where an intangible asset has a readily ascertainable market value, the asset may be revalued to its market value. If one intangible asset is revalued, all other capitalised intangible assets of the same class should be revalued. Once an intangible asset has been revalued, further revaluations should be performed sufficiently often to ensure that the carrying value does not differ materially from the market value at the balance sheet date.

44   Where an external event caused the recognition of an impairment loss in previous periods, and subsequent external events clearly and demonstrably reverse the effects of that event in a way that was not foreseen in the original impairment calculations, any resulting reversal of the impairment loss that increases the recoverable amount of the goodwill or intangible asset above its current carrying value should be recognised in the current period.

45   Except as permitted or required by paragraphs 43 and 44, goodwill and intangible assets should not be revalued, either to increase the carrying value above original cost or to reverse prior period losses arising from impairment or amortisation.

46   An impairment review may identify that an impairment loss recognised in an earlier period has reversed in the current period. In general, such reversals will be the result of the internal generation of goodwill or intangible asset value. The FRS does not permit such restorations to be reflected in the financial statements. However, where the original impairment of goodwill or an intangible asset was caused by an external event and reverses because the external event reverses in a way that was not foreseen when the original impairment calculations were performed, the FRS requires the resulting restoration to be reflected in the financial statements.

47   The amortisation charge for revalued assets should be based on the revalued amounts and the remaining useful economic lives of the assets. Amortisation charged before the revaluation should not be written back in the profit and loss account.

NEGATIVE GOODWILL

48   If an acquisition appears to give rise to negative goodwill, the fair values of the acquired assets should be tested for impairment and the fair values of the acquired liabilities

checked carefully to ensure that none has been omitted or understated. Negative goodwill remaining after the fair values of the assets and liabilities have been checked should be recognised and separately disclosed on the face of the balance sheet, immediately below the goodwill heading and followed by a subtotal showing the net amount of the positive and negative goodwill.

Negative goodwill up to the fair values of the non-monetary assets acquired should be recognised in the profit and loss account in the periods in which the non-monetary assets are recovered, whether through depreciation or sale.   49

Any negative goodwill in excess of the fair values of the non-monetary assets acquired should be recognised in the profit and loss account in the periods expected to be benefited.   50

Purchased goodwill (positive or negative) arising on a single transaction should not be divided into positive and negative components.   51

DISCLOSURES

Recognition and measurement

The financial statements should describe the method used to value intangible assets.   52

The following information should be disclosed separately for positive goodwill, negative goodwill and each class of intangible asset capitalised on the balance sheet: 53

(a) the cost or revalued amount at the beginning of the financial period and at the balance sheet date;
(b) the cumulative amount of provisions for amortisation or impairment at the beginning of the financial period and at the balance sheet date;
(c) a reconciliation of the movements, separately disclosing additions, disposals, revaluations, transfers, amortisation, impairment losses, reversals of past impairment losses and amounts of negative goodwill written back in the financial period; and
(d) the net carrying amount at the balance sheet date.*

The financial statements should disclose the profit or loss on each material disposal of a previously acquired business or business segment.   54

Amortisation of positive goodwill and intangible assets

The financial statements should disclose the methods and periods of amortisation of goodwill and intangible assets and the reasons for choosing those periods.†   55

Where an amortisation period is shortened or extended following a review of the remaining useful economic lives of goodwill and intangible assets, the reason and the effect, if material, should be disclosed in the year of change.   56

Where there has been a change in the amortisation method used, the reason and the effect, if material, should be disclosed in the year of change.   57

*See paragraph 18 of Appendix 1 'Note on Legal Requirements'.

†See paragraph 6 of Appendix 1 'Note on Legal Requirements'.

58   **Where goodwill or an intangible asset is amortised over a period that exceeds 20 years from the date of acquisition or is not amortised, the grounds for rebutting the 20-year presumption should be given. This should be a reasoned explanation based on the specific factors contributing to the durability of the acquired business or intangible asset.**

59   **In addition, where goodwill in the financial statements of companies is not amortised, the financial statements should state that they depart from the specific requirement of companies legislation to amortise goodwill over a finite period* for the overriding purpose of giving a true and fair view. Particulars of the departure, the reasons for it and its effect should be given in sufficient detail to convey to the reader of the financial statements the circumstances justifying the use of the true and fair override† The reasons for the departure should incorporate the explanation of the specific factors contributing to the durability of the acquired business or intangible asset required by paragraph 58.**

60   Companies legislation requires goodwill that is treated as an asset to be amortised systematically over a finite period. Where a company's financial statements depart from the specific requirements of companies legislation for the overriding purpose of providing a true and fair view, they are required to disclose particulars of the departure, the reasons for it and its effect. Paragraphs 62–65 of FRS 18 'Accounting policies' specify disclosures that should be made in order to provide the reader of the financial statements with a clear and unambiguous account of the reasons for the departure from the statutory requirement. The specific factors will be unique to the circumstances of each case. The requirements of FRS 18 encompass the disclosures necessary when it is not possible to quantify the effect of the departure, as will be the case when goodwill is not amortised.

Revaluation

61   **Where a class of assets has been revalued, the financial statements should disclose:**

   (a)   **the year in which the assets were valued, the values and the bases of valuation; and**
   (b)   **the original cost (or original fair value) of the assets and the amount of any provision for amortisation that would have been recognised if the assets had been valued at their original cost or fair value.‡**

62   **Where any asset has been revalued during the year, the name and qualifications of the person who valued it should be disclosed.§**

Negative goodwill

63   **The financial statements should disclose the period(s) in which negative goodwill is being written back in the profit and loss account.**

64   **Where negative goodwill exceeds the fair values of the non-monetary assets, the amount and source of the 'excess' negative goodwill and the period(s) in which it is being written back should be explained.**

*See paragraph 6 of Appendix 1 'Note on Legal Requirements'.

†See paragraph 20 of Appendix 1 'Note on Legal Requirements'.

‡See paragraph 19 of Appendix 1 'Note on Legal Requirements'.

§See paragraph 19 of Appendix 1 'Note on Legal Requirements'.

DATE FROM WHICH EFFECTIVE

The accounting practices set out in the FRS should be regarded as standard in respect of   65
financial statements relating to accounting periods ending on or after 23 December
1998. Earlier adoption is encouraged but not required.

TRANSITIONAL ARRANGEMENTS

Subject to the provisions of paragraphs 68 and 69, changes in accounting policy   66
required to implement the requirements of the FRS should be applied retrospectively.

The way in which prior period adjustments are made and disclosed is set out in FRS 3   67
'Reporting Financial Performance' and FRS 18 'Accounting policies'.

Ideally, all goodwill that had previously been eliminated against reserves but would   68
not have been fully written down under the requirements of the FRS would be reinstated by means of prior year adjustment on implementation of the FRS. However,
the Board recognises that this will not be practicable in all circumstances, and
therefore does not require reinstatement.

In those cases where all goodwill previously eliminated against reserves is not reinstated   69
on implementation of the FRS, the goodwill remaining eliminated against reserves should
comprise one of the following:

(a)   goodwill relating to acquisitions made before 23 December 1989 where the
       necessary information is unavailable or cannot be obtained without unreasonable
       expense or delay; or
(b)   all goodwill eliminated before the implementation of FRS 7; or
(c)   all goodwill previously eliminated.

Where goodwill that was previously eliminated against reserves is reinstated on   70
implementation of the FRS:

(a)   any impairment that is attributed to prior periods must be determined on the basis
       of impairment reviews performed in accordance with the FRS on impairment of
       fixed assets and goodwill;
(b)   the notes to the financial statements should disclose the original cost of the
       goodwill and the amounts attributed to prior period amortisation and, separately,
       prior period impairment;
(c)   it is not necessary to identify separately intangible assets that are subsumed within
       the goodwill.

If goodwill remains eliminated against reserves: 71

(a)   the financial statements should state:

       (i)   the accounting policy followed in respect of that goodwill;
       (ii)   the cumulative amounts of positive goodwill eliminated against reserves and
              negative goodwill added to reserves, net of any goodwill attributable to
              businesses disposed of before the balance sheet date*; and

---

*In the UK, disclosure of amounts pertaining to an overseas business need not be given if it would be seriously
prejudicial to the business and official agreement has been obtained. For acquisitions before 23 December 1989
(in Northern Ireland, 1 April 1990), disclosure need not be made if the information necessary to calculate the
amount with material accuracy is unavailable or cannot be obtained without unreasonable expense or delay. The
exclusion of such amounts and the grounds for the exclusion should be stated. See also paragraph 8 of Appendix
1 'Note on Legal Requirements'.

     (iii)   the fact that this goodwill had been eliminated as a matter of accounting policy and would be charged or credited in the profit and loss account on subsequent disposal of the business to which it related.

(b)   the eliminated goodwill should not be shown as a debit balance on a separate goodwill write-off reserve but should be offset against the profit and loss account or another appropriate reserve. The amount by which the reserve has been reduced by the elimination of goodwill (or increased by the addition of negative goodwill) should not be shown separately on the face of the balance sheet.

(c)   in the reporting period in which the business with which the goodwill was acquired is disposed of or closed:

     (i)   the amount included in the profit or loss account in respect of the profit or loss on disposal or closure should include attributable goodwill to the extent that it has not previously been charged in the profit and loss account; and

     (ii)   the financial statements should disclose as a component of the profit or loss on disposal or closure the attributable amount of goodwill so included.

Where it is impractical or impossible to ascertain the goodwill attributable to a business that was acquired before 1 January 1989, this should be stated and the reasons given.

72   SSAP 22 provided guidance on the circumstances in which goodwill arising in the accounts of an individual company and eliminated against reserves should be regarded as a reduction in realised reserves. This guidance continues to apply to goodwill that remains eliminated against reserves under the transitional arrangements of the FRS. It is reproduced in Appendix V.

73   [Withdrawn].

74   **Any impairment loss relating to previously capitalised goodwill and intangible assets that is recognised on first implementing the FRS should be charged as an expense in the period.**

75   Companies legislation already requires a provision to be made for any permanent diminution in the value of a fixed asset. Therefore, any impairment loss relating to previously capitalised goodwill and intangible assets that is recognised on first implementing the FRS represents a change in an accounting estimate, which is charged as a loss in the period.

76   Examples of the adjustments that will be required under the transitional arrangements are summarised as follows:

Circumstances	Requirements	Method
(a) Goodwill previously eliminated against reserves	1 Leave eliminated against reserves until business disposed of.	If necessary, transfer from separate goodwill write-off reserve to another reserve. Deduct from profit on any future disposal.
	2 Capitalise at cost less amortisation or impairment attributed to previous periods. Amortise thereafter where appropriate.	Make prior year adjustment.
(b) Internally developed intangible assets that do not meet new recognition criteria	Write off.	Make prior year adjustment.
(c) Revalued purchased intangible assets	1 If asset has a readily ascertainable market value, update value.	Report value change as current year gain or loss.
	2 If asset does not have a readily ascertainable market value, restate at cost less amortisation or impairment attributed to previous periods.	Make prior year adjustment.

WITHDRAWAL OF SSAP 22 AND UITF ABSTRACT 3 AND AMENDMENT OF FRS 2

[*Not reproduced as it has been reflected in* FRS 2 *reproduced in this volume.*]

Adoption of FRS 10 by the Board

Financial Reporting Standard 10 - 'Goodwill and Intangible Assets' was approved for issue by a vote of nine of the ten members of the Accounting Standards Board. Mr Hinton dissented. His dissenting view is set out in Appendix IV.

Members of the Accounting Standards Board

Sir David Tweedie	(Chairman)
Allan Cook	(Technical Director)
David Allvey	
Ian Brindle	
Dr John Buchanan	
John Coombe	
Raymond Hinton	
Huw Jones	
Professor Geoffrey Whittington	
Ken Wild	

Appendix I
Note on legal requirements

GREAT BRITAIN

In Great Britain, the statutory requirements relating to accounting for goodwill and   **1**
intangible assets are set out in the Companies Act 1985. The main requirements that
are directly relevant to goodwill and intangible assets and the requirements of FRS 10
are set out in Schedules 4 and 4A and are summarised below.

Schedule 4 does not apply to banking and insurance companies and groups.   **2**
Requirements equivalent to those of Schedule 4 are contained in Schedule 9 (for
banking companies and groups) and in Schedule 9A (for insurance companies and
groups).

Goodwill

The acquisition method of accounting and the calculation of goodwill are described   **3**
by paragraph 9(4) and (5) of Schedule 4A. The interest of the parent company and its
subsidiaries in the adjusted capital and reserves of an acquired subsidiary undertaking must be offset against the acquisition cost. The resulting amount if positive
must be treated as goodwill, and if negative as a negative consolidation difference.

The balance sheet formats in Schedule 4 require purchased goodwill, to the extent   **4**
that it has not been written off, to be included under the heading of intangible fixed
assets, and shown separately from other intangible assets. Note (3) to the formats
states that amounts representing goodwill should be included only to the extent that
the goodwill was acquired for valuable consideration. Internally generated goodwill
may not be capitalised.

Paragraph 5 of Schedule 4 states that amounts in respect of items representing assets   **5**
may not be set off against amounts in respect of items representing liabilities. For
this reason, the FRS requires negative goodwill to be shown separately from positive
goodwill on the face of the balance sheet.

Paragraph 21 of Schedule 4 requires that, where goodwill is treated as an asset, it   **6**
must be depreciated systematically over a period chosen by the directors. The period
chosen must not exceed the useful economic life of the goodwill. The period chosen
and the reason for choosing that period must be disclosed in a note. (No residual
value is permitted for goodwill.)

Paragraph 31(1) of Schedule 4 prohibits the revaluation of goodwill.   **7**

Paragraph 14 of Schedule 4A requires the notes to the accounts to state the cumu-   **8**
lative amount of goodwill resulting from acquisitions in that and earlier financial
years that has been written off. That figure must be net of any goodwill attributable
to subsidiary undertakings or businesses disposed of before the balance sheet date.
Paragraph 16 of Schedule 4A states that disclosure of amounts pertaining to an
overseas business need not be given if it would be seriously prejudicial to the group's
business and agreement has been obtained from the Secretary of State. Further, for
acquisitions before 23 December 1989, disclosure need not be made if the information necessary to calculate the amount with material accuracy is unavailable or
cannot be obtained without unreasonable expense or delay (paragraph 9 of Schedule
2 to the Companies Act 1989 (Commencement No. 4 and Transitional and Saving

Provisions) Order 1990). The exclusion of such amounts and the grounds for the exclusion must be stated.

Intangible assets

9   Paragraph 9(2) of Schedule 4A requires, under the acquisition method of accounting, the identifiable assets and liabilities of an acquired undertaking to be included in the consolidated balance sheet at their fair values as at the date of acquisition. It defines "identifiable" as capable of being disposed of or discharged separately, without disposing of a business of the undertaking.

10   The following headings for intangible assets are set out in the balance sheet formats in Schedule 4:

B   Fixed assets
I   Intangible assets
   1.   Development costs
   2.   Concessions, patents, licences, trade marks and similar rights and assets
   3.   Goodwill
   4.   Payments on account.

11   Note (2) on the balance sheet formats permits amounts in respect of assets to be included in a company's balance sheet under the heading of concessions, patents, licences, trade marks and similar rights and assets only if either (a) the assets were acquired for valuable consideration and are not required to be shown under goodwill; or (b) the assets in question were created by the company itself.

12   Paragraph 18 requires that, where a fixed asset has a limited useful economic life, the purchase price or production cost less any residual value is reduced by provisions for depreciation calculated to write off that amount systematically over the period of the asset's useful economic life.

13   Paragraph 31(1) permits intangible assets, other than goodwill, to be included at their current cost. Where an intangible asset is valued at its current cost, the depreciation rules are to be applied by substituting the most recently determined value for the purchase price or production cost (paragraph 32(1)).

Provisions for diminution in value

14   Paragraph 19(2) of Schedule 4 requires provisions for diminution in value to be made in respect of any fixed asset that has diminished in value if the reduction in its value is expected to be permanent. Any provisions that are not shown in the profit and loss account must be disclosed (either separately or in aggregate) in a note to the accounts.

15   Paragraph 19(3) of Schedule 4 requires that where the reasons for which a provision was made have ceased to apply to any extent, the provision must be written back to the extent that it is no longer necessary. Where any amounts written back are not shown in the profit and loss account, they must be disclosed (either separately or in aggregate) in a note to the accounts.

Amortisation and other amounts written off fixed assets

16   The formats set out in Schedule 4 prescribe the headings under which depreciation and other amounts written off tangible and intangible fixed assets are to be included

in the profit and loss account. Under Formats 1 and 3, such amounts are to be included in cost of sales, distribution costs and administrative expenses. Under Formats 2 and 4, such amounts are to be shown as a separate heading.

Disclosure requirements

Disclosure of the accounting policies adopted by a company (including the policies regarding the depreciation and diminution in value of assets) is required by paragraph 36 of Schedule 4. **17**

Paragraph 42 of Schedule 4 details the disclosures required of the movement on goodwill and intangible asset balances. The same level of detail is required as for other fixed assets. **18**

Paragraphs 33 and 43 of Schedule 4 prescribe additional information to be given for any assets that have been revalued. This includes comparable amounts determined according to the historical cost accounting rules and details of the basis and date of the valuation and the qualifications of the valuer. **19**

True and fair override

Sections 226(3) and 227(4) require the individual and group accounts of a company to comply with the provisions of Schedules 4 and 4A respectively. If, in exceptional circumstances, compliance with any of the provisions is inconsistent with the requirement to give a true and fair view, sections 226(5) and 227(6) require the directors to depart from those provisions to the extent necessary to give a true and fair view. Particulars of any such departure, the reasons for it and its effect are to be given in a note to the accounts. **20**

NORTHERN IRELAND

The statutory requirements in Northern Ireland are set out in the Companies (Northern Ireland) Order 1986. They are similar to those in Great Britain. Most of the references cited above have parallel references in the Companies (Northern Ireland) Order 1986. The only exceptions are that: **21**

(a) the requirements of sections 226 and 227 of the Companies Act 1985 are found in Articles 234 and 235 of the Companies (Northern Ireland) Order 1986; and

(b) the transitional arrangements permitted by paragraph 9 of Schedule 2 to the Companies Act 1989 (Commencement No. 4 and Transitional and Saving Provisions) Order 1990 are found in paragraph 9 of the Companies (1990 Order) (Commencement No. 1) Order (Northern Ireland) 1990. They apply to acquisitions made before 1 April 1990.

REPUBLIC OF IRELAND

The statutory requirements in the Republic of Ireland that correspond to those listed above for Great Britain are shown in the following table. **22**

Great Britain	*Republic of Ireland*
Section 226 of the Companies Act 1985	Section 3(1) of the Companies (Amendment) Act 1986
Section 227(4) and (6) of the Companies Act 1985	Regulations 15(1) and 14(4) of the European Communities (Companies: Group Accounts) Regulations 1992
Paragraph 5 of Schedule 4 to the Companies Act 1985	Section 4(11) of the Companies (Amendment) Act 1986
Schedule 4 to the Companies Act 1985:	The Schedule to the Companies (Amendment) Act 1986:
- notes (2) and (3) on the formats	- notes (1) and (2) on the formats
- paragraph 18	- paragraph 6
- paragraph 19(2) and (3)	- paragraph 7(1) and (2)
- paragraph 21	- paragraph 9
- paragraphs 31(1) and 32(1)	- paragraphs 19(1) and 20(1)
- paragraphs 33 and 36	- paragraphs 21 and 24
- paragraphs 42 and 43	- paragraphs 29 and 30
Schedule 4A to the Companies Act 1985:	European Communities (Companies: Group Accounts) Regulations 1992:
- paragraph 9(2), (4) and (5)	- Regulation 19(2), (4), (5) and (6)
- paragraphs 14 and 16	- no corresponding references

23   There are no transitional provisions in the Republic of Ireland that correspond to those given in paragraph 9 of Schedule 2 to the Companies Act 1989 (Commencement No. 4 and Transitional and Saving Provisions) Order 1990.

Appendix II
Compliance with International Accounting Standards

At present, accounting for goodwill is addressed in International Accounting **1** Standard (IAS) 22 'Business Combinations'. Other than IAS 9 'Research and Development Costs', there are at present no IASs addressing intangible assets.*

The objective of IAS 22 is to write off goodwill over the estimated useful economic **2** life of the original purchased goodwill. The difference between this approach and the approach adopted in the FRS gives rise to a number of differences in the detailed requirements. IAS 22 states that:

(a)   purchased goodwill should be amortised over its estimated useful economic life in all circumstances.
(b)   the amortisation period should not exceed five years unless a longer period, not exceeding 20 years from the date of acquisition, can be justified.
(c)   the unamortised balance of goodwill should be reviewed at each balance sheet date and, to the extent that it is not expected to be recoverable, it should be written down. The write-down may not subsequently be reversed.
(d)   one of two treatments should be adopted for negative goodwill. The benchmark treatment requires the fair values of the non-monetary assets acquired to be reduced proportionately until the negative goodwill is eliminated. The permitted alternative treatment requires negative goodwill to be shown as deferred income in the balance sheet and released to the profit and loss account on a systematic basis over a period that does not exceed five years, unless a longer period not exceeding 20 years can be justified.

In August 1997, the International Accounting Standards Committee (IASC) pub- **3** lished two Exposure Drafts, E60 'Intangible Assets' and E61 'Business Combinations'. The proposals in those Exposure Drafts would align the international requirements for goodwill with those for intangible assets and would reduce the extent of the differences between the FRS and IASs.

Like the FRS, E60 and E61 propose a rebuttable presumption that goodwill and **4** intangible assets have useful economic lives of 20 years or less. They also propose that if the presumption can be rebutted, the goodwill or intangible asset may be amortised over a longer period providing that annual impairment reviews are also performed. The most significant difference between IASC's proposals and the requirements of the FRS is that, under the proposals in E60 and E61, goodwill and intangible assets cannot be regarded as having an indefinite life and must be amortised in all circumstances.

Other aspects of E60 and E61 that would give rise to differences between the FRS and **5** international requirements include proposals that:

●   internally developed intangible assets may be capitalised whenever their costs can be measured reliably, rather than only when they are of a type that is traded on an active market. E60 specifically states that the costs of generating brands, mastheads and other similar assets cannot be measured reliably. Given this, it is

*__*Editor's Note:__ IAS 38 "Intangible Assets" was issued in October 1998. This has since been superseded by a revised version of the standard. IAS 22 has been withdrawn and replaced by IFRS 3. Goodwill is no longer amortized, but subject to an annual impairment review. Negative goodwill, although that term is not used, is first checked and then taken to income.*

expected that there will be few intangible assets which, in practice, can be capitalised under the proposals in E60 that could not be capitalised under the FRS.

- details of intangible assets whose individual values exceed 5 per cent of total assets should be disclosed.
- costs of research and development, software, advertising, pre-opening costs, and any other significant costs incurred on intangible items charged in the profit and loss account in the year should be disclosed.
- negative goodwill attributable to future costs or losses that were identified in the acquirer's purchase plan (and not provided for as identifiable liabilities) should be released as these costs or losses occur.
- other negative goodwill should be released on a systematic basis over the useful lives of the non-monetary assets acquired. Where such negative goodwill exceeds the value of the non-monetary assets, the excess should be released to the profit and loss account immediately.

E60 and E61 do not propose to require the values assigned to intangible assets to be capped at amounts that do not create or increase negative goodwill. Neither do they propose to require first year impairment reviews to be performed.

Appendix III
The development of the FRS

THE NEED FOR A REVIEW

The FRS, when implemented, replaces SSAP 22 'Accounting for goodwill'. The SSAP **1** permitted a choice of two approaches to accounting for purchased goodwill. The preferred approach was immediate elimination against reserves. The permitted alternative approach was capitalisation as an asset, with subsequent write-off by systematic amortisation through the profit and loss account. SSAP 22 prohibited the recognition of internally generated goodwill.

In the late 1980s, the Accounting Standards Board's predecessor body, the **2** Accounting Standards Committee, started a project to replace SSAP 22. On its inception, the Board decided to continue this project. The decision was taken for several reasons. First, the Board took the view that there was a need to restrict accounting for goodwill to a single method. Secondly, it believed that with the growing practice of separating intangible assets from goodwill, there was a need to codify best practice in accounting for intangible assets. The similarities between goodwill and certain types of intangible assets acquired with a business made it appropriate to review the two together. Finally, the Board recognised that SSAP 22's preferred method of accounting for goodwill, whereby it was eliminated immediately against reserves, attracted criticism and was becoming less accepted internationally. Following its revision in 1993, IAS 22, the International Accounting Standard on accounting for business combinations, prohibited SSAP 22's preferred approach.

DIFFERENT APPROACHES TO ACCOUNTING FOR GOODWILL

Elimination against reserves

The preferred method of accounting for purchased goodwill under SSAP 22 was **3** immediate elimination against reserves. The principal rationale for this treatment was that it was consistent with the accepted practice of not including internally generated goodwill on the balance sheet. It can further be argued that goodwill is not an asset that should be recognised by a reporting entity since it is not a right to future economic benefits controlled by the entity.

However, the practice of eliminating goodwill against reserves has weaknesses: **4**

- immediate elimination of goodwill gives the impression that the acquirer's net worth has been depleted or even eliminated.
- the problem of equity depletion has encouraged companies to reduce amounts attributed to purchased goodwill by separately valuing brands and similar intangible assets at the date of purchase. Given that such intangible assets are very similar in nature to goodwill and the allocation of value between the two can be subjective, it is widely thought to be inappropriate that the goodwill should be accounted for differently.
- management is not held accountable for the amount that it has invested in goodwill: it is not taken into account when measuring the assets on which a return must be earned, and there is no requirement to disclose a loss if the value of the goodwill is not maintained.
- although there is consistency in the balance sheet treatment of purchased and internally generated goodwill, there is no consistency in the profit and loss account treatment: the costs that can be attributed to building up internally

generated goodwill are offset against profits in the profit and loss account, whereas the costs of acquired goodwill are not charged against profits in this way unless the acquired business is sold.

● this inconsistency serves to make companies that grow by acquisition appear more profitable than those that grow organically.

Capitalisation and compulsory amortisation

5   An alternative approach to accounting for purchased goodwill, permitted by SSAP 22 and widely adopted internationally, is to capitalise it and amortise it on a systematic basis over a finite period. This approach is based on the rationale that purchased goodwill has a value at the time of recognition but that this value diminishes over time as the purchased goodwill is gradually replaced by internally generated goodwill.

6   This approach is also open to criticism. In 1990, the Accounting Standards Committee issued Exposure Drafts ED 47 'Accounting for goodwill' and ED 52 'Accounting for intangible assets'. They proposed that purchased goodwill and intangible assets should be capitalised and amortised systematically over their estimated useful economic lives, which in general should not exceed 20 years and in no circumstance could exceed 40 years. Opposition to the proposals was strong: 93 per cent of corporate respondents and 73 per cent of all respondents opposed ED 47; 80 per cent of corporate respondents and 62 per cent of all respondents opposed ED 52.

7   Those opposing the proposals argued primarily that, where large sums were spent on maintaining and developing the value of an acquired business, a requirement to amortise a significant part of the investment over an arbitrary period had no economic meaning.

Capitalisation and annual impairment reviews

8   Many of the respondents opposed to amortisation of purchased goodwill agreed that it should be capitalised but thought that it should subsequently be written down only if and to the extent that the carrying value of the goodwill was not supported by the current value of goodwill in the acquired business.

9   This approach is based on the premise that purchased goodwill is neither an identifiable asset like other assets nor an immediate loss in value. Rather, it represents the balance of the purchase consideration that remains after recognising all the identifiable assets and liabilities in the consolidated financial statements. Essentially, it forms a bridge between the cost of the investment shown as an asset in the acquirer's individual financial statements and the identifiable assets and liabilities recognised in the consolidated financial statements of the combined entities. Although purchased goodwill is not in itself an asset, its inclusion amongst the assets of the reporting entity, rather than as a deduction from shareholders' equity, recognises that goodwill is part of a larger asset, the investment, for which management remains accountable.

10   This method ensures that the financial statements reflect management's success in maintaining the value of the goodwill and generating a return from its investment. It can be criticised for treating purchased goodwill differently from internally generated goodwill, although this is true for all methods of accounting for purchased goodwill. Other issues are that:

- impairment reviews, which rely on forecasts of future cash flows, can be subjective.
- impairment reviews are onerous and may not be feasible on an annual basis. Where goodwill has a finite life, amortisation may provide a much simpler, yet adequate, method of reflecting the depletion in value of the goodwill.
- amortisation of goodwill is required by companies legislation.

THE FRS's APPROACH TO ACCOUNTING FOR GOODWILL

The Board recognised when it started its review that goodwill is something of an **11** accounting anomaly. It arises from a distinct transaction that must be accounted for, yet – as illustrated above – each method of accounting for it results in inconsistencies with other aspects of financial reporting. No single method is universally accepted as being the correct one. Preferences for one method or another tend to be determined by the conceptual and practical issues deemed to be the most important in the light of each individual's particular experience.

To gather as many arguments as possible, the Board issued a Discussion Paper that **12** explored a number of options.* Six possible methods were discussed:

1   Capitalisation and amortisation over a finite period.
2   Capitalisation and annual impairment reviews.
3   A combination of methods 1 and 2, with method 2 being used only in the special circumstances where goodwill had an indefinite life believed to exceed 20 years.
4   Immediate elimination against reserves.
5   Immediate elimination to a separate goodwill write-off reserve.
6   Transfer to a separate goodwill write-off reserve, with annual reviews of recoverability and any impairments being charged to the profit and loss account.

Methods 2, 3 and 6 represented a departure from traditional methods of accounting **13** for goodwill. Their aim was to recognise the cost of goodwill as a loss only to the extent that the value of goodwill within the acquired business had reduced below the carrying value of the purchased goodwill.

No overall consensus emerged from the responses to the Discussion Paper. The **14** method that individually achieved greatest support was method 5—immediate transfer to a separate write-off reserve. However, more respondents favoured capitalisation methods than favoured elimination methods.

Given the arguments made by respondents, and in the light of both the direction **15** being taken internationally and the previous opposition to ED 47's proposals for compulsory amortisation, the Board decided to develop proposals based on method 3—capitalisation with a combination of amortisation for goodwill with a finite life and annual impairment reviews for goodwill with an indefinite life expected to exceed 20 years. In combining the amortisation and impairment options, the Board was seeking to overcome the practical and legal issues that would arise under method 2.

In favouring capitalisation rather than elimination against reserves, the Board was **16** influenced in particular by the arguments that:

(a)   a method requiring elimination against reserves would treat goodwill very differently from brands and similar intangible assets. Given that such assets are

Discussion Paper 'Goodwill and intangible assets', December 1993.

very similar in nature to goodwill and that the allocation of a purchase cost between the two can be subjective, it would be possible for a reporting entity's results to be shown in a more favourable light merely by classifying expenditure as an intangible asset rather than goodwill, or vice versa.

(b)   immediate elimination of goodwill against reserves fails to demonstrate management's accountability for goodwill as part of the investment in an acquired business. The goodwill is not included in the assets on which a return must be earned, and under methods 4 and 5 no charge would be made in the profit and loss account if the value of the goodwill were not maintained.

17   The Board acknowledged that under method 6, whereby goodwill would be transferred to a separate goodwill write-off reserve and reviewed annually for impairment, there would be greater accountability. However, some companies told the Board that a requirement to perform detailed impairment reviews every year would be unacceptably onerous. An alternative could have been to require impairment reviews only when there was an indication that the goodwill had become impaired. But the Board took the view that, in the absence of amortisation, such a requirement would be insufficient to ensure that all impairment losses would be recognised on a timely basis. Losses could remain undetected until a major problem came to light.

18   In developing its chosen approach, the Board conducted extensive consultations with preparers, users and auditors of financial statements, in particular addressing concerns that the procedures proposed for impairment reviews were too complicated. The simplified proposals were field-tested by seven large acquisitive groups and, after further refinement, formed the basis of the Working Paper* for subsequent debate at a public hearing.

19   The proposals received broad support from the majority of those responding to the Working Paper. They formed the basis of the proposals for accounting for goodwill exposed in FRED 12 and the requirements subsequently included in the FRS.

THE FRS's APPROACH TO ACCOUNTING FOR INTANGIBLE ASSETS

20   Intangible assets lie on a spectrum ranging from those that can readily be identified and measured separately from goodwill to those that are essentially very similar to goodwill. Companies legislation permits intangible assets to be recognised separately from goodwill only where they are capable of being disposed of separately from a business of the reporting entity.†

21   In its Discussion Paper, the Board expressed a view that certain intangible assets such as brands and publishing titles could not be disposed of separately from a business and, further, that there was no generally accepted method of valuing such intangible assets. Given this, and given that the dividing line between goodwill and intangible assets can be unclear, the Board proposed in the Discussion Paper that intangible assets acquired as part of the acquisition of a business should be subsumed within the value attributed to goodwill.

22   This proposal met with strong opposition. Corporate respondents stressed that intangible assets could be critical to their businesses and that it was important to account for them separately.

*Working Paper 'Goodwill and intangible assets', June 1995.

†See paragraph 9 of Appendix 1 'Note on Legal Requirements'.

The Board accepted these arguments and in its subsequent Working Paper proposed **23** that intangible assets could be recognised separately from goodwill if they met the legal and conceptual requirements for identifiability and could be measured reliably on initial recognition. But to prevent the results of the reporting entity being shown in a more or less favourable light merely by classifying expenditure as an intangible asset rather than goodwill, or vice versa, the Board proposed that the accounting for intangible assets should be aligned with that for goodwill.

This proposal was accepted by most respondents to the Working Paper. It formed **24** the basis of the accounting for intangible assets exposed in FRED 12 and subsequently required by the FRS.

THE DETAILED PROPOSALS FOR POSITIVE GOODWILL AND INTANGIBLE ASSETS

Capitalisation of internally generated intangible assets

In general, the FRS requires the costs of developing intangible assets internally to be **25** charged as an expense as they are incurred. This requirement primarily reflects the Board's objective of aligning the treatment of intangible assets that are similar in nature to goodwill with the treatment of goodwill. The requirement also acknowledges that, at present, the measurement of the value of an intangible asset is often subjective. This is especially true in the absence of a transaction price, which establishes a ceiling on the value attributed to a purchased intangible asset.

The exception that permits capitalisation of intangible assets with readily ascer- **26** tainable market values recognises that such assets are clearly distinguishable from goodwill and readily measurable. It is appropriate to treat those assets in the same way as tangible fixed assets, the costs of which can be capitalised whether they are purchased or self-constructed.

The Board acknowledges that there may be other intangible assets that would be **27** more appropriately treated in the same way as tangible fixed assets, ie with the costs being capitalised even where the asset is developed internally. However, the Board believes that it would be very difficult to define the basis on which they could be distinguished from intangible assets that are similar in nature to goodwill. Hence, it would be difficult to ensure that only those assets that are genuinely different in nature from goodwill were treated as falling within this 'other' category. The approach that the Board has adopted is simpler and more objective.

Valuation of purchased intangible assets

There are two reasons for restricting the fair values that can be assigned to intangible **28** assets to those that do not create or increase negative goodwill: first, the restriction aligns the treatment of purchased intangible assets with that of purchased goodwill and, secondly, it recognises that the values of intangible assets can be subject to a significant degree of uncertainty. Given this subjectivity, the Board regards it as appropriate to restrict the values to those that do not exceed the ceiling established by the purchase price.

Amortisation of goodwill

The required approach seeks to charge goodwill in the profit and loss account only to **29** the extent that the carrying value of the goodwill is not supported by the current value of the goodwill within the acquired business. Systematic amortisation is a practical means of recognising the reduction in value of goodwill that has a limited useful economic life. It is also a means of ensuring that where goodwill is not capable of continued measurement (so that annual impairment reviews would not be feasible), its depletion is recognised over a prudent but not unrealistically short period.

30 The FRS defines the useful economic life of goodwill as the period over which the value of the underlying business is expected to exceed the values of the identifiable net assets. This reflects the link between the carrying value of the goodwill and the continuing value of the goodwill in the acquired investment.

Useful economic lives in excess of 20 years

31 The economic benefits that goodwill and intangible assets represent are generally more nebulous than those of tangible assets. The useful economic lives of goodwill and intangible assets are correspondingly less certain than those of tangible assets and the Board believes that there should be a presumption that they do not exceed a specified maximum period, chosen to be 20 years. The Board recognises that there will be circumstances where there are valid grounds for rebutting the presumption. Such grounds will be based on the nature of the intangible asset or of the investment underlying a goodwill balance.

32 Given the uncertainty in the useful economic life of goodwill or an intangible asset, the Board believes that it would be inappropriate to assume that it exceeds 20 years unless it will be possible to monitor the reasonableness of the resulting amortisation charge. For this reason, the ability to perform impairment reviews is one of the conditions that must be met in order to rebut the 20-year presumption.

33 The choice of 20 years as the presumed maximum useful economic life of goodwill and intangible assets is based largely on judgement. This period was first proposed in the Working Paper. Most respondents to the Working Paper and FRED 12 regarded it as reasonable and accordingly the Board has not changed it in the FRS. Twenty years is not entirely consistent with IAS 22, the International Accounting Standard on goodwill: IAS 22 contains a presumption that the useful economic life of goodwill does not exceed five years and sets 20 years as the absolute maximum. Nevertheless, the alignment of the presumed maximum life in the FRS with the maximum life specified by IAS 22 avoids the unnecessary complexities created by introducing a third arbitrary period.*

34 The inconsistency between IAS 22's presumed maximum life of five years and the FRS's presumed maximum life of 20 years reflects different underlying approaches. Whilst IAS 22 defines the useful economic life of goodwill as the period benefiting from the original purchased goodwill, the FRS defines it as the period over which the value of the underlying business continues to exceed the values of the identifiable net assets. The latter will normally be longer.

Indefinite useful economic lives

35 There may be circumstances in which goodwill or an intangible asset can be regarded as having an indefinite life. In such circumstances, amortisation over an arbitrary period may not be an appropriate method of reflecting the depletion of the goodwill or intangible asset. This will be the case where the value of the goodwill or intangible

---

*At the date of publishing the FRS, IASC has published proposals that would remove the 20-year limit. For further details see Appendix II. **Editor's note:** There is no longer a presumption of twenty year life under IAS 38, the relevant international standard.*

asset is expected to be capable of continued measurement in future. In such circumstances, the Board believes that a true and fair view will be given only if the goodwill or intangible asset is not amortised, but is instead subject to annual reviews for impairment.

The Board has been advised that non-amortisation of goodwill constitutes a **36** departure from the specific requirement of companies legislation to depreciate the value attributed to goodwill over a limited period that does not exceed its useful economic life. However, departure from specific requirements such as this one is permitted by companies legislation in exceptional circumstances where it is necessary for the overriding purpose of providing a true and fair view.* Accordingly, the Board has limited the circumstances in which it proposes that goodwill is not amortised to those circumstances where systematic amortisation would not provide a true and fair view. It has also incorporated within the disclosure requirements the disclosures that are required by companies legislation where advantage has been taken of the true and fair override provisions.

Impairment reviews

It is accepted practice that an asset should not be carried at more than its recoverable **37** amount, i.e. the higher of the amount for which it could be sold and the amount recoverable from its future use.

Systematic amortisation ensures that the carrying value of an asset is reduced to **38** reflect any gradual reduction in the asset's recoverable amount over its useful economic life. An asset that is amortised in an appropriate manner is unlikely to become materially impaired unless it is impaired on initial recognition or subsequent events or changes in circumstances cause a sudden reduction in the estimate of the recoverable amount. Thus, where goodwill and intangible assets are amortised over a period not exceeding 20 years, a requirement for an impairment review to be performed each period would be unnecessary and unduly onerous. The Board believes that, in such circumstances, impairment reviews are necessary only at the end of the first full financial year following initial recognition and, thereafter, if subsequent events or changes in circumstances indicate that the carrying value may not be recoverable.

The requirement to perform an impairment review at the end of the first full financial **39** year following the initial recognition of goodwill and intangible assets ensures that any impairment arising on acquisition (ie any overpayment) is recognised as a loss at that time, rather than being amortised over the life of the asset.

The longer the useful economic lives assigned to goodwill and intangible assets, the **40** greater is the risk that the recoverable amounts will fall below the carrying values in future. Where an amortisation period exceeds 20 years, the Board believes that the risk is sufficiently high to require amortisation to be supplemented by annual reviews for impairment.

Revaluations and restoration of past losses

The FRS prohibits capitalisation of internally generated goodwill and permits **41** internally developed intangible assets to be capitalised only if they have readily ascertainable market values. Revaluation of goodwill and intangible assets has the

---

*Editor's Note: Note the withdrawal of IAS 22 since the date of this statement and its replacement by IFRS 3. See paragraphs 6 and 20 of Appendix 1 'Note on Legal Requirements'.

effect of recognising values that have been internally developed. Hence, the FRS permits revaluation only of intangible assets that have readily ascertainable market values.

42   Following the recognition of an impairment loss, the value of the impaired goodwill or intangible asset may return towards its previous carrying value. Such an increase will usually be attributable to the internal generation of goodwill or intangible asset value, and as such should not be recognised as a restoration of a past loss.

43   Less frequently, the increase in value may be attributable to the unexpected reversal of an external event that caused the original impairment to be recognised. In these limited circumstances, the reversal of the impairment loss can be measured more reliably (by reference to the original impairment) and is required by companies legislation to be recognised in the financial statements.* Accordingly, the FRS permits restoration of past losses in such circumstances.

NEGATIVE GOODWILL

44   Negative goodwill can be attributed to two causes:

- a bargain purchase—the assets have been purchased for less than the aggregate of their individual fair values, perhaps because the vendor needs to achieve a quick sale
- future costs or losses—the purchase price has been reduced to take account of future costs, such as reorganisation costs, or losses that do not represent identifiable liabilities at the balance sheet date.

45   There are a number of methods of accounting for negative goodwill that can be regarded as consistent with the FRS's approach to positive goodwill. Those methods and the Board's reasons for choosing the method required by the FRS are discussed below.

Goodwill attributable to a bargain purchase

46   Where negative goodwill is attributed to a bargain purchase, the acquirer can be viewed as having purchased the group of assets at a discount to their individual fair values.

47   In these circumstances, the value of the business acquired is not less than the fair values of its net assets. It may therefore be argued that the negative goodwill should be recognised as an immediate gain, reflecting the advantageous transaction that the acquirer has undertaken. Since the gain is unrealised, it cannot be recognised in the profit and loss account. Instead, like other revaluation gains, it should be recognised in the statement of total recognised gains and losses.

48   The Board believes that, in the same way as a revaluation reserve is treated as being realised as the asset is depreciated or sold, so negative goodwill becomes a realised gain as the asset purchased at a bargain price and valued at fair value is depreciated or sold. An alternative option is therefore to require negative goodwill to be recognised as a gain only when that asset is charged against realised profits, either through depreciation or cost of sales. At this point, the gain may be recognised in the profit and loss account.

*See paragraph 15 of Appendix 1 'Note on Legal Requirements'.

FRED 12 proposed that negative goodwill attributed to a bargain purchase should be   **49**
released immediately in the statement of total recognised gains and losses. The Board
took the view that this approach would be more consistent with the proposal that
positive goodwill should be written down as soon as it became impaired. However, a
majority of the respondents to FRED 12 opposed this proposal, arguing that a
requirement to recognise a gain on non-monetary assets before the gain was realised
was inconsistent with the requirements of other standards. The Board accepted this
argument and the FRS requires negative goodwill to be released as the non-monetary
assets acquired are used or sold.

The assets that are considered in determining the periods in which negative goodwill   **50**
is released in the profit and loss account are the non-monetary assets only. This
reflects the Board's view that, where a business with both monetary and non-
monetary assets is purchased, it is unlikely that the monetary assets would be purchased at an artificially low price, since they can generally be disposed of individually
at their fair values.

The Board considered a method of accounting for negative goodwill that would   **51**
require negative goodwill to be eliminated against the fair values of the non-monetary assets acquired. Those supporting this method argue that it:

● is consistent with the principle that assets should initially be recognised at cost.
● helps to prevent unrealistically high fair values being assigned to assets whose
  values are very subjective. There is a view that true bargain purchases are not as
  common as optimistic purchasers tend to believe them to be and that cost may
  represent a realistic estimate of fair value.
● is objective and simple to apply.

However, the Board has taken the view that fair values can be different from cost   **52**
and that a method that requires assets to be stated at amounts lower than their fair
values is inconsistent with the requirements in FRS 7 'Fair Values in Acquisition
Accounting'. The Board has also taken into consideration the fact that, if such a
method were used, the impact of the negative goodwill on the financial statements
would not be transparent.

The FRS instead requires negative goodwill to be shown separately. But just as   **53**
positive goodwill is not viewed in the FRS as an asset, so negative goodwill is not
viewed as a liability. The Board regards both as the bridge between the consolidated
financial statements and the investment shown as an asset in the acquirer's own
financial statements. Accordingly, negative goodwill is recognised next to positive
goodwill.

Negative goodwill attributable to future reorganisation costs

Where negative goodwill is attributable to future costs and losses that do not   **54**
represent identifiable liabilities at the acquisition date, the value of the acquired
business is being viewed as being no higher than the price paid for it. The assets that
have been acquired are encumbered in such a way that their combined value in use is
less than their individual fair values, until the costs or losses materialise and eliminate
the difference.

One method of accounting for the negative goodwill arising in these circumstances is   **55**
to release it as the reorganisation costs or losses subsequently materialise. The
rationale is that the negative goodwill is released to match the costs that gave rise to
it. But this method raises a number of issues:

(a) the treatment of future reorganisation costs or losses varies depending on whether the acquisition gives rise to positive goodwill or to negative goodwill. Where the net goodwill is positive, the amount by which it has been reduced by an expectation of future costs or losses cannot be written back as the costs or losses are incurred.

(b) both the fair values of non-monetary assets and the allocation of negative goodwill between its two possible causes can be subjective. Stringent conditions would be necessary to ensure that fair values were not overstated thereby attributing too much negative goodwill to future costs and losses. Such conditions would add to the complexity of the requirements.

(c) views have been expressed that the gain in the value of the investment that arises when the future costs or losses have been incurred might not be a realised gain that can be recognised in the profit and loss account. However, respondents to FRED 12 strongly opposed the proposal that negative goodwill attributable to future reorganisation costs or losses should be released in the statement of total recognised gains and losses. They argued in particular that, if a loss of positive goodwill is charged in the profit and loss account, a reversal of negative goodwill should be credited in the same statement.

56 It can further be argued that a separate accounting treatment for negative goodwill arising in expectation of future costs or losses is unnecessary: such negative goodwill, like that arising from a bargain purchase, should be released as the non-monetary assets are recovered. The argument is that the value of the income-generating units acquired (which will be equal to the present value of the expected future cash flows) is less than the aggregate of the values attributed to the individual assets, so the non-monetary assets in their present state and condition can be viewed as being encumbered or impaired.* This impairment is recognised by deferring the release of the negative goodwill until the acquired assets are recovered through depreciation or sale.

57 In requiring negative goodwill to be treated in the same manner, whatever its cause, the Board was influenced by the arguments set out above. It notes that the requirement to perform impairment reviews whenever negative goodwill appears to have arisen will eliminate much of the negative goodwill that would otherwise be attributed to future costs or losses.

Negative goodwill in excess of the fair values of the non-monetary assets

58 As negative goodwill is expected to occur rarely, negative goodwill in excess of the fair values of the non-monetary assets acquired is expected to occur only extremely rarely and in unusual circumstances. Given this, the FRS does not prescribe the period over which 'excess' negative goodwill should be written back.

59 The FRS does not permit purchased goodwill to be divided into positive and negative components. The Board believes that, since goodwill is viewed as a residual, it would be inappropriate to subdivide a net balance into positive and negative components. Thus, the amounts that can be attributed to any factors identified as causing negative goodwill are limited to the total negative goodwill arising on the acquisition.

The monetary assets are unlikely to be impaired, since it is likely that they will be capable of being realised individually at their fair values.

TRANSITIONAL ARRANGEMENTS

Ideally, all goodwill that had previously been eliminated against reserves but would   **60**
not have been fully written down under the requirements of the FRS would be reinstated by means of a prior year adjustment. However, the Board recognises that this
will not be practicable in all circumstances and envisages that some or all of this
goodwill will remain eliminated against reserves. In order to provide some degree of
consistency to the various possibilities for reinstatement that might be chosen, the
Board has limited them to those set out in paragraph 69 of the FRS. The 23 December
1989 cut-off point stems from the transitional provisions in companies legislation.
The FRS 7 cut-off point recognises that goodwill calculated before then was measured
on a different basis.

The Board considered including a requirement to reinstate goodwill acquired in the   **61**
previous year. However, it concluded that, unless acquisitions made in the previous
year were the only acquisitions for which goodwill remained at the balance sheet
date, this limited requirement would not achieve proper comparability based on
consistent application of the FRS's requirements. The profit and loss account would
still reflect only part of the cost of the benefits conveyed by the goodwill of past
acquisitions. Clearly, the further back any adjustments can be made, the greater the
degree of comparability that will be achieved.

CHANGES MADE FOLLOWING EXPOSURE OF FRED 12

The majority of respondents to FRED 12 were broadly supportive of its overall   **62**
approach. The minority who were opposed to the approach divided into those who
would prefer compulsory amortisation and those who would prefer immediate
elimination of goodwill against reserves. Only a small minority supported the
alternative view put forward in Appendix IV of the FRED. The Board's reasons for
rejecting compulsory amortisation and immediate elimination against reserves are set
out above.

A number of changes to the detailed proposals were suggested by respondents and   **63**
considered by the Board. The more significant changes that have been made in the
light of the responses received are:

- the removal of the procedures to be used in performing impairment reviews. They
  are to be published as a separate FRS encompassing the impairment of all fixed
  assets and goodwill. FRED 15 'Impairment of Fixed Assets and Goodwill' sets out
  the procedures to be used for impairment reviews until that FRS is published.
  Changes that have been made to the impairment procedures as a result of
  responses to FRED 12 are explained in FRED 15.
- simplification of the procedures for performing 'first year' impairment reviews.
  The Board accepts the argument that a requirement to perform a full first year
  impairment review for every acquisition would be unduly onerous, particularly
  for smaller companies. The FRS permits the first year impairment review to be
  performed on a simpler basis, with a full review being required only if the simpler
  review indicates a potential impairment.
- a change in the requirements relating to negative goodwill. The changes are
  explained above.
- clarification of the transitional arrangements. A large majority of respondents to
  FRED 12 (including all who were users of financial statements) supported the
  Board's proposal to permit but not require reinstatement of goodwill that had
  previously been eliminated against reserves. However, many felt that it was
  unclear how goodwill would be reinstated and what, if any, constraints would be

placed on the extent and timing of reinstatement. The requirements have been clarified in the FRS.

- the addition of a new requirement for any 'old' goodwill that remains eliminated against reserves to be netted against another reserve and not shown separately on the face of the balance sheet. The Board agrees with respondents who suggested that it could be misleading and confusing to allow goodwill to appear in two places on the face of the balance sheet, with the two balances being subject to different impairment and amortisation requirements. The FRS now requires entities that wish to highlight goodwill as a separate balance to capitalise it as an asset and subject it to the new requirements for amortisation and/or impairment reviews.

64   A small minority of respondents to FRED 12 opposed the proposal that internally developed brands and mastheads could not be capitalised and the related proposal that purchased brands and mastheads could not be revalued. They argued that reliable valuation techniques exist and that, where brands and mastheads are fundamental to a business, their inclusion makes balance sheets more relevant and comparable and is important for accountability.

65   The Board considered these arguments. However, it has concluded that the restrictions on capitalisation and revaluation of brands and mastheads stems more from the view that such assets are very similar in nature to goodwill and so should be treated in the same way as goodwill than from the view that their values cannot be measured reliably. The Board further notes that:

- internationally, there are no moves to permit brands and similar assets to be carried at valuations
- reporting entities are not prevented from disclosing (and are indeed encouraged to disclose) estimated values for key intangible assets within the operating and financial review.

Appendix IV
Dissenting view

Mr Hinton dissents from the FRS because he does not agree that goodwill should be   **1**
capitalised as an asset and amortised, or that revaluation of identifiable intangible
assets should be prohibited. He advocates an alternative approach, which, he
believes, places greater emphasis on the needs of users and the nature of goodwill,
recognising that it is neither an asset nor an immediate loss in value. He concludes
that goodwill should not be presented as an asset or in any way amortised but should
be deducted from shareholders' equity. He notes that over 95 per cent of UK
companies with goodwill at present deduct such goodwill from shareholders' equity
by write-off to reserves or to a goodwill reserve.

NEEDS OF USERS

Users of financial statements in the UK have indicated that whilst they treat any   **2**
amounts attributed to goodwill with considerable scepticism, they are concerned to
hold management accountable for the amounts spent on goodwill. Immediate write-
off with the amounts subsumed within reserves as practised by many companies
reporting goodwill has clouded such accountability. The measure of such accountability is the relationship between the amounts spent and the likelihood and timing of
improved earnings and cash flows. Mr Hinton believes that users are thus concerned
with stewardship and whether goodwill has been impaired, but not with reporting
goodwill as an asset with either indefinite retention or arbitrary amortisation to
operating profit, both of which they have long ignored.

NATURE OF GOODWILL

Goodwill is not an asset as defined in the draft Statement of Principles for Financial   **3**
Reporting and possesses unique characteristics that distinguish it from an asset. It
may or may not have any relationship to the expenditures incurred to create it; there
is no reliable or continuing relationship of value with any historical cost and such
cost frequently and quickly loses any significance it may ever have possessed. Mr
Hinton believes that, if goodwill is not an asset and is qualitatively different from
assets as generally recognised, it is misleading to report it as such.

AMORTISATION

The FRS defines the useful economic life of purchased goodwill as the period over   **4**
which the value of the underlying business acquired is expected to exceed the values
of its identifiable net assets. Mr Hinton notes that this position is unique to the FRS in
that traditional guidance on useful economic life emphasises the factors likely to
impact the goodwill actually acquired. He regards the definition as inconsistent with
the use of a rebuttable presumption that the useful life does not exceed 20 years. He
notes that what is being reported is some measure of the current value of the
acquired business compared with the current value of its identifiable assets and that
this has little to do with the original purchased goodwill.

The original purchased goodwill cannot have an indefinite or long life. In reality,   **5**
purchased goodwill is incapable of being separately measured in the years after
purchase and inevitably wanes, only to be replaced in whole or in part by new
goodwill arising from current expenditures and events. In effect, the FRS allows

internally generated goodwill to be revalued (which is otherwise precluded by the FRS) and offset against declining purchased goodwill.

6   The approach taken in the FRS regards amortisation as necessary to recognise that goodwill has a limited useful life or as a surrogate for annual impairment reviews where such frequent reviews are not feasible. Mr Hinton does not accept this justification. He argues that:

- FRED 17 'Measurement of Tangible Fixed Assets' defines depreciation as the measure of the cost of the economic benefits of tangible fixed assets that have been consumed during the period. Amortisation is the equivalent process for intangible fixed assets. Yet goodwill differs from other costs in that it is not consumed in any way in operations. Although it contributes to earnings, it arises primarily as a result of earnings or the expectation of them. Any decrease in the value of goodwill is not associated with the income of any period or allocable to any period on any rational or systematic basis.
- Where amortisation is viewed as a surrogate for annual impairment reviews, the FRS requires the goodwill (already acknowledged not to be an asset) to be reported in the balance sheet for up to 20 years irrespective of its value, providing that nothing has happened to indicate that the value might be less than that reported. Mr Hinton believes that this fails to hold management sufficiently accountable for the values assigned to the goodwill.
- In both cases, the FRS requires operating profit to be charged with a meaningless cost.

7   Mr Hinton takes the view that a proper matching of costs and revenue does not call for amortisation of every asset: it calls for amortisation of only those assets that can be related to operations on some realistic and systematic basis so that the charge reasonably reflects the cost of the economic benefits consumed during the period. Since goodwill is not consumed or depleted as a matter of course, amortisation is not relevant. Further, he believes that the life of purchased goodwill is indeterminable and not measurable and therefore that any period of amortisation is completely arbitrary.

IDENTIFIABLE INTANGIBLE ASSETS

8   Mr Hinton notes that whilst the FRS recognises the growing importance attached to intangible assets and permits the inclusion at the date of purchase of intangible assets that are measurable on some recognised basis, it is inconsistent in precluding the subsequent revaluation of such intangibles. He takes the view that if an intangible asset is capable of measurement on some recognised basis at acquisition, it must be capable of subsequent measurement on such a basis and subsequent valuation should be permitted. He believes that this would encourage the development of methodology in this area to the ultimate benefit of users.

AN ALTERNATIVE VIEW

9   Irrespective of whether the consideration is cash, shares or debt, purchased goodwill reduces shareholders' current equity for the prospect of enhanced profit in the future. Part of shareholders' funds (in terms of 'hard assets') has been disbursed: if cash is used, it has gone; if shares, the company could have received cash for the share issue as opposed to goodwill. In both cases, something tangible has been exchanged for something intangible.

10   Mr Hinton believes that goodwill should be deducted from shareholders' equity to reflect the fact that shareholders' funds have been used. This treatment would

recognise that goodwill is neither an asset nor an immediate loss in value. In order to facilitate accountability and subsequent monitoring, the deduction should be by way of establishing a goodwill reserve within shareholders' equity. This presentation of goodwill as a separately identified balance (quasi-asset) would stress stewardship for the amounts spent but not in such a way as to suggest it is an asset, which it is not. It would also meet the requirements of the Companies Act as regards amortisation since such goodwill would be viewed as written off, thus avoiding arbitrary allocations to earnings.

While the business continued to be held, the goodwill would be kept under review for permanent impairment. This would be achieved by using high-level impairment indicators to identify possible impairment and using the full impairment reviews outlined in FRED 15 only for goodwill whose value was in doubt. Mr Hinton takes the view that the impairment reviews set forth in FRED 15 are highly subjective but that such subjectivity would be less sensitive where goodwill was not reported as an asset.   **11**

Intangible assets would be identified as set forth in the FRS. Only those intangible assets with a recognised market value or otherwise measurable on some recognised basis would be capitalised as assets at acquisition; the remainder would form part of goodwill. Only those intangible assets with a clear finite economic life and whose use could be related to earnings on a rational basis would be amortised. Intangible assets not amortised would be reviewed for impairment in the same manner as goodwill. Significantly, subsequent revaluation would be permitted.   **12**

Appendix V
Effect on realised profits of elimination of goodwill against reserves

This text reproduces guidance given in Appendix 2 of SSAP 22 'Accounting for goodwill'. The guidance has been reproduced in the FRS because it continues to apply to goodwill acquired before, and not reinstated on, implementation of the FRS. The text is largely unchanged from that contained in SSAP 22 to avoid losing any of the nuances that were considered carefully before SSAP 22 was published.

This appendix is for guidance only and does not form part of the Statement of Standard Accounting Practice.

1   "[The legal definition of realised profits] is relevant only in the case of an individual company. In the case of goodwill arising on consolidation, the distinction between realised and unrealised reserves is not relevant. Distributions are made from the profits of individual companies, not by groups, and hence the elimination of con-solidation goodwill has no effect on the distributable profits of any company.

2   Where it is the policy of an individual company to eliminate goodwill against reserves immediately on acquisition, the question arises whether such elimination constitutes a reduction of realised reserves. To the extent that the goodwill is con-sidered to have suffered an actual diminution in value, the write-off should be charged against realised reserves. In other cases, where goodwill is written off on acquisition as a matter of accounting policy, rather than because of an actual diminution in value, realised reserves should not be reduced immediately. However, the standard is based on the concept in [UK companies legislation] that purchased goodwill has a limited useful life so that ultimately its elimination must constitute a realised loss. It may in some circumstances (e.g., where a company lacks sufficient distributable reserves to cover the purchase cost of the goodwill) be appropriate to charge the elimination of goodwill initially to a suitable unrealised reserve, thereby spreading the effect of the elimination of goodwill on realised reserves over its useful life rather than impairing realised reserves immediately. The Accounting Standards Committee is advised by the Department of Trade and Industry that the restriction regarding the use of the revaluation reserve set out in paragraph 34(3) of Schedule 4 has the effect that this reserve should not be charged with the write-off of goodwill.*
A suitable unrealised reserve may exist as a result of the crediting to reserves of negative goodwill - see paragraph 3 below. To maintain parity of effect as regards distributable reserves with the amortisation method permitted by [ssap 22], the amount written off should then be transferred from unrealised reserves to realised reserves so as to reduce realised reserves on a systematic basis in the same way as if the goodwill had been amortised. In case of doubt on the points in this paragraph, legal advice should be sought.

3   Where negative goodwill arises in the accounts of an individual company it should be credited initially to an unrealised reserve, from which it may be transferred to realised reserves in line with the depreciation or realisation of the assets acquired in the business combination which gave rise to the goodwill in question. On the introduction of this standard, amounts representing negative goodwill which arose on prior acquisitions may already have been credited to reserves. To the extent that the assets acquired have, on the introduction of this standard, been depreciated or realised, the relevant amount or reserves may be regarded as realised."

Companies legislation has since been amended to clarify that the revaluation reserve may not be used for goodwill write-off. Paragraph 34(3B) of Schedule 4 to the Companies Act 1985 prohibits the reduction of the revaluation reserve in any circumstances other than those specified earlier in that paragraph. The specified circumstances do not include the write-off of goodwill.

Financial Reporting Standard 11 is set out in paragraphs 1–82.

The Statement of Standard Accounting Practice, which comprises the paragraphs set in bold type, should be read in the context of the Objective as stated in paragraph 1 and the definitions set out in paragraph 2 and also of the Foreword to Accounting Standards and the Statement of Principles for Financial Reporting currently in issue.

The explanatory paragraphs contained in the FRS shall be regarded as part of the Statement of Standard Accounting Practice insofar as they assist in interpreting that statement.

Appendix IV 'The development of the FRS' reviews considerations and arguments that were thought significant by members of the Board in reaching the conclusions of the FRS.

[FRS 11]
Impairment of fixed assets and goodwill

(Issued July 1998)

Contents

Paragraphs

Summary

Financial Reporting Standard 11

Adoption of FRS 11 by the board

Appendices
  I Determining pre-tax discount rates
  II Note on legal requirements
  III Compliance with international accounting standards
  IV The development of the FRS

Impairment of fixed assets and goodwill

Summary

a Financial Reporting Standard 11 'Impairment of Fixed Assets and Goodwill' sets out the principles and methodology for accounting for impairments of fixed assets and goodwill. Investments covered by the Accounting Standards Board's project on derivatives and other financial instruments are excluded from the scope of the FRS. Also excluded are investment properties, which are being considered further in the light of other Board projects and the international project on investment properties.

b It would be unnecessarily onerous for all fixed assets and goodwill to be tested for impairment every year. In general, fixed assets and goodwill need be reviewed for impairment only if there is some indication that impairment has occurred. (Requirements for additional impairment reviews of goodwill and intangible assets in certain circumstances are included in FRS 10 'Goodwill and Intangible Assets'.)

c Where possible, individual fixed assets should be tested for impairment. However, impairment can often be tested only for groups of assets because the cash flows upon which the calculation is based do not arise from the use of a single asset. In these cases, impairment is measured for the smallest group of assets (the income-generating unit) that produces a largely independent income stream, subject to constraints of practicality and materiality.

d Impairment is measured by comparing the carrying value of the fixed asset or income-generating unit with its recoverable amount. The recoverable amount is the higher of the amounts that can be obtained from selling the fixed asset or income-generating unit (net realisable value) or using the fixed asset or income-generating unit (value in use).

e Net realisable value is the expected proceeds of selling the fixed asset or income-generating unit less any direct selling costs. Value in use is calculated by discounting the expected cash flows arising from the use of the fixed asset or assets in the income-generating unit at the rate of return that the market would expect from an equally risky investment.

f In some cases a detailed calculation of value in use will not be necessary. A simple estimate may be sufficient to demonstrate that either value in use is higher than carrying value, in which case there is no impairment, or value in use is lower than net realisable value, in which case impairment is measured by reference to net realisable value.

g If an acquisition that gives rise to goodwill is merged with an existing business, the requirements of the FRS necessitate the calculation of the amount of any internally generated goodwill in the existing business at the date of the merger because that amount will need to be used in the calculation of any subsequent impairment loss in the merged business.

h The reversal of past impairment losses is recognised when the recoverable amount of a tangible fixed asset or investment in a subsidiary, an associate or a joint venture has increased because of a change in economic conditions or in the expected use of the asset. Increases in the recoverable amount of goodwill and intangible assets are recognised only when an external event caused the recognition of the impairment loss in previous periods, and subsequent external events clearly and demonstrably reverse the effects of that event in a way that was not foreseen in the original impairment calculations.

Impairment losses are recognised in the profit and loss account, unless they arise on a previously revalued fixed asset. Impairment losses on revalued fixed assets are recognised in the statement of total recognised gains and losses until the carrying value of the asset falls below depreciated historical cost unless the impairment is clearly caused by a consumption of economic benefits, in which case the loss is recognised in the profit and loss account. Impairments below depreciated historical cost are recognised in the profit and loss account.

Financial Reporting Standard 11

Objective

1   The objective of this FRS is to ensure that:

(a)   fixed assets and goodwill are recorded in the financial statements at no more than their recoverable amount;

(b)   any resulting impairment loss is measured and recognised on a consistent basis; and

(c)   sufficient information is disclosed in the financial statements to enable users to understand the impact of the impairment on the financial position and performance of the reporting entity.

Definitions

2   The following definitions shall apply in the FRS and in particular in the Statement of Standard Accounting Practice set out **in bold type.**

Impairment:-

A reduction in the recoverable amount of a fixed asset or goodwill below its carrying amount.

Income-generating unit:-

A group of assets, liabilities and associated goodwill that generates income that is largely independent of the reporting entity's other income streams. The assets and liabilities include those directly involved in generating the income and an appropriate portion of those used to generate more than one income stream.

Intangible assets:-

Non-financial fixed assets that do not have physical substance but are identifiable and controlled by the entity through custody or legal rights.

Net realisable value:-

The amount at which an asset could be disposed of, less any direct selling costs.

Purchased goodwill:-

The difference between the cost of an acquired entity and the aggregate of the fair values of that entity's identifiable assets and liabilities.

Readily ascertainable market value:-

In relation to an intangible asset, the value that is established by reference to a market where:

(a)   the asset belongs to a homogeneous population of assets that are equivalent in all material respects; and

(b)   an active market, evidenced by frequent transactions, exists for that population of assets.

Recoverable amount:-

The higher of net realisable value and value in use.

Tangible fixed assets:-

Assets that have physical substance and are held for use in the production or supply of goods or services, for rental to others, or for administrative purposes on a continuing basis in the reporting entity's activities.

Value in use:-

The present value of the future cash flows obtainable as a result of an asset's continued use, including those resulting from its ultimate disposal.

SCOPE

The FRS applies to all financial statements that are intended to give a true and fair view of a reporting entity's financial position and profit or loss (or income and expenditure) for a period.   **3**

Reporting entities applying the Financial Reporting Standard for Smaller Entities (FRSSE) currently applicable are exempt from the FRS unless preparing consolidated financial statements, in which case they should apply the FRS to such statements as required by the FRSSE.*   **4**

The requirements of the FRS apply to purchased goodwill that is recognised in the balance sheet and all fixed assets, except: **5**

(a)   **fixed assets within the scope of the FRS addressing disclosures of derivatives and other financial instruments†;**

(b)   **investment properties as defined in SSAP 19 'Accounting for investment properties';**

(c)   **an entity's own shares held by an ESOP and shown as a fixed asset in the entity's balance sheet under UITF Abstract 13 'Accounting for ESOP Trusts'; and**

(d)   **costs capitalised pending determination (ie costs capitalised while a field is still being appraised) under the Oil Industry Accounting Committee's SORP 'Accounting for oil and gas exploration and development activities'.‡**

Reporting entities applying the FRSSE are generally exempt from applying this FRS. However, if they prepare consolidated financial statements, the FRSSE in force at the date of the publication of this FRS requires them to apply SSAP 22 to purchased goodwill arising on consolidation. It is envisaged that a future revision of the FRSSE will required smaller entities adopting the FRSSE and preparing consolidated financial statements to replace that reference to SSAP 22 with an equivalent reference to FRS 10 and this FRS. (Editor's note:** The FRSSE (effective March 1999) did this.)*

†Editor's note: See FRS 25 and 29.

*‡**Editor's note:** Superseded by updated SORP 'Accounting for oil and gas exploration, development, production and decommissioning activities' issued January 2000.*

6   Many investments are covered by the Accounting Standards Board's project on derivatives and other financial instruments and hence are excluded from this FRS. However, investments in subsidiary undertakings, associates and joint ventures are excluded from the scope of that project and are, therefore, included within the scope of this FRS

7   The FRS does not apply to purchased goodwill that was written off to reserves under SSAP 22 'Accounting for goodwill' and has not been recognised on the balance sheet under FRS 10 'Goodwill and Intangible Assets'.

INDICATIONS OF IMPAIRMENT

8   **A review for impairment of a fixed asset or goodwill should be carried out if events or changes in circumstances indicate that the carrying amount of the fixed asset or goodwill may not be recoverable.**

9   Impairment occurs because something has happened either to the fixed assets themselves or to the economic environment in which the fixed assets are operated. It is possible, therefore, to rely on the use of indicators of impairment to determine when a review for impairment is needed.

10 Examples of events and changes in circumstances that indicate an impairment may have occurred include:

- a current period operating loss in the business in which the fixed asset or goodwill is involved or net cash outflow from the operating activities of that business, combined with either past operating losses or net cash outflows from such operating activities or an expectation of continuing operating losses or net cash outflows from such operating activities
- a significant decline in a fixed asset's market value during the period
- evidence of obsolescence or physical damage to the fixed asset
- a significant adverse change in:
  - either the business or the market in which the fixed asset or goodwill is involved, such as the entrance of a major competitor
  - the statutory or other regulatory environment in which the business operates
  - any 'indicator of value' (for example turnover) used to measure the fair value of a fixed asset on acquisition
- a commitment by management to undertake a significant reorganisation
- a major loss of key employees
- a significant increase in market interest rates or other market rates of return that are likely to affect materially the fixed asset's recoverable amount.

11 The above indicators of impairment will trigger an impairment review only if they are relevant to the measurement of goodwill or fixed assets. For example, short-term market interest rates may increase without affecting the rate of return the market would require on long-term assets, with the result that there is no effect on the recoverable amount of such assets. Such increases in short-term rates would not trigger an impairment review.

12 If any such events or changes in circumstances are identified, a review of the useful economic lives and residual values of the fixed assets or goodwill affected is appropriate: even if the fixed assets or goodwill are not impaired, their remaining useful economic lives and residual values may have changed as a result of the events or changes in circumstances.

The requirements of this FRS are such that if no such events or changes in circum-   **13**
stances are identified, and there are no other indications that a tangible fixed asset or
investment in a subsidiary, associate or joint venture has become impaired, there is
no requirement for an impairment review. For tangible fixed assets, impairments will
therefore be a relatively infrequent addition to depreciation. Additional requirements
to perform impairment reviews for goodwill and intangible assets that are amortised
over periods of more than 20 years or not at all are set out in FRS 10 'Goodwill and
Intangible Assets'.

RECOGNITION AND MEASUREMENT OF IMPAIRMENT LOSSES

The impairment review should comprise a comparison of the carrying amount of the   **14**
fixed asset or goodwill with its recoverable amount (the higher of net realisable value
and value in use). To the extent that the carrying amount exceeds the recoverable
amount, the fixed asset or goodwill is impaired and should be written down. The
impairment loss should be recognised in the profit and loss account unless it arises on a
previously revalued fixed asset, in which case it should be recognised as required by
paragraph 63.

If either net realisable value or value in use is higher than the carrying amount of a   **15**
fixed asset or goodwill, the fixed asset or goodwill is not impaired and there is no
need to calculate the other amount.

If no reliable estimate of net realisable value can be made, the recoverable amount is   **16**
determined by value in use alone.

If net realisable value is lower than the carrying amount of the fixed asset, before   **17**
writing down the asset to net realisable value it is necessary to establish whether
value in use is higher. If it is, the recoverable amount will be based on value in use,
not net realisable value.

Requirements and guidance relating to the calculation of net realisable value and   **18**
value in use are set out in paragraphs 22–46 below. In many cases, a detailed calculation of value in use will not be necessary because a simple estimate will be
sufficient to demonstrate that value in use is either above carrying value, in which
case there is no impairment, or is below net realisable value, in which case the
recoverable amount will not be based on value in use.

In determining whether recoverable amount should be based on value in use or net   **19**
realisable value, the deferred tax balances that would arise in each case need to be
taken into account. For example, if net realisable value is £100 and would give rise to
a deferred tax liability of £30 and value in use is £110 and would give rise to a
deferred tax liability of £45, recoverable amount is based on net realisable value.

If a fixed asset is not held for the purpose of generating cash flows either by itself or   **20**
in conjunction with other assets, for example certain fixed assets held for charitable
purposes, it is not appropriate to measure the asset at an amount based on expected
future cash flows. In such cases it may not be appropriate to write down the fixed
asset to its recoverable amount – an alternative measure of its service potential may
be more relevant.

When an impairment loss on a fixed asset or goodwill is recognised, the remaining   **21**
useful economic life and residual value should be reviewed and revised if necessary. The
revised carrying amount should be depreciated over the revised estimate of the
remaining useful economic life.

CALCULATION OF NET REALISABLE VALUE

22 The net realisable value of an asset that is traded on an active market will be based on market value.

23 Net realisable value is defined as the amount at which an asset could be disposed of, less any direct selling costs. Examples of direct selling costs are legal costs and stamp duty. Any costs relating to the removal of a sitting tenant are also direct selling costs of a building. However, costs associated with reducing or reorganising the business rather than selling the fixed asset, such as redundancy costs incurred when a factory is sold, are not direct selling costs.

CALCULATION OF VALUE IN USE

24 **The value in use of a fixed asset should be estimated individually where reasonably practicable. Where it is not reasonably practicable to identify cash flows arising from an individual fixed asset, value in use should be calculated at the level of income-generating units. The carrying amount of each income-generating unit containing the fixed asset or goodwill under review should be compared with the higher of the value in use and the net realisable value (if it can be measured reliably) of the unit.**

25 The value in use of a fixed asset is the present value of the future cash flows obtainable as a result of the asset's continued use, including those resulting from its ultimate disposal. In practice, it is not normally possible to estimate the value in use of an individual fixed asset: it is the utilisation of groups of assets and liabilities, together with their associated goodwill, that generates cash flows. Hence value in use will usually have to be estimated in total for groups of assets and liabilities. These groups are referred to as income-generating units.

26 Because it is necessary to identify only material impairments, in some cases it may be acceptable to consider a group of income-generating units together rather than on an individual basis.

Income-generating units

27 **Income-generating units should be identified by dividing the total income of the entity into as many largely independent income streams as is reasonably practicable. Except as permitted by paragraph 32, each of the identifiable assets and liabilities of the entity, excluding deferred tax balances, interest-bearing debt, dividends payable and other items relating wholly to financing, should be attributed to (or apportioned between) one (or more) income-generating unit(s).**

28 To perform impairment reviews as accurately as possible:
- the groups of assets and liabilities that are considered together should be as small as is reasonably practicable, but
- the income stream underlying the future cash flows of one group should be largely independent of other income streams of the entity and should be capable of being monitored separately.

Income-generating units are therefore identified by dividing the total income of the business into as many largely independent income streams as is reasonably practicable in the light of the information available to management.

In general terms, the income streams identified are likely to follow the way in which **29** management monitors and makes decisions about continuing or closing the different lines of business of the entity. Unique intangible assets, such as brands and mastheads, are generally seen to generate income independently of each other and are usually monitored separately. Hence they can often be used to identify income-generating units. Other income streams may be identified by reference to major products or services.

Examples 1–4: Identification of income-generating units

Example 1

A transport company runs a network comprising trunk routes fed by a number of supporting routes. Decisions about continuing or closing the supporting routes are not based on the returns generated by the routes in isolation but on the contribution made to the returns generated by the trunk routes.

An income-generating unit comprises a trunk route plus the supporting routes associated with it because the cash inflows generated by the trunk routes are not independent of the supporting routes.

Example 2

A manufacturer can produce a product at a number of different sites. Not all the sites are used to full capacity and the manufacturer can choose how much to make at each site. However, there is not enough surplus capacity to enable any one site to be closed. The cash inflows generated by any one site therefore depend on the allocation of production across all sites.

The income-generating unit comprises all the sites at which the product can be made.

Example 3

A restaurant chain has a large number of restaurants across the country. The cash inflows of each restaurant can be individually monitored and sensible allocations of costs to each restaurant can be made.

Each restaurant is an income-generating unit by itself. However, any impairment of individual restaurants is unlikely to be material. A material impairment is likely to occur only when a number of restaurants are affected together by the same economic factors. It may therefore be acceptable to consider groupings of restaurants affected by the same economic factors rather than each individual restaurant.

Example 4

An entity comprises three stages of production, A (growing and felling trees), B (creating parts of wooden furniture) and C (assembling the parts from B into finished goods). The output of A is timber that is partly transferred to B and partly sold in an external market. If A did not exist, B could buy its timber from the market. The output of B has no external market and is transferred to C at an internal transfer price. C sells the finished product in an external market and the sales revenue achieved by C is not affected by the fact that the three stages of production are all performed by the entity (unlike example 1, where the sales revenue of the trunk routes is affected by the existence of supporting routes run by the same entity).

A forms an income-generating unit and its cash inflows should be based on the market price for its output. B and C together form one income-generating unit because there is no market available for the output of B. In calculating the cash outflows of the income-generating unit B+C, the timber received by B from A should be priced by reference to the market, not any internal transfer price.

30   Income-generating units are defined by allocating the assets and liabilities of the reporting entity, excluding deferred tax balances, interest-bearing debt, dividends payable and other items relating wholly to financing, to the identified income streams. Certain assets and liabilities that are directly involved in the production and distribution of individual products may be attributed directly to one unit. Central assets, such as group or regional head offices, and working capital may have to be apportioned across the units on a logical and systematic basis. The resulting income-generating units will be complete and non-overlapping, so that the sum of the carrying amounts of the units equals the carrying amount of the net assets (excluding tax and financing items) of the entity as a whole, as illustrated in example 5 below.

Example 5: Allocation of head office assets to income-generating units

An entity has three independent income streams, A, B and C, with net assets directly involved in the income streams with carrying amounts of £100 million, £150 million and £200 million respectively. In addition there are head office net assets with a carrying amount totalling £18 million. The relative proportion of the head office resources used by the income streams is 2:3:4. The income-generating units are defined as follows:

Income-generating unit	A	B	C	Total
Net assets directly attributable to income-generating unit (£ million)	100	150	200	450
Head office net assets (£ million)	4	6	8	18
Total (£ million)	104	156	208	468

If there were an indication that a fixed asset in income-generating unit B was impaired, the recoverable amount of B would be compared with £156 million, not £150 million. Similarly, the cash flows upon which the value in use of B is based would include the relevant portion of any cash outflows arising from central overheads.

31   The income stream of a fixed asset to be disposed of will be largely independent of the income stream of other assets. Such an asset therefore forms an income-generating unit of its own and does not belong to any other income-generating unit.

Central assets

32   **If it is not possible to apportion certain central assets meaningfully across the income-generating units to which they contribute, these assets may be excluded from the individual income-generating units. However, an additional impairment review should be performed on the excluded central assets. In this review, the income-generating units**

to which the central assets contribute should be combined and their combined carrying amount (including that of the central assets) should be compared with their combined value in use.

Example 6: Alternative approach to allocation of head office assets to income-generating units

With this approach, in example 5 above the recoverable amount of B would be compared with £150 million, not £156 million. Then a further impairment test would be required on the whole entity comparing its recoverable amount with the total carrying value of £468 million.

If there is any working capital in the balance sheet that will generate cash flows equal to its carrying amount, the carrying amount of the working capital may be excluded from the income-generating units and the cash flows arising from its realisation/settlement excluded from the value in use calculation.   **33**

Capitalised goodwill should be attributed to (or apportioned between) income-generating units or groups of similar units. If they were acquired as part of the same investment and are involved in similar parts of the business, individual units identified for the purpose of monitoring the recoverability of assets may be combined with other units to enable the recoverability of the related goodwill to be assessed.   **34**

Goodwill is allocated to income-generating units in the same way as are the assets and liabilities of the entity. However, where several similar income-generating units are acquired together in one investment, the units may be combined to assess the recoverability of the goodwill. The income-generating units are first reviewed individually for the purposes of assessing the recoverability of any capitalised intangible assets and tangible fixed assets and then, as illustrated in example 7 below, the combined unit is reviewed to assess the recoverability of the goodwill.   **35**

Example 7: Alternative approach to allocation of goodwill to income-generating units

An entity acquires a business comprising three income-generating units, A, B and C. After five years, the carrying amount of the net assets in the income-generating units and the purchased goodwill compares with the value in use as follows (there is no reliable estimate of net realisable value for any of the income-generating units or the business as a whole):

Income-generating unit	A	B	C	Goodwill	Total
Carrying amount (£ million)	80	120	140	50	390
Value in use (£ million)	100	140	120		360

An impairment loss of £20 million is recognised in respect of income-generating unit C, reducing its carrying amount to £120 million and the total carrying amount to £370 million. A further impairment loss of £10 million is then recognised in respect of the goodwill.

Cash flows

The expected future cash flows of the income-generating unit, including any allocation of central overheads but excluding cash flows relating to financing and tax, should be   **36**

based on reasonable and supportable assumptions. The cash flows should be consistent with the most up-to-date budgets and plans that have been formally approved by management. Cash flows for the period beyond that covered by formal budgets and plans should assume a steady or declining growth rate. Only in exceptional circumstances should:

(a) the period before the steady or declining growth rate is assumed extend to more than five years; or

(b) the steady or declining growth rate exceed the long-term average growth rate for the country or countries in which the business operates.*

37 In exceptional circumstances, the use of a long-term growth rate that is higher than the average country growth rate may be justified. This may, for example, be the case where:

(a) the long-term growth rate for the relevant industry is expected to be significantly higher than the relevant country growth rate; and

(b) the business under review is expected to grow as rapidly as the industry as a whole, taking into account the likelihood of new competitors entering such an industry.

38 Subject to paragraph 39 below, future cash flows should be estimated for income-generating units or individual fixed assets in their current condition. They should not include:

(a) future cash outflows or related cost savings (for example reductions in staff costs) or benefits that are expected to arise from a future reorganisation for which provision has not yet been made; or

(b) future capital expenditure that will improve or enhance the income-generating units or assets in excess of their originally assessed standard of performance or the related future benefits of this future expenditure.

39 In the case of a newly acquired income-generating unit such as a subsidiary, the purchase price will reflect the synergies and other opportunities for making more effective use of the assets as a result of the acquisition. In some of these cases, in order to obtain the benefits from its investment, it may be necessary for the purchaser to undertake related capital expenditure and reorganisations. Consequently, in assessing the future cash flows of the investment, the costs and benefits of such reorganisations and capital expenditure anticipated at the time of performing impairment reviews up to the end of the first full year after acquisition and consistent with budgets and plans at that time may be taken into account in those and subsequent impairment reviews, to the extent that the investment or reorganisations are still to be incurred.

40 Failure to undertake capital investment or a reorganisation according to the planned schedule may call into question the validity of continuing to forecast that the investment or reorganisation will be undertaken in the future and may be an indication of impairment as discussed in paragraphs 8-13. The costs and benefits of the investment or reorganisation would then have to be omitted from forecasts performed for subsequent impairment reviews. Additionally, the monitoring of cash flows required by paragraph 54 may indicate that impairment has already occurred.

The UK post-war average growth in gross domestic product, expressed in real terms, is 2.25 per cent (source: Financial Statement and Budget Report March 1998, HM Treasury).

Discount rate

The present value of the income-generating unit under review should be calculated by discounting the expected future cash flows of the unit. The discount rate used should be an estimate of the rate that the market would expect on an equally risky investment. It should exclude the effects of any risk for which the cash flows have been adjusted and should be calculated on a pre-tax basis.   **41**

Estimates of this market rate may be made by a variety of means including reference to: **42**

(a) the rate implicit in market transactions of similar assets;
(b) the current weighted average cost of capital (WACC) of a listed company whose cash flows have similar risk profiles to those of the income-generating unit; or
(c) the WACC for the entity *but only if* adjusted for the particular risks associated with the income-generating unit.

If method (c) is used the following matters are of note.   **43**

- Where the cash flow forecasts assume a real growth rate that exceeds the long-term average growth rate for more than five years, it is likely that the discount rate will be increased to reflect a higher level of risk.
- The discount rates applied to individual income-generating units will always be estimated such that, were they to be calculated for every unit, the weighted average discount rate would equal the entity's overall WACC.

The WACC will be a post-tax rate from the entity's point of view, whereas the required discount rate will be a pre-tax rate. Some of the issues that need to be considered in adjusting from a post-tax rate to a pre-tax rate are discussed in Appendix I.   **44**

Using a discount rate equal to the rate of return that the market would expect on an equally risky investment is a method of reflecting the risk associated with the cash flows in the value in use measurement. It is likely that this method will be the easiest method of reflecting risk. However, an acceptable alternative is to adjust the cash flows for risk and to discount them using a risk-free rate (eg a government bond rate). Whichever method of reflecting risk is adopted, care must be taken that the effect of risk is not double-counted by inclusion in both the cash flows and the discount rate.   **45**

If the cash flows to be discounted are expressed in current prices, a real discount rate will be used. If the cash flows are expressed in expected future prices, a nominal discount rate will be used.   **46**

ALLOCATION OF IMPAIRMENT LOSSES

The carrying amounts of the income-generating units under review should be calculated as the net of the carrying amounts of the assets, liabilities and goodwill allocated to the unit.   **47**

To the extent that the carrying amount of the income-generating unit exceeds its recoverable amount, the unit is impaired. In the absence of an obvious impairment of specific assets within the unit, the impairment should be allocated: **48**

(a) first, to any goodwill in the unit;
(b) thereafter, to any capitalised intangible asset in the unit; and

(c)   finally, to the tangible assets in the unit, on a pro rata or more appropriate basis.

49   In this allocation, which aims to write down the assets with the most subjective valuations first, no intangible asset with a readily ascertainable market value should be written down below its net realisable value. Similarly, no tangible asset with a net realisable value that can be measured reliably should be written down below its net realisable value.

Allocation when acquired businesses are merged with existing operations

50   Where an acquired business is merged with an existing business and results in an income-generating unit that contains both purchased and (unrecognised) internally generated goodwill:

(a)   the value of the internally generated goodwill of the existing business at the date of merging the businesses should be estimated and added to the carrying amount of the income-generating unit for the purposes of performing impairment reviews;*

(b)   any impairment arising on merging the businesses should be allocated solely to the purchased goodwill within the newly acquired business;

(c)   subsequent impairments should be allocated pro rata between the goodwill of the acquired business and that of the existing business;

(d)   the impairment allocated to the existing business should be allocated first to the (notional) internally generated goodwill; and

(e)   only the impairments allocated to purchased goodwill (and, if necessary, to any recognised intangible or tangible assets) should be recognised in the financial statements.

51   An acquired business may be merged with an existing operation of the reporting entity in such a way that a single income-generating unit includes the assets and liabilities of both the acquired and the existing businesses. This combined income-generating unit contains both acquired and internally generated goodwill and any future impairment needs to be apportioned between the two. This can be done by notionally adjusting the carrying amount of the income-generating unit to recognise a notional carrying amount for the internally generated goodwill of the existing operation at the date of merging the two businesses.

52   The notional carrying amount of the internally generated goodwill is estimated by deducting the fair values of the net assets and purchased goodwill within the existing income-generating unit from its estimated value in use before combining the businesses. This calculation will need to be done whenever an acquisition that gives rise to goodwill is merged with an existing business. The notional balance is assumed to be subject to the same pattern of amortisation as is applied to the purchased goodwill.

53   Because the comparison with value in use will have resulted in the recognition of any impairment of the existing business at the time of merging it with the acquired business, any initial impairment in the combined income-generating unit will, by definition, relate to the acquired business. Any subsequent impairment cannot be attributed directly to either the acquired or the existing businesses and is therefore apportioned between the notional internally generated goodwill and the purchased goodwill pro rata to their current carrying values.

*The internally generated goodwill will not be recognised in the financial statements.

Example 8: Allocation of impairment losses when an acquired business is merged with existing operations

Assumptions

An entity acquires for £60 million a business having net assets with a total fair value of £40 million, resulting in purchased goodwill of £20 million. The acquired business is merged with an existing operation that has net assets with a fair value of £100 million and a carrying amount of £70 million. The value in use of the existing operation at the time of the acquisition is £150 million, implying that the existing operation has internally generated goodwill of £50 million.

Five years later, the carrying amount of the net assets of the combined income-generating unit is £105 million and the carrying amount of the purchased goodwill is £10 million (goodwill is being amortised over 10 years). Value in use is £119 million and there is no reliable estimate of net realisable value.

Calculation of impairment loss	£m
Carrying amount of new assets	105
Carrying amount of goodwill	10
Notional carrying amount of the internally generated goodwill at the date of acquisition (assuming notional amortisation on same basis as for purchased goodwill)	25
Total	140
Value in use	119
Impairment	21

The impairment is allocated on a pro rata basis (2:5) to the purchased goodwill and internally generated goodwill, resulting in the recognition of an impairment loss of £6 million and purchased goodwill being written down to £4 million.

If value in use were £98 million, the resulting total impairment loss of £42 million would be allocated first to the goodwill (purchased and notional amount of internally generated) of £35 million, then to any intangible assets, then to the tangible fixed assets in the income-generating unit, resulting in the recognition of an impairment loss of £17 million (write-down of purchased goodwill £10 million, write-down of intangible and tangible assets £7 million).

SUBSEQUENT MONITORING OF CASH FLOWS

For the five years following each impairment review where the recoverable amount has been based on value in use, the cash flows achieved should be compared with those forecast. If the actual cash flows are so much less than those forecast that use of the actual cash flows could have required recognition of an impairment in previous periods, the original impairment calculations should be re-performed using the actual cash flows. Any impairment identified should be recognised in the current period unless the **54**

impairment has reversed and the reversal of the loss is permitted to be recognised by paragraph 56 or 60 below.

55   In order to check whether an impairment would have arisen, the original calculation is re-performed using the cash flows that have actually occurred but without revising any other cash flows or assumptions (except those that change as a direct consequence of the occurrence of the actual cash flows, eg where a major cash inflow has been delayed for a year). If this recalculation identifies an impairment, the loss should be recognised in the current period. However, the entity may also recalculate value in use using revised assumptions in order to assess the current value in use. If this current value in use shows a reversal of the impairment that would have been recognised had the actual cash flows been used in the original calculation, and that reversal is permitted to be recognised under the FRS, recognition of an impairment loss is not required. Instead, the impairment that would have been recognised and its subsequent reversal are disclosed (paragraph 71).

REVERSAL OF PAST IMPAIRMENTS

Tangible fixed assets and investments in subsidiaries, associates and joint ventures

56   **If, after an impairment loss has been recognised, the recoverable amount of a tangible fixed asset or investment increases because of a change in economic conditions or in the expected use of the asset, the resulting reversal of the impairment loss should be recognised in the current period to the extent that it increases the carrying amount of the fixed asset up to the amount that it would have been had the original impairment not occurred. The reversal of the impairment loss should be recognised in the profit and loss account unless it arises on a previously revalued fixed asset, in which case it should be recognised as required by paragraph 66.**

57   Events and circumstances that are the reverse of those set out in paragraph 10 as triggers for an impairment review may indicate that the recoverable amount of a fixed asset has increased. The increase in the recoverable amount must arise from a change in economic conditions or in the expected use of the asset. This would include situations where the recoverable amount increases as a result of further capital investment or a reorganisation, the benefits of which had been excluded from the original measurement of value in use.

58   Increases in value in use may arise simply because of:

(a)   the passage of time: as future cash inflows become closer, their discounted value increases. (Where value in use has been calculated using cash flows based on current prices and a real discount rate, value in use may also increase because of the effect of general inflation on current prices.)

(b)   the occurrence of forecast cash outflows: once the cash outflows are past, they are no longer part of the value in use calculation and value in use therefore increases.

Such increases in value may not be recognised as reversals of an impairment loss.

59   The recognition of an increase in the recoverable amount of a tangible fixed asset above the amount that its carrying amount would have been had the original impairment not occurred is a revaluation, not a reversal of an impairment.

Goodwill and intangible assets

60   **The reversal of an impairment loss on intangible assets and goodwill should be recognised in the current period if, and only if:**

(a)   an external event caused the recognition of the impairment loss in previous periods, and subsequent external events clearly and demonstrably reverse the effects of that event in a way that was not foreseen in the original impairment calculations; or

(b)   the impairment loss arose on an intangible asset with a readily ascertainable market value and the net realisable value based on that market value has increased to above the intangible asset's impaired carrying amount.

The reversal of the impairment loss should be recognised to the extent that it increases the carrying amount of the goodwill or intangible asset up to the amount that it would have been had the original impairment not occurred.   61

The recognition of an increase in the recoverable amount of an intangible asset above the amount that its carrying amount would have been had the original impairment not occurred is a revaluation and is addressed by FRS 10 'Goodwill and Intangible Assets'.   62

Example 9: Allocation and reversal of impairment losses

Assumptions

An income-generating unit comprising a factory, plant and equipment etc and associated purchased goodwill becomes impaired because the product it makes is overtaken by a technologically more advanced model produced by a competitor. The recoverable amount of the income-generating unit falls to £60 million, resulting in an impairment loss of £80 million, allocated as follows:

	Carrying amounts before impairment £m	Carrying amounts after impairment £m
Goodwill	40	–
Patent (with no market value)	20	–
Tangible fixed assets	80	60
Total	140	60

After three years, the entity makes a technological breakthrough of its own, and the recoverable amount of the income-generating unit increases to £90 million. The carrying amount of the tangible fixed assets had the impairment not occurred would have been £70 million.

Calculation of reversal of the impairment loss

The reversal of the impairment loss is recognised to the extent that it increases the carrying amount of the tangible fixed assets to what it would have been had the impairment not taken place, ie a reversal of £10 million of the impairment loss is recognised and the tangible fixed assets written back to £70 million. Reversal of the impairment is not recognised in relation to the goodwill and a patent because the effect of the external event that caused the original impairment has not reversed – the original product is still overtaken by a more advanced model.

REVALUED FIXED ASSETS

63   An impairment loss on a revalued fixed asset should be recognised in the profit and loss account if it is caused by a clear consumption of economic benefits. Other impairments of revalued fixed assets should be recognised in the statement of total recognised gains and losses until the carrying amount of the asset reaches its depreciated historical cost and thereafter in the profit and loss account.

64   An impairment loss arises on a revalued fixed asset whenever the recoverable amount of the asset falls below its carrying amount. In particular, a downward revaluation may comprise, at least in part, an impairment loss. Some of these impairments are caused by a consumption of economic benefits, for example physical damage or a deterioration in the quality of the service provided by the asset, and are operating costs similar to depreciation.

65   Other impairments of revalued fixed assets may result from general changes in prices, for example a general slump in the property market, and are recognised in the statement of total recognised gains and losses as valuation adjustments until the carrying amount of the asset reaches its depreciated historical cost, and thereafter in the profit and loss account.

66   A reversal of an impairment loss should be recognised in the profit and loss account to the extent that the original impairment loss (adjusted for subsequent depreciation) was recognised in the profit and loss account. Any remaining balance of the reversal of an impairment should be recognised in the statement of total recognised gains and losses.

PRESENTATION AND DISCLOSURE

67   Impairment losses recognised in the profit and loss account should be included within operating profit under the appropriate statutory heading, and disclosed as an exceptional item if appropriate. Impairment losses recognised in the statement of total recognised gains and losses should be disclosed separately on the face of that statement.

68   In the notes to the financial statements in accounting periods after the impairment, the impairment loss should be treated as follows:

   (a)   for assets held on a historical cost basis, the impairment loss should be included within cumulative depreciation: the cost of the asset should not be reduced.

   (b)   for revalued assets held at a market value (eg existing use value or open market value), the impairment loss should be included within the revalued carrying amount.

   (c)   for revalued assets held at depreciated replacement cost, an impairment loss charged to the profit and loss account should be included within cumulative depreciation: the carrying amount of the asset should not be reduced; an impairment loss charged to the statement of total recognised gains and losses should be deducted from the carrying amount of the asset.

69   If the impairment loss is measured by reference to value in use of a fixed asset or income-generating unit, the discount rate applied to the cash flows should be disclosed. If a risk-free discount rate is used, some indication of the risk adjustments made to the cash flows should be given.

70   Where an impairment loss recognised in a previous period is reversed in the current period, the financial statements should disclose the reason for the reversal, including any changes in the assumptions upon which the calculation of recoverable amount is based.

Where an impairment loss would have been recognised in a previous period had the   71
forecasts of future cash flows been more accurate but the impairment has reversed and
the reversal of the loss is permitted to be recognised, the impairment now identified and
its subsequent reversal should be disclosed.

Where, in the measurement of value in use, the period before a steady or declining long-   72
term growth rate has been assumed extends to more than five years, the financial
statements should disclose the length of the longer period and the circumstances
justifying it.

Where, in the measurement of value in use, the long-term growth rate used has exceeded   73
the long-term average growth rate for the country or countries in which the business
operates, the financial statements should disclose the growth rate assumed and the
circumstances justifying it.

Date from which effective and transitional arrangements

The accounting practices set out in the FRS should be regarded as standard in respect of   74
financial statements relating to accounting periods ending on or after 23 December
1998. Earlier adoption is encouraged but not required.

Impairment losses recognised when the standard is implemented for the first time are   75
not the result of a change in accounting policy and should be recognised in accordance
with the requirements of the FRS and not as prior period adjustments.

The requirement that fixed assets should not be held at more than recoverable   76
amount is a well-established principle. Achieving this objective by applying the
method prescribed in the FRS is not a change in accounting policy but is similar to a
change in accounting estimate.

AMENDMENT OF OTHER ACCOUNTING STANDARDS

[*Not reproduced as all changes have been reflected in the material reproduced in this*   77–82
volume.]

Adoption of FRS 11 by the board

*Financial Reporting Standard 11 - 'Impairment of Fixed Assets and Goodwill' was
approved for issue by the ten members of the Accounting Standards Board.*

Sir David Tweedie   (Chairman)
Allan Cook   (Technical Director)
David Allvey
Ian Brindle
Dr John Buchanan
John Coombe
Raymond Hinton
Huw Jones
Professor Geoffrey Whittington
Ken Wild

Appendix I
Determining pre-tax discount rates

The discount rate reflects the rate of return required on the assets being reviewed, not   **1**
the way in which they have been financed. Hence it is not affected by any tax relief
available on the cost of financing the asset or by any tax paid by the provider of
finance.

The required pre-tax rate of return is simply the rate of return that will, after tax has   **2**
been deducted, give the required post-tax rate of return. Because the tax consequence
of different cash flows may be different, the pre-tax rate of return is not always the
post-tax rate of return grossed up by a standard rate of tax.

The effect of discounting pre-tax cash flows at a pre-tax discount rate should be   **3**
similar to the effect of discounting post-tax cash flows at a post-tax discount rate.

Example

An asset is required to generate a post-tax return of 14 per cent. If the asset
cost £100, and generated all of its cash flows in one year's time, the required
post-tax cash flows would be £114.

If tax was charged at 30 per cent, pre-tax cash flows of £120 would be required
to generate the required post-tax cash flows of £114:

	£	£
Pre-tax cash flows		120
Tax at 30% of £120	(36)	
Allowance for cost of asset at 30%	30	
		(6)
		114

Thus the required pre-tax cash flows would be £120, making the required pre-
tax rate of return 20 per cent.

The value assigned to the asset would be £100, whether calculated by discounting pre-tax cash flows (£120) by the pre-tax required rate of return (20
per cent) or by discounting post-tax cash flows (£114) by the post-tax required
rate of return (14 per cent).

However, when an asset becomes impaired, the relationship between pre-tax and   **4**
post-tax required rates of return may change. This is because, although future pre-
tax cash flows reduce, the amount of future tax relief may not. This is taken into
account by providing for deferred tax on any timing differences created by the
recognition of the impairment loss, not by making any adjustment to the pre-tax
discount rate.

Example

Suppose that in the previous example, £100 had been paid for the asset in the expectation that it would generate pre-tax cash flows of at lease £120. However, circumstances then changed and the pre-tax cash flows were expected to halve to £60. The cash flows expected in one year's time would therefore be:

	£	£
Pre-tax cash flows		60
Tax at 30% of £60	(18)	
Allowance for cost of asset (£100 at 30%)	30	
		12
		72

Although the pre-tax cash flows have halved, the post-tax cash flows have not reduced so much. Thus discounting the pre-tax cash flows of £60 by 20 per cent (to give a value of £50) no longer produces the same value for the asset as would be achieved by discounting the post-tax cash flows of £72 by 14 per cent (to give a value of £63).

The difference is not eliminated by making any adjustment to the pre-tax rate of return to reflect the tax status of the asset under review. Rather it is eliminated by providing for deferred tax on the timing difference created by the recognition of the impairment loss:

	£
Impaired carrying value of asset (£60 discounted by 20%)	50
Deferred tax asset (impairment of £50 at 30%, discounted by 14%)	13*
Total amount recognised in respect of asset	63

*Under SSAP 15, the deferred tax asset might not be recognised and would not be discounted. (**Editor's note:** SSAP 15 has now been superseded by FRS 19 'Deferred tax'.)

Appendix II
Note on Legal requirements

GREAT BRITAIN

Impairment losses

Paragraph 19(1) of Schedule 4 to the Companies Act 1985 allows provisions for   **1**
diminutions in value of fixed asset investments to be made and the amount to be
included in respect of the fixed asset investment to be reduced accordingly. Any
provisions that are not shown in the profit and loss account must be disclosed (either
separately or in aggregate) in a note to the accounts.

Paragraph 19(2) of Schedule 4 requires provisions for diminution in value to be made   **2**
in respect of any fixed asset that has diminished in value if the reduction in its value is
expected to be permanent. The amount to be included in respect of the asset must be
reduced accordingly. Any provisions that are not shown in the profit and loss
account must be disclosed (either separately or in aggregate) in a note to the
accounts.

Clearly it is a matter of judgement whether any diminution in value should be treated   **3**
as permanent (although there must be reasonable grounds for making such a judgement), as indicated by the requirement, referred to again below, that any provision
subsequently found not to be necessary has to be reversed.

In addition to references to diminutions in value in the paragraphs noted above, the   **4**
Act allows for the revaluation downwards of fixed assets dealt with under the
alternative accounting rules in paragraph 34 of Schedule 4.

The FRS concerns itself with impairment rather than permanent diminutions in value.   **5**
Nevertheless, the distinction between permanent and temporary diminutions in value
is inherently recognised in the FRS. A principle is established that impairments that
are clearly due to consumption of economic benefits are charged to the profit and
loss account. Any such loss is clearly a permanent loss. Other cases of impairment
raise separate considerations.

Where a fixed asset is impaired, it will always be the case that both the value in use   **6**
and the net realisable value will be below the carrying amount. Although this does
not inevitably signify a loss that is permanent, it would be prudent in relation to fixed
assets held at depreciated historical cost to regard such a loss as permanent and,
despite any element of uncertainty, charge it to the profit and loss account. In the
case of a revalued fixed asset, it would be reasonable to reflect the uncertainty of the
permanence of any impairment by treating it as a reversal of any temporary increase
in value previously recognised. Such an impairment would be dealt with through the
statement of total recognised gains and losses (ie as a revaluation reserve movement).
However, if the impairment results in a carrying value below depreciated historical
cost, then, as in a pure historical cost context, it would be prudent and reasonable to
treat that part of the impairment as being permanent and charge it to the profit and
loss account.

Reversals of impairment losses

7   Paragraph 19(3) of Schedule 4 requires that where the reasons for which a provision was made have ceased to apply to any extent, the provision shall be written back to the extent that it is no longer necessary. Where any amounts written back are not shown in the profit and loss account, they must be disclosed (either separately or in aggregate) in a note to the accounts.

8   The FRS requires that, for tangible fixed assets, a reversal of an impairment loss should be recognised when the recoverable amount of an asset increases because of a change in economic conditions – the reason for the impairment was that the asset was not expected to generate sufficient returns to cover its carrying amount. Once it is expected to do so, the reason for the impairment ceases to apply.

9   The FRS explains that the increase in recoverable amount must arise from a change in economic conditions that results in a revised calculation of the recoverable amount. Increases in value in use may arise simply because of:

(a)   the passage of time: as future cash inflows become closer, their discounted value increases; or

(b)   the occurrence of forecast cash outflows: once the cash outflows are past, they are no longer part of the value in use calculation and value in use therefore increases.

The Board believes that these increases should not give rise to a write-back of the impairment loss because the reason for which the provision was made has not ceased to apply – all that has happened is that time has passed and the expected cash flows have occurred.

10   The Board has received legal advice that a reversal of an impairment loss on goodwill should be recognised only where an external event caused the recognition of the impairment loss in previous periods and subsequent external events clearly and demonstrably reverse the effects of that event in a way that was not foreseen in the original impairment calculations. The Board believes that, for the reasons set out in Appendix IV 'The development of the FRS', the same criterion should apply to intangible assets (except those that have a readily ascertainable market value).

NORTHERN IRELAND AND THE REPUBLIC OF IRELAND

11   The references to the equivalent statutory requirements in Northern Ireland and the Republic of Ireland are as follows:

Great Britain	*Northern Ireland*	*Republic of Ireland*
Schedule 4 to the Companies Act 1985:	Schedule 4 to the Companies (Northern Ireland) Order 1986:	The Schedule to the Companies (Amendment) Act 1986:
paragraph 19(1)	paragraph 19(1)	paragraph 7(1)
paragraph 19(2)	paragraph 19(2)	paragraph 7(2)
paragraph 19(3)	paragraph 19(3)	paragraph 7(3)
paragraph 34	paragraph 34	paragraph 22

Appendix III
Compliance with International Accounting Standards

The International Accounting Standards Committee approved its accounting standard IAS 36 'Impairment of Assets' in April 1998.* The basic approach in the IAS is the same as that in the FRS: impairment is measured by comparing the carrying value of fixed assets and goodwill with the higher of net selling price (equivalent to net realisable value) and value in use. Value in use is calculated by discounting the cash flows expected to be generated from the assets. **1**

The detailed requirements of the IAS are also very similar to those of the FRS. They differ insofar as: **2**

(a)   the FRS requires impairments of revalued assets that are clearly caused by the consumption of economic benefits to be recognised in the profit and loss account (paragraph 63). In contrast, the IAS requires such impairments to be recognised in the profit and loss account only to the extent that the loss exceeds the balance on the revaluation reserve relating to the assets in question.

(b)   to be consistent with FRS 10 'Goodwill and Intangible Assets', the FRS aligns the treatment of intangible assets with that of goodwill, whereas the IAS treats intangibles as being more similar to tangible fixed assets. This has two consequences:

  (i)   the FRS allocates impairment losses in an income-generating unit first to goodwill, secondly to intangible assets and then to tangible fixed assets (paragraph 48). The IAS allocates impairment losses first to goodwill and then pro rata to intangible and tangible assets; and

  (ii)   the FRS restricts the recognition of reversals of impairment losses on intangible assets (except those with a readily ascertainable market value) to the same limited circumstances in which reversals of impairments of goodwill are recognised (paragraph 60). The IAS recognises reversals of impairments of intangible assets under the same conditions that apply to reversals of impairments of tangible fixed assets.

(c)   the FRS has a general rule that in all but exceptional circumstances, longer-term cash flow projections should assume that within five years a steady or declining growth rate of no more than the relevant country average growth rate is achieved (paragraph 36). It requires disclosure if these assumptions are not made. The IAS has a similar general rule but:
  • does not require disclosure if the assumptions are not made
  • rather than restricting growth rates to those of the relevant country, restricts them to those of the relevant products, industry or country.

(d)   if an acquired business has been merged with existing operations, the FRS requires any subsequent impairment to be allocated between the acquired goodwill and the goodwill in the existing operations at the time of merging the two businesses (paragraph 50). The IAS does not include this requirement.

(e)   the FRS requires the accuracy of previous estimates of value in use to be monitored for five years following an impairment review (paragraph 54). Any impairment that should have been recognised at the time must be recognised in the current period unless it has since reversed, in which case its non-recognition in past years should be disclosed. The IAS does not include these requirements.

(f)   The IAS requires the amounts recognised as impairment losses and reversals of impairment losses to be disclosed in more detail than does the FRS.

*__Editor's note:__ *A revised version of IAS 36 was issued in March 2004 as part of the IASB's business combinations project.*

3   The rationale for including in the FRS each of the requirements mentioned above is addressed in Appendix IV 'The development of the FRS'.

Appendix IV
The development of the FRS

THE NEED FOR A STANDARD

It is accepted practice that a fixed asset should not be carried in financial statements 1
at more than its recoverable amount, ie the higher of the amount for which it could
be sold and the amount recoverable from its future use. However, there is little
guidance on how recoverable amount should be measured and when impairment
losses should be recognised. As a result, practice is inconsistent and perhaps some
impairments may not be recognised on a timely basis.

The need for a standard on impairment is increased by the requirement in FRS 10 2
'Goodwill and Intangible Assets' that, where goodwill and intangible assets have a
useful life in excess of twenty years (including those exceptional cases where the life is
indefinite), the recoverable amount of the goodwill and intangible assets should be
reviewed every year.

This FRS sets out a method for measuring and recognising impairment. In developing 3
the FRS the Board has considered comments on its initial proposals that were set out
in the Discussion Paper 'Impairment of Tangible Fixed Assets', on the related
proposals on impairment set out in FRED 12 'Goodwill and Intangible Assets' and in
FRED 15 'Impairment of Fixed Assets and Goodwill'.

INDICATIONS OF IMPAIRMENT

Systematic depreciation ensures that the carrying amount of a fixed asset is reduced 4
to reflect over its useful economic life any reduction in the asset's recoverable amount
arising from consumption of economic benefits. A tangible fixed asset that is
depreciated in an appropriate manner is unlikely to become materially impaired
unless events or changes in circumstances cause a sudden reduction in the estimate of
the recoverable amount. Thus, where tangible fixed assets are depreciated, a
requirement for an impairment review to be performed each period would be
unnecessary and unduly onerous. The Board believes that, in such circumstances,
impairment reviews are necessary only if events or changes in circumstances indicate
that the carrying amount may not be recoverable. The additional occasions when
impairment reviews are required for intangible assets and goodwill are set out and
explained in FRS 10.

MEASUREMENT OF IMPAIRMENT

Measurement by reference to recoverable amount

The FRS requires impairment to be measured by comparing the carrying amount of a 5
fixed asset or income-generating unit with its recoverable amount. The recoverable
amount is based on the cash flows that can be generated by the fixed asset or income-
generating unit either by sale (net realisable value) or by continued use (value in use).
When fixed assets or goodwill are written down to the higher of the amount that can
be recovered through sale or continued use, they are recorded at their greatest value
to the entity. If the entity chooses not to use or sell the fixed asset or income-
generating unit so as to recover the greatest value possible, the loss from not doing so
is properly recorded in the period in which the fixed asset or income-generating unit

is sold when more could be recovered through use, or in the period(s) in which it is used when more could be recovered through sale.

6   The Board believes that this presents a faithful representation of the economic decisions that are made when a fixed asset or income-generating unit becomes impaired.

7   An alternative approach would be to measure impairment by reference to fair value, being the amount at which an asset or liability could be exchanged in an arm's length transaction between informed and willing parties, other than in a forced or liquidation sale. This is the approach adopted by the US standard FAS 121 'Accounting for the Impairment of Long-Lived Assets and for Long-Lived Assets to Be Disposed Of'. For many assets with a deep active market, fair value, net realisable value and value in use will not be materially different. Where there is no such market or where the entity uses the asset for a specific purpose not generally open to other participants in the market, there may well be a difference between net realisable value and value in use, and the notion of fair value is less well defined. It might, for example, be assumed that fair value is equal to net realisable value (subject to transaction costs) even if value in use is higher, but such an assumption does not reflect the fact that a willing seller would not dispose of the asset for much less than its value in use. Exactly what is the 'fair value' of the asset is open to question.

8   The Board believes that defining recoverable amount as the higher of net realisable value and value in use gives a more precise and clearer indication of the amount to which the asset should be written down and therefore prefers this terminology to the use of the term 'fair value'.

Constraints on estimates of value in use – growth rates and subsequent monitoring

9   The forecasts of future cash flows used to measure the value in use of a business are inevitably subjective. The FRS contains two key controls designed to reduce the risk of over-optimistic forecasting. First, it requires the longer-term projections of cash flows to assume a growth rate that does not normally exceed the long-term average growth rate for the country in which the business operates (paragraph 36). It allows higher rates to be used in the shorter-term forecasts, but states that only in exceptional (and disclosed) circumstances should these shorter-term forecasts extend beyond five years.

10 The Board recognises that, even in the longer-term, growth rates in certain industries will exceed average growth rates for the country as a whole. However, it takes the view that this does not necessarily mean that individual businesses within such industries will grow as quickly: in the longer-term, high growth industries may attract new businesses, reducing the opportunities for high growth rates in existing businesses. Hence, where an entity believes that it could justify using an industry growth rate for more than five years, it must disclose what it has done.

11 The second constraint placed on estimates of future cash flows is the requirement to monitor the accuracy of cash flow forecasts for the five years following an impairment review: any impairment that should have been recognised at the time must be recognised in the current period unless it has since reversed, in which case its non-recognition in past years should be disclosed. The aim of the disclosure requirement is primarily to ensure that cash flows are reliable: a record of continually falling short of forecast cash flows will tend to cast doubt on the reliability of current estimates; and awareness that this would have to be disclosed will be an incentive to management to build its forecasts on realistic assumptions.

The Board views these two controls as important checks on the reliability of fore- **12** casts. They were proposed early on in the development of the FRS and included within the proposals in both the Discussion Paper and the subsequent FRED. They were accepted by most respondents.

Discounting

Discounting is a method of reflecting the time value of money and the effect of risk in **13** the valuation of a stream of future cash flows. All rational economic decisions and, hence, all arm's length transactions reflect the time value of money and the effect of risk. Given that the Board's definition of recoverable amount is based on the economic decisions made when an impairment occurs, value in use must also reflect these factors. If not, value in use would not be measured on a consistent basis with net realisable value and cost (both of which are based on observable transactions and, hence, reflect the time value of money and the effect of risk). A comparison between carrying amount (based on cost), net realisable value and value in use would be meaningless.

The Board therefore believes that the cash flows on which value in use is based **14** should either be discounted at a risk-adjusted rate, ie the rate of return that the market would expect on an equally risky investment, or should themselves be adjusted for risk before being discounted at a risk-free rate.

Tax

FRED 15 proposed that impairments should be measured on a post-tax basis and **15** the tax element split out for presentation in the financial statements. An alternative approach, adopted by the FASB in FAS 121 and by IASC in IAS 36 'Impairment of Assets', is for value in use to be calculated by discounting the pre-tax cash flows at a pre-tax rate and any further tax consequences recognised by applying a tax standard. The reason behind the approach in FRED 15 was that it discounted the effect of any future capital allowances still to be received, whereas the present tax standard, SSAP 15, does not.

A slight majority of respondents to FRED 15 preferred the pre-tax approach, primarily **16** because it was thought to be easier to apply. Given this view and the desirability of harmonisation with the USA and IASC, the Board has decided to change to a pre-tax approach. The question of discounting deferred tax assets and liabilities will be considered as part of the Board's project on deferred tax.

Measurement of impairment when acquired businesses are merged with existing operations

The FRS includes specific requirements regarding the measurement of an impairment **17** arising after a purchased business has been merged with existing operations. It requires that any subsequent impairment of the combined business is allocated on a pro rata basis between the (unrecognised) goodwill in the existing operations and the acquired goodwill. Had this requirement not been included, the effect would be that any impairment of the acquired goodwill would not be recognised unless, and to the extent that, the impairment of the combined business exceeded the value of the unrecognised goodwill at the time of merging.

IAS 36 does not include this requirement. Although IASC acknowledged that the **18** requirement would be necessary to measure impairment accurately, it took the view that it would be a difficult requirement to apply in practice. The Board considered this argument, but retained the requirement in the FRS on the grounds that:

- without the requirement, impairment losses would be understated in the circumstances where the requirement applied.
- the absence of such a requirement would create an opportunity to avoid the recognition of impairment losses by treating an acquired business as having been merged with a large existing business.
- the requirement will not have to be applied universally: it will have to be applied only when performing an impairment review of purchased goodwill where the acquired business was merged with an existing business and the goodwill has become partly, but not wholly, impaired. Especially where goodwill is being amortised, these circumstances may not arise often.

IMPAIRMENT OF REVALUED FIXED ASSETS

19   The Board believes that, in principle, impairments of revalued fixed assets fall into two general groups – those that are clearly caused by a consumption of economic benefits and those caused by a general fall in prices. The first type is similar to depreciation and is treated as such, whereas the second type is more like a valuation adjustment that would fall to be recognised in the statement of total recognised gains and losses.

20   However, in many cases it is difficult to allocate an impairment to one or other group with certainty. In order to provide objectivity in the treatment of impairments of revalued fixed assets, the FRS requires that where there is doubt whether the impairment is caused by a reduction in the quantum of the service potential, the impairment loss should be recognised in the statement of total recognised gains and losses until the carrying amount of the asset reaches its depreciated historical cost. Any further impairment should be recognised in the profit and loss account.

21   Although this split between the statement of total recognised gains and losses and the profit and loss account where the type of impairment is unclear is necessarily arbitrary, it has the advantage of being consistent with IAS 16 (revised 1993) 'Property, Plant and Equipment' and IAS 36. It is also likely to be perceived as an equitable approach that does not penalise entities that revalue their fixed assets.

REVERSAL OF PAST IMPAIRMENT LOSSES

22   Companies legislation requires provisions for diminutions in value to be written back if the reasons for the provision have ceased to apply. The Board agrees with this principle but is aware that in some cases it will be difficult to distinguish between increases in the value of a fixed asset or income-generating unit that arise because the reasons for the impairment have ceased to apply and increases in value that arise for some other reason.

23   For tangible fixed assets and investments the Board believes it is acceptable for any increase in value that reverses a previous impairment to be recognised, as long as it results from changed economic conditions or the expected use of the asset and not simply the passage of time or the occurrence of forecast cash flows. After all, increases in value arising from changed economic conditions could be recognised by revaluing the assets.

24   In relation to intangible assets that cannot be revalued and goodwill, the Board does not wish to recognise increases in value attributable to the internal generation of intangible asset value or goodwill. Accordingly, the FRS allows recognition of

reversals of past impairments of intangible assets and goodwill only where the increase in value can be clearly attributed to the unexpected reversal of an external event that caused the original impairment to be recognised.

CHANGES MADE TO FRED 15

In the light of comments made by those responding to FRED 15, a number of changes **25** have been made to its proposals. The most significant changes are that:

- investment properties are exempted from the requirements of the FRS. The treatment of investment properties is being considered further in the light of other Board projects and the international project on investment properties. The Board believes that, until this work is complete, it is appropriate to maintain the status quo as set out in SSAP 19 'Accounting for investment properties'.
- an entity's own shares held in an ESOP and shown as a fixed asset in the balance sheet under UITF Abstract 13 'Accounting for ESOP Trusts' are also exempt from the requirements of the FRS. The Board believes that an entity's own shares should be treated in a manner consistent with other investments, rather than as fixed assets. They will, therefore, be considered as part of the financial instruments project.*
- the FRS requires a pre-tax rather than a post-tax approach to measuring impairment (see paragraphs 15 and 16 above).
- examples to clarify the principles underlying the identification of income-generating units have been added.
- an alternative to allocating central assets across income-generating units is allowed – the central assets may instead be tested for impairment by reviewing the combination of all the income-generating units to which they contribute.
- a requirement has been added (paragraph 38 of the FRS) that value in use should reflect the asset or income-generating unit as it exists at the balance sheet date and hence that in general the costs and benefits of future investment should not be included in the value in use calculation.
- explanation has been added regarding the circumstances in which the reversal of past impairment losses may be recognised.

*Editor's note: UITF 13 has been replaced by UITF 38. This treats own shares held in an ESOP as negative equity, rather than assets.

Financial Reporting Standard 12 is set out in paragraphs 1–102.

The Statement of Standard Accounting Practice, which comprises the paragraphs set in bold type, should be read in the context of the Objective as stated in paragraph 1 and the definitions set out in paragraph 2 and also of the Foreword to Accounting Standards and the Statement of Principles for Financial Reporting currently in issue.

The explanatory paragraphs contained in the FRS shall be regarded as part of the Statement of Standard Accounting Practice insofar as they assist in interpreting that statement.

Appendix VII 'The development of the FRS' reviews considerations and arguments that were thought significant by members of the Board in reaching the conclusions on the FRS.

[FRS 12]
Provisions, contingent liabilities and contingent assets*

(Issued September 1998)

Contents

*Editor's note: FRS 12 was amended by FRS 17, FRS 21 and FRS 26.

Provisions, contingent liabilities and contingent assets

Summary

GENERAL

Financial Reporting Standard 12 'Provisions, Contingent Liabilities and Contingent   **a**
Assets' sets out the principles of accounting for provisions, contingent liabilities and
contingent assets. Its objective is to ensure that appropriate recognition criteria and
measurement bases are applied to provisions, contingent liabilities and contingent
assets and that sufficient information is disclosed in the notes to the financial
statements to enable users to understand their nature, timing and amount.

DEFINITIONS

In the FRS a *provision* is a liability that is of uncertain timing or amount, to be settled   **b**
by the transfer of economic benefits. A *contingent liability* is either (i) a possible
obligation arising from past events whose existence will be confirmed only by the
occurrence of one or more uncertain future events not wholly within the entity's
control; or (ii) a present obligation that arises from past events but is not recognised
because it is not probable that a transfer of economic benefits will be required to
settle the obligation or because the amount of the obligation cannot be measured
with sufficient reliability. A *contingent asset* is a possible asset arising from past
events whose existence will be confirmed only by the occurrence of one or more
uncertain future events not wholly within the entity's control.

SCOPE

The FRS applies to all financial statements that are intended to give a true and fair   **c**
view in accounting for provisions, contingent liabilities and contingent assets except:

- those resulting from financial instruments that are carried at fair value
- those resulting from executory contracts, except where the contract is onerous
- those arising in insurance entities from contracts with policy-holders
- those covered by more specific requirements in another FRS or a SSAP.

RECOGNITION

Provisions

A provision should be recognised when an entity has a present obligation (legal or   **d**
constructive) as a result of a past event, it is probable that a transfer of economic
benefits will be required to settle the obligation, and a reliable estimate can be made
of the amount of the obligation. Unless these conditions are met, no provision
should be recognised.

Present obligation

Where it is not clear whether a present obligation exists, a past event is deemed to   **e**
give rise to a present obligation if, taking account of all available evidence, it is more
likely than not that a present obligation exists at the balance sheet date.

Past event

f   For an event to be an obligating event, it is necessary that the entity has no realistic alternative to settling the obligation created by the event. This will be the case only where the settlement of the obligation can be enforced by law or, in the case of a constructive obligation, the event (which may be an action of the entity) creates valid expectations in other parties that the entity will discharge the obligation. The only liabilities recognised in an entity's balance sheet are those that exist at the balance sheet date. Where an entity can avoid future expenditure by its future actions, for example by changing its method of operation, it has no present liability for that future expenditure and no provision is recognised.

g   An event that does not immediately give rise to an obligation may do so at a later date, because of changes in the law or because an act (for example, a sufficiently specific public statement) by the entity gives rise to a constructive obligation. Where details of a proposed new law have yet to be finalised, an obligation arises only when the legislation is virtually certain to be enacted as drafted.

Probable transfer of economic benefits

h   For a liability to qualify for recognition there must be not only a present obligation but also the probability of a transfer of economic benefits to settle that obligation. A transfer of economic benefits in settlement of an obligation is regarded as probable if the outflow is more likely than not to occur. Where there are a number of similar obligations (eg product warranties or similar contracts) the probability that a transfer will be required in settlement is determined by considering the class of obligations as a whole.

Reliable estimate of the obligation

i   An entity will normally be able to determine a range of possible outcomes and can therefore make an estimate of the obligation that is sufficiently reliable to use in recognising a provision. In the extremely rare case where no reliable estimate can be made, a liability exists that cannot be recognised. That liability is therefore disclosed as a contingent liability.

Contingent liabilities

j   An entity should not recognise a contingent liability.

Contingent assets

k   An entity should not recognise a contingent asset.

MEASUREMENT

Best estimate

l   The amount recognised as a provision should be the best estimate of the expenditure required to settle the present obligation at the balance sheet date. The provision is measured before tax, as the tax consequences of the provision, and changes in it, are dealt with under FRS 19 'Deferred tax'.

Risks and uncertainties

The risks and uncertainties that inevitably surround many events and circumstances should be taken into account in reaching the best estimate of the amount of the provision. Care is needed to avoid duplicating adjustments for risk and uncertainty with consequent overstatement of a provision.

m

Present value

Where the effect of the time value of money is material, the amount of a provision should be the present value of the expenditures expected to be required to settle the obligation. The discount rate (or rates) should be a pre-tax rate (or rates) that reflect(s) current market assessments of the time value of money and the risks specific to the liability. The discount rate(s) should not reflect risks for which future cash flow estimates have been adjusted.

n

Future events

Future events that may affect the amount required to settle the entity's obligation should be reflected in the amount of a provision where there is sufficient objective evidence that they will occur. The effect of possible new legislation is taken into consideration in measuring an existing obligation when sufficient objective evidence exists that the legislation is virtually certain to be enacted.

o

Expected disposal of assets

Gains from the expected disposal of assets should not be taken into account in measuring a provision. Instead such gains are assessed for recognition under the principles of asset recognition, which include the requirements in FRS 11 'Impairment of Fixed Assets and Goodwill'.

p

REIMBURSEMENTS

Where some or all of the expenditure required to settle a provision is expected to be reimbursed by another party, the reimbursement should be recognised only when it is virtually certain that reimbursement will be received if the entity settles the obligation. The reimbursement should be treated as a separate asset. The amount recognised for the reimbursement should not exceed that of the provision. In the profit and loss account, the expense relating to a provision may be presented net of the amount recognised for a reimbursement.

q

CHANGES IN PROVISIONS

Provisions should be reviewed at each balance sheet date and adjusted to reflect the current best estimate. If it is no longer probable that a transfer of economic benefits will be required to settle the obligation, the provision should be reversed.

r

Where discounting is used, the size of a provision will change in each period to reflect the passage of time. This change is recognised as interest expense and disclosed separately from other interest on the face of the profit and loss account.

s

USE OF PROVISIONS

t   A provision should be used only for expenditures for which the provision was originally recognised.

DISCLOSURE

u   For each class of provision, an entity should disclose:

- the carrying amount at the beginning and end of the period
- additional provisions made in the period, including increases to existing provisions
- amounts used (ie incurred and charged against the provision)
- amounts reversed unused
- the change in the discounted amount arising from the passage of time and the effect of any change in the discount rate.

Comparative information need not be disclosed for these items. In addition the entity should give:

(i)   a brief description of the nature of the obligation, and the expected timing of any resulting outflows of economic benefits;

(ii)   an indication of the uncertainties about the amount or timing of those outflows; and

(iii)   the amount of any reimbursement, and of any asset that has been recognised for that expected reimbursement.

v   Unless the possibility of any transfer in settlement is remote, for each class of contingent liability at the balance sheet date a brief description of the nature of the contingent liability should be disclosed and, where practicable, an estimate of its financial effect and an indication of the uncertainties relating to the amount or timing of any outflow. The entity should also disclose the possibility of any reimbursement.

w   Where an inflow of economic benefits is probable, the entity should give a brief description of the nature of the contingent assets at the balance sheet date and, where practicable, an estimate of their financial effect.

x   In extremely rare cases, disclosure of some or all of the information required can be expected to prejudice seriously the position of the entity in a dispute with other parties on the subject matter of the provision, contingent liability or contingent asset. In such cases the information need not be disclosed; but the general nature of the dispute should be disclosed, together with the fact that, and reason why, the information has not been disclosed.

Financial Reporting Standard 12

Objective

The objective of this FRS is to ensure that appropriate recognition criteria and measurement bases are applied to provisions, contingent liabilities and contingent assets and that sufficient information is disclosed in the notes to the financial statements to enable users to understand their nature, timing and amount.   1

Definitions

The following definitions shall apply in the FRS and in particular in the Statement of   2
Standard Accounting Practice set out **in bold type.**

Constructive obligation:-

An obligation that derives from an entity's actions where:

(a)   by an established pattern of past practice, published policies or a sufficiently specific current statement, the entity has indicated to other parties that it will accept certain responsibilities; and
(b)   as a result, the entity has created a valid expectation on the part of those other parties that it will discharge those responsibilities.

Contingent asset:-

A possible asset that arises from past events and whose existence will be confirmed only by the occurrence of one or more uncertain future events not wholly within the entity's control.

Contingent liability:-

(a)   A possible obligation that arises from past events and whose existence will be confirmed only by the occurrence of one or more uncertain future events not wholly within the entity's control; or
(b)   a present obligation that arises from past events but is not recognised because:

(i)   it is not probable that a transfer of economic benefits will be required to settle the obligation; or
(ii)   the amount of the obligation cannot be measured with sufficient reliability.

Legal obligation:-

An obligation that derives from:

(a)   a contract (through its explicit or implicit terms);
(b)   legislation; or
(c)   other operation of law.

Liabilities:-

Obligations of an entity to transfer economic benefits as a result of past transactions or events.

Obligating event:-

An event that creates a legal or constructive obligation that results in an entity having no realistic alternative to settling that obligation.

Onerous contract:-

A contract in which the unavoidable costs of meeting the obligations under it exceed the economic benefits expected to be received under it.

Provision:-

A liability of uncertain timing or amount.

Restructuring:-

A programme that is planned and controlled by management, and materially changes either:

(a)   the scope of a business undertaken by an entity; or
(b)   the manner in which that business is conducted.

SCOPE

3   **The FRS applies to all financial statements that are intended to give a true and fair view in accounting for provisions, contingent liabilities and contingent assets, except:**

(a)   **those resulting from financial instruments that are carried at fair value;**
(b)   **those resulting from executory contracts, except where the contract is onerous;**
(c)   **those arising in insurance entities from contracts with policy-holders; or**
(d)   **those covered by another Standard.***

4   **Reporting entities applying the Financial Reporting Standard for Smaller Entities currently applicable are exempt from the FRS.**

Editor's note: The text of FRS 12 has been amended by FRS 26, but only for those companies which are applying the measurement provisions of FRS 26. Where a company is applying FRS 26 then paragraph 3 reads as follows:

This standard shall be applied by all entities in accounting for provisions, contingent liabilities and contingent assets, except:

(a)   those resulting from executory contracts, except where the contract is onerous;
(b)   those arising in insurance entities from contracts with policyholders, and
(c)   those covered by another FRS or a Statement of Standard Accounting Practice (SSAP).

The FRS applies to financial instruments (including guarantees) that are not carried at   **5**
fair value.*

Executory contracts are contracts under which neither party has performed any of its   **6**
obligations or both parties have partially performed their obligations to an equal
extent. The FRS does not apply to executory contracts unless they are onerous.

The FRS applies to provisions, contingent liabilities and contingent assets of insur-   **7**
ance entities other than those arising from contracts with policy-holders.

Where another FRS or a SSAP deals with a more specific type of provision, contingent   **8**
liability or contingent asset, an entity applies that standard instead of this FRS. For
example, certain types of provisions are also addressed in standards on:

- long-term contracts (see SSAP 9 'Stocks and long-term contracts').
- deferred tax (see FRS 19 'Deferred tax').
- leases (see SSAP 21 'Accounting for leases and hire purchase contracts'). However,
  as SSAP 21 contains no specific requirements to deal with operating leases that
  have become onerous, the FRS applies to such cases.
- pension costs (see FRS 17 'Retirement Benefits').

The FRS defines provisions as liabilities of uncertain timing or amount. The term   **9**
'provision' is also used sometimes in the context of items such as depreciation,
impairment of assets and doubtful debts: these are adjustments to the carrying
amounts of assets and are not addressed in the FRS.

The FRS applies to provisions for restructuring (including discontinued operations).   **10**
Where a restructuring meets the definition of a discontinued operation, additional
disclosures may be required by FRS 3 'Reporting Financial Performance'.

PROVISIONS AND OTHER LIABILITIES

Provisions can be distinguished from other liabilities such as trade creditors and   **11**
accruals because there is uncertainty about the timing or amount of the future
expenditure required in settlement. By contrast:

(a)   trade creditors are liabilities to pay for goods or services that have been
      received or supplied and have been invoiced or formally agreed with the sup-
      plier; and
(b)   accruals are liabilities to pay for goods or services that have been received or
      supplied but have not been paid, invoiced or formally agreed with the supplier,
      including amounts due to employees (for example amounts relating to accrued
      holiday pay). Although it is sometimes necessary to estimate the amount or
      timing of accruals, the uncertainty is generally much less than for provisions.

Accruals are often reported as part of trade and other creditors, whereas provisions
are reported separately.

*****Editor's note:** The text of FRS 12 has been amended by FRS 26, but only for those companies which are
applying the measurement provisions of FRS 26. Where a company is applying FRS 26 then paragraph 5 reads
as follows:*

This standard does not apply to financial instruments (including guarantees) that are within the scope of FRS
26 (IAS 39) *Financial Instruments: Measurement.* For financial guarantees excluded from the scope of FRS
26, this Standard applies as set out in paragraph 2(f) of FRS 26.

RELATIONSHIP BETWEEN PROVISIONS AND CONTINGENT LIABILITIES

12   In a general sense, all provisions are contingent because they are uncertain in timing or amount. However, in the FRS the term 'contingent' is used for liabilities and assets that are not recognised because their existence will be confirmed only by the occurrence of one or more uncertain future events not wholly within the entity's control. In addition, the term 'contingent liability' is used for liabilities that do not meet the recognition criteria.

13   The FRS distinguishes between:

(a)   provisions – which are recognised as liabilities (assuming that a reliable estimate can be made) because they are present obligations where it is probable that a transfer of economic benefits will be required to settle the obligations; and

(b)   contingent liabilities – which are not recognised as liabilities because they are either:

   (i)   possible obligations, as it has yet to be confirmed whether the entity has an obligation that could lead to a transfer of economic benefits; or

   (ii)   present obligations that do not meet the recognition criteria in the FRS because either it is not probable that a transfer of economic benefits will be required to settle the obligation, or a sufficiently reliable estimate of the amount of the obligation cannot be made.

RECOGNITION

Provisions

14   **A provision should be recognised when:**

(a)   **an entity has a present obligation (legal or constructive) as a result of a past event;**

(b)   **it is probable that a transfer of economic benefits will be required to settle the obligation; and**

(c)   **a reliable estimate can be made of the amount of the obligation.**

If these conditions are not met, no provision should be recognised.

Present obligation

15   **In rare cases it is not clear whether there is a present obligation. In these cases, a past event is deemed to give rise to a present obligation if, taking account of all available evidence, it is more likely than not that a present obligation exists at the balance sheet date.**

16   In almost all cases it will be clear whether a past event has given rise to a present obligation. In rare cases, for example in a lawsuit, it may be disputed whether certain events have occurred or whether those events result in a present obligation. In such a case, an entity determines whether a present obligation exists at the balance sheet date by taking account of all available evidence, including, for example, the opinion of experts. The evidence considered includes any additional evidence provided by events occurring after the balance sheet date. On the basis of such evidence:

(a)   where it is more likely than not that a present obligation exists at the balance sheet date, the entity recognises a provision (if the recognition criteria are met); and

(b)   where it is more likely that no present obligation exists at the balance sheet date, the entity discloses a contingent liability, unless the possibility of a transfer of economic resources is remote (see paragraph 91).

Past event

A past event that leads to a present obligation is called an obligating event. For an event to be an obligating event, it is necessary that the entity has no realistic alternative to settling the obligation created by the event. This is the case only: **17**

(a)   where the settlement of the obligation can be enforced by law; or
(b)   in the case of a constructive obligation, where the event (which may be an action of the entity) creates valid expectations in other parties that the entity will discharge the obligation.

Financial statements deal with the financial position of an entity at the end of its reporting period and not its possible position in the future. Therefore no provision is recognised for costs that need to be incurred to operate in the future. The only liabilities recognised in an entity's balance sheet are those that exist at the balance sheet date.   **18**

It is only those obligations arising from past events existing independently of an entity's future actions (ie the future conduct of its business) that are recognised as provisions. Examples of such obligations are penalties or clean-up costs for unlawful environmental damage, both of which would lead to a transfer of economic benefits in settlement regardless of the future actions of the entity. Similarly, an entity recognises a provision for the decommissioning costs of an oil installation or a nuclear power station to the extent that the entity is obliged to rectify damage already caused. In contrast, because of commercial pressures or legal requirements, an entity may intend or need to carry out expenditure to operate in a particular way in the future (for example, by fitting smoke filters in a certain type of factory). Because the entity can avoid the future expenditure by its future actions, for example by changing its method of operation, it has no present obligation for that future expenditure and no provision is recognised.   **19**

An obligation always involves another party to whom the obligation is owed. It is not necessary, however, to know the identity of the party to whom the obligation is owed – indeed the obligation may be to the public at large. Because an obligation always involves a commitment to another party, it follows that a management or board decision does not give rise to a constructive obligation at the balance sheet date unless the decision has been communicated before the balance sheet date to those affected by it in a sufficiently specific manner to raise a valid expectation in them that the entity will discharge its responsibilities.   **20**

An event that does not give rise to an obligation immediately may do so at a later date, because of changes in the law or because an act (for example, a sufficiently specific public statement) by the entity gives rise to a constructive obligation. For example, when environmental damage is caused there may be no obligation to remedy the consequences. However, the causing of the damage will become an obligating event when a new law requires the existing damage to be rectified or when the entity publicly accepts responsibility for rectification in a way that creates a constructive obligation.   **21**

Where details of a proposed new law have yet to be finalised, an obligation arises only when the legislation is virtually certain to be enacted as drafted. For the purposes of the FRS, such an obligation is treated as a legal obligation. Differences in   **22** circumstances surrounding enactment make it impossible to specify a single event that would make the enactment of a law virtually certain. In many cases it will be impossible to be virtually certain of the enactment of a law until it is enacted.

Probable transfer of economic benefits

23   For a liability to qualify for recognition there must be not only a present obligation but also the probability of a transfer of economic benefits to settle that obligation. For the purpose of the FRS, a transfer of economic benefits or other event is regarded as probable if the event is more likely than not to occur, ie the probability that the event will occur is greater than the probability that it will not. Where it is not probable that a present obligation exists, an entity discloses a contingent liability, unless the possibility of a transfer of economic resources is remote (see paragraph 91).

24   Where there are a number of similar obligations (eg product warranties or similar contracts) the probability that a transfer will be required in settlement is determined by considering the class of obligations as a whole. Although the likelihood of outflow for any one item may be small, it may well be probable that some transfer of economic benefits will be needed to settle the class of obligations as a whole. If that is the case, a provision is recognised (if the other recognition criteria are met).

Reliable estimate of the obligation

25   The use of estimates is an essential part of the preparation of financial statements and does not undermine their reliability. This is especially true in the case of provisions, which by their nature are more uncertain than most other balance sheet items. Except in extremely rare cases, an entity will be able to determine a range of possible outcomes and can therefore make an estimate of the obligation that is sufficiently reliable to use in recognising a provision.

26   In the extremely rare case where no reliable estimate can be made, a liability exists that cannot be recognised. That liability is disclosed as a contingent liability (see paragraph 91).

Contingent liabilities

27   **An entity should not recognise a contingent liability.**

28   A contingent liability is disclosed, as required by paragraph 91, unless the possibility of a transfer of economic benefits is remote.

29   Where an entity is jointly and severally liable for an obligation, the part of the obligation that is expected to be met by other parties is treated as a contingent liability. The entity recognises a provision for the part of the obligation for which a transfer of economic benefits is probable (except in the extremely rare circumstances where no reliable estimate can be made).

30   Contingent liabilities may develop in a way not initially expected. Therefore, they are assessed continually to determine whether a transfer of economic benefits has become probable. If it becomes probable that a transfer of future economic benefits will be required for an item previously dealt with as a contingent liability, a provision is recognised in the financial statements of the period in which the change in

probability occurs (except in the extremely rare circumstances where no reliable estimate can be made).

Contingent assets

An entity should not recognise a contingent asset.   31

Contingent assets usually arise from unplanned or other unexpected events that give   32
rise to the possibility of an inflow of economic benefits to the entity. An example is a
claim that an entity is pursuing through legal processes, where the outcome is
uncertain.

Contingent assets are not recognised in financial statements because it could result in   33
the recognition of profit that may never be realised. However, when the realisation of
the profit is virtually certain, then the related asset is not a contingent asset and its
recognition is appropriate.

A contingent asset is disclosed, as required by paragraph 94, where an inflow of   34
economic benefits is probable.

Contingent assets are assessed continually to ensure that developments are appro-   35
priately reflected in the financial statements. If it has become virtually certain that an
inflow of economic benefits will arise, the asset and the related profit are recognised
in the financial statements of the period in which the change occurs. If an inflow of
economic benefits has become probable, an entity discloses the contingent asset (see
paragraph 94).

MEASUREMENT

Best estimate

**The amount recognised as a provision should be the best estimate of the expenditure   36
required to settle the present obligation at the balance sheet date.**

The best estimate of the expenditure required to settle the present obligation is the   37
amount that an entity would rationally pay to settle the obligation at the balance
sheet date or to transfer it to a third party at that time. It will often be impossible or
prohibitively expensive to settle or transfer an obligation at the balance sheet date.
However, the estimate of the amount that an entity would rationally pay to settle or
transfer the obligation gives the best estimate of the expenditure required to settle the
present obligation at the balance sheet date.

The estimates of outcome and financial effect are determined by the judgement of the   38
entity's management, supplemented by experience of similar transactions and, in
some cases, reports from independent experts. The evidence considered will include
any additional evidence provided by events after the balance sheet date.

Uncertainties surrounding the amount to be recognised as a provision are dealt with   39
by various means according to the circumstances. Where the provision being measured involves a large population of items, the obligation is estimated by weighting
all possible outcomes by their associated probabilities. The name for this statistical
method of estimation is 'expected value'. The provision will therefore be different
depending on whether the probability of a loss of a given amount is, for example, 60
per cent or 90 per cent. Where there is a continuous range of possible outcomes, and
each point in that range is as likely as any other, the mid-point of the range is used.

> **Example**
>
> An entity sells goods with a warranty under which customers are covered for the cost of repairs of any manufacturing defects that become apparent within the first six months after purchase. If minor defects were detected in all products sold, repair costs of £1 million would result. If major defects were detected in all products sold, repair costs of £4 million would result. The entity's past experience and future expectations indicate that, for the coming year, 75 per cent of the goods sold will have no defects, 20 per cent of the goods sold will have minor defects and 5 per cent of the goods sold will have major defects. In accordance with paragraph 24 an entity assesses the probability of a transfer for the warranty obligations as a whole.
>
> The expected value of the cost of repairs is:
> (75% of nil) + (20% of £1m) + (5% of £4m) = £400,000

40 Where a single obligation is being measured, the individual most likely outcome may be the best estimate of the liability. However, even in such a case, the entity considers other possible outcomes. Where other possible outcomes are either mostly higher or mostly lower than the most likely outcome, the best estimate will be a higher or lower amount. For example, if an entity has to rectify a serious fault in a major plant that it has constructed for a customer, the individual most likely outcome may be for the repair to succeed at the first attempt at a cost of £1 million but a provision for a larger amount is made if there is a significant chance that further attempts will be necessary.

41 The provision is measured before tax, as the tax consequences of the provision, and changes in it, are dealt with under FRS 19 'Deferred tax'.

Risks and uncertainties

42 **The risks and uncertainties that inevitably surround many events and circumstances should be taken into account in reaching the best estimate of a provision.**

43 Risk describes variability of outcome. A risk adjustment may increase the amount at which a liability is measured. Caution is needed in making judgements under conditions of uncertainty, so that profit or assets are not overstated and expenses or liabilities are not understated. However, uncertainty does not justify the creation of excessive provisions or a deliberate overstatement of liabilities. For example, if the projected costs of a particularly adverse outcome are estimated on a prudent basis, that outcome is not then deliberately treated as more probable than is realistically the case. Care is needed to avoid duplicating adjustments for risk and uncertainty with consequent overstatement of a provision.

44 Disclosure of the uncertainties surrounding the amount of the expenditure is made under paragraph 90(b).

Present value

45 **Where the effect of the time value of money is material, the amount of a provision should be the present value of the expenditures expected to be required to settle the obligation.**

Because of the time value of money, provisions relating to cash outflows that arise **46** soon after the balance sheet date are more onerous than those where cash outflows of the same amount arise later. Provisions are therefore discounted, where the effect is material.

The discount rate (or rates) should be a pre-tax rate (or rates) that reflect(s) current **47** **market assessments of the time value of money and the risks specific to the liability. The discount rate(s) should not reflect risks for which future cash flow estimates have been adjusted.**

The unwinding of the discount should be included as other finance costs adjacent to **48** **interest.***

Using a discount rate that reflects current market assessments of the time value of **49** money and the risks specific to the liability is a method of reflecting the risk associated with the cash flows in the present value calculation. It is likely that this method will be the easiest method of reflecting risk. However, an acceptable alternative is to adjust the cash flows for risk and to discount them using a risk-free rate (eg a government bond rate). Whichever method of reflecting risk is adopted, care must be taken that the effect of risk is not double-counted by inclusion in both the cash flows and the discount rate.

If the cash flows to be discounted are expressed in current prices, a real discount rate **50** will be used. If the cash flows are expressed in expected future prices, a nominal discount rate will be used.

Future events

Future events that may affect the amount required to settle an obligation should be **51** **reflected in the amount of a provision where there is sufficient objective evidence that they will occur.**

Expected future events may be particularly important in measuring provisions. For **52** example, an entity may believe that the cost of cleaning up a site at the end of its life will be reduced by future changes in technology. The amount recognised reflects a reasonable expectation of technically qualified, objective observers, taking account of all available evidence as to the technology that will be available at the time of the clean-up. Thus it is appropriate to include, for example, expected cost reductions associated with increased experience in applying existing technology or the expected cost of applying existing technology to a larger or more complex clean-up operation than has previously been carried out. However, an entity does not anticipate the development of a completely new technology for cleaning up unless it is supported by sufficient objective evidence.

The effect of possible new legislation is taken into consideration in measuring an **53** existing obligation when sufficient objective evidence exists that the legislation is virtually certain to be enacted. The variety of circumstances that arise in practice makes it impossible to specify a single event that will provide sufficient, objective evidence in every case. Evidence is required both of what legislation will demand and of whether it is virtually certain to be enacted and implemented in due course. In many cases sufficient objective evidence will not exist until the new legislation is enacted.

*Editor's note: Paragraph amended by FRS 17.

Expected disposal of assets

54   **Gains from the expected disposal of assets should not be taken into account in measuring a provision.**

55   Gains on the expected disposal of assets are not taken into account in measuring a provision, even if the expected disposal is closely linked to the event giving rise to the provision. Instead, an entity assesses such gains for recognition under the principles of asset recognition, which include the requirements in FRS 11 'Impairment of Fixed Assets and Goodwill'.

Reimbursements

56   **Where some or all of the expenditure required to settle a provision is expected to be reimbursed by another party, the reimbursement should be recognised only when it is virtually certain that reimbursement will be received if the entity settles the obligation. The reimbursement should be treated as a separate asset. The amount recognised for the reimbursement should not exceed the amount of the provision.**

57   **In the profit and loss account, the expense relating to a provision may be presented net of the amount recognised for a reimbursement.**

58   Sometimes, an entity is able to look to another party to pay part or all of the expenditure required to settle a provision (for example, through insurance contracts, indemnity clauses or suppliers' warranties). The other party may either reimburse amounts paid by the entity or pay the amounts directly.

59   In most cases, the entity will remain liable for the whole of the amount in question so that the entity would have to settle the full amount if the third party failed to pay for any reason. In this situation, a provision is recognised for the full amount of the liability, and a separate asset for the expected reimbursement is recognised when it is virtually certain that reimbursement will be received if the entity settles the liability.

60   In some cases the entity will not be liable for the costs in question if the third party fails to pay. In such a case the entity has no liability for those costs and they are not included in the provision.

61   As noted in paragraph 29, an obligation for which an entity is jointly and severally liable is a contingent liability to the extent that it is expected that the obligation will be settled by the other parties.

CHANGES IN PROVISIONS

62   **Provisions should be reviewed at each balance sheet date and adjusted to reflect the current best estimate. If it is no longer probable that a transfer of economic benefits will be required to settle the obligation, the provision should be reversed.**

63   Where discounting is used, the carrying amount of a provision increases in each period to reflect the passage of time. As required in paragraph 48, this increase is recognised as an interest expense.

USE OF PROVISIONS

64   **A provision should be used only for expenditures for which the provision was originally recognised.**

Only expenditures that relate to the original provision are set against it. Setting   **65**
expenditures against a provision that was originally recognised for another purpose
would conceal the impact of two different events.

RECOGNISING AN ASSET WHEN RECOGNISING A PROVISION

When a provision or a change in a provision is recognised, an asset should also be   **66**
recognised when, and only when, the incurring of the present obligation recognised as a
provision gives access to future economic benefits; otherwise the setting up of the
provision should be charged immediately to the profit and loss account.

Where a provision is recognised for a present obligation that has been incurred to   **67**
gain rights or other access to future economic benefits that are to be enjoyed over
more than one period, the part of the provision incurred that relates to such future
benefits is capitalised. For example, an obligation for decommissioning costs is
incurred by commissioning an oil rig but the commissioning also gives access to oil
reserves over the years of the oil rig's operation – an asset representing future access
to oil reserves is therefore recognised at the same time as the provision for decommissioning costs.

APPLICATION OF THE RECOGNITION AND MEASUREMENT RULES

Future operating losses

Provisions should not be recognised for future operating losses.   **68**

Future operating losses do not meet the definition of a liability in paragraph 2 and   **69**
the general recognition criteria set out for provisions in paragraph 14.

An expectation of future operating losses is an indication that certain assets of the   **70**
operation may be impaired. An entity tests these assets for impairment under FRS 11.

Onerous contracts

If an entity has a contract that is onerous, the present obligation under the contract   **71**
should be recognised and measured as a provision.

Many contracts (for example, some routine purchase orders) can be cancelled   **72**
without paying compensation to the other party, and therefore there is no obligation.
Other contracts establish both rights and obligations for each of the contracting
parties. Where events make such a contract onerous, the contract falls within the
scope of the FRS and a liability exists which is recognised. Executory contracts that
are not onerous fall outside the scope of the FRS.

The FRS defines an onerous contract as a contract in which the unavoidable costs of   **73**
meeting the obligations under it exceed the economic benefits expected to be received
under it. The unavoidable costs under a contract reflect the least net cost of exiting
from the contract, ie the lower of the cost of fulfilling it and any compensation or
penalties arising from failure to fulfil it.

Before a separate provision for an onerous contract is established, an entity recog-   **74**
nises any impairment loss that has occurred on assets dedicated to that contract.

Restructuring

75   The following are examples of events that may fall under the definition of restructuring:

(a)   sale or termination of a line of business;

(b)   the closure of business locations in a country or region or the relocation of business activities from one country or region to another;

(c)   changes in management structure, for example, eliminating a layer of management; and

(d)   fundamental reorganisations that have a material effect on the nature and focus of the entity's operations.

76   A provision for restructuring costs is recognised only when the general recognition criteria for provisions set out in paragraph 14 are met. Paragraphs 77-88 set out how those criteria apply to restructurings.

77   **A constructive obligation to restructure arises only when an entity:**

(a)   **has a detailed formal plan for the restructuring identifying at least:**

(i)   **the business or part of a business concerned;**

(ii)   **the principal locations affected;**

(iii)   **the location, function, and approximate number of employees who will be compensated for terminating their services;**

(iv)   **the expenditures that will be undertaken; and**

(v)   **when the plan will be implemented; and**

(b)   **has raised a valid expectation in those affected that it will carry out the restructuring by starting to implement that plan or announcing its main features to those affected by it.**

78   Evidence that an entity has started to implement a restructuring plan would be provided, for example, by dismantling plant or selling assets or by the public announcement of the main features of the plan. A public announcement of a detailed plan to restructure constitutes a constructive obligation to restructure only if it is made in such a way and in sufficient detail (ie setting out the main features of the plan) that it gives rise to valid expectations in other parties such as customers, suppliers and employees (or their representatives) that the entity will carry out the restructuring.

79   For a plan to be sufficient to give rise to a constructive obligation when communicated to those affected by it, its implementation needs to be planned to begin as soon as possible and to be completed in a timeframe that makes significant changes to the plan unlikely. If it is expected that there will be a long delay before the restructuring begins or that the restructuring will take an unreasonably long time, it is unlikely that the plan will raise a valid expectation on the part of others that the entity is at present committed to restructuring, because the timeframe allows opportunities for the entity to change its plans.

80   A management or board decision to restructure taken before the balance sheet date does not give rise to a constructive obligation at the balance sheet date unless the entity has, before the balance sheet date:

(a)   started to implement the restructuring plan; or

(b)   announced the main features of the restructuring plan to those affected by it in a sufficiently specific manner to raise a valid expectation in them that the entity will carry out the restructuring.

If an entity starts to implement the restructuring plan, or announces its main features to those affected, only after the balance sheet date, disclosure is required under FRS 21, *Events after the Balance Sheet Date*, if the restructuring is material and non-disclosure could influence the economic decisions of users taken on the basis of the financial statements.*

Although a constructive obligation is not created solely by a management decision, an obligation may result from other earlier events together with such a decision. For example, negotiations with employee representatives for termination payments, or with purchasers for the sale of an operation, may have been concluded subject only to board approval. Once that approval has been obtained and communicated to the other parties, the entity has a constructive obligation to restructure, if the conditions of paragraph 77 are met.   **81**

In some countries the ultimate authority is vested in a board whose membership includes representatives of interests other than management (eg employees); alternatively, notification to such representatives may be necessary before the board decision is taken. Because a decision by the board in these circumstances involves communication to these representatives, it may result in a constructive obligation to restructure.   **82**

No obligation arises for the sale of an operation until the entity is committed to the sale, ie there is a binding sale agreement.   **83**

Even when an entity has taken a decision to sell an operation and announced that decision publicly, it cannot be committed to the sale until a purchaser has been identified and there is a binding sale agreement. Until there is such an agreement, the entity will be able to change its mind and indeed will have to take another course of action if a purchaser cannot be found on acceptable terms. When the sale of an operation is envisaged as part of a restructuring, the assets of the operation are reviewed for impairment, under FRS 11. When a sale is only part of a restructuring, a constructive obligation can arise for the other parts of the restructuring before a binding sale agreement exists.   **84**

A restructuring provision should include only the direct expenditures arising from the restructuring, which are those that are both: **85**

(a)   **necessarily entailed by the restructuring and**
(b)   **not associated with the ongoing activities of the entity.**

A restructuring provision does not include such costs as: **86**

(a)   retraining or relocating continuing staff;
(b)   marketing; or
(c)   investment in new systems and distribution networks.

These expenditures relate to the future conduct of the business and are not liabilities for restructuring at the balance sheet date. Such expenditures are recognised on the same basis as if they arose independently of a restructuring.

Identifiable future operating losses up to the date of a restructuring are not included in a provision, unless they relate to an onerous contract as defined in paragraph 2.   **87**

Editor's note: Last section of paragraph amended by FRS 21.

88   As required by paragraph 54, gains on the expected disposal of assets are not taken into account in measuring a restructuring provision, even if the sale of assets is envisaged as part of the restructuring.

DISCLOSURE

89   For each class of provision, an entity should disclose:

   (a)   the carrying amount at the beginning and end of the period;
   (b)   additional provisions made in the period, including increases to existing provisions;
   (c)   amounts used (ie incurred and charged against the provision) during the period;
   (d)   unused amounts reversed during the period; and
   (e)   the increase during the period in the discounted amount arising from the passage of time and the effect of any change in the discount rate.

   Comparative information is not required.

90   An entity should disclose the following for each class of provision:

   (a)   a brief description of the nature of the obligation, and the expected timing of any resulting transfers of economic benefits;
   (b)   an indication of the uncertainties about the amount or timing of those transfers of economic benefits. Where necessary to provide adequate information, an entity should disclose the major assumptions made concerning future events, as addressed in paragraph 51; and
   (c)   the amount of any expected reimbursement, stating the amount of any asset that has been recognised for that expected reimbursement.

91   Unless the possibility of any transfer in settlement is remote, an entity should disclose for each class of contingent liability at the balance sheet date a brief description of the nature of the contingent liability and, where practicable:

   (a)   an estimate of its financial effect, measured in accordance with paragraphs 36-55;
   (b)   an indication of the uncertainties relating to the amount or timing of any outflow; and
   (c)   the possibility of any reimbursement.

92   In determining which provisions or contingent liabilities may be aggregated to form a class, it is necessary to consider whether the nature of the items is sufficiently similar for a single statement about them to fulfil the requirements of paragraph 90(a) and (b) or 91(a) and (b). Thus it may be appropriate to treat as a single class of provision amounts relating to warranties of different products, but it would not be appropriate to treat as a single class amounts relating to normal warranties and amounts that are subject to legal proceedings.

93   Where a provision and a contingent liability arise from the same set of circumstances, an entity makes the disclosures required by paragraphs 89–91 in a way that shows the link between the provision and the contingent liability.

94   Where an inflow of economic benefits is probable, an entity should disclose a brief description of the nature of the contingent assets at the balance sheet date and, where practicable, an estimate of their financial effect, measured using the principles set out for provisions in paragraphs 36-55.

95   It is important that disclosures for contingent assets avoid giving misleading indications of the likelihood of a profit arising.

Where any of the information required by paragraphs 91 and 94 is not disclosed because   **96**
it is not practicable to do so, that fact should be stated.

In extremely rare cases, disclosure of some or all of the information required by   **97**
paragraphs 89-94 can be expected to prejudice seriously the position of the entity in a
dispute with other parties on the subject matter of the provision, contingent liability or
contingent asset. In such cases an entity need not disclose the information, unless its
disclosure is required by law; but should disclose the general nature of the dispute,
together with the fact that, and reason why, the information has not been disclosed.

DATE FROM WHICH EFFECTIVE

The accounting practices set out in the FRS should be regarded as standard in respect of   **98**
financial statements relating to accounting periods ending on or after 23 March 1999.
Earlier adoption is encouraged but not required.

WITHDRAWAL OF SSAP 18 AND AMENDMENT OF FRS 3

The FRS supersedes SSAP 18 'Accounting for contingencies'.   **99**

In FRS 3 'Reporting Financial Performance' paragraph 18 is amended as follows: **100**

[*Not reproduced as it has been reflected in FRS 3 reproduced in this volume.*]

APPLICATION OF THE NEW REQUIREMENTS

Changes in accounting policy arising from the initial application of the FRS should be   **101**
dealt with as prior period adjustments in accordance with FRS 3 (paragraphs 7, 29 and
62). Corrections of accounting estimates should be dealt with in the profit and loss
account of the period of initial application, and their effect stated where material (FRS 3,
paragraph 60).

The initial application of the FRS will in some circumstances entail a change in   **102**
accounting policy, and, in other cases, a correction of accounting estimate. For
example, where no provision was previously recognised for decommissioning costs
but the FRS requires that a provision is recognised, or where a provision was previously recognised that is not permitted by the FRS (for example, a provision for self-
insurance), the application of the recognition principles set out in the FRS is a change
in accounting policy. In contrast, where, for example, an entity already provides for
its warranties but the initial application of the FRS causes the provision to be measured at a different amount, the change is a change in accounting estimate.

Adoption of FRS 12 by the Board

Financial Reporting Standard 12 – 'Provisions, Contingent Liabilities and Contingent Assets' was approved for issue by the ten members of the Accounting Standards Board.

Sir David Tweedie   (Chairman)
Allan Cook   (Technical Director)
David Allvey
Ian Brindle
Dr John Buchanan
John Coombe
Raymond Hinton
Huw Jones
Professor Geoffrey Whittington
Ken Wild

Appendix I
Tables: main requirements of the FRS

This appendix summarises the main requirements of the FRS. It does not form part of the FRS and should be read in the context of the full text.

Provisions and contingent liabilities

Where, as a result of past events, there may be a transfer of future economic benefits in settlement of (a) a present obligation or (b) a possible obligation whose existence will be confirmed by the occurrence of one or more uncertain future events not wholly within the entity's control, and		
there is a present obligation that probably requires a transfer of economic benefits in settlement,	there is a possible obligation or a present obligation that may, but probably will not, require a transfer of economic benefits in settlement,	there is a possible obligation or a present obligation where the likelihood of a transfer of economic benefits in settlement is remote,
a provision is recognised (paragraph 14); and	no provision is recognised (paragraph 27); but	no provision is recognised (paragraph 27); and
disclosures are required for the provision (paragraphs 89 and 90).	disclosures are required for the contingent liability (paragraph 91).	no disclosure is required (paragraph 91).

A contingent liability also arises in the extremely rare case where there is a liability that cannot be recognised because it cannot be measured reliably (paragraph 2). Disclosures are required for the contingent liability (paragraph 91).

Contingent assets

Where, as a result of past events, there is a possible asset whose existence will be confirmed by the occurrence of one or more uncertain future events not wholly within the entity's control, and		
the inflow of economic benefits is virtually certain,	the inflow of economic benefits is probably but not virtually certain,	the inflow is not probable,
the asset is not contingent (paragraph 33).	no asset is recognised (paragraph 31); but disclosures are required (paragraph 94).	no asset is recognised (paragraph 31); and no disclosure is required (paragraph 94).

Reimbursements

Where some or all of the expenditure required to settle a provision is expected to be reimbursed by another party, and		
the entity has no obligation for the part of the expenditure to be reimbursed by the other party,	the obligation for the amount expected to be reimbursed remains with the entity and it is virtually certain that reimbursement will be received if the entity settles the provision,	the obligation for the amount expected to be reimbursed remains with the entity and the reimbursement is not virtually certain if the entity settles the provision,
the entity has no liability for the amount to be reimbursed (paragraph 60); and no disclosure is required.	the reimbursement is recognised as a separate asset in the balance sheet and may be offset against the charge in the profit and loss account. The amount recognised for the expected reimbursement does not exceed the liability (paragraphs 56 and 57); and the reimbursement is disclosed together with the amount recognised for the reimbursement (paragraph 90(c)).	the expected reimbursement is not recognised as an asset (paragraph 56); but the expected reimbursement is disclosed (paragraph 90(c)).

Appendix II
Decision Tree

This appendix summarises the main requirements of the FRS. *It does not form part of the* FRS *and should be read in the context of the full text.*

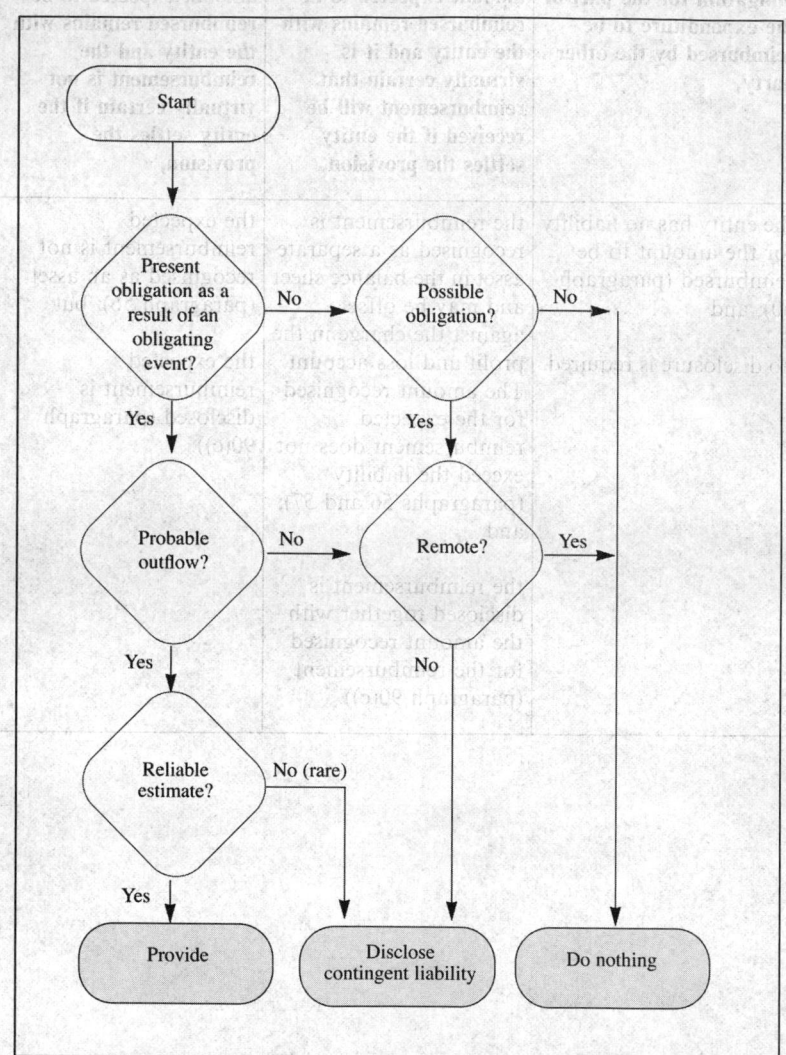

Note: in rare cases it is not clear whether there is a present obligation. In these cases, a past event is deemed to give rise to a present obligation if, taking account of all available evidence, it is more likely than not that a present obligation exists at the balance sheet date (see paragraph 15).

Appendix III
Examples: Recognition

This appendix illustrates the application of the FRS to assist in clarifying its meaning. It does not form part of the FRS.

All the entities in the examples have 31 December year-ends. In all cases it is assumed that a reliable estimate can be made of any outflows expected. In some examples the circumstances described may have resulted in impairment of the assets – this aspect is not dealt with in the examples.

The cross-references in the examples are to paragraphs of the FRS that are particularly relevant. The appendix should be read in the context of the full text of the FRS.

References to 'best estimate' are to the present value amount where the effect of the time value of money is material.

Example 1:

Warranties

A manufacturer gives warranties at the time of sale to purchasers of its product. Under the terms of the contract for sale the manufacturer undertakes to make good, by repair or replacement, manufacturing defects that become apparent within three years from the date of sale. On past experience, it is probable (ie more likely than not) that there will be some claims under the warranties.

Present obligation as a result of a past obligating event – The obligating event is the sale of the product with a warranty, which gives rise to a legal obligation.

Transfer of economic benefits in settlement – Probable for the warranties as a whole (see paragraph 24).

Conclusion – A provision is recognised for the best estimate of the costs of making good under the warranty products sold before the balance sheet date (see paragraphs 14 and 24).

Example 2A:

Contaminated land - legislation virtually certain to be enacted

An entity in the oil industry causes contamination but cleans up only when required to do so under the laws of the particular country in which it operates. One country in which it operates has had no legislation requiring cleaning up, and the entity has been contaminating land in that country for several years. At 31 December it is virtually certain that a draft law requiring a clean-up of land already contaminated will be enacted shortly after the year-end.

Present obligation as a result of a past obligating event – The obligating event is the contamination of the land because of the virtual certainty of legislation requiring cleaning up.

Transfer of economic benefits in settlement – Probable.

Conclusion – A provision is recognised for the best estimate of the costs of the clean-up (see paragraphs 14 and 22).

Example 2B:

Contaminated land and constructive obligation

An entity in the oil industry causes contamination and operates in a country where there is no environmental legislation. However, the entity has a widely published environmental policy in which it undertakes to clean up all contamination that it causes. The entity has a record of honouring this published policy.

Present obligation as a result of a past obligating event – The obligating event is the contamination of the land, which gives rise to a constructive obligation because the conduct of the entity has created a valid expectation on the part of those affected by it that the entity will clean up contamination.

Transfer of economic benefits in settlement – Probable.

Conclusion – A provision is recognised for the best estimate of the costs of clean-up (see paragraphs 2 (the definition of a constructive obligation), 14 and 17).

Example 3:

Offshore oilfield

An entity operates an offshore oilfield where its licensing agreement requires it to remove the oil rig at the end of production and restore the seabed. Ninety per cent of the eventual costs of undertaking this work relate to the removal of the oil rig and restoration of damage caused by building it, and ten per cent arise through the extraction of oil. At the balance sheet date, the rig has been constructed but no oil has been extracted.

Present obligation as a result of a past obligating event – The construction of the oil rig creates a legal obligation under the terms of the licence to remove the rig and restore the seabed and is thus an obligating event. At the balance sheet date, however, there is no obligation to rectify the damage that will be caused by extraction of the oil.

Transfer of economic benefits in settlement – Probable.

Conclusion – A provision is recognised for the best estimate of the ninety per cent of the eventual costs that relate to the removal of the oil rig and restoration of damage caused by building it (see paragraphs 17-19). These costs are included as part of the cost of the oil rig. The ten per cent of costs that arise through the extraction of oil are recognised as a liability when the oil is extracted.

Example 4:

Refunds policy

A retail store has a policy of refunding purchases by dissatisfied customers, even though it is under no legal obligation to do so. Its policy of making refunds is generally known.

Present obligation as a result of a past obligating event – The obligating event is the sale of the product, which gives rise to a constructive obligation because the conduct of the store has created a valid expectation on the part of its customers that the store will refund purchases.

Transfer of economic benefits in settlement – Probable, as a proportion of goods are returned for refund (see paragraph 24).

Conclusion – A provision is recognised for the best estimate of the costs of refunds (see paragraphs 2 (the definition of a constructive obligation), 14, 17 and 24).

Example 5A:

Closure of a division – no implementation before balance sheet date

On 12 December 2000 the board of an entity decided to close down a division. Before the balance sheet date (31 December 2000) the decision was not communicated to any of those affected and no other steps were taken to implement the decision.

Present obligation as a result of a past obligating event – There has been no obligating event and so there is no obligation.

Conclusion – No provision is recognised (see paragraphs 14 and 77).

Example 5B:

Closure of a division – communication/implementation before balance sheet date

On 12 December 2000 the board of an entity decided to close down a division making a particular product. On 20 December 2000 a detailed plan for closing down the division was agreed by the board; letters were sent to customers warning them to seek an alternative source of supply and redundancy notices were sent to the staff of the division.

Present obligation as a result of a past obligating event – The obligating event is the communication of the decision to the customers and employees, which gives rise to a constructive obligation from that date because it creates a valid expectation that the division will be closed.

Transfer of economic benefits in settlement – Probable.

Conclusion – A provision is recognised at 31 December 2000 for the best estimate of the costs of closing the division (see paragraphs 14 and 77).

Example 6:

Legal requirement to fit smoke filters

Under new legislation, an entity is required to fit smoke filters to its factories by 30 June 2000. The entity has not fitted the smoke filters.

(a)   At the balance sheet date of 31 December 1999

Present obligation as a result of a past obligating event – There is no obligation because there is no obligating event either for the costs of fitting smoke filters or for fines under the legislation.

Conclusion – No provision is recognised for the cost of fitting the smoke filters (see paragraphs 14, 17 and 18).

(b)   At the balance sheet date of 31 December 2000

Present obligation as a result of a past obligating event – There is still no obligation for the costs of fitting smoke filters because no obligating event (the fitting of the filters) has occurred. However, an obligation might arise to pay fines or penalties under the legislation because the obligating event has occurred (the non-compliant operation of the factory).

Transfer of economic benefits in settlement – Assessment of probability of incurring fines and penalties by non-compliant operation depends on the details of the legislation and the stringency of the enforcement regime.

Conclusion – No provision is recognised for the costs of fitting smoke filters. However, a provision is recognised for the best estimate of any fines and penalties that are more likely than not to be imposed (see paragraphs 14 and 17-19).

Example 7:

Staff retraining as a result of changes in the income tax system

The government introduces a number of changes to the income tax system. As a result of these changes an entity in the financial services sector will need to retrain a large proportion of its administrative and sales workforce in order to ensure continued compliance with financial services regulation. At the balance sheet date no retraining of staff has taken place.

Present obligation as a result of a past obligating event – There is no obligation because no obligating event (retraining) has taken place.

Conclusion – No provision is recognised (see paragraphs 14 and 17-19).

Example 8:

An onerous contract

An entity operates profitably from a factory that it has leased under an operating lease. During December 2000 the entity relocates its operations to a new factory. The lease on the old factory continues for the next four years, it cannot be cancelled and the factory cannot be re-let to another user.

Present obligation as a result of a past obligating event – The obligating event is the signing of the lease contract, which gives rise to a legal obligation.

Transfer of economic benefits in settlement – When the lease becomes onerous, a transfer of economic benefits is probable. (Until the lease becomes onerous, the entity accounts for the lease by applying SSAP 21 'Accounting for leases and hire purchase contracts'.)

Conclusion – A provision is recognised for the best estimate of the unavoidable lease payments (see paragraphs 14 and 71).

Example 9:

A single guarantee

During 1999 Entity A gives a guarantee of certain borrowings of Entity B, whose financial condition at that time is sound. During 2000, the financial condition of Entity B deteriorates and at 30 June 2000 Entity B files for protection from its creditors.

(a)   At 31 December 1999

Present obligation as a result of a past obligating event – The obligating event is the giving of the guarantee, which gives rise to a legal obligation.

Transfer of economic benefits in settlement – No transfer of benefits is probable at 31 December 1999.

Conclusion – No provision is recognised (see paragraphs 14 and 23). The guarantee is disclosed as a contingent liability unless the probability of any transfer is regarded as remote (see paragraph 91).

(b)   At 31 December 2000

Present obligation as a result of a past obligating event – The obligating event is the giving of the guarantee, which gives rise to a legal obligation.

Transfer of economic benefits in settlement – At 31 December 2000 it is probable that a transfer of economic benefits will be required to settle the obligation.

Conclusion – A provision is recognised for the best estimate of the obligation (see paragraphs 14 and 23).

Note: This example deals with a single guarantee. If an entity has a portfolio of similar guarantees, it will assess that portfolio as a whole in determining whether a transfer of economic benefit is probable (see paragraph 24). Where an entity gives guarantees in exchange for a fee, revenue is recognised only when earned.*

Example 10:

A court case

After a wedding in 2000 ten people died, possibly as a result of food poisoning from products sold by the entity. Legal proceedings are started seeking damages from the entity but it disputes liability. Up to the date of approval of the financial statements for the year to 31 December 2000, the entity's lawyers advise that it is probable that the entity will not be found liable. However, when the entity prepares the financial statements for the year to 31 December 2001 its lawyers advise that, owing to developments in the case, it is probable that the entity will be found liable.

*Editor's note: Example 9 has been amended by FRS 26, but only for those companies which are applying the measurement provisions of FRS 26. Where a company is applying FRS 26 then Example 9 reads as follows:

A single guarantee

On 31 December 1999, Entity A gives a guarantee of certain borrowings of Entity B, whose financial condition at that time is sound. During 2000, the financial condition of Entity B deteriorates and at 30 June 2000 Entity B files for protection from its creditors.

(a)   *At 31 December 1999*

Present obligation as a result of a past obligating event - The obligating event is the giving of the guarantee, which gives rise to a legal obligation.

An outflow of resources embodying economic benefits in settlement - No outflow of benefits is probable at 31 December 1999.

Conclusion - The guarantee is recognised at fair value.

(b)   *At 31 December 2000*

Present obligation as a result of a past obligating event - The obligating event is the giving of the guarantee, which gives rise to a legal obligation.

An outflow of resources embodying economic benefits in settlement - At 31 December 2000, it is probable that an outflow of resources embodying economic benefits will be required to settle the obligation.

Conclusion - The guarantee is subsequently measured at the higher of (a) the best estimate of the obligation (see paragraphs 14 and 23) and (b) the amount initially recognised less, when appropriate, cumulative amortisation.

(a)   At 31 December 2000

Present obligation as a result of a past obligating event – On the basis of the evidence available when the financial statements were approved, there is no obligation as a result of past events.

Conclusion – No provision is recognised (see paragraphs 14-16). The matter is disclosed as a contingent liability unless the probability of any transfer is regarded as remote.

(b)   At 31 December 2001

Present obligation as a result of a past obligating event – On the basis of the evidence available, there is a present obligation.

Transfer of economic benefits in settlement – Probable.

Conclusion – A provision is recognised for the best estimate of the amount needed to settle the present obligation (paragraphs 14-16).

Example 11:

Repairs and maintenance

Some assets require, in addition to routine maintenance, substantial expenditure every few years for major refits or refurbishment and the replacement of major components.

Example 11A:

Refurbishment costs – no legislative requirement

A furnace has a lining that needs to be replaced every five years for technical reasons. At the balance sheet date, the lining has been in use for three years.

Present obligation as a result of a past obligating event – There is no present obligation.

Conclusion – No provision is recognised (see paragraphs 14 and 19).

The cost of replacing the lining is not recognised because, at the balance sheet date, no obligation to replace the lining exists independently of the entity's future actions – even the intention to incur the expenditure depends on the entity deciding to continue operating the furnace or to replace the lining. Instead of a provision being recognised, the depreciation of the lining takes account of its consumption, ie it is depreciated over five years. The re-lining costs then incurred are capitalised with the consumption of each new lining shown by depreciation over the subsequent five years.

Example 11B:

Refurbishment costs – legislative requirement

An airline is required by law to overhaul its aircraft once every three years.

Present obligation as a result of a past obligating event – There is no present obligation.

Conclusion – No provision is recognised (see paragraphs 14 and 19).

The costs of overhauling aircraft are not recognised as a provision for the same reasons as the cost of replacing the lining is not recognised as a provision in example 11A. Even a legal requirement to overhaul does not make the costs of overhaul a liability because no obligation exists to overhaul the aircraft independently of the entity's future actions – the entity could avoid the future expenditure by its future actions, for example by selling the aircraft. Instead of a provision being recognised, the depreciation of the aircraft takes account of the future incidence of maintenance costs, ie an amount equivalent to the expected maintenance costs is depreciated over three years.

Example 12:

Self-insurance

An entity that operates a chain of retail outlets decides not to insure itself in respect of the risk of minor accidents to its customers: instead it will 'self insure'. Based on its past experience, it expects to pay £100,000 a year in respect of these accidents. Should provision be made for the amount expected to arise in a normal year?

Present obligation as a result of a past obligating event – There is no present obligation.

Conclusion – No provision is recognised. There is no present obligation because there is no other party involved in insuring the risks (see paragraph 20).

Appendix IV
Examples: disclosures

These examples are illustrative only and do not form part of the FRS.

Examples 1 and 2 provide examples of the disclosures required by paragraph 90.

Example 1:

Warranties

A manufacturer gives warranties at the time of sale to purchasers of its three product lines. Under the terms of the warranty the manufacturer undertakes to repair or replace items that fail to perform satisfactorily for two years from the date of sale. At the balance sheet date a provision of £60,000 has been recognised. The provision has not been discounted as the effect of discounting is not material. The following information is disclosed:

'*A provision of £60,000 has been recognised for expected warranty claims on products sold during the last three financial years. It is expected that most of this expenditure will be incurred in the next financial year, and all will be incurred within two years of the balance sheet date.*'

Example 2:

Decommissioning costs

In 2000 an entity involved in nuclear activities recognises a provision for decommissioning costs of £300 million. The provision is estimated using the assumption that decommissioning will take place in 60–70 years' time. However, there is a possibility that it will not take place until 100–110 years' time, in which case the present value of the costs will be significantly reduced. The following information is disclosed:

'*A provision of £300 million has been recognised for decommissioning costs. These costs are expected to be incurred between 2060 and 2070. However, there is a possibility that decommissioning will not take place until 2100–2110. If the costs were measured based upon the expectation that they would not be incurred until 2100–2110 the provision would be reduced to £136 million. The provision has been estimated using existing technology, at current prices, and discounted using a real discount rate of 2 per cent.*'

Example 3 provides an example of the disclosures required by paragraph 97, where some of the information required is not given because it can be expected to prejudice seriously the position of the entity.

Example 3:

Disclosure exemption

An entity is involved in a dispute with a competitor, who is alleging that the entity has infringed patents and is seeking damages of £100 million. The entity recognises a provision for its best estimate of the obligation, but discloses none of the information required by paragraphs 89 and 90. The following information is disclosed:

'*Litigation is in process against the company relating to a dispute with a competitor which alleges that the company has infringed patents and which is seeking damages of £100 million. The information usually required by* FRS *12 is not disclosed on the grounds that it can be expected to prejudice seriously the outcome of the litigation. The directors are of the opinion that the claim can be successfully resisted by the company.*'

Appendix V
Note on Legal Requirements

GREAT BRITAIN

The statutory requirements on accounting for provisions and contingencies are set **1** out in the Companies Act 1985. The main requirements that are directly relevant are set out in Schedules 4 and 4A and are summarised below.

Schedule 4 to the Act does not apply to banking and insurance companies and **2** groups. Banking companies and groups are dealt with in Schedule 9 and insurance companies and groups are dealt with in Schedule 9A.

Paragraph 12(b) of Schedule 4 states the general requirement that 'all liabilities and **3** losses which have arisen or are likely to arise in respect of the financial year to which the accounts relate or a previous financial year shall be taken into account ...'

Provisions represent one aspect of the manner in which this general requirement **4** is met. Provisions are defined in paragraph 89 of Schedule 4 in the following manner:

> 'References to provisions for liabilities or charges are to any amount retained as reasonably necessary for the purposes of providing for any liability or loss which is either likely to be incurred, or certain to be incurred but uncertain as to amount or as to the date on which it will arise.'*

The FRS defines a provision as:

> 'A liability of uncertain timing or amount.'

The requirements of the FRS are expressed in more specific terms than the require- **5** ments in Schedule 4. However, although the Act and the FRS define provisions in different terms, the Board believes that, when taken in their respective contexts, the FRS is consistent with the requirements of Schedule 4.

The legal definition refers to '... any amount retained as reasonably necessary for the **6** purposes ...'. The reference to reasonableness recognises that the appropriate amount to set aside as a provision for a specific matter will often be a matter of judgement. The FRS sets out the manner in which this judgement should be exercised in the context of giving a true and fair view.

In addition, the legal definition refers to '... any liability or loss ... [whether likely to **7** be incurred or certain to be incurred]' and this needs to be considered in conjunction with the general requirement that 'liabilities or losses have arisen or are likely to arise in respect of the financial year to which the accounts relate [or a previous financial year]' (paragraph 12(b) of Schedule 4). These requirements are consistent with the Board's approach of requiring there to be a past transaction or event that gives rise to an obligation, before a provision can be recognised. Without a past transaction or event the liability or loss will not have arisen or be likely to arise in respect of the

---

*Editor's note: References to 'provisions for liabilities and charges' in the legislation are now to 'provisions for liabilities'.

financial year or a previous financial year. Before a liability can be recognised, the draft Statement of Principles for Financial Reporting* requires sufficient evidence that a future transfer of benefits will occur.

8   In addition to covering liabilities that are certain to be incurred, the statutory definition also refers to liabilities as losses that are 'likely to be incurred'. This aspect of likelihood is covered in the FRS in two respects. The FRS requires provisions to be recognised arising from 'constructive obligations', which are liabilities that pass the test of sufficient certainty without constituting legal liabilities. The FRS also requires the recognition of provisions where a transfer of economic benefit is more likely than not to occur.

9   Where any amount is transferred to any provision for liabilities and charges or from any provision for liabilities and charges otherwise than for the purpose for which the provision was established, paragraph 46(1) and (2) of Schedule 4 requires the following information to be disclosed:

(a)   the amount of the provisions as at the date of the beginning of the financial year and as at the balance sheet date respectively;

(b)   any amounts transferred to or from provisions during that year; and

(c)   the source and application respectively of any amounts so transferred.

10   Paragraph 46(3) of Schedule 4 requires particulars to be given of each material provision included in the item "other provisions" in the company's balance sheet.

11   Paragraph 50(2) of Schedule 4 requires the following information to be given in respect of any other contingent liability not provided for:

(a)   the amount or estimated amount of that liability;

(b)   its legal nature; and

(c)   whether any valuable security has been provided by the company in connection with that liability and, if so, what.

NORTHERN IRELAND

12   The statutory requirements in Northern Ireland are set out in the Companies (Northern Ireland) Order 1986. They are identical to and parallel the references in the legislation for Great Britain cited above.

REPUBLIC OF IRELAND

13   The statutory requirements in the Republic of Ireland that correspond to those cited above for Great Britain are shown in the following table.

*Exposure Draft, November 1995. (**Editor's note:** also final Statement issued December 1999.)

Great Britain	*Republic of Ireland*
Schedule 4 to the Companies Act 1985	The Schedule to the Companies (Amendment) Act 1986
Schedule 4A to the Companies Act 1985	Regulation 15(1) of the European Communities (Companies: Group Accounts) Regulations 1992
Schedule 9 to the Companies Act 1985	European Communities (Credit Institutions: Accounts) Regulations 1992
Schedule 9A to the Companies Act 1985	European Communities (Insurance Undertakings: Accounts) Regulations 1996
Paragraph 12(b) of Schedule 4 to the Companies Act 1985	Section 5(c)(ii) of the Companies (Amendment) Act 1986
Paragraph 89 of Schedule 4 to the Companies Act 1985	Paragraph 70 of the Schedule to the Companies (Amendment) Act 1986
Paragraph 46(1) and (2) of Schedule 4 to the Companies Act 1985	Paragraph 32(1) and (2) of the Schedule to the Companies (Amendment) Act 1986
Paragraph 46(3) of Schedule 4 to the Companies Act 1985	Paragraph 32(3) of the Schedule to the Companies (Amendment) Act 1986
Paragraph 50(2) of Schedule 4 to the Companies Act 1985	Paragraph 36(2) of the Schedule to the Companies (Amendment) Act 1986

Appendix VI
Compliance with International Accounting Standards

Because the FRS was developed jointly with the international standard on the same topic, IAS 37 'Provisions, Contingent Liabilities and Contingent Assets', all the requirements of the IAS are included in the FRS and there are no differences of substance between these common requirements. The FRS, additionally, deals with the circumstances under which an asset should be recognised when a provision is recognised and gives more guidance than the IAS on the discount rate to be used in the present value calculation.

Appendix VII
The development of the FRS

THE NEED FOR A STANDARD

Provisions often have a substantial effect on an entity's financial position and per-   1
formance. They arise in a wide range of circumstances and businesses covering such
matters as warranties, onerous contracts, restructuring costs, environmental liabilities and decommissioning costs. Published guidance on the subject, however, has
tended to concentrate on particular forms of provision rather than the general
principles underlying all provisions.

To portray the financial position of an entity, it is important that a provision should   2
be recognised whenever a relevant liability exists; but it is equally important to
recognise a provision only when such a liability exists. The basis of a liability is the
existence of an obligation to one or more third parties. It follows that the *intention* to
incur expenditure does not, of itself, result in a liability. This point needs to be made
in an accounting standard because in some cases a mere intention to incur expenditure has been used to justify recognising a provision.

In the absence of an accounting standard on provisions the practice has grown up of   3
aggregating liabilities with expected liabilities of future years, and sometimes even
with expected expenditures related to ongoing operations, in one large provision,
often reported as an exceptional item. The effect of such 'big bath' provisions has
been not only to report excessive liabilities at the outset but also to boost profitability
during the subsequent years, when the liabilities are in fact being incurred.

The FRS addresses these concerns, first by requiring that provisions should be   4
recognised only where a liability exists at the period-end (based on the definition of a
liability in FRS 5 'Reporting the Substance of Transactions' and in the Board's draft
Statement of Principles for Financial Reporting*) and secondly by showing in
examples how this principle should apply to a number of commonly occurring circumstances. The FRS deals with recognition, measurement and disclosure for
provisions. Because contingent liabilities and contingent assets are closely linked to
provisions, the FRS also covers their treatment.

The Board has taken the opportunity to develop a complete framework of disclosure   5
requirements for provisions, contingent liabilities and contingent assets. The new
disclosure requirements give information about the significance of a provision and
any changes in it during the year and show how provisions have been used as
expenditure occurs.

In developing the FRS, the Board has considered the comments on its proposals set   6
out initially in the Discussion Paper 'Provisions' published in November 1995 and
then in FRED 14 'Provisions and Contingencies' issued in June 1997. At both stages
the majority of respondents have supported the issue of an FRS on provisions and the
general principles proposed as its basis.

The FRS has been developed as part of a joint project with the International   7
Accounting Standards Committee. The parallel development of the FRS and IAS 37
'Provisions, Contingent Liabilities and Contingent Assets' has meant that each
standard has been able to benefit from the comments and discussion on the other

*Exposure Draft, November 1995. (**Editor's note:** also final Statement issued December 1999.)

project. Apart from the two minor additions to the FRS noted in Appendix VI, the two standards are identical except for phraseology and structure necessary to conform to established practice in each constituency.

THE GENERAL PRINCIPLES

8   The central principle of the FRS is that a provision should be recognised only where at the period-end a liability exists that can be measured reliably. An entity may feel less well-off at the prospect of future cash flows entailed by its method of operation from the moment it becomes aware that they are likely to be necessary – it may wish to communicate such prospects by a note – but future expenditure, however necessary, does not justify the recognition of a provision unless a liability exists at the period-end. For a liability to exist the entity must have, as a result of past transactions or events, an obligation to transfer economic benefits in settlement. Future expenditure not relating to present obligations should be recognised in the period when the obligation to incur that expenditure arises.

9   FRED 14 distinguished between a legal and a constructive obligation. The responses indicated that it would be helpful to clarify the concept of a constructive obligation as a present obligation arising otherwise than by operation of law. The essence of an obligation is commitment to a third party: for a constructive obligation, that commitment arises through actions of the entity – its establishing a pattern of practice, publishing its policies or making a current statement setting out in detail its intended future actions – that raise in those dealing with it or affected by it a valid expectation that the entity will discharge its responsibilities. A constructive obligation is often the basis for recognising a provision for restructuring. The examples deal also with whether a constructive obligation exists for habitual refunds, cleaning up contamination and the closure of a division.

10   The proposals in FRED 14 defined 'contingency' and dealt with contingent losses and contingent gains rather than contingent liabilities and contingent assets. The draft Statement of Principles deals with the recognition of assets and liabilities and therefore the FRS now bases its analysis on contingent liabilities and contingent assets.

11   The FRS has clarified the relationship between provisions and contingent liabilities, which was the source of some concern to those commenting on the FRED 14 proposals. FRED 14 proposed that some contingent losses should be recognised while others should not. Under the FRS contingent liabilities as defined never qualify for recognition as liabilities – if circumstances change and a provision needs to be recognised there is no longer a contingent liability.

12   Similarly, the effect of the definition of a contingent asset in the FRS is that nothing that meets the criteria for recognition as an asset will count as a contingent asset. This distinction is clearer than the equivalent proposal in FRED 14 that some contingent gains should be recognised while others should not.

SCOPE

13   FRED 14 proposed that the FRS should apply to all financial statements that are intended to give a true and fair view of the reporting entity's financial position and profit or loss for a period. This proposal was widely supported by the respondents. However, because the accounting framework for financial instruments is under review, the Board has decided to exclude financial instruments carried at market value from the scope of the FRS. The special regulatory position of insurance

companies (for which provisions are particularly important) and the review of the accounting framework for insurance companies have led the Board to leave outside the scope of the FRS provisions arising in insurance entities from contracts with policy-holders. Because there are other accounting standards that specifically consider provisions in certain cases (eg pensions), the FRS does not apply to provisions covered by more specific requirements in other standards.

RECOGNITION

A present obligation

As explained above, the FRS follows the general principle proposed in the Discussion **14** Paper and FRED 14 – and already embodied in FRS 3 'Reporting Financial Performance' and FRS 7 'Fair Values in Acquisition Accounting' – that a provision should be recognised only where a liability exists that can be reliably estimated. The recognition criteria in the FRS therefore require that:

(a) an entity has a present obligation (legal or constructive) as a result of a past event;

(b) it is probable that a transfer of economic benefits will be required to settle the obligation; and

(c) a reliable estimate can be made of the amount of the obligation.

Conditions (a) and (b) must be fulfilled for a liability to exist. Condition (c) requires that it should be able to be measured with sufficient reliability. These conditions are therefore consistent with the recognition criteria set out in the draft Statement of Principles.

Past event

For there to be a present obligation the FRS requires that an obligating event has **15** taken place. An obligating event creates a legal or constructive obligation that results in an entity having no realistic alternative to settling that obligation. In FRED 14 the proposals for recognition were also based on the existence of a present obligation, the key notion being that the entity had no realistic alternative to making a transfer of economic benefits. The Board decided that it would be helpful to include more guidance on the obligating event that gives rise to a present obligation. The FRS notes that it is only those obligations arising independently of the entity's future actions that are recognised as provisions. Where the entity can avoid future expenditure by its future actions, it has no present liability for that future expenditure and no provision is recognised. The examples in Appendix III illustrate the effect in practice of applying the FRS in assessing whether an obligating event has taken place – in particular examples 3 (offshore oilfield), 6 (smoke filters), 7 (staff retraining) and 11 (repairs and maintenance).

By basing the recognition of a provision on the existence of a present obligation, the **16** FRS rules out the recognition of any provision made simply to allocate results over more than one period or otherwise to smooth the results reported. For example, in a regulated industry the results achieved in the current period may cause the pricing structure in the next period to be adjusted, eg the higher the profits in this year the lower the prices permitted for next year. There is no justification under the FRS for a provision to be recognised in such circumstances. The purpose of such a provision would be to transfer some of the current year's profit to the following year, which would suffer from lower prices because of the current year's profits. However, there is no present obligation that requires the transfer of economic benefits to settle it and nothing to justify recognition of a provision.

Probable outflow of economic resources

17   An essential part of the definition of a liability is the existence of an obligation to transfer economic benefits. This condition will be met where the transfer of economic benefits is probable, ie more likely than not to occur. Where there are a number of similar obligations the probability of a transfer is determined by considering the class of obligations as a whole.

Reliable estimate of the obligation

18   Some respondents to FRED 14 were concerned that the proposals would allow scope for abuse and the avoidance of proper provision because they permitted the non-recognition of a provision where a reliable estimate of the obligation could not be made. In response to these concerns the FRS notes that, except in extremely rare cases, an entity will be able to determine a range of possible outcomes and can therefore make an estimate that is sufficiently reliable to use in recognising a provision.

CONTINGENT LIABILITIES

19   The recognition of contingent losses on the basis of whether they were probable was supported by the respondents to FRED 14. As explained in paragraphs 10 and 11 above, the FRS bases its analysis on contingent liabilities rather than contingent losses and classifies as a provision, rather than a contingent liability, an obligation that is recognised because it will probably require the transfer of economic benefits in settlement. The effect of these requirements of the FRS on the recognition of losses is the same as proposed in FRED 14.

CONTINGENT ASSETS

20   The recognition of contingent gains on the basis of whether they were virtually certain was supported by the respondents to FRED 14. As explained in paragraphs 10 and 12 above, the FRS bases its analysis on contingent assets, rather than contingent gains, and requires that a contingent asset should not be recognised. When, however, the realisation of a profit becomes virtually certain, the related asset is not a contingent asset and recognition is appropriate. Accordingly, the effect of the requirements of the FRS on the recognition of gains is the same as proposed in FRED 14.

MEASUREMENT

21   The FRS requires a provision to be recognised at the best estimate of the expenditure required to settle the present obligation at the balance sheet date. The risks and uncertainties that surround events should be taken into account in calculating the amount of the provision. Whatever method of estimation is adopted full disclosure of the uncertainties surrounding the amount of the expenditure is required.

22   For a liability where there is a market, the best estimate of that liability at the balance sheet date would be its market value. The FRS recognises that it will often be impossible or prohibitively expensive to settle or transfer an obligation at the balance sheet date because of the uncertainty relating to provisions. By acknowledging this impossibility, the FRS reflects some of the points raised by the respondents to FRED 14.

However, a provision should, in principle, be recognised at the amount of the obligation that existed at the balance sheet date – ie the least cost amount to settle the existing present obligation. Even where it is not possible either to settle or transfer the obligation at the balance sheet date, the process of estimating the amounts at which such hypothetical transactions would take place provides a useful approach to calculating the least cost amount.

Assuming that it is possible to specify all the possible outcomes and their associated probabilities, the amount to be provided for an obligation could be estimated as: **23**

- *the most likely outcome* (ie the outcome with the highest probability). The problem with calculating the estimate using this method is that it ignores the other possible outcomes: for example, where the most likely outcome is nil it could also lead to the inference that an entity has no obligation.
- *the maximum amount* (ie the highest possible outcome). Use of this method to calculate the estimate could result in extremely large amounts being recognised even though the possibility of the outcome is remote.
- *at least the minimum amount in the range* (ie any amount from the lowest possible outcome to the highest possible outcome). This formula results in a wide range of possible estimates and would therefore be likely to impair comparability in financial reporting.
- *the expected value* (ie the amount that takes account of all possible outcomes using probabilities to weight the outcomes). Expected value as a method of estimation has a number of desirable features. The method provides an estimate that reflects the entire probability distribution, ie all the possible outcomes weighted by their probabilities. For a given assessed distribution, the method has the advantage of objectivity in that different measurers would calculate the same estimate. Furthermore, expected value is additive (ie the expected value of a number of items is the sum of the expected values of the individual items).

Where there is a large population of items, the expected value – adjusted as appropriate for risk – will provide the best estimate of a provision.

DISCOUNTING

Some provisions that are to be recognised require outflows of economic benefits in **24** settlement far in the future. For some provisions, therefore, the effect of the time value of money – the greater value of a present sum than the certain payment of the same sum some time in the future – can be material and should be taken into account in estimating the amount to be recognised as a provision. Discounting was proposed for provisions in FRED 14 and received the support of the majority of the respondents. The background to the requirements on discounting is set out in the Working Paper 'Discounting in Financial Reporting' (published in April 1997). The proposals in the FRS are consistent with that Paper.

The FRS requires the unwinding of the discount to be included in the profit and loss **25** account as a financial item adjacent to but shown separately from interest. The respondents to FRED 14 were divided over whether the unwinding discount should be shown as interest or as an operating cost. Those who favoured showing it as an operating cost tended to argue that putting this amount in interest would be misleading and confusing to users of accounts and would distort or obscure the view given by the interest and funding disclosures. The Board has met these concerns by requiring that the unwinding discount should be shown clearly as a separate item from interest. The Board believes that the unwinding discount is a financial item – it relates to the time value of money, reflecting the effect of the passage of time on an amount specified in money terms.

26   Provisions that are calculated at a discounted amount should take into account risk as well as the time value of money. Risk can be taken into account either by discounting at a risk-free rate cash flows that take risk into account or by discounting at a risk-adjusted rate cash flows that take no account of risk. The important point is that risk should be taken into account in the best way possible and that care should be taken not to double-count the effect of risk. Among the considerations to be borne in mind are whether it is feasible to derive an appropriate risk-adjusted rate of interest and whether the incidence of risk over the discount period may follow a different pattern from that of compound interest.

27   Where the amount recognised is discounted, the cash flows to be discounted are the pre-tax cash flows and the discount rate should be the rate of return that will, after tax has been deducted, give the required post-tax rate of return. Because the tax consequences of different cash flows may be different, the pre-tax rate of return is not always the post-tax rate of return grossed up by the standard rate of tax. The Board requires the effect of tax to be shown separately in financial statements rather than netting tax directly off the assets and liabilities. This is in line with the general requirement that tax effects shall be shown separately.

Expected disposal of assets

28   FRED 14 did not refer to the treatment of gains from the expected disposal of assets in measuring provisions. The FRS prohibits such gains from being taken into account in measuring a provision. The principle of the FRS is that provisions should be recognised and measured as liabilities independently of considerations affecting the recognition and measurement of assets held. As a practical matter, if in certain circumstances gains on expected disposals were netted off against the provision to be recognised, it would be difficult to limit the assets whose expected disposal could be set off. There would also need to be guidance on the treatment when the provision was both recognised and used before the gain was achieved.

REIMBURSEMENTS

29   The FRS requires that a provision and any expected reimbursement should be recognised separately as a liability and an asset – although shown net in the profit and loss account. This approach is consistent with the general principle contained in FRS 5 and is designed to reflect the fact that the entity often continues to be liable if the third party from which the reimbursement is due fails to pay. Reimbursement is recognised only when it is virtually certain to be received if the entity settles the liability.

APPLICATION OF THE RECOGNITION AND MEASUREMENT RULES

30   The FRS includes paragraphs applying its recognition and measurement rules to operating losses, onerous contracts and reorganisations. Although the text has changed from FRED 14, the FRS applies the same basic principles as the FRED and has the same effect.

Restructuring provisions

31   The most controversial aspect of the proposals in FRED 14 related to the date on which a provision for restructuring should be recognised – the FRED proposed that the date when the entity became demonstrably committed to a reorganisation should

be the date a provision was recognised. On this principle, no provision should be recognised if the only relevant event before the balance sheet date was a board decision. The majority of those disagreeing with this proposal argued that it was unrealistically strict and that a provision should be recognised where there was a formal board decision before the year-end and either implementation of that decision began before the signing of the financial statements or the decision was communicated in sufficient detail to those affected by it before that date.

The Board has discussed the issues raised by the respondents but has concluded that, **32** for the consistent application of its principles, it must require a constructive obligation to restructure to exist at the balance sheet date for a provision for restructuring to be recognised. This is required also for consistency with the treatment of assets: the entity includes in its financial statements only those assets that it controls at the balance sheet date and does not include assets that come under its control only between the balance sheet date and the signing of the financial statements.

A constructive obligation to restructure arises only when the entity has a detailed **33** formal plan for the reorganisation and, by beginning to implement that plan or communicating it to those affected, raises in them a valid expectation that it will carry out the restructuring as expected. Therefore a board decision alone (unless one of a supervisory board whose members include employees and possibly other affected interests (see paragraph 82 of the FRS)) does not amount to a constructive obligation to restructure.

DISCLOSURE

Respondents raised no major concerns with the disclosures proposed by FRED 14. **34**

The reordering of the FRS to incorporate more fully contingent liabilities and con- **35** tingent assets has led to the disclosure requirements for these to be set out alongside those for provisions, making clear the consistent basis for the requirements. As part of this rearrangement, the dispensation from providing disclosures that can be expected to prejudice seriously the position of the entity in its negotiations with other parties now applies to contingent liabilities and contingent assets as well as to provisions. The respondents to FRED 14 overwhelmingly supported a 'seriously prejudicial' exemption for disclosures on provisions.

DECOMMISSIONING COSTS AND REPAIRS AND MAINTENANCE PROVISIONS

The examples in Appendix III describe two cases where the effect of applying the **36** requirements remains controversial, although the treatment in the examples received general support from the majority of respondents on FRED 14. These are example 3 on decommissioning costs and example 11 on repairs and maintenance.

Decommissioning costs

Before the introduction of the FRS, the treatment generally accorded to decom- **37** missioning costs was to account for them on the 'units of production' method. Under this method, the amount required for decommissioning is built up year by year, in line with production levels, to reach the amount of the expected decommissioning costs by the time production ceases. The FRS requires that, to the extent that decommissioning costs relate to damage already done or goods and services already received, that present obligation should be recognised as a provision. The following points should be noted when considering the effects of the FRS's requirements on decommissioning costs.

- On installation of the oil rig, the effect of the time value of money is that the true measure of the extra cost of the rig represented by decommissioning costs is the discounted amount of the eventual cost.
- Decommissioning costs will be included in the cost of the oil rig only to the extent that they are incurred by the installation of the rig. If any damage is incurred by production, the costs of restoring that damage is a cost of production – the classic case of this in another industry is open-cast mining where the production process itself increases the damage caused and the consequent cost of restoration.
- The unwinding of the discount reflects the effect of the passage of time and that unwinding is matched in principle by interest or income earned as a result of having a liability that has not yet required the transfer of economic resources in settlement. Setting aside a sinking fund equal to the discounted amount of the liability at any time would provide sufficient cumulative interest income to settle the decommissioning liability directly without any additional transfer of resources.
- Some respondents have been concerned that the profile over time of the charge arising for decommissioning costs (lower at first but rising over time) could lead to payments of dividends early in the production process in excess of what the business could bear after taking into account its long-term liability for decommissioning costs. However, provided that the assets in the business earn a return in excess of the interest rate used to discount the decommissioning costs, there will be at least sufficient assets to settle the decommissioning costs liabilities when these need to be paid.

Repairs and maintenance

38   It is the present practice of some entities to recognise as a provision the future costs of repairing or maintaining part of their fixed assets. Example 11 illustrates the application of the FRS to repairs and maintenance for fixed assets. Because future repairs and maintenance are not present obligations of the entity resulting from past events, no provision should be made for them, even if they are required by legislation if the asset is to continue to be used. There are no grounds for recognising a provision for future repairs and maintenance expenditures because these relate to the future operation of the business, the restoration of service potential, and are therefore either to be capitalised as assets or written off as operating expenses when incurred. Where a part of the asset can be identified as declining in service potential because of the need for repairs or maintenance, it should be depreciated to show the declining service potential. Expenditure on repairs and maintenance should be capitalised to show the restoration of service potential.

39   In some operating leases the lessee is required to incur periodic charges for maintenance of the leased asset or to make good dilapidations or other damage occurring during the rental period. The principle illustrated in example 11 does not preclude the recognition of such liabilities once the event giving rise to the obligation under the lease has occurred.

[FRS 13]
Derivatives and other financial instruments: disclosures

FRS 13 is withdrawn with effect for accounting periods beginning on or after 1 January 2007. It is replaced by FRS 29.

Financial Reporting Standard 15 is set out in paragraphs 1–110.

The Statement of Standard Accounting Practice, which comprises the paragraphs set in bold type, should be read in the context of the Objective as stated in paragraph 1 and the definitions set out in paragraph 2 and also of the Foreword to Accounting Standards and the Statement of Principles for Financial Reporting currently in issue.

The explanatory paragraphs contained in the FRS shall be regarded as part of the Statement of Standard Accounting Practice insofar as they assist in interpreting that statement.

Appendix IV 'The development of the FRS' reviews considerations and arguments that were thought significant by members of the Board in reaching the conclusions on the FRS.

[FRS 15]
Tangible fixed assets

(Issued February 1999)

Contents

Summary

GENERAL

a   Financial Reporting Standard 15 'Tangible Fixed Assets' sets out the principles of accounting for the initial measurement, valuation and depreciation of tangible fixed assets, with the exception of investment properties. Investment properties continue to be accounted for in accordance with SSAP 19 'Accounting for investment properties', but are being considered further in the light of other Board projects and the international project on investment properties.

b   The FRS codifies much of existing accounting practice. Its objective is to ensure that tangible fixed assets are accounted for on a consistent basis and, where a policy of revaluation is adopted, that revaluations are kept up-to-date.

INITIAL MEASUREMENT

c   Whether acquired or self-constructed, a tangible fixed asset should initially be measured at its cost. Only costs that are directly attributable to bringing the asset into working condition for its intended use should be included. Such costs should be capitalised only for the period in which the activities that are necessary to get the asset ready for use are in progress.

d   The capitalisation of finance costs, including interest, is optional. However, if an entity adopts such a policy then it should be applied consistently. All finance costs that are directly attributable to the construction of a tangible fixed asset should be capitalised as part of the cost of that asset, subject to the proviso that the total amount of finance costs capitalised during a period should not exceed the amount of finance costs incurred during the period. The FRS also sets limits on the period of capitalisation and specifies certain disclosure requirements.

e   If the amount recognised when a tangible fixed asset is acquired or constructed exceeds its recoverable amount, it should be written down to recoverable amount. However, on initial recognition the asset needs to be reviewed for impairment only if there is an indication of impairment, in accordance with FRS 11 'Impairment of Fixed Assets and Goodwill'.

f   Subsequent expenditure undertaken to ensure that the asset maintains its previously assessed standard of performance, for example routine repairs and maintenance expenditure, should be recognised in the profit and loss account as it is incurred. Without such expenditure the depreciation expense would be increased because the useful economic life or residual value of the asset would be reduced. However, subsequent expenditure should be capitalised in three circumstances, where the expenditure:

    (i)   enhances the economic benefits of the asset in excess of its previously assessed standard of performance; or

    (ii) replaces or restores a component of the asset that has been treated separately for depreciation purposes and depreciated over its individual useful economic life; or

    (iii) relates to a major inspection or overhaul that restores the economic benefits of the asset that have been consumed by the entity and have already been reflected in depreciation.

VALUATION

An entity has the option of revaluing its tangible fixed assets. However, where such a policy is adopted it should be applied consistently to all tangible fixed assets of the same class.

g

Where a tangible fixed asset is revalued its carrying amount should be its current value at the balance sheet date. Generally this requirement is achieved by performing a full valuation at least every five years and an interim valuation in year 3, with an interim valuation in the intervening years where it is likely that there has been a material change in value. Alternatively, for a portfolio of non-specialised properties, a full valuation may be performed on a rolling basis over a five-year cycle, together with an interim valuation on the remaining portfolio where it is likely that there has been a material change in value. For tangible fixed assets other than properties where there is an active second-hand market or appropriate indices, such that the entity's directors can establish the asset's value with reasonable reliability, an annual revaluation by the directors may be sufficient, without necessarily using the services of a qualified valuer.

h

Where tangible fixed assets are revalued the following valuation bases for unimpaired assets should be used:

i

- non-specialised properties – existing use value,* with the addition of notional directly attributable acquisition costs, where material
- specialised properties – depreciated replacement cost
- properties surplus to an entity's requirements – open market value,† after deducting expected directly attributable selling costs, where material
- tangible fixed assets other than properties – market value, or depreciated replacement cost where market value is not available.

Revaluation gains are recognised in the statement of total recognised gains and losses except to the extent that they reverse revaluation losses on the same asset that were previously recognised in the profit and loss account, in which case they, too, should be recognised in the profit and loss account, after adjusting for subsequent depreciation.

j

All revaluation losses that are caused by a clear consumption of economic benefits are recognised in the profit and loss account. Other revaluation losses are recognised in the statement of total recognised gains and losses until the carrying amount of the asset falls below depreciated historical cost. Revaluation losses below depreciated historical cost are recognised in the profit and loss account, except where it can be demonstrated that the recoverable amount of the asset is greater than its revalued amount, in which case the loss is recognised in the statement of total recognised gains and losses to the extent that the recoverable amount of the asset is greater than its revalued amount.

k

Profits and losses on the disposal of tangible fixed assets are treated in accordance with FRS 3 'Reporting Financial Performance' – ie calculated as the difference between the net sale proceeds and the carrying amount and recorded in the profit and loss account in the period in which the disposal occurs.

l

As defined by the Royal Institution of Chartered Surveyors (RICS). These definitions are reproduced in Appendix I.

†As defined by the Royal Institution of Chartered Surveyors (RICS). These definitions are reproduced in Appendix I.*

m Where an entity revalues its tangible fixed assets the FRS requires specific disclosures about the valuation.

DEPRECIATION

n The fundamental objective of depreciation is to reflect in operating profit the cost of use of the tangible fixed assets (ie the amount of economic benefits consumed by the entity) in the period. Therefore, the depreciable amount (ie cost, or revalued amount, less residual value) of a tangible fixed asset should be recognised in the profit and loss account on a systematic basis that reflects as fairly as possible the pattern in which the asset's economic benefits are consumed by the entity, over its useful economic life.

o Where the tangible fixed asset comprises two or more major components with substantially different useful economic lives, each component should be accounted for separately for depreciation purposes and depreciated over its individual useful economic life.

p Subsequent expenditure on a tangible fixed asset that maintains or enhances the previously assessed standard of performance of the asset does not negate the need to charge depreciation, as, other than non-depreciable land, all tangible fixed assets have finite lives. However, where the remaining useful economic life of a tangible fixed asset is estimated to be greater than 50 years or where the depreciation charge is immaterial owing to a long useful economic life or high residual value, then, to ensure that the carrying amount can be supported, the tangible fixed asset should be subjected to impairment reviews at the end of each reporting period, performed in accordance with FRS 11.

q The useful economic life of a tangible fixed asset and its residual value (based on the price level that existed when the asset was purchased or last revalued) where material, should be reviewed at the end of each reporting period. If expectations are significantly different from previous estimates, the change should be accounted for prospectively over the tangible fixed asset's remaining useful economic life, except to the extent that the asset has been impaired at the balance sheet date.

r The FRS requires specific disclosures about the depreciation policies adopted by an entity and changes in those policies.

Financial Reporting Standard 15

Objective

The objective of this FRS is to ensure that:

1

(a) consistent principles are applied to the initial measurement of tangible fixed assets.
(b) where an entity chooses to revalue tangible fixed assets the valuation is performed on a consistent basis and kept up-to-date and gains and losses on revaluation are recognised on a consistent basis.
(c) depreciation of tangible fixed assets is calculated in a consistent manner and recognised as the economic benefits are consumed over the assets' useful economic lives.
(d) sufficient information is disclosed in the financial statements to enable users to understand the impact of the entity's accounting policies regarding initial measurement, valuation and depreciation of tangible fixed assets on the financial position and performance of the entity.

Definitions

The following definitions shall apply in the FRS and in particular in the Statement of Standard Accounting Practice set out **in bold type**.

2

Class of tangible fixed assets:-

A category of tangible fixed assets having a similar nature, function or use in the business of the entity.

Current value:-

The current value of a tangible fixed asset to the business is the lower of replacement cost and recoverable amount.

Depreciable amount:-

The cost of a tangible fixed asset (or, where an asset is revalued, the revalued amount) less its residual value.

Depreciated replacement cost (of property):-

Has the same meaning as in the *Appraisal and Valuation Manual* published by the Royal Institution of Chartered Surveyors (RICS). The definition is reproduced in Appendix I.*

*Editor's note: There are various references to RICS guidance in FRS 15. The RICS guidance has altered since the date of publication of FRS 15, and some of the terms used in FRS 15 are no longer defined by RICS.

Depreciated replacement cost (of tangible fixed assets other than property):-

The cost of replacing an existing tangible fixed asset with an identical or substantially similar new asset having a similar production or service capacity, from which appropriate deductions are made to reflect the value attributable to the remaining portion of the total useful economic life of the asset and the residual value at the end of the asset's useful economic life.

> Costs directly attributable to bringing the tangible fixed asset into working condition for its intended use, such as costs of transport, installation, commissioning, consultants' fees, non-recoverable taxes and duties, are included in depreciated replacement cost. The deductions from gross replacement cost should take into account the age and condition of the asset, economic and functional obsolescence, and environmental and other relevant factors.

Depreciation:-

The measure of the cost or revalued amount of the economic benefits of the tangible fixed asset that have been consumed during the period.

> Consumption includes the wearing out, using up or other reduction in the useful economic life of a tangible fixed asset whether arising from use, effluxion of time or obsolescence through either changes in technology or demand for the goods and services produced by the asset.

Existing use value:-

Has the same meaning as in the *Appraisal and Valuation Manual* published by the RICS. The definition is reproduced in Appendix I.

Finance costs:-

The difference between the net proceeds of an instrument and the total amount of payments (or other transfers of economic benefits) that the issuer may be required to make in respect of the instrument.*

Impairment:-

A reduction in the recoverable amount of a tangible fixed asset below its carrying amount.

> The definition set out above is taken from FRS 11 'Impairment of Fixed Assets and Goodwill'.

Non-specialised properties:-

Has the same meaning as in the *Appraisal and Valuation Manual* published by the RICS. The definition is reproduced in Appendix I.

*Editor's note: The explanatory paragraph on finance costs, which was based on FRS 4, has been deleted by FRS 25.

Open market value:-

Has the same meaning as in the *Appraisal and Valuation Manual* published by the RICS. The definition is reproduced in Appendix I.

Qualified (internal or external) valuer:-

A person conducting the valuation who holds a recognised and relevant professional qualification and having recent post-qualification experience, and sufficient knowledge of the state of the market, in the location and category of the tangible fixed asset being valued. An internal valuer is a director, officer or employee of the entity. An external valuer is not an internal valuer and does not have a significant financial interest in the entity.

Recoverable amount:-

The higher of net realisable value and value in use.*

Residual value:-

The net realisable value of an asset at the end of its useful economic life. Residual values are based on prices prevailing at the date of the acquisition (or revaluation) of the asset and do not take account of expected future price changes.

Specialised properties:-

Has the same meaning as in the *Appraisal and Valuation Manual* published by the RICS. The definition is reproduced in Appendix I.

Tangible fixed assets:-

Assets that have physical substance and are held for use in the production or supply of goods or services, for rental to others, or for administrative purposes on a continuing basis in the reporting entity's activities.

Useful economic life:-

The useful economic life of a tangible fixed asset is the period over which the entity expects to derive economic benefit from that asset.

SCOPE

The FRS applies to all financial statements that are intended to give a true and fair view of a reporting entity's financial position and profit or loss (or income and expenditure) for a period.   3

The requirements of the FRS apply to all tangible fixed assets, with the exception of investment properties as defined in SSAP 19 'Accounting for investment properties'.   4

* Refer to FRS 11 'Impairment of Fixed Assets and Goodwill' for a definition of value in use and details about its calculation.

5   Reporting entities applying the Financial Reporting Standard for Smaller Entities (FRSSE) currently applicable are exempt from the FRS.

INITIAL MEASUREMENT

Cost

6   A tangible fixed asset should initially be measured at its cost.

7   Costs, but only those costs, that are directly attributable to bringing the asset into working condition for its intended use should be included in its measurement.

8   The cost of a tangible fixed asset (whether acquired or self-constructed) comprises its purchase price (after deducting any trade discounts and rebates) and any costs directly attributable to bringing it into working condition for its intended use.

9   Directly attributable costs are:

(a)   the labour costs of own employees (eg site workers, in-house architects and surveyors) arising directly from the construction, or acquisition, of the specific tangible fixed asset; and

(b)   the incremental costs to the entity that would have been avoided only if the tangible fixed asset had not been constructed or acquired.

It follows that administration and other general overhead costs would be excluded from the cost of a tangible fixed asset. Employee costs not related to the specific asset (such as site selection activities) are not directly attributable costs.

10   Examples of directly attributable costs include:

- acquisition costs (such as stamp duty, import duties and non-refundable purchase taxes)
- the cost of site preparation and clearance
- initial delivery and handling costs
- installation costs
- professional fees (such as legal, architects' and engineers' fees)
- the estimated cost of dismantling and removing the asset and restoring the site, to the extent that it is recognised as a provision under FRS 12 'Provisions, Contingent Liabilities and Contingent Assets'. The fact that the prospect of such expenditures emerges only some time after the original capitalisation of the asset (eg because of legislative changes) does not preclude their capitalisation.

11   Abnormal costs (such as those relating to design errors, industrial disputes, idle capacity, wasted materials, labour or other resources and production delays) and costs such as operating losses that occur because a revenue activity has been suspended during the construction of a tangible fixed asset are not directly attributable to bringing the asset into working condition for its intended use.

12   Capitalisation of directly attributable costs should cease when substantially all the activities that are necessary to get the tangible fixed asset ready for use are complete, even if the asset has not yet been brought into use.

13   A tangible fixed asset is ready for use when its physical construction is complete.

The costs associated with a start-up or commissioning period should be included in the   14
cost of the tangible fixed asset only where the asset is available for use but incapable of
operating at normal levels without such a start-up or commissioning period.

A distinction can be made between: 15

(a)   the commissioning period for plant, in which it is impossible for it to operate at
      normal levels because of, for example, the need to run in machinery, to test
      equipment and generally to ensure the proper functioning of the plant; and

(b)   an initial operating period in which, although the plant is available for use and
      capable of running at normal levels, it is operated at below normal levels
      because demand has not yet built up.

The costs of an essential commissioning period are included as part of the cost of   16
bringing the asset up to its normal operating potential, and therefore as part of its
cost. However, there is no justification for regarding costs relating to other start-up
periods, where the asset is available for use but not yet operating at normal levels, for
example because of a lack of demand, as part of the cost of the asset. An example is
the start-up period of a new hotel or bookshop, which could operate at normal levels
almost immediately, but for which experience teaches that demand will build up
slowly and full utilisation or sales levels will be achieved only over a period of several
months.

The initial carrying amount of tangible fixed assets received as gifts and donations by   17
charities should be the current value of the assets at the date they are received.

Donated assets are particularly common in the charity sector. Such organisations   18
often receive tangible fixed assets that the entity cannot dispose of without external
consent and other tangible fixed assets of particular historic, scientific or artistic
importance. On occasion, such assets may present measurement difficulties where
conventional valuation approaches lack sufficient reliability. In addition, even where
valuation is practical, if significant costs are involved they may be onerous compared
with the additional benefit derived by users of the accounts in assessing management's stewardship of the assets. Where it can be demonstrated that these factors are
significant alternative approaches to the valuation of those tangible fixed assets may
be appropriate, provided that adequate disclosure of the reason for the different
treatment, and of the age, nature and scale of the assets is given in the notes to the
accounts. A similar approach is acceptable on the first implementation of the FRS
where, under previously permitted accounting policies, a charity holds tangible fixed
assets that were not capitalised as required by the FRS and for which reliable estimates
of cost or value are not available on a cost-benefit basis. Generally, these issues will
be addressed in the relevant sector-specific guidance and Statements of Recommended Practice (SORPs).

Finance costs

Where an entity adopts a policy of capitalising finance costs, finance costs that are   19
directly attributable to the construction of tangible fixed assets should be capitalised as
part of the cost of those assets. The total amount of finance costs capitalised during a
period should not exceed the total amount of finance costs incurred during that period.

An entity need not capitalise finance costs. However, if an entity adopts a policy of   20
capitalisation of finance costs, then it should be applied consistently to all tangible
fixed assets where finance costs fall to be capitalised in accordance with the above
requirement.

21   Only finance costs that are directly attributable to the construction of a tangible fixed asset, or the financing of progress payments in respect of the construction of a tangible fixed asset by others for the entity, should be capitalised. Directly attributable finance costs are those that would have been avoided (for example by avoiding additional borrowings or by using the funds expended for the asset to repay existing borrowings) if there had been no expenditure on the asset. Finance costs are capitalised on a gross basis, ie before the deduction of any tax relief to which they give rise.

22   Where the entity has borrowed funds specifically for the purpose of financing the construction of a tangible fixed asset, the amount of finance costs capitalised is limited to the actual costs incurred on the borrowings during the period in respect of expenditures to date on the tangible fixed asset. Finance costs in respect of leased tangible fixed assets should be accounted for in accordance with SSAP 21 'Accounting for leases and hire purchase contracts'.

23   Where the funds used to finance the construction of a tangible fixed asset form part of the entity's general borrowings, the amount of finance costs capitalised is determined by applying a capitalisation rate to the expenditure on that asset. For this purpose the expenditure on the asset is the weighted average carrying amount of the asset during the period, including finance costs previously capitalised. The capitalisation rate used in an accounting period is based on the weighted average of rates applicable to the entity's general borrowings that are outstanding during the period. This excludes borrowings by the entity that are specifically for the purpose of constructing or acquiring other tangible fixed assets (eg obligations in respect of finance leases), or for other specific purposes, such as loans used to hedge foreign investments.

24   In determining the borrowings to be included in the weighted average, the objective is a reasonable measure of the finance costs that are directly attributable to the construction of the asset. Accordingly, judgement will be required to make a selection of borrowings that best accomplishes the objective. In some circumstances, it is appropriate to include all borrowings by the parent and its subsidiaries when computing a weighted average of the finance costs; in other circumstances, it is appropriate for each subsidiary to use a weighted average of the finance costs applicable to its own borrowings.

25   **Where finance costs are capitalised, capitalisation should begin when:**

   (a)   finance costs are being incurred; and
   (b)   expenditures for the asset are being incurred; and
   (c)   activities that are necessary to get the asset ready for use are in progress.

26   The activities necessary to get the asset ready for use encompass more than its physical construction. They include technical and administrative work before construction begins, such as obtaining permits. However, such activities exclude the holding of an asset when no production or development that changes the asset's condition is taking place. For example, finance costs incurred while land is under development are capitalised during the period in which activities related to the development are being undertaken. However, finance costs incurred while land acquired for building purposes is held without any associated development activity do not qualify for capitalisation.

27   **Capitalisation of finance costs should be suspended during extended periods in which active development is interrupted.**

Finance costs may be incurred during an extended period in which the activities **28** necessary to get the asset ready for use are interrupted. Such costs are costs of holding partially completed assets and do not qualify for capitalisation.

Capitalisation of finance costs should cease when substantially all the activities that are 29 necessary to get the tangible fixed asset ready for use are complete. When construction of a tangible fixed asset is completed in parts and each part is capable of being used while construction continues on other parts, capitalisation of finance costs relating to a part should cease when substantially all the activities that are necessary to get that part ready for use are completed.

A business park comprising several buildings, each of which can be used individually, **30** is an example of an asset of which parts are usable while construction continues on other parts. An example of an asset that needs to be completed before any part can be used is an industrial plant involving several processes that are carried out in sequence at different parts of the plant within the same site, such as a steel mill.

Disclosures – finance costs

Where a policy of capitalisation of finance costs is adopted, the financial statements 31 should disclose:

(a) **the accounting policy adopted;**
(b) **the aggregate amount of finance costs included in the cost of tangible fixed assets;***
(c) **the amount of finance costs capitalised during the period;**
(d) **the amount of finance costs recognised in the profit and loss account during the period; and**
(e) **the capitalisation rate used to determine the amount of finance costs capitalised during the period.**

Recoverable amount

If the amount recognised when a tangible fixed asset is acquired or constructed exceeds 32 its recoverable amount, it should be written down to its recoverable amount.

A tangible fixed asset needs to be reviewed for impairment on initial recognition only **33** if there is some indication that impairment has occurred, as set out in FRS 11 'Impairment of Fixed Assets and Goodwill'. A tangible fixed asset that is impaired on initial recognition should be written down in accordance with FRS 11.

Subsequent expenditure

Subsequent expenditure to ensure that the tangible fixed asset maintains its previously 34 assessed standard of performance should be recognised in the profit and loss account as it is incurred.

This type of expenditure is often referred to as 'repairs and maintenance' expendi- **35** ture. An entity will assess the standard of performance of an asset (or a component of the asset) to determine its useful economic life and residual value. It will also

---

**This disclosure is required by companies legislation as follows:*
in Great Britain, the Companies Act 1985, Schedule 4, paragraph 26(3).
in Northern Ireland, the Companies (Northern Ireland) Order 1986, Schedule 4, paragraph 26(3).
in the Republic of Ireland, the Companies (Amendment) Act 1986, Schedule, paragraph 14(3).

assume that certain 'repairs and maintenance' expenditure will be carried out to maintain the standard of performance of the asset over its estimated useful economic life. Examples are the cost of servicing or the routine overhauling of plant and equipment and repainting a building structure. Without such expenditure the depreciation expense would be increased because the useful economic life or residual value of the asset would be reduced.

36   Subsequent expenditure should be capitalised in three circumstances:

(a)   where the subsequent expenditure provides an enhancement of the economic benefits of the tangible fixed asset in excess of the previously assessed standard of performance.

(b)   where a component of the tangible fixed asset that has been treated separately for depreciation purposes and depreciated over its individual useful economic life, is replaced or restored.

(c)   where the subsequent expenditure relates to a major inspection or overhaul of a tangible fixed asset that restores the economic benefits of the asset that have been consumed by the entity and have already been reflected in depreciation.

37   Subsequent expenditure on a tangible fixed asset is recognised as an addition to the asset to the extent that the expenditure improves the condition of the asset beyond its previously assessed standard of performance. Examples of subsequent expenditure that results in an enhancement of economic benefits include:

● modification of an item of plant to extend its useful economic life or increase its capacity
● upgrading machine parts to achieve a substantial improvement in the quality of output.

38   Some tangible fixed assets require, in addition to routine repairs and maintenance (which is treated in accordance with paragraph 34), substantial expenditure every few years for major refits or refurbishment or the replacement or restoration of major components. For example, a furnace may require relining every five years. In accordance with paragraph 83, for depreciation purposes an entity accounts separately for major components (eg the furnace lining) that have substantially different useful economic lives from the rest of the asset. In such a case, each component is depreciated over its individual useful economic life, so that the depreciation profile of the whole asset more accurately reflects the actual consumption of the asset's economic benefits. Subsequent expenditure incurred in replacing or renewing the component is accounted for as an addition to the tangible fixed asset and the carrying amount of the replaced component is removed from the balance sheet in accordance with paragraphs 72 and 73.

39   The same approach may also be applied to major inspections and overhauls of tangible fixed assets. For example, an aircraft may be required by law to be overhauled once every three years. Unless the overhaul is undertaken the aircraft cannot continue to be flown. The entity reflects the need to undertake the overhaul or inspection by depreciating an amount of the asset that is equivalent to the expected inspection or overhaul costs over the period until the next inspection or overhaul. In such a case, the cost of the inspection or overhaul is capitalised when incurred because it restores the economic benefits of the tangible fixed asset and the carrying amount representing the cost of the benefits consumed is removed from the balance sheet in accordance with paragraphs 72 and 73.

40   The accounting treatment for subsequent expenditure should reflect the circumstances that were taken into account on the initial recognition of the asset and the depreciation profile adopted (or subsequent revisions thereof). Therefore, when the

carrying amount of the asset already takes into account a consumption of economic benefits, eg by depreciating components of the asset at a faster rate than the asset as a whole (or by a previous impairment of the asset or component), the subsequent expenditure to restore those economic benefits is capitalised. The decision whether to identify separate components or future expenditures on overhauls or inspections for depreciation over a shorter useful economic life than the rest of the tangible fixed asset is likely to reflect:

- whether the useful economic lives of the components are, or the period until the next inspection or overhaul is, substantially different from the useful economic life of the remainder of the asset;
- the degree of irregularity in the level of expenditures required to restate the component or asset in different accounting periods; and
- their materiality in the context of the financial statements.

Where it has been determined not to account for each tangible fixed asset as several **41** different asset components or to depreciate part of the asset over a different timescale from the rest of the asset, the cost of replacing, restoring, overhauling or inspecting the asset or components of the asset is not capitalised, but instead is recognised in the profit and loss account as incurred in accordance with paragraph 34.

Valuation

Tangible fixed assets should be revalued only where the entity adopts a policy of **42** **revaluation. Where such a policy is adopted then it should be applied to individual classes of tangible fixed assets (in accordance with paragraph 61), but need not be applied to all classes of tangible fixed assets held by the entity.**

Frequency

Where a tangible fixed asset is subject to a policy of revaluation* its carrying amount **43** **should be its current value as at the balance sheet date.**

The FRS does not insist on annual revaluations, although the objective of a reva- **44** luation policy is to reflect current values as at the balance sheet date. Paragraphs 45-52 outline the procedures to be adopted in order to satisfy the requirements of paragraph 43, although more frequent valuations may be undertaken where appropriate. However, for cost/benefit reasons, the details specified in paragraphs 45-52 may not be appropriate for charities and other not-for-profit and public sector organisations adopting a revaluation policy, in which case alternative approaches may be acceptable. Generally, these approaches will be addressed in the relevant sector-specific guidance and SORPs.

Where properties are revalued the requirements of paragraph 43 will be met by a full **45** valuation at least every five years and an interim valuation in year 3. Interim valuations in years 1, 2 and 4 should be carried out where it is likely that there has been a material change in value.

Alternatively, for portfolios of non-specialised properties, a full valuation may be **46** performed on a rolling basis designed to cover all the properties over a five-year

*The term 'revaluation' does not encompass either the write-down of the carrying amount of a tangible fixed asset held at historical cost for an impairment in accordance with FRS 11, or determination of the cost of an asset acquired as a result of a business combination stated at its fair value at the date of acquisition, in accordance with FRS 7 'Fair Values in Acquisition Accounting', or, for charities, the initial measurement at current value of a donated tangible fixed asset in accordance with paragraph 17.

cycle, together with an interim valuation on the remaining four-fifths of the portfolio where it is likely that there has been a material change in value. This approach is appropriate only where the property portfolio held by the entity either:

(a)   consists of a number of broadly similar properties whose characteristics are such that their values are likely to be affected by the same market factors; or

(b)   can be divided on a continuing basis into five groups of a broadly similar spread.

47   A full valuation of a property normally involves, inter alia, the following:

(a)   detailed inspection of the interior and exterior of the property (on an initial valuation this will involve detailed measurement of floor space etc, but this would need to be reperformed in future full valuations only if there was evidence of a physical change to the buildings);

(b)   inspection of the locality;

(c)   enquiries of the local planning and similar authorities;

(d)   enquiries of the entity or its solicitors; and

(e)   research into market transactions in similar properties, identification of market trends, and the application of these to determine the value of the property under consideration.

48   A full valuation of a property is conducted by either:

(a)   a qualified external valuer; or

(b)   a qualified internal valuer, provided that the valuation has been subject to review by a qualified external valuer. The review involves the valuation of a sample of the entity's properties by the external valuer and comparison with the internal valuer's figures leading to expression of opinion on the overall accuracy of the valuation, based upon analysis of this sample. The external valuer must be satisfied that the sample represents a genuine cross-section of the entity's portfolio.

49   An interim valuation of a property is conducted by a qualified (external or internal) valuer and consists of:

(a)   research into market transactions in similar properties, identification of market trends, and the application of these to determine the value of the property under consideration (as in paragraph 47(e));

(b)   confirmation that there have been no changes of significance to the physical buildings, the legal rights, or local planning considerations; and

(c)   an inspection of the property or the locality by the valuer to the extent that this is regarded as professionally necessary, having regard to all the circumstances of the case, including recent changes to the property or the locality and the date on which the valuer previously inspected the property.

50   For certain tangible fixed assets other than properties, for example company cars, there may be an active second-hand market for the asset, or appropriate indices may exist, such that the entity's directors can establish the asset's value with reasonable reliability. In such cases it may be unnecessary to use the services of a qualified valuer and the valuation should instead be updated annually by the directors. Otherwise, the valuation should be performed by a qualified valuer at least every five years, with an update in year 3, also performed by a qualified valuer. In addition, the valuation should be updated in the intervening years where it is likely that there has been a material change in value. If a qualified internal valuer is used for the five-yearly valuation, the valuation should be subject to review by a qualified external valuer.

For an index to be appropriate for use by the directors in valuing a tangible fixed **51** asset other than property, the index table will:

(a) be appropriate to the class of asset to which it is to be applied, as well as to the asset's location and condition, and take into account technological change; and
(b) have a proven record of regular publication and use and be expected to be available in the foreseeable future.

As explained in paragraphs 45, 46 and 50, valuations are to be updated where it is **52** likely that there has been a material change in value. A material change in value is a change in value that would reasonably influence the decisions of a user of the accounts. In assessing whether a material change in value is likely, the combined impact of all relevant factors (eg physical deterioration in the property, general movements in market prices in the area etc) should be considered.

Valuation basis

The following valuation bases should be used for revalued properties that are not **53**
impaired:

(a) **non-specialised properties should be valued on the basis of existing use value (EUV),* with the addition of notional directly attributable acquisition costs where material. Where the open market value (OMV) is materially different from EUV, the OMV and the reasons for the difference should be disclosed in the notes to the accounts.**
(b) **specialised properties should be valued on the basis of depreciated replacement cost.**
(c) **properties surplus to an entity's requirements should be valued on the basis of OMV, with expected directly attributable selling costs deducted where material.**

Where there is an indication of impairment, an impairment review should be per- **54** formed in accordance with FRS 11. The asset should be recorded at the lower of the revalued amount, determined in accordance with the above paragraph, and reco- verable amount (which is the higher of net realisable value† and value in use).

Notional directly attributable acquisition costs includes normal dealing costs, such as **55** professional fees, non-recoverable taxes and duties. It does not include expenditure incurred with the objective of enhancing the site value, such as site improvements, costs involved in obtaining planning consent, the cost of site preparation and clearance, or other costs that would already be reflected in EUV. For practical purposes, where notional acquisition costs (or expected selling costs for properties surplus to requirements) are not material they may be ignored.

Certain types of non-specialised properties are bought and sold, and therefore **56** valued, as businesses. The EUV of a property valued as an operational entity is determined by having regard to trading potential, but excludes personal goodwill that has been created in the business by the present owner or management and is not expected to remain with the business in the event of the property being sold.

Some entities make structural changes to their properties or include special fittings **57** within their properties in order to meet the particular needs of their individual businesses

*In the case of registered social landlords the valuation of non-specialised properties is based on Existing Use Value for Social Housing as defined in the RICS Appraisal and Valuation Manual.

†As the revalued amount of a tangible fixed asset is often close to its net realisable value, any further con- sideration of impairment is not generally necessary.

(for example specialised shop fronts on a retail unit). These structural changes and specialised fittings are referred to as 'adaptation works' and have a low or nil market value owing to their specialised nature. In such cases, the adaptation works and shell of the property (ie the property in its state before adaptation) may be treated separately,* with only the shell of the property revalued using EUV. In such a case, the adaptation works are held at depreciated replacement cost or depreciated historical cost.

58   Specialised properties, where a market value is not available, are valued using depreciated replacement cost. The objective of depreciated replacement cost is to make a realistic estimate of the current cost of constructing an asset that has the same service potential as the existing asset.

59   **Tangible fixed assets other than properties should be valued using market value, where possible. Where market value is not obtainable, assets should be valued on the basis of depreciated replacement cost.†**

60   For tangible fixed assets other than property that are used in the business, notional directly attributable acquisition costs should be added to market value where material. For other tangible fixed assets that are surplus to requirements, expected selling costs should be deducted if material. Where market value is not obtainable, depreciated replacement cost, which provides a realistic estimate of the value attributable to the remaining service potential of the total useful economic life of the asset, should be used, with the assistance of a qualified valuer.

Class of assets

61   **Where a tangible fixed asset is revalued all tangible fixed assets of the same class should be revalued. In those rare cases where it is impossible to obtain a reliable valuation of an asset held outside the UK or the Republic of Ireland the asset may be excluded from the class of assets for the purposes of this paragraph. However, the carrying amount of the tangible fixed asset and the fact that it has not been revalued must be stated.**

62   The separate classes of tangible fixed assets that are shown in the formats in companies legislation are:

(a)   land and buildings;
(b)   plant and machinery; and
(c)   fixtures, fittings, tools and equipment.‡

These are broad classes. For the purposes of valuation, entities may, within reason, adopt other, narrower classes that meet the definition of a class of tangible fixed assets and are appropriate to their business. For example, land and buildings may be split into specialised properties, non-specialised properties and short leasehold properties. The disclosures required by paragraphs 74 and 100 should be given for each class of asset adopted by an entity for revaluation purposes.

In accordance with the RICS Appraisal and Valuation Manual, Practice Statement 12.4.

†*In accordance with guidance on the 'Value of Plant and Machinery to the Business' set out in Practice Statement 4 in the RICS Appraisal and Valuation Manual. The definition of Value of Plant and Machinery to the Business is reproduced in Appendix 1.*

‡*In Great Britain, the Companies Act 1985, Schedule 4, Part I.*
In Northern Ireland, the Companies (Northern Ireland) Order 1986, Schedule 4, Part I.
In the Republic of Ireland, the Companies (Amendment) Act 1986, section 4 and Schedule, Part I.

Reporting gains and losses on revaluation

Revaluation gains should be recognised in the profit and loss account only to the extent   **63**
(after adjusting for subsequent depreciation) that they reverse revaluation losses on the
same asset that were previously recognised in the profit and loss account. All other
revaluation gains should be recognised in the statement of total recognised gains and
losses.

Where a revaluation gain reverses a revaluation loss that was previously recognised   **64**
in the profit and loss account, the gain recognised in the profit and loss account is
reduced by the amount of depreciation that would have been charged had the loss
previously taken to the profit and loss account not been recognised in the first place.
This is to achieve the same overall effect that would have been reached had the
original downward revaluation reflected in the profit and loss account not occurred.

All revaluation losses that are caused by a clear consumption of economic benefits   **65**
should be recognised in the profit and loss account. Other revaluation losses should be
recognised:

(a)   **in the statement of total recognised gains and losses until the carrying amount**
       reaches its depreciated historical cost; and
(b)   **thereafter, in the profit and loss account unless it can be demonstrated that the**
       recoverable amount of the asset is greater than its revalued amount, in which case
       the loss should be recognised in the statement of total recognised gains and losses
       to the extent that the recoverable amount of the asset is greater than its revalued
       amount.

For the purposes of paragraph 65(b), the recoverable amount of an asset should be   **66**
calculated in accordance with the requirements of FRS 11.

In determining in which performance statement gains and losses on revaluation should   **67**
be recognised, material gains and losses on individual assets in a class of asset should
not be aggregated.

A downward revaluation may comprise, at least in part, an impairment loss. When it   **68**
is obvious that there has been a consumption of economic benefits (eg physical
damage or a deterioration in the quality of the service provided by the asset), the
asset is clearly impaired and the loss recognised in the profit and loss account, as an
operating cost similar to depreciation.

Other revaluation losses may be due in part to a general fall in prices (eg a general   **69**
slump in the property market) and in part to a consumption of economic benefits.
Unless there is evidence to the contrary, it is assumed that the fall in value from the
asset's previous carrying amount to depreciated historical cost is due to a general fall
in prices (which is recognised in the statement of total recognised gains and losses, as
a valuation adjustment) and the fall in value from depreciated historical cost to the
revalued amount is due to a consumption of economic benefits (and therefore
recognised in the profit and loss account).

However, where it can be demonstrated that recoverable amount is greater than the   **70**
revalued amount, the difference between recoverable amount and the revalued
amount is clearly not an impairment and should therefore be recognised in the
statement of total recognised gains and losses as a valuation adjustment, rather than
the profit and loss account.

71   **Paragraphs 63-70 do not apply to assets held by insurance companies and insurance groups (including assets of the long-term business), as part of their insurance operations, where revaluation changes are included in the profit and loss account.**

Example – Reporting revaluation gains and losses

Assumptions

A non-specialised property costs £1 million and has a useful life of 10 years and no residual value. It is depreciated on a straight-line basis and revalued annually. The entity has a policy of calculating depreciation based on the opening book amount. At the end of years 1 and 2 the asset has an EUV of £1,080,000 and £700,000 respectively. At the end of year 2, the recoverable amount of the asset is £760,000 and its depreciated historical cost is £800,000. There is no obvious consumption of economic benefits in year 2, other than that accounted for through the depreciation charge.

Accounting treatment under modified historical cost

	Year 1	Year 2
	£000	£000
Opening book amount	1,000	1,080
Depreciation	(100)	(120)*
Adjusted book amount	900	960
Revaluation gain (loss)	180	(220)
• recognised in the STRGL		
• recognised in the profit and loss account	–	(40)
Closing book amount	1,080	700

In year 1, after depreciation of £100,000, a revaluation gain of £180,000 is recognised in the statement of total recognised gains and losses, in accordance with paragraph 63.

In year 2, after a depreciation charge of £120,000, the revaluation loss on the property is £260,000. According to paragraph 65, where there is not a clear consumption of economic benefits, revaluation losses should be recognised in the statement of total recognised gains and losses until the carrying amount reaches its depreciated historical cost. Therefore, the fall in value from the adjusted book amount (£960,000) to depreciated historical cost (£800,000) of £160,000 is recognised in the statement of total recognised gains and losses.

The rest of the revaluation loss, £100,000 (ie the fall in value from depreciated historical cost (£800,000) to the revalued amount (£700,000)), should be recognised in the profit and loss account, unless it can be demonstrated that recoverable amount is greater than the revalued amount. In this case, recoverable amount of £760,000 is greater than the revalued amount of £700,000 by £60,000. Therefore £60,000 of the revaluation loss is recognised in the statement of total recognised gains and losses, rather than the profit and loss account – giving rise to a total revaluation loss of £220,000 (£60,000 + £160,000) that is recognised in the statement of total recognised gains and losses. The remaining loss (representing the fall in value from depreciated historical cost of £800,000 to recoverable amount of £760,000) of £40,000 is recognised in the profit and loss account.

---

*As the remaining useful economic life of the asset is nine years, the depreciation charge in year 2 is 1/9th of the opening book amount (£1,080,000/9 = £120,000).

Reporting gains and losses on disposal

The profit or loss on the disposal of a tangible fixed asset should be accounted for in the **72** profit and loss account of the period in which the disposal occurs as the difference between the net sale proceeds and the carrying amount, whether carried at historical cost (less any provisions made) or at a valuation. Profits or losses on the disposal of fixed assets should be shown in accordance with FRS 3 'Reporting Financial Performance'.

Where an asset (or a component of an asset) is replaced, its carrying amount is **73** removed from the balance sheet (by eliminating its cost (or revalued amount) and related accumulated depreciation) and the resulting gain or loss on disposal is recorded in accordance with paragraph 72. For example, a new tangible fixed asset may be acquired from insurance proceeds when a previously held tangible fixed asset has been lost or destroyed. In such cases the lost or destroyed asset is removed from the balance sheet and the resulting gain or loss on disposal (being the difference between the carrying amount and the insurance proceeds) is recognised. The replacement asset is recorded at its cost.

Disclosures

In addition to the disclosures required by paragraphs 53(a), 61 and 72, where any class **74** of tangible fixed assets of an entity has been revalued the following information should be disclosed in each reporting period:

(a) for each class of revalued assets:

   (i)   the name and qualifications of the valuer(s) or the valuer's organisation and a description of its nature;

   (ii) the basis or bases of valuation (including whether notional directly attributable acquisition costs have been included or expected selling costs deducted);

   (iii) the date and amounts of the valuations;

   (iv) where historical cost records are available, the carrying amount that would have been included in the financial statements had the tangible fixed assets been carried at historical cost less depreciation;

   (v)   whether the person(s) carrying out the valuation is (are) internal or external to the entity;

   (vi) where the directors are not aware of any material change in value and therefore the valuation(s) have not been updated, as described in paragraphs 45, 46 and 50, a statement to that effect; and

   (vii) where the valuation has not been updated, or is not a full valuation, the date of the last full valuation.

(b) in addition, for revalued properties:

   (i)   where properties have been valued as fully-equipped operational entities having regard to their trading potential, a statement to that effect and the carrying amount of those properties; and

   (ii) the total amount of notional directly attributable acquisition costs (or the total amount of expected selling costs deducted), included in the carrying amount, where material.

Other professional bodies may require disclosures in the financial statements in **75** addition to the above disclosures. For example, the RICS requires confirmation in a published document containing a reference to a valuation report that the valuation has been made in accordance with the RICS *Appraisal and Valuation Manual* or a (named) alternative pursuant to Practice Statement 1.2.2, or the extent of and reason(s) for departure therefrom.

76   In addition, companies legislation* requires disclosure, in the directors' report, of the difference, with such precision as is practicable, between the carrying amount and market value of interests in land,† where, in the opinion of the directors, it is of such significance that it needs to be drawn to the attention of the members of the entity.

DEPRECIATION

Depreciable amount

77   **The depreciable amount of a tangible fixed asset should be allocated on a systematic basis over its useful economic life. The depreciation method used should reflect as fairly as possible the pattern in which the asset's economic benefits are consumed by the entity. The depreciation charge for each period should be recognised as an expense in the profit and loss account unless it is permitted to be included in the carrying amount of another asset.**

78   The fundamental objective of depreciation is to reflect in operating profit the cost of use of the tangible fixed assets (ie amount of economic benefits consumed) in the period. This requires a charge to operating profit even if the asset has risen in value or been revalued.

79   Where an asset has been revalued the current period's depreciation charge is based on the revalued amount and the remaining useful economic life. Ideally, the average value of the asset for the period should be used to calculate the depreciation charge. In practice, however, either the opening or closing balance may be used instead, provided that it is used consistently each period.

80   The economic benefits embodied in a tangible fixed asset are consumed by the entity principally through the use of the asset. However, other factors often also result in the diminution of the economic benefits that might have been expected to be available from the asset. Consequently, all the following factors need to be considered in determining the useful economic life, residual value and depreciation method of an asset:

- the expected usage of the asset by the entity, assessed by reference to the asset's expected capacity or physical output
- the expected physical deterioration of the asset through use or effluxion of time; this will depend upon the repair and maintenance programme of the entity both when the asset is in use and when it is idle
- economic or technological obsolescence, for example arising from changes or improvements in production, or a change in the market demand for the product or service output of that asset

**In Great Britain, the Companies Act 1985, Schedule 7, paragraph 1(2).*
In Northern Ireland, the Companies (Northern Ireland) Order 1986, Schedule 7, paragraph 1(2).
In the Republic of Ireland, the Companies Act 1963, section 158. (Note: this section includes a general requirement for the directors' report to deal with the state of affairs of the company; there is no specific requirement as in the UK references.)

†*In Great Britain, Schedule 1 to the Interpretation Act 1987 states that '"Land" includes buildings and other structures, land covered with water, and any estate, interest, easement, servitude or right in or over land'.*
In Northern Ireland, section 45 (i)(a) of the Interpretation Act (Northern Ireland) 1954 states that '(a) "Land" shall include- (i) messuages, tenements and hereditaments of any tenure; (ii) land covered by water; (iii) any estate in land or water; and (iv) houses or other buildings or structures whatsoever;'.

- legal or similar limits on the use of the asset, such as the expiry dates of related leases.

A variety of methods can be used to allocate the depreciable amount of a tangible **81** fixed asset on a systematic basis over its useful economic life. The method chosen should result in a depreciation charge throughout the asset's useful economic life and not just towards the end of its useful economic life or when the asset is falling in value. Two of the more common methods are:

(a) Straight-line – Here it is assumed that equal amounts of the asset's economic benefits are consumed in each year of the asset's estimated useful economic life. Therefore the asset is written off in equal instalments over its estimated useful economic life.

(b) Reducing balance – This method more closely reflects the pattern of consumption of the economic benefits of assets that clearly provide greater benefits when new than as they become older – perhaps as a result of general wear causing them to become more prone to breakdown, or less capable of producing a high-quality product, or because they will necessarily be less technologically advanced than the latest model.

Where the pattern of consumption of an asset's economic benefits is uncertain, a straight-line method of depreciation is usually adopted.

A change from one method of providing depreciation to another is permissible only on **82** **the grounds that the new method will give a fairer presentation of the results and of the financial position. Such a change does not, however, constitute a change of accounting policy; the carrying amount of the tangible fixed asset is depreciated using the revised method over the remaining useful economic life, beginning in the period in which the change is made.**

Where the tangible fixed asset comprises two or more major components with sub- **83** **stantially different useful economic lives, each component should be accounted for separately for depreciation purposes and depreciated over its individual useful economic life.**

Land and buildings are separable components and are dealt with separately for **84** accounting purposes, even when they are acquired together. With certain exceptions, such as sites used for extractive purposes or landfill, land has an unlimited life and therefore is not depreciated. Buildings have a limited life and therefore are depreciated. An increase in the existing use value of the land on which a building stands does not affect the determination of the useful economic life or residual value of the building. Another example of separable components that may have substantially different useful economic lives is the structure of a building and items within the structure such as general fittings.

It would not be appropriate, however, to treat the trading potential associated with a **85** property that is valued as an operational entity, such as a public house or hotel, as a separate component, where the value and life of any such trading potential is inherently inseparable from that of the property.

Subsequent expenditure on a tangible fixed asset that maintains or enhances the pre- **86** **viously assessed standard of performance of the asset does not negate the need to charge depreciation.**

In calculating the useful economic life of an asset it is assumed that subsequent **87** expenditure will be undertaken to maintain the previously assessed standard of performance of the asset (for example the cost of servicing or routine overhauling of plant and equipment). Without such expenditure the depreciation expense would be increased because the useful economic life or residual value of the asset would be reduced. This type of expenditure is recognised as an expense when incurred in accordance with paragraph 34.

88   In addition, subsequent expenditure may be undertaken that results in an enhancement of the economic benefits of the asset in excess of the previously assessed standard of performance, or the restoration or replacement of a component of the asset that has been separately depreciated, or the restoration of the economic benefits of a tangible fixed asset where the cost of an overhaul or inspection of the tangible fixed asset has been reflected in previous depreciation. This type of expenditure may result in an extension of the useful economic life of the asset, but cannot extend the useful economic life of the asset indefinitely and does not negate the need to charge depreciation. In accordance with paragraph 36 the subsequent expenditure is capitalised as it is incurred and depreciated over the asset's or the component's useful economic life, or the period to the next major overhaul or inspection, as appropriate.

89   **Tangible fixed assets, other than non-depreciable land, should be reviewed for impairment, in accordance with FRS 11, at the end of each reporting period when either:**

   (a) **no depreciation charge is made on the grounds that it would be immaterial (either because of the length of the estimated remaining useful economic life or because the estimated residual value of the tangible fixed asset is not materially different from the carrying amount of the asset); or**

   (b) **the estimated remaining useful economic life of the tangible fixed asset exceeds 50 years.**

90   For tangible fixed assets other than non-depreciable land, the only grounds for not charging depreciation are that the depreciation charge and accumulated depreciation are immaterial. The depreciation charge and accumulated depreciation are immaterial if they would not reasonably influence the decisions of a user of the accounts.

91   An entity must be able to justify that the uncharged depreciation is not material in aggregate as well as for each tangible fixed asset. Depreciation may be immaterial because of very long useful economic lives or high residual values (or both). A high residual value will reflect the remaining economic value of the asset at the end of its useful economic life to the entity. These conditions may occur when:

   (a) the entity has a policy and practice of regular maintenance and repair (charges for which are recognised in the profit and loss account) such that the asset is kept to its previously assessed standard of performance; and

   (b) the asset is unlikely to suffer from economic or technological obsolescence (eg due to potential changes in demand in the market following changes in fashion); and

   (c) where estimated residual values are material:

        (i)   the entity has a policy and practice of disposing of similar assets well before the end of their economic lives; and

        (ii) the disposal proceeds of similar assets (after excluding the effect of price changes since the date of acquisition or last revaluation) have not been materially less than their carrying amounts.

92   Where it is not reasonably practicable to perform impairment reviews on an individual asset basis, they should be performed for groups of assets, as part of income-generating units, in accordance with FRS 11. After the first period the reviews need only be updated. If expectations of future cash flows and discount rates have not

changed significantly, the updating procedure will be relatively quick to perform. If there have been no adverse changes in the key assumptions and variables, or if the estimated recoverable amount was previously substantially in excess of the carrying amount, it may even be possible to ascertain immediately that the asset or income-generating unit is not impaired.

Review of useful economic life and residual value

The useful economic life of a tangible fixed asset should be reviewed at the end of each reporting period and revised if expectations are significantly different from previous estimates. If a useful economic life is revised, the carrying amount of the tangible fixed asset at the date of revision should be depreciated over the revised remaining useful economic life.   93

If a tangible fixed asset is carried in the balance sheet at a revaluation (particularly if valued using depreciated replacement cost), a reassessment of useful economic life may necessitate a revaluation of the asset, in accordance with paragraphs 43, 45, 46 and 50. The revalued amount should be depreciated over the revised useful economic life.   94

Where the residual value is material it should be reviewed at the end of each reporting period to take account of reasonably expected technological changes based on prices prevailing at the date of acquisition (or revaluation). A change in its estimated residual value should be accounted for prospectively over the asset's remaining useful economic life, except to the extent that the asset has been impaired at the balance sheet date.   95

The reassessed residual value is, where practicable, restated in terms of the price level that existed when the asset was purchased (or revalued). Where such a restatement is not practicable, the residual value is restated in terms of current values only where the residual value at current prices is below the original estimate of residual value. Events or changes in circumstances that cause the residual value to fall may also be indicative of an impairment of the asset (ie when the asset's recoverable amount falls below its carrying amount), in which case an impairment review should be performed in accordance with FRS 11.   96

Renewals accounting

Definable major assets or components within an infrastructure system or network with determinable finite lives should be treated separately and depreciated over their useful economic lives. For the remaining tangible fixed assets within the system or network ('the infrastructure asset'), renewals accounting (as outlined in paragraph 98) may be used as a method of estimating depreciation in the following circumstances: 97

(a)   the infrastructure asset is a system or network that as a whole is intended to be maintained at a specified level of service potential by the continuing replacement and refurbishment of its components; and

(b)   the level of annual expenditure required to maintain the operating capacity (or service capability) of the infrastructure asset is calculated from an asset management plan that is certified by a person who is appropriately qualified and independent; and

(c)   the system or network is in a mature or steady state.

Where renewals accounting is adopted, the level of annual expenditure required to maintain the operating capacity of the infrastructure asset is treated as the depreciation charged for the period and is deducted from the carrying amount of the asset (as part of   98

accumulated depreciation). Actual expenditure is capitalised (as part of the cost of the asset) as incurred.

99   In the above circumstances, it is appropriate to treat the infrastructure asset as a single network of systems (ie one asset, except for definable major components with determinable finite lives), rather than as a number of individual assets. Evidence that a system or network is in a mature and steady state is provided when the annual cost of maintaining that system is relatively constant. In addition, attention should be given to removing the carrying amount of that part of the infrastructure asset that is replaced or restored by the subsequent expenditure. If the above treatment of accounting for infrastructure assets is not adopted, then expenditure to maintain the operating capacity of the infrastructure assets would be recognised in accordance with paragraphs 34 and 36, and depreciation calculated in the conventional manner, in accordance with paragraphs 77-96.

Disclosures

100   **The following information should be disclosed separately in the financial statements for each class of tangible fixed assets:**

(a)   **the depreciation methods used;**

(b)   **the useful economic lives or the depreciation rates used;**

(c)   **total depreciation charged for the period;**

(d)   **where material, the financial effect of a change during the period in either the estimate of useful economic lives (made in accordance with paragraph 93) or the estimate of residual values (made in accordance with paragraph 95);**

(e)   **the cost or revalued amount at the beginning of the financial period and at the balance sheet date;**

(f)   **the cumulative amount of provisions for depreciation or impairment at the beginning of the financial period and at the balance sheet date;**

(g)   **a reconciliation of the movements, separately disclosing additions, disposals, revaluations, transfers, depreciation, impairment losses, and reversals of past impairment losses written back in the financial period; and**

(h)   **the net carrying amount at the beginning of the financial period and at the balance sheet date.**

101   When a tangible fixed asset is revalued, the carrying amount of the asset is restated at its revalued amount. Usually any accumulated depreciation at the date of revaluation is eliminated and the cost or revalued amount of the asset is restated at its revalued amount. Alternatively, where the valuation is calculated on a depreciated replacement cost basis, both the cost or revalued amount and the accumulated depreciation at the date of revaluation may be restated, so that the carrying amount of the asset after revaluation equals its revalued amount.

102   **Where there has been a change in the depreciation method used, the effect, if material, should be disclosed in the period of change. The reason for the change should also be disclosed.**

DATE FROM WHICH EFFECTIVE AND TRANSITIONAL ARRANGEMENTS

103   **The accounting practices set out in the FRS should be regarded as standard in respect of financial statements relating to accounting periods ending on or after 23 March 2000. Earlier adoption is encouraged.**

Where, on implementation of the FRS for the first time, an entity does not adopt a policy **104** of revaluation, but the carrying amount of its tangible fixed assets reflects previous revaluations, it may:

(a) retain the book amounts (subject to the requirement to test the assets for impairment in accordance with FRS 11 where there is an indication that an impairment may have occurred). In these circumstances the entity should disclose the fact that the transitional provisions of the FRS are being followed and that the valuation has not been updated and give the date of the last revaluation; or

(b) restate the carrying amount of the tangible fixed assets to historical cost (less restated accumulated depreciation), as a change in accounting policy.

The transitional arrangement set out in paragraph 104(a) is available only on the first **105** application of the FRS.

Except as provided for in paragraph 108, revisions to the useful economic lives and **106** residual values of tangible fixed assets recognised on adoption of the FRS are not the result of a change in accounting policy and should be treated in accordance with paragraphs 93-96 and not as prior period adjustments.*

Revisions to the useful economic lives or residual values of tangible fixed assets may **107** result in the depreciation of tangible fixed assets that were previously not depreciated by the entity on the grounds of immateriality. In such cases, the carrying amounts of the tangible fixed assets should be depreciated prospectively over the remaining useful economic lives of the assets.

Where, on adoption of the FRS, entities separate tangible fixed assets into different **108** components with significantly different useful economic lives for depreciation purposes, in accordance with paragraphs 36-41 and 83-85, the changes should be dealt with as prior period adjustments, as a change in accounting policy.†

AMENDMENT TO SSAP 19 AND WITHDRAWAL OF SSAP 12

Paragraph 9 of SSAP 19 'Accounting for investment properties' is deleted. **109**

The FRS supersedes SSAP 12 'Accounting for depreciation'. **110**

Adoption of FRS 15 by the Board

Financial Reporting Standard 15 - 'Tangible Fixed Assets' was approved for issue by the ten members of the Accounting Standards Board.

**Editor's note:* See also UITF Abstract 23 'Application of the transitional rules in FRS 15'.

†*In accordance with FRS 3 and FRS 18.*

Appendix I
RICS definitions*

The following definitions have been extracted from the *Appraisal and Valuation Manual* published by RICS Books and are reproduced with the permission of the Royal Institution of Chartered Surveyors, which owns the copyright.

Specialised properties:-

"those which, due to their specialised nature, are rarely, if ever, sold on the open market for single occupation for a continuation of their existing use, except as part of a sale of the business in occupation. Their specialised nature may arise from the construction, arrangement, size or location of the property, or a combination of these factors, or may be due to the nature of the plant and machinery and items of equipment which the buildings are designed to house, or the function, or the purpose for which the buildings are provided. Examples of specialised properties, which are usually valued on the Depreciated Replacement Cost (DRC) basis, are:

(a)   oil refineries and chemical works where, usually, the buildings are no more than housings or cladding for highly specialised plant;

(b)   power stations and dock installations where the buildings and site engineering works are related directly to the business of the owner, it being highly unlikely that they would have a value to anyone other than a company acquiring the undertaking;

(c)   properties of such construction, arrangement, size or specification that there would be no market (for a sale to a single owner occupier for the continuation of existing use) for those buildings;

(d)   standard properties in particular geographical areas and remote from main business centres, located there for operational or business reasons, which are of such an abnormal size for that district, that there would be no market for such buildings there;

(e)   schools, colleges, universities and research establishments where there is no competing market demand from other organisations using these types of property in the locality;

(f)   hospitals, other specialised health care premises and leisure centres where there is no competing market demand from other organisations wishing to use these types of property in the locality; and

(g)   museums, libraries, and other similar premises provided by the public sector."

Non-specialised properties:-

"all properties except those coming within the definition of specialised properties. Hence they are those for which there is a general demand, with or without adaptation, and which are commonly bought, sold or leased on the open market for their existing or similar uses, either with vacant possession for single occupation, or (whether tenanted or vacant) as investments or for development. Residential properties, shops, offices, standard industrial and warehouse buildings, public houses, petrol filling stations, and many others, are usually *non-specialised properties*."

*Editor's note: These definitions are no longer current under RICS guidance.

Open market value:-

"An opinion of the best price at which the sale of an interest in property would have been completed unconditionally for cash consideration on the date of valuation, assuming:

(a) a willing seller;
(b) that, prior to the date of valuation, there had been a reasonable period (having regard to the nature of the property and the state of the market) for the proper marketing of the interest, for the agreement of the price and terms and for the completion of the sale;
(c) that the state of the market, level of values and other circumstances were, on any earlier assumed date of exchange of contracts, the same as on the date of valuation;
(d) that no account is taken of any additional bid by a prospective purchaser with a special interest; and
(e) that both parties to the transaction had acted knowledgeably, prudently and without compulsion."

Existing use value:-

"An opinion of the best price at which the sale of an interest in property would have been completed unconditionally for cash consideration on the date of valuation, assuming:

(a) a willing seller;
(b) that, prior to the date of valuation, there had been a reasonable period (having regard to the nature of the property and the state of the market) for the proper marketing of the interest, for the agreement of the price and terms and for the completion of the sale;
(c) that the state of the market, level of values and other circumstances were, on any earlier assumed date of exchange of contracts, the same as on the date of valuation;
(d) that no account is taken of any additional bid by a prospective purchaser with a special interest;
(e) that both parties to the transaction had acted knowledgeably, prudently and without compulsion;
(f) that the property can be used for the foreseeable future only for the existing use; and
(g) that vacant possession is provided on completion of the sale of all parts of the property occupied by the business."

Depreciated replacement cost (of property):-

"The aggregate amount of the value of the land for the existing use or a notional replacement site in the same locality, and the gross replacement cost of the buildings and other site works, from which appropriate deductions may then be made to allow for the age, condition, economic or functional obsolescence, environmental and other relevant factors; all of these might result in the existing property being worth less to the undertaking in occupation than would a new replacement."

Value of plant and machinery to the business:-

"An opinion of the price at which an interest in the plant and machinery utilised in a business would have been transferred at the date of valuation assuming:

(a)   that the plant and machinery will continue in its present uses in the business;

(b)   adequate potential profitability of the business, or continuing viability of the undertaking, both having due regard to the value of the total assets employed and the nature of the operation; and

(c)   that the transfer is part of an arm's length sale of the business wherein both parties acted knowledgeably, prudently and without compulsion."

Appendix II
Note on legal requirements

GREAT BRITAIN

In Great Britain, the statutory requirements relating to accounting for tangible fixed   **1**
assets are set out in the Companies Act 1985. The main requirements that are directly
relevant to tangible fixed assets and the requirements of FRS 15 are set out in Schedules 4 and 4A and are summarised below.

Schedule 4 does not apply to banking and insurance companies or groups.   **2**
Requirements equivalent to those of Schedule 4 are contained in Schedule 9 (for
banking companies and groups) and in Schedule 9A (for insurance companies and
groups).

Initial cost

Paragraph 17 of Schedule 4 requires the amount to be included in respect of any fixed   **3**
asset to be its purchase price or production cost. The purchase price is to be determined by adding to the actual price any expenses incidental to its acquisition
(paragraph 26(1) of Schedule 4). Paragraph 26(2) requires the cost of production of
an asset to comprise the purchase price of raw materials and consumables used and
the amount of costs incurred by the company that are directly attributable to the
production of that asset. In addition, paragraph 26(3) allows the inclusion of:

(a)   indirectly attributable costs incurred by the company relating to the period of
      production; and
(b)   interest on capital borrowed to finance the production of the asset. (However,
      the amount of the interest capitalised is required to be disclosed in the notes to
      the accounts.)

Where there is no record of the purchase price or production cost of any asset of a   **4**
company, paragraph 28 of Schedule 4 requires the asset value to be determined using
the earliest available record of the value of the asset on or after its acquisition or
production by the company. Such earliest available records may also be used where
there are no relevant prices, expenses or costs against which the purchase price may
be determined or where the record of such purchase price cannot be obtained
without unreasonable expense or delay.

Valuation

The alternative accounting rules set out in paragraph 31(2) of Schedule 4 permit   **5**
tangible fixed assets to be included at a market value determined as at the date of
their last valuation or at their current cost.

Where the alternative accounting rules set out in paragraph 31(2) of Schedule 4 are   **6**
adopted by a company the following additional information is required to be
included in the company's accounts:

(a)   the assets revalued and the basis of valuation (paragraph 33(2) of Schedule 4).
(b)   either the comparable amounts determined according to the historical cost
      accounting rules or the differences between those amounts and the revalued
      amounts (paragraph 33(3) of Schedule 4).
(c)   the year and amount of the valuation (paragraph 43(a) of Schedule 4).

(d)   in the case of assets that have been valued during the financial year, the names of the persons who valued them or particulars of their qualifications for doing so and the bases of valuation used by them (paragraph 43(b) of Schedule 4).

Reporting revaluation gains and losses

7   A revaluation gain is required by the FRS to be recognised in the statement of total recognised gains and losses, unless it reverses a previous revaluation loss that has been recognised in the profit and loss account. This requirement is consistent with paragraph 34(1) of Schedule 4, which requires the "amount of any profit" (ie gain) "or loss" calculated under the alternative accounting rules to be "credited to a separate reserve (the revaluation reserve)". The requirement for a revaluation gain to be recognised in the profit and loss account to the extent that it reverses a revaluation loss previously recognised in the profit and loss account is consistent with paragraph 34(3) of Schedule 4, which explicitly authorises transfers to take place between the revaluation reserve and the profit and loss account provided that the relevant amount was previously charged to that account.

8   The FRS requires all revaluation losses that are clearly due to the consumption of economic benefits to be recognised in the profit and loss account. This requirement is consistent with paragraph 19(2) of Schedule 4, which requires provisions for depreciation or permanent diminution in value to be recognised in the profit and loss account.

9   For other revaluation losses where it *can* be demonstrated that the recoverable amount of the asset is greater than its revalued amount, the FRS requires the difference between recoverable amount and revalued amount to be recognised in the statement of total recognised gains and losses. In this situation there has been no diminution in value under paragraph 19(2) of Schedule 4 and therefore the loss can remain in the revaluation reserve in accordance with paragraph 34(1) of Schedule 4.

10   For other revaluation losses where it *cannot* be demonstrated that the recoverable amount of the asset is greater than its revalued amount, an impairment loss arises. Where a fixed asset is impaired, it will always be the case that both the value in use and the net realisable value will be below the carrying amount. In the case of a revalued fixed asset, it would be reasonable to reflect the uncertainty as to the permanence of any impairment by treating it as a reversal of any revaluation previously recognised. Such an impairment would be dealt with through the statement of total recognised gains and losses (ie as a revaluation reserve movement). However, if the impairment results in a carrying amount below depreciated historical cost, then, as in a pure historical cost context, it would be reasonable to treat that part of the impairment as being of a permanent nature and charge it to the profit and loss account.

Depreciation

11   Where a fixed asset has a limited useful economic life, paragraph 18 of Schedule 4 requires its purchase price or production cost less its estimated residual value to be written off systematically over the period of the asset's useful economic life.

12   Paragraph 32(1) of Schedule 4 requires the depreciation of revalued assets to be calculated on the basis of their latest valuations. Paragraph 32(3) allows a company to include under the relevant profit and loss account heading provisions for depreciation for the revalued assets based only on their historical cost, provided that the difference between that and the provision for depreciation calculated on the revalued

amount is shown separately either in the profit and loss account or in the notes. It is unclear, however, whether the whole depreciation charge is required to be recognised in the profit and loss account (see discussion in Appendix IV 'The development of the FRS').

Disclosure requirements

In addition to the disclosures mentioned in paragraph 6 above in connection with the   **13** revaluation of tangible fixed assets, the following disclosures are required:

(a) Paragraph 36 of Schedule 4 requires the disclosure of the accounting policies adopted by a company (including the policies regarding the depreciation and diminution in value of assets).
(b) Paragraph 26(3) requires the disclosure of the amount of interest capitalised, where such a policy is adopted.
(c) Paragraph 42 details the disclosures required of the movement on tangible fixed asset balances for the items under each of the headings for tangible fixed assets set out in the balance sheet formats in Schedule 4, as follows:
    1. Land and buildings
    2. Plant and machinery
    3. Fixtures, fittings, tools and equipment
    4. Payments on account and assets in the course of construction.
(d) Paragraph 1(2) of Schedule 7 requires disclosure, in the directors' report, of the difference, with such precision as is practicable, between the carrying amount and market value of interests in land, where, in the opinion of the directors, it is of such significance that it needs to be drawn to the attention of the members of the entity.

NORTHERN IRELAND

The statutory requirements in Northern Ireland are set out in the Companies   **14** (Northern Ireland) Order 1986. They are identical to and parallel the references in the legislation for Great Britain cited above.

REPUBLIC OF IRELAND

The statutory requirements in the Republic of Ireland that correspond to those cited   **15** above for Great Britain are shown in the following table.

Great Britain	Republic of Ireland
Schedule 4 to the Companies Act 1985:	The Schedule to the Companies (Amendment) Act 1986:
paragraph 17	paragraph 5
paragraph 18	paragraph 6
paragraph 19(2)	paragraph 7(2)
paragraph 26(1), (2) and (3)	paragraph 14(1), (2) and (3)
paragraph 28	paragraph 16
paragraph 31(2)	paragraph 19(2)
paragraph 32(1) and (3)	paragraph 20(1) and (3)
paragraph 33(2) and (3)	paragraph 21(2) and (3)
paragraph 34(1) and (3)	paragraph 22(1) and (4)
paragraph 36	paragraph 24
paragraph 42	paragraph 29
paragraph 43(a) and (b)	paragraph 30(a) and (b)
Schedule 4A to the Companies Act 1985	European Communities (Companies: Group Accounts) Regulations 1992
Schedule 7 to the Companies Act 1985, paragraph 1(2)	The Companies Act 1963, section 158*
Schedule 9 to the Companies Act 1985	European Communities (Credit Institutions: Accounts) Regulations 1992
Schedule 9A to the Companies Act 1985	European Communities (Insurance Undertakings: Accounts) Regulations 1996

*Note: this section includes a general requirement for the directors' report to deal with the state of affairs of the company; there is no specific requirement as in the UK references.

Appendix III
Compliance with international accounting standards

The main requirements for the recognition, measurement and depreciation of tan- 1
gible fixed assets are included in International Accounting Standard (IAS) 16
(revised 1998) 'Property, Plant and Equipment'. In addition, some other relevant
requirements are included in IAS 23 (revised 1993) 'Borrowing Costs'.*

The requirements in the FRS lead to compliance with IAS 16 and the relevant 2
requirements of IAS 23 in all main respects, except as discussed below.

Fair/current value

Both the FRS and IAS 16 require that, where a policy of revaluation is adopted, the 3
revalued tangible fixed assets should be carried at current values. IAS 16 uses the
term 'fair value' and states that the fair value of land and buildings, plant and
equipment is usually their market value, but where there is no evidence of market
value depreciated replacement cost should be used instead.

As explained in Appendix IV 'The development of the FRS', the valuation require- 4
ments in the FRS are based on the value to the business model and therefore define
current value as the lower of replacement cost and recoverable amount. The Board
believes that this gives a more precise and clearer indication of the amount at which
the asset should be revalued and therefore prefers this terminology to the use of the
term 'fair value'.

Accordingly, the FRS requires non-specialised properties to be valued at existing use 5
value, with the addition of notional directly attributable acquisition costs, if material,
to reflect replacement cost. Similarly, specialised properties should be valued using
depreciated replacement cost. However, properties surplus to requirements should be
valued at net realisable value – ie open market value less expected selling costs, if
material. Similar valuation bases are required for tangible fixed assets other than
property. IAS 16 is silent in respect of whether valuations should be on an existing
use basis and whether material direct acquisition or selling costs should be added/
deducted.

Revaluation gains and losses

The requirements of IAS 16 differ from those in the FRS in two main respects: 6

* To be consistent with FRS 11 'Impairment of Fixed Assets and Goodwill', the FRS
  requires revaluation losses that are clearly caused by the consumption of economic benefits to be recognised in the profit and loss account (paragraph 65). The
  Board believes that such losses are operating costs similar to depreciation and
  should be treated as such by recognition in the profit and loss account. IAS 16
  does not have a similar requirement.
* IAS 16 permits only those losses that reverse revaluation gains that were previously recognised in the statement of total recognised gains and losses to be
  recognised in that statement. The FRS requires other losses to be recognised in the
  statement of total recognised gains and losses to the extent that the asset's

**Editor's note: IAS 16 has been revised, with a new version of the standard issued in December 2003. There are a
number of detailed changes, but one major change is that the IAS no longer has separate principles for initial
measurement of costs and subsequent expenditure.*

recoverable amount is greater than its revalued amount. The Board believes that such losses, which have been demonstrated not to be impairments, are in the nature of losses caused by a general fall in prices.

Depreciation

7   Both the FRS and IAS 16 state that subsequent expenditure does not negate the need for depreciation. However, the FRS takes this one step further by also requiring impairment reviews at the end of each reporting period where depreciation is not charged on the basis of immateriality or where the remaining useful economic life is estimated to be greater than 50 years.

Disclosures

8   IAS 16 requires the following additional disclosures:

(a)   in general:
  - property, plant and equipment pledged as security for liabilities,* and the existence and amounts of restrictions on title
  - the amount of expenditures on account of property, plant and equipment in the course of construction
  - the amount of commitments for the acquisition of property, plant and equipment.*

(b)   in respect of each class of property, plant and equipment:
  - the measurement bases used for determining the gross carrying amount

(c)   in respect of each revalued class of property, plant and equipment:
  - the nature of any indices used to determine replacement cost
  - the revaluation surplus,† indicating the movement for the period and any restrictions on the distribution of the balance to shareholders.

These disclosures are required by companies legislation, as follows:
in Great Britain, the Companies Act 1985, Schedule 4, paragraphs 48(4), 50(1), 50(3) and 50(5).
in Northern Ireland, the Companies (Northern Ireland) Order 1986, Schedule 4, paragraphs 48(4), 50(1), 50(3) and 50(5).
in the Republic of Ireland, the Companies (Amendment) Act 1986, Schedule, paragraphs 34(1), 36(1), 36(3) and 36(6).

†*These disclosures are required by companies legislation, as follows:*
in Great Britain, the Companies Act 1985, Schedule 4, paragraphs 34(2), 42(1) and 46(1).
in Northern Ireland, the Companies (Northern Ireland) Order 1986, Schedule 4, paragraphs 34(2), 42(1) and 46(1).
in the Republic of Ireland, the Companies (Amendment) Act 1986, Schedule, paragraphs 22(3), 29(1) and 32(1).

Appendix IV
The development of the FRS

The need for a standard

Many of the principles for determining the cost of tangible fixed assets when they are   **1**
initially recognised and measured are well known and accepted. However, as no
previous accounting standard dealt with these issues, differences in practice have
arisen.

Many entities adopted a policy of valuing specific tangible fixed assets as permitted   **2**
by the alternative accounting rules in companies legislation.* Previous practices
allowed valuations of assets to be made at an entity's discretion and there was no
requirement for valuations to be updated in subsequent accounting periods.
Replacing the historical cost of an asset with a valuation provides more relevant
information to the user of the accounts. Nevertheless, the relevance of this information diminishes over time as it no longer reflects the current value of the tangible
fixed asset. Finally, an entity could revalue some but not all of its tangible fixed
assets, with little constraint imposed by the need to treat similar assets consistently.
As a result, it was often difficult to understand the amounts attributable to the
entity's assets and accordingly to make comparisons from year to year and between
similar entities.

In respect of depreciation, SSAP 12 'Accounting for depreciation', which this FRS   **3**
supersedes, was generally regarded as broadly satisfactory. However, it became
apparent that some of the requirements of SSAP 12 required clarification. In particular, clarification was sought on the accounting treatment adopted by a number of
entities that did not depreciate certain assets, most commonly properties, on the
grounds that they were either increasing in value or being maintained or refurbished
regularly.

The FRS addresses these concerns by specifying accounting rules for the initial   **4**
recognition, valuation and depreciation of tangible fixed assets, other than investment properties. In developing the FRS, the Board has considered the comments on
its initial proposals which were set out in the Discussion Paper 'Measurement of
Tangible Fixed Assets' and on its subsequent proposals in FRED 17 'Measurement of
Tangible Fixed Assets'.

Initial cost

Decommissioning costs

In accordance with FRS 12 'Provisions, Contingent Liabilities and Contingent Assets'   **5**
a provision may be recognised for a present obligation in respect of decommissioning
costs: such costs may include those relating to the dismantling and removal of a
facility and the restoration of a site. Providing for these costs reflects the obligation
of the entity that arises as a consequence of the construction or acquisition of the
asset, and which cannot be avoided by the entity's future actions.

This FRS states that these costs, to the extent that they qualify for recognition as a   **6**
provision under FRS 12, should be capitalised as a directly attributable cost of the

---

*For example 65 per cent of companies included in the Company Reporting database carried revalued tangible
fixed assets in their accounts. However, Company Reporting noted that half of these companies did not have any
valuations that were more recent than five years old. (Company Reporting No 80 February 1997).

relevant asset (even though they may not be paid until the end of the asset's life). Treating these costs as part of the cost of the relevant asset acknowledges that the entity has undertaken the obligation to meet these costs in order to derive the benefits of the service potential provided by the asset. This has the consequence that these costs are charged to the profit and loss account as depreciation over the asset's life.

Donated tangible fixed assets

7   Charities often receive gifts and donations of assets. Donated tangible fixed assets do not have a cost to the charity, and therefore their initial measurement should be their current value at the date of donation. As this is a particular issue for charities, apart from the above key principle, the FRS leaves more detailed guidance to the relevant sector-specific guidance and Statements of Recommended Practice (SORPs).

Inalienable, historic and similar assets

8   The Board believes that, in principle, inalienable,* historic and similar tangible fixed assets should be recognised in the balance sheet, to reflect that:

(a)   the assets give rise to future economic benefits (although not necessarily in terms of cash inflows),
(b)   the entity has stewardship of the assets, and
(c)   the entity has invested funds in the assets (through acquisition, maintenance, restoration etc).

9   However, the Board accepts that for some assets that were not capitalised in the past and for some donated inalienable, historic and similar assets, the cost of obtaining a valuation (if indeed a reliable valuation is available) may outweigh the benefit to users of the accounts. In such cases, appropriate disclosures should be made in the notes to the accounts instead. Further guidance is available in the relevant sector-specific guidance and SORPs.

Capitalisation of finance costs

10   The FRS permits the optional capitalisation of finance costs, such as interest. The Board acknowledges that it would be preferable either to prohibit or to mandate the capitalisation of finance costs. Conceptually, directly attributable finance costs should be capitalised, for the following reasons:

(a)   finance costs are just as much a cost of constructing the tangible fixed asset as other directly attributable costs.
(b)   capitalising finance costs results in a tangible fixed asset cost that more closely matches the market price of completed assets. Treating the finance costs as an expense distorts the choice between purchasing and constructing a tangible fixed asset.
(c)   the accounts are more likely to reflect the true success or failure of the project.

11   However, the Board was influenced by the argument that if capitalisation is to become mandatory, in theory notional interest should also be capitalised. This is a contentious issue and until an internationally acceptable approach is agreed, the Board favours maintaining the optional capitalisation of finance costs, which is consistent with the approach in IAS 23 'Borrowing Costs'.†

---

*Inalienable assets are tangible fixed assets that an entity cannot dispose of without external consent.

†**Editor's note:** IAS 23 is revised with effect for accounting periods beginning on or after 1 January 2009 and will require the capitalisation of qualifying interest.

Subsequent expenditure

The FRS codifies generally accepted accounting practice that subsequent expenditure on a tangible fixed asset undertaken to ensure that the asset maintains its previously assessed standard of performance (ie 'repairs and maintenance' expenditure) is recognised in the profit and loss account as it is incurred, whereas subsequent expenditure that enhances the previously assessed standard of performance of the tangible fixed asset is capitalised.   **12**

However, the FRS also recognises that it may be appropriate to capitalise certain subsequent expenditure that would have been written off to the profit and loss account in the past as repairs or maintenance expenditure, but to do so only where the depreciation of the asset already reflects the reduction of the service potential of the asset that has been restored by the expenditure. Where appropriate, tangible fixed assets may be divided into two or more major asset components, each component being treated separately for depreciation purposes and depreciated over its own individual useful economic life. Therefore, when a component is restored or replaced, that expenditure should be capitalised.   **13**

The decision to record a tangible fixed asset as several different components with different useful economic lives will depend upon the individual circumstances. In practice the Board expects a commonsense approach, so that only significant, major components with substantially different useful economic lives are identified and treated separately for depreciation purposes.   **14**

Before FRS 12 became applicable, some entities recognised as a provision significant costs of future repairs, maintenance, inspections or overhauls of their tangible fixed assets. Under FRS 12, such future costs are not present obligations of the entity resulting from past events, and therefore no provision should be made for them, even if they are required by legislation if the asset is to continue to be used. In these circumstances, an entity should charge such expenditure to the profit and loss account as it is incurred.   **15**

Alternatively, the entity may depreciate the relevant part of the asset that is declining in service potential to reflect the need for future repairs, maintenance, inspections or overhauls (ie to take account of the actual consumption of the asset's economic benefits) and to capitalise the subsequent expenditure because it results in the restoration of the asset or replacement of some of its components. This latter approach results in a charge being recognised in the profit and loss account that is similar to what would have been recognised under previous (pre-FRS 12) practices. However, the charge takes the form not of a provision for future expenditure but of depreciation, in recognition of the fact that economic benefits of the asset have been consumed at a different rate from that applicable to the remainder of the asset.   **16**

Valuation

Optional valuation

The FRS codifies present practice whereby the valuation of tangible fixed assets is optional. By not imposing a requirement either to revalue or not to revalue, the Board is, exceptionally, leaving to individual preparers of financial statements the task of weighing the costs and benefits of the alternative accounting treatments. However, where a revaluation policy is adopted, the FRS imposes conditions to prevent 'cherry-picking' which assets are revalued and when, by requiring up-to-date valuations of all assets in the same class.   **17**

Frequency of valuation

18   In determining the guidance in the FRS regarding the frequency of revaluations in paragraphs 43-52, the Board had regard to the views of both the Royal Institution of Chartered Surveyors (RICS) and respondents to the earlier proposals in the Discussion Paper and FRED 17. It has balanced the benefits to users of the financial statements of up-to-date and reliable current values with the cost to preparers of obtaining regular, reliable valuations. This guidance was prepared primarily for commercial entities. Therefore, charities, public sector and other not-for-profit organisations, which have different cost/benefit considerations, may find that different approaches are more appropriate. Alternative guidance may be found in the relevant sector-specific guidance and SORPs.

Basis of valuation

19   As mentioned in the Board's draft Statement of Principles for Financial Reporting, the current value of an asset is determined by reference to the value to the business model. The value of an asset to the business (ie its current value) is the value that is relevant to economic decision-making, ie the loss that the entity would suffer if it were deprived of the asset. This can be portrayed diagrammatically as follows:

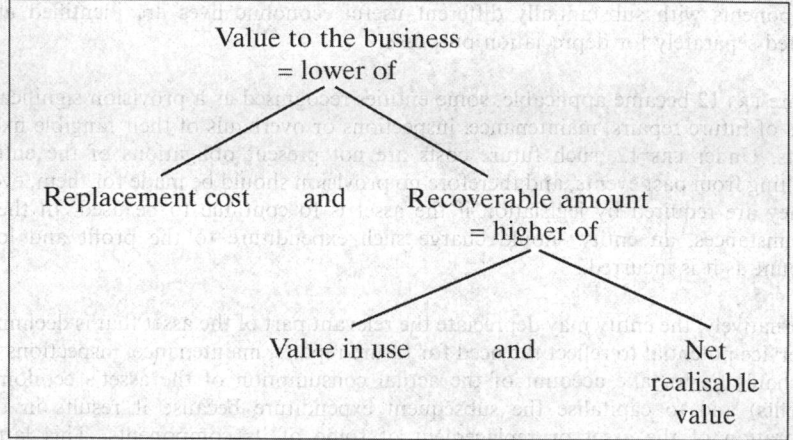

20   If the entity is to continue in its existing business at its current volume (or greater), the value to the business of a tangible fixed asset that is used in the business will normally be its replacement cost. As long as the asset is not impaired (in which case recoverable amount would be less than replacement cost), the entity, if deprived of the asset, would replace it with another similar asset for the same use.

21   For non-specialised properties, existing use value (EUV), with the addition of notional directly attributable acquisition costs (where material), is the basis that more closely approaches the concept of replacement cost (ie the least cost of purchasing the remaining service potential of the asset at the date of valuation). Notional directly attributable acquisition costs are included where material, as they form part of the cost to the entity of replacing the asset. EUV reflects the replacement of the service potential that is used by the owner rather than alternative possible uses.

22   Normally EUV will be no greater than open market value (OMV) as the latter reflects the additional possible uses that are ignored in arriving at EUV (for example,

a factory located on the edge of an expanding town may have greater value as a potential residential property development than as an industrial site). In most cases, where a non-specialised property is fully developed for its most beneficial use, it is expected that the EUV will equal OMV with vacant possession. However, in some circumstances EUV may be higher than OMV. This may be the effect, for example, of restrictive alienation clauses in headleases, planning consents that are personal to the present occupier, or known contamination that does not affect the existing use of the non-specialised property. All of these would lower OMV, but would be disregarded in determining EUV as they do not affect the cost of replacement. Therefore, the FRS requires further information about OMV in the notes to the financial statements where OMV is materially different from EUV.

A concern was raised that in certain limited circumstances EUV may not provide an   **23** adequate measure of the replacement cost of a non-specialised property. This was due, in part, to the following two factors:

- When valuing a property with adaptation works (ie structural changes and specialised fittings made to the shell of a property to meet the particular needs of the individual business), both OMV and EUV are often lower than the original cost of the property. This is because the specialised nature of the adaptation works means that they are either not required by other entities or could not be used by them and therefore they are ascribed a low or nil market value.
- In rare cases, an entity may hold an exceptionally large property that because of its size would be unlikely to be purchased in its present state by a single purchaser but might well be of interest to a number of purchasers if it was divided into components. In this situation it is unlikely that evidence of market transactions of similar exceptionally large properties exists.

The Board has discussed these issues with the RICS. The first issue may be addressed   **24** by treating the adaptation works and shell of the property as separate assets, in accordance with the RICS *Appraisal and Valuation Manual*, Practice Statement 12.4. Because there is no market for the adaptation works they are held at cost or depreciated replacement cost, and the shell of the body (pre-adaptation works) is valued using EUV.

For exceptionally large properties, the RICS has indicated that it is prepared to   **25** consider amending the commentary to the definition of EUV, to include the potential for breaking up such properties into smaller units.

For certain properties no EUV or OMV can be determined, owing to their specia-   **26** lised nature and because they are rarely sold on the open market, except as part of a sale of the business in occupation. Such specialised properties are therefore valued on the basis of depreciated replacement cost.

If an entity were deprived of a tangible fixed asset that was surplus to requirements,   **27** then it would not replace that asset with another similar asset with the same service potential. In this situation, consistently with the value to the business model, the relevant valuation basis is not replacement cost or value in use, but rather net realisable value. Therefore, the FRS requires properties surplus to requirements to be valued using OMV less any material expected directly attributable selling costs. Selling costs are deducted to reflect the net realisable value of the asset to the entity.

Similar valuation bases are to be used for tangible fixed assets other than properties.   **28**

Reporting gains and losses on revaluation

29   The Board believes that, in principle, downward revaluations fall into two general groups – those that are clearly caused by a consumption of economic benefits (eg physical damage or a deterioration in the quality of the service provided by the asset) and those caused by a general fall in prices (eg a general slump in the property market). The first type is similar to depreciation and is treated as such, whereas the second type is more like a valuation adjustment that would fall to be recognised in the statement of total recognised gains and losses.

30   When it is obvious that there has been a consumption of economic benefits, the asset is clearly impaired and the loss recognised in the profit and loss account, which is consistent with the treatment in FRS 11 'Impairment of Fixed Assets and Goodwill'.

31   However, in most cases it is difficult to allocate a downward revaluation to one or other group with certainty. In order to provide objectivity in the treatment of revaluation losses, the FRS requires that where there is doubt whether the fall in value is caused by a reduction in the quantum of the service potential, the loss should be recognised in the statement of total recognised gains and losses until the carrying amount of the asset reaches its depreciated historical cost. Any further fall in value should be recognised in the profit and loss account, except to the extent that it can be demonstrated that the tangible fixed asset is not impaired – ie that the recoverable amount exceeds the revalued amount; such a fall is recognised in the statement of total recognised gains and losses instead.

32   Where the type of fall in value is unclear, splitting the revaluation loss between the statement of total recognised gains and losses and the profit and loss account is necessarily arbitrary, because it depends upon whether the fall in value is above or below depreciated historical cost. However, this treatment has the advantage of being consistent with FRS 11, IAS 16 (revised 1998) 'Property, Plant and Equipment' and IAS 36 'Impairment of Assets' (although some other aspects of the treatment of revaluation gains and losses in the FRS are not consistent with IAS 16, as noted in Appendix III 'Compliance with International Accounting Standards').

33   The Board recognises that the treatment of revaluation losses in the FRS represents a pragmatic solution and, together with the other members of the G4+1,* is developing the above approach further in connection with its project on reporting financial performance. To this end, the Board, as part of the G4+1, intends to issue later in 1999 a Discussion Paper that will consider the development of a new framework for reporting gains and losses with different characteristics.† The Paper will explore the above concepts further and consider ways of refining the approach to revaluation losses. This process may, in due course, lead to revisions to the FRS in this area, in conjunction with future developments in the reporting of financial performance and revisions to FRS 3 'Reporting Financial Performance'.

34   Revaluation gains are most likely to reflect a general rise in prices and therefore are recognised in the statement of total recognised gains and losses as valuation adjustments. Nevertheless, revaluation gains that reverse previous revaluation losses on the same tangible fixed asset are recognised in the same performance statement (after adjusting for subsequent depreciation) as the revaluation loss it reverses.

The G4+1 is a group of representatives from the standard-setting bodies of Australia, Canada, New Zealand, the UK and the USA, and from the International Accounting Standards Committee.

†*Editor's note: The Discussion Paper 'Reporting financial performance: proposals for change' was published in June 1999 and is reproduced in Part Nine of this volume.*

Reporting gains and losses on disposal

FRS 3 requires gains and losses on disposal to be recognised in the profit and loss **35** account in the period in which the disposal took place, calculated as the difference between carrying amount and the net sale proceeds. This treatment of gains and losses on disposals is inconsistent with the treatment of gains and losses on reva- luation. For example, a revaluation gain would be recognised in the statement of total recognised gains and losses, whereas a subsequent gain on disposal would be recognised in the profit and loss account, even though both gains were due to the same factors (ie rising market prices).

FRED 17 therefore proposed amending the requirement in FRS 3, so that immediately **36** before recording the disposal of a tangible fixed asset, the carrying amount of the asset would be adjusted to the disposal proceeds and any gain or loss resulting from such an adjustment would be recognised in accordance with the requirements for reporting revaluation gains and losses. Under these proposals those losses on dis- posal that would be recognised in the profit and loss account are regarded as a form of consumption similar to depreciation. This proposal was to apply to all tangible fixed assets, whether or not a policy of revaluation had been adopted.

The responses to FRED 17 made it clear that this proposal was not acceptable at **37** present. Respondents argued that:

* the development of the role of the statement of total recognised gains and losses in FRED 17 was premature, particularly as the direction and outcome of the Board's intended project to review FRS 3 was unclear.
* the proposal raised anomalies for tangible fixed assets held at historical cost. Gains and losses on disposal reflect the accuracy of depreciation policies and estimated residual values, and therefore it was argued that they should be recognised in the same performance statement as depreciation.
* the proposal is inconsistent with the treatment of gains and losses on disposals of businesses, subsidiaries and investments.

The Board acknowledges that more work needs to be carried out in this area and **38** intends to revisit this aspect in the course of its review of FRS 3. Accordingly the FRS retains the requirements of FRS 3 for the treatment of gains and losses on disposal.

Depreciation

The objective of depreciation

Depreciation is a measure of the cost (historical cost or revalued amount) of the **39** economic benefits of the tangible fixed asset that have been consumed by the entity during the period.

It is sometimes argued that a valuation approach to depreciation should be adopted **40** especially where an entity revalues its tangible fixed assets. The Board disagrees with this approach because it does not distinguish between depreciation (ie the amount consumed) and other sources of value changes and therefore results in a reduced or nil depreciation expense in a period of rising prices, even though there is a cost to the entity of using the asset to generate its revenues.

The Board does not accept that the increase in the value of a tangible fixed asset **41** justifies non-depreciation. Wherever the asset has a finite expected life, part of the asset representing one year's economic benefits of the asset is consumed in the year. The revenues generated by the entity through using the tangible fixed asset in the business justify a charge to the profit and loss account for using that asset. An increase in value, or an increase in residual value, whether arising from external factors or from refurbishment, should impact only on the parts of the asset representing future economic benefits.

Split depreciation

42   Some have argued that the depreciation charge on a revalued tangible fixed asset should be split, and only that part relating to the historical cost of the asset charged to the profit and loss account. The part of the depreciation charge that corresponds to the revaluation movement would be charged instead to the statement of total recognised gains and losses. Such split depreciation would remove a disincentive to revalue fixed assets and the depreciation charged to the profit and loss account would represent an allocation of the actual cash outlay.

43   The issue of split depreciation raises legal considerations. In Great Britain, paragraph 32(3) of Schedule 4 to the Companies Act 1985* states that:

> "Where sub-paragraph (1) applies in the case of any fixed asset the amount of the provision for depreciation in respect of that asset ... may be the *historical cost amount instead of the adjusted amount, provided that the amount of any difference between the two is shown separately in the profit and loss account or in a note to the accounts.*" (emphasis added)

44   It is unclear whether the above-mentioned paragraph permits split depreciation. The Board therefore obtained a legal opinion on this issue. That opinion noted that the practical effect of the paragraph as drafted makes it arguable that the entirety of a given charge need not pass through the profit and loss account. However, the opinion went on to note the implications of the *Marleasing†* decision. This case indicates that national courts of EU Member States are under a Community law obligation to interpret national law so that it conforms, so far as possible, with the underlying directive (in this case, the Fourth Directive). Articles 33.3 and 35.1 (c)(cc) of the Fourth Directive prohibit split depreciation.

45   The Board also considered an alternative method of achieving split depreciation. With this method the full depreciation charge would be included in the profit and loss account along with a credit from the revaluation reserve equal to the depreciation on the revaluation surplus. In Great Britain, section 275(2) of the Companies Act 1985‡ permits depreciation on a revaluation surplus to be treated as a realised profit and paragraph 34(3) of Schedule 4† permits an amount to be transferred from the revaluation reserve to the profit and loss account if it represents a realised profit. However, total depreciation and the credit from the revaluation reserve would be required to be separately disclosed in the profit and loss account (ie the credit from the revaluation reserve would not be permitted to be offset against the charge for depreciation).

*In Northern Ireland, the Companies (Northern Ireland) Order 1986, Schedule 4, paragraph 32(3).
In the Republic of Ireland, the Companies (Amendment) Act 1986, Schedule, paragraph 20(3).

†Marleasing S.A. vs La Commercial Internacional de Alimentation S.A. (C-106/89) [1992 CMLR 305].

‡In Northern Ireland, the Companies (Northern Ireland) Order 1986, article 283(2) and Schedule 4, paragraph 34(3).
In the Republic of Ireland, the Companies (Amendment) Act 1983, section 45(6) and the Companies (Amendment) Act 1986, Schedule, paragraph 22(4).

The Board disagrees with the introduction of this alternative for three reasons: **46**

(a)   It would involve recycling amounts previously recognised in the statement of total recognised gains and losses – ie via a transfer from the revaluation reserve to the profit and loss account. The transfer from the revaluation reserve would result in a charge to the statement of total recognised gains and losses. Such a charge has no meaning.

(b)   It is inconsistent with the Board's view of depreciation as a measure of the cost of the economic benefits consumed during the period.

(c)   An approach that recognises depreciation on the historical amount of an asset in the profit and loss account and depreciation on the revalued amount in the statement of total recognised gains and losses implies that the purpose of the profit and loss account is invariably to report historical cost profits and losses. The Board rejected such an objective during its development of FRS 3. In addition, FRS 3 requires a note of historical cost profits and losses where there is a material difference between the results as disclosed in the profit and loss account and the result on an unmodified historical cost basis.

The Board believes that depreciation measured at current prices represents the best   **47** measure of the operating cost of using the asset in question. This is because the purpose of charging depreciation to the profit and loss account is to show the cost of the economic benefits consumed during the period, and depreciation based on current value reflects the cost that the entity could have avoided if it had not used the asset. In addition, it also provides a consistency between the profit and loss account and the balance sheet and is consistent with companies legislation. Hence, the FRS requires the depreciation charge in the profit and loss account to be based on the revalued amount of the asset, whenever the asset has been revalued.

Non-depreciation of tangible fixed assets

There has been a growing trend towards the non-depreciation of certain tangible   **48** fixed assets, particularly property. The main circumstances in which it is argued that no depreciation need be charged are where maintenance or refurbishment is carried out regularly, significantly extending the useful economic life of the asset or maintaining the residual value of the asset.

The Board believes that the estimate of a tangible fixed asset's useful economic life   **49** cannot be extended limitlessly through maintenance, refurbishment, overhaul or replacement of components of the asset. This is because the physical life of a tangible fixed asset, other than non-depreciable land, cannot be indefinite. At some point in time it will not be economic to continue to maintain and restore the asset and it will have scrap value only. Accordingly, the FRS states that subsequent expenditure on a tangible fixed asset that maintains or enhances the previously assessed standard of performance of the asset does not negate the need to charge depreciation.

The Board acknowledges that, with regular maintenance and restoration and where   **50** economic or technological obsolescence is unlikely, some tangible fixed assets (eg heritage buildings, fine art) may have very long useful economic lives before they need a major refit or restoration or are scrapped. In such cases the periodic depreciation charge may be immaterial.

The useful economic life of a tangible fixed asset is defined as the period in which the   **51** asset is expected to be used by the entity in its business. Therefore the useful economic life to the entity may be substantially shorter than the asset's total economic life, particularly where the asset management policy of the entity involves the disposal of assets after a specified time or after consumption of a limited portion of the economic benefits embodied in the asset. In addition, the asset may have an alternative use that has a longer economic life. In these circumstances, with regular maintenance and repairs, the residual value of the asset at the end of the useful economic life to the entity, which will reflect the remaining economic value of the asset, may not be insignificant or materially different from the carrying amount of the asset.

52   The Board believes that, apart from non-depreciable land, the only grounds for not charging depreciation on a tangible fixed asset are that the depreciation charge and related accumulated depreciation balance are not material, owing to a long estimated remaining useful economic life or high residual value. By not charging depreciation, however, there is greater risk that recoverable amount will fall below the carrying amount in the future. Where depreciation is not charged, therefore, the FRS requires impairment reviews to be undertaken at the end of each reporting period.

53   Similarly, the longer the useful economic lives assigned to tangible fixed assets, the greater is the risk that the recoverable amounts will fall below the carrying amounts in future. Where a depreciation period exceeds 50 years, the Board believes that the risk is sufficiently high to require depreciation to be supplemented by reviews for impairment at the end of each reporting period.

Review of useful economic life and residual value

54   Changes in the useful economic life or residual value of a tangible fixed asset generally arise from new information or developments and therefore do not relate to past periods. For that reason the FRS requires changes in the useful economic life and residual value of an asset to be accounted for prospectively over its remaining useful economic life. Estimates of residual value should be based on prices prevailing at the date of acquisition or latest revaluation. Unless the asset is being revalued, therefore, the estimate of residual value should not be altered simply because of changing prices.

Changes made following exposure of FRED 17

55   The majority of respondents to FRED 17 were broadly supportive of its proposals, with the exception of the proposals in respect of the treatment of gains and losses on disposal and the consequential amendment to FRS 3, which proved controversial. The Board has accepted the argument that the changes to recognition of gains and losses on disposal should not be introduced in isolation from a review of other aspects of FRS 3. It has, therefore, not incorporated these proposals in the requirements of the FRS, maintaining the treatment in FRS 3, as outlined above.*

56   In the light of other comments made by those responding to FRED 17, a number of changes have been made to its proposals. The most significant changes are:

● the exemption of investment properties from the requirements of the FRS. The treatment of investment properties is being considered further by the Board, in tandem with the international project on investment properties. The Board believes that, until this work is complete, it is appropriate to maintain the status quo as set out in SSAP 19 'Accounting for investment properties'.

Editor's note: 'FRED 22 Revision of FRS 3 "Reporting Financial Performance"' was issued by the ASB in December 2000.

- the inclusion of an explanatory paragraph explaining that, when valuing a non-specialised property, the adaptation works may be treated separately from the shell of the building.
- the amendment of the requirements for reporting gains and losses on revaluation that reverse previous losses or gains, to take into account subsequent depreciation. This ensures that the requirements are consistent with the equivalent requirements in FRS 11.
- the deletion of the proposed requirement in FRED 17 to disclose in the notes to the financial statements any significant differences between the current value and the carrying amount of properties that are not revalued. The Board agreed with respondents that the requirement in companies legislation to make a similar disclosure in the directors' report was sufficient.
- the addition of a new requirement for impairment reviews to be performed in each reporting period when either no depreciation charge on a tangible fixed asset is made on the grounds that it would be immaterial or the estimated remaining useful economic life of the asset exceeds 50 years. This replaces the proposal in FRED 17 that it should be assumed that the residual value of a tangible fixed asset was materially different from its carrying amount, unless the entity intends to dispose of the asset within about a year from its date of acquisition. The Board accepted respondents' comments that the assumption in FRED 17 did not reflect economic reality in certain circumstances. The new requirement is explained in paragraphs 48–53 above.
- the addition of a new requirement in respect of the use of renewals accounting as a method of estimating the depreciation of infrastructure assets.
- the addition of a requirement to disclose a reconciliation of the movements on the carrying amount for each class of tangible fixed assets. This is consistent with the equivalent requirement in companies legislation, but is repeated in the FRS for those entities that do not fall within the scope of companies legislation, and to ensure that the reconciliation is given for each class of assets adopted for revaluation purposes.
- the removal of the paragraph in SSAP 19 'Accounting for investment properties' that exempts charities with investment properties from following the requirements of SSAP 19, to be consistent with the SORP 'Accounting by Charities' issued by the Charity Commissioners for England and Wales.

Financial Reporting Standard 16 is set out in paragraphs 1–22.

The Statement of Standard Accounting Practice, which comprises the paragraphs set in bold type, should be read in the context of the Objective as stated in paragraph 1 and the definitions set out in paragraph 2 and also of the Foreword to Accounting Standards and the Statement of Principles for Financial Reporting currently in issue.

The explanatory paragraphs contained in the FRS *shall be regarded as part of the Statement of Standard Accounting Practice insofar as they assist in interpreting that statement.*

Appendix V 'The development of the FRS*' reviews considerations and arguments that were thought significant by members of the Board in reaching the conclusions on the* FRS*.*

[FRS 16]
Current tax

(Issued December 1999)

Contents

Current tax

Summary

a   Financial Reporting Standard 16 'Current Tax' specifies how current tax, in particular withholding tax and tax credits, should be reflected in financial statements.

b   Current tax should be recognised in the profit and loss account for the period, except to the extent that it is attributable to a gain or loss that has been recognised directly in the statement of total recognised gains and losses. Where a gain or loss has been recognised directly in the statement of total recognised gains and losses, the tax relating to that gain or loss should also be recognised directly in that statement.

c   Dividends, interest and other amounts payable or receivable should be recognised at an amount that:

   • includes withholding taxes payable to the tax authorities wholly on behalf of the recipient.
   • excludes any other taxes, such as attributable tax credits, not payable wholly on behalf of the recipient.

d   Subject to the above, income and expenses should be included in the pre-tax results on the basis of the income or expenses actually receivable or payable, without any adjustment to reflect a notional amount of tax that would have been paid or relieved in respect of the transaction if it had been taxable, or allowable for tax purposes, on a different basis.

e   Current tax should be measured using tax rates and laws that have been enacted or substantively enacted by the balance sheet date.

[Financial Reporting Standard 16]

Objective

1   The objective of this FRS is to ensure that reporting entities recognise current taxes in a consistent and transparent manner.

Definitions

2   The following definitions shall apply in the FRS and in particular in the Statement of Standard Accounting Practice set out **in bold type**.

Current tax:-

The amount of tax estimated to be payable or recoverable in respect of the taxable profit or loss for a period, along with adjustments to estimates in respect of previous periods.

Tax credit:-

The tax credit given under UK tax legislation to the recipient of a dividend from a UK company.

The credit is given to acknowledge that the income out of which the dividend has been paid has already been charged to tax, rather than because any withholding tax has been deducted at source. The tax credit may discharge or reduce the recipient's liability to tax on the dividend. Non-taxpayers may or may not be able to recover the tax credit.

Taxable profit or loss:-

The profit or loss for the period, determined in accordance with the rules established by the tax authorities, upon which taxes are assessed.

Withholding tax:-

Tax on dividends or other income that is deducted by the payer of the income and paid to the tax authorities wholly on behalf of the recipient.

SCOPE

The FRS applies to all financial statements that are intended to give a true and fair view   3
of a reporting entity's financial position and profit or loss (or income and expenditure)
for a period.

Reporting entities applying the Financial Reporting Standard for Smaller Entities   4
currently applicable are exempt from the FRS.

RECOGNITION

Current tax should be recognised in the profit and loss account for the period, except to   5
the extent that it is attributable to a gain or loss that is or has been recognised directly
in the statement of total recognised gains and losses.

Where a gain or loss is or has been recognised directly in the statement of total   6
recognised gains and losses, the tax attributable to that gain or loss should also be
recognised directly in that statement.

Accounting standards (or, in their absence, legislation) require or permit certain   7
gains or losses to be credited or charged directly in the statement of total recognised
gains and losses (ie not in the profit and loss account). The FRS requires any attributable tax to be treated in the same way. In exceptional circumstances it may be
difficult to determine the amount of current tax that is attributable to gains or losses
that have been recognised directly in the statement of total recognised gains and
losses. In such circumstances, the attributable tax is based on a reasonable pro rata
allocation, or another allocation that is more appropriate in the circumstances.

Outgoing dividends paid and proposed (or declared and not yet payable), interest and   8
other amounts payable should be recognised at an amount that:

(a)   includes any withholding taxes; but
(b)   excludes any other taxes, such as attributable tax credits, not payable wholly on
      behalf of the recipient.

Incoming dividends, interest or other income receivable should be recognised at an   9
amount that:

(a)   includes any withholding taxes; but

(b)   **excludes any other taxes, such as attributable tax credits, not payable wholly on behalf of the recipient.**

The effect of any withholding tax suffered should be taken into account as part of the tax charge.

10   The amount recognised therefore excludes attributable tax credits of the type defined in the FRS and underlying tax.*

11   **Subject to paragraphs 8 and 9, income and expenses should be included in the pre-tax results on the basis of the income or expenses actually receivable or payable. No adjustment should be made to reflect a notional amount of tax that would have been paid or relieved in respect of the transaction if it had been taxable, or allowable for tax purposes, on a different basis.**

12   The requirement in paragraph 11 applies, for example, to non-taxable income, non-deductible expenditure and income and expenditure subject to non-standard rates of tax.

13   The requirement applies only to notional tax, ie tax that is not actually paid or recovered. In some specialised industries, such as leasing and life insurance, profit from transactions is allocated to accounting periods on a post-tax basis and the tax charge and pre-tax profit relating to the accounting period is found by applying the effective rate of tax to the post-tax profit. Where, as is usually the case, such post-tax methods result in the actual pre-tax profit and the actual tax charge being recorded over the life of the transactions, their use is consistent with the requirements of the FRS.

14   **Current tax should be measured at the amounts expected to be paid (or recovered) using the tax rates and laws that have been enacted or substantively enacted by the balance sheet date.**

15   A UK tax rate can be regarded as having been substantively enacted if it is included in either:

(a)   a Bill that has been passed by the House of Commons and is awaiting only passage through the House of Lords and Royal Assent; or

(b)   a resolution having statutory effect that has been passed under the Provisional Collection of Taxes Act 1968.†

16   A Republic of Ireland tax rate can be regarded as having been substantively enacted if it is included in a Bill that has been passed by the Dail.

DISCLOSURE

17   **The following major components of the current tax expense (or income) for the period in the profit and loss account and the statement of total recognised gains and losses should be disclosed separately:**

---

*In certain circumstances, a UK company receiving dividends from an overseas company obtains relief for the tax (underlying tax) that the overseas company has paid on the profits from which the dividend has been paid. The UK company's taxable income is increased by the amount of underlying tax attributed to the dividend and relief is given against the resulting UK tax charge.

†Such a resolution could be used to collect taxes at a new rate before that rate has been enacted. In practice, corporation tax rates are now set a year ahead to avoid having to invoke the Provisional Collection of Taxes Act for the quarterly payment system.

(a)   UK or Republic of Ireland tax (depending on the companies legislation in accordance with which the entity is reporting); and

(b)   foreign tax.

Both (a) and (b) should be analysed to distinguish tax estimated for the current period and any adjustments recognised in respect of prior periods. The domestic tax should be disclosed before and after double taxation relief.

DATE FROM WHICH EFFECTIVE AND TRANSITIONAL ARRANGEMENTS

The accounting practices set out in the FRS should be regarded as standard in respect of accounting periods ending on or after 23 March 2000. Earlier adoption is encouraged.   18

Non-taxpaying entities that, at the date of implementation of the FRS, are entitled to transitional relief following the removal of their right to reclaim tax credits may continue to present that transitional relief as part of the income to which it relates. The nature and amount of the relief should be separately disclosed.   19

Any unrelieved advance corporation tax (ACT) that at the date of implementation of the FRS is carried forward for relief against future taxable profits should be recognised on the balance sheet only to the extent that it is regarded as recoverable. Any change in the amount of ACT regarded as recoverable should be recognised as part of the tax expense (or income) for the period in the profit and loss account and separately disclosed on the face of the profit and loss account or in a note.   20

Guidance on the circumstances in which ACT can be regarded as recoverable is included in Appendix II.   21

WITHDRAWAL OF SSAP 8 AND UITF ABSTRACT 16

The FRS supersedes SSAP 8 'The treatment of taxation under the imputation system in the accounts of companies' and UITF Abstract 16 'Income and expenses subject to non-standard rates of tax'.   22

Adoption of FRS 16 by the board

Financial Reporting Standard 16 'Current Tax' was approved for issue by the ten members of the Accounting Standards Board.

Sir David Tweedie (Chairman)
Allan Cook CBE (Technical Director)
David Allvey
Ian Brindle
Dr John Buchanan
John Coombe
Raymond Hinton
Huw Jones
Professor Geoffrey Whittington
Ken Wild

Appendix I
Illustration of profit and loss account disclosure
(UK only)

This example illustrates one method of showing (by way of note) the tax items required to be disclosed under companies legislation* and the FRS.

This appendix is for general guidance and does not form part of the Statement of Standard Accounting Practice.

	£000	£000
UK† corporation tax		
Current tax on income for the period		a
Adjustments in respect of prior periods		b
		c
Double taxation relief		(d)
		e
Foreign tax		
Current tax on income for the period		f
Adjustments in respect of prior periods		g
		h
Tax on profit on ordinary activities		i

*In Great Britain, the Companies Act 1985; in Northern Ireland, the Companies (Northern Ireland) Order 1986; and in the Republic of Ireland, the Companies (Amendment) Act 1986.

†Companies reporting in accordance with companies legislation in the Republic of Ireland would instead show the Republic of Ireland tax.

Appendix II
Transitional arrangements for advance corporation tax (UK only)

The definition of recoverable advance corporation tax (ACT) and the treatments for ACT set out below are based on the requirements of SSAP 8. These continue to be relevant for the shadow ACT system, which is designed to ensure that ACT carried forward after April 1999 is recovered only if it could have been recovered had the ACT system still existed.

1   *Recoverable ACT:-*
ACT is regarded as recoverable where the amount of the ACT previously paid on outgoing dividends can be:

(a)   set off against a corporation tax liability on the profits of the period under review or of previous periods;

(b)   properly set off against a credit balance on the deferred tax account; or

(c)   expected to be recoverable taking into account expected profits and dividends—normally those of the next accounting period only.

2   Although ACT can be carried forward indefinitely if necessary, in each year there is an overriding restriction on the use of ACT for set-off imposed by the shadow ACT system. The shadow ACT system is designed to be no more generous than the old ACT system. Its effect is to ensure that ACT that was previously irrecoverable becomes recoverable only to the extent that it would have become recoverable under the old ACT system.

3   In deciding whether ACT should be carried forward as recoverable, regard should be had only to the immediate and foreseeable future. How long this future period should be will depend upon the circumstances of each case, but it is suggested that where there is no deferred tax account it should normally not extend beyond the next accounting period.

4   ACT should be offset against a credit balance on the deferred tax account only if, in the period in which the underlying timing differences are expected to reverse, the reversal will create sufficient taxable profits to enable ACT to be recovered under the shadow ACT system.

5   Subject to the preceding paragraph, if the ACT on dividends relating to previous periods is regarded as recoverable but has not yet been recovered, it should be deducted from the deferred tax account if such an account is available for this purpose. In the absence of a deferred tax account ACT recoverable should be shown as a deferred tax asset.

6   If ACT that was previously regarded as recoverable becomes irrecoverable, it is required to be charged in the profit and loss account as a separately disclosed component of the tax charge.

7   Where the recovery of the ACT was not regarded as reasonably certain and foreseeable, it will have been written off in the profit and loss account. Events may occur under the system applying from April 1999 (the shadow ACT system) causing ACT that has previously been written off as irrecoverable to be recovered. Such ACT is required to be credited in the profit and loss account as a separately disclosed component of the tax charge.

Appendix III
Note on legal requirements

GREAT BRITAIN

The main requirements that are directly relevant are set out in Schedule 4 to the Companies Act 1985 and are summarised below.   **1**

Paragraph 3(7) of Schedule 4 requires every profit and loss account to show separately as additional items the aggregate amount of any dividends paid and proposed.   **2**

The formats in Schedule 4 set out where tax is to be shown in the balance sheet and the profit and loss account.   **3**

Paragraph 54(2) of Schedule 4 requires particulars to be given of any special circumstances that affect liability in respect of taxation of profits, income or capital gains for the financial year or liability in respect of taxation of profits, income or capital gains for succeeding financial years.   **4**

Paragraph 54(3) of Schedule 4 requires the following components of tax on profit or loss on ordinary activities to be stated: **5**

(a) the amount of the charge for UK corporation tax;
(b) if the amount would have been greater but for relief from double taxation, the amount which it would have been but for such relief;
(c) the amount of the charge for UK income tax; and
(d) the amount of the charge for taxation imposed outside the UK of profits, income and (so far as charged to revenue) capital gains.

NORTHERN IRELAND

The statutory requirements in Northern Ireland are set out in the Companies (Northern Ireland) Order 1986. They are identical to and parallel the references for Great Britain in the Companies Act 1985.   **6**

REPUBLIC OF IRELAND

The main requirements that are directly relevant are set out in the Companies (Amendment) Act 1986 and are summarised below.   **7**

Section 4(15)(a) requires every profit and loss account to show separately the aggregate amount of the dividends paid and the aggregate amount of the dividends proposed to be paid.   **8**

The formats in the Schedule set out where taxation is to be shown in the balance sheet and the profit and loss account.   **9**

Paragraph 40(1) of the Schedule requires the basis on which the charge for corporation tax, income tax and other taxation on profits (whether payable in or outside the State) is computed to be stated.   **10**

Paragraph 40(2) of the Schedule requires particulars to be given of any special circumstances which affect liability in respect of taxation on profits, income or   **11** capital gains for the financial year concerned or liability in respect of taxation of profits, income or capital gains for succeeding financial years.

12 Paragraph 40(3) of the Schedule requires that the amount of the charge for corporation tax, income tax and other taxation on profits or capital gains, so far as charged to revenue, including taxation payable outside the State on profits (distinguishing where practicable between corporation tax and other taxation) shall be stated.

13 Any amounts required to be stated under paragraph 40(1)-(3) shall be stated separately in respect of each of the amounts which is or would, but for section 4(6)(b) (items combined in the accounts) of the Act, be shown under the following items in the profit and loss account—'tax on profit or loss on ordinary activities' and 'tax on extraordinary profit or loss'.

14 Paragraph 33 of the Schedule requires that the amount of any provision for taxation other than deferred taxation shall be stated.

15 Paragraph 3 (note 7 on the balance sheet formats) of the Schedule requires the notes to the balance sheet to show separately the combined amounts included under the heading 'Other creditors including tax and social welfare' (format 1, items C8 and F8 and format 2, item C8) in respect of taxation and social welfare, specifying separately the amount due under the different categories of tax payable and the total amount of social welfare due.

Appendix IV
Compliance with international accounting standards

The International Accounting Standard on current tax is IAS 12 (revised 1996)   **1**
'Income Taxes'.*

The main differences between the two standards are that: **2**

- the IAS requires current tax to be presented separately on the face of the balance sheet; the FRS does not.
- the FRS specifies how a reporting entity should account for the tax consequences of outgoing or incoming dividends and other distributions; the IAS does not.
- the FRS requires all current tax income or expense for the period to be included in the statements of performance (ie profit and loss account or statement of total recognised gains and losses). The IAS requires current tax to be charged directly to equity if it relates to items that are also charged or credited directly to equity.
- the IAS requires disclosure of the tax expense relating to discontinued operations; the FRS does not.

Editor's note: IAS 12 was further revised in 2000.

Appendix V
The development of the FRS

BACKGROUND

1   In the last few years there have been important changes in the tax systems of the UK and the Republic of Ireland. Amongst other changes, the reclaimability of tax credits became restricted in July 1997* and advance corporation tax (ACT) was abolished in April 1999. Further, in the Republic of Ireland, the previous imputation system was replaced by a system of withholding taxes.

2   The changes raised questions about the continuing relevance of SSAP 8 'The treatment of taxation under the imputation system in the accounts of companies'. SSAP 8 had been introduced in August 1974 for the UK, with Appendix 3 for the Republic of Ireland added in December 1977. It required incoming dividends to be recognised at the amount received plus the attributable tax credit and contained detailed requirements regarding the treatment of ACT.

3   In response to the earlier change in the UK that restricted the ability of non-tax-payers to reclaim tax credits attributed to dividends received, the Board published proposals for a limited amendment to SSAP 8.† The main proposal was that dividend income should not be grossed up to include tax credits.

4   This proposal received substantial support from commentators. However, in November 1997, the Chancellor of the Exchequer announced a far-reaching review of the UK tax system, part of which was a plan to abolish ACT. Similarly, in December 1997, the Minister for Finance in the Republic of Ireland announced changes to the Irish tax system that included abolition of ACT.

5   The Board therefore accepted a recommendation of its Urgent Issues Task Force that, rather than make a limited amendment to SSAP 8, the whole standard should be reviewed. At the time it was thought that it might be possible to incorporate revised requirements for current tax into the FRS being developed on deferred tax. However, this would have meant a delay in the introduction of the requirements for current tax. To avoid such a delay, the Board decided to issue two separate FRSS.

6   In June 1999, the Board published its proposals for revising SSAP 8 in an Exposure Draft, FRED 18 'Current Taxation'. The basic requirements proposed were widely supported and have remained largely unchanged in the FRS.

CHANGES TO THE REQUIREMENTS OF SSAP 8

7   The main changes introduced by the FRS are in the treatment of tax credits, withholding taxes and similar methods of collecting tax at source:

(a)   the FRS requires dividends to be recognised at an amount that does not include any attributable tax credit or underlying tax. SSAP 8 had required dividends to be recognised at an amount that included the attributable tax credit.

In 1998 in the Republic of Ireland.

†*Exposure Draft: Amendment to SSAP 8 'The treatment of taxation under the imputation system in the accounts of companies', October 1997.*

(b)   the FRS addresses the treatment of withholding taxes, which SSAP 8 did not. It requires dividends to be recognised at an amount that includes any withholding taxes.

The reasons for these changes are discussed further in paragraphs 9-20 below.

Other changes introduced by the FRS are: **8**

(a)   *inclusion of requirements prescribing the circumstances in which current taxes should be recognised directly in the statement of total recognised gains and losses rather than in the profit and loss account.* The requirements reflect the principle underlying the consensus in UITF Abstract 19 'Tax on gains and losses on foreign currency borrowings that hedge an investment in a foreign enterprise' ie that tax should be charged in the same performance statement as the gains and losses on which it arises. The FRS does not fully supersede Abstract 19, which also covers other issues.

(b)   *inclusion of the consensus from UITF Abstract 16, which is now withdrawn.* The FRS thus requires income and expenses to be included in the pre-tax results on the basis of the income or expenses actually receivable or payable. No adjustment is made to reflect a notional amount of tax that would have been paid or relieved had the transaction been taxable or allowable on a different basis.

(c)   *removal of requirements relating to ACT.* With the abolition of ACT in both the UK and the Republic of Ireland, the requirements in SSAP 8 will not be relevant in future. Residual issues arising under the 'shadow' ACT system have been addressed as transitional arrangements in the FRS.

(d)   *a requirement to use 'substantively enacted' tax rates and laws to measure current taxes.* This requirement is discussed further in paragraphs 21 and 22 below.

TAX CREDITS AND WITHHOLDING TAX

Proposals in FRED 18

FRED 18 proposed that incoming dividends should be recognised at the amount   **9**
received or receivable without any attributable tax credit but including any withholding tax deducted at source.

The proposal arose from reconsidering the principles underlying the standard rather   **10**
than as a result of the restriction in the reclaimability of tax credits or the abolition of
ACT. The Board took the view that, whilst these changes affected those entities that
are not taxpayers (through the restrictions on reclaimability*) and the timing of the
tax payments (through ACT†), they did not fundamentally change the underlying
tax system. The central feature of the tax credit system—dividends received with a
tax credit fall outside the corporation tax computation altogether for companies and
have no basic rate tax liability for individuals (and partnerships)—remained
unchanged.

In developing its proposals, the Board considered the three possible amounts at   **11**
which dividends could be recognised, ie:

(a)   *including* withholding taxes but *excluding* tax credits;

Recipients of dividends that are taxpayers receive the benefit from the tax credit through no further tax being payable (except higher rate tax for some individuals). It is only for non-taxpayers that the extent to which the tax credit is recoverable is relevant.

†*ACT, except where irrecoverable, affects only the timing and not the amount of tax due.*

(b)   *including* both withholding taxes and tax credits; or
(c)   *excluding* both withholding taxes and tax credits.

12   In support of (a), it was argued that there is a difference in nature between tax credits and withholding tax. It is not only that a withholding tax is tax that has actually been paid by (or at least on behalf of) the recipient of the dividend. The differences are more than merely technical matters of how the tax is collected, at what rates it is levied and whether the income to which the tax relates is included in a company's corporation tax computation. There are also differences of substance:

   • in many circumstances, no further tax is payable on dividends received with a tax credit: the dividend is treated as non-taxable income. In contrast, income on which withholding tax has been suffered is treated as taxable and subject to further tax, unless (unusually) the amount of the withholding tax is sufficient to discharge the full liability.
   • the amount at which the dividend is measured if it is subject to further tax is different. When dividends are received subject to withholding tax, further tax is levied on the amount received plus the withholding tax. When reporting entities have further tax to pay on dividends received with tax credits (for example, when the investments are held by a bank as part of its trading portfolio), the further tax is levied on the amount received without the tax credit.

13   In support of option (b)—ie including both withholding taxes and tax credits—it was argued that any differences between a tax credit and a withholding tax are a matter of technical form rather than economic substance. Differences arise in the rate of the tax, the method of payment, the system for gaining credit for the tax suffered etc. But in both cases the recipient entity is liable for a reduced or nil amount of tax on the income received as a result of tax paid by the payer of the income. (The payer of the dividend has paid the tax either as corporation tax on the income out of which the dividend is paid or as withholding tax on behalf of the recipient.) Taking this view, it is further argued that the tax credit and the withholding tax have a real effect on the recipient of the dividend or other income and should therefore be reflected in the amount of income received. Grossing up is necessary to reflect the greater value of 100 received as dividend (no tax consequences) compared with 100 earned as trading profit (taxable).

14   In favour of option (c)—ie excluding both withholding taxes and tax credits—it was argued that, given the diversity of tax systems and their implications for different types of recipient, it would be impossible to unravel and account for each system in accordance with its economic substance. Consistency would be achieved, and both the substance and form followed, if this approach were adopted because the financial statements could show that different sources of income had different tax consequences. These could be highlighted in the entity's tax charge.

15   It was further argued that approach (c) can be regarded as consistent with UITF Abstract 16. This is because it applies a consistent rule that tax collections at source are not taken into account by grossing up. This approach also has the advantage of simplicity: it avoids the difficult issue of when such tax collections are 'real' (and should be taken into account) and when they are 'notional' (and should not be taken into account).

16   The majority of the Board found the arguments in favour of option (a)—ie measuring dividends at an amount that included withholding tax but not tax credits—the most persuasive. They took the view that to show only the net amount of income received subject to withholding tax failed to reflect the full amount taxable in the hands of the recipient. And they noted that the distinction between notional and real

tax collections had already received general support in UITF Abstract 16. Hence, option (a) formed the basis of the proposals in the FRED.

Changes to the FRED proposals

The proposal to recognise dividends at an amount that includes withholding taxes **17** but not attributable tax credits received widespread support from respondents to the FRED. Eighty-two per cent of respondents agreed with the proposal, and the pre- ferences of the remaining 18 per cent were spread across a range of options.

However, a number of respondents noted that, by specifying requirements only for **18** withholding taxes and tax credits of the type given to the recipients of dividends from UK companies, the FRS would fail to clarify how other forms of 'tax credit', some of which would have some of the characteristics of withholding taxes, should be treated. Examples included relief for 'underlying' tax and other credits given under double tax treaties.

Most of the respondents who raised this issue thought that underlying taxes and **19** other forms of tax credit should be treated in the same way as UK tax credits. They argued that underlying tax is more like a tax credit than a withholding tax. It is more concerned with the taxes paid by the payer of a dividend rather than those paid by (or on behalf of) the recipient. To gross up a dividend received for the tax on the paying company's profits would fail to represent the substance of the dividend income. They noted that the grossed up amount would be difficult to interpret, being determined on the basis of accounts prepared using different accounting standards from those used in the UK and the Republic of Ireland. They further argued that whilst the measurement of withholding tax is relatively straightforward, underlying tax can be difficult to calculate and often takes time to agree with the Inland Rev- enue. The Board accepted these arguments, and reworded the requirements of the FRS to clarify that dividends should not be grossed up for any taxes other than withholding taxes.

The general proposal that dividends should not be grossed up for UK tax credits has **20** not changed. Rather it has been extended to other taxes that were not addressed by the FRED.

TAX RATES

SSAP 8 required current tax to be measured at the latest known rate. The FRS instead **21** requires current tax to be measured at the amount expected to be payable or reco- verable based on tax rates and laws that have been enacted or substantively enacted by the balance sheet date. The change has been made to increase consistency and align the FRS with the requirements of the international accounting standard, IAS 12 (revised 1996) 'Income Taxes'.

The change was proposed in the FRED and widely supported by those commenting on **22** it. A number of respondents suggested that the requirement should be to use rates that had been substantively enacted by the date of signing the accounts rather than the balance sheet date. The Board acknowledged that this could lead to more accurate measures of the tax that would actually be paid in respect of the period. But it took the view that:

- it was desirable that a universal effect, such as a tax rate, should be applied by all reporting entities from the same date. This would not happen if the cut-off point were the date of signing the accounts.

- practical problems could arise if a new tax rate or law was substantively enacted between the date on which a company announced its results and the date of signing the financial statements.

DISCLOSURES

23   The disclosures required by the FRS are very similar to those required by SSAP 8. A significant difference is the removal of the requirement to disclose certain special reliefs that have been available in the Republic of Ireland. These reliefs are now being phased out.

24   The FRED had proposed a more general requirement to disclose the impact of any special reliefs. However, the Board has removed this proposal, having accepted the views expressed by some respondents that:

- to quantify the effects of all special reliefs obtained would be an onerous requirement for entities with worldwide operations, and
- the effects of significant reliefs are already disclosed because of the general requirement to explain any significant factors affecting the tax charge.

TRANSITIONAL ARRANGEMENTS

25   Charities and other entities at present receive a tapering transitional relief following the changes in the tax system that removed their right to reclaim tax credits. As a concession to these entities, the FRS permits them to continue to show that particular transitional relief as part of the income to which it relates, rather than as a tax refund.

26   The FRS contains no other transitional concessions. The application of the FRS for the first time will therefore be treated as a change in accounting policy, effective from the start of the accounting period in which it was first implemented. The Board chose this approach because the changes required arise from a review of the fundamental principles underlying the standard and not as a result of the changes to the tax system.

Financial Reporting Standard 17 is set out in paragraphs 1–105.

The Statement of Standard Accounting Practice, which comprises the paragraphs set in bold type, should be read in the context of the Objective as stated in paragraph 1 and the definitions set out in paragraph 2 and also of the Foreword to Accounting Standards and the Statement of Principles for Financial Reporting currently in issue.

The explanatory paragraphs contained in the FRS shall be regarded as part of the Statement of Standard Accounting Practice insofar as they assist in interpreting that statement.

Appendix IV 'The development of the FRS' reviews considerations and arguments that were thought significant by members of the Board in reaching the conclusions on the FRS.

[FRS 17]
Retirement benefits

(Issued November 2000)

Contents

Retirement benefits

Summary

Financial Reporting Standard 17 sets out the requirements for accounting for   **a**
retirement benefits.

Defined contribution schemes

The cost of a defined contribution scheme is equal to the contributions payable to the   **b**
scheme for the period.

Measurement of defined benefit scheme assets and liabilities

Defined benefit scheme assets are measured at fair value.   **c**

Defined benefit scheme liabilities are measured using the projected unit method.   **d**

Defined benefit scheme liabilities are discounted at the current rate of return on a   **e**
high quality corporate bond of equivalent term and currency to the liability.

Full actuarial valuations should be obtained at intervals not exceeding three years   **f**
and should be updated at each balance sheet date.

Recognition of defined benefit schemes

An asset is recognised to the extent that an employer can recover a surplus in a   **g**
defined benefit scheme through reduced contributions and refunds. A liability is
recognised to the extent that the deficit reflects the employer's legal or constructive
obligation.

The resulting defined benefit asset or liability is presented separately on the face of   **h**
the balance sheet after other net assets.

The change in the defined benefit asset or liability (other than that arising from   **i**
contributions to the scheme) is analysed into the following components:

(i)   the current service cost
(ii)   the interest cost
(iii)   the expected return on assets
(iv)   actuarial gains and losses
(v)   past service costs (if any)
(vi)   settlements and curtailments (if any).

The current service cost and interest cost are based on the discount rate at the   **j**
beginning of the period. The expected return on assets is based on the expected rate
of return at the beginning of the period. The current service cost is shown within the
appropriate statutory heading for pension costs in the profit and loss account. The
interest cost and expected return on assets are shown as a net amount of other
finance costs (or income) adjacent to interest.

The expected return is calculated by applying the expected rate of return over the   **k**
long term to the market value of scheme assets at the beginning of the year, adjusted
for any contributions received and benefits paid during the year. Although the

expected rate of return will vary according to market conditions it is expected that the amount of the return will normally be relatively stable.

l   Actuarial gains and losses are recognised immediately in the statement of total recognised gains and losses. They are not recycled into the profit and loss account in subsequent periods.

m   Past service costs are recognised in the profit and loss account over the period until the benefits vest. If the benefits vest immediately, the past service cost is recognised immediately.

n   Gains and losses arising on settlements and curtailments are recognised immediately in the profit and loss account.

Disclosures for defined benefit schemes

o   The following disclosures are required:

(i)   the main assumptions underlying the scheme
(ii)   an analysis of the assets in the scheme into broad classes and the expected rate of return on each class
(iii)   an analysis of the amounts included (a) within operating profit, (b) within other finance costs and (c) within the statement of total recognised gains and losses
(iv)   a five-year history of (a) the difference between the expected and actual return on assets, (b) experience gains and losses arising on the scheme liabilities and (c) the total actuarial gain or loss
(v)   an analysis of the movement in the surplus or deficit in the scheme over the period and a reconciliation of the surplus/deficit to the balance sheet asset/ liability.*

Financial Reporting Standard 17

OBJECTIVE

1   The objective of this FRS is to ensure that:

(a)   financial statements reflect at fair value the assets and liabilities arising from an employer's retirement benefit obligations and any related funding;
(b)   the operating costs of providing retirement benefits to employees are recognised in the accounting period(s) in which the benefits are earned by the employees, and the related finance costs and any other changes in value of the assets and liabilities are recognised in the accounting periods in which they arise; and

---

Editor's note: With effect for accounting periods beginning on or after 6 April 2007, and as a result of the Amendment to FRS 17 Retirement Benefits issued in December 2006, this paragraph is amended to read:

"The following disclosures are required:

(i)   the principal assumptions underlying the scheme;
(ii)   a reconciliation of the opening and closing balances of the fair value of scheme assets and the opening and closing balances of scheme liabilities showing effects during the period which gave rise to the movement in the opening and closing balances;
(iii)   for each major category of scheme assets the percentage or the amount that each major category constitutes of the fair value of the total scheme assets;
(iv)   a narrative description of the basis used to determine the overall expected rate of return on assets; and
(v)   the amounts for the current and previous four periods of the present value of the scheme liabilities, the fair value of the scheme assets and the surplus or deficit in the scheme."

(c)   the financial statements contain adequate disclosure of the cost of providing retirement benefits and the related gains, losses, assets and liabilities.

DEFINITIONS

The following definitions shall apply in the FRS and in particular in the Statement of Standard Accounting Practice set out **in bold type**.   **2**

Actuarial gains and losses:-

Changes in actuarial deficits or surpluses that arise because:

(a)   events have not coincided with the actuarial assumptions made for the last valuation (experience gains and losses) or
(b)   the actuarial assumptions have changed.

Current service cost:-

The increase in the present value of the scheme liabilities expected to arise from employee service in the current period.

Curtailment:-

An event that reduces the expected years of future service of present employees or reduces for a number of employees the accrual of defined benefits for some or all of their future service. Curtailments include:

(a)   termination of employees' services earlier than expected, for example as a result of closing a factory or discontinuing a segment of a business, and
(b)   termination of, or amendment to the terms of, a defined benefit scheme so that some or all future service by current employees will no longer qualify for benefits or will qualify only for reduced benefits.

Defined benefit scheme:-

A pension or other retirement benefit scheme other than a defined contribution scheme.

Usually, the scheme rules define the benefits independently of the contributions payable, and the benefits are not directly related to the investments of the scheme. The scheme may be funded or unfunded.

Defined contribution scheme:-

A pension or other retirement benefit scheme into which an employer pays regular contributions fixed as an amount or as a percentage of pay and will have no legal or constructive obligation to pay further contributions if the scheme does not have sufficient assets to pay all employee benefits relating to employee service in the current and prior periods.

An individual member's benefits are determined by reference to contributions paid into the scheme in respect of that member, usually increased by an amount based on the investment return on those contributions.

Defined contribution schemes may also provide death-in-service benefits. For the purposes of this definition, death-in-service benefits are not deemed to relate to employee service in the current and prior periods.

Expected rate of return on assets:-

The average rate of return, including both income and changes in fair value but net of scheme expenses, expected over the remaining life of the related obligation on the actual assets held by the scheme.

Interest cost:-

The expected increase during the period in the present value of the scheme liabilities because the benefits are one period closer to settlement.

Past service cost:-

The increase in the present value of the scheme liabilities related to employee service in prior periods arising in the current period as a result of the introduction of, or improvement to, retirement benefits.

Projected unit method:-

An accrued benefits valuation method in which the scheme liabilities make allowance for projected earnings. An accrued benefits valuation method is a valuation method in which the scheme liabilities at the valuation date relate to:
(a) the benefits for pensioners and deferred pensioners (ie individuals who have ceased to be active members but are entitled to benefits payable at a later date) and their dependants, allowing where appropriate for future increases, and
(b) the accrued benefits for members in service on the valuation date.

The accrued benefits are the benefits for service up to a given point in time, whether vested rights or not.

Guidance on the projected unit method is given in the Guidance Note GN26 issued by the Faculty and Institute of Actuaries.

Retirement benefits:-

All forms of consideration given by an employer in exchange for services rendered by employees that are payable after the completion of employment.

Retirement benefits do not include termination benefits payable as a result of either (i) an employer's decision to terminate an employee's employment before the normal retirement date or (ii) an employee's decision to accept voluntary redundancy in exchange for those benefits, because these are not given in exchange for services rendered by employees.

Scheme liabilities:-

The liabilities of a defined benefit scheme for outgoings due after the valuation date.

Scheme liabilities measured using the projected unit method reflect the benefits that the employer is committed to provide for service up to the valuation date.

Settlement:-

An irrevocable action that relieves the employer (or the defined benefit scheme) of the primary responsibility for a pension obligation and eliminates significant risks relating to the obligation and the assets used to effect the settlement. Settlements include:

(a) a lump-sum cash payment to scheme members in exchange for their rights to receive specified pension benefits;

(b) the purchase of an irrevocable annuity contract sufficient to cover vested benefits; and

(c) the transfer of scheme assets and liabilities relating to a group of employees leaving the scheme.

Vested rights:-

These are:

(a) for active members, benefits to which they would unconditionally be entitled on leaving the scheme;

(b) for deferred pensioners, their preserved benefits;

(c) for pensioners, pensions to which they are entitled.

Vested rights include where appropriate the related benefits for spouses or other dependants.

SCOPE

The FRS applies to all financial statements that are intended to give a true and fair view of a reporting employer's financial position and profit or loss (or income and expenditure) for a period. 3

The FRS covers all retirement benefits that an employer is committed to providing, whether the commitment is statutory, contractual or implicit in the employer's actions. It applies to retirement benefits arising overseas, as well as those arising in the UK and the Republic of Ireland. Retirement benefits include, for example, pensions and medical care during retirement. 4

The FRS covers funded and unfunded retirement benefits, including schemes that are operated on a pay-as-you-go basis, whereby benefits are paid by the employer in the period they fall due and no payments are made to fund benefits earned in the period. The FRS requires a liability to be recognised as the benefits are earned, not when they are due to be paid. The fact that the employer is funded by central government (or any other body) is not a reason for the employer not to recognise its own liabilities arising under the FRS. 5

Reporting entities applying the Financial Reporting Standard for Smaller Entities currently applicable are exempt from the FRS. 6

DEFINED CONTRIBUTION SCHEMES

7   The cost of a defined contribution scheme is equal to the contributions payable to the scheme for the accounting period. The cost should be recognised within operating profit in the profit and loss account.

MULTI-EMPLOYER SCHEMES

8   Where more than one employer participates in a defined contribution scheme, no special problems arise, since the employer's cost is limited to the contributions payable.

9   Where more than one employer participates in a defined benefit scheme the employer should account for the scheme as a defined benefit scheme unless:

(a)   the employer's contributions are set in relation to the current service period only (ie are not affected by any surplus or deficit in the scheme relating to past service of its own employees or any other members of the scheme). If this is the case, the employer should account for the contributions to the scheme as if it were a defined contribution scheme.

(b)   the employer's contributions are affected by a surplus or deficit in the scheme but the employer is unable to identify its share of the underlying assets and liabilities in the scheme on a consistent and reasonable basis. If this is the case, the employer should account for the contributions to the scheme as if it were a defined contribution scheme but, in addition, disclose:

(i)   the fact that the scheme is a defined benefit scheme but that the employer is unable to identify its share of the underlying assets and liabilities; and

(ii)   any available information about the existence of the surplus or deficit in the scheme and the implications of that surplus or deficit for the employer.*

10   Most multi-employer schemes will set contributions from employers so as to make good any deficit in the scheme and may reduce contributions to enable employers to benefit from a surplus. However, in some multi-employer schemes, an employer may have no obligation other than to pay a contribution that reflects only the benefits earned in the current period. In this case, from the point of view of the employer, the scheme is a defined contribution scheme and is accounted for as such. For this to be the case, there must be clear evidence that the employer cannot be required to pay additional contributions to the scheme relating to past service, including the existence of a third party that accepts that it has an obligation to fund the pension payments should the scheme have insufficient assets.

11   An employer may be required to make contributions set at a level to make good any deficit but may be unable to identify its share of the underlying assets and liabilities in the scheme on a consistent and reasonable basis. This may be the case if the scheme exposes the participating employers to actuarial risks associated with the current and former employees of other entities, for example when the contributions

---

*__Editor's note__: With effect for accounting periods beginning on or after 6 April 2007, and as a result of the Amendment to FRS 17 Retirement Benefits issued in December 2006, (i) and (ii) are removed and replaced with:

"(i)   the fact that the scheme is a defined benefit scheme;

(ii)   then reason why sufficient information is not available to enable the employer to account for the scheme as a defined benefit scheme;

(iii)   any available information about that surplus or deficit;

(iv)   the basis used to determine that surplus or deficit;

(v)   the implications, if any, for the employer".

from employers are set at a common level rather than reflecting the characteristics of the workforces of individual employers.

Subsidiaries are not exempt from the FRS and, where possible, will account for defined benefit schemes in accordance with its requirements. However, many group schemes are run on a basis that does not enable individual companies within the group to identify their share of the underlying assets and liabilities. In these circumstances, the individual companies (including the parent company) within the group will account for the scheme as a defined contribution scheme and will give the additional disclosures required above. From the point of view of the group entity, a group defined benefit scheme is not a multi-employer scheme and is treated as any other defined benefit scheme.   **12**

MEASUREMENT OF DEFINED BENEFIT SCHEMES

Paragraphs 14–36 of the FRS set out the requirements for measuring the assets and liabilities within a defined benefit scheme (the scheme assets and the scheme liabilities). The recognition of an asset or liability and the movements therein in the financial statements of the employer arising from the defined benefit scheme measured on this basis is covered in paragraphs 37–74.   **13**

Scheme assets

Assets in a defined benefit scheme should be measured at their fair value at the balance sheet date.   **14**

Scheme assets include current assets as well as investments. Any liabilities such as accrued expenses should be deducted.   **15**

For quoted securities, the mid-market value is taken as the fair value. For unquoted securities, an estimate of fair value is used. The fair value of unitised securities is taken to be the average of the bid and offer prices.*   **16**

Property should be valued at open market value or on another appropriate basis of valuation determined in accordance with the Appraisal and Valuation Manual published by the Royal Institution of Chartered Surveyors and the Practice Statements contained therein.   **17**

Insurance policies that exactly match the amount and timing of some or all of the benefits payable under the scheme should be measured at the same amount as the related obligations. For other insurance policies there are a number of possible valuation methods. A method should be chosen which gives the best approximation to fair value given the circumstances of the scheme.   **18**

Notional funding of a pension scheme does not give rise to assets in a scheme for the purposes of the FRS.   **19**

*****Editor's note**: With effect for accounting periods beginning on or after 6 April 2007, and as a result of the Amendment to FRS 17* Retirement Benefits *issued in December 2006, the reference to "mid-market value" in the first sentence is replaced with 'current bid price'.*

Scheme liabilities

Actuarial method and assumptions

20   **Defined benefit scheme liabilities should be measured on an actuarial basis using the projected unit method. The scheme liabilities comprise:**

    (a)   any benefits promised under the formal terms of the scheme; and

    (b)   any constructive obligations for further benefits where a public statement or past practice by the employer has created a valid expectation in the employees that such benefits will be granted.

21   Where the scheme rules require a surplus arising in the scheme to be shared between the employer and members (perhaps in conjunction with a similar sharing of deficits), or where past practice has established a valid expectation that this will be done, the amount that will be passed to members should be treated as increasing the scheme liabilities.

22   **The benefits should be attributed to periods of service according to the scheme's benefit formula, except where the benefit formula attributes a disproportionate share of the total benefits to later years of service. In such cases, the benefit should be attributed on a straight-line basis over the period during which it is earned.**

23   **The assumptions underlying the valuation should be mutually compatible and lead to the best estimate of the future cash flows that will arise under the scheme liabilities. The assumptions are ultimately the responsibility of the directors (or equivalent) but should be set upon advice given by an actuary. Any assumptions that are affected by economic conditions (financial assumptions) should reflect market expectations at the balance sheet date.**

24   Because of the long-term nature of most defined benefit schemes and the inherent uncertainties affecting them, the liabilities of the scheme are measured on an actuarial basis. This involves estimating the future cash flows arising under the scheme liabilities based on a number of actuarial assumptions such as mortality rates, employee turnover rates and salary growth, then discounting the cash flows at an appropriate rate.

25   Some of these assumptions are affected by the same economic factors. Actuarial assumptions are mutually compatible if they reflect the underlying economic factors consistently. To be consistent with the measurement of the assets of the scheme at fair value, they must also reflect market expectations at the balance sheet date.

26   For example, the rate of increase in salaries and the discount rate must reflect the same rate of general inflation. In jurisdictions where there is a liquid market in long-dated inflation-linked bonds, the yields on such bonds relative to those on fixed interest bonds of similar credit standing will give an indication of the expected rate of general inflation.

27   **The actuarial assumptions should reflect expected future events that will affect the cost of the benefits to which the employer is committed (either legally or through a constructive obligation) at the balance sheet date.**

28   Expected future events that will affect the cost of the benefits include:

    (a)   any expected cost of living increases either provided for in the scheme rules, publicly announced or awarded under an established practice that creates among the employees a valid expectation of receiving them;

    (b)   in the case of pensions based on final salary, any expected salary increases; and

    (c)   expected early retirement where the employee has that right under the scheme rules.

These events affect the measurement of benefits to which the employer is committed at the balance sheet date.

Expected future redundancies are not reflected in the actuarial assumptions because the employer is not committed (either legally or constructively) to making such redundancies in advance. When the employer does become committed to making the redundancies, any impact on the defined benefit scheme is treated as a settlement and/or curtailment (see paragraph 64). **29**

Expected future changes in the cost of retirement healthcare are particularly difficult to estimate—the cost often increases at a faster rate than either the retail price index or national earnings rate. Relevant considerations in determining the assumptions used to arrive at the retirement healthcare obligation include: **30**

(a) advances in medical skills and technologies, often involving more expensive treatment;
(b) the rise in the expectations of prospective patients; and
(c) the effect of the above on companies, governments and insurance schemes in cutting back benefits, or making the patient pay a proportion.

It is not appropriate to assume a reduction in benefits below those currently promised on the grounds that the employer will curtail the scheme at some time in the future. **31**

The discount rate

Defined benefit scheme liabilities should be discounted at a rate that reflects the time value of money and the characteristics of the liability. Such a rate should be assumed to be the current rate of return on a high quality corporate bond of equivalent currency and term to the scheme liabilities. **32**

For this purpose, a high quality corporate bond means a bond that has been rated at the level of AA or equivalent status. The rate of return for such a bond reflects the time value of money and a small premium for risk. That premium is taken to reflect the options that the employer has to reduce the assumed scheme liabilities, including in extremis the option of closing down the scheme. If there is no liquid market in bonds of this type or duration, then a reasonable proxy should be used. This may be government bonds plus a margin for assumed credit risk spreads derived from global bond markets. **33**

Many pension schemes provide benefits at least partly linked to inflation. One way to reflect that characteristic would be to consider the return on an index-linked corporate bond. However, given that there are few such bonds in existence, a more reliable alternative is to consider fixed interest corporate bonds and increase the cash flows to be discounted in line with inflation (ie project the liability to be discounted in nominal terms). Guidance on the inflation assumption is given in paragraph 26. **34**

Frequency of valuations

Full actuarial valuations by a professionally qualified actuary should be obtained for a defined benefit scheme at intervals not exceeding three years. The actuary should review the most recent actuarial valuation at the balance sheet date and update it to reflect current conditions. **35**

36   The actuarial valuations required for the FRS may use different assumptions and measurement methods from those used for a scheme's funding valuation. Full actuarial valuations under the FRS are not needed at every balance sheet date. Some aspects of the valuation will need to be updated at each balance sheet date, for example the fair value of the assets and financial assumptions such as the discount rate. Other assumptions, such as the expected leaving rate and mortality rate, may not need to be updated annually.

RECOGNITION OF DEFINED BENEFIT SCHEMES

Recognition in the balance sheet

37   **The surplus/deficit in a defined benefit scheme is the excess/shortfall of the value of the assets in the scheme over/below the present value of the scheme liabilities. The employer should recognise an asset to the extent that it is able to recover a surplus either through reduced contributions in the future or through refunds from the scheme. The employer should recognise a liability to the extent that it reflects its legal or constructive obligation.**

38   A surplus in the scheme gives rise to an asset of the employer to the extent that:

(a)   the employer controls its use, ie has the ability to use the surplus to generate future economic benefits for itself, either in the form of a reduction in future contributions or a refund from the scheme; and

(b)   that control is a result of past events (contributions paid by the employer and investment growth in excess of rights earned by the employees).

Usually the employer's obligation under the trust deed is to pay such contributions as the actuary believes to be necessary to keep the scheme fully funded but without building up a surplus. When a surplus arises, it is unlikely that the employer can be required to make contributions to maintain the surplus. In addition, the award of benefit improvements is also usually in the hands of the employer. Thus, in general, the employer controls the use of a surplus in the scheme.

39   Conversely, the employer has a liability if it has a legal or constructive obligation to make good a deficit in the defined benefit scheme. In general, the employer will either have a legal obligation under the terms of the scheme trust deed or will have by its past actions and statements created a constructive obligation as defined in FRS 12 'Provisions, Contingent Liabilities and Contingent Assets'. The legal or constructive obligation to fund the deficit should be assumed to apply to the deficit based on assumptions used under the FRS.

40   In a scheme where employees as well as the employer make contributions, any deficit should be assumed to be borne by the employer unless the scheme rules require members' contributions to be increased to help fund a deficit. In this case, the present value of the required additional contributions should be treated as reducing the deficit to be recognised by the employer.

41   **In determining the asset to be recognised in accordance with paragraph 37, the amount that can be recovered through reduced contributions in the future is the present value of the liability expected to arise from future service by current and future scheme members less the present value of future employee contributions. No growth in the number of active scheme members should be assumed but a declining membership should be reflected if appropriate. The amount that can be recovered should be based on the assumptions used under the FRS, not the funding assumptions. The present value of the**

reduction in future contributions is determined using the discount rate applied to measure the defined benefit liability.

The amount to be recovered from refunds from the scheme should reflect only refunds that have been agreed by the pension scheme trustees at the balance sheet date.   **42**

The employer may not control or be able to benefit from the whole of a surplus—it   **43** may be so large that the employer cannot absorb it all through reduced contributions, and refunds from the scheme may be difficult to obtain.

The amount recoverable through reduced contributions reflects the maximum pos-   **44** sible to be recovered without assuming an increase in the number of employees covered by the scheme. There is no restriction on the period over which the reduction in contributions can be obtained, but the effect of discounting will increasingly reduce the impact of the reductions the further into the future they are, leading to an absolute limit on the amount that can be recognised equal to the service cost divided by the discount rate.

In practice, a surplus that potentially could be recovered will instead often be used in   **45** part to provide benefit improvements to members, thereby reducing the amount that the employer recovers through reduced contributions. The use of a potentially recoverable surplus in this way should be treated as a past service cost when it occurs (see paragraph 60) and not anticipated by reducing the amount recognised as an asset.

Paragraphs 67–70 specify how the limit on the amount that can be recognised as an   **46** asset should be recognised in the performance statements.

Any unpaid contributions to the scheme should be presented in the balance sheet as a   **47** **creditor due within one year. The defined benefit asset or liability should be presented separately on the face of the balance sheet:**

(a) **in balance sheets of the type prescribed for companies in Great Britain* by the Companies Act 1985, Schedule 4, format 1: after item J Accruals and deferred income but before item K Capital and reserves; and**

(b) **in balance sheets of the type prescribed for companies in Great Britain* by the Companies Act 1985, Schedule 4, format 2: any asset after ASSETS item D** *Prepayments and accrued income* **and any liability after LIABILITIES item D** *Accruals and deferred income.*

Where an employer has more than one scheme, the total of any defined benefit assets and the total of any defined benefit liabilities should be shown separately on the face of the balance sheet.

An example of the required presentation for the defined benefit asset or liability other   **48** than any unpaid contributions is shown in Appendix I.†

The deferred tax relating to the defined benefit asset or liability should be offset against   **49** **the defined benefit asset or liability and not included with other deferred tax assets or liabilities.**

---

* *The equivalent statutory provisions for Northern Ireland are in the Companies (Northern Ireland) Order 1986, Schedule 4; and for the Republic of Ireland are in the Companies (Amendment) Act 1986, the Schedule.*

† ***Editor's note****: With effect for accounting periods beginning on or after 6 April 2007, and as a result of the Amendment to FRS 17* Retirement Benefits *issued in December 2006, this paragraph is withdrawn.*

Recognition in the performance statements

50   The change in the defined benefit asset or liability (other than that arising from contributions to the scheme) should be analysed into the following components:

PERIODIC COSTS
(a)   the current service cost;
(b)   the interest cost;
(c)   the expected return on assets;
(d)   actuarial gains and losses;

NON-PERIODIC COSTS
(e)   past service costs; and
(f)   gains and losses on settlements and curtailments.

Current service cost, interest cost and expected return on assets

51   The current service cost should be based on the most recent actuarial valuation at the beginning of the period, with the financial assumptions updated to reflect conditions at that date. It should be included within operating profit in the profit and loss account (except insofar as the related employee remuneration is capitalised in accordance with another accounting standard). Any contributions from employees should be set off against the current service cost.

52   The current service cost will be based on the discount rate at the beginning of the period and will therefore reflect current long-term market interest rates at that time.

53   The interest cost should be based on the discount rate and the present value of the scheme liabilities at the beginning of the period. The interest cost should, in addition, reflect changes in the scheme liabilities during the period.

54   The expected return on assets is based on long-term expectations at the beginning of the period and is expected to be reasonably stable. For quoted corporate or government bonds, the expected return should be calculated by applying the current redemption yield at the beginning of the period to the market value of the bonds held by the scheme at the beginning of the period. For other assets (for example, equities), the expected return should be calculated by applying the rate of return expected over the long term at the beginning of the period (given the value of the assets at that date) to the fair value of the assets held by the scheme at the beginning of the period. The expected return on assets should, in addition, reflect changes in the assets in the scheme during the period as a result of contributions paid into and benefits paid out of the scheme. The expected rate of return should be set by the directors (or equivalent) having taken advice from an actuary.

55   For quoted fixed and index-linked securities, the expected return can be observed from the market. For other assets, the expected return has to be based on assumptions about the expected long-term rate of return. The rate of return expected over the long term will vary according to market conditions, but it is expected that the amount of the return will be reasonably stable.

56   The net of the interest cost and the expected return on assets should be included as other finance costs (or income) adjacent to interest.

Actuarial gains and losses

Actuarial gains and losses arising from any new valuation and from updating the latest actuarial valuation to reflect conditions at the balance sheet date should be recognised in the statement of total recognised gains and losses for the period. 57

Actuarial gains and losses may arise on both the defined benefit scheme liabilities and any scheme assets. They comprise: 58

(a) on the scheme assets, differences between the expected return and the actual return (for example, a sudden change in the value of the scheme assets);
(b) on the scheme liabilities, (i) differences between the actuarial assumptions underlying the scheme liabilities and actual experience during the period and (ii) the effect of changes in actuarial assumptions; and
(c) any adjustment necessary in accordance with paragraph 67 resulting from the limit on the amount that can be recognised as an asset in the balance sheet.

Once an actuarial gain or loss has been recognised in the statement of total recognised gains and losses it is not recognised again in the profit and loss account in subsequent periods. 59

Past service costs

Past service costs should be recognised in the profit and loss account on a straight-line basis over the period in which the increases in benefit vest. To the extent that the benefits vest immediately, the past service cost should be recognised immediately. Any unrecognised past service costs should be deducted from the scheme liabilities and the balance sheet asset or liability adjusted accordingly. 60

Past service costs arise when the employer makes a commitment to provide a higher level of benefit than previously promised, for example the creation of a pension benefit for a spouse where such a benefit did not previously exist or a grant of early retirement with added-on years of service. 61

Past service costs do not include increases in the expected cost of benefits that the employer is already statutorily, contractually or implicitly committed to, for example cost of living increases to pensions in payment and deferred pensions. Such increases are covered by the actuarial assumptions and any difference between actual experience and the assumptions or the effects of any changes in the assumptions are actuarial gains and losses. 62

Past service costs include benefit improvements awarded as a result of a surplus arising in the scheme. The fact that they are funded out of a surplus does not result in there being no cost to the employer if the surplus was potentially recoverable by the employer—the use of the surplus for benefit improvements means that the employer cannot then benefit from it in other ways. 63

Settlements and curtailments

Losses arising on a settlement or curtailment not allowed for in the actuarial assumptions should be measured at the date on which the employer becomes demonstrably committed to the transaction and recognised in the profit and loss account covering that date. Gains arising on a settlement or curtailment not allowed for in the actuarial assumptions should be measured at the date on which all parties whose consent 64 is required are irrevocably committed to the transaction and recognised in the profit and loss account covering that date.

65   Where under the scheme rules the employees have the option to retire early or transfer out of the scheme, the resulting settlements and curtailments are allowed for in the normal demographic assumptions made by the actuary and any gains and losses arising are actuarial gains and losses.

66   In contrast, some settlements and curtailments arise from specific decisions made by an employer that are not covered by actuarial assumptions, for example major changes in the circumstances of the scheme instigated by the employer, such as the transfer of accrued benefits of some or all the members into a defined contribution scheme or a reduction in employees because of the sale or termination of an operation. Gains and losses arising from such events are part of the employer's operating results for the period (unless they attach to one of the items shown immediately after operating profit).

Impact of limit on balance sheet asset

67   **The limit set out in paragraph 41 on the amount that can be recognised as an asset may result in there being some part of a defined benefit scheme surplus that is not recognised. Where this is the case, the amounts recognised in the performance statements should be adjusted as follows.**

(a)   **First, if any refund is agreed and is covered by the unrecognised surplus, it should be recognised as other finance income adjacent to interest, with separate disclosure in the notes.**

Refunds from schemes where the whole surplus is regarded as recoverable do not give rise to gains. The cash received simply reduces the balance sheet asset (along with any related tax effect).

(b)   **Next, the unrecognised surplus should be applied to extinguish past service costs or losses on settlements or curtailments that would otherwise be charged in the profit and loss account for the period, with disclosure in the notes of the items and amounts so extinguished.**

(c)   **Next, the expected return on assets should be restricted so that it does not exceed the total of the current service cost, interest cost (and any past service costs and losses on settlements and curtailments not covered by the unrecognised surplus) and any increase in the recoverable surplus.**

(d)   **Finally, any further adjustment necessary should be treated as an actuarial gain or loss.**

68   An increase in the recoverable amount of a surplus arising from an increase in the active membership of the scheme should be recognised as an operating gain.

69   An increase in the active membership can arise either from an increase in general recruitment or from the transfer of employees following an acquisition. The gain arising in the latter case is a post-acquisition operating gain, not an adjustment to the purchase price and goodwill.

70   **A decrease in the recoverable amount of a surplus arising from a fall in the active membership should be treated as an actuarial loss unless it arises from an event not covered by the assumptions underlying the amount originally regarded as recoverable, for example a settlement or curtailment. If it does arise from such an event, it should be treated as part of the loss arising on that event.**

Tax

When current tax relief arises on contributions made to a defined benefit scheme, it should be allocated to the profit and loss account or statement of total recognised gains and losses on the basis that the contribution covers first the items reported in the profit and loss account and then any actuarial losses reported in the statement of total recognised gains and losses, unless it is clear that some other allocation is more appropriate. To the extent that the contribution exceeds these items, the current tax relief attributable to the excess should be allocated to the profit and loss account, again unless it is clearly more appropriate to allocate it to the statement of total recognised gains and losses. **71**

Current tax relief is usually available on contributions paid to the scheme and deferred tax usually arises on the balance of the charges/credits. The tax follows the relevant item, ie tax on the service cost, interest cost and expected return on assets will be recognised in the profit and loss account and tax on the actuarial gains and losses will be recognised in the statement of total recognised gains and losses. FRS 16 'Current Tax' requires disclosure of the current tax recognised in the profit and loss account and statement of total recognised gains and losses. The question arises of where the current tax relief arising on contributions should be deemed to belong. Sometimes it will be clear what the contribution relates to, for example when a special contribution is made to fund a deficit arising from an identifiable cause, say an actuarial loss, in which case the current tax relief should be allocated to the statement of total recognised gains and losses. In the absence of a clear link between the contribution and the items recognised in the performance statements, the allocation in paragraph 71 should be followed. **72**

Death-in-service and incapacity benefits

A charge should be made to operating profit to reflect the expected cost of providing any death-in-service or incapacity benefits for the period. Any difference between that expected cost and amounts actually incurred should be treated as an actuarial gain or loss. **73**

Where a scheme insures the death-in-service costs, the expected cost for the accounting period is simply the premium payable for the period. Where the costs are not insured, the expected cost reflects the probability of any employees dying in the period and the benefit that would then be paid out. **74**

DISCLOSURES

Defined contribution schemes

The following disclosures should be made in respect of a defined contribution scheme: **75**

(a)   the nature of the scheme (ie defined contribution);
(b)   the cost for the period; and
(c)   any outstanding or prepaid contributions at the balance sheet date.

Defined benefit schemes*

The following disclosures should be made in respect of a defined benefit scheme: **76**

*Editor's note: With effect for accounting periods beginning on or after 6 April 2007, and as a result of the Amendment to FRS 17 Retirement Benefits *issued in December 2006, Paragraphs 76 to 93 are withdrawn. The replacement paragraphs have been included at the end of the text of FRS 17.*

(a)   the nature of the scheme (ie defined benefit);

(b)   the date of the most recent full actuarial valuation on which the amounts in the financial statements are based. If the actuary is an employee or officer of the reporting entity, or of the group of which it is a member, this fact should be disclosed;

(c)   the contribution made in respect of the accounting period and any agreed contribution rates for future years; and

(d)   for closed schemes and those in which the age profile of the active membership is rising significantly, the fact that under the projected unit method the current service cost will increase as the members of the scheme approach retirement.

77   Paragraph 9 requires additional disclosures about some multi-employer defined benefit schemes that are accounted for as if they were defined contribution schemes.

Assumptions

78   **Each of the main financial assumptions used at the beginning of the period and at the balance sheet date should be disclosed. They should be disclosed as separate individual figures, not combined or netted. The main financial assumptions include:**

(a)   **the inflation assumption;**

(b)   **the rate of increase in salaries;**

(c)   **the rate of increase for pensions in payment and deferred pensions; and**

(d)   **the rate used to discount scheme liabilities.**

79   The most important assumptions underlying the present value of the scheme liabilities are the rates of increase in salaries and pensions in payment and the rate of interest applied to discount the estimated cash flows arising under the liabilities. The valuation of assets in the scheme is not affected by the actuarial assumptions because the assets are measured at fair value.

Fair value and expected return on assets

80   **The fair value of the assets held by the pension scheme at the beginning and end of the period should be analysed into the following classes and disclosed together with the expected rate of return assumed for each class for the period and the subsequent period:**

(a)   **equities;**

(b)   **bonds; and**

(c)   **other (subanalysed if material).**

81   The assumption made for the expected return on assets does not affect the valuation of the scheme assets because they are measured at fair value. It does, however, determine the amount to be recognised in the profit and loss account.

Components of the defined benefit cost

82   **The following amounts included within operating profit (or capitalised with the relevant employee remuneration) should be disclosed in the notes to the financial statements:**

(a)   **the current service cost;**

(b)   **any past service costs;**

(c)   **any previously unrecognised surplus deducted from the past service costs;**

(d)   **gains and losses on any settlements or curtailments; and**

(e)   **any previously unrecognised surplus deducted from the settlement or curtailment losses.**

Any gains and losses on settlements or curtailments (and any previously unrecognised **83** surplus deducted from the losses) included within a separate item after operating profit should be disclosed in the notes to the financial statements.

The following amounts included as other finance costs (or income) should be disclosed **84** separately in the notes to the financial statements:

(a)   the interest cost; and
(b)   the expected return on assets in the scheme.

The following amounts included within the statement of total recognised gains and **85** losses should be disclosed in the notes to the financial statements:

(a)   the difference between the expected and actual return on assets;
(b)   experience gains and losses arising on the scheme liabilities; and
(c)   the effects of changes in the demographic and financial assumptions underlying the present value of the scheme liabilities.

History of amounts recognised in the statement of total recognised gains and losses

The notes to the financial statements should disclose, for the accounting period and **86** previous four periods:

(a)   the difference between the expected and actual return on assets expressed as (i) an amount and (ii) a percentage of the scheme assets at the balance sheet date;
(b)   the experience gains and losses arising on the scheme liabilities expressed as (i) an amount and (ii) a percentage of the present value of the scheme liabilities at the balance sheet date; and
(c)   the total actuarial gain or loss expressed as (i) an amount and (ii) a percentage of the present value of the scheme liabilities at the balance sheet date.

A consistent trend of experience losses/gains in the statement of total recognised **87** gains and losses may indicate that the assumptions used have been over-optimistic/ over-pessimistic and may cast doubt upon the reliability of the amounts reported in the profit and loss account. Where such a trend has emerged it is important that careful consideration is given to the choice of assumptions in the future.

Reconciliation to the balance sheet

The fair value of the scheme assets, the present value of the scheme liabilities based on **88** the accounting assumptions and the resulting surplus or deficit should be disclosed in a note to the financial statements. Where the asset or liability in the balance sheet differs from the surplus or deficit in the scheme, an explanation of the difference should be given. An analysis of the movements during the period in the surplus or deficit in the scheme should be given.

Differences between the asset or liability in the balance sheet and the surplus or **89** deficit in the scheme will arise because of the related deferred tax balance and also when part of a surplus or deficit has not been recognised in the balance sheet, for example when part of the surplus in the scheme is not recoverable by the employer or when past service awards have not yet vested.

Analysis of reserves

The analysis of reserves in the notes to the financial statements should distinguish the **90** amount relating to the defined benefit asset or liability net of the related deferred tax.

Comparative amounts

91   There is a general requirement in companies legislation and accounting standards for comparative figures to be given. It should be noted that this requirement applies to the disclosures specified in paragraphs 78 and 80 relating to the position at the beginning of the period.

Entities with more than one scheme

92   **Where an employer has more than one defined benefit scheme, disclosures may be made in total, separately for each scheme, or in such groupings as are considered to be the most useful. When an employer provides disclosures in total for a number of schemes, the assumptions should be given in the form of weighted averages or of relatively narrow ranges with any outside the range disclosed separately.**

93   Useful groupings of schemes for disclosure purposes may be based on:

(a)   the geographical location of the schemes, for example by distinguishing UK schemes from overseas schemes; or

(b)   whether the schemes are subject to significantly different risks, for example pension schemes and retirement medical care schemes.

DATE FROM WHICH EFFECTIVE AND TRANSITIONAL ARRANGEMENTS

94   **The following amounts, measured in accordance with the requirements of the FRS, should be disclosed in the notes to the financial statements:**

(a)   **for financial statements relating to accounting periods ending on or after 22 June 2001: the disclosures required by paragraphs 76–81 and 88–93 of the FRS relating to the closing balance sheet (without comparatives for the previous period);**

(b)   **in addition, for financial statements relating to accounting periods ending on or after 22 June 2002:**

   (i)   **the disclosures required by paragraphs 76–81 and 88–93 of the FRS relating to the opening balance sheet (without comparatives for the previous period);**

   (ii)   **the disclosures required by paragraphs 82–85 of the FRS relating to the performance statements (without comparatives for the previous period); and**

   (iii)   **the disclosures required by paragraph 86 for the current period only.**

(c)   **In addition, for financial statements relating to accounting periods ending on or after 22 June 2003, the disclosures required by paragraphs 82–85 for the comparative period and the disclosures required by paragraph 86 for periods ending on or after 22 June 2002.**

   None of these amounts need be recognised in the primary statements in these financial statements.

All the requirements of the FRS should be regarded as standard for accounting periods **95**
beginning on or after 1 January 2005. Earlier adoption is encouraged.*

Gains and losses arising on the initial recognition of items in the primary statements **96**
under the FRS should be dealt with as prior period adjustments in accordance with FRS 3.
It is not required to create retrospectively the five-year history of amounts recognised in
the statement of total recognised gains and losses beyond those figures already disclosed
in financial statements under paragraph 94 above.

FRS 7 requires the fair value of the deficit or surplus to be recognised as part of a **97**
business acquisition. This FRS applies the same policy in requiring the fair value of
the defined benefit asset/liability to be recognised. The method of arriving at fair
value under this FRS may be different from that previously used on acquisition, but
any such difference should be treated as a change in assumptions (ie an actuarial gain
or loss) arising since acquisition. Goodwill arising on the acquisition should not,
therefore, be restated.

WITHDRAWAL OF SSAP 24 AND UITF ABSTRACTS 6 AND 18 AND AMENDMENT OF OTHER ACCOUNTING STANDARDS

When applied in full, the FRS supersedes SSAP 24 'Accounting for pension costs', UITF **98**
Abstract 6 'Accounting for post-retirement benefits other than pensions' and UITF
Abstract 18 'Pension costs following the 1997 tax changes in respect of dividend
income'.

[Not reproduced, as all changes that continue to be relevant have been made to the **99-105**
underlying standards or abstracts.]

Editor's note: The following paragraphs apply with effect for accounting periods
beginning on or after 6 April 2007, as a result of the Amendment to FRS 17
Retirement Benefits issued in December 2006. See note to paragraph 76 of the
standard.

An employer shall disclose information that enables users of financial statements to **76**
evaluate the nature of its defined benefit schemes and the financial effects of changes in
those schemes during the period.

**Editor's note: With effect for accounting periods beginning on or after 6 April 2007, and as a result of the
Amendment to FRS 17Retirement Benefits issued in December 2006, Paragraph 95 is withdrawn and replaced
with:*

*"Subject to the requirements of paragraphs 95A to 95C below, all the requirements of the FRS should be
regarded as standard for accounting periods beginning on or after 1 January 2005. Early adoption is encouraged.*

*95A The requirements of this amendment (which has amended paragraphs 9b, 16 and paragraphs 76 to 82)
become effective for financial statements covering periods beginning on or after 6 April 2007. In accordance with
FRS 28 "Corresponding Amounts" this amendment requires corresponding amounts. Early adoption is
encouraged.*

*95B Paragraph 77(h) of the FRS requires disclosure of the cumulative amount of actuarial gains and losses
recognised in the statement of total recognised gains and losses. The amount to be disclosed should be the amount
recognised in the statement of total recognised gains and losses for accounting periods ending on or after 22 June
2002 and subsequently included by prior year adjustment under paragraph 96 of the FRS.*

*95C Paragraph 77(o) of the FRS requires disclosure for the current accounting period and previous four
accounting periods of the fair value of the scheme assets. This amendment changes paragraph 16 of the FRS and
requires quoted securities to be valued at current bid-price. An entity is not required to restate corresponding
amounts for the first two of the previous four accounting periods required by paragraph 77(o). Where an entity
selects not to restate corresponding amounts it should disclose that corresponding amounts are not restated."*

77   **An employer shall disclose the following information about defined benefit schemes:**

(a)   a general description of the type of scheme.

(b)   a reconciliation of opening and closing balances of the present value of scheme liabilities showing separately, if applicable, the effects during the period attributable to each of the following:

(i)   current service cost,

(ii)   interest cost,

(iii)   contributions by scheme participants,

(iv)   actuarial gains and losses,

(v)   foreign currency exchange rate changes on schemes measured in a currency different from the entity's presentation* currency,

(vi)   benefits paid,

(vii)   past service cost,

(viii)   business combinations,

(ix)   curtailments, and

(x)   settlements.

(c)   an analysis of scheme liabilities into amounts arising from schemes that are wholly unfunded and amounts arising from schemes that are wholly or partly funded.

(d)   a reconciliation of the opening and closing balances of the fair value of scheme assets showing separately, if applicable, the effects during the period attributable to each of the following:

(i)   expected rate of return on scheme assets,

(ii)   actuarial gains and losses,

(iii)   foreign currency exchange rate changes on schemes measured in a currency different from the entity's presentation† currency,

(iv)   contributions by the employer,

(v)   contributions by scheme participants,

(vi)   benefits paid,

(vii)   business combinations and

(viii)   settlements.

(e)   a reconciliation of the present value of scheme liabilities in (b) and the fair value of the scheme assets in (d) to the assets and liabilities recognised in the balance sheet, showing at least:

(i)   any past service cost not recognised in the balance sheet (see paragraph 60);

(ii)   any amount not recognised as an asset, because of the limit in paragraph 41; and

(iii)   any other amounts recognised in the balance sheet.

(f)   the total expense recognised in profit or loss for each of the following, and the line item(s) in which they are included:

(i)   current service cost;

(ii)   interest cost;

(iii)   expected return on scheme assets;

(iv)   past service cost;

(v)   the effect of any curtailment or settlement; and

(vi)   the effect of the limit in paragraph 41.

ASB Note: For entities that apply SSAP 20 'Foreign Currency Translation' the phrase 'entity's presentation currency' should be replaced with 'entity's local currency'.

†ASB Note: For entities that apply SSAP 20 'Foreign Currency Translation' the phrase 'entity's presentation currency' should be replaced with 'entity's local currency'.*

(g) the total amounts recognised in the statement of total recognised gains and losses for each of the following:

   (i) actuarial gains and losses; and
   (ii) the effect of the limit in paragraph 41.

(h) the cumulative amount of actuarial gains and losses recognised in the statement of total recognised gains and losses.

(i) for each major category of scheme assets, which shall include, but is not limited to, equity instruments, debt instruments, property, and all other assets, the percentage or amount that each major category constitutes of the fair value of the total scheme assets.

(j) the amounts included in the fair value of scheme assets for:

   (i) each category of the entity's own financial instruments; and
   (ii) any property occupied by, or other assets used by, the entity.

(k) a narrative description of the basis used to determine the overall expected rate of return on assets, including the effect of the major categories of scheme assets.

(l) the actual return on scheme assets.

(m) the principal actuarial assumptions used as at the balance sheet date, including, when applicable:

   (i)   the discount rates;
   (ii) the expected rates of return on any assets of the scheme for the periods presented in the financial statements*;
   (iii) the expected rates of salary increases (and of changes in an index or other variable specified in the formal or constructive terms of a scheme as the basis for future benefit increases);
   (iv) retirement healthcare cost trend rates; and
   (v)   any other material actuarial assumptions used.

   An employer shall disclose each actuarial assumption in absolute terms (for example, as an absolute percentage) and not just as a margin between different percentages or other variables.

(n) the effect of an increase of one percentage point and the effect of a decrease of one percentage point in the assumed retirement healthcare cost trend rates on:

   (i) the aggregate of the current service cost and interest cost components of net periodic retirement healthcare costs; and
   (ii) the accumulated retirement healthcare obligation for healthcare costs.

   For the purposes of this disclosure, all other assumptions shall be held constant. For schemes operating in a high inflation environment, the disclosure shall be the effect of a percentage increase or decrease in the assumed healthcare cost trend rate of a significance similar to one percentage point in a low inflation environment.

(o) the amounts for the current accounting period and previous four accounting periods of:

   (i) the present value of the scheme liabilities, the fair value of the scheme assets and the surplus or deficit in the scheme; and
   (ii) the experience adjustments arising on:
      (A) the scheme liabilities expressed either as (1) an amount or (2) a percentage of the scheme liabilities at the balance sheet date and
      (B) the assets of the scheme expressed either as (1) an amount or (2) a percentage of the assets of the scheme at the balance sheet date.

*ASB note: This requirement is for information as at the beginning of each period presented.

(p)   **the employer's best estimate, as soon as it can reasonably be determined, of contributions expected to be paid to the scheme during the accounting period beginning after the balance sheet date.**

78   Paragraph 77(a) requires a general description of the type of scheme. Such a description distinguishes, for example, flat salary pension schemes from final salary pension schemes and from retirement healthcare schemes. The description of the scheme shall include informal practices that give rise to constructive obligations included in the measurement of the scheme liabilities in accordance with paragraph 20(b). Further detail is not required.

79   When an employer has more than one defined benefit scheme, disclosures may be made in total, separately for each scheme, or in such groupings as are considered to be the most useful. It may be useful to distinguish groupings by criteria such as the following:

(a)   the geographical location of the schemes, for example, by distinguishing domestic schemes from foreign schemes; or

(b)   whether schemes are subject to materially different risks, for example, by distinguishing flat salary pension schemes from final salary pension schemes and from retirement healthcare schemes.

When an employer provides disclosures in total for a grouping of schemes, such disclosures are provided in the form of weighted averages or of relatively narrow ranges.

80   Paragraph 9(b) requires additional disclosures about multi-employer defined benefit schemes that are treated as if they were defined contribution schemes.

81   Where required by FRS 8 'Related Party Disclosures' an employer discloses information about related party transactions with retirement benefit schemes.

82   Where required by FRS 12 'Provisions, Contingent Liabilities and Contingent Assets' an employer discloses information about contingent liabilities arising from retirement benefit obligations.

Adoption of FRS 17 by the board

Financial Reporting Standard 17 'Retirement Benefits' was approved for issue by the ten members of the Accounting Standards Board.

Sir David Tweedie   (Chairman)
Allan Cook CBE   (Technical Director)
David Allvey
Ian Brindle
Dr John Buchanan
John Coombe
Huw Jones
Isobel Sharp
Professor Geoffrey Whittington
Ken Wild

Appendix I*
Disclosure Example

Balance sheet presentation

	20X2 £ million	20X1 £ million
Net assets excluding pension asset	700	650
Pension asset	335	143
Net assets including pension asset	1,035	793

Reserves note

	20X2 £ million	20X1 £ million
Profit and loss reserve excluding pension asset	400	350
Pension reserve	335	143
Profit and loss reserve	735	493

Pension cost note

Composition of the schemes

The group operates a defined benefit scheme in the UK. A full actuarial valuation was carried out at 31 December 20X1 and updated to 31 December 20X2 by a qualified independent actuary. The major assumptions used by the actuary were:

	At 31/12/X2	At 31/12/X1	At 31/12/X0
Rate of increase in salaries	4.0 %	5.5 %	6.5 %
Rate of increase in pensions in payment	2.0 %	3.0 %	3.5 %
Discount rate	4.5 %	7.0 %	8.5 %
Inflation assumption	2.5 %	4.0 %	5.0 %

The assets in the scheme and the expected rate of return were:

	Long-term rate of return expected at 31/12/X2	Value at 31/12/X2 £ million	Long-term rate of return expected at 31/12/X1	Value at 31/12/X1 £ million	Long-term rate of return expected at 31/12/X0	Value at 31/12/X0 £ million
Equities	7.3%	1116	8.0%	721	9.3%	570
Bonds	5.5%	298	6.0%	192	8.0%	152
Property	6.0%	74	6.1%	49	7.9%	38
Total market value of assets		1,488		962		760
Present value of scheme liabilities		(1,009)		(758)		(668)
Surplus in the scheme		479		204		92
Related deferred tax liability		(144)		(61)		(28)
Net pension asset		335		143		64

[Note: shaded figures not mandatory under the FRS]

Analysis of the amount charged to operating profit

	20X2 £ million	20X1 £ million
Current service cost	34	25
Past service cost	12	—
Total operating charge	46	25

Analysis of the amount credited to other finance income

	20X2 £ million	20X1 £ million
Expected return on pension scheme assets	73	68
Interest on pension scheme liabilities	(53)	(57)
Net return	20	11

Analysis of amount recognised in statement of total recognised gains and losses (STRGL)

	20X2 £ million	20X1 £ million
Actual return less expected return on pension scheme assets	480	138
Experience gains and losses arising on the scheme liabilities	(58)	(6)
Changes in assumptions underlying the present value of the scheme liabilities	(146)	(41)
Actuarial gain recognised in STRGL	276	91

Movement in surplus during the year

	20X2 £ million	20X1 £ million
Surplus in scheme at beginning of the year	204	92
Movement in year:		
Current service cost	(34)	(25)
Contributions	25	35
Past service costs	(12)	–
Other finance income	20	11
Actuarial gain	276	91
Surplus in scheme at end of the year	479	204

The full actuarial valuation at 31 December 20X1 showed an increase in the surplus from £92 million to £204 million. Improvements in benefits costing £12 million were made in 20X2 and contributions reduced to £25 million (8 per cent of pensionable pay). It has been agreed with the trustees that contributions for the next three years will remain at that level.

History of experience gains and losses

	20X2	20X1	20X0	20W9	20W8
Difference between the expected and actual return on scheme assets:					
amount (£ million)	480	138	(6)	94	(73)
percentage of scheme assets	32%	14%	(1%)	16%	(26%)
Experience gains and losses on scheme liabilities:					
amount (£ million)	(58)	(6)	34	25	(23)
percentage of the present value of the scheme liabilities	(6%)	(1%)	5%	2%	(2%)
Total amount recognised in statement of total recognised gains and losses:					
amount (£ million)	276	91	1	66	(158)
percentage of the present value of the scheme liabilities	27%	12%	0%	5%	(14%)

Appendix I*
Illustrative Disclosures

This appendix accompanies, but is not part of, FRS 17. Extracts from notes show how the required disclosures may be aggregated in the case of a large multi-national group that provides a variety of employee benefits. These extracts do not necessarily conform with all the disclosure and presentation requirements of FRS 17 and other Standards. In particular, they do not illustrate the disclosure of:

(a) a general description of the type of plan (paragraph 77(a)).
(b) a narrative description of the basis used to determine the overall expected rate of return on assets (paragraph 77(k)).

Employee benefit obligations

The amounts recognised in the balance sheet are as follows:

	Defined benefit pension plans†		Retirement healthcare benefits	
	20X2	*20X1*	*20X2*	*20X1*
Present value of funded obligations	20,300	17,400	–	–
Fair value of plan assets	(18,420)	(17,280)	–	–
	1,880	120	–	–
Present value of unfunded obligations	2,000	1,000	7,337	6,405
Unrecognised past service cost	(450)	(650)	–	–
Deficit	3,430	470	7,337	6,405
Related deferred tax asset‡:	(1,030)	(140)	(2,200)	(1,922)-
Net liability	2,400	330	5,137	4,483

*Editor's note: This is the replacement example effective for accounting periods beginning on or after 6 April 2007.

†ASB Note: FRS 17 refers to 'defined benefit schemes' whereas IAS 19 uses the term 'defined benefit plans'.

‡ASB Note: Paragraph 49 of FRS 17 requires the deferred tax relating to the defined benefit asset or liability to be offset against the defined benefit asset or liability and not included with other deferred tax assets or liabilities. Differences between the asset or liability in the balance sheet and the surplus or deficit in the scheme will arise because of the related deferred tax balance.

Amounts in the balance sheet

Liabilities	2,400	420	5,137	4,483
Assets	–	(90)	–	–
Net liability	2,400	330	5,137	4,483

The pension plan assets include ordinary shares issued by [name of reporting entity] with a fair value of 317 (20X1: 281). Plan assets also include property occupied by [name of reporting entity] with a fair value of 200 (20X1: 185).

ASB Note: FRS 17 sets out where changes in the defined benefit asset or liability (other than that arising from contributions to the scheme) should be reported in the performance statements.

The amounts recognised in profit or loss are as follows:

	Defined benefit pension plans		Retirement healthcare benefits	
	20X2	*20X1*	*20X2*	*20X1*
Current service cost	850	750	479	411
Interest on obligation	950	1,000	803	705
Expected return on plan assets	(900)	(650)		
Past service cost	200	200		
Losses (gains) on curtailments and settlements	175	(390)		
Total	1,275	910	1,282	1,116
Actual return on plan assets	600	2,250	–	–

Changes in the present value of the defined benefit obligation are as follows:

	Defined benefit pension plans		Retirement healthcare benefits	
	20X2	*20X1*	*20X2*	*20X1*
Opening defined benefit obligation	18,400	11,600	6,405	5,439
Service cost	850	750	479	411
Interest cost	950	1,000	803	705
Actuarial losses (gains)	2,350	950	250	400
Losses (gains) on curtailments	(500)	–		
Liabilities extinguished on settlements	–	(350)		
Liabilities assumed in a business combination	–	5,000		
Exchange differences on foreign plans	900	(150)		
Benefits paid	(650)	(400)	(600)	(550)
Closing defined benefit obligation	22,300	18,400	7,337	6,405

Changes in the fair value of plan assets are as follows:

	Defined benefit pension plans	
	20X2	*20X1*
Opening fair value of plan assets	17,280	9,200
Expected return	900	650
Actuarial gains and (losses)	(300)	1,600
Assets distributed on settlements	(400)	–
Contributions by employer	700	350
Assets acquired in a business combination	–	6,000
Exchange differences on foreign plans	890	(120)
Benefits paid	(650)	(400)
	18,420	17,280

The group expects to contribute 900 to its defined benefit pension plans in 20X3.

The major categories of plan assets as a percentage of total plan assets are as follows:

	20X2	*20X1*
European equities	30%	35%
North American equities	16%	15%
European bonds	31%	28%
North American bonds	18%	17%
Property	5%	5%

Principal actuarial assumptions at the balance sheet date (expressed as weighted averages):

	20X2	*20X1*
Discount rate at 31 December	5.0%	6.5%
Expected return on plan assets at 31 December	5.4%	7.0%
Future salary increases	5%	4%
Future pension increases	3%	2%
Proportion of employees opting for early retirement	30%	30%
Annual increase in healthcare costs	8%	8%
Future changes in maximum state healthcare benefits	3%	2%

Assumed healthcare cost trend rates have a significant effect on the amounts recognised in profit or loss. A one percentage point change in assumed healthcare cost trend rates would have the following effects:

	One percentage point increase	One percentage point decrease
Effect on the aggregate of the service cost and interest cost	190	(150)
Effect on defined benefit obligation	1,000	(900)

Amounts for the current and previous four periods are as follows:

Defined benefit pension plans

	20X2	*20X1*	*20X0*	*20W9*	*20W8*
Defined benefit obligation	(22,300)	(18,400)	(11,600)	(10,582)	(9,144)
Plan assets	18,420	17,280	9,200	8,502	10,000
Surplus/(deficit)	(3,880)	(1,120)	(2,400)	(2,080)	856
Experience adjustments on plan liabilities	(1,111)	(768)	(69)	543	(642)
Experience adjustments on plan assets	(300)	1,600	(1,078)	(2,890)	2,777

~~Post-employment medical~~ Retirement healthcare benefits

	20X2	*20X1*	*20X0*	*20W9*	*20W8*
Defined benefit obligation	7,337	6,405	5,439	4,923	4,221
Experience adjustments on plan liabilities	(232)	829	490	(174)	(103)

The group also participates in an industry-wide defined benefit plan that provides pensions linked to final salaries and is funded on a pay-as-you-go basis. It is not practicable to determine the present value of the group's obligation or the related current service cost as the plan computes its obligations on a basis that differs materially from the basis used in [name of reporting entity's] financial statements. [describe basis] On that basis, the plan's financial statements to 30 June 20X0 show an unfunded liability of 27,525. The unfunded liability will result in future payments by participating employers. The plan has approximately 75,000 members, of whom approximately 5,000 are current or former employees of [name of reporting entity] or their dependants. The expense recognised in the income statement, which is equal to contributions due for the year, and is not included in the above amounts, was 230 (20X1: 215). The group's future contributions may be increased substantially if other entities withdraw from the plan.

Appendix II
Note on legal requirements

Great Britain

1　The statutory requirements relating to the presentation of pension costs in company accounts are set out in the Companies Act 1985. The relevant requirements are contained in Schedule 4 and are summarised below. Schedule 4 to the Act does not apply to banking and insurance companies and groups, nor to small companies to the extent that they choose instead to comply with the reduced requirements set out in Schedule 8. Requirements corresponding to those of Schedule 4 are set out for banking companies and groups in Schedule 9 and for insurance companies and groups in Schedule 9A.

2　The specific references in Schedule 4 include the following:

(a)　the balance sheet formats include a heading:
'Provisions for liabilities and charges:*
1 Pensions and similar obligations'.

(b)　the profit and loss formats 2 and 4 include a heading:
'Staff costs:
(a)　wages and salaries
(b)　social security costs
(c)　other pension costs'.

(c)　When profit and loss formats 1 and 3 are used, paragraph 56(4) requires the information in (b) to be disclosed.

3　Pension costs are defined in paragraph 94 of Schedule 4 as follows:

'"Pension costs" includes any costs incurred by the company in respect of any pension scheme established for the purpose of providing pensions for persons currently or formerly employed by the company, any sums set aside for the future payment of pensions directly by the company to current or former employees and any pensions paid directly to such persons without having first been set aside.'

4　Paragraph 50(4) requires disclosure of particulars of any pension commitments under any provision shown in the company's balance sheet and any such commitments for which no provision has been made.

5　The requirements in the FRS regarding the recognition of the amounts arising from a defined benefit scheme are that:

(a)　the service cost should be presented within operating profit in the profit and loss account;

(b)　the interest cost and expected return on assets should be presented as a net financial item in the profit and loss account;

(c)　actuarial gains and losses should be recognised in the statement of total recognised gains and losses; and

(d)　the net pension asset or liability should be presented separately on the face of the balance sheet following other net assets and before capital and reserves.

Editor's note: Now 'provisions for liabilities'.

The Board has received legal advice that these requirements do not contravene the 6
Companies Act 1985 but that the interest cost and expected return should be presented in a new format heading separate from 'interest and similar charges'.
Accordingly the FRS requires these items to be included as other finance costs (or income) adjacent to interest.

Northern Ireland and the Republic of Ireland

The relevant references to companies legislation in Northern Ireland and the 7
Republic of Ireland are as follows:

Great Britain	Northern Ireland	Republic of Ireland
Companies Act 1985: Schedule 4:	Companies (Northern Ireland) Order 1986: Schedule 4:	The Schedule to the Companies (Amendment) Act 1986:
paragraph 8	paragraph 8	paragraph 3
paragraph 50(4)	paragraph 50(4)	paragraph 36(4)
paragraph 56(4)	paragraph 56(4)	paragraph 42(2)
paragraph 94	paragraph 92	paragraph 74*
Schedule 8	Schedule 8	no equivalent
Schedule 9	Schedule 9	European Communities (Credit Institutions: Accounts) Regulations 1992
Schedule 9A	Schedule 9A	European Communities (Insurance Undertakings: Accounts) Regulations 1996

* *Note* The definition of pension costs in the Republic of Ireland legislation is slightly different from that in UK legislation (see paragraph 3) and is as follows:

'... "pension costs" include any other contributions by a company for the purposes of any pension scheme established for the purpose of providing pensions for persons employed by the company, any sum set aside for that purpose and any amounts paid by the company in respect of pensions without first being so set aside'

Appendix III
Compliance with International Accounting Standards

1   The requirements for retirement benefit costs are included in International Accounting Standard (IAS) 19 (revised 1998) 'Employee Benefits'.* The requirements of the FRS are consistent with IAS 19 (revised) in most respects. The only major difference is the recognition of actuarial gains and losses.†

2   The FRS requires actuarial gains and losses to be recognised, immediately they occur, in the statement of total recognised gains and losses. IAS 19 (revised) requires actuarial gains and losses to be recognised in the profit and loss account to the extent that they exceed 10 per cent of the greater of the gross assets or gross liabilities in the scheme.‡ Recognition of actuarial gains and losses exceeding the 10 per cent corridor may be spread forward over the expected average remaining working lives of the employees participating in the scheme.§

3   The structure for reporting financial performance is more developed in the UK and the Republic of Ireland than under IASs: a second performance statement – the statement of total recognised gains and losses – was introduced by FRS 3 'Reporting Financial Performance' in 1992, whereas no such statement is used in practice under IASs. For the reasons set out in Appendix IV paragraphs 34–47, the Board believes that immediate recognition in the statement of total recognised gains and losses is a major improvement from the traditional treatment of spreading actuarial gains and losses forward in the profit and loss account.

4   There is some indication that the International Accounting Standards Committee (IASC) may also wish to follow this route once it has moved forward with its work on reporting financial performance.¶¶ In IAS 19 (revised), Appendix 3 'Basis for

*Editor's note: IAS 19 was further revised in 2000. It was then revised again in 2004. While not the only treatment possible, IAS 19 can now be applied in such a way as to result in a very similar treatment to that required by FRS 17.

†Editor's note: With effect for accounting periods beginning on or after 6 April 2007, and as a result of the Amendment to FRS 17 Retirement Benefits *issued in December 2006, the final sentence of this paragraph is deleted.*

‡Recognition of actuarial gains and losses within the 10 per cent corridor is allowed but not required.

§Editor's note: With effect for accounting periods beginning on or after 6 April 2007, and as a result of the Amendment to FRS 17 Retirement Benefits *issued in December 2006, paragraphs 2 to 4 are deleted, and replaced with:*

2   The FRS requires actuarial gains and losses to be recognised, immediately they occur, in the statement of total recognised gains and losses. IAS 19 (revised) requires an entity to either:

(i)   recognise a specified portion of the net cumulative actuarial gains and losses in the profit and loss account to the extent that they exceed the greater of 10 per cent of the fair value of the scheme assets and 10 per cent of the present value of the defined benefit obligation (before deducting scheme assets). The portion of the actuarial gains and losses to be recognised for each defined benefit plan is the excess that fell outside the 10 per cent 'corridor' spread forward over the remaining working lives of employees participating in the scheme; or

(ii)   recognise immediately all actuarial gains and losses in the period in which they occur outside the profit and loss account in a statement of recognised income and expense; or

(iii)   use (as permitted by the Standard) systematic methods of faster recognition, provided that the same basis is applied to both gains and losses and the basis is applied consistently from period to period. Such permitted methods include immediate recognition of gains and losses in the profit and loss.

¶¶IASC is currently (November 2000) working on a project on reporting financial performance.

Conclusions' discusses the option of immediate recognition of actuarial gains and losses in a second performance statement. It states that:

> 'the [IASC] Board found the immediate recognition approach attractive. However, the [IASC] Board believes that it is not feasible to use this approach for actuarial gains and losses until the [IASC] Board resolves substantial issues about performance reporting. When the [IASC] Board makes further progress with those issues, it may decide to revisit the treatment of actuarial gains and losses.'

Appendix IV
The development of the FRS

BACKGROUND TO THE FRS

1   The FRS has been developed from the proposals set out in FRED 20 'Retirement Benefits', which was published in November 1999. FRED 20 was itself the result of many years' deliberations by the Board in which a number of factors were influential, in particular:

    (a)   concerns in the UK about the existing standard, SSAP 24 'Accounting for pension costs';

    (b)   the trend internationally towards the use of fair values for pension cost accounting; and

    (c)   the move within the UK actuarial profession away from traditional actuarial valuation methodologies to a greater use of market values.

2   The main concerns about SSAP 24 were:

    (a)   there were too many options available to the preparers of accounts, leading to inconsistency in accounting practice and allowing a great deal of flexibility to adjust results on a short-term basis; and

    (b)   the disclosure requirements did not necessarily ensure that the pension cost and related amounts in the balance sheet were adequately explained.

3   In response to these concerns, in June 1995 the Board published a Discussion Paper 'Pension Costs in the Employer's Financial Statements' which set out two contrasting approaches to accounting for pension costs:

    (a)   an actuarial approach, which relied on actuarial measurement of pension scheme assets but removed many of the options in SSAP 24 and enhanced the disclosure requirements; and

    (b)   a market value approach, which was based on measuring the pension scheme assets at market value.

4   The Discussion Paper noted that the Board's initial view was that the actuarial approach was preferable. The market value approach was included because the Board was aware that the International Accounting Standards Committee (IASC) was likely to propose such an approach and the Board wished to gauge UK reaction to it.

5   IASC published an exposure draft, E54, in October 1996 and a revised standard was issued in February 1998. As expected, IAS 19 (revised 1998) 'Employee Benefits' adopts a market value approach that is very similar to the US standard, FAS 87.

6   The Board set out its views on IAS 19 (revised) in a Discussion Paper 'Aspects of Accounting for Pension Costs', published in July 1998. It explained that the Board did not believe that there were sufficient reasons to stand out against the global trend to a market value approach as long as such an approach could be developed in a way that did not introduce undue volatility into the profit and loss account. It was clear that a pensions standard based on actuarial values for assets would be regarded internationally as weak and would not be an approach that other standard-setters would follow. Given this, and the increasing use of market values by the actuarial profession, it concluded that the UK and the Republic of Ireland should move into line with international practice and use market values rather than actuarial values for

scheme assets. This view was accepted by a majority of the respondents to the Discussion Paper.

The Discussion Paper then set out some options for how the Board might proceed in developing a standard based on market values. FRED 20 took forward some of those options, and they are now embodied in the FRS, as explained below. The resulting main changes from SSAP 24 are: **7**

(a) measuring pension scheme assets: a move from using an actuarial basis to using market values (this is consistent with IAS 19 (revised) and FAS 87*).

(b) the discount rate for scheme liabilities: a move from using the expected rate of return on the scheme assets to a rate that reflects the characteristics of the liabilities (resulting in the use of a high quality corporate bond rate, again consistently with IAS 19 (revised) and FAS 87).

(c) recognition of actuarial gains and losses: a move from gradual recognition of such gains and losses in the profit and loss account to immediate recognition in the statement of total recognised gains and losses (an approach that IAS 19 (revised) indicated a willingness to revisit once further developments have taken place in the IASC project on reporting financial performance (see Appendix III) and which the G4 + 1 has also supported in general terms†).

(d) as a consequence of (c), the balance sheet shows a pension liability or asset equal to the deficit or recoverable surplus in the scheme.

The Board believes that these changes, as well as moving practice in the UK and the Republic of Ireland more into line with international practice, reflect the underlying economics of providing defined benefit promises. The detailed reasoning behind the changes is set out below. **8**

In practical terms, the Board believes that the FRS will, when implemented, make the reported amounts for retirement benefits more transparent and easier to understand. The pension scheme assets and liabilities will be measured at fair value. The balance sheet will show the surplus/deficit in the scheme to the extent that the employer expects to benefit/suffer from it. The profit and loss account will show the ongoing service cost, interest cost and expected return on assets while the market fluctuations will be recorded in the statement of total recognised gains and losses. **9**

MEASUREMENT OF SCHEME ASSETS AND SCHEME LIABILITIES

Scheme assets

As noted above, the Board did not believe that there were sufficient reasons for the UK to differ from the rest of the world by measuring scheme assets at an actuarial value that did not equal fair value. In addition, and perhaps more importantly, it was clear that substantial changes were taking place within the actuarial profession relating to the traditional actuarial methodologies for measuring assets in a pension scheme. Of the actuaries responding to the 1995 Discussion Paper, all but one supported the use of actuarial valuations. Of the actuaries responding to the 1998 Discussion Paper, all but one supported the use of market values. Given this, and the **10**

However, FAS 87 allows the market values to be averaged over a period up to five years, which the FRS and IAS 19 (revised) do not.

†*The G4 + 1 is a group of representatives of the national standard-setters of Australia, Canada, New Zealand, the UK and the USA, and of IASC. In the communiqué issued by the G4 + 1 after its meeting in April 2000, the Group expressed support for the direction of the conclusions in FRED 20.*

advantages of market values in terms of objectivity and understandability, the Board believes there is no credible alternative to their use.

Scheme liabilities

11   Ideally, under a market value approach, the scheme liabilities would, like the scheme assets, be measured at market value. However, there is no active market for most defined benefit scheme liabilities. Their fair value has therefore to be estimated using actuarial techniques. There are two families of actuarial methods for valuing defined benefit liabilities: accrued benefits methods and prospective benefits methods. The difference between them lies in their treatment of the time value of money. Under an accrued benefits method each period is allocated its share of the eventual undiscounted cost, the liability arising from the costs to date is discounted and the discount unwinds in the normal manner over the employee's service life. This results in a higher cost at the end of an employee's service life than at the beginning because the effect of discounting the cost lessens as the employee approaches retirement. Under a prospective benefits method, the total cost including all the interest that will accrue is spread evenly over the employee's service life. This does not represent the economic reality that, because of the time value of money, the cost of providing a defined benefit increases nearer retirement and such valuation methods do not, therefore, approximate the fair value of the liability. For this reason, the FRS requires the use of an accrued benefits method.

12   The FRS requires the defined benefit liability to be the best estimate of the present value of the amount that will actually be paid out. For this to be the case, all expected changes in factors affecting the payments should be taken into account. For final salary liabilities, the liability will therefore be based on the expected final salary, not the current salary. Some argue that this is not consistent with FRS 12 'Provisions, Contingent Liabilities and Contingent Assets' because the employer has some control over the future increases in salary and hence does not have a present obligation relating to those increases. However, there is a difference between a present commitment to pay a pension based on present salary and a present commitment to pay a pension based on final salary, which the Board believes should be reflected in the measurement of the liabilities. The use of expected final salaries is also consistent with IAS 19 (revised) and FAS 87. For retirement healthcare liabilities, calculating the best estimate of the payments to be made in the future means taking into account expected changes in the cost of medical care.

The discount rate

13   In the UK, actuaries have traditionally discounted the liabilities in a defined benefit scheme at the expected rate of return on the assets in the scheme (prudently estimated). IAS 19 (revised) and FAS 87 require the use of a high quality corporate bond rate.

14   The Board believes that the discount rate should reflect the time value of money and the risk associated with the liability. The view put forward in the Discussion Paper published in 1998 was that such a rate could be determined by looking at the rate of return on matching assets. (If the assets exactly matched the liability they must have the same fair value and hence the discount rate appropriate for the liability must be the same as the rate of return on the asset.) Matching assets were expected to be:

(a)   for pensions fixed in monetary terms, fixed rate government bonds;
(b)   for index-linked pensions in payment and deferred pensions, index-linked government bonds;

(c)   for final salary liabilities, a portfolio containing some element of equity investments.

However, later research conducted by the Faculty and Institute of Actuaries **15** demonstrated from past data that the correlation between equities and salaries had not been close and that the best match for final salary liabilities was probably index-linked bonds.

Some argue that even if there is no close correlation between equity and salary **16** growth, it is appropriate to use the expected return on equities as the discount rate if the scheme is invested therein because, over the long term, that return is relatively secure. However, the higher return expected on equities is a reward for the risk involved in equity investment. Unless the risk matches that associated with the liabilities, discounting the liabilities at the higher return anticipates the expected benefit of equity investment without recognising the risks involved. The higher return should instead be recognised as it is earned over the period the equities are held.

On the other hand, although index-linked bonds seem to have been a better match **17** for final salary liabilities, they are not a perfect match and an index-linked bond discount rate would ignore some important aspects of a final salary pension liability, for example the uncertainty of the amounts ultimately to be paid out. The Board has therefore decided not to try to find matching assets but to build up the discount rate from its components. As noted above, it believes that, if possible, the discount rate should reflect:

(a)   the time value of money (given by the rate of return on an investment regarded as being risk-free); and

(b)   the risks associated with the liability because of the uncertainty surrounding the ultimate cash payments due.

The FRS requires the assumptions to reflect the best estimate of the ultimate cash **18** flows. The resulting liability is clearly subject to uncertainty – the ultimate cash flows are not contractually fixed and will depend on final salaries, length of retirement etc. The uncertainty of the future cash outflows might be expected to make the liability more onerous – most entities are risk-averse and would prefer to avoid the possibility that the cash flows might be more than expected.

However, in many defined benefit schemes, the employer has the option of pre- **19** venting the cash flows being greater than expected and even of reducing the cash flows if necessary (eg if investment performance has been consistently poor for a long period). These options exist because the best estimate of the cash flows will include expected benefit increases likely to be granted by the employer such as (i) increases in pensions in payment and deferred pensions at above the minimum required by statute or the scheme rules and (ii) increases in benefits arising from salary increases for active members over and above the rate applicable if they left service (it is assumed that an employer would, over any substantial period, have to increase salaries by at least the indexing rate applied to deferred pensions). Although the employer expects to give these increases, they are not guaranteed. If necessary the employer could, in many cases, give lower than expected increases in benefits and give lower than expected salary increases. In extremis, the employer could even close the scheme down.

These options are a crucial factor in the operation of UK defined benefit schemes and **20** the level of benefits that is given. Employers' willingness to provide the expected benefits is often based, at least partly, on the assumption that the liability can be funded in equities. The expectation is that a higher return on equities compared with that on less risky investments will make such promises affordable. The employer can bear the risk associated with the higher return because, if equities were to under-perform for a long period, the options described above allow the employer to take action to mitigate the financial impact.

21   These options make the liability less onerous and can be reflected by using a discount rate higher than a risk-free rate. In principle, the premium over the risk-free rate should vary from scheme to scheme (and within schemes), reflecting the differing levels of discretion that exist for different scheme liabilities. However, assessing the appropriate premium is difficult and subjective. In the interests of objectivity and international harmonisation, the Board has therefore decided to adopt a standard discount rate: the rate of return on a high quality corporate bond, ie one rated at the level of AA or equivalent status. This includes a small premium above the risk-free rate, which can be regarded as reflecting the options open to the employer to limit the pension scheme liabilities.

22   Reflecting these options in the discount rate is not inconsistent with the proposal in paragraph 31 of the FRS that it is not appropriate to assume a reduction in benefits below those currently promised. It is not appropriate to assume that a curtailment of the scheme will take place in the future but it is appropriate to reflect the value of the *option* to make that curtailment.

Frequency of valuations

23   The FRS requires the actuarial valuation to be updated at each balance sheet date to reflect current conditions. The Board does not believe that this imposes an excessively onerous or impracticable burden on preparers of accounts for two reasons.

(a)   The figures in the profit and loss account are based on assumptions at the beginning of the period, and will therefore be known before the balance sheet date. It is only the figures in the statement of total recognised gains and losses and the balance sheet that depend on the valuation updated at the balance sheet date.

(b)   Unless there have been major changes to the scheme, only the financial assumptions and the fair value of the assets need to be updated at the balance sheet date. The actuarial profession is preparing guidance on what the annual update should involve.

Recognition in the balance sheet

24   Pension schemes will not usually be subsidiary (or quasi-subsidiary) undertakings of the employer because defined benefit schemes are controlled by the trustees, not the employer. It is not, therefore, appropriate to consolidate the scheme into the employer's financial statements. A pension scheme can give rise to assets and liabilities of the employer but these are not the gross amounts of the pension scheme assets and liabilities – the employer does not control the assets nor is it directly liable for the pension payments. Instead, the employer has a pension asset or liability to the extent that it is entitled to benefit from any surplus or has a legal or constructive obligation to make good any deficit.

25   Pension schemes differ in this respect from employee share ownership plans (ESOPs). The key difference lies in the control that the employer has over the trust. ESOP trusts are such that the actions that the trustees can take are very limited – the ESOP exists only to hold the sponsoring company's own shares for future distribution to employees. ESOP trusts are designed to ensure that there is minimal risk in practice

that the trustees would act other than in accordance with the sponsoring company's wishes. The sponsoring company has, in effect, de facto control. In contrast, for a pension scheme, the trustees' rights and duties are much wider. The employer cannot in practice ensure that the trustees will act as it would wish in many significant areas and, hence, does not control the assets and liabilities in the scheme.

Many respondents to FRED 20 questioned whether a surplus in the pension scheme should give rise to any asset in the balance sheet of the employer. Their view was that the employer did not own or control the surplus in the scheme and, hence, it was not appropriate to recognise an asset. The Board's view is that the employer has an asset if it has the right to reduce its contributions in the future. It is unlikely that an employer could be required to make contributions to a scheme in order to maintain a surplus. Accordingly, in general, a surplus will give rise to an asset for the employer. **26**

The amount recognised as an asset cannot, of course, exceed the amount that the employer can recover and such a limit is included in the FRS. The limit reflects the maximum that can be recovered through reduced contributions together with any refunds that have been agreed at the balance sheet date. Some argue that the reductions in contributions must be assessed in relation to the funding assumptions rather than the accounting assumptions because it is in relation to funding assumptions alone that the trustees of the scheme will agree to any such reductions. It is true that the trustees will set the contributions based on the funding assumptions, but over the life of the scheme the accounting and funding assumptions must come together. The delay in accessing the surplus does not affect its measurement because, in the period where the company is still making contributions based on funding assumptions, the accounting surplus will be growing because of the return earned by the excess assets in the scheme with the result that the surplus that the employer will eventually recover through reduced contributions in future will be larger. In present value terms (which is how the surplus is measured), the amount by which the employer can benefit is the same. **27**

Furthermore, the assumptions required by the FRS are a best estimate. Funding assumptions may well build in an element of prudence. It is not appropriate to reflect an arbitrary element of prudence in the measurement of the pension asset for financial reporting purposes. **28**

RECOGNITION IN THE PERFORMANCE STATEMENTS

Analysis of pension cost

The FRS requires the ongoing defined benefit cost to be analysed into (i) the service cost (ii) the interest cost and (iii) the expected return on assets, with (ii) and (iii) presented as finance costs (or income). The Board believes that including the interest cost and the expected return on assets with the service cost within operating activities distorts the operating cost that is shown. For example, the pension cost recorded for an unfunded scheme would be higher than that recorded for a funded scheme with exactly the same pension obligations. This does not properly reflect the fact that the *pension* in both cases costs the same, it is only the funding policy that is different. The interest cost and expected return are matters relating to the financing of the pension promise. The Board believes that the three components of the pension cost and their underlying economic nature are well accepted and understood and, hence, should be reflected in their presentation in the profit and loss account. **29**

Expected return on assets

30   Although the Board wishes to move to market values for retirement benefit accounting, it does not believe that it would be appropriate for the short-term volatility associated with equity returns to be reflected in the profit and loss account. Rather, the profit and loss account should reflect the long-term return that equities are expected to produce with any fluctuations around that return shown in the statement of total recognised gains and losses. The rationale for this view is explained further below (see paragraph 37).

31   In practice, it is difficult to judge the long-term rate of return on equities at any particular date, given that it needs to reflect the current state of the market. The FRS, therefore, requires the disclosure of an analysis of the assets in the scheme and the expected rates of return assumed so that users may assess the assumptions and calculate the effects of making different assumptions. It is to be expected that those using rates at the extremes of the range at any particular date will come under close scrutiny and possible challenge.

32   The higher long-term return expected on equities compensates for the uncertainty over the return. FRED 20 noted that some believe, therefore, that it is not appropriate to recognise the expected higher long-term return in the profit and loss account every year with the fluctuations around the return going to the statement of total recognised gains and losses. Doing so separates the reward for risk (the expected higher return) from the results of taking the risk (the variability in the actual return). It was suggested that an alternative approach would be to record in the profit and loss account a risk-free return on assets (removing the effects of risk to the statement of total recognised gains and losses completely).

33   There was almost no support for this alternative approach in the responses to FRED 20 and it has therefore not been taken forward in the FRS.

Recognition of actuarial gains and losses

34   SSAP 24 required actuarial gains and losses (variations from regular cost) to be recognised gradually over the service lives of the employees. In the 1995 Discussion Paper, under the alternative market value approach, a different treatment was proposed. The profit and loss account would be charged with the cost of pensions earned in the period. Actuarial gains and losses would be recorded in the statement of total recognised gains and losses.

35   This approach was explored in more detail in the 1998 Discussion Paper and in FRED 20. It is based on the view that items of financial performance should be grouped together according to their characteristics. The Board's approach was set out in detail in its Discussion Paper "Reporting Financial Performance: proposals for change' (June 1999). That Paper explained that, where gains and losses arise predominantly from price changes and relate to assets and liabilities that are held not with a view to benefiting directly from changes in their value but because they are needed for the employer's operating activities (eg a head office), it would be misleading to include those gains and losses within operating profit. Instead, they should be reported as "other' gains and losses, ie at present within the statement of total recognised gains and losses rather than the profit and loss account.

36   The Board expects to publish shortly a FRED on reporting financial performance. The proposals in the FRED on the reporting of holding gains and losses will be consistent with those in the Discussion Paper noted above.

The Board regards actuarial gains and losses as similar in nature to revaluation gains **37** and losses on fixed assets. In relation to the assets in the pension scheme, they are held with a view to producing a relatively secure long-term return that will assist in financing the pension cost. The length of the term, coupled with the options available to the employer to restrict the liability in extreme circumstances, mean that much of the fluctuations in market values does not affect the relatively stable cash flows between the employer and its pension scheme. Market fluctuations are incidental to the main purpose of the pension scheme just as the revaluation gains and losses on a fixed asset are incidental to its main operating role. They are therefore best reported within the statement of total recognised gains and losses.

On the scheme liabilities side, the effect of both experience gains and losses and **38** changes in actuarial assumptions is to update the liabilities to reflect current conditions consistent with the current market value used to measure the assets. As with fixed assets, where the profit and loss account reflects the current depreciation charge, so for scheme liabilities the profit and loss account reflects the service cost and interest cost of providing the pension promise. Subsequent changes in the value of the liabilities are generally related to financial assumptions and are caused by general changes in economic conditions. These fluctuations of the liabilities to reflect current market conditions are, like the market value fluctuations of the assets, incidental to the main operating business of the employer.

In the periods after their recognition in the statement of total recognised gains and **39** losses, actuarial gains and losses do not change in nature to become operating costs. They should not, therefore, be "recycled' by recognition in the profit and loss account in later years. (An additional, pragmatic, reason for not recycling the gains and losses is that doing so would introduce volatility into the profit and loss account. Actuarial gains and losses arising under a market value approach are such that, even when spread over the remaining service lives of the employees, they would cause significant fluctuations in the total amount charged to the profit and loss account. Further, there would be problems in knowing how to allocate the recycled amount between operating and financial costs.)

In addition to the fact that this approach is consistent with its views on reporting **40** financial performance, the Board prefers immediate recognition in the statement of total recognised gains and losses to the spreading approach required under SSAP 24 for the following reasons.

(a)   The balance sheet reflects the surplus (to the extent that the employer can benefit from it) or deficit (to the extent that the employer is obliged to fund it) in the scheme based on the latest actuarial valuation. These amounts meet the Board's definitions of assets and liabilities of the employer. In contrast, under SSAP 24, some actuarial gains and losses were not recognised at the balance sheet date. In a market value model, there is no conceptual reason to defer the recognition of these gains and losses. Deferral means that the asset/liability in the balance sheet does not equal the recoverable surplus or the deficit in the scheme. In fact, it was not uncommon under SSAP 24 for a deficit in the scheme to give rise to a supposed asset in the balance sheet which built up as the deficit was funded faster than it was recognised. Such figures do not meet the Board's definition of assets.

(b)   The figures in the balance sheet and performance statements are transparent and easy to understand.

(c)   The complex and arbitrary rules needed to govern spreading gains and losses forward are not required.

41   The main concerns expressed about this approach in the responses to the FRED were the following.

(a)   The figures in the statement of total recognised gains and losses and balance sheet can be large and volatile. They will distort the financial statements of the employer and will not be understood by users of the accounts.

(b)   Some gains and losses are never recorded in the profit and loss account. This concern had two aspects:

(i)   Some believed that all gains and losses (in particular, all losses) should be recorded in the profit and loss account at some point. Doing so is necessary for the profit and loss account to show the true margins achieved by the employer.

(ii)   Others accepted the distinction in principle between actuarial gains and losses and operating costs but were concerned at the possibility of understating the costs that should be reflected in the profit and loss account. Over-optimistic actuarial assumptions could lead to lower service and interest costs in the profit and loss account, while the difference between the assumptions and actual experience would be reflected as a loss in the statement of total recognised gains and losses.

42   In relation to the point (a), the Board believes that users of accounts are sufficiently sophisticated to view the figures in their proper context. It is important to remember that the amounts reported in the statement of total recognised gains and losses *in any one period* have relatively little significance and should not necessarily cause concern. What matters is *the pattern that emerges over a number of years.* For example, if a substantial actuarial loss arises in one year, but then reverses over the next few years, there may well be no impact on future cash flows. If, on the other hand, the loss does not reverse and perhaps even is repeated, then it is more likely that additional contributions to the pension scheme will be required. Repeated gains or losses may also imply that pension costs in the future will be lower or higher as experience causes the actuary to change his assumptions. These trends will be highlighted by the disclosure of a five-year history of actuarial gains and losses.

43   The different context in which the figures in the statement of total recognised gains and losses and balance sheet need to be viewed is also highlighted by their position in the accounts: the actuarial gains and losses are reported in the statement of total recognised gains and losses, not the profit and loss account (or earnings per share), and the pension asset/liability is presented at the foot of the balance sheet separately from and after all other net assets.

44   It is of note that all the users responding to FRED 20 supported the approach in the FRED.

45   The Board's view on the fact that the approach in the FRS does not report actuarial gains and losses in the profit and loss account at any time (paragraph 41(b)(i)) is that this is entirely in line with the approach to reporting financial performance set out in the Board's Discussion Paper on the subject – some gains and losses have different characteristics from those that arise from the employer's mainstream operating activities and it is therefore appropriate for them to be reported separately. This does not imply that they are unimportant or can be disregarded in assessing the employer's performance. It is simply a reflection of the fact that they are different in nature from operating gains and losses.

46   The Board accepts that the concern about understating the costs in the profit and loss account is valid (paragraph 41(b)(ii)), although as, with experience, more attention than hitherto is paid to gains and losses reported in the statement of total recognised gains and losses, such manipulation will become less effective. In the meantime, the five-year history of actuarial gains and losses will separately highlight experience gains and losses so that users of the accounts are aware when actuarial assumptions are consistently not being met. It would be expected that, although the assumptions would probably not be met in each and every year, the experience gains and losses would over time compensate for each other. A consistent trend of experience losses (or gains) should cause the preparers of accounts and the auditors to re-examine the assumptions.

It is worth noting that an approach that spreads the actuarial gains and losses **47** forward in the profit and loss account is equally open to abuse. Although the losses arising from over-optimistic assumptions are recognised in the profit and loss account, only a small proportion is recognised in any one year. The beneficial effects of the over-optimistic assumptions outweigh that small proportion until the effect has built up over many (typically twelve to fifteen) years. Such a delay in the bad news hitting the accounts is likely to be more of an incentive to manipulate the assumptions than immediate recognition of the losses in the statement of total recognised gains and losses.

Recognition of past service costs

Under SSAP 24 past service costs for current employees were spread forward in the **48** profit and loss account and past service costs for former employees were recognised immediately in the profit and loss account to the extent that they were not covered by a surplus in the scheme.

The decision to improve benefits or award new benefits in relation to past service **49** increases the scheme liabilities immediately. If an employee left the day after the increased benefits vested (usually at the time of the award), the transfer value would reflect those increased benefits – no further service from the employee would be required to earn them. The Board does not, therefore, believe that there is any reason to defer recognition of the increased liability beyond the date the benefits vest.

This leaves the question of how the cost should be recognised in the performance **50** statements. Many of the respondents to the FRED believed that the cost of the improved benefits should be offset against any surplus in the scheme, with only the excess cost being recognised in the profit and loss account. They argued that this properly reflects the fact that such benefit improvements may have been awarded only because there was a surplus in the scheme and therefore no cash cost to the employer.

The Board's view is that although there may be no direct cash cost, by using a **51** surplus in this way the employer loses some of the advantages that it could otherwise obtain, for example reduced contributions. Further, by awarding such benefit improvements, it may be able to reduce other aspects of its staff costs. From this perspective, it seems appropriate that the cost of the benefit improvements should be recognised as an employment cost. The manner in which the cost is funded, whether through cash or the use of a surplus that could otherwise have been used to reduce contributions, does not affect that classification. However, sometimes the benefit improvements are funded out of a surplus that the employer could not otherwise benefit from, ie a surplus so large that the employer could not absorb it fully through reduced contributions (or agreed refunds). In these cases, the surplus will not have been recognised in full previously and to the extent that it has been used to fund the past service costs the unrecognised amount should now be offset against the past service cost in the profit and loss account.

52   This treatment of past service costs (including the use of any irrecoverable surplus) is consistent with IAS 19 (revised).

Impact of limit on balance sheet asset

53   The limit on the amount that can be recognised as an asset in the balance sheet may mean that some part of a surplus is not recognised. The effect of the balance sheet limit might be allocated to the various pension components in the performance statements in a number of ways. The allocation required by the FRS is one that preserves the structure of the ongoing items (ie the current service cost, interest cost and expected return on assets) as far as possible but allows one-off costs (eg past service costs) to be offset against the unrecognised surplus.

DISCLOSURES

54   FRED 20 proposed sufficient disclosures for a reader to understand the various elements that constitute the pension cost and the relationship between the actuarial valuation and the amounts recorded in the balance sheet. These disclosures were largely supported by the respondents to the FRED, with the exception of:

(a)   a comment on the difference between the expected rate of return on equities and the AA corporate bond rate; and

(b)   the five-year history of amounts recognised in the statement of total recognised gains and losses.

55   The first of these disclosures has been dropped, because the two rates are required to be disclosed anyway and any comment was likely to be couched in terms that added little extra information.

56   The second disclosure has been retained because the Board believes that it helps place in context the actuarial gains or losses in any one year and hence plays an important role in the FRS.

AMENDMENT TO FRS 17 (2006)*

56A   In 2006 the Accounting Standards Board issued a Financial Reporting Exposure Draft (FRED) that proposed to replace the disclosure requirements of FRS 17 with those of International Accounting Standard 19 (IAS 19) 'Employee Benefits'. In making its proposal the ASB took into consideration the fact that, in December 2004, the International Accounting Standards Board (IASB) amended the disclosure requirements of IAS 19 following a review of national standards on accounting for post-employment benefits.

56B   In replacing the disclosure requirements of FRS 17 with those of IAS 19 the ASB made changes only where the accounting treatment of items differed between the two accounting standards or where necessary to make the terminology consistent.

56C   Respondents to the FRED were generally in agreement with the proposal to replace the disclosure requirements of FRS 17 with those of IAS 19 and so increase convergence between the two standards.

56D   Some respondents did, however, raise a concern regarding disclosures that were required by the current FRS 17 but would no longer be required by the amended

*Editor's note: Inserted by Amendment to FRS 17 issued December 2006.

FRS 17. The ASB considered this view but decided it did not wish to extend the disclosure requirements for entities applying UK Financial Reporting Standards beyond the disclosure requirements of entities applying International Financial Reporting Standards. The ASB therefore decided not to amend the disclosure requirements set out in the amended FRS 17 beyond those of IAS 19. The ASB did, however, note that where an entity considers the information provided by a disclosure that is no longer required by the amended FRS would enhance the understanding of the financial statements to users, the disclosure could be provided on a voluntary basis.

A few respondents to the FRED considered that the amendment should address **56E** some of the other differences that exist between FRS 17 and IAS 19. The ASB gave due consideration to the views of these respondents. However, it decided that in view of the longer term research project that it was undertaking into pension accounting it should not extend the scope of this short-term project. The ASB did, however, decide to include in this amendment its proposal set out in Financial Reporting Exposure Draft 39 'Proposed amendment to FRS 12 Provisions, Contingent Liabilities and Contingent Assets and Amendment to FRS 17 Retirement Benefits' to amendment paragraph 16 of FRS 17. The amendment replaces the term in paragraph 16 'mid-market price' with 'current bid price'.

TRANSITIONAL ARRANGEMENTS

The FRS allows for a long implementation period, with disclosures building up in the **57** notes to the accounts. The reasons for this are:

(a) to avoid companies having to revisit previous actuarial valuations;
(b) to give the Board a chance to persuade IASC to follow the UK approach on the immediate recognition of actuarial gains and losses; and
(c) to give preparers and users of accounts the opportunity to become accustomed to the figures arising under the FRS before they are recognised in the primary statements.

In 2006 the Accounting Standards Board, following convergence of the disclosure **57A** requirements with those of IAS 19, required the new disclosure requirements to be effective for accounting periods beginning on or after 6 April 2007.*

IMPACT ON DISTRIBUTABLE PROFITS

Appendix III to FRED 20 set out a possible approach to mitigate the impact on **58** distributable profits of a pension deficit measured and recognised in accordance with the FRED. Some respondents to FRED 20 thought this approach was unsatisfactory in a number of respects. In the light of these responses and because a distribution problem is unlikely to arise often,† the Board has decided not to proceed with this approach. It believes that it is better for those few companies that are affected to find appropriate solutions with the help of their legal advisers.

*****Editor's note****: Added by the Amendment to FRS 17* Retirement Benefits *issued in December 2006.*

†*A distribution problem will arise only when individual company accounts show a defined benefit liability so large that it reduces distributable reserves to below that needed to cover any intended distribution. In this context, it should be noted that the FRS allows an exemption in some circumstances from the recognition of a defined benefit liability in the accounts of individual companies that are members of a group defined benefit scheme.*

ALTERNATIVE CASH-BASED APPROACH TO PENSION COST ACCOUNTING

59   Throughout the development of the FRS, a number of respondents to the various consultation documents raised the possibility of a return to a cash-based method of accounting for pension costs. It was suggested that in the UK the Pensions Act 1995, together with the existing tax regime, would impose such constraints on the contributions that an employer made to an approved UK pension scheme that, for such schemes, the contributions made in each period could be regarded as an appropriate measure for the pension cost for that period. The argument was that, because the scheme could be neither substantially overfunded (the tax limit) nor underfunded (the minimum funding requirement (MFR) of the Pensions Act), the contributions each year must be equivalent to the increase in the pension obligation that had arisen that year, ie the pension cost. The cost of implementing an accruals-based system, therefore, exceeded the benefits.

60   This argument does not apply to unfunded or overseas schemes, for which an accruals-based method would still need to be prescribed. Also, pension regulation still allows substantial scope for employers and trustees to agree on different and varying contribution schedules.

61   For example, for a typical UK pension scheme, it would not be unusual for a scheme to be regarded as 100 per cent funded when measured using the test for the upper tax limit on funding, but 150 per cent funded using the MFR test. The profile of some schemes may lead to even larger discrepancies than this. A pension scheme funded between the 100 per cent level on the MFR basis and 100 per cent level on the maximum funding basis may be able to justify paying contributions at any level between zero (ie a temporary contribution holiday) and the full regular cost calculated on a conservative basis. With typical regular cost levels being between 10 per cent and 15 per cent of pensionable salaries, the difference between full regular cost and no contributions whatsoever is likely to be material.

62   The Board does not, therefore, believe that a return to a cash-based method would ensure that the proper cost of a pension is measured and recognised as it arises over the service lives of the employees.

ALTERNATIVE ACCOUNTING STANDARDS

63   Some respondents to the consultation papers have suggested that if overseas pension schemes have been accounted for under a "recognised' standard (for example, FAS 87), those figures could be included in UK financial statements without restatement. The same suggestion was made for retirement benefits other than pensions that have been accounted for under FAS 106. The Board does not accept this suggestion. While it may sometimes be possible, using options in standards, to achieve a high degree of convergence between the effect of each, where there are differences the Board's standards must be followed.

Financial Reporting Standard 18 is set out in paragraphs 1–69.

The Statement of Standard Accounting Practice, which comprises the paragraphs set in bold type, should be read in the context of the Objective as stated in paragraph 1 and the definitions set out in paragraph 2 and also of the Foreword to Accounting Standards and the Statement of Principles for Financial Reporting currently in issue.

The explanatory paragraphs contained in the FRS shall be regarded as part of the Statement of Standard Accounting Practice insofar as they assist in interpreting that statement.

Appendix IV 'The development of the FRS' reviews considerations and arguments that were thought significant by members of the Board in reaching the conclusions on the FRS.

FRS 18
Accounting policies*

(Issued December 2000)

Contents

Editor's note: FRS 18 has been amended by FRS 21 with effect for accounting periods beginning on or after 1 January 2005.

Accounting policies

Summary

Financial Reporting Standard 18 sets out the principles to be followed in selecting   **a**
accounting policies and the disclosures needed to help users to understand the
accounting policies adopted and how they have been applied.

The FRS defines accounting policies, and estimation techniques used in implementing   **b**
those policies. Accounting policies should be consistent with accounting standards,
Urgent Issues Task Force (UITF) Abstracts and companies legislation. Where this
requirement allows a choice, the FRS requires an entity to select those accounting
policies judged to be most appropriate to its particular circumstances for the purpose
of giving a true and fair view.

An entity should judge the appropriateness of accounting policies to its particular   **c**
circumstances against the objectives of relevance, reliability, comparability and
understandability. The constraints that an entity should take into account are the
need to balance the different objectives, and the need to balance the cost of providing
information with the likely benefit of such information to users of the entity's
financial statements.

An entity's accounting policies should be reviewed regularly to ensure that they   **d**
remain the most appropriate to its particular circumstances. An entity should
implement a new accounting policy if it is judged more appropriate to the entity's
particular circumstances than the present accounting policy.

The FRS requires specific disclosures about the accounting policies followed and   **e**
changes to those policies. It also requires, in some circumstances, disclosures about
the estimation techniques used in applying those policies.

Financial Reporting Standard 18

OBJECTIVE

The objective of this FRS is to ensure that for all material items: **1**

(a)   an entity adopts the accounting policies most appropriate to its particular
circumstances for the purpose of giving a true and fair view;

(b)   the accounting policies adopted are reviewed regularly to ensure that they
remain appropriate, and are changed when a new policy becomes more
appropriate to the entity's particular circumstances; and

(c)   sufficient information is disclosed in the financial statements to enable users to
understand the accounting policies adopted and how they have been
implemented.

SCOPE

The FRS applies to all financial statements that are intended to give a true and fair view   **2**
of a reporting entity's financial position and profit or loss (or income and expenditure)
for a period.

3   **Reporting entities applying the Financial Reporting Standard for Smaller Entities currently applicable are exempt from the FRS.**

DEFINITIONS

4   The following definitions shall apply in the FRS and in particular in the Statement of Standard Accounting Practice set out **in bold type**.

Accounting policies:-

Those principles, bases, conventions, rules and practices applied by an entity that specify how the effects of transactions and other events are to be reflected in its financial statements through

(i)   recognising,
(ii)   selecting measurement bases for, and
(iii)   presenting

assets, liabilities, gains, losses and changes to shareholders' funds. Accounting policies do not include estimation techniques.

> Accounting policies define the process whereby transactions and other events are reflected in financial statements. For example, an accounting policy for a particular type of expenditure may specify whether an asset or a loss is to be recognised; the basis on which it is to be measured; and where in the profit and loss account or balance sheet it is to be presented.

Estimation techniques:-

The methods adopted by an entity to arrive at estimated monetary amounts, corresponding to the measurement bases selected, for assets, liabilities, gains, losses and changes to shareholders' funds.

> Estimation techniques implement the measurement aspects of accounting policies. An accounting policy will specify the basis on which an item is to be measured; where there is uncertainty over the monetary amount corresponding to that basis, the amount will be arrived at by using an estimation technique.

Estimation techniques include, for example:

(a)   methods of depreciation, such as straight-line and reducing balance, applied in the context of a particular measurement basis, used to estimate the proportion of the economic benefits of a tangible fixed asset consumed in a period;
(b)   different methods used to estimate the proportion of trade debts that will not be recovered, particularly where such methods consider a population as a whole rather than individual balances.

Measurement bases:-

Those monetary attributes of the elements of financial statements – assets, liabilities, gains, losses and changes to shareholders' funds – that are reflected in financial statements.

Where a business holds an asset that was purchased, the asset will have a number of qualities that may be expressed in terms of 'values'. As well as the amount for which it was acquired, it will have a current net realisable value and, if it is capable of being replaced, it will have a current replacement cost. These are examples of monetary attributes of the asset. Other examples arise when different monetary attributes are combined in a formula. For example, in a historical cost system, stocks are stated at the lower of historical cost and net realisable value. Similarly, in a current value measurement system, the current value of an asset, using the value to the business rule, is the lower of replacement cost and recoverable amount.*

Monetary attributes fall into two broad categories – those that reflect current values and those that reflect historical values. Some monetary attributes will be suitable for use in financial statements only in conjunction with others.† A monetary attribute, or combination of attributes, that may be reflected in financial statements is called a measurement basis.

SORP:-

An extant Statement of Recommended Practice (SORP) either developed in accordance with the Board's policy on SORPs, and including a statement by the Board‡, or 'franked' by the former Accounting Standards Committee.

SORPs recommend accounting practices for specialised industries or sectors. They supplement accounting standards and other legal and regulatory requirements in the light of the special factors prevailing or transactions undertaken in a particular industry or sector.

References to companies legislation mean, for a company: 5

(a)   in Great Britain, the Companies Act 1985;
(b)   in Northern Ireland, the Companies (Northern Ireland) Order 1986; and
(c)   in the Republic of Ireland, the Companies Acts 1963–90 and the European Communities (Companies: Group Accounts) Regulations 1992;

and for an entity other than a company, any equivalent legislation.

APPLYING THE DEFINITIONS IN PRACTICE

Distinguishing accounting policies from estimation techniques

Often, accounting standards or companies legislation will prescribe the measurement   6
bases to be used in respect of particular assets and liabilities. Whether prescribed or selected, measurement bases are a matter of accounting policy. Accordingly, if an entity has previously reported certain assets on a historical cost basis, but now reports them on a current value basis, that is a change of accounting policy.

*Recoverable amount is itself the higher of value in use and net realisable value.

†For example, value in use is unlikely to be appropriate for use in financial statements unless the competing claims of alternative monetary attributes are also considered, as in the value to the business rule.

‡The Statement 'SORPs: Policy and Code of Practice' sets out the Board's policy on SORPs and the basis on which a SORP will include a statement by the Board.

7   By contrast, the choice of method used to arrive at a monetary amount corresponding to a measurement basis is not a matter of accounting policy. For example, an entity may wish to measure the current disposal value of an asset. It might estimate this by reference to its own recent disposals of similar assets, or by reference to prices quoted in advertisements. Both methods are intended to arrive at the same unknown figure, and therefore a change from one method to another is a change of estimate, not of accounting policy. These methods are referred to in the FRS as estimation techniques.

8   Financial statements present information about their elements – assets, liabilities, gains, losses and changes to shareholders' funds – but not all the information that is available can be presented in an entity's primary financial statements. For example, although information may be available about two different monetary attributes of a particular asset – its historical cost and its current value under the value to the business rule – it will not be possible to reflect both in the entity's balance sheet. Therefore, accounting policies are used to determine which information is to be presented – ie which attribute of the asset is to be measured – and also how it is to be presented. By contrast, where it is either impossible or impractical to measure directly the amount corresponding to that attribute, estimation techniques are used to arrive at a suitable approximation. In simple terms, accounting policies determine which facts about a business are to be presented in financial statements, and how those facts are to be presented; estimation techniques are used to establish what those facts are. Some examples of changes to accounting policies and to estimation techniques are set out in Appendix I.

Recognition

9   For certain transactions, accounting standards allow a choice of what is to be recognised. Examples arise in FRS 15 'Tangible Fixed Assets', which allows directly attributable interest to be treated either as part of an asset or as an expense, and in SSAP 13 'Accounting for research and development', which allows expenditure satisfying asset recognition criteria to be treated either as an asset or as an expense. Where accounting standards allow a choice over what is to be recognised, that choice is a matter of accounting policy.

Measurement bases for fungible assets

10   Fungible assets are assets that are substantially indistinguishable one from another, in that there is no basis on which to distinguish between them in economic terms. Companies legislation, accounting standards and Urgent Issues Task Force (UITF) Abstracts may specify accounting policies for particular types of fungible asset. Subject to any such constraints, where fungible assets are recorded at historical cost, an entity's accounting policy may be to determine cost on an asset-by-asset basis, or the entity may select an accounting policy that considers those assets in aggregate, rather than individually. Accounting policies that consider fungible assets in aggregate will use measurement bases such as weighted average historical cost and historical cost measured on a 'first in, first out' (FIFO) basis.

11   However, an accounting policy that determines cost for fungible assets on an asset-by-asset basis may not enhance the comparability of financial statements. This is because the results reported under such a policy will be affected by the order in which fungible assets are disposed of or consumed, even though there is no basis on which to distinguish between those assets in economic terms. Accordingly, an accounting policy that considers fungible assets in aggregate will be more consistent with the objective of comparability set out in paragraph 30.

Changes to presentation

When an entity changes the way it presents a particular item in the balance sheet or   **12**
in the profit and loss account, that is a change of accounting policy. However, it is
not a change of accounting policy merely to provide additional information.
Accordingly, where a more detailed analysis of a particular item in the balance sheet
or in the profit and loss account is presented, or where information is disclosed for
the first time, that is not of itself a change of accounting policy. Nevertheless, it will
still be necessary to disclose corresponding amounts in similar detail.

Care is needed when an accounting change involves both a change of presentation   **13**
and a change of estimation technique. The former will be treated as a change of
accounting policy but the latter will not.*

ACCOUNTING POLICIES

Accounting policies and financial statements

An entity should adopt accounting policies that enable its financial statements to give a   **14**
true and fair view. Those accounting policies should be consistent with the requirements
of accounting standards, Urgent Issues Task Force (UITF) Abstracts and companies
legislation.

If in exceptional circumstances compliance with the requirements of an accounting   **15**
standard or UITF Abstract is inconsistent with the requirement to give a true and fair
view, the requirements of the accounting standard or UITF Abstract should be departed
from to the extent necessary to give a true and fair view. In such circumstances, the
disclosures set out in paragraph 62 should be provided.

An entity will not depart from the requirements of an accounting standard or UITF   **16**
Abstract where a true and fair view can be achieved by additional disclosure. In such
circumstances, the requirements of the accounting standard or UITF Abstract are not
inconsistent with the requirement to give a true and fair view.

Where it is necessary to choose between accounting policies that satisfy the conditions   **17**
in paragraph 14, an entity should select whichever of those accounting policies is judged
by the entity to be most appropriate to its particular circumstances for the purpose of
giving a true and fair view.

The provision of additional disclosures will not justify or remedy the adoption of an   **18**
accounting policy other than that which is judged by the entity to be most appropriate to its particular circumstances for the purpose of giving a true and fair view.
The appropriateness of accounting policies to an entity's particular circumstances is
judged by reference to the objectives and constraints set out in paragraphs 30 and 31.

Financial statements need to reflect, in an appropriate manner and as far as is   **19**
practicable, the effects of transactions and other events on an entity's financial
performance and financial position. Accounting policies assist in this process by
providing a framework within which elements of financial statements, such as assets
and liabilities, are recognised, measured and presented. They enhance the comparability of financial statements by helping to ensure that similar transactions are
reflected in a similar way.

This is illustrated in Example 4b in Appendix I.

20   Two concepts – the going concern assumption and accruals – play a pervasive role in financial statements, and hence in the selection of accounting policies.

Going concern

21   **An entity should prepare its financial statements on a going concern basis, unless**

(a)   the entity is being liquidated or has ceased trading, or

(b)   the directors either intend to liquidate the entity or to cease trading, or have no realistic alternative but to do so,

in which circumstances the entity should prepare its financial statements on a basis other than that of a going concern.*

22   The information provided by financial statements is usually most relevant if prepared on the hypothesis that the entity is to continue in operational existence for the foreseeable future. This hypothesis is commonly referred to as the going concern assumption. Financial statements are usually prepared on the basis that the reporting entity is a going concern because measures based on break-up values tend not to be relevant to users seeking to assess the entity's cash-generation ability and financial adaptability.

23   **When preparing financial statements, directors should assess whether there are significant doubts about an entity's ability to continue as a going concern.**

24   If the directors, when making the assessment required by paragraph 23, are aware of material uncertainties related to events or conditions that may cast significant doubt upon the entity's ability to continue as a going concern, paragraph 61 requires them to disclose those uncertainties. In making their assessment, the directors take into account all available information about the foreseeable future.

25   The degree of consideration necessary to make the assessment required by paragraph 23 depends on the facts in each case. When an entity has a history of profitable operations, which are expected to continue, and ready access to financial resources, detailed analysis may not be necessary. In other cases, the directors may, in making their assessment, need to consider a wide range of factors surrounding current and expected profitability, debt repayment schedules and potential sources of replacement financing. Such considerations also govern the length of time in respect of which the assessment should be made.

Accruals

26   **An entity should prepare its financial statements, except for cash flow information, on the accrual basis of accounting.**

27   The accrual basis of accounting requires the non-cash effects of transactions and other events to be reflected, as far as is possible†, in the financial statements for the accounting period in which they occur, and not, for example, in the period in which any cash involved is received or paid. The accruals concept lies at the heart of the definitions of assets and liabilities, which are set out in FRS 5 'Reporting the

---

*Editor's note: Paragraph amended by FRS 21.

†*In rare cases, it may not be possible to reflect the non-cash effects of transactions and other events in the financial statements for the accounting period in which they occur because they are not yet capable of reliable measurement. In such circumstances, recognition will be deferred until reliable measurement is possible.*

Substance of Transactions'. Accordingly, the use of those definitions to determine items to be recognised in an entity's balance sheet is consistent with the accruals concept.

Realisation

In preparing financial statements, an entity will have regard to requirements in **28** companies legislation that only profits realised at the balance sheet date should be included in the profit and loss account. Companies legislation requires realised profits to be determined in accordance with principles generally accepted at the time that financial statements are prepared. It is generally accepted that profits shall be treated as realised,* for these purposes, only when realised in the form either of cash or of other assets the ultimate cash realisation of which can be assessed with reasonable certainty.

The requirements in paragraph 28 relating to realised profits and the profit and loss **29** account apply unless there are special reasons for departing from them. However, such reasons will not exist unless, as a minimum, it is possible to be reasonably certain that, although a gain is unrealised, it nevertheless exists, and to measure it with sufficient reliability.†

Objectives and constraints in selecting accounting policies

The objectives against which an entity should judge the appropriateness of accounting **30** **policies to its particular circumstances are:**

(a)   **relevance;**
(b)   **reliability;**
(c)   **comparability; and**
(d)   **understandability.**

The constraints that an entity should take into account in judging the appropriateness of **31** **accounting policies to its particular circumstances are:**

(a)   **the need to balance the different objectives set out in paragraph 30; and**
(b)   **the need to balance the cost of providing information with the likely benefit of such information to users of the entity's financial statements.**

Although these objectives and constraints are discussed individually below, they are **32** considered together in judging the appropriateness of accounting policies to an entity's particular circumstances.

Relevance

The objective of financial statements is to provide information about an entity's **33** financial performance and financial position that is useful for assessing the stewardship of management and for making economic decisions. Financial information is relevant if it has the ability to influence the economic decisions of users and is

---

In this context, 'realised' may also encompass profits relating to assets that are readily realisable.

†*In addition, where there are special reasons for departing from the requirements described in paragraph 28, directors will also consider whether a departure would result in the use of valuation bases or other accounting treatments not permitted by companies legislation, which would be available only if use of the true and fair override was justified.*

provided in time to influence those decisions. Relevant information possesses either predictive or confirmatory value or both.

34   Appropriate accounting policies will result in financial information being presented that is relevant. Where more than one accounting policy would achieve this result, an entity will consider which of those policies presents the most relevant financial information in the context of the financial statements as a whole. In identifying that accounting policy, an entity will consider which measurement basis is most relevant and how to present information in the most relevant way.

Reliability

35   Financial information is reliable if:

(a)   it can be depended upon by users to represent faithfully what it either purports to represent or could reasonably be expected to represent, and therefore reflects the substance of the transactions and other events that have taken place;

(b)   it is free from deliberate or systematic bias (ie it is neutral);

(c)   it is free from material error;

(d)   it is complete within the bounds of materiality; and

(e)   under conditions of uncertainty, it has been prudently prepared (ie a degree of caution has been applied in exercising judgement and making the necessary estimates).

36   Appropriate accounting policies will result in financial information being presented that is reliable. They will present transactions and other events in a way that reflects their substance. A transaction or other event is faithfully represented in financial statements if the way in which it is recognised, measured and presented in those statements corresponds closely to the effect of that transaction or event.

37   Often there is uncertainty, either about the existence of assets, liabilities, gains, losses and changes to shareholders' funds, or about the amount at which they should be measured. Prudence requires that accounting policies take account of such uncertainty in recognising and measuring those assets, liabilities, gains, losses and changes to shareholders' funds. In conditions of uncertainty, appropriate accounting policies will require more confirmatory evidence about the existence of an asset or gain than about the existence of a liability or loss, and a greater reliability of measurement for assets and gains than for liabilities and losses.

38   However, it is not necessary to exercise prudence where there is no uncertainty. Nor is it appropriate to use prudence as a reason for, for example, creating hidden reserves or excessive provisions, deliberately understating assets or gains, or deliberately overstating liabilities or losses, because that would mean that the financial statements are not neutral and therefore not reliable.

Comparability

39   Information in an entity's financial statements gains greatly in usefulness if it can be compared with similar information about the entity for some other period or point in time, and with similar information about other entities. Such comparability can usually be achieved through a combination of consistency and disclosure. The disclosures required in respect of an entity's accounting policies, and any changes to those policies, are set out in paragraph 55.

Appropriate accounting policies will result in financial information being presented   **40**
in a way that enables users to discern and evaluate similarities in, and differences
between, the nature and effects of transactions and other events taking place over
time. In selecting accounting policies, an entity will assess whether accepted industry
practices are appropriate to its particular circumstances. Such practices will be
particularly persuasive if set out in a SORP that has been generally accepted by an
industry or sector.

Understandability

Information provided by financial statements needs to be capable of being under-   **41**
stood by users having a reasonable knowledge of business and economic activities
and accounting and a willingness to study with reasonable diligence the information
provided. Appropriate accounting policies will result in financial information being
presented in a way that enables its significance to be perceived by such users.

Balancing the different objectives

There can be tensions between the different objectives set out in paragraph 30. In   **42**
particular, sometimes the accounting policy that is most relevant to a particular
entity's circumstances is not the most reliable, and vice versa. In such circumstances,
the most appropriate accounting policy will usually be that which is the most relevant of those that are reliable.

There can also be tension between two aspects of reliability – neutrality and pru-   **43**
dence. Whilst neutrality involves freedom from deliberate or systematic bias,
prudence is a potentially biased concept that seeks to ensure that, under conditions
of uncertainty, gains and assets are not overstated and losses and liabilities are not
understated. This tension exists only where there is uncertainty, because it is only
then that prudence needs to be exercised. In the selection of accounting policies, the
competing demands of neutrality and prudence are reconciled by finding a balance
that ensures that the deliberate and systematic understatement of assets and gains
and overstatement of liabilities and losses do not occur.

Cost and benefit considerations

Paragraph 14 emphasises that accounting policies should be consistent with the   **44**
requirements of accounting standards, UITF Abstracts and companies legislation.
Accordingly, cost and benefit considerations will not justify the adoption of an
accounting policy that is inconsistent with those requirements.

Reviewing and changing accounting policies

An entity's accounting policies should be reviewed regularly to ensure that they remain   **45**
the most appropriate to its particular circumstances for the purpose of giving a true and
fair view. However, in judging whether a new policy is more appropriate than the
existing policy, an entity will give due weight to the impact on comparability, as
explained in paragraph 49.

An entity may take account of recently issued FRSs – ie those for which the effective   **46**
date falls in a later accounting period – in judging whether its present accounting
policies are still the most appropriate to its particular circumstances. Paragraph 45
does not require early adoption of a new FRS, because the effective date of a new FRS
allows an appropriate period for entities to consider and address any issues

surrounding its implementation. However, where it is necessary either to implement a new accounting policy or to change an existing accounting policy, an entity will ensure wherever possible that the new accounting policy is in accordance with recently issued FRSs.

47   An entity may take account of Financial Reporting Exposure Drafts (FREDs) in judging which accounting policies are most appropriate to its particular circumstances. However, in accordance with paragraph 14, an entity will not be free to adopt an accounting policy based on a FRED unless that policy is consistent with the requirements of existing accounting standards and UITF Abstracts. Moreover, there may be changes between a FRED and the ensuing FRS. Accordingly, where an entity believes that an accounting policy based on a FRED may be more appropriate than its existing policy, the entity will, in reaching a judgement, consider the factors discussed in paragraph 49.

48   Unless other accounting standards, UITF Abstracts or companies legislation require otherwise, a material adjustment applicable to prior periods arising from a change to an accounting policy is accounted for as a prior period adjustment, in accordance with the requirements of FRS 3 'Reporting Financial Performance'.

49   Frequent changes to accounting policies will not enhance comparability over the longer term, because they make it more difficult for users to compare an entity's financial statements with those of earlier periods. Consequently, the impact of past and expected future changes is considered when determining whether a potential change is desirable, and accounting policies are not changed unless the benefit to users outweighs the corresponding disadvantages. Nevertheless, consistency is not an end in itself and therefore does not impede the introduction of improved accounting practices that result in an overall benefit to users.

ESTIMATION TECHNIQUES

50   **Where estimation techniques are required to enable the accounting policies adopted to be applied, an entity should select estimation techniques that enable its financial statements to give a true and fair view and are consistent with the requirements of accounting standards, UITF Abstracts and companies legislation.**

51   **Where it is necessary to choose between estimation techniques that satisfy the conditions in paragraph 50, an entity should select whichever of those estimation techniques is judged by the entity to be most appropriate to its particular circumstances for the purpose of giving a true and fair view.**

52   The purpose of an estimation technique is to arrive at a monetary amount corresponding to a particular measurement basis. Accordingly, it is important for estimation techniques to be reliable and, all other things being equal, an entity will ideally select whichever estimation technique best approximates that monetary amount. However, it may not be possible to identify that estimation technique with certainty, at least at the time that financial statements are prepared, because estimation techniques are used only in circumstances where an amount is unknown. Moreover, materiality and cost and benefit considerations will usually play a part; greater accuracy of estimation often comes at an incremental cost, which may not be justified once improvements in accuracy cease to be material.

53   In addition, other factors will sometimes be relevant. In certain circumstances, paragraph 55(b) requires a description of the estimation technique selected to be given, so that users may consider the impact that different judgements might have

had on the entity's financial statements and to enable comparisons to be made with the financial statements of other entities. When choosing between estimation techniques in circumstances where disclosures are likely to be required, an entity will also consider the extent to which each technique may be understood by users, and the extent to which each will facilitate comparisons with other entities.

A change to an estimation technique should not be accounted for as a prior period adjustment, unless   54

(a)   **it represents the correction of a fundamental error, or**
(b)   **another accounting standard, a UITF Abstract or companies legislation requires the change to be accounted for as a prior period adjustment.**

DISCLOSURES

The following information should be disclosed in the financial statements: 55

(a)   **a description of each of the accounting policies that is material in the context of the entity's financial statements.**
(b)   **a description of those estimation techniques adopted that are significant, as explained in paragraph 57.**
(c)   **details of any changes to the accounting policies that were followed in preparing financial statements for the preceding period, including:**

   (i)   **a brief explanation of why each new accounting policy is thought more appropriate;**
   (ii)   **where practicable, the effect of a prior period adjustment on the results for the preceding period, in accordance with FRS 3 'Reporting Financial Performance'; and**
   (iii)   **where practicable, an indication of the effect of a change in accounting policy on the results for the current period.**
   Where it is not practicable to make the disclosures described in (ii) or (iii) above, that fact, together with the reasons, should be stated.

(d)   **where the effect of a change to an estimation technique is material, a description of the change and, where practicable, the effect on the results for the current period.**

The objective of the disclosures required by paragraph 55(a) is to enable the accounting policies adopted by an entity to be understood by users having a reasonable knowledge of business and economic activities and accounting and a willingness to study with reasonable diligence the information provided. Where an accounting policy is prescribed by, and fully described in, an accounting standard, a UITF Abstract or companies legislation, a succinct description of the policy will satisfy the requirements of paragraph 55(a). Where an accounting policy is not prescribed by an accounting standard, a UITF Abstract or companies legislation, or the entity uses an option permitted therein, a fuller description will be provided.   56

Estimation techniques are used where there is uncertainty over the monetary amount at which an item is to be measured. The amount that is determined will depend both on the estimation technique selected and on any assumptions (such as interest rates and useful lives) used in applying that technique. Although many estimation techniques are used in preparing financial statements, most do not require disclosure because, in most instances, the monetary amounts that might reasonably be ascribed to an item will fall within a relatively narrow range. An estimation technique is significant for the purposes of paragraph 55(b) only if the range of reasonable monetary amounts is so large that the use of a different amount from within that   57 range could materially affect the view shown by the entity's financial statements. To judge whether disclosures are required in respect of a particular estimation technique, an entity will consider the impact of varying the assumptions underlying that technique. The description of a significant estimation technique will include details of those underlying assumptions to which the monetary amount is particularly sensitive.

SORPs

58 **Where an entity's financial statements fall within the scope of a SORP, the entity should state the title of the SORP and whether its financial statements have been prepared in accordance with those of the SORP's provisions currently in effect.* In the event of a departure, the entity should give a brief description of how the financial statements depart from the recommended practice set out in the SORP, which should include:**

(a) for any treatment that is not in accordance with the SORP, the reasons why the treatment adopted is judged more appropriate to the entity's particular circumstances, and

(b) details of any disclosures recommended by the SORP that have not been provided, and the reasons why they have not been provided.

59 SORPs recommend particular accounting treatments with the aim of narrowing areas of difference and variety between comparable entities. Compliance with a SORP that has been generally accepted by an industry or sector leads to enhanced comparability between the financial statements of entities in that industry or sector. Comparability is further enhanced if users are made aware of the extent to which an entity complies with a SORP, and the reasons for any departures. The effect of a departure from a SORP need not be quantified, except in those rare cases where such quantification is necessary for the entity's financial statements to give a true and fair view.

60 Entities whose financial statements do not fall within the scope of a SORP may nevertheless choose to comply with the SORP's recommendations when preparing financial statements. Where this is the case, entities are encouraged to disclose that fact.

Going concern

61 **The following information should be disclosed in the financial statements in relation to the going concern assessment required by paragraph 23:**

(a) any material uncertainties, of which the directors are aware in making their assessment, related to events or conditions that may cast significant doubt upon the entity's ability to continue as a going concern.

(b) where the foreseeable future considered by the directors has been limited to a period of less than one year from the date of approval of the financial statements, that fact.

(c) when the financial statements are not prepared on a going concern basis, that fact, together with the basis on which the financial statements are prepared and the reason why the entity is not regarded as a going concern.

*The provisions of a SORP will cease to have effect, for example, to the extent that they conflict with a more recent accounting standard or UITF Abstract.

True and fair view override

For any material departure from the requirements of an accounting standard, a UITF   **62**
Abstract or companies legislation, particulars of the departure, the reasons for it and its
effect should be disclosed. The information disclosed should include:

(a)   a clear and unambiguous statement that there has been a departure from the
      requirements of an accounting standard, a UITF Abstract or companies legislation,
      as the case may be, and that the departure is necessary to give a true and fair view.
(b)   a statement of the treatment that the accounting standard, UITF Abstract or
      companies legislation would normally require in the circumstances and a
      description of the treatment actually adopted.
(c)   a statement of why the treatment prescribed would not give a true and fair view.
(d)   a description of how the position shown in the financial statements is different as a
      result of the departure, normally with quantification, except where

   (i)   quantification is already evident in the financial statements themselves;* or
   (ii)   the effect cannot reasonably be quantified, in which case the directors should
          explain the circumstances.

Where a departure continues in subsequent financial statements, the disclosures should   **63**
be made in all such subsequent statements, and should include corresponding amounts
for the previous year. Where a departure affects only the corresponding amounts, the
disclosures should be given for those corresponding amounts.

Where companies legislation requires an entity to make a statement of whether its   **64**
financial statements have been prepared in accordance with applicable accounting
standards†, that statement should either include or cross-reference any disclosures
required by paragraph 62.

Where companies legislation requires disclosure of particulars of a departure from a   **65**
specific statutory requirement, the reasons for it and its effect, disclosures equivalent to
those set out in paragraph 62 should be provided.‡

DATE FROM WHICH EFFECTIVE

Subject to paragraph 67, the accounting practices set out in the FRS should be regarded   **66**
as standard in respect of accounting periods ending on or after 22 June 2001. Earlier
adoption is encouraged.

Paragraphs 58–60 and the last sentence of paragraph 40 need not be applied in respect   **67**
of accounting periods beginning on or before 23 December 2001, but earlier application
is encouraged.

*An example might be a matter of presentation rather than measurement.

†This disclosure is required by companies legislation as follows:
in Great Britain, the Companies Act 1985, Schedule 4, paragraph 36A; and
in Northern Ireland, the Companies (Northern Ireland) Order 1986, Schedule 4, paragraph 36A. There is no
equivalent requirement in the Republic of Ireland.

‡In Great Britain, such disclosures in connection with a departure are required by the Companies Act 1985,
sections 226(5) and 227(6), Schedule 4 paragraph 15, Schedule 4A paragraph 3(2), Schedule 8 paragraph 15,
Schedule 9 paragraph 22 and Schedule 9A paragraph 19. The equivalent requirements in Northern Ireland and in
the Republic of Ireland are set out in Appendix II.

WITHDRAWAL OF ssap 2 AND uitf ABSTRACTS 7 AND 14 AND AMENDMENT OF OTHER ACCOUNTING STANDARDS AND uitf ABSTRACTS

68   The frs supersedes ssap 2 'Disclosure of accounting policies', uitf Abstract 7 'True and fair view override disclosures' and uitf Abstract 14 'Disclosure of changes in accounting policy'.

69   The frs makes the following changes to other accounting standards and uitf Abstracts:

[Not reproduced as all changes have been reflected in the material reproduced in this volume.]

Adoption of FRS 18 by the Board

Financial Reporting Standard 18 'Accounting Policies' was approved for issue by the ten members of the Accounting Standards Board.

Sir David Tweedie	(Chairman)
Allan Cook CBE	(Technical Director)

David Allvey
Ian Brindle
Dr John Buchanan
John Coombe
Huw Jones
Isobel Sharp
Professor Geoffrey Whittington
Ken Wild

Appendix I
Examples of changes to accounting policies and to estimation techniques

This appendix illustrates the application of the FRS to assist in clarifying its meaning. It does not form part of the FRS.

Example 1:
Capitalised finance costs

An entity has previously charged to the profit and loss account interest incurred in connection with the construction of tangible fixed assets. It now proposes to capitalise such interest, as permitted by FRS 15 'Tangible Fixed Assets', since it believes this better reflects the cost of constructing those assets.

Does this involve a change to:	
Recognition?	✓
Presentation?	✓
Measurement basis?	✗

Explanation – The transaction whose effects are being reflected is the incurring of directly attributable finance costs. That transaction is still being measured in the same way, but there is a change to recognition, in that it is now being recognised as (part of) an asset rather than as an expense.* There is also, consequently, a change to the presentation of the transaction in the balance sheet and the profit and loss account.

Conclusion – This is a change of accounting policy.

Example 2:
Indirect overheads recorded in the value of stock

A manufacturing entity has three indirect cost centres (A, B and C). It has previously assessed that the indirect costs attributable to production are 30 per cent of A and 40 per cent of B. Having reassessed the nature of those cost centres' activities, it now assesses that the indirect costs attributable to production are 25 per cent of A, 40 per cent of B and 10 per cent of C.

Does this involve a change to:	
Recognition?	✗
Presentation?	✗
Measurement basis?	✗

Explanation – This example has similarities with Example 1; cost centre C may be contrasted with interest in that example. The key difference is that, in Example 1, FRS 15 allows the entity a choice of how to treat directly attributable interest – as an asset

---

Paragraph 9 of the FRS notes that where accounting standards allow a choice over what is to be recognised, that choice is a matter of accounting policy.

or as an expense. There is no such choice here; directly attributable costs, once estimated, must be treated as part of an asset. Accordingly there is no change to recognition. In addition, both stocks and overheads continue to be presented in the same way and measured on the same basis (stocks are measured at the amount of directly attributable historical costs).

Conclusion – This is a change of estimation technique.

Example 3:
Classification of overheads

An entity has previously shown certain overheads within cost of sales. It now proposes to show those overheads within administrative expenses.

Does this involve a change to:	
Recognition?	×
Presentation?	✓
Measurement basis?	×

Explanation – Although there is no change to the recognition and measurement of costs, they are being presented differently.

Conclusion – This is a change of accounting policy.

Example 4a:
Depreciation of vehicles

An entity has previously depreciated vehicles using the reducing balance method at 40 per cent per year. It now proposes to depreciate vehicles using the straight-line method over five years, since it believes this better reflects the pattern of consumption of economic benefits.

Does this involve a change to:	
Recognition?	×
Presentation?	×
Measurement basis?	×

Explanation – Vehicles are being recognised and presented in the same way as before, and using the same, historical cost measurement basis. The only change is to the estimation technique used to measure the unexpired portion of each vehicle's economic benefits.

Conclusion – This is not a change of accounting policy.*

Example 4b:
Depreciation of vehicles

As in Example 4a, an entity has previously depreciated vehicles using the reducing balance method at 40 per cent per year and now proposes to depreciate vehicles using the straight-line method over five years. In addition, it has previously recorded the

---

**Paragraph 82 of FRS 15 also states that a change from one method of providing depreciation to another does not constitute a change of accounting policy.*

depreciation charge within cost of sales, but now proposes to include it within administrative expenses.

Does this involve a change to:	
Recognition?	✗
Presentation?	✓
Measurement basis?	✗

Explanation – This accounting change involves both a change to presentation, as in Example 3 above, and a change of estimation technique, as in Example 4a above. For the reasons set out in those examples, the former is a change of accounting policy but the latter is not.

Conclusion – The two changes are accounted for separately. No change is made to the amount of depreciation charged in earlier periods, but the profit and loss account for the preceding period is restated to move the depreciation charge from cost of sales to administrative expenses.

Example 5:
Accounting for fungible stocks

An entity has fungible stocks and its accounting policy has previously been to consider those stocks in aggregate, measuring them at weighted average historical cost. However, it determines that the normal accounting policy in its industry is to measure such stocks at historical cost on a FIFO basis. It concludes, for reasons of comparability, that it should adopt the normal industry policy.

Does this involve a change to:	
Recognition?	✗
Presentation?	✗
Measurement basis?	✓

Explanation – There is explicitly a change of measurement basis.*

Conclusion – This is a change of accounting policy, and it should be disclosed. However, a prior period adjustment will be required only if the difference between weighted average and FIFO is material.

Example 6a:
Discounting

An entity has previously reported deferred tax on an undiscounted basis. However, the norm in its industry is to report deferred tax on a discounted basis. It concludes, for reasons of comparability, that it should adopt the normal industry approach.

---

*As explained in paragraph 10 of the FRS, an entity with fungible assets will make clear, when disclosing its accounting policy, whether it is to consider those assets individually or, if in aggregate, which measurement basis is reflected (FIFO, weighted average etc.). For many entities, however, the difference between measurement bases in value terms may not be material.

Does this involve a change to:	
Recognition?	×
Presentation?	×
Measurement basis?	✓

Explanation – FRS 19 allows entities to report deferred tax on either a discounted or an undiscounted basis. These are two different measurement bases, and it is a matter of accounting policy which an entity chooses to adopt.

Conclusion – This is a change of accounting policy.

Example 6b:
Discounting

An entity has previously measured a particular provision on an undiscounted basis, in accordance with FRS 12 'Provisions, Contingent Liabilities and Contingent Assets', as the effect of discounting was not material. However, this year it has revised upwards its estimates of future cash flows associated with the provision and, as a result, the effect of discounting is now material. FRS 12 therefore requires it to report the provision at the discounted amount.

Does this involve a change to:	
Recognition?	×
Presentation?	×
Measurement basis?	×

Explanation – FRS 12 requires entities to report provisions at the best estimate of the expenditure required to settle the present obligation at the balance sheet date. Where that estimate is based on future cash flows, it is permissible to use undiscounted amounts only where the effect of the time value of money is not material. In such circumstances, the use of undiscounted future cash flows is, in effect, an estimation technique for arriving at the present value.

Conclusion – This is not a change of accounting policy.

Example 7:
Translating the financial statements of a foreign subsidiary

A group has previously translated the profit and loss account of its foreign subsidiary using the closing rate. However, it now proposes to use the average rate for the accounting period, on the basis that this reflects more fairly the group's profits and losses as they arise throughout the accounting period.

Does this involve a change to:	
Recognition?	×
Presentation?	×
Measurement basis?	✓

Explanation – SSAP 20 'Foreign currency translation' allows a group translating the profit and loss account of a foreign subsidiary under the closing rate/net investment method to use either the closing rate or the average rate for the accounting period. These are two different measurement bases for the profit and loss account, and it is a matter of accounting policy which an entity chooses to adopt.

Conclusion – This is a change of accounting policy.

Appendix II
Note on legal requirements

Great Britain

The statutory requirements relating to accounting policies are set out in the Companies Act 1985. The main requirements that are directly relevant are set out in Schedules 4 and 4A and are summarised below.   **1**

Schedules 4 and 4A to the Act do not apply to banking and insurance companies and groups. Corresponding requirements are set out in Schedule 9 for banking companies and groups and in Schedule 9A for insurance companies and groups. Schedule 4 to the Act does not apply to small companies to the extent that they choose instead to comply with the reduced requirements set out in Schedule 8.   **2**

Accounting principles

Paragraph 9 of Schedule 4 requires the amounts to be included in a company's accounts to be determined in accordance with the following principles set out in paragraphs 10–14 of Schedule 4, unless there are special reasons for departing from any of those principles: **3**

(a)   the company shall be presumed to be carrying on business as a going concern;
(b)   accounting policies shall be applied consistently within the same accounts and from one financial year to the next;
(c)   the amount of any item shall be determined on a prudent basis, and in particular–

   (i)   only profits realised at the balance sheet date shall be included in the profit and loss account; and
   (ii)   all liabilities and losses which have arisen or are likely to arise in respect of the financial year to which the accounts relate or a previous financial year shall be taken into account, including those which only become apparent between the balance sheet date and the date on which it is signed on behalf of the board of directors;

(d)   all income and charges relating to the financial year to which the accounts relate shall be taken into account, without regard to the date of receipt or payment; and
(e)   in determining the aggregate amount of any item the amount of each individual asset or liability that falls to be taken into account shall be determined separately.

Paragraph 15 of Schedule 4 permits the directors of a company to depart from any of the principles stated above in preparing the company's accounts in respect of any financial year if it appears to them that there are special reasons for such a departure. Particulars of the departure, the reasons for it and its effect are required to be given in a note to the accounts.   **4**

Although 'prudence' is not defined in the Act, the Act describes the requirement that the amount of any item shall be determined on a prudent basis in a way that differs from the FRS. Nevertheless, the Board believes that the requirements of the FRS are not inconsistent with those of the Act.*   **5**

*This matter is discussed in greater detail in paragraphs 3–8 of Appendix V to FRS 12 'Provisions, Contingent Liabilities and Contingent Assets'.

Disclosure of accounting policies

6   Paragraph 36 of Schedule 4 requires disclosure of the accounting policies adopted by a company (including the policies regarding the depreciation and diminution in value of assets).*

Measurement bases

7   Except to the extent that a company chooses to adopt the alternative accounting rules, the amounts to be included in a company's accounts are to be determined in accordance with the historical cost accounting rules set out in paragraphs 17–28 of Schedule 4. The alternative accounting rules are set out in paragraphs 29–34 of Schedule 4.

8   The following paragraphs of Schedule 4 require disclosures in respect of measurement bases:

(a)   where stocks or other fungible assets are measured using 'first in, first out' (FIFO), 'last in, first out' (LIFO),† weighted average price or a similar method, paragraph 27(3) requires the difference between the amount measured using that method and on the basis of replacement cost at the balance sheet date, or of most recent actual cost, to be disclosed if material.

(b)   where the alternative accounting rules set out in paragraph 31 are adopted as the measurement bases for certain assets, paragraph 33(2) requires disclosure of each item affected and the basis of valuation, and paragraph 33(3) requires disclosure for each item affected (except stocks) either of the amount that would have been determined under the historical cost accounting rules, or of the difference between the amount measured under the historical cost accounting rules and under the alternative accounting rule adopted.

(c)   paragraph 45(2) requires disclosure of the aggregate market value of listed investments where this differs from the amount included in a company's accounts, and of both the market value and the stock exchange value of any investments of which the former value is, for the purposes of a company's accounts, taken as being higher than the latter.

(d)   paragraph 58(1) requires disclosure of the basis on which any amounts originally denominated in foreign currencies have been translated into sterling for inclusion in the balance sheet or profit and loss account.

Comparability

9   Paragraph 4(2) of Schedule 4 requires the corresponding amount for any item in a company's balance sheet or profit and loss account to be adjusted if it is not comparable with the amount for the current financial year. Particulars of the adjustment and the reasons for it are to be disclosed. Paragraph 58(2) of Schedule 4 extends this

---

According to legal advice received by the Financial Reporting Review Panel, a statement that accounts have been prepared in accordance with applicable accounting standards, as required by paragraph 36A, does not satisfy the requirement in paragraph 36. To satisfy that requirement, there must be a brief statement of each relevant accounting policy, either in the accounts themselves or in the notes to the accounts. However, paragraph 36 does not require disclosure of accounting policies that are immaterial in the context of the accounts in question.

†*SSAP 9 'Stocks and long-term contracts' notes that 'the use of the LIFO method can result in the reporting of current assets at amounts that bear little relationship to recent costs. This may result in not only a significant misstatement of balance sheet amounts but also a potential distortion of current and future results. This places a special responsibility on the directors to be assured that the circumstances of the company require the adoption of such a valuation method in order for the accounts to give a true and fair view.'*

requirement to corresponding amounts stated in notes to the accounts, with the exception of the items listed in paragraph 58(3) of Schedule 4.

Group accounts

Where assets and liabilities to be included in group accounts have been valued or otherwise determined according to accounting rules differing from those used for the group accounts, paragraph 3 of Schedule 4A requires the values or amounts to be adjusted so as to accord with the rules used for the group accounts, unless it appears to the directors of the parent company that there are special reasons for departing from this rule. Particulars of any such departure, the reasons for it and its effect shall be given in a note to the accounts. **10**

Paragraph 4 of Schedule 4A requires any differences of accounting rules as between a parent company's individual accounts for a financial year and its group accounts to be disclosed in a note to the group accounts and the reasons for the difference to be given. **11**

The true and fair view override

In special circumstances, compliance with a provision of the Act on the matters to be included in a company's accounts (or notes thereto) may be inconsistent with the requirement to give a true and fair view of the state of affairs and profit or loss. Sections 226(5) and 227(6) of the Act provide, for individual company accounts and for group accounts, that in such circumstances the directors shall depart from that provision to the extent necessary to give a true and fair view* Where this true and fair view override is used, the Act requires particulars of the departure, the reasons for it and its effect to be given in a note to the accounts. **12**

Realisation

Part VIII of the Act sets limits on a company's ability to make distributions to its members. Different rules apply to public companies, private companies, investment companies and insurance companies, but those rules are in part concerned with whether gains and losses have been realised. Realised profits and realised losses are defined in section 262(3) of the Act: **13**

'References in this Part to "realised profits" and "realised losses", in relation to a company's accounts, are to such profits or losses of the company as fall to be treated as realised in accordance with principles generally accepted, at the time when the accounts are prepared, with respect to the determination for accounting purposes of realised profits or losses.

This is without prejudice to –

(a) the construction of any other expression (where appropriate) by reference to accepted accounting principles or practice, or

(b) any specific provision for the treatment of profits or losses of any description as realised.'

The concept of realisation is discussed further in paragraphs 15–20 of Appendix IV. **14**

However, if a true and fair view can be achieved by the provision of additional information, there is no inconsistency. No departure is allowed in such circumstances.

Northern Ireland

15   The statutory requirements in Northern Ireland are set out in the Companies (Northern Ireland) Order 1986. Those requirements are identical to the legislation for Great Britain cited above.

Republic of Ireland

16   The statutory requirements in the Republic of Ireland that correspond to those cited above for Great Britain are shown in the following table.

Great Britain	Republic of Ireland
section 226(5) of the Companies Act 1985	section 3(1) of the Companies (Amendment) Act 1986
section 227(6) of the Companies Act 1985	Regulation 14(3) and (4) of the European Communities (Companies: Group Accounts) Regulations 1992
section 262(3) of the Companies Act 1985	paragraph 72 of the Schedule to the Companies (Amendment) Act 1986
Part VIII of the Companies Act 1985	Part IV of the Companies (Amendment) Act 1983
Schedule 4 to the Companies Act 1985:	The Companies (Amendment) Act 1986:
paragraph 4(2)	section 4(8)
paragraph 9	section 5
paragraph 10	section 5(a)
paragraph 11	section 5(b)
paragraph 12	section 5(c)
paragraph 13	section 5(d)
paragraph 14	section 5(e)
paragraph 15	section 6
Schedule 4 to the Companies Act 1985:	The Schedule to the Companies (Amendment) Act 1986:
paragraphs 17—28	paragraphs 5—16*
paragraph 27(3)	paragraph 15(3)
paragraphs 29—34	paragraphs 17—22†
paragraph 33(2)	paragraph 21(2)
paragraph 33(3)	paragraph 21(3)
paragraph 36	paragraph 24
paragraph 36A	no equivalent
paragraph 45(2)	paragraph 31(2)
paragraph 58(1)	paragraph 44(1)
paragraph 58(2)	paragraph 44(2)
paragraph 58(3)(a)–(c)	no equivalent
paragraph 58(3)(d)	paragraph 44(3)

*Note: there is no requirement corresponding to paragraph 27(2)(b) of Schedule 4.

†Note: there is no requirement corresponding to paragraph 34(3A) of Schedule 4.

Schedule 4A to the Companies Act 1985: European Communities(Companies: Group Accounts) Regulations 1992:

   paragraph 3   Regulation 30

   paragraph 4   Regulation 29

Schedule 8 to the Companies Act 1985   no equivalent

Schedule 9 to the Companies Act 1985   European Communities (Credit Institutions: Accounts) Regulations 1992

Schedule 9A to the Companies Act 1985   European Communities (Insurance Undertakings: Accounts) Regulations 1996

Appendix III
Compliance with International Accounting Standards

1   The International Accounting Standards Committee deals with accounting policies in its standards IAS 1 (revised 1997) 'Presentation of Financial Statements' and IAS 8 (revised 1993) 'Net Profit or Loss for the Period, Fundamental Errors and Changes in Accounting Policies'. The general requirements for accounting policies in the FRS are consistent with those standards, except as discussed below.*

2   IAS 8 (revised 1993) defines accounting policies as the specific principles, bases, conventions, rules and practices adopted by an enterprise in preparing and presenting financial statements. The definition in the FRS also refers to principles, bases, conventions, rules and practices, but it is more specific about the role that accounting policies play in the preparation and presentation of financial statements. Specifically, accounting policies are applied by an entity in order to reflect the effects of transactions and other events through recognising, selecting measurement bases for, and presenting assets, liabilities, gains, losses and changes to shareholders' funds.

3   The FRS defines estimation techniques and distinguishes them from accounting policies. IAS 8 (revised 1993) distinguishes between a change of accounting policy and a change of accounting estimate, but does not include an equivalent definition.

4   IAS 1 (revised 1997) requires management to develop accounting policies that provide information that is relevant and reliable, and that provide the most useful information to users, but only in the absence both of a specific IAS and of an interpretation of the Standing Interpretations Committee.† Accordingly, where specific IASs or interpretations of the Standing Interpretations Committee allow different treatments, an entity is permitted a free choice; it is not required in such circumstances to choose whichever policy will provide the most useful information to users. By contrast, the FRS requires that, where more than one treatment is allowed, an entity should use the criteria of relevance, reliability, comparability and understandability to select the policy that is the most appropriate of those allowed.

5   IAS 1 (revised 1997) requires management to make an assessment of an enterprise's ability to continue as a going concern, taking into account all available information for the foreseeable future, which should be at least, but is not limited to, twelve months from the balance sheet date. The FRS includes a similar requirement but, like the UK Auditing Standard SAS 130 'The going concern basis in financial statements', it does not specify a minimum length for the foreseeable future. Instead, it requires disclosure where the directors have considered a period of less than twelve months from the date of approval of the financial statements.‡

6   IAS 1 (revised 1997) requires financial statements to be prepared on a going concern basis unless management either intends to liquidate the enterprise or to cease trading, or has no realistic alternative but to do so. The FRS includes a requirement that is similar except that management intent is not sufficient to justify a departure from the going concern basis. Accordingly, the FRS requires an entity's financial statements to be prepared on a going concern basis unless the entity is being liquidated or has ceased trading, or the directors have no realistic alternative but to liquidate the entity or to cease trading.

---

*Editor's note: IAS 1 and IAS 8 have both been revised. IAS 8 now contains all guidance on accounting policies.

†Editor's note: The Standard Interpretations Committee has now been replaced by the International Financial Reporting Interpretations Committee.

‡Editor's note: SAS 130 is no longer applicable, and has now been replaced by ISA (UK and Ireland) 570, Going Concern.

Appendix IV
The development of the FRS

History

The FRS sets out the principles to be followed in selecting accounting policies and the   1
disclosures needed to help users to understand the accounting policies adopted and
how they have been implemented. It supersedes SSAP 2 'Disclosure of accounting
policies', which was issued in November 1971.

The objective of SSAP 2 was to ensure disclosure in an entity's financial statements of   2
clear explanations of the accounting policies followed insofar as they were significant
for the purpose of giving a true and fair view. At the time it was issued, no statement
of principles existed in the UK and the Republic of Ireland to provide a framework
within which 'accounting policies' might be defined. Accordingly, SSAP 2 introduced
and defined 'fundamental accounting concepts', singling out four – going concern,
accruals, consistency and prudence – which have since been reflected in the EC
Accounting Directives and in companies legislation in the UK and the Republic of
Ireland.*

SSAP 2 made clear that this approach was expedient rather than theoretical. The   3
fundamental accounting concepts were to be regarded as working assumptions
having general acceptance at the time of issue of the standard – practical rules rather
than theoretical ideals. It was envisaged that, as accounting thought and practice
developed, the concepts would be capable of variation and evolution.

In December 1999, the Board issued its Statement of Principles for Financial   4
Reporting, which reflected, among other things, how accounting developments in the
28 years since SSAP 2 was issued had affected the fundamental accounting concepts
identified in that standard. Although the Statement of Principles discussed each of
the concepts individually, they were no longer referred to as 'fundamental accounting
concepts' and their respective roles had changed, as explained further below.

A number of respondents to the Revised Exposure Draft of the Statement of Prin-   5
ciples commented that SSAP 2 should be amended in the light of that document. The
Board agreed and in December 1999 it published FRED 21 'Accounting Policies',
which set out proposals to update the concepts underpinning SSAP 2. In other
respects, the Board regarded SSAP 2 as broadly satisfactory, retaining many of its
requirements in FRED 21, but it took the opportunity to clarify and to expand on
certain matters. Accordingly, the FRED:

- sought to make the distinction between a change of accounting policy and a
  change of estimate more robust, by including a more specific definition of
  accounting policies and a new definition of estimation techniques
- set out clearly a requirement, implied but not explicit in SSAP 2, that an entity
  should adopt those accounting policies that are most appropriate to its particular
  circumstances for the purpose of giving a true and fair view
- set out the objectives and constraints to be considered when selecting and
  changing accounting policies
- set out circumstances in which an entity should also disclose details of the estimation techniques used in implementing its accounting policies

---

*See paragraphs 3 and 4 of Appendix II 'Note on legal requirements' (and paragraph 16 for the Republic of Ireland).

6   The Board has considered the comments of respondents to FRED 21 in developing the FRS. The most significant comments, and the resulting changes made to the proposals in FRED 21, are discussed in the following sections.

The fundamental accounting concepts in SSAP 2

7   As SSAP 2 envisaged, the meanings attaching to the fundamental accounting concepts, and their individual importance relative to one another, have developed and evolved over time. Accordingly, they are treated somewhat differently in the FRS from the way in which they were treated in SSAP 2.

Going concern and accruals

8   Two of the concepts – going concern and accruals – have a particularly prominent role in the FRS. That is because they are part of the bedrock of accounting, and hence critical to the selection of accounting policies. The going concern assumption determines the perspective from which the objectives and constraints set out in the FRS should be viewed, particularly with regard to measurement. The accruals concept lies at the heart of the definitions of assets, liabilities, gains, losses and changes to shareholders' funds, and both notions play an important role in the recognition of those items.

9   In discussing the accruals concept, SSAP 2 explained that revenues and costs should be matched with one another so far as their relationship can be established or justifiably assumed, and dealt with in the profit and loss account of the period to which they relate. The FRS takes a slightly different approach to the accruals concept. Rather than focusing on when a relationship can be established or justifiably assumed, it emphasises instead that the non-cash effects of transactions and other events should be reflected, as far as is possible, in the financial statements for the accounting period in which they occur, and not, for example, in the period in which any cash involved is received or paid.* Together with the definitions of assets and liabilities, set out in FRS 5 'Reporting the Substance of Transactions', this provides a discipline within which the matching process can operate, while still resulting in the simultaneous recognition of revenues and costs that result from the same transactions or events.

10   SSAP 2 did not require financial statements to be prepared in accordance with the going concern and accruals concepts; rather, where this was not the case, it required the facts to be disclosed and explained. This approach was also taken in FRED 21, but several respondents suggested that the role of these concepts should be strengthened. Respondents also suggested that disclosure should be required of any material uncertainties that might cast doubt on an entity's ability to continue as a going concern, as is the case under the International Accounting Standard IAS 1 (revised 1997) 'Presentation of Financial Statements'.

11   The Board has accepted these proposals. Accordingly the FRS requires financial statements to be prepared on a going concern basis† and on the accruals basis. The FRS also requires directors to assess whether there are significant doubts about the entity's ability to continue as a going concern and to disclose any material

---

*This approach is consistent with that taken in the Statement of Principles.

†Except where an entity is being liquidated or has ceased trading, or the directors have no realistic alternative but to liquidate the entity or to cease trading.

uncertainties, of which they are aware, related to events or conditions that may raise such doubts.*

FRS 21 'Events after the Balance Sheet Date' was issued in May 2004. It was based on IAS 10 'Events after the Balance Sheet Date' and is effective for accounting periods beginning on or after 1 January 2005. To conform with FRS 21 and international accounting standards a consequential amendment was made to paragraph 21.   **11A**

21   An entity should prepare its financial statements on a going concern basis, unless

(a)   the entity is being liquidated or has ceased trading, or

(b)   the directors either intend to liquidate the entity or to cease trading, or have no realistic alternative but to do so,

in which circumstances the entity should prepare its financial statements on a basis other than that of a going concern.†

Consistency and prudence

The other two concepts from SSAP 2 – consistency and prudence – are rather different in that they are desirable qualities of financial information rather than part of the bedrock of accounting. The FRS therefore discusses them in the context of the objectives against which an entity should judge the appropriateness of accounting policies to its particular circumstances.   **12**

Like the Statement of Principles, the FRS regards comparability as a more fundamental objective than consistency. Information in financial statements should be prepared and presented in a way that enables users to discern and evaluate similarities in, and differences between, the nature and effects of transactions and other events taking place over time and across different reporting entities. Although comparability is usually achieved through consistency, the latter is not an end in itself and there will be circumstances in which it needs to be sacrificed. In particular, whilst consistency is important, it should not be allowed to prevent improvements in accounting. Where the introduction of a new accounting policy would result in an overall benefit to users, an entity should not use consistency to justify retaining an existing policy that is no longer the most appropriate to its particular circumstances.   **13**

The FRS also reflects how the prudence concept has evolved from the way in which it was described in SSAP 2. Since SSAP 2 was issued, the smoothing of reported profits has become as great a concern as their overstatement and, as a result, the deliberate understatement of assets and gains and the deliberate overstatement of liabilities are no longer seen as a virtue. Accordingly, like the Statement of Principles, the FRS treats prudence as one aspect of the overall objective of reliability. In conditions of uncertainty, prudence requires more confirmatory evidence about the existence of an asset or gain than about the existence of a liability or loss, and a greater reliability of measurement for assets and gains than for liabilities and losses.   **14**

---

*Differences between the requirements of the FRS and of IAS 1 (revised 1997) are discussed in Appendix III.

†Editor's note: Paragraph inserted by FRS 21.

Realisation

15   One aspect of prudence as described in SSAP 2 was that revenue and profits should be included in the profit and loss account only when realised in the form either of cash or of other assets the ultimate cash realisation of which could be assessed with reasonable certainty. However, the FRS does not refer to the notion of realisation in discussing prudence.

16   The realisation notion was originally concerned with the conversion into cash of non-cash resources and rights, and was intended to ensure that sufficient cash was available to distribute profits without an entity becoming insolvent. By the time SSAP 2 was issued, the notion had evolved so that it was also concerned with claims to cash, and was used to ensure that only gains that were reasonably certain, and unlikely to reverse, were included in the profit and loss account.

17   By the time that FRED 21 was being developed, however, the linking of prudence to realisation in SSAP 2 had itself become out of date. Markets have developed so that it is often possible to be reasonably certain that a gain exists, and to measure it with sufficient reliability, even if no disposal has occurred. One approach to this problem might have been to try to update the notion of realisation. However, the Board believes that it is preferable to focus on the underlying objective. In the Board's view, this is that a gain should be recognised only if there is reasonable certainty that it exists and if it can be measured reliably. Accordingly, the FRED and the FRS both discuss the concept of prudence in these terms, rather than in terms of realisation.

18   This approach provoked much comment from respondents to the FRED, with some supportive but many expressing concern. Two themes emerged strongly from the responses:

- although the Board does not believe that it is useful to link prudence and realisation, requirements based on the notion of realisation are nevertheless part of companies legislation. Respondents were concerned that the Board appeared, in effect, to be encouraging entities to ignore or flout those requirements.
- rather than fixing the interpretation of the notion of realisation, companies legislation requires it to be determined in accordance with principles generally accepted at the time when financial statements are prepared. The description of realisation in SSAP 2 provided a strong underpinning to those principles, and respondents were concerned that its omission from the FRED would lead to that underpinning being removed.

19   As regards the first concern, it was never the Board's intention to encourage entities to ignore or flout requirements of companies legislation. Certain paragraphs from the FRED have been redrafted to reduce any risk of ambiguity in that regard. In particular, paragraph 14 of the FRS makes clear that entities should adopt accounting policies that are consistent with the requirements of other accounting standards and of companies legislation, which will include any requirements relating to realisation. Paragraph 29 and its footnote have also been redrafted to avoid wrongly giving the impression that the Board is encouraging entities to depart from such requirements.

20   The words from SSAP 2 describing the notion of realisation have been included in paragraph 28 of the FRS in order to address the second concern. Although the FRS does not maintain the link between prudence and realisation from SSAP 2, the Board had not intended to create uncertainty in respect of existing realisation requirements, and the inclusion of these words is intended to preserve the status quo.

Definitions

Accounting bases

SSAP 2 defined both accounting bases and accounting policies. It explained that accounting bases are the methods developed for applying fundamental accounting concepts to financial transactions and items, while accounting policies are the specific accounting bases adopted by an entity. In developing the FRS, the Board considered whether the concept of accounting bases was useful in defining accounting policies. **21**

The Board noted that definitions of accounting policies adopted by other standard-setters do not refer to accounting bases in this way. In addition, it noted that there are no other UK accounting standards in which the phrase 'accounting bases' is used, and that a distinction between accounting bases and accounting policies does not appear to have any practical consequences for recognition, measurement or disclosure in financial statements. Finally, it noted that references in SSAP 2 to accounting bases had led in some instances to confusion, for example about whether a choice of depreciation method was an accounting basis. **22**

For these reasons, the Board concluded that it is not necessary, and might be confusing, to continue to define accounting policies as the specific accounting bases adopted by an entity. Instead, the FRS makes clear by its context whether the phrase 'accounting policies' refers to such policies in general or to the specific policies adopted by an entity. **23**

Accounting policies and estimation techniques

Having recognised that it is not always easy to distinguish between a change of accounting policy and a change of estimate, the Board also looked again at the definition of an accounting policy. SSAP 2 referred to 'the methods developed for applying fundamental accounting concepts to financial transactions and items', but it is clear that some methods adopted by an entity are merely estimates rather than accounting policies. **24**

Accordingly, the FRS introduces a more specific definition of an accounting policy. As defined in the FRS, accounting policies are concerned with the recognition and presentation of assets, liabilities, gains, losses and changes to shareholders' funds, and with the selection of measurement bases for those items. However, methods used to arrive at a monetary amount corresponding to the measurement basis selected are in the nature of estimates rather than accounting policies. Accordingly, the FRS defines such methods as 'estimation techniques' and makes clear that they are not accounting policies. **25**

The Board believes that this approach will make it easier to distinguish between a change of accounting policy and a change of accounting estimate. Where an accounting change leads to an asset, liability or other item being measured in a different way, an important question is whether this involves a change of measurement basis – ie whether a different attribute of the item is being measured. If so, it will be a change of accounting policy. Otherwise, it will be merely a change of estimation technique. **26**

FRS 3 'Reporting Financial Performance'

Some respondents suggested that material relating to prior period adjustments included in FRS 3 'Reporting Financial Performance' might more appropriately be **27** included in an FRS developed from FRED 21. However, in June 1999 the Board published a Discussion Paper entitled 'Reporting Financial Performance: proposals for change', which included a proposal that might affect the circumstances in which errors in earlier financial statements would lead to prior period adjustments. Accordingly, while the Board agrees that, in the longer term, it may be appropriate for material relating to prior period adjustments to be included with the material in this FRS, it does not believe it is appropriate to move material from FRS 3 at present.

Adopting and changing accounting policies

Requiring adoption of the most appropriate accounting policies

28   The standard accounting practice required by SSAP 2 was concerned, explicitly, only with disclosure. Nevertheless, the explanatory note to SSAP 2 described accounting policies as being those 'judged by business enterprises to be most appropriate to their circumstances', while the definition of an enterprise's accounting policies referred to them being 'best suited to present fairly its results and financial position'. The FRS makes explicit that an entity should adopt those accounting policies judged to be the most appropriate to its particular circumstances for the purpose of giving a true and fair view.

29   A minority of respondents suggested that an FRS developed from FRED 21 should require only that accounting policies be appropriate, rather than most appropriate. The Board rejected this as being a step backwards from the position under SSAP 2. Other respondents suggested that the approach set out in the FRED would be more onerous than SSAP 2; however, although the FRS uses the phrase 'most appropriate' whereas the SSAP sometimes used the phrase 'best suited', the Board believes both phrases reflect the same underlying objective.

30   In addition, some respondents expressed concern that the approach taken in the FRED might create difficulties for directors and auditors, particularly if similar entities adopt different accounting policies or if an entity's choice of accounting policies is subsequently challenged. The Board does not believe that such difficulties should arise. The FRS makes clear that the most appropriate accounting policies are to be judged in the context of an entity's particular circumstances; different policies may be most appropriate in different circumstances. Further, the choice of accounting policies is only one of many judgements involved in the preparation of financial statements. For any such judgement it may become clear, with the benefit of hindsight, that a different judgement would have been more appropriate, but that does not invalidate an earlier judgement arrived at in good faith. In particular, where an entity changes accounting policies it does not follow that its former accounting policies were in some sense wrong, or that financial statements prepared under those former policies did not give a true and fair view.

31   Finally, a small number of respondents thought the FRED was proposing that an entity should disregard or overrule the requirements of other accounting standards and legislation in determining the most appropriate accounting policies. As explained below, this was not the case; however, the FRS has been amended to avoid any confusion in this respect.

Identifying the most appropriate accounting policies

32   In identifying the accounting policies to be followed, directors need to ensure that an entity complies with the provisions of other accounting standards and specific statutory requirements. This will often mean that the policies available to an entity are

restricted, and on occasions there may be only one acceptable accounting policy to be followed. However, where more than one policy is acceptable the FRS requires the entity to adopt whichever of those policies is judged to be the most appropriate.

The Board acknowledges that the judgement of which accounting policy is most **33** appropriate for the purpose of giving a true and fair view will to an extent be subjective, since it must take into account an entity's particular circumstances. Nevertheless, it is important that different entities have the same goal in sight when selecting policies, which is that they should reflect, as far as is practicable, the effects of transactions and other events on the entity's financial performance and financial position in an appropriate manner. Accordingly, the FRS specifies objectives and constraints that an entity should take into account in judging which accounting policies are most appropriate.

The FRS does not prescribe measurement bases, but some examples of changes to **34** accounting policies and to estimation techniques are set out in Appendix I. However, some respondents suggested that the proposals in FRED 21 implied that the Board was seeking to require entities to make greater use of current values and to restrict legitimate options to report assets at historical cost. This was not the Board's intention, nor does it believe that this will be the effect of the FRS. Where it is permissible to report an asset on either a historical cost or a current value basis, as under FRS 15 'Tangible Fixed Assets' for example, an entity will judge which of those policies is most appropriate to its particular circumstances. Factors to be taken into account will include, among others, the relevance of the information to users, comparability with other entities and also the relative costs and benefits of the different policies. Moreover, different judgements may be likely depending on the nature both of the asset and of the reporting entity.

Changing accounting policies

The FRS requires accounting policies to be reviewed regularly to ensure that they **35** remain the most appropriate to an entity's particular circumstances, and a new accounting policy to be implemented if judged more appropriate. Although the objectives and constraints to be considered by an entity will not change, the relative merits of a particular accounting policy, and of the associated measurement basis, may change over time.

Many respondents expressed the view that it is unhelpful to users for an entity to **36** change accounting policy too frequently, and that the FRED had placed insufficient emphasis on this longer-term aspect of comparability. The Board agrees that there is a balance to be achieved in this regard. Accordingly, paragraph 49 of the FRS makes clear that, in judging whether a change of accounting policy is appropriate, an entity will assess whether the benefit to users arising from the new policy outweighs the corresponding disadvantages.

Disclosures: estimation techniques

In developing the FRED, the Board considered whether disclosures should be required **37** in respect of estimation techniques. Very often, such disclosures will not be necessary because it is sufficient for users to understand the measurement basis that is being reflected. This is particularly the case where an amount may be estimated with reasonable certainty, ie whichever estimation technique is used the amount estimated will fall within a relatively narrow range. Accordingly, the FRED did not propose to require disclosures in respect of an estimation technique merely because it produces an amount that is material.

38   Instead, the FRED proposed that a description of an estimation technique should be provided where the use of that technique is material. It explained that this would be the case where another estimation technique, other than that adopted, is also relevant and reliable and, had that other estimation technique instead been adopted, the figures presented in the financial statements would have been materially different. Where a range of methods and estimates would be acceptable, the entity would need to consider the range of amounts resulting from using those different estimates and methods.

39   Many respondents disliked this approach, objecting that it was too complex and that it was onerous to expect entities to assess amounts using many different estimation techniques. Some respondents suggested that disclosures should be required in respect of all estimation techniques used for material items. However, the Board believes that this alternative approach would also be onerous, in that many estimation techniques are used in the preparation of financial statements, and that it would result in users being swamped with irrelevant information.

40   Estimation techniques are used where there is uncertainty over the monetary amount to be associated with the measurement basis chosen for a particular item. The Board believes that information about estimation techniques should be provided where that uncertainty is significant in the context of the accounts as a whole. Nevertheless, it accepts the criticisms of the FRED's proposals, and has reconsidered how this objective should be encapsulated. Accordingly, the FRS instead focuses on the degree to which judgement is needed in applying whichever estimation technique has been chosen, and the sensitivity of the resulting amounts to such judgement.

FRED 21 Supplement 'Accounting Policies: Compliance with Statements of Recommended Practice'

41   In March 2000, the Board published a Supplement to FRED 21, which proposed additional disclosures where a significant part of an entity's activities falls within the scope of a Statement of Recommended Practice (SORP). The Supplement's proposals were well received by most respondents, and they have been reflected in the FRS. However, respondents raised a number of practical issues, particularly relating to the scope of SORPs and to possible conflicts between SORPs. In response to these, the FRS:

- requires disclosures where an entity's financial statements fall within the scope of a SORP, rather than where a significant part of its activities falls within the scope of a SORP
- makes clear that where an entity fails to provide disclosures recommended by a SORP, it should describe those disclosures and explain why they have been omitted
- emphasises that quantification of a departure from a SORP is not required except in those rare cases where such quantification is necessary for the entity's financial statements to give a true and fair view.

42   In July 2000 the Board issued a Statement 'SORPs: Policy and Code of Practice'. The Code of Practice requires, amongst other things, that a SORP should state its scope by indicating the types of entity to whose financial statements the SORP is intended to apply. However, the Board recognises that some SORPs may need to be updated in order to comply with this requirement. Until that updating has taken place, it may not be possible for an entity to determine whether it falls within the scope of a SORP and, hence, is required to make disclosures under the FRS. Accordingly, those paragraphs of the FRS that relate directly to the Supplement's proposals need not be applied in respect of accounting periods beginning on or before 23 December 2001, though earlier application is encouraged.

Financial Reporting Standard 19 'Deferred Tax' is issued by the Accounting Standards Board in respect of its application in the United Kingdom and by the Institute of Chartered Accountants in Ireland in respect of its application in the Republic of Ireland.

Financial Reporting Standard 19 is set out in paragraphs 1–72.

The Statement of Standard Accounting Practice, which comprises the paragraphs set in bold type, should be read in the context of the Objective as stated in paragraph 1 and the definitions set out in paragraph 2 and also of the Foreword to Accounting Standards and the Statement of Principles for Financial Reporting currently in issue.

The explanatory paragraphs contained in the FRS shall be regarded as part of the Statement of Standard Accounting Practice insofar as they assist in interpreting that statement.

Appendix V 'The development of the FRS' reviews considerations and arguments that were thought significant by members of the Board in reaching the conclusions on the FRS.

[FRS 19]
Deferred tax

(Issued December 2000)

Contents

Summary

a   Financial Reporting Standard 19 'Deferred Tax' requires full provision to be made for deferred tax assets and liabilities arising from timing differences between the recognition of gains and losses in the financial statements and their recognition in a tax computation.

b   The general principle underlying the requirements is that deferred tax should be recognised as a liability or asset if the transactions or events that give the entity an obligation to pay more tax in future or a right to pay less tax in future have occurred by the balance sheet date. The FRS:

(a) *requires deferred tax to be recognised on most types of timing difference, including those attributable to:*
  - accelerated capital allowances
  - accruals for pension costs and other post-retirement benefits that will be deductible for tax purposes only when paid
  - elimination of unrealised intragroup profits on consolidation unrelieved tax losses
  - other sources of short-term timing differences.

(b) *prohibits the recognition of deferred tax on timing differences arising when:*
  - a fixed asset is revalued without there being any commitment to sell the asset
  - the gain on sale of an asset is rolled over into replacement assets
  - the remittance of a subsidiary, associate or joint venture's earnings would cause tax to be payable, but no commitment has been made to the remittance of the earnings.

(c) *requires deferred tax assets to be recognised to the extent that it is regarded as more likely than not that they will be recovered.*

c   As an exception to the general requirement not to recognise deferred tax on revaluation gains and losses, the FRS requires deferred tax to be recognised when assets are continuously revalued to fair value, with changes in fair value being recognised in the profit and loss account.

d   The FRS permits but does not require entities to adopt a policy of discounting deferred tax assets and liabilities.

e   The FRS includes other requirements regarding the measurement and presentation of deferred tax assets and liabilities. These include requirements for the deferred tax to be:

  - measured using tax rates that have been enacted or substantively enacted
  - presented separately on the face of the balance sheet if the amounts are so material that, in the absence of such disclosure, readers may misinterpret the financial statements.

f   The FRS requires information to be disclosed about factors affecting current and future tax charges. A key element of this is a requirement to disclose a reconciliation of the current tax charge for the period to the charge that would arise if the profits reported in the financial statements were charged at a standard rate of tax.

g   The FRS amends FRS 7 'Fair Values in Acquisition Accounting'. The amendment requires deferred tax recognised in a fair value exercise to be measured in accordance with the requirements of the FRS. Thus, deferred tax would not be recognised on an adjustment to recognise a non-monetary asset acquired with the business at its fair value on acquisition.

Financial Reporting Standard 19

OBJECTIVE

The objective of this FRS is to ensure that:

(a) future tax consequences of past transactions and events are recognised as liabilities or assets in n the financial statements; and

(b) the financial statements disclose any other special circumstances that may have an effect on future tax charges.

1

DEFINITIONS

The following definitions shall apply in the FRS and in particular in the Statement of Standard Accounting Practice set out **in bold type**.

2

Current tax:

The amount of tax estimated to be payable or recoverable in respect of the taxable profit or loss for a period, along with adjustments to estimates in respect of previous periods.

Deferred tax:

Estimated future tax consequences of transactions and events recognised in the financial statements of the current and previous periods.

Permanent differences:

Differences between an entity's taxable profits and its results as stated in the financial statements that arise because certain types of income and expenditure are non-taxable or disallowable, or because certain tax charges or allowances have no corresponding amount in the financial statements.

Timing differences:

Differences between an entity's taxable profits and its results as stated in the financial statements that arise from the inclusion of gains and losses in tax assessments in periods different from those in which they are recognised in financial statements. Timing differences originate in one period and are capable of reversal in one or more subsequent periods.

Timing differences arise when, for example:

- tax deductions for the cost of a fixed asset* are accelerated or decelerated, ie received before or after the cost of the fixed asset is recognised in the profit and loss account
- pension liabilities are accrued in the financial statements but are allowed for tax purposes only when paid or contributed at a later date
- interest charges or development costs are capitalised on the balance sheet but are treated as revenue expenditure and allowed as incurred for tax purposes
- intragroup profits in stock, unrealised at group level, are reversed on consolidation
- an asset is revalued in the financial statements but the revaluation gain becomes taxable only if and when the asset is sold
- a tax loss is not relieved against past or present taxable profits but can be carried forward to reduce future taxable profits
- the unremitted earnings of subsidiary and associated undertakings and joint ventures are recognised in the group results but will be subject to further taxation only if and when remitted to the parent undertaking.

SCOPE

3   **The FRS applies to all financial statements that are intended to give a true and fair view of a reporting entity's financial position and profit or loss (or income and expenditure) for a period.**

4   **The FRS applies to taxes calculated on the basis of taxable profits, including withholding taxes paid on behalf of the reporting entity.**

5   In the UK and the Republic of Ireland, the taxes that are calculated on the basis of taxable profits are primarily corporation tax and income tax. Other taxes, such as value added tax and petroleum revenue tax, that are not assessed directly on profits for an accounting period are not within the scope of the FRS.

6   **Reporting entities applying the Financial Reporting Standard for Smaller Entities (FRSSE) currently applicable are exempt from the FRS.**

RECOGNITION OF DEFERRED TAX ASSETS AND LIABILITIES

General requirements

7   **Except as set out in paragraphs 9–33, deferred tax:**

(a)   **should be recognised in respect of all timing differences that have originated but not reversed by the balance sheet date;**

(b)   **should not be recognised on permanent differences.**

8   The requirements of paragraph 7 are not intended to prevent lessors preparing financial statements in accordance with SSAP 21 'Accounting for leases and hire purchase contracts' from allocating profit from transactions over the term of the lease on a post-tax basis and measuring the tax charge and pre-tax profit relating to the accounting period by applying the effective rate of tax to the post-tax profit. The way in which finance lessors should determine the amount of deferred tax to be provided for is illustrated in Part II of the Guidance Notes on SSAP 21.

Including deductions for expenditure on infrastructure assets capitalised and depreciated using renewals accounting.

Allowances for fixed asset expenditure

Deferred tax should be recognised when the allowances for the cost of a fixed asset are received before or after the cost of the fixed asset is recognised in the profit and loss account. However, if and when all conditions for retaining the allowances have been met, the deferred tax should be reversed. 9

If an asset is not being depreciated (and has not otherwise been written down to a carrying value less than cost), the timing difference is the amount of capital allowances received. 10

Most capital allowances are received on a conditional basis, ie they are repayable (for example, via a balancing charge) if the assets to which they relate are sold for more than their tax written-down value. However, some, such as industrial buildings allowances, are repayable only if the assets to which they relate are sold within a specified period. Once that period has expired, all conditions for retaining the allowance have been met. At that point, deferred tax that has been recognised (ie on the excess of the allowance over any depreciation) is reversed. 11

Non-monetary assets – revaluations and gains on disposal

Assets continuously revalued to fair value with changes in fair value recognised in the profit and loss account

Deferred tax should be recognised on timing differences arising when an asset is continuously revalued to fair value with changes in fair value being recognised in the profit and loss account. 12

The assets to which paragraph 12 applies are typically investments and current assets that are 'marked to market' with fluctuations being recognised in the profit and loss account. In many circumstances, the gains and losses are subject to current tax when they are recognised, and no timing difference (and hence no deferred tax) arises. Paragraph 12 is relevant only if the gains and losses are not taxed until realised at a later date. 13

Other non-monetary assets

Deferred tax should not be recognised on timing differences arising when other non-monetary assets are revalued, unless, by the balance sheet date, the reporting entity has: 14

(a)   entered into a binding agreement to sell the revalued assets; and
(b)   recognised the gains and losses expected to arise on sale.

Deferred tax should not be recognised on timing differences arising when non-monetary assets (other than those referred to in paragraph 12) are revalued or sold if, on the basis of all available evidence, it is more likely than not that the taxable gain will be rolled over, being charged to tax only if and when the assets into which the gain has been rolled over are sold.* 15

Where an entity has entered into a binding agreement to sell a fixed asset, such as land and buildings, and has revalued the fixed asset at the net sale proceeds, it will have recognised the expected gain or loss on sale. To the extent that rollover relief is 16

**or are deemed to have been sold for tax purposes.*

not expected to be obtained and a timing difference has arisen – ie the gain will not be chargeable to current tax – the FRS requires deferred tax to be recognised.

17   An asset may have been purchased with a view to resale. Stock, for example, may be purchased for the sole purpose of resale. But this does not in itself mean that the entity has entered into a binding agreement to sell the asset.

18   Stock may be adjusted to its fair value on the acquisition of a business. However, even where such stock has been manufactured under the terms of a binding contract, that contract will generally be treated as an executory contract. The rights and obligations under that contract (and hence the gain on sale) will not have been recognised. In adjusting the value of the stock, the entity is merely recognising a movement in the replacement cost of the stock. In such circumstances, the FRS does not allow provision to be made for deferred tax on the adjustment.

19   The requirement not to provide for deferred tax if it is more likely than not that a taxable gain will be rolled over into replacement assets applies only if the terms of the relief are such that the gain will not be taxed unless and until the replacement assets are themselves sold (rollover relief). It does not apply if the terms of the relief are such that taxation of the gain is merely postponed (held over) for a finite period (holdover relief).* Sometimes, holdover relief can be converted into rollover relief if qualifying replacement assets are purchased before the held-over gain crystallises. Where this is the case, the requirements regarding rollover relief apply. However, it may be more difficult to arrive at the conclusion that it is more likely than not that the gain will be rolled over and, in consequence, that no provision is required.

20   The need to make a judgement regarding the availability of rollover relief will arise when the entity has not yet reinvested the proceeds of sale in qualifying replacement assets but may still do so within the period allowed by the tax authorities.† All available evidence, including that provided by events occurring after the balance sheet date, is considered when judging whether it is more likely than not that the gain will be rolled over. The available evidence will change with time and will therefore be reassessed continually until the entity either claims rollover relief or loses its right to do so. Any adjustment to recognise a previously unrecognised deferred tax provision (or to release a provision previously recognised) is a change in estimate, which, in accordance with the requirements of FRS 3 'Reporting Financial Performance', is charged or credited as part of the tax charge for the period in the profit and loss account or statement of total recognised gains and losses.

Unremitted earnings of subsidiaries, associates and joint ventures

21   **Tax that could be payable (taking account of any double taxation relief) on any future remittance of the past earnings of a subsidiary, associate or joint venture should be provided for only to the extent that, at the balance sheet date:**

      (a)   dividends have been accrued as receivable; or

      (b)   a binding agreement to distribute the past earnings in future has been entered into by the subsidiary, associate or joint venture.

22   It is unlikely that there will be a binding agreement for the future distribution of the past earnings of a subsidiary, associate or joint venture. In most circumstances,

---

*At present (December 2000), holdover relief can postpone the payment of tax for up to ten years from acquisition of the replacement asset.

†At present (December 2000), within three years of the sale of the original asset.

therefore, the deferred tax provision comprises only tax that will become payable (taking account of double taxation relief) on receipt of dividends accrued at the balance sheet date.

Deferred tax assets

General requirements

Deferred tax assets should be recognised to the extent that they are regarded as   **23**
recoverable. They should be regarded as recoverable to the extent that, on the basis of
all available evidence, it can be regarded as more likely than not that there will be
suitable taxable profits from which the future reversal of the underlying timing dif-
ferences can be deducted.

Suitable taxable profits

Suitable taxable profits from which the future reversal of timing differences could be   **24**
deducted are those that are:

(a)   generated in the same taxable entity (or in an entity whose profits would be available via group relief) and assessed by the same taxation authority as the income or expenditure giving rise to the deferred tax asset;

(b)   generated in the same period as that in which the deferred tax asset is expected to reverse, or in a period to which a tax loss arising from the reversal of the deferred tax asset may be carried back or forward; and

(c)   of a type (such as capital or trading) from which the taxation authority allows the reversal of the timing difference to be deducted.

Account may be taken of tax planning opportunities, ie actions that the entity would   **25**
take if necessary to create suitable taxable profits. Such actions could include:

(a)   accelerating taxable amounts or deferring claims for writing down allowances to recover losses being carried forward (perhaps before they expire);

(b)   changing the character of taxable or deductible amounts from trading gains or losses to capital gains or losses or vice versa; or

(c)   switching from tax-free to taxable investments.

Deferred tax assets that can be recovered against deferred tax liabilities

It can be assumed that the future reversal of any deferred tax liabilities recognised at   **26**
the balance sheet date will give rise to taxable profits. To the extent that those profits
will be suitable for the deduction of the reversing deferred tax asset, the asset can
always be regarded as recoverable.

Deferred tax assets that cannot be recovered against deferred tax liabilities

To the extent that the deferred tax asset cannot be recovered against the reversal of   **27**
deferred tax liabilities, it is necessary to consider the likelihood of there being other
suitable taxable profits.

All available evidence is considered. Historical information about the entity's   **28**
financial performance and position may provide the most objective evidence. Other
evidence may be important if historical information is either not available or of
limited relevance because of recent or forthcoming changes in circumstances.

29   The existence of unrelieved tax losses of a certain character (for example, trading or capital) at the balance sheet date is strong evidence that there will not be suitable taxable profits of that character in future against which the losses (and other deferred tax assets) can be recovered. In such circumstances, the unrelieved losses (and other deferred tax assets affected) are recognised only if there is other persuasive and reliable evidence suggesting that suitable taxable profits will be generated in future.

30   In the case of unrelieved trading losses, such evidence may exist if the loss resulted from an identifiable and non-recurring cause and the reporting entity has otherwise been consistently profitable over a long period, with any past losses being more than offset by income in later periods.

31   If an unrelieved capital loss can be relieved only against future capital gains, there is likely to be persuasive and reliable evidence that there will be suitable taxable gains against which the loss can be relieved only to the extent that:

    (a)   a potential chargeable gain not expected to be covered by rollover relief is present in assets but has not been recognised as a deferred tax liability;
    (b)   plans are in place for the sale of these assets; and
    (c)   the carried-forward loss will be offset against the resulting chargeable gain for tax purposes.

32   If it is expected that it will take some time for tax losses to be relieved, the recoverability of the resulting deferred tax asset is likely to be relatively uncertain. In such circumstances, it may not be appropriate to recognise the deferred tax asset at all.

Reassessment of recoverability

33   Changes in circumstances from one balance sheet date to the next might affect the extent to which a deferred tax asset is regarded as recoverable and therefore require an adjustment to the amount recognised. For example, an improvement in trading conditions or the acquisition of a new subsidiary might make it more likely that a previously unrecognised tax loss in the acquiring entity will be recovered. As changes in estimates, the resulting movements in the deferred tax balance are required by FRS 3 'Reporting Financial Performance' to be reflected in the results for the period.

RECOGNITION IN THE STATEMENTS OF PERFORMANCE

34   **Deferred tax should be recognised in the profit and loss account for the period, except to the extent that it is attributable to a gain or loss that is or has been recognised directly in the statement of total recognised gains and losses.**

35   **Where a gain or loss is or has been recognised directly in the statement of total recognised gains and losses, deferred tax attributable to that gain or loss should also be recognised directly in that statement.**

36   Accounting standards (or, in their absence, legislation) require or permit certain gains or losses to be credited or charged directly in the statement of total recognised gains and losses (ie not in the profit and loss account). The FRS requires any attributable deferred tax to be treated in the same way. In exceptional circumstances it may be difficult to determine the amount of deferred tax that is attributable to gains or losses that have been recognised directly in the statement of total recognised gains and losses. In such circumstances, the attributable deferred tax is based on a reasonable pro rata allocation, or another allocation that is more appropriate in the circumstances.

MEASUREMENT

Tax rates

Deferred tax should be measured at the average tax rates that are expected to apply in   37
the periods in which the timing differences are expected to reverse, based on tax rates
and laws that have been enacted or substantively enacted by the balance sheet date.

It will normally be necessary to calculate an average tax rate only if the enacted or   38
substantively enacted tax rates are graduated, ie if different rates apply to different
levels of taxable income. To calculate the average tax rate it is necessary to estimate
the levels of profits expected in the periods in which the timing differences reverse.

The requirement to calculate an average tax rate is not intended to lead to averaging   39
of different rates expected to apply to different types of taxable profit or in different
tax jurisdictions. If different rates of tax apply to different types of taxable profits
(for example, trading profits and capital gains), the rate used will reflect the nature of
the timing difference. The rates used for measuring deferred tax arising in a specific
tax jurisdiction will be the rates expected to apply in that jurisdiction.

A UK tax rate can be regarded as having been substantively enacted if it is included   40
in either:

(a)   a Bill that has been passed by the House of Commons and is awaiting only
      passage through the House of Lords and Royal Assent; or
(b)   a resolution having statutory effect that has been passed under the Provisional
      Collection of Taxes Act 1968.*

A Republic of Ireland tax rate can be regarded as having been substantively enacted   41
if it is included in a Bill that has been passed by the Dail.

Discounting

Criteria for discounting

Reporting entities are permitted but not required to discount deferred tax assets and   42
liabilities to reflect the time value of money.

Requirements and guidance on selecting and changing accounting policies are set out   43
in FRS 18 'Accounting Policies'. Factors that are likely to be especially relevant to
selecting a policy of either discounting or not discounting deferred tax include:

(a)   how material the impact of discounting would tend to be to the overall results
      and position reported in the entity's financial statements;
(b)   whether the benefits of discounting to users would outweigh the costs of col-
      lating the necessary information and performing discounting calculations; and
(c)   whether there is an established industry practice, adherence to which would
      enhance comparability.

---

*Such a resolution could be used to collect taxes at a new rate before that rate has been enacted. In practice,
corporation tax rates are now set a year ahead to avoid having to invoke the Provisional Collection of Taxes Act
for the quarterly payment system.*

44   If a reporting entity adopts a policy of discounting, all deferred tax (and recoverable advance corporation tax*) balances that have been measured by reference to undiscounted cash flows and for which the impact of discounting is material should be discounted.

45   Certain timing differences, such as those arising on:
- provisions for pension costs and other long-term liabilities
- a lessor's investment in finance leases,

are measured by reference to cash flows that have already been discounted. The deferred tax provisions to which they give rise already incorporate discounting. They are not eligible for further discounting and are not subject to any of the detailed requirements for discounting, or disclosures of amounts arising from discounting, in the FRS. They are disclosed as if they were undiscounted amounts.

46   Timing differences that are eligible for discounting include those arising from accelerated capital allowances, revaluation gains and losses and carried- forward tax losses. (However, as noted in paragraph 32, if it is expected that it will take some time for tax losses to be relieved, it may not be appropriate to recognise the losses as an asset at all.)

Scheduling the cash flows to be discounted

47   **If deferred tax balances are discounted, the discount period(s) should be the number of years between the balance sheet date and the date(s) on which it is estimated that the underlying timing differences will reverse. Assumptions made when estimating the date(s) of reversal should be consistent with those made elsewhere in the financial statements. The scheduling of the reversal(s) should take into account the remaining tax effects of transactions that have already been reflected in the financial statements. However, no account should be taken either of other timing differences expected to arise on future transactions or of future tax losses.**

48   Where, for example, assets are depreciated over their useful economic lives but receive capital allowances early in their lives, the timing of the reversal of accelerated capital allowances is determined:
    (a)   by scheduling all expected future movements (increases as well as decreases) in the accelerated capital allowances on assets that are held at the balance sheet date, taking account of both future depreciation patterns and the expected timing of remaining capital allowances to be received on these assets; but
    (b)   without taking into consideration timing differences that might arise on fixed assets to be purchased in future.

The assumptions about future depreciation charges and residual value should be consistent with those used to account for the related fixed assets. It may be possible to use approximations or averages to simplify the calculations without introducing material errors. Illustrative examples are given below and in Appendix I.

49   A timing difference might be expected to reverse in a period in which it is also expected that the entity will make tax losses. In this situation, the reversal of the timing difference may not have an incremental effect on a tax payment until an even

---

*Advance corporation tax (ACT) was abolished in 1999. ACT that had been paid but not relieved by that date may still be recoverable under the shadow ACT system. FRS 16 'Current Tax' sets out requirements and guidance regarding the recognition of recoverable ACT.

later period, when the future losses are relieved. However, the FRS requires deferred tax to be discounted without taking into consideration the possibility of future losses.

Simple example illustrating the scheduling of the reversal of accelerated capital allowances on a single asset

An entity purchases an asset for £100,000 at the start of 20X0. It is estimated that the asset will have a useful economic life of ten years and no residual value. Capital allowances can be claimed at a rate of 25 per cent of cost in each of the first four years.

At the end of 20X0, there is a timing difference of £15,000, which is the difference between the allowances of £25,000 received and the depreciation of £10,000. The timing difference is treated as reversing according to the following schedule (even if the entity expects to make losses at some point during the life of the asset):

Years from now:	1	2	3	4	5	6	7	8	9	Total
Depreciation (£000)	10	10	10	10	10	10	10	10	10	90
Allowances (£000)	25	25	25	–	–	–	–	–	–	75
(Increase)/Reversal	(15)	(15)	(15)	10	10	10	10	10	10	15

Where deferred tax is recognised on changes in the carrying amount of an asset that is revalued to fair value (ie as required by paragraph 12), the objective is to provide for the incremental tax that the entity will pay or recover on selling the asset, above the amount that it would have paid if it had purchased the asset at its carrying amount at the balance sheet date. The timing difference is therefore discounted from the future date on which it is estimated that the tax will become payable, taking account of any available reliefs. **50**

The amount of tax that will be payable and the time at which it is likely to be paid may be uncertain and, hence, may have to be estimated on the basis of available evidence. Where the entity holds a portfolio of assets for investment or trading purposes, evidence can be obtained from historical data regarding average turnover periods, average amounts of tax paid as a percentage of the book gain and other variables. But evidence of how these variables are likely to change in future also has to be considered. **51**

Discount rates

If deferred tax balances are discounted, the discount rates used should be the post-tax yields to maturity that could be obtained at the balance sheet date on government bonds with maturity dates and in currencies similar to those of the deferred tax assets or liabilities. **52**

The yields to maturity on government bonds can be obtained from published sources. The post-tax yield is estimated by deducting tax at the rate at which it would be paid by an entity holding the bond, based on enacted or substantively enacted tax rates and laws. **53**

The need to match the discount rate with the maturity date and currency of the deferred tax asset or liability in theory requires a different discount rate to be applied to each year in which a timing difference is forecast to reverse and for each different tax jurisdiction. It may, however, be possible to use approximations and averages to simplify the calculations without introducing material errors. This is illustrated in the example in Appendix I. **54**

PRESENTATION

Presentation in the balance sheet

55   With the exception of deferred tax relating to a defined benefit asset or liability recognised in accordance with FRS 17 'Retirement Benefits'*:

(a)   net deferred tax liabilities should be classified as provisions for liabilities and charges.

(b)   net deferred tax assets should be classified as debtors, as a separate subheading of debtors where material.

56   Deferred tax debit and credit balances should be offset within the above headings to the extent, and only to the extent, that they:

(a)   relate to taxes levied by the same tax authority; and

(b)   arise in the same taxable entity or in a group of taxable entities where the tax losses of one entity can reduce the taxable profits of another.

57   Typically, each company in the UK is a single taxable entity and can offset current corporation tax payable to the Inland Revenue against current corporation tax due from the Inland Revenue. Where this is the case, deferred tax balances relating to the corporation tax of a single company are offset on the balance sheet. It may be appropriate to offset the deferred tax assets and liabilities of different entities within the same tax jurisdiction. This will be the case if and to the extent that the entities are treated as a group for tax purposes, being able to use the tax losses of one entity to reduce the amount of tax paid by another. The deferred tax assets and liabilities of different entities cannot be offset when they relate to taxes levied in different jurisdictions.

58   Deferred tax liabilities and assets should be disclosed separately on the face of the balance sheet if the amounts are so material in the context of the total net current assets or net assets that, in the absence of such disclosure, readers may misinterpret the financial statements.

Presentation in the statements of performance

59   All deferred tax recognised in the profit and loss account should be included within the heading 'tax on profit or loss on ordinary activities'.

DISCLOSURES

Deferred tax included in the statements of performance

60   The notes to the financial statements should disclose the amount of deferred tax charged or credited within:

(a)   tax on ordinary activities in the profit and loss account, separately disclosing material components, including those attributable to:

(i)   changes in deferred tax balances (before discounting, where applicable) arising from:

● the origination and reversal of timing differences;

● changes in tax rates and laws; and

*FRS 17 requires such deferred tax to be offset against the defined benefit asset or liability to which it relates.

- adjustments to the estimated recoverable amount of deferred tax assets arising in previous periods.

(ii) where applicable, changes in the amounts of discount deducted in arriving at the deferred tax balance.

(b) tax charged or credited directly in the statement of total recognised gains and losses for the period, separately disclosing material components, including those listed in (a) above.

Deferred tax included in the balance sheet

The financial statements should disclose: **61**

(a) the total deferred tax balance (before discounting, where applicable), showing the amount recognised for each significant type of timing difference separately;

(b) the impact of discounting on, and the discounted amount of, the deferred tax balance; and

(c) the movement between the opening and closing net deferred tax balance, analysing separately:

(i) the amount charged or credited in the profit and loss account for the period;

(ii) the amount charged or credited directly in the statement of total recognised gains and losses for the period; and

(iii) movements arising from the acquisition or disposal of businesses.

The financial statements should disclose the amount of a deferred tax asset and the   **62**
nature of the evidence supporting its recognition if:

(a) the recoverability of the deferred tax asset is dependent on future taxable profits in excess of those arising from the reversal of deferred tax liabilities; and

(b) the reporting entity has suffered a loss in either the current or preceding period in the tax jurisdiction to which the deferred tax asset relates.

The evidence supporting the recognition of the deferred tax asset is the specific   **63**
circumstances that make it reasonable to forecast that there will be future profits against which the deferred tax assets can be recovered. Such circumstances are discussed in paragraphs 28–31.

Circumstances affecting current and future tax charges

The notes to the financial statements should highlight circumstances that affect the   **64**
current and total tax charges or credits for the current period or may affect the current and total tax charges or credits in future periods. This disclosure (illustrated in Appendix II) should include:

(a) a reconciliation of the current tax charge or credit on ordinary activities for the period reported in the profit and loss account to the current tax charge that would result from applying a relevant standard rate of tax to the profit on ordinary activities before tax. Either the monetary amounts or the rates (as a percentage of profits on ordinary activities before tax) may be reconciled. Where material, positive amounts should not be offset against negative amounts or vice versa: they should be shown as separate reconciling items. The basis on which the standard rate of tax has been determined should be disclosed.

(b) – if assets have been revalued in the financial statements without deferred tax having been recognised on the revaluation gain or loss, or if the market values of assets that have not been revalued have been disclosed in a note – an estimate of tax that could be payable or recoverable if the assets were sold at the values shown, the circumstances in which the tax would be payable or recoverable and an indication of the amount that may become payable or recoverable in the foreseeable future.

(c)   – if the reporting entity has sold (or entered into a binding agreement to sell) an asset but has not recognised deferred tax on a taxable gain because the gain has been or is expected to be rolled over into replacement assets – the conditions that will have to be met to obtain the rollover relief and an estimate of the tax that would become payable if those conditions were not met.

(d)   – if a deferred tax asset has not been recognised on the grounds that there is insufficient evidence that the asset will be recoverable – the amount that has not been recognised and the circumstances in which the asset would be recovered.

(e)   – if any other deferred tax has not been recognised – the nature of the amounts not recognised, the circumstances in which the tax would become payable or recoverable and an indication of the amount that may become payable or recoverable in the foreseeable future.

65   Relevant 'standard' tax rates vary from entity to entity. A relevant rate for a group whose profits are earned primarily in the UK is the standard rate of corporation tax in the UK, even if some of the group's operations are conducted in other countries. The impact of different rates of tax applied to profits earned in other countries would be shown as a reconciling item. The standard rate of tax in the UK might be regarded as being of limited relevance for a group that operates primarily outside the UK. For such a group, it may be more appropriate to use the average rate of tax (weighted in proportion to accounting profits) applicable across the group. Such a reconciliation could be performed by preparing and aggregating separate reconciliations for each country using the local rate of tax as the standard tax rate for each reconciliation.

DATE FROM WHICH EFFECTIVE

66   The accounting practices set out in the FRS should be regarded as standard for financial statements relating to accounting periods ending on or after 23 January 2002. Earlier adoption is encouraged.

WITHDRAWAL OF SSAP 15 AND AMENDMENT OF OTHER ACCOUNTING STANDARDS

67   The FRS supersedes SSAP 15 'Accounting for deferred tax'.

68–71   [*Not reproduced as all changes have been reflected in the material reproduced in this volume.*]

72   The Guidance Notes to SSAP 21 'Accounting for leases and hire purchase contracts' were issued by the former Accounting Standards Committee of the CCAB and were not adopted by the Board. Nonetheless, it would be consistent with the FRS if paragraphs 170 and 173–175 of the Notes, and the references to them in paragraphs 47, 101 and 110, were deemed to be deleted.

Adoption of FRS 19 by the board

Financial Reporting Standard 19 'Deferred Tax' was approved for issue by a vote of nine of the ten members of the Accounting Standards Board. Ms Sharp, recognising that she had not participated in the Board's key earlier debates in the development of this standard and its important role in promoting international convergence, abstained from voting in accordance with the Board's agreed procedure for newly appointed members.

Sir David Tweedie	(Chairman)
Allan Cook CBE	(Technical Director)
David Allvey	
Ian Brindle	
Dr John Buchanan	
John Coombe	
Huw Jones	
Professor Geoffrey Whittington	
Ken Wild	

Appendix I
Discounting example

1   This appendix illustrates how deferred tax arising from accelerated capital allowances on a plant and machinery pool is discounted.

Assumptions

2   A company that operates solely in the UK depreciates its plant and machinery on a straight-line basis over 10 years. Residual value is estimated to be $1/11^{th}$ of cost. The company receives capital allowances at a rate of 25 per cent per year on a reducing balance basis. It is taxed on its profits at 30 per cent.

3   The company has three groups of assets costing £1,100 each, purchased six years, three years and one year ago (in each case at the end of the financial year). The net book value of plant and machinery at the balance sheet date (year 0) is:

	£
Original cost	3,300
Cumulative depreciation	(1,000)
Net book value	2,300

4   The tax written-down values of the plant and machinery pool, and the consequential timing difference, at the balance sheet date are:

	£
Net book value	2,300
Tax written-down value	(1,114)
Timing difference at end of year 0	1,114

Scheduling the reversal of the deferred tax liability

5   The future reversals of the liability are scheduled in Table 1 below. The future depreciation of the existing pool of fixed assets (column b) is compared with the future writing-down allowances available on the pool (column c) to determine the years of reversal of the capital allowances (column d). When forecasting capital allowances for future periods, it is assumed that allowances will be claimed as early as possible and that the residual values of the assets will equal those forecast for depreciation purposes.

TABLE 1

Years from now	Depreciation	Capital allowances	Reversal of timing difference	Deferred tax liability (undiscounted)
	£	£	£	£
a	b	c	d = b−c	e = d × 30%
1	300	278	22	7
2	300	209	91	27
3	300	157	143	43
4	300	93	207	62
5	200	69	131	39
6	200	52	148	44
7	200	14	186	56
8	100	11	89	27
9	100	(17)*	117	35
10+	–	(52)	52	16
Total	2,000†	814	1,186	356

Discount rates

The prices of and yields on UK Treasury gilts are published in the Financial Times. An appropriate post-tax rate is obtained by deducting the rate of tax that the entity pays on investment income (30 per cent) from these returns. 6

TABLE 2

	Published information			Post-tax return (Bid yield less tax of 30%)
Years to maturity	Coupon rate %	Bid Price	Bid Yield %	
1	6	99.37	6.67	4.7
3	7	102.82	6.01	4.2
5	6.5	104.27	5.55	3.9
9	7.2	114.16	5.29	3.7
30	6	114.00	5.09	3.6

Appropriate rates of return for other maturity dates are estimated by interpolation. See column f of Table 3 below.

It is assumed that the plant and machinery pool on which the writing-down allowances are claimed will continue beyond year 9 and hence that the incremental effect of the sale of the third asset in year 9 will be to reduce the writing-down allowances obtained in that and following years.

†The future depreciation and capital allowances are £300 less than the net book value and tax written-down value respectively owing to the assumption that assets will be sold for £100 in each of years 4, 7 and 9.

Discounting the liability

7   Table 3 below illustrates how the discounted liability of £290 is calculated. The guidance in the FRS notes that it may be possible to use simplifying assumptions without introducing material errors into the measurement of the discounted liability. In this example, all timing differences reversing in years 10 onwards are treated as reversing in year 10.

TABLE 3

Years from now	Deferred tax liability (undiscounted) £	Discount rate %		Deferred tax liability (discounted) £
a	**e** (from Table 1)	**f** (from Table 2)		$g = e/[(1 + f)^a]$
1	7	4.7		7
2	27	4.4	i	25
3	43	4.2		38
4	62	4.0	i	53
5	39	3.9		33
6	44	3.8	i	35
7	56	3.8	i	43
8	27	3.7	i	20
9	35	3.7		25
10+	16	3.7	i	11
Total	356			290

i = estimate based on interpolation of rates known for years 1, 3, 5, 9 and 30*

8   The discount reduces the deferred tax liability at year 0 by £66, ie from £356 to £290.

In practice, it might be possible to limit the number of rates used without introducing material differences. For example, in the above illustration, the rates could be simplified to:
4.5 per cent for short-term reversals (years 1–4)
3.8 per cent for medium-term reversals (years 5–9)
3.7 per cent for long-term reversals (years 10+).

Appendix II
Disclosure illustrations

The following illustrates how the disclosures required by paragraphs 60-65 of the FRS could be presented in the notes to the accounts. (Not illustrated is the disclosure that would be required of any deferred tax that had been charged or credited in the statement of total recognised gains and losses for the period.)

In this illustration, the analysis of the deferred tax charge for the period required by paragraph 60 (a) of the FRS has been combined with the analysis of the current tax charge for the period required by paragraph 17 of FRS 16 'Current Tax'.

The reconciliation of the tax charge, illustrated as a reconciliation of monetary amounts in note 1 (b) below, could alternatively be given as a reconciliation of the standard rate of tax to the effective rate.

1 TAX ON PROFIT ON ORDINARY ACTIVITIES

(a) Analysis of charge in period	200Y		200X	
	£m	£m	£m	£m
Current tax:				
UK corporation tax on profits of the period	**40**		26	
Adjustments in respect of previous periods	**4**		(6)	
		44		20
Foreign tax		**12**		16
Total current tax (note 1(b))		**56**		36
Deferred tax:				
Origination and reversal of timing differences	**67**		60	
Effect of increased tax rate on opening liability	**12**		–	
Increase in discount	**(14)**		(33)	
Total deferred tax (note 2)		**65**		27
Tax on profit on ordinary activities		**121**		63

(b) Factors affecting tax charge for period

The tax assessed for the period is lower than the standard rate of corporation tax in the UK (31 per cent). The differences are explained below:

	200Y £m	200X £m
Profit on ordinary activities before tax	361	327

	200Y £m	200X £m
Profit on ordinary activities multiplied by standard rate of corporation tax in the UK of 31% (200X: 30%)	112	98
Effects of:		
Expenses not deductible for tax purposes (primarily goodwill amortisation)	22	10
Capital allowances for period in excess of depreciation	(58)	(54)
Utilisation of tax losses	(17)	(18)
Rollover relief on profit on disposal of property	(10)	–
Higher tax rates on overseas earnings	3	6
Adjustments to tax charge in respect of previous periods	4	(6)
Current tax charge for period (note 1(a))	56	36

(c) Factors that may affect future tax charges

Based on current capital investment plans, the group expects to continue to be able to claim capital allowances in excess of depreciation in future years but at a slightly lower level than in the current year.

The group has now used all brought-forward tax losses, which have significantly reduced tax payments in recent years.

No provision has been made for deferred tax on gains recognised on revaluing property to its market value or on the sale of properties where potentially taxable gains have been rolled over into replacement assets. Such tax would become payable only if the property were sold without it being possible to claim rollover relief. The total amount unprovided for is £21 million. At present, it is not envisaged that any tax will become payable in the foreseeable future.

The group's overseas tax rates are higher than those in the UK primarily because the profits earned in country X are taxed at a rate of 45 per cent. The group expects a reduction in future tax rates following a recent announcement that the rate of tax in that country is to reduce to 40 per cent.

No deferred tax is recognised on the unremitted earnings of overseas subsidiaries, associates and joint ventures. As the earnings are continually reinvested by the group, no tax is expected to be payable on them in the foreseeable future.

2 PROVISION FOR DEFERRED TAX

	31.12.200Y	31.12.200X
	£m	£m
Accelerated capital allowances	426	356
Tax losses carried forward	–	(9)
Undiscounted provision for deferred tax	426	347
Discount	(80)	(66)
Discounted provision for deferred tax	346	281

Provision at start of period	281
Deferred tax charge in profit and loss account for period (note 1)	65
Provision at end of period	346

Appendix III
Note on legal requirements

Great Britain

1   The Companies Act 1985 sets out requirements for companies on accounting for provisions and current assets in general and deferred tax in particular. The main requirements that are directly relevant are set out in Schedule 4 and are summarised below.

2   Schedule 4 does not apply to banking and insurance companies and groups, nor to small companies to the extent that they choose instead to comply with the reduced requirements set out in Schedule 8. Requirements corresponding to those of Schedule 4 are set out for banking companies and groups in Schedule 9 and for insurance companies and groups in Schedule 9A.

Recognition and measurement

3   Paragraph 12(b) of Schedule 4 states the general requirement to provide for all liabilities that have arisen in respect of the financial year to which the accounts relate or a previous financial year. Under the full provision method of accounting for deferred tax a timing difference is viewed as creating a liability because, as a result of that timing difference, a future tax assessment will be higher than it would otherwise have been (whether or not the timing difference will be replaced).

4   Paragraph 89 of Schedule 4 defines provisions as:

'any amount retained as reasonably necessary for the purposes of providing for any liability or loss which is either likely to be incurred, or certain to be incurred but uncertain as to amount or as to the date on which it will arise.'

The deferred tax liabilities provided for in accordance with the FRS, which are typically uncertain in terms of both timing and amount, are categorised as provisions in the balance sheet formats prescribed by Schedule 4.

5   The reference to 'liability or loss' in the definition of provisions needs to be considered in conjunction with the general requirement that the liabilities have arisen or are likely to arise *in respect of the financial year to which the accounts relate [or a previous financial year]*. Thus deferred tax can be regarded as giving rise to a liability that is required to be provided for only if the events causing the future reversal of a timing difference (such as a commitment to sell a revalued asset or to remit overseas earnings) have occurred before the end of the financial year. Without that past event the future 'liability' does not relate to the financial year or a previous financial year.

6   In addition to covering liabilities that are certain to be incurred the statutory definition also refers to liabilities as losses that are likely to be incurred. Typically, if the events causing the future reversal of a timing difference have occurred, the deferred tax liability, although not certain, is likely to be incurred. An exception is the deferred tax that might be payable following the sale of a fixed asset, if it is not yet certain whether rollover relief will be obtained. The FRS requires such deferred tax to be provided for only if it is likely that rollover relief will not be obtained. The amount unprovided for is regarded as a contingent liability.

Paragraph 34(3)(b) of Schedule 4 allows taxation to be transferred to or from the   7
revaluation reserve if it relates to any profit or loss credited or debited to that reserve.
Paragraph 34(4) requires the treatment for taxation purposes of amounts credited or
debited to the revaluation reserve to be disclosed. The FRS requires the deferred tax to
be included either in the profit and loss account or directly in the statement of total
recognised gains and losses and requires the amounts to be disclosed.

Presentation and disclosure

Paragraph 3(6) of Schedule 4 requires the profit and loss accounts of companies to   8
show the profit or loss on ordinary activities before taxation.

The balance sheet formats set out in Schedule 4 require provisions for taxation,   9
including deferred taxation, to be included within the total for provisions for
liabilities and charges. Provisions for taxation need not be shown separately on the
face of the balance sheet (paragraph 3(4)), providing that material amounts are
disclosed in a note to the accounts. Paragraph 47 requires the provision for deferred
taxation to be shown separately from any other tax provision. Paragraph 46 requires
the movements on provisions for taxation to be disclosed in a note to the accounts.

Paragraph 5 of Schedule 4 states that assets and income should not be offset against   10
liabilities and expenditure in the balance sheet and profit and loss account. Deferred
tax debit and credit balances that arise with the same taxation authority and that the
entity would have a right to settle on a net basis are not separate assets and liabilities
and should therefore be shown on a net basis in the financial statements. Net debit
balances, however, must be shown as assets rather than as negative amounts within
provisions. The formats set out in Schedule 4 do not specify a heading for net
deferred tax assets but paragraph 3(2) permits assets not covered by the prescribed
headings to be included in the balance sheet. The FRS requires material deferred tax
assets to be included as a separate subheading within debtors. Note (5) on the
balance sheet formats requires the amount falling due after more than one year to be
shown separately for each item included under debtors.

Paragraph 50(2) of Schedule 4 requires the following information to be given in   11
respect of any contingent liability not provided for:

(a)   the amount or estimated amount of that liability;
(b)   its legal nature; and
(c)   whether any valuable security has been provided by the company in connection
       with that liability, and if so, what.

Any deferred tax not provided for because it is expected that rollover relief will be
obtained is a contingent liability. The FRS requires the estimated amount and the
circumstances in which it will become payable to be disclosed.

Paragraph 54(2) of Schedule 4 requires any special circumstances affecting the lia-   12
bility to tax on profits, income or capital gains for the current or future years to be
disclosed. The FRS details specific circumstances that should be disclosed.

Impact on distributable profits

As discussed in paragraphs 3 and 4 above, the deferred tax provisions that are   13
required to be recognised by the FRS are, in general, regarded as liabilities that arise
from past events and, hence, as 'provisions for liabilities and charges' of the type
given in paragraph 89 of Schedule 4. Section 275(1) requires provisions of the type

mentioned in paragraph 89 of Schedule 4 to be treated as realised losses for the purposes of determining a company's profits available for distribution.

14   The FRS additionally requires deferred tax to be provided for when assets are revalued to their fair values with changes being recorded in the profit and loss account. In such circumstances, the purpose of the deferred tax is to recognise the tax attributable to the gain resulting from the change in fair value. As such a gain on which deferred tax is provided for is regarded as unrealised, the deferred tax on that gain should be treated as a reduction in that unrealised gain rather than a realised loss. The fact that the deferred tax is presented with other tax provisions within the heading 'provisions for liabilities and charges' does not alter that position.

Northern Ireland

15   The statutory requirements in Northern Ireland are set out in Schedule 4 to the Companies (Northern Ireland) Order 1986. They are identical to and have the same paragraph references as those cited above for Great Britain.

Republic of Ireland

16   The statutory requirements in the Republic of Ireland that correspond to those listed above for Great Britain are shown in the following table.

Great Britain	*Republic of Ireland*
Section 275(1) of the Companies Act 1985	section 45(4) of the Companies (Amendment) Act 1983 and paragraphs 69 and 70 of the Schedule to the Companies (Amendment) Act 1986.
Schedule 4 to the Companies Act 1985:	Companies (Amendment) Act 1986:
paragraph 3(2), 3(4) and 3(6)	section 4(12), 4(6) and 4(16)
paragraph 5	section 4(11)
paragraph 12(b)	section 5(c)(ii)
Schedule 4 to the Companies Act 1985:	The Schedule to the Companies (Amendment) Act 1986:
note (5) on the formats	note 4 on the formats
paragraph 34(4)	paragraph 22(5)
paragraph 46	paragraph 32
paragraph 47	paragraph 33
paragraph 50(2)	paragraph 36(2)
paragraph 54(2)	paragraph 40(2)
paragraph 89	paragraph 70
Schedule 8 to the Companies Act 1985	no equivalent

| Schedule 9 to the Companies Act 1985 | European Communities (Credit Institutions: Accounts) Regulations 1992 |
| Schedule 9A to the Companies Act 1985 | European Communities (Insurance Undertakings: Accounts) Regulations 1996 |

There is no equivalent to paragraph 34(3)(b) of Schedule 4 to The Companies Act 1985.   **17**

Appendix IV
Compliance with International Accounting Standards

1   The International Accounting Standard (IAS) that addresses deferred tax is IAS 12 (revised 1996) 'Income Taxes'.* Like the FRS, IAS 12 (revised) requires deferred tax to be recognised on a full provision basis. But it requires deferred tax to be recognised on the basis of 'temporary differences' rather than on the basis of obligations arising from timing differences. The conceptual differences between temporary differences and timing differences are explained in Appendix V 'The development of the FRS'. This appendix sets out the resulting differences in the requirements of the two standards.

2   The circumstances in which deferred tax is provided for are wider under IAS 12 (revised) than under the FRS. This is for two reasons: temporary differences can arise from both timing and permanent differences; and IAS 12 (revised) requires provisions to be made even when the critical events causing the deferred tax to become payable in future have not occurred by the balance sheet date. The main areas where compliance with IAS 12 (revised) could require additional provisions to be recognised by UK and Irish companies are set out in the following table.

Differences between the recognition requirements of IAS 12 (revised 1996) and those of the FRS

Circumstances giving rise to deferred tax	Deferred tax required to be recognised:	
	by FRS 19	by IAS 12 (revised 1996)
1 Revaluation of non-monetary assets	Provision is required only if either: (a) the asset is revalued to fair value each period with changes in fair value being recognised in the profit and loss account; or (b) the entity has entered into a binding agreement to sell the revalued asset, has revalued the asset to its selling price and does not expect to obtain rollover relief.	Provision is required whether or not it is intended that the asset will be sold and whether or not rollover relief could be claimed.
2 Sale of assets, where gain has been or might be rolled over into replacement assets.	Provision is required only if rollover relief has not been obtained and is not expected to be obtained.	Provision is required. The deferred tax is measured on the difference between the replacement asset's cost and its tax base (ie cost less taxable gain rolled over).

Editor's note: IAS 12 was further revised in 2000.

Circumstances giving rise to deferred tax	Deferred tax required to be recognised:	
	by FRS 19	by IAS 12 (revised 1996)
3 Adjustments to recognise assets and liabilities at their fair values on the acquisition of a business.	The amendment to FRS 7 'Fair Values in Acquisition Accounting' introduced by FRS 19 requires deferred tax to be provided for as if the adjustments had been gains or losses recognised before the acquisition. Deferred tax would not normally be recognised on adjusting non-monetary assets to market values. No provision is recognised in respect of acquired goodwill.	Provision is made for all differences between the fair values recognised for assets and liabilities and their tax bases. The only exception is that no provision is required in respect of the temporary difference arising on the recognition of non-deductible goodwill.
4 Unremitted earnings of subsidiaries, associates and joint ventures.	Provision is required only to the extent that dividends payable by a subsidiary, associate or joint venture have been accrued at the balance sheet date or a binding agreement to distribute the past earnings in future has been made.	Provision is required on the unremitted earnings of associates in all circumstances. Provision is required on the unremitted profits of subsidiaries, branches and joint ventures if either the parent/investor is unable to control the timing of the remittance of the earnings or it is probable that remittance will take place in the foreseeable future.
5 Exchange differences arising on consolidation of non-monetary assets of an entity accounted for under the temporal method.	No provision is required because there is no timing difference.	Provision is required on the temporary difference between the carrying amount (at historical exchange rates) and the tax base (at balance sheet date exchange rates).

Circumstances giving rise to deferred tax	Deferred tax required to be recognised:	
	by FRS 19	by IAS 12 (revised 1996)
6 Unrealised intragroup profits (for example, in stock) are eliminated on consolidation.	Provision is required on the timing difference, ie the profit that has been taxed but not recognised in the consolidated financial statements. It is therefore measured using the supplying company's rate of tax.	Provision is required on the temporary difference. IAS 12 (revised) states that this is the difference between the (reduced) carrying amount of the stock in the balance sheet and its higher tax base (the amount paid by the receiving company). The provision is measured using the receiving company's rate of tax.

3 The requirements in the FRS regarding the rates of tax used to measure deferred tax assets and liabilities are very similar to those in IAS 12 (revised). However, IAS 12 (revised) does not permit deferred tax balances to be discounted.

4 The FRS requires deferred tax to be shown separately on the face of the balance sheet if the amounts are so material that failure to do so could cause readers to mis-interpret the financial statements. IAS 12 (revised) requires all (material) deferred tax balances to be shown separately on the face of the balance sheet.

5 The amendment to FRS 7 'Fair Values in Acquisition Accounting' introduced by FRS 19 refers to previously unrecognised deferred tax assets (typically carried forward losses) that meet the criteria for recognition as a result of the acquisition. The amendment requires the benefit of the assets to be recognised as part of the fair value exercise only if the assets have arisen in the acquired entity: if the assets have arisen in the acquiring entity, the benefit is required to be recognised as part of post-acquisition performance. IAS 22 'Business Combinations' requires the benefit to be recognised as part of the fair value exercise whether the assets have arisen in the acquired or the acquiring entities.

6 The disclosures required by the FRS are similar overall to those required by IAS 12 (revised). The main differences comprise:

(a) *disclosures required by IAS 12 (revised) but not by FRS 19:*

  – the aggregate amount of temporary differences associated with invest-ments in subsidiaries, branches, associates and joint ventures for which deferred tax liabilities have not been recognised
  – the tax expense relating to discontinued operations;

(b) *disclosures required by FRS 19 but not by IAS 12 (revised):*

  – disclosures of the effects of discounting
  – a general explanation of circumstances that have affected the current and total tax charges for the current period or that may affect the charges in future periods
  – the circumstances in which deferred tax relating to revaluation and rolled over gains (and other deferred tax unprovided for) would become payable and an indication of the amounts that are expected to become payable in the foreseeable future;

(c) other differences:

IAS 12 (revised) requires disclosure of a reconciliation of the entity's actual tax charge (current and deferred) for the period to the tax that would be payable using a standard rate of tax. The FRS requires a different reconciliation to be disclosed: a reconciliation of the *current* tax assessed for the period to a standard rate of tax. (It is of note, however, that although the two reconciliations are different, the IAS 12 (revised) reconciliation can be constructed from information required to be disclosed by the FRS.)

Appendix V
The development of the FRS

Contents

Changes to requirements proposed in FRED 19

The development of the FRS

REQUIREMENT FOR FULL PROVISION

The source of deferred tax

In most tax jurisdictions, including the UK and the Republic of Ireland, the starting | **1**
point for computing corporation tax is the accounting profit as reported in the
financial statements. However, adjustments are made to the accounting profit to
arrive at taxable profits. These differences can be analysed into two types: 'permanent' and 'timing'.

Permanent differences arise because certain gains or losses that are recognised in the | **2**
financial statements are not taxable or tax-deductible at all. An example is a non-taxable government grant. Timing differences arise when gains or losses are recognised in accounting profits in periods different from those in which they are
recognised in taxable profits. An example is a capital allowance that is obtained
before the depreciation of the asset to which it relates is recognised in the financial
statements.

Because timing differences reverse, tax charged in later periods may be increased or | **3**
reduced as a result of transactions or events that have taken place before the balance
sheet date. The issue in accounting for deferred tax is the extent to which provision
should be made for the future tax consequences of past transactions and events.
Three different methods – flow-through accounting, full provision and partial provision – exist.

Three methods of accounting for tax

Flow-through accounting

Flow-through accounting makes no provision at all for deferred tax. Rather, tax is | **4**
accounted for as it is assessed.

The rationale for this method of accounting is that tax is assessed annually on profits | **5**
as determined for tax purposes, not on accounting profits. The tax authorities impose
a single tax assessment on the entity and that is its only liability to tax for that period.
Any tax assessed in future years will depend on future events and hence is not a present
liability as defined in the Board's Statement of Principles for Financial Reporting.

Supporters of flow-through accounting also argue that it is the most transparent and | **6**
intuitively sensible way of communicating an entity's tax position. The financial
statements show the actual tax charge for the year in the clearest possible manner,
and the associated notes (which would disclose such matters as accumulated timing
differences and the items reconciling the actual tax charge to a standard rate) would
be no more detailed and possibly more intelligible than those resulting from other
possible accounting methods.

Some supporters of flow-through accounting further argue that even if, in principle, | **7**
timing differences did give rise to tax liabilities,* in practice such liabilities could not
always be measured reliably. The future tax consequences of current transactions
depend upon a complex interaction of future events, such as the profitability,
investment and financing transactions of the entity, and changes in tax rates and
laws. Only those that could be measured reliably – typically very short-term discrete

---

*To avoid making the text unduly cumbersome, this discussion focuses on deferred tax liabilities (which tend to
be more significant and frequent than deferred tax assets). The same principles extend to deferred tax assets,
although the precise arguments may be slightly different.*

timing differences – should be provided for. Thus they advocate a modified flow-through approach.

Full provision method

8   The full provision method is based on the view that every transaction has a tax consequence and it is possible to make a reasonable estimate of the future tax consequences of transactions that have occurred by the balance sheet date. Such future tax consequences cannot be avoided: whatever happens in future, the entity will pay less or more tax as a result of the reversal of a timing difference that exists at the balance sheet date than it would have done in the absence of that timing difference. Deferred tax should therefore be provided for in full on timing differences.

Partial provision method

9   The partial provision method also starts from the premise that the future reversal of timing differences gives rise to a tax asset or liability. However, rather than focusing on the individual components of the tax computation, the partial provision method emphasises the interaction of those components in a single net assessment. To the extent that timing differences are expected to continue in future (ie the existing timing differences being replaced by future timing differences as they reverse), the tax is viewed as being deferred permanently.

10   Where, for example, fixed asset expenditure attracts tax deductions before the fixed assets are depreciated, timing differences arise. The timing differences increase with time under conditions of inflation or expansion, with the result that new timing differences more than replace those that reverse. In consequence, effective tax rates are reduced. The partial provision method allows the lower effective tax rates to be reflected in the profit and loss account, to the extent that the reduction is not expected to reverse in future years.

11   The attraction of the partial provision method is that it reflects an entity's ongoing effective tax rate. It results in tax charges that reflect the amount of tax that it is expected will actually be paid and excludes amounts that are expected to be deferred 'permanently'.

Reasons for rejecting the partial provision method

12   The FRS supersedes SSAP 15 'Accounting for deferred tax'. SSAP 15 required deferred tax to be accounted for using the partial provision method.

13   SSAP 15 and the partial provision method were first implemented in the UK and the Republic of Ireland in 1978, when they were viewed as a pragmatic response to the corporation tax system of the time. A key feature of that system was very generous capital and stock allowances: companies could deduct for tax purposes 100 per cent of the cost of plant and equipment in the year of purchase and inflationary increases in the value of stock. The effect of these deductions was that companies could indefinitely postpone payment of some or all of their deferred tax and paid tax at well below the enacted rate of 52 per cent.

14   The partial provision method allowed companies to avoid creating provisions for tax that they argued they were unlikely to pay. However, by the early 1990s, concerns were being expressed about the method and the way in which it was being applied. It was noted in particular that:

- the recognition rules and anticipation of future events were subjective and inconsistent with the principles underlying other aspects of accounting.
- the partial provision method had not been regarded as appropriate for dealing with the long-term deferred tax assets associated with provisions for post-retirement benefits. As a result, SSAP 15 had been amended in 1992 to permit such assets to be accounted for on a full provision basis. The amendment introduced inconsistencies into SSAP 15.
- there were variations in the way in which SSAP 15 was applied in practice. Different entities within the same industry and with similar prospects seemed to take quite different views on the levels of provisions necessary. There was evidence that some companies provided for deferred tax in full for simplicity's sake rather than because their circumstances required it. The different approaches being taken reduced the comparability of financial statements.
- because of its recognition rules and anticipation of future events, the partial provision method was increasingly being rejected by standard-setters in other countries. The US Financial Accounting Standards Board (FASB) had issued a standard FAS 109 'Accounting for Income Taxes' requiring full provision. The International Accounting Standards Committee (IASC) had published proposals for similar requirements and other standard-setters had started to move in the same direction.

When rejecting the partial provision method, the FASB and IASC argued in particular that: **15**

(a) every tax timing difference represented a real liability, since every one would reverse and, whatever else happened, an entity would pay more tax in future as a result of the reversal than it would have done in the absence of the timing difference.

(b) it was only the impact of new timing differences arising in future that prevented the total liability from reducing. It was inappropriate (and inconsistent with other areas of accounting) to take account of future transactions when measuring an existing liability.

(c) the assessment of the liability using the partial provision method relied on management intentions regarding future events. Standard-setters were uncomfortable with this, having already embodied in a number of other standards the principle that liabilities should be determined on the basis of obligations rather than management decisions or intentions.

In view of the criticisms of the partial provision method, the Board decided to review **16** SSAP 15. In 1995 it published a Discussion Paper 'Accounting for Tax'. The Discussion Paper proposed that SSAP 15 should be replaced with an FRS requiring full provision for deferred tax.

Most respondents to the Discussion Paper opposed the move to full provision at that **17** stage, preferring instead to retain the partial provision method. In the meantime, however, IASC had approved its standard, IAS 12 (revised 1996) 'Income Taxes', which required use of the full provision method. The Board reconsidered the arguments and arrived at the view that:

- whilst it did not agree with all of the criticisms of the partial provision method expressed internationally and could see the logic for all three methods of accounting for tax, it shared some of the concerns regarding the subjectivity of the partial provision method and its reliance on future events; and
- as more companies adopted international accounting standards, the partial provision method would become less well understood and accepted, particularly as it was regarded as less prudent than the internationally accepted method.

Hence, the retention of the partial provision method in the UK could damage the credibility of UK financial reporting.

18   For these reasons, the Board took the view that deferred tax was not an area where a good case could be made for departing from principles that had been widely accepted internationally. Following informal consultations, it developed a draft FRS, FRED 19 'Deferred Tax', which proposed requirements based more closely on a full provision method. The FRED was published for consultation in August 1999.

19   The responses to FRED 19 indicated that, whilst many amongst the financial community remained disappointed that there had not been international acceptance of the partial provision method, most accepted the arguments for greater harmonisation with international practice and supported the proposed move to a full provision method.

Reasons for rejecting flow-through accounting

20   For the reasons outlined in paragraphs 5–7 above, a number of Board members believe that the clearest and most transparent method of communicating an entity's tax position is by flow-through accounting combined with detailed disclosures. The possibility of moving to flow-through accounting was therefore suggested in the Board's Discussion Paper.

21   However, flow-through accounting would not have moved UK accounting more into line with international practice and received little support from those responding to the Board's Discussion Paper. Most respondents agreed with the view that taxable profit was, in both form and substance, an adjusted accounting profit and that it was possible to attribute tax effects to individual transactions. Further, they regarded tax systems as sufficiently stable to allow reasonable estimates to be made of the deferred tax consequences of events reported up to the balance sheet date. They added their concerns that flow-through accounting would make their results more volatile, could sometimes understate an entity's liability to tax and that any modification to it would require arbitrary cut-off points that could be difficult to rationalise.

22   In view of the lack of support from respondents and the Board's commitment to international harmonisation, Board members who would have preferred flow-through accounting accepted that the FRS should instead require full provision for deferred tax.

RECOGNITION CRITERIA – INCREMENTAL LIABILITY APPROACH

Overview

23   Traditionally, deferred tax has been identified and recognised on the basis of timing differences. And, even under full provision methods, not all types of timing difference have necessarily been provided for. Varying approaches have been taken, depending on views regarding the nature and purpose of deferred tax.

24   A completely different approach, which requires deferred tax to be recognised on 'temporary' rather than timing differences, was developed for FAS 109 and adopted in IAS 12 (revised).

25   Given that the move to full provision accounting in the UK was driven primarily by international harmonisation, it would have been ideal if the requirements of the FRS could have mirrored those of IAS 12 (revised). However, the Board did not accept

some of the assumptions underlying the temporary difference approach and opposed some of the practical consequences of the approach. The Board therefore considered alternative approaches that did not rely on the same assumptions and were designed to be consistent with its Statement of Principles for Financial Reporting.

The Board developed two approaches. The first required deferred tax to be recognised only when it could be regarded as meeting the definition of an asset or a liability in its own right (the 'incremental liability' approach). The second required deferred tax to be recognised as a necessary adjustment to the values at which other assets and liabilities were recognised (the 'valuation adjustment' approach). **26**

Most Board members preferred the incremental liability approach and based the requirements of FRED 19 on this approach. A majority of respondents who expressed a preference supported the proposed approach, with the rest supporting either a valuation adjustment approach or full harmonisation with IAS 12 (revised). The incremental liability approach therefore remains the approach on which the requirements in the FRS have been based. **27**

Reasons for rejecting the temporary difference approach

The meaning of 'temporary difference'

A temporary difference is defined as any difference between the amount at which an asset or liability is recognised in financial statements and its tax base. The tax base is the amount that will be deductible or taxable in respect of the asset or liability in the future. **28**

Most temporary differences are created by timing differences. For example, the tax base of a fixed asset that attracts capital allowances is its cost less allowances received. A temporary difference arises if the tax base is less than the net book value recognised in the financial statements. The temporary difference equals the timing difference created if the allowances received have exceeded depreciation. **29**

But temporary differences can also be created by permanent differences between accounting profits and taxable profits. If a government grant is non-taxable, any portion that is deferred as a liability has a tax base of zero. Similarly, a non-deductible cost capitalised as an asset has a tax base of zero. In some tax jurisdictions, certain fixed asset expenditure is 'super- deductible' and qualifies for tax allowances for, say, 150 per cent of cost. The tax base will initially be greater than cost. In each of these cases, a temporary difference arises as soon as the asset or liability is recognised. **30**

Rationale for the temporary difference approach

The rationale for recognising deferred tax on temporary differences is that the entity should provide for the unavoidable tax consequences of recovering the carrying values of assets or settling liabilities at the amounts shown in the accounts. It is argued that it is inherent in the carrying value of an asset that the asset will generate pre-tax cash flows at least equal to that carrying value. Any tax payable on generating such cash flows is therefore inherently a liability of the entity. The temporary difference measures the amount on which tax will be payable. **31**

Reasons for rejecting the temporary difference approach

The Board did not accept one of the fundamental assumptions underlying the temporary difference approach, ie that the carrying value of an asset represented the **32** minimum pre-tax cash flows that the asset would generate. It identified circumstances in which tax cash flows might also be reflected in the carrying value. For example, if an entity had bought a non-deductible asset for 100 and carried it at its historical cost of 100, this would not be because it had expected to generate pre-tax cash flows of 100, on which it would pay tax of 33. Rather it would have expected to generate pre-tax cash flows of at least 150, on which it would pay tax of 50. The carrying value of 100 would therefore have already taken account of future tax cash flows.

33   The circumstances in which future tax cash flows are not reflected in the carrying value of an asset (and hence should potentially be provided for) are those in which there has been a timing difference. This could arise when one of the future tax cash flows inherent in the original cost of an asset had been received without the asset having been depreciated (as would be the case on receipt of an accelerated capital allowance). Or it could arise when an asset had been revalued to a market value that assumed the whole cost was deductible.

34   Thus the Board concluded that deferred tax should be provided for on timing but not permanent differences.

35   IASC board members also had concerns about the need to provide for deferred tax on permanent differences. They decided that, as an exception to the general rule that deferred tax should be provided for on all temporary differences, IAS 12 (revised) should not require recognition of deferred tax arising on initial recognition of an asset or liability (ie permanent differences).

36   In the Board's view, a standard based on timing differences would be preferable to IAS 12 (revised), which is based on temporary differences but permits exceptions for temporary differences that are not timing differences. In the Board's view, a timing difference approach would not only be easier to justify conceptually, it would also be simpler to understand and apply. Timing differences are relatively easily identified from tax computations. Temporary differences can be more difficult to identify and measure. A substantial amount of guidance was required in IAS 12 (revised).

37   A substantial majority of respondents to FRED 19 supported the Board's decision not to adopt the temporary difference approach.

Reasons for adopting the incremental liability approach

Overview

38   There are two different views on how an approach based on timing differences should be implemented. The first view is that deferred tax should be recognised only when it meets the strict criteria for recognition as a liability (or asset) in its own right – the incremental liability approach. The alternative view is that deferred tax should be recognised even if it does not itself meet the strict recognition criteria if it can be regarded as a necessary adjustment to the values at which other assets and liabilities are recognised – the valuation adjustment approach. The requirements of the FRS are based on an incremental liability approach.

Incremental liability approach

39   The Board's Statement of Principles for Financial Reporting defines liabilities as 'obligations of an entity to transfer economic benefits as a result of past transactions

or events'.* The assessment of whether deferred tax is a liability requires conclusions to be reached about whether the transactions and events giving rise to an obligation to pay tax in future (the obligating events) are past events, ie have occurred at the balance sheet date.

Typically, a series of events must take place before an entity becomes required to pay **40** tax: the entity must undertake a potentially taxable transaction, generate taxable profits and be required by tax laws to pay tax on these profits. The Statement of Principles provides guidance:

> 'Sometimes a series of events must take place before the entity will have an obligation to transfer economic benefits. In such circumstances, whether the obligation exists depends on whether any of the events that have still to take place are under the entity's control. If they are, the entity retains discretion to avoid the transfer, so no obligation exists.'†

Thus the obligating event is the one that leaves the entity with no realistic alternative to paying tax, or in other words the event that will trigger the reversal of a timing difference in future.

For most types of timing difference, the events that trigger the reversal of the timing **41** difference can be regarded as having taken place by the year-end. Suppose, for example, that the entity has accrued interest on cash deposits, but will pay tax on that interest only when it is received. Having placed the funds on deposit, it has a right to the interest they will generate. And by recognising the right to the interest, it also has to recognise the obligation to pay tax on that interest. The entity no longer has the discretion to avoid paying the tax. And as the future events that will confirm the existence of the liability (ie the inclusion of the interest received in a future tax computation and a request for the payment of tax based on that computation) are relatively certain, they do not affect its recognition.

However, this is not the case with timing differences arising when assets are revalued. **42** In the UK, the revaluation of a fixed asset to its replacement cost is not a taxable event. The taxable event is the sale of the revalued asset. Therefore, as long as the management of the entity has the discretion not to sell the fixed asset, the entity does not have an obligation to pay any tax as a result of the increase in value. An obligation can arise only when the reporting entity enters into a binding sale agreement.

Similarly, a parent company can incur a tax liability when the earnings of overseas **43** subsidiaries, associates and joint ventures are remitted to it, for example by the payment of a dividend. Therefore, the existence of unremitted earnings can be regarded as giving rise to a tax timing difference. However, their existence does not give rise to an obligation to pay tax, as long as the entity has the discretion to avoid remitting the earnings. The obligating event is the distribution of earnings. Hence, the liability arises, and, under an incremental liability approach, should be recognised, only when a dividend is accrued as receivable or a binding agreement has been made for the sale of the investment.

Following the incremental liability approach, therefore, leads to a conclusion that **44** deferred tax should not be provided for on timing differences arising from revaluation of assets or non-remittance of earnings to the parent entity. The obligating

---

Paragraph 4.23, Statement of Principles for Financial Reporting.

†*Paragraph 4.32, Statement of Principles for Financial Reporting.*

event has not occurred and the entity does not have a liability at the balance sheet date.

Valuation adjustment approach

45   An alternative view is that, even where timing differences do not give rise to obligations in their own right, recognition of deferred tax could still be argued to be consistent with the Board's Statement of Principles. The argument would be that the deferred tax might need to be provided for in order to ensure that other assets were not valued at more than their economic (ie post-tax) values to the business.

46   Suppose, for example, that a company revalued an asset such as a building to its market value of 100. A timing difference would arise because the revaluation gain would be taxable only if and when the asset was sold. This timing difference would not in itself give rise to an obligation to pay more tax in future. But the valuation adjustment argument would be that deferred tax should be provided for to reflect the fact that the economic value to the business was not the market value of 100. Rather, in principle, it was the market value of 100 less the present value of the tax that would be payable on selling the asset for 100.

47   The valuation adjustment argument would apply even when the purpose of revaluing the asset to market value was to recognise its replacement cost rather than its net realisable value. It would be argued that the market values were established in the expectation that the full market value would be tax-deductible on sale (or earlier, if capital allowances were available). Unadjusted market value would not reflect that there would be more tax payable on the sale of the existing asset than there would be on the sale of an asset purchased at the market value. The true economic replacement cost of the existing asset would be measured by valuing the asset at the market value of an 'equivalent' asset and then adjusting it by providing for deferred tax.

48   The present value of the additional tax paid on the sale of a revalued asset would depend on when that tax was paid. Hence, deferred tax provided for on revaluation gains would in theory be discounted. Where an asset was not eligible for capital allowances and there was an assumption that it would be retained in the business (or replaced only when rollover relief could be claimed), the difference in the future tax deductions would materialise only very far into the future or perhaps not at all. In such cases it could be argued that the present value of the tax on the revaluation gain was negligible. A valuation adjustment approach could be simplified to require deferred tax to be provided for on revaluation gains only if it were expected that the timing difference would reverse without rollover relief being obtained.

49   In theory, deferred tax provided for as a valuation adjustment rather than as a liability might most appropriately be reflected by netting the tax provision against the value of the asset. However, it is generally accepted, both in the UK and internationally, that an entity's results and position are more clearly communicated if tax effects are shown separately from the items or transactions to which they relate.

Reasons for adopting the incremental liability approach

50   A minority of Board members favoured the valuation adjustment approach. They regarded it as important that assets recognised at their fair values – and in particular financial assets and assets adjusted to their fair values on acquisition – should be recognised at their true economic fair values, taking into consideration all future cash flows, including tax. Unless a valuation adjustment approach was adopted, assets could be valued at more than their economic (ie post-tax) recoverable

amounts. The Board members also noted that an FRS based on a valuation adjustment approach would more closely align UK accounting requirements with those of IAS 12 (revised).

However, most Board members favoured the incremental liability approach. They **51** took the view that:

- the incremental liability approach was more clearly consistent with FRS 12 'Provisions, Contingent Liabilities and Contingent Assets' than one that recognised deferred tax liabilities that were not obligations.
- the valuation adjustment approach relied on theoretical models of the way in which asset values were determined. The fact that these models did not always hold in practice, combined with the difficulty in estimating the amount and timing of tax that was likely to be paid on the possible future sale of an asset, meant that the deferred tax provisions could be somewhat artificial. The tax position would be communicated much more clearly to users by recognising the amounts payable only when the entity became obliged to pay them.
- the effect of the creation and reversal of provisions under a valuation adjustment approach could be simply to standardise the tax charge rather than reflect the accrual and eventual payment of tax. For example, if a revalued asset was recovered through use in the business (ie depreciation) rather than sale, any deferred tax provision recognised on revaluing the asset would simply be reversed over the life of the asset, without any tax having become payable.

Accepting the views of the majority, the Board chose to base the FRS's requirements **52** on the incremental liability approach. The way in which the detailed requirements fit into that approach is explained below.

Detailed aspects of the recognition requirements

Accelerated capital allowances

Capital allowances in excess of depreciation (accelerated capital allowances) give rise **53** to timing differences, the reversals of which occur automatically in future and cannot be avoided by the reporting entity.

It was suggested to the Board that the receipt of an accelerated capital allowance for **54** the purchase of an asset did not give rise to a deferred tax obligation since it would not in itself increase a future tax assessment. The entity had no more than a contingent liability to repay the allowance – it would be repayable only if the fixed asset was sold. Any future sale was a future event that should not be taken into account at the balance sheet date.

However, the Board took the view that, in commercial and economic terms, capital **55** allowances were given for the loss arising from the consumption of the service potential of an asset – not simply for the purchase of the asset. An entity that had received capital allowances in excess of depreciation had received allowances in advance, ie on service potential that would be consumed in future. As with any consideration received in advance of performance, the entity had an obligation either to perform or to repay the consideration. This obligation remained until, as a result of future events, the service potential was consumed.

Hence, the Board concluded that under an incremental liability approach, deferred **56** tax should be provided for on accelerated capital allowances.

Industrial buildings allowances

57   In general, allowances for capital expenditure are repayable to the tax authorities if the assets purchased are sold for more than their tax written-down value. However, this is not always the case. Industrial buildings allowances (IBAs),* for example, are repayable only if the building is sold within a certain time – 25 years of purchase.

58   FRED 19 did not specify whether and for how long deferred tax should be provided for on accelerated IBAs (or similar non-repayable allowances). Several respondents asked for clarification.

59   Some argued that, from the outset, the deferred tax was not a liability (or at least was no more than a contingent liability) because, like the deferred tax on a revaluation gain, it would be repayable only upon an uncertain future event within management's control, ie sale within 25 years. It should therefore be provided for only if and when there was an intention or commitment to sell.

60   However, the Board noted that in this respect an IBA was no different from other capital allowances – all were repayable only if the asset was sold rather than being consumed within the business. The argument (in paragraph 55 above) for requiring accelerated capital allowances to be recognised as liabilities was that, until the conditions for retaining the allowances had been met (ie through consumption of the asset), they remained unearned – a liability had not been discharged – and hence should be provided for. The deferred tax on an accelerated capital allowance was different from that on a revaluation gain because it arose from a past event. Applying the same argument to accelerated IBAs led the Board to conclude that the deferred tax thereon should be provided for until the condition for retaining the IBAs (ie the expiry of 25 years) had been met. Thus, the FRS clarifies that accelerated capital allowances of all types should be recognised as liabilities until the conditions for retaining them (ie the expiry of 25 years) have been met.

61   One respondent further noted that if industrial buildings were not being depreciated (for example, if they were investment properties), and there was no intention of selling them within 25 years, the allowances could be regarded as giving rise to permanent differences. FRED 19 had proposed that deferred tax should not be provided for on permanent differences. The Board considered this suggestion but concluded that the obligation to repay an IBA remained until all conditions for retaining it had been met, irrespective of whether the asset was being depreciated. The requirement to provide for accelerated IBAs until the conditions for retaining them have been met therefore applies to depreciating and non-depreciating assets.

Infrastructure assets

62   The FRS requires deferred tax to be provided for on all accelerated capital allowances, including those arising on infrastructure assets that, in accordance with the requirements of FRS 15 'Tangible Fixed Assets', are accounted for using renewals accounting. As clarified in the definitions section of the FRS, capital allowances obtained for such assets can give rise to timing differences in the same way as capital allowances obtained for any other assets.

IBAs are given for expenditure on some buildings – factories, warehouses and hotels, and any commercial buildings in enterprise zones. Buildings in enterprise zones can qualify for 100 per cent first year allowances. Other industrial buildings receive IBAs at a rate of 4 per cent per year.

Assets continuously revalued to fair value with changes recognised in profit and loss account

In line with the incremental liability approach on which it was based, FRED 19 **63** proposed that deferred tax should not be recognised on revaluation gains. The rationale was that the rise in value of an asset was not an event that in itself obliged an entity to pay more tax in future.

A significant number of respondents, whilst accepting this approach for most types **64** of revalued asset, regarded it as inappropriate where assets were 'marked to market', ie continuously revalued to fair value with changes being recognised in the profit and loss account. Such assets could include the investments of financial institutions and some commodities.

The respondents took the view that when assets were marked to market in this way, **65** the gains and losses were recognised in the profit and loss account because, although not necessarily realised, they were readily realisable. To give a true and fair view of the entity's performance, any tax that would be payable on realising the gains should also be recognised. The respondents suggested that the arguments that deferred tax provisions on revaluation gains were somewhat artificial (paragraph 51 above) did not hold in these circumstances.

The Board accepted this view and amended the FRS to require deferred tax to be **66** provided for if it arose when assets were marked to market with gains and losses being recognised in the profit and loss account.

Current assets (other than those that are marked to market)

It is rare for current assets (other than those, such as commodities, that are marked **67** to market with gains and losses being recognised in the profit and loss account) to be held at fair value. But they are more frequently adjusted to their fair values on the acquisition of a business.

The FRS permits deferred tax to be recognised on the adjustment only if there is a **68** binding agreement for the sale of the asset at the acquisition date and the gains and losses on selling the asset have also been recognised in the fair value exercise.

It was suggested to the Board that an entity always had a constructive or commercial **69** commitment to sell stock, since that was the whole purpose of purchasing it in the first place. But the Board took the view that, whilst there could be an expectation that stock would be sold, the expectation alone did not give rise to a binding commitment.

It acknowledged that a binding agreement to sell stock could exist if goods were **70** being manufactured under the terms of a binding contract. In such circumstances, one of the obligations associated with the contract was the obligation to pay tax on the profits made. But if the contract was being accounted for as an executory contract (ie if neither the rights nor the obligations had yet been recognised because both parties had yet to perform), it would be inappropriate to recognise the tax obligation alone.

Rollover relief

As an extension of the requirement not to provide for deferred tax on revaluation **71** gains and losses, the FRS does not require deferred tax to be provided for on taxable gains that have been deferred via 'rollover relief'.

72   Rollover relief can be claimed in a number of tax jurisdictions when the proceeds of sale of 'qualifying' assets (such as land and buildings) are reinvested in other qualifying assets within a specified period. The taxable gain is not charged to tax immediately but is instead rolled over into the replacement assets, becoming chargeable only if and when the replacement assets are sold.

73   The Board took the view that, where such rollover relief had been obtained, the entity retained the discretion to avoid paying tax on the chargeable gain. That tax would be paid only if and when the replacement assets were sold. Hence, where an entity had sold or agreed to sell an asset and had recognised the gain on sale, it still did not have a liability for any tax if it had already met the conditions for rolling the gain over into a replacement asset. (This would not be the case if the terms of the relief were different and merely postponed the payment of tax for a specified period.)

74   It was suggested that the justification for not providing for rolled-over gains (ie that the tax was not a liability because it would be deferred by the purchase of new assets) should also justify providing on a partial basis for accelerated capital allowances. However, the arguments are different. When a gain is rolled over into a replacement asset, it does not enter a tax computation and will not do so unless and until a decision is made to sell the replacement asset. It might not make future tax charges higher than they would otherwise have been. The tax authorities are in effect recognising successive assets as if they were a single asset. So, even using full provision arguments, the deferred tax should not be provided for. In contrast, an accelerated capital allowance will reverse automatically over the life of the asset, entering into a future tax computation and making a future tax assessment higher than it would otherwise have been, whether or not more assets are purchased. The purchase of another asset does not prevent the original accelerated capital allowance from reversing, it merely originates a new one that offsets it.

75   Tax legislation may allow rollover relief to be claimed even if the proceeds of sale are not reinvested immediately, but are reinvested within a specified period. In such circumstances, an entity could have sold or entered into a binding agreement to sell one asset by the balance sheet date without being certain that it would be able to roll the gain over into a replacement asset. The Board took the view that in such circumstances the deferred tax represented a contingent liability as defined in FRS 12 'Provisions, Contingent Liabilities and Contingent Assets'. Consistently with the recognition requirements in FRS 12, the FRS requires that for as long as it appears more likely than not that the entity will be able to roll over the gain, the deferred tax on that gain should not be provided for.

RECOVERABILITY OF DEFERRED TAX ASSETS

General recognition requirement – transfer of economic benefits

76   Assets or liabilities are recognised only if there is sufficient evidence that the rights or obligations that give rise to them will result in the transfer of economic benefits in future.* In respect of deferred tax assets and liabilities, there would be such a transfer of economic benefits only if the future reversal of the timing difference had an incremental effect on a future tax payment or receipt. This would be the case only if the reporting entity generated taxable profits in future (or tax losses that could be relieved against past taxable profits). If, instead, it were to generate unrelieved tax losses, the reversal of the timing differences would not result in any cash flows: it would simply alter the amount of losses for which no relief had been received. Deferred tax assets and liabilities should therefore be recognised only when there is

*Chapter 4, Statement of Principles for Financial Reporting.

evidence that the entity will make sufficient taxable profits in future for the reversal of the timing difference to affect the amount of tax actually paid.

Deferred tax liabilities

In theory, therefore, there could be circumstances in which entities need not recog-   77
nise deferred tax liabilities. However, the FRS requires all deferred tax liabilities to be recognised, without referring at all to future tax losses. The Board's rationale for this proposal was that:

- it was very unlikely that there would be persuasive evidence on which to base a prudent and reliable prediction that an entity that was a going concern was more likely than not to make tax losses in future that would remain unrelieved; and
- a requirement to make a judgement on this matter would make the FRS more difficult to understand and apply.

Deferred tax assets

With deferred tax assets, the situation is slightly different. To recover a deferred tax   78
asset, an entity would have to do more than simply *not make losses* in future: it would have to *make sufficient profits* that would be charged to tax if it were not for the reversal of the timing difference. Further, the need for prudence would suggest that more evidence of the likelihood of future profits was needed for recognition of a deferred tax asset than for recognition of a deferred tax liability. For these reasons, the FRS permits deferred tax assets to be recognised only when, on the basis of available evidence, it is more likely than not that there will be taxable profits in future against which the deferred tax asset can be offset. The requirements are the same as those of both FAS 109 and IAS 12 (revised).

SSAP 15 permitted deferred tax assets arising from tax losses to be recognised only if   79
the availability of future taxable profits against which the losses could be offset was 'assured beyond reasonable doubt'. The Board agreed that the recognition of tax losses as assets should be restricted, since the very existence of losses provided strong evidence that they would not be recovered. However, in the Board's view, it was more appropriate to restrict the recognition of the losses by emphasising that the 'more likely than not' threshold must be met rather than by setting a recognition threshold that was higher than that set for other deferred tax assets (such as those arising on accruals for retirement benefits).

MEASUREMENT – TAX RATES

The FRS follows IAS 12 (revised) in requiring deferred tax to be measured using tax   80
rates that have been enacted or substantively enacted by the balance sheet date.

Although it could be argued that the rates used should instead be the best estimates   81
of the future rates that would apply, the Board concluded that:

- given that future tax rates are influenced by political and economic considera-tions that are very difficult to predict, the best estimates of future tax rates would normally be the most recently enacted or substantively enacted rates
- where there was evidence of possible future changes (for example, when propo-sals had been announced for consultation), it was generally difficult for individuals to assess the likelihood that the changes would be enacted. Different views could be taken and different rates used by different entities. Given that these entities would actually be paying tax at the same rate, such inconsistencies would be unhelpful.

82   Guidance has been given on the meaning of 'substantively enacted' in the UK and the Republic of Ireland to help ensure that the requirement is interpreted consistently. In developing this guidance the Board considered, but rejected, suggestions that a Budget announcement should be viewed as substantive enactment in the UK providing that the changes were very likely to be enacted. The Board took the view that 'substantive enactment' meant that the process of enactment was substantively complete. Whilst in some circumstances it could be very likely that a change proposed at the first reading of a Finance Bill would be enacted, the process of enactment was not at that stage substantively complete. In particular, the Bill still had to pass through committee and two further readings in the House of Commons. Similarly, in the Republic of Ireland, the process of enactment would not be substantively complete until the Bill had been passed by the Dail.

83   The FRS requires that, where tax rates are graduated – ie where different tax rates apply to different bands of taxable profit – entities should use the *average* rate expected to be paid in the year in which the timing difference reverses. IAS 12 (revised) has the same requirement. The Board was aware that arguments could be made for using instead the rate that applied to the bottom, or the top, band of taxable profits. However, it believed that there were insufficient grounds for departing from international practice in this respect, in particular because most UK companies were unaffected by graduated tax rates.

MEASUREMENT – DISCOUNTING

Overview

84   FRED 19 tentatively proposed that deferred tax balances should be discounted where the effect of discounting was material and asked for respondents' views on the proposal. In the light of the responses received, the Board decided that the FRS should neither prohibit nor require discounting but should allow entities a choice of accounting policy.

Arguments for and against discounting

Conceptual validity

85   A key feature of the UK tax system is that there can be a significant delay between the recognition of certain items in the accounts and their recognition in a tax computation and vice versa. The delay suggests that there would be a case for discounting deferred tax assets and liabilities where the effect was material. However, views differ on whether there is a conceptual justification for discounting certain deferred tax balances, such as those arising from accelerated capital allowances.

86   The purpose of discounting is to measure future cash flows at their present value. It is therefore valid to discount deferred tax balances only if they can be viewed as representing future cash flows that are not already measured at their present value.

87   There are some types of timing differences that clearly represent future tax cash flows. Where, for example, an accrual is made for expenses that are to be paid far into the future and tax relief will be received only when the expenses are paid, the tax relief represents a future tax cash flow that should be discounted to its present value. In practice, however, it is rarely necessary to perform separate discounting calculations for this type of deferred tax, since long-term accruals, such as those for retirement benefits, are usually themselves measured on a discounted basis. Thus the

timing differences already incorporate discounting and it is not appropriate to discount the resulting deferred tax as well.

Separate discounting would, however, be required if the timing difference giving rise **88** to a future tax cash flow were not discounted. An example of such a timing difference is that provided for (in the limited circumstances set out in paragraph 12 of the FRS) on revaluation gains. Discounting of deferred tax on revaluation gains is discussed in paragraphs 47 and 48 above.

More controversial is the issue of whether it is valid to discount deferred tax when **89** tax cash flows have already occurred. This situation arises most commonly when capital allowances have been received before an asset has been depreciated.

Undoubtedly, an entity that receives a capital allowance as soon as it purchases an **90** asset is better off than one that receives the same allowance as it depreciates the asset. *Without discounting*, this benefit materialises in the form of higher interest income over the period in which the asset is being depreciated. *With discounting*, the benefit of the additional interest income is pulled forward and recognised immediately.

The question is whether the benefit should be recognised immediately by discounting. **91** One view – typically held by those who regard deferred tax as an adjustment to the values at which other assets are recognised rather than as a liability in its own right – is that it should not. Those holding this view argue that:

- the deferred tax provision represents a cash inflow that has already been received. It is therefore already stated at its present value. There are no future tax cash flows to occur.
- the carrying value of an asset reflects the present value of the future economic benefits that it will generate. At the outset, one of these future benefits is the present value of the capital allowance that will be received (including the value of receiving it early in the life of the asset). Once the capital allowance has been received, the remaining future benefits are reduced by that amount. The reduction in the value of the asset is recognised by providing for deferred tax. If the amount provided for is discounted, the entity is recognising a 'gain' that has not necessarily been earned.
- the cash outflow arising from the purchase of a fixed asset is recognised as depreciation evenly over the life of the asset. If the cash inflow arising from a capital allowance is seen as an adjustment to the value of the asset, it too should be recognised evenly over the life of the asset.

However, a different view can be taken under the incremental liability approach **92** required by the FRS. Under this approach, an accelerated capital allowance is viewed as a liability that will be repaid in the form of higher tax assessments in the future. Although one tax cash flow has already occurred, creating the timing difference, it can be argued that there will be a second tax cash flow when, on reversal of the timing difference, a future tax payment is higher than it would otherwise have been. And, where the higher future tax payment will occur some distance into the future, it is valid to discount it to reflect the fact that, at the balance sheet date, it represents a lower obligation than a liability that is payable immediately.

Another way of viewing the accelerated capital allowance is as an interest-free loan **93** from the tax authorities. And just as it can be argued that an interest-free loan is a smaller obligation than a loan paying a commercial rate of interest, so it can be argued that a deferred tax liability should be discounted.

The different conclusions on discounting that are reached depending on whether **94** deferred tax is rationalised as a liability or a valuation adjustment can be reconciled. When a capital allowance is received, the cash-generating capability of the fixed asset (and hence its value in *absolute* terms) is reduced by the amount of that past tax cash flow. A valuation adjustment approach seeks to recognise that absolute reduction in future cash flows. However, if deferred tax is rationalised as a liability, all that is being provided for is the additional tax cash flows that the entity will pay *relative* to the tax that it would have paid had it not received capital allowances until they were earned. The liability is being measured without reference to changes in the values of fixed assets.

Cost/benefit considerations

95   One of the messages that emerged strongly from the responses to FRED 19 was that for most industries the benefits of discounting were not perceived to outweigh the costs.

96   Significant time and effort may be required to collate the information required to discount accelerated capital allowances and perform the discounting calculations, especially for large organisations with operations spread across a wide range of tax jurisdictions. Some respondents argued that they would have to collate substantial amounts of information even if only to establish that the impact of discounting was not material in that period.

97   There were also reservations expressed about the benefit of discounting to users of financial statements. Users who responded to the FRED were divided in their opinions. And preparers were concerned that the impact on the profit and loss account would be difficult to understand: movements caused, for example, by changes in discount rate from one period to the next could be difficult to explain to users.

98   Support for discounting was strong only from companies for which the effect of discounting would be fundamental.

International practice

99   Both IAS 12 (revised) and the US accounting standard FAS 109 prohibit discounting of deferred tax balances. IASC took the view that the scheduling of the reversal of timing differences was often impracticable or highly complex and hence that it should not be made mandatory. It rejected the possibility of permitting discounting without requiring it, because the option would make the results of different entities less comparable. It is, however, now reconsidering, as part of a general project on discounting, whether deferred tax should be discounted. *Reasons for making discounting optional*

100   One Board member opposed discounting, primarily on the grounds that it impeded international harmonisation. The Board member also took the view (explained in paragraphs 89-91 above) that discounting was conceptually wrong for timing differences – such as accelerated capital allowances – where tax cash flows had already occurred.

101   The rest of the Board supported discounting in principle, regarding it as consistent with the incremental liability approach on which the FRS requirements were based and as a means of providing more relevant information to users. However, taking into consideration the practical arguments made by respondents, the Board concluded that:

(a)   in many circumstances, the costs were widely perceived to outweigh the benefits. Discounting should not be required in those circumstances.

(b)   this was especially the case given that discounting was not yet well established in the context of deferred tax (either in theory or in practice). A methodology was being introduced in the UK before an international consensus had been reached.

(c)   providing that discounting was applied consistently from one period to the next, and the impact of discounting on the financial statements was highlighted clearly, there would not be a serious loss of comparability if not all entities discounted deferred tax.

The Board considered first whether it could achieve its aims by emphasising that discounting was required only where the effect was genuinely material to the overall results and performance portrayed in the financial statements. It considered whether 'indicators of materiality' could be prescribed to make it easier for companies to determine that the effect would not be material.   **102**

However, it took the view that such indicators would be difficult to define other than in vague (and hence not very useful) terms. Further, basing decisions on discounting purely on materiality would not entirely eliminate the practical problems. First, there would remain some companies for which the effect of discounting deferred tax would border on being material. Such companies would certainly have to perform discounting calculations and would probably take the view that they should report discounted amounts, even though they would probably regard the costs as exceeding the benefits.   **103**

The second problem would be that by concentrating only on materiality, it would be difficult to emphasise the importance of consistency. For some companies, the effect of discounting could be material in some periods but not others. In such circumstances, it could be argued that it was more important that the company reported consistently from one period to the next (either discounting or not) than that it discounted only when the effect was material.   **104**

For these reasons, the Board concluded that the FRS should not require all entities to discount deferred tax. Instead, it should allow them a choice of accounting policy that they would then apply consistently. In taking this approach, the FRS has followed a precedent set in FRS 15 'Tangible Fixed Assets', which allows entities a choice of policies with regard to capitalisation of finance costs attributable to the construction of a fixed asset. The factors set out in paragraph 101 above are very similar to those that led the Board to permit a choice of policies in FRS 15.   **105**

Detailed requirements for discounting

The 'full reversal' approach to scheduling reversals

To discount a deferred tax liability or asset, it is necessary to forecast the timing of the future cash flows that the deferred tax represents. Two alternative approaches were considered by the Board: **106**

- *the full reversal basis*, whereby the future cash flows are treated as occurring when the timing differences constituting the deferred tax balance at the year-end are expected to reverse
- *the net reversal basis*, whereby the future cash flows are treated as occurring when the timing differences as a whole (ie after taking account of new timing differences to replace those that reverse) are expected to reduce.

The rationale for the full reversal basis is the same as that for full provision accounting: every individual timing difference reverses and, when it does so, has an   **107** incremental or decremental effect on future cash flows. Similarly, the rationale for the net reversal basis is the same as that for the partial provision method: the deferred tax is viewed as a homogeneous whole and is regarded as giving rise to a future cash flow only to the extent that reversing timing differences will not be replaced by new originating timing differences.

108   The Board took the view that the net reversal basis for discounting could be justified only within a partial provision framework. Within a full provision framework, it would be inconsistent not to treat the cash flows as occurring when the individual timing differences reversed. The FRS therefore requires that where deferred tax is discounted, it is to be discounted on a full reversal basis.

109   The FRS does, however, require the scheduling of reversals to take account of the remaining capital allowances to be received on the existing assets on which the timing differences have arisen. It was suggested that the remaining capital allowances should be ignored on the grounds that they were future events that created further timing differences (rather than delaying the reversal of the existing timing differences). The existing timing differences would be viewed as reversing as soon as further depreciation occurred. However, the Board did not view the remaining capital allowances as arising from future events. Rather it regarded the allowances, like depreciation, as one of the expected consequences of a past event (the purchase of an asset) that had to be taken into account in measuring the tax liability arising from that event.

Future losses

110   Future tax losses could affect the time at which deferred tax liabilities and assets were paid or recovered. Suppose, for example, that an accelerated capital allowance was expected to reverse over the next five years but that the entity expected to generate in that period tax losses that would themselves be relieved only in later periods. The deferred tax liability would not have an incremental effect on the amount of tax actually paid until the future losses were relieved. It could therefore be argued that the liability should be discounted further to reflect the expected delay.

111   However, in addition to possible conceptual reasons, the Board concluded that there were practical reasons why possible future losses should not be taken into account when assessing the period over which deferred tax assets and liabilities were discounted:

(a)   whilst little judgement was required to schedule the reversal of timing differences, far more judgement would be required if predictions regarding future tax losses had to be made. It would be difficult to forecast patterns of future losses reliably, especially those expected to arise in later years (ie those for which discounting would be most relevant). The discounting calculations could be more difficult to perform and the discounted amount could be significantly less reliable.

(b)   whilst there was a theoretical risk that deferred tax assets would be overstated if future losses were not taken into consideration when estimating the timing of the recovery of the assets, this risk was unlikely to give rise to problems in practice. The overstatement would arise only if future losses were expected to delay significantly the recovery of a deferred tax asset. In such circumstances, it is unlikely that there would be sufficient evidence to support the recognition of the deferred tax asset at all. Guidance to this effect is included in the FRS.

For these reasons, the Board concluded that future losses should not be taken into consideration when determining the period over which deferred tax assets and liabilities should be discounted. **112**

Discount rate

General conclusions on discounting were set out in the Board's Working Paper 'Discounting in Financial Reporting', published in April 1997. The requirements of the FRS are consistent with the conclusions reached in that Paper. **113**

Chapter 4 of the Working Paper concluded that the discount rate for a liability should reflect only the characteristics of the liability. Hence the discount rate used to measure a liability should not be based on the entity's cost of capital. Rather it should aim to measure the least cost of settling the liability, which would be either: **114**

(a) the amount that a third party would have to be paid to take over the liability; or
(b) the amount that would have to be invested in assets that would grow to match the amount due and settle the liability at the due date.

In practice, it is unlikely that there would be a third party willing to take over a deferred tax liability. Hence it is necessary to determine the amount that the entity would have to invest at the balance sheet date in assets that would grow to match the liability. **115**

When deferred tax liabilities are discounted on a full reversal basis, the future cash flows that they represent are relatively certain. In most circumstances, they are fixed at the amount of the timing difference multiplied by the rate of tax paid by the entity. The most appropriate 'matching assets' are therefore those that provide a fixed income that is taxable at the same rate. This is most likely to be government bonds of a maturity date and in a currency similar to those of the deferred tax liability. **116**

The Working Paper suggested that the rate at which assets should be discounted was the rate that the market would expect on an equally risky investment. The rate would be reduced to the extent that any of the risk had been taken into account by lowering the estimates of future cash flows. The FRS requires uncertainty about the recoverability of a deferred tax asset to be taken into account in determining the extent to which the undiscounted asset is recognised. This uncertainty should not therefore be reflected in the discount rate. In other respects, the future cash flows associated with a deferred tax asset are relatively certain. For this reason the return that would be expected by the market is approximately equal to the effective return on a government bond. **117**

The FRS therefore requires both deferred tax assets and liabilities to be discounted at the effective rates of return on government bonds of maturity dates and in currencies similar to those of the deferred tax. These rates are not only consistent with the conclusions reached in the Working Paper on discounting, they also have the advantage of being simpler to determine and less subjective than other possible rates. **118**

The FRS requires the government bond rates used to discount deferred tax to be measured on a post-tax basis, ie after taking account of the tax that the reporting entity would pay on income generated by the bonds. This is because the cost of the reversing timing differences is not tax-deductible. The whole reversing timing difference would therefore have to be funded from the post-tax yield on the government bond. **119**

Presentation of movement in discount

120   When deferred tax is discounted, there is a charge or credit to the profit and loss account each period that represents the movement on the discount. The net movement has three components:

(a)   changes in the underlying timing differences and tax rates;

(b)   an 'unwinding' of the discount on timing differences that had existed at the start of the period (because these differences are now one year closer to reversal); and

(c)   changes in the rates at which the opening deferred tax balance is discounted.

121   The Board takes the view that, in principle, an expense should be measured in the profit and loss account at the present value (when the expense is recognised) of the amount to be paid. Thus, an operating expense that was not payable immediately would be recognised in the profit and loss account at a discounted amount. The additional charge attributable to the unwinding of the discount as the payment date approached would not be presented as an additional operating expense. Rather, because it arose as a consequence of not settling the liability immediately, it would be presented as a financing item, ie next to interest payable and receivable. An argument in support of such an approach is that it avoids the amounts reported as operating profit being distorted by funding decisions: an operating expense that was not payable immediately would be recorded at the same amount whether or not it had been funded. The Board believes that such an approach, which it regards as correct in principle, should be required when it is practicable and results in a presentation that corresponds to the reader's understanding of the underlying economic nature of the transaction.

122   However, even though the unwinding of the discount on a deferred tax liability (or asset) can be regarded in principle as a financing item, the FRS does not require it to be shown as part of the financing section in the profit and loss account. The reason is that profit and loss account formats require all of the tax consequences of pre-tax profits to be shown separately, below the subtotal 'profits on ordinary activities before taxation'. The unwinding of a discount on a deferred tax balance, whether viewed conceptually as part of the tax expense or as a finance item, is not part of profits before tax. Hence, it is shown after the subtotal of profits before tax.

123   For similar reasons the FRS also requires the movement in the discount attributable to a change in the rate at which the opening deferred tax liability or asset has been discounted to be shown as part of the tax charge.

PRESENTATION OF DEFERRED TAX BALANCES

Offset of deferred tax assets and liabilities

124   The Board's Statement of Principles* states that:

'If a right to receive future economic benefits and an obligation to transfer future economic benefits exist and the reporting entity has the ability – which is assured – to insist on net settlement of the balances, the right and obligation together form a single net asset or liability regardless of how the parties intend to settle the balances.'

*Paragraph 4.34, Statement of Principles for Financial Reporting.

If this principle is applied, deferred tax debit and credit balances might be regarded   **125**
as being capable of being offset and presented as a single net asset or liability only if:

(a)   they relate to the same tax authority;
(b)   they arise within the same taxable entities or within different taxable entities
      that are entitled to settle their tax liabilities on a net basis; and
(c)   the timing differences giving rise to a deferred tax asset reverse before or at the
      same time as those giving rise to a deferred tax liability. (If those giving rise to
      the liability reverse first, there will be a requirement to pay tax before any
      entitlement to recover tax.)

However, the requirements in the FRS do not restrict the offsetting of deferred tax   **126**
debit and credit balances to circumstances where the above criteria are met. The
Board took the view that:

(a)   it could be argued that all deferred tax balances of a single taxable entity* with
      a single tax authority were adjustments to future liabilities of that entity (rather
      than assets or liabilities in their own right) and so should be shown as a single
      balance;
(b)   the costs of scheduling the timings of reversals to measure the extent to which
      the balances should be offset would greatly exceed any benefit to users. Indeed,
      the needs of many users would probably best be served by presenting the
      deferred tax in as uncomplicated a manner as possible.

The view that a requirement to take account of the timing of reversals would be   **127**
impracticable has also been taken in IAS 12 (revised). The offset requirements required
by the FRS are therefore very similar to those of IAS 12 (revised). A significant difference is that IAS 12 (revised) adds a criterion based on whether or not it is intended
that current tax balances will be settled on a net basis. The difference reflects differences between the Board's and IASC's general principles regarding offset.

Presentation on the face of the balance sheet

The requirements for separate presentation of deferred tax (at least in the notes to   **128**
the accounts) reflect the Board's view that deferred tax is different from most other
debtors and provisions. In general it does not have a direct relationship with future
cash receipts or payments. Rather than being a payment or receipt in its own right, it
affects other (possibly very distant) future payments, which will also be affected by a
number of other factors.

To identify the deferred tax assets and provisions that should be presented separately   **129**
on the face of the balance sheet, the Board followed the consensus reached in UITF
Abstract 4 in respect of any long- term debtor included within current assets:

      'In most cases, it will be satisfactory to disclose the size ... in the notes to the
      accounts. There will be some instances, however, where the amount is so
      material in the context of the total net current assets that in the absence of
      disclosure ... on the face of the balance sheet readers may misinterpret the
      accounts.'

The FRS does not go as far as IAS 12 (revised), which requires all (material) deferred   **130**
tax balances to be presented separately from other debtors and provisions on the face
of the balance sheet. In the Board's view, such a requirement would add unnecessary

---

*or of entities within a single tax group, where the losses of one entity could be used to reduce the taxable profits
of another.*

detail when deferred tax assets and liabilities did not have a fundamental impact on the company's net asset or net current asset position.

DISCLOSURES

Unrecognised deferred tax

131   The FRS requires disclosure of the amounts of deferred tax not provided for on the unremitted earnings of subsidiaries, associates and joint ventures only to the extent that the earnings are expected to be remitted in the foreseeable future. Unlike IAS 12 (revised), it does not require any quantification of the total timing differences arising from unremitted earnings because the Board was not persuaded that such a disclosure would provide relevant information to users of financial statements. (In most circumstances, the possibility of all of the earnings being remitted is remote, and the tax that would become payable would be subject to a number of uncertainties.)

Other factors affecting future tax charges

132   Companies legislation requires information to be given about special circumstances that have affected the tax charge for the current period and might affect the tax charges of future periods. Users of financial statements frequently told the Board that they particularly valued information that helped them to make more accurate predictions about future tax payments. The FRED therefore specifies the information that an entity should include.

133   The Board decided that the requirement to disclose a reconciliation of the entity's current tax charge for the period to an 'expected' charge – ie the charge that would result if accounting profits were taxed at a standard rate – was especially important. The reconciliation would provide users of financial statements with a complete picture of the factors that had influenced the current tax charge for the period. They could then use other information about the company (for example, the nature of its deferred tax liabilities and its capital investment plans) to arrive at a judgement about the extent to which the reconciling items would recur. The requirement received strong support from those responding to the FRED on behalf of institutional investors.

134   IAS 12 (revised) and FAS 109 also require reconciliations to be disclosed. However, both of those standards require a reconciliation of the total tax charge for the period (ie the total of current and deferred tax) to a standard tax charge. The Board chose to focus the reconciliation on the current tax charge instead because it believed that that was the element of the total tax charge that was of most importance to users. A reconciliation based on the current tax charge was the clearest and most direct way of providing information on the factors that might affect future current tax charges.

135   FAS 109 requires the reconciliation to be given only by listed companies. Other entities need disclose only the nature of significant reconciling items. The Board considered whether it should propose a similar distinction in FRED 19. It concluded that a full reconciliation would be of use to the users of the financial statements of all entities. And, since the information would normally be readily available from tax computations, it ought not to be an onerous requirement.

Other disclosures required by IAS 12 (revised)

IAS 12 (revised) requires entities that have recently made losses to explain (where **136** relevant) why they have recognised deferred tax assets.

It could be argued that this disclosure is not necessary: the recognition of the asset in **137** itself shows that the directors and auditors have satisfied themselves that it is more likely than not that the asset will be recovered.

However, the Board took the view that additional information about the assump- **138** tions underlying the recognition of a deferred tax asset alerted users to the uncertainties surrounding the asset's recoverability and helped them to assess the financial position of the entity. The FRS therefore includes a disclosure requirement identical to that included in IAS 12 (revised).

AMENDMENT TO FRS 7

General changes

FRS 7 'Fair Values in Acquisition Accounting' aims to recognise in a fair value **139** exercise only the identifiable assets and liabilities of the acquired entity that existed at the date of acquisition. It aims to measure them based on their condition at that date, independent of the intentions of the acquirer. However, its requirements regarding deferred tax (ie to measure the extent to which the liabilities would crystallise con- sidering the enlarged group as a whole) were slightly inconsistent with this general aim, since they had to be consistent with the partial provision method of accounting for deferred tax required by SSAP 15.

With the replacement of SSAP 15 it is no longer necessary to consider the enlarged **140** group when measuring deferred tax liabilities. The amendment to FRS 7 implemented by the FRS clarifies that this is the case. And it ensures that deferred tax recognised in a fair value exercise is recognised on the same basis as it is recognised in the group financial statements thereafter.

Previously unrecognised deferred tax assets

The amendment to FRS 7 adds guidance on how to treat deferred tax assets – typi- **141** cally, unrelieved tax losses – that were not regarded as recoverable before the acquisition but, as a result of the acquisition, become sufficiently recoverable within the enlarged group to be recognised as assets after the acquisition. FRS 7 previously gave no guidance on whether such assets should be recognised in the fair value exercise or as a credit in the post-acquisition profit and loss account. The Board received anecdotal evidence that practice varied.

The Board concluded that, if the losses had arisen in the acquiring group, it would be **142** inconsistent with the principles of FRS 7 to require them to be recognised as part of the fair value exercise. They could not be regarded as assets of the acquired entity. Rather, as a result of the acquisition, the acquiring group was expected to be more profitable in future. The FRS 7 therefore requires the benefit to be recognised as a credit in the post-acquisition profit and loss account.

It was less clear how any previously unrecognised losses in the acquired entity should **143** be recognised. One view was that the recoverability of the acquired entity's deferred tax asset stemmed from the future actions of the acquiring group. In its condition before acquisition, the asset had not been recoverable. Hence it was argued that it would be inconsistent with the principles underlying FRS 7 to recognise an asset as part of the fair value exercise. This was the view taken in FRED 19, which proposed that the losses should not be recognised as assets in the fair value exercise.

144   However, another view was that deferred tax losses (unlike, say, provisions for future reorganisations) were identifiable contingent assets of the acquired entity that had existed before the acquisition. Especially if a large proportion of the purchase price related to the losses, a requirement not to reflect them as an asset (but to recognise a larger goodwill balance instead) seemed not to reflect the economics of the purchase.

145   Those taking this view noted that paragraph 37 of FRS 7 specifically addressed such contingent assets:

> 'Certain contingent assets and liabilities that crystallise as a result of the acquisition would also be recognised, provided that the underlying contingency was in existence before the acquisition. An example is where the acquired entity has previously entered into a contract that contains a clause under which the obligations are triggered in the event of a change of ownership.'

146   After consideration of the arguments, the Board decided that it would be consistent with the treatment of other contingent assets to recognise the recoverable tax losses of an acquired entity in the fair value exercise. The requirements proposed in FRED 19 have therefore been amended in the FRS.

CHANGES TO REQUIREMENTS PROPOSED IN FRED 19

Change	Paragraph reference: FRS (Requirement)	This Appendix (Explanation)
1 New requirement clarifying that deferred tax should be provided for on capital allowances until all conditions for retaining them have been met. Applies in practice to industrial buildings allowances.	9	57–61
2 New exception to general requirement that deferred tax should not be recognised on revaluation gains and losses. Exception requires deferred tax to be recognised on timing differences arising when an asset or liability is continuously revalued to its fair value with revaluation gains and losses being recognised in the profit and loss account.	12	63–66
3 Discounting made optional (rather than mandatory as had been proposed).	42	100–105
4 Removal of requirement to present as finance costs the movement in deferred tax balances in the year resulting from unwinding of discounts and changes in discount rates. These are now required to be shown as part of the deferred tax charge.	59	120–123
5 Amendment of proposal regarding recognition of deferred tax assets on the acquisition of a business. The FRS requires deferred tax assets of the acquired entity to be included in the fair value exercise, even if they had not been recognised before the acquisition. The FRED had proposed that they should be recognised as credits to post-acquisition profits.	71	141–146

Financial Reporting Standard 20 embodies IFRS 2 'Share-based Payment' and some amendments to that standard adopted for entities subject to UK accounting standards.

The Statement of Standard Accounting Practice in FRS 20 is set out in paragraphs 1-60 and Appendices A-C. All the paragraphs have equal authority. Paragraphs in bold type state the main principles. Terms defined in Appendix A are in italics the first time they appear.

Accompanying the Statement of Standard Accounting Practice is the basis for the conclusions reached in the Statement and some implementation guidance, neither of which forms part of the Statement.

The Statement of Standard Accounting Practice should be read in the context of its objective as stated in paragraph 1, the Basis for Conclusions set out in paragraphs BC1-BC333, and the Accounting Standards Board's 'Foreword to Accounting Standards' and 'Statement of Principles for Financial Reporting'.

FRS 20
(IFRS 2) Share-based payment

(Issued April 2004)

Contents

Appendices

A   Defined terms
B   Application guidance
C   Amendments to other standards and UITF Abstracts

Preface by the Accounting Standards Board

This Financial Reporting Standard (FRS) has the effect of implementing the   **a**
International Accounting Standards Board's (IASB's) International Financial
Reporting Standard (IFRS) 2 *Share-based Payment* in the UK and the Republic of
Ireland for entities not preparing their financial statements in accordance with
international accounting standards adopted pursuant to the Regulation of the
European Parliament and of the Council on the Application of International
Accounting Standards.

IFRS 2 sets out requirements on the accounting treatment of share-based payment   **b**
transactions. It applies to all entities and to all share-based payment transactions,
and it comes into effect for accounting periods beginning on or after 1 January 2005.
The requirements, scope and effective date of FRS 20 are identical to IFRS 2 with
two exceptions:

- entities applying the FRSSE will be exempt from the FRS, and
- for unlisted entities that are not applying the FRSSE, the FRS will come into
  effect for accounting periods beginning on or after 1 January 2006, rather than
  2005.

For this purpose an unlisted entity is an entity that has neither shares nor debt
admitted to trading on a regulated market in the EU.

The text of IFRS 2 contains various references to other IFRSs. In FRS 20 those   **c**
references have been amended where necessary to enable the Standard to be applied
in a UK context. The Accounting Standards Board believes that those amendments
do not change the requirements of IFRS 2 in any way.

Appendix C of IFRS 2 contains amendments that the IASB has made to existing   **d**
IFRS in the light of the main requirements in IFRS 2. In FRS 20 this material has
been amended and added to so that the FRS can be applied in a UK context. In
particular, from the relevant effective date of the Standard paragraphs C9 and C10
withdraw UITF Abstract 17 *Employee share schemes* and UITF Abstract 30 *Date of
award to employees of shares or rights to shares* and amend UITF Abstract 38
Accounting for ESOP trusts.

In all other respects the FRS is identical to IFRS 2.   **e**

Introduction

REASONS FOR ISSUING THE IFRS*

IN1   Entities often grant shares or share options to employees or other parties. Share plans and share option plans are a common feature of employee remuneration, for directors, senior executives and many other employees. Some entities issue shares or share options to pay suppliers, such as suppliers of professional services.

IN2   Until this IFRS was issued, there was no IFRS covering the recognition and measurement of these transactions. Concerns were raised about this gap in IFRSs, given the increasing prevalence of share-based payment transactions in many countries.

MAIN FEATURES OF THE IFRS

IN3   The IFRS requires an entity to recognise share-based payment transactions in its financial statements, including transactions with employees or other parties to be settled in cash, other assets, or equity instruments of the entity. There are no exceptions to the IFRS, other than for transactions to which other Standards apply.

IN4   The IFRS sets out measurement principles and specific requirements for three types of share-based payment transactions:

   (a)   equity-settled share-based payment transactions, in which the entity receives goods or services as consideration for equity instruments of the entity (including shares or share options);
   (b)   cash-settled share-based payment transactions, in which the entity acquires goods or services by incurring liabilities to the supplier of those goods or services for amounts that are based on the price (or value) of the entity's shares or other equity instruments of the entity; and
   (c)   transactions in which the entity receives or acquires goods or services and the terms of the arrangement provide either the entity or the supplier of those goods or services with a choice of whether the entity settles the transaction in cash or by issuing equity instruments.

IN5   For equity-settled share-based payment transactions, the IFRS requires an entity to measure the goods or services received, and the corresponding increase in equity, directly, at the fair value of the goods or services received, unless that fair value cannot be estimated reliably. If the entity cannot estimate reliably the fair value of the goods or services received, the entity is required to measure their value, and the corresponding increase in equity, indirectly, by reference to the fair value of the equity instruments granted. Furthermore:

   (a)   for transactions with employees and others providing similar services, the entity is required to measure the fair value of the equity instruments granted, because it is typically not possible to estimate reliably the fair value of employee services received. The fair value of the equity instruments granted is measured at grant date.
   (b)   for transactions with parties other than employees (and those providing similar services), there is a rebuttable presumption that the fair value of the goods or services received can be estimated reliably. That fair value is measured at the

---

*ASB footnote: Although references to specific IFRSs have been amended so that the standard can be applied in a UK context, the standard's references to itself as an 'IFRS' and its references to other extant accounting standards as 'other IFRS' have been left unchanged. They should though be taken to be references to this FRS and to extant standards issued in the UK and the Republic of Ireland respectively.

date the entity obtains the goods or the counterparty renders service. In rare cases, if the presumption is rebutted, the transaction is measured by reference to the fair value of the equity instruments granted, measured at the date the entity obtains the goods or the counterparty renders service.

(c)   for goods or services measured by reference to the fair value of the equity instruments granted, the IFRS specifies that vesting conditions, other than market conditions, are not taken into account when estimating the fair value of the shares or options at the relevant measurement date (as specified above). Instead, vesting conditions are taken into account by adjusting the number of equity instruments included in the measurement of the transaction amount so that, ultimately, the amount recognised for goods or services received as consideration for the equity instruments granted is based on the number of equity instruments that eventually vest. Hence, on a cumulative basis, no amount is recognised for goods or services received if the equity instruments granted do not vest because of failure to satisfy a vesting condition (other than a market condition).

(d)   the IFRS requires the fair value of equity instruments granted to be based on market prices, if available, and to take into account the terms and conditions upon which those equity instruments were granted. In the absence of market prices, fair value is estimated, using a valuation technique to estimate what the price of those equity instruments would have been on the measurement date in an arm's length transaction between knowledgeable, willing parties.

(e)   the IFRS also sets out requirements if the terms and conditions of an option or share grant are modified (eg an option is repriced) or if a grant is cancelled, repurchased or replaced with another grant of equity instruments. For example, irrespective of any modification, cancellation or settlement of a grant of equity instruments to employees, the IFRS generally requires the entity to recognise, as a minimum, the services received measured at the grant date fair value of the equity instruments granted.

For cash-settled share-based payment transactions, the IFRS requires an entity to **IN6** measure the goods or services acquired and the liability incurred at the fair value of the liability. Until the liability is settled, the entity is required to remeasure the fair value of the liability at each reporting date and at the date of settlement, with any changes in value recognised in profit or loss for the period.

For share-based payment transactions in which the terms of the arrangement provide **IN7** either the entity or the supplier of goods or services with a choice of whether the entity settles the transaction in cash or by issuing equity instruments, the entity is required to account for that transaction, or the components of that transaction, as a cash-settled share-based payment transaction if, and to the extent that, the entity has incurred a liability to settle in cash (or other assets), or as an equity-settled share-based payment transaction if, and to the extent that, no such liability has been incurred.

The IFRS prescribes various disclosure requirements to enable users of financial **IN8** statements to understand:

(a)   the nature and extent of share-based payment arrangements that existed during the period;

(b)   how the fair value of the goods or services received, or the fair value of the equity instruments granted, during the period was determined; and

(c)   the effect of share-based payment transactions on the entity's profit or loss for the period and on its financial position.

Financial Reporting Standard 20 (IFRS 2)

'Share-based Payment'

OBJECTIVE

1   The objective of this IFRS is to specify the financial reporting by an entity when it undertakes a *share-based payment transaction*. In particular, it requires an entity to reflect in its profit or loss and financial position the effects of share-based payment transactions, including expenses associated with transactions in which *share options* are granted to employees.

SCOPE

1A   This IFRS applies to all financial statements that are intended to give a true and fair view of a reporting entity's financial position and profit or loss (or income or expenditure), except that reporting entities applying the Financial Reporting Standard for Smaller Entities (FRSSE) currently applicable are exempt from the IFRS.

2   An entity shall apply this IFRS in accounting for all share-based payment transactions including:

    (a)   *equity-settled share-based payment transactions*, in which the entity receives goods or services as consideration for *equity instruments* of the entity (including shares or share options),

    (b)   *cash-settled share-based payment transactions*, in which the entity acquires goods or services by incurring liabilities to the supplier of those goods or services for amounts that are based on the price (or value) of the entity's shares or other equity instruments of the entity, and

    (c)   transactions in which the entity receives or acquires goods or services and the terms of the arrangement provide either the entity or the supplier of those goods or services with a choice of whether the entity settles the transaction in cash (or other assets) or by issuing equity instruments,

except as noted in paragraphs 5 and 6.

3   For the purposes of this IFRS, transfers of an entity's equity instruments by its shareholders to parties that have supplied goods or services to the entity (including employees) are share-based payment transactions, unless the transfer is clearly for a purpose other than payment for goods or services supplied to the entity. This also applies to transfers of equity instruments of the entity's parent, or equity instruments of another entity in the same group as the entity, to parties that have supplied goods or services to the entity.

4   For the purposes of this IFRS, a transaction with an employee (or other party) in his/her capacity as a holder of equity instruments of the entity is not a share-based payment transaction. For example, if an entity grants all holders of a particular class of its equity instruments the right to acquire additional equity instruments of the entity at a price that is less than the fair value of those equity instruments, and an employee receives such a right because he/she is a holder of equity instruments of that particular class, the granting or exercise of that right is not subject to the requirements of this IFRS.

As noted in paragraph 2, this IFRS applies to share-based payment transactions in which an entity acquires or receives goods or services. Goods includes inventories, consumables, property, plant and equipment, intangible assets and other non-financial assets. However, an entity shall not apply this IFRS to transactions in which the entity acquires goods as part of the net assets acquired in a business combination to which FRS 6 *Acquisitions and Mergers* applies. Hence, equity instruments issued in a business combination in exchange for control of the acquiree are not within the scope of this IFRS. However, equity instruments granted to employees of the acquiree in their capacity as employees (eg in return for continued service) are within the scope of this IFRS. Similarly, the cancellation, replacement or other modification of *share-based payment arrangements* because of a business combination or other equity restructuring shall be accounted for in accordance with this IFRS.

This IFRS does not apply to share-based payment transactions in which the entity receives or acquires goods or services under a contract to buy or sell a non-financial item that can be settled net in cash or another financial instrument, or by exchanging financial instruments, as if the contracts were financial instruments, except that it does apply to contracts that were entered into and continue to be held for the purpose of the receipt or delivery of a non-financial item in accordance with the entity's expected purchase, sale or usage requirements.

RECOGNITION

An entity shall recognise the goods or services received or acquired in a share-based payment transaction when it obtains the goods or as the services are received. The entity shall recognise a corresponding increase in equity if the goods or services were received in an equity-settled share-based payment transaction, or a liability if the goods or services were acquired in a cash-settled share-based payment transaction.

When the goods or services received or acquired in a share-based payment transaction do not qualify for recognition as assets, they shall be recognised as expenses.

Typically, an expense arises from the consumption of goods or services. For example, services are typically consumed immediately, in which case an expense is recognised as the counterparty renders service. Goods might be consumed over a period of time or, in the case of inventories, sold at a later date, in which case an expense is recognised when the goods are consumed or sold. However, sometimes it is necessary to recognise an expense before the goods or services are consumed or sold, because they do not qualify for recognition as assets. For example, an entity might acquire goods as part of the research phase of a project to develop a new product. Although those goods have not been consumed, they might not qualify for recognition as assets under the applicable IFRS.

EQUITY-SETTLED SHARE-BASED PAYMENT TRANSACTIONS

Overview

For equity-settled share-based payment transactions, the entity shall measure the goods or services received, and the corresponding increase in equity, directly, at the *fair value* of the goods or services received, unless that fair value cannot be estimated reliably. If the entity cannot estimate reliably the fair value of the goods or services received, the

entity shall measure their value, and the corresponding increase in equity, indirectly, by reference to* the fair value of the *equity instruments granted.*

11   To apply the requirements of paragraph 10 to transactions with *employees and others providing similar services,*† the entity shall measure the fair value of the services received by reference to the fair value of the equity instruments granted, because typically it is not possible to estimate reliably the fair value of the services received, as explained in paragraph 12. The fair value of those equity instruments shall be measured at *grant date.*

12   Typically, shares, share options or other equity instruments are granted to employees as part of their remuneration package, in addition to a cash salary and other employment benefits. Usually, it is not possible to measure directly the services received for particular components of the employee's remuneration package. It might also not be possible to measure the fair value of the total remuneration package independently, without measuring directly the fair value of the equity instruments granted. Furthermore, shares or share options are sometimes granted as part of a bonus arrangement, rather than as a part of basic remuneration, eg as an incentive to the employees to remain in the entity's employ or to reward them for their efforts in improving the entity's performance. By granting shares or share options, in addition to other remuneration, the entity is paying additional remuneration to obtain additional benefits. Estimating the fair value of those additional benefits is likely to be difficult. Because of the difficulty of measuring directly the fair value of the services received, the entity shall measure the fair value of the employee services received by reference to the fair value of the equity instruments granted.

13   To apply the requirements of paragraph 10 to transactions with parties other than employees, there shall be a rebuttable presumption that the fair value of the goods or services received can be estimated reliably. That fair value shall be measured at the date the entity obtains the goods or the counterparty renders service. In rare cases, if the entity rebuts this presumption because it cannot estimate reliably the fair value of the goods or services received, the entity shall measure the goods or services received, and the corresponding increase in equity, indirectly, by reference to the fair value of the equity instruments granted, measured at the date the entity obtains the goods or the counterparty renders service.

Transactions in which services are received

14   If the equity instruments granted *vest* immediately, the counterparty is not required to complete a specified period of service before becoming unconditionally entitled to those equity instruments. In the absence of evidence to the contrary, the entity shall presume that services rendered by the counterparty as consideration for the equity instruments have been received. In this case, on grant date the entity shall recognise the services received in full, with a corresponding increase in equity.

15   If the equity instruments granted do not vest until the counterparty completes a specified period of service, the entity shall presume that the services to be rendered by the counterparty as consideration for those equity instruments will be received in the future, during the *vesting period.* The entity shall account for those services as they

---

*This IFRS uses the phrase 'by reference to' rather than 'at', because the transaction is ultimately measured by multiplying the fair value of the equity instruments granted, measured at the date specified in paragraph 11 or 13 (whichever is applicable), by the number of equity instruments that vest, as explained in paragraph 19.

†In the remainder of this IFRS, all references to employees also includes others providing similar services.

are rendered by the counterparty during the vesting period, with a corresponding increase in equity. For example:

(a) if an employee is granted share options conditional upon completing three years' service, then the entity shall presume that the services to be rendered by the employee as consideration for the share options will be received in the future, over that three-year vesting period.

(b) if an employee is granted share options conditional upon the achievement of a performance condition and remaining in the entity's employ until that performance condition is satisfied, and the length of the vesting period varies depending on when that performance condition is satisfied, the entity shall presume that the services to be rendered by the employee as consideration for the share options will be received in the future, over the expected vesting period. The entity shall estimate the length of the expected vesting period at grant date, based on the most likely outcome of the performance condition. If the performance condition is a *market condition*, the estimate of the length of the expected vesting period shall be consistent with the assumptions used in estimating the fair value of the options granted, and shall not be subsequently revised. If the performance condition is not a market condition, the entity shall revise its estimate of the length of the vesting period, if necessary, if subsequent information indicates that the length of the vesting period differs from previous estimates.

Transactions measured by reference to the fair value of the equity instruments granted

Determining the fair value of equity instruments granted

For transactions measured by reference to the fair value of the equity instruments granted, an entity shall measure the fair value of equity instruments granted at the *measurement date*, based on market prices if available, taking into account the terms and conditions upon which those equity instruments were granted (subject to the requirements of paragraphs 19–22). **16**

If market prices are not available, the entity shall estimate the fair value of the equity instruments granted using a valuation technique to estimate what the price of those equity instruments would have been on the measurement date in an arm's length transaction between knowledgeable, willing parties. The valuation technique shall be consistent with generally accepted valuation methodologies for pricing financial instruments, and shall incorporate all factors and assumptions that knowledgeable, willing market participants would consider in setting the price (subject to the requirements of paragraphs 19–22). **17**

Appendix B contains further guidance on the measurement of the fair value of shares and share options, focusing on the specific terms and conditions that are common features of a grant of shares or share options to employees. **18**

Treatment of vesting conditions

A grant of equity instruments might be conditional upon satisfying specified *vesting conditions*. For example, a grant of shares or share options to an employee is typically conditional on the employee remaining in the entity's employ for a specified period of time. There might be performance conditions that must be satisfied, such as the entity achieving a specified growth in profit or a specified increase in the entity's share price. Vesting conditions, other than market conditions, shall not be taken into **19** account when estimating the fair value of the shares or share options at the measurement date. Instead, vesting conditions shall be taken into account by adjusting the number of equity instruments included in the measurement of the transaction amount so that, ultimately, the amount recognised for goods or services received as consideration for the equity instruments granted shall be based on the number of equity instruments that eventually vest. Hence, on a cumulative basis, no amount is recognised for goods or services received if the equity instruments granted do not vest because of failure to satisfy a vesting condition, eg the counterparty fails to complete a specified service period, or a performance condition is not satisfied, subject to the requirements of paragraph 21.

20   To apply the requirements of paragraph 19, the entity shall recognise an amount for the goods or services received during the vesting period based on the best available estimate of the number of equity instruments expected to vest and shall revise that estimate, if necessary, if subsequent information indicates that the number of equity instruments expected to vest differs from previous estimates. On vesting date, the entity shall revise the estimate to equal the number of equity instruments that ultimately vested, subject to the requirements of paragraph 21.

21   Market conditions, such as a target share price upon which vesting (or exercisability) is conditioned, shall be taken into account when estimating the fair value of the equity instruments granted. Therefore, for grants of equity instruments with market conditions, the entity shall recognise the goods or services received from a counterparty who satisfies all other vesting conditions (eg services received from an employee who remains in service for the specified period of service), irrespective of whether that market condition is satisfied.

Treatment of a reload feature

22   For options with a *reload feature*, the reload feature shall not be taken into account when estimating the fair value of options granted at the measurement date. Instead, a *reload option* shall be accounted for as a new option grant, if and when a reload option is subsequently granted.

After vesting date

23   Having recognised the goods or services received in accordance with paragraphs 10–22, and a corresponding increase in equity, the entity shall make no subsequent adjustment to total equity after vesting date. For example, the entity shall not subsequently reverse the amount recognised for services received from an employee if the vested equity instruments are later forfeited or, in the case of share options, the options are not exercised. However, this requirement does not preclude the entity from recognising a transfer within equity, ie a transfer from one component of equity to another.

If the fair value of the equity instruments cannot be estimated reliably

24   The requirements in paragraphs 16–23 apply when the entity is required to measure a share-based payment transaction by reference to the fair value of the equity instruments granted. In rare cases, the entity may be unable to estimate reliably the fair value of the equity instruments granted at the measurement date, in accordance with the requirements in paragraphs 16–22. In these rare cases only, the entity shall instead:

(a)   measure the equity instruments at their *intrinsic value*, initially at the date the entity obtains the goods or the counterparty renders service and subsequently at each reporting date and at the date of final settlement, with any change in intrinsic value recognised in profit or loss. For a grant of share options, the share-based payment arrangement is finally settled when the options are exercised, are forfeited (eg upon cessation of employment) or lapse (eg at the end of the option's life).

(b)   recognise the goods or services received based on the number of equity instruments that ultimately vest or (where applicable) are ultimately exercised. To apply this requirement to share options, for example, the entity shall recognise the goods or services received during the vesting period, if any, in accordance with paragraphs 14 and 15, except that the requirements in paragraph 15(b) concerning a market condition do not apply. The amount recognised for goods or services received during the vesting period shall be based on the number of share options expected to vest. The entity shall revise that estimate, if necessary, if subsequent information indicates that the number of share options expected to vest differs from previous estimates. On vesting date, the entity shall revise the estimate to equal the number of equity instruments that ultimately vested. After vesting date, the entity shall reverse the amount recognised for goods or services received if the share options are later forfeited, or lapse at the end of the share option's life.

If an entity applies paragraph 24, it is not necessary to apply paragraphs 26-29,   **25** because any modifications to the terms and conditions on which the equity instruments were granted will be taken into account when applying the intrinsic value method set out in paragraph 24. However, if an entity settles a grant of equity instruments to which paragraph 24 has been applied:

(a)   if the settlement occurs during the vesting period, the entity shall account for the settlement as an acceleration of vesting, and shall therefore recognise immediately the amount that would otherwise have been recognised for services received over the remainder of the vesting period.

(b)   any payment made on settlement shall be accounted for as the repurchase of equity instruments, ie as a deduction from equity, except to the extent that the payment exceeds the intrinsic value of the equity instruments, measured at the repurchase date. Any such excess shall be recognised as an expense.

Modifications to the terms and conditions on which equity instruments were granted, including cancellations and settlements

An entity might modify the terms and conditions on which the equity instruments   **26** were granted. For example, it might reduce the exercise price of options granted to employees (ie reprice the options), which increases the fair value of those options. The requirements in paragraphs 27–29 to account for the effects of modifications are expressed in the context of share-based payment transactions with employees. However, the requirements shall also be applied to share-based payment transactions with parties other than employees that are measured by reference to the fair value of the equity instruments granted. In the latter case, any references in paragraphs 27–29 to grant date shall instead refer to the date the entity obtains the goods or the counterparty renders service.

The entity shall recognise, as a minimum, the services received measured at the grant   **27** date fair value of the equity instruments granted, unless those equity instruments do not vest because of failure to satisfy a vesting condition (other than a market condition) that was specified at grant date. This applies irrespective of any modifications to the terms and conditions on which the equity instruments were granted, or a cancellation or settlement of that grant of equity instruments. In addition, the entity shall recognise the effects of modifications that increase the total fair value of the share-based payment arrangement or are otherwise beneficial to the employee. Guidance on applying this requirement is given in Appendix B.

28　If the entity cancels or settles a grant of equity instruments during the vesting period (other than a grant cancelled by forfeiture when the vesting conditions are not satisfied):

   (a)　the entity shall account for the cancellation or settlement as an acceleration of vesting, and shall therefore recognise immediately the amount that otherwise would have been recognised for services received over the remainder of the vesting period.

   (b)　any payment made to the employee on the cancellation or settlement of the grant shall be accounted for as the repurchase of an equity interest, ie as a deduction from equity, except to the extent that the payment exceeds the fair value of the equity instruments granted, measured at the repurchase date. Any such excess shall be recognised as an expense.

   (c)　if new equity instruments are granted to the employee and, on the date when those new equity instruments are granted, the entity identifies the new equity instruments granted as replacement equity instruments for the cancelled equity instruments, the entity shall account for the granting of replacement equity instruments in the same way as a modification of the original grant of equity instruments, in accordance with paragraph 27 and the guidance in Appendix B. The incremental fair value granted is the difference between the fair value of the replacement equity instruments and the net fair value of the cancelled equity instruments, at the date the replacement equity instruments are granted. The net fair value of the cancelled equity instruments is their fair value, immediately before the cancellation, less the amount of any payment made to the employee on cancellation of the equity instruments that is accounted for as a deduction from equity in accordance with (b) above. If the entity does not identify new equity instruments granted as replacement equity instruments for the cancelled equity instruments, the entity shall account for those new equity instruments as a new grant of equity instruments.

29　If an entity repurchases vested equity instruments, the payment made to the employee shall be accounted for as a deduction from equity, except to the extent that the payment exceeds the fair value of the equity instruments repurchased, measured at the repurchase date. Any such excess shall be recognised as an expense.

CASH-SETTLED SHARE-BASED PAYMENT TRANSACTIONS

30　**For cash-settled share-based payment transactions, the entity shall measure the goods or services acquired and the liability incurred at the fair value of the liability. Until the liability is settled, the entity shall remeasure the fair value of the liability at each reporting date and at the date of settlement, with any changes in fair value recognised in profit or loss for the period.**

31　For example, an entity might grant share appreciation rights to employees as part of their remuneration package, whereby the employees will become entitled to a future cash payment (rather than an equity instrument), based on the increase in the entity's share price from a specified level over a specified period of time. Or an entity might grant to its employees a right to receive a future cash payment by granting to them a right to shares (including shares to be issued upon the exercise of share options) that are redeemable, either mandatorily (eg upon cessation of employment) or at the employee's option.

The entity shall recognise the services received, and a liability to pay for those **32** services, as the employees render service. For example, some share appreciation rights vest immediately, and the employees are therefore not required to complete a specified period of service to become entitled to the cash payment. In the absence of evidence to the contrary, the entity shall presume that the services rendered by the employees in exchange for the share appreciation rights have been received. Thus, the entity shall recognise immediately the services received and a liability to pay for them. If the share appreciation rights do not vest until the employees have completed a specified period of service, the entity shall recognise the services received, and a liability to pay for them, as the employees render service during that period.

The liability shall be measured, initially and at each reporting date until settled, at **33** the fair value of the share appreciation rights, by applying an option pricing model, taking into account the terms and conditions on which the share appreciation rights were granted, and the extent to which the employees have rendered service to date.

SHARE-BASED PAYMENT TRANSACTIONS WITH CASH ALTERNATIVES

For share-based payment transactions in which the terms of the arrangement provide **34** **either the entity or the counterparty with the choice of whether the entity settles the transaction in cash (or other assets) or by issuing equity instruments, the entity shall account for that transaction, or the components of that transaction, as a cash-settled share-based payment transaction if, and to the extent that, the entity has incurred a liability to settle in cash or other assets, or as an equity-settled share-based payment transaction if, and to the extent that, no such liability has been incurred.**

Share-based payment transactions in which the terms of the arrangement provide the counterparty with a choice of settlement

If an entity has granted the counterparty the right to choose whether a share-based **35** payment transaction is settled in cash* or by issuing equity instruments, the entity has granted a compound financial instrument, which includes a debt component (ie the counterparty's right to demand payment in cash) and an equity component (ie the counterparty's right to demand settlement in equity instruments rather than in cash). For transactions with parties other than employees, in which the fair value of the goods or services received is measured directly, the entity shall measure the equity component of the compound financial instrument as the difference between the fair value of the goods or services received and the fair value of the debt component, at the date when the goods or services are received.

For other transactions, including transactions with employees, the entity shall **36** measure the fair value of the compound financial instrument at the measurement date, taking into account the terms and conditions on which the rights to cash or equity instruments were granted.

To apply paragraph 36, the entity shall first measure the fair value of the debt **37** component, and then measure the fair value of the equity component – taking into account that the counterparty must forfeit the right to receive cash in order to receive the equity instrument. The fair value of the compound financial instrument is the sum of the fair values of the two components. However, share-based payment transactions in which the counterparty has the choice of settlement are often structured so that the fair value of one settlement alternative is the same as the other.

In paragraphs 35-43, all references to cash also include other assets of the entity.

For example, the counterparty might have the choice of receiving share options or cash-settled share appreciation rights. In such cases, the fair value of the equity component is zero, and hence the fair value of the compound financial instrument is the same as the fair value of the debt component. Conversely, if the fair values of the settlement alternatives differ, the fair value of the equity component usually will be greater than zero, in which case the fair value of the compound financial instrument will be greater than the fair value of the debt component.

38   The entity shall account separately for the goods or services received or acquired in respect of each component of the compound financial instrument. For the debt component, the entity shall recognise the goods or services acquired, and a liability to pay for those goods or services, as the counterparty supplies goods or renders service, in accordance with the requirements applying to cash-settled share-based payment transactions (paragraphs 30–33). For the equity component (if any), the entity shall recognise the goods or services received, and an increase in equity, as the counterparty supplies goods or renders service, in accordance with the requirements applying to equity-settled share-based payment transactions (paragraphs 10–29).

39   At the date of settlement, the entity shall remeasure the liability to its fair value. If the entity issues equity instruments on settlement rather than paying cash, the liability shall be transferred direct to equity, as the consideration for the equity instruments issued.

40   If the entity pays in cash on settlement rather than issuing equity instruments, that payment shall be applied to settle the liability in full. Any equity component previously recognised shall remain within equity. By electing to receive cash on settlement, the counterparty forfeited the right to receive equity instruments. However, this requirement does not preclude the entity from recognising a transfer within equity, ie a transfer from one component of equity to another.

Share-based payment transactions in which the terms of the arrangement provide the entity with a choice of settlement

41   For a share-based payment transaction in which the terms of the arrangement provide an entity with the choice of whether to settle in cash or by issuing equity instruments, the entity shall determine whether it has a present obligation to settle in cash and account for the share-based payment transaction accordingly. The entity has a present obligation to settle in cash if the choice of settlement in equity instruments has no commercial substance (eg because the entity is legally prohibited from issuing shares), or the entity has a past practice or a stated policy of settling in cash, or generally settles in cash whenever the counterparty asks for cash settlement.

42   If the entity has a present obligation to settle in cash, it shall account for the transaction in accordance with the requirements applying to cash-settled share-based payment transactions, in paragraphs 30–33.

43   If no such obligation exists, the entity shall account for the transaction in accordance with the requirements applying to equity-settled share-based payment transactions, in paragraphs 10–29. Upon settlement:

(a)   if the entity elects to settle in cash, the cash payment shall be accounted for as the repurchase of an equity interest, ie as a deduction from equity, except as noted in (c) below.

(b)   if the entity elects to settle by issuing equity instruments, no further accounting is required (other than a transfer from one component of equity to another, if necessary), except as noted in (c) below.

(c)   if the entity elects the settlement alternative with the higher fair value, as at the date of settlement, the entity shall recognise an additional expense for the excess value given, ie the difference between the cash paid and the fair value of the equity instruments that would otherwise have been issued, or the difference between the fair value of the equity instruments issued and the amount of cash that would otherwise have been paid, whichever is applicable.

DISCLOSURES

An entity shall disclose information that enables users of the financial statements to   **44**
understand the nature and extent of share-based payment arrangements that existed
during the period.

To give effect to the principle in paragraph 44, the entity shall disclose at least the   **45**
following:

(a)   a description of each type of share-based payment arrangement that existed at any time during the period, including the general terms and conditions of each arrangement, such as vesting requirements, the maximum term of options granted, and the method of settlement (eg whether in cash or equity). An entity with substantially similar types of share-based payment arrangements may aggregate this information, unless separate disclosure of each arrangement is necessary to satisfy the principle in paragraph 44.

(b)   the number and weighted average exercise prices of share options for each of the following groups of options:

  (i)   outstanding at the beginning of the period;
  (ii)   granted during the period;
  (iii)   forfeited during the period;
  (iv)   exercised during the period;
  (v)   expired during the period;
  (vi)   outstanding at the end of the period; and
  (vii) exercisable at the end of the period.

(c)   for share options exercised during the period, the weighted average share price at the date of exercise. If options were exercised on a regular basis throughout the period, the entity may instead disclose the weighted average share price during the period.

(d)   for share options outstanding at the end of the period, the range of exercise prices and weighted average remaining contractual life. If the range of exercise prices is wide, the outstanding options shall be divided into ranges that are meaningful for assessing the number and timing of additional shares that may be issued and the cash that may be received upon exercise of those options.

An entity shall disclose information that enables users of the financial statements to   **46**
understand how the fair value of the goods or services received, or the fair value of the
equity instruments granted, during the period was determined.

If the entity has measured the fair value of goods or services received as con-   **47**
sideration for equity instruments of the entity indirectly, by reference to the fair value
of the equity instruments granted, to give effect to the principle in paragraph 46, the
entity shall disclose at least the following:

(a)   for share options granted during the period, the weighted average fair value of those options at the measurement date and information on how that fair value was measured, including:

(i)   the option pricing model used and the inputs to that model, including the weighted average share price, exercise price, expected volatility, option life, expected dividends, the risk-free interest rate and any other inputs to the model, including the method used and the assumptions made to incorporate the effects of expected early exercise;

(ii) how expected volatility was determined, including an explanation of the extent to which expected volatility was based on historical volatility; and

(iii) whether and how any other features of the option grant were incorporated into the measurement of fair value, such as a market condition.

(b) for other equity instruments granted during the period (ie other than share options), the number and weighted average fair value of those equity instruments at the measurement date, and information on how that fair value was measured, including:

(i)   if fair value was not measured on the basis of an observable market price, how it was determined;

(ii) whether and how expected dividends were incorporated into the measurement of fair value; and

(iii) whether and how any other features of the equity instruments granted were incorporated into the measurement of fair value.

(c) for share-based payment arrangements that were modified during the period:

(i)   an explanation of those modifications;

(ii) the incremental fair value granted (as a result of those modifications); and

(iii) information on how the incremental fair value granted was measured, consistently with the requirements set out in (a) and (b) above, where applicable.

48   If the entity has measured directly the fair value of goods or services received during the period, the entity shall disclose how that fair value was determined, eg whether fair value was measured at a market price for those goods or services.

49   If the entity has rebutted the presumption in paragraph 13, it shall disclose that fact, and give an explanation of why the presumption was rebutted.

50   **An entity shall disclose information that enables users of the financial statements to understand the effect of share-based payment transactions on the entity's profit or loss for the period and on its financial position.**

51   To give effect to the principle in paragraph 50, the entity shall disclose at least the following:

(a) the total expense recognised for the period arising from share-based payment transactions in which the goods or services received did not qualify for recognition as assets and hence were recognised immediately as an expense, including separate disclosure of that portion of the total expense that arises from transactions accounted for as equity-settled share-based payment transactions;

(b) for liabilities arising from share-based payment transactions:

(i)   the total carrying amount at the end of the period; and

(ii) the total intrinsic value at the end of the period of liabilities for which the counterparty's right to cash or other assets had vested by the end of the period (eg vested share appreciation rights).

If the information required to be disclosed by this IFRS does not satisfy the principles in paragraphs 44, 46 and 50, the entity shall disclose such additional information as is necessary to satisfy them. **52**

TRANSITIONAL PROVISIONS

For equity-settled share-based payment transactions, the entity shall apply this IFRS **53** to grants of shares, share options or other equity instruments that were granted after 7 November 2002 and had not yet vested at the relevant effective date of this IFRS.

The entity is encouraged, but not required, to apply this IFRS to other grants of **54** equity instruments if the entity has disclosed publicly the fair value of those equity instruments, determined at the measurement date.

For all grants of equity instruments to which this IFRS is applied, the entity shall **55** restate comparative information and, where applicable, adjust the opening balance of retained earnings for the earliest period presented.

For all grants of equity instruments to which this IFRS has not been applied (eg **56** equity instruments granted on or before 7 November 2002), the entity shall nevertheless disclose the information required by paragraphs 44 and 45.

If, after the IFRS becomes effective, an entity modifies the terms or conditions of a **57** grant of equity instruments to which this IFRS has not been applied, the entity shall nevertheless apply paragraphs 26–29 to account for any such modifications.

For liabilities arising from share-based payment transactions existing at the effective **58** date of this IFRS, the entity shall apply the IFRS retrospectively. For these liabilities, the entity shall restate comparative information, including adjusting the opening balance of retained earnings in the earliest period presented for which comparative information has been restated, except that the entity is not required to restate comparative information to the extent that the information relates to a period or date that is earlier than 7 November 2002.

The entity is encouraged, but not required, to apply retrospectively the IFRS to other **59** liabilities arising from share-based payment transactions, for example, to liabilities that were settled during a period for which comparative information is presented.

EFFECTIVE DATE

A *listed entity* shall apply this IFRS for accounting periods beginning on or after **60** 1 January 2005; and an *unlisted entity* shall apply it for accounting periods beginning on or after 1 January 2006. In both cases earlier application is encouraged. If an entity applies the IFRS before the relevant effective date, it shall disclose that fact.

Appendix A
Defined terms

This appendix is an integral part of the IFRS.

cash-settled share-based payment transaction	A **share-based payment transaction** in which the entity acquires goods or services by incurring a liability to transfer cash or other assets to the supplier of those goods or services for amounts that are based on the price (or value) of the entity's shares or other **equity instruments** of the entity.
employees and others providing similar services	Individuals who render personal services to the entity and either (a) the individuals are regarded as employees for legal or tax purposes, (b) the individuals work for the entity under its direction in the same way as individuals who are regarded as employees for legal or tax purposes, or (c) the services rendered are similar to those rendered by employees. For example, the term encompasses all management personnel, ie those persons having authority and responsibility for planning, directing and controlling the activities of the entity, including non-executive directors.
equity instrument	A contract that evidences a residual interest in the assets of an entity after deducting all of its liabilities.*
equity instrument granted	The right (conditional or unconditional) to an **equity instrument** of the entity conferred by the entity on another party, under a **share-based payment arrangement**.
equity-settled share-based payment transaction	A **share-based payment transaction** in which the entity receives goods or services as consideration for **equity instruments** of the entity (including shares or **share options**).
fair value	The amount for which an asset could be exchanged, a liability settled, or an **equity instrument granted** could be exchanged, between knowledgeable, willing parties in an arm's length transaction.
grant date	The date at which the entity and another party (including an employee) agree to a **share-based payment arrangement**, being when the entity and the counterparty have a shared understanding of the terms and conditions of the arrangement. At grant date the entity confers on the counterparty the right to cash, other assets, or **equity instruments** of the entity, provided the specified **vesting conditions**, if any, are met. If that agreement is subject to an approval process (for example, by shareholders), grant date is the date when that approval is obtained.

*The Framework defines a liability as a present obligation of the entity arising from past events, the settlement of which is expected to result in an outflow from the entity of resources embodying economic benefits (ie an outflow of cash or other assets of the entity).

intrinsic value	The difference between the **fair value** of the shares to which the counterparty has the (conditional or unconditional) right to subscribe or which it has the right to receive, and the price (if any) the counterparty is (or will be) required to pay for those shares. For example, a **share option** with an exercise price of CU15,* on a share with a **fair value** of CU20, has an intrinsic value of CU5.
listed entity	An entity that has in issue one or more securities that are admitted to trading on a regulated market of any Member State within the meaning of Article 1(13) of Council Directive 93/22/EEC of 10 May 1993 on investment services in the securities field.
market condition	A condition upon which the exercise price, vesting or exercisability of an **equity instrument** depends that is related to the market price of the entity's **equity instruments**, such as attaining a specified share price or a specified amount of **intrinsic value** of a **share option**, or achieving a specified target that is based on the market price of the entity's **equity instruments** relative to an index of market prices of **equity instruments** of other entities.
measurement date	The date at which the **fair value** of the **equity instruments granted** is measured for the purposes of this IFRS. For transactions with **employees and others providing similar services**, the measurement date is **grant date**. For transactions with parties other than employees (and those providing similar services), the measurement date is the date the entity obtains the goods or the counterparty renders service.
reload feature	A feature that provides for an automatic grant of additional **share options** whenever the option holder exercises previously granted options using the entity's shares, rather than cash, to satisfy the exercise price.
reload option	**A new share option** granted when a share is used to satisfy the exercise price of a previous **share option**.
share-based payment arrangement	An agreement between the entity and another party (including an employee) to enter into a **share-based payment transaction**, which thereby entitles the other party to receive cash or other assets of the entity for amounts that are based on the price of the entity's shares or other **equity instruments** of the entity, or to receive **equity instruments** of the entity, provided the specified **vesting conditions**, if any, are met.
share-based payment transaction	A transaction in which the entity receives goods or services as consideration for **equity instruments** of the entity (including shares or **share options**), or acquires goods or services by incurring liabilities to the supplier of those goods or services for amounts that are based on the price of the entity's shares or other **equity instruments** of the entity.

*In this appendix, monetary amounts are denominated in 'currency units' (CU).

share option   A contract that gives the holder the right, but not the obligation, to subscribe to the entity's shares at a fixed or determinable price for a specified period of time.

unlisted entity   An entity that is not a **listed entity**.

vest   To become an entitlement. Under a **share-based payment arrangement**, a counterparty's right to receive cash, other assets, or **equity instruments** of the entity vests upon satisfaction of any specified **vesting conditions**.

vesting conditions   The conditions that must be satisfied for the counterparty to become entitled to receive cash, other assets or **equity instruments** of the entity, under a **share-based payment arrangement**. Vesting conditions include service conditions, which require the other party to complete a specified period of service, and performance conditions, which require specified performance targets to be met (such as a specified increase in the entity's profit over a specified period of time).

vesting period   The period during which all the specified **vesting conditions** of a **share-based payment arrangement** are to be satisfied.

Appendix B
Application Guidance

This appendix is an integral part of the IFRS.

ESTIMATING THE FAIR VALUE OF EQUITY INSTRUMENTS GRANTED

Paragraphs B2–B41 of this appendix discuss measurement of the fair value of shares **B1** and share options granted, focusing on the specific terms and conditions that are common features of a grant of shares or share options to employees. Therefore, it is not exhaustive. Furthermore, because the valuation issues discussed below focus on shares and share options granted to employees, it is assumed that the fair value of the shares or share options is measured at grant date. However, many of the valuation issues discussed below (eg determining expected volatility) also apply in the context of estimating the fair value of shares or share options granted to parties other than employees at the date the entity obtains the goods or the counterparty renders service.

Shares

For shares granted to employees, the fair value of the shares shall be measured at the **B2** market price of the entity's shares (or an estimated market price, if the entity's shares are not publicly traded), adjusted to take into account the terms and conditions upon which the shares were granted (except for vesting conditions that are excluded from the measurement of fair value in accordance with paragraphs 19–21).

For example, if the employee is not entitled to receive dividends during the vesting **B3** period, this factor shall be taken into account when estimating the fair value of the shares granted. Similarly, if the shares are subject to restrictions on transfer after vesting date, that factor shall be taken into account, but only to the extent that the post-vesting restrictions affect the price that a knowledgeable, willing market participant would pay for that share. For example, if the shares are actively traded in a deep and liquid market, post-vesting transfer restrictions may have little, if any, effect on the price that a knowledgeable, willing market participant would pay for those shares. Restrictions on transfer or other restrictions that exist during the vesting period shall not be taken into account when estimating the grant date fair value of the shares granted, because those restrictions stem from the existence of vesting conditions, which are accounted for in accordance with paragraphs 19–21.

Share options

For share options granted to employees, in many cases market prices are not **B4** available, because the options granted are subject to terms and conditions that do not apply to traded options. If traded options with similar terms and conditions do not exist, the fair value of the options granted shall be estimated by applying an option pricing model.

The entity shall consider factors that knowledgeable, willing market participants **B5** would consider in selecting the option pricing model to apply. For example, many employee options have long lives, are usually exercisable during the period between vesting date and the end of the options' life, and are often exercised early. These factors should be considered when estimating the grant date fair value of the options.

For many entities, this might preclude the use of the Black-Scholes-Merton formula, which does not allow for the possibility of exercise before the end of the option's life and may not adequately reflect the effects of expected early exercise. It also does not allow for the possibility that expected volatility and other model inputs might vary over the option's life. However, for share options with relatively short contractual lives, or that must be exercised within a short period of time after vesting date, the factors identified above may not apply. In these instances, the Black-Scholes-Merton formula may produce a value that is substantially the same as a more flexible option pricing model.

B6   All option pricing models take into account, as a minimum, the following factors:

    (a)   the exercise price of the option;

    (b)   the life of the option;

    (c)   the current price of the underlying shares;

    (d)   the expected volatility of the share price;

    (e)   the dividends expected on the shares (if appropriate); and

    (f)   the risk-free interest rate for the life of the option.

B7   Other factors that knowledgeable, willing market participants would consider in setting the price shall also be taken into account (except for vesting conditions and reload features that are excluded from the measurement of fair value in accordance with paragraphs 19–22).

B8   For example, a share option granted to an employee typically cannot be exercised during specified periods (eg during the vesting period or during periods specified by securities regulators). This factor shall be taken into account if the option pricing model applied would otherwise assume that the option could be exercised at any time during its life. However, if an entity uses an option pricing model that values options that can be exercised only at the end of the options' life, no adjustment is required for the inability to exercise them during the vesting period (or other periods during the options' life), because the model assumes that the options cannot be exercised during those periods.

B9   Similarly, another factor common to employee share options is the possibility of early exercise of the option, for example, because the option is not freely transferable, or because the employee must exercise all vested options upon cessation of employment. The effects of expected early exercise shall be taken into account, as discussed in paragraphs B16-B21.

B10   Factors that a knowledgeable, willing market participant would not consider in setting the price of a share option (or other equity instrument) shall not be taken into account when estimating the fair value of share options (or other equity instruments) granted. For example, for share options granted to employees, factors that affect the value of the option from the individual employee's perspective only are not relevant to estimating the price that would be set by a knowledgeable, willing market participant.

Inputs to option pricing models

B11   In estimating the expected volatility of and dividends on the underlying shares, the objective is to approximate the expectations that would be reflected in a current market or negotiated exchange price for the option. Similarly, when estimating the effects of early exercise of employee share options, the objective is to approximate the expectations that an outside party with access to detailed information about employees' exercise behaviour would develop based on information available at the grant date.

Often, there is likely to be a range of reasonable expectations about future volatility, **B12** dividends and exercise behaviour. If so, an expected value should be calculated, by weighting each amount within the range by its associated probability of occurrence.

Expectations about the future are generally based on experience, modified if the **B13** future is reasonably expected to differ from the past. In some circumstances, identifiable factors may indicate that unadjusted historical experience is a relatively poor predictor of future experience. For example, if an entity with two distinctly different lines of business disposes of the one that was significantly less risky than the other, historical volatility may not be the best information on which to base reasonable expectations for the future.

In other circumstances, historical information may not be available. For example, a **B14** newly listed entity will have little, if any, historical data on the volatility of its share price. Unlisted and newly listed entities are discussed further below.

In summary, an entity should not simply base estimates of volatility, exercise **B15** behaviour and dividends on historical information without considering the extent to which the past experience is expected to be reasonably predictive of future experience.

Expected early exercise

Employees often exercise share options early, for a variety of reasons. For example, **B16** employee share options are typically non-transferable. This often causes employees to exercise their share options early, because that is the only way for the employees to liquidate their position. Also, employees who cease employment are usually required to exercise any vested options within a short period of time, otherwise the share options are forfeited. This factor also causes the early exercise of employee share options. Other factors causing early exercise are risk aversion and lack of wealth diversification.

The means by which the effects of expected early exercise are taken into account **B17** depends upon the type of option pricing model applied. For example, expected early exercise could be taken into account by using an estimate of the option's expected life (which, for an employee share option, is the period of time from grant date to the date on which the option is expected to be exercised) as an input into an option pricing model (eg the Black-Scholes-Merton formula). Alternatively, expected early exercise could be modelled in a binomial or similar option pricing model that uses contractual life as an input.

Factors to consider in estimating early exercise include: **B18**

(a) the length of the vesting period, because the share option typically cannot be exercised until the end of the vesting period. Hence, determining the valuation implications of expected early exercise is based on the assumption that the options will vest. The implications of vesting conditions are discussed in paragraphs 19–21.

(b) the average length of time similar options have remained outstanding in the past.

(c) the price of the underlying shares. Experience may indicate that the employees tend to exercise options when the share price reaches a specified level above the exercise price.

(d) the employee's level within the organisation. For example, experience might indicate that higher-level employees tend to exercise options later than lower-level employees (discussed further in paragraph B21).

(e) expected volatility of the underlying shares. On average, employees might tend to exercise options on highly volatile shares earlier than on shares with low volatility.

B19 As noted in paragraph B17, the effects of early exercise could be taken into account by using an estimate of the option's expected life as an input into an option pricing model. When estimating the expected life of share options granted to a group of employees, the entity could base that estimate on an appropriately weighted average expected life for the entire employee group or on appropriately weighted average lives for subgroups of employees within the group, based on more detailed data about employees' exercise behaviour (discussed further below).

B20 Separating an option grant into groups for employees with relatively homogeneous exercise behaviour is likely to be important. Option value is not a linear function of option term; value increases at a decreasing rate as the term lengthens. For example, if all other assumptions are equal, although a two-year option is worth more than a one-year option, it is not worth twice as much. That means that calculating estimated option value on the basis of a single weighted average life that includes widely differing individual lives would overstate the total fair value of the share options granted. Separating options granted into several groups, each of which has a relatively narrow range of lives included in its weighted average life, reduces that overstatement.

B21 Similar considerations apply when using a binomial or similar model. For example, the experience of an entity that grants options broadly to all levels of employees might indicate that top-level executives tend to hold their options longer than middle-management employees hold theirs and that lower-level employees tend to exercise their options earlier than any other group. In addition, employees who are encouraged or required to hold a minimum amount of their employer's equity instruments, including options, might on average exercise options later than employees not subject to that provision. In those situations, separating options by groups of recipients with relatively homogeneous exercise behaviour will result in a more accurate estimate of the total fair value of the share options granted.

Expected volatility

B22 Expected volatility is a measure of the amount by which a price is expected to fluctuate during a period. The measure of volatility used in option pricing models is the annualised standard deviation of the continuously compounded rates of return on the share over a period of time. Volatility is typically expressed in annualised terms that are comparable regardless of the time period used in the calculation, for example, daily, weekly or monthly price observations.

B23 The rate of return (which may be positive or negative) on a share for a period measures how much a shareholder has benefited from dividends and appreciation (or depreciation) of the share price.

B24 The expected annualised volatility of a share is the range within which the continuously compounded annual rate of return is expected to fall approximately two-thirds of the time. For example, to say that a share with an expected continuously compounded rate of return of 12 per cent has a volatility of 30 per cent means that the probability that the rate of return on the share for one year will be between −18 per cent (12% − 30%) and 42 per cent (12% + 30%) is approximately two-thirds. If the share price is CU100 at the beginning of the year and no dividends are paid, the year-end share price would be expected to be between CU83.53 (CU100 × e$^{-0.18}$) and CU152.20 (CU100 × e$^{0.42}$) approximately two-thirds of the time.

Factors to consider in estimating expected volatility include: **B25**

(a) implied volatility from traded share options on the entity's shares, or other traded instruments of the entity that include option features (such as convertible debt), if any.

(b) the historical volatility of the share price over the most recent period that is generally commensurate with the expected term of the option (taking into account the remaining contractual life of the option and the effects of expected early exercise).

(c) the length of time an entity's shares have been publicly traded. A newly listed entity might have a high historical volatility, compared with similar entities that have been listed longer. Further guidance for newly listed entities is given below.

(d) the tendency of volatility to revert to its mean, ie its long-term average level, and other factors indicating that expected future volatility might differ from past volatility. For example, if an entity's share price was extraordinarily volatile for some identifiable period of time because of a failed takeover bid or a major restructuring, that period could be disregarded in computing historical average annual volatility.

(e) appropriate and regular intervals for price observations. The price observations should be consistent from period to period. For example, an entity might use the closing price for each week or the highest price for the week, but it should not use the closing price for some weeks and the highest price for other weeks. Also, the price observations should be expressed in the same currency as the exercise price.

Newly listed entities

As noted in paragraph B25, an entity should consider historical volatility of the share **B26** price over the most recent period that is generally commensurate with the expected option term. If a newly listed entity does not have sufficient information on historical volatility, it should nevertheless compute historical volatility for the longest period for which trading activity is available. It could also consider the historical volatility of similar entities following a comparable period in their lives. For example, an entity that has been listed for only one year and grants options with an average expected life of five years might consider the pattern and level of historical volatility of entities in the same industry for the first six years in which the shares of those entities were publicly traded.

Unlisted entities

An unlisted entity will not have historical information to consider when estimating **B27** expected volatility. Some factors to consider instead are set out below.

In some cases, an unlisted entity that regularly issues options or shares to employees **B28** (or other parties) might have set up an internal market for its shares. The volatility of those share prices could be considered when estimating expected volatility.

Alternatively, the entity could consider the historical or implied volatility of similar **B29** listed entities, for which share price or option price information is available, to use when estimating expected volatility. This would be appropriate if the entity has based the value of its shares on the share prices of similar listed entities.

B30 If the entity has not based its estimate of the value of its shares on the share prices of similar listed entities, and has instead used another valuation methodology to value its shares, the entity could derive an estimate of expected volatility consistent with that valuation methodology. For example, the entity might value its shares on a net asset or earnings basis. It could consider the expected volatility of those net asset values or earnings.

Expected dividends

B31 Whether expected dividends should be taken into account when measuring the fair value of shares or options granted depends on whether the counterparty is entitled to dividends or dividend equivalents.

B32 For example, if employees were granted options and are entitled to dividends on the underlying shares or dividend equivalents (which might be paid in cash or applied to reduce the exercise price) between grant date and exercise date, the options granted should be valued as if no dividends will be paid on the underlying shares, ie the input for expected dividends should be zero.

B33 Similarly, when the grant date fair value of shares granted to employees is estimated, no adjustment is required for expected dividends if the employee is entitled to receive dividends paid during the vesting period.

B34 Conversely, if the employees are not entitled to dividends or dividend equivalents during the vesting period (or before exercise, in the case of an option), the grant date valuation of the rights to shares or options should take expected dividends into account. That is to say, when the fair value of an option grant is estimated, expected dividends should be included in the application of an option pricing model. When the fair value of a share grant is estimated, that valuation should be reduced by the present value of dividends expected to be paid during the vesting period.

B35 Option pricing models generally call for expected dividend yield. However, the models may be modified to use an expected dividend amount rather than a yield. An entity may use either its expected yield or its expected payments. If the entity uses the latter, it should consider its historical pattern of increases in dividends. For example, if an entity's policy has generally been to increase dividends by approximately 3 per cent per year, its estimated option value should not assume a fixed dividend amount throughout the option's life unless there is evidence that supports that assumption.

B36 Generally, the assumption about expected dividends should be based on publicly available information. An entity that does not pay dividends and has no plans to do so should assume an expected dividend yield of zero. However, an emerging entity with no history of paying dividends might expect to begin paying dividends during the expected lives of its employee share options. Those entities could use an average of their past dividend yield (zero) and the mean dividend yield of an appropriately comparable peer group.

Risk-free interest rate

B37 Typically, the risk-free interest rate is the implied yield currently available on zero-coupon government issues of the country in whose currency the exercise price is expressed, with a remaining term equal to the expected term of the option being valued (based on the option's remaining contractual life and taking into account the effects of expected early exercise). It may be necessary to use an appropriate substitute, if no such government issues exist or circumstances indicate that the implied yield on zero-coupon government issues is not representative of the risk-free interest rate (for example, in high inflation economies). Also, an appropriate substitute should be used if market participants would typically determine the risk-free interest rate by using that substitute, rather than the implied yield of zero-coupon government issues, when estimating the fair value of an option with a life equal to the expected term of the option being valued.

Capital structure effects

Typically, third parties, not the entity, write traded share options. When these share options are exercised, the writer delivers shares to the option holder. Those shares are acquired from existing shareholders. Hence the exercise of traded share options has no dilutive effect. **B38**

In contrast, if share options are written by the entity, new shares are issued when those share options are exercised (either actually issued or issued in substance, if shares previously repurchased and held in treasury are used). Given that the shares will be issued at the exercise price rather than the current market price at the date of exercise, this actual or potential dilution might reduce the share price, so that the option holder does not make as large a gain on exercise as on exercising an otherwise similar traded option that does not dilute the share price. **B39**

Whether this has a significant effect on the value of the share options granted depends on various factors, such as the number of new shares that will be issued on exercise of the options compared with the number of shares already issued. Also, if the market already expects that the option grant will take place, the market may have already factored the potential dilution into the share price at the date of grant. **B40**

However, the entity should consider whether the possible dilutive effect of the future exercise of the share options granted might have an impact on their estimated fair value at grant date. Option pricing models can be adapted to take into account this potential dilutive effect. **B41**

Modifications to equity-settled share-based payment arrangements

Paragraph 27 requires that, irrespective of any modifications to the terms and conditions on which the equity instruments were granted, or a cancellation or settlement of that grant of equity instruments, the entity should recognise, as a minimum, the services received measured at the grant date fair value of the equity instruments granted, unless those equity instruments do not vest because of failure to satisfy a vesting condition (other than a market condition) that was specified at grant date. In addition, the entity should recognise the effects of modifications that increase the total fair value of the share-based payment arrangement or are otherwise beneficial to the employee. **B42**

To apply the requirements of paragraph 27: **B43**

(a)   if the modification increases the fair value of the equity instruments granted (eg by reducing the exercise price), measured immediately before and after the modification, the entity shall include the incremental fair value granted in the measurement of the amount recognised for services received as consideration for the equity instruments granted. The incremental fair value granted is the difference between the fair value of the modified equity instrument and that of the original equity instrument, both estimated as at the date of the modification. If the modification occurs during the vesting period, the incremental fair value granted is included in the measurement of the amount recognised for services received over the period from the modification date until the date when the modified equity instruments vest, in addition to the amount based on the grant date fair value of the original equity instruments, which is recognised over the remainder of the original vesting period. If the modification occurs after vesting date, the incremental fair value granted is recognised immediately, or over the vesting period if the employee is required to complete an additional period of service before becoming unconditionally entitled to those modified equity instruments.

(b)   similarly, if the modification increases the number of equity instruments granted, the entity shall include the fair value of the additional equity instruments granted, measured at the date of the modification, in the measurement of the amount recognised for services received as consideration for the equity instruments granted, consistently with the requirements in (a) above. For example, if the modification occurs during the vesting period, the fair value of the additional equity instruments granted is included in the measurement of the amount recognised for services received over the period from the modification date until the date when the additional equity instruments vest, in addition to the amount based on the grant date fair value of the equity instruments originally granted, which is recognised over the remainder of the original vesting period.

(c)   if the entity modifies the vesting conditions in a manner that is beneficial to the employee, for example, by reducing the vesting period or by modifying or eliminating a performance condition (other than a market condition, changes to which are accounted for in accordance with (a) above), the entity shall take the modified vesting conditions into account when applying the requirements of paragraphs 19–21.

B44   Furthermore, if the entity modifies the terms or conditions of the equity instruments granted in a manner that reduces the total fair value of the share-based payment arrangement, or is not otherwise beneficial to the employee, the entity shall nevertheless continue to account for the services received as consideration for the equity instruments granted as if that modification had not occurred (other than a cancellation of some or all the equity instruments granted, which shall be accounted for in accordance with paragraph 28). For example:

(a)   if the modification reduces the fair value of the equity instruments granted, measured immediately before and after the modification, the entity shall not take into account that decrease in fair value and shall continue to measure the amount recognised for services received as consideration for the equity instruments based on the grant date fair value of the equity instruments granted.

(b)   if the modification reduces the number of equity instruments granted to an employee, that reduction shall be accounted for as a cancellation of that portion of the grant, in accordance with the requirements of paragraph 28.

(c)   if the entity modifies the vesting conditions in a manner that is not beneficial to the employee, for example, by increasing the vesting period or by modifying or adding a performance condition (other than a market condition, changes to which are accounted for in accordance with (a) above), the entity shall not take the modified vesting conditions into account when applying the requirements of paragraphs 19–21.

Appendix C
Amendments to other standards and UITF Abstracts

[Not reproduced, as all changes have been made to the underlying standards and abstracts]

Adoption of the standard
Approval of IFRS 2 by the International Accounting Standards Board

International Financial Reporting Standard 2 Share-based Payment was approved for issue by the fourteen members of the International Accounting Standards Board.

Sir David Tweedie	Chairman
Thomas E Jones	Vice-Chairman
Mary E Barth	
Hans-Georg Bruns	
Anthony T Cope	
Robert P Garnett	
Gilbert Gélard	
James J Leisenring	
Warren J McGregor	
Patricia L O'Malley	
Harry K Schmid	
John T Smith	
Geoffrey Whittington	
Tatsumi Yamada	

Adoption of FRS 20 by the Accounting Standards Board

Financial Reporting Standard 20 (IFRS 2) Share-based Payment was approved for issue by the nine members of the Accounting Standards Board.

Mary Keegan	Chairman
Andrew Lennard	Technical Director
Michael Ashley	
Douglas Flint	
Huw Jones	
Roger Marshall	
Isobel Sharp	
John Smith	
Jonathan Symonds	

Notes on the standard's application in the UK and the Republic of Ireland

THE NEED FOR AN FRS ON SHARE-BASED PAYMENTS

In November 2002, the IASB published a draft International Financial Reporting **N1**
Standard (IFRS) on share-based payments. It indicated that it expected the final
IFRS to come into effect for accounting periods beginning on or after 1 January
2004. The ASB (the Board) proposed in FRED 31 that a Financial Reporting
Standard (FRS) based on the draft IFRS should be implemented in the UK and the
Republic of Ireland* from that same date.

The Board had for many years been concerned about the accounting treatment of **N2**
share-based payment transactions. In its view, such transactions give rise to an
expense and that expense should be measured at fair value and recognised in full in
the profit and loss account (or included as part of the cost of an asset recognised on
the balance sheet). Unless and until that is done, the financial statements will not
fully reflect the substance of the transactions the reporting entity has entered into. A
standard like the draft IFRS that requires all entities to recognise an expense,
measured at fair value, in relation to all their share-based payments was therefore
needed urgently to improve the UK financial reporting framework.

Some respondents to FRED 31 thought it wrong to require recognition of a fair **N3**
value expense, either because the entity was not thought to incur an expense or
because fair value was not believed to be the appropriate measure. The Board was
not persuaded by these arguments for the same reasons the IASB was not persuaded
(see paragraphs BC34-BC60).

Some respondents argued that there was no need for the Board to issue an FRS **N4**
because listed entities preparing consolidated financial statements would be required
by the EU Regulation on International Accounting Standards† to apply EU adopted
IFRS rather than the UK financial reporting framework from 2005. Notwithstanding the EU Regulation, the Board's responsibility continues to be to establish
and improve the UK financial reporting framework for the benefit of users, preparers, and auditors of financial information. Therefore, if it believes that a material
aspect of accounting practice in the UK is deficient and is capable of improvement –
as it does with share-based payments – its responsibility is to achieve the necessary
improvement.

Some respondents disagreed with the timetable proposed in the FRED. **N5**

(a) Some thought the FRS should be implemented in 2005 to coincide with the
substantial changes that many UK entities would be making to their financial
reporting to comply with the EU Regulation.

---

*For simplicity, the remainder of this section uses 'UK' to mean 'UK and the Republic of Ireland' unless the
context indicates otherwise.*

†*Regulation (EC) No 1606/2002 of the European Parliament and of the Council of 19 July 2002 on the
application of international accounting standards.*

(b)   Others thought it inappropriate for the UK to implement the IFRS in advance of an equivalent standard being implemented in the USA because to do so would put UK entities at a competitive disadvantage.* The Board does not accept this argument, not least because it implies that no improvement – however worthy and necessary – should be made to the UK's accounting requirements unless those same improvements are being made at the same time, or have already been made, in the USA. The Board also believes that users are generally sufficiently sophisticated to take superior accounting practices into account in evaluating an entity's financial statements, even if those superior accounting practices result in the recognition of additional expenses.

N6   In February 2004, the IASB issued its standard as IFRS 2 *Share-based Payment*. Having considered the responses received to FRED 31, the Board decided it should implement an FRS based on that IFRS as soon as possible. It took the view that, for listed entities, that means implementation for accounting periods beginning on or after 1 January 2005.

SCOPE EXEMPTIONS FROM FRS 20

N7   The Board has followed its usual practice by exempting from the FRS all entities falling within the scope of the Financial Reporting Standard for Smaller Entities (FRSSE).

All-employee schemes

N8   A number of respondents argued for some sort of exemption for broadly-based employee schemes such as Save-As-You-Earn (SAYE) schemes. In their view:

(a)   even though other share-based payment arrangements involve the sponsoring entity incurring an expense, broadly-based employee schemes do not;

(b)   requiring entities to recognise a fair value expense for such schemes would involve them taking on a burden that was not commensurate with the benefits derived from such an accounting treatment; and

(c)   the Board should take into account that, if entities were required to recognise a fair value expense for broadly-based employee schemes, many would discontinue the schemes which would not be a good thing.

N9   As the IASB makes clear in its Basis for Conclusions, it does not find such arguments persuasive. In its view, broadly-based schemes such as all-employee schemes *do* involve an expense and the benefits of recognising that expense in the financial statements justify the costs involved. Furthermore, the role of accounting is to report transactions and events in a neutral manner, not to permit or require favourable treatments of particular transactions so as to encourage entities to engage in those transactions. The Board shares those views.

At the moment, the USA has a non-mandatory standard that adopts a fair value approach to share-based payment expense recognition. It also has an active project that involves working with the IASB on a single, high-quality global accounting standard on share-based payments. A US exposure draft on equity-settled share-based payments is expected soon, with a final standard scheduled by the end of the year. The draft standard is expected to be similar to IFRS 2 in many important respects, although there will be some differences. The intention is that a convergence project will be undertaken as soon as is reasonably possible to bring the IFRS and the eventual US standard fully into line.

Unlisted entities

Some respondents suggested that unlisted entities also needed some sort of exemp- **N10** tion. Some stated that the public's interest in such entities was not as great as for listed entities, so the benefits of recognising a fair value expense would not be as great. Furthermore, unlisted entities would often have difficulty fair valuing their share-based payments. Therefore, unlisted entities should be exempt from the Standard or permitted to use some sort of simplified methodology. Other respondents thought unlisted entities needed more time to prepare for the FRS.

The IASB received similar comments in response to its draft IFRS and responded by **N11** amending its proposals to permit a simplified methodology to be used in circumstances in which an entity is unable to estimate reliably the measurement date fair value of the equity instruments granted (see paragraphs 24 and 25 of FRS 20). No specific exemption for unlisted entities was granted.

The Board agrees that there is no conceptual or practical reason for excluding **N12** unlisted entities from the scope of the FRS. However, anecdotal evidence suggests that many of the unlisted entities that make share-based payments will not be ready to implement the Standard in 2005; they need more time to gather the necessary information and develop the necessary systems and valuation techniques. The Board has decided therefore to delay implementation of FRS 20 for unlisted entities by one year until accounting periods beginning on or after 1 January 2006.

This decision meant it was necessary to include definitions of 'listed entity' and **N13** 'unlisted entity' in the FRS. Existing FRSs and FREDs suggested some possible definitions: FRS 13 *Derivatives and other Financial Instruments: Disclosures* refers to instruments that are "listed or publicly traded on a stock exchange or market" and FRS 22 (IAS 33) *Earnings per share* refers also to entities that are in the process of issuing instruments in public securities markets. However, the Board thought it would be best, and also least confusing, if it adopted the definition of a listed entity set out in the EU Regulation.

Parents' and subsidiaries' single entity financial statements

The other exemption that the Board considered concerns the single entity financial **N14** statements of parent and subsidiary entities whose financial information is also included in consolidated financial statements.

IFRS 2 does not differentiate between individual entity financial statements and **N15** consolidated financial statements, nor between subsidiaries or parents; the Standard applies to all entities and to all their financial statements.

The Board recognises that there is generally less interest from users in an entity's **N16** single entity financial statements if its financial information is also included in consolidated financial statements. However, it does not believe that is sufficient reason to justify exempting single entity financial statements from the scope of the Standard. The expense that arises on a share-based payment is no different from any other expense an entity incurs and should be treated in exactly the same way regardless of the type of financial statements being prepared.

IAS 32

N17   One of the issues that the Board will need to consider whenever it is implementing an FRS based on an IFRS is whether that IFRS relies on other IFRSs that have not yet been implemented in the UK.

N18   In the case of IFRS 2 it would appear that the only IFRS it assumes is already in place is IAS 32 *Financial Instruments: Disclosure and Presentation*; in particular the material in that standard on the equity/liability classification (the so-called 'presentation requirements'). The Board has recently announced* that it intends to implement those presentation requirements in the UK for all entities for accounting periods beginning on or after 1 January 2005.†

CONSEQUENTIAL AMENDMENTS TO EXISTING STANDARDS AND UITF ABSTRACTS

N19-N26   [Not reproduced, as all changes have been made to the underlying standards and abstracts]

THE FRS' IMPLICATIONS FOR DISTRIBUTABLE PROFITS

N27   A number of those responding to FRED 31 raised questions about the effect that the proposals would have on distributable profits. The Board's general policy is not to comment on distribution matters of this kind because, if they are material to the amount that an entity may wish to distribute, the entity will need to take its own legal advice.

N28   As explained above, FRS 20 supersedes UITF 17. When developing the original version of that Abstract, the UITF took legal advice on the implications of the required accounting treatment for the share premium account. A summary of the advice received was included in the Abstract. Some respondents have suggested that, although the Abstract itself is to be withdrawn, that legal advice will still have relevance in the context of FRS 20 and should therefore be repeated in the FRS. UITF 17's summary of the legal advice the UITF received is set out below, although it needs to be borne in mind that the accounting treatment required by FRS 20 is very different from that required by UITF 17, as is the rationale that underpins the respective requirements.

> "The UITF has received legal advice on the implications for share premium account when the accounting treatment required by this Abstract is followed. It has been advised that where new shares are issued in connection with an employee share scheme the share premium account will normally have to reflect only the cash subscribed for the shares (eg by the employee or by an ESOP). In such cases, any difference between the cash subscribed for the shares (which must be at least as much as the nominal value, as shares cannot be issued at a discount) and the fair value at the date of grant of rights should be credited to reserves other than the share premium account. This is on the basis that the services of the employee do not, as a matter of law, form part of the consideration received for the shares issued, and the UITF has been advised that this would be the usual legal interpretation of such transactions. Exceptionally,

---

*In its *UK Accounting Standards: A Strategy for Convergence with IFRS Discussion Paper*, which was issued in March 2004.

†*Editor's note:* Now FRS 25.

however, the terms of a transaction might be such as to lead to the opposite interpretation, and companies may need to take legal advice on this point. In such a case, the operation of section 99(2) of the Companies Act 1985 [prohibition of public company accepting undertaking to perform services in payment up of its shares] and section 103 [non-cash consideration to be valued before allotment of shares] would also have to be considered."

Basis for conclusions

Contents

Basis for conclusions

This Basis for Conclusions accompanies, but is not part of, IFRS 2.

> *ASB note:* The IASB's Basis for Conclusions, which accompanies IFRS 2, is set out below in full. It should be noted though that some of the discussion it contains concerns IASB requirements that have no equivalent in the UK or Republic of Ireland. Footnotes have been used to highlight those parts of the discussion.
>
> All references in this section to 'the Board' and 'Board members' are references to the IASB Board and IASB Board members.

INTRODUCTION

BC1 This Basis for Conclusions summarises the International Accounting Standards Board's considerations in reaching the conclusions in IFRS 2 *Share-based Payment*. Individual Board members gave greater weight to some factors than to others.

BC2 Entities often issue* shares or share options to pay employees or other parties. Share plans and share option plans are a common feature of employee remuneration, not only for directors and senior executives, but also for many other employees. Some entities issue shares or share options to pay suppliers, such as suppliers of professional services.

BC3 Until the issue of IFRS 2, there has been no International Financial Reporting Standard (IFRS) covering the recognition and measurement of these transactions. Concerns have been raised about this gap in international standards. For example, the International Organization of Securities Commissions (IOSCO), in its 2000 report on international standards, stated that IASC (the IASB's predecessor body) should consider the accounting treatment of share-based payment.

BC4 Few countries have standards on the topic. This is a concern in many countries, because the use of share-based payment has increased in recent years and continues to spread. Various standard-setting bodies have been working on this issue. At the time the IASB added a project on share-based payment to its agenda in July 2001, some standard-setters had recently published proposals. For example, the German Accounting Standards Committee published a draft accounting standard *Accounting for Share Option Plans and Similar Compensation Arrangements* in June 2001. The UK Accounting Standards Board led the development of the Discussion Paper *Accounting for Share-based Payment*, published in July 2000 by IASC, the ASB and other bodies represented in the G4+1.† The Danish Institute of State Authorised Public Accountants issued a Discussion Paper *The Accounting Treatment of Share-Based Payment* in April 2000. More recently, in December 2002, the Accounting Standards Board of Japan published a Summary Issues Paper on share-based payment. In March 2003, the US Financial Accounting Standards Board (FASB) added

---

The word 'issue' is used in a broad sense. For example, a transfer of shares held in treasury (own shares held) to another party is regarded as an 'issue' of equity instruments. Some argue that if options or shares are granted with vesting conditions, they are not 'issued' until those vesting conditions have been satisfied. However, even if this argument is accepted, it does not change the Board's conclusions on the requirements of the IFRS, and therefore the word 'issue' is used broadly, to include situations in which equity instruments are conditionally transferred to the counterparty, subject to the satisfaction of specified vesting conditions.

†*The G4+1 comprised members of the national accounting standard-setting bodies of Australia, Canada, New Zealand, the UK and the US, and IASC.*

to its agenda a project to review US accounting requirements on share-based payment. Also, the Canadian Accounting Standards Board (AcSB) recently completed its project on share-based payment. The AcSB standard requires recognition of all share-based payment transactions, including transactions in which share options are granted to employees (discussed further in paragraphs BC281 and BC282).

Users of financial statements and other commentators are calling for improvements **BC5** in the accounting treatment of share-based payment. For example, the proposal in the IASC/G4 + 1 Discussion Paper and ED 2 *Share-based Payment*, that share-based payment transactions should be recognised in the financial statements, resulting in an expense when the goods or services are consumed, received strong support from investors and other users of financial statements. Recent economic events have emphasised the importance of high quality financial statements that provide neutral, transparent and comparable information to help users make economic decisions. In particular, the omission of expenses arising from share-based payment transactions with employees has been highlighted by investors, other users of financial statements and other commentators as causing economic distortions and corporate governance concerns.

As noted above, the Board began a project to develop an IFRS on share-based **BC6** payment in July 2001. In September 2001, the Board invited additional comment on the IASC/G4 + 1 Discussion Paper, with a comment deadline of 15 December 2001. The Board received over 270 letters. During the development of ED 2, the Board was also assisted by an Advisory Group, consisting of individuals from various countries and with a range of backgrounds, including persons from the investment, corporate, audit, academic, compensation consultancy, valuation and regulatory communities. The Board received further assistance from other experts at a panel discussion held in New York in July 2002. In November 2002, the Board published an Exposure Draft, ED 2 *Share-based Payment*, with a comment deadline of 7 March 2003. The Board received over 240 letters. The Board also worked with the FASB after that body added to its agenda a project to review US accounting requirements on share-based payment. This included participating in meetings of the FASB's Option Valuation Group and meeting the FASB to discuss convergence issues.

SCOPE

Much of the controversy and complexity surrounding the accounting for share-based **BC7** payment relates to employee share options. However, the scope of IFRS 2 is broader than that. It applies to transactions in which shares or other equity instruments are granted to employees. It also applies to transactions with parties other than employees, in which goods or services are received as consideration for the issue of shares, share options or other equity instruments. The term 'goods' includes inventories, consumables, property, plant and equipment, intangible assets and other non-financial assets. Lastly, the IFRS applies to payments in cash (or other assets) that are 'share-based' because the amount of the payment is based on the price of the entity's shares or other equity instruments, eg cash share appreciation rights.

Broad-based employee share plans, including employee share purchase plans

Some employee share plans are described as 'broad-based' or 'allemployee' plans, in **BC8** which all (or virtually all) employees have the opportunity to participate, whereas other plans are more selective, covering individual or specific groups of employees (eg senior executives). Employee share purchase plans are often broad-based plans. Typically, employee share purchase plans provide employees with an opportunity to buy a specific number of shares at a discounted price, ie at an amount that is less than the fair value of the shares. The employee's entitlement to discounted shares is usually conditional upon specific conditions being satisfied, such as remaining in the service of the entity for a specified period.

BC9   The issues that arise with respect to employee share purchase plans are:

(a)   are these plans somehow so different from other employee share plans that a different accounting treatment is appropriate?

(b)   even if the answer to the above question is 'no', are there circumstances, such as when the discount is very small, when it is appropriate to exempt employee share purchase plans from an accounting standard on share-based payment?

BC10   Some respondents to ED 2 argued that broad-based employee share plans should be exempt from an accounting standard on share-based payment. The reason usually given was that these plans are different from other types of employee share plans and, in particular, are not a part of remuneration for employee services. Some argued that requiring the recognition of an expense in respect of these types of plans was perceived to be contrary to government policy to encourage employee share ownership. In contrast, other respondents saw no difference between employee share purchase plans and other employee share plans, and argued that the same accounting requirements should therefore apply. However, some suggested that there should be an exemption if the discount is small.

BC11   The Board concluded that, in principle, there is no reason to treat broad-based employee share plans, including broad-based employee share purchase plans, differently from other employee share plans (the issue of 'small' discounts is considered later). The Board noted that the fact that these schemes are available only to employees is in itself sufficient to conclude that the benefits provided represent employee remuneration. Moreover, the term 'remuneration' is not limited to remuneration provided as part of an individual employee's contract: it encompasses all benefits provided to employees. Similarly, the term services encompasses all benefits provided by the employees in return, including increased productivity, commitment or other enhancements in employee work performance as a result of the incentives provided by the share plan.

BC12   Moreover, distinguishing regular employee services from the additional benefits received from broad-based employee share plans would not change the conclusion that it is necessary to account for such plans. No matter what label is placed on the benefits provided by employees – or the benefits provided by the entity – the transaction should be recognised in the financial statements.

BC13   Furthermore, that governments in some countries have a policy of encouraging employee share ownership is not a valid reason for according these types of plans a different accounting treatment, because it is not the role of financial reporting to give favourable accounting treatment to particular transactions to encourage entities to enter into them. For example, governments might wish to encourage entities to provide pensions to their employees, to lessen the future burden on the state, but that does not mean that pension costs should be excluded from the financial statements. To do so would impair the quality of financial reporting. The purpose of financial reporting is to provide information to users of financial statements, to assist them in making economic decisions. The omission of expenses from the financial statements does not change the fact that those expenses have been incurred. The omission of expenses causes reported profits to be overstated and hence the financial statements are not neutral, are less transparent and comparable, and are potentially misleading to users.

There remains the question whether there should be an exemption for some plans, **BC14** when the discount is small. For example, FASB Statement of Financial Accounting Standards No. 123 *Accounting for Stock-Based Compensation* contains an exemption for employee share purchase plans that meet specified criteria, of which one is that the discount is small.

On the one hand, it seems reasonable to exempt an employee share purchase plan if it **BC15** has substantially no option features and the discount is small. In such situations, the rights given to the employees under the plan probably do not have a significant value, from the entity's perspective.

On the other hand, even if one accepts that an exemption is appropriate, specifying **BC16** its scope is problematic, eg deciding what constitutes a small discount. Some argue that a 5 per cent discount from the market price (as specified in SFAS 123) is too high, noting that a block of shares can be sold on the market at a price close to the current share price. Furthermore, it could be argued that it is unnecessary to exempt these plans from the standard. If the rights given to the employees do not have a significant value, this suggests that the amounts involved are immaterial. Because it is not necessary to include immaterial information in the financial statements, there is no need for a specific exclusion in an accounting standard.

For the reasons given in the preceding paragraph, the Board concluded that broad- **BC17** based employee share plans, including broad-based employee share purchase plans, should not be exempted from the IFRS.

However, the Board noted that there might be instances when an entity engages in a **BC18** transaction with an employee in his/her capacity as a holder of equity instruments, rather than in his/her capacity as an employee. For example, an entity might grant all holders of a particular class of its equity instruments the right to acquire additional equity instruments of the entity at a price that is less than the fair value of those equity instruments. If an employee receives such a right because he/she is a holder of that particular class of equity instruments, the Board concluded that the granting or exercise of that right should not be subject to the requirements of the IFRS, because the employee has received that right in his/her capacity as a shareholder, rather than as an employee.

Transfers of equity instruments to employees

In some situations, an entity might not issue shares or share options to employees (or **BC19** other parties) direct. Instead, a shareholder (or shareholders) might transfer equity instruments to the employees (or other parties).

Under this arrangement, the entity has received services (or goods) that were paid for **BC20** by its shareholders. The arrangement could be viewed as being, in substance, two transactions – one transaction in which the entity has reacquired equity instruments for nil consideration, and a second transaction in which the entity has received services (or goods) as consideration for equity instruments issued to the employees (or other parties).

The second transaction is a share-based payment transaction. Therefore, the Board **BC21** concluded that the entity should account for transfers of equity instruments by shareholders to employees or other parties in the same way as other share-based payment transactions. The Board reached the same conclusion with respect to transfers of equity instruments of the entity's parent, or of another entity within the same group as the entity, to the entity's employees or other suppliers.

BC22 However, such a transfer is not a share-based payment transaction if the transfer of equity instruments to an employee or other party is clearly for a purpose other than payment for goods or services supplied to the entity. This would be the case, for example, if the transfer is to settle a shareholder's personal obligation to an employee that is unrelated to employment by the entity, or if the shareholder and employee are related and the transfer is a personal gift because of that relationship.

Transactions within the scope of IAS 22 *Business Combinations**

BC23 An entity might acquire goods (or other non-financial assets) as part of the net assets acquired in a business combination for which the consideration paid included shares or other equity instruments issued by the entity. Because IAS 22 applies to the acquisition of assets and issue of shares in connection with a business combination, that is the more specific standard that should be applied to that transaction.

BC24 Therefore, equity instruments issued in a business combination in exchange for control of the acquiree are not within the scope of IFRS 2. However, equity instruments granted to employees of the acquiree in their capacity as employees, eg in return for continued service, are within the scope of IFRS 2. Also, the cancellation, replacement, or other modifications to share-based payment arrangements because of a business combination or other equity restructuring should be accounted for in accordance with IFRS 2.

Transactions within the scope of IAS 32 *Financial Instruments: Disclosure and Presentation* and IAS 39 *Financial Instruments: Recognition and Measurement*†

BC25 The IFRS includes consequential amendments to IAS 32 and IAS 39 to exclude from their scope transactions within the scope of IFRS 2.

BC26 For example, suppose the entity enters into a contract to purchase cloth for use in its clothing manufacturing business, whereby it is required to pay cash to the counterparty in an amount equal to the value of 1,000 of the entity's shares at the date of delivery of the cloth. The entity will acquire goods and pay cash at an amount based on its share price. This meets the definition of a share-based payment transaction. Moreover, because the contract is to purchase cloth, which is a non-financial item, and the contract was entered into for the purpose of taking delivery of the cloth for use in the entity's manufacturing business, the contract is not within the scope of IAS 32 and IAS 39.

BC27 The scope of IAS 32 and IAS 39 includes contracts to buy non-financial items that can be settled net in cash or another financial instrument, or by exchanging financial instruments, with the exception of contracts that were entered into and continue to be held for the purpose of the receipt or delivery of a non-financial item in accordance with the entity's expected purchase, sale or usage requirements. A contract that can be settled net in cash or another financial instrument or by exchanging financial instruments includes (a) when the terms of the contract permit either party

*ASB footnote: The equivalent standard in the UK and Republic of Ireland to IAS 22 is FRS 6 Acquisitions and Mergers. The reference in paragraph 5 of IFRS 2 to IAS 22 has therefore been replaced in FRS 20 with a reference to FRS 6.

†ASB footnote: There is no equivalent standard in the UK and Republic of Ireland to IAS 39. The equivalent standards to IAS 32 are FRS 4 Capital Instruments and FRS 13 Derivatives and other Financial Instruments: Disclosures. The implications of FRS 20 for those standards is explained in 'Notes on the standard's application in the UK and the Republic of Ireland' section.

to settle it net in cash or another financial instrument or by exchanging financial instruments; (b) when the ability to settle net in cash or another financial instrument, or by exchanging financial instruments, is not explicit in the terms of the contract, but the entity has a practice of settling similar contracts net in cash or another financial instrument, or by exchanging financial instruments (whether with the counterparty, by entering into offsetting contracts, or by selling the contract before its exercise or lapse); (c) when, for similar contracts, the entity has a practice of taking delivery of the underlying and selling it within a short period after delivery for the purpose of generating a profit from short-term fluctuations in price or dealer's margin; and (d) when the non-financial item that is the subject of the contract is readily convertible to cash (IAS 32, paragraphs 8-10 and IAS 39, paragraphs 5-7).

The Board concluded that the contracts discussed in paragraph BC27 should remain within the scope of IAS 32 and IAS 39 and they are therefore excluded from the scope of IFRS 2. **BC28**

RECOGNITION OF EQUITY-SETTLED SHARE-BASED PAYMENT TRANSACTIONS

When it developed ED 2, the Board first considered conceptual arguments relating to the recognition of an expense arising from equity-settled share-based payment transactions, including arguments advanced by respondents to the Discussion Paper and other commentators. Some respondents who disagreed with the recognition of an expense arising from particular share-based payment transactions (ie those involving employee share options) did so for practical, rather than conceptual, reasons. The Board considered those practical issues later (see paragraphs BC294-BC310). **BC29**

The Board focused its discussions on employee share options, because that is where most of the complexity and controversy lies, but the question of whether expense recognition is appropriate is broader than that it covers all transactions involving the issue of shares, share options or other equity instruments to employees or suppliers of goods and services. For example, the Board noted that arguments made by respondents and other commentators against expense recognition are directed solely at employee share options. However, if conceptual arguments made against recognition of an expense in relation to employee share options are valid (eg that there is no cost to the entity), those arguments ought to apply equally to transactions involving other equity instruments (eg shares) and to equity instruments issued to other parties (eg suppliers of professional services). **BC30**

The rationale for recognising all types of share-based payment transactions – irrespective of whether the equity instrument is a share or a share option, and irrespective of whether the equity instrument is granted to an employee or to some other party – is that the entity has engaged in a transaction that is in essence the same as any other issue of equity instruments. In other words, the entity has received resources (goods or services) as consideration for the issue of shares, share options or other equity instruments. It should therefore account for the inflow of resources (goods or services) and the increase in equity. Subsequently, either at the time of receipt of the goods or services or at some later date, the entity should also account for the expense arising from the consumption of those resources. **BC31**

Many respondents to ED 2 agreed with this conclusion. Of those who disagreed, some disagreed in principle, some disagreed for practical reasons, and some disagreed for both reasons. The arguments against expense recognition in principle were considered by the Board when it developed ED 2, as were the arguments against **BC32** expense recognition for practical reasons, as explained below and in paragraphs BC294-BC310.

BC33   Arguments commonly made against expense recognition include:

(a)   the transaction is between the shareholders and the employees, not the entity and the employees.

(b)   the employees do not provide services for the options.

(c)   there is no cost to the entity, because no cash or other assets are given up; the shareholders bear the cost, in the form of dilution of their ownership interests, not the entity.

(d)   the recognition of an expense is inconsistent with the definition of an expense in the conceptual frameworks used by accounting standard-setters, including the IASB's *Framework for the Preparation and Presentation of Financial Statements.**

(e)   the cost borne by the shareholders is recognised in the dilution of earnings per share (EPS); if the transaction is recognised in the entity's accounts, the resulting charge to the income statement would mean that EPS is 'hit twice'.

(f)   requiring the recognition of a charge would have adverse economic consequences, because it would discourage entities from introducing or continuing employee share plans.

'The entity is not a party to the transaction'

BC34   Some argue that the effect of employee share plans is that the existing shareholders transfer some of their ownership interests to the employees and that the entity is not a party to this transaction.

BC35   The Board did not accept this argument. Entities, not shareholders, set up employee share plans and entities, not shareholders, issue share options to their employees. Even if that were not the case, eg if shareholders transferred shares or share options direct to the employees, this would not mean that the entity is not a party to the transaction. The equity instruments are issued in return for services rendered by the employees and the entity, not the shareholders, receives those services. Therefore, the Board concluded that the entity should account for the services received in return for the equity instruments issued. The Board noted that this is no different from other situations in which equity instruments are issued. For example, if an entity issues warrants for cash, the entity recognises the cash received in return for the warrants issued. Although the effect of an issue, and subsequent exercise, of warrants might be described as a transfer of ownership interests from the existing shareholders to the warrant holders, the entity nevertheless is a party to the transaction because it receives resources (cash) for the issue of warrants and further resources (cash) for the issue of shares upon exercise of the warrants. Similarly, with employee share options, the entity receives resources (employee services) for the issue of the options and further resources (cash) for the issue of shares on the exercise of options.

'The employees do not provide services'

BC36   Some who argue that the entity is not a party to the transaction counter the points made above with the argument that employees do not provide services for the options, because the employees are paid in cash (or other assets) for their services.

* *ASB footnote:* The equivalent document in the UK and Republic of Ireland to the IASB's Framework is the ASB's Statement of Principles for Financial Reporting. Although the Statement of Principles is very similar to the Framework, it is not identical.

Again, the Board was not convinced by this argument. If it were true that employees **BC37** do not provide services for their share options, this would mean that entities are issuing valuable share options and getting nothing in return. Employees do not pay cash for the share options they receive. Hence, if they do not provide services for the options, the employees are providing nothing in return. If this were true, by issuing such options the entity's directors would be in breach of their fiduciary duties to their shareholders.

Typically, shares or share options granted to employees form one part of their **BC38** remuneration package. For example, an employee might have a remuneration package consisting of a basic cash salary, company car, pension, healthcare benefits, and other benefits including shares and share options. It is usually not possible to identify the services received in respect of individual components of that remuneration package, eg the services received in respect of healthcare benefits. But that does not mean that the employee does not provide services for those healthcare benefits. Rather, the employee provides services for the entire remuneration package.

In summary, shares, share options or other equity instruments are granted to **BC39** employees because they are employees. The equity instruments granted form a part of their total remuneration package, regardless of whether that represents a large part or a small part.

'There is no cost to the entity, therefore there is no expense'

Some argue that because share-based payments do not require the entity to sacrifice **BC40** any cash or other assets, there is no cost to the entity, and therefore no expense should be recognised.

The Board regards this argument as unsound, because it overlooks that: **BC41**

(a) every time an entity receives resources as consideration for the issue of equity instruments, there is no outflow of cash or other assets, and on every other occasion the resources received as consideration for the issue of equity instruments are recognised in the financial statements; and

(b) the expense arises from the consumption of those resources, not from an outflow of assets.

In other words, irrespective of whether one accepts that there is a cost to the entity, **BC42** an accounting entry is required to recognise the resources received as consideration for the issue of equity instruments, just as it is on other occasions when equity instruments are issued. For example, when shares are issued for cash, an entry is required to recognise the cash received. If a non-monetary asset, such as plant and machinery, is received for those shares instead of cash, an entry is required to recognise the asset received. If the entity acquires another business or entity by issuing shares in a business combination, the entity recognises the net assets acquired.

The recognition of an expense arising out of such a transaction represents the con- **BC43** sumption of resources received, ie the 'using up' of the resources received for the shares or share options. In the case of the plant and machinery mentioned above, the asset would be depreciated over its expected life, resulting in the recognition of an expense each year. Eventually, the entire amount recognised for the resources received when the shares were issued would be recognised as an expense (including any residual value, which would form part of the measurement of the gain or loss on disposal of the asset). Similarly, if another business or entity is acquired by an issue of shares, an expense is recognised when the assets acquired are consumed. For example, inventories acquired will be recognised as an expense when sold, even though no cash or other assets were disbursed to acquire those inventories.

BC44   The only difference in the case of employee services (or other services) received as consideration for the issue of shares or share options is that usually the resources received are consumed immediately upon receipt. This means that an expense for the consumption of resources is recognised immediately, rather than over a period of time. The Board concluded that the timing of consumption does not change the principle; the financial statements should recognise the receipt and consumption of resources, even when consumption occurs at the same time as, or soon after, receipt. This point is discussed further in paragraphs BC45-BC53.

'Expense recognition is inconsistent with the definition of an expense'

BC45   Some have questioned whether recognition of an expense arising from particular share-based payment transactions is consistent with accounting standard-setters' conceptual frameworks, in particular, the *Framework*, which states:

> Expenses are decreases in economic benefits during the accounting period in the form of outflows or *depletions of assets* or incurrences of liabilities that result in decreases in equity, other than those relating to distributions to equity participants. (paragraph 70, emphasis added)

BC46   Some argue that if services are received in a share-based payment transaction, there is no transaction or event that meets the definition of an expense. They contend that there is no outflow of assets and that no liability is incurred. Furthermore, because services usually do not meet the criteria for recognition as an asset, it is argued that the consumption of those services does not represent a depletion of assets.

BC47   The *Framework* defines an asset and explains that the term 'asset' is not limited to resources that can be recognised as assets in the balance sheet (*Framework*, paragraphs 49 and 50). Although services to be received in the future might not meet the definition of an asset,* services are assets when received. These assets are usually consumed immediately. This is explained in FASB Statement of Financial Accounting Concepts No. 6 *Elements of Financial Statements*:

> Services provided by other entities, including personal services, cannot be stored and are received and used simultaneously. They can be assets of an entity only momentarily as the entity receives and uses them although their use may create or add value to other assets of the entity... (paragraph 31)

BC48   This applies to all types of services, eg employee services, legal services and telephone services. It also applies irrespective of the form of payment. For example, if an entity purchases services for cash, the accounting entry is:

Dr   Services received

Cr   Cash paid

BC49   Sometimes, those services are consumed in the creation of a recognisable asset, such as inventories, in which case the debit for services received is capitalised as part of a recognised asset. But often the services do not create or form part of a recognisable asset, in which case the debit for services received is charged immediately to the income statement as an expense. The debit entry above (and the resulting expense)

---

*For example, the entity might not have control over future services.

does not represent the cash outflow that is what the credit entry was for. Nor does it represent some sort of balancing item, to make the accounts balance. The debit entry above represents the resources received, and the resulting expense represents the consumption of those resources.

The same analysis applies if the services are acquired with payment made in shares or share options. The resulting expense represents the consumption of services, ie a depletion of assets. **BC50**

To illustrate this point, suppose that an entity has two buildings, both with gas heating, and the entity issues shares to the gas supplier instead of paying cash. Suppose that, for one building, the gas is supplied through a pipeline, and so is consumed immediately upon receipt. Suppose that, for the other building, the gas is supplied in bottles, and is consumed over a period of time. In both cases, the entity has received assets as consideration for the issue of equity instruments, and should therefore recognise the assets received, and a corresponding contribution to equity. If the assets are consumed immediately (the gas received through the pipeline), an expense is recognised immediately; if the assets are consumed later (the gas received in bottles), an expense is recognised later when the assets are consumed. **BC51**

Therefore, the Board concluded that the recognition of an expense arising from share-based payment transactions is consistent with the definition of an expense in the *Framework*. **BC52**

The FASB considered the same issue and reached the same conclusion in SFAS 123: **BC53**

> Some respondents pointed out that the definition of expenses in FASB Concepts Statement No. 6, *Elements of Financial Statements*, says that expenses result from outflows or using up of assets or incurring of liabilities (or both). They asserted that because the issuance of stock options does not result in the incurrence of a liability, no expense should be recognised. The Board agrees that employee stock options are not a liability – like stock purchase warrants, employee stock options are equity instruments of the issuer. However, equity instruments, including employee stock options, are valuable financial instruments and thus are issued for valuable consideration, which...for employee stock options is employee services. Using in the entity's operations the benefits embodied in the asset received results in an expense... (Concepts Statement 6, paragraph 81, footnote 43, notes that, in concept most expenses decrease assets. However, if receipt of an asset, such as services, and its use occur virtually simultaneously, the asset often is not recorded.) [paragraph 88]

'Earnings per share is "hit twice"'

Some argue that any cost arising from share-based payment transactions is already recognised in the dilution of earnings per share (EPS). If an expense were recognised in the income statement, EPS would be 'hit twice'. **BC54**

However, the Board noted that this result is appropriate. For example, if the entity paid the employees in cash for their services and the cash was then returned to the entity, as consideration for the issue of share options, the effect on EPS would be the same as issuing those options direct to the employees. **BC55**

The dual effect on EPS simply reflects the two economic events that have occurred: the entity has issued shares or share options, thereby increasing the number of shares included in the EPS calculation – although, in the case of options, only to the extent **BC56** that the options are regarded as dilutive – and it has also consumed the resources it received for those options, thereby decreasing earnings. This is illustrated by the plant and machinery example mentioned in paragraphs BC42 and BC43. Issuing shares affects the number of shares in the EPS calculation, and the consumption (depreciation) of the asset affects earnings.

BC57   In summary, the Board concluded that the dual effect on diluted EPS is not doublecounting the effects of a share or share option grant – the same effect is not counted twice. Rather, two different effects are each counted once.

'Adverse economic consequences'

BC58   Some argue that to require recognition (or greater recognition) of employee share-based payment would have adverse economic consequences, in that it might discourage entities from introducing or continuing employee share plans.

BC59   Others argue that if the introduction of accounting changes did lead to a reduction in the use of employee share plans, it might be because the requirement for entities to account properly for employee share plans had revealed the economic consequences of such plans. They argue that this would correct the present economic distortion, whereby entities obtain and consume resources by issuing valuable shares or share options without accounting for those transactions.

BC60   In any event, the Board noted that the role of accounting is to report transactions and events in a neutral manner, not to give 'favourable' treatment to particular transactions to encourage entities to engage in those transactions. To do so would impair the quality of financial reporting. The omission of expenses from the financial statements does not change the fact that those expenses have been incurred. Hence, if expenses are omitted from the income statement, reported profits are overstated. The financial statements are not neutral, are less transparent and are potentially misleading to users. Comparability is impaired, given that expenses arising from employee share-based payment transactions vary from entity to entity, from sector to sector, and from year to year. More fundamentally, accountability is impaired, because the entities are not accounting for transactions they have entered into and the consequences of those transactions.

MEASUREMENT OF EQUITY-SETTLED SHARE-BASED PAYMENT TRANSACTIONS

BC61   To recognise equity-settled share-based payment transactions, it is necessary to decide how the transactions should be measured. The Board began by considering how to measure share-based payment transactions in principle. Later, it considered practical issues arising from the application of its preferred measurement approach. In terms of accounting principles, there are two basic questions:

(a)   which measurement basis should be applied?
(b)   when should that measurement basis be applied?

BC62   To answer these questions, the Board considered the accounting principles applying to equity transactions. The *Framework* states:

> Equity is the residual interest in the assets of the enterprise after deducting all of its liabilities...The amount at which equity is shown in the balance sheet is dependent upon the measurement of assets and liabilities. Normally, the aggregate amount of equity only by coincidence corresponds with the aggregate market value of the shares of the enterprise... (paragraphs 49 and 67).

The accounting equation that corresponds to this definition of equity is:　　　　**BC63**

　　assets minus liabilities equals equity

Equity is a residual interest, dependent on the measurement of assets and liabilities. **BC64**
Therefore, accounting focuses on recording changes in the left side of the equation
(assets minus liabilities, or net assets), rather than the right side. Changes in equity
arise from changes in net assets. For example, if an entity issues shares for cash, it
recognises the cash received and a corresponding increase in equity. Subsequent
changes in the market price of the shares do not affect the entity's net assets and
therefore those changes in value are not recognised.

Hence, the Board concluded that, when accounting for an equity-settled share-based **BC65**
payment transaction, the primary accounting objective is to account for the goods or
services received as consideration for the issue of equity instruments. Therefore,
equity-settled share-based payment transactions should be accounted for in the same
way as other issues of equity instruments, by recognising the consideration received
(the change in net assets), and a corresponding increase in equity.

Given this objective, the Board concluded that, in principle, the goods or services **BC66**
received should be measured at their fair value at the date when the entity obtains
those goods or as the services are received. In other words, because a change in net
assets occurs when the entity obtains the goods or as the services are received, the fair
value of those goods or services at that date provides an appropriate measure of the
change in net assets.

However, for share-based payment transactions with employees, it is usually difficult **BC67**
to measure directly the fair value of the services received. As noted earlier, typically
shares or share options are granted to employees as one component of their remuneration package. It is usually not possible to identify the services rendered in respect
of individual components of that package. It might also not be possible to measure
independently the fair value of the total package, without measuring directly the fair
value of the equity instruments granted. Furthermore, options or shares are sometimes granted as part of a bonus arrangement, rather than as a part of basic
remuneration, eg as an incentive to the employees to remain in the entity's employ,
or to reward them for their efforts in improving the entity's performance. By
granting share options, in addition to other remuneration, the entity is paying
additional remuneration to obtain additional benefits. Estimating the fair value of
those additional benefits is likely to be difficult.

Given these practical difficulties in measuring directly the fair value of the employee **BC68**
services received, the Board concluded that it is necessary to measure the other side
of the transaction, ie the fair value of the equity instruments granted, as a surrogate
measure of the fair value of the services received. In this context, the Board considered the same basic questions, as mentioned above:

(a)　which measurement basis should be applied?
(b)　when should that measurement basis be applied?

Measurement basis

The Board discussed the following measurement bases, to decide which should be **BC69**
applied in principle:

(a)　historical cost
(b)　intrinsic value

(c)   minimum value

(d)   fair value.

Historical cost

BC70   In jurisdictions where legislation permits, entities commonly repurchase their own shares, either directly or through a vehicle such as a trust, which are used to fulfil promised grants of shares to employees or the exercise of employee share options. A possible basis for measuring a grant of options or shares would be the historical cost (purchase price) of its own shares that an entity holds (own shares held), even if they were acquired before the award was made.

BC71   For share options, this would entail comparing the historical cost of own shares held with the exercise price of options granted to employees. Any shortfall would be recognised as an expense. Also, presumably, if the exercise price exceeded the historical cost of own shares held, the excess would be recognised as a gain.

BC72   At first sight, if one simply focuses on the cash flows involved, the historical cost basis appears reasonable: there is a cash outflow to acquire the shares, followed by a cash inflow when those shares are transferred to the employees (the exercise price), with any shortfall representing a cost to the entity. If the cash flows related to anything other than the entity's own shares, this approach would be appropriate. For example, suppose ABC Ltd bought shares in another entity, XYZ Ltd, for a total cost of CU500,000,* and later sold the shares to employees for a total of CU400,000. The entity would recognise an expense for the CU100,000 shortfall.

BC73   But when this analysis is applied to the entity's own shares, the logic breaks down. The entity's own shares are not an asset of the entity.† Rather, the shares are an interest in the entity's assets. Hence, the distribution of cash to buy back shares is a return of capital to shareholders, and should therefore be recognised as a decrease in equity. Similarly, when the shares are subsequently reissued or transferred, the inflow of cash is an increase in shareholders' capital, and should therefore be recognised as an increase in equity. It follows that no revenue or expense should be recognised. Just as the issue of shares does not represent revenue to the entity, the repurchase of those shares does not represent an expense.

BC74   Therefore, the Board concluded that historical cost is not an appropriate basis upon which to measure equity-settled share-based payment transactions.

---

*All monetary amounts in this Basis for Conclusions are denominated in 'currency units' (CU).

†The Discussion Paper discusses this point:

Accounting practice in some jurisdictions may present own shares acquired as an asset, but they lack the essential feature of an asset – the ability to provide future economic benefits. The future economic benefits usually provided by an interest in shares are the right to receive dividends and the right to gain from an increase in value of the shares. When a company has an interest in its own shares, it will receive dividends on those shares only if it elects to pay them, and such dividends do not represent a gain to the company, as there is no change in net assets: the flow of funds is simply circular. Whilst it is true that a company that holds its own shares in treasury may sell them and receive a higher amount if their value has increased, a company is generally able to issue shares to third parties at (or near) the current market price. Although there may be legal, regulatory or administrative reasons why it is easier to sell shares that are held as treasury shares than it would be to issue new shares, such considerations do not seem to amount to a fundamental contrast between the two cases. (Footnote to paragraph 4.7)

Intrinsic value

An equity instrument could be measured at its intrinsic value. The intrinsic value of a **BC75** share option at any point in time is the difference between the market price of the underlying shares and the exercise price of the option.

Often, employee share options have zero intrinsic value at the date of grant – **BC76** commonly the exercise price is at the market value of the shares at grant date. Therefore, in many cases, valuing share options at their intrinsic value at grant date is equivalent to attributing no value to the options.

However, the intrinsic value of an option does not fully reflect its value. Options sell **BC77** in the market for more than their intrinsic value. This is because the holder of an option need not exercise it immediately and benefits from any increase in the value of the underlying shares. In other words, although the ultimate benefit realised by the option holder is the option's intrinsic value at the date of exercise, the option holder is able to realise that future intrinsic value because of having held the option. Thus, the option holder benefits from the right to participate in future gains from increases in the share price. In addition, the option holder benefits from the right to defer payment of the exercise price until the end of the option term. These benefits are commonly referred to as the option's 'time value'.

For many options, time value represents a substantial part of their value. As noted **BC78** earlier, many employee share options have zero intrinsic value at grant date, and hence the option's value consists entirely of time value. In such cases, ignoring time value by applying the intrinsic value method at grant date understates the value of the option by 100 per cent.

The Board concluded that, in general, the intrinsic value measurement basis is not **BC79** appropriate for measuring share-based payment transactions, because omitting the option's time value ignores a potentially substantial part of an option's total value. Measuring share-based payment transactions at such an understated value would fail to represent those transactions faithfully in the financial statements.

Minimum value

A share option could be measured at its minimum value. Minimum value is based on **BC80** the premise that someone who wants to buy a call option on a share would be willing to pay at least (and the option writer would demand at least) the value of the right to defer payment of the exercise price until the end of the option's term. Therefore, minimum value can be calculated using a present value technique. For a dividend-paying share, the calculation is:

(a)   the current price of the share, minus
(b)   the present value of expected dividends on that share during the option term (if the option holder does not receive dividends), minus
(c)   the present value of the exercise price.

Minimum value can also be calculated using an option pricing model with an **BC81** expected volatility of effectively zero (not exactly zero, because some option pricing models use volatility as a divisor, and zero cannot be a divisor).

The minimum value measurement basis captures part of the time value of options, **BC82** being the value of the right to defer payment of the exercise price until the end of the option's term. It does not capture the effects of volatility. Option holders benefit from volatility because they have the right to participate in gains from increases in the share price during the option term without having to bear the full risk of loss from decreases in the share price. By ignoring volatility, the minimum value method produces a value that is lower, and often much lower, than values produced by methods designed to estimate the fair value of an option.

BC83   The Board concluded that minimum value is not an appropriate measurement basis, because ignoring the effects of volatility ignores a potentially large part of an option's value. As with intrinsic value, measuring share-based payment transactions at the option's minimum value would fail to represent those transactions faithfully in the financial statements.

Fair value

BC84   Fair value is already used in other areas of accounting, including other transactions in which noncash resources are acquired through the issue of equity instruments. For example, a business acquisition is measured at the fair value of the consideration given, including the fair value of any equity instruments issued by the entity.

BC85   Fair value, which is the amount at which an equity instrument granted could be exchanged between knowledgeable, willing parties in an arm's length transaction, captures both intrinsic value and time value and therefore provides a measure of the share option's total value (unlike intrinsic value or minimum value). It is the value that reflects the bargain between the entity and its employees, whereby the entity has agreed to grant share options to employees for their services to the entity. Hence, measuring share-based payment transactions at fair value ensures that those transactions are represented faithfully in the financial statements, and consistently with other transactions in which the entity receives resources as consideration for the issue of equity instruments.

BC86   Therefore, the Board concluded that shares, share options or other equity instruments granted should be measured at their fair value.

BC87   Of the respondents to ED 2 who addressed this issue, many agreed with the proposal to measure the equity instruments granted at their fair value. Some respondents who disagreed with the proposal, or who agreed with reservations, expressed concerns about measurement reliability, particularly in the case of smaller or unlisted entities. The issues of measurement reliability and unlisted entities are discussed in paragraphs BC294-BC310 and BC137-BC144, respectively.

Measurement date

BC88   The Board first considered at which date the fair value of equity instruments should be determined for the purpose of measuring share-based payment transactions with employees (and others providing similar services).* The possible measurement dates

*When the Board developed the proposals in ED 2, it focused on the measurement of equity-settled transactions with employees and with parties other than employees. ED 2 did not propose a definition of the term 'employees'. When the Board reconsidered the proposals in ED 2 in the light of comments received, it discussed whether the term might be interpreted too narrowly. This could result in a different accounting treatment of services received from individuals who are regarded as employees (eg for legal or tax purposes) and substantially similar services received from other individuals. The Board therefore concluded that the requirements of the IFRS for transactions with employees should also apply to transactions with other parties providing similar services. This includes services received from (1) individuals who work for the entity under its direction in the same way as individuals who are regarded as employees for legal or tax purposes and (2) individuals who are not employees but who render personal services to the entity similar to those rendered by employees. All references to employees therefore includes other parties providing similar services.

discussed were grant date, service date, vesting date and exercise date. Much of this discussion was in the context of share options rather than shares or other equity instruments, because only options have an exercise date.

In the context of an employee share option, grant date is when the entity and the **BC89** employee enter into an agreement, whereby the employee is granted rights to the share option, provided that specified conditions are met, such as the employee's remaining in the entity's employ for a specified period. Service date is the date when the employee renders the services necessary to become entitled to the share option.* Vesting date is the date when the employee has satisfied all the conditions necessary to become entitled to the share option. For example, if the employee is required to remain in the entity's employ for three years, vesting date is at the end of that threeyear period. Exercise date is when the share option is exercised.

To help determine the appropriate measurement date, the Board applied the **BC90** accounting concepts in the *Framework* to each side of the transaction. For transactions with employees, the Board concluded that grant date is the appropriate measurement date, as explained in paragraphs BC91-BC105. The Board also considered some other issues, as explained in paragraphs BC106-BC118. For transactions with parties other than employees, the Board concluded that delivery date is the appropriate measurement date (ie the date the goods or services are received, referred to as service date in the context of transactions with employees), as explained in paragraphs BC119-BC128.

The debit side of the transaction

Focusing on the debit side of the transaction means focusing on measuring the fair **BC91** value of the resources received. This measurement objective is consistent with the primary objective of accounting for the goods or services received as consideration for the issue of equity instruments (see paragraphs BC64-BC66). The Board therefore concluded that, in principle, the goods or services received should be measured at their fair value at the date when the entity obtains those goods or as the services are received.

However, if the fair value of the services received is not readily determinable, then a **BC92** surrogate measure must be used, such as the fair value of the share options or shares granted. This is the case for employee services.

If the fair value of the equity instruments granted is used as a surrogate measure of **BC93** the fair value of the services received, both vesting date and exercise date measurement are inappropriate because the fair value of the services received during a particular accounting period is not affected by subsequent changes in the fair value of the equity instrument. For example, suppose that services are received during years 13 as the consideration for share options that are exercised at the end of year 5. For services received in year 1, subsequent changes in the value of the share option in years 25 are unrelated to, and have no effect on, the fair value of those services when received.

Service date measurement measures the fair value of the equity instrument at the **BC94** same time as the services are received. This means that changes in the fair value of the

*Service date measurement theoretically requires the entity to measure the fair value of the share option at each date when services are received. For pragmatic reasons, an approximation would probably be used, such as the fair value of the share option at the end of each accounting period, or the value of the share option measured at regular intervals during each accounting period.

equity instrument during the vesting period affect the amount attributed to the services received. Some argue that this is appropriate, because, in their view, there is a correlation between changes in the fair value of the equity instrument and the fair value of the services received. For example, they argue that if the fair value of a share option falls, so does its incentive effects, which causes employees to reduce the level of services provided for that option, or demand extra remuneration. Some argue that when the fair value of a share option falls because of a general decline in share prices, remuneration levels also fall, and therefore service date measurement reflects this decline in remuneration levels.

BC95   The Board concluded, however, that there is unlikely to be a high correlation between changes in the fair value of an equity instrument and the fair value of the services received. For example, if the fair value of a share option doubles, it is unlikely that the employees work twice as hard, or accept a reduction in the rest of their remuneration package. Similarly, even if a general rise in share prices is accompanied by a rise in remuneration levels, it is unlikely that there is a high correlation between the two. Furthermore, it is likely that any link between share prices and remuneration levels is not universally applicable to all industry sectors.

BC96   The Board concluded that, at grant date, it is reasonable to presume that the fair value of both sides of the contract are substantially the same, ie the fair value of the services expected to be received is substantially the same as the fair value of the equity instruments granted. This conclusion, together with the Board's conclusion that there is unlikely to be a high correlation between the fair value of the services received and the fair value of the equity instruments granted at later measurement dates, led the Board to conclude that grant date is the most appropriate measurement date for the purposes of providing a surrogate measure of the fair value of the services received.

The credit side of the transaction

BC97   Although focusing on the debit side of the transaction is consistent with the primary accounting objective, some approach the measurement date question from the perspective of the credit side of the transaction, ie the issue of an equity instrument. The Board therefore considered the matter from this perspective too.

Exercise date

BC98   Under exercise date measurement, the entity recognises the resources received (eg employee services) for the issue of share options, and also recognises changes in the fair value of the option until it is exercised or lapses. Thus, if the option is exercised, the transaction amount is ultimately 'trued up' to equal the gain made by the option holder on exercise of the option. However, if the option lapses at the end of the exercise period, any amounts previously recognised are effectively reversed, hence the transaction amount is ultimately trued up to equal zero. The Board rejected exercise date measurement because it requires share options to be treated as liabilities, which is inconsistent with the definition of liabilities in the *Framework*. Exercise date measurement requires share options to be treated as liabilities because it requires the remeasurement of share options after initial recognition, which is inappropriate if the share options are equity instruments. A share option does not meet the definition of a liability, because it does not contain an obligation to transfer cash or other assets.

Vesting date, service date and grant date

The Board noted that the IASC/G4 + 1 Discussion Paper supported vesting date measurement, and rejected grant date and service date measurement, because it concluded that the share option is not issued until vesting date. It noted that the employees must perform their side of the arrangement by providing the necessary services and meeting any other performance criteria before the entity is obliged to perform its side of the arrangement. The provision of services by the employees is not merely a condition of the arrangement, it is the consideration they use to 'pay' for the share option. Therefore, the Discussion Paper concluded, in economic terms the share option is not issued until vesting date. Because the entity performs its side of the arrangement on vesting date, that is the appropriate measurement date.   **BC99**

The Discussion Paper also proposed recognising an accrual in equity during the vesting period to ensure that the services are recognised when they are received. It proposed that this accrual should be revised on vesting date to equal the fair value of the share option at that date. This means that amounts credited to equity during the vesting period will be subsequently remeasured to reflect changes in the value of that equity interest before vesting date. That is inconsistent with the *Framework* because equity interests are not subsequently remeasured, ie any changes in their value are not recognised. The Discussion Paper justified this remeasurement by arguing that because the share option is not issued until vesting date, the option is not being remeasured. The credit to equity during the vesting period is merely an interim measure that is used to recognise the partially completed transaction.   **BC100**

However, the Board noted that even if one accepts that the share option is not issued until vesting date, this does not mean that there is no equity interest until then. If an equity interest exists before vesting date, that interest should not be remeasured. Moreover, the conversion of one type of equity interest into another should not, in itself, cause a change in total equity, because no change in net assets has occurred.   **BC101**

Some supporters of vesting date suggest that the accrual during the performance period meets the definition of a liability. However, the basis for this conclusion is unclear. The entity is not required to transfer cash or other assets to the employees. Its only commitment is to issue equity instruments.   **BC102**

The Board concluded that vesting date measurement is inconsistent with the *Framework*, because it requires the remeasurement of equity.   **BC103**

Service date measurement does not require remeasurement of equity interests after initial recognition. However, as explained earlier, the Board concluded that incorporating changes in the fair value of the share option into the transaction amount is unlikely to produce an amount that fairly reflects the fair value of the services received, which is the primary objective.   **BC104**

The Board therefore concluded that, no matter which side of the transaction one focuses upon (ie the receipt of resources or the issue of an equity instrument), grant date is the appropriate measurement date under the *Framework*, because it does not require remeasurement of equity interests and it provides a reasonable surrogate measure of the fair value of the services received from employees.   **BC105**

Other issues

IAS 32 Financial Instruments: Disclosure and Presentation

BC106   As discussed above, under the definitions of liabilities and equity in the *Framework*, both shares and share options are equity instruments, because neither instrument requires the entity to transfer cash or other assets. Similarly, all contracts or arrangements that will be settled by the entity issuing shares or share options are classified as equity. However, this differs from the distinction between liabilities and equity applied in IAS 32. Although IAS 32 also considers, in its debt/equity distinction, whether an instrument contains an obligation to transfer cash or other assets, this is supplemented by a second criterion, which considers whether the number of shares to be issued (and cash to be received) on settlement is fixed or variable. IAS 32 classifies a contract that will or may be settled in the entity's own equity instruments as a liability if the contract is a non-derivative for which the entity is or may be obliged to deliver a variable number of the entity's own equity instruments; or a derivative that will or may be settled other than by the exchange of a fixed amount of cash or another financial asset for a fixed number of the entity's own equity instruments.

BC107   In some cases, the number of share options to which employees are entitled varies. For example, the number of share options to which the employees will be entitled on vesting date might vary depending on whether, and to the extent that, a particular performance target is exceeded. Another example is share appreciation rights settled in shares. In this situation, a variable number of shares will be issued, equal in value to the appreciation of the entity's share price over a period of time.

BC108   Therefore, if the requirements of IAS 32 were applied to equity-settled share-based payment transactions, in some situations an obligation to issue equity instruments would be classified as a liability. In such cases, final measurement of the transaction would be at a measurement date later than grant date.

BC109   The Board concluded that different considerations applied in developing IFRS 2. For example, drawing a distinction between fixed and variable option plans and requiring a later measurement date for variable option plans has undesirable consequences, as discussed in paragraphs BC272-BC275.

BC110   The Board concluded that the requirements in IAS 32, whereby some obligations to issue equity instruments are classified as liabilities, should not be applied in the IFRS on share-based payment. The Board recognises that this creates a difference between IFRS 2 and IAS 32. Before deciding whether and how that difference should be eliminated, the Board concluded that it is necessary to address this issue in a broader context, as part of a fundamental review of the definitions of liabilities and equity in the *Framework*, particularly because this is not the only debt/ equity classification issue that has arisen in the share-based payment project, as explained below.

Suggestions to change the definitions of liabilities and equity

BC111   In concluding that, for transactions with employees, grant date is the appropriate measurement date under the *Framework*, the Board noted that some respondents to ED 2 and the Discussion Paper support other measurement dates because they believe that the definitions of liabilities and equity in the *Framework* should be revised.

For example, some supporters of vesting date argue that receipt of employee services **BC112** between grant date and vesting date creates an obligation for the entity to pay for those services, and that the method of settlement should not matter. In other words, it should not matter whether that obligation is settled in cash or in equity instruments – both ought to be treated as liabilities. Therefore, the definition of a liability should be modified so that all types of obligations, however settled, are included in liabilities. But it is not clear that this approach would necessarily result in vesting date measurement. A share option contains an obligation to issue shares. Hence, if all types of obligations are classified as liabilities, then a share option would be a liability, which would result in exercise date measurement.

Some support exercise date measurement on the grounds that it produces the same **BC113** accounting result as 'economically similar' cash-settled share-based payments. For example, it is argued that share appreciation rights (SARs) settled in cash are substantially similar to SARs settled in shares, because in both cases the employee receives consideration to the same value. Also, if the SARs are settled in shares and the shares are immediately sold, the employee ends up in exactly the same position as under a cash-settled SAR, ie with cash equal to the appreciation in the entity's share price over the specified period. Similarly, some argue that share options and cash-settled SARs are economically similar. This is particularly true when the employee realises the gain on the exercise of share options by selling the shares immediately after exercise, as commonly occurs. Either way, the employee ends up with an amount of cash that is based on the appreciation of the share price over a period of time. If cash-settled transactions and equity-settled transactions are economically similar, the accounting treatment should be the same.

However, it is not clear that changing the distinction between liabilities and equity to **BC114** be consistent with exercise date measurement is the only way to achieve the same accounting treatment. For example, the distinction could be changed so that cash-settled employee share plans are measured at grant date, with the subsequent cash payment debited directly to equity, as a distribution to equity participants.

Others who support exercise date measurement do not regard share option holders as **BC115** part of the ownership group, and therefore believe that options should not be classified as equity. Option holders, some argue, are only potential owners of the entity. But it is not clear whether this view is held generally, ie applied to all types of options. For example, some who support exercise date measurement for employee share options do not necessarily advocate the same approach for share options or warrants issued for cash in the market. However, any revision to the definitions of liabilities and equity in the *Framework* would affect the classification of all options and warrants issued by the entity.

Given that there is more than one suggestion to change the definitions of liabilities **BC116** and equity, and these suggestions have not been fully explored, it is not clear exactly what changes to the definitions are being proposed.

Moreover, the Board concluded that these suggestions should not be considered in **BC117** isolation, because changing the distinction between liabilities and equity affects all sorts of financial interests, not just those relating to employee share plans. All of the implications of any suggested changes should be explored in a broader project to review the definitions of liabilities and equity in the *Framework*. If such a review resulted in changes to the definitions, the Board would then consider whether the IFRS on share-based payment should be revised.

Therefore, after considering the issues discussed above, the Board confirmed its **BC118** conclusion that grant date is the appropriate date at which to measure the fair value of the equity instruments granted for the purposes of providing a surrogate measure of the fair value of services received from employees.

Share-based payment transactions with parties other than employees

BC119   In many share-based payment transactions with parties other than employees, it should be possible to measure reliably the fair value of the goods or services received. The Board therefore concluded that the IFRS should require an entity to presume that the fair value of the goods or services received can be measured reliably.* However, in rare cases in which the presumption is rebutted, it is necessary to measure the transaction at the fair value of the equity instruments granted.

BC120   Some measurement issues that arise in respect of share-based payment transactions with employees also arise in transactions with other parties. For example, there might be performance (ie vesting) conditions that must be met before the other party is entitled to the shares or share options. Therefore, any conclusions reached on how to treat vesting conditions in the context of share-based payment transactions with employees also apply to transactions with other parties.

BC121   Similarly, performance by the other party might take place over a period of time, rather than on one specific date, which again raises the question of the appropriate measurement date.

BC122   SFAS 123 does not specify a measurement date for share-based payment transactions with parties other than employees, on the grounds that this is usually a minor issue in such transactions. However, the date at which to estimate the fair value of equity instruments issued to parties other than employees is specified in the US interpretation EITF 9618 *Accounting for Equity Instruments That Are Issued to Other Than Employees for Acquiring, or in Conjunction with Selling, Goods or Services*:

> [The measurement date is] the earlier of the following:
>
> 1.   The date at which a commitment for performance by the counterparty to earn the equity instruments is reached (a "performance commitment"), or
>
> 2.   The date at which the counterparty's performance is complete. (extract from Issue 1, footnotes excluded)

BC123   The second of these two dates corresponds to vesting date, because vesting date is when the other party has satisfied all the conditions necessary to become unconditionally entitled to the share options or shares. The first of the two dates does not necessarily correspond to grant date. For example, under an employee share plan, the employees are (usually) not committed to providing the necessary services, because they are usually able to leave at any time. Indeed, EITF 9618 makes it clear

---

*ED 2 proposed that equity-settled share-based payment transactions should be measured at the fair value of the goods or services received, or by reference to the fair value of the equity instruments granted, whichever fair value is more readily determinable. For transactions with parties other than employees, ED 2 proposed that there should be a rebuttable presumption that the fair value of the goods or services received is the more readily determinable fair value. The Board reconsidered these proposed requirements when finalising the IFRS. It concluded that it would be more consistent with the primary accounting objective (explained in paragraphs BC64-BC66) to require equity-settled share-based payment transactions to be measured at the fair value of the goods or services received, unless that fair value cannot be estimated reliably (eg in transactions with employees). For transactions with parties other than employees, the Board concluded that, in many cases, it should be possible to measure reliably the fair value of the goods or services received, as noted above. Hence, the Board concluded that the IFRS should require an entity to presume that the fair value of the goods or services received can be measured reliably.

that the fact that the equity instrument will be forfeited if the counterparty fails to perform is not sufficient evidence of a performance commitment (Issue 1, footnote 3). Therefore, in the context of share-based payment transactions with parties other than employees, if the other party is not committed to perform, there would be no performance commitment date, in which case the measurement date would be vesting date.

Accordingly, under SFAS 123 and EITF 9618, the measurement date for share-based payment transactions with employees is grant date, but for transactions with other parties the measurement date could be vesting date, or some other date between grant date and vesting date.   **BC124**

In developing the proposals in ED 2, the Board concluded that for transactions with parties other than employees that are measured by reference to the fair value of the equity instruments granted, the equity instruments should be measured at grant date, the same as for transactions with employees.   **BC125**

However, the Board reconsidered this conclusion during its redeliberations of the proposals in ED 2. The Board considered whether the delivery (service) date fair value of the equity instruments granted provided a better surrogate measure of the fair value of the goods or services received from parties other than employees than the grant date fair value of those instruments. For example, some argue that if the counterparty is not firmly committed to delivering the goods or services, the counterparty would consider whether the fair value of the equity instruments at the delivery date is sufficient payment for the goods or services when deciding whether to deliver the goods or services. This suggests that there is a high correlation between the fair value of the equity instruments at the date the goods or services are received and the fair value of those goods or services. The Board noted that it had considered and rejected a similar argument in the context of transactions with employees (see paragraphs BC94 and BC95). However, the Board found the argument more compelling in the case of transactions with parties other than employees, particularly for transactions in which the counterparty delivers the goods or services on a single date (or over a short period of time) that is substantially later than grant date, compared with transactions with employees in which the services are received over a continuous period that typically begins on grant date.   **BC126**

The Board was also concerned that permitting entities to measure transactions with parties other than employees on the basis of the fair value of the equity instruments at grant date would provide opportunities for entities to structure transactions to achieve a particular accounting result, causing the carrying amount of the goods or services received, and the resulting expense for the consumption of those goods or services, to be understated.   **BC127**

The Board therefore concluded that for transactions with parties other than employees in which the entity cannot measure reliably the fair value of the goods or services received at the date of receipt, the fair value of those goods or services should be measured indirectly, based on the fair value of the equity instruments granted, measured at the date the goods or services are received.   **BC128**

FAIR VALUE OF EMPLOYEE SHARE OPTIONS

The Board spent much time discussing how to measure the fair value of employee share options, including how to take into account common features of employee share options, such as vesting conditions and non-transferability. These discussions focused on measuring fair value at grant date, not only because the Board regarded   **BC129** grant date as the appropriate measurement date for transactions with employees, but also because more measurement issues arise at grant date than at later measurement dates. In reaching its conclusions in ED 2, the Board received assistance from the project's Advisory Group and from a panel of experts. During its redeliberations of the proposals in ED 2, the Board considered comments by respondents and advice received from valuation experts on the FASB's Option Valuation Group.

BC130 Market prices provide the best evidence of the fair value of share options. However, share options with terms and conditions similar to employee share options are seldom traded in the markets. The Board therefore concluded that, if market prices are not available, it will be necessary to apply an option pricing model to estimate the fair value of share options.

BC131 The Board decided that it is not necessary or appropriate to prescribe the precise formula or model to be used for option valuation. There is no particular option pricing model that is regarded as theoretically superior to the others, and there is the risk that any model specified might be superseded by improved methodologies in the future. Entities should select whichever model is most appropriate in the circumstances. For example, many employee share options have long lives, are usually exercisable during the period between vesting date and the end of the option's life, and are often exercised early. These factors should be considered when estimating the grant date fair value of share options. For many entities, this might preclude the use of the Black-Scholes-Merton formula, which does not take into account the possibility of exercise before the end of the share option's life and may not adequately reflect the effects of expected early exercise. This is discussed further below (paragraphs BC160-BC162).

BC132 All option pricing models take into account the following option features:

- the exercise price of the option
- the current market price of the share
- the expected volatility of the share price
- the dividends expected to be paid on the shares
- the rate of interest available in the market
- the term of the option.

BC133 The first two items define the intrinsic value of a share option; the remaining four are relevant to the share option's time value. Expected volatility, dividends and interest rate are all based on expectations over the option term. Therefore, the option term is an important part of calculating time value, because it affects the other inputs.

BC134 One aspect of time value is the value of the right to participate in future gains, if any. The valuation does not attempt to predict what the future gain will be, only the amount that a buyer would pay at the valuation date to obtain the right to participate in any future gains. In other words, option pricing models estimate the value of the share option at the measurement date, not the value of the underlying share at some future date.

BC135 The Board noted that some argue that any estimate of the fair value of a share option is inherently uncertain, because it is not known what the ultimate outcome will be, eg whether the share option will expire worthless or whether the employee (or other party) will make a large gain on exercise. However, the valuation objective is to measure the fair value of the rights granted, not to predict the outcome of having granted those rights. Hence, irrespective of whether the option expires worthless or the employee makes a large gain on exercise, that outcome does not mean that the grant date estimate of the fair value of the option was unreliable or wrong.

A similar analysis applies to the argument that share options do not have any value until they are in the money, ie the share price is greater than the exercise price. This argument refers to the share option's intrinsic value only. Share options also have a time value, which is why they are traded in the markets at prices greater than their intrinsic value. The option holder has a valuable right to participate in any future increases in the share price. So even share options that are at the money have a value when granted. The subsequent outcome of that option grant, even if it expires worthless, does not change the fact that the share option had a value at grant date. **BC136**

Application of option pricing models to unlisted and newly listed entities

As explained above, two of the inputs to an option pricing model are the entity's share price and the expected volatility of its share price. For an unlisted entity, there is no published share price information. The entity would therefore need to estimate the fair value of its shares (eg based on the share price of similar entities that are listed, or on a net assets or earnings basis). It would also need to estimate the expected volatility of that value. **BC137**

The Board considered whether unlisted entities should be permitted to use the minimum value method instead of a fair value measurement method. The minimum value method is explained earlier, in paragraphs BC80-BC83. Because it excludes the effects of expected volatility, the minimum value method produces a value that is lower, often much lower, than that produced by methods designed to estimate the fair value of an option. Therefore, the Board discussed how an unlisted entity could estimate expected volatility. **BC138**

An unlisted entity that regularly issues share options or shares to employees (or other parties) might have an internal market for its shares. The volatility of the internal market share prices provides a basis for estimating expected volatility. Alternatively, an entity could use the historical or implied volatility of similar entities that are listed, and for which share price or option price information is available, as the basis for an estimate of expected volatility. This would be appropriate if the entity has estimated the value of its shares by reference to the share prices of these similar listed entities. If the entity has instead used another methodology to value its shares, the entity could derive an estimate of expected volatility consistent with that methodology. For example, the entity might value its shares on the basis of net asset values or earnings, in which case it could use the expected volatility of those net asset values or earnings as a basis for estimating expected share price volatility. **BC139**

The Board acknowledged that these approaches for estimating the expected volatility of an unlisted entity's shares are somewhat subjective. However, the Board thought it likely that, in practice, the application of these approaches would result in underestimates of expected volatility, rather than overestimates, because entities were likely to exercise caution in making such estimates, to ensure that the resulting option values are not overstated. Therefore, estimating expected volatility is likely to produce a more reliable measure of the fair value of share options granted by unlisted entities than an alternative valuation method, such as the minimum value method. **BC140**

Newly listed entities would not need to estimate their share price. However, like unlisted entities, newly listed entities could have difficulties in estimating expected volatility when valuing share options, because they might not have sufficient historical share price information upon which to base an estimate of expected volatility. **BC141**

BC142　SFAS 123 requires such entities to consider the historical volatility of similar entities during a comparable period in their lives:

> For example, an entity that has been publicly traded for only one year that grants options with an average expected life of five years might consider the pattern and level of historical volatility of more mature entities in the same industry for the first six years the stock of those entities were publicly traded. (paragraph 285b)

BC143　The Board concluded that, in general, unlisted and newly listed entities should not be exempt from a requirement to apply fair value measurement and that the IFRS should include implementation guidance on estimating expected volatility for the purposes of applying an option pricing model to share options granted by unlisted and newly listed entities.

BC144　However, the Board acknowledged that there might be some instances in which an entity – such as (but not limited to) an unlisted or newly listed entity – cannot estimate reliably the grant date fair value of share options granted. In this situation, the Board concluded that the entity should measure the share option at its intrinsic value, initially at the date the entity obtains the goods or the counterparty renders service and subsequently at each reporting date until the final settlement of the share-based payment arrangement, with the effects of the remeasurement recognised in profit or loss. For a grant of share options, the share-based payment arrangement is finally settled when the options are exercised, forfeited (eg upon cessation of employment) or lapse (eg at the end of the option's life). For a grant of shares, the share-based payment arrangement is finally settled when the shares vest or are forfeited.

Application of option pricing models to employee share options

BC145　Option pricing models are widely used in, and accepted by, the financial markets. However, there are differences between employee share options and traded share options. The Board considered the valuation implications of these differences, with assistance from its Advisory Group and other experts, including experts in the FASB's Option Valuation Group, and comments made by respondents to ED 2. Employee share options usually differ from traded options in the following ways, which are discussed further below:

(a)　there is a vesting period, during which time the share options are not exercisable;

(b)　the options are non-transferable;

(c)　there are conditions attached to vesting which, if not satisfied, cause the options to be forfeited; and

(d)　the option term is significantly longer.

Inability to exercise during the vesting period

BC146　Typically, employee share options have a vesting period, during which the options cannot be exercised. For example, a share option might be granted with a ten-year life and a vesting period of three years, so the option is not exercisable for the first three years and can then be exercised at any time during the remaining seven years. Employee share options cannot be exercised during the vesting period because the employees must first 'pay' for the options, by providing the necessary services. Furthermore, there might be other specified periods during which an employee share option cannot be exercised (eg during a closed period).

In the finance literature, employee share options are sometimes called Bermudian **BC147** options, being partly European and partly American. An American share option can be exercised at any time during the option's life, whereas a European share option can be exercised only at the end of the option's life. An American share option is more valuable than a European share option, although the difference in value is not usually significant.

Therefore, other things being equal, an employee share option would have a higher **BC148** value than a European share option and a lower value than an American share option, but the difference between the three values is unlikely to be significant.

If the entity uses the Black-Scholes-Merton formula, or another option pricing model **BC149** that values European share options, there is no need to adjust the model for the inability to exercise an option in the vesting period (or any other period), because the model already assumes that the option cannot be exercised during that period.

If the entity uses an option pricing model that values American share options, such **BC150** as the binomial model, the inability to exercise an option during the vesting period can be taken into account in applying such a model.

Although the inability to exercise the share option during the vesting period does **BC151** not, in itself, have a significant effect on the value of the option, there is still the question whether this restriction has an effect when combined with non-transferability. This is discussed in the following section.

The Board therefore concluded that: **BC152**

(a) if the entity uses an option pricing model that values European share options, such as the Black-Scholes-Merton formula, no adjustment is required for the inability to exercise the options during the vesting period, because the model already assumes that they cannot be exercised during that period.

(b) if the entity uses an option pricing model that values American share options, such as a binomial model, the application of the model should take account of the inability to exercise the options during the vesting period.

Non-transferability

From the option holder's perspective, the inability to transfer a share option limits **BC153** the opportunities available when the option has some time yet to run and the holder wishes either to terminate the exposure to future price changes or to liquidate the position. For example, the holder might believe that over the remaining term of the share option the share price is more likely to decrease than to increase. Also, employee share option plans typically require employees to exercise vested options within a fixed period of time after the employee leaves the entity, or to forfeit the options.

In the case of a conventional share option, the holder would sell the option rather **BC154** than exercise it and then sell the shares. Selling the share option enables the holder to receive the option's fair value, including both its intrinsic value and remaining time value, whereas exercising the option enables the holder to receive intrinsic value only.

However, the option holder is not able to sell a non-transferable share option. **BC155** Usually, the only possibility open to the option holder is to exercise it, which entails forgoing the remaining time value. (This is not always true. The use of other derivatives, in effect, to sell or gain protection from future changes in the value of the option is discussed later.)

BC156   At first sight, the inability to transfer a share option could seem irrelevant from the entity's perspective, because the entity must issue shares at the exercise price upon exercise of the option, no matter who holds it. In other words, from the entity's perspective, its commitments under the contract are unaffected by whether the shares are issued to the original option holder or to someone else. Therefore, in valuing the entity's side of the contract, from the entity's perspective, non-transferability seems irrelevant.

BC157   However, the lack of transferability often results in early exercise of the share option, because that is the only way for the employees to liquidate their position. Therefore, by imposing the restriction on transferability, the entity has caused the option holder to exercise the option early, thereby resulting in the loss of time value. For example, one aspect of time value is the value of the right to defer payment of the exercise price until the end of the option term. If the option is exercised early because of non-transferability, the entity receives the exercise price much earlier than it would otherwise have done.

BC158   Non-transferability is not the only reason why employees might exercise share options early. Other reasons include risk aversion, lack of wealth diversification, and termination of employment (typically, employees must exercise vested options soon after termination of employment; otherwise the options are forfeited).

BC159   Recent accounting standards and proposed standards (including ED 2) address the issue of early exercise by requiring the expected life of a non-transferable share option to be used in valuing it, rather than the contractual option term. Expected life can be estimated either for the entire share option plan or for subgroups of employees participating in the plan. The estimate takes into account factors such as the length of the vesting period, the average length of time similar options have remained outstanding in the past and the expected volatility of the underlying shares.

BC160   However, comments from respondents to ED 2 and advice received from valuation experts during the Board's redeliberations led the Board to conclude that using a single expected life as an input into an option pricing model (eg the Black-Scholes-Merton formula) was not the best solution for reflecting in the share option valuation the effects of early exercise. For example, such an approach does not take into account the correlation between the share price and early exercise. It would also mean that the share option valuation does not take into account the possibility that the option might be exercised at a date that is later than the end of its expected life. Therefore, in many instances, a more flexible model, such as a binomial model, that uses the share option's contractual life as an input and takes into account the possibility of early exercise on a range of different dates in the option's life, allowing for factors such as the correlation between the share price and early exercise and expected employee turnover, is likely to produce a more accurate estimate of the option's fair value.

BC161   Binomial lattice and similar option pricing models also have the advantage of permitting the inputs to the model to vary over the share option's life. For example, instead of using a single expected volatility, a binomial lattice or similar option pricing model can allow for the possibility that volatility might change over the share option's life. This would be particularly appropriate when valuing share options granted by entities experiencing higher than usual volatility, because volatility tends to revert to its mean over time.

BC162   For these reasons, the Board considered whether it should require the use of a more flexible model, rather than the more commonly used Black-Scholes-Merton formula. However, the Board concluded that it was not necessary to prohibit the use of the

Black-Scholes-Merton formula, because there might be instances in which the formula produces a sufficiently reliable estimate of the fair value of the share options granted. For example, if the entity has not granted many share options, the effects of applying a more flexible model might not have a material impact on the entity's financial statements. Also, for share options with relatively short contractual lives, or share options that must be exercised within a short period of time after vesting date, the issues discussed in paragraph BC160 may not be relevant, and hence the Black-Scholes-Merton formula may produce a value that is substantially the same as that produced by a more flexible option pricing model. Therefore, rather than prohibit the use of the Black-Scholes-Merton formula, the Board concluded that the IFRS should include guidance on selecting the most appropriate model to apply. This includes the requirement that the entity should consider factors that knowledgeable, willing market participants would consider in selecting the option pricing model to apply.

Although non-transferability often results in the early exercise of employee share **BC163** options, some employees can mitigate the effects of non-transferability, because they are able, in effect, to sell the options or protect themselves from future changes in the value of the options by selling or buying other derivatives. For example, the employee might be able, in effect, to sell an employee share option by entering into an arrangement with an investment bank whereby the employee sells a similar call option to the bank, ie an option with the same exercise price and term. A zero-cost collar is one means of obtaining protection from changes in the value of an employee share option, by selling a call option and buying a put option.

However, it appears that such arrangements are not always available. For example, **BC164** the amounts involved have to be sufficiently large to make it worthwhile for the investment bank, which would probably exclude many employees (unless a collective arrangement was made). Also, it appears that investment banks are unlikely to enter into such an arrangement unless the entity is a top listed company, with shares traded in a deep and active market, to enable the investment bank to hedge its own position.

It would not be feasible to stipulate in an accounting standard that an adjustment to **BC165** take account of non-transferability is necessary only if the employees cannot mitigate the effects of non-transferability through the use of other derivatives. However, using expected life as an input into an option pricing model, or modelling early exercise in a binomial or similar model, copes with both situations. If employees were able to mitigate the effects of non-transferability by using derivatives, this would often result in the employee share options being exercised later than they would otherwise have been. By taking this factor into account, the estimated fair value of the share option would be higher, which makes sense, given that non-transferability is not a constraint in this case. If the employees cannot mitigate the effects of non-transferability through the use of derivatives, they are likely to exercise the share options much earlier than is optimal. In this case, allowing for the effects of early exercise would significantly reduce the estimated value of the share option.

This still leaves the question whether there is a need for further adjustment for the **BC166** combined effect of being unable to exercise or transfer the share option during the vesting period. In other words, the inability to exercise a share option does not, in itself, appear to have a significant effect on its value. But if the share option cannot be transferred and cannot be exercised, and assuming that other derivatives are not available, the holder is unable to extract value from the share option or protect its value during the vesting period.

However, it should be noted why these restrictions are in place: the employee has not **BC167** yet 'paid' for the share option by providing the required services (and fulfilling any other performance conditions). The employee cannot exercise or transfer a share option to which he/she is not yet entitled. The share option will either vest or fail to vest, depending on whether the vesting conditions are satisfied. The possibility of forfeiture resulting from failure to fulfil the vesting conditions is taken into account through the application of the modified grant date method (discussed in paragraphs BC170-BC184).

BC168   Moreover, for accounting purposes, the objective is to estimate the fair value of the share option, not the value from the employee's perspective. The fair value of any item depends on the expected amounts, timing, and uncertainty of the future cash flows relating to the item. The share option grant gives the employee the right to subscribe to the entity's shares at the exercise price, provided that the vesting conditions are satisfied and the exercise price is paid during the specified period. The effect of the vesting conditions is considered below. The effect of the share option being nonexercisable during the vesting period has already been considered above, as has the effect of non-transferability. There does not seem to be any additional effect on the expected amounts, timing or uncertainty of the future cash flows arising from the combination of nonexercisability and non-transferability during the vesting period.

BC169   After considering all of the above points, the Board concluded that the effects of early exercise, because of non-transferability and other factors, should be taken into account when estimating the fair value of the share option, either by modelling early exercise in a binomial or similar model, or using expected life rather than contracted life as an input into an option pricing model, such as the Black-Scholes-Merton formula.

Vesting conditions

BC170   Employee share options usually have vesting conditions. The most common condition is that the employee must remain in the entity's employ for a specified period, say three years. If the employee leaves during that period, the options are forfeited. There might also be other performance conditions, eg that the entity achieves a specified growth in share price or earnings.

BC171   Vesting conditions ensure that the employees provide the services required to 'pay' for their share options. For example, the usual reason for imposing service conditions is to retain staff; the usual reason for imposing other performance conditions is to provide an incentive for the employees to work towards specified performance targets.

BC172   Some argue that the existence of vesting conditions does not necessarily imply that the value of employee share options is significantly less than the value of traded share options. The employees have to satisfy the vesting conditions to fulfil their side of the arrangement. In other words, the employees' performance of their side of the arrangement is what they do to pay for their share options. Employees do not pay for the options with cash, as do the holders of traded share options; they pay with their services. Having to pay for the share options does not make them less valuable. On the contrary, it proves that the share options are valuable.

BC173   Others argue that the possibility of forfeiture without compensation for part-performance suggests that the share options are less valuable. The employees might partly perform their side of the arrangement, eg by working for part of the period, then have to leave for some reason, and forfeit the share options without compensation for that part performance. If there are other performance conditions, such as achieving a specified growth in the share price or earnings, the employees might work for the entire vesting period, but fail to meet the vesting conditions and therefore forfeit the share options.

Similarly, some argue that the entity would take into account the possibility of **BC174** forfeiture when entering into the agreement at grant date. In other words, in deciding how many share options to grant in total, the entity would allow for expected forfeitures. Hence, if the objective is to estimate at grant date the fair value of the entity's commitments under the share option agreement, that valuation should take into account that the entity's commitment to fulfil its side of the option agreement is conditional upon the vesting conditions being satisfied.

In developing the proposals in ED 2, the Board concluded that the valuation of **BC175** rights to share options or shares granted to employees (or other parties) should take into account all types of vesting conditions, including both service conditions and performance conditions. In other words, the grant date valuation should be reduced to allow for the possibility of forfeiture due to failure to satisfy the vesting conditions.

Such a reduction might be achieved by adapting an option pricing model to incor- **BC176** porate vesting conditions. Alternatively, a more simplistic approach might be applied. One such approach is to estimate the possibility of forfeiture at grant date, and reduce the value produced by an option pricing model accordingly. For example, if the valuation calculated using an option pricing model was CU15, and the entity estimated that 20 per cent of the share options would be forfeited because of failure to satisfy the vesting conditions, allowing for the possibility of forfeiture would reduce the grant date value of each option granted from CU15 to CU12.

The Board decided against proposing detailed guidance on how the grant date value **BC177** should be adjusted to allow for the possibility of forfeiture. This is consistent with the Board's objective of setting principles-based standards. The measurement objective is to estimate fair value. That objective might not be achieved if detailed, prescriptive rules were specified, which would probably become outdated by future developments in valuation methodologies.

However, respondents to ED 2 raised a variety of concerns about the inclusion of **BC178** vesting conditions in the grant date valuation. Some respondents were concerned about the practicality and subjectivity of including non-market performance con- ditions in the share option valuation. Some were also concerned about the practicality of including service conditions in the grant date valuation, particularly in conjunction with the units of service method proposed in ED 2 (discussed further in paragraphs BC203-BC217).

Some respondents suggested the alternative approach applied in SFAS 123, referred **BC179** to as the modified grant date method. Under this method, service conditions and non-market performance conditions are excluded from the grant date valuation (ie the possibility of forfeiture is not taken into account when estimating the grant date fair value of the share options or other equity instruments, thereby producing a higher grant date fair value), but are instead taken into account by requiring the transaction amount to be based on the number of equity instruments that eventually vest. Under this method, on a cumulative basis, no amount is recognised for goods or services received if the equity instruments granted do not vest because of failure to satisfy a vesting condition (other than a market condition), eg the counterparty fails to complete a specified service period, or a performance condition (other than a market condition) is not satisfied.

BC180 After considering respondents' comments and obtaining further advice from valuation experts, the Board decided to adopt the modified grant date method applied in SFAS 123. However, the Board decided that it should not permit the choice available in SFAS 123 to account for the effects of expected or actual forfeitures of share options or other equity instruments because of failure to satisfy a service condition. For a grant of equity instruments with a service condition, SFAS 123 permits an entity to choose at grant date to recognise the services received based on an estimate of the number of share options or other equity instruments expected to vest, and to revise that estimate, if necessary, if subsequent information indicates that actual forfeitures are likely to differ from previous estimates. Alternatively, an entity may begin recognising the services received as if all the equity instruments granted that are subject to a service requirement are expected to vest. The effects of forfeitures are then recognised when those forfeitures occur, by reversing any amounts previously recognised for services received as consideration for equity instruments that are forfeited.

BC181 The Board decided that the latter method should not be permitted. Given that the transaction amount is ultimately based on the number of equity instruments that vest, it is appropriate to estimate the number of expected forfeitures when recognising the services received during the vesting period. Furthermore, by ignoring expected forfeitures until those forfeitures occur, the effects of reversing any amounts previously recognised might result in a distortion of remuneration expense recognised during the vesting period. For example, an entity that experiences a high level of forfeitures might recognise a large amount of remuneration expense in one period, which is then reversed in a later period.

BC182 Therefore, the Board decided that the IFRS should require an entity to estimate the number of equity instruments expected to vest and to revise that estimate, if necessary, if subsequent information indicates that actual forfeitures are likely to differ from previous estimates.

BC183 Under SFAS 123, market conditions (eg a condition involving a target share price, or specified amount of intrinsic value on which vesting or exercisability is conditioned) are included in the grant date valuation, without subsequent reversal. That is to say, when estimating the fair value of the equity instruments at grant date, the entity takes into account the possibility that the market condition may not be satisfied. Having allowed for that possibility in the grant date valuation of the equity instruments, no adjustment is made to the number of equity instruments included in the calculation of the transaction amount, irrespective of the outcome of the market condition. In other words, the entity recognises the goods or services received from a counterparty that satisfies all other vesting conditions (eg services received from an employee who remains in service for the specified service period), irrespective of whether that market condition is satisfied. The treatment of market conditions therefore contrasts with the treatment of other types of vesting conditions. As explained in paragraph BC179, under the modified grant date method, vesting conditions are not taken into account when estimating the fair value of the equity instruments at grant date, but are instead taken into account by requiring the transaction amount to be based on the number of equity instruments that eventually vest.

BC184 The Board considered whether it should apply the same approach to market conditions as is applied in SFAS 123. It might be argued that it is not appropriate to distinguish between market conditions and other types of performance conditions, because to do so could create opportunities for arbitrage, or cause an economic distortion by encouraging entities to favour one type of performance condition over another. However, the Board noted that it is not clear what the result would be. On the one hand, some entities might prefer the 'truing up' aspect of the modified grant date method, because it permits a reversal of remuneration expense if the condition is not met. On the other hand, if the performance condition is met, and it has not been incorporated into the grant date valuation (as is the case when the modified grant date method is used), the expense will be higher than it would otherwise have been (ie if the performance condition had been incorporated into the grant date valuation). Furthermore, some entities might prefer to avoid the potential volatility caused by the truing up mechanism. Therefore, it is not clear whether having a different treatment for market and non-market performance conditions will necessarily cause entities to favour market conditions over non-market performance conditions, or vice versa. Furthermore, the practical difficulties that led the Board to conclude that non-market performance conditions should be dealt with via the modified grant date method rather than being included in the grant date valuation do not apply to market conditions, because market conditions can be incorporated into option pricing models. Moreover, it is difficult to distinguish between market conditions, such as a target share price, and the market condition that is inherent in the option itself, ie that the option will be exercised only if the share price on the date of exercise exceeds the exercise price. For these reasons, the Board concluded that the IFRS should apply the same approach as is applied in SFAS 123.

Option term

Employee share options often have a long contractual life, eg ten years. Traded **BC185** options typically have short lives, often only a few months. Estimating the inputs required by an option pricing model, such as expected volatility, over long periods can be difficult, giving rise to the possibility of significant estimation error. This is not usually a problem with traded share options, given their much shorter lives.

However, some share options traded over the counter have long lives, such as ten or **BC186** fifteen years. Option pricing models are used to value them. Therefore, contrary to the argument sometimes advanced, option pricing models can be (and are being) applied to long-lived share options.

Moreover, the potential for estimation error is mitigated by using a binomial or **BC187** similar model that allows for changes in model inputs over the share option's life, such as expected volatility, and interest and dividend rates, that could occur and the probability of those changes occurring during the term of the share option. The potential for estimation error is further mitigated by taking into account the possibility of early exercise, either by using expected life rather than contracted life as an input into an option pricing model or by modelling exercise behaviour in a binomial or similar model, because this reduces the expected term of the share option. Because employees often exercise their share options relatively early in the share option's life, the expected term is usually much shorter than contracted life.

Other features of employee share option plans

Whilst the features discussed above are common to most employee share options, **BC188** some might include other features. For example, some share options have a reload feature. This entitles the employee to automatic grants of additional share options whenever he/she exercises previously granted share options and pays the exercise price in the entity's shares rather than in cash. Typically, the employee is granted a new share option, called a reload option, for each share surrendered when exercising the previous share option. The exercise price of the reload option is usually set at the market price of the shares on the date the reload option is granted.

BC189   When SFAS 123 was developed, the FASB concluded that, ideally, the value of the reload feature should be included in the valuation of the original share option at grant date. However, at that time the FASB believed that it was not possible to do so. Accordingly, SFAS 123 does not require the reload feature to be included in the grant date valuation of the original share option. Instead, reload options granted upon exercise of the original share options are accounted for as a new share option grant.

BC190   However, recent academic research indicates that it is possible to value the reload feature at grant date, eg Saly, Jagannathan and Huddart (1999).* However, if significant uncertainties exist, such as the number and timing of expected grants of reload options, it might not be practicable to include the reload feature in the grant date valuation.

BC191   When it developed ED 2, the Board concluded that the reload feature should be taken into account, where practicable, when measuring the fair value of the share options granted. However, if the reload feature was not taken into account, then when the reload option is granted, it should be accounted for as a new share option grant.

BC192   Many respondents to ED 2 agreed with the proposals in ED 2. However, some disagreed. For example, some disagreed with there being a choice of treatments. Some respondents supported always treating reload options granted as new grants whereas others supported always including the reload feature in the grant date valuation. Some expressed concerns about the practicality of including the reload feature in the grant date valuation. After reconsidering this issue, the Board concluded that the reload feature should not be included in the grant date valuation and therefore all reload options granted should be accounted for as new share option grants.

BC193   There may be other features of employee (and other) share options that the Board has not yet considered. But even if the Board were to consider every conceivable feature of employee (and other) share options that exist at present, new features might be developed in the future.

BC194   The Board therefore concluded that the IFRS should focus on setting out clear principles to be applied to share-based payment transactions, and provide guidance on the more common features of employee share options, but should not prescribe extensive application guidance, which would be likely to become outdated.

BC195   Nevertheless, the Board considered whether there are share options with such unusual or complex features that it is too difficult to make a reliable estimate of their fair value and, if so, what the accounting treatment should be.

BC196   SFAS 123 states that "it should be possible to reasonably estimate the fair value of most stock options and other equity instruments at the date they are granted" (paragraph 21). However, it states that, "in unusual circumstances, the terms of the stock option or other equity instrument may make it virtually impossible to reasonably estimate the instrument's fair value at the date it is granted". The standard requires that, in such situations, measurement should be delayed until it is possible to estimate reasonably the instrument's fair value. It notes that this is likely to be the date at which the number of shares to which the employee is entitled and the exercise price are determinable. This could be vesting date. The standard requires that

P J Saly, R Jagannathan and S J Huddart. 1999. Valuing the Reload Features of Executive Stock Options. Accounting Horizons 13 (3): 219240.

estimates of compensation expense for earlier periods (ie until it is possible to estimate fair value) should be based on current intrinsic value.

The Board thought it unlikely that entities could not reasonably determine the fair value of share options at grant date, particularly after excluding vesting conditions* and reload features from the grant date valuation. The share options form part of the employee's remuneration package, and it seems reasonable to presume that an entity's management would consider the value of the share options to satisfy itself that the employee's remuneration package is fair and reasonable. **BC197**

When it developed ED 2, the Board concluded that there should be no exceptions to the requirement to apply a fair value measurement basis, and therefore it was not necessary to include in the proposed IFRS specific accounting requirements for share options that are difficult to value. **BC198**

However, after considering respondents' comments, particularly with regard to unlisted entities, the Board reconsidered this issue. The Board concluded that, in rare cases only, in which the entity could not estimate reliably the grant date fair value of the equity instruments granted, the entity should measure the equity instruments at intrinsic value, initially at grant date and subsequently at each reporting date until the final settlement of the share-based payment arrangement, with the effects of the remeasurement recognised in profit or loss. For a grant of share options, the share-based payment arrangement is finally settled when the share options are exercised, are forfeited (eg upon cessation of employment) or lapse (eg at the end of the option's life). For a grant of shares, the share-based payment arrangement is finally settled when the shares vest or are forfeited. This requirement would apply to all entities, including listed and unlisted entities. **BC199**

RECOGNITION AND MEASUREMENT OF SERVICES RECEIVED IN AN EQUITY-SETTLED SHARE-BASED PAYMENT TRANSACTION

During the vesting period

In an equity-settled share-based payment transaction, the accounting objective is to recognise the goods or services received as consideration for the entity's equity instruments, measured at the fair value of those goods or services when received. For transactions in which the entity receives employee services, it is often difficult to measure directly the fair value of the services received. In this case, the Board concluded that the fair value of the equity instruments granted should be used as a surrogate measure of the fair value of the services received. This raises the question how to use that surrogate measure to derive an amount to attribute to the services received. Another related question is how the entity should determine when the services are received. **BC200**

Starting with the latter question, some argue that shares or share options are often granted to employees for past services rather than future services, or mostly for past services, irrespective of whether the employees are required to continue working for the entity for a specified future period before their rights to those shares or share options vest. Conversely, some argue that shares or share options granted provide a future incentive to the employees and those incentive effects continue after vesting date, which implies that the entity receives services from employees during a period that extends beyond vesting date. For share options in particular, some argue that **BC201**

ie vesting conditions other than market conditions.

employees render services beyond vesting date, because employees are able to benefit from an option's time value between vesting date and exercise date only if they continue to work for the entity (since usually a departing employee must exercise the share options within a short period, otherwise they are forfeited).

BC202 However, the Board concluded that if the employees are required to complete a specified service period to become entitled to the shares or share options, this requirement provides the best evidence of when the employees render services in return for the shares or share options. Consequently, the Board concluded that the entity should presume that the services are received during the vesting period. If the shares or share options vest immediately, it should be presumed that the entity has already received the services, in the absence of evidence to the contrary. An example of when immediately vested shares or share options are not for past services is when the employee concerned has only recently begun working for the entity, and the shares or share options are granted as a signing bonus. But in this situation, it might nevertheless be necessary to recognise an expense immediately, if the future employee services do not meet the definition of an asset.

BC203 Returning to the first question in paragraph BC200, when the Board developed ED 2 it developed an approach whereby the fair value of the shares or share options granted, measured at grant date and allowing for all vesting conditions, is divided by the number of units of service expected to be received to determine the deemed fair value of each unit of service subsequently received.

BC204 For example, suppose that the fair value of share options granted, before taking into account the possibility of forfeiture, is CU750,000. Suppose that the entity estimates the possibility of forfeiture because of failure of the employees to complete the required threeyear period of service is 20 per cent (based on a weighted average probability), and hence it estimates the fair value of the options granted at CU600,000 (CU750,000 × 80%). The entity expects to receive 1,350 units of service over the threeyear vesting period.

BC205 Under the units of service method proposed in ED 2, the deemed fair value per unit of service subsequently received is CU444.44 (CU600,000/ 1,350). If everything turns out as expected, the amount recognised for services received is CU600,000 (CU444.44 × 1,350).

BC206 This approach is based on the presumption that there is a fairly bargained contract at grant date. Thus the entity has granted share options valued at CU600,000 and expects to receive services valued at CU600,000 in return. It does not expect all share options granted to vest because it does not expect all employees to complete three years' service. Expectations of forfeiture because of employee departures are taken into account when estimating the fair value of the share options granted, and when determining the fair value of the services to be received in return.

BC207 Under the units of service method, the amount recognised for services received during the vesting period might exceed CU600,000, if the entity receives more services than expected. This is because the objective is to account for the services subsequently received, not the fair value of the share options granted. In other words, the objective is not to estimate the fair value of the share options granted and then spread that amount over the vesting period. Rather, the objective is to account for the services subsequently received, because it is the receipt of those services that causes a change in net assets and hence a change in equity. Because of the practical difficulty of valuing those services directly, the fair value of the share options granted is used as a surrogate measure to determine the fair value of each unit of service subsequently received, and therefore the transaction amount is dependent upon the number of units of service actually received. If more are received than expected, the transaction amount will be greater than CU600,000. If fewer services are received, the transaction amount will be less than CU600,000.

Hence, a grant date measurement method is used as a practical expedient to achieve **BC208** the accounting objective, which is to account for the services actually received in the vesting period. The Board noted that many who support grant date measurement do so for reasons that focus on the entity's commitments under the contract, not the services received. They take the view that the entity has conveyed to its employees valuable equity instruments at grant date and that the accounting objective should be to account for the equity instruments conveyed. Similarly, supporters of vesting date measurement argue that the entity does not convey valuable equity instruments to the employees until vesting date, and that the accounting objective should be to account for the equity instruments conveyed at vesting date. Supporters of exercise date measurement argue that, ultimately, the valuable equity instruments conveyed by the entity to the employees are the shares issued on exercise date and the objective should be to account for the value given up by the entity by issuing equity instruments at less than their fair value.

Hence all of these arguments for various measurement dates are focused entirely on **BC209** what the entity (or its shareholders) has given up under the share-based payment arrangement, and accounting for that sacrifice. Therefore, if 'grant date measurement' were applied as a matter of principle, the primary objective would be to account for the value of the rights granted. Depending on whether the services have already been received and whether a prepayment for services to be received in the future meets the definition of an asset, the other side of the transaction would either be recognised as an expense at grant date, or capitalised as a prepayment and amortised over some period of time, such as over the vesting period or over the expected life of the share option. Under this view of grant date measurement, there would be no subsequent adjustment for actual outcomes. No matter how many share options vest or how many share options are exercised, that does not change the value of the rights given to the employees at grant date.

Therefore, the reason why some support grant date measurement differs from the **BC210** reason why the Board concluded that the fair value of the equity instruments granted should be measured at grant date. This means that some will have different views about the consequences of applying grant date measurement. Because the units of service method is based on using the fair value of the equity instruments granted, measured at grant date, as a surrogate measure of the fair value of the services received, the total transaction amount is dependent upon the number of units of service received.

Some respondents to ED 2 disagreed with the units of service method in principle, **BC211** because they did not accept that the fair value of the services received should be the accounting focus. Rather, the respondents focused on accounting for the 'cost' of the equity instruments issued (ie the credit side of the transaction rather than the debit side), and took the view that if the share options or shares are forfeited, no cost was incurred, and thus any amounts recognised previously should be reversed, as would happen with a cash-settled transaction.

Some respondents also disagreed with the treatment of performance conditions **BC212** under the units of service method, because if the employee completes the required service period but the equity instruments do not vest because of the performance condition not being satisfied, there is no reversal of amounts recognised during the vesting period. Some argue that this result is unreasonable because, if the performance condition is not satisfied, then the employee did not perform as required, hence it is inappropriate to recognise an expense for services received or consumed, because the entity did not receive the specified services.

BC213 The Board considered and rejected the above arguments made against the units of service method in principle. For example, the Board noted that the objective of accounting for the services received, rather than the cost of the equity instruments issued, is consistent with the accounting treatment of other issues of equity instruments, and with the IASB *Framework*. With regard to performance conditions, the Board noted that the strength of the argument in paragraph BC212 depends on the extent to which the employee has control or influence over the achievement of the performance target. One cannot necessarily conclude that the nonattainment of the performance target is a good indication that the employee has failed to perform his/her side of the arrangement (ie failed to provide services).

BC214 Therefore, the Board was not persuaded by those respondents who disagreed with the units of service method in principle. However, the Board also noted that some respondents raised practical concerns about the method. Some respondents regarded the units of service method as too complex and burdensome to apply in practice. For example, if an entity granted share options to a group of employees but did not grant the same number of share options to each employee (eg the number might vary according to their salary or position in the entity), it would be necessary to calculate a different deemed fair value per unit of service for each individual employee (or for each subgroup of employees, if there are groups of employees who each received the same number of options). Then the entity would have to track each employee, to calculate the amount to recognise for each employee. Furthermore, in some circumstances, an employee share or share option scheme might not require the employee to forfeit the shares or share options if the employee leaves during the vesting period in specified circumstances. Under the terms of some schemes, employees can retain their share options or shares if they are classified as a 'good leaver', eg a departure resulting from circumstances not within the employee's control, such as compulsory retirement, ill health or redundancy. Therefore, in estimating the possibility of forfeiture, it is not simply a matter of estimating the possibility of employee departure during the vesting period. It is also necessary to estimate whether those departures will be 'good leavers' or 'bad leavers'. And because the share options or shares will vest upon departure of 'good leavers', the expected number of units to be received and the expected length of the vesting period will be shorter for this group of employees. These factors would need to be incorporated into the application of the units of service method.

BC215 Some respondents also raised practical concerns about applying the units of service method to grants with performance conditions. These concerns include the difficulty of incorporating non-market and complex performance conditions into the grant date valuation, the additional subjectivity that this introduces, and that it was unclear how to apply the method when the length of the vesting period is not fixed, because it depends on when a performance condition is satisfied.

BC216 The Board considered the practical concerns raised by respondents, and obtained further advice from valuation experts concerning the difficulties highlighted by respondents of including non-market performance conditions in the grant date valuation. Because of these practical considerations, the Board concluded that the units of service method should not be retained in the IFRS. Instead, the Board decided to adopt the modified grant date method applied in SFAS 123. Under this method, service conditions and non-market performance conditions are excluded from the grant date valuation (ie the possibility of forfeiture is not taken into account when estimating the grant date fair value of the share options or other equity instruments, thereby producing a higher grant date fair value), but are instead taken into account by requiring that the transaction amount be based on the number of equity instruments that eventually vest.* Under this method, on a cumulative basis, no amount is recognised for goods or services received if the equity instruments granted do not vest because of failure to satisfy a vesting condition (other than a market condition), eg the counterparty fails to complete a specified service period, or a performance condition (other than a market condition) is not satisfied.

However, as discussed earlier (paragraphs BC180-BC182), the Board decided that it should not permit the choice available in SFAS 123 to account for the effects of expected or actual forfeitures of share options or other equity instruments because of failure to satisfy a service condition. The Board decided that the IFRS should require an entity to estimate the number of equity instruments expected to vest and to revise that estimate, if necessary, if subsequent information indicates that actual forfeitures are likely to differ from previous estimates. **BC217**

Share options that are forfeited or lapse after the end of the vesting period

Some share options might not be exercised. For example, a share option holder is unlikely to exercise a share option if the share price is below the exercise price throughout the exercise period. Once the last date for exercise is passed, the share option will lapse. **BC218**

The lapse of a share option at the end of the exercise period does not change the fact that the original transaction occurred, ie goods or services were received as consideration for the issue of an equity instrument (the share option). The lapsing of the share option does not represent a gain to the entity, because there is no change to the entity's net assets. In other words, although some might see such an event as being a benefit to the remaining shareholders, it has no effect on the entity's financial position. In effect, one type of equity interest (the share option holders' interest) becomes part of another type of equity interest (the shareholders' interest). The Board therefore concluded that the only accounting entry that might be required is a movement within equity, to reflect that the share options are no longer outstanding (ie as a transfer from one type of equity interest to another). **BC219**

This is consistent with the treatment of other equity instruments, such as warrants issued for cash. When warrants subsequently lapse unexercised, this is not treated as a gain; instead the amount previously recognised when the warrants were issued remains within equity.† **BC220**

The same analysis applies to equity instruments that are forfeited after the end of the vesting period. For example, an employee with vested share options typically must exercise those options within a short period after cessation of employment, otherwise the options are forfeited. If the share options are not in the money, the employee is unlikely to exercise the options and hence they will be forfeited. For the same reasons as are given in paragraph BC219, no adjustment is made to the amounts previously recognised for services received as consideration for the share options. The only **BC221**

The treatment of market conditions is discussed in paragraphs BC183 and BC184. As noted in paragraph BC184, the practical difficulties that led the Board to conclude that non-market conditions should be dealt with via the modified grant date method rather than being included in the grant date valuation do not apply to market conditions, because market conditions can be incorporated into option pricing models.

†*However, an alternative approach is followed in some jurisdictions (eg Japan and the UK), where the entity recognises a gain when warrants lapse. But under the Framework, recognising a gain on the lapse of warrants would be appropriate only if warrants were liabilities, which they are not.*

accounting entry that might be required is a movement within equity, to reflect that the share options are no longer outstanding.

MODIFICATIONS TO THE TERMS AND CONDITIONS OF SHARE-BASED PAYMENT ARRANGEMENTS

BC222 An entity might modify the terms of or conditions under which the equity instruments were granted. For example, the entity might reduce the exercise price of share options granted to employees (ie reprice the options), which increases the fair value of those options. During the development of ED 2, the Board focused mainly on the repricing of share options.

BC223 The Board noted that the IASC/G4+1 Discussion Paper argued that if the entity reprices its share options it has, in effect, replaced the original share option with a more valuable share option. The entity presumably believes that it will receive an equivalent amount of benefit from doing so, because otherwise the directors would not be acting in the best interests of the entity or its shareholders. This suggests that the entity expects to receive additional or enhanced employee services equivalent in value to the incremental value of the repriced share options. The Discussion Paper therefore proposed that the incremental value given (ie the difference between the value of the original share option and the value of the repriced share option, as at the date of repricing) should be recognised as additional remuneration expense. Although the Discussion Paper discussed repricing in the context of vesting date measurement, SFAS 123, which applies a grant date measurement basis for employee share-based payment, contains reasoning similar to that in the Discussion Paper.

BC224 This reasoning seems appropriate if grant date measurement is applied on the grounds that the entity made a payment to the employees on grant date by granting them valuable rights to equity instruments of the entity. If the entity is prepared to replace that payment with a more valuable payment, it must believe it will receive an equivalent amount of benefit from doing so.

BC225 The same conclusion is drawn if grant date measurement is applied on the grounds that some type of equity interest is created at grant date, and thereafter changes in the value of that equity interest accrue to the option holders as equity participants, not as employees. Repricing is inconsistent with the view that share option holders bear changes in value as equity participants. Hence it follows that the incremental value has been granted to the share option holders in their capacity as employees (rather than equity participants), as part of their remuneration for services to the entity. Therefore additional remuneration expense arises in respect of the incremental value given.

BC226 It could be argued that if (a) grant date measurement is used as a surrogate measure of the fair value of the services received and (b) the repricing occurs between grant date and vesting date and (c) the repricing merely restores the share option's original value at grant date, then the entity may not receive additional services. Rather, the repricing might simply be a means of ensuring that the entity receives the services it originally expected to receive when the share options were granted. Under this view, it is not appropriate to recognise additional remuneration expense to the extent that the repricing restores the share option's original value at grant date.

BC227 Some argue that the effect of a repricing is to create a new deal between the entity and its employees, and therefore the entity should estimate the fair value of the repriced share options at the date of repricing to calculate a new measure of the fair value of the services received subsequent to repricing. Under this view, the entity would cease using the grant date fair value of the share options when measuring services received after the repricing date, but without reversal of amounts recognised previously. The entity would then measure the services received between the date of repricing and the end of the vesting period by reference to the fair value of the modified share options, measured at the date of repricing. If the repricing occurs after the end of the vesting period, the same process applies. That is to say, there is no adjustment to previously recognised amounts, and the entity recognises – either immediately or over the vesting period, depending on whether the employees are required to complete an additional period of service to become entitled to the repriced share options – an amount equal to the fair value of the modified share options, measured at the date of repricing.

In the context of measuring the fair value of the equity instruments as a surrogate measure of the fair value of the services received, after considering the above points, the Board concluded when it developed ED 2 that the incremental value granted on repricing should be taken into account when measuring the services received, because: **BC228**

(a) there is an underlying presumption that the fair value of the equity instruments, at grant date, provides a surrogate measure of the fair value of the services received. That fair value is based on the share option's original terms and conditions. Therefore, if those terms or conditions are modified, the modification should be taken into account when measuring the services received.

(b) a share option that will be repriced if the share price falls is more valuable than one that will not be repriced. Therefore, by presuming at grant date that the share option will not be repriced, the entity underestimated the fair value of that option. The Board concluded that, because it is impractical to include the possibility of repricing in the estimate of fair value at grant date, the incremental value granted on repricing should be taken into account as and when the repricing occurs.

Many of the respondents to ED 2 who addressed the issue of repricing agreed with the proposed requirements. After considering respondents' comments, the Board decided to retain the approach to repricing as proposed in ED 2, ie recognise the incremental value granted on repricing, in addition to continuing to recognise amounts based on the fair value of the original grant. **BC229**

The Board also discussed situations in which repricing might be effected by cancelling share options and issuing replacement share options. For example, suppose an entity grants atthemoney share options with an estimated fair value of CU20 each. Suppose the share price falls, so that the share options become significantly out of the money, and are now worth CU2 each. Suppose the entity is considering repricing, so that the share options are again at the money, which would result in them being worth, say, CU10 each. (Note that the share options are still worth less than at grant date, because the share price is now lower. Other things being equal, an atthemoney option on a low priced share is worth less than an atthemoney option on a high priced share.) **BC230**

Under ED 2's proposed treatment of repricing, the incremental value given on repricing (CU10 – CU2 = CU8 increment in fair value per share option) would be accounted for when measuring the services rendered, resulting in the recognition of additional expense, ie additional to any amounts recognised in the future in respect of the original share option grant (valued at CU20). If the entity instead cancelled the existing share options and then issued what were, in effect, replacement share options, but treated the replacement share options as a new share option grant, this **BC231** could reduce the expense recognised. Although the new grant would be valued at CU10 rather than incremental value of CU8, the entity would not recognise any further expense in respect of the original share option grant, valued at CU20. Although some regard such a result as appropriate (and consistent with their views on repricing, as explained in paragraph BC227), it is inconsistent with the Board's treatment of repricing.

BC232   By this means, the entity could, in effect, reduce its remuneration expense if the share price falls, without having to increase the expense if the share price rises (because no repricing would be necessary in this case). In other words, the entity could structure a repricing so as to achieve a form of service date measurement if the share price falls and grant date measurement if the share price rises, ie an asymmetrical treatment of share price changes.

BC233   When it developed ED 2, the Board concluded that if an entity cancels a share or share option grant during the vesting period (other than cancellations because of employees' failing to satisfy the vesting conditions), it should nevertheless continue to account for services received, as if that share or share option grant had not been cancelled. In the Board's view, it is very unlikely that a share or share option grant would be cancelled without some compensation to the counterparty, either in the form of cash or replacement share options. Moreover, the Board saw no difference between a repricing of share options and a cancellation of share options followed by the granting of replacement share options at a lower exercise price, and therefore concluded that the accounting treatment should be the same. If cash is paid on the cancellation of the share or share option grant, the Board concluded that the payment should be accounted for as the repurchase of an equity interest, ie as a deduction from equity.

BC234   The Board noted that its proposed treatment means that an entity would continue to recognise services received during the remainder of the original vesting period, even though the entity might have paid cash compensation to the counterparty upon cancellation of the share or share option grant. The Board discussed an alternative approach applied in SFAS 123: if an entity settles unvested shares or share options in cash, those shares or share options are treated as having immediately vested. The entity is required to recognise immediately an expense for the amount of compensation expense that would otherwise have been recognised during the remainder of the original vesting period. Although the Board would have preferred to adopt this approach, it would have been difficult to apply in the context of the proposed accounting method in ED 2, given that there is not a specific amount of unrecognised compensation expense – the amount recognised in the future would have depended on the number of units of service received in the future.

BC235   Many respondents who commented on the treatment of cancellations disagreed with the proposals in ED 2. They commented that it was inappropriate to continue recognising an expense after a grant has been cancelled. Some suggested other approaches, including the approach applied in SFAS 123. After considering these comments, and given that the Board had decided to replace the units of service method with the modified grant date method in SFAS 123, the Board concluded that it should adopt the same approach as applied in SFAS 123 to cancellations and settlements. Under SFAS 123, a settlement (including a cancellation) is regarded as resulting in the immediate vesting of the equity instruments. The amount of remuneration expense measured at grant date but not yet recognised is recognised immediately at the date of settlement or cancellation.

In addition to the above issues, during its redeliberation of the proposals in ED 2 the **BC236** Board also considered more detailed issues relating to modifications and cancellations. Specifically, the Board considered:

(a) a modification that results in a decrease in fair value (ie the fair value of the modified instrument is less than the fair value of the original instrument, measured at the date of the modification).
(b) a change in the number of equity instruments granted (increase and decrease).
(c) a change in services conditions, thereby changing the length of the vesting period (increase and decrease).
(d) a change in performance conditions, thereby changing the probability of vesting (increase and decrease).
(e) a change in the classification of the grant, from equity to liabilities.

The Board concluded that having adopted a grant date measurement method, the **BC237** requirements for modifications and cancellations should ensure that the entity cannot, by modifying or cancelling the grant of shares or share options, avoid recognising remuneration expense based on the grant date fair values. Therefore, the Board concluded that, for arrangements that are classified as equity-settled arrangements (at least initially), the entity must recognise the grant date fair value of the equity instruments over the vesting period, unless the employee fails to vest in those equity instruments under the terms of the original vesting conditions.

SHARE APPRECIATION RIGHTS SETTLED IN CASH

Some transactions are 'share-based', even though they do not involve the issue of **BC238** shares, share options or any other form of equity instrument. Share appreciation rights (SARs) settled in cash are transactions in which the amount of cash paid to the employee (or another party) is based upon the increase in the share price over a specified period, usually subject to vesting conditions, such as the employee's remaining with the entity during the specified period. (Note that the following discussion focuses on SARs granted to employees, but also applies to SARs granted to other parties.)

In terms of accounting concepts, share-based payment transactions involving an **BC239** outflow of cash (or other assets) are different from transactions in which goods or services are received as consideration for the issue of equity instruments.

In an equity-settled transaction, only one side of the transaction causes a change in **BC240** assets, ie an asset (services) is received but no assets are disbursed. The other side of the transaction increases equity; it does not cause a change in assets. Accordingly, not only is it not necessary to remeasure the transaction amount upon settlement, it is not appropriate, because equity interests are not remeasured.

In contrast, in a cash-settled transaction, both sides of the transaction cause a change **BC241** in assets, ie an asset (services) is received and an asset (cash) is ultimately disbursed. Therefore, no matter what value is attributed to the first asset (services received), eventually it will be necessary to recognise the change in assets when the second asset (cash) is disbursed. Thus, no matter how the transaction is accounted for between the receipt of services and the settlement in cash, it will be 'trued up' to equal the amount of cash paid out, to account for both changes in assets.

Because cash-settled SARs involve an outflow of cash (rather than the issue of equity **BC242** instruments) cash SARs should be accounted for in accordance with the usual accounting for similar liabilities. That sounds straightforward, but there are some questions to consider:

(a)   should a liability be recognised before vesting date, ie before the employees have fulfilled the conditions to become unconditionally entitled to the cash payment?

(b)   if so, how should that liability be measured?

(c)   how should the expense be presented in the income statement?

Is there a liability before vesting date?

BC243   It could be argued that the entity does not have a liability until vesting date, because the entity does not have a present obligation to pay cash to the employees until the employees fulfil the conditions to become unconditionally entitled to the cash; between grant date and vesting date there is only a contingent liability.

BC244   The Board noted that this argument applies to all sorts of employee benefits settled in cash, not just SARs. For example, it could be argued that an entity has no liability for pension payments to employees until the employees have met the specified vesting conditions. This argument was considered by IASC in IAS 19 *Employee Benefits*. The Basis for Conclusions states:

> Paragraph 54 of the new IAS 19 summarises the recognition and measurement of liabilities arising from defined benefit plans...Paragraph 54 of the new IAS 19 is based on the definition of, and recognition criteria for, a liability in IASC's Framework...The Board believes that an enterprise has an obligation under a defined benefit plan when an employee has rendered service in return for the benefits promised under the plan...The Board believes that an obligation exists even if a benefit is not vested, in other words if the employee's right to receive the benefit is conditional upon future employment. For example, consider an enterprise that provides a benefit of 100 to employees who remain in service for two years. At the end of the first year, the employee and the enterprise are not in the same position as at the beginning of the first year, because the employee will only need to work for one year, instead of two, before becoming entitled to the benefit. Although there is a possibility that the benefit may not vest, that difference is an obligation and, in the Board's view, should result in the recognition of a liability at the end of the first year. The measurement of that obligation at its present value reflects the enterprise's best estimate of the probability that the benefit may not vest. (IAS 19, Basis for Conclusions, paragraphs 11-14)

BC245   Therefore, the Board concluded that, to be consistent with IAS 19, which covers other cash-settled employee benefits, a liability should be recognised in respect of cash-settled SARs during the vesting period, as services are rendered by the employees. Thus, no matter how the liability is measured, the Board concluded that it should be accrued over the vesting period, to the extent that the employees have performed their side of the arrangement. For example, if the terms of the arrangement require the employees to perform services over a threeyear period, the liability would be accrued over that threeyear period, consistently with the treatment of other cash-settled employee benefits.

How should the liability be measured?

BC246   A simple approach would be to base the accrual on the entity's share price at the end of each reporting period. If the entity's share price increased over the vesting period, expenses would be larger in later reporting periods compared with earlier reporting periods. This is because each reporting period will include the effects of (a) an increase in the liability in respect of the employee services received during that reporting period and (b) an increase in the liability attributable to the increase in the entity's share price during the reporting period, which increases the amount payable in respect of past employee services received.

This approach is consistent with SFAS 123 (paragraph 25) and FASB Interpretation No. 28 *Accounting for Stock Appreciation Rights and Other Variable Stock Option or Award Plans.*   **BC247**

However, this is not a fair value approach. Like share options, the fair value of SARs includes both their intrinsic value (the increase in the share price to date) and their time value (the value of the right to participate in future increases in the share price, if any, that may occur between the valuation date and the settlement date). An option pricing model can be used to estimate the fair value of SARs.   **BC248**

Ultimately, however, no matter how the liability is measured during the vesting period, the liability – and therefore the expense – will be remeasured, when the SARs are settled, to equal the amount of the cash paid out. The amount of cash paid will be based on the SARs' intrinsic value at the settlement date. Some support measuring the SAR liability at intrinsic value for this reason, and because intrinsic value is easier to measure.   **BC249**

The Board concluded that measuring SARs at intrinsic value would be inconsistent with the fair value measurement basis applied, in most cases, in the rest of the IFRS. Furthermore, although a fair value measurement basis is more complex to apply, it was likely that many entities would be measuring the fair value of similar instruments regularly, eg new SAR or share option grants, which would provide much of the information required to remeasure the fair value of the SAR at each reporting date. Moreover, because the intrinsic value measurement basis does not include time value, it is not an adequate measure of either the SAR liability or the cost of services consumed.   **BC250**

The question of how to measure the liability is linked with the question how to present the associated expense in the income statement, as explained below.   **BC251**

How should the associated expense be presented in the income statement?

SARs are economically similar to share options. Hence some argue that the accounting treatment of SARs should be the same as the treatment of share options, as discussed earlier (paragraph BC113). However, as noted in paragraphs BC240 and BC241, in an equity-settled transaction there is one change in net assets (the goods or services received) whereas in a cash-settled transaction there are two changes in net assets (the goods or services received and the cash or other assets paid out). To differentiate between the effects of each change in net assets in a cash-settled transaction, the expense could be separated into two components: **BC252**

- an amount based on the fair value of the SARs at grant date, recognised over the vesting period, in a manner similar to accounting for equity-settled share-based payment transactions, and
- changes in estimate between grant date and settlement date, ie all changes required to remeasure the transaction amount to equal the amount paid out on settlement date.

In developing ED 2, the Board concluded that information about these two com-   **BC253**
ponents would be helpful to users of financial statements. For example, users of financial statements regard the effects of remeasuring the liability as having little predictive value. Therefore, the Board concluded that there should be separate disclosure, either on the face of the income statement or in the notes, of that portion of

the expense recognised during each accounting period that is attributable to changes in the estimated fair value of the liability between grant date and settlement date.

BC254　However, some respondents to ED 2 disagreed with the proposed disclosure, arguing that it was burdensome and inappropriate to require the entity to account for the transaction as a cash-settled transaction and also calculate, for the purposes of the disclosure, what the transaction amount would have been if the arrangement was an equity-settled transaction.

BC255　The Board considered these comments and also noted that its decision to adopt the SFAS 123 modified grant date method will make it more complex for entities to determine the amount to disclose, because it will be necessary to distinguish between the effects of forfeitures and the effects of fair value changes when calculating the amount to disclose. The Board therefore concluded that the disclosure should not be retained as a mandatory requirement, but instead should be given as an example of an additional disclosure that entities should consider providing. For example, entities with a significant amount of cash-settled arrangements that experience significant share price volatility will probably find that the disclosure is helpful to users of their financial statements.

SHARE-BASED PAYMENT TRANSACTIONS WITH CASH ALTERNATIVES

BC256　Under some employee share-based payment arrangements the employees can choose to receive cash instead of shares or share options, or instead of exercising share options. There are many possible variations of share-based payment arrangements under which a cash alternative may be paid. For example, the employees may have more than one opportunity to elect to receive the cash alternative, eg the employees may be able to elect to receive cash instead of shares or share options on vesting date, or elect to receive cash instead of exercising the share options. The terms of the arrangement may provide the entity with a choice of settlement, ie whether to pay the cash alternative instead of issuing shares or share options on vesting date or instead of issuing shares upon the exercise of the share options. The amount of the cash alternative may be fixed or variable and, if variable, may be determinable in a manner that is related, or unrelated, to the price of the entity's shares.

BC257　The IFRS contains different accounting methods for cash-settled and equity-settled share-based payment transactions. Hence, if the entity or the employee has the choice of settlement, it is necessary to determine which accounting method should be applied. The Board considered situations when the terms of the arrangement provide (a) the employee with a choice of settlement and (b) the entity with a choice of settlement.

The terms of the arrangement provide the employee with a choice of settlement

BC258　Share-based payment transactions without cash alternatives do not give rise to liabilities under the *Framework*, because the entity is not required to transfer cash or other assets to the other party. However, this is not so if the contract between the entity and the employee gives the employee the contractual right to demand the cash alternative. In this situation, the entity has an obligation to transfer cash to the employee and hence a liability exists. Furthermore, because the employee has the right to demand settlement in equity instead of cash, the employee also has a conditional right to equity instruments. Hence, on grant date the employee was granted rights to a compound financial instrument, ie a financial instrument that includes both debt and equity components.

It is common for the alternatives to be structured so that the fair value of the cash **BC259** alternative is always the same as the fair value of the equity alternative, eg where the employee has a choice between share options and SARs. However, if this is not so, then the fair value of the compound financial instrument will usually exceed both the individual fair value of the cash alternative (because of the possibility that the shares or share options may be more valuable than the cash alternative) and that of the shares or options (because of the possibility that the cash alternative may be more valuable than the shares or options).

Under IAS 32, a financial instrument that is accounted for as a compound instru- **BC260** ment is separated into its debt and equity components, by allocating the proceeds received for the issue of a compound instrument to its debt and equity components. This entails determining the fair value of the liability component and then assigning the remainder of the proceeds received to the equity component. This is possible if those proceeds are cash or noncash consideration whose fair value can be reliably measured. If that is not the case, it will be necessary to estimate the fair value of the compound instrument itself.

The Board concluded that the compound instrument should be measured by first **BC261** valuing the liability component (the cash alternative) and then valuing the equity component (the equity instrument) – with that valuation taking into account that the employee must forfeit the cash alternative to receive the equity instrument – and adding the two component values together. This is consistent with the approach adopted in IAS 32, whereby the liability component is measured first and the residual is allocated to equity. If the fair value of each settlement alternative is always the same, then the fair value of the equity component of the compound instrument will be zero and hence the fair value of the compound instrument will be the same as the fair value of the liability component.

The Board concluded that the entity should separately account for the services **BC262** rendered in respect of each component of the compound financial instrument, to ensure consistency with the IFRS's requirements for equity-settled and cash-settled share-based payment transactions. Hence, for the debt component, the entity should recognise the services received, and a liability to pay for those services, as the employees render services, in the same manner as other cash-settled share-based payment transactions (eg SARs). For the equity component (if any), the entity should recognise the services received, and an increase in equity, as the employees render services, in the same way as other equity-settled share-based payment transactions.

The Board concluded that the liability should be remeasured to its fair value as at the **BC263** date of settlement, before accounting for the settlement of the liability. This ensures that, if the entity settles the liability by issuing equity instruments, the resulting increase in equity is measured at the fair value of the consideration received for the equity instruments issued, being the fair value of the liability settled.

The Board also concluded that, if the entity pays cash rather than issuing equity **BC264** instruments on settlement, any contributions to equity previously recognised in respect of the equity component should remain in equity. By electing to receive cash rather than equity instruments, the employee has surrendered his/her rights to receive equity instruments. That event does not cause a change in net assets and hence there is no change in total equity. This is consistent with the Board's conclusions on other lapses of equity instruments (see paragraphs BC218-BC221).

The terms of the arrangement provide the entity with a choice of settlement

BC265   For share-based payment transactions in which the terms of the arrangement provide the entity with a choice of whether to settle in cash or by issuing equity instruments, the entity would need first to determine whether it has an obligation to settle in cash and therefore does not, in effect, have a choice of settlement. Although the contract might specify that the entity can choose whether to settle in cash or by issuing equity instruments, the Board concluded that the entity will have an obligation to settle in cash if the choice of settlement in equity has no commercial substance (eg because the entity is legally prohibited from issuing shares), or if the entity has a past practice or a stated policy of settling in cash, or generally settles in cash whenever the counterparty asks for cash settlement. The entity will also have an obligation to settle in cash if the shares issued (including shares issued upon the exercise of share options) are redeemable, either mandatorily (eg upon cessation of employment) or at the counterparty's option.

BC266   During its redeliberations of the proposals in ED 2, the Board noted that the classification as liabilities or equity of arrangements in which the entity appears to have the choice of settlement differs from the classification under IAS 32, which requires such an arrangement to be classified either wholly as a liability (if the contract is a derivative contract) or as a compound instrument (if the contract is a non-derivative contract). However, consistently with its conclusions on the other differences between IFRS 2 and IAS 32 (see paragraphs BC106-BC110), the Board decided to retain this difference, pending the outcome of its longer-term Concepts project, which includes reviewing the definitions of liabilities and equity.

BC267   Even if the entity is not obliged to settle in cash until it chooses to do so, at the time it makes that election a liability will arise for the amount of the cash payment. This raises the question how to account for the debit side of the entry. It could be argued that any difference between (a) the amount of the cash payment and (b) the total expense recognised for services received and consumed up to the date of settlement (which would be based on the grant date value of the equity settlement alternative) should be recognised as an adjustment to the employee remuneration expense. However, given that the cash payment is to settle an equity interest, the Board concluded that it is consistent with the *Framework* to treat the cash payment as the repurchase of an equity interest, ie as a deduction from equity. In this case, no adjustment to remuneration expense is required on settlement.

BC268   However, the Board concluded that an additional expense should be recognised if the entity chooses the settlement alternative with the higher fair value because, given that the entity has voluntarily paid more than it needed to, presumably it expects to receive (or has already received) additional services from the employees in return for the additional value given.

OVERALL CONCLUSIONS ON ACCOUNTING FOR EMPLOYEE SHARE OPTIONS

BC269   The Board first considered all major issues relating to the recognition and measurement of share-based payment transactions, and reached conclusions on those issues. It then drew some overall conclusions, particularly on the treatment of employee share options, which is one of the most controversial aspects of the project. In arriving at those conclusions, the Board considered the following issues:

- convergence with US GAAP
- recognition versus disclosure of expenses arising from employee share-based payment transactions

- reliability of measurement of the fair value of employee share options.

Convergence with US GAAP

Some respondents to the Discussion Paper and ED 2 urged the Board to develop an IFRS that was based on existing requirements under US generally accepted accounting principles (US GAAP). **BC270**

More specifically, respondents urged the Board to develop a standard based on SFAS 123. However, given that convergence of accounting standards was commonly given as a reason for this suggestion, the Board considered US GAAP overall, not just one aspect of it. The main pronouncements of US GAAP on share-based payment are Accounting Principles Board Opinion No. 25 *Accounting for Stock Issued to Employees*, and SFAS 123. **BC271**

APB 25

APB 25 was issued in 1972. It deals with employee share plans only, and draws a distinction between nonperformance-related (fixed) plans and performance-related and other variable plans. **BC272**

For fixed plans, an expense is measured at intrinsic value (ie the difference between the share price and the exercise price), if any, at grant date. Typically, this results in no expense being recognised for fixed plans, because most share options granted under fixed plans are granted at the money. For performance-related and other variable plans, an expense is measured at intrinsic value at the measurement date. The measurement date is when both the number of shares or share options that the employee is entitled to receive and the exercise price are fixed. Because this measurement date is likely to be much later than grant date, any expense is subject to uncertainty and, if the share price is increasing, the expense for performance-related plans would be larger than for fixed plans. **BC273**

In SFAS 123, the FASB noted that APB 25 is criticised for producing anomalous results and for lacking any underlying conceptual rationale. For example, the requirements of APB 25 typically result in the recognition of an expense for performance-related share options but usually no expense is recognised for fixed share options. This result is anomalous because fixed share options are usually more valuable at grant date than performance-related share options. Moreover, the omission of an expense for fixed share options impairs the quality of financial statements: **BC274**

> The resulting financial statements are less credible than they could be, and the financial statements of entities that use fixed employee share options extensively are not comparable to those of entities that do not make significant use of fixed options. (SFAS 123, paragraph 56)

The Discussion Paper, in its discussion of US GAAP, noted that the different accounting treatments for fixed and performance-related plans also had the perverse effect of discouraging entities from setting up performance-related employee share plans. **BC275**

SFAS 123

BC276   SFAS 123 was issued in 1995. It requires recognition of share-based payment transactions with parties other than employees, based on the fair value of the shares or share options issued or the fair value of the goods or services received, whichever is more reliably measurable. Entities are also encouraged, but not required, to apply the fair value accounting method in SFAS 123 to share-based payment transactions with employees. Generally speaking, SFAS 123 draws no distinction between fixed and performance-related plans.

BC277   If an entity applies the accounting method in APB 25 rather than that in SFAS 123, SFAS 123 requires disclosures of pro forma net income and earnings per share in the annual financial statements, as if the standard had been applied. Recently, a significant number of major US companies have voluntarily adopted the fair value accounting method in SFAS 123 for transactions with employees.

BC278   The FASB regards SFAS 123 as superior to APB 25, and would have preferred recognition based on the fair value of employee options to be mandatory, not optional. SFAS 123 makes it clear that the FASB decided to permit the disclosurebased alternative for political reasons, not because it thought that it was the best accounting solution:

> ...the Board...continues to believe that disclosure is not an adequate substitute for recognition of assets, liabilities, equity, revenues and expenses in financial statements...The Board chose a disclosurebased solution for stockbased employee compensation to bring closure to the divisive debate on this issuenot because it believes that solution is the best way to improve financial accounting and reporting. (SFAS 123, paragraphs 61 and 62)

BC279   Under US GAAP, the accounting treatment of share-based payment transactions differs, depending on whether the other party to the transaction is an employee or non-employee, and whether the entity chooses to apply SFAS 123 or APB 25 to transactions with employees. Having a choice of accounting methods is generally regarded as undesirable. Indeed, the Board recently devoted much time and effort to developing improvements to existing international standards, one of the objectives of which is to eliminate choices of accounting methods.

BC280   Research in the US demonstrates that choosing one accounting method over the other has a significant impact on the reported earnings of US entities. For example, research by Bear Stearns and Credit Suisse First Boston on the S&P 500 shows that, had the fair value measurement method in SFAS 123 been applied for the purposes of recognising an expense for employee stockbased compensation, the earnings of the S&P 500 companies would have been significantly lower, and that the effect is growing. The effect on reported earnings is substantial in some sectors, where companies make heavy use of share options.

BC281   The Canadian Accounting Standards Board (AcSB) recently completed its project on share-based payment. In accordance with the AcSB's policy of harmonising Canadian standards with those in the US, the AcSB initially proposed a standard that was based on US GAAP, including APB 25. After considering respondents' comments, the AcSB decided to delete the guidance drawn from APB 25. The AcSB reached this decision for various reasons, including that, in its view, the intrinsic value method is flawed. Also, incorporating the requirements of APB 25 into an accounting standard would result in preparers of financial statements incurring substantial costs for which users of financial statements would derive no benefit – entities would spend a great deal of time and effort on understanding the rules and then redesigning option plans, usually by deleting existing performance conditions, to avoid recognising an expense in respect of such plans, thereby producing no improvement in the accounting for share option plans.

The Canadian standard was initially consistent with SFAS 123. That included per- **BC282** mitting a choice between fair valuebased accounting for employee stockbased compensation expense in the income statement and disclosure of pro forma amounts in the notes to both interim and annual financial statements. However, the AcSB recently amended its standard to remove the choice between recognition and disclosure, and therefore expense recognition is mandatory for financial periods beginning on or after 1 January 2004.

Because APB 25 contains serious flaws, the Board concluded that basing an IFRS on **BC283** it is unlikely to represent much, if any, improvement in financial reporting. Moreover, the perverse effects of APB 25, particularly in discouraging performance-related share option plans, may cause economic distortions. Accounting standards are intended to be neutral, not to give favourable or unfavourable accounting treatments to particular transactions to encourage or discourage entities from entering into those transactions. APB 25 fails to achieve that objective. Performance-related employee share plans are common in Europe (performance conditions are often required by law) and in other parts of the world outside the US, and investors are calling for greater use of performance conditions. Therefore, the Board concluded that introducing an accounting standard based on APB 25 would be inconsistent with its objective of developing high quality accounting standards.

That leaves SFAS 123. Comments from the FASB, in the SFAS 123 Basis for **BC284** Conclusions, and from the Canadian AcSB when it developed a standard based on SFAS 123, indicate that both standard-setters regard it as inadequate, because it permits a choice between recognition and disclosure. (This issue is discussed further below.) The FASB added to its agenda in March 2003 a project to review US accounting requirements on share-based payment, including removing the disclosure alternative in SFAS 123, so that expense recognition is mandatory. The Chairman of the FASB commented:

> Recent events have served as a reminder to all of us that clear, credible and comparable financial information is essential to the health and vitality of our capital market system. In the wake of the market meltdown and corporate reporting scandals, the FASB has received numerous requests from individual and institutional investors, financial analysts and many others urging the Board to mandate the expensing of the compensation cost relating to employee stock options...While a number of major companies have voluntarily opted to reflect these costs as an expense in reporting their earnings, other companies continue to show these costs in the footnotes to their financial statements. In addition, a move to require an expense treatment would be consistent with the FASB's commitment to work toward convergence between U.S. and international accounting standards. In taking all of these factors into consideration, the Board concluded that it was critical that it now revisit this important subject. (FASB News Release, 12 March 2003)

During the Board's redeliberations of the proposals in ED 2, the Board worked with **BC285** the FASB to achieve convergence of international and US standards, to the extent possible, bearing in mind that the FASB was at an earlier stage in its project – the FASB was developing an Exposure Draft to revise SFAS 123 whereas the IASB was finalising its IFRS. The Board concluded that, although convergence is an important objective, it would not be appropriate to delay the issue of the IFRS, because of the pressing need for a standard on share-based payment, as explained in paragraphs

BC2BC5. In any event, at the time the IASB concluded its deliberations, a substantial amount of convergence had been achieved. For example, the FASB agreed with the IASB that all share-based payment transactions should be recognised in the financial statements, measured on a fair value measurement basis, including transactions in which share options are granted to employees. Hence, the FASB agreed that the disclosure alternative in SFAS 123 should be eliminated.

BC286   The IASB and FASB also agreed that, once both boards have issued final standards on share-based payment, the two boards will consider undertaking a convergence project, with the objective of eliminating any remaining areas of divergence between international and US standards on this topic.

Recognition versus disclosure

BC287   A basic accounting concept is that disclosure of financial information is not an adequate substitute for recognition in the financial statements. For example, the *Framework* states:

> Items that meet the recognition criteria should be recognised in the balance sheet or income statement. The failure to recognise such items is not rectified by disclosure of the accounting policies used nor by notes or explanatory material. (paragraph 82)

BC288   A key aspect of the recognition criteria is that the item can be measured with reliability. This issue is discussed further below. Therefore, this discussion focuses on the 'recognition versus disclosure' issue in principle, not on measurement reliability. Once it has been determined that an item meets the criteria for recognition in the financial statements, failing to recognise it is inconsistent with the basic concept that disclosure is not an adequate substitute for recognition.

BC289   Some disagree with this concept, arguing that it makes no difference whether information is recognised in the financial statements or disclosed in the notes. Either way, users of financial statements have the information they require to make economic decisions. Hence, they believe that note disclosure of expenses arising from particular employee share-based payment transactions (ie those involving awards of share options to employees), rather than recognition in the income statement, is acceptable.

BC290   The Board did not accept this argument. The Board noted that if note disclosure is acceptable, because it makes no difference whether the expense is recognised or disclosed, then recognition in the financial statements must also be acceptable for the same reason. If recognition is acceptable, and recognition rather than mere disclosure accords with the accounting principles applied to all other expense items, it is not acceptable to leave one particular expense item out of the income statement.

BC291   The Board also noted that there is significant evidence that there is a difference between recognition and disclosure. First, academic research indicates that whether information is recognised or merely disclosed affects market prices (eg Barth, Clinch and Shibano, 2003).* If information is disclosed only in the notes, users of financial statements have to expend time and effort to become sufficiently expert in accounting to know (a) that there are items that are not recognised in the financial statements, (b) that there is information about those items in the notes, and (c) how to assess the note disclosures. Because gaining that expertise comes at a cost, and not all users of

*M E Barth, G Clinch and T Shibano. 2003. Market Effects of Recognition and Disclosure. Journal of Accounting Research 41(4): 581609.

financial statements will become accounting experts, information that is merely disclosed may not be fully reflected in share prices.

Second, both preparers and users of financial statements appear to agree that there is an important difference between recognition and disclosure. Users of financial statements have strongly expressed the view that all forms of share-based payment, including employee share options, should be recognised in the financial statements, resulting in the recognition of an expense when the goods or services received are consumed, and that note disclosure alone is inadequate. Their views have been expressed by various means, including: **BC292**

(a) users' responses to the Discussion Paper and ED 2.
(b) the 2001 survey by the Association for Investment Management and Research of analysts and fund managers – 83 per cent of survey respondents said the accounting method for all share-based payment transactions should require recognition of an expense in the income statement.
(c) public comments by users of financial statements, such as those reported in the press or made at recent US Senate hearings.

Preparers of financial statements also see a major difference between recognition and disclosure. For example, some preparers who responded to the Discussion Paper and ED 2 were concerned that unless expense recognition is required in all countries, entities that are required to recognise an expense would be at a competitive disadvantage compared with entities that are permitted a choice between recognition and disclosure. Comments such as these indicate that preparers of financial statements regard expense recognition as having consequences that are different from those of disclosure. **BC293**

Reliability of measurement

One reason commonly given by those who oppose the recognition of an expense arising from transactions involving grants of share options to employees is that it is not possible to measure those transactions reliably. **BC294**

The Board discussed these concerns about reliability, after first putting the issue into context. For example, the Board noted that when estimating the fair value of share options, the objective is to measure that fair value at the measurement date, not the value of the underlying share at some future date. Some regard the fair value estimate as inherently uncertain because it is not known, at the measurement date, what the final outcome will be, ie how much the gain on exercise (if any) will be. However, the valuation does not attempt to estimate the future gain, only the amount that the other party would pay to obtain the right to participate in any future gains. Therefore, even if the share option expires worthless or the employee makes a large gain on exercise, this does not mean that the grant date estimate of the fair value of that option was unreliable or wrong. **BC295**

The Board also noted that accounting often involves making estimates, and therefore reporting an estimated fair value is not objectionable merely because that amount represents an estimate rather than a precise measure. Examples of other estimates made in accounting, which may have a material effect on the income statement and the balance sheet, include estimates of the collectability of doubtful debts, estimates of the useful life of fixed assets and the pattern of their consumption, and estimates of employee pension liabilities. **BC296**

However, some argue that including in the financial statements an estimate of the fair value of employee share options is different from including other estimates, because **BC297** there is no subsequent correction of the estimate. Other estimates, such as employee pension costs, will ultimately be revised to equal the amount of the cash paid out. In contrast, because equity is not remeasured, if the estimated fair value of employee share options is recognised, there is no remeasurement of the fair value estimate – unless exercise date measurement is used – so any estimation error is permanently embedded in the financial statements.

BC298   The FASB considered and rejected this argument in developing SFAS 123. For example, for employee pension costs, the total cost is never completely trued up unless the scheme is terminated, the amount attributed to any particular year is never trued up, and it can take decades before the amounts relating to particular employees are trued up. In the meantime, users of financial statements have made economic decisions based on the estimated costs.

BC299   Moreover, the Board noted that if no expense (or an expense based on intrinsic value only, which is typically zero) is recognised in respect of employee share options, that also means that there is an error that is permanently embedded in the financial statements. Reporting zero (or an amount based on intrinsic value, if any) is never trued up.

BC300   The Board also considered the meaning of reliability. Arguments about whether estimates of the fair value of employee share options are sufficiently reliable focus on one aspect of reliability only – whether the estimate is free from material error. The *Framework*, in common with the conceptual frameworks of other accounting standard-setters, makes it clear that another important aspect of reliability is whether the information can be depended upon by users of financial statements to represent faithfully what it purports to represent. Therefore, in assessing whether a particular accounting method produces reliable financial information, it is necessary to consider whether that information is representationally faithful. This is one way in which reliability is linked to another important qualitative characteristic of financial information, relevance.

BC301   For example, in the context of share-based payment, some commentators advocate measuring employee share options at intrinsic value rather than fair value, because intrinsic value is regarded as a much more reliable measure. Whether intrinsic value is a more reliable measure is doubtful – it is certainly less subject to estimation error, but is unlikely to be a representationally faithful measure of remuneration. Nor is intrinsic value a relevant measure, especially when measured at grant date. Many employee share options are issued at the money, so have no intrinsic value at grant date. A share option with no intrinsic value consists entirely of time value. If a share option is measured at intrinsic value at grant date, zero value is attributed to the share option. Therefore, by ignoring time value, the amount attributed to the share option is 100 per cent understated.

BC302   Another qualitative characteristic is comparability. Some argue that, given the uncertainties relating to estimating the fair value of employee share options, it is better for all entities to report zero, because this will make financial statements more comparable. They argue that if, for example, for two entities the 'true' amount of expense relating to employee share options is CU500,000, and estimation uncertainties cause one entity to report CU450,000 and the other to report CU550,000, the two entities' financial statements would be more comparable if both reported zero, rather than these divergent figures.

BC303   However, it is unlikely that any two entities will have the same amount of employee share-based remuneration expense. Research (eg by Bear Stearns and Credit Suisse First Boston) indicates that the expense varies widely from industry to industry, from entity to entity, and from year to year. Reporting zero rather than an estimated amount is likely to make the financial statements much less comparable, not more comparable. For example, if the estimated employee share-based remuneration expense of Company A, Company B and Company C is CU10,000, CU100,000 and CU1,000,000 respectively, reporting zero for all three companies will not make their financial statements comparable.

In the context of the foregoing discussion of reliability, the Board addressed the question whether transactions involving share options granted to employees can be measured with sufficient reliability for the purpose of recognition in the financial statements. The Board noted that many respondents to the Discussion Paper asserted that this is not possible. They argue that option pricing models cannot be applied to employee share options, because of the differences between employee options and traded options. **BC304**

The Board considered these differences, with the assistance of the project's Advisory Group and other experts, and has reached conclusions on how to take account of these differences when estimating the fair value of employee share options, as explained in paragraphs BC145-BC199. In doing so, the Board noted that the objective is to measure the fair value of the share options, ie an estimate of what the price of those equity instruments would have been on grant date in an arm's length transaction between knowledgeable, willing parties. The valuation methodology applied should therefore be consistent with valuation methodologies that market participants would use for pricing similar financial instruments, and should incorporate all factors and assumptions that knowledgeable, willing market participants would consider in setting the price. **BC305**

Hence, factors that a knowledgeable, willing market participant would not consider in setting the price of an option are not relevant when estimating the fair value of shares, share options or other equity instruments granted. For example, for share options granted to employees, factors that affect the value of the option from the individual employee's perspective only are not relevant to estimating the price that would be set by a knowledgeable, willing market participant. Many respondents' comments about measurement reliability, and the differences between employee share options and traded options, often focused on the value of the option from the employee's perspective. Therefore, the Board concluded that the IFRS should emphasise that the objective is to estimate the fair value of the share option, not an employee specific value. **BC306**

The Board noted that there is evidence to support a conclusion that it is possible to make a reliable estimate of the fair value of employee share options. First, there is academic research to support this conclusion (eg Carpenter 1998, Maller, Tan and Van De Vyver 2002).* Second, users of financial statements regard the estimated fair values as sufficiently reliable for recognition in the financial statements. Evidence of this can be found in a variety of sources, such as the comment letters received from users of financial statements who responded to the Discussion Paper and ED 2. Users' views are important, because the objective of financial statements is to provide high quality, transparent and comparable information to help users make economic decisions. In other words, financial statements are intended to meet the needs of users, rather than preparers or other interest groups. The purpose of setting accounting standards is to ensure that, wherever possible, the information provided **BC307**

*J N Carpenter. 1998. *The exercise and valuation of executive stock options. Journal of Financial Economics* 48: 127158.
R A Maller, R Tan and M Van De Vyver. 2002. How Might Companies Value ESOs? Australian Accounting Review 12 (1): 1124.

in the financial statements meets users' needs. Therefore, if the people who use the financial statements in making economic decisions regard the fair value estimates as sufficiently reliable for recognition in the financial statements, this provides strong evidence of measurement reliability.

BC308   The Board also noted that, although the FASB decided to permit a choice between recognition and disclosure of expenses arising from employee share-based payment transactions, it did so for nontechnical reasons, not because it agreed with the view that reliable measurement was not possible:

> The Board continues to believe that use of optionpricing models, as modified in this statement, will produce estimates of the fair value of stock options that are sufficiently reliable to justify recognition in financial statements. Imprecision in those estimates does not justify failure to recognize compensation cost stemming from employee stock options. That belief underlies the Board's encouragement to entities to adopt the fair value based method of recognizing stockbased employee compensation cost in their financial statements. (SFAS 123, Basis for Conclusions, paragraph 117)

BC309   In summary, if expenses arising from grants of share options to employees are omitted from the financial statements, or recognised using the intrinsic value method (which typically results in zero expense) or the minimum value method, there will be a permanent error embedded in the financial statements. So the question is, which accounting method is more likely to produce the smallest amount of error and the most relevant, comparable information – a fair value estimate, which might result in some understatement or overstatement of the associated expense, or another measurement basis, such as intrinsic value (especially if measured at grant date), that will definitely result in substantial understatement of the associated expense?

BC310   Taking all of the above into consideration, the Board concluded that, in virtually all cases, the estimated fair value of employee share options at grant date can be measured with sufficient reliability for the purposes of recognising employee share-based payment transactions in the financial statements. The Board therefore concluded that, in general, the IFRS on share-based payment should require a fair value measurement method to be applied to all types of share-based payment transactions, including all types of employee share-based payment. Hence, the Board concluded that the IFRS should not allow a choice between a fair value measurement method and an intrinsic value measurement method, and should not permit a choice between recognition and disclosure of expenses arising from employee share-based payment transactions.

CONSEQUENTIAL AMENDMENTS TO OTHER STANDARDS*

Tax effects of share-based payment transactions

BC311   Whether expenses arising from share-based payment transactions are deductible, and if so, whether the amount of the tax deduction is the same as the reported expense and whether the tax deduction arises in the same accounting period, varies from country to country.

*ASB footnote: The section of IFRS 2 dealing with the consequential amendments to other standards needed to be amended very significantly before being included in FRS 20 so that it can be applied in a UK context. In the context of the discussion in paragraphs BC311-BC333, it should be noted that the ASB has decided not to make amendments to its tax standards (FRS 16 Current Tax and FRS 19 Deferred Tax) equivalent to those made in IFRS 2 to IAS 12 Income Taxes. The ASB's rationale is explained in the 'Notes on the standard's application in the UK and the Republic of Ireland' section.

If the amount of the tax deduction is the same as the reported expense, but the tax deduction arises in a later accounting period, this will result in a deductible temporary difference under IAS 12 *Income Taxes*. Temporary differences usually arise from differences between the carrying amount of assets and liabilities and the amount attributed to those assets and liabilities for tax purposes. However, IAS 12 also deals with items that have a tax base but are not recognised as assets and liabilities in the balance sheet. It gives an example of research costs that are recognised as an expense in the financial statements in the period in which the costs are incurred, but are deductible for tax purposes in a later accounting period. The Standard states that the difference between the tax base of the research costs, being the amount that will be deductible in a future accounting period, and the carrying amount of nil is a deductible temporary difference that results in a deferred tax asset (IAS 12, paragraph 9).   **BC312**

Applying this guidance indicates that if an expense arising from a share-based payment transaction is recognised in the financial statements in one accounting period and is taxdeductible in a later accounting period, this should be accounted for as a deductible temporary difference under IAS 12. Under that Standard, a deferred tax asset is recognised for all deductible temporary differences to the extent that it is probable that taxable profit will be available against which the deductible temporary difference can be used (IAS 12, paragraph 24).   **BC313**

Whilst IAS 12 does not discuss reverse situations, the same logic applies. For example, suppose the entity is able to claim a tax deduction for the total transaction amount at the date of grant but the entity recognises an expense arising from that transaction over the vesting period. Applying the guidance in IAS 12 suggests that this should be accounted for as a taxable temporary difference, and hence a deferred tax liability should be recognised.   **BC314**

However, the amount of the tax deduction might differ from the amount of the expense recognised in the financial statements. For example, the measurement basis applied for accounting purposes might not be the same as that used for tax purposes, eg intrinsic value might be used for tax purposes and fair value for accounting purposes. Similarly, the measurement date might differ. For example, US entities receive a tax deduction based on intrinsic value at the date of exercise in respect of some share options, whereas for accounting purposes an entity applying SFAS 123 would recognise an expense based on the option's fair value, measured at the date of grant. There could also be other differences in the measurement method applied for accounting and tax purposes, eg differences in the treatment of forfeitures or different valuation methodologies applied.   **BC315**

SFAS 123 requires that, if the amount of the tax deduction exceeds the total expense recognised in the financial statements, the tax benefit for the excess deduction should be recognised as additional paidin capital, ie as a direct credit to equity. Conversely, if the tax deduction is less than the total expense recognised for accounting purposes, the write-off of the related deferred tax asset in excess of the benefits of the tax deduction is recognised in the income statement, except to the extent that there is remaining additional paidin capital from excess tax deductions from previous share-based payment transactions (SFAS 123, paragraph 44).   **BC316**

At first sight, it may seem questionable to credit or debit directly to equity amounts that relate to differences between the amount of the tax deduction and the total recognised expense. The tax effects of any such differences would ordinarily flow through the income statement. However, some argue that the approach in SFAS 123 is appropriate if the reason for the difference between the amount of the tax deduction and the recognised expense is that a different measurement date is applied.   **BC317**

BC318   For example, suppose grant date measurement is used for accounting purposes and exercise date measurement is used for tax purposes. Under grant date measurement, any changes in the value of the equity instrument after grant date accrue to the employee (or other party) in their capacity as equity participants. Therefore, some argue that any tax effects arising from those valuation changes should be credited to equity (or debited to equity, if the value of the equity instrument declines).

BC319   Similarly, some argue that the tax deduction arises from an equity transaction (the exercise of options), and hence the tax effects should be reported in equity. It can also be argued that this treatment is consistent with the requirement in IAS 12 to account for the tax effects of transactions or events in the same way as the entity accounts for those transactions or events themselves. If the tax deduction relates to both an income statement item and an equity item, the associated tax effects should be allocated between the income statement and equity.

BC320   Others disagree, arguing that the tax deduction relates to employee remuneration expense, ie an income statement item only, and therefore all of the tax effects of the deduction should be recognised in the income statement. The fact that the taxing authority applies a different method in measuring the amount of the tax deduction does not change this conclusion. A further argument is that this treatment is consistent with the *Framework*, because reporting amounts directly in equity would be inappropriate, given that the government is not an owner of the entity.

BC321   The Board noted that, if one accepts that it might be appropriate to debit/ credit to equity the tax effect of the difference between the amount of the tax deduction and the total recognised expense where that difference relates to changes in the value of equity interests, there could be other reasons why the amount of the tax deduction differs from the total recognised expense. For example, grant date measurement may be used for both tax and accounting purposes, but the valuation methodology used for tax purposes might produce a higher value than the methodology used for accounting purposes (eg the effects of early exercise might be ignored when valuing an option for tax purposes). The Board saw no reason why, in this situation, the excess tax benefits should be credited to equity.

BC322   In developing ED 2, the Board concluded that the tax effects of share-based payment transactions should be recognised in the income statement by being taken into account in the determination of tax expense. It agreed that this should be explained in the form of a worked example in a consequential amendment to IAS 12.

BC323   During the Board's redeliberation of the proposals in ED 2, the Board reconsidered the points above, and concluded that the tax effects of an equity-settled share-based payment transaction should be allocated between the income statement and equity. The Board then considered how this allocation should be made and related issues, such as the measurement of the deferred tax asset.

BC324   Under IAS 12, the deferred tax asset for a deductible temporary difference is based on the amount the taxation authorities will permit as a deduction in future periods. Therefore, the Board concluded that the measurement of the deferred tax asset should be based on an estimate of the future tax deduction. If changes in the share price affect that future tax deduction, the estimate of the expected future tax deduction should be based on the current share price.

BC325   These conclusions are consistent with the proposals in ED 2 concerning the measurement of the deferred tax asset. However, this approach differs from SFAS 123, which measures the deferred tax asset on the basis of the cumulative recognised expense. The Board rejected the SFAS 123 method of measuring the deferred tax asset because it is inconsistent with IAS 12. As noted above, under IAS 12, the deferred tax asset for a deductible temporary difference is based on the amount the taxation authorities will permit as a deduction in future periods. If a later measurement date is applied for tax purposes, it is very unlikely that the tax deduction will ever equal the cumulative expense, except by coincidence. For example, if share options are granted to employees, and the entity receives a tax deduction measured as the difference between the share price and the exercise price at the date of exercise, it is extremely unlikely that the tax deduction will ever equal the cumulative expense. By basing the measurement of the deferred tax asset on the cumulative expense, the SFAS 123 method is likely to result in the understatement or overstatement of the deferred tax asset. In some situations, such as when share options are significantly out of the money, SFAS 123 requires the entity to continue to recognise a deferred tax asset even when the possibility of the entity recovering that asset is remote. Continuing to recognise a deferred tax asset in this situation is not only inconsistent with IAS 12, it is inconsistent with the definition of an asset in the *Framework*, and the requirements of other IFRSs for the recognition and measurement of assets, including requirements to assess impairment.

The Board also concluded that: **BC326**

(a) if the tax deduction received (or expected to be received, measured as described in paragraph BC324) is less than or equal to the cumulative expense, the associated tax benefits received (or expected to be received) should be recognised as tax income and included in profit or loss for the period.

(b) if the tax deduction received (or expected to be received, measured as described in paragraph BC324) exceeds the cumulative expense, the excess associated tax benefits received (or expected to be received) should be recognised directly in equity.

The above allocation method is similar to that applied in SFAS 123, with some **BC327** exceptions. First, the above allocation method ensures that the total tax benefits recognised in the income statement in respect of a particular share-based payment transaction do not exceed the tax benefits ultimately received. The Board disagreed with the approach in SFAS 123, which sometimes results in the total tax benefits recognised in the income statement exceeding the tax benefits ultimately received because, in some situations, SFAS 123 permits the unrecovered portion of the deferred tax asset to be written off to equity.

Second, the Board concluded that the above allocation method should be applied **BC328** irrespective of why the tax deduction received (or expected to be received) differs from the cumulative expense. The SFAS 123 method is based on US tax legislation, under which the excess tax benefits credited to equity (if any) arise from the use of a later measurement date for tax purposes. The Board agreed with respondents who commented that the accounting treatment must be capable of being applied in various tax jurisdictions. The Board was concerned that requiring entities to examine the reasons why there is a difference between the tax deduction and the cumulative expense, and then account for the tax effects accordingly, would be too complex to be applied consistently across a wide range of different tax jurisdictions.

The Board noted that it might need to reconsider its conclusions on accounting for **BC329** the tax effects of share-based payment transactions in the future, for example, if the Board reviews IAS 12 more broadly.

Accounting for own shares held

BC330   IAS 32 requires the acquisition of treasury shares to be deducted from equity, and no gain or loss is to be recognised on the sale, issue or cancellation of treasury shares. Consideration received on the subsequent sale or issue of treasury shares is credited to equity.

BC331   This is consistent with the *Framework*. The repurchase of shares and their subsequent reissue or transfer to other parties are transactions with equity participants that should be recognised as changes in equity. In accounting terms, there is no difference between shares that are repurchased and cancelled, and shares that are repurchased and held by the entity. In both cases, the repurchase involves an outflow of resources to shareholders (ie a distribution), thereby reducing shareholders' investment in the entity. Similarly, there is no difference between a new issue of shares and an issue of shares previously repurchased and held in treasury. In both cases, there is an inflow of resources from shareholders, thereby increasing shareholders' investment in the entity. Although accounting practice in some jurisdictions treats own shares held as assets, this is not consistent with the definition of assets in the *Framework* and the conceptual frameworks of other standard-setters, as explained in the Discussion Paper (footnote to paragraph 4.7 of the Discussion Paper, reproduced earlier in the footnote to paragraph BC73).

BC332   Given that treasury shares are treated as an asset in some jurisdictions, it will be necessary to change that accounting treatment when this IFRS is applied, because otherwise an entity would be faced with two expense items – an expense arising from the share-based payment transaction (for the consumption of goods and services received as consideration for the issue of an equity instrument) and another expense arising from the write-down of the 'asset' for treasury shares issued or transferred to employees at an exercise price that is less than their purchase price.

BC333   Hence, the Board concluded that the requirements in the relevant paragraphs of IAS 32 regarding treasury shares should also be applied to treasury shares purchased, sold, issued or cancelled in connection with employee share plans or other share-based payment arrangements.

Implementation guidance

Contents

Implementation Guidance

This guidance accompanies, but is not part of, IFRS 2.

> *ASB note:* This Implementation Guidance was prepared by the IASB.

Definition of grant date

IG1   IFRS 2 defines grant date as the date at which the entity and the employee (or other party providing similar services) agree to a share-based payment arrangement, being when the entity and the counterparty have a shared understanding of the terms and conditions of the arrangement. At grant date the entity confers on the counterparty the right to cash, other assets, or equity instruments of the entity, provided the specified vesting conditions, if any, are met. If that agreement is subject to an approval process (for example, by shareholders), grant date is the date when that approval is obtained.

IG2   As noted above, grant date is when both parties agree to a share-based payment arrangement. The word 'agree' is used in its usual sense, which means that there must be both an offer and acceptance of that offer. Hence, the date at which one party makes an offer to another party is not grant date. The date of grant is when that other party accepts the offer. In some instances, the counterparty explicitly agrees to the arrangement, eg by signing a contract. In other instances, agreement might be implicit, eg for many share-based payment arrangements with employees, the employees' agreement is evidenced by their commencing to render services.

IG3   Furthermore, for both parties to have agreed to the share-based payment arrangement, both parties must have a shared understanding of the terms and conditions of the arrangement. Therefore, if some of the terms and conditions of the arrangement are agreed on one date, with the remainder of the terms and conditions agreed on a later date, then grant date is on that later date, when all of the terms and conditions have been agreed. For example, if an entity agrees to issue share options to an employee, but the exercise price of the options will be set by a compensation committee that meets in three months' time, grant date is when the exercise price is set by the compensation committee.

IG4   In some cases, grant date might occur after the employees to whom the equity instruments were granted have begun rendering services. For example, if a grant of equity instruments is subject to shareholder approval, grant date might occur some months after the employees have begun rendering services in respect of that grant. The IFRS requires the entity to recognise the services when received. In this situation, the entity should estimate the grant date fair value of the equity instruments (eg by estimating the fair value of the equity instruments at the end of the reporting period), for the purposes of recognising the services received during the period between service commencement date and grant date. Once the date of grant has been established, the entity should revise the earlier estimate so that the amounts recognised for services received in respect of the grant are ultimately based on the grant date fair value of the equity instruments.

Measurement date for transactions with parties other than employees

For transactions with parties other than employees (and others providing similar services) that are measured by reference to the fair value of the equity instruments granted, paragraph 13 of IFRS 2 requires the entity to measure that fair value at the date the entity obtains the goods or the counterparty renders service. **IG5**

If the goods or services are received on more than one date, the entity should measure the fair value of the equity instruments granted on each date when goods or services are received. The entity should apply that fair value when measuring the goods or services received on that date. **IG6**

However, an approximation could be used in some cases. For example, if an entity received services continuously during a three-month period, and its share price did not change significantly during that period, the entity could use the average share price during the three-month period when estimating the fair value of the equity instruments granted. **IG7**

Transitional arrangements

In paragraph 54 of IFRS 2, the entity is encouraged, but not required, to apply the requirements of the IFRS to other grants of equity instruments (ie grants other than those specified in paragraph 53 of the IFRS), if the entity has disclosed publicly the fair value of those equity instruments, measured at the measurement date. For example, such equity instruments include equity instruments for which the entity has disclosed in the notes to its financial statements the information required in the US by SFAS 123 *Accounting for Stock-Based Compensation.* **IG8**

Illustrative examples

Equity-settled share-based payment transactions

For equity-settled transactions measured by reference to the fair value of the equity instruments granted, paragraph 19 of IFRS 2 states that vesting conditions, other than market conditions,* are not taken into account when estimating the fair value of the shares or share options at the measurement date (ie grant date, for transactions with employees and others providing similar services). Instead, vesting conditions are taken into account by adjusting the number of equity instruments included in the measurement of the transaction amount so that, ultimately, the amount recognised for goods or services received as consideration for the equity instruments granted is based on the number of equity instruments that eventually vest. Hence, on a cumulative basis, no amount is recognised for goods or services received if the equity instruments granted do not vest because of failure to satisfy a vesting condition, eg the counterparty fails to complete a specified service period, or a performance condition is not satisfied. This accounting method is known as the modified grant date method, because the number of equity instruments included in the determination of the transaction amount is adjusted to reflect the outcome of the vesting conditions, but no adjustment is made to the fair value of those equity instruments. That fair value is estimated at grant date (for transactions with employees and others providing similar services) and not subsequently revised. Hence, neither increases nor decreases in the fair value of the equity instruments after grant date are taken into account when determining the transaction amount (other **IG9**

*In the remainder of this paragraph, the discussion of vesting conditions excludes market conditions, which are subject to the requirements of paragraph 21 of IFRS 2.

than in the context of measuring the incremental fair value transferred if a grant of equity instruments is subsequently modified).

IG10   To apply these requirements, paragraph 20 of IFRS 2 requires the entity to recognise the goods or services received during the vesting period based on the best available estimate of the number of equity instruments expected to vest and to revise that estimate, if necessary, if subsequent information indicates that the number of equity instruments expected to vest differs from previous estimates. On vesting date, the entity revises the estimate to equal the number of equity instruments that ultimately vested (subject to the requirements of paragraph 21 concerning market conditions).

IG11   In the examples below, the share options granted all vest at the same time, at the end of a specified period. In some situations, share options or other equity instruments granted might vest in instalments over the vesting period. For example, suppose an employee is granted 100 share options, which will vest in instalments of 25 share options at the end of each year over the next four years. To apply the requirements of the IFRS, the entity should treat each instalment as a separate share option grant, because each instalment has a different vesting period, and hence the fair value of each instalment will differ (because the length of the vesting period affects, for example, the likely timing of cash flows arising from the exercise of the options).

IG Example 1

BACKGROUND

An entity grants 100 share options to each of its 500 employees. Each grant is conditional upon the employee working for the entity over the next three years. The entity estimates that the fair value of each share option is CU15.*

On the basis of a weighted average probability, the entity estimates that 20 per - cent of employees will leave during the three-year period and therefore forfeit their rights to the share options.

APPLICATION OF REQUIREMENTS

Scenario 1

If everything turns out exactly as expected, the entity recognises the following amounts during the vesting period, for services received as consideration for the share options.

Year	Calculation	Remuneration expense for period CU	Cumulative remuneration expense CU
1	50,000 options × 80% × CU15 × 1/3 years	200,000	200,000
2	(50,000 options × 80% × CU15 × 2/3 years) – CU200,000	200,000	400,000
3	(50,000 options × 80% × CU15 × 3/3 years) – CU400,000	200,000	600,000

In this example, and in all other examples in this guidance, monetary amounts are denominated in 'currency units' (CU).

Scenario 2

During year 1, 20 employees leave. The entity revises its estimate of total employee departures over the three-year period from 20 per cent (100employees) to 15 per cent (75 employees). During year 2, a further 22employees leave. The entity revises its estimate of total employee departures over the three-year period from 15 per cent to 12 per cent (60 employees). During year 3, a further 15 employees leave. Hence, a total of 57 employees forfeited their rights to the share options during the three-year period, and a total of 44,300 share options (443 employees × 100 options per employee) vested at the end of year 3.

Year	Calculation	Remuneration expense for period CU	Cumulative remuneration expense CU
1	50,000 options × 85% × CU15 × 1/3 years	212,500	212,500
2	(50,000 options × 88% × CU15 × 2/3 years) CU212,500	227,500	440,000
3	(44,300 options × CU15) CU440,000	224,500	664,500

In Example 1, the share options were granted conditionally upon the employees' **IG12** completing a specified service period. In some cases, a share option or share grant might also be conditional upon the achievement of a specified performance target. Examples 2, 3 and 4 illustrate the application of the IFRS to share option or share grants with performance conditions (other than market conditions, which are discussed in paragraph IG5 and illustrated in Examples 5 and 6). In Example 2, the length of the vesting period varies, depending on when the performance condition is satisfied. Paragraph 15 of the IFRS requires the entity to estimate the length of the expected vesting period, based on the most likely outcome of the performance condition, and to revise that estimate, if necessary, if subsequent information indicates that the length of the vesting period is likely to differ from previous estimates.

IG Example 2

Grant with a performance condition, in which the length of the vesting period varies

BACKGROUND

At the beginning of year 1, the entity grants 100 shares each to 500 employees, conditional upon the employees' remaining in the entity's employ during the vesting period. The shares will vest at the end of year 1 if the entity's earnings increase by more than 18 per cent; at the end of year 2 if the entity's earnings increase by more than an average of 13 per cent per year over the two-year period; and at the end of year 3 if the entity's earnings increase by more than an average of 10 per cent per year over the three-year period. The shares have a fair value of CU30 per share at the start of year 1, which equals the share price at grant date. No dividends are expected to be paid over the three-year period.

By the end of year 1, the entity's earnings have increased by 14 per cent, and 30 employees have left. The entity expects that earnings will continue to increase at a similar rate in year 2, and therefore expects that the shares will vest at the end of year 2. The entity expects, on the basis of a weighted average probability, that a further 30 employees will leave during year 2, and therefore expects that 440 employees will vest in 100 shares each at the end of year 2.

By the end of year 2, the entity's earnings have increased by only 10 per cent and therefore the shares do not vest at the end of year 2. 28 employees have left during the year. The entity expects that a further 25 employees will leave during year 3, and that the entity's earnings will increase by at least 6 per cent, thereby achieving the average of 10 per cent per year.

By the end of year 3, 23 employees have left and the entity's earnings had increased by 8 per cent, resulting in an average increase of 10.67 per cent per year. Therefore, 419 employees received 100 shares at the end of year 3.

APPLICATION OF REQUIREMENTS

Year	Calculation	Remuneration expense for period CU	Cumulative remuneration expense CU
1	440 employees × 100 shares × CU30 × 1/2	660,000	660,000
2	(417 employees × 100 shares × CU30 × 2/3) – CU660,000	174,000	834,000
3	(419 employees × 100 shares × CU30 × 3/3) – CU834,000	423,000	1,257,000

IG Example 3

Grant with a performance condition, in which the number of equity instruments varies

BACKGROUND

At the beginning of year 1, Entity A grants share options to each of its 100 employees working in the sales department. The share options will vest at the end of year 3, provided that the employees remain in the entity's employ, and provided that the volume of sales of a particular product increases by at least an average of 5 per cent per year. If the volume of sales of the product increases by an average of between 5 per cent and 10 per cent per year, each employee will receive 100 share options. If the volume of sales increases by an average of between 10 per cent and 15 per cent each year, each employee will receive 200 share options. If the volume of sales increases by an average of 15 per cent or more, each employee will receive 300 share options.

On grant date, Entity A estimates that the share options have a fair value of CU20 per option. Entity A also estimates that the volume of sales of the product will increase by an average of between 10 per cent and 15 per cent per year, and therefore expects that, for each employee who remains in service until the end of year 3, 200 share options will vest. The entity also estimates, on the basis of a weighted average probability, that 20 per cent of employees will leave before the end of year 3.

By the end of year 1, seven employees have left and the entity still expects that a total of 20 employees will leave by the end of year 3. Hence, the entity expects that 80 employees will remain in service for the three-year period. Product sales have increased by 12 per cent and the entity expects this rate of increase to continue over the next 2 years.

By the end of year 2, a further five employees have left, bringing the total to 12 to date. The entity now expects only three more employees will leave during year 3, and therefore expects a total of 15 employees will have left during the three-year period, and hence 85 employees are expected to remain. Product sales have increased by 18 per cent, resulting in an average of 15 per cent over the two years to date. The entity now expects that sales will average 15 per cent or more over the three-year period, and hence expects each sales employee to receive 300 share options at the end of year 3.

By the end of year 3, a further two employees have left. Hence, 14 employees have left during the three-year period, and 86 employees remain. The entity's sales have increased by an average of 16 per cent over the three years. Therefore, each of the 86 employees receive 300 share options.

APPLICATION OF REQUIREMENTS

Year	Calculation	Remuneration expense for period CU	Cumulative remuneration expense CU
1	80 employees × 200 options × CU20 × 1/3	106,667	106,667
2	(85 employees × 300 options × CU20 × 2/3) − CU106,667	233,333	340,000
3	(86 employees × 300 options × CU20 × 3/3) − CU340,000	176,000	516,000

IG Example 4

Grant with a performance condition, in which the exercise price varies

BACKGROUND

At the beginning of year 1, an entity grants to a senior executive 10,000 share options, conditional upon the executive's remaining in the entity's employ until the end of year 3. The exercise price is CU40. However, the exercise price drops to CU30 if the entity's earnings increase by at least an average of 10 per cent per year over the three-year period.

On grant date, the entity estimates that the fair value of the share options, with an exercise price of CU30, is CU16 per option. If the exercise price is CU40, the entity estimates that the share options have a fair value of CU12 per option.

During year 1, the entity's earnings increased by 12 per cent, and the entity expects that earnings will continue to increase at this rate over the next two years. The entity therefore expects that the earnings target will be achieved, and hence the share options will have an exercise price of CU30.

During year 2, the entity's earnings increased by 13 per cent, and the entity continues to expect that the earnings target will be achieved.

During year 3, the entity's earnings increased by only 3 per cent, and therefore the earnings target was not achieved. The executive completes three years' service, and therefore satisfies the service condition. Because the earnings target was not achieved, the 10,000 vested share options have an exercise price of CU40.

APPLICATION OF REQUIREMENTS

Because the exercise price varies depending on the outcome of a performance condition that is not a market condition, the effect of that performance condition (ie the possibility that the exercise price might be CU40 and the possibility that the exercise price might be CU30) is not taken into account when estimating the fair value of the share options at grant date. Instead, the entity estimates the fair value of the share options at grant date under each scenario (ie exercise price of CU40 and exercise price of CU30) and ultimately revises the transaction amount to reflect the outcome of that performance condition, as illustrated below.

Year	Calculation	Remuneration expense for period CU	Cumulative remuneration expense CU
1	10,000 options × CU16 × 1/3	53,333	53,333
2	(10,000 options × CU16 × 2/3) − CU53,333	53,334	106,667
3	(10,000 options × CU12 × 3/3) − CU106,667	13,333	120,000

IG13 Paragraph 21 of the IFRS requires market conditions, such as a target share price upon which vesting (or exercisability) is conditional, to be taken into account when estimating the fair value of the equity instruments granted. Therefore, for grants of equity instruments with market conditions, the entity recognises the goods or services received from a counterparty who satisfies all other vesting conditions (eg services received from an employee who remains in service for the specified period of service), irrespective of whether that market condition is satisfied. Example 5 illustrates these requirements.

IG Example 5

Grant with a market condition

BACKGROUND

At the beginning of year 1, an entity grants to a senior executive 10,000 share options, conditional upon the executive remaining in the entity's employ until the end of year 3. However, the share options cannot be exercised unless the share price has increased from CU50 at the beginning of year 1 to above CU65 at the end of year 3. If the share price is above CU65 at the end of year 3, the share options can be exercised at any time during the next seven years, ie by the end of year 10.

The entity applies a binomial option pricing model, which takes into account the possibility that the share price will exceed CU65 at the end of year 3 (and hence the share options become exercisable) and the possibility that the share price will not exceed CU65 at the end of year 3 (and hence the options will be forfeited). It estimates the fair value of the share options with this market condition to be CU24 per option.

APPLICATION OF REQUIREMENTS

Because paragraph 21 of the IFRS requires the entity to recognise the services received from a counterparty who satisfies all other vesting conditions (eg services received from an employee who remains in service for the specified service period), irrespective of whether that market condition is satisfied, it makes no difference whether the share price target is achieved. The possibility that the share price target might not be achieved has already been taken into account when estimating the fair value of the share options at grant date. Therefore, if the entity expects the executive to complete the three-year service period, and the executive does so, the entity recognises the following amounts in years 1, 2 and 3:

Year	Calculation	Remuneration expense for period CU	Cumulative remuneration expense CU
1	10,000 options × CU24 × 1/3	80,000	80,000
2	(10,000 options × CU24 × 2/3) – CU80,000	80,000	160,000
3	(10,000 options × CU24) – CU160,000	80,000	240,000

As noted above, these amounts are recognised irrespective of the outcome of the market condition. However, if the executive left during year 2 (or year 3), the amount recognised during year 1 (and year 2) would be reversed in year 2 (or year 3). This is because the service condition, in contrast to the market condition, was not taken into account when estimating the fair value of the share options at grant date. Instead, the service condition is taken into account by adjusting the transaction amount to be based on the number of equity instruments that ultimately vest, in accordance with paragraphs 19 and 20 of the IFRS.

In Example 5, the outcome of the market condition did not change the length of the vesting period. However, if the length of the vesting period varies depending on when a performance condition is satisfied, paragraph 15 of the IFRS requires the entity to presume that the services to be rendered by the employees as consideration for the equity instruments granted will be received in the future, over the expected vesting period. The entity is required to estimate the length of the expected vesting period at grant date, based on the most likely outcome of the performance condition. If the performance condition is a market condition, the estimate of the length of the expected vesting period must be consistent with the assumptions used in estimating the fair value of the share options granted, and is not subsequently revised. Example 6 illustrates these requirements. **IG14**

IG Example 6

Grant with a market condition, in which the length of the vesting period varies

BACKGROUND

At the beginning of year 1, an entity grants 10,000 share options with a ten-year life to each of ten senior executives. The share options will vest and become exercisable immediately if and when the entity's share price increases from CU50 to CU70, provided that the executive remains in service until the share price target is achieved.

The entity applies a binomial option pricing model, which takes into account the possibility that the share price target will be achieved during the ten-year life of the options, and the possibility that the target will not be achieved. The entity estimates that the fair value of the share options at grant date is CU25 per option. From the option pricing model, the entity determines that the mode of the distribution of possible vesting dates is five years. In other words, of all the possible outcomes, the most likely outcome of the market condition is that the share price target will be achieved at the end of year 5. Therefore, the entity estimates that the expected vesting period is five years. The entity also estimates that two executives will have left by the end of year 5, and therefore expects that 80,000 share options (10,000 share options x 8 executives) will vest at the end of year 5.

Throughout years 1–4, the entity continues to estimate that a total of two executives will leave by the end of year 5. However, in total three executives leave, one in each of years 3, 4 and 5. The share price target is achieved at the end of year 6. Another executive leaves during year 6, before the share price target is achieved.

Application of requirements

Paragraph 15 of the IFRS requires the entity to recognise the services received over the expected vesting period, as estimated at grant date, and also requires the entity not to revise that estimate. Therefore, the entity recognises the services received from the executives over years 1–5. Hence, the transaction amount is ultimately based on 70,000 share options (10,000 share options × 7 executives who remain in service at the end of year 5). Although another executive left during year 6, no adjustment is made, because the executive had already completed the expected vesting period of 5 years. Therefore, the entity recognises the following amounts in years 1–5:

Year	Calculation	Remuneration expense for period CU	Cumulative remuneration expense CU
1	80,000 options × CU25 × 1/5	400,000	400,000
2	(80,000 options × CU25 × 2/5) − CU400,000	400,000	800,000
3	(80,000 options × CU25 × 3/5) − CU800,000	400,000	1,200,000
4	(80,000 options × CU25 × 4/5) − CU1,200,000	400,000	1,600,000
5	(70,000 options × CU25) − CU1,600,000	150,000	1,750,000

IG15   Paragraphs 26–29 and B42–B44 of the IFRS set out requirements that apply if a share option is repriced (or the entity otherwise modifies the terms or conditions of a share-based payment arrangement). Examples 7–9 illustrate some of these requirements.

IG Example 7

Grant of share options that are subsequently repriced

BACKGROUND

At the beginning of year 1, an entity grants 100 share options to each of its 500 employees. Each grant is conditional upon the employee remaining in service over the next three years. The entity estimates that the fair value of each option is CU15. On the basis of a weighted average probability, the entity estimates that 100 employees will leave during the three-year period and therefore forfeit their rights to the share options.

Suppose that 40 employees leave during year 1. Also suppose that by the end of year 1, the entity's share price has dropped, and the entity reprices its share options, and that the repriced share options vest at the end of year 3. The entity estimates that a further 70 employees will leave during years 2 and 3, and hence the total expected employee departures over the three-year vesting period is 110 employees. During year 2, a further 35 employees leave, and the entity estimates that a further 30 employees will leave during year 3, to bring the total expected employee departures over the three-year vesting period to 105 employees. During year 3, a total of 28 employees leave, and hence a total of 103 employees ceased employment during the vesting period. For the remaining 397 employees, the share options vested at the end of year 3.

The entity estimates that, at the date of repricing, the fair value of each of the original share options granted (ie before taking into account the repricing) is CU5 and that the fair value of each repriced share option is CU8.

APPLICATION OF REQUIREMENTS

Paragraph 27 of the IFRS requires the entity to recognise the effects of modifications that increase the total fair value of the share-based payment arrangement or are otherwise beneficial to the employee. If the modification increases the fair value of the equity instruments granted (eg by reducing the exercise price), measured immediately before and after the modification, paragraph B43(a) of Appendix B requires the entity to include the incremental fair value granted (ie the difference between the fair value of the modified equity instrument and that of the original equity instrument, both estimated as at the date of the modification) in the measurement of the amount recognised for services received as consideration for the equity instruments granted. If the modification occurs during the vesting period, the incremental fair value granted is included in the measurement of the amount recognised for services received over the period from the modification date until the date when the modified equity instruments vest, in addition to the amount based on the grant date fair value of the original equity instruments, which is recognised over the remainder of the original vesting period.

The incremental value is CU3 per share option (CU8 – CU5). This amount is recognised over the remaining two years of the vesting period, along with remuneration expense based on the original option value of CU15.

The amounts recognised in years 1–3 are as follows:

Year	Calculation	Remuneration expense for period CU	Cumulative remuneration expense CU
1	(500 – 110) employees × 100 options × CU15 × 1/3	195,000	195,000
2	(500 – 105) employees × 100 options × (CU15 × 2/3 + CU3 × 1/2) – CU195,000	259,250	454,250
3	(500 – 103) employees × 100 options × (CU15 + CU3) – CU454,250	260,350	714,600

IG Example 8

Grant of share options with a vesting condition that is subsequently modified

BACKGROUND

At the beginning of year 1, the entity grants 1,000 share options to each member of its sales team, conditional upon the employee's remaining in the entity's employ for three years, and the team selling more than 50,000 units of a particular product over the three-year period. The fair value of the share options is CU15 per option at the date of grant.

During year 2, the entity increases the sales target to 100,000 units. By the end of year 3, the entity has sold 55,000 units, and the share options are forfeited. Twelve members of the sales team have remained in service for the three-year period.

APPLICATION OF REQUIREMENTS

Paragraph 20 of the IFRS requires, for a performance condition that is not a market condition, the entity to recognise the services received during the vesting period based on the best available estimate of the number of equity instruments expected to vest and to revise that estimate, if necessary, if subsequent information indicates that the number of equity instruments expected to vest differs from previous estimates. On vesting date, the entity revises the estimate to equal the number of equity instruments that ultimately vested. However, paragraph 27 of the IFRS requires, irrespective of any modifications to the terms and conditions on which the equity instruments were granted, or a cancellation or settlement of that grant of equity instruments, the entity to recognise, as a minimum, the services received, measured at the grant date fair value of the equity instruments granted, unless those equity instruments do not vest because of failure to satisfy a vesting condition (other than a market condition) that was specified at grant date. Furthermore, paragraph B44(c) of Appendix B specifies that, if the entity modifies the vesting conditions in a manner that is not beneficial to the employee, the entity does not take the modified vesting conditions into account when applying the requirements of paragraphs 19–21 of the IFRS.

Therefore, because the modification to the performance condition made it less likely that the share options will vest, which was not beneficial to the employee, the entity takes no account of the modified performance condition when recognising the services received. Instead, it continues to recognise the services received over the three-year period based on the original vesting conditions. Hence, the entity ultimately recognises cumulative remuneration expense of CU180,000 over the three-year period (12 employees × 1,000 options × CU15).

The same result would have occurred if, instead of modifying the performance target, the entity had increased the number of years of service required for the share options to vest from three years to ten years. Because such a modification would make it less likely that the options will vest, which would not be beneficial to the employees, the entity would take no account of the modified service condition when recognising the services received. Instead, it would recognise the services received from the twelve employees who remained in service over the original three-year vesting period.

IG Example 9

Grant of shares, with a cash alternative subsequently added

BACKGROUND

At the beginning of year 1, the entity grants 10,000 shares with a fair value of CU33 per share to a senior executive, conditional upon the completion of three years' service. By the end of year 2, the share price has dropped to CU25 per share. At that date, the entity adds a cash alternative to the grant, whereby the executive can choose whether to receive 10,000 shares or cash equal to the value of 10,000 shares on vesting date. The share price is CU22 on vesting date.

APPLICATION OF REQUIREMENTS

Paragraph 27 of the IFRS requires, irrespective of any modifications to the terms and conditions on which the equity instruments were granted, or a cancellation or settlement of that grant of equity instruments, the entity to recognise, as a minimum, the services received measured at the grant date fair value of the equity instruments granted, unless those equity instruments do not vest because of failure to satisfy a vesting condition (other than a market condition) that was specified at grant date. Therefore, the entity recognises the services received over the three-year period, based on the grant date fair value of the shares.

Furthermore, the addition of the cash alternative at the end of year 2 creates an obligation to settle in cash. In accordance with the requirements for cash-settled share-based payment transactions (paragraphs 30–33 of the IFRS), the entity recognises the liability to settle in cash at the modification date, based on the fair value of the shares at the modification date and the extent to which the specified services have been received. Furthermore, the entity remeasures the fair value of the liability at each reporting date and at the date of settlement, with any changes in fair value recognised in profit or loss for the period. Therefore, the entity recognises the following amounts:

Year	Calculation	Expense CU	Equity CU	Liability CU
1	Remuneration expense for year: 10,000 shares × CU33 × 1/3	110,000	110,000	
2	Remuneration expense for year: (10,000 shares × CU33 × 2/3) – CU110,000	110,000	110,000	
	Reclassify equity to liabilities: 10,000 shares × CU25 × 2/3		(166,667)	166,667
3	Remuneration expense for year: (10,000 shares × CU33 × 3/3) – CU220,000	110,000	26,667*	83,333*
	Adjust liability to closing fair value: (CU166,667 + CU83,333) – (CU22 × 10,000 shares)	(30,000)		(30,000)
	Total	300,000	80,000	220,000

Allocated between liabilities and equity, to bring in the final third of the liability based on the fair value of the shares as at the date of the modification.

IG16   Paragraph 24 of the IFRS requires that, in rare cases only, in which the IFRS requires the entity to measure an equity-settled share-based payment transaction by reference to the fair value of the equity instruments granted, but the entity is unable to estimate reliably that fair value at the specified measurement date (eg grant date, for transactions with employees), the entity shall instead measure the transaction using an intrinsic value measurement method. Paragraph 24 also contains requirements on how to apply this method. The following example illustrates these requirements.

IG Example 10

Grant of share options that is accounted for by applying the intrinsic value method

BACKGROUND

At the beginning of year 1, an entity grants 1,000 share options to 50 employees. The share options will vest at the end of year 3, provided the employees remain in service until then. The share options have a life of 10 years. The exercise price is CU60 and the entity's share price is also CU60 at the date of grant.

At the date of grant, the entity concludes that it cannot estimate reliably the fair value of the share options granted.

At the end of year 1, three employees have ceased employment and the entity estimates that a further seven employees will leave during years 2 and 3. Hence, the entity estimates that 80 per cent of the share options will vest.

Two employees leave during year 2, and the entity revises its estimate of the number of share options that it expects will vest to 86 per cent.

Two employees leave during year 3. Hence, 43,000 share options vested at the end of year 3.

The entity's share price during years 1-10, and the number of share options exercised during years 4-10, are set out below. Share options that were exercised during a particular year were all exercised at the end of that year.

Year	Share price at year-end	Number of share options exercised at year-end
1	63	0
2	65	0
3	75	0
4	88	6,000
5	100	8,000
6	90	5,000
7	96	9,000
8	105	8,000
9	108	5,000
10	115	2,000

APPLICATION OF REQUIREMENTS

In accordance with paragraph 24 of the IFRS, the entity recognises the following amounts in years 1-10.

Year	Calculation	Expense for period CU	Cumulative expense CU
1	50,000 options × 80% × (CU63 – CU60) × 1/3 years	40,000	40,000
2	50,000 options × 86% × (CU65 – CU60) × 2/3 years – CU40,000	103,333	143,333
3	43,000 options × (CU75 – CU60) – CU143,333	501,667	645,000
4	37,000 outstanding options × (CU88 – CU75) + 6,000 exercised options × (CU88 – CU75)	559,000	1,204,000
5	29,000 outstanding options × (CU100 – CU88) + 8,000 exercised options × (CU100 – CU88)	444,000	1,648,000
6	24,000 outstanding options × (CU90 – CU100) + 5,000 exercised options × (CU90 – CU100)	(290,000)	1,358,000
7	15,000 outstanding options × (CU96 – CU90) + 9,000 exercised options × (CU96 – CU90)	144,000	1,502,000
8	7,000 outstanding options × (CU105 – CU96) + 8,000 exercised options × (CU105 – CU96)	135,000	1,637,000
9	2,000 outstanding options × (CU108 – CU105) + 5,000 exercised options × (CU108 – CU105)	21,000	1,658,000
10	2,000 exercised options × (CU115 – CU108)	14,000	1,672,000

There are many different types of employee share and share option plans. The following example illustrates the application of IFRS 2 to one particular type of plan – an employee share purchase plan. Typically, an employee share purchase plan provides employees with the opportunity to purchase the entity's shares at a discounted price. The terms and conditions under which employee share purchase plans operate differ from country to country. That is to say, not only are there many different types of employee share and share options plans, there are also many different types of employee share purchase plans. Therefore, the following example illustrates the application of IFRS 2 to one specific employee share purchase plan. **IG17**

IG Example 11

Employee share purchase plan

BACKGROUND

An entity offers all its 1,000 employees the opportunity to participate in an employee share purchase plan. The employees have two weeks to decide whether to accept the offer. Under the terms of the plan, the employees are entitled to purchase a maximum of 100 shares each. The purchase price will be 20 per cent less than the market price of the entity's shares at the date the offer is accepted, and the purchase price must be paid immediately upon acceptance of the offer. All shares purchased must be held in trust for the employees, and cannot be sold for five years. The employee is not permitted to withdraw from the plan during that period. For example, if the employee ceases employment during the five-year period, the shares must nevertheless remain in the plan until the end of the five-year period. Any dividends paid during the five-year period will be held in trust for the employees until the end of the five-year period.

In total, 800 employees accept the offer and each employee purchases, on average, 80 shares, ie the employees purchase a total of 64,000 shares. The weighted-average market price of the shares at the purchase date is CU30 per share, and the weighted-average purchase price is CU24 per share.

APPLICATION OF REQUIREMENTS

For transactions with employees, IFRS 2 requires the transaction amount to be measured by reference to the fair value of the equity instruments granted (IFRS 2, paragraph 11). To apply this requirement, it is necessary first to determine the type of equity instrument granted to the employees. Although the plan is described as an employee share purchase plan (ESPP), some ESPPs include option features and are therefore, in effect, share option plans. For example, an ESPP might include a 'lookback feature', whereby the employee is able to purchase shares at a discount, and choose whether the discount is applied to the entity's share price at the date of grant or its share price at the date of purchase. Or an ESPP might specify the purchase price, and then allow the employees a significant period of time to decide whether to participate in the plan. Another example of an option feature is an ESPP that permits the participating employees to cancel their participation before or at the end of a specified period and obtain a refund of amounts previously paid into the plan.

However, in this example, the plan includes no option features. The discount is applied to the share price at the purchase date, and the employees are not permitted to withdraw from the plan.

Another factor to consider is the effect of post-vesting transfer restrictions, if any. Paragraph B3 of IFRS 2 states that, if shares are subject to restrictions on transfer after vesting date, that factor should be taken into account when estimating the fair value of those shares, but only to the extent that the postvesting restrictions affect the price that a knowledgeable, willing market participant would pay for that share. For example, if the shares are actively traded in a deep and liquid market, post-vesting transfer restrictions may have little, if any, effect on the price that a knowledgeable, willing market participant would pay for those shares.

In this example, the shares are vested when purchased, but cannot be sold for five years after the date of purchase. Therefore, the entity should consider the valuation effect of the five-year post-vesting transfer restriction. This entails using a valuation technique to estimate what the price of the restricted share would have been on the purchase date in an arm's length transaction between knowledgeable, willing parties. Suppose that, in this example, the entity estimates that the fair value of each restricted share is CU28. In this case, the fair value of the equity instruments granted is CU4 per share (being the fair value of the restricted share of CU28 less the purchase price of CU24). Because 64,000 shares were purchased, the total fair value of the equity instruments granted is CU256,000.

In this example, there is no vesting period. Therefore, in accordance with paragraph 14 of IFRS 2, the entity should recognise an expense of CU256,000 immediately.

However, in some cases, the expense relating to an ESPP might not be material. IAS 8 *Accounting Policies, Changes in Accounting Policies and Errors* states that the accounting policies in IFRSs need not be applied when the effect of applying them is immaterial (IAS 8, paragraph 8). IAS 8 also states that an omission or mis-statement of an item is material if it could, individually or collectively, influence the economic decisions of users taken on the basis of the financial statements. Mate-riality depends on the size and nature of the omission or misstatement judged in the surrounding circumstances. The size or nature of the item, or a combination of both, could be the determining factor (IAS 8, paragraph 5). Therefore, in this example, the entity should consider whether the expense of CU256,000 is material.

Cash-settled share-based payment transactions

Paragraphs 30–33 of the IFRS set out requirements for transactions in which an entity acquires goods or services by incurring liabilities to the supplier of those goods or services in amounts based on the price of the entity's shares or other equity instruments. The entity is required to recognise initially the goods or services acquired, and a liability to pay for those goods or services, when the entity obtains the goods or as the services are rendered, measured at the fair value of the liability. Thereafter, until the liability is settled, the entity is required to recognise changes in the fair value of the liability. **IG18**

For example, an entity might grant share appreciation rights to employees as part of their remuneration package, whereby the employees will become entitled to a future cash payment (rather than an equity instrument), based on the increase in the entity's share price from a specified level over a specified period of time. If the share appreciation rights do not vest until the employees have completed a specified period of service, the entity recognises the services received, and a liability to pay for them, as the employees render service during that period. The liability is measured, initially and at each reporting date until settled, at the fair value of the share appreciation rights, by applying an option pricing model, and the extent to which the employees have rendered service to date. Changes in fair value are recognised in profit or loss. Therefore, if the amount recognised for the services received was included in the carrying amount of an asset recognised in the entity's balance sheet (eg inventory), the carrying amount of that asset is not adjusted for the effects of the liability remeasurement. Example 12 illustrates these requirements. **IG19**

IG Example 12

BACKGROUND

An entity grants 100 cash share appreciation rights (SARs) to each of its 500 employees, on condition that the employees remain in its employ for the next three years.

During year 1, 35 employees leave. The entity estimates that a further 60 will leave during years 2 and 3. During year 2, 40 employees leave and the entity estimates that a further 25 will leave during year 3. During year 3, 22 employees leave. At the end of year 3, 150 employees exercise their SARs, another 140 employees exercise their SARs at the end of year 4 and the remaining 113 employees exercise their SARs at the end of year 5.

The entity estimates the fair value of the SARs at the end of each year in which a liability exists as shown below. At the end of year 3, all SARs held by the remaining employees vest. The intrinsic values of the SARs at the date of exercise (which equal the cash paid out) at the end of years 3, 4 and 5 are also shown below.

Year	Fair value	Intrinsic value
1	CU14.40	
2	CU15.50	
3	CU18.20	CU15.00
4	CU21.40	CU20.00
5		CU25.00

APPLICATION OF REQUIREMENTS

Year	Calculation	Expense CU	Liability CU
1	(500 − 95) employees × 100 SARs × CU14.40 × 1/3	194,400	194,400
2	(500 − 100) employees × 100 SARs × CU15.50 × 2/3 − CU194,400	218,933	413,333
3	(500 − 97 − 150) employees × 100 SARs × CU18.20 − CU413,333	47,127	460,460
	+ 150 employees × 100 SARs × CU15.00	225,000	
	Total	272,127	
4	(253 − 140) employees × 100 SARs × CU21.40 − CU460,460	(218,640)	241,820
	+ 140 employees × 100 SARs × CU20.00	280,000	
	Total	61,360	
5	CU0 − CU241,820	(241,820)	0
	+ 113 employees × 100 SARs × CU25.00	282,500	
	Total	40,680	
	Total	787,500	

Share-based payment arrangements with cash alternatives

IG20   Some employee share-based payment arrangements permit the employee to choose whether to receive cash or equity instruments. In this situation, a compound financial instrument has been granted, ie a financial instrument with debt and equity components. Paragraph 37 of the IFRS requires the entity to estimate the fair value of the compound financial instrument at grant date, by first measuring the fair value of the debt component, and then measuring the fair value of the equity component – taking into account that the employee must forfeit the right to receive cash to receive the equity instrument.

IG21   Typically, share-based payment arrangements with cash alternatives are structured so that the fair value of one settlement alternative is the same as the other. For example, the employee might have the choice of receiving share options or cash share appreciation rights. In such cases, the fair value of the equity component will be zero, and hence the fair value of the compound financial instrument will be the same as the fair value of the debt component. However, if the fair values of the settlement alternatives differ, usually the fair value of the equity component will be greater than zero, in which case the fair value of the compound financial instrument will be greater than the fair value of the debt component.

Paragraph 38 of the IFRS requires the entity to account separately for the services received in respect of each component of the compound financial instrument. For the debt component, the entity recognises the services received, and a liability to pay for those services, as the counterparty renders service, in accordance with the requirements applying to cash-settled share-based payment transactions. For the equity component (if any), the entity recognises the services received, and an increase in equity, as the counterparty renders service, in accordance with the requirements applying to equity-settled share-based payment transactions. Example 13 illustrates these requirements.

IG Example 13

BACKGROUND

An entity grants to an employee the right to choose either 1,000 phantom shares, ie a right to a cash payment equal to the value of 1,000 shares, or 1,200 shares. The grant is conditional upon the completion of three years' service. If the employee chooses the share alternative, the shares must be held for three years after vesting date.

At grant date, the entity's share price is CU50 per share. At the end of years 1, 2 and 3, the share price is CU52, CU55 and CU60 respectively. The entity does not expect to pay dividends in the next three years. After taking into account the effects of the post-vesting transfer restrictions, the entity estimates that the grant date fair value of the share alternative is CU48 per share.

At the end of year 3, the employee chooses:

Scenario 1: The cash alternative

Scenario 2: The equity alternative

APPLICATION OF REQUIREMENTS

The fair value of the equity alternative is CU57,600 (1,200 shares × CU48). The fair value of the cash alternative is CU50,000 (1,000 phantom shares × CU50). Therefore, the fair value of the equity component of the compound instrument is CU7,600 (CU57,600 – CU50,000).

The entity recognises the following amounts:

Year		Expense CU	Equity CU	Liability CU
1	Liability component: (1,000 × CU52 × 1/3)	17,333		17,333
	Equity component: (CU7,600 × 1/3)	2,533	2,533	
2	Liability component: (1,000 × CU55 × 2/3) – CU17,333	19,333		19,333
	Equity component: (CU7,600 × 1/3)	2,533	2,533	
3	Liability component: (1,000 × CU60) – CU36,666	23,334		23,334
		2,534	2,534	

	Equity component: (CU7,600 × 1/3)			
End Year 3	Scenario 1: cash of CU60,000 paid			(60,000)
	Scenario 1 totals	67,600	7,600	0
	Scenario 2: 1,200 shares issued		60,000	(60,000)
	Scenario 2 totals	67,600	67,600	0

ILLUSTRATIVE DISCLOSURES

IG23   The following example illustrates the disclosure requirements in paragraphs 44-52 of the IFRS.*

Extract from the Notes to the Financial Statements of Company Z for the year ended 31 December 2005.

Share-based Payment

During the period ended 31 December 2005, the Company had four share-based payment arrangements, which are described below.

Type of arrangement	Senior management share option plan	General employee share option plan	Executive share plan	Senior management share appreciation cash plan
Date of grant	1 January 2004	1 January 2005	1 January 2005	1 July 2005
Number granted	50,000	75,000	50,000	25,000
Contractual life	10 years	10 years	N/A	10 years
Vesting conditions	1.5 years' service and achievement of a share price target, which was achieved.	Three years' service.	Three years' service and achievement of a target growth in earnings per share.	Three years' service and achievement of a target increase in market share.

The estimated fair value of each share option granted in the general employee share option plan is CU23.60. This was calculated by applying a binomial option pricing model. The model inputs were the share price at grant date of CU50, exercise price of CU50, expected volatility of 30 per cent, no expected dividends, contractual life of ten years, and a risk-free interest rate of 5 per cent. To allow for the effects of early exercise, it was assumed that the employees would exercise the options after vesting date when the share price was twice the exercise price. Historical volatility was 40 per cent, which includes the early

Note that the illustrative example is not intended to be a template or model and is therefore not exhaustive. For example, it does not illustrate the disclosure requirements in paragraphs 47(c), 48 and 49 of the IFRS.

years of the Company's life; the Company expects the volatility of its share price to reduce as it matures.

The estimated fair value of each share granted in the executive share plan is CU50.00, which is equal to the share price at the date of grant.

Further details of the two share option plans are as follows:

	2004		2005	
	Number of options	Weighted average exercise price	Number of options	Weighted average exercise price
Outstanding at start of year	0	–	45,000	CU40
Granted	50,000	CU40	75,000	CU50
Forfeited	(5,000)	CU40	(8,000)	CU46
Exercised	0	–	(4,000)	CU40
Outstanding at end of year	45,000	CU40	108,000	CU46
Exercisable at end of year	0	CU40	38,000	CU40

The weighted average share price at the date of exercise for share options exercised during the period was CU52. The options outstanding at 31 December 2005 had an exercise price of CU40 or CU50, and a weighted average remaining contractual life of 8.64 years.

	2004 CU	2005 CU
Expense arising from share-based payment transactions	495,000	1,105,867
Expense arising from share and share option plans	495,000	1,007,000
Closing balance of liability for cash share appreciation plan	-	98,867
Expense arising from increase in fair value of liability for cash share appreciation plan	-	9,200

Financial Reporting Standard 21 embodies IAS 10 (revised 2003) 'Events after the Balance Sheet Date' and some amendments to that standard adopted for entities subject to UK accounting standards.

The Statement of Standard Accounting Practice in FRS 21 is set out in paragraphs 1-23 and the Appendix. All the paragraphs have equal authority. Paragraphs in bold type state the main principles.

Accompanying the Statement of Standard Accounting Practice is the basis for the conclusions reached in the Statement which does not form part of the Statement.

The Statement of Standard Accounting Practice should be read in the context of its objective as stated in paragraph 1, the Basis for Conclusions set out in paragraphs BC1-BC4, and the Accounting Standards Board's 'Foreword to Accounting Standards' and 'Statement of Principles for Financial Reporting'.

FRS 21
(IAS 10) Events after the balance sheet date

(Issued May 2004)

Contents

Preface by the Accounting Standards Board

a This Financial Reporting Standard (FRS) has the effect of implementing the International Accounting Standards Board's (IASB's) International Accounting Standard (IAS) 10 (revised 2003) *Events after the Balance Sheet Date* in the UK and the Republic of Ireland for entities not preparing their financial statements in accordance with international accounting standards adopted pursuant to the Regulation of the European Parliament and of the Council on the Application of International Accounting Standards. It replaces SSAP 17 *Accounting for post balance sheet events,* and reflects the proposals of FRED 27 which was published in May 2002.

b In March 2004 the Department of Trade and Industry (DTI) issued a consultation document 'Modernisation of Accounting Directives/IAS Infrastructure'. These proposals include draft Regulations amending the Companies Act 1985 which will apply in respect of companies' financial years which begin on or after 1 January 2005*. The proposals remove the requirement to report proposed dividends in the profit and loss account. This is in accordance with the now generally accepted view that dividends declared after the balance sheet date should not be reported as liabilities. This is reflected in this FRS and is the principal difference between this FRS and SSAP 17.

c The accounting practice set out in this FRS should be applied for accounting periods beginning on or after 1 January 2005 which is consistent with the proposed legislative changes.

d The requirements, scope and effective date of FRS 21 are identical to IAS 10 except that:

- entities applying the FRSSE will be exempt from the FRS, and
- early adoption is not permitted because proposed changes to the legal requirements for recognising dividend payments come into effect for accounting periods beginning on or after 1 January 2005 and compliance with the FRS before then will not be compatible with the law.

e The text of IAS 10 contains various references to other IASs and IFRSs. In FRS 21 those references have been amended where necessary to enable the Standard to be applied in the UK context. Deleted text has been struck through and inserted text is underlined. The Accounting Standards Board believes that those amendments do not change the requirements of IAS 10 in any way.

f The Appendix of IAS 10 contains amendments that the IASB has made to existing IASs in the light of the main requirements in IAS 10. In FRS 21 this material has been amended and added to so that the FRS can be applied in a UK context. In particular, from the relevant effective date of the Standard, paragraphs A5 to A8 withdraw SSAP 17 *Accounting for post balance sheet events* and amend FRS 12 *Provisions, Contingent Liabilities and Contingent Assets* and FRS 18 *Accounting Policies.*

g In all other respects the FRS is identical to IAS 10.

**Similar amendments are proposed to the statutory requirements in Northern Ireland and the Republic of Ireland.*

Introduction

International Accounting Standard 10 *Events after the Balance Sheet Date* (IAS 10) **IN1**
replaces IAS 10 *Events after the Balance Sheet Date* (revised in 1999)* and should be
applied for accounting periods beginning on or after 1 January 2005.

REASONS FOR REVISING IAS 10

The International Accounting Standards Board developed this revised IAS 10 as part **IN2**
of its project on Improvements to International Accounting Standards. The project
was undertaken in the light of queries and criticisms raised in relation to the Standards by securities regulators, professional accountants and other interested parties.
The objectives of the project were to reduce or eliminate alternatives, redundancies
and conflicts within the Standards, to deal with some convergence issues and to make
other improvements.

For IAS 10 the Board's main objective was a limited clarification of the accounting **IN3**
for dividends declared after the balance sheet date. The Board did not reconsider the
fundamental approach to the accounting for events after the balance sheet date
contained in IAS 10.

THE MAIN CHANGES

The main change from the previous version of IAS 10 was a limited clarification of **IN4**
paragraphs 12 and 13 (paragraphs 11 and 12 of the previous version of IAS 10). As
revised, those paragraphs state that if an entity declares dividends after the balance
sheet date, the entity shall not recognise those dividends as a liability at the balance
sheet date.

---

*ASB footnote: This previous version of IAS 10 was not adopted by the Accounting Standards Board.

Financial Reporting Standard 21 (IAS 10)

'Events after the Balance Sheet Date'

OBJECTIVE

1   The objective of this Standard is to prescribe:

(a)   when an entity should adjust its financial statements for events after the balance sheet date; and

(b)   the disclosures that an entity should give about the date when the financial statements were authorised for issue and about events after the balance sheet date.

The Standard also requires that an entity should not prepare its financial statements on a going concern basis if events after the balance sheet date indicate that the going concern assumption is not appropriate.

SCOPE

1A   This Standard applies to all financial statements that are intended to give a true and fair view of a reporting entity's financial position and profit or loss (or income and expenditure), except that reporting entities applying the Financial Reporting Standard for Smaller Entities (FRSSE) currently applicable are exempt.

2   This Standard shall be applied in the accounting for, and disclosure of, events after the balance sheet date.

DEFINITIONS

3   **The following terms are used in this Standard with the meanings specified:**

Events after the balance sheet date are those events, favourable and unfavourable, that occur between the balance sheet date and the date when the financial statements are authorised for issue. Two types of events can be identified:

(a)   **those that provide evidence of conditions that existed at the balance sheet date (adjusting events after the balance sheet date); and**

(b)   **those that are indicative of conditions that arose after the balance sheet date (non-adjusting events after the balance sheet date).**

4   The process involved in authorising the financial statements for issue will vary depending upon the management structure, statutory requirements and procedures followed in preparing and finalising the financial statements.

5   In some cases, an entity is required to submit its financial statements to its shareholders for approval after the financial statements have been issued. In such cases, the financial statements are authorised for issue on the date of issue, not the date when shareholders approve the financial statements.

> **Example**
>
> The management of an entity completes draft financial statements for the year to 31 December 20X1 on 28 February 20X2. On 18 March 20X2, the board of directors reviews the financial statements and authorises them for issue. The entity announces its profit and selected other financial information on 19 March 20X2. The financial statements are made available to shareholders and others on 1 April 20X2. The shareholders approve the financial statements at their annual meeting on 15 May 20X2 and the approved financial statements are then filed with a regulatory body on 17 May 20X2.
>
> *The financial statements are authorised for issue on 18 March 20X2 (date of board authorisation for issue).*

In some cases, the management of an entity is required to issue its financial state-   6
ments to a supervisory board (made up solely of non-executives) for approval. In such cases, the financial statements are authorised for issue when the management authorises them for issue to the supervisory board.

> **Example**
>
> On 18 March 20X2, the management of an entity authorises financial statements for issue to its supervisory board. The supervisory board is made up solely of non-executives and may include representatives of employees and other outside interests. The supervisory board approves the financial statements on 26 March 20X2. The financial statements are made available to shareholders and others on 1 April 20X2. The shareholders approve the financial statements at their annual meeting on 15 May 20X2 and the financial statements are then filed with a regulatory body on 17 May 20X2.
>
> *The financial statements are authorised for issue on 18 March 20X2 (date of management authorisation for issue to the supervisory board).*

Events after the balance sheet date include all events up to the date when the   7
financial statements are authorised for issue, even if those events occur after the public announcement of profit or of other selected financial information.

RECOGNITION AND MEASUREMENT

Adjusting Events after the Balance Sheet Date

**An entity shall adjust the amounts recognised in its financial statements to reflect   8
adjusting events after the balance sheet date.**

The following are examples of adjusting events after the balance sheet date that   9
require an entity to adjust the amounts recognised in its financial statements, or to recognise items that were not previously recognised:

(a)   the settlement after the balance sheet date of a court case that confirms that the entity had a present obligation at the balance sheet date. The entity adjusts any previously recognised provision related to this court case in accordance with

FRS 12 *Provisions, Contingent Liabilities and Contingent Assets* or recognises a new provision. The entity does not merely disclose a contingent liability because the settlement provides additional evidence that would be considered in accordance with paragraph 16 of FRS 12.

(b)   the receipt of information after the balance sheet date indicating that an asset was impaired at the balance sheet date, or that the amount of a previously recognised impairment loss for that asset needs to be adjusted. For example:

  (i)   the bankruptcy of a customer that occurs after the balance sheet date usually confirms that a loss existed at the balance sheet date on a trade receivable and that the entity needs to adjust the carrying amount of the trade receivable; and

  (ii)   the sale of inventories after the balance sheet date may give evidence about their net realisable value at the balance sheet date.

(c)   the determination after the balance sheet date of the cost of assets purchased, or the proceeds from assets sold, before the balance sheet date.

(d)   the determination after the balance sheet date of the amount of profit-sharing or bonus payments, if the entity had a present legal or constructive obligation at the balance sheet date to make such payments as a result of events before that date.

(e)   the discovery of fraud or errors that show that the financial statements are incorrect.

Non-adjusting Events after the Balance Sheet Date

10   An entity shall not adjust the amounts recognised in its financial statements to reflect non-adjusting events after the balance sheet date.

11   An example of a non-adjusting event after the balance sheet date is a decline in market value of investments between the balance sheet date and the date when the financial statements are authorised for issue. The decline in market value does not normally relate to the condition of the investments at the balance sheet date, but reflects circumstances that have arisen subsequently. Therefore, an entity does not adjust the amounts recognised in its financial statements for the investments. Similarly, the entity does not update the amounts disclosed for the investments as at the balance sheet date, although it may need to give additional disclosure under paragraph 21.

Dividends

12   If an entity declares dividends to holders of equity instruments (as defined in FRS 25 (*IAS 32*) *Financial Instruments: Disclosure and Presentation**) after the balance sheet date, the entity shall not recognise those dividends as a liability at the balance sheet date.

13   If dividends are declared (ie the dividends are appropriately authorised and no longer at the discretion of the entity) after the balance sheet date but before the financial statements are authorised for issue, the dividends are not recognised as a liability at the balance sheet date because they do not meet the criteria of a present obligation in FRS 12. Such dividends are disclosed in the notes to the financial statements.

ASB Footnote: The ASB will introduce a UK standard adopting IAS 32 for accounting periods beginning on or after 1 January 2005. **Editor's note: this is now FRS 25.*

GOING CONCERN

**An entity shall not prepare its financial statements on a going concern basis if man- 14
agement determines after the balance sheet date either that it intends to liquidate the
entity or to cease trading, or that it has no realistic alternative but to do so.**

Deterioration in operating results and financial position after the balance sheet date   15
may indicate a need to consider whether the going concern assumption is still
appropriate. If the going concern assumption is no longer appropriate, the effect is so
pervasive that this Standard requires a fundamental change in the basis of
accounting, rather than an adjustment to the amounts recognised within the original
basis of accounting.

FRS 18 *Accounting Policies* specifies required disclosures in relation to the assess-   16
ment of going concern:

(a)   any material uncertainties, of which the directors are aware in making their
      assessment, related to events or conditions that may cast significant doubt upon
      the entity's ability to continue as a going concern;
(b)   where the foreseeable future considered by the directors has been limited to a
      period of less than one year from the date of approval of the financial state-
      ments, that fact;
(c)   when the financial statements are not prepared on a going concern basis, that
      fact, together with the basis on which the financial statements are prepared and
      the reason why the entity is not regarded as a going concern.

DISCLOSURE

Date of Authorisation for Issue

**An entity shall disclose the date when the financial statements were authorised for issue   17
and who gave that authorisation. If the entity's owners or others have the power to
amend the financial statements after issue, the entity shall disclose that fact.**

It is important for users to know when the financial statements were authorised for   18
issue, because the financial statements do not reflect events after this date.

Updating Disclosure about Conditions at the Balance Sheet Date

**If an entity receives information after the balance sheet date about conditions that   19
existed at the balance sheet date, it shall update disclosures that relate to those conditions, in the light of the new information.**

In some cases, an entity needs to update the disclosures in its financial statements to   20
reflect information received after the balance sheet date, even when the information
does not affect the amounts that it recognises in its financial statements. One example
of the need to update disclosures is when evidence becomes available after the balance sheet date about a contingent liability that existed at the balance sheet date. In
addition to considering whether it should recognise or change a provision under
FRS 12 *Provisions, Contingent Liabilities and Contingent Assets*, an entity updates its
disclosures about the contingent liability in the light of that evidence.

Non-adjusting Events after the Balance Sheet Date

21   If non-adjusting events after the balance sheet date are material, non-disclosure could influence the economic decisions of users taken on the basis of the financial statements. Accordingly, an entity shall disclose the following for each material category of non-adjusting event after the balance sheet date:

(a)   the nature of the event; and

(b)   an estimate of its financial effect, or a statement that such an estimate cannot be made.

22   The following are examples of non-adjusting events after the balance sheet date that would generally result in disclosure:

(a)   a major business combination after the balance sheet date or disposing of a major subsidiary;

(b)   announcing a plan to discontinue an operation;

(c)   major purchases and disposals of assets, or expropriation of major assets by government;

(d)   the destruction of a major production plant by a fire after the balance sheet date;

(e)   announcing, or commencing the implementation of, a major restructuring (see FRS 12);

(f)   major ordinary share transactions and potential ordinary share transactions after the balance sheet date (FRS 22 (IAS 33) *Earnings per Share* requires an entity to disclose a description of such transactions, other than when such transactions involve capitalisation or bonus issues, share splits or reverse share splits all of which are required to be adjusted under FRS 22);

(g)   abnormally large changes after the balance sheet date in asset prices or foreign exchange rates;

(h)   changes in tax rates or tax laws enacted or announced after the balance sheet date that have a significant effect on current and deferred tax assets and liabilities;

(i)   entering into significant commitments or contingent liabilities, for example, by issuing significant guarantees; and

(j)   commencing major litigation arising solely out of events that occurred after the balance sheet date.

EFFECTIVE DATE

23   An entity shall apply this Standard for accounting periods beginning on or after 1 January 2005.

Appendix
Amendments to other Standards

[Not reproduced, as all changes have been made to the underlying standards]

Adoption of the standard
Approval of IAS 10 by the International Accounting Standards Board

International Accounting Standard 10 *Events after the Balance Sheet Date* was approved for issue by the fourteen members of the International Accounting Standards Board.

Sir David Tweedie	Chairman
Thomas E Jones	Vice-Chairman
Mary E Barth	
Hans-Georg Bruns	
Anthony T Cope	
Robert P Garnett	
Gilbert Gélard	
James J Leisenring	
Warren J McGregor	
Patricia L O'Malley	
Harry K Schmid	
John T Smith	
Geoffrey Whittington	
Tatsumi Yamada	

Adoption of FRS 21 by the Accounting Standards Board

Financial Reporting Standard 21 (IAS 10) *Events after the Balance Sheet Date* was approved for issue by the nine members of the Accounting Standards Board.

Mary Keegan	Chairman
Andrew Lennard	Technical Director
Michael Ashley	
Douglas Flint	
Huw Jones	
Roger Marshall	
Isobel Sharp	
John Smith	
Jonathan Symonds	

Notes on the standard's application in the UK and the Republic of Ireland

NOTE ON LEGAL REQUIREMENTS

Great Britain

Paid and proposed dividends

The statutory requirements relating to paid and proposed dividends are set out in Schedule 4 paragraph 3(7) to the Companies Act 1985. Schedule 4 does not apply to banking and insurance groups. Corresponding requirements are set out in Schedule 9 paragraph 8 for banking companies and groups and in Schedule 9A paragraph 5 for insurance companies and groups. **N1**

The UK Government has recently published its proposals* to amend the Companies Act 1985 through a draft Statutory Instrument – *The Companies Act 1985 (International Accounting Standards and Other Accounting Amendments) Regulations 2004*. The draft Regulations will apply in respect of companies' financial years which begin on or after 1 January 2005.† **N2**

The draft Regulations amend paragraph 3(7) of Schedule 4 to the 1985 Act, by replacing the requirement for companies to show the aggregate amount of any dividends paid and proposed in the profit and loss account, with a requirement to show dividends which are paid or liable to be paid at the balance sheet date. The draft Regulations introduce a new requirement, as paragraph 3(7A), to disclose in the notes to the accounts the aggregate amount of dividends proposed before the date of approval of the accounts, which have not been shown in the profit and loss account in accordance with the requirement in paragraph 3(7). **N3**

The draft Regulations make corresponding amendments to Schedules 9 and 9A to the 1985 Act. **N4**

The accounting practice set out in paragraphs 12 and 13 of the FRS is consistent with the proposed changes to the 1985 Act and will take effect from the same date. **N5**

Going Concern

Paragraph 10 of Schedule 4 to the Companies Act 1985 requires that the company shall be presumed to be carrying on business as a going concern. Paragraph 15 of Schedule 4 permits the directors of a company to depart from this principle in preparing the company's accounts in respect of any financial year if it appears to them that there are special reasons for such a departure. Particulars of the departure, the reasons for it and its effect are required to be given in a note to the accounts. Schedule 4 does not apply to banking and insurance groups. Corresponding requirements are set out in Schedule 9 paragraphs 17 and 22 for banking companies and groups and in Schedule 9A paragraphs 14 and 19 for insurance companies and groups. **N6**

*DTI/HM Treasury – Modernisation of accounting directives/IAS infrastructure – a consultation document. March 2004.

†**Editor's note**: This statutory instrument was issued as SI 2004 No. 2947.

Northern Ireland

N7   The statutory requirements in Northern Ireland are set out in the Companies (Northern Ireland) Order 1986. These requirements are identical to the legislation for Great Britain cited above. Under the Northern Ireland Act 1998 company law is a transferred matter. Northern Ireland will therefore make Statutory Regulations, with provisions similar to those in the Statutory Instrument being prepared in Great Britain to amend the Companies (Northern Ireland) Order 1986. It is intended that these should be effective from 1 January 2005.

Republic of Ireland

N8   The statutory requirements in the Republic of Ireland that correspond to those cited above for Great Britain are shown in the following table:

Great Britain	*Republic of Ireland*
Schedule 4 to the Companies Act 1985:	The Companies (Amendment) Act 1986:
paragraph 3(7)	Section 4(15)(a)
paragraph 10	Section 5(a)
paragraph 15	Section 6
Schedule 9 to the Companies Act 1985	European Communities (Credit Institutions: Accounts) Regulations 1992
Schedule 9A to the Companies Act 1985	European Communities (Insurance Undertakings: Accounts) Regulations 1996

The Republic of Ireland has under consideration similar amendments to those proposed for Great Britain.

DEVELOPMENT OF THE FRS

N9   This FRS is based on IAS 10 (revised 2003) *Events after the Balance Sheet Date* and it supersedes SSAP 17 *Accounting for post balance sheet events*, which was issued in August 1980. The draft standard was published as FRED 27 in May 2002. Respondents were concerned that the proposed reference to FRS 4 in paragraph 12 was unhelpful. In light of the ASB's decision to introduce a standard based on IAS 32 *Financial Instruments: Disclosure and Presentation* effective from 1 January 2005 the reference has been amended to refer to this standard. Respondents also raised practical issues regarding the proposed removal of references to Going Concern and possible deficiencies in FRS 18 *Accounting Policies*; and if the references to Going Concern were retained, possible conflicts with FRS 18. In response to this the FRS retains references to Going Concern in paragraphs 1, 14 and 15 to minimise divergence from IAS 10. As a consequence an amendment has been made to FRS 18 paragraph 21 to bring the assessment of going concern into line with that used in paragraph 14 of IAS 10. Paragraph 16 of the FRS is amended to refer to the disclosure requirements of FRS 18

Basis for Conclusions

This Basis for Conclusions accompanies, but is not part of IAS 10.

ASB note: All references in this section to 'the Board' and 'Board members' are references to the IASB Board and IASB Board members.

INTRODUCTION

This Basis for Conclusions summarises the International Accounting Standards **BC1** Board's considerations in reaching its conclusions on revising IAS 10 *Events After the Balance Sheet Date* in 2003. Individual Board members gave greater weight to some factors than to others.

In July 2001 the Board announced that, as part of its initial agenda of technical **BC2** projects, it would undertake a project to improve a number of Standards, including IAS 10. The project was undertaken in the light of queries and criticisms raised in relation to the Standards by securities regulators, professional accountants and other interested parties. The objectives of the Improvements project were to reduce or eliminate alternatives, redundancies and conflicts within Standards, to deal with some convergence issues and to make other improvements. In May 2002 the Board published its proposals in an Exposure Draft of *Improvements to International Accounting Standards*, with a comment deadline of 16 September 2002. The Board received over 160 comment letters on the Exposure Draft.

Because the Board's intention was not to reconsider the fundamental approach to the **BC3** accounting for events after the balance sheet date established by IAS 10, this Basis for Conclusions does not discuss requirements in IAS 10 that the Board has not reconsidered.

LIMITED CLARIFICATION

For this limited clarification of IAS 10 the main change made is in paragraphs 12 and **BC4** 13 (paragraphs 11 and 12 of the previous version of IAS 10). As revised, those paragraphs state that if dividends are declared after the balance sheet date, an entity shall not recognise those dividends as a liability at the balance sheet date. This is because undeclared dividends do not meet the criteria of a present obligation in IAS 37 *Provisions, Contingent Liabilities and Contingent Assets.* The Board discussed whether or not an entity's past practice of paying dividends could be considered a constructive obligation. The Board concluded that such practices do not give rise to a liability to pay dividends.

Financial Reporting Standard 22 embodies IAS 33 (revised 2003) 'Earnings per Share' and some amendments to that standard adopted for entities subject to UK accounting standards.

The Statement of Standard Accounting Practice in FRS 22 is set out in paragraphs 1-75 and Appendices A-C. All the paragraphs have equal authority. Paragraphs in bold type state the main principles.

Accompanying the Statement of Standard Accounting Practice is the basis for the conclusions reached in the Statement and some illustrative examples, which do not form part of the Statement.

The Statement of Standard Accounting Practice should be read in the context of its objective as stated in paragraph 1, the Basis for Conclusions set out in paragraphs BC1-BC15, and the Accounting Standards Board's 'Foreword to Accounting Standards' and 'Statement of Principles for Financial Reporting'.

FRS 22
(IAS 33) Earnings per share

(Issued December 2004)

Contents

Preface by the Accounting Standards Board

a   This Financial Reporting Standard (FRS) prescribes the basis for calculating and presenting earnings per share in the financial statements of entities whose shares are, or will be, publicly traded and other entities that choose to disclose earnings per share. It has the effect of implementing the International Accounting Standards Board's (IASB's) International Accounting Standard (IAS) 33 (revised 2003) *Earnings per Share* in the UK and the Republic of Ireland for such entities not preparing their financial statements in accordance with international accounting standards adopted pursuant to the Regulation of the European Parliament and of the Council on the Application of International Accounting Standards. It replaces FRS 14 *Earnings per Share*.

b   An exposure draft of the proposed standard, FRED 26 *Earnings per Share*, was published in May 2002. FRED 26 was based on the IASB's exposure draft of a proposed revision of IAS 33 but under the assumption that the UK and Republic of Ireland equivalent standards of IAS 32 *Financial Instruments: Disclosure and Presentation* and IAS 39 *Financial Instruments: Recognition and Measurement* would not be effective and that the requirements of FRS 4 *Capital Instruments* would therefore remain. The UK and Republic of Ireland equivalent standards of IAS 32 and IAS 39 have now been issued and therefore this standard no longer contains the differences from IAS 33 that it was necessary to propose in FRED 26. The IASB made a number of changes to the exposure draft of IAS 33 when it issued IAS 33 (revised 2003) in addressing comments received from respondents. This standard contains only limited differences from IAS 33 (revised 2003).

c   The accounting practice set out in this FRS should be applied for accounting periods beginning on or after 1 January 2005.

MAIN CHANGES TO EXISTING UK REQUIREMENTS

d   This standard requires that basic and diluted earnings per share should be disclosed on the face of the profit and loss account both for net profit or loss for the period and also for profit or loss from continuing operations. Basic and diluted earnings per share for discontinued operations (if reported) should be reported either on the face of the profit and loss account or in a note to the accounts. Entities will be permitted to present additional per share amounts in the notes to the accounts. Under FRS 14, basic and diluted earnings per share for net profit or loss were required on the face of the profit and loss account. Companies were encouraged to provide additional per share amounts which they could disclose where they wished, providing they were no more prominent than the per share amounts required by FRS 14.

e   Where additional earnings per share amounts were presented, FRS 14 required a reconciliation to the amounts required by FRS 14, listing the items for which an adjustment was being made and their individual effect on the calculation. The reason for the additional per share amount was also required to be given. This standard requires less disclosure than FRS 14 where additional per share amounts are presented – if the component of the income statement used for the additional earnings per share amount is not reported as a line item in the income statement, a reconciliation should be provided between the component and a line item.

f   This standard gives more guidance than FRS 14 did on the adjustments required in calculating basic earnings per share for transactions involving preference shares.

FRS 14 and this standard both use profit or loss from continuing operations as the   g
control number that is used to establish whether potential ordinary shares are
dilutive or anti-dilutive. However, as FRS 3 *Reporting Financial Performance*
requires an analysis of continuing operations, acquisitions and discontinued operations only to the level of profit before interest, FRS 14 gave additional guidance on
how to allocate interest and tax in order to achieve a reasonable estimate of profit or
loss from continuing operations. This standard does not provide any guidance on
how to estimate this number, which is also required for basic earnings per share
disclosure purposes. The guidance in FRS 14, which entities applying FRS 3 may
find a useful reference, is reproduced in Appendix D, as non-mandatory application
guidance.

For contracts that may be settled in ordinary shares or cash, the treatment under   h
FRS 14 depended on the facts available each period. Unless past experience or a
stated policy provided a basis for concluding how the contract would be satisfied, it
was presumed that the contract would be settled by the more dilutive method. This
standard distinguishes between those contracts where settlement is to be determined
by the entity and those by the holder. For those contracts that may be settled at the
holder's option, the more dilutive of cash or share settlement should be used. For
those contracts that may be settled in cash or shares at the entity's option, it should
be presumed for the purpose of calculating diluted earnings per share that the
contract will be settled in shares, and this presumption is not rebuttable.

This standard provides a specific requirement in respect of written put options   i
(contracts that require the entity to repurchase its own shares). These are included in
the calculation of diluted earnings per share if the effect is dilutive (ie the contracts
are 'in the money' during the period). Although not specified in FRS 14, the guidance
is consistent with its principles.

The standard requires disclosure of securities that could potentially dilute basic   j
earnings per share in the future but which were not included in the calculation
because they were anti-dilutive for the periods presented.

FRS 14 included additional guidance in respect of the presentation of financial   k
statistics in historical summaries. There is no equivalent guidance in this standard.

MAIN DIFFERENCES BETWEEN UK REQUIREMENTS AND IAS 33

The requirements, scope and effective date of FRS 22 are identical to IAS 33 except   l
that:

- early adoption is not permitted consistent with FRS 25 (IAS 32) *Financial
  Instruments: Disclosure and Presentation.*
- The guidance on earnings per share for business combinations accounted for as
  mergers under FRS 6 *Acquisitions and Mergers* that was exposed in FRED 26 has
  been retained in Appendix C.
- The text of IAS 33 contains various references to other IASs and IFRSs. In
  FRS 22 those references have been amended where necessary to enable the
  Standard to be applied in the UK context. Deleted text has been struck through
  and inserted text is underlined. The Accounting Standards Board believes that
  those amendments do not change the requirements of IAS 33 in any way.

AMENDMENTS TO OTHER UK STANDARDS AND UITF ABSTRACTS

m   Implementation of this standard requires, from the relevant effective date of the standard, amendment to FRS 3 *Reporting Financial Performance* and amendment of references to FRS 14 in FRS 20 *Share-Based Payment*, FRS 21 *Events after the Balance Sheet Date*, the Financial Reporting Standard for Smaller Entities (FRSSE), UITF 37 *Purchases and Sales of Own Shares* and UITF 38 *Accounting for ESOP Trusts*.

Introduction

[Not reproduced].   **IN1**

REASONS FOR REVISING IAS 33

The International Accounting Standards Board has developed this revised IAS 33 as   **IN2**
part of its project on Improvements to International Accounting Standards. The
project was undertaken in the light of queries and criticisms raised in relation to the
Standards by securities regulators, professional accountants and other interested
parties. The objectives of the project were to reduce or eliminate alternatives,
redundancies and conflicts within the Standards, to deal with some convergence
issues and to make other improvements.

For IAS 33 the Board's main objective was a limited revision to provide additional   **IN3**
guidance and illustrative examples on selected complex matters, such as the effects of
contingently issuable shares; potential ordinary shares of subsidiaries, joint ventures
or associates; participating equity instruments; written put options; purchased put
and call options; and mandatorily convertible instruments. The Board did not
reconsider the fundamental approach to the determination and presentation of
earnings per share contained in IAS 33.

Financial Reporting Standard 22 (IAS 33)

'Earnings per Share'

OBJECTIVE

1   The objective of this Standard is to prescribe principles for the determination and presentation of earnings per share, so as to improve performance comparisons between different entities in the same reporting period and between different reporting periods for the same entity. Even though earnings per share data have limitations because of the different accounting policies that may be used for determining 'earnings', a consistently determined denominator enhances financial reporting. The focus of this Standard is on the denominator of the earnings per share calculation.

SCOPE

2   *This Standard shall be applied by entities whose ordinary shares or potential ordinary shares are publicly traded, and by entities that are in the process of issuing ordinary shares or potential ordinary shares in public markets.*

2A *Reporting entities applying the Financial Reporting Standard for Smaller Entities currently applicable are exempt from the FRS.*

3   *An entity that discloses earnings per share shall calculate and disclose earnings per share in accordance with this Standard.*

3A *Entities that use merger accounting as required or permitted by FRS 6 'Acquisitions and Mergers' should follow the requirements in Appendix C 'Application to Merger Accounting'.*

4   *When an entity presents both consolidated financial statements and separate financial statements, the disclosures required by this Standard need be presented only on the basis of the consolidated information. An entity that chooses to disclose earnings per share based on its separate financial statements shall present such earnings per share information only on the face of its separate income statement. An entity shall not present such earnings per share information in the consolidated financial statements.*

DEFINITIONS

5   *The following terms are used in this Standard with the meanings specified:*

Antidilution is an increase in earnings per share or a reduction in loss per share resulting from the assumption that convertible instruments are converted, that options or warrants are exercised, or that ordinary shares are issued upon the satisfaction of specified conditions.

A contingent share agreement is an agreement to issue shares that is dependent on the satisfaction of specified conditions.

Contingently issuable ordinary shares are ordinary shares issuable for little or no cash or other consideration upon the satisfaction of specified conditions in a contingent share agreement.

Dilution is a reduction in earnings per share or an increase in loss per share resulting from the assumption that convertible instruments are converted, that options or warrants are exercised, or that ordinary shares are issued upon the satisfaction of specified conditions.

Options, warrants and their equivalents are financial instruments that give the holder the right to purchase ordinary shares.

An ordinary share is an equity instrument that is subordinate to all other classes of equity instruments.

A potential ordinary share is a financial instrument or other contract that may entitle its holder to ordinary shares.

Put options on ordinary shares are contracts that give the holder the right to sell ordinary shares at a specified price for a given period.

Ordinary shares participate in profit for the period only after other types of shares   **6** such as preference shares have participated. An entity may have more than one class of ordinary shares. Ordinary shares of the same class have the same rights to receive dividends.

Examples of potential ordinary shares are: **7**

(a)   financial liabilities or equity instruments, including preference shares, that are convertible into ordinary shares;
(b)   options and warrants;
(c)   shares that would be issued upon the satisfaction of conditions resulting from contractual arrangements, such as the purchase of a business or other assets.

Terms defined in FRS 25 (IAS 32) *Financial Instruments: Disclosure and Presentation*   **8** are used in this Standard with the meanings specified in paragraph 11 of FRS 25 (IAS 32), unless otherwise noted. FRS 25 (IAS 32) defines financial instrument, financial asset, financial liability, equity instrument and fair value, and provides guidance on applying those definitions.

MEASUREMENT

Basic Earnings per Share

An entity shall calculate basic earnings per share amounts for profit or loss attributable   **9** *to ordinary equity holders of the parent entity and, if presented, profit or loss from continuing operations attributable to those equity holders.*

Basic earnings per share shall be calculated by dividing profit or loss attributable to   **10** *ordinary equity holders of the parent entity (the numerator) by the weighted average number of ordinary shares outstanding (the denominator) during the period.*

The objective of basic earnings per share information is to provide a measure of the   **11** interests of each ordinary share of a parent entity in the performance of the entity over the reporting period.

Earnings

12   *For the purpose of calculating basic earnings per share, the amounts attributable to ordinary equity holders of the parent entity in respect of:*

   (a)   profit or loss from continuing operations attributable to the parent entity; and
   (b)   profit or loss attributable to the parent entity

   shall be the amounts in (a) and (b) adjusted for the after-tax amounts of preference dividends, differences arising on the settlement of preference shares, and other similar effects of preference shares classified as equity.

13   All items of income and expense attributable to ordinary equity holders of the parent entity that are recognised in a period, including tax expense and dividends on preference shares classified as liabilities are included in the determination of profit or loss for the period attributable to ordinary equity holders of the parent entity.

14   The after-tax amount of preference dividends that is deducted from profit or loss is:

   (a)   the after-tax amount of any preference dividends on noncumulative preference shares declared in respect of the period; and
   (b)   the after-tax amount of the preference dividends for cumulative preference shares required for the period, whether or not the dividends have been declared. The amount of preference dividends for the period does not include the amount of any preference dividends for cumulative preference shares paid or declared during the current period in respect of previous periods.

15   Preference shares that provide for a low initial dividend to compensate an entity for selling the preference shares at a discount, or an above market dividend in later periods to compensate investors for purchasing preference shares at a premium, are sometimes referred to as increasing rate preference shares. Any original issue discount or premium on increasing rate preference shares is amortised to retained earnings using the effective interest method and treated as a preference dividend for the purposes of calculating earnings per share.

16   Preference shares may be repurchased under an entity's tender offer to the holders. The excess of the fair value of the consideration paid to the preference shareholders over the carrying amount of the preference shares represents a return to the holders of the preference shares and a charge to retained earnings for the entity. This amount is deducted in calculating profit or loss attributable to ordinary equity holders of the parent entity.

17   Early conversion of convertible preference shares may be induced by an entity through favourable changes to the original conversion terms or the payment of additional consideration. The excess of the fair value of the ordinary shares or other consideration paid over the fair value of the ordinary shares issuable under the original conversion terms is a return to the preference shareholders, and is deducted in calculating profit or loss attributable to ordinary equity holders of the parent entity.

18   Any excess of the carrying amount of preference shares over the fair value of the consideration paid to settle them is added in calculating profit or loss attributable to ordinary equity holders of the parent entity.

Shares

For the purpose of calculating basic earnings per share, the number of ordinary shares   **19**
shall be the weighted average number of ordinary shares outstanding during the period.

Using the weighted average number of ordinary shares outstanding during the period   **20**
reflects the possibility that the amount of shareholders' capital varied during the
period as a result of a larger or smaller number of shares being outstanding at any
time. The weighted average number of ordinary shares outstanding during the period
is the number of ordinary shares outstanding at the beginning of the period, adjusted
by the number of ordinary shares bought back or issued during the period multiplied
by a time-weighting factor. The timeweighting factor is the number of days that the
shares are outstanding as a proportion of the total number of days in the period; a
reasonable approximation of the weighted average is adequate in many
circumstances.

Shares are usually included in the weighted average number of shares from the date   **21**
consideration is receivable (which is generally the date of their issue), for example:

(a) ordinary shares issued in exchange for cash are included when cash is
    receivable;
(b) ordinary shares issued on the voluntary reinvestment of dividends on ordinary
    or preference shares are included when dividends are reinvested;
(c) ordinary shares issued as a result of the conversion of a debt instrument to
    ordinary shares are included from the date that interest ceases to accrue;
(d) ordinary shares issued in place of interest or principal on other financial
    instruments are included from the date that interest ceases to accrue;
(e) ordinary shares issued in exchange for the settlement of a liability of the entity
    are included from the settlement date;
(f) ordinary shares issued as consideration for the acquisition of an asset other
    than cash are included as of the date on which the acquisition is recognised; and
(g) ordinary shares issued for the rendering of services to the entity are included as
    the services are rendered.

The timing of the inclusion of ordinary shares is determined by the terms and
conditions attaching to their issue. Due consideration is given to the substance of
any contract associated with the issue.

Ordinary shares issued as part of the cost of a business combination are included in   **22**
the weighted average number of shares from the acquisition date. This is because the
acquirer incorporates into its income statement the acquiree's profits and losses from
that date.

Ordinary shares that will be issued upon the conversion of a mandatorily convertible   **23**
instrument are included in the calculation of basic earnings per share from the date
the contract is entered into.

Contingently issuable shares are treated as outstanding and are included in the   **24**
calculation of basic earnings per share only from the date when all necessary conditions are satisfied (ie the events have occurred). Shares that are issuable solely after
the passage of time are not contingently issuable shares, because the passage of time
is a certainty.

Outstanding ordinary shares that are contingently returnable (ie subject to recall) are   **25**
not treated as outstanding and are excluded from the calculation of basic earnings
per share until the date the shares are no longer subject to recall.

26 *The weighted average number of ordinary shares outstanding during the period and for all periods presented shall be adjusted for events, other than the conversion of potential ordinary shares, that have changed the number of ordinary shares outstanding without a corresponding change in resources.*

27 Ordinary shares may be issued, or the number of ordinary shares outstanding may be reduced, without a corresponding change in resources. Examples include:

(a) a capitalisation or bonus issue (sometimes referred to as a stock dividend);
(b) a bonus element in any other issue, for example a bonus element in a rights issue to existing shareholders;
(c) a share split; and
(d) a reverse share split (consolidation of shares).

28 In a capitalisation or bonus issue or a share split, ordinary shares are issued to existing shareholders for no additional consideration. Therefore, the number of ordinary shares outstanding is increased without an increase in resources. The number of ordinary shares outstanding before the event is adjusted for the pro-portionate change in the number of ordinary shares outstanding as if the event had occurred at the beginning of the earliest period presented. For example, on a two for-one bonus issue, the number of ordinary shares outstanding before the issue is multiplied by three to obtain the new total number of ordinary shares, or by two to obtain the number of additional ordinary shares.

29 A consolidation of ordinary shares generally reduces the number of ordinary shares outstanding without a corresponding reduction in resources. However, when the overall effect is a share repurchase at fair value, the reduction in the number of ordinary shares outstanding is the result of a corresponding reduction in resources. An example is a share consolidation combined with a special dividend. The weighted average number of ordinary shares outstanding for the period in which the combined transaction takes place is adjusted for the reduction in the number of ordinary shares from the date the special dividend is recognised.

Diluted Earnings per Share

30 *An entity shall calculate diluted earnings per share amounts for profit or loss attribu-table to ordinary equity holders of the parent entity and, if presented, profit or loss from continuing operations attributable to those equity holders.*

31 *For the purpose of calculating diluted earnings per share, an entity shall adjust profit or loss attributable to ordinary equity holders of the parent entity, and the weighted average number of shares outstanding, for the effects of all dilutive potential ordinary shares.*

32 The objective of diluted earnings per share is consistent with that of basic earnings per share—to provide a measure of the interest of each ordinary share in the per-formance of an entity—while giving effect to all dilutive potential ordinary shares outstanding during the period. As a result:

(a) profit or loss attributable to ordinary equity holders of the parent entity is increased by the after-tax amount of dividends and interest recognised in the period in respect of the dilutive potential ordinary shares and is adjusted for any other changes in income or expense that would result from the conversion of the dilutive potential ordinary shares; and

(b)   the weighted average number of ordinary shares outstanding is increased by the weighted average number of additional ordinary shares that would have been outstanding assuming the conversion of all dilutive potential ordinary shares.

Earnings

For the purpose of calculating diluted earnings per share, an entity shall adjust profit or **33** *loss attributable to ordinary equity holders of the parent entity, as calculated in accordance with paragraph 12, by the after-tax effect of:*

(a)   any dividends or other items related to dilutive potential ordinary shares deducted in arriving at profit or loss attributable to ordinary equity holders of the parent entity as calculated in accordance with paragraph 12;

(b)   any interest recognised in the period related to dilutive potential ordinary shares; and

(c)   any other changes in income or expense that would result from the conversion of the dilutive potential ordinary shares.

After the potential ordinary shares are converted into ordinary shares, the items **34** identified in paragraph 33(a)-(c) no longer arise. Instead, the new ordinary shares are entitled to participate in profit or loss attributable to ordinary equity holders of the parent entity. Therefore, profit or loss attributable to ordinary equity holders of the parent entity calculated in accordance with paragraph 12 is adjusted for the items identified in paragraph 33(a)-(c) and any related taxes. The expenses associated with potential ordinary shares include transaction costs and discounts accounted for in accordance with the effective interest method (see paragraph 9 of FRS 26 (Part of IAS 39) *Financial Instruments: Measurement*).

The conversion of potential ordinary shares may lead to consequential changes in **35** income or expenses. For example, the reduction of interest expense related to potential ordinary shares and the resulting increase in profit or reduction in loss may lead to an increase in the expense related to a nondiscretionary employee profit sharing plan. For the purpose of calculating diluted earnings per share, profit or loss attributable to ordinary equity holders of the parent entity is adjusted for any such consequential changes in income or expense.

Shares

For the purpose of calculating diluted earnings per share, the number of ordinary shares **36** *shall be the weighted average number of ordinary shares calculated in accordance with paragraphs 19 and 26, plus the weighted average number of ordinary shares that would be issued on the conversion of all the dilutive potential ordinary shares into ordinary shares. Dilutive potential ordinary shares shall be deemed to have been converted into ordinary shares at the beginning of the period or, if later, the date of the issue of the potential ordinary shares.*

Dilutive potential ordinary shares shall be determined independently for each period **37** presented. The number of dilutive potential ordinary shares included in the year-to-date period is not a weighted average of the dilutive potential ordinary shares included in each interim computation.

Potential ordinary shares are weighted for the period they are outstanding. Potential **38** ordinary shares that are cancelled or allowed to lapse during the period are included in the calculation of diluted earnings per share only for the portion of the period during which they are outstanding. Potential ordinary shares that are converted into ordinary shares during the period are included in the calculation of diluted earnings per share from the beginning of the period to the date of conversion; from the date of conversion, the resulting ordinary shares are included in both basic and diluted earnings per share.

39   The number of ordinary shares that would be issued on conversion of dilutive potential ordinary shares is determined from the terms of the potential ordinary shares. When more than one basis of conversion exists, the calculation assumes the most advantageous conversion rate or exercise price from the standpoint of the holder of the potential ordinary shares.

40   A subsidiary, joint venture or associate may issue to parties other than the parent, venturer or investor potential ordinary shares that are convertible into either ordinary shares of the subsidiary, joint venture or associate, or ordinary shares of the parent, venturer or investor (the reporting entity). If these potential ordinary shares of the subsidiary, joint venture or associate have a dilutive effect on the basic earnings per share of the reporting entity, they are included in the calculation of diluted earnings per share.

Dilutive Potential Ordinary Shares

41   **Potential ordinary shares shall be treated as dilutive when, and only when, their conversion to ordinary shares would decrease earnings per share or increase loss per share from continuing operations.**

42   An entity uses profit or loss from continuing operations attributable to the parent entity as the control number to establish whether potential ordinary shares are dilutive or antidilutive. Profit or loss from continuing operations attributable to the parent entity is adjusted in accordance with paragraph 12 and excludes items relating to discontinued operations*

43   Potential ordinary shares are antidilutive when their conversion to ordinary shares would increase earnings per share or decrease loss per share from continuing operations. The calculation of diluted earnings per share does not assume conversion, exercise, or other issue of potential ordinary shares that would have an antidilutive effect on earnings per share.

44   In determining whether potential ordinary shares are dilutive or antidilutive, each issue or series of potential ordinary shares is considered separately rather than in aggregate. The sequence in which potential ordinary shares are considered may affect whether they are dilutive. Therefore, to maximise the dilution of basic earnings per share, each issue or series of potential ordinary shares is considered in sequence from the most dilutive to the least dilutive, ie dilutive potential ordinary shares with the lowest 'earnings per incremental share' are included in the diluted earnings per share calculation before those with a higher earnings per incremental share. Options and warrants are generally included first because they do not affect the numerator of the calculation.

Options, warrants and their equivalents

45   **For the purpose of calculating diluted earnings per share, an entity shall assume the exercise of dilutive options and warrants of the entity. The assumed proceeds from these instruments shall be regarded as having been received from the issue of ordinary shares**

*ASB footnote: Discontinued operations are defined in FRS 3 Reporting Financial Performance

at the average market price of ordinary shares during the period. The difference between the number of ordinary shares issued and the number of ordinary shares that would have been issued at the average market price of ordinary shares during the period shall be treated as an issue of ordinary shares for no consideration.

Options and warrants are dilutive when they would result in the issue of ordinary shares for less than the average market price of ordinary shares during the period. The amount of the dilution is the average market price of ordinary shares during the period minus the issue price. Therefore, to calculate diluted earnings per share, potential ordinary shares are treated as consisting of both the following: **46**

(a) a contract to issue a certain number of the ordinary shares at their average market price during the period. Such ordinary shares are assumed to be fairly priced and to be neither dilutive nor antidilutive. They are ignored in the calculation of diluted earnings per share.

(b) a contract to issue the remaining ordinary shares for no consideration. Such ordinary shares generate no proceeds and have no effect on profit or loss attributable to ordinary shares outstanding. Therefore, such shares are dilutive and are added to the number of ordinary shares outstanding in the calculation of diluted earnings per share.

Options and warrants have a dilutive effect only when the average market price of ordinary shares during the period exceeds the exercise price of the options or warrants (ie they are 'in the money'). Previously reported earnings per share are not retroactively adjusted to reflect changes in prices of ordinary shares. **47**

For share options and other share-based payment arrangement to which FRS 20 (IFRS 2) *Share-based Payment* applies, the issue price referred to in paragraph 46 and the exercise price referred to in paragraph 47 shall include the fair value of any goods or services to be supplied to the entity in the future under the share option or other share-based payment arrangement. **47A**

Employee share options with fixed or determinable terms and nonvested ordinary shares are treated as options in the calculation of diluted earnings per share, even though they may be contingent on vesting. They are treated as outstanding on the grant date. Performance-based employee share options are treated as contingently issuable shares because their issue is contingent upon satisfying specified conditions in addition to the passage of time. **48**

Convertible instruments

The dilutive effect of convertible instruments shall be reflected in diluted earnings per share in accordance with paragraphs 33 and 36. **49**

Convertible preference shares are antidilutive whenever the amount of the dividend on such shares declared in or accumulated for the current period per ordinary share obtainable on conversion exceeds basic earnings per share. Similarly, convertible debt is antidilutive whenever its interest (net of tax and other changes in income or expense) per ordinary share obtainable on conversion exceeds basic earnings per share. **50**

The redemption or induced conversion of convertible preference shares may affect only a portion of the previously outstanding convertible preference shares. In such cases, any excess consideration referred to in paragraph 17 is attributed to those shares that are redeemed or converted for the purpose of determining whether the remaining outstanding preference shares are dilutive. The shares redeemed or **51** converted are considered separately from those shares that are not redeemed or converted.

Contingently issuable shares

52   As in the calculation of basic earnings per share, contingently issuable ordinary shares are treated as outstanding and included in the calculation of diluted earnings per share if the conditions are satisfied (ie the events have occurred). Contingently issuable shares are included from the beginning of the period (or from the date of the contingent share agreement, if later). If the conditions are not satisfied, the number of contingently issuable shares included in the diluted earnings per share calculation is based on the number of shares that would be issuable if the end of the period were the end of the contingency period. Restatement is not permitted if the conditions are not met when the contingency period expires.

53   If attainment or maintenance of a specified amount of earnings for a period is the condition for contingent issue and if that amount has been attained at the end of the reporting period but must be maintained beyond the end of the reporting period for an additional period, then the additional ordinary shares are treated as outstanding, if the effect is dilutive, when calculating diluted earnings per share. In that case, the calculation of diluted earnings per share is based on the number of ordinary shares that would be issued if the amount of earnings at the end of the reporting period were the amount of earnings at the end of the contingency period. Because earnings may change in a future period, the calculation of basic earnings per share does not include such contingently issuable ordinary shares until the end of the contingency period because not all necessary conditions have been satisfied.

54   The number of ordinary shares contingently issuable may depend on the future market price of the ordinary shares. In that case, if the effect is dilutive, the calculation of diluted earnings per share is based on the number of ordinary shares that would be issued if the market price at the end of the reporting period were the market price at the end of the contingency period. If the condition is based on an average of market prices over a period of time that extends beyond the end of the reporting period, the average for the period of time that has lapsed is used. Because the market price may change in a future period, the calculation of basic earnings per share does not include such contingently issuable ordinary shares until the end of the contingency period because not all necessary conditions have been satisfied.

55   The number of ordinary shares contingently issuable may depend on future earnings and future prices of the ordinary shares. In such cases, the number of ordinary shares included in the diluted earnings per share calculation is based on both conditions (ie earnings to date and the current market price at the end of the reporting period). Contingently issuable ordinary shares are not included in the diluted earnings per share calculation unless both conditions are met.

56   In other cases, the number of ordinary shares contingently issuable depends on a condition other than earnings or market price (for example, the opening of a specific number of retail stores). In such cases, assuming that the present status of the condition remains unchanged until the end of the contingency period, the contingently issuable ordinary shares are included in the calculation of diluted earnings per share according to the status at the end of the reporting period.

57   Contingently issuable potential ordinary shares (other than those covered by a contingent share agreement, such as contingently issuable convertible instruments) are included in the diluted earnings per share calculation as follows:

(a)   an entity determines whether the potential ordinary shares may be assumed to be issuable on the basis of the conditions specified for their issue in accordance with the contingent ordinary share provisions in paragraphs 52-56; and

(b)   if those potential ordinary shares should be reflected in diluted earnings per share, an entity determines their impact on the calculation of diluted earnings per share by following the provisions for options and warrants in paragraphs 45-48, the provisions for convertible instruments in paragraphs 49-51, the provisions for contracts that may be settled in ordinary shares or cash in paragraphs 58-61, or other provisions, as appropriate.

However, exercise or conversion is not assumed for the purpose of calculating diluted earnings per share unless exercise or conversion of similar outstanding potential ordinary shares that are not contingently issuable is assumed.

Contracts that may be settled in ordinary shares or cash

When an entity has issued a contract that may be settled in ordinary shares or cash at   **58**
the entity's option, the entity shall presume that the contract will be settled in ordinary shares, and the resulting potential ordinary shares shall be included in diluted earnings per share if the effect is dilutive.

When such a contract is presented for accounting purposes as an asset or a liability,   **59**
or has an equity component and a liability component, the entity shall adjust the numerator for any changes in profit or loss that would have resulted during the period if the contract had been classified wholly as an equity instrument. That adjustment is similar to the adjustments required in paragraph 33.

For contracts that may be settled in ordinary shares or cash at the holder's option, the   **60**
more dilutive of cash settlement and share settlement shall be used in calculating diluted earnings per share.

An example of a contract that may be settled in ordinary shares or cash is a debt   **61**
instrument that, on maturity, gives the entity the unrestricted right to settle the principal amount in cash or in its own ordinary shares. Another example is a written put option that gives the holder a choice of settling in ordinary shares or cash.

Purchased options

Contracts such as purchased put options and purchased call options (ie options held   **62**
by the entity on its own ordinary shares) are not included in the calculation of diluted earnings per share because including them would be antidilutive. The put option would be exercised only if the exercise price were higher than the market price and the call option would be exercised only if the exercise price were lower than the market price.

Written put options

Contracts that require the entity to repurchase its own shares, such as written put   **63**
options and forward purchase contracts, are reflected in the calculation of diluted earnings per share if the effect is dilutive. If these contracts are 'in the money' during the period (ie the exercise or settlement price is above the average market price for that period), the potential dilutive effect on earnings per share shall be calculated as follows:

(a) *it shall be assumed that at the beginning of the period sufficient ordinary shares will be issued (at the average market price during the period) to raise proceeds to satisfy the contract;*

(b) *it shall be assumed that the proceeds from the issue are used to satisfy the contract (ie to buy back ordinary shares); and*

(c) *the incremental ordinary shares (the difference between the number of ordinary shares assumed issued and the number of ordinary shares received from satisfying the contract) shall be included in the calculation of diluted earnings per share.*

RETROSPECTIVE ADJUSTMENTS

64   *If the number of ordinary or potential ordinary shares outstanding increases as a result of a capitalisation, bonus issue or share split, or decreases as a result of a reverse share split, the calculation of basic and diluted earnings per share for all periods presented shall be adjusted retrospectively. If these changes occur after the balance sheet date but before the financial statements are authorised for issue, the per share calculations for those and any prior period financial statements presented shall be based on the new number of shares. The fact that per share calculations reflect such changes in the number of shares shall be disclosed. In addition, basic and diluted earnings per share of all periods presented shall be adjusted for the effects of errors and adjustments resulting from changes in accounting policies accounted for retrospectively.*

65   An entity does not restate diluted earnings per share of any prior period presented for changes in the assumptions used in earnings per share calculations or for the conversion of potential ordinary shares into ordinary shares.

PRESENTATION

66   *An entity shall present on the face of the income statement basic and diluted earnings per share for profit or loss from continuing operations attributable to the ordinary equity holders of the parent entity and for profit or loss attributable to the ordinary equity holders of the parent entity for the period for each class of ordinary shares that has a different right to share in profit for the period. An entity shall present basic and diluted earnings per share with equal prominence for all periods presented.*

67   Earnings per share is presented for every period for which an income statement is presented. If diluted earnings per share is reported for at least one period, it shall be reported for all periods presented, even if it equals basic earnings per share. If basic and diluted earnings per share are equal, dual presentation can be accomplished in one line on the income statement.

68   *An entity that reports a discontinued operation shall disclose the basic and diluted amounts per share for the discontinued operation either on the face of the income statement or in the notes to the financial statements.*

69   *An entity shall present basic and diluted earnings per share, even if the amounts are negative (ie a loss per share).*

DISCLOSURE

70   *An entity shall disclose the following:*

(a) *the amounts used as the numerators in calculating basic and diluted earnings per share, and a reconciliation of those amounts to profit or loss attributable to the parent entity for the period. The reconciliation shall include the individual effect of each class of instruments that affects earnings per share.*

(b)   the weighted average number of ordinary shares used as the denominator in calculating basic and diluted earnings per share, and a reconciliation of these denominators to each other. The reconciliation shall include the individual effect of each class of instruments that affects earnings per share.

(c)   instruments (including contingently issuable shares) that could potentially dilute basic earnings per share in the future, but were not included in the calculation of diluted earnings per share because they are antidilutive for the period(s) presented.

(d)   a description of ordinary share transactions or potential ordinary share transactions, other than those accounted for in accordance with paragraph 64, that occur after the balance sheet date and that would have changed significantly the number of ordinary shares or potential ordinary shares outstanding at the end of the period if those transactions had occurred before the end of the reporting period.

Examples of transactions in paragraph 70(d) include: **71**

(a)   an issue of shares for cash;

(b)   an issue of shares when the proceeds are used to repay debt or preference shares outstanding at the balance sheet date;

(c)   the redemption of ordinary shares outstanding;

(d)   the conversion or exercise of potential ordinary shares outstanding at the balance sheet date into ordinary shares;

(e)   an issue of options, warrants, or convertible instruments; and

(f)   the achievement of conditions that would result in the issue of contingently issuable shares.

Earnings per share amounts are not adjusted for such transactions occurring after the balance sheet date because such transactions do not affect the amount of capital used to produce profit or loss for the period.

Financial instruments and other contracts generating potential ordinary shares may   **72**
incorporate terms and conditions that affect the measurement of basic and diluted earnings per share. These terms and conditions may determine whether any potential ordinary shares are dilutive and, if so, the effect on the weighted average number of shares outstanding and any consequent adjustments to profit or loss attributable to ordinary equity holders. The disclosure of the terms and conditions of such financial instruments and other contracts is encouraged, if not otherwise required (see FRS 29 (IFRS 7) Financial Instruments: Disclosures).*

If an entity discloses, in addition to basic and diluted earnings per share, amounts per   **73**
share using a reported component of the income statement other than one required by this Standard, such amounts shall be calculated using the weighted average number of ordinary shares determined in accordance with this Standard. Basic and diluted amounts per share relating to such a component shall be disclosed with equal prominence and presented in the notes to the financial statements. An entity shall indicate the basis on which the numerator(s) is (are) determined, including whether amounts per share are before tax or after tax. If a component of the income statement is used that is not reported as a line item in the income statement, a reconciliation shall be provided between the component used and a line item that is reported in the income statement.

*Editor's note: Amended by FRS 29.

EFFECTIVE DATE

74   ***An entity shall apply this Standard for accounting periods beginning on or after 1 January 2005.***

WITHDRAWAL OF OTHER PRONOUNCEMENTS

75   This Standard supersedes FRS 14 *Earnings per Share*.

Appendix A
Application Guidance

This appendix is an integral part of the Standard.

Profit or Loss Attributable to the Parent Entity

For the purpose of calculating earnings per share based on the consolidated financial statements, profit or loss attributable to the parent entity refers to profit or loss of the consolidated entity after adjusting for minority interests. **A1**

Rights Issues

The issue of ordinary shares at the time of exercise or conversion of potential **A2** ordinary shares does not usually give rise to a bonus element. This is because the potential ordinary shares are usually issued for full value, resulting in a proportionate change in the resources available to the entity. In a rights issue, however, the exercise price is often less than the fair value of the shares. Therefore, as noted in paragraph 27(b), such a rights issue includes a bonus element. If a rights issue is offered to all existing shareholders, the number of ordinary shares to be used in calculating basic and diluted earnings per share for all periods before the rights issue is the number of ordinary shares outstanding before the issue, multiplied by the following factor:

$$\frac{\text{Fair value per share immediately before the exercise of rights}}{\text{Theoretical ex-rights fair value per share}}$$

The theoretical ex-rights fair value per share is calculated by adding the aggregate market value of the shares immediately before the exercise of the rights to the proceeds from the exercise of the rights, and dividing by the number of shares outstanding after the exercise of the rights. Where the rights are to be publicly traded separately from the shares before the exercise date, fair value for the purposes of this calculation is established at the close of the last day on which the shares are traded together with the rights.

Control Number

To illustrate the application of the control number notion described in paragraphs 42 **A3** and 43, assume that an entity has profit from continuing operations attributable to the parent entity of CU4,800,* a loss from discontinued operations attributable to the parent entity of (CU7,200), a loss attributable to the parent entity of (CU2,400), and 2,000 ordinary shares and 400 potential ordinary shares outstanding. The entity's basic earnings per share is CU2.40 for continuing operations, (CU3.60) for discontinued operations and (CU1.20) for the loss. The 400 potential ordinary shares are included in the diluted earnings per share calculation because the resulting CU2.00 earnings per share for continuing operations is dilutive, assuming no profit or loss impact of those 400 potential ordinary shares. Because profit from continuing operations attributable to the parent entity is the control number, the entity also includes those 400 potential ordinary shares in the calculation of the other earnings per share amounts, even though the resulting earnings per share amounts are anti-dilutive to their comparable basic earnings per share amounts, ie the loss per share is

*In this guidance, monetary amounts are denominated in 'currency units' (CU).

less [(CU3.00) per share for the loss from discontinued operations and (CU1.00) per share for the loss].

Average Market Price of Ordinary Shares

A4   For the purpose of calculating diluted earnings per share, the average market price of ordinary shares assumed to be issued is calculated on the basis of the average market price of the ordinary shares during the period. Theoretically, every market transaction for an entity's ordinary shares could be included in the determination of the average market price. As a practical matter, however, a simple average of weekly or monthly prices is usually adequate.

A5   Generally, closing market prices are adequate for calculating the average market price. When prices fluctuate widely, however, an average of the high and low prices usually produces a more representative price. The method used to calculate the average market price is used consistently unless it is no longer representative because of changed conditions. For example, an entity that uses closing market prices to calculate the average market price for several years of relatively stable prices might change to an average of high and low prices if prices start fluctuating greatly and the closing market prices no longer produce a representative average price.

Options, Warrants and Their Equivalents

A6   Options or warrants to purchase convertible instruments are assumed to be exercised to purchase the convertible instrument whenever the average prices of both the convertible instrument and the ordinary shares obtainable upon conversion are above the exercise price of the options or warrants. However, exercise is not assumed unless conversion of similar outstanding convertible instruments, if any, is also assumed.

A7   Options or warrants may permit or require the tendering of debt or other instruments of the entity (or its parent or a subsidiary) in payment of all or a portion of the exercise price. In the calculation of diluted earnings per share, those options or warrants have a dilutive effect if (a) the average market price of the related ordinary shares for the period exceeds the exercise price or (b) the selling price of the instrument to be tendered is below that at which the instrument may be tendered under the option or warrant agreement and the resulting discount establishes an effective exercise price below the market price of the ordinary shares obtainable upon exercise. In the calculation of diluted earnings per share, those options or warrants are assumed to be exercised and the debt or other instruments are assumed to be tendered. If tendering cash is more advantageous to the option or warrant holder and the contract permits tendering cash, tendering of cash is assumed. Interest (net of tax) on any debt assumed to be tendered is added back as an adjustment to the numerator.

A8   Similar treatment is given to preference shares that have similar provisions or to other instruments that have conversion options that permit the investor to pay cash for a more favourable conversion rate.

A9   The underlying terms of certain options or warrants may require the proceeds received from the exercise of those instruments to be applied to redeem debt or other instruments of the entity (or its parent or a subsidiary). In the calculation of diluted earnings per share, those options or warrants are assumed to be exercised and the proceeds applied to purchase the debt at its average market price rather than to purchase ordinary shares. However, the excess proceeds received from the assumed exercise over the amount used for the assumed purchase of debt are considered (ie assumed to be used to buy back ordinary shares) in the diluted earnings per share calculation. Interest (net of tax) on any debt assumed to be purchased is added back as an adjustment to the numerator.

Written Put Options

To illustrate the application of paragraph 63, assume that an entity has outstanding   **A10**
120 written put options on its ordinary shares with an exercise price of CU35. The average market price of its ordinary shares for the period is CU28. In calculating diluted earnings per share, the entity assumes that it issued 150 shares at CU28 per share at the beginning of the period to satisfy its put obligation of CU4,200. The difference between the 150 ordinary shares issued and the 120 ordinary shares received from satisfying the put option (30 incremental ordinary shares) is added to the denominator in calculating diluted earnings per share.

Instruments of Subsidiaries, Joint Ventures or Associates

Potential ordinary shares of a subsidiary, joint venture or associate convertible into   **A11**
either ordinary shares of the subsidiary, joint venture or associate, or ordinary shares of the parent, venturer or investor (the reporting entity) are included in the calculation of diluted earnings per share as follows:

(a)   instruments issued by a subsidiary, joint venture or associate that enable their holders to obtain ordinary shares of the subsidiary, joint venture or associate are included in calculating the diluted earnings per share data of the subsidiary, joint venture or associate. Those earnings per share are then included in the reporting entity's earnings per share calculations based on the reporting entity's holding of the instruments of the subsidiary, joint venture or associate.
(b)   instruments of a subsidiary, joint venture or associate that are convertible into the reporting entity's ordinary shares are considered among the potential ordinary shares of the reporting entity for the purpose of calculating diluted earnings per share. Likewise, options or warrants issued by a subsidiary, joint venture or associate to purchase ordinary shares of the reporting entity are considered among the potential ordinary shares of the reporting entity in the calculation of consolidated diluted earnings per share.

For the purpose of determining the earnings per share effect of instruments issued by   **A12**
a reporting entity that are convertible into ordinary shares of a subsidiary, joint venture or associate, the instruments are assumed to be converted and the numerator (profit or loss attributable to ordinary equity holders of the parent entity) adjusted as necessary in accordance with paragraph 33. In addition to those adjustments, the numerator is adjusted for any change in the profit or loss recorded by the reporting entity (such as dividend income or equity method income) that is attributable to the increase in the number of ordinary shares of the subsidiary, joint venture or associate outstanding as a result of the assumed conversion. The denominator of the diluted earnings per share calculation is not affected because the number of ordinary shares of the reporting entity outstanding would not change upon assumed conversion.

Participating Equity Instruments and Two-Class Ordinary Shares

The equity of some entities includes: **A13**

(a)   instruments that participate in dividends with ordinary shares according to a predetermined formula (for example, two for one) with, at times, an upper limit on the extent of participation (for example, up to, but not beyond, a specified amount per share).

(b) a class of ordinary shares with a different dividend rate from that of another class of ordinary shares but without prior or senior rights.

A14 For the purpose of calculating diluted earnings per share, conversion is assumed for those instruments described in paragraph A13 that are convertible into ordinary shares if the effect is dilutive. For those instruments that are not convertible into a class of ordinary shares, profit or loss for the period is allocated to the different classes of shares and participating equity instruments in accordance with their dividend rights or other rights to participate in undistributed earnings. To calculate basic and diluted earnings per share:

(a) profit or loss attributable to ordinary equity holders of the parent entity is adjusted (a profit reduced and a loss increased) by the amount of dividends declared in the period for each class of shares and by the contractual amount of dividends (or interest on participating bonds) that must be paid for the period (for example, unpaid cumulative dividends).

(b) the remaining profit or loss is allocated to ordinary shares and participating equity instruments to the extent that each instrument shares in earnings as if all of the profit or loss for the period had been distributed. The total profit or loss allocated to each class of equity instrument is determined by adding together the amount allocated for dividends and the amount allocated for a participation feature.

(c) the total amount of profit or loss allocated to each class of equity instrument is divided by the number of outstanding instruments to which the earnings are allocated to determine the earnings per share for the instrument.

For the calculation of diluted earnings per share, all potential ordinary shares assumed to have been issued are included in outstanding ordinary shares.

Partly Paid Shares

A15 Where ordinary shares are issued but not fully paid, they are treated in the calculation of basic earnings per share as a fraction of an ordinary share to the extent that they were entitled to participate in dividends during the period relative to a fully paid ordinary share.

A16 To the extent that partly paid shares are not entitled to participate in dividends during the period they are treated as the equivalent of warrants or options in the calculation of diluted earnings per share. The unpaid balance is assumed to represent proceeds used to purchase ordinary shares. The number of shares included in diluted earnings per share is the difference between the number of shares subscribed and the number of shares assumed to be purchased.

Appendix B
Amendments to other Standards and UITF Abstracts

[Not reproduced, as all changes have been made to the underlying standards and abstracts].

Appendix C

ASB note: This Appendix has been prepared by the ASB

APPLICATION TO MERGER ACCOUNTING

Entities that use merger accounting as required by FRS 6 **Acquisitions and Mergers** *should apply FRS 22 in full with the following amendments:*

C1 Paragraph 22 of FRS 22 should not be applied. Instead:

Ordinary shares issued as part of a business combination that is merger accounted under FRS 6 *Acquisitions and Mergers* are included in the calculation of the weighted average number of shares for all periods presented because the financial statements of the combined entity are prepared as if the combined entity had always existed. Therefore, the number of ordinary shares used for the calculation of basic earnings per share in a business combination that is merger accounted under FRS 6 is the aggregate of the weighted average number of shares of the combined entities, adjusted to equivalent shares of the entity whose shares are outstanding after the combination.

C2 Basic and diluted earnings per share of all periods presented shall be adjusted for the effects of a business combination that is merger accounted under FRS 6.

Appendix D

NON-MANDATORY APPLICATION GUIDANCE

This appendix does not form part of the standard

Net profit from continuing operations

This Appendix reproduces the text of paragraphs 59 and 60 of FRS 14 *Earnings per Share*. Entities applying FRS 3 *Reporting Financial Performance* may find this guidance to be a useful reference.

FRS 3 'Reporting Financial Performance' requires an analysis of continuing   **D1**
operations, acquisitions (as a component of continuing operations) and discontinued operations only to the level of profit before interest, because interest payable often reflects an entity's overall financing policy rather than an aggregation of the particular types of finance allocated to its operations. Although FRS 3 does not encourage further allocation without disclosure of the method and underlying assumptions adopted, many entities will have the data necessary to allocate interest and tax between continuing and discontinued operations. In particular, it will often be possible to allocate a specific amount of tax and interest to exceptional items that are reported after operating profit under paragraph 20 of FRS 3. Where practicable, such an allocation is adopted for determination of the 'control number'.

In the absence of a practical, more reliable method of allocation, however, net profit   **D2**
from continuing operations will need to be estimated. In these restricted circumstances, and following any specific allocation of tax and interest that may be possible in respect of exceptional items shown after operating profit, it is permitted to allocate interest and taxation in the proportion of profits from continuing operations to total profit at the operating profit level. In practice a profit-based allocation method may be more suitable for taxation, which is levied on profits, than for interest, which finances capital.

Adoption of the Standard

APPROVAL OF IAS 33 BY THE INTERNATIONAL ACCOUNTING STANDARDS BOARD

International Accounting Standard 33 *Earnings per Share* was approved for issue by the fourteen members of the International Accounting Standards Board.

Sir David Tweedie   Chairman
Thomas E Jones   Vice-Chairman
Mary E Barth
Hans-Georg Bruns
Anthony T Cope
Robert P Garnett
Gilbert Gélard
James J Leisenring
Warren J McGregor
Patricia L O'Malley
Harry K Schmid
John T Smith
Geoffrey Whittington
Tatsumi Yamada

ADOPTION OF FRS 22 BY THE ACCOUNTING STANDARDS BOARD

Financial Reporting Standard 22 (IAS33) *Earnings per Share* was approved for issue by the ten members of the Accounting Standards Board.

Ian Mackintosh   Chairman
Andrew Lennard   Technical Director
Michael Ashley
Douglas Flint
Anthony Good
Roger Marshall
Isobel Sharp
John Smith
Jonathan Symonds
Peter Westlake

DEVELOPMENT OF THE FRS

This FRS is based on IAS 33 (revised 2003) *Earnings per Share* and supersedes FRS   **1**
14 *Earnings per Share*, which was issued in October 1998. The draft standard was
published as FRED 26 in May 2002. Respondents expressed a number of concerns
over the proposed standard, and many also expressed their concerns directly with the
IASB, but the majority stated that they did not want the ASB to make any additional
amendments to the IASB's final standard over and above those necessary for cross-
referencing and consequential amendments to align the standard to UK GAAP and
legal requirements. The IASB addressed many of the concerns raised when it issued
IAS 33 (revised 2003) as explained in their basis for conclusions which accompanies
this FRS.

Many UK respondents objected to IAS 33 (revised 2003) paragraphs 66 and 73   **2**
which require an entity to present additional per share amounts in the notes to the
financial statements, but the respondents also stated that they did not want the ASB
to make changes to IAS 33 (revised 2003) because this would hinder convergence.
The ASB has not therefore amended the requirements in IAS 33 (revised 2003).

The accounting practices set out in this FRS require an entity to have adopted FRS   **3**
25 (IAS 32) and, therefore, this FRS takes effect from the same date, being
accounting periods beginning on or after 1 January 2005, and earlier application is
not permitted.

Basis for Conclusions

This Basis for Conclusions accompanies, but is not part of, IAS 33.

> *ASB note:* The IASB's Basis for Conclusions, which accompanies IAS 33, is set out below in full. All references in this section to 'the Board' and 'Board members' are references to the IASB Board and IASB Board members.

INTRODUCTION

BC1   This Basis for Conclusions summarises the International Accounting Standards Board's considerations in reaching its conclusions on revising IAS 33 *Earnings Per Share* in 2003. Individual Board members gave greater weight to some factors than to others.

BC2   In July 2001 the Board announced that, as part of its initial agenda of technical projects, it would undertake a project to improve a number of Standards, including IAS 33. The project was undertaken in the light of queries and criticisms raised in relation to the Standards by securities regulators, professional accountants and other interested parties. The objectives of the Improvements project were to reduce or eliminate alternatives, redundancies and conflicts within Standards, to deal with some convergence issues and to make other improvements. In May 2002 the Board published its proposals in an Exposure Draft of *Improvements to International Accounting Standards*, with a comment deadline of 16 September 2002. The Board received over 160 comment letters on the Exposure Draft.

BC3   Because the Board's intention was not to reconsider the fundamental approach to the determination and presentation of earnings per share established by IAS 33, this Basis for Conclusions does not discuss requirements in IAS 33 that the Board has not reconsidered.

PRESENTATION OF PARENT'S SEPARATE EARNINGS PER SHARE

BC4   The Exposure Draft published in May 2002 proposed deleting paragraphs 2 and 3 of the previous version of IAS 33, which stated that when the parent's separate financial statements and consolidated financial statements are presented, earnings per share need be presented only on the basis of consolidated information.

BC5   Some respondents expressed concern that the presentation of two earnings per share figures (one for the parent's separate financial statements and one for the consolidated financial statements) might be misleading.

BC6   The Board noted that disclosing the parent's separate earnings per share amount is useful in limited situations, and therefore decided to retain the option. However, the Board decided that the Standard should prohibit presentation of the parent's separate earnings per share amounts in the consolidated financial statements (either on the face of the financial statements or in the notes).

CONTRACTS THAT MAY BE SETTLED IN ORDINARY SHARES OR CASH

The Exposure Draft proposed that an entity should include in the calculation of the **BC7** number of potential ordinary shares in the diluted earnings per share calculation contracts that may be settled in ordinary shares or cash, at the issuer's option, based on a rebuttable presumption that the contracts will be settled in shares. This proposed presumption could be rebutted if the issuer had acted through an established pattern of past practice, published policies, or by having made a sufficiently specific current statement indicating to other parties the manner in which it expected to settle, and, as a result, the issuer had created a valid expectation on the part of those other parties that it would settle in a manner other than by issuing shares.

The majority of the respondents on the Exposure Draft agreed with the proposed **BC8** treatment of contracts that may be settled in ordinary shares or cash at the issuer's option. However, the Board decided to withdraw the notion of a rebuttable presumption and to incorporate into the Standard the requirements of SIC-24 *Earnings Per Share—Financial Instruments and Other Contracts that May Be Settled in Shares*. SIC24 requires financial instruments or other contracts that may result in the issue of ordinary shares of the entity to be considered potential ordinary shares of the entity.

Although the proposed treatment would have converged with that required by **BC9** several liaison standard-setters, for example, in US SFAS 128 *Earnings per Share*, the Board concluded that the notion of a rebuttable presumption is inconsistent with the stated objective of diluted earnings per share. The US Financial Accounting Standards Board has agreed to consider this difference as part of the joint shortterm convergence project with the IASB.

CALCULATION OF YEAR-TO-DATE DILUTED EARNINGS PER SHARE

The Exposure Draft proposed the following approach to the yeartodate calculation **BC10** of diluted earnings per share:

(a)   The number of potential ordinary shares is a year-to-date weighted average of the number of potential ordinary shares included in each interim diluted earnings per share calculation, rather than a year-to-date weighted average of the number of potential ordinary shares weighted for the period they were outstanding (ie without regard for the diluted earnings per share information reported during the interim periods).

(b)   The number of potential ordinary shares is computed using the average market price during the interim periods, rather than using the average market price during the year-to-date period.

(c)   Contingently issuable shares are weighted for the interim periods in which they were included in the computation of diluted earnings per share, rather than being included in the computation of diluted earnings per share (if the conditions are satisfied) from the beginning of the year-to-date reporting period (or from the date of the contingent share agreement, if later).

The majority of the respondents on the Exposure Draft disagreed with the proposed **BC11** approach to the year-to-date calculation of diluted earnings per share. The most significant argument against the proposed approach was that the proposed calculation of diluted earnings per share could result in an amount for year-to-date diluted earnings per share that was different for entities that report more frequently, for example, on a quarterly or half-yearly basis, and for entities that report only annually. It was also noted that this problem would be exacerbated for entities with seasonal businesses.

BC12   The Board considered whether to accept that differences in the frequency of interim reporting would result in different earnings per share amounts being reported. However, IAS 34 *Interim Financial Reporting* states "the frequency of an entity's reporting (annual, halfyearly, or quarterly) should not affect the measurement of its annual results. To achieve that objective, measurements for interim reporting purposes should be made on a year-to-date basis."

BC13   The Board also considered whether it could mandate the frequency of interim reporting to ensure consistency between all entities preparing financial statements in accordance with IFRSs, ie those that are brought within the scope of IAS 33 by virtue of issuing publicly traded instruments or because they elect to present earnings per share. However, IAS 34 states that, "This Standard does not mandate which entities should be required to publish interim financial reports, how frequently, or how soon after the end of an interim period." The frequency of interim reporting is mandated by securities regulators, stock exchanges, governments, and accountancy bodies, and varies by jurisdiction.

BC14   Although the proposed approach for the calculation of year-to-date diluted earnings per share would have converged with US SFAS 128, the Board concluded that the approach was inconsistent with IAS 34 and that it could not mandate the frequency of interim reporting. The US Financial Accounting Standards Board has agreed to consider this difference as part of the joint shortterm convergence project with the IASB as well as the issue noted in paragraph BC9.

OTHER CHANGES

BC15   Implementation questions have arisen since the previous version of IAS 33 was issued, typically concerning the application of the Standard to complex capital structures and arrangements. In response, the Board decided to provide additional application guidance in the Appendix as well as illustrative examples on more complex matters that were not addressed in the previous version of IAS 33. These matters include the effects of contingently issuable shares, potential ordinary shares of subsidiaries, joint ventures or associates, participating equity instruments, written put options, and purchased put and call options.

Illustrative Examples

These examples accompany, but are not part of, IAS 33.

> *ASB note:* These Illustrative Examples have been prepared by the IASB

Contents

Example 1 - Increasing Rate Preference Shares

Reference: FRS 22 (IAS 33), paragraphs 12 and 15

Entity D issued non-convertible, non-redeemable class A cumulative preference shares of CU100 par value on 1 January 20X1. The class A preference shares are entitled to a cumulative annual dividend of CU7 per share starting in 20X4.

At the time of issue, the market rate dividend yield on the class A preference shares was 7 per cent a year. Thus, Entity D could have expected to receive proceeds of approximately CU100 per class A preference share if the dividend rate of CU7 per share had been in effect at the date of issue.

In consideration of the dividend payment terms, however, the class A preference shares were issued at CU81.63 per share, ie at a discount of CU18.37 per share. The issue price can be calculated by taking the present value of CU100, discounted at 7 per cent over a three-year period.

Because the shares are classified as equity, the original issue discount is amortised to retained earnings using the effective interest method and treated as a preference dividend for earnings per share purposes. To calculate basic earnings per share, the following imputed dividend per class A preference share is deducted to determine the profit or loss attributable to ordinary equity holders of the parent entity:

Year	Carrying amount of class A preference shares 1 January	Imputed dividend[1]	Carrying amount of class A preference shares 31 December[2]	Dividend paid
	CU	CU	CU	CU
20X1	81.63	5.71	87.34	-
20X2	87.34	6.12	93.46	-
20X3	93.46	6.54	100.00	-
Thereafter:	100.00	7.00	107.00	(7.00)

[1]   at 7%
[2]   This is before dividend payment.

Example 2 - Weighted Average Number of Ordinary Shares

Reference: FRS 22 (IAS 33), paragraphs 19-21

		Shares issued	*Treasury shares*[3]	*Shares outstanding*
1 January 20X1	Balance at beginning of year	2,000	300	1,700
31 May 20X1	Issue of new shares for cash	800	–	2,500
1 December 20X1	Purchase of treasury shares for cash	–	250	2,250
31 December 20X1	Balance at yearend	2,800	550	2,250

Calculation of weighted average:

$(1,700 \times 5/12) + (2,500 \times 6/12) + (2,250 \times 1/12) = 2,146$ shares   *or*
$(1,700 \times 12/12) + (800 \times 7/12) - (250 \times 1/12) = 2,146$ shares

---

[3] Treasury shares are equity instruments reacquired and held by the issuing entity itself or by its subsidiaries.

Example 3 - Bonus Issue

Reference: FRS 22 (IAS 33), paragraphs 26, 27(a) and 28

Profit attributable to ordinary equity holders of the parent entity 20X0   CU180

Profit attributable to ordinary equity holders of the parent entity 20X1   CU600

Ordinary shares outstanding until 30 September 20X1   200

Bonus issue 1 October 20X1   2 ordinary shares for
each ordinary share
outstanding at
30 September 20X1
$200 \times 2 = 400$

Basic earnings per share 20X1
$$\frac{CU600}{(200 + 400)} = CU1.00$$

Basic earnings per share 20X0
$$\frac{CU600}{(200 + 400)} = CU0.30$$

Because the bonus issue was without consideration, it is treated as if it had occurred before the beginning of 20X0, the earliest period presented.

Example 4 - Rights Issue

Reference: FRS 22 (IAS 33), paragraphs 26, 27(b) and A2

	20X0	20X1	20X2
Profit attributable to ordinary equity holders of the parent entity	CU1,100	CU1,500	CU1,800

Shares outstanding before rights issue	500 shares
Rights issue	One new share for each five outstanding shares (100 new shares total) Exercise price: CU5.00 Date of rights issue: 1 January 20X1 Last date to exercise rights: 1 March 20X1
Market price of one ordinary share immediately before exercise on 1 March 20X1:	CU11.00
Reporting date	31 December

Calculation of theoretical ex-rights value per share

$$\frac{\text{Fair value of all outstanding shares before the exercise of rights} + \text{total amount received from exercise of rights}}{\text{Number of shares outstanding before exercise} + \text{number of shares issued in the exercise}}$$

$$\frac{(\text{CU11.00} \times 500 \text{ shares}) + (\text{CU5.00} \times 100 \text{ shares})}{500 \text{ shares} + 100 \text{ shares}}$$

Theoretical ex-rights value per share $=$ CU10.00

Calculation of adjustment factor

$$\frac{\text{Fair value per share before exercise of rights}}{\text{Theoretical ex-rights value per share}} \qquad \frac{\text{CU11.00}}{\text{CU10.00}} = 1.10$$

continued...

Calculation of basic earnings per share

		20X0	20X1	20X2
20X0 basic EPS as originally reported:	CU 1,100 ÷ 500 shares	CU2.20		
20X0 basic EPS restated for rights issue:	$\dfrac{CU1,100}{(500 \text{ shares} \times 1.1)}$	CU2.00		
20X1 basic EPS including effects of rights issue:			CU2.54	
20X2 basic EPS:	CU1,800 ÷ 600 shares			CU3.00

Example 5 - Effects of Share Options on Diluted Earnings per Share

Reference: FRS 22 (IAS 33), paragraphs 45-47

Profit attributable to ordinary equity holders of the parent entity for year 20X1	CU1,200,000
Weighted average number of ordinary shares outstanding during year 20X1	500,000 shares
Average market price of one ordinary share during year 20X1	CU20.00
Weighted average number of shares under option during year 20X1	100,000 shares
Exercise price for shares under option during year 20X1	CU15.00

Calculation of earnings per share

	Earnings	*Shares*	*Per share*
Profit attributable to ordinary equity holders of the parent entity for year 20X1	CU1,200,000		
Weighted average shares outstanding during year 20X1		500,000	
Basic earnings per share			CU2.40
Weighted average number of shares under option		100,000	
Weighted average number of shares that would have been issued at average market price: (100,000 × CU15.00) ÷ CU20.00		*(75,000)	
Diluted earnings per share	CU1,200,000	525,000	CU2.29

---

* Earnings have not increased because the total number of shares has increased only by the number of shares (25,000) deemed to have been issued for no consideration (see paragraph 46(b) of the Standard).

Example 5A - Determining the Exercise Price of Employee Share Options

Weighted average number of unvested share options per employee	1,000
Weighted average amount per employee to be recognised over the remainder of the vesting period for employee services to be rendered as consideration for the share options, determined in accordance with FRS 20 (IFRS 2) *Share-based Payment*	CU1,200
Cash exercise price of unvested share options	CU15

Calculation of adjusted exercise price

Fair value of services yet to be rendered per employee: CU1,200

Fair value of services yet to be rendered per option: (CU1,200/   CU1.20
1,000)

Total exercise price of share options: (CU 15.00 + CU1.20)   CU16.20

Example 6 - Convertible Bonds[4]

Reference: FRS 22 (IAS 33), paragraphs 33, 34, 36 and 49

Profit attributable to ordinary equity holders of the parent entity	CU1,004
Ordinary shares outstanding	1,000
Basic earnings per share	CU1.00
Convertible bonds	100
Each block of 10 bonds is convertible into three ordinary shares	
Interest expense for the current year relating to the liability component of the convertible bonds	CU10
Current and deferred tax relating to that interest expense	CU4

Note: the interest expense includes amortisation of the discount arising on initial recognition of the liability component (see FRS 25 (IAS 32) Financial Instruments: Disclosure and Presentation).

Adjusted profit attributable to ordinary equity holders of the parent entity	CU1,004 + CU10 − CU4 = CU1,010
Number of ordinary shares resulting from conversion of bonds	30
Number of ordinary shares used to calculate diluted earnings per share	1,000 + 30 = 1,030
Diluted earnings per share	$\dfrac{CU1,010}{1,030} = CU0.98$

---

[4] This example does not illustrate the classification of the components of convertible financial instruments as liabilities and equity or the classification of related interest and dividends as expenses and equity as required by *FRS 25* (IAS 32).

Example 7 - Contingently Issuable Shares

Reference: FRS 22 (IAS 33), paragraphs 19, 24, 36, 37, 41-43 and 52

Ordinary shares outstanding during 20X1	1,000,000 (there were no options, warrants or convertible instruments outstanding during the period)

An agreement related to a recent business combination provides for the issue of additional ordinary shares based on the following conditions:

	5,000 additional ordinary shares for each new retail site opened during 20X1
	1,000 additional ordinary shares for each CU1,000 of consolidated profit in excess of CU2,000,000 for the year ended 31 December 20X1
Retail sites opened during the year:	one on 1 May 20X1
	one on 1 September 20X1
Consolidated year-to-date profit attributable to ordinary equity holders of the parent entity:	CU1,100,000 as of 31 March 20X1
	CU2,300,000 as of 30 June 20X1
	CU1,900,000 as of 30 September 20X1 (including a CU450,000 loss from a discontinued operation)
	CU2,900,000 as of 31 December 20X1

continued...

Basic earnings per share

	First quarter	Second quarter	Third quarter	Fourth quarter	Full year
Numerator (CU)	1,100,000	1,200,000	(400,000)	1,000,000	2,900,000
Denominator:					
Ordinary shares outstanding	1,000,000	1,000,000	1,000,000	1,000,000	1,000,000
Retail site contingency	–	3,333[a]	6,667[b]	10,000	5,000[c]
Earnings contingency [d]	–	–	–	–	–
Total shares	1,000,000	1,003,333	1,006,667	1,010,000	1,005,000
Basic earnings per share (CU)	1.10	1.20	(0.40)	0.99	2.89

[a] 5,000 shares × 2/3
[b] 5,000 shares + (5,000 shares × 1/3)
[c] (5,000 shares × 8/12) + (5,000 shares × 4/12)
[d] The earnings contingency has no effect on basic earnings per share because it is not certain that the condition is satisfied until the end of the contingency period. The effect is negligible for the fourth-quarter and full-year calculations because it is not certain that the condition is met until the last day of the period.

Diluted earnings per share

	First quarter	Second quarter	Third quarter	Fourth quarter	Full year
Numerator (CU)	1,100,000	1,200,000	(400,000)	1,000,000	2,900,000
Denominator:					
Ordinary shares outstanding	1,000,000	1,000,000	1,000,000	1,000,000	1,000,000
Retail site contingency	–	5,000	10,000	10,000	10,000
Earnings contingency	–[e]	300,000[f]	–[g]	900,000[h]	900,000[h]
Total shares	1,000,000	1,305,000	1,010,000	1,910,000	1,910,000
Diluted earnings per share (CU)	1.10	0.92	(0.40)[i]	0.52	1.52

[e] Company A does not have year-to-date profit exceeding CU2,000,000 at 31 March 20X1. The Standard does not permit projecting future earnings levels and including the related contingent shares.

[f] [(CU2,300,000 − CU2,000,000) ÷ 1,000] × 1,000 shares = 300,000 shares.

[g] Year-to-date profit is less than CU2,000,000.

[h] [(CU2,900,000 − CU2,000,000) ÷ 1,000] × 1,000 shares = 900,000 shares.

[i] Because the loss during the third quarter is attributable to a loss from a discontinued operation, the antidilution rules do not apply. The control number (ie profit or loss from continuing operations attributable to the equity holders of the parent entity) is positive. Accordingly, the effect of potential ordinary shares is included in the calculation of diluted earnings per share.

Example 8 – Convertible Bonds Settled in Shares or Cash at the Issuer's Option

Reference: FRS 22 (IAS 33), paragraphs 31-33, 36, 58 and 59

An entity issues 2,000 convertible bonds at the beginning of Year 1. The bonds have a three year term, and are issued at par with a face value of CU1,000 per bond, giving total proceeds of CU2,000,000. Interest is payable annually in arrears at a nominal annual interest rate of 6 per cent. Each bond is convertible at any time up to maturity into 250 common shares. The entity has an option to settle the principal amount of the convertible bonds in ordinary shares or in cash.

When the bonds are issued, the prevailing market interest rate for similar debt without a conversion option is 9 per cent. At the issue date, the market price of one common share is CU3. Income tax is ignored.

Profit attributable to ordinary equity holders of the parent entity Year 1	CU1,000,000 1,000,000
Ordinary shares outstanding	1,200,000
Convertible bonds outstanding	2,000

Allocation of proceeds of the bond issue:

Liability component	CU1,848,122[5]
Equity component	CU151,878
	CU2,000,000

The liability and equity components would be determined in accordance with *FRS 25* (IAS 32) *Financial Instruments: Disclosure and Presentation*. These amounts are recognised as the initial carrying amounts of the liability and equity components. The amount assigned to the issuer conversion option equity element is an addition to equity and is not adjusted.

continued...

---

[5] This represents the present value of the principal and interest discounted at 9% – CU2,000,000 payable at the end of three years; CU120,000 payable annually in arrears for three years.

Basic earnings per share Year 1:

$$\frac{CU1,000,000}{1,200,000} = CU0.83 \text{ per ordinary share}$$

Diluted earnings per share Year 1:

It is presumed that the issuer will settle the contract by the issue of ordinary shares. The dilutive effect is therefore calculated in accordance with paragraph 59 of the Standard.

$$\frac{CU1,000,000 + CU166,331^{(a)}}{1,200,000 + 500,000^{(b)}} = CU0.69 \text{ per ordinary share}$$

[a] Profit is adjusted for the accretion of CU166,331 (CU1,848,122 × 9%) of the liability because of the passage of time.

[b] 500,000 ordinary shares = 250 ordinary shares × 2,000 convertible bonds

Example 9 – Calculation of Weighted Average Number of Shares: Determining the Order in Which to Include Dilutive Instruments[6]

Primary reference: FRS 22 (IAS 33), paragraph 44

Secondary reference: FRS 22 (IAS 33), paragraphs 10, 12, 19, 31-33, 36, 41-47, 49 and 50

Earnings	CU
Profit from continuing operations attributable to the parent entity	16,400,000
Less dividends on preference shares	(6,400,000)
Profit from continuing operations attributable to ordinary equity holders of the parent entity	10,000,000
Loss from discontinued operations attributable to the parent entity	(4,000,000)
Profit attributable to ordinary equity holders of the parent entity	6,000,000
Ordinary shares outstanding	2,000,000
Average market price of one ordinary share during year	CU75.00

Potential Ordinary Shares

Options	100,000 with exercise price of CU60
Convertible preference shares	800,000 shares with a par value of CU100 entitled to a cumulative dividend of CU8 per share. Each preference share is convertible to two ordinary shares.
5% convertible bonds	Nominal amount CU100,000,000. Each CU1,000 bond is convertible to 20 ordinary shares. There is no amortisation of premium or discount affecting the determination of interest expense.
Tax rate	40%

continued...

---

[6] This example does not illustrate the classification of the components of convertible financial instruments as liabilities and equity or the classification of related interest and dividends as expenses and equity as required by *FRS 25* (IAS 32).

Increase in Earnings Attributable to Ordinary Equity Holders on Conversion of Potential Ordinary Shares

		Increase in earnings	Increase in number of ordinary shares	Earnings per incremental share
		CU		CU
Options				
Increase in earnings		Nil		
Incremental shares issued for no consideration	100,000 ×(CU75 − CU60) ÷ CU75		20,000	Nil
Convertible preference shares				
Increase in profit	CU800,000 × 100 × 0.08	6,400,000		
Incremental shares	2 × 800,000		1,600,000	4.00
5% convertible bonds				
Increase in profit	CU100,000,000 × 0.05 × (1 − 0.40)	3,000,000		
Incremental shares	100,000 × 20		2,000,000	1.50

The order in which to include the dilutive instruments is therefore:

(1) Options
(2) 5% convertible bonds
(3) Convertible preference shares

continued...

Calculation of Diluted Earnings per Share

	Profit from continuing operations attributable to ordinary equity holders of the parent entity (control number) CU	Ordinary shares	Per share CU	
As reported	10,000,000	2,000,000	5.00	
Options	-	20,000		
	10,000,000	2,020,000	4.95	Dilutive
5% convertible bonds	3,000,000	2,000,000		
	13,000,000	4,020,000	3.23	Dilutive
Convertible preference shares	6,400,000	1,600,000		
	19,400,000	5,620,000	3.45	Antidilutive

Because diluted earnings per share is increased when taking the convertible preference shares into account (from CU3.23 to CU3.45), the convertible preference shares are antidilutive and are ignored in the calculation of diluted earnings per share. Therefore, diluted earnings per share for profit from continuing operations is CU3.23:

	Basic EPS CU	Diluted EPS CU
Profit from continuing operations attributable to ordinary equity holders of the parent entity	5.00	3.23
Loss from discontinued operations attributable to ordinary equity holders of the parent entity	(2.00)[a]	(0.99)[b]
Profit attributable to ordinary equity holders of the parent entity	3.00[c]	2.24[d]

[a] (CU4,000,000) ÷ 2,000,000 = (CU2.00)
[b] (CU4,000,000) ÷ 4,020,000 = (CU0.99)
[c] CU6,000,000 ÷ 2,000,000 = CU3.00
[d] (CU6,000,000 + CU3,000,000) ÷ 4,020,000 = CU2.24

Example 10 - Instruments of a Subsidiary: Calculation of Basic and Diluted Earnings per Share[7]

Reference: FRS 22 (IAS 33), paragraphs 40, A11 and A12

Parent:

Profit attributable to ordinary equity holders of the parent entity	CU12,000 (excluding any earnings of, or dividends paid by, the subsidiary)
Ordinary shares outstanding	10,000
Instruments of subsidiary owned by the parent	800 ordinary shares 30 warrants exercisable to purchase ordinary shares of subsidiary 300 convertible preference shares

Subsidiary:

Profit	CU5,400
Ordinary shares outstanding	1,000
Warrants	150, exercisable to purchase ordinary shares of the subsidiary
Exercise price	CU10
Average market price of one ordinary share	CU20
Convertible preference shares	400, each convertible into one ordinary share
Dividends on preference shares	CU1 per share

No inter-company eliminations or adjustments were necessary except for dividends.

For the purposes of this illustration, income taxes have been ignored.

continued...

[7] This example does not illustrate the classification of the components of convertible financial instruments as liabilities and equity or the classification of related interest and dividends as expenses and equity as required by *FRS 25* (IAS 32).

Subsidiary's earnings per share

Basic EPS   CU5.00 calculated: $$\frac{CU5,400^{(a)} - CU400^{(b)}}{1,000^{(c)}}$$

Diluted EPS   CU3.66 calculated: $$\frac{CU5,400^{(d)}}{(1,000 + 75^{(e)} + 400^{(f)})}$$

(a) Subsidiary's profit attributable to ordinary equity holders.
(b) Dividends paid by subsidiary on convertible preference shares.
(c) Subsidiary's ordinary shares outstanding.
(d) Subsidiary's profit attributable to ordinary equity holders (CU5,000) increased by CU400 preference dividends for the purpose of calculating diluted earnings per share.
(e) Incremental shares from warrants, calculated: [(CU20 − CU10) ÷ CU20] × 150.
(f) Subsidiary's ordinary shares assumed outstanding from conversion of convertible preference shares, calculated: 400 convertible preference shares × conversion factor of 1.

Consolidated earnings per share

Basic EPS   CU1.63 calculated: $$\frac{CU12,000^{(g)} + CU4,300^{(h)}}{10,000^{(i)}}$$

Diluted EPS   CU1.61 calculated:
$$\frac{CU12,000 + CU2,928^{(j)} + CU55^{(k)} + CU1,098^{(l)}}{10,000}$$

(g) Parent's profit attributable to ordinary equity holders of the parent entity.
(h) Portion of subsidiary's profit to be included in consolidated basic earnings per share, calculated: (800 × CU5.00) + (300 × CU1.00).
(i) Parent's ordinary shares outstanding.
(j) Parent's proportionate interest in subsidiary's earnings attributable to ordinary shares, calculated: (800 ÷ 1,000) × (1,000 shares × CU3.66 per share).
(k) Parent's proportionate interest in subsidiary's earnings attributable to warrants, calculated: (30 ÷ 150) × (75 incremental shares × CU3.66 per share).
(l) Parent's proportionate interest in subsidiary's earnings attributable to convertible preference shares, calculated: (300 ÷ 400) × (400 shares from conversion × CU3.66 per share).

Example 11 - Participating Equity Instruments and Two-class Ordinary Shares[8]

Reference: FRS 22 (IAS 33), paragraphs A13 and A14

Profit attributable to equity holders of the parent entity	CU100,000
Ordinary shares outstanding	10,000
Non-convertible preference shares	6,000
Non-cumulative annual dividend on preference shares (before any dividend is paid on ordinary shares)	CU5.50 per share

After ordinary shares have been paid a dividend of CU2.10 per share, the preference shares participate in any additional dividends on a 20:80 ratio with ordinary shares (ie after preference and ordinary shares have been paid dividends of CU5.50 and CU2.10 per share, respectively, preference shares participate in any additional dividends at a rate of one-fourth of the amount paid to ordinary shares on a per-share basis).

Dividends on preference shares paid	CU33,000	(CU5.50 per share)
Dividends on ordinary shares paid	CU21,000	(CU2.10 per share)

continued...

---

[8]   This example does not illustrate the classification of the components of convertible financial instruments as liabilities and equity or the classification of related interest and dividends as expenses and equity as required by *FRS 25* (IAS 32).

Basic earnings per share is calculated as follows:

	CU	CU
Profit attributable to equity holders of the parent entity		100,000
Less dividends paid:		
Preference	33,000	
Ordinary	21,000	
		(54,000)
Undistributed earnings		46,000

Allocation of undistributed earnings:

Allocation per ordinary share = A
Allocation per preference share = B; B = 1/4 A

$$(A \times 10,000) + (1/4 \times A \times 6,000) = CU46,000$$
$$A = CU46,000 \div (10,000 + 1,500)$$
$$A = CU4.00$$
$$B = 1/4\ A$$
$$B = CU1.00$$

Basic per share amounts:

	Preference shares	*Ordinary shares*
Distributed earnings	CU5.50	CU2.10
Undistributed earnings	CU1.00	CU4.00
Totals	CU6.50	CU6.10

Example 12 - Calculation of Basic and Diluted Earnings per Share and Income Statement Presentation (Comprehensive Example)[9]

This example illustrates the quarterly and annual calculations of basic and diluted earnings per share in the year 20X1 for Company A, which has a complex capital structure. The control number is profit or loss from continuing operations attributable to the parent entity. Other facts assumed are as follows:

Average market price of ordinary shares: The average market prices of ordinary shares for the calendar year 20X1 were as follows:

First quarter	CU49
Second quarter	CU60
Third quarter	CU67
Fourth quarter	CU67

The average market price of ordinary shares from 1 July to 1 September 20X1 was CU65.

Ordinary shares: The number of ordinary shares outstanding at the beginning of 20X1 was 5,000,000. On 1 March 20X1, 200,000 ordinary shares were issued for cash.

Convertible bonds: In the last quarter of 20X0, 5 per cent convertible bonds with a principal amount of CU12,000,000 due in 20 years were sold for cash at CU1,000 (par). Interest is payable twice a year, on 1 November and 1 May. Each CU1,000 bond is convertible into 40 ordinary shares. No bonds were converted in 20X0. The entire issue was converted on 1 April 20X1 because the issue was called by Company A.

Convertible preference shares: In the second quarter of 20X0, 800,000 convertible preference shares were issued for assets in a purchase transaction. The quarterly dividend on each convertible preference share is CU0.05, payable at the end of the quarter for shares outstanding at that date. Each share is convertible into one ordinary share. Holders of 600,000 convertible preference shares converted their preference shares into ordinary shares on 1 June 20X1.

continued...

---

[9]   This example does not illustrate the classification of the components of convertible financial instruments as liabilities and equity or the classification of related interest and dividends as expenses and equity as required by *FRS 25* (IAS 32).

Warrants: Warrants to buy 600,000 ordinary shares at CU55 per share for a period of five years were issued on 1 January 20X1. All outstanding warrants were exercised on 1 September 20X1.

Options: Options to buy 1,500,000 ordinary shares at CU75 per share for a period of 10 years were issued on 1 July 20X1. No options were exercised during 20X1 because the exercise price of the options exceeded the market price of the ordinary shares.

Tax rate: The tax rate was 40 per cent for 20X1.

20X1	*Profit (loss) from continuing operations attributable to the parent entity*[a]	*Profit (loss) attributable to the parent entity*
	CU	CU
First quarter	5,000,000	5,000,000
Second quarter	6,500,000	6,500,000
Third quarter	1,000,000	(1,000,000)[b]
Fourth quarter	(700,000)	(700,000)
Full year	11,800,000	9,800,000

First Quarter 20X1

Basic EPS calculation	CU
Profit from continuing operations attributable to the parent entity	5,000,000
Less: preference shares dividends	(40,000)[c]
Profit attributable to ordinary equity holders of the parent entity	4,960,000

continued...

---

[a] This is the control number (before adjusting for preference dividends).
[b] Company A had a CU2,000,000 loss (net of tax) from discontinued operations in the third quarter.
[c] 800,000 shares × CU0.05

Dates	Shares Outstanding	Fraction of period	Weighted- average shares
1 January–28 February	5,000,000	2/3	3,333,333
Issue of ordinary shares on 1 March	200,000		
1 March–31 March	5,200,000	1/3	1,733,333
Weighted-average shares			5,066,666

Basic EPS   **CU0.98**

Diluted EPS calculation

Profit attributable to ordinary equity holders of the parent entity	CU4,960,000
Plus: profit impact of assumed conversions	

Preference share dividends	CU40,000[(d)]
Interest on 5% convertible bonds	CU90,000[(e)]
Effect of assumed conversions	**CU130,000**

Profit attributable to ordinary equity holders of the parent entity including assumed conversions	CU5,090,000
Weighted-average shares	5,066,666
Plus: incremental shares from assumed conversions	
Warrants	0[(f)]

continued...

[(d)] 800,000 shares × CU0.05
[(e)] (CU12,000,000 × 5%) ÷ 4; less taxes at 40%
[(f)] The warrants were not assumed to be exercised because they were antidilutive in the period (CU55 [exercise price] > CU49 [average price]).

Convertible preference shares	800,000
5% convertible bonds	480,000
Dilutive potential ordinary shares	1,280,000
Adjusted weighted-average shares	6,346,666
Diluted EPS	***CU0.80***

Second Quarter 20X1

Basic EPS calculation   <u>CU</u>

Profit from continuing operations attributable to the parent
entity   6,500,000

Less: preference shares dividends   <u>(10,000)</u>[(g)]

Profit attributable to ordinary equity holders of the parent entity

6,490,000

Dates	Shares outstanding	Fraction of period	Weighted-average shares
1 April	5,200,000		
Conversion of 5% bonds on 1 April	<u>480,000</u>		
1 April–31 May	5,680,000	2/3	3,786,666
Conversion of preference shares on 1 June	<u>600,000</u>		
1 June–30 June	6,280,000	1/3	<u>2,093,333</u>
Weighted-average shares			<u><u>5,880,000</u></u>

Basic EPS   <u><u>CU1.10</u></u>

[(g)] 200,000 shares × CU0.05

continued...

Diluted EPS calculation

Profit attributable to ordinary equity holders of the parent entity		CU6,490,000
Plus: profit impact of assumed conversions		
Preference share dividends	CU10,000[(h)]	
Effect of assumed conversions		CU10,000
Profit attributable to ordinary equity holders of the parent entity including assumed conversions		CU6,500,000
Weighted-average shares		5,880,000
Plus: incremental shares from assumed conversions		
Warrants	50,000[(i)]	
Convertible preference shares	600,000[(j)]	
Dilutive potential ordinary shares		650,000
Adjusted weighted-average shares		6,530,000
Diluted EPS		*CU1.00*

[(h)] 200,000 shares × CU0.05
[(i)] CU55 × 600,000 = CU33,000,000; CU33,000,000 ÷ CU60 = 550,000;
600,000 − 550,000 = 50,000 shares OR [(CU60 − CU55) ÷ CU60] × 600,000 shares = 50,000 shares
[(j)] (800,000 shares × 2/3) + (200,000 shares × 1/3)

continued...

Third Quarter 20X1

Basic EPS calculation	<u>CU</u>
Profit from continuing operations attributable to the parent entity	1,000,000
Less: preference shares dividends	<u>(10,000)</u>
Profit from continuing operations attributable to ordinary equity holders of the parent entity	990,000
Loss from discontinued operations attributable to the parent entity	<u>(2,000,000)</u>
Loss attributable to ordinary equity holders of the parent entity	<u>(1,010,000)</u>

Dates	*Shares outstanding*	*Fraction of period*	*Weighted- average shares*
1 July–31 August	6,280,000	2/3	4,186,666
Exercise of warrants on 1 September	<u>600,000</u>		
1 September-30 September	6,880,000	1/3	<u>2,293,333</u>
Weighted-average shares			6,480,000

Basic EPS

Profit from continuing operations	***CU0.15***
Loss from discontinued operations	***(CU0.31)***
Loss	***(CU0.16)***

continued...

Diluted EPS calculation

Profit from continuing operations attributable to ordinary equity holders of the parent entity	CU990,000
Plus: profit impact of assumed conversions	
Preference shares dividends	CU10,000
Effect of assumed conversions	CU10,000
Profit from continuing operations attributable to ordinary equity holders of the parent entity including assumed conversions	CU1,000,000
Loss from discontinued operations attributable to the parent entity	(CU2,000,000)
Loss attributable to ordinary equity holders of the parent entity including assumed conversions	(CU1,000,000)
Weighted-average shares	6,480,000
Plus: incremental shares from assumed conversions	
Warrants	61,538[(k)]
Convertible preference shares	200,000
Dilutive potential ordinary shares	
	261,538
Adjusted weighted-average shares	6,741,538
Diluted EPS	
Profit from continuing operations	***CU0.15***
Loss from discontinued operations	***(CU0.30)***
Loss	***(CU0.15)***

[(k)] [(CU65 − CU55) ÷ CU65] × 600,000 = 92,308 shares; 92,308 × 2/3 = 61,538 shares

Note: The incremental shares from assumed conversions are included in calculating the diluted per-share amounts for the loss from discontinued operations and loss even though they are antidilutive. This is because the control number (profit from continuing operations attributable to ordinary equity holders of the parent entity, adjusted for preference dividends) was positive (ie profit, rather than loss).

continued...

Fourth Quarter 20X1

Basic and diluted EPS calculation	CU
Loss from continuing operations attributable to the parent entity	(700,000)
Add: preference shares dividends	(10,000)
Loss attributable to ordinary equity holders of the parent entity	(710,000)

Dates	*Shares outstanding*	*Fraction of period*	*Weighted-average shares*
1 October–31 December	6,880,000	3/3	6,880,000
Weighted-average shares			6,880,000

Basic and diluted EPS

Loss attributable to ordinary equity holders of the parent entity	*(CU0.10)*

Note: The incremental shares from assumed conversions are not included in calculating the diluted per-share amounts because the control number (loss from continuing operations attributable to ordinary equity holders of the parent entity adjusted for preference dividends) was negative (ie a loss, rather than profit).

continued...

Full Year 20X1

			CU
Basic EPS calculation			
Profit from continuing operations attributable to the parent entity			11,800,000
Less: preference shares dividends			(70,000)
Profit from continuing operations attributable to ordinary equity holders of the parent entity			11,730,000
Loss from discontinued operations attributable to the parent entity			(2,000,000)
Profit attributable to ordinary equity holders of the parent entity			9,730,000

Dates	*Shares Outstanding*	*Fraction of period*	*Weighted-average shares*
1 January-28 February	5,000,000	2/12	833,333
Issue of ordinary shares on 1 March	200,000		
1 March-31 March	5,200,000	1/12	433,333
Conversion of 5% bonds on 1 April	480,000		
1 April-31 May	5,680,000	2/12	946,667
Conversion of preference shares on 1 June	600,000		
1 June-31 August	6,280,000	3/12	1,570,000
Exercise of warrants on 1 September	600,000		
1 September-31 December	6,880,000	4/12	2,293,333
Weighted-average shares			6,076,667

Basic EPS	
Profit from continuing operations	*CU1.93*
Loss from discontinued operations	*(CU0.33)*
Profit	*CU 1.60*

continued...

Diluted EPS calculation

Profit from continuing operations attributable to ordinary equity holders of the parent entity		CU11,730,000
Plus: profit impact of assumed conversions		
Preference share dividends	CU70,000	
Interest on 5% convertible bonds	CU90,000[(l)](#)	
Effect of assumed conversions		CU160,000
Profit from continuing operations attributable to ordinary equity holders of the parent entity including assumed conversions		CU11,890,000
Loss from discontinued operations attributable to the parent entity		(CU2,000,000)
Profit attributable to ordinary equity holders of the parent entity including assumed conversions		CU9,890,000
Weighted-average shares		6,076,667
Plus: incremental shares from assumed conversions		
Warrants	14,880[(m)](#)	
Convertible preference shares	450,000[(n)](#)	
5% convertible bonds	120,000[(o)](#)	
Dilutive potential ordinary shares		584,880
Adjusted weighted-average shares		6,661,547

Diluted EPS

Profit from continuing operations	*CU1.78*
Loss from discontinued operations	*(CU0.30)*
Profit	*CU1.48*

[(l)] (CU12,000,000 × 5%) ÷ 4; less taxes at 40%
[(m)] [(CU57.125* − CU55) ÷ CU57.125] × 600,000 = 22,320 shares; 22,320 × 8/12 = 14,880 shares
  * The average market price from 1 January 20X1 to 1 September 20X1
[(n)] (800,000 shares × 5/12) + (200,000 shares × 7/12)
[(o)] 480,000 shares × 3/12

continued...

The following illustrates how Company A might present its earnings per share data on its income statement. Note that the amounts per share for the loss from discontinued operations are not required to be presented on the face of the income statement.

	For the year ended 20X1
	CU
Earnings per ordinary share	
Profit from continuing operations	1.93
Loss from discontinued operations	(0.33)
Profit	1.60
Diluted earnings per ordinary share	
Profit from continuing operations	1.78
Loss from discontinued operations	(0.30)
Profit	1.48

The following table includes the quarterly and annual earnings per share data for Company A. The purpose of this table is to illustrate that the sum of the four quarters' earnings per share data will not necessarily equal the annual earnings per share data. The Standard does not require disclosure of this information.

	First quarter	Second quarter	Third quarter	Fourth quarter	Full year
	CU	CU	CU	CU	CU
Basic EPS					
Profit (loss) from continuing operations	0.98	1.10	0.15	(0.10)	1.93
Loss from discontinued operations	–	–	(0.31)	–	(0.33)
Profit (loss)	0.98	1.10	(0.16)	(0.10)	1.60
Diluted EPS					
Profit (loss) from continuing operations	0.80	1.00	0.15	(0.10)	1.78
Loss from discontinued operations	–	–	(0.30)	–	(0.30)
Profit (loss)	0.80	1.00	(0.15)	(0.10)	1.48

Financial Reporting Standard 23 embodies IAS 21 'The Effects of Changes in Foreign Exchange Rates' and some amendments to that standard adopted for entities subject to UK accounting standards.

The Statement of Standard Accounting Practice in FRS 23 is set out in paragraphs 1-62 and the appendix. All the paragraphs have equal authority. Paragraphs in bold type state the main principles.

Accompanying the Statement of Standard Accounting Practice is the basis for the conclusions reached in the Statement. This does not form part of the Statement.

The Statement of Standard Accounting Practice should be read in the context of its objective as stated in paragraphs 1-2, the Basis for Conclusions set out in paragraphs BC1-BC32, and the Accounting Standards Board's 'Foreword to Accounting Standards' and 'Statement of Principles for Financial Reporting'.

FRS 23
(IAS 21) The effects of changes in foreign exchange rates

(Issued December 2004)

Contents

Preface by the Accounting Standards Board

a   This Financial Reporting Standard (FRS) has the effect, for those entities that are applying it, of:

- implementing in the UK and the Republic of Ireland the International Accounting Standards Board's (IASB's) International Accounting Standard (IAS) 21 *The Effects of Changes in Foreign Exchange Rates*;
- withdrawing an existing UK standard, SSAP 20 *Foreign currency translation*; and
- making consequential amendments to certain other UK standards and UITF Abstracts.

SSAP 20 remains in place unamended—and the various other UK standards and UITF Abstracts amended by this FRS remain in place unamended—for entities not applying this FRS.

b   This FRS is, in effect, part of a package of UK standards comprising:

- this FRS,
- FRS 24 (IAS 29) *Financial Reporting in Hyperinflationary Economies*,
- the disclosure requirements of FRS 25 (IAS 32) *Financial Instruments: Disclosure and Presentation*,*; and
- FRS 26 (IAS 39) *Financial Instruments: Measurement*.

c   The application of the package of standards is determined by reference to FRS 26's application.

- For accounting periods beginning on or after 1 January 2005, FRS 26—and therefore the entire package of standards listed above, including this FRS—applies to all listed entities preparing their financial statements in accordance with UK requirements—including listed parent undertakings preparing individual financial statements in accordance with those requirements.† Other entities are permitted to apply the entire package of standards from that date, although entities are not permitted to apply some of the standards in the package but not others—except that FRS 25 exempts certain entities from applying the disclosure requirements and also permits entities to apply those disclosure requirements in advance of the other standards in the package if they wish.
- For accounting periods beginning on or after 1 January 2006, unlisted entities using accounting policies that are consistent with the fair value measurement rules incorporated into the Companies Act 1985 (or equivalent legislation) to implement the Fair Value Directive will also be required to comply with FRS 26—and therefore the entire package of standards including this one.

d   The Accounting Standards Board (the Board) will in due course be issuing proposals for the application of the standards to other unlisted entities.

e   The text of IAS 21 contains various references to other International Financial Reporting Standards (IFRSs). In the FRS those references have been amended where necessary to enable the Standard to be applied in a UK context. The Board

---

The other requirements of FRS 25 apply to all entities—regardless of whether they are listed or unlisted— for accounting periods beginning on or after 1 January 2005.

†*For this purpose a listed entity is an entity that has shares or debt admitted to trading on a regulated market in the EU.*

believes that those amendments do not change the requirements of IAS 21 in any way.

The appendix of IAS 21 contains amendments that the IASB has made to existing   **d**
IFRSs in the light of the main requirements in IAS 21. In the FRS that material has
been amended and added to so that the FRS can be applied in a UK context.

IFRS 1 *First-time Adoption of International Financial Reporting Standards* sets out   **e**
additional transitional provisions for the application of IAS 21 by a first-time
adopter of IFRSs. Those transitional provisions have been incorporated into the
FRS as paragraph 59A.

In all other respects the FRS is identical to IAS 21.   **f**

In December 2005 the Board amended FRS 23 to incorporate changes made to IAS   **g**
21 by the IASB in the Amendments to IAS 21 *The Effect of Changes In Foreign
Exchange Rates* – Net Investment in a Foreign Operation, also issued in December
2005.*

Editor's note: *Made by 'Amendment to FRS 23 (IAS 21) The Effects of Changes In Foreign Exchange Rates*
– Net Investment in a Foreign Operation.'

Introduction*

> *ASB note:* The IASB's Introduction to IAS 21 is set out in full below. It should be noted that the discussion focuses on the changes that the IASB made in December 2003 to the previous version of IAS 21. Neither that previous version of IAS 21 nor the various SIC Interpretations that were incorporated in the December 2003 revision of IAS 21 had been implemented as UK standards.
>
> Footnotes have been used to provide some UK context to the discussion.

IN1 International Accounting Standard 21 *The Effects of Changes in Foreign Exchange Rates* (IAS 21) replaces IAS 21 *The Effects of Changes in Foreign Exchange Rates* (revised in 1993), and should be applied for annual periods beginning on or after 1 January 2005. Earlier application is encouraged. The Standard also replaces the following Interpretations:†

- SIC-11 *Foreign Exchange—Capitalisation of Losses Resulting from Severe Currency Devaluations*
- SIC-19 *Reporting Currency—Measurement and Presentation of Financial Statements under IAS 21 and IAS 29*
- SIC-30 *Reporting Currency—Translation from Measurement Currency to Presentation Currency.*

REASONS FOR REVISING IAS 21

IN2 The International Accounting Standards Board developed this revised IAS 21 as part of its project on Improvements to International Accounting Standards. The - project was undertaken in the light of queries and criticisms raised in relation to the Standards by securities regulators, professional accountants and other interested parties. The objectives of the project were to reduce or eliminate alternatives, redundancies and conflicts within the Standards, to deal with some convergence issues and to make other improvements.

IN3 For IAS 21 the Board's main objective was to provide additional guidance on the translation method and on determining the functional and presentation currencies. The Board did not reconsider the fundamental approach to accounting for the effects of changes in foreign exchange rates contained in IAS 21.

THE MAIN CHANGES

IN4 The main changes from the previous version of IAS 21 are described below.

---

*ASB Footnote: Throughout this standard, although references to specific IFRSs have been amended so that the standard can be applied in a UK context, the standard's references to itself as an 'IFRS' and its references to other extant accounting standards as 'other IFRS' have been left unchanged. They should though be taken to be references to this FRS and to extant standards issued in the UK and the Republic of Ireland respectively.

†ASB footnote: None of these SIC Interpretations had a UK equivalent.

Scope

The Standard excludes from its scope foreign currency derivatives that are within the scope of IAS 39 *Financial Instruments: Recognition and Measurement*.* Similarly, the material on hedge accounting has been moved to IAS 39.   **IN5**

Definitions

The notion of 'reporting currency' has been replaced with two notions: **IN6**

- functional currency, ie the currency of the primary economic environment in which the entity operates. The term 'functional currency' is used in place of 'measurement currency' (the term used in SIC-19) because it is the more commonly used term, but with essentially the same meaning.
- presentation currency, ie the currency in which financial statements are presented.

Definitions—Functional Currency

When a reporting entity prepares financial statements, the Standard requires each individual entity included in the reporting entity   whether it is a stand-alone entity, an entity with foreign operations (such as a parent) or a foreign operation (such as a subsidiary or branch)—to determine its functional currency and measure its results and financial position in that currency. The new material on functional currency incorporates some of the guidance previously included in SIC-19 on how to determine a measurement currency. However, the Standard gives greater emphasis than SIC-19 gave to the currency of the economy that determines the pricing of transactions, as opposed to the currency in which transactions are denominated.   **IN7**

As a result of these changes and the incorporation of guidance previously in SIC19:   **IN8**

- an entity (whether a stand-alone entity or a foreign operation) does not have a free choice of functional currency.
- an entity cannot avoid restatement in accordance with IAS 29 *Financial Reporting in Hyperinflationary Economies* by, for example, adopting a stable currency (such as the functional currency of its parent) as its functional currency.†

The Standard revises the requirements in the previous version of IAS 21 for distinguishing between foreign operations that are integral to the operations of the reporting entity (referred to below as 'integral foreign operations') and foreign entities. The requirements are now among the indicators of an entity's functional currency. As a result: **IN9**

- there is no distinction between integral foreign operations and foreign entities. Rather, an entity that was previously classified as an integral foreign operation will have the same functional currency as the reporting entity.
- only one translation method is used for foreign operations—namely that described in the previous version of IAS 21 as applying to foreign entities (see paragraph IN13).

*ASB footnote: The measurement and hedge accounting requirements of IAS 39 (but not its requirements on recognition and derecognition) have been implemented in the UK and the Republic of Ireland as FRS 26 (IAS 39) Financial Instruments: Measurement.

†IAS 29 has been implemented in the UK and the Republic of Ireland as FRS 24 (IAS 29) Financial Reporting in Hyperinflationary Economies.

- the paragraphs dealing with the distinction between an integral foreign operation and a foreign entity and the paragraph specifying the translation method to be used for the former have been deleted.

Reporting Foreign Currency Transactions in the Functional Currency—Recognition of Exchange Differences

IN10   The Standard removes the limited option in the previous version of IAS 21 to capitalise exchange differences resulting from a severe devaluation or depreciation of a currency against which there is no means of hedging. Under the Standard, such exchange differences are now recognised in profit or loss. Consequently, SIC-11, which outlined restricted circumstances in which such exchange differences may be capitalised, has been superseded since capitalisation of such exchange differences is no longer permitted in any circumstances.

Reporting Foreign Currency Transactions in the Functional Currency—Change in Functional Currency

IN11   The Standard replaces the previous requirement for accounting for a change in the classification of a foreign operation (which is now redundant) with a requirement that a change in functional currency is accounted for prospectively.

Use of a Presentation Currency other than the Functional Currency—Translation to the Presentation Currency

IN12   The Standard permits an entity to present its financial statements in any currency (or currencies). For this purpose, an entity could be a standalone entity, a parent preparing consolidated financial statements or a parent, an investor or a venturer preparing separate financial statements in accordance with IAS 27 *Consolidated and Separate Financial Statements*.

IN13   An entity is required to translate its results and financial position from its functional currency into a presentation currency (or currencies) using the method required for translating a foreign operation for inclusion in the reporting entity's financial statements. Under this method, assets and liabilities are translated at the closing rate, and income and expenses are translated at the exchange rates at the dates of the transactions (or at the average rate for the period when this is a reasonable approximation).

IN14   The Standard requires comparative amounts to be translated as follows:

(a)   for an entity whose functional currency is not the currency of a hyperinflationary economy:

(i)   assets and liabilities in each balance sheet presented are translated at the closing rate at the date of that balance sheet (ie last year's comparatives are translated at last year's closing rate).

(ii)   income and expenses in each income statement presented are translated at exchange rates at the dates of the transactions (ie last year's comparatives are translated at last year's actual or average rate).

(b)   for an entity whose functional currency is the currency of a hyperinflationary economy, and for which the comparative amounts are translated into the currency of a different hyperinflationary economy, all amounts (eg balance sheet and income statement amounts) are translated at the closing rate of the most recent balance sheet presented (ie last year's comparatives, as adjusted for subsequent changes in the price level, are translated at this year's closing rate).

(c)   for an entity whose functional currency is the currency of a hyperinflationary economy, and for which the comparative amounts are translated into the currency of a nonhyperinflationary economy, all amounts are those presented in the prior year financial statements (ie not adjusted for subsequent changes in the price level or subsequent changes in exchange rates).

This translation method, like that described in paragraph IN13, applies when translating the financial statements of a foreign operation for inclusion in the financial statements of the reporting entity, and when translating the financial statements of an entity into a different presentation currency.

Use of a Presentation Currency other than the Functional Currency—Translation of a Foreign Operation

The Standard requires goodwill and fair value adjustments to assets and liabilities that arise on the acquisition of a foreign entity to be treated as part of the assets and liabilities of the acquired entity and translated at the closing rate.   **IN15**

Disclosure

The Standard includes most of the disclosure requirements of SIC-30. These apply when a translation method different from that described in paragraphs IN13 and IN14 is used or other supplementary information (such as an extract from the full financial statements) is displayed in a currency other than the functional currency or the presentation currency.   **IN16**

In addition, entities must disclose when there has been a change in functional currency, and the reasons for the change.   **IN17**

Financial Reporting Standard 23 (IAS 21)

The Effects of Changes in Foreign Exchange Rates

OBJECTIVE

1   An entity may carry on foreign activities in two ways. It may have transactions in foreign currencies or it may have foreign operations. In addition, an entity may present its financial statements in a foreign currency. The objective of this Standard is to prescribe how to include foreign currency transactions and foreign operations in the financial statements of an entity and how to translate financial statements into a presentation currency.

2   The principal issues are which exchange rate(s) to use and how to report the effects of changes in exchange rates in the financial statements.

SCOPE

2A   *This Standard applies to all financial statements that are intended to give a true and fair view of a reporting entity's financial position and profit or loss (or income or expenditure), except that:*

   (a)   it should not be applied to any financial statements to which FRS 26 (IAS 39) **Financial Instruments: Recognition and Measurement** *has not also been applied; and*

   (b)   entities applying the **Financial Reporting Standard for Smaller Entities** *(FRSSE) currently applicable are exempt from the Standard.**

2B   For accounting periods beginning on or after 1 January 2005, FRS 26—and therefore this Standard—will apply to listed entities. Other entities have the option of applying the Standard, though only if they also apply FRS 26 (and certain other Standards). From 2006 unlisted entities using accounting policies that are consistent with the fair value measurement rules incorporated into the Companies Act or equivalent legislation will also be required to apply FRS 26, and therefore this Standard.

3   *This Standard shall be applied:†*

   (a)   in accounting for transactions and balances in foreign currencies, except for those derivative transactions and balances that are within the scope of FRS 26;

   (b)   in translating the results and financial position of foreign operations that are included in the financial statements of the entity by consolidation, proportionate consolidation or the equity method;‡ and

   (c)   in translating an entity's results and financial position into a presentation currency.

4   FRS 26 applies to many foreign currency derivatives and, accordingly, these are excluded from the scope of this Standard. However, those foreign currency

---

*Editor's note: Reference to FRS 26 altered by amendments to FRS 26, to reflect the change in its title.

†See also UITF Abstract 21 Accounting issues arising from the proposed introduction of the euro.

‡ASB footnote: Although IFRSs permit proportional consolidation in certain circumstances, existing FRSs do not so the reference here and elsewhere in the standard to proportional consolidation can be disregarded. Also, for the avoidance of doubt the reference here and elsewhere in the standard to 'the equity method' should be taken to include the gross equity method.

derivatives that are not within the scope of FRS 26 (eg some foreign currency derivatives that are embedded in other contracts) are within the scope of this Standard. In addition, this Standard applies when an entity translates amounts relating to derivatives from its functional currency to its presentation currency.

This Standard does not apply to hedge accounting for foreign currency items, including the hedging of a net investment in a foreign operation. FRS 26 applies to hedge accounting. **5**

This Standard applies to the presentation of an entity's financial statements in a foreign currency and sets out requirements for the resulting financial statements to be described as complying with Financial Reporting Standards. For translations of financial information into a foreign currency that do not meet these requirements, this Standard specifies information to be disclosed. **6**

This Standard does not apply to the presentation in a cash flow statement of cash flows arising from transactions in a foreign currency, or to the translation of cash flows of a foreign operation (see FRS 1 *Cash Flow Statements*). **7**

DEFINITIONS

The following terms are used in this Standard with the meanings specified: **8**

Closing rate is the spot exchange rate at the balance sheet date.

Exchange difference is the difference resulting from translating a given number of units of one currency into another currency at different exchange rates.

Exchange rate is the ratio of exchange for two currencies.

Fair value is the amount for which an asset could be exchanged, or a liability settled, between knowledgeable, willing parties in an arm's length transaction.

Foreign currency is a currency other than the functional currency of the entity.

Foreign operation is an entity that is a subsidiary, associate, joint venture or branch of a reporting entity, the activities of which are based or conducted in a country or currency other than those of the reporting entity.

Functional currency is the currency of the primary economic environment in which the entity operates.

A group is a parent and all its subsidiaries.

Monetary items are units of currency held and assets and liabilities to be received or paid in a fixed or determinable number of units of currency.

Net investment in a foreign operation is the amount of the reporting entity's interest in the net assets of that operation.

Presentation currency is the currency in which the financial statements are presented.

Spot exchange rate is the exchange rate for immediate delivery.

Elaboration on the Definitions

Functional Currency

9   The primary economic environment in which an entity operates is normally the one in which it primarily generates and expends cash. An entity considers the following factors in determining its functional currency:

(a)   the currency:

   (i)   that mainly influences sales prices for goods and services (this will often be the currency in which sales prices for its goods and services are denominated and settled); and

   (ii)   of the country whose competitive forces and regulations mainly determine the sales prices of its goods and services.

(b)   the currency that mainly influences labour, material and other costs of providing goods or services (this will often be the currency in which such costs are denominated and settled).

10   The following factors may also provide evidence of an entity's functional currency:

(a)   the currency in which funds from financing activities (ie issuing debt and equity instruments) are generated.

(b)   the currency in which receipts from operating activities are usually retained.

11   The following additional factors are considered in determining the functional currency of a foreign operation, and whether its functional currency is the same as that of the reporting entity (the reporting entity, in this context, being the entity that has the foreign operation as its subsidiary, branch, associate or joint venture):

(a)   whether the activities of the foreign operation are carried out as an extension of the reporting entity, rather than being carried out with a significant degree of autonomy. An example of the former is when the foreign operation only sells goods imported from the reporting entity and remits the proceeds to it. An example of the latter is when the operation accumulates cash and other monetary items, incurs expenses, generates income and arranges borrowings, all substantially in its local currency.

(b)   whether transactions with the reporting entity are a high or a low proportion of the foreign operation's activities.

(c)   whether cash flows from the activities of the foreign operation directly affect the cash flows of the reporting entity and are readily available for remittance to it.

(d)   whether cash flows from the activities of the foreign operation are sufficient to service existing and normally expected debt obligations without funds being made available by the reporting entity.

12   When the above indicators are mixed and the functional currency is not obvious, management uses its judgement to determine the functional currency that most faithfully represents the economic effects of the underlying transactions, events and conditions. As part of this approach, management gives priority to the primary indicators in paragraph 9 before considering the indicators in paragraphs 10 and 11, which are designed to provide additional supporting evidence to determine an entity's functional currency.

13   An entity's functional currency reflects the underlying transactions, events and conditions that are relevant to it. Accordingly, once determined, the functional currency is not changed unless there is a change in those underlying transactions, events and conditions.

If the functional currency is the currency of a hyperinflationary economy, the entity's **14** financial statements are restated in accordance with FRS 24 (IAS 29) *Financial Reporting in Hyperinflationary Economies*. An entity cannot avoid restatement in accordance with FRS 24 by, for example, adopting as its functional currency a currency other than the functional currency determined in accordance with this Standard (such as the functional currency of its parent).

Net Investment in a Foreign Operation

An entity may have a monetary item that is receivable from or payable to a foreign **15** operation. An item for which settlement is neither planned nor likely to occur in the foreseeable future is, in substance, a part of the entity's net investment in that foreign operation, and is accounted for in accordance with paragraphs 32 and 33. Such monetary items may include long-term receivables or loans. They do not include trade receivables or trade payables.

The entity that has a monetary item receivable from or payable to a foreign **15A** operation described in paragraph 15 may be any subsidiary of the group. For example, an entity has two subsidiaries, A and B. Subsidiary B is a foreign operation. Subsidiary A grants a loan to Subsidiary B. Subsidiary A's loan receivable from Subsidiary B would be part of the entity's net investment in Subsidiary B if settlement of the loan is neither planned nor likely to occur in the foreseeable future. This would also be true if Subsidiary A were itself a foreign operation.*

Monetary Items

The essential feature of a monetary item is a right to receive (or an obligation to **16** deliver) a fixed or determinable number of units of currency. Examples include: pensions and other employee benefits to be paid in cash; provisions that are to be settled in cash; and cash dividends that are recognised as a liability. Similarly, a contract to receive (or deliver) a variable number of the entity's own equity instruments or a variable amount of assets in which the fair value to be received (or delivered) equals a fixed or determinable number of units of currency is a monetary item. Conversely, the essential feature of a non-monetary item is the absence of a right to receive (or an obligation to deliver) a fixed or determinable number of units of currency. Examples include: amounts prepaid for goods and services (eg prepaid rent); goodwill; intangible assets; inventories; property, plant and equipment; and provisions that are to be settled by the delivery of a non-monetary asset.

SUMMARY OF THE APPROACH REQUIRED BY THIS STANDARD

In preparing financial statements, each entity—whether a stand-alone entity, an **17** entity with foreign operations (such as a parent) or a foreign operation (such as a subsidiary or branch)—determines its functional currency in accordance with paragraphs 9-14. The entity translates foreign currency items into its functional currency and reports the effects of such translation in accordance with paragraphs 20-37 and 50.

Many reporting entities comprise a number of individual entities (eg a group is made **18** up of a parent and one or more subsidiaries). Various types of entities, whether members of a group or otherwise, may have investments in associates or joint ventures. They may also have branches. It is necessary for the results and financial

*__*Editor's note:__ Paragraph 15A added by 'Amendment to FRS 23 (IAS 21) The Effects of Changes In Foreign Exchange Rates – Net Investment in a Foreign Operation' with effect for accounting periods beginning on or after 1 January 2006, although early adoption is encouraged.*

position of each individual entity included in the reporting entity to be translated into the currency in which the reporting entity presents its financial statements. This Standard permits the presentation currency of a reporting entity to be any currency (or currencies). The results and financial position of any individual entity within the reporting entity whose functional currency differs from the presentation currency are translated in accordance with paragraphs 38-50.

19   This Standard also permits a stand-alone entity preparing financial statements or an entity that has an investment in a subsidiary, a jointly-controlled entity or an associate and is preparing separate financial statements to present its financial statements in any currency (or currencies). If the entity's presentation currency differs from its functional currency, its results and financial position are also translated into the presentation currency in accordance with paragraphs 38-50.

REPORTING FOREIGN CURRENCY TRANSACTIONS IN THE FUNCTIONAL CURRENCY

Initial Recognition

20   A foreign currency transaction is a transaction that is denominated or requires settlement in a foreign currency, including transactions arising when an entity:

(a)   buys or sells goods or services whose price is denominated in a foreign currency;

(b)   borrows or lends funds when the amounts payable or receivable are denominated in a foreign currency; or

(c)   otherwise acquires or disposes of assets, or incurs or settles liabilities, denominated in a foreign currency.

21   *A foreign currency transaction shall be recorded, on initial recognition in the functional currency, by applying to the foreign currency amount the spot exchange rate between the functional currency and the foreign currency at the date of the transaction.*

22   The date of a transaction is the date on which the transaction first qualifies for recognition in accordance with Financial Reporting Standards. For practical reasons, a rate that approximates the actual rate at the date of the transaction is often used, for example, an average rate for a week or a month might be used for all transactions in each foreign currency occurring during that period. However, if exchange rates fluctuate significantly, the use of the average rate for a period is inappropriate.

Reporting at Subsequent Balance Sheet Dates

23   *At each balance sheet date:*

(a)   *foreign currency monetary items shall be translated using the closing rate;*

(b)   *non-monetary items that are measured in terms of historical cost in a foreign currency shall be translated using the exchange rate at the date of the transaction; and*

(c)   *non-monetary items that are measured at fair value in a foreign currency shall be translated using the exchange rates at the date when the fair value was determined.*

24   The carrying amount of an item is determined in conjunction with other relevant Standards. For example, property, plant and equipment may be measured in terms of current value or historical cost in accordance with FRS 15 *Tangible fixed assets.* Whether the carrying amount is determined on the basis of historical cost or on the

basis of current value, if the amount is determined in a foreign currency it is then translated into the functional currency in accordance with this Standard.

The carrying amount of some items is determined by comparing two or more **25** amounts. For example, the carrying amount of inventories is the lower of cost and net realisable value in accordance with SSAP 9 *Stocks and long-term contracts.* Similarly, in accordance with FRS 11 *Impairment of fixed assets and goodwill,* the carrying amount of an asset for which there is an indication of impairment is the lower of its carrying amount before considering possible impairment losses and its recoverable amount. When such an asset is nonmonetary and is measured in a foreign currency, the carrying amount is determined by comparing:

(a) the cost or carrying amount, as appropriate, translated at the exchange rate at the date when that amount was determined (ie the rate at the date of the transaction for an item measured in terms of historical cost); and
(b) the net realisable value or recoverable amount, as appropriate, translated at the exchange rate at the date when that value was determined (eg the closing rate at the balance sheet date).

The effect of this comparison may be that an impairment loss is recognised in the functional currency but would not be recognised in the foreign currency, or vice versa.

When several exchange rates are available, the rate used is that at which the future **26** cash flows represented by the transaction or balance could have been settled if those cash flows had occurred at the measurement date. If exchangeability between two currencies is temporarily lacking, the rate used is the first subsequent rate at which exchanges could be made.

Recognition of Exchange Differences

As noted in paragraph 3, FRS 26 applies to hedge accounting for foreign currency **27** items. The application of hedge accounting requires an entity to account for some exchange differences differently from the treatment of exchange differences required by this Standard. For example, FRS 26 requires that exchange differences on monetary items that qualify as hedging instruments in a cash flow hedge are recognised initially through the statement of total recognised gains and losses to the extent that the hedge is effective.*

Exchange differences arising on the settlement of monetary items or on translating **28** *monetary items at rates different from those at which they were translated on initial recognition during the period or in previous financial statements shall be recognised in profit or loss in the period in which they arise, except as described in paragraph 32.*

When monetary items arise from a foreign currency transaction and there is a change **29** in the exchange rate between the transaction date and the date of settlement, an exchange difference results. When the transaction is settled within the same accounting period as that in which it occurred, all the exchange difference is recognised in that period. However, when the transaction is settled in a subsequent accounting period, the exchange difference recognised in each period up to the date of settlement is determined by the change in exchange rates during each period.

*ASB footnote: There are a number of references in this standard to certain exchange differences being "reported initially in equity", "recognised directly in equity" or being "recognised initially in a separate component of equity". Under UK standards such exchange differences are recognised in the statement of total recognised gains and losses.

30   *When a gain or loss on a non-monetary item is recognised through the statement of total recognised gains and losses, any exchange component of that gain or loss shall be recognised through the statement of total recognised gains and losses. Conversely, when a gain or loss on a non-monetary item is recognised in profit or loss, any exchange component of that gain or loss shall be recognised in profit or loss.*

31   Other Standards require some gains and losses to be recognised through the statement of total recognised gains and losses. For example, FRS 15 requires some gains and losses arising on a revaluation of property, plant and equipment to be recognised through the statement of total recognised gains and losses. When such an asset is measured in a foreign currency, paragraph 23(c) of this Standard requires the revalued amount to be translated using the rate at the date the value is determined, resulting in an exchange difference that is also recognised through the statement of total recognised gains and losses.

32   *Exchange differences arising on a monetary item that forms part of a reporting entity's net investment in a foreign operation (see paragraph 15) shall be recognised in profit or loss in the separate financial statements of the reporting entity or the individual financial statements of the foreign operation, as appropriate. In the financial statements that include the foreign operation and the reporting entity (eg consolidated financial statements when the foreign operation is a subsidiary), such exchange differences shall be recognised initially through the statement of total recognised gains and losses and recognised in profit or loss on disposal of the net investment in accordance with paragraph 48.*

33   When a monetary item forms part of a reporting entity's net investment in a foreign operation and is denominated in the functional currency of the reporting entity, an exchange difference arises in the foreign operation's individual financial statements in accordance with paragraph 28. If such an item is denominated in the functional currency of the foreign operation, an exchange difference arises in the reporting entity's separate financial statements in accordance with paragraph 28. If such an item is denominated in a currency other the functional currency of either the reporting entity or the foreign operation, an exchange difference arises in the reporting entity's separate financial statements and in the foreign operation's individual financial statements in accordance with paragraph 28. Such exchange differences are recognised through the statement of total recognised gains and losses in the financial statements that include the foreign operation and the reporting entity (ie financial statements in which the foreign operation is consolidated, proportionately consolidated or accounted for using the equity method).*

34   When an entity keeps its books and records in a currency other than its functional currency, at the time the entity prepares its financial statements all amounts are translated into the functional currency in accordance with paragraphs 20-26. This produces the same amounts in the functional currency as would have occurred had the items been recorded initially in the functional currency. For example, monetary items are translated into the functional currency using the closing rate, and nonmonetary items that are measured on a historical cost basis are translated using the exchange rate at the date of the transaction that resulted in their recognition.

Editor's note: Paragraph 33 amended by 'Amendment to FRS 23 (IAS 21) The Effects of Changes In Foreign Exchange Rates – Net Investment in a Foreign Operation' *with effect for accounting periods beginning on or after 1 January 2006, although early adoption is encouraged.*

Change in Functional Currency

When there is a change in an entity's functional currency, the entity shall apply the translation procedures applicable to the new functional currency prospectively from the date of the change.   **35**

As noted in paragraph 13, the functional currency of an entity reflects the underlying   **36** transactions, events and conditions that are relevant to the entity. Accordingly, once the functional currency is determined, it can be changed only if there is a change to those underlying transactions, events and conditions. For example, a change in the currency that mainly influences the sales prices of goods and services may lead to a change in an entity's functional currency.

The effect of a change in functional currency is accounted for prospectively. In other   **37** words, an entity translates all items into the new functional currency using the exchange rate at the date of the change. The resulting translated amounts for non-monetary items are treated as their historical cost. Exchange differences arising from the translation of a foreign operation previously recognised through the statement of total recognised gains and losses in accordance with paragraphs 32 and 39(c) are not recognised in profit or loss until the disposal of the operation.

USE OF A PRESENTATION CURRENCY OTHER THAN THE FUNCTIONAL CURRENCY

Translation to the Presentation Currency

An entity may present its financial statements in any currency (or currencies). If the   **38** presentation currency differs from the entity's functional currency, it translates its results and financial position into the presentation currency. For example, when a group contains individual entities with different functional currencies, the results and financial position of each entity are expressed in a common currency so that con-solidated financial statements may be presented.

The results and financial position of an entity whose functional currency is not the   **39** *currency of a hyperinflationary economy shall be translated into a different presentation currency using the following procedures:*

(a)   assets and liabilities for each balance sheet presented (ie including comparatives) shall be translated at the closing rate at the date of that balance sheet;

(b)   income and expenses for each income statement (ie including comparatives) shall be translated at exchange rates at the dates of the transactions; and

(c)   all resulting exchange differences shall be recognised through the statement of total recognised gains and losses.

For practical reasons, a rate that approximates the exchange rates at the dates of the   **40** transactions, for example an average rate for the period, is often used to translate income and expense items. However, if exchange rates fluctuate significantly, the use of the average rate for a period is inappropriate.

The exchange differences referred to in paragraph 39(c) result from: **41**

(a)   translating income and expenses at the exchange rates at the dates of the transactions and assets and liabilities at the closing rate. Such exchange dif-ferences arise both on income and expense items recognised in profit or loss and on those recognised through the statement of total recognised gains and losses.

(b)   translating the opening net assets at a closing rate that differs from the previous closing rate.

These exchange differences are not recognised in profit or loss because the changes in exchange rates have little or no direct effect on the present and future cash flows from operations. When the exchange differences relate to a foreign operation that is consolidated but not wholly-owned, accumulated exchange differences arising from translation and attributable to minority interests are allocated to, and recognised as part of, minority interest in the consolidated balance sheet.

42   *The results and financial position of an entity whose functional currency is the currency of a hyperinflationary economy shall be translated into a different presentation currency using the following procedures:*

(a)   *all amounts (ie assets, liabilities, amounts recognised through the statement of total recognised gains and losses, income and expenses, including comparatives) shall be translated at the closing rate at the date of the most recent balance sheet, except that*

(b)   *when amounts are translated into the currency of a nonhyperinflationary economy, comparative amounts shall be those that were presented as current year amounts in the relevant prior year financial statements (ie not adjusted for subsequent changes in the price level or subsequent changes in exchange rates).*

43   *When an entity's functional currency is the currency of a hyperinflationary economy, the entity shall restate its financial statements in accordance with FRS 24 before applying the translation method set out in paragraph 42, except for comparative amounts that are translated into a currency of a non-hyperinflationary economy (see paragraph 42(b)). When the economy ceases to be hyperinflationary and the entity no longer restates its financial statements in accordance with FRS 24, it shall use as the historical costs for translation into the presentation currency the amounts restated to the price level at the date the entity ceased restating its financial statements.*

Translation of a Foreign Operation

44   Paragraphs 45-47, in addition to paragraphs 38-43, apply when the results and financial position of a foreign operation are translated into a presentation currency so that the foreign operation can be included in the financial statements of the reporting entity by consolidation, proportionate consolidation or the equity method.

45   The incorporation of the results and financial position of a foreign operation with those of the reporting entity follows normal consolidation procedures, such as the elimination of intragroup balances and intragroup transactions of a subsidiary (see FRS 2 *Accounting for subsidiary undertakings*). However, an intragroup monetary asset (or liability), whether short-term or long-term, cannot be eliminated against the corresponding intragroup liability (or asset) without showing the results of currency fluctuations in the consolidated financial statements. This is because the monetary item represents a commitment to convert one currency into another and exposes the reporting entity to a gain or loss through currency fluctuations. Accordingly, in the consolidated financial statements of the reporting entity, such an exchange difference continues to be recognised in profit or loss or, if it arises from the circumstances described in paragraph 32, it is recognised through the statement of total recognised gains and losses until the disposal of the foreign operation.

46   When the financial statements of a foreign operation are as of a date different from that of the reporting entity, the foreign operation often prepares additional statements as of the same date as the reporting entity's financial statements. When this is

not done, FRS 2 allows the use of a different reporting date provided that the difference is no greater than three months before the relevant period-end of the parent of the group and adjustments are made for the effects of any significant transactions or other events that occur between the different dates. In such a case, the assets and liabilities of the foreign operation are translated at the exchange rate at the balance sheet date of the foreign operation. Adjustments are made for significant changes in exchange rates up to the balance sheet date of the reporting entity in accordance with FRS 2. The same approach is used in applying the equity method to associates and joint ventures and in applying proportionate consolidation to joint ventures in accordance with FRS 9 *Associates and joint ventures*, except that if using these statements would release restricted, price-sensitive information, financial statements prepared for a period that ended not more than six months before the investor's period-end may be used.

Any goodwill arising on the acquisition of a foreign operation and any fair value   47
adjustments to the carrying amounts of assets and liabilities arising on the acquisition of that foreign operation shall be treated as assets and liabilities of the foreign operation. Thus they shall be expressed in the functional currency of the foreign operation and shall be translated at the closing rate in accordance with paragraphs 39 and 42.

Disposal of a Foreign Operation

On the disposal of a foreign operation, the cumulative amount of the exchange dif-   48
ferences recognised through the statement of total recognised gains and losses relating to that foreign operation shall be recognised in profit or loss when the gain or loss on disposal is recognised.*

An entity may dispose of its interest in a foreign operation through sale, liquidation,   49
repayment of share capital or abandonment of all, or part of, that entity. The payment of a dividend is part of a disposal only when it constitutes a return of the investment, for example when the dividend is paid out of pre-acquisition profits. In the case of a partial disposal, only the proportionate share of the related accumulated exchange difference is included in the gain or loss. A write-down of the carrying amount of a foreign operation does not constitute a partial disposal. Accordingly, no part of the deferred foreign exchange gain or loss is recognised in profit or loss at the time of a write-down.

TAX EFFECTS OF ALL EXCHANGE DIFFERENCES

Gains and losses on foreign currency transactions and exchange differences arising   50
on translating the results and financial position of an entity (including a foreign operation) into a different currency may have tax effects. FRS 16 *Current tax* and FRS 19 *Deferred tax* apply to these tax effects.

DISCLOSURE

In paragraphs 53 and 55-57 references to 'functional currency' apply, in the case of a   51
group, to the functional currency of the parent.

*ASB footnote: As explained already in the footnote to paragraph 27, references in this standard to exchange differences and other gains and losses being taken to equity are, under the standards that apply in the UK and the Republic of Ireland, references to the items being recognised in the statement of recognised gains and losses (STRGL). Therefore paragraph 48, when applied in the context of other UK standards, requires the cumulative amount of the exchange differences recognised in the STRGL in respect of the foreign operation disposed of to be reversed out of the STRGL and recognised in the profit and loss account.

52   *An entity shall disclose:*

    (a)   the amount of exchange differences recognised in profit or loss except for those arising on financial instruments measured at fair value through profit or loss in accordance with FRS 26; and

    (b)   net exchange differences recognised through the statement of total recognised gains and losses, and a reconciliation of the amount of such exchange differences at the beginning and end of the period.

53   *When the presentation currency is different from the functional currency, that fact shall be stated, together with disclosure of the functional currency and the reason for using a different presentation currency.*

54   *When there is a change in the functional currency of either the reporting entity or a significant foreign operation, that fact and the reason for the change in functional currency shall be disclosed.*

55   *When an entity presents its financial statements in a currency that is different from its functional currency, it shall describe the financial statements as complying with Financial Reporting Standards only if they comply with all the requirements of each applicable Standard and each applicable Interpretation of those Standards including the translation method set out in paragraphs 39 and 42.*

56   An entity sometimes presents its financial statements or other financial information in a currency that is not its functional currency without meeting the requirements of paragraph 55. For example, an entity may convert into another currency only selected items from its financial statements. Or, an entity whose functional currency is not the currency of a hyperinflationary economy may convert the financial statements into another currency by translating all items at the most recent closing rate. Such conversions are not in accordance with Financial Reporting Standards and the disclosures set out in paragraph 57 are required.

57   *When an entity displays its financial statements or other financial information in a currency that is different from either its functional currency or its presentation currency and the requirements of paragraph 55 are not met, it shall:*

    (a)   clearly identify the information as supplementary information to distinguish it from the information that complies with Financial Reporting Standards;

    (b)   disclose the currency in which the supplementary information is displayed; and

    (c)   disclose the entity's functional currency and the method of translation used to determine the supplementary information.

EFFECTIVE DATE AND TRANSITION

58   *An entity shall apply this Standard for accounting periods in which they also apply FRS 26 but not in any other accounting period.*

58A   **Net Investment in a Foreign Operation** *(Amendment to FRS 23), issued in December 2005, added paragraph 15A and amended paragraph 33. An entity shall apply those amendments for accounting periods beginning on or after 1 January 2006. Earlier application is encouraged.**

*Editor's note: Added by the amendment to which reference is made. The current paragraph 58B was previously paragraph 58A.

Unless and until an entity applies FRS 26 it is not permitted to adopt this Standard; **58B** and if it applies FRS 26 it must also apply this Standard. Listed entities are required to apply FRS 26 for accounting periods beginning on or after 1 January 2005 (and other entities are permitted to apply it from that same date). As explained in paragraph 2B, certain unlisted entities are required to apply FRS 26 for accounting periods beginning on or after 1 January 2006.

An entity shall apply paragraph 47 prospectively to all acquisitions occurring after the **59** *beginning of the financial reporting period in which this Standard is first applied. Retrospective application of paragraph 47 to earlier acquisitions is permitted. For an acquisition of a foreign operation treated prospectively but which occurred before the date on which this Standard is first applied, the entity shall not restate prior years and accordingly may, when appropriate, treat goodwill and fair value adjustments arising on that acquisition as assets and liabilities of the entity rather than as assets and liabilities of the foreign operation. Therefore, those goodwill and fair value adjustments either are already expressed in the entity's functional currency or are non-monetary foreign currency items, which are reported using the exchange rate at the date of the acquisition.*

Paragraphs 48 and 49 require an entity to recognise some translation differences **59A†** *through the statement of total recognised gains and losses as a separate component of equity and, on disposal of a foreign operation, to transfer the cumulative translation difference for that foreign operation (including, if applicable, gains and losses on related hedges) to the income statement as part of the gain or loss on disposal. However, on first applying this standard an entity need not comply with these requirements for cumulative translation differences that existed at the effective date. If an entity uses this exemption:*

(a) the cumulative translation differences for all foreign operations are deemed to be zero at the effective date; and

(b) the gain or loss on a subsequent disposal of any foreign operation shall exclude translation differences that arose before the effective date and shall include later translation differences.

All other changes resulting from the application of this Standard shall be accounted for **60** *in accordance with the requirements of FRS 18* Accounting policies.

WITHDRAWAL OF OTHER PRONOUNCEMENTS

For entities applying this Standard, it supersedes SSAP 20 *Foreign currency* **61** *translation.*

[*ASB note:* Deleted] **62**

---

† *ASB footnote: This ASB amendment inserts into the FRS paragraphs 21 and 22 of IFRS 1* First-time Adoption of International Financial Reporting Standards. *Those paragraphs have been amended to refer to recognising translation differences 'through the statement of total recognised gains and losses' rather than 'as a separate component of equity'.*

Appendix
Amendments to other pronouncements

[Not reproduced, as all changes have been made to the underlying standards and abstracts].

Adoption of the standard

APPROVAL OF IAS 21 BY THE INTERNATIONAL ACCOUNTING STANDARDS BOARD

International Accounting Standard 21 *The Effects of Changes in Foreign Exchange Rates* was approved for issue by the fourteen members of the International Accounting Standards Board.

Sir David Tweedie	Chairman
Thomas E Jones	Vice-Chairman
Mary E Barth	
Hans-Georg Bruns	
Anthony T Cope	
Robert P Garnett	
Gilbert Gélard	
James J Leisenring	
Warren J McGregor	
Patricia L O'Malley	
Harry K Schmid	
John T Smith	
Geoffrey Whittington	
Tatsumi Yamada	

ADOPTION OF FRS 23 BY THE ACCOUNTING STANDARDS BOARD

Financial Reporting Standard 23 (IAS 21) *The Effects of Changes in Foreign Exchange Rates* was approved for issue by the ten members of the Accounting Standards Board.

Ian Mackintosh	Chairman
Andrew Lennard	Technical Director
Michael Ashley	
Douglas Flint	
Anthony Good	
Roger Marshall	
Isobel Sharp	
John Smith	
Jonathan Symonds	
Peter Westlake	

Notes on the standard's application in the UK and the Republic of Ireland

N1　SSAP 20 *Foreign currency translation* was issued in April 1983. It was developed at the same time as the original version of IAS 21 and the US Financial Accounting Standard (FAS) 52 *Foreign Currency Translation* as part of an international convergence project on accounting for foreign currency. As a result, the main requirements of the three standards were similar, although they differed somewhat in the terminology used and the matters of emphasis.

THE IASB'S IMPROVEMENTS PROJECT

N2　In 2001 the IASB announced that it would be reviewing a number of existing standards, including IAS 21. The revised IAS 21 was issued in December 2003.

N3　The main changes made are summarised in the IASB's Introduction to the standard; and the rationale behind the changes made is set out in the Basis for Conclusions material that the IASB prepared to accompany the standard.

FRED 24

N4　In recent years, the Accounting Standards Board (the Board) has been placing increasing emphasis on the convergence aspects of its standard-setting role: listed entities in the UK and the Republic of Ireland preparing consolidated financial statements will from 2005 be required to prepare those statements in accordance with EU-adopted international accounting standards (International Financial Reporting Standards or IFRSs) and, although entities can continue to prepare other financial statements in accordance with the requirements of the UK and the Republic of Ireland, the Board's view is that there can be no case for the use of two sets of wholly different standards in the medium term.

N5　As part of this convergence strategy, the Board issued FRED 24 *The Effects of Changes in Foreign Exchange Rates & Financial Reporting in Hyperinflationary Economies*. FRED 24 set out for comment two proposed UK standards, based on the IASB's proposals for a revised IAS 21 and the IASB's existing IAS 29. The FRED proposed that, with certain amendments, both IFRSs should be implemented as standards in the UK and the Republic of Ireland and should apply to all UK and Republic of Ireland entities. At the same time the FRED proposed withdrawing the existing UK requirements in this area, which are mainly in SSAP 20 *Foreign currency translation*.

N6　Those responding to FRED 24 were broadly supportive of the Board's strategy to converge its standards in this area with those of the IASB. However, concerns were raised about recycling, hedge accounting and some detailed aspects of the UK implementation plan proposed.

Recycling

N7　'Recycling' is the term commonly used to describe the practice of reversing out of the statement of total recognised gains and losses (STRGL) gains and losses that have been recognised in prior periods and recognising them instead in the profit and loss account (P&L).

IAS 21 requires exchange differences on a monetary item that is part of a net **N8** investment in a foreign operation to be recognised initially in the STRGL, then recycled to the P&L on disposal of the foreign operation. Existing UK standards, on the other hand, do not permit such gains and losses to be recycled; indeed, they do not permit any gains and losses to be recycled.

FRED 24 proposed to retain the prohibition on recycling, primarily because the **N9** IASB was reviewing its use of recycling as part of its comprehensive income project and it was understood at the time that the result of that review was likely to be that the IASB would converge on UK practice and prohibit recycling.

Respondents were split on how the Board should deal with recycling in implementing **N10** IAS 21. Some agreed with the approach taken in the FRED; others thought that if the Board decides to implement an IFRS in the UK it should not amend that IFRS. The issue was discussed again in the Board's recent Discussion Paper *UK Accounting Standards: A Strategy for Convergence with IFRS* and this time the clear majority of respondents favoured making no amendment to IAS 21.

The Board continues to have concerns about recycling, primarily because it is not **N11** consistent with the *Statement of Principles*. That is because it involves (depending precisely on how one looks at it) either the recognition in the performance statements of items that are not gains and losses or the recognition in the performance statements of the same gains and losses twice.

The IASB is actively considering the future of recycling in its comprehensive income **N12** project, and the Board intends to continue to argue strongly for the practice's prohibition. Nevertheless, the Board has concluded that it would be inconsistent with its stated policy of convergence were it to amend IAS 21's recycling provisions simply because it does not like them and thinks the UK has a better solution. It is therefore implementing IAS 21 unamended.

Hedge accounting

SSAP 20 sets out the UK requirements on the accounting treatment of hedges of net **N13** investments in foreign operations. IAS 21 contains no equivalent requirements, because hedge accounting is dealt with in another standard (IAS 39). Therefore, when developing the proposals in FRED 24 the Board had a choice.

(a)   It could include in the UK version of IAS 21 (or issue as some form of standalone standard) some hedge accounting requirements. Those requirements could be those set out in SSAP 20, those set out in IAS 39, or some other hedge accounting requirements.

(b)   It could allow entities to adopt the UK version of IAS 21 (rather than SSAP 20) only if they are apply the UK version of IAS 39.

(c)   It could implement IAS 21 without any hedge accounting requirements, take a separate independent decision on UK implementation of IAS 39, and accept that some entities may—for an interim period—no longer be subject to any requirements concerning the accounting treatment of hedges of net investments in foreign operations.

The Board decided to adopt option (a) in FRED 24. Furthermore, rather than **N14** import either SSAP 20's requirements or IAS 39's requirements, it proposed (in FRED 23 *Financial instruments: Hedge accounting*) issuing a standalone hedge accounting standard, albeit one based on the principles set out in IAS 39. This proposal was not supported by respondents who thought that the development of a UK standard on hedge accounting was not consistent with the convergence objective. Others thought the proposal introduced additional complexity in the financial reporting framework at a time when what was needed most of all was simplicity. As a result, the Board announced in its Convergence Strategy Discussion Paper that, although it has not withdrawn FRED 23, it has no present intention to develop it into a standard.

N15   The Board has now decided to address the issue described in paragraph N13 by adopting option (b)—in other words, implementing IAS 21 (as FRS 23) and the hedge accounting requirements of IAS 39 (as FRS 26) in the UK and the Republic of Ireland at the same time and for the same entities.

Application of the FRS

N16   Having reached this conclusion, the Board then decided that it was sensible to implement the UK standard based on IAS 29 *Financial Reporting in Hyperinflationary Economies* at the same time as this standard, and that it was sensible to implement the disclosure aspects of the UK standard based on IAS 32 *Financial Instruments: Disclosures and Presentation* at the same time as the measurement aspects of the UK standard based on IAS 39. This approach has the advantage of simplicity—entities are either applying the financial instruments and foreign currency standards or they are not—and simplicity is a desirable attribute at this time. The Board recognises that the approach does mean though that there will be some entities that wanted to start applying FRS 23 in 2005 but will not now do so because they are not ready to implement the whole package of standards.

Timetable

N17   FRED 24 proposed that IAS 21 should be implemented as a standard in the UK and the Republic of Ireland as soon as the IASB had finalised its revisions to IAS 21—which the IASB expected at the time to be in early 2003. In fact, the revised standard was not issued until December 2003. In any event, many respondents to FRED 24—and to the other convergence proposals the Board issued at the time in FREDs 25-30—argued that it would be more appropriate to implement the proposed new standards from 2005.

N18   As just explained, the Board has decided to implement IAS 21 and IAS 39 in the UK together and for the same entities. The Board furthermore decided that the implementation timetable for both standards should be determined by reference to the UK version of IAS 39 (FRS 26). FRS 26 will apply to all listed entities for accounting periods starting on or after 1 January 2005 and to all unlisted [fair value volunteers] for accounting periods beginning on or after 1 January 2006. It follows that FRS 23 will apply to the same entities from the same dates. Earlier adoption is permitted, as long as both standards (together with the other standards that the Board has decided should be implemented at the same time*) are implemented at the same time.

N19   The Board intends to issue proposals on the implementation of the standards for other entities in due course.

N20   Another issue raised by respondents concerned the transitional provisions. Some respondents suggested that the transitional arrangements proposed in the IASB's exposure draft of a revised IAS 21 (and therefore in FRED 24) were not practicable and that additional transitional relief needed to be given in respect of the treatment

FRSs 23-26, excluding the presentation requirements of FRS 25. Entities are permitted to apply the disclosure requirements of FRS 25 ahead of the other FRSs.

of purchased goodwill (paragraph 47 of the FRS) and the treatment of disposals of foreign operations (paragraphs 48 and 49). In finalising the standard the IASB included in its standard additional relief on the first point; it also included transitional relief on the second point in IFRS 1 *First-time Adoption of International Financial Reporting Standards* and the Board has incorporated that relief into FRS 23.

CHANGES TO EXISTING UK REQUIREMENTS

As already mentioned, SSAP 20 and IAS 21 were developed together and, as a result, their main requirements are similar. In its improvement project, the IASB did not reconsider the fundamental approach adopted in IAS 21—the main objective was to provide additional guidance on the translation method and on determining the functional and presentation currencies—so the main requirements of the revised version of IAS 21 (and therefore of this standard) are also similar to SSAP 20's requirements. The main differences between FRS 23 and SSAP 20 are described in the following paragraphs.

N21

Preparing the individual entity financial statements

Presentation currency

SSAP 20 and FRS 23 both require each entity to determine its functional currency and measure its results in that currency (although SSAP 20 refers to the 'functional currency' as the 'local currency'). FRS 23, but not SSAP 20, also deals explicitly with the currency in which financial statements are then presented (the presentation currency).

N22

(a) The implication in SSAP 20 is that the presentation currency will be the entity's local currency (or, in the case of consolidated financial statements, the parent entity's local currency).

(b) FRS 23, on the other hand, states that an entity may present its financial statements in any currency or currencies. The standard also specifies the method to be used to translate the results and financial position into that presentation currency when the functional currency and presentation currency are different.

Use of contracted rates of exchange

The terms on which some foreign currency transactions are carried out specify the rate of exchange that is to be used for settlement purposes and SSAP 20 permits such transactions and any resulting assets and liabilities to be translated into the functional currency at that contracted rate. FRS 23, on the other hand, requires the transaction to be measured on initial recognition at the then spot rate; subsequently, if a monetary item is involved it should be retranslated each balance sheet date at the relevant closing rate.

N23

Monetary items forming part of a net investment in a foreign operation

SSAP 20 permits exchange differences arising on an entity's net investment in a foreign operation to be recognised in the STRGL of the individual financial statements of that investing entity. FRS 23, however, requires some of these exchange differences—in particular those that arise on monetary items that are part of the investing entity's net investment—to be recognised in the P&L of the investee's individual financial statements.

N24

Exchange gains on long-term monetary items

N25   SSAP 20 generally requires exchange gains and losses on monetary items to be recognised immediately in the profit and loss account. However, when long-term monetary items are involved, SSAP 20 permits the recognition of some or all of such gains (but not losses) to be deferred if there are doubts as to the convertibility or marketability of the currency in question. Deferring the recognition of such gains is not permitted under FRS 23.

Preparing the consolidated financial statements

Net investment method or temporal method?

N26   If an entity is preparing consolidated financial statements for a group that includes one or more foreign operations, SSAP 20 generally requires the net investment method to be used to incorporate the results and financial position of a foreign operation. (SSAP 20 called this method the 'closing rate/net investment method'.) However, if the foreign operation is deemed to be an integral part of the investing company (ie the affairs of a foreign entity are so closely interlinked with those of the investing company that its results are regarded as being more dependent on the economic environment of the investing company's currency than on that of its own currency), the temporal method should be used.* FRS 23 permits only one method to be used: the net investment method.

N27   This difference in the requirements ought not, however, to result in a difference in accounting practice. As explained in paragraph BC6 of the Basis for Conclusions, if a foreign operation is integral to the investing company, the functional currency of the foreign operation will be the same as the investing company's, so the overall effect will be the same in the consolidated financial statements as under SSAP 20 when the temporal method was applied.

Exchange rate to be used for P&L items under the net investment method

N28   Under SSAP 20's version of the net investment method, the profit and loss account (the P&L) of the foreign operation is translated at either the closing rate or an appropriate average rate. FRS 23, on the other hand, requires the rate of exchange at the transaction date to be used, although it accepts that an average rate will often be a good approximation of that rate.

Translation of goodwill and fair value adjustments

N29   SSAP 20 does not specifically address the treatment of goodwill and fair value adjustments to the carrying amounts of assets and liabilities on the acquisition of a foreign operation. FRS 23 requires such items to be treated as assets and liabilities of the foreign operation and translated at the closing rate.

Put another way, the net investment method is used under SSAP 20 when a foreign operation is largely self-contained and is not dependent upon the economic environment of the investing company's functional currency. In such circumstances, the foreign currency exposure that the investing company has relates to its net investment in the foreign operation, rather than in the individual assets and liabilities of the foreign operation. The net investment method reflects this by translating the net investment at the closing rate of exchange. The temporal method treats the foreign operation's transactions as if they had been entered into by the investing company itself in its own currency.

Disposal of a foreign operation

SSAP 20 does not explicitly deal with the disposal of a foreign operation. However, the implication of the standard (when taken together with other UK standards) is that, when a foreign operation is sold, no adjustment should be made to the cumulative amount of the exchange differences previously recognised in the STRGL in respect of that foreign operation—other than perhaps moving the amounts from one reserve to another. FRS 23 requires the cumulative amount of those exchange differences to be reversed out of the STRGL and recognised in full in the P&L (in other words, they should be recycled to the P&L).   **N30**

Hedge accounting

SSAP 20 sets out the requirements to be followed in accounting for hedges of net investments in foreign operations. As already explained, FRS 23 does not contain equivalent requirements; instead, they are set out in FRS 26. FRS 26's requirements are also different from SSAP 20's. The main differences are   **N31**

(a)   Although the net investment hedging provisions of SSAP 20 apply both to individual financial statements and consolidated financial statements, under FRS 26 they apply only to consolidated financial statements. To be able to use hedge accounting in the individual financial statements to account for a hedge of a net investment in a foreign operation, the hedge will need to qualify as a fair value hedge of the foreign exchange risk involved. Under FRS 26, gains and losses arising on the hedging instrument and hedged item in a net investment hedge are recognised in the STRGL; and gains and losses arising on the hedging instrument and hedged item in a fair value hedge are recognised in the P&L.

(b)   FRS 26 is more restrictive than SSAP 20 on what will qualify for hedge accounting,

(b)   Unlike SSAP 20, FRS 26 requires entities to recognise gains and losses on any ineffective element of a hedge in the P&L immediately.

(c)   Although both standards require gains and losses on a net investment hedge to be recognised in the consolidated financial statements in the STRGL, FRS 26 requires those gains and losses to be recycled to the P&L on disposal of the foreign operation. SSAP 20 does not.

Disclosure requirements

The disclosure requirements of the two standards are also somewhat different.   **N32**

Basis for Conclusions

ASB note: The IASB's Basis for Conclusions, which accompanies IAS 21, is set out below in full. It should be noted though that some of the discussion it contains concerns IASB requirements that have no equivalent in the UK or Republic of Ireland. Footnotes have been used to highlight those parts of the discussion.

Paragraph BC1 is amended and paragraph BC25A-BC25F are added in relation to the amendment to IAS 21 issued in December 2005.*

All references in this section to 'the Board' and 'Board members' are references to the IASB Board and IASB Board members.

This Basis for Conclusions accompanies, but is not part of, IAS 21.

INTRODUCTION

BC1   This Basis for Conclusions summarises the International Accounting Standards Board's considerations in reaching its conclusions on revising IAS 21 *The Effects of Changes in Foreign Exchange Rates* in 2003, and on the amendment to IAS 21 *Net Investment in a Foreign Operation* in December 2005. Individual Board members gave greater weight to some factors than to others.†

BC2   In July 2001 the Board announced that, as part of its initial agenda of technical projects, it would undertake a project to improve a number of Standards, including IAS 21. The project was undertaken in the light of queries and criticisms raised in relation to the Standards by securities regulators, professional accountants and other interested parties. The objectives of the Improvements project were to reduce or eliminate alternatives, redundancies and conflicts within Standards, to deal with some convergence issues and to make other improvements. In May 2002 the Board published its proposals in an Exposure Draft of *Improvements to International Accounting Standards*, with a comment deadline of 16 September 2002. The Board received over 160 comment letters on the Exposure Draft.

BC3   Because the Board's intention was not to reconsider the fundamental approach to accounting for the effects of changes in foreign exchange rates established by IAS 21, this Basis for Conclusions does not discuss requirements in IAS 21 that the Board has not reconsidered.

FUNCTIONAL CURRENCY

BC4   The term 'reporting currency' was previously defined as "the currency used in presenting the financial statements". This definition comprises two separate notions (which were identified in SIC-19 *Reporting Currency—Measurement and Presentation of Financial Statements under IAS 21 and IAS 29*):

- the measurement currency (the currency in which the entity measures the items in the financial statements); and

---

**Editor's note: Added by the amendment to which reference is made.*

†*Editor's note: Amended by 'Amendment to FRS 23 (IAS 21) The Effects of Changes In Foreign Exchange Rates – Net Investment in a Foreign Operation'.*

- the presentation currency (the currency in which the entity presents its financial statements).

The Board decided to revise the previous version of IAS 21 to incorporate the SIC19 approach of separating these two notions. The Board also noted that the term 'functional currency' is more commonly used than 'measurement currency' and decided to adopt the more common term.

The Board noted a concern that the guidance in SIC-19 on determining a mea-   **BC5**
surement currency could permit entities to choose one of several currencies, or to select an inappropriate currency. In particular, some believed that SIC-19 placed too much emphasis on the currency in which transactions are denominated and too little emphasis on the underlying economy that determines the pricing of those transactions. To meet these concerns, the Board defined functional currency as "the currency of the primary economic environment in which the entity operates". The Board also provided guidance on how to determine the functional currency (see paragraphs 9-14 of the Standard). This guidance draws heavily on SIC-19 and equivalent guidance in US and other national standards, but also reflects the Board's decision that some factors merit greater emphasis than others.

The Board also discussed whether a foreign operation that is integral to the reporting   **BC6**
entity (as described in the previous version of IAS 21) could have a functional currency that is different from that of its 'parent'.* The Board decided that the functional currencies will always be the same, because it would be contradictory for an integral foreign operation that "carries on business as if it were an extension of the reporting enterprise's operations"† to operate in a primary economic environment different from its parent.

It follows that it is not necessary to translate the results and financial position of an   **BC7**
integral foreign operation when incorporating them into the financial statements of the parent—they will already be measured in the parent's functional currency. Furthermore, it is not necessary to distinguish between an integral foreign operation and a foreign entity. When a foreign operation's functional currency is different from that of its parent, it is a foreign entity, and the translation method in paragraphs 38-49 of the Standard applies.

The Board also decided that the principles in the previous version of IAS 21 for   **BC8**
distinguishing an integral foreign operation from a foreign entity are relevant in determining an operation's functional currency. Hence it incorporated these principles into the Standard in that context.

The Board agreed that the indicators in paragraph 9 are the primary indicators for   **BC9**
determining the functional currency and that paragraphs 10 and 11 are secondary. This is because the indicators in paragraphs 10 and 11 are not linked to the primary economic environment in which the entity operates but provide additional supporting evidence to determine an entity's functional currency.

PRESENTATION CURRENCY

A further issue is whether an entity should be permitted to present its financial   **BC10**
statements in a currency (or currencies) other than its functional currency. Some

---

*The term 'parent' is used broadly in this context to mean an entity that has a branch, associate or joint venture, as well as one with a subsidiary.

†IAS 21 (revised 1993), paragraph 24

believe it should not. They believe that the functional currency, being the currency of the primary economic environment in which the entity operates, most usefully portrays the economic effect of transactions and events on the entity. For a group that comprises operations with a number of functional currencies, they believe that the consolidated financial statements should be presented in the functional currency that management uses when controlling and monitoring the performance and financial position of the group. They also believe that allowing an entity to present its financial statements in more than one currency may confuse, rather than help, users of those financial statements. Supporters of this view believe that any presentation in a currency other than that described above should be regarded as a 'convenience translation' that is outside the scope of IFRSs.

BC11   Others believe that the choice of presentation currency should be limited, for example, to the functional currency of one of the substantive entities within a group. However, such a restriction might be easily overcome—an entity that wished to present its financial statements in a different currency might establish a substantive, but relatively small operation with that functional currency.

BC12   Still others believe that, given the rising trend towards globalisation, entities should be permitted to present their financial statements in any currency. They note that most large groups do not have a single functional currency, but rather comprise operations with a number of functional currencies. For such entities, they believe it is not clear which currency should be the presentation currency, or why one currency is preferable to another. They also point out that management may not use a single currency when controlling and monitoring the performance and financial position of such a group. In addition, they note that in some jurisdictions, entities are required to present their financial statements in the local currency, even when this is not the functional currency.* Hence, if IFRSs required the financial statements to be presented in the functional currency, some entities would have to present two sets of financial statements: financial statements that comply with IFRSs presented in the functional currency and financial statements that comply with local regulations presented in a different currency.

BC13   The Board was persuaded by the arguments in the previous paragraph. Accordingly, it decided that entities should be permitted to present their financial statements in any currency (or currencies).

BC14   The Board also clarified that the Standard does not prohibit the entity from providing, as supplementary information, a 'convenience translation'. Such a 'convenience translation' may display financial statements (or selected portions of financial statements) in a currency other than the presentation currency, as a convenience to some users. The 'convenience translation' may be prepared using a translation method other than that required by the Standard. These types of 'convenience translations' should be clearly identified as supplementary information to distinguish them from information required by IFRSs and translated in accordance with the Standard.

TRANSLATION METHOD

BC15   The Board debated which method should be used to translate financial statements from an entity's functional currency into a different presentation currency.

This includes entities operating in another country and, for example, publishing financial statements to comply with a listing requirement of that country.

The Board agreed that the translation method should not have the effect of sub- **BC16** stituting another currency for the functional currency. Put another way, presenting the financial statements in a different currency should not change the way in which the underlying items are measured. Rather, the translation method should merely express the underlying amounts, as measured in the functional currency, in a different currency.

Given this, the Board considered two possible translation methods. The first is to **BC17** translate all amounts (including comparatives) at the most recent closing rate. This method has several advantages: it is simple to apply; it does not generate any new gains and losses; and it does not change ratios such as return on assets. This method is supported by those who believe that the process of merely expressing amounts in a different currency should preserve the relationships among amounts as measured in the functional currency and, as such, should not lead to any new gains or losses.

The second method considered by the Board is the one that the previous version of **BC18** IAS 21 required for translating the financial statements of a foreign operation.* This method results in the same amounts in the presentation currency regardless of whether the financial statements of a foreign operation are:

(a)   first translated into the functional currency of another group entity (eg the parent) and then into the presentation currency, or
(b)   translated directly into the presentation currency.

This method avoids the need to decide the currency in which to express the financial **BC19** statements of a multinational group before they are translated into the presentation currency. As noted above, many large groups do not have a single functional currency, but comprise operations with a number of functional currencies. For such entities it is not clear which functional currency should be chosen in which to express amounts before they are translated into the presentation currency, or why one currency is preferable to another. In addition, this method produces the same amounts in the presentation currency for a standalone entity as for an identical subsidiary of a parent whose functional currency is the presentation currency.

The Board decided to require the second method, ie that the financial statements of **BC20** any entity (whether a stand-alone entity, a parent or an operation within a group) whose functional currency differs from the presentation currency used by the reporting entity are translated using the method set out in paragraphs 3849 of the Standard.

With respect to translation of comparative amounts, the Board adopted the **BC21** approach required by SIC-30 for:

(a)   an entity whose functional currency is not the currency of the hyperinflationary economy (assets and liabilities in the comparative balance sheet are translated at the closing rate at the date of that balance sheet and income and expenses in the comparative income statement are translated at exchange rates at the dates of the transactions); and
(b)   an entity whose functional currency is the currency of a hyperinflationary economy, and for which the comparative amounts are being translated into the currency of a hyperinflationary economy (both balance sheet and income statement items are translated at the closing rate of the most recent balance sheet presented).

This is to translate balance sheet items at the closing rate and income and expense items at actual (or average) rates, except for an entity whose functional currency is that of a hyperinflationary economy.

BC22   However, the Board decided not to adopt the SIC-30 approach for the translation of comparatives for an entity whose functional currency is the currency of a hyperinflationary economy, and for which the comparative amounts are being translated into a presentation currency of a nonhyperinflationary economy. The Board noted that in such a case, the SIC30 approach requires restating the comparative amounts from those shown in last year's financial statements for both the effects of inflation and for changes in exchange rates. If exchange rates fully reflect differing price levels between the two economies to which they relate, the SIC-30 approach will result in the same amounts for the comparatives as were reported as current year amounts in the prior year financial statements. Furthermore, the Board noted that in the prior year, the relevant amounts had been already expressed in the non-hyperinflationary presentation currency, and there was no reason to change them. For these reasons the Board decided to require that all comparative amounts are those presented in the prior year financial statements (ie there is no adjustment for either subsequent changes in the price level or subsequent changes in exchange rates).

BC23   The Board decided to incorporate into the Standard most of the disclosure requirements of SIC-30 *Reporting Currency—Translation from Measurement Currency to Presentation Currency* that apply when a different translation method is used or other supplementary information, such as an extract from the full financial statements, is displayed in a currency other than the functional currency (see paragraph 57 of the Standard). These disclosures enable users to distinguish information prepared in accordance with IFRSs from information that may be useful to users but is not the subject of IFRSs, and also tell users how the latter information has been prepared.

CAPITALISATION OF EXCHANGE DIFFERENCES

BC24   The previous version of IAS 21 allowed a limited choice of accounting for exchange differences that arise "from a severe devaluation or depreciation of a currency against which there is no practical means of hedging and that affects liabilities which cannot be settled and which arise directly on the recent acquisition of an asset".* The benchmark treatment was to recognise such exchange differences in profit or loss. The allowed alternative was to recognise them as an asset.

BC25   The Board noted that the allowed alternative (of recognition as an asset) was not in accordance with the *Framework for the Preparation and Presentation of Financial Statements* because exchange losses do not meet the definition of an asset.† Moreover, recognition of exchange losses as an asset is neither allowed nor required by any liaison standard-setter, so its deletion would improve convergence. Finally, in many cases when the conditions for recognition as an asset are met, the asset would be restated in accordance with IAS 29 *Financial Reporting in Hyperinflationary Economies*.‡ Thus, to the extent that an exchange loss reflects hyperinflation, this effect is taken into account by IAS 29. For all of these reasons, the Board removed the allowed alternative treatment and the related SIC Interpretation is superseded.

IAS 21 (revised 1993), paragraph 21

†*ASB footnote:* *The equivalent document in the UK and the Republic of Ireland to the IASB's* Framework for the Preparation and Presentation of Financial Statements *is the* Statement of Principles for Financial Reporting. *Exchange losses do not meet the* Statement of Principles' *asset definition either.*

‡*ASB footnote:* *IAS 29 is being implemented in the UK and the Republic of Ireland at the same time as this standard as FRS 24 (IAS 29)* Financial Reporting in Hyperinflationary Economies.

Net investment in a foreign operation

The principle in paragraph 32 is that exchange differences arising on a monetary item   **BC25A**
that is, in substance, part of the reporting entity's net investment in a foreign
operation are initially recognised in a separate component of equity in the consolidated financial statements of the reporting entity. Among the revisions to IAS 21
made in 2003 was the provision of guidance on this principle that required the
monetary item to be denominated in the functional currency of either the reporting
entity or the foreign operation. The previous version of IAS 21 did not include such
guidance.

The requirements can be illustrated by the following example. Parent P owns 100 per   **BC25B**
cent of Subsidiary S. Parent P has a functional currency of UK sterling. Subsidiary S
has a functional currency of Mexican pesos. Parent P grants a loan of 100 US dollars
to Subsidiary S, for which settlement is neither planned nor likely to occur in the
foreseeable future. IAS 21 (as revised in 2003) requires the exchange differences
arising on the loan to be recognised in profit or loss in the consolidated financial
statements of Parent P, whereas those differences would be recognised initially in
equity in the consolidated financial statements of Parent P, if the loan were to be
denominated in sterling or Mexican pesos.

After the revised IAS 21 was issued in 2003, constituents raised the following   **BC25C**
concerns:

(a)   It is common practice for a monetary item that forms part of an entity's
      investment in a foreign operation to be denominated in a currency that is not
      the functional currency of either the reporting entity or the foreign operation.
      An example is a monetary item denominated in a currency that is more readily
      convertible than the local domestic currency of the foreign operation.
(b)   An investment in a foreign operation denominated in a currency that is not the
      functional currency of the reporting entity or the foreign operation does not
      expose the group to a greater foreign currency exchange difference than arises
      when the investment is denominated in the functional currency of the reporting
      entity or the foreign operation. It simply results in exchange differences arising
      in the foreign operation's individual financial statements and the reporting
      entity's separate financial statements.
(c)   It is not clear whether the term 'reporting entity' in paragraph 32 should be
      interpreted as the single entity or the group comprising a parent and all its
      subsidiaries. As a result, constituents questioned whether the monetary item
      must be transacted between the foreign operation and the reporting entity, or
      whether it could be transacted between the foreign operation and any member
      of the consolidated group, ie the reporting entity or any of its subsidiaries.

The Board noted that the nature of the monetary item referred to in paragraph 15 is   **BC25D**
similar to an equity investment in a foreign operation, ie settlement of the monetary
item is neither planned nor likely to occur in the foreseeable future. Therefore, the
principle in paragraph 32 to recognise exchange differences arising on a monetary
item initially in a separate component of equity effectively results in the monetary
item being accounted for in the same way as an equity investment in the foreign
operation when consolidated financial statements are prepared. The Board concluded that the accounting treatment in the consolidated financial statements should
not be dependent on the currency in which the monetary item is denominated, nor on
which entity within the group conducts the transaction with the foreign operation.

Accordingly, in 2005 the Board decided to amend IAS 21. The amendment requires   **BC25E**
exchange differences arising on a monetary item that forms part of a reporting

entity's net investment in a foreign operation to be recognised initially in a separate component of equity in the consolidated financial statements. This requirement applies irrespective of the currency of the monetary item and of whether the monetary item results from a transaction with the reporting entity or any of its subsidiaries.

BC25F   The Board also proposed amending IAS 21 to clarify that an investment in a foreign operation made by an associate of the reporting entity is not part of the reporting entity's net investment in that foreign operation. Respondents to the exposure draft disagreed with this proposal. Many respondents said that the proposed amendment added a detailed rule that was not required because the principle in paragraph 15 was clear. In redeliberations, the Board agreed with those comments and decided not to proceed with that proposed amendment.*

GOODWILL AND FAIR VALUE ADJUSTMENTS

BC26   The previous version of IAS 21 allowed a choice of translating goodwill and fair value adjustments to assets and liabilities that arise on the acquisition of a foreign entity at (a) the closing rate or (b) the historical transaction rate.

BC27   The Board agreed that, conceptually, the correct treatment depends on whether goodwill and fair value adjustments are part of:

(a)   the assets and liabilities of the acquired entity (which would imply translating them at the closing rate); or

(b)   the assets and liabilities of the parent (which would imply translating them at the historical rate).

BC28   The Board agreed that fair value adjustments clearly relate to the identifiable assets and liabilities of the acquired entity and should therefore be translated at the closing rate.

BC29   Goodwill is more complex, partly because it is measured as a residual. In addition, the Board noted that difficult issues can arise when the acquired entity comprises businesses that have different functional currencies (eg if the acquired entity is a multinational group). The Board discussed how to assess any resulting goodwill for impairment and, in particular, whether the goodwill would need to be 'pushed down' to the level of each different functional currency or could be accounted for and assessed at a higher level.

BC30   One view is that when the parent acquires a multinational operation comprising businesses with many different functional currencies, any goodwill may be treated as an asset of the parent/acquirer and tested for impairment at a consolidated level. Those who support this view believe that, in economic terms, the goodwill is an asset of the parent because it is part of the acquisition price paid by the parent. Thus, they believe, it would be incorrect to allocate the goodwill to the many acquired businesses and translate it into their various functional currencies. Rather, the goodwill, being treated as an asset of the parent, is not exposed to foreign currency risks, and translation differences associated with it should not be recognised. In addition, they believe that such goodwill should be tested for impairment at a consolidated level. Under this view, allocating or 'pushing down' the goodwill to a lower level, such as each different functional currency within the acquired foreign operation, would not serve any purpose.

Editor's note: Paragraphs BC25A to BC25F added by 'Amendment to FRS 23 (IAS 21) The Effects of Changes in Foreign Exchange Rates – Net Investment in a Foreign Operation'.

Others take a different view. They believe that the goodwill is part of the parent's net investment in the acquired entity. In their view, goodwill should be treated no differently from other assets of the acquired entity, in particular intangible assets, because a significant part of the goodwill is likely to comprise intangible assets that do not qualify for separate recognition. They also note that goodwill arises only because of the investment in the foreign entity and has no existence apart from that entity. Lastly, they point out that when the acquired entity comprises a number of businesses with different functional currencies, the cash flows that support the continued recognition of goodwill are generated in those different functional currencies.

BC31

The Board was persuaded by the reasons set out in the preceding paragraph and decided that goodwill is treated as an asset of the foreign operation and translated at the closing rate. Consequently, goodwill should be allocated to the level of each functional currency of the acquired foreign operation. This means that the level to which goodwill is allocated for foreign currency translation purposes may be different from the level at which the goodwill is tested for impairment. Entities follow the requirements in IAS 36 *Impairment of Assets* to determine the level at which goodwill is tested for impairment.*

BC32

*ASB footnote: The equivalent standard in the UK and the Republic of Ireland to IAS 36 is FRS 11 Impairment of fixed assets and goodwill.

Financial Reporting Standard 24 embodies IAS 29 'Financial Reporting in Hyperinflationary Economies' and some amendments to that standard adopted for entities subject to UK accounting standards.

The Statement of Standard Accounting Practice in FRS 24 is set out in paragraphs 1-42. All the paragraphs have equal authority. Paragraphs in bold type state the main principles.

The Statement of Standard Accounting Practice should be read in the context of the Accounting Standards Board's 'Foreword to Accounting Standards' and 'Statement of Principles for Financial Reporting'.

FRS 24
(IAS 29) Financial reporting in hyperinflationary economies

(Issued December 2004)

Contents

Preface by the Accounting Standards Board

a   This Financial Reporting Standard (FRS) has the effect, for those entities that are applying it, of:

- implementing in the UK and the Republic of Ireland the International Accounting Standards Board's (IASB's) International Accounting Standard (IAS) 29 *Financial Reporting in Hyperinflationary Economies*; and
- withdrawing the existing UK requirements on the subject, which are contained in UITF Abstract 9 *Accounting for operations in hyper-inflationary economies*.

UITF Abstract 9 remains in place unamended for entities not applying this FRS.

b   This FRS is, in effect, part of a package of UK standards comprising:

- this FRS,
- FRS 23 (IAS 21) *The Effects of Changes in Foreign Exchange Rates*,
- the disclosure requirements of FRS 25 (IAS 32) *Financial Instruments: Disclosure and Presentation*,* and
- FRS 26 (IAS 39) *Financial Instruments: Measurement*.

c   The applicability of the package of standards is determined by reference to FRS 26's application.

- For accounting periods beginning on or after 1 January 2005, FRS 26—and therefore the entire package of standards listed above, including this FRS—applies to all listed entities preparing their financial statements in accordance with UK requirements—including listed parent undertakings preparing individual financial statements in accordance with those requirements.† Other entities are permitted to apply the entire package of standards from that date, although entities are not permitted to apply some of the standards in the package but not others—except that FRS 25 exempts certain entities from applying its disclosure requirements and also permits entities to apply those disclosure requirements in advance of the other standards in the package if they wish.
- For accounting periods beginning on or after 1 January 2006, unlisted entities using accounting policies that are consistent with the fair value measurement rules incorporated into the Companies Act 1985 (or equivalent legislation) to implement the Fair Value Directive will also be required to comply with FRS 26—and therefore the entire package of standards including this one.

d   The Accounting Standards Board (the Board) will in due course be issuing proposals for the application of the standards to other unlisted entities.

e   The text of IAS 29 contains various references to other International Financial Reporting Standards (IFRSs). In the FRS those references have been amended where necessary to enable the Standard to be applied in a UK context. The text has also been amended to remove the material relating to current cost financial statements, because that material is not relevant in the UK. The Board believes that those amendments do not change the basic requirements of IAS 29 in any way.

f   In all other respects the FRS is identical to IAS 29.

---

*The other requirements of FRS 25 apply to all entities—regardless of whether they are listed or unlisted—for accounting periods beginning on or after 1 January 2005.

†For this purpose a listed entity is an entity that has shares or debt admitted to trading on a regulated market in the EU.

International Accounting Standard 29 (IAS 29)

Financial Reporting in Hyperinflationary Economies

SCOPE

This Standard applies to all financial statements that are intended to give a true and fair   **1**
view of a reporting entity's financial position and profit or loss (or income or expenditure) and which are the financial statements of a reporting entity whose functional currency is the currency of a hyperinflationary economy, except that:

(a) *it should not be applied to any financial statements to which FRS 26 (IAS 39)* **Financial Instruments: Recognition and Measurement** *has not also been applied;* *and*

(b) *entities applying the* **Financial Reporting Standard for Smaller Entities** *(FRSSE)* *currently applicable are exempt from the Standard.**

For accounting periods beginning on or after 1 January 2005, FRS 26—and there-   **1A**
fore this Standard—will apply to listed entities; other entities have the option of applying the Standard, though only if they also apply FRS 26 (and certain other Standards). From 2006, unlisted entities using accounting policies that are consistent with the fair value measurement rules incorporated into the Companies Act or equivalent legislation will also be required to apply FRS 26 and, therefore, this Standard.

In a hyperinflationary economy, reporting of operating results and financial position   **2**
in the local currency without restatement is not useful. Money loses purchasing power at such a rate that comparison of amounts from transactions and other events that have occurred at different times, even within the same accounting period, is misleading.

This Standard does not establish an absolute rate at which hyperinflation is deemed   **3**
to arise. It is a matter of judgement when restatement of financial statements in accordance with this Standard becomes necessary. Hyperinflation is indicated by characteristics of the economic environment of a country which include, but are not limited to, the following:

(a)   the general population prefers to keep its wealth in non-monetary assets or in a relatively stable foreign currency. Amounts of local currency held are immediately invested to maintain purchasing power;

(b)   the general population regards monetary amounts not in terms of the local currency but in terms of a relatively stable foreign currency. Prices may be quoted in that currency;

(c)   sales and purchases on credit take place at prices that compensate for the expected loss of purchasing power during the credit period, even if the period is short;

(d)   interest rates, wages and prices are linked to a price index; and

(e)   the cumulative inflation rate over three years is approaching, or exceeds, 100%.

It is preferable that all entities that report in the currency of the same hyperinfla-   **4**
tionary economy apply this Standard from the same date. Nevertheless, this Standard applies to the financial statements of any entity from the beginning of the reporting period in which it identifies the existence of hyperinflation in the country in whose currency it reports.

*Editor's note: Reference to FRS 26 altered by amendments to FRS 26, to reflect the change in its title.

THE RESTATEMENT OF FINANCIAL STATEMENTS

5   Prices change over time as the result of various specific or general political, economic and social forces. Specific forces such as changes in supply and demand and technological changes may cause individual prices to increase or decrease significantly and independently of each other. In addition, general forces may result in changes in the general level of prices and therefore in the general purchasing power of money.

6   In most countries, financial statements are prepared on the historical cost basis of accounting without regard either to changes in the general level of prices or to increases in specific prices of assets held, except to the extent that property, plant and equipment and investments may be revalued. Some entities, however, present financial statements that are based on a current cost approach that reflects the effects of changes in the specific prices of assets held.

7   In a hyperinflationary economy, financial statements, whether they are based on a historical cost approach or a current cost approach, are useful only if they are expressed in terms of the measuring unit current at the balance sheet date. As a result, this Standard applies to the financial statements of entities reporting in the currency of a hyperinflationary economy. Presentation of the information required by this Standard as a supplement to unrestated financial statements is not permitted. Furthermore, separate presentation of the financial statements before restatement is discouraged.

8   *The financial statements of an entity whose functional currency is the currency of a hyperinflationary economy shall be stated in terms of the measuring unit current at the balance sheet date. The required corresponding figures for the previous period and any information in respect of earlier periods shall also be stated in terms of the measuring unit current at the balance sheet date. For the purpose of presenting comparative amounts in a different presentation currency, paragraphs 42(b) and 43 of FRS 23 (IAS 21)* **The Effects of Changes in Foreign Exchange Rates** *apply.*

9   *The gain or loss on the net monetary position shall be included in profit or loss and separately disclosed.*

10   The restatement of financial statements in accordance with this Standard requires the application of certain procedures as well as judgement. The consistent application of these procedures and judgements from period to period is more important than the precise accuracy of the resulting amounts included in the restated financial statements.

Historical Cost Financial Statements

Balance Sheet

11   Balance sheet amounts not already expressed in terms of the measuring unit current at the balance sheet date are restated by applying a general price index.

12   Monetary items are not restated because they are already expressed in terms of the monetary unit current at the balance sheet date. Monetary items are money held and items to be received or paid in money.

13   Assets and liabilities linked by agreement to changes in prices, such as index linked bonds and loans, are adjusted in accordance with the agreement in order to ascertain

the amount outstanding at the balance sheet date. These items are carried at this adjusted amount in the restated balance sheet.

All other assets and liabilities are non-monetary. Some non-monetary items are **14** carried at amounts current at the balance sheet date, such as net realisable value and market value, so they are not restated. All other non-monetary assets and liabilities are restated.

Most non-monetary items are carried at cost or cost less depreciation; hence they are **15** expressed at amounts current at their date of acquisition. The restated cost, or cost less depreciation, of each item is determined by applying to its historical cost and accumulated depreciation the change in a general price index from the date of acquisition to the balance sheet date. Hence, property, plant and equipment, investments, inventories of raw materials and merchandise, goodwill, patents, trademarks and similar assets are restated from the dates of their purchase. Inventories of partly-finished and finished goods are restated from the dates on which the costs of purchase and of conversion were incurred.

Detailed records of the acquisition dates of items of property, plant and equipment **16** may not be available or capable of estimation. In these rare circumstances, it may be necessary, in the first period of application of this Standard, to use an independent professional assessment of the value of the items as the basis for their restatement.

A general price index may not be available for the periods for which the restatement **17** of property, plant and equipment is required by this Standard. In these circumstances, it may be necessary to use an estimate based, for example, on the movements in the exchange rate between the functional currency and a relatively stable foreign currency.

Some non-monetary items are carried at amounts current at dates other than that of **18** acquisition or that of the balance sheet, for example property, plant and equipment that has been revalued at some earlier date. In these cases, the carrying amounts are restated from the date of the revaluation.

The restated amount of a non-monetary item is reduced, in accordance with **19** appropriate Standards, when it exceeds the amount recoverable from the item's future use (including sale or other disposal). Hence, in such cases, restated amounts of property, plant and equipment, goodwill, patents and trademarks are reduced to recoverable amount, restated amounts of inventories are reduced to net realisable value and restated amounts of current investments are reduced to market value.

An investee that is accounted for under the equity method may report in the currency **20** of a hyperinflationary economy. The balance sheet and income statement of such an investee are restated in accordance with this Standard in order to calculate the investor's share of its net assets and results of operations. Where the restated financial statements of the investee are expressed in a foreign currency they are translated at closing rates.

The impact of inflation is usually recognised in borrowing costs. It is not appropriate **21** both to restate the capital expenditure financed by borrowing and to capitalise that part of the borrowing costs that compensates for the inflation during the same period. This part of the borrowing costs is recognised as an expense in the period in which the costs are incurred.

An entity may acquire assets under an arrangement that permits it to defer payment **22** without incurring an explicit interest charge. Where it is impracticable to impute the amount of interest, such assets are restated from the payment date and not the date of purchase.

23   [Deleted]

24   At the beginning of the first period of application of this Standard, the components of owners' equity, except retained earnings and any revaluation surplus, are restated by applying a general price index from the dates the components were contributed or otherwise arose. Any revaluation surplus that arose in previous periods is eliminated. Restated retained earnings are derived from all the other amounts in the restated balance sheet.

25   At the end of the first period and in subsequent periods, all components of owners' equity are restated by applying a general price index from the beginning of the period or the date of contribution, if later. The movements for the period in owners' equity are disclosed in accordance with FRS 3 *Reporting Financial Performance*.

Income Statement

26   This Standard requires that all items in the income statement are expressed in terms of the measuring unit current at the balance sheet date. Therefore all amounts need to be restated by applying the change in the general price index from the dates when the items of income and expenses were initially recorded in the financial statements.

Gain or Loss on Net Monetary Position

27   In a period of inflation, an entity holding an excess of monetary assets over monetary liabilities loses purchasing power and an entity with an excess of monetary liabilities over monetary assets gains purchasing power to the extent the assets and liabilities are not linked to a price level. This gain or loss on the net monetary position may be derived as the difference resulting from the restatement of non-monetary assets, owners' equity and income statement items and the adjustment of index linked assets and liabilities. The gain or loss may be estimated by applying the change in a general price index to the weighted average for the period of the difference between monetary assets and monetary liabilities.

28   The gain or loss on the net monetary position is included in net income. The adjustment to those assets and liabilities linked by agreement to changes in prices made in accordance with paragraph 13 is offset against the gain or loss on net monetary position. Other income statement items, such as interest income and expense, and foreign exchange differences related to invested or borrowed funds, are also associated with the net monetary position. Although such items are separately disclosed, it may be helpful if they are presented together with the gain or loss on net monetary position in the income statement.

29-31   [*ASB note:* Deleted]

Taxes

32   The restatement of financial statements in accordance with this Standard may give rise to differences between the carrying amount of individual assets and liabilities in the balance sheet and their tax bases. Consequential timing differences are accounted for in accordance with FRS 19 *Deferred Tax*.

Cash Flow Statement

This Standard requires that all items in the cash flow statement are expressed in   **33**
terms of the measuring unit current at the balance sheet date.

Corresponding Figures

Corresponding figures for the previous reporting period, whether they were based on   **34**
a historical cost approach or a current cost approach, are restated by applying a
general price index so that the comparative financial statements are presented in
terms of the measuring unit current at the end of the reporting period. Information
that is disclosed in respect of earlier periods is also expressed in terms of the measuring unit current at the end of the reporting period. For the purpose of presenting
comparative amounts in a different presentation currency, paragraphs 42(b) and 43
of FRS 23 apply.

Consolidated Financial Statements

A parent that reports in the currency of a hyperinflationary economy may have   **35**
subsidiaries that also report in the currencies of hyperinflationary economies.
The financial statements of any such subsidiary need to be restated by applying a
general price index of the country in whose currency it reports before they are
included in the consolidated financial statements issued by its parent. Where such a
subsidiary is a foreign subsidiary, its restated financial statements are translated at
closing rates. The financial statements of subsidiaries that do not report in the
currencies of hyperinflationary economies are dealt with in accordance with FRS 23.

If financial statements with different reporting dates are consolidated, all items,   **36**
whether non-monetary or monetary, need to be restated into the measuring unit
current at the date of the consolidated financial statements.

Selection and Use of the General Price Index

The restatement of financial statements in accordance with this Standard requires the   **37**
use of a general price index that reflects changes in general purchasing power. It is
preferable that all entities that report in the currency of the same economy use the
same index.

ECONOMIES CEASING TO BE HYPERINFLATIONARY

When an economy ceases to be hyperinflationary and an entity discontinues the pre-   **38**
paration and presentation of financial statements prepared in accordance with this
Standard, it shall treat the amounts expressed in the measuring unit current at the end
of the previous reporting period as the basis for the carrying amounts in its subsequent
financial statements.

DISCLOSURES

The following disclosures shall be made: **39**

(a)   the fact that the financial statements and the corresponding figures for previous
periods have been restated for the changes in the general purchasing power of the
functional currency and, as a result, are stated in terms of the measuring unit
current at the balance sheet date;

(b)   whether the financial statements are based on a historical cost approach or a current cost approach; and

(c)   the identity and level of the price index at the balance sheet date and the movement in the index during the current and the previous reporting period.

40   The disclosures required by this Standard are needed to make clear the basis of dealing with the effects of inflation in the financial statements. They are also intended to provide other information necessary to understand that basis and the resulting amounts.

EFFECTIVE DATE

41   *An entity shall apply this Standard for accounting periods in which they also apply FRS 26 but not in any other accounting period.*

41A   Unless and until an entity applies FRS 26 it is not permitted to adopt this Standard; and if it applies FRS 26 it must also apply this Standard. Listed entities are required to apply FRS 26 for accounting periods beginning on or after 1 January 2005 (and other entities are permitted to apply it from that date). As explained in paragraph 1A, certain unlisted entities are required to apply FRS 26 for accounting periods beginning on or after 1 January 2006.

WITHDRAWAL OF OTHER PRONOUNCEMENTS

42   *For entities applying this Standard, it supersedes UITF Abstract 9* Accounting for operations in hyper-inflationary economies.

Adoption of the standard

APPROVAL OF IAS 21 BY THE INTERNATIONAL ACCOUNTING STANDARDS BOARD

[*ASB note:*   IAS 29 was originally approved by the International Accounting Standards Committee, the IASB's predecessor body, in 1989. It was subsequently reformatted and, in 2001, was adopted by the IASB.]

ADOPTION OF FRS 24 BY THE ACCOUNTING STANDARDS BOARD

Financial Reporting Standard 24 (IAS 29) *Financial Reporting in Hyperinflationary Economies* was approved for issue by the ten members of the Accounting Standards Board.

Ian Mackintosh   Chairman
Andrew Lennard   Technical Director
Michael Ashley
Douglas Flint
Anthony Good
Roger Marshall
Isobel Sharp
John Smith
Jonathan Symonds
Peter Westlake

Notes on the standard's application in the UK and the Republic of Ireland

FRED 24

N1   In recent years, the Accounting Standards Board (the Board) has been placing increasing emphasis on the convergence aspects of its standard-setting role: listed entities in the UK and the Republic of Ireland preparing consolidated financial statements will from 2005 be required to prepare those statements in accordance with EU-adopted international accounting standards (International Financial Reporting Standards or IFRSs) and, although entities can continue to prepare other financial statements in accordance with the requirements of the UK and the Republic of Ireland, the Board's view is that there can be no case for the use of two sets of wholly different standards in the medium term.

N2   As part of this convergence strategy, the Board issued in May 2002 FRED 24 *The Effects of Changes in Foreign Exchange Rates & Financial Reporting in Hyperinflationary Economies*. FRED 24 proposed replacing the existing UK material on accounting for foreign currency (set out in SSAP 20 *Foreign currency translation*) and accounting in inflationary economies (set out in UITF Abstract 9 *Accounting for operations in hyper-inflationary economies*) with two new UK standards based on IAS 21 *The Effects of Changes in Foreign Exchange Rates* and IAS 29 *Financial Reporting in Hyperinflationary Economies*.

N3   Those responding to FRED 24 were broadly supportive of the Board's strategy to converge its standards in this area with those of the IASB, and there was in particular relatively little negative comment on the proposal to implement IAS 29 in the UK and the Republic of Ireland. The issue raised by most of those who did comment on the proposal concerned the main proposed change:

(a)   UITF 9 specifies two methods of eliminating the distortions caused by hyper-inflation—the current price level approach and the stable currency approach*—but also permits entities to adopt an alternative approach if neither of those methods is considered appropriate.

(b)   IAS 29, on the other hand, is much more prescriptive in that it requires use of the current price level approach.

N4   Some respondents thought that the proposed new standard should be amended to incorporate the stable currency approach. Some argued that this should be done because the stable currency approach was better than (or as good as) the current price level approach, and some argued that some flexibility was needed because it would not always be practicable to apply IAS 29's current price level approach.

N5   The Board noted that IAS 29 has been in place for fifteen years and has apparently proved workable. It was therefore unconvinced that an amendment was needed for practicability reasons. It also noted that, having decided to adopt a convergence objective, it is difficult to justify an amendment to an international accounting standard on the grounds that some other approach is better. It therefore decided not to amend the IAS 29 requirements in the way suggested.

The current price level approach involves adjusting the functional currency financial statements to reflect current price levels before the translation process is undertaken. The stable currency approach involves using a relatively stable currency as the functional currency of the relevant foreign operation.

FRED 24 proposed that a UK standard based on IAS 29 should be implemented for **N6** all entities in 2004. That proposal was however based on the assumption that a UK standard based on the revised version of IAS 21 that the IASB was then developing would also be implemented in 2004 for all entities. It also assumed that the UK standard based on IAS 21 would be supplemented in some way by a hedge accounting standard based on the principles underlying the hedge accounting requirements in the revised version of IAS 39 that the IASB was developing. However, the revised versions of IASs 21 and 39 were not issued until December 2003, making their application in the UK for 2004 impracticable. In any event, as explained more fully in the UK version of IAS 21 which has now been issued (FRS 23), the Board decided to change its approach to the implementation of IAS 21 in the light of the comments received in response to FRED 24. IAS 21 will now be implemented in the UK in tandem with IAS 39—in other words, all entities applying the UK version of IAS 39 (ie FRS 26) must also apply FRS 23 and an entity that is not applying FRS 26 is not permitted to apply FRS 23.

The Board has also decided that IAS 29 should be implemented in the UK in tandem **N7** with FRS 23.

The Board further decided that it should be the implementation of FRS 26 that **N8** should determine when the other standards are implemented. In other words, because all listed entities are required to apply FRS 26 for all accounting periods beginning on or after 1 January 2005, all listed entities will be required to apply FRS 23 and this standard from that date as well. Similarly, certain unlisted entities will be required to apply FRS 26 for all accounting periods beginning on or after 1 January 2006, so they will also be required to apply FRS 23 and this standard from that date.

Changes to existing UK requirements

As mentioned already, the existing UK requirements on accounting for operations in **N9** hyperinflationary economies are set out in UITF Abstract 9. The main differences between that Abstract and FRS 24 are as follows:

(a) The scope of FRS 24 is wider than UITF 9. UITF 9 applies only to "group financial statements". FRS 24, on the other hand, also deals with the accounting to be adopted in individual financial statements when the entity has a functional currency that is the currency of a hyperinflationary economy.

(b) As explained in paragraph N3 above, UITF 9 is considerably less prescriptive than IAS 29 as to the method to be used to eliminate the distortions caused by hyperinflation.

(c) FRS 24 is in other ways also more detailed and more prescriptive than UITF 9. FRS 24's disclosure requirements are also a little more extensive.

Financial Reporting Standard 25 embodies IAS 32 'Financial Instruments: Disclosure and Presentation' and some amendments to that standard adopted for entities subject to UK accounting standards.

The Statement of Standard Accounting Practice in FRS 25 is set out in paragraphs 1 to 100D and the application guidance set out in the appendix. All the paragraphs have equal authority. Paragraphs in bold type state the main principles.

Accompanying the Statement of Standard Accounting Practice is the basis for the conclusions reached in the Statement and illustrative examples. These do not form part of the Statement.

The Statement of Standard Accounting Practice should be read in the context of its objective as stated in paragraphs 1-3, the Basis for Conclusions set out in paragraphs BC1-BC49, and the Accounting Standards Board's 'Foreword to Accounting Standards' and 'Statement of Principles for Financial Reporting'.

FRS 25
(IAS 32) Financial instruments: Presentation*

(Issued December 2004)

Contents

*Editor's note: The disclosure requirements of FRS 25 are replaced by FRS 29 with effect for accounting periods beginning on or after 1 January 2007.

Preface by the Accounting Standards Board

This Financial Reporting Standard (FRS) has the effect of implementing the **a**
International Accounting Standards Board's (IASB's) International Accounting
Standard (IAS) 32 'Financial Instruments: Disclosure and Presentation' in the UK
and the Republic of Ireland for entities not preparing their financial statements in
accordance with international accounting standards adopted pursuant to the Regulation of the European Parliament and of the Council on the Application of
International Accounting Standards.

IAS 32 sets out requirements for the presentation of, and disclosures relating to, **b**
financial instruments. FRS 25 is based on the text of IAS 32 as at 31 March 2004,
incorporating the revised version of IAS 32 issued by the IASB in December 2003
and includes amendments made by IFRS 4 'Insurance Contracts'.

The presentation requirements of FRS 25 are applicable to all entities other than **c**
entities applying the FRSSE, and apply for accounting periods beginning on or after
1 January 2005, corresponding to the effective date of amendments to the Companies
Act 1985 implementing the EU Modernisation Directive*; early adoption is not
permitted for this part of the standard.

The disclosure requirements of the FRS are, in effect, part of a package of UK **d**
standards comprising

- the disclosure requirements of this FRS,
- FRS 23 (IAS 21) *The Effects of Changes in Foreign Exchange Rates*, and
- FRS 24 (IAS 29) *Financial Reporting in Hyperinflationary Economies*,
- FRS 26 (IAS 39) *Financial Instruments: Measurement*.

Listed entities preparing their financial statements in accordance with UK and **e**
Republic of Ireland requirements—including listed parent undertakings preparing
individual financial statements in accordance with those requirements—are required
to comply with the entire package of standards for accounting periods beginning on
or after 1 January 2005.† Other entities are permitted to apply the entire package of
standards from that date, although entities are not permitted to apply some of the
standards in the package but not others—except that FRS 25 exempts certain entities
from applying its disclosure requirements and also permits entities to apply those
disclosure requirements in advance of the other standards in the package if they wish.

For accounting periods beginning on or after 1 January 2006, unlisted entities using **f**
accounting policies that are consistent with the fair value measurement rules incorporated into the Companies Act to implement the EU Fair Value Directive‡ will also
be required to comply with the entire package of standards.

The Accounting Standards Board (the Board) will in due course be issuing proposals **g**
for the application of the standards to other unlisted entities.

**Directive 2003/51/EC, implemented by The Companies Act 1985 (International Accounting Standards and
Other Accounting Amendments) Regulations 2004; similar amendments are to be made to the equivalent
Northern Ireland and Republic of Ireland legislation.*

*†For this purpose a listed entity is an entity that has shares or debt admitted to trading on a regulated market in
the EU.*

*‡Section D of Schedule 4, and equivalents in other schedules, inserted by the Companies Act 1985 (International
Accounting Standards and Other Accounting Amendments) Regulations 2004, and equivalent Northern Ireland
and Republic of Ireland legislation.*

h   The Board expects in due course to issue revised disclosure requirements, as proposed in FRED 33 and the IASB's ED 7 'Financial Instruments: Disclosures', amending those set out in FRS 25. It is envisaged that these revised disclosures would be required from 2007, but entities would have the option to adopt them early in place of the requirements of FRS 25.

i   The requirements of FRS 25 are identical to the revised IAS 32 with the following exceptions in addition to the differences in scope and implementation date set out above:

- disclosures are not required for certain subsidiaries where at least 90 per cent of the voting rights are held within the group, and parent companies in their single-entity financial statements;
- the Board has added certain requirements for those entities not applying the requirements of FRS 26 (IAS 39) 'Financial Instruments: Measurement' but who wish to comply with the disclosure requirements of this standard voluntarily;
- *
- material relating to the classification of liabilities as current or non-current has been incorporated from IAS 1 'Presentation of Financial Statements';
- the Board has added transitional provisions from IFRS 1 'First-time Adoption of International Financial Reporting Standards' allowing entities not to separate elements of equity for compound instruments no longer in outstanding; the ASB has not included transitional provisions permitting non-restatement of comparatives in relation to the presentation requirements of the FRS; and
- the Board has also added transitional provisions from IFRS 1 permitting entities that apply this standard for accounting periods commencing before 1 January 2007 not to restate comparatives to comply with this standard.

j   The text of IAS 32 contains various references to other International Financial Reporting Standards (IFRSs). In FRS 25 those references have been amended where necessary to enable the standard to be applied in a UK context. The ASB believes that those amendments do not change the requirements of IAS 32 in any way.

k   The FRS withdraws parts of FRS 4 'Capital Instruments'. For convenience, the text of FRS 4 following these amendments is set out in the appendix to the FRS.

l   The FRS also has the effect of withdrawing FRS 13 for those entities complying with the disclosure requirements of the FRS. It also supersedes UITF Abstract 33 'Obligations in capital instruments' and Abstract 37 'Purchases and sales of own shares'. Consequential amendments to other UK standards are also made.

m   IAS 32 sets out amendments to other IFRSs. These amendments are not relevant in a UK context and have not been included in FRS 25.

n   In October 2005 the Board amended FRS 25 to incorporate consequential amendments made to IAS 32 by the IASB in amendments to IAS 39:

- The Fair Value Option (June 2005)
- Financial Guarantee Contracts and Credit Insurance (August 2005).

Editor's note: Bullet point deleted by amendments to FRS 26 for those entities applying the revised version of FRS 26 which also deals with derecognition requirements.

The Board did not include certain disclosure requirements relating to the designation   o
of financial assets and financial liabilities as at fair value through profit and loss
account as it does not consider them to be necessary.*

In April 2006 the Board amended FRS 26 to include the IAS 39 material on   p
recognition and derecognition into the Standard. Accordingly, on implementation of
this amendment the corresponding disclosure requirements of IAS 32 are implemented in FRS 25. Those new disclosure requirements replace disclosures required
for financial assets and liabilities by FRS 5 'Reporting the Substance of Transactions'. These amendments are effective for accounting periods on or after 1 January
2007, with earlier adoption permitted.†

__Editor's note:__ Paragraph n and o added in October 2005.

†*__Editor's note:__ Paragraph p added in April 2006.*

Introduction

Reasons for Revising IAS 32*

IN1   International Accounting Standard 32 *Financial Instruments: Disclosure and Presentation* (IAS 32) replaces IAS 32 *Financial Instruments: Disclosure and Presentation*† (revised in 2000), and should be applied for annual periods beginning on or after 1 January 2005. Earlier application is permitted. The Standard also replaces the following Interpretations and draft Interpretation:

- SIC-5 *Classification of Financial Instruments—Contingent Settlement Provisions*;
- SIC-16 *Share Capital—Reacquired Own Equity Instruments (Treasury Shares)*;
- SIC-17 *Equity—Costs of an Equity Transaction*; and
- draft SIC-D34 *Financial Instruments—Instruments or Rights Redeemable by the Holder*.

IN2   The International Accounting Standards Board developed this revised IAS 32 as part of its project to improve IAS 32 and IAS 39 *Financial Instruments: Recognition and Measurement*. The objective of the project was to reduce complexity by clarifying and adding guidance, eliminating internal inconsistencies and incorporating into the Standards elements of Standing Interpretations Committee (SIC) Interpretations and IAS 39 implementation guidance published by the Implementation Guidance Committee (IGC).

IN3   For IAS 32, the Board's main objective was a limited revision to provide additional guidance on selected matters—such as the measurement of the components of a compound financial instrument on initial recognition, and the classification of derivatives based on an entity's own shares—and to locate all disclosures relating to financial instruments in one Standard.‡ The Board did not reconsider the fundamental approach to the presentation and disclosure of financial instruments contained in IAS 32.

The Main Changes

IN4   The main changes from the previous version of IAS 32 are described below.

Scope

IN5   The scope of IAS 32 has, where appropriate, been conformed to the scope of IAS 39.

Principle

IN6   In summary, when an issuer determines whether a financial instrument is a financial liability or an equity instrument, the instrument is an equity instrument if, and only if, both conditions (a) and (b) are met.

ASB footnote: Although references to specific IFRSs have been amended in the main section of the Standard, references in the Introduction, which describes the revision of IAS 32, have been left unchanged.

†*This Introduction refers to IAS 32 as revised in December 2003. In August 2005 the IASB amended IAS 32 by relocating all disclosures relating to financial instruments to IFRS 7 Financial Instruments: Disclosures. **Editor's note:** This footnote was added by FRS 29.*

‡*In August 2005 the IASB relocated all disclosures relating to financial instruments to IFRS 7 Financial Instruments: Disclosures. **Editor's note:** This footnote was added by FRS 29.*

(a) The instrument includes no contractual obligation:

   (i)   to deliver cash or another financial asset to another entity; or
   (ii) to exchange financial assets or financial liabilities with another entity under conditions that are potentially unfavourable to the issuer.

(b) If the instrument will or may be settled in the issuer's own equity instruments, it is:

   (i)   a non-derivative that includes no contractual obligation for the issuer to deliver a variable number of its own equity instruments; or
   (ii) a derivative that will be settled by the issuer exchanging a fixed amount of cash or another financial asset for a fixed number of its own equity instruments. For this purpose, the issuer's own equity instruments do not include instruments that are themselves contracts for the future receipt or delivery of the issuer's own equity instruments.

In addition, when an issuer has an obligation to purchase its own shares for cash or another financial asset, there is a liability for the amount that the issuer is obliged to pay. **IN7**

The definitions of a financial asset and a financial liability, and the description of an equity instrument, are amended consistently with this principle. **IN8**

Classification of Contracts Settled in an Entity's Own Equity Instruments

The classification of derivative and non-derivative contracts indexed to, or settled in, an entity's own equity instruments has been clarified consistently with the principle in paragraph IN6 above. In particular, when an entity uses its own equity instruments 'as currency' in a contract to receive or deliver a variable number of shares whose value equals a fixed amount or an amount based on changes in an underlying variable (eg a commodity price), the contract is not an equity instrument, but is a financial asset or a financial liability. **IN9**

Puttable Instruments

IAS 32 incorporates the guidance previously proposed in draft SIC Interpretation 34 *Financial Instruments—Instruments or Rights Redeemable by the Holder*. Consequently, a financial instrument that gives the holder the right to put the instrument back to the issuer for cash or another financial asset (a 'puttable instrument') is a financial liability of the issuer. In response to comments received on the Exposure Draft, the Standard provides additional guidance and illustrative examples for entities that, because of this requirement, have no equity or whose share capital is not equity as defined in IAS 32. **IN10**

Contingent Settlement Provisions

IAS 32 incorporates the conclusion previously in SIC-5 *Classification of Financial Instruments—Contingent Settlement Provisions* that a financial instrument is a financial liability when the manner of settlement depends on the occurrence or nonoccurrence of uncertain future events or on the outcome of uncertain circumstances that are beyond the control of both the issuer and the holder. Contingent settlement provisions are ignored when they apply only in the event of liquidation of the issuer or are not genuine. **IN11**

Settlement Options

IN12   Under IAS 32, a derivative financial instrument is a financial asset or a financial liability when it gives one of the parties to it a choice of how it is settled unless all of the settlement alternatives would result in it being an equity instrument.

Measurement of the Components of a Compound Financial Instrument on Initial Recognition

IN13   The revisions eliminate the option previously in IAS 32 to measure the liability component of a compound financial instrument on initial recognition either as a residual amount after separating the equity component, or by using a relative-fairvalue method. Thus, any asset and liability components are separated first and the residual is the amount of any equity component. These requirements for separating the liability and equity components of a compound financial instrument are conformed to both the definition of an equity instrument as a residual and the measurement requirements in IAS 39.

Treasury Shares

IN14   IAS 32 incorporates the conclusion previously in SIC-16 *Share Capital—Reacquired Own Equity Instruments (Treasury Shares)* that the acquisition or subsequent resale by an entity of its own equity instruments does not result in a gain or loss for the entity. Rather it represents a transfer between those holders of equity instruments who have given up their equity interest and those who continue to hold an equity instrument.

Interest, Dividends, Losses and Gains

IN15   IAS 32 incorporates the guidance previously in SIC-17 *Equity—Costs of an Equity Transaction*. Transaction costs incurred as a necessary part of completing an equity transaction are accounted for as part of that transaction and are deducted from equity.

*Disclosure**

IN16–19   [Withdrawn]

IN19A   In August 2005 the Board revised disclosures about financial instruments and relocated them to IFRS 7 *Financial Instruments: Disclosures.*

Withdrawal of Other Pronouncements

IN20   As a consequence of the revisions to this Standard, the Board withdrew the three Interpretations and one draft Interpretation of the former Standing Interpretations Committee noted in paragraph IN1.

Potential Impact of Proposals in Exposure Drafts

IN21   [Deleted]

***Editor's note:** Paragraphs IN16 to IN19 deleted by FRS 29, with effect for accounting periods beginning on or after 1 January 2007, and replaced with IN19A.*

Financial Instruments: Disclosure and Presentation

Objective

[Withdrawn]   1*

The objective of this Standard is to establish principles for presenting financial   2†
instruments as liabilities or equity and for offsetting financial assets and financial
liabilities. It applies to the classification of financial instruments, from the perspective
of the issuer, into financial assets, financial liabilities and equity instruments; the
classification of related interest, dividends, losses and gains; and the circumstances in
which financial assets and financial liabilities should be offset.

The principles in this Standard complement the principles for measuring financial   3‡
assets and financial liabilities in FRS 26 (IAS 39) *Financial Instruments: Measure-*
ment, and for disclosing information about them in FRS 29 (IFRS 7) *Financial*
Instruments: Disclosures.§

SCOPE

This Standard applies to all financial statements that are intended to give a true and fair   3A
view of a reporting entity's financial position and profit or loss (or income and
expenditure). Reporting entities applying the Financial Reporting Standard for Smaller
Entities (FRSSE) are exempt from this Standard.

                                                                               3B§§

This Standard shall be applied by all entities to all types of financial instruments except: ‖4

(a)   those interests in subsidiary, quasi-subsidiary and associated undertakings, part-
      nerships and joint ventures that are accounted for under FRS 2 *Accounting for*
      Subsidiary Undertakings; FRS 5 *Reporting the Substance of Transactions*; and
      FRS 9 *Associates and Joint Ventures*. However when entities apply this standard
      to an interest in a subsidiary, quasi-subsidiary or associated undertaking, part-
      nership or joint venture that is accounted for using FRS 26 or is otherwise
      accounted for as held for resale; in those cases entities shall apply the disclosure
      requirements in FRSs 2, 5 and 9 in addition to those in this Standard. Entities
      shall also apply this Standard to all derivatives linked to interests in subsidiaries,
      quasi-subsidiary or associated undertakings, partnerships or joint ventures.

*Editor's note: Paragraph 1 deleted by FRS 29 with effect for accounting periods beginning on or after 1
January 2007.

†Editor's note: Paragraph 2 amended by FRS 29 with effect for accounting periods beginning on or after 1
January 2007.

‡Editor's note: Paragraph 3 amended by FRS 29 with effect for accounting periods beginning on or after 1
January 2007.

§Editor's note: Reference to FRS 26 altered by amendments to FRS 26, to reflect the change in its title.

§§Editor's note: Paragraphs 3B to 3D deleted by FRS 29 with effect for accounting periods beginning on or after
1 January 2007.

‖Editor's note: Paragraph 4 amended by FRS 29 with effect for accounting periods beginning on or after 1
January 2007.

(b) *employers' rights and obligations under employee benefit plans, to which FRS 17* Retirement Benefits, *applies.*

(c) *contracts for contingent consideration in a business combination (see FRS 7* Fair Values in Acquisition Accounting*). This exemption applies only to the acquirer.*

(d) *insurance contracts as defined in* Appendix C to FRS 26. However, this Standard applies to derivatives that are embedded in insurance contracts if FRS 26 requires the entity to account for them separately. Moreover, an issuer shall apply this Standard to financial guarantee contracts if the issuer applies FRS 26 in measuring the contracts.*

(e) *financial instruments that an entity issues with a discretionary participation feature as defined in Appendix C to FRS 26). The issuer of these instruments is exempt from applying to these features paragraphs 15-32 and AG25-AG35 of this Standard regarding the distinction between financial liabilities and equity instruments. However, these instruments are subject to all other requirements of this Standard. Furthermore, this Standard applies to derivatives that are embedded in these instruments (see FRS 26).*

(f) *financial instruments, contracts and obligations under share-based payment transactions to which FRS 20* Share-based Payment *applies, except for*

    (i) *contracts within the scope of paragraphs 8-10 of this Standard, to which this Standard applies,*

    (ii) *paragraphs 33 and 34 of this Standard, which shall be applied to treasury shares purchased, sold, issued or cancelled in connection with employee share option plans, employee share purchase plans, and all other share-based payment arrangements.*

5†   [Withdrawn]

6   [Deleted]

7   [Withdrawn]

8   *This Standard shall be applied to those contracts to buy or sell a nonfinancial item that can be settled net in cash or another financial instrument, or by exchanging financial instruments, as if the contracts were financial instruments, with the exception of contracts that were entered into and continue to be held for the purpose of the receipt or delivery of a non-financial item in accordance with the entity's expected purchase, sale or usage requirements.*

9   There are various ways in which a contract to buy or sell a non-financial item can be settled net in cash or another financial instrument or by exchanging financial instruments. These include:

(a)   when the terms of the contract permit either party to settle it net in cash or another financial instrument or by exchanging financial instruments;

(b)   when the ability to settle net in cash or another financial instrument, or by exchanging financial instruments, is not explicit in the terms of the contract, but the entity has a practice of settling similar contracts net in cash or another financial instrument, or by exchanging financial instruments (whether with the counterparty, by entering into offsetting contracts or by selling the contract before its exercise or lapse);

---

*Editor's note: Amended with effect from 1 January 2005.

†Editor's note: Paragraphs 5 and 7 deleted by FRS 29 with effect for accounting periods beginning on or after 1 January 2007.

(c)   when, for similar contracts, the entity has a practice of taking delivery of the underlying and selling it within a short period after delivery for the purpose of generating a profit from shortterm fluctuations in price or dealer's margin; and

(d)   when the non-financial item that is the subject of the contract is readily convertible to cash.

A contract to which (b) or (c) applies is not entered into for the purpose of the receipt or delivery of the non-financial item in accordance with the entity's expected purchase, sale or usage requirements, and, accordingly, is within the scope of this Standard. Other contracts to which paragraph 8 applies are evaluated to determine whether they were entered into and continue to be held for the purpose of the receipt or delivery of the non-financial item in accordance with the entity's expected purchase, sale or usage requirement, and accordingly, whether they are within the scope of this Standard.

A written option to buy or sell a non-financial item that can be settled net in cash or another financial instrument, or by exchanging financial instruments, in accordance with paragraph 9(a) or (d) is within the scope of this Standard. Such a contract cannot be entered into for the purpose of the receipt or delivery of the nonfinancial item in accordance with the entity's expected purchase, sale or usage requirements.   **10**

DEFINITIONS (see also paragraphs AG3-AG24)

The following terms are used in this Standard with the meanings specified: **11**

A *financial instrument* is any contract that gives rise to a financial asset of one entity and a financial liability or equity instrument of another entity.

A *financial asset* is any asset that is:

(a)   cash;

(b)   an equity instrument of another entity;

(c)   a contractual right:

   (i)   to receive cash or another financial asset from another entity; or

   (ii)   to exchange financial assets or financial liabilities with another entity under conditions that are potentially favourable to the entity; or

(d)   a contract that will or may be settled in the entity's own equity instruments and is:

   (i)   a non-derivative for which the entity is or may be obliged to receive a variable number of the entity's own equity instruments; or

   (ii)   a derivative that will or may be settled other than by the exchange of a fixed amount of cash or another financial asset for a fixed number of the entity's own equity instruments. For this purpose the entity's own equity instruments do not include instruments that are themselves contracts for the future receipt or delivery of the entity's own equity instruments.

A *financial liability* is any liability that is:

(a)   a contractual obligation:

   (i)   to deliver cash or another financial asset to another entity; or

   (ii)   to exchange financial assets or financial liabilities with another entity under conditions that are potentially unfavourable to the entity; or

(b)   a contract that will or may be settled in the entity's own equity instruments and is:

> *(i)* a non-derivative for which the entity is or may be obliged to deliver a variable number of the entity's own equity instruments; or
>
> *(ii)* a derivative that will or may be settled other than by the exchange of a fixed amount of cash or another financial asset for a fixed number of the entity's own equity instruments. For this purpose the entity's own equity instruments do not include instruments that are themselves contracts for the future receipt or delivery of the entity's own equity instruments.

An equity instrument is any contract that evidences a residual interest in the assets of an entity after deducting all of its liabilities.

Fair value is the amount for which an asset could be exchanged, or a liability settled, between knowledgeable, willing parties in an arm's length transaction.

12   The following terms are defined in paragraph 9 of FRS 26 and are used in this Standard with the meaning specified in FRS 26.

- amortised cost of a financial asset or financial liability
- available-for-sale financial assets
- derecognition
- derivative
- effective interest method
- financial asset or financial liability at fair value through profit or loss
- financial guarantee contract*
- firm commitment
- forecast transaction
- hedge effectiveness
- hedged item
- hedging instrument
- held-to-maturity investments
- loans and receivables
- regular way purchase or sale
- transaction costs.

13   In this Standard, 'contract' and 'contractual' refer to an agreement between two or more parties that has clear economic consequences that the parties have little, if any, discretion to avoid, usually because the agreement is enforceable by law. Contracts, and thus financial instruments, may take a variety of forms and need not be in writing.

14   In this Standard, 'entity' includes individuals, partnerships, incorporated bodies, trusts and government agencies.

PRESENTATION

Liabilities and Equity (see also paragraphs AG25-AG29)

15   *The issuer of a financial instrument shall classify the instrument, or its component parts, on initial recognition as a financial liability, a financial asset or an equity instrument in accordance with the substance of the contractual arrangement and the definitions of a financial liability, a financial asset and an equity instrument.*

*Editor's note: Added with effect from 1 January 2006.

When an issuer applies the definitions in paragraph 11 to determine whether a **16** financial instrument is an equity instrument rather than a financial liability, the instrument is an equity instrument if, and only if, both conditions (a) and (b) below are met.

(a) The instrument includes no contractual obligation:

   (i)   to deliver cash or another financial asset to another entity; or
   (ii) to exchange financial assets or financial liabilities with another entity under conditions that are potentially unfavourable to the issuer.

(b) If the instrument will or may be settled in the issuer's own equity instruments, it is:

   (i)   a non-derivative that includes no contractual obligation for the issuer to deliver a variable number of its own equity instruments; or
   (ii) a derivative that will be settled only by the issuer exchanging a fixed amount of cash or another financial asset for a fixed number of its own equity instruments. For this purpose the issuer's own equity instruments do not include instruments that are themselves contracts for the future receipt or delivery of the issuer's own equity instruments.

A contractual obligation, including one arising from a derivative financial instrument, that will or may result in the future receipt or delivery of the issuer's own equity instruments, but does not meet conditions (a) and (b) above, is not an equity instrument.

No Contractual Obligation to Deliver Cash or Another Financial Asset (paragraph 16(a))

A critical feature in differentiating a financial liability from an equity instrument is **17** the existence of a contractual obligation of one party to the financial instrument (the issuer) either to deliver cash or another financial asset to the other party (the holder) or to exchange financial assets or financial liabilities with the holder under conditions that are potentially unfavourable to the issuer. Although the holder of an equity instrument may be entitled to receive a pro rata share of any dividends or other distributions of equity, the issuer does not have a contractual obligation to make such distributions because it cannot be required to deliver cash or another financial asset to another party.

The substance of a financial instrument, rather than its legal form, governs its **18** classification on the entity's balance sheet. Substance and legal form are commonly consistent, but not always. Some financial instruments take the legal form of equity but are liabilities in substance and others may combine features associated with equity instruments and features associated with financial liabilities. For example:

(a) a preference share that provides for mandatory redemption by the issuer for a fixed or determinable amount at a fixed or determinable future date, or gives the holder the right to require the issuer to redeem the instrument at or after a particular date for a fixed or determinable amount, is a financial liability.

(b) a financial instrument that gives the holder the right to put it back to the issuer for cash or another financial asset (a 'puttable instrument') is a financial liability. This is so even when the amount of cash or other financial assets is determined on the basis of an index or other item that has the potential to increase or decrease, or when the legal form of the puttable instrument gives the holder a right to a residual interest in the assets of an issuer. The existence of an option for the holder to put the instrument back to the issuer for cash or another financial asset means that the puttable instrument meets the definition of a financial liability. For example, open-ended mutual funds, unit trusts, partnerships and some co-operative entities may provide their unitholders or members with a right to redeem their interests in the issuer at any time for cash equal to their proportionate share of the asset value of the issuer. However, classification as a financial liability does not preclude the use of descriptors such as 'net asset value attributable to unitholders' and 'change in net asset value attributable to unitholders' on the face of the financial statements of an entity that has no contributed equity (such as some mutual funds and unit trusts, see Illustrative Example 7) or the use of additional disclosure to show that total members' interests comprise items such as reserves that meet the definition of equity and puttable instruments that do not (see Illustrative Example 8).

19   If an entity does not have an unconditional right to avoid delivering cash or another financial asset to settle a contractual obligation, the obligation meets the definition of a financial liability. For example:

(a)   a restriction on the ability of an entity to satisfy a contractual obligation, such as lack of access to foreign currency or the need to obtain approval for payment from a regulatory authority, does not negate the entity's contractual obligation or the holder's contractual right under the instrument.

(b)   a contractual obligation that is conditional on a counterparty exercising its right to redeem is a financial liability because the entity does not have the unconditional right to avoid delivering cash or another financial asset.

20   A financial instrument that does not explicitly establish a contractual obligation to deliver cash or another financial asset may establish an obligation indirectly through its terms and conditions. For example:

(a)   a financial instrument may contain a non-financial obligation that must be settled if, and only if, the entity fails to make distributions or to redeem the instrument. If the entity can avoid a transfer of cash or another financial asset only by settling the non-financial obligation, the financial instrument is a financial liability.

(b)   a financial instrument is a financial liability if it provides that on settlement the entity will deliver either:

(i)   cash or another financial asset; or

(ii)   its own shares whose value is determined to exceed substantially the value of the cash or other financial asset.

Although the entity does not have an explicit contractual obligation to deliver cash or another financial asset, the value of the share settlement alternative is such that the entity will settle in cash. In any event, the holder has in substance been guaranteed receipt of an amount that is at least equal to the cash settlement option (see paragraph 21).

Settlement in the Entity's Own Equity Instruments (paragraph 16(b))

21   A contract is not an equity instrument solely because it may result in the receipt or delivery of the entity's own equity instruments. An entity may have a contractual right or obligation to receive or deliver a number of its own shares or other equity instruments that varies so that the fair value of the entity's own equity instruments to be received or delivered equals the amount of the contractual right or obligation. Such a contractual right or obligation may be for a fixed amount or an amount that fluctuates in part or in full in response to changes in a variable other than the market price of the entity's own equity instruments (eg an interest rate, a commodity price or

a financial instrument price). Two examples are (a) a contract to deliver as many of the entity's own equity instruments as are equal in value to CU100,* and (b) a contract to deliver as many of the entity's own equity instruments as are equal in value to the value of 100 ounces of gold. Such a contract is a financial liability of the entity even though the entity must or can settle it by delivering its own equity instruments. It is not an equity instrument because the entity uses a variable number of its own equity instruments as a means to settle the contract. Accordingly, the contract does not evidence a residual interest in the entity's assets after deducting all of its liabilities.

A contract that will be settled by the entity (receiving or) delivering a fixed number of **22** its own equity instruments in exchange for a fixed amount of cash or another financial asset is an equity instrument. For example, an issued share option that gives the counterparty a right to buy a fixed number of the entity's shares for a fixed price or for a fixed stated principal amount of a bond is an equity instrument. Changes in the fair value of a contract arising from variations in market interest rates that do not affect the amount of cash or other financial assets to be paid or received, or the number of equity instruments to be received or delivered, on settlement of the contract do not preclude the contract from being an equity instrument. Any consideration received (such as the premium received for a written option or warrant on the entity's own shares) is added directly to equity. Any consideration paid (such as the premium paid for a purchased option) is deducted directly from equity. Changes in the fair value of an equity instrument are not recognised in the financial statements.

A contract that contains an obligation for an entity to purchase its own equity **23** instruments for cash or another financial asset gives rise to a financial liability for the present value of the redemption amount (for example, for the present value of the forward repurchase price, option exercise price or other redemption amount). This is the case even if the contract itself is an equity instrument. One example is an entity's obligation under a forward contract to purchase its own equity instruments for cash. When the financial liability is recognised initially under FRS 26, its fair value (the present value of the redemption amount) is reclassified from equity. Subsequently, the financial liability is measured in accordance with FRS 26. If the contract expires without delivery, the carrying amount of the financial liability is reclassified to equity. If the contract subsequently expires without delivery, the carrying amount of the financial liability is reclassified to equity. An entity's contractual obligation to purchase its own equity instruments gives rise to a financial liability for the present value of the redemption amount even if the obligation to purchase is conditional on the counterparty exercising a right to redeem (eg a written put option that gives the counterparty the right to sell an entity's own equity instruments to the entity for a fixed price).†

A contract that will be settled by the entity delivering or receiving a fixed number of **24** its own equity instruments in exchange for a variable amount of cash or another financial asset is a financial asset or financial liability. An example is a contract for the entity to deliver 100 of its own equity instruments in return for an amount of cash calculated to equal the value of 100 ounces of gold.

*In this Standard, monetary amounts are denominated in 'currency units' (CU).

†*Editor's note:* Amended by FRS 26.

Contingent Settlement Provisions

25   A financial instrument may require the entity to deliver cash or another financial asset, or otherwise to settle it in such a way that it would be a financial liability, in the event of the occurrence or non-occurrence of uncertain future events (or on the outcome of uncertain circumstances) that are beyond the control of both the issuer and the holder of the instrument, such as a change in a stock market index, consumer price index, interest rate or taxation requirements, or the issuer's future revenues, net income or debt-to-equity ratio. The issuer of such an instrument does not have the unconditional right to avoid delivering cash or another financial asset (or otherwise to settle it in such a way that it would be a financial liability). Therefore, it is a financial liability of the issuer unless:

(a)   the part of the contingent settlement provision that could require settlement in cash or another financial asset (or otherwise in such a way that it would be a financial liability) is not genuine; or

(b)   the issuer can be required to settle the obligation in cash or another financial asset (or otherwise to settle it in such a way that it would be a financial liability) only in the event of liquidation of the issuer.

Settlement Options

26   *When a derivative financial instrument gives one party a choice over how it is settled (eg the issuer or the holder can choose settlement net in cash or by exchanging shares for cash), it is a financial asset or a financial liability unless all of the settlement alternatives would result in it being an equity instrument.*

27   An example of a derivative financial instrument with a settlement option that is a financial liability is a share option that the issuer can decide to settle net in cash or by exchanging its own shares for cash. Similarly, some contracts to buy or sell a non-financial item in exchange for the entity's own equity instruments are within the scope of this Standard because they can be settled either by delivery of the non-financial item or net in cash or another financial instrument (see paragraphs 810). Such contracts are financial assets or financial liabilities and not equity instruments.

Compound Financial Instruments
(see also paragraphs AG30-AG35 and Illustrative Examples 9-12)

28   *The issuer of a non-derivative financial instrument shall evaluate the terms of the financial instrument to determine whether it contains both a liability and an equity component. Such components shall be classified separately as financial liabilities, financial assets or equity instruments in accordance with paragraph 15.*

29   An entity recognises separately the components of a financial instrument that (a) creates a financial liability of the entity and (b) grants an option to the holder of the instrument to convert it into an equity instrument of the entity. For example, a bond or similar instrument convertible by the holder into a fixed number of ordinary shares of the entity is a compound financial instrument. From the per-spective of the entity, such an instrument comprises two components: a financial liability (a contractual arrangement to deliver cash or another financial asset) and an equity instrument (a call option granting the holder the right, for a specified period of time, to convert it into a fixed number of ordinary shares of the entity). The eco-nomic effect of issuing such an instrument is substantially the same as issuing simultaneously a debt instrument with an early settlement provision and warrants to purchase ordinary shares, or issuing a debt instrument with detachable share

purchase warrants. Accordingly, in all cases, the entity presents the liability and equity components separately on its balance sheet.

Classification of the liability and equity components of a convertible instrument is **30** not revised as a result of a change in the likelihood that a conversion option will be exercised, even when exercise of the option may appear to have become economically advantageous to some holders. Holders may not always act in the way that might be expected because, for example, the tax consequences resulting from conversion may differ among holders. Furthermore, the likelihood of conversion will change from time to time. The entity's contractual obligation to make future payments remains outstanding until it is extinguished through conversion, maturity of the instrument or some other transaction.

IAS 39 deals with the measurement of financial assets and financial liabilities. Equity **31** instruments are instruments that evidence a residual interest in the assets of an entity after deducting all of its liabilities. Therefore, when the initial carrying amount of a compound financial instrument is allocated to its equity and liability components, the equity component is assigned the residual amount after deducting from the fair value of the instrument as a whole the amount separately determined for the liability component. The value of any derivative features (such as a call option) embedded in the compound financial instrument other than the equity component (such as an equity conversion option) is included in the liability component. The sum of the carrying amounts assigned to the liability and equity components on initial recognition is always equal to the fair value that would be ascribed to the instrument as a whole. No gain or loss arises from initially recognising the components of the instrument separately.*

Under the approach described in paragraph 31, the issuer of a bond convertible into **32** ordinary shares first determines the carrying amount of the liability component by measuring the fair value of a similar liability (including any embedded non-equity derivative features) that does not have an associated equity component. The carrying amount of the equity instrument represented by the option to convert the instrument into ordinary shares is then determined by deducting the fair value of the financial liability from the fair value of the compound financial instrument as a whole.

Treasury Shares (see also paragraph AG36)

If an entity reacquires its own equity instruments, those instruments ('treasury shares') **33** *shall be deducted from equity. No gain or loss shall be recognised in profit or loss on the purchase, sale, issue or cancellation of an entity's own equity instruments. Such treasury shares may be acquired and held by the entity or by other members of the consolidated group. Consideration paid or received shall be recognised directly in equity.*

The amount of treasury shares held is disclosed separately either on the face of the **34** balance sheet or in the notes. An entity provides disclosure in accordance with FRS 8 *Related Party Disclosures* if the entity reacquires its own equity instruments from related parties.

Interest, Dividends, Losses and Gains (see also paragraph AG37)

Interest, dividends, losses and gains relating to a financial instrument or a component **35** *that is a financial liability shall be recognised as income or expense in profit or loss.*

---

*Editor's note: Amended by amendments to FRS 26. Reference to IAS 39 should be read as reference to FRS 26.

Distributions to holders of an equity instrument shall be debited by the entity directly to equity, net of any related income tax benefit. Transaction costs of an equity transaction, other than costs of issuing an equity instrument that are directly attributable to the acquisition of a business (which shall be accounted for under FRS 6 **Acquisitions and Mergers***), shall be accounted for as a deduction from equity, net of any related income tax benefit.*

36   The classification of a financial instrument as a financial liability or an equity instrument determines whether interest, dividends, losses and gains relating to that instrument are recognised as income or expense in profit or loss. Thus, dividend payments on shares wholly recognised as liabilities are recognised as expenses in the same way as interest on a bond. Similarly, gains and losses associated with redemptions or refinancings of financial liabilities are recognised in profit or loss, whereas redemptions or refinancings of equity instruments are recognised as changes in equity. Changes in the fair value of an equity instrument are not recognised in the financial statements.

37   An entity typically incurs various costs in issuing or acquiring its own equity instruments. Those costs might include registration and other regulatory fees, amounts paid to legal, accounting and other professional advisers, printing costs and stamp duties. The transaction costs of an equity transaction are accounted for as a deduction from equity (net of any related income tax benefit) to the extent they are incremental costs directly attributable to the equity transaction that otherwise would have been avoided. The costs of an equity transaction that is abandoned are recognised as an expense.

38   Transaction costs that relate to the issue of a compound financial instrument are allocated to the liability and equity components of the instrument in proportion to the allocation of proceeds. Transaction costs that relate jointly to more than one transaction (for example, costs of a concurrent offering of some shares and a stock exchange listing of other shares) are allocated to those transactions using a basis of allocation that is rational and consistent with similar transactions.

39   The amount of transaction costs accounted for as a deduction from equity in the period shall be disclosed separately.

40   Dividends classified as an expense may be presented in the income statement either with interests on other liabilities or as a separate item. In addition to the requirements of this Standard, disclosure of interests and dividends is subject to the requirements of FRS 29. In some circumstances, because of the differences between interest and dividends with respect to matters such as tax deductibility, it is desirable to disclose them separately in the income statement.*

41   Gains and losses related to changes in the carrying amount of a financial liability are recognised as income or expense in profit or loss even when they relate to an instrument that includes a right to the residual interest in the assets of the entity in exchange for cash or another financial asset (see paragraph 18(b)).

Offsetting a Financial Asset and a Financial Liability
(see also paragraphs AG38 and AG39)

42   *A financial asset and a financial liability shall be offset and the net amount presented in the balance sheet when, and only when, an entity:*

Editor's note: Amended by FRS 29 with effect for accounting periods beginning on or after 1 January 2007.

(a) currently has a legally enforceable right to set off the recognised amounts; and
(b) intends either to settle on a net basis, or to realise the asset and settle the liability simultaneously.

In accounting for a transfer of a financial asset that does not qualify for derecognition, the entity shall not offset the transferred asset and the associated liability (see IAS 39, paragraph 36).*

This Standard requires the presentation of financial assets and financial liabilities on a net basis when doing so reflects an entity's expected future cash flows from settling two or more separate financial instruments. When an entity has the right to receive or pay a single net amount and intends to do so, it has, in effect, only a single financial asset or financial liability. In other circumstances, financial assets and financial liabilities are presented separately from each other consistently with their characteristics as resources or obligations of the entity. **43**

Offsetting a recognised financial asset and a recognised financial liability and presenting the net amount differs from the derecognition of a financial asset or a financial liability. Although offsetting does not give rise to recognition of a gain or loss, the derecognition of a financial instrument not only results in the removal of the previously recognised item from the balance sheet but also may result in recognition of a gain or loss. **44**

A right of set-off is a debtor's legal right, by contract or otherwise, to settle or otherwise eliminate all or a portion of an amount due to a creditor by applying against that amount an amount due from the creditor. In unusual circumstances, a debtor may have a legal right to apply an amount due from a third party against the amount due to a creditor provided that there is an agreement between the three parties that clearly establishes the debtor's right of set-off. Because the right of setoff is a legal right, the conditions supporting the right may vary from one legal jurisdiction to another and the laws applicable to the relationships between the parties need to be considered. **45**

The existence of an enforceable right to set off a financial asset and a financial liability affects the rights and obligations associated with a financial asset and a financial liability and may affect an entity's exposure to credit and liquidity risk. However, the existence of the right, by itself, is not a sufficient basis for offsetting. In the absence of an intention to exercise the right or to settle simultaneously, the amount and timing of an entity's future cash flows are not affected. When an entity intends to exercise the right or to settle simultaneously, presentation of the asset and liability on a net basis reflects more appropriately the amounts and timing of the expected future cash flows, as well as the risks to which those cash flows are exposed. An intention by one or both parties to settle on a net basis without the legal right to do so is not sufficient to justify offsetting because the rights and obligations associated with the individual financial asset and financial liability remain unaltered. **46**

An entity's intentions with respect to settlement of particular assets and liabilities may be influenced by its normal business practices, the requirements of the financial markets and other circumstances that may limit the ability to settle net or to settle simultaneously. When an entity has a right of set-off, but does not intend to settle net **47**

---

*Editor's note: Last sentence added by amendments to FRS 26. Reference to IAS 39 should be read as reference to FRS 26.

or to realise the assets and settle the liability simultaneously, the effect of the right on the credit risk exposure is disclosed in accordance with paragraph 36 of FRS 29.*

48   Simultaneous settlement of two financial instruments may occur through, for example, the operation of a clearing house in an organised financial market or a face-to-face exchange. In these circumstances the cash flows are, in effect, equivalent to a single net amount and there is no exposure to credit or liquidity risk. In other circumstances, an entity may settle two instruments by receiving and paying separate amounts, becoming exposed to credit risk for the full amount of the asset or liquidity risk for the full amount of the liability. Such risk exposures may be significant even though relatively brief. Accordingly, realisation of a financial asset and settlement of a financial liability are treated as simultaneous only when the transactions occur at the same moment.

49   The conditions set out in paragraph 42 are generally not satisfied and offsetting is usually inappropriate when:

(a)   several different financial instruments are used to emulate the features of a single financial instrument (a 'synthetic instrument');

(b)   financial assets and financial liabilities arise from financial instruments having the same primary risk exposure (for example, assets and liabilities within a portfolio of forward contracts or other derivative instruments) but involve different counterparties;

(c)   financial or other assets are pledged as collateral for nonrecourse financial liabilities;

(d)   financial assets are set aside in trust by a debtor for the purpose of discharging an obligation without those assets having been accepted by the creditor in settlement of the obligation (for example, a sinking fund arrangement); or

(e)   obligations incurred as a result of events giving rise to losses are expected to be recovered from a third party by virtue of a claim made under an insurance contract.

50   An entity that undertakes a number of financial instrument transactions with a single counterparty may enter into a 'master netting arrangement' with that counterparty. Such an agreement provides for a single net settlement of all financial instruments covered by the agreement in the event of default on, or termination of, any one contract. These arrangements are commonly used by financial institutions to provide protection against loss in the event of bankruptcy or other circumstances that result in a counterparty being unable to meet its obligations. A master netting arrangement commonly creates a right of set-off that becomes enforceable and affects the realisation or settlement of individual financial assets and financial liabilities only following a specified event of default or in other circumstances not expected to arise in the normal course of business. A master netting arrangement does not provide a basis for offsetting unless both of the criteria in paragraph 42 are satisfied. When financial assets and financial liabilities subject to a master netting arrangement are not offset, the effect of the arrangement on an entity's exposure to credit risk is disclosed in accordance with paragraph 36 of FRS 29.†

Current liabilities

50A   An entity regards its financial liabilities as due to be settled within twelve months after the balance sheet date, and classifies them as current, even if:

*Editor's note: Amended by FRS 29 with effect for accounting periods beginning on or after 1 January 2007.

†Editor's note: Amended by FRS 29 with effect for accounting periods beginning on or after 1 January 2007.

(a) the original term was for a period longer than twelve months; and
(b) an agreement to refinance, or to reschedule payments, on a long-term basis is completed after the balance sheet date and before the financial statements are authorised for issue.

If an entity expects, and has the discretion, to refinance or roll over an obligation for at least twelve months after the balance sheet date under an existing loan facility, it classifies the obligation as non-current, even if it would otherwise be due within a shorter period. However, when refinancing or rolling over the obligation is not at the discretion of the entity (for example, there is no agreement to refinance), the potential to refinance is not considered and the obligation is classified as current. **50B**

When an entity breaches an undertaking under a long-term loan agreement on or before the balance sheet date with the effect that the liability becomes payable on demand, the liability is classified as current, even if the lender has agreed, after the balance sheet date and before the authorisation of the financial statements for issue, not to demand payment as a consequence of the breach. The liability is classified as current because, at the balance sheet date, the entity does not have an unconditional right to defer its settlement for at least twelve months after that date. **50C**

However, the liability is classified as non-current if the lender agreed by the balance sheet date to provide a period of grace ending at least twelve months after the balance sheet date, within which the entity can rectify the breach and during which the lender cannot demand immediate repayment. **50D**

In respect of loans classified as current liabilities, if the following events occur between the balance sheet date and the date the financial statements are authorised for issue, those events qualify for disclosure as non-adjusting events in accordance with FRS 21 (IAS 10) *Events after the Balance Sheet Date*: **50E**

(a) refinancing on a long-term basis;
(b) rectification of a breach of a long-term loan agreement; and
(c) the receipt from the lender of a period of grace to rectify a breach of a long-term loan agreement ending at least twelve months after the balance sheet date.

DISCLOSURE*

EFFECTIVE DATE

An entity shall apply paragraphs 15 to 50 of this Standard for accounting periods beginning on or after 1 January 2005. Earlier application of these paragraphs of the Standard is not permitted. An entity shall apply paragraphs 51 to 95 of the Standard no later than the accounting period the entity is applying FRS 26. Where, in an accounting period commencing before 1 January 2007, an entity applies the measurement provisions of FRS 26 but not the derecognition provisions of that Standard, it is not required to make the disclosures required by paragraph 94(a).† **96**

This Standard shall be applied retrospectively, subject to paragraphs 97A and 97B. **97**

This Standard requires an entity to split a compound financial instrument at inception into separate liability and equity components. If the liability component is **97A**

---

*Editor's note: Paragraphs 51 to 95 are deleted by FRS 29 with effect for accounting periods beginning on or after 1 January 2007.

†Editor's note: Last sentence added by amendments to FRS 26.

no longer outstanding, retrospective application of this Standard involves separating two portions of equity. The first portion is in retained earnings and represents the cumulative interest accreted on the liability component. The other portion represents the original equity component. On first applying this Standard, an entity need not separate these two portions if the liability component is no longer outstanding at the date of transition to this Standard. The date of transition to this standard is the beginning of the earliest period for which an entity presents comparative information in compliance with this standard.

97B   An entity that first adopts the presentation requirements in paragraphs 15 to 50 of this Standard for an accounting period that commences before 1 January 2006, or that adopts the disclosure requirements in paragraphs 51 to 95 of this Standard for an accounting period that commences before 1 January 2007, need not restate comparative information to comply with those requirements An entity that chooses to present comparative information that does not comply with those requirements in their first year of adoption shall:

(a)   apply its existing accounting policies to financial instruments within the scope of this standard and FRS 25 in the comparative information;

(b)   disclose this fact together with the basis used to prepare this information; and

(c)   disclose the nature of the main adjustments that would make the information comply with this Standard. The entity need not quantify those adjustments. However, the entity shall treat any adjustment between the balance sheet at the comparative period's reporting date (ie the balance sheet that includes comparative information under previous accounting policies) and the balance sheet at the start of the first reporting period that includes information that complies with this Standard and FRS 25 as arising from a change in accounting policy and give the disclosures required by FRS 18 *Accounting Policies.*

98A   In December 2005 the ASB relocated all disclosures relating to financial instruments to FRS 29 (IFRS 7) *Financial Instruments: Disclosures.**

___

**Editor's note: This paragraph is added by FRS 29 with effect for accounting periods beginning on or after 1 January 2007.*

Withdrawal of, and amendments to, existing UK Standards and UITF Abstracts

[Not reproduced, as all changes have been made to the underlying standards and abstracts].

Appendix
Application Guidance
FRS 25 Financial Instruments: Disclosure and Presentation

This appendix is an integral part of the Standard.

AG1   This Application Guidance explains the application of particular aspects of the Standard.

AG2   The Standard does not deal with the recognition or measurement of financial instruments. Requirements about the recognition and measurement of financial assets and financial liabilities are set out in FRS 26 (IAS 39) *Financial Instruments: Recognition and Measurement.**

Definitions (paragraphs 11-14)

Financial Assets and Financial Liabilities

AG3   Currency (cash) is a financial asset because it represents the medium of exchange and is therefore the basis on which all transactions are measured and recognised in financial statements. A deposit of cash with a bank or similar financial institution is a financial asset because it represents the contractual right of the depositor to obtain cash from the institution or to draw a cheque or similar instrument against the balance in favour of a creditor in payment of a financial liability.

AG4   Common examples of financial assets representing a contractual right to receive cash in the future and corresponding financial liabilities representing a contractual obligation to deliver cash in the future are:

(a)   trade accounts receivable and payable;
(b)   notes receivable and payable;
(c)   loans receivable and payable; and
(d)   bonds receivable and payable.

In each case, one party's contractual right to receive (or obligation to pay) cash is matched by the other party's corresponding obligation to pay (or right to receive).

AG5   Another type of financial instrument is one for which the economic benefit to be received or given up is a financial asset other than cash. For example, a note payable in government bonds gives the holder the contractual right to receive and the issuer the contractual obligation to deliver government bonds, not cash. The bonds are financial assets because they represent obligations of the issuing government to pay cash. The note is, therefore, a financial asset of the note holder and a financial liability of the note issuer.

AG6   'Perpetual' debt instruments (such as 'perpetual' bonds, debentures and capital notes) normally provide the holder with the contractual right to receive payments on account of interest at fixed dates extending into the indefinite future, either with no right to receive a return of principal or a right to a return of principal under terms that make it very unlikely or very far in the future. For example, an entity may issue

Editor's note: Reference to FRS 26 altered by amendments to FRS 26 to reflect the change in its title.

a financial instrument requiring it to make annual payments in perpetuity equal to a stated interest rate of 8 per cent applied to a stated par or principal amount of CU1,000.* Assuming 8 per cent to be the market rate of interest for the instrument when issued, the issuer assumes a contractual obligation to make a stream of future interest payments having a fair value (present value) of CU1,000 on initial recognition. The holder and issuer of the instrument have a financial asset and a financial liability, respectively.

A contractual right or contractual obligation to receive, deliver or exchange financial instruments is itself a financial instrument. A chain of contractual rights or contractual obligations meets the definition of a financial instrument if it will ultimately lead to the receipt or payment of cash or to the acquisition or issue of an equity instrument.   **AG7**

The ability to exercise a contractual right or the requirement to satisfy a contractual obligation may be absolute, or it may be contingent on the occurrence of a future event. For example, a financial guarantee is a contractual right of the lender to receive cash from the guarantor, and a corresponding contractual obligation of the guarantor to pay the lender, if the borrower defaults. The contractual right and obligation exist because of a past transaction or event (assumption of the guarantee), even though the lender's ability to exercise its right and the requirement for the guarantor to perform under its obligation are both contingent on a future act of default by the borrower. A contingent right and obligation meet the definition of a financial asset and a financial liability, even though such assets and liabilities are not always recognised in the financial statements. Some of their contingent rights and obligations may be insurance contracts as defined in Appendix C to FRS 26.   **AG8**

Under SSAP 21 *Accounting for leases and hire purchase contracts* a finance lease is regarded as primarily an entitlement of the lessor to receive, and an obligation of the lessee to pay, a stream of payments that are substantially the same as blended payments of principal and interest under a loan agreement. The lessor accounts for its investment in the amount receivable under the lease contract rather than the leased asset itself. An operating lease, on the other hand, is regarded as primarily an uncompleted contract committing the lessor to provide the use of an asset in future periods in exchange for consideration similar to a fee for a service. The lessor continues to account for the leased asset itself rather than any amount receivable in the future under the contract. Accordingly, a finance lease is regarded as a financial instrument and an operating lease is not regarded as a financial instrument (except as regards individual payments currently due and payable).   **AG9**

Physical assets (such as inventories, property, plant and equipment), leased assets and intangible assets (such as patents and trademarks) are not financial assets. Control of such physical and intangible assets creates an opportunity to generate an inflow of cash or another financial asset, but it does not give rise to a present right to receive cash or another financial asset.   **AG10**

Assets (such as prepaid expenses) for which the future economic benefit is the receipt of goods or services, rather than the right to receive cash or another financial asset, are not financial assets. Similarly, items such as deferred revenue and most warranty obligations are not financial liabilities because the outflow of economic benefits associated with them is the delivery of goods and services rather than a contractual obligation to pay cash or another financial asset.   **AG11**

---

*In this guidance, monetary amounts are denominated in 'currency units' (CU).

AG12   Liabilities or assets that are not contractual (such as income taxes that are created as a result of statutory requirements imposed by governments) are not financial liabilities or financial assets. Accounting for income taxes is dealt with in FRS 16 *Current Tax* and FRS 19 *Deferred Tax*. Similarly, constructive obligations, as defined in FRS 12 *Provisions, Contingent Liabilities and Contingent Assets*, do not arise from contracts and are not financial liabilities.

Equity Instruments

AG13   Examples of equity instruments include non-puttable ordinary shares, some types of preference shares (see paragraphs AG25 and AG26), and warrants or written call options that allow the holder to subscribe for or purchase a fixed number of non-puttable ordinary shares in the issuing entity in exchange for a fixed amount of cash or another financial asset. An entity's obligation to issue or purchase a fixed number of its own equity instruments in exchange for a fixed amount of cash or another financial asset is an equity instrument of the entity. However, if such a contract contains an obligation for the entity to pay cash or another financial asset, it also gives rise to a liability for the present value of the redemption amount (see paragraph AG27(a)). An issuer of nonputtable ordinary shares assumes a liability when it formally acts to make a distribution and becomes legally obligated to the shareholders to do so. This may be the case following the declaration of a dividend or when the entity is being wound up and any assets remaining after the satisfaction of liabilities become distributable to shareholders.

AG14   A purchased call option or other similar contract acquired by an entity that gives it the right to reacquire a fixed number of its own equity instruments in exchange for delivering a fixed amount of cash or another financial asset is not a financial asset of the entity. Instead, any consideration paid for such a contract is deducted from equity.

Derivative Financial Instruments

AG15   Financial instruments include primary instruments (such as receivables, payables and equity instruments) and derivative financial instruments (such as financial options, futures and forwards, interest rate swaps and currency swaps). Derivative financial instruments meet the definition of a financial instrument and, accordingly, are within the scope of this Standard.

AG16   Derivative financial instruments create rights and obligations that have the effect of transferring between the parties to the instrument one or more of the financial risks inherent in an underlying primary financial instrument. On inception, derivative financial instruments give one party a contractual right to exchange financial assets or financial liabilities with another party under conditions that are potentially favourable, or a contractual obligation to exchange financial assets or financial liabilities with another party under conditions that are potentially unfavourable. However, they generally* do not result in a transfer of the underlying primary financial instrument on inception of the contract, nor does such a transfer necessarily take place on maturity of the contract. Some instruments embody both a right and an obligation to make an exchange. Because the terms of the exchange are determined on inception of the derivative instrument, as prices in financial markets change those terms may become either favourable or unfavourable.

**This is true of most, but not all derivatives, eg in some cross-currency interest rate swaps principal is exchanged on inception (and re-exchanged on maturity).*

A put or call option to exchange financial assets or financial liabilities (ie financial instruments other than an entity's own equity instruments) gives the holder a right to obtain potential future economic benefits associated with changes in the fair value of the financial instrument underlying the contract. Conversely, the writer of an option assumes an obligation to forgo potential future economic benefits or bear potential losses of economic benefits associated with changes in the fair value of the underlying financial instrument. The contractual right of the holder and obligation of the writer meet the definition of a financial asset and a financial liability, respectively. The financial instrument underlying an option contract may be any financial asset, including shares in other entities and interestbearing instruments. An option may require the writer to issue a debt instrument, rather than transfer a financial asset, but the instrument underlying the option would constitute a financial asset of the holder if the option were exercised. The option-holder's right to exchange the financial asset under potentially favourable conditions and the writer's obligation to exchange the financial asset under potentially unfavourable conditions are distinct from the underlying financial asset to be exchanged upon exercise of the option. The nature of the holder's right and of the writer's obligation are not affected by the likelihood that the option will be exercised. **AG17**

Another example of a derivative financial instrument is a forward contract to be settled in six months' time in which one party (the purchaser) promises to deliver CU1,000,000 cash in exchange for CU1,000,000 face amount of fixed rate government bonds, and the other party (the seller) promises to deliver CU1,000,000 face amount of fixed rate government bonds in exchange for CU1,000,000 cash. During the six months, both parties have a contractual right and a contractual obligation to exchange financial instruments. If the market price of the government bonds rises above CU1,000,000, the conditions will be favourable to the purchaser and unfavourable to the seller; if the market price falls below CU1,000,000, the effect will be the opposite. The purchaser has a contractual right (a financial asset) similar to the right under a call option held and a contractual obligation (a financial liability) similar to the obligation under a put option written; the seller has a contractual right (a financial asset) similar to the right under a put option held and a contractual obligation (a financial liability) similar to the obligation under a call option written. As with options, these contractual rights and obligations constitute financial assets and financial liabilities separate and distinct from the underlying financial instruments (the bonds and cash to be exchanged). Both parties to a forward contract have an obligation to perform at the agreed time, whereas performance under an option contract occurs only if and when the holder of the option chooses to exercise it. **AG18**

Many other types of derivative instruments embody a right or obligation to make a future exchange, including interest rate and currency swaps, interest rate caps, collars and floors, loan commitments, note issuance facilities and letters of credit. An interest rate swap contract may be viewed as a variation of a forward contract in which the parties agree to make a series of future exchanges of cash amounts, one amount calculated with reference to a floating interest rate and the other with reference to a fixed interest rate. Futures contracts are another variation of forward contracts, differing primarily in that the contracts are standardised and traded on an exchange. **AG19**

Contracts to Buy or Sell Non-Financial Items (paragraphs 8-10)

Contracts to buy or sell non-financial items do not meet the definition of a financial instrument because the contractual right of one party to receive a nonfinancial asset or service and the corresponding obligation of the other party do not establish a present right or obligation of either party to receive, deliver or exchange a financial **AG20** asset. For example, contracts that provide for settlement only by the receipt or delivery of a non-financial item (eg an option, futures or forward contract on silver) are not financial instruments. Many commodity contracts are of this type. Some are standardised in form and traded on organised markets in much the same fashion as some derivative financial instruments. For example, a commodity futures contract may be bought and sold readily for cash because it is listed for trading on an exchange and may change hands many times. However, the parties buying and selling the contract are, in effect, trading the underlying commodity. The ability to buy or sell a commodity contract for cash, the ease with which it may be bought or sold and the possibility of negotiating a cash settlement of the obligation to receive or deliver the commodity do not alter the fundamental character of the contract in a way that creates a financial instrument. Nevertheless, some contracts to buy or sell nonfinancial items that can be settled net or by exchanging financial instruments, or in which the nonfinancial item is readily convertible to cash, are within the scope of the Standard as if they were financial instruments (see paragraph 8).

AG21   A contract that involves the receipt or delivery of physical assets does not give rise to a financial asset of one party and a financial liability of the other party unless any corresponding payment is deferred past the date on which the physical assets are transferred. Such is the case with the purchase or sale of goods on trade credit.

AG22   Some contracts are commodity-linked, but do not involve settlement through the physical receipt or delivery of a commodity. They specify settlement through cash payments that are determined according to a formula in the contract, rather than through payment of fixed amounts. For example, the principal amount of a bond may be calculated by applying the market price of oil prevailing at the maturity of the bond to a fixed quantity of oil. The principal is indexed by reference to a commodity price, but is settled only in cash. Such a contract constitutes a financial instrument.

AG23   The definition of a financial instrument also encompasses a contract that gives rise to a non-financial asset or non-financial liability in addition to a financial asset or financial liability. Such financial instruments often give one party an option to exchange a financial asset for a non-financial asset. For example, an oil-linked bond may give the holder the right to receive a stream of fixed periodic interest payments and a fixed amount of cash on maturity, with the option to exchange the principal amount for a fixed quantity of oil. The desirability of exercising this option will vary from time to time depending on the fair value of oil relative to the exchange ratio of cash for oil (the exchange price) inherent in the bond. The intentions of the bond-holder concerning the exercise of the option do not affect the substance of the component assets. The financial asset of the holder and the financial liability of the issuer make the bond a financial instrument, regardless of the other types of assets and liabilities also created.

AG24   [Withdrawn]*

Editor's note: AG24 deleted by FRS 29 with effect for accounting periods beginning on or after 1 January 2007.

PRESENTATION

Liabilities and Equity (paragraphs 15-27)

No Contractual Obligation to Deliver Cash or Another Financial Asset (paragraphs 17-20)

Preference shares may be issued with various rights. In determining whether a pre- **AG25** ference share is a financial liability or an equity instrument, an issuer assesses the particular rights attaching to the share to determine whether it exhibits the fundamental characteristic of a financial liability. For example, a preference share that provides for redemption on a specific date or at the option of the holder contains a financial liability because the issuer has an obligation to transfer financial assets to the holder of the share. The potential inability of an issuer to satisfy an obligation to redeem a preference share when contractually required to do so, whether because of a lack of funds, a statutory restriction or insufficient profits or reserves, does not negate the obligation. An option of the issuer to redeem the shares for cash does not satisfy the definition of a financial liability because the issuer does not have a present obligation to transfer financial assets to the shareholders. In this case, redemption of the shares is solely at the discretion of the issuer. An obligation may arise, however, when the issuer of the shares exercises its option, usually by formally notifying the shareholders of an intention to redeem the shares.

When preference shares are non-redeemable, the appropriate classification is deter- **AG26** mined by the other rights that attach to them. Classification is based on an assessment of the substance of the contractual arrangements and the definitions of a financial liability and an equity instrument. When distributions to holders of the preference shares, whether cumulative or non-cumulative, are at the discretion of the issuer, the shares are equity instruments. The classification of a preference share as an equity instrument or a financial liability is not affected by, for example:

(a) a history of making distributions;
(b) an intention to make distributions in the future;
(c) a possible negative impact on the price of ordinary shares of the issuer if distributions are not made (because of restrictions on paying dividends on the ordinary shares if dividends are not paid on the preference shares);
(d) the amount of the issuer's reserves;
(e) an issuer's expectation of a profit or loss for a period; or
(f) an ability or inability of the issuer to influence the amount of its profit or loss for the period.

Settlement in the Entity's Own Equity Instruments (paragraphs 21-24)

The following examples illustrate how to classify different types of contracts on an **AG27** entity's own equity instruments:

(a) A contract that will be settled by the entity receiving or delivering a fixed number of its own shares for no future consideration, or exchanging a fixed number of its own shares for a fixed amount of cash or another financial asset, is an equity instrument. Accordingly, any consideration received or paid for such a contract is added directly to or deducted directly from equity. One example is an issued share option that gives the counterparty a right to buy a fixed number of the entity's shares for a fixed amount of cash. However, if the contract requires the entity to purchase (redeem) its own shares for cash or another financial asset at a fixed or determinable date or on demand, the entity also recognises a financial liability for the present value of the redemption amount. One example is an entity's obligation under a forward contract to repurchase a fixed number of its own shares for a fixed amount of cash.

(b) An entity's obligation to purchase its own shares for cash gives rise to a financial liability for the present value of the redemption amount even if the number of shares that the entity is obliged to repurchase is not fixed or if the obligation is conditional on the counterparty exercising a right to redeem. One example of a conditional obligation is an issued option that requires the entity to repurchase its own shares for cash if the counterparty exercises the option.

(c) A contract that will be settled in cash or another financial asset is a financial asset or financial liability even if the amount of cash or another financial asset that will be received or delivered is based on changes in the market price of the entity's own equity. One example is a net cash-settled share option.

(d) A contract that will be settled in a variable number of the entity's own shares whose value equals a fixed amount or an amount based on changes in an underlying variable (eg a commodity price) is a financial asset or a financial liability. An example is a written option to buy gold that, if exercised, is settled net in the entity's own instruments by the entity delivering as many of those instruments as are equal to the value of the option contract. Such a contract is a financial asset or financial liability even if the underlying variable is the entity's own share price rather than gold. Similarly, a contract that will be settled in a fixed number of the entity's own shares, but the rights attaching to those shares will be varied so that the settlement value equals a fixed amount or an amount based on changes in an underlying variable, is a financial asset or a financial liability.

Contingent Settlement Provisions (paragraph 25)

AG28 Paragraph 25 requires that if a part of a contingent settlement provision that could require settlement in cash or another financial asset (or in another way that would result in the instrument being a financial liability) is not genuine, the settlement provision does not affect the classification of a financial instrument. Thus, a contract that requires settlement in cash or a variable number of the entity's own shares only on the occurrence of an event that is extremely rare, highly abnormal and very unlikely to occur is an equity instrument. Similarly, settlement in a fixed number of an entity's own shares may be contractually precluded in circumstances that are outside the control of the entity, but if these circumstances have no genuine possibility of occurring, classification as an equity instrument is appropriate.

Treatment in Consolidated Financial Statements

AG29 In consolidated financial statements, an entity presents minority interests—ie the interests of other parties in the equity and income of its subsidiaries—in accordance with FRS 2 *Subsidiary Undertakings*. When classifying a financial instrument (or a component of it) in consolidated financial statements, an entity considers all terms and conditions agreed between members of the group and the holders of the instrument in determining whether the group as a whole has an obligation to deliver cash or another financial asset in respect of the instrument or to settle it in a manner that results in liability classification. When a subsidiary in a group issues a financial instrument and a parent or other group entity agrees additional terms directly with the holders of the instrument (eg a guarantee), the group may not have discretion over distributions or redemption. Although the subsidiary may appropriately classify the instrument without regard to these additional terms in its individual financial statements, the effect of other agreements between members of the group and the holders of the instrument is considered in order to ensure that consolidated financial statements reflect the contracts and transactions entered into by the group as a whole. To the extent that there is such an obligation or settlement provision, the instrument (or the component of it that is subject to the obligation) is classified as a financial liability in consolidated financial statements.

Compound Financial Instruments (paragraphs 28-32)

Paragraph 28 applies only to issuers of non-derivative compound financial instruments. Paragraph 28 does not deal with compound financial instruments from the perspective of holders. IAS 39 deals with the separation of embedded derivatives from the perspective of holders of compound financial instruments that contain debt and equity features.   **AG30**

A common form of compound financial instrument is a debt instrument with an embedded conversion option, such as a bond convertible into ordinary shares of the issuer, and without any other embedded derivative features. Paragraph 28 requires the issuer of such a financial instrument to present the liability component and the equity component separately on the balance sheet, as follows: **AG31**

(a)   The issuer's obligation to make scheduled payments of interest and principal is a financial liability that exists as long as the instrument is not converted. On initial recognition, the fair value of the liability component is the present value of the contractually determined stream of future cash flows discounted at the rate of interest applied at that time by the market to instruments of comparable credit status and providing substantially the same cash flows, on the same terms, but without the conversion option.

(b)   The equity instrument is an embedded option to convert the liability into equity of the issuer. The fair value of the option comprises its time value and its intrinsic value, if any. This option has value on initial recognition even when it is out of the money.

On conversion of a convertible instrument at maturity, the entity derecognises the liability component and recognises it as equity. The original equity component remains as equity (although it may be transferred from one line item within equity to another). There is no gain or loss on conversion at maturity.   **AG32**

When an entity extinguishes a convertible instrument before maturity through an early redemption or repurchase in which the original conversion privileges are unchanged, the entity allocates the consideration paid and any transaction costs for the repurchase or redemption to the liability and equity components of the instrument at the date of the transaction. The method used in allocating the consideration paid and transaction costs to the separate components is consistent with that used in the original allocation to the separate components of the proceeds received by the entity when the convertible instrument was issued, in accordance with paragraphs 28-32.   **AG33**

Once the allocation of the consideration is made, any resulting gain or loss is treated in accordance with accounting principles applicable to the related component, as follows: **AG34**

(a)   the amount of gain or loss relating to the liability component is recognised in profit or loss; and

(b)   the amount of consideration relating to the equity component is recognised in equity.

An entity may amend the terms of a convertible instrument to induce early conversion, for example by offering a more favourable conversion ratio or paying other   **AG35** additional consideration in the event of conversion before a specified date. The difference, at the date the terms are amended, between the fair value of the consideration the holder receives on conversion of the instrument under the revised terms and the fair value of the consideration the holder would have received under the original terms is recognised as a loss in profit or loss.

Treasury Shares (paragraphs 33 and 34)

AG36   An entity's own equity instruments are not recognised as a financial asset regardless of the reason for which they are reacquired. Paragraph 33 requires an entity that reacquires its own equity instruments to deduct those equity instruments from equity. However, when an entity holds its own equity on behalf of others, eg a financial institution holding its own equity on behalf of a client, there is an agency relationship and as a result those holdings are not included in the entity's balance sheet.

Interest, Dividends, Losses and Gains (paragraphs 35-41)

AG37   The following example illustrates the application of paragraph 35 to a compound financial instrument. Assume that a non-cumulative preference share is mandatorily redeemable for cash in five years, but that dividends are payable at the discretion of the entity before the redemption date. Such an instrument is a compound financial instrument, with the liability component being the present value of the redemption amount. The unwinding of the discount on this component is recognised in profit or loss and classified as interest expense. Any dividends paid relate to the equity component and, accordingly, are recognised as a distribution of profit or loss. A similar treatment would apply if the redemption was not mandatory but at the option of the holder, or if the share was mandatorily convertible into a variable number of ordinary shares calculated to equal a fixed amount or an amount based on changes in an underlying variable (eg commodity). However, if any unpaid dividends are added to the redemption amount, the entire instrument is a liability. In such a case, any dividends are classified as interest expense.

Offsetting a Financial Asset and a Financial Liability (paragraphs 42-50)

AG38   To offset a financial asset and a financial liability, an entity must have a currently enforceable legal right to set off the recognised amounts. An entity may have a conditional right to set off recognised amounts, such as in a master netting agreement or in some forms of nonrecourse debt, but such rights are enforceable only on the occurrence of some future event, usually a default of the counterparty. Thus, such an arrangement does not meet the conditions for offset.

AG39   The Standard does not provide special treatment for so-called 'synthetic instruments', which are groups of separate financial instruments acquired and held to emulate the characteristics of another instrument. For example, a floating rate long-term debt combined with an interest rate swap that involves receiving floating payments and making fixed payments synthesises a fixed rate long-term debt. Each of the individual financial instruments that together constitute a 'synthetic instrument' represents a contractual right or obligation with its own terms and conditions and each may be transferred or settled separately. Each financial instrument is exposed to risks that may differ from the risks to which other financial instruments are exposed. Accordingly, when one financial instrument in a 'synthetic instrument' is an asset and another is a liability, they are not offset and presented on an entity's balance sheet on a net basis unless they meet the criteria for offsetting in paragraph 42. Disclosures are provided about the significant terms and conditions of each financial instrument, although an entity may indicate in addition the nature of the relationship between the individual instruments (see paragraph 65).*

DISCLOSURE

Financial Assets and Financial Liabilities at Fair Value Through Profit or Loss (paragraph 94(f))

[Withdrawn]†   **AG40**

---

*Editor's note: The last sentence of this paragraph is deleted by FRS 29 with effect for accounting periods beginning on or after 1 January 2007, or where FRS 29 is adopted early.

†Editor's note: Paragraph deleted by FRS 29.

APPROVAL OF IAS 32 BY THE BOARD

International Accounting Standard 32 *Financial Instruments: Disclosure and Presentation* was approved for issue by thirteen of the fourteen members of the International Accounting Standards Board. Mr Leisenring dissented. His dissenting opinion is set out after the Basis for Conclusions.

Sir David Tweedie   Chairman
Thomas E Jones   Vice-Chairman
Mary E Barth
Hans-Georg Bruns
Anthony T Cope
Robert P Garnett
Gilbert Gélard
James J Leisenring
Warren J McGregor
Patricia L O'Malley
Harry K Schmid
John T Smith
Geoffrey Whittington
Tatsumi Yamada

ADOPTION OF FRS 25 BY THE ACCOUNTING STANDARDS BOARD

Financial Reporting Standard 25 (IAS 32) *Financial Instruments: Disclosure and Presentation* was approved for issue by the ten members of the Accounting Standards Board.

Ian Mackintosh   Chairman
Andrew Lennard   Technical Director
Michael Ashley
Douglas Flint
Anthony Good
Roger Marshall
Isobel Sharp
John Smith
Jonathan Symonds
Peter Westlake

Notes on the standard's application in the UK and the Republic of Ireland

The need for an FRS on financial instruments disclosure and presentation

In June 2002 the Accounting Standards Board (the Board) issued FRED 30 'Financial Instruments: Disclosure and Presentation & Recognition and Measurement'. In August 2003, April 2004 and July 2004 it issued three supplements to that FRED. Together, the four documents proposed that: **N1**

(a) a standard for use in the UK and Republic or Ireland based on IAS 32 'Financial Instruments: Disclosure and Presentation' should be implemented for all entities, other than those that apply the FRSSE, for accounting periods beginning on or after 1 January 2005; and

(b) a standard for use in the UK and the Republic of Ireland based on the measurement and hedge accounting requirements of IAS 39 'Financial Instruments: Recognition and Measurement' (but not its recognition and derecognition requirements) should be implemented from the same date for all listed entities and for any unlisted entity that chooses to apply fair value accounting in its financial statements.

The Board has now decided to issue FRS 25 which, together with FRS 26 (IAS 39) 'Financial Instruments: Measurement', implements these proposals.

The issue of these two standards forms part of the Board's programme to bring about convergence between its accounting standards and International Accounting Standards (IFRSs). Under this programme, the Board is seeking to bring its standards into line with IFRS over the medium term, dealing first with areas where implementation of an international standard would enhance existing UK and Republic of Ireland financial reporting requirements and keep them in step with changes in the law. **N2**

The Board is strongly of the view that a standard on disclosures relating to financial instruments including derivatives is important beyond the limited scope of the existing UK standard on these disclosures, FRS 13 'Derivatives and Other Financial Instruments'. **N3**

Furthermore, the Board considers it necessary to implement the presentation requirements of the IASB's standard on financial instruments in place of the requirements of FRS 4 'Capital Instruments' to correspond with the amendments to the Companies Act 1985 resulting from the Modernisation Directive*. These amendments will require the classification of items on the balance sheet to have regard to their substance, and as a result preference shares that contain obligations to transfer economic benefits will be classified as liabilities rather than shareholders' funds. The Board therefore believes that it is necessary to issue a standard providing guidance on the application of these new requirements in the Companies Act, to be effective from the same date as the amendments to the Act. **N4**

**Directive 2003/51/EC; similar amendments are to be made to the equivalent Northern Ireland and Republic of Ireland legislation.*

Effective date

N5   The presentation requirements of the FRS are effective for accounting periods beginning on or after 1 January 2005, to correspond to the effective date of the regulations amending the Companies Act to implement the Modernisation Directive, and accordingly early implementation is not permitted. The disclosure requirements apply for accounting periods beginning on or after 1 January 2007; earlier compliance is required for entities that are required, or choose, to comply with FRS 26, as explained in the notes on application of that standard.

Exemptions from FRS 25

N6   The Board has followed its usual practice of exempting from the FRS all entities falling within the scope of the Financial Reporting Standard for Smaller Entities (FRSSE).

N7   The Board did not consider any other exemptions from the presentation requirements of the standard were necessary. The Board did, however, decide that some exemptions were appropriate from the disclosure requirements.

Disclosure exemptions

N8   The Board first developed disclosure requirements for financial instruments in FRS 13, which applied only to banks and listed entities. Since the issue of that standard, experience in disclosing information relating to financial instruments has developed, and in FRED 30 Third Supplement the Board expressed its view that it was time for disclosures on financial instruments to be required from a wider range of entities.

N9   However, many respondents pointed out the considerable burden these disclosures would place on entities, particularly smaller ones. They also pointed out the major changes to the disclosure requirements proposed by the IASB in its exposure draft ED 7 'Financial Instruments: Disclosures' (issued by the Board as FRED 33). The Board has decided to require the IAS 32 disclosures from 2005 only for those entities that applied the measurement rules set out in FRS 26 (IAS 39) 'Financial Instruments: Measurement'. Other entities are required to adopt the amended requirements of FRS 25 from 2007, although early adoption is encouraged. Furthermore, if the IASB and ASB issue a standard based on ED 7 and FRED 33 during 2005, as is expected, it is envisaged that entities will be permitted to implement the requirements of this new standard in place of the FRS 25 disclosure requirements.

N10   The Board also noted that the amendments to the Companies Act that are being introduced to implement the Fair Value Directive include additional disclosure requirements for all companies on financial instruments. Most of these requirements are similar to those set out in FRS 25. The Board would encourage those entities outside the scope of the disclosure requirements of FRS 25 to have regard to the standard to guide them in applying the new requirements of the Companies Act.

N11   In FRED 30 the Board proposed additional disclosure requirements for those entities applying the disclosure provisions of IAS 32 but not the measurement provisions of IAS 39. These additional requirements called for additional detail of accounting policies for financial instruments to be given. Although the disclosures are no longer required for those entities not adopting FRS 26, the Board has retained these additional requirements, in paragraphs 66A and 66B, for those entities voluntarily making FRS 25 disclosures, to emphasise the importance of full disclosure of accounting policies. The Board has also, in paragraph 3C, included clarification that entities not applying the measurement requirements set out in FRS

26 but voluntarily giving the FRS 25 disclosures should adapt these disclosure requirements in line with the entity's accounting policies for the relevant transactions. In particular, an entity would disclose the interest rate used for accruing interest under its accounting policies, rather than the effective interest rate calculated in accordance with IAS 39; would classify contracts as insurance contracts for disclosure purposes in line with their accounting treatment rather than in accordance with the definition in IFRS 4; and would make disclosures relating to hedge accounting that correspond to its accounting policies for hedging transactions.

Parents and subsidiaries

IAS 39 does not differentiate between individual entity financial statements and consolidated financial statements, nor between subsidiaries and parents; it applies to all entities and to all their financial statements. **N12**

Several respondents expressed the view that applying the disclosure requirements to the single-entity financial statements of parent companies and wholly-owned subsidiaries may result in lengthy disclosures for little benefit, particularly where the financial risks of the entity were managed as part of the risks of the group. The Board agreed that there was a balance to be struck between the value of this information and the additional burden of requiring it to be published, and in many such cases this information is likely to be of less importance. It also noted that the legislative amendments implementing the Fair Value Directive would require disclosure of some, though not all, of the information. It therefore agreed that the benefits of applying the full disclosure requirements to all such entities were outweighed by the likely costs of so doing, and has included an exemption in the FRS. This exemption applies to parent companies in their own single-entity financial statements, and to subsidiaries where at least 90 per cent of the voting rights are controlled within the group. In each case it is dependent on the entity being included in consolidated financial statements that are publicly available and which include the disclosures on a group basis. **N13**

However, the arguments for full disclosure were stronger in the case of certain entities where there is a substantial public interest – banks and insurance companies – and the Board has therefore not included these in the above exemption. **N14**

Derecognition

[Deleted]* **N15**

Material on current liabilities

In FRED 30 the Board also proposed that the requirements in IAS 1 'Presentation of Financial Statements' on the classification of financial liabilities as current or non-current should be implemented in the UK and Republic of Ireland to support the disclosures in IAS 32, and these have been included in the standard, with minor drafting amendments. **N16**

Transitional provisions

The Board considered whether to allow entities adopting this FRS to be able to take advantage of the same transitional provisions as entities adopting the corresponding **N17**

Editor's note: Paragraph deleted by amendments to FRS 26.

international standard as part of their transition to IFRS, which are set out in IFRS 1 'First-time Adoption of International Financial Reporting Standards'. Under IFRS 1, entities first adopting IFRS for an accounting period commencing before 1 January 2006 are not required to restate comparatives to comply with IAS 32 and IAS 39, subject to additional disclosure requirements. The Board agreed to include this exemption for those entities adopting both this FRS and FRS 26 for that accounting period. The relevant paragraphs from IFRS 1 have therefore been incorporated in FRS 26 and referred to in this FRS. The FRS does not prohibit restatement and entities are encouraged to restate comparatives for the presentation changes where practicable.

N18   The Board intends that entities adopting this FRS should be able to take advantage of the same transitional provisions as entities adopting the corresponding international standards as part of their transition to IFRS, which are set out in IFRS 1 'First-time Adoption of International Financial Reporting Standards', and consistently with its reasons for deferring the effective date for some entities to 2006, has extended the period for which these transitional provisions apply. Restatement of comparatives is therefore not required for an entity adopting the presentation requirements of this standard for an accounting period commencing before 1 January 2006, or adopting the disclosure requirements of the standard together with the requirements of FRS 26 for an accounting period commencing before 1 January 2007.

N19   The Board has, in adopting the transition requirements in IFRS 1, followed the practice adopted in several previous UK standards that applied prospectively and therefore not required corresponding amounts on a comparable basis. Some commentators have recently raised concerns that this might not be in compliance with the requirements of the Companies Act. The Board does not believe that it was ever the intention that prospective application of a new standard should be prevented. However, in view of these concerns, it has noted that a minor change to the Act could clarify the issue by explicitly permitting entities not to restate comparatives in certain circumstances; the DTI has agreed to consider such an amendment if this would remove uncertainty over the application of the transitional provisions of the FRS.

N20   Where an entity has previously issued a convertible instrument that the FRS requires to be split into its equity and liability components, and the instrument is not longer outstanding, retrospective application of the FRS would require separating two portions of equity. The Board has included the transitional provision in IFRS 1 that permits entities not to make this allocation if the liability component is no longer outstanding at the beginning of the earliest period for which comparative information is given.

ASB consequential amendments

N21   Amendments to existing UK standards and UITF Abstracts are set out in paragraphs 100A to 100D.

N22   The existing UK standard on financial instrument disclosures, FRS 13, applies only to listed entities and to banks and similar institutions. Most of these entities will be required to adopt the measurement rules of FRS 26 and accordingly fall within the scope of FRS 25's disclosure requirements. For such entities, FRS 13 is withdrawn. However, it remains in force for any banking or similar institution that does not fall within the scope of FRS 26 and does not voluntarily adopt that standard.

The FRS also has the effect of withdrawing FRS 4, except for material on measurement of debt and gains and loses on repurchase of debt. This material is withdrawn for those entities applying the measurement requirements set out in FRS 26, but remains applicable for other entities. In addition, a UITF Abstract interpreting the requirements of FRS 4 is withdrawn: Abstract 33 'Obligations in capital instruments'. Abstract 11 'Capital instruments: issue call options' relates to the measurement requirements of FRS 4 and continues in force for those entities not applying the requirements of FRS 26.

N23

A further UITF Abstract, Abstract 37 'Purchase and sales of own shares' is also withdrawn as these requirements are incorporated in the FRS.

N24

The offset rules in FRS 5 'Reporting the Substance of Transactions' are withdrawn, as these are replaced by requirements in the FRS.

N25

Minor consequential amendments to other UK standards are set out in paragraph 100D.

N26

Other consequential amendments set out in IAS 32 do not affect UK standards and are not included in FRS 25.

N27

In October 2005 the Board amended FRS 25 to incorporate consequential amendments made to IAS 32 by the IASB in amendments to IAS 39:

N28

- The Fair Value Option (June 2005)
- Financial Guarantee Contracts and Credit Insurance (August 2005)

Fair Value Option

In June 2005 the IASB amended IAS 39 to restrict the circumstances in which a financial asset or financial liability could be designated as at fair value through profit and loss, and incorporated additional disclosure requirements in IAS 32 for information on the circumstances in which an entity designated items at fair value through profit and loss, and on the items so designated.

N29

The ASB has amended FRS 25 to include certain of these additional disclosure requirements. The ASB does, however, have considerable reservations over the value of some of the disclosures introduced by the IASB's amendment which in its view are intended to provide information that is relevant to regulatory returns rather than general purpose financial statements. The ASB has not, therefore, implemented all the disclosure requirements inserted in IAS 32.*

N30

Implementation of derecognition material

In April 2006 the Board amended FRS 26 to include the IAS 39 material on recognition and derecognition into the Standard. Accordingly, on implementation of this amendment the corresponding disclosure requirements of IAS 32 are implemented in FRS 25. These new disclosure requirements replace disclosures required for financial assets and liabilities by FRS 5 'Reporting the Substance of Transactions'. These amendments are effective for accounting periods on or after 1 January 2007, with earlier adoption permitted.†

N31

---

*Editor's note: Paragraphs N28 to N30 added in October 2005.

†Editor's note: Paragraph N31 added in April 2006.

Basis for Conclusions

Basis for Conclusions

This Basis for Conclusions accompanies, but is not part of, IAS 32.

> *ASB note:* The IASB's Basis for Conclusions, which accompanies IAS 32, is set out below in full. It should be noted though that some of the discussion it contains concerns IASB requirements that have no equivalent in the UK or Republic of Ireland. Footnotes have been used to indicate corresponding requirements in the UK and Republic of Ireland where applicable.

All references in this section to 'the Board' and 'Board members' are references to the IASB Board and IASB Board members.

BC1 This Basis for Conclusions summarises the International Accounting Standards Board's considerations in reaching its conclusions on revising IAS 32 *Financial Instruments: Disclosure and Presentation* in 2003*. Individual Board members gave greater weight to some factors than to others.

BC2 In July 2001 the Board announced that, as part of its initial agenda of technical projects, it would undertake a project to improve a number of Standards, including IAS 32 and IAS 39 *Financial Instruments: Recognition and Measurement*. The objectives of the Improvements project were to reduce the complexity in the Standards by clarifying and adding guidance, eliminating internal inconsistencies, and incorporating into the Standards elements of Standing Interpretations Committee (SIC) Interpretations and IAS 39 implementation guidance. In June 2002 the Board published its proposals in an Exposure Draft of proposed amendments to IAS 32 *Financial Instruments: Disclosure and Presentation* and IAS 39 *Financial Instruments: Recognition and Measurement*, with a comment deadline of 14 October 2002. The Board received over 170 comment letters on the Exposure Draft.

BC3 Because the Board did not reconsider the fundamental approach to the accounting for financial instruments established by IAS 32 and IAS 39, this Basis for Conclusions does not discuss requirements in IAS 32 that the Board has not reconsidered.

DEFINITIONS (PARAGRAPHS 11-14 AND AG3AG24)

Financial Asset, Financial Liability and Equity Instrument (paragraphs 11 and AG3 – AG 14)

BC4 The revised IAS 32 addresses the classification as financial assets, financial liabilities or equity instruments of financial instruments that are indexed to, or settled in, an entity's own equity instruments. As discussed further in paragraphs BC6–BC15, the Board decided to preclude equity classification for such contracts when they (a) involve an obligation to deliver cash or another financial asset or to exchange financial assets or financial liabilities under conditions that are potentially unfavourable to the entity, (b) in the case of a nonderivative, are not for the receipt or delivery of a fixed number of shares or (c) in the case of a derivative, are not for the exchange of a fixed number of shares for a fixed amount of cash or another financial asset. The Board also decided to preclude equity classification for contracts that are derivatives on derivatives on an entity's own equity. Consistently with this decision,

---

**ASB footnote: The Basis for Conclusions discusses the changes from the previous version of IAS 32 issued in 2000. This version of IAS 32 was not implemented in the UK.*

the Board also decided to amend the definitions of financial asset, financial liability and equity instrument in IAS 32 to make them consistent with the guidance about contracts on an entity's own equity instruments. The Board did not reconsider other aspects of the definitions as part of this project to revise IAS 32, for example the other changes to the definitions proposed by the Joint Working Group in its Draft Standard *Financial Instruments and Similar Items* published by the Board's predecessor body, IASC, in 2000*.

PRESENTATION (PARAGRAPHS 15-50 AND AG25AG39)

Liabilities and Equity (paragraphs 15-27 and AG25-AG29)

BC5   The revised IAS 32 addresses whether derivative and non-derivative contracts indexed to, or settled in, an entity's own equity instruments are financial assets, financial liabilities or equity instruments. The original IAS 32 dealt with aspects of this issue piecemeal and it was not clear how various transactions (eg net share settled contracts and contracts with settlement options) should be treated under the Standard. The Board concluded that it needed to clarify the accounting treatment for such transactions.

BC6   The approach agreed by the Board can be summarised as follows:

A contract on an entity's own equity is an equity instrument if, and only if:

(a)   it contains no contractual obligation to transfer cash or another financial asset, or to exchange financial assets or financial liabilities with another entity under conditions that are potentially unfavourable to the entity; and

(b)   if the instrument will or may be settled in the entity's own equity instruments, it is either (i) a non-derivative that includes no contractual obligation for the entity to deliver a variable number of its own equity instruments, or (ii) a derivative that will be settled by the entity exchanging a fixed amount of cash or another financial asset for a fixed number of its own equity instruments.

No Contractual Obligation to Deliver Cash or Another Financial Asset (paragraphs 17-20 and AG25-AG26)

Puttable Instruments (paragraph 18(b))

BC7   The Board decided that a financial instrument that gives the holder the right to put the instrument back to the entity for cash or another financial asset is a financial liability of the entity. Such financial instruments are commonly issued by mutual funds, unit trusts, co-operative and similar entities, often with the redemption amount being equal to a proportionate share in the net assets of the entity. Although the legal form of such financial instruments often includes a right to the residual interest in the assets of an entity available to holders of such instruments, the inclusion of an option for the holder to put the instrument back to the entity for cash or another financial asset means that the instrument meets the definition of a financial liability. The classification as a financial liability is independent of considerations such as when the right is exercisable, how the amount payable or receivable upon exercise of the right is determined, and whether the puttable instrument has a fixed maturity.

BC8   The Board noted that the classification of a puttable instrument as a financial liability does not preclude the use of descriptors such as 'net assets attributable to

*ASB footnote: This document was also published by the ASB.

unitholders' and 'change in net assets attributable to unitholders' on the face of the financial statements of an entity that has no equity (such as some mutual funds and unit trusts) or whose share capital is a financial liability under IAS 32 (such as some cooperatives). The Board also agreed that it should provide examples of how such entities might present their income statement and balance sheet (see Illustrative Examples 7 and 8).

Implicit Obligations (paragraph 20)

The Board did not debate whether an obligation can be established implicitly rather than explicitly because this is not within the scope of an improvements project. This question will be considered by the Board in its project on revenue, liabilities and equity. Consequently, the Board retained the existing notion that an instrument may establish an obligation indirectly through its terms and conditions (see paragraph 20). However, it decided that the example of a preference share with a contractually accelerating dividend which, within the foreseeable future, is scheduled to yield a dividend so high that the entity will be economically compelled to redeem the instrument, was insufficiently clear. The example was therefore removed and replaced with others that are clearer and deal with situations that have proved problematic in practice. **BC9**

Settlement in the Entity's Own Equity Instruments (paragraphs 21-24 and AG27)

The approach taken in the revised IAS 32 includes two main conclusions: **BC10**

(a)   When an entity has an obligation to purchase its own shares for cash (such as under a forward contract to purchase its own shares), there is a financial liability for the amount of cash that the entity has an obligation to pay.

(b)   When an entity uses its own equity instruments 'as currency' in a contract to receive or deliver a variable number of shares whose value equals a fixed amount or an amount based on changes in an underlying variable (eg a - commodity price), the contract is not an equity instrument, but is a financial asset or a financial liability. In other words, when a contract is settled in a variable number of the entity's own equity instruments, or by the entity exchanging a fixed number of its own equity instruments for a variable amount of cash or another financial asset, the contract is not an equity instrument but is a financial asset or a financial liability.

When an entity has an obligation to purchase its own shares for cash, there is a financial liability for the amount of cash that the entity has an obligation to pay.

An entity's obligation to purchase its own shares establishes a maturity date for the shares that are subject to the contract. Therefore, to the extent of the obligation, those shares cease to be equity instruments when the entity assumes the obligation. This treatment under IAS 32 is consistent with the treatment of shares that provide for mandatory redemption by the entity. Without a requirement to recognise a financial liability for the present value of the share redemption amount, entities with identical obligations to deliver cash in exchange for their own equity instruments could report different information in their financial statements depending on whether the redemption clause is embedded in the equity instrument or is a free-standing derivative contract. **BC11**

Some respondents to the Exposure Draft suggested that when an entity writes an option that, if exercised, will result in the entity paying cash in return for receiving its own shares, it is incorrect to treat the full amount of the exercise price as a financial **BC12** liability because the obligation is conditional upon the option being exercised. The Board rejected this argument because the entity has an obligation to pay the full redemption amount and cannot avoid settlement in cash or another financial asset for the full redemption amount unless the counterparty decides not to exercise its redemption right or specified future events or circumstances beyond the control of the entity occur or do not occur. The Board also noted that a change would require a reconsideration of other provisions in IAS 32 that require liability treatment for obligations that are conditional on events or choices that are beyond the entity's control. These include, for example, (a) the treatment of financial instruments with contingent settlement provisions as financial liabilities for the full amount of the conditional obligation, (b) the treatment of preference shares that are redeemable at the option of the holder as financial liabilities for the full amount of the conditional obligation, and (c) the treatment of financial instruments (puttable instruments) that give the holder the right to put the instrument back to the issuer for cash or another financial asset, the amount of which is determined by reference to an index, and which therefore has the potential to increase and decrease, as financial liabilities for the full amount of the conditional obligation.

When an entity uses its own equity instruments as currency in a contract to receive or deliver a variable number of shares, the contract is not an equity instrument, but is a financial asset or a financial liability.

BC13   The Board agreed that it would be inappropriate to account for a contract as an equity instrument when an entity's own equity instruments are used as currency in a contract to receive or deliver a variable number of shares whose value equals a fixed amount or an amount based on changes in an underlying variable (eg a net share-settled derivative contract on gold or an obligation to deliver as many shares as are equal in value to CU10,000). Such a contract represents a right or obligation of a specified amount rather than a specified equity interest. A contract to pay or receive a specified amount (rather than a specified equity interest) is not an equity instrument. For such a contract, the entity does not know, before the transaction is settled, how many of its own shares (or how much cash) it will receive or deliver and the entity may not even know whether it will receive or deliver its own shares.

BC14   In addition, the Board noted that precluding equity treatment for such a contract limits incentives for structuring potentially favourable or unfavourable transactions to obtain equity treatment. For example, the Board believes that an entity should not be able to obtain equity treatment for a transaction simply by including a share settlement clause when the contract is for a specified value, rather than a specified equity interest.

BC15   The Board rejected the argument that a contract that is settled in the entity's own shares must be an equity instrument because no change in assets or liabilities, and thus no gain or loss, arises on settlement of the contract. The Board noted that any gain or loss arises before settlement of the transaction, not when it is settled.

Contingent Settlement Provisions (paragraphs 25 and AG28)

BC16   The revised Standard incorporates the conclusion previously in SIC-5 *Classification of Financial Instruments—Contingent Settlement Provisions** that a financial instrument for which the manner of settlement depends on the occurrence or non-occurrence of uncertain future events, or on the outcome of uncertain circumstances

****ASB footnote***: *no equivalent requirement in the UK and Republic of Ireland.*

that are beyond the control of both the issuer and the holder (ie a 'contingent settlement provision'), is a financial liability.

The amendments do not include the exception previously provided in paragraph 6 of SIC5 for circumstances in which the possibility of the entity being required to settle in cash or another financial asset is remote at the time the financial instrument is issued. The Board concluded that it is not consistent with the definitions of financial liabilities and equity instruments to classify an obligation to deliver cash or another financial asset as a financial liability only when settlement in cash is probable. There is a contractual obligation to transfer economic benefits as a result of past events because the entity is unable to avoid a settlement in cash or another financial asset unless an event occurs or does not occur in the future. **BC17**

However, the Board also concluded that contingent settlement provisions that would apply only in the event of liquidation of an entity should not influence the classification of the instrument because to do so would be inconsistent with a going concern assumption. A contingent settlement provision that provides for payment in cash or another financial asset only on the liquidation of the entity is similar to an equity instrument that has priority in liquidation and therefore should be ignored in classifying the instrument. **BC18**

Additionally, the Board decided that if the part of a contingent settlement provision that could require settlement in cash or a variable number of own shares is not genuine, it should be ignored for the purposes of classifying the instrument. The Board also agreed to provide guidance on the meaning of 'genuine' in this context (see paragraph AG28). **BC19**

Settlement Options (paragraphs 26 and 27)

The revised Standard requires that if one of the parties to a contract has one or more options as to how it is settled (eg net in cash or by exchanging shares for cash), the contract is a financial asset or a financial liability unless all of the settlement alternatives would result in equity classification. The Board concluded that entities should not be able to circumvent the accounting requirements for financial assets and financial liabilities simply by including an option to settle a contract through the exchange of a fixed number of shares for a fixed amount. The Board had proposed in the Exposure Draft that past practice and management intentions should be considered in determining the classification of such instruments. However, respondents to the Exposure Draft noted that such requirements can be difficult to apply because some entities do not have any history of similar transactions and the assessment of whether an established practice exists and of what is management's intention can be subjective. The Board agreed with these comments and accordingly concluded that past practice and management intentions should not be determining factors. **BC20**

Alternative Approaches Considered

In finalising the revisions to IAS 32 the Board considered, but rejected, a number of alternative approaches: **BC21**

(a) To classify as an equity instrument any contract that will be settled in the entity's own shares. The Board rejected this approach because it does not deal adequately with transactions in which an entity is using its own shares as currency, eg when an entity has an obligation to pay a fixed or determinable amount that is settled in a variable number of its own shares.

(b)   To classify a contract as an equity instrument only if (i) the contract will be settled in the entity's own shares, and (ii) the changes in the fair value of the contract move in the same direction as the changes in the fair value of the shares from the perspective of the counterparty. Under this approach, contracts that will be settled in the entity's own shares would be financial assets or financial liabilities if, from the perspective of the counterparty, their value moves inversely with the price of the entity's own shares. An example is an entity's obligation to buy back its own shares. The Board rejected this approach because its adoption would represent a fundamental shift in the concept of equity. The Board also noted that it would result in a change to the classification of some transactions, compared with the existing *Framework** and IAS 32, that had not been exposed for comment.

(c)   To classify as an equity instrument a contract that will be settled in the entity's own shares unless its value changes in response to something other than the price of the entity's own shares. The Board rejected this approach to avoid an exception to the principle that non-derivative contracts that are settled in a variable number of an entity's own shares should be treated as financial assets or financial liabilities.

(d)   To limit classification as equity instruments to outstanding ordinary shares, and classify as financial assets or financial liabilities all contracts that involve future receipt or delivery of the entity's own shares. The Board rejected this approach because its adoption would represent a fundamental shift in the concept of equity. The Board also noted that it would result in a change to the classification of some transactions compared with the existing IAS 32 that had not been exposed for comment.

Compound Financial Instruments (paragraphs 28-32 and AG30-AG35)

BC22   The Standard requires the separate presentation on an entity's balance sheet of liability and equity components of a single financial instrument. It is more a matter of form than a matter of substance that both liabilities and equity interests are created by a single financial instrument rather than two or more separate instruments. The Board believes that an entity's financial position is more faithfully represented by separate presentation of liability and equity components contained in a single instrument.

Allocation of the initial carrying amount to the liability and equity components (paragraphs 31 and 32, AG36-AG38 and Illustrative Examples 9-12)

BC23   The previous version of IAS 32 did not prescribe a particular method for assigning the initial carrying amount of a compound financial instrument to its separated liability and equity components. Rather, it suggested approaches that might be considered, such as:

(a)   assigning to the less easily measurable component (often the equity component) the residual amount after deducting from the instrument as a whole the amount separately determined for the component that is more easily determinable (a 'withandwithout' method); and

(b)   measuring the liability and equity components separately and, to the extent necessary, adjusting these amounts pro rata so that the sum of the components equals the amount of the instrument as a whole (a 'relative fair value' method).

**ASB footnote: The equivalent document in the UK and Republic of Ireland to the IASB's* Framework *is the ASB's* Statement of Principles for Financial Reporting. *Although the Statement of Principles is very similar to the* Framework, *it is not identical.*

This choice was originally justified on the grounds that IAS 32 did not deal with the measurement of financial assets, financial liabilities and equity instruments.   **BC24**

However, since the issue of IAS 39*, IFRSs contain requirements for the measurement of financial assets and financial liabilities. Therefore, the view that IAS 32 should not prescribe a particular method for separating compound financial instruments because of the absence of measurement requirements for financial instruments is no longer valid. IAS 39, paragraph 43, requires a financial liability to be measured on initial recognition at its fair value. Therefore, a relative fair value method could result in an initial measurement of the liability component that is not in compliance with IAS 39.   **BC25**

After initial recognition, a financial liability that is classified as at fair value through profit or loss is measured at fair value under IAS 39, and other financial liabilities are measured at amortised cost. If the liability component of a compound financial instrument is classified as at fair value through profit or loss, an entity could recognise an immediate gain or loss after initial recognition if it applies a relative fair value method. This is contrary to IAS 32, paragraph 31, which states that no gain or loss arises from recognising the components of the instrument separately.   **BC26**

Under the *Framework*, and IASs 32 and 39, an equity instrument is defined as any contract that evidences a residual interest in the assets of an entity after deducting all of its liabilities. Paragraph 67 of the *Framework* further states that the amount at which equity is recognised in the balance sheet is dependent on the measurement of assets and liabilities.   **BC27**

The Board concluded that the alternatives in IAS 32 to measure on initial recognition the liability component of a compound financial instrument as a residual amount after separating the equity component or on the basis of a relative fair value method should be eliminated. Instead the liability component should be measured first (including the value of any embedded non-equity derivative features, such as an embedded call feature), and the residual amount assigned to the equity component.   **BC28**

The objective of this amendment is to make the requirements about the entity's separation of the liability and equity components of a single compound financial instrument consistent with the requirements about the initial measurement of a financial liability in IAS 39 and the definitions in IAS 32 and the *Framework* of an equity instrument as a residual interest.   **BC29**

This approach removes the need to estimate inputs to, and apply, complex option pricing models to measure the equity component of some compound financial instruments. The Board also noted that the absence of a prescribed approach led to a lack of comparability among entities applying IAS 32 and that it therefore was desirable to specify a single approach.   **BC30**

The Board noted that a requirement to use the with-and-without method, under which the liability component is determined first, is consistent with the proposals of the Joint Working Group of Standard Setters in its Draft Standard and Basis for Conclusions in *Financial Instruments and Similar Items,* published by IASC in December 2000 (see Draft Standard, paragraphs 74 and 75 and Application Supplement, paragraph 318).   **BC31**

---

*ASB footnote: now being implemented in the UK as FRS 26.

Treasury Shares (paragraphs 33, 34 and AG36)

BC32   The revised Standard incorporates the guidance in SIC-16 *Share Capital—Reacquired Own Equity Instruments (Treasury Shares)**. The acquisition and subsequent resale by an entity of its own equity instruments represents a transfer between those holders of equity instruments who have given up their equity interest and those who continue to hold an equity instrument, rather than a gain or loss to the entity.

Interest, Dividends, Losses and Gains (paragraphs 35-41 and AG37)

Costs of an equity transaction (paragraphs 35 and 37-39)

BC33   The revised Standard incorporates the guidance in SIC-17 *Equity—Costs of an Equity Transaction†*. *Transaction costs incurred as a necessary part of completing an equity transaction are accounted for as part of the transaction to which they relate. Linking the equity transaction and costs of the transaction reflects in equity the total cost of the transaction.*

DISCLOSURE (PARAGRAPHS 51-95)‡

SUMMARY OF CHANGES FROM THE EXPOSURE DRAFT

BC49   The main changes from the Exposure Draft's proposals are as follows:

(a)   The Exposure Draft proposed to define a financial liability as a contractual obligation to deliver cash or another financial asset to another entity or to exchange financial instruments with another entity under conditions that are potentially unfavourable. The definition in the Standard has been expanded to include some contracts that will or may be settled in the entity's own equity instruments. The Standard's definition of a financial asset has been similarly expanded.

(b)   The Exposure Draft proposed that a financial instrument that gives the holder the right to put it back to the entity for cash or another financial asset is a financial liability. The Standard retains this conclusion, but provides additional guidance and illustrative examples to assist entities that, as a result of this requirement, either have no equity as defined in IAS 32 or whose share capital is not equity as defined in IAS 32.

(c)   The Standard retains and clarifies the proposal in the Exposure Draft that terms and conditions of a financial instrument may indirectly create an obligation.

(d)   The Exposure Draft proposed to incorporate in IAS 32 the conclusion previously in SIC-5 *Classification of Financial Instruments—Contingent Settlement Provisions*. This is that a financial instrument for which the manner of settlement depends on the occurrence or non-occurrence of uncertain future events or on the outcome of uncertain circumstances that are beyond the control of both the issuer and the holder is a financial liability. The Standard clarifies this conclusion by requiring contingent settlement provisions that apply only in the event of liquidation of an entity or are not genuine to be ignored.

*ASB footnote: similar provisions were included in UITF Abstract 37 Purchases and sales of own shares.

†ASB footnote: similar provisions were included in FRS 4 Capital Instruments.

‡Editor's note: BC34 to BC48 withdrawn by FRS 29.

(e)   The Exposure Draft proposed that a derivative contract that contains an option as to how it is settled meets the definition of an equity instrument if the entity had all of the following: (i) an unconditional right and ability to settle the contract gross; (ii) an established practice of such settlement; and (iii) the intention to settle the contract gross. These conditions have not been carried forward into the Standard. Rather, a derivative with settlement options is classified as a financial asset or a financial liability unless all the settlement alternatives would result in equity classification.

(f)   The Standard provides explicit guidance on accounting for the repurchase of a convertible instrument.

(g)   The Standard provides explicit guidance on accounting for the amendment of the terms of a convertible instrument to induce early conversion.

(h)   The Exposure Draft proposed that a financial instrument that is an equity instrument of a subsidiary should be eliminated on consolidation when held by the parent, or presented in the consolidated balance sheet within equity when not held by the parent (as a minority interest separate from the equity of the parent). The Standard requires all terms and conditions agreed between members of the group and the holders of the instrument to be considered when determining if the group as a whole has an obligation that would give rise to a financial liability. To the extent there is such an obligation, the instrument (or component of the instrument that is subject to the obligation) is a financial liability in consolidated financial statements.

(i)   [Withdrawn]

(j)   [Withdrawn]

(k)   In August 2005, the IASB issued IFRS 7 Financial Instruments: Disclosures. As a result, disclosures relating to financial instruments, if still relevant, were relocated to IFRS 7.

DISSENTING OPINION

Dissent of James J Leisenring

Mr Leisenring dissents from IAS 32 because, in his view, the conclusions about the accounting for forward purchase contracts and written put options on an issuer's equity instruments that require physical settlement in exchange for cash are inappropriate. IAS 32 requires a forward purchase contract to be recognised as though the future transaction had already occurred. Similarly it requires a written put option to be accounted for as though the option had already been exercised. Both of these contracts result in combining the separate forward contract and the written put option with outstanding shares to create a synthetic liability.   **DO1**

Recording a liability for the present value of the fixed forward price as a result of a forward contract is inconsistent with the accounting for other forward contracts. Recording a liability for the present value of the strike price of an option results in recording a liability that is inconsistent with the *Framework* as there is no present obligation for the strike price. In both instances the shares considered to be subject to the contracts are outstanding, have the same rights as any other shares and should be accounted for as outstanding. The forward and option contracts meet the definition of a derivative and should be accounted for as derivatives rather than create an exception to the accounting required by IAS 39. Similarly, if the redemption feature is embedded in the equity instrument (for example, a redeemable preference share) rather than being a free-standing derivative contract, the redemption feature should be accounted for as a derivative.   **DO2**

DO3   Mr Leisenring also objects to the conclusion that a purchased put or call option on a fixed number of an issuer's equity instruments is not an asset. The rights created by these contracts meet the definition of an asset and should be accounted for as assets and not as a reduction in equity. These contracts also meet the definition of derivatives that should be accounted for as such consistently with IAS 39.

Illustrative Examples

Illustrative Examples

These examples accompany, but are not part of, FRS 25.

Accounting for Contracts on Equity Instruments of an Entity

IE1   The following examples* illustrate the application of paragraphs 15-27 and FRS 26 to the accounting for contracts on an entity's own equity instruments.

Example 1: Forward to buy shares

IE2   This example illustrates the journal entries for forward purchase contracts on an entity's own shares that will be settled (a) net in cash, (b) net in shares or (c) by delivering cash in exchange for shares. It also discusses the effect of settlement options (see (d) below). To simplify the illustration, it is assumed that no dividends are paid on the underlying shares (ie the 'carry return' is zero) so that the present value of the forward price equals the spot price when the fair value of the forward contract is zero. The fair value of the forward has been computed as the difference between the market share price and the present value of the fixed forward price.

Assumptions:

Contract date	1 February 2002
Maturity date	31 January 2003
Market price per share on 1 February 2002	CU100
Market price per share on 31 December 2002	CU110
Market price per share on 31 January 2003	CU106
Fixed forward price to be paid on 31 January 2003	CU104
Present value of forward price on 1 February 2002	CU100
Number of shares under forward contract	1,000
Fair value of forward on 1 February 2002	CU0
Fair value of forward on 31 December 2002	CU6,300
Fair value of forward on 31 January 2003	CU2,000

(a)   Cash for cash ('net cash settlement')

IE3   In this subsection, the forward purchase contract on the entity's own shares will be settled net in cash, ie there is no receipt or delivery of the entity's own shares upon settlement of the forward contract.

On 1 February 2002, Entity A enters into a contract with Entity B to receive the fair value of 1,000 of Entity A's own outstanding ordinary shares as of 31 January 2003 in exchange for a payment of CU104,000 in cash (ie CU104 per share) on 31 January 2003. The contract will be settled net in cash. Entity A records the following journal entries.

In these examples, monetary amounts are denominated in 'currency units' (CU).

1 February 2002

The price per share when the contract is agreed on 1 February 2002 is CU100. The initial fair value of the forward contract on 1 February 2002 is zero.

No entry is required because the fair value of the derivative is zero and no cash is paid or received.

31 December 2002

On 31 December 2002, the market price per share has increased to CU110 and, as a result, the fair value of the forward contract has increased to CU6,300.

Dr	Forward asset	CU6,300	
Cr	Gain		CU6,300

To record the increase in the fair value of the forward contract.

31 January 2003

On 31 January 2003, the market price per share has decreased to CU106. The fair value of the forward contract is CU2,000
([CU106 x 1,000] – CU104,000).

On the same day, the contract is settled net in cash. Entity A has an obligation to deliver CU104,000 to Entity B and Entity B has an obligation to deliver CU106,000 (CU106 x 1,000) to Entity A, so Entity B pays the net amount of CU2,000 to Entity A.

Dr	Loss	CU4,300	
Cr	Forward asset		CU4,300

To record the decrease in the fair value of the forward contract (ie CU4,300 = CU6,300 – CU2,000).

Dr	Cash	CU2,000	
Cr	Forward asset		CU2,000

To record the settlement of the forward contract.

(b) Shares for shares ('net share settlement')

Assume the same facts as in (a) except that settlement will be made net in shares instead of net in cash. Entity A's journal entries are the same as those shown in (a) above, except for recording the settlement of the forward contract, as follows: **IE4**

31 January 2003

The contract is settled net in shares. Entity A has an obligation to deliver CU104,000 (CU104 x 1,000) worth of its shares to Entity B and Entity B has an obligation to deliver CU106,000 (CU106 x 1,000) worth of shares to Entity A. Thus, Entity B delivers a net amount of CU2,000 (CU106,000 – CU104,000) worth of shares to Entity A, ie 18.9 shares (CU2,000 / CU106).

Dr	Equity	CU2,000	
Cr	Forward asset		CU2,000

To record the settlement of the forward contract.

(c)   Cash for shares ('gross physical settlement')

IE5   Assume the same facts as in (a) except that settlement will be made by delivering a fixed amount of cash and receiving a fixed number of Entity A's shares. Similarly to (a) and (b) above, the price per share that Entity A will pay in one year is fixed at CU104. Accordingly, Entity A has an obligation to pay CU104,000 in cash to Entity B (CU104 x 1,000) and Entity B has an obligation to deliver 1,000 of Entity A's outstanding shares to Entity A in one year. Entity A records the following journal entries.

1 February 2002

Dr	Equity	CU100,000	
Cr	Liability		CU100,000

To record the obligation to deliver CU104,000 in one year at its present value of CU100,000 discounted using an appropriate interest rate (see IAS 39, paragraph AG64).

31 December 2002

Dr	Interest expense	CU3,660	
Cr	Liability		CU3,660

To accrue interest in accordance with the effective interest method on the liability for the share redemption amount.

31 January 2003

Dr	Interest expense	CU340	
Cr	Liability		CU340

To accrue interest in accordance with the effective interest method on the liability for the share redemption amount.

Entity A delivers CU104,000 in cash to Entity B and Entity B delivers 1,000 of Entity A's shares to Entity A.

Dr	Liability	CU104,000	
Cr	Cash		CU104,000

To record the settlement of the obligation to redeem Entity A's own shares for cash.

(d)   Settlement options

IE6   The existence of settlement options (such as net in cash, net in shares or by an exchange of cash and shares) has the result that the forward repurchase contract is a financial asset or a financial liability. If one of the settlement alternatives is to exchange cash for shares ((c) above), Entity A recognises a liability for the obligation to deliver cash, as illustrated in (c) above. Otherwise, Entity A accounts for the forward contract as a derivative.

Example 2: Forward to sell shares

This example illustrates the journal entries for forward sale contracts on an entity's **IE7** own shares that will be settled (a) net in cash, (b) net in shares or (c) by receiving cash in exchange for shares. It also discusses the effect of settlement options (see (d) below). To simplify the illustration, it is assumed that no dividends are paid on the underlying shares (ie the 'carry return' is zero) so that the present value of the forward price equals the spot price when the fair value of the forward contract is zero. The fair value of the forward has been computed as the difference between the market share price and the present value of the fixed forward price.

Assumptions:

Contract date	1 February 2002
Maturity date	31 January 2003

Market price per share on 1 February 2002	CU100
Market price per share on 31 December 2002	CU110
Market price per share on 31 January 2003	CU106
Fixed forward price to be received on 31 January 2003	CU104
Present value of forward price on 1 February 2002	CU100
Number of shares under forward contract	1,000

Fair value of forward on 1 February 2002	CU0
Fair value of forward on 31 December 2002	CU(6,300)
Fair value of forward on 31 January 2003	CU(2,000)

(a) Cash for cash ('net cash settlement')

On 1 February 2002, Entity A enters into a contract with Entity B to pay the fair **IE8** value of 1,000 of Entity A's own outstanding ordinary shares as of 31 January 2003 in exchange for CU104,000 in cash (ie CU104 per share) on 31 January 2003. The contract will be settled net in cash. Entity A records the following journal entries.

1 February 2002

No entry is required because the fair value of the derivative is zero and no cash is paid or received.

31 December 2002

Dr	Loss	CU6,300	
Cr	Forward liability		CU6,300

To record the decrease in the fair value of the forward contract.

31 January 2003

Dr	Forward liability	CU4,300	
Cr	Gain		CU4,300

To record the increase in the fair value of the forward contract (ie CU4,300 = CU6,300 − CU2,000).

The contract is settled net in cash. Entity B has an obligation to deliver CU104,000 to Entity A, and Entity A has an obligation to deliver CU106,000 (CU106 x 1,000) to Entity B. Thus, Entity A pays the net amount of CU2,000 to Entity B.

Dr	Forward liability	CU2,000
Cr	Cash	CU2,000

To record the settlement of the forward contract.

(b)   Shares for shares ('net share settlement')

IE9   Assume the same facts as in (a) except that settlement will be made net in shares instead of net in cash. Entity A's journal entries are the same as those shown in (a), except:

31 January 2003

The contract is settled net in shares. Entity A has a right to receive CU104,000 (CU104 x 1,000) worth of its shares and an obligation to deliver CU106,000 (CU106 x 1,000) worth of its shares to Entity A. Thus, Entity A delivers a net amount of CU2,000 (CU106,000 – CU104,000) worth of its shares to Entity B, ie 18.9 shares (CU2,000 / CU106).

Dr	Forward liability	CU2,000
Cr	Equity	CU2,000

To record the settlement of the forward contract. The issue of the entity's own shares is treated as an equity transaction.

(c)   Shares for cash ('gross physical settlement')

IE10   Assume the same facts as in (a), except that settlement will be made by receiving a fixed amount of cash and delivering a fixed number of the entity's own shares. Similarly to (a) and (b) above, the price per share that Entity A will pay in one year is fixed at CU104. Accordingly, Entity A has a right to receive CU104,000 in cash (CU104 x 1,000) and an obligation to deliver 1,000 of its own shares in one year. Entity A records the following journal entries.

1 February 2002

No entry is made on 1 February. No cash is paid or received because the forward has an initial fair value of zero. A forward contract to deliver a fixed number of Entity A's own shares in exchange for a fixed amount of cash or another financial asset meets the definition of an equity instrument because it cannot be settled otherwise than through the delivery of shares in exchange for cash.

31 December 2002

No entry is made on 31 December because no cash is paid or received and a contract to deliver a fixed number of Entity A's own shares in exchange for a fixed amount of cash meets the definition of an equity instrument of the entity.

31 January 2003

On 31 January 2003, Entity A receives CU104,000 in cash and delivers 1,000 shares.

Dr	Cash	CU104,000	
Cr	Equity		CU104,000

To record the settlement of the forward contract.

(d) Settlement options

The existence of settlement options (such as net in cash, net in shares or by an **IE11** exchange of cash and shares) has the result that the forward contract is a financial asset or a financial liability. It does not meet the definition of an equity instrument because it can be settled otherwise than by Entity A repurchasing a fixed number of its own shares in exchange for paying a fixed amount of cash or another financial asset. Entity A recognises a derivative asset or liability, as illustrated in (a) and (b) above. The accounting entry to be made on settlement depends on how the contract is actually settled.

Example 3: Purchased call option on shares

This example illustrates the journal entries for a purchased call option right on the **IE12** entity's own shares that will be settled (a) net in cash, (b) net in shares or (c) by delivering cash in exchange for the entity's own shares. It also discusses the effect of settlement options (see (d) below):

Assumptions:

Contract date	1 February 2002
Exercise date	31 January 2003
	(European terms, ie it can be
	exercised only at maturity)
Exercise right holder	Reporting entity
	(Entity A)

Market price per share on 1 February 2002	CU100
Market price per share on 31 December 2002	CU104
Market price per share on 31 January 2003	CU104

Fixed exercise price to be paid on 31 January 2003	CU102
Number of shares under option contract	1,000

Fair value of option on 1 February 2002	CU5,000
Fair value of option on 31 December 2002	CU3,000
Fair value of option on 31 January 2003	CU2,000

(a) Cash for cash ('net cash settlement')

On 1 February 2002, Entity A enters into a contract with Entity B that gives Entity B **IE13** the obligation to deliver, and Entity A the right to receive the fair value of 1,000 of Entity A's own ordinary shares as of 31 January 2003 in exchange for CU102,000 in cash (ie CU102 per share) on 31 January 2003, if Entity A exercises that right. The contract will be settled net in cash. If Entity A does not exercise its right, no payment will be made. Entity A records the following journal entries.

1 February 2002

The price per share when the contract is agreed on 1 February 2002 is CU100. The initial fair value of the option contract on 1 February 2002 is CU5,000, which Entity A pays to Entity B in cash on that date. On that date, the option has no intrinsic value, only time value, because the exercise price of CU102 exceeds the market price per share of CU100 and it would therefore not be economic for Entity A to exercise the option. In other words, the call option is out of the money.

Dr	Call option asset	CU5,000	
Cr	Cash		CU5,000

To recognise the purchased call option.

31 December 2002

On 31 December 2002, the market price per share has increased to CU104. The fair value of the call option has decreased to CU3,000, of which CU2,000 is intrinsic value ([CU104 – CU102] x 1,000), and CU1,000 is the remaining time value.

Dr	Loss	CU2,000	
Cr	Call option asset		CU2,000

To record the decrease in the fair value of the call option.

31 January 2003

On 31 January 2003, the market price per share is still CU104. The fair value of the call option has decreased to CU2,000, which is all intrinsic value ([CU104 – CU102] x 1,000) because no time value remains.

Dr	Loss	CU1,000	
Cr	Call option asset		CU1,000

To record the decrease in the fair value of the call option.

On the same day, Entity A exercises the call option and the contract is settled net in cash. Entity B has an obligation to deliver CU104,000 (CU104 x 1,000) to Entity A in exchange for CU102,000 (CU102 x 1,000) from Entity A, so Entity A receives a net amount of CU2,000.

Dr	Cash	CU2,000	
Cr	Call option asset		CU2,000

To record the settlement of the option contract.

(b)   Shares for shares ('net share settlement')

IE14   Assume the same facts as in (a) except that settlement will be made net in shares instead of net in cash. Entity A's journal entries are the same as those shown in (a) except for recording the settlement of the option contract as follows:

31 January 2003

Entity A exercises the call option and the contract is settled net in shares. Entity B has an obligation to deliver CU104,000 (CU104 x 1,000) worth of Entity A's shares to Entity A in exchange for CU102,000 (CU102 x 1,000) worth of Entity A's shares. Thus, Entity B delivers the net amount of CU2,000 worth of shares to Entity A, ie 19.2 shares (CU2,000 / CU104).

Dr	Equity	CU2,000	
Cr	Call option asset		CU2,000

To record the settlement of the option contract. The settlement is accounted for as a treasury share transaction (ie no gain or loss).

(c)   Cash for shares ('gross physical settlement')

Assume the same facts as in (a) except that settlement will be made by receiving a fixed number of shares and paying a fixed amount of cash, if Entity A exercises the option. Similarly to (a) and (b) above, the exercise price per share is fixed at CU102. Accordingly, Entity A has a right to receive 1,000 of Entity A's own outstanding shares in exchange for CU102,000 (CU102 x 1,000) in cash, if Entity A exercises its option. Entity A records the following journal entries.   **IE15**

1 February 2002

Dr	Equity	CU5,000	
Cr	Cash		CU5,000

To record the cash paid in exchange for the right to receive Entity A's own shares in one year for a fixed price. The premium paid is recognised in equity.

31 December 2002

No entry is made on 31 December because no cash is paid or received and a contract that gives a right to receive a fixed number of Entity A's own shares in exchange for a fixed amount of cash meets the definition of an equity instrument of the entity.

31 January 2003

Entity A exercises the call option and the contract is settled gross. Entity B has an obligation to deliver 1,000 of Entity A's shares in exchange for CU102,000 in cash.

Dr	Equity	CU102,000	
Cr	Cash		CU102,000

To record the settlement of the option contract.

(d)   Settlement options

The existence of settlement options (such as net in cash, net in shares or by an exchange of cash and shares) has the result that the call option is a financial asset. It does not meet the definition of an equity instrument because it can be settled otherwise than by Entity A repurchasing a fixed number of its own shares in exchange for paying a fixed amount of cash or another financial asset. Entity A recognises a derivative asset, as illustrated in (a) and (b) above. The accounting entry to be made on settlement depends on how the contract is actually settled.   **IE16**

Example 4: Written call option on shares

IE17   This example illustrates the journal entries for a written call option obligation on the entity's own shares that will be settled (a) net in cash, (b) net in shares or (c) by delivering cash in exchange for shares. It also discusses the effect of settlement options (see (d) below).

Assumptions:

Contract date	1 February 2002
Exercise date	31 January 2003
	(European terms, ie it can be
	exercised only at maturity)
Exercise right holder	Counterparty
	(Entity B)
Market price per share on 1 February 2002	CU100
Market price per share on 31 December 2002	CU104
Market price per share on 31 January 2003	CU104
Fixed exercise price to be received on 31 January 2003	CU102
Number of shares under option contract	1,000
Fair value of option on 1 February 2002	CU5,000
Fair value of option on 31 December 2002	CU3,000
Fair value of option on 31 January 2003	CU2,000

(a)   Cash for cash ('net cash settlement')

IE18   Assume the same facts as in Example 3(a) above except that Entity A has written a call option on its own shares instead of having purchased a call option on them. Accordingly, on 1 February 2002 Entity A enters into a contract with Entity B that gives Entity B the right to receive and Entity A the obligation to pay the fair value of 1,000 of Entity A's own ordinary shares as of 31 January 2003 in exchange for CU102,000 in cash (ie CU102 per share) on 31 January 2003, if Entity B exercises that right. The contract will be settled net in cash. If Entity B does not exercise its right, no payment will be made. Entity A records the following journal entries.

1 February 2002

Dr	Cash		CU5,000	
Cr	Call	option		CU5,000
	obligation			

To recognise the written call option.

31 December 2002

Dr	Call	option	CU2,000	
	obligation			
Cr	Gain			CU2,000

To record the decrease in the fair value of the call option.

31 January 2003

Dr	Call option obligation	CU1,000	
Cr	Gain		CU1,000

To record the decrease in the fair value of the option.

On the same day, Entity B exercises the call option and the contract is settled net in cash. Entity A has an obligation to deliver CU104,000 (CU104 x 1,000) to Entity B in exchange for CU102,000 (CU102 x 1,000) from Entity B, so Entity A pays a net amount of CU2,000.

Dr	Call option obligation	CU2,000	
Cr	Cash		CU2,000

To record the settlement of the option contract.

(b)   Shares for shares ('net share settlement')

Assume the same facts as in (a) except that settlement will be made net in shares   **IE19**
instead of net in cash. Entity A's journal entries are the same as those shown in (a),
except for recording the settlement of the option contract, as follows:

31 January 2003

Entity B exercises the call option and the contract is settled net in shares. Entity A has an obligation to deliver CU104,000 (CU104 x 1,000) worth of Entity A's shares to Entity B in exchange for CU102,000 (CU102 x 1,000) worth of Entity A's shares. Thus, Entity A delivers the net amount of CU2,000 worth of shares to Entity B, ie 19.2 shares (CU2,000 / CU104).

Dr	Call option obligation	CU2,000	
Cr	Equity		CU2,000

To record the settlement of the option contract. The settlement is accounted for as an equity transaction.

(c)   Cash for shares ('gross physical settlement')

Assume the same facts as in (a) except that settlement will be made by delivering a   **IE20**
fixed number of shares and receiving a fixed amount of cash, if Entity B exercises the
option. Similarly to (a) and (b) above, the exercise price per share is fixed at CU102.
Accordingly, Entity B has a right to receive 1,000 of Entity A's own outstanding
shares in exchange for CU102,000 (CU102 x 1,000) in cash, if Entity B exercises its
option. Entity A records the following journal entries.

1 February 2002

Dr	Cash	CU5,000	
Cr	Equity		CU5,000

To record the cash received in exchange for the obligation to deliver a fixed number of Entity A's own shares in one year for a fixed price. The premium received is recognised in equity. Upon exercise, the call would result in the issue of a fixed number of shares in exchange for a fixed amount of cash.

31 December 2002

No entry is made on 31 December because no cash is paid or received and a contract to deliver a fixed number of Entity A's own shares in exchange for a fixed amount of cash meets the definition of an equity instrument of the entity.

31 January 2003

Entity B exercises the call option and the contract is settled gross. Entity A has an obligation to deliver 1,000 shares in exchange for CU102,000 in cash.

Dr	Cash	CU102,000	
Cr	Equity		CU102,000

To record the settlement of the option contract.

(d)   Settlement options

IE21   The existence of settlement options (such as net in cash, net in shares or by an exchange of cash and shares) has the result that the call option is a financial liability. It does not meet the definition of an equity instrument because it can be settled otherwise than by Entity A issuing a fixed number of its own shares in exchange for receiving a fixed amount of cash or another financial asset. Entity A recognises a derivative liability, as illustrated in (a) and (b) above. The accounting entry to be made on settlement depends on how the contract is actually settled.

Example 5: Purchased put option on shares

IE22   This example illustrates the journal entries for a purchased put option on the entity's own shares that will be settled (a) net in cash, (b) net in shares or (c) by delivering cash in exchange for shares. It also discusses the effect of settlement options (see (d) below).

Assumptions:

Contract date	1 February 2002
Exercise date	31 January 2003
	(European terms, ie it can be
	exercised only at maturity)
Exercise right holder	Reporting entity
	(Entity A)

Market price per share on 1 February 2002	CU100
Market price per share on 31 December 2002	CU95
Market price per share on 31 January 2003	CU95
Fixed exercise price to be received on 31 January 2003	CU98
Number of shares under option contract	1,000
Fair value of option on 1 February 2002	CU5,000
Fair value of option on 31 December 2002	CU4,000
Fair value of option on 31 January 2003	CU3,000

(a) Cash for cash ('net cash settlement')

On 1 February 2002, Entity A enters into a contract with Entity B that gives Entity A **IE23** the right to sell, and Entity B the obligation to buy the fair value of 1,000 of Entity A's own outstanding ordinary shares as of 31 January 2003 at a strike price of CU98,000 (ie CU98 per share) on 31 January 2003, if Entity A exercises that right. The contract will be settled net in cash. If Entity A does not exercise its right, no payment will be made. Entity A records the following journal entries.

1 February 2002

The price per share when the contract is agreed on 1 February 2002 is CU100. The initial fair value of the option contract on 1 February 2002 is CU5,000, which Entity A pays to Entity B in cash on that date. On that date, the option has no intrinsic value, only time value, because the exercise price of CU98 is less than the market price per share of CU100. Therefore it would not be economic for Entity A to exercise the option. In other words, the put option is out of the money.

Dr	Put option asset	CU5,000	
Cr	Cash		CU5,000

To recognise the purchased put option.

31 December 2002

On 31 December 2002 the market price per share has decreased to CU95. The fair value of the put option has decreased to CU4,000, of which CU3,000 is intrinsic value ([CU98 – CU95] x 1,000) and CU1,000 is the remaining time value.

Dr	Loss	CU1,000	
Cr	Put option asset		CU1,000

To record the decrease in the fair value of the put option.

31 January 2003

On 31 January 2003 the market price per share is still CU95. The fair value of the put option has decreased to CU3,000, which is all intrinsic value ([CU98 – CU95] x 1,000) because no time value remains.

| Dr | Loss | CU1,000 | |
| Cr | Put option asset | | CU1,000 |

To record the decrease in the fair value of the option.

On the same day, Entity A exercises the put option and the contract is settled net in cash. Entity B has an obligation to deliver CU98,000 to Entity A and Entity A has an obligation to deliver CU95,000 (CU95 x 1,000) to Entity B, so Entity B pays the net amount of CU3,000 to Entity A.

| Dr | Cash | CU3,000 | |
| Cr | Put option asset | | CU3,000 |

To record the settlement of the option contract.

(b)   Shares for shares ('net share settlement')

IE24   Assume the same facts as in (a) except that settlement will be made net in shares instead of net in cash. Entity A's journal entries are the same as shown in (a), except:

31 January 2003

Entity A exercises the put option and the contract is settled net in shares. In effect, Entity B has an obligation to deliver CU98,000 worth of Entity A's shares to Entity A, and Entity A has an obligation to deliver CU95,000 worth of Entity A's shares (CU95 x 1,000) to Entity B, so Entity B delivers the net amount of CU3,000 worth of shares to Entity A, ie 31.6 shares (CU3,000 / CU95).

| Dr | Equity | CU3,000 | |
| Cr | Put option asset | | CU3,000 |

To record the settlement of the option contract.

(c)   Cash for shares ('gross physical settlement')

IE25   Assume the same facts as in (a) except that settlement will be made by receiving a fixed amount of cash and delivering a fixed number of Entity A's shares, if Entity A exercises the option. Similarly to (a) and (b) above, the exercise price per share is fixed at CU98. Accordingly, Entity B has an obligation to pay CU98,000 in cash to Entity A (CU98 x 1,000) in exchange for 1,000 of Entity A's outstanding shares, if Entity A exercises its option. Entity A records the following journal entries.

1 February 2002

| Dr | Equity | CU5,000 | |
| Cr | Cash | | CU5,000 |

To record the cash received in exchange for the right to deliver Entity A's own shares in one year for a fixed price. The premium paid is recognised directly in equity. Upon exercise, it results in the issue of a fixed number of shares in exchange for a fixed price.

31 December 2002

No entry is made on 31 December because no cash is paid or received and a contract to deliver a fixed number of Entity A's own shares in exchange for a fixed amount of cash meets the definition of an equity instrument of Entity A.

31 January 2003

Entity A exercises the put option and the contract is settled gross. Entity B has an obligation to deliver CU98,000 in cash to Entity A in exchange for 1,000 shares.

Dr	Cash	CU98,000	
Cr	Equity		CU98,000

To record the settlement of the option contract.

(d) Settlement options

The existence of settlement options (such as net in cash, net in shares or by an exchange of cash and shares) has the result that the put option is a financial asset. It does not meet the definition of an equity instrument because it can be settled otherwise than by Entity A issuing a fixed number of its own shares in exchange for receiving a fixed amount of cash or another financial asset. Entity A recognises a derivative asset, as illustrated in (a) and (b) above. The accounting entry to be made on settlement depends on how the contract is actually settled.

IE26

Example 6: Written put option on shares

This example illustrates the journal entries for a written put option on the entity's own shares that will be settled (a) net in cash, (b) net in shares or (c) by delivering cash in exchange for shares. It also discusses the effect of settlement options (see (d) below).

IE27

Assumptions:

Contract date	1 February 2002
Exercise date	31 January 2003
	(European terms, ie it can be
	exercised only at maturity)
Exercise right holder	Counterparty
	(Entity B)

Market price per share on 1 February 2002	CU100
Market price per share on 31 December 2002	CU95
Market price per share on 31 January 2003	CU95
Fixed exercise price to be paid on 31 January 2003	CU98
Present value of exercise price on 1 February 2002	CU95
Number of shares under option contract	1,000
Fair value of option on 1 February 2002	CU5,000
Fair value of option on 31 December 2002	CU4,000
Fair value of option on 31 January 2003	CU3,000

(a)   Cash for cash ('net cash settlement')

IE28   Assume the same facts as in Example 5(a) above, except that Entity A has written a put option on its own shares instead of having purchased a put option on its own shares. Accordingly, on 1 February 2002, Entity A enters into a contract with Entity B that gives Entity B the right to receive and Entity A the obligation to pay the fair value of 1,000 of Entity A's outstanding ordinary shares as of 31 January 2003 in exchange for CU98,000 in cash (ie CU98 per share) on 31 January 2003, if Entity B exercises that right. The contract will be settled net in cash. If Entity B does not exercise its right, no payment will be made. Entity A records the following journal entries.

1 February 2002

Dr	Cash	CU5,000	
Cr	Put option liability		CU5,000

To recognise the written put option.

31 December 2002

Dr	Put option liability	CU1,000	
Cr	Gain		CU1,000

To record the decrease in the fair value of the put option.

31 January 2003

Dr	Put option liability	CU1,000	
Cr	Gain		CU1,000

To record the decrease in the fair value of the put option.

On the same day, Entity B exercises the put option and the contract is settled net in cash. Entity A has an obligation to deliver CU98,000 to Entity B, and Entity B has an obligation to deliver CU95,000 (CU95 x 1,000) to Entity A. Thus, Entity A pays the net amount of CU3,000 to Entity B.

Dr	Put option liability	CU3,000	
Cr	Cash		CU3,000

To record the settlement of the option contract.

(b)   Shares for shares ('net share settlement')

IE29   Assume the same facts as in (a) except that settlement will be made net in shares instead of net in cash. Entity A's journal entries are the same as those in (a), except for the following:

31 January 2003

Entity B exercises the put option and the contract is settled net in shares. In effect, Entity A has an obligation to deliver CU98,000 worth of shares to Entity B, and Entity B has an obligation to deliver CU95,000 worth of Entity A's shares (CU95 x 1,000) to Entity A. Thus, Entity A delivers the net amount of CU3,000 worth of Entity A's shares to Entity B, ie 31.6 shares (3,000 / 95).

Dr	Put option liability	CU3,000
Cr	Equity	CU3,000

To record the settlement of the option contract. The issue of Entity A's own shares is accounted for as an equity transaction.

(c) Cash for shares ('gross physical settlement')

Assume the same facts as in (a) except that settlement will be made by delivering a **IE30** fixed amount of cash and receiving a fixed number of shares, if Entity B exercises the option. Similarly to (a) and (b) above, the exercise price per share is fixed at CU98. Accordingly, Entity A has an obligation to pay CU98,000 in cash to Entity B (CU98 x 1,000) in exchange for 1,000 of Entity A's outstanding shares, if Entity B exercises its option. Entity A records the following journal entries.

1 February 2002

Dr	Cash	CU5,000
Cr	Equity	CU5,000

To recognise the option premium received of CU5,000 in equity.

Dr	Equity	CU95,000
Cr	Liability	CU95,000

To recognise the present value of the obligation to deliver CU98,000 in one year, ie CU95,000, as a liability.

31 December 2002

Dr	Interest expense	CU2,750
Cr	Liability	CU2,750

To accrue interest in accordance with the effective interest method on the liability for the share redemption amount.

31 January 2003

Dr	Interest expense	CU250
Cr	Liability	CU250

To accrue interest in accordance with the effective interest method on the liability for the share redemption amount.

On the same day, Entity B exercises the put option and the contract is settled gross. Entity A has an obligation to deliver CU98,000 in cash to Entity B in exchange for CU95,000 worth of shares (CU95 x 1,000).

Dr	Liability	CU98,000
Cr	Cash	CU98,000

To record the settlement of the option contract.

(d) Settlement options

IE31　The existence of settlement options (such as net in cash, net in shares or by an exchange of cash and shares) has the result that the written put option is a financial liability. If one of the settlement alternatives is to exchange cash for shares ((c) above), Entity A recognises a liability for the obligation to deliver cash, as illustrated in (c) above. Otherwise, Entity A accounts for the put option as a derivative liability.

Entities such as Mutual Funds and Co-operatives whose Share Capital is not Equity as Defined in IAS 32

Example 7: Entities with no equity

The following example illustrates an income statement and balance sheet format that may be used by entities such as mutual funds that do not have equity as defined in FRS 25. Other formats are possible.

IE32

Income statement for the year ended 31 December 20x1

	20x1 CU	20x0 CU
Revenue	2,956	1,718
Expenses (classified by nature or function)	(644)	(614)
Profit from operating activities	2,312	1,104
Finance costs – other finance costs	(47)	(47)
– distributions to unitholders	(50)	(50)
Change in net assets attributable to unitholders		
	2,215	1,007

Balance sheet at 31 December 20x1

	20x1		20x0	
	CU	CU	CU	CU
ASSETS				
Non-current assets (classified in accordance with IAS 1)	91,374		78,484	
Total non-current assets		91,374		78,484
Current assets (classified in accordance with IAS 1)	1,422		1,769	
Total current assets		1,422		1,769
Total assets		92,796		80,253
LIABILITIES				
Current liabilities (classified in accordance with IAS 1)	647		66	
Total current liabilities		(647)		(66)
Non-current liabilities excluding net assets attributable to unitholders (classified in accordance with IAS 1)	280		136	
		(280)		(136)
Net assets attributable to unitholders		91,869		80,051

Example 8: Entities with some equity

The following example illustrates an income statement and balance sheet format that **IE33** may be used by entities whose share capital is not equity as defined in FRS 25 because the entity has an obligation to repay the share capital on demand. Other formats are possible.

Income statement for the year ended 31 December 20x1

	20x1	*20x0*
	CU	CU
Revenue	472	498
Expenses (classified by nature or function)	(367)	(396)
Profit from operating activities	105	102
Finance costs – other finance costs	(4)	(4)
– distributions to members	(50)	(50)
Change in net assets attributable to members	51	48

Balance sheet at 31 December 20x1

	20x1 CU	CU	CU	20x0 CU
ASSETS				
Non-current assets (classified in accordance with IAS 1)	908		830	
Total non-current assets		908		830
Current assets (classified in accordance with IAS 1)	383			350
Total current assets		383		350
Total assets		1,291		1,180
LIABILITIES				
Current liabilities (classified in accordance with IAS 1)	372			338
Share capital repayable on demand	202			161
Total current liabilities		(574)		(499)
Total assets less current liabilities		717		681
Non-current liabilities (classified in accordance with IAS 1)	187		196	
		187		196
RESERVES*				
Reserves eg revaluation reserve, retained earnings etc	530		485	
		530		485
		717		681

*In this example, the entity has no obligation to deliver a share of its reserves to its members.

MEMORANDUM NOTE – Total Members' Interests

Share capital repayable on demand	202	161
Reserves	530	485
	732	646

Accounting for Compound Financial Instruments

Example 9: Separation of a compound financial instrument on initial recognition

Paragraph 28 describes how the components of a compound financial instrument are separated by the entity on initial recognition. The following example illustrates how such a separation is made. **IE34**

An entity issues 2,000 convertible bonds at the start of year 1. The bonds have a three-year term, and are issued at par with a face value of CU1,000 per bond, giving total proceeds of CU2,000,000. Interest is payable annually in arrears at a nominal annual interest rate of 6 per cent. Each bond is convertible at any time up to maturity into 250 ordinary shares. When the bonds are issued, the prevailing market interest rate for similar debt without conversion options is 9 per cent. **IE35**

The liability component is measured first, and the difference between the proceeds of the bond issue and the fair value of the liability is assigned to the equity component. The present value of the liability component is calculated using a discount rate of 9 per cent, the market interest rate for similar bonds having no conversion rights, as shown below. **IE36**

	CU
Present value of the principal – CU2,000,000 payable at the end of three years	1,544,367
Present value of the interest – CU120,000 payable annually in arrears for three years	303,755
Total liability component	1,848,122
Equity component (by deduction)	151,878
Proceeds of the bond issue	2,000,000

Example 10: Separation of a compound financial instrument with multiple embedded derivative features

IE37   The following example illustrates the application of paragraph 31 to the separation of the liability and equity components of a compound financial instrument with multiple embedded derivative features.

IE38   Assume that the proceeds received on the issue of a callable convertible bond are CU60. The value of a similar bond without a call or equity conversion option is CU57. Based on an option pricing model, it is determined that the value to the entity of the embedded call feature in a similar bond without an equity conversion option is CU2. In this case, the value allocated to the liability component under paragraph 31 is CU55 (CU57 – CU2) and the value allocated to the equity component is CU5 (CU60 – CU55).

Example 11: Repurchase of a convertible instrument

IE39   The following example illustrates how an entity accounts for a repurchase of a convertible instrument. For simplicity, at inception, the face amount of the instrument is assumed to be equal to the aggregate carrying amount of its liability and equity components in the financial statements, ie no original issue premium or discount exists. Also, for simplicity, tax considerations have been omitted from the example.

IE40   On 1 January 1999, Entity A issued a 10 per cent convertible debenture with a face value of CU1,000 maturing on 31 December 2008. The debenture is convertible into ordinary shares of Entity A at a conversion price of CU25 per share. Interest is payable half-yearly in cash. At the date of issue, Entity A could have issued non-convertible debt with a ten-year term bearing a coupon interest rate of 11 per cent.

IE41   In the financial statements of Entity A the carrying amount of the debenture was allocated on issue as follows:

	CU
Liability component	
Present value of 20 half-yearly interest payments of CU50, discounted at 11%	597
Present value of CU1,000 due in 10 years, discounted at 11%, compounded half-yearly	343
	940
Equity component	
(difference between CU1,000 total proceeds and CU940 allocated above)	60
Total proceeds	1,000

IE42   On 1 January 2004, the convertible debenture has a fair value of CU1,700.

IE43   Entity A makes a tender offer to the holder of the debenture to repurchase the debenture for CU1,700, which the holder accepts. At the date of repurchase, Entity A could have issued non-convertible debt with a five-year term bearing a coupon interest rate of 8 per cent.

IE44   The repurchase price is allocated as follows:

	Carrying Value	Fair Value	Difference
Liability component:	CU	CU	CU
Present value of 10 remaining halfyearly interest payments of CU50, discounted at 11% and 8%, respectively	377	405	
Present value of CU1,000 due in 5 years, discounted at 11% and 8%, compounded half-yearly, respectively	585	676	
	962	1,081	(119)
Equity component	60	619*	(559)
Total	1,022	1,700	(678)

Entity A recognises the repurchase of the debenture as follows: **IE45**

Dr	Liability component	CU962	
Dr	Debt settlement expense (income statement)	CU119	
Cr	Cash		CU1,081

To recognise the repurchase of the liability component.

Dr	Equity	CU619	
Cr	Cash		CU619

To recognise the cash paid for the equity component.

The equity component remains as equity, but may be transferred from one line item   **IE46**
within equity to another.

Example 12: Amendment of the terms of a convertible instrument to induce early conversion

The following example illustrates how an entity accounts for the additional con-   **IE47**
sideration paid when the terms of a convertible instrument are amended to induce
early conversion.

On 1 January 1999, Entity A issued a 10 per cent convertible debenture with a face   **IE48**
value of CU1,000 with the same terms as described in Example 11. On 1 January
2000, to induce the holder to convert the convertible debenture promptly, Entity A
reduces the conversion price to CU20 if the debenture is converted before 1 March
2000 (ie within 60 days).

Assume the market price of Entity A's ordinary shares on the date the terms are   **IE49**
amended is CU40 per share. The fair value of the incremental consideration paid by
Entity A is calculated as follows:

Number of ordinary shares to be issued to debenture holders under
***amended** conversion terms:*

**This amount represents the difference between the fair value amount allocated to the liability component and
the repurchase price of CU1,700.*

Face amount	CU1,000	
New conversion price	/CU20	per share
Number of ordinary shares to be issued on conversion	50	shares

Number of ordinary shares to be issued to debenture holders under **original** *conversion terms:*

Face amount	CU1,000	
Original conversion price	/CU25	per share
Number of ordinary shares issued upon conversion	40	shares

Number of **incremental** *ordinary shares issued upon conversion*	10	shares

Value of incremental ordinary shares issued upon conversion

CU40 per share x 10 incremental shares	CU400

IE50   The incremental consideration of CU400 is recognised as a loss in profit or loss.

Financial Reporting Standard 26 embodies part of IAS 39 'Financial Instruments: Recognition and Measurement' and some amendments to that standard adopted for entities subject to UK accounting standards.

The Statement of Standard Accounting Practice in FRS 26 is set out in paragraphs 1-110A and the appendices. All the paragraphs have equal authority. Paragraphs in bold type state the main principles.

Accompanying the Statement of Standard Accounting Practice is the basis for the conclusions reached in the Statement. This does not form part of the Statement.

The Statement of Standard Accounting Practice should be read in the context of its objective as stated in paragraph 1, the Basis for Conclusions set out in paragraphs BC1-BC222, and the Accounting Standards Board's 'Foreword to Accounting Standards' and 'Statement of Principles for Financial Reporting'.

FRS 26
(IAS 39) Financial instruments: recognition and measurement*

(Issued December 2004)

Contents

Editor's note: Title changed in April 2006.

Appendix B: Amendments to other pronouncements

Appendix C: Insurance Contracts

Preface by the Accounting Standards Board

This Financial Reporting Standard (FRS) has the effect, for those entities applying   **a**
it, of implementing the International Accounting Standards Board's (IASB's)
International Accounting Standard (IAS) 39 'Financial Instruments: Recognition
and Measurement' in the UK and the Republic of Ireland.

IAS 39 sets out requirements for the measurement, recognition and derecognition of   **b**
financial instruments. FRS 26 is based on the text of IAS 39 as at 31 March 2004,
incorporating the revised version of IAS 39 issued by the IASB in December 2003
together with the amendments to IAS 39 on 'Fair Value Hedge Accounting for a
Portfolio Hedge of Interest Rate Risk' and those made by IFRS 4 'Insurance
Contracts', both issued in March 2004.

The FRS is, in effect, part of a package of UK standards comprising: **c**

- this FRS,
- FRS 23 (IAS 21) *The Effects of Changes in Foreign Exchange Rates*,
- FRS 24 (IAS 29) *Financial Reporting in Hyperinflationary Economies*, and
- the disclosure requirements of FRS 25 (IAS 32) *Financial Instruments: Disclosure
  and Presentation.**

Listed entities preparing their financial statements in accordance with UK requir-   **d**
ements—including listed parent undertakings preparing individual financial
statements in accordance with those requirements—are required to comply with the
entire package of standards for accounting periods beginning on or after 1 January
2005.† Other entities are permitted to apply the entire package of standards from
that date, although entities are not permitted to apply some of the standards in the
package but not others—except that FRS 25 exempts certain entities from applying
its disclosure requirements and also permits entities to apply those disclosure
requirements in advance of the other standards in the package if they wish.

For accounting periods beginning on or after 1 January 2006, unlisted entities using   **e**
accounting policies that are consistent with the fair value measurement rules incorporated into the Companies Act‡ to implement the EU Fair Value Directive§ will
also be required to comply with the entire package of standards.

The Board will in due course be issuing proposals for the application of the entire   **f**
package of standards to other unlisted entities.

The requirements, scope and effective date of FRS 26 are identical to the revised IAS   **g**
39 with the following exceptions:

- entities applying the FRSSE are exempt from the FRS;

**The other requirements of FRS 25 apply to all entities—regardless of whether they are listed or unlisted— for
accounting periods beginning on or after 1 January 2005.*

†*For this purpose a listed entity is an entity that has shares or debt admitted to trading on a regulated market in
the EU.*

‡*Section D of Schedule 4, and equivalents in other schedules, inserted by The Companies Act 1985 (International Accounting Standards and Other Accoutning Amendments) Regulations 2004; and equivalent Northern
Ireland and Republic of Ireland legislation.*

§*Directive 2001/65/EC.*

- only those entities that are listed entities or whose financial statements are prepared in accordance with the fair value accounting rules set out in the Companies Act 1985* are required to adopt the standard;
- changes in fair value that are recognised directly in equity under IAS 39 are required by FRS 26 to be recognised in the statement of total recognised gains and losses;
- commencement of the FRS for listed entities corresponds to the effective date of amendments to the Companies Act implementing the Fair Value Directive†, and earlier adoption is not permitted; other entities required to apply the FRS are permitted to defer its application for one year from this date;
- the Board has added transitional provisions from IFRS 1 'First-time Adoption of International Financial Reporting Standards' to enable prospective application of the requirements of the FRS without the need for full restatement of comparatives; and
- the scope of IAS 39 includes a reference to the definition of an insurance contract, as set out in IFRS 4; the ASB has included, in an appendix forming an integral part of FRS 26, this definition and supporting material from IFRS 4.

h The text of IAS 39 and the material included from IFRS 4 contain various references to other International Financial Reporting Standards (IFRSs). In FRS 26 those references have been amended where necessary to enable the standard to be applied in a UK context. The ASB believes that those amendments do not change the requirements of IAS 39 or the definition of insurance contract in IFRS 4 in any way.

i IAS 39 sets out amendments to other IFRSs. The Board has made amendments to FRS 12 'Provisions, Contingent Liabilities and Contingent Assets' corresponding to those made by IAS 39 to IAS 37 'Provisions, Contingent Liabilities and Contingent Assets'. The amendments clarify the interaction between FRS 12 and FRS 26, and apply only to those entities applying FRS 26. Other amendments set out in IAS 39 are not relevant in a UK context and have not been included in FRS 26.

j This FRS supersedes, for those entities applying the standard, UITF Abstract 11 'Capital instruments: issuer call options'.

k The illustrative example and implementation guidance issued by the IASB, which accompanies but does not form part of IAS 39, has also been issued by the ASB. Implementation guidance from IFRS 1 that relates to IAS 39 has also been included.

l In October 2005 the Board amended FRS 26 to incorporate five amendments made to IAS 39 by the IASB:

- Transition and Initial Recognition of Financial Assets and Financial Liabilities (December 2004)
- Cash Flow Hedge Accounting of Forecast Intragroup Transactions (April 2005)
- The Fair Value Option (June 2005)
- Financial Guarantee Contracts and Credit Insurance (August 2005)
- IFRIC Interpretation 5 'Rights to Interests arising from Decommissioning, Restoration and Environmental Rehabilitation Funds' (December 2004).

m The requirements of these amendments to FRS 26 are identical to the amendments to IAS 39 except that for the Fair Value Option the Board has:

**and equivalent Northern Ireland and Republic of Ireland legislation.*

†*Similar amendments are to be made to Northern Ireland and Republic of Ireland legislation.*

- added transitional provisions that IASB has inserted in IFRS 1 'First-time Adoption of International Financial Reporting Standards'
- amended the date by which transitional designations must be made from 1 September 2005 to 1 December 2005. This applies only to those entities adopting the amended fair value option for accounting periods commencing before 1 January 2006.

The Board has agreed, in response to a request from the Irish Government, to permit a limited deferral of the effective date of the standard for certain securitisation entities in the Republic of Ireland with listed debt securities but no listed equity.* **n**

In the exposure drafts preceding FRS 26 the Board had decided not to implement in the UK the sections of IAS 39 relating to recognition and derecognition of financial instruments. The Board had taken this approach as it doubted the validity of the method of derecognition that the IASB had been considering at the time and had exposed to its constituents in June 2002. The IASB did not proceed with that approach to derecognition and issued a clarified version of its existing derecognition model in 2003. This Board has therefore decided to bring FRS 26 fully into line with IAS 39 by implementing the IAS 39 recognition and derecognition material into the Standard. **o**

In April 2006 the Board amended FRS 26 to include the IAS 39 material on recognition and derecognition into the Standard. Upon implementation of the amendment the requirements and scope of FRS 26 will be identical to that of IAS 39 except as described in paragraphs g and m above. **p**

Upon implementation of this amendment entities within the scope of FRS 26 will apply the derecognition requirements in FRS 26 to financial assets and liabilities and the derecognition principles of FRS 5 to non-financial assets and liabilities. **q**

For entities within the scope of FRS 26 the recognition and derecognition material is applicable to accounting periods commencing on or after 1 January 2007; earlier adoption is permitted. **r**

The Board took into consideration that on initial application of the new requirements, it may not be practicable to obtain the necessary information to restate all past transactions and that to require such restatement would also be inconsistent with international standards. It has, therefore, permitted transitional provisions similar to those set out in international standards, allowing an entity to choose to apply the requirements either: **s**

(a) only to transactions entered into after the beginning of the comparative period for the accounting period the entity first applied the derecognition requirements of the standard; or
(b) only to transactions entered into after an earlier date of the entity's choosing, provided information sufficient to apply the standard was obtained at the time of initial accounting for each transaction.

The Board has allowed the application of the derecognition provisions from a date related to the entity's first application of the standard rather than a fixed date; but notes that entities wishing to adopt IFRS in due course may wish to choose an earlier date for this purpose, for example 1 January 2004, the equivalent transition provisions of IFRS 1, for this purpose. **t**

Editor's note: Paragraphs l to n added in October 2005.

u   At the same time the Board made consequential amendments to FRS 25 which incorporate into that Standard the corresponding disclosure requirements relating to the recognition and derecognition material from IAS 32; to FRS 29 'Financial Instruments: Disclosures' to reinstate the disclosure requirements relating to recognition and derecognition; and to FRS 5 to exclude from its scope those transactions falling within FRS 26.

v   In the FRED the Board had proposed to extend the scope of FRS 26 to all entities, excluding those applying the FRSSE, in the UK. The Board has decided to defer a decision on the extension of scope until it has decided on the wider issue of convergence of UK standards with IFRS.*

Editor's note: Paragraphs o to v added in April 2006.

Introduction

Reasons for Revising IAS 39*

International Accounting Standard 39 *Financial Instruments: Recognition and Measurement* (IAS 39) replaces IAS 39 *Financial Instruments: Recognition and Measurement* (revised in 2000) and should be applied for annual periods beginning on or after 1 January 2005. Earlier application is permitted. Implementation Guidance accompanying this revised IAS 39 replaces the Questions and Answers published by the former Implementation Guidance Committee (IGC). **IN1**

The International Accounting Standards Board has developed this revised IAS 39 as part of its project to improve IAS 32 *Financial Instruments: Disclosure and Presentation* and IAS 39. The objective of this project was to reduce complexity by clarifying and adding guidance, eliminating internal inconsistencies and incorporating into the Standard elements of Standing Interpretations Committee (SIC) Interpretations and Questions and Answers published by the IGC. **IN2**

For IAS 39, the Board's main objective was a limited revision to provide additional guidance on selected matters such as derecognition, when financial assets and financial liabilities may be measured at fair value, how to assess impairment, how to determine fair value and some aspects of hedge accounting. The Board did not reconsider the fundamental approach to the accounting for financial instruments contained in IAS 39. **IN3**

The Main Changes

The main changes from the previous version of IAS 39 are described below. **IN4**

Scope

A scope exclusion has been made for loan commitments that are not designated as at fair value through profit or loss, cannot be settled net, and do not involve loan at a below-market interest rate. A commitment to provide a loan at a below-market interest rate is initially recognised at fair value, and subsequently measured at the higher of (a) the amount that would be recognised in accordance with IAS 37 *Provisions, Contingent Liabilities and Contingent Assets* and (b) the amount initially recognised less, when appropriate, cumulative amortisation recognised in accordance with IAS 18 *Revenue*. **IN5**

The scope of the Standard includes financial guarantee contracts issued. However, if an issuer of financial guarantee contracts has previously asserted explicitly that it regards such contracts as insurance contracts and has used accounting applicable to insurance contracts, the issuer may elect to apply either this Standard or IFRS 4 to such financial guarantee contracts. Under this Standard, a financial guarantee contract is initially recognised at fair value and is subsequently measured at the higher of (a) the amount determined in accordance with IAS 37 and (b) the amount initially recognised less, when appropriate, cumulative amortisation recognised in accordance with IAS 18. Different requirements apply for the subsequent measurement of financial guarantee contracts that prevent derecognition of financial assets or result **IN6**

*ASB footnote: Although references to specific IFRSs have been amended in the main section of the Standard, references in the Introduction, which describes the revision of IAS 39, have been left unchanged.

in continuing involvement. Financial guarantee contracts held are not within the scope of the Standard.*

IN7   The Standard continues to require that a contract to buy or sell a nonfinancial item is within the scope of IAS 39 if it can be settled net in cash or another financial instrument, unless it is entered into and continues to be held for the purpose of receipt or delivery of a non- financial item in accordance with the entity's expected purchase, sale or usage requirements. However, the Standard clarifies that there are various ways in which a contract to buy or sell a nonfinancial asset can be settled net. These include: when the entity has a practice of settling similar contracts net in cash or another financial instrument, or by exchanging financial instruments; when the entity has a practice of taking delivery of the underlying and selling it within a short period after delivery for the purpose of generating a profit from shortterm fluctuations in price or dealer's margin; and when the non-financial item that is the subject of the contract is readily convertible to cash. The Standard also clarifies that a written option that can be settled net in cash or another financial instrument, or by exchanging financial instruments, is within the scope of the Standard.

Definitions

IN8   The Standard amends the definition of 'originated loans and receivables' to become 'loans and receivables'. Under the revised definition, an entity is permitted to classify as loans and receivables purchased loans that are not quoted in an active market.

Derecognition of a Financial Asset

IN9   Under the original IAS 39, several concepts governed when a financial asset should be derecognised. Although the revised Standard retains the two main concepts of *risks and rewards* and *control*, it clarifies that the evaluation of the transfer of risks and rewards of ownership precedes the evaluation of the transfer of control for all derecognition transactions.

IN10 Under the Standard, an entity determines what asset is to be considered for derecognition. The Standard requires a part of a larger financial asset to be considered for derecognition if, and only if, the part is one of:

(a)   specifically identified cash flows from a financial asset; or
(b)   a fully proportionate (pro rata) share of the cash flows from a financial asset; or
(c)   a fully proportionate (pro rata) share of specifically identified cash flows from a financial asset.

In all other cases, the Standard requires the financial asset to be considered for derecognition in its entirety.

IN11 The Standard introduces the notion of a 'transfer' of a financial asset. A financial asset is derecognised when (a) an entity has transferred a financial asset and (b) the transfer qualifies for derecognition.

IN12 The Standard states that an entity has transferred a financial asset if, and only if, it either:

(a)   retains the contractual rights to receive the cash flows of the financial asset, but assumes a contractual obligation to pay those cash flows to one or more recipients in an arrangement that meets three specified conditions; or

*Editor's Note: Paragraphs IN5 and IN6 amended with effect from 1 January 2006.

(b) transfers the contractual rights to receive the cash flows of a financial asset.

Under the Standard, if an entity has transferred a financial asset, it assesses whether **IN13** it has transferred substantially all the risks and rewards of ownership of the transferred asset. If an entity has retained substantially all such risks and rewards, it continues to recognise the transferred asset. If it has transferred substantially all such risks and rewards, it derecognises the transferred asset.

The Standard specifies that if an entity has neither transferred nor retained sub- **IN14** stantially all the risks and rewards of ownership of the transferred asset, it assesses whether it has retained control over the transferred asset. If it has retained control, the entity continues to recognise the transferred asset to the extent of its continuing involvement in the transferred asset. If it has not retained control, the entity derecognises the transferred asset.

The Standard provides guidance on how to apply the concepts of risks and rewards **IN15** and of control.*

Measurement: Fair Value Option

The Standard permits an entity to designate any financial asset or financial liability **IN16** on initial recognition as one to be measured at fair value, with changes in fair value recognised in profit or loss. To impose discipline on this categorisation, an entity is precluded from reclassifying financial instruments into or out of this category.

The option previously contained in IAS 39 to recognise in profit or loss gains and **IN17** losses on available-for-sale financial assets has been eliminated. Such an option is no longer necessary because under the amendments to IAS 39 an entity is now permitted by designation to measure any financial asset or financial liability at fair value with gains and losses recognised in profit or loss.

How to Determine Fair Value

The Standard provides the following additional guidance about how to determine **IN18** fair values using valuation techniques.

● The objective is to establish what the transaction price would have been on the measurement date in an arm's length exchange motivated by normal business considerations.

● A valuation technique (a) incorporates all factors that market participants would consider in setting a price and (b) is consistent with accepted economic methodologies for pricing financial instruments.

● In applying valuation techniques, an entity uses estimates and assumptions that are consistent with available information about the estimates and assumptions that market participants would use in setting a price for the financial instrument.

● The best estimate of fair value at initial recognition of a financial instrument that is not quoted in an active market is the transaction price unless the fair value of the instrument is evidenced by other observable market transactions or is based on a valuation technique whose variables include only data from observable markets.

Editor's note: Paragraphs IN9 to IN15 added in April 2006.

IN19   The Standard also clarifies that the fair value of a liability with a demand feature, eg a demand deposit, is not less than the amount payable on demand, discounted from the first date that the amount could be required to be paid.

Impairment of Financial Assets

IN20   The Standard clarifies that an impairment loss is recognised only when it has been incurred. It also provides additional guidance on what events provide objective evidence of impairment for investments in equity instruments.

IN21   The Standard provides additional guidance about how to evaluate impairment that is inherent in a group of loans, receivables or heldtomaturity investments, but cannot yet be identified with any individual financial asset in the group, as follows:

- An asset that is individually assessed for impairment and found to be impaired should not be included in a group of assets that are collectively assessed for impairment.
- An asset that has been individually assessed for impairment and found *not* to be individually impaired should be included in a collective assessment of impairment. The occurrence of an event or a combination of events should not be a precondition for including an asset in a group of assets that are collectively evaluated for impairment.
- When performing a collective assessment of impairment, an entity groups assets by similar credit risk characteristics that are indicative of the debtors' ability to pay all amounts due according to the contractual terms.
- Contractual cash flows and historical loss experience provide the basis for estimating expected cash flows. Historical loss rates are adjusted on the basis of relevant observable data that reflect current economic conditions.
- The methodology for measuring impairment should ensure that an impairment loss is not recognised on the initial recognition of an asset.

IN22   The Standard requires that impairment losses on available-for-sale equity instruments cannot be reversed through profit or loss, ie any subsequent increase in fair value is recognised in equity.

Hedge Accounting

IN23   Hedges of firm commitments are now treated as fair value hedges rather than cash flow hedges. However, the Standard clarifies that a hedge of the foreign currency risk of a firm commitment can be treated as either a cash flow hedge or a fair value hedge.

IN24   The Standard requires that when a hedged forecast transaction occurs and results in the recognition of a *financial* asset or a *financial* liability, the gain or loss deferred in equity does not adjust the initial carrying amount of the asset or liability (ie basis adjustment is prohibited), but remains in equity and is recognised in profit or loss consistently with the recognition of gains and losses on the asset or liability. For - hedges of forecast transactions that result in the recognition of a *non-financial* asset or a *non-financial* liability, the entity has a choice of whether to apply basis adjustment or retain the hedging gain or loss in equity and report it in profit or loss when the asset or liability affects profit or loss.

IN24A   This Standard permits fair value hedge accounting to be used more readily for a portfolio hedge of interest rate risk than previous versions of IAS 39. In particular, for such a hedge, it allows:

(a)   the hedged item to be designated as an amount of a currency (eg an amount of dollars, euro, pounds or rand) rather than as individual assets (or liabilities).

(b)   the gain or loss attributable to the hedged item to be presented either:

    (i)   in a single separate line item within assets, for those repricing time periods for which the hedged item is an asset; or

    (ii) in a single separate line item within liabilities, for those repricing time periods for which the hedged item is a liability.

(c)   prepayment risk to be incorporated by scheduling prepayable items into repricing time periods based on expected, rather than contractual, repricing dates. However, when the portion hedged is based on expected repricing dates, the effect that changes in the hedged interest rate have on those expected repricing dates are included when determining the change in the fair value of the hedged item. Consequently, if a portfolio that contains prepayable items is hedged with a non-prepayable derivative, ineffectiveness arises if the dates on which items in the hedged portfolio are expected to prepay are revised, or actual prepayment dates differ from those expected.

Disclosure

The disclosure requirements previously in IAS 39 have been moved to IAS 32.* **IN25**

Amendments to and Withdrawal of Other Pronouncements

As a consequence of the revisions to this Standard, the Implementation Guidance   **IN26**
developed by IASC's IAS 39 Implementation Guidance Committee is superseded by
this Standard and its accompanying Implementation Guidance.

Potential Impact of Proposals in Exposure Drafts

[Deleted]   **IN27**

In August 2005 the IASB relocated all disclosures relating to financial instruments to IFRS 7 Financial
Instruments: Disclosures. **Editor's note:** *Footnote added by FRS 29.*

Financial Instruments: Measurement

OBJECTIVE

1   The objective of this Standard is to establish principles for recognising and measuring financial assets, financial liabilities and some contracts to buy or sell non-financial items. Requirements for presenting information about financial instruments are in FRS 25 (IAS 32) *Financial Instruments: Presentation.* Requirements for disclosing information about financial instruments are in FRS 29 (IFRS 7) *Financial Instruments: Disclosures.* *

SCOPE

1A   *This Standard applies to all financial statements that are intended to give a true and fair view of a reporting entity's financial position and profit or loss (or income and expenditure) and are:*

   (a) for an entity that is a listed entity, or

   (b) prepared in accordance with the fair value accounting rules set out in the Companies Act 1985

   except that reporting entities applying the Financial Reporting Standard for Smaller Entities currently applicable are exempt.

1B   The fair value accounting rules are those set out in paragraphs 34A and 34C of Schedule 4 to the Companies Act 1985†, and their equivalents in other schedules. For the purposes of interpreting paragraph 1A, an entity prepares its accounts in accordance with the fair value accounting rules if it applies an accounting policy that measures financial instruments at fair value through profit and loss account and this is not explicitly permitted by the historical cost accounting rules or the alternative accounting rules set out in that schedule (or equivalents in other schedules as appropriate). In particular:

   (a)   an entity under Schedule 4 that uses fair value accounting through profit and loss account for trading book financial instruments or other financial instruments, or

   (b)   a banking entity under Schedule 9 that uses fair value accounting through profit and loss account for derivatives, or other financial instruments for which this is not specifically permitted under the historical accounting rules in that schedule, or

   (c)   an insurance entity under Schedule 9A that uses fair value accounting for derivatives, or other financial instruments for which this is not specifically permitted under the current value accounting rules in that schedule

   falls within the scope of FRS 26.

2   *This Standard shall be applied to all types of financial instruments except:*

   (a) those interests in subsidiary, quasi-subsidiary and associated undertakings, partnerships and joint ventures that are accounted for under FRS 2 Accounting for Subsidiary Undertakings; FRS 5 Reporting the Substance of Transactions; and

---

*Editor's note: Amended by FRS 29 with effect for accounting periods beginning on or after 1 January 2007.

†In this paragraph, all references to schedules of the Companies Act should be read as including equivalent Northern Ireland and Republic of Ireland legislation.

FRS 9 Associates and Joint Ventures. *However, entities shall apply this Standard to an interest in a subsidiary, quasi-subsidiary or associated undertaking, partnership or joint venture that is accounted for as held for resale. Entities shall also apply this Standard to derivatives on an interest in a subsidiary, quasi-subsidiary or associated undertaking, partnership or joint venture unless the derivative meets the definition of an equity instrument of the entity in FRS 25.*

(b) rights and obligations under leases to which *SSAP 21* Accounting for leases and hire purchase contracts *applies. However:*

    (i)   *lease receivables recognised by a lessor are subject to the derecognition and impairment provisions of this Standard (see paragraphs 15-37, 58, 59, 63-65 and Appendix A paragraphs AG36-AG52 and AG84-AG93); and*

    (ii)   *finance lease payables recognised by a lessee are subject to the derecognition provisions of this Standard (see paragraphs 39-42 and Appendix A paragraphs AG57-AG63); and**

    (iii) *derivatives that are embedded in leases are subject to the embedded derivatives provisions of this Standard (see paragraphs 10-13 and Appendix A paragraphs AG27-AG33).*

(c) *employers' rights and obligations under employee benefit plans, to which FRS 17* Retirement Benefits *applies.*

(d) *financial instruments issued by the entity that meet the definition of an equity instrument in FRS 25 (including options and warrants). However, the holder of such equity instruments shall apply this Standard to those instruments, unless they meet the exception in (a) above.*

(e) *rights and obligations arising under (i) an insurance contract as defined in Appendix C to FRS 26, other than an issuer's rights and obligations arising under an insurance contract that meets the definition of a financial guarantee contract in paragraph 9, or (ii) a contract that contains a discretionary participation feature as defined in that Appendix. However, this Standard applies to a derivative that is embedded in such a contract if the derivative is not itself an insurance contract (see paragraphs 10–13 and Appendix A paragraphs AG27–AG33). Moreover, if an issuer of financial guarantee contracts has previously asserted explicitly that it regards such contracts as insurance contracts and has used accounting applicable to insurance contracts, the issuer may elect to apply either this Standard or continue to use accounting applicable to insurance contracts to such financial guarantee contracts (see paragraphs AG4 and AG4A). The issuer may make that election contract by contract, but the election for each contract is irrevocable.*

(f) *contracts for contingent consideration in a business combination (see paragraphs 81-84 of FRS 7* Fair Values in Acquisition Accounting*). This exemption applies only to the acquirer.*

(g) *contracts between an acquirer and a vendor in a business combination to buy or sell an acquiree at a future date.*

(h) *loan commitments other than those loan commitments described in paragraph 4. An issuer of loan commitments shall apply FRS 12 to loan commitments that are not within the scope of this Standard.†*

(i) *financial instruments, contracts and obligations under share- based payment transactions to which FRS 20* Share-based Payment *applies, except for contracts within the scope of paragraphs 5-7 of this Standard, to which this Standard applies.*

(j) *rights to payments to reimburse the entity for expenditure it is required to make to settle a liability it recognises as a provision in accordance with FRS 12 Provisions,*

---

*Editor's note: (i) amended and (ii) added in April 2006.

†Editor's note: (e) and (h) amended with effect from 1 January 2006.

Contingent Liabilities and Contingent Assets, or for which, in an earlier period, it recognised a provision in accordance with FRS 12.*

3　[†]

4　The following loan commitments are within the scope of this Standard:

(a)　loan commitments that the entity designates as financial liabilities at fair value through profit or loss. An entity that has a past practice of selling the assets resulting from its loan commitments shortly after origination shall apply this Standard to all its loan commitments in the same class.

(b)　loan commitments that can be settled net in cash or by delivering or issuing another financial instrument. These loan commitments are derivatives. A loan commitment is not regarded as settled net merely because the loan is paid out in instalments (for example, a mortgage construction loan that is paid out in instalments in line with the progress of construction).

(c)　commitments to provide a loan at a below-market interest rate. Paragraph 47(d) specifies the subsequent measurement of liabilities arising from these loan commitments.

5　*This Standard shall be applied to those contracts to buy or sell a nonfinancial item that can be settled net in cash or another financial instrument, or by exchanging financial instruments, as if the contracts were financial instruments, with the exception of contracts that were entered into and continue to be held for the purpose of the receipt or delivery of a non-financial item in accordance with the entity's expected purchase, sale or usage requirements.*

6　There are various ways in which a contract to buy or sell a non-financial item can be settled net in cash or another financial instrument or by exchanging financial instruments. These include:

(a)　when the terms of the contract permit either party to settle it net in cash or another financial instrument or by exchanging financial instruments;

(b)　when the ability to settle net in cash or another financial instrument, or by exchanging financial instruments, is not explicit in the terms of the contract, but the entity has a practice of settling similar contracts net in cash or another financial instrument or by exchanging financial instruments (whether with the counterparty, by entering into offsetting contracts or by selling the contract before its exercise or lapse);

(c)　when, for similar contracts, the entity has a practice of taking delivery of the underlying and selling it within a short period after delivery for the purpose of generating a profit from shortterm fluctuations in price or dealer's margin; and

(d)　when the non-financial item that is the subject of the contract is readily convertible to cash.

A contract to which (b) or (c) applies is not entered into for the purpose of the receipt or delivery of the non-financial item in accordance with the entity's expected purchase, sale or usage requirements and, accordingly, is within the scope of this Standard. Other contracts to which paragraph 5 applies are evaluated to determine whether they were entered into and continue to be held for the purpose of the receipt or delivery of the non-financial item in accordance with the entity's expected purchase, sale or usage requirements and, accordingly, whether they are within the scope of this Standard.

*Editor's note: Added with effect from 1 January 2006.

†Editor's note: Paragraph 3 deleted with effect from 1 January 2006.

A written option to buy or sell a non-financial item that can be settled net in cash or **7**
another financial instrument, or by exchanging financial instruments, in accordance
with paragraph 6(a) or (d) is within the scope of this Standard. Such a contract
cannot be entered into for the purpose of the receipt or delivery of the non-financial
item in accordance with the entity's expected purchase, sale or usage requirements.

DEFINITIONS

The terms defined in FRS 25 are used in this Standard with the meanings specified in **8**
paragraph 11 of FRS 25. FRS 25 defines the following terms:

- financial instrument
- financial asset
- financial liability
- equity instrument

and provides guidance on applying those definitions.

The following terms are used in this Standard with the meanings specified: **9**

Definition of a Derivative

*A <u>derivative</u> is a financial instrument or other contract within the scope of this Standard
(see paragraphs 2-7) with all three of the following characteristics:*

*(a) its value changes in response to the change in a specified interest rate, financial
instrument price, commodity price, foreign exchange rate, index of prices or rates,
credit rating or credit index, or other variable, provided in the case of a non-
financial variable that the variable is not specific to a party to the contract
(sometimes called the 'underlying');*

*(b) it requires no initial net investment or an initial net investment that is smaller than
would be required for other types of contracts that would be expected to have a
similar response to changes in market factors; and*

(c) it is settled at a future date.

Definitions of Four Categories of Financial Instruments

*A <u>financial asset or financial liability at fair value through profit or loss</u> is a financial
asset or financial liability that meets either of the following conditions.*

*(a) It is classified as held for trading. A financial asset or financial liability is clas-
sified as held for trading if it is:*

   *(i)   acquired or incurred principally for the purpose of selling or repurchasing it
   in the near term;*

   *(ii) part of a portfolio of identified financial instruments that are managed
   together and for which there is evidence of a recent actual pattern of short-
   term profit taking; or*

   *(iii) a derivative (except for a derivative that is a financial guarantee contract or
   a designated and effective hedging instrument).*

*(b) Upon initial recognition it is designated by the entity as at fair value through
profit or loss. An entity may use this designation only when permitted by paragraph 11A, or when doing so results in more relevant information, because either*

   *(i)   it eliminates or significantly reduces a measurement or recognition incon-
   sistency (sometimes referred to as 'an accounting mismatch') that would*

otherwise arise from measuring assets or liabilities or recognising the gains and losses on them on different bases; or

(ii) *a group of financial assets, financial liabilities or both is managed and its performance is evaluated on a fair value basis, in accordance with a documented risk management or investment strategy, and information about the group is provided internally on that basis to the entity's key management personnel. For the purposes of this standard, key management personnel are those persons having authority and responsibility for planning, directing and controlling the activities of the entity, directly or indirectly, including any director (whether executive or otherwise) of that entity. For example the entity's board of directors and chief executive officer.**

In FRS 29, paragraphs 9–11 and B4 require the entity to provide disclosures about financial assets and financial liabilities it has designated as at fair value through profit or loss, including how it has satisfied these conditions. For instruments qualifying in accordance with (ii) above, that disclosure includes a narrative description of how designation as at fair value through profit or loss is consistent with the entity's documented risk management or investment strategy.

Investments in equity instruments that do not have a quoted market price in an active market, and whose fair value cannot be reliably measured (see paragraph 46(c) and Appendix A paragraphs AG80 and AG81), shall not be designated as at fair value through profit or loss.

It should be noted that paragraphs 48, 48A, 49 and Appendix A paragraphs AG69-AG82, which set out requirements for determining a reliable measure of the fair value of a financial asset or financial liability, apply equally to all items that are measured at fair value, whether by designation or otherwise, or whose fair value is disclosed.†

Held-to-maturity investments *are non-derivative financial assets with fixed or determinable payments and fixed maturity that an entity has the positive intention and ability to hold to maturity (see Appendix A paragraphs AG16-AG25) other than:*

(a) *those that the entity upon initial recognition designates as at fair value through profit or loss;*

(b) *those that the entity designates as available for sale; and*

(c) *those that meet the definition of loans and receivables.*

An entity shall not classify any financial assets as held to maturity if the entity has, during the current financial year or during the two preceding financial years, sold or reclassified more than an insignificant amount of held-to-maturity investments before maturity (more than insignificant in relation to the total amount of heldtomaturity investments) other than sales or reclassifications that:

(i) *are so close to maturity or the financial asset's call date (for example, less than three months before maturity) that changes in the market rate of interest would not have a significant effect on the financial asset's fair value;*

(ii) *occur after the entity has collected substantially all of the financial asset's original principal through scheduled payments or prepayments; or*

(iii) *are attributable to an isolated event that is beyond the entity's control, is non-recurring and could not have been reasonably anticipated by the entity.*

*ASB Footnote: The IASB's definition of key management personnel is contained in IAS 24 Related Party Disclosures. In the UK key management is defined in FRS 8 Related Party Disclosures. For the purposes of this standard the ASB Board considered it appropriate to use the IASB's definition.

†Editor's note: Definition amended October 2005, with effect from 1 January 2006.

<u>Loans and receivables</u> *are non-derivative financial assets with fixed or determinable payments that are not quoted in an active market, other than:*

(a)   those that the entity intends to sell immediately or in the near term, which shall be classified as held for trading, and those that the entity upon initial recognition designates as at fair value through profit or loss;

(b)   those that the entity upon initial recognition designates as available for sale; or

(c)   those for which the holder may not recover substantially all of its initial investment, other than because of credit deterioration, which shall be classified as available for sale.

An interest acquired in a pool of assets that are not loans or receivables (for example, an interest in a mutual fund or a similar fund) is not a loan or receivable.

<u>Available-for-sale financial assets</u> *are those non-derivative financial assets that are designated as available for sale or are not classified as (a) loans and receivables, (b) held-to-maturity investments or (c) financial assets at fair value through profit or loss.*

Definition of a financial guarantee contract

A *financial guarantee contract* is a contract that requires the issuer to make specified payments to reimburse the holder for a loss it incurs because a specified debtor fails to make payment when due in accordance with the original or modified terms of a debt instrument.*

Definitions Relating to Recognition and Measurement

For the purposes of paragraph 19, cash comprises cash on hand and demand deposits, and cash equivalents are short-term, highly liquid investments that are readily convertible to known amounts of cash and which are subject to insignificant risk of changes in value.†

<u>The amortised cost of a financial asset or financial liability</u> *is the amount at which the financial asset or financial liability is measured at initial recognition minus principal repayments, plus or minus the cumulative amortisation using the effective interest method of any difference between that initial amount and the maturity amount, and minus any reduction (directly or through the use of an allowance account) for impairment or uncollectibility.*

<u>The effective interest method</u> *is a method of calculating the amortised cost of a financial asset or a financial liability (or group of financial assets or financial liabilities) and of allocating the interest income or interest expense over the relevant period. The <u>effective interest rate</u> is the rate that exactly discounts estimated future cash payments or receipts through the expected life of the financial instrument or, when appropriate, a shorter period to the net carrying amount of the financial asset or financial liability. When calculating the effective interest rate, an entity shall estimate cash flows considering all contractual terms of the financial instrument (for example, prepayment, call and similar options) but shall not consider future credit losses. The calculation includes all fees and points paid or received between parties to the contract that are an integral part of the effective interest rate (see IAS 18), transaction costs, and all other premiums or discounts. There is a presumption that the cash flows and the expected life*

**Editor's note: Definition added with effect from 1 January 2006.*

†*Editor's note: Definition added in April 2006.*

of a group of similar financial instruments can be estimated reliably. However, in those rare cases when it is not possible to estimate reliably the cash flows or the expected life of a financial instrument (or group of financial instruments), the entity shall use the contractual cash flows over the full contractual term of the financial instrument (or group of financial instruments).

Derecognition is the removal of a previously recognised financial asset or financial liability from an entity's balance sheet.*

Fair value is the amount for which an asset could be exchanged, or a liability settled, between knowledgeable, willing parties in an arm's length transaction.†

A regular way purchase or sale is a purchase or sale of a financial asset under a contract whose terms require delivery of the asset within the time frame established generally by regulation or convention in the marketplace concerned.

Transaction costs are incremental costs that are directly attributable to the acquisition, issue or disposal of a financial asset or financial liability (see Appendix A paragraph AG13). An incremental cost is one that would not have been incurred if the entity had not acquired, issued or disposed of the financial instrument.

Definitions Relating to Hedge Accounting

A firm commitment is a binding agreement for the exchange of a specified quantity of resources at a specified price on a specified future date or dates.

A forecast transaction is an uncommitted but anticipated future transaction.

A hedging instrument is a designated derivative or (for a hedge of the risk of changes in foreign currency exchange rates only) a designated nonderivative financial asset or non-derivative financial liability whose fair value or cash flows are expected to offset changes in the fair value or cash flows of a designated hedged item (paragraphs 72-77 and Appendix A paragraphs AG94-AG97 elaborate on the definition of a hedging instrument).

A hedged item is an asset, liability, firm commitment, highly probable forecast transaction or net investment in a foreign operation that (a) exposes the entity to risk of changes in fair value or future cash flows and (b) is designated as being hedged (paragraphs 78-84 and Appendix A paragraphs AG98-AG101 elaborate on the definition of hedged items).

Hedge effectiveness is the degree to which changes in the fair value or cash flows of the hedged item that are attributable to a hedged risk are offset by changes in the fair value or cash flows of the hedging instrument (see Appendix A paragraphs AG105-AG113).

9A   *A listed entity is an entity that has in issue one or more securities that are admitted to trading on a regulated market of any Member State within the meaning of Article 1(13) of Council Directive 93/22/EEC of 10 May 1993 on investment services in the securities field.*

*Editor's note: Definition added in April 2006.

†Paragraphs 48, 49 and AG69-AG82 of Appendix A contain requirements for determining the fair value of a financial asset or financial liability.

The date of transition to this standard is the beginning of the earliest period for which **9B**
an entity presents comparative information in compliance with this standard. In the case
of an entity that chooses to apply the option in paragraph 108D not to restate com-
parative information, the date of transition is the beginning of the accounting period in
which the standard is first applied.

EMBEDDED DERIVATIVES

An embedded derivative is a component of a hybrid (combined) instrument that also **10**
includes a non-derivative host contract—with the effect that some of the cash flows
of the combined instrument vary in a way similar to a stand-alone derivative.
An embedded derivative causes some or all of the cash flows that otherwise would be
required by the contract to be modified according to a specified interest rate,
financial instrument price, commodity price, foreign exchange rate, index of prices or
rates, credit rating or credit index, or other variable, provided in the case of a non-
financial variable that the variable is not specific to a party to the contract. A derivative that is attached to a financial instrument but is contractually transferable
independently of that instrument, or has a different counterparty from that instrument, is not an embedded derivative, but a separate financial instrument.

An embedded derivative shall be separated from the host contract and accounted for as **11**
a derivative under this Standard if, and only if:

(a)   the economic characteristics and risks of the embedded derivative are not closely
*   related to the economic characteristics and risks of the host contract (see*
*   Appendix A paragraphs AG30 and AG33);*
(b)   a separate instrument with the same terms as the embedded derivative would meet
*   the definition of a derivative; and*
(c)   the hybrid (combined) instrument is not measured at fair value with changes in
*   fair value recognised in profit or loss (ie a derivative that is embedded in a*
*   financial asset or financial liability at fair value through profit or loss is not*
*   separated).*

If an embedded derivative is separated, the host contract shall be accounted for under
this Standard if it is a financial instrument, and in accordance with other appropriate
Standards if it is not a financial instrument. This Standard does not address whether an
embedded derivative shall be presented separately on the face of the financial
statements.

Notwithstanding paragraph 11, if a contract contains one or more embedded deriva- **11A**
tives, an entity may designate the entire hybrid (combined) contract as a financial asset
or financial liability at fair value through profit or loss unless:

(a)   the embedded derivative(s) does not significantly modify the cash flows that
*   otherwise would be required by the contract; or*
(b)   it is clear with little or no analysis when a similar hybrid (combined) instrument is
*   first considered that separation of the embedded derivative(s) is prohibited, such*
*   as a prepayment option embedded in a loan that permits the holder to prepay the*
*   loan for approximately its amortised cost.*

If an entity is required by this Standard to separate an embedded derivative from its **12**
host contract, but is unable to measure the embedded derivative separately either at
acquisition or at a subsequent financial reporting date, it shall designate the entire
hybrid (combined) contract as at fair value through profit or loss.

13   If an entity is unable to determine reliably the fair value of an embedded derivative on the basis of its terms and conditions (for example, because the embedded derivative is based on an unquoted equity instrument), the fair value of the embedded derivative is the difference between the fair value of the hybrid (combined) instrument and the fair value of the host contract, if those can be determined under this Standard. If the entity is unable to determine the fair value of the embedded derivative using this method, paragraph 12 applies and the hybrid (combined) instrument is designated as at fair value through profit or loss.*

Recognition and Derecognition

Initial Recognition

14   *An entity shall recognise a financial asset or a financial liability on its balance sheet when, and only when, the entity becomes a party to the contractual provisions of the instrument. (See paragraph 38 with respect to regular way purchases of financial assets.)*

Derecognition of a Financial Asset

15   In consolidated financial statements, paragraphs 16–23 and Appendix A paragraphs AG34–AG52 are applied at a consolidated level. Hence, an entity first consolidates all subsidiaries in accordance with FRS 2 and quasi-subsidiaries in accordance with FRS 5† and then applies paragraphs 16–23 and Appendix A paragraphs AG34–AG52 to the resulting group.

16   *Before evaluating whether, and to what extent, derecognition is appropriate under paragraphs 17–23, an entity determines whether those paragraphs should be applied to a part of a financial asset (or a part of a group of similar financial assets) or a financial asset (or a group of similar financial assets) in its entirety, as follows.*

(a)   *Paragraphs 17–23 are applied to a part of a financial asset (or a part of a group of similar financial assets) if, and only if, the part being considered for derecognition meets one of the following three conditions.*

(i)   *The part comprises only specifically identified cash flows from a financial asset (or a group of similar financial assets). For example, when an entity enters into an interest rate strip whereby the counterparty obtains the right to the interest cash flows, but not the principal cash flows from a debt instrument, paragraphs 17–23 are applied to the interest cash flows.*

(ii)   *The part comprises only a fully proportionate (pro rata) share of the cash flows from a financial asset (or a group of similar financial assets). For example, when an entity enters into an arrangement whereby the counterparty obtains the rights to a 90 per cent share of all cash flows of a debt instrument, paragraphs 17–23 are applied to 90 per cent of those cash flows. If there is more than one counterparty, each counterparty is not required to have a proportionate share of the cash flows provided that the transferring entity has a fully proportionate share.*

(iii)   *The part comprises only a fully proportionate (pro rata) share of specifically identified cash flows from a financial asset (or a group of similar*

Editor's note: Paragraph 11A added, and 12 and 13 amended, with effect from 1 January 2006.

†*ASB footnote: Where an entity has a quasi-subsidiary but no subsidiary undertakings and therefore does not prepare group financial statements, it should provide in its financial statements consolidated financial statements of itself and its quasi-subsidiary in accordance with paragraph 35 of FRS 5.*

financial assets). For example, when an entity enters into an arrangement whereby the counterparty obtains the rights to a 90 per cent share of interest cash flows from a financial asset, paragraphs 17–23 are applied to 90 per cent of those interest cash flows. If there is more than one counterparty, each counterparty is not required to have a proportionate share of the specifically identified cash flows provided that the transferring entity has a fully proportionate share.

(b) *In all other cases, paragraphs 17–23 are applied to the financial asset in its entirety (or to the group of similar financial assets in their entirety). For e-xample, when an entity transfers (i) the rights to the first or the last 90 per cent of cash collections from a financial asset (or a group of financial assets), or (ii) the rights to 90 per cent of the cash flows from a group of receivables, but provides a guarantee to compensate the buyer for any credit losses up to 8 per cent of the principal amount of the receivables, paragraphs 17–23 are applied to the financial asset (or a group of similar financial assets) in its entirety.*

In paragraphs 17–26, the term 'financial asset' refers to either a part of a financial asset (or a part of a group of similar financial assets) as identified in (a) above or, otherwise, a financial asset (or a group of similar financial assets) in its entirety.

An entity shall derecognise a financial asset when, and only when: **17**

(a) *the contractual rights to the cash flows from the financial asset expire; or*
(b) *it transfers the financial asset as set out in paragraphs 18 and 19 and the transfer qualifies for derecognition in accordance with paragraph 20.*

(See paragraph 38 for regular way sales of financial assets.)

An entity transfers a financial asset if, and only if, it either: **18**

(a) *transfers the contractual rights to receive the cash flows of the financial asset; or*
(b) *retains the contractual rights to receive the cash flows of the financial asset, but assumes a contractual obligation to pay the cash flows to one or more recipients in an arrangement that meets the conditions in paragraph 19.*

When an entity retains the contractual rights to receive the cash flows of a financial **19** *asset (the 'original asset'), but assumes a contractual obligation to pay those cash flows to one or more entities (the 'eventual recipients'), the entity treats the transaction as a transfer of a financial asset if, and only if, all of the following three conditions are met.*

(a) *The entity has no obligation to pay amounts to the eventual recipients unless it collects equivalent amounts from the original asset. Short-term advances by the entity with the right of full recovery of the amount lent plus accrued interest at market rates do not violate this condition.*
(b) *The entity is prohibited by the terms of the transfer contract from selling or pledging the original asset other than as security to the eventual recipients for the obligation to pay them cash flows.*
(c) *The entity has an obligation to remit any cash flows it collects on behalf of the eventual recipients without material delay. In addition, the entity is not entitled to reinvest such cash flows, except for investments in cash or cash equivalents (as defined in paragraph 9) during the short settlement period from the collection date to the date of required remittance to the eventual recipients, and interest earned on such investments is passed to the eventual recipients.*

When an entity transfers a financial asset (see paragraph 18), it shall evaluate the **20** *extent to which it retains the risks and rewards of ownership of the financial asset. In this case:*

(a)   *if the entity transfers substantially all the risks and rewards of ownership of the financial asset, the entity shall derecognise the financial asset and recognise separately as assets or liabilities any rights and obligations created or retained in the transfer.*

(b)   *if the entity retains substantially all the risks and rewards of ownership of the financial asset, the entity shall continue to recognise the financial asset.*

(c)   *if the entity neither transfers nor retains substantially all the risks and rewards of ownership of the financial asset, the entity shall determine whether it has retained control of the financial asset. In this case:*

   (i)   *if the entity has not retained control, it shall derecognise the financial asset and recognise separately as assets or liabilities any rights and obligations created or retained in the transfer.*

   (ii)   *if the entity has retained control, it shall continue to recognise the financial asset to the extent of its continuing involvement in the financial asset (see paragraph 30).*

21   The transfer of risks and rewards (see paragraph 20) is evaluated by comparing the entity's exposure, before and after the transfer, with the variability in the amounts and timing of the net cash flows of the transferred asset. An entity has retained substantially all the risks and rewards of ownership of a financial asset if its exposure to the variability in the present value of the future net cash flows from the financial asset does not change significantly as a result of the transfer (eg because the entity has sold a financial asset subject to an agreement to buy it back at a fixed price or the sale price plus a lender's return). An entity has transferred substantially all the risks and rewards of ownership of a financial asset if its exposure to such variability is no longer significant in relation to the total variability in the present value of the future net cash flows associated with the financial asset (eg because the entity has sold a financial asset subject only to an option to buy it back at its fair value at the time of repurchase or has transferred a fully proportionate share of the cash flows from a larger financial asset in an arrangement, such as a loan sub-participation, that meets the conditions in paragraph 19).

22   Often it will be obvious whether the entity has transferred or retained substantially all risks and rewards of ownership and there will be no need to perform any computations. In other cases, it will be necessary to compute and compare the entity's exposure to the variability in the present value of the future net cash flows before and after the transfer. The computation and comparison is made using as the discount rate an appropriate current market interest rate. All reasonably possible variability in net cash flows is considered, with greater weight being given to those outcomes that are more likely to occur.

23   Whether the entity has retained control (see paragraph 20(c)) of the transferred asset depends on the transferee's ability to sell the asset. If the transferee has the practical ability to sell the asset in its entirety to an unrelated third party and is able to exercise that ability unilaterally and without needing to impose additional restrictions on the transfer, the entity has not retained control. In all other cases, the entity has retained control.

Transfers that Qualify for Derecognition (see paragraph 20(a) and (c)(i))

24   *If an entity transfers a financial asset in a transfer that qualifies for derecognition in its entirety and retains the right to service the financial asset for a fee, it shall recognise either a servicing asset or a servicing liability for that servicing contract. If the fee to be received is not expected to compensate the entity adequately for performing the servicing, a servicing liability for the servicing obligation shall be recognised at its fair*

value. If the fee to be received is expected to be more than adequate compensation for the servicing, a servicing asset shall be recognised for the servicing right at an amount determined on the basis of an allocation of the carrying amount of the larger financial asset in accordance with paragraph 27.

If, as a result of a transfer, a financial asset is derecognised in its entirety but the transfer results in the entity obtaining a new financial asset or assuming a new financial liability, or a servicing liability, the entity shall recognise the new financial asset, financial liability or servicing liability at fair value. **25**

On derecognition of a financial asset in its entirety, the difference between: **26**

(a) the carrying amount and
(b) the sum of (i) the consideration received (including any new asset obtained less any new liability assumed) and (ii) any cumulative gain or loss that had been recognised directly in equity (see paragraph 55(b))

shall be recognised in profit or loss.

If the transferred asset is part of a larger financial asset (eg when an entity transfers interest cash flows that are part of a debt instrument, see paragraph 16(a)) and the part transferred qualifies for derecognition in its entirety, the previous carrying amount of the larger financial asset shall be allocated between the part that continues to be recognised and the part that is derecognised, based on the relative fair values of those parts on the date of the transfer. For this purpose, a retained servicing asset shall be treated as a part that continues to be recognised. The difference between: **27**

(a) the carrying amount allocated to the part derecognised and
(b) the sum of (i) the consideration received for the part derecognised (including any new asset obtained less any new liability assumed) and (ii) any cumulative gain or loss allocated to it that had been recognised directly in equity (see paragraph 55(b))

shall be recognised in profit or loss. A cumulative gain or loss that had been recognised in equity is allocated between the part that continues to be recognised and the part that is derecognised, based on the relative fair values of those parts.

When an entity allocates the previous carrying amount of a larger financial asset between the part that continues to be recognised and the part that is derecognised, the fair value of the part that continues to be recognised needs to be determined. When the entity has a history of selling parts similar to the part that continues to be recognised or other market transactions exist for such parts, recent prices of actual transactions provide the best estimate of its fair value. When there are no price quotes or recent market transactions to support the fair value of the part that continues to be recognised, the best estimate of the fair value is the difference between the fair value of the larger financial asset as a whole and the consideration received from the transferee for the part that is derecognised. **28**

Transfers that Do Not Qualify for Derecognition (see paragraph 20(b))

If a transfer does not result in derecognition because the entity has retained substantially all the risks and rewards of ownership of the transferred asset, the entity shall continue to recognise the transferred asset in its entirety and shall recognise a financial liability for the consideration received. In subsequent periods, the entity shall recognise any income on the transferred asset and any expense incurred on the financial liability. **29**

Continuing Involvement in Transferred Assets *(see paragraph 20(c)(ii))*

30   *If an entity neither transfers nor retains substantially all the risks and rewards of ownership of a transferred asset, and retains control of the transferred asset, the entity continues to recognise the transferred asset to the extent of its continuing involvement. The extent of the entity's continuing involvement in the transferred asset is the extent to which it is exposed to changes in the value of the transferred asset. For example:*

(a)   *when the entity's continuing involvement takes the form of guaranteeing the transferred asset, the extent of the entity's continuing involvement is the lower of (i) the amount of the asset and (ii) the maximum amount of the consideration received that the entity could be required to repay ('the guarantee amount').*

(b)   *when the entity's continuing involvement takes the form of a written or purchased option (or both) on the transferred asset, the extent of the entity's continuing involvement is the amount of the transferred asset that the entity may repurchase. However, in case of a written put option on an asset that is measured at fair value, the extent of the entity's continuing involvement is limited to the lower of the fair value of the transferred asset and the option exercise price (see paragraph AG48).*

(c)   *when the entity's continuing involvement takes the form of a cash-settled option or similar provision on the transferred asset, the extent of the entity's continuing involvement is measured in the same way as that which results from non-cash settled options as set out in (b) above.*

31   *When an entity continues to recognise an asset to the extent of its continuing involvement, the entity also recognises an associated liability. Despite the other measurement requirements in this Standard, the transferred asset and the associated liability are measured on a basis that reflects the rights and obligations that the entity has retained. The associated liability is measured in such a way that the net carrying amount of the transferred asset and the associated liability is:*

(a)   *the amortised cost of the rights and obligations retained by the entity, if the transferred asset is measured at amortised cost; or*

(b)   *equal to the fair value of the rights and obligations retained by the entity when measured on a stand-alone basis, if the transferred asset is measured at fair value.*

32   *The entity shall continue to recognise any income arising on the transferred asset to the extent of its continuing involvement and shall recognise any expense incurred on the associated liability.*

33   *For the purpose of subsequent measurement, recognised changes in the fair value of the transferred asset and the associated liability are accounted for consistently with each other in accordance with paragraph 55, and shall not be offset.*

34   *If an entity's continuing involvement is in only a part of a financial asset (eg when an entity retains an option to repurchase part of a transferred asset, or retains a residual interest that does not result in the retention of substantially all the risks and rewards of ownership and the entity retains control), the entity allocates the previous carrying amount of the financial asset between the part it continues to recognise under continuing involvement, and the part it no longer recognises on the basis of the relative fair values of those parts on the date of the transfer. For this purpose, the requirements of paragraph 28 apply. The difference between:*

(a)   *the carrying amount allocated to the part that is no longer recognised; and*

(b)   *the sum of (i) the consideration received for the part no longer recognised and (ii) any cumulative gain or loss allocated to it that had been recognised directly in equity (see paragraph 55(b)) shall be recognised in profit or loss. A cumulative gain or loss that had been recognised in equity is allocated between the part that continues to be recognised and the part that is no longer recognised on the basis of the relative fair values of those parts.*

If the transferred asset is measured at amortised cost, the option in this Standard to   **35**
designate a financial liability as at fair value through profit or loss is not applicable to
the associated liability.

All Transfers

If a transferred asset continues to be recognised, the asset and the associated liability   **36**
shall not be offset. Similarly, the entity shall not offset any income arising from the
transferred asset with any expense incurred on the associated liability (see FRS 25
paragraph 42).

If a transferor provides non-cash collateral (such as debt or equity instruments) to the   **37**
transferee, the accounting for the collateral by the transferor and the transferee depends
on whether the transferee has the right to sell or repledge the collateral and on whether
the transferor has defaulted. The transferor and transferee shall account for the col-
lateral as follows:

(a)   If the transferee has the right by contract or custom to sell or repledge the
collateral, then the transferor shall reclassify that asset in its balance sheet (eg as
a loaned asset, pledged equity instruments or repurchase receivable) separately
from other assets.
(b)   If the transferee sells collateral pledged to it, it shall recognise the proceeds from
the sale and a liability measured at fair value for its obligation to return the
collateral.
(c)   If the transferor defaults under the terms of the contract and is no longer entitled
to redeem the collateral, it shall derecognise the collateral, and the transferee shall
recognise the collateral as its asset initially measured at fair value or, if it has
already sold the collateral, derecognise its obligation to return the collateral.
(d)   Except as provided in (c), the transferor shall continue to carry the collateral as
its asset, and the transferee shall not recognise the collateral as an asset.

Regular Way Purchase or Sale of a Financial Asset

A regular way purchase or sale of financial assets shall be recognised and derecognised,   **38**
as applicable, using trade date accounting or settlement date accounting (see Appendix
A paragraphs AG53–AG56).

Derecognition of a Financial Liability

An entity shall remove a financial liability (or a part of a financial liability) from its   **39**
balance sheet when, and only when, it is extinguished—ie when the obligation specified
in the contract is discharged or cancelled or expires.

An exchange between an existing borrower and lender of debt instruments with sub-   **40**
stantially different terms shall be accounted for as an extinguishment of the original
financial liability and the recognition of a new financial liability. Similarly, a substantial
modification of the terms of an existing financial liability or a part of it (whether or not
attributable to the financial difficulty of the debtor) shall be accounted for as an
extinguishment of the original financial liability and the recognition of a new financial
liability.

41   *The difference between the carrying amount of a financial liability (or part of a financial liability) extinguished or transferred to another party and the consideration paid, including any non-cash assets transferred or liabilities assumed, shall be recognised in profit or loss.*

42   If an entity repurchases a part of a financial liability, the entity shall allocate the previous carrying amount of the financial liability between the part that continues to be recognised and the part that is derecognised based on the relative fair values of those parts on the date of the repurchase. The difference between (a) the carrying amount allocated to the part derecognised and (b) the consideration paid, including any non-cash assets transferred or liabilities assumed, for the part derecognised shall be recognised in profit or loss.

MEASUREMENT

Initial Measurement of Financial Assets and Financial Liabilities

43   *When a financial asset or financial liability is recognised initially, an entity shall measure it at its fair value plus, in the case of a financial asset or financial liability not at fair value through profit or loss, transaction costs that are directly attributable to the acquisition or issue of the financial asset or financial liability.*

44   When an entity uses settlement date accounting for an asset that is subsequently measured at cost or amortised cost, the asset is recognised initially at its fair value on the trade date (see Appendix A paragraphs AG53-AG56).

Subsequent Measurement of Financial Assets

45   For the purpose of measuring a financial asset after initial recognition, this Standard classifies financial assets into the following four categories defined in paragraph 9:

(a)   financial assets at fair value through profit or loss;
(b)   held-to-maturity investments;
(c)   loans and receivables; and
(d)   available-for-sale financial assets.

These categories apply to measurement and profit or loss recognition under this Standard. The entity may use other descriptors for these categories or other categorisations when presenting information on the face of the financial statements. The entity shall disclose in the notes the information required by FRS 29.*

46   *After initial recognition, an entity shall measure financial assets, including derivatives that are assets, at their fair values, without any deduction for transaction costs it may incur on sale or other disposal, except for the following financial assets:*

(a)   loans and receivables as defined in paragraph 9, which shall be measured at amortised cost using the effective interest method;
(b)   held-to-maturity investments as defined in paragraph 9, which shall be measured at amortised cost using the effective interest method; and
(c)   investments in equity instruments that do not have a quoted market price in an active market and whose fair value cannot be reliably measured and derivatives that are linked to and must be settled by delivery of such unquoted equity

---

**Editor's note: Reference to FRS 25 replaced with a reference to FRS 29 with effect for accounting periods beginning on or after 1 January 2007.*

instruments, which shall be measured at cost (see Appendix A paragraphs AG80 and AG81).

Financial assets that are designated as hedged items are subject to measurement under the hedge accounting requirements in paragraphs 89-102. All financial assets except those measured at fair value through profit or loss are subject to review for impairment in accordance with paragraphs 58-70 and Appendix A paragraphs AG84-AG93.

Subsequent Measurement of Financial Liabilities

After initial recognition, an entity shall measure all financial liabilities at amortised cost using the effective interest method, except for: **47**

(a) financial liabilities at fair value through profit or loss. Such liabilities, including derivatives that are liabilities, shall be measured at fair value except for a derivative liability that is linked to and must be settled by delivery of an unquoted equity instrument whose fair value cannot be reliably measured which shall be measured at cost.

(b) financial liabilities that arise when a transfer of a financial asset does not qualify for derecognition.

(c) financial liabilities that arise when a transfer of a non-financial asset does not qualify for derecognition.*

(c) financial guarantee contracts as defined in paragraph 9. After initial recognition, an issuer of such a contract shall (unless paragraph 47(a) or (b) applies) measure it at the higher of:

   (i) the amount determined in accordance with FRS 12 *Provisions, Contingent Liabilities and Contingent Assets*; and
   (ii) the amount initially recognised (see paragraph 43) less, when appropriate, cumulative amortisation.

(d) commitments to provide a loan at a below-market interest rate. After initial recognition, an issuer of such a commitment shall (unless paragraph 47(a) applies) measure it at the higher of:

   (i) the amount determined in accordance with FRS 12; and
   (ii) the amount initially recognised (see paragraph 43) less, when appropriate, cumulative amortisation.†

Fair Value Measurement Considerations

In determining the fair value of a financial asset or a financial liability for the purpose of applying this Standard or FRS 25, an entity shall apply paragraphs AG69-AG82 of Appendix A.‡ **48**

The best evidence of fair value is quoted prices in an active market. If the market for a financial instrument is not active, an entity establishes fair value by using a valuation technique. The objective of using a valuation technique is to establish what the transaction price would have been on the measurement date in an arm's length **48A**

---

*Editor's note: Added in April 2006. There would now appear to be two sub-paragraphs (c).

†*Editor's note: Paragraph amended with effect from 1 January 2006.*

‡*Editor's note: This paragraph is replaced with the following by FRS 29 with effect for accounting periods beginning on or after 1 January 2007, or where FRS 29 is adopted early.*
   'In determining the fair value of a financial asset or a financial liability for the purpose of applying this Standard, FRS 25 or FRS 29, an entity shall apply paragraphs AG69-AG82 of Appendix A.'

exchange motivated by normal business considerations. Valuation techniques include using recent arm's length market transactions between knowledgeable, willing parties, if available, reference to the current fair value of another instrument that is substantially the same, discounted cash flow analysis and option pricing models. If there is a valuation technique commonly used by market participants to price the instrument and that technique has been demonstrated to provide reliable estimates of prices obtained in actual market transactions, the entity uses that technique. The chosen valuation technique makes maximum use of market inputs and relies as little as possible on entity-specific inputs. It incorporates all factors that market participants would consider in setting a price and is consistent with accepted economic methodologies for pricing financial instruments. Periodically, an entity calibrates the valuation technique and tests it for validity using prices from any observable current market transactions in the same instrument (ie without modification or repackaging) or based on any available observable market data.*

49   The fair value of a financial liability with a demand feature (eg a demand deposit) is not less than the amount payable on demand, discounted from the first date that the amount could be required to be paid.

Reclassifications

50   *An entity shall not reclassify a financial instrument into or out of the fair value through profit or loss category while it is held or issued.*

51   *If, as a result of a change in intention or ability, it is no longer appropriate to classify an investment as held to maturity, it shall be reclassified as available for sale and remeasured at fair value, and the difference between its carrying amount and fair value shall be accounted for in accordance with paragraph 55(b).*

52   *Whenever sales or reclassification of more than an insignificant amount of heldto-maturity investments do not meet any of the conditions in paragraph 9, any remaining held-to-maturity investments shall be reclassified as available for sale. On such reclassification, the difference between their carrying amount and fair value shall be accounted for in accordance with paragraph 55(b).*

53   *If a reliable measure becomes available for a financial asset or financial liability for which such a measure was previously not available, and the asset or liability is required to be measured at fair value if a reliable measure is available (see paragraphs 46(c) and 47), the asset or liability shall be remeasured at fair value, and the difference between its carrying amount and fair value shall be accounted for in accordance with paragraph 55.*

54   *If, as a result of a change in intention or ability or in the rare circumstance that a reliable measure of fair value is no longer available (see paragraphs 46(c) and 47) or because the 'two preceding financial years' referred to in paragraph 9 have passed, it becomes appropriate to carry a financial asset or financial liability at cost or amortised cost rather than at fair value, the fair value carrying amount of the financial asset or the financial liability on that date becomes its new cost or amortised cost, as applicable. Any previous gain or loss on that asset that has been recognised directly in equity in accordance with paragraph 55(b) shall be accounted for as follows:*

   (a)   In the case of a financial asset with a fixed maturity, the gain or loss shall be amortised to profit or loss over the remaining life of the held-to-maturity investment using the effective interest method. Any difference between the new

Editor's note: Paragraph 48A added with effect from 1 January 2006.

amortised cost and maturity amount shall also be amortised over the remaining life of the financial asset using the effective interest method, similar to the amortisation of a premium and a discount. If the financial asset is subsequently impaired, any gain or loss that has been recognised directly in equity is recognised in profit or loss in accordance with paragraph 67.

(b)   In the case of a financial asset that does not have a fixed maturity, the gain or loss shall remain in equity until the financial asset is sold or otherwise disposed of, when it shall be recognised in profit or loss. If the financial asset is subsequently impaired any previous gain or loss that has been recognised directly in equity is recognised in profit or loss in accordance with paragraph 67.

Gains and Losses

A gain or loss arising from a change in the fair value of a financial asset or financial liability that is not part of a hedging relationship (see paragraphs 89102), shall be recognised, as follows.   **55**

(a)   A gain or loss on a financial asset or financial liability classified as at fair value through profit or loss shall be recognised in profit or loss.

(b)   A gain or loss on an available-for-sale financial asset shall be recognised through the statement of total recognised gains and losses, except for impairment losses (see paragraphs 67-70) and foreign exchange gains and losses (see Appendix A paragraph AG83), until the financial asset is derecognised, at which time the cumulative gain or loss previously recognised through the statement of total recognised gains and losses shall be recognised in profit or loss. However, interest calculated using the effective interest method (see paragraph 9) is recognised in profit or loss. Dividends on an available-for-sale equity instrument are recognised in profit or loss when the entity's right to receive payment is established.

For financial assets and financial liabilities carried at amortised cost (see paragraphs 46 and 47), a gain or loss is recognised in profit or loss when the financial asset or financial liability is derecognised or impaired, and through the amortisation process. However, for financial assets or financial liabilities that are hedged items (see paragraphs 78-84 and Appendix A paragraphs AG98-AG101) the accounting for the gain or loss shall follow paragraphs 89-102.   **56**

If an entity recognises financial assets using settlement date accounting (see paragraph 38 and Appendix A paragraphs AG53 and AG56), any change in the fair value of the asset to be received during the period between the trade date and the settlement date is not recognised for assets carried at cost or amortised cost (other than impairment losses). For assets carried at fair value, however, the change in fair value shall be recognised in profit or loss or through the statement of total recognised gains and losses, as appropriate under paragraph 55.   **57**

Impairment and Uncollectibility of Financial Assets

An entity shall assess at each balance sheet date whether there is any objective evidence that a financial asset or group of financial assets is impaired. If any such evidence exists, the entity shall apply paragraph 63 (for financial assets carried at amortised cost), paragraph 66 (for financial assets carried at cost) or paragraph 67 (for available-for-sale financial assets) to determine the amount of any impairment loss.   **58**

A financial asset or a group of financial assets is impaired and impairment losses are incurred if, and only if, there is objective evidence of impairment as a result of one or more events that occurred after the initial recognition of the asset (a 'loss event') and that loss event (or events) has an impact on the estimated future cash flows of the   **59** financial asset or group of financial assets that can be reliably estimated. It may not be possible to identify a single, discrete event that caused the impairment. Rather the combined effect of several events may have caused the impairment. Losses expected as a result of future events, no matter how likely, are not recognised. Objective evidence that a financial asset or group of assets is impaired includes observable data that comes to the attention of the holder of the asset about the following loss events:

(a)   significant financial difficulty of the issuer or obligor;

(b)   a breach of contract, such as a default or delinquency in interest or principal payments;

(c)   the lender, for economic or legal reasons relating to the borrower's financial difficulty, granting to the borrower a concession that the lender would not otherwise consider;

(d)   it becoming probable that the borrower will enter bankruptcy or other financial reorganisation;

(e)   the disappearance of an active market for that financial asset because of financial difficulties; or

(f)   observable data indicating that there is a measurable decrease in the estimated future cash flows from a group of financial assets since the initial recognition of those assets, although the decrease cannot yet be identified with the individual financial assets in the group, including:

    (i)   adverse changes in the payment status of borrowers in the group (eg a-n increased number of delayed payments or an increased number of credit card borrowers who have reached their credit limit and are paying the minimum monthly amount); or

    (ii)   national or local economic conditions that correlate with defaults on the assets in the group (eg an increase in the unemployment rate in the geographical area of the borrowers, a decrease in property prices for mortgages in the relevant area, a decrease in oil prices for loan assets to oil producers, or adverse changes in industry conditions that affect the borrowers in the group).

60   The disappearance of an active market because an entity's financial instruments are no longer publicly traded is not evidence of impairment. A downgrade of an entity's credit rating is not, of itself, evidence of impairment, although it may be evidence of impairment when considered with other available information. A decline in the fair value of a financial asset below its cost or amortised cost is not necessarily evidence of impairment (for example, a decline in the fair value of an investment in a debt instrument that results from an increase in the risk-free interest rate).

61   In addition to the types of events in paragraph 59, objective evidence of impairment for an investment in an equity instrument includes information about significant changes with an adverse effect that have taken place in the technological, market, economic or legal environment in which the issuer operates, and indicates that the cost of the investment in the equity instrument may not be recovered. A significant or prolonged decline in the fair value of an investment in an equity instrument below its cost is also objective evidence of impairment.

62   In some cases the observable data required to estimate the amount of an impairment loss on a financial asset may be limited or no longer fully relevant to current circumstances. For example, this may be the case when a borrower is in financial difficulties and there are few available historical data relating to similar borrowers. In such cases, an entity uses its experienced judgement to estimate the amount of any impairment loss. Similarly an entity uses its experienced judgement to adjust observable data for a group of financial assets to reflect current circumstances (see paragraph AG89). The use of reasonable estimates is an essential part of the preparation of financial statements and does not undermine their reliability.

Financial Assets Carried at Amortised Cost

If there is objective evidence that an impairment loss on loans and receivables or held-to-maturity investments carried at amortised cost has been incurred, the amount of the loss is measured as the difference between the asset's carrying amount and the present value of estimated future cash flows (excluding future credit losses that have not been incurred) discounted at the financial asset's original effective interest rate (ie the effective interest rate computed at initial recognition). The carrying amount of the asset shall be reduced either directly or through use of an allowance account. The amount of the loss shall be recognised in profit or loss.   **63**

An entity first assesses whether objective evidence of impairment exists individually   **64** for financial assets that are individually significant, and individually or collectively for financial assets that are not individually significant (see paragraph 59). If an entity determines that no objective evidence of impairment exists for an individually assessed financial asset, whether significant or not, it includes the asset in a group of financial assets with similar credit risk characteristics and collectively assesses them for impairment. Assets that are individually assessed for impairment and for which an impairment loss is or continues to be recognised are not included in a collective assessment of impairment.

If, in a subsequent period, the amount of the impairment loss decreases and the decrease   **65** *can be related objectively to an event occurring after the impairment was recognised (such as an improvement in the debtor's credit rating), the previously recognised impairment loss shall be reversed either directly or by adjusting an allowance account. The reversal shall not result in a carrying amount of the financial asset that exceeds what the amortised cost would have been had the impairment not been recognised at the date the impairment is reversed. The amount of the reversal shall be recognised in profit or loss.*

Financial Assets Carried at Cost

If there is objective evidence that an impairment loss has been incurred on an unquoted   **66** *equity instrument that is not carried at fair value because its fair value cannot be reliably measured, or on a derivative asset that is linked to and must be settled by delivery of such an unquoted equity instrument, the amount of the impairment loss is measured as the difference between the carrying amount of the financial asset and the present value of estimated future cash flows discounted at the current market rate of return for a similar financial asset (see paragraph 46(c) and Appendix A paragraphs AG80 and AG81). Such impairment losses shall not be reversed.*

Available-for-Sale Financial Assets

When a decline in the fair value of an available-for-sale financial asset has been   **67** *recognised through the statement of total recognised gains and losses and there is objective evidence that the asset is impaired (see paragraph 59), the cumulative loss that had been recognised through the statement of total recognised gains and losses shall be removed from reserves and recognised in profit or loss even though the financial asset has not been derecognised.*

68   *The amount of the cumulative loss that is removed from reserves and recognised in profit or loss under paragraph 67 shall be the difference between the acquisition cost (net of any principal repayment and amortisation) and current fair value, less any impairment loss on that financial asset previously recognised in profit or loss.*

69   *Impairment losses recognised in profit or loss for an investment in an equity instrument classified as available for sale shall not be reversed through profit or loss.*

70   *If, in a subsequent period, the fair value of a debt instrument classified as available for sale increases and the increase can be objectively related to an event occurring after the impairment loss was recognised in profit or loss, the impairment loss shall be reversed, with the amount of the reversal recognised in profit or loss.*

HEDGING

71   *If there is a designated hedging relationship between a hedging instrument and a hedged item as described in paragraphs 85-88 and Appendix A paragraphs AG102-AG104, accounting for the gain or loss on the hedging instrument and the hedged item shall follow paragraphs 89-102.*

Hedging Instruments

Qualifying Instruments

72   This Standard does not restrict the circumstances in which a derivative may be designated as a hedging instrument provided the conditions in paragraph 88 are met, except for some written options (see Appendix A paragraph AG94). However, a non-derivative financial asset or non-derivative financial liability may be designated as a hedging instrument only for a hedge of a foreign currency risk.

73   For hedge accounting purposes, only instruments that involve a party external to the reporting entity (ie external to the group, segment or individual entity that is being reported on) can be designated as hedging instruments. Although individual entities within a consolidated group or divisions within an entity may enter into hedging transactions with other entities within the group or divisions within the entity, any such intragroup transactions are eliminated on consolidation. Therefore, such hedging transactions do not qualify for hedge accounting in the consolidated financial statements of the group. However, they may qualify for hedge accounting in the individual or separate financial statements of individual entities within the group or in segment reporting provided that they are external to the individual entity or segment that is being reported on.

Designation of Hedging Instruments

74   There is normally a single fair value measure for a hedging instrument in its entirety, and the factors that cause changes in fair value are codependent. Thus, a hedging relationship is designated by an entity for a hedging instrument in its entirety. The only exceptions permitted are:

(a)   separating the intrinsic value and time value of an option contract and designating as the hedging instrument only the change in intrinsic value of an option and excluding change in its time value; and

(b)   separating the interest element and the spot price of a forward contract.

These exceptions are permitted because the intrinsic value of the option and the premium on the forward can generally be measured separately. A dynamic hedging strategy that assesses both the intrinsic value and time value of an option contract can qualify for hedge accounting.

A proportion of the entire hedging instrument, such as 50 per cent of the notional amount, may be designated as the hedging instrument in a hedging relationship. However, a hedging relationship may not be designated for only a portion of the time period during which a hedging instrument remains outstanding.   **75**

A single hedging instrument may be designated as a hedge of more than one type of risk provided that (a) the risks hedged can be identified clearly; (b) the effectiveness of the hedge can be demonstrated; and (c) it is possible to ensure that there is specific designation of the hedging instrument and different risk positions.   **76**

Two or more derivatives, or proportions of them (or, in the case of a hedge of currency risk, two or more non-derivatives or proportions of them, or a combination of derivatives and non-derivatives or proportions of them), may be viewed in combination and jointly designated as the hedging instrument, including when the risk(s) arising from some derivatives offset(s) those arising from others. However, an interest rate collar or other derivative instrument that combines a written option and a purchased option does not qualify as a hedging instrument if it is, in effect, a net written option (for which a net premium is received). Similarly, two or more instruments (or proportions of them) may be designated as the hedging instrument only if none of them is a written option or a net written option.   **77**

Hedged Items

Qualifying Items

A hedged item can be a recognised asset or liability, an unrecognised firm commitment, a highly probable forecast transaction or a net investment in a foreign operation. The hedged item can be (a) a single asset, liability, firm commitment, highly probable forecast transaction or net investment in a foreign operation, (b) a group of assets, liabilities, firm commitments, highly probable forecast transactions or net investments in foreign operations with similar risk characteristics or (c) in a portfolio hedge of interest rate risk only, a portion of the portfolio of financial assets or financial liabilities that share the risk being hedged.   **78**

Unlike loans and receivables, a held-to-maturity investment cannot be a hedged item with respect to interest-rate risk or prepayment risk because designation of an investment as held to maturity requires an intention to hold the investment until maturity without regard to changes in the fair value or cash flows of such an investment attributable to changes in interest rates. However, a held-to-maturity investment can be a hedged item with respect to risks from changes in foreign currency exchange rates and credit risk.   **79**

For hedge accounting purposes, only assets, liabilities, firm commitments or highly probable forecast transactions that involve a party external to the entity can be designated as hedged items. It follows that hedge accounting can be applied to transactions between entities or segments in the same group only in the individual or separate financial statements of those entities or segments and not in the consolidated financial statements of the group. As an exception, the foreign currency risk of an intragroup monetary item (eg a payable/receivable between two subsidiaries) may qualify as a hedged item in the consolidated financial statements if it   **80** results in an exposure to foreign exchange rate gains or losses that are not fully eliminated on consolidation in accordance with FRS 23 (IAS 21) *The Effects of Changes in Foreign Exchange Rates.* In accordance with FRS 23 (IAS 21), foreign exchange rate gains and losses on intragroup monetary items are not fully eliminated on consolidation when the intragroup monetary item is transacted between two group entities that have different functional currencies. In addition, the foreign currency risk of a highly probable forecast intragroup transaction may qualify as a hedged item in consolidated financial statements provided that the transaction is denominated in a currency other than the functional currency of the entity entering into that transaction and the foreign currency risk will affect consolidated profit or loss.*

Designation of Financial Items as Hedged Items

81　If the hedged item is a financial asset or financial liability, it may be a hedged item with respect to the risks associated with only a portion of its cash flows or fair value (such as one or more selected contractual cash flows or portions of them or a percentage of the fair value) provided that effectiveness can be measured. For example, an identifiable and separately measurable portion of the interest rate exposure of an interest-bearing asset or interest-bearing liability may be designated as the hedged risk (such as a risk-free interest rate or benchmark interest rate component of the total interest rate exposure of a hedged financial instrument).

81A　In a fair value hedge of the interest rate exposure of a portfolio of financial assets or financial liabilities (and only in such a hedge), the portion hedged may be designated in terms of an amount of a currency (eg an amount of dollars, euro, pounds or rand) rather than as individual assets (or liabilities). Although the portfolio may, for risk management purposes, include assets and liabilities, the amount designated is an amount of assets or an amount of liabilities. Designation of a net amount including assets and liabilities is not permitted. The entity may hedge a portion of the interest rate risk associated with this designated amount. For example, in the case of a hedge of a portfolio containing prepayable assets, the entity may hedge the change in fair value that is attributable to a change in the hedged interest rate on the basis of expected, rather than contractual, repricing dates. When the portion hedged is based on expected repricing dates, the effect that changes in the hedged interest rate have on those expected repricing dates shall be included when determining the change in the fair value of the hedged item. Consequently, if a portfolio that contains prepayable items is hedged with a non-prepayable derivative, ineffectiveness arises if the dates on which items in the hedged portfolio are expected to prepay are revised, or actual prepayment dates differ from those expected.

Designation of Non-Financial Items as Hedged Items

82　*If the hedged item is a non-financial asset or non-financial liability, it shall be designated as a hedged item (a) for foreign currency risks, or (b) in its entirety for all risks, because of the difficulty of isolating and measuring the appropriate portion of the cash flows or fair value changes attributable to specific risks other than foreign currency risks.*

Editor's note: Paragraph amended October 2005.

Designation of Groups of Items as Hedged Items

Similar assets or similar liabilities shall be aggregated and hedged as a group only if **83** the individual assets or individual liabilities in the group share the risk exposure that is designated as being hedged. Furthermore, the change in fair value attributable to the hedged risk for each individual item in the group shall be expected to be approximately proportional to the overall change in fair value attributable to the hedged risk of the group of items.

Because an entity assesses hedge effectiveness by comparing the change in the fair **84** value or cash flow of a hedging instrument (or group of similar hedging instruments) and a hedged item (or group of similar hedged items), comparing a hedging instrument with an overall net position (eg the net of all fixed rate assets and fixed rate liabilities with similar maturities), rather than with a specific hedged item, does not qualify for hedge accounting.

Hedge Accounting

Hedge accounting recognises the offsetting effects on profit or loss of changes in the **85** fair values of the hedging instrument and the hedged item.

Hedging relationships are of three types: **86**

(a) *fair value hedge: a hedge of the exposure to changes in fair value of a recognised asset or liability or an unrecognised firm commitment, or an identified portion of such an asset, liability or firm commitment, that is attributable to a particular risk and could affect profit or loss.*
(b) *cash flow hedge: a hedge of the exposure to variability in cash flows that (i) is attributable to a particular risk associated with a recognised asset or liability (such as all or some future interest payments on variable rate debt) or a highly probable forecast transaction and (ii) could affect profit or loss.*
(c) *hedge of a net investment in a foreign operation as defined in FRS 23.*

A hedge of the foreign currency risk of a firm commitment may be accounted for as a **87** fair value hedge or as a cash flow hedge.

A hedging relationship qualifies for hedge accounting under paragraphs 89-102 if, and **88** *only if, all of the following conditions are met.*

(a) *At the inception of the hedge there is formal designation and documentation of the hedging relationship and the entity's risk management objective and strategy for undertaking the hedge. That documentation shall include identification of the hedging instrument, the hedged item or transaction, the nature of the risk being hedged and how the entity will assess the hedging instrument's effectiveness in offsetting the exposure to changes in the hedged item's fair value or cash flows attributable to the hedged risk.*
(b) *The hedge is expected to be highly effective (see Appendix A paragraphs AG105-AG113) in achieving offsetting changes in fair value or cash flows attributable to the hedged risk, consistently with the originally documented risk management strategy for that particular hedging relationship.*
(c) *For cash flow hedges, a forecast transaction that is the subject of the hedge must be highly probable and must present an exposure to variations in cash flows that could ultimately affect profit or loss.*
(d) *The effectiveness of the hedge can be reliably measured, ie the fair value or cash flows of the hedged item that are attributable to the hedged risk and the fair value of the hedging instrument can be reliably measured (see paragraphs 46 and 47*

> *and Appendix A paragraphs AG80 and AG81 for guidance on determining fair value).*
>
> *(e)   The hedge is assessed on an ongoing basis and determined actually to have been highly effective throughout the financial reporting periods for which the hedge was designated.*

Fair Value Hedges

89   *If a fair value hedge meets the conditions in paragraph 88 during the period, it shall be accounted for as follows:*

> *(a)   the gain or loss from remeasuring the hedging instrument at fair value (for a derivative hedging instrument) or the foreign currency component of its carrying amount measured in accordance with FRS 23 (for a non-derivative hedging instrument) shall be recognised in profit or loss; and*
>
> *(b)   the gain or loss on the hedged item attributable to the hedged risk shall adjust the carrying amount of the hedged item and be recognised in profit or loss. This applies if the hedged item is otherwise measured at cost. Recognition of the gain or loss attributable to the hedged risk in profit or loss applies if the hedged item is an available-for-sale financial asset.*

89A   For a fair value hedge of the interest rate exposure of a portion of a portfolio of financial assets or financial liabilities (and only in such a hedge), the requirement in paragraph 89(b) may be met by presenting the gain or loss attributable to the hedged item either:

> (a)   in a single separate line item within assets, for those repricing time periods for which the hedged item is an asset; or
>
> (b)   in a single separate line item within liabilities, for those repricing time periods for which the hedged item is a liability.

The separate line items referred to in (a) and (b) above shall be presented next to financial assets or financial liabilities. Amounts included in these line items shall be removed from the balance sheet when the assets or liabilities to which they relate are derecognised.

90   If only particular risks attributable to a hedged item are hedged, recognised changes in the fair value of the hedged item unrelated to the hedged risk are recognised as set out in paragraph 55.

91   *An entity shall discontinue prospectively the hedge accounting specified in paragraph 89 if:*

> *(a)   the hedging instrument expires or is sold, terminated or exercised (for this purpose, the replacement or rollover of a hedging instrument into another hedging instrument is not an expiration or termination if such replacement or rollover is part of the entity's documented hedging strategy);*
>
> *(b)   the hedge no longer meets the criteria for hedge accounting in paragraph 88; or*
>
> *(c)   the entity revokes the designation.*

92   *Any adjustment arising from paragraph 89(b) to the carrying amount of a hedged financial instrument for which the effective interest method is used (or, in the case of a portfolio hedge of interest rate risk, to the separate balance sheet line item described in paragraph 89A) shall be amortised to profit or loss. Amortisation may begin as soon as an adjustment exists and shall begin no later than when the hedged item ceases to be adjusted for changes in its fair value attributable to the risk being hedged. The adjustment is based on a recalculated effective interest rate at the date amortisation* *begins. However, if, in the case of a fair value hedge of the interest rate exposure of a portfolio of financial assets or financial liabilities (and only in such a hedge), amortising using a recalculated effective interest rate is not practicable, the adjustment shall be amortised using a straightline method. The adjustment shall be amortised fully by maturity of the financial instrument or, in the case of a portfolio hedge of interest rate risk, by expiry of the relevant repricing time period.*

When an unrecognised firm commitment is designated as a hedged item, the subsequent cumulative change in the fair value of the firm commitment attributable to the hedged risk is recognised as an asset or liability with a corresponding gain or loss recognised in profit or loss (see paragraph 89(b)). The changes in the fair value of the hedging instrument are also recognised in profit or loss.   **93**

When an entity enters into a firm commitment to acquire an asset or assume a liability that is a hedged item in a fair value hedge, the initial carrying amount of the asset or liability that results from the entity meeting the firm commitment is adjusted to include the cumulative change in the fair value of the firm commitment attributable to the hedged risk that was recognised in the balance sheet.   **94**

Cash Flow Hedges

If a cash flow hedge meets the conditions in paragraph 88 during the period, it shall be accounted for as follows: **95**

(a)   *the portion of the gain or loss on the hedging instrument that is determined to be an effective hedge (see paragraph 88) shall be recognised through the statement of total recognised gains and losses; and*
(b)   *the ineffective portion of the gain or loss on the hedging instrument shall be recognised in profit or loss.*

More specifically, a cash flow hedge is accounted for as follows: **96**

(a)   the separate amount recognised through the statement of total recognised gains and losses associated with the hedged item is adjusted to the lesser of the following (in absolute amounts):
  (i)   the cumulative gain or loss on the hedging instrument from inception of the hedge; and
  (ii)   the cumulative change in fair value (present value) of the expected future cash flows on the hedged item from inception of the hedge;
(b)   any remaining gain or loss on the hedging instrument or designated component of it (that is not an effective hedge) is recognised in profit or loss; and
(c)   if an entity's documented risk management strategy for a particular hedging relationship excludes from the assessment of hedge effectiveness a specific component of the gain or loss or related cash flows on the hedging instrument (see paragraphs 74, 75 and 88(a)), that excluded component of gain or loss is recognised in accordance with paragraph 55.

If a hedge of a forecast transaction subsequently results in the recognition of a financial asset or a financial liability, the associated gains or losses that were recognised directly in reserves in accordance with paragraph 95 shall be reclassified into profit or loss in the same period or periods during which the asset acquired or liability assumed affects profit or loss (such as in the periods that interest income or interest expense is recognised). However, if an entity expects that all or a portion of a loss recognised directly in reserves will not be recovered in one or more future periods, it shall reclassify into profit or loss the amount that is not expected to be recovered.   **97**

98 *If a hedge of a forecast transaction subsequently results in the recognition of a non-financial asset or a non-financial liability, or a forecast transaction for a non-financial asset or non-financial liability becomes a firm commitment for which fair value hedge accounting is applied, then the entity shall adopt (a) or (b) below:*

(a) *It reclassifies the associated gains and losses that were recognised directly in reserves in accordance with paragraph 95 into profit or loss in the same period or periods during which the asset acquired or liability assumed affects profit or loss (such as in the periods that depreciation expense or cost of sales is recognised). However, if an entity expects that all or a portion of a loss recognised directly in reserves will not be recovered in one or more future periods, it shall reclassify into profit or loss the amount that is not expected to be recovered.*

(b) *It removes the associated gains and losses that were recognised directly in reserves in accordance with paragraph 95, and includes them in the initial cost or other carrying amount of the asset or liability.*

99 *An entity shall adopt either (a) or (b) in paragraph 98 as its accounting policy and shall apply it consistently to all hedges to which paragraph 98 relates.*

100 *For cash flow hedges other than those covered by paragraphs 97 and 98, amounts that had been recognised directly in reserves shall be recognised in profit or loss in the same period or periods during which the hedged forecast transaction affects profit or loss (for example, when a forecast sale occurs).*

101 *In any of the following circumstances an entity shall discontinue prospectively the hedge accounting specified in paragraphs 95-100:*

(a) *The hedging instrument expires or is sold, terminated or exercised (for this purpose, the replacement or rollover of a hedging instrument into another hedging instrument is not an expiration or termination if such replacement or rollover is part of the entity's documented hedging strategy). In this case, the cumulative gain or loss on the hedging instrument that remains recognised directly in reserves from the period when the hedge was effective (see paragraph 95(a)) shall remain separately recognised in reserves until the forecast transaction occurs. When the transaction occurs, paragraph 97, 98 or 100 applies.*

(b) *The hedge no longer meets the criteria for hedge accounting in paragraph 88. In this case, the cumulative gain or loss on the hedging instrument that remains recognised directly in reserves from the period when the hedge was effective (see paragraph 95(a)) shall remain separately recognised in reserves until the forecast transaction occurs. When the transaction occurs, paragraph 97, 98 or 100 applies.*

(c) *The forecast transaction is no longer expected to occur, in which case any related cumulative gain or loss on the hedging instrument that remains recognised directly in reserves from the period when the hedge was effective (see paragraph 95(a)) shall be recognised in profit or loss. A forecast transaction that is no longer highly probable (see paragraph 88(c)) may still be expected to occur.*

(d) *The entity revokes the designation. For hedges of a forecast transaction, the cumulative gain or loss on the hedging instrument that remains recognised directly in reserves from the period when the hedge was effective (see paragraph 95(a)) shall remain separately recognised in reserves until the forecast transaction occurs or is no longer expected to occur. When the transaction occurs, paragraph 97, 98 or 100 applies. If the transaction is no longer expected to occur, the cumulative gain or loss that had been recognised directly in reserves shall be recognised in profit or loss.*

Hedges of a Net Investment

Hedges of a net investment in a foreign operation, including a hedge of a monetary item   **102**
that is accounted for as part of the net investment (see FRS 23), shall be accounted for
similarly to cash flow hedges:

(a)   *the portion of the gain or loss on the hedging instrument that is determined to be*
    an effective hedge (see paragraph 88) shall be recognised through the statement
    of total recognised gains and losses; and
(b)   *the ineffective portion shall be recognised in profit or loss.*

The gain or loss on the hedging instrument relating to the effective portion of the hedge
that has been recognised directly in reserves shall be recognised in profit or loss on
disposal of the foreign operation.

EFFECTIVE DATE AND TRANSITION

A listed entity shall apply this Standard for accounting periods beginning on or after 1   **103**
January 2005. Other entities falling within the scope of this Standard shall apply it for
accounting periods beginning on or after 1 January 2006, and may voluntarily apply it
for accounting periods beginning on or after 1 January 2005. Earlier application is not
permitted.

An entity shall apply the amendment in paragraph 2(j) for annual periods beginning on   **103A**
or after 1 January 2006.

The amendments to the standard made in March 2006, including the insertion of   **103A**
paragraphs 14 to 42 and AG34 to AG63, are effective for accounting periods
commencing on or after 1 January 2007. Earlier implementation of this amendment
is permitted.*

This amendment to FRS 26 amended paragraphs 2(e) and (h), 4, 47 and AG4, added   **103B**
paragraph AG4A, added a new definition of financial guarantee contracts in paragraph
9, and deleted paragraph 3. An entity shall apply those amendments for annual periods
beginning on or after 1 January 2006. Earlier application is encouraged. If an entity
applies these changes for an earlier period, it shall disclose that fact and apply the
related amendments to FRS 25 at the same time.

For accounting periods commencing before 1 January 2006, the definition of listed   **103C**
entity in paragraph 9A shall not be treated as including entities in the Republic of
Ireland that (i) have debt securities but not equity securities admitted to trading on a
regulated market as referred to in that paragraph and (ii) are qualifying companies
within the meaning of Section 110 of the Taxes Consolidation Act 1997 of the Republic
of Ireland.

This Standard shall be applied retrospectively except as specified in paragraphs 105-   **104**
108D. The opening balance of retained earnings for the earliest prior period presented
and all other comparative amounts shall be adjusted as if this Standard had always been
in use unless restating the information would be impracticable. If restatement is
impracticable, the entity shall disclose that fact and indicate the extent to which the
information was restated.

When this Standard is first applied, an entity is permitted to designate a previously   **105**
recognised financial asset as available for sale. For any such financial asset the entity

Editor's note: There now appear to be two paragraphs 103A.

shall recognise all cumulative changes in fair value in a separate component of equity until subsequent derecognition or impairment, when the entity shall transfer that cumulative gain or loss to profit or loss. The entity shall also:

(a) *restate the financial asset using the new designation in the comparative financial statements; and*

(b) *disclose the fair value of the financial assets at the date of designation and their classification and carrying amount in the previous financial statements.*

105A *An entity shall apply paragraphs 11A, 48A, AG4B-AG4K, AG33A and AG33B and the 2005 amendments in paragraphs 9, 12 and 13 for accounting periods beginning on or after 1 January 2006. Earlier application is encouraged.*

105C *An entity that is not adopting the standard for the first time that first applies paragraphs 11A, 48A, AG4B-AG4K, AG33A and AG33B and the 2005 amendments in paragraphs 9, 12 and 13 in its accounting period beginning on or after 1 January 2006:*

(a) *shall de-designate any financial asset or financial liability previously designated as at fair value through profit or loss only if it does not qualify for such designation in accordance with those new and amended paragraphs. When a financial asset or financial liability will be measured at amortised cost after de-designation, the date of de-designation is deemed to be its date of initial recognition.*

(b) *shall not designate as at fair value through profit or loss any previously recognised financial assets or financial liabilities.*

(c) *shall disclose the fair value of any financial assets or financial liabilities de-designated in accordance with subparagraph (a) at the date of de-designation and their new classifications.*

105D *An entity falling within paragraph 105C shall restate its comparative financial statements using the new designations in that paragraph provided that, in the case of a financial asset, financial liability, or group of financial assets, financial liabilities or both, designated as at fair value through profit or loss, those items or groups would have met the criteria in paragraph 9(b)(i), 9(b)(ii) or 11A at the beginning of the comparative period or, if acquired after the beginning of the comparative period, would have met the criteria in paragraph 9(b)(i), 9(b)(ii) or 11A at the date of initial recognition.*

105E *An entity that first adopts this Standard for an accounting period beginning on or after 1 January 2006*—such an entity is permitted to designate, at the date of transition to this standard, any financial asset or financial liability as at fair value through profit or loss provided the asset or liability meets the criteria in paragraph 9(b)(i), 9(b)(ii) or 11A of FRS 26 at that date.

105F When the date of transition to this standard is before 1 December 2005, such designations need not be completed until 1 December 2005 and may also include financial assets and financial liabilities recognised between the date of transition to this standard and 1 December 2005.

105G *An entity that first adopts this Standard for an accounting period beginning before 1 January 2006 and applies paragraphs 11A, 48A, AG4B-AG4K, AG33A and AG33B and the 2005 amendments in paragraphs 9, 12 and 13 of FRS 26*—such an entity is permitted at the start of the first period in which it adopts the standard to designate as at fair value through profit or loss any financial asset or financial liability that qualifies for such designation in accordance with these new and amended paragraphs at that date. When the entity's period of first adopting the Standard begins before 1 December 2005, such designations need not be completed until 1 December 2005 and may also include financial assets and financial liabilities recognised between the beginning of that period and 1 December 2005. If the entity restates comparative information for FRS 26 it shall restate that information for the financial assets, financial liabilities, or group of financial assets, financial liabilities or both, designated at the start of the period in which the Standard is adopted. Such restatement of comparative information shall be made only if the designated items or groups would have met the criteria for such designation in paragraph 9(b)(i), 9(b)(ii) or 11A of FRS 26 at the date of transition to this standard or, if acquired after the date of transition to this standard, would have met the criteria in paragraph 9(b)(i), 9(b)(ii) or 11A at the date of initial recognition.

Where any financial assets and financial liabilities are designated as at fair value through profit or loss in accordance with subparagraph 105F or 105G above and were previously designated as the hedged item in fair value hedge accounting relationships, they shall be de-designated from those hedging relationships at the same time they are designated as at fair value through profit or loss, notwithstanding the requirements of paragraph 91 of FRS 26.   **105H**

Notwithstanding paragraph 104, an entity may apply the requirements in the last sentence of paragraph AG76, and paragraph AG76A, in either of the following ways: **107A**

(a)   prospectively to transactions entered into after 25 October 2002; or

(b)   prospectively to transactions entered into after 1 January 2004.*

An entity shall not adjust the carrying amount of non-financial assets and non-financial liabilities to exclude gains and losses related to cash flow hedges that were included in the carrying amount before the beginning of the financial year in which this Standard is first applied. At the beginning of the financial period in which this Standard is first applied, any amount recognised directly in equity for a hedge of a firm commitment that under this Standard is accounted for as a fair value hedge shall be reclassified as an asset or liability, except for a hedge of foreign currency risk that continues to be treated as a cash flow hedge.   **108**

At the date of transition to this Standard, an entity shall: **108A**

(a)   measure all derivatives at fair value; and

(b)   eliminate all deferred losses and gains arising on derivatives that were reported under its previous accounting policies as if they were assets or liabilities.

An entity shall not reflect in its opening balance sheet at the date of transition to this standard a hedging relationship of a type that does not qualify for hedge accounting under this Standard (for example, many hedging relationships where the hedging instrument is a cash instrument or written option; where the hedged item is a net position; or where the hedge covers interest risk in a held-to-maturity investment). However, if an entity designated a net position as a hedged item under its previous accounting policies, it may designate an individual item within that net position as a hedged item under this Standard, provided that it does so no later than the date of transition to this Standard.   **108B**

If, before the date of transition to this Standard, an entity had designated a transaction as a hedge but the hedge does not meet the conditions for hedge accounting in this Standard the entity shall apply paragraphs 91 and 101 to discontinue hedge accounting. Transactions entered into before the date of transition to this Standard shall not be retrospectively designated as hedges.   **108C**

An entity that first adopts this Standard for an accounting period that commences before 1 January 2007 need not restate comparative information to comply with this   **108D**

Editor's note: Paragraph added October 2005.

Standard and FRS 25. An entity that chooses to present comparative information that does not comply with this Standard and FRS 25 in its first year of adoption shall:

(a) apply its existing accounting policies to financial instruments within the scope of this standard and FRS 25 in the comparative information;

(b) disclose this fact together with the basis used to prepare this information; and

(c) disclose the nature of the main adjustments that would make the information comply with this Standard and FRS 25. The entity need not quantify those adjustments. However, the entity shall treat any adjustment between the balance sheet at the comparative period's reporting date (ie the balance sheet that includes comparative information under previous accounting policies) and the balance sheet at the start of the first reporting period that includes information that complies with this Standard and FRS 25 as arising from a change in accounting policy and give the disclosures required by FRS 18 *Accounting Policies.*

108E Except as permitted by paragraph 108F, an entity adopting paragraphs 15-37 and AG36-AG52 for the first time shall apply these requirements prospectively for transactions occurring on or after the beginning of the comparative period for the accounting period in which the entity first applies these paragraphs. In other words, if the entity derecognised non-derivative financial assets or non-derivative financial liabilities under its previous accounting policies as a result of a transaction that occurred before that date, if shall not recognise those assets and liabilities (unless they qualify for recognition as a result of a later transaction or event). When an entity has previously shown a transaction using the linked presentation of FRS 5, it shall not treat this as derecognition for the purposes of this paragraph.

...

108E An entity shall apply the last sentence of paragraph 80, and paragraphs AG99A and AG99B, for accounting periods beginning on or after 1 January 2006. Earlier application is encouraged. If an entity has designated as the hedged item an external forecast transaction that

(a) is denominated in the functional currency of the entity entering into the transaction,

(b) gives rise to an exposure that will have an effect on consolidated profit or loss (ie is denominated in a currency other than the group's presentation currency), and

(c) would have qualified for hedge accounting had it not been denominated in the functional currency of the entity entering into it,

it may apply hedge accounting in the consolidated financial statements in the period(s) before the date of application of the last sentence of paragraph 80, and paragraphs AG99A and AG99B.

108F Notwithstanding paragraph 108F, an entity may apply the derecognition requirements in paragraphs 15-37 and AG36-52 retrospectively from a date of the entity's choosing, provided that the information needed to apply these paragraphs to financial assets and financial liabilities derecognised as a result of past transactions was obtained at the time of initially accounting for those transactions.

An entity need not apply paragraph AG99B to comparative information relating to   **108F**
periods before the date of application of the last sentence of paragraph 80 and
paragraph AG99A.*

WITHDRAWAL OF OTHER PRONOUNCEMENTS

This Standard supersedes UITF Abstract 11 **Capital instruments: issuer call options** *for*   **110A**
those entities applying this Standard.

*Editor's note: There now appear to be two paragraphs 108E and 108F.

Appendix A
Application Guidance

This appendix is an integral part of the Standard.

SCOPE (PARAGRAPHS 2-7)

AG1   Some contracts require a payment based on climatic, geological or other physical variables. (Those based on climatic variables are sometimes referred to as 'weather derivatives'.) If those contracts are not insurance contracts as defined in Appendix C to FRS 26, they are within the scope of this Standard.

AG2   This Standard does not change the requirements relating to employee benefit plans that comply with FRS 17 *Retirement Benefits* and royalty agreements based on the volume of sales or service revenues.

AG3   Sometimes, an entity makes what it views as a 'strategic investment' in equity instruments issued by another entity, with the intention of establishing or maintaining a long-term operating relationship with the entity in which the investment is made. The investor entity uses FRS 9 *Associates and Joint Ventures* to determine whether the equity method of accounting, gross equity method, or treatment as a joint arrangement that is not an entity is appropriate for such an investment. If none of these is appropriate, the entity applies this Standard to that strategic investment.

AG3A   This Standard applies to the financial assets and financial liabilities of insurers, other than rights and obligations that paragraph 2(e) excludes because they arise under contracts that are insurance contracts as defined in Appendix C to FRS 26.

AG4   Financial guarantee contracts may have various legal forms, such as a guarantee, some types of letter of credit, a credit default contract or an insurance contract. Their accounting treatment does not depend on their legal form. The following are examples of the appropriate treatment (see paragraph 2(e)):

(a)   Although a financial guarantee contract meets the definition of an insurance contract in Appendix C to FRS 26 if the risk transferred is significant, the issuer applies this Standard. Nevertheless, if the issuer has previously asserted explicitly that it regards such contracts as insurance contracts and has used accounting applicable to insurance contracts, the issuer may elect to apply this Standard to such financial guarantee contracts. If this Standard applies, paragraph 43 requires the issuer to recognise a financial guarantee contract initially at fair value. If the financial guarantee contract was issued to an unrelated party in a stand-alone arm's length transaction, its fair value at inception is likely to equal the premium received, unless there is evidence to the contrary. Subsequently, unless the financial guarantee contract was designated at inception as at fair value through profit or loss, the issuer measures it at the higher of:

(i)   the amount determined in accordance with FRS 12; and
(ii)   the amount initially recognised less, when appropriate, cumulative amortisation (see paragraph 47(c)).

(b)   Some credit-related guarantees do not, as a precondition for payment, require that the holder is exposed to, and has incurred a loss on, the failure of the debtor to make payments on the guaranteed asset when due. An example of such a guarantee is one that requires payments in response to changes in a specified credit rating or credit index. Such guarantees are not financial guarantee contracts, as defined in this Standard, and are not insurance contracts, as defined in Appendix C to FRS 26. Such guarantees are derivatives and the issuer applies this Standard to them.

(c) If a financial guarantee contract was issued in connection with the sale of goods, the issuer applies Application Note G to FRS 5 *Reporting the Substance of Transactions* in determining when it recognises the revenue from the sale of goods.

Assertions that an issuer regards contracts as insurance contracts are typically found throughout the issuer's communications with customers and regulators, contracts, business documentation and financial statements. Furthermore, insurance contracts are often subject to accounting requirements that are distinct from the requirements for other types of transaction, such as contracts issued by banks or commercial companies. In such cases, an issuer's financial statements typically include a statement that the issuer has used those accounting requirements.* **AG4A**

Paragraph 9 of this Standard allows an entity to designate a financial asset, a financial liability, or a group of financial instruments (financial assets, financial liabilities or both) as at fair value through profit or loss provided that doing so results in more relevant information. **AG4B**

The decision of an entity to designate a financial asset or financial liability as at fair value through profit or loss is similar to an accounting policy choice (although, unlike an accounting policy choice, it is not required to be applied consistently to all similar transactions). Paragraph 30 of FRS 18 *Accounting Policies* states that the objectives against which an entity should judge the appropriateness of accounting policies include relevance and reliability. In the case of designation as at fair value through profit or loss paragraph 9 sets out the two circumstances in which more relevant information will be provided. Accordingly, to choose such designation in accordance with paragraph 9, the entity needs to demonstrate that it falls within one (or both) of these two circumstances. **AG4C**

Paragraph 9(b)(i): Designation eliminates or significantly reduces a measurement or recognition inconsistency that would otherwise arise

Under FRS 26, measurement of a financial asset or financial liability and classification of recognised changes in its value are determined by the item's classification and whether the item is part of a designated hedging relationship. Those requirements can create a measurement or recognition inconsistency (sometimes referred to as an 'accounting mismatch') when, for example, in the absence of designation as at fair value through profit or loss, a financial asset would be classified as available for sale (with most changes in fair value recognised directly in equity) and a liability the entity considers related would be measured at amortised cost (with changes in fair value not recognised). In such circumstances, an entity may conclude that its financial statements would provide more relevant information if both the asset and the liability were classified as at fair value through profit or loss. **AG4D**

The following examples show when this condition could be met. In all cases, an entity may use this condition to designate financial assets or financial liabilities as at fair value through profit or loss only if it meets the principle in paragraph 9(b)(i). **AG4E**

(a) An entity has liabilities whose cash flows are contractually based on the performance of assets that would otherwise be classified as available for sale. For

Editor's note: AG4 amended and AG4A added with effect from 1 January 2006.

example, an insurer may have liabilities containing a discretionary participation feature that pay benefits based on realised and/or unrealised investment returns of a specified pool of the insurer's assets. If the measurement of those liabilities reflects current market prices, classifying the assets as at fair value through profit or loss means that changes in the fair value of the financial assets are recognised in profit or loss in the same period as related changes in the value of the liabilities.

(b) An entity has liabilities under insurance contracts whose measurement incorporates current information and financial assets it considers related that would otherwise be classified as available for sale or measured at amortised cost.

(c) An entity has financial assets, financial liabilities or both that share a risk, such as interest rate risk, that gives rise to opposite changes in fair value that tend to offset each other. However, only some of the instruments would be measured at fair value through profit or loss (ie are derivatives, or are classified as held for trading). It may also be the case that the requirements for hedge accounting are not met, for example because the requirements for effectiveness in paragraph 88 are not met.

(d) An entity has financial assets, financial liabilities or both that share a risk, such as interest rate risk, that gives rise to opposite changes in fair value that tend to offset each other and the entity does not qualify for hedge accounting because none of the instruments is a derivative. Furthermore, in the absence of hedge accounting there is a significant inconsistency in the recognition of gains and losses. For example:

(i) the entity has financed a portfolio of fixed rate assets that would otherwise be classified as available for sale with fixed rate debentures whose changes in fair value tend to offset each other. Reporting both the assets and the debentures at fair value through profit or loss corrects the inconsistency that would otherwise arise from measuring the assets at fair value with changes reported in equity and the debentures at amortised cost.

(ii) the entity has financed a specified group of loans by issuing traded bonds whose changes in fair value tend to offset each other. If, in addition, the entity regularly buys and sells the bonds but rarely, if ever, buys and sells the loans, reporting both the loans and the bonds at fair value through profit or loss eliminates the inconsistency in the timing of recognition of gains and losses that would otherwise result from measuring them both at amortised cost and recognising a gain or loss each time a bond is repurchased.

AG4F In cases such as those described in the preceding paragraph, to designate, at initial recognition, the financial assets and financial liabilities not otherwise so measured as at fair value through profit or loss may eliminate or significantly reduce the measurement or recognition inconsistency and produce more relevant information. For practical purposes, the entity need not enter into all of the assets and liabilities giving rise to the measurement or recognition inconsistency at exactly the same time. A reasonable delay is permitted provided that each transaction is designated as at fair value through profit or loss at its initial recognition and, at that time, any remaining transactions are expected to occur.

AG4G It would not be acceptable to designate only some of the financial assets and financial liabilities giving rise to the inconsistency as at fair value through profit or loss if to do so would not eliminate or significantly reduce the inconsistency and would therefore not result in more relevant information. However, it would be acceptable to designate only some of a number of similar financial assets or similar financial liabilities if doing so achieves a significant reduction (and possibly a greater reduction than other allowable designations) in the inconsistency. For example, assume an entity has a number of similar financial liabilities that sum to CU100* and a number of similar financial assets that sum to CU50 but are measured on a different basis. The entity may significantly reduce the measurement inconsistency by designating at initial recognition all of the assets but only some of the liabilities (for example, individual liabilities with a combined total of CU45) as at fair value through profit or loss. However, because designation as at fair value through profit or loss can be applied only to the whole of a financial instrument, the entity in this example must designate one or more liabilities in their entirety. It could not designate either a component of a liability (eg changes in value attributable to only one risk, such as changes in a benchmark interest rate) or a proportion (ie percentage) of a liability.

Paragraph 9(b)(ii): A group of financial assets, financial liabilities or both is managed and its performance is evaluated on a fair value basis, in accordance with a documented risk management or investment strategy

An entity may manage and evaluate the performance of a group of financial assets, financial liabilities or both in such a way that measuring that group at fair value through profit or loss results in more relevant information. The focus in this instance is on the way the entity manages and evaluates performance, rather than on the nature of its financial instruments.   **AG4H**

The following examples show when this condition could be met. In all cases, an entity may use this condition to designate financial assets or financial liabilities as at fair value through profit or loss only if it meets the principle in paragraph 9(b)(ii).   **AG4I**

(a)   The entity is a venture capital organisation, mutual fund, unit trust or similar entity whose business is investing in financial assets with a view to profiting from their total return in the form of interest or dividends and changes in fair value.†

(b)   The entity has financial assets and financial liabilities that share one or more risks and those risks are managed and evaluated on a fair value basis in accordance with a documented policy of asset and liability management. An example could be an entity that has issued 'structured products' containing multiple embedded derivatives and manages the resulting risks on a fair value basis using a mix of derivative and non-derivative financial instruments. A similar example could be an entity that originates fixed interest rate loans and manages the resulting benchmark interest rate risk using a mix of derivative and non-derivative financial instruments.

(c)   The entity is an insurer that holds a portfolio of financial assets, manages that portfolio so as to maximise its total return (ie interest or dividends and changes in fair value), and evaluates its performance on that basis. The portfolio may be held to back specific liabilities, equity or both. If the portfolio is held to back specific liabilities, the condition in paragraph 9(b)(ii) may be met for the assets regardless of whether the insurer also manages and evaluates the liabilities on a fair value basis. The condition in paragraph 9(b)(ii) may be met when the insurer's objective is to maximise total return on the assets over the longer term even if amounts paid to holders of participating contracts depend on other factors such as the amount of gains realised in a shorter period (eg a year) or are subject to the insurer's discretion.

In this Standard, monetary amounts are denominated in 'currency units' (CU)

†ASB Footnote: *Under FRS 9 Associates and Joint Ventures, investment funds account for their investments at cost or market value. Unlike IFRS, where a market value approach is taken it is not a requirement for the period movement in market value to be recorded in the profit and loss account. Accordingly the second sentence of paragraph AG 41(a) has been deleted for the purposes of FRS 26.*

AG4J As noted above, this condition relies on the way the entity manages and evaluates performance of the group of financial instruments under consideration. Accordingly, (subject to the requirement of designation at initial recognition) an entity that designates financial instruments as at fair value through profit or loss on the basis of this condition shall so designate all eligible financial instruments that are managed and evaluated together.

AG4K Documentation of the entity's strategy need not be extensive but should be sufficient to demonstrate compliance with paragraph 9(b)(ii). Such documentation is not required for each individual item, but may be on a portfolio basis. For example, if the performance management system for a department—as approved by the entity's key management personnel (as defined in paragraph 9(b)(ii))—clearly demonstrates that its performance is evaluated on a total return basis, no further documentation is required to demonstrate compliance with paragraph 9(b)(ii).*

DEFINITIONS (PARAGRAPHS 8 AND 9)

Effective Interest Rate

AG5 In some cases, financial assets are acquired at a deep discount that reflects incurred credit losses. Entities include such incurred credit losses in the estimated cash flows when computing the effective interest rate.

AG6 When applying the effective interest method, an entity generally amortises any fees, points paid or received, transaction costs and other premiums or discounts included in the calculation of the effective interest rate over the expected life of the instrument. However, a shorter period is used if this is the period to which the fees, points paid or received, transaction costs, premiums or discounts relate. This will be the case when the variable to which the fees, points paid or received, transaction costs, premiums or discounts relate is repriced to market rates before the expected maturity of the instrument. In such a case, the appropriate amortisation period is the period to the next such repricing date. For example, if a premium or discount on a floating rate instrument reflects interest that has accrued on the instrument since interest was last paid, or changes in market rates since the floating interest rate was reset to market rates, it will be amortised to the next date when the floating interest is reset to market rates. This is because the premium or discount relates to the period to the next interest reset date because, at that date, the variable to which the premium or discount relates (ie interest rates) is reset to market rates. If, however, the premium or discount results from a change in the credit spread over the floating rate specified in the instrument, or other variables that are not reset to market rates, it is amortised over the expected life of the instrument.

AG7 For floating rate financial assets and floating rate financial liabilities, periodic reestimation of cash flows to reflect movements in market rates of interest alters the effective interest rate. If a floating rate financial asset or floating rate financial liability is recognised initially at an amount equal to the principal receivable or payable on maturity, re-estimating the future interest payments normally has no significant effect on the carrying amount of the asset or liability.

AG8 If an entity revises its estimates of payments or receipts, the entity shall adjust the carrying amount of the financial asset or financial liability (or group of financial instruments) to reflect actual and revised estimated cash flows. The entity recalculates the carrying amount by computing the present value of estimated future cash flows at

Editor's note: AG4B to AG4K added with effect from 1 January 2006.

the financial instrument's original effective interest rate. The adjustment is recognised as income or expense in profit or loss.

Derivatives

Typical examples of derivatives are futures and forward, swap and option contracts. **AG9**
A derivative usually has a notional amount, which is an amount of currency, a
number of shares, a number of units of weight or volume or other units specified in
the contract. However, a derivative instrument does not require the holder or writer
to invest or receive the notional amount at the inception of the contract. Alternatively, a derivative could require a fixed payment or payment of an amount that
can change (but not proportionally with a change in the underlying) as a result of
some future event that is unrelated to a notional amount. For example, a contract
may require a fixed payment of CU1,000* if sixmonth LIBOR increases by 100 basis
points. Such a contract is a derivative even though a notional amount is not specified.

The definition of a derivative in this Standard includes contracts that are settled gross **AG10**
by delivery of the underlying item (eg a forward contract to purchase a fixed rate
debt instrument). An entity may have a contract to buy or sell a nonfinancial item
that can be settled net in cash or another financial instrument or by exchanging
financial instruments (eg a contract to buy or sell a commodity at a fixed price at a
future date). Such a contract is within the scope of this Standard unless it was entered
into and continues to be held for the purpose of delivery of a non-financial item in
accordance with the entity's expected purchase, sale or usage requirements (see
paragraphs 5-7).

One of the defining characteristics of a derivative is that it has an initial net **AG11**
investment that is smaller than would be required for other types of contracts that
would be expected to have a similar response to changes in market factors.
An option contract meets that definition because the premium is less than the
investment that would be required to obtain the underlying financial instrument to
which the option is linked. A currency swap that requires an initial exchange of
different currencies of equal fair values meets the definition because it has a zero
initial net investment.

A regular way purchase or sale gives rise to a fixed price commitment between trade **AG12**
date and settlement date that meets the definition of a derivative. However, because
of the short duration of the commitment it is not recognised as a derivative financial
instrument. Rather, this Standard provides for special accounting for such regular
way contracts (see paragraphs 38 and AG53-AG56).

The definition of a derivative refers to non-financial variables that are not specific to **AG12A**
a party to the contract. These include an index of earthquake losses in a particular
region and an index of temperatures in a particular city. Nonfinancial variables
specific to a party to the contract include the occurrence or nonoccurrence of a fire
that damages or destroys an asset of a party to the contract. A change in the fair
value of a nonfinancial asset is specific to the owner if the fair value reflects not only
changes in market prices for such assets (a financial variable) but also the condition
of the specific nonfinancial asset held (a nonfinancial variable). For example, if a
guarantee of the residual value of a specific car exposes the guarantor to the risk of
changes in the car's physical condition, the change in that residual value is specific to
the owner of the car.

*In this Standard, monetary amounts are denominated in 'currency units' (CU).

Transaction Costs

AG13   Transaction costs include fees and commissions paid to agents (including employees acting as selling agents), advisers, brokers and dealers, levies by regulatory agencies and securities exchanges, and transfer taxes and duties. Transaction costs do not include debt premiums or discounts, financing costs or internal administrative or holding costs.

Financial Assets and Financial Liabilities Held for Trading

AG14   Trading generally reflects active and frequent buying and selling, and financial instruments held for trading generally are used with the objective of generating a profit from short-term fluctuations in price or dealer's margin.

AG15   Financial liabilities held for trading include:

(a)   derivative liabilities that are not accounted for as hedging instruments;

(b)   obligations to deliver financial assets borrowed by a short seller (ie an entity that sells financial assets it has borrowed and does not yet own);

(c)   financial liabilities that are incurred with an intention to repurchase them in the near term (eg a quoted debt instrument that the issuer may buy back in the near term depending on changes in its fair value); and

(d)   financial liabilities that are part of a portfolio of identified financial instruments that are managed together and for which there is evidence of a recent pattern of short-term profit-taking.

The fact that a liability is used to fund trading activities does not in itself make that liability one that is held for trading.

Held-to-Maturity Investments

AG16   An entity does not have a positive intention to hold to maturity an investment in a financial asset with a fixed maturity if:

(a)   the entity intends to hold the financial asset for an undefined period;

(b)   the entity stands ready to sell the financial asset (other than if a situation arises that is non-recurring and could not have been reasonably anticipated by the entity) in response to changes in market interest rates or risks, liquidity needs, changes in the availability of and the yield on alternative investments, changes in financing sources and terms or changes in foreign currency risk; or

(c)   the issuer has a right to settle the financial asset at an amount significantly below its amortised cost.

AG17   A debt instrument with a variable interest rate can satisfy the criteria for a heldto-maturity investment. Equity instruments cannot be heldtomaturity investments either because they have an indefinite life (such as ordinary shares) or because the amounts the holder may receive can vary in a manner that is not predetermined (such as for share options, warrants and similar rights). With respect to the definition of heldtomaturity investments, fixed or determinable payments and fixed maturity mean that a contractual arrangement defines the amounts and dates of payments to the holder, such as interest and principal payments. A significant risk of non-payment does not preclude classification of a financial asset as held to maturity as long as its contractual payments are fixed or determinable and the other criteria for that classification are met. If the terms of a perpetual debt instrument provide for interest payments for an indefinite period, the instrument cannot be classified as held to maturity because there is no maturity date.

The criteria for classification as a held-to-maturity investment are met for a financial **AG18** asset that is callable by the issuer if the holder intends and is able to hold it until it is called or until maturity and the holder would recover substantially all of its carrying amount. The call option of the issuer, if exercised, simply accelerates the asset's maturity. However, if the financial asset is callable on a basis that would result in the holder not recovering substantially all of its carrying amount, the financial asset cannot be classified as a held-to-maturity investment. The entity considers any premium paid and capitalised transaction costs in determining whether the carrying amount would be substantially recovered.

A financial asset that is puttable (ie the holder has the right to require that the issuer **AG19** repay or redeem the financial asset before maturity) cannot be classified as a held-to-maturity investment because paying for a put feature in a financial asset is inconsistent with expressing an intention to hold the financial asset until maturity.

For most financial assets, fair value is a more appropriate measure than amortised **AG20** cost. The held-to-maturity classification is an exception, but only if the entity has a positive intention and the ability to hold the investment to maturity. When an entity's actions cast doubt on its intention and ability to hold such investments to maturity, paragraph 9 precludes the use of the exception for a reasonable period of time.

A disaster scenario that is only remotely possible, such as a run on a bank or a **AG21** similar situation affecting an insurer, is not something that is assessed by an entity in deciding whether it has the positive intention and ability to hold an investment to maturity.

Sales before maturity could satisfy the condition in paragraph 9—and therefore not **AG22** raise a question about the entity's intention to hold other investments to maturity—if they are attributable to any of the following:

(a) a significant deterioration in the issuer's creditworthiness. For example, a sale following a downgrade in a credit rating by an external rating agency would not necessarily raise a question about the entity's intention to hold other investments to maturity if the downgrade provides evidence of a significant deterioration in the issuer's creditworthiness judged by reference to the credit rating at initial recognition. Similarly, if an entity uses internal ratings for assessing exposures, changes in those internal ratings may help to identify issuers for which there has been a significant deterioration in creditworthiness, provided the entity's approach to assigning internal ratings and changes in those ratings give a consistent, reliable and objective measure of the credit quality of the issuers. If there is evidence that a financial asset is impaired (see paragraphs 58 and 59), the deterioration in creditworthiness is often regarded as significant.

(b) a change in tax law that eliminates or significantly reduces the tax-exempt status of interest on the held-to-maturity investment (but not a change in tax law that revises the marginal tax rates applicable to interest income).

(c) a major business combination or major disposition (such as a sale of a segment) that necessitates the sale or transfer of heldto-maturity investments to maintain the entity's existing interest rate risk position or credit risk policy (although the business combination is an event within the entity's control, the changes to its investment portfolio to maintain an interest rate risk position or credit risk policy may be consequential rather than anticipated).

(d) a change in statutory or regulatory requirements significantly modifying either what constitutes a permissible investment or the maximum level of particular types of investments, thereby causing an entity to dispose of a heldto-maturity investment.

(e)   a significant increase in the industry's regulatory capital requirements that causes the entity to downsize by selling heldto-maturity investments.

(f)   a significant increase in the risk weights of held-to-maturity investments used for regulatory risk-based capital purposes.

AG23   An entity does not have a demonstrated ability to hold to maturity an investment in a financial asset with a fixed maturity if:

(a)   it does not have the financial resources available to continue to finance the investment until maturity; or

(b)   it is subject to an existing legal or other constraint that could frustrate its intention to hold the financial asset to maturity. (However, an issuer's call option does not necessarily frustrate an entity's intention to hold a financial asset to maturity—see paragraph AG18.)

AG24   Circumstances other than those described in paragraphs AG16-AG23 can indicate that an entity does not have a positive intention or the ability to hold an investment to maturity.

AG25   An entity assesses its intention and ability to hold its held-to-maturity investments to maturity not only when those financial assets are initially recognised, but also at each subsequent balance sheet date.

Loans and Receivables

AG26   Any non-derivative financial asset with fixed or determinable payments (including loan assets, trade receivables, investments in debt instruments and deposits held in banks) could potentially meet the definition of loans and receivables. However, a financial asset that is quoted in an active market (such as a quoted debt instrument, see paragraph AG71) does not qualify for classification as a loan or receivable. Financial assets that do not meet the definition of loans and receivables may be classified as held-to-maturity investments if they meet the conditions for that classification (see paragraphs 9 and AG16-AG25). On initial recognition of a financial asset that would otherwise be classified as a loan or receivable, an entity may designate it as a financial asset at fair value through profit or loss, or available for sale.

EMBEDDED DERIVATIVES (PARAGRAPHS 10-13)

AG27   If a host contract has no stated or predetermined maturity and represents a residual interest in the net assets of an entity, then its economic characteristics and risks are those of an equity instrument, and an embedded derivative would need to possess equity characteristics related to the same entity to be regarded as closely related. If the host contract is not an equity instrument and meets the definition of a financial instrument, then its economic characteristics and risks are those of a debt instrument.

AG28   An embedded non-option derivative (such as an embedded forward or swap) is separated from its host contract on the basis of its stated or implied substantive terms, so as to result in it having a fair value of zero at initial recognition. An embedded option-based derivative (such as an embedded put, call, cap, floor or swaption) is separated from its host contract on the basis of the stated terms of the option feature. The initial carrying amount of the host instrument is the residual amount after separating the embedded derivative.

Generally, multiple embedded derivatives in a single instrument are treated as a **AG29** single compound embedded derivative. However, embedded derivatives that are classified as equity (see FRS 25 *Financial Instruments: Disclosure and Presentation*) are accounted for separately from those classified as assets or liabilities. In addition, if an instrument has more than one embedded derivative and those derivatives relate to different risk exposures and are readily separable and independent of each other, they are accounted for separately from each other.

The economic characteristics and risks of an embedded derivative are not closely **AG30** related to the host contract (paragraph 11(a)) in the following examples. In these examples, assuming the conditions in paragraph 11(b) and (c) are met, an entity accounts for the embedded derivative separately from the host contract.

(a) A put option embedded in an instrument that enables the holder to require the issuer to reacquire the instrument for an amount of cash or other assets that varies on the basis of the change in an equity or commodity price or index is not closely related to a host debt instrument.

(b) A call option embedded in an equity instrument that enables the issuer to reacquire that equity instrument at a specified price is not closely related to the host equity instrument from the perspective of the holder (from the issuer's perspective, the call option is an equity instrument provided it meets the conditions for that classification under FRS 25, in which case it is excluded from the scope of this Standard).

(c) An option or automatic provision to extend the remaining term to maturity of a debt instrument is not closely related to the host debt instrument unless there is a concurrent adjustment to the approximate current market rate of interest at the time of the extension. If an entity issues a debt instrument and the holder of that debt instrument writes a call option on the debt instrument to a third party, the issuer regards the call option as extending the term to maturity of the debt instrument provided the issuer can be required to participate in or facilitate the remarketing of the debt instrument as a result of the call option being exercised.

(d) Equity-indexed interest or principal payments embedded in a host debt instrument or insurance contract—by which the amount of interest or principal is indexed to the value of equity instruments—are not closely related to the host instrument because the risks inherent in the host and the embedded derivative are dissimilar.

(e) Commodity-indexed interest or principal payments embedded in a host debt instrument or insurance contract—by which the amount of interest or principal is indexed to the price of a commodity (such as gold)—are not closely related to the host instrument because the risks inherent in the host and the embedded derivative are dissimilar.

(f) An equity conversion feature embedded in a convertible debt instrument is not closely related to the host debt instrument from the perspective of the holder of the instrument (from the issuer's perspective, the equity conversion option is an equity instrument and excluded from the scope of this Standard provided it meets the conditions for that classification under FRS 25).

(g) A call, put, or prepayment option embedded in a host debt contract or host insurance contract is not closely related to the host contract unless the option's exercise price is approximately equal on each exercise date to the amortised cost of the host debt instrument or the carrying amount of the host insurance contract. From the perspective of the issuer of a convertible debt instrument with an embedded call or put option feature, the assessment of whether the call or put option is closely related to the host debt contract is made before separating the equity element under FRS 25.

(h)   Credit derivatives that are embedded in a host debt instrument and allow one party (the 'beneficiary') to transfer the credit risk of a particular reference asset, which it may not own, to another party (the 'guarantor') are not closely related to the host debt instrument. Such credit derivatives allow the guarantor to assume the credit risk associated with the reference asset without directly owning it.

AG31   An example of a hybrid instrument is a financial instrument that gives the holder a right to put the financial instrument back to the issuer in exchange for an amount of cash or other financial assets that varies on the basis of the change in an equity or commodity index that may increase or decrease (a 'puttable instrument'). Unless the issuer on initial recognition designates the puttable instrument as a financial liability at fair value through profit or loss, it is required to separate an embedded derivative (ie the indexed principal payment) under paragraph 11 because the host contract is a debt instrument under paragraph AG27 and the indexed principal payment is not closely related to a host debt instrument under paragraph AG30(a). Because the principal payment can increase and decrease, the embedded derivative is a non-option derivative whose value is indexed to the underlying variable.

AG32   In the case of a puttable instrument that can be put back at any time for cash equal to a proportionate share of the net asset value of an entity (such as units of an openended mutual fund or some unitlinked investment products), the effect of separating an embedded derivative and accounting for each component is to measure the combined instrument at the redemption amount that is payable at the balance sheet date if the holder exercised its right to put the instrument back to the issuer.

AG33   The economic characteristics and risks of an embedded derivative are closely related to the economic characteristics and risks of the host contract in the following examples. In these examples, an entity does not account for the embedded derivative separately from the host contract.

(a)   An embedded derivative in which the underlying is an interest rate or interest rate index that can change the amount of interest that would otherwise be paid or received on an interest-bearing host debt contract or insurance contract is closely related to the host contract unless the combined instrument can be settled in such a way that the holder would not recover substantially all of its recognised investment or the embedded derivative could at least double the holder's initial rate of return on the host contract and could result in a rate of return that is at least twice what the market return would be for a contract with the same terms as the host contract.

(b)   An embedded floor or cap on the interest rate on a debt contract or insurance contract is closely related to the host contract, provided the cap is at or above the market rate of interest and the floor is at or below the market rate of interest when the contract is issued, and the cap or floor is not leveraged in relation to the host contract. Similarly, provisions included in a contract to purchase or sell an asset (eg a commodity) that establish a cap and a floor on the price to be paid or received for the asset are closely related to the host contract if both the cap and floor were out of the money at inception and are not leveraged.

(c)   An embedded foreign currency derivative that provides a stream of principal or interest payments that are denominated in a foreign currency and is embedded in a host debt instrument (eg a dual currency bond) is closely related to the host debt instrument. Such a derivative is not separated from the host instrument because FRS 23 *The Effects of Changes in Foreign Exchange Rates* requires foreign currency gains and losses on monetary items to be recognised in profit or loss.

(d)   An embedded foreign currency derivative in a host contract that is an insurance contract or not a financial instrument (such as a contract for the purchase or sale of a non-financial item where the price is denominated in a foreign currency) is closely related to the host contract provided it is not leveraged, does not contain an option feature, and requires payments denominated in one of the following currencies:

    (i)   the functional currency of any substantial party to that contract;

    (ii) the currency in which the price of the related good or service that is acquired or delivered is routinely denominated in commercial transactions around the world (such as the US dollar for crude oil transactions); or

    (iii) a currency that is commonly used in contracts to purchase or sell non-financial items in the economic environment in which the transaction takes place (eg a relatively stable and liquid currency that is commonly used in local business transactions or external trade).

(e)   An embedded prepayment option in an interest-only or principal-only strip is closely related to the host contract provided the host contract (i) initially resulted from separating the right to receive contractual cash flows of a financial instrument that, in and of itself, did not contain an embedded derivative, and (ii) does not contain any terms not present in the original host debt contract.

(f)   An embedded derivative in a host lease contract is closely related to the host contract if the embedded derivative is (i) an inflation-related index such as an index of lease payments to a consumer price index (provided that the lease is not leveraged and the index relates to inflation in the entity's own economic environment), (ii) contingent rentals based on related sales or (iii) contingent rentals based on variable interest rates.

(g)   A unit-linking feature embedded in a host financial instrument or host insurance contract is closely related to the host instrument or host contract if the unit-denominated payments are measured at current unit values that reflect the fair values of the assets of the fund. A unit-linking feature is a contractual term that requires payments denominated in units of an internal or external investment fund.

(h)   A derivative embedded in an insurance contract is closely related to the host insurance contract if the embedded derivative and host insurance contract are so interdependent that an entity cannot measure the embedded derivative separately (ie without considering the host contract).

AG33A When an entity becomes a party to a hybrid (combined) instrument that contains one or more embedded derivatives, paragraph 11 requires the entity to identify any such embedded derivative, assess whether it is required to be separated from the host contract and, for those that are required to be separated, measure the derivatives at fair value at initial recognition and subsequently. These requirements can be more complex, or result in less reliable measures, than measuring the entire instrument at fair value through profit or loss. For that reason this Standard permits the entire instrument to be designated as at fair value through profit or loss.

AG33B Such designation may be used whether paragraph 11 requires the embedded derivatives to be separated from the host contract or prohibits such separation. However, paragraph 11A would not justify designating the hybrid (combined) instrument as at fair value through profit or loss in the cases set out in paragraph 11A(a) and (b) because doing so would not reduce complexity or increase reliability.*

*Editor's note: AG33A and AG33B added with effect from 1 January 2006.

RECOGNITION AND DERECOGNITION (PARAGRAPHS 14–42)

Initial Recognition (paragraph 14)

AG34   As a consequence of the principle in paragraph 14, an entity recognises all of its contractual rights and obligations under derivatives in its balance sheet as assets and liabilities, respectively, except for derivatives that prevent a transfer of financial assets from being accounted for as a sale (see paragraph AG49). If a transfer of a financial asset does not qualify for derecognition, the transferee does not recognise the transferred asset as its asset (see paragraph AG50).

AG35   The following are examples of applying the principle in paragraph 14:

(a)   unconditional receivables and payables are recognised as assets or liabilities when the entity becomes a party to the contract and, as a consequence, has a legal right to receive or a legal obligation to pay cash.

(b)   assets to be acquired and liabilities to be incurred as a result of a firm commitment to purchase or sell goods or services are generally not recognised until at least one of the parties has performed under the agreement. For example, an entity that receives a firm order does not generally recognise an asset (and the entity that places the order does not recognise a liability) at the time of the commitment but, rather, delays recognition until the ordered goods or services have been shipped, delivered or rendered. If a firm commitment to buy or sell non-financial items is within the scope of this Standard under paragraphs 5–7, its net fair value is recognised as an asset or liability on the commitment date (see (c) below). In addition, if a previously unrecognised firm commitment is designated as a hedged item in a fair value hedge, any change in the net fair value attributable to the hedged risk is recognised as an asset or liability after the inception of the hedge (see paragraphs 93 and 94).

(c)   a forward contract that is within the scope of this Standard (see paragraph 27) is recognised as an asset or a liability on the commitment date, rather than on the date on which settlement takes place. When an entity becomes a party to a forward contract, the fair values of the right and obligation are often equal, so that the net fair value of the forward is zero. If the net fair value of the right and obligation is not zero, the contract is recognised as an asset or liability.

(d)   option contracts that are within the scope of this Standard (see paragraph 27) are recognised as assets or liabilities when the holder or writer becomes a party to the contract.

(e)   planned future transactions, no matter how likely, are not assets and liabilities because the entity has not become a party to a contract.

Derecognition of a Financial Asset (paragraphs 15–37)

The following flow chart illustrates the evaluation of whether and to what extent a   **AG36**
financial asset is derecognised.

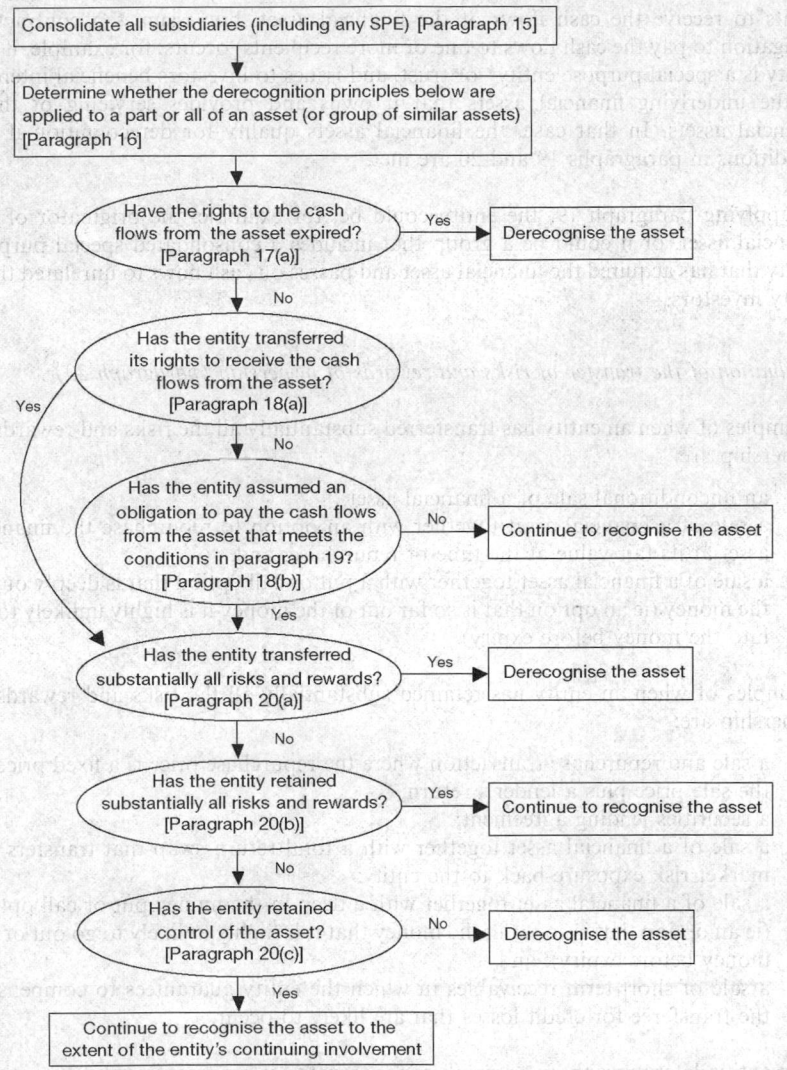

Arrangements under which an entity retains the contractual rights to receive the cash flows of a financial asset, but assumes a contractual obligation to pay the cash flows to one or more recipients (paragraph 18(b))

AG37   The situation described in paragraph 18(b) (when an entity retains the contractual rights to receive the cash flows of the financial asset, but assumes a contractual obligation to pay the cash flows to one or more recipients) occurs, for example, if the entity is a special purpose entity* or trust, and issues to investors beneficial interests in the underlying financial assets that it owns and provides servicing of those financial assets. In that case, the financial assets qualify for derecognition if the conditions in paragraphs 19 and 20 are met.

AG38   In applying paragraph 19, the entity could be, for example, the originator of the financial asset, or it could be a group that includes a consolidated special purpose entity that has acquired the financial asset and passes on cash flows to unrelated third party investors.

Evaluation of the transfer of risks and rewards of ownership (paragraph 20)

AG39   Examples of when an entity has transferred substantially all the risks and rewards of ownership are:

(a)   an unconditional sale of a financial asset;
(b)   a sale of a financial asset together with an option to repurchase the financial asset at its fair value at the time of repurchase; and
(c)   a sale of a financial asset together with a put or call option that is deeply out of the money (ie an option that is so far out of the money it is highly unlikely to go into the money before expiry).

AG40   Examples of when an entity has retained substantially all the risks and rewards of ownership are:

(a)   a sale and repurchase transaction where the repurchase price is a fixed price or the sale price plus a lender's return;
(b)   a securities lending agreement;
(c)   a sale of a financial asset together with a total return swap that transfers the market risk exposure back to the entity;
(d)   a sale of a financial asset together with a deep in-the-money put or call option (ie an option that is so far in the money that it is highly unlikely to go out of the money before expiry); and
(e)   a sale of short-term receivables in which the entity guarantees to compensate the transferee for credit losses that are likely to occur.

AG41   If an entity determines that as a result of the transfer, it has transferred substantially all the risks and rewards of ownership of the transferred asset, it does not recognise the transferred asset again in a future period, unless it reacquires the transferred asset in a new transaction.

Evaluation of the transfer of control

AG42   An entity has not retained control of a transferred asset if the transferee has the practical ability to sell the transferred asset. An entity has retained control of a transferred asset if the transferee does not have the practical ability to sell the

*ASB footnote: a special purpose entity is consolidated if it meets the definition of subsidiary undertaking in FRS 2 or quasi-subsidiary in FRS 5.

transferred asset. A transferee has the practical ability to sell the transferred asset if it is traded in an active market because the transferee could repurchase the transferred asset in the market if it needs to return the asset to the entity. For example, a transferee may have the practical ability to sell a transferred asset if the transferred asset is subject to an option that allows the entity to repurchase it, but the transferee can readily obtain the transferred asset in the market if the option is exercised. A transferee does not have the practical ability to sell the transferred asset if the entity retains such an option and the transferee cannot readily obtain the transferred asset in the market if the entity exercises its option.

The transferee has the practical ability to sell the transferred asset only if the   **AG43**
transferee can sell the transferred asset in its entirety to an unrelated third party and is able to exercise that ability unilaterally and without imposing additional restrictions on the transfer. The critical question is what the transferee is able to do in practice, not what contractual rights the transferee has concerning what it can do with the transferred asset or what contractual prohibitions exist. In particular:

(a)   a contractual right to dispose of the transferred asset has little practical effect if there is no market for the transferred asset; and

(b)   an ability to dispose of the transferred asset has little practical effect if it cannot be exercised freely. For that reason:

   (i)   the transferee's ability to dispose of the transferred asset must be independent of the actions of others (ie it must be a unilateral ability); and

   (ii)   the transferee must be able to dispose of the transferred asset without needing to attach restrictive conditions or 'strings' to the transfer (eg conditions about how a loan asset is serviced or an option giving the transferee the right to repurchase the asset).

That the transferee is unlikely to sell the transferred asset does not, of itself, mean   **AG44**
that the transferor has retained control of the transferred asset. However, if a put option or guarantee constrains the transferee from selling the transferred asset, then the transferor has retained control of the transferred asset. For example, if a put option or guarantee is sufficiently valuable it constrains the transferee from selling the transferred asset because the transferee would, in practice, not sell the transferred asset to a third party without attaching a similar option or other restrictive conditions. Instead, the transferee would hold the transferred asset so as to obtain payments under the guarantee or put option. Under these circumstances the transferor has retained control of the transferred asset.

Transfers that Qualify for Derecognition

An entity may retain the right to a part of the interest payments on transferred assets   **AG45**
as compensation for servicing those assets. The part of the interest payments that the entity would give up upon termination or transfer of the servicing contract is allocated to the servicing asset or servicing liability. The part of the interest payments that the entity would not give up is an interest-only strip receivable. For example, if the entity would not give up any interest upon termination or transfer of the servicing contract, the entire interest spread is an interest-only strip receivable. For the purposes of applying paragraph 27, the fair values of the servicing asset and interest-only strip receivable are used to allocate the carrying amount of the receivable between the part of the asset that is derecognised and the part that continues to be recognised. If there is no servicing fee specified or the fee to be received is not expected to compensate the entity adequately for performing the servicing, a liability for the servicing obligation is recognised at fair value.

AG46   In estimating the fair values of the part that continues to be recognised and the part that is derecognised for the purposes of applying paragraph 27, an entity applies the fair value measurement requirements in paragraphs 48, 49 and AG69–AG82 in addition to paragraph 28.

Transfers that Do Not Qualify for Derecognition

AG47   The following is an application of the principle outlined in paragraph 29. If a guarantee provided by the entity for default losses on the transferred asset prevents a transferred asset from being derecognised because the entity has retained substantially all the risks and rewards of ownership of the transferred asset, the transferred asset continues to be recognised in its entirety and the consideration received is recognised as a liability.

Continuing Involvement in Transferred Assets

AG48   The following are examples of how an entity measures a transferred asset and the associated liability under paragraph 30.

All assets

(a)   If a guarantee provided by an entity to pay for default losses on a transferred asset prevents the transferred asset from being derecognised to the extent of the continuing involvement, the transferred asset at the date of the transfer is measured at the lower of (i) the carrying amount of the asset and (ii) the maximum amount of the consideration received in the transfer that the entity could be required to repay ('the guarantee amount'). The associated liability is initially measured at the guarantee amount plus the fair value of the guarantee (which is normally the consideration received for the guarantee). Subsequently, the initial fair value of the guarantee is recognised in profit or loss on a time proportion basis (see IAS 18) and the carrying value of the asset is reduced by any impairment losses.

Assets measured at amortised cost

(b)   If a put option obligation written by an entity or call option right held by an entity prevents a transferred asset from being derecognised and the entity measures the transferred asset at amortised cost, the associated liability is measured at its cost (ie the consideration received) adjusted for the amortisation of any difference between that cost and the amortised cost of the transferred asset at the expiration date of the option. For example, assume that the amortised cost and carrying amount of the asset on the date of the transfer is CU98 and that the consideration received is CU95. The amortised cost of the asset on the option exercise date will be CU100. The initial carrying amount of the associated liability is CU95 and the difference between CU95 and CU100 is recognised in profit or loss using the effective interest method. If the option is exercised, any difference between the carrying amount of the associated liability and the exercise price is recognised in profit or loss.

Assets measured at fair value

(c)   If a call option right retained by an entity prevents a transferred asset from being derecognised and the entity measures the transferred asset at fair value, the asset continues to be measured at its fair value. The associated liability is measured at (i) the option exercise price less the time value of the option if the option is in or at the money, or (ii) the fair value of the transferred asset less the time value of the option if the option is out of the money. The adjustment to the measurement of the associated liability ensures that the net carrying amount of the asset and the associated liability is the fair value of the call option right. For example, if the fair value of the underlying asset is CU80, the option exercise price is CU95 and the time value of the option is CU5, the carrying amount of the associated liability is CU75 (CU80 – CU5) and the carrying amount of the transferred asset is CU80 (ie its fair value).

(d) If a put option written by an entity prevents a transferred asset from being derecognised and the entity measures the transferred asset at fair value, the associated liability is measured at the option exercise price plus the time value of the option. The measurement of the asset at fair value is limited to the lower of the fair value and the option exercise price because the entity has no right to increases in the fair value of the transferred asset above the exercise price of the option. This ensures that the net carrying amount of the asset and the associated liability is the fair value of the put option obligation. For example, if the fair value of the underlying asset is CU120, the option exercise price is CU100 and the time value of the option is CU5, the carrying amount of the associated liability is CU105 (CU100 + CU5) and the carrying amount of the asset is CU100 (in this case the option exercise price).

(e) If a collar, in the form of a purchased call and written put, prevents a transferred asset from being derecognised and the entity measures the asset at fair value, it continues to measure the asset at fair value. The associated liability is measured at (i) the sum of the call exercise price and fair value of the put option less the time value of the call option, if the call option is in or at the money, or (ii) the sum of the fair value of the asset and the fair value of the put option less the time value of the call option if the call option is out of the money. The adjustment to the associated liability ensures that the net carrying amount of the asset and the associated liability is the fair value of the options held and written by the entity. For example, assume an entity transfers a financial asset that is measured at fair value while simultaneously purchasing a call with an exercise price of CU120 and writing a put with an exercise price of CU80. Assume also that the fair value of the asset is CU100 at the date of the transfer. The time value of the put and call are CU1 and CU5 respectively. In this case, the entity recognises an asset of CU100 (the fair value of the asset) and a liability of CU96 [(CU100 + CU1) – CU5]. This gives a net asset value of CU4, which is the fair value of the options held and written by the entity.

All Transfers

To the extent that a transfer of a financial asset does not qualify for derecognition, the transferor's contractual rights or obligations related to the transfer are not accounted for separately as derivatives if recognising both the derivative and either the transferred asset or the liability arising from the transfer would result in recognising the same rights or obligations twice. For example, a call option retained by the transferor may prevent a transfer of financial assets from being accounted for as a sale. In that case, the call option is not separately recognised as a derivative asset. **AG49**

To the extent that a transfer of a financial asset does not qualify for derecognition, the transferee does not recognise the transferred asset as its asset. The transferee derecognises the cash or other consideration paid and recognises a receivable from the transferor. If the transferor has both a right and an obligation to reacquire control of the entire transferred asset for a fixed amount (such as under a repurchase agreement), the transferee may account for its receivable as a loan or receivable. **AG50**

Examples

AG51   The following examples illustrate the application of the derecognition principles of this Standard.

(a)   *Repurchase agreements and securities lending.* If a financial asset is sold under an agreement to repurchase it at a fixed price or at the sale price plus a lender's return or if it is loaned under an agreement to return it to the transferor, it is not derecognised because the transferor retains substantially all the risks and rewards of ownership. If the transferee obtains the right to sell or pledge the asset, the transferor reclassifies the asset on its balance sheet, for example, as a loaned asset or repurchase receivable.

(b)   *Repurchase agreements and securities lending—assets that are substantially the same.* If a financial asset is sold under an agreement to repurchase the same or substantially the same asset at a fixed price or at the sale price plus a lender's return or if a financial asset is borrowed or loaned under an agreement to return the same or substantially the same asset to the transferor, it is not derecognised because the transferor retains substantially all the risks and rewards of ownership.

(c)   *Repurchase agreements and securities lending—right of substitution.* If a repurchase agreement at a fixed repurchase price or a price equal to the sale price plus a lender's return, or a similar securities lending transaction, provides the transferee with a right to substitute assets that are similar and of equal fair value to the transferred asset at the repurchase date, the asset sold or lent under a repurchase or securities lending transaction is not derecognised because the transferor retains substantially all the risks and rewards of ownership.

(d)   *Repurchase right of first refusal at fair value.* If an entity sells a financial asset and retains only a right of first refusal to repurchase the transferred asset at fair value if the transferee subsequently sells it, the entity derecognises the asset because it has transferred substantially all the risks and rewards of ownership.

(e)   *Wash sale transaction.* The repurchase of a financial asset shortly after it has been sold is sometimes referred to as a wash sale. Such a repurchase does not preclude derecognition provided that the original transaction met the derecognition requirements. However, if an agreement to sell a financial asset is entered into concurrently with an agreement to repurchase the same asset at a fixed price or the sale price plus a lender's return, then the asset is not derecognised.

(f)   *Put options and call options that are deeply in the money.* If a transferred financial asset can be called back by the transferor and the call option is deeply in the money, the transfer does not qualify for derecognition because the transferor has retained substantially all the risks and rewards of ownership. Similarly, if the financial asset can be put back by the transferee and the put option is deeply in the money, the transfer does not qualify for derecognition because the transferor has retained substantially all the risks and rewards of ownership.

(g)   *Put options and call options that are deeply out of the money.* A financial asset that is transferred subject only to a deep out-of-the-money put option held by the transferee or a deep out-of-the-money call option held by the transferor is derecognised. This is because the transferor has transferred substantially all the risks and rewards of ownership.

(h)   *Readily obtainable assets subject to a call option that is neither deeply in the money nor deeply out of the money.* If an entity holds a call option on an asset that is readily obtainable in the market and the option is neither deeply in the money nor deeply out of the money, the asset is derecognised. This is because the entity (i) has neither retained nor transferred substantially all the risks and rewards of ownership, and (ii) has not retained control. However, if the asset is not readily obtainable in the market, derecognition is precluded to the extent of the amount of the asset that is subject to the call option because the entity has retained control of the asset.

(i) *A not readily obtainable asset subject to a put option written by an entity that is neither deeply in the money nor deeply out of the money.* If an entity transfers a financial asset that is not readily obtainable in the market, and writes a put option that is not deeply out of the money, the entity neither retains nor transfers substantially all the risks and rewards of ownership because of the written put option. The entity retains control of the asset if the put option is sufficiently valuable to prevent the transferee from selling the asset, in which case the asset continues to be recognised to the extent of the transferor's continuing involvement (see paragraph AG44). The entity transfers control of the asset if the put option is not sufficiently valuable to prevent the transferee from selling the asset, in which case the asset is derecognised.

(j) *Assets subject to a fair value put or call option or a forward repurchase agreement.* A transfer of a financial asset that is subject only to a put or call option or a forward repurchase agreement that has an exercise or repurchase price equal to the fair value of the financial asset at the time of repurchase results in derecognition because of the transfer of substantially all the risks and rewards of ownership.

(k) *Cash settled call or put options.* An entity evaluates the transfer of a financial asset that is subject to a put or call option or a forward repurchase agreement that will be settled net in cash to determine whether it has retained or transferred substantially all the risks and rewards of ownership. If the entity has not retained substantially all the risks and rewards of ownership of the transferred asset, it determines whether it has retained control of the transferred asset. That the put or the call or the forward repurchase agreement is settled net in cash does not automatically mean that the entity has transferred control (see paragraphs AG44 and (g), (h) and (i) above).

(l) *Removal of accounts provision.* A removal of accounts provision is an unconditional repurchase (call) option that gives an entity the right to reclaim assets transferred subject to some restrictions. Provided that such an option results in the entity neither retaining nor transferring substantially all the risks and rewards of ownership, it precludes derecognition only to the extent of the amount subject to repurchase (assuming that the transferee cannot sell the assets). For example, if the carrying amount and proceeds from the transfer of loan assets are CU100,000 and any individual loan could be called back but the aggregate amount of loans that could be repurchased could not exceed CU10,000, CU90,000 of the loans would qualify for derecognition.

(m) *Clean-up calls.* An entity, which may be a transferor, that services transferred assets may hold a clean-up call to purchase remaining transferred assets when the amount of outstanding assets falls to a specified level at which the cost of servicing those assets becomes burdensome in relation to the benefits of servicing. Provided that such a clean-up call results in the entity neither retaining nor transferring substantially all the risks and rewards of ownership and the transferee cannot sell the assets, it precludes derecognition only to the extent of the amount of the assets that is subject to the call option.

(n) *Subordinated retained interests and credit guarantees.* An entity may provide the transferee with credit enhancement by subordinating some or all of its interest retained in the transferred asset. Alternatively, an entity may provide the transferee with credit enhancement in the form of a credit guarantee that could be unlimited or limited to a specified amount. If the entity retains substantially all the risks and rewards of ownership of the transferred asset, the asset continues to be recognised in its entirety. If the entity retains some, but not substantially all, of the risks and rewards of ownership and has retained control, derecognition is precluded to the extent of the amount of cash or other assets that the entity could be required to pay.

(o) *Total return swaps.* An entity may sell a financial asset to a transferee and enter into a total return swap with the transferee, whereby all of the interest payment cash flows from the underlying asset are remitted to the entity in exchange for a fixed payment or variable rate payment and any increases or declines in the fair value of the underlying asset are absorbed by the entity. In such a case, derecognition of all of the asset is prohibited.

(p) *Interest rate swaps.* An entity may transfer to a transferee a fixed rate financial asset and enter into an interest rate swap with the transferee to receive a fixed interest rate and pay a variable interest rate based on a notional amount that is equal to the principal amount of the transferred financial asset. The interest rate swap does not preclude derecognition of the transferred asset provided the payments on the swap are not conditional on payments being made on the transferred asset.

(q) *Amortising interest rate swaps.* An entity may transfer to a transferee a fixed rate financial asset that is paid off over time, and enter into an amortising interest rate swap with the transferee to receive a fixed interest rate and pay a variable interest rate based on a notional amount. If the notional amount of the swap amortises so that it equals the principal amount of the transferred financial asset outstanding at any point in time, the swap would generally result in the entity retaining substantial prepayment risk, in which case the entity either continues to recognise all of the transferred asset or continues to recognise the transferred asset to the extent of its continuing involvement. Conversely, if the amortisation of the notional amount of the swap is not linked to the principal amount outstanding of the transferred asset, such a swap would not result in the entity retaining prepayment risk on the asset. Hence, it would not preclude derecognition of the transferred asset provided the payments on the swap are not conditional on interest payments being made on the transferred asset and the swap does not result in the entity retaining any other significant risks and rewards of ownership on the transferred asset.

AG52 This paragraph illustrates the application of the continuing involvement approach when the entity's continuing involvement is in a part of a financial asset.

Assume an entity has a portfolio of prepayable loans whose coupon and effective interest rate is 10 per cent and whose principal amount and amortised cost is CU10,000. It enters into a transaction in which, in return for a payment of CU9,115, the transferee obtains the right to CU9,000 of any collections of principal plus interest thereon at 9.5 per cent. The entity retains rights to CU1,000 of any collections of principal plus interest thereon at 10 per cent, plus the excess spread of 0.5 per cent on the remaining CU9,000 of principal. Collections from prepayments are allocated between the entity and the transferee proportionately in the ratio of 1:9, but any defaults are deducted from the entity's interest of CU1,000 until that interest is exhausted. The fair value of the loans at the date of the transaction is CU10,100 and the estimated fair value of the excess spread of 0.5 per cent is CU40.

The entity determines that it has transferred some significant risks and rewards of ownership (for example, significant prepayment risk) but has also retained some significant risks and rewards of ownership (because of its subordinated retained interest) and has retained control. It therefore applies the continuing involvement approach.

To apply this Standard, the entity analyses the transaction as (a) a retention of a fully proportionate retained interest of CU1,000, plus (b) the subordination of that retained interest to provide credit enhancement to the transferee for credit losses.

The entity calculates that CU9,090 (90 per cent × CU10,100) of the consideration received of CU9,115 represents the consideration for a fully proportionate 90 per cent share. The remainder of the consideration received (CU25) represents consideration received for subordinating its retained interest to provide credit enhancement to the transferee for credit losses. In addition, the excess spread of 0.5 per cent represents consideration received for the credit enhancement. Accordingly, the total consideration received for the credit enhancement is CU65 (CU25 + CU40).

The entity calculates the gain or loss on the sale of the 90 per cent share of cash flows. Assuming that separate fair values of the 10 per cent part transferred and the 90 per cent part retained are not available at the date of the transfer, the entity allocates the carrying amount of the asset in accordance with paragraph 28 as follows:

	Estimated Fair Value	Percentage	Allocated Carrying Amount
Portion transferred	9,090	90%	9,000
Portion retained	1,010	10%	1,000
Total	**10,100**		**10,000**

The entity computes its gain or loss on the sale of the 90 per cent share of the cash flows by deducting the allocated carrying amount of the portion transferred from the consideration received, ie CU90 (CU9,090 – CU9,000). The carrying amount of the portion retained by the entity is CU1,000.

In addition, the entity recognises the continuing involvement that results from the subordination of its retained interest for credit losses. Accordingly, it recognises an asset of CU1,000 (the maximum amount of the cash flows it would not receive under the subordination), and an associated liability of CU1,065 (which is the maximum amount of the cash flows it would not receive under the subordination, ie CU1,000 plus the fair value of the subordination of CU65). The entity uses all of the above information to account for the transaction as follows:

	Debit	Credit
Original asset	-	9,000
Asset recognised for subordination or the residual interest	1,000	-
Asset for the consideration received in the form of excess spread	40	-
Profit or loss (gain on transfer)	-	90
Liability	-	1,065
Cash received	9,115	-
Total	**10,155**	**10,155**

Immediately following the transaction, the carrying amount of the asset is CU2,040 comprising CU1,000, representing the allocated cost of the portion retained, and CU1,040, representing the entity's additional continuing involvement from the subordination of its retained interest for credit losses (which includes the excess spread of CU40).

In subsequent periods, the entity recognises the consideration received for the credit enhancement (CU65) on a time proportion basis, accrues interest on the recognised asset using the effective interest method and recognises any credit impairment on the recognised assets. As an example of the latter, assume that in the following year there is a credit impairment loss on the underlying loans of CU300. The entity reduces its recognised asset by CU600 (CU300 relating to its retained interest and CU300 relating to the additional continuing involvement that arises from the subordination of its retained interest for credit losses), and reduces its recognised liability by CU300. The net result is a charge to profit or loss for credit impairment of CU300.

Regular Way Purchase or Sale of a Financial Asset (paragraph 38)

AG53   A regular way purchase or sale of financial assets is recognised using either trade date accounting or settlement date accounting as described in paragraphs AG55 and AG56. The method used is applied consistently for all purchases and sales of financial assets that belong to the same category of financial assets defined in paragraph 9. For this purpose assets that are held for trading form a separate category from assets designated at fair value through profit and loss.

AG54   A contract that requires or permits net settlement of the change in the value of the contract is not a regular way contract. Instead, such a contract is accounted for as a derivative in the period between the trade date and the settlement date.

AG55   The trade date is the date that an entity commits itself to purchase or sell an asset. Trade date accounting refers to (a) the recognition of an asset to be received and the liability to pay for it on the trade date, and (b) derecognition of an asset that is sold, recognition of any gain or loss on disposal and the recognition of a receivable from the buyer for payment on the trade date. Generally, interest does not start to accrue on the asset and corresponding liability until the settlement date when title passes.

AG56   The settlement date is the date that an asset is delivered to or by an entity. Settlement date accounting refers to (a) the recognition of an asset on the day it is received by the entity, and (b) the derecognition of an asset and recognition of any gain or loss on disposal on the day that it is delivered by the entity. When settlement date accounting is applied an entity accounts for any change in the fair value of the asset to be received during the period between the trade date and the settlement date in the same way as it accounts for the acquired asset. In other words, the change in value is not recognised for assets carried at cost or amortised cost; it is recognised in profit or loss for assets classified as financial assets at fair value through profit or loss; and it is recognised in equity for assets classified as available for sale.

Derecognition of a Financial Liability (paragraphs 39–42)

AG57   A financial liability (or part of it) is extinguished when the debtor either:

(a)   discharges the liability (or part of it) by paying the creditor, normally with cash, other financial assets, goods or services; or

(b) is legally released from primary responsibility for the liability (or part of it) either by process of law or by the creditor. (If the debtor has given a guarantee this condition may still be met.)

If an issuer of a debt instrument repurchases that instrument, the debt is extinguished even if the issuer is a market maker in that instrument or intends to resell it in the near term.   **AG58**

Payment to a third party, including a trust (sometimes called 'insubstance defeasance'), does not, by itself, relieve the debtor of its primary obligation to the creditor, in the absence of legal release.   **AG59**

If a debtor pays a third party to assume an obligation and notifies its creditor that the third party has assumed its debt obligation, the debtor does not derecognise the debt obligation unless the condition in paragraph AG57(b) is met. If the debtor pays a third party to assume an obligation and obtains a legal release from its creditor, the debtor has extinguished the debt. However, if the debtor agrees to make payments on the debt to the third party or direct to its original creditor, the debtor recognises a new debt obligation to the third party.   **AG60**

Although legal release, whether judicially or by the creditor, results in derecognition of a liability, the entity may recognise a new liability if the derecognition criteria in paragraphs 15–37 are not met for the financial assets transferred. If those criteria are not met, the transferred assets are not derecognised, and the entity recognises a new liability relating to the transferred assets.   **AG61**

For the purpose of paragraph 40, the terms are substantially different if the discounted present value of the cash flows under the new terms, including any fees paid net of any fees received and discounted using the original effective interest rate, is at least 10 per cent different from the discounted present value of the remaining cash flows of the original financial liability. If an exchange of debt instruments or modification of terms is accounted for as an extinguishment, any costs or fees incurred are recognised as part of the gain or loss on the extinguishment. If the exchange or modification is not accounted for as an extinguishment, any costs or fees incurred adjust the carrying amount of the liability and are amortised over the remaining term of the modified liability.   **AG62**

In some cases, a creditor releases a debtor from its present obligation to make payments, but the debtor assumes a guarantee obligation to pay if the party assuming primary responsibility defaults. In this circumstance the debtor: **AG63**

(a) recognises a new financial liability based on the fair value of its obligation for the guarantee; and
(b) recognises a gain or loss based on the difference between (i) any proceeds paid and (ii) the carrying amount of the original financial liability less the fair value of the new financial liability.

MEASUREMENT (PARAGRAPHS 43-70)

Initial Measurement of Financial Assets and Financial Liabilities (paragraph 43)

The fair value of a financial instrument on initial recognition is normally the transaction price (ie the fair value of the consideration given or received, see also paragraph AG76). However, if part of the consideration given or received is for something other than the financial instrument, the fair value of the financial   **AG64** instrument is estimated, using a valuation technique (see paragraphs AG74-AG79). For example, the fair value of a long-term loan or receivable that carries no interest can be estimated as the present value of all future cash receipts discounted using the prevailing market rate(s) of interest for a similar instrument (similar as to currency, term, type of interest rate and other factors) with a similar credit rating. Any additional amount lent is an expense or a reduction of income unless it qualifies for recognition as some other type of asset.

AG65   If an entity originates a loan that bears an off-market interest rate (eg 5 per cent when the market rate for similar loans is 8 per cent), and receives an up-front fee as compensation, the entity recognises the loan at its fair value, ie net of the fee it receives. The entity accretes the discount to profit or loss using the effective interest rate method.

Subsequent Measurement of Financial Assets (paragraphs 45 and 46)

AG66   If a financial instrument that was previously recognised as a financial asset is measured at fair value and its fair value falls below zero, it is a financial liability in accordance with paragraph 47.

AG67   The following example illustrates the accounting for transaction costs on the initial and subsequent measurement of an available-for-sale financial asset. An asset is acquired for CU100 plus a purchase commission of CU2. Initially, the asset is recognised at CU102. The next financial reporting date occurs one day later, when the quoted market price of the asset is CU100. If the asset were sold, a commission of CU3 would be paid. On that date, the asset is measured at CU100 (without regard to the possible commission on sale) and a loss of CU2 is recognised in equity. If the availableforsale financial asset has fixed or determinable payments, the transaction costs are amortised to profit or loss using the effective interest method. If the available-for-sale financial asset does not have fixed or determinable payments, the transaction costs are recognised in profit or loss when the asset is derecognised or becomes impaired.

AG68   Instruments that are classified as loans and receivables are measured at amortised cost without regard to the entity's intention to hold them to maturity.

Fair Value Measurement Considerations (paragraphs 48 and 49)

AG69   Underlying the definition of fair value is a presumption that an entity is a going concern without any intention or need to liquidate, to curtail materially the scale of its operations or to undertake a transaction on adverse terms. Fair value is not, therefore, the amount that an entity would receive or pay in a forced transaction, involuntary liquidation or distress sale. However, fair value reflects the credit quality of the instrument.

AG70   This Standard uses the terms 'bid price' and 'asking price' (sometimes referred to as 'current offer price') in the context of quoted market prices, and the term 'the bid-ask spread' to include only transaction costs. Other adjustments to arrive at fair value (eg for counterparty credit risk) are not included in the term 'bid-ask spread'.

Active Market: Quoted Price

AG71   A financial instrument is regarded as quoted in an active market if quoted prices are readily and regularly available from an exchange, dealer, broker, industry group, pricing service or regulatory agency, and those prices represent actual and regularly occurring market transactions on an arm's length basis. Fair value is defined in terms of a price agreed by a willing buyer and a willing seller in an arm's length transaction. The objective of determining fair value for a financial instrument that is traded in an active market is to arrive at the price at which a transaction would occur at the balance sheet date in that instrument (ie without modifying or repackaging the instrument) in the most advantageous active market to which the entity has immediate access. However, the entity adjusts the price in the more advantageous market to reflect any differences in counterparty credit risk between instruments traded in that market and the one being valued. The existence of published price quotations in an active market is the best evidence of fair value and when they exist they are used to measure the financial asset or financial liability.

The appropriate quoted market price for an asset held or liability to be issued is usually the current bid price and, for an asset to be acquired or liability held, the asking price. When an entity has assets and liabilities with offsetting market risks, it may use mid-market prices as a basis for establishing fair values for the offsetting risk positions and apply the bid or asking price to the net open position as appropriate. When current bid and asking prices are unavailable, the price of the most recent transaction provides evidence of the current fair value as long as there has not been a significant change in economic circumstances since the time of the transaction. If conditions have changed since the time of the transaction (eg a change in the risk-free interest rate following the most recent price quote for a corporate bond), the fair value reflects the change in conditions by reference to current prices or rates for similar financial instruments, as appropriate. Similarly, if the entity can demonstrate that the last transaction price is not fair value (eg because it reflected the amount that an entity would receive or pay in a forced transaction, involuntary liquidation or distress sale), that price is adjusted. The fair value of a portfolio of financial instruments is the product of the number of units of the instrument and its quoted market price. If a published price quotation in an active market does not exist for a financial instrument in its entirety, but active markets exist for its component parts, fair value is determined on the basis of the relevant market prices for the component parts. **AG72**

If a rate (rather than a price) is quoted in an active market, the entity uses that market-quoted rate as an input into a valuation technique to determine fair value. If the market-quoted rate does not include credit risk or other factors that market participants would include in valuing the instrument, the entity adjusts for those factors. **AG73**

No Active Market: Valuation Technique

If the market for a financial instrument is not active, an entity establishes fair value by using a valuation technique. Valuation techniques include using recent arm's length market transactions between knowledgeable, willing parties, if available, reference to the current fair value of another instrument that is substantially the same, discounted cash flow analysis and option pricing models. If there is a valuation technique commonly used by market participants to price the instrument and that technique has been demonstrated to provide reliable estimates of prices obtained in actual market transactions, the entity uses that technique. **AG74**

The objective of using a valuation technique is to establish what the transaction price would have been on the measurement date in an arm's length exchange motivated by normal business considerations. Fair value is estimated on the basis of the results of a valuation technique that makes maximum use of market inputs, and relies as little as possible on entity-specific inputs. A valuation technique would be expected to arrive at a realistic estimate of the fair value if (a) it reasonably reflects how the market **AG75** could be expected to price the instrument and (b) the inputs to the valuation technique reasonably represent market expectations and measures of the risk-return factors inherent in the financial instrument.

AG76   Therefore, a valuation technique (a) incorporates all factors that market participants would consider in setting a price and (b) is consistent with accepted economic methodologies for pricing financial instruments. Periodically, an entity calibrates the valuation technique and tests it for validity using prices from any observable current market transactions in the same instrument (ie without modification or repackaging) or based on any available observable market data. An entity obtains market data consistently in the same market where the instrument was originated or purchased. The best evidence of the fair value of a financial instrument at initial recognition is the transaction price (ie the fair value of the consideration given or received) unless the fair value of that instrument is evidenced by comparison with other observable current market transactions in the same instrument (ie without modification or repackaging) or based on a valuation technique whose variables include only data from observable markets.

AG76A The subsequent measurement of the financial asset or financial liability and the subsequent recognition of gains and losses shall be consistent with the requirements of this Standard. The application of paragraph AG76 may result in no gain or loss being recognised on the initial recognition of a financial asset or financial liability. In such a case, FRS 26 requires that a gain or loss shall be recognised after initial recognition only to the extent that it arises from a change in a factor (including time) that market participants would consider in setting a price.*

AG77   The initial acquisition or origination of a financial asset or incurrence of a financial liability is a market transaction that provides a foundation for estimating the fair value of the financial instrument. In particular, if the financial instrument is a debt instrument (such as a loan), its fair value can be determined by reference to the market conditions that existed at its acquisition or origination date and current market conditions or interest rates currently charged by the entity or by others for similar debt instruments (ie similar remaining maturity, cash flow pattern, currency, credit risk, collateral and interest basis). Alternatively, provided there is no change in the credit risk of the debtor and applicable credit spreads after the origination of the debt instrument, an estimate of the current market interest rate may be derived by using a benchmark interest rate reflecting a better credit quality than the underlying debt instrument, holding the credit spread constant, and adjusting for the change in the benchmark interest rate from the origination date. If conditions have changed since the most recent market transaction, the corresponding change in the fair value of the financial instrument being valued is determined by reference to current prices or rates for similar financial instruments, adjusted as appropriate, for any differences from the instrument being valued.

AG78   The same information may not be available at each measurement date. For example, at the date that an entity makes a loan or acquires a debt instrument that is not actively traded, the entity has a transaction price that is also a market price. However, no new transaction information may be available at the next measurement date and, although the entity can determine the general level of market interest rates, it may not know what level of credit or other risk market participants would consider in pricing the instrument on that date. An entity may not have information from recent transactions to determine the appropriate credit spread over the basic interest rate to use in determining a discount rate for a present value computation. It would be reasonable to assume, in the absence of evidence to the contrary, that no changes

Editor's note: Paragraph added in October 2005.

have taken place in the spread that existed at the date the loan was made. However, the entity would be expected to make reasonable efforts to determine whether there is evidence that there has been a change in such factors. When evidence of a change exists, the entity would consider the effects of the change in determining the fair value of the financial instrument.

In applying discounted cash flow analysis, an entity uses one or more discount rates   **AG79** equal to the prevailing rates of return for financial instruments having substantially the same terms and characteristics, including the credit quality of the instrument, the remaining term over which the contractual interest rate is fixed, the remaining term to repayment of the principal and the currency in which payments are to be made. Short-term receivables and payables with no stated interest rate may be measured at the original invoice amount if the effect of discounting is immaterial.

No Active Market: Equity Instruments

The fair value of investments in equity instruments that do not have a quoted market   **AG80** price in an active market and derivatives that are linked to and must be settled by delivery of such an unquoted equity instrument (see paragraphs 46(c) and 47) is reliably measurable if (a) the variability in the range of reasonable fair value estimates is not significant for that instrument or (b) the probabilities of the various estimates within the range can be reasonably assessed and used in estimating fair value.

There are many situations in which the variability in the range of reasonable fair   **AG81** value estimates of investments in equity instruments that do not have a quoted market price and derivatives that are linked to and must be settled by delivery of such an unquoted equity instrument (see paragraphs 46(c) and 47) is likely not to be significant. Normally it is possible to estimate the fair value of a financial asset that an entity has acquired from an outside party. However, if the range of reasonable fair value estimates is significant and the probabilities of the various estimates cannot be reasonably assessed, an entity is precluded from measuring the instrument at fair value.

Inputs to Valuation Techniques

An appropriate technique for estimating the fair value of a particular financial   **AG82** instrument would incorporate observable market data about the market conditions and other factors that are likely to affect the instrument's fair value. The fair value of a financial instrument will be based on one or more of the following factors (and perhaps others).

(a)   *The time value of money (ie interest at the basic or risk-free rate).* Basic interest rates can usually be derived from observable government bond prices and are often quoted in financial publications. These rates typically vary with the expected dates of the projected cash flows along a yield curve of interest rates for different time horizons. For practical reasons, an entity may use a well-accepted and readily observable general rate, such as LIBOR or a swap rate, as the benchmark rate. (Because a rate such as LIBOR is not the riskfree interest rate, the credit risk adjustment appropriate to the particular financial instrument is determined on the basis of its credit risk in relation to the credit risk in this benchmark rate.) In some countries, the central government's bonds may carry a significant credit risk and may not provide a stable benchmark basic interest rate for instruments denominated in that currency. Some entities in these countries may have a better credit standing and a lower borrowing rate than the central government. In such a case, basic interest rates may be more appropriately determined by reference to interest rates for the highest rated corporate bonds issued in the currency of that jurisdiction.

(b) *Credit risk.* The effect on fair value of credit risk (ie the premium over the basic interest rate for credit risk) may be derived from observable market prices for traded instruments of different credit quality or from observable interest rates charged by lenders for loans of various credit ratings.

(c) *Foreign currency exchange prices.* Active currency exchange markets exist for most major currencies, and prices are quoted daily in financial publications.

(d) *Commodity prices.* There are observable market prices for many commodities.

(e) *Equity prices.* Prices (and indexes of prices) of traded equity instruments are readily observable in some markets. Present value based techniques may be used to estimate the current market price of equity instruments for which there are no observable prices.

(f) *Volatility (ie magnitude of future changes in price of the financial instrument or other item).* Measures of the volatility of actively traded items can normally be reasonably estimated on the basis of historical market data or by using volatilities implied in current market prices.

(g) *Prepayment risk and surrender risk.* Expected prepayment patterns for financial assets and expected surrender patterns for financial liabilities can be estimated on the basis of historical data. (The fair value of a financial liability that can be surrendered by the counterparty cannot be less than the present value of the surrender amount—see paragraph 49.)

(h) *Servicing costs for a financial asset or a financial liability.* Costs of servicing can be estimated using comparisons with current fees charged by other market participants. If the costs of servicing a financial asset or financial liability are significant and other market participants would face comparable costs, the issuer would consider them in determining the fair value of that financial asset or financial liability. It is likely that the fair value at inception of a contractual right to future fees equals the origination costs paid for them, unless future fees and related costs are out of line with market comparables.

Gains and Losses (paragraphs 55-57)

AG83 An entity applies FRS 23 to financial assets and financial liabilities that are monetary items in accordance with FRS 23 and denominated in a foreign currency. Under FRS 23, any foreign exchange gains and losses on monetary assets and monetary liabilities are recognised in profit or loss. An exception is a monetary item that is designated as a hedging instrument in either a cash flow hedge (see paragraphs 95-101) or a hedge of a net investment (see paragraph 102). For the purpose of recognising foreign exchange gains and losses under FRS 23, a monetary available-for-sale financial asset is treated as if it were carried at amortised cost in the foreign currency. Accordingly, for such a financial asset, exchange differences resulting from changes in amortised cost are recognised in profit or loss and other changes in carrying amount are recognised in accordance with paragraph 55(b). For available-for-sale financial assets that are not monetary items under FRS 23 (for example, equity instruments), the gain or loss that is recognised directly in equity under paragraph 55(b) includes any related foreign exchange component. If there is a hedging relationship between a non-derivative monetary asset and a non-derivative monetary liability, changes in the foreign currency component of those financial instruments are recognised in profit or loss.

Impairment and Uncollectibility of Financial Assets (paragraphs 58-70)

Financial Assets Carried at Amortised Cost (paragraphs 63-65)

Impairment of a financial asset carried at amortised cost is measured using the financial instrument's original effective interest rate because discounting at the current market rate of interest would, in effect, impose fair value measurement on financial assets that are otherwise measured at amortised cost. If the terms of a loan, receivable or held-to-maturity investment are renegotiated or otherwise modified because of financial difficulties of the borrower or issuer, impairment is measured using the original effective interest rate before the modification of terms. Cash flows relating to short-term receivables are not discounted if the effect of discounting is immaterial. If a loan, receivable or held-to-maturity investment has a variable interest rate, the discount rate for measuring any impairment loss under paragraph 63 is the current effective interest rate(s) determined under the contract. As a practical expedient, a creditor may measure impairment of a financial asset carried at amortised cost on the basis of an instrument's fair value using an observable market price. The calculation of the present value of the estimated future cash flows of a collateralised financial asset reflects the cash flows that may result from foreclosure less costs for obtaining and selling the collateral, whether or not foreclosure is probable. **AG84**

The process for estimating impairment considers all credit exposures, not only those of low credit quality. For example, if an entity uses an internal credit grading system it considers all credit grades, not only those reflecting a severe credit deterioration. **AG85**

The process for estimating the amount of an impairment loss may result either in a single amount or in a range of possible amounts. In the latter case, the entity recognises an impairment loss equal to the best estimate within the range* taking into account all relevant information available before the financial statements are issued about conditions existing at the balance sheet date. **AG86**

For the purpose of a collective evaluation of impairment, financial assets are grouped on the basis of similar credit risk characteristics that are indicative of the debtors' ability to pay all amounts due according to the contractual terms (for example, on the basis of a credit risk evaluation or grading process that considers asset type, industry, geographical location, collateral type, past-due status and other relevant factors). The characteristics chosen are relevant to the estimation of future cash flows for groups of such assets by being indicative of the debtors' ability to pay all amounts due according to the contractual terms of the assets being evaluated. However, loss probabilities and other loss statistics differ at a group level between (a) assets that have been individually evaluated for impairment and found not to be impaired and (b) assets that have not been individually evaluated for impairment, with the result that a different amount of impairment may be required. If an entity does not have a group of assets with similar risk characteristics, it does not make the additional assessment. **AG87**

Impairment losses recognised on a group basis represent an interim step pending the identification of impairment losses on individual assets in the group of financial assets that are collectively assessed for impairment. As soon as information is available that specifically identifies losses on individually impaired assets in a group, those assets are removed from the group. **AG88**

*IAS 37, paragraph 39 contains guidance on how to determine the best estimate in a range of possible outcomes.

AG89   Future cash flows in a group of financial assets that are collectively evaluated for impairment are estimated on the basis of historical loss experience for assets with credit risk characteristics similar to those in the group. Entities that have no entity-specific loss experience or insufficient experience, use peer group experience for comparable groups of financial assets. Historical loss experience is adjusted on the basis of current observable data to reflect the effects of current conditions that did not affect the period on which the historical loss experience is based and to remove the effects of conditions in the historical period that do not exist currently. Estimates of changes in future cash flows reflect and are directionally consistent with changes in related observable data from period to period (such as changes in unemployment rates, property prices, commodity prices, payment status or other factors that are indicative of incurred losses in the group and their magnitude). The methodology and assumptions used for estimating future cash flows are reviewed regularly to reduce any differences between loss estimates and actual loss experience.

AG90   As an example of applying paragraph AG89, an entity may determine, on the basis of historical experience, that one of the main causes of default on credit card loans is the death of the borrower. The entity may observe that the death rate is unchanged from one year to the next. Nevertheless, some of the borrowers in the entity's group of credit card loans may have died in that year, indicating that an impairment loss has occurred on those loans, even if, at the year-end, the entity is not yet aware which specific borrowers have died. It would be appropriate for an impairment loss to be recognised for these 'incurred but not reported' losses. However, it would not be appropriate to recognise an impairment loss for deaths that are expected to occur in a future period, because the necessary loss event (the death of the borrower) has not yet occurred.

AG91   When using historical loss rates in estimating future cash flows, it is important that information about historical loss rates is applied to groups that are defined in a manner consistent with the groups for which the historical loss rates were observed. Therefore, the method used should enable each group to be associated with information about past loss experience in groups of assets with similar credit risk characteristics and relevant observable data that reflect current conditions.

AG92   Formula-based approaches or statistical methods may be used to determine impairment losses in a group of financial assets (eg for smaller balance loans) as long as they are consistent with the requirements in paragraphs 63-65 and AG87-AG91. Any model used would incorporate the effect of the time value of money, consider the cash flows for all of the remaining life of an asset (not only the next year), consider the age of the loans within the portfolio and not give rise to an impairment loss on initial recognition of a financial asset.

Interest Income After Impairment Recognition

AG93   Once a financial asset or a group of similar financial assets has been written down as a result of an impairment loss, interest income is thereafter recognised using the rate of interest used to discount the future cash flows for the purpose of measuring the impairment loss.

HEDGING (PARAGRAPHS 71-102)

Hedging Instruments (paragraphs 72-77)

Qualifying Instruments (paragraphs 72 and 73)

The potential loss on an option that an entity writes could be significantly greater than the potential gain in value of a related hedged item. In other words, a written option is not effective in reducing the profit or loss exposure of a hedged item. Therefore, a written option does not qualify as a hedging instrument unless it is designated as an offset to a purchased option, including one that is embedded in another financial instrument (for example, a written call option used to hedge a callable liability). In contrast, a purchased option has potential gains equal to or greater than losses and therefore has the potential to reduce profit or loss exposure from changes in fair values or cash flows. Accordingly, it can qualify as a hedging instrument. **AG94**

A held-to-maturity investment carried at amortised cost may be designated as a hedging instrument in a hedge of foreign currency risk. **AG95**

An investment in an unquoted equity instrument that is not carried at fair value because its fair value cannot be reliably measured or a derivative that is linked to and must be settled by delivery of such an unquoted equity instrument (see paragraphs 46(c) and 47) cannot be designated as a hedging instrument. **AG96**

An entity's own equity instruments are not financial assets or financial liabilities of the entity and therefore cannot be designated as hedging instruments. **AG97**

Hedged Items (paragraphs 78-84)

Qualifying Items (paragraphs 78-80)

A firm commitment to acquire a business in a business combination cannot be a hedged item, except for foreign exchange risk, because the other risks being hedged cannot be specifically identified and measured. These other risks are general business risks. **AG98**

An equity method investment cannot be a hedged item in a fair value hedge because the equity method recognises in profit or loss the investor's share of the associate's profit or loss, rather than changes in the investment's fair value. For a similar reason, an investment in a consolidated subsidiary cannot be a hedged item in a fair value hedge because consolidation recognises in profit or loss the subsidiary's profit or loss, rather than changes in the investment's fair value. A hedge of a net investment in a foreign operation is different because it is a hedge of the foreign currency exposure, not a fair value hedge of the change in the value of the investment. **AG99**

Designation of Financial Items as Hedged Items (paragraphs 81 and 81A)

Paragraph 80 states that in consolidated financial statements the foreign currency risk of a highly probable forecast intragroup transaction may qualify as a hedged item in a cash flow hedge, provided the transaction is denominated in a currency other than the functional currency of the entity entering into that transaction and the foreign currency risk will affect consolidated profit or loss. For this purpose an entity can be a parent, subsidiary, associate, joint venture or branch. If the foreign currency risk of a forecast intragroup transaction does not affect consolidated profit or loss, **AG99A** the intragroup transaction cannot qualify as a hedged item. This is usually the case for royalty payments, interest payments or management charges between members of the same group unless there is a related external transaction. However, when the foreign currency risk of a forecast intragroup transaction will affect consolidated profit or loss, the intragroup transaction can qualify as a hedged item. An example is forecast sales or purchases of inventories between members of the same group if there is an onward sale of the inventory to a party external to the group. Similarly, a forecast intragroup sale of plant and equipment from the group entity that manufactured it to a group entity that will use the plant and equipment in its operations may affect consolidated profit or loss. This could occur, for example, because the plant and equipment will be depreciated by the purchasing entity and the amount initially recognised for the plant and equipment may change if the forecast intragroup transaction is denominated in a currency other than the functional currency of the purchasing entity.

AG99B   If a hedge of a forecast intragroup transaction qualifies for hedge accounting, any gain or loss that is recognised directly through the statement of total recognised gains and losses in accordance with paragraph 95(a) shall be reclassified into profit or loss in the same period or periods during which the foreign currency risk of the hedged transaction affects consolidated profit or loss.

AG99C   If a portion of the cash flows of a financial asset or financial liability is designated as the hedged item, that designated portion must be less than the total cash flows of the asset or liability. For example, in the case of a liability whose effective interest rate is below LIBOR, an entity cannot designate (a) a portion of the liability equal to the principal amount plus interest at LIBOR and (b) a negative residual portion. However, the entity may designate all of the cash flows of the entire financial asset or financial liability as the hedged item and hedge them for only one particular risk (eg only for changes that are attributable to changes in LIBOR). For example, in the case of a financial liability whose effective interest rate is 100 basis points below LIBOR, an entity can designate as the hedged item the entire liability (ie principal plus interest at LIBOR minus 100 basis points) and hedge the change in the fair value or cash flows of that entire liability that is attributable to changes in LIBOR. The entity may also choose a hedge ratio of other than one to one in order to improve the effectiveness of the hedge as described in paragraph AG100.

AG99D   In addition, if a fixed rate financial instrument is hedged some time after its origination and interest rates have changed in the meantime, the entity can designate a portion equal to a benchmark rate that is higher than the contractual rate paid on the item. The entity can do so provided that the benchmark rate is less than the effective interest rate calculated on the assumption that the entity had purchased the instrument on the day it first designates the hedged item. For example, assume an entity originates a fixed rate financial asset of CU100 that has an effective interest rate of 6 per cent at a time when LIBOR is 4 per cent. It begins to hedge that asset some time later when LIBOR has increased to 8 per cent and the fair value of the asset has decreased to CU90. The entity calculates that if it had purchased the asset on the date it first designates it as the hedged item for its then fair value of CU90, the effective yield would have been 9.5 per cent. Because LIBOR is less than this effective yield, the entity can designate a LIBOR portion of 8 per cent that consists partly of the contractual interest cash flows and partly of the difference between the current fair value (ie CU90) and the amount repayable on maturity (ie CU100).

Designation of Non-Financial Items as Hedged Items (paragraph 82)

Changes in the price of an ingredient or component of a non-financial asset or non-financial liability generally do not have a predictable, separately measurable effect on the price of the item that is comparable to the effect of, say, a change in market interest rates on the price of a bond. Thus, a non-financial asset or nonfinancial liability is a hedged item only in its entirety or for foreign exchange risk. If there is a difference between the terms of the hedging instrument and the hedged item (such as for a hedge of the forecast purchase of Brazilian coffee using a forward contract to purchase Colombian coffee on otherwise similar terms), the hedging relationship nonetheless can qualify as a hedge relationship provided all the conditions in paragraph 88 are met, including that the hedge is expected to be highly effective. For this purpose, the amount of the hedging instrument may be greater or less than that of the hedged item if this improves the effectiveness of the hedging relationship. For example, a regression analysis could be performed to establish a statistical relationship between the hedged item (eg a transaction in Brazilian coffee) and the hedging instrument (eg a transaction in Colombian coffee). If there is a valid statistical relationship between the two variables (ie between the unit prices of Brazilian coffee and Colombian coffee), the slope of the regression line can be used to establish the hedge ratio that will maximise expected effectiveness. For example, if the slope of the regression line is 1.02, a hedge ratio based on 0.98 quantities of hedged items to 1.00 quantities of the hedging instrument maximises expected effectiveness. However, the hedging relationship may result in ineffectiveness that is recognised in profit or loss during the term of the hedging relationship.

AG100

Designation of Groups of Items as Hedged Items (paragraphs 83 and 84)

A hedge of an overall net position (eg the net of all fixed rate assets and fixed rate liabilities with similar maturities), rather than of a specific hedged item, does not qualify for hedge accounting. However, almost the same effect on profit or loss of hedge accounting for this type of hedging relationship can be achieved by designating as the hedged item part of the underlying items. For example, if a bank has CU100 of assets and CU90 of liabilities with risks and terms of a similar nature and hedges the net CU10 exposure, it can designate as the hedged item CU10 of those assets. This designation can be used if such assets and liabilities are fixed rate instruments, in which case it is a fair value hedge, or if they are variable rate instruments, in which case it is a cash flow hedge. Similarly, if an entity has a firm commitment to make a purchase in a foreign currency of CU100 and a firm commitment to make a sale in the foreign currency of CU90, it can hedge the net amount of CU10 by acquiring a derivative and designating it as a hedging instrument associated with CU10 of the firm purchase commitment of CU100.

AG101

Hedge Accounting (paragraphs 85-102)

An example of a fair value hedge is a hedge of exposure to changes in the fair value of a fixed rate debt instrument as a result of changes in interest rates. Such a hedge could be entered into by the issuer or by the holder.

AG102

An example of a cash flow hedge is the use of a swap to change floating rate debt to fixed rate debt (ie a hedge of a future transaction where the future cash flows being hedged are the future interest payments).

AG103

A hedge of a firm commitment (eg a hedge of the change in fuel price relating to an unrecognised contractual commitment by an electric utility to purchase fuel at a fixed price) is a hedge of an exposure to a change in fair value. Accordingly, such a hedge

AG104

is a fair value hedge. However, under paragraph 87 a hedge of the foreign currency risk of a firm commitment could alternatively be accounted for as a cash flow hedge.

Assessing Hedge Effectiveness

AG105   A hedge is regarded as highly effective only if both of the following conditions are met:

(a)   At the inception of the hedge and in subsequent periods, the hedge is expected to be highly effective in achieving offsetting changes in fair value or cash flows attributable to the hedged risk during the period for which the hedge is designated. Such an expectation can be demonstrated in various ways, including a comparison of past changes in the fair value or cash flows of the hedged item that are attributable to the hedged risk with past changes in the fair value or cash flows of the hedging instrument, or by demonstrating a high statistical correlation between the fair value or cash flows of the hedged item and those of the hedging instrument. The entity may choose a hedge ratio of other than one to one in order to improve the effectiveness of the hedge as described in paragraph AG100.

(b)   The actual results of the hedge are within a range of 80-125 per cent. For example, if actual results are such that the loss on the hedging instrument is CU120 and the gain on the cash instrument is CU100, offset can be measured by 120 / 100, which is 120 per cent, or by 100 / 120, which is 83 per cent. In this example, assuming the hedge meets the condition in (a), the entity would conclude that the hedge has been highly effective.

AG106   Effectiveness is assessed, at a minimum, at the time an entity prepares its annual or interim financial statements.

AG107   This Standard does not specify a single method for assessing hedge effectiveness. The method an entity adopts for assessing hedge effectiveness depends on its risk management strategy. For example, if the entity's risk management strategy is to adjust the amount of the hedging instrument periodically to reflect changes in the hedged position, the entity needs to demonstrate that the hedge is expected to be highly effective only for the period until the amount of the hedging instrument is next adjusted. In some cases, an entity adopts different methods for different types of hedges. An entity's documentation of its hedging strategy includes its procedures for assessing effectiveness. Those procedures state whether the assessment includes all of the gain or loss on a hedging instrument or whether the instrument's time value is excluded.

AG107A   If an entity hedges less than 100 per cent of the exposure on an item, such as 85 per cent, it shall designate the hedged item as being 85 per cent of the exposure and shall measure ineffectiveness based on the change in that designated 85 per cent exposure. However, when hedging the designated 85 per cent exposure, the entity may use a hedge ratio of other than one to one if that improves the expected effectiveness of the hedge, as explained in paragraph AG100.

AG108   If the principal terms of the hedging instrument and of the hedged asset, liability, firm commitment or highly probable forecast transaction are the same, the changes in fair value and cash flows attributable to the risk being hedged may be likely to offset each other fully, both when the hedge is entered into and afterwards. For example, an interest rate swap is likely to be an effective hedge if the notional and principal amounts, term, repricing dates, dates of interest and principal receipts and payments, and basis for measuring interest rates are the same for the hedging instrument and the hedged item. In addition, a hedge of a highly probable forecast purchase of a commodity with a forward contract is likely to be highly effective if:

(a) the forward contract is for the purchase of the same quantity of the same commodity at the same time and location as the hedged forecast purchase;
(b) the fair value of the forward contract at inception is zero; and
(c) either the change in the discount or premium on the forward contract is excluded from the assessment of effectiveness and recognised in profit or loss or the change in expected cash flows on the highly probable forecast transaction is based on the forward price for the commodity.

AG109 Sometimes the hedging instrument offsets only part of the hedged risk. For example, a hedge would not be fully effective if the hedging instrument and hedged item are denominated in different currencies that do not move in tandem. Also, a hedge of interest rate risk using a derivative would not be fully effective if part of the change in the fair value of the derivative is attributable to the counterparty's credit risk.

AG110 To qualify for hedge accounting, the hedge must relate to a specific identified and designated risk, and not merely to the entity's general business risks, and must ultimately affect the entity's profit or loss. A hedge of the risk of obsolescence of a physical asset or the risk of expropriation of property by a government is not eligible for hedge accounting; effectiveness cannot be measured because those risks are not measurable reliably.

AG111 In the case of interest rate risk, hedge effectiveness may be assessed by preparing a maturity schedule for financial assets and financial liabilities that shows the net interest rate exposure for each time period, provided that the net exposure is associated with a specific asset or liability (or a specific group of assets or liabilities or a specific portion of them) giving rise to the net exposure, and hedge effectiveness is assessed against that asset or liability.

AG112 In assessing the effectiveness of a hedge, an entity generally considers the time value of money. The fixed interest rate on a hedged item need not exactly match the fixed interest rate on a swap designated as a fair value hedge. Nor does the variable interest rate on an interest-bearing asset or liability need to be the same as the variable interest rate on a swap designated as a cash flow hedge. A swap's fair value derives from its net settlements. The fixed and variable rates on a swap can be changed without affecting the net settlement if both are changed by the same amount.

AG113 If an entity does not meet hedge effectiveness criteria, the entity discontinues hedge accounting from the last date on which compliance with hedge effectiveness was demonstrated. However, if the entity identifies the event or change in circumstances that caused the hedging relationship to fail the effectiveness criteria, and demonstrates that the hedge was effective before the event or change in circumstances occurred, the entity discontinues hedge accounting from the date of the event or change in circumstances.

Fair Value Hedge Accounting for a Portfolio Hedge of Interest Rate Risk

AG114 For a fair value hedge of interest rate risk associated with a portfolio of financial assets or financial liabilities, an entity would meet the requirements of this Standard if it complies with the procedures set out in (a)-(i) and paragraphs AG115-AG132 below.

(a) As part of its risk management process the entity identifies a portfolio of items whose interest rate risk it wishes to hedge. The portfolio may comprise only assets, only liabilities or both assets and liabilities. The entity may identify two or more portfolios (eg the entity may group its available-for-sale assets into a separate portfolio), in which case it applies the guidance below to each portfolio separately.

(b) The entity analyses the portfolio into repricing time periods based on expected, rather than contractual, repricing dates. The analysis into repricing time periods may be performed in various ways including scheduling cash flows into the periods in which they are expected to occur, or scheduling notional principal amounts into all periods until repricing is expected to occur.

(c) On the basis of this analysis, the entity decides the amount it wishes to hedge. The entity designates as the hedged item an amount of assets or liabilities (but not a net amount) from the identified portfolio equal to the amount it wishes to designate as being hedged. This amount also determines the percentage measure that is used for testing effectiveness in accordance with paragraph AG126(b).

(d) The entity designates the interest rate risk it is hedging. This risk could be a portion of the interest rate risk in each of the items in the hedged position, such as a benchmark interest rate (eg LIBOR).

(e) The entity designates one or more hedging instruments for each repricing time period.

(f) Using the designations made in (c)-(e) above, the entity assesses at inception and in subsequent periods, whether the hedge is expected to be highly effective during the period for which the hedge is designated.

(g) Periodically, the entity measures the change in the fair value of the hedged item (as designated in (c)) that is attributable to the hedged risk (as designated in (d)), on the basis of the expected repricing dates determined in (b). Provided that the hedge is determined actually to have been highly effective when assessed using the entity's documented method of assessing effectiveness, the entity recognises the change in fair value of the hedged item as a gain or loss in profit or loss and in one of two line items in the balance sheet as described in paragraph 89A. The change in fair value need not be allocated to individual assets or liabilities.

(h) The entity measures the change in fair value of the hedging instrument(s) (as designated in (e)) and recognises it as a gain or loss in profit or loss. The fair value of the hedging instrument(s) is recognised as an asset or liability in the balance sheet.

(i) Any ineffectiveness* will be recognised in profit or loss as the difference between the change in fair value referred to in (g) and that referred to in (h).

AG115   This approach is described in more detail below. The approach shall be applied only to a fair value hedge of the interest rate risk associated with a portfolio of financial assets or financial liabilities.

AG116   The portfolio identified in paragraph AG114(a) could contain assets and liabilities. Alternatively, it could be a portfolio containing only assets, or only liabilities. The portfolio is used to determine the amount of the assets or liabilities the entity wishes to hedge. However, the portfolio is not itself designated as the hedged item.

AG117   In applying paragraph AG114(b), the entity determines the expected repricing date of an item as the earlier of the dates when that item is expected to mature or to reprice to market rates. The expected repricing dates are estimated at the inception of the hedge and throughout the term of the hedge, based on historical experience and

The same materiality considerations apply in this context as apply throughout IFRSs.

other available information, including information and expectations regarding pre-payment rates, interest rates and the interaction between them. Entities that have no entity-specific experience or insufficient experience use peer group experience for comparable financial instruments. These estimates are reviewed periodically and updated in the light of experience. In the case of a fixed rate item that is prepayable, the expected repricing date is the date on which the item is expected to prepay unless it reprices to market rates on an earlier date. For a group of similar items, the analysis into time periods based on expected repricing dates may take the form of allocating a percentage of the group, rather than individual items, to each time period. An entity may apply other methodologies for such allocation purposes. For example, it may use a prepayment rate multiplier for allocating amortising loans to time periods based on expected repricing dates. However, the methodology for such an allocation shall be in accordance with the entity's risk management procedures and objectives.

As an example of the designation set out in paragraph AG114(c), if in a particular repricing time period an entity estimates that it has fixed rate assets of CU100 and fixed rate liabilities of CU80 and decides to hedge all of the net position of CU20, it designates as the hedged item assets in the amount of CU20 (a portion of the assets).* The designation is expressed as an 'amount of a currency' (eg an amount of dollars, euro, pounds or rand) rather than as individual assets. It follows that all of the assets (or liabilities) from which the hedged amount is drawn—ie all of the CU100 of assets in the above example—must be: **AG118**

(a)   items whose fair value changes in response to changes in the interest rate being hedged; and

(b)   items that could have qualified for fair value hedge accounting if they had been designated as hedged individually. In particular, because the Standard† specifies that the fair value of a financial liability with a demand feature (such as demand deposits and some types of time deposits) is not less than the amount payable on demand, discounted from the first date that the amount could be required to be paid, such an item cannot qualify for fair value hedge accounting for any time period beyond the shortest period in which the holder can demand payment. In the above example, the hedged position is an amount of assets. Hence, such liabilities are not a part of the designated hedged item, but are used by the entity to determine the amount of the asset that is designated as being hedged. If the position the entity wished to hedge was an amount of liabilities, the amount representing the designated hedged item must be drawn from fixed rate liabilities other than liabilities that the entity can be required to repay in an earlier time period, and the percentage measure used for assessing hedge effectiveness in accordance with paragraph AG126(b) would be calculated as a percentage of these other liabilities. For example, assume that an entity estimates that in a particular repricing time period it has fixed rate liabilities of CU100, comprising CU40 of demand deposits and CU60 of liabilities with no demand feature, and CU70 of fixed rate assets. If the entity decides to hedge all of the net position of CU30, it designates as the hedged item liabilities of CU30 or 50 per cent‡ of the liabilities with no demand feature.

The entity also complies with the other designation and documentation requirements set out in paragraph 88(a). For a portfolio hedge of interest rate risk, this designation   **AG119**

**The Standard permits an entity to designate any amount of the available qualifying assets or liabilities, ie in this example any amount of assets between CU0 and CU100.*

†*see paragraph 49*

‡*CU30 ÷ (CU100 − CU40) = 50 per cent*

and documentation specifies the entity's policy for all of the variables that are used to identify the amount that is hedged and how effectiveness is measured, including the following:

(a)   which assets and liabilities are to be included in the portfolio hedge and the basis to be used for removing them from the portfolio.

(b)   how the entity estimates repricing dates, including what interest rate assumptions underlie estimates of prepayment rates and the basis for changing those estimates. The same method is used for both the initial estimates made at the time an asset or liability is included in the hedged portfolio and for any later revisions to those estimates.

(c)   the number and duration of repricing time periods.

(d)   how often the entity will test effectiveness and which of the two methods in paragraph AG126 it will use.

(e)   the methodology used by the entity to determine the amount of assets or liabilities that are designated as the hedged item and, accordingly, the percentage measure used when the entity tests effectiveness using the method described in paragraph AG126(b).

(f)   when the entity tests effectiveness using the method described in paragraph AG126(b), whether the entity will test effectiveness for each repricing time period individually, for all time periods in aggregate, or by using some combination of the two.

The policies specified in designating and documenting the hedging relationship shall be in accordance with the entity's risk management procedures and objectives. Changes in policies shall not be made arbitrarily. They shall be justified on the basis of changes in market conditions and other factors and be founded on and consistent with the entity's risk management procedures and objectives.

AG120   The hedging instrument referred to in paragraph AG114(e) may be a single derivative or a portfolio of derivatives all of which contain exposure to the hedged interest rate risk designated in paragraph AG114(d) (eg a portfolio of interest rate swaps all of which contain exposure to LIBOR). Such a portfolio of derivatives may contain offsetting risk positions. However, it may not include written options or net written options, because the Standard* does not permit such options to be designated as hedging instruments (except when a written option is designated as an offset to a purchased option). If the hedging instrument hedges the amount designated in paragraph AG114(c) for more than one repricing time period, it is allocated to all of the time periods that it hedges. However, the whole of the hedging instrument must be allocated to those repricing time periods because the Standard† does not permit a hedging relationship to be designated for only a portion of the time period during which a hedging instrument remains outstanding.

AG121   When the entity measures the change in the fair value of a prepayable item in accordance with paragraph AG114(g), a change in interest rates affects the fair value of the prepayable item in two ways: it affects the fair value of the contractual cash flows and the fair value of the prepayment option that is contained in a prepayable item. Paragraph 81 of the Standard permits an entity to designate a portion of a financial asset or financial liability, sharing a common risk exposure, as the hedged item, provided effectiveness can be measured. For prepayable items, paragraph 81A permits this to be achieved by designating the hedged item in terms of the change in the fair value that is attributable to changes in the designated interest rate on the

*see paragraphs 77 and AG94

†see paragraph 75

basis of *expected*, rather than *contractual*, repricing dates. However, the effect that changes in the hedged interest rate have on those expected repricing dates shall be included when determining the change in the fair value of the hedged item. Consequently, if the expected repricing dates are revised (eg to reflect a change in expected prepayments), or if actual repricing dates differ from those expected, ineffectiveness will arise as described in paragraph AG126. Conversely, changes in expected repricing dates that (a) clearly arise from factors other than changes in the hedged interest rate, (b) are uncorrelated with changes in the hedged interest rate and (c) can be reliably separated from changes that are attributable to the hedged interest rate (eg changes in prepayment rates clearly arising from a change in demographic factors or tax regulations rather than changes in interest rate) are excluded when determining the change in the fair value of the hedged item, because they are not attributable to the hedged risk. If there is uncertainty about the factor that gave rise to the change in expected repricing dates or the entity is not able to separate reliably the changes that arise from the hedged interest rate from those that arise from other factors, the change is assumed to arise from changes in the hedged interest rate.

The Standard does not specify the techniques used to determine the amount referred to in paragraph AG114(g), namely the change in the fair value of the hedged item that is attributable to the hedged risk. If statistical or other estimation techniques are used for such measurement, management must expect the result to approximate closely that which would have been obtained from measurement of all the individual assets or liabilities that constitute the hedged item. It is not appropriate to assume that changes in the fair value of the hedged item equal changes in the value of the hedging instrument.   **AG122**

Paragraph 89A requires that if the hedged item for a particular repricing time period is an asset, the change in its value is presented in a separate line item within assets. Conversely, if the hedged item for a particular repricing time period is a liability, the change in its value is presented in a separate line item within liabilities. These are the separate line items referred to in paragraph AG114(g). Specific allocation to individual assets (or liabilities) is not required.   **AG123**

Paragraph AG114(i) notes that ineffectiveness arises to the extent that the change in the fair value of the hedged item that is attributable to the hedged risk differs from the change in the fair value of the hedging derivative. Such a difference may arise for a number of reasons, including: **AG124**

(a)   actual repricing dates being different from those expected, or expected repricing dates being revised;

(b)   items in the hedged portfolio becoming impaired or being derecognised;

(c)   the payment dates of the hedging instrument and the hedged item being different; and

(d)   other causes (eg when a few of the hedged items bear interest at a rate below the benchmark rate for which they are designated as being hedged, and the resulting ineffectiveness is not so great that the portfolio as a whole fails to qualify for hedge accounting).

Such ineffectiveness* shall be identified and recognised in profit or loss.

Generally, the effectiveness of the hedge will be improved: **AG125**

(a)   if the entity schedules items with different prepayment characteristics in a way that takes account of the differences in prepayment behaviour.

*The same materiality considerations apply in this context as apply throughout IFRSs.

(b)   when the number of items in the portfolio is larger. When only a few items are contained in the portfolio, relatively high ineffectiveness is likely if one of the items prepays earlier or later than expected. Conversely, when the portfolio contains many items, the prepayment behaviour can be predicted more accurately.

(c)   when the repricing time periods used are narrower (eg 1-month as opposed to 3-month repricing time periods). Narrower repricing time periods reduces the effect of any mismatch between the repricing and payment dates (within the repricing time period) of the hedged item and those of the hedging instrument.

(d)   the greater the frequency with which the amount of the hedging instrument is adjusted to reflect changes in the hedged item (eg because of changes in prepayment expectations).

AG126   An entity tests effectiveness periodically. If estimates of repricing dates change between one date on which an entity assesses effectiveness and the next, it shall calculate the amount of effectiveness either:

(a)   as the difference between the change in the fair value of the hedging instrument (see paragraph AG114(h)) and the change in the value of the entire hedged item that is attributable to changes in the hedged interest rate (including the effect that changes in the hedged interest rate have on the fair value of any embedded prepayment option); or

(b)   using the following approximation. The entity:

  (i)   calculates the percentage of the assets (or liabilities) in each repricing time period that was hedged, on the basis of the estimated repricing dates at the last date it tested effectiveness.

  (ii)   applies this percentage to its revised estimate of the amount in that repricing time period to calculate the amount of the hedged item based on its revised estimate.

  (iii)   calculates the change in the fair value of its revised estimate of the hedged item that is attributable to the hedged risk and presents it as set out in paragraph AG114(g).

  (iv)   recognises ineffectiveness equal to the difference between the amount determined in (iii) and the change in the fair value of the hedging instrument (see paragraph AG114(h)).

AG127   When measuring effectiveness, the entity distinguishes revisions to the estimated repricing dates of existing assets (or liabilities) from the origination of new assets (or liabilities), with only the former giving rise to ineffectiveness. All revisions to estimated repricing dates (other than those excluded in accordance with paragraph AG121), including any reallocation of existing items between time periods, are included when revising the estimated amount in a time period in accordance with paragraph AG126(b)(ii) and hence when measuring effectiveness. Once ineffectiveness has been recognised as set out above, the entity establishes a new estimate of the total assets (or liabilities) in each repricing time period, including new assets (or liabilities) that have been originated since it last tested effectiveness, and designates a new amount as the hedged item and a new percentage as the hedged percentage. The procedures set out in paragraph AG126(b) are then repeated at the next date it tests effectiveness.

AG128   Items that were originally scheduled into a repricing time period may be derecognised because of earlier than expected prepayment or writeoffs caused by impairment or sale. When this occurs, the amount of change in fair value included in the separate line item referred to in paragraph AG114(g) that relates to the derecognised item shall be removed from the balance sheet, and included in the gain or loss that arises on derecognition of the item. For this purpose, it is necessary to know the repricing time period(s) into which the derecognised item was scheduled, because this determines the repricing time period(s) from which to remove it and hence the amount to remove from the separate line item referred to in paragraph AG114(g). When an item is derecognised, if it can be determined in which time period it was included, it is removed from that time period. If not, it is removed from the earliest time period if the derecognition resulted from higher than expected prepayments, or allocated to all time periods containing the derecognised item on a systematic and rational basis if the item was sold or became impaired.

In addition, any amount relating to a particular time period that has not been **AG129** derecognised when the time period expires is recognised in profit or loss at that time (see paragraph 89A). For example, assume an entity schedules items into three repricing time periods. At the previous redesignation, the change in fair value reported in the single line item on the balance sheet was an asset of CU25. That amount represents amounts attributable to periods 1, 2 and 3 of CU7, CU8 and CU10, respectively. At the next redesignation, the assets attributable to period 1 have been either realised or rescheduled into other periods. Therefore, CU7 is derecognised from the balance sheet and recognised in profit or loss. CU8 and CU10 are now attributable to periods 1 and 2, respectively. These remaining periods are then adjusted, as necessary, for changes in fair value as described in paragraph AG114(g).

As an illustration of the requirements of the previous two paragraphs, assume that **AG130** an entity scheduled assets by allocating a percentage of the portfolio into each repricing time period. Assume also that it scheduled CU100 into each of the first two time periods. When the first repricing time period expires, CU110 of assets are derecognised because of expected and unexpected repayments. In this case, all of the amount contained in the separate line item referred to in paragraph AG114(g) that relates to the first time period is removed from the balance sheet, plus 10 per cent of the amount that relates to the second time period.

If the hedged amount for a repricing time period is reduced without the related assets **AG131** (or liabilities) being derecognised, the amount included in the separate line item referred to in paragraph AG114(g) that relates to the reduction shall be amortised in accordance with paragraph 92.

An entity may wish to apply the approach set out in paragraphs AG114-AG131 to a **AG132** portfolio hedge that had previously been accounted for as a cash flow hedge in accordance with IAS 39. Such an entity would revoke the previous designation of a cash flow hedge in accordance with paragraph 101(d), and apply the requirements set out in that paragraph. It would also redesignate the hedge as a fair value hedge and apply the approach set out in paragraphs AG114-AG131 prospectively to subsequent accounting periods.

An entity may have designated a forecast intragroup transaction as a hedged item at **AG133** the start of an annual period beginning on or after 1 January 2005 (or, for the purpose of restating comparative information, the start of an earlier comparative period) in a hedge that would qualify for hedge accounting in accordance with this Standard (as amended by the last sentence of paragraph 80). Such an entity may use that designation to apply hedge accounting in consolidated financial statements from the start of the annual period beginning on or after 1 January 2005 (or the start of the earlier comparative period). Such an entity shall also apply paragraphs AG99A and AG99B from the start of the annual period beginning on or after 1 January 2005. However, in accordance with paragraph 108F, it need not apply paragraph AG99B to comparative information for earlier periods.*

Editor's note: Paragraph added October 2005.

Appendix B
Amendments to Other Pronouncements

[Not reproduced, as all changes have been made to the underlying standards and abstracts].

Appendix C

This appendix is an integral part of the Standard.

Insurance Contracts – extracts from IFRS 4

Paragraphs C2 to C4 are taken from the Standard section of IFRS 4, paragraphs 7 to 9.   **C1**

Embedded derivatives

IAS 39 requires an entity to separate some embedded derivatives from their host   **C2**
contract, measure them at *fair value* and include changes in their fair value in profit
or loss. IAS 39 applies to derivatives embedded in an insurance contract unless the
embedded derivative is itself an insurance contract.

As an exception to the requirement in IAS 39, an insurer need not separate, and   **C3**
measure at fair value, a policyholder's option to surrender an insurance contract for
a fixed amount (or for an amount based on a fixed amount and an interest rate), even
if the exercise price differs from the carrying amount of the host *insurance liability*.
However, the requirement in IAS 39 does apply to a put option or cash surrender
option embedded in an insurance contract if the surrender value varies in response to
the change in a financial variable (such as an equity or commodity price or index), or
a non-financial variable that is not specific to a party to the contract. Furthermore,
that requirement also applies if the holder's ability to exercise a put option or cash
surrender option is triggered by a change in such a variable (for example, a put
option that can be exercised if a stock market index reaches a specified level).

Paragraph 8 applies equally to options to surrender a financial instrument containing   **C4**
a discretionary participation feature.

The following definitions are taken from Appendix A of IFRS 4 'Defined Terms'.   **C5**
This appendix is an integral part of IFRS 4.

Discretionary participation feature	A contractual right to receive, as a supplement to guaranteed benefits, additional benefits:
	(a) that are likely to be a significant portion of the total contractual benefits;
	(b) whose amount or timing is contractually at the discretion of the issuer; and
	(c) that are contractually based on:
	(i) the performance of a specified pool of contracts or a specified type of contract;
	(ii) realised and/or unrealised investment returns on a specified pool of assets held by the issuer; or
	(iii) the profit or loss of the company, fund or other entity that issues the contract.
Financial risk	The risk of a possible future change in one or more of a specified interest rate, financial instrument price, commodity price, foreign exchange rate, index of prices or rates, credit rating or credit index or other

	variable, provided in the case of a non-financial variable that the variable is not specific to a party to the contract.
Guaranteed benefits	Payments or other benefits to which a particular policyholder or investor has an unconditional right that is not subject to the contractual discretion of the issuer.
Insurance contract	A contract under which one party (the insurer) accepts significant insurance risk from another party (the policyholder) by agreeing to compensate the policyholder if a specified uncertain future event (the insured event) adversely affects the policyholder. (See Appendix B for guidance on this definition.)
Insurance liability	An insurer's net contractual obligations under an insurance contract.
Insurance risk	Risk, other than financial risk, transferred from the holder of a contract to the issuer.
Insured event	An uncertain future event that is covered by an insurance contract and creates insurance risk.
Insurer	The party that has an obligation under an insurance contract to compensate a policyholder if an insured event occurs.
Policyholder	A party that has a right to compensation under an insurance contract if an insured event occurs.

C6   Paragraphs C7 to C36 are taken from Appendix B of IFRS 4 'Definition of an insurance contract', paragraphs B1 to B30; this appendix is an integral part of IFRS 4.

C7   Paragraphs C8 to C36 give guidance on the definition of an insurance contract in paragraph C5. They addresses the following issues:

(a)   the term 'uncertain future event' (paragraphs C8-C10);
(b)   payments in kind (paragraphs C11-C13);
(c)   insurance risk and other risks (paragraphs C14-C23);
(d)   examples of insurance contracts (paragraphs C24-C27);
(e)   significant insurance risk (paragraphs C28-C34); and
(f)   changes in the level of insurance risk (paragraphs C35 and C36).

Uncertain future event

C8   Uncertainty (or risk) is the essence of an insurance contract. Accordingly, at least one of the following is uncertain at the inception of an insurance contract:

(a)   whether an *insured event* will occur;
(b)   when it will occur; or
(c)   how much the insurer will need to pay if it occurs.

C9   In some insurance contracts, the insured event is the discovery of a loss during the term of the contract, even if the loss arises from an event that occurred before the inception of the contract. In other insurance contracts, the insured event is an event that occurs during the term of the contract, even if the resulting loss is discovered after the end of the contract term.

Some insurance contracts cover events that have already occurred, but whose financial effect is still uncertain. An example is a reinsurance contract that covers the direct insurer against adverse development of claims already reported by policy-holders. In such contracts, the insured event is the discovery of the ultimate cost of those claims.

C10

Payments in kind

Some insurance contracts require or permit payments to be made in kind. An example is when the insurer replaces a stolen article directly, instead of reimbursing the policyholder. Another example is when an insurer uses its own hospitals and medical staff to provide medical services covered by the contracts.

C11

Some fixed-fee service contracts in which the level of service depends on an uncertain event meet the definition of an insurance contract in this Appendix but are not regulated as insurance contracts in some countries. One example is a maintenance contract in which the service provider agrees to repair specified equipment after a malfunction. The fixed service fee is based on the expected number of malfunctions, but it is uncertain whether a particular machine will break down. The malfunction of the equipment adversely affects its owner and the contract compensates the owner (in kind, rather than cash). Another example is a contract for car breakdown services in which the provider agrees, for a fixed annual fee, to provide roadside assistance or tow the car to a nearby garage. The latter contract could meet the definition of an insurance contract even if the provider does not agree to carry out repairs or replace parts.

C12

Distinction between insurance risk and other risks

The definition of an insurance contract refers to insurance risk, which this Appendix defines as risk, other than *financial risk*, transferred from the holder of a contract to the issuer. A contract that exposes the issuer to financial risk without significant insurance risk is not an insurance contract.

C14

The definition of financial risk in paragraph C5 includes a list of financial and non-financial variables. That list includes non-financial variables that are not specific to a party to the contract, such as an index of earthquake losses in a particular region or an index of temperatures in a particular city. It excludes non-financial variables that are specific to a party to the contract, such as the occurrence or nonoccurrence of a fire that damages or destroys an asset of that party. Furthermore, the risk of changes in the fair value of a non-financial asset is not a financial risk if the fair value reflects not only changes in market prices for such assets (a financial variable) but also the condition of a specific non-financial asset held by a party to a contract (a non-financial variable). For example, if a guarantee of the residual value of a specific car exposes the guarantor to the risk of changes in the car's physical condition, that risk is insurance risk, not financial risk.

C15

Some contracts expose the issuer to financial risk, in addition to significant insurance risk. For example, many life insurance contracts both guarantee a minimum rate of return to policyholders (creating financial risk) and promise death benefits that at some times significantly exceed the policyholder's account balance (creating insur-ance risk in the form of mortality risk). Such contracts are insurance contracts.

C16

Under some contracts, an insured event triggers the payment of an amount linked to a price index. Such contracts are insurance contracts, provided the payment that is contingent on the insured event can be significant. For example, a life-contingent

C17

annuity linked to a cost-of-living index transfers insurance risk because payment is triggered by an uncertain event—the survival of the annuitant. The link to the price index is an embedded derivative, but it also transfers insurance risk. If the resulting transfer of insurance risk is significant, the embedded derivative meets the definition of an insurance contract, in which case it need not be separated and measured at fair value (see paragraph C2 of this Appendix).

C18   The definition of insurance risk refers to risk that the insurer accepts from the policyholder. In other words, insurance risk is a pre-existing risk transferred from the policyholder to the insurer. Thus, a new risk created by the contract is not insurance risk.

C19   The definition of an insurance contract refers to an adverse effect on the policy-holder. The definition does not limit the payment by the insurer to an amount equal to the financial impact of the adverse event. For example, the definition does not exclude 'new-for-old' coverage that pays the policyholder sufficient to permit replacement of a damaged old asset by a new asset. Similarly, the definition does not limit payment under a term life insurance contract to the financial loss suffered by the deceased's dependants, nor does it preclude the payment of predetermined amounts to quantify the loss caused by death or an accident.

C20   Some contracts require a payment if a specified uncertain event occurs, but do not require an adverse effect on the policyholder as a precondition for payment. Such a contract is not an insurance contract even if the holder uses the contract to mitigate an underlying risk exposure. For example, if the holder uses a derivative to hedge an underlying non-financial variable that is correlated with cash flows from an asset of the entity, the derivative is not an insurance contract because payment is not conditional on whether the holder is adversely affected by a reduction in the cash flows from the asset. Conversely, the definition of an insurance contract refers to an uncertain event for which an adverse effect on the policyholder is a contractual precondition for payment. This contractual precondition does not require the insurer to investigate whether the event actually caused an adverse effect, but permits the insurer to deny payment if it is not satisfied that the event caused an adverse effect.

C21   Lapse or persistency risk (ie the risk that the counterparty will cancel the contract earlier or later than the issuer had expected in pricing the contract) is not insurance risk because the payment to the counterparty is not contingent on an uncertain future event that adversely affects the counterparty. Similarly, expense risk (ie the risk of unexpected increases in the administrative costs associated with the servicing of a contract, rather than in costs associated with insured events) is not insurance risk because an unexpected increase in expenses does not adversely affect the counterparty.

C22   Therefore, a contract that exposes the issuer to lapse risk, persistency risk or expense risk is not an insurance contract unless it also exposes the issuer to insurance risk. However, if the issuer of that contract mitigates that risk by using a second contract to transfer part of that risk to another party, the second contract exposes that other party to insurance risk.

C23   An insurer can accept significant insurance risk from the policyholder only if the insurer is an entity separate from the policyholder. In the case of a mutual insurer, the mutual accepts risk from each policyholder and pools that risk. Although pol-icyholders bear that pooled risk collectively in their capacity as owners, the mutual has still accepted the risk that is the essence of an insurance contract.

Examples of insurance contracts

The following are examples of contracts that are insurance contracts, if the transfer of insurance risk is significant: **C24**

(a)   insurance against theft or damage to property.

(b)   insurance against product liability, professional liability, civil liability or legal expenses.

(c)   life insurance and prepaid funeral plans (although death is certain, it is uncertain when death will occur or, for some types of life insurance, whether death will occur within the period covered by the insurance).

(d)   life-contingent annuities and pensions (ie contracts that provide compensation for the uncertain future event—the survival of the annuitant or pensioner—to assist the annuitant or pensioner in maintaining a given standard of living, which would otherwise be adversely affected by his or her survival).

(e)   disability and medical cover.

(f)   surety bonds, fidelity bonds, performance bonds and bid bonds (ie contracts that provide compensation if another party fails to perform a contractual obligation, for example an obligation to construct a building).

(g)   credit insurance that provides for specified payments to be made to reimburse the holder for a loss it incurs because a specified debtor fails to make payment when due under the original or modified terms of a debt instrument. These contracts could have various legal forms, such as that of a guarantee, some types of letter of credit, a credit derivative default contract or an insurance contract. However, although these contracts meet the definition of an insurance contract, they also meet the definition of a financial guarantee contract in FRS 26 and are within the scope of FRS 25 and FRS 26. Nevertheless, if an issuer of financial guarantee contracts has previously asserted explicitly that it regards such contracts as insurance contracts and has used accounting applicable to insurance contracts, the issuer may elect to apply FRS 26 and FRS 25 to such financial guarantee contracts.*

(h)   product warranties. Product warranties issued by another party for goods sold by a manufacturer, dealer or retailer are within the scope of this IFRS. However, product warranties issued directly by a manufacturer, dealer or retailer are outside its scope, because they are within the scope of FRS 12 *Provisions, Contingent Liabilities and Contingent Assets*.

(i)   title insurance (ie insurance against the discovery of defects in title to land that were not apparent when the insurance contract was written). In this case, the insured event is the discovery of a defect in the title, not the defect itself.

(j)   travel assistance (ie compensation in cash or in kind to policyholders for losses suffered while they are travelling). Paragraphs C11 and C12 discuss some contracts of this kind.

(k)   catastrophe bonds that provide for reduced payments of principal, interest or both if a specified event adversely affects the issuer of the bond (unless the specified event does not create significant insurance risk, for example if the event is a change in an interest rate or foreign exchange rate).

(l)   insurance swaps and other contracts that require a payment based on changes in climatic, geological or other physical variables that are specific to a party to the contract.

(m)   reinsurance contracts.

The following are examples of items that are not insurance contracts: **C25**

(a)   investment contracts that have the legal form of an insurance contract but do not expose the insurer to significant insurance risk, for example life insurance

*Editor's note: Amended with effect from 1 January 2006.

contracts in which the insurer bears no significant mortality risk (such contracts are noninsurance financial instruments or service contracts, see paragraphC26).

(b)   contracts that have the legal form of insurance, but pass all significant insurance risk back to the policyholder through non-cancellable and enforceable mechanisms that adjust future payments by the policyholder as a direct result of insured losses, for example some financial reinsurance contracts or some group contracts (such contracts are normally non-insurance financial instruments or service contracts, see paragraph C26).

(c)   self-insurance, in other words retaining a risk that could have been covered by insurance (there is no insurance contract because there is no agreement with another party).

(d)   contracts (such as gambling contracts) that require a payment if a specified uncertain future event occurs, but do not require, as a contractual precondition for payment, that the event adversely affects the policyholder. However, this does not preclude the specification of a predetermined payout to quantify the loss caused by a specified event such as death or an accident (see also paragraph C19).

(e)   derivatives that expose one party to financial risk but not insurance risk, because they require that party to make payment based solely on changes in one or more of a specified interest rate, financial instrument price, commodity price, foreign exchange rate, index of prices or rates, credit rating or credit index or other variable, provided in the case of a non-financial variable that the variable is not specific to a party to the contract (see FRS 26).

(f)   a credit-related guarantee (or letter of credit, credit derivative default contract or credit insurance contract) that requires payments even if the holder has not incurred a loss on the failure of the debtor to make payments when due.*

(g)   contracts that require a payment based on a climatic, geological or other physical variable that is not specific to a party to the contract (commonly described as weather derivatives).

(h)   catastrophe bonds that provide for reduced payments of principal, interest or both, based on a climatic, geological or other physical variable that is not specific to a party to the contract.

C26   If the contracts described in paragraph C25 create financial assets or financial liabilities, they are within the scope of FRS 26. Among other things, this means that the parties to the contract use what is sometimes called deposit accounting, which involves the following:

(a)   one party recognises the consideration received as a financial liability, rather than as revenue.

(b)   the other party recognises the consideration paid as a financial asset, rather than as an expense.

Significant insurance risk

C28   A contract is an insurance contract only if it transfers significant insurance risk. Paragraphs C13-C26 discuss insurance risk. The following paragraphs discuss the assessment of whether insurance risk is significant.

C29   Insurance risk is significant if, and only if, an insured event could cause an insurer to pay significant additional benefits in any scenario, excluding scenarios that lack commercial substance (ie have no discernible effect on the economics of the transaction). If significant additional benefits would be payable in scenarios that have commercial substance, the condition in the previous sentence may be met even if the

Editor's note: Amended with effect from 1 January 2006.

insured event is extremely unlikely or even if the expected (ie probability-weighted) present value of contingent cash flows is a small proportion of the expected present value of all the remaining contractual cash flows.

The additional benefits described in paragraph C29 refer to amounts that exceed those that would be payable if no insured event occurred (excluding scenarios that lack commercial substance). Those additional amounts include claims handling and claims assessment costs, but exclude: **C30**

(a)   the loss of the ability to charge the policyholder for future services. For example, in an investment-linked life insurance contract, the death of the policyholder means that the insurer can no longer perform investment management services and collect a fee for doing so. However, this economic loss for the insurer does not reflect insurance risk, just as a mutual fund manager does not take on insurance risk in relation to the possible death of the client. Therefore, the potential loss of future investment management fees is not relevant in assessing how much insurance risk is transferred by a contract.

(b)   waiver on death of charges that would be made on cancellation or surrender. Because the contract brought those charges into existence, the waiver of these charges does not compensate the policyholder for a pre-existing risk. Hence, they are not relevant in assessing how much insurance risk is transferred by a contract.

(c)   a payment conditional on an event that does not cause a significant loss to the holder of the contract. For example, consider a contract that requires the issuer to pay one million currency units if an asset suffers physical damage causing an insignificant economic loss of one currency unit to the holder. In this contract, the holder transfers to the insurer the insignificant risk of losing one currency unit. At the same time, the contract creates non-insurance risk that the issuer will need to pay 999,999 currency units if the specified event occurs. Because the issuer does not accept significant insurance risk from the holder, this contract is not an insurance contract.

(d)   possible reinsurance recoveries. The insurer accounts for these separately.

An insurer shall assess the significance of insurance risk contract by contract, rather than by reference to materiality to the financial statements.* Thus, insurance risk may be significant even if there is a minimal probability of material losses for a whole book of contracts. This contract-by-contract assessment makes it easier to classify a contract as an insurance contract. However, if a relatively homogeneous book of small contracts is known to consist of contracts that all transfer insurance risk, an insurer need not examine each contract within that book to identify a few non-derivative contracts that transfer insignificant insurance risk.   **C31**

It follows from paragraphs C29-C31 that if a contract pays a death benefit exceeding the amount payable on survival, the contract is an insurance contract unless the additional death benefit is insignificant (judged by reference to the contract rather than to an entire book of contracts). As noted in paragraph B24(b), the waiver on death of cancellation or surrender charges is not included in this assessment if this waiver does not compensate the policyholder for a pre-existing risk. Similarly, an annuity contract that pays out regular sums for the rest of a policyholder's life is an insurance contract, unless the aggregate lifecontingent payments are insignificant.   **C32**

Paragraph C29 refers to additional benefits. These additional benefits could include a requirement to pay benefits earlier if the insured event occurs earlier and the payment   **C33**

For this purpose, contracts entered into simultaneously with a single counterparty (or contracts that are otherwise interdependent) form a single contract.

is not adjusted for the time value of money. An example is whole life insurance for a fixed amount (in other words, insurance that provides a fixed death benefit whenever the policyholder dies, with no expiry date for the cover). It is certain that the policyholder will die, but the date of death is uncertain. The insurer will suffer a loss on those individual contracts for which policyholders die early, even if there is no overall loss on the whole book of contracts.

C34   If an insurance contract is unbundled into a deposit component and an insurance component, the significance of insurance risk transfer is assessed by reference to the insurance component. The significance of insurance risk transferred by an embedded derivative is assessed by reference to the embedded derivative.

Changes in the level of insurance risk

C35   Some contracts do not transfer any insurance risk to the issuer at inception, although they do transfer insurance risk at a later time. For example, consider a contract that provides a specified investment return and includes an option for the policyholder to use the proceeds of the investment on maturity to buy a life-contingent annuity at the current annuity rates charged by the insurer to other new annuitants when the policyholder exercises the option. The contract transfers no insurance risk to the issuer until the option is exercised, because the insurer remains free to price the annuity on a basis that reflects the insurance risk transferred to the insurer at that time. However, if the contract specifies the annuity rates (or a basis for setting the annuity rates), the contract transfers insurance risk to the issuer at inception.

C36   A contract that qualifies as an insurance contract remains an insurance contract until all rights and obligations are extinguished or expire.

APPROVAL OF IAS 39 BY THE BOARD

International Accounting Standard 39 *Financial Instruments: Recognition and Measurement* was approved for issue by eleven of the fourteen members of the International Accounting Standards Board. Messrs Cope, Leisenring and McGregor dissented. Their dissenting opinions are set out after the Basis for Conclusions.

The amendments made in March 2004 in International Accounting Standard 39 Financial Instruments: Recognition and Measurement *Fair Value Hedge Accounting for a Portfolio Hedge of Interest Rate Risk* were approved for issue by thirteen of the fourteen members of the International Accounting Standards Board. Mr Smith dissented. His dissenting opinion is set out after the Basis for Conclusions.

Sir David Tweedie   Chairman
Thomas E Jones   Vice-Chairman
Mary E Barth
Hans-Georg Bruns
Anthony T Cope
Robert P Garnett
Gilbert Gélard
James J Leisenring
Warren J McGregor
Patricia L O'Malley
Harry K Schmid
John T Smith
Geoffrey Whittington
Tatsumi Yamada

ADOPTION OF FRS 26 BY THE ACCOUNTING STANDARDS BOARD

Financial Reporting Standard 26 (IAS 39) *Financial Instruments: Measurement* was approved for issue by the ten members of the Accounting Standards Board.

Ian Mackintosh   Chairman
Andrew Lennard   Technical Director
Michael Ashley
Douglas Flint
Anthony Good
Roger Marshall
Isobel Sharp
John Smith
Jonathan Symonds
Peter Westlake

Notes on the standard's application in the UK and the Republic of Ireland

The need for an FRS on measurement of financial instruments

N1 In June 2002 the Accounting Standards Board (the Board) issued FRED 30 'Financial Instruments: Disclosure and Presentation & Recognition and Measurement'. In August 2003, April 2004 and July 2004 it issued three supplements to that FRED. Together, the four documents proposed that:

(a) a standard for use in the UK and Republic of Ireland based on IAS 32 'Financial Instruments: Disclosure and Presentation' should be implemented for all entities, other than those that apply the FRSSE, for accounting periods beginning on or after 1 January 2005; and

(b) a standard for use in the UK and Republic of Ireland based on the measurement and hedge accounting requirements of IAS 39 'Financial Instruments: Recognition and Measurement' (but not its recognition and derecognition requirements) should be implemented from the same date for all listed entities and for any unlisted entity that chooses to apply fair value accounting in its financial statements (so-called 'fair value volunteers').

The Board has now decided to issue FRS 26 which, together with FRS 25 (IAS 32) 'Financial Instruments: Disclosure and Presentation', implements these proposals.

N2 The issue of these two standards forms part of the Accounting Standards Board's programme to bring about convergence between UK accounting standards and International Accounting Standards (IFRSs). Under this programme, the Board is seeking to bring UK standards into line with IFRS over the medium term, dealing first with areas where implementation of an international standard would enhance existing UK financial reporting requirements and keep them in step with changes in the law.

N3 The Board is strongly of the view that a standard on measurement of derivatives and other financial instruments is important, and that the initial implementation of this standard in the UK and Republic of Ireland should not be delayed.

N4 Furthermore, amendments that have been made to the Companies Act 1985 (the Act) to implement the Fair Value Directive* will enable companies to adopt fair value accounting for some types of asset and liability. In the Board's view the application of the fair value rules set out in the Act should be governed by an accounting standard.

Application of FRS 26

N5 The Board's phased approach to implementation of IAS 39 envisages that in due course all the sections of IAS 39 will be applied generally in the UK and Republic of Ireland. However, the initial application of IAS 39, as implemented by FRS 26, is limited in two major respects; in relation to its scope, and in relation to the exclusion of the part of the standard dealing with recognition and derecognition.

**Similar amendments are to be made to Northern Ireland and Republic of Ireland legislation.*

Scope

The Board considers that because of the complexity of the measurement requirements of IAS 39, and the delays in IASB issuing a final version of this standard, these
requirements should be implemented on a phased basis in the UK and Republic of
Ireland. The Board has restricted the scope of FRS 25 to apply as follows:

N6

(a)   for accounting periods beginning on or after 1 January 2005, to all listed
      entities (other than those implementing IFRS under the IAS Regulation), and
(b)   for accounting periods beginning on or after 1 January 2006, to other entities
      only if they adopt an accounting policy that complies with the fair value
      accounting rules in the Act.

The Board has explained the definition of the scope of (b) to make it clear that this is
to be interpreted widely, to include all entities whose accounting policies for financial
instruments are consistent with the fair value rules of the Act. This includes any
entity that accounts for financal instruments at fair value through profit and loss
account, except where this practice is specifically permitted under rules other than the
fair value accounting rules in the Act.

N7

For those entities reporting under Schedule 4 of the Act, no provision is made in the
historical cost or alternative accounting rules* for fair value accounting with the
gains and losses recognised in the profit and loss account for financial instruments of
any kind. An accounting policy to measure any financial instruments (for example,
trading book securities) at fair value and recognise the resulting gains and losses in
the profit and loss account (for example, marking to market trading positions in
securities, derivatives or other financial instruments) falls within the fair value rules
in the Schedule. Accordingly, an entity using such an accounting policy will be
required to adopt FRS 26.

N8

For banking entities reporting under Schedule 9, the historical cost accounting rules†
permit fair value accounting through the profit and loss account for some classes of
financial instrument. Where such an entity applies fair value accounting only to those
financial instruments which those rules specifically permit to be fair valued through
the profit and loss account, it does not fall within the scope of FRS 26. However, if
an entity reporting under these Schedules uses fair value accounting through the
profit and loss account for financial instruments that are not specifically covered by
the historical cost rules but are within the scope of the fair value rules – such as
derivatives or loans and advances – the entity will be required to adopt FRS 26.The
standard will therefore apply inter alia to banks and similar entities that use mark to
market or fair value accounting through profit and loss account for derivatives, for
example those held for trading.

N9

Similarly, for insurance entities under Schedule 9A, the current value rules‡ permit
or require fair value accounting through the profit and loss account for investments
and certain other assets. Where an insurance entity applies fair value accounting only
to those financial instruments for which it is specifically permitted under these rules,
it does not fall within the scope of FRS 26. However, the standard will apply to

N10

*Paragraphs 16 to 34 of Schedule 4, and equivalent requirements in Northern Ireland and Republic of Ireland
legislation.*

†*Paragraphs 23 to 38 of Schedule 9 and equivalent requirements in Northern Ireland and Republic of Ireland
legislation.*

‡*Paragraphs 20 to 29 of Schedule 9A and equivalent requirements in Northern Ireland and Republic of Ireland
legislation.*

insurance entities that use fair value accounting through profit and loss account for any derivatives, or for any other financial instruments that are not specifically covered by the current value rules in Schedule 9A.

N11   The Board decided that, in the light of uncertainties expressed by some respondents over the interpretation of the scope set out in the exposure draft, that the effective date of entities falling within paragraph (b) above should be deferred for one year, to 2006. However, it confirmed the proposed effective date of 2005 for listed entities falling under paragraph (a) above.

N12   The Board intends bringing forward proposals extending the scope of application of the FRS to other entities after 2006, and intends to issue an exposure draft shortly.

Recycling

N15   IAS 39 requires gains and losses on remeasurement of available for sale assets to be recognised in equity and subsequently included in profit and loss on derecognition of the assets (e.g. on sale). Similarly gains and losses arising on a hedging instrument under cash flow hedging are recognised in equity and subsequently reclassified to profit and loss in accordance with the cash flow hedge accounting requirements. Existing UK standards, however, do not permit such gains and losses to be recycled.

N16   In FRED 30 the Board proposed amending the IAS 39 requirements to prohibit recycling, as the IASB was at that time reviewing its use of recycling as part of its comprehensive income project. Respondents were concerned that this would result in a UK standard that was not consistent with the equivalent international standard, and in the amended version of the draft FRS set out in FRED 30 Second Supplement the Board amended its approach to retain the IAS 39 requirements for recycling, although gains and losses recognised directly in equity under IAS 39 would be reflected in the statement of total recognised gains and losses under UK standards.

N17   The Board continues to have concerns over recycling, primarily because it is not consistent with the *Statement of Principles*. The IASB is actively considering the future of recycling in its comprehensive income project, and the Board intends to continue to argue strongly for the practice's prohibition. Nevertheless, the Board has concluded that it would be inconsistent with its stated policy of convergence were it to amend IAS 39's recycling provisions, and it is therefore implementing this aspect of IAS 39 unamended.

Relationship of the UK standard to the Fair Value Directive

N18   The Fair Value Directive, adopted in 2001, was drafted to correspond to the version of IAS 39 issued in 2000. Since then, IAS 39 has been revised, but these revisions have not been reflected in the directive, nor in the amendments to the Companies Act implementing the directive. In particular, IAS 39 now allows a reporting entity to designate *any* financial asset or financial liability to be measured at fair value through profit or loss. This unrestricted 'fair value option' is not available under the amendments to the Act implementing the directive, which limit the use of fair values to specified categories of asset and liability. In FRS 26 the Board has implemented the current version of IAS 39 rather than the 2000 version; since the inconsistencies with the Act relate to an optional designation rather than a requirement, entities may comply with both the FRS and the Act by not choosing to use this option.

N19   There may be circumstances in which an entity's financial statements will not present a true and fair view if certain financial liabilities are not accounted for at fair value. In such circumstances the entity should use the true and fair override and adopt an accounting policy that measures these liabilities at fair value in accordance with the FRS. It is difficult for the Board to provide guidance as to the circumstances that might merit the use of such an override because the use of the override must be justified by the particular circumstances of the entity in question. The Board would envisage that:

(a) if the override is to be applied there would need to be potential for substantial artificial volatility to arise otherwise. 'Artificial volatility' in this context means that the financial statements show volatility that would not be present were the financial liabilities concerned measured at fair value through profit or loss like the financial assets they are managed with. The Board believes that the *potential* for volatility, rather than the existence of actual volatility, is important in order to ensure that consistency in accounting practice from year to year is to be achieved.

(b) it would not generally be appropriate to apply the override if the result would be the recognition in the profit and loss account of a substantial gain arising from a fall in the fair value of financial liabilities caused by a deterioration in the entity's own credit standing.

The IASB issued an exposure draft proposing an amendment to IAS 39 to restrict the circumstances in which the fair value option may be adopted, and this exposure draft was issued by the Board as part of FRED 30 Third Supplement. If implemented, this proposal would reduce the significance of the difference between IAS 39 and the Fair Value Directive referred to in the previous paragraph. The Board will issue any IASB amendment to IAS 39 as an amendment to this FRS.   **N20**

Transitional provisions

The Board intends that entities adopting this FRS should be able to take advantage of the same transitional provisions as entities adopting the corresponding international standards as part of their transition to IFRS, which are set out in IFRS 1 'First-time Adoption of International Financial Reporting Standards', and consistently with its reasons for deferring the effective date for some entities to 2006, has extended the period for which these transitional provisions apply. An entity that first applies the requirements of the FRS for accounting periods commencing before 1 January 2007 need not restate comparatives to comply with the requirements of the FRS or those of FRS 25.   **N21**

The relevant paragraphs from IFRS 1 have been incorporated in the FRS, including the implementation guidance in IFRS 1 that relates to IAS 39 which is included at the end of the implementation guidance section of this FRS.   **N22**

The Board has, in adopting the transition requirements in IFRS 1, followed the practice adopted in several previous UK standards that applied prospectively and therefore not required corresponding amounts on a comparable basis. Some commentators have recently raised concerns that this might not be in compliance with the requirements of the Companies Act. The Board does not believe that it was ever the intention that prospective application of a new standard should be prevented. However, in view of these concerns, it has noted that a minor change to the Act could clarify the issue by explicitly permitting entities not to restate comparatives in certain circumstances; the DTI has agreed to consider such an amendment if this would remove uncertainty over the application of the transitional provisions of the FRS.   **N23**

Consequential amendments

N24   Measurement of financial instruments is addressed in FRS 4 'Capital Instruments'. Most of the requirements of FRS are superseded by FRS 25; the remaining paragraphs of FRS 4, relating to measurement of debt instruments, are superseded by this FRS. UITF Abstract 11 'Capital instruments: issuer call options' is also superseded by this FRS. No other amendments of substance are required to these on issue of FRS 26.

N25   IAS 39 made minor changes to IAS 37 'Provisions, Contingent Liabilities and Contingent Assets' clarifying the interaction between the two standards. IAS 37 is substantially the same as FRS 12 37 'Provisions, Contingent Liabilities and Contingent Assets', and the Board has implemented the same changes to FRS 12, applicable only to those entities applying FRS 26.

N26   Other amendments set out in IAS 39 do not affect UK standards and are not included in FRS 26.

N27   In July 2004 the ASB issued an exposure draft FRED 30 Third Supplement 'Further Amendments to the Proposed Standards on Financial Instruments'. This set out, inter alia, four exposure drafts issued by the IASB of proposed amendments to IAS 39.

N28   Subsequent to those exposure drafts, the IASB has made five amendments to IAS 39:

- Transition and Initial Recognition of Financial Assets and Financial Liabilities (December 2004)
- Cash Flow Hedge Accounting of Forecast Intragroup Transactions (April 2005)
- The Fair Value Option (June 2005)
- Financial Guarantee Contracts and Credit Insurance (August 2005)
- IFRIC Interpretation 5 'Rights to Interests arising from Decommissioning, Restoration and Environmental Rehabilitation Funds' (December 2004).

N29   The ASB has considered those amendments and decided to make corresponding changes to FRS 26.

Transition and initial recognition of financial assets and financial liabilities

N30   FRS 26 requires that the fair value of a financial instrument on its initial recognition should be the transaction price unless a different fair value can be evidenced by observable market data – thus limiting the circumstances in which a 'day one' profit or loss is recognised. On initial application of FRS 26 prior to the amendment, all financial instruments held by the entity would need to be assessed to determine any profit or loss recognised on initial recognition, even if this occurred in previous accounting periods. The amendment permits entities to restrict this reassessment to transactions that occurred after 1 January 2004, or to those that occurred after 25 October 2002 (the effective date for equivalent US GAAP requirements).

N31   The ASB agreed that the IASB's amendment was an appropriate simplification and should be incorporated into FRS 26.

N32   In line with the amendment to IAS 39, the amendment is effective for accounting periods commencing on or after 1 January 2005. The transitional provisions of FRS 26 are consistent with the provisions for first-time adopters under IFRS 1 *First-time Adoption of International Reporting Standards*.

Cash flow hedge accounting of forecast intragroup transactions

Prior to the amendment, FRS 26 did not permit hedge accounting to be used where **N33**
the hedged risk arises on a forecast intragroup transaction; hedge accounting is only
permitted for risks arising from transactions with parties external to the group.
However, in some circumstances forecast intragroup transactions denominated in a
currency other than the functional currency of one or both of the parties to the
transaction can give rise to a foreign currency risk that affects consolidated profit
and loss. The IASB have amended IAS 39 to permit cash flow hedge accounting of
forecast intragroup transactions in these circumstances.

The ASB agreed that it was appropriate to amend FRS 26 in line with the amend- **N34**
ment to IAS 39.

In line with the amendment to IAS 39, the amendment is effective for accounting **N35**
periods commencing on or after 1 January 2006. Earlier adoption is encouraged.

The Fair Value Option

Prior to the amendment, IAS 39 permitted entities to designate any financial asset or **N36**
financial liability as at fair value through profit and loss. The amendment restricted
this to circumstances where fair value accounting provided more relevant information, either by eliminating or reducing a measurement inconsistency or where a group
of financial items is managed, and its performance evaluated, on a fair value basis in
accordance with documented risk management or investment strategy. Fair value
measurement is also permitted for certain contracts that contain embedded
derivatives.

The ASB stated, when it issued FRED 30 Third Supplement, that it had considerable **N37**
reservations about the proposed restriction on the use of the fair value option.
However, it now agrees that, although the restricted amendment results in greater
complexity in implementation, there are unlikely to be cases where the use of fair
value accounting would be appropriate but not permitted by the amended standard,
and that the disadvantages of implementing these restrictions are outweighed by the
benefits of keeping UK standards in line with IFRS. It has therefore agreed to
implement the changes by amending FRS 26.

Under the amendment to IAS 39, an entity must take into account criteria set out in **N38**
IAS 8 'Accounting Policies' when deciding whether to designate items as at fair value
through profit and loss. As there is no UK standard equivalent to IAS 8, the ASB
has amended the guidance in AG4C and subsequent paragraphs to refer to the need
to consider objectives against which an entity should judge the appropriateness of
accounting policies as set out in FRS 18 'Accounting Policies'.

Paragraph 9(b)(ii) of the amended standard refers to information provided internally **N39**
to the entity's key management personnel, as defined in IAS 24 'Related Party
Disclosures'. This definition is not identical to the definition of key management in
FRS 8 'Related Party Disclosures' and has therefore been included in the amended
standard.

In line with the amendment to IAS 39, the amendment is effective for accounting **N40**
periods commencing on or after 1 January 2006. Earlier adoption is permitted. The
ASB has also amended the transitional provisions of FRS 26 to remain consistent
with the provisions for first-time adopters under IFRS 1.

N41 The ASB has also amended FRS 25 to include certain additional disclosure requirements. The ASB does, however, have considerable reservations over the value of some of the disclosures introduced by the IASB's amendment. These include disclosures introduced as paragraph 94 (g) relating to the credit risk of loans and receivables designated as at fair value through profit and loss which in the ASB's view are intended to provide information that is relevant to regulatory returns rather than general purpose financial statements. The ASB has not, therefore, implemented all the disclosure requirements inserted in IAS 32.

N42 The ASB has, however, amended the date by which transitional designations must be made from 1 September 2005 to 1 December 2005. This applies only to those entities adopting the amended fair value option for accounting periods commencing before 1 January 2006.

Credit insurance and financial guarantees

N43 Before the amendment, IAS 39 excluded credit insurance and financial guarantee contracts from its scope where these met the definition of an insurance contract. The IASB considered that although there may be differences in the way insurance entities and banks currently account for these contracts, there was no fundamental difference between credit insurance and financial guarantees, although those entered into by insurance companies were often longer term and more complex arrangements. The IASB considered that financial guarantees are similar in nature to financial instruments, and should be within the scope of IAS 39. However, some aspects of the more complex types of contract issued by insurance companies were not dealt with in IAS 39; furthermore, applying IAS 39 to these contracts would cause insurance companies to change their systems in advance of the completion of the IASB's insurance project. The IASB agreed that all such contracts should be included in the scope of IAS 39 except where these have been regarded by the issuer as an insurance contract and previously accounted for as such.

N44 The ASB has considered the amendment and agreed that it was appropriate to make a corresponding amendment to FRS 26.

N45 In line with the amendment to IAS 39, the amendment is effective for accounting periods commencing on or after 1 January 2006. Earlier adoption is encouraged.

N46 The IASB amended example 9 in Appendix C to IAS 37 *Provisions, Contingent Liabilities and Contingent Assets* so that it refers to accounting in accordance with IAS 39. The equivalent example is contained in FRS 12 and the ASB has made a corresponding amendment. However, as the amendment is only applicable to entities adopting FRS 26 the change is noted in Appendix B to the Standard.

IFRIC Interpretation 5

N47 In IFRIC Interpretation 5 'Rights to Interests arising from Decommissioning, Restoration and Environmental Rehabilitation Funds' (December 2004) the IASB amended the scope of IAS 39 to exclude rights to payments to reimburse the entity for expenditure required to settle a liability that it recognises as a provision in accordance with IAS 37 *Provisions, Contingent Liabilities and Contingent Assets*. The ASB has made a corresponding amendment to FRS 26.

N48 In line with the amendment to IAS 39, the amendment is effective for accounting periods commencing on or after 1 January 2006. Earlier adoption is encouraged.

Securitisation entities in the Republic of Ireland

The Board notes that the implementation of the IAS Regulation in the Republic of   **N49**
Ireland took advantage of the member state option to defer the effective date of the
Regulation to accounting periods commencing on or after 1 January 2007 for entities
with listed debt but no listed equity. The Board considered a request from the Irish
Government for an equivalent exemption from the Standard on the ground of
practicalities. It agreed to permit a deferral for one year for Irish securitisation
entities, as defined in Irish tax legislation, that have listed debt but no listed equities.*

Recognition and derecognition of financial assets and liabilities

In April 2006 the Board amended FRS 26 to include the IAS 39 material on   **N50**
recognition and derecognition into the Standard. Upon implementation of this
amendment entities within the scope of FRS 26 will apply the derecognition
requirements in FRS 26 to financial assets and liabilities and the derecognition
principles of FRS 5 to non-financial assets and liabilities.

Consolidation requirements – subsidiaries and quasi-subsidiaries

The first step in considering derecognition for a particular transaction is to ensure   **N51**
that all subsidiaries and quasi-subsidiaries are consolidated. Some respondents to the
Exposure Draft noted that the consolidation requirements relating to subsidiaries
and quasi-subsidiaries in FRS 2 and FRS 5 are not completely equivalent to those
in IAS 27 and SIC 12, leading to differences in accounting for subsidiaries under
IFRS and UK GAAP. The Board considered whether it would be appropriate to
amend the requirements in the UK to make them compliant with IFRS. It decided to
postpone this due to the following considerations: a number of the FRS 2
requirements are derived from company law (until this is amended entities applying
UK standards would also need to consider the Companies Act definition of a subsidiary); and the IASB is currently considering the long term future of SIC 12 which
may lead to an amendment of IAS 27 to clarify the situation of SPEs.

Transactions that result in assets being transferred but not derecognised

The amendment also sets out a clarification of the treatment of liabilities that are   **N52**
recognised when a transaction is entered into that transfers an asset but does not
result in derecognition; for example, where the entity retains a call option over the
asset. Application of the subsequent measurement provisions of FRS 26 to such
liabilities may not be appropriate, as there may not be any contracted cash outflows.
Paragraph 47 of FRS 26 currently exempts such liabilities from the continuing
measurement provisions of the standard where they arise from a transaction in
financial assets. The amendment would extend this exception to financial liabilities
that arise as a result of not derecognising a *non-financial* asset, under FRS 5.

Overlap between the requirements of FRS 26 and FRS 5

Some respondents to the FRED were concerned about the interaction between   **N53**
FRS 5 and FRS 26. For example Application Note F of FRS 5 can sometimes lead
to a financial asset being recognised, which the Application Note requires should be
recorded at fair value. Some constituents noted that this financial asset may need to
be recognised under the 'available for sale' category of FRS 26, thus leading to

*Editor's note: Paragraph N27 to N49 added in October 2005.

confusion as to the accounting for such assets. The Board considered paragraph 13 of FRS 5 and in its view the accounting is clear in that an entity would comply with FRS 5 in determining what assets and liabilities should be recognised. If, as a result of applying FRS 5, a financial asset or liability arises this should be accounted for in accordance with FRS 26.

N54   The Board also noted that where a transaction in a non-financial asset incorporates options, these might also be within the scope of FRS 26 and it might be unclear which standard applies. The Board's view is that such options will often fall outside the definition of derivative, as the option will be based on a non-financial variable that is specific to a party to the contract. However, where a transaction includes an option that falls within the scope of FRS 26, it should be accounted for under that standard as well as taken into account in determining the substance of the transaction in the non-financial asset.

Treatment of transactions previously accounted for under linked presentation

N55   In its deliberations over the transitional arrangements the Board considered the issue of transactions previously accounted for under linked presentation. As a result, the Board decided that if a transaction that occurred before the transition date resulted in linked presentation under FRS 5, the derecognition of the gross asset and liability must be re-examined under the new derecognition requirements of FRS 26.

Explanatory material describing non-financial assets in FRS 5

N56   As a consequence of excluding derecognition of financial assets and liabilities from the scope of FRS 5, some material in the explanation section and application notes which addresses transactions involving financial assets is no longer relevant. The consequential amendment has the effect of deleting this material, including the illustrations of the linked presentation, and application notes dealing with factoring of debt, securitised assets (which is discussed only in terms of securitisation of financial assets) and loan transfers.

N57   Some respondents to the Exposure Draft requested that the deleted material be replaced with explanatory material describing transactions in non-financial assets. The Board did not incorporate such material in this amendment. In doing so it took the following into consideration: it believes that the principles in FRS 5 are now widely understood so the examples are less necessary; and until the scope of FRS 26 is extended to all entities in the UK the examples will not completely disappear from UK standards. It also noted that additional material in FRS 5 would need to be exposed to the UK constituents which would mean a further delay in issuing this amendment.

Effective date and transitional provisions

N58   For entities within the scope of FRS 26 the recognition and derecognition material would be applicable to accounting periods commencing on or after 1 January 2007; earlier adoption is permitted.

N59   The Board took into consideration that on initial application of the new requirements, it may not be practicable to obtain the necessary information to restate all past transactions and that to require such restatement would also be inconsistent with international standards. It has, therefore, included transitional provisions equivalent to those set out in IFRS 1 – First–time Adoption of International

Financial Reporting Standards, allowing an entity to choose to apply the requirements either:

(a)   only to transactions entered into after the beginning of the comparative period for the accounting period the entity first applied the derecognition requirements of the standard; or

(b)   only to transactions entered into after an earlier date of the entity's choosing, provided information sufficient to apply the standard was obtained at the time of initial accounting for each transaction.

The Board has allowed the application of the derecognition provisions from a date related to the entity's first application of the standard rather than a fixed date; but notes that entities wishing to adopt IFRS in due course may wish to choose 1 January 2004 (or an earlier date), the equivalent transition provisions of IFRS 1, for this purpose.*   **N60**

Editor's note: Paragraphs N50 to N60 added in April 2006.

Basis for Conclusions

Basis for Conclusions

This Basis for Conclusions accompanies, but is not part of, FRS 26.

> *ASB note:* The IASB's Basis for Conclusions, which accompanies IAS 39, is set out below in full. It should be noted though that some of the discussion it contains concerns IASB requirements that have no equivalent in the UK or Republic of Ireland. Footnotes have been used to indicate corresponding requirements in the UK and Republic of Ireland where applicable.
>
> All references in this section to 'the Board' and 'Board members' are references to the IASB Board and IASB Board members.

BC1　This Basis for Conclusions summarises the International Accounting Standards Board's considerations in reaching the conclusions on revising IAS 39 *Financial Instruments: Recognition and Measurement* in 2003. Individual Board members gave greater weight to some factors than to others.

BC2　In July 2001 the Board announced that, as part of its initial agenda of technical projects, it would undertake a project to improve a number of Standards, including IAS 32 *Financial Instruments: Disclosure and Presentation* and IAS 39 *Financial Instruments: Recognition and Measurement*. The objectives of the Improvements project were to reduce the complexity in the Standards by clarifying and adding guidance, eliminating internal inconsistencies and incorporating into the Standards elements of Standing Interpretations Committee (SIC) Interpretations and IAS 39 implementation guidance. In June 2002 the Board published its proposals in an Exposure Draft of Proposed Amendments to IAS 32 *Financial Instruments: Disclosure and Presentation* and IAS 39 *Financial Instruments: Recognition and Measurement*, with a comment deadline of 14 October 2002. In August 2003 the Board published a further Exposure Draft of Proposed Amendments to IAS 39 on *Fair Value Hedge Accounting for a Portfolio Hedge of Interest Rate Risk*, with a comment deadline of 14 November 2003.

BC3　Because the Board's intention was not to reconsider the fundamental approach to the accounting for financial instruments established by IAS 32 and IAS 39, this Basis for Conclusions does not discuss requirements in IAS 39 that the Board has not reconsidered.

BACKGROUND

BC4　The original version of IAS 39 became effective for financial statements covering financial years beginning on or after 1 January 2001. It reflected a mixed measurement model in which some financial assets and financial liabilities are measured at fair value and others at cost or amortised cost, depending in part on an entity's intention in holding an instrument.

BC5　The Board recognises that accounting for financial instruments is a difficult and controversial subject. The Board's predecessor body, the International Accounting Standards Committee (IASC) began its work on the issue some 15 years ago, in 1988. During the next eight years it published two Exposure Drafts, culminating in the issue of IAS 32 on disclosure and presentation in 1995. IASC decided that its initial proposals on recognition and measurement should not be progressed to a Standard, in view of:

- the critical response they had attracted;
- evolving practices in financial instruments; and
- the developing thinking by national standard-setters.

Accordingly, in 1997 IASC published, jointly with the Canadian Accounting Standards Board, a discussion paper that proposed a different approach, namely that all financial assets and financial liabilities should be measured at fair value. The responses to that paper indicated both widespread unease with some of its proposals and that more work needed to be done before a standard requiring a full fair value approach could be contemplated.   **BC6**

In the meantime, IASC concluded that a standard on the recognition and measurement of financial instruments was needed urgently. It noted that although financial instruments were widely held and used throughout the world, few countries apart from the United States had any recognition and measurement standards for them. In addition, IASC had agreed with the International Organization of Securities Commissions (IOSCO) that it would develop a set of 'core' International Accounting Standards that could be endorsed by IOSCO for the purpose of cross-border capital raising and listing in all global markets. Those core standards included one on the recognition and measurement of financial instruments. Accordingly, IASC developed the version of IAS 39 that was issued in 2000.   **BC7**

In December 2000 a Financial Instruments Joint Working Group of Standard Setters (JWG), comprising representatives or members of accounting standardsetters and professional organisations from a range of countries, published a Draft Standard and Basis for Conclusions entitled *Financial Instruments and Similar Items*. That Draft Standard proposed far-reaching changes to accounting for financial instruments and similar items, including the measurement of virtually all financial instruments at fair value. In the light of feedback on the JWG's proposals, it is evident that much more work is needed before a comprehensive fair value accounting model could be introduced.   **BC8**

In July 2001 the Board announced that it would undertake a project to improve the existing requirements on the accounting for financial instruments in IAS 32 and IAS 39. The improvements deal with practice issues identified by audit firms, national standard-setters, regulators and others, and issues identified in the IAS 39 implementation guidance process or by IASB staff.   **BC9**

In June 2002 the Board published an Exposure Draft of proposed amendments to IAS 32 and IAS 39 for a 116-day comment period. More than 170 comment letters were received.   **BC10**

Subsequently, the Board took steps to enable constituents to inform it better about the main issues arising out of the comment process, and to enable the Board to explain its views of the issues and its tentative conclusions. These consultations included: **BC11**
(a)   discussions with the Standards Advisory Council on the main issues raised in the comment process.
(b)   nine roundtable discussions with constituents during March 2003 conducted in Brussels and London. Over 100 organisations and individuals took part in those discussions.
(c)   discussions with the Board's liaison standard-setters of the issues raised in the roundtable discussions.

(d)   meetings between members of the Board and its staff and various groups of constituents to explore further issues raised in comment letters and at the roundtable discussions.

BC11A   Some of the comment letters on the June 2002 Exposure Draft and participants in the roundtables raised a significant issue for which the June 2003 Exposure Draft had not proposed any changes. This was hedge accounting for a portfolio hedge of interest rate risk (sometimes referred to as 'macro hedging') and the related question of the treatment in hedge accounting of deposits with a demand feature (sometimes referred to as 'demand deposits' or 'demandable liabilities'). In particular, some were concerned that it was very difficult to achieve fair value hedge accounting for a macro hedge in accordance with previous versions of IAS 39.

BC11B   In the light of these concerns, the Board decided to explore whether and how IAS 39 might be amended to enable fair value hedge accounting to be used more readily for a portfolio hedge of interest rate risk. This resulted in a further Exposure Draft of Proposed Amendments to IAS 39 that was published in August 2003 and on which more than 120 comment letters were received. The amendments proposed in the Exposure Draft were finalised in March 2004.

BC11C   After those amendments were issued in March 2004 the Board received further comments from constituents calling for further amendments to the Standard. In particular, as a result of continuing discussions with constituents, the Board became aware that some, including prudential supervisors of banks, securities companies and insurers, were concerned that the fair value option might be used inappropriately. These constituents were concerned that:

(a)   entities might apply the fair value option to financial assets or financial liabilities whose fair value is not verifiable. If so, because the valuation of these financial assets and financial liabilities is subjective, entities might determine their fair value in a way that inappropriately affects profit or loss.

(b)   the use of the option might increase, rather than decrease, volatility in profit or loss, for example if an entity applied the option to only one part of a matched position.

(c)   if an entity applied the fair value option to financial liabilities, it might result in an entity recognising gains or losses in profit or loss associated with changes in its own creditworthiness.

In response to those concerns, the Board published in April 2004 an Exposure Draft of proposed restrictions to the fair value option*. In March 2005 the Board held a series of round-table meetings to discuss proposals with invited constituents. As a result of this process, the Board issued an amendment to IAS 39 in June 2005 relating to the fair value option.†

BC12   The Board did not reconsider the fundamental approach to accounting for financial instruments contained in IAS 39. Some of the complexity in existing requirements is inevitable in a mixed measurement model based in part on management's intentions for holding financial instruments and given the complexity of finance concepts and fair value estimation issues. The amendments reduce some of the complexity by clarifying the Standard, eliminating internal inconsistencies and incorporating additional guidance into the Standard.

*ASB Footnote: *equivalent proposals were published in the UK by the ASB as part of FRED 30 Third Supplement.*

†*Editor's note: BC11C added with effect from 1 January 2006.*

The amendments also eliminate or mitigate some differences between IAS 39 and **BC13** US GAAP related to the measurement of financial instruments. Already, the measurement requirements in IAS 39 are, to a large extent, similar to equivalent requirements in US GAAP, in particular, those in FASB SFAS 114 *Accounting by Creditors for Impairment of a Loan*, SFAS 115 *Accounting for Certain Investments in Debt and Equity Securities* and SFAS 133 *Accounting for Derivative Instruments and Hedging Activities*.

The Board will continue its consideration of issues related to the accounting for **BC14** financial instruments. However, it expects that the basic principles in the improved IAS 39 will be in place for a considerable period.

SCOPE

Loan Commitments (paragraphs 2(i) and 4)

Loan commitments are firm commitments to provide credit under prespecified terms **BC15** and conditions. In the IAS 39 implementation guidance process, the question was raised whether a bank's loan commitments are derivatives accounted for at fair value under IAS 39. This question arises because a commitment to make a loan at a specified rate of interest during a fixed period of time meets the definition of a derivative. In effect, it is a written option for the potential borrower to obtain a loan at a specified rate.

To simplify the accounting for holders and issuers of loan commitments, the Board **BC16** decided to exclude particular loan commitments from the scope of IAS 39. The effect of the exclusion is that an entity will not recognise and measure changes in fair value of these loan commitments that result from changes in market interest rates or credit spreads. This is consistent with the measurement of the loan that results if the holder of the loan commitment exercises its right to obtain financing, because changes in market interest rates do not affect the measurement of an asset measured at amortised cost (assuming it is not designated in a category other than loans and receivables).

However, the Board decided that an entity should be permitted to measure a loan **BC17** commitment at fair value with changes in fair value recognised in profit or loss on the basis of designation at inception of the loan commitment as a financial liability through profit or loss. This may be appropriate, for example, if the entity manages risk exposures related to loan commitments on a fair value basis.

The Board further decided that a loan commitment should be excluded from the **BC18** scope of IAS 39 only if it cannot be settled net. If the value of a loan commitment can be settled net in cash or another financial instrument, including when the entity has a past practice of selling the resulting loan assets shortly after origination, it is difficult to justify its exclusion from the requirement in IAS 39 to measure at fair value similar instruments that meet the definition of a derivative.

Some comments received on the Exposure Draft disagreed with the Board's proposal **BC19** that an entity that has a past practice of selling the assets resulting from its loan commitments shortly after origination should apply IAS 39 to all of its loan commitments. The Board considered this concern and agreed that the words in the Exposure Draft did not reflect the Board's intention. Thus, the Board clarified that if an entity has a past practice of selling the assets resulting from its loan commitments shortly after origination, it applies IAS 39 only to its loan commitments in the same class.

BC20 Finally, the Board decided that commitments to provide a loan at a below-market interest rate should be initially measured at fair value, and subsequently measured at the higher of (a) the amount that would be recognised under IAS 37* and (b) the amount initially recognised less, where appropriate, cumulative amortisation recognised in accordance with IAS 18 *Revenue*†. It noted that without such a requirement, liabilities that result from such commitments might not be recognised in the balance sheet, because in many cases no cash consideration is received.

BC20A As discussed in paragraphs BC21–BC23E, the Board amended IAS 39 in 2005 to address financial guarantee contracts. In making those amendments, the Board moved the material on loan commitments from the scope section of the Standard to the section on subsequent measurement (paragraph 47(d)). The purpose of this change was to rationalise the presentation of this material without making substantive changes.

Financial guarantee contracts
(paragraphs 2(e), 9, 47(c), AG4 and AG4A)

BC21 In finalising IFRS 4 *Insurance Contracts*‡ in early 2004, the Board reached the following conclusions:

(a) Financial guarantee contracts can have various legal forms, such as that of a guarantee, some types of letter of credit, a credit default contract or an insurance contract. However, although this difference in legal form may in some cases reflect differences in substance, the accounting for these instruments should not depend on their legal form.

(b) If a financial guarantee contract is not an insurance contract, as defined in IFRS 4, it should be within the scope of IAS 39. This was the case before the Board finalised IFRS 4.

(c) As required before the Board finalised IFRS 4, if a financial guarantee contract was entered into or retained on transferring to another party financial assets or financial liabilities within the scope of IAS 39, the issuer should apply IAS 39 to that contract even if it is an insurance contract, as defined in IFRS 4.

(d) Unless (c) applies, the following treatment is appropriate for a financial guarantee contract that meets the definition of an insurance contract:

    (i) At inception, the issuer of a financial guarantee contract has a recognisable liability and should measure it at fair value. If a financial guarantee contract was issued in a stand-alone arm's length transaction to an unrelated party, its fair value at inception is likely to equal the premium received, unless there is evidence to the contrary.

    (ii) Subsequently, the issuer should measure the contract at the higher of the amount determined in accordance with IAS 37 *Provisions, Contingent Liabilities and Contingent Assets*§ and the amount initially recognised less,

---

*ASB footnote: the equivalent standard in the UK and the Republic of Ireland is FRS 12 Provisions, Contingent Liabilities and Contingent Assets.

†ASB footnote: the requirements of IAS 18 are more specific than those of the equivalent in the UK and Republic of Ireland, Application Note G Revenue Recognition *to FRS 5* Reporting the Substance of Transactions.

‡ASB footnote: There is no UK standard equivalent to IFRS 4; the IFRS 4 definition of insurance contract is set out in Appendix C to FRS 26.

§ASB footnote: The equivalent standard in the UK and the Republic of Ireland is FRS 12 Provisions, Contingent Liabilities and Contingent Assets.

when appropriate, cumulative amortisation recognised in accordance with IAS 18 *Revenue*.*

Mindful of the need to develop a 'stable platform' of Standards for 2005, the Board finalised IFRS 4 in early 2004 without specifying the accounting for these contracts and then published an Exposure Draft *Financial Guarantee Contracts and Credit Insurance* in July 2004 to expose for public comment the conclusion set out in paragraph BC21(d). The Board set a comment deadline of 8 October 2004 and received more than 60 comment letters. Before reviewing the comment letters, the Board held a public education session at which it received briefings from representatives of the International Credit Insurance & Surety Association and of the Association of Financial Guaranty Insurers. **BC22**

Some respondents to the Exposure Draft of July 2004 argued that there were important economic differences between credit insurance contracts and other forms of contract that met the proposed definition of a financial guarantee contract. However, both in developing the Exposure Draft and in subsequently discussing the comments received, the Board was unable to identify differences that would justify differences in accounting treatment. **BC23**

Some respondents to the Exposure Draft of July 2004 noted that some credit insurance contracts contain features, such as cancellation and renewal rights and profit-sharing features, that the Board will not address until phase II of its project on insurance contracts. They argued that the Exposure Draft did not give enough guidance to enable them to account for these features. The Board concluded it could not address such features in the short term. The Board noted that when credit insurers issue credit insurance contracts, they typically recognise a liability measured as either the premium received or an estimate of the expected losses. However, the Board was concerned that some other issuers of financial guarantee contracts might argue that no recognisable liability existed at inception. To provide a temporary solution that balances these competing concerns, the Board decided the following: **BC23A**

(a) If the issuer of financial guarantee contracts has previously asserted explicitly that it regards such contracts as insurance contracts and has used accounting applicable to insurance contracts, the issuer may elect to apply either IAS 39 or IFRS 4 to such financial guarantee contracts.

(b) In all other cases, the issuer of a financial guarantee contract should apply IAS 39.

The Board does not regard criteria such as those described in paragraph BC23A(a) as suitable for the long term, because they can lead to different accounting for contracts that have similar economic effects. However, the Board could not find a more compelling approach to resolve its concerns for the short term. Moreover, although the criteria described in paragraph BC23A(a) may appear imprecise, the Board believes that the criteria would provide a clear answer in the vast majority of cases. Paragraph AG4A gives guidance on the application of those criteria. **BC23B**

The Board considered convergence with US GAAP. In US GAAP, the requirements for financial guarantee contracts (other than those covered by US standards specific to the insurance sector) are in FASB Interpretation 45 *Guarantor's Accounting and Disclosure Requirements for Guarantees, Including Indirect Guarantees of Indebtedness of Others* (FIN 45). The recognition and measurement requirements of FIN 45 **BC23C**

*ASB footnote: *The requirements of IAS 18 are more specific than those of the equivalent in the UK and Republic of Ireland, Application Note G* Revenue recognition *to FRS 5* Reporting the Substance of transactions.

do not apply to guarantees issued between parents and their subsidiaries, between entities under common control, or by a parent or subsidiary on behalf of a subsidiary or the parent. Some respondents to the Exposure Draft of July 2004 asked the Board to provide a similar exemption. They argued that the requirement to recognise these financial guarantee contracts in separate or individual financial statements would cause costs disproportionate to the likely benefits, given that intragroup transactions are eliminated on consolidation. However, to avoid the omission of material liabilities from separate or individual financial statements, the Board did not create such an exemption.

BC23D   The Board issued the amendments for financial guarantee contracts in August 2005. After those amendments, the recognition and measurement requirements for financial guarantee contracts within the scope of IAS 39 are consistent with FIN 45 in some areas, but differ in others:

(a)   Like FIN 45, IAS 39 requires initial recognition at fair value.

(b)   IAS 39 requires systematic amortisation, in accordance with IAS 18, of the liability recognised initially. This is compatible with FIN 45, though FIN 45 contains less prescriptive requirements on subsequent measurement. Both IAS 39 and FIN 45 include a liability adequacy (or loss recognition) test, although the tests differ because of underlying differences in the Standards to which those tests refer (IAS 37 and SFAS 5).

(c)   Like FIN 45, IAS 39 permits a different treatment for financial guarantee contracts issued by insurers.

(d)   Unlike FIN 45, IAS 39 does not contain exemptions for parents, subsidiaries or other entities under common control. However, any differences are reflected only in the separate or individual financial statements of the parent, subsidiaries or common control entities.

BC23E   Some respondents to the Exposure Draft of July 2004 asked for guidance on the treatment of financial guarantee contracts by the holder. However, this was beyond the limited scope of the project.*

Contracts to Buy or Sell a Non-Financial Item (paragraphs 5-7 and AG10)

BC24   Before the amendments, IAS 39 and IAS 32 were not consistent with respect to the circumstances in which a commodity-based contract meets the definition of a financial instrument and is accounted for as a derivative. The Board concluded that the amendments should make them consistent on the basis of the notion that a contract to buy or sell a non-financial item should be accounted for as a derivative when it (i) can be settled net or by exchanging financial instruments and (ii) is not held for the purpose of receipt or delivery of the non-financial item in accordance with the entity's expected purchase, sale or usage requirements (a 'normal' purchase or sale). In addition, the Board concluded that the notion of when a contract can be settled net should include contracts:

(a)   where the entity has a practice of settling similar contracts net in cash or another financial instrument or by exchanging financial instruments;

(b)   for which the entity has a practice of taking delivery of the underlying and selling it within a short period after delivery for the purpose of generating a profit from short-term fluctuations in price or dealer's margin; and

(c)   in which the non-financial item that is the subject of the contract is readily convertible to cash.

*Editor's note: BC20A to BC23E added with effect from 1 January 2006.

Because practices of settling net or taking delivery of the underlying and selling it within a short period after delivery also indicate that the contracts are not 'normal' purchases or sales, such contracts are within the scope of IAS 39 and are accounted for as derivatives. The Board also decided to clarify that a written option that can be settled net in cash or another financial instrument, or by exchanging financial instruments, is within the scope of the Standard and cannot qualify as a 'normal' purchase or sale.

DEFINITIONS

Loans and Receivables (paragraphs 9, 46(a) and AG26)

The principal difference between loans and receivables and other financial assets is that loans and receivables are not subject to the tainting provisions that apply to held-to-maturity investments. Loans and receivables that are not held for trading may be measured at amortised cost even if an entity does not have the positive intention and ability to hold the loan asset until maturity. **BC25**

The Board decided that the ability to measure a financial asset at amortised cost without consideration of the entity's intention and ability to hold the asset until maturity is most appropriate when there is no liquid market for the asset. It is less appropriate to extend the category to debt instruments traded in liquid markets. The distinction for measurement purposes between liquid debt instruments that are acquired upon issue and liquid debt instruments that are acquired shortly afterwards is difficult to justify on conceptual grounds. Why should a liquid debt instrument that is purchased on the day of issue be treated differently from a liquid debt instrument that is purchased one week after issue? Why should it not be possible to classify a liquid debt instrument that is acquired directly from the issuer as available for sale, with fair value gains and losses recognised in equity? Why should a liquid debt instrument that is bought shortly after it is issued be subject to tainting provisions, if a liquid debt instrument that is bought at the time of issue is not subject to tainting provisions? **BC26**

The Board therefore decided to add a condition to the definition of a loan or receivable. More specifically, an entity should not be permitted to classify as a loan or receivable an investment in a debt instrument that is quoted in an active market. For such an investment, an entity should be required to demonstrate its positive intention and ability to hold the investment until maturity to be permitted to measure the investment at amortised cost by classifying it as held to maturity. **BC27**

The Board considered comments received on the proposal in the Exposure Draft (which was unchanged from the requirement in the original IAS 39) that 'loans and receivables' must be originated (rather than purchased) to meet that classification. Such comments suggested that purchased loans should be eligible for classification as loans and receivables, for example, if an entity buys a loan portfolio, and the purchased loans meet the definition other than the fact that they were purchased. Such comments also noted that (a) some entities typically manage purchased and originated loans together, and (b) there are systems problems of segregating purchased loans from originated loans given that a distinction between them is likely to be made only for accounting purposes. In the light of these concerns, the Board decided to remove the requirement that loans or receivables must be originated by the entity to meet the definition of 'loans and receivables'. **BC28**

However, the Board was concerned that removing this requirement might result in some instruments that should be measured at fair value meeting the definition of **BC29** loans and receivables and thus being measured at amortised cost. In particular, the Board was concerned that this would be the case for a debt instrument in which the purchaser may not recover its investment, for example a fixed rate interest-only strip created in a securitisation and subject to prepayment risk. The Board therefore decided to exclude from the definition of loans and receivables instruments for which the holder may not recover substantially all of its initial investment, other than because of credit deterioration. Such assets are accounted for as available for sale or at fair value through profit or loss.

Effective Interest Rate (paragraphs 9 and AG5-AG8)

BC30   The Board considered whether the effective interest rate for all financial instruments should be calculated on the basis of estimated cash flows (consistently with the original IAS 39) or whether the use of estimated cash flows should be restricted to groups of financial instruments with contractual cash flows being used for individual financial instruments. The Board agreed to reconfirm the position in the original IAS 39 because it achieves consistent application of the effective interest method throughout the Standard.

BC31   The Board noted that future cash flows and the expected life can be reliably estimated for most financial assets and financial liabilities, in particular for a group of similar financial assets or similar financial liabilities. However, the Board acknowledged that in some rare cases it might not be possible to estimate the timing or amount of future cash flows reliably. It therefore decided to require that if it is not possible to estimate reliably the future cash flows or the expected life of a financial instrument, the entity should use contractual cash flows over the full contractual term of the financial instrument.

BC32   The Board also decided to clarify that expected future defaults should not be included in estimates of cash flows because this would be a departure from the incurred loss model for impairment recognition. At the same time, the Board noted that in some cases, for example, when a financial asset is acquired at a deep discount, credit losses have occurred and are reflected in the price. If an entity does not take into account such credit losses in the calculation of the effective interest rate, the entity would recognise a higher interest income than that inherent in the price paid. The Board therefore decided to clarify that such credit losses are included in the estimated cash flows when computing the effective interest rate.

BC33   The revised IAS 39 refers to all fees "that are an integral part of the effective interest rate". The Board included this reference to clarify that IAS 39 relates only to those fees that are determined to be an integral part of the effective interest rate in accordance with IAS 18.

BC34   Some commentators noted that it was not always clear how to interpret the requirement in the original IAS 39 that the effective interest rate must be based on discounting cash flows through maturity or the next market-based repricing date. In particular, it was not always clear whether fees, transaction costs and other premiums or discounts included in the calculation of the effective interest rate should be amortised over the period until maturity or the period to the next market-based repricing date.

BC35   For consistency with the estimated cash flows approach, the Board decided to clarify that the effective interest rate is calculated over the expected life of the instrument or, when applicable, a shorter period. A shorter period is used when the variable (eg interest rates) to which the fee, transaction costs, discount or premium relates is repriced to market rates before the expected maturity of the instrument. In such a case, the appropriate amortisation period is the period to the next such repricing date.

Accounting for a Change in Estimates

The Board considered the accounting for a change in the estimates used in calcu- **BC36** lating the effective interest rate. The Board agreed that if an entity revises its estimates of payments or receipts, it should adjust the carrying amount of the financial instrument to reflect actual and revised estimated cash flows. The adjustment is recognised as income or expense in profit or loss. The entity recalculates the carrying amount by computing the present value of remaining cash flows at the original effective interest rate of the financial instrument. The Board noted that this approach has the practical advantage that it does not require recalculation of the effective interest rate, ie the entity simply recognises the remaining cash flows at the original rate. As a result, this approach avoids a possible conflict with the requirement when assessing impairment to discount estimated cash flows using the original effective interest rate.

EMBEDDED DERIVATIVES

Embedded Foreign Currency Derivatives (paragraphs 10 and AG33(d))

A rationale for the embedded derivatives requirements is that an entity should not be **BC37** able to circumvent the recognition and measurement requirements for derivatives merely by embedding a derivative in a non-derivative financial instrument or other contract, for example, a commodity forward in a debt instrument. To achieve consistency in accounting for such embedded derivatives, all derivatives embedded in financial instruments that are not measured at fair value with gains and losses recognised in profit or loss ought to be accounted for separately as derivatives. However, as a practical expedient IAS 39 provides that an embedded derivative need not be separated if it is regarded as closely related to its host contract. When the embedded derivative bears a close economic relationship to the host contract, such as a cap or a floor on the interest rate on a loan, it is less likely that the derivative was embedded to achieve a desired accounting result.

The original IAS 39 specified that a foreign currency derivative embedded in a non- **BC38** financial host contract (such as a supply contract denominated in a foreign currency) was not separated if it required payments denominated in the currency of the primary economic environment in which any substantial party to the contract operates (their functional currencies) or the currency in which the price of the related good or service that is acquired or delivered is routinely denominated in international commerce (such as the US dollar for crude oil transactions). Such foreign currency derivatives are regarded as bearing such a close economic relationship to their host contracts that they do not have to be separated.

The requirement to separate embedded foreign currency derivatives may be bur- **BC39** densome for entities that operate in economies in which business contracts denominated in a foreign currency are common. For example, entities domiciled in small countries may find it convenient to denominate business contracts with entities from other small countries in an internationally liquid currency (such as the US dollar, euro or yen) rather than the local currency of any of the parties to the transaction. In addition, an entity operating in a hyperinflationary economy may use a price list in a hard currency to protect against inflation, for example, an entity that has a foreign operation in a hyperinflationary economy that denominates local contracts in the functional currency of the parent.

BC40   In revising IAS 39, the Board concluded that an embedded foreign currency derivative may be integral to the contractual arrangements in the cases mentioned in the previous paragraph. It decided that a foreign currency derivative in a contract should not be required to be separated if it is denominated in a currency that is commonly used in business transactions (that are not financial instruments) in the environment in which the transaction takes place. A foreign currency derivative would be viewed as closely related to the host contract if the currency is commonly used in local business transactions, for example, when monetary amounts are viewed by the general population not in terms of the local currency but in terms of a relatively stable foreign currency, and prices may be quoted in that foreign currency (see IAS 29 *Financial Reporting in Hyperinflationary Economies**).

RECOGNITION AND DERECOGNITION

Derecognition of a Financial Asset (paragraphs 15–37)

The Original IAS 39

BC41   Under the original IAS 39, several concepts governed when a financial asset should be derecognised. It was not always clear when and in what order to apply these concepts. As a result, the derecognition requirements in the original IAS 39 were not applied consistently in practice.

BC42   As an example, the original IAS 39 was unclear about the extent to which risks and rewards of a transferred asset should be considered for the purpose of determining whether derecognition is appropriate and how risks and rewards should be assessed. In some cases (eg transfers with total returns swaps or unconditional written put options), the Standard specifically indicated whether derecognition was appropriate, whereas in others (eg credit guarantees) it was unclear. Also, some questioned whether the assessment should focus on risks and rewards or only risks and how different risks and rewards should be aggregated and weighed.

BC43   To illustrate, assume an entity sells a portfolio of short-term receivables of CU100† and provides a guarantee to the buyer for credit losses up to a specified amount (say CU20) that is less than the total amount of the receivables, but higher than the amount of expected losses (say CU5). In this case, should (a) the entire portfolio continue to be recognised, (b) the portion that is guaranteed continue to be recognised or (c) the portfolio be derecognised in full and a guarantee be recognised as a financial liability? The original IAS 39 did not give a clear answer and the IAS 39 Implementation Guidance Committee—a group set up by the Board's predecessor body to resolve interpretive issues raised in practice—was unable to reach an agreement on how IAS 39 should be applied in this case. In developing proposals for improvements to IAS 39, the Board concluded that it was important that IAS 39 should provide clear and consistent guidance on how to account for such a transaction.

*****ASB footnote**: the ASB is implementing IAS 29 as FRS 24 (IAS 29) Financial Reporting in Hyperinflationary Economies.

†*In this Basis for Conclusions, monetary amounts are denominated in 'currency units' (CU).*

Exposure Draft

To resolve the problems, the Exposure Draft proposed an approach to derecognition **BC44** under which a transferor of a financial asset continues to recognise that asset to the extent the transferor has a continuing involvement in it. Continuing involvement could be established in two ways: (a) a reacquisition provision (such as a call option, put option or repurchase agreement) and (b) a provision to pay or receive compensation based on changes in value of the transferred asset (such as a credit guarantee or net cash settled option).

The purpose of the approach proposed in the Exposure Draft was to facilitate **BC45** consistent implementation and application of IAS 39 by eliminating conflicting concepts and establishing an unambiguous, more internally consistent and workable approach to derecognition. The main benefits of the proposed approach were that it would greatly clarify IAS 39 and provide transparency on the face of the balance sheet about any continuing involvement in a transferred asset.

Comments Received

Many respondents agreed that there were inconsistencies in the existing derecogni- **BC46** tion requirements in IAS 39. However, there was limited support for the continuing involvement approach proposed in the Exposure Draft. Respondents expressed conceptual and practical concerns, including:

(a)   any benefits of the proposed changes did not outweigh the burden of adopting a different approach that had its own set of (as yet unidentified and unsolved) problems;
(b)   the proposed approach was a fundamental change from that in the original IAS 39;
(c)   the proposal did not achieve convergence with US GAAP;
(d)   the proposal was untested; and
(e)   the proposal was not consistent with the *Framework**

Many respondents expressed the view that the basic approach in the original IAS 39 **BC47** should be retained in the revised Standard and the inconsistencies removed. The reasons included: (a) the existing IAS 39 was proven to be reasonable in concept and operational in practice and (b) the approach should not be changed until the Board developed an alternative comprehensive approach.

Revisions to IAS 39

In response to the comments received, the Board decided to revert to the derecog- **BC48** nition concepts in the original IAS 39 and to clarify how and in what order the concepts should be applied. In particular, the Board decided that an evaluation of the transfer of risks and rewards should precede an evaluation of the transfer of control for all types of transactions.

Although the structure and wording of the derecognition requirements have been **BC49** substantially amended, the Board concluded that the requirements in the revised IAS 39 are not substantially different from those in the original IAS 39. In support of this conclusion, it noted that the application of the requirements in the revised IAS 39 generally results in answers that could have been obtained under the original

---

*ASB footnote: *The equivalent document in the UK and Republic of Ireland to the IASB's* Framework *is the ASB's* Statement of Principles for Financial Reporting. *Although the Statement of Principles is very similar to the* Framework, *it is not identical.*

IAS 39. In addition, although there will be a need to apply judgement to evaluate whether substantially all risks and rewards have been retained, this type of judgement is not new compared with the original IAS 39. However, the revised requirements clarify the application of the concepts in circumstances in which it was previously unclear how IAS 39 should be applied. The Board concluded that it would be inappropriate to revert to the original IAS 39 without such clarifications.

BC50 The Board also decided to include guidance in the Standard that clarifies how to evaluate the concepts of risks and rewards and of control. The Board regards such guidance as important to provide a framework for applying the concepts in IAS 39. Although judgement is still necessary to apply the concepts in practice, the guidance should increase consistency in how the concepts are applied.

BC51 More specifically, the Board decided that the transfer of risks and rewards should be evaluated by comparing the entity's exposure before and after the transfer to the variability in the amounts and timing of the net cash flows of the transferred asset. If the entity's exposure, on a present value basis, has not changed significantly, the entity would conclude that it has retained substantially all risks and rewards. In this case, the Board concluded that the asset should continue to be recognised. This accounting treatment is consistent with the treatment of repurchase transactions and some assets subject to deep in-the-money options under the original IAS 39. It is also consistent with how some interpreted the original IAS 39 when an entity sells a portfolio of short-term receivables but retains all substantive risks through the issue of a guarantee to compensate for all expected credit losses (see the example in paragraph BC43).

BC52 The Board decided that control should be evaluated by looking to whether the transferee has the practical ability to sell the asset. If the transferee can sell the asset (eg because the asset is readily obtainable in the market and the transferee can obtain a replacement asset should it need to return the asset to the transferor), the transferor has not retained control because the transferor does not control the transferee's use of the asset. If the transferee cannot sell the asset (eg because the transferor has a call option and the asset is not readily obtainable in the market, so that the transferee cannot obtain a replacement asset), the transferor has retained control because the transferee is not free to use the asset as its own.

BC53 The original IAS 39 also did not contain guidance on when a part of a financial asset could be considered for derecognition. The Board decided to include such guidance in the Standard to clarify the issue. It decided that an entity should apply the derecognition principles to a part of a financial asset only if that part contains no risks and rewards relating to the part not being considered for derecognition. Accordingly, a part of a financial asset is considered for derecognition only if it comprises:

(a)   only specifically identified cash flows from a financial asset (or a group of similar financial assets);

(b)   only a fully proportionate (pro rata) share of the cash flows from a financial asset (or a group of similar financial assets); or

(c)   only a fully proportionate (pro rata) share of specifically identified cash flows from a financial asset (or a group of similar financial assets).

In all other cases the derecognition principles are applied to the financial asset in its entirety.

Arrangements Under Which an Entity Retains the Contractual Rights to Receive the Cash Flows of a Financial Asset but Assumes a Contractual Obligation to Pay the Cash Flows to One or More Recipients (paragraph 19)

The original IAS 39 did not provide explicit guidance about the extent to which **BC54** derecognition is appropriate for contractual arrangements in which an entity retains its contractual right to receive the cash flows from an asset, but assumes a contractual obligation to pay those cash flows to another entity (a 'pass-through arrangement'). Questions were raised in practice about the appropriate accounting treatment and divergent interpretations evolved for more complex structures.

To illustrate the issue using a simple example, assume the following. Entity A makes **BC55** a five-year interest-bearing loan (the 'original asset') of CU100 to Entity B. Entity A then enters into an agreement with Entity C in which, in exchange for a cash payment of CU90, Entity A agrees to pass to Entity C 90 per cent of all principal and interest payments collected from Entity B (as, when and if collected). Entity A accepts no obligation to make any payments to Entity C other than 90 per cent of exactly what has been received from Entity B. Entity A provides no guarantee to Entity C about the performance of the loan and has no rights to retain 90 per cent of the cash collected from Entity B nor any obligation to pay cash to Entity C if cash has not been received from Entity B. In the example above, does Entity A have a loan asset of CU100 and a liability of CU90 or does it have an asset of CU10? To make the example more complex, what if Entity A first transfers the loan to a consolidated special purpose entity (SPE), which in turn passes through to investors the cash flows from the asset? Does the accounting treatment change because Entity A first sold the asset to an SPE?

To address these issues, the Exposure Draft of proposed amendments to IAS 39 **BC56** included guidance to clarify under which conditions pass-through arrangements can be treated as a transfer of the underlying financial asset. The Board concluded that an entity does not have an asset and a liability, as defined in the *Framework*, when it enters into an arrangement to pass through cash flows from an asset and that arrangement meets specified conditions. In these cases, the entity acts more as an agent of the eventual recipients of the cash flows than as an owner of the asset. Accordingly, to the extent that those conditions are met the arrangement is treated as a transfer and considered for derecognition even though the entity may continue to collect cash flows from the asset. Conversely, to the extent the conditions are not met, the entity acts more as an owner of the asset with the result that the asset should continue to be recognised.

Respondents to the Exposure Draft were generally supportive of the proposed **BC57** changes. Some respondents asked for further clarification of the requirements and the interaction with the requirements for consolidation of special purpose entities (in SIC-12)*. Respondents in the securitisation industry noted that under the proposed guidance many securitisation structures would not qualify for derecognition.

Considering these and other comments, the Board decided to proceed with its pro- **BC58** posals to issue guidance on pass-through arrangements and to clarify that guidance in finalising the revised IAS 39.

ASB footnote: under FRS 26, special purpose entities are consolidated if they meet the definition of subsidiary undertaking in FRS 2 'Accounting for Subsidiary Undertakings' or quasi-subsidiary in FRS 5 'Reporting the Substance of Transactions'.

BC59   The Board concluded that the following three conditions must be met for treating a contractual arrangement to pass through cash flows from a financial asset as a transfer of that asset:

(a)   The entity has no obligation to pay amounts to the eventual recipients unless it collects equivalent amounts from the original asset. However, the entity is allowed to make short-term advances to the eventual recipient so long as it has the right of full recovery of the amount lent plus accrued interest.

(b)   The entity is prohibited by the terms of the transfer contract from selling or pledging the original asset other than as security to the eventual recipients for the obligation to pay them cash flows.

(c)   The entity has an obligation to remit any cash flows it collects on behalf of the eventual recipients without material delay. In addition, during the short settlement period, the entity is not entitled to reinvest such cash flows except for investments in cash or cash equivalents and where any interest earned from such investments is remitted to the eventual recipients.

BC60   These conditions follow from the definitions of assets and liabilities in the *Framework*. Condition (a) indicates that the transferor has no liability (because there is no present obligation to pay cash), and conditions (b) and (c) indicate that the transferor has no asset (because the transferor does not control the future economic benefits associated with the transferred asset).

BC61   The Board decided that the derecognition tests that apply to other transfers of financial assets (ie the tests of transferring substantially all the risks and rewards and control) should also apply to arrangements to pass through cash flows that meet the three conditions but do not involve a fully proportional share of all or specifically identified cash flows. Thus, if the three conditions are met and the entity passes on a fully proportional share, either of all cash flows (as in the example in paragraph BC55) or of specifically identified cash flows (eg 10 per cent of all interest cash flows), the proportion sold is derecognised, provided the entity has transferred substantially all the risks and rewards of ownership. Thus, in the example in paragraph BC55, Entity A would report a loan asset of CU10 and derecognise CU90. Similarly, if an entity enters into an arrangement that meets the three conditions above, but the arrangement is not on a fully proportionate basis, the contractual arrangement would have to meet the general derecognition conditions to qualify for derecognition. This ensures consistency in the application of the derecognition model, whether a transaction is structured as a transfer of the contractual right to receive the cash flows of a financial asset or as an arrangement to pass through cash flows.

BC62   To illustrate a disproportionate arrangement using a simple example, assume the following. Entity A originates a portfolio of five-year interest-bearing loans of CU10,000. Entity A then enters into an agreement with Entity C in which, in exchange for a cash payment of CU9,000, Entity A agrees to pay to Entity C the first CU9,000 (plus interest) of cash collected from the loan portfolio. Entity A retains rights to the last CU1,000 (plus interest), ie it retains a subordinated residual interest. If Entity A collects, say, only CU8,000 of its loans of CU10,000 because some debtors default, Entity A would pass on to Entity C all of the CU8,000 collected and Entity A keeps nothing of the CU8,000 collected. If Entity A collects CU9,500, it passes CU9,000 to Entity C and retains CU500. In this case, if Entity A retains substantially all the risks and rewards of ownership because the subordinated retained interest absorbs all of the likely variability in net cash flows, the loans continue to be recognised in their entirety even if the three pass-through conditions are met.

The Board recognises that many securitisations may fail to qualify for derecognition either because one or more of the three conditions in paragraph 19 are not met or because the entity has retained substantially all the risks and rewards of ownership. **BC63**

Whether a transfer of a financial asset qualifies for derecognition does not differ depending on whether the transfer is direct to investors or through a consolidated SPE or trust that obtains the financial assets and, in turn, transfers a portion of those financial assets to third party investors. **BC64**

Transfers that Do Not Qualify for Derecognition (paragraph 29)

The original IAS 39 did not provide guidance about how to account for a transfer of a financial asset that does not qualify for derecognition. The amendments include such guidance. To ensure that the accounting reflects the rights and obligations that the transferor has in relation to the transferred asset, there is a need to consider the accounting for the asset as well as the accounting for the associated liability. **BC65**

When an entity retains substantially all the risks and rewards of the asset (eg in a repurchase transaction), there are generally no special accounting considerations because the entity retains upside and downside exposure to gains and losses resulting from the transferred asset. Therefore, the asset continues to be recognised in its entirety and the proceeds received are recognised as a liability. Similarly, the entity continues to recognise any income from the asset along with any expense incurred on the associated liability. **BC66**

Continuing Involvement in a Transferred Asset (paragraphs 30–35)

The Board decided that if the entity determines that it has neither retained nor transferred substantially all of the risks and rewards of an asset and that it has retained control, the entity should continue to recognise the asset to the extent of its continuing involvement. This is to reflect the transferor's continuing exposure to the risks and rewards of the asset and that this exposure is not related to the entire asset, but is limited in amount. The Board noted that precluding derecognition to the extent of the continuing involvement is useful to users of financial statements in such cases, because it reflects the entity's retained exposure to the risks and rewards of the financial asset better than full derecognition. **BC67**

When the entity transfers some significant risks and rewards and retains others and derecognition is precluded because the entity retains control of the transferred asset, the entity no longer retains all the upside and downside exposure to gains and losses resulting from the transferred asset. Therefore, the revised IAS 39 requires the asset and the associated liability to be measured in a way that ensures that any changes in value of the transferred asset that are not attributed to the entity are not recognised by the entity. **BC68**

For example, special measurement and income recognition issues arise if derecognition is precluded because the transferor has retained a call option or written a put option and the asset is measured at fair value. In those situations, in the absence of additional guidance, application of the general measurement and income recognition requirements for financial assets and financial liabilities in IAS 39 may result in accounting that does not represent the transferor's rights and obligations related to the transfer. **BC69**

As another example, if the transferor retains a call option on a transferred available-for-sale financial asset and the fair value of the asset decreases below the exercise **BC70** price, the transferor does not suffer a loss because it has no obligation to exercise the call option. In that case, the Board decided that it is appropriate to adjust the measurement of the liability to reflect that the transferor has no exposure to decreases in the fair value of the asset below the option exercise price. Similarly, if a transferor writes a put option and the fair value of the asset exceeds the exercise price, the transferee need not exercise the put. Because the transferor has no right to increases in the fair value of the asset above the option exercise price, it is appropriate to measure the asset at the lower of (a) the option exercise price and (b) the fair value of the asset.

MEASUREMENT

Fair Value Option (paragraph 9)*

BC71   The Board concluded that it could simplify the application of IAS 39 (as revised in 2000) for some entities by permitting the use of fair value measurement for any financial instrument. With one exception (see paragraph 9), this greater use of fair value is optional. The fair value option does not require entities to measure more financial instruments at fair value.

BC72   IAS 39 (as revised in 2000) did not permit an entity to measure particular categories of financial instruments at fair value with changes in fair value recognised in profit or loss. Examples included:

(a)   originated loans and receivables, including a debt instrument acquired directly from the issuer, unless they met the conditions for classification as held for trading in paragraph 9.

(b)   financial assets classified as available for sale, unless as an accounting policy choice gains and losses on all available-for-sale financial assets were recognised in profit or loss or they met the conditions for classification as held for trading in paragraph 9.

(c)   non-derivative financial liabilities, even if the entity had a policy and practice of actively repurchasing such liabilities or they formed part of an arbitrage/customer facilitation strategy or fund trading activities.

BC73   The Board decided in IAS 39 (as revised in 2003) to permit entities to designate irrevocably on initial recognition any financial instruments as ones to be measured at fair value with gains and losses recognised in profit or loss ('fair value through profit or loss'). To impose discipline on this approach, the Board decided that financial instruments should not be reclassified into or out of the category of fair value through profit or loss. In particular, some comments received on the Exposure Draft of proposed amendments to IAS 39 published in June 2002 suggested that entities could use the fair value option to recognise selectively changes in fair value in profit or loss. The Board noted that the requirement to designate irrevocably on initial recognition the financial instruments for which the fair value option is to be applied results in an entity being unable to 'cherry pick' in this way. This is because it will not be known at initial recognition whether the fair value of the instrument will increase or decrease.

BC73A   Following the issue of IAS 39 (as revised in 2003), as a result of continuing discussions with constituents on the fair value option, the Board became aware that some, including prudential supervisors of banks, securities companies and insurers, were concerned that the fair value option might be used inappropriately (as discussed in paragraph BC11C). In response to those concerns, the Board published in

Editor's note: whole section amended with effect from 1 January 2006.

April 2004 an Exposure Draft of proposed restrictions to the fair value option contained in IAS 39 (as revised in 2003). After discussing comments received from constituents and a series of public roundtable meetings, the Board issued an amendment to IAS 39 in June 2005 permitting entities to designate irrevocably on initial recognition financial instruments that meet one of three conditions (see paragraphs 9(b)(i), 9(b)(ii) and 11A) as ones to be measured at fair value through profit or loss.

In the amendment to the fair value option, the Board identified three situations in which permitting designation at fair value through profit or loss either results in more relevant information (cases (a) and (b) below) or is justified on the grounds of reducing complexity or increasing measurement reliability (case (c) below). These are: **BC74**

(a)   when such designation eliminates or significantly reduces a measurement or recognition inconsistency (sometimes referred to as an 'accounting mismatch') that would otherwise arise (paragraphs BC75-BC75B);

(b)   when a group of financial assets, financial liabilities or both is managed and its performance is evaluated on a fair value basis, in accordance with a documented risk management or investment strategy (paragraphs BC76-BC76B); and

(c)   when an instrument contains an embedded derivative that meets particular conditions (paragraphs BC77-BC78).

The ability for entities to use the fair value option simplifies the application of IAS 39 by mitigating some anomalies that result from the different measurement attributes in the Standard. In particular, for financial instruments designated in this way: **BC74A**

(a)   it eliminates the need for hedge accounting for hedges of fair value exposures when there are natural offsets, and thereby eliminates the related burden of designating, tracking and analysing hedge effectiveness.

(b)   it eliminates the burden of separating embedded derivatives.

(c)   it eliminates problems arising from a mixed measurement model when financial assets are measured at fair value and related financial liabilities are measured at amortised cost. In particular, it eliminates volatility in profit or loss and equity that results when matched positions of financial assets and financial liabilities are not measured consistently.

(d)   the option to recognise unrealised gains and losses on available for-sale financial assets in profit or loss is no longer necessary.

(e)   it de-emphasises interpretative issues around what constitutes trading.

Designation as at fair value through profit or loss eliminates or significantly reduces a measurement or recognition inconsistency (paragraph 9(b)(i))

IAS 39, like comparable standards in some national jurisdictions, imposes a mixed-attribute measurement model. It requires some financial assets and liabilities to be measured at fair value, and others to be measured at amortised cost. It requires some gains and losses to be recognised in profit or loss, and others to be recognised initially as a component of equity. This combination of measurement and recognition requirements can result in inconsistencies, which some refer to as 'accounting mismatches', between the accounting for an asset (or group of assets) and a liability (or group of liabilities). The notion of an accounting mismatch necessarily involves two propositions. First, an entity has particular assets and liabilities that are measured, or on which gains and losses are recognised, inconsistently; second, there is a perceived economic relationship between those assets and liabilities. For example, a   **BC75** liability may be considered to be related to an asset when they share a risk that gives rise to opposite changes in fair value that tend to offset, or when the entity considers that the liability funds the asset.

BC75A   Some entities can overcome measurement or recognition inconsistencies by using hedge accounting or, in the case of insurers, shadow accounting. However, the Board recognises that those techniques are complex and do not address all situations. In developing the amendment to the fair value option, the Board considered whether it should impose conditions to limit the situations in which an entity could use the option to eliminate an accounting mismatch. For example, it considered whether entities should be required to demonstrate that particular assets and liabilities are managed together, or that a management strategy is effective in reducing risk (as is required for hedge accounting to be used), or that hedge accounting or other ways of overcoming the inconsistency are not available.

BC75B   The Board concluded that accounting mismatches arise in a wide variety of circumstances. In the Board's view, financial reporting is best served by providing entities with the opportunity to eliminate perceived accounting mismatches whenever that results in more relevant information. Furthermore, the Board concluded that the fair value option may validly be used in place of hedge accounting for hedges of fair value exposures, thereby eliminating the related burden of designating, tracking and analysing hedge effectiveness. Hence, the Board decided not to develop detailed prescriptive guidance about when the fair value option could be applied (such as requiring effectiveness tests similar to those required for hedge accounting) in the amendment on the fair value option. Rather, the Board decided to require disclosures in IAS 32* about:

- the criteria an entity uses for designating financial assets and financial liabilities as at fair value through profit or loss
- how the entity satisfies the conditions in this Standard for such designation
- the nature of the assets and liabilities so designated
- the effect on the financial statement of using this designation, namely the carrying amounts and net gains and losses on assets and liabilities so designated, information about the effect of changes in a financial liability's credit quality on changes in its fair value, and information about the credit risk of loans or receivables and any related credit derivatives or similar instruments.

A group of financial assets, financial liabilities or both is managed and its performance is evaluated on a fair value basis, in accordance with a documented risk management or investment strategy (paragraph 9(b)(ii))

BC76   The Standard requires financial instruments to be measured at fair value through profit or loss in only two situations, namely when an instrument is held for trading or when it contains an embedded derivative that the entity is unable to measure separately. However, the Board recognised that some entities manage and evaluate the performance of financial instruments on a fair value basis in other situations. Furthermore, for instruments managed and evaluated in this way, users of financial statements may regard fair value measurement as providing more relevant information. Finally, it is established practice in some industries in some jurisdictions to recognise all financial assets at fair value through profit or loss. (This practice was permitted for many assets in IAS 39 (as revised in 2000) as an accounting policy choice in accordance with which gains and losses on all available-for-sale financial assets were reported in profit or loss.)

*ASB Footnote: In the UK IAS 32 is implemented as FRS 25 Financial Instruments: Disclosure and Presentation.

In the amendment to IAS 39 relating to the fair value option issued in June 2005, the **BC76A** Board decided to permit financial instruments managed and evaluated on a fair value basis to be measured at fair value through profit or loss. The Board also decided to introduce two requirements to make this category operational. These requirements are that the financial instruments are managed and evaluated on a fair value basis in accordance with a documented risk management or investment strategy, and that information about the financial instruments is provided internally on that basis to the entity's key management personnel.

In looking to an entity's documented risk management or investment strategy, the **BC76B** Board makes no judgement on what an entity's strategy should be. However, the Board noted that users, in making economic decisions, would find useful both a description of the chosen strategy and how designation at fair value through profit or loss is consistent with it. Accordingly, IAS 32 requires such disclosures. The Board also noted that the required documentation of the entity's strategy need not be on an item-by-item basis, nor need it be in the level of detail required for hedge accounting. However, it should be sufficient to demonstrate that using the fair value option is consistent with the entity's risk management or investment strategy. In many cases, the entity's existing documentation, as approved by its key management personnel, should be sufficient for this purpose.

The instrument contains an embedded derivative that meets particular conditions (paragraph 11A)

The Standard requires virtually all derivative financial instruments to be measured at **BC77** fair value. This requirement extends to derivatives that are *embedded* in an instrument that also includes a non-derivative host contract if the embedded derivative meets the conditions in paragraph 11. Conversely, if the embedded derivative does not meet those conditions, separate accounting with measurement of the embedded derivative at fair value is prohibited. Therefore, to satisfy these requirements, the entity must:

(a)   identify whether the instrument contains one or more embedded derivatives,
(b)   determine whether each embedded derivative is one that must be separated from the host instrument or one for which separation is prohibited, and
(c)   if the embedded derivative is one that must be separated, determine its fair value at initial recognition and subsequently.

For some embedded derivatives, like the prepayment option in an ordinary resi- **BC77A** dential mortgage, this process is fairly simple. However, entities with more complex instruments have reported that the search for and analysis of embedded derivatives (steps (a) and (b) in paragraph BC77) significantly increase the cost of complying with the Standard. They report that this cost could be eliminated if they had the option to fair value the combined contract.

Other entities report that one of the most common uses of the fair value option is **BC77B** likely to be for structured products that contain several embedded derivatives. Those structured products will typically be hedged with derivatives that offset all (or nearly all) of the risks they contain, whether or not the embedded derivatives that give rise to those risks are separated for accounting purposes. Hence, the simplest way to account for such products is to apply the fair value option so that the combined contract (as well as the derivatives that hedge it) is measured at fair value through profit or loss. Furthermore, for these more complex instruments, the fair value of the combined contract may be significantly easier to measure and hence be more reliable than the fair value of only those embedded derivatives that IAS 39 requires to be separated.

BC78   The Board sought to strike a balance between reducing the costs of complying with the embedded derivatives provisions of this Standard and the need to respond to the concerns expressed regarding possible inappropriate use of the fair value option. The Board determined that allowing the fair value option to be used for *any* instrument with an embedded derivative would make other restrictions on the use of the option ineffective, because many financial instruments include an embedded derivative. In contrast, limiting the use of the fair value option to situations in which the embedded derivative must otherwise be separated would not significantly reduce the costs of compliance and could result in less reliable measures being included in the financial statements. Therefore, the Board decided to specify situations in which an entity cannot justify using the fair value option in place of assessing embedded derivatives—when the embedded derivative does not significantly modify the cash flows that would otherwise be required by the contract or is one for which it is clear with little or no analysis when a similar hybrid instrument is first considered that separation is prohibited.

The role of prudential supervisors

BC78A   The Board considered the circumstances of regulated financial institutions such as banks and insurers in determining the extent to which conditions should be placed on the use of the fair value option. The Board recognised that regulated financial institutions are extensive holders and issuers of financial instruments and so are likely to be among the largest potential users of the fair value option. However, the Board noted that some of the prudential supervisors that oversee these entities expressed concern that the fair value option might be used inappropriately.

BC79   The Board noted that the primary objective of prudential supervisors is to maintain the financial soundness of individual financial institutions and the stability of the financial system as a whole. Prudential supervisors achieve this objective partly by assessing the risk profile of each regulated institution and imposing a risk-based capital requirement.

BC79A   The Board noted that these objectives of prudential supervision differ from the objectives of general purpose financial reporting. The latter is intended to provide information about the financial position, performance and changes in financial position of an entity that is useful to a wide range of users in making economic decisions. However, the Board acknowledged that for the purposes of determining what level of capital an institution should maintain, prudential supervisors may wish to understand the circumstances in which a regulated financial institution has chosen to apply the fair value option and evaluate the rigour of the institution's fair value measurement practices and the robustness of its underlying risk management strategies, policies and practices. Furthermore, the Board agreed that certain disclosures would assist both prudential supervisors in their evaluation of capital requirements and investors in making economic decisions. In particular, the Board decided to require an entity to disclose how it has satisfied the conditions in paragraphs 9(b), 11A and 12 for using the fair value option, including, for instruments within paragraph 9(b)(ii), a narrative description of how designation at fair value through profit or loss is consistent with the entity's documented risk management or investment strategy.

Other matters

BC80   IAS 39 (as revised in 2000) contained an accounting policy choice for the recognition of gains and losses on available-for-sale financial assets—such gains and losses could be recognised either in equity or in profit or loss. The Board concluded that the fair value option removed the need for such an accounting policy choice. An entity can achieve recognition of gains and losses on such assets in profit or loss in appropriate cases by using the fair value option. Accordingly, the Board decided that the choice that was in IAS 39 (as revised in 2000) should be removed and that gains and losses on available-for-sale financial assets should be recognised in equity when IAS 39 was revised in 2003.

The fair value option permits (but does not require) entities to measure financial **BC80A** instruments at fair value with changes in fair value recognised in profit or loss. Accordingly, it does not restrict an entity's ability to use other accounting methods (such as amortised cost). Some respondents to the Exposure Draft of proposed amendments to IAS 39 published in June 2002 would have preferred more pervasive changes to expand the use of fair values and limit the choices available to entities, such as the elimination of the held-to-maturity category or the cash flow hedge accounting approach. Although such changes have the potential to make the principles in IAS 39 more coherent and less complex, the Board did not consider such changes as part of the project to improve IAS 39.

Comments received on the Exposure Draft of proposed amendments to IAS 39 **BC81** published in June 2002 also questioned the proposal that all items measured at fair value through profit or loss should have the descriptor 'held for trading'. Some comments noted that 'held for trading' is commonly used with a narrower meaning, and it may be confusing for users if instruments designated at fair value through profit or loss are also called 'held for trading'. Therefore, the Board considered using a fifth category of financial instruments—'fair value through profit or loss'—to distinguish those instruments to which the fair value option was applied from those classified as held for trading. The Board rejected this possibility because it believed that adding a fifth category of financial instruments would unnecessarily complicate the Standard. Rather, the Board concluded that 'fair value through profit or loss' should be used to describe a category that encompasses financial instruments classified as held for trading and those to which the fair value option is applied.

The Board also decided to include in IAS 39 (as revised in 2003) the ability for **BC84** entities to designate a loan or receivable as available for sale (see paragraph 9). The Board decided that, in the context of the existing mixed measurement model, there are no reasons to limit to any particular type of asset the ability to designate an asset as available for sale.

Application of the Fair Value Option to a Component or a Proportion (Rather than the Entirety) of a Financial Asset or a Financial Liability

Some comments received on the Exposure Draft of proposed amendments to IAS 39 **BC85** published in June 2002 argued that the fair value option should be extended so that it could also be applied to a component of a financial asset or a financial liability (eg changes in fair value attributable to one risk such as changes in a benchmark interest rate). The arguments included (a) concerns regarding inclusion of own credit risk in the measurement of financial liabilities and (b) the prohibition on using non-derivatives as hedging instruments (cash instrument hedging).

The Board concluded that IAS 39 should not extend the fair value option to com- **BC86** ponents of financial assets or financial liabilities. It was concerned (a) about difficulties in measuring the change in value of the component because of ordering issues and joint effects (ie if the component is affected by more than one risk, it may be difficult to isolate accurately and measure the component); (b) that the amounts recognised in the balance sheet would be neither fair value nor cost; and (c) that a fair value adjustment for a component may move the carrying amount of an instrument away from its fair value. In finalising the 2003 amendments to IAS 39, the Board separately considered the issue of cash instrument hedging (see paragraphs BC144 and BC145).

BC86A   Other comments received on the April 2004 Exposure Draft of proposed restrictions to the fair value option contained in IAS 39 (as revised in 2003) suggested that the fair value option should be extended so that it could be applied to a proportion (ie a percentage) of a financial asset or financial liability. The Board was concerned that such an extension would require prescriptive guidance on how to determine a proportion. For example if an entity were to issue a bond totalling CU100 million in the form of 100 certificates each of CU1 million, would a proportion of 10 per cent be identified as 10 per cent of each certificate, 10 million specified certificates, the first (or last) 10 million certificates to be redeemed, or on some other basis? The Board was also concerned that the remaining proportion, not being subject to the fair value option, could give rise to incentives for an entity to 'cherry pick' (ie to realise financial assets or financial liabilities selectively so as to achieve a desired accounting result). For these reasons, the Board decided not to allow the fair value option to be applied to a proportion of a single financial asset or financial liability. However, if an entity simultaneously issues two or more identical financial instruments, it is not precluded from designating only some of those instruments as being subject to the fair value option (for example, if doing so achieves a significant reduction in a recognition or measurement inconsistency, as explained in paragraph AG4G). Thus, in the above example, the entity could designate 10 million specified certificates if to do so would meet one of the three criteria in paragraph BC74.

Credit Risk of Liabilities

BC87   The Board discussed the issue of including changes in the credit risk of a financial liability in its fair value measurement. It considered responses to the Exposure Draft of proposed amendments to IAS 39 published in June 2002 that expressed concern about the effect of including this component in the fair value measurement and that suggested the fair value option should be restricted to exclude all or some financial liabilities. However, the Board concluded that the fair value option could be applied to any financial liability, and decided not to restrict the option in the Standard (as revised in 2003) because to do so would negate some of the benefits of the fair value option set out in paragraph BC74A.

BC88   The Board considered comments on the same Exposure Draft that disagreed with the view that, in applying the fair value option to financial liabilities, an entity should recognise income as a result of deteriorating credit quality (and a loan expense as a result of improving credit quality). Commentators noted that it is not useful to report lower liabilities when an entity is in financial difficulty precisely because its debt levels are too high, and that it would be difficult to explain to users of financial statements the reasons why income would be recognised when a liability's creditworthiness deteriorates. These comments suggested that fair value should exclude the effects of changes in the instrument's credit risk.

BC89   However, the Board noted that because financial statements are prepared on a going concern basis, credit risk affects the value at which liabilities could be repurchased or settled. Accordingly, the fair value of a financial liability reflects the credit risk relating to that liability. Therefore, it decided to include credit risk relating to a financial liability in the fair value measurement of that liability for the following reasons:

(a)   entities realise changes in fair value, including fair value attributable to the liability's credit risk, for example, by renegotiating or repurchasing liabilities or by using derivatives;
(b)   changes in credit risk affect the observed market price of a financial liability and hence its fair value;
(c)   it is difficult from a practical standpoint to exclude changes in credit risk from an observed market price; and
(d)   the fair value of a financial liability (ie the price of that liability in an exchange between a knowledgeable, willing buyer and a knowledgeable, willing seller) on initial recognition reflects its credit risk. The Board believes that it is inappropriate to include credit risk in the initial fair value measurement of financial liabilities, but not subsequently.

The Board also considered whether the component of the fair value of a financial liability attributable to changes in credit quality should be specifically disclosed, separately presented in the income statement, or separately presented in equity. The Board decided that whilst separately presenting or disclosing such changes might be difficult in practice, disclosure of such information would be useful to users of financial statements and would help alleviate the concerns expressed. Therefore, it decided to include in IAS 32 a disclosure to help identify the changes in the fair value of a financial liability that arise from changes in the liability's credit risk. The Board believes this is a reasonable proxy for the change in fair value that is attributable to changes in the liability's credit risk, in particular when such changes are large, and will provide users with information with which to understand the profit or loss effect of such a change in credit risk.   **BC90**

The Board decided to clarify that this issue relates to the credit risk of the financial liability, rather than the creditworthiness of the entity. The Board noted that this more appropriately describes the objective of what is included in the fair value measurement of financial liabilities.   **BC91**

The Board also noted that the fair value of liabilities secured by valuable collateral, guaranteed by third parties or ranking ahead of virtually all other liabilities is generally unaffected by changes in the entity's creditworthiness.   **BC92**

Measurement of Financial Liabilities with a Demand Feature

Some comments received on the Exposure Draft requested clarification of how to determine fair value for financial liabilities with a demand feature (eg demand deposits), when the fair value measurement option is applied or the liability is otherwise measured at fair value. In other words, could the fair value be less than the amount payable on demand, discounted from the first date that an amount could be required to be paid (the 'demand amount'), such as the amount of the deposit discounted for the period that the entity expects the deposit to be outstanding? Some commentators believe that the fair value of financial liabilities with a demand feature is less than the demand amount, for reasons that include the consistency of such measurement with how those financial liabilities are treated for risk management purposes.   **BC93**

The Board agreed that this issue should be clarified in IAS 39. It confirmed that the fair value of a financial liability with a demand feature is not less than the amount payable on demand discounted from the first date that the amount could be required to be paid. This conclusion is the same as in the original IAS 32. The Board noted that in many cases, the market price observed for such financial liabilities is the price at which they are originated between the customer and the deposit-taker—ie the   **BC94** demand amount. It also noted that recognising a financial liability with a demand feature at less than the demand amount would give rise to an immediate gain on the origination of such a deposit, which the Board believes is inappropriate.

Fair Value Measurement Guidance (paragraphs AG69-AG82)

BC95   The Board decided to include in the revised IAS 39 expanded guidance about how to determine fair values, in particular for financial instruments for which no quoted market price is available (Appendix A paragraphs AG74-AG82). The Board decided that it is desirable to provide clear and reasonably detailed guidance about the objective and use of valuation techniques to achieve reliable and comparable fair value estimates when financial instruments are measured at fair value.

Use of Quoted Prices in Active Markets (paragraphs AG71-AG73)

BC96   The Board considered comments received that disagreed with the proposal in the Exposure Draft that a quoted price is the appropriate measure of fair value for an instrument quoted in an active market. Some respondents argued that (a) valuation techniques are more appropriate for measuring fair value than a quoted price in an active market (eg for derivatives) and (b) valuation models are consistent with industry best practice, and are justified because of their acceptance for regulatory capital purposes.

BC97   However, the Board confirmed that a quoted price is the appropriate measure of fair value for an instrument quoted in an active market, notably because (a) in an active market, the quoted price is the best evidence of fair value, given that fair value is defined in terms of a price agreed by a knowledgeable, willing buyer and a knowledgeable, willing seller; (b) it results in consistent measurement across entities; and (c) fair value as defined in the Standard does not depend on entityspecific factors. The Board further clarified that a quoted price includes market-quoted rates as well as prices.

Entities that have access to more than one active market (paragraph AG71)

BC98   The Board considered situations in which entities operate in different markets. An example is a trader that originates a derivative with a corporate in an active corporate retail market and offsets the derivative by taking out a derivative with a dealer in an active dealers' wholesale market. The Board decided to clarify that the objective of fair value measurement is to arrive at the price at which a transaction would occur at the balance sheet date in the same instrument (ie without modification or repackaging) in the most advantageous active market to which an entity has immediate access. Thus, if a dealer enters into a derivative instrument with the corporate, but has immediate access to a more advantageously priced dealers' market, the entity recognises a profit on initial recognition of the derivative instrument. However, the entity adjusts the price observed in the dealer market for any differences in counterparty credit risk between the derivative instrument with the corporate and that with the dealers' market.

Bid-ask spreads in active markets (paragraph AG72)

BC99   The Board confirmed the proposal in the Exposure Draft that the appropriate quoted market price for an asset held or liability to be issued is usually the current bid price and, for an asset to be acquired or liability held, the asking price. It concluded that applying midmarket prices to an individual instrument is not appropriate because it would result in entities recognising up-front gains or losses for the difference between the bid-ask price and the mid-market price.

The Board discussed whether the bid-ask spread should be applied to the net open position of a portfolio containing offsetting market risk positions, or to each instrument in the portfolio. It noted the concerns raised by constituents that applying the bid-ask spread to the net open position better reflects the fair value of the risk retained in the portfolio. The Board concluded that for offsetting risk positions, entities could use mid-market prices to determine fair value, and hence may apply the bid or asking price to the net open position as appropriate. The Board believes that when an entity has offsetting risk positions, using the mid-market price is appropriate because the entity (a) has locked in its cash flows from the asset and liability and (b) potentially could sell the matched position without incurring the bid-ask spread. **BC100**

Comments received on the Exposure Draft revealed that some interpret the term 'bid-ask spread' differently from others and from the Board. Thus, IAS 39 clarifies that the spread represents only transaction costs. **BC101**

No Active Market (paragraphs AG74-AG82)

The Exposure Draft proposed a three-tier fair value measurement hierarchy as follows: **BC102**

(a) For instruments traded in active markets, use a quoted price.
(b) For instruments for which there is not an active market, use a recent market transaction.
(c) For instruments for which there is neither an active market nor a recent market transaction, use a valuation technique.

The Board decided to simplify the proposed fair value measurement hierarchy by requiring the fair value of financial instruments for which there is not an active market to be determined on the basis of valuation techniques, including the use of recent market transactions between knowledgeable, willing parties in an arm's length transaction. **BC103**

The Board also considered constituents' comments regarding whether an instrument should always be recognised on initial recognition at the transaction price or whether gains or losses may be recognised on initial recognition when an entity uses a valuation technique to estimate fair value. The Board concluded that an entity may recognise a gain or loss at inception only if fair value is evidenced by comparison with other observable current market transactions in the same instrument (ie without modification or repackaging) or is based on a valuation technique incorporating only observable market data. The Board concluded that those conditions were necessary and sufficient to provide reasonable assurance that fair value was other than the transaction price for the purpose of recognising up-front gains or losses. The Board decided that in other cases, the transaction price gave the best evidence of fair value. The Board also noted that its decision achieved convergence with US GAAP. **BC104**

Impairment and Uncollectibility of Financial Assets

Impairment of Investments in Equity Instruments (paragraph 61)

Under IAS 39, investments in equity instruments that are classified as available for sale and investments in unquoted equity instruments whose fair value cannot be **BC105** reliably measured are subject to an impairment assessment. The original IAS 39 did not include guidance about impairment indicators that are specific to investments in equity instruments. Questions were raised about when in practice such investments become impaired.

BC106 The Board agreed that for marketable investments in equity instruments any impairment trigger other than a decline in fair value below cost is likely to be arbitrary to some extent. If markets are reasonably efficient, today's market price is the best estimate of the discounted value of the future market price. However, the Board also concluded that it is important to provide guidance to address the questions raised in practice.

BC107 The revised IAS 39 includes impairment triggers that the Board concluded were reasonable in the case of investments in equity instruments (paragraph 61). They apply in addition to those specified in paragraph 59, which focus on the assessment of impairment in debt instruments.

Incurred versus expected losses

BC108 Some respondents to the Exposure Draft were confused about whether the Exposure Draft reflected an 'incurred loss' model or an 'expected loss' model. Others expressed concern about the extent to which 'future losses' could be recognised as impairment losses. They suggested that losses should be recognised only when they are incurred (ie a deterioration in the credit quality of an asset or a group of assets after their initial recognition). Other respondents favoured the use of an expected loss approach. They suggested that expected future losses should be considered in the determination of the impairment loss for a group of assets even if the credit quality of a group of assets has not deteriorated from original expectations.

BC109 In considering these comments, the Board decided that impairment losses should be recognised only if they have been incurred. The Board reasoned that it was inconsistent with an amortised cost model to recognise impairment on the basis of expected future transactions and events. The Board also decided that guidance should be provided about what 'incurred' means when assessing whether impairment exists in a group of financial assets. The Board was concerned that, in the absence of such guidance, there could be a range of interpretations about when a loss is incurred or what events cause a loss to be incurred in a group of assets.

BC110 Therefore, the Board included guidance in IAS 39 that specifies that for a loss to be incurred, an event that provides objective evidence of impairment must have occurred after the initial recognition of the financial asset, and IAS 39 now identifies types of such events. Possible or expected future trends that may lead to a loss in the future (eg an expectation that unemployment will rise or a recession will occur) do not provide objective evidence of impairment. In addition, the loss event must have a reliably measurable effect on the present value of estimated future cash flows and be supported by current observable data.

Assets assessed individually and found not to be impaired (paragraphs 59(f) and 64)

BC111 It was not clear in the original IAS 39 whether loans and receivables and some other financial assets, when reviewed for impairment and determined not to be impaired, could or should subsequently be included in the assessment of impairment for a group of financial assets with similar characteristics.

BC112 The Exposure Draft proposed that a loan asset or other financial asset that is measured at amortised cost and has been individually assessed for impairment and found not to be impaired should be included in a collective assessment of impairment. The Exposure Draft also included proposed guidance about how to evaluate impairment inherent in a group of financial assets.

The comment letters received on the Exposure Draft indicated considerable support for the proposal to include in a collective evaluation of impairment an individually assessed financial asset that is found not to be impaired.   **BC113**

The Board noted the following arguments in favour of an additional portfolio assessment for individually assessed assets that are found not to be impaired.   **BC114**

(a)   Impairment that cannot be identified with an individual loan may be identifiable on a portfolio basis. The *Framework** states that for a large population of receivables, some degree of nonpayment is normally regarded as probable. In that case, an expense representing the expected reduction in economic benefits is recognised (*Framework*, paragraph 85). For example, a lender may have some concerns about identified loans with similar characteristics, but not have sufficient evidence to conclude that an impairment loss has occurred on any of those loans on the basis of an individual assessment. Experience may indicate that some of those loans are impaired even though an individual assessment may not reveal this. The amount of loss in a large population of items can be estimated on the basis of experience and other factors by weighing all possible outcomes by their associated probabilities.

(b)   Some time may elapse between an event that affects the ability of a borrower to repay a loan and actual default of the borrower. For example, if the market forward price for wheat decreases by 10 per cent, experience may indicate that the estimated payments from borrowers that are wheat farmers will decrease by 1 per cent over a one-year period. When the forward price decreases, there may be no objective evidence that any individual wheat farmer will default on an individually significant loan. On a portfolio basis, however, the decrease in the forward price may provide objective evidence that the estimated future cash flows on loans to wheat farmers have decreased by 1 per cent over a one-year period.

(c)   Under IAS 39, impairment of loans is measured on the basis of the present value of estimated future cash flows. Estimations of future cash flows may change because of economic factors affecting a group of loans, such as country and industry factors, even if there is no objective evidence of impairment of an individual loan. For example, if unemployment increases by 10 per cent in a quarter in a particular region, the estimated future cash flows from loans to borrowers in that region for the next quarters may have decreased even though no objective evidence of impairment exists that is based on an individual assessment of loans to borrowers in that region. In that case, objective evidence of impairment exists for the group of financial assets, even though it does not exist for an individual asset. A requirement for objective evidence to exist to recognise and measure impairment in individually significant loans might result in delayed recognition of loan impairment that has already occurred.

(d)   Accepted accounting practice in some countries is to establish a provision to cover impairment losses that, although not specifically identified to individual assets, are known from experience to exist in a loan portfolio as of the balance sheet date.

(e)   If assets that are individually not significant are collectively assessed for impairment and assets that are individually significant are not, assets will not be

---

ASB footnote: The equivalent document in the UK and Republic of Ireland to the IASB's Framework is the ASB's Statement of Principles for Financial Reporting. Although the Statement of Principles is very similar to the Framework, it is not identical.

measured on a consistent basis because impairment losses are more difficult to identify asset by asset.

(f)   What is an individually significant loan that is assessed on its own will differ from one entity to another. Thus, identical exposures will be evaluated on different bases (individually or collectively), depending on their significance to the entity holding them. If a collective evaluation were not to be required, an entity that wishes to minimise its recognised impairment losses could elect to assess all loans individually. Requiring a collective assessment of impairment for all exposures judged not to be impaired individually enhances consistency between entities rather than reduces it.

BC115   Arguments against an additional portfolio assessment for individually assessed loans that are found not to be impaired are as follows.

(a)   It appears illogical to make an impairment provision on a group of loans that have been assessed for impairment on an individual basis and have been found not to be impaired.

(b)   The measurement of impairment should not depend on whether a lender has only one loan or a group of similar loans. If the measurement of impairment is affected by whether the lender has groups of similar loans, identical loans may be measured differently by different lenders. To ensure consistent measurement of identical loans, impairment in individually significant financial assets should be recognised and measured asset by asset.

(c)   The *Framework* specifies that financial statements are prepared on the accrual basis of accounting, according to which the effects of transactions and events are recognised when they occur and are recognised in the financial statements in the periods to which they relate. Financial statements should reflect the outcome of events that took place before the balance sheet date and should not reflect events that have not yet occurred. If an impairment loss cannot be attributed to a specifically identified financial asset or a group of financial assets that are not individually significant, it is questionable whether an event has occurred that justifies the recognition of impairment. Even though the risk of loss may have increased, a loss has not yet materialised.

(d)   The *Framework*, paragraph 94, requires an expense to be recognised only if it can be measured reliably. The process of estimating impairment in a group of loans that have been individually assessed for impairment but found not to be impaired may involve a significant degree of subjectivity. There may be a wide range of reasonable estimates of impairment. In practice, the establishment of general loan loss provisions is sometimes viewed as more of an art than a science. This portfolio approach should be applied only if it is necessary on practical grounds and not to override an assessment made on an individual loan, which must provide a better determination of whether an allowance is necessary.

(e)   IAS 39 requires impairment to be measured on a present value basis using the original effective interest rate. Mechanically, it may not be obvious how to do this for a group of loans with similar characteristics that have different effective interest rates. In addition, measurement of impairment in a group of loans based on the present value of estimated cash flows discounted using the original effective interest rate may result in doublecounting of losses that were expected on a portfolio basis when the loans were originated because the lender included compensation for those losses in the contractual interest rate charged. As a result, a portfolio assessment of impairment may result in the recognition of a loss almost as soon as a loan is issued. (This question arises also in measuring impairment on a portfolio basis for loans that are not individually assessed for impairment under IAS 39.)

The Board was persuaded by the arguments in favour of a portfolio assessment for **BC116** individually assessed assets that are found not to be impaired and decided to confirm that a loan or other financial asset measured at amortised cost that is individually assessed for impairment and found not to be impaired should be included in a group of similar financial assets that are assessed for impairment on a portfolio basis. This is to reflect that, in the light of the law of large numbers, impairment may be evident in a group of assets, but not yet meet the threshold for recognition when any individual asset in that group is assessed. The Board also confirmed that it is important to provide guidance about how to assess impairment on a portfolio basis to introduce discipline into a portfolio assessment. Such guidance promotes consistency in practice and comparability of information across entities. It should also mitigate concerns that collective assessments of impairment should not be used to conceal changes in asset values or as a cushion for potential future losses.

Some respondents expressed concerns about some of the detailed guidance proposed **BC117** in the Exposure Draft, such as the guidance about adjusting the discount rate for expected losses. Many entities indicated that they do not have the data and systems necessary to implement the proposed approach. The Board decided to eliminate some of the detailed application guidance (eg whether to make an adjustment of the discount rate for originally expected losses and an illustration of the application of the guidance).

Assets that are assessed individually and found to be impaired (paragraph 64)

In making a portfolio assessment of impairment, one issue that arises is whether the **BC118** collective assessment should include assets that have been individually evaluated and identified as impaired.

One view is that methods used to estimate impairment losses on a portfolio basis are **BC119** equally valid whether or not an asset has been specifically identified as impaired. Those who support this view note that the law of large numbers applies equally whether or not an asset has been individually identified as impaired and that a portfolio assessment may enable a more accurate prediction to be made of estimated future cash flows.

Another view is that there should be no need to complement an individual assess- **BC120** ment of impairment for an asset that is specifically identified as impaired by an additional portfolio assessment, because objective evidence of impairment exists on an individual basis and expectations of losses can be incorporated in the measurement of impairment for the individual assets. Double-counting of losses in terms of estimated future cash flows should not be permitted. Moreover, recognition of impairment losses for groups of assets should not be a substitute for the recognition of impairment losses on individual assets.

The Board decided that assets that are individually assessed for impairment and **BC121** identified as impaired should be excluded from a portfolio assessment of impairment. Excluding assets that are individually identified as impaired from a portfolio assessment of impairment is consistent with the view that collective evaluation of impairment is an interim step pending the identification of impairment losses on individual assets. A collective evaluation identifies losses that have been incurred on a group basis as of the balance sheet date, but cannot yet be identified with individual assets. As soon as information is available to identify losses on individually impaired assets, those assets are removed from the group that is collectively assessed for impairment.

Grouping of assets that are collectively evaluated for impairment(paragraphs 64 and AG87)

BC122   The Board considered how assets that are collectively assessed for impairment should be grouped for the purpose of assessing impairment on a portfolio basis. In practice, different methods are conceivable for grouping assets for the purposes of assessing impairment and computing historical and expected loss rates. For example, assets may be grouped on the basis of one or more of the following characteristics: (a) estimated default probabilities or credit risk grades; (b) type (for example, mortgage loans or credit card loans); (c) geographical location; (d) collateral type; (e) counterparty type (for example, consumer, commercial or sovereign); (f) past-due status; and (g) maturity. More sophisticated credit risk models or methodologies for estimating expected future cash flows may combine several factors, for example, a credit risk evaluation or grading process that considers asset type, industry, geographical location, collateral type, past-due status, and other relevant characteristics of the assets being evaluated and associated loss data.

BC123   The Board decided that for the purpose of assessing impairment on a portfolio basis, the method employed for grouping assets should, as a minimum, ensure that individual assets are allocated to groups of assets that share similar credit risk characteristics. It also decided to clarify that when assets that are assessed individually and found not to be impaired are grouped with assets with similar credit risk characteristics that are assessed only on a collective basis, the loss probabilities and other loss statistics differ between the two types of asset with the result that a different amount of impairment may be required.

Estimates of future cash flows in groups (paragraphs AG89-AG92)

BC124   The Board decided that to promote consistency in the estimation of impairment on groups of financial assets that are collectively evaluated for impairment, guidance should be provided about the process for estimating future cash flows in such groups. It identified the following elements as critical to an adequate process:

(a)   Historical loss experience should provide the basis for estimating future cash flows in a group of financial assets that are collectively assessed for impairment.

(b)   Entities that have no loss experience of their own or insufficient experience should use peer group experience for comparable groups of financial assets.

(c)   Historical loss experience should be adjusted, on the basis of observable data, to reflect the effects of current conditions that did not affect the period on which the historical loss experience is based and to remove the effects of conditions in the historical period that do not exist currently.

(d)   Changes in estimates of future cash flows should be directionally consistent with changes in underlying observable data.

(e)   Estimation methods should be adjusted to reduce differences between estimates of future cash flows and actual cash flows.

Impairment of investments in available-for-sale financial assets (paragraphs 67-70)

BC125   In the Exposure Draft, the Board proposed that impairment losses on debt and equity instruments classified as available for sale should not be reversed through profit or loss if conditions changed after the recognition of the impairment loss. The Board arrived at this decision because of the difficulties in determining objectively when impairment losses on debt and equity instruments classified as available-for-sale have been recovered and hence of distinguishing a reversal of an impairment (recognised in profit or loss) from other increases in value (recognised in equity). Accordingly, the Board proposed that any increase in the fair value of an available-for-sale financial asset would be recognised directly in equity even though the entity had previously recognised an impairment loss on that asset. The Board noted that this was consistent with the recognition of changes in the fair value of available-for-sale financial assets directly in equity (see paragraph 55(b)).

The Board considered the comments received on its proposal to preclude reversals of impairment on available-for-sale financial assets. It concluded that available-for-sale debt instruments and available-for-sale equity instruments should be treated differently.   **BC126**

Reversals of impairment on available-for-sale debt instruments (paragraph 70)

For available-for-sale debt instruments, the Board decided that impairment should be reversed through profit or loss when fair value increases and the increase can be objectively related to an event occurring after the loss was recognised.   **BC127**

The Board noted that (a) other Standards require the reversal of impairment losses if circumstances change (eg IAS 2 *Inventories*, IAS 16 *Property, Plant and Equipment* and IAS 38 *Intangible Assets**); (b) the decision provides consistency with the requirement to reverse impairment losses on loans and receivables, and on assets classified as held to maturity; and (c) reversals of impairment in debt instruments (ie determining an increase in fair value attributable to an improvement in credit standing) are more objectively determinable than those in equity instruments.   **BC128**

Reversals of impairment on available-for-sale equity instruments (paragraph 69)

For available-for-sale equity instruments, the Board concluded that if impairment is recognised, and the fair value subsequently increases, the increase in value should be recognised in equity (and not as a reversal of the impairment loss through profit or loss).   **BC129**

The Board could not find an acceptable way to distinguish reversals of impairment losses from other increases in fair value. Therefore, it decided that precluding reversals of impairment on available-for-sale equity instruments was the only appropriate solution. In its deliberations, the Board considered: **BC130**

(a)   limiting reversals to those cases in which specific facts that caused the original impairment reverse. However, the Board questioned the operationality of applying this approach (ie how to decide whether the same event that caused the impairment caused the reversal).

(b)   recognising all changes in fair value below cost as impairments and reversals of impairment through profit or loss, ie all changes in fair value below cost would be recognised in profit or loss, and all changes above cost would be recognised in equity. Although this approach achieves consistency with IAS 16 and IAS 38, and eliminates any subjectivity involved in determining what constitutes impairment or reversal of impairment, the Board noted that it would significantly change the notion of 'available for sale' in practice. The Board believed that introducing such a change to the available-for-sale category was not appropriate at this time.

**ASB footnote: the corresponding requirements in the UK and the Republic of Ireland are in SSAP 9 Stocks and long-term contracts and FRS 11 Impairment of Fixed Assets and Goodwill.*

HEDGING

BC131 The Exposure Draft proposed few changes to the hedge accounting guidance in the original IAS 39. The comments on the Exposure Draft raised several issues in the area of hedge accounting suggesting that the Board should consider these issues in the revised IAS 39. The Board's decisions with regard to these issues are presented in the following paragraphs.

Consideration of the Shortcut Method in SFAS 133

BC132 SFAS 133 *Accounting for Derivative Instruments and Hedging Activities* issued by the FASB allows an entity to assume no ineffectiveness in a hedge of interest rate risk using an interest rate swap as the hedging instrument, provided specified criteria are met (the 'shortcut method').

BC133 The original IAS 39 and the Exposure Draft precluded the use of the shortcut method. Many comments received on the Exposure Draft argued that IAS 39 should permit use of the shortcut method. The Board considered the issue in developing the Exposure Draft, and discussed it in the roundtable discussions that were held in the process of finalising IAS 39.

BC134 The Board noted that, if the shortcut method were permitted, an exception would have to be made to the principle in IAS 39 that ineffectiveness in a hedging relationship is measured and recognised in profit or loss. The Board agreed that no exception to this principle should be made, and therefore concluded that IAS 39 should not permit the shortcut method.

BC135 Additionally, IAS 39 permits the hedging of portions of financial assets and financial liabilities in cases when US GAAP does not. The Board noted that under IAS 39 an entity may hedge a portion of a financial instrument (eg interest rate risk or credit risk), and that if the critical terms of the hedging instrument and the hedged item are the same, the entity would, in many cases, recognise no ineffectiveness.

Hedges of Portions of Financial Assets and Financial Liabilities (paragraphs 81, 81A, AG99A and AG99B)

BC135A IAS 39 permits a hedged item to be designated as a portion of the cash flows or fair value of a financial asset or financial liability. In finalising the Exposure Draft *Fair Value Hedge Accounting for a Portfolio Hedge of Interest Rate Risk*, the Board received comments that demonstrated that the meaning of a 'portion' was unclear in this context. Accordingly, the Board decided to amend IAS 39 to provide further guidance on what may be designated as a hedged portion, including confirmation that it is not possible to designate a portion that is greater than the total cash flows of the asset or liability.

Expected Effectiveness (paragraphs AG105–AG113)

BC136 Qualification for hedge accounting is based on expectations of future effectiveness (prospective) and evaluation of actual effectiveness (retrospective). In the original IAS 39, the prospective test was expressed as "almost fully offset", whereas the retrospective test was "within a range of 80-125 per cent". The Board considered whether to amend IAS 39 to permit the prospective effectiveness to be within the range of 80-125 per cent rather than "almost fully offset". The Board noted that an undesirable consequence of such an amendment could be that entities would deliberately underhedge a hedged item in a cash flow hedge so as to reduce recognised ineffectiveness. Therefore, the Board initially decided to retain the guidance in the original IAS 39.

However, when subsequently finalising the requirements for portfolio hedges of interest rate risk, the Board received representations from constituents that some hedges would fail the "almost fully offset" test in IAS 39, including some hedges that would qualify for the short-cut method in US GAAP and thus be assumed to be 100 per cent effective. The Board was persuaded that the concern described in the previous paragraph that an entity might deliberately underhedge would be met by an explicit statement that an entity could not deliberately hedge less than 100 per cent of the exposure on an item and designate the hedge as a hedge of 100 per cent of the exposure. Therefore, the Board decided to amend IAS 39: **BC136A**

(a)   to remove the words "almost fully offset" from the prospective effectiveness test, and replace them by a requirement that the hedge is expected to be "highly effective". (This amendment is consistent with the wording in US GAAP.)

(b)   to include a statement in the Application Guidance in IAS 39 that if an entity hedges less than 100 per cent of the exposure on an item, such as 85 per cent, it shall designate the hedged item as being 85 per cent of the exposure and shall measure ineffectiveness on the basis of the change in the whole of that designated 85 per cent exposure.

Additionally, comments made in response to the Exposure Draft *Fair Value Hedge Accounting for a Portfolio Hedge of Interest Rate Risk* demonstrated that it was unclear how the prospective effectiveness test was to be applied. The Board noted that the objective of the test was to ensure there was firm evidence to support an expectation of high effectiveness. Therefore, the Board decided to amend the Standard to clarify that an expectation of high effectiveness may be demonstrated in various ways, including a comparison of past changes in the fair value or cash flows of the hedged item that are attributable to the hedged risk with past changes in the fair value or cash flows of the hedging instrument, or by demonstrating a high statistical correlation between the fair value of cash flows of the hedged item and those of the hedging instrument. The Board noted that the entity may choose a hedge ratio of other than one to one in order to improve the effectiveness of the hedge as described in paragraph AG100. **BC136B**

Hedges of Portions of Non-Financial Assets and Non-Financial Liabilities for Risk Other Than Foreign Currency Risk *(paragraph 82)*

The Board considered comments on the Exposure Draft that suggested that IAS 39 should permit designating as the hedged risk a risk portion of a non-financial item other than foreign currency risk. **BC137**

The Board concluded that IAS 39 should not be amended to permit such designation. It noted that in many cases, changes in the cash flows or fair value of a portion of a non-financial hedged item are difficult to isolate and measure. Moreover, the Board noted that permitting portions of non-financial assets and non-financial liabilities to be designated as the hedged item for risk other than foreign currency risk would compromise the principles of identification of the hedged item and effectiveness testing that the Board has confirmed because the portion could be designated so that no ineffectiveness would ever arise. **BC138**

The Board confirmed that non-financial items may be hedged in their entirety when the item the entity is hedging is not the standard item underlying contracts traded in the market. In this context, the Board decided to clarify that a hedge ratio of other **BC139** than one-to-one may maximise expected effectiveness, and to include guidance on how the hedge ratio that maximises expected effectiveness can be determined.

Loan Servicing Rights

BC140   The Board also considered whether IAS 39 should permit the interest rate risk portion of loan servicing rights to be designated as the hedged item.

BC141   The Board considered the argument that interest rate risk can be separately identified and measured in loan servicing rights, and that changes in market interest rates have a predictable and separately measurable effect on the value of loan servicing rights. The Board also considered the possibility of treating loan servicing rights as financial assets (rather than non-financial assets).

BC142   However, the Board concluded that no exceptions should be permitted for this matter. The Board noted that (a) the interest rate risk and prepayment risk in loan servicing rights are interdependent, and thus inseparable, (b) the fair values of loan servicing rights do not change in a linear fashion as interest rates increase or decrease, and (c) concerns exist about how to isolate and measure the interest rate risk portion of a loan servicing right. Moreover, the Board expressed concern that in jurisdictions in which loan servicing right markets are not developed, the interest rate risk portion may not be measurable.

BC143   The Board also considered whether IAS 39 should be amended to allow, on an elective basis, the inclusion of loan servicing rights in its scope provided that they are measured at fair value with changes in fair value recognised immediately in profit or loss. The Board noted that this would create two exceptions to the general principles in IAS 39. First, it would create a scope exception because IAS 39 applies only to financial assets and financial liabilities; loan servicing rights are non-financial assets. Second, *requiring* an entity to measure loan servicing rights at fair value through profit or loss would create a further exception, because this treatment is optional (except for items that are held for trading). The Board therefore decided not to amend the scope of IAS 39 for loan servicing rights.

Whether to Permit Hedge Accounting Using Cash Instruments

BC144   In finalising the amendments to IAS 39, the Board discussed whether an entity should be permitted to designate a financial asset or financial liability other than a derivative (ie a 'cash instrument') as a hedging instrument in hedges of risks other than foreign currency risk. The original IAS 39 precluded such designation because of the different bases for measuring derivatives and cash instruments. The Exposure Draft did not propose a change to this limitation. However, some commentators suggested a change, noting that entities do not distinguish between derivative and non-derivative financial instruments in their hedging and other risk management activities and that entities may have to use a non-derivative financial instrument to hedge risk if no suitable derivative financial instrument exists.

BC145   The Board acknowledged that some entities use non-derivatives to manage risk. However, it decided to retain the restriction against designating non-derivatives as hedging instruments in hedges of risks other than foreign currency risk. It noted the following arguments in support of this conclusion:

(a)   The need for hedge accounting arises in part because derivatives are measured at fair value, whereas the items they hedge may be measured at cost or not recognised at all. Without hedge accounting, an entity might recognise volatility in profit or loss for matched positions. For non-derivative items that are not measured at fair value or for which changes in fair value are not recognised in profit or loss, there is generally no need to adjust the accounting of the hedging instrument or the hedged item to achieve matched recognition of gains and losses in profit or loss.

(b) To allow designation of cash instruments as hedging instruments would diverge from US GAAP: SFAS 133 precludes the designation of non-derivative instruments as hedging instruments except for some foreign currency hedges.

(c) To allow designation of cash instruments as hedging instruments would add complexity to the Standard. More financial instruments would be measured at an amount that represents neither amortised cost nor fair value. Hedge accounting is, and should be, an exception to the normal measurement requirements.

(d) If cash instruments were permitted to be designated as hedging instruments, there would be much less discipline in the accounting model because, in the absence of hedge accounting, a non-derivative may not be selectively measured at fair value. If the entity subsequently decides that it would rather not apply fair value measurement to a cash instrument that had been designated as a hedging instrument, it can breach one of the hedge accounting requirements, conclude that the non-derivative no longer qualifies as a hedging instrument and selectively avoid recognising the changes in fair value of the non-derivative instrument in equity (for a cash flow hedge) or profit or loss (for a fair value hedge).

(e) The most significant use of cash instruments as hedging instruments is to hedge foreign currency exposures, which is permitted under IAS 39.

Whether to Treat Hedges of Forecast Transactions as Fair Value Hedges

The Board considered a suggestion made in some of the comment letters received on the Exposure Draft that a hedge of a forecast transaction should be treated as a fair value hedge, rather than as a cash flow hedge. Some argued that the hedge accounting provisions should be simplified by having only one type of hedge accounting. Some also raised concern about an entity's ability, in some cases, to choose between two hedge accounting methods for the same hedging strategy (ie the choice between designating a forward contract to sell an existing asset as a fair value hedge of the asset or a cash flow hedge of a forecast sale of the asset).   **BC146**

The Board acknowledged that the hedge accounting provisions would be simplified, and their application more consistent in some situations, if the Standard permitted only one type of hedge accounting. However, the Board concluded that IAS 39 should continue to distinguish between fair value hedge accounting and cash flow hedge accounting. It noted that removing either type of hedge accounting would narrow the range of hedging strategies that could qualify for hedge accounting.   **BC147**

The Board also noted that treating a hedge of a forecast transaction as a fair value hedge is not appropriate for the following reasons: (a) it would result in the recognition of an asset or liability before the entity has become a party to the contract; (b) amounts would be recognised in the balance sheet that do not meet the definitions of assets and liabilities in the *Framework*; and (c) transactions in which there is no fair value exposure would be treated as if there were a fair value exposure.   **BC148**

Hedges of Firm Commitments (paragraphs 93 and 94)

The previous version of IAS 39 required a hedge of a firm commitment to be accounted for as a cash flow hedge. In other words, hedging gains and losses, to the   **BC149** extent that the hedge is effective, were initially recognised in equity and were subsequently 'recycled' to profit or loss in the same period(s) that the hedged firm commitment affected profit or loss (although, when basis adjustment was used, they adjusted the initial carrying amount of an asset or liability recognised in the meantime). Some believe this is appropriate because cash flow hedge accounting for hedges of firm commitments avoids partial recognition of the firm commitment that would otherwise not be recognised. Moreover, some believe it is conceptually incorrect to recognise the hedged fair value exposure of a firm commitment as an asset or liability merely because it has been hedged.

BC150   The Board considered whether hedges of firm commitments should be treated as cash flow hedges or fair value hedges. The Board concluded that hedges of firm commitments should be accounted for as fair value hedges.

BC151   The Board noted that, in concept, a hedge of a firm commitment is a fair value hedge. This is because the fair value of the item being hedged (the firm commitment) changes with changes in the hedged risk.

BC152   The Board was not persuaded by the argument that it is conceptually incorrect to recognise an asset or liability for a firm commitment merely because it has been hedged. It noted that for all fair value hedges, applying hedge accounting has the effect that amounts are recognised as assets or liabilities that would otherwise not be recognised. For example, assume an entity hedges a fixed rate loan asset with a payfixed, receive-variable interest rate swap. If there is a loss on the swap, applying fair value hedge accounting requires the offsetting gain on the loan to be recognised, ie the carrying amount of the loan is increased. Thus, applying hedge accounting has the effect of recognising a part of an asset (the increase in the loan's value attributable to interest rate movements) that would otherwise not have been recognised. The only difference in the case of a firm commitment is that, without hedge accounting, none of the commitment is recognised, ie the carrying amount is zero. However, this difference merely reflects that the historical cost of a firm commitment is usually zero. It is not a fundamental difference in concept.

BC153   Furthermore, the Board's decision converges with SFAS 133, and thus eliminates practical problems and eases implementation for entities that report under both standards.

BC154   However, the Board clarified that a hedge of the foreign currency risk of a firm commitment may be treated as either a fair value hedge or a cash flow hedge because foreign currency risk affects both the cash flows and the fair value of the hedged item. Accordingly a foreign currency cash flow hedge of a forecast transaction need not be re-designated as a fair value hedge when the forecast transaction becomes a firm commitment.

Basis Adjustments (paragraphs 97–99)

BC155   The question of basis adjustment arises when an entity hedges the future purchase of an asset or the future issue of a liability. One example is that of a US entity that expects to make a future purchase of a German machine that it will pay for in euro. The entity enters into a derivative to hedge against possible future changes in the US dollar / euro exchange rate. Such a hedge is classified as a cash flow hedge under IAS 39, with the effect that gains and losses on the hedging instrument (to the extent that the hedge is effective) are initially recognised in equity. The question the Board considered is what the accounting should be once the future transaction takes place. In its deliberations on this issue, the Board discussed the following approaches:

(a) to remove the hedging gain or loss from equity and recognise it as part of the initial carrying amount of the asset or liability (in the example above, the machine). In future periods, the hedging gain or loss is automatically recognised in profit or loss by being included in amounts such as depreciation expense (for a fixed asset), interest income or expense (for a financial asset or financial liability), or cost of sales (for inventories). This treatment is commonly referred to as 'basis adjustment'.

(b) to leave the hedging gain or loss in equity. In future periods, the gain or loss on the hedging instrument is 'recycled' to profit or loss in the same period(s) as the acquired asset or liability affects profit or loss. This recycling requires a separate adjustment and is not automatic.

It should be noted that both approaches have the same effect on profit or loss and net assets for all periods affected, so long as the hedge is accounted for as a cash flow hedge. The difference relates to balance sheet presentation and, possibly, the line item in the income statement.   **BC156**

In the Exposure Draft, the Board proposed that the 'basis adjustment' approach for forecast transactions (approach (a)) should be eliminated and replaced by approach (b) above. It further noted that eliminating the basis adjustment approach would enable IAS 39 to converge with SFAS 133.   **BC157**

Many of the comments received from constituents disagreed with the proposal in the Exposure Draft. Those responses argued that it would unnecessarily complicate the accounting to leave the hedging gain or loss in equity when the hedged forecast transaction occurs. They particularly noted that tracking the effects of cash flow hedges after the asset or liability is acquired would be complicated and would require systems changes. They also pointed out that treating hedges of firm commitments as fair value hedges has the same effect as a basis adjustment when the firm commitment results in the recognition of an asset or liability. For example, for a perfectly effective hedge of the foreign currency risk of a firm commitment to buy a machine, the effect is to recognise the machine initially at its foreign currency price translated at the forward rate in effect at the inception of the hedge rather than the spot rate. Therefore, they questioned whether it is consistent to treat a hedge of a firm commitment as a fair value hedge while precluding basis adjustments for hedges of forecast transactions.   **BC158**

Others believe that a basis adjustment is difficult to justify in principle for forecast transactions, and also argue that such basis adjustments impair comparability of financial information. In other words, two identical assets that are purchased at the same time and in the same way, except for the fact that one was hedged, should not be recognised at different amounts.   **BC159**

The Board concluded that IAS 39 should distinguish between hedges of forecast transactions that will result in the recognition of a *financial* asset or a *financial* liability and those that will result in the recognition of a *non-financial* asset or a *non-financial* liability.   **BC160**

Basis adjustments for hedges of forecast transactions that will result in the recognition of a financial asset or a financial liability

For hedges of forecast transactions that will result in the recognition of a financial asset or a financial liability, the Board concluded that basis adjustments are not appropriate. Its reason was that basis adjustments cause the initial carrying amount of acquired assets (or assumed liabilities) arising from forecast transactions to move   **BC161** away from fair value and hence would override the requirement in IAS 39 to measure a financial instrument initially at its fair value.

Basis adjustments for hedges of forecast transactions that will result in the recognition of a non-financial asset or a non-financial liability

BC162   For hedges of forecast transactions that will result in the recognition of a non-financial asset or a non-financial liability, the Board decided to permit entities a choice of whether to apply basis adjustment.

BC163   The Board considered the argument that changes in the fair value of the hedging instrument are appropriately included in the initial carrying amount of the recognised asset or liability because such changes represent a part of the "cost" of that asset or liability. Although the Board has not yet considered the broader issue of what costs may be capitalised at initial recognition, the Board believes that its decision to provide an option for basis adjustments in the case of non-financial items will not pre-empt that future discussion. The Board also recognised that financial items and non-financial items are not necessarily measured at the same amount on initial recognition, because financial items are measured at fair value and non-financial items are measured at cost.

BC164   The Board concluded that, on balance, providing entities with a choice in this case was appropriate. The Board took the view that allowing basis adjustments addresses the concern that precluding basis adjustments complicates the accounting for hedges of forecast transactions. In addition, the number of balance sheet line items that could be affected is quite small, generally being only property, plant and equipment, inventory and the cash flow hedge line item in equity. The Board also noted that US GAAP precludes basis adjustments and that applying a basis adjustment is inconsistent with the accounting for hedges of forecast transactions that will result in the recognition of a financial asset or a financial liability. The Board acknowledged the merits of these arguments, and recognised that by permitting a choice in IAS 39, entities could apply the accounting treatment required by US GAAP.

Hedging Using Internal Contracts

BC165   IAS 39 does not preclude entities from using internal contracts as a risk management tool, or as a tracking device in applying hedge accounting for external contracts that hedge external positions. Furthermore, IAS 39 permits hedge accounting to be applied to transactions between entities in the same group or between segments in the *separate reporting* of those entities or segments. However, IAS 39 does not permit hedge accounting for transactions between entities in the same group in consolidated financial statements. The reason is the fundamental requirement of consolidation that the accounting effects of internal contracts should be eliminated in consolidated financial statements, including any internally generated gains or losses. Designating internal contracts as hedging instruments could result in non-elimination of internal gains and losses and have other accounting effects. The Exposure Draft did not propose any change in this area.

BC166   To illustrate, assume the banking book division of Bank A enters into an internal interest rate swap with the trading book division of the same bank. The purpose is to hedge the net interest rate risk exposure in the banking book of a group of similar fixed rate loan assets funded by floating rate liabilities. Under the swap, the banking book pays fixed interest payments to the trading book and receives variable interest rate payments in return. The bank wants to designate the internal interest rate swap in the banking book as a hedging instrument in its consolidated financial statements.

If the internal swap in the banking book is designated as a hedging instrument in a **BC167** cash flow hedge of the liabilities, and the internal swap in the trading book is classified as held for trading, internal gains and losses on that internal swap would not be eliminated. This is because the gains and losses on the internal swap in the banking book would be recognised in equity to the extent the hedge is effective and the gains and losses on the internal swap in the trading book would be recognised in profit or loss.

If the internal swap in the banking book is designated as a hedging instrument in a **BC168** fair value hedge of the loan assets and the internal swap in the trading book is classified as held for trading, the changes in the fair value of the internal swap would offset both in total net assets in the balance sheet and profit or loss. However, without elimination of the internal swap, there would be an adjustment to the carrying amount of the hedged loan asset in the banking book to reflect the change in the fair value attributable to the risk hedged by the internal contract. Moreover, to reflect the effect of the internal swap the bank would in effect recognise the fixed rate loan at a floating interest rate and recognise an offsetting trading gain or loss in the income statement. Hence the internal swap would have accounting effects.

Some respondents to the Exposure Draft and some participants in the roundtables **BC169** objected to not being able to obtain hedge accounting in the consolidated financial statements for internal contracts between subsidiaries or between a subsidiary and the parent (as illustrated above). Among other things, they emphasised that the use of internal contracts is a key risk management tool and that the accounting should reflect the way in which risk is managed. Some suggested that IAS 39 should be changed to make it consistent with US GAAP, which allows the designation of internal derivative contracts as hedging instruments in cash flow hedges of forecast foreign currency transactions in specified, limited circumstances.

In considering these comments, the Board noted that the following principles apply **BC170** to consolidated financial statements:

(a) financial statements provide financial information about an entity or group as a whole (as that of a single entity). Financial statements do not provide financial information about an entity as if it were two separate entities.

(b) a fundamental principle of consolidation is that intragroup balances and intragroup transactions are eliminated in full. Permitting the designation of internal contracts as hedging instruments would require a change to the consolidation principles.

(c) it is conceptually wrong to permit an entity to recognise internally generated gains and losses or make other accounting adjustments because of internal transactions. No external event has occurred.

(d) an ability to recognise internally generated gains and losses could result in abuse in the absence of requirements about how entities should manage and control the associated risks. It is not the purpose of accounting standards to prescribe how entities should manage and control risks.

(e) permitting the designation of internal contracts as hedging instruments violates the following requirements in IAS 39:

(i) the prohibition against designating as a hedging instrument a non-derivative financial asset or non-derivative financial liability for other than foreign currency risk. To illustrate, if an entity has two offsetting internal contracts and one is the designated hedging instrument in a fair value hedge of a non-derivative asset and the other is the designated hedging instrument in a fair value hedge of a non-derivative liability, from the entity's perspective the effect is to designate a hedging relationship between the asset and the liability (ie a non-derivative asset or non-derivative liability is used as the hedging instrument).

(ii)   the prohibition on designating a net position of assets and liabilities as the hedged item. To illustrate, an entity has two internal contracts. One is designated in a fair value hedge of an asset and the other in a fair value hedge of a liability. The two internal contracts do not fully offset, so the entity lays off the net risk exposure by entering into a net external derivative. In that case, the effect from the entity's perspective is to designate a hedging relationship between the net external derivative and a net position of an asset and a liability.

(iii) the option to fair value assets and liabilities does not extend to portions of assets and liabilities.

(f)   the Board is considering separately whether to make an amendment to IAS 39 to facilitate fair value hedge accounting for portfolio hedges of interest rate risk. The Board believes that that is a better way to address the concerns raised about symmetry with risk management systems than permitting the designation of internal contracts as hedging instruments.

(g)   the Board decided to permit an option to measure any financial asset or financial liability at fair value with changes in fair value recognised in profit or loss. This enables an entity to measure matching asset/liability positions at fair value without a need for hedge accounting.

BC171   The Board reaffirmed that it is a fundamental principle of consolidation that any accounting effect of internal contracts is eliminated on consolidation. The Board decided that no exception to this principle should be made in IAS 39. Consistently with this decision, the Board also decided not to explore an amendment to permit internal derivative contracts to be designated as hedging instruments in hedges of some forecast foreign currency transactions, as is permitted by SFAS 138 *Accounting for Certain Derivative Instruments and Certain Hedging Activities.*

BC172   The Board also decided to clarify that IAS 39 does not preclude hedge accounting for transactions between entities in the same group or transactions between segments in individual or separate financial statements of those entities or reporting segments because they are not internal to the entity (ie the individual entity or segment).

Fair Value Hedge Accounting for a Portfolio Hedge of Interest Rate Risk

Background

BC173   The Exposure Draft of proposed improvements to IAS 39 published in June 2002 did not propose any substantial changes to the requirements for hedge accounting as they applied to a portfolio hedge of interest rate risk. However, some of the comment letters on the Exposure Draft and participants in the roundtable discussions raised this issue. In particular, some were concerned that portfolio hedging strategies they regarded as effective hedges would not have qualified for fair value hedge accounting in accordance with previous versions of IAS 39. Rather, they would have either:

(a)   not qualified for hedge accounting at all, with the result that reported profit or loss would be volatile; or

(b)   qualified only for cash flow hedge accounting, with the result that reported equity would be volatile.

BC174   In the light of these concerns, the Board decided to explore whether and how IAS 39 could be amended to enable fair value hedge accounting to be used more readily for portfolio hedges of interest rate risk. As a result, in August 2003 the Board published a second Exposure Draft, *Fair Value Hedge Accounting for a Portfolio Hedge of Interest Rate Risk*, with a comment deadline of 14 November 2003. More than 120 comment letters were received. The amendments proposed in this second Exposure Draft were finalised in March 2004. Paragraphs BC135A-BC136B and BC175-BC220 summarise the Board's considerations in reaching conclusions on the issues raised.

Scope

The Board decided to limit any amendments to IAS 39 to applying fair value hedge accounting to a hedge of interest rate risk on a portfolio of items. In making this decision it noted that:

    BC175

(a) implementation guidance on IAS 39* explains how to apply cash flow hedge accounting to a hedge of the interest rate risk on a portfolio of items.

(b) the issues that arise for a portfolio hedge of interest rate risk are different from those that arise for hedges of individual items and for hedges of other risks. In particular, the three issues discussed in paragraph BC176 do not arise in combination for such other hedging arrangements.

The issue: why fair value hedge accounting was difficult to achieve in accordance with previous versions of IAS 39

The Board identified the following three main reasons why a portfolio hedge of interest rate risk might not have qualified for fair value hedge accounting in accordance with previous versions of IAS 39.

    BC176

(a) Typically, many of the assets that are included in a portfolio hedge are pre-payable, ie the counterparty has a right to repay the item before its contractual repricing date. Such assets contain a prepayment option whose fair value changes as interest rates change. However, the derivative that is used as the hedging instrument typically is not prepayable, ie it does not contain a pre-payment option. When interest rates change, the resulting change in the fair value of the hedged item (which is prepayable) differs from the change in fair value of the hedging derivative (which is not prepayable), with the result that the hedge may not meet IAS 39's effectiveness tests.† Furthermore, prepayment risk may have the effect that the items included in a portfolio hedge fail the requirement‡ that a group of hedged assets or liabilities must be "similar" and the related requirement§ that "the change in fair value attributable to the hedged risk for each individual item in the group shall be expected to be approximately proportional to the overall change in fair value attributable to the hedged risk of the group of items".

(b) IAS 39¶¶ prohibits the designation of an overall net position (eg the net of fixed rate assets and fixed rate liabilities) as the hedged item. Rather, it requires individual assets (or liabilities), or groups of similar assets (or similar liabilities), that share the risk exposure equal in amount to the net position to be designated as the hedged item. For example, if an entity has a portfolio of CU100 of assets and CU80 of liabilities, IAS 39 requires that individual assets

---

*see Q&A F.6.1 and F.6.2

†see IAS 39, paragraph AG105

‡see IAS 39, paragraph 78

§see IAS 39, paragraph 83

¶¶see IAS 39, paragraph AG101

or a group of similar assets of CU20 are designated as the hedged item. However, for risk management purposes, entities often seek to hedge the net position. This net position changes each period as items are repriced or derecognised and as new items are originated. Hence, the individual items designated as the hedged item also need to be changed each period. This requires de- and redesignation of the individual items that constitute the hedged item, which gives rise to significant systems needs.

(c)   Fair value hedge accounting requires the carrying amount of the hedged item to be adjusted for the effect of changes in the hedged risk.* Applied to a portfolio hedge, this could involve changing the carrying amounts of many thousands of individual items. Also, for any items subsequently de-designated from being hedged, the revised carrying amount must be amortised over the item's remaining life.† This, too, gives rise to significant systems needs.

BC177   The Board decided that any change to IAS 39 must be consistent with the principles that underlie IAS 39's requirements on derivatives and hedge accounting. The three principles that are most relevant to a portfolio hedge of interest rate risk are:

(a)   derivatives should be measured at fair value;

(b)   hedge ineffectiveness should be identified and recognised in profit or loss;‡ and

(c)   only items that are assets and liabilities should be recognised as such in the balance sheet. Deferred losses are not assets and deferred gains are not liabilities. However, if an asset or liability is hedged, any change in its fair value that is attributable to the hedged risk should be recognised in the balance sheet.

Prepayment risk

BC178   In considering the issue described in paragraph BC176(a), the Board noted that a prepayable item can be viewed as a combination of a non-prepayable item and a prepayment option. It follows that the fair value of a fixed rate prepayable item changes for two reasons when interest rates move:

(a)   the fair value of the contracted cash flows to the contractual repricing date changes (because the rate used to discount them changes); and

(b)   the fair value of the prepayment option changes (reflecting, among other things, that the likelihood of prepayment is affected by interest rates).

BC179   The Board also noted that, for risk management purposes, many entities do not consider these two effects separately. Instead they incorporate the effect of prepayments by grouping the hedged portfolio into repricing time periods based on *expected* repayment dates (rather than contractual repayment dates). For example, an entity with a portfolio of 25-year mortgages of CU100 may expect 5 per cent of that portfolio to repay in one year's time, in which case it schedules an amount of CU5 into a 12-month time period. The entity schedules all other items contained in its portfolio in a similar way (ie on the basis of expected repayment dates) and hedges all or part of the resulting overall net position in each repricing time period.

BC180   The Board decided to permit the scheduling that is used for risk management purposes, ie on the basis of expected repayment dates, to be used as a basis for the designation necessary for hedge accounting. As a result, an entity would not be required to compute the effect that a change in interest rates has on the fair value of

*see IAS 39, paragraph 89 (b)

†see IAS 39, paragraph 92

‡Subject to the same materiality considerations that apply in this context as throughout IFRSs.

the prepayment option embedded in a prepayable item. Instead, it could incorporate the effect of a change in interest rates on prepayments by grouping the hedged portfolio into repricing time periods based on expected repayment dates. The Board noted that this approach has significant practical advantages for preparers of financial statements, because it allows them to use the data they use for risk management. The Board also noted that the approach is consistent with paragraph 81 of IAS 34, which permits hedge accounting for a portion of a financial asset or financial liability. However, as discussed further in paragraphs BC193-BC206, the Board also concluded that if the entity changes its estimates of the time periods in which items are expected to repay (eg in the light of recent prepayment experience), ineffectiveness will arise, regardless of whether the revision in estimates results in more or less being scheduled in a particular time period.

The Board also noted that if the items in the hedged portfolio are subject to different **BC181** amounts of prepayment risk, they may fail the test in paragraph 78 of being similar and the related requirement in paragraph 83 that the change in fair value attributable to the hedged risk for each individual item in the group is expected to be approximately proportional to the overall change in fair value attributable to the hedged risk of the group of items. The Board decided that, in the context of a portfolio hedge of interest rate risk, these requirements could be inconsistent with the Board's decision, set out in the previous paragraph, on how to incorporate the effects of prepayment risk. Accordingly, the Board decided that they should not apply. Instead, the financial assets or financial liabilities included in a portfolio hedge of interest rate risk need only share the risk being hedged.

Designation of the hedged item and liabilities with a demand feature

The Board considered two main ways to overcome the issue noted in paragraph **BC182** BC176(b). These were:

(a) to designate the hedged item as the overall net position that results from a portfolio containing assets and liabilities. For example, if a repricing time period contains CU100 of fixed rate assets and CU90 of fixed rate liabilities, the net position of CU10 would be designated as the hedged item.
(b) to designate the hedged item as a portion of the assets (ie assets of CU10 in the above example), but not to require individual assets to be designated.

Some of those who commented on the Exposure Draft favoured designation of the **BC183** overall net position in a portfolio that contains assets and liabilities. In their view, existing asset-liability management (ALM) systems treat the identified assets and liabilities as a natural hedge. Management's decisions about additional hedging focus on the entity's remaining net exposure. They observe that designation based on a portion of either the assets or the liabilities is not consistent with existing ALM systems and would entail additional systems costs.

In considering questions of designation, the Board was also concerned about questions **BC184** of measurement. In particular, the Board observed that fair value hedge accounting requires measurement of the change in fair value of the hedged item attributable to the risk being hedged. Designation based on the net position would require the assets and the liabilities in a portfolio each to be measured at fair value (for the risk being hedged) in order to compute the fair value of the net position. Although statistical and other techniques can be used to estimate these fair values, the Board concluded that it is not appropriate to assume that the change in fair value of the hedging instrument is equal to the change in fair value of the net position.

BC185   The Board noted that under the first approach in paragraph BC182 (designating an overall net position), an issue arises if the entity has liabilities that are repayable on demand or after a notice period (referred to below as 'demandable liabilities'). This includes items such as demand deposits and some types of time deposits. The Board was informed that, when managing interest rate risk, many entities that have demandable liabilities include them in a portfolio hedge by scheduling them to the date when they *expect* the total amount of demandable liabilities in the portfolio to be due because of net withdrawals from the accounts in the portfolio. This expected repayment date is typically a period covering several years into the future (eg 0-10 years hence). The Board was also informed that some entities wish to apply fair value hedge accounting based on this scheduling, ie they wish to include demandable liabilities in a fair value portfolio hedge by scheduling them on the basis of their expected repayment dates. The arguments for this view are:

(a)   it is consistent with how demandable liabilities are scheduled for risk management purposes. Interest rate risk management involves hedging the interest rate margin resulting from assets and liabilities and not the fair value of all or part of the assets and liabilities included in the hedged portfolio. The interest rate margin of a specific period is subject to variability as soon as the amount of fixed rate assets in that period differs from the amount of fixed rate liabilities in that period.

(b)   it is consistent with the treatment of prepayable assets to include demandable liabilities in a portfolio hedge based on expected repayment dates.

(c)   as with prepayable assets, expected maturities for demandable liabilities are based on the historical behaviour of customers.

(d)   applying the fair value hedge accounting framework to a portfolio that includes demandable liabilities would not entail an immediate gain on origination of such liabilities because all assets and liabilities enter the hedged portfolio at their carrying amounts. Furthermore, IAS 39* requires the carrying amount of a financial liability on its initial recognition to be its fair value, which normally equates to the transaction price (ie the amount deposited).

(e)   historical analysis shows that a base level of a portfolio of demandable liabilities, such as chequing accounts, is very stable. Whilst a portion of the demandable liabilities varies with interest rates, the remaining portion—the base level—does not. Hence, entities regard this base level as a long-term fixed rate item and include it as such in the scheduling that is used for risk management purposes.

(f)   the distinction between 'old' and 'new' money makes little sense at a portfolio level. The portfolio behaves like a long-term item even if individual liabilities do not.

BC186   The Board noted that this issue is related to that of how to measure the fair value of a demandable liability. In particular, it interrelates with the requirement in IAS 39† that the fair value of a liability with a demand feature is not less than the amount payable on demand, discounted from the first date that the amount could be required to be paid. This requirement applies to all liabilities with a demand feature, not only to those included in a portfolio hedge.

BC187   The Board also noted that:

(a)   although entities, when managing risk, may schedule demandable liabilities based on the expected repayment date of the total balance of a portfolio of accounts, the deposit liabilities included in that balance are unlikely to be

---

*see IAS 39, paragraph AG76

†see IAS 39, paragraph 49

outstanding for an extended period (eg several years). Rather, these deposits are usually expected to be withdrawn within a short time (eg a few months or less), although they may be replaced by new deposits. Put another way, the balance of the portfolio is relatively stable only because withdrawals on some accounts (which usually occur relatively quickly) are offset by new deposits into others. Thus, the liability being hedged is actually the forecast replacement of existing deposits by the receipt of new deposits. IAS 39 does not permit a hedge of such a forecast transaction to qualify for fair value hedge accounting. Rather, fair value hedge accounting can be applied only to the liability (or asset) or firm commitment that exists today.

(b)   a portfolio of demandable liabilities is similar to a portfolio of trade payables. Both comprise individual balances that usually are expected to be paid within a short time (eg a few months or less) and replaced by new balances. Also, for both, there is an amount—the base level—that is expected to be stable and present indefinitely. Hence, if the Board were to permit demandable liabilities to be included in a fair value hedge on the basis of a stable base level created by expected replacements, it should similarly allow a hedge of a portfolio of trade payables to qualify for fair value hedge accounting on this basis.

(c)   a portfolio of similar core deposits is not different from an individual deposit, other than that, in the light of the 'law of large numbers', the behaviour of the portfolio is more predictable. There are no diversification effects from aggregating many similar items.

(d)   it would be inconsistent with the requirement in IAS 39 that the fair value of a liability with a demand feature is not less than the amount payable on demand, discounted from the first date that the amount could be required to be paid, to schedule such liabilities for hedging purposes using a different date. For example, consider a deposit of CU100 that can be withdrawn on demand without penalty. IAS 39 states that the fair value of such a deposit is CU100. That fair value is unaffected by interest rates and does not change when interest rates move. Accordingly, the demand deposit cannot be included in a fair value hedge of interest rate risk—there is no fair value exposure to hedge.

For these reasons, the Board concluded that demandable liabilities should not be included in a portfolio hedge on the basis of the expected repayment date of the *total balance of a portfolio* of demandable liabilities, ie including expected rollovers or replacements of existing deposits by new ones. However, as part of its consideration of comments received on the Exposure Draft, the Board also considered whether a demandable liability, such as a demand deposit, could be included in a portfolio hedge based on the expected repayment date of the *existing balance of individual deposits*, ie ignoring any rollovers or replacements of existing deposits by new deposits. The Board noted the following.   **BC188**

(a)   For many demandable liabilities, this approach would imply a much earlier expected repayment date than is generally assumed for risk management purposes. In particular, for chequing accounts it would probably imply an expected maturity of a few months or less. However, for other demandable liabilities, such as fixed term deposits that can be withdrawn only by the depositor incurring a significant penalty, it might imply an expected repayment date that is closer to that assumed for risk management.

(b)   This approach implies that the *fair value* of the demandable liability should also reflect the expected repayment date of the existing balance, ie that the fair value of a demandable deposit liability is the present value of the amount of the deposit discounted from the expected repayment date. The Board noted that it would be inconsistent to permit fair value hedge accounting to be based on the expected repayment date, but to measure the fair value of the liability on initial recognition on a different basis. The Board also noted that this approach would give rise to a difference on initial recognition between the amount deposited and the fair value recognised in the balance sheet. This, in turn, gives rise to the issue of what the difference represents. Possibilities the Board considered include (i) the value of the depositor's option to withdraw its money before the expected maturity, (ii) prepaid servicing costs or (iii) a gain. The Board did not reach a conclusion on what the difference represents, but agreed that if it were to require such differences to be recognised, this would apply to all demandable liabilities, not only to those included in a portfolio hedge. Such a requirement would represent a significant change from present practice.

(c)   If the fair value of a demandable deposit liability at the date of initial recognition is deemed to equal the amount deposited, a fair value portfolio hedge based on an expected repayment date is unlikely to be effective. This is because such deposits typically pay interest at a rate that is significantly lower than that being hedged (eg the deposits may pay interest at zero or at very low rates, whereas the interest rate being hedged may be LIBOR or a similar benchmark rate). Hence, the fair value of the deposit will be significantly less sensitive to interest rate changes than that of the hedging instrument.

(d)   The question of how to fair value a demandable liability is closely related to issues being debated by the Board in other projects, including Insurance (phase II), Revenue Recognition, Leases and Measurement. The Board's discussions in these other projects are continuing and it would be premature to reach a conclusion in the context of portfolio hedging without considering the implications for these other projects.

BC189   As a result, the Board decided:

(a)   to confirm the requirement in IAS 39* that "the fair value of a financial liability with a demand feature (eg a demand deposit) is not less than the amount payable on demand, discounted from the first date that the amount could be required to be paid", and

(b)   consequently, that a demandable liability cannot qualify for fair value hedge accounting for any time period beyond the shortest period in which the counterparty can demand payment.

The Board noted that, depending on the outcome of its discussions in other projects (principally Insurance (phase II), Revenue Recognition, Leases and Measurement), it might reconsider these decisions at some time in the future.

BC190   The Board also noted that what is designated as the hedged item in a portfolio hedge affects the relevance of this issue, at least to some extent. In particular, if the hedged item is designated as a portion *of the assets* in a portfolio, this issue is irrelevant. To illustrate, assume that in a particular repricing time period an entity has CU100 of fixed rate assets and CU80 of what it regards as fixed rate liabilities and the entity wishes to hedge its net exposure of CU20. Also assume that all of the liabilities are demandable liabilities and the time period is later than that containing the earliest date on which the items can be repaid. If the hedged item is designated as CU20 of *assets*, then the demandable *liabilities* are not included in the hedged item, but rather are used only to determine how much of the assets the entity wishes to designate as being hedged. In such a case, whether the demandable liabilities can be designated as a hedged item in a fair value hedge is irrelevant. However, if the overall net position were to be designated as the hedged item, because the net position comprises CU100 of assets and CU80 of demandable liabilities, whether the demandable liabilities can be designated as a hedged item in a fair value hedge becomes critical.

*see paragraph 49

Given the above points, the Board decided that a portion of assets or liabilities (rather than an overall net position) may be designated as the hedged item, to overcome part of the demandable liabilities issue. It also noted that this approach is consistent with IAS 39*, whereas designating an overall net position is not. IAS 39† prohibits an overall net position from being designated as the hedged item, but permits a similar effect to be achieved by designating an amount of assets (or liabilities) equal to the net position. **BC191**

However, the Board also recognised that this method of designation would not fully resolve the demandable liabilities issue. In particular, the issue is still relevant if, in a particular repricing time period, the entity has so many demandable liabilities whose earliest repayment date is before that time period that (a) they comprise nearly all of what the entity regards as its fixed rate liabilities and (b) its fixed rate liabilities (including the demandable liabilities) exceed its fixed rate assets in this repricing time period. In this case, the entity is in a net liability position. Thus, it needs to designate an amount of the *liabilities* as the hedged item. But unless it has sufficient fixed rate liabilities other than those that can be demanded before that time period, this implies designating the demandable liabilities as the hedged item. Consistently with the Board's decision discussed above, such a hedge does not qualify for fair value hedge accounting. (If the liabilities are non-interest bearing, they cannot be designated as the hedged item in a cash flow hedge because their cash flows do not vary with changes in interest rates, ie there is no cash flow exposure to interest rates.‡ However, the hedging relationship may qualify for cash flow hedge accounting if designated as a hedge of associated assets.) **BC192**

What portion of assets should be designated and the impact on ineffectiveness

Having decided that a portion of assets (or liabilities) could be designated as the hedged item, the Board considered how to overcome the systems problems noted in paragraph BC176(b) and (c). The Board noted that these problems arise from designating individual assets (or liabilities) as the hedged item. Accordingly, the Board decided that the hedged item could be expressed as an *amount* (of assets or liabilities) rather than as individual assets or liabilities. **BC193**

The Board noted that this decision—that the hedged item may be designated as an amount of assets or liabilities rather than as specified items—gives rise to the issue of how the amount designated should be specified. The Board considered comments received on the Exposure Draft that it should not specify any method for designating the hedged item and hence measuring effectiveness. However, the Board concluded that if it provided no guidance, entities might designate in different ways, resulting in little comparability between them. The Board also noted that its objective, when permitting an amount to be designated, was to overcome the systems problems associated with designating individual items whilst achieving a very similar accounting result. Accordingly, it concluded that it should require a method of designation that closely approximates the accounting result that would be achieved by designating individual items. **BC194**

Additionally, the Board noted that designation determines how much, if any, ineffectiveness arises if actual repricing dates in a particular repricing time period vary from those estimated or if the estimated repricing dates are revised. Taking the above **BC195**

*see IAS 39, paragraph 84

†see IAS 39, paragraph AG101

‡see Guidance on Implementing IAS 39, Question and Answer F.6.3.

example of a repricing time period in which there are CU100 of fixed rate assets and the entity designates as the hedged item an amount of CU20 of assets, the Board considered two approaches (a layer approach and a percentage approach) that are summarised below.

Layer approach

BC196   The first of these approaches, illustrated in figure 1, designates the hedged item as a 'layer' (eg (a) the bottom layer, (b) the top layer or (c) a portion of the top layer) of the assets (or liabilities) in a repricing time period. In this approach, the portfolio of CU100 in the above example is considered to comprise a hedged layer of CU20 and an unhedged layer of CU80.

Figure 1: Illustrating the designation of an amount of assets as a layer

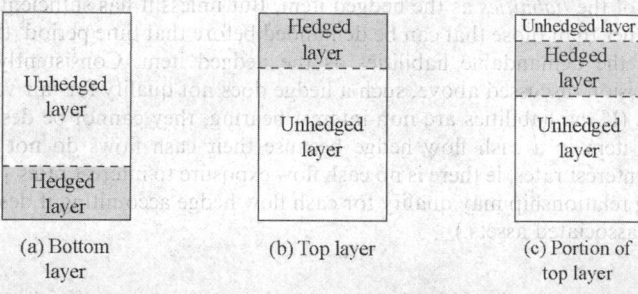

| | | |
| (a) Bottom layer | (b) Top layer | (c) Portion of top layer |

BC197   The Board noted that the layer approach does not result in the recognition of ineffectiveness in all cases when the estimated amount of assets (or liabilities) changes. For example, in a bottom layer approach (see figure 2), if some assets prepay earlier than expected so that the entity revises downward its estimate of the amount of assets in the repricing time period (eg from CU100 to CU90), these reductions are assumed to come first from the unhedged top layer (figure 2(b)). Whether any ineffectiveness arises depends on whether the downward revision reaches the hedged layer of CU20. Thus, if the bottom layer is designated as the hedged item, it is unlikely that the hedged (bottom) layer will be reached and that any ineffectiveness will arise. Conversely, if the top layer is designated (see figure 3), any downward revision to the estimated amount in a repricing time period will reduce the hedged (top) layer and ineffectiveness will arise (figure 3(b)).

Figure 2: Illustrating the effect on changes in prepayments in a bottom layer approach

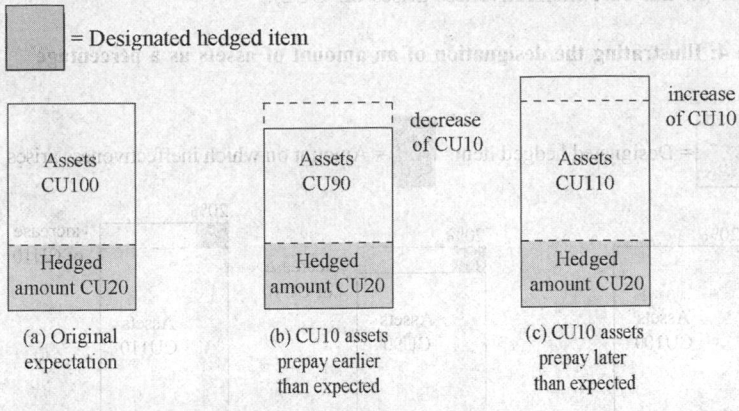

Figure 3: Illustrating the effect on changes in prepayments in a top layer approach

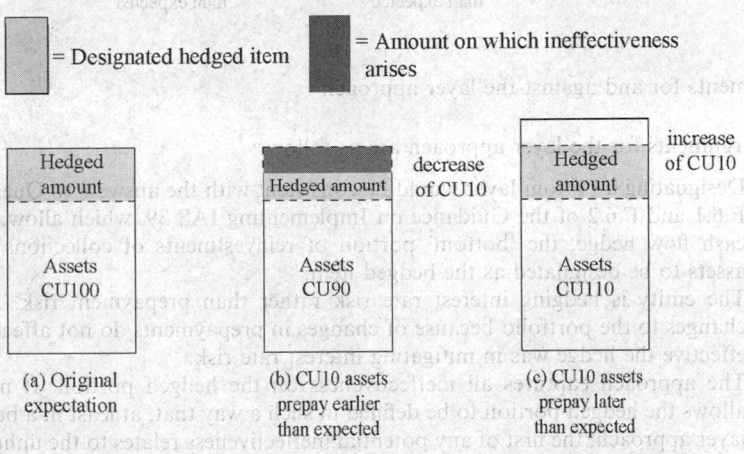

Finally, if some assets prepay *later* than expected so that the entity revises *upward* its estimate of the amount of assets in this repricing time period (eg from CU100 to CU110, see figures 2(c) and 3(c)), no ineffectiveness arises no matter how the layer is designated, on the grounds that the hedged layer of CU20 is still there and that was all that was being hedged.   **BC198**

Percentage approach

The percentage approach, illustrated in figure 4, designates the hedged item as a **BC199** percentage of the assets (or liabilities) in a repricing time period. In this approach, in the portfolio in the above example, 20 per cent of the assets of CU100 in this repricing time period is designated as the hedged item (figure 4(a)). As a result, if some assets prepay *earlier* than expected so that the entity revises *downwards* its estimate of the amount of assets in this repricing time period (eg from CU100 to CU90, figure 4(b)), ineffectiveness arises on 20 per cent of the decrease (in this case ineffectiveness arises on CU2). Similarly, if some assets prepay *later* than expected so that the entity revises *upwards* its estimate of the amount of assets in this repricing time period (eg from CU100 to CU110, figure 4(c)), ineffectiveness arises on 20 per cent of the increase (in this case ineffectiveness arises on CU2).

Figure 4: Illustrating the designation of an amount of assets as a percentage

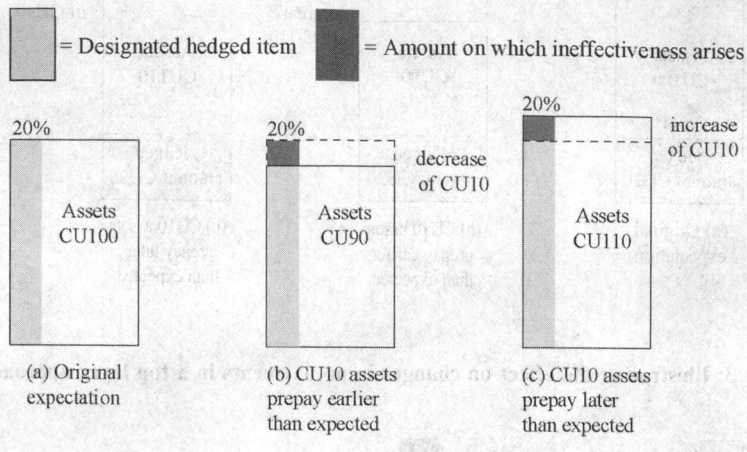

Arguments for and against the layer approach

BC200   The arguments for the layer approach are as follows:

(a)   Designating a bottom layer would be consistent with the answers to Questions F.6.1 and F.6.2 of the Guidance on Implementing IAS 39, which allow, for a cash flow hedge, the 'bottom' portion of reinvestments of collections from assets to be designated as the hedged item.

(b)   The entity is hedging interest rate risk rather than prepayment risk. Any - changes to the portfolio because of changes in prepayments do not affect how effective the hedge was in mitigating interest rate risk.

(c)   The approach captures all ineffectiveness on the hedged portion. It merely allows the hedged portion to be defined in such a way that, at least in a bottom layer approach, the first of any potential ineffectiveness relates to the unhedged portion.

(d)   It is correct that no ineffectiveness arises if changes in prepayment estimates cause more assets to be scheduled into that repricing time period. So long as assets equal to the hedged layer remain, there is no ineffectiveness and upward revisions of the amount in a repricing time period do not affect the hedged layer.

(e)   A prepayable item can be viewed as a combination of a non-prepayable item and a prepayment option. The designation of a bottom layer can be viewed as hedging a part of the life of the non-prepayable item, but none of the pre-payment option. For example, a 25-year prepayable mortgage can be viewed as a combination of (i) a non-prepayable, fixed term, 25-year mortgage and (ii) a written prepayment option that allows the borrower to repay the mortgage early. If the entity hedges this asset with a 5year derivative, this is equivalent to hedging the first five years of component (i). If the position is viewed in this way, no ineffectiveness arises when interest rate changes cause the value of the prepayment option to change (unless the option is exercised and the asset prepaid) because the prepayment option was not hedged.

BC201   The arguments against the layer approach are as follows:

(a)   The considerations that apply to a fair value hedge are different from those that apply to a cash flow hedge. In a cash flow hedge, it is the cash flows associated with the reinvestment of probable future collections that are hedged. In a fair value hedge it is the fair value of the assets that currently exist.

(b)   The fact that no ineffectiveness is recognised if the amount in a repricing time period is re-estimated upwards (with the effect that the entity becomes underhedged) is not in accordance with IAS 39. For a fair value hedge, IAS 39 requires that ineffectiveness is recognised both when the entity becomes over-hedged (ie the derivative exceeds the hedged item) and when it becomes underhedged (ie the derivative is smaller than the hedged item).

(c)   As noted in paragraph BC200(e), a prepayable item can be viewed as a com-bination of a non-prepayable item and a prepayment option. When interest rates change, the fair value of both of these components changes.

(d)   The objective of applying fair value hedge accounting to a hedged item designated in terms of an amount (rather than as individual assets or liabilities) is to obtain results that closely approximate those that would have been obtained if individual assets or liabilities had been designated as the hedged item. If individual prepayable assets had been designated as the hedged item, the change in both the components noted in (c) above (to the extent they are attributable to the hedged risk) would be recognised in profit or loss, both when interest rates increase and when they decrease. Accordingly, the change in the fair value of the hedged asset would differ from the change in the fair value of the hedging derivative (unless that derivative includes an equivalent prepay-ment option) and ineffectiveness would be recognised for the difference. It follows that in the simplified approach of designating the hedged item as an amount, ineffectiveness should similarly arise.

(e)   *All* prepayable assets in a repricing time period, and not just a layer of them, contain a prepayment option whose fair value changes with changes in interest rates. Accordingly, when interest rates change, the fair value of the hedged assets (which include a prepayment option whose fair value has changed) will change by an amount different from that of the hedging derivative (which typically does not contain a prepayment option), and ineffectiveness will arise. This effect occurs regardless of whether interest rates increase or decrea-se—ie regardless of whether re-estimates of prepayments result in the amount in a time period being more or less.

(f)   Interest rate risk and prepayment risk are so closely interrelated that it is not appropriate to separate the two components referred to in paragraph BC200(e) and designate only one of them (or a part of one of them) as the hedged item. Often the biggest single cause of changes in prepayment rates is changes in interest rates. This close relationship is the reason why IAS 39* prohibits a held-to-maturity asset from being a hedged item with respect to either interest rate risk or prepayment risk. Furthermore, most entities do not separate the two components for risk management purposes. Rather, they incorporate the prepayment option by scheduling amounts based on expected maturities. When entities choose to use risk management practices—based on not separ-ating prepayment and interest rate risk—as the basis for designation for hedge accounting purposes, it is not appropriate to separate the two components referred to in paragraph BC200(e) and designate only one of them (or a part of one of them) as the hedged item.

(g)   If interest rates change, the effect on the fair value of a portfolio of prepayable items will be different from the effect on the fair value of a portfolio of otherwise identical but non-prepayable items. However, using a layer approach, this difference would not be recognised—if both portfolios were

*see IAS 39, paragraph 79

hedged to the same extent, both would be recognised in the balance sheet at the same amount.

BC202   The Board was persuaded by the arguments in paragraph BC201 and rejected layer approaches. In particular, the Board concluded that the hedged item should be designated in such a way that if the entity changes its estimates of the repricing time periods in which items are expected to repay or mature (eg in the light of recent prepayment experience), ineffectiveness arises. It also concluded that ineffectiveness should arise both when estimated prepayments decrease, resulting in more assets in a particular repricing time period, and when they increase, resulting in fewer.

Arguments for a third approach—measuring directly the change in fair value of the entire hedged item

BC203   The Board also considered comments on the Exposure Draft that:

(a)   some entities hedge prepayment risk and interest rate risk separately, by hedging to the expected prepayment date using interest rate swaps, and hedging possible variations in these expected prepayment dates using swaptions.

(b)   the embedded derivatives provisions of IAS 39 require some prepayable assets to be separated into a prepayment option and a non-prepayable host contract* (unless the entity is unable to measure separately the prepayment option, in which case it treats the entire asset as held for trading†). This seems to conflict with the view in the Exposure Draft that the two risks are too difficult to separate for the purposes of a portfolio hedge.

BC204   In considering these arguments, the Board noted that the percentage approach described in paragraph AG126(b) is a proxy for measuring the change in the fair value of the *entire* asset (or liability)—including any embedded prepayment option—that is attributable to changes in interest rates. The Board had developed this proxy in the Exposure Draft because it had been informed that most entities (a) do not separate interest rate risk and prepayment risk for risk management purposes and hence (b) were unable to value the change in the value of the entire asset (including any embedded prepayment option) that is attributable to changes in the hedged interest rates. However, the comments described in BC203 indicated that in some cases, entities may be able to measure this change in value directly. The Board noted that such a direct method of measurement is conceptually preferable to the proxy described in paragraph AG126(b) and, accordingly, decided to recognise it explicitly. Thus, for example, if an entity that hedges prepayable assets using a combination of interest rate swaps and swaptions is able to measure directly the change in fair value of the entire asset, it could measure effectiveness by comparing the change in the value of the swaps and swaptions with the change in the fair value of the entire asset (including the change in the value of the prepayment option embedded in them) that is attributable to changes in the hedged interest rate. However, the Board also decided to permit the proxy proposed in the Exposure Draft for those entities that are unable to measure directly the change in the fair value of the entire asset.

Consideration of systems requirements

BC205   Finally, the Board was informed that, to be practicable in terms of systems needs, any approach should not require tracking of the amount in a repricing time period

---

*see IAS 39, paragraphs 11 and AG30(g)

†see IAS 39, paragraph 12

for multiple periods. Therefore it decided that ineffectiveness should be calculated by determining the change in the estimated amount in a repricing time period between one date on which effectiveness is measured and the next, as described more fully in paragraphs AG126 and AG127. This requires the entity to track how much of the change in each repricing time period between these two dates is attributable to revisions in estimates and how much is attributable to the origination of new assets (or liabilities). However, once ineffectiveness has been determined as set out above, the entity in essence starts again, ie it establishes the new amount in each repricing time period (including new items that have been originated since it last tested effectiveness), designates a new hedged item, and repeats the procedures to determine ineffectiveness at the next date it tests effectiveness. Thus the tracking is limited to movements between one date when effectiveness is measured and the next. It is not necessary to track for multiple periods. However, the entity will need to keep records relating to each repricing time period (a) to reconcile the amounts for each repricing time period with the total amounts in the two separate line items in the balance sheet (see paragraph AG114(f)), and (b) to ensure that amounts in the two separate line items are derecognised no later than when the repricing time period to which they relate expires.

The Board also noted that the amount of tracking required by the percentage approach is no more than what would be required by any of the layer approaches. Thus, the Board concluded that none of the approaches was clearly preferable from the standpoint of systems needs. **BC206**

The carrying amount of the hedged item

The last issue noted in paragraph BC176 is how to present in the balance sheet the change in fair value of the hedged item. The Board noted the concern of respondents that the hedged item may contain many—even thousands of—individual assets (or liabilities) and that to change the carrying amounts of each of these individual items would be impracticable. The Board considered dealing with this concern by permitting the change in value to be presented in a single line item in the balance sheet. However, the Board noted that this could result in a decrease in the fair value of a financial asset (financial liability) being recognised as a financial liability (financial asset). Furthermore, for some repricing time periods the hedged item may be an asset, whereas for others it may be a liability. The Board concluded that it would be incorrect to present together the changes in fair value for such repricing time periods, because to do so would combine changes in the fair value of assets with changes in the fair value of liabilities. **BC207**

Accordingly, the Board decided that two line items should be presented, as follows: **BC208**

(a) for those repricing time periods for which the hedged item is an asset, the change in its fair value is presented in a single separate line item within assets; and

(b) for those repricing time periods for which the hedged item is a liability, the change in its fair value is presented in a single separate line item within liabilities.

The Board noted that these line items represent changes in the fair value of the hedged item. For this reason, the Board decided that they should be presented next to financial assets or financial liabilities. **BC209**

Derecognition of amounts included in the separate line items

Derecognition of an asset (or liability) in the hedged portfolio

BC210   The Board discussed how and when amounts recognised in the separate balance sheet line items should be removed from the balance sheet. The Board noted that the objective is to remove such amounts from the balance sheet in the same periods as they would have been removed had individual assets or liabilities (rather than an amount) been designated as the hedged item.

BC211   The Board noted that this objective could be fully met only if the entity schedules individual assets or liabilities into repricing time periods and tracks both for how long the scheduled individual items have been hedged and how much of each item was hedged in each time period. In the absence of such scheduling and tracking, some assumptions would need to be made about these matters and, hence, about how much should be removed from the separate balance sheet line items when an asset (or liability) in the hedged portfolio is derecognised. In addition, some safeguards would be needed to ensure that amounts included in the separate balance sheet line items are removed from the balance sheet over a reasonable period and do not remain in the balance sheet indefinitely. With these points in mind, the Board decided to require that:

(a)   whenever an asset (or liability) in the hedged portfolio is derecognised—whether through earlier than expected prepayment, sale or write-off from impairment—any amount included in the separate balance sheet line item relating to that derecognised asset (or liability) should be removed from the balance sheet and included in the gain or loss on derecognition.

(b)   if an entity cannot determine into which time period(s) a derecognised asset (or liability) was scheduled:

(i)   it should assume that higher than expected prepayments occur on assets scheduled into the first available time period; and

(ii)   it should allocate sales and impairments to assets scheduled into all time periods containing the derecognised item on a systematic and rational basis.

(c)   the entity should track how much of the total amount included in the separate line items relates to each repricing time period, and should remove the amount that relates to a particular time period from the balance sheet no later than when that time period expires.

Amortisation

BC212   The Board also noted that if the designated hedged amount for a repricing time period is reduced, IAS 39* requires that the separate balance sheet line item described in paragraph 89A relating to that reduction is amortised on the basis of a recalculated effective interest rate. The Board noted that for a portfolio hedge of interest rate risk, amortisation based on a recalculated effective interest rate could be complex to determine and could demand significant additional systems requirements. Consequently, the Board decided that in the case of a portfolio hedge of interest rate risk (and only in such a hedge), the line item balance may be amortised using a straight-line method when a method based on a recalculated effective interest rate is not practicable.

---

*see paragraph 92

The hedging instrument

The Board was asked by commentators to clarify whether the hedging instrument may be a portfolio of derivatives containing offsetting risk positions. Commentators noted that previous versions of IAS 39 were unclear on this point. **BC213**

The issue arises because the assets and liabilities in each repricing time period change over time as prepayment expectations change, as items are derecognised and as new items are originated. Thus the net position, and the amount the entity wishes to designate as the hedged item, also changes over time. If the hedged item decreases, the hedging instrument needs to be reduced. However, entities do not normally reduce the hedging instrument by disposing of some of the derivatives contained in it. Instead, entities adjust the hedging instrument by entering into new derivatives with an offsetting risk profile. **BC214**

The Board decided to permit the hedging instrument to be a portfolio of derivatives containing offsetting risk positions for both individual and portfolio hedges. It noted that all of the derivatives concerned are measured at fair value. It also noted that the two ways of adjusting the hedging instrument described in the previous paragraph can achieve substantially the same effect. Therefore the Board clarified paragraph 77 to this effect. **BC215**

Hedge effectiveness for a portfolio hedge of interest rate risk

Some respondents to the Exposure Draft questioned whether IAS 39's effectiveness tests* should apply to a portfolio hedge of interest rate risk. The Board noted that its objective in amending IAS 39 for a portfolio hedge of interest rate risk is to permit fair value hedge accounting to be used more easily, whilst continuing to meet the principles of hedge accounting. One of these principles is that the hedge is highly effective. Thus, the Board concluded that the effectiveness requirements in IAS 39 apply equally to a portfolio hedge of interest rate risk. **BC216**

Some respondents to the Exposure Draft sought guidance on how the effectiveness tests are to be applied to a portfolio hedge. In particular, they asked how the prospective effectiveness test is to be applied when an entity periodically 'rebalances' a hedge (ie adjusts the amount of the hedging instrument to reflect changes in the hedged item). The Board decided that if the entity's risk management strategy is to change the amount of the hedging instrument periodically to reflect changes in the hedged position, that strategy affects the determination of the term of the hedge. Thus, the entity needs to demonstrate that the hedge is expected to be highly effective only for the period until the amount of the hedging instrument is next adjusted. The Board noted that this decision does not conflict with the requirement in paragraph 75 that "a hedging relationship may not be designated for only a portion of the time period during which a hedging instrument remains outstanding". This is because the entire hedging instrument is designated (and not only some of its cash flows, for example, those to the time when the hedge is next adjusted). However, expected effectiveness is assessed by considering the change in the fair value of the entire hedging instrument only for the period until it is next adjusted. **BC217**

A third issue raised in the comment letters was whether, for a portfolio hedge, the retrospective effectiveness test should be assessed for all time buckets in aggregate or individually for each time bucket. The Board decided that entities could use any method to assess retrospective effectiveness, but noted that the chosen method would **BC218**

*see paragraph AG105

form part of the documentation of the hedging relationship made at the inception of the hedge in accordance with paragraph 88(a) and hence could not be decided at the time the retrospective effectiveness test is performed.

Transition to fair value hedge accounting for portfolios of interest rate risk

BC219　In finalising the amendments to IAS 39, the Board considered whether to provide additional guidance for entities wishing to apply fair value hedge accounting to a portfolio hedge that had previously been accounted for using cash flow hedge accounting. The Board noted that such entities could apply paragraph 101(d) to revoke the designation of a cash flow hedge and re-designate a new fair value hedge using the same hedged item and hedging instrument, and decided to clarify this in the Application Guidance. Additionally, the Board concluded that clarification was not required for first-time adopters because IFRS 1 already contained sufficient guidance.

BC220　The Board also considered whether to permit retrospective designation of a portfolio hedge. The Board noted that this would conflict with the principle in paragraph 88(a) that "at the inception of the hedge there is formal designation and documentation of the hedging relationship" and accordingly, decided not to permit retrospective designation.

ELIMINATION OF SELECTED DIFFERENCES FROM US GAAP

BC221　The Board considered opportunities to eliminate differences between IAS 39 and US GAAP. The guidance on measurement and hedge accounting under revised IAS 39 is generally similar to that under US GAAP. The amendments will further reduce or eliminate differences between IAS 39 and US GAAP in the areas listed below. In some other areas, a difference will remain. For example, US GAAP in many, but not all, areas is more detailed, which may result in a difference in accounting when an entity applies an accounting approach under IAS 39 that would not be permitted under US GAAP.

Contracts to buy or sell a non-financial item

(a)　The Board decided that a contract to buy or sell a non-financial item is a derivative within the scope of IAS 39 if the non-financial item that is the subject of the contract is readily convertible to cash and the contract is not a 'normal' purchase or sale. This requirement is comparable to the definition of a derivative in SFAS 133, which also includes contracts for which the underlying is readily convertible to cash, and to the scope exclusion in SFAS 133 for 'normal' purchases and sales.

Scope: loan commitments

(b)　The Board decided to add a paragraph to IAS 39 to exclude particular loan commitments that are not settled net. Such loan commitments were within the scope of the original IAS 39. The amendment moves IAS 39 closer to US GAAP.

Unrealised gains and losses on available-for-sale financial assets

(c)　The Board decided to eliminate the option to recognise in profit or loss gains and losses on available-for-sale financial assets (IAS 39, paragraph 55(b)), and thus require such gains and losses to be recognised in equity. The change is consistent with SFAS 115, which does not provide the option in the original IAS 39 to recognise gains and losses on available-for-sale financial assets in profit or loss. SFAS 115 requires those unrealised gains and losses to be recognised in other comprehensive income (not profit or loss).

Fair value in active markets

(d)   The Board decided to amend the wording in IAS 39, paragraph AG71, to state that, instead of a quoted market price *normally* being the best evidence of fair value, a quoted market price *is* the best evidence of fair value. This is similar to SFAS 107 *Disclosures about Fair Value of Financial Instruments.*

Fair value in inactive markets

(e)   The Board decided to include in IAS 39 a requirement that the best evidence of the fair value of an instrument that is not traded in an active market is the transaction price, unless the fair value is evidenced by comparison with other observable current market transactions in the same instrument (ie without modification or repackaging) or based on a valuation technique incorporating only observable market data. This is similar to the requirements of EITF 02-3 *Issues Involved in Accounting for Derivative Contracts Held for Trading Purposes and Contracts Involved in Energy Trading and Risk Management Activities.*

Impaired fixed rate loans: observable market price

(f)   The Board decided to permit an impaired fixed interest rate loan to be measured using an observable market price. SFAS 114 allows impairment to be measured on the basis of a loan's observable market price.

Reversal of impairment losses on investments in equity instruments

(g)   The Board decided that if an entity recognises an impairment loss on an available-for-sale equity investment and the fair value of the investment subsequently increases, the increase in fair value should be recognised in equity. This is comparable to US GAAP under which reversals of impairment losses are not permitted.

Hedges of firm commitments

(h)   The Board decided to require hedges of firm commitments to be treated as fair value hedges instead of cash flow hedges as was required under the original IAS 39 (except foreign currency risk when the hedge may be designated as either a cash flow hedge or a fair value hedge). This change brings IAS 39 closer to SFAS 133.

Basis adjustments to financial assets or financial liabilities resulting from hedges of forecast transactions

(i)   Basis adjustments to financial assets or financial liabilities resulting from hedges of forecast transactions are not permitted under SFAS 133. The revised IAS 39 also precludes such basis adjustments.

Basis adjustments to non-financial assets or non-financial liabilities resulting from hedges of forecast transactions

(j)   The Board decided to permit entities to apply basis adjustments to non-financial assets or non-financial liabilities that result from hedges of forecast transactions. Although US GAAP precludes basis adjustments, permitting a choice in IAS 39 allows entities to meet the US GAAP requirements.

SUMMARY OF CHANGES FROM THE EXPOSURE DRAFT

BC222   The main changes from the Exposure Draft's proposals are as follows:

Scope

(a)   The Standard adopts the proposal in the Exposure Draft that loan commitments that cannot be settled net and are not classified at fair value through profit or loss are excluded from the scope of the Standard. The Standard requires, however, that a commitment to extend a loan at a below-market interest rate is initially recognised at fair value, and subsequently measured at the higher of (i) the amount determined under IAS 37 and (ii) the amount initially recognised, less where appropriate, cumulative amortisation recognised in accordance with IAS 18.

(b)   The Standard adopts the proposal in the Exposure Draft that financial guarantees are initially recognised at fair value, but clarifies that subsequently they are measured at the higher of (a) the amount determined under IAS 37 and (b) the amount initially recognised, less, where appropriate, cumulative amortisation recognised in accordance with IAS 18.

Definitions

(c)   The Standard amends the definition of 'originated loans and receivables' to 'loans and receivables'. Under the revised definition, an entity is permitted to classify as loans and receivables purchased loans that are not quoted in an active market.

(d)   The Standard amends the definition of transaction costs in the Exposure Draft to include internal costs, provided they are incremental and directly attributable to the acquisition, issue or disposal of a financial asset or financial liability.

(e)   The Standard amends the definition of the effective interest rate proposed in the Exposure Draft so that the effective interest rate is calculated using estimated cash flows for all instruments. An exception is made for those rare cases in which it is not possible to estimate cash flows reliably, when the Standard requires the use of contractual cash flows over the contractual life of the instrument. The Standard further stipulates that when accounting for a change in estimates, entities adjust the carrying amount of the instrument in the period of change with a corresponding gain or loss recognised in profit or loss. To calculate the new carrying amount, entities discount revised estimated cash flows at the original effective rate.

Derecognition of a financial asset

(f)   The Exposure Draft proposed that an entity would continue to recognise a financial asset to the extent of its continuing involvement in that asset. Hence, an entity would derecognise a financial asset only if it did not have any continuing involvement in that asset. The Standard uses the concepts of control and of risks and rewards of ownership to determine whether, and to what extent, a financial asset is derecognised. The continuing involvement approach applies only if an entity retains some, but not substantially all, the risks and rewards of ownership and also retains control (see also (i) below).

(g) Unlike the Exposure Draft, the Standard clarifies when a part of a larger financial asset should be considered for derecognition. The Standard requires a part of a larger financial asset to be considered for derecognition if, and only if, the part is one of:

- only specifically identified cash flows from a financial asset;
- only a fully proportionate (pro rata) share of the cash flows from a financial asset; or
- only a fully proportionate (pro rata) share of specifically identified cash flows from a financial asset.

In all other cases, the Standard requires the financial asset to be considered for derecognition in its entirety.

(h) The Standard retains the conditions proposed in the Exposure Draft for 'pass-through arrangements' in which an entity retains the contractual rights to receive cash flows of a financial asset, but assumes a contractual obligation to pay those cash flows to one or more entities. However, because of confusion over the meaning of the term 'pass-through arrangements', the Standard does not use this term.

(i) The Standard requires that an entity first assesses whether it has transferred substantially all the risks and rewards of ownership. If an entity has retained substantially all such risks and rewards, it continues to recognise the transferred asset. If it has transferred substantially all such risks and rewards, it derecognises the transferred asset. If an entity has neither transferred nor retained substantially all the risks and rewards of ownership of the transferred asset, it assesses whether it has retained control over the transferred asset. If it has retained control, the Standard requires the entity to continue recognising the transferred asset to the extent of its continuing involvement in the transferred asset. If it has not retained control, the entity derecognises the transferred asset.

(j) The Standard provides guidance on how to evaluate the concepts of risks and rewards and of control for derecognition purposes.

Measurement

(k) The Standard adopts the option proposed in the Exposure Draft to permit designation of any financial asset or financial liability on initial recognition as one to be measured at fair value, with changes in fair value recognised in profit or loss. However, the Standard clarifies that the fair value of liabilities with a demand feature, for example, demand deposits, is not less than the amount payable on demand discounted from the first date that the amount could be required to be paid.

(l) The Standard adopts the proposal in the Exposure Draft that quoted prices in active markets should be used to determine fair value in preference to other valuation techniques. The Standard adds guidance that if a rate (rather than a price) is quoted, these quoted rates are used as inputs into valuation techniques to determine the fair value. The Standard further clarifies that if an entity operates in more than one active market, the entity uses the price at which a transaction would occur at the balance sheet date in the same instrument (ie without modification or repackaging) in the most advantageous active market to which the entity has immediate access.

(m) The Standard simplifies the fair value measurement hierarchy in an inactive market so that recent market transactions do not take precedence over a valuation technique. Rather, when there is not a price in an active market, a valuation technique is used. Such valuation techniques include using recent arm's length market transactions.

(n) The Standard also clarifies that the best estimate of fair value at initial recognition of a financial instrument that is not quoted in an active market is the transaction price, unless the fair value of the instrument is evidenced by other observable market transactions or is based on a valuation technique whose variables include only data from observable markets.

Impairment of financial assets

(o) The Standard clarifies that an impairment loss is recognised only when it has been incurred. The Standard eliminates some of the detailed guidance in the Exposure Draft, in particular, the example of how to calculate the discount rate for the purpose of measuring impairment in a group of financial assets.

(p) The Exposure Draft proposed that impairment losses recognised on investments in debt or equity instruments that are classified as available for sale cannot be reversed through profit or loss. The Standard requires that for available-for-sale debt instruments, an impairment loss is reversed through profit or loss when fair value increases and the increase can be objectively related to an event occurring after the loss was recognised. Impairment losses recognised on available-for-sale equity instruments cannot be reversed through profit or loss, ie any subsequent increase in fair value is recognised in equity.

Hedge accounting

(q) The Standard requires that when a hedged forecast transaction actually occurs and results in the recognition of a financial asset or a financial liability, the gain or loss deferred in equity does not adjust the initial carrying amount of the asset or liability (ie 'basis adjustment' is prohibited), but remains in equity and is recognised in profit or loss consistently with the recognition of gains and losses on the asset or liability. For hedges of forecast transactions that will result in the recognition of a non-financial asset or a non-financial liability, the entity has a choice of whether to apply basis adjustment or retain the hedging gain or loss in equity and recognise it in profit or loss when the asset or liability affects profit or loss.

(r) The Exposure Draft proposed to treat hedges of firm commitments as fair value hedges (rather than as cash flow hedges). The Standard adopts this requirement but clarifies that a hedge of the foreign currency risk of a firm commitment may be accounted for as either a fair value hedge or a cash flow hedge.

Transition

(s) The Exposure Draft maintained the prior guidance that a forecast intragroup transaction may be designated as the hedged item in a foreign currency cash flow hedge provided the transaction is highly probable, meets all other hedge accounting criteria, and will result in the recognition of an intragroup monetary item. The Standard (as revised in 2003) did not include this guidance in the light of comments received from some constituents questioning its conceptual basis. After the revised Standard was issued, constituents raised concerns that it was common practice for entities to designate a forecast intragroup transaction as the hedged item and that the revised IAS 39 created a difference from

US GAAP. In response to these concerns, the Board published an Exposure Draft in July 2004*. That Exposure Draft proposed to allow an entity to apply hedge accounting in the consolidated financial statements to a highly probable forecast external transaction denominated in the functional currency of the entity entering into the transaction, provided the transaction gave rise to an exposure that would have an effect on the consolidated profit or loss (ie was denominated in a currency other than the group's presentation currency). After discussing the comment letters received on that Exposure Draft, the Board decided to permit the foreign currency risk of a forecast intragroup transaction to be the hedged item in a cash flow hedge in consolidated financial statements provided the transaction is denominated in a currency other than the functional currency of the entity entering into that transaction and the foreign currency risk will affect consolidated profit or loss. In issuing this amendment the Board concluded that:

(i) allowing a forecast intragroup transaction to be designated as the hedged item in consolidated financial statements is consistent with the functional currency framework in IAS 21 *The Effects of Changes in Foreign Exchange Rates*†, which recognises a functional currency exposure whenever a transaction (including a forecast transaction) is denominated in a currency different from the functional currency of the entity entering into the transaction.

(ii) allowing a forecast transaction (intragroup or external) to be designated as the hedged item in consolidated financial statements would not be consistent with the functional currency framework in IAS 21 if the transaction is denominated in the functional currency of the entity entering into it. Accordingly, such transactions should not be permitted to be designated as hedged items in a foreign currency cash flow hedge.

(iii) it is consistent with paragraphs 97 and 98 that any gain or loss that is recognised directly in equity in a cash flow hedge of a forecast intragroup transaction should be reclassified into consolidated profit or loss in the same period or periods during which the foreign currency risk of the hedged transaction affects consolidated profit or loss.‡

(t) The revised Standard adopts the proposal in the Exposure Draft that, on transition, an entity is permitted to designate a previously recognised financial asset or financial liability as a financial asset or a financial liability at fair value through profit or loss or available for sale. However, a disclosure requirement has been added to IAS 32 to provide information about the fair value of the financial assets or financial liabilities designated into each category and the classification and carrying amount in the previous financial statements.

(u) The Exposure Draft proposed retrospective application of the derecognition provisions of the revised IAS 39 to financial assets derecognised under the original IAS 39. The Standard requires prospective application, namely that entities do not recognise those assets that were derecognised under the original Standard, but permits retrospective application from a date of the entity's choosing, provided that the information needed to apply IAS 39 to assets and liabilities derecognised as a result of past transactions was obtained at the time of initially accounting for those transactions.

---

*ASB footnote: *In the UK equivalent proposed amendments were contained in FRED 30 Third Supplement published in July 2004.*

†ASB footnote: *The corresponding requirements in the UK and the Republic of Ireland are in FRS 23 (IAS 21)* The Effects of Changes in Foreign Exchange Rates.

‡*Editor's note: section (s) added October 2005, with consequential re-referencing.*

(v)   The Exposure Draft proposed, and the revised Standard originally required, retrospective application of the 'day 1' gain or loss recognition requirements in paragraph AG76. After the revised Standard was issued, constituents raised concerns that retrospective application would diverge from the requirements of US GAAP, would be difficult and expensive to implement, and might require subjective assumptions about what was observable and what was not. In response to these concerns, the Board decided:

(i)   to permit entities to apply the requirements in the last sentence of paragraph AG76 in any one of the following ways:

- retrospectively, as previously required by IAS 39
- prospectively to transactions entered into after 25 October 2002, the effective date of equivalent US GAAP requirements
- prospectively to transactions entered into after 1 January 2004, the date of transition to IFRSs for many entities.

(ii)   to clarify that a gain or loss should be recognised after initial recognition only to the extent that it arises from a change in a factor (including time) that market participants would consider in setting a price. Some constituents asked the Board to clarify that straight-line amortisation is an appropriate method of recognising the difference between a transaction price (used as fair value in accordance with paragraph AG76) and a valuation made at the time of the transaction that was not based solely on data from observable markets. The Board decided not to do this. It concluded that although straight-line amortisation may be an appropriate method in some cases, it will not be appropriate in others.*

DISSENTING OPINIONS

Dissent of Anthony T Cope, James J Leisenring and Warren J McGregor from the issue of IAS 39 in December 2003

DO1   Messrs Cope, Leisenring and McGregor dissent from the issue of this Standard.

DO2   Mr Leisenring dissents because he disagrees with the conclusions concerning derecognition, impairment of certain assets and the adoption of basis adjustment hedge accounting in certain circumstances.

DO3   The Standard requires in paragraphs 30 and 31 that to the extent of an entity's continuing involvement in an asset, a liability should be recognised for the consideration received. Mr Leisenring believes that the result of that accounting is to recognise assets that fail to meet the definition of assets and to record liabilities that fail to meet the definition of liabilities. Furthermore, the Standard fails to recognise forward contracts, puts or call options and guarantees that are created, but instead records a fictitious 'borrowing' as a result of rights and obligations created by those contracts. There are other consequences of the continuing involvement approach that has been adopted. For transferors, it results in very different accounting by two entities when they have identical contractual rights and obligations only because one entity once owned the transferred financial asset. Furthermore, the 'borrowing' that is recognised is not accounted for like other loans, so no interest expense may be recorded. Indeed, implementing the proposed approach requires the specific override of measurement and presentation standards applicable to other similar financial instruments that do not arise from derecognition transactions. For example, derivatives created by derecognition transactions are not accounted for at fair value. For

*Editor's note: Section V added in October 2005.

transferees, the approach also requires the override of the recognition and measurement requirements applicable to other similar financial instruments. If an instrument is acquired in a transfer transaction that fails the derecognition criteria, the transferee recognises and measures it differently from an instrument that is acquired from the same counterparty separately.

Mr Leisenring also disagrees with the requirement in paragraph 64 to include an **DO4** asset that has been individually judged not to be impaired in a portfolio of similar assets for an additional portfolio assessment of impairment. Once an asset is judged not to be impaired, it is irrelevant whether the entity owns one or more similar assets as those assets have no implications for whether the asset that was individually considered for impairment is or is not impaired. The result of this accounting is that two entities could each own 50 per cent of a single loan. Both entities could conclude the loan is not impaired. However, if one of the two entities happens to have other loans that are similar, it would be allowed to recognise an impairment with respect to the loan where the other entity is not. Accounting for identical exposures differently is unacceptable. Mr Leisenring believes that the arguments in paragraph BC115 are compelling.

Mr Leisenring also dissents from paragraph 98 which allows but does not require **DO5** basis adjustment for hedges of forecast transactions that result in the recognition of non-financial assets or liabilities. This accounting results in always adjusting the recorded asset or liability at the date of initial recognition away from its fair value. It also records an asset, if the basis adjustment alternative is selected, at an amount other than its cost as defined in IAS 16 *Property, Plant and Equipment* and further described in paragraph 16 of that Standard. If a derivative were to be considered a part of the cost of acquiring an asset, hedge accounting in these circumstances should not be elective to be consistent with IAS 16. Mr Leisenring also objects to creating this alternative as a result of an improvement project that ostensibly had as an objective the reduction of alternatives. The noncomparability that results from this alternative is both undesirable and unnecessary.

Mr Leisenring also dissents from the application guidance in paragraph AG71 and in **DO6** particular the conclusion contained in paragraph BC98. He does not believe that an entity that originates a contract in one market should measure the fair value of the contract by reference to a different market in which the transaction did not take place. If prices change in the transacting market, that price change should be recognised when subsequently measuring the fair value of the contract. However, there are many implications of switching between markets when measuring fair value that the Board has not yet addressed. Mr Leisenring believes a gain or loss should not be recognised based on the fact a transaction could occur in a different market.

Mr Cope dissents from paragraph 64 and agrees with Mr Leisenring's analysis and **DO7** conclusions on loan impairment as set out above in paragraph DO4. He finds it counter-intuitive that a loan that has been determined not to be impaired following careful analysis should be subsequently accounted for as if it were impaired when included in a portfolio.

Mr Cope also dissents from paragraph 98, and, in particular, the Board's decision to **DO8** allow a free choice over whether basis adjustment is used when accounting for hedges of forecast transactions that result in the recognition of non-financial assets or non-financial liabilities. In his view, of the three courses of action open to the Board— retaining IAS 39's requirement to use basis adjustment, prohibiting basis adjustment as proposed in the June 2002 Exposure Draft, or providing a choice—the Board has selected the worst course. Mr Cope believes that the best approach would have been to prohibit basis adjustment, as proposed in the Exposure Draft, because, in his opinion, basis adjustments result in the recognition of assets and liabilities at inappropriate amounts.

DO9 Mr Cope believes that increasing the number of choices in international standards is bad policy. The Board's decision potentially creates major differences between entities choosing one option and those choosing the other. This lack of comparability will adversely affect users' ability to make sound economic decisions.

D10 In addition, Mr Cope notes that entities that are US registrants may choose not to adopt basis adjustment in order to avoid a large reconciling difference to US GAAP. Mr Cope believes that increasing differences between IFRS-compliant entities that are US registrants and those that are not is undesirable.

DO11 Mr McGregor dissents from paragraph 98 and agrees with Mr Cope's and Mr Leisenring's analyses and conclusions as set out above in paragraphs DO5 and DO8-DO10.

DO12 Mr McGregor also dissents from this Standard because he disagrees with the conclusions about impairment of certain assets.

DO13 Mr McGregor disagrees with paragraphs 67 and 69, which deal with the impairment of equity investments classified as available for sale. These paragraphs require impairment losses on such assets to be recognised in profit or loss when there is objective evidence that the asset is impaired. Previously recognised impairment losses are not to be reversed through profit and loss when the assets' fair value increases. Mr McGregor notes that the Board's reasoning for prohibiting reversals through profit or loss of previously impaired available-for-sale equity investments, set out in paragraph BC130 of the Basis for Conclusions, is that it "..could not find an acceptable way to distinguish reversals of impairment losses from other increases in fair value". He agrees with this reasoning but believes that it applies equally to the recognition of impairment losses in the first place. Mr McGregor believes that the significant subjectivity involved in assessing whether a reduction in fair value represents an impairment (and thus should be recognised in profit or loss) or another decrease in value (and should be recognised directly in equity) will at best lead to a lack of comparability within an entity over time and between entities, and at worst provide an opportunity for entities to manage reported profit or loss.

DO14 Mr McGregor believes that all changes in the fair value of assets classified as available for sale should be recognised in profit or loss. However, such a major change to the Standard would need to be subject to the Board's full due process. At this time, to overcome the concerns expressed in paragraph DO13, he believes that for equity investments classified as available for sale, the Standard should require all changes in fair value below cost to be recognised in profit or loss as impairments and reversals of impairments and all changes in value above cost to be recognised in equity. This approach treats all changes in value the same way, no matter what their cause. The problem of how to distinguish an impairment loss from another decline in value (and of deciding whether there is an impairment in the first place) is eliminated because there is no longer any subjectivity involved. In addition, the approach is consistent with IAS 16 *Property, Plant and Equipment* and IAS 38 *Intangible Assets*.

DO15 Mr McGregor disagrees with paragraph 106 of the Standard and with the consequential amendments to paragraph 27 of IFRS 1 *First-time Adoption of International Financial Reporting Standards*. Paragraph 106 requires entities to apply the derecognition provisions prospectively to financial assets. Paragraph 27 of IFRS 1 requires first-time adopters to apply the derecognition provisions of IAS 39 (as revised in 2003) prospectively to non-derivative financial assets and financial liabilities. Mr McGregor believes that existing IAS 39 appliers should apply the derecognition provisions retrospectively to financial assets, and that first-time adopters should apply the derecognition provisions of IAS 39 retrospectively to all financial assets and financial liabilities. He is concerned that financial assets may have been derecognised under the original IAS 39 by entities that were subject to it, which might not have been derecognised under the revised IAS 39. He is also concerned that non-derivative financial assets and financial liabilities may have been derecognised by first-time adopters under previous GAAP that would not have been derecognised under the revised IAS 39. These amounts may be significant in many cases. Not requiring recognition of such amounts will result in the loss of relevant information and will impair the ability of users of financial statements to make sound economic decisions.

Dissent of John T Smith from the issue in March 2004 of amendments to International Accounting Standard IAS 39 on Fair Value Hedge Accounting for a Portfolio Hedge of Interest Rate Risk

Mr Smith dissents from these Amendments to IAS 39 Financial Instruments: **DO1**
Recognition and Measurement *Fair Value Hedge Accounting for a Portfolio Hedge of Interest Rate Risk*. He agrees with the objective of finding a macro hedging solution that would reduce systems demands without undermining the fundamental accounting principles related to derivative instruments and hedging activities. However, Mr Smith believes that some respondents' support for these Amendments and their willingness to accept IAS 39 is based more on the extent to which the Amendments reduce recognition of ineffectiveness, volatility of profit or loss, and volatility of equity than on whether the Amendments reduce systems demands without undermining the fundamental accounting principles.

Mr Smith believes some decisions made during the Board's deliberations result in an **DO2**
approach to hedge accounting for a portfolio hedge that does not capture what was originally intended, namely a result that is substantially equivalent to designating an individual asset or liability as the hedged item. He understands some respondents will not accept IAS 39 unless the Board provides still another alternative that will further reduce reported volatility. Mr Smith believes that the Amendments already go beyond their intended objective. In particular, he believes that features of these Amendments can be applied to smooth out ineffectiveness and achieve results substantially equivalent to the other methods of measuring ineffectiveness that the Board considered when developing the Exposure Draft. The Board rejected those methods because they did not require the immediate recognition of all ineffectiveness. He also believes those features could be used to manage earnings.

FRS 26 'Financial Instruments: Measurement'

ILLUSTRATIVE EXAMPLE

This example accompanies, but is not part of, FRS 26.

Facts

IE1   On 1 January 20x1, Entity A identifies a portfolio comprising assets and liabilities whose interest rate risk it wishes to hedge. The liabilities include demandable deposit liabilities that the depositor may withdraw at any time without notice. For risk management purposes, the entity views all of the items in the portfolio as fixed rate items.

IE2   For risk management purposes, Entity A analyses the assets and liabilities in the portfolio into repricing time periods based on expected repricing dates. The entity uses monthly time periods and schedules items for the next five years (ie it has 60 separate monthly time periods).* The assets in the portfolio are prepayable assets that Entity A allocates into time periods based on the expected prepayment dates, by allocating a percentage of all of the assets, rather than individual items, into each time period. The portfolio also includes demandable liabilities that the entity expects, on a portfolio basis, to repay between one month and five years and, for risk management purposes, are scheduled into time periods on this basis. On the basis of this analysis, Entity A decides what amount it wishes to hedge in each time period.

IE3   This example deals only with the repricing time period expiring in three months' time, ie the time period maturing on 31 March 20x1 (a similar procedure would be applied for each of the other 59 time periods). Entity A has scheduled assets of CU100 million and liabilities of CU80 million into this time period. All of the liabilities are repayable on demand.

IE4   Entity A decides, for risk management purposes, to hedge the net position of CU20 million and accordingly enters into an interest rate swap† on 1 January 20x1 to pay a fixed rate and receive LIBOR, with a notional principal amount of CU20 million and a fixed life of three months.

IE5   This Example makes the following simplifying assumptions:

(a)   the coupon on the fixed leg of the swap is equal to the fixed coupon on the asset;

(b)   the coupon on the fixed leg of the swap becomes payable on the same dates as the interest payments on the asset; and

(c)   the interest on the variable leg of the swap is the overnight LIBOR rate. As a result, the entire fair value change of the swap arises from the fixed leg only, because the variable leg is not exposed to changes in fair value due to changes in interest rates.

In this Example principal cash flows have been scheduled into time periods but the related interest cash flows have been included when calculating the change in the fair value of the hedged item. Other methods of scheduling assets and liabilities are also possible. Also, in this Example, monthly repricing time periods have been used. An entity may choose narrower or wider time periods.

†The Example uses a swap as the hedging instrument. An entity may use forward rate agreements or other derivatives as hedging instruments.*

In cases when these simplifying assumptions do not hold, greater ineffectiveness will arise.

The ineffectiveness arising from (a) could be eliminated by designating as the hedged item a portion of the cash flows on the asset that are equivalent to the fixed leg of the swap.)

It is also assumed that Entity A tests effectiveness on a monthly basis.   **IE6**

The fair value of an equivalent non-prepayable asset of CU20 million, ignoring   **IE7**
changes in value that are not attributable to interest rate movements, at various times during the period of the hedge is as follows:

	1 Jan 20x1	31 Jan 20x1	1 Feb 20x1	28 Feb 20x1	31 Mar 20x1
Fair value (asset) (CU)	20,000,000	20,047,408	20,047,408	20,023,795	Nil

The fair value of the swap at various times during the period of the hedge is as   **IE8**
follows.

	1 Jan 20x1	31 Jan 20x1	1 Feb 20x1	28 Feb 20x1	31 Mar 20x1
Fair value (liability) (CU)	Nil	(47,408)	(47,408)	(23,795)	Nil

Accounting Treatment

On 1 January 20x1, Entity A designates as the hedged item an amount of CU20   **IE9**
million of assets in the three-month time period. It designates as the hedged risk the change in the value of the hedged item (ie the CU20 million of assets) that is attributable to changes in LIBOR. It also complies with the other designation requirements set out in paragraphs 88(d) and AG119 of the Standard.

Entity A designates as the hedging instrument the interest rate swap described in   **IE10**
paragraph IE4.

End of month 1 (31 January 20x1)

On 31 January 20x1 (at the end of month 1) when Entity A tests effectiveness,   **IE11**
LIBOR has decreased. Based on historical prepayment experience, Entity A estimates that, as a consequence, prepayments will occur faster than previously estimated. As a result it re-estimates the amount of assets scheduled into this time period (excluding new assets originated during the month) as CU96 million.

The fair value of the designated interest rate swap with a notional principal of CU20   **IE12**
million is (CU47,408)* (the swap is a liability).

Entity A computes the change in the fair value of the hedged item, taking into   **IE13**
account the change in estimated prepayments, as follows.

(a)   First, it calculates the percentage of the initial estimate of the assets in the time period that was hedged. This is 20 per cent (CU20 million ÷ CU100 million).

(b)   Second, it applies this percentage (20 per cent) to its revised estimate of the amount in that time period (CU96 million) to calculate the amount that is the hedged item based on its revised estimate. This is CU19.2 million.

*see paragraph IE8.

(c) Third, it calculates the change in the fair value of this revised estimate of the hedged item (CU19.2 million) that is attributable to changes in LIBOR. This is CU45,511 (CU47,408* × (CU19.2 million ÷ CU20 million)).

IE14   Entity A makes the following accounting entries relating to this time period: †

Dr	Cash	CU172,097	
Cr	Income statement (interest income)§		CU172,097

To recognise the interest received on the hedged amount

Dr	Income statement (interestexpense)	CU179,268	
Cr	Income statement (interest income)		CU179,268
Cr	Cash		Nil

To recognise the interest received and paid on the swap designated as the hedging instrument.

Dr	Income statement (loss)	CU47,408
Cr	Derivative liability	CU47,408

To recognise the change in the fair value of the swap.

Dr	Separate balance sheet lineitem	CU45,511
Cr	Income statement (gain)	CU45,511

To recognise the change in the fair value of the hedged amount.

IE15   The net result on profit or loss (excluding interest income and interest expense) is to recognise a loss of (CU1,897). This represents ineffectiveness in the hedging relationship that arises from the change in estimated prepayment dates.

Beginning of month 2

IE16   On 1 February 20x1 Entity A sells a proportion of the assets in the various time periods. Entity A calculates that it has sold $8^{1}/_{3}$ per cent of the entire portfolio of assets. Because the assets were allocated into time periods by allocating a percentage of the assets (rather than individual assets) into each time period, Entity A determines that it cannot ascertain into which specific time periods the sold assets were scheduled. Hence it uses a systematic and rational basis of allocation. Based on the fact that it sold a representative selection of the assets in the portfolio, Entity A allocates the sale proportionately over all time periods.

IE17   On this basis, Entity A computes that it has sold $8^{1}/_{3}$ per cent of the assets allocated to the three-month time period, ie CU8 million ($8^{1}/_{3}$ per cent of CU96 million). The proceeds received are CU8,018,400, equal to the fair value of the assets.‡ On derecognition of the assets, Entity A also removes from the separate balance sheet line item an amount that represents the change in the fair value of the hedged assets that

---

*ie CU20,047,408 − CU20,000,000. See paragraph IE7.

†This Example does not show how amounts of interest income and interest expense are calculated.

‡The amount realised on sale of the asset is the fair value of a prepayable asset, which is less than the fair value of the equivalent non-prepayable asset shown in paragraph IE7.

it has now sold. This is $8^1/_3$ per cent of the total line item balance of CU45,511, ie CU3,793.

Entity A makes the following accounting entries to recognise the sale of the asset and the removal of part of the balance in the separate balance sheet line item.   **IE18**

Dr	Cash	CU8,018,400	
Cr	Asset		CU8,000,000
Cr	Separate balance sheet line item		CU3,793
Cr	Income statement (gain)		CU14,607

To recognise the sale of the asset at fair value and to recognise a gain on sale.

Because the change in the amount of the assets is not attributable to a change in the hedged interest rate no ineffectiveness arises.

Entity A now has CU88 million of assets and CU80 million of liabilities in this time period. Hence the net amount Entity A wants to hedge is now CU8 million and, accordingly, it designates CU8 million as the hedged amount.   **IE19**

Entity A decides to adjust the hedging instrument by designating only a proportion of the original swap as the hedging instrument. Accordingly, it designates as the hedging instrument CU8 million or 40 per cent of the notional amount of the original swap with a remaining life of two months and a fair value of CU18,963.* It also complies with the other designation requirements in paragraphs 88(a) and AG119 of the Standard. The CU12 million of the notional amount of the swap that is no longer designated as the hedging instrument is either classified as held for trading with changes in fair value recognised in profit or loss, or is designated as the hedging instrument in a different hedge. †   **IE20**

As at 1 February 20x1 and after accounting for the sale of assets, the separate balance sheet line item is CU41,718 (CU45,511 – CU3,793), which represents the cumulative change in fair value of CU17.6‡ million of assets. However, as at 1 February 20x1, Entity A is hedging only CU8 million of assets that have a cumulative change in fair value of CU18,963.§ The remaining separate balance sheet line item of CU22,755¶¶ relates to an amount of assets that Entity A still holds but is no longer hedging. Accordingly Entity A amortises this amount over the remaining life of the time period, ie it amortises CU22,755 over two months.   **IE21**

Entity A determines that it is not practicable to use a method of amortisation based on a recalculated effective yield and hence uses a straight-line method.   **IE22**

---

*CU47,408 ∞ 40 per cent

†The entity could instead enter into an offsetting swap with a notional principal of CU12 million to adjust its position and designate as the hedging instrument all CU20 million of the existing swap and all CU12 million of the new offsetting swap.

‡CU19.2 million-($8^1/_3$% ∞ CU19.2 million)

§CU41,718 ∞ (CU8 million ≥ CU17.6 million)

¶¶CU41,718 – CU18,963

End of month 2 (28 February 20x1)

IE23   On 28 February 20x1 when Entity A next tests effectiveness, LIBOR is unchanged. Entity A does not revise its prepayment expectations. The fair value of the designated interest rate swap with a notional principal of CU8 million is (CU9,518)* (the swap is a liability). Also, Entity A calculates the fair value of the CU8 million of the hedged assets as at 28 February 20x1 as CU8,009,518†.

IE24   Entity A makes the following accounting entries relating to the hedge in this time period:

Dr	Cash	CU71,707	
Cr	Income statement (interest income)		CU71,707

To recognise the interest received on the hedged amount (CU8 million).

Dr	Income statement (interest expense)	CU71,707	
Cr	Income statement (interest income)		CU62,115
Cr	Cash		CU9,592

To recognise the interest received and paid on the portion of the swap designated as the hedging instrument (CU8 million).

Dr	Derivative liability	CU9,445	
Cr	Income statement (gain)		CU9,445

To recognise the change in the fair value of the portion of the swap designated as the hedging instrument (CU8 million) (CU9,518 – CU18,963).

Dr	Income statement (loss)	CU9,445	
Cr	Separate balance sheet line item		CU9,445

To recognise the change in the fair value of the hedged amount (CU8,009,518 – CU8,018,963).

IE25   The net effect on profit or loss (excluding interest income and interest expense) is nil reflecting that the hedge is fully effective.

IE26   Entity A makes the following accounting entry to amortise the line item balance for this time period: ‡

Dr	Income statement (loss)	CU11,378	
Cr	Separate balance sheet line item		CU11,378*

To recognise the amortisation charge for the period.

End of month 3

IE27   During the third month there is no further change in the amount of assets or liabilities in the three-month time period. On 31 March 20x1 the assets and the swap mature and all balances are recognised in profit or loss.

---

*CU23,795 [see paragraph IE8] ∞ (CU8 million ≥ CU20 million)

†CU20,023,795 [see paragraph IE7] ∞ (CU8 million ≥ CU20 million)

‡CU22,755 ≥ 2

Entity A makes the following accounting entries relating to this time period: **IE28**

Dr	Cash	CU8,071,707	
Cr	Asset (balance sheet)		CU8,000,000
Cr	Income statement (interest income)		CU71,707

To recognise the interest and cash received on maturity of the hedged amount (CU8 million).

Dr	Income statement (interest expense)	CU71,707	
Cr	Income statement (interest income)		CU62,115
Cr	Cash		CU9,592

To recognise the interest received and paid on the portion of the swap designated as the hedging instrument (CU8 million).

| Dr | Derivative liability | CU9,518 | |
| Cr | Income statement (gain) | | CU9,518 |

To recognise the expiry of the portion of the swap designated as the hedging instrument (CU8 million).

| Dr | Income statement (loss) | CU9,518 | |
| Cr | Separate balance sheet line item | | CU9,518 |

To remove the remaining line item balance on expiry of the time period.

The net effect on profit or loss (excluding interest income and interest expense) is nil   **IE29**
reflecting that the hedge is fully effective.

Entity A makes the following accounting entry to amortise the line item balance for   **IE30**
this time period: *

| Dr | Income statement (loss) | CU11,377 | |
| Cr | Separate balance sheet line item | | CU11,377* |

To recognise the amortisation charge for the period.

Summary

The tables below summarise: **IE31**

(a)   changes in the separate balance sheet line item;
(b)   the fair value of the derivative;
(c)   the profit or loss effect of the hedge for the entire three-month period of the hedge; and
(d)   interest income and interest expense relating to the amount designated as hedged.

*CU22,755 ≥ 2

Description	1 Jan 20x1	31 Jan 20x1	1 Feb 20x1	28 Feb 20x1	31 Mar 20x1
	CU	CU	CU	CU	CU
Amount of asset hedged	**20,000,000**	**19,200,000**	**8,000,000**	**8,000,000**	**8,000,000**

(a) Changes in the separate balance sheet line item

Brought forward:					
Balance to be amortised	Nil	Nil	Nil	22,755	11,377
Remaining balance	Nil	Nil	45,511	18,963	9,518
Less: Adjustment on sale of asset	Nil	Nil	(3,793)	Nil	Nil
Adjustment for change in fair value of the hedged asset	Nil	45,511	Nil	(9,445)	(9,518)
Amortisation	Nil	Nil	Nil	(11,378)	(11,377)

Carried forward:					
Balance to be amortised	**Nil**	**Nil**	**22,755**	**11,377**	**Nil**
Remaining balance	**Nil**	**45,511**	**18,963**	**9,518**	**Nil**

(b) The fair value of the derivative

	1 Jan 20x1	31 Jan 20x1	1 Feb 20x1	28 Feb 20x1	31 Mar 20x1
CU20,000,000	Nil	47,408	-	-	-
CU12,000,000	Nil	-	28,445	No longer designated as the hedging instrument.	
CU8,000,000	Nil	-	18,963	9,518	Nil
Total	**Nil**	**47,408**	**47,408**	**9,518**	**Nil**

(c) Profit or loss effect of the hedge

	1 Jan 20x1	31 Jan 20x1	1 Feb 20x1	28 Feb 20x1	31 Mar 20x1
Change in line item: asset	Nil	45,511	N/A	(9,445)	(9,518)
Change in derivative fair value	Nil	(47,408)	N/A	9,445	9,518
Net effect	**Nil**	**(1,897)**	**N/A**	**Nil**	**Nil**
Amortisation	**Nil**	**Nil**	**N/A**	**(11,378)**	**(11,377)**

In addition, there is a gain on sale of assets of CU14,607 at 1 February 20x1.

(d) Interest income and interest expense relating to the amount designated as hedged

Profit or loss recognised for the amount hedged Interest income	1 Jan20x1	31 Jan20x1	1 Feb20x1	28 Feb 20x1	31 Mar20x1
- on the asset	Nil	172,097	N/A	71,707	71,707
- on the swap	Nil	179,268	N/A	62,115	62,115
Interest expense					
- on the swap	Nil	(179,268)	N/A	(71,707)	(71,707)

Guidance on Implementing International Accounting Standard 39

Financial Instruments: Recognition and Measurement

Contents

Guidance on Implementing IAS 39
Financial Instruments: Recognition and Measurement

Implementation guidance relating to IAS 39 extracted from IFRS 1 *First-time Application of International Financial Reporting Standards*

Guidance on Implementing

IAS 39 *Financial Instruments: Recognition and Measurement*

This guidance accompanies, but is not part of, IAS 39.

SECTION A: SCOPE

A.1 Practice of settling net: forward contract to purchase a commodity

Entity XYZ enters into a fixed price forward contract to purchase one million kilograms of copper in accordance with its expected usage requirements. The contract permits XYZ to take physical delivery of the copper at the end of twelve months or to pay or receive a net settlement in cash, based on the change in fair value of copper. Is the contract accounted for as a derivative?

While such a contract meets the definition of a derivative, it is not necessarily accounted for as a derivative. The contract is a derivative instrument because there is no initial net investment, the contract is based on the price of copper, and it is to be settled at a future date. However, if XYZ intends to settle the contract by taking delivery and has no history for similar contracts of settling net in cash or of taking delivery of the copper and selling it within a short period after delivery for the purpose of generating a profit from short-term fluctuations in price or dealer's margin, the contract is not accounted for as a derivative under IAS 39. Instead, it is accounted for as an executory contract.

A.2 Option to put a non-financial asset

Entity XYZ owns an office building. XYZ enters into a put option with an investor that permits XYZ to put the building to the investor for CU150 million. The current value of the building is CU175* million. The option expires in five years. The option, if exercised, may be settled through physical delivery or net cash, at XYZ's option. How do both XYZ and the investor account for the option?

XYZ's accounting depends on XYZ's intention and past practice for settlement. Although the contract meets the definition of a derivative, XYZ does not account for it as a derivative if XYZ intends to settle the contract by delivering the building if XYZ exercises its option and there is no past practice of settling net (IAS 39.5 and IAS 39.AG10).

The investor, however, cannot conclude that the option was entered into to meet the investor's expected purchase, sale or usage requirements because the investor does not have the ability to require delivery (IAS 39.7). In addition, the option may be settled net in cash. Therefore, the investor has to account for the contract as a derivative. Regardless of past practices, the investor's intention does not affect whether settlement is by delivery or in cash. The investor has written an option, and a written option in which the holder has a choice of physical settlement or net cash settlement can never satisfy the normal delivery requirement for the exemption from IAS 39 because the option writer does not have the ability to require delivery.

However, if the contract were a forward contract rather than an option, and if the contract required physical delivery and the reporting entity had no past practice of settling net in cash or of taking delivery of the building and selling it within a short period after delivery for the purpose of generating a profit from short-term fluctuations in price or dealer's margin, the contract would not be accounted for as a derivative.

**In this Guidance, monetary amounts are denominated in 'currency units' (CU).*

SECTION B: DEFINITIONS

B.1 Definition of a financial instrument: gold bullion

Is gold bullion a financial instrument (like cash) or is it a commodity?

It is a commodity. Although bullion is highly liquid, there is no contractual right to receive cash or another financial asset inherent in bullion.

B.2 Definition of a derivative: examples of derivatives and underlyings

What are examples of common derivative contracts and the identified underlying?

IAS 39 defines a derivative as follows:

"A derivative is a financial instrument or other contract within the scope of this Standard with all three of the following characteristics:

(a) *its value changes in response to the change in a specified interest rate, financial instrument price, commodity price, foreign exchange rate, index of prices or rates, credit rating or credit index, or other variable, provided in the case of a non-financial variable that the variable is not specific to a party to the contract (sometimes called the 'underlying');*

(b) *it requires no initial net investment or an initial net investment that is smaller than would be required for other types of contracts that would be expected to have a similar response to changes in market factors; and*

(c) *it is settled at a future date."*

Type of Contract	Main Pricing-Settlement Variable (Underlying Variable)
Interest Rate Swap	Interest rates
Currency Swap (Foreign Exchange Swap)	Currency rates
Commodity Swap	Commodity prices
Equity Swap	Equity prices (equity of another entity)
Credit Swap	Credit rating, credit index or credit price
Total Return Swap	Total fair value of the reference asset and interest rates
Purchased or Written Treasury Bond Option (call or put)	Interest rates
Purchased or Written Currency Option (call or put)	Currency rates
Purchased or Written Commodity Option (call or put)	Commodity prices
Purchased or Written Stock Option (call or put)	Equity prices (equity of another entity)
Interest Rate Futures Linked to Government Debt (Treasury Futures)	Interest rates
Currency Futures	Currency rates
Commodity Futures	Commodity prices
Interest Rate Forward Linked to Government Debt (Treasury Forward)	Interest rates
Currency Forward	Currency rates

Commodity Forward	Commodity prices
Equity Forward	Equity prices (equity of another entity)

The above list provides examples of contracts that normally qualify as derivatives under IAS 39. The list is not exhaustive. Any contract that has an underlying may be a derivative. Moreover, even if an instrument meets the definition of a derivative contract, special provisions of IAS 39 may apply, for example, if it is a weather derivative (see IAS 39.AG1), a contract to buy or sell a non-financial item such as commodity (see IAS 39.5 and IAS 39.AG10) or a contract settled in an entity's own shares (see IAS 32.21-IAS 32.24). Therefore, an entity must evaluate the contract to determine whether the other characteristics of a derivative are present and whether special provisions apply.

B.3 Definition of a derivative: settlement at a future date, interest rate swap with net or gross settlement

For the purpose of determining whether an interest rate swap is a derivative financial instrument under IAS 39, does it make a difference whether the parties pay the interest payments to each other (gross settlement) or settle on a net basis?

No. The definition of a derivative does not depend on gross or net settlement.

To illustrate: Entity ABC enters into an interest rate swap with a counterparty (XYZ) that requires ABC to pay a fixed rate of 8 per cent and receive a variable amount based on threemonth LIBOR, reset on a quarterly basis. The fixed and variable amounts are determined based on a CU100 million notional amount. ABC and XYZ do not exchange the notional amount. ABC pays or receives a net cash amount each quarter based on the difference between 8 per cent and three-month LIBOR. Alternatively, settlement may be on a gross basis.

The contract meets the definition of a derivative regardless of whether there is net or gross settlement because its value changes in response to changes in an underlying variable (LIBOR), there is no initial net investment, and settlements occur at future dates.

B.4 Definition of a derivative: prepaid interest rate swap (fixed rate payment obligation prepaid at inception or subsequently)

If a party prepays its obligation under a pay-fixed, receive-variable interest rate swap at inception, is the swap a derivative financial instrument?

Yes.

To illustrate: Entity S enters into a CU100 million notional amount five-year pay-fixed, receive-variable interest rate swap with Counterparty C. The interest rate of the variable part of the swap is reset on a quarterly basis to threemonth LIBOR. The interest rate of the fixed part of the swap is 10 per cent per year. Entity S prepays its fixed obligation under the swap of CU50 million (CU100 million · 10 per cent · 5 years) at inception, discounted using market interest rates, while retaining the right to receive interest payments on the CU100 million reset quarterly based on three-month LIBOR over the life of the swap.

The initial net investment in the interest rate swap is significantly less than the notional amount on which the variable payments under the variable leg will be calculated. The contract requires an initial net investment that is smaller than would be required for other types of contracts that would be expected to have a similar response to changes in market factors, such as a variable rate bond. Therefore, the contract fulfils the "no initial net investment or an initial net investment that is smaller than would be required for other types of contracts that would be expected to have a similar response to changes in market factors" provision of IAS 39. Even though Entity S has no future performance obligation, the ultimate settlement of the contract is at a future date and the value of the contract changes in response to changes in the LIBOR index. Accordingly, the contract is regarded as a derivative contract.

Would the answer change if the fixed rate payment obligation is prepaid subsequent to initial recognition?

If the fixed leg is prepaid during the term, that would be regarded as a termination of the old swap and an origination of a new instrument that is evaluated under IAS 39.

B.5 Definition of a derivative: prepaid pay-variable, receive-fixed interest rate swap

If a party prepays its obligation under a pay-variable, receive-fixed interest rate swap at inception of the contract or subsequently, is the swap a derivative financial instrument?

No. A prepaid pay-variable, receive-fixed interest rate swap is not a derivative if it is prepaid at inception and it is no longer a derivative if it is prepaid after inception because it provides a return on the prepaid (invested) amount comparable to the return on a debt instrument with fixed cash flows. The prepaid amount fails the "no initial net investment or an initial net investment that is smaller than would be required for other types of contracts that would be expected to have a similar response to changes in market factors" criterion of a derivative.

To illustrate: Entity S enters into a CU100 million notional amount five-year pay-variable, receive-fixed interest rate swap with Counterparty C. The variable leg of the swap is reset on a quarterly basis to three-month LIBOR. The fixed interest payments under the swap are calculated as 10 per cent times the swap's notional amount, ie CU10 million per year. Entity S prepays its obligation under the variable leg of the swap at inception at current market rates, while retaining the right to receive fixed interest payments of 10 per cent on CU100 million per year.

The cash inflows under the contract are equivalent to those of a financial instrument with a fixed annuity stream since Entity S knows it will receive CU10 million per year over the life of the swap. Therefore, all else being equal, the initial investment in the contract should equal that of other financial instruments that consist of fixed annuities. Thus, the initial net investment in the pay-variable, receive-fixed interest rate swap is equal to the investment required in a non-derivative contract that has a similar response to changes in market conditions. For this reason, the instrument fails the "no initial net investment or an initial net investment that is smaller than would be required for other types of contracts that would be expected to have a similar response to changes in market factors" criterion of IAS 39. Therefore, the contract is not accounted for as a derivative under IAS 39. By discharging the obligation to pay variable interest rate payments, Entity S in effect provides a loan to Counterparty C.

B.6 Definition of a derivative: offsetting loans

Entity A makes a five-year fixed rate loan to Entity B, while B at the same time makes a five-year variable rate loan for the same amount to A. There are no transfers of principal at inception of the two loans, since A and B have a netting agreement. Is this a derivative under IAS 39?

Yes. This meets the definition of a derivative (that is to say, there is an underlying variable, no initial net investment or an initial net investment that is smaller than would be required for other types of contracts that would be expected to have a similar response to changes in market factors, and future settlement). The contractual effect of the loans is the equivalent of an interest rate swap arrangement with no initial net investment. Non-derivative transactions are aggregated and treated as a derivative when the transactions result, in substance, in a derivative. Indicators of this would include:

- they are entered into at the same time and in contemplation of one another
- they have the same counterparty
- they relate to the same risk
- there is no apparent economic need or substantive business purpose for structuring the transactions separately that could not also have been accomplished in a single transaction.

The same answer would apply if Entity A and Entity B did not have a netting agreement, because the definition of a derivative instrument in IAS 39.9 does not require net settlement.

B.7 Definition of a derivative: option not expected to be exercised

The definition of a derivative in IAS 39.9 requires that the instrument "is settled at a future date". Is this criterion met even if an option is expected not to be exercised, for example, because it is out of the money?

Yes. An option is settled upon exercise or at its maturity. Expiry at maturity is a form of settlement even though there is no additional exchange of consideration.

B.8 Definition of a derivative: foreign currency contract based on sales volume

Entity XYZ, whose functional currency is the US dollar, sells products in France denominated in euro. XYZ enters into a contract with an investment bank to convert euro to US dollars at a fixed exchange rate. The contract requires XYZ to remit euro based on its sales volume in France in exchange for US dollars at a fixed exchange rate of 6.00. Is that contract a derivative?

Yes. The contract has two underlying variables (the foreign exchange rate and the volume of sales), no initial net investment or an initial net investment that is smaller than would be required for other types of contracts that would be expected to have a similar response to changes in market factors, and a payment provision. IAS 39 does not exclude from its scope derivatives that are based on sales volume.

B.9 Definition of a derivative: prepaid forward

An entity enters into a forward contract to purchase shares of stock in one year at the forward price. It prepays at inception based on the current price of the shares. Is the forward contract a derivative?

No. The forward contract fails the "no initial net investment or an initial net investment that is smaller than would be required for other types of contracts that would be expected to have a similar response to changes in market factors" test for a derivative.

To illustrate: Entity XYZ enters into a forward contract to purchase one million T ordinary shares in one year. The current market price of T is CU50 per share; the one-year forward price of T is CU55 per share. XYZ is required to prepay the forward contract at inception with a CU50 million payment. The initial investment in the forward contract of CU50 million is less than the notional amount applied to the underlying, one million shares at the forward price of CU55 per share, ie CU55 million. However, the initial net investment approximates the investment that would be required for other types of contracts that would be expected to have a similar response to changes in market factors because T's shares could be purchased at inception for the same price of CU50. Accordingly, the prepaid forward contract does not meet the initial net investment criterion of a derivative instrument.

B.10 Definition of a derivative: initial net investment

Many derivative instruments, such as futures contracts and exchange traded written options, require margin accounts. Is the margin account part of the initial net investment?

No. The margin account is not part of the initial net investment in a derivative instrument. Margin accounts are a form of collateral for the counterparty or clearing house and may take the form of cash, securities or other specified assets, typically liquid assets. Margin accounts are separate assets that are accounted for separately.

B.11 Definition of held for trading: portfolio with a recent actual pattern of short-term profit taking

The definition of a financial asset or financial liability held for trading states that "a financial asset or financial liability is classified as held for trading if it is ... part of a portfolio of identified financial instruments that are managed together and for which there is evidence of a recent actual pattern of short-term profit taking". What is a 'portfolio' for the purposes of applying this definition?

Although the term 'portfolio' is not explicitly defined in IAS 39, the context in which it is used suggests that a portfolio is a group of financial assets or financial liabilities that are managed as part of that group (IAS 39.9). If there is evidence of a recent actual pattern of short-term profit taking on financial instruments included in such a portfolio, those financial instruments qualify as held for trading even though an individual financial instrument may in fact be held for a longer period of time.

B.12 Definition of held for trading: balancing a portfolio

Entity A has an investment portfolio of debt and equity instruments. The documented portfolio management guidelines specify that the equity exposure of the portfolio should be limited to between 30 and 50 per cent of total portfolio value. The investment manager of the portfolio is authorised to balance the portfolio within the designated guidelines by buying and selling equity and debt instruments. Is Entity A permitted to classify the instruments as available for sale?

It depends on Entity A's intentions and past practice. If the portfolio manager is authorised to buy and sell instruments to balance the risks in a portfolio, but there is no intention to trade and there is no past practice of trading for short-term profit, the instruments can be classified as available for sale. If the portfolio manager actively buys and sells instruments to generate short-term profits, the financial instruments in the portfolio are classified as held for trading.

B.13 Definition of held-to-maturity financial assets: index-linked principal

Entity A purchases a five-year equity-index-linked note with an original issue price of CU10 at a market price of CU12 at the time of purchase. The note requires no interest payments before maturity. At maturity, the note requires payment of the original issue price of CU10 plus a supplemental redemption amount that depends on whether a specified share price index exceeds a predetermined level at the maturity date. If the share index does not exceed or is equal to the predetermined level, no supplemental redemption amount is paid. If the share index exceeds the predetermined level, the supplemental redemption amount equals the product of 1.15 and the difference between the level of the share index at maturity and the level of the share index when the note was issued divided by the level of the share index at the time of issue. Entity A has the positive intention and ability to hold the note to maturity. Can Entity A classify the note as a held-to-maturity investment?

Yes. The note can be classified as a held-to-maturity investment because it has a fixed payment of CU10 and fixed maturity and Entity A has the positive intention and ability to hold it to maturity (IAS 39.9). However, the equity index feature is a call option not closely related to the debt host, which must be separated as an embedded derivative under IAS 39.11. The purchase price of CU12 is allocated between the host debt instrument and the embedded derivative. For example, if the fair value of the embedded option at acquisition is CU4, the host debt instrument is measured at CU8 on initial recognition. In this case, the discount of CU2 that is implicit in the host bond (principal of CU10 minus the original carrying amount of CU8) is amortised to profit or loss over the term to maturity of the note using the effective interest method.

B.14 Definition of held-to-maturity financial assets: index-linked interest

Can a bond with a fixed payment at maturity and a fixed maturity date be classified as a held-to-maturity investment if the bond's interest payments are indexed to the price of a commodity or equity, and the entity has the positive intention and ability to hold the bond to maturity?

Yes. However, the commodity-indexed or equity-indexed interest payments result in an embedded derivative that is separated and accounted for as a derivative at fair value (IAS 39.11). IAS 39.12 is not applicable since it should be straightforward to separate the host debt investment (the fixed payment at maturity) from the embedded derivative (the index-linked interest payments).

B.15 Definition of held-to-maturity financial assets: sale following rating downgrade

Would a sale of a held-to-maturity investment following a downgrade of the issuer's credit rating by a rating agency raise a question about the entity's intention to hold other investments to maturity?

Not necessarily. A downgrade is likely to indicate a decline in the issuer's creditworthiness. IAS 39 specifies that a sale due to a significant deterioration in the issuer's creditworthiness could satisfy the condition in IAS 39 and therefore not raise a question about the entity's intention to hold other investments to maturity. However, the deterioration in creditworthiness must be significant judged by reference to the credit rating at initial recognition. Also, the rating downgrade must not have been reasonably anticipated when the entity classified the investment as held to maturity in order to meet the condition in IAS 39. A credit downgrade of a notch within a class or from one rating class to the immediately lower rating class could often be regarded as reasonably anticipated. If the rating downgrade in combination with other information provides evidence of impairment, the deterioration in creditworthiness often would be regarded as significant.

B.16 Definition of held-to-maturity financial assets: permitted sales

Would sales of held-to-maturity financial assets due to a change in management compromise the classification of other financial assets as held to maturity?

Yes. A change in management is not identified under IAS 39.AG22 as an instance where sales or transfers from held-to-maturity do not compromise the classification as held to maturity. Sales in response to such a change in management would, therefore, call into question the entity's intention to hold investments to maturity.

To illustrate: Entity X has a portfolio of financial assets that is classified as held to maturity. In the current period, at the direction of the board of directors, the senior management team has been replaced. The new management wishes to sell a portion of the held-to-maturity financial assets in order to carry out an expansion strategy designated and approved by the board. Although the previous management team had been in place since the entity's inception and Entity X had never before undergone a major restructuring, the sale nevertheless calls into question Entity X's intention to hold remaining held-to- maturity financial assets to maturity.

B.17 Definition of held-to-maturity investments: sales in response to entity-specific capital requirements

In some countries, regulators of banks or other industries may set *entityspecific* capital requirements that are based on an assessment of the risk in that particular entity. IAS 39.AG22(e) indicates that an entity that sells held-to-maturity investments in response to an unanticipated significant increase by the regulator in the *industry's* capital requirements may do so under IAS 39 without necessarily raising a question about its intention to hold other investments to maturity. Would sales of held-to-maturity investments that are due to a significant increase in *entityspecific* capital requirements imposed by regulators (ie capital requirements applicable to a particular entity, but not to the industry) raise such doubt?

Yes, such sales 'taint' the entity's intention to hold other financial assets as held to maturity unless it can be demonstrated that the sales fulfil the condition in IAS 39.9 in that they result from an increase in capital requirements, which is an isolated event that is beyond the entity's control, is nonrecurring and could not have been reasonably anticipated by the entity.

B.18 Definition of held-to-maturity financial assets: pledged collateral, repurchase agreements (repos) and securities lending agreements

An entity cannot have a demonstrated ability to hold to maturity an investment if it is subject to a constraint that could frustrate its intention to hold the financial asset to maturity. Does this mean that a debt instrument that has been pledged as collateral, or transferred to another party under a repo or securities lending transaction, and continues to be recognised cannot be classified as a held-to-maturity investment?

No. An entity's intention and ability to hold debt instruments to maturity is not necessarily constrained if those instruments have been pledged as collateral or are subject to a repurchase agreement or securities lending agreement. However, an entity does not have the positive intention and ability to hold the debt instruments until maturity if it does not expect to be able to maintain or recover access to the instruments.

B.19 Definition of held-to-maturity financial assets: 'tainting'

In response to unsolicited tender offers, Entity A sells a significant amount of financial assets classified as held to maturity on economically favourable terms. Entity A does not classify any financial assets acquired after the date of the sale as held to maturity. However, it does not reclassify the remaining held-to-maturity investments since it maintains that it still intends to hold them to maturity. Is Entity A in compliance with IAS 39?

No. Whenever a sale or transfer of more than an insignificant amount of financial assets classified as held to maturity (HTM) results in the conditions in IAS 39.9 and IAS 39.AG22 not being satisfied, no instruments should be classified in that category. Accordingly, any remaining HTM assets are reclassified as available-for-sale financial assets. The reclassification is recorded in the reporting period in which the sales or transfers occurred and is accounted for as a change in classification under IAS 39.51. IAS 39.9 makes it clear that at least two full financial years must pass before an entity can again classify financial assets as HTM.

B.20 Definition of held-to-maturity investments: sub-categorisation for the purpose of applying the 'tainting' rule

Can an entity apply the conditions for held-to-maturity classification in IAS 39.9 separately to different categories of held-to-maturity financial assets, such as debt instruments denominated in US dollars and debt instruments denominated in euro?

No. The 'tainting rule' in IAS 39.9 is clear. If an entity has sold or reclassified more than an insignificant amount of held-to-maturity investments, it cannot classify any financial assets as held-to-maturity financial assets.

B.21 Definition of held-to-maturity investments: application of the 'tainting' rule on consolidation

Can an entity apply the conditions in IAS 39.9 separately to held-to-maturity financial assets held by different entities in a consolidated group, for example, if those group entities are in different countries with different legal or economic environments?

No. If an entity has sold or reclassified more than an insignificant amount of investments classified as held-to-maturity in the consolidated financial statements, it cannot classify any financial assets as held-to-maturity financial assets in the consolidated financial statements unless the conditions in IAS 39.9 are met.

B.22 Definition of loans and receivables: equity instrument

Can an equity instrument, such as a preference share, with fixed or determinable payments be classified within loans and receivables by the holder?

Yes. If a non-derivative equity instrument would be recorded as a liability by the issuer, and it has fixed or determinable payments and is not quoted in an active market, it can be classified within loans and receivables by the holder, provided the definition is otherwise met. IAS 32.15-IAS 32.22 provide guidance about the classification of a financial instrument as a liability or as equity from the perspective of the issuer of a financial instrument. If an instrument meets the definition of an equity instrument under IAS 32, it cannot be classified within loans and receivables by the holder.

B.23 Definition of loans and receivables: banks' deposits in other banks

Banks make term deposits with a central bank or other banks. Sometimes, the proof of deposit is negotiable, sometimes not. Even if negotiable, the depositor bank may or may not intend to sell it. Would such a deposit fall within loans and receivables under IAS 39.9?

Such a deposit meets the definition of loans and receivables, whether or not the proof of deposit is negotiable, unless the depositor bank intends to sell the instrument immediately or in the near term, in which case the deposit is classified as a financial asset held for trading.

B.24 Definition of amortised cost: perpetual debt instruments with fixed or market-based variable rate

Sometimes entities purchase or issue debt instruments that are required to be measured at amortised cost and in respect of which the issuer has no obligation to repay the principal amount. Interest may be paid either at a fixed rate or at a variable rate. Would the difference between the initial amount paid or received and zero ('the maturity amount') be amortised immediately on initial recognition for the purpose of determining amortised cost if the rate of interest is fixed or specified as a market-based variable rate?

No. Since there are no repayments of principal, there is no amortisation of the difference between the initial amount and the maturity amount if the rate of interest is fixed or specified as a market-based variable rate. Because interest payments are fixed or market-based and will be paid in perpetuity, the amortised cost (the present value of the stream of future cash payments discounted at the effective interest rate) equals the principal amount in each period (IAS 39.9).

B.25 Definition of amortised cost: perpetual debt instruments with decreasing interest rate

If the stated rate of interest on a perpetual debt instrument decreases over time, would amortised cost equal the principal amount in each period?

No. From an economic perspective, some or all of the interest payments are repayments of the principal amount. For example, the interest rate may be stated as 16 per cent for the first ten years and as zero per cent in subsequent periods. In that case, the initial amount is amortised to zero over the first ten years using the effective interest method, since a portion of the interest payments represents repayments of the principal amount. The amortised cost is zero after year 10 because the present value of the stream of future cash payments in subsequent periods is zero (there are no further cash payments of either principal or interest in subsequent periods).

B.26 Example of calculating amortised cost: financial asset

Financial assets that are excluded from fair valuation and have a fixed maturity should be measured at amortised cost. How is amortised cost calculated?

Under IAS 39, amortised cost is calculated using the effective interest method. The effective interest rate inherent in a financial instrument is the rate that exactly discounts the estimated cash flows associated with the financial instrument through the expected life of the instrument or, where appropriate, a shorter period to the net carrying amount at initial recognition. The computation includes all fees and points paid or received that are an integral part of the effective interest rate, directly attributable transaction costs and all other premiums or discounts.

The following example illustrates how amortised cost is calculated using the effective interest method. Entity A purchases a debt instrument with five years remaining to maturity for its fair value of CU1,000 (including transaction costs). The instrument has a principal amount of CU1,250 and carries fixed interest of 4.7 per cent that is paid annually (CU1,250 · 4.7 per cent = CU59 per year). The contract also specifies that the borrower has an option to prepay the instrument and that no penalty will be charged for prepayment. At inception, the entity expects the borrower not to prepay.

It can be shown that in order to allocate interest receipts and the initial discount over the term of the debt instrument at a constant rate on the carrying amount, they must be accrued at the rate of 10 per cent annually. The table below provides information about the amortised cost, interest income and cash flows of the debt instrument in each reporting period.

Year	(a) Amortised cost at the beginning of the year	(b = a 10%) Interest income	(c) Cash flows	(d = a + b - c) Amortised cost at the end of the year
20x0	1,000	100	59	1,041
20x1	1,041	104	59	1,086
20x2	1,086	109	59	1,136
20x3	1,136	113	59	1,190
20x4	1,190	119	1,250 + 59	-

On the first day of 20x2 the entity revises its estimate of cash flows. It now expects that 50 per cent of the principal will be prepaid at the end of 20x2 and the remaining 50 per cent at the end of 20x4. In accordance with IAS 39.AG8, the opening balance of the debt instrument in 20x2 is adjusted. The adjusted amount is calculated by discounting the amount the entity expects to receive in 20x2 and subsequent years using the original effective interest rate (10 per cent). This results in the new opening balance in 20x2 of CU1,138. The adjustment of CU52 (CU1,138 − CU1,086) is recorded in profit or loss in 20x2. The table below provides information about the amortised cost, interest income and cash flows as they would be adjusted taking into account the change in estimate.

Year	(a) Amortised cost at the beginning of the year	(b = a × 10%) Interest income	(c) Cash flows	(d = a + b - c) Amortised cost at the end of the year
20x0	1,000	100	59	1,041
20x1	1,041	104	59	1,086
20x2	1,086 + 52	114	625 + 59	568
20x3	568	57	30	595
20x4	595	60	625 + 30	-

If the debt instrument becomes impaired, say, at the end of 20x3, the impairment loss is calculated as the difference between the carrying amount (CU595) and the present value of estimated future cash flows discounted at the original effective interest rate (10 per cent).

B.27 Example of calculating amortised cost: debt instruments with stepped interest payments

Sometimes entities purchase or issue debt instruments with a predetermined rate of interest that increases or decreases progressively ('stepped interest') over the term of the debt instrument. If a debt instrument with stepped interest and no embedded derivative is issued at CU1,250 and has a maturity amount of CU1,250, would the amortised cost equal CU1,250 in each reporting period over the term of the debt instrument?

No. Although there is no difference between the initial amount and maturity amount, an entity uses the effective interest method to allocate interest payments over the term of the debt instrument to achieve a constant rate on the carrying amount (IAS 39.9).

The following example illustrates how amortised cost is calculated using the effective interest method for an instrument with a predetermined rate of interest that increases or decreases over the term of the debt instrument ('stepped interest').

On 1 January 2000, Entity A issues a debt instrument for a price of CU1,250. The principal amount is CU1,250 and the debt instrument is repayable on 31 December 2004. The rate of interest is specified in the debt agreement as a percentage of the principal amount as follows: 6.0 per cent in 2000 (CU75), 8.0 per cent in 2001 (CU100), 10.0 per cent in 2002 (CU125), 12.0 per cent in 2003 (CU150), and 16.4 per cent in 2004 (CU205). In this case, the interest rate that exactly discounts the stream of future cash payments through maturity is 10 per cent. Therefore, cash interest payments are reallocated over the term of the debt instrument for the purposes of determining amortised cost in each period. In each period, the amortised cost at the beginning of the period is multiplied by the effective interest rate of 10 per cent and added to the amortised cost. Any cash payments in the period are deducted from the resulting number. Accordingly, the amortised cost in each period is as follows:

Year	(a) Amortised cost at the beginning of the year	(b = a 10%) Reported interest	(c) Cash flows	(d = a+b-c) Amortised cost at the end of the year
2000	1,250	125	75	1,300
2001	1,300	130	100	1,330
2002	1,330	133	125	1,338
2003	1,338	134	150	1,322
2004	1,322	133	1,250 + 205	-

B.28 Regular way contracts: no established market

Can a contract to purchase a financial asset be a regular way contract if there is no established market for trading such a contract?

Yes. IAS 39.9 refers to terms that require delivery of the asset within the time frame established generally by regulation or convention in the marketplace concerned. Marketplace, as that term is used in IAS 39.9, is not limited to a formal stock exchange or organised over-the-counter market. Rather, it means the environment in which the financial asset is customarily exchanged. An acceptable time frame would be the period reasonably and customarily required for the parties to complete the transaction and prepare and execute closing documents.

For example, a market for private issue financial instruments can be a marketplace.

B.29 Regular way contracts: forward contract

Entity ABC enters into a forward contract to purchase one million of M's ordinary shares in two months for CU10 per share. The contract is with an individual and is not an exchange-traded contract. The contract requires ABC to take physical delivery of the shares and pay the counterparty CU10 million in cash. M's shares trade in an active public market at an average of 100,000 shares a day. Regular way delivery is three days. Is the forward contract regarded as a regular way contract?

No. The contract must be accounted for as a derivative because it is not settled in the way established by regulation or convention in the marketplace concerned.

B.30 Regular way contracts: which customary settlement provisions apply?

If an entity's financial instruments trade in more than one active market, and the settlement provisions differ in the various active markets, which provisions apply in assessing whether a contract to purchase those financial instruments is a regular way contract?

The provisions that apply are those in the market in which the purchase actually takes place.

To illustrate: Entity XYZ purchases one million shares of Entity ABC on a US stock exchange, for example, through a broker. The settlement date of the contract is six business days later. Trades for equity shares on US exchanges customarily settle in three business days. Because the trade settles in six business days, it does not meet the exemption as a regular way trade.

However, if XYZ did the same transaction on a foreign exchange that has a customary settlement period of six business days, the contract would meet the exemption for a regular way trade.

B.31 Regular way contracts: share purchase by call option

Entity A purchases a call option in a public market permitting it to purchase 100 shares of Entity XYZ at any time over the next three months at a price of CU100 per share. If Entity A exercises its option, it has 14 days to settle the transaction according to regulation or convention in the options market. XYZ shares are traded in an active public market that requires three-day settlement. Is the purchase of shares by exercising the option a regular way purchase of shares?

Yes. The settlement of an option is governed by regulation or convention in the marketplace for options and, therefore, upon exercise of the option it is no longer accounted for as a derivative because settlement by delivery of the shares within 14 days is a regular way transaction.

B.32 Recognition and derecognition of financial liabilities using trade date or settlement date accounting

IAS 39 has special rules about recognition and derecognition of financial assets using trade date or settlement date accounting. Do these rules apply to transactions in financial instruments that are classified as financial liabilities, such as transactions in deposit liabilities and trading liabilities?

No. IAS 39 does not contain any specific requirements about trade date accounting and settlement date accounting in the case of transactions in financial instruments that are classified as financial liabilities. Therefore, the general recognition and derecognition requirements in IAS 39.14 and IAS 39.39 apply. IAS 39.14 states that financial liabilities are recognised on the date the entity "becomes a party to the contractual provisions of the instrument". Such contracts generally are not recognised unless one of the parties has performed or the contract is a derivative contract not exempted from the scope of IAS 39. IAS 39.39 specifies that financial liabilities are derecognised only when they are extinguished, ie when the obligation specified in the contract is discharged or cancelled or expires.

SECTION C: EMBEDDED DERIVATIVES

C.1 Embedded derivatives: separation of host debt instrument

If an embedded non-option derivative is required to be separated from a host debt instrument, how are the terms of the host debt instrument and the embedded derivative identified? For example, would the host debt instrument be a fixed rate instrument, a variable rate instrument or a zero coupon instrument?

The terms of the host debt instrument reflect the stated or implied substantive terms of the hybrid instrument. In the absence of implied or stated terms, the entity makes its own judgement of the terms. However, an entity may not identify a component that is not specified or may not establish terms of the host debt instrument in a manner that would result in the separation of an embedded derivative that is not already clearly present in the hybrid instrument, that is to say, it cannot create a cash flow that does not exist. For example, if a five-year debt instrument has fixed interest payments of CU40,000 annually and a principal payment at maturity of CU1,000,000 multiplied by the change in an equity price index, it would be inappropriate to identify a floating rate host contract and an embedded equity swap that has an offsetting floating rate leg in lieu of identifying a fixed rate host. In that example, the host contract is a fixed rate debt instrument that pays CU40,000 annually because there are no floating interest rate cash flows in the hybrid instrument.

In addition, the terms of an embedded non-option derivative, such as a forward or swap, must be determined so as to result in the embedded derivative having a fair value of zero at the inception of the hybrid instrument. If it were permitted to separate embedded non-option derivatives on other terms, a single hybrid instrument could be decomposed into an infinite variety of combinations of host debt instruments and embedded derivatives, for example, by separating embedded derivatives with terms that create leverage, asymmetry or some other risk exposure not already present in the hybrid instrument. Therefore, it is inappropriate to separate an embedded non-option derivative on terms that result in a fair value other than zero at the inception of the hybrid instrument. The determination of the terms of the embedded derivative is based on the conditions existing when the financial instrument was issued.

C.2 Embedded derivatives: separation of embedded option

The response to Question C.1 states that the terms of an embedded nonoption derivative should be determined so as to result in the embedded derivative having a fair value of zero at the initial recognition of the hybrid instrument. When an embedded option-based derivative is separated, must the terms of the embedded option be determined so as to result in the embedded derivative having either a fair value of zero or an intrinsic value of zero (that is to say, be at the money) at the inception of the hybrid instrument?

No. The economic behaviour of a hybrid instrument with an option-based embedded derivative depends critically on the strike price (or strike rate) specified for the option feature in the hybrid instrument, as discussed below. Therefore, the separation of an option-based embedded derivative (including any embedded put, call, cap, floor, caption, floortion or swaption feature in a hybrid instrument) should be based on the stated terms of the option feature documented in the hybrid instrument. As a result, the embedded derivative would not necessarily have a fair value or intrinsic value equal to zero at the initial recognition of the hybrid instrument.

If an entity were required to identify the terms of an embedded option-based derivative so as to achieve a fair value of the embedded derivative of zero, the strike price (or strike rate) generally would have to be determined so as to result in the option being infinitely out of the money. This would imply a zero probability of the option feature being exercised. However, since the probability of the option feature in a hybrid instrument being exercised generally is not zero, it would be inconsistent with the likely economic behaviour of the hybrid instrument to assume an initial fair value of zero. Similarly, if an entity were required to identify the terms of an embedded option-based derivative so as to achieve an intrinsic value of zero for the embedded derivative, the strike price (or strike rate) would have to be assumed to equal the price (or rate) of the underlying variable at the initial recognition of the hybrid instrument. In this case, the fair value of the option would consist only of time value. However, such an assumption would not be consistent with the likely economic behaviour of the hybrid instrument, including the probability of the option feature being exercised, unless the agreed strike price was indeed equal to the price (or rate) of the underlying variable at the initial recognition of the hybrid instrument.

The economic nature of an option-based embedded derivative is fundamentally different from a forward-based embedded derivative (including forwards and swaps), because the terms of a forward are such that a payment based on the difference between the price of the underlying and the forward price will occur at a specified date, while the terms of an option are such that a payment based on the difference between the price of the underlying and the strike price of the option may or may not occur depending on the relationship between the agreed strike price and the price of the underlying at a specified date or dates in the future. Adjusting the strike price of an option-based embedded derivative, therefore, alters the nature of the hybrid instrument. On the other hand, if the terms of a non-option embedded derivative in a host debt instrument were determined so as to result in a fair value of any amount other than zero at the inception of the hybrid instrument, that amount would essentially represent a borrowing or lending. Accordingly, as discussed in the answer to Question C.1, it is not appropriate to separate a non-option embedded derivative in a host debt instrument on terms that result in a fair value other than zero at the initial recognition of the hybrid instrument.

C.3 Embedded derivatives: accounting for a convertible bond

What is the accounting treatment of an investment in a bond (financial asset) that is convertible into shares of the issuing entity or another entity before maturity?

An investment in a convertible bond that is convertible before maturity generally cannot be classified as a held-to-maturity investment because that would be inconsistent with paying for the conversion feature—the right to convert into equity shares before maturity.

An investment in a convertible bond can be classified as an available-for-sale financial asset provided it is not purchased for trading purposes. The equity conversion option is an embedded derivative.

If the bond is classified as available for sale (ie fair value changes recognised directly in equity until the bond is sold), the equity conversion option (the embedded derivative) is separated. The amount paid for the bond is split between the debt instrument without the conversion option and the equity conversion option. Changes in the fair value of the equity conversion option are recognised in profit or loss unless the option is part of a cash flow hedging relationship.

If the convertible bond is measured at fair value with changes in fair value recognised in profit or loss, separating the embedded derivative from the host bond is not permitted.

C.4 Embedded derivatives: equity kicker

In some instances, venture capital entities providing subordinated loans agree that if and when the borrower lists its shares on a stock exchange, the venture capital entity is entitled to receive shares of the borrowing entity free of charge or at a very low price (an 'equity kicker') in addition to interest and repayment of principal. As a result of the equity kicker feature, the interest on the subordinated loan is lower than it would otherwise be. Assuming that the subordinated loan is not measured at fair value with changes in fair value recognised in profit or loss (IAS 39.11(c)), does the equity kicker feature meet the definition of an embedded derivative even though it is contingent upon the future listing of the borrower?

Yes. The economic characteristics and risks of an equity return are not closely related to the economic characteristics and risks of a host debt instrument (IAS 39.11(a)). The equity kicker meets the definition of a derivative because it has a value that changes in response to the change in the price of the shares of the borrower, it requires no initial net investment or an initial net investment that is smaller than would be required for other types of contracts that would be expected to have a similar response to changes in market factors, and it is settled at a future date (IAS 39.11(b) and IAS 39.9(a)). The equity kicker feature meets the definition of a derivative even though the right to receive shares is contingent upon the future listing of the borrower. IAS 39.AG9 states that a derivative could require a payment as a result of some future event that is unrelated to a notional amount. An equity kicker feature is similar to such a derivative except that it does not give a right to a fixed payment, but an option right, if the future event occurs.

C.5 Embedded derivatives: debt or equity host contract

Entity A purchases a five-year 'debt' instrument issued by Entity B with a principal amount of CU1 million that is indexed to the share price of Entity C. At maturity, Entity A will receive from Entity B the principal amount plus or minus the change in the fair value of 10,000 shares of Entity C. The current share price is CU110. No separate interest payments are made by Entity B. The purchase price is CU1 million. Entity A classifies the debt instrument as available for sale. Entity A concludes that the instrument is a hybrid instrument with an embedded derivative because of the equity-indexed principal. For the purposes of separating an embedded derivative, is the host contract an equity instrument or a debt instrument?

The host contract is a debt instrument because the hybrid instrument has a stated maturity, ie it does not meet the definition of an equity instrument (IAS 32.11 and IAS 32.16). It is accounted for as a zero coupon debt instrument. Thus, in accounting for the host instrument, Entity A imputes interest on CU1 million over five years using the applicable market interest rate at initial recognition. The embedded non-option derivative is separated so as to have an initial fair value of zero (see Question C.1).

C.6 Embedded derivatives: synthetic instruments

Entity A acquires a five-year floating rate debt instrument issued by Entity B. At the same time, it enters into a five-year pay-variable, receive-fixed interest rate swap with Entity C. Entity A regards the combination of the debt instrument and swap as a synthetic fixed rate instrument and classifies the instrument as a held-to-maturity investment, since it has the positive intention and ability to hold it to maturity. Entity A contends that separate accounting for the swap is inappropriate since IAS 39.AG33(a) requires an embedded derivative to be classified together with its host instrument if the derivative is linked to an interest rate that can change the amount of interest that would otherwise be paid or received on the host debt contract. Is the entity's analysis correct?

No. Embedded derivative instruments are terms and conditions that are included in non-derivative host contracts. It is generally inappropriate to treat two or more separate financial instruments as a single combined instrument ('synthetic instrument' accounting) for the purpose of applying IAS 39. Each of the financial instruments has its own terms and conditions and each may be transferred or settled separately. Therefore, the debt instrument and the swap are classified separately. The transactions described here differ from the transactions discussed in Question B.6, which had no substance apart from the resulting interest rate swap.

C.7 Embedded derivatives: purchases and sales contracts in foreign currency instruments

A supply contract provides for payment in a currency other than (a) the functional currency of either party to the contract, (b) the currency in which the product is routinely denominated in commercial transactions around the world and (c) the currency that is commonly used in contracts to purchase or sell non-financial items in the economic environment in which the transaction takes place. Is there an embedded derivative that should be separated under IAS 39?

Yes. To illustrate: a Norwegian entity agrees to sell oil to an entity in France. The oil contract is denominated in Swiss francs, although oil contracts are routinely denominated in US dollars in commercial transactions around the world, and Norwegian krone are commonly used in contracts to purchase or sell non-financial items in Norway. Neither entity carries out any significant activities in Swiss francs. In this case, the Norwegian entity regards the supply contract as a host contract with an embedded foreign currency forward to purchase Swiss francs. The French entity regards the supply contact as a host contract with an embedded foreign currency forward to sell Swiss francs. Each entity includes fair value changes on the currency forward in profit or loss unless the reporting entity designates it as a cash flow hedging instrument, if appropriate.

C.8 Embedded foreign currency derivatives: unrelated foreign currency provision

Entity A, which measures items in its financial statements on the basis of the euro (its functional currency), enters into a contract with Entity B, which has the Norwegian krone as its functional currency, to purchase oil in six months for 1,000 US dollars. The host oil contract is not within the scope of IAS 39 because it was entered into and continues to be for the purpose of delivery of a non-financial item in accordance with the entity's expected purchase, sale or usage requirements (IAS 39.5 and IAS 39.AG10). The oil contract includes a leveraged foreign exchange provision that states that the parties, in addition to the provision of, and payment for, oil will exchange an amount equal to the fluctuation in the exchange rate of the US dollar and Norwegian krone applied to a notional amount of 100,000 US dollars. Under IAS 39.11, is that embedded derivative (the leveraged foreign exchange provision) regarded as closely related to the host oil contract?

No, that leveraged foreign exchange provision is separated from the host oil contract because it is not closely related to the host oil contract (IAS 39.33(d)).

The payment provision under the host oil contract of 1,000 US dollars can be viewed as a foreign currency derivative because the US dollar is neither Entity A's nor Entity B's functional currency. This foreign currency derivative would not be separated because it follows from IAS 39.AG33(d) that a crude oil contract that requires payment in US dollars is not regarded as a host contract with a foreign currency derivative.

The leveraged foreign exchange provision that states that the parties will exchange an amount equal to the fluctuation in the exchange rate of the US dollar and Norwegian krone applied to a notional amount of 100,000 US dollars is in addition to the required payment for the oil transaction. It is unrelated to the host oil contract and therefore separated from the host oil contract and accounted for as an embedded derivative under IAS 39.11.

C.9 Embedded foreign currency derivatives: currency of international commerce

IAS 39.AG33(d) refers to the currency in which the price of the related goods or services is routinely denominated in commercial transactions around the world. Could it be a currency that is used for a certain product or service in commercial transactions within the local area of one of the substantial parties to the contract?

No. The currency in which the price of the related goods or services is routinely denominated in commercial transactions around the world is only a currency that is used for similar transactions all around the world, not just in one local area. For example, if crossborder transactions in natural gas in North America are routinely denominated in US dollars and such transactions are routinely denominated in euro in Europe, neither the US dollar nor the euro is a currency in which the goods or services is routinely denominated in commercial transactions around the world.

C.10 Embedded derivatives: holder permitted, but not required, to settle without recovering substantially all of its recognised investment

If the terms of a combined instrument permit, but do not require, the holder to settle the combined instrument in a manner that causes it not to recover substantially all of its recognised investment and the issuer does not have such a right (for example, a puttable debt instrument), does the contract satisfy the condition in IAS 39.AG33(a) that the holder would not recover substantially all of its recognised investment?

No. The condition that "the holder would not recover substantially all of its recognised investment" is not satisfied if the terms of the combined instrument permit, but do not require, the investor to settle the combined instrument in a manner that causes it not to recover substantially all of its recognised investment and the issuer has no such right. Accordingly, an interest-bearing host contract with an embedded interest rate derivative with such terms is regarded as closely related to the host contract. The condition that "the holder would not recover substantially all of its recognised investment" applies to situations in which the holder can be forced to accept settlement at an amount that causes the holder not to recover substantially all of its recognised investment.

C.11 Embedded derivatives: reliable determination of fair value

If an embedded derivative that is required to be separated cannot be reliably measured because it will be settled by an unquoted equity instrument whose fair value cannot be reliably measured, is the embedded derivative measured at cost?

No. In this case, the entire combined contract is treated as a financial instrument held for trading (IAS 39.12). If the fair value of the combined instrument can be reliably measured, the combined contract is measured at fair value. The entity might conclude, however, that the equity component of the combined instrument may be sufficiently significant to preclude it from obtaining a reliable estimate of the entire instrument. In that case, the combined instrument is measured at cost less impairment.

SECTION D: RECOGNITION AND DERECOGNITION

D.1 Initial Recognition

D.1.1 Recognition: cash collateral

Entity B transfers cash to Entity A as collateral for another transaction with Entity A (for example, a securities borrowing transaction). The cash is not legally segregated from Entity A's assets. Should Entity A recognise the cash collateral it has received as an asset?

Yes. The ultimate realisation of a financial asset is its conversion into cash and, therefore, no further transformation is required before the economic benefits of the cash transferred by Entity B can be realised by Entity A. Therefore, Entity A recognises the cash as an asset and a payable to Entity B while Entity B derecognises the cash and recognises a receivable from Entity A.

D.2 Regular Way Purchase or Sale of a Financial Asset

D.2.1 Trade date vs settlement date: amounts to be recorded for a purchase

How are the trade date and settlement date accounting principles in the Standard applied to a purchase of a financial asset?

The following example illustrates the application of the trade date and settlement date accounting principles in the Standard for a purchase of a financial asset. On 29 December 20x1, an entity commits itself to purchase a financial asset for CU1,000, which is its fair value on commitment (trade) date. Transaction costs are immaterial. On 31 December 20x1 (financial year-end) and on 4 January 20x2 (settlement date) the fair value of the asset is CU1,002 and CU1,003, respectively. The amounts to be recorded for the asset will depend on how it is classified and whether trade date or settlement date accounting is used, as shown in the two tables below.

SETTLEMENT DATE ACCOUNTING			
Balances	**Held-to-Maturity Investments Carried at Amortised Cost**	**Available-for-Sale Assets Remeasured to Fair Value with Changes in Equity**	**Assets at Fair Value through Profit or Loss Remeasured to Fair Value with Changes in Profit or Loss**
29 December 20x1			
Financial asset	-	-	-
Financial liability	-	-	-
31 December 20x1	-		
Receivable	-	2	2
Financial asset	-	-	-
Financial liability	-	-	-
Equity (fair value adjustment)	-	(2)	-
Retained earnings (through profit or loss)	-	-	(2)
4 January 20x2			
Receivable	-	-	-
Financial asset	1,000	1,003	1,003
Financial liability	-	-	-
Equity (fair value adjustment)	-	(3)	-
Retained earnings (through profit or loss)	-	-	(3)

TRADE DATE ACCOUNTING			
Balances	**Held-to-Maturity Investments Carried at Amortised Cost**	**Available-for-Sale Assets Remeasured to Fair Value with Changes in Equity**	**Assets at Fair Value through Profit or Loss Remeasured to Fair Value with Changes in Profit or Loss**
29 December 20x1			
Financial asset	1,000	1,000	1,000
Financial liability	(1,000)	(1,000)	(1,000)
31 December 20x1			
Receivable	-	-	-
Financial asset	1,000	1,002	1,002
Financial liability	(1,000)	(1,000)	(1,000)
Equity (fair value adjustment)	-	(2)	-
Retained earnings (through profit or loss)	-	-	(2)
4 January 20x2			
Receivable	-	-	-
Financial asset	1,000	1,003	1,003
Financial liability	-	-	-
Equity (fair value adjustment)	-	(3)	-
Retained earnings (through profit or loss)	-	-	(3)

D.2.2 Trade date vs settlement date: amounts to be recorded for a sale

How are the trade date and settlement date accounting principles in the Standard applied to a sale of a financial asset?

The following example illustrates the application of the trade date and settlement date accounting principles in the Standard for a sale of a financial asset. On 29 December 20x2 (trade date) an entity enters into a contract to sell a financial asset for its current fair value of CU1,010. The asset was acquired one year earlier for CU1,000 and its amortised cost is CU1,000. On 31 December 20x2 (financial year-end), the fair value of the asset is CU1,012. On 4 January 20x3 (settlement date), the fair value is CU1,013. The amounts to be recorded will depend on how the asset is classified and whether trade date or settlement date accounting is used as shown in the two tables below (any interest that might have accrued on the asset is disregarded).

A change in the fair value of a financial asset that is sold on a regular way basis is not recorded in the financial statements between trade date and settlement date even if the entity applies settlement date accounting because the seller's right to changes in the fair value ceases on the trade date.

SETTLEMENT DATE ACCOUNTING			
Balances	**Held-to-Maturity Investments Carried at Amortised Cost**	**Available-for-Sale Assets Remeasured to Fair Value with Changes in Equity**	**Assets at Fair Value through Profit or Loss Remeasured to Fair Value with Changes in Profit or Loss**
29 December 20x2			
Receivable	-	-	-
Financial asset	1,000	1,010	1,010
Equity (fair value adjustment)	-	10	-
Retained earnings (through profit or loss)	-	-	10
31 December 20x2			
Receivable	-	-	-
Financial asset	1,000	1,010	1,010
Equity (fair value adjustment)	-	10	-
Retained earnings (through profit or loss)	-	-	10
4 January 20x3			
Equity (fair value adjustment)	-	-	-
Retained earnings (through profit or loss)	10	10	10

TRADE DATE ACCOUNTING			
Balances	Held-to-Maturity Investments Carried at Amortised Cost	Available-for-Sale Assets Remeasured to Fair Value with Changes in Equity	Assets at Fair Value through Profit or Loss Remeasured to Fair Value with Changes in Profit or Loss
29 December 20x2			
Receivable	1,010	1,010	1,010
Financial asset	-	-	-
Equity (fair value adjustment)		-	
Retained earnings (through profit or loss)	10	10	10
31 December 20x2			
Receivable	1,010	1,010	1,010
Financial asset	-	-	-
Equity (fair value adjustment)		-	
Retained earnings (through profit or loss)	10	10	10
4 January 20x3			
Equity (fair value adjustment)		-	
Retained earnings (through profit or loss)	10	10	10

D.2.3 Settlement date accounting: exchange of non-cash financial assets

If an entity recognises sales of financial assets using settlement date accounting, would a change in the fair value of a financial asset to be received in exchange for the noncash financial asset that is sold be recognised in accordance with IAS 39.57?

It depends. Any change in the fair value of the financial asset to be received would be accounted for under IAS 39.57 if the entity applies settlement date accounting for that category of financial assets. However, if the entity classifies the financial asset to be received in a category for which it applies trade date accounting, the asset to be received is recognised on the trade date as described in IAS 39.AG55. In that case, the entity recognises a liability of an amount equal to the carrying amount of the financial asset to be delivered on settlement date.

To illustrate: on 29 December 20x2 (trade date) Entity A enters into a contract to sell Note Receivable A, which is carried at amortised cost, in exchange for Bond B, which will be classified as held for trading and measured at fair value. Both assets have a fair value of CU1,010 on 29 December, while the amortised cost of Note Receivable A is CU1,000. Entity A uses settlement date accounting for loans and receivables and trade date accounting for assets held for trading. On 31 December 20x2 (financial year-end), the fair value of Note Receivable A is CU1,012 and the fair value of Bond B is CU1,009. On 4 January 20x3, the fair value of Note Receivable A is CU1,013 and the fair value of Bond B is CU1,007. The following entries are made:

29 December 20x2

Dr Bond B	CU1,010	
Cr Payable		CU1,010

31 December 20x2

Dr Trading loss	CU1	
Cr Bond B		CU1

4 January 20x3

Dr Payable	CU1,010	
Dr Trading loss	CU2	
Cr Note Receivable A		CU1,000
Cr Bond B		CU2
Cr Realisation gain		CU10

SECTION E: MEASUREMENT

E.1 Initial Measurement of Financial Assets and Financial Liabilities

E.1.1 Initial measurement: transaction costs

Transaction costs should be included in the initial measurement of financial assets and financial liabilities other than those at fair value through profit or loss. How should this requirement be applied in practice?

For financial assets, incremental costs that are directly attributable to the acquisition of the asset, for example fees and commissions, are added to the amount originally recognised. For financial liabilities, directly related costs of issuing debt are deducted from the amount of debt originally recognised. For financial instruments that are measured at fair value through profit or loss, transaction costs are not added to the fair value measurement at initial recognition.

For financial instruments that are carried at amortised cost, such as held-to-maturity investments, loans and receivables, and financial liabilities that are not at fair value through profit or loss, transaction costs are included in the calculation of amortised cost using the effective interest method and, in effect, amortised through profit or loss over the life of the instrument.

For available-for-sale financial assets, transaction costs are recognised in equity as part of a change in fair value at the next remeasurement. If an available-for-sale financial asset has fixed or determinable payments and does not have an indefinite life, the transaction costs are amortised to profit or loss using the effective interest method. If an available-for-sale financial asset does not have fixed or determinable payments and has an indefinite life, the transaction costs are recognised in profit or loss when the asset is derecognised or becomes impaired.

Transaction costs expected to be incurred on transfer or disposal of a financial instrument are not included in the measurement of the financial instrument.

E.2 Fair Value Measurement Considerations

E.2.1 Fair value measurement considerations for investment funds

IAS 39.AG72 states that the current bid price is usually the appropriate price to be used in measuring the fair value of an asset held. The rules applicable to some investment funds require net asset values to be reported to investors on the basis of mid-market prices. In these circumstances, would it be appropriate for an investment fund to measure its assets on the basis of mid-market prices?

No. The existence of regulations that require a different measurement for specific purposes does not justify a departure from the general requirement in IAS 39.AG72 to use the current bid price in the absence of a matching liability position. In its financial statements, an investment fund measures its assets at current bid prices. In reporting its net asset value to investors, an investment fund may wish to provide a reconciliation between the fair values recognised on its balance sheet and the prices used for the net asset value calculation.

E.2.2 Fair value measurement: large holding

Entity A holds 15 per cent of the share capital in Entity B. The shares are publicly traded in an active market. The currently quoted price is CU100. Daily trading volume is 0.1 per cent of outstanding shares. Because Entity A believes that the fair value of the Entity B shares it owns, if sold as a block, is greater than the quoted market price, Entity A obtains several independent estimates of the price it would obtain if it sells its holding. These estimates indicate that Entity A would be able to obtain a price of CU105, ie a 5 per cent premium above the quoted price. Which figure should Entity A use for measuring its holding at fair value?

Under IAS 39.AG71, a published price quotation in an active market is the best estimate of fair value. Therefore, Entity A uses the published price quotation (CU100). Entity A cannot depart from the quoted market price solely because independent estimates indicate that Entity A would obtain a higher (or lower) price by selling the holding as a block.

E.3 Gains and Losses

E.3.1 Available-for-sale financial assets: exchange of shares

Entity A holds a small number of shares in Entity B. The shares are classified as available for sale. On 20 December 2000, the fair value of the shares is CU120 and the cumulative gain recognised in equity is CU20. On the same day, Entity B is acquired by Entity C, a large public entity. As a result, Entity A receives shares in Entity C in exchange for those it had in Entity B of equal fair value. Under IAS 39.55(b), should Entity A recognise the cumulative gain of CU20 recognised in equity in profit or loss?

Yes. The transaction qualifies for derecognition under IAS 39. IAS 39.55(b) requires that the cumulative gain or loss that has been recognised in equity on an available-for-sale financial asset be recognised in profit or loss when the asset is derecognised. In the exchange of shares, Entity A disposes of the shares it had in Entity B and receives shares in Entity C.

E.3.2 IAS 39 and IAS 21 – Available-for-sale financial assets: separation of currency component

For an available-for-sale monetary financial asset, the entity reports changes in the carrying amount relating to changes in foreign exchange rates in profit or loss in accordance with IAS 21.23(a) and IAS 21.28 and other changes in the carrying amount in equity in accordance with IAS 39. How is the cumulative gain or loss that is recognised in equity determined?

It is the difference between the amortised cost (adjusted for impairment, if any) and fair value of the available-for-sale monetary financial asset in the functional currency of the reporting entity. For the purpose of applying IAS 21.28 the asset is treated as an asset measured at amortised cost in the foreign currency.

To illustrate: on 31 December 2001 Entity A acquires a bond denominated in a foreign currency (FC) for its fair value of FC1,000. The bond has five years remaining to maturity and a principal amount of FC1,250, carries fixed interest of 4.7 per cent that is paid annually (FC1,250 · 4.7 per cent = FC59 per year), and has an effective interest rate of 10 per cent. Entity A classifies the bond as available for sale, and thus recognises gains and losses in equity. The entity's functional currency is its local currency (LC). The exchange rate is FC1 to LC1.5 and the carrying amount of the bond is LC1,500 (= FC1,000 · 1.5).

Dr Bond		LC1,500	
	Cr Cash		LC1,500

On 31 December 2002, the foreign currency has appreciated and the exchange rate is FC1 to LC2. The fair value of the bond is FC1,060 and thus the carrying amount is LC2,120 (= FC1,060 · 2). The amortised cost is FC1,041 (= LC2,082). In this case, the cumulative gain or loss to be recognised directly in equity is the difference between the fair value and the amortised cost on 31 December 2002, ie LC38 (= LC2,120 – LC2,082).

Interest received on the bond on 31 December 2002 is FC59 (= LC118). Interest income determined in accordance with the effective interest method is FC100 (= 1,000☐· 10 per cent). The average exchange rate during the year is FC1 to LC1.75. For the purpose of this question, it is assumed that the use of the average exchange rate provides a reliable approximation of the spot rates applicable to the accrual of interest income during the year (IAS 21.22). Thus, reported interest income is LC175 (= FC100 · 1.75) including accretion of the initial discount of LC72 (= [FC100 – FC59] · 1.75). Accordingly, the exchange difference on the bond that is recognised in profit or loss is LC510 (= LC2,082 – LC1,500 – LC72). Also, there is an exchange gain on the interest receivable for the year of LC15 (= LC59 · [2.00 – 1.75]).

Dr Bond		LC620	
Dr Cash		LC118	
	Cr Interest income		LC175
	Cr Exchange gain		LC525
	Cr Fair value change in equity		LC38

On 31 December 2003, the foreign currency has appreciated further and the exchange rate is FC1 to LC2.50. The fair value of the bond is FC1,070 and thus the carrying amount is LC2,675 (= FC1,070 · 2.50). The amortised cost is FC1,086 (= LC2,715).

The cumulative gain or loss to be recognised directly in equity is the difference between the fair value and the amortised cost on 31 December 2003, ie negative LC40 (= LC2,675 – LC2,715). Thus, there is a debit to equity equal to the change in the difference during 2003 of LC78 (= LC40 + LC38).

Interest received on the bond on 31 December 2003 is FC59 (= LC148). Interest income determined in accordance with the effective interest method is FC104 (= FC1,041· 10 per cent). The average exchange rate during the year is FC1 to LC2.25. For the purpose of this question, it is assumed that the use of the average exchange rate provides a reliable approximation of the spot rates applicable to the accrual of interest income during the year (IAS 21.22). Thus, recognised interest income is LC234 (= FC104 · 2.25) including accretion of the initial discount of LC101 (= [FC104 – FC59] · 2.25). Accordingly, the exchange difference on the bond that is recognised in profit or loss is LC532 (= LC2,715 – LC2,082 – LC101). Also, there is an exchange gain on the interest receivable for the year of LC15 (= FC59 · [2.50 – 2.25]).

Dr Bond	LC555	
Dr Cash	LC148	
Dr Fair value change in equity	LC78	
Cr Interest income		LC234
Cr Exchange gain		LC547

E.3.3 IAS 39 and IAS 21 – Exchange differences arising on translation of foreign entities: equity or income?

IAS 21.32 and IAS 21.48 states that all exchange differences resulting from translating the financial statements of a foreign operation should be recognised in equity until disposal of the net investment. This would include exchange differences arising from financial instruments carried at fair value, which would include both financial assets classified as at fair value through profit or loss and financial assets that are available for sale.

IAS 39.55 requires that changes in fair value of financial assets classified as at fair value through profit or loss should be recognised in profit or loss and changes in fair value of available-for-sale investments should be reported in equity.

If the foreign operation is a subsidiary whose financial statements are consolidated with those of its parent, in the consolidated financial statements how are IAS 39.55 and IAS 21.39 applied?

IAS 39 applies in the accounting for financial instruments in the financial statements of a foreign operation and IAS 21 applies in translating the financial statements of a foreign operation for incorporation in the financial statements of the reporting entity.

To illustrate: Entity A is domiciled in Country X and its functional currency and presentation currency are the local currency of Country X (LCX). A has a foreign subsidiary (Entity B) in Country Y whose functional currency is the local currency of Country Y (LCY). B is the owner of a debt instrument, which is held for trading and therefore carried at fair value under IAS 39.

In B's financial statements for year 20x0, the fair value and carrying amount of the debt instrument is LCY100 in the local currency of Country Y. In A's consolidated financial statements, the asset is translated into the local currency of Country X at the spot exchange rate applicable at the balance sheet date (2.00). Thus, the carrying amount is LCX200 (= LCY100 · 2.00) in the consolidated financial statements.

At the end of year 20x1, the fair value of the debt instrument has increased to LCY110 in the local currency of Country Y. B recognises the trading asset at LCY110 in its balance sheet and recognises a fair value gain of LCY10 in its income statement. During the year, the spot exchange rate has increased from 2.00 to 3.00 resulting in an increase in the fair value of the instrument from LCX200 to LCX330 (= LCY110 · 3.00) in the currency of Country X. Therefore, Entity A recognises the trading asset at LCX330 in its consolidated financial statements.

Entity A translates the income statement of B "at the exchange rates at the dates of the transactions" (IAS 21.39(b)). Since the fair value gain has accrued through the year, A uses the average rate as a practical approximation ([3.00 + 2.00] / 2 = 2.50, in accordance with IAS 21.22). Therefore, while the fair value of the trading asset has increased by LCX130 (= LCX330 - LCX200), Entity A recognises only LCX25 (= LCY10 · 2.5) of this increase in consolidated profit or loss to comply with IAS 21.39(b). The resulting exchange difference, ie the remaining increase in the fair value of the debt instrument (LCX130 – LCX25 = LCX105), is classified as equity until the disposal of the net investment in the foreign operation in accordance with IAS 21.48.

E.3.4 IAS 39 and IAS 21 – Interaction between IAS 39 and IAS 21

IAS 39 includes requirements about the measurement of financial assets and financial liabilities and the recognition of gains and losses on remeasurement in profit or loss. IAS 21 includes rules about the reporting of foreign currency items and the recognition of exchange differences in profit or loss. In what order are IAS 21 and IAS 39 applied?

Balance sheet

Generally, the measurement of a financial asset or financial liability at fair value, cost or amortised cost is first determined in the foreign currency in which the item is denominated in accordance with IAS 39. Then, the foreign currency amount is translated into the functional currency using the closing rate or a historical rate in accordance with IAS 21 (IAS 39.AG83). For example, if a monetary financial asset (such as a debt instrument) is carried at amortised cost under IAS 39, amortised cost is calculated in the currency of denomination of that financial asset. Then, the foreign currency amount is recognised using the closing rate in the entity's financial statements (IAS 21.23). That applies regardless of whether a monetary item is measured at cost, amortised cost or fair value in the foreign currency (IAS 21.24). A non-monetary financial asset (such as an investment in an equity instrument) is translated using the closing rate if it is carried at fair value in the foreign currency (IAS 21.23(c)) and at a historical rate if it is not carried at fair value under IAS 39 because its fair value cannot be reliably measured (IAS 21.23(b) and IAS 39.46(c)).

As an exception, if the financial asset or financial liability is designated as a hedged item in a fair value hedge of the exposure to changes in foreign currency rates under IAS 39, the hedged item is remeasured for changes in foreign currency rates even if it would otherwise have been recognised using a historical rate under IAS 21 (IAS 39.89), ie the foreign currency amount is recognised using the closing rate. This exception applies to non-monetary items that are carried in terms of historical cost in the foreign currency and are hedged against exposure to foreign currency rates (IAS 21.23(b)).

Income statement

The recognition of a change in the carrying amount of a financial asset or financial liability in profit or loss depends on a number of factors, including whether it is an exchange difference or other change in carrying amount, whether it arises on a monetary item (for example, most debt instruments) or non-monetary item (such as most equity investments), whether the associated asset or liability is designated as a cash flow hedge of an exposure to changes in foreign currency rates, and whether it results from translating the financial statements of a foreign operation. The issue of recognising changes in the carrying amount of a financial asset or financial liability held by a foreign operation is addressed in a separate question (see Question E.3.3).

Any exchange difference arising on recognising a *monetary item* at a rate different from that at which it was initially recognised during the period, or recognised in previous financial statements, is recognised in profit or loss or in equity in accordance with IAS 21 (IAS 39.AG83, IAS 21.28 and IAS 21.32), unless the monetary item is designated as a cash flow hedge of a highly probable forecast transaction in foreign currency, in which case the requirements for recognition of gains and losses on cash flow hedges in IAS 39 apply (IAS 39.95). Differences arising from recognising a monetary item at a foreign currency amount different from that at which it was previously recognised are accounted for in a similar manner, since all changes in the carrying amount relating to foreign currency movements should be treated consistently. All other changes in the balance sheet measurement of a monetary item are recognised in profit or loss or in equity in accordance with IAS 39. For example, although an entity recognises gains and losses on availablefor-sale monetary financial assets in equity (IAS 39.55(b)), the entity nevertheless recognises the changes in the carrying amount relating to changes in foreign exchange rates in profit or loss (IAS 21.23(a)).

Any changes in the carrying amount of a *non-monetary item* are recognised in profit or loss or in equity in accordance with IAS 39 (IAS 39.AG83). For example, for available-for-sale financial assets the entire change in the carrying amount, including the effect of changes in foreign currency rates, is reported in equity. If the non-monetary item is designated as a cash flow hedge of an unrecognised firm commitment or a highly probable forecast transaction in foreign currency, the requirements for recognition of gains and losses on cash flow hedges in IAS 39 apply (IAS 39.95).

When some portion of the change in carrying amount is recognised in equity and some portion is recognised in profit or loss, for example, if the amortised cost of a foreign currency bond classified as available for sale has increased in foreign currency (resulting in a gain in profit or loss) but its fair value has decreased in the functional currency (resulting in a loss in equity), an entity cannot offset those two components for the purposes of determining gains or losses that should be recognised in profit or loss or in equity.

E.4 Impairment and Uncollectibility of Financial Assets

E.4.1 Objective evidence of impairment

Does IAS 39 require that an entity be able to identify a single, distinct past causative event to conclude that it is probable that an impairment loss on a financial asset has been incurred?

No. IAS 39.59 states "It may not be possible to identify a single, discrete event that caused the impairment. Rather the combined effect of several events may have caused the impairment." Also, IAS 39.60 states that "a downgrade of an entity's credit rating is not, of itself, evidence of impairment, although it may be evidence of impairment when considered with other available information". Other factors that an entity considers in determining whether it has objective evidence that an impairment loss has been incurred include information about the debtors' or issuers' liquidity, solvency and business and financial risk exposures, levels of and trends in delinquencies for similar financial assets, national and local economic trends and conditions, and the fair value of collateral and guarantees. These and other factors may, either individually or taken together, provide sufficient objective evidence that an impairment loss has been incurred in a financial asset or group of financial assets.

E.4.2 Impairment: future losses

Does IAS 39 permit the recognition of an impairment loss through the establishment of an allowance for future losses when a loan is given? For example, if Entity A lends CU1,000 to Customer B, can it recognise an immediate impairment loss of CU10 if Entity A, based on historical experience, expects that 1 per cent of the principal amount of loans given will not be collected?

No. IAS 39.14 requires a financial asset to be initially measured at fair value. For a loan asset, the fair value is the amount of cash lent adjusted for any fees and costs (unless a portion of the amount lent is compensation for other stated or implied rights or privileges). In addition, IAS 39.58 requires that an impairment loss is recognised only if there is objective evidence of impairment as a result of a past event that occurred after initial recognition. Accordingly, it is inconsistent with IAS 39.14 and IAS 39.58 to reduce the carrying amount of a loan asset on initial recognition through the recognition of an immediate impairment loss.

E.4.3 Assessment of impairment: principal and interest

Because of Customer B's financial difficulties, Entity A is concerned that Customer B will not be able to make all principal and interest payments due on a loan in a timely manner. It negotiates a restructuring of the loan. Entity A expects that Customer B will be able to meet its obligations under the restructured terms. Would Entity A recognise an impairment loss if the restructured terms are as reflected in any of the following cases?

(a)   Customer B will pay the full principal amount of the original loan five years after the original due date, but none of the interest due under the original terms.

(b)   Customer B will pay the full principal amount of the original loan on the original due date, but none of the interest due under the original terms.

(c)   Customer B will pay the full principal amount of the original loan on the original due date with interest only at a lower interest rate than the interest rate inherent in the original loan.

(d)   Customer B will pay the full principal amount of the original loan five years after the original due date and all interest accrued during the original loan term, but no interest for the extended term.

(e)   Customer B will pay the full principal amount of the original loan five years after the original due date and all interest, including interest for both the original term of the loan and the extended term.

IAS 39.58 indicates that an impairment loss has been incurred if there is objective evidence of impairment. The amount of the impairment loss for a loan measured at amortised cost is the difference between the carrying amount of the loan and the present value of future principal and interest payments discounted at the loan's original effective interest rate. In cases (a)-(d) above, the present value of the future principal and interest payments discounted at the loan's original effective interest rate will be lower than the carrying amount of the loan. Therefore, an impairment loss is recognised in those cases.

In case (e), even though the timing of payments has changed, the lender will receive interest on interest, and the present value of the future principal and interest payments discounted at the loan's original effective interest rate will equal the carrying amount of the loan. Therefore, there is no impairment loss. However, this fact pattern is unlikely given Customer B's financial difficulties.

E.4.4 Assessment of impairment: fair value hedge

A loan with fixed interest rate payments is hedged against the exposure to interest rate risk by a receive-variable, pay-fixed interest rate swap. The hedge relationship qualifies for fair value hedge accounting and is reported as a fair value hedge. Thus, the carrying amount of the loan includes an adjustment for fair value changes attributable to movements in interest rates. Should an assessment of impairment in the loan take into account the fair value adjustment for interest rate risk?

Yes. The loan's original effective interest rate before the hedge becomes irrelevant once the carrying amount of the loan is adjusted for any changes in its fair value attributable to interest rate movements. Therefore, the original effective interest rate and amortised cost of the loan are adjusted to take into account recognised fair value changes. The adjusted effective interest rate is calculated using the adjusted carrying amount of the loan.

An impairment loss on the hedged loan is calculated as the difference between its carrying amount after adjustment for fair value changes attributable to the risk being hedged and the estimated future cash flows of the loan discounted at the adjusted effective interest rate. When a loan is included in a portfolio hedge of interest rate risk, the entity should allocate the change in the fair value of the hedged portfolio to the loans (or groups of similar loans) being assessed for impairment on a systematic and rational basis.

E.4.5 Impairment: provision matrix

A financial institution calculates impairment in the unsecured portion of loans and receivables on the basis of a provision matrix that specifies fixed provision rates for the number of days a loan has been classified as nonperforming (zero per cent if less than 90 days, 20 per cent if 90-180 days, 50 per cent if 181-365 days and 100 per cent if more than 365 days). Can the results be considered to be appropriate for the purpose of calculating the impairment loss on loans and receivables under IAS 39.63?

Not necessarily. IAS 39.63 requires impairment or bad debt losses to be calculated as the difference between the asset's carrying amount and the present value of estimated future cash flows discounted at the financial instrument's original effective interest rate.

E.4.6 Impairment: excess losses

Does IAS 39 permit an entity to recognise impairment or bad debt losses in excess of impairment losses that are determined on the basis of objective evidence about impairment in identified individual financial assets or identified groups of similar financial assets?

No. IAS 39 does not permit an entity to recognise impairment or bad debt losses in addition to those that can be attributed to individually identified financial assets or identified groups of financial assets with similar credit risk characteristics (IAS 39.64) on the basis of objective evidence about the existence of impairment in those assets (IAS 39.58). Amounts that an entity might want to set aside for additional possible impairment in financial assets, such as reserves that cannot be supported by objective evidence about impairment, are not recognised as impairment or bad debt losses under IAS 39. However, if an entity determines that no objective evidence of impairment exists for an individually assessed financial asset, whether significant or not, it includes the asset in a group of financial assets with similar credit risk characteristics (IAS 39.64).

E.4.7 Recognition of impairment on a portfolio basis

IAS 39.63 requires that impairment be recognised for financial assets carried at amortised cost. IAS 39.64 states that impairment may be measured and recognised individually or on a portfolio basis for a group of similar financial assets. If one asset in the group is impaired but the fair value of another asset in the group is above its amortised cost, does IAS 39 allow non-recognition of the impairment of the first asset?

No. If an entity knows that an individual financial asset carried at amortised cost is impaired, IAS 39.63 requires that the impairment of that asset should be recognised. It states: "the amount of the loss is measured as the difference between *the asset's* carrying amount and the present value of estimated future cash flows (excluding future credit losses that have not been incurred) discounted at the financial asset's original effective interest rate" (emphasis added). Measurement of impairment on a portfolio basis under IAS 39.64 may be applied to groups of small balance items and to financial assets that are individually assessed and found not to be impaired when there is indication of impairment in a group of similar assets and impairment cannot be identified with an individual asset in that group.

E.4.8 Impairment: recognition of collateral

If an impaired financial asset is secured by collateral and foreclosure is probable, is the collateral recognised as an asset separate from the impaired financial asset?

No. The measurement of the impaired financial asset reflects the fair value of the collateral. The collateral would generally not meet the recognition criteria until it is transferred to the lender. Accordingly, the collateral is not recognised as an asset separate from the impaired financial asset before foreclosure.

E.4.9 Impairment of non-monetary available-for-sale financial asset

If a non-monetary financial asset, such as an equity instrument, measured at fair value with gains and losses recognised in equity becomes impaired, should the cumulative net loss recognised in equity, including any portion attributable to foreign currency changes, be recognised in profit or loss?

Yes. IAS 39.67 states that when a decline in the fair value of an available-for-sale financial asset has been recognised directly in equity and there is objective evidence that the asset is impaired, the cumulative net loss that had been recognised directly in equity should be removed from equity and recognised in profit or loss even though the asset has not been derecognised. Any portion of the cumulative net loss that is attributable to foreign currency changes on that asset that had been recognised in equity is also recognised in profit or loss. Any subsequent losses, including any portion attributable to foreign currency changes, are also recognised in profit or loss until the asset is derecognised.

E.4.10 Impairment: whether the available-for-sale reserve in equity can be negative

IAS 39.67 requires that gains and losses arising from changes in fair value on available-for-sale financial assets are recognised directly in equity. If the aggregate fair value of such assets is less than their carrying amount, should the aggregate net loss that has been recognised directly in equity be removed from equity and recognised in profit or loss?

Not necessarily. The relevant criterion is not whether the aggregate fair value is less than the carrying amount, but whether there is objective evidence that a financial asset or group of assets is impaired. An entity assesses at each balance sheet date whether there is any objective evidence that a financial asset or group of assets may be impaired, in accordance with IAS 39.59-61. IAS 39.60 states that a downgrade of an entity's credit rating is not, of itself, evidence of impairment, although it may be evidence of impairment when considered with other available information. Additionally, a decline in the fair value of a financial asset below its cost or amortised cost is not necessarily evidence of impairment (for example, a decline in the fair value of an investment in a debt instrument that results from an increase in the basic, riskfree interest rate).

SECTION F HEDGING

F.1 Hedging Instruments

F.1.1 Hedging the fair value exposure of a bond denominated in a foreign currency

Entity J, whose functional currency is the Japanese yen, has issued 5 million five-year US dollar fixed rate debt. Also, it owns a 5 million five-year fixed rate US dollar bond which it has classified as available for sale. Can Entity J designate its US dollar liability as a hedging instrument in a fair value hedge of the entire fair value exposure of its US dollar bond?

No. IAS 39.72 permits a non-derivative to be used as a hedging instrument only for a hedge of a foreign currency risk. Entity J's bond has a fair value exposure to foreign currency and interest rate changes and credit risk.

Alternatively, can the US dollar liability be designated as a fair value hedge or cash flow hedge of the foreign currency component of the bond?

Yes. However, hedge accounting is unnecessary because the amortised cost of the hedging instrument and the hedged item are both remeasured using closing rates. Regardless of whether Entity J designates the relationship as a cash flow hedge or a fair value hedge, the effect on profit or loss is the same. Any gain or loss on the non-derivative hedging instrument designated as a cash flow hedge is immediately recognised in profit or loss to correspond with the recognition of the change in spot rate on the hedged item in profit or loss as required by IAS 21.

F.1.2 Hedging with a non-derivative financial asset or liability

Entity J's functional currency is the Japanese yen. It has issued a fixed rate debt instrument with semi-annual interest payments that matures in two years with principal due at maturity of 5 million US dollars. It has also entered into a fixed price sales commitment for 5 million US dollars that matures in two years and is not accounted for as a derivative because it meets the exemption for normal sales in paragraph 5. Can Entity J designate its US dollar liability as a fair value hedge of the entire fair value exposure of its fixed price sales commitment and qualify for hedge accounting?

No. IAS 39.72 permits a non-derivative asset or liability to be used as a hedging instrument only for a hedge of a foreign currency risk.

Alternatively, can Entity J designate its US dollar liability as a cash flow hedge of the foreign currency exposure associated with the future receipt of US dollars on the fixed price sales commitment?

Yes. IAS 39 permits the designation of a non-derivative asset or liability as a hedging instrument in either a cash flow hedge or a fair value hedge of the exposure to changes in foreign exchange rates of a firm commitment (IAS 39.87). Any gain or loss on the non-derivative hedging instrument that is recognised in equity during the period preceding the future sale is recognised in profit or loss when the sale takes place (IAS 39.95).

Alternatively, can Entity J designate the sales commitment as the hedging instrument instead of the hedged item?

No. Only a derivative instrument or a non-derivative financial asset or liability can be designated as a hedging instrument in a hedge of a foreign currency risk. A firm commitment cannot be designated as a hedging instrument. However, if the foreign currency component of the sales commitment is required to be separated as an embedded derivative under IAS 39.11 and IAS 39.AG33(d), it could be designated as a hedging instrument in a hedge of the exposure to changes in the fair value of the maturity amount of the debt attributable to foreign currency risk.

F.1.3 Hedge accounting: use of written options in combined hedging instruments

Issue (a) - Does IAS 39.AG94 preclude the use of an interest rate collar or other derivative instrument that combines a written option component and a purchased option component as a hedging instrument?

It depends. An interest rate collar or other derivative instrument that includes a written option cannot be designated as a hedging instrument if it is a net written option, because IAS 39.AG94 precludes the use of a written option as a hedging instrument unless it is designated as an offset to a purchased option. An interest rate collar or other derivative instrument that includes a written option may be designated as a hedging instrument, however, if the combination is a net purchased option or zero cost collar.

Issue (b) - What factors indicate that an interest rate collar or other derivative instrument that combines a written option component and a purchased option component is not a net written option?

The following factors taken together suggest that an interest rate collar or other derivative instrument that includes a written option is not a net written option.

(a)   No net premium is received either at inception or over the life of the combination of options. The distinguishing feature of a written option is the receipt of a premium to compensate the writer for the risk incurred.

(b)   Except for the strike prices, the critical terms and conditions of the written option component and the purchased option component are the same (including underlying variable or variables, currency denomination and maturity date). Also, the notional amount of the written option component is not greater than the notional amount of the purchased option component.

F.1.4 Internal hedges

Some entities use internal derivative contracts (internal hedges) to transfer risk exposures between different companies within a group or divisions within a single legal entity. Does IAS 39.73 prohibit hedge accounting in such cases?

Yes, if the derivative contracts are internal to the entity being reported on. IAS 39 does not specify how an entity should manage its risk. However, it states that internal hedging transactions do not qualify for hedge accounting. This applies both (a) in consolidated financial statements for intragroup hedging transactions, and (b) in the individual or separate financial statements of a legal entity for hedging transactions between divisions in the entity. The principles of preparing consolidated financial statements in IAS 27.24 require that "intragroup balances, transactions, income and expenses shall be eliminated in full".

On the other hand, an intragroup hedging transaction may be designated as a hedge in the individual or separate financial statements of a group entity, if the intragroup transaction is an external transaction from the perspective of the group entity. In addition, if the internal contract is offset with an external party the external contract may be regarded as the hedging instrument and the hedging relationship may qualify for hedge accounting.

The following summarises the application of IAS 39 to internal hedging transactions.

- IAS 39 does not preclude an entity from using internal derivative contracts for risk management purposes and it does not preclude internal derivatives from being accumulated at the treasury level or some other central location so that risk can be managed on an entitywide basis or at some higher level than the separate legal entity or division.
- Internal derivative contracts between two separate entities within a consolidated group can qualify for hedge accounting by those entities in their individual or separate financial statements, even though the internal contracts are not offset by derivative contracts with a party external to the consolidated group.
- Internal derivative contracts between two separate divisions within the same legal entity can qualify for hedge accounting in the individual or separate financial statements of that legal entity only if those contracts are offset by derivative contracts with a party external to the legal entity.
- Internal derivative contracts between separate divisions within the same legal entity and between separate entities within the consolidated group can qualify for hedge accounting in the consolidated financial statements only if the internal contracts are offset by derivative contracts with a party external to the consolidated group.
- If the internal derivative contracts are not offset by derivative contracts with external parties, the use of hedge accounting by group entities and divisions using internal contracts must be reversed on consolidation.

To illustrate: the banking division of Entity A enters into an internal interest rate swap with the trading division of the same entity. The purpose is to hedge the interest rate risk exposure of a loan (or group of similar loans) in the loan portfolio. Under the swap, the banking division pays fixed interest payments to the trading division and receives variable interest rate payments in return.

If a hedging instrument is not acquired from an external party, IAS 39 does not allow hedge accounting treatment for the hedging transaction undertaken by the banking and trading divisions. IAS 39.73 indicates that only derivatives that involve a party external to the entity can be designated as hedging instruments and, further, that any gains or losses on intragroup or intra-entity transactions should be eliminated on consolidation. Therefore, transactions between different divisions within Entity A do not qualify for hedge accounting treatment in the financial statements of Entity A. Similarly, transactions between different entities within a group do not qualify for hedge accounting treatment in consolidated financial statements.

However, if in addition to the internal swap in the above example the trading division enters into an interest rate swap or other contract with an external party that offsets the exposure hedged in the internal swap, hedge accounting is permitted under IAS 39. For the purposes of IAS 39, the hedged item is the loan (or group of similar loans) in the banking division and the hedging instrument is the external interest rate swap or other contract.

The trading division may aggregate several internal swaps or portions of them that are not offsetting each other and enter into a single third party derivative contract that offsets the aggregate exposure. Under IAS 39, such external hedging transactions may qualify for hedge accounting treatment provided that the hedged items in the banking division are identified and the other conditions for hedge accounting are met. It should be noted, however, that IAS 39.79 does not permit hedge accounting treatment for held-to-maturity investments if the hedged risk is the exposure to interest rate changes.

F.1.5 Offsetting internal derivative contracts used to manage interest rate risk

If a central treasury function enters into internal derivative contracts with subsidiaries and various divisions within the consolidated group to manage interest rate risk on a centralised basis, can those contracts qualify for hedge accounting in the consolidated financial statements if, before laying off the risk, the internal contracts are first netted against each other and only the net exposure is offset in the marketplace with external derivative contracts?

No. An internal contract designated at the subsidiary level or by a division as a hedge results in the recognition of changes in the fair value of the item being hedged in profit or loss (a fair value hedge) or in the recognition of the changes in the fair value of the internal derivative in equity (a cash flow hedge). There is no basis for changing the measurement attribute of the item being hedged in a fair value hedge unless the exposure is offset with an external derivative. There is also no basis for including the gain or loss on the internal derivative in equity for one entity and recognising it in profit or loss by the other entity unless it is offset with an external derivative. In cases where two or more internal derivatives are used to manage interest rate risk on assets or liabilities at the subsidiary or division level and those internal derivatives are offset at the treasury level, the effect of designating the internal derivatives as hedging instruments is that the hedged non-derivative exposures at the subsidiary or division levels would be used to offset each other on consolidation. Accordingly, since IAS 39.72 does not permit designating non-derivatives as hedging instruments, except for foreign currency exposures, the results of hedge accounting from the use of internal derivatives at the subsidiary or division level that are not laid off with external parties must be reversed on consolidation.

It should be noted, however, that there will be no effect on profit or loss and equity of reversing the effect of hedge accounting in consolidation for internal derivatives that offset each other at the consolidation level if they are used in the same type of hedging relationship at the subsidiary or division level and, in the case of cash flow hedges, where the hedged items affect profit or loss in the same period. Just as the internal derivatives offset at the treasury level, their use as fair value hedges by two separate entities or divisions within the consolidated group will also result in the offset of the fair value amounts recognised in profit or loss, and their use as cash flow hedges by two separate entities or divisions within the consolidated group will also result in the fair value amounts being offset against each other in equity. However, there may be an effect on individual line items in both the consolidated income statement and the consolidated balance sheet, for example when internal derivatives that hedge assets (or liabilities) in a fair value hedge are offset by internal derivatives that are used as a fair value hedge of other assets (or liabilities) that are recognised in a different balance sheet or income statement line item. In addition, to the extent that one of the internal contracts is used as a cash flow hedge and the other is used in a fair value hedge, the effect on profit or loss and equity would not offset since the gain (or loss) on the internal derivative used as a fair value hedge would be recognised in profit or loss and the corresponding loss (or gain) on the internal derivative used as a cash flow hedge would be recognised in equity.

Question F.1.4 describes the application of IAS 39 to internal hedging transactions.

F.1.6 Offsetting internal derivative contracts used to manage foreign currency risk

If a central treasury function enters into internal derivative contracts with subsidiaries and various divisions within the consolidated group to manage foreign currency risk on a centralised basis, can those contracts be used as a basis for identifying external transactions that qualify for hedge accounting in the consolidated financial statements if, before laying off the risk, the internal contracts are first netted against each other and only the net exposure is offset by entering into a derivative contract with an external party?

It depends. IAS 27 *Consolidated and Separate Financial Statements* requires all internal transactions to be eliminated in consolidated financial statements. As stated in IAS 39.73, internal hedging transactions do not qualify for hedge accounting in the consolidated financial statements of the group. Therefore, if an entity wishes to achieve hedge accounting in the consolidated financial statements, it must designate a hedging relationship between a qualifying external hedging instrument and a qualifying hedged item.

As discussed in Question F.1.5, the accounting effect of two or more internal derivatives that are used to manage interest rate risk at the subsidiary or division level and are offset at the treasury level is that the hedged non-derivative exposures at those levels would be used to offset each other on consolidation. There is no effect on profit or loss or equity if (a) the internal derivatives are used in the same type of hedge relationship (ie fair value or cash flow hedges) and (b), in the case of cash flow hedges, any derivative gains and losses that are initially recognised in equity are recognised in profit or loss in the same period(s). When these two conditions are met, the gains and losses on the internal derivatives that are recognised in profit or loss or in equity will offset on consolidation resulting in the same profit or loss and equity as if the derivatives had been eliminated. However, there may be an effect on individual line items, in both the consolidated income statement and the consolidated balance sheet, that would need to be eliminated. In addition, there is an effect on profit or loss and equity if some of the offsetting internal derivatives are used in cash flow hedges, while others are used in fair value hedges. There is also an effect on profit or loss and equity for offsetting internal derivatives that are used in cash flow hedges if the derivative gains and losses that are initially recognised in equity are recognised in profit or loss in different periods (because the hedged items affect profit or loss in different periods).

As regards foreign currency risk, provided that the internal derivatives represent the transfer of foreign currency risk on underlying non-derivative financial assets or liabilities, hedge accounting can be applied because IAS 39.72 permits a non-derivative financial asset or liability to be designated as a hedging instrument for hedge accounting purposes for a hedge of a foreign currency risk. Accordingly, in this case the internal derivative contracts can be used as a basis for identifying external transactions that qualify for hedge accounting in the consolidated financial statements even if they are offset against each other. However, for consolidated financial statements, it is necessary to designate the hedging relationship so that it involves only external transactions.

Furthermore, the entity cannot apply hedge accounting to the extent that two or more offsetting internal derivatives represent the transfer of foreign currency risk on underlying forecast transactions or unrecognised firm commitments. This is because an unrecognised firm commitment or forecast transaction does not qualify as a hedging instrument under IAS 39. Accordingly, in this case the internal derivatives cannot be used as a basis for identifying external transactions that qualify for hedge accounting in the consolidated financial statements. As a result, any cumulative net gain or loss on an internal derivative that has been included in the initial carrying amount of an asset or liability (basis adjustment) or deferred in equity would have to be reversed on consolidation if it cannot be demonstrated that the offsetting internal derivative represented the transfer of a foreign currency risk on a financial asset or liability to an external hedging instrument.

F.1.7 Internal derivatives: examples of applying Question F.1.6

In each case, FC = foreign currency, LC = local currency (which is the entity's functional currency), and TC = treasury centre.

Case 1: Offset of fair value hedges

Subsidiary A has trade receivables of FC100, due in 60 days, which it hedges using a forward contract with TC. Subsidiary B has payables of FC50, also due in 60 days, which it hedges using a forward contact with TC.

TC nets the two internal derivatives and enters into a net external forward contract to pay FC50 and receive LC in 60 days.

At the end of month 1, FC weakens against LC. A incurs a foreign exchange loss of LC10 on its receivables, offset by a gain of LC10 on its forward contract with TC. B makes a foreign exchange gain of LC5 on its payables offset by a loss of LC5 on its forward contract with TC. TC makes a loss of LC10 on its internal forward contract with A, a gain of LC5 on its internal forward contract with B, and a gain of LC5 on its external forward contract.

At the end of month 1, the following entries are made in the individual or separate financial statements of A, B and TC. Entries reflecting intragroup transactions or events are shown in italics.

A's entries

Dr	Foreign exchange loss	LC10	
	Cr Receivables		LC10
Dr	*Internal contract TC*	*LC10*	
	Cr Internal gain TC		*LC10*

B's entries

Dr	Payables	LC5	
	Cr Foreign exchange gain		LC5
Dr	*Internal loss TC*	*LC5*	
	Cr Internal contract TC		*LC5*

TC's entries

Dr	*Internal loss A*	*LC10*	
	Cr Internal contract A		*LC10*
Dr	*Internal contract B*	*LC5*	
	Cr Internal gain B		*LC5*
Dr	External forward contract	LC5	
	Cr Foreign exchange gain		LC5

Both A and B could apply hedge accounting in their individual financial statements provided all conditions in IAS 39 are met. However, in this case, no hedge accounting is required because gains and losses on the internal derivatives and the offsetting losses and gains on the hedged receivables and payables are recognised immediately in the income statements of A and B without hedge accounting.

In the consolidated financial statements, the internal derivative transactions are eliminated. In economic terms, the payable in B hedges FC50 of the receivables in A. The external forward contract in TC hedges the remaining FC50 of the receivable in A. Hedge accounting is not necessary in the consolidated financial statements because monetary items are measured at spot foreign exchange rates under IAS 21 irrespective of whether hedge accounting is applied.

The net balances before and after elimination of the accounting entries relating to the internal derivatives are the same, as set out below. Accordingly, there is no need to make any further accounting entries to meet the requirements of IAS 39.

	Debit	Credit
Receivables	-	LC10
Payables	LC5	-
External forward contract	LC5	-
Gains and losses	-	-
Internal contracts	-	-

Case 2: Offset of cash flow hedges

To extend the example, A also has highly probable future revenues of FC200 on which it expects to receive cash in 90 days. B has highly probable future expenses of FC500 (advertising cost), also to be paid for in 90 days. A and B enter into separate forward contracts with TC to hedge these exposures and TC enters into an external forward contract to receive FC300 in 90 days.

As before, FC weakens at the end of month 1. A incurs a 'loss' of LC20 on its anticipated revenues because the LC value of these revenues decreases. This is offset by a 'gain' of LC20 on its forward contract with TC.

B incurs a 'gain' of LC50 on its anticipated advertising cost because the LC value of the expense decreases. This is offset by a 'loss' of LC50 on its transaction with TC.

TC incurs a 'gain' of LC50 on its internal transaction with B, a 'loss' of LC20 on its internal transaction with A and a loss of LC30 on its external forward contract.

A and B complete the necessary documentation, the hedges are effective, and both A and B qualify for hedge accounting in their individual financial statements. A defers the gain of LC20 on its internal derivative transaction in a hedging reserve in equity and B defers the loss of LC50 in its hedging reserve in equity. TC does not claim hedge accounting, but measures both its internal and external derivative positions at fair value, which net to zero.

At the end of month 1, the following entries are made in the individual or separate financial statements of A, B and TC. Entries reflecting intragroup transactions or events are shown in italics.

A's entries

| Dr | Internal contract TC | LC20 | |
| | Cr Equity | | LC20 |

B's entries

| Dr | Equity | LC50 | |
| | Cr Internal contract TC | | LC50 |

TC's entries

Dr	Internal loss A	LC20	
	Cr Internal contract A		LC20
Dr	Internal contract B	LC50	
	Cr Internal gain B		LC50
Dr	Foreign exchange loss	LC30	
	Cr External forward contract		LC30

For the consolidated financial statements, TC's external forward contract on FC300 is designated, at the beginning of month 1, as a hedging instrument of the first FC300 of B's highly probable future expenses. IAS 39 requires that in the consolidated financial statements at the end of month 1, the accounting effects of the internal derivative transactions must be eliminated.

However, the net balances before and after elimination of the accounting entries relating to the internal derivatives are the same, as set out below. Accordingly, there is no need to make any further accounting entries in order for the requirements of IAS 39 to be met.

	Debit	Credit
External forward contract	–	LC30
Equity	LC30	–
Gains and losses	–	–
Internal contracts	–	–

Case 3: Offset of fair value and cash flow hedges

Assume that the exposures and the internal derivative transactions are the same as in cases 1 and 2. However, instead of entering into two external derivatives to hedge separately the fair value and cash flow exposures, TC enters into a single net external derivative to receive FC250 in exchange for LC in 90 days.

TC has four internal derivatives, two maturing in 60 days and two maturing in 90 days. These are offset by a net external derivative maturing in 90 days. The interest rate differential between FC and LC is minimal, and therefore the ineffectiveness resulting from the mismatch in maturities is expected to have a minimal effect on profit or loss in TC.

As in cases 1 and 2, A and B apply hedge accounting for their cash flow hedges and TC measures its derivatives at fair value. A defers a gain of LC20 on its internal derivative transaction in equity and B defers a loss of LC50 on its internal derivative transaction in equity.

At the end of month 1, the following entries are made in the individual or separate financial statements of A, B and TC. Entries reflecting intragroup transactions or events are shown in italics.

A's entries

Dr	Foreign exchange loss	LC10	
	Cr Receivables		LC10
Dr	*Internal contract TC*	*LC10*	
	Cr Internal gain TC		*LC10*
Dr	*Internal contract TC*	*LC20*	
	Cr Equity		*LC20*

B's entries

Dr	Payables	LC5	
	Cr Foreign exchange gain		LC5
Dr	*Internal loss TC*	*LC5*	
	Cr Internal contract TC		*LC5*
Dr	*Equity*	*LC50*	
	Cr Internal contract TC		*LC50*

TC's entries

Dr	*Internal loss A*	*LC10*	
	Cr Internal contract A		*LC10*
Dr	*Internal loss A*	*LC20*	
	Cr Internal contract A		*LC20*
Dr	*Internal contract B*	*LC5*	
	Cr Internal gain B		*LC5*
Dr	*Internal contract B*	*LC50*	
	Cr Internal gain B		*LC50*
Dr	Foreign exchange loss	LC25	
	Cr External forward contract		LC25

TOTAL (for the internal derivatives)	A LC	B LC	Total LC
Income (fair value hedges)	10	(5)	5
Equity (cash flow hedges)	20	(50)	(30)
Total	30	(55)	(25)

Combining these amounts with the external transactions (ie those not marked in italics above) produces the total net balances before elimination of the internal derivatives as follows:

	Debit	Credit
Receivables	-	LC10
Payables	LC5	-
Forward contract	-	LC25
Equity	LC30	-
Gains and losses	-	-
Internal contracts	-	-

For the consolidated financial statements, the following designations are made at the beginning of month 1:

- the payable of FC50 in B is designated as a hedge of the first FC50 of the highly probable future revenues in A. Therefore, at the end of month 1, the following entries are made in the consolidated financial statements: Dr Payable LC5; Cr Equity LC5;
- the receivable of FC100 in A is designated as a hedge of the first FC100 of the highly probable future expenses in B. Therefore, at the end of month 1, the following entries are made in the consolidated financial statements: Dr Equity LC10, Cr Receivable LC10; and
- the external forward contract on FC250 in TC is designated as a hedge of the next FC250 of highly probable future expenses in B. Therefore, at the end of month 1, the following entries are made in the consolidated financial statements: Dr Equity LC25; Cr External forward contract LC25.

In the consolidated financial statements at the end of month 1, IAS 39 requires the accounting effects of the internal derivative transactions to be eliminated.

However, the total net balances before and after elimination of the accounting entries relating to the internal derivatives are the same, as set out below. Accordingly, there is no need to make any further accounting entries to meet the requirements of IAS 39.

	Debit	Credit
Receivables	-	LC10
Payables	LC5	-
Forward contract	-	LC25
Equity	LC30	-
Gains and losses	-	-
Internal contracts	-	-

Case 4: Offset of fair value and cash flow hedges with adjustment to carrying amount of inventory

Assume similar transactions as in case 3, except that the anticipated cash outflow of FC500 in B relates to the purchase of inventory that is delivered after 60 days. Assume also that the entity has a policy of basis-adjusting hedged forecast non-financial items. At the end of month 2, there are no further changes in exchange rates or fair values. At that date, the inventory is delivered and the loss of LC50 on B's internal derivative, deferred in equity in month 1, is adjusted against the carrying amount of inventory in B. The gain of LC20 on A's internal derivative is deferred in equity as before.

In the consolidated financial statements, there is now a mismatch compared with the result that would have been achieved by unwinding and redesignating the hedges. The external derivative (FC250) and a proportion of the receivable (FC50) offset FC300 of the anticipated inventory purchase. There is a natural hedge between the remaining FC200 of anticipated cash outflow in B and the anticipated cash inflow of FC200 in A. This relationship does not qualify for hedge accounting under IAS 39 and this time there is only a partial offset between gains and losses on the internal derivatives that hedge these amounts.

At the end of months 1 and 2, the following entries are made in the individual or separate financial statements of A, B and TC. Entries reflecting intragroup transactions or events are shown in italics.

A's entries (all at the end of month 1)

Dr	Foreign exchange loss	LC10	
	Cr Receivables		LC10
Dr	*Internal contract TC*	*LC10*	
	Cr Internal gain TC		*LC10*
Dr	*Internal contract TC*	*LC20*	
	Cr Equity		*LC20*

B's entries

At the end of month 1:

Dr	Payables	LC5	
	Cr Foreign exchange gain		LC5
Dr	*Internal loss TC*	*LC5*	
	Cr *Internal contract TC*		*LC5*
Dr	Equity	LC50	
	Cr *Internal contract TC*		*LC50*

At the end of month 2:

| Dr | Inventory | LC50 | |
| | Cr   Equity | | LC50 |

TC's entries (all at the end of month 1)

Dr	*Internal loss A*	*LC10*	
	Cr *Internal contract A*		*LC10*
Dr	*Internal loss A*	*LC20*	
	Cr *Internal contract A*		*LC20*
Dr	*Internal contract B*	*LC5*	
	Cr *Internal gain B*		*LC5*
Dr	*Internal contract B*	*LC50*	
	Cr *Internal gain B*		*LC50*
Dr	Foreign exchange loss	LC25	
	Cr Forward		LC25

TOTAL *(for the internal derivatives)*	A LC	B LC	Total LC
Income (fair value hedges)	10	(5)	5
Equity (cash flow hedges)	20		20
Basis adjustment (inventory)	-	(50)	(50)
Total	30	(55)	(25)

Combining these amounts with the external transactions (ie those not marked in italics above) produces the total net balances before elimination of the internal derivatives as follows:

	Debit	Credit
Receivables	-	LC10
Payables	LC5	-
Forward contract	-	LC25
Equity	-	LC20
Basis adjustment (inventory)	LC50	-
Gains and losses	-	-
Internal contracts	-	-

For the consolidated financial statements, the following designations are made at the beginning of month 1:

- the payable of FC50 in B is designated as a hedge of the first FC50 of the highly probable future revenues in A. Therefore, at the end of month 1, the following entry is made in the consolidated financial statements: Dr Payables LC5; Cr Equity LC5.
- the receivable of FC100 in A is designated as a hedge of the first FC100 of the highly probable future expenses in B. Therefore, at the end of month 1, the following entries are made in the consolidated financial statements: Dr Equity LC10; Cr Receivable LC10; and at the end of month 2, Dr Inventory LC10; Cr Equity LC10.
- the external forward contract on FC250 in TC is designated as a hedge of the next FC250 of highly probable future expenses in B. Therefore, at the end of month 1, the following entry is made in the consolidated financial statements: Dr Equity LC25; Cr External forward contract LC25; and at the end of month 2, Dr Inventory LC25; Cr Equity LC25.

The total net balances after elimination of the accounting entries relating to the internal derivatives are as follows:

	Debit	Credit
Receivables	-	LC10
Payables	LC5	-
Forward contract	-	LC25
Equity	-	LC5
Basis adjustment (inventory)	LC35	-
Gains and losses	-	-
Internal contracts	-	-

These total net balances are different from those that would be recognised if the internal derivatives were not eliminated, and it is these net balances that IAS 39 requires to be included in the consolidated financial statements. The accounting entries required to adjust the total net balances before elimination of the internal derivatives are as follows:

(a)   to reclassify LC15 of the loss on B's internal derivative that is included in inventory to reflect that FC150 of the forecast purchase of inventory is not hedged by an external instrument (neither the external forward contract of FC250 in TC nor the external payable of FC100 in A); and

(b)   to reclassify the gain of LC15 on A's internal derivative to reflect that the forecast revenues of FC150 to which it relates is not hedged by an external instrument.

The net effect of these two adjustments is as follows:

Dr   Equity   LC15
     Cr   Inventory   LC15

F.1.8 Combination of written and purchased options

In most cases, IAS 39.AG94 prohibits the use of written options as hedging instruments. If a combination of a written option and purchased option (such as an interest rate collar) is transacted as a single instrument with one counterparty, can an entity split the derivative instrument into its written option component and purchased option component and designate the purchased option component as a hedging instrument?

No. IAS 39.74 specifies that a hedging relationship is designated by an entity for a hedging instrument in its entirety. The only exceptions permitted are splitting the time value and intrinsic value of an option and splitting the interest element and spot price on a forward. Question F.1.3 addresses the issue of whether and when a combination of ptions is considered as a written option.

F.1.9 Delta-neutral hedging strategy

Does IAS 39 permit an entity to apply hedge accounting for a 'deltaneutral' hedging strategy and other dynamic hedging strategies under which the quantity of the hedging instrument is constantly adjusted in order to maintain a desired hedge ratio, for example, to achieve a deltaneutral position insensitive to changes in the fair value of the hedged item?

Yes. IAS 39.74 states that "a dynamic hedging strategy that assesses both the intrinsic value and time value of an option contract can qualify for hedge accounting". For example, a portfolio insurance strategy that seeks to ensure that the fair value of the hedged item does not drop below a certain level, while allowing the fair value to increase, may qualify for hedge accounting.

To qualify for hedge accounting, the entity must document how it will monitor and update the hedge and measure hedge effectiveness, be able to track properly all terminations and redesignations of the hedging instrument, and demonstrate that all other criteria for hedge accounting in IAS 39.88 are met. Also, it must be able to demonstrate an expectation that the hedge will be highly effective for a specified short period of time during which the hedge is not expected to be adjusted.

F.1.10 Hedging instrument: out of the money put option

Entity A has an investment in one share of Entity B, which it has classified as available for sale. To give itself partial protection against decreases in the share price of Entity B, Entity A acquires a put option on one share of Entity B and designates the change in the intrinsic value of the put as a hedging instrument in a fair value hedge of changes in the fair value of its share in Entity B. The put gives Entity A the right to sell one share of Entity B at a strike price of CU90. At the inception of the hedging relationship, the share has a quoted price of CU100. Since the put option gives Entity A the right to dispose of the share at a price of CU90, the put should normally be fully effective in offsetting price declines below CU90 on an intrinsic value basis. Price changes above CU90 are not hedged. In this case, are changes in the fair value of the share of Entity B for prices above CU90 regarded as hedge ineffectiveness under IAS 39.88 and recognised in profit or loss under IAS 39.89?

No. IAS 39.74 permits Entity A to designate changes in the intrinsic value of the option as the hedging instrument. The changes in the intrinsic value of the option provide protection against the risk of variability in the fair value of one share of Entity B below or equal to the strike price of the put of CU90. For prices above CU90, the option is out of the money and has no intrinsic value. Accordingly, gains and losses on one share of Entity B for prices above CU90 are not attributable to the hedged risk for the purposes of assessing hedge effectiveness and recognising gains and losses on the hedged item.

Therefore, Entity A reports changes in the fair value of the share in equity if it is associated with variation in its price above CU90 (IAS 39.55 and IAS 39.90). Changes in the fair value of the share associated with price declines below CU90 form part of the designated fair value hedge and are recognised in profit or loss under IAS 39.89(b). Assuming the hedge is effective, those changes are offset by changes in the intrinsic value of the put, which are also recognised in profit or loss (IAS 39.89(a)). Changes in the time value of the put are excluded from the designated hedging relationship and recognised in profit or loss under IAS 39.55(a).

F.1.11 Hedging instrument: proportion of the cash flows of a cash instrument

In the case of foreign exchange risk, a non-derivative financial asset or non-derivative financial liability can potentially qualify as a hedging instrument. Can an entity treat the cash flows for specified periods during which a financial asset or financial liability that is designated as a hedging instrument remains outstanding as a proportion of the hedging instrument under IAS 39.75, and exclude the other cash flows from the designated hedging relationship?

No. IAS 39.75 indicates that a hedging relationship may not be designated for only a portion of the time period in which the hedging instrument is outstanding. For example, the cash flows during the first three years of a tenyear borrowing denominated in a foreign currency cannot qualify as a hedging instrument in a cash flow hedge of the first three years of revenue in the same foreign currency. On the other hand, a non-derivative financial asset or financial liability denominated in a foreign currency may potentially qualify as a hedging instrument in a hedge of the foreign currency risk associated with a hedged item that has a remaining time period until maturity that is equal to or longer than the remaining maturity of the hedging instrument (see Question F.2.17).

F.1.12 Hedges of more than one type of risk

Issue (a) - Normally a hedging relationship is designated between an entire hedging instrument and a hedged item so that there is a single measure of fair value for the hedging instrument. Does this preclude designating a single financial instrument simultaneously as a hedging instrument in both a cash flow hedge and a fair value hedge?

No. For example, entities commonly use a combined interest rate and currency swap to convert a variable rate position in a foreign currency to a fixed rate position in the functional currency. IAS 39.76 allows the swap to be designated separately as a fair value hedge of the currency risk and a cash flow hedge of the interest rate risk provided the conditions in IAS 39.76 are met.

Issue (b) - If a single financial instrument is a hedging instrument in two different hedges, is special disclosure required?

IAS 32.58 requires disclosures separately for designated fair value hedges, cash flow hedges and hedges of a net investment in a foreign operation. The instrument in question would be reported in the IAS 32.58 disclosures separately for each type of hedge.

F.1.13 Hedging instrument: dual foreign currency forward exchange contract

Entity A's functional currency is the Japanese yen. Entity A has a fiveyear floating rate US dollar liability and a ten-year fixed rate pound sterling-denominated note receivable. The principal amounts of the asset and liability when converted into the Japanese yen are the same. Entity A enters into a single foreign currency forward contract to hedge its foreign currency exposure on both instruments under which it receives US dollars and pays pounds sterling at the end of five years. If Entity A designates the forward exchange contract as a hedging instrument in a cash flow hedge against the foreign currency exposure on the principal repayments of both instruments, can it qualify for hedge accounting?

Yes. IAS 39.76 permits designating a single hedging instrument as a hedge of multiple types of risk if three conditions are met. In this example, the derivative hedging instrument satisfies all of these conditions, as follows.

(a)   The risks hedged can be identified clearly. The risks are the exposures to changes in the exchange rates between US dollars and yen, and yen and pounds, respectively.

(b)   The effectiveness of the hedge can be demonstrated. For the pound sterling loan, the effectiveness is measured as the degree of offset between the fair value of the principal repayment in pounds sterling and the fair value of the pound sterling payment on the forward exchange contract. For the US dollar liability, the effectiveness is measured as the degree of offset between the fair value of the principal repayment in US dollars and the US dollar receipt on the forward exchange contract. Even though the receivable has a ten-year life and the forward protects it for only the first five years, hedge accounting is permitted for only a portion of the exposure as described in Question F.2.17.

(c)   It is possible to ensure that there is specific designation of the hedging instrument and different risk positions. The hedged exposures are identified as the principal amounts of the liability and the note receivable in their respective currency of denomination.

F.1.14 Concurrent offsetting swaps and use of one as a hedging instrument

Entity A enters into an interest rate swap and designates it as a hedge of the fair value exposure associated with fixed rate debt. The fair value hedge meets the hedge accounting criteria of IAS 39. Entity A simultaneously enters into a second interest rate swap with the same swap counterparty that has terms that fully offset the first interest rate swap. Is Entity A required to view the two swaps as one unit and therefore precluded from applying fair value hedge accounting to the first swap?

It depends. IAS 39 is transaction-based. If the second swap was not entered into in contemplation of the first swap or there is a substantive business purpose for structuring the transactions separately, then the swaps are not viewed as one unit.

For example, some entities have a policy that requires a centralised dealer or treasury subsidiary to enter into third-party derivative contracts on behalf of other subsidiaries within the organisation to hedge the subsidiaries' interest rate risk exposures. The dealer or treasury subsidiary also enters into internal derivative transactions with those subsidiaries in order to track those hedges operationally within the organisation. Because the dealer or treasury subsidiary also enters into derivative contracts as part of its trading operations, or because it may wish to rebalance the risk of its overall portfolio, it may enter into a derivative contract with the same third party during the same business day that has substantially the same terms as a contract entered into as a hedging instrument on behalf of another subsidiary. In this case, there is a valid business purpose for entering into each contract.

Judgement is applied to determine whether there is a substantive business purpose for structuring the transactions separately. For example, if the sole purpose is to obtain fair value accounting treatment for the debt, there is no substantive business purpose.

F.2 Hedged Items

F.2.1 Whether a derivative can be designated as a hedged item

Does IAS 39 permit designating a derivative instrument (whether a standalone or separately recognised embedded derivative) as a hedged item either individually or as part of a hedged group in a fair value or cash flow hedge, for example, by designating a pay-variable, receive-fixed Forward Rate Agreement (FRA) as a cash flow hedge of a pay-fixed, receive-variable FRA?

No. Derivative instruments are always deemed held for trading and measured at fair value with gains and losses recognised in profit or loss unless they are designated and effective hedging instruments (IAS 39.9). As an exception, IAS 39.AG94 permits the designation of a purchased option as the hedged item in a fair value hedge.

F.2.2 Cash flow hedge: anticipated issue of fixed rate debt

Is hedge accounting allowed for a hedge of an anticipated issue of fixed rate debt?

Yes. This would be a cash flow hedge of a highly probable forecast transaction that will affect profit or loss (IAS 39.86) provided that the conditions in IAS 39.88 are met.

To illustrate: Entity R periodically issues new bonds to refinance maturing bonds, provide working capital and for various other purposes. When Entity R decides it will be issuing bonds, it may hedge the risk of changes in the long-term interest rate from the date it decides to issue the bonds to the date the bonds are issued. If long-term interest rates go up, the bond will be issued either at a higher rate or with a higher discount or smaller premium than was originally expected. The higher rate being paid or decrease in proceeds is normally offset by the gain on the hedge. If long-term interest rates go down, the bond will be issued either at a lower rate or with a higher premium or a smaller discount than was originally expected. The lower rate being paid or increase in proceeds is normally offset by the loss on the hedge.

For example, in August 2000 Entity R decided it would issue CU200 million seven-year bonds in January 2001. Entity R performed historical correlation studies and determined that a seven-year treasury bond adequately correlates to the bonds Entity R expected to issue, assuming a hedge ratio of 0.93 futures contracts to one debt unit. Therefore, Entity R hedged the anticipated issue of the bonds by selling (shorting) CU186 million worth of futures on seven-year treasury bonds. From August 2000 to January 2001 interest rates increased. The short futures positions were closed in January 2001, the date the bonds were issued, and resulted in a CU1.2 million gain that will offset the increased interest payments on the bonds and, therefore, will affect profit or loss over the life of the bonds. The hedge qualifies as a cash flow hedge of the interest rate risk on the forecast issue of debt.

F.2.3 Hedge accounting: core deposit intangibles

Is hedge accounting treatment permitted for a hedge of the fair value exposure of core deposit intangibles?

It depends on whether the core deposit intangible is generated internally or acquired (eg as part of a business combination).

Internally generated core deposit intangibles are not recognised as intangible assets under IAS 38. Because they are not recognised, they cannot be designated as a hedged item.

If a core deposit intangible is acquired together with a related portfolio of deposits, the core deposit intangible is required to be recognised separately as an intangible asset (or as part of the related acquired portfolio of deposits) if it meets the recognition criteria in paragraph 21 of IAS 38 *Intangible Assets*. A recognised core deposit intangible asset could be designated as a hedged item, but only if it meets the conditions in paragraph 88, including the requirement in paragraph 88(b) that the effectiveness of the hedge can be measured reliably. Because it is often difficult to measure reliably the fair value of a core.

F.2.4 Hedge accounting: hedging of future foreign currency revenue streams

Is hedge accounting permitted for a currency borrowing that hedges an expected but not contractual revenue stream in foreign currency?

Yes, if the revenues are highly probable. Under IAS 39.86(b) a hedge of an anticipated sale may qualify as a cash flow hedge. For example, an airline entity may use sophisticated models based on experience and economic data to project its revenues in various currencies. If it can demonstrate that forecast revenues for a period of time into the future in a particular currency are "highly probable", as required by IAS 39.88, it may designate a currency borrowing as a cash flow hedge of the future revenue stream. The portion of the gain or loss on the borrowing that is determined to be an effective hedge is recognised directly in equity through the statement of changes in equity until the revenues occur.

It is unlikely that an entity can reliably predict 100 per cent of revenues for a future year. On the other hand, it is possible that a portion of predicted revenues, normally those expected in the short term, will meet the "highly probable" criterion.

F.2.5 Cash flow hedges: 'all in one' hedge

If a derivative instrument is expected to be settled gross by delivery of the underlying asset in exchange for the payment of a fixed price, can the derivative instrument be designated as the hedging instrument in a cash flow hedge of that gross settlement assuming the other cash flow hedge accounting criteria are met?

Yes. A derivative instrument that will be settled gross can be designated as the hedging instrument in a cash flow hedge of the variability of the consideration to be paid or received in the future transaction that will occur on gross settlement of the derivative contract itself because there would be an exposure to variability in the purchase or sale price without the derivative. This applies to all fixed price contracts that are accounted for as derivatives under IAS 39.

For example, if an entity enters into a fixed price contract to sell a commodity and that contract is accounted for as a derivative under IAS 39 (for example, because the entity has a practice of settling such contracts net in cash or of taking delivery of the underlying and selling it within a short period after delivery for the purpose of generating a profit from short-term fluctuations in price or dealer's margin), the entity may designate the fixed price contract as a cash flow hedge of the variability of the consideration to be received on the sale of the asset (a future transaction) even though the fixed price contract is the contract under which the asset will be sold. Also, if an entity enters into a forward contract to purchase a debt instrument that will be settled by delivery, but the forward contract is a derivative because its term exceeds the regular way delivery period in the marketplace, the entity may designate the forward as a cash flow hedge of the variability of the consideration to be paid to acquire the debt instrument (a future transaction), even though the derivative is the contract under which the debt instrument will be acquired.

F.2.6 Hedge relationships: entity-wide risk

An entity has a fixed rate asset and a fixed rate liability, each having the same principal amount. Under the terms of the instruments, interest payments on the asset and liability occur in the same period and the net cash flow is always positive because the interest rate on the asset exceeds the interest rate on the liability. The entity enters into an interest rate swap to receive a floating interest rate and pay a fixed interest rate on a notional amount equal to the principal of the asset and designates the interest rate swap as a fair value hedge of the fixed rate asset. Does the hedging relationship qualify for hedge accounting even though the effect of the interest rate swap on an entity-wide basis is to create an exposure to interest rate changes that did not previously exist?

Yes. IAS 39 does not require risk reduction on an entity-wide basis as a condition for hedge accounting. Exposure is assessed on a transaction basis and, in this instance, the asset being hedged has a fair value exposure to interest rate increases that is offset by the interest rate swap.

F.2.7 Cash flow hedge: forecast transaction related to an entity's equity

Can a forecast transaction in the entity's own equity instruments or forecast dividend payments to shareholders be designated as a hedged item in a cash flow hedge?

No. To qualify as a hedged item, the forecast transaction must expose the entity to a particular risk that can affect profit or loss (IAS 39.86). The classification of financial instruments as liabilities or equity generally provides the basis for determining whether transactions or other payments relating to such instruments are recognised in profit or loss (IAS 32). For example, distributions to holders of an equity instrument are debited by the issuer directly to equity (IAS 32.35). Therefore, such distributions cannot be designated as a hedged item. However, a declared dividend that has not yet been paid and is recognised as a financial liability may qualify as a hedged item, for example, for foreign currency risk if it is denominated in a foreign currency.

F.2.8 Hedge accounting: risk of a transaction not occurring

Does IAS 39 permit an entity to apply hedge accounting to a hedge of the risk that a transaction will not occur, for example, if that would result in less revenue to the entity than expected?

No. The risk that a transaction will not occur is an overall business risk that is not eligible as a hedged item. Hedge accounting is permitted only for risks associated with recognised assets and liabilities, firm commitments, highly probable forecast transactions and net investments in foreign operations (IAS 39.86).

F.2.9 Held-to-maturity investments: hedging variable interest rate payments

Can an entity designate a pay-variable, receive-fixed interest rate swap as a cash flow hedge of a variable rate, held-to-maturity investment?

No. It is inconsistent with the designation of a debt investment as being held to maturity to designate a swap as a cash flow hedge of the debt investment's variable interest rate payments. IAS 39.79 states that a held-to-maturity investment cannot be a hedged item with respect to interest rate risk or prepayment risk "because designation of an investment as held to maturity requires an intention to hold the investment until maturity without regard to changes in the fair value or cash flows of such an investment attributable to changes in interest rates".

F.2.10 Hedged items: purchase of held-to-maturity investment

An entity forecasts the purchase of a financial asset that it intends to classify as held to maturity when the forecast transaction occurs. It enters into a derivative contract with the intent to lock in the current interest rate and designates the derivative as a hedge of the forecast purchase of the financial asset. Can the hedging relationship qualify for cash flow hedge accounting even though the asset will be classified as a held-to-maturity investment?

Yes. With respect to interest rate risk, IAS 39 prohibits hedge accounting for financial assets that are classified as held-to-maturity (IAS 39.79). However, even though the entity intends to classify the asset as held to maturity, the instrument is not classified as such until the transaction occurs.

F.2.11 Cash flow hedges: reinvestment of funds obtained from held-to-maturity investments

An entity owns a variable rate asset that it has classified as held to maturity. It enters into a derivative contract with the intention to lock in the current interest rate on the reinvestment of variable rate cash flows, and designates the derivative as a cash flow hedge of the forecast future interest receipts on debt instruments resulting from the reinvestment of interest receipts on the held-to-maturity asset. Assuming that the other hedge accounting criteria are met, can the hedging relationship qualify for cash flow hedge accounting even though the interest payments that are being reinvested come from an asset that is classified as held to maturity?

Yes. IAS 39.79 states that a held-to-maturity investment cannot be a hedged item with respect to interest rate risk. Question F.2.9 specifies that this applies not only to fair value hedges, ie hedges of the exposure to fair value interest rate risk associated with held-to-maturity investments that pay fixed interest, but also to cash flow hedges, ie hedges of the exposure to cash flow interest rate risk associated with held-to-maturity investments that pay variable interest at current market rates. However, in this instance, the derivative is designated as an offset of the exposure to cash flow risk associated with forecast future interest receipts on debt instruments resulting from the forecast reinvestment of variable rate cash flows on the held-to-maturity investment. The source of the funds forecast to be reinvested is not relevant in determining whether the reinvestment risk can be hedged. Accordingly, designation of the derivative as a cash flow hedge is permitted. This answer applies also to a hedge of the exposure to cash flow risk associated with the forecast future interest receipts on debt instruments resulting from the reinvestment of interest receipts on a fixed rate asset classified as held to maturity.

F.2.12 Hedge accounting: prepayable financial asset

If the issuer has the right to prepay a financial asset, can the investor designate the cash flows after the prepayment date as part of the hedged item?

Cash flows after the prepayment date may be designated as the hedged item to the extent it can be demonstrated that they are "highly probable" (IAS 39.88). For example, cash flows after the prepayment date may qualify as highly probable if they result from a group or pool of similar assets (for example, mortgage loans) for which prepayments can be estimated with a high degree of accuracy or if the prepayment option is significantly out of the money. In addition, the cash flows after the pre-payment date may be designated as the hedged item if a comparable option exists in the hedging instrument.

F.2.13 Fair value hedge: risk that could affect profit or loss

Is fair value hedge accounting permitted for exposure to interest rate risk in fixed rate loans that are classified as loans and receivables?

Yes. Under IAS 39, loans and receivables are carried at amortised cost. Banking institutions in many countries hold the bulk of their loans and receivables until maturity. Thus, changes in the fair value of such loans and receivables that are due to changes in market interest rates will not affect profit or loss. IAS 39.86 specifies that a fair value hedge is a hedge of the exposure to changes in fair value that is attributable to a particular risk and that can affect profit or loss. Therefore, IAS 39.86 may appear to preclude fair value hedge accounting for loans and receivables. However, it follows from IAS 39.79 that loans and receivables can be hedged items with respect to interest rate risk since they are not designated as held-to-maturity investments. The entity could sell them and the change in fair values would affect profit or loss. Thus, fair value hedge accounting is permitted for loans and receivables.

F.2.14 Intragroup and intra-entity hedging transactions

An Australian entity, whose functional currency is the Australian dollar, has forecast purchases in Japanese yen that are highly probable. The Australian entity is wholly owned by a Swiss entity, which prepares consolidated financial statements (which include the Australian subsidiary) in Swiss francs. The Swiss parent entity enters into a forward contract to hedge the change in yen relative to the Australian dollar. Can that hedge qualify for hedge accounting in the consolidated financial statements, or must the Australian subsidiary that has the foreign currency exposure be a party to the hedging transaction?

Yes. The hedge can qualify for hedge accounting provided the other hedge accounting criteria in IAS 39 are met. Since the Australian entity did not hedge the foreign currency exchange risk associated with the forecast purchases in yen, the effects of exchange rate changes between the Australian dollar and the yen will affect the Australian entity's profit or loss and, therefore, would also affect consolidated profit or loss. IAS 39 does not require that the operating unit that is exposed to the risk being hedged be a party to the hedging instrument.

F.2.15 *Internal contracts: single offsetting external derivative*

An entity uses what it describes as internal derivative contracts to document the transfer of responsibility for interest rate risk exposures from individual divisions to a central treasury function. The central treasury function aggregates the internal derivative contracts and enters into a single external derivative contract that offsets the internal derivative contracts on a net basis. For example, if the central treasury function has entered into three internal receive-fixed, pay-variable interest rate swaps that lay off the exposure to variable interest cash flows on variable rate liabilities in other divisions and one internal receive-variable, pay-fixed interest rate swap that lays off the exposure to variable interest cash flows on variable rate assets in another division, it would enter into an interest rate swap with an external counterparty that exactly offsets the four internal swaps. Assuming that the hedge accounting criteria are met, in the entity's financial statements would the single offsetting external derivative qualify as a hedging instrument in a hedge of a part of the underlying items on a gross basis?

Yes, but only to the extent the external derivative is designated as an offset of cash inflows or cash outflows on a gross basis. IAS 39.84 indicates that a hedge of an overall net position does not qualify for hedge accounting. However, it does permit designating a part of the underlying items as the hedged position on a gross basis. Therefore, even though the purpose of entering into the external derivative was to offset internal derivative contracts on a net basis, hedge accounting is permitted if the hedging relationship is defined and documented as a hedge of a part of the underlying cash inflows or cash outflows on a gross basis. An entity follows the approach outlined in IAS 39.84 and IAS 39.AG101 to designate part of the underlying cash flows as the hedged position.

F.2.16 Internal contracts: external derivative contracts that are settled net

Issue (a) - An entity uses internal derivative contracts to transfer interest rate risk exposures from individual divisions to a central treasury function. For each internal derivative contract, the central treasury function enters into a derivative contract with a single external counterparty that offsets the internal derivative contract. For example, if the central treasury function has entered into a receive-5 per cent-fixed, pay-LIBOR interest rate swap with another division that has entered into the internal contract with central treasury to hedge the exposure to variability in interest cash flows on a pay-LIBOR borrowing, central treasury would enter into a pay-5 per cent-fixed, receive-LIBOR interest rate swap on the same principal terms with the external counterparty. Although each of the external derivative contracts is formally documented as a separate contract, only the net of the payments on all of the external derivative contracts is settled since there is a netting agreement with the external counterparty. Assuming that the other hedge accounting criteria are met, can the individual external derivative contracts, such as the pay5 per cent-fixed, receive-LIBOR interest rate swap above, be designated as hedging instruments of underlying gross exposures, such as the exposure to changes in variable interest payments on the pay-LIBOR borrowing above, even though the external derivatives are settled on a net basis?

Generally, yes. External derivative contracts that are legally separate contracts and serve a valid business purpose, such as laying off risk exposures on a gross basis, qualify as hedging instruments even if those external contracts are settled on a net basis with the same external counterparty, provided the hedge accounting criteria in IAS 39 are met. See also Question F.1.14.

Issue (b) - Treasury observes that by entering into the external offsetting contracts and including them in the centralised portfolio, it is no longer able to evaluate the exposures on a net basis. Treasury wishes to manage the portfolio of offsetting external derivatives separately from other exposures of the entity. Therefore, it enters into an additional, single derivative to offset the risk of the portfolio. Can the individual external derivative contracts in the portfolio still be designated as hedging instruments of underlying gross exposures even though a single external derivative is used to offset fully the market exposure created by entering into the external contracts?

Generally, yes. The purpose of structuring the external derivative contracts in this manner is consistent with the entity's risk management objectives and strategies. As indicated above, external derivative contracts that are legally separate contracts and serve a valid business purpose qualify as hedging instruments. Moreover, the answer to Question F.1.14 specifies that hedge accounting is not precluded simply because the entity has entered into a swap that mirrors exactly the terms of another swap with the same counterparty if there is a substantive business purpose for structuring the transactions separately.

F.2.17 Partial term hedging

IAS 39.75 indicates that a hedging relationship may not be designated for only a portion of the time period during which a hedging instrument remains outstanding. Is it permitted to designate a derivative as hedging only a portion of the time period to maturity of a hedged item?

Yes. A financial instrument may be a hedged item for only a portion of its cash flows or fair value, if effectiveness can be measured and the other hedge accounting criteria are met.

To illustrate: Entity A acquires a 10 per cent fixed rate government bond with a remaining term to maturity of ten years. Entity A classifies the bond as available for sale. To hedge itself against fair value exposure on the bond associated with the present value of the interest rate payments until year 5, Entity A acquires a five-year pay-fixed, receive-floating swap. The swap may be designated as hedging the fair value exposure of the interest rate payments on the government bond until year 5 and the change in value of the principal payment due at maturity to the extent affected by changes in the yield curve relating to the five years of the swap.

F.2.18 Hedging instrument: cross-currency interest rate swap

Entity A's functional currency is the Japanese yen. Entity A has a fiveyear floating rate US dollar liability and a 10-year fixed rate pound sterling-denominated note receivable. Entity A wishes to hedge the foreign currency exposure on its asset and liability and the fair value interest rate exposure on the receivable and enters into a matching cross-currency interest rate swap to receive floating rate US dollars and pay fixed rate pounds sterling and to exchange the dollars for the pounds at the end of five years. Can Entity A designate the swap as a hedging instrument in a fair value hedge against both foreign currency risk and interest rate risk, although both the pound sterling and US dollar are foreign currencies to Entity A?

Yes. IAS 39.81 permits hedge accounting for components of risk, if effectiveness can be measured. Also, IAS 39.76 permits designating a single hedging instrument as a hedge of more than one type of risk if the risks can be identified clearly, effectiveness can be demonstrated, and specific designation of the hedging instrument and different risk positions can be ensured. Therefore, the swap may be designated as a hedging instrument in a fair value hedge of the pound sterling receivable against exposure to changes in its fair value associated with changes in UK interest rates for the initial partial term of five years and the exchange rate between pounds and US dollars. The swap is measured at fair value with changes in fair value recognised in profit or loss. The carrying amount of the receivable is adjusted for changes in its fair value caused by changes in UK interest rates for the first fiveyear portion of the yield curve. The receivable and payable are remeasured using spot exchange rates under IAS 21 and the changes to their carrying amounts recognised in profit or loss.

F.2.19 Hedged items: hedge of foreign currency risk of publicly traded shares

Entity A acquires shares in Entity B on a foreign stock exchange for their fair value of 1,000 in foreign currency (FC). It classifies the shares as available for sale. To protect itself from the exposure to changes in the foreign exchange rate associated with the shares, it enters into a forward contract to sell FC750. Entity A intends to roll over the forward exchange contract for as long as it retains the shares. Assuming that the other hedge accounting criteria are met, could the forward exchange contract qualify as a hedge of the foreign exchange risk associated with the shares?

Yes, but only if there is a clear and identifiable exposure to changes in foreign exchange rates. Therefore, hedge accounting is permitted if (a) the equity instrument is not traded on an exchange (or in another established marketplace) where trades are denominated in the same currency as the functional currency of Entity A and (b) dividends to Entity A are not denominated in that currency. Thus, if a share is traded in multiple currencies and one of those currencies is the functional currency of the reporting entity, hedge accounting for the foreign currency component of the share price is not permitted.

If so, could the forward exchange contract be designated as a hedging instrument in a hedge of the foreign exchange risk associated with the portion of the fair value of the shares up to FC750 in foreign currency?

Yes. IAS 39 permits designating a portion of the cash flow or fair value of a financial asset as the hedged item if effectiveness can be measured (IAS 39.81). Therefore, Entity A may designate the forward exchange contract as a hedge of the foreign exchange risk associated with only a portion of the fair value of the shares in foreign currency. It could either be designated as a fair value hedge of the foreign exchange exposure of FC750 associated with the shares or as a cash flow hedge of a forecast sale of the shares, provided the timing of the sale is identified. Any variability in the fair value of the shares in foreign currency would not affect the assessment of hedge effectiveness unless the fair value of the shares in foreign currency was to fall below FC750.

F.2.20 Hedge accounting: stock index

An entity may acquire a portfolio of shares to replicate a stock index and a put option on the index to protect itself from fair value losses. Does IAS 39 permit designating the put on the stock index as a hedging instrument in a hedge of the portfolio of shares?

No. If similar financial instruments are aggregated and hedged as a group, IAS 39.83 states that the change in fair value attributable to the hedged risk for each individual item in the group is expected to be approximately proportional to the overall change in fair value attributable to the hedged risk of the group. In the scenario above, the change in the fair value attributable to the hedged risk for each individual item in the group (individual share prices) is not expected to be approximately proportional to the overall change in fair value attributable to the hedged risk of the group.

F.2.21 Hedge accounting: netting of assets and liabilities

May an entity group financial assets together with financial liabilities for the purpose of determining the net cash flow exposure to be hedged for hedge accounting purposes?

An entity's hedging strategy and risk management practices may assess cash flow risk on a net basis but IAS 39.84 does not permit designating a net cash flow exposure as a hedged item for hedge accounting purposes. IAS 39.AG101 provides an example of how a bank might assess its risk on a net basis (with similar assets and liabilities grouped together) and then qualify for hedge accounting by hedging on a gross basis.

F.3 Hedge Accounting

F.3.1 Cash flow hedge: fixed interest rate cash flows

An entity issues a fixed rate debt instrument and enters into a receive-fixed, pay-variable interest rate swap to offset the exposure to interest rate risk associated with the debt instrument. Can the entity designate the swap as a cash flow hedge of the future interest cash outflows associated with the debt instrument?

No. IAS 39.86(b) states that a cash flow hedge is "a hedge of the exposure to variability in cash flows". In this case, the issued debt instrument does not give rise to any exposure to variability in cash flows since the interest payments are fixed. The entity may designate the swap as a fair value hedge of the debt instrument, but it cannot designate the swap as a cash flow hedge of the future cash outflows of the debt instrument.

F.3.2 Cash flow hedge: reinvestment of fixed interest rate cash flows

An entity manages interest rate risk on a net basis. On 1 January 2001, it forecasts aggregate cash inflows of CU100 on fixed rate assets and aggregate cash outflows of CU90 on fixed rate liabilities in the first quarter of 2002. For risk management purposes it uses a receive-variable, pay-fixed Forward Rate Agreement (FRA) to hedge the forecast net cash inflow of CU10. The entity designates as the hedged item the first CU10 of cash inflows on fixed rate assets in the first quarter of 2002. Can it designate the receive-variable, pay-fixed FRA as a cash flow hedge of the exposure to variability to cash flows in the first quarter of 2002 associated with the fixed rate assets?

No. The FRA does not qualify as a cash flow hedge of the cash flow relating to the fixed rate assets because they do not have a cash flow exposure. The entity could, however, designate the FRA as a hedge of the fair value exposure that exists before the cash flows are remitted.

In some cases, the entity could also hedge the interest rate exposure associated with the forecast reinvestment of the interest and principal it receives on fixed rate assets (see Question F.6.2). However, in this example, the FRA does not qualify for cash flow hedge accounting because it increases rather than reduces the variability of interest cash flows resulting from the reinvestment of interest cash flows (for example, if market rates increase, there will be a cash inflow on the FRA and an increase in the expected interest cash inflows resulting from the reinvestment of interest cash inflows on fixed rate assets). However, potentially it could qualify as a cash flow hedge of a portion of the refinancing of cash outflows on a gross basis.

F.3.3 Foreign currency hedge

Entity A has a foreign currency liability payable in six months' time and it wishes to hedge the amount payable on settlement against foreign currency fluctuations. To that end, it takes out a forward contract to buy the foreign currency in six months' time. Should the hedge be treated as:

(a)   a fair value hedge of the foreign currency liability with gains and losses on revaluing the liability and the forward contract at the year-end both recognised in the income statement; or

(b)   a cash flow hedge of the amount to be settled in the future with gains and losses on revaluing the forward contract recognised in equity?

IAS 39 does not preclude either of these two methods. If the hedge is treated as a fair value hedge, the gain or loss on the fair value remeasurement of the hedging instrument and the gain or loss on the fair value remeasurement of the hedged item for the hedged risk are recognised immediately in profit or loss. If the hedge is treated as a cash flow hedge with the gain or loss on remeasuring the forward contract recognised in equity, that amount is recognised in profit or loss in the same period or periods during which the hedged item (the liability) affects profit or loss, ie when the liability is remeasured for changes in foreign exchange rates. Therefore, if the hedge is effective, the gain or loss on the derivative is released to profit or loss in the same periods during which the liability is remeasured, not when the payment occurs. See Question F.3.4.

F.3.4 Foreign currency cash flow hedge

An entity exports a product at a price denominated in a foreign currency. At the date of the sale, the entity obtains a receivable for the sale price payable in 90 days and takes out a 90-day forward exchange contract in the same currency as the receivable to hedge its foreign currency exposure.

Under IAS 21, the sale is recorded at the spot rate at the date of sale, and the receivable is restated during the 90-day period for changes in exchange rates with the difference being taken to profit or loss (IAS 21.23 and IAS 21.28).

If the foreign exchange contract is designated as a hedging instrument, does the entity have a choice whether to designate the foreign exchange contract as a fair value hedge of the foreign currency exposure of the receivable or as a cash flow hedge of the collection of the receivable?

Yes. If the entity designates the foreign exchange contract as a fair value hedge, the gain or loss from remeasuring the forward exchange contract at fair value is recognised immediately in profit or loss and the gain or loss on remeasuring the receivable is also recognised in profit or loss.

If the entity designates the foreign exchange contract as a cash flow hedge of the foreign currency risk associated with the collection of the receivable, the portion of the gain or loss that is determined to be an effective hedge is recognised directly in equity, and the ineffective portion in profit or loss (IAS 39.95). The amount recognised directly in equity is transferred to profit or loss in the same period or periods during which changes in the measurement of the receivable affect profit or loss (IAS 39.100).

F.3.5 Fair value hedge: variable rate debt instrument

Does IAS 39 permit an entity to designate a portion of the risk exposure of a variable rate debt instrument as a hedged item in a fair value hedge?

Yes. A variable rate debt instrument may have an exposure to changes in its fair value due to credit risk. It may also have an exposure to changes in its fair value relating to movements in the market interest rate in the periods between which the variable interest rate on the debt instrument is reset. For example, if the debt instrument provides for annual interest payments reset to the market rate each year, a portion of the debt instrument has an exposure to changes in fair value during the year.

F.3.6 Fair value hedge: inventory

IAS 39.86(a) states that a fair value hedge is "a hedge of the exposure to changes in fair value of a recognised asset or liability ... that is attributable to a particular risk and could affect profit or loss". Can an entity designate inventories, such as copper inventory, as the hedged item in a fair value hedge of the exposure to changes in the price of the inventories, such as the copper price, although inventories are measured at the lower of cost and net realisable value under IAS 2 *Inventories*?

Yes. The inventories may be hedged for changes in fair value due to changes in the copper price because the change in fair value of inventories will affect profit or loss when the inventories are sold or their carrying amount is written down. The adjusted carrying amount becomes the cost basis for the purpose of applying the lower of cost and net realisable value test under IAS 2. The hedging instrument used in a fair value hedge of inventories may alternatively qualify as a cash flow hedge of the future sale of the inventory.

F.3.7 Hedge accounting: forecast transaction

For cash flow hedges, a forecast transaction that is subject to a hedge must be "highly probable". How should the term "highly probable" be interpreted?

The term "highly probable" indicates a much greater likelihood of happening than the term "more likely than not". An assessment of the likelihood that a forecast transaction will take place is not based solely on management's intentions because intentions are not verifiable. A transaction's probability should be supported by observable facts and the attendant circumstances.

In assessing the likelihood that a transaction will occur, an entity should consider the following circumstances:

(a) the frequency of similar past transactions;
(b) the financial and operational ability of the entity to carry out the transaction;
(c) substantial commitments of resources to a particular activity (for example, a manufacturing facility that can be used in the short run only to process a particular type of commodity);
(d) the extent of loss or disruption of operations that could result if the transaction does not occur;
(e) the likelihood that transactions with substantially different characteristics might be used to achieve the same business purpose (for example, an entity that intends to raise cash may have several ways of doing so, ranging from a short-term bank loan to an offering of ordinary shares); and
(f) the entity's business plan.

The length of time until a forecast transaction is projected to occur is also a factor in determining probability. Other factors being equal, the more distant a forecast transaction is, the less likely it is that the transaction would be regarded as highly probable and the stronger the evidence that would be needed to support an assertion that it is highly probable.

For example, a transaction forecast to occur in five years may be less likely to occur than a transaction forecast to occur in one year. However, forecast interest payments for the next 20 years on variable rate debt would typically be highly probable if supported by an existing contractual obligation.

In addition, other factors being equal, the greater the physical quantity or future value of a forecast transaction in proportion to the entity's transactions of the same nature, the less likely it is that the transaction would be regarded as highly probable and the stronger the evidence that would be required to support an assertion that it is highly probable. For example, less evidence generally would be needed to support forecast sales of 100,000 units in the next month than 950,000 units in that month when recent sales have averaged 950,000 units per month for the past three months.

A history of having designated hedges of forecast transactions and then determining that the forecast transactions are no longer expected to occur would call into question both an entity's ability to predict forecast transactions accurately and the propriety of using hedge accounting in the future for similar forecast transactions.

F.3.8 Retrospective designation of hedges

Does IAS 39 permit an entity to designate hedge relationships retrospectively?

No. Designation of hedge relationships takes effect prospectively from the date all hedge accounting criteria in IAS 39.88 are met. In particular, hedge accounting can be applied only from the date the entity has completed the necessary documentation of the hedge relationship, including identification of the hedging instrument, the related hedged item or transaction, the nature of the risk being hedged, and how the entity will assess hedge effectiveness.

F.3.9 Hedge accounting: designation at the inception of the hedge

Does IAS 39 permit an entity to designate and formally document a derivative contract as a hedging instrument after entering into the derivative contract?

Yes, prospectively. For hedge accounting purposes, IAS 39 requires a hedging instrument to be designated and formally documented as such from the inception of the hedge relationship (IAS 39.88); in other words, a hedge relationship cannot be designated retrospectively. Also, it precludes designating a hedging relationship for only a portion of the time period during which the hedging instrument remains outstanding (IAS 39.75). However, it does not require the hedging instrument to be acquired at the inception of the hedge relationship.

F.3.10 Hedge accounting: identification of hedged forecast transaction

Can a forecast transaction be identified as the purchase or sale of the last 15,000 units of a product in a specified period or as a percentage of purchases or sales during a specified period?

No. The hedged forecast transaction must be identified and documented with sufficient specificity so that when the transaction occurs, it is clear whether the transaction is or is not the hedged transaction. Therefore, a forecast transaction may be identified as the sale of the first 15,000 units of a specific product during a specified three-month period, but it could not be identified as the last 15,000 units of that product sold during a three-month period because the last 15,000 units cannot be identified when they are sold. For the same reason, a forecast transaction cannot be specified solely as a percentage of sales or purchases during a period.

F.3.11 Cash flow hedge: documentation of timing of forecast transaction

For a hedge of a forecast transaction, should the documentation of the hedge relationship that is established at inception of the hedge identify the date on, or time period in which, the forecast transaction is expected to occur?

Yes. To qualify for hedge accounting, the hedge must relate to a specific identified and designated risk (IAS 39.AG110) and it must be possible to measure its effectiveness reliably (IAS 39.88(d)). Also, the hedged forecast transaction must be highly probable (IAS 39.88(c)). To meet these criteria, an entity is not required to predict and document the exact date a forecast transaction is expected to occur. However, it is required to identify and document the time period during which the forecast transaction is expected to occur within a reasonably specific and generally narrow range of time from a most probable date, as a basis for assessing hedge effectiveness. To determine that the hedge will be highly effective in accordance with IAS 39.88(d), it is necessary to ensure that changes in the fair value of the expected cash flows are offset by changes in the fair value of the hedging instrument and this test may be met only if the timing of the cash flows occur within close proximity to each other. If the forecast transaction is no longer expected to occur, hedge accounting is discontinued in accordance with IAS 39.101(c).

F.4 Hedge Effectiveness

F.4.1 Hedging on an after-tax basis

Hedging is often done on an after-tax basis. Is hedge effectiveness assessed after taxes?

IAS 39 permits, but does not require, assessment of hedge effectiveness on an after-tax basis. If the hedge is undertaken on an after-tax basis, it is so designated at inception as part of the formal documentation of the hedging relationship and strategy.

F.4.2 Hedge effectiveness: assessment on cumulative basis

IAS 39.88(b) requires that the hedge is expected to be highly effective. Should expected hedge effectiveness be assessed separately for each period or cumulatively over the life of the hedging relationship?

Expected hedge effectiveness may be assessed on a cumulative basis if the hedge is so designated, and that condition is incorporated into the appropriate hedging documentation. Therefore, even if a hedge is not expected to be highly effective in a particular period, hedge accounting is not precluded if effectiveness is expected to remain sufficiently high over the life of the hedging relationship. However, any ineffectiveness is required to be recognised in profit or loss as it occurs.

To illustrate: an entity designates a LIBOR-based interest rate swap as a hedge of a borrowing whose interest rate is a UK base rate plus a margin. The UK base rate changes, perhaps, once each quarter or less, in increments of 25-50 basis points, while LIBOR changes daily. Over a period of 1-2 years, the hedge is expected to be almost perfect. However, there will be quarters when the UK base rate does not change at all, while LIBOR has changed significantly. This would not necessarily preclude hedge accounting.

F.4.3 Hedge effectiveness: counterparty credit risk

Must an entity consider the likelihood of default by the counterparty to the hedging instrument in assessing hedge effectiveness?

Yes. An entity cannot ignore whether it will be able to collect all amounts due under the contractual provisions of the hedging instrument. When assessing hedge effectiveness, both at the inception of the hedge and on an ongoing basis, the entity considers the risk that the counterparty to the hedging instrument will default by failing to make any contractual payments to the entity. For a cash flow hedge, if it becomes probable that a counterparty will default, an entity would be unable to conclude that the hedging relationship is expected to be highly effective in achieving offsetting cash flows. As a result, hedge accounting would be discontinued. For a fair value hedge, if there is a change in the counterparty's creditworthiness, the fair value of the hedging instrument will change, which affects the assessment of whether the hedge relationship is effective and whether it qualifies for continued hedge accounting.

F.4.4 Hedge effectiveness: effectiveness tests

How should hedge effectiveness be measured for the purposes of initially qualifying for hedge accounting and for continued qualification?

IAS 39 does not provide specific guidance about how effectiveness tests are performed. IAS 39.AG105 specifies that a hedge is normally regarded as highly effective only if at inception and in subsequent periods, the hedge is expected to be highly effective in achieving offsetting changes in fair value or cash flows attributable to the hedged risk during the period for which the hedge is designated, and (b) the actual results are within a range of 80125 per cent. IAS 39.AG105 also states that the expectation in (a) can be demonstrated in various ways.

The appropriateness of a given method of assessing hedge effectiveness will depend on the nature of the risk being hedged and the type of hedging instrument used. The method of assessing effectiveness must be reasonable and consistent with other similar hedges unless different methods are explicitly justified. An entity is required to document at the inception of the hedge how effectiveness will be assessed and then to apply that effectiveness test on a consistent basis for the duration of the hedge.

Several mathematical techniques can be used to measure hedge effectiveness, including ratio analysis, ie a comparison of hedging gains and losses with the corresponding gains and losses on the hedged item at a point in time, and statistical measurement techniques such as regression analysis. If regression analysis is used, the entity's documented policies for assessing effectiveness must specify how the results of the regression will be assessed.

F.4.5 Hedge effectiveness: less than 100 per cent offset

If a cash flow hedge is regarded as highly effective because the actual risk offset is within the allowed 80-125 per cent range of deviation from full offset, is the gain or loss on the ineffective portion of the hedge recognised in equity?

No. IAS 39.95(a) indicates that only the effective portion is recognised directly in equity. IAS 39.95(b) requires the ineffective portion to be recognised in profit or loss.

F.4.7 Assuming perfect hedge effectiveness

If the principal terms of the hedging instrument and of the entire hedged asset or liability or hedged forecast transaction arc the same, can an entity assume perfect hedge effectiveness without further effectiveness testing?

No. IAS 39.88(e) requires an entity to assess hedges on an ongoing basis for hedge effectiveness. It cannot assume hedge effectiveness even if the principal terms of the hedging instrument and the hedged item are the same, since hedge ineffectiveness may arise because of other attributes such as the liquidity of the instruments or their credit risk (IAS 39.AG109). It may, however, designate only certain risks in an overall exposure as being hedged and thereby improve the effectiveness of the hedging relationship. For example, for a fair value hedge of a debt instrument, if the derivative hedging instrument has a credit risk that is equivalent to the AA-rate, it may designate only the risk related to AA-rated interest rate movements as being hedged, in which case changes in credit spreads generally will not affect the effectiveness of the hedge.

F.5 Cash Flow Hedges

F.5.1 Hedge accounting: non-derivative monetary asset or non-derivative monetary liability used as a hedging instrument

If an entity designates a non-derivative monetary asset as a foreign currency cash flow hedge of the repayment of the principal of a non-derivative monetary liability, would the exchange differences on the hedged item be recognised in profit or loss (IAS 21.28) and the exchange differences on the hedging instrument be recognised in equity until the repayment of the liability (IAS 39.95)?

No. Exchange differences on the monetary asset and the monetary liability are both recognised in profit or loss in the period in which they arise (IAS 21.28). IAS 39.AG83 specifies that if there is a hedge relationship between a non-derivative monetary asset and a non-derivative monetary liability, changes in fair values of those financial instruments are recognised in profit or loss.

F.5.2 Cash flow hedges: performance of hedging instrument (1)

Entity A has a floating rate liability of CU1,000 with five years remaining to maturity. It enters into a five-year pay-fixed, receive-floating interest rate swap in the same currency and with the same principal terms as the liability to hedge the exposure to variable cash flow payments on the floating rate liability attributable to interest rate risk. At inception, the fair value of the swap is zero. Subsequently, there is an increase of CU49 in the fair value of the swap. This increase consists of a change of CU50 resulting from an increase in market interest rates and a change of minus CU1 resulting from an increase in the credit risk of the swap counterparty. There is no change in the fair value of the floating rate liability, but the fair value (present value) of the future cash flows needed to offset the exposure to variable interest cash flows on the liability increases by CU50. Assuming that Entity A determines that the hedge is still highly effective, is there ineffectiveness that should be recognised in profit or loss?

No. A hedge of interest rate risk is not fully effective if part of the change in the fair value of the derivative is attributable to the counterparty's credit risk (IAS 39.AG109). However, because Entity A determines that the hedge relationship is still highly effective, it credits the effective portion of the change in fair value of the swap, ie the net change in fair value of CU49, to equity. There is no debit to profit or loss for the change in fair value of the swap attributable to the deterioration in the credit quality of the swap counterparty, because the cumulative change in the present value of the future cash flows needed to offset the exposure to variable interest cash flows on the hedged item, ie CU50, exceeds the cumulative change in value of the hedging instrument, ie CU49.

Dr	Swap	CU49
	Cr Equity	CU49

If Entity A concludes that the hedge is no longer highly effective, it discontinues hedge accounting prospectively as from the date the hedge ceased to be highly effective in accordance with IAS 39.101.

Would the answer change if the fair value of the swap instead increases to CU51 of which CU50 results from the increase in market interest rates and CU1 from a decrease in the credit risk of the swap counterparty?

Yes. In this case, there is a credit to profit or loss of CU1 for the change in fair value of the swap attributable to the improvement in the credit quality of the swap counterparty. This is because the cumulative change in the value of the hedging instrument, ie CU51, exceeds the cumulative change in the present value of the future cash flows needed to offset the exposure to variable interest cash flows on the hedged item, ie CU50. The difference of CU1 represents the excess ineffectiveness attributable to the derivative hedging instrument, the swap, and is recognised in profit or loss.

Dr	Swap	CU51
	Cr Equity	CU50
	Cr Profit or loss	CU1

F.5.3 Cash flow hedges: performance of hedging instrument (2)

On 30 September 2001, Entity A hedges the anticipated sale of 24 tonnes of pulp on 1 March 2002 by entering into a short forward contract on 24 tonnes of pulp. The contract requires net settlement in cash determined as the difference between the future spot price of pulp on a specified commodity exchange and CU1,000. Entity A expects to sell the pulp in a different, local market. Entity A determines that the forward contract is an effective hedge of the anticipated sale and that the other conditions for hedge accounting are met. It assesses hedge effectiveness by comparing the entire change in the fair value of the forward contract with the change in the fair value of the expected cash inflows. On 31 December, the spot price of pulp has increased both in the local market and on the exchange. The increase in the local market exceeds the increase on the exchange. As a result, the present value of the expected cash inflow from the sale on the local market is CU1,100. The fair value of Entity A's forward contract is negative CU80. Assuming that Entity A determines that the hedge is still highly effective, is there ineffectiveness that should be recognised in profit or loss?

No. In a cash flow hedge, ineffectiveness is not recognised in the financial statements when the cumulative change in the fair value of the hedged cash flows exceeds the cumulative change in the value of the hedging instrument. In this case, the cumulative change in the fair value of the forward contract is CU80, while the fair value of the cumulative change in expected future cash flows on the hedged item is CU100. Since the fair value of the cumulative change in expected future cash flows on the hedged item from the inception of the hedge exceeds the cumulative change in fair value of the hedging instrument (in absolute amounts), no portion of the gain or loss on the hedging instrument is recognised in profit or loss (IAS 39.95(a)). Because Entity A determines that the hedge relationship is still highly effective, it debits the entire change in fair value of the forward contract (CU80) to equity.

Dr   Equity   CU80
     Cr   Forward   CU80

If Entity A concludes that the hedge is no longer highly effective, it discontinues hedge accounting prospectively as from the date the hedge ceases to be highly effective in accordance with IAS 39.101.

F.5.4 Cash flow hedges: forecast transaction occurs before the specified period

An entity designates a derivative as a hedging instrument in a cash flow hedge of a forecast transaction, such as a forecast sale of a commodity. The hedging relationship meets all the hedge accounting conditions, including the requirement to identify and document the period in which the transaction is expected to occur within a reasonably specific and narrow range of time (see Question F.1.17). If, in a subsequent period, the forecast transaction is expected to occur in an earlier period than originally anticipated, can the entity conclude that this transaction is the same as the one that was designated as being hedged?

Yes. The change in timing of the forecast transaction does not affect the validity of the designation. However, it may affect the assessment of the effectiveness of the hedging relationship. Also, the hedging instrument would need to be designated as a hedging instrument for the whole remaining period of its existence in order for it to continue to qualify as a hedging instrument (see IAS 39.75 and Question F.2.17).

F.5.5 Cash flow hedges: measuring effectiveness for a hedge of a forecast transaction in a debt instrument

A forecast investment in an interest-earning asset or forecast issue of an interest-bearing liability creates a cash flow exposure to interest rate changes because the related interest payments will be based on the market rate that exists when the forecast transaction occurs. The objective of a cash flow hedge of the exposure to interest rate changes is to offset the effects of future changes in interest rates so as to obtain a single fixed rate, usually the rate that existed at the inception of the hedge that corresponds with the term and timing of the forecast transaction. During the period of the hedge, it is not possible to determine what the market interest rate for the forecast transaction will be at the time the hedge is terminated or when the forecast transaction occurs. In this case, how is the effectiveness of the hedge assessed and measured?

During this period, effectiveness can be measured on the basis of changes in interest rates between the designation date and the interim effectiveness measurement date. The interest rates used to make this measurement are the interest rates that correspond with the term and occurrence of the forecast transaction that existed at the inception of the hedge and that exist at the measurement date as evidenced by the term structure of interest rates.

Generally it will not be sufficient simply to compare cash flows of the hedged item with cash flows generated by the derivative hedging instrument as they are paid or received, since such an approach ignores the entity's expectations of whether the cash flows will offset in subsequent periods and whether there will be any resulting ineffectiveness.

The discussion that follows illustrates the mechanics of establishing a cash flow hedge and measuring its effectiveness. For the purpose of the illustrations, assume that an entity expects to issue a CU100,000 one-year debt instrument in three months. The instrument will pay interest quarterly with principal due at maturity. The entity is exposed to interest rate increases and establishes a hedge of the interest cash flows of the debt by entering into a forward starting interest rate swap. The swap has a term of one year and will start in three months to correspond with the terms of the forecast debt issue. The entity will pay a fixed rate and receive a variable rate, and the entity designates the risk being hedged as the LIBOR-based interest component in the forecast issue of the debt.

Yield curve

The yield curve provides the foundation for computing future cash flows and the fair value of such cash flows both at the inception of, and during, the hedging relationship. It is based on current market yields on applicable reference bonds that are traded in the marketplace. Market yields are converted to spot interest rates ('spot rates' or 'zero coupon rates') by eliminating the effect of coupon payments on the market yield. Spot rates are used to discount future cash flows, such as principal and interest rate payments, to arrive at their fair value. Spot rates also are used to compute forward interest rates that are used to compute variable and estimated future cash flows. The relationship between spot rates and one-period forward rates is shown by the following formula:

Spot–forward relationship

$$F = \frac{(1 + SR)}{(1 + SR)} - 1$$

where F = forward rate (%)
      SR = spot rate (%)
      t = period in time (eg 1, 2, 3, 4, 5)

Also, for the purpose of this illustration, assume that the following quarterlyperiod term structure of interest rates using quarterly compounding exists at the inception of the hedge.

Yield curve at inception – (beginning of period 1)

Forward periods	1	2	3	4	5
Spot rates	3.75%	4.50%	5.50%	6.00%	6.25%
Forward rates	3.75%	5.25%	7.51%	7.50%	7.25%

The one-period forward rates are computed on the basis of spot rates for the applicable maturities. For example, the current forward rate for Period 2 calculated using the formula above is equal to $[1.0450^2 / 1.0375] - 1 = 5.25$ per cent. The current one-period forward rate for Period 2 is different from the current spot rate for Period 2, since the spot rate is an interest rate from the beginning of Period 1 (spot) to the end of Period 2, while the forward rate is an interest rate from the beginning of Period 2 to the end of Period 2.

Hedged item

In this example, the entity expects to issue a CU100,000 one-year debt instrument in three months with quarterly interest payments. The entity is exposed to interest rate increases and would like to eliminate the effect on cash flows of interest rate changes that may happen before the forecast transaction takes place. If that risk is eliminated, the entity would obtain an interest rate on its debt issue that is equal to the one-year forward coupon rate currently available in the marketplace in three months. That forward coupon rate, which is different from the forward (spot) rate, is 6.86 per cent, computed from the term structure of interest rates shown above. It is the market rate of interest that exists at the inception of the hedge, given the terms of the forecast debt instrument. It results in the fair value of the debt being equal to par at its issue.

At the inception of the hedging relationship, the expected cash flows of the debt instrument can be calculated on the basis of the existing term structure of interest rates. For this purpose, it is assumed that interest rates do not change and that the debt would be issued at 6.86 per cent at the beginning of Period 2. In this case, the cash flows and fair value of the debt instrument would be as follows at the beginning of Period 2.

Issue of fixed rate debt

Beginning of period 2 - No rate changes (Spot based on forward rates)

	Total					
		1	*2*	*3*	*4*	*5*
Original forward periods						
Remaining periods			*1*	*2*	*3*	*4*
Spot rates			5.25%	6.38%	6.75%	6.88%
Forward rates			5.25%	7.51%	7.50%	7.25%
	CU		*CU*	*CU*	*CU*	*CU*
Cash flows:						
Fixed interest @ 6.86%			1,716	1,716	1,716	1,716
Principal						100,000
Fair value:						
Interest	6,592		1,694	1,663	1,632	1,603
Principal	93,408					93,408*
Total						100,000

* CU100,000 / (1 + [0.0688 / 4])^4

Since it is assumed that interest rates do not change, the fair value of the interest and principal amounts equals the par amount of the forecast transaction. The fair value amounts are computed on the basis of the spot rates that exist at the inception of the hedge for the applicable periods in which the cash flows would occur had the debt been issued at the date of the forecast transaction. They reflect the effect of discounting those cash flows on the basis of the periods that will remain after the debt instrument is issued. For example, the spot rate of 6.38 per cent is used to discount the interest cash flow that is expected to be paid in Period 3, but it is discounted for only two periods because it will occur two periods after the forecast transaction.

The forward interest rates are the same as shown previously, since it is assumed that interest rates do not change. The spot rates are different but they have not actually changed. They represent the spot rates one period forward and are based on the applicable forward rates.

Hedging instrument

The objective of the hedge is to obtain an overall interest rate on the forecast transaction and the hedging instrument that is equal to 6.86 per cent, which is the market rate at the inception of the hedge for the period from Period 2 to Period 5. This objective is accomplished by entering into a forward starting interest rate swap that has a fixed rate of 6.86 per cent. Based on the term structure of interest rates that exist at the inception of the hedge, the interest rate swap will have such a rate. At the inception of the hedge, the fair value of the fixed rate payments on the interest rate swap will equal the fair value of the variable rate payments, resulting in the interest rate swap having a fair value of zero. The expected cash flows of the interest rate swap and the related fair value amounts are shown as follows.

Interest rate swap

	Total	1	2	3	4	5
Original forward periods						
Remaining periods			1	2	3	4
	CU		*CU*	*CU*	*CU*	*CU*
Cash flows: Fixed interest @ 6.86%			1,716	1,716	1,716	1,716
Forecast variable interest			1,313	1,877	1,876	1,813
Forecast based on forward rate			5.25%	7.51%	7.50%	7.25%
Net interest			(403)	161	160	97
Fair value: Discount rate *(spot)*			5.25%	6.38%	6.75%	6.88%
Fixed interest	6,592		1,694	1,663	1,632	1,603
Forecast variable interest	6,592		1,296	1,819	1,784	1,693
Fair value of interest rate swap	0		(398)	156	152	90

At the inception of the hedge, the fixed rate on the forward swap is equal to the fixed rate the entity would receive if it could issue the debt in three months under terms that exist today.

Measuring hedge effectiveness

If interest rates change during the period the hedge is outstanding, the effectiveness of the hedge can be measured in various ways.

Assume that interest rates change as follows immediately before the debt is issued at the beginning of Period 2.

Yield curve - Rates increase 200 basis points

Forward periods	1	2	3	4	5
Remaining periods		1	2	3	4
Spot rates		5.75%	6.50%	7.50%	8.00%
Forward rates		5.75%	7.25%	9.51%	9.50%

Under the new interest rate environment, the fair value of the pay-fixed at 6.86 per cent, receive-variable interest rate swap that was designated as the hedging instrument would be as follows.

Fair value of interest rate swap

	Total	1	2	3	4	5
Original forward periods						
Remaining periods			1	2	3	4
	CU	CU	CU	CU	CU	CU
Cash flows: Fixed interest @ 6.86%			1,716	1,716	1,716	1,716
Forecast variable interest			1,438	1,813	2,377	2,376
Forecast based on new forward rate			5.75%	7.25%	9.51%	9.50%
Net interest			(279)	97	661	660
Fair value:						
New discount rate (spot)			5.75%	6.50%	7.50%	8.00%
Fixed interest	6,562		1,692	1,662	1,623	1,585
Forecast variable interest	7,615		1,417	1,755	2,248	2,195
Fair value of net interest	1,053		(275)	93	625	610

In order to compute the effectiveness of the hedge, it is necessary to measure the change in the present value of the cash flows or the value of the hedged forecast transaction. There are at least two methods of accomplishing this measurement.

Method A – Compute change in fair value of debt

	Total	1	2	3	4	5
Original forward periods		*1*	*2*	*3*	*4*	*5*
Remaining periods			*1*	*2*	*3*	*4*
	CU		*CU*	*CU*	*CU*	*CU*
Cash flows:						
Fixed interest @ 6.86%			1,716	1,716	1,716	1,716
Principal				100,000		
Fair value:						
New discount rate *(spot)*			5.75%	6.50%	7.50%	8.00%
Interest	6,562		1,692	1,662	1,623	1,585
Principal	92,385					92,385*
Total	98,947					
Fair value at inception	100,000					
Fair value difference	(1,053)					

* $= \text{CU}100,000 / (1 + [0.08 / 4])^4$

Under Method A, a computation is made of the fair value in the new interest rate environment of debt that carries interest that is equal to the coupon interest rate that existed at the inception of the hedging relationship (6.86 per cent). This fair value is compared with the expected fair value as of the beginning of Period 2 that was calculated on the basis of the term structure of interest rates that existed at the inception of the hedging relationship, as illustrated above, to determine the change in the fair value. Note that the difference between the change in the fair value of the swap and the change in the expected fair value of the debt exactly offset in this example, since the terms of the swap and the forecast transaction match each other.

Method B - Compute change in fair value of cash flows

	Total	1	2	3	4	5
Original forward periods		1	2	3	4	5
Remaining periods			1	2	3	4
Market rate at inception			6.86%	6.86%	6.86%	6.86%
Current forward rate			5.75%	7.25%	9.51%	9.50%
Rate difference			1.11%	(0.39%)	(2.64%)	(2.64%)
Cash flow difference (principal rate)			CU279	(CU97)	(CU661)	(CU660)
Discount rate (spot)			5.75%	6.50%	7.50%	8.00%
Fair value of difference	(CU1,053)		CU 275	(CU93)	(CU625)	(CU610)

Under Method B, the present value of the change in cash flows is computed on the basis of the difference between the forward interest rates for the applicable periods at the effectiveness measurement date and the interest rate that would have been obtained if the debt had been issued at the market rate that existed at the inception of the hedge. The market rate that existed at the inception of the hedge is the one-year forward coupon rate in three months. The present value of the change in cash flows is computed on the basis of the current spot rates that exist at the effectiveness measurement date for the applicable periods in which the cash flows are expected to occur. This method also could be referred to as the 'theoretical swap' method (or 'hypothetical derivative' method) because the comparison is between the hedged fixed rate on the debt and the current variable rate, which is the same as comparing cash flows on the fixed and variable rate legs of an interest rate swap.

As before, the difference between the change in the fair value of the swap and the change in the present value of the cash flows exactly offset in this example, since the terms match.

Other considerations

There is an additional computation that should be performed to compute ineffectiveness before the expected date of the forecast transaction that has not been considered for the purpose of this illustration. The fair value difference has been determined in each of the illustrations as of the expected date of the forecast transaction immediately before the forecast transaction, ie at the beginning of Period 2. If the assessment of hedge effectiveness is done before the forecast transaction occurs, the difference should be discounted to the current date to arrive at the actual amount of ineffectiveness. For example, if the measurement date were one month after the hedging relationship was established and the forecast transaction is now expected to occur in two months, the amount would have to be discounted for the remaining two months before the forecast transaction is expected to occur to arrive at the actual fair value. This step would not be necessary in the examples provided above because there was no ineffectiveness. Therefore, additional discounting of the amounts, which net to zero, would not have changed the result.

Under Method B, ineffectiveness is computed on the basis of the difference between the forward coupon interest rates for the applicable periods at the effectiveness measurement date and the interest rate that would have been obtained if the debt had been issued at the market rate that existed at the inception of the hedge. Computing the change in cash flows based on the difference between the forward interest rates that existed at the inception of the hedge and the forward rates that exist at the effectiveness measurement date is inappropriate if the objective of the hedge is to establish a single fixed rate for a series of forecast interest payments. This objective is met by hedging the exposures with an interest rate swap as illustrated in the above example. The fixed interest rate on the swap is a blended interest rate composed of the forward rates over the life of the swap. Unless the yield curve is flat, the comparison between the forward interest rate exposures over the life of the swap and the fixed rate on the swap will produce different cash flows whose fair values are equal only at the inception of the hedging relationship. This difference is shown in the table below.

	Total	*1*	*2*	*3*	*4*	*5*
Original forward periods						
Remaining periods			*1*	*2*	*3*	*4*
Forward rate at inception			5.25%	7.51%	7.50%	7.25%
Current forward rate			5.75%	7.25%	9.51%	9.50%
Rate difference			(0.50%)	0.26%	(2.00%)	(2.25%)
Cash flow difference (principal rate)			(CU125)	CU 64	(CU501)	(CU563)
Discount rate (spot)			5.75%	6.50%	7.50%	8.00%
Fair value of difference	(CU1,055)		(CU123)	CU 62	(CU474)	(CU520)
Fair value of interest rate swap	CU 1,053					
Ineffectiveness	(CU2)					

If the objective of the hedge is to obtain the forward rates that existed at the inception of the hedge, the interest rate swap is ineffective because the swap has a single blended fixed coupon rate that does not offset a series of different forward interest rates. However, if the objective of the hedge is to obtain the forward coupon rate that existed at the inception of the hedge, the swap is effective, and the comparison based on differences in forward interest rates suggests ineffectiveness when none may exist. Computing ineffectiveness based on the difference between the forward interest rates that existed at the inception of the hedge and the forward rates that exist at the effectiveness measurement date would be an appropriate measurement of ineffectiveness if the hedging objective is to lock in those forward interest rates. In that case, the appropriate hedging instrument would be a series of forward contracts each of which matures on a repricing date that corresponds with the date of the forecast transactions.

It also should be noted that it would be inappropriate to compare only the variable cash flows on the interest rate swap with the interest cash flows in the debt that would be generated by the forward interest rates. That methodology has the effect of measuring ineffectiveness only on a portion of the derivative, and IAS 39 does not permit the bifurcation of a derivative for the purposes of assessing effectiveness in this situation (IAS 39.74). It is recognised, however, that if the fixed interest rate on the interest rate swap is equal to the fixed rate that would have been obtained on the debt at inception, there will be no ineffectiveness assuming that there are no differences in terms and no change in credit risk or it is not designated in the hedging relationship.

F.5.6 Cash flow hedges: firm commitment to purchase inventory in a foreign currency

Entity A has the Local Currency (LC) as its functional currency and presentation currency. On 30 June 2001, it enters into a forward exchange contract to receive Foreign Currency (FC) 100,000 and deliver LC109,600 on 30 June 2002 at an initial cost and fair value of zero. It designates the forward exchange contract as a hedging instrument in a cash flow hedge of a firm commitment to purchase a certain quantity of paper on 31 March 2002 and the resulting payable of FC100,000, which is to be paid on 30 June 2002. All hedge accounting conditions in IAS 39 are met.

As indicated in the table below, on 30 June 2001, the spot exchange rate is LC1.072 to FC1, while the twelve-month forward exchange rate is LC1.096 to FC1. On 31 December 2001, the spot exchange rate is LC1.080 to FC1, while the six-month forward exchange rate is LC1.092 to FC1. On 31 March 2002, the spot exchange rate is LC1.074 to FC1, while the three-month forward rate is LC1.076 to FC1. On 30 June 2002, the spot exchange rate is LC1.072 to FC1. The applicable yield curve in the local currency is flat at 6 per cent per year throughout the period. The fair value of the forward exchange contract is negative LC388 on 31 December 2001 $\{([1.092 \cdot 100,000] - 109,600) / 1.06^{(6/12)}\}$, negative LC1,971 on 31 March 2002 $\{([1.076 \cdot 100,000] - 109,600) / 1.06^{(3/12)}\}$, and negative LC2,400 on 30 June 2002 $\{1.072 \cdot 100,000 - 109,600\}$.

Date	Spot rate	Forward rate to 30 June 2002	Fair value of forward contract
30 June 2001	1.072	1.096	
31 December 2001	1.080	1.092	(388)
31 March 2002	1.074	1.076	(1,971)
30 June 2002	1.072	-	(2,400)

Issue (a) - What is the accounting for these transactions if the hedging relationship is designated as being for changes in the fair value of the forward exchange contract and the entity's accounting policy is to apply basis adjustment to non-financial assets that result from hedged forecast transactions?

The accounting entries are as follows.

30 June 2001

Dr   Forward   LC0

   Cr   Cash   LC0

To record the forward exchange contract at its initial amount of zero (IAS 39.43). The hedge is expected to be fully effective because the critical terms of the forward exchange contract and the purchase contract and the assessment of hedge effectiveness are based on the forward price (IAS 39.AG108).

31 December 2001

Dr   Equity   LC388

   Cr   Forward liability   LC388

To record the change in the fair value of the forward exchange contract between 30 June 2001 and 31 December 2001, ie LC388 − 0 = LC388, directly in equity (IAS 39.95). The hedge is fully effective because the loss on the forward exchange contract (LC388) exactly offsets the change in cash flows associated with the purchase contract based on the forward price [(LC388) = {([1.092 · 100,000] − 109,600)/1.06$^{(6/12)}$} − {([1.096 · 100,000] − 109,600) / 1.06}].

31 March 2002

Dr Equity	LC1,583	
Cr Forward liability		LC1,583

To record the change in the fair value of the forward exchange contract between 1 January 2002 and 31 March 2002 (ie LC1,971 − LC388 = LC1,583), directly in equity (IAS 39.94). The hedge is fully effective because the loss on the forward exchange contract (LC1,583) exactly offsets the change in cash flows associated with the purchase contract based on the forward price [(LC1,583) = {([1.076 · 100,000] − 109,600)/1.06$^{(3/12)}$} − {([1.092 · 100,000] − 109,600) /1.06$^{(6/12)}$}].

Dr Paper (purchase price)	LC107,400	
Dr Paper (hedging loss)	LC1,971	
Cr Equity		LC1,971
Cr Payable		LC107,400

To recognise the purchase of the paper at the spot rate (1.074 · FC100,000) and remove the cumulative loss on the forward exchange contract that has been recognised directly in equity (LC1,971) and include it in the initial measurement of the purchased paper. Accordingly, the initial measurement of the purchased paper is LC109,371 consisting of a purchase consideration of LC107,400 and a hedging loss of LC1,971.

30 June 2002

Dr Payable	LC107,400	
Cr Cash		LC107,200
Cr Profit or loss		LC200

To record the settlement of the payable at the spot rate (FC100,000 · 1.072 = 107,200) and the associated exchange gain of LC200 (LC107,400- LC107,200).

Dr Profit or loss	LC429	
Cr Forward liability		LC429

To record the loss on the forward exchange contract between 1 April 2002 and 30 June 2002 (ie LC2,400 − LC1,971 = LC429) in profit or loss. The hedge is regarded as fully effective because the loss on the forward exchange contract (LC429) exactly offsets the change in the fair value of the payable based on the forward price (LC429 = ([1.072· 100,000] − 109,600 − {([1.076 · 100,000] − 109,600)/1.06$^{(3/12)}$}).

Dr Forward liability	LC2,400	
Cr Cash		LC2,400

To record the net settlement of the forward exchange contract.

Issue (b) - What is the accounting for these transactions if the hedging relationship instead is designated as being for changes in the spot element of the forward exchange contract and the interest element is excluded from the designated hedging relationship (IAS 39.74)?

The accounting entries are as follows.

30 June 2001

Dr   Forward   LC0

    Cr   Cash   LC0

To record the forward exchange contract at its initial amount of zero (IAS 39.43). The hedge is expected to be fully effective because the critical terms of the forward exchange contract and the purchase contract are the same and the change in the premium or discount on the forward contract is excluded from the assessment of effectiveness (IAS 39.AG108).

31 December 2001

Dr   Profit or loss (interest element)   LC1,165

    Cr   Equity (spot element)   LC777

    Cr   Forward liability   LC388

To record the change in the fair value of the forward exchange contract between 30 June 2001 and 31 December 2001, ie LC388 – 0 = LC388. The change in the present value of spot settlement of the forward exchange contract is a gain of LC777 ($\{\{([1.080 \cdot 100,000] - 107,200)/1.06^{(6/12)}\} - \{([1.072 \cdot 100,000] - 107,200)/1.06\})$, which is recognised directly in equity (IAS 39.95(a)). The change in the interest element of the forward exchange contract (the residual change in fair value) is a loss of LC1,165 (388 + 777), which is recognised in profit or loss (IAS 39.74 and IAS 39.55(a)). The hedge is fully effective because the gain in the spot element of the forward contract (LC777) exactly offsets the change in the purchase price at spot rates (LC777 = $\{([1.080 \cdot 100,000] - 107,200)/1.06^{(6/12)}\} - \{([1.072 \cdot 100,000] - 107,200)/1.06\}$).

31 March 2002

Dr   Equity (spot element)   LC580

Dr   Profit or loss (interest element)   LC1,003

    Cr   Forward liability   LC1,583

To record the change in the fair value of the forward exchange contract between 1 January 2002 and 31 March 2002, ie LC1,971 – LC388 = LC1,583. The change in the present value of the spot settlement of the forward exchange contract is a loss of LC580 ($\{\{([1.074 \cdot 100,000] - 107,200)/1.06^{(3/12)}\} - \{([1.080 \cdot 100,000] - 107,200) / 1.06^{(6/12)}\})$, which is recognised directly in equity (IAS 39.95(a)). The change in the interest element of the forward exchange contract (the residual change in fair value) is a loss of LC1,003 (LC1,583 – LC580), which is recognised in profit or loss (IAS 39.74 and IAS 39.55(a)). The hedge is fully effective because the loss in the spot element of the forward contract (LC580) exactly offsets the change in the purchase price at spot rates [(580) = $\{([1.074 \cdot 100,000] - 107,200)/1.06^{(3/12)}\} - \{([1.080 \cdot 100,000] - 107,200) /1.06^{(6/12)}\}$].

Dr   Paper (purchase price)   LC107,400
Dr   Equity   LC197
   Cr   Paper (hedging gain)   LC197
   Cr   Payable   LC107,400

To recognise the purchase of the paper at the spot rate (= 1.074 · FC100,000) and remove the cumulative gain on the spot element of the forward exchange contract that has been recognised directly in equity (LC777 – LC580 = LC197) and include it in the initial measurement of the purchased paper. Accordingly, the initial measurement of the purchased paper is LC107,203, consisting of a purchase consideration of LC107,400 and a hedging gain of LC197.

30 June 2002

Dr   Payable   LC107,400
   Cr   Cash   LC107,200
   Cr   Profit or loss   LC200

To record the settlement of the payable at the spot rate (FC100,000 · 1.072 = LC107,200) and the associated exchange gain of LC200 (– [1.072 – 1.074] · FC100,000).

Dr   Profit or loss (spot element)   LC197
Dr   Profit or loss (interest element) LC232
   Cr   Forward liability   LC429

To record the change in the fair value of the forward exchange contract between 1 April 2002 and 30 June 2002 (ie LC2,400 – LC1,971 = LC429). The change in the present value of the spot settlement of the forward exchange contract is a loss of LC197 ([1.072 · 100,000] – 107,200 – {([1.074 · 100,000] – 107,200)/1.06$^{(3/12)}$}), which is recognised in profit or loss. The change in the interest element of the forward exchange contract (the residual change in fair value) is a loss of LC232 (LC429 – LC197), which is recognised in profit or loss. The hedge is fully effective because the loss in the spot element of the forward contract (LC197) exactly offsets the change in the present value of the spot settlement of the payable [(LC197) = {[1.072 · 100,000] – 107,200 – {([1.074 · 100,000] – 107,200)/1.06$^{(3/12)}$}].

Dr   Forward liability   LC2,400
   Cr   Cash   LC2,400

To record the net settlement of the forward exchange contract.

The following table provides an overview of the components of the change in fair value of the hedging instrument over the term of the hedging relationship. It illustrates that the way in which a hedging relationship is designated affects the subsequent accounting for that hedging relationship, including the assessment of hedge effectiveness and the recognition of gains and losses.

Period ending	Change in spot settlement LC	Fair value of change in spot settlement LC	Change in forward settlement LC	Fair value of change in forward settlement LC	Fair value of change in interest element LC
June 2001	–	–	–	–	–
December 2001	800	777	(400)	(388)	(1,165)
March 2002	(600)	(580)	(1,600)	(1,583)	(1,003)
June 2002	(200)	(197)	(400)	(429)	(232)
Total	–	(2,400)	(2,400)	(2,400)	

F.6 Hedges: Other issues

F.6.1 Hedge accounting: management of interest rate risk in financial institutions

Banks and other financial institutions often manage their exposure to interest rate risk on a net basis for all or parts of their activities. They have systems to accumulate critical information throughout the entity about their financial assets, financial liabilities and forward commitments, including loan commitments. This information is used to estimate and aggregate cash flows and to schedule such estimated cash flows into the applicable future periods in which they are expected to be paid or received. The systems generate estimates of cash flows based on the contractual terms of the instruments and other factors, including estimates of prepayments and defaults. For risk management purposes, many financial institutions use derivative contracts to offset some or all exposure to interest rate risk on a net basis.

If a financial institution manages interest rate risk on a net basis, can its activities potentially qualify for hedge accounting under IAS 39?

Yes. However, to qualify for hedge accounting the derivative hedging instrument that hedges the net position for risk management purposes must be designated for accounting purposes as a hedge of a gross position related to assets, liabilities, forecast cash inflows or forecast cash outflows giving rise to the net exposure (IAS 39.84, IAS 39.AG101 and IAS 39.AG111). It is not possible to designate a net position as a hedged item under IAS 39 because of the inability to associate hedging gains and losses with a specific item being hedged and, correspondingly, to determine objectively the period in which such gains and losses should be recognised in profit or loss.

Hedging a net exposure to interest rate risk can often be defined and documented to meet the qualifying criteria for hedge accounting in IAS 39.88 if the objective of the activity is to offset a specific, identified and designated risk exposure that ultimately affects the entity's profit or loss (IAS 39.AG110) and the entity designates and documents its interest rate risk exposure on a gross basis. Also, to qualify for hedge accounting the information systems must capture sufficient information about the amount and timing of cash flows and the effectiveness of the risk management activities in accomplishing their objective.

The factors an entity must consider for hedge accounting purposes if it manages interest rate risk on a net basis are discussed in Question F.6.2.

F.6.2 Hedge accounting considerations when interest rate risk is managed on a net basis

If an entity manages its exposure to interest rate risk on a net basis, what are the issues the entity should consider in defining and documenting its interest rate risk management activities to qualify for hedge accounting and in establishing and accounting for the hedge relationship?

Issues (a)-(l) below deal with the main issues. First, Issues (a) and (b) discuss the designation of derivatives used in interest rate risk management activities as fair value hedges or cash flow hedges. As noted there, hedge accounting criteria and accounting consequences differ between fair value hedges and cash flow hedges. Since it may be easier to achieve hedge accounting treatment if derivatives used in interest rate risk management activities are designated as cash flow hedging instruments, Issues (c)-(l) expand on various aspects of the accounting for cash flow hedges. Issues (c)-(f) consider the application of the hedge accounting criteria for cash flow hedges in IAS 39, and Issues (g) and (h) discuss the required accounting treatment. Finally, Issues (i)-(l) elaborate on other specific issues relating to the accounting for cash flow hedges.

Issue (a) – Can a derivative that is used to manage interest rate risk on a net basis be designated under IAS 39 as a hedging instrument in a fair value hedge or a cash flow hedge of a gross exposure?

Both types of designation are possible under IAS 39. An entity may designate the derivative used in interest rate risk management activities either as a fair value hedge of assets, liabilities and firm commitments or as a cash flow hedge of forecast transactions, such as the anticipated reinvestment of cash inflows, the anticipated refinancing or rollover of a financial liability, and the cash flow consequences of the resetting of interest rates for an asset or a liability.

In economic terms, it does not matter whether the derivative instrument is regarded as a fair value hedge or as a cash flow hedge. Under either perspective of the exposure, the derivative has the same economic effect of reducing the net exposure. For example, a receive-fixed, pay-variable interest rate swap can be considered to be a cash flow hedge of a variable rate asset or a fair value hedge of a fixed rate liability. Under either perspective, the fair value or cash flows of the interest rate swap offset the exposure to interest rate changes. However, accounting consequences differ depending on whether the derivative is designated as a fair value hedge or a cash flow hedge, as discussed in Issue (b).

To illustrate: a bank has the following assets and liabilities with a maturity of two years.

	Variable interest	*Fixed interest*
	CU	*CU*
Assets	60	100
Liabilities	(100)	(60)
Net	(40)	40

The bank takes out a two-year swap with a notional principal of CU40 to receive a variable interest rate and pay a fixed interest rate to hedge the net exposure. As discussed above, this may be regarded and designated either as a fair value hedge of CU40 of the fixed rate assets or as a cash flow hedge of CU40 of the variable rate liabilities.

Issue (b) – What are the critical considerations in deciding whether a derivative that is used to manage interest rate risk on a net basis should be designated as a hedging instrument in a fair value hedge or a cash flow hedge of a gross exposure?

Critical considerations include the assessment of hedge effectiveness in the presence of prepayment risk and the ability of the information systems to attribute fair value or cash flow changes of hedging instruments to fair value or cash flow changes, respectively, of hedged items, as discussed below.

For accounting purposes, the designation of a derivative as hedging a fair value exposure or a cash flow exposure is important because both the qualification requirements for hedge accounting and the recognition of hedging gains and losses for these categories are different. It is often easier to demonstrate high effectiveness for a cash flow hedge than for a fair value hedge.

Effects of prepayments

Prepayment risk inherent in many financial instruments affects the fair value of an instrument and the timing of its cash flows and impacts on the effectiveness test for fair value hedges and the highly probable test for cash flow hedges, respectively.

Effectiveness is often more difficult to achieve for fair value hedges than for cash flow hedges when the instrument being hedged is subject to prepayment risk. For a fair value hedge to qualify for hedge accounting, the changes in the fair value of the derivative hedging instrument must be expected to be highly effective in offsetting the changes in the fair value of the hedged item (IAS 39.88(b)). This test may be difficult to meet if, for example, the derivative hedging instrument is a forward contract having a fixed term and the financial assets being hedged are subject to prepayment by the borrower. Also, it may be difficult to conclude that, for a portfolio of fixed rate assets that are subject to prepayment, the changes in the fair value for each individual item in the group will be expected to be approximately proportional to the overall changes in fair value attributable to the hedged risk of the group. Even if the risk being hedged is a benchmark interest rate, to be able to conclude that fair value changes will be proportional for each item in the portfolio, it may be necessary to disaggregate the asset portfolio into categories based on term, coupon, credit, type of loan and other characteristics.

In economic terms, a forward derivative instrument could be used to hedge assets that are subject to prepayment but it would be effective only for small movements in interest rates. A reasonable estimate of prepayments can be made for a given interest rate environment and the derivative position can be adjusted as the interest rate environment changes. If an entity's risk management strategy is to adjust the amount of the hedging instrument periodically to reflect changes in the hedged position, the entity needs to demonstrate that the hedge is expected to be highly effective only for the period until the amount of the hedging instrument is next adjusted. However, for that period, the expectation of effectiveness has to be based on existing fair value exposures and the potential for interest rate movements without consideration of future adjustments to those positions. Furthermore, the fair value exposure attributable to prepayment risk can generally be hedged with options.

For a cash flow hedge to qualify for hedge accounting, the forecast cash flows, including the reinvestment of cash inflows or the refinancing of cash outflows, must be highly probable (IAS 39.88(c)) and the hedge expected to be highly effective in achieving offsetting changes in the cash flows of the hedged item and hedging instrument (IAS 39.88(b)). Prepayments affect the timing of cash flows and, therefore, the probability of occurrence of the forecast transaction. If the hedge is established for risk management purposes on a net basis, an entity may have sufficient levels of highly probable cash flows on a gross basis to support the designation for accounting purposes of forecast transactions associated with a portion of the gross cash flows as the hedged item. In this case, the portion of the gross cash flows designated as being hedged may be chosen to be equal to the amount of net cash flows being hedged for risk management purposes.

Systems considerations

The accounting for fair value hedges differs from that for cash flow hedges. It is usually easier to use existing information systems to manage and track cash flow hedges than it is for fair value hedges.

Under fair value hedge accounting, the assets or liabilities that are designated as being hedged are remeasured for those changes in fair values during the hedge period that are attributable to the risk being hedged. Such changes adjust the carrying amount of the hedged items and, for interest sensitive assets and liabilities, may result in an adjustment of the effective interest rate of the hedged item (IAS 39.89). As a consequence of fair value hedging activities, the changes in fair value have to be allocated to the assets or liabilities being hedged in order for the entity to be able to recompute their effective interest rate, determine the subsequent amortisation of the fair value adjustment to profit or loss, and determine the amount that should be recognised in profit or loss when assets are sold or liabilities extinguished (IAS 39.89 and IAS 39.92). To comply with the requirements for fair value hedge accounting, it will generally be necessary to establish a system to track the changes in the fair value attributable to the hedged risk, associate those changes with individual hedged items, recompute the effective interest rate of the hedged items, and amortise the changes to profit or loss over the life of the respective hedged item.

Under cash flow hedge accounting, the cash flows relating to the forecast transactions that are designated as being hedged reflect changes in interest rates. The adjustment for changes in the fair value of a hedging derivative instrument is initially recognised in equity (IAS 39.95). To comply with the requirements for cash flow hedge accounting, it is necessary to determine when the adjustments to equity from changes in the fair value of a hedging instrument should be recognised in profit or loss (IAS 39.100 and IAS 39.101). For cash flow hedges, it is not necessary to create a separate system to make this determination. The system used to determine the extent of the net exposure provides the basis for scheduling the changes in the cash flows of the derivative and the recognition of such changes in profit or loss.

The timing of the recognition in profit or loss can be predetermined when the hedge is associated with the exposure to changes in cash flows. The forecast transactions that are being hedged can be associated with a specific principal amount in specific future periods composed of variable rate assets and cash inflows being reinvested or variable rate liabilities and cash outflows being refinanced, each of which creates a cash flow exposure to changes in interest rates. The specific principal amounts in specific future periods are equal to the notional amount of the derivative hedging instruments and are hedged only for the period that corresponds to the repricing or maturity of the derivative hedging instruments so that the cash flow changes resulting from changes in interest rates are matched with the derivative hedging instrument. IAS 39.100 specifies that the amounts recognised in equity should be recognised in profit or loss in the same period or periods during which the hedged item affects profit or loss.

Issue (c) – If a hedging relationship is designated as a cash flow hedge relating to changes in cash flows resulting from interest rate changes, what would be included in the documentation required by IAS 39.88(a)?

The following would be included in the documentation.

The hedging relationship - The maturity schedule of cash flows used for risk management purposes to determine exposures to cash flow mismatches on a net basis would provide part of the documentation of the hedging relationship.

The entity's risk management objective and strategy for undertaking the hedge - The entity's overall risk management objective and strategy for hedging exposures to interest rate risk would provide part of the documentation of the hedging objective and strategy.

The type of hedge - The hedge is documented as a cash flow hedge.

The hedged item - The hedged item is documented as a group of forecast transactions (interest cash flows) that are expected to occur with a high degree of probability in specified future periods, for example, scheduled on a monthly basis. The hedged item may include interest cash flows resulting from the reinvestment of cash inflows, including the resetting of interest rates on assets, or from the refinancing of cash outflows, including the resetting of interest rates on liabilities and rollovers of financial liabilities. As discussed in Issue (e), the forecast transactions meet the probability test if there are sufficient levels of highly probable cash flows in the specified future periods to encompass the amounts designated as being hedged on a gross basis.

The hedged risk - The risk designated as being hedged is documented as a portion of the overall exposure to changes in a specified market interest rate, often the risk-free interest rate or an interbank offered rate, common to all items in the group. To help ensure that the hedge effectiveness test is met at inception of the hedge and subsequently, the designated hedged portion of the interest rate risk could be documented as being based on the same yield curve as the derivative hedging instrument.

The hedging instrument - Each derivative hedging instrument is documented as a hedge of specified amounts in specified future time periods corresponding with the forecast transactions occurring in the specified future time periods designated as being hedged.

The method of assessing effectiveness - The effectiveness test is documented as being measured by comparing the changes in the cash flows of the derivatives allocated to the applicable periods in which they are designated as a hedge to the changes in the cash flows of the forecast transactions being hedged. Measurement of the cash flow changes is based on the applicable yield curves of the derivatives and hedged items.

Issue (d) – If the hedging relationship is designated as a cash flow hedge, how does an entity satisfy the requirement for an expectation of high effectiveness in achieving offsetting changes in IAS 39.88(b)?

An entity may demonstrate an expectation of high effectiveness by preparing an analysis demonstrating high historical and expected future correlation between the interest rate risk designated as being hedged and the interest rate risk of the hedging instrument. Existing documentation of the hedge ratio used in establishing the derivative contracts may also serve to demonstrate an expectation of effectiveness.

Issue (e) – If the hedging relationship is designated as a cash flow hedge, how does an entity demonstrate a high probability of the forecast transactions occurring as required by IAS 39.88(c)?

An entity may do this by preparing a cash flow maturity schedule showing that there exist sufficient aggregate gross levels of expected cash flows, including the effects of the resetting of interest rates for assets or liabilities, to establish that the forecast transactions that are designated as being hedged are highly probable to occur. Such a schedule should be supported by management's stated intentions and past practice of reinvesting cash inflows and refinancing cash outflows.

For example, an entity may forecast aggregate gross cash inflows of CU100 and aggregate gross cash outflows of CU90 in a particular time period in the near future. In this case, it may wish to designate the forecast reinvestment of gross cash inflows of CU10 as the hedged item in the future time period. If more than CU10 of the forecast cash inflows are contractually specified and have low credit risk, the entity has strong evidence to support an assertion that gross cash inflows of CU10 are highly probable to occur and to support the designation of the forecast reinvestment of those cash flows as being hedged for a particular portion of the reinvestment period. A high probability of the forecast transactions occurring may also be demonstrated under other circumstances.

Issue (f) – If the hedging relationship is designated as a cash flow hedge, how does an entity assess and measure effectiveness under IAS 39.88(d) and IAS 39.88(e)?

Effectiveness is required to be measured at a minimum at the time an entity prepares its annual or interim financial reports. However, an entity may wish to measure it more frequently on a specified periodic basis, at the end of each month or other applicable reporting period. It is also measured whenever derivative positions designated as hedging instruments are changed or hedges are terminated to ensure that the recognition in profit or loss of the changes in the fair value amounts on assets and liabilities and the recognition of changes in the fair value of derivative instruments designated as cash flow hedges are appropriate.

Changes in the cash flows of the derivative are computed and allocated to the applicable periods in which the derivative is designated as a hedge and are compared with computations of changes in the cash flows of the forecast transactions. Computations are based on yield curves applicable to the hedged items and the derivative hedging instruments and applicable interest rates for the specified periods being hedged.

The schedule used to determine effectiveness could be maintained and used as the basis for determining the period in which the hedging gains and losses recognised initially in equity are reclassified out of equity and recognised in profit or loss.

Issue (g) – If the hedging relationship is designated as a cash flow hedge, how does an entity account for the hedge?

The hedge is accounted for as a cash flow hedge in accordance with the provisions in IAS 39.95-IAS 39.100, as follows:

(i)   the portion of gains and losses on hedging derivatives determined to result from effective hedges is recognised in equity whenever effectiveness is measured; and

(ii) the ineffective portion of gains and losses resulting from hedging derivatives is recognised in profit or loss.

IAS 39.100 specifies that the amounts recognised in equity should be recognised in profit or loss in the same period or periods during which the hedged item affects profit or loss. Accordingly, when the forecast transactions occur, the amounts previously recognised in equity are recognised in profit or loss. For example, if an interest rate swap is designated as a hedging instrument of a series of forecast cash flows, the changes in the cash flows of the swap are recognised in profit or loss in the periods when the forecast cash flows and the cash flows of the swap offset each other.

Issue (h) – If the hedging relationship is designated as a cash flow hedge, what is the treatment of any net cumulative gains and losses recognised in equity if the hedging instrument is terminated prematurely, the hedge accounting criteria are no longer met, or the hedged forecast transactions are no longer expected to take place?

If the hedging instrument is terminated prematurely or the hedge no longer meets the criteria for qualification for hedge accounting, for example, the forecast transactions are no longer highly probable, the net cumulative gain or loss recognised in equity remains in equity until the forecast transaction occurs (IAS 39.101(a) and IAS 39.101(b)). If the hedged forecast transactions are no longer expected to occur, the net cumulative gain or loss is recognised in profit or loss (IAS 39.101(c)).

Issue (i) – IAS 39.75 states that a hedging relationship may not be designated for only a portion of the time period in which a hedging instrument is outstanding. If the hedging relationship is designated as a cash flow hedge, and the hedge subsequently fails the test for being highly effective, does IAS 39.75 preclude redesignating the hedging instrument?

No. IAS 39.75 indicates that a derivative instrument may not be designated as a hedging instrument for only a portion of its remaining period to maturity. IAS 39.75 does not refer to the derivative instrument's original period to maturity. If there is a hedge effectiveness failure, the ineffective portion of the gain or loss on the derivative instrument is recognised immediately in profit or loss (IAS 39.95(b)) and hedge accounting based on the previous designation of the hedge relationship cannot be continued (IAS 39.101). In this case, the derivative instrument may be redesignated prospectively as a hedging instrument in a new hedging relationship provided this hedging relationship satisfies the necessary conditions. The derivative instrument must be redesignated as a hedge for the entire time period it remains outstanding.

Issue (j) – For cash flow hedges, if a derivative is used to manage a net exposure to interest rate risk and the derivative is designated as a cash flow hedge of forecast interest cash flows or portions of them on a gross basis, does the occurrence of the hedged forecast transaction give rise to an asset or liability that will result in a portion of the hedging gains and losses that were recognised in equity remaining in equity?

No. In the hedging relationship described in Issue (c) above, the hedged item is a group of forecast transactions consisting of interest cash flows in specified future periods. The hedged forecast transactions do not result in the recognition of assets or liabilities and the effect of interest rate changes that are designated as being hedged is recognised in profit or loss in the period in which the forecast transactions occur. Although this is not relevant for the types of hedges described here, if instead the derivative is designated as a hedge of a forecast purchase of a financial asset or issue of a financial liability, the associated gains or losses that were recognised directly in equity are reclassified into profit or loss in the same period or periods during which the asset acquired or liability incurred affects profit or loss (such as in the periods that interest expenses are recognised). However, if an entity expects at any time that all or a portion of a net loss recognised directly in equity will not be recovered in one or more future periods, it shall reclassify immediately into profit or loss the amount that is not expected to be recovered.

Issue (k) – In the answer to Issue (c) above it was indicated that the designated hedged item is a portion of a cash flow exposure. Does IAS 39 permit a portion of a cash flow exposure to be designated as a hedged item?

Yes. IAS 39 does not specifically address a hedge of a portion of a cash flow exposure for a forecast transaction. However, IAS 39.81 specifies that a financial asset or liability may be a hedged item with respect to the risks associated with only a portion of its cash flows or fair value, if effectiveness can be measured. The ability to hedge a portion of a cash flow exposure resulting from the resetting of interest rates for assets and liabilities suggests that a portion of a cash flow exposure resulting from the forecast reinvestment of cash inflows or the refinancing or rollover of financial liabilities can also be hedged. The basis for qualification as a hedged item of a portion of an exposure is the ability to measure effectiveness. This is further supported by IAS 39.82, which specifies that a non-financial asset or liability can be hedged only in its entirety or for foreign currency risk but not for a portion of other risks because of the difficulty of isolating and measuring the appropriate portion of the cash flows or fair value changes attributable to a specific risk. Accordingly, assuming effectiveness can be measured, a portion of a cash flow exposure of forecast transactions associated with, for example, the resetting of interest rates for a variable rate asset or liability can be designated as a hedged item.

Issue (l) – In the answer to Issue (c) above it was indicated that the hedged item is documented as a group of forecast transactions. Since these transactions will have different terms when they occur, including credit exposures, maturities and option features, how can an entity satisfy the tests in IAS 39.78 and IAS 39.83 requiring the hedged group to have similar risk characteristics?

IAS 39.78 provides for hedging a group of assets, liabilities, firm commitments or forecast transactions with similar risk characteristics. IAS 39.83 provides additional guidance and specifies that portfolio hedging is permitted if two conditions are met, namely: the individual items in the portfolio share the same risk for which they are designated, and the change in the fair value attributable to the hedged risk for each individual item in the group will be expected to be approximately proportional to the overall change in fair value.

When an entity associates a derivative hedging instrument with a gross exposure, the hedged item typically is a group of forecast transactions. For hedges of cash flow exposures relating to a group of forecast transactions, the overall exposure of the forecast transactions and the assets or liabilities that are repriced may have very different risks. The exposure from forecast transactions may differ depending on the terms that are expected as they relate to credit exposures, maturities, options and other features. Although the overall risk exposures may be different for the individual items in the group, a specific risk inherent in each of the items in the group can be designated as being hedged.

The items in the portfolio do not necessarily have to have the same overall exposure to risk, provided they share the same risk for which they are designated as being hedged. A common risk typically shared by a portfolio of financial instruments is exposure to changes in the risk-free or benchmark interest rate or to changes in a specified rate that has a credit exposure equal to the highest credit-rated instrument in the portfolio (ie the instrument with the lowest credit risk). If the instruments that are grouped into a portfolio have different credit exposures, they may be hedged as a group for a portion of the exposure. The risk they have in common that is designated as being hedged is the exposure to interest rate changes from the highest credit rated instrument in the portfolio. This ensures that the change in fair value attributable to the hedged risk for each individual item in the group is expected to be approximately proportional to the overall change in fair value attributable to the hedged risk of the group. It is likely there will be some ineffectiveness if the hedging instrument has a credit quality that is inferior to the credit quality of the highest credit-rated instrument being hedged, since a hedging relationship is designated for a hedging instrument in its entirety (IAS 39.74). For example, if a portfolio of assets consists of assets rated A, BB and B, and the current market interest rates for these assets are LIBOR + 20 basis points, LIBOR + 40 basis points and LIBOR + 60 basis points, respectively, an entity may use a swap that pays fixed interest rate and for which variable interest payments based on LIBOR are made to hedge the exposure to variable interest rates. If LIBOR is designated as the risk being hedged, credit spreads above LIBOR on the hedged items are excluded from the designated hedge relationship and the assessment of hedge effectiveness.

F.6.3 Illustrative example of applying the approach in Question F.6.2

The purpose of this example is to illustrate the process of establishing, monitoring and adjusting hedge positions and of qualifying for cash flow hedge accounting in applying the approach to hedge accounting described in Question F.6.2 when a financial institution manages its interest rate risk on an entity-wide basis. To this end, this example identifies a methodology that allows for the use of hedge accounting and takes advantage of existing risk management systems so as to avoid unnecessary changes to it and to avoid unnecessary bookkeeping and tracking.

The approach illustrated here reflects only one of a number of risk management processes that could be employed and could qualify for hedge accounting. Its use is not intended to suggest that other alternatives could not or should not be used. The approach being illustrated could also be applied in other circumstances (such as for cash flow hedges of commercial entities), for example, hedging the rollover of commercial paper financing.

Identifying, assessing and reducing cash flow exposures

The discussion and illustrations that follow focus on the risk management activities of a financial institution that manages its interest rate risk by analysing expected cash flows in a particular currency on an entity-wide basis. The cash flow analysis forms the basis for identifying the interest rate risk of the entity, entering into hedging transactions to manage the risk, assessing the effectiveness of risk management activities, and qualifying for and applying cash flow hedge accounting.

The illustrations that follow assume that an entity, a financial institution, had the following expected future net cash flows and hedging positions outstanding in a specific currency, consisting of interest rate swaps, at the beginning of Period X0. The cash flows shown are expected to occur at the end of the period and, therefore, create a cash flow interest exposure in the following period as a result of the reinvestment or repricing of the cash inflows or the refinancing or repricing of the cash outflows.

The illustrations assume that the entity has an ongoing interest rate risk management programme. Schedule I shows the expected cash flows and hedging positions that existed at the beginning of Period X0. It is included here to provide a starting point in the analysis. It provides a basis for considering existing hedges in connection with the evaluation that occurs at the beginning of Period X1.

Schedule I – End of period – Expected cash flows and hedging positions

Quarterly period (units)	X0 CU	X1 CU	X2 CU	X3 CU	X4 CU	X5 CU	...n CU
Expected net cash flows		1,100	1,500	1,200	1,400	1,500	x,xxx
Outstanding interest rate swaps:							
Receive-fixed, pay-variable (notional amounts)	2,000	2,000	2,000	1,200	1,200	1,200	x,xxx
Pay-fixed, receive-variable (notional amounts)	(1,000)	(1,000)	(1,000)	(500)	(500)	(500)	x,xxx
Net exposure after outstanding swaps		100	500	500	700	800	x,xxx

The schedule depicts five quarterly periods. The actual analysis would extend over a period of many years, represented by the notation '...n'. A financial institution that manages its interest rate risk on an entity-wide basis re-evaluates its cash flow exposures periodically. The frequency of the evaluation depends on the entity's risk management policy.

For the purposes of this illustration, the entity is re-evaluating its cash flow exposures at the end of Period X0. The first step in the process is the generation of forecast net cash flow exposures from existing interest-earning assets and interest-bearing liabilities, including the rollover of short-term assets and short-term liabilities. Schedule II below illustrates the forecast of net cash flow exposures. A common technique for assessing exposure to interest rates for risk management purposes is an interest rate sensitivity gap analysis showing the gap between interest rate-sensitive assets and interest rate-sensitive liabilities over different time intervals. Such an analysis could be used as a starting point for identifying cash flow exposures to interest rate risk for hedge accounting purposes.

Schedule II – Forecast net cash flow and repricing exposures

Quarterly period (units)	Notes	X1 CU	X2 CU	X3 CU	X4 CU	X5 CU	...n CU
CASH INFLOW AND REPRICING EXPOSURES - from assets							
Principal and interest payments:							
Long-term fixed rate	(1)	2,400	3,000	3,000	1,000	1,200	x,xxx
Short-term (roll over)	(1)(2)	1,575	1,579	1,582	1,586	1,591	x,xxx
Variable rate - principal payments	(1)	2,000	1,000	-	500	500	x,xxx
Variable rate - estimated interest	(2)	125	110	105	114	118	x,xxx
Total expected cash inflows		*6,100*	*5,689*	*4,687*	*3,200*	*3,409*	*x,xxx*
Variable rate asset balances	(3)	8,000	7,000	7,000	6,500	6,000	x,xxx
Cash inflows and repricings	**(4)**	**14,100**	**12,689**	**11,687**	**9,700**	**9,409**	**x,xxx**
CASH OUTFLOW AND REPRICING EXPOSURES - from liabilities							
Principal and interest payments:							
Long-term fixed rate	(1)	2,100	400	500	500	301	x,xxx
Short-term (roll over)	(1)(2)	735	737	738	740	742	x,xxx
Variable rate - principal payments	(1)	-	-	2,000	-	1,000	x,xxx
Variable rate - estimated interest	(2)	100	110	120	98	109	x,xxx
Total expected cash outflows		*2,935*	*1,247*	*3,358*	*1,338*	*2,152*	*x,xxx*
Variable rate liability balances	(3)	8,000	8,000	6,000	6,000	5,000	x,xxx
Cash outflows and repricings	**(4)**	**10,935**	**9,247**	**9,358**	**7,338**	**7,152**	**x,xxx**
NET EXPOSURES	*(5)*	*3,165*	*3,442*	*2,329*	*2,362*	*2,257*	*x,xxx*

(1) The cash flows are estimated using contractual terms and assumptions based on management's intentions and market factors. It is assumed that short-term assets and liabilities will continue to be rolled over in succeeding periods. Assumptions about prepayments and defaults and the withdrawal of deposits are based on market and historical data. It is assumed that principal and interest inflows and outflows will be reinvested and refinanced, respectively, at the end of each period at the then current market interest rates and share the benchmark interest rate risk to which they are exposed.

(2) Forward interest rates obtained from Schedule VI are used to forecast interest payments on variable rate financial instruments and expected rollovers of short-term assets and liabilities. All forecast cash flows are associated with the specific time periods (3 months, 6 months, 9 months and 12 months) in which

they are expected to occur. For completeness, the interest cash flows resulting from reinvestments, refinancings and repricings are included in the schedule and shown gross even though only the net margin may actually be reinvested. Some entities may choose to disregard the forecast interest cash flows for risk management purposes because they may be used to absorb operating costs and any remaining amounts would not be significant enough to affect risk management decisions.

(3)   The cash flow forecast is adjusted to include the variable rate asset and liability balances in each period in which such variable rate asset and liability balances are repriced. The principal amounts of these assets and liabilities are not actually being paid and, therefore, do not generate a cash flow. However, since interest is computed on the principal amounts each period based on the then current market interest rate, such principal amounts expose the entity to the same interest rate risk as if they were cash flows being reinvested or refinanced.

(4)   The forecast cash flow and repricing exposures that are identified in each period represent the principal amounts of cash inflows that will be reinvested or repriced and cash outflows that will be refinanced or repriced at the market interest rates that are in effect when those forecast transactions occur.

(5)   The net cash flow and repricing exposure is the difference between the cash inflow and repricing exposures from assets and the cash outflow and repricing exposures from liabilities. In the illustration, the entity is exposed to interest rate declines because the exposure from assets exceeds the exposure from liabilities and the excess (ie the net amount) will be reinvested or repriced at the current market rate and there is no offsetting refinancing or repricing of outflows.

Note that some banks regard some portion of their non-interest bearing demand deposits as economically equivalent to long-term debt. However, these deposits do not create a cash flow exposure to interest rates and would therefore be excluded from this analysis for accounting purposes.

Schedule II *Forecast net cash flow and repricing exposures* provides no more than a starting point for assessing cash flow exposure to interest rates and for adjusting hedging positions. The complete analysis includes outstanding hedging positions and is shown in Schedule III *Analysis of expected net exposures and hedging positions*. It compares the forecast net cash flow exposures for each period (developed in Schedule II) with existing hedging positions (obtained from Schedule I), and provides a basis for considering whether adjustment of the hedging relationship should be made.

Schedule III – Analysis of expected net exposures and hedging positions

Quarterly period (units)	X1 CU	X2 CU	X3 CU	X4 CU	X5 CU	...n CU
Net cash flow and repricing exposures (Schedule II)	3,165	3,442	2,329	2,362	2,257	x,xxx
Pre-existing swaps outstanding:						
Receive-fixed, pay-variable (notional amounts)	2,000	2,000	1,200	1,200	1,200	x,xxx
Pay-fixed, receive-variable (notional amounts)	(1,000)	(1,000)	(500)	(500)	(500)	x,xxx
Net exposure after pre-existing swaps	*2,165*	*2,442*	*1,629*	*1,662*	*1,557*	*x,xxx*
Transactions to adjust outstanding hedging positions:						
Receive-fixed, pay variable swap 1 (notional amount, 10-years)	2,000	2,000	2,000	2,000	2,000	x,xxx
Pay-fixed, receive-variable swap 2 (notional amount, 3-years)			(1,000)	(1,000)	(1,000)	x,xxx
Swaps ...X						x,xxx
Unhedged cash flow and repricing exposure	*165*	*442*	*629*	*662*	*557*	*x,xxx*

The notional amounts of the interest rate swaps that are outstanding at the analysis date are included in each of the periods in which the interest rate swaps are outstanding to illustrate the impact of the outstanding interest rate swaps on the identified cash flow exposures. The notional amounts of the outstanding interest rate swaps are included in each period because interest is computed on the notional amounts each period, and the variable rate components of the outstanding swaps are repriced to the current market rate quarterly. The notional amounts create an exposure to interest rates that in part is similar to the principal balances of variable rate assets and variable rate liabilities.

The exposure that remains after considering the existing positions is then evaluated to determine the extent to which adjustments of existing hedging positions are necessary. The bottom portion of Schedule III shows the beginning of Period X1 using interest rate swap transactions to reduce the net exposures further to within the tolerance levels established under the entity's risk management policy.

Note that in the illustration, the cash flow exposure is not entirely eliminated. Many financial institutions do not fully eliminate risk but rather reduce it to within some tolerable limit.

Various types of derivative instruments could be used to manage the cash flow exposure to interest rate risk identified in the schedule of forecast net cash flows (Schedule II). However, for the purpose of the illustration, it is assumed that interest rate swaps are used for all hedging activities. It is also assumed that in periods in which interest rate swaps should be reduced, rather than terminating some of the outstanding interest rate swap positions, a new swap with the opposite return characteristics is added to the portfolio.

In the illustration in Schedule III above, swap 1, a receive-fixed, pay-variable swap, is used to reduce the net exposure in Periods X1 and X2. Since it is a 10year swap, it also reduces exposures identified in other future periods not shown. However, it has the effect of creating an over-hedged position in Periods X3-X5. Swap 2, a forward starting pay-fixed, receive-variable interest rate swap, is used to reduce the notional amount of the outstanding receive-fixed, pay-variable interest rate swaps in Periods X3-X5 and thereby reduce the over-hedged positions.

It also is noted that in many situations, no adjustment or only a single adjustment of the outstanding hedging position is necessary to bring the exposure to within an acceptable limit. However, when the entity's risk management policy specifies a very low tolerance of risk a greater number of adjustments to the hedging positions over the forecast period would be needed to further reduce any remaining risk.

To the extent that some of the interest rate swaps fully offset other interest rate swaps that have been entered into for hedging purposes, it is not necessary to include them in a designated hedging relationship for hedge accounting purposes. These offsetting positions can be combined, de-designated as hedging instruments, if necessary, and reclassified for accounting purposes from the hedging portfolio to the trading portfolio. This procedure limits the extent to which the gross swaps must continue to be designated and tracked in a hedging relationship for accounting purposes. For the purposes of this illustration it is assumed that CU500 of the pay-fixed, receive-variable interest rate swaps fully offset CU500 of the receive-fixed, pay-variable interest rate swaps at the beginning of Period X1 and for Periods X1-X5, and are dedesignated as hedging instruments and reclassified to the trading account.

After reflecting these offsetting positions, the remaining gross interest rate swap positions from Schedule III are shown in Schedule IV as follows.

Schedule IV – Interest rate swaps designated as hedges

Quarterly period (units)	X1 CU	X2 CU	X3 CU	X4 CU	X5 CU	...n CU
Receive-fixed, pay-variable (notional amounts)	3,500	3,500	2,700	2,700	2,700	x,xxx
Pay-fixed, receive-variable (notional amounts)	(500)	(500)	(1,000)	(1,000)	(1,000)	x,xxx
Net outstanding swaps positions	*3,000*	*3,000*	*1,700*	*1,700*	*1,700*	*x,xxx*

For the purposes of the illustrations, it is assumed that Swap 2, entered into at the beginning of Period X1, only partially offsets another swap being accounted for as a hedge and therefore continues to be designated as a hedging instrument.

Hedge accounting considerations

Illustrating the designation of the hedging relationship

The discussion and illustrations thus far have focused primarily on economic and risk management considerations relating to the identification of risk in future periods and the adjustment of that risk using interest rate swaps. These activities form the basis for designating a hedging relationship for accounting purposes.

The examples in IAS 39 focus primarily on hedging relationships involving a single hedged item and a single hedging instrument, but there is little discussion and guidance on portfolio hedging relationships for cash flow hedges when risk is being managed centrally. In this illustration, the general principles are applied to hedging relationships involving a component of risk in a portfolio having multiple risks from multiple transactions or positions.

Although designation is necessary to achieve hedge accounting, the way in which the designation is described also affects the extent to which the hedging relationship is judged to be effective for accounting purposes and the extent to which the entity's existing system for managing risk will be required to be modified to track hedging activities for accounting purposes. Accordingly, an entity may wish to designate the hedging relationship in a manner that avoids unnecessary systems changes by taking advantage of the information already generated by the risk management system and avoids unnecessary bookkeeping and tracking. In designating hedging relationships, the entity may also consider the extent to which ineffectiveness is expected to be recognised for accounting purposes under alternative designations.

The designation of the hedging relationship needs to specify various matters. These are illustrated and discussed here from the perspective of the hedge of the interest rate risk associated with the cash inflows, but the guidance can also be applied to the hedge of the risk associated with the cash outflows. It is fairly obvious that only a portion of the gross exposures relating to the cash inflows is being hedged by the interest rate swaps. Schedule V *The general hedging relationship* illustrates the designation of the portion of the gross reinvestment risk exposures identified in Schedule II as being hedged by the interest rate swaps.

Schedule V – The general hedging relationship

Quarterly period (units)	X1 CU	X2 CU	X3 CU	X4 CU	X5 CU	...n CU
Cash inflow repricing exposure (Schedule II)	14,100	12,689	11,687	9,700	9,409	x,xxx
Receive-fixed, pay-variable swaps (Schedule IV)	3,500	3,500	2,700	2,700	2,700	x,xxx
Hedged exposure percentage	24.8%	27.6%	23.1%	27.8%	28.7%	xx.x%

The hedged exposure percentage is computed as the ratio of the notional amount of the receive-fixed, pay-variable swaps that are outstanding divided by the gross exposure. Note that in Schedule V there are sufficient levels of forecast reinvestments in each period to offset more than the notional amount of the receive-fixed, pay-variable swaps and satisfy the accounting requirement that the forecast transaction is highly probable.

It is not as obvious, however, how the interest rate swaps are specifically related to the cash flow interest risks designated as being hedged and how the interest rate swaps are effective in reducing that risk. The more specific designation is illustrated in Schedule VI *The specific hedging relationship* below. It provides a meaningful way of depicting the more complicated narrative designation of the hedge by focusing on the hedging objective to eliminate the cash flow variability associated with future changes in interest rates and to obtain an interest rate equal to the fixed rate inherent in the term structure of interest rates that exists at the commencement of the hedge.

The expected interest from the reinvestment of the cash inflows and repricings of the assets is computed by multiplying the gross amounts exposed by the forward rate for the period. For example, the gross exposure for Period X2 of CU14,100 is multiplied by the forward rate for Periods X2-X5 of 5.50 per cent, 6.00 per cent, 6.50 per cent and 7.25 per cent, respectively, to compute the expected interest for those quarterly periods based on the current term structure of interest rates. The hedged expected interest is computed by multiplying the expected interest for the applicable three-month period by the hedged exposure percentage.

Schedule VI – The specific hedging relationship

Quarterly period	Term structure of interest rates					
	X1	X2	X3	X4	X5	...n
Spot rates	5.00%	5.25%	5.50%	5.75%	6.05%	x.xx%
Forward rates*	5.00%	5.50%	6.00%	6.50%	7.25%	x.xx%

Cash flow exposures and expected interest amounts

Repricing period	Time to forecast transaction	Gross amounts exposed	Expected interest					
			CU	CU	CU	CU	CU	CU
2	3 months	14,100	→	194	212	229	256	
3	6 months	12,689			190	206	230	xxx
4	9 months	11,687				190	212	xxx
5	12 months	9,700					176	xxx
6	15 months	9,409						xxx
Hedged percentage (Schedule V) in the previous period				24.8%	27.6%	23.1%	27.8%	xx.x%
Hedged expected interest				48	52	44	49	xx

* The forward interest rates are computed from the spot interest rates and rounded for the purposes of the presentation. Computations that are based on the forward interest rates are made based on the actual computed forward rate and then rounded for the purposes of the presentation.

It does not matter whether the gross amount exposed is reinvested in long-term fixed rate debt or variable rate debt, or in short-term debt that is rolled over in each subsequent period. The exposure to changes in the forward interest rate is the same. For example, if the CU14,100 is reinvested at a fixed rate at the beginning of Period X2 for six months, it will be reinvested at 5.75 per cent. The expected interest is based on the forward interest rates for Period X2 of 5.50 per cent and for Period X3 of 6.00 per cent, equal to a blended rate of 5.75 per cent $(1.055 \cdot 1.060)^{0.5}$, which is the Period X2 spot rate for the next six months.

However, only the expected interest from the reinvestment of the cash inflows or repricing of the gross amount for the first three-month period after the forecast transaction occurs is designated as being hedged. The expected interest being hedged is represented by the shaded cells. The exposure for the subsequent periods is not hedged. In the example, the portion of the interest rate exposure being hedged is the forward rate of 5.50 per cent for Period X2. In order to assess hedge effectiveness and compute actual hedge ineffectiveness on an ongoing basis, the entity may use the information on hedged interest cash inflows in Schedule VI and compare it with updated estimates of expected interest cash inflows (for example, in a table that looks like Schedule II). As long as expected interest cash inflows exceed hedged interest cash inflows, the entity may compare the cumulative change in the fair value of the hedged cash inflows with the cumulative change in the fair value of the hedging instrument to compute actual hedge effectiveness. If there are insufficient expected interest cash inflows, there will be ineffectiveness. It is measured by comparing the cumulative change in the fair value of the expected interest cash flows to the extent they are less than the hedged cash flows with the cumulative change in the fair value of the hedging instrument.

Describing the designation of the hedging relationship

As mentioned previously, there are various matters that should be specified in the designation of the hedging relationship that complicate the description of the designation but are necessary to limit ineffectiveness to be recognised for accounting purposes and to avoid unnecessary systems changes and bookkeeping. The example that follows describes the designation more fully and identifies additional aspects of the designation not apparent from the previous illustrations.

Example designation

Hedging objective

The hedging objective is to eliminate the risk of interest rate fluctuations over the hedging period, which is the life of the interest rate swap, and in effect obtain a fixed interest rate during this period that is equal to the fixed interest rate on the interest rate swap.

Type of hedge

Cash flow hedge.

Hedging instrument

The receive-fixed, pay-variable swaps are designated as the hedging instrument. They hedge the cash flow exposure to interest rate risk.
Each repricing of the swap hedges a three-month portion of the interest cash inflows that results from:

- the forecast reinvestment or repricing of the principal amounts shown in Schedule V.
- unrelated investments or repricings that occur after the repricing dates on the swap over its life and involve different borrowers or lenders.

The hedged item - General

The hedged item is a portion of the gross interest cash inflows that will result from the reinvestment or repricing of the cash flows identified in Schedule V and are expected to occur within the periods shown on such schedule. The portion of the interest cash inflow that is being hedged has three components:

- the principal component giving rise to the interest cash inflow and the period in which it occurs,
- the interest rate component, and
- the time component or period covered by the hedge.

The hedged item The principal component

The portion of the interest cash inflows being hedged is the amount that results from the first portion of the principal amounts being invested or repriced in each period:

- that is equal to the sum of the notional amounts of the received-fixed, pay-variable interest rate swaps that are designated as hedging instruments and outstanding in the period of the reinvestment or repricing, and
- that corresponds to the first principal amounts of cash flow exposures that are invested or repriced at or after the repricing dates of the interest rate swaps.

> *The hedged item The interest rate component*
>
> The portion of the interest rate change that is being hedged is the change in both of the following:
>
> - the credit component of the interest rate being paid on the principal amount invested or repriced that is equal to the credit risk inherent in the interest rate swap. It is that portion of the interest rate on the investment that is equal to the interest index of the interest rate swap, such as LIBOR, and
> - the yield curve component of the interest rate that is equal to the repricing period on the interest rate swap designated as the hedging instrument.
>
> *The hedged item The hedged period*
>
> The period of the exposure to interest rate changes on the portion of the cash flow exposures being hedged is:
>
> - the period from the designation date to the repricing date of the interest rate swap that occurs within the quarterly period in which, but not before, the forecast transactions occur, and
> - its effects for the period after the forecast transactions occur equal to the repricing interval of the interest rate swap.

It is important to recognise that the swaps are not hedging the cash flow risk for a single investment over its entire life. The swaps are designated as hedging the cash flow risk from different principal investments and repricings that are made in each repricing period of the swaps over their entire term. The swaps hedge only the interest accruals that occur in the first period following the reinvestment. They are hedging the cash flow impact resulting from a change in interest rates that occurs up to the repricing of the swap. The exposure to changes in rates for the period from the repricing of the swap to the date of the hedged reinvestment of cash inflows or repricing of variable rate assets is not hedged. When the swap is repriced, the interest rate on the swap is fixed until the next repricing date and the accrual of the net swap settlements is determined. Any changes in interest rates after that date that affect the amount of the interest cash inflow are no longer hedged for accounting purposes.

Designation objectives

Systems considerations

Many of the tracking and bookkeeping requirements are eliminated by designating each repricing of an interest rate swap as hedging the cash flow risk from forecast reinvestments of cash inflows and repricings of variable rate assets for only a portion of the lives of the related assets. Much tracking and bookkeeping would be necessary if the swaps were instead designated as hedging the cash flow risk from forecast principal investments and repricings of variable rate assets over the entire lives of these assets.

This type of designation avoids keeping track of deferred derivative gains and losses in equity after the forecast transactions occur (IAS 39.97 and IAS 39.98) because the portion of the cash flow risk being hedged is that portion that will be recognised in profit or loss in the period immediately following the forecast transactions that corresponds with the periodic net cash settlements on the swap. If the hedge were to cover the entire life of the assets being acquired, it would be necessary to associate a specific interest rate swap with the asset being acquired. If a forecast transaction is the acquisition of a fixed rate instrument, the fair value of the swap that hedged that transaction would be reclassified out of equity to adjust the interest income on the asset when the interest income is recognised. The swap would then have to be terminated or redesignated in another hedging relationship. If a forecast transaction is the acquisition of a variable rate asset, the swap would continue in the hedging relationship but it would have to be tracked back to the asset acquired so that any fair value amounts on the swap recognised in equity could be recognised in profit or loss upon the subsequent sale of the asset.

It also avoids the necessity of associating with variable rate assets any portion of the fair value of the swaps that is recognised in equity. Accordingly, there is no portion of the fair value of the swap that is recognised in equity that should be reclassified out of equity when a forecast transaction occurs or upon the sale of a variable rate asset.

This type of designation also permits flexibility in deciding how to reinvest cash flows when they occur. Since the hedged risk relates only to a single period that corresponds with the repricing period of the interest rate swap designated as the hedging instrument, it is not necessary to determine at the designation date whether the cash flows will be reinvested in fixed rate or variable rate assets or to specify at the date of designation the life of the asset to be acquired.

Effectiveness considerations

Ineffectiveness is greatly reduced by designating a specific portion of the cash flow exposure as being hedged.

- Ineffectiveness due to credit differences between the interest rate swap and hedged forecast cash flow is eliminated by designating the cash flow risk being hedged as the risk attributable to changes in the interest rates that correspond with the rates inherent in the swap, such as the AA rate curve. This type of designation prevents changes resulting from changes in credit spreads from being considered as ineffectiveness.
- Ineffectiveness due to duration differences between the interest rate swap and hedged forecast cash flow is eliminated by designating the interest rate risk being hedged as the risk relating to changes in the portion of the yield curve that corresponds with the period in which the variable rate leg of the interest rate swap is repriced.
- Ineffectiveness due to interest rate changes that occur between the repricing date of the interest rate swap and the date of the forecast transactions is eliminated by simply not hedging that period of time. The period from the repricing of the swap and the occurrence of the forecast transactions in the period immediately following the repricing of the swap is left unhedged. Therefore, the difference in dates does not result in ineffectiveness.

Accounting considerations

The ability to qualify for hedge accounting using the methodology described here is founded on provisions in IAS 39 and on interpretations of its requirements. Some of those are described in the answer to Question F.6.2 *Hedge accounting considerations when interest rate risk is managed on a net basis*. Some additional and supporting provisions and interpretations are identified below.

Hedging a portion of the risk exposure

The ability to identify and hedge only a portion of the cash flow risk exposure resulting from the reinvestment of cash flows or repricing of variable rate instruments is found in IAS 39.81 as interpreted in the answers to Questions F.6.2 Issue (k) and F.2.17 *Partial term hedging*.

Hedging multiple risks with a single instrument

The ability to designate a single interest rate swap as a hedge of the cash flow exposure to interest rates resulting from various reinvestments of cash inflows or repricings of variable rate assets that occur over the life of the swap is founded on IAS 39.76 as interpreted in the answer to Question F.1.12 *Hedges of more than one type of risk*.

Hedging similar risks in a portfolio

The ability to specify the forecast transaction being hedged as a portion of the cash flow exposure to interest rates for a portion of the duration of the investment that gives rise to the interest payment without specifying at the designation date the expected life of the instrument and whether it pays a fixed or variable rate is founded on the answer to Question F.6.2 Issue (l), which specifies that the items in the portfolio do not necessarily have to have the same overall exposure to risk, providing they share the same risk for which they are designated as being hedged.

Hedge terminations

The ability to de-designate the forecast transaction (the cash flow exposure on an investment or repricing that will occur after the repricing date of the swap) as being hedged is provided for in IAS 39.101 dealing with hedge terminations. While a portion of the forecast transaction is no longer being hedged, the interest rate swap is not de-designated, and it continues to be a hedging instrument for the remaining transactions in the series that have not occurred. For example, assume that an interest rate swap having a remaining life of one year has been designated as hedging a series of three quarterly reinvestments of cash flows. The next forecast cash flow reinvestment occurs in three months. When the interest rate swap is repriced in three months at the then current variable rate, the fixed rate and the variable rate on the interest rate swap become known and no longer provide hedge protection for the next three months. If the next forecast transaction does not occur until three months and ten days, the ten-day period that remains after the repricing of the interest rate swap is not hedged.

F.6.4 Hedge accounting: premium or discount on forward exchange contract

A forward exchange contract is designated as a hedging instrument, for example, in a hedge of a net investment in a foreign operation. Is it permitted to amortise the discount or premium on the forward exchange contract to profit or loss over the term of the contract?

No. The premium or discount on a forward exchange contract may not be amortised to profit or loss under IAS 39. Derivatives are always measured at fair value in the balance sheet. The gain or loss resulting from a change in the fair value of the forward exchange contract is always recognised in profit or loss unless the forward exchange contract is designated and effective as a hedging instrument in a cash flow hedge or in a hedge of a net investment in a foreign operation, in which case the effective portion of the gain or loss is recognised in equity. In that case, the amounts recognised in equity are released to profit or loss when the hedged future cash flows occur or on the disposal of the net investment, as appropriate. Under IAS 39.74(b), the interest element (time value) of the fair value of a forward may be excluded from the designated hedge relationship. In that case, changes in the interest element portion of the fair value of the forward exchange contract are recognised in profit or loss.

F.6.5 IAS 39 and IAS 21 – Fair value hedge of asset measured at cost

If the future sale of a ship carried at historical cost is hedged against the exposure to currency risk by foreign currency borrowing, does IAS 39 require the ship to be remeasured for changes in the exchange rate even though the basis of measurement for the asset is historical cost?

No. In a fair value hedge, the hedged item is remeasured. However, a foreign currency borrowing cannot be classified as a fair value hedge of a ship since a ship does not contain any separately measurable foreign currency risk. If the hedge accounting conditions in IAS 39.88 are met, the foreign currency borrowing may be classified as a cash flow hedge of an anticipated sale in that foreign currency. In a cash flow hedge, the hedged item is not remeasured.

To illustrate: a shipping entity in Denmark has a US subsidiary that has the same functional currency (the Danish krone). The shipping entity measures its ships at historical cost less depreciation in the consolidated financial statements. In accordance with IAS 21.23(b), the ships are recognised in Danish krone using the historical exchange rate. To hedge, fully or partly, the potential currency risk on the ships at disposal in US dollars, the shipping entity normally finances its purchases of ships with loans denominated in US dollars.

In this case, a US dollar borrowing (or a portion of it) may be designated as a cash flow hedge of the anticipated sale of the ship financed by the borrowing provided the sale is highly probable, for example, because it is expected to occur in the immediate future, and the amount of the sales proceeds designated as being hedged is equal to the amount of the foreign currency borrowing designated as the hedging instrument. The gains and losses on the currency borrowing that are determined to constitute an effective hedge of the anticipated sale are recognised directly in equity through the statement of changes in equity in accordance with IAS 39.95(a).

SECTION G: OTHER

G.1 Disclosure of changes in fair value

IAS 39 requires financial assets classified as available for sale (AFS) and financial assets and financial liabilities at fair value through profit or loss to be remeasured to fair value. Unless a financial asset or a financial liability is designated as a cash flow hedging instrument, fair value changes for financial assets and financial liabilities at fair value through profit or loss are recognised in profit or loss, and fair value changes for AFS assets are recognised in equity. What disclosures are required regarding the amounts of the fair value changes during a reporting period?

IAS 32.94(h) requires material items of income, expense and gains and losses to be disclosed whether included in profit or loss or in equity. This disclosure requirement encompasses material items of income, expense and gains and losses that arise on remeasurement to fair value. Therefore, an entity provides disclosures of material fair value changes, distinguishing between changes that are recognised in profit or loss and changes that are recognised in equity. Further breakdown is provided of changes that relate to:

(a)   AFS assets;

(b)   financial assets and financial liabilities at fair value through profit or loss; and

(c)   hedging instruments.

IAS 32 neither requires nor prohibits disclosure of components of the change in fair value by the way items are classified for internal purposes. For example, an entity may choose to disclose separately the change in fair value of those derivatives that IAS 39 classifies as held for trading but the entity classifies as part of risk management activities outside the trading portfolio.

In addition, IAS 32.94(e) requires disclosure of the carrying amounts of financial assets and financial liabilities that: (i) are classified as held for trading and (ii) were, upon initial recognition, designated by the entity as financial assets and financial liabilities at fair value through profit or loss (ie those not financial instruments classified as held for trading).

Implementation guidance relating to IAS 39 extracted from IFRS 1 *First-time Application of International Financial Reporting Standards*

An entity recognises and measures all financial assets and financial liabilities in its opening IFRS balance sheet in accordance with IAS 39, except as specified in paragraphs 27-30 of the IFRS, which address derecognition and hedge accounting, and paragraph 36A, which permits an exemption from restating comparative information.

IG52

Recognition

An entity recognises all financial assets and financial liabilities (including all derivatives) that qualify for recognition under IAS 39 and have not yet qualified for derecognition under IAS 39, except non-derivative financial assets and nonderivative financial liabilities derecognised under previous GAAP before 1 January 2004, to which the entity does not choose to apply paragraph 27A (see paragraphs 27 and 27A of the IFRS). For example, an entity that does not apply paragraph 27A does not recognise assets transferred in a securitisation, transfer or other derecognition transaction that occurred before 1 January 2004 if those transactions qualified for derecognition under previous GAAP. However, if the entity uses the same securitisation arrangement or other derecognition arrangement for further transfers after 1 January 2004, those further transfers qualify for derecognition only if they meet the derecognition criteria of IAS 39.

IG53

An entity does not recognise financial assets and financial liabilities that do not qualify for recognition under IAS 39, or have already qualified for derecognition under IAS 39.

IG54

Embedded derivatives

When IAS 39 requires an entity to separate an embedded derivative from a host contract, the initial carrying amounts of the components at the date when the instrument first satisfies the recognition criteria in IAS 39 reflect circumstances at that date (IAS 39, paragraph 11). If the entity cannot determine the initial carrying amounts of the embedded derivative and host contract reliably, it treats the entire combined contract as a financial instrument held for trading (IAS 39, paragraph 12). This results in fair value measurement (except when the entity cannot determine a reliable fair value, see IAS 39, paragraph 46(c)), with changes in fair value recognised in profit or loss.

IG55

Measurement

In preparing its opening IFRS balance sheet, an entity applies the criteria in IAS 39 to identify those financial assets and financial liabilities that are measured at fair value and those that are measured at amortised cost. In particular:

IG56

(a) to comply with IAS 39, paragraph 51, classification of financial assets as heldto-maturity investments relies on a designation made by the entity in applying IAS 39 reflecting the entity's intention and ability at the date of transition to IFRSs. It follows that sales or transfers of held-to-maturity investments before the date of transition to IFRSs do not trigger the 'tainting' rules in IAS 39, paragraph 9.

(b)   to comply with IAS 39, paragraph 9, the category of 'loans and receivables' refers to the circumstances when the financial asset first satisfied the recognition criteria in IAS 39.

(c)   under IAS 39, paragraph 9, derivative financial assets and derivative financial liabilities are always deemed held for trading (except for a derivative that is a designated and effective hedging instrument). The result is that an entity measures all derivative financial assets and derivative financial liabilities at fair value.

(d)   to comply with IAS 39, paragraph 50, an entity classifies a nonderivative financial asset or non-derivative financial liability in its opening IFRS balance sheet as at fair value through profit or loss if, and only if, the asset or liability was:

   (i)   acquired or incurred principally for the purpose of selling or repurchasing it in the near term;
   (ii)   at the date of transition to IFRSs, part of a portfolio of identified financial instruments that were managed together and for which there was evidence of a recent actual pattern of shortterm profit-taking; or
   (iii) designated as at fair value through profit or loss at the date of transition to IFRS, for an entity that presents its first IFRS financial statements for an annual period beginning on or after 1 January 2006.
   (iv)   designated as at fair value through profit or loss at the start of its first IFRS reporting period, for an entity that presents its first IFRS financial statements for an annual period beginning before 1 January 2006 and applies paragraphs 11A, 48A, AG4B-AG4K, AG33A and AG33B and the 2005 amendments in paragraphs 9, 12 and 13 of IAS 39. If the entity restates comparative information for IAS 39 it shall restate the comparative information only if the financial assets or financial liabilities designated at the start of its first IFRS reporting period would have met the criteria for such designation in paragraph 9(b)(i), 9(b)(ii) or 11A of IAS 39 at the date of transition to IFRS or, if acquired after the date of transition to IFRSs, would have met the criteria in paragraph 9(b)(i), 9(b)(ii) or 11A at the date of initial recognition. For groups of financial assets, financial liabilities or both that are designated in accordance with paragraph 9(b)(ii) of IAS 39 at the start of the first IFRS reporting period, the comparative financial statements should be restated for all the financial assets and financial liabilities within the groups at the date of transition to IFRSs even if individual financial assets or liabilities within a group were derecognised during the comparative period.*

(e)   to comply with IAS 39, paragraph 9, available-for-sale financial assets are those non-derivative financial assets that are designated as available for sale and those non-derivative financial assets that are not in any of the previous categories.

IG57   For those financial assets and financial liabilities measured at amortised cost in the opening IFRS balance sheet, an entity determines their cost on the basis of circumstances existing when the assets and liabilities first satisfied the recognition criteria in IAS 39. However, if the entity acquired those financial assets and financial liabilities in a past business combination, their carrying amount under previous GAAP immediately following the business combination is their deemed cost under IFRSs at that date (paragraph B2(e) of the IFRS).

__Editor's note:__ Paragraph amended with effect from 1 January 2006.

An entity's estimates of loan impairments at the date of transition to IFRSs are **IG58** consistent with estimates made for the same date under previous GAAP (after adjustments to reflect any difference in accounting policies), unless there is objective evidence that those assumptions were in error (paragraph 31 of the IFRS). The entity treats the impact of any later revisions to those estimates as impairment losses (or, if the criteria in IAS 39 are met, reversals of impairment losses) of the period in which it makes the revisions.

Transition adjustments

An entity shall treat an adjustment to the carrying amount of a financial asset or **IG58A** financial liability as a transition adjustment to be recognised in the opening balance of retained earnings at the date of transition to IFRSs only to the extent that it results from adopting IAS 39. Because all derivatives, other than those that are designated and effective hedging instruments, are classified as held for trading, the differences between the previous carrying amount (which may have been zero) and the fair value of the derivatives are recognised as an adjustment of the balance of retained earnings at the beginning of the financial year in which IAS 39 is initially applied (other than for a derivative that is a designated and effective hedging instrument).

IAS 8 (as revised in 2003) applies to adjustments resulting from changes in estimates. **IG58B** If an entity is unable to determine whether a particular portion of the adjustment is a transition adjustment or a change in estimate, it treats that portion as a change in accounting estimate under IAS 8, with appropriate disclosures (IAS 8, paragraphs 32-40).

An entity may, under its previous GAAP, have measured investments at fair value **IG59** and recognised the revaluation gain directly in equity. If an investment is classified as at fair value through profit or loss, the preIAS 39 revaluation gain that had been recognised in equity is reclassified into retained earnings on initial application of IAS 39. If, on initial application of IAS 39, an investment is classified as available for sale, then the preIAS 39 revaluation gain is recognised in a separate component of equity. Subsequently, the entity recognises gains and losses on the availableforsale financial asset in that separate component of equity until the investment is impaired, sold, collected or otherwise disposed of. On subsequent derecognition or impairment of the available-for-sale financial asset, the entity transfers to profit or loss the cumulative gain or loss remaining in equity (IAS 39, paragraph 55(b)).

Hedge accounting

Paragraphs 28-30 of the IFRS deal with hedge accounting. The designation and **IG60** documentation of a hedge relationship must be completed on or before the date of transition to IFRSs if the hedge relationship is to qualify for hedge accounting from that date. Hedge accounting can be applied prospectively only from the date that the hedge relationship is fully designated and documented.

An entity may, under its previous GAAP, have deferred or not recognised gains and **IG60A** losses on a fair value hedge of a hedged item that is not measured at fair value. For such a fair value hedge, an entity adjusts the carrying amount of the hedged item at the date of transition to IFRSs. The adjustment is the lower of:

(a)   that portion of the cumulative change in the fair value of the hedged item that reflects the designated hedged risk and was not recognised under previous GAAP; and

(b)   that portion of the cumulative change in the fair value of the hedging instrument that reflects the designated hedged risk and, under previous GAAP, was either (i) not recognised or (ii) deferred in the balance sheet as an asset or liability.

IG60B   An entity may, under its previous GAAP, have deferred gains and losses on a cash flow hedge of a forecast transaction. If, at the date of transition to IFRSs, the hedged forecast transaction is not highly probable, but is expected to occur, the entire deferred gain or loss is recognised in equity. Any net cumulative gain or loss that has been reclassified to equity on initial application of IAS 39 remains in equity until (a) the forecast transaction subsequently results in the recognition of a nonfinancial asset or non-financial liability, (b) the forecast transaction affects profit or loss or (c) subsequently circumstances change and the forecast transaction is no longer expected to occur, in which case any related net cumulative gain or loss that had been recognised directly in equity is recognised in profit or loss. If the hedging instrument is still held, but the hedge does not qualify as a cash flow hedge under IAS 39, hedge accounting is no longer appropriate starting from the date of transition to IFRSs.

Financial Reporting Standard 27 'Life Assurance' is set out in paragraphs 1-67.

The Statement of Standard Accounting Practice, which comprises the paragraphs set in bold type, should be read in the context of the Objective as stated in paragraph 1 and the definitions set out in paragraph 2 and also of the Foreword to Accounting Standards and the Statement of Principles for Financial Reporting currently in issue.

The explanatory paragraphs contained in the FRS shall be regarded as part of the Statement of Standard Accounting Practice insofar as they assist in interpreting that statement.

Appendix IV 'The development of the FRS' reviews considerations and arguments that were thought significant by members of the Board in reaching the conclusions on the FRS.

FRS 27
Life assurance

(Issued December 2004)

Contents

Summary

Financial Reporting Standard 27 applies to all entities that have a life assurance **a**
business, including a life reinsurance business.

For large UK with-profits life assurance businesses falling within the scope of the **b**
FSA's realistic capital regime, liabilities to policyholders are required by the FRS to
be measured on the basis determined in accordance with that regime, subject to
adjustments specified in the FRS. Further adjustments are made to related assets and
deferred tax for consistency with the measurement of the realistic liabilities, and the
resulting effect on profit and loss account is offset by a corresponding transfer to the
fund for future appropriations or, in the case of a mutual, to retained surplus.

For all entities within the scope of the FRS, the fund for future appropriations must **c**
be separately presented on the balance sheet and an explanation given of a negative
FFA balance.

The FRS restricts the recognition of the value of in-force business, but permits **d**
entities that currently recognise such value to continue to do so, subject to limitations
on the way this value may be determined.

A capital statement is required setting out the total available capital for sections of **e**
the life assurance business of the entity.

The capital statement is required to be supported by information on regulatory **f**
capital requirements or management's capital targets, the basis of determining regulatory capital, the sensitivity of liabilities and capital to changes in market variables
and key assumptions, and the entity's capital management policies.

Information is also required to be disclosed on the assumptions used in the mea- **g**
surement of liabilities, and the terms and conditions of options and guarantees
relating to life assurance contracts. For those liabilities to policyholders resulting
from options and guarantees that are not measured at fair value or on a statistical
basis that takes into account all possible outcomes of the option or guarantee,
entities must provide additional information on the nature and extent of the options
and guarantees and the possible liabilities that may arise.

A movements table is also required to show the changes in capital from one reporting **h**
date to the next.

Financial Reporting Standard

OBJECTIVE

1   The objective of this FRS is to require appropriate measurement of, and disclosures relating to, liabilities and assets of life assurance business; and disclosures relating to the financial strength of entities carrying on life assurance business.

DEFINITIONS

2   The following definitions shall apply in the FRS and in particular in the Statement of Standard Accounting Practice set out in **bold type**.

The **Financial Services Authority (FSA) realistic capital regime** is that set out in section 7.4 of its integrated prudential sourcebook.*

The **realistic value of liabilities** is that element of the amount defined by rule 7.4.40 in the FSA's integrated prudential sourcebook, excluding current liabilities falling within the definition in rule 7.4.190 that are recognised separately on the entity's balance sheet.

An entity's **existing accounting policies** are the accounting policies adopted in its last annual financial statements before adoption of this FRS.

The **modified statutory solvency basis (MSSB)** for determining insurance liabilities is the statutory solvency basis adjusted, in accordance with the Statement of Recommended Practice of the Association of British Insurers (the ABI SORP), for the following items:

(a)   to defer new business acquisition costs incurred where the benefit of such costs will be obtained in subsequent accounting periods; and

(b)   to treat investment, resilience and similar reserves, or reserves held in respect of general contingencies or the specific contingency that the fund will be closed to new business, where such items are held within the long term business fund, as reserves rather than provisions. These are included, as appropriate, within shareholders' capital and reserves or the Fund for Future Appropriations.

The **statutory solvency basis** is the basis of determination of insurance liabilities in accordance with rule 7.4.27 of the FSA's integrated prudential sourcebook.

The **Principles and Practices of Financial Management (PPFM)** is the statement that the FSA requires each with-profits life fund to make available to its policyholders containing, inter alia, a description of the fund's investment management and bonus distribution policies.

The **Fund for Future Appropriations (FFA)** is the balance sheet item required by Schedule 9A to the Companies Act 1985 to comprise all funds the allocation of which, either to policyholders or to shareholders, has not been determined by the end of the accounting period.

References to the FSA's integrated prudential sourcebook for insurers, and to individual rules therein, are to the rules made on 18 November 2004 by the Integrated Prudential Sourcebook (Insurers and Other Amendments) Instrument 2004.

Directive friendly societies and **non-directive friendly societies** are as defined in section 7 of the FSA Interim Prudential Sourcebook for Friendly Societies.

SCOPE

The FRS applies to all financial statements that are intended to give a true and fair view   3
of a reporting entity's financial position and profit and loss (or income and expenditure) for a period, where the reporting entity includes a business that is a life assurance business (including reinsurance business).

LIFE ASSURANCE LIABILITIES AND ASSETS

Measurement of with-profits liabilities and related assets

For with-profits life funds falling within the scope of the FSA realistic capital regime: 4

(a)   liabilities to policyholders arising from with-profits life assurance business shall be stated at the amount of the realistic value of liabilities adjusted to exclude the shareholders' share of projected future bonuses;
(b)   acquisition costs shall not be deferred;
(c)   reinsurance recoveries that are recognised shall be measured on a basis that is consistent with the value of the policyholder liabilities to which the reinsurance applies;
(d)   an amount may be recognised for the present value of future profits on non-participating business written in a with-profits fund if:

  (i)   the non-participating business is measured on this basis for the purposes of the regulatory returns made under the FSA realistic capital regime;
  (ii)   the value is determined in accordance with the FSA regulations*; and
  (iii) the determination of the realistic value of liabilities in that with-profits fund takes account, directly or indirectly, of this value;

(e)   where a with-profits life fund has an interest in a subsidiary or associated entity that is valued for FSA regulatory purposes at an amount in excess of the net amounts included in the entity's consolidated accounts, an amount may be recognised representing this excess if the determination of the realistic value of liabilities to with-profits policyholders takes account of this value; and
(f)   adjustments to reflect the consequential tax effects of (a) to (e) above shall be made.

Adjustments from the modified statutory solvency basis necessary to meet the above requirements, including the recognition of an amount in accordance with paragraph 4(d) or 4(e), shall be included in the profit and loss account. An amount equal and opposite to the net amount of these adjustments shall be transferred to or from the FFA (or, in the case of a mutual, its retained surplus) and also included in the profit and loss account.

Amounts recognised under paragraph 4(d) or 4(e) shall be presented in one of the   5
following ways:

(a)   Where it is possible to apportion the amount recognised under paragraph 4(d) or 4(e) between an amount relating to liabilities to policyholders and an amount relating to the FFA, these portions shall be presented in the balance sheet as a deduction in arriving at the amount of liabilities to policyholders and the FFA respectively.

*FSA rule PRU 7.4.37

(b)   **Where it is not possible to make a reasonably approximate apportionment of the amount recognised under paragraph 4(d) or 4(e), the amount shall be presented on the balance sheet as a separate item deducted from a sub-total of liabilities to policyholders and the FFA.**

(c)   **Where the presentation under 5(a) or 5(b) does not comply with statutory requirements for balance sheet presentation applying to the entity, the amount recognised under paragraph 4(d) or 4(e) shall be recognised as an asset.**

6   The established accounting treatment for UK life assurance business is to measure liabilities for policyholder benefits on the modified statutory solvency basis (MSSB). The FRS does not require any change to the accounting for those funds not within the scope of the FSA realistic capital regime, but requires those UK with-profits funds that fall under that regime to use the realistic value of liabilities as the basis for the estimated value of the liabilities to be included in the financial statements. Where the entity's returns to the FSA have not been completed at the time of completion of the financial statements, an estimate of the amount may be used provided it is in accordance with the FSA regulations.

7   An entity may, but is not required to, adopt the requirements of paragraph 4 for UK* with-profits funds that do not fall within the scope of the FSA realistic capital regime or for which the FSA has granted a full waiver from compliance with this regime.

8   Overseas insurance businesses that do not fall within the FSA's regulatory remit may determine insurance liabilities in accordance with local regulatory and accounting requirements. Adjustments on consolidation may be made to take account of the different bases of reporting, although insurance entities are exempt from the requirement in the Companies Act 1985† applicable to other businesses to adjust amounts recognised in the financial statements of subsidiary undertakings onto a consistent basis for the purposes of consolidated financial statements. The FRS does not require any change to the accounting treatment of the liabilities of overseas businesses, but voluntary adoption of the requirements of paragraph 4 is permitted.

9   Liabilities determined in accordance with the FSA realistic capital regime include, in addition to amounts attributable to declared bonuses, amounts in respect of future bonuses, estimated in accordance with the entity's published Principles and Practices of Financial Management and representing a constructive obligation to policyholders. A liability is also included for policyholders' options and guarantees, measured at fair value or estimated using a stochastic model that has been calibrated to give market-consistent estimates of option and guarantee values.

10   An adjustment is made to the realistic value of liabilities to exclude the portion attributed to shareholders, which represents the shareholders' share of future bonuses. Similar adjustments should be made if other amounts due to shareholders would otherwise be included in the realistic value of liabilities.

11   Acquisition costs are deferred under MSSB to offset the effects of 'new business strain', being the requirement to establish liabilities on a statutory solvency basis on inception of a policy in excess of the premiums received. When liabilities are restated in accordance with the FSA realistic capital regime, there is no longer any justification for treating such costs as an asset. The FRS does not alter the treatment of deferred acquisition costs relating to business outside the scope of the FSA realistic

---

*and Republic of Ireland with-profits funds

†and equivalent Republic of Ireland and Northern Ireland legislation

capital regime (other than adjustments that may be made to deferred acquisition costs relating to business for which the value of in-force business is recognised under paragraph 4(d) or (e)).

Amounts recoverable under reinsurance contracts relating to life assurance shall be measured on a basis consistent with the measurement of the related liability, so that the net amount reflects the exposure of the entity. Changing the measurement of the liability may therefore give rise to a change in the related reinsurance asset. The amount of the change in the asset will depend on the terms of the reinsurance contract. **12**

Under the FSA realistic capital regime, a with-profits life fund includes within assets the value of future profits expected to arise from non-participating business (ie life assurance policies that do not have a with-profits feature, such as term assurance, annuities and unit-linked policies) that form part of the with-profits fund—sometimes referred to as the value of in-force business. In the FSA realistic capital regime, this value is also taken into account in determining the returns earned by the fund and its financial strength, and thus gives rise to an increase in the estimated value of future bonuses included in the realistic value of liabilities, although there is not necessarily a direct link between the value of in-force business and the additional amount included in liabilities. To exclude from the balance sheet the value of in-force business whilst recognising the realistic value of liabilities in full, and valuing non-participating liabilities on a statutory basis, would give rise to an inconsistency in the fund's net assets. An entity is therefore permitted to recognise the value of in-force business if that business has been taken into account in measuring the liability, in the circumstances of paragraph 4(d), even though there is not a direct link between the value of the asset and the amount of the liabilities. Where there is not a direct link between the value of the business and the amount of realistic liabilities, but the value is taken into account in determining those liabilities, it is appropriate to recognise the total value of the business. Although not separately identifiable, any excess value over that included in realistic liabilities will be taken to the FFA. Paragraph 4(d) applies only to non-participating business written in a with-profits fund and not to such business outside a with-profits fund. **13**

The amount recognised under paragraph 4(d) or 4(e) may be regarded either as an additional asset, representing the value of future cash flows from the related insurance business; or as an adjustment to the measurement of liabilities and the FFA, being the deduction from these items of the obligation to transfer an unrecognised asset or other source of value. The FRS requires entities to adopt the latter interpretation, unless this would not be in compliance with the statutory requirements that apply to the entity, in which case it permits the amount to be recognised as an asset. Where the amount is treated as an adjustment to a liability, the FRS requires an entity to apportion, if practicable, the amount between the amounts that have been taken into account in the measurement of liabilities and other amounts that should be shown as an adjustment to the FFA. Where this is not practicable, the amount recognised should be shown as an adjustment to a sub-total of the FFA and liabilities to policyholders. **14**

The value of in-force non-participating business recognised within assets for regulatory purposes as described in paragraph 13 is determined as the discounted value of future profits expected to arise from the policies, taking into account liabilities relating to the policies measured on a statutory solvency basis. When adjustments are made onto an MSSB basis for the purposes of the financial statements (for example, to adjust liabilities to exclude certain additional reserves included in the liabilities for regulatory purposes, or where future income included in the value of in-force business covers deferred acquisition costs included in the MSSB balance sheet), a **15** corresponding adjustment to the value of in-force policies will need to be made in order to ensure a consistent valuation.

16   A similar situation may arise where an entity chooses to value an interest in a subsidiary that is held directly in the with-profits fund at a value that includes the value of in-force business within the subsidiary in addition to its net asset value, as permitted by the FSA regulations. In such a case, the value taken into account in determining the realistic value of liabilities is greater than the net assets included in the consolidated accounts. To exclude from the balance sheet the additional value of the investment in the subsidiary whilst recognising the realistic value of liabilities in full would result in an inconsistency in the fund's net assets. An entity is therefore permitted to recognise the excess of the market value of the subsidiary over the net amounts included in the consolidated financial statements as a deduction from the sub-total of the FFA and liabilities to policyholders in the same way as the value of in-force business described in paragraph 13.

17   Where the amounts on a 'realistic' basis determined in accordance with paragraph 4 above are different from the amounts on a modified statutory solvency basis, a corresponding amount is transferred to or from the FFA, so that there is no effect on shareholders' funds. However, individual lines in the revenue (technical) account, including the line item for transfers to or from the FFA, will be affected. The potential shareholders' share corresponding to additional bonuses to policyholders that have been included in the policyholders' liability should be accounted for in the FFA. As a result, there will generally be no change in the profit for the financial year and, in the case of an entity that is not a mutual, generally no change to shareholders' funds. However, this will not be the case where the adjustments result in a negative balance on the FFA and the entity determines that this negative balance should result in a deduction from shareholders' funds through the profit and loss account.

18   In the case of a mutual, which has no shareholders, an FFA or retained surplus account is maintained that represents amounts that have not yet been allocated to specific policyholders. For such entities, the adjustments required by paragraph 4 will be offset within the profit and loss account by a transfer directly to or from this FFA or retained surplus account, with the result that overall profit or loss for the year will be unchanged.

Policyholders' options and guarantees

19   Entities with with-profits funds within the scope of the FSA's realistic capital regime are required to measure the liability of those funds in respect of options and guarantees relating to policyholders either at fair value or at an amount estimated using a market-consistent stochastic model in accordance with FSA regulations.

20   For all life assurance businesses, the best basis for measuring policyholders' options and guarantees is one that includes their time value*. Any deterministic approach to valuation of a policy with a guarantee or optionality feature will generally fail to deal appropriately with the time value of the option. In order to capture this time value it is necessary to use stochastic modelling techniques to evaluate the range of potential outcomes unless a market value for the option is available. The FSA realistic capital regime includes a requirement to value options and guarantees on this basis. For the

---

The value of an option or guarantee comprises two elements, the intrinsic value and the time value. The intrinsic value is the amount that would be payable if the option or guarantee were exercised immediately – that is, the amount it is currently 'in the money', or nil if it is 'out of the money'. The time value is the additional value that reflects the possibility of the intrinsic value increasing in future, before the expiry date of the option or guarantee.

liabilities of businesses not falling within the scope of the FSA realistic capital regime, entities are encouraged, but not required, to adopt these valuation techniques. Where options are not valued on this basis, additional disclosures are required; these are set out in paragraph 48(c).

Under the FSA realistic capital regime, a market-consistent stochastic method for estimating the value of guarantees and options involves: **21**

(a) determining the market variables whose value will affect the additional amount payable under the guarantee or option, and the period in which they have such effect;

(b) determining the likely distribution of each of those variables within that time period, using assumptions calibrated to market observations;

(c) constructing a large number of possible scenarios combining different changes in each variable over the time period, reflecting the expected distribution of values determined in accordance with (b);

(d) evaluating the additional amounts payable under the option or guarantee under each scenario; and

(e) combining these, weighted according to the probability of each scenario occurring, to determine the expected value of the liability.

In determining the amount payable under each scenario, the entity will take into account management actions it anticipates would be taken in response to variations in market variables (such as changing the balance of the investment portfolio between debt instruments and equity, varying the amount charged to policyholders, or varying its bonus policy) that will affect the amount payable under the guarantee or option. Such actions must be realistically capable of being implemented within the time-scale assumed in the scenario analysis, and be consistent with the entity's published Principles and Practice of Financial Management.

Disclosure and presentation relating to with-profits business

Entities shall present the FFA on the balance sheet separately from technical provisions and other liabilities.   **22**

Where the balance on the FFA of a with-profits life fund is negative, as a result of the transfer made in accordance with paragraph 4 or otherwise, the entity shall include in the notes to the financial statements an explanation of the nature of the negative balance and the circumstances in which it arose, and why no action to eliminate it has been considered necessary.   **23**

The FFA should be disclosed separately on the balance sheet, and not combined with technical provisions. Entities that consolidate interests in a life assurance entity on a basis that combines the FFA and technical provisions into a single amount of liabilities to policyholders are required to show these elements separately.   **24**

A negative balance on the FFA may arise, either under MSSB or as a result of adjustments made under paragraph 4. Sometimes this will result in the entity taking action that results in the elimination of the negative balance. Where no such action has been considered necessary, details of the negative balance are required by paragraph 23, including an explanation of why the entity considers it appropriate not to take action to eliminate this balance. Where an entity has more than one with-profits fund, a negative balance on the FFA in one fund should not be offset against a positive balance in another.   **25**

Value of in-force life assurance business

26   Where, other than under paragraph 4(d) or 4(e) above, an entity's existing accounting policies include the recognition of the value of in-force life assurance business as an asset (or as a deduction from a liability), it may continue to recognise such an item as an asset, but shall exclude from the value of that asset any value of in-force policies that reflects future investment margins.

27   Banking and other non-insurance entities with insurance subsidiaries* sometimes account for the insurance business in their consolidated financial statements on an embedded value or similar basis under which, in addition to the value of the retained surplus in the insurance subsidiary, an asset is recognised for the discounted value of the future profit to shareholders expected to arise from existing insurance business. The FRS permits the continuation of such a practice only if the existing policy is amended, if necessary, to exclude from the measurement of the value of the in-force business any value attributable to future investment margins. Investment margins are the amounts by which assumed investment returns exceed the risk-free return on assets. As a consequence of excluding these margins, the embedded value will not vary with the choice of assets in which the fund is invested (ignoring different tax treatments of various types of asset). An example of an accounting policy that reflects those margins, and is not permitted under the FRS, is projecting the returns on the insurer's assets at an estimated rate of return in excess of the risk-free rate, discounting those projected returns at a lower rate and including the result as part of the measurement of the value of in-force business.

28   No value shall be attributed to in-force life assurance business other than:

   (a)   in accordance with paragraphs 4(d), 4(e) or 26 above; or

   (b)   amounts recognised as an intangible asset as part of the allocation of fair values under acquisition accounting in accordance with FRS 7 'Fair Values in Acquisition Accounting', which are subject to the measurement requirements of that standard and not paragraph 26 above.

29   Where the value attributable to in-force life assurance business recognised under paragraph 26 or paragraph 28(b) includes an amount in relation to non-participating business for which the entity also recognises an amount under paragraph 4(d) or 4(e), the amount recognised under paragraph 4(d) or 4(e) shall be reduced to exclude the amount that is included in relation to that business under paragraph 26 or paragraph 28(b).

CAPITAL AND LIABILITIES

30   An entity shall present quantitative and narrative disclosures of its regulatory capital position, as set out below.

31   An entity is not required to include the disclosures required by paragraphs 32 to 47 and 53 to 60 if it is:

   (a)   a subsidiary undertaking where 90 per cent or more of the voting rights are controlled within the group; or

   (b)   a parent entity, in relation to its individual financial statements

   provided the entity is included in publicly available group financial statements which provide information on a group basis complying with the FRS.

*and insurance entities and groups in the Republic of Ireland

Capital statement

An entity shall present a statement setting out its total capital resources relating to life assurance business. The statement shall show, for each section of that business as defined in paragraph 34:   **32**

(a) **shareholders' funds (or in the case of a mutual, the equivalent, often described as disclosed surplus);**
(b) **adjustments to restate these amounts in accordance with regulatory requirements;**
(c) **each additional component of capital included for regulatory purposes, including capital retained within a life fund whether attributable to shareholders, policy-holders or not yet allocated between shareholders and policyholders; and**
(d) **the total capital available to meet regulatory capital requirements.**

Available capital will comprise a number of distinct elements, each of which will be separately disclosed, including: **33**

(a) shareholders' funds as included in the published balance sheet, represented by surplus held within a life fund or by assets held separately from those of the fund itself;
(b) amounts that are wholly attributable to shareholders, but held within a life fund and where the distribution out of the fund is restricted by regulatory or other considerations;
(c) surplus held in life funds that has yet to be attributed or allocated between shareholders and policyholders (in the case of a mutual all such surplus is attributable to policyholders but is not treated as a liability); and
(d) qualifying debt capital, whether issued by the life entity itself or by another entity within the group.

The capital statement shall show as separate sections: **34**

(a) **each UK* with-profits life fund that is material to the group; and**
(b) **the entity's other life assurance business, showing the extent to which the various components of capital are subject to constraints such that they are available to meet requirements in only part of the entity's business, or are available to meet risks and regulatory capital requirements in all parts of the business.**

The purpose of the capital statement is to set out the financial strength of the entity and to provide an analysis of the disposition and constraints over the availability of the capital to meet risks and regulatory requirements. It is particularly important to show the various sources of capital separately and the extent to which the capital in each section is subject to constraint as to its ability to meet requirements in other parts of the entity. Such constraints can arise for any of the following reasons: **35**

(a) ownership—the capital may be subject to specific ownership considerations (for example, the FFA of a UK with-profits fund, for which the allocation between policyholders and shareholders has not been determined);
(b) regulatory—local regulatory limitations may require the maintenance of solvency margins in particular funds or countries; or
(c) financial—the availability of capital in certain cases can be restricted due to the imposition of taxes or other financial penalty in the event of the capital being required to be redeployed across the group.

An entity must consider how best to present information to meet the requirements of paragraph 34(b) in the particular circumstances of its own business. For example, those requirements might be met by sub-analysis of the part of the entity's life   **36**

*or, for an entity in the Republic of Ireland, each with-profits fund in the Republic of Ireland.

assurance business, other than the UK with-profit life funds, into two sections in the statement, one including amounts of capital that are constrained and the other amounts that are freely available to meet risks and regulatory capital requirements in all parts of the business. Alternatively, this information could be presented by means of a sub-analysis by the nature of the capital constraints applying to each business unit: one section in the capital statement would include those business units where there were no constraints on transferring surplus capital to other parts of the group, and another section in the statement would include those business units where surplus capital was constrained. Under either approach, the information would need to be supplemented by narrative explaining the nature and effect of the constraints. Where the capital constraints are more complex, it may be necessary to add additional sections in the capital statement providing further analysis of the different types of constraint that apply. Another way of meeting this requirement would be to provide aggregated information supplemented by fuller narrative disclosure of the constraints and their effect.

37   **The aggregate amount of regulatory capital resources included in the capital statement shall be reconciled to the shareholders' funds, FFA and other amounts shown in the entity's balance sheet, showing separately for each component of capital the amount relating to the entity's business other than life assurance. Where such other business is significant, an explanation shall be given of the extent to which this capital can be used to meet the requirements of the life assurance business.**

38   Although the detailed requirements apply to life assurance business, entities will need to incorporate information on other parts of the business, together with consolidation adjustments, in order to demonstrate how the aggregated capital attributed to the life assurance business reconciles to the total shown in the consolidated balance sheet, and the extent to which capital outside the life assurance business may be made available to meet the capital requirements of the life assurance business. This reconciliation applies to each different type of capital shown in the capital statement.

39   **Where the reporting entity is a subsidiary undertaking, narrative supporting the capital statement shall explain the extent to which the capital of the entity is able to be transferred to the parent or fellow subsidiaries, or the extent to which it is required to be retained within the reporting entity.**

40   For life funds within the scope of the FSA realistic capital regime, in determining available capital, liabilities will be taken into account at their 'realistic' amount (unless the capital requirement is higher on the regulatory basis). Further adjustments are necessary to adjust the capital shown in the balance sheet to the amount for regulatory purposes. The most significant differences are:

(a)   the inclusion in capital of the fund for future appropriations;
(b)   the exclusion from capital of the shareholders' share of accrued bonus;
(c)   the exclusion of goodwill and other intangible assets, such as an amount attributed to the acquired value of in-force business; and
(d)   changes to the valuation of assets and the exclusion of certain non-admissible assets for regulatory purposes, for example any regulatory adjustment to a pension fund deficit that is recognised as a liability.

Disclosure of these adjustments should be sufficient to give a clear picture of the capital position from a regulatory perspective and its relationship to the shareholders' funds shown in the consolidated balance sheet.

41   **Where the amount of a capital instrument that qualifies for inclusion as regulatory capital is restricted (for example, where a limited percentage of total regulatory capital**

may be in the form of debt) the full amount of the instrument shall be included, with a separate deduction for the amount in excess of the restriction.

Disclosure shall be made of any formal intra-group arrangements to provide capital to particular funds or business units, including intra-group loans and contingent arrangements. Where the reporting entity is a subsidiary undertaking, disclosure shall also be made of similar arrangements between the entity and its parent or fellow subsidiary undertakings. **42**

Regulatory capital can include both shareholders' funds and surplus within the fund. Such surplus may be wholly attributable to shareholders, or form part of the fund that has not yet been appropriated and allocated between shareholders and policy-holders. In a mutual fund, all surplus is attributable to policyholders. Debt instruments qualifying as capital may also be issued from the fund itself, or may form part of the shareholders' net assets outside the life fund; and a debt instrument issued by the fund to the shareholders may effectively transfer capital from the shareholders to the fund. Separate disclosure of each class of capital is important to an understanding of the funding of the business and the way any future losses would be absorbed or new business financed. **43**

Intra-group arrangements should be included in the regulatory capital of a section only where they are subject to formal arrangements. Where capital in other parts of a group is available to meet the requirements of a particular section of the business, but no formal arrangement has been entered into to do so, no allocation of this capital to the section of the business should be shown in the capital position statement. **44**

Disclosures relating to liabilities and capital

The capital statement shall be supported by the following disclosures: **45**
(a) narrative or quantified information on the regulatory capital requirements applying to each section of the business shown in the capital statement, or on the capital targets set by management for that section;
(b) narrative disclosure of the basis of determining regulatory capital and the corresponding regulatory capital requirements and any major inconsistencies in this basis between the different sections of the business;
(c) narrative disclosure addressing the sensitivity of liabilities and the components of total capital to changes in market conditions, key assumptions and other variables, and assumptions about future management actions in response to changes in market conditions; and
(d) narrative disclosure of the entity's capital management policies and objectives, and its approach to managing the risks that would affect the capital position.

Although the capital statement itself deals only with capital available to meet regulatory requirements, the narrative discussion should address both this and the related regulatory requirements. Narrative explanation of the capital position, setting out its capital management objectives and risk management policies and the sensitivity to changes in assumptions, is important to the user's ability to understand the management of capital by the entity, its financial adaptability in changing circumstances, and the resources available to each group of policyholders. **46**

Narrative discussion of sensitivity to changes in market conditions, assumptions and other variables is required to address both liabilities, including options and guarantees given to policyholders, and the components of total capital. Measurement of liabilities, including options and guarantees, may be determined using stochastic **47** methods that take into account actions that are assumed would be taken by management in response to changes in market conditions. Incorporating management actions in this way can substantially alter the value of liabilities and disclosure of the effect of changes in such assumptions is required. In relation to UK life funds, management actions that are taken into account should be consistent with those disclosed in the life fund's Principles and Practices of Financial Management available to policyholders.

48   **In relation to life assurance liabilities, the entity shall include the following additional information:**

(a)   **the process used to determine the assumptions that have the greatest effect on the measurement of liabilities including options and guarantees and, where practicable, quantified disclosure of those assumptions;**

(b)   **those terms and conditions of options and guarantees relating to life assurance contracts that could in aggregate have a material effect on the amount, timing and uncertainty of the entity's future cash flows; and**

(c)   **information about exposures to interest rate risk or market risk under options and guarantees if the entity does not measure these at fair value or at an amount estimated using a market-consistent stochastic model.**

49   It may be relatively easy to quantify some assumptions that are used in the measurement of liabilities – for example, discount rates or general inflation, where the rate used should be disclosed. For other assumptions, such as mortality tables, it may not be practicable to disclose quantified assumptions because there are too many, or they cannot be expressed as single values, in which case it is more important to describe the process used to generate the assumptions. The description of the process would include the objective – whether a best-estimate or a given level of assurance is intended; the sources of data; whether assumptions are consistent with observable market data or other published information; how past experience, current conditions and future trends are taken into account; correlations between different assumptions; management's policy for future bonuses; and the nature and extent of uncertainties affecting the assumptions.

50   Options and guarantees are features of life assurance contracts that confer potentially valuable guarantees underlying the level or nature of policyholder benefits, or options to change these benefits exercisable at the discretion of the policyholder. For the purposes of this FRS, the term is used to refer only to those options and guarantees whose potential value is affected by the behaviour of financial variables, and not to those features of life assurance contracts where the potential changes in policyholder benefits arise solely from insurance risk (including mortality and morbidity), or from changes in the entity's creditworthiness. It includes a financial guarantee or option that applies if a policy lapses, but does not include the option to surrender or allow a policy to lapse.

51   **The requirements of 48(c) will require, for options and guarantees that are not measured at fair value or at an amount estimated using a market-consistent stochastic model, the following disclosures:**

(a)   **a description of the nature and extent of the options and guarantees;**

(b)   **the basis of measurement for the amount at which these options and guarantees are stated, and the extent to which an amount is included for the additional payment that may arise under the option or guarantee in excess of the amounts expected to be paid under the relevant policies if they did not include the option or guarantee feature;**

(c)   **the main variables that determine the amount payable under the option or guarantee; and**

(d) **information on the potential effects of adverse changes in those market conditions that affect the entity's obligations under options and guarantees.**

The requirement of 51(d) may be met by disclosing: 52

(a) for options and guarantees that would result in additional payments to policyholders if current asset values and market rates continued unchanged (ie those that are 'in the money'), an indication of the change in these amounts if the variables moved adversely by a stated amount;

(b) for options and guarantees that would result in additional payments to policyholders only if there was an adverse change in current asset values and market rates (ie those that are 'out of the money'):

(i) an indication of the change in these variables, from current levels, which would cause material amounts to become payable under the options and guarantees; and

(ii) an indication of the amount that would result from a specified adverse change in these variables from the levels at which amounts first become payable under the options and guarantees.

The above disclosures may be made in aggregate for classes of options and guarantees that do not differ materially, or which are not individually material.

Disclosure of analysis of liabilities

The capital statement shall show the amount of policyholder liabilities attributed to each section of the business shown in the statement, analysed between: 53

(a) **with-profits business;**
(b) **unit-linked business;**
(c) **other life assurance business; and**
(d) **insurance business accounted for as financial instruments in accordance with the requirements of FRS 26 (IAS 39) 'Financial Instruments: Measurement'.**

The total of these policyholder liabilities shall be the amounts shown in the entity's balance sheet.

The relationship between capital requirements and policyholder liabilities for each fund or business unit provides additional information on the interrelationship between the capital position and the extent of liabilities. 54

Movements in capital

An entity shall include an explanation of the movements in the total amount of available capital for life assurance business shown in the capital statement with the corresponding amounts at the end of the previous accounting period. This disclosure shall cover individually each UK life fund* that is separately shown in the capital statement required under paragraph 32, and other life assurance business in aggregate. 55

This disclosure shall set out in tabular form the effect of changes resulting from: 56

(a) **changes in assumptions used to measure life assurance liabilities, showing separately the effect of each change in an assumption that has had a material effect on the group;**

(b) **changes in management policy;**

*or, for an entity in the Republic of Ireland, each life fund in the Republic of Ireland.

(c)　changes in regulatory requirements and similar external developments; and

(d)　new business and other factors, describing any material items.

57　An understanding of the underlying causes of changes in the capital position is valuable, giving an insight into the development of the entity's life assurance business. It is important to separate movements relating to changes in assumptions and management policy from other movements arising from the business. Those other movements might arise from changing market prices affecting assets and liabilities and movements resulting from surrenders, lapses and maturities of existing policies and new business written, and would be identified, where material, in accordance with paragraph 56(d).

58　The movements analysis distinguishes between assumption changes, changes in management policy, and other factors. Changes in management policy relate to significant changes in the management of the fund such as changes in investment policy or changes in the use of the estate. Where management actions are clearly directly related to changes in assumptions or other factors, it will be appropriate to show the net impact but the narrative should discuss the constituent factors. An example might be the combined effect of a reduced level of bonuses assumed as a result of a reduction in the assumed level of future investment return and a reduction in investment returns earned in the period.

59　Although it is important to explain all movements in liabilities and capital during the period that are material to the group, this does not imply that the impact of each assumption change needs to be shown separately. Where there is a common cause for the change of assumption the impact can be grouped together. As an example, the impact of changes in investment return attributable to changing market circumstances does not need to be broken down between the various classes of investment.

60　Determination of the effect of assumption changes involves considerable recalculation of valuations using both old and new assumptions and, particularly in the case of option and guarantee models, this may result in impracticable demands on computer systems. This is especially so in the first year of applying the FRS, when the FSA realistic valuation methodology is relatively new and untried, and estimation and approximation methods for analysing and explaining movements for management purposes are in the early stages of development. Accordingly, less detailed analysis of changes, and less quantification of movements, may be expected in the first year of applying the FRS as a result of these practical difficulties; paragraph 66 permits entities to present this information in non-tabular form for an accounting period ending before 23 December 2006.

DATE FROM WHICH EFFECTIVE AND TRANSITIONAL ARRANGEMENTS

61　**Subject to paragraphs 62 and 63, the accounting practices set out in the FRS shall be regarded as standard for financial statements relating to accounting periods ending on or after 23 December 2005. Earlier adoption of all or part of the FRS is permitted.**

62　**Entities that are directive friendly societies and are not within the scope of the FSA realistic capital regime are not required to apply the FRS for accounting periods ending before 23 December 2006.**

63　**Entities that are non-directive friendly societies are not required to apply the FRS for accounting periods ending before 23 December 2007.**

Changes in accounting policy resulting from the adoption of the FRS shall be accounted **64** for by restating prior periods in accordance with FRS 3 'Reporting Financial Performance', except that comparatives in the profit and loss account need not be restated for changes arising from the adoption of a new accounting policy in accordance with paragraph 4 where this is not practicable.

For those entities that adopt the measurement requirements of paragraph 4, **65** including adoption of the realistic value of liabilities as the basis of measurement, or adoption of stochastic methods for the measurement of options and guarantees, it may not be practicable to restate profit and loss account comparatives for the first year of adoption. Accordingly, the FRS permits such comparatives not to be restated. FRS 18 'Accounting Policies' sets out requirements for disclosures relating to changes in accounting policies.

For accounting periods ending before 23 December 2006, an entity is not required to set **66** out the analysis of movements in tabular form as required by paragraph 56, but should include quantified disclosure of changes where practicable. The narrative disclosure required by paragraph 55 should address the movements as categorised in paragraph 56. For the first accounting period for which a table of movements is presented, comparatives for the previous period are not required.

Comparatives should be disclosed for the capital position statement, for the table of **67** movements in the capital position and for the related disclosures. However, this may not be practicable in the case of the movements table for the first accounting period in which the FRS comes into effect. Accordingly, such disclosure is not required for that period, although it is encouraged if information is available.

Adoption of FRS 27 by the Board

Financial Reporting Standard 27 *Life Assurance* was approved for issue by the nine members of the Accounting Standards Board.

Ian Mackintosh	Chairman
Andrew Lennard	Technical Director
Michael Ashley	
Douglas Flint	
Anthony Good	
Roger Marshall	
Isobel Sharp	
Jonathan Symonds	
Peter Westlake	

Appendix I
Illustration of the Capital Statement

The following illustration of a capital statement and its supporting narrative is provided for general guidance only and does not form part of the FRS. It is intended to show a possible format for the capital statement, but is not intended to imply that this is the only form such a statement could take. Entities will need to consider the format for the statement that best meets their individual circumstances.

Available capital resources	A UK (with-profits)	B UK (with-profits)	UK non-participating	Overseas	Life Business Shareholders' Funds	TOTAL LIFE BUSINESS	Other Activities	Consol. adjusts.	GROUP TOTAL
Shareholders' funds outside fund					850	850	200	(50)	1,000
Shareholders' funds held in fund			350			350			350
Total shareholders' funds			350		850	1,200	200	(50)	1,350
Adjustments onto regulatory basis:									
FFA	350	150				500			500
Adjustment to assets	(25)	(20)				(45)			(45)
Shareholders' share in realistic liabilities	(25)	(30)				(55)			(55)
Other adjustments									
	300	100	350		850	1,600	200	(50)	1,750
Other qualifying capital:									
Loan capital							750		750
Internal loans		150			(150)				
Allocation of group capital		300		300	(600)				
Total available capital resources	300	550	350	300	100	1,600	950	(50)	2,500

With-profits liabilities on realistic basis:				
Options and guarantees	200	100		300
Other policyholder obligations	1,800	4,000	1,900	7,700
Total with-profits liabilities	**2,000**	**4,100**	**1,900**	**8,000**
Unit-linked	1,000	500	800	2,300
Non-participating life assurance	800	1,800	500	3,100
Technical provisions in balance sheet	3,800	6,400	3,200	13,400

The following paragraphs illustrate the explanation of the regulatory capital requirements required by paragraph 45(a) and (b), together with the analysis of liabilities required by paragraph 53. Further details of the determination of the regulatory capital position, including discussion of the sensitivity to changes in assumptions and management's policies and objectives, would need to be included to meet the requirements of paragraph 45(c) and (d) of the FRS.

The Group has two UK with-profit funds, A and B, shown separately in the capital position statement. The Group's UK non-participating business is shown in aggregate. The Group's overseas life businesses are also aggregated for the purposes of the statement.

For the Group's two UK with-profit funds the available capital is determined in accordance with the 'realistic balance sheet' regime prescribed by the FSA's regulations, under which liabilities to policyholders include both declared bonuses and the constructive obligation for future bonuses not yet declared. The available capital resources include an estimate of the value of their respective estates, included as part of the FFA. The estate represents the surplus in the fund that is in excess of any constructive obligation to policyholders. The allocation of the estate between policyholders and shareholders has not been determined. It represents capital resources of the individual with-profits fund to which it relates and is available to meet regulatory and other solvency requirements of the fund and, in certain circumstances, additional liabilities that may arise.

For these with-profit funds, the liabilities included in the balance sheet include only amounts relating to policyholders and do not include the amount representing the shareholders' share of future bonuses. However, the shareholders' share is treated as a deduction from capital that is available to meet regulatory requirements and is therefore shown as a separate adjustment in the capital statement.

Shareholders' funds held outside the life funds and overseas businesses are shown separately in the capital statement. In the case of Fund B and certain overseas funds the capital requirements are met in part from centrally-held Group capital, by means of internal loans, contingent loans and share capital. To the extent that this support is made under a formal arrangement, it is shown as an allocation of Group capital between the sections of the statement.

The total available capital resources for each section of the statement shows the capital on a regulatory basis that is available to meet the regulatory capital requirements of that part of the business, and the targets for the surplus capital management regards as appropriate protection against future adverse changes in circumstances. Such capital is generally subject to restrictions as to its availability to meet requirements that arise elsewhere in the Group. The principal restrictions are:

(a)   *UK with-profits funds A and B –* the available surplus held in the fund can only be applied to meet the requirements of the fund itself or be distributed to policyholders and shareholders. Shareholders are entitled to an amount not exceeding one ninth of the amount distributed to policyholders in the form of bonuses, and the shareholders' share of distributions would also be subject to a tax charge.

(b)   *UK non-participating funds –* the available surplus held in the fund is attributable to shareholders and, subject to meeting the regulatory requirements of these businesses, this capital is available to meet requirements elsewhere in the Group. Any transfer of the surplus would give rise to a tax charge.

(c)   *Overseas businesses –* these include several smaller participating and non-participating businesses. In all cases the available capital resources are subject to local regulatory restrictions which restrict management's ability to redeploy these amounts in other parts of the Group and in most cases such transfers would also give rise to a tax charge. Because of the complex nature of these restrictions, the Group's management does not regard this capital as available to meet requirements in other parts of the Group.

For the UK life funds the group is required to hold sufficient capital to meet the FSA capital requirements, based on the 'risk capital margin' (RCM) determined in accordance with the FSA's regulatory rules under its realistic capital regime, together with the Individual Capital Assessment (ICA) which takes into account certain business risks not reflected in the RCM. The determination of the RCM depends on various actuarial and other assumptions about potential changes in market prices, and the actions management would take in the event of particular adverse changes in market conditions.

Management intends to maintain surplus capital in excess of the RCM and ICA to meet the FSA's total requirements, and to maintain an appropriate additional margin over this to absorb changes in both capital and capital requirements. For life fund A, the capital was 171% of the RCM of £175 million and for life fund B the capital was 140% of the RCM of £390 million, in line with management's target of maintaining a margin of at least 35% of the RCM.

For UK non-participating business, the relevant capital requirement is the minimum solvency requirement determined in accordance with FSA regulations. For this business, a lower capital surplus is targeted by management, since the capital requirement is less subject to fluctuation and the capital amount is after deducting liabilities that include additional prudential margins. At 31 December the available capital was 130% of the capital requirement £270 million, in excess of management's target minimum of 120%.

For overseas businesses the amount shown is the minimum requirement under the locally applicable regulatory regimes. These are determined on various bases, and in practice the local regulators expect a significant margin over these minima to be maintained. Management also carries out its own assessment of the level of capital resources it regards as appropriate, in excess of these regulatory minima. Overall, overseas businesses held capital substantially in excess of management's target minimum capital level of £250 million. No individual overseas business held less that 150% of its regulatory capital requirement.

Additional narrative disclosures will cover:

* *sensitivity of liabilities (including options and guarantees) and components of capital (paragraph 45(c));*
* *capital management policies and the approach to managing risks (paragraph 45(d));*
* *information on liabilities, including information on assumptions, terms and conditions relating to options and guarantees, and exposure to risk in relation to options and guarantees not measured at fair value or by using a stochastic modelling method (paragraphs 48 and 51);*
* *information on movements in capital, including a movements table (paragraphs 55 and 56); and*
* *an explanation of the reasons for a negative balance on an FFA of any with-profits fund of the entity, and why no action to eliminate it has been considered necessary (paragraph 23).*

Appendix II
Note on Legal Requirements

GREAT BRITAIN

Insurance companies and insurance groups

1   For accounting periods beginning prior to 1 January 2005, all insurance companies and insurance groups (as defined by the Companies Act 1985) are required to prepare their financial statements in accordance with Schedule 9A to the Companies Act 1985 (the Schedule). For accounting periods beginning on or after 1 January 2005, the financial statements of some insurance companies and insurance groups will continue to be prepared in accordance with the Schedule. However, other financial statements of insurance companies and insurance groups will be prepared in accordance with EU-adopted IFRS and will, as a result, not be subject to any detailed legal requirements as to their form and content.

2   The requirements of the Schedule that are relevant to the FRS are set out in paragraphs 3-10 below. It is the requirement in the FRS for some entities to recognise 'realistic' liabilities for certain policyholder liabilities that is most relevant to the Schedule's requirements, and the implications of that are analysed in paragraphs 4.47-4.65 of Appendix IV 'The Development of the FRS'. That analysis is not relevant to entities not required to recognise 'realistic' liabilities, nor is it relevant to entities that *are* required to recognise 'realistic' liabilities but, because they prepare their financial statements in accordance with EU-adopted IFRS, are not subject to the requirements of the Schedule.

The FFA

3   The Schedule requires disclosure, as a separate item on the face of the balance sheet immediately below 'Subordinated liabilities' and immediately above 'Technical provisions', of an item called 'Fund for future appropriations'. Note 19 on the balance sheet format in the Schedule states that the item shall comprise "all funds the allocation of which either to policy holders or shareholders has not been determined by the end of the financial year."

Technical provisions

4   The Schedule requires disclosure, as a separate item on the face of the balance sheet, of an item entitled 'Technical provisions'. That item is to be analysed between the provision for unearned premiums, long-term business provisions, claims outstanding, the provision for bonuses and rebates, the equalisation provision, and other technical provisions.

5   Note 21 on the balance sheet format in the Schedule requires that the long-term business provision shall comprise the actuarially estimated value of the company's liabilities (excluding technical provisions included under 'Technical provisions for linked liabilities'), including bonuses already declared and after deducting the actuarial value of future premiums.

   (a)   A technical provision should be included under 'Technical provisions for linked liabilities' if it is constituted to cover liabilities relating to investment in the context of long-term policies under which the benefits payable to policyholders are wholly or partly to be determined by reference to the value of, or the income from, property of any description or by reference to fluctuations in, or in an index of, the value of property of any description. Any additional technical provisions constituted to cover death risks, operating expenses or other risks (such as benefits payable at the maturity date or guaranteed surrender values) shall be included under 'Technical provisions—Long-term business provision'.

(b)   Note 20 permits the provision for unearned premiums to be included within the long-term business provision rather than the provision for unearned premiums.

Paragraph 43 of the Schedule requires that the amount of technical provisions must at all times be sufficient to cover any liabilities arising out of insurance contracts as far as can reasonably be foreseen.   **6**

Paragraph 46 of the Schedule goes on to require that: **7**

"(1)   The long term business provision shall in principle be computed separately for each long term contract, save that statistical or mathematical methods may be used where they may be expected to give approximately the same results as individual calculations.

(2)   A summary of the principal assumptions in making the provision under sub-paragraph (1) shall be given in the notes to the accounts.

(3)   The computation shall be made annually by a Fellow of the Institute or Faculty of Actuaries on the basis of recognised actuarial methods, with due regard to the actuarial principles laid down in Council Directive 92/96/EEC."

The reference in paragraph 46(3) to Council Directive 92/96/EEC is, in effect, a reference to Directive 2002/83/EC of the European Parliament and of the Council.* That Directive is concerned with prudential regulation, and many parts of the Directive have no relevance to the true and fair financial statements. However, the following parts of Article 20 appear to have indirect relevance to the financial statements by virtue of the cross reference in paragraph 46(3):   **8**

"Establishment of technical provisions

1.   The home Member State shall require every assurance undertaking to establish sufficient technical provisions, including mathematical provisions, in respect of its entire business.
      The amount of such technical provisions shall be determined according to the following principles.

      A. (i)   the amount of the technical life-assurance provisions shall be calculated by a sufficiently prudent prospective actuarial valuation, taking account of all future liabilities as determined by the policy conditions for each existing contract, including:
      -      all guaranteed benefits, including guaranteed surrender values,
      -      bonuses to which policy holders are already either collectively or individually entitled, however those bonuses are described - vested, declared or allotted,
      -      all options available to the policy holder under the terms of the contract,
      -      expenses, including commissions, taking credit for future premiums due;

Directive 2002/83/EC has replaced Council Directive 92/96/EEC, which has been repealed. The cross-reference in paragraph 46(3) has not yet been updated, but it is understood that it will be shortly.

(ii) the use of a retrospective method is allowed, if it can be shown that the resulting technical provisions are not lower than would be required under a sufficiently prudent prospective calculation or if a prospective method cannot be used for the type of contract involved;

(iii) a prudent valuation is not a 'best estimate' valuation, but shall include an appropriate margin for adverse deviation of the relevant factors;

(iv) the method of valuation for the technical provisions must not only be prudent in itself, but must also be so having regard to the method of valuation for the assets covering those provisions;

(v) technical provisions shall be calculated separately for each contract. The use of appropriate approximations or generalisations is allowed, however, where they are likely to give approximately the same result as individual calculations. The principle of separate calculation shall in no way prevent the establishment of additional provisions for general risks which are not individualised;

(vi) where the surrender value of a contract is guaranteed, the amount of the mathematical provisions for the contract at any time shall be at least as great as the value guaranteed at that time;

B. the rate of interest used shall be chosen prudently. It shall be determined in accordance with the rules of the competent authority in the home Member State, applying the following principles:

(a) for all contracts, the competent authority of the assurance undertaking's home Member State shall fix one or more maximum rates of interest, in particular in accordance with the following rules:

(i) when contracts contain an interest rate guarantee, the competent authority in the home Member State shall set a single maximum rate of interest. It may differ according to the currency in which the contract is denominated, provided that it is not more than 60% of the rate on bond issues by the State in whose currency the contract is denominated.

If a Member State decides, pursuant to the second sentence of the first subparagraph, to set a maximum rate of interest for contracts denominated in another Member State's currency, it shall first consult the competent authority of the Member State in whose currency the contract is denominated;

(ii) however, when the assets of the assurance undertaking are not valued at their purchase price, a Member State may stipulate that one or more maximum rates may be calculated taking into account the yield on the corresponding assets currently held, minus a prudential margin and, in particular for contracts with periodic premiums, furthermore taking into account the anticipated yield on future assets. The prudential margin and the maximum rate or rates of interest applied to the anticipated yield on future assets shall be fixed by the competent authority of the home Member State;

(b) the establishment of a maximum rate of interest shall not imply that the assurance undertaking is bound to use a rate as high as that;

(c) the home Member State may decide not to apply paragraph (a) to the following categories of contracts:
- unit-linked contracts,
- single-premium contracts for a period of up to eight years,
- without-profits contracts, and annuity contracts with no surrender value.

In the cases referred to in the second and third indents of the first subparagraph, in choosing a prudent rate of interest, account may be taken of the currency in which the contract is denominated and corresponding assets currently held and where the undertaking's assets are valued at their current value, the anticipated yield on future assets.

Under no circumstances may the rate of interest used be higher than the yield on assets as calculated in accordance with the accounting rules in the home Member State, less an appropriate deduction;

(d) the Member State shall require an assurance undertaking to set aside in its accounts a provision to meet interest-rate commitments vis-à-vis policy holders if the present or foreseeable yield on the undertaking's assets is insufficient to cover those commitments;

(e) the Commission and the competent authorities of the Member States which so request shall be notified of the maximum rates of interest set under (a);

C. the statistical elements of the valuation and the allowance for expenses used shall be chosen prudently, having regard to the State of the commitment, the type of policy and the administrative costs and commissions expected to be incurred;

D. in the case of participating contracts, the method of calculation for technical provisions may take into account, either implicitly or explicitly, future bonuses of all kinds, in a manner consistent with the other assumptions on future experience and with the current method of distribution of bonuses;

E. allowance for future expenses may be made implicitly, for instance by the use of future premiums net of management charges. However, the overall allowance, implicit or explicit, shall be not less than a prudent estimate of the relevant future expenses;

F. the method of calculation of technical provisions shall not be subject to discontinuities from year to year arising from arbitrary changes to the method or the bases of calculation and shall be such as to recognise the distribution of profits in an appropriate way over the duration of each policy."

Deferred acquisition costs

The Schedule includes an item entitled 'deferred acquisition costs' to be shown **9** separately on the balance sheet under the heading 'Prepayments and accrued income'. Note 17 on the balance sheet format requires that the item shall comprise the costs of acquiring insurance policies which are incurred during a financial year but relate to a subsequent financial year, except in so far as:

(a) allowance has been made in the computation of the long-term business provision made under paragraph 46 of the Schedule and shown under 'Technical provisions—Long-term business provisions' or 'Technical provisions for linked liabilities' in the balance sheet, for:

(i) the explicit recognition of such costs,

(ii) the implicit recognition of such costs by virtue of the anticipation of future income from which such costs may prudently be expected to be recovered, or

(b) allowance has been made for such costs in respect of general business policies by a deduction from the provision for unearned premiums made under paragraph 44 of the Schedule and shown under 'Technical provisions—Provision for unearned premiums' in the balance sheet.

10   Note 17 also requires that:

(a)   deferred acquisition costs arising in general business shall be distinguished from those arising in long-term business;

(b)   there shall be disclosed in the notes how the deferral of acquisition costs has been treated (unless otherwise expressly stated in the accounts);

(c)   where such costs are included as a deduction from 'Technical provisions —Provision for unearned premiums', the amount of such deduction; and

(d)   where the actuarial method used in the calculation of the 'Technical provisions —Long-term business provisions' or 'Technical provisions for linked liabilities' has made allowance for the explicit recognition of such costs, the amount of the costs so recognised.

Other entities

11   Paragraphs 1–10 above describe the accounting requirements in the legislation that apply to insurance companies or insurance groups as defined in the Companies Act 1985. The FRS also applies to:

(a)   groups reporting under the Companies Act 1985 that are not insurance groups, including bancassurers and retail groups with life assurance subsidiaries. Bancassurers are required to prepare their financial statements in accordance with Schedule 9 of the Act; retail groups in accordance with Schedule 4 of the Act. Neither Schedule contains specific requirements on how to account for life assurance activities.

(b)   friendly societies. Friendly societies are required to prepare their financial statements in accordance with The Friendly Societies (Accounts and Related Provisions) Regulations 1994.

(i)   The financial statements of directive friendly societies are required to prepare in accordance with Schedules 1 - 6 of the Regulations. The requirements on the form and content of the balance sheet are set out in Schedule 2 and are almost identical to the Companies Act requirements summarised above.

(ii)   The financial statements of non-directive friendly societies are required to prepare in accordance with Schedule 7 of the Regulations. Although Schedule 7 requires a prescribed analysis of liabilities to be provided, that prescribed analysis is, compared to the analysis required by Schedule 9A of the Companies Act, highly abbreviated.

(c)   various other entities that prepare their financial statements in accordance with The Insurance Accounts Directive (Miscellaneous Insurance Undertakings) Regulations 1993. Those Regulations require the entities to which they apply to comply with the requirements of Schedule 9A of the Companies Act in preparing their financial statements.

NORTHERN IRELAND

12   The statutory requirements in Northern Ireland that apply to insurance companies and insurance groups are set out in Schedule 9A to the Companies (Northern Ireland) Order 1986. Those requirements are identical to the legislation for Great Britain cited above.

REPUBLIC OF IRELAND

The statutory requirements in the Republic of Ireland that correspond to those cited above for Great Britain are shown in the following table. **13**

Great Britain	Republic of Ireland
Schedule 9A to the Companies Act 1985 (the Schedule)	European Communities (Insurance Undertakings: Accounts) Regulations, 1996
Note 17 on the balance sheet format in the Schedule	Schedule, Part I, Chapter 2, Section A, Note 17
Note 19 on the balance sheet format in the Schedule	Schedule, Part I, Chapter 2, Section A, Note 21
Note 20 on the balance sheet format in the Schedule	Schedule, Part I, Chapter 2, Section A, Note 23
Note 21 on the balance sheet format in the Schedule	Schedule, Part I, Chapter 2, Section A, Note 25
Paragraph 43 of the Schedule	Schedule, Part II, Chapter 3 – Paragraph 23
Paragraph 44 of the Schedule	Schedule, Part II, Chapter 3 – Paragraph 24
Paragraph 46 of the Schedule	Schedule, Part II, Chapter 3 – Paragraph 26
Paragraph 46(3) of the Schedule	Schedule, Part II, Chapter 3 – Paragraph 26(4)

Appendix III
Compliance with International Accounting Standards

1   Some of the entities applying the FRS will do so in financial statements prepared in accordance with EU-adopted IFRS; others will be applying it in financial statements prepared in accordance with UK standards and legal requirements.

(a)   Paragraphs 10.1-10.4 of Appendix IV 'The Development of the FRS' discuss the implications of the FRS for the former entities.

(b)   This appendix is addressed to the entities preparing their financial statements in accordance with UK standards and legal requirements. The appendix explains the extent to which compliance with the FRS will ensure compliance with the international accounting standard on insurance, IFRS 4 'Insurance Contracts'.

2   IFRS 4 contains definitions of 'insurance contracts' and various other insurance-related terms. Although those definitions are not included in the FRS, those that define the scope of IFRS 4, IAS 32 and IAS 39—including the definition of 'insurance contracts'—are included in FRS 26 and will therefore apply to entities complying with that standard.

3   Paragraph 10 of IFRS 4 notes that some insurance contracts contain both an insurance contract and a deposit component. Paragraphs 10-12 require those components in certain specified circumstances to be accounted for as if they were separate contracts (in other words, unbundled); permits, but does not require, them to be unbundled in certain other specified circumstances; and prohibits them from being unbundled in certain other specified circumstances. There is nothing in this FRS or any other UK standard requiring, permitting or prohibiting the unbundling of insurance contracts, save the general principle in FRS 5 'Reporting the Substance of Transactions' that transactions should be accounted for in accordance with their substance.

4   All accounting policies adopted by an insurer are required to meet the criteria set out in paragraph 14 of IFRS 4. Neither this FRS nor any other extant UK standard contains similar criteria. The accounting policies that the FRS requires to be adopted all meet the criteria, but some of the entity's other accounting policies might not.

5   Paragraphs 21-23 of IFRS 4 prohibit an insurer from changing its accounting policies for insurance contracts unless two criteria are met.

(a)   The first criterion is that the new accounting policy shall make the financial statements more relevant to the economic decision-making needs of users and no less reliable, or more reliable and no less relevant to those needs. Although there is no similar requirement in the FRS, compliance with FRS 18 'Accounting Policies' would ensure compliance with this criterion.

(b)   The second criterion is that the change shall be consistent with the requirements set out in paragraphs 24-30 of IFRS 4, which relate to changes of certain specific accounting policies. Compliance with the FRS would ensure compliance with the requirements in paragraphs 27 and 28 of IFRS 4 concerning the inclusion of future investment margins in the measurement of insurance contracts. However, compliance with the FRS and extant UK standards would not necessarily ensure compliance in all respects with the other requirements in paragraphs 24-30 of IFRS 4.

6   Paragraph 34(d) of IFRS 4 requires that, if an insurance contract contains a discretionary feature, a guaranteed element and an embedded derivative that is within

the scope of IAS 39 'Financial Instruments: Recognition and Measurement', that embedded derivative shall be accounted for in accordance with IAS 39. For accounting periods beginning on or after 1 January 2005, some entities are required—and all entities may choose—to apply FRS 26 (IAS 39) 'Financial Instruments: Measurement'.

(a) Compliance with FRS 26 would ensure compliance with paragraph 34(d) of IFRS 4.

(b) For entities not complying with FRS 26, neither this FRS nor any other extant UK standard currently requires embedded derivatives to be separated from their host contract.

Paragraphs 36-39 of IFRS 4 contain disclosure requirements. The disclosure requirements in paragraphs 37(c), 39(b), 39(e) and 37(d) are virtually identical to requirements in the FRS (paragraphs 48(a), (b) and (c) and paragraph 56(a) respectively), although the scope of the FRS' disclosures is more limited.

7

Appendix IV
The Development of the FRS

BACKGROUND

Life assurance accounting today

1.1　In Great Britain, financial reporting by most types of insurance entity is governed by the legislation implementing the EU Insurance Accounts Directive.*·† These requirements are derived in the main from regulatory solvency requirements. The requirements are relatively prescriptive, leaving only a limited amount of scope for accounting developments, although a number of modifications to the underlying solvency principles have been made for the purposes of accounting for life assurance by the Statement of Recommended Practice of the Association of British Insurers (the ABI SORP)—resulting in the financial statements of life assurers being prepared on the so-called Modified Statutory Solvency Basis (MSSB).

1.2　The MSSB basis of accounting has a number of distinctive features. They include:

(a)　*A non-standard liability model*—The liability model differs from the model that applies to other entities in at least three important respects:

　　(i)　Liabilities are recognised for legal obligations but not constructive obligations (such as constructive obligations in respect of terminal bonuses in with-profits funds). FRS 12 'Provisions, Contingent Liabilities and Contingent Assets' requires liabilities to be recognised both for legal obligations and constructive obligations.

　　(ii)　Recognised liabilities are measured on a particularly prudent basis. FRS 12 requires a best estimate measurement to be used.

　　(iii)　The Fund for Future Appropriations (FFA) is classified as a liability even though parts of it do not meet the definition of a liability set out in accounting standards.‡

(b)　*Deferred acquisition costs*—In part to compensate for this liability model, life assurance policy selling costs are recognised as assets (deferred acquisition costs).

(c)　*Profit recognition model*—The MSSB profit recognition model involves the use of statutory transfers from the with-profits fund and profit smoothing techniques such as the amortisation of deferred acquisition costs in line with margin earned. This is a very different profit recognition from the asset/liability framework that is now informing most developments in financial reporting.

---

*For example, Schedule 9A of the Companies Act 1985 implements the Directive for insurance companies and insurance groups. Schedules 1-6 of The Friendly Societies (Accounts and Related Provisions) Regulations 1994 implement the Directive for certain friendly societies.

†The legal framework in Great Britain is, as explained more fully in Appendix II, broadly similar to the framework that exists in Northern Ireland and the Republic of Ireland. However, for simplicity this appendix refers only to British legislation. Similarly, although the intention is that the FRS should apply in Great Britain, Northern Ireland and the Republic of Ireland, the text tends for simplicity to refer to 'UK entities', 'UK standards' etc rather than 'entities in the UK and the Republic of Ireland' and 'standards that apply in the UK and the Republic of Ireland'. However, the system of prudential regulation that applies in the UK differs from that that applies in the Republic of Ireland. so in that context 'UK' is not used to include 'the Republic of Ireland'.

‡The FFA represents the balance of surplus of a with-profits fund that has neither been declared as a bonus to policyholders nor distributed as profit to shareholders. The eventual allocation of the FFA between shareholders and policyholders will depend on future appropriations of bonus and profit, hence the name.

This reporting framework also does not reflect well the distinctive features of with-profits life assurance: the participatory nature of the entity's relationship with its policyholders; policyholders' expectations about future bonus declarations; the nature of the options granted and guarantees given; and the ownership and nature of any estate* and of the capital more generally.   **1.3**

The resulting financial statements do not report on life assurance activities in as meaningful a way as they might.   **1.4**

The Penrose Report

In March 2004 the Accounting Standards Board (the Board or the ASB) received a request from the Financial Secretary to the Treasury to initiate an urgent study into accounting for with-profits business by life insurers. That request was part of the Financial Secretary's response to the Report of the Equitable Life Inquiry, prepared by the Right Honourable Lord Penrose (the Penrose Report).   **1.5**

The Penrose Report criticised a number of aspects of existing with-profits accounting: **1.6**

(a) *The treatment of future bonuses.* The report found that the current practice of recognising (as part of the technical provision) a liability for bonuses declared, but not recognising a specific liability for accrued terminal bonuses was unsatisfactory. The conclusion was that the financial statements would not show a realistic position of the life office unless a liability was recognised for the constructive obligation in respect of terminal bonuses.

(b) *Reserves available to cover bonuses.* Insufficient information was provided about the amount of reserves available to meet expected future bonuses. The conclusion was that financial statements should include a disclosure that compares the value of the liability for such bonuses with the reserves available to cover them.

(c) *Changes during the period.* It was unsatisfactory that, under existing practice, life assurers could make important changes affecting policyholders without those changes being apparent from the financial statements. In particular, the report highlighted in this context changes in actuarial assumptions and reductions made to guaranteed benefits as a result of:

  (i) altering the mix of bonus between declared and final elements progressively towards terminal bonus; and
  (ii) changing policy conditions to reduce the scope of contractual benefits and increase the scope for allotting terminal bonus.

  It was suggested that the financial statements should provide an analysis of the movements over the year in the amount of realistic liabilities.

(d) *Complexity.* Addressing the complexity of life assurers' regulatory returns and financial statements and the inter-relationship between them, the report suggested that policyholders and other users should be provided with simplified summary versions of both reports. Furthermore, the objective in the longer-term should be to move to a single accounting basis for both reports.

(e) *The information needs of policyholders.* There was a danger in focusing exclusively on the information needs of investors when preparing financial statements covering life assurance products. Policyholders' interests needed to be taken into account; they were investors in the entity's products and their

---

*The estate of a with-profits fund is the excess of a fund's assets over its obligations—legal and constructive—to policyholders.

interests, in financial terms in with-profits funds, usually exceeded those of shareholders by a factor of about 9:1.

1.7   The Financial Secretary's letter to the Board requested that the Board's study into accounting for with-profits business should be made against the background of the developments in the Financial Services Authority's (FSA's) regulatory regime and the requirement for listed companies to use EU-adopted International Financial Reporting Standards (IFRS) in their consolidated financial statements from 1 January 2005.

The FSA's regulatory regime

1.8   Until recently, the system of prudential regulation for UK with-profits funds has been the basis that underlies Schedule 9A—the Statutory Solvency Basis (SSB). The FSA has, however, introduced a new system of prudential regulation for UK with-profits funds, which applies from 31 December 2004 to the UK with-profits funds of entities with UK with-profits liabilities of £500m or more. This new methodology is known as the Realistic Balance Sheet (RBS) approach.*†

1.9   The FSA has designed the RBS approach to be based on notions that are much closer than existing regulatory practice to the liability model in general financial reporting standards. For example, the policyholder liabilities are required to take into account both legal and constructive obligations, and they are required to be measured on a basis that is much closer than the current MSSB liability to FRS 12's best estimate approach.

1.10   The development of the RBS approach has implications for the way in which the existing legal requirements are interpreted and, as a result, means the Board has been able to contemplate making changes to life assurance accounting that would not have been possible hitherto. (This is explained more fully in paragraphs 4.47-4.65.)

1.11   The RBS approach therefore appears to provide both an opportunity and a means for the Board to improve life assurance accounting.

The move to IFRS

1.12   From 1 January 2005, listed UK entities will be required‡ to prepare their consolidated financial statements in accordance with EU-adopted IFRS, rather than UK standards and legal requirements. In addition, from that date most unlisted entities will be permitted to use EU-adopted IFRS, rather than UK standards and legal requirements, in their financial statements.

1.13   Entities reporting under EU-adopted IFRS are, by definition, not reporting under the existing UK legal requirements and, as such, are free of the constraints imposed on their accounting policies by the Companies Act 1985 (the Act). Thus, the move to

---

*'Realistic' is the FSA's term for the methodology it has developed. In using the term in the FRS, the Board is not intending to imply anything other than that the items involved have been calculated by applying the FSA's RBS methodology. There is, for example, no suggestion that entities should be required to use the term in their true and fair financial statements.

†The RBS approach has been implemented alongside the existing SSB) as part of a 'twin peaks' approach under which the higher of the RBS approach's 'realistic peak' and the SSB's 'regulatory peak' will be the regulatory requirement.

‡By EU Regulation 1606/2002.

EU-adopted IFRS provides a further opportunity for improvements in insurance accounting to be made. However, during the initial stages of this project the Board took the view that from 2005 those improvements would have to be made by the industry or by the International Accounting Standards Board (IASB) because the Board's standards would not apply to entities following EU-adopted IFRS. For that reason, the Board's focus initially was on the changes it could make in 2004 that would remain in place after 2005.

For UK reporting entities with life assurance activities, one of the key standards in 2005 for those following EU-adopted IFRS will be IFRS 4 'Insurance Contracts', which was issued in March 2004. Under IFRS 4, issuers of insurance contracts are permitted in the main to continue to use their pre-2005 accounting policies in preparing their financial statements from 2005 even if those policies do not meet the requirements of other IASB standards ('the grandfathering provisions'). However, if the entity wishes to change an accounting policy, it can do provided that the new accounting policy will make the financial statements more relevant to the economic decision-making needs of users and no less reliable, or more reliable and no less relevant to those needs. **1.14**

The Board viewed these grandfathering provisions as highly relevant to its project because they provided a means by which the Board could make changes to life assurance accounting policies that would remain in place for some time after 2005. In other words, although IFRS 4 itself makes few improvements to insurance accounting, the timing of its introduction provided a one-year window of opportunity for a national standard-setter to do so. **1.15**

IFRS 4 fulfils another important role. By setting out the criteria that need to be met if a new accounting policy is to be adopted, it provides an indication of the direction in which the IASB expects insurance accounting to develop. This enabled the UK Board to make changes to life assurance accounting and be reasonably confident that those changes would not be reversed by the IASB in the near future. **1.16**

APPROACH ADOPTED BY THE BOARD

A two-part project

Bearing in mind the opportunity offered by the development of the RBS approach to prudential regulation of with-profits insurance business and the timing constraint imposed by the move to EU-adopted IFRS in 2005, the Board concluded that its project should comprise two parts: **2.1**

(a) *To consider what improvements could be made to life assurance accounting in time for the 2004 accounts and to develop a standard requiring those improvements.* Within this timescale, it would not be realistic to make wholesale change to the existing insurance accounting framework nor would it be appropriate to do so ahead of phase 2 of the IASB's insurance project. However, it would be realistic to make limited improvements which could be implemented for 2004 reporting and would point in the direction of the further improvements the IASB has indicated it would like to see.

(b) *To develop views on the direction in which insurance accounting more generally should develop over the next few years and on the key issues that will need to be addressed in securing the changes necessary.* Although the Board may have less direct influence on the shape of insurance accounting from 2005, it intends to continue to play an active and influential role in phase 2 of the IASB's project and will therefore continue to develop its thinking on the issues that need to be addressed. Where the Board identifies potential improvements that it cannot introduce across the industry as a whole, it will recommend them to the IASB for consideration. In some cases, it might also incorporate them into UK standards.

2.2   In considering which issues it should attempt to address in the first part of the project, the Board recognised that, although the issues raised by Lord Penrose would represent an important part of its work, it would need to consider addressing other issues and concerns as well. The broad issues and concerns that the Board considered initially are summarised briefly in paragraphs 2.3-2.17 and those dealt with in this Financial Reporting Standard (the FRS) are explored more fully in sections 3-8 of this appendix.

Financial strength

2.3   As mentioned in paragraph 1.3, the existing reporting framework struggles to reflect in the financial statements a number of the distinctive features of with-profits life assurance. One of those features is the rather unusual nature of the capital resources involved. Although some of the capital is fungible, much of it is subject to a variety of restrictions as to its availability and use. Some of the capital is shareholders' capital but the ownership of some other capital—and for with-profits funds this capital can be very significant—is uncertain and is perhaps best viewed as being jointly owned by policyholders and shareholders. Unless the nature, fungibility and extent of the capital available to a life assurer is properly explained in the financial statements, users of those financial statements will struggle to understand the insurer's prospective ability to continue to treat customers fairly whilst meeting all other obligations to third parties and providing an appropriate and secure return to shareholders. In other words, they will struggle to understand the insurer's financial strength.

2.4   The Penrose Report also raised some concerns in this area, emphasising the importance of disclosing the amount of the reserves the insurer is holding against actual and contingent liabilities.

2.5   The Board therefore concluded that one of the issues it should seek to address through its limited improvements project was the provision of information about the financial strength of UK with-profits funds.

Liability accounting

2.6   The Board decided that another priority was to consider ways of improving the existing liability recognition, measurement and presentation model. This is one of the areas in which existing life assurance accounting is most out-of-step with general accounting principles. It is an issue that the Board highlighted in the statement it attached to the November 2003 revision of the ABI SORP; it is mentioned in the Penrose Report as a significant concern; and it is the aspect of with-profits life assurance accounting for which the FSA's new RBS approach has the most implications.

2.7   Another of the issues raised by the Board in its statement attached to the November 2003 revision of the ABI SORP concerned the balance sheet classification of the FFA. The Board decided to consider this issue in its limited improvements project (although it eventually decided not to address the matter in the FRS).

Options and guarantees

Many life funds over the last few years have experienced major reductions in their **2.8** capital position as a consequence of the need to fund options and guarantees provided to policyholders. These options and guarantees can take a variety of forms, and some expose the entity to insurance variables such as mortality and morbidity, while others expose the entity to financial variables such as market prices.

Historically, UK entities with life assurance activities have tended to recognise a **2.9** liability for an option or guarantee that exposes it to financial variables only if it is 'in the money'. The financial statements have, as a result, reported the impact on the estate and net assets of such options and guarantees as being more sudden and severe than might have been the case had the liability measurement basis taken appropriate account of the potential for future changes (for example, through stochastic modelling of possible outcomes or some form of fair valuing).*

The RBS approach requires the options and guarantees liabilities of large UK with- **2.10** profits funds to be measured at fair value or at a stochastically modelled value. This makes it reasonable to consider whether the liability should be measured on the same basis in the true and fair financial statements, and also whether the treatment in the financial statements of other options and guarantees (for example, those granted on overseas life assurance contracts) could be improved. As the Board has previously made clear the importance it attaches to treating options and guarantees properly, it decided to consider these issues further in its limited improvements project.

Profit recognition and performance reporting

The Board recognised that the existing profit recognition, measurement and pre- **2.11** sentation model used by insurers is in need of improvement. It was also conscious though that, in looking predominately at with-profits reporting, any improvements it made to the model would inevitably be only a partial solution to a wider problem. It therefore decided that, to the extent that changes to the balance sheet were to be proposed, it would address the consequential profit recognition and performance reporting issues but, that apart, profit recognition and performance reporting issues would not be considered in the first part of the project.

Complexity and lack of transparency

The financial statements of an insurance company or group are complex and difficult **2.12** for anyone who is not an expert to use. This complexity only partly derives from the nature of the business. The terminology used is not always helpful and the presentation of information calculated on different bases—without proper disclosure of how these different sets of information relate to each other—can be very confusing.

The complexity and lack of transparency of insurance financial statements was **2.13** highlighted in the Penrose Report, which criticised both the regulatory returns and the financial statements for not being readily understandable.

This is an important issue. The purpose of financial statements is to communicate **2.14** information. Financial statements that cannot be understood by a user with general financial knowledge, applying reasonable diligence, do not fulfil their purpose. However, the Board decided that it should not carry out a study of how the existing

*A stochastic modelling approach involves valuing the item by reference to the weighted average value under a large number of possible future market price scenarios.

formats and terminology might be improved during the first part of its work because the formats and terminology used were largely determined by legislation and legislative change was not feasible in 2004.

2.15   The Penrose Report concluded that another source of complexity was the existence of multiple statements—regulatory returns, true and fair financial statements, and embedded value supplementary information—prepared on different bases with no means for the user to navigate their way between the statements. This is a matter which the Board considered in its limited improvements project.

The use of embedded value in the primary financial statements

2.16   Generally speaking, entities with life assurance activities respond to the perceived inadequacies of MSSB financial statements by trying to focus users' attention on the value of in-force business. Some do this by supplementing the MSSB financial statements with information prepared on an embedded value basis. Some others recognise assets based on those embedded values in their primary financial statements and use them to drive the profit recognition model. This means that the same transactions are accounted for in the financial statements of different entities in fundamentally different ways.

2.17   Such inconsistencies are unsatisfactory, so the Board decided to consider the use of embedded value—even though the matter is a more general concern and is not specifically linked to with-profits reporting—in its limited improvements project in order to determine whether it was appropriate and possible to achieve greater consistency..

Summary

2.18   In summary, the Board decided to focus on the following issues in the first part—the limited improvements project part—of its work:

    (a)   the provision of information that helps users to assess the financial strength of UK with-profits funds (section 3);

    (b)   the liability model for with-profits policyholder liabilities (section 4);

    (c)   the balance sheet classification of the FFA (section 5);

    (d)   the treatment of options and guarantees not taken appropriately into account in measuring policyholder liabilities (section 6);

    (e)   recognising the value of in-force life assurance business (ie embedded value) in the primary financial statements (section 7); and

    (f)   the complexity caused by multiple statements prepared on different bases (section 8).

2.19   In July 2004 the Board issued Financial Reporting Exposure Draft (FRED) 34 'Life Assurance'. Sections 3 to 8 explain the issues the Board considered in developing the proposals in the FRED, as well as how the Board has addressed the main comments made on those issues by those responding to the FRED.

2.20   The other sections of this appendix discuss:

    (a)   other issues arising from the FRED 34 consultations (section 9);

    (b)   the memorandum of understanding and the application of the FRS by entities applying EU-adopted IFRS (section 10);

    (c)   future developments (section 11); and

    (d)   the ASB's advisory panel on life assurance (section 12).

FINANCIAL STRENGTH

Generally speaking, it is possible for users of financial statements to develop a good understanding of the financial strength of most entities from their balance sheet and supporting disclosures. This is possible because the capital of such entities is largely fungible. However, one of the unique features of with-profits life assurers is that their capital often comprises elements that exhibit widely different characteristics. These characteristics—which relate to the ownership, certainty of valuation and availability of use—mean that some analysis of the components of capital is needed to enable the entity's financial strength to be understood by both policyholders and shareholders. This is not information that the financial statements currently provide. **3.1**

At first, the Board considered the possibility of changing the presentation of the balance sheet to provide this information. For example, the entity's capital could be shown as a series of layers each subject to a different set of restrictions. However, the Board concluded that such a presentation would not be able to do justice to the capital structures that currently exist. What was needed was a disclosure that focused on the amount and nature of capital held by, or available to, the life assurer, and that showed where the capital is held and the extent to which it is available to other parts of the business. (The FRS refers to this disclosure as a 'capital statement'.) **3.2**

The remainder of section 3 discusses the main issues that the Board considered in developing its requirements on the capital statement. **3.3**

ED 7

The Board issued the FRED that preceded this FRS in the same month that the IASB issued ED 7 'Financial Instruments: Disclosures'. ED 7 proposed, inter alia, that entities should be required to disclose certain information about the amount of their capital resources, their target capital levels and the way they manage their capital. The proposal was that the final standard would be published early in 2005 and would be mandatory from 2007, although entities could adopt it from 2005 if they wished. The Board issued ED 7 as a UK exposure draft (FRED 33 'Financial Instruments: Disclosures') and proposed that it should be implemented as a UK standard when it is implemented internationally. **3.4**

A number of respondents to FRED 34 argued that, in view of the proposals in ED 7, the capital statement proposals in FRED 34 were superfluous. Some argued that the two sets of proposals merely set out alternative ways of achieving the same objective and, in the interests of convergence, FRED 34's proposals should be withdrawn in favour of ED 7's. However, the Board does not consider the proposals to be inter-changeable; although the disclosures described in FRED 34 would meet most of the proposed capital disclosure requirements set out in ED 7, the opposite would not be the case because an entity could comply with proposed requirements in ED 7 without providing any information about the fungibility of its capital. During the development of the FRED the Board saw the two sets of proposals as complementary because, while ED 7 proposed some important, extremely useful general disclosures, FRED 34 proposed extending those disclosures to highlight some specific factors of particular importance in the life assurance industry. In finalising the FRS, the Board has emphasised the complementary nature of the two sets of disclosures. **3.5**

Entity level or group level?

The Board took the view in developing the proposals in the FRED that, if a good understanding is to be obtained of a UK with-profits fund's overall financial **3.6** strength, its capital position needs to be put in the context of the consolidated group of which it is a part. In the Board's view, such a presentation ensures that due account is taken of the extent to which shareholder or other finance exists in other parts of the Group and might be available to the UK with-profits funds. The FRED proposed therefore that, if the reporting entity has general insurance and other activities, these should be included in the disclosure—grouped together but shown separately from the life funds—with an indication of the availability or otherwise of this capital. In doing so, the Board recognised that the complex structure of many of the largest insurance and bancassurer groups, with intra-group and inter-fund lending and investing arrangements, made it likely that the consolidation of the various individual capital positions would be complicated and consolidation adjustments could be significant. It believed however that this was itself relevant to an understanding of the different aspects of the entity's capital position. The contrast between the simplicity of the capital position of the large, single fund of a traditional UK mutual and the complex capital structure of a diversified global group was important and was of relevance to users.

3.7   Some of those responding to the FRED disagreed with this focus on group-wide information, particularly as the FRED also exempted some single entities that are part of groups from the need to include the capital disclosures in their individual financial statements. Those respondents argued that what policyholders needed was information about financial strength at the level of their individual fund and, because of materiality and the inevitable need to aggregate, the information provided at the entity level was the nearest policyholders would get to that. Some respondents also argued a group-wide presentation could be misleading if the funds are ring-fenced.

3.8   The Board has not been persuaded by these arguments for the following reasons:

(a)   Although prima facie a policyholders' interest lies at the individual fund level, it does not follow that policyholders are not interested in the financial strength of the group as a whole. Many groups seek to market on the basis of their group level financial strength and it is therefore reasonable to provide policyholders with an analysis that relates the position of the individual funds to the overall group capital position. Even if a group manages its individual funds on a strictly ring-fenced basis, it is of value to the policyholder to see the overall financial strength of the group and how 'their' fund fits in, thereby gaining some understanding of the likely financial imperatives that are going to govern the fund's management. Indeed, it is important for policyholders to know whether the group manages their fund on the basis of strict ring-fencing or on the basis of group-level financial strength (taking advantage of the benefit of financial diversification, for example). During discussions with major life assurers, the Board had both these diametrically opposing positions explained to it as the basis on which the capital position of that particular group was managed. Setting out which approach applies would be a key part of the narrative disclosures that should accompany the capital statement.

(b)   Most insurers manage their capital both at the individual fund level and at the group level. For example, an entity with most of its available capital resources tied up in funds that it cannot easily access (for example a UK with-profits fund) might need a capital injection to raise capital for other purposes even if the capital resources within particular funds are substantial. Users need information that helps them understand the interrelationship between the financial position of individual funds and the group's capital position. The great variety of intra-group financial arrangements (such as reinsurance, contingent loans, guarantees etc) that can apply means there will often need to be careful explanation of the consolidation adjustments that are made in producing the group level information.

Some respondents recognised the objective behind the capital statement but argued **3.9**
that the objective would not be achievable unless the statement reflected the benefits
of diversification. However, the fact that diversification benefits *are* particularly
important for some groups—though not for those that manage their funds on a
strictly ring-fenced basis—is one of the main reasons why it is essential for the
aggregate of the individual entities' capital positions to be clearly reconciled to the
group position as shown in the balance sheet. Without this reconciliation, there is a
significant risk of the capital statement being unable to be related to other aspects of
the group financial position.

As mentioned earlier, the FRED not only proposed that the capital statement should **3.10**
be prepared at a group level, it also proposed that some single entities should be
exempt from the requirement to provide the statement. The proposal was that the
exemption would apply to:

(a) an entity that is a wholly-owned subsidiary undertaking, if its ultimate or
intermediate parent entity includes a capital statement complying with the FRS
in its consolidated financial statements; and

(b) in a parent entity's own financial statements when presented together with the
parent's consolidated financial statements.

In the light of the comments received in response to the FRED, the Board recon- **3.11**
sidered the appropriateness of this exemption. The Board noted that, without the
exemptions, much of the information provided by the subsidiary or parent company
would be available to policyholders in the consolidated financial statements and, as
such, there would be some duplication if the exemptions were deleted. On the other
hand, it recognised that the information would often be provided at a higher level of
aggregation in the consolidated financial statements than in, say, the subsidiary's
financial statements and that some smaller funds would be 'visible' only at a subsidiary level.

In the Board's view, neither of the options available to it was ideal. It nevertheless **3.12**
decided, for pragmatic reasons, to retain the exemptions; entities would not be forced
to provide disclosures at a subsidiary level but also would not be prevented from
doing so if they considered the benefit of doing so justified the cost.

For consistency with other standards, the Board decided to amend the exemption for **3.13**
subsidiaries so that it applies to 90%-owned subsidiaries, rather than just wholly-
owned subsidiaries.

Level of aggregation

As the focus of the capital statement should be on the different types of capital the **3.14**
entity has, the statement needed to show a disaggregated view of capital. On the
other hand, showing each segment of capital and each restriction separately would,
in some cases, make the disclosure so voluminous that it would be of little value. A
balance needed to be found.

The Board took the view in the FRED that the primary focus should be on the **3.15**
individual UK with-profits funds (or, for an entity in the Republic of Ireland, on the
individual with-profits funds in the Republic of Ireland) because it is in that context
that the need for detailed information about financial strength is greatest. Respondents largely agreed with this view. Paragraph 34(a) of the FRS therefore requires
information about each UK with-profits fund to be shown separately if the fund is
material.

3.16   The FRED proposed that the information about the entity's other life assurance business should be provided separately for each material section of that business. It went on to propose that, for this purpose, a fund or business unit would be a separate section if the capital attributable to that business was subject to material restriction or limitation as to its availability to other parts of the business.

3.17   A number of respondents criticised this proposal. Some argued that the level and manner of aggregation it implied was not appropriate for their business; some argued that, bearing in mind that the capital in most business sections would be subject to some constraints, the aggregation principle proposed was not particularly useful. Some respondents were concerned about how the information on the separate sections would be interpreted, with some arguing that the aggregation of fungible capital should be permitted to avoid confusion and others arguing that aggregating capital that is subject to different restrictions implies it is fungible when it is not. Concerns were also raised about whether showing funds that had interdependencies separately would be helpful. It was also clear that there was some confusion as to how the restrictions over the use of capital would be portrayed.

3.18   The Board reconsidered its proposals in the light of the comments received, and decided that the FRS should be more flexible as to how the information about life assurance activities other than UK with-profits funds is presented. Paragraphs 34(b), 35 and 36 of the FRS now require that the disclosures show the extent to which the various components of capital are subject to constraints or are available to other parts of the business—how that is done is up to each entity. The result is that entities will be able to adopt a presentation that best suits their particular circumstances.

Should the capital statement focus on capital resources, or also show capital requirements or targets?

3.19   The FRED proposed that the capital statement should show not only an analysis of the entity's capital resources but also the regulatory capital requirements relevant to each section of that capital. Disclosing the regulatory capital requirements provided context for the information about capital resources. Furthermore, as the regulatory capital requirements impose restrictions on the use of capital in other parts of the business, including them in the disclosure helped focus attention on available capital *after meeting regulatory capital requirements*.

3.20   The proposal to require disclosure of the regulatory capital requirements in the capital statement was criticised by a significant number of respondents.

    (a)   Some commentators argued that the target capital levels set by management, rather than the regulatory capital requirements, should be disclosed because what matters most is the basis on which the business is being managed and that would be by reference to target capital. These commentators also pointed out that ED 7 proposed the disclosure of information about internally-set capital target levels.

    (b)   Some commentators argued, in a similar vein, that disclosing a single regulatory capital requirement for each section would be misleading in jurisdictions where there was more than one regulatory requirement or where the requirements comprise a series of action levels or trigger points. In such jurisdictions, it is not immediately clear which regulatory requirement would be the most useful to use in the capital statement. The FRED's suggestion—that in such circumstances the disclosure should focus on the minimum requirement—was thought by many to be inappropriate.

(c) Under the proposals in the FRED, the regulatory requirements shown would be calculated on different bases. This, some respondents argued, meant they were inconsistent and, as a result, not additive.

(d) Some commentators suggested that the Board should not adopt a regulatory approach because it would not be practicable to prepare the relevant numbers to the required quality until after the end of the annual statutory reporting process.

The Board has not accepted all these arguments. For example, although those arguing that the requirements are not calculated on a consistent basis and are therefore not additive are right in pointing out that the insurance industry is not as fortunate as the banks in having a common approach, the numbers nevertheless *are* the regulatory capital requirements and hence *are* relevant. Similarly, although there may be some practical difficulties in preparing the relevant numbers to the required quality at short notice, this is an argument for deferring the disclosure, not for abandoning it. **3.21**

The Board nevertheless concluded that the role of the regulatory capital require- **3.22** ments in the capital statement should be downgraded because a surplus of capital over the regulatory minimum is not a true surplus, and could even represent a shortfall below the target capital level; as a result, complex and lengthy notes would need to be provided to enable users to understand the true position. The regulatory capital requirements are just one of the constraints placed on the free use of capital. Therefore, rather than insist on the amount of the requirement to be disclosed for each business section disclosed separately in the capital statement, paragraph 45(a) of the FRS requires the capital statement to be supported by "narrative or quantified information on the regulatory capital requirements applying to each section of the business shown in the capital statement, or on the capital targets set by management for that section."

Clarity

In developing its proposals on the capital statement, the Board was very aware of the **3.23** comments in the Penrose Report about different pieces of information in the financial statements being prepared on different bases with no explanation of those differences. For that reason the Board considered it important to ensure that the information in the capital statement could be reconciled to the balance sheet. This matter is discussed in more detail in section 8.

Practicalities of obtaining information

The proposal in the FRED was that the capital statement should be provided for the **3.24** first time in the 2004 year-end financial statements. Some commentators expressed the view that, due in particular to the sequential process that is adopted by com-panies in the preparation of their year-end financial information—with the preliminary announcement and published financial statements preceding the reg-ulatory returns—it would not be possible to include in their 2004 year-end financial statements information that, currently, is only required to be disclosed in the reg-ulatory returns. This would be an issue in 2004 for information calculated on the FSA's RBS basis and for overseas regulatory information (which is often not pro-duced until much later in the year).

Although the decision to downgrade the role of the regulatory capital requirements **3.25** in the capital statement (see paragraph 3.22 above) changed the significance of this issue, it did not mean it was no longer a concern because:

(a)   the Board still envisaged that the available capital amounts shown in the capital statement would be calculated on a regulatory basis; and

(b)   some disclosures about the regulatory capital requirements would still be required.

3.26   The Board decided to defer the implementation of its capital statement disclosure requirement by one year to accounting periods ending on or after 23 December 2005.

(a)   As explained more fully in paragraphs 4.67–4.72 and section 10 of this appendix, the Board decided to defer for a year the changes it is making to the UK with-profits liability model. Having taken that decision, there were strong arguments for deferring the capital statement requirement as well.

(b)   Allowing entities a year in which to prepare for this disclosure would, the Board believed, give them time to experiment with different forms of presentation and find a presentation that best fits their circumstances.

(c)   The current expectation is that a standard based on ED 7 will be issued in 2005 and will be available for early adoption in accounting periods beginning on or after 1 January 2005. Deferring the capital statement requirements a year enables entities to implement the capital statement requirements at the same time as their ED 7 capital disclosures should they wish to do so.

Commercial sensitivity

3.27   Another concern that respondents raised was the commercial sensitivity of the information. The financial strength of an insurer is a key aspect of its customer proposition and is often used in marketing products. It is also of interest to shareholders. Requiring UK entities to disclose detailed information about the fungibility of their available capital when non-UK competitors in a similar position can remain silent or can point to an inappropriate indicator (such as the value of funds under management) would put UK entities at a disadvantage. Financial strength matters to current and prospective investors and policyholders, so putting an insurer at a competitive disadvantage could impact both on new business levels and on perception amongst the investor community.

3.28   The Board did not find these arguments persuasive. Given the importance of financial strength to the commercial success of an insurer, it is inevitable that the requirement for a capital statement will be viewed as sensitive by companies (and very relevant and important by users). It is true that different standards of financial reporting requirements have been and continue to be a problem. It does not follow, however, that entities that are more forthcoming in their disclosures are at a disadvantage compared to those that remain wrapped in a cloak of silence and ambiguity. The principal reason for the movement in Europe to the use of improved and international accounting standards is that markets have rewarded companies that have been open about their financial position and performance and discussed frankly the strategy options facing them. Regulators, too, have moved from believing that secrecy was an essential means of maintaining public confidence in the financial system to acknowledging that early identification and public discussion of problems is a surer way of avoiding potential crises. Experience also shows that better disclosures and management discussion by leading entities serve to educate users and create pressures on their competitors to emulate their example.

Communication to policyholders

3.29   The Penrose Report urged that policyholders, as well as shareholders, should be kept better informed on the financial strength of an insurer. It is outside the Board's remit to require this directly. However, the capital statement required by the FRS has been designed with the idea that it could be extracted from the financial statements and sent to policyholders on an annual basis—or included as an annual annex to the Principles and Practices of Financial Management (PPFM)*—together with an appropriate introduction as to its purpose and explanation as to its form.

Movements analysis

One of the concerns expressed in the Penrose Report was that financial statements **3.30** contain insufficient information on the changes over the accounting period in key numbers (such as liabilities) and the causes of those changes. As a result, changes that an insurer has made to assumptions and in policy might not be apparent to users of those financial statements.

The Board shares those concerns and, as a result, it proposed in the FRED that a **3.31** movements analysis should be provided in support of the proposed capital statement. That analysis should show how the capital position had developed in the period in the light of changes in assumptions and policies; the impact of new business, surrenders and maturities; and changes in asset mix. It should also be show a separate analysis for each category of capital or fund set out in the capital statement.

A number of respondents expressed concerns about the practicality of what the **3.32** FRED proposed. There were three common concerns. Two related to how the FRED proposed the movement during the year should be analysed.

(a) Respondents thought the difference between a change in assumption and a change in a management policy needed to be clarified and that guidance was needed on how to distinguish between the effect of an assumption change and the effect of a management policy caused by an assumption change. Additional guidance has now been provided in the FRS.

(b) Respondents also argued that the complexities of the stochastic models involved made it difficult to isolate the effect of new business on available capital and liability levels and that this would not be information they would need for management purposes. The FRS now does not require the effects of new business to be shown separately.

The third concern related to the difficulty of isolating the effect of any specific change **3.33** when the numbers involved are calculated on a stochastic basis. For example, the Board has been told by some entities that it will take them nearly a month to run the stochastic models necessary to estimate their 'realistic' liabilities. Their intention had been to run these models just at the end of each accounting period. However, in order to produce the FRED's proposed movements analysis it would be necessary to run the models after every change. That would involve a substantial amount of additional work.

(a) The Board considered this to be a short-term difficulty caused by an understandable reluctance on the part of preparers to use short-cut methods to estimate the effects of changes until the stochastic models used are better understood.

(b) In the Board's view, even if some relief needs to be given for a year or so until preparers are comfortable using short-cut methods, the longer-term objective should still be to require entities to provide a full, quantitative analysis of the reasons for the movements in available capital.

The PPFM is a new document that the FSA requires UK with-profits life funds to make available to their policyholders. It contains a description of the fund's investment management and bonus distribution policies.

3.34   The FRS therefore retains the disclosure proposed in the FRED (subject to the amendment described in paragraph 3.32(b) above). However, for the first year (ie for 2005 year-ends), significant flexibility is given as to the form the disclosure should take. The Board believed that this additional flexibility would ease significantly the practical difficulties that would otherwise arise in the first year of implementation.

LIABILITY ACCOUNTING

Existing accounting practice

4.1   As explained in Appendix II 'Note on legal requirements', most UK entities with life assurance activities are required to follow either the accounting requirements set out in Schedule 9A of the Companies Act 1985 (Schedule 9A) or requirements that are almost identical to those in Schedule 9A (for example, The Friendly Societies (Accounts and Related Provisions) Regulations 1994) in presenting their balance sheet information. The items in the prescribed format that relate in whole or in part to with-profits activities are:

Debit balances

(a)   *Investments*. Included within this item will be the aggregate fair value of the investments held within the with-profits fund.

(b)   *Prepayments and accrued income: Deferred acquisition costs (DACs)*. Selling a with-profits policy typically involves the insurer incurring significant up-front costs (acquisition costs). Under existing accounting practice, those costs are usually not charged immediately to the profit and loss account; instead, they are carried forward on the balance sheet and amortised over the period in which they are expected to be recoverable out of margins earned by the insurer from the policy at a rate commensurate with the pattern of such margins. The unamortised costs are shown on the balance sheet as 'deferred acquisition costs'.

(c)   *Reinsurers' share of technical provisions*. If the exposure on a with-profits policy has been reinsured, an asset may be recognised under this heading. The amount of any such asset will be determined by reference to the amount recognised as a liability for that reinsured risk and the nature of the reinsurance.

Credit balances

(d)   *Technical provision for long-term business*. Currently this item represents an extremely prudent provision for bonuses already declared and claims incurred but not yet reported. It is calculated in accordance with regulatory guidance (the MSSB basis).

(e)   *The FFA*. The FFA comprises all funds the allocation of which either to policyholders or shareholders has not been determined by the end of the financial year.

4.2   In its work on insurance liability accounting, the Board focused on:

(a)   *Recognition*—The technical provision for long-term business currently recognised takes into account the insurer's legal obligations to policyholders (for example, to pay declared bonuses), but not its constructive obligations (for example, in respect of future bonuses).

(b)   *Measurement*—The liability to policyholders that is recognised (under technical provisions for long-term business) is measured using extremely prudent (and therefore biased) estimates; under general accounting principles a best estimate measurement basis is usually used.

(c) *Presentation*—The FFA is presented in the balance sheet amongst liabilities, even though significant elements of the FFA appear not to meet the definition of a liability.

Reporting entities that have insurance business but are not subject to Schedule 9A requirements or the equivalent—for example, bancassurers and some retail groups—tend to include the assets arising from their insurance business on one line of the balance sheet and the liabilities arising from their insurance business on another. Those recognising the value of in-force life assurance business in their primary financial statements also recognise, on a separate line in the balance sheet, an asset that represents the value of in-force business.* The analysis included in the notes of liabilities tends to follow Schedule 9A conventions, so a technical provision for long-term business and an FFA are shown. As such, the recognition, measurement and presentation liability issues that arise in Schedule 9A financial statements also arise in the context of these statements. **4.3**

The remainder of this section focuses on the recognition and measurement issues; the presentation issue is addressed in section 5. **4.4**

FRS 12

The liability recognition and measurement principles that apply to most entities are those set out in FRS 12. Liabilities are required to be recognised when: **4.5**

(a) an entity has a present obligation (legal or constructive) as a result of a past event;

(b) it is probable that a transfer of economic benefits will be required to settle the obligation; and

(c) a best estimate of the expenditure required to settle the present obligation at the balance sheet date can be determined reliably.

However, FRS 12 does not apply to provisions, contingent liabilities and contingent assets that arise in insurance entities from contracts with policyholders. There were two main reasons for this exemption: the constraints imposed by Schedule 9A and the uncertainty as to how to apply the notion of a constructive obligation to with-profits business because of the ill-defined nature of the obligations owed to with-profits policyholders. **4.6**

Although there may have been difficulties in applying FRS 12 to with-profits obligations, the Board has never doubted that the principles in the standard are just as applicable to those obligations as to any other obligation. In its view, policyholder liabilities should be recognised for constructive obligations, not just legal obligations, and those liabilities should be measured on a best estimate basis, rather than on an overly prudent basis. **4.7**

The objective of the Board's work on insurance liability accounting has been to identify improvements that point in the direction in which insurance accounting is likely to develop and are capable of being implemented quickly. In the Board's view it is clear that the direction in which insurance liability accounting will develop will be to converge on the principles in FRS 12. However, the Board did not believe that it was possible to remove the FRS 12 scope exemption for insurance contracts without developing a substantial amount of additional guidance and without **4.8**

Embedded value is discussed further in section 7 of this appendix.

addressing certain key issues—neither of which the Board would have been able to do in the time available for this project.

The RBS approach

4.9   Having concluded that it was not practicable in the short-term to remove the FRS 12 exemption for with-profits business, the Board considered what other options were available to it. In its view, any approach adopted needed to meet the following criteria:

(a)   If improvements are to be made in the near-future, time constraints suggest that they would have to be based either on a method that already exists and is widely used or on a new method for which preparations for implementation are already well underway.

(b)   If the direction in which insurance liability accounting should develop is towards the principles in FRS 12, it seems reasonable to suppose that any change in the liability model that is in the direction of those principles will be an improvement, as long as it does not bring with it offsetting disadvantages. Any change being considered therefore needs to be closer to FRS 12 than the existing basis.

(c)   Any proposed new liability model would need to be consistent with the relevant legal requirements and capable of being implemented in true and fair financial statements in the timescales envisaged by the project.

4.10   The Board saw the FSA's RBS approach as the only approach that might meet all these criteria.

Is the 'realistic' liability closer to the FRS 12 basis than the existing basis?

4.11   The Board therefore examined the RBS method in detail to determine whether it was, in theory at least, an improvement on the existing basis.

4.12   The RBS method involves restating the assets and liabilities of a with-profits fund onto a 'realistic' basis. The FSA's rules envisage that the 'realistic' liability* will comprise the 'with-profits benefits reserve' and 'future policy-related liabilities'.

(a)   The most significant element is the with-profits benefits reserve, which can be calculated in one of two ways: the retrospective method (ie asset share) or the prospective benefit method (ie the bonus reserve approach).

(b)   Where not already taken into account in the with-profits benefits reserve, the future policy-related liabilities, among other things, add to the benefits reserve provisions for:

(i)   future costs of options and guarantees, of smoothing, and of non-contractual commitments and other amounts needed to ensure that customers are treated fairly;

(ii)   any past miscellaneous surplus or deficit that the entity intends to attribute to the benefits reserve and any future planned enhancements to the benefits reserve; and

(iii)   other long-term insurance liabilities.

4.13   The objective of the calculation is to estimate the discounted value of future payments on policies in force.

This appendix uses the term "'realistic' liability" as short-hand for the 'realistic value of liabilities', which is the term used in the FRS.

Thus, the liability is not restricted to legal obligations—constructive obligations are **4.14** taken into account as well—and the liability is not measured on an extremely prudent basis. This is similar to FRS 12's approach. However:

(a) there are a number of detailed differences in approach that the Board explored before concluding that the 'realistic' liability is an improvement, for accounting purposes, on the existing basis. These are considered in paragraphs 4.15-4.19;

(b) the estimate of future payments to be made on in-force policies used in the 'realistic' liabilities calculation takes into account the fair value of the investments held in the with-profits fund (because the future payments will, by-and-large, in normal circumstances be a distribution of the part of the fund that does not represent the estate). If some assets are taken into account in calculating the 'realistic' liability but are not recognised in the financial statements—or are not measured on the same basis—it could be argued that there will be a mismatch between the asset and liability sides of the balance sheet. The Board's approach to this issue is set out in paragraphs 4.20-4.31; and

(c) the FSA is requiring initially only some with-profits funds—those UK with-profits funds of entities with UK with-profits liabilities that are at least £500m in size—to implement the RBS method. RBS information is likely therefore to be available initially for only those funds. The implications of this are considered in paragraphs 4.32-4.35.

Differences between a 'realistic' liability and an FRS 12 liability

With most UK with-profits policies, when a bonus is declared an allocation is made **4.15** both to policyholders and to shareholders. (For example, assume that policyholders and shareholders share fund profits on a 90:10 basis: if a bonus to policyholders of £90 is declared, an allocation of £10 will be made to shareholders.) When calculating the provision to be made for constructive obligations in respect of additional undeclared bonuses, the RBS approach requires both the constructive obligation to policyholders and the related shareholder allocation (the shareholders' share of undeclared bonus) to be included in the 'realistic' liability. Under FRS 12, the shareholders' share of undeclared bonus would not be treated as a liability. If the shareholders' share of undeclared bonus was to be left in the amount recognised for policyholder liabilities, that liability would always be overstated and in many cases that overstatement would be significant. However, as it appears to be a relatively straightforward matter to eliminate the shareholders' share of the undeclared bonus from the 'realistic' liability, this appears not to create any difficulties for the possible use of 'realistic' liabilities in true and fair financial statements.

The FSA's rules make it clear that, in estimating future payments to be made on in- **4.16** force policies in order to estimate the 'realistic' liability, account should be taken of any intention of management to enhance (or reduce) permanently allocations to policyholders. Under FRS 12 such an intention would create a constructive obligation only where:

(a) an established pattern of past practice, published policies or a sufficiently specific current statement has meant that the entity has indicated to other parties that it will accept certain responsibilities; and

(b) as a result, the entity has created a valid expectation on the part of those other parties that it will discharge those responsibilities.

Thus a management intention to enhance (or reduce) allocations to policyholders might be reflected in the 'realistic' liability even though it does not give rise to a constructive obligation as defined by FRS 12.

4.17   There are also potential differences in the way that options and guarantees are measured. Under existing generally applicable accounting principles, options and guarantees giving rise to liabilities would usually be measured either on a best estimate basis or at fair value; under the RBS method they can be measured at either fair value or at a stochastically modelled value. Although the stochastically modelled value will often be the closest approximation to fair value that is available, it is not the same thing.*

4.18   Another apparent difference between the 'realistic' liability and the FRS 12 liability is the treatment of future premiums and future investment gains. Under the RBS method, if the 'realistic' liability is being determined by estimating the future payments to be made on in-force business, the entity will project the eventual outcome (using, inter alia, the expected rate of future investment gains) and deduct from that the expected future premiums. Although this is the technically most accurate way of estimating the future payments to be made on in-force business, it does involve the anticipation of future events.

4.19   The Board's understanding is that there is no easy way to adjust for the potential differences described in paragraphs 4.16-4.18 because the differences go to the core of the methodology used. Therefore, if the RBS method is to be used as a basis for insurance liability accounting, it has to be used with the 'potential differences' unresolved. The Board's judgement in developing the FRED was that, despite the potential differences, the 'realistic' liability would still be closer than the existing liability to FRS 12 and is therefore to be preferred. Few of those responding to the FRED disagreed with this view.

Potential balance sheet mismatches

4.20   In order to estimate the 'realistic' liability, it is necessary to estimate the future payments to be made on in-force policies. That estimate will need to take into account the fair value of all the investments in the with-profits fund since it is the overall financial strength of the fund that will be taken into account when determining bonuses. If non-participating business has been written in the with-profits fund, that business will be one of the with-profits fund's investments, and the fair value of that investment will be one of the fair values to be taken into account in estimating the amount of the 'realistic' liability. It seems to follow from this that, if 'realistic' liabilities are to be recognised, the fair value of non-participating business written in the with-profits fund—referred to in this appendix as the value of in-force, non-participating business (or the VIF of non-participating business)—needs to be recognised as well.

4.21   The VIF of non-participating business is, in effect, an embedded value. The Board has been asked to consider the merits of embedded value methodologies several times in the past and on each occasion has concluded that it could not support their use in true and fair financial statements. For that reason, when faced with the VIF of non-participating business issue, the Board's response was to consider whether recognition of the VIF could be avoided.

4.22   It could be argued that the basis on which the assets were being recognised and measured ought not to matter. FRS 12 takes no account of the basis of asset recognition and measurement; it focuses exclusively on the present obligations the entity has as a result of a past event to transfer economic benefits. On that analysis, the notion of a mismatch between assets and liabilities would not exist and there

The measurement of options and guarantees is discussed further in section 6.

would be no reason why the VIF of non-participating business would need to be recognised just because the 'realistic' liability is recognised.

Another way to look at the issue is to ask how one should account for an obligation **4.23** to transfer to another party some or all of the valuable benefit to be derived from an item that is not recognised on the balance sheet—because, unless either the item was recognised on the asset side of the balance sheet or that element of the obligation is measured at nil, there would be a mismatch. For example, assume that an entity enters into an arrangement that involves it agreeing to pay a specified percentage of the next five years' profits to a third party. As future profits are not usually considered to be assets, they would not be recognised on the balance sheet; nor therefore is the liability under generally accepted practice.

The simplest treatment to adopt would be to show the VIF of non-participating **4.24** business as an asset and to recognise as a liability the full amount of the 'realistic' liabilities. Under this approach the 'realistic' liabilities would be clearly shown, and the fair value of the investments being held against that liability would be shown on the asset side of the balance sheet. This was the approach proposed in the FRED.

Some respondents argued however that the VIF asset does not meet the definition of **4.25** an asset and therefore should not be recognised on the balance sheet. Others argued that an insurance contract might meet the definition of an asset; the key question for them was whether measuring that asset by reference to the VIF of non-participating business would be appropriate bearing in mind that the value was an embedded value and the Board had not previously permitted the use of embedded values in the financial statements. As will be explained later in this section of the appendix, the Board has decided to defer implementation of the FRS until 2005, which has meant that the implications for the FRS of EU-adopted IFRS need also to be taken into account.

(a) The Board's view is that it may be difficult to recognise the VIF asset in full—and perhaps even at all—in financial statements prepared in accordance with EU-adopted IFRS if that VIF asset is recognised for the first time in 2005 financial statements.

    (i) IFRS 4 does not permit the introduction of new accounting policies in 2005 that involve including a value for future investment risk margins (and for investment management fees in excess of fair value) in an embedded value. It is possible that the amount at which the VIF asset has been measured for regulatory purposes would include some amounts for such items.

    (ii) The effect of paragraph 11 of IAS 8 'Accounting Policies, Changes in Accounting Estimates and Errors' is that entities are required to refer to and consider the applicability of "the definitions, recognition criteria and measurement concepts for assets" set out in the IASB's 'Framework for the Preparation and Presentation of Financial Statements' (the IASB's Framework). The VIF asset probably would not qualify for recognition on the balance sheet as an asset under the IASB's Framework, although some might argue that the reference to the need to "consider the applicability of" the IASB's Framework, coupled with IFRS 4's acceptance of the recognition of embedded value assets makes the position much less clear cut than that.

(b) In theory similar difficulties would arise for an entity preparing its financial statements in accordance with UK standards and legal requirements as the FRS would contain IFRS 4's embedded value restrictions and the Board's Framework (the 'Statement of Principles for Financial Reporting') is similar to the IASB's. However, the Board's Framework does not form part of the hierarchy of authoritative accounting literature that preparers are required to take into account.

4.26   An alternative approach more in keeping with the discussion in paragraph 4.23 would be to deduct the VIF of non-participating business from liabilities. Such an approach could be justified on the grounds that the liabilities would be calculated by taking into account the value of the fund's investments (including the VIF of non-participating business); if it is not appropriate to recognise the VIF of non-participating business as an asset, its effect on the liabilities should be removed. As one element of the VIF of non-participating business is often an amount to compensate for the excessive prudence included in the measurement of the non-participating business liabilities, deducting the VIF of non-participating business from liabilities would have the effect of netting off that compensation for over-prudence against the over-prudent liability, which seems reasonable.

(a)   In an ideal world, when applying this approach one would deduct that part of the VIF of non-participating business included in the policyholder liabilities from the 'realistic' liability number, that part of the VIF of non-participating business included in the FFA from the FFA, and that part of the VIF of non-participating business relating to the excessive prudence included in the non-participating liabilities from those liabilities. However, the Board's understanding is that it will seldom be practicable to allocate the VIF of non-participating business in this way.

(b)   Another approach might be to deduct the whole of the VIF of non-participating business from policyholder liabilities, or alternatively to deduct the whole of the VIF from the FFA. The Board rejected both these alternatives, believing that neither method represented faithfully the actual underlying position (unless by coincidence). As such, the resulting information could be misleading.

(c)   The Board then considered the possibility of deducting the VIF of non-participating business from the aggregate of policyholder liabilities and the FFA, while still displaying separately on the face of the balance sheet all three items. The Board concluded that such a presentation—showing the three elements separately—was superior to showing a single (net) number of the balance sheet (supported by a breakdown of the net number in the notes) because the three elements are so different in nature.

4.27   Such an approach appears consistent with the requirements of EU-adopted IFRS, especially as those standards contain flexibility as to the liability model to be adopted in accounting for insurance. However, it is not clear that such an approach could be reconciled with the requirements set out in Schedule 9A , which appear not to contemplate that amounts not calculated in accordance with the legal requirements could be shown as deductions from balance sheet items that have been calculated in accordance with those requirements (ie policyholder liabilities and the FFA).

4.28   On the basis of the above analysis, it would appear that the 'asset presentation' approach described in paragraphs 4.24 and 4.25 might be the only option available for financial statements prepared in accordance with UK standards and legal requirements, while the 'liability presentation' approach described in paragraphs 4.26 and 4.27 might be the appropriate option for entities prepared in accordance with EU-adopted IFRS. Faced with the prospect of having to permit a choice on the issue, the Board considered whether it might be preferable to abandon the proposal to include 'realistic' liabilities on the balance sheet.

The Board has always understood that the improvement it is seeking to make to **4.29** insurance accounting through the recognition of 'realistic' liabilities on the balance sheet is just one step on what will be a long journey for insurance accounting. The improvement tackles a number of issues (such as the recognition of liabilities based on legal obligations only and not constructive obligations, the use of overly prudent measures and the recognition as assets of deferred acquisition costs), but leaves some other issues to be addressed another day. The objective throughout has been to ensure that the benefits (ie the advantages gained by tackling the various issues) continue to outweigh the disadvantages (ie the unresolved issues). The Board believes that this continues to be the case regardless of whether the asset or liability presentation approach is adopted.

The other issue that arose from FRED 34 concerned the extent to which the VIF of **4.30** non-participating business has actually been taken into account in determining the amount of the 'realistic' liabilities. The FRED stated that the VIF of non-participating business could be recognised "to the extent that...the determination of the realistic value of liabilities ...takes account of this value". The objective of this statement was to prevent entities from recognising the VIF of non-participating business if it was not taken into account in determining 'realistic' liabilities. However, a number of respondents pointed out that there would generally be no direct link between the value of the VIF of non-participating business and the value of 'realistic' liabilities; in other words, if the former increased by a certain amount, it would not follow that the latter would increase by the same amount. The relationship between the two would be rather more indirect. Respondents were concerned that the FRED expected a direct link between the two to be present before it permitted the VIF of non-participating business to be recognised. The FRS has been amended to make it clear that a direct link of this kind is not expected and that the amount of the VIF to be recognised is not restricted to the value taken into account in determining the amount at which to measure the liabilities.

A similar potential mismatch situation to the VIF issue discussed above arises where **4.31** the with-profits fund has an investment in a subsidiary undertaking. In some cases that subsidiary will be valued for the purposes of estimating the 'realistic' liability at a market value or other value in excess of the net amount at which the subsidiary is included in the consolidated balance sheet. For similar reasons to those outlined above, the Board concluded that in such circumstances a mismatch could be avoided only by allowing the recognition as part of the with-profits fund of the excess of the amount at which it is valued for regulatory purposes over the amount at which it would normally be included in the consolidated balance sheet.

Implications of the FSA limiting the application of its RBS method

Initially, only entities with UK with-profits life liabilities of at least £500m will be **4.32** required by the FSA to implement the RBS method, and then only for their UK with-profits funds; the method will not have to be adopted for smaller firms or for other UK life funds or any overseas life funds. It is understood that this means initially between thirty and forty large UK funds will be applying the RBS method. They will together represent approximately 95% in value of UK with-profits funds, but probably less than 50% in value of all UK life office funds.

When the Board was developing FRED 34, it considered the possibility of including **4.33** within the scope of its 'realistic' liability requirement some or all of the funds that are not within the scope of the FSA's RBS regime. However, at that time the proposal was that the Board's requirement would be implemented for 2004 year-ends and the Board took the view that the FSA was in the best position to judge how practicable it is to expect a fund to apply the RBS method in 2004 and had the FSA thought it possible to apply the RBS method more widely in 2004, it would have done so.

4.34　Later, when it became apparent that the FRS would not be implemented until 2005 year-ends, the Board considered the possibility again. However, the FSA had no immediate plans at that time to extend the scope of its RBS requirements or of the other FSA requirements that make it possible to apply the notion of a constructive obligation to with-profits business. That would have meant that the Board would have had to develop substantial additional guidance of its own. While that was feasible given time, it was not feasible given that the Board had decided that the FRS had to be finalised before the end of 2004.

4.35　That meant that, if the Board were to require 'realistic' liabilities to be used in the true and fair financial statements, it would have to accept that 'realistic' liabilities would be used only for the funds required by the FSA to prepare RBS information. The Board considered whether a 'partial' implementation of this kind of accounting was appropriate. If the amount currently recognised for policyholder liabilities had been calculated on a consistent basis, that might have represented a powerful argument for not adopting a partial implementation approach. However, Schedule 9A does not require uniform accounting policies to be adopted, and local regulatory constraints mean that full advantage of this relief is often taken. As such, requiring the UK with-profits liabilities of some entities to be calculated using the RBS method would therefore not introduce inconsistency or additional diversity in those entities' accounting. It would, however, mean that an important element of the amount of the total liability would be calculated on a basis closer to that of FRS 12.

Summary

4.36　The Board examined the RBS method to determine whether it was, in theory at least, an improvement on the existing basis. It concluded that:

(a)　there were differences between the 'realistic' liability basis (as amended to exclude the shareholders' share of undeclared bonus) and FRS 12;

(b)　in order to state the with-profits assets and liabilities on the same basis, if a 'realistic' liability is to be recognised on the balance sheet it will be necessary also to recognise the value of in-force business written in the with-profits fund if that business has been taken into account in determining the 'realistic' liability. A similar adjustment would also be made if the amount of the 'realistic' liability takes into account, for an investment that the with-profits fund has in a subsidiary undertaking, a value that is in excess of the amount at which that investment is shown in the consolidated balance sheet; and

(c)　it is not practicable initially to require the whole of the policyholder liability to be calculated on an RBS basis.

4.37　In the Board's view it would nevertheless still be an improvement for 'realistic' liability amounts to be used wherever they were available.

Implications of recognising 'realistic' liabilities in the balance sheet for other balance sheet and profit and loss items

4.38　Recognising 'realistic' liabilities in the balance sheet has implications for a number of other balance sheet items and, potentially, the profit and loss account.

Reinsurers' share of technical provisions

If the exposure on a with-profits policy has been reinsured, an asset called **4.39** "Reinsurers' share of technical provisions" will be recognised. That asset will be measured at an amount that reflects the amount recognised as a liability for that reinsured risk. Therefore, if the basis used to determine the amount of the liability is to change, so must the basis used for the reinsurance asset.

Deferred acquisition costs

Under MSSB accounting, where liabilities are measured on an excessively prudent **4.40** basis, acquisition costs are deferred in order to reduce the distortion to reported financial performance that results from overly prudent provisioning. Under the RBS approach, the need to recover acquisition costs incurred is taken into account in the estimate of future bonus levels used to calculate the amount of the 'realistic' liability, so it would be inappropriate to continue to defer such costs.

Tax effects of the proposed changes

It would also be necessary to account fully for the tax effects of the changes described **4.41** above.

Implications for the FFA and for the profit and loss account

The implications of the changes suggested for the FFA and the profit and loss **4.42** account also needed to be considered. (To summarise, those suggestions involve, for the balance sheet items relating to a UK with-profits fund falling within the scope of the FSA's RBS method:

(a) adjusting the liability onto a 'realistic' basis and making consequential adjustments to any reinsurance assets;

(b) removing the related deferred acquisition costs from the balance sheet;

(c) recognising the value of non-participating in-force business written in the with-profits fund;

(d) recognising the amount by which the value of an interest in a subsidiary undertaking held in the with-profits fund as estimated for the purposes of the 'realistic' liability calculation exceeds the net amount that would otherwise have been included in the consolidated balance sheet; and

(e) adjustments to reflect the consequential tax effects of the above adjustments.)

The Board took the view in developing the FRED that, in the case of an entity with **4.43** shareholders, all these adjustments should be made to the profit and loss account with an offsetting transfer to the FFA. That would mean that, for such an entity, the proposals would have no direct net effect on the profit and loss account or share-holders' funds. Mutuals have no shareholders, and all the surplus is attributable to policyholders (though not yet allocated to specific policyholders). In some cases that retained surplus account is called 'the FFA'. The FRED therefore proposed for mutuals that the adjustment to liabilities should be offset by a direct transfer to or from this retained surplus account. Few of those responding to the FRED disagreed.

Shareholders' interest in the liability for undeclared bonuses

The RBS method requires a liability to be set up for a life assurer's constructive **4.44** obligation in respect of additional bonuses. For the FSA's purposes, that liability is required to include the shareholders' share of the undeclared additional bonus but, as explained in 4.15, the FRS requires this shareholders' share to be excluded from the liability recognised in the financial statements. The effect of this is that for financial reporting the shareholders' share would remain in the FFA.

4.45 Some commentators argue that the shareholders' share should be treated as part of shareholders' funds. They reason that:

(a) if the FFA is supposed to contain only funds the allocation of which has not been determined, and

(b) the undeclared additional bonuses to which the constructive obligation relates is deemed to have had its allocation,

the shareholders' interest in those undeclared bonuses should also be deemed to have been allocated—which means it should be excluded from the FFA.

4.46 However, in most cases the amount that would be allocated to shareholders is not fixed until the bonus is declared. The terms of the policy often state that the entitlement of shareholders is up to 10% but there are examples of shareholders taking less than 10% and in some cases not taking anything at all. In addition, as explained in more detail in section 5, providing for the 'realistic' liability does not mean that the balance of the FFA represents equity. After meeting policyholders' reasonable expectations the FFA will still include material elements of surplus the ownership of which remains uncertain. For that reason the Board believes it appropriate to leave the shareholders' share in the FFA.

The legal position

4.47 The form and content of insurance financial statements are the subject of detailed legal requirements.* A number of those requirements have in the past been cited as constraining the ability of insurance entities to improve their liability model. Therefore, when the Board was developing the FRED it considered the implications of those requirements for the balance sheet changes it was contemplating making. In particular it considered the following issues:

(a) If 'realistic' liabilities are to be recognised in the balance sheet for some UK with-profits funds, for some funds the technical provision would comprise just liabilities arising out of legal obligations and in other cases it would also include liabilities arising out of constructive obligations. Does the law permit the inclusion of liabilities arising out of constructive obligations in the technical provision and, if so, does it also permit the inclusion of such liabilities for some funds but not others?

(b) Another implication of recognising 'realistic' liabilities in the balance sheet for some UK with-profits funds is that some liabilities included in the technical provision would be measured using an extremely prudent basis and some would not. Does the law permit liabilities to be included in the technical provision on a less prudent basis than at present and, if so, does it also permit some liabilities to be measured on that less prudent basis while some others are measured on the existing extremely prudent basis?

(c) If a 'realistic' liability is being recognised for a particular fund, the intention is that the recognition of an asset for deferred acquisition costs arising on that fund would be prohibited. Is that consistent with the legal requirements?

As explained more fully in Appendix II, the detailed requirements that apply to British insurance entities are either contained in or almost identical to those contained in Schedule 9A of the Companies Act 1985. Similar requirements apply to insurance entities in Northern Ireland and the Republic of Ireland.

(d)   Are there any legal difficulties in recognising the value of in-force non-parti-
      cipating business written in the with-profits fund or the value of an interest in a
      subsidiary undertaking in excess of the net amount that would otherwise have
      been included in the consolidated balance sheet?

The Board's view at the time that it was developing the FRED was that there were no   **4.48**
legal difficulties arising from any of those issues. The Board has since received legal
advice that confirms that view. It has also considered the views expressed by
respondents as to the meaning of some of Schedule 9A's requirements but has not
changed its view that the changes it is making to the insurance liability model (and
the consequential changes that are being made to other balance sheet items) are
consistent with Schedule 9A's requirements.

The Board's detailed analysis of the issues highlighted above is set out in the   **4.49**
paragraphs that follow.

Including constructive obligations in the technical provision

Currently, the liability to policyholders recognised in the technical provision for   **4.50**
long-term business relates only to legal obligations owed to policyholders; it does
not include constructive obligations in respect of additional bonuses. Some
commentators argue that the law prohibits the inclusion in the technical provision of
liabilities for bonuses not yet declared. That may well have been the case in the past,
but the Board believes that the development of the RBS method and, with it, a means
of applying FRS 12's constructive obligations notion to UK with-profits business has
had the effect of making possible a wider range of interpretations of the legal
restrictions than hitherto. One consequence of this is that it is now reasonable to
interpret the law as permitting the inclusion of liabilities for additional bonuses in the
technical provision. The analysis leading to this conclusion is set out in the following
paragraphs.

Paragraph 16 of Schedule 9A requires "all liabilities and losses which have arisen or   **4.51**
are likely to arise in respect of the financial year" to be taken into account in
determining the amount at which to show items in the financial statements. This
makes it clear that a liability should not be ignored; the Board believes it also means
that all liabilities that have been identified should be recognised on the balance sheet.
This interpretation seems to be supported by note 21 of the balance sheet format in
Schedule 9A, which states that the long-term business provision shall comprise "the
actuarially estimated value of the company's liabilities (excluding technical provisions
[included under 'Technical provisions for linked liabilities']), including bonuses
already declared and after deducting the actuarial value of future premiums."

(a)   The reference to "bonuses already declared" appears not to be restrictive
      because it is preceded by the word 'including', which implies that the list is not
      exhaustive.
(b)   The reference to the provision comprising "the company's liabilities" suggests
      that, if a liability is identified, note 21 expects it to be included in the long-term
      business provision. Under the MSSB basis the only liabilities identified were for
      bonuses already declared; under the RBS method liabilities are also identified in
      respect of additional bonuses not yet declared.

Paragraph 46(3) of Schedule 9A states that the computation of the long-term busi-   **4.52**
ness provision "shall be made annually by a Fellow of the Institute or Faculty of
Actuaries on the basis of recognised actuarial methods, with due regard to the
actuarial principles laid down in Council Directive 92/96/EEC." This reference to

Council Directive 92/96/EEC is in effect a reference to Directive 2002/83/EC.*
Article 20 of that Directive states, inter alia, that the amount of such technical
provisions "shall be calculated by a sufficiently prudent prospective actuarial
valuation, taking account of all future liabilities as determined by the policy
conditions for each existing contract, including: all guaranteed benefits, including
guaranteed surrender values; bonuses to which policy holders are already either
collectively or individually entitled, however those bonuses are described—vested,
declared or allotted; all options available to the policy holder under the terms of the
contract; expenses, including commissions, taking credit for future premiums due..."

(a) Again, the use of the word 'including' means that the list at the end of this
quote is not restrictive and, therefore, not significant. The technical provision
must include bonuses to which policyholders are already entitled, but could
also include other amounts relating to future bonuses. This is reinforced by the
explanation in the Article (paragraph 1D) that "in the case of participating
contracts, the method of calculation for technical provisions may take into
account, either implicitly or explicitly, future bonuses of all kinds, in a manner
consistent with the other assumptions on future experience and with the current
method of distribution of bonuses."

(b) The reference to "taking account of all future liabilities" is significant in that it
makes it clear that no liability should be ignored. 'Taking account of' is
however a rather imprecise term open to interpretation in different ways. One
interpretation which the Board believes is reasonable—though not necessarily
the *only* interpretation that is reasonable—is that the paragraph requires all
liabilities to be recognised in the balance sheet.

4.53 Paragraphs 4.50-4.52 analyse the legal requirements dealing with the items to be
included in the long-term business provision. The legal requirements as to the
content of the FFA are also relevant because, if an item is required to be included in
the FFA, it cannot also be included in the long-term business provision. Note 19 of
the balance sheet format in Schedule 9A states that the FFA should comprise "all
funds the allocation of which either to policyholders or shareholders has not been
determined by the end of the financial year." This means that amounts for which the
allocation has not been determined should not be recognised in the long-term
business provision. Some commentators have suggested that an allocation is
determined only when a bonus is declared. Such a view would mean that amounts
relating to constructive obligations for additional bonuses would be required to be
included in the FFA rather than the technical provision. However, although the
reference to 'allocations being determined' could be interpreted in that way, it could
also be interpreted in other ways—for example, it could be that an allocation can be
determined through the identification of a constructive obligation—and there is no
reason to believe that the first interpretation is more appropriate than the second.†

4.54 So, to summarise, a reasonable interpretation of:

(a) paragraph 16 of Schedule 9A is that all liabilities that have been identified
should be recognised on the balance sheet;

(b) note 21 of Schedule 9A's balance sheet formats is that the long-term business
provision is required to show the company's liabilities; and

(c) paragraph 46(3) of Schedule 9A requires all future liabilities to be recognised in
the long-term business provision.

---

*Directive 2002/83/EC has replaced Council Directive 92/96/EEC, which has been repealed. The cross-reference
in paragraph 46(3) has not yet been updated, but it is understood that it will be shortly.

†The discussion, in paragraphs 4.44-4.46, on the balance sheet treatment of the shareholders' interest in the
liability for undeclared bonuses is also relevant here.

None of these paragraphs—nor indeed any other legal requirements—suggest that 'liabilities' can comprise only liabilities for bonuses already declared. Furthermore, it is reasonable to interpret the description of the contents of the FFA in note 19 of Schedule 9A's balance sheet formats as not prohibiting liabilities for additional bonuses not yet declared from being included in the long-term business provision.

As a result, there appears no legal restriction on including liabilities for additional bonuses in the long-term business provision. Indeed: **4.55**

(a)   in the case of funds for which 'realistic' liabilities are determined, constructive obligations (for additional bonuses not yet declared) that give rise to liabilities have been identified, so those liabilities should be recognised in the technical provision.
(b)   for other funds, the only liabilities that have been identified are those based on legal obligations. As such, it seems reasonable to recognise only those amounts in the technical provision.

As explained more fully later in this appendix, the FRS requires entities to start   **4.56** recognising 'realistic' liabilities in their financial statements from December 2005 year-ends. This raises a further issue: is there an inconsistency between the conclusion (in subparagraph (a) above) that all liabilities that have been identified should be recognised in the financial statements and the Board's decision not to require recognition of 'realistic' liabilities for 2004 year-ends even though the FSA requires the RBS method to be used in prudential returns from December 2004? The Board does not believe so. In its view, there are issues surrounding the recognition of 'realistic' liabilities in financial statements that mean, for many entities, that it is not yet practicable for them to be recognised in financial statements for 2004 year-ends—and there seems no reason to suppose that Schedule 9A would require their use in such circumstances. However, if they are not recognised, as explained more fully under the next heading it will be necessary to take that into account in determining the amount of prudence to include in the measurement of the liabilities that are recognised.

Less prudent measurement bases

Currently those liabilities recognised in the technical provision are measured on an   **4.57** extremely prudent basis. 'Realistic' liabilities are measured on a less prudent basis and it has been suggested that the existing legal requirements prevent these 'less prudent' measures from being used in the financial statements. The Board does not agree. Its analysis is set out below.

The legal requirements are that the long-term business provision is measured at "the   **4.58** actuarially estimated value" (note 21 of the balance sheet format in Schedule 9A), the computation of the technical provision to be made "on the basis of recognised actuarial methods" (paragraph 46(3) of Schedule 9A), the amount of the technical life-assurance provisions shall be calculated "by a sufficiently prudent prospective actuarial valuation" (Directive 2002/83/EC). Legislation also makes clear that "a prudent valuation is not a 'best estimate' valuation, but shall include an appropriate margin for adverse deviation of the relevant factors". There is therefore no requirement that an extremely prudent measurement basis should be used.

(a)   Both an MSSB measure and a RBS measure would meet the requirement that the liability be measured at the "actuarially estimated value" and on the basis of "recognised actuarial methods". Similarly, both would meet the requirement that a prudent measurement basis should be used rather than a best estimate measurement basis. (Although the RBS measure is closer than the MSSB measure to a best estimate, it still includes certain margins for adverse deviations.)

(b)   Although the law requires that the measurement basis should be "sufficiently prudent" and that the measure should include "an appropriate margin" for adverse deviation, it provides no further guidance and, in particular, does not make clear the purpose for which the measure should be sufficiently prudent or for which the margin needs to be appropriate. For example, it has been argued that more prudence has been needed to date in arriving at a measure that is to be used for prudential regulatory purposes than in arriving at a measure for true and fair financial statements. It seems reasonable to argue therefore that what is sufficient and appropriate should be judged in the context in which the measurement is to be used.

In an accounting framework in which liabilities are not recognised for constructive obligations in respect of additional bonuses, substantial margins are necessary to take account of those obligations. However, in an accounting system in which liabilities are recognised for those constructive obligations, a less (possibly much less) prudent measurement basis can be used because the prudence 'margin' does not need to take account of those obligations.

4.59   Paragraph 43 of Schedule 9A states that "the amount of technical provisions must at all times be sufficient to cover any liabilities arising out of insurance contracts as far as can reasonably be foreseen." The meaning of this paragraph is open to different interpretations.

(a)   For example, some commentators suggest that it requires the maximum liability that might arise from an uncertain event to be recognised. This, they suggest, means that using a measurement basis in the financial statements that is as close to a best estimate basis as the RBS method would not be consistent with the law. Others point out that, if this interpretation were correct, options and guarantees would be measured by reference to the worst case scenario, assuming a catastrophe. Such a measurement approach is impractical and potentially misleading. It is also not how options and guarantees are measured currently.

(b)   In the absence of any other indications as to its meaning, it seems reasonable to assume that the requirement has the same objective in mind as the requirements discussed in paragraph 4.53-4.54–a liability amount should be determined on a basis that is sufficiently prudent for the purpose to which the number is to be used, bearing in mind the context in which it is to be placed and taking appropriate account of the various risks and uncertainties in arriving at the measure.

Deferred acquisition costs

4.60   Note 17 of the balance sheet format in Schedule 9A states that the deferred acquisition costs line of the balance sheet shall comprise "the costs of acquiring insurance policies which are incurred during a financial year but relate to a subsequent financial year" (except for certain allowances not relevant to this discussion). Some commentators have suggested that this means that any accounting standard that prohibits deferral of acquisition costs (as the FRS does) is not consistent with the law.

4.61   When costs are incurred is largely a matter of fact and nothing in the FRS seeks to change the existing view on when acquisition costs are incurred. However, which period such costs relate to is a matter of accounting convention and is therefore something that standards help determine. In effect, the FRS requires that, for funds required by the FSA to prepare RBS information, the acquisition costs should be treated as relating to the period in which they were incurred. For other funds, the FRS does not prevent acquisition costs from being treated as relating to future periods.

Recognising the value of in-force non-participating business and the excess value of any investment that the with-profits fund has in a subsidiary

As explained above, the FRS permits entities to recognise the value of in-force (VIF of) non-participating business written in the with-profits fund as an asset or as a deduction from liabilities, although in both cases only if it has been taken into account in determining a 'realistic' liability that is recognised on the balance sheet. Some commentators have questioned whether the recognition of this amount is permitted by Schedule 9A. **4.62**

Considering first the 'asset presentation' approach, Schedule 9A sets out in some detail the items that should be disclosed on the balance sheet and where they should be disclosed. An implication of this is that, if an entity intends to recognise a particular type of asset that has a line item allocated to it by Schedule 9A—for example, deferred acquisition costs—the only place that asset can be recognised on the balance sheet is on the deferred acquisition costs line. Some have suggested that the value of in-force non-participating business includes items that should more properly be disclosed under Schedule 9A's prescribed line items; and as such recognising the value separately is not consistent with the law. The Board does not share these concerns. Although the VIF of non-participating business may well be derived, inter alia, from the use of assets and liabilities shown on other lines in Schedule 9A's format that is not the same as saying the value comprises those other assets and liabilities and should therefore be shown on the lines allocated for those assets and liabilities by Schedule 9A. **4.63**

The Board believes that a similar argument applies to the recognition of the excess value of any investment that the with-profits fund has in a subsidiary. **4.64**

The FRS describes two different approaches to 'liability presentation'. **4.65**

(a) The first approach will usually not be feasible but should be adopted if it is. It requires that part of the VIF of non-participating business included in the policyholder liabilities to be deducted from the 'realistic' liability number, and that part of the VIF of non-participating business included in the FFA to be deducted from the FFA. The Board believes that this approach would be consistent with Schedule 9A's requirements analysed above in that it is still a prudent measure derived from an actuarial valuation—it is just that no value has been attributed to an obligation to transfer an item that is not recognised as an asset.

(b) On the other hand, the Board believes that the 'liability presentation' approach that is usually feasible—deducting the VIF of non-participating business from the aggregate of policyholder liabilities and the FFA, although showing each of the three items separately on the face of the balance sheet—might not meet Schedule 9A's requirements. That is because Schedule 9A requires policyholder liabilities and the FFA to be shown separately, and that seems to require the VIF of non-participating business to be allocated between them rather than deducted from the sum of them.

Practicality

To summarise the discussion in section 4 so far: **4.66**

(a)   Although there were certain conceptual difficulties with 'realistic' liabilities, the Board still considers their use where available preferable to the continued use of the existing MSSB basis.

(b)   If 'realistic' liabilities were to be used, it would be necessary to make certain consequential changes to other balance sheet items. However, those changes would not be problematical.

(c)   It was possible to use 'realistic' liabilities where available and make the consequential balance sheet amendments deemed necessary and still comply with the requirements of Schedule 9A (and equivalent requirements).

Deferral until 2005

4.67   During the development of the FRED, the Board heard from a number of commentators who suggested that, regardless of the technical merits of recognising 'realistic' liabilities, there are practical considerations that mean that such a change should either not be made at all or should not be made for 2004 year-ends.

(a)   Some commentators questioned whether the FSA's rules on the RBS method will be sufficiently robust to bear the burden that the Board is proposing to put on them. These commentators characterised the RBS method as involving a negotiation with the FSA and this, they argued, was not a good basis for an accounting standard. It would also mean that the reporting timetable would become crucially dependent on the FSA's ability to provide timely input into the estimation process. They also argued that the estimation of the 'realistic' liability amount was a highly subjective exercise; too subjective for the information to be included in financial statements intended to show a true and fair view.

(b)   Some had fewer doubts about the long-term practicality of the proposals, but questioned the wisdom of implementing the proposals for 2004 reporting. They argued that, as with any major change in practice, the RBS method would take time to 'bed down' and would be very approximate until it does. They also suggested it would take longer to implement in the first year than in subsequent years. In their view it would be better to defer implementation for a year rather than jeopardise the timeliness of the financial statements and significantly increase the risk of those statements containing errors or misstatements.

(c)   Some argued that, even though auditors would be required to give an opinion on the FSA's 2004 regulatory returns which would include RBS information, the FRED's proposals would raise important audit issues that were not capable of resolution in time for 2004.

4.68   At the time the Board was developing the FRED, it did not find these arguments persuasive. In its view, 'realistic' liability numbers would be no less subjective than other numbers—such as loan loss provisions, provisions for decommissioning costs, perhaps even pension liabilities. Furthermore, although the Board recognised that the proposed FRS would set preparers and auditors a challenge—particularly in the first year of implementation—it was not convinced that this would be any more difficult to overcome than the difficulties that some other entities have had to overcome in preparing their financial statements. In its view it would not be credible for entities to publish financial statements including liabilities measured on the existing basis whilst, at the same time, measuring liabilities in publicly available regulatory returns on a basis that is generally perceived to be better. The Board therefore proposed in the FRED that the changes to the liability model should be implemented for 2004 year-ends.

4.69   Implementation in 2004 also had the advantage of ensuring that the FRS would apply to the whole industry in 2004 and would, in the main, continue to be applied by the whole industry in subsequent periods—including, because of the grandfathering provisions in IFRS 4, entities preparing their financial statements in accordance with EU-adopted IFRS. On the other hand, if the FRS was not implemented until 2005, entities preparing their financial statements in accordance with EU-adopted IFRS would not fall within its scope. The Board considered it important that the FRS should be applied across the industry.

Most of those responding to FRED 34 criticised the proposal that the FRS should be implemented for 2004 year-ends. Some simply stated that the timetable was impracticable; others suggested a one year deferral. **4.70**

The Board noted that a number of entities due to be preparing their financial statements in accordance with EU-adopted IFRS from 2005 had offered, either in their formal responses to FRED 34 or in their discussions with the Board's staff, to implement the FRS from 2005 if the Board decided not to require its adoption in 2004. It therefore had discussions with the Association of British Insurers, the British Banking Association and some of those bodies' members about that possibility. As explained more fully in section 10 of this appendix, those discussions were positive, thus enabling the Board to consider the proposed implementation timetable in isolation from its desire to issue a standard that would be adopted across the industry as a whole. **4.71**

The Board then reconsidered its proposal to implement this part of the FRS in 2004 and concluded that implementation should be deferred by a year. The advantage to be gained by implementing this part of the FRS in 2004 rather than 2005 were marginal and there was a risk that, if more time for implementation was not allowed, the information provided could prove misleading. **4.72**

Implications of IFRS 4 for a delay in implementation of the proposed standard

IFRS 4 imposes restrictions on the accounting policies that can be used from 2005 in financial statements prepared in accordance with EU-adopted IFRS. Those restrictions differ depending on whether the accounting policy is an existing policy (ie was also used in 2004) or a new policy (ie is being implemented for the first time in 2005). When the Board was developing the proposals in FRED 34, it kept its eye firmly fixed on the former restrictions but ignored the latter restrictions. The decision to delay implementation of the proposed FRS until 2005 meant that the latter restrictions were now relevant. **4.73**

The Board believed there were three restrictions to consider. The first is set out in paragraph 22 of IFRS 4. That paragraph requires that, subject to certain exceptions (none of which are relevant here), an accounting policy can be changed only if it represents an improvement; in other words, if the change makes the financial statements more relevant and no less reliable, or more reliable and no less relevant. Does a change of accounting policy to one that involves the recognition of 'realistic' liabilities represent an improvement under IFRS 4? The Board believes that it does and its reasons for reaching that conclusion are as follows: **4.74**

(a) The Board believes that it is beyond dispute that 'realistic' liabilities are a more relevant measure of the obligation to policyholders than the existing MSSB basis. The question is therefore whether they are less reliable.

(b) IFRS 4 requires reliability to be judged by the criteria in IAS 8. Paragraph 10(b) of IAS 8 makes it clear that reliability should be judged by considering whether an accounting policy results in financial statements that:

(i)   represent faithfully the financial position, financial performance and cash flows of the entity;

(ii) reflect the economic substance of transactions, other events and conditions, and not merely the legal form;

(iii) are neutral; in other words, free from bias;

(iv) are prudent; and

(v)   are complete in all material respects.

There is no doubt that 'realistic' liabilities are generally 'softer' numbers than MSSB liabilities (because they are significantly affected by assumptions and non-market inputs). However, as IAS 8 makes clear, the reliability test is not about the softness (or otherwise) of the numbers per se. Rather it is about attributes such as faithful representation (the MSSB number is not a faithful representation of policyholder liabilities because it omits a major element of the obligation to the policyholders—the constructive obligation for future bonuses); neutrality (the 'realistic' liability is a more neutral number than the MSSB liability because the latter is prepared on a very prudent basis), and prudence (both bases are prudent, it is just that the MSSB basis is overly prudent). On that analysis, 'realistic' liabilities are also more reliable than MSSB liabilities.

4.75   The second restriction relates to paragraph 25(c) of IFRS 4, which stipulates that, except as permitted by paragraph 24 of the IFRS, an accounting policy change cannot be made if it would involve the use of non-uniform accounting policies for the insurance liabilities of subsidiaries. The question here is, is a requirement to change the basis of recognising and measuring the policyholder liabilities of some entities' UK with-profits liabilities—and at the same time making changes to the treatment of the deferred acquisition costs and reinsurance assets arising from such funds— without changing the basis for all with-profits liabilities permitted by IFRS 4? The Board believes that it does; its reasoning is as follows:

(a)   Most groups with UK life assurance activities currently adopt a wide diversity of accounting policies in determining their policyholder liabilities, especially in respect of various overseas subsidiaries. For them, the change from the MSSB basis to the 'realistic' basis can be described as changing one basis that is used for UK with-profits policyholder liabilities but no other policyholder liabilities to another basis that is used for UK with-profits policyholder liabilities but no other policyholder liabilities.

(b)   An alternative way of viewing the change to 'realistic' liabilities is a move from applying a partial recognition basis to the recognition of with-profits liabilities (because it takes account only of declared bonuses) to a basis that attempts to recognise constructive obligations for future bonuses as well. Viewed in this way the change can be seen as improving the uniformity of accounting policies used in the group, because the recognition bases used in other parts of the group—including non-participating business and general insurance business—will also be close to a full recognition basis.

(c)   The exemption in paragraph 24 of the IFRS also appears relevant and clearly demonstrates that partial changes are not prohibited by the standard:
      "An insurer is permitted, but not required to change its accounting policies so that it remeasures designated insurance liabilities to reflect current market interest rates and recognises changes in those liabilities in profit or loss. At that time, it may also introduce accounting policies that require other current estimates and assumptions for the designated liabilities. The election in this paragraph permits an insurer to change its accounting policies for designated liabilities, without applying those policies to all similar liabilities as IAS 8 would otherwise require."

The adoption of realistic liabilities would represent the introduction of an accounting policy that requires the use of current estimates and assumptions and as such is envisaged by the IFRS.

The third restriction relates to the recognition of the VIF of non-participating business written in a with-profits fund. The FRS permits the whole of the amount to be recognised if the non-participating business is measured on that basis for the purpose of the regulatory returns, the value is determined in accordance with the FSA's requirements, and the 'realistic' liabilities amount took account of the value. However, most UK entities recognising this VIF amount in their balance sheet will be doing so for the first time in their 2005 financial statements, which means that entities preparing their financial statements in accordance with EU-adopted IFRS will need to be able to implement the changes the FRS requires under EU-adopted IFRS. The Board believes that they can. That is because paragraph 5 of the FRS gives entities a choice of ways in which to incorporate the VIF amount on the balance sheet and although recognising the VIF as an asset will not be possible under IFRS 4 unless that amount includes neither future investment risk margins or excess investment management fees—and may not be possible under the IASB's Framework—the other two approaches allowed by the FRS envisage the VIF amount being taken into account in determining liabilities and IFRS 4's embedded value restrictions will have no implications for such a treatment. **4.76**

The Board's view is therefore that it is possible to implement the requirements of the FRS in full in 2005 in a set of financial statements that comply fully with EU-adopted IFRS. **4.77**

BALANCE SHEET CLASSIFICATION OF THE FFA

What is the FFA?

As already explained, under existing UK requirements entities with with-profits funds recognise an item called the Fund for Future Appropriations (or FFA) amongst their liabilities. The FFA is the cumulative amount that is available for allocation to policyholders (current and future) and, where applicable, shareholders but remains unallocated at the balance sheet date. Therefore, for an entity with shareholders one of the issues concerning the FFA is its ownership. For all entities there will also be the inter-generational issue: how much of the FFA belongs to which generation of policyholders? **5.1**

Currently the FFA includes amounts relating to obligations (for example, amounts relating to the constructive obligations that exist in respect of additional bonuses) . However, in many cases it also includes an 'estate'. The ownership and future application of the estate is uncertain; although the expectation might be that 90% or so of it will be allocated to policyholders, there is no current obligation to allocate or pay any of the estate to anyone—it can be held indefinitely or used for any or all of the following purposes: **5.2**

(a) meeting the expenses incurred in writing new business;
(b) meeting investment or other losses arising on the assets backing the estate;
(c) meeting losses arising from non-participating business written by the with-profit fund;
(d) meeting liabilities to the with-profit policyholders arising from non-participating features of the policies (such as options or guarantees);

(e) distribution to current and or future policyholders through the declaration of bonuses in excess of their measured obligations. (This could, for example, be as a consequence of a marketing initiative or a tontine effect*); or

(f) distribution to shareholders in accordance with their rights of participation in bonus declaration or by way of a scheme of arrangement agreed with policyholders.†

5.3   The FRS requires changes to the existing liability model that would have the effect, inter alia, of removing from the FFA, for those funds required by the FSA to prepare RBS information, amounts relating to the fund's constructive obligations in respect of additional bonuses and amounts relating to options and guarantees. As a result, it seems reasonable to consider whether for those funds the FFA should continue to be classified, as it is currently in the UK, amongst liabilities. (Many entities will also have funds not required to prepare RBS information and the FFA for those funds will continue to have an element that is related to constructive obligations in respect of additional bonuses.)

5.4   IFRS 4, which applies from 2005 to those entities preparing their financial statements in accordance with EU-adopted IFRS, requires the FFA to be classified as either equity or liability or in part as equity and in part as a liability. The standard allows almost total flexibility as to how the classification (and any split) is done and does not, for example, appear to require it to be based on the existing equity and liability definitions. However, it does require that all guaranteed elements are classified as liabilities and that, if the guaranteed element is not distinguished from other parts of the with-profits contract, all the amounts relating to the contract should be classified as a liability.

5.5   Under most US GAAP approaches and under embedded value principles the FFA is classified on the assumption that it is to be shared between policyholders and shareholders, generally in a 90:10 ratio. In other words, 90% of the FFA is treated as a liability and the balance is classified as equity.

Should the FRS address the classification of the FFA?

5.6   Against this background, the Board considered whether the FRS should address the classification of the FFA. Bearing in mind that the FFA appears to comprise both equity and liability elements, it seemed unlikely that accounting would be improved by requiring the entire FFA to be treated as a liability or to be classified as equity.‡ The options the Board considered were:

(a) to require the FFA to be classified as equity to the extent that no liability is involved (in other words, classify the estate as equity) and as a liability to the extent that the liability definition is met; or

---

*If a closed fund has a surplus but those leaving the fund are paid an amount that is equal to the constructive obligation, the value of the fund per remaining policyholder will increase as policyholders leave until there is only one remaining policyholder, who would be entitled to the entire surplus. (The principle of the tontine is that the last remaining policyholder is entitled to the surplus.) To avoid the tontine effect, funds over-distribute when they foresee a tontine arising.

†Normally in a life company that has shareholders, when a surplus is declared as a bonus, 10% of the surplus involved is attributed to shareholders and 90% to policyholders. A scheme of arrangement may allow a higher amount to be attributed to shareholders. This is generally as part of an agreement to share the surplus with current policyholders.

‡The Board's Framework envisages that credit balances will be classified as liabilities if they meet the definition of a liability and as part of the ownership interest (which might be called by a number of different names, including 'equity') otherwise. The FRS uses the term 'equity'.

(b)   to adopt a similar approach to that set out in IFRS 4.

In order to apply the change described in option (a) to entities preparing their **5.7** financial statements in accordance with UK standards and legal requirements, a change would be required to the law and the Board understands there is little prospect of such a change in the near-future. However, rather than dismissing this option out of hand because of the legal difficulties, the Board considered whether it would want to make the change, legal requirements permitting.

(a)   The case for classifying the estate as equity is simply stated: the estate (if correctly calculated) is not a liability as defined and any credit balance that is not a liability is equity under the Board's Framework. Arguments that the estate does not have the characteristics that one would normally associate with something that is equity miss the point: the only characteristic that equity has is that it is a residual and the estate possesses that characteristic. However, as the Board's Framework itself admits, definitions of items like liabilities are developed with current and past accounting problems in mind and, although they will often help in tackling new accounting problems, those new problems will sometimes point up shortcomings that need to be addressed. Indeed, recent work by a number of standard-setters has revealed the need for the principles that underlie the equity/liability classification to be reviewed. The US standard-setter, FASB, is carrying out a review for the IASB and that project is likely to inform the IASB's work in phase 2 of its insurance project.

(b)   In order to classify as equity all of the FFA other than the portion identified as a liability, the Board would want to be confident that its definitions of 'liabilities' and of 'equity' were appropriate in the context of with-profits activities. It would also want to be confident that all the liabilities had been recognised and appropriately measured because it would not be appropriate to classify as equity a balance that might contain some element of liabilities. Although the development of the FSA's RBS approach has made it possible to get much closer to identifying the liability element (as defined by FRS 12) for the funds to which the methodology relates, 'realistic' liabilities are not the same as 'liabilities calculated on an FRS 12 basis'. There also remains considerable difficulty in attempting to identify the liability element for other funds.

(c)   A consequence of classifying some or all of the FFA as equity would be a fundamental change to the profit recognition model. The Board would not want to make changes of this kind without a more detailed consideration of the profit recognition model than has been possible in this project.

The Board therefore decided not to propose the reclassification of some or all of the FFA as equity.

The other change the Board could have made was to adopt a similar approach to **5.8** that set out in IFRS 4. However, such a change would have no effect on entities preparing their financial statements under UK standards and legal requirements unless there was a change of law—and there is no prospect of that in the near-future. Adopting the IFRS 4 approach in the UK would also have created the possibility of a diversity of practice where currently there is uniformity. The Board therefore decided not to pursue this option.

The FRS therefore remains silent on the classification of the FFA. This means that: **5.9**

(a)   in financial statements prepared in accordance with UK standards and legal requirements, the FFA will be classified as a liability; and

(b)   in financial statements prepared in accordance with EU-adopted IFRS, there will be almost complete flexibility as to how the FFA is classified, subject only to the caveats explained in paragraph 5.4 above and pending completion of phase 2 of the IASB's insurance project.

Showing the technical provision and the FFA separately on the balance sheet

5.10   Currently Schedule 9A requires that the FFA and the technical provision are shown on separate lines of the balance sheet. However, for entities applying EU-adopted IFRS are not subject to that legal requirement. Furthermore, IFRS 4 permits, but does not require, entities to combine the technical provision and FFA on a single line of the balance sheet.

5.11   Combining the technical provision and the FFA on a single line of the balance sheet would lose the improvements that the FRS is requiring because, rather than a technical provision that is prepared on a basis that is closer than the existing basis to FRS 12 and an FFA, there would just be an aggregated liability that would bear no resemblance whatsoever to the FRS 12 liability. The Penrose Report's desire to see the financial statements show a realistic position of the life office would also have been frustrated.

5.12   Furthermore, although the Board decided that it should not for the time being propose reclassification of any of the FFA, it did not consider the FFA to be like any other liability and believed it would be inappropriate for the FFA and the technical provision to be combined together on a single line of the balance sheet.

5.13   The Board therefore took steps to preserve the improvement the FRS makes to insurance liability accounting and to preserve the distinction between the FFA and other liabilities by including in the FRS a requirement that the technical provision and FFA should always be shown separately on the face of the balance sheet.

5.14   The Board recognised that this would involve a change in balance sheet presentation for those non-insurance entities with insurance activities that show the FFA and the technical provision, together with all other insurance liabilities, on a single line of the consolidated balance sheet. However, it believed the change to be justified for the reasons explained above.

OPTIONS AND GUARANTEES

6.1   Many life assurance policies include option or guarantee features, such as guaranteed surrender values or guaranteed annuity options on vesting of a pension accumulation product. Such options and guarantees are, furthermore, not unique to UK with-profits funds. They can also arise, for example, in non-participating funds and overseas funds.

6.2   Some of these options and guarantees expose the entity to insurance variables (for example, mortality or morbidity); some to financial variables (for example, market prices). The latter are similar to financial options in that the amount payable will depend on the level of a variable, relative to a predetermined value, on a specified maturity date (or in a specified time period).

(a)   If at the specified time the variable is lower than the predetermined value, an amount is payable—the exact amount depending on the amount of the variable—and, if the variable is higher than the predetermined value, no amount is payable.

(b)   An option contract is 'in the money' if the current level of the variable is below the predetermined value such that, were the current value to remain unchanged, an amount would be payable under the option. It is 'out of the money' if, were the current value to remain unchanged, no amount would be payable on maturity. Of course, a contract that is in the money prior to maturity may be out of the money when it matures, and vice versa.

(c) The fair value of such a contract at any time prior to its maturity will reflect both the amount (if any) by which the option is in the money at that time (its 'intrinsic value') and the risk that the intrinsic value will change in the period to maturity (its 'time value'). A contract that is out of the money will still have value, unless there is no possibility that it could be in the money when it matures. Therefore, an accounting practice that considers merely the extent to which the contract is in the money at the valuation date (or on a single forecast of the position at maturity date)—and thus ignores the time value of the contract—does not reflect the fair value of the contract.

The Board has long held the view that in principle all financial derivatives should be measured in the primary financial statements at an amount that takes into account both intrinsic value and time value (ie typically fair value),* and it sees no reason why options and guarantees exposing the life assurer to financial variables life assurers should be any different.   **6.3**

The Board noted in this context that, in calculating the 'realistic' liability arising from options and guarantees on UK with-profits policies within the scope of its RBS approach, the FSA requires the options and guarantees to be measured at an amount that takes into account both intrinsic value and time value. Currently, there are two ways of doing this: **6.4**

(a) *Fair value derived from a market value comparison.* Contracts traded on financial markets are traded at their fair value so, if an option or guarantee feature of a with-profits policy is similar to a traded contract (or is similar to a combination of traded contracts), its fair value can be estimated by reference to that (those) observable market value(s).

(b) *A probabilistic or stochastic valuation method.* For many option and guarantee features incorporated in with-profits policies, equivalent traded instruments do not exist. In such circumstances, in order to capture the time value involved a probabilistic or stochastic modelling approach has to be adopted. Under such an approach, all possible outcomes are considered and weighted according to the probability of that outcome occurring, and the weighted average of the outcomes calculated.

Stochastic models need careful calibration, with the probabilities used in the model being adjusted to ensure that the values produced are consistent with observable market values for similar traded instruments. The models are further complicated by the need to reflect future management actions that may be taken in response to changes in conditions. For example, it may be that, were equity market prices to fall by 10% from current levels, the intention would be to change the mix of the fund's investment portfolio so that a greater proportion of bonds is held. It may alternatively be that management would respond by varying bonus rates or charges to policyholders. Both these courses of action could reduce the cost of the options. Stochastically modelled values need to take account of such management actions to the extent that such actions are realistically possible in the timescale envisaged and are consistent with the PPFM.   **6.5**

Although the Board believed that options and guarantees written by life assurers should in principle be included in the balance sheet at amounts that take into account both intrinsic value and time value, it accepted that major difficulties would arise in   **6.6**

*See 'Derivatives and other Financial Instruments' Discussion Paper, which was issued in July 1996.

the short-term were it to require that time value should be taken into account for options and guarantees which do not have to be measured on that basis currently.* Accordingly, it decided that it should not at this stage *require* all options and guarantees to be measured on that basis.

6.7   Instead the proposal in the FRED was that detailed disclosure should be provided about all the options and guarantees written by a life assurer that are not measured at amounts that include time value, including options and guarantees written in non-participating funds and overseas funds. Disclosure is a poor substitute for proper accounting, but it helps ensure that users of accounts are aware of such options and guarantees.

6.8   One option open to the Board was to implement in the UK some or all of IFRS 4's disclosure requirements. Such an approach would achieve convergence with international standards. The Board took the view that, although the IFRS 4 requirements set out the high-level disclosure principle involved, they were not detailed enough to ensure that the disclosure would be focused on the aspects of the options and guarantees on which the Board thought the disclosure should focus. It therefore developed its own disclosure proposals.

6.9   Mixed views were expressed about the FRED's proposals, with some respondents expressing the view that their scope should be extended to include options and guarantees that were shown in the balance sheet at fair value or at market-consistent stochastic values, and others arguing that the disclosure should be narrowly scoped. A number of respondents also thought the proposed disclosures would be onerous to produce and should be simplified.

6.10   On the question of scope:

(a)   the Board reconsidered whether it was appropriate to restrict the scope of the disclosures just to those options and guarantees not shown on the balance sheet at fair value or at a market-consistent stochastic value. It noted that, for those entities preparing their financial statements in accordance with EU-adopted IFRS, the IFRS 4 disclosure requirements would apply to all options and guarantees. The Board thought there was a need for some general disclosures (similar to some of those required by IFRS 4) for all options and guarantees, and that those disclosures should be supplemented with some more targeted disclosures (similar to those in FRED 34) for options and guarantees not shown on the balance sheet at fair value or at a market-consistent stochastic value. Therefore, in the FRS the general disclosure principle (in paragraph 48) is based on requirements in IFRS 4, and the disclosure requirement for options and guarantees not shown on the balance sheet at fair value or at a market-consistent stochastic value (in paragraph 51) is based on FRED 34; and

(b)   the Board recognised that the FRED had not been clear as to what exactly was meant by 'options and guarantees' and, as a result, it was possible to interpret the phrase much more widely than the Board intended. The intention had been for the disclosures to focus on the financial risk aspects of the options and guarantees granted, rather than the insurance risk. Paragraph 50 of the FRS now makes this clear.

6.11   As already mentioned, some respondents thought the disclosures would be extremely burdensome. This was thought to be a particular problem if the information provided had to be audited at the 2004 year-end, because there was little time to put in place the systems needed to gather the necessary information.

---

*ie non-participatory funds, the smaller UK with-profits funds and some overseas with-profits funds. It is understood that some overseas regulators already require the use of a measurement basis that takes into account both intrinsic value and time value.

(a) In the light of these comments, the Board reconsidered its disclosure proposals but concluded that it was essential that there should be disclosures that enable users to understand the main variables that determine the amount payable under options and guarantees granted and the potential effects of adverse changes in those variables. However, it accepted that there are different ways of presenting that information and that the most appropriate presentation would often depend on the circumstances involved. The FRS is therefore more flexible than the FRED on the detailed nature of the disclosures to be provided.

(b) Furthermore, to give preparers more time to put in place the necessary systems (and in line with the decisions taken on other aspects of the FRS), the Board decided to defer implementation of the options and guarantee disclosure requirements until 2005 year-ends. At the same time, a number of the biggest entities with life assurance activities have volunteered to provide the FRS's disclosures on options and guarantees in their OFR (or equivalent statements) for 2004 year-ends (see section 10 of this appendix).

RECOGNISING THE VALUE OF IN-FORCE LIFE ASSURANCE IN FINANCIAL STATEMENTS

Background

One aspect of the embedded value debate—the recognition of an asset that represents **7.1** the VIF of non-participating business written in a with-profits fund—has already been discussed in this appendix (see paragraphs 4.20-4.30 and 4.62-4.65). A different but related issue was also considered in this project: the recognition in the primary financial statements as an asset of the value of in-force life assurance business (the VIF of life assurance business). In other words, the recognition on the balance sheet by some entities of an asset that represents the value to shareholders of in-force life assurance business and (usually) the recognition in the profit and loss account of changes in the value of this asset (after adjustment for any capital transfers into or out of the fund in the period).*

The objective of embedded value techniques is to reflect the estimated economic **7.2** value of the existing in-force life business and of any existing surplus in the life fund from the shareholders' perspective. For example, for a with-profit life fund, VIF comprises two elements:

(a) *The shareholders' share of any surplus of the assets of the fund over the 'realistic' liabilities to current policyholders.* This surplus represents the estate of the fund and is usually held to meet solvency requirements and as working capital.

(b) *The net present value of the shareholders' share of the future bonuses expected to be declared in respect of in-force policies.* This represents the capitalised future returns on existing business and, as such, is derived from expected future profits and, in some cases, assumptions about the distribution of the estate.

There is not one single, precisely designed embedded value methodology; there are a **7.3** number of similar, but different techniques.†

This use of embedded values in the primary financial statements is most commonly—though not exclusively—seen in consolidated financial statements when a non-insurance group is consolidating an insurance subsidiary.

†A number of different terms are also used, some of which describe different techniques and some of which do not. These include: embedded value, European embedded value, market-consistent embedded value, certainty equivalent embedded value, achieved profits, and value of in-force business. The discussion that follows uses the term 'embedded value' in its widest sense.

The issue

7.4   Existing insurance accounting focuses more on the needs of prudential regulation than on the information needs of investors. As a result, the true and fair financial statements are not very good at providing shareholders with useful information about the value of their interest in the business. Many entities have sought to address this by including in the annual report information prepared on an embedded value basis. Some entities provide this embedded value information as supplementary information. Others include embedded values in the primary financial statements.

7.5   When the ABI was carrying out its latest revision of its SORP, it discussed with the Board the then practice of several insurance groups of recognising the VIF of life assurance business in the primary financial statements. The Board's view was that an asset for the internally-generated VIF of life assurance business should not be recognised in a balance sheet prepared on an MSSB basis, and that was the view that prevailed in the 2003 revision of the SORP. As a result, entities within the scope of the SORP—British insurance companies and insurance groups—no longer recognise the internally-generated VIF of life assurance business in their primary statements. Instead, they usually provide supplementary embedded value information.

7.6   However, there are entities that have insurance activities but do not fall within the scope of the SORP (for example, bancassurers, Irish insurance entities and some retail groups), and a number of them still recognise the VIF of life assurance business in their primary financial statements. Thus, the same transactions are accounted for in fundamentally different ways depending on the type of entity involved. Although the effect on the profit and loss account is only a timing difference, the impact can be significant and the periods involved can be very long.

7.7   The Board believes that there is no reason in principle why all entities should not account for life assurance in the same way. It has therefore been considering how it should respond to this inconsistency.

Courses of action open to the Board

7.8   One possible option was to reverse the position the Board took during its discussions with the ABI and allow entities falling within the scope of the SORP to recognise the VIF of life assurance business in their primary financial statements without restriction. The Board rejected this approach. It has long-standing concerns about aspects of the embedded value approach and was not prepared to put aside those concerns—at least not without undertaking a comprehensive analysis of embedded value methodologies.*

7.9   Another possible option was to prohibit all entities from recognising the VIF of life assurance business in their financial statements. Such an approach would achieve consistency between different types of entity, and appears to be consistent with the position the Board took in its discussions with the ABI in 2003. It would however mean forcing entities that currently recognise the VIF of life assurance business back on to a basis of accounting that the Board has acknowledged is very unsatisfactory—the MSSB basis (albeit modified by the FRS). A standard that achieves convergence by requiring some entities to move from a useful basis of accounting to a less useful basis is not a good accounting standard.

*The Board intends to carry out a more thorough analysis of embedded value methods in the second half of this project. That work will include a review of the European CFO Forum paper 'European Embedded Value Principles' (issued May 2004).

The Board concluded therefore that its approach should lie somewhere between these two extremes. **7.10**

The aspect of embedded value that has caused the Board greatest concern in the past is the inclusion of future investment risk margins in the VIF of life assurance business.* Under 'traditional' embedded value methodologies, the expected future bonuses element of the VIF of life assurance business is determined after estimating the projected investment returns on each of the asset classes held in the funds, then discounting those returns using a single discount rate. Thus, the projected differential investment risk premium from asset classes is included in the embedded value; in other words, as the investment mix of the fund's portfolio changes, so will the amount of the VIF. This, the Board believes, is not appropriate. **7.11**

For that reason, the Board was interested to see that a recent development of an embedded value methodology (known as market-consistent embedded value or MCEV) under which the expected future investment return on each asset class is discounted using a discount rate that is equal to that assumed return—thus ensuring that the future investment risk margins for the different asset classes are not anticipated in the VIF of life assurance business recognised as an asset. The Board might view more favourably embedded values that exclude those margins. **7.12**

Before the Board would be able to form a view on embedded value methods that exclude future investment risk margins, it would need to study carefully a number of other aspects of the methodology. Those aspects include: **7.13**

(a)   *Future bonus assumptions*—Embedded value approaches for with-profits business generally make a number of simplifying assumptions in respect of future bonuses. For example, it is generally assumed that the whole of the estate will be distributed to existing policyholders, and that this distribution will be achieved by a proportionate uplift in the projected level of bonuses. The effect of this assumption is to spread the distribution of the estate over the run off period of the existing policies. It could be argued that this is not appropriate because it in effect assumes artificially that the fund is going to go into run off with no new policies being written and therefore no need to maintain an estate to meet future solvency or other requirements.

(b)   *'Lock in'*—Embedded value calculations generally reduce the value of the shareholders' interest in the life business if that capital is considered to be 'locked in' the fund by the requirement to maintain regulatory solvency margins and prudential margins. For example, some—though not all—life assurers assume under that basis that the amounts are available for shareholders only as the solvency margins decline and therefore apply a discount. It could be argued that this reduction in value is inconsistent with usual accounting practice, which generally does not impose measurement limitations when there are restrictions as to distributability.

(c)   *'Burn through' of the estate*—Generally embedded value calculations do not at present stochastically model all possible outcomes for the fund, and in particular do not take full account of the asymmetry of the shareholders' interest. For example, although embedded value methodologies generally assume that the shareholders' interest is 10% (with the policyholders taking 90%), they do not necessarily take account of extreme adverse circumstances in which the estate is exhausted (burnt through) and the shareholders' exposure might increase. (The shareholders' exposure can become 100% of the increase in the

---

*IFRS 4 uses the term 'future investment margins'. The FRS does as well because it is implementing IFRS 4 requirements. This appendix uses 'future investment risk margin' because that is a more precise description of what is being discussed.

liability, although the exact exposure will depend on the contract terms and the PPFM of the fund concerned.) Taking these extreme circumstances into account in the stochastic model will reduce the embedded value.

(d)   *Movements analysis*—Currently there are a number of differing conventions as to how the movement in the VIF of life assurance business in a period—particularly the impact of changing assumptions—is presented. This movements analysis is an important part of the embedded value information set.

7.14   The suggestion at the end of paragraph 7.12—that embedded value with future investment risk margins excluded might be the way forward—seems to be echoed in IFRS 4. Although IFRS 4 does not require an entity already recognising an embedded value that includes future investment risk margins to change that accounting policy, it makes it difficult for an entity not recognising future investment risk margins to start recognising them. (It adopts a similar approach to excess investment management fees—see paragraph 7.19 below.)

7.15   The Board decided that it should propose a prohibition on including, as part of an asset of the VIF of life assurance business, any value attributed to future investment risk margins. Such a proposal had three advantages:

(a)   It addressed the aspect of embedded value that most concerns the Board.

(b)   It appeared to be in line with the direction IFRS 4 indicates the IASB is taking.

(c)   If applied to all entities prior to them preparing their financial statements under EU-adopted IFRS, it would ensure that under EU-adopted IFRS they were all subject to the same restriction on the use of future investment risk margins (rather than different restrictions depending on whether the entity is already recognising such margins).

7.16   When the FRED was being developed, the intention was to implement the above proposal for 2004 year-ends. Against this background some commentators suggested that, in the interests of achieving immediate convergence on future investment risk margins, the Board should allow the ABI to amend its SORP to permit the recognition by insurance entities of assets representing the VIF of life assurance business. That amendment, plus the proposal in the FRED, would mean that all entities—whether or not they were within the scope of the SORP and whether reporting under UK standards or EU-adopted IFRS—would be subject to the same restrictions in 2004. However, the Board decided instead that the FRED should propose that:

(a)   those entities currently recognising an asset that represents the VIF of life assurance business could continue to recognise such an asset as long as, from 2004, that VIF did not include future investment risk margins; and

(b)   there should be no change in the Board's position towards entities preparing their financial statements in accordance with UK standards and not currently recognising the VIF of life assurance business unless and until the Board had studied embedded value methodologies that do not include future investment risk margins and concluded that they were acceptable for use in financial statements.

7.17   These proposals allowed an inconsistency in existing practice to persist for 2004 but, because of IFRS 4's grandfathering provisions, would mean that all entities preparing their financial statements in accordance with EU-adopted IFRS would be subject to the same restrictions from 2005.

7.18   The proposal to prohibit a value being attributed to future investment risk margins received a mixed response.

(a) Some respondents claimed that embedded value was outside the scope of the life assurance project, because the Financial Secretary to the Treasury had made no reference to the subject in her letter to the Board. However, it is the Board that decides the scope of its project work and it decided in this case that, as the objective was to improve life assurance accounting, the scope of its work should not be limited to the concerns raised in the Penrose Report—the use of embedded value in the primary financial statements should also be considered.

(b) Some respondents argued that the restriction should be omitted because it would have no effect on the amount at which the VIF asset was recognised. On the other hand, others argued that, even if it had no effect on the amount recognised, the restriction would ensure that a more disciplined approach would be taken to the valuation of the VIF asset.

(c) Some respondents argued that the Board was misdirecting itself by seeking to achieve convergence on the restrictions that apply to the recognition of the VIF asset; it would not result in practice converging because recognising the VIF asset was optional. The Board was aware that convergence would not be achieved in the short-term, but did not believe that invalidated the proposal.

(d) Some respondents criticised the proposal that the restriction should be implemented for 2004 year-ends, arguing that it was too late in the year to require entities already recognising the VIF of life assurance business to make a potentially major change to their basis of profit recognition. They also pointed out that they would have to make changes to the VIF of life assurance business in 2005 when they implemented IAS 39 'Financial Investments: Recognition and Measurement' and it would be preferable if they could make all the changes at the same time. One reason the Board was seeking to implement the change in 2004 was because it would not be able to mandate the change in 2005 for entities preparing their financial statements in accordance with EU-adopted IFRS. The Board therefore had discussions with the largest entities currently recognising a VIF asset in their financial statements about the possibility of deferring the implementation of the restriction in exchange for a commitment to implement the restriction in 2005. Those discussions proved positive and the Board decided that the FRS should apply for accounting periods ending on or after 23 December 2005.

As mentioned in paragraph 7.14, IFRS 4 also prohibits entities from changing their accounting policies to start recognising in their VIF for life assurance business a value attributed to future investment management fees that exceeds the fair value of those future fees. In line with the Board's objective of trying to ensure that all types of entity would be subject from 2005 to the same restrictions on the use of embedded value, the Board proposed in the FRED that the FRS should include a similar restriction. However, it was clear from the comments received that the restriction was not being interpreted consistently and that the differences in interpretation could have a significant effect on the amount at which the VIF asset was recognised. As the source of the ambiguity seemed to be the wording taken from IFRS 4 and the Board was reluctant to include a clarification of that wording in the FRS (because that would involve interpreting an IFRS), it was eventually decided that the restriction should be omitted from the FRS. **7.19**

MULTIPLE STATEMENTS PREPARED ON DIFFERENT BASES

The financial statements of life assurers are not easy to follow. Partly that is because life assurance is a complex business that has to date proved difficult to represent faithfully and simply in financial statements—the uncertainty of ownership of the estate is, for example, difficult to portray simply, as is the measurement uncertainty that is involved in any insurance entity. This is not a matter that is easily fixed. Partly **8.1** the complexity stems from the unfamiliar technical jargon and formats used. However, for entities preparing their financial statements in accordance with UK standards and legal requirements, that terminology and those formats are largely dictated by law and the Board understands that there is no prospect of the law being changed in the near future. Entities preparing their financial statements in accordance with EU-adopted IFRS are not constrained in the same way, but the Board has no ability to mandate change for such entities.

8.2   For these reasons, the Board believes that there is little it can do about the unfamiliar technical jargon and formats used in the short-term.

8.3   Another source of complexity is the publication of multiple statements: the true and fair financial statements, the supplementary embedded value statements, and the regulatory returns—each of which is prepared on a different basis, designed to serve a distinct (but often unexplained) purpose, and all of which are typically presented with little or no means for the users to navigate their way from one statement to another. The complexity this creates was a particular concern noted in the Penrose Report. It is also an issue that the Board believes it can do something about.

8.4   The Penrose Report makes the case for convergence of true and fair financial statements with regulatory returns. However, the statements and returns serve different purposes—regulatory returns are primarily focused on solvency whereas true and fair financial statements have a broader remit—and statements that have different purposes will in their optimal form often involve different structures and bases. Therefore, although alignment of regulatory and financial reporting is desirable, this is best achieved through convergence around the structure and basis that are 'right' for the true and fair financial statements. The Board has been able to base so much of the FRS on the FSA's methodology because that methodology is to some extent an attempt by the FSA to converge aspects of regulatory returns with the approach applied generally in financial statements.

8.5   Where differences between the statements remain, the Board's preference is to seek to improve the clarity of the information provided by requiring reconciliations between the statements.

8.6   If two statements have been prepared on bases that have nothing in common, a reconciliation between them is not very useful because it tends to involve simply the substitution of one set of numbers with a second set. Therefore, reconciliations between statements should be required only if they would be meaningful.

8.7   The Board believes that, although the various statements currently prepared are each serving a different purpose, there is an underlying convergence of approach which means that it is reasonable to expect reconciliations between the true and fair financial statements and the prudential returns to be meaningful. For example:

(a)   apart from a few isolated exceptions, the same asset recognition and measurement model is used in all the statements;

(b)   as a result of the changes in the liability model required by the FRS, the same basic liability model will underlie the big UK with-profits funds' policyholder liability numbers in the true and fair financial statements, the regulatory returns, and in many cases (depending on the exact methodology used) the embedded value information; and

(c)   embedded value methodology seems to be developing in the direction of valuing options and guarantees written in policies in a manner consistent with that required for 'realistic' balance sheets (ie on a fair value or stochastic basis).

These developments mean that reconciliations can provide a useful service in high-   **8.8**
lighting the remaining issues of difference between the various statements. On
implementing the FRS, the main areas of difference would be:

(a)   any adjustments to asset valuation required by solvency regulation; and
(b)   the treatment as a liability for RBS regulatory returns of the shareholders'
      share of future bonus.

The Board believes that the proposed capital statement lends itself well to a recon-   **8.9**
ciliation requirement, which is why paragraph 37 of the FRS requires the aggregate
amount of the capital resources included in the capital statement to be reconciled to
the shareholders' funds, FFA and other amounts shown in the entity's balance sheet.
The effect is that the capital statement provides a reconciliation between regulatory
and financial reporting at the available capital level.

The Board has not included in the FRS any requirement to provide a reconciliation   **8.10**
between the supplementary embedded value information and the other statements.
That is primarily it seems likely that such a reconciliation would have to be included
in the supplementary information rather than the financial statements (because
otherwise at least some of the embedded value information would be brought within
the scope of the true and fair view requirement and the implications of that have not
yet been fully explored). The Board has no means of insisting on a reconciliation if it
is not to be included in the financial statements.

OTHER ISSUES ARISING FROM THE FRED 34 CONSULTATIONS

Scope

FRED 34 proposed that the FRS should apply to all entities that include a life   **9.1**
assurance business, regardless of how they are constituted, whether life assurance is
their main business and their size.

A number of respondents thought the proposals were inappropriate for some   **9.2**
friendly societies or for smaller entities. Some suggested exemptions; others suggested deferred implementation.

Friendly societies are either 'directive friendly societies' or 'non-directive friendly   **9.3**
societies'.

(a)   Directive friendly societies are those whose premium income exceeds 5 million
      euro. They are required to prepare true and fair financial statements and, in
      doing so, to comply with detailed legal requirements that are almost identical to
      those set out in Schedule 9A .
(b)   Non-directive friendly societies are also subject to a true and fair requirement,
      although the requirements as to the form and content of their financial state-
      ments are much less onerous and less prescriptive than those applying to
      directive friendly societies.

Another way of categorising friendly societies is as either 'incorporated friendly   **9.4**
societies' or 'registered friendly societies'.

(a)   An incorporated friendly society is a friendly society constituted under the
      Friendly Societies Act 1992. That Act accords a friendly society a separate legal
      identity.
(b)   A registered friendly society is a friendly society constituted under the Friendly
      Societies Act 1974. Such friendly societies have no separate legal identity and,

as a result, they carry out their transactions in the name of the appointed trustees.

9.5   The main implications of the FRS for friendly societies and for smaller entities can be summarised as follows.

(a)   The recognition of 'realistic' liabilities—Only a few of the biggest friendly societies are required by the FSA to adopt the RBS method in their prudential returns and will therefore be required by the FRS to recognise 'realistic' liabilities in their balance sheets. Unless and until the FSA extends the scope of its regulations to entities that have UK with-profits liabilities of less than £500m, this aspect of the FRS will not apply to other friendly societies or to the other smaller entities with life assurance activities.

(b)   Capital statement—Policyholders have the same level of interest in financial strength, and fungibility of capital, in the case of a friendly society as for any other life assurer. The same is true regardless of the entity's size. As such, there seems to be no reason why the capital statement and its supporting disclosures would not be relevant for a friendly society or for a smaller entity.

(c)   Options and guarantees—The objective of these disclosures is to highlight the existence of any options and guarantees, to provide information that helps users to understand the extent to which the options and guarantees granted expose the entity to risk, and to explain what that exposure is. This objective is valid regardless of the size or type of entity involved.

9.6   There seems therefore to be no technical reason why the requirements of the FRS are any less applicable to friendly societies than to any other type of entity with a life assurance business. Nor does there seem to be any technical reason why the requirements should not be applied to smaller entities.

9.7   However, directive friendly societies do not have to submit prudential returns to the FSA until six months after their year-end. (From 2006 this will be reduced to four months, and from 2007 to three months.) As a result, their current practice tends to be to publish their true and fair financial statements and hold their AGMs long before the completion and submission of their prudential returns.

9.8   If an FRS were to require the inclusion in the 2005 financial statements of regulatory information, it will be necessary either to delay the financial statements (perhaps until six months after the year-end) or to accelerate the computation of regulatory numbers. , which could be difficult for some friendly societies. The Board weighed this against the advantages to be gained by applying the FRS as soon as possible. It also noted that, by issuing the FRS in December 2004 for application to December 2005 year-ends, it was giving entities more time to prepare for the standard's implementation than the FRED had proposed. The Board decided:

(a)   to require friendly societies applying the RBS approach for the FSA's regulatory returns to implement the FRS from the same date that all other life assurers applying the RBS approach were implementing it; and

(b)   for purely pragmatic grounds, to defer the FRS's application to all other directive friendly societies for a further year (ie until 2006 year-ends).

9.9   The smallest friendly societies—non-directive friendly societies—are subject to a less rigorous prudential reporting regime than directive friendly societies. For example, a full actuarial valuation for the prudential return is computed only triennially and, although interim valuations are made for the purposes of the financial statements, they are often no more than 'no material change' confirmations. Although the Board can see no reason why policyholders and other users of the financial statements of such friendly societies should not be as well-informed as any other policyholders about the financial position of their life assurer, it accepts that the application of the FRS will cause considerable practical difficulties for these friendly societies and they will struggle to overcome those difficulties quickly. For that reason, the Board decided to give such friendly societies a further year to prepare for the FRS; in other words, it will not apply to non-directive friendly societies until 2007 year-ends.

Terminology

The FRS uses the term "'realistic' liabilities" to describe the basis of liability   **9.10**
recognition and measurement that it requires to be adopted for certain with-profits funds. That term has been used because it is the term that the FSA also uses (and it *was* the FSA that developed the basis).Although there is little doubt that the new basis is "more realistic" than the existing (MSSB) basis, some of those responding to the FRED thought it was an exaggeration—and therefore potentially misleading—to call it the 'realistic' basis. They suggested that the Board use a different term.

One of the things that makes insurance accounting difficult for many users to   **9.11**
understand is the terminology used. The Board does not wish to add to that difficulty. However, the FSA's new methodology *is* universally known as the 'realistic' basis, and the Board believed it would be unhelpful to use any other term in the FRS. However, entities are not required by the FRS to use the term in their financial statements.

Changes to the FSA's 'realistic' capital regime

The FRS requires what is, in effect, a slightly amended regulatory number (the   **9.12**
'realistic' liabilities number) to be recognised in the financial statements. When this was proposed in the FRED, several respondents sought clarification as to the implications of a change in the regulations from which the number is derived.

There are two possible types of regulatory change that could be made: **9.13**

(a) The scope of the regulations could change, so that they apply to funds or entities not currently within their scope. The FRED was worded so that, if the FSA extends the scope of its regulations to include other with-profits funds, entities would automatically be required by the FRS to show 'realistic' liabilities for those funds in their financial statements. However, if the scope was extended to include non-with-profits funds, that change would be treated in the same way as the changes described in (b). This approach has also been adopted in the FRS.
(b) The basis of the calculation could be changed. Although the Board believes the current 'realistic' capital regime is a satisfactory basis to use in the financial statements, it recognises that—because prudential regulation and true and fair financial statements serve different purposes—a future version of the 'realistic' capital regime may not be a satisfactory basis for the financial statements. For that reason, the FRS makes it clear (through the footnote to the definition of the 'Financial Services Authority realistic capital regime') that the FRS is based on the original version of the regime (ie the 18 November 2004 version) and will continue to be based on that version if the 'realistic' capital regime is amended unless and until the FRS is amended. Similarly, if the scope of the 'realistic' capital regime is extended by the FSA to include non-with-profits funds, the scope of the FRS would not extend to such funds unless and until the FRS is amended.

Negative FFAs

9.14   Some funds currently have a negative FFA—in other words, the aggregate of the fund-related debits recognised on the balance sheet is lower than the aggregate of the fund-related credits (other than the FFA) recognised. As a result of the changes the FRS requires to be made to the liability model, it is likely that more negative FFAs will arise in the future.

9.15   There are a number of reasons why a negative FFA might arise, and only some of those reasons would result in the entity taking action to eliminate the negative FFA. For example, if the negative FFA was caused by the measurement of a liability at an amount that takes into account unrecognised assets or by the excessive prudence that will continue to be incorporated in many policyholder liabilities, it may be that corrective action would be deemed unnecessary. However, in other cases corrective action might be expected. Some types of corrective action would address the cause of the negative FFA but would not be accounted for in a way that would result in the negative FFA as shown in the balance sheet being eliminated, some would not.

9.16   A number of respondents noted that FRED 34 was silent on the accounting treatment of negative FFAs and suggested that the FRS should make clear the treatment to be adopted. Some suggested that a negative FFA should always be eliminated as soon as it arises by making a charge to the profit or loss account.

9.17   The Board considered these comments, but concluded that the FRS should remain silent on the accounting treatment. To adopt a blanket requirement that a negative FFA should always be written off to profit and loss account would not be appropriate in all cases. On the other hand, it would be difficult to identify all the circumstances in which it *would* be appropriate.

9.18   The FRS requires entities with a negative FFA to explain how the negative balance arose and why it is that corrective action is not considered necessary.

ABI SORP

9.19   Because of the FRS, the ABI's SORP will, for accounting periods ending on or after 23 December 2005, no longer be consistent in all respects with UK standards. The Board intends to discuss with the ABI how best to amend the SORP to eliminate the inconsistencies.

Corresponding amounts

9.20   The FRED's proposals on the restatement of the corresponding amounts were based on the FRS being implemented for 2004 year-ends, and are therefore not relevant to the final FRS, which is to be implemented for 2005 year-ends.

9.21   Currently the Act requires corresponding amounts to be presented for all the amounts included in the primary financial statements and for those corresponding amounts to be calculated on the same basis as the amounts for the current period. However, paragraph 64 of the FRS states that, when the FRS is first adopted, it will not be necessary to restate certain corresponding amounts in the profit and loss account. That is because, if all the corresponding amounts in the profit and loss account are to be restated, it will be necessary to produce a restated opening balance sheet for 2004. The Board accepts that this will often not be practicable.

EU-adopted IFRS permit entities not to restate corresponding amounts if it is impracticable to do so. Although there is no equivalent provision in UK standards or legislation, the Board has asked the Department of Trade and Industry to consider amending the legal requirements to achieve the same effect.   **9.22**

THE MEMORANDUM OF UNDERSTANDING AND EU-ADOPTED IFRS

As has already been mentioned, the proposal in FRED 34 was that the FRS would be implemented for accounting periods beginning on or after 23 December 2004. There were two main reasons for this: **10.1**

(a)   The Board believed that improvements to life assurance accounting were needed urgently and that the improvements it was proposing were capable of being implemented for 2004 year-ends.

(b)   The Board wished the improvements to be adopted by all UK entities with life assurance activities. If it did not implement the FRS until 2005 year-ends, its standard would not apply to entities preparing their financial statements in accordance with EU-adopted IFRS. On the other hand, if it implemented the FRS in 2004, the grandfathering provisions of IFRS 4 meant that entities preparing their financial statements in accordance with EU-adopted IFRS were likely to be required to continue to adopt the accounting policy changes required in the FRS in 2005 and thereafter.

Almost all respondents questioned whether implementation of the proposals for 2004 year-ends was as practicable as the FRED suggested. In the light of those comments, the Board decided to discuss with the largest entities with life assurance activities a suggestion that they had made to the Board on several occasions: the possibility of the Board deferring its FRS until 2005 and entities preparing EU-adopted IFRS financial statements still complying with the FRS as if it applied directly to them.   **10.2**

The Board has entered into a memorandum of understanding with a number of large entities and with the ABI along exactly those lines. The preparers signing the memorandum have also volunteered to provide most of the information that the FRS requires to be provided in the financial statements from 2005 in the OFR (or equivalent document) in 2004. A copy of the memorandum of understanding, together with details of the entities that have signed it, can be downloaded from the Board's website (www.frc.org.uk/asb).   **10.3**

When the FRED was being developed, the Board considered how the standard would work in the context of existing UK standards and what the implications of IFRS 4 would be for those entities applying the FRS in 2004, then moving onto EU-adopted IFRS in 2005. The implications of IFRS 4 differ depending on whether an accounting policy is being changed in 2004 (and is therefore an existing accounting policy in 2005) or 2005. This meant that, before it could consider deferring the FRS, the Board had to consider the implications of EU-adopted IFRS for a 2005 implementation of the FRS.   **10.4**

(a)   One issue that the Board considered was whether the changes that the FRS requires to be made to accounting policies could be made in 2005, bearing in mind IFRS 4's restrictions on changing accounting policies. As explained in paragraphs 4.73-4.77, the Board concluded that they could.

(b)   Another issue concerned the implications for the FRS of IAS 39's requirement that contracts that have in the past been viewed as insurance but actually meet the definition of a financial instrument (savings business) should be accounted for in accordance with IAS 39 rather than IFRS 4. The question the Board asked itself was would the changes required by IAS 39 have any effect on the accounting and disclosures required by the FRS and, if they would, was that effect troublesome?

(i)   The FRS's 'realistic' liability requirements apply only to certain UK with-profits funds and, under IFRS 4, all UK with-profits activities would be 'insurance contracts that contain discretionary participation features' and would be accounted for in accordance with IFRS 4 rather than IAS 39. As mentioned in subparagraph (a), there is nothing in IFRS 4 that prevents the FRS's 'realistic' liabilities requirements from being complied with. Therefore, IAS 39 has no significant effect on the FRS's 'realistic' liability requirements.

(ii)   IAS 39 appears to have no significant impact on the capital statement disclosures.

(iii)   The FRS requires certain disclosures to be provided in respect of those options and guarantees described in paragraph 50 of the FRS that are not measured at fair value or on the basis of a market-consistent stochastic model. Some of the options and guarantees described in paragraph 50 (and not merely those not measured at fair value or on the basis of a market-consistent stochastic model) will fall within the scope of IAS 39 and will therefore be covered by the disclosure requirements in IAS 32 'Financial Instruments: Disclosure and Presentation' as well.

(iv)   Entities already recognising the value of in-force life assurance business that are reporting under EU-adopted IFRS in 2005 but wishing to comply with this FRS at the same time will find they may have to make three changes to the VIF asset in 2005: in order to comply with IAS 39 they will need to exclude any embedded value that arises on the contracts that IFRS treats as savings business rather than insurance business; in order to comply with IFRS 4 they will need to comply with that standard's restriction on excess investment management fees and, in order to comply with this FRS they will need to exclude any amounts attributed to future investment risk margins.

None of this seemed to suggest that implementing the FRS would be particularly troublesome.

FUTURE DEVELOPMENTS

11.1   The Board recognises that the FRS will not be the final word on insurance accounting. Further improvements are still necessary, but the Board has taken the view that it is not reasonable for it to require further substantial changes in accounting policy at this time.

11.2   The Board has, over the last seven years, taken a close interest in the international project on insurance accounting which was started by the International Accounting Standards Committee (IASC) and was taken up by the IASC's successor body, the IASB. The Board continues to see this international project as the best chance of achieving a fundamental and long-lasting improvement in insurance accounting. It intends to do all that it can, working with the IASB, the FSA and others, to secure that improvement.

11.3   In this context, the FRS can be seen as outlining the direction in which the Board believes insurance accounting should develop over the next few years—away from the excessively prudent, deferral, matching and smoothing model of today towards a model consistent with the reporting framework that applies more generally, supplemented in ways that ensure that the distinctive features of insurance activities can properly be reflected in financial statements. The Board hopes that the industry, freed as most of the biggest UK entities with life assurance activities are from the constraints of Schedules 9 and 9A, will make further improvements in their accounting in this direction.

The FRS is the first output from the Board's insurance project. The Board will also **11.4** be making a formal response to the Financial Secretary on some issues not addressed in the FRS. It intends also to develop its thinking on a range of insurance-related issues and to use that thinking to help the IASB in its work.

THE ASB'S ADVISORY PANEL ON LIFE ASSURANCE

To assist the Board in the development of the FRS and in its ongoing consideration **12.1** of improvements needed to insurance accounting, the Board set up an Advisory Panel, chaired by Mr Julian Hance. Although the Board reached its own conclusions and those conclusions were not necessarily the same as those of individual Panel members, it reached those conclusions only after taking fully into account the advice of Panel members. The Board found the Panel's advice and expertise invaluable during the development of the FRS, and it wishes to place on record its gratitude to Panel members for their work over the last eight months.

Financial Reporting Standard 28 'Corresponding Amounts' is set out in paragraphs 1-18.

The Statement of Standard Accounting Practice, which comprises the paragraphs set in bold type, should be read in the context of the Objective as stated in paragraph 1 and also of the Foreword to Accounting Standards and the Statement of Principles for Financial Reporting currently in issue.

The explanatory paragraphs contained in the FRS shall be regarded as part of the Statement of Standard Accounting Practice insofar as they assist in interpreting that statement.

Appendix III 'The development of the FRS' reviews considerations and arguments that were thought significant by members of the Board in reaching the conslusions on the FRS.

FRS 28
Corresponding amounts

Summary

Financial Reporting Standard 28 sets out the requirements for the disclosure of   **a**
corresponding amounts* for items shown in an entity's primary financial statements
and notes to the financial statements.

The requirements of the FRS apply to financial statements that are intended to give a   **b**
true and fair view except where an accounting standard or Urgent Issues Task Force
Abstract requires or permits an alternative treatment.

Corresponding amounts should be shown for items in the primary financial state-   **c**
ments and the notes to the financial statements.

Where the corresponding amounts are not directly comparable with the amount to   **d**
be shown in respect of the current financial year, they should be adjusted and the
basis for adjustment disclosed in a note to the financial statements.

The FRS permits a reporting entity not to show corresponding amounts for certain   **e**
items in the notes to the financial statements that were previously exempted under
company law. It also does not require corresponding amounts for the earliest period
presented where financial statements for two or more consecutive periods are presented together.

*Also described as 'comparative figures' or 'comparative information' in other accounting standards.

Financial Reporting Standard

OBJECTIVE

1   The objective of this FRS is to require appropriate disclosures of corresponding amounts for items shown in an entity's primary financial statements and notes to the financial statements.

SCOPE

2   **The FRS applies to all financial statements that are intended to give a true and fair view of a reporting entity's financial position and profit and loss (or income and expenditure) for a period.**

3   **The requirements of the FRS apply except where an accounting standard or an Urgent Issues Task Force Abstract requires or permits an alternative treatment.**

4   **Where financial statements intended to give a true and fair view for two or more consecutive periods are presented together this FRS does not require corresponding amounts for the earliest period presented.**

5   **Reporting entities applying the Financial Reporting Standard for Smaller Entities currently applicable are exempt from the FRS.**

DISCLOSURE REQUIREMENTS

Primary financial statements

6   **In respect of every item shown in an entity's primary financial statements the corresponding amount for the accounting period immediately preceding that to which the primary financial statements relate shall also be shown.**

7   Primary financial statements generally comprise statements of financial performance (for example, profit and loss account and statement of total recognised gains and losses); a statement of financial position (for example, balance sheet) and a cash flow statement. FRS 3 'Reporting financial performance' notes that the reconciliation of movements in shareholders' funds may be presented as a primary statement. Other terminology may be used to describe these primary financial statements in some industries and sectors.

8   **Where there is no amount to be shown for an item in respect of the accounting period to which the primary financial statements relate but a corresponding amount can be shown for the item in question for the accounting period immediately preceding that to which the primary financial statements relate, the corresponding amount shall be shown.**

9   **Where a corresponding amount given in accordance with paragraph 6 or 8 of this FRS is not comparable with the amount to be shown for the item in question in respect of the accounting period to which the primary financial statements relate, the former amount shall be adjusted and particulars of the adjustment and the reasons for it shall be disclosed in a note to the financial statements.**

Notes to the financial statements

In respect of every item stated in a note to the financial statements: **10**

(a)   the corresponding amount for the accounting period immediately preceding that to which the financial statements relate shall also be stated, unless not required by paragraph 11 of this FRS; and

(b)   where a corresponding amount is not comparable, it shall be adjusted and particulars of the adjustment and the reasons for it shall be given.

A reporting entity is not required to apply paragraph 10(a) in relation to any amounts   **11** stated for the items listed below which correspond to the requirements of the Companies Act 1985 identified in the marginal notes:

(a)   details of additions, disposals, revaluations, transfers and cumulative depreciation of fixed assets;   *[From Sch 4 42*]*

(b)   transfers to or from reserves and provisions and the source and application of any transfers;   *[From Sch 4 46†]*

(c)   accounting treatment of acquisitions;   *[From Sch 4A 13]*

(d)   details of shareholdings in subsidiary undertakings held by a company or, where group accounts are prepared, held by the parent company and by the group;   *[From Sch 5 2 and 16]*

(e)   significant holdings in undertakings other than subsidiary undertakings where group accounts are not prepared, details of the identity of each class of share in the undertaking held by the company, and the proportion of the nominal value of the shares of that class represented by those shares;   *[From Sch 5 8(3)]*

(f)   the proportion of the capital of the joint venture held by undertakings included in the consolidation;   *[From Sch 5 21(1) (d))]*

(g)   details of shareholdings of associated undertakings held by the parent company and group; and   *[From Sch 5 22(4) and 22(5)]*

(h)   details of other significant shareholdings of the parent company or the group.   *[From Sch 5 24(3), 24(4), 27(3) and 27(4)]*

*The corresponding requirement is set out in Schedule 9 paragraph 55 for banking companies and Schedule 9A paragraph 62 for insurance companies.

†The corresponding requirement is set out in Schedule 9 paragraph 59 for banking companies and Schedule 9A paragraph 66 for insurance companies.

DATE FROM WHICH EFFECTIVE

12   The accounting practices set out in the FRS should be regarded as standard for financial statements relating to accounting periods which begin on or after 1 January 2005 and which end on or after 1 October 2005.

AMENDMENTS TO THE FINANCIAL REPORTING STANDARD FOR SMALLER ENTITIES (EFFECTIVE JANUARY 2005)

[Not reproduced, as all changes have been made to the FRSSE]

Adoption of FRS 28 by the Board

Financial Reporting Standard 28 *Corresponding Amounts* was approved for issue by the ten members of the Accounting Standards Board.

Ian Mackintosh   Chairman
Andrew Lennard   Technical Director
Michael Ashley
Marisa Cassoni
Anthony Good
Roger Marshall
Isobel Sharp
Jonathan Symonds
Helen Weir
Peter Westlake

Appendix I
Note on Legal Requirements

GREAT BRITAIN

1 The statutory requirements relating to the disclosure of corresponding amounts for items presented in the balance sheet or profit and loss account are set out in paragraph 3(5) and paragraph 4 of Schedule 4 to the Companies Act 1985. Corresponding requirements are set out in Schedule 9 paragraphs 3(4) and 4 for banking companies and groups and in Schedule 9A paragraphs 2(4) and 3 for insurance companies and groups. Schedule 4 to the Act does not apply to small companies to the extent that they choose instead to comply with the reduced requirements set out in Schedule 8.

2 The UK Government has recently amended the Companies Act 1985 by a statutory instrument – SI 2005 No. 2280 'Companies Act 1985 (Investment Companies and Accounting and Audit Amendments) Regulations 2005'. The statutory instrument will apply in respect of companies' financial years which begin on or after 1 January 2005 and which end on or after 1 October 2005.

3 The statutory instrument amends paragraph 4(2) of Schedule 4 by removing the requirement to restate corresponding amounts in the balance sheet and profit and loss account where they are not comparable. The statutory instrument deletes paragraph 58(2) of Schedule 4 thereby removing the requirement to provide corresponding amounts for items disclosed in the notes to the financial statements. As a consequence paragraph 58(3) of Schedule 4, which previously provided certain exemptions from the requirement to provide corresponding amounts for items disclosed in the notes to the financial statements, is also deleted.

4 The Regulations make corresponding amendments to Schedule 9 for banking companies and groups and Schedule 9A for insurance companies and groups to the 1985 Act.

NORTHERN IRELAND

5 The statutory requirements in Northern Ireland are set out in the Companies (Northern Ireland) Order 1986. These requirements are identical to the legislation for Great Britain cited above. Under the Northern Ireland Act 1998 company law is a transferred matter. Northern Ireland is expected to make Statutory Regulations, with provisions similar to those in the statutory instrument SI 2005 No. 2280 to amend the Companies (Northern Ireland) Order 1986. It is intended these Regulations should take effect before the end of 2005.

REPUBLIC OF IRELAND

6 The statutory requirements in the Republic of Ireland that correspond to those cited above for Great Britain are shown in the following table.

Great Britain Companies Act	*Republic of Ireland*
Schedule 4, paragraph 3(5)	Companies (Amendment) Act 1986, section 4(9)
Schedule 4, paragraph 4(1)	Companies (Amendment) Act 1986, section 4(8)
Schedule 4, paragraph 4(2)	Companies (Amendment) Act 1986, section 4(8)
Schedule 4, paragraph 4(3)	Companies (Amendment) Act 1986, section 4(10)
Schedule 4, paragraph 42	Companies (Amendment) Act 1986, Schedule paragraph 29
Schedule 4, paragraph 46	Companies (Amendment) Act 1986, Schedule paragraph 32
Schedule 4A, paragraph 13	No specific equivalent in Republic of Ireland legislation
Schedule 5, paragraph 2	Companies (Amendment) Act 1986, section 16(1)
Schedule 5, paragraph 16	Companies (Amendment) Act 1986, section 16(1), and
	European Communities (Companies: Group Accounts) Regulations 1992, Schedule paragraph 18
Schedule 5, paragraph 8(3)	Companies (Amendment) Act 1986, section 16(1)
Schedule 5, paragraph 21(1)(d)	No equivalent reference
Schedule 5, paragraphs 22(4) and 22(5)	Companies (Amendment) Act 1986, section 16(1)
Schedule 5, paragraphs 24(3) and 24(4)	Companies (Amendment) Act 1986, section 16(1)
Schedule 5, paragraphs 27(3) and 27(4)	
Schedule 9	European Communities (Credit Institutions: Accounts) Regulations 1992
Schedule 9A	European Communities (Insurance Undertakings: Accounts) Regulations, 1996

The Department of Enterprise, Trade and Employment in the Republic of Ireland is **7**
considering similar amendments to those made in Great Britain.

Appendix II
Compliance with International Accounting Standards

1   The International Accounting Standards Board deals with corresponding amounts in its standards IAS 1 'Presentation of Financial Statements', IAS 8 'Accounting Policies, Changes in Accounting Estimates and Errors' and IFRS 1 'First-time Adoption of International Financial Reporting Standards'.

2   IAS 1 'Presentation of Financial Statements' paragraphs 36 to 41 set out requirements for comparative information. IFRS 1 'First-time adoption of IFRS' paragraph 36A provides exemption from the requirement to restate comparative information for IAS 32, IAS 39 and IFRS 4 for entities adopting IFRSs before 1 January 2006. IAS 8 'Accounting Policies, Changes in Accounting Estimates and Errors' deals in general with adjustments to comparative information required when an entity changes an accounting policy or corrects an error. It also discusses the impracticability of retrospective restatement.

3   The requirements of the FRS are consistent with international accounting standards in most cases except that:

(a)   the FRS does not explicitly require comparative information for narrative and descriptive information required under paragraph 36 of IAS 1;

(b)   the FRS does not permit non-restatement of comparative amounts on first time adoption of certain accounting standards or require disclosures of this as set out in paragraph 36A of IFRS 1;

(c)   IAS 1 paragraph 38 does not require reclassification of comparative amounts where reclassification is impractical. This FRS does not contain a similar exemption; and

(d)   paragraph 11 of the FRS provides specific exemptions from the requirement to disclose corresponding amounts for certain items disclosed in a note to the financial statements, not all of which have equivalent exemptions in IFRS.

Appendix III
The development of the FRS

BACKGROUND

In March 2005 the Department of Trade and Industry (DTI) issued a Consultation   **1**
Document 'A consultation on extending use of summary financial statements and
other minor changes'. In parallel the ASB issued Financial Reporting Exposure
Draft 35 'Corresponding Amounts'. FRED 35 related to one aspect of the Consultation Document: the proposals in respect of corresponding amounts.

Following the consultation period the Companies Act 1985 was amended by a   **2**
statutory instrument SI 2005 No. 2280 'Companies Act 1985 (Investment Companies
and Accounting and Audit Amendments) Regulations 2005'.

The amendments made by the statutory instrument removed from the law the   **3**
requirement to restate corresponding amounts where they are not comparable –
although it remains a legal requirement to provide corresponding amounts in respect
of the balance sheet and the profit and loss account, and the law permits them to be
restated where they are not comparable. The amendments also removed from the law
the requirement to provide corresponding amounts for items disclosed in the notes to
the financial statements.

As a consequence of the amendments to the Companies Act 1985 it falls to   **4**
accounting standards to prescribe whether corresponding amounts should be
restated and whether corresponding amounts should be provided for amounts disclosed in the notes to the financial statements. FRED 35 set out the Board's proposal
for a new FRS to require disclosure of corresponding amounts, generally adjusted
onto a comparable basis, in an entity's primary financial statements and items disclosed in the notes to the financial statements.

APPROACH ADOPTED BY THE BOARD

The Board considers that the disclosure of corresponding amounts, generally   **5**
adjusted onto a comparable basis, is an important part of accepted accounting
practice. This Financial Reporting Standard is intended to secure this. In the main,
the FRS replicates the legal requirements on corresponding amounts that existed
prior to amendments made by the statutory instrument.

The Board intends that entities using UK IFRS-based accounting standards should   **6**
be able to take advantage of the same exemptions as entities adopting IFRS. To
enable the Board to incorporate these exemptions in UK IFRS-based standards the
requirements of this FRS do not apply where a UK accounting standard or Urgent
Issues Task Force Abstract requires or permits an alternative accounting treatment.
This will allow the Board to consider exemptions for IFRS-based UK standards as
the individual standards are developed.

CONVERGENCE WITH INTERNATIONAL FINANCIAL
REPORTING STANDARDS

The Board considered adopting the requirements of International Financial   **7**
Reporting Standards for corresponding amounts. These are set out in IAS 1 'Presentation of Financial Statements', IFRS 1 'First-time Adoption of International

Financial Reporting Standards' and IAS 8 'Accounting Policies, Changes in Accounting Estimates and Errors'. However, the Board concluded it was undesirable to introduce on a piecemeal basis elements of individual international accounting standards. This might introduce unintended consequences for other UK standards, whilst not achieving a substantive step towards convergence.

8   The Board also considered whether to introduce a general exemption from restating corresponding amounts on a comparable basis on grounds of practicality. The Board noted there is no such exemption under present or past requirements and considered that practicality is better addressed as each new accounting standard is developed.

9   In considering the comments made by respondents to FRED 35 the Board noted that most respondents supported the Board's approach in respect of these matters and the proposals have been retained in the FRS.

SCOPE OF THE FRS

10   The requirements of the FRS to disclose corresponding amounts apply to all entities and not just entities reporting under the Companies Act 1985. In its Statement of Principles* the Board notes that information in an entity's financial statements gains greatly in usefulness if it can be compared with similar information about the entity for some other period or point in time in order to identify trends in financial performance and financial position. It has become widely accepted practice to provide corresponding amounts in the financial statements of all entities. The FRS requires that where corresponding amounts are not comparable they should be restated unless an accounting standard or Urgent Issues Task Force Abstract permits or requires an alternative treatment.

11   During its redeliberations of FRED 35 the Board became aware that the requirements proposed in FRED 35 could, in certain circumstances, be considered to extend regulatory requirements. One possible example was where a regulator requires a three year financial record and that the information given for each of the three years is required to give a true and fair view. The impact of FRED 35 would be to require a further year of corresponding amounts (ie corresponding amounts for the earliest year presented and thereby a further year presented). The Board decided it would be appropriate to amend the scope of the FRS such that where financial statements intended to give a true and fair view for two or more consecutive periods are presented together the FRS does not require corresponding amounts for the earliest period presented. This would avoid the potential extension of reporting requirements, as set out in the example above, but preserve the requirement to present corresponding amounts for at least one period.

EXEMPTIONS

12   As noted FRED 35 was issued in parallel with the DTI's Consultation Document; 'A consultation on extending use of summary financial statements and other minor changes'. The Consultation Document did not propose to amend the legal requirements relating to corresponding amounts required for the notes to the financial statements. The DTI sought views on whether the requirements for disclosure in the notes should be retained in the Companies Act 1985, or should be removed and any future requirements be a matter for the ASB.

Statement of Principles for Financial Reporting; December 1999.

Previously the Companies Act 1985 (paragraph 58 of Schedule 4) required corresponding amounts for every item stated in a note to the accounts for the financial year immediately preceding that to which the accounts relate. It also provided a number of specific exemptions from this requirement. The amendments made by the statutory instrument deleted the requirement to provide corresponding amounts for every item stated in a note to the accounts and thereby the exemptions from this requirement. **13**

FRED 35 replicated the legal requirements and exemptions to these requirements previously set out in paragraph 58 of Schedule 4 to the Companies Act 1985 and corresponding schedules for banking and insurance and companies, except that it did not include an exemption from the requirement to provide corresponding amounts for loans and other dealings in favour of directors and others*. This was on the basis that the corresponding amounts for these items can often be easily provided and inclusion would enhance the usefulness of the financial statements. It is also difficult to justify these specific exemptions as there is no general exemption for related party transactions. Respondents to FRED 35 were generally in favour of the Board's proposals and these have been retained. **14**

DATE FROM WHICH EFFECTIVE

The Regulations are effective in respect of financial years which begin on or after 1 January 2005 and which end on or after 1 October 2005. The FRS is effective from the same date. **15**

---

*Part II and III of Schedule 6 (loans and other dealings in favour of directors and others) to the Companies Act 1985.

Financial Reporting Standard 29 embodies IFRS 7 'Financial Instruments: Disclosures' and some amendments to that standard adopted for entities subject to UK accounting standards.

The Statement of Standard Accounting Practice in FRS 29 is set out in paragraphs 1-45A and the appendices. All paragraphs have equal authority. Paragraphs in bold type state the main principles.

Accompanying the Statement of Standard Accounting Practice is the basis for the conclusions reached in the Statement and some implementation guidance, neither of which forms part of the Statement.

The Statement of Standard Accounting Practice should be read in the context of its objectives as stated in paragraph 1, the Basis for Conclusions set out in paragraphs BC1-EBC16, and the Accounting Standard Board's 'Foreword to Accounting Standards' and 'Statement of Principles for Financial Reporting'.

Preface by the Accounting Standards Board

This Financial Reporting Standard (FRS) has the effect of implementing the International Accounting Standards Board's (IASB's) International Financial Reporting Standard (IFRS) 7 'Financial Instruments: Disclosures' in the UK and Republic of Ireland for entities not preparing their financial statements in accordance with international financial reporting standards pursuant to the Regulation of the European Parliament and of the Council on the Application of International Accounting Standards.

This Standard sets out requirements for disclosures relating to financial instruments and capital. Unlike IFRS 7, it only applies to entities within the scope of FRS 26 'Financial Instruments: Measurement' and comes into effect for accounting periods beginning on or after 1 January 2007. This Standard replaces the disclosure requirements of FRS 25 'Financial Instruments: Disclosure and Presentation'.

Entities not applying FRS 26 are not required to comply with this Standard, although voluntary compliance is permitted.*

The Board has issued FRS 29 to enable entities within the current scope of FRS 26 to adopt this standard in 2005 or 2006 if they so wish, with identical scope exemptions for subsidiaries and parent companies to those for the disclosure requirements of FRS 25. However, the FRS may be amended at a later date to remove some or all scope exemptions.

In addition to the differences in scope set out above, the following differences exist between the requirements, scope and effective date of FRS 29 and IFRS 7:

- entities applying the FRSSE will be exempt from the FRS;
- disclosures are not required for certain subsidiary undertakings where at least 90 percent of the voting rights are held within the group, and parent companies in their single-entity financial statements provided the entity is included in publicly available consolidated financial statements which include disclosures that comply with this Standard;
- the FRS contains certain additional requirements for those entities not applying the requirements of FRS 26 (IAS 39) 'Financial Instruments: Measurement' but who wish to comply with the disclosure requirements of this standard voluntarily;
- certain disclosure requirements relating to the designation of financial assets and financial liabilities as at fair value through profit and loss account were not included as they were not considered necessary;
- disclosure requirements relating to capital that the IASB made as an amendment to IAS 1 'Presentation of Financial Statements' have been included in Appendix E to FRS 29; and
- certain transitional provisions from IFRS 1 'First-time Adoption of International Financial Reporting Standards' permitting entities applying the requirements of the FRS before 1 January 2007 not to restate comparatives to comply with this standard have been added.

*The Board is currently considering proposals to extend the scope of FRS 26, as set out in the exposure draft 'Amendment to FRS 26: Extension of Scope and Recognition and Derecognition' (April 2005), and may decide to: extend the scope of FRS 26 and thus the effective scope of FRS 29; require some or all of the disclosures of FRS 29 to be made by entities not within the scope of FRS 26; and amend the scope exemption for subsidiary undertakings and parent companies. The Board may also implement the derecognition parts of IAS 39, in which case it will also implement the related disclosures in IFRS 7 (and paragraph 13 in particular). **Editor's note**: These changes have now been made.*

The text of IFRS 7 contains various references to other IFRSs. In FRS 29 those references have been amended where necessary to enable the Standard to be applied in a UK context. The Accounting Standards Board believes that those amendments do not change the requirements of IFRS 7 in any way.

IFRS 7 sets out amendments to other IFRSs. The Board has made amendments to FRS 26 corresponding to those made by IFRS 7 to IAS 39 'Financial Instruments: Recognition and Measurement'. Other amendments set out in IFRS 7 are not relevant in a UK context and have not been included in FRS 29.

For entities applying this Standard, it supersedes the disclosure requirements of FRS 25 and FRS 13 'Derivatives and Other Financial Instruments: Disclosures'.

In April 2006 the Board amended FRS 26 to include the IAS 39 material on recognition and derecognition in the Standard. Accordingly, on implementation of this amendment the corresponding disclosure requirements of IAS 32 are implemented in FRS 25. These new disclosure requirements replace disclosures required for financial assets and liabilities by FRS 5 'Reporting the Substance of Transactions'. These amendments are effective for accounting periods on or after 1 January 2007, with earlier adoption permitted.

FRS 29
(IFRS 7) Financial instruments: disclosures

(Issued December 2005)

Contents

paragraphs

Introduction*

Reasons for issuing the IFRS

IN1   In recent years, the techniques used by entities for measuring and managing exposure to risks arising from financial instruments have evolved and new risk management concepts and approaches have gained acceptance. In addition, many public and private sector initiatives have proposed improvements to the disclosure framework for risks arising from financial instruments.

IN2   The International Accounting Standards Board believes that users of financial statements need information about an entity's exposure to risks and how those risks are managed. Such information can influence a user's assessment of the financial position and financial performance of an entity or of the amount, timing and uncertainty of its future cash flows. Greater transparency regarding those risks allows users to make more informed judgements about risk and return.

IN3   Consequently, the Board concluded that there was a need to revise and enhance the disclosures in IAS 30 *Disclosures in the Financial Statements of Banks and Similar Financial Institutions†* and IAS 32 *Financial Instruments: Disclosure and Presentation‡*. As part of this revision, the Board removed duplicative disclosures and simplified the disclosures about concentrations of risk, credit risk, liquidity risk and market risk in IAS 32.

Main features of the IFRS

IN4   IFRS 7 applies to all risks arising from all financial instruments, except those instruments listed in paragraph 3. The IFRS applies to all entities, including entities that have few financial instruments (eg a manufacturer whose only financial instruments are accounts receivable and accounts payable) and those that have many financial instruments (eg a financial institution most of whose assets and liabilities are financial instruments). However, the extent of disclosure required depends on the extent of the entity's use of financial instruments and of its exposure to risk.

IN5   The IFRS requires disclosure of:

(a)   the significance of financial instruments for an entity's financial position and performance. These disclosures incorporate many of the requirements previously in IAS 32.

(b)   qualitative and quantitative information about exposure to risks arising from financial instruments, including specified minimum disclosures about credit risk, liquidity risk and market risk. The qualitative disclosures describe management's objectives, policies and processes for managing those risks. The quantitative disclosures provide information about the extent to which the entity is exposed to risk, based on information provided internally to the entity's key management personnel. Together, these disclosures provide an

*ASB Footnote: *Although references to specific IFRSs have been amended in the main section of the Standard, references in the Introduction, which describes the issue of IFRS 7, have been left unchanged.*

†ASB Footnote: *IAS 30 has no equivalent in the UK and Republic of Ireland.*

‡ASB Footnote: *The equivalent standard in the UK and Republic of Ireland is FRS 25 (IAS 32) Financial Instruments: Disclsoure and Presentation.*

overview of the entity's use of financial instruments and the exposures to risks they create.

The IFRS includes in Appendix B mandatory application guidance that explains how to apply the requirements in the IFRS. The IFRS is accompanied by non-mandatory Implementation Guidance that describes how an entity might provide the disclosures required by the IFRS. **IN6**

The IFRS supersedes IAS 30 and the disclosure requirements of IAS 32. The presentation requirements of IAS 32 remain unchanged. **IN7**

The IFRS is effective for annual periods beginning on or after 1 January 2007. Earlier application is encouraged. **IN8**

Financial Instruments: Disclosures

OBJECTIVE

1   The objective of this Standard is to require entities to provide disclosures in their financial statements that enable users to evaluate:

(a)   the significance of financial instruments for the entity's financial position and performance; and

(b)   the nature and extent of risks arising from financial instruments to which the entity is exposed during the period and at the reporting date, and how the entity manages those risks.

2   The principles in this Standard complement the principles for recognising, measuring and presenting financial assets and financial liabilities in FRS 25 (IAS 32) *Financial Instruments: Presentation* and FRS 26 (IAS 39) *Financial Instruments: Recognition and Measurement*.

SCOPE

2A   This Standard applies to all financial statements that are intended to give a true and fair view of a reporting entity's financial position and profit or loss (or income and expenditure), subject to the exemptions in 2B to 2E below.

2B   Reporting entities applying the Financial Reporting Standard for Smaller Entities (FRSSE) currently applicable are exempt from this Standard.

2C   Entities that are not applying FRS 26 are exempt from this Standard.

2D   The following entities are exempted from this Standard:

(a)   subsidiary undertakings, other than banks or insurance companies, 90 percent or more of whose voting rights are controlled within the group; and

(b)   parent companies in respect of their single-entity financial statements

provided the entity is included in publicly available consolidated financial statements which include disclosures that comply with this Standard.

2E   Although not mandatory, entities that are not applying FRS 26 are encouraged to comply with the disclosure requirements of this Standard, adapting these in line with the entity's accounting policies for the relevant transactions, and describing those accounting policies as required by paragraphs 21, 21A and 21B. In particular:

(a)   interest rate disclosures should be based on the rates at which interest is accounted for under the entity's accounting policies if this is different from the effective interest rate defined in FRS 26;

(b)   disclosures on hedge accounting set out in paragraphs 22 to 24 should be applied to the entity's own hedge accounting policies; and

(c)   instruments should be treated as insurance contracts for the purposes of disclosure if they are accounted for as such under the entity's accounting policies, even if they meet the definition of a financial instrument in FRS 26.

3   This Standard shall be applied by all entities to all types of financial instruments, except:

(a) those interests in subsidiary, quasi-subsidiary and associated undertakings, partnerships and joint ventures that are accounted for under FRS 2 *Accounting for Subsidiary Undertakings*; FRS 5 *Reporting the Substance of Transactions*; and FRS 9 *Associates and Joint Ventures*. However, when entities apply this standard to an interest in a subsidiary, quasi-subsidiary or associated undertaking, partnership or joint venture that is accounted for using FRS 26 or is otherwise accounted for as held for resale; in those cases, entities shall apply the disclosure requirements in FRSs 2, 5 and 9 in addition to those in this Standard. Entities shall also apply this Standard to all derivatives linked to interests in subsidiaries, quasi-subsidiary or associated undertakings, partnerships or joint ventures unless the derivative meets the definition of an equity instrument in FRS 25.

(b) employers' rights and obligations arising from employee benefit plans, to which FRS 17 *Retirement Benefits* applies.

(c) contracts for contingent consideration in a business combination (see paragraphs 81—84 of FRS 7 *Fair Values in Acquisition Accounting*). This exemption applies only to the acquirer.

(d) insurance contracts as defined in Appendix C to FRS 26. However, this Standard applies to derivatives that are embedded in insurance contracts if FRS 26 requires the entity to account for them separately. Moreover, an issuer shall apply this Standard to *financial guarantee contracts* if the issuer applies FRS 26 in measuring the contracts.

(e) financial instruments, contracts and obligations under share-based payment transactions to which FRS 20 (IFRS 2) *Share-based Payment* applies, except that this Standard applies to contracts within the scope of paragraphs 5–7 of FRS 26.

This Standard applies to recognised and unrecognised financial instruments. **4** Recognised financial instruments include financial assets and financial liabilities that are within the scope of FRS 26. Unrecognised financial instruments include some financial instruments that, although outside the scope of FRS 26, are within the scope of this Standard (such as some loan commitments).

This Standard applies to contracts to buy or sell a non-financial item that are within **5** the scope of FRS 26 (see paragraphs 5–7 of FRS 26).

CLASSES OF FINANCIAL INSTRUMENTS AND LEVEL OF DISCLOSURE

When this Standard requires disclosures by class of financial instrument, an entity **6** shall group financial instruments into classes that are appropriate to the nature of the information disclosed and that take into account the characteristics of those financial instruments. An entity shall provide sufficient information to permit reconciliation to the line items presented in the balance sheet.

SIGNIFICANCE OF FINANCIAL INSTRUMENTS FOR FINANCIAL POSITION AND PERFORMANCE

An entity shall disclose information that enables users of its financial statements to **7** evaluate the significance of financial instruments for its financial position and performance.

Balance sheet

Categories of financial assets and financial liabilities

8   The carrying amounts of each of the following categories, as defined in FRS 26, shall be disclosed either on the face of the balance sheet or in the notes:

(a) financial assets at fair value through profit or loss, showing separately (i) those designated as such upon initial recognition and (ii) those classified as held for trading in accordance with FRS 26;
(b) held-to-maturity investments;
(c) loans and receivables;
(d) available-for-sale financial assets;
(e) financial liabilities at fair value through profit or loss, showing separately (i) those designated as such upon initial recognition and (ii) those classified as held for trading in accordance with FRS 26; and
(f) financial liabilities measured at amortised cost.

Financial assets or financial liabilities at fair value through profit or loss

10   If the entity has designated a financial liability as at fair value through profit or loss in accordance with paragraph 9 of FRS 26, it shall disclose:

(a) the amount of change, during the period and cumulatively, in the fair value of the financial liability that is attributable to changes in the credit risk of that liability determined either:

   (i) as the amount of change in its fair value that is not attributable to changes in market conditions that give rise to market risk (see Appendix B, paragraph B4); or
   (ii) using an alternative method the entity believes more faithfully represents the amount of change in its fair value that is attributable to changes in the credit risk of the liability.

   Changes in market conditions that give rise to market risk include changes in a benchmark interest rate, the price of another entity's financial instrument, a commodity price, a foreign exchange rate or an index of prices or rates. For contracts that include a unit-linking feature, changes in market conditions include changes in the performance of the related internal or external investment fund.

(b) the difference between the financial liability's carrying amount and the amount the entity would be contractually required to pay at maturity to the holder of the obligation.

11   The entity shall disclose:

(a) the methods used to comply with the requirements in paragraph 10(a).
(b) if the entity believes that the disclosure it has given to comply with the requirements in paragraph 10(a) does not faithfully represent the change in the fair value of the financial asset or financial liability attributable to changes in its credit risk, the reasons for reaching this conclusion and the factors it believes are relevant.

Reclassification

12   If the entity has reclassified a financial asset as one measured:

(a) at cost or amortised cost, rather than at fair value; or

(b)   at fair value, rather than at cost or amortised cost,

it shall disclose the amount reclassified into and out of each category and the reason for that reclassification (see paragraphs 51–54 of FRS 26).

Derecognition

An entity may have transferred financial assets in such a way that part or all of the   **13**
financial assets do not qualify for derecognition (see paragraphs 15–37 of IAS 39). The entity shall disclose for each class of such financial assets:

(a)   the nature of the assets;
(b)   the nature of the risks and rewards of ownership to which the entity remains exposed;
(c)   when the entity continues to recognise all of the assets, the carrying amounts of the assets and of the associated liabilities; and
(d)   when the entity continues to recognise the assets to the extent of its continuing involvement, the total carrying amount of the original assets, the amount of the assets that the entity continues to recognise, and the carrying amount of the associated liabilities.

Collateral

An entity shall disclose: **14**

(a)   the carrying amount of financial assets it has pledged as collateral for liabilities or contingent liabilities; and
(b)   the terms and conditions relating to its pledge.

When an entity holds collateral (of financial or non-financial assets) and is permitted   **15**
to sell or repledge the collateral in the absence of default by the owner of the collateral, it shall disclose:

(a)   the fair value of the collateral held;
(b)   the fair value of any such collateral sold or repledged, and whether the entity has an obligation to return it; and
(c)   the terms and conditions associated with its use of the collateral.

Allowance account for credit losses

When financial assets are impaired by credit losses and the entity records the   **16**
impairment in a separate account (eg an allowance account used to record individual impairments or a similar account used to record a collective impairment of assets) rather than directly reducing the carrying amount of the asset, it shall disclose a reconciliation of changes in that account during the period for each class of financial assets.

Compound financial instruments with multiple embedded derivatives

If an entity has issued an instrument that contains both a liability and an equity   **17**
component (see paragraph 28 of FRS 25) and the instrument has multiple embedded derivatives whose values are interdependent (such as a callable convertible debt instrument), it shall disclose the existence of those features.

Defaults and breaches

18   For *loans payable* recognised at the reporting date, an entity shall disclose:

(a)   details of any defaults during the period of principal, interest, sinking fund, or redemption terms of those loans payable;

(b)   the carrying amount of the loans payable in default at the reporting date; and

(c)   whether the default was remedied, or the terms of the loans payable were renegotiated, before the financial statements were authorised for issue.

19   If, during the period, there were breaches of loan agreement terms other than those described in paragraph 18, an entity shall disclose the same information as required by paragraph 18 if those breaches permitted the lender to demand accelerated repayment (unless the breaches were remedied, or the terms of the loan were renegotiated, on or before the reporting date).

Income statement and equity

Items of income, expense, gains or losses

20   An entity shall disclose the following items of income, expense, gains or losses either on the face of the financial statements or in the notes:

(a)   net gains or net losses on:

(i)   financial assets or financial liabilities at fair value through profit or loss, showing separately those on financial assets or financial liabilities designated as such upon initial recognition, and those on financial assets or financial liabilities that are classified as held for trading in accordance with FRS 26;

(ii)   available-for-sale financial assets, showing separately the amount of gain or loss recognised directly in equity during the period and the amount removed from equity and recognised in profit or loss for the period;

(iii)   held-to-maturity investments;

(iv)   loans and receivables; and

(v)   financial liabilities measured at amortised cost;

(b)   total interest income and total interest expense (calculated using the effective interest method) for financial assets or financial liabilities that are not at fair value through profit or loss;

(c)   fee income and expense (other than amounts included in determining the effective interest rate) arising from:

(i)   financial assets or financial liabilities that are not at fair value through profit or loss; and

(ii)   trust and other fiduciary activities that result in the holding or investing of assets on behalf of individuals, trusts, retirement benefit plans, and other institutions;

(d)   interest income on impaired financial assets accrued in accordance with paragraph AG93 of FRS 26; and

(e)   the amount of any impairment loss for each class of financial asset.

An issuer applying paragraph 20(b) of this Standard to contracts with a discretionary **20A** participation feature shall disclose the total interest expense recognised in profit or loss, but need not calculate such interest expense using the effective interest method.*

Accounting policies

In accordance with paragraph 55 of FRS 18 *Accounting Policies*, an entity discloses **21** the accounting policies that are material in the context of the entity's financial statements.

†For entities that choose to apply this Standard but do not apply FRS 26, it will be **21A** particularly important to provide adequate information for users of financial statements to understand the basis on which financial assets and financial liabilities have been measured. Therefore, disclosures of accounting policies indicate not only whether cost, fair value or some other basis of measurement has been applied to a specific class of asset or liability but also the method of applying that basis. For example, for financial instruments carried on the cost basis, an entity may be required to disclose how it accounts for:

(a) costs of acquisition or issuance;
(b) premiums and discounts on monetary financial assets and financial liabilities;
(c) changes in the estimated amount of determinable future cash flows associated with a monetary financial instrument such as a bond indexed to a commodity price;
(d) changes in circumstances that result in significant uncertainty about the timely collection of all contractual amounts due from monetary financial assets;
(e) declines in the fair value of financial assets below their carrying amount; and
(f) restructured financial liabilities.

For financial assets and financial liabilities carried at fair value, an entity indicates whether carrying amounts are determined from quoted market prices, independent appraisals, discounted cash flow analysis or another appropriate method, and discloses any significant assumptions made in applying those methods.

An entity discloses the basis for reporting in the income statement realised and **21B** unrealised gains and losses, interest and other items of income and expense associated with financial assets and financial liabilities. The disclosure includes information about the basis on which income and expense arising from financial instruments held for hedging purposes are recognised. When an entity presents income and expense items on a net basis even though the corresponding financial asset and financial liabilities on the balance sheet have not been offset, the reason for that presentation is disclosed if the effect is significant.

---

*ASB Footnote: *The IASB have incorporated this exemption from the effective interest rate method for issuers of financial instruments with discretionary participation features in IFRS 4* Insurance Contracts. *The ASB have replicated the text here to afford UK GAAP preparers the same exemption.*

†ASB footnote: *This paragraph is identical (apart from a necessary but cosmetic change to the introductory text) to paragraph 54 of the 1998 version of IAS 32, which the IASB has subsequently deleted. The ASB has reinstated it because compliance with FRS 26 is not mandatory for all companies initially. Similarly, paragraph 21B is identical to paragraph 55 of the 1998 version of IAS 32, which the IASB has subsequently deleted but the ASB has reinstated.*

Hedge accounting

22   An entity shall disclose the following separately for each type of hedge described in FRS 26 (ie fair value hedges, cash flow hedges, and hedges of net investments in foreign operations):

(a)   a description of each type of hedge;

(b)   a description of the financial instruments designated as hedging instruments and their fair values at the reporting date; and

(c)   the nature of the risks being hedged.

23   For cash flow hedges, an entity shall disclose:

(a)   the periods when the cash flows are expected to occur and when they are expected to affect profit or loss;

(b)   a description of any forecast transaction for which hedge accounting had previously been used, but which is no longer expected to occur;

(c)   the amount that was recognised in equity during the period;

(d)   the amount that was removed from equity and included in profit or loss for the period, showing the amount included in each line item in the income statement; and

(e)   the amount that was removed from equity during the period and included in the initial cost or other carrying amount of a non-financial asset or non-financial liability whose acquisition or incurrence was a hedged highly probable forecast transaction.

24   An entity shall disclose separately:

(a)   in fair value hedges, gains or losses:

(i)   on the hedging instrument; and

(ii)   on the hedged item attributable to the hedged risk.

(b)   the ineffectiveness recognised in profit or loss that arises from cash flow hedges; and

(c)   the ineffectiveness recognised in profit or loss that arises from hedges of net investments in foreign operations.

Fair value

25   Except as set out in paragraph 29, for each class of financial assets and financial liabilities (see paragraph 6), an entity shall disclose the fair value of that class of assets and liabilities in a way that permits it to be compared with its carrying amount.

26   In disclosing fair values, an entity shall group financial assets and financial liabilities into classes, but shall offset them only to the extent that their carrying amounts are offset in the balance sheet.

27   An entity shall disclose:

(a)   the methods and, when a valuation technique is used, the assumptions applied in determining fair values of each class of financial assets or financial liabilities. For example, if applicable, an entity discloses information about the assumptions relating to prepayment rates, rates of estimated credit losses, and interest rates or discount rates.

(b)   whether fair values are determined, in whole or in part, directly by reference to published price quotations in an active market or are estimated using a valuation technique (see paragraphs AG71–AG79 of FRS 26).
(c)   whether the fair values recognised or disclosed in the financial statements are determined in whole or in part using a valuation technique based on assumptions that are not supported by prices from observable current market transactions in the same instrument (ie without modification or repackaging) and not based on available observable market data. For fair values that are recognised in the financial statements, if changing one or more of those assumptions to reasonably possible alternative assumptions would change fair value significantly, the entity shall state this fact and disclose the effect of those changes. For this purpose, significance shall be judged with respect to profit or loss, and total assets or total liabilities, or, when changes in fair value are recognised in equity, total equity.
(d)   if (c) applies, the total amount of the change in fair value estimated using such a valuation technique that was recognised in profit or loss during the period.

If the market for a financial instrument is not active, an entity establishes its fair **28** value using a valuation technique (see paragraphs AG74–AG79 of FRS 26). Nevertheless, the best evidence of fair value at initial recognition is the transaction price (ie the fair value of the consideration given or received), unless conditions described in paragraph AG76 of FRS 26 are met. It follows that there could be a difference between the fair value at initial recognition and the amount that would be determined at that date using the valuation technique. If such a difference exists, an entity shall disclose, by class of financial instrument:

(a)   its accounting policy for recognising that difference in profit or loss to reflect a change in factors (including time) that market participants would consider in setting a price (see paragraph AG76A of FRS 26); and
(b)   the aggregate difference yet to be recognised in profit or loss at the beginning and end of the period and a reconciliation of changes in the balance of this difference.

Disclosures of fair value are not required: **29**

(a)   when the carrying amount is a reasonable approximation of fair value, for example, for financial instruments such as short-term trade receivables and payables;
(b)   for an investment in equity instruments that do not have a quoted market price in an active market, or derivatives linked to such equity instruments, that is measured at cost in accordance with FRS 26 because its fair value cannot be measured reliably; or
(c)   for a contract containing a discretionary participation feature (as described in Appendix C to FRS 26) if the fair value of that feature cannot be measured reliably.

In the cases described in paragraph 29(b) and (c), an entity shall disclose information **30** to help users of the financial statements make their own judgements about the extent of possible differences between the carrying amount of those financial assets or financial liabilities and their fair value, including:

(a)   the fact that fair value information has not been disclosed for these instruments because their fair value cannot be measured reliably;
(b)   a description of the financial instruments, their carrying amount, and an explanation of why fair value cannot be measured reliably;
(c)   information about the market for the instruments;

(d)   information about whether and how the entity intends to dispose of the financial instruments; and

(e)   if financial instruments whose fair value previously could not be reliably measured are derecognised, that fact, their carrying amount at the time of derecognition, and the amount of gain or loss recognised.

Nature and extent of risks arising from financial instruments

31   An entity shall disclose information that enables users of its financial statements to evaluate the nature and extent of risks arising from financial instruments to which the entity is exposed at the reporting date.

32   The disclosures required by paragraphs 33–42 focus on the risks that arise from financial instruments and how they have been managed. These risks typically include, but are not limited to, credit risk, *liquidity risk* and market risk.

QUALITATIVE DISCLOSURES

33   For each type of risk arising from financial instruments, an entity shall disclose:

(a)   the exposures to risk and how they arise;

(b)   its objectives, policies and processes for managing the risk and the methods used to measure the risk; and

(c)   any changes in (a) or (b) from the previous period.

QUANTITATIVE DISCLOSURES

34   For each type of risk arising from financial instruments, an entity shall disclose:

(a)   summary quantitative data about its exposure to that risk at the reporting date. This disclosure shall be based on the information provided internally to key management personnel of the entity , for example the entity's board of directors or chief executive officer. For the purposes of this standard key management personnel are those persons having authority and responsibility for planning, directing and controlling the activities of the entity directly or indirectly, including any director (whether executive or otherwise) of that entity.*

(b)   the disclosures required by paragraphs 36–42, to the extent not provided in (a), unless the risk is not material .†

(c)   concentrations of risk if not apparent from (a) and (b).

35   If the quantitative data disclosed as at the reporting date are unrepresentative of an entity's exposure to risk during the period, an entity shall provide further information that is representative.

Credit risk

36   An entity shall disclose by class of financial instrument:

(a)   the amount that best represents its maximum exposure to credit risk at the reporting date without taking account of any collateral held or other credit

*ASB footnote: *Amendment made to ensure consistent definition of key management personnel; the equivalent definition in FRS 8* Related Parties *differs slightly.*

†ASB footnote: *A discussion of materiality is provided in the ASB's* Statement of principles for financial reporting *at paragraphs 3.28 to 3.32.*

enhancements (eg netting agreements that do not qualify for offset in accordance with FRS 25);

(b)   in respect of the amount disclosed in (a), a description of collateral held as security and other credit enhancements;

(c)   information about the credit quality of financial assets that are neither *past due* nor impaired; and

(d)   the carrying amount of financial assets that would otherwise be past due or impaired whose terms have been renegotiated.

Financial assets that are either past due or impaired

An entity shall disclose by class of financial asset: **37**

(a)   an analysis of the age of financial assets that are past due as at the reporting date but not impaired;

(b)   an analysis of financial assets that are individually determined to be impaired as at the reporting date, including the factors the entity considered in determining that they are impaired; and

(c)   for the amounts disclosed in (a) and (b), a description of collateral held by the entity as security and other credit enhancements and, unless impracticable, an estimate of their fair value.

Collateral and other credit enhancements obtained

When an entity obtains financial or non-financial assets during the period by taking   **38**
possession of collateral it holds as security or calling on other credit enhancements (eg guarantees), and such assets meet the recognition criteria in other Standards, an entity shall disclose:

(a)   the nature and carrying amount of the assets obtained; and

(b)   when the assets are not readily convertible into cash, its policies for disposing of such assets or for using them in its operations.

Liquidity risk

An entity shall disclose: **39**

(a)   a maturity analysis for financial liabilities that shows the remaining contractual maturities; and

(b)   a description of how it manages the liquidity risk inherent in (a).

Market risk

Sensitivity analysis

Unless an entity complies with paragraph 41, it shall disclose: **40**

(a)   a sensitivity analysis for each type of market risk to which the entity is exposed at the reporting date, showing how profit or loss and equity would have been affected by changes in the relevant risk variable that were reasonably possible at that date;

(b)   the methods and assumptions used in preparing the sensitivity analysis; and

(c)   changes from the previous period in the methods and assumptions used, and the reasons for such changes.

If an entity prepares a sensitivity analysis, such as value-at-risk, that reflects inter-   **41**
dependencies between risk variables (eg interest rates and exchange rates) and uses it

to manage financial risks, it may use that sensitivity analysis in place of the analysis specified in paragraph 40. The entity shall also disclose:

(a)   an explanation of the method used in preparing such a sensitivity analysis, and of the main parameters and assumptions underlying the data provided; and

(b)   an explanation of the objective of the method used and of limitations that may result in the information not fully reflecting the fair value of the assets and liabilities involved.

Other market risk disclosures

42   When the sensitivity analyses disclosed in accordance with paragraph 40 or 41 are unrepresentative of a risk inherent in a financial instrument (for example because the year-end exposure does not reflect the exposure during the year), the entity shall disclose that fact and the reason it believes the sensitivity analyses are unrepresentative.

Capital disclosures

42A   An entity shall make disclosures about its capital as required by Appendix E, which is an integral part of this Standard.

Effective date and transition

43   An entity shall apply this Standard for accounting periods beginning on or after 1 January 2007. Earlier application is encouraged. If an entity applies this Standard for an earlier period, it shall disclose that fact.

44A   An entity that chooses to adopt this Standard for accounting periods beginning before 1 January 2007 may elect to:

(i)   adopt the requirements of Appendix E only;

(ii)   adopt the Standard with the exception of Appendix E; or

(iii) adopt the whole Standard.*

44B   If an entity that has not previously adopted the disclosure requirements of FRS 25 applies this Standard for an accounting period beginning before 1 January 2007 it need not present the comparative disclosures required by this Standard in its first financial statements prepared in accordance with this Standard. This exemption from the requirement to present comparative information does not extend to the requirements of Appendix E.†

*ASB Footnote: *A consequence of putting the Capital Disclosures in IAS 1 is the ability of IFRS preparers to adopt IFRS 7 and the amendments to IAS 1 separately. Paragraph 44B of FRS 29 enables UK GAAP preparers to likewise adopt the Capital Disclosures separately from the other disclosures of the Standard.*

†ASB Footnote: *This paragraph implements transitional provisions of IFRS 1 for entities that voluntarily adopt the requirements of this Standard prior to its effective date. As a result, the exemption in paragraph 44 is not applicable and has been deleted. Appendix E contains the Capital Disclosures requirements developed by the IASB as part of the IFRS 7 project but introduced as an amendment to IAS 1 rather than in IFRS 7. IFRS 1 has been amended to provide certain reliefs from the need to restate comparative information for the requirements of IFRS 7 but not IAS 1. This approach has been replicated by the ASB.*

WITHDRAWAL OF FRS 13

For entities applying this Standard, it supersedes FRS 13 *Derivatives and other*   **45A**
financial instruments: disclosures.

Appendix A
Defined terms

This appendix is an integral part of the Standard.

credit risk	The risk that one party to a financial instrument will cause a financial loss for the other party by failing to discharge an obligation.
currency risk	The risk that the fair value or future cash flows of a financial instrument will fluctuate because of changes in foreign exchange rates.
interest rate risk	The risk that the fair value or future cash flows of a financial instrument will fluctuate because of changes in market interest rates.
liquidity risk	The risk that an entity will encounter difficulty in meeting obligations associated with financial liabilities.
loans payable	Loans payable are financial liabilities, other than short-term trade payables on normal credit terms.
market risk	The risk that the fair value or future cash flows of a financial instrument will fluctuate because of changes in market prices. Market risk comprises three types of risk: **currency risk**, **interest rate risk** and **other price risk**.
other price risk	The risk that the fair value or future cash flows of a financial instrument will fluctuate because of changes in market prices (other than those arising from **interest rate risk** or **currency risk**), whether those changes are caused by factors specific to the individual financial instrument or its issuer, or factors affecting all similar financial instruments traded in the market.
past due	A financial asset is past due when a counterparty has failed to make a payment when contractually due.

The following terms are defined in paragraph 11 of FRS 25 or paragraph 9 of FRS 26 and are used in the Standard with the meaning specified in FRS 25 and FRS 26

- amortised cost of a financial asset or financial liability
- available-for-sale financial assets
- derivative
- effective interest method
- equity instrument
- fair value
- financial asset
- financial instrument
- financial liability
- financial asset or financial liability at fair value through profit or loss
- financial guarantee contract
- financial asset or financial liability held for trading

- forecast transaction
- hedging instrument
- held-to-maturity investments
- loans and receivables
- regular way purchase or sale

Appendix B
Application guidance

This appendix is an integral part of the Standard.

CLASSES OF FINANCIAL INSTRUMENTS AND LEVEL OF DISCLOSURE (PARAGRAPH 6)

B1   Paragraph 6 requires an entity to group financial instruments into classes that are appropriate to the nature of the information disclosed and that take into account the characteristics of those financial instruments. The classes described in paragraph 6 are determined by the entity and are, thus, distinct from the categories of financial instruments specified in FRS 26 (which determine how financial instruments are measured and where changes in fair value are recognised).

B2   In determining classes of financial instrument, an entity shall, at a minimum:

(a)   distinguish instruments measured at amortised cost from those measured at fair value

(b)   treat as a separate class or classes those financial instruments outside the scope of this Standard.

B3   An entity decides, in the light of its circumstances, how much detail it provides to satisfy the requirements of this Standard, how much emphasis it places on different aspects of the requirements and how it aggregates information to display the overall picture without combining information with different characteristics. It is necessary to strike a balance between overburdening financial statements with excessive detail that may not assist users of financial statements and obscuring important information as a result of too much aggregation. For example, an entity shall not obscure important information by including it among a large amount of insignificant detail. Similarly, an entity shall not disclose information that is so aggregated that it obscures important differences between individual transactions or associated risks.

SIGNIFICANCE OF FINANCIAL INSTRUMENTS FOR FINANCIAL POSITION AND PERFORMANCE

Financial liabilities at fair value through profit or loss (paragraphs 10 and 11)

B4   If an entity designates a financial liability as at fair value through profit or loss, paragraph 10(a) requires it to disclose the amount of change in the fair value of the financial liability that is attributable to changes in the liability's credit risk. Paragraph 10(a)(i) permits an entity to determine this amount as the amount of change in the liability's fair value that is not attributable to changes in market conditions that give rise to market risk. If the only relevant changes in market conditions for a liability are changes in an observed (benchmark) interest rate, this amount can be estimated as follows:

(a)   First, the entity computes the liability's internal rate of return at the start of the period using the observed market price of the liability and the liability's contractual cash flows at the start of the period. It deducts from this rate of return the observed (benchmark) interest rate at the start of the period, to arrive at an instrument-specific component of the internal rate of return.

(b)   Next, the entity calculates the present value of the cash flows associated with the liability using the liability's contractual cash flows at the end of the period and a discount rate equal to the sum of (i) the observed (benchmark) interest rate at the end of the period and (ii) the instrument-specific component of the internal rate of return as determined in (a).

(c) The difference between the observed market price of the liability at the end of the period and the amount determined in (b) is the change in fair value that is not attributable to changes in the observed (benchmark) interest rate. This is the amount to be disclosed.

This example assumes that changes in fair value arising from factors other than changes in the instrument's credit risk or changes in interest rates are not significant. If the instrument in the example contains an embedded derivative, the change in fair value of the embedded derivative is excluded in determining the amount to be disclosed in accordance with paragraph 10(a).

OTHER DISCLOSURE – ACCOUNTING POLICIES (PARAGRAPH 21)

Paragraph 21 requires disclosure of the measurement basis (or bases) used in preparing the financial statements and the other accounting policies used that are relevant to an understanding of the financial statements. For financial instruments, such disclosure may include:

B5

(a) for financial assets or financial liabilities designated as at fair value through profit or loss:

(i) the nature of the financial assets or financial liabilities the entity has designated as at fair value through profit or loss;

(ii) the criteria for so designating such financial assets or financial liabilities on initial recognition; and

(iii) how the entity has satisfied the conditions in paragraph 9, 11A or 12 of FRS 26 for such designation. For instruments designated in accordance with paragraph (b)(i) of the definition of a financial asset or financial liability at fair value through profit or loss in FRS 26, that disclosure includes a narrative description of the circumstances underlying the measurement or recognition inconsistency that would otherwise arise. For instruments designated in accordance with paragraph (b)(ii) of the definition of a financial asset or financial liability at fair value through profit or loss in FRS 26, that disclosure includes a narrative description of how designation at fair value through profit or loss is consistent with the entity's documented risk management or investment strategy.

(b) the criteria for designating financial assets as available for sale.

(c) whether regular way purchases and sales of financial assets are accounted for at trade date or at settlement date (see paragraph 38 of IAS 39).

(d) when an allowance account is used to reduce the carrying amount of financial assets impaired by credit losses:

(i) the criteria for determining when the carrying amount of impaired financial assets is reduced directly (or, in the case of a reversal of a write-down, increased directly) and when the allowance account is used; and

(ii) the criteria for writing off amounts charged to the allowance account against the carrying amount of impaired financial assets (see paragraph 16).

(e) how net gains or net losses on each category of financial instrument are determined (see paragraph 20(a)), for example, whether the net gains or net losses on items at fair value through profit or loss include interest or dividend income.

(f)   the criteria the entity uses to determine that there is objective evidence that an impairment loss has occurred (see paragraph 20(e)).

(g)   when the terms of financial assets that would otherwise be past due or impaired have been renegotiated, the accounting policy for financial assets that are the subject of renegotiated terms (see paragraph 36(d)).

NATURE AND EXTENT OF RISKS ARISING FROM FINANCIAL INSTRUMENTS (PARAGRAPHS 31–42)

B6   The disclosures required by paragraphs 31–42 shall be either given in the financial statements or incorporated by cross-reference from the financial statements to some other statement, such as a management commentary or risk report, that is available to users of the financial statements on the same terms as the financial statements and at the same time. Without the information incorporated by cross-reference, the financial statements are incomplete.

Quantitative disclosures (paragraph 34)

B7   Paragraph 34(a) requires disclosures of summary quantitative data about an entity's exposure to risks based on the information provided internally to key management personnel of the entity. When an entity uses several methods to manage a risk exposure, the entity shall disclose information using the method or methods that provide the most relevant and reliable information. FRS 18 *Accounting Policies* discusses relevance and reliability.

B8   Paragraph 34(c) requires disclosures about concentrations of risk. Concentrations of risk arise from financial instruments that have similar characteristics and are affected similarly by changes in economic or other conditions. The identification of concentrations of risk requires judgement taking into account the circumstances of the entity. Disclosure of concentrations of risk shall include:

(a)   a description of how management determines concentrations;

(b)   a description of the shared characteristic that identifies each concentration (eg counterparty, geographical area, currency or market); and

(c)   the amount of the risk exposure associated with all financial instruments sharing that characteristic.

Maximum credit risk exposure (paragraph 36(a))

B9   Paragraph 36(a) requires disclosure of the amount that best represents the entity's maximum exposure to credit risk. For a financial asset, this is typically the gross carrying amount, net of:

(a)   any amounts offset in accordance with FRS 25; and

(b)   any impairment losses recognised in accordance with FRS 26.

B10   Activities that give rise to credit risk and the associated maximum exposure to credit risk include, but are not limited to:

(a)   granting loans and receivables to customers and placing deposits with other entities. In these cases, the maximum exposure to credit risk is the carrying amount of the related financial assets.

(b)   entering into derivative contracts, eg foreign exchange contracts, interest rate swaps and credit derivatives. When the resulting asset is measured at fair value, the maximum exposure to credit risk at the reporting date will equal the carrying amount.

(c)   granting financial guarantees. In this case, the maximum exposure to credit risk is the maximum amount the entity could have to pay if the guarantee is called on, which may be significantly greater than the amount recognised as a liability.

(d)   making a loan commitment that is irrevocable over the life of the facility or is revocable only in response to a material adverse change. If the issuer cannot settle the loan commitment net in cash or another financial instrument, the maximum credit exposure is the full amount of the commitment. This is because it is uncertain whether the amount of any undrawn portion may be drawn upon in the future. This may be significantly greater than the amount recognised as a liability.

CONTRACTUAL MATURITY ANALYSIS (PARAGRAPH 39(A))

In preparing the contractual maturity analysis for financial liabilities required by paragraph 39(a), an entity uses its judgement to determine an appropriate number of time bands. For example, an entity might determine that the following time bands are appropriate: **B11**

(a)   not later than one month;
(b)   later than one month and not later than three months;
(c)   later than three months and not later than one year; and
(d)   later than one year and not later than five years.

When a counterparty has a choice of when an amount is paid, the liability is included on the basis of the earliest date on which the entity can be required to pay. For example, financial liabilities that an entity can be required to repay on demand (eg demand deposits) are included in the earliest time band.   **B12**

When an entity is committed to make amounts available in instalments, each instalment is allocated to the earliest period in which the entity can be required to pay. For example, an undrawn loan commitment is included in the time band containing the earliest date it can be drawn down.   **B13**

The amounts disclosed in the maturity analysis are the contractual undiscounted cash flows, for example: **B14**

(a)   gross finance lease obligations (before deducting finance charges);
(b)   prices specified in forward agreements to purchase financial assets for cash;
(c)   net amounts for pay-floating/receive-fixed interest rate swaps for which net cash flows are exchanged;
(d)   contractual amounts to be exchanged in a derivative financial instrument (eg a currency swap) for which gross cash flows are exchanged; and
(e)   gross loan commitments.

Such undiscounted cash flows differ from the amount included in the balance sheet because the balance sheet amount is based on discounted cash flows.

If appropriate, an entity shall disclose the analysis of derivative financial instruments separately from that of non-derivative financial instruments in the contractual maturity analysis for financial liabilities required by paragraph 39(a). For example, it would be appropriate to distinguish cash flows from derivative financial instruments and non-derivative financial instruments if the cash flows arising from the derivative financial instruments are settled gross. This is because the gross cash outflow may be accompanied by a related inflow.   **B15**

B16   When the amount payable is not fixed, the amount disclosed is determined by reference to the conditions existing at the reporting date. For example, when the amount payable varies with changes in an index, the amount disclosed may be based on the level of the index at the reporting date.

Market risk – sensitivity analysis (paragraphs 40 and 41)

B17   Paragraph 40(a) requires a sensitivity analysis for each type of market risk to which the entity is exposed. In accordance with paragraph B3, an entity decides how it aggregates information to display the overall picture without combining information with different characteristics about exposures to risks from significantly different economic environments. For example:

(a)   an entity that trades financial instruments might disclose this information separately for financial instruments held for trading and those not held for trading.

(b)   an entity would not aggregate its exposure to market risks from areas of hyperinflation with its exposure to the same market risks from areas of very low inflation.

If an entity has exposure to only one type of market risk in only one economic environment, it would not show disaggregated information.

B18   Paragraph 40(a) requires the sensitivity analysis to show the effect on profit or loss and equity of reasonably possible changes in the relevant risk variable (eg prevailing market interest rates, currency rates, equity prices or commodity prices). For this purpose:

(a)   entities are not required to determine what the profit or loss for the period would have been if relevant risk variables had been different. Instead, entities disclose the effect on profit or loss and equity at the balance sheet date assuming that a reasonably possible change in the relevant risk variable had occurred at the balance sheet date and had been applied to the risk exposures in existence at that date. For example, if an entity has a floating rate liability at the end of the year, the entity would disclose the effect on profit or loss (ie interest expense) for the current year if interest rates had varied by reasonably possible amounts.

(b)   entities are not required to disclose the effect on profit or loss and equity for each change within a range of reasonably possible changes of the relevant risk variable. Disclosure of the effects of the changes at the limits of the reasonably possible range would be sufficient.

B19   In determining what a reasonably possible change in the relevant risk variable is, an entity should consider:

(a)   the economic environments in which it operates. A reasonably possible change should not include remote or 'worst case' scenarios or 'stress tests'. Moreover, if the rate of change in the underlying risk variable is stable, the entity need not alter the chosen reasonably possible change in the risk variable. For example, assume that interest rates are 5 per cent and an entity determines that a fluctuation in interest rates of ± 50 basis points is reasonably possible. It would disclose the effect on profit or loss and equity if interest rates were to change to 4.5 per cent or 5.5 per cent. In the next period, interest rates have increased to 5.5 per cent. The entity continues to believe that interest rates may fluctuate by ± 50 basis points (ie that the rate of change in interest rates is stable). The entity would disclose the effect on profit or loss and equity if interest rates were to change to 5 per cent or 6 per cent. The entity would not be required to revise its assessment that interest rates might reasonably fluctuate by ±50 basis points, unless there is evidence that interest rates have become significantly more volatile.

(b)   the time frame over which it is making the assessment. The sensitivity analysis shall show the effects of changes that are considered to be reasonably possible over the period until the entity will next present these disclosures, which is usually its next annual reporting period.

Paragraph 41 permits an entity to use a sensitivity analysis that reflects inter-   **B20**
dependencies between risk variables, such as a value-at-risk methodology, if it uses this analysis to manage its exposure to financial risks. This applies even if such a methodology measures only the potential for loss and does not measure the potential for gain. Such an entity might comply with paragraph 41(a) by disclosing the type of value-at-risk model used (eg whether the model relies on Monte Carlo simulations), an explanation about how the model works and the main assumptions (eg the holding period and confidence level). Entities might also disclose the historical observation period and weightings applied to observations within that period, an explanation of how options are dealt with in the calculations, and which volatilities and correlations (or, alternatively, Monte Carlo probability distribution simulations) are used.

An entity shall provide sensitivity analyses for the whole of its business, but may   **B21**
provide different types of sensitivity analysis for different classes of financial instruments.

Interest rate risk

Interest rate risk arises on interest-bearing financial instruments recognised in the   **B22**
balance sheet (eg loans and receivables and debt instruments issued) and on some financial instruments not recognised in the balance sheet (eg some loan commitments).

Currency risk

Currency risk (or foreign exchange risk) arises on financial instruments that are   **B23**
denominated in a foreign currency, ie in a currency other than the functional currency in which they are measured. For the purpose of this Standard, currency risk does not arise from financial instruments that are non-monetary items or from financial instruments denominated in the functional currency.

A sensitivity analysis is disclosed for each currency to which an entity has significant   **B24**
exposure.

Other price risk

Other price risk arises on financial instruments because of changes in, for example,   **B25**
commodity prices or equity prices. To comply with paragraph 40, an entity might disclose the effect of a decrease in a specified stock market index, commodity price, or other risk variable. For example, if an entity gives residual value guarantees that are financial instruments, the entity discloses an increase or decrease in the value of the assets to which the guarantee applies.

Two examples of financial instruments that give rise to equity price risk are a holding   **B26**
of equities in another entity, and an investment in a trust, which in turn holds investments in equity instruments. Other examples include forward contracts and

options to buy or sell specified quantities of an equity instrument and swaps that are indexed to equity prices. The fair values of such financial instruments are affected by changes in the market price of the underlying equity instruments.

B27 In accordance with paragraph 40(a), the sensitivity of profit or loss (that arises, for example, from instruments classified as at fair value through profit or loss and impairments of available-for-sale financial assets) is disclosed separately from the sensitivity of equity (that arises, for example, from instruments classified as available for sale).

B28 Financial instruments that an entity classifies as equity instruments are not remeasured. Neither profit or loss nor equity will be affected by the equity price risk of those instruments. Accordingly, no sensitivity analysis is required.

Appendix C
Amendments to other Standards

[Not reproduced, as all changes have been made to the underlying standards]

Appendix D
Amendments to FRS 29 if the Amendments to FRS 26 (IAS 39) Financial Instruments: Measurement—*The Fair Value Option* have not been applied

In October 2005, the ASB issued Amendments to FRS 26 (IAS 39): Financial Instruments: Measurement Part III – The Fair Value Option, to be applied for accounting periods beginning on or after 1 January 2006. If an entity applies FRS 29 for accounting periods beginning before 1 January 2006 and it does not apply these amendments to FRS 26, it shall amend FRS 29 for that period, as follows.

D1   The heading above paragraph 9 and paragraph 11 are amended to read as follows.

Financial liabilities at fair value through profit or loss

11   The entity shall disclose:

(a)   the methods used to comply with the requirements in paragraph 10(a).

(b)   if the entity believes that the disclosure it has given to comply with the requirement in paragraph 10(a) does not faithfully represent the change in the fair value of the financial liability attributable to changes in its credit risk, the reasons for reaching this conclusion and the factors it believes to be relevant.

Paragraph B5(a) is amended as follows:

(a)   the criteria for designating, on initial recognition, financial assets or financial liabilities as at fair value through profit or loss.

Appendix E
Capital disclosures

ASB Note: This appendix reproduces the IASB's Capital Disclosures requirements developed by the IASB as part of the IFRS 7 project and issued as amendments to IAS 1. The IASB's Basis for Conclusions that relate to the Capital Disclosures have been reproduced in the Basis for Conclusions at paragraphs EBC 1 to EBC 16. The IASB's Implementation Guidance has been reproduced in the Implementation Guidance at paragraphs EIG 1–EIG 2.

Paragraphs E1 to E3 are an integral part of the Standard. Subject to the transitional provisions contained in paragraphs 43 to 46 the requirements of this Appendix should be applied for accounting periods beginning on or after 1 January 2007.

Capital Disclosures

Capital

An entity shall disclose information that enables users of its financial statements to evaluate the entity's objectives, policies and processes for managing capital.   E1

To comply with paragraph E1, the entity discloses the following: E2

(a)   qualitative information about its objectives, policies and processes for managing capital, including (but not limited to):

    (i)   a description of what it manages as capital;

    (ii)   when an entity is subject to externally imposed capital requirements, the nature of those requirements and how those requirements are incorporated into the management of capital; and

    (iii)   how it is meeting its objectives for managing capital.

(b)   summary quantitative data about what it manages as capital. Some entities regard some financial liabilities (eg some forms of subordinated debt) as part of capital. Other entities regard capital as excluding some components of equity (eg components arising from cash flow hedges).

(c)   any changes in (a) and (b) from the previous period.

(d)   whether during the period it complied with any externally imposed capital requirements to which it is subject.

(e)   when the entity has not complied with such externally imposed capital requirements, the consequences of such noncompliance.

These disclosures shall be based on the information provided internally to the entity's key management personnel.

An entity may manage capital in a number of ways and be subject to a number of different capital requirements. For example, a conglomerate may include entities that undertake insurance activities and banking activities, and those entities may also operate in several jurisdictions. When an aggregate disclosure of capital requirements and how capital is managed would not provide useful information or distorts a financial statement user's understanding of an entity's capital resources, the entity shall disclose separate information for each capital requirement to which the entity is subject.   E3

Adoption of the standard

Approval of IFRS 7 by the Board

International Financial Reporting Standard 7 *Financial Instruments: Disclosures* was approved for issue by the fourteen members of the International Accounting Standards Board.

Sir David Tweedie	Chairman
Thomas E Jones	Vice-Chairman
Mary E Barth	
Hans-Georg Bruns	
Anthony T Cope	
Jan Engström	
Robert P Garnett	
Gilbert Gélard	
James J Leisenring	
Warren J McGregor	
Patricia L O'Malley	
John T Smith	
Geoffrey Whittington	
Tatsumi Yamada	

Approval of Amendments to IAS 1 by the Board

These Amendments to International Accounting Standard 1 *Presentation of Financial Statements: Capital Disclosures** were approved for issue by thirteen of the fourteen members of the International Accounting Standards Board. Mr Leisenring dissented. His dissenting opinion is set out on page 116.

Sir David Tweedie	Chairman
Thomas E Jones	Vice-Chairman
Mary E Barth	
Hans-Georg Bruns	
Anthony T Cope	
Jan Engström	
Robert P Garnett	
Gilbert Gélard	
James J Leisenring	
Warren J McGregor	
Patricia L O'Malley	
John T Smith	
Geoffrey Whittington	
Tatsumi Yamada	

*ASB Footnote: *The equivalent requirements have been reproduced in Appendix E of this Standard.*

Adoption of FRS 29 by the Accounting Standards Board

Financial Reporting Standard 29 (IFRS 7) 'Financial Instruments: Disclosures' was approved for issue by the ten members of the Accounting Standards Board.

Ian Mackintosh	Chairman
Andrew Lennard	Technical Director
Michael Ashley	
Marisa Cassoni	
Anthony Good	
Roger Marshall	
Isobel Sharp	
Jonathan Symonds	
Helen Weir	
Peter Westlake	

Notes on the Standard's Application in the UK and the Republic of Ireland

N1   In July 2004, the IASB published exposure draft ED7 'Financial Instruments: Disclosures', setting out proposals for a new IFRS that would:

- contain some new disclosure requirements as well as disclosures already required by IAS 32, and
- require additional capital disclosure requirements in the new IFRS.

N2   The ASB issued these proposals as FRED 33 'Financial Instruments: Disclosures' at the same time as the IASB.

N3   As part of its convergence programme, the ASB then issued FRS 25 (IAS 32) 'Financial Instruments: Disclosure and Presentation' in December 2004.

N4   Respondents to the FRED generally supported the implementation of the IFRS in the UK, although some expressed concern over the details of the proposals, and in particular aspects of the capital disclosures. Similar concerns were expressed to IASB, who agreed some changes in their redeliberation of the proposed standard.

N5   In August 2005, the IASB issued its standard as IFRS 7 *Financial Instruments: Disclosures*, and the ASB then agreed to issue a UK standard based on that IFRS.

GENERAL

N6   The requirements of Schedules 4 and 4A* to the Companies Act 1985 (and Schedules 4 and 4A* to the Companies (Northern Ireland) Order 1986 (S.I. 1986/1032 N.I. 6)) relating to the form and content of company and group financial statements set out formats for the balance sheet and profit and loss account which allow some flexibility in certain circumstances in the manner in which the information is presented. The provisions of the FRS supplement those legal requirements, while remaining within their bounds.

SCOPE

N7   The ASB has followed its usual practice of exempting from the FRS all entities applying the Financial Reporting Standard for Smaller Entities (FRSSE).

Entities not applying FRS 26 measurement requirements

N8   As with FRS 25, the Board has exempted entities not applying FRS 26 measurement requirements from the disclosure requirements of this FRS. The Board is currently discussing the possibility of extending the scope of FRS 26 which may lead to an extension in the scope of this Standard. However, the Board is also aware that some entities falling within the scope of FRS 26 may wish to adopt the disclosure requirements of this Standard, rather than those contained in FRS 25, in 2005 or

---

*The requirements relating to banking and insurance companies are set out in Schedules 9 and 9A respectively. The equivalent Northern Ireland requirements are set out in Schedules 4, 4A, 9 and 9A of the Companies (Northern Ireland) Order 1986. The equivalent Republic of Ireland requirements are set out in the Sixth Schedule of the Companies Act 1963, and Section 3 and the Schedule of the Companies (Amendment) Act 1986, the European Communities (Companies: Group Accounts) Regulations 1992, the European Communities (Credit Institutions: Accounts) Regulations 1992 and the European Communities (Insurance Undertakings: Accounts) Regulations 1992.

2006 thus avoiding the need to make two changes in quick succession. It has, therefore, decided to issue this Standard in advance of a decision on the scope of FRS 26 with the provision that it may amend the scope of the Standard at a later date.

Parents and subsidiaries

As for FRS 25, the Board has granted certain exemptions for parent companies and wholly-owned subsidiaries from complying with the disclosure requirements of this Standard. The exemption applies to parent companies in their own single-entity financial statements and to subsidiaries where at least 90 percent of the voting rights are controlled within the group. In each case it is dependent on the entity being included in consolidated financial statements that are publicly available and which include the disclosures on a group basis. The Board takes the view that applying the disclosure requirements to the single entity financial statements of parent companies and wholly-owned subsidiaries may result in lengthy disclosures for little benefit. Entities falling within the scope of this exemption may still be subject to the disclosure requirements of the Companies Act referred to in paragraph N13 below.

N9

EFFECTIVE DATE

The new standard is effective from the same date as the IFRS, for accounting periods commencing on or after 1 January 2007. Early adoption is permitted; in particular, entities required to adopt FRS 25 for periods commencing in 2005 or 2006 are permitted instead to adopt the requirements of the new FRS, thereby avoiding two changes in disclosure requirements in quick succession.

N10

DISCLOSURES RELATING TO CAPITAL

The standard proposed in ED 7 and FRED 33 included a requirement for certain disclosures relating to capital. The IASB has not included these in IFRS 7, but has amended IAS 1 to incorporate these disclosure requirements on the basis that they are not directly related to financial instruments. As the UK does not have a standard that corresponds to IAS 1, these requirements have been added as a separate appendix to FRS 29, with the same scope and scope exemptions as the main standard.

N11

DISCLOSURES RELATING TO THE FAIR VALUE OPTION

The ASB has considerable reservations over the value of some of the consequential disclosures introduced by the IASB's Fair Value Option amendment to IAS 39. These include disclosures introduced as paragraph 9 relating to the credit risk of loans and receivables designated as at fair value through profit and loss which in the ASB's view are intended to provide information that is relevant to regulatory returns rather than general purpose financial statements. The ASB has not, therefore, implemented all the disclosure requirements inserted in IAS 32.

N12

FAIR VALUE DIRECTIVE

The Companies Act includes certain disclosure requirements relating to financial instruments, in particular those inserted in Schedules 4, 9 and 9A, as a result of implementing the Fair Value Directive. These requirements apply to all entities within the scope of the Act, whether or not they are within the scope of the FRS; they are generally similar, but not identical, to certain requirements of the FRS. Entities

N13

within the scope of both the Act and the FRS will need to ensure that they comply with the requirements of both.

N14 The table below provides an overview of the disclosure requirements contained in the Companies Act and their relationship to those in the Standard.

Financial Statements

Companies Act*	Republic of Ireland Companies Legislation	FRS 29
Sch 4 Paragraph 45A (2) (a) (2) There must be stated- (a) where the fair value of the instruments has been determined in accordance with paragraph 34B(4), the significant assumptions underlying the valuation models and techniques used;	Para 31A (2)(a), Schedule, Companies (Amendment) Act, 1986 Regulation 16A(2)(a), European Communities (Companies: Group Accounts) Regulations 1992	Paragraph 27(a) An entity shall disclose: (a) the methods and, when a valuation technique is used, the assumptions applied in determining fair values of each class of financial assets or financial liabilities. For example, if applicable, an entity discloses information about the assumptions relating to prepayment rates, rates of estimated credit losses, and interest rates or discount rates.

* ASB Footnote: *The numbering provided here follows that contained in the amendments to Schdules 4 and 7 of the Companies Act 1985 as described in Statutory Instrument 2004 No. 2947 and the Companies (Northern Ireland) Order 1986 as described in S. R. 2004 No. 496. The requirements relating to banking and insurance companies are set out in Schedules 9 and 9A respectively.*

Companies Act	Republic of Ireland Companies Legislation	FRS 29
Sch 4 Paragraph 45A (2) (b) (2) There must be stated- (b) for each category of financial instrument, the fair value of the instruments in that category and the changes in value – (i) included in the profit and loss account, or (ii) credited to or (as the case my be) debited from the fair value reserve, in respect of those instruments.	Para 31A (2)(b), Schedule, Companies (Amendment) Act, 1986 Regulation 16A(2)(b), European Communities (Companies: Group Accounts) Regulations 1992	Paragraphs 20 and 25 **Paragraph 20**: An entity shall disclose the following items of income, expense, gains or losses either on the face of the financial statements or in the notes: (a) net gains or net losses on: (i) financial assets or financial liabilities at fair value through profit or loss, showing separately those on financial assets or financial liabilities designated as such upon initial recognition, and those on financial assets or financial liabilities that are classified as held for trading in accordance with FRS 26; (ii) available-for-sale financial assets, showing separately the amount of gain or loss recognised directly in equity during the period and the amount removed from equity and recognised in profit or loss for the period; (iii) held-to-maturity investments; and (iv) loans and receivables; and

Companies Act	Republic of Ireland Companies Legislation	FRS 29
		(v) financial liabilities measured at amortised cost;
		(b) total interest income and total interest expense (calculated using the effective interest method) for financial assets or financial liabilities that are not at fair value through profit or loss;
		(c) fee income and expense (other than amounts included in determining the effective interest rate) arising from:
		(i) financial assets or financial liabilities that are not at fair value through profit or loss; and
		(ii) trust and other fiduciary activities that result in the holding or investing of assets on behalf of individuals, trusts, retirement benefit plans, and other institutions;
		(d) interest income on impaired financial assets accrued in accordance with paragraph AG93 of IAS 39; and
		(e) the amount of any impairment loss for each class of financial asset.

Companies Act	Republic of Ireland Companies Legislation	FRS 29
		Paragraph 25: Except as set out in paragraph 29, for each class of financial assets and financial liabilities (see paragraph 6), an entity shall disclose the fair value of that class of assets and liabilities in a way that permits it to be compared with its carrying amount.
Sch 4 Paragraph 45A (2) (c) (2) There must be stated- (c) for each class of derivatives, the extent and nature of the instruments, including significant terms and conditions that may affect the amount, timing and certainty of future cash flows.	Para 31 A (2) (a), Schedule, Companies (Amendment) Act, 1986 Regulations 16A(2)(c), European Communities (Companies: Group Accounts) Regulations 1992	[the Standard does not specifically require these disclosures]
Sch 4 Paragraph 45A (3) (3) Where any amount is transferred to or from the fair value reserve during the financial year, there must be stated in tabular form: (a) the amount of the reserve as at the date of the beginning of the financial year and as at the balance sheet date respectively;	–	[the Standard does not specifically require these disclosures]

Companies Act	Republic of Ireland Companies Legislation	FRS 29
(b) the amount transferred to or from the reserve during that year; and (c) the source and application respectively of the amounts so transferred.		
Sch 4 Paragraph 45B Where the company has derivatives that it has not included at fair value, there must be stated for each class of such derivative - (a) the fair value of the derivatives in that class, if such a value can be determined in accordance with paragraph 34B, and (b) the extent and nature of the derivatives.	Para 31B, Schedule, Companies (Amendment) Act, 1986 Regulation 16B, European Communities (Companies: Group Accounts) Regulations 1992	Paragraph 25 Except as set out in paragraph 29, for each class of financial assets and financial liabilities (see paragraph 6), an entity shall disclose the fair value of that class of assets and liabilities in a way that permits it to be compared with its carrying amount.
Sch 4 Paragraph 45C (1) Sub-paragraph (2) applies if – (a) the company has financial fixed assets which could be included at fair value by virtue of paragraph 34A, (b) the amount at which those assets are included under any item in the company's accounts is in excess of their fair value, and	Para 31C, Schedule, Companies (Amendment) Act, 1986 Regulation 16C, European Communities (Companies: Group Accounts) Regulations 1992	[the Standard does not specifically require these disclosures]

Companies Act	Republic of Ireland Companies Legislation	FRS 29
(c) the company has not made provision for diminution in value of those assets in accordance with paragraph 19(1) of this Schedule.		
(2) There must be stated—		
(a) the amount at which either the individual assets or appropriate groupings of those individual assets are included in the company's accounts,		
(b) the fair value of those assets or groupings, and		
(c) the reasons for not making a provision for diminution in value of those assets, including the nature of the evidence that provides the basis for the belief that the amount at which they are stated in the accounts will be recovered.		

Directors' Report

Companies Act	Republic of Ireland Companies Legislation	FRS 29
Sch 7 Paragraph 5A (1) (1) In relation to the use of financial instruments by a company and by its subsidiary undertakings, the directors' report must also contain an indication of - (a) the financial risk management objectives and policies of the company and its subsidiary undertakings included in the consolidation, including the policy for hedging each major type of forecasted transaction for which hedge accounting is used, and (b) the exposure of the company and its subsidiary undertakings included in the consolidation to price risk, credit risk, liquidity risk and cashflow risk, unless such information is not material for the assessment of the assets, liabilities, financial position and profit or loss of the company and its subsidiary undertakings included in the consolidation.	Section 13(f), Companies (Amendment) Act 1986 Regulation 37 (1)(f), European Communities (Companies: Group Accounts) Regulations 1992	See paragraphs 31, 33 and 34-42 for disclosures in the financial statement relating to the nature and extent of risks arising from financial instruments

Implementation of derecognition material

N15   In April 2006 the Board amended FRS 26 to include the IAS 39 material on recognition and derecognition into the Standard. Accordingly, on implementation of this amendment the corresponding disclosure requirements of IAS 32 are implemented in FRS 25. These new disclosure requirements replace disclosures required for financial assets and liabilities by FRS 5 'Reporting the Substance of Transactions'. These amendments are effective for accounting periods on or after 1 January 2007, with earlier adoption permitted.

Basis for Conclusions

Basis for Conclusions

This Basis for Conclusions accompanies, but is not part of, FRS 29.

> ASB Note: The IASB's Basis for Conclusion, which accompanies IFRS 7, is set out below in full. It should be noted though that some of the discussion it contains concerns IASB requirements that have no equivalent in the UK or Republic of Ireland. Footnotes have been used to indicate corresponding requirements in the UK and Republic of Ireland where applicable.
>
> All references to 'the Board' and 'Board members' are references to the IASB Board and IASB Board members.

INTRODUCTION

This Basis for Conclusions summarises the International Accounting Standards Board's considerations in reaching the conclusions in IFRS 7 *Financial Instruments: Disclosures*. Individual Board members gave greater weight to some factors than to others. **BC1**

During the late 1990s, the need for a comprehensive review of IAS 30 *Disclosures in the Financial Statements of Banks and Similar Financial Institutions** became apparent. The Board's predecessor, the International Accounting Standards Committee (IASC), issued a number of Standards that addressed, more comprehensively, some of the topics previously addressed only for banks in IAS 30. Also, fundamental changes were taking place in the financial services industry and in the way in which financial institutions manage their activities and risk exposures. This made it increasingly difficult for users of banks' financial statements to assess and compare their financial position and performance, their associated risk exposures, and their processes for measuring and managing those risks. **BC2**

In 1999 IASC added a project to its agenda to revise IAS 30 and in 2000 it appointed a steering committee. **BC3**

In 2001 the Board added this project to its agenda. To assist and advise it, the Board retained the IAS 30 steering committee, renamed the Financial Activities Advisory Committee (FAAC), as an expert advisory group. FAAC members had experience and expertise in banks, finance companies and insurance companies and included auditors, financial analysts, preparers and regulators. The FAAC's role was: **BC4**

(a) to provide input from the perspective of preparers and auditors of financial statements of entities that have significant exposures to financial instruments; and

(b) to assist the Board in developing a standard and implementation guidance for risk disclosures arising from financial instruments and for other related disclosures.

The Board published its proposals in July 2004 as ED 7 *Financial Instruments: Disclosures*†. The deadline for comments was 27 October 2004. The Board received **BC5**

---

*ASB Footnote: *The Basis for Conclusions discusses the IAS 30 revision project. IAS 30 was not implemented in the UK.*

†ASB Footnote: *FRED 33 was based on ED 7 and was issued by the ASB in July 2004.*

105 comment letters. After reviewing the responses, the Board issued IFRS 7 in August 2005.

SCOPE (PARAGRAPHS 3–5)

The entities to which the IFRS applies

BC6   Although IFRS 7 arose from a project to revise IAS 30 (a Standard that applied only to banks and similar financial institutions), it applies to all entities that have financial instruments. The Board observed that the reduction in regulatory barriers in many countries and increasing competition between banks, non-bank financial services firms, and financial conglomerates have resulted in many entities providing financial services that were traditionally provided only by entities regulated and supervised as banks. The Board concluded that this development would make it inappropriate to limit this project to banks and similar financial institutions.

BC7   The Board considered whether entities that undertake specified activities commonly undertaken by banks and other financial institutions, namely deposit-taking, lending and securities activities, face unique risks that would require a standard specific to them. However, the Board decided that the scope of this project should include disclosures about risks arising from financial instruments in all entities for the following reasons:

(a)   disclosures about risks associated with financial instruments are useful to users of the financial statements of all entities.

(b)   the Board found it could not satisfactorily define deposit-taking, lending, and securities activities. In particular, it could not satisfactorily differentiate an entity with securities activities from an entity holding a portfolio of financial assets for investment and liquidity management purposes.

(c)   responses to the Exposure Draft of Improvements to IAS 32 *Financial Instruments: Disclosure and Presentation**, published in June 2002, indicated that IAS 32's risk disclosure requirements, applicable to all entities, could be improved.

(d)   the exclusion of some financial instruments would increase the danger that risk disclosures could be incomplete and possibly misleading. For example, a debt instrument issued by an entity could significantly affect its exposures to liquidity risk, interest rate risk and currency risk even if that instrument is not held as part of deposit-taking, lending and securities activities.

(e)   users of financial statements need to be able to compare similar activities, transactions and events of different entities on a consistent basis. Hence, the disclosure principles that apply to regulated entities should not differ from those that apply to non-regulated, but otherwise similar, entities.

BC8   The Board decided that the scope of the IFRS should be the same as that of IAS 32 with one exception. The Board concluded that the IFRS should not apply to derivatives based on interests in subsidiaries, associates or joint ventures if the derivatives meet the definition of an equity instrument in IAS 32. This is because equity instruments are not remeasured and hence:

(a)   they do not expose the issuer to balance sheet and income statement risk; and

(b)   the disclosures about the significance of financial instruments for financial position and performance are not relevant to equity instruments.

*ASB Footnote: *FRS 25 implemented the IAS 32 requirements in the UK.*

Although these instruments are excluded from the scope of IFRS 7, they are within the scope of IAS 32 for the purpose of determining whether they meet the definition of equity instruments.

Exemptions considered by the Board

Insurers

The Board considered whether the IFRS should apply to entities that both have   **BC9**
financial instruments and issue insurance contracts. The Board did not exempt these
entities because financial instruments expose all entities to risks regardless of what
other assets and liabilities they have. Accordingly, an entity that both issues insurance contracts and has financial instruments applies IFRS 4 *Insurance Contracts** to
its insurance contracts and IFRS 7 to its financial assets and financial liabilities.
However, many of the disclosure requirements in IFRS 4 were applications of, or
relatively straightforward analogies with, existing requirements in IAS 32. Therefore,
the Board also updated the disclosures required by IFRS 4 to make them consistent
with IFRS 7, with modifications that reflect the interim nature of IFRS 4.

Small and medium-sized entities

The Board considered whether it should exempt small and medium-sized entities   **BC10**
from the scope of the IFRS†. The Board noted that the extent of disclosures required
by the IFRS will depend on the extent to which the entity uses financial instruments
and the extent to which it has assumed associated risks. The IFRS requires entities
with few financial instruments and few risks to give few disclosures. Also, many of
the requirements in the IFRS are based on information provided internally to the
entity's key management personnel. This helps to avoid unduly onerous requirements that would not be appropriate for smaller entities. Accordingly, the Board
decided not to exempt such entities from the scope of IFRS 7. However, it will keep
this decision under review in its project on financial reporting for small and medium-
sized entities.

Subsidiaries

Some respondents to ED 7 stated that there is little public interest in the financial   **BC11**
statements of some entities, such as a wholly-owned subsidiary whose parent issues
publicly available financial statements. These respondents stated that such subsidiaries should be exempt from some of the requirements of IFRS 7 in their
individual financial statements. However, deciding whether such an entity should
prepare general purpose financial statements is a matter for the entity and local
legislators and regulators. If such an entity prepares financial statements in accordance with IFRSs, users of those statements should receive information of the same
quality as users of any general purpose financial statements prepared in accordance
with IFRSs. The Board confirmed its view that no exemptions from the general
requirements of any Standard should be given for the financial statements of
subsidiaries.

**ASB Footnote: IFRS 4 has not been implemented in the UK but its definition of insurance contract was
implemented as Appendix C to FRS 26. As a result the disclosure requirements for insurance contracts remain as
those in FRS 27* Life Assurance *and in Schedule 9A of Companies Act 1985, supplemented by guidance in the
SORP on Insurance Business issued by the Association of British Insurers.*

*†ASB Footnote: Reporting entities in the UK applying the Financial Reporting Standard for Smaller Entities
(FRSSE) currently applicable are exempt from this Standard.*

DISCLOSURES ABOUT THE SIGNIFICANCE OF FINANCIAL INSTRUMENTS FOR FINANCIAL POSITION AND PERFORMANCE (PARAGRAPHS 7–30, B4 AND B5)

BC12   The Board relocated disclosures from IAS 32 to IFRS 7, so that all disclosure requirements for financial instruments are in one Standard. Many of the disclosure requirements about the significance of financial instruments for an entity's financial position and performance were previously in IAS 32. For these disclosures, the relevant paragraphs from the Basis for Conclusions on IAS 32 have been incorporated into this Basis for Conclusions. This Basis for Conclusions does not discuss requirements that the Board did not reconsider either in revising IAS 32 in 2003 or in developing IFRS 7.

The principle (paragraph 7)

BC13   The Board decided that the disclosure requirements of IFRS 7 should result from the explicit disclosure principle in paragraph 7. The Board also decided to specify disclosures to satisfy this principle. In the Board's view, entities could not satisfy the principle in paragraph 7 unless they disclose the information required by paragraphs 8–30.

Balance sheet disclosures (paragraphs 8–19 and B4)

Categories of financial assets and financial liabilities (paragraph 8)

BC14   Paragraph 8 requires entities to disclose financial assets and financial liabilities by the measurement categories in IAS 39 *Financial Instruments: Recognition and Measurement**. The Board concluded that the disclosure for each measurement category would assist users in understanding the extent to which accounting policies affect the amounts at which financial assets and financial liabilities are recognised.

BC15   The Board also concluded that separate disclosure of the carrying amounts of financial assets and financial liabilities that are classified as held for trading and those designated upon initial recognition as financial assets and financial liabilities at fair value through profit or loss is useful because such designation is at the discretion of the entity.

Financial assets or financial liabilities at fair value through profit or loss (paragraphs 9–11, B4 and B5)

BC16   IAS 39 permits entities to designate a non-derivative financial liability as at fair value through profit or loss, if specified conditions are met. If entities do so, they are required to provide the disclosures in paragraphs 10 and 11. The Board's reasons for these disclosures are set out in the Basis for Conclusions on IAS 39, paragraphs BC87–BC92.

BC17   The requirements in paragraphs 9, 11 and B5(a) are related to the Amendments to IAS 39 Financial Instruments: Recognition and Measurement—*The Fair Value*

---

*ASB Footnote: *FRS 26 implemented the equivalent measurement categories in the UK.*

Option*, issued in June 2005. The reasons for those requirements are discussed in the Basis for Conclusions on those Amendments.

Paragraph 10(a) requires disclosure of the change in fair value of a financial liability designated as at fair value through profit or loss that is attributable to changes in the liability's credit risk. The Board previously considered this disclosure in its deliberations on the fair value measurement of financial liabilities in IAS 39.

BC18

Although quantifying such changes might be difficult in practice, the Board concluded that disclosure of such information would be useful to users of financial statements and would help alleviate concerns that users may misinterpret the profit or loss effects of changes in credit risk, especially in the absence of disclosures. Therefore, in finalising the revisions to IAS 32 in 2003, it decided to require disclosure of the change in fair value of the financial liability that is not attributable to changes in a benchmark interest rate. The Board believed that this is often a reasonable proxy for the change in fair value that is attributable to changes in the liability's credit risk, in particular when such changes are large, and would provide users with information with which to understand the profit or loss effect of such a change in credit risk.

BC19

However, some respondents to ED 7 stated that they did not agree that the IAS 32 disclosure provided a reasonable proxy, except for straightforward debt instruments. In particular, there could be other factors involved in the change in an instrument's fair value unrelated to the benchmark interest rate, such as the effect of an embedded derivative. Respondents also cited difficulties for unit-linked insurance contracts, for which the amount of the liability reflects the performance of a defined pool of assets. The Board noted that the proxy that was developed in IAS 32 assumed that it is not practicable for entities to determine directly the change in fair value arising from changes in credit risk. However, the Board acknowledged and shared these concerns.

BC20

As a result, the Board amended this requirement to focus directly on the objective of providing information about the effects of changes in credit risk:

BC21

(a) by permitting entities to provide a more faithful representation of the amount of change in fair value that is attributable to changes in credit risk if they could do so. However, such entities are also required to disclose the methods used and provide their justification for concluding that those methods give a more faithful representation than the proxy in paragraph 10(a)(i).

(b) by amending the proxy disclosure to be the amount of change in fair value that is not attributable to changes in market conditions that give rise to market risk. For example, some entities may be able to identify part of the change in the fair value of the liability as attributable to a change in an index. In these cases, the proxy disclosure would exclude the amount of change attributable to a change in an index. Similarly, excluding the amount attributable to a change in an internal or external investment fund makes the proxy more suitable for unit-linked insurance contracts.

The Board decided that when an entity has designated a financial liability as at fair value through profit or loss, it should disclose the difference between the carrying amount and the amount the entity would contractually be required to pay at maturity to the holders of the liability (see paragraph 10(b)). The fair value may differ significantly from the settlement amount, in particular for financial liabilities with a long duration when an entity has experienced a significant deterioration in

BC22

*ASB Footnote: The Fair Value Option amendment was issued in the UK as part of the amendments to FRS 26 issued in October 2005.

creditworthiness since their issue. The Board concluded that knowledge of this difference would be useful to users of financial statements. Also, the settlement amount is important to some financial statement users, particularly creditors.

Reclassification (paragraph 12)

BC23   IAS 32 required disclosure of the reason for reclassification of financial assets at cost or amortised cost rather than at fair value. The Board extended this requirement to include disclosure of the reason for reclassifications and of the amount reclassified into and out of each category. As noted in paragraph BC14, the Board regards such information as useful because the categorisation of financial instruments has a significant effect on their measurement.

Derecognition (paragraph 13)

BC24   An entity may have transferred financial assets in such a way that part or all of them do not qualify for derecognition (see paragraphs 15–37 of IAS 39). If the entity either continues to recognise all of the assets or continues to recognise the assets to the extent of its continuing involvement, paragraph 13 requires disclosure of the nature of the financial assets, the extent of the entity's continuing involvement, and any associated liabilities. Such disclosure helps users of the financial statements evaluate the significance of the risks retained.

Collateral (paragraphs 14 and 15)

BC25   Paragraph 15 requires disclosures about collateral that the entity holds if it is permitted to sell or repledge the collateral in the absence of default by the owner. Some respondents to ED 7 argued for an exemption from this disclosure if it is impracticable to obtain the fair value of the collateral held. However, the Board concluded that it is reasonable to expect an entity to know the fair value of collateral that it holds and can sell even if there is no default.

Allowance account for credit losses (paragraph 16)

BC26   When a separate account is used to record impairment losses (such as an allowance account or similar account used to record a collective impairment of assets), paragraph 16 requires a reconciliation of that account to be disclosed. The Board was informed that analysts and other users find this information useful in assessing the adequacy of the allowance for impairment losses for such entities and when comparing one entity with another. However, the Board decided not to specify the components of the reconciliation. This allows entities flexibility in determining the most appropriate format for their needs.

BC27   Respondents to ED 7 asked the Board to require entities to provide equivalent information if they do not use an allowance account. The Board decided not to add this disclosure in finalising the IFRS. It concluded that, for virtually all entities, IAS 39's requirement to consider impairment on a group basis would necessitate the use of an allowance or similar account. The accounting policy disclosures required by paragraph B5(d) also include information about the use of direct adjustments to carrying amounts of financial assets.

Compound financial instruments with multiple embedded derivatives (paragraph 17)

IAS 32 requires the separation of the liability and equity components of a compound **BC28** financial instrument. The Board notes that this is more complicated for compound financial instruments with multiple embedded derivative features whose values are interdependent (for example, a convertible debt instrument that gives the issuer a right to call the instrument back from the holder, or the holder a right to put the instrument back to the issuer) than for those without such features. If the embedded equity and non-equity derivative features are interdependent, the sum of the separately determined values of the liability and equity components will not equal the value of the compound financial instrument as a whole.

For example, the values of an embedded call option feature and an equity conversion **BC29** option feature in a callable convertible debt instrument depend in part on each other if the holder's equity conversion option is extinguished when the entity exercises the call option or vice versa. The following diagram illustrates the joint value arising from the interaction between a call option and an equity conversion option in a callable convertible bond. Circle L represents the value of the liability component, ie the value of the straight debt and the embedded call option on the straight debt, and Circle E represents the value of the equity component, ie the equity conversion option on the straight debt. The total area of the two circles represents the value of the callable convertible bond. The difference between the value of the callable convertible bond as a whole and the sum of the separately determined values for the liability and equity components is the joint value attributable to the interdependence between the call option feature and the equity conversion feature. It is represented by the intersection between the two circles.

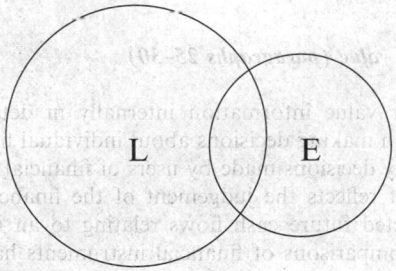

Under the approach in IAS 32, the joint value attributable to the interdependence **BC30** between multiple embedded derivative features is included in the liability component. A numerical example is set out as Illustrative Example 10 accompanying IAS 32.

Even though this approach is consistent with the definition of equity as a residual **BC31** interest, the Board recognises that the allocation of the joint value to either the liability component or the equity component is arbitrary because it is, by its nature, joint. Therefore, the Board concluded that it is important to disclose the existence of issued compound financial instruments with multiple embedded derivative features that have interdependent values. Such disclosure highlights the effect of multiple embedded derivative features on the amounts recognised as liabilities and equity.

Defaults and breaches (paragraphs 18 and 19)

Paragraphs 18 and 19 require disclosures about defaults and breaches of loans **BC32** payable and other loan agreements. The Board concluded that such disclosures provide relevant information about the entity's creditworthiness and its prospects of obtaining future loans.

Income statement and equity (paragraph 20)

Items of income, expenses, gains or losses (paragraph 20(a))

BC33   Paragraph 20(a) requires disclosure of income statement gains and losses by the measurement categories in IAS 39 (which complement the balance sheet disclosure requirement described in paragraph BC14). The Board concluded that the disclosure is needed for users to understand the financial performance of an entity's financial instruments, given the different measurement bases in IAS 39.

BC34   Some entities include interest and dividend income in gains and losses on financial assets and financial liabilities held for trading and others do not. To assist users in comparing income arising from financial instruments across different entities, the Board decided that an entity should disclose how the income statement amounts are determined. For example, an entity should disclose whether net gains and losses on financial assets or financial liabilities held for trading include interest and dividend income (see Appendix B, paragraph B5(e)).

Fee income and expense (paragraph 20(c))

BC35   Paragraph 20(c) requires disclosure of fee income and expense (other than amounts included in determining the effective interest rate) arising from financial assets or financial liabilities and from trust and other fiduciary activities that result in the entity holding or placing assets on behalf of individuals, trusts, retirement benefit plans, and other institutions. This information indicates the level of such activities and helps users to estimate possible future income of the entity.

Other disclosures—fair value (paragraphs 25–30)

BC36   Many entities use fair value information internally in determining their overall financial position and in making decisions about individual financial instruments. It is also relevant to many decisions made by users of financial statements because, in many circumstances, it reflects the judgement of the financial markets about the present value of expected future cash flows relating to an instrument. Fair value information permits comparisons of financial instruments having substantially the same economic characteristics, regardless of why they are held and when and by whom they were issued or acquired. Fair values provide a neutral basis for assessing management's stewardship by indicating the effects of its decisions to buy, sell or hold financial assets and to incur, maintain or discharge financial liabilities. The Board decided that when an entity does not measure a financial asset or financial liability in its balance sheet at fair value, it should provide fair value information through supplementary disclosures to assist users to compare entities on a consistent basis.

BC37   Disclosure of fair value is not required for investments in unquoted equity instruments and derivatives linked to such equity instruments if their fair value cannot be measured reliably. Similarly, IFRS 4 does not specify the accounting required for contracts containing a discretionary participation feature pending phase II of the Board's project on insurance contracts. Accordingly, disclosure of fair value is not required for contracts containing a discretionary participation feature, if the fair value of that feature cannot be measured reliably. For all other financial assets and financial liabilities, it is reasonable to expect that fair value can be determined with sufficient reliability within constraints of timeliness and cost. Therefore, the Board concluded that there should be no other exception from the requirement to disclose fair value information for financial assets or financial liabilities.

To provide users of financial statements with a sense of the potential variability of **BC38** fair value estimates, the Board decided that information about the use of valuation techniques should be disclosed, in particular the sensitivities of fair value estimates to the main valuation assumptions. In forming this conclusion, the Board considered the view that disclosure of sensitivities could be difficult, particularly when there are many assumptions to which the disclosure would apply and these assumptions are interdependent. However, the Board noted that a detailed quantitative disclosure of sensitivity to all assumptions is not required (only those that could result in a significantly different estimate of fair value are required) and that the disclosure does not require the entity to reflect interdependencies between assumptions when making the disclosure. Additionally, the Board considered whether this disclosure might imply that a fair value established by a valuation technique is less reliable than one established by other means. However, the Board noted that fair values estimated by valuation techniques are more subjective than those established from an observable market price, and concluded that users need information to help them assess the extent of this subjectivity.

Paragraph 28 requires disclosure about the difference that arises if the transaction **BC39** price differs from the fair value of a financial instrument that is determined in accordance with paragraph AG76 of IAS 39. Those disclosures relate to matters addressed in the December 2004 amendment to IAS 39 *Transition and Initial Recognition of Financial Assets and Financial Liabilities**. That amendment does not specify how entities should account for those initial differences in subsequent periods. The disclosures required by paragraph 28 inform users about the amount of gain or loss that will be recognised in profit or loss in future periods. The Board noted that the information required to provide these disclosures would be readily available to the entities affected.

DISCLOSURES ABOUT THE NATURE AND EXTENT OF RISKS ARISING FROM FINANCIAL INSTRUMENTS (PARAGRAPHS 31–42 AND B6–B28)

The Board was informed that users of financial statements value information about **BC40** the risks arising from financial instruments, such as credit risk, liquidity risk and market risk, to which entities are exposed, and the techniques used to identify, measure, monitor and control those risks. Therefore, the Board decided to require disclosure of this information. The Board also decided to balance two objectives:

(a)   consistent requirements should apply to all entities so that users receive comparable information about the risks to which entities are exposed.
(b)   the disclosures provided should depend on the extent of an entity's use of financial instruments and the extent to which it assumes associated risks. Entities with many financial instruments and related risks should provide more disclosure to communicate those risks to users of financial statements. Conversely, entities with few financial instruments and related risks may provide less extensive disclosure.

The Board decided to balance these two objectives by developing an IFRS that sets **BC41** out principles and minimum requirements applicable to all entities, supported by guidance on implementing the IFRS. The requirements in paragraphs 33–42 combine qualitative disclosures of the entity's exposure to risks arising from financial instruments, and the way in which management views and manages these risks, with quantitative disclosures about material risks arising from financial instruments. The

*ASB Footnote: This amendment was issued in the UK as part of the amendments to FRS 26 issued in October 2005.

extent of disclosure depends on the extent of the entity's exposure to risks arising from financial instruments. The guidance on implementing the IFRS illustrates how an entity might apply the IFRS. This guidance is consistent with the disclosure requirements for banks developed by the Basel Committee (known as Pillar 3), so that banks can prepare, and users receive, a single co-ordinated set of disclosures about financial risk.

BC42   The Board noted that because entities view and manage risk in different ways, disclosures based on how an entity manages risk are unlikely to be comparable between entities. In addition, for an entity that undertakes limited management of risks arising from financial instruments, such disclosures would convey little or no information about the risks the entity has assumed. To overcome these limitations, the Board decided to specify disclosures about risk exposures applicable to all entities. These disclosures provide a common benchmark for financial statement users when comparing risk exposures across different entities and are expected to be relatively easy for entities to prepare. Entities with more developed risk management systems would provide more detailed information.

Location of disclosures of risks arising from financial instruments (paragraph B6)

BC43   Many respondents to ED 7 argued that disclosures about risks in paragraphs 31–42 should not be part of the financial statements for the following reasons:

(a)   the information would be difficult and costly to audit.

(b)   the information is different from information generally included in financial statements because it is subjective, forward-looking and based on management's judgement. Thus, the information does not meet the criteria of comparability, faithful representation and completeness.

(c)   inclusion of such information in a management commentary section outside the financial statements would be consistent with practice in other jurisdictions, including the US. Having this information in the financial statements would put IFRS preparers at a disadvantage relative to their US peers.

BC44   Respondents raised concerns that the disclosure of sensitivity analysis in particular should not be part of the financial statements. Respondents stated that sensitivity analysis cannot be prepared with the degree of reliability expected of information in the financial statements, and that the subjectivity in the sensitivity analysis and the hypothetical alternative values could undermine the credibility of the fair values recognised in the financial statements.

BC45   The Board considered whether the disclosures should be part of the information provided by management outside the financial statements. The Board noted that respondents generally regarded the disclosures proposed in ED 7 as useful, even if they did not agree that they should be located in the financial statements. The Board's view is that financial statements would be incomplete and potentially misleading without disclosures about risks arising from financial instruments. Hence, it concluded that such disclosures should be part of the financial statements. The Board rejected the argument that increased transparency puts an entity at a disadvantage; greater certainty on the part of investors can provide a significant advantage by lowering the entity's cost of capital.

BC46   The Board also noted that some entities might prefer to present the information required by the IFRS together with material such as a management commentary or risk report that is not part of the financial statements. Some entities might be required by regulatory authorities to provide in a separate report information similar to that required by the IFRS. Accordingly, the Board decided these disclosures should be given in the financial statements or incorporated by cross-reference from the financial statements to some other statement that is available to users of the financial statements on the same terms as the financial statements and at the same time.

Quantitative disclosures (paragraphs 34–42 and B7–B28)

Information based on how the entity manages risk (paragraphs 34 and B7)

The Board concluded that disclosures about an entity's exposure to risks arising from financial instruments should be required, and should be based on how the entity views and manages its risks, ie using the information provided to key management personnel (for example, its board of directors or chief executive officer). This approach: **BC47**

(a)   provides a useful insight into how the entity views and manages risk;
(b)   results in information that has more predictive value than information based on assumptions and methods that management does not use, for instance, in considering the entity's ability to react to adverse situations;
(c)   is more effective in adapting to changes in risk measurement and management techniques and developments in the external environment;
(d)   has practical advantages for preparers of financial statements, because it allows them to use the data they use in managing risk; and
(e)   is consistent with the approach used in IAS 14 *Segment Reporting**.

Information on averages

The Board considered whether it should require quantitative information about average risk exposures during the period. It noted that information about averages is more informative if the risk exposure at the reporting date is not typical of the exposure during the period. However, information about averages is also more onerous to prepare. On balance, the Board decided to require disclosure of the exposures at the reporting date in all cases and to require additional information only if the information provided at the reporting date is unrepresentative of the entity's exposure to risk during the period. **BC48**

Credit risk (paragraphs 36–38, B9 and B10)

Maximum exposure to credit risk (paragraphs 36(a), B9 and B10)

Paragraph 36(a) requires disclosure of an entity's maximum exposure to credit risk at the reporting date. Some respondents to ED 7 stated that these disclosures would not provide useful information when there are no identified problems in a loan portfolio, and it is not likely that collateral would be called on. However, the Board disagreed because it believes that such information: **BC49**

(a)   provides users of financial statements with a consistent measure of an entity's exposure to credit risk; and
(b)   takes into account the possibility that the maximum exposure to loss may differ from the amount recognised in the balance sheet.

*ASB Footnote: *IAS 14 has not been implemented in the UK.* SSAP 25 Segmental Reporting *addresses issues that are addressed in some parts of IAS 14.*

BC50 Some respondents to ED 7 questioned whether the maximum exposure to credit risk for a derivative contract is its carrying amount because fair value does not always reflect potential future exposure to credit risk (see paragraph B10(b)). However, the Board noted that paragraph 36(a) requires disclosure of the amount that best represents the maximum exposure to credit risk *at the reporting date*, which is the carrying amount.

Collateral held as security and other credit enhancements
(paragraphs 36(b) and 37(c))

BC51 ED 7 proposed that, unless impracticable, the entity should disclose the fair value of collateral held as security and other credit enhancements, to provide information about the loss the entity might incur in the event of default. However, many respondents to ED 7 disagreed with this proposal on cost/benefit grounds. Respondents indicated that fair value information might not be available for:

(a) small entities and entities other than banks, which may find it onerous to acquire information about collateral;

(b) banks that collect precise information on the value of collateral only on origination, for loans whose payments are made on time and in full (for example a mortgage portfolio secured by properties, for which valuations are not kept up to date on an asset-by-asset basis);

(c) particular types of collateral, such as a floating charge on all the assets of an entity; and

(d) insurers that hold collateral for which fair value information is not readily available.

BC52 The Board also noted respondents' concerns that an aggregate disclosure of the fair value of collateral held would be misleading when some loans in a portfolio are over-collateralised, and other loans have insufficient collateral. In these circumstances, netting the fair value of the two types of collateral would under-report the amount of credit risk. The Board agreed with respondents that the information useful to users is not the total amount of credit exposure less the total amount of collateral, but rather is the amount of credit exposure that is left after available collateral is taken into account.

BC53 Therefore, the Board decided not to require disclosure of the fair value of collateral held, but to require disclosure of only a description of collateral held as security and other credit enhancements. The Board noted that such disclosure does not require an entity to establish fair values for all its collateral (in particular when the entity has determined that the fair value of some collateral exceeds the carrying amount of the loan) and, thus, would be less onerous for entities to provide than fair values.

Credit quality of financial assets that are neither past due nor impaired (paragraph 36(c))

BC54 The Board noted that information about credit quality gives a greater insight into the credit risk of assets and helps users assess whether such assets are more or less likely to become impaired in the future. Because this information will vary between entities, the Board decided not to specify a particular method for giving this information, but rather to allow each entity to devise a method that is appropriate to its circumstances.

Financial assets that are either past due or impaired (paragraph 37)

The Board decided to require separate disclosure of financial assets that are past due   **BC55**
or impaired to provide users with information about financial assets with the greatest
credit risk (paragraph 37). This includes:

(a)   an analysis of the age of financial assets, including trade receivables, that are
      past due at the reporting date, but not impaired (paragraph 37(a)). This
      information provides users with information about those financial assets that
      are more likely to become impaired and helps users to estimate the level of
      future impairment losses.
(b)   an analysis of financial assets that are individually determined to be impaired at
      the reporting date, including the factors the entity considered in determining
      that the financial assets are impaired (paragraph 37(b)). The Board concluded
      that an analysis of impaired financial assets by factors other than age (eg nature
      of the counterparty, or geographical analysis of impaired assets) would be
      useful because it helps users to understand why the impairment occurred.

Collateral and other credit enhancements obtained (paragraph 38)

Paragraph 38 requires the entity to disclose the nature and carrying amount of assets   **BC56**
obtained by taking possession of collateral held as security or calling on other credit
enhancements and its policy for disposing of such assets. The Board concluded that
this information is useful because it provides information about the frequency of
such activities and the entity's ability to obtain and realise the value of the collateral.
ED 7 had proposed that the entity should disclose the fair value of the assets
obtained less the cost of selling them, rather than the carrying amount. The Board
noted that this amount might be more relevant in the case of collateral obtained that
is expected to be sold. However, it also noted that such an amount would be included
in the impairment calculation that is reflected in the amount recognised in the balance sheet and the purpose of the disclosure is to indicate the amount recognised in
the balance sheet for such assets.

Liquidity risk (paragraphs 39 and B11–B16)

The Board decided to require disclosure of a maturity analysis for financial liabilities   **BC57**
showing the remaining earliest contractual maturities (paragraph 39(a) and paragraphs B11–B16 of Appendix B). Liquidity risk, ie the risk that the entity will
encounter difficulty in meeting commitments associated with financial liabilities,
arises because of the possibility (which may often be remote) that the entity could be
required to pay its liabilities earlier than expected. The Board decided to require
disclosure based on the earliest contractual maturity date because this disclosure
shows a worst case scenario.

Some respondents expressed concerns that such a contractual maturity analysis does   **BC58**
not reveal the expected maturity of liabilities, which, for some entities—eg banks
with many demand deposits—may be very different. They suggested that a contractual maturity analysis alone does not provide information about the conditions
expected in normal circumstances or how the entity manages deviations from
expected maturity. Therefore, the Board decided to require a description of how the
entity manages the liquidity risk portrayed by the contractual maturity analysis.

Market risk (paragraphs 40–42 and B17–B28)

BC59   The Board decided to require disclosure of a sensitivity analysis for each type of market risk (paragraph 40) because:

(a)   users have consistently emphasised the fundamental importance of sensitivity analysis;

(b)   a sensitivity analysis can be disclosed for all types of market risk and by all entities, and is relatively easy to understand and calculate; and

(c)   it is suitable for all entities—including non-financial entities—that have financial instruments. It is supported by disclosures of how the entity manages the risk. Thus, it is a simpler and more suitable disclosure than other approaches, including the disclosures of terms and conditions and the gap analysis of interest rate risk previously required by IAS 32.

The Board noted that information provided by a simple sensitivity analysis would not be comparable across entities. This is because the methodologies used to prepare the sensitivity analysis and the resulting disclosures would vary according to the nature of the entity and the complexity of its risk management systems.

BC60   The Board acknowledged that a simple sensitivity analysis that shows a change in only one variable has limitations. For example, the analysis may not reveal non-linearities in sensitivities or the effects of interdependencies between variables. The Board decided to meet the first concern by requiring additional disclosure when the sensitivity analysis is unrepresentative of a risk inherent in a financial instrument (paragraph 42). The Board noted that it could meet the second concern by requiring a more complex sensitivity analysis that takes into account the interdependencies between risks. Although more informative, such an analysis is also more complex and costly to prepare. Accordingly, the Board decided not to require such an analysis, but to permit its disclosure as an alternative to the minimum requirement when it is used by management to manage risk.

BC61   Respondents to ED 7 noted that a value-at-risk amount would not show the effect on profit or loss or equity. However, entities that manage on the basis of value at risk would not want to prepare a separate sensitivity analysis solely for the purpose of this disclosure. The Board's objective was to require disclosures about sensitivity, not to mandate a particular form of sensitivity disclosure. Therefore, the Board decided not to require disclosure of the effects on profit or loss and equity if an alternative disclosure of sensitivity is made.

BC62   Respondents to ED 7 requested the Board to provide more guidance and clarification about the sensitivity analysis, in particular:

(a)   what is a reasonably possible change in the relevant risk variable?

(b)   what is the appropriate level of aggregation in the disclosures?

(c)   what methodology should be used in preparing the sensitivity analysis?

BC63   The Board concluded that it would not be possible to provide comprehensive guidance on the methodology to be used in preparing the sensitivity analysis. The Board noted that more comparable information would be obtained if it imposed specific requirements about the inputs, process and methodology of the analysis, for example disclosure of the effects of a parallel shift of the yield curve by 100 basis points. However, the Board decided against such a specific requirement because a reasonably possible change in a relevant risk variable (such as interest rates) in one economic environment may not be reasonably possible in another (such as an economy with higher inflation). Moreover, the effect of a reasonably possible change will vary depending on the entity's risk exposures. As a result, entities are required to judge what those reasonably possible changes are.

However, the Board decided that it would provide high level application guidance **BC64** about how the entity should assess what is a reasonably possible change and on the appropriate level of aggregation in the disclosures. In response to comments received on ED 7, the Board also decided to clarify that:

(a) an entity should not aggregate information about material exposures to risk from significantly different economic environments. However, if it has exposure to only one type of market risk in only one economic environment, it might not show disaggregated information.

(b) the sensitivity analysis does not require entities to determine what the profit or loss for the period would have been had the relevant risk variable been different. The sensitivity analysis shows the effect on current period profit or loss and equity if a reasonably possible change in the relevant risk variable had been applied to the risk exposures in existence at the balance sheet date.

(c) a reasonably possible change is judged relative to the economic environments in which the entity operates, and does not include remote or 'worst case' scenarios or 'stress tests'.

(d) entities are required to disclose only the effects of the changes at the limits of the reasonably possible range of the relevant risk variable, rather than all reasonably possible changes.

(e) the time frame for which entities should make an assessment about what is reasonably possible is the period until the entity next presents these disclosures, usually its next annual reporting period.

The Board also decided to add a simple example of what a sensitivity analysis might look like.

Operational risk

The Board discussed whether it should require disclosure of information about **BC65** operational risk. However, the Board noted that the definition and measurement of operational risk are in their infancy and are not necessarily related to financial instruments. It also decided that such disclosures would be more appropriately located outside the financial statements. Therefore, the Board decided to defer this issue to its research project on management commentary.

EFFECTIVE DATE AND TRANSITION (PARAGRAPHS 43 AND 44)

The Board is committed to maintaining a 'stable platform' of substantially **BC66** unchanged Standards for annual periods beginning on or before 1 January 2005, when many entities will adopt IFRSs for the first time. In addition, some preparers will need time to make the system changes necessary to comply with the IFRS. Therefore, the Board decided that the effective date of IFRS 7 should be annual periods beginning on or after 1 January 2007, with earlier application encouraged.

The Board noted that entities that apply IFRS 7 only when it becomes mandatory **BC67** will have sufficient time to prepare comparative information. This conclusion does not apply to entities that apply IFRS 7 early. In particular, the time would be extremely short for those entities that would like to apply IFRS 7 when they first adopt IFRSs in 2005, to avoid changing from local GAAP to IAS 32 and IAS 30 when they adopt IFRSs and then changing again to IFRS 7 only one or two years later. Therefore, the Board gave an exemption from providing comparative disclosure in the first year of application of IFRS 7 to any entity that both (a) is a first-time adopter of IFRSs and (b) applies IFRS 7 before 1 January 2006. The Board noted that such an exemption for first-time adopters exists in IAS 32 and IFRS 4 and that the reasons for providing the exemption apply equally to IFRS 7.

BC68   The Board also considered whether it should provide an exemption from presenting all or some of the comparative information to encourage early adoption of IFRS 7 by entities that already apply IFRSs.

BC69   The Board noted that IFRS 7 contains two types of disclosures: accounting disclosures (in paragraphs 7–30) that are based on requirements previously in IAS 32 and new risk disclosures (in paragraphs 31–42). The Board concluded that existing users of IFRSs already will have complied with the requirements of IAS 32 and will not encounter difficulty in providing comparative information for the accounting disclosures.

BC70   The Board noted that most of the risk disclosures, in particular those about market risk, are based on information collected at the end of the reporting period. The Board concluded that although IFRS 7 was published in August 2005, it will still be possible for entities to collect the information that they require to comply with IFRS 7 for accounting periods beginning in 2005. However, it would not always be possible to collect the information needed to provide comparative information about accounting periods that began in 2004. As a result, the Board decided that entities that apply IFRS 7 for accounting periods beginning in 2005 (ie before 1 January 2006) need not present comparative information about the risk disclosures.

BC71   The Board also noted that comparative disclosures about risk are less relevant because these disclosures are intended to have predictive value. As a result information about risk loses relevance more quickly than other types of disclosure, and any disclosures required by previous GAAP are unlikely to be comparable with those required by IFRS 7. Accordingly, the Board decided that an entity that is not a first-time adopter and applies IFRS 7 for annual periods beginning before 1 January 2006 need not present comparative disclosures about the nature and extent of risks arising from financial instruments. In reaching this conclusion, the Board noted that the advantages of encouraging more entities to apply IFRS 7 early outweighed the disadvantage of the reduced information provided.

BC72   The Board considered and rejected arguments that it should extend the exemption:

   (a)   from providing comparative information to first-time adopters that applied IFRS 7 before 1 January 2007 (rather than only those that applied IFRS 7 before 1 January 2006). The Board concluded that an entity that intends to adopt IFRSs for the first time on or after 1 January 2006 will have sufficient time to collect information for its accounting period beginning on or after 1 January 2005 and, thus, should not have difficulty in providing the comparative disclosures for accounting periods beginning on or after 1 January 2006.

   (b)   from providing comparative disclosures about the significance of financial instruments to all entities adopting the IFRS for annual periods beginning before 1 January 2006 (rather than only to first-time adopters). The Board concluded that only first-time adopters warranted special relief so that they would be able to adopt IFRS 7 early without first having to adopt IAS 32 and IAS 30 for only one period. Entities that are not first-time adopters already apply IAS 32 and IAS 30 and have no particular need to adopt IFRS 7 before 1 January 2007.

(c)   from providing comparative disclosures about risk to periods beginning before 1 January 2007 (rather than 2006). The Board noted that entities adopting IFRS 7 after 1 January 2006 would have a full calendar year to prepare after the publication of the IFRS.

Summary of main changes from the Exposure Draft

BC73   The main changes to the proposals in ED 7 are:

(a)   ED 7 proposed disclosure of the amount of change in the fair value of a financial liability designated as at fair value through profit or loss that is not attributable to changes in a benchmark interest rate as a proxy for the amount of change in fair value attributable to changes in the instrument's credit risk. The IFRS permits entities to determine the amount of change in fair value attributable to changes in the instrument's credit risk using an alternative method if the entity believes that its alternative method gives more faithful representation. The proxy disclosure has been amended to be the amount of change in fair value that is not attributable to changes in market conditions that give rise to market risk. As a result, entities may exclude factors other than a change in a benchmark interest rate when calculating the proxy.

(b)   a requirement has been added for disclosures about the difference between the transaction price at initial recognition (used as fair value in accordance with paragraph AG76 of IAS 39) and the results of a valuation technique that will be used for subsequent measurement.

(c)   no disclosure is required of the fair value of collateral pledged as security and other credit enhancements as was proposed in ED 7.

(d)   the sensitivity analysis requirements have been clarified.

(e)   the exemption from presenting comparatives has been widened.

(f)   the capital disclosures are a stand-alone amendment to IAS 1, rather than part of the IFRS. No disclosure is required of whether the entity has complied with capital targets set by management and of the consequences of any non-compliance with those targets.

(g)   the amendments to IFRS 4 related to IFRS 7 have been modified to reduce systems changes for insurers.

Disclosures about capital

ASB Note: The following is a reproduction of the IASB's Basis for Conclusions and related Dissenting Opinion in relation to the Capital Disclosures that were developed as part of the IFRS 7 project but implemented as amendments to IAS 1. The ASB has implemented the amendments to IAS 1 as Appendix E to FRS 29.

EBC1   In July 2004, the Board published an Exposure Draft—ED 7 *Financial Instruments: Disclosures*. As part of that project, the Board considered whether it should require disclosures about capital.

EBC2   The level of an entity's capital and how it manages capital are important factors for users to consider in assessing the risk profile of an entity and its ability to withstand unexpected adverse events. The level of capital might also affect the entity's ability to pay dividends. Consequently, ED 7 proposed disclosures about capital.

EBC3   In ED 7, the Board decided that it should not limit its requirements for disclosures about capital to entities that are subject to external capital requirements (eg regulatory capital requirements established by legislation or other regulation). The Board believes that information about capital is useful for all entities, as is evidenced by the fact that some entities set internal capital requirements and norms have been established for some industries. The Board noted that the capital disclosures are not intended to replace disclosures required by regulators. The Board also noted that the financial statements should not be regarded as a substitute for disclosures to regulators (which may not be available to all users) because the function of disclosures made to regulators may differ from those to other users. Therefore, the Board decided that information about capital should be required of all entities because it is useful to users of general purpose financial statements. Accordingly, the Board did not distinguish between the requirements for regulated and nonregulated entities.

Some respondents to ED 7 questioned the relevance of the capital disclosures in a Standard dealing with disclosures relating to financial instruments. The Board noted that an entity's capital does not relate solely to financial instruments and, thus, capital disclosures have more general relevance. Accordingly, the Board included these disclosures in IAS 1, rather than IFRS 7.   **EBC4**

The Board also decided that an entity's decision to adopt the amendments to IAS 1 should be independent of the entity's decision to adopt IFRS 7. The Board noted that issuing a separate amendment facilitates separate adoption decisions.   **EBC5**

Objectives, policies and processes for managing capital

The Board decided that disclosure about capital should be placed in the context of a discussion of the entity's objectives, policies and processes for managing capital. This is because the Board believes that such a discussion both communicates important information about the entity's capital strategy and provides the context for other disclosures.   **EBC6**

The Board considered whether an entity can have a view of capital that differs from what IFRSs define as equity. The Board noted that, although for the purposes of this disclosure capital would often equate with equity as defined in IFRSs, it might also include or exclude some components. The Board also noted that this disclosure is intended to give entities the opportunity to describe how they view the components of capital they manage, if this is different from what IFRSs define as equity.   **EBC7**

Externally imposed capital requirements

The Board considered whether it should require disclosure of any externally imposed capital requirements. Such a capital requirement could be: **EBC8**

(a) an industrywide requirement with which all entities in the industry must comply; or
(b) an entityspecific requirement imposed on a particular entity by its prudential supervisor or other regulator.

The Board noted that some industries and countries have industrywide capital requirements, and others do not. Thus, the Board concluded that it should not require disclosure of industrywide requirements, or compliance with such requirements, because such disclosure would not lead to comparability between different entities or between similar entities in different countries.   **EBC9**

The Board concluded that disclosure of the existence and level of entityspecific capital requirements is important information for users, because it informs them about the risk assessment of the regulator. Such disclosure improves transparency and market discipline.   **EBC10**

However, the Board noted the following arguments against requiring disclosure of externally imposed entityspecific capital requirements.   **EBC11**

(a) Users of financial statements might rely primarily on the regulator's assessment of solvency risk without making their own risk assessment.

(b) The focus of a regulator's risk assessment is for those whose interests the regulations are intended to protect (eg depositors or policyholders). This emphasis is different from that of a shareholder. Thus, it could be misleading to suggest that the regulator's risk assessment could, or should, be a substitute for independent analysis by investors.

(c) The disclosure of entityspecific capital requirements imposed by a regulator might undermine that regulator's ability to impose such requirements. For example, the information could cause depositors to withdraw funds. Hence, this might discourage regulators from imposing requirements. Furthermore, an entity's regulatory dialogue would become public, which might not be appropriate in all circumstances.

(d) Because different regulators have different tools available, for example formal requirements and moral suasion, a requirement to disclose entityspecific capital requirements could not be framed in a way that would lead to the provision of information that is comparable across entities.

(e) Disclosure of capital requirements (and hence, regulatory judgements) could hamper clear communication to the entity of the regulator's assessment by creating incentives to use moral suasion and other informal mechanisms.

(f) Disclosure requirements should not focus on entityspecific capital requirements in isolation, but should focus on how entityspecific capital requirements affect how an entity manages and determines the adequacy of its capital resources.

(g) A requirement to disclose entityspecific capital requirements imposed by a regulator is not part of Pillar 3 of the Basel II Framework developed by the Basel Committee on Banking Supervision.

EBC12 Taking into account all of the above arguments, the Board decided not to require quantitative disclosure of externally imposed capital requirements. Rather, it decided to require disclosures about whether the entity complied with any externally imposed capital requirements during the period and, if not, the consequences of noncompliance. This retains confidentiality between regulators and the entity, but alerts users to breaches of capital requirements and their consequences.

EBC13 Some respondents to ED 7 did not agree that breaches of externally imposed capital requirements should be disclosed. They argued that disclosure about breaches of externally imposed capital requirements and the associated regulatory measures subsequently imposed could be disproportionately damaging to entities. The Board was not persuaded by these arguments because it believes that such concerns indicate that information about breaches of externally imposed capital requirements may often be material by its nature. The *Framework* states that 'Information is material if its omission or misstatement could influence the economic decisions of users taken on the basis of the financial statements.' Similarly, the Board decided not to provide an exemption for temporary noncompliance with regulatory requirements during the year. Information that an entity is sufficiently close to its limits to breach them, even on a temporary basis, is useful for users.

Internal capital targets

EBC14 The Board proposed in ED 7 that the requirement to disclose information about breaches of capital requirements should apply equally to breaches of internally imposed requirements, because it believed the information is also useful to a user of the financial statements.

However, this proposal was criticised by respondents to ED 7 for the following reasons: **EBC15**

(a) the information is subjective and, thus, not comparable between entities. In particular, different entities will set internal targets for different reasons, so a breach of a requirement might signify different things for different entities. In contrast, a breach of an external requirement has similar implications for all entities required to comply with similar requirements.

(b) capital targets are not more important than other internally set financial targets, and to require disclosure only of capital targets would provide users with incomplete and, perhaps, misleading information.

(c) internal targets are estimates that are subject to change by the entity. It is not appropriate to require the entity's performance against this benchmark to be disclosed.

(d) an internally set capital target can be manipulated by management. The disclosure requirement could cause management to set the target so that it would always be achieved, providing little useful information to users and potentially reducing the effectiveness of the entity's capital management.

As a result, the Board decided not to require disclosure of the capital targets set by management, whether the entity has complied with those targets, or the consequences of any noncompliance. However, the Board confirmed its view that when an entity has policies and processes for managing capital, qualitative disclosures about these policies and processes are useful. The Board also concluded that these disclosures, together with disclosure of the components of equity and their changes during the year (required by paragraphs 96–101)*, would give sufficient information about entities that are not regulated or subject to externally imposed capital requirements. **EBC16**

DISSENTING OPINION

Dissent of James J Leisenring

Mr Leisenring dissents from the amendments to IAS 1 Presentation of Financial Statements—*Capital Disclosures*. He disagrees with the assertion in paragraph BC43 that the information required by this amendment is useful for all entities. He notes that nothing would prohibit an entity making these disclosures if specific circumstances suggested the disclosures were particularly useful. Therefore he would not impose the disclosure requirements of paragraphs 124A–124C on entities that are not subject to external capital requirements.† **EDO1**

---

*ASB Footnote: *IAS 1 has no equivalent in the UK.*

†ASB Footnote: *The ASB has included these amendments to IAS 1 in this Standard and these are contained within Appendix E. Paragraph BC43 in IAS 1 has been incorporated at EBC3 in this Standard and the IAS 1 disclosure requirements in paragraphs 124A – 124C have been incorporated at E1 – E3 in Appendix C.*

Appendix
Amendments to Basis for Conclusions
on other IFRSs

This appendix contains amendments to the Basis for Conclusions on other Standards that are necessary in order to ensure consistency with FRS 29. In the amended paragraphs, new text is underlined and deleted text is struck through.

BCA1   The Basis for Conclusions on FRS 25 *Financial Instruments: Disclosure and Presentation* is amended as described below.

The reference to FRS 25 in paragraph BC1 is footnoted as follows:

> In August 2005, the IASB relocated all disclosures relating to financial instruments to IFRS 7. The paragraphs relating to disclosures that were originally published in this Basis for Conclusions were relocated, if still relevant, to the Basis for Conclusions on IFRS 7.

An ASB footnote is also added as follows:

> The ASB issued FRS 29 in December 2005. All disclosures relating to financial instruments, and so all relevant paragraphs from this Basis for Conclusions were similarly relocated.

The headings above paragraph BC34 and paragraphs BC34–BC48 are deleted.

In paragraph BC49, subparagraphs (i) and (j) are deleted and new subparagraph (k) is added as follows:

(k)   In August 2005, the IASB issued IFRS 7 *Financial Instruments: Disclosures*. As a result, disclosures relating to financial instruments, if still relevant, were relocated to IFRS 7.

The new subparagraph (k) is footnoted as follows:

> The ASB issued FRS 29 in December 2005. All disclosures relating to financial instruments were similarly relocated.

BCA2   In the Basis for Conclusions on FRS 26 (IAS 39) *Financial Instruments: Measurement*, the references to FRS 25 in paragraphs BC90 and BC222(s) are footnoted as follows:

> In August 2005, the IASB relocated all disclosures relating to financial instruments to IFRS 7 *Financial Instruments: Disclosures*.

An ASB footnote is also added as follows:

> In December 2005, the ASB similarly relocated all disclosures relating to financial instruments to FRS 29.

BCA3   Deleted by ASB (IAS 41)

BCA4   Deleted by ASB (IFRS 4)

Guidance on implementing FRS 29 (IFRS 7)
Financial instruments: disclosures

Guidance on Implementing FRS 29 (IFRS 7)
Financial Instruments: Disclosures

This guidance accompanies, but is not part of, FRS 29.

INTRODUCTION

IG1   This guidance suggests possible ways to apply some of the disclosure requirements in *FRS 29*. The guidance does not create additional requirements.

IG2   For convenience, each disclosure requirement in the FRS is discussed separately. In practice, disclosures would normally be presented as an integrated package and individual disclosures might satisfy more than one requirement. For example, information about concentrations of risk might also convey information about exposure to credit or other risk.

Materiality

IG3   The concept of materiality is set out in the ASB's Statement of principles for financial reporting in paragraphs 3.28 to 3.32.

CLASSES OF FINANCIAL INSTRUMENTS AND LEVEL OF DISCLOSURE (PARAGRAPHS 6 AND B1–B3)

IG5   Paragraph B3 states that 'an entity decides in the light of its circumstances how much detail it provides to satisfy the requirements of this FRS, how much emphasis it places on different aspects of the requirements and how it aggregates information to display the overall picture without combining information with different characteristics.' To satisfy the requirements, an entity may not need to disclose all the information suggested in this guidance.

SIGNIFICANCE OF FINANCIAL INSTRUMENTS FOR FINANCIAL POSITION AND PERFORMANCE (PARAGRAPHS 7–30, B4 AND B5)

Financial liabilities at fair value through profit or loss (paragraphs 10(a)(i) and B4)

IG7   The following example illustrates the calculation that an entity might perform in accordance with paragraph B4 of Appendix B of the FRS.

IG8   On 1 January 20X1, an entity issues a 10-year bond with a par value of CU150,000 and an annual fixed coupon rate of 8 per cent, which is consistent with market rates for bonds with similar characteristics.

IG9   The entity uses LIBOR as its observable (benchmark) interest rate. At the date of inception of the bond, LIBOR is 5 per cent. At the end of the first year:

(a)   LIBOR has decreased to 4.75 per cent.
(b)   the fair value for the bond is CU153,811, consistent with an interest rate of 7.6 per cent.*

---

*This reflects a shift in LIBOR from 5 per cent to 4.75 per cent and a movement of 0.15 per cent which, in the absence of other relevant changes in market conditions, is assumed to reflect changes in credit risk of the instrument.

The entity assumes a flat yield curve, all changes in interest rates result from a parallel shift in the yield curve, and the changes in LIBOR are the only relevant changes in market conditions. **IG10**

The entity estimates the amount of change in the fair value of the bond that is not attributable to changes in market conditions that give rise to market risk as follows: **IG11**

[paragraph B4(a)]	
First, the entity computes the liability's internal rate of return at the start of the period using the observed market price of the liability and the liability's contractual cash flows at the start of the period. It deducts from this rate of return the observed (benchmark) interest rate at the start of the period, to arrive at an instrument-specific component of the internal rate of return.	At the start of the period of a 10-year bond with a coupon of 8 per cent, the bond's internal rate of return is 8 per cent. Because the observed (benchmark) interest rate (LIBOR) is 5 per cent, the instrument-specific component of the internal rate of return is 3 per cent.
[paragraph B4(b)]	
Next, the entity calculates the present value of the cash flows associated with the liability using the liability's contractual cash flows at the end of the period and a discount rate equal to the sum of (i) the observed (benchmark) interest rate at the end of the period and (ii) the instrument-specific component of the internal rate of return as determined in accordance with paragraph B4(a).	The contractual cash flows of the instrument at the end of the period are: • interest: CU12,000[(a)] per year for each of years 2–10. • principal: CU150,000 in year 10. The discount rate to be used to calculate the present value of the bond is thus 7.75 per cent, which is 4.75 per cent end of period LIBOR rate, plus the 3 per cent instrument-specific component. This gives a present value of CU152,367.[(b)]
[paragraph B4(c)]	
The difference between the observed market price of the liability at the end of the period and the amount determined in accordance with paragraph B4(b) is the change in fair value that is not attributable to changes in the observed (benchmark) interest rate. This is the amount to be disclosed.	The market price of the liability at the end of the period is CU153,811.[(c)] Thus, the entity discloses CU1,444, which is CU153,811–CU152,367, as the increase in fair value of the bond that is not attributable to changes in market conditions that give rise to market risk.
(a) $CU150,000 \times 8\% = CU12,000$ (b) $PV = [CU12,000 \times (1-(1+0.0775)^{-9})/0.0775] + CU150,000 \times (1+0.0775)^{-9}$ (c) market price $= [CU12,000 \times (1-(1+0.076)^{-9})/0.076] + CU150,000 \times (1+0.076)^{-9}$	

Defaults and breaches (paragraphs 18 and 19)

IG12   Paragraphs 18 and 19 require disclosures when there are any defaults or breaches of loans payable. Any defaults or breaches may affect the classification of the liability as current or non-current in accordance with paragraphs 50A to 50E of FRS 25.

Total interest income and total interest expense (paragraph 20(b))

IG13   The total interest income and total interest expense disclosed in accordance with paragraph 20(b) is a component of the line item for finance costs which may also include amounts that arise on non-financial assets or non-financial liabilities.

Fair value (paragraph 28)

IG14   The fair value at initial recognition of financial instruments that are not traded in active markets is determined in accordance with paragraph AG76 of FRS26. However, when, after initial recognition, an entity will use a valuation technique that incorporates data not obtained from observable markets, there may be a difference between the transaction price at initial recognition and the amount determined at initial recognition using that valuation technique. In these circumstances, the difference will be recognised in profit or loss in subsequent periods in accordance with FRS26 and the entity's accounting policy. Such recognition reflects changes in factors (including time) that market participants would consider in setting a price (see paragraph AG76A of FRS26). Paragraph 28 requires disclosures in these circumstances. An entity might disclose the following to comply with paragraph 28:

Background

On 1 January 20X1 an entity purchases for CU15 million financial assets that are not traded in an active market. The entity has only one class of such financial assets.

The transaction price of CU15 million is the fair value at initial recognition.

After initial recognition, the entity will apply a valuation technique to establish the financial assets' fair value. This valuation technique includes variables other than data from observable markets.

At initial recognition, the same valuation technique would have resulted in an amount of CU14 million, which differs from fair value by CU1 million.

The entity has existing differences of CU5 million at 1 January 20X1.

Application of requirements

The entity's 20X2 disclosure would include the following:

Accounting policies

The entity uses the following valuation technique to determine the fair value of financial instruments that are not traded in an active market: [description of technique, not included in this example]. Differences may arise between the fair

---

value at initial recognition (which, in accordance with FRS26, is generally the transaction price) and the amount determined at initial recognition using the valuation technique. Any such differences are [description of the entity's accounting policy].

In the notes to the financial statements

As discussed in note X, the entity uses [name of valuation technique] to measure the fair value of the following financial instruments that are not traded in an active market. However, in accordance with FRS26, the fair value of an instrument at inception is generally the transaction price. If the transaction price differs from the amount determined at inception using the valuation technique, that difference is [description of the entity's accounting policy]. The differences yet to be recognised in profit or loss are as follows:

	31 Dec X2 CU million	31 Dec X1 CU million
Balance at beginning of year	5.3	5.0
New transactions	–	1.0
Amounts recognised in profit or loss during the year	(0.7)	(0.8)
Other increases	–	0.2
Other decreases	(0.1)	(0.1)
Balance at end of year	4.5	5.3

NATURE AND EXTENT OF RISKS ARISING FROM FINANCIAL INSTRUMENTS (PARAGRAPHS 31–42 AND B6–B28)

Qualitative disclosures (paragraph 33)

The type of qualitative information an entity might disclose to meet the requirements in paragraph 33 includes, but is not limited to, a narrative description of: **IG15**

(a) the entity's exposures to risk and how they arose. Information about risk exposures might describe exposures both gross and net of risk transfer and other risk-mitigating transactions.
(b) the entity's policies and processes for accepting, measuring, monitoring and controlling risk, which might include:
   (i) the structure and organisation of the entity's risk management function(s), including a discussion of independence and accountability;
   (ii) the scope and nature of the entity's risk reporting or measurement systems;
   (iii) the entity's policies for hedging or mitigating risk, including its policies and procedures for taking collateral; and
   (iv) the entity's processes for monitoring the continuing effectiveness of such hedges or mitigating devices.
(c) the entity's policies and procedures for avoiding excessive concentrations of risk.

Information about the nature and extent of risks arising from financial instruments is more useful if it highlights any relationship between financial instruments that can affect the amount, timing or uncertainty of an entity's future cash flows. The extent to which a risk exposure is altered by such relationships might be apparent to users **IG16** from the disclosures required by this Standard, but in some cases further disclosures might be useful.

IG17 In accordance with paragraph 33(c), entities disclose any change in the qualitative information from the previous period and explain the reasons for the change. Such changes may result from changes in exposure to risk or from changes in the way those exposures are managed.

Quantitative disclosures (paragraphs 34–42 and B7–B28)

IG18 Paragraph 34 requires disclosure of quantitative data about concentrations of risk. For example, concentrations of credit risk may arise from:

(a) industry sectors. Thus, if an entity's counterparties are concentrated in one or more industry sectors (such as retail or wholesale), it would disclose separately exposure to risks arising from each concentration of counterparties.

(b) credit rating or other measure of credit quality. Thus, if an entity's counterparties are concentrated in one or more credit qualities (such as secured loans or unsecured loans) or in one or more credit ratings (such as investment grade or speculative grade), it would disclose separately exposure to risks arising from each concentration of counterparties.

(c) geographical distribution. Thus, if an entity's counterparties are concentrated in one or more geographical markets (such as Asia or Europe), it would disclose separately exposure to risks arising from each concentration of counterparties.

(d) a limited number of individual counterparties or groups of closely related counterparties.

Similar principles apply to identifying concentrations of other risks, including liquidity risk and market risk. For example, concentrations of liquidity risk may arise from the repayment terms of financial liabilities, sources of borrowing facilities or reliance on a particular market in which to realise liquid assets. Concentrations of foreign exchange risk may arise if an entity has a significant net open position in a single foreign currency, or aggregate net open positions in several currencies that tend to move together.

IG19 In accordance with paragraph B8, disclosure of concentrations of risk includes a description of the shared characteristic that identifies each concentration. For example, the shared characteristic may refer to geographical distribution of counterparties by groups of countries, individual countries or regions within countries.

IG20 When quantitative information at the reporting date is unrepresentative of the entity's exposure to risk during the period, paragraph 35 requires further disclosure. To meet this requirement, an entity might disclose the highest, lowest and average amount of risk to which it was exposed during the period. For example, if an entity typically has a large exposure to a particular currency, but at year-end unwinds the position, the entity might disclose a graph that shows the exposure at various times during the period, or disclose the highest, lowest and average exposures.

Credit risk (paragraphs 36–38, B9 and B10)

IG21 Paragraph 36 requires an entity to disclose information about its exposure to credit risk by class of financial instrument. Financial instruments in the same class share economic characteristics with respect to the risk being disclosed (in this case, credit risk). For example, an entity might determine that residential mortgages, unsecured consumer loans, and commercial loans each have different economic characteristics.

Collateral and other credit enhancements pledged (paragraph 36(b))

Paragraph 36(b) requires an entity to describe collateral available as security for assets it holds and other credit enhancements obtained. An entity might meet this requirement by disclosing: **IG22**

(a)   the policies and processes for valuing and managing collateral and other credit enhancements obtained;
(b)   a description of the main types of collateral and other credit enhancements (examples of the latter being guarantees, credit derivatives, and netting agreements that do not qualify for offset in accordance with FRS 25);
(c)   the main types of counterparties to collateral and other credit enhancements and their creditworthiness; and
(d)   information about risk concentrations within the collateral or other credit enhancements.

Credit quality (paragraph 36(c))

Paragraph 36(c) requires an entity to disclose information about the credit quality of financial assets with credit risk that are neither past due nor impaired. In doing so, an entity might disclose the following information: **IG23**

(a)   an analysis of credit exposures using an external or internal credit grading system;
(b)   the nature of the counterparty;
(c)   historical information about counterparty default rates; and
(d)   any other information used to assess credit quality.

When the entity considers external ratings when managing and monitoring credit quality, the entity might disclose information about: **IG24**

(a)   the amounts of credit exposures for each external credit grade;
(b)   the rating agencies used;
(c)   the amount of an entity's rated and unrated credit exposures; and
(d)   the relationship between internal and external ratings.

When the entity considers internal credit ratings when managing and monitoring credit quality, the entity might disclose information about: **IG25**

(a)   the internal credit ratings process;
(b)   the amounts of credit exposures for each internal credit grade; and
(c)   the relationship between internal and external ratings.

Financial assets that are either past due or impaired (paragraph 37)

A financial asset is past due when the counterparty has failed to make a payment when contractually due. As an example, an entity enters into a lending agreement that requires interest to be paid every month. On the first day of the next month, if interest has not been paid, the loan is past due. Past due does not mean that a counterparty will never pay, but it can trigger various actions such as renegotiation, enforcement of covenants, or legal proceedings.   **IG26**

IG27   When the terms and conditions of financial assets that have been classified as past due are renegotiated, the terms and conditions of the new contractual arrangement apply in determining whether the financial asset remains past due.

IG28   Paragraph 37(a) requires an analysis by class of the age of financial assets that are past due but not impaired. An entity uses its judgement to determine an appropriate number of time bands. For example, an entity might determine that the following time bands are appropriate:

(a)   not more than three months;

(b)   more than three months and not more than six months;

(c)   more than six months and not more than one year; and

(d)   more than one year.

IG29   Paragraph 37(b) requires an analysis of impaired financial assets by class. This analysis might include:

(a)   the carrying amount, before deducting any impairment loss;

(b)   the amount of any related impairment loss; and

(c)   the nature and fair value of collateral available and other credit enhancements obtained.

Liquidity risk (paragraphs 39 and B11)

Liquidity management (paragraph 39(b))

IG30   If an entity manages liquidity risk on the basis of expected maturity dates, it might disclose a maturity analysis of the expected maturity dates of both financial liabilities and financial assets. If an entity discloses such an expected maturity analysis, it might clarify that expected dates are based on estimates made by management, and explain how the estimates are determined and the principal reasons for differences from the contractual maturity analysis that is required by paragraph 39(a).

IG31   Paragraph 39(b) requires the entity to describe how it manages the liquidity risk inherent in the maturity analysis of financial liabilities required in paragraph 39(a). The factors that the entity might consider in providing this disclosure include, but are not limited to, whether the entity:

(a)   expects some of its liabilities to be paid later than the earliest date on which the entity can be required to pay (as may be the case for customer deposits placed with a bank);

(b)   expects some of its undrawn loan commitments not to be drawn;

(c)   holds financial assets for which there is a liquid market and that are readily saleable to meet liquidity needs;

(d)   has committed borrowing facilities (eg commercial paper facilities) or other lines of credit (eg stand-by credit facilities) that it can access to meet liquidity needs;

(e)   holds financial assets for which there is not a liquid market, but which are expected to generate cash inflows (principal or interest) that will be available to meet cash outflows on liabilities;

(f)   holds deposits at central banks to meet liquidity needs;

(g)   has very diverse funding sources; or

(h)   has significant concentrations of liquidity risk in either its assets or its funding sources.

Market risk (paragraphs 40-42 and B17-B28)

Paragraph 40(a) requires a sensitivity analysis for each type of market risk to which   **IG32**
the entity is exposed. There are three types of market risk: interest rate risk, currency
risk and other price risk. Other price risk may include risks such as equity price risk,
commodity price risk, prepayment risk (ie the risk that one party to a financial asset
will incur a financial loss because the other party repays earlier or later than
expected), and residual value risk (eg a lessor of motor cars that writes residual value
guarantees is exposed to residual value risk). Risk variables that are relevant to
disclosing market risk include, but are not limited to:

(a)   the yield curve of market interest rates. It may be necessary to consider both
      parallel and non-parallel shifts in the yield curve.
(b)   foreign exchange rates.
(c)   prices of equity instruments.
(d)   market prices of commodities.

Paragraph 40(a) requires the sensitivity analysis to show the effect on profit or loss   **IG33**
and equity of reasonably possible changes in the relevant risk variable. For example,
relevant risk variables might include:

(a)   prevailing market interest rates, for interest-sensitive financial instruments such
      as a variable-rate loan; or
(b)   currency rates and interest rates, for foreign currency financial instruments
      such as foreign currency bonds.

For interest rate risk, the sensitivity analysis might show separately the effect of a   **IG34**
change in market interest rates on:

(a)   interest income and expense;
(b)   other line items of profit or loss (such as trading gains and losses); and
(c)   when applicable, equity.

An entity might disclose a sensitivity analysis for interest rate risk for each currency
in which the entity has material exposures to interest rate risk.

Because the factors affecting market risk vary depending on the specific circum-   **IG35**
stances of each entity, the appropriate range to be considered in providing a
sensitivity analysis of market risk varies for each entity and for each type of market
risk.

The following example illustrates the application of the disclosure requirement in   **IG36**
paragraph 40(a):

Interest rate risk

At 31 December 20X2, if interest rates at that date had been 10 basis points lower
with all other variables held constant, post-tax profit for the year would have
been CU1.7 million (20X1—CU2.4 million) higher, arising mainly as a result of
lower interest expense on variable borrowings, and other components of equity
would have been CU2.8 million (20X1—CU3.2 million) higher, arising mainly as
a result of an increase in the fair value of fixed rate financial assets classified as
available for sale. If interest rates had been 10 basis points higher, with all other
variables held constant, post-tax profit would have been CU1.5 million
(20X1—CU2.1 million) lower, arising mainly as a result of higher interest expense
on variable borrowings, and other components of equity would have been CU3.0

million (20X1—CU3.4 million) lower, arising mainly as a result of a decrease in the fair value of fixed rate financial assets classified as available for sale. Profit is more sensitive to interest rate decreases than increases because of borrowings with capped interest rates. The sensitivity is lower in 20X2 than in 20X1 because of a reduction in outstanding borrowings that has occurred as the entity's debt has matured (see note X).[a]

Foreign currency exchange rate risk

At 31 December 20X2, if the CU had weakened 10 per cent against the US dollar with all other variables held constant, post-tax profit for the year would have been CU2.8 million (20X1—CU6.4 million) lower, and other components of equity would have been CU1.2 million (20X1—CU1.1 million) higher. Conversely, if the CU had strengthened 10 per cent against the US dollar with all other variables held constant, post-tax profit would have been CU2.8 million (20X1—CU6.4 million) higher, and other components of equity would have been CU1.2 million (20X1—CU1.1 million) lower. The lower foreign currency exchange rate sensitivity in profit in 20X2 compared with 20X1 is attributable to a reduction in foreign currency denominated debt. Equity is more sensitive in 20X2 than in 20X1 because of the increased use of hedges of foreign currency purchases, offset by the reduction in foreign currency debt.

(a) Paragraph 39(a) requires disclosure of a maturity analysis of liabilities.

Other market risk disclosures (paragraph 42)

IG37   Paragraph 42 requires the disclosure of additional information when the sensitivity analysis disclosed is unrepresentative of a risk inherent in a financial instrument. For example, this can occur when:

(a)   a financial instrument contains terms and conditions whose effects are not apparent from the sensitivity analysis, eg options that remain out of (or in) the money for the chosen change in the risk variable;

(b)   financial assets are illiquid, eg when there is a low volume of transactions in similar assets and an entity finds it difficult to find a counterparty; or

(c)   an entity has a large holding of a financial asset that, if sold in its entirety, would be sold at a discount or premium to the quoted market price for a smaller holding.

IG38   In the situation in paragraph IG37(a), additional disclosure might include:

(a)   the terms and conditions of the financial instrument (eg the options);

(b)   the effect on profit or loss if the term or condition were met (ie if the options were exercised); and

(c)   a description of how the risk is hedged.

For example, an entity may acquire a zero-cost interest rate collar that includes an out-of-the-money leveraged written option (eg the entity pays ten times the amount of the difference between a specified interest rate floor and the current market interest rate). The entity may regard the collar as an inexpensive economic hedge against a reasonably possible increase in interest rates. However, an unexpectedly large decrease in interest rates might trigger payments under the written option that, because of the leverage, might be significantly larger than the benefit of lower interest rates. Neither the fair value of the collar nor a sensitivity analysis based on reasonably possible changes in market variables would indicate this exposure. In this case, the entity might provide the additional information described above.

In the situation described in paragraph IG37(b), additional disclosure might include **IG39** the reasons for the lack of liquidity and how the entity hedges the risk.

In the situation described in paragraph IG37(c), additional disclosure might include: **IG40**

(a)   the nature of the security (eg entity name);
(b)   the extent of holding (eg 15 per cent of the issued shares);
(c)   the effect on profit or loss; and
(d)   how the entity hedges the risk.

TRANSITION (PARAGRAPH 44)

The following table* summarises the effect of the exemption from presenting com- **IG41** parative accounting and risk disclosures for accounting periods beginning before 1 January 2006, before 1 January 2007, and on or after 1 January 2007. In this table:

(a)   a **first-time adopter** is an entity that is adopting FRS 26 for the first time in preparing its financial statements.
(b)   an **existing user** is an entity that applies this standard when preparing its second or subsequent financial statements in accordance with FRS 26.

*ASB Footnote: *The ASB has removed an IASB table, providing the effect of exemption from presenting comparatives for accounting and risk disclosures for entities producing IFRS financial statements, and replaced it with the table on the following page which summarises the various transition options availble to UK entities applying this standard.*

	Accounting and Risk disclosures	**Capital Disclosures**
Accounting periods beginning before 1 January 2006		
First-time adopter not applying FRS 29 early	Applies FRS 25 but exempt from providing FRS 25 comparative information.	May choose to provide capital disclosures contained within Appendix E. Must provide comparative information if Appendix E adopted.
First-time adopter applying FRS 29 early	Exempt from presenting FRS 29 comparative information[(a)]	May choose to provide capital disclosures contained within Appendix E. Must provide comparative information if Appendix E adopted.
Accounting periods beginning on or after 1 January 2006 and before 1 January 2007		
First-time adopter not applying FRS 29 early	Applies FRS 25 but exempt from providing FRS 25 comparative information.	May choose to provide capital disclosures contained within Appendix E. Must provide comparative information if Appendix E adopted.
First-time adopter applying FRS 29 early	Exempt from presenting FRS 29 comparative information.	Has the option to provide capital disclosures contained within Appendix E but is not required to do so.
Existing user not applying FRS 29 early	Applies FRS 25. Provides full FRS 25 comparative information.	Has the option to provide capital disclosures contained within Appendix E.
Existing user applying FRS 29 early	Provides full FRS 29 comparative information.	Has the option to provide capital disclosures contained within Appendix E but is not required to do so.
Accounting periods beginning on or after 1 January 2007 (mandatory application of FRS 29)		
First-time adopter	Provides full FRS 29 comparative information.	Provides full FRS 29 capital disclosures.
Existing user	Provides full FRS 29 comparative information.	Provides full FRS 29 capital disclosures.
(a) See paragraph 44B of FRS 29.		

Disclosures about capital

> ASB Note: the following is a reproduction of the IASB's guidance on implementing disclosures on capital that were developed as part of the IFRS 7 project but implemented an amendment to IAS 1. The ASB has implemented the amendments to IAS 1 as Appendix E to FRS 29.

ILLUSTRATIVE EXAMPLES OF CAPITAL DISCLOSURES (PARAGRAPHS E1–E3)

This implementation guidance accompanies but is not part of the standard

An entity that is not a regulated financial institution

The following example illustrates the application of paragraphs E1 and E3 for an entity that is not a financial institution and is not subject to an externally imposed capital requirement. In this example, the entity monitors capital using a debt-to-adjusted capital ratio. Other entities may use different methods to monitor capital. The example is also relatively simple. An entity decides, in the light of its circumstances, how much detail it provides to satisfy the requirements of paragraphs E1 and E3.

E1G1

> **Facts**
>
> Group A manufactures and sells cars. Group A includes a finance subsidiary that provides finance to customers, primarily in the form of leases. Group A is not subject to any externally imposed capital requirements.
>
> **Example disclosure**
>
> The Group's objectives when managing capital are:
> - to safeguard the entity's ability to continue as a going concern, so that it can continue to provide returns for shareholders and benefits for other stakeholders, and
> - to provide an adequate return to shareholders by pricing products and services commensurately with the level of risk.
>
> The Group sets the amount of capital in proportion to risk. The Group manages the capital structure and make adjustments to it in the light of changes in economic conditions and the risk characteristics of the underlying assets. In order to maintain or adjust the capital structure, the Group may adjust the amount of dividends paid to shareholders, return capital to shareholders, issue new shares, or sell assets to reduce debt.
>
> Consistently with others in the industry, the Group monitors capital on the basis of the debt-to-adjusted capital ratio. This ratio is calculated as net debt ÷ adjusted capital. Net debt is calculated as total debt (as shown in the balance sheet) less cash and cash equivalents. Adjusted capital comprises all components of equity (ie share capital, share premium, minority interest, retained earnings, and revaluation reserve) other than amounts recognised in equity relating to cash flow hedges, and includes some forms of subordinated debt.

During 20X4, the Group's strategy, which was unchanged from 20X3, was to maintain the debt-to-adjusted capital ratio at the lower end of the range 6:1 to 7:1, in order to secure access to finance at a reasonable cost by maintaining a BB credit rating. The debt-to-adjusted capital ratios at 31 December 20X4 and at 31 December 20X3 were as follows:

	31 Dec X4 CU million	31 Dec X3 CU million
Total debt	1,000	1,100
Less: cash and cash equivalents	(90)	(150)
Net debt	910	950
Total equity	110	105
Add: subordinated debt instruments	38	38
Less: amounts recognised in equity relating to cash flow hedges	(10)	(5)
Adjusted capital	138	138
Debt-to-adjusted capital ratio	6.6	6.9

The decrease in the debt-to-adjusted capital ratio during 20X4 resulted primarily from the reduction in net debt that occurred on the sale of subsidiary Z. As a result of this reduction in net debt, improved profitability and lower levels of managed receivables, the dividend payment was increased to CU2.8 million for 20X4 (from CU2.5 million for 20X3).

An entity that has not complied with externally imposed capital requirements

EIG2   The following example illustrates the application of paragraph E2(e) when an entity has not complied with externally imposed capital requirements during the period. Other disclosures would be provided to comply with the other requirements of paragraphs E1 and E2.

Facts
Entity A provides financial services to its customers and is subject to capital requirements imposed by Regulator B. During the year ended 31 December 20X7, Entity A did not comply with the capital requirements imposed by Regulator B. In its financial statements for the year ended 31 December 20X7, Entity A provides the following disclosure relating to its noncompliance.

Example disclosure
Entity A filed its quarterly regulatory capital return for 30 September 20X7 on 20 October 20X7. At that date, Entity A's regulatory capital was below the capital requirement imposed by Regulator B by CU1 million. As a result, Entity A was required to submit a plan to the regulator indicating how it would increase its regulatory capital to the amount required. Entity A submitted a plan that entailed selling part of its unquoted equities portfolio with a carrying amount of CU11.5 million in the fourth quarter of 20X7. In the fourth quarter of 20X7, Entity A sold its fixed interest investment portfolio for CU12.6 million and met its regulatory capital requirement.

Appendix
Amendments to guidance on other IFRSs

This appendix contains amendments to guidance on other Standards that are necessary in order to ensure consistency with FRS 29. In the amended paragraphs, new text is underlined and deleted text is struck through.

The Guidance on Implementing FRS 26 (IAS 39) *Financial Instruments: Recognition*   **IGA1**
and Measurement is amended to read below.

Q&A E.4.8 is amended as follows:

> If an impaired financial asset is secured by collateral that does not meet the recognition criteria for assets in other Standards, is the collateral recognised as an asset separate from the impaired financial asset?

> No. The measurement of the impaired financial asset reflects the fair value of the collateral. The collateral is not recognised as an asset separate from the impaired financial asset unless it meets the recognition criteria for an asset in another Standard.

In Q&A F.1.12 issue (b), both references to 'IAS 32.58' are replaced by 'IFRS 7.22'.

In Q&A G.1, the answer is amended as follows:

> IFRS 7.20 requires items of income, expense and gains and losses to be disclosed. This disclosure requirement encompasses items of income, expense and gains and losses that arise on remeasurement to fair value. Therefore, an entity provides disclosures of fair value changes, distinguishing between changes that are recognised in profit or loss and changes that are recognised in equity. Further breakdown is provided of changes that relate to:
> (a)   AFS assets, showing separately the amount of gain or loss recognised directly in equity during the period and the amount that was removed from equity and recognised in profit or loss for the period;
> (b)   financial assets or financial liabilities at fair value through profit or loss, showing separately those fair value changes on financial assets or financial liabilities (i) designated as such upon initial recognition and (ii) classified as held for trading in accordance with IAS 39; and
> (c)   hedging instruments.

> IFRS 7 neither requires nor prohibits disclosure of components of the change in fair value by the way items are classified for internal purposes. For example, an entity may choose to disclose separately the change in fair value of those derivatives that in accordance with IAS 39 it categorises as held for trading, but the entity classifies as part of risk management activities outside the trading portfolio.

> In addition, IFRS 7.8 requires disclosure of the carrying amounts of financial assets or financial liabilities at fair value through profit or loss, showing separately : (i) those designated as such upon initial recognition and (ii) those held for trading in accordance with IAS 39.

Financial Reporting Standard for Smaller Entities (effective January 2007) is set out in parts A-D.

The Statement of Standard Accounting Practice set out in sections 1-20 of Part B should be read in the context of the Objective as stated in Part A, the Definitions set out in Part C and the Foreword to Accounting Standards. In addition, recommended Voluntary Disclosures, which do not form part of the Statement of Standard Accounting Practice, are set out in Part D.

As stated in the Foreword to Accounting Standards, accounting standards, which include the FRSSE, need not be applied to immaterial items.

Appendix IV 'The development of the FRSSE' reviews considerations and arguments that were thought significant by members of the Board in reaching the conclusions on the document.

The Financial Reporting Standard for Smaller Entities (effective January 2007) updates and supersedes the FRSSE (effective January 2005). It should be regarded as standard for financial statements relating to accounting periods beginning on or after 1 January 2007. The revised and new paragraphs in Parts B-D are highlighted by the use of sidelines. The FRSSE (effective January 2005) remains in force for financial statements relating to accounting periods beginning on or after 1 January 2005, although early adoption of the FRSSE (effective January 2007) is permitted.

Financial Reporting Standard for Smaller Entities (effective January 2007)

(Issued January 2007)

Contents

Status of the FRSSE

GENERAL

1   The Financial Reporting Standard for Smaller Entities (effective January 2007) – the FRSSE – prescribes the basis, for those entities within its scope that have chosen to adopt it, for preparing and presenting their financial statements. The definitions and accounting treatments are consistent with the requirements of companies legislation and, for the generality of small entities, are the same as those required by other accounting standards or a simplified version of those requirements. The disclosure requirements exclude a number of those stipulated in other accounting standards.

2   Reporting entities that apply the FRSSE are exempt from complying with other accounting standards (Statements of Standard Accounting Practice and Financial Reporting Standards) and Urgent Issues Task Force (UITF) Abstracts, unless preparing consolidated financial statements, in which case certain other accounting standards apply, as set out in paragraph 16.1.

3   For the convenience of companies using the FRSSE, the requirements of company law in Great Britain and Northern Ireland on full financial statements have been reflected in this standard. THESE ARE SHOWN IN SMALL CAPITALS TO DISTINGUISH THEM FROM THE REQUIREMENTS OF THE FRSSE*. The legal requirements set out in the FRSSE are intended to reflect company law effective on 1 January 2007. This does not affect directors' responsibilities regarding compliance with company law and in all matters regarding interpretation of the legal requirements reference should be to the relevant legislation.

4   Financial statements will generally be prepared using accepted practice and, accordingly, for transactions or events not dealt with in the FRSSE, smaller entities should have regard to other accounting standards and UITF Abstracts, not as mandatory documents, but as a means of establishing current practice.

CRITERIA

5   When considering the application of accounting standards and UITF Abstracts to smaller entities, the Accounting Standards Board has had, and will continue to have, regard to the following criteria:†

(a)   The standard or requirement is likely to be regarded as having general application and as an essential element of generally accepted accounting practice for all entities.

*The detail of the requirements in company law in the Republic of Ireland in many cases differs from the UK requirements reflected in the FRSSE. Tables showing the source of legislative requirements in British law and the equivalent sources in Northern Ireland and the Republic of Ireland are available on the ASB website (www.frc-asb.org.uk) In addition, there are a number of Republic of Ireland legal requirements that are not reflected in the FRSSE. There is no equivalent to Schedule 8 of the Companies Act 1985 providing certain exemptions for small companies when preparing annual accounts for shareholders. Exemptions from company law requirements for small companies in the Republic of Ireland are therefore limited and relate primarily to information that must be filed with the Companies Registration Office. This does not affect directors' responsibilities regarding compliance with company law and in all matters regarding interpretation of the legal requirements in the Republic of Ireland reference should be made to the relevant legislation.

†Legal advice has been obtained that in accounting standards smaller entities may properly be allowed exemptions or differing treatments provided that there are rational grounds for doing so: see Appendix I.

(b)   The standard or requirement is likely to lead to a transaction being treated in a way that would be readily recognised by the proprietor or manager of the business as corresponding to his or her understanding of the transaction.

(c)   The standard or requirement is likely to meet the information needs and legitimate expectations of a user of a small entity's accounts.

(d)   The standard or requirement results in disclosures that are likely to be meaningful and comprehensive to such a user. Where disclosures are aimed at a particular group of users, that group would be likely to receive the information, given that they may have access only to abbreviated accounts.

(e)   The requirements of the standard significantly augment the treatment prescribed by legislation.

(f)   The treatment prescribed by the standard or requirement is compatible with that already used, or expected to be used, by HM Revenue & Customs in computing taxable profits.

(g)   The standard or requirement provides the least cumbersome method of achieving the desired accounting treatment and/or disclosure for an entity that is not complex.

(h)   The standard provides guidance that is expected to be widely relevant to the transactions of small entities and is written in terms that can be understood by such businesses.

(i)   The measurement methods prescribed in the standard are likely to be reasonably practical for small entities.

The satisfaction of a majority of the above criteria would suggest that the standard   **6**
or requirement under consideration may also be appropriate for application to smaller entities, whereas failure to satisfy a majority of the above criteria would suggest that exemption, or differing treatment, from the standard, or a specific requirement within that standard, may be more appropriate.

SCOPE

The FRSSE may be applied to all financial statements intended to give a true and fair   **7**
view of the financial position and profit or loss (or income and expenditure) of all entities* that are:

(a)   small companies or small groups as defined in companies legislation† preparing Companies Act individual or group accounts; or

(b)   entities that would also qualify under (a) if they had been incorporated under companies legislation, with the exception of building societies.

Accordingly, the FRSSE does not apply to: **8**

(i)   large or medium-sized companies, groups and other entities;
(ii)   public companies;
(iii)   banks, building societies or insurance companies;

Some older accounting standards are drafted in terms of application to companies. References to companies and associated terms, such as board of directors and shareholders, in the FRSSE should therefore be taken to apply also to unincorporated entities.

†The legal definitions of small companies and small groups in the UK are set out in Appendix I. In the Republic of Ireland the FRSSE can be applied to those companies meeting the criteria as set out in companies legislation that allow them to be treated as 'small' for the purposes of filing information with the Companies Registration Office.

(iv) certain authorised persons under the Financial Services and Markets Act 2000 (in the UK)* or, notwithstanding the definition of a small company in the legislation, companies authorised under the Investment Intermediaries Act 1995 (in the Republic of Ireland);

(v) members of groups that contain companies falling under (ii)-(iv) above;

(vi) companies preparing individual or group accounts in accordance with international accounting standards; or

(vii) companies preparing individual or group accounts in accordance with the fair value accounting rules for certain assets and liabilities set out in Part D of Schedule 8 to the 1985 Companies Act. †

9　Reporting entities that are entitled to adopt the FRSSE, but choose not to do so, should apply Statements of Standard Accounting Practice (SSAPs), other Financial Reporting Standards (FRSs) and UITF Abstracts when preparing financial statements intended to give a true and fair view of the financial position and profit or loss of the entity.

Statements of Recommended Practice

10　Statements of Recommended Practice (SORPs) and other equivalent guidance developed or revised after the FRSSE was first issued (in November 1997) may specify the circumstances, if any, in which entities in the industry or sector addressed in the SORP or equivalent guidance may adopt the current version of the FRSSE. Financial statements that purport to comply with existing SORPs that are drafted on the basis that the financial statements comply with the requirements of SSAPs, FRSs (other than the FRSSE) and UITF Abstracts, should also observe those requirements, rather than adopt the FRSSE.

*The Companies Act 1985 (Small Companies' Accounts and Audit) Regulations 2006 came into force on 8 November 2006 and applies for financial years ending on or after 31 December 2006. The Regulations allow more categories of small financial services companies to qualify as small and take advantage of the small company exemptions. However companies that are required to have an audit based on a requirement in a European directive are still prohibited from taking advantage of the small company exemptions. In case of doubt, reference should be made to the Regulations.

†Companies accounting for fixed assets and investments at valuation are not precluded from using the FRSSE.

Financial Reporting Standard for Smaller Entities (effective January 2007)

A – Objective

The objective of the FRSSE is to ensure that reporting entities falling within its scope provide in their financial statements information about the financial position, performance and financial adaptability of the entity that is useful to users in assessing the stewardship of management and for making economic decisions, recognising that the balance between users' needs in respect of stewardship and economic decision-making for smaller entities is different from that for other reporting entities.

1

B – Statement of Standard Accounting Practice

1   SCOPE

1.1   The FRSSE may be applied to all financial statements intended to give a true and fair view of the financial position and profit or loss (or income and expenditure) of all entities that are:

(a)   companies incorporated under **companies legislation*** and entitled to the exemptions available in the legislation for small companies when filing accounts with the Registrar of Companies;† or

(b)   entities that would have come into category (a) above had they been companies incorporated under **companies legislation,** excluding building societies. While not bound by the requirements of **companies legislation** reflected in the FRSSE (set out in SMALL CAPITALS), such entities shall have regard to the **accounting principles,** presentation and disclosure requirements in **companies legislation** (or other equivalent legislation) that, taking into account the FRSSE, are necessary to present a true and fair view.

2   GENERAL

Requirement to prepare financial statements

2.1   THE **DIRECTORS** SHALL PREPARE FOR EACH **FINANCIAL YEAR** OF THE COMPANY‡ –

(A)   A BALANCE SHEET AS AT THE LAST DAY OF THE **FINANCIAL YEAR**, AND

(B)   A PROFIT AND LOSS ACCOUNT.

True and fair view

2.2   THE BALANCE SHEET MUST GIVE A TRUE AND FAIR VIEW OF THE STATE OF AFFAIRS OF THE COMPANY AS AT THE END OF THE **FINANCIAL YEAR**; AND THE PROFIT AND LOSS ACCOUNT MUST GIVE A TRUE AND FAIR VIEW OF THE PROFIT OR LOSS OF THE COMPANY FOR THE **FINANCIAL YEAR**. THE DIRECTORS OF A COMPANY MUST, IN DETERMINING HOW AMOUNTS ARE PRESENTED WITHIN ITEMS IN THE PROFIT AND LOSS ACCOUNT AND BALANCE SHEET, HAVE REGARD TO THE SUBSTANCE OF THE REPORTED TRANSACTION OR ARRANGEMENT, IN ACCORDANCE WITH GENERALLY ACCEPTED ACCOUNTING PRINCIPLES OR PRACTICE. To determine the substance of a transaction it is necessary to identify whether the transaction has given rise to new **assets** or **liabilities** for the reporting entity and whether it has changed the entity's existing **assets** or **liabilities**.

2.3   IF IN SPECIAL CIRCUMSTANCES COMPLIANCE WITH ANY OF THE PROVISIONS OF THE FRSSE OR COMPANIES ACT IS INCONSISTENT WITH THE REQUIREMENT TO GIVE A TRUE AND FAIR VIEW, THE **DIRECTORS** MUST DEPART FROM THAT PROVISION TO THE EXTENT NECESSARY TO GIVE A TRUE AND FAIR VIEW. PARTICULARS OF THE DEPARTURE, THE REASONS FOR IT AND ITS EFFECT MUST BE GIVEN IN A NOTE TO THE ACCOUNTS as follows:

Terms appearing in* **bold *in the text are explained in the Definitions set out in Part C.*

†*The legal definitions of small companies and small groups in the UK are set out in Appendix I. In the Republic of Ireland the FRSSE can be applied to those companies meeting the criteria as set out in companies legislation that allow them to be treated as 'small' for the purposes of filing information with the Companies Registration Office.*

‡*Text appearing in* SMALL CAPITALS *refers to UK company legislation requirements.*

(a) a statement that there has been a departure from the requirements of the FRSSE or Companies Act and that the departure is necessary to give a true and fair view;

(b) a statement of the treatment that the FRSSE or Companies Act would normally require and a description of the treatment adopted;

(c) a statement of the reasons why the treatment prescribed would not give a true and fair view; and

(d) a description of how the position shown in the financial statements is different as a result of the departure, normally with quantification, except where:

(i) quantification is already evident in the financial statements themselves; or

(ii) the effect cannot be reasonably quantified, in which case the **directors** shall explain the circumstances.

Where a departure continues in subsequent financial statements, the disclosures shall be made in all subsequent statements and shall include comparative amounts for the previous period. Where a departure affects only the comparative amounts, the disclosures shall be given for those comparative amounts. **2.4**

Where there is doubt whether applying provisions of the FRSSE would be sufficient to give a true and fair view, adequate explanation shall be given in the notes to the accounts of the transaction or arrangement concerned and the treatment adopted. **2.5**

Accounting principles and policies

The financial statements shall state that they have been prepared in accordance with the Financial Reporting Standard for Smaller Entities (effective January 2007)*. **2.6**

Financial statements shall include: **2.7**

(a) a description of each material **accounting policy** followed;

(b) details of any changes to the **accounting policies** followed in the preceding period including, in addition to the disclosures necessary for **prior period adjustments**, a brief explanation of why each new **accounting policy** is thought more appropriate and, where practicable, an indication of the effect of the change on the results for the current period; and

(c) where the effect of a change to an **estimation technique** is material, a description of the change and, where practicable, the effect on the results for the current period.

THE ACCOUNTING POLICIES ADOPTED BY THE COMPANY IN DETERMINING THE AMOUNTS TO BE INCLUDED IN RESPECT OF ITEMS SHOWN IN THE BALANCE SHEET AND IN DETERMINING THE PROFIT OR LOSS OF THE COMPANY SHALL BE STATED (INCLUDING SUCH POLICIES WITH RESPECT TO THE DEPRECIATION AND DIMINUTION IN VALUE OF ASSETS). **2.8**

Accounting policies and **estimation techniques** shall be consistent with the requirements of the FRSSE and of **companies legislation** (or other equivalent legislation). Where this permits a choice, an entity shall select the policies and techniques most appropriate to its particular circumstances for the purpose of giving a true and fair **2.9**

This statement may be included with the note of accounting policies or, for those entities taking advantage of the exemptions for small companies in companies legislation, in the statement required by companies legislation to be given on the balance sheet. For example, in Great Britain the combined statement could read as follows "These accounts have been prepared in accordance with the special provisions relating to small companies within Part VII of the Companies Act 1985 and with the Financial Reporting Standard for Smaller Entities (effective January 2007)." If abbreviated accounts are also to be prepared, the statement referring to the Financial Reporting Standard for Smaller Entities (effective January 2007) shall be included with the note of accounting policies so that it is reproduced in the abbreviated accounts.

view, taking account of the objectives of relevance, **reliability**, comparability and understandability.

2.10   **Accounting policies** SHALL BE APPLIED CONSISTENTLY WITHIN THE SAME ACCOUNTS AND FROM ONE **FINANCIAL YEAR** TO THE NEXT. They shall be reviewed regularly to ensure that they remain the most appropriate to the entity's particular circumstances for the purpose of giving a true and fair view. However, in judging whether a new policy is more appropriate than the existing policy, due weight shall be given to the impact on consistency and comparability. Following a change in **accounting policy**, the amounts for the current and corresponding periods shall be restated on the basis of the new policies.

2.11   IN DETERMINING THE AGGREGATE AMOUNT OF ANY ITEM, THE AMOUNT OF EACH INDIVI-DUAL ASSET OR LIABILITY THAT FALLS TO BE TAKEN INTO ACCOUNT SHALL BE DETERMINED SEPARATELY. AMOUNTS IN RESPECT OF ASSETS OR INCOME MAY NOT BE SET OFF AGAINST AMOUNTS IN RESPECT OF LIABILITIES OR EXPENDITURE (AS THE CASE MAY BE), OR VICE VERSA.

Going concern

2.12   THE COMPANY SHALL BE PRESUMED TO BE CARRYING ON BUSINESS AS A GOING CONCERN. When preparing financial statements, **directors** shall assess whether there are significant doubts about the entity's ability to continue as a going concern. Any material uncertainties, of which the **directors** are aware in making their assessment, shall be disclosed. Where the period considered by the **directors** in making this assessment has been limited to a period of less than one year from the date of approval of the financial statements, that fact shall be stated. The financial statements shall not be prepared on a going concern basis if the **directors** determine after the balance sheet date either that they intend to liquidate the entity or to cease trading, or that they have no realistic alternative but to do so.

Prudence

2.13   THE AMOUNT OF ANY ITEM SHALL BE DETERMINED ON A PRUDENT BASIS. Prudence is the inclusion of a degree of caution in the exercise of the judgements needed in making the estimates required under conditions of uncertainty, such that gains and assets are not overstated and liabilities are not understated. However it is not necessary to exercise prudence where there is no uncertainty. Nor is it appropriate to use prudence as a reason to understate deliberately assets or gains or overstate liabilities or losses.

Accruals

2.14   The financial statements, with the exception of cash flow information, shall be prepared on the accruals basis of accounting. HENCE, ALL INCOME AND CHARGES RELATING TO THE **FINANCIAL YEAR** TO WHICH THE ACCOUNTS RELATE SHALL BE TAKEN INTO ACCOUNT, WITHOUT REGARD TO THE DATE OF PAYMENT OR RECEIPT.

Prior period adjustments

2.15   **Prior period adjustments** shall be accounted for by restating the comparative figures for the preceding period in the primary statements and notes and adjusting the opening balance of reserves for the cumulative effect. The cumulative effect of the adjustments shall also be noted at the foot of the statement of **total recognised gains**

and losses of the current period. The effect of **prior period adjustments** on the results for the preceding period shall be disclosed where practicable.

Formats – general rules

THE FORMATS FOR THE BALANCE SHEET AND PROFIT AND LOSS ACCOUNT ARE SET OUT BELOW. A COMPANY'S INDIVIDUAL ACCOUNTS SHALL COMPLY WITH THE PROVISIONS SET OUT BELOW AS TO THE FORM AND CONTENT OF THE BALANCE SHEET AND PROFIT AND LOSS ACCOUNT AND ADDITIONAL INFORMATION TO BE PROVIDED BY WAY OF NOTES TO THE ACCOUNTS.   **2.16**

THE DIRECTORS OF THE COMPANY SHALL ADOPT THE SAME FORMAT IN PREPARING THE ACCOUNTS FOR SUBSEQUENT FINANCIAL YEARS OF THE COMPANY UNLESS IN THEIR OPINION THERE ARE SPECIAL REASONS FOR A CHANGE. PARTICULARS OF ANY CHANGE IN THE FORMAT ADOPTED IN A COMPANY'S PROFIT AND LOSS ACCOUNT SHALL BE DISCLOSED, AND THE REASONS FOR THE CHANGE SHALL BE EXPLAINED IN A NOTE TO THE ACCOUNTS IN WHICH THE NEW FORMAT IS FIRST ADOPTED.   **2.17**

WHERE COMPLIANCE WITH THE PROVISIONS OF COMPANIES LEGISLATION AS TO THE MATTERS TO BE INCLUDED IN A COMPANY'S INDIVIDUAL ACCOUNTS OR IN NOTES TO THOSE ACCOUNTS WOULD NOT BE SUFFICIENT TO GIVE A TRUE AND FAIR VIEW, THE NECESSARY ADDITIONAL INFORMATION MUST BE GIVEN IN THE ACCOUNTS OR IN A NOTE TO THEM.   **2.18**

ANY ITEM REQUIRED TO BE SHOWN IN THE ACCOUNTS MAY BE SHOWN IN GREATER DETAIL THAN REQUIRED BY THE FORMAT ADOPTED. THE ACCOUNTS MAY INCLUDE AN ITEM REPRESENTING OR COVERING THE AMOUNT OF ANY ASSET OR LIABILITY, INCOME OR EXPENDITURE NOT OTHERWISE COVERED BY ANY OF THE ITEMS LISTED IN THE FORMAT ADOPTED*.   **2.19**

ITEMS LISTED IN THE FORMATS SHALL NOT BE INCLUDED IF THERE IS NO AMOUNT TO BE SHOWN FOR THAT ITEM IN RESPECT OF THE FINANCIAL YEAR TO WHICH THE ACCOUNT RELATES AND FOR THE IMMEDIATELY PRECEDING FINANCIAL YEAR.   **2.20**

IN PREPARING THE BALANCE SHEET OR PROFIT AND LOSS ACCOUNT, THE DIRECTORS SHALL ADAPT THE ARRANGEMENT AND HEADINGS AND SUBHEADINGS OF ITEMS TO WHICH AN ARABIC NUMBER IS ASSIGNED IN THE FORMATS, WHERE THE SPECIAL NATURE OF THE COMPANY'S BUSINESS REQUIRES SUCH ADAPTATION.   **2.21**

ITEMS TO WHICH ARABIC NUMBERS ARE ASSIGNED IN ANY OF THE FORMATS MAY BE COMBINED FOR ANY FINANCIAL YEAR IF: **2.22**

(A) THEIR INDIVIDUAL AMOUNTS ARE NOT MATERIAL TO ASSESSING THE STATE OF AFFAIRS OR PROFIT AND LOSS OF THE COMPANY FOR THAT YEAR; OR
(B) THEIR COMBINATION FACILITATES THAT ASSESSMENT OF THE BALANCE SHEET OR PROFIT AND LOSS ACCOUNT. WHERE THIS APPLIES, THE INDIVIDUAL AMOUNTS SHALL BE DISCLOSED IN A NOTE TO THE ACCOUNTS.

Corresponding amounts for the previous accounting period shall be shown for every item disclosed in the balance sheet, profit and loss account and notes to the financial statements. Where there is no amount to be shown for an item in the balance sheet or profit and loss account for the current accounting period but a corresponding amount can be shown for the previous accounting period, the corresponding amount shall be shown. Where a corresponding amount is not comparable with that for the   **2.23**

PRELIMINARY EXPENSES, EXPENSES OF AND COMMISSION ON ANY ISSUE OF SHARES OR DEBENTURES AND COSTS OF RESEARCH SHALL NOT BE TREATED AS ASSETS.

current accounting period, it shall be adjusted and particulars of the adjustment and the reasons for it shall be disclosed in a note to the financial statements. Corresponding amounts are not required in relation to any amounts stated in the notes to the financial statements for the items listed below:

(a) details of additions, disposals, revaluations, transfers and cumulative depreciation of fixed assets;

(b) transfers to or from reserves and provisions and the source and application of any transfers;

(c) details of a company's shareholdings in subsidiary undertakings;

(d) details of a company's significant holdings in undertakings other than subsidiary undertakings.

2.24   IF NOT GIVEN IN THE COMPANY'S ACCOUNTS THERE MUST BE STATED BY WAY OF A NOTE TO THOSE ACCOUNTS ANY AMOUNT SET ASIDE OR PROPOSED TO BE SET ASIDE, OR WITHDRAWN OR PROPOSED TO BE WITHDRAWN FROM RESERVES. FOR EACH RESERVE DISCLOSED SEPARATELY IN THE ACCOUNTS, THE FOLLOWING INFORMATION SHALL BE PROVIDED:

(A) THE AMOUNT OF THE RESERVE AT THE BEGINNING AND THE END OF THE FINANCIAL YEAR;

(B) ANY AMOUNTS TRANSFERRED TO OR FROM THE RESERVES DURING THE YEAR; AND

(C) THE SOURCE AND APPLICATION OF THE AMOUNTS TRANSFERRED.

2.25   FOR THE AGGREGATE OF ALL ITEMS SHOWN AS CREDITORS IN THE BALANCE SHEET, THE AGGREGATE OF THE AMOUNTS WHICH FALL DUE FOR PAYMENT MORE THAN FIVE YEARS AFTER THE END OF THE CURRENT PERIOD SHALL BE DISCLOSED. AMOUNTS PAYABLE OR REPAYABLE BY INSTALMENTS AND THOSE PAYABLE OR REPAYABLE OTHERWISE THAN BY INSTALMENTS SHALL BE SEPARATELY DISCLOSED.

2.26   FOR EACH ITEM SHOWN UNDER CREDITORS, THE AGGREGATE OF ANY DEBTS INCLUDED WHERE ANY SECURITY HAS BEEN GIVEN BY THE COMPANY SHALL BE DISCLOSED.

Balance sheet format*

2.27   THE BALANCE SHEET SHALL SHOW THE ITEMS LISTED IN THE ORDER, AND UNDER THE HEADINGS AND SUB-HEADINGS, SHOWN IN THE FORMAT BELOW†.

---

*An alternative format is available under companies legislation and may be adopted.

†Note: this does not mean that the items, headings and sub-headings need be identified by the letters and numbers assigned to them in the format.

BALANCE SHEET FORMAT*

A. CALLED UP SHARE CAPITAL NOT PAID

B. FIXED ASSETS
   - I. INTANGIBLE ASSETS
     1. GOODWILL
     2. OTHER INTANGIBLE ASSETS
   - II. TANGIBLE ASSETS
     1. LAND AND BUILDINGS
     2. PLANT AND MACHINERY ETC
   - III. INVESTMENTS
     1. SHARES IN GROUP UNDERTAKINGS AND PARTICIPATING INTERESTS
     2. LOANS TO GROUP UNDERTAKINGS AND UNDERTAKINGS IN WHICH THE COMPANY HAS A PARTICIPATING INTEREST
     3. OTHER INVESTMENTS OTHER THAN LOANS
     4. OTHER INVESTMENTS

C. CURRENT ASSETS
   - I. STOCKS
     1. STOCKS
     2. PAYMENTS ON ACCOUNT
   - II. DEBTORS†
     1. TRADE DEBTORS
     2. AMOUNTS OWED BY GROUP UNDERTAKINGS AND UNDERTAKINGS IN WHICH THE COMPANY HAS A PARTICIPATING INTEREST
     3. OTHER DEBTORS
   - III. INVESTMENTS
     1. SHARES IN GROUP UNDERTAKINGS
     2. OTHER INVESTMENTS
   - IV. CASH AT BANK AND IN HAND

D. PREPAYMENTS AND ACCRUED INCOME‡

E. CREDITORS: AMOUNTS FALLING DUE WITHIN ONE YEAR
   1. BANK LOANS AND OVERDRAFTS
   2. TRADE CREDITORS
   3. AMOUNTS OWED TO GROUP UNDERTAKINGS AND UNDERTAKINGS IN WHICH THE COMPANY HAS A PARTICIPATING INTEREST
   4. OTHER CREDITORS §

F. NET CURRENT ASSETS/LIABILITIES¶¶

G. TOTAL ASSETS LESS CURRENT LIABILITIES

H. CREDITORS: AMOUNTS FALLING DUE AFTER MORE THAN ONE YEAR
   1. BANK LOANS AND OVERDRAFTS
   2. TRADE CREDITORS

*There are certain differences in the format requirements for the balance sheet under companies legislation in the Republic of Ireland. The format requirements are contained in Part 1 of the Schedule to the Companies (Amendment) Act 1986 with references available in the derivation tables on the ASB website.

†THE AMOUNT FALLING DUE AFTER MORE THAN ONE YEAR SHALL BE SHOWN SEPARATELY FOR EACH ITEM INCLUDED UNDER DEBTORS UNLESS THE AGGREGATE AMOUNT OF DEBTORS FALLING DUE AFTER MORE THAN ONE YEAR IS DISCLOSED IN THE NOTES TO THE ACCOUNTS.

‡THIS ITEM MAY ALTERNATIVELY BE INCLUDED UNDER ITEM C.II.3.

§ITEMS E4, H4 AND J: THERE SHALL BE SHOWN SEPARATELY THE AMOUNT OF ANY CONVERTIBLE LOANS AND THE AMOUNT OF CREDITORS IN RESPECT OF TAXATION AND SOCIAL SECURITY.

¶¶IN DETERMINING THE AMOUNT TO BE SHOWN UNDER THIS ITEM ANY PREPAYMENTS AND ACCRUED INCOME SHALL BE TAKEN INTO ACCOUNT.

> 3.   AMOUNTS OWED TO GROUP UNDERTAKINGS AND UNDERTAKINGS IN WHICH
>   THE COMPANY HAS A PARTICIPATING INTEREST
> 4.   OTHER CREDITORS
> I.   PROVISIONS FOR LIABILITIES
> J.   ACCRUALS AND DEFERRED INCOME*
> K.   CAPITAL AND RESERVES
>   I.   CALLED UP SHARE CAPITAL
>   II.   SHARE PREMIUM ACCOUNT
>   III.   REVALUATION RESERVE
>   IV.   OTHER RESERVES
>   V.   PROFIT AND LOSS ACCOUNT

Profit and loss account formats

2.28   THE FORMAT OF THE PROFIT AND LOSS ACCOUNT SHALL COMPLY WITH ONE OF THE FORMATS SET OUT BELOW.

2.29   THE ACCOUNT SHALL SHOW THE ITEMS LISTED IN THE ORDER, AND UNDER THE HEADINGS AND SUB-HEADINGS, SHOWN IN THE FORMATS SET OUT BELOW†.

> ## PROFIT AND LOSS ACCOUNT FORMAT 1‡
> 1. TURNOVER
> 2. COST OF SALES§
> 3. GROSS PROFIT OR LOSS
> 4. DISTRIBUTION COSTS
> 5. ADMINISTRATIVE EXPENSES
> 6. OTHER OPERATING INCOME
> 7. INCOME FROM SHARES IN GROUP UNDERTAKINGS
> 8. INCOME FROM PARTICIPATING INTERESTS
> 9. INCOME FROM OTHER FIXED ASSET INVESTMENTS
> 10. OTHER INTEREST RECEIVABLE AND SIMILAR INCOME
> 11. AMOUNTS WRITTEN OFF INVESTMENTS
> 12. INTEREST PAYABLE AND SIMILAR CHARGES
> 12A. PROFIT OR LOSS ON ORDINARY ACTIVITIES BEFORE TAXATION
> 13. TAX ON PROFIT OR LOSS ON ORDINARY ACTIVITIES
> 14. PROFIT OR LOSS ON ORDINARY ACTIVITIES AFTER TAXATION¶¶
> 19. OTHER TAXES NOT SHOWN UNDER THE ABOVE ITEMS
> 20. PROFIT OR LOSS FOR THE FINANCIAL YEAR

*THIS ITEM MAY ALTERNATIVELY BE INCLUDED UNDER ITEM E4 OR H4 OR BOTH (AS THE CASE MAY REQUIRE).

†*Note, this does not mean that the items, headings and sub-headings need be identified by the letters and numbers assigned to them in the formats.*

‡*There are certain differences in the format requirements for the profit and loss account under companies legislation in the Republic of Ireland. The format requirements are contained in Part 1 of the Schedule to the Companies (Amendment) Act 1986. References are available in the derivation tables on the ASB's website.*

§COST OF SALES, DISTRIBUTION COSTS AND ADMINISTRATIVE EXPENSES SHALL INCLUDE THE PROVISIONS FOR DEPRECIATION AND WRITE-DOWNS OF TANGIBLE AND INTANGIBLE FIXED ASSETS. THESE AMOUNTS SHALL ALSO BE SEPARATELY DISCLOSED IN A NOTE TO THE ACCOUNTS.

¶¶*Extraordinary items, which are extremely rare, shall be shown separately after the profit or loss on ordinary activities after taxation.*

PROFIT AND LOSS ACCOUNT FORMAT 2
1. TURNOVER
2. CHANGE IN STOCKS OF FINISHED GOODS AND IN WORK IN PROGRESS
3. OWN WORK CAPITALISED
4. OTHER OPERATING INCOME
5. A. RAW MATERIALS AND CONSUMABLES
B. OTHER EXTERNAL CHARGES
6. STAFF COSTS:
A. WAGES AND SALARIES
B. SOCIAL SECURITY COSTS
C. OTHER PENSION COSTS
7. A. DEPRECIATION AND OTHER AMOUNTS WRITTEN OFF TANGIBLE AND INTANGIBLE
FIXED ASSETS
B. EXCEPTIONAL AMOUNTS WRITTEN OFF CURRENT ASSETS
8. OTHER OPERATING CHARGES
9. INCOME FROM SHARES IN GROUP UNDERTAKINGS
10. INCOME FROM PARTICIPATING INTERESTS
11. INCOME FROM OTHER FIXED ASSET INVESTMENTS
12. OTHER INTEREST RECEIVABLE AND SIMILAR INCOME
13. AMOUNTS WRITTEN OFF INVESTMENTS
14. INTEREST PAYABLE AND SIMILAR CHARGES
14A. PROFIT OR LOSS ON ORDINARY ACTIVITIES BEFORE TAXATION
15. TAX ON PROFIT OR LOSS ON ORDINARY ACTIVITIES
16. PROFIT OR LOSS ON ORDINARY ACTIVITIES AFTER TAXATION*
21. OTHER TAXES NOT SHOWN UNDER THE ABOVE ITEMS
22. PROFIT OR LOSS FOR THE FINANCIAL YEAR

Approval and signing of accounts

A COMPANY'S ANNUAL ACCOUNTS SHALL BE APPROVED BY THE BOARD OF **DIRECTORS** AND **2.30**
SIGNED ON BEHALF OF THE BOARD BY A DIRECTOR OF THE COMPANY. THE SIGNATURE SHALL
BE ON THE COMPANY'S BALANCE SHEET. The date on which the financial statements are
approved by the board of **directors** shall be disclosed in the financial statements. THE
BALANCE SHEET SHALL CONTAIN, IN A PROMINENT POSITION, A STATEMENT THAT THE
ACCOUNTS HAVE BEEN PREPARED IN ACCORDANCE WITH THE SPECIAL PROVISIONS IN PART
VII OF THE COMPANIES ACT 1985 RELATING TO SMALL COMPANIES.

EVERY COPY OF THE BALANCE SHEET WHICH IS LAID BEFORE THE COMPANY IN GENERAL **2.31**
MEETING, OR WHICH IS OTHERWISE CIRCULATED, PUBLISHED OR ISSUED, SHALL STATE THE
NAME OF THE PERSON WHO SIGNED THE BALANCE SHEET ON BEHALF OF THE BOARD.

THE COPY OF THE COMPANY'S BALANCE SHEET WHICH IS DELIVERED TO THE REGISTRAR **2.32**
SHALL BE SIGNED ON BEHALF OF THE BOARD BY A DIRECTOR OF THE COMPANY.

IF ANNUAL ACCOUNTS ARE APPROVED WHICH DO NOT COMPLY WITH THE REQUIREMENTS OF **2.33**
THE COMPANIES ACT, EVERY DIRECTOR OF THE COMPANY WHO IS PARTY TO THEIR APPROVAL
AND WHO KNOWS THAT THEY DO NOT COMPLY OR IS RECKLESS AS TO WHETHER THEY
COMPLY IS GUILTY OF AN OFFENCE AND LIABLE TO A FINE. FOR THIS PURPOSE EVERY
DIRECTOR OF THE COMPANY AT THE TIME THE ACCOUNTS ARE APPROVED SHALL BE TAKEN
TO BE A PARTY TO THEIR APPROVAL UNLESS HE SHOWS THAT HE TOOK ALL REASONABLE
STEPS TO PREVENT THEIR BEING APPROVED.

**Extraordinary items, which are extremely rare, shall be shown separately after the profit or loss on ordinary
activities after taxation.*

2.34   IF A COPY OF THE BALANCE SHEET –

(A)   IS LAID BEFORE THE COMPANY, OR OTHERWISE CIRCULATED, PUBLISHED OR ISSUED, WITHOUT THE BALANCE SHEET HAVING BEEN SIGNED OR WITHOUT THE REQUIRED STATEMENT OF THE SIGNATORY'S NAME BEING INCLUDED; OR

(B)   IS DELIVERED TO THE REGISTRAR WITHOUT BEING SIGNED,

THE COMPANY AND EVERY OFFICER OF IT WHO IS IN DEFAULT IS GUILTY OF AN OFFENCE AND LIABLE TO A FINE.

Delivery to the registrar

2.35   THE COPY OF THE FINANCIAL STATEMENTS DELIVERED TO THE REGISTRAR MUST STATE IN A PROMINENT POSITION THE REGISTERED NUMBER OF THE COMPANY, BE SIGNED BY, AND STATE THE NAME OF, THE **DIRECTORS** AND REGISTERED AUDITORS AS APPROPRIATE AND COMPLY WITH ANY REQUIREMENTS SPECIFIED BY THE REGISTRAR TO ENABLE CLEAR COPIES TO BE MADE.

2.36   THE FINANCIAL STATEMENTS MUST ALSO CONTAIN A STATEMENT IN A PROMINENT POSITION ON THE BALANCE SHEET THAT THEY HAVE BEEN PREPARED IN ACCORDANCE WITH THE SPECIAL PROVISIONS IN PART VII OF THE COMPANIES ACT 1985 RELATING TO SMALL COMPANIES.

Exemptions from audit

2.37   WHERE A COMPANY MEETS THE CONDITIONS FOR EXEMPTION FROM AUDIT, AND HAS TAKEN ADVANTAGE OF THAT EXEMPTION, THE BALANCE SHEET MUST CONTAIN A STATEMENT BY THE **DIRECTORS** THAT:

(A)   FOR THE YEAR IN QUESTION, THE COMPANY WAS ENTITLED TO EXEMPTION (UNDER SUBSECTION (1) OR (2) (AS THE CASE MAY BE) OF SECTION 249A OF THE COMPANIES ACT 1985);

(B)   NO MEMBER OR MEMBERS ELIGIBLE TO DO SO HAVE DEPOSITED A NOTICE REQUESTING AN AUDIT WITHIN THE SPECIFIED TIME PERIOD; AND

(C)   THE **DIRECTORS** ACKNOWLEDGE THEIR RESPONSIBILITY FOR ENSURING THAT THE COMPANY KEEPS ACCOUNTING RECORDS WHICH COMPLY WITH SECTION 221 (DUTY TO KEEP ACCOUNTING RECORDS) AND FOR PREPARING ACCOUNTS WHICH GIVE A TRUE AND FAIR VIEW OF THE STATE OF AFFAIRS OF THE COMPANY AS AT THE END OF THE **FINANCIAL YEAR** AND OF ITS PROFIT OR LOSS FOR THE **FINANCIAL YEAR** IN ACCORDANCE WITH THE REQUIREMENTS OF SECTION 226 (DUTY TO PREPARE INDIVIDUAL COMPANY ACCOUNTS), AND WHICH OTHERWISE COMPLY WITH THE REQUIREMENTS OF THE COMPANIES ACT 1985 RELATING TO ACCOUNTS, SO FAR AS APPLICABLE TO THE COMPANY.

2.38   WHERE THE **DIRECTORS** HAVE TAKEN ADVANTAGE OF THE EXEMPTION FROM AUDIT DUE TO THE FACT THAT THE COMPANY IS DORMANT, AND THE COMPANY HAS DURING THE **FINANCIAL YEAR** IN QUESTION ACTED AS AN AGENT FOR ANY PERSON, THE FACT THAT IT HAS SO ACTED MUST BE STATED.

3   PROFIT AND LOSS ACCOUNT

General

3.1   All gains and losses **recognised** in the financial statements for the period shall be included in the profit and loss account or the statement of **total recognised gains and**

losses. ONLY PROFITS THAT ARE REALISED AT THE BALANCE SHEET DATE SHALL BE INCLUDED IN THE PROFIT AND LOSS ACCOUNT. ALL LIABILITIES WHICH HAVE ARISEN IN RESPECT OF THE PERIOD SHALL BE TAKEN INTO ACCOUNT, INCLUDING THOSE WHICH ONLY BECOME APPARENT BETWEEN THE BALANCE SHEET DATE AND THE DATE ON WHICH IT IS SIGNED.

Gains and losses may be excluded from the profit and loss account only if they are specifically permitted or required to be taken direct to reserves by this standard or by **companies legislation** or equivalent legislation.   **3.2**

WHERE AN AMOUNT RELATING TO ANY PRECEDING FINANCIAL YEAR IS INCLUDED IN THE PROFIT AND LOSS ACCOUNT, THE EFFECT OF ITS INCLUSION SHALL BE STATED.   **3.3**

IF THE COMPANY HAS SUPPLIED GEOGRAPHICAL MARKETS OUTSIDE THE UNITED KINGDOM DURING THE FINANCIAL YEAR, THE PERCENTAGE OF TURNOVER THAT IS ATTRIBUTABLE TO THOSE MARKETS SHALL BE SEPARATELY DISCLOSED. IN ANALYSING THE SOURCE OF TURN-OVER, REGARD SHALL BE PAID TO THE MANNER IN WHICH THE COMPANY'S ACTIVITIES ARE ORGANISED.   **3.4**

Exceptional items

All **exceptional items**, other than those included in the items listed in the next paragraph, shall be credited or charged in arriving at the profit or loss on **ordinary activities** by inclusion under the statutory format headings to which they relate. The amount of each **exceptional item**, either individually or as an aggregate of items of a similar type, shall be disclosed separately by way of a note, or on the face of the profit and loss account if that degree of prominence is necessary in order to give a true and fair view. An adequate description of each **exceptional item** shall be given to enable its nature to be understood. THE EFFECT SHALL BE STATED OF ANY TRANSACTIONS THAT ARE EXCEPTIONAL BY VIRTUE OF SIZE OR INCIDENCE THOUGH THEY FALL WITHIN THE ORDINARY ACTIVITIES OF THE COMPANY.   **3.5**

The following items, including provisions in respect of such items, shall be shown separately on the face of the profit and loss account after operating profit (which is normally profit before income from shares in group undertakings) and before interest: **3.6**
(a) profits or losses on the sale or termination of an operation;
(b) costs of a fundamental reorganisation or restructuring having a material effect on the nature and focus of the reporting entity's operations; and
(c) profits or losses on the disposal of fixed assets.

Profit or loss on disposal

The profit or loss on the disposal of an asset shall be accounted for in the profit and loss account of the period in which the disposal occurs as the difference between the net sale proceeds and the net carrying amount, whether carried at historical cost (less any provisions made) or at a valuation. Profit or loss on disposal of a previously acquired business shall include the attributable amount of **purchased goodwill** that has previously been eliminated against reserves as a matter of **accounting policy** and has not previously been charged in the profit and loss account.   **3.7**

Auditors' remuneration

3.8   THE REMUNERATION OF THE COMPANY'S AUDITORS, INCLUDING SUMS PAID IN RESPECT OF EXPENSES, SHALL BE DISCLOSED IN A NOTE TO THE ACCOUNTS. THE NATURE AND ESTIMATED MONETARY VALUE OF ANY BENEFITS IN KIND SHALL ALSO BE STATED.

4   REVENUE RECOGNITION

*Basic principles**

4.1   A seller recognises revenue under an **exchange transaction** with a customer, when, and to the extent that, it obtains the **right to consideration** in exchange for its **performance**. At the same time, it typically recognises a new asset, usually a debtor.

4.2   When a seller receives payment from a customer in advance of **performance**, it recognises a liability equal to the amount received, representing its **obligation** under the contract. When the seller obtains the **right to consideration** through its **performance**, that liability is reduced and the amount of the reduction in the liability is simultaneously reported as revenue.

4.3   A seller may obtain a **right to consideration** when some, but not all, of its contractual **obligations** have been fulfilled. Where a seller has partially performed its contractual **obligations**, it recognises revenue to the extent that it has obtained the **right to consideration** through its **performance**.

4.4   Revenue shall be measured at the **fair value** of the **right to consideration**. Subject to paragraphs 4.5–4.6 or other evidence to the contrary, this will normally be the price specified in the contractual arrangement, net of discounts, value added tax and similar sales taxes.

4.5   Where the effect of the time value of money is material to reported revenue, the amount of revenue **recognised** shall be the present value of the cash inflows expected to be received from the customer in settlement. The unwinding of the discount shall be credited to finance income as this represents a gain from a financing transaction.

4.6   Where at the time revenue is **recognised** on a transaction there is a significant risk that there will be default on the amount of consideration due and the effect is material to reported revenue, an adjustment to the price specified in the contractual arrangement will be necessary to arrive at the amount of revenue to be **recognised**.

4.7   Subsequent adjustments to a debtor as a result of changes in the time value of money and credit risk shall not be included within revenue.

Turnover

4.8   Turnover (which may be described as 'sales' in a seller's financial statements) is the revenue resulting from **exchange transactions** under which a seller supplies to customers the goods or services that it is in business to provide.†

*Guidance on the practical considerations for recognising revenue in respect of service contracts, bill and hold arrangements, presentation of turnover as principal or as agent and sales with rights of return is given in Appendix III.

†These transactions are often referred to as being part of the seller's operating activities.

A seller may enter into other **exchange transactions** such as the sale of fixed assets. Such transactions do not normally give rise to turnover, as they do not normally fall within the class of transactions set out in paragraph 4.8. **4.9**

Contracts for services

Where there are distinguishable phases of a single contract it may be appropriate to account for the contract as two or more separate transactions, provided the value of each phase can be reliably estimated. **4.10**

Contracts for services should not be accounted for as long-term contracts unless they involve the provision of a single service, or a number of services that constitute a single project. **4.11**

A contract for services should be accounted for as a long-term contract where contract activity falls into different accounting periods and it is concluded that the effect is material. In determining whether contracts should be accounted for as long-term contracts, the aggregate effect of all such contracts on the financial statements as a whole should be considered. **4.12**

Where the substance of a contract is that the seller's contractual obligations are performed gradually over time, revenue should be recognised as contract activity progresses to reflect the seller's partial performance of its contractual obligations. The amount of revenue should reflect the accrual of the right to consideration as contract activity progresses by reference to value of the work performed. **4.13**

Where the substance of a contract is that a right to consideration does not arise until the occurrence of a critical event, revenue is not recognised until that event occurs. This only applies where the right to consideration is conditional or contingent on a specified future event or outcome, the occurrence of which is outside the control of the seller. **4.14**

The amount of revenue recognised on any contract for services should reflect any uncertainties as to the amount that the customer will accept and pay. **4.15**

5 STATEMENT OF TOTAL RECOGNISED GAINS AND LOSSES

A primary statement shall be presented, with the same prominence as the profit and loss account, showing the **total of recognised gains and losses** and its components. The components shall be the gains and losses that are **recognised** in the period insofar as they are attributable to shareholders, excluding transactions with shareholders.* Where the only **recognised** gains and losses are the results included in the profit and loss account no separate statement to this effect need be made. **5.1**

6 FIXED ASSETS AND GOODWILL

Disclosure

THE FOLLOWING INFORMATION SHALL BE PROVIDED FOR ALL FIXED ASSETS AND GOODWILL: **6.1**

(A) THE COST OR VALUATION AT THE BEGINNING AND THE END OF THE YEAR; AND

(B) THE EFFECT OF ANY:

  (I) REVALUATION MADE DURING THE YEAR;

An illustration of a statement of total recognised gains and losses is given in Appendix III.

(II)   ACQUISITIONS DURING THE YEAR;
(III) DISPOSALS DURING THE YEAR; AND
(IV)   TRANSFERS DURING THE YEAR.

6.2   THE FOLLOWING INFORMATION SHALL BE PROVIDED IN RESPECT OF PROVISIONS FOR DEPRECIATION OR DIMINUTION IN VALUE:

(A)   THE CUMULATIVE AMOUNT OF SUCH PROVISIONS AS AT THE BEGINNING AND END OF THE YEAR;
(B)   THE AMOUNT OF ANY SUCH PROVISIONS MADE DURING THE YEAR;
(C)   THE AMOUNT OF ANY ADJUSTMENTS MADE ON DISPOSAL DURING THE YEAR; AND
(D)   THE AMOUNT OF ANY OTHER ADJUSTMENTS MADE DURING THE YEAR.

Research and development

6.3   The cost of fixed assets acquired or constructed in order to provide facilities for **research and development** activities over a number of accounting periods shall be capitalised and written off over their useful lives through the profit and loss account.

6.4   Expenditure on **pure** and **applied research** shall be written off in the period of expenditure through the profit and loss account.

6.5   **Development** expenditure shall be written off in the period of expenditure except in the following circumstances when it may be deferred to future periods:

(a)   there is a clearly defined project; and
(b)   the related expenditure is separately identifiable; and
(c)   the outcome of such a project has been assessed with reasonable certainty as to:
(i)   its technical feasibility; and
(ii)   its ultimate commercial viability considered in the light of factors such as likely market conditions (including competing products), public opinion, consumer and environmental legislation; and
(d)   the aggregate of the deferred **development** costs, any further **development** costs, and related production, selling and administration costs is reasonably expected to be exceeded by related future sales or other revenues; and
(e)   adequate resources exist, or are reasonably expected to be available, to enable the project to be completed and to provide any consequential increases in working capital.

6.6   In the foregoing circumstances **development** expenditure may be deferred to the extent that its recovery can be reasonably regarded as assured.

6.7   If an **accounting policy** of deferral of **development** expenditure is adopted, it shall be applied to all **development** projects that meet the criteria in paragraph 6.5.

6.8   If **development** costs are deferred to future periods, they shall be amortised. The amortisation shall commence with the commercial production or application of the product, service, process or system and shall be allocated on a systematic basis to each accounting period, by reference to either the sale or use of the product, service, process or system or the period over which these are expected to be sold or used.

6.9   Deferred **development** expenditure for each product shall be reviewed at the end of each accounting period and where the circumstances that justified the deferral of expenditure no longer apply, or are considered doubtful, the expenditure, to the extent to which it is considered to be irrecoverable, shall be written off immediately project by project.

The amount of deferred **development** expenditure carried forward at the beginning **6.10** and end of the period shall be disclosed under **intangible assets** in the balance sheet or in the notes to the balance sheet. THE REASON FOR CAPITALISING THESE COSTS AND THE PERIOD OVER WHICH THEY ARE BEING DEPRECIATED SHALL BE DISCLOSED IN A NOTE TO THE ACCOUNTS. IF **DEVELOPMENT** COSTS ARE NOT TREATED AS A REALISED LOSS OR REALISED REVENUE LOSS THIS SHALL BE STATED TOGETHER WITH AN EXPLANATION OF THE CIRCUM- STANCES RELIED UPON BY THE **DIRECTORS** TO JUSTIFY THEIR DECISION.

Other intangible assets and goodwill

Positive **purchased goodwill** and purchased **intangible assets** shall be capitalised. **6.11** Internally generated goodwill and intangible assets shall not be capitalised.

An **intangible asset** purchased with a business shall be **recognised** separately from the **6.12** **purchased goodwill** if its value can be measured reliably.

Capitalised goodwill and **intangible assets** shall be **depreciated** on a straight-line (or **6.13** more appropriate) basis over their **useful economic lives**, which shall not exceed 20 years. THE PERIOD CHOSEN FOR DEPRECIATING GOODWILL AND THE REASONS FOR CHOOS- ING THAT PERIOD SHALL BE DISCLOSED IN A NOTE TO THE ACCOUNTS.

The **residual value** assigned to goodwill shall be zero. A higher **residual value** may be .**6.14** assigned to an **intangible asset** only when this value can be established reliably, for example when it has been agreed contractually.

Useful economic lives shall be reviewed at the end of each reporting period and **6.15** revised if necessary, subject to the constraint that the revised life shall not exceed 20 years from the date of acquisition. The carrying amount at the date of revision shall be **depreciated** over the revised estimate of remaining **useful economic life**.

Goodwill and **intangible assets** shall not be revalued. **6.16**

If an acquisition appears to give rise to negative goodwill, **fair values** shall be checked **6.17** to ensure that those of the acquired **assets** have not been overstated and those of the acquired **liabilities** have not been understated. Once this has been done, remaining negative goodwill up to the **fair values** of the non-monetary **assets** acquired shall be released in the profit and loss account over the lives of those assets. Any additional negative goodwill shall be **recognised** in the profit and loss account over the period expected to benefit from it. The amount of negative goodwill on the balance sheet and the period(s) in which it is being written back shall be disclosed.

Tangible fixed assets

Paragraphs 6.19–6.26 apply to all **tangible fixed assets** other than **investment** **6.18** **properties**.

A **tangible fixed asset** shall initially be measured at its cost, then written down to its **6.19** **recoverable amount** if necessary. The initial carrying amount of a **tangible fixed asset** received as a gift or donation by a charity shall be its current value, i.e. the lower of replacement cost and **recoverable amount**, at the date it is received.* WHERE THERE IS NO RECORD OF THE PURCHASE PRICE OR PRODUCTION COST OF AN ASSET, OR ANY SUCH RECORD CANNOT BE OBTAINED WITHOUT UNREASONABLE EXPENSE OR DELAY, THE VALUE

Generally, where issues of practicality or of cost-benefit arise, these will be addressed in the relevant sector- specific guidance and Statements of Recommended Practice (SORPs).

ASCRIBED SHALL BE THE EARLIEST AVAILABLE RECORD OF ITS VALUE. PARTICULARS SHALL BE GIVEN OF ANY CASE WHERE THE PURCHASE PRICE OR PRODUCTION COST OF ANY ASSET IS FOR THE FIRST TIME DETERMINED IN THIS WAY.

6.20   Costs that are directly attributable to bringing the **tangible fixed asset** into working condition for its intended use shall be included in its measurement. Other costs shall not be included. An entity may adopt an **accounting policy** of capitalising **finance costs** (such as interest). Where such a policy is adopted, **finance costs** that are directly attributable to the construction of **tangible fixed assets** shall be capitalised as part of the cost of those assets. The total amount of **finance costs** capitalised during a period shall not exceed the total amount of **finance costs** incurred during that period. WHERE APPLICABLE, THE NOTES TO THE ACCOUNTS SHALL DISCLOSE THAT FINANCE COSTS ARE INCLUDED IN DETERMINING THE COST OF THE ASSET AND THE AMOUNT OF FINANCE COSTS SO INCLUDED.

6.21   Capitalisation of directly attributable costs, including **finance costs**, shall be suspended during extended periods in which active **development** is interrupted. Capitalisation shall cease when substantially all the activities that are necessary to get the **tangible fixed asset** ready for use are complete, even if the asset has not yet been brought into use.

6.22   Subsequent expenditure shall be capitalised only if:
(a)   it enhances the economic benefits of a **tangible fixed asset** in excess of the previously assessed standard of performance (i.e. if it is an 'improvement'); or
(b)   it replaces or restores a component that has been separately depreciated over its **useful economic life**.

Otherwise it shall be **recognised** in the profit and loss account as it is incurred.

6.23   Where an entity adopts an **accounting policy** of revaluation in respect of a **tangible fixed asset**, its carrying amount shall be its market value (or the best estimate thereof) as at the balance sheet date. Where the **directors** believe that market value is not an appropriate basis, current value (i.e. the lower of replacement cost and **recoverable amount**) may be used instead. Where a **tangible fixed asset** is revalued, all **tangible fixed assets** of the same class (i.e. having a similar nature, function or use in the business) shall be revalued, but a policy of revaluation need not be applied to all classes of **tangible fixed assets**.

6.24   It may be possible to establish with reasonable **reliability** the values of certain **tangible fixed assets**, other than properties, by reference to active second-hand markets or appropriate publicly available indices. For other **tangible fixed assets**, including properties, a valuation shall be performed by an experienced valuer (i.e. one who has recognised and relevant recent professional experience, and sufficient knowledge of the state of the market, in the location and category of the **tangible fixed asset** being valued) at least every five years. It shall be updated by an experienced valuer in the intervening years where it is likely that there has been a material change in value.*

6.25   Revaluation losses caused only by changing market prices shall be **recognised** in the statement of **total recognised gains and losses** until the carrying amount of the asset reaches its depreciated historical cost. Other revaluation losses shall be **recognised** in the profit and loss account.

*Where, for cost/benefit reasons, alternative approaches are set out in relevant sector-specific guidance and SORPs, these may be adopted instead of the approach in paragraph 6.24.

Revaluation gains shall be **recognised** in the statement of **total recognised gains and losses**, except to the extent (after adjusting for subsequent **depreciation**) that they reverse revaluation losses on the same asset that were previously **recognised** in the profit and loss account. To that extent they shall be **recognised** in the profit and loss account. The adjustment for subsequent **depreciation** is to achieve the same overall effect that would have been reached had the original downward revaluation reflected in the profit and loss account not occurred.   **6.26**

WHERE **TANGIBLE FIXED ASSETS** HAVE BEEN REVALUED EITHER − THE COMPARABLE AMOUNTS DETERMINED UNDER THE HISTORICAL COST ACCOUNTING RULES (i.e. the aggregate historical cost amount that would have been included had the **assets** not been revalued, reflecting any write-downs to **recoverable amount** that would have been necessary); OR THE DIFFERENCES BETWEEN THOSE AMOUNTS AND THE CORRESPONDING AMOUNTS ACTUALLY SHOWN IN THE BALANCE SHEET SHALL BE SHOWN SEPARATELY IN THE BALANCE SHEET OR IN A NOTE TO THE ACCOUNTS.   **6.27**

WHERE TANGIBLE FIXED ASSETS ARE CONSTANTLY BEING REPLACED AND THEIR VALUE IS NOT MATERIAL TO ASSESSING THE COMPANY'S STATE OF AFFAIRS AND THEIR QUANTITY, VALUE AND COMPOSITION ARE NOT SUBJECT TO MATERIAL VARIATION, THEY MAY BE INCLUDED AT A FIXED QUANTITY AND VALUE.   **6.28**

WHERE TANGIBLE FIXED ASSETS HAVE BEEN REVALUED, THE YEAR IN WHICH THEY WERE VALUED SHALL BE DISCLOSED. IN THE CASE OF ASSETS THAT HAVE BEEN REVALUED DURING THE CURRENT **FINANCIAL YEAR**, THE NAMES OF THE PERSONS WHO VALUED THEM OR PARTICULARS OF THEIR QUALIFICATIONS FOR DOING SO AND THE BASES OF THE VALUATION SHALL BE DISCLOSED.   **6.29**

Investments

FIXED ASSET INVESTMENTS SHALL INITIALLY BE MEASURED AT COST. ALTERNATIVELY, THEY MAY BE MEASURED AT A MARKET VALUE DETERMINED AS AT THE DATE OF THEIR LAST VALUATION OR ON ANY OTHER VALUE DETERMINED ON A BASIS WHICH APPEARS TO THE **DIRECTORS** TO BE APPROPRIATE IN THE CIRCUMSTANCES OF THE COMPANY (IN THE LATTER CASE, THE METHOD OF VALUATION ADOPTED AND OF THE REASONS FOR ADOPTING IT SHALL BE DISCLOSED IN A NOTE TO THE ACCOUNTS). Gains and losses shall be **recognised** (in the profit and loss account or statement of **total recognised gains and losses**) using the same basis applied to **tangible fixed assets** in paragraphs 6.25 and 6.26 above.   **6.30**

WHERE FIXED ASSET INVESTMENTS HAVE BEEN REVALUED EITHER - THE COMPARABLE AMOUNTS DETERMINED UNDER THE HISTORICAL COST ACCOUNTING RULES (i.e. the aggregate historical cost amount that would have been included had the **assets** not been revalued, reflecting any write-downs to **recoverable amount** that would have been necessary); OR THE DIFFERENCES BETWEEN THOSE AMOUNTS AND THE CORRESPONDING AMOUNTS ACTUALLY SHOWN IN THE BALANCE SHEET SHALL BE SHOWN SEPARATELY IN THE BALANCE SHEET OR IN A NOTE TO THE ACCOUNTS.   **6.31**

THE AGGREGATE AMOUNT OF LISTED INVESTMENTS INCLUDED UNDER EACH ITEM OF INVESTMENTS SHOWN IN THE BALANCE SHEET SHALL BE DISCLOSED. FOR EACH ITEM WHICH INCLUDES LISTED INVESTMENTS, THE FOLLOWING SHALL BE DISCLOSED: **6.32**

(A)   THE AGGREGATE MARKET VALUE OF THE LISTED INVESTMENTS WHERE IT DIFFERS FROM THEIR BALANCE SHEET AMOUNT; AND

(B)   BOTH THE MARKET VALUE AND THE STOCK EXCHANGE VALUE OF ANY INVESTMENTS, OF WHICH THE MARKET VALUE IS TAKEN AS BEING HIGHER THAN THE STOCK EXCHANGE VALUE.

6.33   WHERE THE COMPANY HAS AT THE END OF THE FINANCIAL YEAR A SIGNIFICANT HOLDING IN
AN UNDERTAKING (WHICH IS NOT A SUBSIDIARY UNDERTAKING OF THE COMPANY) WHICH
REPRESENTS 20% OR MORE OF THE NOMINAL VALUE OF ANY CLASS OF SHARES IN THE
UNDERTAKING, OR MORE THAN 20% OF THE BOOK VALUE OF THE INVESTING COMPANY'S
TOTAL ASSETS, THE FOLLOWING SHALL BE STATED IN RELATION TO THAT UNDERTAKING:* † ‡

(A)   THE NAME OF THE UNDERTAKING;

(B)   IF THE COMPANY IS INCORPORATED OUTSIDE GREAT BRITAIN, THE COUNTRY IN WHICH
IT IS INCORPORATED;

(C)   IF IT IS UNINCORPORATED, THE ADDRESS OF ITS PRINCIPAL PLACE OF BUSINESS;

(D)   THE IDENTITY AND PROPORTION OF THE NOMINAL VALUE OF EACH CLASS OF SHARES
HELD;

(E)   THE AGGREGATE AMOUNT OF THE CAPITAL AND RESERVES OF THE UNDERTAKING AS
AT THE END OF THE MOST RECENT FINANCIAL YEAR ENDING WITH OR BEFORE THAT OF
THE INVESTING COMPANY; AND

(F)   ITS PROFIT OR LOSS FOR THAT YEAR.

Revaluation reserve

6.34   GAINS AND LOSSES ARISING ON THE REVALUATION OF ASSETS that have been **recognised** in
the statement of **total recognised gains and losses** SHALL BE CREDITED, OR DEBITED, TO A
SEPARATE REVALUATION RESERVE.

6.35   AMOUNTS MAY BE TRANSFERRED FROM THE REVALUATION RESERVE TO THE PROFIT AND
LOSS ACCOUNT WHEN THEY ARE REALISED. For **tangible fixed assets**, this will normally
result in an annual transfer from the revaluation reserve to the profit and loss
account over the **useful economic life** of the **asset** (i.e. in line with the **depreciation**
charge). Realisation may also occur on the eventual disposal of the **asset**.

6.36   THE TREATMENT FOR TAXATION PURPOSES OF AMOUNTS CREDITED OR DEBITED TO THE
REVALUATION RESERVE SHALL BE DISCLOSED IN A NOTE TO THE ACCOUNTS.

Depreciation

6.37   Paragraphs 6.38-6.43 apply to all **tangible fixed assets** other than **investment
properties**.

6.38   The cost (or revalued amount) less estimated **residual value** of a **tangible fixed asset**
shall be depreciated on a systematic basis over its **useful economic life**. The **depreciation** method used shall reflect as fairly as possible the pattern in which the asset's
economic benefits are consumed by the entity. The **depreciation** charge for each

---

*If the directors of the company are of opinion the number of undertakings in respect of which the company is
required to disclose information is such that compliance would result in information of excessive length being
given, the information need only be given in respect of the undertakings principally affecting the figures shown in
the company's annual accounts. Where the disclosures are limited in this way, the notes shall include a statement
that the information is given only with respect to such undertakings and full details must be annexed to the
company's next annual return.

†Information need not be disclosed with respect to an undertaking which is established under the law of a country
outside the United Kingdom or carries on business outside the United Kingdom, if in the opinion of the directors
of the company the disclosure would be seriously prejudicial to the business of that undertaking, or to the
business of the company or any of its subsidiary undertakings, and the DTI agrees that the information need not
be disclosed. Where advantage is taken of this, that fact shall be stated in a note to the company's annual
accounts. This statutory exemption is not available in the Republic of Ireland.

‡Disclosure requirements for holdings in subsidiary undertakings are set out in paragraph 15.17.

period shall be **recognised** as an expense in the profit and loss account unless it is permitted to be included in the carrying amount of another **asset**.

Where a **tangible fixed asset** comprises two or more major components with sub- **6.39** stantially different **useful economic lives**, each component shall be accounted for separately for **depreciation** purposes and depreciated over its individual **useful economic life**. With certain exceptions, such as sites used for extractive purposes or landfill, land has an unlimited life and therefore is not depreciated.

The **useful economic lives** and **residual values** of **tangible fixed assets** shall be reviewed **6.40** regularly and, when necessary, revised. On revision, the carrying amount of the **tangible fixed asset** at the date of revision less the revised **residual value** shall be depreciated over the revised remaining **useful economic life**.

A change from one method of providing **depreciation** to another is permissible only **6.41** on the grounds that the new method will give a fairer presentation of the results and of the financial position. Such a change does not, however, constitute a change of **accounting policy**; the carrying amount of the **tangible fixed asset** is depreciated using the revised method over the remaining **useful economic life**, beginning in the period in which the change is made.

The following shall be disclosed in the financial statements for (1) land and buildings **6.42** and (2) other **tangible fixed assets** in aggregate:

(a)   the **depreciation** methods used;
(b)   the **useful economic lives** or the **depreciation** rates used; and
(c)   where material, the financial effect of a change during the period in either the estimate of **useful economic lives** or the estimate of **residual values**.

Where there has been a change in the **depreciation** method used, the effect, if **6.43** material, shall be disclosed in the period of change. The reason for the change shall also be disclosed.

Write-downs to recoverable amount

Paragraphs 6.45-6.48 apply to capitalised goodwill and all fixed assets (i.e. **tangible** **6.44** **fixed assets**, **intangible assets** and **investments**) except **investment properties** and financial instruments (other than investments in subsidiaries, associates and joint ventures).

Fixed assets and goodwill shall be carried in the balance sheet at no more than **6.45** **recoverable amount**. If the net book amount of a fixed asset or goodwill is considered not to be recoverable in full at the balance sheet date (perhaps as a result of obsolescence or a fall in demand for a product), the net book amount shall be written down to the estimated **recoverable amount**, which shall then be written off over the remaining **useful economic life** of the asset.

If the **recoverable amount** of a **tangible fixed asset** or investment subsequently **6.46** increases as a result of a change in economic conditions or in the expected use of the asset, the net book amount shall be written back to the lower of **recoverable amount** and the amount at which the asset would have been recorded had the original write-down not been made.

If the **recoverable amount** of an **intangible asset** or capitalised goodwill subsequently **6.47** increases, the net book amount shall be written back only if an external event caused the original write-down and subsequent external events clearly and demonstrably reverse the effects of that event in a way that was not foreseen when the original write-down was calculated.

6.48   Write-downs (and any reversals) to **recoverable amount** shall be charged (or credited) in the profit and loss account for the period. However, write-downs of revalued **tangible fixed assets** that reverse previous revaluation gains simply as a result of changing market prices shall instead be **recognised** in the statement of **total recognised gains and losses**, to the extent that the carrying amount of the asset is greater than its depreciated historical cost. ANY AMOUNTS WHICH ARE NOT SHOWN IN THE PROFIT AND LOSS ACCOUNT SHALL BE DISCLOSED (EITHER SEPARATELY OR IN AGGREGATE) IN A NOTE TO THE ACCOUNTS.

6.49   WHERE FIXED ASSETS ARE NOT ACTUALLY REVALUED IN THE BALANCE SHEET BUT THEIR VALUE IS CONSIDERED BY THE **DIRECTORS**, A NOTE TO THE ACCOUNTS SHALL STATE THE FOLLOWING:

(A)   THAT THE **DIRECTORS** HAVE CONSIDERED THE VALUE OF FIXED ASSETS, WITHOUT ACTUALLY REVALUING THOSE ASSETS;

(B)   THAT THE **DIRECTORS** ARE SATISFIED THAT THE AGGREGATE VALUE OF THOSE ASSETS AT THE TIME IN QUESTION IS OR WAS NOT LESS THAN THE AGGREGATE AMOUNT AT WHICH THEY WERE FOR THE TIME BEING STATED IN THE COMPANY'S ACCOUNTS; AND

(C)   THE ASSETS AFFECTED ARE ACCORDINGLY STATED IN THE ACCOUNTS ON THE BASIS THAT A REVALUATION OF THE COMPANY'S FIXED ASSETS TOOK PLACE AT THAT TIME.

Investment properties

6.50   **Investment properties** shall not be subject to periodic charges for **depreciation** except for properties held on lease, which shall be **depreciated** at least over the period when the unexpired term is 20 years or less.

6.51   **Investment properties** shall be included in the balance sheet at their market value and the carrying value shall be displayed prominently either on the face of the balance sheet or in the notes.

6.52   The names of the persons making the valuation, or particulars of their qualifications, shall be disclosed together with the bases of valuation used by them. If a person making a valuation is an employee or officer of the company or group that owns the property this fact shall be disclosed.

6.53   Changes in the market value of **investment properties** shall not be taken to the profit and loss account but shall be taken to the statement of **total recognised gains and losses** (being a movement on an investment revaluation reserve), unless a deficit (or its reversal) on an individual **investment property** is expected to be permanent, in which case it shall be charged (or credited) in the profit and loss account of the period.

Government grants*

6.54   Subject to paragraph 6.55, **government grants** shall be **recognised** in the profit and loss account so as to match them with the expenditure towards which they are intended to contribute. To the extent that the grant is made as a contribution towards expenditure on a fixed asset, in principle it may be deducted from the purchase price

*Additional specific legal requirements relating to government grants in the Republic of Ireland are included in the derivation tables on the ASB website.

or production cost of that asset. However, the option to deduct **government grants** from the purchase price or production costs of fixed assets is not available to companies governed by the accounting and reporting requirements of UK **companies legislation.** In such cases, the amount so deferred shall be treated as deferred income.

A **government grant** shall not be **recognised** in the profit and loss account until the **6.55** conditions for its receipt have been complied with and there is reasonable assurance that the grant will be received.

Potential liabilities to repay grants either in whole or in part in specified circum- **6.56** stances shall be provided for only to the extent that repayment is probable. The repayment of a **government grant** shall be accounted for by setting off the repayment against any unamortised deferred income relating to the grant. Any excess shall be charged immediately to the profit and loss account.

The following information shall be disclosed in the financial statements: **6.57**
(a)   the effects of **government grants** on the results for the period and/or the financial position of the entity; and
(b)   where the results of the period are affected materially by the receipt of forms of **government** assistance other than grants, the nature of that assistance and, to the extent that the effects on the financial statements can be measured, an estimate of those effects.

7   LEASES

Hire purchase and leasing

Those **hire purchase contracts** which are of a financing nature shall be accounted for **7.1** on a basis similar to that set out below for **finance leases**. Conversely, other **hire purchase contracts** shall be accounted for on a basis similar to that set out below for **operating leases**.

Accounting by lessees

A **finance lease** shall be recorded in the balance sheet of a lessee as an asset and as an **7.2** **obligation** to pay future rentals. At the **inception** of the lease the sum to be recorded both as an asset and as a liability shall normally be the **fair value** of the asset.

In those cases where the **fair value** of the asset does not give a realistic estimate of the **7.3** cost to the lessee of the asset and of the **obligation** entered into, a better estimate shall be used. In principle this shall approximate to the present value of the **minimum lease payments**, derived by discounting them at the interest rate implicit in the lease. An example of where this might be used would be where the lessee has benefited from grants and capital allowances that enable the **minimum lease payments** under a **finance lease** to be adjusted to a total that is less than the **fair value** of the asset. A negative **finance charge** shall not be shown.

The total **finance charge** under a **finance lease** shall be allocated to accounting periods **7.4** during the **lease term** so as to produce a constant periodic rate of charge on the remaining balance of the **obligation** for each accounting period, or a reasonable approximation thereto. The straight-line method may provide such a reasonable approximation.

7.5 The rental under an **operating lease** shall be charged on a straight-line basis over the **lease term** even if the payments are not made on such a basis, unless another systematic and rational basis is more appropriate.

7.6 Incentives to sign a lease, in whatever form they may take, shall be spread by the lessee on a straight-line basis over the **lease term** or, if shorter than the full **lease term**, over the period to the review date on which the rent is first expected to be adjusted to the prevailing market rate.

7.7 An **asset** leased under a **finance lease** shall be depreciated over the shorter of the **lease term** or its useful life. However, in the case of a **hire purchase contract** that has the characteristics of a **finance lease** the asset shall be depreciated over its useful life.

Accounting by lessors

7.8 The amount due from the lessee under a **finance lease** shall be recorded in the balance sheet of a lessor as a debtor at the amount of the **net investment** in the lease after making provisions for items such as bad and doubtful rentals receivable.

7.9 The total **gross earnings** under **finance leases** shall be **recognised** on a systematic and rational basis. This will normally be a constant periodic rate of return on the lessor's **net investment**.

7.10 Rental income from an **operating lease** shall be **recognised** on a straight-line basis over the period of the lease, even if the payments are not made on such a basis, unless another systematic and rational basis is more representative of the time pattern in which the benefit from the **leased** asset is receivable.

7.11 An asset held for use in **operating leases** by a lessor shall be recorded as a fixed **asset** and **depreciated** over its useful life.

Manufacturer/dealer lessor

7.12 A manufacturer or dealer lessor shall not **recognise** a selling profit under an **operating lease**. The selling profit under a **finance lease** shall be restricted to the excess of the **fair value** of the **asset** over the manufacturer's or dealer's cost less any grants receivable by the manufacturer or dealer towards the purchase, construction or use of the **asset**.

Sale and leaseback transactions - accounting by the seller/lessee

7.13 In a sale and leaseback transaction that results in a **finance lease**, any apparent profit or loss (i.e. the difference between the sale price and the previous carrying value) shall be deferred and amortised in the financial statements of the seller/lessee over the shorter of the **lease term** and the useful life of the **asset**.

7.14 If the leaseback is an **operating lease**:

(a) any profit or loss shall be **recognised** immediately, provided it is clear that the transaction is established at **fair value**;

(b) if the sale price is below **fair value** any profit or loss shall be **recognised** immediately, except that if the apparent loss is compensated for by future rentals at below market price it shall to that extent be deferred and amortised over the remainder of the **lease term** (or, if shorter, the period during which the reduced rentals are chargeable); or

(c)   if the sale price is above **fair value**, the excess over **fair value** shall be deferred and amortised over the shorter of the remainder of the **lease term** and the period to the next rent review (if any).

Sale and leaseback transactions - accounting by the buyer/lessor

A buyer/lessor shall account for a sale and leaseback in the same way as other leases   **7.15**
are accounted for, i.e. using the methods set out in paragraphs 7.8-7.12.

Disclosure by lessees

Disclosure shall be made of: **7.16**

(a)   either:

    (i)   the gross amounts of **assets** that are held under **finance leases** together with the related accumulated **depreciation** for (1) land and buildings and (2) other fixed **assets** in aggregate; or

    (ii)   alternatively to being shown separately from that in respect of owned fixed **assets**, the information in (i) above may be integrated with it, such that the totals of gross amount, accumulated **depreciation**, net amount and **depreciation** allocated for the period for (1) land and buildings and (2) other fixed **assets** in aggregate for **assets** held under **finance leases** are included with similar amounts for owned fixed **assets**. Where this alternative treatment is adopted, the net amount of **assets** held under **finance leases** and the amount of **depreciation** allocated for the period in respect of **assets** under **finance leases** included in the overall total shall be disclosed separately.

(b)   the amounts of **obligations** related to **finance leases** (net of **finance charges** allocated to future periods). These shall be disclosed separately from other **obligations** and liabilities, either on the face of the balance sheet or in the notes to the accounts.

(c)   the amount of any commitments existing at the balance sheet date in respect of **finance leases** that have been entered into but whose **inception** occurs after the year end.

In respect of **operating leases**, the lessee shall disclose the payments that it is com-   **7.17**
mitted to make during the next year, analysed into those in which the commitment expires within that year, those expiring in the second to fifth years inclusive, and those expiring over five years from the balance sheet date.

Disclosure by lessors

Disclosure shall be made of: **7.18**

(a)   the gross amounts of **assets** held for use in **operating leases** and the related accumulated **depreciation** charges;

(b)   the cost of assets acquired, whether by purchase or **finance lease**, for the purpose of letting under **finance leases**; and

(c)   the **net investment** in (i) **finance leases** and (ii) **hire purchase contracts** at each balance sheet date.

8   CURRENT ASSETS

Stocks and long-term contracts*

8.1   The amount at which stocks are stated in the financial statements shall be the total of the lower of cost and **net realisable value** of the separate items of stock or of groups of similar items.

8.2   WHERE THERE IS NO RECORD OF THE PURCHASE PRICE OR PRODUCTION COST OF STOCK THE VALUE ASCRIBED SHALL BE THE EARLIEST AVAILABLE RECORD OF ITS VALUE. PARTICULARS SHALL BE GIVEN OF ANY CASE WHERE THE PURCHASE PRICE OR PRODUCTION COST OF ANY ASSET IS FOR THE FIRST TIME DETERMINED IN THIS WAY.

8.3   FINANCE COSTS (SUCH AS INTEREST) THAT ARE DIRECTLY ATTRIBUTABLE TO THE ACQUISITION, CONSTRUCTION OR PRODUCTION OF STOCK MAY BE INCLUDED AS PART OF THE COST. IN SUCH CIRCUMSTANCES, THE NOTES TO THE ACCOUNTS SHALL DISCLOSE THAT FINANCE COSTS ARE INCLUDED IN DETERMINING THE COST OF THE ASSET AND THE AMOUNT OF FINANCE COSTS SO INCLUDED.

8.4   WHERE STOCKS ARE CONSTANTLY BEING REPLACED AND THEIR VALUE IS NOT MATERIAL TO ASSESSING THE COMPANY'S STATE OF AFFAIRS AND THEIR QUANTITY, VALUE AND COMPOSITION ARE NOT SUBJECT TO MATERIAL VARIATION, THEY MAY BE INCLUDED AT A FIXED QUANTITY AND VALUE.

8.5   DISTRIBUTION COSTS MAY NOT BE INCLUDED IN THE PRODUCTION COSTS OF STOCKS.

8.6   **Long-term contracts** shall be assessed on a contract-by-contract basis and reflected in the profit and loss account by recording turnover and related costs as contract activity progresses. Turnover is ascertained in a manner appropriate to the stage of completion of the contract, the business and the industry in which it operates.

8.7   Where it is considered that the outcome of a **long-term contract** can be assessed with reasonable certainty before its conclusion, the prudently calculated **attributable profit** shall be **recognised** in the profit and loss account as the difference between the reported turnover and related costs for that contract.

8.8   **Long-term contracts** shall be disclosed in the balance sheet as follows:

(a)   The amount by which recorded turnover is in excess of payments on account shall be classified as 'amounts recoverable on contracts' and separately disclosed within debtors.

(b)   The balance of payments on account (in excess of the amounts (i) matched with turnover and (ii) offset against **long-term contract** balances) shall be classified as payments on account and separately disclosed within creditors.

(c)   The amount of **long-term contracts**, at costs incurred, net of amounts transferred to cost of sales, after deducting **foreseeable losses** and payments on account not matched with turnover, shall be classified as 'long-term contract balances' and separately disclosed within the balance sheet heading 'stocks'. The balance sheet note shall disclose separately the balances of:

(i)   net cost less **foreseeable losses**; and
(ii)   applicable payments on account.

Guidance on the practical considerations of arriving at amounts at which stocks and long-term contracts are stated in financial statements is given in Appendix III.

(d) The amount by which the provision or accrual for **foreseeable losses** exceeds the costs incurred (after transfers to cost of sales) shall be included within either 'provisions for liabilities' or 'creditors' as appropriate.

Consignment stock*

Where **consignment stock** is in substance an **asset** of the dealer, the stock shall be **recognised** as such on the dealer's balance sheet, together with a corresponding liability to the manufacturer. Any deposit shall be deducted from the **liability** and the excess classified as a trade creditor. Where stock is not in substance an **asset** of the dealer, the stock shall not be included on the dealer's balance sheet until the transfer of title has crystallised. Any deposit shall be included under 'other debtors'.

8.9

Debt factoring†

Where the entity has transferred to the factor all significant benefits (i.e. the future cash flows from payment by the debtors) and all significant risks (i.e. slow payment risk and the risk of bad debts) relating to the debts, and has no **obligation** to repay the factor, the debts shall be removed from the entity's balance sheet and no **liability** shall be shown in respect of the proceeds received from the factor. A profit or loss shall be **recognised,** calculated as the difference between the carrying amount of the debts and the proceeds received.

8.10

Where the entity has retained significant benefits and risks relating to factored debts, and all the following conditions are met:

8.11

(a) there is absolutely no doubt that the entity's exposure to loss is limited to a fixed monetary amount (e.g. because there is no recourse or such recourse has a fixed monetary ceiling);

(b) amounts received from the factor are secured only on the debts factored;

(c) the debts factored are capable of separate identification;

(d) the debt factor has no recourse to other debts or assets;

(e) the entity has no right to reacquire the debts in the future;

(f) the factor has no right to return the debts even in the event of the cessation of the factoring agreement,

then the factored debts shall be shown gross (after providing for bad debts, credit protection charges and any accrued interest) separately on the face of the balance sheet. Any amounts received from the factor in respect of those debts, to the extent that they are not returnable, shall be shown as deductions therefrom on the face of the balance sheet (a 'linked presentation'). The financial statements shall include a note stating that the entity is not required to support bad debts in respect of factored debts and that the factors have stated in writing that they will not seek recourse other than out of factored debts. The interest element of the factor's charges shall be **recognised** as it accrues and included in the profit and loss account with other interest charges.

In all other cases a separate presentation shall be adopted. A gross **asset** (equivalent in amount to the gross amount of the debts) shall be shown on the balance sheet of the entity within **assets** and a corresponding **liability** in respect of the proceeds

8.12

*A table illustrating the considerations affecting the treatment of consignment stock is given in Appendix III.

†Similar arrangements, such as invoice discounting, shall be accounted for in the same way as debt factoring. A table illustrating the considerations affecting the treatment of debt factoring is given in Appendix III.

received from the factor shall be shown within **liabilities**. The interest element of the factor's charges and other factoring costs shall be **recognised** as they accrue and included in the profit and loss account with other interest charges.

Current asset investments

8.13   CURRENT ASSET INVESTMENTS SHALL INITIALLY BE STATED IN THE FINANCIAL STATEMENTS AT THE LOWER OF COST AND NET REALISABLE VALUE. ALTERNATIVELY, THEY MAY BE MEASURED AT THEIR CURRENT COST. Gains and losses shall be **recognised** (in the profit and loss account or statement of **total recognised gains and losses**) using the same basis applied to **tangible fixed assets** in paragraphs 6.25 and 6.26 above.

8.14   WHERE LISTED SHARES ARE HELD AS A CURRENT ASSET INVESTMENT, THE FOLLOWING INFORMATION SHALL BE DISCLOSED:

(A)   THE AGGREGATE MARKET VALUE OF THOSE LISTED INVESTMENTS WHERE IT DIFFERS FROM THEIR BALANCE SHEET AMOUNT; AND

(B)   BOTH THE MARKET VALUE AND THE STOCK EXCHANGE VALUE OF ANY INVESTMENTS, OF WHICH THE MARKET VALUE IS TAKEN AS BEING HIGHER THAN THE STOCK EXCHANGE VALUE.

Start-up costs and pre-contract costs

8.15   **Start-up costs** shall be accounted for on a basis consistent with the accounting treatment of similar costs incurred as part of the entity's on-going activities. In cases where there are no such similar costs, **start-up** costs that do not meet the criteria for **recognition** as **assets** under another specific requirement of the FRSSE shall be **recognised** as an expense when they are incurred. They shall not be carried forward as an **asset**.

8.16   **Pre-contract costs** shall be expensed as incurred, except that **directly attributable costs** shall be **recognised** as an **asset** when it is virtually certain that a contract will be obtained and the contract is expected to result in future net cash inflows with a present value no less than all amounts **recognised** as an **asset**. Costs incurred before the **asset recognition** criteria are met shall not be **recognised** as an **asset**.

9   TAXATION

General

9.1   **Tax** (current and **deferred**) shall be **recognised** in the profit and loss account, except to the extent that it is attributable to a gain or loss that is or has been **recognised** directly in the statement of **total recognised gains and losses** (in which case the tax shall also be **recognised** directly in that statement).

9.2   The material components of the (current and **deferred**) **tax** charge (or credit) for the period shall be disclosed separately.

9.3   Any special circumstances that affect the overall tax charge or credit for the period, or may affect those of future periods, shall be disclosed by way of a note to the profit and loss account and their individual effects quantified. The effects of a fundamental change in the basis of taxation shall be included in the tax charge or credit for the period and separately disclosed on the face of the profit and loss account.

Deferred tax

Deferred tax shall be **recognised** in respect of all **timing differences** that have origi-   **9.4**
nated but not reversed by the balance sheet date; however, **deferred tax** shall not be
recognised on:

(a) revaluation gains and losses unless, by the balance sheet date, the entity has
entered into a binding agreement to sell the **asset** and has revalued the **asset** to
the selling price; or

(b) taxable gains arising on revaluations or sales if it is more likely than not that
the gain will be rolled over into a replacement **asset**.

Unrelieved tax losses and other **deferred tax assets** shall be **recognised** only to the   **9.5**
extent that it is more likely than not that they will be recovered against the reversal of
deferred tax liabilities or other future taxable profits (the very existence of unrelieved
tax losses is strong evidence that there may not be 'other future taxable profits'
against which the losses will be relieved).

Deferred tax shall be **recognised** when the tax allowances for the cost of a fixed **asset**   **9.6**
are received before or after the **depreciation** of the fixed **asset** is **recognised** in the
profit and loss account. However, if and when all conditions for retaining the tax
allowances have been met, the **deferred tax** shall be reversed.

Deferred tax shall not be **recognised** on **permanent differences**.   **9.7**

Deferred tax shall be measured at the average tax rates that would apply when the   **9.8**
timing differences are expected to reverse, based on tax rates and laws that have been
enacted by the balance sheet date.

The discounting of **deferred tax assets** and **liabilities** is not required. However, if an   **9.9**
entity does adopt a policy of discounting, all **deferred tax** balances that have been
measured by reference to undiscounted cash flows and for which the impact of
discounting is material shall be discounted. Where discounting is used, the
unwinding of the discount shall be shown as a component of the tax charge and
disclosed separately.

The **deferred tax** balance and its material components shall be disclosed.   **9.10**

The movement between the opening and closing net **deferred tax** balances, and the   **9.11**
material components of this movement, shall be disclosed.

If **assets** have been revalued, or if their market values have been disclosed in a note,   **9.12**
the amount of tax that would be payable or recoverable if the **assets** were sold at the
values shown shall be disclosed.

Tax on dividends

Outgoing dividends and similar amounts payable shall be **recognised** at an amount   **9.13**
that includes any **withholding tax** but excludes other taxes, such as attributable **tax
credits**.

Incoming dividends and similar income receivable shall be **recognised** at an amount   **9.14**
that includes any **withholding tax** but excludes other taxes, such as attributable **tax
credits**. Any **withholding tax** suffered shall be shown as part of the tax charge.

Value added tax (VAT)

9.15 Turnover shown in the profit and loss account shall exclude either VAT on taxable outputs or VAT imputed under the flat rate VAT scheme. Irrecoverable VAT allocable to fixed **assets** and to other items disclosed separately in the financial statements shall be included in their cost where practicable and material.

10   PENSIONS

10.1 The cost of a **defined contribution scheme** is equal to the contributions payable to the scheme for the accounting period. The cost shall be **recognised** within operating profit in the profit and loss account.

10.2 PARTICULARS SHALL BE GIVEN OF ANY PENSION COMMITMENTS INCLUDED UNDER ANY PROVISION SHOWN IN THE COMPANY'S BALANCE SHEET AND ANY SUCH COMMITMENTS FOR WHICH NO PROVISION HAS BEEN MADE. WHERE ANY SUCH COMMITMENT RELATES WHOLLY OR PARTLY TO PENSIONS PAYABLE TO PAST **DIRECTORS** OF THE COMPANY, SEPARATE PARTICULARS SHALL BE GIVEN OF THAT COMMITMENT, SO FAR AS IT RELATES TO SUCH PENSIONS.

10.3 The following disclosures shall be made in respect of a **defined contribution scheme**:

(a)   the nature of the scheme (i.e. defined contribution);
(b)   the cost for the period; and
(c)   any outstanding or prepaid contributions at the balance sheet date.

10.4 An employer participating in a **defined benefit scheme** shall refer to Appendix II 'Accounting for retirement benefits: defined benefit schemes'.

11   PROVISIONS, CONTINGENT LIABILITIES AND CONTINGENT ASSETS

11.1 The requirements in paragraphs 11.2-11.8 do not apply to pensions, **deferred tax** and leases, which are covered by more specific requirements of the FRSSE.

Provisions

11.2 A **provision** shall be **recognised** when, and only when, it is probable (i.e. more likely than not) that a present **obligation** exists, as a result of a past event, and that it will require a transfer of economic benefits in settlement that can be estimated reliably. The amount **recognised** as a **provision** shall be the best estimate of the expenditure required to settle the **obligation** at the balance sheet date. Where the effect of the time value of money is material, the amount of a **provision** shall be the present value of the expenditures expected to be required to settle the **obligation**. Where discounting is used, the unwinding of the discount shall be shown as other finance costs adjacent to interest.*

11.3 Where some or all of the expenditure required to settle a **provision** may be reimbursed by another party (e.g. through an insurance claim), the reimbursement shall be **recognised**, as a separate **asset**, only when it is virtually certain to be received if the entity settles the **obligation**. In the profit and loss account, the expense relating to the

There are a number of acceptable methods of discounting, and the appropriate discount rate depends on the method adopted. However, if cash flows are expressed in future prices and have been adjusted for risk, it will be appropriate to discount them at a risk-free rate such as a market rate on relevant government bonds. An illustrative example of a provision calculated using discounting is given in Appendix III.

provision may be presented net of the recovery. Gains from the expected disposal of **assets** shall be excluded from the measurement of a provision.

Provisions shall be reviewed at each balance sheet date and adjusted to reflect the current best estimate. **11.4**

A **provision** shall be used only for expenditures for which the **provision** was originally **recognised**. **11.5**

FOR EACH CLASS OF **PROVISION** THE FOLLOWING INFORMATION SHALL BE PROVIDED: **11.6**

(A) THE AMOUNT OF THE **PROVISION** AT THE BEGINNING AND THE END OF THE **FINANCIAL YEAR**;
(B) ANY AMOUNTS TRANSFERRED TO OR FROM THE **PROVISION** DURING THE YEAR;
(C) THE SOURCE AND APPLICATION OF THE AMOUNTS TRANSFERRED; AND
(D) PARTICULARS OF EACH MATERIAL **PROVISION** INCLUDED UNDER 'OTHER PROVISIONS' IN THE COMPANY'S BALANCE SHEET IN ANY CASE WHERE THE AMOUNT OF THAT **PROVISION** IS MATERIAL.

THE DISCLOSURES SET OUT ABOVE ARE NOT REQUIRED WHERE THE MOVEMENT CONSISTS OF THE APPLICATION OF A **PROVISION** FOR THE PURPOSE FOR WHICH IT WAS ESTABLISHED.

Contingent liabilities and contingent assets

Contingent liabilities and **contingent assets** shall not be **recognised.** **11.7**

The following shall be disclosed for **contingent liabilities**, except where their existence is remote, and for probable **contingent assets**: **11.8**

(a) a brief description of the nature of the contingent item; and
(b) where practicable, an estimate of its financial effect; and
(c) ITS LEGAL NATURE.

DETAILS SHALL BE PROVIDED WHERE ANY VALUABLE SECURITY HAS BEEN PROVIDED BY THE COMPANY IN CONNECTION WITH A **CONTINGENT LIABILITY** AND IF SO, WHAT. **11.9**

WHERE PRACTICABLE, THE AGGREGATE AMOUNT, OR ESTIMATED AMOUNT, OF CONTRACTS FOR CAPITAL EXPENDITURE NOT PROVIDED FOR SHALL BE DISCLOSED. DETAILS OF ANY OTHER FINANCIAL COMMITMENTS NOT PROVIDED FOR WHICH ARE RELEVANT TO ASSESSING THE COMPANY'S STATE OF AFFAIRS SHALL ALSO BE DISCLOSED. **11.10**

PARTICULARS SHALL BE GIVEN OF ANY CHARGE ON THE ASSETS OF THE COMPANY TO SECURE THE LIABILITIES OF ANY OTHER PERSON, INCLUDING WHERE PRACTICABLE, THE AMOUNT SECURED. **11.11**

12 FINANCIAL INSTRUMENTS, SHARE CAPITAL AND SHARE-BASED PAYMENTS

General

A **financial instrument**, or its component parts, shall be classified as a **financial liability**, a **financial asset** or an **equity instrument** in accordance with the substance of the contractual arrangement rather than its legal form. Some **financial instruments** take the legal form of equity but are **liabilities** in substance and others may combine features associated with **equity instruments** and features associated with **financial liabilities**. For example a preference share that provides for mandatory redemption **12.1** by the issuer for a fixed or determinable amount at a fixed or determinable future date, or gives the holder the right to require the issuer to redeem the instrument at or after a particular date for a fixed or determinable amount, is a **financial liability**.

12.2   The **finance costs** of **borrowings** shall be allocated to periods over the **term** of the **borrowings** at a constant rate on the carrying amount. All **finance costs** shall be charged in the profit and loss account.

12.3   **Borrowings** shall be initially stated in the balance sheet at the **fair value** of consideration received. The carrying amount of **borrowings** shall be increased by the **finance cost** in respect of the reporting period and reduced by payments made in respect of the **borrowings** in that period.

12.4   Where an **arrangement fee** is such as to represent a significant additional cost of finance when compared with the interest payable over the life of the instrument, the treatment set out in paragraph 12.2 shall be followed. Where this is not the case it shall be charged in the profit and loss account immediately it is incurred.

12.5   THE AMOUNT OF ANY CONVERTIBLE DEBT ISSUED SHALL BE SEPARATELY DISCLOSED FROM OTHER LIABILITIES.

12.6   Dividends relating to a **financial instrument** or a component that is a **financial liability** shall be recognised as expense in profit or loss. Distributions to holders of an **equity instrument** shall be debited by the entity directly to equity, net of any related income tax benefit. If an entity declares dividends after the balance sheet date, the dividends shall not be **recognised** as a **liability** at the balance sheet date.

12.7   THE NOTES TO THE ACCOUNTS MUST STATE:

(A)   THE AGGREGATE AMOUNT OF DIVIDENDS PAID IN THE FINANCIAL YEAR (OTHER THAN THOSE FOR WHICH A LIABILITY EXISTED AT THE IMMEDIATELY PRECEDING BALANCE SHEET DATE);

(B)   THE AGGREGATE AMOUNT OF DIVIDENDS THAT THE COMPANY IS LIABLE TO PAY AT THE BALANCE SHEET DATE; AND

(C)   THE AGGREGATE AMOUNT OF DIVIDENDS THAT ARE PROPOSED BEFORE THE DATE OF APPROVAL OF THE ACCOUNTS, AND NOT OTHERWISE DISCLOSED UNDER PARAGRAPH (A) OR (B) ABOVE.

12.8   IF ANY FIXED CUMULATIVE DIVIDENDS ON THE COMPANY'S SHARES ARE IN ARREARS, THE AMOUNT OF THE ARREARS AND THE PERIOD FOR WHICH EACH CLASS OF DIVIDENDS IS IN ARREARS SHALL BE DISCLOSED.

The company's share capital

12.9   THE FOLLOWING INFORMATION SHALL BE DISCLOSED WITH RESPECT TO THE COMPANY'S SHARE CAPITAL:

(A)   THE AUTHORISED SHARE CAPITAL;

(B)   WHERE SHARES OF MORE THAN ONE CLASS HAVE BEEN ALLOTTED, THE NUMBER AND AGGREGATE NOMINAL VALUE OF SHARES OF EACH CLASS ALLOTTED;

(C)   FOR ANY PART OF THE ALLOTTED SHARE CAPITAL THAT CONSISTS OF REDEEMABLE SHARES:

(I)   THE EARLIEST AND LATEST DATES ON WHICH THE COMPANY HAS THE POWER TO REDEEM THOSE SHARES;

(II)   WHETHER THOSE SHARES MUST BE REDEEMED IN ANY EVENT OR ARE LIABLE TO BE REDEEMED AT THE OPTION OF THE COMPANY OR OF THE SHAREHOLDER; AND

(III) WHETHER ANY (AND, IF SO, WHAT) PREMIUM IS PAYABLE ON REDEMPTION.

IF THE COMPANY HAS ALLOTTED ANY SHARES DURING THE PERIOD, THE FOLLOWING INFORMATION SHALL BE DISCLOSED: **12.10**

(A) THE CLASSES OF SHARES ALLOTTED; AND

(B) FOR EACH CLASS, THE NUMBER ALLOTTED, THEIR AGGREGATE NOMINAL VALUE, AND THE CONSIDERATION RECEIVED BY THE COMPANY FOR THE ALLOTMENT.

THE AMOUNT OF ALLOTTED SHARE CAPITAL AND THE AMOUNT OF CALLED UP SHARE CAPITAL WHICH HAS BEEN PAID UP SHALL BE SEPARATELY DISCLOSED. **12.11**

THE NUMBER, DESCRIPTION AND AMOUNT OF SHARES IN THE COMPANY HELD BY OR ON BEHALF OF ITS **SUBSIDIARY UNDERTAKINGS** SHALL BE DISCLOSED UNLESS THE SUBSIDIARY UNDERTAKING IS CONCERNED AS A PERSONAL REPRESENTATIVE OR A TRUSTEE **12.12**

Share-based Payments

An entity which undertakes **share-based payment arrangements**, including transactions with **employees or others providing similar services** shall account for them as follows **12.13**

Cash-settled share-based payment transactions

(a) An entity shall **recognise** the goods or services received or acquired when it obtains the goods or as the services are received. If the goods or services received or acquired do not qualify for recognition as **assets**, they shall be **recognised** as expenses. The entity shall **recognise** a corresponding **liability.**

(b) The amount of the goods or services and the corresponding **liability recognised** shall be the best estimate of the expenditure required to settle the **liability** at the balance sheet date. The **liability** shall be remeasured at each balance sheet date and at the date of settlement.

(c) Information shall be disclosed in a note to describe the principal terms and conditions of cash settled share-based payment transactions that exist during the period, including their current and potential financial effect.

Equity-settled share-based payment arrangements

(d) Information shall be disclosed in a note to describe the principal terms and conditions of any equity settled share-based payment arrangements that exist during the period including, the number of shares and the number of employees and others potentially involved, the grant date, any performance conditions and over what periods these apply and, where applicable, any option exercise prices.

Where the terms of the arrangement provide the counterparty with the choice of whether the entity settles the transaction in cash (or other assets) or by issuing **equity instruments**, the transaction, shall be accounted for as a cash settled transaction in accordance with paragraph 12.13 (a) to (c) above. The liability shall be measured at the best estimate of the amount required to settle it at the balance sheet date if the counterparty were to opt for cash settlement. If the obligation is eventually settled by the issue of equity instruments, the liability previously recognised should be treated as the proceeds of issue of those instruments. **12.14**

Where the entity and not the counterparty has the choice of settlement method, the arrangement shall be treated as either an equity settled transaction in accordance **12.15** with paragraph 12.13 (d) or a cash settled transaction in accordance with paragraph 12.13 (a) to (c), as appropriate, in the entity's circumstances.

13   FOREIGN CURRENCY TRANSLATION

Transactions in foreign currencies

13.1   WHERE SUMS ORIGINALLY DENOMINATED IN FOREIGN CURRENCIES HAVE BEEN BROUGHT INTO ACCOUNT UNDER ANY ITEMS SHOWN IN THE BALANCE SHEET OR PROFIT AND LOSS ACCOUNT, THE BASIS ON WHICH THOSE SUMS HAVE BEEN TRANSLATED INTO **LOCAL CURRENCY** SHALL BE DISCLOSED.

13.2   Subject to the provisions of paragraphs 13.4 and 13.6 each **asset**, **liability**, revenue or cost arising from a transaction denominated in a foreign currency shall be translated into the **local currency** at the **exchange rate** in operation on the date on which the transaction occurred; if the rates do not fluctuate significantly, an average rate for a period may be used as an approximation. Where the transaction is to be settled at a contracted rate, that rate shall be used. Where a trading transaction is covered by a related or matching **forward contract**, the rate of exchange specified in that contract may be used.

13.3   Subject to the special provisions of paragraph 13.6, which relate to the treatment of foreign equity investments financed by foreign currency **borrowings**, no subsequent **translations** shall normally be made once non-monetary **assets** have been translated and recorded.

13.4   At each balance sheet date, monetary **assets** and **liabilities** denominated in a foreign currency shall be translated by using the **closing rate** or, where appropriate, the rates of exchange fixed under the terms of the relevant transactions. Where there are related or matching **forward contracts** in respect of trading transactions, the rates of exchange specified in those contracts may be used.

13.5   All exchange gains or losses on settled transactions and unsettled **monetary items** shall be reported as part of the profit or loss for the period from **ordinary activities**.

13.6   Where a company has used foreign currency **borrowings** to finance, or to provide a hedge against, its foreign equity investments and the conditions set out in this paragraph apply, the equity investments may be denominated in the appropriate foreign currencies and the carrying amounts translated at the end of each accounting period at **closing rates** for inclusion in the investing company's financial statements. Where investments are treated in this way, any exchange differences arising shall be taken to reserves and the exchange gains or losses on the foreign currency **borrowings** shall then be offset, as a reserve movement, against these exchange differences. The conditions that must apply are as follows:

(a)   in any accounting period, exchange gains or losses arising on the **borrowings** may be offset only to the extent of exchange differences arising on the equity investments;

(b)   the foreign currency **borrowings**, whose exchange gains or losses are used in the offset process, shall not exceed, in the aggregate, the total amount of cash that the investments are expected to be able to generate, whether from profits or otherwise; and

(c)   the accounting treatment adopted shall be applied consistently from period to period.

Incorporating accounts of foreign entities

When preparing accounts for a company and its **foreign entities** (which includes the   **13.7**
incorporation of the results of associated companies or foreign branches into those
of an investing company) the **closing rate/net investment** method of translating the
local currency financial statements shall normally be used.

Exchange differences arising from the retranslation of the opening **net investment** in a   **13.8**
foreign entity at the **closing rate** shall be recorded as a movement on reserves.

The profit and loss account of a **foreign entity** accounted for under the **closing rate/**   **13.9**
net investment method shall be translated at the **closing rate** or at an average rate for
the period. Where an average rate is used, the difference between the profit and loss
account translated at an average rate and at the **closing rate** shall be recorded as a
movement on reserves. The average rate used shall be calculated by the method
considered most appropriate for the circumstances of the **foreign entity**.

In those circumstances where the trade of the **foreign entity** is more dependent on the   **13.10**
economic environment of the investing company's currency than that of its own
reporting currency, the transactions of the foreign operation shall be reported as
though all of its transactions had been entered into by the investing company itself in
its own currency, as stated in paragraphs 13.2-13.5.

The method used for translating the financial statements of each **foreign entity** shall   **13.11**
be applied consistently from period to period unless its financial and other operational relationships with the investing company change.

Where foreign currency **borrowings** have been used to finance, or provide a hedge   **13.12**
against, group equity investments in **foreign entities**, exchange gains or losses on the
borrowings, which would otherwise have been taken to the profit and loss account,
may be offset as reserve movements against exchange differences arising on the
retranslation of the **net investments** provided that:

(a)   the relationships between the investing company and the **foreign entities** con-
      cerned justify the use of the **closing rate** method for consolidation purposes;
(b)   in any accounting period, the exchange gains and losses arising on foreign
      currency **borrowings** are offset only to the extent of the exchange differences
      arising on the **net investments** in **foreign entities**;
(c)   the foreign currency **borrowings**, whose exchange gains or losses are used in the
      offset process, shall not exceed, in the aggregate, the total amount of cash that
      the **net investments** are expected to be able to generate, whether from profits or
      otherwise; and
(d)   the accounting treatment is applied consistently from period to period.

Where the provisions of paragraph 13.6 have been applied in the investing company's financial statements to a foreign equity investment that is neither a subsidiary
nor an associated company, the same offset procedure may be applied in the **consolidated financial statements**.

14   POST BALANCE SHEET EVENTS

An entity shall adjust the amounts **recognised** in its financial statements to reflect   **14.1**
adjusting **events after the balance sheet date**.

An entity shall not adjust the amounts **recognised** in its financial statements to reflect   **14.2**
non-adjusting **events after the balance sheet date**.

14.3   If non-adjusting **events after the balance sheet date** are material, non-disclosure could influence the economic decisions of users taken on the basis of the financial statements. Accordingly, an entity shall disclose the following for each material category of non-adjusting event after the balance sheet date:

(a)   the nature of the event; and

(b)   an estimate of its financial effect, or a statement that such an estimate cannot be made.

14.4   The date on which the financial statements are approved for issue and who gave that approval shall be disclosed in the financial statements.

15   RELATED PARTY DISCLOSURES

15.1   Where the reporting entity:

(a)   purchases, sells or transfers goods and other **assets** or **liabilities**; or

(b)   renders or receives services; or

(c)   provides or receives finance or financial support; (irrespective of whether a price is charged) to, from or on behalf of a **related party**, then such material* transactions shall be disclosed, including:

(i)   the names of the transacting **related parties**;

(ii)   a description of the relationship between the parties;

(iii)   a description of the transactions;

(iv)   the amounts involved;

(v)   any other elements of the transactions necessary for an under-standing of the financial statements;

(vi)   the amounts due to or from **related parties** at the balance sheet date and provisions for doubtful debts due from such parties at that date; and

(vii)   amounts written off in the period in respect of debts due to or from **related parties**.

15.2   Personal guarantees given by **directors** in respect of **borrowings** by the reporting entity shall be disclosed in the notes to the financial statements.

15.3   AMOUNTS INCLUDED IN THE PROFIT AND LOSS ACCOUNT UNDER 'INVESTMENT INCOME' AND 'OTHER INTEREST RECEIVABLE AND SIMILAR INCOME' THAT WERE RECEIVED, OR ARE RECEIVABLE FROM GROUP UNDERTAKINGS, SHALL BE DISCLOSED SEPARATELY.

15.4   'INTEREST PAYABLE AND SIMILAR CHARGES' PAID, OR PAYABLE, TO GROUP UNDERTAKINGS, SHALL BE SHOWN SEPARATELY.

15.5   COMMITMENTS WHICH ARE UNDERTAKEN ON BEHALF OF OR FOR THE BENEFIT OF (A) ANY PARENT UNDERTAKING OR FELLOW **SUBSIDIARY UNDERTAKING**, OR (B) ANY **SUBSIDIARY UNDERTAKING** OF THE COMPANY, SHALL BE DISCLOSED SEPARATELY FROM THOSE COMMITMENTS DISCLOSED UNDER PARAGRAPHS 10.2 AND 11.8 TO 11.11, AND COMMITMENTS UNDERTAKEN UNDER (A) SHALL BE DISCLOSED SEPARATELY FROM THOSE UNDERTAKEN UNDER (B).

15.6   Other transactions with **related parties** may be disclosed on an aggregated basis (aggregation of similar transactions by type of **related party**) unless disclosure of an individual transaction, or connected transactions, is necessary for an understanding of the impact of the transactions on the financial statements of the reporting entity or is required by law.

The materiality of a related party transaction shall be judged in terms of its significance to the reporting entity.

Disclosure, as a **related party** transaction, is not required of: **15.7**

(a) pension contributions paid to a pension fund;
(b) emoluments in respect of services as an employee of the reporting entity; or
(c) transactions with the parties listed below simply as a result of their role as:

    (i) providers of finance in the course of their business in that regard;
    (ii) utility companies;
    (iii) **government** departments and their sponsored bodies; or
    (iv) a customer, supplier, franchiser, distributor or general agent.

When the reporting entity is controlled by another party, there shall be disclosure of **15.8** the **related party** relationship and the name of that party and, if different, that of the ultimate controlling party. If the controlling party or ultimate controlling party of the reporting entity is not known, that fact shall be disclosed. This information shall be disclosed irrespective of whether any transactions have taken place between the controlling parties and the reporting entity.

WHERE THE COMPANY IS A **SUBSIDIARY UNDERTAKING**, THE FOLLOWING INFORMATION SHALL **15.9** BE GIVEN WITH RESPECT TO THE COMPANY (IF ANY) REGARDED BY THE DIRECTORS AS BEING THE COMPANY'S ULTIMATE PARENT COMPANY:

(A) THE NAME OF THAT COMPANY; AND
(B) ITS COUNTRY OF INCORPORATION IF OUTSIDE GREAT BRITAIN.

*Parent undertaking drawing up accounts for larger group**

WHERE THE COMPANY IS A **SUBSIDIARY UNDERTAKING**, THE FOLLOWING INFORMATION SHALL **15.10** BE GIVEN WITH RESPECT TO THE PARENT UNDERTAKING OF:

(A) THE LARGEST GROUP OF WHICH IT IS A MEMBER FOR WHICH GROUP ACCOUNTS ARE DRAWN UP; AND
(B) THE SMALLEST SUCH GROUP OF UNDERTAKINGS:

    (I) THE NAME OF THE PARENT UNDERTAKING,
    (II) THE COUNTRY OF INCORPORATION, IF OUTSIDE GREAT BRITAIN;
    (III) IF UNINCORPORATED, THE ADDRESS OF ITS PRINCIPAL PLACE OF BUSINESS; AND
    (IV) IF COPIES OF EITHER OF THE GROUP ACCOUNTS REFERRED TO IN (A) OR (B) ABOVE ARE AVAILABLE TO THE PUBLIC, THE ADDRESS FROM WHICH THEY MAY BE OBTAINED.

Transactions with directors

DISCLOSURE SHALL BE PROVIDED IN RESPECT OF ANY OF THE FOLLOWING TRANSACTIONS **15.11** WITH **DIRECTORS** (INCLUDING SHADOW DIRECTORS):

(A) ANY LOANS, **QUASI-LOANS**, CREDIT TRANSACTIONS AND ANY GUARANTEE OR SECURITY IN CONNECTION THEREWITH;
(B) ANY AGREEMENT (BY THE COMPANY OR A SUBSIDIARY) TO ENTER INTO ANY SUCH TRANSACTION;

*INFORMATION NEED NOT BE DISCLOSED WITH RESPECT TO AN UNDERTAKING WHICH IS ESTABLISHED UNDER THE LAW OF A COUNTRY OUTSIDE THE UNITED KINGDOM OR CARRIES ON BUSINESS OUTSIDE THE UNITED KINGDOM, IF IN THE OPINION OF THE DIRECTORS OF THE COMPANY THE DISCLOSURE WOULD BE SERIOUSLY PREJUDICIAL TO THE BUSINESS OF THAT UNDERTAKING, OR TO THE BUSINESS OF THE COMPANY OR ANY OF ITS SUBSIDIARY UNDERTAKINGS, AND THE DTI AGREES THAT THE INFORMATION NEED NOT BE DISCLOSED. WHERE ADVANTAGE IS TAKEN OF THIS EXEMPTION, THAT FACT SHALL BE STATED IN A NOTE TO THE COMPANY'S ANNUAL ACCOUNTS. This statutory exemption is not available in the Republic of Ireland.

(c)   ANY ASSIGNMENT TO THE COMPANY OR AN ASSUMPTION BY IT OF RIGHTS, **OBLIGATIONS** OR LIABILITIES UNDER ANY SUCH TRANSACTION WHICH, HAD IT BEEN ENTERED INTO BY THE COMPANY WOULD HAVE CONTRAVENED THE ACT; AND

(d)   ANY ARRANGEMENT BY THE COMPANY WHEREBY ANOTHER PARTY ENTERS INTO ANY SUCH TRANSACTION WHICH IF ENTERED INTO BY THE COMPANY WOULD HAVE CONTRAVENED THE ACT AND WHEREBY THAT OTHER PARTY OBTAINS ANY BENEFIT FROM THE COMPANY OR OTHER GROUP COMPANY.

15.12   FOR EACH TRANSACTION, ARRANGEMENT OR AGREEMENT, SEPARATE DISCLOSURE SHALL BE PROVIDED OF:

(A)   A STATEMENT THAT IT WAS MADE OR SUBSISTED DURING THE PERIOD;
(B)   THE NAME OF THE **DIRECTOR** AND, WHERE APPLICABLE, THE CONNECTED PERSON; AND
(C)   ITS PRINCIPAL TERMS.

15.13   ADDITIONALLY, DISCLOSURE SHALL BE PROVIDED:

(A)   FOR A LOAN OR AGREEMENT FOR A LOAN OR AN ARRANGEMENT UNDER (C) OR (D) ABOVE IN RELATION TO A LOAN:

(I)   AMOUNT OF THE LIABILITY (PRINCIPAL AND INTEREST) AT THE BEGINNING AND END OF THE **FINANCIAL YEAR**;
(II)   THE MAXIMUM AMOUNT OF THE LIABILITY AT ANY TIME DURING THE PERIOD;
(III)   AMOUNT OF INTEREST DUE BUT UNPAID; AND
(IV)   ANY PROVISION IN THE ACCOUNTS FOR NON-RECOVERY OF ALL OR PART OF THE LOAN OR ANY INTEREST THEREON; AND

(B)   FOR A GUARANTEE OR SECURITY OR AN ARRANGEMENT UNDER (C) ABOVE IN RELATION TO A GUARANTEE OR SECURITY:

(I)   AMOUNT OF THE LIABILITY OF THE COMPANY (OR SUBSIDIARY) AT BEGINNING AND END OF THE **FINANCIAL YEAR**;
(II)   MAXIMUM AMOUNT FOR WHICH THE COMPANY (OR SUBSIDIARY) MAY BECOME LIABLE; AND
(III)   ANY AMOUNT PAID OR LIABILITY INCURRED BY THE COMPANY (OR A SUBSIDIARY) IN FULFILLING A GUARANTEE OR IN DISCHARGING ANY SECURITY; AND

(C)   FOR ANY OTHER TRANSACTION (I.E. INCLUDING **QUASI-LOANS** AND CREDIT TRANSACTIONS), THE VALUE OF THE TRANSACTION OR ARRANGEMENT.

15.14   FOR ANY TRANSACTION OR ARRANGEMENT (OTHER THAN LOANS) IN WHICH A **DIRECTOR** (INCLUDING A SHADOW DIRECTOR) OR CONNECTED PERSON HAD DIRECTLY OR INDIRECTLY A MATERIAL INTEREST, DISCLOSE :

(A)   A STATEMENT THAT IT WAS MADE OR SUBSISTED DURING THE PERIOD;
(B)   ITS PRINCIPAL TERMS;
(C)   THE NAME OF THE PERSON FOR WHOM IT WAS MADE (I.E. THE OTHER PARTIES TO THE TRANSACTIONS) AND WHERE THAT PERSON IS CONNECTED WITH A **DIRECTOR**, THE NAME OF THE **DIRECTOR**;
(D)   THE NAME OF THE **DIRECTOR** WITH THE MATERIAL INTEREST AND THE NATURE OF THE INTEREST; AND
(E)   THE VALUE OF THE TRANSACTION OR ARRANGEMENT.

15.15   IN RESPECT OF TRANSACTIONS, ARRANGEMENTS AND AGREEMENTS BY THE COMPANY AND, FOR HOLDING COMPANIES, BY THEIR SUBSIDIARIES, FOR PERSONS WHO AT ANY TIME DURING THE **FINANCIAL YEAR** WERE OFFICERS OF THE COMPANY (BUT NOT **DIRECTORS**), UNDER EACH OF:

(A)   LOANS;
(B)   **QUASI-LOANS**;

(c)   CREDIT TRANSACTIONS,

IN EACH CASE INCLUDING RELATED GUARANTEES, SECURITY, ARRANGEMENTS FOR ASSIGNMENT OR ASSUMPTION, AND INDIRECT ARRANGEMENTS, THE FOLLOWING SHALL BE DISCLOSED FOR EACH CATEGORY:

(I)   THE AGGREGATE AMOUNTS OUTSTANDING AT THE END OF THE **FINANCIAL YEAR** (COMPARATIVE AMOUNTS NOT REQUIRED); AND

(II)   THE NUMBER OF OFFICERS FOR WHOM THEY WERE MADE.

Subsidiary undertakings

THE FOLLOWING INFORMATION SHALL BE GIVEN WHERE AT THE END OF THE **FINANCIAL YEAR** THE COMPANY HAS **SUBSIDIARY UNDERTAKINGS**;   **15.16**

(A)   THE NAME OF EACH **SUBSIDIARY UNDERTAKING** SHALL BE STATED;

(B)   WITH RESPECT TO EACH **SUBSIDIARY UNDERTAKING** IF IT IS INCORPORATED OUTSIDE GREAT BRITAIN, THE COUNTRY IN WHICH IT IS INCORPORATED; IF IT IS UNINCORPORATED, THE ADDRESS OF ITS PRINCIPAL PLACE OF BUSINESS; AND

(C)   THE REASON WHY THE COMPANY IS NOT REQUIRED TO PREPARE GROUP ACCOUNTS SHALL BE STATED. IF THE REASON IS THAT ALL THE **SUBSIDIARY UNDERTAKINGS** OF THE COMPANY FALL WITHIN THE EXCLUSIONS PROVIDED FOR IN SECTION 229 OF THE COMPANIES ACT 1985*, IT SHALL BE STATED WITH RESPECT TO EACH **SUBSIDIARY UNDERTAKING** WHICH OF THOSE EXCLUSIONS APPLIES.

Holdings in subsidiary undertakings†

THERE SHALL BE STATED IN RELATION TO SHARES OF EACH CLASS HELD BY THE COMPANY IN   **15.17**
A **SUBSIDIARY UNDERTAKING** -

(A)   THE IDENTITY OF THE CLASS; AND

(B)   THE PROPORTION OF THE NOMINAL VALUE OF THE SHARES OF THAT CLASS REPRESENTED BY THOSE SHARES.

THE SHARES HELD BY THE COMPANY ITSELF SHALL BE DISTINGUISHED FROM THOSE ATTRIBUTED BY THE COMPANY WHICH ARE HELD BY OR ON BEHALF OF THE SUBSIDIARY UNDERTAKING

Financial information about subsidiary undertakings

THERE SHALL BE DISCLOSED WITH RESPECT TO EACH **SUBSIDIARY UNDERTAKING** -   **15.18**

(A)   THE AGGREGATE AMOUNT OF ITS CAPITAL AND RESERVES AS AT THE END OF ITS RELEVANT **FINANCIAL YEAR**; AND

(B)   ITS PROFIT OR LOSS FOR THAT YEAR.

THAT INFORMATION NEED NOT BE GIVEN IF: **15.19**

A SUBSIDIARY UNDERTAKING MAY BE EXCLUDED FROM CONSOLIDATION IF ONE OF THE FOLLOWING CONDITIONS APPLIES: (1) THE SUBSIDIARY IS NOT MATERIAL, (2) SEVERE LONG-TERM RESTRICTIONS SUBSTANTIALLY HINDER THE EXERCISE OF THE RIGHTS OF THE PARENT COMPANY OVER THE ASSETS OR MANAGEMENT OF THE UNDERTAKING, (3) INFORMATION FOR THE PREPARATION OF GROUP ACCOUNTS CANNOT BE OBTAINED WITHOUT DISPROPORTIONATE EXPENSE OR UNDUE DELAY, (4) THE INTEREST OF THE PARENT COMPANY IS HELD EXCLUSIVELY WITH A VIEW TO SUBSEQUENT RESALE.

†DISCLOSURE REQUIREMENTS FOR HOLDINGS IN UNDERTAKINGS OTHER THAN SUBSIDIARY UNDERTAKINGS ARE SET OUT IN PARAGRAPH 6.33

(A)   THE COMPANY IS EXEMPT BY VIRTUE OF SECTION 228 OF THE COMPANIES ACT 1985 FROM THE REQUIREMENT TO PREPARE GROUP ACCOUNTS;

(B)   THE COMPANY'S INVESTMENT IN THE SUBSIDIARY UNDERTAKING IS INCLUDED IN THE COMPANY'S ACCOUNTS BY WAY OF THE EQUITY METHOD OF VALUATION;

(C)   THE SUBSIDIARY UNDERTAKING IS NOT REQUIRED BY ANY PROVISION OF THE COMPANIES ACT 1985 TO DELIVER A COPY OF ITS BALANCE SHEET FOR ITS RELEVANT FINANCIAL YEAR AND DOES NOT OTHERWISE PUBLISH THAT BALANCE SHEET IN GREAT BRITAIN OR ELSEWHERE, AND THE COMPANY'S HOLDING IS LESS THAN 50 PER CENT OF THE NOMINAL VALUE OF THE SHARES IN THE UNDERTAKING; OR

(D)   IT IS NOT MATERIAL.

15.20   THE "RELEVANT FINANCIAL YEAR" OF A SUBSIDIARY UNDERTAKING IS -

(A)   IF ITS FINANCIAL YEAR ENDS WITH THAT OF THE COMPANY, THAT YEAR; AND

(B)   IF NOT, ITS FINANCIAL YEAR ENDING LAST BEFORE THE END OF THE COMPANY'S FINANCIAL YEAR.

Membership of certain undertakings

15.21   THE FOLLOWING INFORMATION SHALL BE GIVEN WHERE AT THE END OF THE FINANCIAL YEAR THE COMPANY IS A MEMBER OF A QUALIFYING UNDERTAKING:

(A)   THE NAME AND LEGAL FORM OF THE UNDERTAKING; AND

(B)   THE ADDRESS OF THE UNDERTAKING'S REGISTERED OFFICE (WHETHER IN OR OUTSIDE GREAT BRITAIN) OR, IF IT DOES NOT HAVE SUCH AN OFFICE, ITS HEAD OFFICE (WHETHER IN OR OUTSIDE GREAT BRITAIN).

15.22   WHERE THE UNDERTAKING IS A QUALIFYING PARTNERSHIP THERE SHALL ALSO BE STATED EITHER -

(A)   THAT A COPY OF THE LATEST ACCOUNTS OF THE UNDERTAKING HAS BEEN OR IS TO BE APPENDED TO THE COPY OF THE COMPANY'S ACCOUNTS SENT TO THE REGISTRAR; OR

(B)   THE NAME OF AT LEAST ONE BODY CORPORATE (WHICH MAY BE THE COMPANY) IN WHOSE GROUP ACCOUNTS THE UNDERTAKING HAS BEEN OR IS TO BE DEALT WITH ON A CONSOLIDATED BASIS.

15.23   INFORMATION OTHERWISE REQUIRED BY PARAGRAPH 15.21 ABOVE NEED NOT BE GIVEN IF IT IS NOT MATERIAL.

15.24   INFORMATION OTHERWISE REQUIRED BY PARAGRAPH 15.22 (B) ABOVE NEED NOT BE GIVEN IF THE NOTES TO THE COMPANY'S ACCOUNTS DISCLOSE THAT THE COMPANY IS EXEMPT BECAUSE THE PARTNERSHIP IS DEALT WITH ON A CONSOLIDATED BASIS IN GROUP ACCOUNTS PEPARED BY (I) A MEMBER OF THE PARTNERSHIP ESTABLISHED UNDER LAW, OR (II) A PARENT UNDERTAKING OF SUCH A MEMBER.

16   CONSOLIDATED FINANCIAL STATEMENTS

16.1   Where the reporting entity is preparing **consolidated financial statements**, it should regard as standard the accounting practices and disclosure requirements set out in FRSs 2, 6, 7 and, as they apply in respect of **consolidated financial statements**, FRSs 5, 9, 10*, 11. and 28. Where the reporting entity is part of a group that prepares publicly available **consolidated financial statements**, it is entitled to the exemptions given in FRS 8 paragraph 3(a)-(c).

*FRS 10 and, as directed by FRS 10, FRS 11 need be applied only in respect of purchased goodwill arising on consolidation.

Form and content of small group accounts*

WHERE A SMALL COMPANY IIAS PREPARED INDIVIDUAL ACCOUNTS IN ACCORDANCE WITH **16.2**
THE LEGAL REQUIREMENTS REFLECTED IN THE FRSSE AND IS PREPARING GROUP ACCOUNTS
IN RESPECT OF THE SAME YEAR PARAGRAPHS 16.3 TO 16.5 SHALL APPLY.

IN PREPARING GROUP ACCOUNTS, A COMPANY SHALL HAVE REGARD TO THE LEGAL **16.3**
REQUIREMENTS REFLECTED IN THE FRSSE AND SCHEDULE 4A OF THE COMPANIES ACT
1985. ANY REFERENCES IN THAT SCHEDULE TO COMPLIANCE WITH THE PROVISIONS OF
'SCHEDULE 4' SHALL BE CONSTRUED AS REFERENCES TO THE LEGAL REQUIREMENTS
REFLECTED IN THE FRSSE.

THE BALANCE SHEET FORMAT SET OUT IN PARAGRAPH 2.27 SHALL BE MODIFIED AS FOL- **16.4**
LOWS. FOR ITEM B.III 'INVESTMENTS' SUBSTITUTE:

"B.III INVESTMENTS

1. SHARES IN GROUP UNDERTAKINGS
2. INTERESTS IN ASSOCIATED UNDERTAKINGS
3. OTHER PARTICIPATING INTERESTS
4. LOANS TO GROUP UNDERTAKINGS AND UNDERTAKINGS IN WHICH A PARTICIPATING
INTEREST IS HELD
5. OTHER INVESTMENTS OTHER THAN LOANS
6. OTHERS."

WHERE GROUP ACCOUNTS ARE PREPARED THE BALANCE SHEET SHALL CONTAIN IN A PRO- **16.5**
MINENT POSITION ON THE BALANCE SHEET, ABOVE THE SIGNATURE REQUIRED BY PARAGRAPH
2.30, THAT THEY ARE PREPARED IN ACCORDANCE WITH THE SPECIAL PROVISIONS IN PART
VII OF THE COMPANIES ACT RELATING TO SMALL COMPANIES.

17 DIRECTORS' EMOLUMENTS

THE AGGREGATE TOTAL OF THE FOLLOWING ITEMS SHALL BE DISCLOSED IN RESPECT OF **17.1**
DIRECTORS' EMOLUMENTS:

(A) THE AGGREGATE AMOUNT OF EMOLUMENTS PAID TO OR RECEIVABLE BY **DIRECTORS** IN
RESPECT OF **QUALIFYING SERVICES**;
(B) THE AGGREGATE OF THE AMOUNT OF MONEY PAID TO OR RECEIVABLE BY **DIRECTORS**
UNDER LONG-TERM INCENTIVE SCHEMES AND THE NET VALUE OF ASSETS (OTHER THAN
MONEY, SHARES AND SHARE OPTIONS) RECEIVED OR RECEIVABLE UNDER SUCH
SCHEMES IN RESPECT OF SUCH SERVICES; AND
(C) THE VALUE OF ANY COMPANY CONTRIBUTIONS PAID, OR TREATED AS PAID, TO A
PENSION SCHEME IN RESPECT OF **DIRECTORS' QUALIFYING SERVICES**, TO A **MONEY
PURCHASE SCHEME**.

IN THE CASE OF **MONEY PURCHASE SCHEMES** AND **DEFINED BENEFIT SCHEMES**, DISCLOSE THE
NUMBER OF **DIRECTORS** (IF ANY) TO WHOM **RETIREMENT BENEFITS** ARE ACCRUING IN RESPECT
OF **QUALIFYING SERVICES**.

DISCLOSURE SHALL BE PROVIDED OF THE AGGREGATE AMOUNTS OF ANY COMPENSATION TO **17.2**
DIRECTORS OR PAST **DIRECTORS** IN RESPECT OF LOSS OF OFFICE, INCLUDING THE ESTIMATED
AMOUNT OF BENEFITS IN KIND AND STATING THE NATURE OF SUCH BENEFITS.

**There are no special provisions in Republic of Ireland company law that relate to the preparation of group
accounts by small companies. See Appendix I.*

17.3   DISCLOSURE SHALL BE PROVIDED OF THE AGGREGATE AMOUNT OF ANY CONSIDERATION PAID TO, OR RECEIVABLE BY, THIRD PARTIES* FOR MAKING AVAILABLE THE SERVICES OF ANY PERSON:

(A)   AS A **DIRECTOR** OF THE COMPANY; OR

(B)   WHILE **DIRECTOR** OF THE COMPANY, AS **DIRECTOR** OF ANY SUBSIDIARY UNDERTAKING, OR OTHERWISE IN CONNECTION WITH THE MANAGEMENT OF THE AFFAIRS OF THE COMPANY OR ANY OF ITS **SUBSIDIARY UNDERTAKINGS.**

THE REFERENCE TO CONSIDERATION INCLUDES BENEFITS IN KIND AND THE ESTIMATED MONEY VALUE OF SUCH BENEFITS AND THEIR NATURE SHALL BE STATED.

18   THE DIRECTORS' REPORT

Introduction

18.1   THE FOLLOWING DISCLOSURES SHALL BE PROVIDED IN THE DIRECTORS' REPORT:

(A)   THE PRINCIPAL ACTIVITIES OF THE COMPANY;

(B)   DETAILS OF THE COMPANY'S **DIRECTORS** AND THEIR INTERESTS IN THE COMPANY;

(C)   POLITICAL AND CHARITABLE GIFTS;

(D)   ACQUISITION OF OWN SHARES; AND

(E)   EMPLOYMENT OF DISABLED PERSONS.

18.2   THE REPORT SHALL BE APPROVED BY THE BOARD AND SIGNED ON THEIR BEHALF. IT SHALL STATE THE NAME OF THE PERSON WHO HAS SIGNED THE REPORT.

The principal activities of the company

18.3   THE REPORT SHALL STATE THE PRINCIPAL ACTIVITIES OF THE COMPANY AND ITS SUB-SIDIARIES DURING THE YEAR. These activities will be the various classes of business in which the company operates.

Details of the company's directors and their interests in the company†

18.4   THE REPORT SHALL STATE THE NAMES OF THE PERSONS WHO, AT ANY TIME DURING THE **FINANCIAL YEAR**, WERE **DIRECTORS** OF THE COMPANY.

18.5   THE REPORT SHALL STATE FOR EACH PERSON WHO AT THE END OF THE **FINANCIAL YEAR** WAS A DIRECTOR, DETAILS OF ANY SHARES OR DEBENTURES HELD AT THE END OF THE **FINANCIAL YEAR**. WHERE SUCH AN INTEREST ARISES, THE REPORT SHALL STATE:

(A)   THE NAME OF THE COMPANY;

(B)   THE NUMBER OF SHARES AND THE AMOUNT OF DEBENTURES;

(C)   A DESCRIPTION OF SHARES; AND

(D)   A COMPARATIVE FIGURE AT THE BEGINNING OF THE YEAR OR DATE OF APPOINTMENT IF LATER (OR A NEGATIVE STATEMENT).

IF NO INTEREST ARISES THE REPORT SHALL PROVIDE A NEGATIVE STATEMENT.

Third parties are persons other than (1) the director himself or a person connected with him or body corporate controlled by him, and (2) the company or any of its subsidiary undertakings. Amounts paid to or receivable by a person connected with a director, or a body corporate controlled by a director, shall be included instead within the disclosures set out in paragraph 17.1.

†THE INFORMATION REQUIRED BY PARAGRAPHS 18.6 AND 18.7 MAY ALTERNATIVELY BE GIVEN BY WAY OF NOTES TO THE ANNUAL ACCOUNTS.

THE REPORT SHALL DISCLOSE WHETHER A DIRECTOR, OR MEMBERS OF THEIR **IMMEDIATE** **18.6** **FAMILY**, WAS GRANTED OR EXERCISED THE RIGHT TO SUBSCRIBE TO SHARES IN RESPECT OF EACH GROUP COMPANY DURING THE YEAR. IF SUCH RIGHTS WERE GRANTED OR EXERCISED, THE REPORT SHALL NOTE THE NUMBER OF SHARES INVOLVED.

Disclosure of qualifying third party indemnity provisions

IF A DIRECTORS' REPORT IS APPROVED ON OR AFTER 6 APRIL 2005 AND IF AT THE TIME **18.7** WHEN THE REPORT IS APPROVED ANY QUALIFYING THIRD PARTY INDEMNITY PROVISION (WHETHER MADE BY THE COMPANY OR OTHERWISE) IS IN FORCE OR WAS IN FORCE DURING THE FINANCIAL YEAR FOR THE BENEFIT OF ONE OR MORE DIRECTORS OF THE COMPANY (OR OF AN ASSOCIATED COMPANY), THE REPORT SHALL STATE THAT ANY SUCH PROVISION IS OR WAS IN FORCE.

Political and charitable gifts

IF THE COMPANY, OR THE COMPANY AND ITS SUBSIDIARIES, MADE ANY DONATIONS TO A **18.8** REGISTERED POLITICAL PARTY OR OTHER POLITICAL ORGANISATION IN THE EU (INCLUDING THE UK) OR INCURRED EU POLITICAL EXPENDITURE EXCEEDING £200 IN AGGREGATE IN THE **FINANCIAL YEAR** THEN DISCLOSE:

(A) FOR EU DONATIONS – THE TOTAL AMOUNT GIVEN TO EACH NAMED POLITICAL PARTY, BY THE COMPANY AND EACH SUBSIDIARY THAT HAS DONATED OR INCURRED SUCH EXPENDITURE; AND

(B) FOR EU POLITICAL EXPENDITURE – THE TOTAL AMOUNT INCURRED BY THE COMPANY AND EACH SUBSIDIARY INDIVIDUALLY.

IF THE COMPANY, OR THE COMPANY AND ITS SUBSIDIARIES MADE ANY CONTRIBUTIONS TO NON-EU POLITICAL PARTIES, DISCLOSE THE TOTAL CONTRIBUTIONS MADE BY THE COMPANY AND ITS SUBSIDIARIES.

IF THE COMPANY, OR THE COMPANY AND ITS SUBSIDIARIES, HAS GIVEN MONEY FOR CHARITABLE PURPOSES EXCEEDING £200 DISCLOSE THE TOTAL AMOUNT GIVEN FOR EACH PURPOSE.

*Acquisition of own shares**

WHERE THE COMPANY ACQUIRES ITS OWN SHARES, EITHER BY PURCHASE OR ACQUISITION BY **18.9** FORFEITURE, THE FOLLOWING SHALL BE DISCLOSED:

(A) THE NUMBER AND NOMINAL VALUE OF SHARES PURCHASED, THE AGGREGATE CON-SIDERATION PAID FOR THE SHARES AND THE REASONS FOR THE PURCHASE;

(B) THE NUMBER AND NOMINAL VALUE OF SHARES ACQUIRED;

(C) THE MAXIMUM NUMBER AND NOMINAL VALUE OF SHARES ACQUIRED OR CHARGED DURING THE YEAR; AND

(D) THE NUMBER AND NOMINAL VALUE OF SUCH SHARES ACQUIRED WHICH WERE DIS-POSED OF IN THE YEAR. THE AMOUNT OF MONEY RECEIVED SHALL BE DISCLOSED WHERE THE SHARES WERE DISPOSED OF FOR MONEY.

*THESE DISCLOSURE REQUIREMENTS APPLY WHERE OWN SHARES ARE: (I) PURCHASED BY THE COMPANY OR ACQUIRED BY THE COMPANY BY FORFEITURE OR SURRENDER IN LIEU OF FORFEITURE; (II) ACQUIRED BY THE COMPANY OTHERWISE THAN FOR VALUABLE CONSIDERATION; (III) ACQUIRED BY A NOMINEE OF THE COMPANY WITHOUT FINANCIAL ASSISTANCE FROM THE COMPANY, OR BY ANY PERSON WITH FINANCIAL ASSISTANCE FROM THE COMPANY, AND, IN EITHER CASE, THE COMPANY HAS A BENEFICIAL INTEREST IN THE SHARES; OR (IV) MADE SUBJECT TO A LIEN OR CHARGE UNDER s150 OR s6(3) OF THE CONSEQUENTIAL PROVISIONS ACT 1985.

IN EACH OF THE ABOVE CASES, THE PERCENTAGE OF THE CALLED-UP SHARE CAPITAL WHICH THEY REPRESENT AND, IN EACH CASE WHERE SHARES HAVE BEEN CHARGED, THE AMOUNT OF THE CHARGE.

Employment of disabled persons

18.10   WHERE THE AVERAGE NUMBER OF EMPLOYEES EXCEEDS 250 THE DIRECTORS' REPORT SHALL INCLUDE A STATEMENT DESCRIBING THE POLICY WHICH THE COMPANY HAS ADOPTED FOR:

(A)   GIVING FULL AND FAIR CONSIDERATION TO APPLICATIONS FOR EMPLOYMENT BY DISABLED PERSONS, HAVING REGARD TO THEIR PARTICULAR APTITUDES AND ABILITIES;

(B)   CONTINUING EMPLOYMENT AND APPROPRIATE TRAINING FOR EMPLOYEES OF THE COMPANY WHO BECAME DISABLED DURING THE PERIOD WHEN THEY WERE EMPLOYED BY THE COMPANY; AND

(C)   OTHERWISE FOR THE TRAINING, CAREER DEVELOPMENT AND PROMOTION OF DISABLED PERSONS EMPLOYED BY THE COMPANY.

Statement as to disclosure of information to auditors

18.11   THE DIRECTORS' REPORT SHALL CONTAIN A STATEMENT THAT, SO FAR AS EACH OF THE DIRECTORS AT THE TIME THE REPORT IS APPROVED ARE AWARE:

(A)   THERE IS NO RELEVANT AUDIT INFORMATION OF WHICH THE COMPANY'S AUDITORS ARE UNAWARE, AND

(B)   THE DIRECTORS HAVE TAKEN ALL STEPS THAT THEY OUGHT TO HAVE TAKEN TO MAKE THEMSELVES AWARE OF ANY RELEVANT AUDIT INFORMATION AND TO ESTABLISH THAT THE AUDITORS ARE AWARE OF THAT INFORMATION.

Approval and signing of the Directors' Report

18.12   THE DIRECTORS' REPORT SHALL BE APPROVED BY THE BOARD OF **DIRECTORS** AND SIGNED ON BEHALF OF THE BOARD BY A **DIRECTOR** OR THE SECRETARY OF THE COMPANY. EVERY COPY OF THE DIRECTORS' REPORT WHICH IS LAID BEFORE THE COMPANY IN GENERAL MEETING, OR WHICH IS OTHERWISE CIRCULATED, PUBLISHED OR ISSUED, SHALL STATE THE NAME OF THE PERSON WHO SIGNED IT ON BEHALF OF THE BOARD.

18.13   THE COPY OF THE DIRECTORS' REPORT WHICH IS DELIVERED TO THE REGISTRAR SHALL BE SIGNED ON BEHALF OF THE BOARD BY A **DIRECTOR** OR THE SECRETARY OF THE COMPANY.

18.14   THE DIRECTORS' REPORT SHALL CONTAIN A STATEMENT THAT THE ACCOUNTS HAVE BEEN PREPARED IN ACCORDANCE WITH THE SPECIAL PROVISIONS IN PART VII OF THE COMPANIES ACT 1985 RELATING TO SMALL COMPANIES.

18.15   IF A COPY OF THE DIRECTORS' REPORT -

(A)   IS LAID BEFORE THE COMPANY, OR OTHERWISE CIRCULATED, PUBLISHED OR ISSUED, WITHOUT THE REPORT HAVING BEEN SIGNED AS REQUIRED BY THIS SECTION OR WITHOUT THE REQUIRED STATEMENT OF THE SIGNATORY'S NAME BEING INCLUDED; OR

(B)   IS DELIVERED TO THE REGISTRAR WITHOUT BEING SIGNED AS REQUIRED BY THIS SECTION,

THE COMPANY AND EVERY OFFICER OF IT WHO IS IN DEFAULT IS GUILTY OF AN OFFENCE AND LIABLE TO A FINE.

19 DATE FROM WHICH EFFECTIVE AND TRANSITIONAL ARRANGEMENTS

The accounting practices set out in this Financial Reporting Standard for Smaller **19.1** Entities (effective January 2007) shall be regarded as standard in respect of financial statements relating to accounting periods beginning on or after 1 January 2007. Earlier application is permitted.*

Transitional arrangements - goodwill

All goodwill that was eliminated against reserves in accordance with an **accounting** **19.2** **policy** permitted until 23 March 1999 may remain eliminated against reserves thereafter.† Alternatively, in its first accounting period beginning on or after 23 March 1999, an entity may reinstate by prior period adjustment all goodwill previously eliminated against reserves.

Transitional arrangements - tangible fixed assets

Where, for its first accounting period ending on or after 23 March 2000, an entity **19.3** does not adopt an **accounting policy** of revaluation, but the carrying amount of its **tangible fixed assets** reflects previous revaluations, it may:

(a) retain the book amounts. In these circumstances the entity shall disclose the fact that the transitional provisions of the FRSSE are being followed and that the valuation has not been updated and give the date of the last revaluation; or

(b) restate the carrying amount of the **tangible fixed assets** to historical cost (less restated accumulated **depreciation**), as a change in **accounting policy**.

Where, for its first accounting period ending on or after 23 March 2000, an entity **19.4** separates **tangible fixed assets** into different components with significantly different useful economic lives for **depreciation** purposes, the changes shall be dealt with as a prior period adjustment, as a change in **accounting policy**. Other revisions to the useful economic lives and **residual values** of **tangible fixed assets** are not the result of a change in **accounting policy** and shall be treated in accordance with paragraph 6.40 and not as **prior period adjustments**.

20 WITHDRAWAL OF THE FRSSE (EFFECTIVE JANUARY 2005)

The Financial Reporting Standard for Smaller Entities (effective January 2007) **20.1** supersedes the FRSSE (effective January 2005).

In permitting earlier application, directors will need to ensure that accounts prepared in accordance with this version of the FRSSE comply with company law requirements relevant to the period of account, particularly where these requirements may have since been amended.

†*The treatment of such amounts on disposal of a business is set out in paragraph 3.7.*

C – Definitions

The following definitions shall apply in the FRSSE and in particular in the Statement of Standard Accounting Practice set out in sections 1-20 of Part B.

Accounting policies:-

Those principles, bases, conventions, rules and practices applied by an entity that specify how the effects of transactions and other events are to be reflected in its financial statements through:

(i)   **recognising**;
(ii) selecting measurement bases for; and
(iii) presenting

assets, **liabilities**, gains, losses and changes to shareholders' funds. Accounting policies do not include **estimation techniques**.

Accounting policies define the process whereby transactions and other events are reflected in financial statements. For example, an accounting policy for a particular type of expenditure may specify whether an **asset** or a loss is to be **recognised**; the basis on which it is to be measured; and where in the profit and loss account or balance sheet it is to be presented.

Actuarial gains and losses:-

Changes in actuarial deficits or surpluses that arise because events have not coincided with the actuarial assumptions made for the last valuation or because the actuarial assumptions have changed.

Applied research:-

Original or critical investigation undertaken in order to gain new scientific or technical knowledge and directed towards a specific practical aim or objective.

Arrangement fees:-

The costs that are incurred directly in connection with the issue of a **capital instrument**, i.e. those costs that would not have been incurred if the specific instrument in question had not been issued.

Assets:-

Rights or other access to future economic benefits controlled by an entity as a result of past transactions or events.

Attributable profit (on long-term contracts):-

That part of the total profit currently estimated to arise over the duration of the contract, after allowing for estimated remedial and maintenance costs and increases in costs so far as not recoverable under the terms of the contract, that fairly reflects the profit attributable to that part of the work performed at the accounting date. (There can be no attributable profit until the profitable outcome of the contract can be assessed with reasonable certainty.)

Borrowings:-

Capital instruments that are classified as **liabilities**.

Capital instruments:-

All instruments that are issued (or arrangements entered into) by reporting entities as a means of raising finance, including shares, debentures, loans and debt instruments, options and warrants that give the holder the right to subscribe for or obtain capital instruments. In the case of **consolidated financial statements** the term includes capital instruments issued by subsidiaries except those that are held by another member of the group that is included in the consolidation.

Cash-settled share-based payment transaction:-

A **share-based payment transaction** in which the entity acquires goods or services by incurring a **liability** to transfer cash or other **assets** to the supplier of those goods or services for amounts that are based on the price (or value) of the entity's shares or other **equity instruments** of the entity.

Close family:-

Close members of the family of an individual are those family members, or members of the same household, who may be expected to influence, or be influenced by, that person in their dealings with the reporting entity.

Closing rate:-

The closing rate is the **exchange rate** for spot transactions ruling at the balance sheet date and is the mean of the buying and selling rates at the close of business on the day for which the rate is to be ascertained.

Companies legislation:-

(a)   In Great Britain, the Companies Act 1985 as amended by the Companies Act 1989;
(b)   in Northern Ireland, the Companies (Northern Ireland) Order 1986 as amended; and
(c)   in the Republic of Ireland, the Companies Acts 1963-2003 and all other Regulations to be read as one with the Companies Acts.

Consignment stock:-

Consignment stock is stock held by one party (the 'dealer') but legally owned by another (the 'manufacturer'), on terms that give the dealer the right to sell the stock in the normal course of its business or, at its option, to return it unsold to the legal owner.

Consolidated financial statements:-

The financial statements of a group prepared by consolidation. A group is a parent undertaking and its subsidiary undertakings. Consolidation is the process of adjusting and combining financial information from the individual financial statements of a parent undertaking and its subsidiary undertakings to prepare consolidated financial statements that present financial information for the group as a single economic entity.

Contingent asset:-

A possible **asset** that arises from past events and whose existence will be confirmed only by the occurrence of one or more uncertain future events not wholly within the entity's control.

Contingent liability:-

(a)   A possible **obligation** that arises from past events and whose existence will be confirmed only by the occurrence of one or more uncertain future events not wholly within the entity's control; or

(b)   an **obligation** at the balance sheet date that arises from past events but is not **recognised** as a **provision** because:

    (i)   it is not probable that a transfer of economic benefits will be required to settle the **obligation**; or

    (ii)   the amount of the **obligation** cannot be measured with sufficient **reliability**.

Cost (of stock):-

Cost is defined as being that expenditure which has been incurred in the normal course of business in bringing the product or service to its present location and condition. This expenditure should include, in addition to cost of purchase, such costs of conversion (including, for example, attributable overheads) as are appropriate to that location and condition. BORROWING COSTS THAT ARE DIRECTLY ATTRIBUTABLE TO THE ACQUISITION, CONSTRUCTION OR PRODUCTION OF STOCK MAY BE INCLUDED AS PART OF THE COST.

Current service cost:-

The increase in the present value of the **scheme liabilities** expected to arise from employee service in the current period.

Current tax:-

The amount of tax estimated to be payable or recoverable in respect of the taxable profit or loss for a period, along with adjustments to estimates in respect of previous periods.

Curtailment:-

An event that reduces the expected years of future service of present employees or reduces for a number of employees the accrual of defined benefits for some or all of their future service.

Deferred tax:-

Estimated future tax consequences of transactions and events **recognised** in the financial statements of the current and previous periods.

Defined benefit scheme:-

A pension or other **retirement benefit** scheme other than a **defined contribution scheme**. Normally, the scheme rules define the benefits independently of the contributions payable, and the benefits are not directly related to the investments of the scheme.

Defined contribution scheme:-

A pension or other **retirement benefit** scheme into which an employer pays regular contributions fixed as an amount or as a percentage of pay. The employer will have no legal or constructive **obligation** to pay further contributions if the scheme does not have sufficient **assets** to pay all employee benefits relating to employee service in the current and prior periods.

Depreciation:-

The measure of the cost or revalued amount of the economic benefits of a fixed **asset** that have been consumed during the period. Consumption includes the wearing out, using up or other reduction in the **useful economic life** of a fixed **asset** whether arising from use, effluxion of time or obsolescence through either changes in technology or demand for the goods and services produced by the **asset**.

Development:-

Use of scientific or technical knowledge in order to produce new or substantially improved materials, devices, products or services, to install new processes or systems before the commencement of commercial production or commercial applications, or to improve substantially those already produced or installed.

Directly attributable costs:-

The costs that relate directly to securing the specific contract after the asset recognition criteria for **pre-contract costs** are met, if they can be separately identified and measured reliably.

Directors:-

The directors of a company or other body, the partners, proprietors, committee of management or trustees of other forms of entity, or equivalent persons responsible for directing the entity's affairs and preparing its financial statements.

Employees and others providing similar services:-

Individuals who render personal services to the entity and either (a) the individuals are regarded as employees for legal or tax purposes, (b) the individuals work for the entity under its direction in the same way as individuals who are regarded as employees for legal or tax purposes, or (c) the services rendered are similar to those rendered by employees. For example, the term encompasses all management personnel, ie those persons having authority and responsibility for planning, directing and controlling the activities of the entity, including non-executive directors.

Equity instrument:-

Any contract that evidences a residual interest in the assets of an entity after deducting all of its liabilities.

Equity instrument granted:-

The right (conditional or unconditional) to an equity instrument of the entity conferred by the entity on another party, under a share-based payment arrangement.

Equity-settled share-based payment transaction:-

A **share-based payment transaction** in which the entity receives goods or services as consideration for **equity instruments** of the entity (including shares or share options).

Estimation techniques:-

The methods adopted by an entity to arrive at estimated monetary amounts, corresponding to the measurement bases selected, for **assets**, **liabilities**, gains, losses and changes to shareholders' funds.

Estimation techniques implement the measurement aspects of **accounting policies**. An **accounting policy** will specify the basis on which an item is to be measured; where there is uncertainty over the monetary amount corresponding to that basis, the amount will be arrived at by using an estimation technique.

Estimation techniques include, for example:-

(a)   methods of **depreciation**, such as straight-line and reducing balance, applied in the context of a particular measurement basis, used to estimate the proportion of the economic benefits of a tangible fixed asset consumed in a period; and

(b)   different methods used to estimate the proportion of trade debts that will not be recovered, particularly where such methods consider a population as a whole rather than individual balances.

Events after the balance sheet date:-

Those events, both favourable and unfavourable, that occur between the balance sheet date and the date when financial statements are authorised for issue. Two types of events can be identified:

Adjusting events

(a)   those that provide evidence of conditions that existed at the balance sheet date; and

Non-adjusting events

(b)   those that are indicative of conditions that arose after the balance sheet date.

Exceptional items:-

Material items that derive from events or transactions that fall within the **ordinary activities** of the reporting entity and individually or, if of a similar type, in aggregate need to be disclosed by virtue of their size or incidence if the financial statements are to give a true and fair view.

Exchange rate:-

An exchange rate is a rate at which two currencies may be exchanged for each other at a particular point in time; different rates apply for spot and forward transactions.

Exchange transaction:-

A transaction in which one party supplies goods or services to another party in exchange for a consideration, usually monetary.

Fair value:-

Fair value is the amount at which an **asset** or **liability** could be exchanged in an arm's length transaction between informed and willing parties, other than in a forced or liquidation sale, less, where applicable, any grants receivable towards the purchase or use of an **asset**.

Finance charge (on a lease):-

The finance charge is the amount borne by the lessee over the **lease term**, representing the difference between the total of the **minimum lease payments** (including any residual amounts guaranteed by the lessee) and the amount at which the lessee records the leased asset at the **inception** of the lease.

Finance costs (of a capital instrument):-

The difference between the net proceeds of a **capital instrument** and the total amount of the payments (or other transfer of economic benefits) that the issuer may be required to make in respect of the instrument other than **arrangement fees**.

Finance lease:-

A finance lease is a lease that transfers substantially all the risks and rewards of ownership of an asset to the lessee. It should be presumed that such a transfer of risks and rewards occurs if at the **inception** of a lease the present value of the **minimum lease payments**, including any initial payment, amounts to substantially all (normally 90 per cent or more) of the **fair value** of the leased asset. The present value should be calculated by using the interest rate implicit in the lease. If the **fair value** of the asset is not determinable an estimate thereof should be used.

Financial asset:-

Any asset that is:

(a) cash;
(b) an equity instrument of another entity;
(c) a contractual right:

    (i) to receive cash or another financial asset from another entity; or
    (ii) to exchange financial assets or financial liabilities with another entity under conditions that are potentially favourable to the entity; or

(d) a contract that will or may be settled in the entity's own equity instruments and is:

    (i) a non-derivative for which the entity is or may be obliged to receive a variable number of the entity's own equity instruments; or
    (ii) a derivative that will or may be settled other than by the exchange of a fixed amount of cash or another financial asset for a fixed number of the entity's own equity instruments. For this purpose the entity's own equity instruments do not include instruments that are themselves contracts for the future receipt or delivery of the entity's own equity instruments.

Financial instrument:-

Any contract that gives rise to a **financial asset** of one entity and a **financial liability** or equity instrument of another entity.

Financial liability:-

Any liability that is:

(a)   a contractual obligation:

   (i)   to deliver cash or another financial asset to another entity; or
   (ii)   to exchange financial assets or financial liabilities with another entity under conditions that are potentially unfavourable to the entity; or

(b)   a contract that will or may be settled in the entity's own equity instruments and is:

   (i)   a non-derivative for which the entity is or may be obliged to deliver a variable number of the entity's own equity instruments; or
   (ii)   a derivative that will or may be settled other than by the exchange of a fixed amount of cash or another financial asset for a fixed number of the entity's own equity instruments. For this purpose the entity's own equity instruments do not include instruments that are themselves contracts for the future receipt or delivery of the entity's own equity instruments.

FINANCIAL YEAR:-

A COMPANY'S **FINANCIAL YEAR** BEGINS WITH THE FIRST DAY OF ITS ACCOUNTING REFERENCE PERIOD AND ENDS WITH THE LAST DAY OF THAT PERIOD OR SUCH OTHER DATE, NOT MORE THAN SEVEN DAYS BEFORE OR AFTER THE END OF THAT PERIOD, AS THE **DIRECTORS** MAY DETERMINE.

Foreign entity:-

A foreign entity is a subsidiary, associated company or branch whose operations are based in a country other than that of the investing company or whose **assets** and **liabilities** are denominated mainly in a foreign currency.

Foreseeable losses (on a long-term contract):-

Losses that are currently estimated to arise over the duration of the contract (after allowing for estimated remedial and maintenance costs and increases in costs so far as not recoverable under the terms of the contract). This estimate is required irrespective of:

(a)   whether work has yet commenced on such contracts;
(b)   the proportion of work carried out at the accounting date; or
(c)   the amount of profits expected to arise on other contracts.

Forward contract:-

A forward contract is an agreement to exchange different currencies at a specified future date and at a specified rate. The difference between the specified rate and the spot rate ruling on the date the contract was entered into is the discount or premium on the forward contract.

Government:-

Government includes government and inter-governmental agencies and similar bodies whether local, national or international.

Government grants:-

Government grants are assistance by **government** in the form of cash or transfers of assets to an entity in return for past or future compliance with certain conditions relating to the operating activities of the entity.

Grant date for share-based payment arrangements:-

The date at which the entity and another party (including an employee) agree to a share-based payment arrangement, being when the entity and the counterparty have a shared understanding of the terms and conditions of the arrangement. At grant date the entity confers on the counterparty the right to cash, other **assets**, or **equity instruments** of the entity, provided the specified vesting conditions, if any, are met. If that agreement is subject to an approval process (for example, by shareholders), grant date is the date when that approval is obtained.

Gross earnings (from a lease):-

Gross earnings comprise the lessor's gross finance income over the **lease term**, representing the difference between its gross investment in the lease and the cost of the leased **asset** less any grants receivable towards the purchase or use of the **asset**.

Hire purchase contract:-

A hire purchase contract is a contract for the hire of an **asset** that contains a **provision** giving the hirer an option to acquire legal title to the **asset** upon the fulfilment of certain conditions stated in the contract.

Identifiable assets and liabilities:-

Identifiable assets and liabilities are the **assets** and **liabilities** of an entity that are capable of being disposed of or settled separately, without disposing of a business of the entity.

IMMEDIATE FAMILY:-

A DIRECTOR'S SPOUSE AND INFANT CHILDREN, INCLUDING STEP-CHILDREN AND PERSONS UNDER THE AGE OF 18 YEARS. IT EXCLUDES A PERSON WHO IS A DIRECTOR OF THE COMPANY.

Inception (of a lease):-

The inception of a lease is the earlier of the time the asset is brought into use and the date from which rentals first accrue.

Intangible assets:-

Intangible assets are non-financial fixed **assets** that do not have physical substance but are **identifiable** and are controlled by the entity through custody or legal rights.

Interest cost:-

The expected increase during the period in the present value of the **scheme liabilities** because the benefits are one period closer to **settlement**.

Investment property:-

An investment property is an interest in land and/or buildings:

(a)   in respect of which construction work and development have been completed; and

(b)   which is held for its investment potential, any rental income being negotiated at arm's length, but excluding:

(c)   a property that is owned and occupied by a company for its own purposes; and

(d)   a property let to and occupied by another group company.

Lease term:-

The lease term is the period for which the lessee has contracted to lease the **asset** and any further terms for which the lessee has the option to continue to lease the **asset** with or without further payment, which option it is reasonably certain at the **inception** of the lease that the lessee will exercise.

Liabilities:-

An entity's **obligations** to transfer economic benefits as a result of past transactions or events.

Local currency:-

An entity's local currency is the currency of the primary economic environment in which it operates and generates net cash flows.

Long-term contract:-

A contract entered into for the design, manufacture or construction of a single substantial **asset** or the provision of a service (or of a combination of **assets** or services that together constitute a single project) where the time taken substantially to complete the contract is such that the contract activity falls into different accounting periods. A contract that is required to be accounted for as long-term by the FRSSE will usually extend for a period exceeding one year. However, a duration exceeding one year is not an essential feature of a long-term contract. Some contracts with a shorter duration than one year should be accounted for as long-term contracts if they are sufficiently material to the activity of the period that not to record turnover and **attributable profit** would lead to distortion of the period's turnover and results such that the financial statements would not give a true and fair view, provided that the policy is applied consistently within the reporting entity and from year to year.

Minimum lease payments:-

The minimum lease payments are the minimum payments over the remaining part of the **lease term** (excluding charges for services and taxes to be paid by the lessor) and:

(a)   in the case of the lessee any residual amounts guaranteed by it or by a party related to it; or

(b) in the case of the lessor any residual amounts guaranteed by the lessee or by an independent third party.

Monetary items:-

Monetary items are money held and amounts to be received or paid in money and should be categorised as either short-term or long-term. Short-term monetary items are those that fall due within one year of the balance sheet date.

MONEY PURCHASE SCHEME:-

A DEFINED CONTRIBUTION SCHEME UNDER WHICH ALL OF THE BENEFITS THAT MAY BECOME PAYABLE ARE CALCULATED BY REFERENCE TO THE PAYMENTS MADE OR TREATED AS MADE BY THE SCHEME MEMBER AND WHICH ARE NOT AVERAGE SALARY BENEFITS.

Net investment (in a foreign entity):-

The net investment that a company has in a **foreign entity** is its effective equity stake and comprises its proportion of such **foreign entity's** net assets; in appropriate circumstances, intragroup loans and other deferred balances may be regarded as part of the effective equity stake.

Net investment (in a lease):-

The net investment in a lease at a point in time comprises:

(a) the gross investment in a lease (i.e. the total of the **minimum lease payments** and that portion of the **residual value** of the **leased asset**, the realisation of which by the lessor is not assured or is guaranteed solely by a party related to the lessor); less

(b) **gross earnings** allocated to future periods.

Net realisable value (of fixed assets):-

Net realisable value of a fixed asset is the amount at which the asset could be disposed of, less any direct selling costs.

Net realisable value (of stocks and long-term contracts):-

The actual or estimated selling price (net of trade but before settlement discounts) less:

(a) all further costs to completion; and

(b) all costs to be incurred in marketing, selling and distributing.

Obligation:-

An obligation may be either a legal obligation (derived, for example, from a contract or legislation) or a constructive obligation, where the entity has indicated to other parties that it will accept certain responsibilities and has created valid expectations in those other parties that it will discharge those responsibilities.

Operating lease:-

An operating lease is a lease other than a **finance lease**.

Ordinary activities:-

Any activities that are undertaken by a reporting entity as part of its business and such related activities in which the reporting entity engages in furtherance of, incidental to, or arising from, these activities. Ordinary activities include the effects on the reporting entity of any event in the various environments in which it operates, including the political, regulatory, economic and geographical environments, irrespective of the frequency or unusual nature of the events.

Past service cost:-

The increase in the present value of the **scheme liabilities** related to employee service in prior periods arising in the current period as a result of the introduction of, or improvement to, **retirement benefits.**

Pension schemes:-

A pension scheme is an arrangement (other than accident insurance) to provide pension and/or other benefits for members on leaving service or retiring and, after a member's death, for his/her dependants.

Performance:-

The fulfilment of the seller's contractual **obligations** to a customer through the supply of goods and services.

Permanent differences:-

Differences between an entity's taxable profits and its results as stated in the financial statements that arise because certain types of income and expenditure are non-taxable or disallowable, or because certain tax charges or allowances have no corresponding amount in the financial statements.

Pre-contract costs:-

The costs of tendering for and securing contracts to supply products or services.

Prior period adjustments:-

Material adjustments applicable to prior periods arising from changes in **accounting policies** or from the correction of fundamental errors. They do not include normal recurring adjustments or corrections of accounting estimates made in prior periods.

Projected unit method:-

An accrued benefits valuation method in which the **scheme liabilities** make allowance for projected earnings. An accrued benefits valuation method is a valuation method in which the **scheme liabilities** at the valuation date relate to:

(a)   the benefits for pensioners and deferred pensioners (i.e. individuals who have ceased to be active members but are entitled to benefits payable at a later date) and their dependants, allowing where appropriate for future increases; and

(b)   the accrued benefits for members in service on the valuation date.

The accrued benefits are the benefits for service up to a given point in time, whether vested rights or not. Guidance on the projected unit method is given in the Guidance Note GN26 issued by the Faculty and Institute of Actuaries.

Provision:-

A **liability** of uncertain timing or amount.

Purchased goodwill:-

Purchased goodwill is goodwill that is established as a result of the purchase of a business accounted for as an acquisition. It represents the difference between the cost of the acquired business and the aggregate of the **fair values** recorded for the **identifiable assets and liabilities** acquired. Positive goodwill arises when the acquisition cost exceeds the aggregate **fair values** of the **identifiable assets and liabilities**. Negative goodwill arises when the aggregate **fair values** of the **identifiable assets and liabilities** of the entity exceed the acquisition cost.

Pure (or basic) research:-

Experimental or theoretical work undertaken primarily to acquire new scientific or technological knowledge for its own sake rather than directed towards any specific aim or application.

QUALIFYING SERVICES:-

SERVICES AS A DIRECTOR OF THE COMPANY OR SERVICES WHILE DIRECTOR OF THE COMPANY AND AS DIRECTOR OF ANY OF ITS SUBSIDIARY UNDERTAKINGS OR OTHERWISE IN CONNECTION WITH THE MANAGEMENT OF THE AFFAIRS OF THE COMPANY OR ANY OF ITS SUBSIDIARIES.

QUALIFYING THIRD PARTY INDEMNITY PROVISION:-

A PROVISION BY WHICH A COMPANY DIRECTLY OR INDIRECTLY PROVIDES AN INDEMNITY FOR A DIRECTOR OF THE COMPANY OR AN ASSOCIATED COMPANY WHICH SATISFIES THE FOLLOWING THREE CONDITIONS:

(A) THE PROVISION DOES NOT PROVIDE ANY INDEMNITY AGAINST ANY LIABILITY INCURRED BY THE DIRECTOR TO THE COMPANY OR ANY ASSOCIATED COMPANY;

(B) THE PROVISION DOES NOT PROVIDE ANY INDEMNITY AGAINST ANY LIABILITY INCURRED BY THE DIRECTOR TO PAY A FINE IMPOSED BY CRIMINAL PROCEEDINGS OR PAY A PENALTY TO A REGULATORY AUTHORITY IN RESPECT OF NON-COMPLIANCE;

(C) THE PROVISION DOES NOT PROVIDE ANY INDEMNITY AGAINST ANY LIABILITY INCURRED BY THE DIRECTOR (I) IN DEFENDING ANY CRIMINAL PROCEEDINGS IN WHICH HE IS CONVICTED OR (II) IN DEFENDING ANY CIVIL PROCEEDINGS BROUGHT BY THE COMPANY OR AN ASSOCIATED COMPANY IN WHICH JUDGEMENT IS GIVEN AGAINST HIM, OR (III) IN WHICH THE COURT REFUSES TO GRANT RELIEF IN CONNECTION WITH ANY APPLICATION UNDER THE FOLLOWING PROVISIONS: ACQUISITION OF SHARES BY INNOCENT NOMINEE, OR GENERAL POWER TO GRANT RELIEF IN CSE OF HONEST AND REASONABLE CONDUCT.

QUALIFYING UNDERTAKING:-

A QUALIFYING PARTNERSHIP OR A QUALIFYING COMPANY GOVERNED BY THE LAWS OF ANY PART OF GREAT BRITAIN WHERE EACH OF ITS MEMBERS IS (I) A LIMITED COMPANY, OR (II)

ANOTHER LIMITED COMPANY OR A SCOTTISH FIRM, EACH OF WHOSE MEMBERS IS A LIMITED COMPANY.

THIS INCLUDES ANY COMPARABLE UNDERTAKING INCORPORATED IN OR FORMED UNDER THE LAW OF ANY COUNTRY OR TERRITORY OUTSIDE GREAT BRITAIN.

QUASI-LOAN:-

A TRANSACTION UNDER WHICH ONE PARTY ('THE CREDITOR') AGREES TO PAY A SUM FOR ANOTHER PARTY ('THE BORROWER'), OR AGREES TO REIMBURSE EXPENDITURE INCURRED BY ANOTHER PARTY FOR 'THE BORROWER' SUCH THAT 'THE CREDITOR' WILL BE REIMBURSED.

Recognised:-

Recognition is the process of incorporating an item into the primary financial statements under the appropriate heading. It involves depiction of the item in words and by a monetary amount and inclusion of that amount in the statement totals.

Recoverable amount:-

Recoverable amount of an **asset** is the higher of the amounts that can be obtained from selling the **asset** (i.e. **net realisable value**) or continuing to use the **asset** in the business (i.e. value in use). Value in use is calculated as the present value of the future cash flows* obtainable as a result of the **asset's** continued use (including those resulting from its ultimate disposal), or a reasonable estimate thereof.

Regular (pension) cost:-

The consistent ongoing cost **recognised** under the actuarial method used.

Related parties:-

Two or more parties are related parties when at any time during the financial period:

(a) one party has direct or indirect control of the other party; or
(b) the parties are subject to common control from the same source; or
(c) one party has significant influence over the financial and operating policies of the other party. Significant influence would occur if that other party is inhibited from pursuing its own separate interests.

For the avoidance of doubt, related parties of the reporting entity include the following:

(i)   parent undertakings, subsidiary and fellow subsidiary undertakings;
(ii)   associates and joint ventures;
(iii) investors with significant influence and their **close families**; and
(iv)   **directors** of the reporting entity and of its parent undertakings and their **close families**.

Reliability:-

Financial information is reliable if:

**This calculation may not be relevant for fixed assets held by charities and other not-for-profit entities, where they are not held for the purpose of generating cash flows.*

(a) it can be depended upon by users to represent faithfully what it either purports to represent or could reasonably be expected to represent, and therefore reflects the substance of the transactions and other events that have taken place;

(b) it is free from deliberate or systematic bias (i.e. it is neutral);

(c) it is free from material error;

(d) it is complete within the bounds of materiality; and

(e) under conditions of uncertainty, it has been prudently prepared (i.e. a degree of caution has been applied in exercising judgement and making the necessary estimates).

Research and development expenditure:-

Research and development expenditure means expenditure falling into one or more of the broad categories of **pure (or basic) research**, **applied research** and **development** (except to the extent that it relates to locating or exploiting oil, gas or mineral deposits or is reimbursable by third parties either directly or under the terms of a firm contract to develop and manufacture at an agreed price calculated to reimburse both elements of expenditure).

Residual value:-

Residual value is the realisable value of an **asset** at the end of its **useful economic life**, based on prices prevailing at the date of acquisition or revaluation, where this has taken place. Residual values do not take account of future price changes Realisation costs should be deducted in arriving at the residual value.

Retirement benefits:-

All forms of consideration given by an employer in exchange for services rendered by employees that are payable after the completion of employment. Retirement benefits do not include termination benefits payable as a result of either (i) an employer's decision to terminate an employee's employment before the normal retirement date or (ii) an employee's decision to accept voluntary redundancy in exchange for those benefits, because these are not given in exchange for services rendered by employees.

Right to consideration:-

A seller's right to the amount received or receivable in exchange for its **performance**. This right does not necessarily correspond to amounts falling due in accordance with a schedule of stage payments which may be specified in a contractual arrangement. Whilst stage payments will often be timed to coincide with **performance**, they may not correspond exactly. Stage payments reflect only the agreed timing of payment, whereas a right to consideration arises through the seller's **performance**.

Scheme liabilities:-

The **liabilities** of a defined benefit scheme for outgoings due after the valuation date. Scheme liabilities measured using the **projected unit method** reflect the benefits that the employer is committed to provide for service up to the valuation date.

Settlement:-

An irrevocable action that relieves the employer (or the **defined benefit scheme**) of the primary responsibility for a pension **obligation** and eliminates significant risks relating to the **obligation** and the **assets** used to effect the settlement.

Share-based payment transaction:-

A transaction in which the entity receives goods or services as consideration for **equity instruments** of the entity (including shares or share options), or acquires goods or services by incurring **liabilities** to the supplier of those goods or services for amounts that are based on the price of the entity's shares or other **equity instruments** of the entity.

SOCIAL SECURITY COSTS:-

ANY CONTRIBUTIONS BY THE ENTITY TO ANY STATE SOCIAL SECURITY OR PENSION SCHEME, FUND OR ARRANGEMENT.

Start-up costs:-

Costs arising from those one-time activities related to opening a new facility, introducing a new product or service, conducting business in a new territory, conducting business with a new class of customer, initiating a new process in an existing facility, starting some new operation and similar items. They include costs of relocating or reorganising part or all of an entity, costs related to organising a new entity, and expenses and losses incurred both before and after opening.

SUBSIDIARY UNDERTAKINGS*

AN UNDERTAKING IS A SUBSIDIARY OF A PARENT UNDERTAKING WHERE THE PARENT:

(A)   HOLDS A MAJORITY OF THE VOTING RIGHTS IN THE UNDERTAKING, OR

(B)   IS A MEMBER OF THE UNDERTAKING AND HAS THE RIGHT TO APPOINT OR REMOVE A MAJORITY OF ITS BOARD OF DIRECTORS, OR

(C)   HAS THE RIGHT TO EXERCISE A DOMINANT INFLUENCE OVER THE UNDERTAKING BY VIRTUE OF PROVISIONS CONTAINED IN ITS MEMORANDUM OR ARTICLES OR BY VIRTUE OF A CONTROL CONTRACT, OR

(D)   IS A MEMBER OF THE UNDERTAKING AND CONTROLS ALONE, PURSUANT TO AN AGREEMENT WITH OTHER SHAREHOLDERS OR MEMBERS, A MAJORITY OF THE VOTING RIGHTS IN THE UNDERTAKING; OR.

(E)   HAS THE POWER TO EXERCISE, OR ACTUALLY EXERCISES, DOMINANT INFLUENCE OR CONTROL OVER THE UNDERTAKING; OR

(F)   THE PARENT AND THE SUBSIDIARY UNDERTAKING ARE MANAGED ON A UNIFIED BASIS.

Tangible fixed **assets:-**

Assets that have physical substance and are held for use in the production or supply of goods or services, for rental to others, or for administrative purposes on a continuing basis in the reporting entity's activities.

Tax credit:-

The tax credit given under UK legislation to the recipient of a dividend from a UK company.

In case of doubt, reference should be made to the full definition in section 258 of the Companies Act 1985

Term (of a capital instrument):-

The period from the date of issue of the **capital instrument** to the date at which it will expire, be redeemed, or be cancelled. If either party has the option to require the instrument to be redeemed or cancelled and, under the terms of the instrument, it is uncertain whether such an option will be exercised, the term should be taken to end on the earliest date at which the instrument would be redeemed or cancelled on exercise of such an option. If either party has the right to extend the period of an instrument, the term should not include the period of the extension if there is a genuine commercial possibility that the period will not be extended.

Timing differences:-

Differences between taxable profits and the results as stated in the financial statements that arise from the inclusion of gains and losses in tax assessments in periods different from those in which they are **recognised** in financial statements. For example, a timing difference would arise when tax allowances for the cost of a fixed asset are accelerated or decelerated, i.e. received before or after the **depreciation** of the fixed asset is **recognised** in the profit and loss account.

Total recognised gains and losses:-

The total of all gains and losses of the reporting entity that are **recognised** in a period and are attributable to the shareholders.

Translation:-

Translation is the process whereby financial data denominated in one currency are expressed in terms of another currency. It includes both the expression of individual transactions in terms of another currency and the expression of a complete set of financial statements prepared in one currency in terms of another currency.

Useful economic life:-

The useful economic life of a tangible fixed asset is the period over which the entity expects to derive economic benefit from that asset.

Withholding tax:-

Tax on dividends or other income that is deducted by the payer of the income and paid to the tax authorities wholly on behalf of the recipient.

D – Voluntary disclosures

The disclosures below are not mandatory and do not form part of the Statement of Standard Accounting Practice. The Board, however, encourages reporting entities voluntarily to include the following disclosures in their financial statements.

CASH FLOW INFORMATION*

1   Reporting entities are encouraged, but not required, to provide a cash flow statement using the indirect method as explained below.†

2   The indirect method starts with operating profit (which is normally profit before income from shares in group undertakings) and adjusts it for non-cash charges and credits to reconcile it with cash generated from operations. Other sources and applications of cash are shown to arrive at total cash generated (or utilised) in the period.

3   Cash is taken as 'cash at bank and in hand' less overdrafts repayable on demand, which should be reconciled to the balance sheet.

4   Cash flows are shown net of any attributable value added tax or other sales tax unless the tax is irrecoverable by the reporting entity.

5   It is recommended that material transactions not resulting in movements of cash of the reporting entity are disclosed by way of note, if disclosure is necessary for an understanding of the underlying transactions.

---

*The Board's reasoning for including a voluntary recommendation for cash flow information is set out in Appendix IV.

†An illustrative example of a cash flow statement using the indirect method is given in Appendix III.

E – Adoption of the FRSSE (effective January 2007) by the Board

Financial Reporting Standard for Smaller Entities (effective January 2007) was approved for issue by the ten members of the Accounting Standards Board.

Ian Mackintosh	Chairman
David Loweth	Technical Director (Acting)
Michael Ashley	
Marisa Cassoni	
Peter Elwin	
Roger Marshall	
Robert Overend	
Helen Weir	
Peter Westlake	
Geoffrey Whittington	

Appendix I
Note on legal requirements for companies

GREAT BRITAIN

Companies Act 1985, sections 247-249

1   The definition of a small company is contained in sections 247 and 247A of the Companies Act 1985. The qualifying conditions are met by a company in a year in which it does not exceed two or more of the following criteria:

Turnover	£5,600,000
Balance sheet total	£2,800,000
Average number of employees	50

For any company, other than a newly incorporated company, to qualify as small, the qualifying conditions must be met for two consecutive years. A company will cease to qualify as small if it fails to meet the qualifying conditions for two consecutive years.

2   Certain companies are excluded by section 247A from the 'small company' criteria for reasons of public interest. These are any entity that is, or is in a group that includes:

(a)   a public company;
(b)   a banking or insurance company;
(c)   a body corporate that (not being a company) has the power to offer its shares or debentures to the public and may lawfully exercise that power;
(d)   a person who carries on an insurance market related activity; or
(e)   certain authorised persons under Part 4 of the Financial Services and Markets Act 2000.*

3   A parent company shall not be treated as qualifying as a small company in relation to a financial year unless the group headed by it qualifies as a small group.

4   The definition of a small group is contained in sections 248 and 249. The qualifying conditions are met by a group in a year in which it does not exceed two or more of the following criteria:

Aggregate turnover	£5,600,000 net (or £6,720,000 gross)
Aggregate balance sheet total	£2,800,000 net (or £3,360,000 gross)
Aggregate number of employees	50

'Net' means after the set-offs and other adjustments required by Schedule 4A in the case of group accounts, and 'gross' means without those set-offs and adjustments. A

The Companies Act 1985 (Small Companies' Accounts and Audit) Regulations 2006 came into force on 8 November 2006 and applies for financial years ending on or after 31 December 2006. The Regulations allow more categories of small financial services companies to qualify as small and take advantage of the small company exemptions. However companies that are required to have an audit based on a requirement in a European directive are still prohibited from taking advantage of the small company exemptions. In case of doubt, reference should be made to the Regulations.

company may satisfy the relevant requirements on the basis of either the net or the gross figure.

NORTHERN IRELAND

The statutory requirements in Northern Ireland are set out in Articles 255-257 of the   5
Companies (Northern Ireland) Order 1986. The qualifying conditions for the definition of a small company may be met by a company in a year in which it does not exceed two or more of the following criteria:

Turnover	£5,600,000
Balance sheet total	£2,800,000
Average number of employees	50

REPUBLIC OF IRELAND

The following table shows the references in companies legislation in the Republic of   6
Ireland that correspond to the references in paragraphs 1-4 above.

GREAT BRITAIN	REPUBLIC OF IRELAND
Sections 247 and 247A	Companies (Amendment) Act 1986, sections 2, 8 and 9
Sections 248 and 249	No equivalent
Schedule 8	No equivalent

The qualifying conditions for the definition of a small company may be met by a company in a year in which it does not exceed two or more of the following criteria:

Turnover	€3.81 million
Balance sheet total	€1.9 million
Average number of employees	50

The FRSSE can be applied to those companies meeting the criteria as set out in the Republic of Ireland Companies Acts that allow them to be treated as "small" for the purposes of filing information with the Companies Registration Office. Small groups are not defined in Republic of Ireland legislation. However, in the Republic of Ireland, for the purposes of the FRSSE, small groups should meet, on a consolidated basis, the same legal conditions as are required for small companies. If a group does not qualify as small, then the parent undertaking of that group, even if it qualifies as a small company under Republic of Ireland legislation, is not entitled to adopt the FRSSE.

DERIVATION TABLES FOR LEGAL REQUIREMENTS REFERRED TO IN THE FRSSE*

Derivation tables for all the legal requirements referred to in the FRSSE are available   7
from the ASB website at www.frc.org.uk/asb/technical/frsse.cfm in the derivation tables which indicates the source of company law in Great Britain, Northern Ireland and the Republic of Ireland.

*To help make the FRSSE a more manageable document, derivation tables have been removed from the published version but are instead available on the ASB website at www.frc.org.uk/asb/technical/frsse.cfm.

8   Republic of Ireland users of the FRSSE should note that the requirements of company law as shown in SMALL CAPITALS in the text of the FRSSE relate to UK company law as applicable to small companies. The corresponding reference to Republic of Ireland companies legislation is shown in Table 1 of the derivation tables . However, Republic of Ireland users should note that the detail of the Republic of Ireland legal requirements in many cases differs from UK company law.

9   In addition, there are a number of Republic of Ireland legal requirements that are not reflected in the FRSSE. There is no equivalent to Schedule 8 of the Companies Act 1985 providing certain exemptions for small companies when preparing annual accounts for shareholders. Exemptions from company law requirements for small companies in the Republic of Ireland are limited and relate primarily to information that must be filed with the Companies Registration Office. These additional requirements are referenced in Table 2 of the derivation tables.

10   There are no special provisions in Republic of Ireland company law that relate to the preparation of group accounts by small entities. The general requirement for the preparation of group accounts is contained in section 150 of the Companies Act 1963. Regulation 7 of the EC (Companies: Group Accounts) Regulations 1992, SI 201/1992, contains an exemption from the requirement to prepare group accounts for certain undertakings to whom the above Regulation applies. The legal references are given in Table 2 of the derivation tables.

11   Republic of Ireland users should refer to the underlying legislation when using the FRSSE. The Republic of Ireland legal requirements set out in the derivation tables are intended to reflect company law as applicable to accounting periods beginning on or after 1 January 2007.

STATUS OF THE FRSSE

12   Legal advice has been obtained that in accounting standards smaller entities may properly be allowed exemptions or different treatment provided that such differences are justified on rational grounds. The Board will have regard to the criteria given in the 'Status of the FRSSE' section in determining whether such rational grounds exist.

13   The summary of advice regarding the status of the FRSSE given by Richard Sykes QC in December 1995 is reproduced below:

"I do not see any conflict with the law or likely weakening of the authority of ASB or FRRP* as respects the upholding of Standards provided that

(i)   the treatment required by the FRSSE is the same as that required by existing Standards or is a simplified version of that treatment; or

(ii)   in a case where a future Standard calls for a new treatment for Big GAAP† Companies only and which is also likely to be significant to small companies, ASB is able to justify on rational grounds any lack of a change in treatment for smaller entities when the FRSSE is in due course revised;

(iii)   in a case where in the future the FRSSE requires a treatment which is materially different from then existing Standards on a significant matter ASB is able to justify on rational grounds such different treatment in the case of smaller entities.

Financial Reporting Review Panel

†*Generally Accepted Accounting Practice*

(iv) it is recognised that the starting point for deciding how a smaller entity will account for something not covered by the FRSSE will be existing practice and that the smaller entity must be able to justify its departure from such practice on rational grounds related to its size. Where the matter is covered by a Big GAAP Standard, that Standard would provide the obvious source in determining existing practice.

Rational grounds for justifying different treatments might include:

(i) the different nature of entities;

(ii) particularly if the different treatment is in the area of disclosure, the different users of their financial statements; and

(iii) established practices existing at the time of issue of a Standard or FRSSE revision."

Appendix II
Accounting for retirement benefits: defined benefit schemes

1   The following requirements should be regarded as standard in respect of financial statements relating to accounting periods ending on or after 22 June 2006, although earlier adoption is encouraged:

(a)   **Assets** in a **defined benefit scheme** should be measured at their **fair value** at the balance sheet date.

(b)   **Defined benefit scheme liabilities** should be measured on an actuarial basis using the **projected unit method**. The **scheme liabilities** comprise both any benefits promised under the formal terms of the scheme and any constructive **obligations** for further benefits.

(c)   The assumptions underlying the valuation should be mutually compatible and lead to the best estimate of the future cash flows that will arise under the **scheme liabilities**. The assumptions are ultimately the responsibility of the **directors** (or equivalent) but should be set upon advice given by an actuary. Any assumptions that are affected by economic conditions (financial assumptions) should reflect market expectations at the balance sheet date.

(d)   **Defined benefit scheme liabilities** should be discounted at the current rate of return on a high quality corporate bond of equivalent currency and term.

(e)   Full actuarial valuations by a professionally qualified actuary should be obtained for a **defined benefit scheme** at intervals not exceeding three years. The actuary should review the most recent actuarial valuation at the balance sheet date and update it to reflect current conditions.

(f)   The surplus/deficit in a **defined benefit scheme** is the excess/shortfall of the value of the **assets** in the scheme over/below the present value of the **scheme liabilities**. The employer should **recognise** an **asset** to the extent that it is able to recover a surplus either through reduced contributions in the future or through refunds from the scheme. The employer should **recognise** a **liability** to the extent that it reflects its legal or constructive **obligation**.

(g)   Any unpaid contributions to the scheme should be presented in the balance sheet as a creditor due within one year. The defined benefit **asset** or **liability** should be presented separately on the face of the balance sheet:

(i)   in balance sheets of the type prescribed for small companies in Great Britain* by the Companies Act 1985, Schedule 8, format 1: after item J Accruals and deferred income but before item K Capital and reserves; and

(ii)   in balance sheets of the type prescribed for small companies in Great Britain by the Companies Act 1985, Schedule 8, format 2: any **asset** after ASSETS item D Prepayments and accrued income and any **liability** after LIABILITIES item D Accruals and deferred income.

(h)   The **deferred tax** relating to the defined benefit **asset** or **liability** should be offset against the defined benefit **asset** or **liability** and not included with other **deferred tax assets** or **liabilities**:

(i)   The components of the change in the defined benefit **asset** or **liability** (other than those arising from contributions to the scheme) should be presented separately in the performance statements as follows:

The equivalent legislation in Northern Ireland is Schedule 8 to the Companies (Northern Ireland) Order 1986. There is no equivalent to Schedule 8 in companies legislation in the Republic of Ireland. See Appendix VII for Republic of Ireland legal requirements.

(i)   the **current service cost** should be included within operating profit in the profit and loss account;

(ii)   the net of the **interest cost** and the expected return on assets should be included as other finance costs (or income) adjacent to interest;

(iii) **actuarial gains and losses** should be **recognised** in the statement of **total recognised gains and losses**;

(iv) **past service costs** should be **recognised** in the profit and loss account in the period in which the increases in benefit vest; and

(v)   losses arising on a **settlement** or **curtailment** should be **recognised** in the profit and loss account when the employer becomes demonstrably committed to the transaction (gains should only be **recognised** once all parties whose consent is required are irrevocably committed).

(j)   The following disclosures should be made in respect of a **defined benefit scheme**:

(i)   the nature of the scheme (i.e. **defined benefit**);

(ii)   the date of the most recent full actuarial valuation on which the amounts in the financial statements are based. If the actuary is an employee or officer of the reporting entity, or of the group of which it is a member, this fact should be disclosed;

(iii) the contribution made in respect of the accounting period and any agreed contribution rates for future years; and

(iv) for closed schemes and those in which the age profile of the active membership is rising significantly, the fact that under the **projected unit method** the **current service cost** will increase as the members of the scheme approach retirement.

(k)   The **fair value** of the scheme **assets**, the present value of the scheme **liabilities** based on the accounting assumptions and the resulting surplus or deficit should be disclosed in a note to the financial statements. Where the **asset** or **liability** in the balance sheet differs from the surplus or deficit in the scheme, an explanation of the difference should be given. An analysis of the movements during the period in the surplus or deficit in the scheme should be given.

Appendix III
Illustrative examples and practical considerations

This Appendix contains illustrative examples and practical considerations for general guidance and does not form part of the Financial Reporting Standard. The best form of reporting will depend on individual circumstances.

Example: Statement of total recognised gains and losses

	2002	2001 as restated
	£	£
Profit for the financial year	29,000	7,000
Unrealised surplus on revaluation of property	4,000	6,000
Unrealised (loss) /gain on trade investment	(3,000)	7,000
Total recognised gains and losses relating to the year	30,000	20,000
Prior year adjustment (as explained in note x)	(10,000)	
Total gains and losses recognised since last annual report	20,000	

Example: Disclosure - defined contribution pension scheme

The company operates a defined contribution pension scheme. The assets of the scheme are held separately from those of the company in an independently administered fund. The pension cost charge represents contributions payable by the company to the fund and amounted to £50,000 (2001 £45,000). Contributions totalling £2,500 (2001 £1,500) were payable to the fund at the year-end and are included in creditors.

Example: Disclosure - defined benefit pension scheme*

The company operates a pension scheme providing benefits based on final pensionable pay. The assets of the scheme are held separately from those of the company, being invested with insurance companies.

The contributions are determined by a qualified actuary on the basis of triennial valuations using the projected unit method. The most recent valuation was as at 31 December 2005 which has been updated to reflect conditions at the balance sheet date. The assumptions that have the most significant effect on the results of the valuation are those relating to the rate of return on investments and the rate of increase in salaries and pensions. It was assumed that the investment returns would

*This example reflects the disclosure requirements of paragraph 2 of Appendix II which become mandatory in full for years ending on or after 22 June 2006.

be 6 per cent per year, that salary increases would average 4 per cent per year and that present and future pensions would increase at the rate of 3 per cent per year.

The pension charge for the year was £46,000 (2005 £25,000). This included £12,000 (2005 £nil) in respect of past service costs. The contributions of the company and employees will remain at 10 per cent and 5 per cent of earnings respectively.

The defined benefit scheme is closed to new members and so under the projected unit method the current service cost would be expected to increase over time as members of the scheme approach retirement.

Value of scheme assets and liabilities	2006 £	2005 £
Market value of assets	1,488,000	962,000
Present value of scheme liabilities	(1,009,000)	(758,000)
Pension scheme surplus/(deficit)	479,000	204,000
Related deferred tax asset/(liability)	(144,000)	(61,000)
Net pension scheme asset/(liability)	335,000	143,000

Movements in year	2006 £	2005 £
Pension scheme surplus/(deficit) at beginning of year	204,000	92,000
Current service cost	(34,000)	(25,000)
Cash contribution	25,000	35,000
Past service costs	(12,000)	0
Other finance income	20,000	11,000
Actuarial gain	276,000	91,000
Pension scheme surplus/(deficit) at end of year	479,000	204,000

This example reflects the disclosure requirements of paragraph 2 of Appendix II which become mandatory in full for years ending on or after 22 June 2006.

PRACTICAL CONSIDERATIONS: STOCKS AND LONG-TERM CONTRACTS

Many of the problems involved in arriving at the amount at which stocks and long-term contracts are stated in financial statements are of a practical nature rather than resulting from matters of principle. The following paragraphs discuss some particular areas in which difficulty may be encountered.

The allocation of overheads

Production overheads are included in the cost of conversion together with direct labour, direct expenses and subcontracted work. This inclusion is a necessary corollary of the principle that expenditure should be included to the extent to which it has been incurred in bringing the product 'to its present location and condition'. However, all abnormal conversion costs (such as exceptional spoilage, idle capacity and other losses) that are avoidable under normal operating conditions need, for the same reason, to be excluded.

2   Where firm sales contracts have been entered into for the provision of goods or services to customer's specification, overheads relating to design, and marketing and selling costs incurred before manufacture, may be included in arriving at cost.

3   The costing methods adopted by a business are usually designed to ensure that all direct material, direct labour, direct expenses and subcontracted work are identified and charged on a reasonable and consistent basis, but problems arise on the allocation of overheads, which must usually involve the exercise of personal judgement in the selection of an appropriate convention.

4   The classification of overheads necessary to achieve this allocation takes the function of the overhead as its distinguishing characteristic (e.g. whether it is a function of production, marketing, selling or administration), rather than whether the overhead tends to vary with time or with volume.

5   The costs of general management, as distinct from functional management, are not directly related to current production and are, therefore, excluded from the cost of conversion and, hence, from the cost of stocks and long-term contracts.

6   In the case of smaller organisations whose management may be involved in the daily administration of each of the various functions, particular problems may arise in practice in distinguishing these general management overheads. In such organisations the costs of management may fairly be allocated on suitable bases to the functions of production, marketing, selling and administration.

7   Problems may also arise in allocating the costs of central service departments, the allocation of which should depend on the function or functions that the department is serving. For example, the accounts department will normally support the following functions:

(a)   production - by paying direct and indirect production wages and salaries, by controlling purchases and by preparing periodic financial statements for the production units;
(b)   marketing and distribution - by analysing sales and by controlling the sales ledger;
(c)   general administration - by preparing management accounts and annual financial statements and budgets, by controlling cash resources and by planning investments.

Only those costs of the accounts department that can reasonably be allocated to the production function fall to be included in the cost of conversion.

8   The allocation of overheads included in the valuation of stocks and long-term contracts needs to be based on the company's normal level of activity, taking one year with another. The governing factor is that the cost of unused capacity should be written off in the current year. In determining what constitutes 'normal' the following factors need to be considered:

(a)   the volume of production that the production facilities are intended by their designers and by management to produce under the working conditions (e.g. single or double shift) prevailing during the year;
(b)   the budgeted level of activity for the year under review and for the ensuing year;

(c) the level of activity achieved both in the year under review and in previous years.

Although temporary changes in the load of activity may be ignored, persistent variation should lead to revision of the previous norm.

Where management accounts are prepared on a marginal cost basis, it will be **9** necessary to add to the figure of stocks so arrived at the appropriate proportion of those production overheads not already included in the marginal cost.

The adoption of a conservative approach to the valuation of stocks and long-term **10** contracts has sometimes been used as one of the reasons for omitting selected production overheads. In so far as the circumstances of the business require an element of prudence in determining the amount at which stocks and long-term contracts are stated, this needs to be taken into account in the determination of net realisable value and not by the exclusion from cost of selected overheads.

Methods of costing

It is frequently not practicable to relate expenditure to specific units of stocks and **11** long-term contracts. The ascertainment of the nearest approximation to cost gives rise to two problems:

(a) the selection of an appropriate method for relating costs to stocks and long-term contracts (e.g. job costing, batch costing, process costing, standard costing);

(b) the selection of an appropriate method for calculating the related costs where a number of identical items have been purchased or made at different times (e.g. unit cost, average cost or 'first in, first out' (FIFO)).

In selecting the methods referred to in paragraph 11(a) and (b), management must **12** exercise judgement to ensure that the methods chosen provide the fairest practicable approximation to cost. Furthermore, where standard costs are used they need to be reviewed frequently to ensure that they bear a reasonable relationship to actual costs obtaining during the period. Methods such as base stock and 'last in, first out' (LIFO) are not usually appropriate methods of stock valuation because they often result in stocks being stated in the balance sheet at amounts that bear little relationship to recent cost levels. When this happens, not only is the presentation of current assets misleading, but there is potential distortion of subsequent results if stock levels reduce and out-of-date costs are drawn into the profit and loss account.

The method of arriving at cost by applying the latest purchase price to the total **13** number of units in stock is unacceptable in principle because it is not necessarily the same as actual cost and, in times of rising prices, will result in the taking of a profit that has not been realised.

One method of arriving at cost, in the absence of a satisfactory costing system, is the **14** use of selling price less an estimated profit margin. This is acceptable only if it can be demonstrated that the method gives a reasonable approximation of the actual cost.

In industries where the cost of minor by-products is not separable from the cost of **15** the principal products, stocks of such by-products may be stated in accounts at their net realisable value. In this case the costs of the main products are calculated after deducting the net realisable value of the by-products.

The determination of net realisable value

16   The initial calculation of provisions to reduce stocks from cost to net realisable value may often be made by the use of formulae based on predetermined criteria. The formulae normally take account of the age, movements in the past, expected future movements and estimated scrap values of the stock, as appropriate. Whilst the use of such formulae establishes a basis for making a provision that can be consistently applied, it is still necessary for the results to be reviewed in the light of any special circumstances that cannot be anticipated in the formulae, such as changes in the state of the order book.

17   Where a provision is required to reduce the value of finished goods below cost, the stocks of the parts and subassemblies held for the purpose of the manufacture of such products, together with stocks on order, need to be reviewed to determine if provision is also required against such items.

18   Where stocks of spares are held for sale, special consideration of the factors in paragraph 16 will be required in the context of:

(a)   the number of units sold to which they are applicable;
(b)   the estimated frequency with which a replacement spare is required;
(c)   the expected useful life of the unit to which they are applicable.

19   Events occurring between the balance sheet date and the date of completion of the financial statements need to be considered in arriving at the net realisable value at the balance sheet date (e.g. a subsequent reduction in selling prices). However, no reduction falls to be made when the realisable value of material stocks is less than the purchase price, provided that the goods into which the materials are to be incorporated can still be sold at a profit after incorporating the materials at cost price.

The application of net realisable value

20   The principal situations in which net realisable value is likely to be less than cost are where there has been:

(a)   an increase in costs or a fall in selling price;
(b)   physical deterioration of stocks;
(c)   obsolescence of products;
(d)   a decision as part of a company's marketing strategy to manufacture and sell products at a loss;
(e)   errors in production or purchasing.

Furthermore, when stocks are held that are unlikely to be sold within the turnover period normal in that company (i.e. excess stocks), the impending delay in realisation increases the risk that the situations outlined in (a)-(c) above may occur before the stocks are sold and needs to be taken into account in assessing net realisable value.

Long-term contracts

21   In ascertaining costs of long-term contracts it is not normally appropriate to include interest payable on borrowed money. However, in circumstances where sums borrowed can be identified as financing specific long-term contracts, it may be appropriate to include such related interest in cost, in which circumstances the inclusion of interest and the amount of interest so included should be disclosed in a note to the financial statements.

In some businesses, long-term contracts for the supply of services or manufacture **22** and supply of goods exist where the prices are determined and invoiced according to separate parts of the contract. In these businesses the most appropriate method of reflecting profits on each contract is usually to match costs against performance of the separable parts of the contract, treating each such separable part as a separate contract. In such instances, however, future revenues from the contract need to be compared with future estimated costs and provision made for any foreseen loss.

Turnover (ascertained in a manner appropriate to the industry, the nature of the **23** contracts concerned and the contractual relationship with the customer) and related costs should be recorded in the profit and loss account as contract activity progresses. Turnover may sometimes be ascertained by reference to valuation of the work carried out to date. In other cases, there may be specific points during a contract at which individual elements of work done with separately ascertainable sales and values and costs can be identified and appropriately recorded as turnover (e.g. because delivery or customer acceptance has taken place

In determining whether the stage has been reached at which it is appropriate to **24** recognise profit, account should be taken of the nature of the business concerned. It is necessary to define the earliest point for each particular contract before which no profit is taken up, the overriding principle being that there can be no attributable profit until the outcome of a contract can reasonably be foreseen. Of the profit that in the light of all the circumstances can be foreseen with a reasonable degree of certainty to arise on completion of the contract, there should be regarded as earned to date only that part which prudently reflects the amount of work performed to date. The method used for taking up such profit needs to be consistently applied.

In calculating the total estimated profit on the contract, it is necessary to take into **25** account not only the total costs to date and the total estimated further costs to completion (calculated by reference to the same principles as were applied to cost to date) but also the estimated future costs of rectification and guarantee work, and any other future work to be undertaken under the terms of the contract. These are then compared with the total sales value of the contract. In considering future costs, it is necessary to have regard to likely increases in wages and salaries, to likely increases in the price of raw materials and to rises in general overheads, so far as these items are not recoverable from the customer under the terms of the contract.

Where approved variations have been made to a contract in the course of it and the **26** amount to be received in respect of these variations has not yet been settled and is likely to be a material factor in the outcome, it is necessary to make a conservative estimate of the amount likely to be received and this is then treated as part of the total sales value. On the other hand, allowance needs to be made for foreseen claims or penalties payable arising out of delays in completion or from other causes.

The settlement of claims arising from circumstances not envisaged in the contract or **27** arising as an indirect consequence of approved variations is subject to a high level of uncertainty relating to the outcome of future negotiations. In view of this, it is generally prudent to recognise receipts in respect of such claims only when negotiations have reached an advanced stage and there is sufficient evidence of the acceptability of the claim in principle to the purchaser, with an indication of the amount involved also being available.

The amounts to be included in the year's profit and loss account will be both the **28** appropriate amount of turnover and the associated costs of achieving that turnover, to the extent that these amounts exceed corresponding amounts recognised in previous years. The estimated outcome of a contract that extends over several accounting years will nearly always vary in the light of changes in circumstances and for this reason the result of the year will not necessarily represent the proportion of the total profit on the contract that is appropriate to the amount of work carried out in the period; it may also reflect the effect of changes in circumstances during the year that affect the total profit estimated to accrue on completion.

PRACTICAL CONSIDERATIONS - CONSIGNMENT STOCK

29   In determining whether consignment stock is in substance an asset of the dealer, it is necessary to identify whether the dealer has access to the benefits of the stock and exposure to the risks inherent in those benefits. Therefore, to assist in using paragraph 8.9 of the FRSSE, the following table is provided.

Indications that the stock is not an asset of the dealer at delivery	Indications that the stock is an asset of the dealer at delivery
The manufacturer can require the dealer to return stock (or to transfer stock to another dealer) without compensation *or* Penalty paid by the dealer to prevent returns/transfers of stock at the manufacturer's request.	The manufacturer cannot require the dealer to return or transfer stock *or* Financial incentives given to persuade the dealer to transfer stock at the manufacturer's request.
The dealer has unfettered right to return stock to the manufacturer without penalty and actually exercises the right in practice.	The dealer has no right to return stock or is commercially compelled not to exercise its right of return.
The manufacturer bears obsolescence risk, e.g.: - obsolete stock is returned to the manufacturer without penalty *or* - financial incentives given by the manufacturer to prevent stock being returned to it (e.g. on model change or if it becomes obsolete).	The dealer bears obsolescence risk, e.g.: - penalty charged if the dealer returns stock to the manufacturer *or* - obsolete stock cannot be returned to the manufacturer and no compensation is paid by the manufacturer for losses due to obsolescence.
Stock transfer price charged by the manufacturer is based on the manufacturer's list price at date of transfer of legal title.	Stock transfer price charged by the manufacturer is based on the manufacturer's list price at date of delivery.
The manufacturer bears slow movement risk, e.g.: - transfer price set independently of time for which the dealer holds stock, and there is no deposit.	The dealer bears slow movement risk, e.g.: - the dealer is effectively charged interest as transfer price or other payments to the manufacturer vary with time for which the dealer holds stock *or* - the dealer makes a substantial interest-free deposit that varies with the levels of stock held.

PRACTICAL CONSIDERATIONS - DEBT FACTORING

To assist in using paragraphs 8.10-8.12 of the FRSSE, the following table is pro-   **30**
vided.

Indications that derecognition is appropriate (debts are not an asset of the seller)	Indications that a linked presentation is appropriate	Indications that a separate presentation is appropriate (debts are an asset of the seller)
Transfer is for a single, non-returnable fixed sum.	Some non-returnable proceeds received, but the seller has rights to further sums from the factor (or vice versa) whose amount depends on whether or when debtors pay.	Finance cost varies with speed of collection of debts, e.g.: - by adjustment to consideration for original transfer *or* - subsequent transfers priced to recover costs of earlier transfers.
There is no recourse to the seller for losses.	There is either no recourse for losses, or such recourse has a fixed monetary ceiling.	There is full recourse to the seller for losses.
The factor is paid all amounts received from the factored debts (and no more). The seller has no rights to further sums from the factor.	The factor is paid only out of amounts collected from the factored debts, and the seller has no right or obligation to repurchase debts.	The seller is required to repay amounts received from the factor on or before a set date, regardless of timing or amounts of collections from debtors.

PRACTICAL CONSIDERATIONS – BILL AND HOLD ARRANGEMENTS

Under a bill and hold arrangement, a seller enters into a contractual arrangement   **31**
with a customer for the supply of goods where there is transfer of title but physical
delivery is deferred to a later date.

Analysis

The purpose of the analysis below is to determine whether, in the circumstances   **32**
described in paragraph 37, the seller should:

(a)   recognise turnover and a **right to consideration**; or
(b)   continue to recognise the goods as stock.

In accordance with the general principles set out in Section 4 of the FRSSE the goods   **33**
cease to be assets of the seller and become assets of the customer (and in exchange
the seller obtains the **right to consideration**) when the seller transfers to the customer
access to the significant benefits relating to the goods and exposure to the risks
inherent in those benefits. From the customer's perspective, the principal benefits and
risks include:

Benefits

(a)   the right to obtain the goods as and when required;
(b)   the sole right to the goods for their sale to a third party and the future cash flows from such a sale; and
(c)   insulation from changes in prices charged by the seller (e.g. because the seller has revised its standard price list).

Risks

(a)   slow movement, resulting in increased costs of financing and holding of the goods, and an increased risk of obsolescence; and
(b)   being compelled to take delivery of goods that have become obsolete or not readily saleable, resulting in no onward sale or a sale at a reduced price.

34   In order for the seller to have the right to recognise changes in its assets or liabilities, and turnover, arising from its **right to consideration** in respect of the bill and hold arrangement, the terms of the contractual arrangement between the seller and the customer should include all of the following characteristics:

(a)   the goods should be complete and ready for delivery;
(b)   the seller should not have retained any significant **performance obligations** other than the safekeeping of the goods and their shipment when the customer requests this;
(c)   subject to any rights of return, the seller should have obtained the **right to consideration** regardless of whether the goods are shipped, at the customer's request, to its delivery address. Where rights of return are granted, particular consideration is required of the commercial substance of the related sales, especially the transfer of risk. Rights of return are addressed at paragraphs 43-53 below;
(d)   the goods should be identified separately from the seller's other stock and should not be capable of being used to fill other orders that are received between the date of the bill and hold sale and shipment of the goods to the customer; and
(e)   the bill and hold terms should be in accordance with the commercial objectives of the customer and not the seller. For example, where the delay in the delivery of the goods is to meet the customer's need for flexibility in the timing and location of delivery, and the conditions set out in paragraphs (a) to (d) above are met, it will be appropriate for the seller to recognise changes in assets or liabilities, and turnover.

Accounting

Substance of the transaction is that the goods represent an asset of the customer

35   Where it is concluded that the stock is an asset of the customer, resulting in the seller having a **right to consideration**, the seller should recognise the related changes in its assets or liabilities, and turnover.

Substance of the transaction is that the goods represent an asset of the seller

36   Where it is concluded that the stock remains an asset of the seller, it should be retained on the seller's balance sheet. Any amounts received from the customer should be included within creditors in accordance with paragraph 4.2 of the FRSSE.

PRACTICAL CONSIDERATIONS – SALES WITH RIGHTS OF RETURN

Features

The terms of contractual arrangements may allow customers to return goods that they have purchased and obtain a refund or release from the **obligation** to pay.   37

Rights of return may be included explicitly or implicitly within contractual arrangements. Alternatively, they may arise through statutory requirements.   38

Analysis

The purpose of the analysis below is to determine the effect of rights of return on a seller's recognition of changes in its assets or liabilities, and turnover.   39

The inclusion of rights of return in a contractual arrangement may affect both the quantification of the seller's **right to consideration**, compared to an otherwise identical arrangement which does not have these rights, and the point at which the seller should recognise that right. This is because rights of return give rise to a contractual **obligation** on the part of the seller to transfer economic benefits to its customer and in some cases oblige the seller to defer recognition of the sales transaction so long as substantially all of the risks associated with the goods are retained.   40

The seller's recognition of its **right to consideration** and contractual **obligation** to transfer economic benefits to its customer in respect of rights of return are linked transactions. In consequence, changes in the seller's assets or liabilities should reflect the loss expected to arise from the rights of return. Turnover should exclude the sales value of estimated returns.   41

A seller will generally be able to estimate reliably the sales value of returns, having regard to risk, which may be less than its maximum potential **obligation**. It will generally be possible to derive a **reliable** estimate from historical experience of the amount of comparable goods returned as a proportion of comparable sales.   42

If a seller is unable to estimate reliably the expected value of returns, the maximum potential amount should be calculated in accordance with the terms of its contractual arrangement with the customer and excluded from turnover.   43

In some cases, the risk of return may be so significant that substantially all of the risks associated with the goods are retained by the seller and accordingly the seller does not have the **right to consideration**. In such circumstances the seller should not recognise any changes in its assets or liabilities, and turnover, from the transaction. Any amounts received from the customer should be accounted for as a payment in advance, in accordance with paragraph 4.2 of the FRSSE.   44

Accounting

A seller should record changes in its assets or liabilities, and turnover, to the extent that its **performance** has earned it the **right to consideration**, taking account of any expected loss. The amount recorded as turnover should exclude the sales value of estimated returns from the total sales value of the goods supplied to customers.   45

46   At each reporting date, the seller should review its estimate of returns, having regard to changes in expectations and the expiry of contractual rights of return. Subsequent adjustments to the estimate should be recorded within revenue.

47   Where a seller has been precluded from recognising changes in its assets or liabilities, and turnover, because substantially all of the risks associated with the goods are retained and so it has not earned the **right to consideration**, it should recognise these changes and turnover on the earlier of the dates on which:

(a)   it is capable of estimating the level of returns with **reliability**; and
(b)   the right of return expires or is surrendered.

PRACTICAL CONSIDERATIONS – PRESENTATION OF TURNOVER AS PRINCIPAL OR AS AGENT

Features

48   A seller may act on its own account when contracting with its customers for the supply of goods in return for the right to consideration. In such transactions the seller is frequently referred to as a principal.

49   Alternatively, a seller may act as an intermediary, earning a fee or commission in return for arranging the provision of goods or services on behalf of a principal. In such transactions, the seller is frequently referred to as an agent.

Analysis

50   The purpose of the analysis below is to determine whether a seller obtains the right to consideration by performing its contractual obligations:

(a)   as principal in an exchange transaction with its customer; or
(b)   as agent in relation to a transaction between its principal and the principal's customer.

51   The general principles of the standard require that, in order for a seller to account for exchange transactions as principal, it should normally have exposure to all significant benefits and risks associated with at least one of the following:

(a)   Selling price: the ability, within economic constraints, to establish the selling price with the customer, either directly or, where the selling price of an item is fixed, indirectly by providing additional goods or services or adjusting the terms of a linked transaction; or
(b)   Stock: exposure to the risks of damage, slow movement and obsolescence, and changes in suppliers' prices.

52   Where the seller has not disclosed that it is acting as agent, there is a rebuttable presumption that it is acting as principal.

53   Additional factors which indicate that a seller may be acting as principal include:

(a)   performance of part of the services, or modification to the goods supplied;
(b)   assumption of credit risk; and
(c)   discretion in supplier selection.

54   In contrast, where a seller acts as agent it will not normally be exposed to the majority of the benefits and risks associated with the exchange transaction. Agency arrangements will typically include the following characteristics:

(a)   the seller has disclosed the fact that it is acting as agent;
(b)   once the seller has confirmed its customer's order with a third party, the seller will normally have no further involvement in the performance of the ultimate supplier's contractual obligations;
(c)   the amount that the seller earns is predetermined, being either a fixed fee per transaction or a stated percentage of the amount billed to the customer; and
(d)   the seller bears no stock or credit risk, other than in circumstances where it receives additional consideration from the ultimate supplier in return for its assumption of this risk.

Accounting

Seller acts as principal

Where the substance of a transaction is that the seller acts as principal, it should report turnover based on the gross amount received or receivable in return for its performance under the contractual arrangement.   **55**

Seller acts as agent

Where the substance of a transaction is that the seller acts as agent, it should report   **56**
as turnover the commission or other amounts received or receivable in return for its performance under the contractual arrangement. Any amounts received or receivable from the customer that are payable to the principal should not be included in the agent's turnover.

Illustrations

A seller acts as a building contractor for the construction of a new office block. An   **57**
analysis of the arrangement shows that the terms of the seller's contract with its customer include a negotiated selling price, credit risk for amounts due from the customer, primary responsibility for the construction and quality of the new building and discretion as to whether it carries out the work itself or employs subcontractors. The seller is acting as principal and should account for the gross amount of turnover, regardless of whether it carries out the work itself or employs subcontractors to carry out part or all of the construction activities.

A seller acts as an online retailer from a website, where it advertises holidays. An   **58**
analysis of the arrangement shows that it acts as an intermediary between its customers and the ultimate sellers of the holidays and that it does not set the selling price. Its contractual terms of business include an exclusion of any liability to its customers once they have been put in touch with the ultimate sellers. The seller is paid a fee for each customer that purchases a holiday from an ultimate seller and has no involvement in the transaction after it has put the customer in touch with the ultimate seller. The seller is acting as agent and its turnover should include only the fees it receives from the ultimate seller.

A department store provides space for concessionaires to sell products and receives a   **59**
fixed amount of rental income from the concessionaire. An analysis of the factors discussed in paragraphs 57-60 shows that the concessionaire is acting as principal in an exchange transaction with its customers and is entitled to the amounts received from the sale of the goods and services. In these circumstances, the concessionaire should include within its turnover the amounts received or receivable in respect of the

sale of the goods and services. The department store should not include within its turnover the value of the concessionaire's sales.

Disclosure - seller acts as agent

60   Where a seller acts as agent, it is encouraged, where practicable, to disclose the gross value of sales throughput as additional, non-statutory information. Where such disclosure is given, a brief explanation of the relationship of recognised turnover to the gross value of sales throughput should be given.

PRACTICAL CONSIDERATIONS – CLASSIFICATION OF PREFERENCE SHARES

61   Paragraph 12.1 of the FRSSE provides an example of a preference share that is classified as a financial liability. The following analysis provides further guidance on the classification of preference shares as financial liabilities or equity instruments.

Illustrative features of preference shares

62   A company issues preference shares that:

- carry a fixed right to cumulative dividends;
- have the same voting rights as the ordinary shares;
- the issuer is under no obligation to redeem these shares (but may be able to choose to redeem them); and
- in a formal winding up the preference shares rank above the ordinary shares and receive par value.

Analysis

63   In determining whether the preference shares are a financial liability or an equity instrument the issuer will need to assess the particular rights attaching to the shares.

64   In the straightforward case where the preference shares provide for redemption on a set date they would be classified as financial liabilities. The classification is clear from looking at the rights attached to the shares i.e. at the set redemption date the issuer has an obligation to transfer financial assets to the holder of the preference shares.

65   For preference shares that the issuer is not obliged to redeem the appropriate classification is determined by the other rights that attach to them i.e. based on an assessment of the substance of the contractual arrangements and by reference to the definitions of financial liabilities and equity instruments. Therefore only when the distributions to the holders of the preference shares are at the discretion of the issuer will such shares be classified as equity instruments. It should be noted there is a difference between an expectation of dividend payments and an obligation.

66   One feature of the above preference shares is that the holders are entitled to fixed rights to cumulative dividends which are not at the discretion of the issuer. This would indicate that the issuer has an obligation to transfer financial assets to the holders of the preference shares. The shares would therefore be classified as financial liabilities*.

*In arriving at this conclusion, it is assumed that the dividend represents a market rate of return and that the instrument was issued at fair value.

EXAMPLE: CASH FLOW STATEMENT

Entities are encouraged, but not required, to report some cash flow information using the indirect method. An example of a presentation of an indirect method of cash flow statement is given overleaf, as an indication of the type of statements that smaller entities may wish to include in their financial statements. Comparative figures are not shown in the example.

	£	£
Cash generated from operations		
Operating profit/(loss)	**(5,050)**	
Reconciliation to cash generated from operations:		
Depreciation	245	
Increase in stocks	(194)	
Decrease in trade debtors	67,440	
Decrease in trade creditors	(4,678)	
Increase in other creditors	3,127	
		60,890
Cash from other sources		
Interest received	150	
Issues of shares for cash	5,500	
New long-term bank borrowings	4,500	
Proceeds from sale of tangible fixed assets	50	
		10,200
Application of cash		
Interest paid	(3,000)	
Tax paid	(29,220)	
Dividends paid	(10,000)	
Purchase of fixed assets	(10,500)	
Repayment of amounts borrowed		
	(3,000)	
		(55,720)
Net increase in cash		**15,370**
Cash at bank and in hand less overdrafts at beginning of year		(4,321)
Cash at bank and in hand less overdrafts at end of year		
		11,049
Consisting of:		
Cash at bank and in hand		11,549
Overdrafts included in 'bank loans and overdrafts falling due within one year'		
		(500)
		11,049

Major non-cash transactions: finance leases
During the year the company entered into finance lease arrangements in respect of assets with a total capital value at the inception of the leases of £2,850.

EXAMPLE: DISCOUNTING WHEN MAKING A PROVISION

A company faces a fine for operating without due regard to safety legislation. The company has been notified of the case and expects to lose it but does not expect the fine (of £100,000) to be payable for five years. How much should be provided for if the amount and timing of the fine is assumed to be certain and the market rate on relevant government bonds is 5 per cent?

The discounted amount for the payment of £100,000 to be made in five years' time is:

$$\frac{£100,000}{(1 + (5/100))^5} = £78,353$$

Therefore, in the current year £78,353 is recorded as an expense and a provision in the company's books, rather than £100,000.

In the subsequent years the discount will unwind, increasing the amount of the provision and resulting in a debit to the profit and loss account (shown as a financial expense separate from interest) as follows:

		£
year 1	(78,353 x 5%)	3,918
year 2	((78,353 + 3,918) x 5%)	4,113
year 3	etc	4,319
year 4	etc	4,535
year 5	etc	4,762
		21,647
Add amount originally recorded		78,353
Total provision at end of year 5		100,000

Appendix IV
The development of the FRSSE

For many years there has been different reporting by different types of company: the   **1**
requirements for listed public companies have been more onerous than for private
companies and those for larger companies more onerous than for smaller companies. In particular, the provisions of the EC Fourth and Seventh Company Law
Directives have been adopted in the UK and the Republic of Ireland, through which
the disclosure requirements for large, medium-sized and small companies have been
varied, allowing small companies more extensive exemptions both in the abbreviated
accounts to be filed with the registrar of companies and in the statutory accounts for
shareholders.

The application of accounting standards for smaller companies has also been an   **2**
issue for standard-setters. The Board, prompted by the concern to reduce burdens
on business, asked the Consultative Committee of Accountancy Bodies (CCAB) to
establish a Working Party to examine the issue and to undertake wide consultation
with a view to recommending criteria for exempting certain types of entity from
accounting standards on the grounds of size or relative lack of public interest.

The CCAB Working Party published a Consultative Document in November 1994.   **3**
This proposed that the Board should exempt all entities that met the Companies Act
definition of a small company from compliance with all but the five accounting
standards and the UITF Abstract noted below, which would continue to apply.

SSAP 4   'Accounting for government grants'

SSAP 9   'Stocks and long-term contracts'

SSAP 13   'Accounting for research and development'

SSAP 17   'Accounting for post balance sheet events'

SSAP 18   'Accounting for contingencies'

UITF   'True and fair view override disclosures'.
Abstract 7

Comments in response to that Consultative Document supported the use of the small   **4**
companies threshold and a change in the present system whereby small entities were
required to comply with almost all accounting standards. However, there was no
clear support for the proposal of piecemeal application of a limited number of
standards. Analysis of the comments identified a number of recurrent themes,
including the need for guidance on measurement issues and the suggestion that a
codification of all standards should be undertaken as well as a comprehensive review
of those standards that were perceived as needing revision or updating, particularly
in the context of their application to smaller entities. On the latter point, the amount
of time needed for this codification and review was recognised, as was the observation that it might not provide a complete solution for the issues faced by smaller
entities.

Prompted by the comments received, the proposals in the DTI's Consultative   **5**
Document 'Accounting Simplifications' published in May 1995 and the wish to focus
on the needs of smaller entities, the CCAB Working Party proposed in its Paper
'Designed to fit', published in December 1995, that there should be a specific
Financial Reporting Standard for Smaller Entities. To demonstrate that this

approach was feasible, practical and capable of delivering benefits to those involved with financial statements for smaller entities, a draft FRSSE was included in 'Designed to fit'.

6   Letters of comment received in response to 'Designed to fit' indicated general support for a FRSSE that would apply to small companies and groups, as defined in companies legislation. Accordingly, the CCAB Working Party recommended to the Board that it should publish, as part of its due process, an Exposure Draft containing the proposed FRSSE, amended as appropriate to incorporate comments made on the draft contained in 'Designed to fit'.

7   The Board, largely accepting the CCAB Working Party's recommendations, duly published an Exposure Draft of the proposed FRSSE in December 1996, based on the proposals in 'Designed to fit', but with three main differences. First, the proposed FRSSE in the Exposure Draft was capable of application to small groups, unlike the proposals in 'Designed to fit'. Secondly, guidance on debt factoring arrangements was included in the Exposure Draft. Lastly, the requirement in 'Designed to fit' for a summarised cash flow statement was omitted. This led to the issue of the FRSSE in November 1997.

LINK WITH COMPANIES LEGISLATION

8   The FRSSE is linked with accounts drawn up in Great Britain under Schedule 8 to the Companies Act 1985* for the following reasons:

(a)   it allows the establishment of a clearly distinguishable regime, i.e. the relevant statutory Schedule and the FRSSE. The importance of this was enhanced by the implementation of the Companies Act 1985 (Accounts of Small and Medium-Sized Companies and Minor Accounting Amendments) Regulations 1997 (SI 1997/220), which established a revised Schedule 8, containing all of the provisions applying to small companies; and

(b)   it creates the link with the Schedule 8 provisions on a true and fair view, which may be of assistance to standard-setters and others in justifying different disclosure and any simplified measurement regime.

MATTERS CONSIDERED IN THE DEVELOPMENT OF THE FRSSE ISSUED IN NOVEMBER 1997

Application to small groups

9   Small groups are not required by law to prepare consolidated accounts, and therefore in practice not many do so, at least on a statutory basis. The Board, however, agreed that it would be unfair to those small groups that voluntarily prepare group accounts, if they were not able to take advantage of the provisions in the FRSSE. To import all the necessary requirements from accounting standards and UITF Abstracts into the FRSSE to deal with consolidated accounts would have added substantially to its length and complexity, even though it would have been of interest to only a small percentage of entities. Accordingly, the Board preferred to extend the FRSSE in certain areas and then require small groups adopting the FRSSE to follow those accounting standards and UITF Abstracts that deal with consolidated financial statements. This approach was supported by the majority of respondents to the Exposure Draft commenting on the matter.

The equivalent legislation in Northern Ireland is Schedule 8 to the Companies (Northern Ireland) Order 1986. There is no equivalent to Schedule 8 in companies legislation in the Republic of Ireland. See Appendix VII for Republic of Ireland legal requirements.

Cash flow statements

Consistently with the views of the majority of respondents to 'Designed to fit', the   **10**
Exposure Draft did not propose any cash flow disclosures based on FRS 1 (Revised
1996) 'Cash Flow Statements'. The majority of respondents to the Exposure Draft
supported the deletion of the cash flow requirements. However, given that management of cash is fundamental to the success of small businesses, the Board agreed
with the minority of respondents, mainly representing users of the financial statements, that a cash flow statement is important. It provides a useful focus for
discussions with management, as well as a reference point for subsequent more
detailed analysis that users might require. Despite this, the Board recognised the
difficulty of mandating a cash flow requirement when, previously, small entities had
been exempt from such a requirement. Furthermore, the Board acknowledged that a
cash flow format based on FRS 1 (Revised 1996) was not necessarily suitable or
appropriate for smaller businesses.

The Board, therefore, while not mandating cash flow statements, strongly   **11**
encourages smaller entities to provide such a statement voluntarily. Consultations
suggested that it would be preferable to advocate only one method of cash flow
presentation, for consistency and comparability. The direct method of cash flow
statement, in a format similar to an entity's own cash forecasts and management
accounts, may provide a link between management's cash projections and the
financial statements. However, the indirect method is helpful in understanding the
connection between the cash generated during a period and the resulting profit.
Following consultation, the Board encourages the presentation of a cash flow
statement using the indirect method as it is generally held to be more useful and
better understood by many users of financial statements, as well as less costly to
prepare.

Related party disclosures

About half of the respondents to the Board's Exposure Draft of the FRSSE believed   **12**
that the FRSSE should not include any of the provisions from FRS 8 'Related Party
Disclosures'. They argued that they were unnecessary, given that Parts II and III of
Schedule 6 to the Companies Act 1985 require the disclosure of dealings in favour of
directors and connected persons. Furthermore, if there was a material transaction
with a related party, possibly executed at other than fair value, then, where there was
any doubt whether applying any provision of the FRSSE would be sufficient to give
a true and fair view, adequate explanation in the notes to the accounts of the
transaction or arrangement concerned and the treatment adopted would be required
(paragraph 2.5).

The Board, however, shared the view of the other respondents that related party   **13**
disclosures are needed for a proper understanding of an entity's operations and for a
true and fair view, given that material related party transactions are generally more
prevalent in smaller businesses. It also noted that, in respect of dealings in favour of
directors and connected persons, the statutory provisions apply equally to companies
of all sizes and although the provisions overlapped the disclosure requirements in
FRS 8 in many respects, the FRS was broader in scope and, in particular, expressed
more clearly than the Act the spirit of Schedule 6. It also clarified, to the benefit of
both preparers and auditors, the disclosures necessary to meet the fundamental
requirement that accounts should give a true and fair view.

The Board, however, accepted that the full requirements of FRS 8 were unduly   **14**
onerous and could be reduced for smaller entities, without compromising the benefit

of the disclosures. Accordingly, the FRSSE requires that only those related party transactions that are material to the reporting entity need be disclosed in the notes to the financial statements, even though the FRS requires the disclosure of some transactions that are material only in relation to the other related party.

FRS 5

15   The FRSSE requires regard to be had to the substance of any arrangement or transaction, or series of such, into which an entity has entered. But it does not contain the extensive discussion in FRS 5 'Reporting the Substance of Transactions' on reflecting the substance of transactions. This is because small entities generally do not enter into complex transactions. However, the Board was advised that debt factoring and consignment stock may be a common feature of such entities and accordingly the provisions, principally in FRS 5's Application Notes, are likely to be of value to small entities. The relevant guidance in FRS 5 has therefore been included in the FRSSE.

SUBSEQUENT AMENDMENTS TO THE FRSSE

The FRSSE (effective March 1999)

16   On issuing the FRSSE, the Board acknowledged that it would need to be revised and updated periodically to reflect developments in financial reporting. The first such revision was issued in December 1998, and incorporated the relevant aspects of FRSs 9-11 and UITF Abstracts 18-22. The main changes were to align the requirements for entities applying the FRSSE with the basic measurement requirements of FRS 10 'Goodwill and Intangible Assets', which was issued in December 1997, and FRS 11 'Impairment of Fixed Assets and Goodwill', which was issued in July 1998.

17   The measurement requirements in the FRSSE were simplified, compared with those of FRS 10 and FRS 11, by:

- setting 20 years as a maximum, rather than a presumed maximum that may be rebutted, for the useful economic lives assigned to intangible assets and goodwill arising on the acquisition of unincorporated businesses, thereby removing the need for annual exercises to forecast and discount future cash flows
- removing the exception that allows recognition of internally developed intangible assets with market values and revaluation of any intangible asset with a market value
- omitting the detailed requirements for calculating value in use (as part of reco-verable amount) and the subsequent monitoring of cash flows for five years following an impairment review where recoverable amount has been based on value in use.

18   The Board acknowledged that in principle the options for smaller entities applying the FRSSE would be more restricted than those for entities applying FRS 10. However, the Board is of the opinion that it would not, in practice, be restricting the options, as smaller entities would rarely be in a position to take advantage of them. The Board has not incorporated the detailed requirements from FRS 11 in the FRSSE, in order to allow smaller entities greater flexibility by enabling simpler calculations to be used where appropriate, given that detailed cash flow projections of smaller businesses are often not readily available.

The FRSSE (effective March 2000)

The second revision of the FRSSE was issued in December 1999. It incorporated the **19** relevant aspects, modified and simplified where appropriate for smaller entities, of the four Financial Reporting Standards (FRSs 12-15) that were issued between July 1998 and June 1999.

The main changes were to update and add to the material relating to provisions and **20** fixed assets, to reflect the issue of FRSs 12 'Provisions, contingent liabilities and contingent assets' and 15 'Tangible fixed assets'. FRSs 13 and 14, which deal with financial instruments and earnings per share, respectively, were not addressed.

The detailed rules of FRS 12 relating to discounting were omitted from the FRSSE, **21** as were the majority of the disclosure requirements. The requirements of FRS 15 were also simplified for inclusion in the FRSSE, particularly those relating to revaluations and the disclosure requirements.

The FRSSE (effective June 2002)

The third revision of the FRSSE was issued in December 2001. It incorporated the **22** relevant aspects, modified and simplified where appropriate for smaller entities of the four Financial Reporting Standards (FRSs 16-19) that were issued between July 1999 and June 2001.

The main changes were to update the requirements relating to current and deferred **23** tax to reflect the issue of FRS 16 'Current tax' and FRS 19 'Deferred tax'. The requirement for discounting of deferred tax balances in FRS 19 was not included and a number of presentational and disclosure requirements were omitted.

A new Appendix II was added to the FRSSE setting out the requirements for **24** accounting for defined benefit schemes included in FRS 17 'Retirement benefits'. Some of the requirements of FRS 18 'Accounting policies' were incorporated into the FRSSE to ensure the framework underpinning the definition, selection and disclosure of accounting policies by FRSSE entities is consistent with that applied by other companies.

The FRSSE (effective January 2005)

The fourth edition of the FRSSE was issued in April 2005. In developing this revi- **25** sion, the Board considered the relevant aspects, modified and simplified as appropriate for smaller entities, of the two Financial Reporting Standards (FRS 20 and 21), amendments to FRS 5 and FRS 17 and eight UITF Abstracts (UITF Abstracts 31 to 38) that were issued between June 2001 and November 2004. The Board also considered the requirements of relevant companies legislation.

The main changes were to update the requirements for post balance sheet events to **26** be consistent with FRS 21 and to incorporate the principles on revenue recognition from Application Note G to FRS 5. Specific guidance on "bill and hold arrangements", "sales with rights of return" and "presentation of turnover as principal or as agent" were also included in Appendix III as these are transactions commonly undertaken by smaller entities. An additional disclosure example for a defined contribution pension scheme was also included in Appendix III.

The Board decided not introduce any of the requirements from FRS 20 (IFRS 2) **27** Share-based Payment into the FRSSE but proposed to consider further in a future update. It also decided not to reflect the requirements of UITF Abstracts 31 to 38 other than UITF Abstract 34 "Pre-contract costs" which deals with the costs incurred in bidding for and securing contracts to supply goods or services. of the FRSSE. The Board also incorporated the requirements of UITF Abstract 40 as guidance in Appendix III.

The FRSSE (effective January 2007)

28   The amendments made to the January 2005 version of the FRSSE are largely based upon those proposed in the Exposure Draft on amending the FRSSE that was published in April 2006. In developing this revision, the Board was again advised by its specialist Committee on Accounting for Smaller Entities (CASE).

29   This fifth revision of the FRSSE was published in January 2007 and incorporates the relevant aspects, modified and simplified where appropriate for smaller entities, of the eight new Financial Reporting Standards (FRS 22 to FRS 29), two amendments to FRSs (FRS 2 and FRS 26) and two UITF Abstracts (UITF 39 and UITF 40) that have been issued since October 2004, when the last Exposure Draft of amendments to the FRSSE was published. It also considers FRS 20 "Share-based payment", which was not addressed in the last amendment of the FRSSE, and changes in the company law financial reporting requirements affecting smaller entities.

30   The main question asked by the Board in publishing the Exposure Draft was whether the FRSSE should require smaller entities to apply the key principles of FRS20 for share-based payment arrangements. The majority of respondents argued against this proposal on the grounds that share-based payments were relatively uncommon for smaller entities and that the costs of complying with FRS20 are likely to outweigh the benefits obtained by users of small company accounts. The Board acknowledged these arguments and accepted CASE's proposals that cash settled transactions should be reported at the entity's best estimate of the expenditure required to settle the liability at the balance sheet date and that equity settled arrangements should be reported on a disclosure only basis.

31   The other main issue arising from consultation relates to the FRS 25 requirements for classifying capital instruments as either debt or equity. Respondents commented this was a difficult issue for smaller entities, particularly in terms of preference shares, and one where illustrative guidance in the FRSSE would be welcomed. The FRSSE (effective January 2007) therefore includes practical guidance that is intended to assist smaller entities in applying the presentation requirements of FRS 25.

32   A number of other minor changes have been made to the FRSSE (effective January 2007), which now permits early adoption, to reflect recent changes in company law and to make some presentational changes. The most significant presentational change has been to remove Appendices V to VII, thereby helping to make the FRSSE a more manageable document. The Board acknowledges that smaller entities find the derivation information included in these Appendices helpful and is therefore committed to making it freely available on the ASB website.

RELATIONSHIP WITH OTHER ASB DOCUMENTS

33   The FRSSE is designed to provide smaller entities with a single accounting standard that is focused on their particular circumstances. Smaller entities that choose to adopt the FRSSE are exempt from other accounting standards and UITF Abstracts (with certain exceptions for those small groups preparing consolidated financial statements). The Board accepts that the FRSSE is not comprehensive and that there

may be issues of general application on which guidance will be sought. Preparers may come across transactions on which accounting guidance is not provided in the FRSSE. This raises the question of whether, in the absence of guidance within the FRSSE, preparers and auditors would be required to follow all SSAPs, other FRSs and UITF Abstracts to the extent that they provide guidance on transactions of relevance to the smaller entity. The Board's view, formulated after consultation with legal advisers and others, is that users expect financial statements to be prepared using accepted practice. If a practice was clearly established and accepted, it should be followed unless there were good reasons to depart from it. Accordingly, preparers and auditors should have regard to SSAPs, FRSs and UITF Abstracts, not as mandatory documents, but as a means of establishing current practice.

The Board rejected suggestions that there should be specific cross-references within the FRSSE to SSAPs, other FRSs and UITF Abstracts. This is because the inclusion of cross-references would lead to preparers and auditors having to consider those other pronouncements in all cases, as well as the FRSSE, thereby lengthening checklists and adding to the burden. Furthermore, it is recognised that as new FRSs are issued that amend generally accepted accounting practice as it applies to larger entities, it may not be appropriate for such rules to apply to smaller entities. An example that has been frequently cited, but on which the Board has not established a firm position, is that some of the likely proposals on marking to market fixed interest instruments, while appropriate for larger entities, would not be appropriate for smaller entities. Because generally accepted accounting practice had not been established for all in this area then there would not be an expectation that smaller entities should have regard to such a new rule.

34

Appendix V
Amendment to the FRSSE (effective January 2007)

1   In publishing this updated version of the Financial Reporting Standard for Smaller Entities (effective January 2007), the Board was advised by its specialist Committee on Accounting for Smaller Entities (CASE).

2   The Board and CASE considered FRS 20 on share-based payment (which was not considered as part of the last FRSSE update) and all new Financial Reporting Standards (since FRS 21 which was considered as part of the 2005 FRSSE update), amendments to FRSs and UITF Abstracts that have been issued since the last Exposure Draft of amendments to the FRSSE was published. These are listed in the table below.

New FRSs, amendments to FRSs and UITF abstracts	Title	Issued
Amendment to FRS 2	Accounting for subsidiary undertakings	December 2004
FRS 22	(IAS 33) Earnings per share	December 2004
FRS 23	(IAS 21) The effects of changes in foreign exchange rates	December 2004
FRS 24	(IAS 29) Financial reporting in hyperinflationary economies	December 2004
FRS 25	(IAS 32) Financial Instruments: disclosure and presentation	December 2004
FRS 26	(IAS 39) Financial Instruments: measurement	December 2004
FRS 27	Life Assurance	December 2004
Amendment to FRS 26	(IAS 39) Financial Instruments: measurement – various amendments	October 2005
FRS 28	Corresponding amounts	October 2005
FRS 29	(IFRS 7) Financial Instruments: disclosures	December 2005
Amendment to FRS 23	(IAS 21) The effects of changes in foreign exchange rates – net investment in a foreign operation	December 2005
UITF Abstract 39	(IFRIC interpretation 2) Members shares in cooperative entities and similar instruments	February 2005
UITF Abstract 40	Revenue recognition and service contracts	March 2005

3   This appendix sets out all the changes to Part B 'Statement of Standard Accounting Practice' and Part C 'Definitions' of the FRSSE (effective January 2005) that have been incorporated into this version of the FRSSE. New paragraphs or significant

revisions have been highlighted in parts B and C by sidelining the text. Most amendments arise from incorporation of the relevant aspects of recent FRSs and UITF Abstracts, modified and simplified where appropriate for smaller entities. The Board has also included within this version of the FRSSE requirements for accounting for share based payment (FRS 20). Early adoption is also now permitted.

In addition, and now that the full requirements of FRS 17 are mandatory, an **4** updated illustrative example for the disclosure of a defined benefit pension scheme is provided in Appendix III. Also included in Appendix III is new guidance on the FRS 25 requirements for the classification of capital instruments as debt or equity.

The other changes to note include a change to paragraph 19.1 of the Statement of **5** Standard Accounting Practice that now permits early application and changes to the scope of the FRSSE in paragraph 8 of the Status section which :

- no longer precludes certain authorised persons under the Financial Services and Markets Act 2000* from using the FRSSE; but
- does now preclude companies preparing group or individual accounts in accordance with the fair value rules for certain assets and liabilities from using the FRSSE.

There are also a number of minor changes arising from updates in company law **6** financial reporting for smaller entities and, with a view to making the FRSSE a more manageable document, the derivation information that was included from Appendices V to VII in FRSSE (effective January 2005) has been removed and is now being separately maintained (and is freely available) on the ASB website (www.frc-asb.org.uk).

FRS 28 CORRESPONDING AMOUNTS

Amendments to Statement of Standard Accounting Practice

As a consequence of changes to the Companies Act 1985, it falls to accounting **7** standards to set out the requirements for corresponding amounts. FRS 28 sets out these requirements which require consequential amendments to the FRSSE. Paragraph 2.23 of the Statement of Standard Accounting Practice has been replaced with the following text (which is now in lower case).

2.23 Corresponding amounts for the previous accounting period shall be shown for every item disclosed in the balance sheet, profit and loss account and notes to the financial statements. Where there is no amount to be shown for an item in the balance sheet or profit and loss account for the current accounting period but a corresponding amount can be shown for the previous accounting period, the corresponding amount shall be shown. Where a corresponding amount is not comparable with that for the current accounting period, it shall be adjusted and particulars of the adjustment and the reasons for it shall be disclosed in a note to the financial statements. Corresponding amounts are not required in relation to any amounts stated in the notes to the financial statements for the items listed below:

The Companies Act 1985 (Small Companies' Accounts and Audit) Regulations 2006 came into force on 8 November 2006 and applies for financial years ending on or after 31 December 2006. The Regulations allow more categories of small financial services companies to qualify as small and take advantage of the small company exemptions. However companies that are required to have an audit based on a requirement in a European directive are still prohibited from taking advantage of the small company exemptions. In case of doubt, reference should be made to the Regulations.

(e)   details of additions, disposals, revaluations, transfers and cumulative depreciation of fixed assets;

(f)   transfers to or from reserves and provisions and the source and application of any transfers;

(g)   details of a company's shareholdings in subsidiary undertakings;

(h)   details of a company's significant holdings in undertakings other than subsidiary undertakings

FRS 20 SHARE-BASED PAYMENT

Amendments to Statement of Standard Accounting Practice

8   New paragraphs 12.13 and 12.14 have been inserted into section 12 of the Statement of Standard Accounting Practice which now covers "financial instruments, share capital and share-based payments". The new paragraphs come after a new sub-title "Share-based payments":

Share-based payments

12.13   An entity which undertakes **share-based payment arrangements**, including transactions with **employees or others providing similar services** shall account for them as follows

Cash-settled share-based payment transactions

(a)   An entity shall **recognise** the goods or services received or acquired when it obtains the goods or as the services are received. If the goods or services received or acquired do not qualify for recognition as **assets**, they shall be **recognised** as expenses. The entity shall **recognise** a corresponding **liability.**

(b)   The amount of the goods or services and the corresponding **liability recognised** shall be the best estimate of the expenditure required to settle the **liability** at the balance sheet date. The **liability** shall be remeasured at each balance sheet date and at the date of settlement.

(c)   Information shall be disclosed in a note to describe the principal terms and conditions of cash settled share-based payment transactions that exist during the period, including their current and potential financial effect.

Equity-settled share-based payment arrangements

Information shall be disclosed in a note to describe the principal terms and conditions of any equity settled share-based payment arrangements that exist during the period including, the number of shares and the number of employees and others potentially involved, the grant date, any performance conditions and over what periods these apply and, where applicable, any option exercise prices.

12.14   Where the terms of the arrangement provide the counterparty with the choice of whether the entity settles the transaction in cash (or other assets) or by issuing **equity instruments**, the transaction, shall be accounted for as a cash settled transaction in accordance with paragraph 12.13 (a) to (c) above. The liability shall be measured at the best estimate of the amount required to settle it at the balance sheet date if the counterparty were to opt for cash settlement. If the obligation is eventually settled by the issue of equity instruments, the liability previously recognised should be treated as the proceeds of issue of those instruments.

12.15 Where the entity and not the counterparty has the choice of settlement method, the arrangement shall be treated as either an equity settled transaction in accordance with paragraph 12.13 (d) or a cash settled transaction in accordance with paragraph 12.13 (a) to (c), as appropriate and in the entity's circumstances.

Amendments to definitions

The following definitions are inserted into Part C 'Definitions' of the FRSSE: **9**

Cash-settled share-based payment transaction:-

A **share-based payment transaction** in which the entity acquires goods or services by incurring a **liability** to transfer cash or other **assets** to the supplier of those goods or services for amounts that are based on the price (or value) of the entity's shares or other **equity instruments** of the entity.

Employees and others providing similar services:-

Individuals who render personal services to the entity and either (a) the individuals are regarded as employees for legal or tax purposes, (b) the individuals work for the entity under its direction in the same way as individuals who are regarded as employees for legal or tax purposes, or (c) the services rendered are similar to those rendered by employees. For example, the term encompasses all management personnel, ie those persons having authority and responsibility for planning, directing and controlling the activities of the entity, including non-executive directors.

Equity Instrument granted:-

The right (conditional or unconditional) to an equity instrument of the entity conferred by the entity on another party, under a share-based payment arrangement.

Equity-settled share-based payment transaction:-

A **share-based payment transaction** in which the entity receives goods or services as consideration for **equity instruments** of the entity (including shares or share options).

Grant date for share-based payment arrangements:-

The date at which the entity and another party (including an employee) agree to a share-based payment arrangement, being when the entity and the counterparty have a shared understanding of the terms and conditions of the arrangement. At grant date the entity confers on the counterparty the right to cash, other **assets**, or **equity instruments** of the entity, provided the specified vesting conditions, if any, are met. If that agreement is subject to an approval process (for example, by shareholders), grant date is the date when that approval is obtained.

Share-based payment transaction:-

A transaction in which the entity receives goods or services as consideration for **equity instruments** of the entity (including shares or share options), or acquires goods or services by incurring **liabilities** to the supplier of those goods or services for amounts that are based on the price of the entity's shares or other **equity instruments** of the entity.

CONTRACTS FOR SERVICES (UITF ABSTRACT 40)

Amendments to Statement of Standard Accounting Practice

10   The consensus paragraphs from UITF Abstract 40 have been moved from Appendix III into section 4 of the Statement of Standard Accounting Practice on Revenue Recognition. The new paragraphs are from 4.10 to 4.15 and come after a new subtitle Contracts for services. The critical event requirement from paragraph 19 of UITF Abstract 40 has also been inserted as part of the new paragraph 4.14.

Contracts for services

4.10   Where there are distinguishable phases of a single contract it may be appropriate to account for the contract as two or more separate transactions, provided the value of each phase can be reliably estimated.

4.11   Contracts for services should not be accounted for as long-term contracts unless they involve the provision of a single service, or a number of services that constitute a single project.

4.12   A contract for services should be accounted for as a long-term contract where contract activity falls into different accounting periods and it is concluded that the effect is material. In determining whether contracts should be accounted for as long-term contracts, the aggregate effect of all such contracts on the financial statements as a whole should be considered.

4.13   Where the substance of a contract is that the seller's contractual obligations are performed gradually over time, revenue should be recognised as contract activity progresses to reflect the seller's partial performance of its contractual obligations. The amount of revenue should reflect the accrual of the right to consideration as contract activity progresses by reference to value of the work performed.

4.14   Where the substance of a contract is that a right to consideration does not arise until the occurrence of a critical event, revenue is not recognised until that event occurs. This only applies where the right to consideration is conditional or contingent on a specified future event or outcome, the occurrence of which is outside the control of the seller.

4.15   The amount of revenue recognised on any contract for services should reflect any uncertainties as to the amount that the customer will accept and pay.

SUBSIDIARY UNDERTAKINGS

Amendment to Definitions

11   The FOLLOWING DEFINITIONS ARE INSERTED INTO PART C "DEFINITIONS" OF THE FRSSE:

SUBSIDIARY UNDERTAKINGS*

AN UNDERTAKING IS A SUBSIDIARY OF A PARENT UNDERTAKING WHERE THE PARENT:

(A)   HOLDS A MAJORITY OF THE VOTING RIGHTS IN THE UNDERTAKING, OR

*In case of doubt, reference should be made to the full definition in section 258 of the Companies Act 1985

(B) IS A MEMBER OF THE UNDERTAKING AND HAS THE RIGHT TO APPOINT OR REMOVE A MAJORITY OF ITS BOARD OF DIRECTORS, OR

(C) HAS THE RIGHT TO EXERCISE A DOMINANT INFLUENCE OVER THE UNDERTAKING BY VIRTUE OF PROVISIONS CONTAINED IN ITS ARTICLES OR BY VIRTUE OF A CONTROL CONTRACT, OR

(D) IS A MEMBER OF THE UNDERTAKING AND CONTROLS ALONE, PURSUANT TO AN AGREEMENT WITH OTHER SHAREHOLDERS OR MEMBERS, A MAJORITY OF THE VOTING RIGHTS; OR.

(E) HAS THE POWER TO EXERCISE, OR ACTUALLY EXERCISES, DOMINANT INFLUENCE OR CONTROL OVER THE UNDERTAKING;OR

(F) THE PARENT AND THE SUBSIDIARY UNDERTAKING ARE MANAGED ON A UNIFIED BASIS.

Definitions in respect of SSAP24 "Accounting for pension costs" have been deleted **12** from Part C "Definitions" of the FRSSE as this standard has been withdrawn for accounting periods ending on or after 22 June 2006 with the requirements of FRS 17, "Retirement benefits" applying in full.

Part Four

Statements by the
Accounting Standards Board

Reporting Statement:
Operating and financial review

Contents

Reporting statement:
Operating and Financial Review (OFR)

Introduction

1   The Accounting Standards Board (ASB) originally issued the Statement 'Operating and Financial Review' in July 1993. The Statement built on the foundations of existing best practice by providing a framework within which directors could discuss the main factors underlying the company's performance and financial position. The Statement was updated and a revised version issued in January 2003 to reflect later improvements in narrative reporting.

2   Following a recommendation in the final report of the Company Law Review (CLR) Steering Group (2001) and the Government response on the White Paper 'Modernising Company Law' (2002), the Government decided to require quoted companies to prepare and publish OFRs. In May 2004, the Government issued proposals on the detailed implementation of this new requirement in a consultation document 'Draft Regulations on the Operating and Financial Review and Directors' Report'. The consultation document contained draft secondary legislation to implement a new statutory OFR as well as certain provisions of the EU Accounts Modernisation Directive requiring an enhanced review of a company's business (the Business Review) in the directors' report. Following consultation, the final OFR Regulations were passed into law in March 2005, taking effect for financial years beginning on or after 1 April 2005.

3   The Government also gave the ASB a statutory power to make reporting standards for the OFR. In November 2004, the ASB issued Reporting Exposure Draft (RED) 1 'The Operating and Financial Review'. Following consultation, Reporting Standard (RS) 1 was issued in May 2005.

4   On 28 November 2005, the Chancellor of the Exchequer announced the Government's intention to remove the statutory requirement on quoted companies to publish OFRs, on the grounds that the central requirements of the Business Review are largely identical to those of the statutory OFR and the Government has a general policy not to impose regulatory requirements on UK businesses over and above the relevant EU Directive requirements. Regulations to repeal the requirement for the OFR were laid in December 2005 and came into force on 12 January 2006.

5   The statutory underpinning for RS 1 has been removed as a result of the removal of the statutory requirement for the OFR. As a consequence, RS 1 has now been formally withdrawn and the ASB has 'converted' RS 1 into a statement of best practice on the OFR, which is set out in this document. In preparing this statement, the ASB has sought to limit the changes to those required as a consequence of the repeal of the OFR legislation and to make the language consistent with a voluntary statement of best practice rather than a standard. Given the extensive consultation that took place in developing RS 1, and the need to continue to give entities guidance in preparing OFRs, the ASB is issuing this as a final Reporting Statement, rather than engaging in a further round of consultation.

Reporting statement:
Operating and Financial Review (OFR)

Summary

The Reporting Statement is designed as a formulation and development of best **a** practice; it is intended to have persuasive rather than mandatory force. This Statement has been written with quoted companies in mind, but is also applicable to any other entities that purport to prepare an OFR.

The Reporting Statement recommends that directors prepare an OFR addressed to **b** members, setting out their analysis of the business, with a forward-looking orientation in order to assist members to assess the strategies adopted by the entity and the potential for those strategies to succeed. The information disclosed in the OFR will also be of relevance to other stakeholders. The OFR should not, however, be seen as a replacement for other forms of reporting addressed to a wider stakeholder group.

The Reporting Statement sets out a number of other principles regarded as best **c** practice in the preparation of an OFR, namely that the review should: both complement and supplement the financial statements; be comprehensive and understandable; be balanced and neutral; and be comparable over time.

The Reporting Statement sets out the key elements of the disclosure framework that **d** directors should address in an OFR, including details on particular matters that should be disclosed to the extent necessary to meet the objective of the OFR.

Those Key Performance Indicators (KPIs) judged by the directors to be effective in **e** measuring the development, performance and position of the business of the entity should be disclosed, together with information that should enable members to understand and evaluate each KPI.

The Reporting Statement recommends the inclusion of other measures and evidence **f** to support the information included in the OFR.

The Reporting Statement is accompanied by Implementation Guidance that provides **g** illustrative examples of KPIs that might be disclosed in an OFR, as well as further guidance as to what is envisaged with regard to particular matters.

Reporting statement:
Operating and Financial Review (OFR)

OBJECTIVE

1   The objective of this Reporting Statement is to specify the best practice for an OFR, which should be a balanced and comprehensive analysis, consistent with the size and complexity of the business, of:

a.   the development and performance of the business of the entity during the financial year;

b.   the position of the entity at the end of the year;

c.   the main trends and factors underlying the development, performance and position of the business of the entity during the financial year; and

d.   the main trends and factors which are likely to affect the entity's future development, performance and position,

prepared so as to assist members to assess the strategies adopted by the entity and the potential for those strategies to succeed.

SCOPE

2   The Reporting Statement has been written with quoted companies in mind, but is also applicable to any other entities that purport to prepare an OFR.

DEFINITIONS

3   The following terms are used in this Reporting Statement with the meanings specified:

Directors

Reference to either "directors" or "board of directors" within the Reporting Statement is taken to be the entity's governing body where the entity is not a company.

Key Performance Indicators (KPIs)

KPIs are factors by reference to which the development, performance or position of the business of the entity can be measured effectively. They are quantified measurements that reflect the critical success factors of an entity and disclose progress towards achieving a particular objective or objectives.

Operating and Financial Review (OFR)

An OFR is a narrative explanation, provided in or accompanying the annual report, of the main trends and factors underlying the development, performance and position of an entity during the financial year covered by the financial statements, and those which are likely to affect the entity's future development, performance and position.

PRINCIPLES

The OFR should set out an analysis of the business through the eyes of the board of directors. 4

The OFR should reflect the directors' view of the business. Accordingly, the entity 5
should disclose appropriate elements of information used in managing the entity, including its subsidiary undertakings. Where appropriate, the review may give greater emphasis to those matters which are significant to the entity and its subsidiary undertakings taken as a whole. Such matters may include issues specific to business segments where relevant to the understanding of the business as a whole. Directors should develop the presentation of their OFR in a way that complements the format of their annual report as a whole.

The OFR should focus on matters that are relevant to the interests of members. 6

Members' needs are paramount when directors consider what information should be 7
contained in the OFR. Information in the OFR will also be of interest to users other than members, for example other investors, potential investors, creditors, customers, suppliers, employees and society more widely. The directors should consider the extent to which they should report on issues relevant to those other users where, because of those issues influence on the performance of the business and its value, they are also of significance to members. The OFR should not, however, be seen as a replacement for other forms of reporting addressed to a wider stakeholder group.

The OFR should have a forward-looking orientation, identifying those trends and 8
factors relevant to the members' assessment of the current and future performance of
the business and the progress towards the achievement of long-term business objectives.

The particular factors discussed should be those that have affected development, 9
performance, and position during the financial year and those which are likely to affect the entity's future development, performance and position.

Given the nature of some forward-looking information, in particular elements that 10
cannot be objectively verified but have been made in good faith, directors may want to include a statement in the OFR to treat such elements with caution, explaining the uncertainties underpinning such information.

The OFR should comment on the impact on future performance of significant events 11
after the balance sheet date.

The OFR should also discuss predictive comments, both positive and negative, made 12
in previous reviews whether or not these have been borne out by events.

The OFR should complement as well as supplement the financial statements, in order to 13
enhance the overall corporate disclosure.

In complementing the financial statements, the OFR should provide useful financial 14
and non-financial information about the business and its performance that is not reported in financial statements but which, the directors' judge, might be relevant to the members' evaluation of past results and assessment of future prospects.

In supplementing the financial statements, the OFR should where relevant: 15

- provide additional explanations of amounts recorded in the financial statements;

- explain the conditions and events that shaped the information contained in the financial statements.

Where amounts from the financial statements have been adjusted for inclusion in the OFR, that fact should be highlighted and a reconciliation provided.

16 **The OFR should be comprehensive and understandable.**

17 Directors should consider whether the omission of information might reasonably be expected to influence significantly the assessment made by members.

18 The recommendation for the OFR to be comprehensive does not mean that the OFR should cover all possible matters: the objective is quality, not quantity of content. It is neither possible nor desirable for a Reporting Statement to list all the elements that might need to be included, since these will vary depending on the nature and circumstances of the particular business and how the business is run.

19 Directors should consider the evidence underpinning the information to be included in the OFR. Where relevant, directors should explain the source of the information and the degree to which the information is objectively supportable, to allow members to assess the reliability of the information presented for themselves.

20 Directors should consider the key issues to include in the OFR that will provide members with focused and relevant information. The inclusion of too much information may obscure judgements and will not promote understanding. Where additional information is discussed elsewhere in the annual report, or in other reports, cross-referencing to those sources will assist members.

21 The OFR should be written in a clear and readily understandable style.

22 **The OFR should be balanced and neutral, dealing even-handedly with both good and bad aspects.**

23 The directors should ensure that the OFR retains balance and that members are not misled as a result of the omission of any information on unfavourable aspects.

24 **The OFR should be comparable over time.**

25 Disclosure should be sufficient for the members to be able to compare the information presented with similar information about the entity for previous financial years. Comparability enables identification of the main trends and factors, and their analysis, over successive financial years. Directors may wish to consider the extent to which the OFR is comparable with reviews prepared by other entities in the same industry or sector.

DISCLOSURE FRAMEWORK

26 Paragraphs 27 to 74 below set out a framework for the disclosures to be provided by directors in an OFR. This framework is not a template, nor should the elements in paragraph 27 be taken as headings that should be included within an OFR. Its purpose is to set out the key content elements that should be addressed within an OFR. It is for directors to consider how best to use the framework to structure the OFR and the precise content, including the level of detail to be disclosed, relating to the key elements, given the particular circumstances of the entity. These circumstances may include:

a.   the industry or industries in which it operates;
b.   the range of products, services or processes it offers;
c.   the number of markets it serves.

The OFR should provide information to assist members to assess the strategies adopted   **27**
by the entity and the potential for those strategies to succeed. The key elements of the
disclosure framework recommended to achieve this are:

a.   **the nature of the business, including a description of the market, competitive and**
      regulatory environment in which the entity operates, and the entity's objectives
      and strategies;
b.   **the development and performance of the business, both in the financial year under**
      review and in the future;
c.   **the resources, principal risks and uncertainties and relationships that may affect**
      the entity's long-term value; and
d.   **position of the business including a description of the capital structure, treasury**
      policies and objectives and liquidity of the entity, both in the financial year under
      review and the future.

Details of particular matters

To the extent necessary to meet the recommendations set out in paragraph 27 above,   **28**
the OFR should include information about:

a.   **environmental matters (including the impact of the business of the entity on the**
      environment);
b.   **the entity's employees;**
c.   **social and community issues;**
d.   **persons with whom the entity has contractual or other arrangements with are**
      essential to the business of the entity;
e.   **receipts from, and returns to, members of the entity in respect of shares held by**
      them; and
f.   **all other matters the directors consider to be relevant.**

For items (a) to (c) in paragraph 28, the OFR should, in particular, include: **29**

a.   **the policies of the entity in each area mentioned; and**
b.   **the extent to which those policies have been successfully implemented.**

The nature, objectives and strategies of the business

The OFR should include a description of the business and the external environment in   **30**
which it operates as context for the directors' discussion and analysis of performance
and financial position.

A description of the business is recommended in order to provide members with an   **31**
understanding of the industry or industries in which the entity operates, its main
products, services, customers, business processes and distribution methods, the
structure of the business, and its economic model, including an overview of the main
operating facilities and their location.

Every entity is affected by its external environment. Depending on the nature of the   **32**
business, the OFR should include discussion of matters such as the entity's major
markets and competitive position within those markets and the significant features of
the legal, regulatory, macro-economic and social environment that influence the
business. For example, an entity may disclose the fact that it has significant

operations in a number of different countries, which could have an impact on the future development and performance of the business.

33   **The OFR should discuss the objectives of the business to generate or preserve value over the longer-term.**

34   Objectives will often be defined in terms of financial performance; however, objectives in non-financial areas should also be discussed where appropriate.

35   The nature of the industry will affect the directors' determination of an appropriate time perspective for reporting in the OFR. For example, a business that focuses on large long-term projects must carry out its strategic planning over the full project lifecycle, which may be 20 years or more. Furthermore, where a project has a long-term impact on the environment, this is likely to affect long-term value and should therefore determine the time perspective for reporting in the OFR. By contrast, a service industry with few physical assets and depending on the supply of particular employee skills for its source of competitive advantage, will plan over a period consistent with its ability to recruit, train and develop its staff, which may be much shorter.

36   **The OFR should set out the directors' strategies for achieving the objectives of the business.**

37   Disclosure of the directors' strategies is recommended in order for members to assess the current and past action undertaken by directors in respect of the stated objectives.

38   **To the extent necessary to meet the recommendations set out in paragraph 27 above, the OFR should include the key performance indicators, both financial and, where appropriate, non-financial, used by the directors to assess progress against their stated objectives.**

39   The KPIs disclosed should be those that the directors judge are effective in measuring the delivery of their strategies and managing their business. Regular measurement using KPIs should enable an entity to set and communicate its performance targets and to measure whether it is achieving them.

40   Comparability will be enhanced if the KPIs disclosed are accepted and widely used, either within the industry sector or more generally.

41   **Directors should also consider the extent to which other measures and evidence should be included in the OFR.**

42   These could be narrative evidence describing how the directors manage the business or quantified measures used to monitor the entity's external environment and/or progress towards the achievement of its objectives.

Current and future development and performance

43   **The OFR should describe the significant features of the development and performance of the business in the financial year covered by the financial statements, focusing on those business segments that are relevant to an understanding of the development and performance as a whole.**

Trends and factors in development and performance suggested by an analysis of the current and previous financial years should be highlighted. Development and performance should be described in the context of the strategic objectives of the business. **44**

The OFR should cover significant aspects of the statements of financial performance and where appropriate should be linked to other aspects of performance. **45**

The OFR should set out the directors' analysis of the effect on current development and performance of changes during the financial year in the industry or the external environment in which the business operates and of developments within the business. For example, changes in market conditions could have an impact on the development and performance of the entity during the period, as could the introduction, or announcement, of new products and services. **46**

The OFR should analyse the main trends and factors that directors consider likely to impact future prospects. **47**

The main trends and factors likely to affect the future development and performance will vary according to the nature of the business, but could include the development of known new products and services or the benefits expected from capital investment. The OFR should discuss the current level of investment expenditure together with planned future expenditure and should explain how that investment is directed to assist the achievement of business objectives. Any assumptions underlying the main trends and factors should be disclosed. **48**

Directors should consider the potential future significance of issues in deciding whether or not to include an analysis of them in the OFR. **49**

Resources

The OFR should include a description of the resources available to the entity and how they are managed. **50**

The OFR should set out the key strengths and resources, tangible and intangible, available to the business, which will assist it in the pursuit of its objectives and, in particular, those items that are not reflected in the balance sheet. Depending on the nature of the business, these may include: corporate reputation and brand strength; natural resources; employees; research and development; intellectual capital; licences, patents, copyright and trademarks; and market position. **51**

Principal risks and uncertainties

The OFR should include a description of the principal risks and uncertainties facing the entity, together with a commentary on the directors' approach to them. **52**

While different industries and entities use different risk models or approaches for identifying and managing risk, all entities face and should disclose strategic, commercial, operational and financial risks where these may significantly affect the entity's strategies and development of the entity's value. **53**

The principal risks and uncertainties facing entities will vary according to the nature of the business, although it is expected that some risks, such as reputational risk, will be common to all. **54**

55   The description of the principal risks and uncertainties should cover both the exposure to negative consequences as well as potential opportunities. The directors' policy for managing principal risks should be disclosed.

56   The OFR should cover the principal risks and uncertainties necessary for an understanding of the objectives and strategies of the business, both where they constitute a significant external risk to the entity, and where the entity's impact on other parties through its activities, products or services, affects its performance. Directors should consider the full range of business risks.

Relationships

57   **To the extent necessary to meet the recommendations set out in paragraph 27 above, the OFR should include information about significant relationships with stakeholders other than members, which are likely, directly or indirectly, to influence the performance of the business and its value.**

58   Directors, in deciding what should be included in the OFR, should take a broad view in considering the extent to which the actions of stakeholders other than members can affect an entity's performance and thus its value. For example, for many entities, relationships with customers, suppliers, employees, contractors, lenders, creditors and regulators will be important, as will the entity's broader impact on society and the communities affected by its activities. Strategic alliances with other entities can also affect the performance of the entity and its value.

59   **Where necessary for an understanding of the business, the OFR should describe receipts from, and returns to, shareholders in relation to shares held by them. This should include a description of any distributions, capital raising and share repurchases.**

Financial position

60   **The OFR should contain an analysis of the financial position of the entity.**

61   The analysis, whilst based upon the financial statements, should comment on the events that have impacted the financial position of the entity during the financial year, and future factors that are likely to affect the financial position going forward. The analysis should supplement the disclosures required in accounting standards, in particular those required by FRS 25 (IAS 32) 'Financial Instruments: Disclosure and Presentation' or FRS 29 (IFRS 7) 'Financial Instruments: Disclosures'.

62   The OFR should highlight accounting policies set out in the notes to the financial statements and discuss those accounting policies that are critical to an understanding of the performance and financial position of the entity, focusing on those which have required the particular exercise of judgement in their application and to which the results are most sensitive. In addition, it should draw attention to the accounting policies which have changed during the financial year under review.

63   **The OFR should contain a discussion of the capital structure of the entity.**

64   This could include the balance between equity and debt, the maturity profile of debt, type of capital instruments used, currency, regulatory capital and interest rate structure. The discussion should include comments on short and longer-term funding plans to support the directors' strategies to achieve the entity's objectives. In addition, the discussion should comment on why the entity has adopted its particular capital structure.

The OFR should set out the entity's treasury policies and objectives.   65

The OFR should also discuss the implementation of these policies in the financial   66
year under review.

The purpose and effect of major financing transactions undertaken up to the date of   67
approval of the financial statements should be explained. The effect of interest costs
on profits and the potential impact of interest rate changes should also be discussed.

Cash flows

The OFR should discuss the cash inflows and outflows during the financial year, along   68
with the entity's ability to generate cash, to meet known or probable cash requirements
and to fund growth.

Any discussion should supplement the information provided in the financial state-   69
ments by, for example, commenting on any special factors that have influenced cash
flows in the financial year and those that may have a significant effect on future cash
flows. This could include, for example, the existence and timing of commitments for
capital expenditures and other known or probable cash requirements. Where entities
have cash that is surplus to future operating requirements and current levels of
distribution, the discussion should include future plans for making use of the excess
cash.

Although segmental analysis of profit may be indicative of the cash flow generated   70
by each segment, this will not always be so – for example, because of fluctuations in
capital expenditure and depreciation. Where segmental cash flows are significantly
out of line with segmental revenues or profits, this should be indicated and explained.

Liquidity

The OFR should discuss the entity's current and prospective liquidity. Where relevant,   71
this should include commentary on the level of borrowings, the seasonality of borrowing
requirements (indicated by the peak level of borrowings during that period) and the
maturity profile of both borrowings and undrawn committed borrowing facilities.

The discussion on liquidity should discuss the ability of the entity to fund its current   72
and future operations and stated strategies.

The discussion should cover internal sources of liquidity, referring to any restrictions   73
on the ability to transfer funds from one part of the group to meet the obligations of
another part of the group, where these represent, or might foreseeably come to
represent, a significant restraint on the group. Such constraints would include
exchange controls and taxation consequences of transfers.

Where the entity has entered into covenants in financing contracts which could have   74
the effect of restricting the use of financing arrangements or credit facilities, and
negotiations with the lenders on the operation of these covenants are taking place or
are expected to take place, this fact should be indicated in the OFR. Where a breach
of a covenant has occurred or is expected to occur, the OFR should give details of
the measures taken or proposed to remedy the situation.

KEY PERFORMANCE INDICATORS

75 An entity should provide information that enables members to understand each KPI disclosed in the OFR.

76 For each KPI disclosed in the OFR:
- the definition and its calculation method should be explained;
- its purpose should be explained;
- the source of underlying data should be disclosed and, where relevant, assumptions explained;
- quantification or commentary on future targets should be provided;
- where information from the financial statements has been adjusted for inclusion in the OFR, that fact should be highlighted and a reconciliation provided;
- where available, corresponding amount for the financial year immediately preceding the current year should be disclosed; and
- any changes to KPIs should be disclosed and the calculation method used compared to previous financial years, including significant changes in the underlying accounting policies adopted in the financial statements, should be identified and explained.

77 Quantification or commentary on future targets is about communicating the direction the entity is taking by, for example, setting out future strategies and goals.

OTHER PERFORMANCE INDICATORS

78 Where a quantified measure, other than a KPI, is included, the OFR should disclose:
- the definition and its calculation method; and
- where available, corresponding amount for the financial year immediately preceding the current year.

SERIOUSLY PREJUDICIAL

79 Consistent with existing practice in informing the markets on such matters, no disclosure of information should be made about impending developments or about matters in the course of negotiation if the disclosure would, in the opinion of the directors, be seriously prejudicial to the interests of the entity.

STATEMENT OF COMPLIANCE

80 As this is a Reporting Statement of voluntary best practice, directors are not required to include in the annual report any formal confirmation that they have complied with this Reporting Statement. That said, as a matter of best practice, the OFR should include a statement as to whether it has been prepared in accordance with this Reporting Statement.

Implementation guidance

This guidance accompanies, but is not part of, the Reporting Statement.

INTRODUCTION

This Implementation Guidance: IG1

a.   Outlines some suggestions and illustrations of the content recommended to be covered in the OFR with regard to the disclosure framework as set out in paragraph 27 of the Reporting Statement, and related Key Performance Indicators (KPIs) (paragraphs 38 to 40).

b.   Provides some further "signposting" guidance as to the areas directors should consider with regard to the particular matters identified in paragraph 28 (a)-(e) of the Reporting Statement.

> The format used for the illustrative examples of KPIs featured in IG Examples 1-23 should not be taken as a template. Its purpose is simply to demonstrate the information that could be provided for a particular measure. It is not envisaged that the layout presented in the Implementation Guidance will be replicated by an entity preparing an OFR. It is for the directors to consider how best to present the information, perhaps by providing some of the details within in footnotes, or in a separate section of the OFR.
>
> Furthermore, these suggestions are non-exhaustive. Many further KPIs exist within different industries.
>
> In addition, the definitions and other criteria set out in IG Examples 1-23 are illustrative and should not be taken to imply generally accepted definitions or calculations.

CONTENT RELATED TO THE DISCLOSURE FRAMEWORK AND RELATED KPIS

The guidance in paragraphs IG11-IG35 suggests possible content envisaged for each element of the disclosure framework, whilst IG Examples 1-23 provide illustrative examples of KPIs and the disclosure recommended under paragraphs 75 and 76 of the Reporting Statement.   IG2

Paragraph 27 of the Reporting Statement requires that the OFR should provide the information to assist members to assess the strategies adopted by the entity and the potential for those strategies to succeed. To this end, the Reporting Statement provides a disclosure framework which sets out the areas to be considered by directors in preparing their entity's OFR. As acknowledged in the Reporting Statement, it is for directors to consider how best to use the framework to structure the OFR.   IG3

Paragraphs 75 and 76 set out the disclosure requirements relating to each KPI, which are dealt with in paragraphs 38 to 40 of the Reporting Statement.   IG4

Whilst IG Examples 1-23 are expressed as KPIs, they could also be considered as examples of quantified other measures as set out in paragraphs 41 and 42 of the Reporting Statement. If any of these examples were disclosed as quantified other measures, then the recommended disclosure would only cover the measures definition, its calculation method and the corresponding amount as set out in paragraph 78 of the Reporting Statement.   IG5

IG6   Other trends and factors monitored by the entity may also be considered quantified other measures, although they would not ever be KPIs as they are outside of the control of the entity. For example, an insurance company might monitor changing demographics as a key trend in the external operating environment, due to the impact of demographics on future demand for its products. Accordingly, in such circumstances, quantified demographic information would be included in the OFR as an example of a quantified other measure.

IG7   Definitions and other criteria set out in IG Examples 1-23 are illustrative and should not be taken to imply generally accepted definitions or calculations. They are simply provided to demonstrate the information that could be provided for a particular measure. It is important that the information provided in the OFR with regard to any KPIs or quantified other measures makes explicit the definition and precise calculation method used by the entity.

PARTICULAR MATTERS

IG8   **The guidance below includes some background material that might be useful to consider when developing an entity's OFR with regard to the specific "particular matters" set out in paragraph 28 (a)-(e) of the Reporting Statement. In addition, where the management of a particular matter has been identified as being essential to the successful implementation of a stated strategy or could have an effect on the entity's short or long-term value, the guidance provides some illustrations of areas that might be covered.**

IG9   **Paragraph 28 (a)-(e) of the Reporting Statement requires that, to the extent necessary to meet the requirements set out in paragraph 27 of the Reporting Statement, the OFR should include information about a number of particular matters, e.g. employees, and environment. As explained in paragraph 27 of the Reporting Statement, the OFR should provide the information necessary to assist members to assess the strategies adopted by the entity and the potential for those strategies to succeed. Accordingly, where the management of a particular matter could significantly affect the entity's ability to successfully implement its strategies or the entity's short or long-term value, that matter should be addressed within the OFR.**

IG10   **Paragraph 28 (a)-(e) contains a non-exhaustive list of topics that directors should consider for inclusion in their OFR to the extent necessary. Accordingly, paragraph 28 (f) provides a further recommendation that directors, to the extent necessary, include within the OFR "all other relevant matters." The directors should consider what other topics also should be included in the OFR, as these will be specific to the entity, its objectives and strategies, as well as dependent on the industry in which it operates.**

Nature, objectives and strategies of the business

IG11   The Reporting Statement recommends the provision of meaningful contextual information regarding the directors' objectives and strategies, along with a description of the business and its external environment, to assist members to assess the strategies adopted and the potential for those strategies to succeed.

IG12   Specifically, the OFR should set out the objectives of the business and the directors' strategies for generating or preserving value for members over the long term. A number of economic measures exist that are commonly used by companies in order to assess the company's ability to create value over time, and which are likely to be considered a KPI. These include:

- Return on capital employed.

- Incremental returns on investments.
- Economic profit type measures.
- Organic rates of growth and returns thereon.

IG Example 1: Return on capital employed (ROCE)

As an example of a measure of the creation of value, the recommended disclosure should incorporate the following:

- Definition and calculation: ROCE, measures the profit as a percentage of the total capital employed (invested) in the business.
- Purpose: The company's aim is to increase shareholder value. This is measured by the extent to which this goal has been achieved by using ROCE, as it is a measure of how well the money invested in the business is providing a return to investors.
- Source of underlying data: GAAP financial statement figures as adjusted below.
- Reconciliation of financial statement information:
  Operating result for calculation of ROCE =
  Operating result as per financial statements
  Plus interest from sales financing
  Capital employed =
  Intangible assets/property, plant and equipment
  Plus investments
  Plus accumulated goodwill amortisation
  Plus inventories
  Plus trade accounts receivable
  Plus other assets including prepaid expenses
  Less non-interesting bearing provisions/liabilities
- Quantified target: 10%.
- Quantified data: 2005 – Consolidated ROCE – 10.4%, 2004 – 10.2%, 2003 – 9.8%.
- No changes have been made to the source of data or calculation methods used.

IG Example 2: "Economic profit"

Economic profit is a further example of a measure that a company might use to quantify the creation of value. The recommended disclosure should incorporate the following:

- Definition and calculation: Economic profit, being a measure of capital adjusted profit. Based upon operating profit after tax, adjusted for one-off items and the cost of capital.
- Purpose: The company's key objective is to increase shareholder value, which is measured and managed using economic profit.
- Source of underlying data: GAAP financial statement figures as adjusted below.
- Quantified target: Economic profit for 2006 of £200 million, 2005 target was £150 million.
- Reconciliation of financial statement information:
  Profit after tax and minority interests, excluding goodwill amortisation =
  Operating profit after tax and minority interests
  Plus goodwill amortisation
  Less tax credit on goodwill
  Economic profit =
  Profit after tax and minority interests, excluding
  goodwill amortisation
  Less cost of capital
- Quantified data: 2005 – £160 million, 2004 – £145 million, 2003 – £140 million.
- No changes have been made to the source of data or calculation methods used.

Market positioning

IG13   Directors may also set their long term objectives around market positioning. In such cases, KPIs commonly used by the board, and accordingly included in the OFR might include:

- Market position.
- Market share.

IG Example 3: Market Share

For a company reporting market share as a KPI, the recommended disclosure should incorporate the following:

- Definition and calculation: Market share, being company revenue over estimated market revenue.
- Purpose: To assess how the company is performing in its particular market.
- Source of underlying data: No external verifiable source for market share exists; accordingly data are internal estimates.
- Quantified target: Achieve market share of 25% within 5 years.
- Quantified data: Five year trend data, 2001 – 17%, 2002 –18%, 2003 – 17%, 2004 – 19%, 2005 – 20%.
- No changes have been made to the source of data or calculation methods used.

Development, performance and position

The Reporting Statement recommends that the OFR should set out an historical and **IG14** prospective analysis of the development, performance and position of the company. Whilst a number of the measures used to monitor the development, performance and position of the company may be traditional financial measures, directors often supplement these with other measures common to their industry to monitor their progress towards stated objectives.

IG Example 4: Average revenue per user (customer)

A telecoms company may measure average revenue per user (ARPU) by types of product offerings as a KPI. By doing this, the directors are able to monitor customer buying patterns as this is a key factor that is likely to affect the development of future revenues. Recommended disclosure should incorporate the following information:

- Definition and calculation: Average revenue per user (ARPU) by major product segments, e.g. pre-pay and post-pay customers.
- Purpose: In the mobile network industry, ARPU is one of the key drivers for future revenue growth.
- Source of underlying data: Internal company data.
- Quantified target: To increase ARPU by 15% per annum for pre-pay customers and 5% per annum for post-pay customers.
- Quantified data: ARPU graph showing comparatives and percentage change year on year e.g. Pre-pay 2004 – £121, 2005 – £141, growth of 16.5%, Post-pay 2004 – £503, 2005   £525, growth of 4.4%.
- No changes have been made to the source of data or calculation methods used.

IG Example 5: Number of subscribers

A pay TV company with an objective of achieving revenue growth may monitor the effectiveness of their actions and progress towards their goal through measuring of the number of subscribers as a KPI. Recommended disclosure should incorporate the following information:

- Definition and calculation: Number of subscribers by type of connection, i.e. direct to home (DTH) and cable.
- Purpose: In the pay TV industry, the level of subscribers is the key driver for future revenue growth.
- Source of underlying data: Internal company data.
- Quantified target: To increase the number of subscribers by 10% per annum for each type of connection.
- Quantified data: Table of number of subscribers and percentage increase from year to year e.g. 2005 – DTH 4,532 million, cable 3,241 million, 2004 – DTH 4,013, cable 3,004, growth of 12.9% and 7.9%.
- No changes have been made to the source of data or calculation methods used.

IG Example 6: Sales per square foot

A retail company with an objective of increasing revenues may monitor and measure revenue per square foot as a KPI. Recommended disclosure should incorporate the following information:

- Definition and calculation: Average revenue per square foot (£ per week), with square footage measured as store space excluding storage/delivery space, checkout and administrative space.
- Purpose: In the retail industry, sales per square foot is one of the key drivers for future revenue growth.
- Source of underlying data: Internal company data.
- Quantified target: To increase sales per square foot to £20 per square foot/ week.
- Quantified data: Graph showing weekly sales per square foot over the past five years, 2005 – £18.53, 2004 – £17.56, 2003 – £16.99, 2002 – £16.04, 2001 – £15.67
- No changes have been made to the source of data or calculation methods used.

IG Example 7: Percentage of revenue from new products

A consumer products company that has a strategy of providing innovation products to its customers may measure and monitor the percentage of revenue from new products as a KPI. Recommended disclosure should incorporate the following information:

- Definition and calculation: Percentage of revenue from new products = revenue from those products launched over the past two years over total revenue for the year.
- Purpose: In order to continue to grow in the fast paced market of consumer products, the company needs to ensure that it is continually renewing its product portfolio. One way of measuring success is to look at the percentage of revenue generated by new products.
- Source of underlying data: Internal company data.
- Quantified target: To achieve 35% of revenue from new products per annum.
- Quantified data: Percentage of revenue from new products, 2005 – 37%, 2004 – 33%, 2003 – 36%.
- No changes have been made to the source of data or calculation methods used.

IG Example 8: Number of products sold per customer

In the financial services industry, a company may have an objective to increase margins by increasing the number of products sold to existing customers. Directors may monitor the number of products sold per customer, or "customer penetration" rates as a KPI. Recommended disclosure should incorporate the following information:

- Definition and calculation: Customer penetration rates by geographic segment. Penetration rates are measured by taking the number of products sold to each customer on an annual basis.
- Purpose: Increasing customer penetration rates, leads to increased revenues without incurring significant customer handling costs.
- Source of underlying data: Company data from UK and South Africa.
- Quantified target: To increase customer penetration rates to 5.0 products per customer territory.
- Quantified data: Penetration, 2005 – UK 4.3, South Africa 4.9, 2004 – UK 4.5, South Africa 4.5, 2003 – UK 4.0, South Africa 4.1.
- No changes have been made to the source of data or calculation methods used.

IG Example 9: Products in the development pipeline

In the pharmaceutical industry, for example, future revenues may be greatly affected by the launch of new products from the company's product development pipeline. Directors may monitor number of products at each stage of development and the markets/timing for future launches as a KPI. Recommended disclosure should incorporate the following information:

- Definition and calculation: Product development pipeline being the key products currently under development, and the stage of development (Phase I, II or III). Phase I initial evaluation, Phase II determination of dose and initial evaluation of efficacy, Phase III large comparative study in patients to establish clinical benefit and safety.
- Purpose: In order to achieve a strategy of continuing growth, the company must have a productive product development pipeline.
- Source of underlying data: Company data.
- Quantified target: To have 5 new products launched annually.
- Quantified data: Phase I – 25 projects, Phase II – 18 projects, Phase III – 12 projects, number of new products launched this year 4. Detailed information for those projects in Phase III and those launched during the year, e.g. name of product, description, projected market launch dates by territory.
- No changes have been made to the source of data or calculation methods used.

IG Example 10: Cost per unit produced

The directors in a utility company may measure costs per unit produced as a KPI in order to monitor progress towards becoming a low cost producer. Recommended disclosure should incorporate the following information:

- Definition and calculation: Exploration and production finding and development unit costs, being costs per £ per boe (E&P F&D costs (£/boe)). Boe means barrel of oil equivalent, which is a standard method of equating oil, gas and natural gas liquids by converting gas and natural gas liquids to oil based on their relative energy contents.
- Purpose: One of the key drivers to strong economic returns is to reduce E&P F&D costs.
- Source of underlying data: Internal company data.
- Quantified target: To be in the top quartile of low cost producers in Europe as compared to benchmarking studies produced by Evaluate Energy for 2004.
- Quantified data: E&P F&D unit costs (£ per boe) graph showing comparatives for three years e.g. 2003 − 3.22, 2004 − 3.20, 2005 − 3.08.
- No changes have been made to the source of data or calculation methods used.

Resources, principal risks and uncertainties and relationships

IG15   The Reporting Statement recommends that the OFR should set out the resources, principal risks and uncertainties and relationships that may significantly affect the company's short and long-term value. A number of the examples highlighted in the Reporting Statement could be considered either resources, risks or a relationship, or all three. Key resources of an entity may also be key stakeholders and accordingly lead to risks and uncertainties.

IG16   The KPIs used by directors will be those used to monitor the effective management of their resources, risks and relationships, as these will be the areas that may significantly affect the company's short and long-term value.

Persons with whom the entity has relations

IG17   The decisions of those with whom the entity has relations – regulators, customers, suppliers, employees, community and society at large – can affect a company's prospective performance and accordingly its value. For example, in regulated sectors, the risk of non-compliance with regulatory requirements could lead to the loss of a licence to operate. Accordingly the effective management of these relationships could significantly impact on the success of the entity's strategies and affect the long-term value of the entity.

IG18   The directors should consider whether such relationships could have a significant impact. The directors could do this by seeking the answers to a number of key questions, such as:

a.   How do our customers view the service we provide?
b.   How do our employees' feel about the entity?
c.   How do our suppliers view the entity?
d.   How do our regulators view the entity?

IG19   For example, in considering the first question above, IG Example 11 provides an illustration of how an entity could measure the customers' relationship with the entity, by measuring "customer churn" rates as a KPI. Ultimately, the selection of appropriate customer measures will depend on the nature of the business and the strategies adopted by the board.

Areas of importance relating to employees, the community and society at large, **IG20** including environmental matters, are addressed in paragraphs IG25-IG33. For other stakeholders with which the entity has relations, such as customers, suppliers, regulators, contractors and pensioners, some areas of interest might be:

- Profile of the stakeholder and nature of the relationship (length of relationship, is it subject to contract, if so when does the contract expire).
- Level of dependency.
- Satisfaction with relationship – feedback results, levels of complaints, fines etc.

IG Example 11: "Customer churn"

In the telecoms industry, future prospects are greatly affected by the number of customers they can retain. Directors may monitor "customer churn" rates by the types of products offered as a KPI. Recommended disclosure should incorporate the following information:

- Definition and calculation: Churn rates by geographical market. Churn measured as the percentage of customers who do not renew their contract with the company at the end of the contract, over the total number of customers under that contract type.
- Purpose: Reducing churn rates means there is less pressure to increase customer acquisitions in order to improve revenues. Lower churn rates lead to direct savings in the form of savings in marketing, sales, installation and disconnection costs.
- Source of underlying data: Company data from UK, Germany and France.
- Quantified target: To reduce customer churn by 5% per annum in each territory.
- Quantified data: Churn rate, 2003 – UK 15%, Germany 18%, France 22%, 2002 – UK 14%, Germany 21%, France 25%, 2001 – UK 15%, Germany 24%, France 26%.
- No changes have been made to the source of data or calculation methods used.

Environmental matters

Environmental matters, particularly environmental risks and uncertainties, impact to **IG21** some extent on all businesses, as they can affect investment decisions, consumer behaviour and Government policy. Poor management of energy, natural resources or waste can affect current performance; failure to plan for a future in which environmental factors are likely to be increasingly significant may risk the long-term future of the business. Proper attention to the environmental impacts of supply chains and products and to regulatory compliance of the company's own operations are both important for a business' public reputation and for its licence to operate.

Environmental matters cover a very wide range of areas. The matters that will be of **IG22** concern to a particular entity will vary depending on both the industry in which it operates and the strategies it has adopted. However, some consensus as to the generic environmental concerns facing all companies has been reached*, which might serve as a useful reference point for directors:

*UN Conference on Trade and Development (2000) Integrating Environmental and Financial Performance at the Enterprise Level

- Water use;
- Energy use;
- Waste;
- Climate change, including global warming contribution or emissions management;
- Ozone depleting substances.

IG23   Entities in industries that have a significant environmental footprint may set objectives and adopt strategies to specifically address key environmental risks, as illustrated in IG Examples 12 to 14. For others, whilst the management of environmental risks will impact the company's reputation, monitoring of performance in this area will not be considered a KPI. However, as set out in paragraph 19 of the Reporting Statement, the directors should support the information provided in the OFR with other evidence, for example consumption rates of scarce resources (energy and/or water) if this significantly impacts the entity's reputation, by providing the information recommended in paragraphs 41 and 42 of the Reporting Statement.

IG Example 12: Environmental spillage

A company involved in the transportation of hazardous materials may monitor "significant spills" as a KPI due to the potential impact of a spill on the reputation of the company. Recommended disclosure should incorporate the following information:

- Definition and calculation: Significant spills, being spills exceeding 100,000 litres.
- Purpose: To assess the effectiveness of the management of hazardous waste.
- Source of underlying data: All data from 100% controlled companies, representing 85% of the total group on a revenue basis.
- Quantified target: Reduce significant spills to below 10 per annum within 3 years.
- Quantified data: In 2005 there were 25 significant spills, in 2004 there were 30 spills, all due to leaking tanks.
- No changes have been made to the source of data or calculation methods used.

IG Example 13: CO_2 emissions

A company involved in energy production may monitor CO_2 equivalent emissions due to both potential fines and the impact of growing emissions on the reputation of the company. Recommended disclosure should incorporate the following information:

- Definition and calculation: CO_2 emissions, being on-site greenhouse gas emissions measured in million of tonnes of CO_2 equivalents (CO_2-e)
- Purpose: To assess the effectiveness of the management of the company's impact on greenhouse gas emissions.
- Source of underlying data: Data from 100% controlled companies within Europe and Africa, representing 95% of the company on a revenue basis.
- Quantified target: A 5% annual reduction in CO_2 equivalents
- Quantified data: 2005 CO_2-e 5.7, 2004 6.0, 2003 6.2
- No changes have been made to the source of data or calculation methods used.

IG Example 14: Waste

A retail group that promotes its 'green credentials' might monitor waste due to packaging, as this may impact on the reputation of the company. Recommended disclosure should incorporate the following information:

- Definition and calculation: Amount of waste (measured in kg) arising from packaging on each £1,000 of products we sell.
- Purpose: As the retail businesses in the group handle large amounts of packaging for transporting and presenting the goods sold, the group has established processes to minimise packaging waste.
- Source of underlying data: Data from all retail businesses in the group, representing 80% of the company on a revenue basis.
- Quantified target: To reduce the trend of increasing the amount of packaging to at least, or below, the levels in 2000, being 11.1kg packaging waste per £1,000 of sales.
- Quantified data: 2005 13.4, 2004 14.0, 2003 13.8, 2002 12.9, 2001, 12.1
- No changes have been made to the source of data or calculation methods used.

Employees

Employees may be a particularly key resource – and accordingly a key risk – for many entities. The strengths of a company's workforce and the ways it is managed can play a major role in both current and future company performance. Entities will need to be able to recruit and retain the staff they need to achieve their business strategies. Accordingly, the risks and uncertainties associated with the management of recruitment and retention of staff with the particular skills required for the entity's strategies could have a significant impact on the entity's future development and performance. For example, poor employment relationships can carry the risk of costly litigation, low workforce morale and ultimately affect company reputation. In addition, directors should consider their employment policies and practices and to assess which aspects are relevant to an understanding of the entity. For example, the degree to which the human resources of the entity represent a significant competitive advantage or are critical to a key product, service or process.
IG24

The employee matters that will be of concern to directors will vary from entity to entity, depending on the industry in which the entity operates and the strategies it has adopted.
IG25

In order to assess employee performance and development, the following areas, along with related performance measures, may be helpful:
IG26

- Employee health and safety (which could also be considered a "social matter" see paragraph IG30) – details of RIDDOR (Reporting of injuries, diseases and dangerous occurrences regulations 1995), lost days to injury, levels of occupational related diseases in the workforce, compliance levels with working hours directives;
- Recruitment and retention – employee turnover, retention rates, remuneration policies, number of applicants per post, offer/acceptance statistics, levels of skills shortages;
- Training and development – hours spent on training, number of courses taken, leadership/career development;
- Morale/motivation – employee feedback results, absence rates, levels of employee engagement;

- Workforce performance and profile – employee productivity, revenue/profit per employee, diversity (see also IG30), number of professionally qualified employees.

IG27   IG Examples 15 and 16 provide some illustrations of where entities might set objectives relative to employees and monitor their progress as KPIs. Alternatively, the board may monitor employee measures to assess how effectively the entity is managing its employees' resources, development and performance to ensure that adequate resources are available to the entity, even though these performance measures are not considered KPIs. In such circumstances, it would be appropriate for the OFR to include these performance measures as other evidence, as set out in paragraphs 41 and 42 of the Reporting Statement.

IG Example 15: Employee morale

A professional services company may measure "employee satisfaction" in order to monitor employee morale, as decreasing levels of morale indicate higher levels of leavers in the future. Recommended disclosure should incorporate the following information:

- Definition and calculation: Employee satisfaction on a scale of 1 to 5 where 1 is low and 5 is high.
- Purpose: A professional services company needs to ensure it retains its best and brightest employees in order to properly service clients.
- Source of underlying data: Annual employee surveys in the UK, France and Germany, representing 85% of the total client facing employees.
- Quantified target: For 2006 to achieve a rating of 4.5, with the populations surveyed to cover at least 95% of client facing employees.
- Quantified data: Employee satisfaction graph showing comparatives e.g. 2004 – 4.1 rating, 2005 – 4.4 rating.
- Comparability: The 2004 survey results were based on surveys in the UK and France, representing 65% of total client facing employees.

IG Example 16: Employee health and safety

In an industry such as mining, where the "licence to operate" is based on effectively managing a myriad of issues, including health and safety, the directors may monitor "lost time injury frequency rate" as a KPI. Recommended disclosure should incorporate the following:

- Definition and calculation: Lost time injury frequency rate (LTIFR) – the number of lost-time injuries per million hours worked.
- Purpose: As the industry involves large equipment and working with hazardous materials, safety is a core value and a major priority.
- Source of underlying data: Injury data returns from 100% owned facilities only.
- Quantified target: To reduce LTIFR by 10% per annum.
- Quantified data: LTIFR table showing comparatives e.g. 2004 – 10 injuries/million hours worked, 2005 – 8.4 injuries/million hours worked.
- No changes have been made to the source of data or calculation methods used.

Social and community matters

The management of an entity's social and community matters can affect its repu- **IG28**
tation and licence to operate in a similar way to the management of environmental
matters. Social concerns with regard to product safety, e.g. genetically modified
foods, product responsibility, e.g. underage drinking or smoking, and the ethical
management of the supply chain are all examples of issues that can significantly
impact on the reputation of an entity. Furthermore, disregard for local community
concerns can result in successful opposition to development applications.

As with the other areas noted under particular matters, the areas that will be of **IG29**
concern to a particular entity will vary depending on both the industry in which it
operates and the strategies it has adopted.

Currently, there is no commonly held definition of social and community matters*, **IG30**
nor is there a common understanding of the generic issues. It is also the case that
specific matters within the broad social and community category can change as new
issues arise. However, areas that directors might want to consider include:

- Public health issues, such as obesity, perceived safety issues related to high use of
  mobile phones, smoking;
- Employee health and safety (can also be considered an area under employees, see
  IG26);
- Social risks existing in the supply chain, for example the use of child labour and
  payments of "fair wages";
- Diversity in either the employee (see IG26) or customer base;
- Impact on the local community, for example noise, pollution, transport con-
  gestion (these areas could also link to environmental matters);
- Indigenous and human right issues relating to communities local to overseas
  operations.

Entities where reputation is a key concern might set objectives and adopt strategies **IG31**
that specifically address key social or community concerns, as illustrated in IG
Examples 17 and 18. Alternatively, the monitoring of social and community matters
may not be considered a KPI, however, directors will still monitor their performance
in these areas. In such situations, it would be appropriate for the OFR to include
these performance measures, as set out in paragraphs 41 and 42.

*As noted in the International Organisation for Standardization (ISO) document 'Working Report on Social
Responsibility' (2004), page 67.*

IG Example 17: Monitoring of social risks in the supply chain

A company that sources its branded products from overseas could face additional risks relating to stakeholder, in particular customer, concerns around local labour practices. In this situation, a company might have put in place a system to validate and monitor supply chain performance, specifically related to adherence to stated policies. The directors may monitor the extent of the programme and compliance rates as KPIs. Recommended disclosure should incorporate the following:

- Definition and calculation: Number of factories subject to ratings by independent accredited monitors, number of factories in each rating category, where one star signifies numerous severe non-compliance issues and four stars reflects those factories with no non-compliance issues.
- Purpose: Whilst the company has outsourced its supply chain, it wants to reassure customers that it has not outsourced its moral responsibility for the way its products are made. The objective is for all parts of the business – including suppliers – to share a common set of values and live up to them.
- Source of underlying data: Results of assessments made by accredited monitors in the current year.
- Quantified target: To increase the number of suppliers monitored by 20% per annum and reduce non-compliance to below 3%.
- Quantified data: Geographical split (for current year and prior year) of results for overseas suppliers, by Asia, Americas and Europe. Total factories in each of the four rating categories.
- No changes have been made to the source of data or calculation methods used.

IG Example 18: Noise infringements

An airport operator might want to measure the number of noise infringements as a KPI in order to monitor the success of its management of this "licence to operate" and reputational risk issue. Recommended disclosure should incorporate the following information:

- Definition and calculation: Number of noise infringements being the number of aircraft exceeding Department of Transport take-off noise limits.
- Purpose: Our ability to expand any airport is dependent on continuing support from local communities. If we fail to ensure aircraft using our airports comply with local noise limits, we are putting at risk future developments which are necessary given the growth in the airline industry in the country.
- Source of underlying data: Internal company data.
- Quantified target: Reduce noise infringements by 5% per annum.
- Quantified data: Annual noise infringements table showing comparatives, e.g. 2005 – 55, 2004 – 57, 2003 – 60, 2002 – 64, 2001 – 63.
- No changes have been made to the source of data or calculation methods used.

Receipts from, and returns to, shareholders

IG32   Paragraph 59 of the Reporting Statement recommends that the OFR should include information relating to receipts from, and returns to, shareholders. This would include details of, and the rationale behind, any of the following:

1.   Receipts from shareholders resulting from capital raising activities;
2.   Distribution via dividends or special dividends;
3.   Return of capital by means of share repurchases and share reconstructions.

Other resources

Paragraph 50 of the Reporting Statement recommends that the OFR should include   **IG33**
a description of the resources available to the entity and how they are managed. In
addition to employee and customers already featured in IG Examples 11 to 13, other
resources could include areas such as corporate reputation and brand strength; the
condition of infrastructure; research and development; intellectual capital; licenses,
patents, copyright and trademarks; market position and reserves of natural resources, as illustrated in IG Example 19.

IG Example 19: Reserves

In an extractive industry, future revenues are greatly affected by the reserves
controlled by the company. Accordingly, proven and probable reserves may be
monitored by the directors as a KPI. Recommended disclosure should incorporate
the following:

- Definition and calculation: Reserves are defined as those quantities of petroleum which are anticipated to be commercially recoverable from known
  accumulations from a given date forward. Reserves are reported net of the gas
  required for processing and transportation to the customer. The reporting
  process is in line with reserves definitions and resource classification systems
  published by the Society of Petroleum Engineers (SPE) and the World Petroleum Congress (WPC).
- Purpose: The most critical driver of growth of any oil and gas company is
  reserve replacement.
- Source of underlying data: Internal company data reviewed by an independent
  expert (who should be named, along with professional qualifications).
- Target: To replace current year's sales volume through reserve growth in the
  year.
- Quantified data:
  Proven at end of 2004 = 316, less production 57, add revisions 27, add
  exploration additions 41, Proven at end of 2005 = 327.
  Proven and probable at end of 2004 = 724, less production 57, add revisions -
  4, add exploration additions 69, Proven and probable at end of 2005 = 732.
- No changes have been made to the source of data or calculations methods
  used.

Other business risks

As set out in paragraph 52 of the Reporting Statement, the OFR should include a   **IG34**
description of the principal risks and uncertainties facing the entity, together with a
commentary on the directors' approach to them. In addition to risks related to
environmental, social and community matters addressed in IG Examples 12 to 14,
and 17 and 18, other risks might arise due to the external environment, dependencies
on others, and the management of resources, both non-financial and financial, as
illustrated in IG Examples 20 and 21.

IG Example 20: Market risk

A bank might measure market risks arising from uncertainty about changes in market prices and rates, such as interest rates, equity prices, exchange rates, commodity prices) by using "value-at-risk" approaches as a KPI. Recommended disclosure should incorporate the following information:

- Definition and calculation: Value-at-risk (VaR) uses a Monte Carlo simulation process. Volatilities and correlations of market parameters are observed over the most recent twelve-month period and used on an unweighted basis. The VaR estimates are made at a 99% confidence level for a one-day time horizon.
- Purpose: Tracking the daily VaR allows the bank to derive a quantitative measure of market risk in order to monitor the risk profile it has taken on related to all market risk areas.
- Source of underlying data: VaR of trading units in the UK and of the units responsible for management of interest rate and foreign exchange risks of non-trading units.
- Target: The goal is not to exceed the limit set by the VaR calculation on any day of trading during any year.
- Quantified data: VaR histogram, showing the number of days VaR was at certain levels.
- No changes have been made to the source of data or calculation methods used.

IG Example 21: Business Continuity Management

A company providing computer services may monitor its compliance with business continuity plans. Recommended disclosure should incorporate the following information:

- Definition and calculation: Number of business units in each rating category, where an 'Pass' rating signifies full compliance with stated business continuity plans, whilst 'Fail' rating signifies numerous non-compliance issues.
- Purpose: As the provider of computer services, the company wishes to provide assurance of their ability to withstand events that would interrupt the provisions of such services.
- Source of underlying data: Data from all business units within the company.
- Quantified target: To achieve full compliance with stated business continuity plans, ie nil 'fail' ratings.
- Quantified data: 2005 98% Pass, 2% Fail, 2004 95% Pass, 5% Fail, 2003 93% Pass, 7% Fail.
- No changes have been made to the source of data or calculation methods used.

Financial position

IG35   The Reporting Statement recommends that the OFR should set out an analysis of the position of the entity both in the financial year and the future, including a description of the capital structure, treasury policies and objectives, and liquidity of the entity. Whilst a number of the measures used to monitor the position of the company may be traditional financial measures, directors often supplement these with other measures common to their industry to monitor their progress towards stated objectives. Such disclosures may include sensitivity analysis in respect of financial instrument disclosures.

IG Example 22: "Economic capital"

The directors of a financial institution may measure economic capital, in addition to regulatory capital, as a risk management tool and to monitor risk positions in individual business units. Recommended disclosure should incorporate the following information:

- Definition and calculation: Economic capital is the amount of capital that a transaction or business unit requires in order to support the economic risks it creates. A 99.95% confidence interval and a one-year time horizon are used to calculate economic capital. The economic capital calculation is subdivided into five distinct risk types: credit risk, market risk, transfer risk, business risk and operational risk.
- Purpose: The directors measure economic capital in order to monitor the efficient use of group's capital base.
- Source of underlying data: Internal company data.
- Quantified data: Economic capital for each business unit, reconciling to total economic capital for 2004 and 2005.
- No changes have been made to the source of data or calculation methods used.

IG Example 23: Cash conversion rate

To supplement the cash flow information provided in the financial statements, directors may measure operating profit cash conversion rates as a KPI. Recommended disclosure should incorporate the following information:

- Definition and calculation: Cash conversion rate being cash flow from operations as a percentage of operating profit.
- Purpose: One of the key drivers to strong economic returns is the ability to convert operating profits into cash.
- Source of underlying data: Internal company data.
- Quantified target: A minimum target of 85% cash conversion for any year.
- Quantified data: Cash conversion 2001 – 74%, 2002 – 101%, 2003 – 92%, 2004 – 85%, 2005 – 92%.
- No changes have been made to the source of data or calculation methods used.

Reporting Statement:
Retirement Benefits – Disclosures

Contents

Reporting Statement:
Retirement Benefits – Disclosures

Introduction

This document sets out a Reporting Statement 'Retirement Benefits – Disclosures'. **1** The Reporting Statement builds on Financial Reporting Standard (FRS) 17 'Retirement Benefits' (as amended in December 2006) and sets out additional disclosures that complement the disclosure requirements of FRS 17. It is a best practice guide and is not mandatory.

The Accounting Standards Board (ASB) published FRS 17 in November 2000, **2** although its full requirements only became mandatory for accounting periods beginning on or after 1 January 2005. Following its implementation, some commentators expressed a concern that the financial statements do not contain sufficient information in relation to defined benefit schemes to allow users of the financial statements to obtain a clear view of the risks and rewards arising from defined benefit schemes.

In May 2006 the ASB issued for comment a Financial Reporting Exposure Draft **3** (FRED) of a proposed amendment to FRS 17 and a draft Reporting Statement 'Retirement Benefits – Disclosures'. In finalising this document the ASB has taken into consideration the comments received in respect to the FRED.

The ASB considered the amended FRS 17 addressed many, but not all, of the **4** concerns of commentators and so decided to develop the Reporting Statement. As the amendment to FRS 17 replaced the disclosure requirements set out in the previous version of FRS 17 with those of International Accounting Standards (IAS) 19 'Employee Benefits' the ASB noted the Reporting Statement can be applied by entities adopting either UK or International Financial Reporting Standards (IFRS).

The ASB was conscious that any additional disclosure requirements, beyond those **5** set out in the amended FRS 17, should address the needs of users whilst not being cumbersome to preparers. The ASB is of the view a Reporting Statement which sets out principles for disclosure, rather than specific requirements, allows entities the flexibility to provide disclosures that are appropriate to their exposure to risks and rewards arising from defined benefit schemes.

Summary

The Reporting Statement is designed as a formulation of best practice; it is intended **a** to have persuasive rather than mandatory force. The Reporting Statement is written for any entity that operates or sponsors a defined benefit scheme.

The Reporting Statement recommends that the directors provide disclosures in the **b** notes to the financial statements that complement the disclosure requirements set out in FRS 17 'Retirement Benefits'. The extent of disclosure depends on the significance to the entity of its participation in defined benefit schemes and of its exposure to risk arising from those schemes.

The Reporting Statement sets out six principles to be considered when providing **c** disclosures for defined benefit schemes in the financial statements. The six areas addressed by the principles are:

i the relationship between the entity and trustees (managers) of the defined benefit scheme;

ii the principal assumptions used to measure scheme liabilities;

iii the sensitivity of the principal assumptions used to measure the scheme liabilities;

iv how the liabilities arising from defined benefit schemes are measured;

v the future funding obligations in relation to the defined benefit scheme; and

vi the nature and extent of the risks arising from financial instruments held by the defined benefit scheme.

d The principles set out in the Reporting Statement aim to assist the users of financial statements in understanding the risks and rewards, and funding obligations, arising from defined benefit schemes.

Reporting Statement:
Retirement Benefits – Disclosures

OBJECTIVE

The objective of this Reporting Statement is to recommend disclosures for defined **1** benefit schemes such that:

a. the financial statements contain adequate disclosure of the cost of providing retirement benefits and the related gains, losses, assets and liabilities;
b. the users of financial statements can obtain a clear view of the risks and rewards arising from defined benefit schemes; and
c. the funding obligations of the entity in relation to liabilities of a defined benefit scheme are clearly identified.

SCOPE

This Reporting Statement may be applied to financial statements that are intended to **2** give a true and fair view of a reporting entity's financial position and profit or loss (or income and expenditure) for a period the reporting entity operates or sponsors a defined benefit scheme.

DEFINITIONS

The following definitions shall apply in this Reporting Statement: **3**

Accumulated Benefits Obligation – the liability calculated on the projected unit method as defined in FRS 17 'Retirement Benefits' where no allowance is made for projected earnings.

Cost of buying out scheme benefits – this cost is based on an actual insolvency amount where this is available, or estimated using a suitable method based on the guidance contained in Guidance Note 9 'Funding Defined Benefits – Presentation of Actuarial Advice' adopted by the Board of Actuarial Standards.

Duration of scheme liabilities – The duration of the scheme liabilities is a measure of how long on average it is until the benefits of the scheme fall due. This is the weighted average time to payment of the cash flows, weighted by the present value of the cash flows (ie on a discounted basis).

Duration is calculated by adding the results of multiplying the present value of each cash flow by the time it is received (paid) and then dividing by the total present value of all the cash flows.

PRINCIPLES

The financial statements should disclose information that enables the users of the **4** **financial statements to understand the relationship between the reporting entity and the trustees (managers) of defined benefit schemes.**

FRS 17* 'Retirement Benefits', paragraph 76 (IAS 19 'Employee Benefits' para- **5** graph 120), requires an employer to disclose information that enables users of

As amended December 2006.

financial statements to evaluate the nature of its defined benefits schemes and the
financial effects of changes in those schemes during the period.

6   Many retirement benefit schemes are established as trusts. The basis of trust law is
that one group (the trustees) hold assets for the benefit of another group (the beneficiaries). The relationship between the entity and the trust is normally governed by
a trust deed and/or trust rules. In addition to trust law itself, the powers of trustees
may be regulated by legislation. The powers conferred on trustees by regulation may
enhance their authority compared to that of the trust deed and/or trust rules.

7   The relationship between the reporting entity and the trustees (managers) of the
scheme will determine how an entity manages and arranges its affairs with regard to
the defined benefit scheme, including: determination of the investment strategy for
the assets held by the scheme, arrangements to determine principles for funding the
scheme including how contribution levels to the scheme are agreed. The management
and arrangement of affairs may be affected by the powers vested in the trustees
(managers). The financial statements should explain significant and unusual powers
that have been granted to the trustees (managers) of the scheme that could have a
material financial effect on the reporting entity.

8   **The financial statements should include sufficient information about the principal
assumptions the entity has used to measure scheme liabilities to allow users to understand the inherent uncertainties affecting the measurement of scheme liabilities. These
assumptions should include, where this is not otherwise required by FRS 17 (or IAS 19),
mortality rates.**

9   FRS 17 paragraph 77(m) (IAS 19 paragraph 120A(n)) requires the entity to disclose
the principal actuarial assumptions used as at the balance sheet date. This Reporting
Statement recommends, where otherwise not required, that the assumptions disclosed include mortality rates.

10   Information provided in the financial statements should communicate in a clear and
effective manner the number of years post retirement it is anticipated pensions will be
paid to members of the defined benefit scheme. Where the number of years assumed
differs depending on geographical, demographical or other significant reasons, the
different mortality rates should be separately disclosed.

11   Where it is anticipated a change in mortality rates could have a material effect on the
measurement of the scheme liabilities a sensitivity analysis, as recommended by
paragraph 12 of this Reporting Statement, should be provided.

12   **The financial statements should disclose a sensitivity analysis for the principal
assumptions used to measure the scheme liabilities, showing how the measurement of
scheme liabilities would have been affected by changes in the relevant assumption that
were reasonably possible at the balance sheet date.**

For the purposes of this disclosure, all other assumptions should be held constant.

13   The inherent uncertainties affecting the measurement of scheme liabilities require the
liabilities to be measured on an actuarial basis. This involves estimating the future
cash flows arising under the scheme liabilities based on a number of actuarial
assumptions. The measurement of scheme liabilities can be materially affected by
changes in assumptions. The financial statements should disclose how changes in the
assumptions could affect the measurement of scheme liabilities.

Where an entity chooses not to provide a sensitivity analysis, it may decide to **14** provide alternative disclosures that provide greater information about the nature of scheme liabilities. Such information may include an analysis of liabilities between pensioners, deferred pensioners and employed members.

The financial statements should disclose information that enables users to understand **15** **the method of measurement used to measure scheme liabilities arising from defined benefit schemes.**

FRS 17 requires defined benefit scheme liabilities to be measured on an actuarial **16** basis using the projected unit method. The scheme liabilities should be discounted at a rate that reflects the time value of money and the characteristics of the liability (assumed to be the current rate of return of a high quality corporate bond). There are, however, alternative approaches to the measurement of defined benefit scheme liabilities*.

One such alternative approach is the cost of buying out benefits. In certain jur- **17** isdictions this amount may be disclosed to trustees (managers) and/or members of defined benefit schemes. Where the cost of buying out benefits is made available to trustees (managers) and/or members of defined benefit schemes it is recommended that the financial statements also disclose the cost of buying out benefits.

Another alternative approach for measuring defined benefit scheme liabilities is the **18** accumulated benefits obligation (ABO). The ABO is similar to measuring defined benefit scheme liabilities using the projected unit method but does not take into consideration future salary increases. An entity may consider it useful to disclose the ABO when explaining how scheme liabilities are measured.

The financial statements should disclose information that enables the users of financial **19** **statements to understand the funding obligations (estimated where applicable) that the entity has in relation to defined benefit schemes.**

FRS 17 paragraph 77(p) (IAS 19 paragraph 120A(q)) requires the employer's best **20** estimate, as soon as it can reasonably be determined, of contributions expected to be paid to the scheme during the accounting period beginning after the balance sheet date. Scheme liabilities are, however, often of a long term nature and contributions expected to be paid in the next accounting period may not provide sufficient information to allow the users of the financial statements to understand how the scheme liabilities affect the economic resources available to the entity, including its cash flow.

The financial statements should disclose rates or amounts of contributions which **21** have been agreed with the trustees (managers) of the scheme and are payable to the scheme by or on behalf of the reporting entity.

The funding requirements for defined benefit schemes are often regulated by legis- **22** lation. An entity may be required or may choose to agree principles for funding scheme liabilities with the trustees (managers) of the scheme. The financial statements should disclose the funding principles the entity has agreed or operates with regard to defined benefit schemes.

---

*The measurement of defined benefit scheme liabilities is discussed in paragraphs 11 to 22 of The Development of the FRS to FRS 17 'Retirement Benefits'.

23   Where a defined benefit scheme is in deficit* and the entity has entered into an agreement with the trustees (managers) of the scheme to make additional contributions to reduce or recover the deficit, in addition to normal levels of funding, the financial statements should disclose separately the additional contributions. The financial statements should also disclose separately the number of years over which it is anticipated the additional contributions will be paid to the defined benefit scheme in order to recover or reduce the deficit.

24   In order to evaluate the economic resources available to the entity, users of financial statements are particularly interested in the period of time over which the liabilities of the defined benefit scheme mature. A measure of this is the duration of scheme liabilities, which should be disclosed in the financial statements.

25   The duration of the scheme's liabilities may not alone provide users with information as to how the cash flows of defined benefit schemes fall due. In addition to the duration of liabilities, the financial statements should disclose information that allows users to understand the projected cash flows of defined benefit schemes. This information might usefully be presented in graphical form.

26   **The financial statements should disclose information that enables users of financial statements to evaluate the nature and extent of the risks and rewards arising from the financial instruments held by defined benefit schemes at the balance sheet date.**

27   For each type of risk arising from financial instruments held by defined benefit schemes, an entity may disclose:

    a.   the exposures to risk and how they arise;

    b.   the objectives, policies and processes undertaken by the defined benefits scheme or the entity for managing the risk and the methods used to measure the risk; and

    c.   any changes in (a) or (b) from the previous period.

28   An entity may disclose a sensitivity analysis, such as value-at-risk, for types of risks to which the defined benefit scheme is exposed. Where an entity discloses such sensitivity analysis it should also disclose the method and assumptions used in preparing this analysis and any changes from the previous period in the methods and assumptions used.

29   FRS 17 paragraph 77(i) (IAS 19 paragraph 120A(j)) requires an entity to disclose for each major category of scheme assets the percentage or amount that each major category constitutes of the fair value of the total scheme assets. It is recommended that this disclosure includes the expected rate of return assumed for each major category of scheme assets for the period presented.

30   The assumption made for the expected return on assets does not affect the valuation of the scheme assets because they are measured at fair value. It does, however, determine the amount to be recognised in the profit and loss account.

A deficit/surplus in a defined benefit scheme is the shortfall/excess of the value of the assets in the scheme below/over the present value of the scheme liabilities.

Illustrative examples of disclosures

The following illustrations of possible disclosure examples for defined benefit schemes are provided for general guidance only and do not form part of the Reporting Statement. The disclosures provided should supplement those disclosures provided in accordance with FRS 17 and IAS 19.

Illustration 1 – Explanation of the relationship between the reporting entity and the trustees (managers) of the defined benefit scheme
(Paragraphs 4 to 7)

The pension scheme assets are held in a separate Trustee-administered fund to meet long-term pension liabilities to past and present employees. The trustees of the fund are required to act in the best interest of the fund's beneficiaries. The appointment of trustees to the fund is determined by the scheme's trust documentation. The Group has a policy that one-third of all trustees should be nominated by members of the fund, including at least one member by current pensioners.

*In addition to its statutory duties the board of trustees have been granted the power to 'call' for additional contributions in the event of certain circumstances. The circumstances in which the trustees can exercise this power include a disposal that accounts for more than 15% of the net assets, as reported in the consolidated Balance Sheet or when the funding position of the scheme falls below 65% of the scheme liabilities.

*This disclosure is also provided in accordance with FRS 12 'Provisions, Contingent Liabilities and Contingent Assets' and IAS 37 'Provisions, Contingent Liabilities and Contingent Assets'.

Illustration 2 - Disclosure of principal assumptions
(Paragraphs 8 to 11)

Principal actuarial assumptions at the balance sheet date:

	UK		USA	
	2006	*2005*	*2006*	*2005*
Discount rate at 31 December	5%	5.7%	5.25%	6.25%
Expected return on plan assets at 31 December	5.4%	7.0%	6%	7.5%
Future salary increases	5%	4%	4.5%	3.8%
Future pension increases	3%	2%	2.9%	3.0%
Proportion of employees opting for early retirement	30%	30%	25%	25%

Investigations have been carried out within the past three years into the mortality experience of the Group's major schemes. These investigations concluded that the current mortality assumptions include sufficient allowance for future improvements in mortality rates. The assumed life expectations on retirement at age 65 are:

	UK		USA	
	2006	*2005*	*2006*	*2005*
Retiring today				
Males	20.1	20.1	19.5	19.5
Females	22.9	22.9	21.8	21.8
Retiring in 20 years				
Males	21.4	21.3	21.1	21.0
Females	24.1	24.0	23.0	23.0

Illustration 3 - Sensitivity analysis of the principal assumptions used to measure scheme liabilities
(Paragraphs 12 to 14)

The sensitivities regarding the principal assumptions used to measure the scheme liabilities are set out below:

Assumption	Change in assumption	Impact on scheme liabilities
Discount rate	Increase/decrease by 0.5%	Increase/decrease by 9.5%
Rate of inflation	Increase/decrease by 0.5%	Increase/decrease by 5.5%
Rate of salary growth	Increase/decrease by 0.5%	Increase/decrease by 3%
Rate of mortality	Increase by 1 year	Increase by 4.5%

Illustration 4 - How the liabilities arising from defined benefit schemes are measured
(Paragraphs 15 to 18)

The Group provides retirement benefits to some of its former and approximately 60% of current employees through defined benefit schemes. The level of retirement benefit is principally based on salary earned in the last five years of employment.

The liabilities of the defined benefit scheme are measured by discounting the best estimate of future cash flows to be paid out by the scheme using the projected unit method. This amount is reflected in the deficit in the balance sheet*. The projected unit method is an accrued benefits valuation method in which the scheme liabilities make allowance for projected earnings. The accumulated benefit obligation is an actuarial measure of the present value of benefits for service already rendered but differs from the projected unit method in that it includes no assumption for future salary increases. At the balance sheet date the accumulated benefit obligation was £xm.

An alternative method of valuation to the projected unit method is a solvency basis, often estimated using the cost of buying out benefits at the balance sheet date with a suitable insurer. This amount represents the amount that would be required to settle the scheme liabilities at the balance sheet date rather than the Group continuing to fund the on-going liabilities of the scheme. The Group estimates the amount required to settle the scheme's liabilities at the balance sheet date is £xm.

---

*An entity that prepares financial statements in accordance with IAS 19 'Employee Benefits' should explain the method of recognition for actuarial gains and losses.

Illustration 5 – Future funding obligations in relation to defined benefit schemes
(Paragraph 19 to 25)

The most recently completed triennial actuarial valuation of the Group's main retirement benefits fund was performed by an independent actuary for the trustees of the scheme and was carried out as at 31 December 2005. Following the valuation the Group's ordinary contributions rate increased, with effect from 1 January 2006, from 12.9% of pensionable salaries to 13.4% representing regular contributions. In addition the Group contributed a further £8m to the scheme as a contribution towards the current deficit. The Group has agreed with the trustees it will aim to eliminate the deficit over the next 8 years. The Group will monitor funding levels on an annual basis. The next triennial valuation is due to be completed as at 31 December 2008. The Group considers that the contribution rates agreed with trustees at the last valuation date are sufficient to eliminate the deficit over the agreed period and that regular contributions, which are based on service costs, will not increase significantly.

The Group has agreed the following funding objectives with trustees:

1.   To return the on-going funding level of the scheme to 100% of the projected past service liabilities within a period of 8 years measured in accordance with FRS 17;
2.   Once the funding level of the scheme is 100% of the projected past service liabilities to maintain funding at least at this level; and
3.   To meet the liabilities of the scheme in the event that the scheme is wound-up.

The levels of contributions are based on the current service costs and the expected future cash flows of the defined benefit scheme. The Group estimates the present value of the duration of UK scheme liabilities on average fall due over Y years and foreign schemes over X years.

The benefits payable by the defined benefit scheme are expected to be paid as follows:

£m

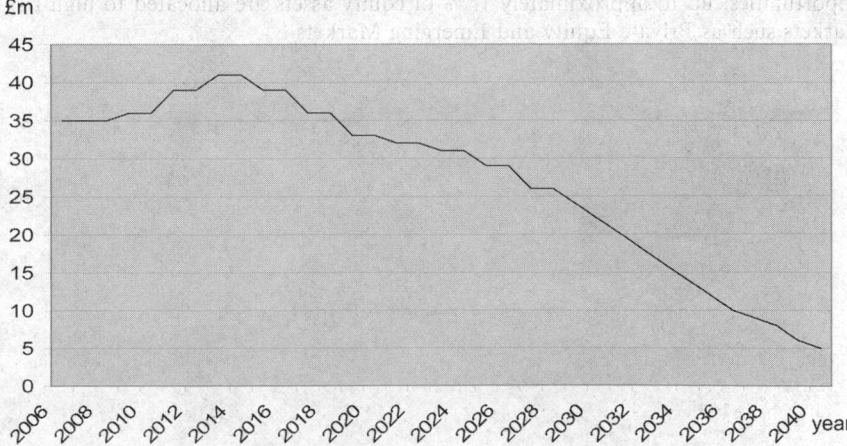

Illustration 6 – Nature and extent of the risks arising from financial instruments held by the defined benefit scheme
(Paragraphs 26 to 30)

At 31 December 2006 the scheme assets were invested in a diversified portfolio that consisted primarily of equity and debt securities. The fair value of the scheme assets as a percentage of total scheme assets and target allocations are set out below:

	Planned 2007	2006	2005
(as a percentage of total scheme assets)			
Equity securities	60	62	65
Debt	25	22	19
Property	10	9	12
Other	5	7	4

In conjunction with the trustees, the Group has recently conducted an asset-liability review for its major schemes. These studies are used to assist the trustees and the Group to determine the optimal long-term asset allocation with regard to the structure of liabilities within the scheme. The results of the study are used to assist the trustees in managing the volatility in the underlying investment performance and risk of a significant increase in the scheme deficit by providing information used to determine the pension schemes investment strategy.

The majority of the equities held by the scheme are in international blue chip entities. The aim is to hold a globally diversified portfolio of equities, with a target of 60% of equities being held in UK and Europe, 30% in US equities and the remainder in emerging markets. To maintain a wide range of diversification and to improve return opportunities, up to approximately 15% of equity assets are allocated to high risk markets such as Private Equity and Emerging Markets.

Appendix A
The development of the reporting statement

This development of the Reporting Statement accompanies, but is not part of the Reporting Statement.

INTRODUCTION

This development of the Reporting Statement summarises the Accounting Standards Board's (ASB) considerations in reaching its conclusions in the Reporting Statement for 'Retirement Benefits - Disclosures'.   **A1**

BACKGROUND

The ASB published Financial Reporting Standard (FRS) 17 'Retirement Benefits' in November 2000, although its requirements have only become mandatory in full for accounting periods beginning on or after 1 January 2005.   **A2**

Following the implementation of FRS 17 a number of comments concerning the accounting for pensions have arisen. In particular, there is a general concern that financial statements do not include sufficient information to allow users of the financial statements to obtain a clear view of the risks and rewards arising from defined benefit schemes.   **A3**

In addition the UK legal and regulatory environment for retirement benefit schemes has changed significantly since FRS 17 was published, which could not have been anticipated when FRS 17 was developed. Regulatory changes arising from the Pensions Act 2004 include the following: **A4**

- establishment of The Pensions Regulator (TPR), a new regulator with significant new powers;
- the establishment of the Pension Protection Fund (PPF) to pay compensation to members of eligible defined benefits schemes where there is a qualifying insolvency event in relation to the employer; and
- a new statutory obligation on solvent companies to meet their pension obligations.

In October 2005 the ASB announced a research project into the financial reporting of pensions. The project is wide ranging and is reconsidering the fundamental principles of accounting for retirement benefits. The ASB aims to issue a Discussion Paper outlining its findings during 2007.   **A5**

In December 2005 the Financial Reporting Council (FRC) published its Regulatory Strategy (version 2) and its Plan & Budget 2006/07. As part of its objective to promote high quality corporate reporting, the FRC undertook to review best practice for the disclosure of pension liabilities by UK companies in the context of the regulatory regime for UK pension schemes.   **A6**

In view of comments received following the implementation of FRS 17 the ASB decided to undertake a review of disclosures for retirement benefit schemes as set out in FRS 17. The review was distinct from the wider research project and had a narrow focus on how disclosures for defined benefit schemes could be improved in the short-term giving particular consideration to the changes made in the UK regulatory regime.   **A7**

APPROACH TO THE REVIEW

A8   To assist in its research project the ASB formed a Pensions Advisory Panel in the UK, with members who could provide a variety of expert perspectives on pensions accounting, including those of actuaries, regulators, auditors, the preparers and users of financial statements. In addition the research project is supported by a Working Group from the European Financial Reporting Advisory Group (EFRAG). The role of the Panel and the Working Group is to ensure that a number of knowledgeable points of view are fully considered. The ASB wished to progress the short-term review of disclosures as quickly as possibly and considered the Panel and the Working Group would provide a unique resource to assist the ASB in its short-term review. The Panel and Working Group agreed to assist the ASB in its short-term review. The ASB would like to thank the members of the Panel and Working Group for their contribution to the Reporting Statement.

A9   Following research on possible improvements to disclosures for defined benefit schemes a number of recommendations were made to the ASB for consideration. The ASB then considered how these recommendations could be implemented within the context of existing UK Financial Reporting Standards.

A10   In May 2006 the ASB issued a Financial Reporting Exposure Draft (FRED) that proposed to replace the disclosure requirements set out in FRS 17 with those of IAS 19 'Employee Benefits.' In addition the FRED set out a draft Reporting Statement which proposed disclosures that would complement those disclosures required by the amended FRS 17.

A11   Respondents to the FRED were generally in agreement with its proposals to replace the disclosure requirements of FRS 17 with those of IAS 19. In December 2006 the ASB published an amendment to FRS 17. Respondents, however, expressed mixed views in relation to the proposals set out in the draft Reporting Statement. These views have been considered in developing the Reporting Statement.

OBJECTIVE

A12   The objective of the Reporting Statement is to recommend disclosures that provide the users of financial statements with information, in addition to the disclosure required by the amended FRS 17 (or IAS 19), which enables them to evaluate the risks and rewards arising from defined benefit schemes including the funding requirements placed on the entity by those schemes.

SCOPE OF THE REPORTING STATEMENT

A13   In reaching its decision to issue a Reporting Statement the ASB gave due consideration to the needs of users of financial statements. The ASB was also conscious that any additional disclosure requirements, that went beyond those set out in the amended FRS 17, should not be cumbersome to preparers. Some respondents to the FRED, however, questioned the ASB's decision to propose a Reporting Statement. The ASB decided it should set out clearly its considerations in deciding to propose a Reporting Statement.

A14   When the ASB decided to propose a Reporting Statement it considered that the needs of the users of UK financial statements had been influenced by changes in the UK regulatory environment. However, it noted UK quoted entities generally apply International Financial Reporting Standards (IFRS) and therefore an amendment to the disclosure requirements in FRS 17 alone may not address the needs of users. The

ASB sought to find a solution which improved disclosures provided by UK entities whether the entity applied International or UK Financial Reporting Standards.

The ASB noted, in January 2006, it had published a non-mandatory Reporting **A15** Statement: 'Operating and Financial Review' which is a formulation of best practice and is intended to have persuasive rather than mandatory force. The ASB considered it could achieve its objective of improving disclosures for defined benefit schemes by publishing a Reporting Statement that addressed the disclosure requirements for defined benefit schemes.

In reaching its decision to publish a Reporting Statement the ASB gave due con- **A16** sideration to its strategy for convergence of UK Financial Reporting Standards with those of International Financial Reporting Standards. Although the ASB is still considering its convergence plan, it had previously stated*:

> In general there is little case for UK accounting standards being more prescriptive than IFRS. However, the ASB will not, as a matter of policy, preclude the possibility of promulgating standards that go beyond IFRS where, in its judgement, the need for this is demonstrable.

The ASB gave due consideration to this statement and decided that there was a clear demonstrable need to encourage improvements in the disclosure relating to defined benefit schemes.

During its redeliberation of the proposals in the draft Reporting Statement, the ASB **A17** reconsidered its decision to propose a Reporting Statement. The ASB affirmed its decision, noting that the amendment to FRS 17 alone would not address the needs of users and that the Reporting Statement was complementary to the amendment made to FRS 17.

Some respondents to the FRED expressed a concern that the role of the Reporting **A18** Statement was not clear. During its redeliberations the ASB noted that it had, in the past, issued not only the Reporting Statement – 'Operating and Financial Review' but it had also issued Statements on 'Interim Reports' and 'Preliminary Announcements'. These statements all specified that they were designed as a formulation and development of best practice and are intended to have persuasive rather than mandatory force.

The ASB considers that the role of the Reporting Statement is that of a best practice **A19** guide. The ASB also reaffirmed its early view that a Reporting Statement, which sets out principles for disclosure, rather than specific requirements, allows entities the flexibility to provide disclosures that are appropriate to their exposure to risks arising from defined benefit schemes.

PRINCIPLES

Relationship between the entity and trustees (managers) of the defined benefit scheme

The draft Reporting Statement proposed that the directors disclose information that **A20** enabled users of financial statements to understand the relationship between the entity (employer) and trustees (managers) of the defined benefit scheme. This

---

*Draft Policy Statement (2005) – Accounting Standard Setting in a Changing Environment: the Role of the Accounting Standards Board.

information would allow users of financial statements to understand the extent to which an entity is able to influence arrangements with the scheme.

A21   In making this proposal the ASB was conscious of the importance of the independent role of trustees (managers) of many defined benefit schemes and how the extent of this independence might vary between individual schemes and between schemes in different legal jurisdictions. The ASB consider that the relationship between the trustees (managers) of defined benefit schemes and the reporting entity affects how an entity is able to manage its affairs with regard to the defined benefit scheme and, that users of financial statements would benefit from having a greater understanding of this relationship.

A22   A number of respondents were concerned that the proposals as set out in the draft Reporting Statement would lead to cumbersome disclosures that were complex and difficult to understand. These respondents considered that the level of complexity could lead to 'boilerplate' disclosures that provided very little information to the users of financial statements.

A23   Some respondents, however, accepted there was a need for greater disclosures regarding the relationship between the entity and trustees (managers) and considered the disclosures recommended in the draft Reporting Statement should focus on any 'out-of-the ordinary' powers of, or constraints on the trustees, or schemes for which the trustees' position differs significantly from that for other UK schemes.

A24   The ASB considered the alternative views of respondents. The ASB, however, retained its view that there was a need for financial statements to provide information that assisted a user to understand the relationship between the entity and the trustees (managers) of the scheme but agreed that the wording in the Reporting Statement should make clear that disclosure should address powers that were both significant and unusual in relation to the legal and regulatory framework to which the entity operated. It also noted that disclosure was only recommended where these powers could have a material financial affect on the reporting entity.

Principal assumptions used to measure scheme liabilities

A25   A particular concern highlighted by commentators in relation to the previous FRS 17 was the absence of the requirement to disclose mortality rates used to calculate scheme liabilities. In developing the FRED, issued in May 2006, the ASB noted that IAS 19 requires the principal actuarial assumptions of the scheme to be disclosed (and therefore requires disclosure of mortality rates where it is considered to be a principal assumption) whereas FRS 17 required only the principal financial assumptions to be disclosed. In the FRED the ASB decided, consistent with its policy of convergence, not to amend the text of IAS 19 (as adopted into FRS 17) to specify the disclosure of mortality rates but to recommend in the draft Reporting Statement that mortality rates be disclosed.

A26   Respondents to the FRED were generally in agreement with the proposal to disclose mortality rates. A number of respondents did, however, question the illustrative example set out in the draft Reporting Statement. Those that questioned the illustrative example noted that the example was not consistent with the recommendation in the draft Reporting Statement. The ASB thereby amended the illustrative example in the Reporting Statement.

The ASB, in amending the illustrative example in the Reporting Statement, also took into consideration the views of some respondents that too much emphasis was placed on the disclosure of mortality rates and that other assumptions may be significant.   A27

In addition, some respondents asked for greater clarification as to how disclosures for mortality rates should be set out in the financial statements. In view of respondents' comments, the ASB considered whether it should provide more prescriptive guidance than that set out in the draft Reporting Statement.   A28

In considering whether to provide more prescriptive guidance for the disclosure of mortality rates the ASB took into consideration the report issued by the Financial Reporting Review Panel which noted the inconsistency in disclosure of mortality rates gave rise to a lack of comparability between reporting entities.   A29

The ASB was also mindful of the ongoing research project into pension accounting and considered it should not provide prescriptive guidance while the research work was ongoing. The ASB did, however, reiterate its earlier view that disclosure of the number of years post retirement (mortality rate) it is anticipated pensions will be paid to members of the scheme would provide more useful information to users of financial statements than details of a mortality standard table used, or details of a cohort factor, which may require a user to undertake further research to determine the actual number of years.   A30

The ASB also noted that the 'Statement of Principles for Financial Reporting' notes that good presentation ensures that the essential messages of the financial statements are communicated clearly and effectively in a simple and straightforward manner as is possible.   A31

The draft Reporting Statement also carried forward as a recommendation a requirement from the previous FRS 17 that where an entity has a closed scheme or a scheme in which the age profile of the active membership is rising significantly, the fact that under the projected unit method, the current service costs will increase as the members of the scheme approach retirement. The ASB took into consideration the views from respondents who considered the disclosure was misleading. In view of the comments received the ASB decided to remove the recommendation from the Reporting Statement.   A32

Sensitivity analysis of the principal assumptions used to measure scheme liabilities

In developing the draft Reporting Statement the ASB had taken into consideration that the measurement of scheme liabilities is inherently uncertain and based on assumptions selected by the entity's managers (directors). The ASB also noted that neither the previous FRS 17 nor IAS 19 required a sensitivity analysis that disclosed the effect that changes in assumptions made to the measurement of scheme liabilities. The ASB decided to recommend in the draft Reporting Statement that the financial statements include a sensitivity analysis for the principal assumptions used to measure the scheme liabilities.   A33

In forming this view the ASB gave due consideration to the views of some commentators that greater information should be provided about the defined benefit scheme to allow users to undertake their own sensitivity analysis, whilst others considered that the reporting entity should prepare the sensitivity analysis. The ASB considered these two views and concluded that a sensitivity analysis prepared by the reporting entity would provide more reliable information than an external user of the financial statements could prepare.   A34

A35   Although respondents to this recommendation noted the benefit of the disclosure, some expressed a concern regarding the additional costs incurred in the preparation of the sensitivity analysis. They noted the additional costs might outweigh the benefits of disclosure.

A36   The ASB considered this concern but noted that the Reporting Statement is a best practice statement and is not mandatory. The ASB considered therefore the reporting entity should decide whether on cost/benefit or other grounds to include such an analysis. The ASB also considered that where an entity decided not to include a sensitivity analysis it could provide alternative disclosures that enable users to understand scheme liabilities.

How the liabilities arising from defined benefit schemes are measured

A37   The draft Reporting Statement recommends that the financial statements should disclose information that enable users to understand the nature of the liabilities arising from defined benefit schemes. In making this recommendation the ASB noted that FRS 17 requires scheme liabilities to be measured using the projected unit method. There are, however, alternative approaches to the measurement of defined benefit scheme liabilities*.

A38   In the draft Reporting Statement it was noted one alternative approach was the cost of buying out benefits with a suitable insurance entity at the balance sheet date.

A39   In setting out its proposals in the draft Reporting Statement the ASB considered a number of points of view on this disclosure. The ASB, noted that with the improved disclosures proposed in the draft Reporting Statement, users of financial statements may be able to estimate the cost of buying out scheme benefits with a suitable insurance entity at the Balance Sheet date. The ASB was concerned that this could give rise to a number of estimates being made that may be inaccurate. The ASB therefore decided to recommend disclosure of the cost of buying out scheme liabilities in the draft Reporting Statement but to specifically seek the views of constituents on whether this disclosure should be included in the final Reporting Statement.

A40   The majority of respondents to the draft Reporting Statement did not support the recommendation to disclose the cost of buying out scheme liabilities. The principal arguments put forward by these respondents were:

- users would misunderstand the disclosure, particularly regarding future funding requirements;
- this misunderstanding will lead to more scheme closures;
- there is limited actuarial guidance on how to calculate this amount – as a consequence the calculation is subjective;
- The Pension Regulator (TPR) had removed buy-out as a scheme trigger for funding regulations and therefore disclosure is inconsistent; and
- the insurance market is not sufficiently homogenous to assure reliable measurement.

These respondents supported the concerns the ASB had set out in The Development of the Draft Reporting Statement, namely:

The measurement of defined benefit scheme liabilities is discussed in paragraphs 11 to 22 of The Development of the FRS to FRS 17 'Retirement Benefits'.

- that the disclosure of a buy-out cost is not consistent with the going-concern concept;
- the buy-out cost may not be easily available for non-UK schemes; and
- the amount is merely an estimate and an active market does not exist for these obligations.

During its redeliberation of this proposal the ASB noted that in the UK under the **A41** Occupational Pension Schemes (Employer Debt) Regulations 2005 (SI 2005/678), the debt on the employer on the winding up of a pension scheme will be determined on a full buy-out basis. In addition the ASB noted:

(i) S224 of Pensions Act 2004 requires that the trustees or managers obtain valuations:

    a.   at intervals of not more than one year or, if they obtain actuarial reports for the intervening years, at intervals of not more than three years, and

    b.   in such circumstances and on such other occasions as may be prescribed.

(ii) summary funding statements disclose the buy-out amount.

The ASB considered the comment made by respondents that there was a lack of **A42** guidance on how to disclose the cost of buying out scheme liabilities. The ASB, however, noted that Guidance Note 9 'Funding Defined Benefits – Presentation of Actuarial Advice' as adopted by the Board of Actuarial Standards provided some guidance on how to calculate this amount. The Board therefore decided to specifically refer to the Guidance Note in the Reporting Statement.

The ASB took into consideration the views of respondents very carefully but could **A43** find no justification that information made available to members of defined benefit schemes and/or trustees (managers of schemes), should not be made available to members (investors) of the entity. However the ASB noted the concern of respondents and decided to amend the recommendation in the draft Reporting Statement to only recommend disclosure where the cost of buying out benefits is made available to trustees (managers) and/or members of defined benefit schemes.

In considering the comments from respondents regarding this disclosure the ASB **A44** noted that some commentators had highlighted that the illustrative example discussed the Accumulated Benefits Obligation (ABO) in addition to the amount that would be required to buy out benefits. Respondents had noted that it might be useful for users of financial statements to understand the effect on scheme liabilities arising from future salary growth assumptions but, that the Reporting Statement should define the terms and provide clarification that the term is a suitable alternative. The ASB agreed with respondents and amended the Reporting Statement accordingly.

Future funding obligations in relation to defined benefit schemes

The amended FRS 17 requires an entity to disclose details of any contributions **A45** agreed to be paid in the next accounting period to the defined benefit scheme. Scheme liabilities are, however, often of a long-term nature and contributions expected to be paid in the next accounting period may not provide sufficient information to allow the users of the financial statements to understand how the funding requirements for scheme liabilities impact the economic resources available to the entity, including its cash flow. In developing its proposals in the draft Reporting Statement the ASB, supported by the views of its Advisory Panel, considered that greater information regarding funding would allow users to evaluate how funding obligations affect an entity's economic resources.

A46   In recommending that greater information be provided regarding funding obligations the ASB considered the regulations introduced in the UK setting out a new funding regime for defined benefit schemes. The new funding regime proposes a partnership approach between employers and trustees (managers) of defined benefit schemes. The ASB formed the view that users of financial statements would gain from a greater understanding of agreements reached between the trustees (managers) of defined benefit schemes and the reporting entity regarding not only agreed contributions but also funding principles.

A47   The ASB gave consideration to the number of defined benefit schemes that are, at present, in deficit. Some entities have entered into agreements with the trustees (managers) of the defined benefit scheme to make additional ('special') contributions to the scheme in order to reduce the current level of deficit. These 'special' contributions are often separate from 'regular' contributions and are to be made over a specified period of years. The ASB considered that disclosure of both 'regular' and 'special' contributions would provide the users of financial statements with information about how an entity's cash flows are affected by 'regular' and 'special' contributions.

A48   Respondents to the draft Reporting Statement were generally in agreement with the need for greater information requiring funding obligations but were concerned that funding requirements are reviewed regularly between the entity and the trustees (managers) of retirement benefit schemes. They therefore considered that detailed funding projections may be misleading and would not provide useful information to users of financial statements. The Board took the views of respondents into consideration and decided that details of funding obligations should be of a narrative nature.

A49   In addition to understanding agreed contribution levels for defined benefit schemes, it was noted by some commentators that it is important also to understand how long on average the liabilities of a retirement benefit scheme mature. The Reporting Statement recommends that the financial statements should disclose the duration of the scheme liabilities.

A50   The Reporting Statement also recommends that information should be provided with regard to how the liabilities of the defined benefit scheme fall due. Some respondents questioned this recommendation, arguing that these are the cash flows of the scheme and are separate from those of the reporting entity. Consequentially, they had no direct impact on the cash flows of the entity and should not therefore be disclosed in the reporting entity's financial statements. The ASB, however, considered that the cash flow information provided useful information to users of financial statements as it allowed users to understand the profile of cash flows including peak cash flows. The ASB therefore decided to retain the disclosure but agreed a graphical presentation of the information may be of more use to users of financial statements.

Nature and extent of the risks arising from financial instruments held by the defined benefit scheme

A51   FRS 17 as amended requires scheme assets to be analysed only by class of asset. This classification does not enable users to evaluate the risks arising from financial assets or liabilities that might be held by the scheme. The Reporting Statement therefore recommends that the financial statements disclose information that enables users of financial statements to evaluate the nature and extent of the risks arising from the financial assets or liabilities held by the defined benefits scheme.

In making this recommendation the Board took into consideration the growing trend **A52** of 'Liability Driven Investment' which aims to reduce the risk by focusing on the significant risks and narrowing the range of possible outcomes, using financial instruments.

Interim reports*

(Issued September 1997)

This Statement is designed as a formulation and development of best practice; it is intended to have persuasive rather than mandatory force and is not an accounting standard. In the interests of good financial reporting its use is commended by the Financial Reporting Council, the Hundred Group of Finance Directors, the London Stock Exchange and the Irish Stock Exchange.

Contents

*****Editor's note**: The ASB has issued an exposure draft of a proposed statement dealing with Half-Yearly Financial Reports (see exposure drafts). If implemented, this will replace this statement.*

Foreword by the Financial Reporting Council

The Financial Reporting Council (FRC) regards interim reports as an important aspect of financial reporting. Shareholders and potential shareholders rely on interim reports to obtain relevant and timely information about a company's financial position and performance. Such reports, together with other information available through the press or company reports throughout the year, are a necessary input to the making of informed investment decisions.

Many companies find that there are advantages in expanding their published interim information beyond the minimum required by the London Stock Exchange as this enables key issues to be openly discussed with less risk of accidental disclosure of unpublished price–sensitive information. Increased information at the interim stage also benefits shareholders and potential shareholders as it can improve their understanding or give reassurance at an earlier stage in the reporting process than the year–end figures.

The FRC believes that the Accounting Standards Board's Statement has an important role to play in assisting directors to develop their presentation of interim reports by emulating the achievements of best practice. The FRC therefore welcomes the Board's Statement and invites the directors of all listed companies, and such other organisations as prepare interim reports, to adopt its recommendations.

Sydney Lipworth

Sir Sydney Lipworth QC
Chairman, Financial Reporting Council
September 1997

Introduction

The Committee on the Financial Aspects of Corporate Governance (the Cadbury Committee) recommended in 1992 that the Accounting Standards Board, in conjunction with the London Stock Exchange, should clarify the accounting principles to be adopted by companies when preparing their interim reports. It also recommended that balance sheet information should be included with the interim report and suggested that the inclusion of cash flow information should also be considered.*

More recently, the International Accounting Standards Committee (IASC) has been developing a new International Accounting Standard, scheduled for publication in the spring of 1998,† on recognising, measuring and reporting interim financial information. IASC's initial proposals, published in September 1996, and its subsequent Exposure Draft E57, issued in August 1997, were considered during the preparation of the Statement.

In response to the Cadbury initiative, the Financial Reporting Committee of the Institute of Chartered Accountants in England and Wales undertook a project focusing on the accounting aspects of interim accounts, in particular their content, measurement basis and extent of disclosure. The Committee published a consultative paper 'Interim Financial Reporting' in 1993 which led to formal proposals being presented to the Board. This Statement is developed from those proposals and presents its recommendations as best practice in the reporting of interim information.

SCOPE

The Statement recommends principles for interim financial reporting which are intended to apply to all entities that are required or voluntarily choose to issue general purpose interim financial reports (interim reports) directed towards the common information needs of a wide range of users.

Special purpose financial reports prepared as of an interim date, for example computations prepared for taxation purposes and reports prepared for parties to a business combination, are outside the scope of this Statement. Nevertheless, the principles within this Statement may well be relevant to the preparation of such special purpose reports.

Whilst the Statement is designed in the context of a half–yearly reporting requirement, the key principles may also be applied to first and third quarters' statements made by companies that report on a quarterly basis, subject to additional considerations that would apply, for example, to the selection of appropriate comparative data. However, where companies choose to report quarterly, it is recognised that the content of first and third quarterly reports may not be as detailed as half–yearly reports.

Furthermore, in the Republic of Ireland, the Report of the Financial Reporting Commission published in 1992 (the Ryan Report) also advocated half-yearly interim reporting and recommended that interim reports should include details of items of an exceptional nature such as capital profits or losses, depreciation and interest charges, and segmental data, together with a balance sheet in sufficient detail for financial position to be assessed.

†*Editor's note: IAS 34 'Interim financial reporting' was issued in March 1998.*

Interim reports

ROLE OF THE INTERIM REPORT

Interim reports were introduced by the London Stock Exchange as a requirement for listing, mainly because the interval between annual reports was considered to be too long a period for shareholders and the investing public to be without financial information, particularly when developments were affecting trading conditions. **1**

Interim reports play an important role as a progress report in the continuing reporting process of the operating, financing and investing activities of a business. Like annual financial statements they fulfil a confirmatory and predictive function. Within the constraints of time and cost, interim reports are designed to enable users to monitor the progress of a business from its financial position as stated in the last set of annual financial statements and to assess the impact of recent events on operating performance and financial position. **2**

TIMESCALE

The benefits of providing users of accounts with interim information need to be balanced against the practical problems of collecting it at an acceptable cost and within a reasonable timeframe. For information to be of value in updating users' knowledge of a company it must be timely. The Board therefore encourages companies to make their interim reports available within 60 days of the interim period–end. **3**

BASIS OF PRESENTATION

Interim reports, like annual financial statements, are presented in respect of a distinct reporting period. A fair assessment of the progress of the business can be made only if the interim accounts are prepared on a consistent and comparable basis taking one reporting period with another. **4**

Traditionally, two rather different methods have been used in the preparation of interim reports: the 'integral method' and the 'discrete method'. **5**

The integral method views the interim period as a part of the larger annual reporting cycle. Its function is predominantly to predict and explain the financial information for the full financial year. Items are therefore recognised in interim periods on the basis of estimating the total annual revenue and expenses and allocating accordingly. **6**

Under the discrete method, the interim period is treated as an accounting period distinct from the annual cycle. Incomplete transactions are treated according to the same principles as are applied at the year–end. This has the advantage that the elements of financial statements are defined in the same way as for the annual financial statements. **7**

The Board recommends an approach whereby items of income and expense are measured and recognised on a basis consistent with that used in the preparation of annual financial statements (the discrete method). It is nevertheless consistent with this method that for certain specific items of income and expense that occur on an annual basis (taxation for example) it is necessary to take into account the estimated income or expense for the whole year to determine the appropriate amount to be recognised in the interim period. Depending on the item, this might be for example, **8** on the basis of the time expired, the benefit received or the activity associated with the period.

Accounting policies

9   The London Stock Exchange* requires the accounting policies and presentation of figures in interim reports to be consistent with those in the annual financial statements. Accordingly, interim reports should be prepared using the same measurement basis and adopting the same accounting principles and practices as are employed in the annual financial statements.

10   Interim reports should include a statement that they are prepared on the basis of the accounting policies set out in the most recent set of annual financial statements. Interim reports are often reviewed in conjunction with the previous year's financial statements and therefore their accounting policies need to be stated and explained only where they differ from those previously adopted.

Changes in accounting policy and prior period adjustments

11   When it is known at the time that interim accounts are prepared that an accounting policy change (or a presentation change) will be made in the annual accounts (including voluntary changes in accounting policy, not resulting from a new or revised accounting standard, UITF abstract or a change in companies legislation), the change should preferably be implemented in the interim accounts rather than deferred to the year–end. This ensures that the interim results are presented on the same basis as those for the full financial year. Where a known accounting policy change in the current year is not implemented in the interim report an estimate of its effect should be shown; if that is not possible, a statement of explanation should be included.

12   Following a change in accounting policy, the amounts for the current and prior periods should be stated on the basis of the new policies. The cumulative effect of the policy change on opening reserves (ie at the beginning of the financial year) should be disclosed at the foot of the statement of total recognised gains and losses of the period. Similar disclosures should be made in respect of other prior period adjustments arising from the discovery of fundamental errors. A description should be given to help users understand the nature of each change or adjustment.

Annually determined income and expenditure

13   Certain items of income and expenditure are determined on a formal basis once a year when the full financial statements are prepared; examples include bonuses, profit–sharing arrangements, volume discounts, sales commissions and rent based on income or sales criteria.

14   In each case it is necessary to determine whether an obligation to transfer economic benefits as a result of past transactions or events exists at the interim period–end. Only if there is such an obligation (either contractual or constructive), should a

*The Irish Stock Exchange follows the same Listing Rules as the London Stock Exchange. Therefore, all references to the Listing Rules of the London Stock Exchange should also be taken as including those of the Irish Stock Exchange. (**Editor's note:** In the UK, the Listing Rules are now issued by the Financial Services Authority in its capacity as UK Listing Authority.)

provision be made at the period end. An intention to transfer economic benefits is, by itself, not sufficient to recognise future costs and income in the interim period.

For example, a genuinely discretionary one–off bonus given at the end of the year 15
would be recognised only in the final interim accounting period. On the other hand, a profit–related bonus paid at the year–end, although non–contractual, would be recognised in an earlier interim period, on the basis of profits earned in that period, if past practice indicated that there was a constructive obligation. Similarly, a contractual supplier's volume discount, based on an annual target for the year, would also be recognised in an earlier interim period on the basis of a proportion of the expected annual discount.

Seasonal revenues

A business is seasonal where there is a substantial and recurring variation between 16
the levels of profit in the interim period and the remainder of the year. Fluctuating revenues of seasonal businesses are generally understood by the marketplace and it is appropriate to report them as they arise.

Taxation

Treating the interim date as if it were a year–end for tax purposes would require the 17
interim tax charge to be calculated without taking account of capital allowances and other adjustments that affect the effective annual rate. The resulting number would not be meaningful as it would not reflect the fact that tax is an annual charge that cannot finally be determined until the end of the financial year.

The interim tax charge should be based on an estimate of the likely effective tax rate 18
for the year, expressed as a percentage of the expected results for the year and then applied to the interim profit or loss arising. This approach results in taxation, including permanent and timing tax differences, being recognised rateably over the year as a whole in common with other contractual, annually determined items of income and expenditure as noted in paragraphs 14 and 15.

To the extent practicable and where more meaningful, a separate estimated effective 19
annual tax rate should be determined for each material tax jurisdiction and applied individually to the interim period pre–tax income of each jurisdiction. Similarly, if different income tax rates apply to different categories of income (such as capital gains tax), to the extent practicable, a separate rate should be applied to each individual category of interim period pre–tax income, where material. In many cases a weighted average of rates across jurisdictions or across categories of income may be a reasonable approximation of the effect of using more specific rates.

Exceptional items are, by definition, material to the accounts and can often distort 20
the overall tax charge if the tax rate applying to the exceptional item differs significantly from the likely effective tax rate. Therefore, where material, the tax effect of exceptional items should not be included in the likely effective annual tax rate but should be recognised in the same period(s) as the relevant exceptional item. In such circumstances, the estimated annual effective tax rate (excluding exceptional items) will be applied to the interim profits or losses before exceptional items.

Events and expenditure that are expected to fall in the second part of the year and 21
would affect the effective annual tax rate should be brought into the estimate on a prudent basis. Capital expenditure is usually planned in advance; it is, therefore, usually possible to take account of the expected capital allowances in calculating the

effective tax rate for the year. It would not normally be appropriate, however, to take account of the tax effects of other significant events that, although expected to arise in the second part of the year, are subject to considerable uncertainty.

22   The interim report should give a brief explanation of the basis of the effective tax rate in the narrative commentary where such events are anticipated.

23   The general approach of making an estimate of the effective tax rate for the year should be employed even where, for example, a company's result in the first half–year is expected to be completely offset by its result in the second half–year. Even if the overall result is break–even, there will still be an effective tax rate (say 30 per cent). The full year's tax of nil is, conceptually, 30 per cent of no profit, rather than zero per cent. Thus that tax rate is applied to both profits and losses. However, a tax credit should be booked (and a deferred tax asset recognised) for interim tax losses only if there is reasonable assurance that it will reverse in the foreseeable future (in accordance with the accounting standard on deferred tax).

24   In determining the amount of tax losses and recoverable advance corporation tax to recognise in the interim period, an estimate should be made of the utilisation expected over the whole tax year. The amount recognised in the interim period should be proportional to the profit before tax of the interim period and the estimated annual profit before tax, but limited to the amount recoverable for the year as a whole.*

Foreign exchange

25   The profit and loss account of a foreign entity accounted for under the net investment or closing rate method should be translated either at the average rate for the interim period or at the closing rate at the end of that period, whichever is consistent with the company's accounting policy.†

Valuations

26   Whether value changes of assets held at a valuation are recognised depends upon the nature of the assets and the difficulty of obtaining valuations. Revaluation would be

---

For example, if there was a tax loss brought forward of £75,000; estimated first half-year taxable profits of £100,000; and an expected second half-year tax loss of £40,000; then tax losses of £60,000 would be absorbed in the first half of the year (being the maximum annual utilisation of tax losses brought forward, based on expected taxable profits for the year), leaving £40,000 first half-year taxable profits to be set against second half-year tax losses of £40,000. This would result in a tax charge (at, say, an effective tax rate of 30%) of £12,000 in the first half-year and a tax credit of £12,000 in the second half-year, giving a nil overall tax charge for the year.

†*Editor's note: For companies complying with FRS 23, paragraph 25 is amended, and paragraph 25A added, as follows:*

25   FRS 23 (IAS 21) *The Effects of Changes in Foreign Exchange rates* specifies how to translate the financial statements for foreign operations into the presentation currency, including guidelines for using average or closing foreign exchange rates and guidelines for recognising the resulting adjustments in profit or loss or in the statement of total recognised gains and losses. Consistently, with FRS 23, the actual average rate and closing rates for the interim period are used. Entities do not anticipate some future changes in foreign exchange rates in the remainder of the current financial year in translating foreign operations at an interim date.

25A If FRS 23 requires translation adjustments to be recognised as income or expense in the period in which they arise, that principle is applied during each interim period. Entities do not defer some foreign currency translation adjustments at an interim date if the adjustments are expected to reverse before the end of the financial year.

necessary, for example, in respect of quoted stocks carried at market value, but not, as a matter of course, in respect of properties, where revaluations on the basis used in the previous annual financial statements would suffice, subject to the following:

(a)   the most recent valuations available should be used;

(b)   where valuations have been brought forward, without amendment from the previous annual accounts, a statement to that effect should be given; and

(c)   where significant, the directors are encouraged to comment on price movements since the last valuation.

Similarly, it should not usually be necessary to obtain a new actuarial valuation for pension costs, unless a significant event, such as a change in benefits, has rendered the previous estimate misleading. If, however, a more recent actuarial valuation is available at an interim date, this should be used in the interim accounts.   **27**

Materiality

Consistently with the discrete approach, materiality should be assessed with refer-   **28** ence to the results and financial position for the interim period rather than in relation to expected results and financial position for the full year.

CONTENT OF INTERIM REPORT

Interim reports provide an update on the latest set of annual financial statements   **29** and, accordingly, should focus on new activities, events and circumstances.

An informed assessment of financial position and performance does not focus solely   **30** on the profit (or loss) for the period, but requires comparison of information from the profit and loss account, statement of total recognised gains and losses, balance sheet and cash flow statement. Whilst not all information in the four primary statements is critical to such an analysis, it is useful to present the significant information within the context of the four statements, along with a narrative commentary that highlights and explains these elements in the context of events since the previous annual report and accounts.

It is therefore recommended that an interim report should include a narrative   **31** commentary, summarised profit and loss account, statement of total recognised gains and losses, summarised balance sheet and summarised cash flow statement.

Significant events and trends mentioned in the commentary should be supported by   **32** the underlying figures given either on the face of the primary statements or by way of note. Sufficient supplementary information should be given, where appropriate to the nature of the company's business and as the directors see fit, to permit an understanding of the significant items contained within the primary statements. For example, in certain cases it may be useful to analyse fixed assets into component parts, provide more detail about the company's borrowings, or state the equity and non–equity interests in shareholders' funds, in accordance with FRS 4 'Capital Instruments'.

The information should be presented in a concise manner, should be consistent and   **33** comparable with that previously reported (the annual report) and should facilitate comparison between like companies.

MANAGEMENT COMMENTARY

34   The London Stock Exchange requires interim reports to include 'an explanatory statement including any significant information enabling investors to make an informed assessment of the trend of the group's activities and profit or loss' (The Listing Rules Chapter 12.56). Interim reports should focus attention on areas of change since the last set of annual financial statements. A balanced narrative commentary that explains the reasons for significant movements in key indicators and indicates perceived trends within the business is an important feature of an interim report, providing management with the opportunity to report on its stewardship of the business as a whole.

35   The commentary should enable users to appreciate the main factors influencing the company's performance during the interim period and its position at the period–end. For example, gross margins are an important factor in the success of retailing businesses and should be adequately disclosed and explained in such cases. It may sometimes be necessary to explain that the greater part of an improvement in performance was due to an event that occurred in the second half of the previous year. Attention should be drawn to events and changes within the period that are likely to have a significant effect on the succeeding period despite having had relatively little impact in the current period.

36   The commentary is not intended to be as comprehensive as an operating and financial review (OFR). However, management should consider whether key issues normally referred to in the OFR should be included within the interim report (albeit in less detail and focusing on areas of change) in order to meet these recommendations and to help users gain a better understanding of the company's business.

37   The commentary should describe the nature of any seasonal activity and, together with other disclosures, provide adequate information for the performance of the business and its financial position at the end of the period to be understood in the context of the annual cycle. The principles by which seasonal results are reflected in the interim report should be stated, particularly where there are any expected changes in the effects of seasonality.

38   As well as referring to trading performance, the commentary should draw attention to a summarised balance sheet and cash flow statement. It should also highlight and explain significant changes since the last annual financial statements, particularly regarding movements in working capital, liquidity and net debt that are likely to be of value to users in their assessment of the business.

39   The narrative commentary should explain any other matter that management thinks would help users to understand the report. This would include for example, where relevant:

- acquisitions and disposals of major fixed assets or investments during the period covered by the report
- changes in contingencies, commitments and off balance sheet financial instruments* since the previous year–end
- material changes in capital structure or financing
- events arising after the end of the period covered by the report.

The Board is reviewing the accounting treatment of off balance sheet financial instruments as part of its project on derivatives and other financial instruments.

PROFIT AND LOSS ACCOUNT

An interim report should include a summarised profit and loss account that includes   **40**
the following information where relevant (with separate identification of amounts
relating to associates and joint ventures):

- Turnover
- Operating profit or loss
- Interest payable less interest receivable (net)
- Profit or loss on ordinary activities before tax
- Tax on profit or loss on ordinary activities
- Profit or loss on ordinary activities after tax
- Minority interests
- Profit or loss for the period
- Dividends paid and proposed.

Acquisitions and discontinued operations

Turnover and operating profit of acquisitions and discontinued operations (as   **41**
defined in FRS 3 'Reporting Financial Performance') should be disclosed separately
on the face of the profit and loss account in the period in accordance with FRS 3. For
this purpose, operations are regarded as discontinued when the sale or termination is
completed either in the interim period or before the earlier of three months after the
end of the interim period and the date on which the interim report is approved.

It may be appropriate to disclose separately, either by way of note or in the   **42**
management commentary, the results of operations which, although not
discontinued, are in the process of discontinuing or are expected to be classified as
discontinued in the current year's financial statements. Where it is not practicable to
determine the post–acquisition results of an operation to the end of the interim
period, an indication should be given of the contribution of the acquisition to the
turnover and operating profit of the continuing operations.

Segmental information

To improve the quality of trend analysis and inter–company comparisons, compa-   **43**
nies required to present segmental information in their annual financial statements
should adopt the same business and geographical classifications in their interim
reports and disclose:

- segment turnover, distinguishing inter–segment sales if significant
- segment profit or loss as disclosed in the annual financial statements – normally
  profit or loss before accounting for interest, taxation and minority interests.

The basis of presentation of segmental information in the interim report should,   **44**
where possible, be consistent with that to be used at the current year–end in order to
assist users in making predictions that will be readily comparable with the annual
results. Any significant differences in presentation from that used in the latest annual
financial statements should be disclosed and explained.

Exceptional items

By definition, exceptional items are unusual in nature and significant in amount.   **45**
They rarely extend over more than one year and it is not generally appropriate to
allocate their effect to different parts of the reporting period. They should be

recognised and disclosed in the profit and loss account of the interim period in which they occur. Certain exceptional items should be shown separately after operating profit and before interest as required by paragraph 20 of FRS 3.

46   Other exceptional items should be charged or credited in arriving at the profit or loss on ordinary activities by inclusion under the statutory headings to which they relate. In addition, they should be disclosed and described by way of a note.

47   The tax effects of exceptional items disclosed on the face of the profit and loss account, in accordance with paragraph 45 above, should be separately disclosed in the profit and loss account or a related note.

Earnings per share

48   The London Stock Exchange requires listed companies to disclose earnings per share expressed as pence per share. Basic earnings per share should be derived from the results for the interim period and calculated and disclosed in the same manner as at the year–end. Companies that choose to present in their annual financial statements additional amounts per share based on another level of earnings should present them also in their interim accounts, calculated and disclosed in accordance with FRS 3.

STATEMENT OF TOTAL RECOGNISED GAINS AND LOSSES

49   A statement of total recognised gains and losses should be included where material gains or losses, other than profit or loss for the interim period, as reported in the profit and loss account, are recognised in the period.

50   The recognition of foreign currency translation differences, for example, would require a statement of total recognised gains and losses only where the aggregate difference is material to the results of the period. By contrast, a statement of total recognised gains and losses would always be required in respect of an investment company that continuously revalued its investments. Where assets are revalued only at the year–end, there would be no valuation movement to report and hence, subject to there being no other reported gains or losses, no such statement would be required.

51   A reconciliation of movements in shareholders' funds is required only where movements other than those in the statement of total recognised gains and losses need to be explained.

BALANCE SHEET

52   A summarised balance sheet (together with comparatives) should highlight significant movements in key indicators of the company's financial position. For consistency, similar classifications to those used in the annual financial statements should be adopted. It is recommended that, for example, a Schedule 4 company or Schedule 4A* group should give the following balance sheet information:

- Fixed assets
- Current assets

*In Great Britain, Schedule 4 or 4A to the Companies Act 1985; in Northern Ireland, Schedule 4 or 4A to the Companies (Northern Ireland) Order 1986; in the Republic of Ireland, Part I of the Schedule to the Companies (Amendment) Act 1986 or Part I of the Schedule to the European Communities (Companies: Group Accounts) Regulations 1992.

- Stocks
- Debtors
- Cash at bank and in hand
- Other current assets
- Creditors: amounts falling due within one year
- Net current assets (liabilities)
- Total assets less current liabilities
- Creditors: amounts falling due after more than one year
- Provisions for liabilities and charges
- Capital and reserves
- Minority interests.

CASH FLOW STATEMENT

Information on the amounts and sources of cash flows provides an additional   **53** perspective to the performance of a company through the interim period. Total amounts for the categories of cash flows specified by FRS 1 (Revised 1996) 'Cash Flow Statements' should be presented as follows:

- Net cash inflow/outflow from operating activities
- Returns on investments and servicing of finance
- Taxation
- Capital expenditure and financial investment
- Acquisitions and disposals
- Equity dividends paid
- Management of liquid resources
- Financing
- Increase/decrease in cash.

A reconciliation of operating profit to operating cash flow should be given in suf-   **54** ficient detail for users to appreciate its chief components. A reconciliation should also be given of the movement of cash in the period to the movement in net debt, as required by FRS 1 (Revised 1996), including the effect of movements on short–term and long–term borrowings, cash and other components of net debt, unless disclosed elsewhere.

COMPARATIVE FIGURES

Comparative figures for the summarised profit and loss account, the statement of   **55** total recognised gains and losses and summarised cash flow statement should be presented for the corresponding interim period and the previous full financial year. This provides a meaningful view of performance to date, particularly where the business is seasonal. Users may then compare figures on a year–on–year basis, or use them in the evaluation of trends and estimations of annual results.

Balance sheet information is included in interim reports to highlight changes in key   **56** indicators of financial performance in the context of the entity's operating envir- onment since the entity's last accounting year–end. The critical comparative figures are, therefore, those from the last annual financial statements, which may be accompanied by those from the previous corresponding interim period to highlight the effect of seasonality.

OTHER DISCLOSURES

57   Subject to the limited exceptions noted in this Statement, disclosures demanded by Financial Reporting Standards and Statements of Standard Accounting Practice are not generally required in the presentation of interim reports.

58   There are, however, certain disclosures specific to interim reports that are helpful to users in assessing the relevance and reliability with which the reports might be used. They are:

- the period covered by the report
- the date on which it is approved by the board of directors
- the extent to which the information it contains has been audited or reviewed.

Appendix I
Explanation

MEASUREMENT AND RECOGNITION BASES

One of the major issues, from a theoretical viewpoint, is whether the period on which **1**
an interim report is made should be treated as a distinct, stand–alone reporting
period in its own right (the discrete method) or as part of the larger annual reporting
period (the integral method). The Board believes that the key principle should be that
the same measurement and recognition bases are used at the interim reporting date
as are used at the year–end. This ensures that the definitions of the elements of the
financial statements—assets, liabilities, revenues and expenses—apply equally to
interim reports, and has the added advantages of consistency and understandability.

Under this approach, as adopted in the Statement, expenses and revenues are **2**
recognised in their proper period and matched where appropriate. Unlike the integral method, it does not aim to smooth the results across the year. Instead, any
volatility in the interim report, for example as a result of seasonality or a large one–
off expenditure at the beginning of the year, needs to be explained in the narrative
commentary. This helps users' understanding of the business, so enhancing their
ability to assess the financial performance and position of the company.

The consequence is that the Statement adopts the discrete method, whilst recognising **3**
that this incorporates elements of the integral method for certain annually determined items. This approach reflects the fact that, whatever the length of the
accounting period chosen, it would rarely be an entirely independent period in that
some items of income or expense will always be incomplete. Calculating the interim
tax charge by performing a full tax computation on the interim period, for example,
could result in a meaningless number because it does not take into account all the
factors influencing the level of taxation being charged for that period in the context
of the year's events.

CONTENT

The objectives of interim reports are consistent with those of annual reports. Interim **4**
reports play an important role in the financial reporting calendar and, like annual
financial statements, are often fundamental to the making of investment decisions,
enabling these to be made on the basis of more timely financial information than
would otherwise be available. Hence, largely similar information is required at the
interim date as at the year–end, although the balance of benefit and cost on the
reliability and timeliness of information may differ.

Whilst sufficient information should be given in an interim report to permit an **5**
informed assessment of the company's performance and financial position, as a
progress report within the annual reporting cycle, it need not be as extensive as that
required by annual financial statements. Avoiding unnecessary detail will normally
increase the cost–effectiveness of an interim report, bearing in mind that such
statements are used to update information contained in previously published
financial statements. A recommendation for summarised information is therefore
consistent with the role of interim reports in a continuing reporting process.

A summarised profit and loss account, statement of total recognised gains and losses, **6**
balance sheet and cash flow statement provides information about the financial

position, performance and financial adaptability of a company that is useful to a wide range of users for making economic decisions.

7   The requirement for the summarised profit and loss account reflects the London Stock Exchange Listing Rules.* Additionally, in response to the frequently expressed needs of users, the Statement calls for segmental information and, in recognition of recent developments in year–end reporting, it also recommends the analysis of turnover and operating profit into continuing and discontinued operations, identifying the effect of acquisitions where possible.

8   The recommended format of the summarised balance sheet analyses current assets into their main constituent parts because the different characteristics (including liquidity) of these items vary significantly. Other items in the balance sheet may be expanded further if they add to the understanding of the events and trends in the interim period. For example, a company with significant additions to intangible fixed assets in an interim period may usefully disclose that information.

9   Cash flow information is of great potential value to the user of an interim report. It gives an indication of the relationship between profitability and cash–generating ability, and thus of the quality of the profit earned. It is helpful to be able to understand cash flows within the context of the other primary statements and therefore the reconciliation of operating profit to operating cash flow in an interim report is recommended.

10   Information on the net debt (essentially borrowings less cash and liquid resources) of a company is often important to an understanding of how the company finances its activities. The Statement therefore proposes that a reconciliation of cash movements to movements in net debt should be given. This highlights any significant movements in net debt during the period, providing information on the company's liquidity, solvency and financial adaptability that may otherwise not be highlighted in the interim report.

Editor's note: Now the Listing Rules of the Financial Services Authority as the UK Listing Authority.

Appendix II
Compliance with International Accounting Standards

The International Accounting Standards Committee (IASC) published an Exposure Draft, E57, of its proposed International Accounting Standard on Interim Financial Reporting in August 1997, and intends to vote on the final Standard in March 1998.*

Although the ASB's Statement is drafted primarily in the context of half–yearly reporting, whereas the IASC's proposals cover aspects relating to quarterly reporting in more detail, the key elements of the two sets of proposals are consistent in all material respects.

Like the ASB's Statement, E57 states that the same accounting recognition and measurement principles should be applied in the interim report as are applied in the annual financial statements. E57 also states that measurements for interim reporting purposes should be made on a year–to–date basis, which ensures that an entity's frequency of reporting (annual, half–yearly, or quarterly) does not affect the measurement of its annual results. However, as a consequence, amounts reported in prior interim periods of the current financial year may need to be remeasured at a later date, as new information becomes available. E57 requires significant remeasurements of previously reported interim data to be disclosed in the interim report, or, if there is no separate interim report for the final interim period of the year, in a note to the annual financial statements.

Editor's note: IAS 34 'Interim financial reporting' was issued in March 1998.

Preliminary announcements

(Issued July 1998)

This Statement is designed as a formulation and development of best practice; it is intended to have persuasive rather than mandatory force and is not an accounting standard. In the interests of good financial reporting its use is commended by the Financial Reporting Council, the Hundred Group of Finance Directors, the London Stock Exchange and the Irish Stock Exchange.

Contents

Foreword by the Financial Reporting Council

The Financial Reporting Council (FRC) recognises that, for listed companies, preliminary announcements play a key part in the annual financial reporting cycle, being the first public communication of companies' full-year results and year-end financial position. Preliminary announcements are relied upon to provide timely, sufficient and accurate information to ensure an orderly and efficient market.

Preliminary announcements form one of the focal points for investor interest, primarily because they confirm or update market expectations. Because of this, many companies are choosing to include more information in their preliminary announcements than is strictly required under the London Stock Exchange's Listing Rules – so that they convey the essential thrust of the full financial statements and the operating and financial review. This policy ensures that price-sensitive information is properly disseminated to the market and can therefore be openly discussed at analysts' briefings, which for many companies are playing an increasingly significant role in the public explanation of their performance and financial position.

The FRC believes that the Accounting Standards Board's Statement provides valuable guidance for directors wishing to embrace best practice when preparing their preliminary announcements. The FRC therefore welcomes the Board's Statement and encourages directors of all listed companies, and other such organisations as prepare preliminary announcements, to adopt its recommendations.

Sydney Lipworth

Sir Sydney Lipworth QC
Chairman, Financial Reporting Council
July 1998

Introduction

In the UK preliminary announcements are a requirement of the Listing Rules of the London Stock Exchange, under which listed companies are required to notify the Exchange of their preliminary statement of annual results and dividends (generally known as the preliminary announcement) without delay after board approval.* The Exchange requires companies to include in their preliminary announcement at least the items required by it for a half-yearly report (ie interim report), as well as any significant information necessary for the purpose of assessing the results being announced.

Preliminary announcements are companies' primary vehicle for the first public communication of their full-year results and year-end financial position to the markets. As such they often contain more information than the minimum required by the Exchange. This Statement provides voluntary guidance, which is intended to supplement the mandatory requirements of the Exchange, in respect of preliminary announcements.

The objective of the Statement is to improve the timeliness, quality, relevance and consistency of preliminary announcements within the constraints of reliability. Compliance with the Statement would both promote best practice within the context of the present reporting environment and increase comparability between preliminary announcements and previously published accounts.

Interim reports and preliminary announcements have much in common. They both communicate new information about the company's financial performance and position to the market, fulfilling confirmatory and predictive functions, although at different stages in the annual reporting cycle. The contents of interim reports and preliminary announcements, therefore, are likely to be similar. Accordingly, this Statement builds on the Statement of best practice 'Interim Reports' recently issued by the Accounting Standards Board.

Discussions about the role of preliminary announcements naturally lead to questions about their interaction with other year-end financial reports (ie the full report and accounts and summary financial statements). Indeed, comments on the exposure draft of this Statement included suggestions for reforming the year-end reporting package.

These ideas and the wider issues connected with the year-end financial reporting structure as a whole are being explored further by the Board, with the help of its working party.† This is intended to be a relatively long-term project to allow time for debate and future consultations on the overall reporting regime and for changes in practice to become accepted. In this context, the Board notes and welcomes the Government's announcement in March 1998 of its review of company law.

---

*A similar position exists in the Republic of Ireland, since the Irish Stock Exchange has the same Listing Rules as the London Stock Exchange. All references to the Listing Rules of the London Stock Exchange should be taken as also including those of the Irish Stock Exchange. (**Editor's note:** In the UK, the Listing Rules are now issued by the Financial Services Authority in its capacity as UK Listing Authority.)*

†**Editor's note:** A Discussion Paper was published in February 2000 and is reproduced in Part Nine of this volume.

SCOPE

The Statement recommends principles for the preparation of preliminary announcements which are intended to apply to all entities that are required by the Exchange to issue preliminary statements of annual results.

Preliminary Announcements

ROLE OF THE PRELIMINARY ANNOUNCEMENT

As the first external communication by companies of their financial performance and **1** position for the financial year, the preliminary announcement plays a key part in the reporting cycle. It enables the market to assess whether the company's annual results have met, exceeded or fallen short of expectations.

To be of value in updating the market's knowledge of a company, preliminary **2** announcements must be issued on a timely basis. Timely publication also helps to minimise the possibility of insider dealing.

The information in the preliminary announcement must be reliable and sufficient to **3** permit an immediate, informed assessment of the company's overall performance.

DISTRIBUTION

Preliminary announcements tend to be targeted at financial analysts and institutional **4** shareholders, as the persons or organisations most likely to influence a company's share price.

Under the Listing Rules of the Exchange, listed companies must notify the Exchange **5** of their preliminary announcements. In turn, the Exchange disseminates the information given to it by electronic means using its Regulatory News Service.

It is not mandatory for preliminary announcements to be sent to shareholders; in **6** practice, often only financial analysts and institutional shareholders receive them. Other shareholders are less likely to be in a position to take advantage of the information on a timely basis. However, in principle, to be equitable, all shareholders should be entitled, on request, to have access to the preliminary announcement as soon as it becomes available, although it should be noted that information required by the Exchange must not be given to another party before it has been notified to the Exchange.

Receiving a preliminary announcement after the market has reacted to that infor- **7** mation is of limited use. In practical terms, apart from press advertisements, information can be made available to a wider audience contemporaneously, and at the earliest possible moment that it becomes available, only through the use of electronic means (eg the Internet). Companies are therefore strongly encouraged to make further use of electronic means as a way of disseminating financial information, and in particular the preliminary announcement, to a wider audience.

Notwithstanding the emerging use of the Internet, companies are encouraged to **8** provide some means to ensure that all shareholders can, if they wish, readily obtain a copy of the preliminary announcement as soon as possible after its issue. There are various different methods (as well as electronic means) for achieving this and companies should consider and adopt methods that are appropriate to their share-holder base. Examples include:

- press advertisements containing the essential details of the preliminary announcement;
- pre-registration schemes (for example with reply cards that could be sent out with interim reports);
- publicising an address or telephone number by which shareholders can obtain copies of the announcement;
- notifying shareholders (eg with the last interim report of the period) of the exact date that the announcement is expected to be issued, so that they can take appropriate action to receive the preliminary announcement if they choose to do so.

Some of the above arrangements may be particularly useful for shareholders in companies whose results are not reported in detail in the press.

TIMESCALE

9   The benefits of providing the market with early notification of the annual results need to be balanced against the practical problems of collecting and processing information at an acceptable cost and with the same reliability as is required of the full financial statements. With this balance in mind, companies should consider ways of accelerating their year-end reporting timetable, so that they can issue their preliminary announcement as soon as possible after the year-end. Whilst recognising that individual circumstances may make it impracticable for some companies to achieve, the Board nevertheless encourages companies to issue their preliminary announcements within 60 days of the year-end.

10   Furthermore, companies should issue the full report and accounts (and the summary financial statement, if prepared) as soon as practicable after the preliminary announcement has been issued.

RELIABILITY

11   To ensure reliability, the Exchange requires the company's auditors to agree with the release of the preliminary announcement. Therefore the directors should publish the preliminary announcement only when it has been approved by the board and agreement, as required by the Listing Rules, has been obtained from the auditors.* In addition, if the auditors' report on the full financial statements is likely to be qualified, the Listing Rules require details of the nature of the qualification to be given in the preliminary announcement.

12   There is an expectation that the information in a preliminary announcement will be consistent with that in the audited financial statements. To achieve this:

(a)   the audit of the financial statements should be complete or at least at an advanced stage at the date of the preliminary announcement.

(b)   all the figures appearing in the preliminary announcement should agree with the figures in the audited financial statements or in the draft financial statements on which the audit is at an advanced stage.

*Further guidance for auditors has been issued by the Auditing Practices Board in Bulletin 1998/7 'The auditors' association with preliminary announcements'.

(c)   the other information and commentary in the preliminary announcement
      should be consistent with the figures in the preliminary announcement and with
      the audited or draft financial statements.

The guidance in paragraph 12 above balances the need for timeliness and reliability.   **13**
The overriding consideration is that the information in the preliminary announcement should be reliable and not subject to later alterations. The risk of later changes
to the figures in the preliminary announcement is not completely extinguished unless
the preliminary announcement is issued at the same time that the full financial
statements are approved by the directors and the auditors have signed their opinion
on them.

Against this there lies the need for the timely publication of price-sensitive infor-   **14**
mation once it is available, as evidenced in the Exchange's Listing Rules that the
preliminary announcement must be notified to the Exchange without delay after
board approval. It is accepted practice, therefore, that, where the reliability of the
information in the announcement is not compromised, the main figures and highlights from the financial statements are issued as the preliminary announcement
when the audit is at an advanced stage (ie when any outstanding audit matters are
unlikely to have a material impact on the financial statements or disclosures in the
preliminary announcement), but before the audit report on the financial statements
has been signed.

Section 240(3)(c) of the Companies Act 1985* requires companies to make a state-   **15**
ment whether the company's auditors have made an audit report on the statutory
accounts dealing with any financial year with which the non-statutory accounts (ie
the preliminary announcement, in this case) purport to deal. To prevent misunderstandings about whether the underlying financial statements have been
reported upon by the auditors, it would also be helpful if the preliminary
announcement clearly stated that the audit report on the full financial statements has
yet to be signed, if that is the case.

ACCOUNTING POLICIES AND PRIOR YEAR ADJUSTMENTS

The accounting policies and presentation of figures in preliminary announcements   **16**
should be consistent with those in the full financial statements, that have yet to be
published.

Preliminary announcements should include a statement that, subject to specified   **17**
exceptions, they are prepared on the basis of the accounting policies as set out in the
most recently published set of annual financial statements. Preliminary announcements are often reviewed in conjunction with the previous year's financial statements
and therefore the accounting policies need to be stated and explained only where they
differ from those adopted in the previous year's annual financial statements.

Following a change in accounting policy, the amounts for the current and prior years   **18**
should be stated on the basis of the new policies, consistently with the annual
financial statements. The cumulative effect of the policy change on opening reserves
(ie at the beginning of the financial year) should be disclosed at the foot of the
statement of total recognised gains and losses of the year. Similar disclosures should
be made in respect of other prior year adjustments arising from the discovery of

*The equivalent legislation in Northern Ireland is Article 248(3)(c) in Part VIII of the Companies (Northern
Ireland) Order 1986 and in the Republic of Ireland is section 19(2)(c) of the Companies (Amendment) Act
1986.

fundamental errors. A description should be given to help users understand the nature of each change or adjustment.

CONTENT

19   Under the Listing Rules of the Exchange, a preliminary announcement must contain profit and loss information and any significant information necessary for the purpose of assessing the results being announced. Present practice, however, indicates a trend towards lengthier preliminary announcements and the disclosure of much more information than the minimum required by the Exchange.

20   The disclosure of more detailed information in preliminary announcements is driven by both demands from financial analysts and a desire on the part of companies to communicate effectively and efficiently with the market.

21   In addition, companies are keen to ensure that all price-sensitive information likely to be given at analysts' briefings is included in the preliminary announcement. By giving analysts more information, companies are also safeguarding against misunderstandings and misinterpretation of the information in the preliminary announcement, which would otherwise be detected only at a later date when the full report and accounts are published.

22   An informed assessment of financial position and performance requires comparison of information from the profit and loss account, statement of total recognised gains and losses, balance sheet and cash flow statement together with a narrative commentary that explains the primary statements in the context of events and trends since the previous annual report and accounts and the previous interim report.

23   It is therefore recommended that a preliminary announcement should include a narrative commentary, a summarised profit and loss account, a statement of total recognised gains and losses, a summarised balance sheet and a summarised cash flow statement.

24   Sufficient supplementary information should be given, where helpful, given the nature of the company's business, and as the directors see fit, to permit an understanding of the significant items contained within the primary statements. For example, in certain cases it may be useful to analyse fixed assets into component parts, provide more detail about the company's borrowings, or state the equity and non-equity interests in shareholders' funds, in accordance with FRS 4 'Capital Instruments'.

25   Significant events and trends mentioned in the commentary should be supported by the underlying figures given either on the face of the primary statements or by way of note.

26   The information should be presented in a succinct manner and should be consistent with that in the yet to be published full report and accounts and comparable with previously published reports.

MANAGEMENT COMMENTARY

27   An important feature of a preliminary announcement is a balanced narrative commentary that explains the reasons for significant movements in key indicators and indicates perceived trends within the business. The management commentary should enable users to appreciate the main factors influencing the company's performance

during the financial year and its position at the year-end. For example, gross margins are an important factor in the success of retailing businesses and should be adequately disclosed and explained in such cases.

Attention should also be drawn to events and changes within the year that are likely **28** to have a significant effect on the succeeding year despite having had relatively little impact in the current year.

The commentary is not intended to be as comprehensive as an operating and **29** financial review (OFR). However, management should consider whether key issues normally referred to in the OFR should be included within the preliminary announcement (albeit in less detail and focusing on areas of change) in order to provide a balanced view and help users gain a better understanding of the company's business.

The commentary should describe the nature of any seasonal activity and, together **30** with other disclosures, provide adequate information for the performance of the business and its financial position at the end of the year to be assessed.

As well as referring to trading performance, the commentary should draw attention **31** to a summarised balance sheet and a cash flow statement and should highlight and explain significant changes since the last annual financial statements and interim report, particularly regarding movements in working capital, liquidity and net debt, that are likely to be of value to users in their assessment of the business.

The commentary and/or notes to the preliminary announcement should explain any **32** other matter that the directors think would help users to understand the report. This would include, for example, where relevant:

- acquisitions and disposals of major fixed assets or investments during the year;
- changes in contingencies, commitments and off balance sheet financial instruments* since the previous year-end and/or half year-end;
- material changes in capital structure or financing;
- events arising after the end of the year;
- the effect of foreign exchange movements during the year;
- the impact of revised actuarial valuations on pension costs.

FINAL INTERIM PERIOD

The market normally tends to react only to new information arising from the final **33** interim period (ie the second half or, if quarterly reporting is adopted, the fourth quarter of the year) that has not been previously reported upon. However, the preliminary announcement and the annual results have traditionally focused on the results for the year, generally without presenting or discussing the results for the final interim period of the year. This means that the results for this period are subsumed within those for the year and not generally reported to shareholders.

It is, therefore, particularly important that the salient events and features of the final **34** interim period are referred to and explained as part of the management commentary.

Given the importance attached by users to the most current information, including **35** adequate management commentary thereon, preparers are encouraged to comment specifically on the final interim period's results in the preliminary announcement.

The Board is reviewing the accounting treatment of off balance sheet financial instruments as part of its project on derivatives and other financial instruments.

Separate presentation of the final interim period figures, together with their corresponding amounts, is also encouraged to the extent necessary to support the commentary and to facilitate an understanding of current performance. The extent of information on the final interim period will vary from company to company – in some cases a reference to the key figures in the narrative commentary will be sufficient. This may entail the disclosure and explanation of significant changes to previously reported interim figures for the current year (which would occur only if the change qualified as a prior period adjustment) and of significant changes in estimates of amounts in previously reported interim figures (which are recognised in the final interim period).

PROFIT AND LOSS ACCOUNT

36   A preliminary announcement should include a summarised profit and loss account that includes at least the following information where relevant (with separate identification of significant amounts relating to associates and joint ventures):

- Turnover
- Operating profit or loss
- Interest payable less interest receivable (net)
- Profit or loss on ordinary activities before tax
- Tax on profit or loss on ordinary activities
- Profit or loss on ordinary activities after tax
- Minority interests
- Profit or loss for the period
- Dividends paid and proposed.

Acquisitions and discontinued operations

37   Turnover and operating profit of acquisitions and discontinued operations (as defined in FRS 3 'Reporting Financial Performance') should be disclosed separately on the face of the profit and loss account in the period in accordance with FRS 3.

Segmental information

38   Segmental analysis of trading performance is often crucial to understanding the performance of a company or group. Therefore, where significant, segmental information should be disclosed in the preliminary announcement, for business and/ or geographical classifications (using the same classifications as given in the full report and accounts for the year) as follows:

- segment turnover, distinguishing inter-segment sales if significant;
- segment profit or loss on the same basis as in the annual financial statements – normally profit or loss before accounting for interest, taxation and minority interests.

Taxation

39   Sufficient information should be given to understand any significant changes in the effective tax rate from the prior year. It may be necessary to analyse the tax charge into its significant components (eg UK and overseas tax; and/or current and deferred tax).

Exceptional items

Exceptional items should be disclosed in the preliminary announcement, either on **40** the face of the profit and loss account or in a note in accordance with FRS 3, together with an adequate description.

Earnings per share

The Exchange requires listed companies to disclose earnings per share expressed as **41** pence per share. Basic and diluted earnings per share should, therefore, be calculated and disclosed in the same manner as in the full financial statements. Companies that choose to present in their annual financial statements additional amounts per share based on another level of earnings should present them also in their preliminary announcements, in accordance with FRS 3.

STATEMENT OF TOTAL RECOGNISED GAINS AND LOSSES

A statement of total recognised gains and losses should be included where material **42** gains or losses, other than profit or loss for the financial year as reported in the profit and loss account, are recognised in the period.

A reconciliation of movements in shareholders' funds should be included in the **43** preliminary announcement only where movements other than those in the statement of total recognised gains and losses need to be explained.

BALANCE SHEET

A summarised balance sheet should highlight significant movements in key indica- **44** tors of the company's financial position. For consistency, similar classifications to those used in the annual financial statements should be adopted. It is recommended that, for example, a Schedule 4 company or Schedule 4A* group should give at least the following balance sheet information:

- Fixed assets
- Current assets
  - Stocks
  - Debtors
  - Cash at bank and in hand
  - Other current assets
- Creditors: amounts falling due within one year
- Net current assets (liabilities)
- Total assets less current liabilities
- Creditors: amounts falling due after more than one year
- Provisions for liabilities and charges
- Capital and reserves
- Minority interests.

---

*In Great Britain, Schedule 4 or 4A to the Companies Act 1985; in Northern Ireland, Schedule 4 or 4A to the Companies (Northern Ireland) Order 1986; in the Republic of Ireland, the Schedule to the Companies (Amendment) Act 1986 and the Schedule to the European Communities (Companies: Group Accounts) Regulations 1992.

CASH FLOW STATEMENT

45   Cash flow information helps users to assess the company's liquidity, viability and financial adaptability. Therefore, total amounts for the categories of cash flows specified by FRS 1 (Revised 1996) 'Cash Flow Statements' should include, at least, the following headings:

- Net cash inflow/outflow from operating activities
- Dividends received from joint ventures and associates
- Returns on investments and servicing of finance
- Taxation
- Capital expenditure and financial investment
- Acquisitions and disposals
- Equity dividends paid
- Management of liquid resources
- Financing
- Increase/decrease in cash.

46   A reconciliation of operating profit to operating cash flow should be given in sufficient detail for users to appreciate its chief components. A reconciliation should also be given of the movement of cash in the period to the movement in net debt, as required by FRS 1 (Revised 1996), including the effect of movements on short-term and long-term borrowings, cash and other components of net debt, unless disclosed elsewhere in the preliminary announcement.

COMPARATIVE FIGURES

47   Comparative figures for the summarised profit and loss account, the statement of total recognised gains and losses, the summarised balance sheet and the summarised cash flow statement should be presented for the previous full financial year.

OTHER DISCLOSURES

48   Subject to the limited exceptions noted in this Statement, disclosures demanded by Financial Reporting Standards and Statements of Standard Accounting Practice are not generally required in the presentation of preliminary announcements.

49   The preliminary announcement should state:

- the period covered by the report;
- the date on which it is approved by the board of directors.

50   In Great Britain, the preliminary announcement should contain a statement that satisfies the provisions of section 240 of the Companies Act 1985* regarding the publication of non-statutory accounts.

The equivalent legislation in Northern Ireland is Article 248 in Part VIII of the Companies (Northern Ireland) Order 1986 and in the Republic of Ireland is section 19 of the Companies (Amendment) Act 1986.

Part Five

UITF abstracts

Part Five

UHF abstracts

Foreword to UITF abstracts

(Issued February 1994)

Contents

Foreword to UITF abstracts

INTRODUCTION

1   This Foreword explains the authority, scope and application of the 'UITF Abstracts' issued by the Accounting Standards Board (ASB) that set out the consensus reached by its Urgent Issues Task Force (UITF) on particular issues. The composition and procedures of the UITF are set out in the Appendix to this Foreword.

2   The UITF's main role is to assist the ASB with important or significant accounting issues where there exists an accounting standard or a provision of companies legislation* (including the requirement to give a true and fair view) and where unsatisfactory or conflicting interpretations have developed or seem likely to develop. In such circumstances it operates by seeking a consensus as to the accounting treatment that should be adopted. Such a consensus is reached against the background of the ASB's declared aim of relying on principles rather than detailed prescription.

3   The UITF forms its view as to the appropriate accounting treatment for any particular issue within the framework of the law and the principles established in the accounting standards and other statements issued or adopted by the ASB. It also has due regard to international developments.

4   Given the standing of the UITF's membership, the ASB normally expects to accept the UITF's consensus, subject only to the ASB's overriding duty to ensure that nothing is done that conflicts with the law, accounting standards, or the ASB's present or future policy or plans. The rules of procedure have been designed accordingly.

AUTHORITY OF UITF ABSTRACTS

5   The establishment of the UITF and its aim of avoiding the development of unsatisfactory or conflicting interpretations of law or accounting standards have the strong support of the Consultative Committee of Accountancy Bodies (CCAB). The Councils of the CCAB bodies expect their members who assume responsibilities in respect of financial statements to observe UITF Abstracts until they are replaced by accounting standards or otherwise withdrawn by the ASB. The Councils have agreed that:

(a)   where this responsibility is evidenced by the association of members' names with such financial statements in the capacity of directors or other officers other than auditors, the onus will be on them to ensure that the existence and purpose of UITF Abstracts are fully understood by fellow directors and other officers. Members should also use their best endeavours to ensure that UITF Abstracts are observed and that any significant departures found to be necessary are adequately disclosed and explained in the financial statements.

(b)   where members act as auditors or reporting accountants, they should be in a position to justify significant departures to the extent that their concurrence with the departures is stated or implied. They are not, however, required to refer in their report to departures with which they concur, provided that adequate disclosure has been made in the notes to the financial statements.

References to companies legislation are to: in Great Britain, the Companies Act 1985; in Northern Ireland, the Companies (Northern Ireland) Order 1986; and in the Republic of Ireland, the Companies Acts 1963–90 and the European Communities (Companies: Group Accounts) Regulations 1992.

The CCAB bodies, through appropriate committees, may enquire into apparent 6
failures by their members to observe UITF Abstracts or to ensure adequate disclosure of significant departures.

The UITF notes the intention of the Institute of Chartered Accountants in Ireland of 7
maintaining close liaison with the UITF on promulgating, with appropriate modifications for legal differences, UITF Abstracts for application in the Republic of
Ireland.

SCOPE AND APPLICATION OF UITF ABSTRACTS

Directors of companies incorporated under companies legislation are required to 8
prepare accounts that give a true and fair view of the state of affairs of the company,
and where applicable the group, at the end of the financial year and of the profit or
loss of the company or group for the financial year.

UITF Abstracts are applicable to financial statements of a reporting entity that are 9
intended to give a true and fair view of its state of affairs at the balance sheet date
and of its profit or loss (or income and expenditure) for the financial period ending
on that date. UITF Abstracts need not be applied to immaterial items. Nothing in
the UITF Abstracts is to be construed as amending or overriding the accounting
standards or other statements adopted or issued by the ASB.

As with accounting standards it is important when applying UITF Abstracts to be 10
guided by the spirit and reasoning behind them. The spirit and reasoning are set out
in the individual UITF Abstracts (and are based on the ASB's Statement of Principles for Financial Reporting). UITF Abstracts are intended to be as concise as the
nature of a particular topic allows rather than detailed rules dealing with every
conceivable circumstance.

UITF Abstracts should be applied to United Kingdom and Republic of Ireland 11
group financial statements (including any amounts relating to overseas entities that
are included in those financial statements). UITF Abstracts are not intended to apply
to financial statements of overseas entities prepared for local purposes.

Where UITF Abstracts prescribe information to be contained in financial state- 12
ments, such requirements do not override exemptions from disclosure given by law
to, and utilised by, certain types of entity.

COMPLIANCE WITH UITF ABSTRACTS

UITF Abstracts should be regarded as part of the corpus of practices forming the 13
basis for determining what constitutes a true and fair view and should be read in
conjunction with accounting standards. UITF Abstracts consequently may be taken
into consideration by the Financial Reporting Review Panel (the Review Panel) in
deciding whether financial statements call for review.

In the United Kingdom, the Review Panel and, in Great Britain the Department of 14
Trade and Industry, in Northern Ireland the Department of Economic Development,
have procedures for receiving and investigating complaints regarding the annual
accounts of companies in respect of apparent departures from the accounting
requirements of companies legislation including the requirement to give a true and
fair view. The Review Panel is authorised under the legislation to apply to the court
for a declaration or declarator that the annual accounts of a company do not comply
with the statutory requirements and an order requiring the directors of the company

to prepare revised accounts. The Department of Trade and Industry and the Department of Economic Development have similar powers.*

15   The requirement to give a true and fair view may in special circumstances require a departure from UITF Abstracts. However, because UITF Abstracts are formulated with the objective of ensuring that the information resulting from their application faithfully represents the underlying commercial activity, the ASB envisages that only in exceptional circumstances will departure from the requirements of a UITF Abstract be necessary in order for the financial statements to give a true and fair view.

16   If in exceptional circumstances compliance with the requirements of a UITF Abstract is inconsistent with the requirement to give a true and fair view, the requirements of the UITF Abstract should be departed from to the extent necessary to give a true and fair view. In such cases informed and unbiased judgement should be used to devise an appropriate alternative treatment, which should be consistent with the economic and commercial characteristics of the circumstances concerned. Particulars of any material departure from a UITF Abstract, the reasons for it and its financial effects should be disclosed in the financial statements. The disclosure made should be equivalent to that given in respect of departures from specific accounting provisions of companies legislation.

APPLICABILITY OF A UITF ABSTRACT TO TRANSACTIONS ENTERED INTO BEFORE THE ABSTRACT WAS ISSUED

17   When a new UITF Abstract is issued the question arises whether its provisions should be applied to transactions that took place before the promulgation of the Abstract. The general policy of the ASB is that the provisions of UITF Abstracts should apply to all material transactions irrespective of the date at which they are entered into. The reasons for this policy are set out more fully in paragraphs 27–30 of the 'Foreword to Accounting Standards'. All references in those paragraphs to 'accounting standards' should in the present context be read as references to 'UITF Abstracts'.

UITF ABSTRACTS AND THE LEGAL FRAMEWORK

18   The status of UITF Abstracts in United Kingdom legislation is addressed in the Opinion by Miss Mary Arden QC† 'The true and fair requirement', which is published as an appendix to the 'Foreword to Accounting Standards' and should be read in conjunction with this Foreword.

DISSEMINATION AND IMPLEMENTATION

19   The UITF Abstracts are made publicly available by the ASB for the guidance of users, preparers and auditors of financial information. They include a discussion of the matter, the accounting issues identified, reference sources, and a summary of the UITF's deliberations, and clearly indicate what conclusion has been reached.

20   If the UITF is unable to reach a consensus, or if a consensus is not ratified by the ASB, an explanation of the circumstances will be published.

*In the Republic of Ireland the Department of Enterprise and Employment has powers to investigate generally the affairs of companies. The Review Panel does not operate in the Republic of Ireland.

†Now the Honourable Mrs Justice Arden.

A UITF Abstract takes effect from the effective date in the published Abstract, and **21** is thereafter to be regarded as accepted practice in the area in question. Accordingly, all reporting entities will be expected to conform to it, if necessary by changing previously adopted accounting policies, unless the consensus explicitly states otherwise.

Appendix
Composition and procedures of the UITF

(revised September 1995)

COMPOSITION

A1 The UITF is a committee of the ASB comprising a number of people of standing in the field of financial reporting. Its purpose is to enlist the experience and influence of its members to assist the ASB in its task of establishing and improving standards of financial accounting and reporting, for the benefit of users, preparers and auditors of financial information.

A2 The UITF consists of up to fifteen members experienced in the technicalities of financial reporting. The membership includes:

up to seven senior representatives from the largest accounting firms;

one member from a medium-sized or small accounting firm;

four members from industry or commerce; and

up to three further members chosen on a personal basis.

A3 The ASB may adjust the size and composition of the UITF from time to time.

A4 Members are appointed by the ASB for periods of up to two years. Membership is personal. Each member is entitled to appoint a named alternate; any such appointment and subsequent changes of appointment shall be notified to the Secretary of the ASB before the named alternate acts in the place of the member. The named alternate may attend and vote at any meetings that the member is unable to attend. If neither the member nor his named alternate is able to attend, the member may appoint another alternate to attend the meeting and shall inform the Secretary of the ASB in advance of the meeting, but such alternate does not have the right to vote.

A5 The office of Chairman of the UITF shall be held by the Chairman of the ASB.

A6 Members of the ASB are free to attend UITF meetings and have the right to speak, but do not have the right to vote.

A7 The Chairman may invite others to attend UITF meetings as observers.

ADMISSION OF ITEMS TO THE AGENDA

A8 Auditors and companies, and others with an interest in financial reporting, are invited to refer substantial new issues to the UITF where there is doubt about the most appropriate accounting treatment leading to a true and fair view and it is important that a standard treatment should be established before a precedent is set by practice.

A9 The Councils of the CCAB bodies invite their members to raise for possible consideration by the UITF any substantial accounting issues of general concern that arise in connection with the preparation and audit of financial statements. In raising such issues members should not disclose information of a confidential nature either directly or by implication to anyone likely to be aware of the background.

The UITF will not consider any issue that the ASB indicates falls within its own agenda unless specifically requested to do so by the ASB. **A10**

CONSULTATION

The urgent nature of the matters deal with by the UITF necessarily means that it is not possible for it to follow an extended consultation and due process procedure. The ASB therefore takes special measures to publicise the matters on the UITF's agenda. Preliminary decisions reached by the UITF are circulated for comment to recipients for the ASB Bulletin and to finance directors of listed companies. **A11**

QUORUM

The quorum for a meeting of the UITF is eleven voting members or their named alternates. **A12**

MEETINGS AND VOTING

Voting may take place either at meetings or by post. A consensus is necessary for the approval of an Abstract for ratification and issue by the ASB. **A13**

A consensus will have been attained at a meeting where not more than two voting members of the UITF, or their named alternates, present at the meeting dissent from the treatment proposed as the appropriate accounting practice for the matter in question. **A14**

A consensus will have been attained in a postal vote of the UITF where **A15**

(a)   at least eleven of those eligible to participate in the vote (see below) return their votes by the relevant deadline and

(b)   not more than two of those eligible to vote have registered, by the relevant deadline, a vote against the treatment proposed as the appropriate accounting practice for the matter in question. Participating in a postal vote is open only to those members and named alternates who were present at the last meeting of the UITF at which the topic was considered as an agenda item. Where a member was represented at that meeting by his named alternate, either he or the named alternate may register a vote.

When voting slips are dispatched for a postal vote, the Chairman of the UITF shall specify the deadline (being not less than seven calendar days from the date of dispatch) by which votes are to be returned. At his discretion the Chairman may, if the deadline has not yet been reached, extend it by up to seven further calendar days. If the Chairman is unable for any reason to specify the deadline, the deadline shall be specified by the Technical Director of the ASB. **A16**

A member of the UITF is expected to support any vote of his alternate and to agree to be bound by it. **A17**

The Chairman has no vote. **A18**

Meetings of the UITF shall be chaired by the Chairman of the UITF or in his absence the Technical Director of the ASB, or such other person as the Chairman may nominate, shall preside as chairman of the meeting. **A19**

RATIFICATION BY THE ASB

A20   As indicated in paragraph 4 of the 'Foreword to UITF Abstracts', the ASB will normally expect to accept the UITF's consensus. However, the ASB retains the right to decline to accept any consensus that it believes is contrary to law or to its extant or intended accounting standards. Where such a situation arises the ASB will set out its views to the UITF in writing for consideration as soon as practicable thereafter with the objective if possible of achieving a mutually acceptable solution.

A21   A consensus that has been ratified by the ASB will be published by the ASB as a UITF Abstract.

UITF abstract 4: Presentation of long-term debtors in current assets

(Issued July 1992)

THE ISSUE

Both for liabilities and for debtors the Companies Act requires a distinction to be 1
drawn between the amounts payable or receivable within one year and those due to
be settled or received after more than one year. Although the distinction is disclosed
in the notes for each of the items forming part of debtors (including prepayments and
accrued income if included in debtors), unlike in the case of liabilities it is not
required to be carried through to the total of current assets nor to the significant
Format 1 sub-total of net current assets (liabilities).

In consequence, there is a certain imbalance between the items that the formats 2
require to be classified under current assets or current liabilities. For example, a
pension fund surplus (to the extent recognised in the balance sheet) could give rise to
a prepayment forming part of net current assets (liabilities), whereas a deficiency
would normally be shown as a provision under long-term liabilities.* In some cases
the period expected to be required for recovery of such an asset may be considerable,
perhaps in excess of ten years. Other examples of long-term debtor items include
much of the trade debtors of lessors and deferred consideration in respect of the sale
of an investment or other fixed asset.

APPLICATION TO SMALLER ENTITIES

Reporting entities applying the Financial Reporting Standard for Smaller Entities 2A
currently applicable are exempt from this Abstract.

UITF CONSENSUS

In most cases it will be satisfactory to disclose the size of debtors due after more than 3
one year in the notes to the accounts. There will be some instances, however, where
the amount is so material in the context of the total net current assets that in the
absence of disclosure of debtors due after more than one year on the face of the
balance sheet readers may misinterpret the accounts. The Task Force have agreed
that, in such circumstances, the amount should be disclosed on the face of the
balance sheet.

DATE FROM WHICH EFFECTIVE

The disclosure required by this consensus should be adopted in financial statements 4
relating to accounting periods ending on or after 23 August 1992, but earlier
adoption is encouraged.

REFERENCES

Companies Act 1985 and Companies (Northern Ireland) Order 1986 – Schedule 4
Balance Sheet Formats 1 and 2 including notes 5 and 6.

*Under FRS 17 'Retirement benefits', the pension asset or liability will be shown separately rather than under
these format headings. (**Editor's note:** FRS 17 came into effect fully with effect from 2005.)*

Republic of Ireland – Companies (Amendment) Act 1986, the Schedule, Balance Sheet Formats 1 and 2 including note 4.

Statement of Standard Accounting Practice 21 – Accounting for leases and hire purchase contracts.

Statement of Standard Accounting Practice 24 – Accounting for pension costs.*

International Accounting Standard 13 – Presentation of Current Assets and Current Liabilities.†

Editor's note: FRS 17 'Retirement benefits' superseded SSAP 24 fully with effect from 2005.

†*Editor's note: Replaced by IAS 1 (revised) 'Presentation of financial statements' issued August 1997. Further revised in December 2003.*

UITF abstract 5: Transfers from current assets to fixed assets

(Issued July 1992)

THE ISSUE

The Companies Act 1985 defines a fixed asset as one intended for use on a continuing basis in the company's activities and any which are not intended for such use are current assets (section 262(1)CA 1985). Where at a date subsequent to its original acquisition a current asset is retained for use on a continuing basis in the company's activities it becomes a fixed asset and the question arises as to the appropriate transfer value. An example is a property which is reclassified from trading properties to investment properties.   **1**

Of particular concern is the possibility that companies could avoid charging the profit and loss account with write-downs to net realisable value arising on unsold trading assets. This could be done by transferring the relevant assets from current assets to fixed assets at above net realisable value, as a result of which any later write down might be debited to revaluation reserve.   **2**

This abstract deals only with situations where current assets are included in the balance sheet at the lower of cost and net realisable value under paragraphs 22 and 23 of Schedule 4 to the Companies Act 1985.   **3**

The timing of the transfer of current assets to fixed assets should reflect the timing of management's change of intent and should not be backdated (for example to the start of the financial year). Since the date of the management decision is unlikely to correspond with the balance sheet date at which a full review of carrying values would be made, consideration must be given to the appropriate amounts at which such assets should be transferred at the time of transfer.   **4**

APPLICATION TO SMALLER ENTITIES

Reporting entities applying the Financial Reporting Standard for Smaller Entities currently applicable are exempt from this Abstract.   **4A**

UITF CONSENSUS

The Task Force reached a consensus that where assets are transferred from current to fixed, the current asset accounting rules should be applied up to the effective date of transfer, which is the date of management's change of intent. Consequently the transfer should be made at the lower of cost and net realisable value, and accordingly an assessment should be made of the net realisable value at the date of transfer and if this is less than its previous carrying value the diminution should be charged in the profit and loss account, reflecting the loss to the company while the asset was held as a current asset.   **5**

Whether assets are transferred at cost or at net realisable value in accordance with paragraph 5 above, fixed asset accounting rules will apply to the assets subsequent to the date of transfer. In cases where the transfer is at net realisable value, the asset should be accounted for as a fixed asset at a valuation (under the alternative accounting rules of the Act) as at the date of the transfer; at subsequent balance sheet dates it may or may not be revalued, but in either event the disclosure requirements appropriate to a valuation should be given.   **6**

DATE FROM WHICH EFFECTIVE

7   The accounting treatment required by this consensus should be adopted in financial statements relating to accounting periods ending on or after 23 December 1992, but earlier adoption is encouraged. In order to ensure consistency of treatment, corresponding amounts for preceding years should be restated where applicable.

REFERENCES

Companies Act 1985 Section 222(1) and Schedule 4 paragraphs 17 to 19, 22 to 23, 30 to 34 and 43.

Northern Ireland—Companies (Northern Ireland) Order 1986, articles 229(1) and 270(1) and Schedule 4 paragraphs 17 to 19, 22 to 23, 30 to 34 and 43.

Republic of Ireland—Companies Act 1990 section 202(1) and the Companies (Amendment) Act 1986, the Schedule paragraphs 5 to 7, 10 to 11, 18 to 22, 30 and 60.

FRS 3 'Reporting Financial Performance'—paragraph 13.

Statement of Standard Accounting Practice 9—'Stocks and long-term contracts—paragraph 26.

Statement of Standard Accounting Practice 19—'Accounting for investment properties—paragraphs 11 and 13.

NOTE ON LEGAL REQUIREMENTS

The Task Force has been advised by leading Counsel that assets can be treated as having been transferred from current assets to fixed assets at a value equal to the lower of cost and net realisable value. Counsel indicated that the above advice is based on the assumption that where the transfer takes place at net realisable value, the asset will be accounted for as a fixed asset as at the date of transfer in accordance with the accounting rules in Schedule 4 to the Companies Act (that is, included at a current value rather than historical cost).

UITF abstract 9: Accounting for operations in hyper-inflationary economies*

(Issued June 1993)

THE ISSUE

SSAP 20 'Foreign currency translation' states that 'where a foreign enterprise operates   1
in a country in which a very high rate of inflation exists it may not be possible to
present fairly in historical cost accounts the financial position of a foreign enterprise
simply by a translation process. In such circumstances the local currency financial
statements should be adjusted where possible to reflect current price levels before the
translation process is undertaken'. However there is some uncertainty as to when and
how this guidance should be applied in practice.

The overriding requirement to give a true and fair view of the profit or loss and state   2
of affairs can be considered to require appropriate adjustments to be made where
significant distortions arise from very high rates of inflation ('hyper-inflation').
Because it is a common condition, users of financial statements have developed
tolerance for some inflation and in varying degrees allow for it in their analyses. The
distortions caused by hyper-inflation may in practice be diluted by the relative rates
of inflation in the reporting country and in other countries where the reporting entity
operates, when taken together with the relative size of the operations in hyperinflationary economies in the context of the reporting group.

The question of what constitutes hyper-inflation is necessarily judgmental. Interna-   3
tional Accounting Standard No.29 'Financial Reporting in Hyperinflationary
Economies' describes a number of characteristics of the economic environment of a
country which indicate hyper-inflation (see the Appendix to this Abstract). Failure to
adjust for hyper-inflation before application of the SSAP 20 closing rate/net investment method of translation produces a significant debit to group reserves, whilst at
the same time inflated profits are included in the group profit and loss account
(whether from high interest income on deposits in a rapidly depreciating local currency or from trading operations at what could be considered unrealistically high
profitability).

Methods adopted to eliminate distortions caused by hyper-inflation need to take   4
account of the following factors:

(a)   the lack of reliable and timely inflation indices in a number of hyper-infla-
      tionary economies can pose a major practical problem to adjusting local
      currency financial statements;
(b)   it is necessary to have regard to the particular local circumstances as these can
      vary significantly between countries in terms of how real profitability should be
      measured.

APPLICATION TO SMALLER ENTITIES

Reporting entities applying the Financial Reporting Standard for Smaller Entities   4A
currently applicable are exempt from this Abstract.

*Editor's note: For companies complying with FRS 24, UITF 9 is superseded. It remains in force for other
companies.*

UITF CONSENSUS

5   The Task Force reached a consensus that adjustments are required where the distortions caused by hyper-inflation are such as to affect the true and fair view given by the group financial statements. In any event adjustments are required where the cumulative inflation rate over three years is approaching, or exceeds, 100% and the operations in the hyper-inflationary economies are material.

6   The Task Force considered that the following two methods of eliminating the distortions were consistent with SSAP 20 and therefore acceptable:

(a)   adjusting the local currency financial statements to reflect current price levels before the translation process is undertaken, as suggested in paragraph 26 of SSAP 20. This includes taking any gain or loss on the net monetary position through the profit and loss account.

(b)   using a relatively stable currency (which would not necessarily be sterling) as the functional currency (i.e., the currency of measurement) for the relevant foreign operations. For example in certain businesses operating in Latin American territories the US dollar acts effectively as the functional currency for business operations. The functional currency would in effect be the 'local currency' as defined in paragraph 39 of SSAP 20. In such circumstances, if the transactions are not recorded initially in that stable currency, they must first be remeasured into that currency by applying the temporal method described in SSAP 20 (but based on the dollar or other stable currency rather than sterling). The effect is that the movement between the original currency of record and the stable currency is used as a proxy for an inflation index.

7   If neither of the above methods is considered appropriate for material operations, then the reasons should be stated and alternative methods to eliminate the distortions should be adopted.

8   Where group operations in areas of hyper-inflation are material in the context of group results or net assets, the accounting policy adopted to eliminate the distortions of such inflation should be disclosed.

DATE FROM WHICH EFFECTIVE

9   The accounting treatment required by this consensus should be adopted in financial statements relating to accounting periods ending on or after 23 August 1993, but earlier adoption is encouraged. In order to ensure consistency of treatment, corresponding amounts for preceding years should be restated where applicable.

REFERENCES

Statement of Standard Accounting Practice 20 – Foreign Currency Translation – paragraphs 26, 39 and 55.

International Accounting Standard 29 – Financial Reporting in Hyper-inflationary Economies.

Appendix

Extract from IAS 29 'Financial Reporting in Hyper-inflationary Economies'

'3   This Statement does not establish an absolute rate at which hyperinflation is deemed to arise. It is a matter of judgement when restatement of financial statements in accordance with this Statement becomes necessary. Hyperinflation is indicated by characteristics of the economic environment of a country which include, but are not limited to, the following:

(a)   the general population prefers to keep its wealth in nonmonetary assets or in a relatively stable foreign currency. Amounts of local currency held are immediately invested to maintain purchasing power;

(b)   the general population regards monetary amounts not in terms of the local currency but in terms of a relatively stable foreign currency. Prices may be quoted in that currency;

(c)   sales and purchases on credit take place at prices that compensate for the expected loss of purchasing power during the credit period, even if the period is short;

(d)   interest rates, wages and prices are linked to a price index; and

(e)   the cumulative inflation rate over three years is approaching, or exceeds, 100%'.

UITF abstract 11: Capital instruments: issuer call options*

(Issued September 1994)

THE ISSUE

1   The terms of a capital instrument sometimes include an issuer call option, that is, a right of the issuer (but not the investor) to redeem the instrument early, usually on the payment of a premium. Such an option is included primarily to preserve the financial flexibility of the issuer. The question arises as to the appropriate accounting for an instrument that includes an issuer call option following the issue of FRS 4 'Capital Instruments'.

2   FRS 4 requires the finance costs of debt and non-equity shares to be charged in the profit and loss account and allocated to periods over the term of the instrument at a constant rate on the carrying amount. Finance costs are defined as 'The difference between the net proceeds of an instrument and the total amount of the payments (or other transfers of economic benefits) that the issuer may be required to make in respect of the instrument' (paragraph 8). However, paragraph 16 states that 'If either party has the option to require the instrument to be redeemed or cancelled and, under the terms of the instrument, it is uncertain whether such an option will be exercised, the term should be taken to end on the earliest date at which the instrument would be redeemed or cancelled on exercise of such an option.' The Explanation of FRS 4 states that this is the case 'unless there is no genuine commercial possibility that the option will be exercised' (paragraph 73). This could be construed as requiring the accounting to be based on the assumption that the call option will be exercised and hence that the premium will be paid. Nevertheless, except in the special circumstances envisaged in paragraph 5 below, the amount payable under an issuer call option is not a payment 'that the issuer may be required to make in respect of the instrument' (part of the definition of 'finance costs' quoted above).

3   FRS 4 also contains a requirement that 'Gains and losses arising on the repurchase or early settlement of debt should be recognised in the profit and loss account in the period during which the repurchase or early settlement is made' (paragraph 32). Further, FRS 4 requires that where shares are redeemed, shareholders' funds should be reduced by the value of the consideration given (paragraph 39).

4   Issuers of instruments should not have to account for possible payments that they are not obliged to make, and may very well elect not to make. Payment of a premium on exercise of an issuer call option is a cost that stems directly from the decision to exercise the option and may therefore fairly be reported in the period in which exercise takes place.

5   Issuer call options as contemplated in this Abstract do not include those cases where the effective rate of interest (or the margin above a base rate by which interest is calculated) increases after the date at which the option is exercisable. In these cases the exercise price may be deemed to compensate the investor for forgoing such increased interest.

Editor's note: For companies complying with FRS 26, UITF 11 is superseded. It remains in force for other companies.

APPLICATION TO SMALLER ENTITIES

Reporting entities applying the Financial Reporting Standard for Smaller Entities   **5A**
currently applicable are exempt from this Abstract.

UITF CONSENSUS

The Task Force reached a consensus that where an instrument includes a call option   **6**
that can be exercised only by the issuer, the payment required on exercise of that
option does not form part of the finance costs of the instrument in accordance with
the requirements of FRS 4 'Capital Instruments'. In the case of debt, the gain or loss
arising on any repurchase or early settlement will reflect the amount payable on
exercise. In the case of shares, the amount payable on exercise will be used to reduce
the amount of shareholders' funds.

The Task Force noted that in the case of an instrument with an issuer call option   **7**
exercise of which is uncertain, the term of the instrument, as defined in paragraph 16
of FRS 4, would end on the date that the option was exercisable.

The Task Force agreed that, in accordance with paragraph 16 of FRS 4, this consensus   **8**
should apply only to genuine options, and would not therefore apply to cases where,
under the terms of the instrument, it was clear that the issuer would be commercially
obliged to exercise its call option. An example of such a case would be where the
terms of a debt instrument give the issuer the 'option' of early redemption but it is
clear from the outset that in all conceivable circumstances it would be advantageous
to the issuer to exercise the option rather than allow the debt to remain in issue.

The Task Force also agreed that the consensus should not apply to those cases   **9**
described in paragraph 5 above. The Task Force agreed that in those cases, 'the total
amount of the payments . . . that the issuer may be required to make in respect of the
instrument' must include the amount payable on exercise of the option.

DATE FROM WHICH EFFECTIVE

The accounting treatment required by this abstract should be adopted in financial   **10**
statements relating to accounting periods ending on or after 23 October 1994, but
earlier adoption is encouraged.

REFERENCES

Financial Reporting Standard 4 - Capital Instruments - paragraphs 8, 16, 32, 39 and
73.

UITF abstract 15: (revised 1999) Disclosure of substantial acquisitions

(Issued February 1999)

THE ISSUE

1   FRS 6 'Acquisitions and Mergers' specifies additional disclosures that are required in respect of substantial acquisitions. For listed companies, these disclosures are required for business combinations that are Class 1 or Super Class 1 transactions under the London Stock Exchange Listing Rules.*

2   The Listing Rules classify transactions by assessing their size relative to that of the company proposing to make the transaction. It does this by reference to whether any of a number of ratios (eg the assets of the target to those of the offeror) exceeds a given amount when expressed as a percentage. At the time FRS 6 was issued, Class 1 transactions were defined as those where the ratio exceeded 15 per cent, and Super Class 1 were those where the ratio exceeded 25 per cent. As a result of changes to the Listing Rules, Class 1 transactions are now defined as those where the ratio exceeds 25 per cent and the term 'Super Class 1' is no longer used.

3   For non-listed entities FRS 6 requires the disclosures in respect of substantial acquisitions where any of certain ratios exceeds 15 per cent.

APPLICATION TO SMALLER ENTITIES

4   Reporting entities applying the Financial Reporting Standard for Smaller Entities currently applicable are exempt from this Abstract.

UITF CONSENSUS

5   The UITF reached a consensus that, in order to retain the Accounting Standards Board's original intentions for FRS 6, the reference in paragraph 37(a) to Class 1 transactions should be interpreted as meaning those business combinations in which any of the ratios set out in the London Stock Exchange Listing Rules for the classification of transactions exceeds 15 per cent.

DATE FROM WHICH EFFECTIVE AND WITHDRAWAL OF UITF ABSTRACT 15 (as issued on 30 January 1996)

6   As this consensus maintains the status quo it is effective immediately.

7   This abstract supersedes UITF Abstract 15 (as issued on 30 January 1996) 'Disclosure of substantial acquisitions'.

References

Financial Reporting Standard 6 'Acquisitions and Mergers' paragraph 37.
The Listing Rules of the London Stock Exchange Chapter 10 'Transactions'.

Editor's note: In the UK, the Listing Rules are now issued by the Financial Services Authority in its capacity as UK Listing Authority.

UITF abstract 19: Tax on gains and losses on foreign currency borrowings that hedge an investment in a foreign enterprise

(Issued February 1998)

BACKGROUND

Where certain conditions are met, SSAP 20 'Foreign currency translation' permits **1** certain gains and losses on foreign currency borrowings that have been used to finance or provide a hedge against equity investments in foreign enterprises to be reported as reserve movements. As a result of the subsequent introduction of FRS 3 'Reporting Financial Performance' these gains and losses are now reported in the statement of total recognised gains and losses.*

Until recently, neither the retranslation of the net investment in a foreign enterprise **2** nor the gain or loss on foreign borrowings had any consequences for tax. Owing to recent changes in UK tax legislation this is no longer always the case and in some circumstances, for example where a matching election is not made for tax purposes, the gain or loss on retranslation of the borrowings is taxable.

THE ISSUES

The UITF considered how any tax effect of gains and losses on exchange differences **3** on borrowings that are reported in the statement of total recognised gains and losses should be recognised. It concluded that such tax effects should also be reported in the statement of total recognised gains and losses.

The UITF considered the restrictions of SSAP 20 on the gains and losses that are dealt **4** with in the statement of total recognised gains and losses. It concluded that the restriction that the gains and losses should not exceed the exchange differences on the equity investments (in individual accounts) or net investments in foreign enterprises (in consolidated accounts) should be applied after taking account of any tax charge or credit relating to the gain or loss on the borrowings. It noted that SSAP 20 also requires that the borrowings whose exchange gains and losses are dealt with in the statement of total recognised gains and losses should not exceed the amount of cash that the equity investment or net investment is expected to be able to generate, whether from profits or otherwise. The UITF believed that it would be consistent with its view on the restrictions on gains and losses that this test should also be performed on a net-of-tax basis.†

SSAP 20 also requires that the amount of exchange gains and losses on borrowings **5** that are taken to the statement of total recognised gains and losses should be reported. The UITF concluded that it was necessary to disclose the amount of the related tax.

*Editor's note: For companies complying with FRS 23 this paragraph now reads as follows:
Where certain conditions are met, FRS 26 (IAS 39) 'Financial Instruments: Measurement' permits certain gains and losses on foreign currency borrowings that have been used to provide a hedge of net investments in foreign operations to be reported initially in the statement of total recognised gains and losses.

†Editor's note: For companies complying with FRS 23 this paragraph is deleted.

APPLICATION TO SMALLER ENTITIES

6   Reporting entities applying the Financial Reporting Standard for Smaller Entities currently applicable are exempt from this Abstract.

UITF CONSENSUS

7   The UITF reached a consensus that where exchange differences on foreign currency borrowings that have been used to finance, or provide a hedge against, equity investments in foreign enterprises are taken to reserves and reported in the statement of total recognised gains and losses, in accordance with paragraphs 51, 57 and 58 of SSAP 20 and paragraph 27 of FRS 3, tax charges or credits that are directly and solely attributable to such exchange differences should also be taken to reserves and reported in that statement.*†

8   The restriction on the amount of the gains or losses arising on the borrowings that are dealt with in the statement of total recognised gains and losses set out in paragraphs 51(a) and 57(b) of SSAP 20 should be applied after taking account of any tax charge or credit directly and solely attributable to the borrowings. Similarly, the comparison with the total amount of cash that the investments are expected to be able to generate and the exposure created by the borrowings (paragraphs 51(b) and 57(c) of SSAP 20) should be considered in after-tax terms.‡

9   The amount of tax charges and credits accounted for as described in paragraph 7 above should be disclosed, in addition to the gross amount of the exchange differences.

DATE FROM WHICH EFFECTIVE

10   The accounting treatment required by this consensus should be adopted in financial statements relating to accounting periods ending on or after 23 March 1998, but earlier adoption is encouraged.

REFERENCES

Statement of Standard Accounting Practice 20 'Foreign currency translation', paragraphs 51, 57, 58 and 60.

FRS 3 'Reporting Financial Performance', paragraph 27.

Editor's note: See also paragraph 6 of FRS 16 'Current tax'.

†*Editor's note:* For companies complying with FRS 23 this paragraph now reads as follows:
The UITF reached a consensus that where exchange differences on foreign currency borrowings that have been used to provide a hedge against a net investment in a foreign operation are taken to reserves and reported in the statement of total recognised gains and losses, in accordance with FRS 26, tax charges or credits that are directly and solely attributable to such exchange differences should also be taken to reserves and reported in that statement.

‡*Editor's note:* For companies complying with FRS 23 this paragraph is deleted.

UITF abstract 21: Accounting issues arising from the proposed introduction of the euro

(Issued March 1998)

BACKGROUND

The advent of stage 3 of the Economic and Monetary Union (EMU) will necessitate   **1**
significant expenditure by many business entities to adapt their operations and
information systems to accommodate the single currency, the euro. This will be the
case irrespective of whether a Member State participates in the single currency, since
all those in, or trading with, participating Member States are potentially affected.

Entities will incur a variety of costs, which may include administrative planning, staff   **2**
training, the provision of information to customers, modification of software and the
adaptation of hardware, such as vending machines, retail outlets' cash registers or
banks' automatic teller machines.

Apart from additional costs arising from the introduction of the euro there will be   **3**
other consequences with potential accounting implications. For example, all foreign
exchange differences that have arisen on balances denominated in participating
currencies will become permanent and the exchange risk between currency units of
participating Member States will disappear.

In June 1997 the European Commission published a paper 'Accounting for the   **4**
introduction of the euro'. This Abstract is consistent with the relevant guidance
included in that paper in relation to the euro.

THE ISSUES

The UITF has considered three issues: **5**

(a) Should costs incurred in connection with the introduction of the euro be
    charged as an expense or capitalised as an asset and what disclosure is
    appropriate?
(b) What impact will the irrevocable locking of national currencies of participating
    Member States to the euro have on cumulative foreign exchange translation
    differences that have been recognised in periods before the introduction of the
    euro?
(c) What impact will the irrevocable locking of national currencies of participating
    Member States to the euro have on anticipatory hedging instruments existing at
    the date of introduction of the euro in respect of future transactions?

COSTS ASSOCIATED WITH THE INTRODUCTION OF THE EURO

Costs may be capitalised only if they give rise to an asset. Assets are defined in FRS 5   **6**
'Reporting the Substance of Transactions' as:

> 'Rights or other access to future economic benefits controlled by an entity as a
> result of past transactions or events.'

Many of the costs of preparing for the euro will not give rise to assets, for example   **7**
the costs of staff training, giving information to customers etc. Where costs are
incurred on adapting existing assets, it is necessary to assess whether the expenditure
simply maintains the asset's originally assessed standard of performance or whether

the expenditure results in an enhancement of economic benefits by extending the service potential of the asset concerned. In the former case, there is no access to additional future economic benefits and the costs should be written off as incurred. In the latter case, the costs should be capitalised and depreciated over the asset's useful economic life.

8   Regarding the timing of recognition of a provision for costs associated with the introduction of the euro, the UITF noted that FRS 5 defines liabilities (of which provisions are one type) as 'An entity's obligations to transfer economic benefits as a result of past transactions or events.' One aspect of this is exemplified in FRED 14 (the Exposure Draft of a Financial Reporting Standard on accounting for provisions and contingencies, issued in June 1997). If the envisaged FRS* implements the proposals in FRED 14 a provision would be recognised when and only when an entity has a legal or constructive obligation to transfer economic benefits as a result of past events: the mere intention or even necessity to undertake expenditure related to the future would not be sufficient to give rise to an obligation. Thus costs associated with the introduction of the euro would be recognised in the accounting period in which the work is carried out and no provision would be made for estimated future costs.

9   A further issue concerns the disclosure of information regarding the nature and potential impact of the introduction of the euro, including the related costs incurred and likely to be incurred. In this connection the UITF believes that existing requirements, such as FRS 3 in respect of exceptional costs and companies legislation in respect of significant commitments (including revenue commitments), may apply in some cases. Where the potential impact is likely to be significant, the UITF recommends that entities should give disclosures as indicated in this Abstract.

10   This Abstract addresses the accounting for external and internal costs of the changeover to the euro.† It does not address the costs of modifying software or hardware produced for sale, nor does it address purchases of replacement software or hardware.

CUMULATIVE FOREIGN EXCHANGE TRANSLATION DIFFERENCES

11   Under the closing rate/net investment method of translating the financial statements of foreign entities, the amounts in the balance sheet of a foreign entity are translated into the reporting currency using the rate of exchange ruling at the balance sheet date. Translation differences arise if this rate differs from that ruling at the previous balance sheet date or at the date of any subsequent capital injection or reduction. Such translation differences are taken to reserves and reported in the statement of total recognised gains and losses in accordance with paragraph 53 of SSAP 20 'Foreign currency translation' and paragraph 27 of FRS 3 'Reporting financial performance'.

12   Where the parent undertaking and the subsidiary undertaking report at present in different national currencies of participating Member States the question arises as to what impact the irrevocable locking of national currencies of participating Member States to the euro will have on cumulative translation differences that have been recognised in periods before the introduction of the euro.

__Editor's note:__ FRS 12 'Provisions, Contingent Liabilities and Contingent Assets', issued September 1998, implemented these proposals of FRED 14.

†*The entity and the country in which it reports may not, themselves, be changing over to the euro.*

FRS 3 makes it clear that the same gains and losses should not be recognised twice. **13** The exchange differences have already been recognised through the statement of total recognised gains and losses and consequently there is no question of reporting them in the profit and loss account when such cumulative differences become permanent.*

ANTICIPATORY HEDGES EXISTING AT THE DATE OF INTRODUCTION OF THE EURO

Foreign exchange contracts (and other financial instruments) are often used to hedge **14** currency risk. With the introduction of the euro the exchange risk between currency units of two participating Member States will disappear. The issue concerns the impact this would have on hedges of future transactions existing at the date the euro is introduced.

There is no accounting standard dealing with anticipatory hedges. The UITF con- **15** sidered the issue in the context of an entity with an accounting policy of deferring gains and losses on anticipatory hedges and recognising them in the profit and loss account in the same period as the related income or expense being hedged. The UITF concluded that the introduction of the euro would have no impact on the accounting treatment adopted at present and accordingly gains and losses would continue to be deferred.†

APPLICATION TO SMALLER ENTITIES

Reporting entities applying the Financial Reporting Standard for Smaller Entities **16** currently applicable are exempt from this Abstract. However, where the impact of the changeover to the euro is likely to be significant, smaller entities are encouraged to consider the matters addressed in this Abstract.

UITF CONSENSUS

The UITF reached a consensus that the costs of making the necessary modifications **17** to assets to deal with the euro should be written off to the profit and loss account except in those cases where (a) an entity already has an accounting policy to capitalise assets of the relevant type and (b) to the extent that the expenditure clearly results in an enhancement of an asset beyond that originally assessed rather than merely maintaining its service potential. Other costs associated with the introduction of the euro should also be written off to the profit and loss account.

Expenditure incurred in preparing for the changeover to the euro and regarded as **18** exceptional should be disclosed in accordance with FRS 3. Particulars of commitments at the balance sheet date in respect of costs to be incurred (whether to be treated as capital or revenue) should be disclosed where they are regarded as relevant to assessing the entity's state of affairs. Where the potential impact is likely to be significant to the entity, the UITF recommends that other information and

---

*Editor's note: For companies complying with FRS 23 this paragraph now reads as follows:
Although the introduction of the euro will have made the exchange differences that have already been recognised through the statement of total recognised gains and losses permanent, there is no resulting change in their accounting treatment. It will not, for example, result in the cumulative differences being reported in the profit and loss account.

†Editor's note: For companies complying with FRS 23 this paragraph now reads as follows:
Anticipatory hedges are dealt with in FRS 26. the introduction of the Euro would, under that standard, have no impact on the accounting treatment adopted for anticipatory hedges.

discussion should be given, including an indication of the total costs likely to be incurred. This information may be more appropriately located in the directors' report or any operating and financial review or other statement included in the annual report published by the entity.

19   Following the principle set out in FRS 3, cumulative foreign exchange translation differences recognised in the statement of total recognised gains and losses in accordance with SSAP 20 should remain in reserves after the introduction of the euro and should not be reported in the profit and loss account.*

20   Where gains and losses on financial instruments used as anticipatory hedges are at present deferred and matched with the related income or expense in a future period, the introduction of the euro should not alter this deferral and matching treatment.

DATE FROM WHICH EFFECTIVE

21   This consensus should be adopted as soon as practicable, but in any event for accounting periods ending on or after 23 March 1998.

REFERENCES

Legislation

Great Britain and Northern Ireland

Companies Act 1985 and Companies (Northern Ireland) Order 1986:
Schedule 4 – paragraph 50(5)
Schedule 8 – paragraph 46(5)
Schedule 9 – paragraph 66(3)
Schedule 9A – paragraph 70(5)

Republic of Ireland

Companies (Amendment) Act 1986: Schedule paragraph 36(6)
European Communities (Credit Institutions: Accounts) Regulations 1992: Schedule, Part 1, paragraph 66(4)
European Communities (Insurance Undertakings: Accounts) Regulations 1996: Schedule, Part III, paragraph 18(5)

Accounting Standards and ASB Statements

FRS 3 'Reporting Financial Performance' – paragraphs 2, 5, 19, 27 and 56
FRS 5 'Reporting the Substance of Transactions' – paragraphs 2 and 4
SSAP 20 'Foreign currency translation' – paragraphs 51, 53 and 57
ASB Statement 'Operating and Financial Review' – paragraphs 13–18.

Editor's note: For companies complying with FRS 23 this paragraph now reads as follows:
Cumulative foreign exchange translation differences recognised in the statement of total recognised gains and losses in accordance with FRS 23 should remain in reserves on the introduction of the euro; they should not be reported in the profit and loss account simply because of the euro's introduction.

Appendix
Further accounting issues arising from the introduction of the euro

(Issued August 1998)

The UITF has been asked for its views on how certain requirements should be applied in the context of the introduction of the euro. The opportunity has been taken to provide clarification in this Appendix, as many entities are likely to be affected, including some that are outside participating Member States. However, this Appendix deals mainly with issues that arise for those companies with a functional (or in SSAP 20's terms 'local') currency that is participating in monetary union. This Appendix has the same status as the Abstract itself.

Introduction

Although the euro had not been envisaged when SSAP 20 was published in 1983, the underlying principles of the SSAP nevertheless remain applicable following the introduction of the euro. It needs to be remembered that the introduction of the euro does not alter the reality that participating Member States had, in the periods before the introduction of the euro, exchange rates between themselves that were different from the fixed conversion rates applicable from 1 January 1999. Users of financial information therefore need to be aware that an exchange rate effect may be embodied in information related to periods before the introduction of the euro and that relationships between figures, although they may be stated in euro for the convenience of readers ('a convenience translation'), will vary depending on whether figures in the previous reporting currency were themselves the result of translation at the time. This aspect is considered further below (see question 1).

The following questions and answers elaborate on issues that have been raised.

1   What translation rate should be used where an entity chooses to provide a convenience translation of its financial statements, including comparative amounts in respect of accounting periods before the introduction of the euro?

The euro will be the continuation of each national currency of participating Member States from 1 January 1999. Where an entity presents a convenience translation of its financial statements into euro, including comparative amounts for accounting periods ending before the introduction of the euro, the original reporting currency amounts should be translated at that currency's conversion rate to the euro established at 1 January 1999. It is not appropriate to rework the translations underlying the preparation of the original financial statements in the relevant national currency of the Member State. For example, a French subsidiary of an Irish company may have had level profits for two consecutive years when expressed in francs. However, when expressed in punts the figures will have reflected the change in the punt/franc exchange rate over the two years and the profits expressed in punts are unlikely to be level. Translation of the franc figures into euro should be carried out by first translating them into punts at the exchange rates ruling at the relevant dates and then translating those figures into euro.

It would be helpful if the notes to the financial statements explained that the trends over the years are exactly the same as if the financial statements for all periods had been expressed in the previous national denomination. Expression of these historical amounts in euro does not eliminate or alter any translation effect that existed when they were originally reported in the currency of the Member State. The UITF recommends that entities should disclose the previous national denomination applicable when information on periods before 1 January 1999 is presented in euro.

2   What exchange rate should be used for financial statements with year-ends other than 31 December (for example, should the fixed conversion rates be anticipated in respect of balances at dates earlier than the date of introduction of the euro)?

The normal rules in SSAPs 17 and 20 should apply and exchange rate changes between the year-end (say September 1998) and 1 January 1999 should continue to be treated as non-adjusting events. At present it is possible for an exchange gain on an unsettled amount at a year-end to be recognised, although subsequently the gain could turn into a loss when the amount is settled. Both periods report what has happened in the relevant period. If, for example, a company with a September 1998 year-end includes in its assets and liabilities foreign currency amounts with participating Member States (amounts that may not be settled until after 1 January 1999) it would not be appropriate to record the balances at other than the closing rate at the end of September 1998.

3   Is any special treatment needed for apparent differences arising from the use of the temporal method as, for example, the same asset may be reported at a different euro figure in a subsidiary's own accounts and in the group accounts?

The temporal method is described in paragraphs 21-24 of SSAP 20. It is possible that there could be a different euro figure for the same asset (acquired before 1 January 1999) in a subsidiary's own accounts and in the group accounts, but this is a natural consequence of the temporal method, which preserves in group accounts the historical rates of exchange at which transactions were undertaken. If the functional currency of a subsidiary changes or becomes the same as the functional currency of its parent because exchange rates become fixed, it is not appropriate to restate prior year figures as if the functional currency had been different from what it actually was at the relevant time. If a revaluation of the asset was incorporated in the financial statements, it would be translated at the rate ruling at the date of revaluation. If that date were at or after the changeover to the euro the asset would appear in the financial statements of both the subsidiary and the group accounts at the same amount.

4   Does the introduction of the euro and the fixing of exchange rates mean that exchange gains on unsettled items (in respect of currencies of countries in participating Member States) become realised?

The UITF notes that the European Commission's paper 'Accounting for the introduction of the euro', published in June 1997, concludes that such gains should be treated as realised. However, SSAP 20 requires continuous recognition of gains and losses on all monetary items, even long-term ones, whether realised or not. There is no cause to recognise any further gain or loss when realisation takes place.

UITF abstract 22: The acquisition of a Lloyd's business

(Issued June 1998)

BACKGROUND

In accordance with the requirements of Lloyd's, Lloyd's syndicates adopt a fund   1
basis of accounting, under which underwriting accounts are not closed for at least
three years. Syndicates are managed by managing agents who are usually entitles,
under the management agreement, to commissions equivalent to a shore in the
syndicates' profits, which will not be known with certainty until the accounts are
closed.

THE ISSUE

The issue concerns the recognition of assets and liabilities when a business such as a   2
Lloyd's managing agent is acquired. FRS 7 'Fair Values in Acquisition Accounting'
required that, on an acquisition, the assets and liabilities that are recognised 'should
be those of the acquired entity that existed at the date of the acquisition' (paragraph
5). The issue is whether profit commissions receivable in respect of years that are not
yet closed should be included in these assets.

One view is that such commissions should not be included. This is because they are   3
inherently uncertain and would not be reflected in the agent's accounts (or those of
its acquirer) until the syndicates' accounts are closed. If these commissions were
included as assets on acquisition, there would be a hiatus in the amount of profit
reported in the acquirer's accounts in the years following the acquisition.

Another view is that the commissions are clearly an asset of the acquired business.   4
They will normally be reflected in the price paid to acquire the business. Supporters
of this view point out that it is a basic principle of acquisition accounting that profits
earned before the date of acquisition are not reported as post-acquisition profits. It is
a normal consequence of accounting for the acquisition of a business with a long
operating cycle (for example a life assurance business) that there is some discontinuity in the stream of reported profits, and Lloyd's simply provides an extreme
example of this.

FRS 7 states that contingent assets are amongst the identifiable assets and liabilities   5
recognised on an acquisition, and that assets and liabilities not normally recognised
in accounts in the absence of an acquisition may be included in those assets. In
particular, FRS 7 states that the recognition of an acquired contingent asset represents
the expectation that the amount expended on its acquisition will be recovered, and
does not anticipate a future gain. Recognition of an asset in respect of commissions
receivable would be consistent with this view.

A similar issue arises in respect of the acquisition of Lloyd's members agents or   6
Lloyd's corporate capital vehicles. The principles of FRS 7 would again require the
identifiable assets and liabilities recognised to reflect an estimate of the profit or loss
of the business that had arisen in respect of periods before the acquisition.

FRS 7 permits provisional valuations to be used if it has not been possible to complete   7
the investigation of fair values by the date on which the first post-acquisition
financial statements of the acquirer are approved by the directors. These provisional
valuations should be amended if necessary in the next financial statements with a
corresponding adjustment to goodwill.

APPLICATION TO SMALLER ENTITIES

8   Reporting entities applying the Financial Reporting Standard for Smaller Entities currently applicable are exempt from this Abstract.

UITF CONSENSUS

9   The UITF reached a consensus that, on the acquisition of a Lloyd's managing agent, the identifiable assets and liabilities to be recognised include all profit commissions receivable in respect of periods before the acquisition, including those relating to years that are not yet closed.

10   Such profit commissions receivable should be recognised at their fair value, based on the best estimate of the likely outcome based on profits earned before the date of acquisition.*

11   Similarly, the UITF reached a consensus that, on the acquisition of a business with analogous circumstances to those of a Lloyd's managing agent, such as a Lloyd's member agent or Lloyd's corporate capital vehicle, the identifiable assets and liabilities to be recognised should reflect an estimate of the profit or loss of the business that had arisen in respect of periods before the acquisition, including those relating to years that are not yet closed. The fair value of the acquired assets and liabilities should again be based on the best estimate of the likely outcome.

DATE FROM WHICH EFFECTIVE

12   The accounting treatment required by this consensus should be adopted in respect of acquisitions first accounted for in financial statements relating to accounting periods ending on or after 23 December 1998. Earlier adoption is encouraged but not required.

REFERENCES

Legislation

Great Britain and Northern Ireland

Companies Act 1985 and Companies (Northern Ireland) Order 1986
Schedule 4A paragraph 9

Republic of Ireland

European Communities (Companies: Group Accounts) Regulations, 1992 Regulation 19

Accounting Standards

FRS 7 'Fair Values in Acquisition Accounting' paragraphs 5, 6, 15, 23-25 and 34-37.

---

*Editor's note: A Technical Release issued by the Institute of Chartered Accountants in England & Wales in January 1999 (Tech 1/99 — Accounting by Lloyd's Corporate Capital Vehicles) provides guidance on how this estimate should be made.

UITF abstract 23: Application of the transitional rules in FRS 15

(Issued May 2000)

THE ISSUE

An issue has been raised on the application of paragraphs 106 and 108 of FRS 15 **1**
'Tangible fixed assets' and how widely the prior period adjustment approach may be
used. The relevant basic requirement of FRS 15 is paragraph 83, which states:

'83   Where the tangible fixed asset comprises two or more major components with
       substantially different useful economic lives, each component should be
       accounted for separately for depreciation purposes and depreciated over its
       individual useful economic life.'

Paragraphs 36–41 also discuss the treatment of expenditure on components.

The transitional rules in paragraphs 106 and 108 are as follows: **2**

'106 Except as provided for in paragraph 108, revisions to the useful economic lives
      and residual values of tangible fixed assets recognised on adoption of the FRS
      are not the result of a change in accounting policy and should be treated in
      accordance with paragraphs 93–96 [i.e. prospectively] and, not as prior period
      adjustments.'

'108 Where, on adoption of the FRS, entities separate tangible fixed assets into dif-
      ferent components with significantly different useful economic lives for
      depreciation purposes, in accordance with paragraphs 36–41 and 83–85, the
      changes should be dealt with as prior period adjustments, as a change in
      accounting policy.'

Prior to the adoption of FRS 15 an entity may have based its depreciation policy on **3**
the whole of an asset, such as property, while recognising that certain components,
such as lifts, had a substantially shorter life than the property as a whole: the cost of
replacement of such components would have been provided for by means of a
provision (prior to FRS 12) or written off as incurred. On adoption of FRS 15 an entity
may at the same time (a) identify one or more separate components with significantly
different useful economic lives from the remainder of the asset and (b) amend the
residual value and/or economic useful life of the remainder of the asset. A typical
example would be where the lifts within a building are to be treated as a separate
component and depreciated separately and at the same time the building itself is to
be depreciated for the first time. The question is whether the effect of both aspects
can be combined into a single prior period adjustment under paragraph 108.

Since paragraph 106 is expressed as being subject to paragraph 108, it could be read **4**
as placing no limits on the extent to which prior period adjustments could be set up
in respect of changes to depreciation rates on the introduction of component
accounting. The UITF took the view that paragraph 108 should not be taken as
disapplying paragraph 106 with regard to all elements of an asset in which one or
more components had been identified on the adoption of FRS 15, but rather as
introducing a limited exemption to deal with the situation discussed in paragraph 3
above. The UITF noted that paragraph 106 itself reflects the ongoing requirements
for revisions of residual values and/or economic lives (set out in paragraphs 93–96)
which is that they should be reflected prospectively over the remaining useful life of
the asset. Allocating a shorter life to components of an asset does not itself involve
changing the life/residual value placed previously on the asset as a whole. However,

reviewing the asset as a whole may also give rise to changes in the estimates of its life/ residual value: such changes should be dealt with prospectively.

5   FRS 15 notes that land and buildings are separable components and are dealt with separately for accounting purposes, even when they are acquired together (paragraph 84). Where they had not previously been treated separately and there had been no charge for depreciation, any depreciation of the buildings component arising from the introduction of FRS 15 should be dealt with prospectively.

6   Before the adoption of FRS 12 'Provisions, contingent liabilities and contingent assets' and FRS 15, the fact that some components deteriorated faster than the asset as a whole might have been recognised by a provision for repairs and maintenance (including major refits or refurbishment and the replacement of major components) rather than by different depreciation rates on the components. On adoption of FRS 12 any such provision would have been eliminated by a prior period adjustment. It follows that it was necessary in FRS 15 to allow prior period treatment in respect of the corresponding adjustment resulting from recomputing cumulative depreciation by reference to components of an asset rather than the asset as a whole.

APPLICATION TO SMALLER ENTITIES

7   Reporting entities applying the Financial Reporting Standard for Smaller Entities currently applicable are exempt from this Abstract.

UITF CONSENSUS

8   The UITF reached a consensus that the prior period adjustment required by paragraph 108 of FRS 15, where components of an asset are identified, should be restricted to the effects of treating separately only those components in respect of which:

(a)   any provision for repairs and maintenance (including replacement expenditure) was itself eliminated by prior period adjustment on adoption of FRS 12 or

(b)   there has been a change from a previous policy of writing off as incurred relevant repairs and maintenance expenditure (including replacement expenditure) to a policy whereby such expenditure is capitalised because it replaces a separately depreciated component.

In particular, any prior period adjustment should not embrace any changes to the useful economic lives or residual values of the remainder of the asset.

DATE FROM WHICH EFFECTIVE

9   The accounting treatment required by this consensus should be adopted as soon as practicable, but in any event in financial statements relating to accounting periods ending on or after 23 March 2000 (the effective date of FRS 15).

REFERENCES

FRS 15 'Tangible fixed assets' – paragraphs 36–41, 83–4, 93–96, 106 and 108.
FRS 12 'Provisions, contingent liabilities and contingent assets' – paragraphs 14, 101 and Example 11 in Appendix III.

Appendix
Illustrative Example

Assume a building with a cost of £1 million, on which before FRS 15 no depreciation had been charged on the ground that any depreciation was immaterial. Inflation is ignored.

Ten years after the purchase of the building FRS 15 is adopted and the lifts within the building are identified as a separate component with a cost of £150,000 and a 20-year life. Assume (as an example of a paragraph 8 (a) situation) that a provision for the replacement of the lifts had been built up, amounting to £75,000 (10/20 2 £150,000). However, on the adoption of FRS 12 the provision is eliminated as a prior period adjustment.

Clearly the lifts have been in existence since the date of purchase and have always had a cost and a life (and possibly a residual value, assumed to be nil in this case).

On adoption of FRS 15 the lifts are formally recognised as a separate component in accordance with the standard and cumulative depreciation of £75,000 (being the difference between the amount of depreciation previously charged, i.e., nil in this case, and the recalculated amount) is charged in respect of that component by way of prior period adjustment in accordance with paragraph 108. In this case, this is equal and opposite to the prior period adjustment required on the adoption of FRS 12 (for simplicity it has been assumed that FRS 12 and FRS 15 were adopted at the same time, which may not have been the case in practice). This adjustment, of itself, should not result in revision of any depreciation previously charged in respect of the building excluding the lifts (nil in this example).

If (as an example of a paragraph 8 (b) situation) no provision had been made for replacement of the lifts, but the policy had been to write off as incurred the replacement of major components such as lifts, then the prior period adjustment on the adoption of FRS 15 would be £75,000 cumulative depreciation as above. When the lift is eventually replaced the new lift will be capitalised as it replaces a separately depreciated component.

In both examples above, any change to the life (or residual value) of the building as a whole should be accounted for prospectively under paragraph 106. Thus if the building was given a revised useful economic life of 50 years (i.e., a remaining useful economic life of 40 years) on adoption of FRS 15, the depreciation on the building (excluding the separately depreciated lift) would be accounted for prospectively, i.e., £21,250 per year (1/40 × £850,000).

UITF abstract 24: Accounting for start-up costs

(Issued June 2000)

THE ISSUE

1   The issue is whether start-up costs that cannot be included in the cost of a fixed asset may nevertheless be carried forward, for example as a prepayment, deferred expenditure or other kind of asset. FRS 15 'Tangible fixed assets' addresses the accounting for costs associated with a start-up or commissioning period. Paragraph 14 states that such costs should be included in the cost of a tangible fixed asset only where the asset is available for use but incapable of operating at normal levels without such a start-up or commissioning period.

2   FRS 15 includes a section on other start-up costs which notes that:

'there is no justification for regarding costs relating to other start-up periods [i.e., other than essential commissioning costs, which are regarded as part of the cost of the asset], where the asset is available for use but not yet operating at normal levels, for example because of a lack of demand, as part of the cost of the asset. An example is the start-up period of a new hotel or bookshop, which could operate at normal levels almost immediately, but for which experience teaches that demand will build up slowly and full utilisation or sales levels will be achieved only over a period of several months.' (paragraph 16)

FRS 15 does not specify how the costs of a start-up period that cannot be included in the cost of a tangible fixed asset should be accounted for.

3   This Abstract addresses whether an entity may apply an accounting treatment in respect of certain costs arising in a start-up period that differs from the treatment it would normally apply to similar costs incurred as part of its on-going activities. In particular, may costs that would usually be recognised as expenses when incurred be capitalised, or otherwise deferred, simply on the grounds that they relate to a new activity? Conversely, may costs that would usually be capitalised, or otherwise deferred, be recognised as expenses when incurred, simply on the grounds that they relate to a new activity?

4   For the purpose of this Abstract 'start-up costs' should be construed broadly so as to include costs arising from those one-time activities related to opening a new facility, introducing a new product or service, conducting business in a new territory, conducting business with a new class of customer, initiating a new process in an existing facility, starting some new operation and similar items. They include costs of relocating or reorganising part or all of an entity, costs related to organising a new entity, and expenses and losses incurred both before and after opening.

5   The UITF took the view that start-up costs should be treated in the same manner as similar costs incurred as part of the entity's on-going activities.

6   In the case of costs that are regarded as peculiar to a start-up activity, such that there are no similar costs incurred as part of the entity's on-going activities, the issue is whether the costs should be recognised as an asset or as an expense when incurred. Assets are defined as 'rights or other access to future economic benefits controlled by an entity as a result of past transactions or events'. Assets are recognised in financial statements only if certain criteria are met. The UITF took the view that, in general, start-up costs do not meet these criteria because the relationship between the expenditure and any future economic benefits that may be derived from that

expenditure is usually not sufficiently certain to warrant recognising start-up costs as assets and that, in particular, in most cases it is inappropriate to carry forward start-up costs as prepayments or deferred expenditure. Accordingly, the UITF concluded that start-up costs should be recognised as an expense when incurred unless they meet the specific conditions for recognition as assets under a relevant accounting standard, such as FRS 15, FRS 10 'Goodwill and intangible assets' or SSAP 13 'Accounting for research and development'.

The UITF noted that this conclusion is consistent with IAS 38 'Intangible Assets' **7**
paragraphs 56 and 57 and is similar to the requirements on start-up costs in the USA.

APPLICATION TO SMALLER ENTITIES

Reporting entities applying the Financial Reporting Standard for Smaller Entities **8**
currently applicable are exempt from this Abstract.

UITF CONSENSUS

The UITF reached a consensus that: **9**

(a) start-up costs should be accounted for on a basis consistent with the accounting treatment of similar costs incurred as part of the entity's on-going activities; and

(b) in cases where there are no such similar costs, start-up costs that do not meet the criteria for recognition as assets under a relevant accounting standard, such as FRS 15 'Tangible fixed assets', FRS 10 'Goodwill and intangible assets' or SSAP 13 'Accounting for research and development', should be recognised as an expense when they are incurred. They should not be carried forward as an asset.

Where start-up costs meet the definition of exceptional items in FRS 3 'Reporting **10**
financial performance' they should be disclosed in accordance with that Standard. Entities are encouraged to give additional disclosures regarding start-up costs in accordance with paragraphs 16-18 of the ASB Statement 'Operating and Financial Review'.

DATE FROM WHICH EFFECTIVE

The accounting treatment required by this consensus should be adopted in financial **11**
statements relating to accounting periods ending on or after 23 July 2000, but earlier adoption is encouraged.

REFERENCES

ASB pronouncements
FRS 3 'Reporting financial performance' – paragraph 19
FRS 5 'Reporting the substance of transactions' – paragraphs 2 and 20
FRS 10 'Goodwill and intangible assets' – paragraph 14
FRS 15 'Tangible fixed assets' – paragraphs 14–16
SSAP 13 'Accounting for research and development' – paragraphs 25 and 26
ASB Statement 'Operating and financial review' – paragraphs 16–18

Other pronouncements
IAS 38 'Intangible assets' – paragraphs 56 and 57
AICPA (USA) Statement of Position 98–5 'Reporting on the costs of start-up activities'

UITF abstract 25: National Insurance contributions on share option gains

(Issued July 2000)

BACKGROUND

1   The Social Security Act 1998 introduced a National Insurance charge on UK employers on the gains made by employees upon exercise of options issued under unapproved share option schemes (i.e., those not approved by the Inland Revenue). The charge applies to options granted after 5 April 1999. The gain on which National Insurance contributions are payable is the difference between the share price at the date the options are exercised and the exercise price paid by the employee. This applies to those schemes where the shares are 'readily convertible assets', i.e., they can be sold on a stock exchange or there are arrangements in place that allow the employees to obtain cash for the shares.

THE ISSUE

2   The issue is whether the employer should accrue for the estimated liability between the grant date and the exercise date, which is when it becomes payable, and, if so, how the liability should be calculated.

3   FRS 12 'Provisions, contingent liabilities and contingent assets' requires a provision to be recognised when:

(a)   an entity has a present obligation (legal or constructive) as a result of a past event;

(b)   it is probable that a transfer of economic benefits will be required to settle the obligation; and

(c)   a reliable estimate can be made of the amount of the obligation.

4   The UITF regards the granting of the option as the past event that gives rise to a present obligation to pay National Insurance when the option is exercised. By granting the option, the employer has exposed itself to an obligation to pay National Insurance, which exists independently of the employer's future actions. Only the amount payable is uncertain, as it is not possible to make a reliable estimate of what the employer's share price will be at a future date when the option may be exercised. However, when the amount of the obligation at an intervening balance sheet date is considered FRS 12 requires the amount recognised as a provision to be the best estimate of the expenditure required to settle the present obligation at the balance sheet date (paragraph 36). The market price of the shares provides a reliable basis for making such an estimate.

5   Where it is thought probable that a cash outflow will occur, a liability should be accrued over the performance period in respect of that probable future cash outflow, to the extent that the employees have performed their side of the arrangement. For example, if the terms of the arrangement require the employees to perform services over a three-year period, the liability should be accrued over that three-year period. The UITF therefore agreed that provision should be made systematically by reference to the market value of the shares at the balance sheet dates over the period from the date of grant to the end of the performance period; from that date to the date of actual exercise, the provision should be adjusted by reference to changes in market value. Where there is no performance period full provision should be made immediately. The performance period is the period during which the employee performs

the services necessary to become unconditionally entitled to the options, which may entail satisfying specified performance criteria or remaining in the company's employment for a specified period of time.

Legislation now before Parliament (the Child Support, Pensions and Social Security   **6**
Bill) would permit the employer's National Insurance contributions to be recovered from or transferred to the employee. Where there is an agreement between employer and employee under which the employee agrees to reimburse all or part of the employer's National Insurance contributions, FRS 12 requires a provision for the full amount to be made and the expected reimbursement to be treated as a separate asset if receipt is virtually certain, with a net presentation permitted in the profit and loss account. Where there is a joint election by employer and employee under which the liability is formally transferred to the employee there is no liability to appear in the employer's accounts.

FRS 12 requires, for each class of provision, disclosure of an indication of the   **7**
uncertainties about the amount or timing of the eventual transfer of economic benefits and, where necessary to provide adequate information, the major assumptions made concerning future events (paragraph 90). In the case of a provision for National Insurance on share options, disclosure of the share price and of the effect of a significant movement in that price may be necessary to provide a full understanding of these factors.

This Abstract addresses National Insurance contributions on share option gains.   **8**
However, the principles apply to other analogous situations that give rise to employer's National Insurance liabilities.

APPLICATION TO SMALLER ENTITIES

Reporting entities applying the Financial Reporting Standard for Smaller Entities   **9**
currently applicable are exempt from this Abstract.

UITF CONSENSUS

The UITF reached a consensus that provision should be made for National Insur-   **10**
ance contributions on outstanding share options that are expected to be exercised. It should be calculated at the latest enacted National Insurance rate applied to the difference between the market value of the underlying shares at the balance sheet date and the option exercise price and allocated over the period from the date of grant* to the end of the performance period; from that date to the date of actual exercise the provision should be adjusted by using the current market value of the shares. Where there is no performance period full provision should be made immediately.

All amounts provided for in respect of National Insurance contributions in accor-   **11**
dance with paragraph 10 should be charged to the profit and loss account, except insofar as they form part of staff costs capitalised under companies legislation and accounting standards. Any reimbursement by employees should be accounted for in accordance with paragraphs 56–61 of FRS 12.

*Editor's note: See also UITF Abstract 30 'Date of award to employees of shares or rights to shares'.

DATE FROM WHICH EFFECTIVE

12   The accounting treatment required by this consensus should be adopted in financial statements relating to accounting periods ending on or after 22 September 2000, but earlier adoption is encouraged.

REFERENCES AND LEGAL CONSIDERATIONS

FRS 12 'Provisions, contingent liabilities and contingent assets' – paragraphs 14, 36, 37, 56–61 and 90.

The effect of paragraph 94 of Schedule 4 to the Companies Act 1985* is that the National Insurance charge required by this Abstract is included as part of staff costs in the profit and loss account.

The UITF has received legal advice that National Insurance contributions on share option gains do not constitute an expense of an issue of shares such as to allow the share premium account to be applied in writing off the expense in terms of the Companies Act 1985 section 130(2).†

*In Northern Ireland – the Companies (Northern Ireland) Order 1986 Schedule 4 paragraph 92; in the Republic of Ireland – the Companies (Amendment) Act 1986 Schedule paragraph 74

†In Northern Ireland – the Companies (Northern Ireland) Order 1986 Article 140; in the Republic Ireland – the Companies Act 1963 section 62(2)

Appendix
Illustrative example of the consensus in paragraphs 10 and 11

The company's year-end is 31 December.

A maximum of 10,000 share options are granted at 1 July 1999, when the market value is £1, at an exercise price of £1, dependent upon performance from 1 July 1999 to 30 June 2002. The options are exercisable from 1 July 2002 to 1 July 2003.

Employer's National Insurance contributions, currently at 12.2 per cent, are payable on exercise of the options.

31 December 1999
The market value of a share is £1.80. It is estimated that the maximum entitlement of options will be exercised.

National Insurance charge for the year: one-sixth of 12.2% of 10,000 x (£1.80 - £1) = £163.

31 December 2000
The market value of a share is £3.00. Again the full entitlement is expected to be exercised.

National Insurance cumulative charge: one-half of 12.2% of 10,000 x (£3.00 - £1) = £1,220
[Charge for the year : £1,220 - £163 = £1,057]

31 December 2001
The market value of a share is £2.80. It is now expected that only 8,000 share options will be exercised.

National Insurance cumulative charge: five-sixths of 12.2% x 8,000 x (£2.80 - £1) = £1,464
[Charge for the year: £1,464 - £1,220 = £244]

31 December 2002
The market value of a share is £2.20. Only 6,000 share options vested; none of these have been exercised.

National Insurance cumulative charge: 12.2% x 6,000 x (£2.20 - £1) = £878
[Credit for the year : £1,464 - £878 = £586]

31 December 2003
The 6,000 share options were exercised on 17 May 2003 when the market value of a share was £2.65.

The National Insurance liability was therefore: 12.2% x 6,000 x (£2.65 - £1) = £1,208
[Charge for the year: £1,208 - £878 = £330]

UITF abstract 26: Barter transactions for advertising

(Issued 9 November 2000)

THE ISSUE

1   An entity such as a publisher or broadcaster may agree to provide advertising in exchange for advertising services provided by its customer, rather than for a cash consideration. For example, it has recently become common for companies that provide commercial websites to display advertisements in exchange for advertising of their own services on another website. Such an exchange gives rise to the question of what amount, if any, should be included in reported turnover and expense.

2   Although this issue has no overall effect on the total profit or loss, it does affect the amount of turnover, which is often cited as a significant measure of performance for internet companies.

3   The recognition criteria in the Statement of Principles for Financial Reporting require (a) sufficient evidence and (b) measurement at a monetary amount with sufficient reliability. Where advertising services are provided for a cash consideration, the transaction evidences the value of the services provided. In contrast, where advertising is provided in exchange for advertising received, the arrangement provides little or no evidence of the value of the services provided.

4   The UITF decided that it would be appropriate to recognise turnover and costs in respect of barter transactions for advertising only if there is persuasive evidence of the value at which, if the advertising had not been exchanged, it would have been sold for cash in a similar transaction. The UITF believed that such circumstances would be rare.

5   The UITF noted that this conclusion is consistent with a recent consensus of the Emerging Issues Task Force in the USA (Accounting for Advertising Barter Transactions – Issue No 99-17).

6   This Abstract applies to barter transactions for advertising, whether on the internet, or on television, in magazines, on poster sites or by another medium.

7   FRS 5 'Reporting the substance of transactions' requires that, in determining the substance of a transaction to be reported, all its aspects and implications should be identified and greater weight given to those more likely to have commercial effect in practice. Accordingly, an arrangement should be regarded as a barter transaction where that fairly reflects its substance. This may be the case where a contract to provide advertising for a cash consideration is made on the understanding that a similar reciprocal contract is entered into. It may also be the case where the purchaser of advertising agrees to procure advertising services from another party in exchange rather than provide them itself.

8   This Abstract has been developed in the context of barter transactions for advertising. A distinctive feature of such transactions is that they involve little or no marginal cost. Application of this Abstract is not mandatory for barter transactions for services other than advertising, although its principles may be relevant to such transactions.

APPLICATION TO SMALLER ENTITIES

Reporting entities applying the Financial Reporting Standard for Smaller Entities currently applicable are exempt from this Abstract.　　**9**

UITF CONSENSUS

The UITF reached a consensus that turnover and costs in respect of barter trans-　**10** actions for advertising should not be recognised unless there is persuasive evidence of the value at which, if the advertising had not been exchanged, it would have been sold for cash in a similar transaction. In these circumstances, that value should be included in turnover and costs.

Persuasive evidence of the value of advertising exchanged will exist only where it can　**11** be demonstrated that similar advertising has been sold for cash. This will be the case only where the entity has a history of selling similar advertising for cash, and where substantially all of the turnover from advertising within the accounting period is represented by cash sales.

To provide evidence of the value of advertising exchanged, cash sales of advertising　**12** must be similar in all significant respects. This requires that the cash sales are of advertising space in the same vehicle (for example, the same website or magazine) as that exchanged, and must have taken place within a reasonably short period of the exchange transaction (in no case more than six months before or after it). There must also be no other factors that would be expected to make the value of the advertising sold for cash significantly different from that exchanged. Specific factors to consider include:

● circulation, exposure, or saturation within an intended market;
● timing (time of day, day of week, daily, weekly, 24 hours a day/7 days a week, and season of the year);
● prominence (page on website, section of periodical, location on page, and size of advertisement);
● demographics of readers, viewers, or customers;
● duration (length of time advertising will be displayed).

The above list is not intended to be exhaustive.

Even where similar advertising has been sold for cash, it is necessary to consider　**13** whether in the light of all available information there is persuasive evidence of the value at which the advertising exchanged would have been sold if not exchanged. Specific factors that may be relevant include:

● the entity's practice in setting prices for the advertising it provides, and the circumstances in which discounts are offered;
● the probability that, if the advertising were not exchanged, a cash sale would have taken place;
● the value to the entity of the advertising received in exchange, and the evidence that the entity would have been willing to buy that advertising for cash if it had not been able to obtain it through an exchange transaction.

Entities should disclose in the notes to the financial statements the total amount of　**14** barter transactions for advertising that is included in turnover. Entities are encouraged to disclose information on the volume and type of such transactions and other kinds of barter transaction (whether or not included in turnover).

DATE FROM WHICH EFFECTIVE

15   The accounting treatment required by the consensus should be adopted in financial statements relating to accounting periods ending on or after 23 December 2000, but earlier adoption is encouraged.

REFERENCES

ASB pronouncements

FRS 5 'Reporting the Substance of Transactions' – paragraph 14

ASB Statement of Principles for Financial Reporting – Chapter 5

Other pronouncements

EITF Consensus (USA) 'Accounting for Advertising Barter Transactions' (Issue No 99–17)

UITF abstract 27: Revision to estimates of the useful economic life of goodwill and intangible assets

(Issued December 2000)

THE ISSUE

Paragraph 19 of FRS 10 states that 'There is a rebuttable presumption that the useful 1 economic lives of purchased goodwill and intangible assets are limited to periods of 20 years or less.' Paragraph 33 states that 'The useful economic lives of goodwill and intangible assets should be reviewed at the end of each reporting period and revised if necessary. If a useful economic life is revised, the carrying value ... should be amortised over the revised remaining useful economic life.'

An entity may rebut the presumption because there is evidence that its goodwill (or 2 intangible asset) has an indefinite life: in these circumstances no amortisation is charged. In a subsequent year, the entity may decide that it no longer wishes or is now unable to rebut the presumption. Amortisation over a period of up to 20 years from the date of acquisition would be necessary. The issue is whether such a change should be treated as a change of accounting policy (with a consequential prior period adjustment) or a change of useful economic life (and thus accounted for prospectively in accordance with paragraph 33 of FRS 10).

The UITF took the view that a decision not to rebut the presumption is not a change 3 of accounting policy but rather a change in the way in which useful economic life is estimated. This is because the FRS does not allow a choice of policies; goodwill should be amortised unless its life is indefinite. What the FRS does allow is two different sets of assumptions for estimating useful economic life. The change referred to in paragraph 2 above is simply from one permitted way of estimating useful economic life to another, more prudent, one.

APPLICATION TO SMALLER ENTITIES

Reporting entities applying the Financial Reporting Standard for Smaller Entities 4 currently applicable are exempt from this Abstract.

UITF CONSENSUS

The UITF reached a consensus that, other than on the initial implementation of FRS 5 10:

(a) where estimates of the useful economic lives of goodwill or intangible assets are revised, the carrying value should be amortised over the revised remaining useful economic life, as required by paragraph 33 of FRS 10; and
(b) this requirement applies equally where the presumption of a 20-year life has previously been rebutted, as it does to other revisions of estimates of the useful economic lives of goodwill and intangible assets.

DATE FROM WHICH EFFECTIVE

The accounting treatment required by this consensus should be adopted with 6 immediate effect. Where applicable, corresponding amounts should be restated.

REFERENCES

FRS 10 'Goodwill and intangible assets' – paragraphs 19 and 33

UITF abstract 28: Operating lease incentives

(Issued February 2001)

THE ISSUE

In negotiating a new or renewed operating lease, a lessor may provide incentives for the lessee to enter into the agreement. Examples of such incentives are an up-front cash payment to the lessee or the reimbursement or assumption by the lessor of costs of the lessee (such as relocation costs, and costs associated with a pre-existing lease commitment of the lessee). Alternatively, initial periods of the lease term may be agreed to be rent-free or at a reduced rent.   **1**

The issue is how an incentive for an operating lease should be recognised in the financial statements of the lessee and of the lessor.   **2**

A payment (or other transfer of value) from a lessor to (or for the benefit of) a lessee should be regarded as a lease incentive when that fairly reflects its substance. A payment to reimburse a lessee for fitting-out costs should be regarded as a lease incentive where the fittings are suitable only for the lessee and accordingly do not add to the value of the property to the lessor. On the other hand, insofar as a reimbursement of expenditure enhances a property generally and causes commensurate benefit to flow to the lessor, it should be treated as reimbursement of expenditure on the property. For example, where the lifts in a building are to be renewed and a lease has only five years to run, a payment made by the lessor may not be an inducement to enter into a lease but payment for an improvement to the lessor's property.   **3**

This Abstract does not deal with incentives to surrender leases. However, such incentives should be examined to determine whether in substance the incentive relates to the new lease, particularly where the offer of the incentive is linked to an arrangement to vacate a property under lease from a different lessor. Such consideration should take into account the market rentals applicable to the old and new leases. If it is determined that the incentive, or part of it, relates in substance to the new lease, the provisions of this Abstract apply.   **4**

SSAP 21 'Accounting for leases and hire purchase contracts' does not deal specifically with accounting for lease incentives. However, it requires lessees to charge operating lease rentals 'on a straight-line basis over the lease term, even if the payments are not made on such a basis, unless another systematic and rational basis is more appropriate.' (paragraph 37)   **5**

As regards lessors, SSAP 21 requires that 'Rental income from an operating lease, excluding charges for services such as insurance and maintenance, should be recognised on a straight-line basis over the period of the lease, even if the payments are not made on such a basis, unless another systematic and rational basis is more representative of the time pattern in which the benefit from the leased asset is receivable.' (paragraph 43)   **6**

A lease may be structured in a way that accords with the cash flow needs of the lessee, for example by providing for rental reductions or payments from the lessor when certain costs are incurred by the lessee. An up-front incentive creates a presumption that the subsequent rentals are above the level acceptable to the parties in the market current at the time (even though they may be termed 'market rate'). This is because a lessor's main objective is to obtain the best rent available from the lessee for the property in question and the lessor has no interest in how a lessee spends any up-front incentive paid.   **7**

8   In accordance with the accruals concept, any incentive should be allocated to match the effect of the increased rentals payable in later periods, so that the financial statements reflect the true effective rental for the premises, irrespective of the particular cash flow arrangements agreed between the parties. The accounting treatment should be similar, however the arrangement is structured.

9   Many leases provide for periodic reviews whereby the rental can be adjusted to the prevailing market rate. In such a case it is necessary to recognise the incentive over the period in which, before taking account of the incentive, the rentals will be other than the market rate. This will generally be the period up to the first review date at which the rental being paid is expected to come into line with the prevailing market rate. Neither SSAP 21 nor the Guidance Notes specifically address the situation where rentals are periodically reviewed.

10   SSAP 19 'Accounting for investment properties' requires investment properties to be reported in the balance sheet at their open market value. That value should not include any amount that is reported as a separate asset, for example as accrued rent receivable, if there would be double-counting of assets. For example, a property might have a value of £20 million reflecting, in part, the rents on a lease that has been negotiated with a tenant. However, if a lease incentive (of say £1 million) was given as part of the negotiation of that rent, the open market value to be reported under investment properties would be £19 million, as the other £1 million would be reported as a separate asset.

11   Where a debtor is recognised in respect of an operating lease incentive, the requirements of UITF Abstract 4 'Presentation of long-term debtors in current assets' may be relevant.

APPLICATION TO SMALLER ENTITIES

12   Reporting entities applying the Financial Reporting Standard for Smaller Entities currently applicable are exempt from this Abstract.

UITF CONSENSUS

13   All incentives for the agreement of a new or renewed operating lease should be recognised as an integral part of the net payment agreed for the use of the leased asset, irrespective of the incentive's nature or form or the timing of payments.

Accounting by lessees

14   A lessee should recognise the aggregate benefit of incentives as a reduction of rental expense. The benefit should be allocated over the shorter of the lease term and a period ending on a date from which it is expected the prevailing market rental will be payable. The allocation should be on a straight-line basis unless another systematic basis is more representative of the time pattern of the lessee's benefit from the use of the leased asset.

Accounting by lessors

15   A lessor should recognise the aggregate cost of incentives as a reduction of rental income. The cost of the incentives should be allocated over the lease term or a shorter period ending on a date from which it is expected the prevailing market rental will be payable. The allocation should be on a straight-line basis unless another systematic basis is more representative of the time pattern in which the benefit from the leased asset is receivable.

Where a building is accounted for as an investment property, the value at which it is   **16**
stated in the balance sheet should not include any amount that is reported as a separate asset, for example, as accrued rent receivable.

In accordance with normal accounting practice, an amount recognised as a debtor in   **17**
respect of an operating lease incentive should be written down to the extent that it is not expected to be recovered.

DATE FROM WHICH EFFECTIVE AND WITHDRAWAL OF UITF ABSTRACT 12

The accounting practices set out in this Abstract should be adopted for financial   **18**
statements relating to accounting periods ending on or after 22 September 2001 (including corresponding amounts for the immediately preceding period) in respect of lease agreements commencing in the current or the preceding accounting period. Adoption in respect of earlier lease agreements is permitted but not required.

This Abstract supersedes UITF Abstract 12 'Lessee accounting for reverse premiums   **19**
and similar incentives'.*

REFERENCES

ASB pronouncements
SSAP 19 'Accounting for investment properties', paragraph 11
SSAP 21 'Accounting for leases and hire purchase contracts', paragraphs 37 and 43
FRS 18 'Accounting Policies', paragraphs 26 and 27
UITF Abstract 4 'Presentation of long-term debtors in current assets'

IASC pronouncements
Standing Interpretations Committee, SIC-15 'Operating Leases - Incentives'
IAS 40 'Investment Property', paragraph 44†

---

*UITF Abstract 12 superseded that part of the guidance given in paragraph 16 of the Guidance Notes on SSAP 21 which suggests that the total rentals should be charged 'over the period in which the assets are in use'.

†Editor's note: This is now paragraph 50 of IAS 40 as revised in December 2003.

APPENDIX

Illustrative examples of the consensus in paragraphs 13-17

The examples each assume a lease for five years. It is assumed that a straight-line allocation basis is the most representative of the benefits. The accounting is illustrated from the perspective of the lessor. The lessee's expense would be equivalent to the lessor's income.

(a)   First year rent-free, then four annual rentals of £500

Year	£ Income		£ Cash		£ Debtor	
	For year	Cumulative	Movement in year	Cumulative	Movement in year	Cumulative
1	400	400	—	—	400	400
2	400	800	500	500	(100)	300
3	400	1,200	500	1,000	(100)	200
4	400	1,600	500	1,500	(100)	100
5	400	2,000	500	2,000	(100)	—

(b)   Cash incentive of £1,000 paid, and five rentals of £600

Year	£ Income		£ Cash		£ Debtor	
	For year	Cumulative	Movement in year	Cumulative	Movement in year	Cumulative
1			(1,000) 600		1,000 (600)	
	400	400		(400)	400	800
2			600		(600)	
	400	800		200	400	600
3			600		(600)	
	400	1,200		800	400	400
4			600		(600)	
	400	1,600		1,400	400	200
5			600		(600)	
	400	2,000		2,000	400	—

UITF abstract 29: Website development costs

(Issued February 2001)

THE ISSUE

Websites are used for a wide variety of business purposes, including promotion and   1
advertising of products and services; taking orders for products or services; and
selling access to information that is contained on the Website. Many companies incur
significant costs in developing such Websites.

This Abstract addresses the accounting for the development costs of a Website for a   2
company's own use: it does not address the accounting for the costs of developing a
Website for another entity.

The costs of developing a Website include: 3

(a) *planning costs*—including, for example, the costs of undertaking feasibility
    studies, determining the objectives and functionalities of the Website, exploring
    ways of achieving the desired functionalities, identifying appropriate hardware
    and Web applications and selecting suppliers and consultants.
(b) *application and infrastructure development costs*—including the costs of
    obtaining and registering a domain name and of buying or developing hard-
    ware and operating software that relate to the functionality of the site (for
    example, updateable content management systems and e-commerce systems,
    including encryption software, and interfaces with other IT systems used by the
    entity).
(c) *design costs*—expenditure to develop the design and appearance of individual
    Website pages, including the creation of graphics.
(d) *content costs*—expenditure incurred on preparing, accumulating and posting
    the Website content.

Planning costs do not in themselves give rise to future economic benefits that are   4
controlled by the entity. Such costs should not therefore be capitalised as an asset but
should be charged to the profit and loss account as incurred.

In contrast, the remaining costs of Website development (paragraph 3(b)-(d)) could   5
give rise to an asset, which should be capitalised if the relationship between the
expenditure and the future economic benefits is sufficiently certain.

However, there is often substantial uncertainty regarding the viability, useful eco-   6
nomic life and value of a Website. The UITF took the view that, in relation to
amounts spent on the design and content of a Website (paragraph 3(c) and (d)),
criteria should be established that ensured that the costs would be capitalised only to
the extent that they created an enduring asset and there were reasonable grounds for
supposing that future economic benefits in excess of the amounts capitalised would
be generated by the Website. In the UITF's opinion, this would be the case only if the
Website was capable of generating revenues directly, for example by enabling orders
to be placed.

The UITF considered whether capitalised Website development costs should be   7
regarded as tangible or as intangible fixed assets. It noted that Websites fitted neither
classification perfectly. It also noted the statement in paragraph 2 of FRS 10
'Goodwill and Intangible Assets' that:

'Software development costs that are directly attributable to bringing a computer system or other computer-operated machinery into working condition for its intended use within the business are treated as part of the cost of the related hardware rather than as a separate intangible asset.'

8   The UITF decided that certain Website development costs were of the type that FRS 10 envisaged should be treated as tangible fixed assets. It took the view that the reference to the capitalisation of software development costs applied irrespective of whether the hardware on which the software ran was owned by the entity. It further decided that, in the interests of consistency and clarity, all Website development costs should be classified in the same way – separating the costs into tangible and intangible components could be difficult and would serve no practical purpose.

9   Website development costs are subject to the capitalisation, depreciation and impairment review requirements set out in FRS 15 and FRS 11 'Impairment of Fixed Assets and Goodwill'. They are not regarded as 'development costs' of the type referred to in companies legislation.*

APPLICATION TO SMALLER ENTITIES

10   Reporting entities applying the Financial Reporting Standard for Smaller Entities currently applicable are exempt from this Abstract.

UITF CONSENSUS

11   The UITF reached a consensus that:

(a)   Website *planning* costs should be charged to the profit and loss account as incurred.

(b)   subject to paragraph 12 below, *other Website development costs* should be capitalised as tangible fixed assets, in accordance with the requirements of FRS 15 'Tangible Fixed Assets'.

(c)   expenditure to maintain or operate a Website once it has been developed should be charged to the profit and loss account as incurred, in accordance with the requirements of FRS 15.

12   *Design and content* development costs should be capitalised only to the extent that they lead to the creation of an enduring asset delivering benefits at least as great as the amount capitalised. This will be the case only to the extent that

(a)   the expenditure is separately identifiable;

(b)   the technical feasibility and commercial viability of the Website have been assessed with reasonable certainty in the light of factors such as likely market conditions (including competing products), public opinion, and possible legislation;

(c)   the Website will generate sales or other revenues directly† and the expenditure makes an enduring contribution to the development of the revenue-generating capabilities of the Website;

(d)   there is a reasonable expectation that the present value of the future cash flows (ie future revenues less attributable costs) to be generated by the Website will be

In Great Britain, the Companies Act 1985; in Northern Ireland, the Companies (Northern Ireland) Order 1986; and in the Republic of Ireland, the Companies (Amendment) Act 1986.

†*For not-for-profit entities, an alternative measure of service potential may be more relevant, in which case paragraphs 12, 14 and 15 should be interpreted as permitting capitalisation only to the extent that the primary purpose of the Website is to provide a means of delivery of the specific services offered by the entity in fulfilment of its principal objectives.*

no less than the amounts capitalised in respect of that revenue-generating activity; and

(e) adequate resources exist, or are reasonably expected to be available, to enable the Website project to be completed and to meet any consequential need for increased working capital.

If there is insufficient evidence on which to base reasonable estimates of the economic **13** benefits that will be generated in the period until the design and content are next updated, the costs of developing the design and content should be charged to the profit and loss account as incurred.

Revenues that can be regarded as arising directly from the Website could include **14** those attributable to orders placed via the Website, amounts paid by subscribers for access to information contained on the Website or advertising revenues obtained by selling advertising space on the Website. If a Website is used only for advertising or promotion of the entity's own products or services, it is unlikely to be possible to provide sufficient evidence to demonstrate that future sales or revenue will be generated directly by the Website.

It is possible that revenues expected to arise directly from the Website will include **15** some that would have been achieved by other means in the absence of the Website. In such circumstances, it will be necessary to consider whether other fixed assets have become impaired as a result of the development of the Website.

As required by paragraph 8 of FRS 11 'Impairment of Fixed Assets and Goodwill', **16** capitalised Website development costs should be reviewed for impairment if events or changes in circumstances indicate that the carrying amount may not be recoverable.

Capitalised Website development costs should be depreciated over their estimated **17** useful economic life, which should be selected and reviewed each period in accordance with the requirements of FRS 15. Given the rapid rate of technological innovation, the useful economic life of a Website is likely to be short. Further, where the design or content of a Website requires more frequent replacement than the Website as a whole, it may be appropriate to select a depreciation period for the cost of the design or content that is shorter than the depreciation period selected for the remainder of the asset.

DATE FROM WHICH EFFECTIVE

The accounting treatment required by this Abstract should be adopted in financial **18** statements relating to accounting periods ending on or after 23 March 2001, but earlier adoption is encouraged.

REFERENCES

ASB pronouncements

FRS 10 'Goodwill and Intangible Assets' paragraph 2
FRS 11 'Impairment of Fixed Assets and Goodwill' paragraph 8
FRS 15 'Tangible Fixed Assets'

Other pronouncements

EITF (USA) Abstract No. 00-2 'Accounting for Web Site Development Costs' March 2000

UITF abstract 31: Exchanges of businesses or other non-monetary assets for an interest in a subsidiary, joint venture or associate

(Issued 18 October 2001

BACKGROUND

1   It is becoming increasingly common for reporting entities to exchange businesses for equity, for example by forming a joint venture combining one of their existing businesses with that of another entity. The UITF has been asked to develop guidance on certain issues that arise in accounting for such transactions.

THE ISSUES

2   This Abstract deals with the treatment in consolidated financial statements of transactions in which an entity (A) exchanges a business or other non-monetary assets for an interest in another entity (B) which thereby becomes A's subsidiary or which is or thereby becomes A's joint venture or associate. The Abstract does not prescribe the treatment of barter transactions in general.

3   The issues discussed in this Abstract are:

(a)   should businesses or other non-monetary assets exchanged for an interest in a subsidiary, joint venture or associate be accounted for at fair value at the date of the transaction or at previous book values?

(b)   how should any gain or loss arising on the transaction be reported?

4   The UITF has considered different approaches to these kinds of exchanges and has decided that they should be analysed in terms of net changes in ownership interests. For example, the exchange of a wholly-owned business for a 50 per cent interest in another entity which absorbs that business should be characterised as an exchange of that part of the business where ownership is wholly given up (the 50 per cent interest now belonging to the other party) for the 50 per cent ownership interest acquired in the other entity's pre-transaction business. Under this approach, any part of the business exchanged that is owned by the transferor both directly before the exchange and indirectly thereafter is treated as having been owned throughout the transaction, and therefore remains at book value. The consideration for the interest acquired in the entity will include that part of the business or non-monetary assets no longer owned by the transferor.* The assets acquired consist of the transferor's 50 per cent share in the pre-transaction net assets of the other entity. Where it is difficult to value the consideration given, the best estimate of its value may be given by valuing what is acquired.

5   The UITF noted that in acquisition accounting, accounting standards and companies legislation require the consideration to be stated at fair value and fair values to be ascribed to the separable assets and liabilities acquired, any difference arising being goodwill. This applies whether the investee is a subsidiary, an associate or a joint venture.

6   If the fair value of the consideration received exceeds the book value of the part of the business or non-monetary assets no longer owned by the transferor (and any related goodwill) together with any cash given up, the transferor will record a gain.

The consideration may also include cash or monetary assets to achieve equalisation of values.

In the reverse case, the transferor will record a loss. To the extent that the transferor group retains an interest in a business or non-monetary assets after a transaction covered by this Abstract, even if then held through a different subsidiary or a joint venture or associate, that interest should be included at its pre-transaction carrying amount. The assets acquired through the interest in the entity will be accounted for at fair value and any goodwill arising will be recorded.

The UITF noted that International Accounting Standards require recognition of the   7
portion of a gain or loss attributable to the equity interests of other venturers when non-monetary assets are contributed to a jointly controlled entity in exchange for an equity interest in that entity (SIC-13 'Jointly Controlled Entities – Non-Monetary Contributions by Venturers'). This is subject to limited exceptions, one of which is where the non-monetary assets contributed are 'similar' to those contributed by the other venturers. However, the UITF noted the intended narrowness of the exception because 'similar' is restrictively defined to mean having a similar nature, a similar use in the same line of business and a similar fair value.

The UITF concluded that the only exception to the use of fair values in the trans-   8
actions covered by this Abstract would be rare cases where the transaction is artificial or has no substance such that a gain or loss would be recognised that could not be justified. For example, an exchange might purport to give rise to a recognisable gain even though the assets exchanged would be unlikely otherwise to be saleable. In such a case, no gain should be recognised. Where a gain or loss on exchange is not taken into account because of special circumstances, those circumstances should be explained.

The UITF took the view that any unrealised gain arising on the transactions that are   9
the subject of the Abstract should be reported in the statement of total recognised gains and losses. Where a loss arises, all relevant assets should first be reviewed for impairment with any impairment identified accounted for as required by FRS 11 'Impairment of Fixed Assets and Goodwill'. Any remaining loss should be recorded in the profit and loss account. Where an impairment has been identified, similar assets should also be reviewed for impairment.

APPLICATION TO SMALLER ENTITIES

Reporting entities applying the Financial Reporting Standard for Smaller Entities   10
currently applicable are exempt from this Abstract.

UITF CONSENSUS

The UITF reached a consensus that where an entity (A) exchanges a business or   11
other non-monetary assets for an interest in another entity (B), which thereby becomes A's subsidiary or which is or thereby becomes A's joint venture or associate, the following accounting treatment should apply in A's consolidated financial statements:

(a) to the extent that A retains an ownership interest in a business or non-monetary assets exchanged for an interest in B after such a transaction, even if that business or non-monetary assets is then held through B as a subsidiary, joint venture or associate, that retained interest, including any related goodwill, should be included at its pre-transaction carrying amount.

(b) A's share of net assets acquired through its new interest in B should be accounted for at fair value, with the difference between these and the fair value of the consideration given being accounted for as goodwill.

(c)   to the extent that the fair value of the consideration received by A exceeds the book value of the part of the business or non-monetary assets no longer owned by A (and any related goodwill*) together with any cash given up, A should recognise a gain. Any gain arising on the exchange that is not realised should be reported in A's statement of total recognised gains and losses.

(d)   where the fair value of the consideration received by A is less than the book value of the part of the business or non-monetary assets no longer owned by A (and any related goodwill) together with any cash given up, A should recognise a loss, either as an impairment in accordance with FRS 11 or, for any loss remaining after an impairment review of the relevant assets, in A's profit and loss account.

12   No gain or loss should be recognised in those rare cases where the artificiality or lack of substance of the transaction is such that any gain or loss on the exchange could not be justified. Where a gain or loss on the exchange is not taken into account because the transaction is artificial or has no substance, the circumstances should be explained.

DATE FROM WHICH EFFECTIVE

13   The accounting treatment required by this Abstract should be adopted in respect of transactions first accounted for in financial statements relating to accounting periods commencing on or after 23 December 2001, but earlier adoption is encouraged.

REFERENCES

Legislation

Great Britain and Northern Ireland
Companies Act 1985 and Companies (Northern Ireland) Order 1986
Schedule 4A paragraph 9

Republic of Ireland
European Communities (Companies: Group Accounts) Regulations 1992 Regulation 19

Accounting standards

FRS 2 'Accounting for Subsidiary Undertakings' paragraphs 51 and 91
FRS 6 'Acquisitions and Mergers' paragraph 20
FRS 7 'Fair Values in Acquisition Accounting' paragraph 26
FRS 9 'Associates and Joint Ventures' paragraph 31(a)
FRS 10 'Goodwill and Intangible Assets' paragraph 68

Other pronouncements
IASC Standing Interpretations Committee SIC-13 'Jointly Controlled Entities – Non-Monetary Contributions by Venturers'

**These amounts will include any related goodwill written off under SSAP 22 'Accounting for goodwill' and not reinstated in accordance with the transitional arrangements of FRS 10 'Goodwill and Intangible Assets'.*

UITF abstract 32: Employee benefit trusts and other intermediate payment arrangements

(Issued December 2001)

SCOPE

This Abstract deals with intermediate payment arrangements as described in para- **1** graphs 2-3 below. Although employee share ownership plans (ESOPs) are an example of intermediate payment arrangements, this Abstract does not apply to them because there is already a UITF Abstract on the subject (UITF Abstract 13 'Accounting for ESOP Trusts'). Similarly, pension funds, another example of intermediate payment arrangements, are not dealt with in this Abstract because they are the subject of an accounting standard (FRS 17 'Retirement Benefits').*

BACKGROUND

In a typical employee benefit trust, an entity makes payments to a trust, the bene- **2** ficiaries of which are to be the entity's employees, and the trust then uses assets accumulated from those payments to pay the entity's employees for some or all of the employee services they have rendered to the entity.

The arrangement described in paragraph 2 is only one example of an 'intermediate **3** payment arrangement'. Such arrangements may take a variety of forms.

(a) Although the intermediary is usually constituted as a trust, other arrangements are possible.

(b) Although such arrangements are most commonly used to pay employees, they are sometimes used to compensate suppliers of goods and services other than employee services. Sometimes the sponsoring entity's employees and other suppliers are not the only beneficiaries of the arrangement. Other beneficiaries may include past employees and their dependants, and the intermediary may be entitled to make charitable donations.

(c) Usually, the precise identity of the persons or entities that will receive payments from the intermediary, and the amounts that they will receive, are not agreed at the outset.

(d) The relationship between the sponsoring entity and the intermediary may take different forms. For example, when the intermediary is constituted as a trust, the sponsoring entity will not have a right to direct the intermediary's activities. However, in these and other cases the sponsoring entity may give advice to the intermediary or may be relied on by the intermediary to provide the infor- mation it needs to carry out its activities. Sometimes, the way the intermediary has been set up gives it little discretion in the broad nature of its activities.

(e) Often, the sponsoring entity has the right to appoint or veto the appointment of the intermediary's trustees (or its directors or the equivalent).

(f) The payments made to the intermediary and the payments made by the intermediary are often cash payments but may involve other transfers of value.

THE ISSUES

This Abstract addresses two accounting issues that arise when intermediate payment **4** arrangements are entered into:

Editor's note: UITF 13 has now been replaced by UITF 38. FRS 17 came into force in 2005.

(a)   whether the sponsoring entity's payments to the intermediary represent an immediate expense of the entity; and

(b)   if the payments do not represent an immediate expense, what is the nature and extent of the sponsoring entity's assets and liabilities after making the payment to the intermediary.

Does the sponsoring entity's payment to the intermediary represent an immediate expense?

5   Generally speaking, most expenses are incurred not when they are paid for but when a liability arises. For example, when an entity receives cleaning services the expense arises as it receives those services not when it pays for them, regardless of whether the services are paid for before they are received or after they have been received.

6   That is also the case for goods and services (including employee services) paid for through an intermediate payment arrangement. For example, with an employee benefit trust, generally speaking:

(a)   the expense will be incurred when a liability for the employee costs arises. This will only coincidentally be when payment is made to the intermediary;

(b)   the payment made by the intermediary will either settle a liability or will be made in advance of the liability arising (ie it will be a prepayment); and

(c)   the payment made to the intermediary will involve the exchange of one asset for another.

7   A payment made to an intermediary will represent an immediate expense of the sponsoring entity only if the payment neither results in the acquisition of another asset (for example, restricted cash or a prepayment) nor settles a liability. Whether a payment involves the full or partial settlement of a liability is a matter of fact and is not considered in this Abstract. The Abstract focuses instead on whether the payment involves the acquisition of another asset.

8   An asset is defined in the Statement of Principles for Financial Reporting as a right or other access to future economic benefits that is controlled by the entity as a result of a past transaction or event. The attributes of an asset are therefore the access to future economic benefits and the control of that access.

(a)   Future economic benefit can be obtained in a variety of forms. In the context of intermediate payment arrangements, probably the most common form the benefit takes is meeting some or all of the cost of goods or services provided to the sponsoring entity. That benefit can be the basis for an asset even though it is not capable of being turned into cash or of being distributed in a liquidation.

(b)   Control comprises two abilities, the ability to direct and the ability to benefit from that direction. Although control is probably most visible when it is exerted through intervention and instruction on an ongoing day-to-day basis, it can be present in a variety of other guises. For example, even though a sponsoring entity of an intermediate payment arrangement involving a trust does not have the right to dictate to trustees how they should exercise their responsibilities under a trust, it may still, as Abstract 13 makes clear, have de facto control of that trust's assets and liabilities. Although Abstract 13 focuses on ESOP trusts, it is based upon the wider principles of FRS 5 'Reporting the Substance of Transactions' and its analysis, explanations and conclusions are relevant in analogous circumstances such as when other intermediate payment arrangements are involved.

FRS 5 requires that, when determining whether an entity has an asset, one should   **9**
look beyond the structure of the transaction to consider its substance; in other
words, consideration should be given to the commercial effect of the transaction in
practice. Recognising that it is highly unusual for an entity to pay a significant
amount to a third party without receiving something in return, the UITF takes the
view that, when an entity transfers funds to an intermediary, there should be a
rebuttable presumption that the sponsoring entity will obtain future economic
benefit from the amounts transferred and that it has control of the rights or other
access to those future economic benefits.

To rebut this presumption at the time the payment is made to the intermediary, it will   **10**
be necessary to demonstrate that either:

(a)   the sponsoring entity will not obtain future economic benefit from the amounts
      transferred. For example, it may be that the only beneficiaries of the inter-
      mediary are registered charities or a benevolent fund that is in no way linked to
      amounts otherwise due from the entity; or
(b)   the sponsoring entity does not have control of the rights or other access to the
      future economic benefits it is expected to receive. This will involve evidence that
      the payments made by the intermediary are not habitually made in a way that is
      in accordance with the sponsoring entity's wishes.

The presumption of future economic benefit would not be rebutted where payments   **11**
by the intermediary served to relieve the sponsoring entity from paying for such
items as retirement benefit increases or benefits in kind (for example, medical
insurance cover).

The presumption of control would be rebutted at the time the payment is made to the   **12**
intermediary if at that time the asset(s) transferred to the intermediary vest unconditionally in identified beneficiaries.

If, and to the extent that, the sponsoring entity has obtained rights or other access to   **13**
future economic benefit over which it has control through its payment to the
intermediary, the payment will involve an exchange of one asset for another and no
immediate expense will be incurred.

***If the sponsoring entity's payment to the intermediary does not represent an immediate
expense, what is the nature and extent of its assets and liabilities after the payment?***

As explained above, if a payment made by a sponsoring entity to an intermediary   **14**
involves an exchange of one asset for another, that will be because, despite paying
money to the intermediary, the sponsoring entity continues to have the benefit of that
money and to have control of that benefit; in other words, the amount paid to the
intermediary remains an asset of the sponsoring entity despite being in the intermediary's possession. That will remain the case if the intermediary then exchanges
some or all of that amount for other assets. The UITF takes the view that, in such
circumstances, the sponsoring entity has de facto control of the intermediary's assets
and should, as a result, account for the intermediary as an extension of its own
business. The intermediary's assets, and any liabilities that it has, should therefore be
recognised as assets and liabilities of the sponsoring entity. The subsequent
accounting for those assets and liabilities and for expense recognition should follow
the normal accounting rules. Accordingly, an asset held by the intermediary would
cease to be recognised as an asset of the sponsoring entity when, for example, it vests
unconditionally in identified beneficiaries.

15   Abstract 13 concludes that the assets and liabilities of most ESOP trusts are under the de facto control of the sponsoring company. The UITF is of the view that the reasoning that leads to that conclusion—and the conclusion itself—applies equally to the assets and liabilities of most employee benefit trusts.

APPLICATION TO SMALLER ENTITIES

16   Reporting entities applying the Financial Reporting Standard for Smaller Entities currently applicable are exempt from this Abstract.

UITF CONSENSUS

17   This UITF consensus applies to all intermediate payment arrangements other than those dealt with in Abstract 13 or FRS 17.*

18   The UITF reached a consensus that, when an entity transfers funds to an intermediary, there should be a rebuttable presumption that the sponsoring entity has exchanged one asset for another and that the payment itself does not represent an immediate expense.

19   Where a payment to an intermediary is an exchange by the sponsoring entity of one asset for another, any assets that the intermediary acquires in a subsequent exchange transaction will also be under the de facto control of the sponsoring entity. The intermediary's assets, and any liabilities that it has, should therefore be recognised as assets and liabilities of the sponsoring entity. The subsequent accounting for those assets and liabilities and for expense recognition should follow the normal accounting rules. Accordingly, an asset held by the intermediary would cease to be recognised as an asset of the sponsoring entity when, for example, it vests unconditionally in identified beneficiaries.

20   When an entity recognises the assets and liabilities held by an intermediary on its balance sheet, it should disclose sufficient information in the notes to its financial statements to enable readers to understand any restrictions relating to those assets and liabilities.

DATE FROM WHICH EFFECTIVE

21   The accounting treatment required by this Abstract should be adopted in financial statements relating to accounting periods ending on or after 23 December 2001, but earlier adoption is encouraged. Where applicable, corresponding amounts should be restated.

REFERENCES

ASB pronouncements

Statement of Principles for Financial Reporting, paragraphs 4.6 and 4.39
FRS 5 'Reporting the Substance of Transactions', paragraphs 14, 16, 20 and 54
FRS 17 'Retirement Benefits'
UITF Abstract 13 'Accounting for ESOP Trusts', paragraph 2(d) and the appendix†

Editor's note: UITF 13 has now been replaced by UITF 38. FRS 17 came into force in 2005.

†*Editor's note: UITF 13 has now been replaced by UITF 38.*

UITF abstract 34: Pre-contract costs

(Issued May 2002)

THE ISSUE

Entities in some industries incur significant costs in bidding for and securing con- **1**
tracts to supply products or services. Examples are entities that supply property and
services under the Private Finance Initiative, Public-Private Partnerships, out-
sourcing and similar arrangements. Where a bid is successful, the entity will often
have incurred significant costs before the contract is signed. There has been uncertainty over whether such costs should be recognised as an asset (and charged as
expenses during the period of the contract) or charged as immediate expenses, and
diverse accounting treatments have developed in practice.

The issues are: **2**

(a)   Should pre-contract costs be recognised as an asset?
(b)   If so, how should the asset be measured?

This Abstract addresses the accounting by the supplier for the costs of tendering for **3**
and securing contracts (referred to herein as pre-contract costs). The Abstract applies
to costs relating to contracts for the design, construction, manufacture or operation
of assets or for the provision of services or a combination of assets and services. The
Abstract does not, however, prescribe the accounting treatment of

(a)   costs that are subject to the more specific requirements of accounting standards
      (such as FRS 4 *Capital Instruments*, FRS 10 *Goodwill and Intangible Assets*, FRS 15
      Tangible Fixed Assets or SSAP 13 *Accounting for research and development*) or
(b)   the costs of acquiring insurance policies in the financial statements of insurance
      entities (covered by Schedule 9A to the Companies Act 1985).

Prospective amendment: The draft FRS 'Financial Instruments: Disclosure and presentation' in FRED 30 'Financial Instruments: Disclosure and presentation,
Recognition and measurement' supersedes FRS 4, following publication in final form.

SHOULD PRE-CONTRACT COSTS BE RECOGNISED AS AN ASSET?

Assets are defined in the Statement of Principles for Financial Reporting as 'rights or **4**
other access to future economic benefits controlled by an entity as a result of past
transactions or events'. An asset is recognised in financial statements only if there is
sufficient evidence that the asset has been created (including, where appropriate, that
a future inflow of benefit will occur) and it can be measured with sufficient reliability.

The UITF takes the view that pre-contract costs are not start-up costs covered by **5**
UITF Abstract 24 *Accounting for start-up costs*; rather they are part of the ongoing
costs of obtaining contracts. The activity of bidding for contracts does not necessarily, however, give rise to rights or access to future economic benefits that are
controlled by the entity. Control is defined in FRS 5 as 'the ability to obtain the future
economic benefits relating to an asset and to restrict the access of others to those
benefits'. Where it is merely possible that a contract will be awarded there is no
control over future economic benefits, although there may well be an expectation
that such benefits will accrue to the entity.

6   It follows that, at the stage where an entity has obtained the right to bid for a contract, it does not yet have an asset that should be recognised in the financial statements. That is the case even where a bid is part of a portfolio of bids that an entity undertakes in the expectation that at least some will result in profitable contracts. The recognition of an asset in the financial statements reflects an economically significant event, being the point at which control is obtained over the rights or access to future economic benefits from the award of a contract. Expenditure that is invested in tendering for a contract before that event occurs is not an asset that is recognised in financial statements.

7   The UITF took the view that, in this context, control does not arise before it is virtually certain that a contract will be awarded. Until the award of a contract is virtually certain there will not be sufficient evidence that an asset has been created. The exact point when the award of a contract becomes virtually certain – and pre-contract costs should be recognised as an asset – will depend on the particular circumstances of the case. The requirement for control means that only one competing bidder can recognise an asset that reflects rights or access to the future economic benefits from a contract. It would therefore be essential, but not necessarily sufficient, that there are no other bidders in competition – for example, where the entity has been appointed sole preferred bidder giving it exclusive rights to negotiate the contract terms with the purchaser. In addition, the award of the contract should be expected within a reasonable timescale and the proposed contractual arrangements should have been specified in sufficient detail to provide evidence that the pre-contract costs recognised as an asset will be recovered from the contract's net cash inflows. Virtual certainty is not achieved if the award of a contract is subject to uncertain future events not wholly within the control of the entity or the purchaser (such as the need for regulatory approval or the likelihood of legal challenge).

HOW SHOULD THE ASSET BE MEASURED?

8   The UITF takes the view that costs should be recognised as an asset only if they are directly attributable to a specific contract, can be separately identified and can be measured reliably.

9   The UITF considered three approaches to measuring an asset when the recognition criteria are met:

(i)   Only pre-contract costs incurred from the date the asset recognition criteria are met are recognised as an asset. This means that pre-contract costs incurred before then (for example, during the competitive tendering stage) are recognised as expenses as incurred and are not subsequently reinstated as an asset.

(ii)   All previously incurred pre-contract costs (ie including those charged as expenses in previous years' financial statements) are reinstated as part of the cost of the asset when the asset recognition criteria are met.

(iii)   All pre-contract costs incurred within the accounting period in which the asset recognition criteria are met are recognised as part of the cost of the asset. This means that costs that have been charged as expenses in previous years' financial statements are not reinstated as part of the cost of the asset when the contract is obtained in a subsequent financial year.

10   Some commentators believe that all previously incurred pre-contract costs should be reinstated as part of the cost of the asset (and credited in the profit and loss account) when the asset recognition criteria are met. In their view, it is more meaningful to recognise as an asset all the costs that have been incurred in creating it than to recognise only those costs incurred in the later stages of the bid. Some proponents of that view believe that in essence an asset arises from the start of the bidding process but that full provision is made against the asset until there is sufficient certainty of recovery, when the provision is released. As noted earlier, the UITF took the view that no recognisable asset arises until there is virtual certainty that a contract will be awarded. Costs incurred before then are recognised as expenses, not as assets (or assets that are fully provided against); once an item is recognised as an expense in the profit and loss account, it is not subsequently credited in the profit and loss account in order to be charged as an expense again (as cost of sales) in future periods. The UITF also noted that International Accounting Standards do not allow costs incurred in securing a contract that are recognised as expenses when they are incurred to be recognised as part of the cost of an asset when the contract is obtained in a subsequent period.

Some other commentators agree that it is not appropriate to allow costs that have **11** been recognised as expenses in previous accounting periods to be recognised as an asset in a subsequent period, but believe that all directly attributable costs incurred during the period in which the asset recognition criteria are met should be recognised as part of the cost of the asset. The UITF took the view that this approach too is inconsistent with the principles for asset recognition. Furthermore, under such a system the accounting information would lack comparability where the bidding process extended over more than one accounting period; that is because the amounts of costs reported as expenses or assets would vary depending on how early or late in the accounting period the asset recognition criteria were met.

The UITF took the view that the approach in paragraph 9(i) is consistent with the **12** criteria for asset recognition set out in paragraphs 4 to 7 above. Costs incurred before the event that gives rise to a recognisable asset in relation to the award of a contract are recognised as expenses because they do not meet the definition of an asset when they are incurred.

Sometimes a consortium of bidders will form a special-purpose entity to undertake **13** the contract and the consortium members may transfer pre-contract costs to that entity when the contract is signed. The amount recovered by a consortium member from the special-purpose entity at the inception of the contract may exceed the amount of pre-contract costs that have been recognised as an asset under the principles in this Abstract (as, for example, where the amount recovered takes account of pre-contract costs incurred before the asset recognition criteria were met). The accounting by the consortium members for the recovery of pre-contract costs from the special-purpose entity should reflect the principles in this Abstract (in particular, that costs incurred and written off as an expense before the asset recognition criteria are met are not subsequently reinstated as an asset), having regard to the substance of the arrangement. Where the special-purpose entity is an associate or joint venture, the recovery of an amount that exceeds the amount of pre-contract costs recognised as an asset does not result in an immediate gain in a consortium member's consolidated financial statements to the extent that the substance is a financing arrangement. This will usually be the case unless the original consortium members rearrange or dispose of their interests in the special-purpose entity.

APPLICATION TO SMALLER ENTITIES

Reporting entities applying the Financial Reporting Standard for Smaller Entities **14** currently applicable are exempt from this Abstract.

UITF CONSENSUS

The UITF reached a consensus that: **15**

(a)   Pre-contract costs should be recognised as expenses as incurred, except that directly attributable costs should be recognised as an asset when it is virtually certain that a contract will be obtained and the contract is expected to result in future net cash inflows (ie future revenues less attributable costs) with a present value no less than all amounts recognised as an asset.

(b)   Costs incurred before the asset recognition criteria in (a) above are met should not be recognised as an asset then or later.

(c)   Directly attributable costs are costs that relate directly to securing the specific contract after the asset recognition criteria in (a) above are met, if they can be separately identified and measured reliably.

(d)   The accounting by consortium members for the recovery of pre-contract costs from a special-purpose entity should reflect the principles set out in (a) to (c) above.

DATE FROM WHICH EFFECTIVE

16   The accounting treatment required by this Abstract should be adopted in financial statements relating to accounting periods ending on or after 22 June 2002, but earlier adoption is encouraged.

REFERENCES

ASB pronouncements

Statement of Principles for Financial Reporting, Chapters 4 and 5
FRS 5 *Reporting the Substance of Transactions*, paragraphs 2 and 20
UITF Abstract 24 *Accounting for start-up costs*

Other pronouncements

IAS 11 'Construction Contracts', paragraph 21
IAS 38 'Intangible Assets', paragraphs 53–55 and 59*

---

*Editor's note: These have been moved to paragraphs 65-67 and 71 of IAS 38, as amended in March 2004.

UITF abstract 35: Death-in-service and incapacity benefits

(Issued May 2002)

THE ISSUE

An issue has been raised on the application of paragraphs 73 and 74 of FRS 17   **1**
'Retirement Benefits'. The issue is how an entity should recognise the cost of providing death-in-service and incapacity benefits where the benefits are provided
through a defined benefit pension scheme. Such benefits may include lump sum
payments and pensions that become payable to employees' dependants.

The principles of FRS 17 view the obligation to pay pensions as covering the period of   **2**
an employee's service; the scheme liability is an accrual at the reporting date of a
portion of those total benefits. Those principles are reflected in the requirement in
paragraphs 20 and 22 of FRS 17 for defined benefit scheme liabilities to be measured
on an actuarial basis using the projected unit method. If those principles were
applied to accounting for death-in-service and incapacity benefits that are provided
through a defined benefit pension scheme, the scheme liability would include a
portion of the estimated cost of paying benefits in respect of employees who are
expected to die or become incapacitated between the reporting date and the date of
leaving service.

Paragraphs 73 and 74 of FRS 17 are as follows: **3**

73 A charge should be made to operating profit to reflect the expected cost of
providing any death-in-service or incapacity benefits for the period. Any difference
between that expected cost and amounts actually incurred should be treated as an
actuarial gain or loss.

74 Where a scheme insures the death-in-service costs, the expected cost for the
accounting period is simply the premium payable for the period. Where the costs are
not insured, the expected cost reflects the probability of any employees dying in the
period and the benefit that would then be paid out.

The effect of applying paragraphs 73 and 74 is that the liability for death-in-service
and incapacity benefits would include the estimated cost of paying benefits only in
respect of employees that have died or become incapacitated by the reporting date.

The UITF was asked to consider the application of these paragraphs where death-in-   **4**
service and incapacity benefits are provided through a defined benefit pension
scheme. The UITF took the view that where the costs of death-in-service and
incapacity benefits are not insured and are provided through a defined benefit pension scheme, the scheme liability and the cost should be measured in accordance with
paragraphs 20 and 22 of FRS 17, ie using the projected unit method. The effect is that
the valuation of uninsured benefits reflects the current period's portion of the full
benefits ultimately payable in respect of current members of the scheme; the cost of
insured benefits is determined by the relevant insurance premiums. The UITF considered that, in valuing the scheme liability for a defined benefit pension scheme, the
actuary will allow for the possibility that some employees will die or become incapacitated before they leave service (and that future pension payments will be reduced
accordingly). The UITF concluded that it would be inappropriate for the benefits
that would then become payable to be excluded from the valuation.

UITF CONSENSUS

5   The UITF reached a consensus that the cost of providing death-in-service and incapacity benefits should be recognised in accordance with paragraphs 73 and 74 of FRS 17, except where the benefits are provided through a defined benefit pension scheme and are not wholly insured, in which case the uninsured scheme liability and the cost for the accounting period should be measured by applying the principles in paragraphs 20 and 22 of FRS 17.

DATE FROM WHICH EFFECTIVE

6   The accounting treatment required by this consensus should be adopted as soon as practicable, but in any event in financial statements relating to accounting periods ending on or after 22 June 2002.

REFERENCES

FRS 17 'Retirement Benefits' – paragraphs 20, 22, 73, 74.

UITF abstract 36: Contracts for sales of capacity

(Issued March 2003)

THE ISSUE

Entities in some industries enter into contracts that convey the right to use some or   **1**
all of the capacity of a physical asset. Examples are found in the telecommunications
and electricity industries where entities buy and sell capacity on each others' networks. Whilst the capacity provider will retain ownership of the network assets,
some contracts convey indefeasible rights of use (usually referred to as IRUs) to the
buyer for an agreed period of time. Some contracts convey the right to use identifiable physical assets (or identifiable physical components of larger infrastructure
assets); others convey the right to use a specified amount of capacity, defined in terms
of an asset's output, rather than the right to use a specific physical item. The UITF
decided that it should develop guidance on certain issues that arise in accounting for
such transactions.

In this Abstract the parties to a contract that conveys a right of use are referred to as   **2**
'seller' and 'buyer', notwithstanding that analysis of the transaction may have the
effect that the 'seller' continues to recognise the asset in its balance sheet.

The issues addressed in this Abstract are: **3**

(a) Should the seller report the transaction as a sale (thereby derecognising an asset
    or a component of a larger asset), or should the seller continue to recognise
    existing assets in their entirety (thereby recognising income over the life of the
    contract)?
(b) In the performance statements, should the seller present gains and losses arising
    from the transaction as operating revenues and costs or as gains and losses on
    the disposal of fixed assets?
(c) How should transactions be accounted for where, rather than selling capacity
    for cash (or the right to receive cash), an entity exchanges capacity on its own
    network for capacity on another entity's network?

DERECOGNITION ISSUE

Contracts that convey rights of use are in many respects akin to leases. SSAP 21   **4**
Accounting for leases and hire purchase contracts defines a lease as:

> 'a contract between a lessor and a lessee for the hire of a specific asset. The lessor
> retains ownership of the asset but conveys the right to the use of the asset to the
> lessee for an agreed period of time in return for the payment of specified rentals.
> The term 'lease' as used in this statement also applies to other arrangements in
> which one party retains ownership of an asset but conveys the right to the use of
> the asset to another party for an agreed period of time in return for specified
> payments'.

From the lessor's perspective, SSAP 21 precludes accounting for the lease as a sale
(thereby derecognising the asset that is the subject of the lease) unless the lease is a
finance lease, ie 'a lease that transfers substantially all the risks and rewards of
ownership of an asset to the lessee'. Assets held under operating leases should
continue to be recognised in their entirety (as fixed assets) and rental income from the
lease should be recognised (normally on a straight-line basis) over the period of the
lease.

5   The derecognition principles in FRS 5 *Reporting the Substance of Transactions* (paragraph 22) require that a previously recognised asset should cease to be recognised (and should, therefore, be accounted for as an outright sale) where the transaction transfers (a) all significant rights or other access to benefits relating to that asset, and (b) all significant exposure to the risks inherent in those benefits. FRS 5 also addresses (in paragraph 23) special cases where transactions do not completely transfer all significant benefits and risks, but nonetheless result in a significant change in an entity's rights to benefits and exposure to risks. In such cases an entity needs to consider whether the description or monetary amount of the asset needs to be changed and also whether a liability needs to be recognised for any obligations assumed or risks retained. A contract that transfers an item for all of its life but where the seller retains some significant right to benefits or exposure to risk is an example of such special cases. Paragraph 24 of FRS 5 emphasises that where the amount of any resulting gain or loss is uncertain, full provision should be made for any probable loss but recognition of any gain, to the extent it is in doubt, should be deferred.

6   Derecognition of an asset by the seller and recognition of the same asset by the buyer implies that control is transferred to the buyer. Control is defined in FRS 5 as 'the ability to obtain the future economic benefits relating to an asset and to restrict the access of others to those benefits'.

7   It follows from the principles in FRS 5 and SSAP 21 that the criteria for derecognition in relation to a contract for rights of use cannot be satisfied unless a specific asset component can be identified as having been 'sold' to the buyer. The UITF considers that the purchaser's right of use should be exclusive and irrevocable, such that no other party, including the seller, would have the right to use the capacity that is the subject of the contract, even if the buyer is not using it. The term of the contract should be for a major part of the asset's useful economic life. An asset component might be tangibly separable (such as a specific cable or specific fibres) or the technology might allow an asset component to be intangibly separable (such as a specific wavelength); however, in either case the buyer's exclusivity must be guaranteed. If the seller had the right to perform its contractual obligations to deliver capacity by substituting other assets, the contract would not convey the right to use a specific asset and would not, therefore, qualify to be reported as the sale of an asset.

8   Where the capacity 'sold' is part of a larger infrastructure, it may be difficult to measure its cost or carrying value reliably, with the result that any gain or loss that would be recognised would be uncertain. Where the cost or carrying value cannot be measured reliably, the UITF takes the view that a specific asset component cannot be identified and the seller should not report the transaction as the sale of an asset.

9   In contracts for rights to use components of networks, the seller will often have some continuing involvement in making the asset available to the buyer, which may result in the seller retaining significant risks. In practical terms, this means there is no sale. The following are examples of risks that, if they are significant and are borne by the seller, serve as indicators that the seller should continue to recognise an asset in its entirety:
    (a)   risk of changes in asset value;
    (b)   risk of obsolescence or changes in technology;
    (c)   risk of damage;
    (d)   risk of unsatisfactory performance (arising, for example, from performance guarantees);

(e)   risks relating to the seller's obligations to provide continuing access by operating and maintaining the assets (arising, for example, from exposure to costs that cannot be recovered from the buyer).

PERFORMANCE REPORTING ISSUE

As discussed above, some contracts for sales of capacity result in the seller continuing to recognise existing assets in their entirety. Income from the contract is then recognised over the life of the contract. Both income and expenses (including depreciation of the relevant fixed assets) are reported in operating results in accordance with FRS3 *Reporting Financial Performance*.

10

Other contracts are reported as sales of assets. It is necessary to determine whether the asset that is the subject of such a contract is a fixed asset or a current asset (ie stock). The classification determines whether any gain or loss is reported as a profit or loss on the disposal of a fixed asset or whether the sale proceeds and the costs of sale are reported respectively as turnover and operating costs.*

11

FRS 15's definition of tangible fixed assets refers to assets 'held for use in the production or supply of goods or services, for rental to others, or for administrative purposes on a continuing basis in the reporting entity's activities'. The business models of some entities include investment in capacity for resale as well as for use in the supply of services, such that similar assets may be held as current assets and fixed assets. The UITF takes the view that proceeds from disposals should not be reported in turnover unless the assets were designated as held for resale (and classified as stock) when they were acquired or on completion of construction. Capacity that was acquired or constructed to be used to supply ongoing services should not be transferred from fixed assets to stocks if capacity subsequently becomes surplus to the business' own requirements.

12

If sales of assets are reported in operating results, and within the same reportable segment as the supply of ongoing services, the UITF takes the view that an analysis of turnover and profits should be clearly disclosed.

13

EXCHANGE TRANSACTIONS

An entity may sell capacity on a network in exchange for receiving capacity on another entity's network. In some cases the two capacities are of a similar value and little or no cash is exchanged. In other cases, capacity is sold wholly or in part for cash (or the right to receive cash) and a separate agreement is entered into with the buyer at approximately the same time to purchase capacity of a similar value. Such cases are referred to in this Abstract as 'reciprocal transactions' where this reflects the substance of the transaction, even though the agreements may contain no reference to reciprocity.

14

No accounting recognition should be given to transactions that are artificial or lacking in substance, which would be the case, for example, if exchange or reciprocal transactions were entered into for capacity for which the transacting parties had no current need and which would be unlikely otherwise to be saleable. Accordingly, in the following discussion it is assumed that there is a proper commercial rationale for

15

Treating proceeds of sale of fixed assets as turnover would contravene FRS 3. Paragraph 20 requires profit or losses on the disposal of fixed assets (except for marginal adjustments to depreciation) to be shown after operating profit.

entering into exchange or reciprocal transactions and that they provide economic benefits to the transacting parties.

16   The derecognition issues considered in paragraphs 4 to 9 above are relevant in determining whether or not capacity provided in an exchange transaction should be accounted for as the sale of an asset or the provision of a service. If the appropriate treatment is to report the sale of an asset, the presentation issues considered in paragraphs 10 to 13 above are relevant in determining how recognised gains and losses, if any, should be presented in the performance statements. If continued recognition is the appropriate treatment, turnover, if any, is recognised over the life of the contract. Recognition of gains and turnover is, however, subject to the criteria set out below.

17   The recognition criteria in the *Statement of Principles for Financial Reporting* require (a) sufficient evidence and (b) measurement at a monetary amount with sufficient reliability. Where a contract to provide capacity is for a cash consideration, the transaction evidences the fair value of the asset or services provided. In contrast, measurement of the fair value of the asset or services provided (and received) is much more difficult where capacity is provided in exchange for capacity received. Where reciprocal transactions are entered into, an exchange of cash between the transacting parties for equal or substantially equal amounts does not provide reliable evidence of fair value. An exchange that involves part cash consideration does not provide reliable evidence of the fair value of the entire transaction.

18   The UITF decided that it would be appropriate to recognise turnover or gains in respect of exchange and reciprocal transactions only if fair value can be determined by reference to observable transactions in an active market, ie where the assets or services provided or received have a readily ascertainable market value as defined in FRS10 *Goodwill and Intangible Assets*.

APPLICATION TO SMALLER ENTITIES

19   Reporting entities applying the *Financial Reporting Standard for Smaller Entities* currently applicable are exempt from this Abstract.

UITF CONSENSUS

20   A seller of a right to use capacity should not report the transaction as the sale of an asset, or of a component of a larger asset, unless:

   (a)   the purchaser's right of use is exclusive and irrevocable;
   (b)   the asset component is specific and separable (such that the buyer's exclusivity is guaranteed and the seller has no right to substitute other assets);
   (c)   the term of the contract is for a major part of the asset's useful economic life;
   (d)   the attributable cost or carrying value can be measured reliably; and
   (e)   no significant risks, as indicated in paragraph 9, are retained by the seller.

21   Where a transaction is reported as the sale of an asset, the proceeds should be reported as turnover only if the assets were designated as held for resale (and classified as stock) when they were acquired or on completion of construction. Otherwise such transactions should be reported as disposals of fixed assets.

22   Where transactions are reported as asset sales in operating results, amounts included in turnover and profits from these transactions should be clearly disclosed.

Turnover or gains in respect of contracts to provide capacity in exchange for   **23**
receiving capacity should be recognised only if the assets or services provided or
received have a readily ascertainable market value. The same principle applies to
reciprocal transactions to provide capacity entered into wholly or in part for a cash
consideration. No accounting recognition should be given to transactions that are
artificial or lacking in substance.

DATE FROM WHICH EFFECTIVE

The accounting treatment required by this Abstract should be adopted in financial   **24**
statements relating to accounting periods ending on or after 22 June 2003, but earlier
adoption is encouraged.

REFERENCES

ASB pronouncements

FRS 3 *Reporting Financial Performance*
FRS 5 *Reporting the Substance of Transactions* paragraphs 14, 21–25, 67–75
FRS 10 *Goodwill and Intangible Assets* paragraph 2
FRS 15 *Tangible Fixed Assets* paragraph 2
SSAP 21 *Accounting for leases and hire purchase contracts* paragraphs 14–15
UITF Abstract 26 *Barter transactions for advertising*
ASB *Statement of Principles for Financial Reporting* Chapter 5

UITF abstract 38
Accounting for ESOP trusts

(Issued December 2003)

INTRODUCTION

1   This Abstract supersedes UITF Abstract 13 'Accounting for ESOP trusts' (issued on 8 June 1995).

2   Abstract 13 addressed:

(a)   the nature and extent of the sponsoring company's assets and liabilities that should be recognised under employee share ownership plans (ESOPs); and

(b)   the timing of expense recognition under such arrangements.

3   This Abstract addresses issue (a) above. The principal change from Abstract 13 concerns the treatment of an interest in an entity's own shares arising through an ESOP trust. Abstract 13 required that such shares should be recognised as assets of the sponsoring entity. This Abstract reflects the principle in UITF Abstract 37 'Purchases and sales of own shares', which is consistent with International Financial Reporting Standards (IFRSs), that an entity that reacquires its own equity instruments should present them as a deduction in arriving at shareholders' funds rather than as assets.

4   This Abstract does not include any requirements concerning the recognition of the cost of awards to employees that take the form of shares or rights to shares. Those accounting requirements are dealt with in UITF Abstract 17 'Employee share schemes', which is amended by this Abstract. This Abstract does not include any requirements concerning the recognition of the cost of awards to employees that take the form of shares or rights to shares. Those accounting requirements are dealt with in FRS 20 (IFRS 2) Share-based Payment.*

THE ISSUE

5   ESOPs are designed to facilitate employee shareholdings and are often used as vehicles for distributing shares to employees under remuneration schemes.

6   The detailed structures of individual ESOPs are many and varied, as are the reasons for establishing them. However, the main features are often as follows:

(a)   The ESOP trust provides a warehouse for the sponsoring company's shares, for example by acquiring and holding shares that are to be sold or transferred to employees in the future. The trustees may purchase the shares with finance provided by the sponsoring company (by way of cash contributions or loans), or by a third-party bank loan, or by a combination of the two. Loans from the company are usually interest-free. In other cases, the ESOP trust may subscribe directly for shares issued by the sponsoring company or acquire shares held as treasury shares.

(b)   Where the ESOP trust borrows from a third party, the sponsoring company will usually guarantee the loan, ie it will be responsible for any shortfall if the trust's assets are insufficient to meet its debt repayment obligations. The company will also generally make regular contributions to the trust to enable the trust to meet its interest payments, ie to make good any shortfall between

---

Editor's note: Amended by FRS 20.

the dividend income of the trust (if any) and the interest payable. As part of this arrangement the trustees usually waive their right to dividends on the shares held by the trust.

(c) Shares held by the ESOP trust are distributed to employees through an employee share scheme. There are many different arrangements – these include: the purchase of shares by employees when exercising their share options under a share option scheme; the purchase of shares by the trustees of an approved profit-sharing scheme for allocation to employees under the rules of the scheme; or the transfer of shares to employees under some other incentive scheme.

(d) Although the trustees of the ESOP trust must act at all times in accordance with the interests of the beneficiaries under the trust, most ESOP trusts (particularly those established as a means of remunerating employees) are specifically designed so as to serve the purposes of the sponsoring company, and to ensure that there will be minimal risk of any conflict arising between the duties of the trustees and the interest of the company. Where this is so, the sponsoring company has de facto control and there will be nothing to encumber implementation of its wishes in practice.

FRS 5 'Reporting the Substance of Transactions' requires a reporting entity's **7** financial statements to report the substance of the transactions into which it has entered (paragraph 14). In determining the substance of a transaction all its aspects and implications should be identified and greater weight given to those more likely to have a commercial effect in practice. To determine the substance of a transaction it is necessary to identify whether the transaction has given rise to new assets or liabilities for the reporting entity and whether it has changed the entity's existing assets or liabilities (paragraph 16). In the circumstances described above, the commercial effect is that the sponsoring company is, for all practical purposes, in the same position as if it had purchased the shares directly and it should account for them as such. As is explained below, shares of the company are presented in the balance sheet as a deduction in arriving at shareholders' funds, not as assets.

Where a company holds its own equity shares, IFRSs* require them to be accounted **8** for as a deduction from equity in all circumstances; they should not be recognised as assets. The ASB's Statement of Principles for Financial Reporting is consistent with IFRSs in this regard. Paragraph 4.45 states "a purchase by a company of its own shares is an example of a return of capital and is therefore reflected in financial statements by reducing the amount of ownership interest". This accounting treatment of own shares is reflected in Abstract 37, which requires that consideration paid or received for the purchase or sale of an entity's own shares should be shown in the reconciliation of movements in shareholders' funds and that no gain or loss should be recognised in the profit and loss account or statement of total recognised gains and losses on the purchase, sale, or cancellation of an entity's own shares. The UITF takes the view that the same accounting treatment should apply where an entity's own shares are held by an ESOP trust.

APPLICATION TO SMALLER ENTITIES

Reporting entities applying the Financial Reporting Standard for Smaller Entities **9** currently applicable are exempt from this Abstract.

*SIC-16 'Share Capital – Reacquired Own Equity Instruments (Treasury Shares)'.

UITF CONSENSUS

10   The UITF reached a consensus that the sponsoring company of an ESOP trust should recognise the assets and liabilities of the trust in its own accounts whenever it has de facto control of those assets and liabilities. This will generally be the case when the trust is established in order to hold shares for an employee remuneration scheme and may be so in other circumstances. Where this consensus applies:

(a)   Until such time as the company's own shares held by the ESOP trust vest unconditionally in employees, the consideration paid for the shares should be deducted in arriving at shareholders' funds.

(b)   Other assets and liabilities (including borrowings) of the ESOP trust should be recognised as assets and liabilities of the sponsoring company.

(c)   Consideration paid or received for the purchase or sale of the company's own shares in an ESOP trust should be shown as separate amounts in the reconciliation of movements in shareholders' funds.

(d)   No gain or loss should be recognised in the profit and loss account or statement of total recognised gains and losses on the purchase, sale, issue or cancellation of the company's own shares.

(e)   Finance costs and any administration expenses should be charged as they accrue and not as funding payments are made to the ESOP trust.

(f)   Any dividend income arising on own shares should be excluded in arriving at profit before tax and deducted from the aggregate of dividends paid and proposed. The deduction should be disclosed if material. In accordance with the principles of FRS 22 (IAS 33) *Earnings per share*, the shares should be treated as if they were cancelled when calculating earnings per share.

11   Sufficient information should be disclosed in the financial statements of the sponsoring company to enable readers to understand the significance of the ESOP trust in the context of the sponsoring company. This should include:

(a)   a description of the main features of the ESOP trust including the arrangements for distributing shares to employees;

(b)   the amounts of reductions to shareholders' funds and the number and (for companies that have shares listed or publicly traded on a stock exchange or market) market value of shares held by the ESOP trust which have not yet vested unconditionally in employees; and

(c)   the extent to which these shares are under option to employees, or have been conditionally gifted to them.

DATE FROM WHICH EFFECTIVE

12   The accounting treatment required by this Abstract should be adopted in financial statements relating to accounting periods ending on or after 22 June 2004, but earlier adoption is encouraged.

Corresponding amounts

13   Where applicable, corresponding balance sheet amounts should be restated to reclassify the company's own shares as deductions in arriving at shareholders' funds at the amount of the consideration paid for the shares. Amounts in the profit and loss account should also be restated, where applicable, for comparative periods presented.

WITHDRAWAL OF UITF ABSTRACT 13 (AS ISSUED ON 8 JUNE 1995)

This Abstract supersedes UITF Abstract 13 'Accounting for ESOP trusts' (issued on   **14**
8 June 1995).

AMENDMENT TO UITF ABSTRACT 17

[Withdrawn]   **15**

REFERENCES

ASB pronouncements
FRS 5 'Reporting the Substance of Transactions' – paragraphs 2, 4, 14, 16, 17, 20
and 46
Statement of Principles for Financial Reporting – Chapter 4
UITF Abstract 37 'Purchases and sales of own shares'

ASB exposure drafts
FRED 30 'Financial Instruments: Disclosure and Presentation' – paragraphs 29A–
29B
FRED 31 'Share-based Payment' – Appendix E, paragraph E1

International Financial Reporting Standards
SIC-16 'Share Capital – Reacquired Own Equity Instruments (Treasury Shares)'

LEGAL CONSIDERATIONS

FRS 5 is not intended to affect the legal characterisation of a transaction, or to
change the situation at law achieved by the parties to it (paragraph 46). Shares
acquired by ESOP trusts and included in the balance sheet under this Abstract are
not treasury shares as defined in the Companies Act 1985 (as amended by the
Companies (Acquisition of Own Shares) (Treasury Shares) Regulations 2003) or as
defined by the Companies Act 1990 in the Republic of Ireland. Nor does the
inclusion of the shares in the company's balance sheet as a deduction in arriving at
shareholders' funds imply that they have been purchased by the company as a matter
of law or that they are required to be cancelled, which would be the consequence of
such a purchase except for shares held as treasury shares (in Great Britain sections
162(2) and 160(4) of the Companies Act 1985).*

The UITF has received legal advice on the implications for companies' distributable
profits when the accounting treatment required by this Abstract is followed. It has
been advised that in Great Britain:

(a) Section 264 of the Companies Act 1985 provides that a public company may
    only make a distribution if, and to the extent that, this will not reduce the
    company's net assets to less than an amount equal to the aggregate of its called
    up share capital and undistributable reserves. Section 270 applies for the pur-
    poses of determining whether a distribution can be made without contravening
    sections 263, 264 or 265. It provides that the amount of a distribution which

---

*The corresponding references in Northern Ireland are to articles 172(2) and 170(4) of the Companies
(Northern Ireland) Order 1986 and in the Republic of Ireland to sections 211(2) and 208(a) of the Companies
Act 1990. The corresponding references for the Republic of Ireland indicate the provisions dealing with the same
topic as the sections in the Companies Act 1985 and are not identical in all cases. The Republic of Ireland
references should be consulted for further information.*

can be made is determined by reference, inter alia, to the company's assets and liabilities as stated in the company's accounts. These are normally the company's last annual accounts (but may be initial or interim accounts). As the effect of the accounting treatment required by this Abstract would be that, in drawing up the accounts in question, any shares held by an ESOP would be recorded as a deduction in arriving at shareholders' funds rather than as an asset, it follows that the relevant aggregate asset value for the purposes of the definition of net assets in section 264(2) would be reduced by a corresponding amount.

(b)   In calculating a company's distributable profits, it is necessary to determine its "accumulated, realised profits so far as not previously utilised by distribution or capitalisation, less its accumulated, realised losses, so far as not previously written off in a reduction or reorganisation of capital duly made" (section 263(3) of the Companies Act 1985).

The acquisition of shares by an ESOP does not, of itself, affect the company's realised profits or realised losses. The accounting treatment required by this Abstract, which requires a deduction in arriving at shareholders' funds and that no gain or loss should be recognised in the profit and loss account, is consistent with this analysis. This analysis holds good notwithstanding that an acquisition of treasury shares, with which an acquisition of shares by an ESOP has similarities, involves a deduction from distributable profits.

Although the acquisition of shares by an ESOP will not, of itself, result in a realised profit or loss for the company concerned, a company will still need to consider other transactions with the ESOP, for example a loan to the ESOP to fund acquisitions of shares, and these may affect the company's realised profits and losses.

(c)   In determining whether a company has sufficient distributable profits and net assets in order lawfully to pay a dividend to its shareholders, under section 270(2) of the Companies Act 1985 the relevant accounts are the company's own individual accounts and not its consolidated accounts.

Appendix I
Further explanation of consensus in terms of the principles of FRS 5

UITF Abstract 13 (issued on 8 June 1995)

The UITF's consensus in Abstract 13 required that the sponsoring company of an ESOP trust should recognise certain assets and liabilities of the trust as its own whenever it had de facto control of the shares held by the ESOP trust and bore their benefits or risks. Appendix 1 to Abstract 13 explained the consensus further in terms of the principles of FRS 5 and, in particular, the attributes of assets (as defined in FRS 5) which are access to future economic benefits and control of that access. The UITF concluded that, where the arrangements were such that the sponsoring company had de facto control, the ESOP trust fell within the consensus of Abstract 13. Moreover, the UITF noted that where an ESOP trust was established as a means of remunerating employees, the sponsoring company would generally bear the risks and many of the benefits of the shares held by the trust until such time as they vested unconditionally in employees (eg through gifts becoming unconditional or options being exercised).

Distinction between ESOP trusts and pension schemes

The UITF considered that the substance of ESOP trusts was different from that of pension schemes (where, under the requirements of FRS 17 'Retirement Benefits', the gross assets and liabilities of the scheme are not required to be included in the balance sheet) in that pension schemes have a longer time-frame and are wider in scope with the result that the obligations imposed by trust law and statute have a much greater commercial effect in practice.

The present Abstract

The UITF's consensus in this Abstract (Abstract 38) also requires the sponsoring company of an ESOP trust to recognise the assets and liabilities of the trust in its own accounts whenever it has de facto control of those assets and liabilities. In that respect, the requirements are unchanged from Abstract 13. However, whereas Abstract 13 required that a sponsoring company's own shares held by an ESOP trust should be recognised as assets of the company, this Abstract requires the company's own shares to be presented as a deduction in arriving at shareholders' funds rather than as assets. This change follows the changes to the accounting treatment of own shares in Abstract 37. Other assets and liabilities of an ESOP trust continue to be recognised as assets and liabilities of the sponsoring entity.

Appendix II
Illustrative examples

The examples do not form part of the Abstract and are given for illustrative purposes only. In particular, the period of service to which an employee benefit relates can be determined only having regard to all the facts and circumstances of any particular case. Whilst the examples illustrate how this question might be approached, they should not be regarded as definitive.

In examples 1-6 below it is assumed that the ESOP trust is established for the purpose of remunerating employees and that the sponsoring company has de facto control of the assets and liabilities held by the ESOP trust. The detailed legal arrangements are not discussed since the purpose of the examples is to focus on the accounting principles.

1   *The ESOP trust holds unallocated shares costing 100, funded by a bank loan. The sponsoring company undertakes to make contributions to the trust whenever the loan-to-value ratio falls below a set figure. At the reporting date market value is at least 100.*

The company deducts the consideration paid for the shares of 100 in arriving at shareholders' funds. The company also recognises a liability of 100. Interest expense is accrued in the usual way. The amount of the reduction to shareholders' funds (100) and the market value of the shares held are disclosed.

2   *As 1 but the market value of the shares falls to 80.*

The fall in the market value of the shares does not give rise to a recognised loss. The amount of the reduction to shareholders' funds (100) and the market value of the shares held is disclosed.

3   *As 1 but options are granted over the shares at 80, when the market value is 100.*

The company recognises an expense over the period to which the employee's performance relates, in accordance with FRS 20. The amount recognised as an expense is credited in arriving at shareholders' funds. The reduction to shareholders' funds of 100 in respect of the consideration paid for the shares, and the market value of the shares, are disclosed until the shares vest unconditionally in employees.

4   *As 3 but subsequent to the grant of the options the market value of the shares falls to 50.*

The accounting is the same as in Example 3. The fall in the market value of the shares does not give rise to a recognised loss.

5   *An annual profit share of 100 is paid to a profit-sharing share trust in order that it may buy and hold shares for specified employees for a tax-efficient period. Dividends on the shares are passed through to the employees.*

If the shares have vested unconditionally in the employees, they are not accounted for as the company's own shares since the shares are in substance those of the employees. If the entitlement will lapse in the event that the employees do not remain with the company for a specified period, the shares do not yet belong to the employees. The consideration paid for the shares is deducted in arriving at shareholders' funds and disclosed until the shares vest unconditionally in the employees.

[Withdrawn]   **6**

A company is a co-operative, owned by its employees. All of its shares are held in a trust   **7**
for the benefit of the employees collectively and the trust receives dividends from the
company which are distributed to employees in accordance with the provisions of the
trust deed. The shares never vest in individual employees. The company does not have de
facto control of the trust shares.

The shares held by the trust are not in substance the company's own shares and are
not accounted for as such.

UITF abstract 39 (IFRIC Interpretation 2)
Members' shares in co-operative entities and similar instruments

(Issued 10 February 2005)

Preface by the Urgent Issues Task Force

a   This Abstract has the effect of implementing the International Accounting Standards Board's (IASB's) International Financial Reporting Interpretations Committee (IFRIC) Interpretation 2 'Members' Shares in Co-operative Entities and Similar Instruments' in the UK and the Republic of Ireland for entities preparing their financial statements in accordance with UK accounting standards.

b   IFRIC 2 applies to financial instruments within the scope of IAS 32 'Financial Instruments: Disclosure and Presentation'. FRS 25 (IAS 32) 'Financial Instruments: Disclosure and Presentation' implemented the presentation requirements of IAS 32 for entities subject to UK accounting standards. The requirements, scope and effective date of Abstract 39 are identical to IFRIC 2 except that:

- entities applying the FRSSE will be exempt from the Abstract, and
- the effective date and transitional provisions have been amended to be consistent with FRS 25.

c   This Abstract incorporates the text of IFRIC 2.* The text of IFRIC 2 contains various references to International Financial Reporting Standards (IFRSs). In this Abstract those references have been amended to enable the Interpretation to be applied in a UK context. The UITF believes that those amendments do not change the requirements of IFRIC 2 in any way.

---

*Deleted text has been struck through and inserted text is underlined.

Contents

UITF abstract 39 (IFRIC Interpretation 2)
Members' Shares in Co-operative Entities and Similar Instruments

paragraphs

REFERENCES

- FRS 25 (IAS 32) *Financial Instruments: Disclosure and Presentation*
- FRS 26 (IAS 39) *Financial Instruments: Measurement*

BACKGROUND

1   Co-operatives and other similar entities are formed by groups of persons to meet common economic or social needs. National laws typically define a co-operative as a society endeavouring to promote its members' economic advancement by way of a joint business operation (the principle of self-help). Members' interests in a co-operative are often characterised as members' shares, units or the like, and are referred to below as 'members' shares'.

2   IAS 32 establishes principles for the classification of financial instruments as financial liabilities or equity. In particular, those principles apply to the classification of puttable instruments that allow the holder to put those instruments to the issuer for cash or another financial instrument. The application of those principles to members' shares in cooperative entities and similar instruments is difficult. Some of the International Accounting Standards Board's constituents have asked for help in understanding how the principles in IAS 32 apply to members' shares and similar instruments that have certain features, and the circumstances in which those features affect the classification as liabilities or equity.

SCOPE

3   This Abstract applies to financial instruments within the scope of FRS 25, including financial instruments issued to members of co-operative entities that evidence the members' ownership interest in the entity. This Abstract does not apply to financial instruments that will or may be settled in the entity's own equity instruments.

3A   Reporting entities applying the Financial Reporting Standard for Smaller Entities 3A currently applicable are exempt from this Abstract.

ISSUE

4   Many financial instruments, including members' shares, have characteristics of equity, including voting rights and rights to participate in dividend distributions. Some financial instruments give the holder the right to request redemption for cash or another financial asset, but may include or be subject to limits on whether the financial instruments will be redeemed. How should those redemption terms be evaluated in determining whether the financial instruments should be classified as liabilities or equity?

UITF CONSENSUS

5   The contractual right of the holder of a financial instrument (including members' shares in co-operative entities) to request redemption does not, in itself, require that financial instrument to be classified as a financial liability. Rather, the entity must consider all of the terms and conditions of the financial instrument in determining its classification as a financial liability or equity. Those terms and conditions include relevant local laws, regulations and the entity's governing charter in effect at the date of classification, but not expected future amendments to those laws, regulations or charter.

Members' shares that would be classified as equity if the members did not have a   **6**
right to request redemption are equity if either of the conditions described in paragraphs 7 and 8 is present. Demand deposits, including current accounts, deposit
accounts and similar contracts that arise when members act as customers are
financial liabilities of the entity.

Members' shares are equity if the entity has an unconditional right to refuse   **7**
redemption of the members' shares.

Local law, regulation or the entity's governing charter can impose various types of   **8**
prohibitions on the redemption of members' shares, eg unconditional prohibitions or
prohibitions based on liquidity criteria. If redemption is unconditionally prohibited
by local law, regulation or the entity's governing charter, members' shares are equity.
However, provisions in local law, regulation or the entity's governing charter that
prohibit redemption only if conditions-such as liquidity constraints-are met (or are
not met) do not result in members' shares being equity.

An unconditional prohibition may be absolute, in that all redemptions are pro-   **9**
hibited. An unconditional prohibition may be partial, in that it prohibits redemption
of members' shares if redemption would cause the number of members' shares or
amount of paid-in capital from members' shares to fall below a specified level.
Members' shares in excess of the prohibition against redemption are liabilities, unless
the entity has the unconditional right to refuse redemption as described in paragraph
7. In some cases, the number of shares or the amount of paid-in capital subject to a
redemption prohibition may change from time to time. Such a change in the
redemption prohibition leads to a transfer between financial liabilities and equity.

At initial recognition, the entity shall measure its financial liability for redemption at   **10**
fair value. In the case of members' shares with a redemption feature, the entity
measures the fair value of the financial liability for redemption at no less than the
maximum amount payable under the redemption provisions of its governing charter
or applicable law discounted from the first date that the amount could be required to
be paid (see example 3).

As required by paragraph 35 of FRS 25, distributions to holders of equity instru-   **11**
ments are recognised directly in equity, net of any income tax benefits. Interest,
dividends and other returns relating to financial instruments classified as financial
liabilities are expenses, regardless of whether those amounts paid are legally characterised as dividends, interest or otherwise.

The Appendix, which is an integral part of the consensus, provides examples of the   **12**
12 application of this consensus.

DISCLOSURE

When a change in the redemption prohibition leads to a transfer between financial   **13**
liabilities and equity, the entity shall disclose separately the amount, timing and
reason for the transfer.

EFFECTIVE DATE

The effective date and transition requirements of this Abstract are the same as those   **14**
for FRS 25 (paragraphs 96 to 97B). An entity shall apply this Interpretation Abstract
for annual periods beginning on or after 1 January 2005. Earlier application is not
permitted.

Appendix
Examples of application of the consensus

This appendix is an integral part of the Abstract.

A1   This appendix sets out seven examples of the application of the IFRIC UITF consensus. The examples do not constitute an exhaustive list; other fact patterns are possible. Each example assumes that there are no conditions other than those set out in the facts of the example that would require the financial instrument to be classified as a financial liability.

UNCONDITIONAL RIGHT TO REFUSE REDEMPTION (paragraph 7)

Example 1

Facts

A2   The entity's charter states that redemptions are made at the sole discretion of the entity. The charter does not provide further elaboration or limitation on that discretion. In its history, the entity has never refused to redeem members' shares, although the governing board has the right to do so.

Classification

A3   The entity has the unconditional right to refuse redemption and the members' shares are equity. FRS 25 establishes principles for classification that are based on the terms of the financial instrument and notes that a history of, or intention to make, discretionary payments does not trigger liability classification. Paragraph AG26 of FRS 25 states:

> When preference shares are non-redeemable, the appropriate classification is determined by the other rights that attach to them. Classification is based on an assessment of the substance of the contractual arrangements and the definitions of a financial liability and an equity instrument. When distributions to holders of the preference shares, whether cumulative or non-cumulative, are at the discretion of the issuer, the shares are equity instruments. The classification of a preference share as an equity instrument or a financial liability is not affected by, for example:
>
> (a)   a history of making distributions;
> (b)   an intention to make distributions in the future;
> (c)   a possible negative impact on the price of ordinary shares of the issuer if distributions are not made (because of restrictions on paying dividends on the ordinary shares if dividends are not paid on the preference shares);
> (d)   the amount of the issuer's reserves;
> (e)   an issuer's expectation of a profit or loss for a period; or
> (f)   an ability or inability of the issuer to influence the amount of its profit or loss for the period.

Example 2

Facts

The entity's charter states that redemptions are made at the sole discretion of the   **A4**
entity. However, the charter further states that approval of a redemption request is
automatic unless the entity is unable to make payments without violating local
regulations regarding liquidity or reserves.

Classification

The entity does not have the unconditional right to refuse redemption and the   **A5**
members' shares are a financial liability. The restrictions described above are based
on the entity's ability to settle its liability. They restrict redemptions only if the
liquidity or reserve requirements are not met and then only until such time as they
are met. Hence, they do not, under the principles established in FRS 25, result in the
classification of the financial instrument as equity. Paragraph AG25 of FRS 25
states:

> Preference shares may be issued with various rights. In determining whether a
> preference share is a financial liability or an equity instrument, an issuer assesses
> the particular rights attaching to the share to determine whether it exhibits the
> fundamental characteristic of a financial liability. For example, a preference
> share that provides for redemption on a specific date or at the option of the
> holder contains a financial liability because the issuer has an obligation to
> transfer financial assets to the holder of the share. *The potential inability of an
> issuer to satisfy an obligation to redeem a preference share when contractually
> required to do so, whether because of a lack of funds, a statutory restriction or
> insufficient profits or reserves, does not negate the obligation.* [Emphasis added]

PROHIBITIONS AGAINST REDEMPTION (PARAGRAPHS 8 AND 9)

Example 3

Facts

A co-operative entity has issued shares to its members at different dates and for   **A6**
different amounts in the past as follows:

(a)   1 January 20x1 100,000 shares at CU10 each (CU1,000,000);
(b)   1 January 20x2 100,000 shares at CU20 each (a further CU2,000,000, so that
      the total for shares issued is CU3,000,000).

Shares are redeemable on demand at the amount for which they were issued.

The entity's charter states that cumulative redemptions cannot exceed 20 per cent of   **A7**
the highest number of its members' shares ever outstanding. At 31 December 20x2
the entity has 200,000 of outstanding shares, which is the highest number of members' shares ever outstanding and no shares have been redeemed in the past. On 1
January 20x3 the entity amends its governing charter and increases the permitted
level of cumulative redemptions to 25 per cent of the highest number of its members'
shares ever outstanding.

Classification

Before the governing charter is amended

A8   Members' shares in excess of the prohibition against redemption are financial liabilities. The co-operative entity measures this financial liability at fair value at initial recognition. Because these shares are redeemable on demand, the co-operative entity determines the fair value of such financial liabilities as required by paragraph 49 of FRS 26*, which states: 'The fair value of a financial liability with a demand feature (eg a demand deposit) is not less than the amount payable on demand ...' Accordingly, the co-operative entity classifies as financial liabilities the maximum amount payable on demand under the redemption provisions.

A9   On 1 January 20x1 the maximum amount payable under the redemption provisions is 20,000 shares at CU10 each and accordingly the entity classifies CU200,000 as financial liability and CU800,000 as equity. However, on 1 January 20x2 because of the new issue of shares at CU20, the maximum amount payable under the redemption provisions increases to 40,000 shares at CU20 each. The issue of additional shares at CU20 creates a new liability that is measured on initial recognition at fair value. The liability after these shares have been issued is 20 per cent of the total shares in issue (200,000), measured at CU20, or CU800,000. This requires recognition of an additional liability of CU600,000. In this example no gain or loss is recognised. Accordingly the entity now classifies CU800,000 as financial liabilities and CU2,200,000 as equity. This example assumes these amounts are not changed between 1 January 20x1 and 31 December 20x2.

After the governing charter is amended

A10   Following the change in its governing charter the co-operative entity can now be required to redeem a maximum of 25 per cent of its outstanding shares or a maximum of 50,000 shares at CU20 each. Accordingly, on 1 January 20x3 the co-operative entity classifies as financial liabilities an amount of CU1,000,000 being the maximum amount payable on demand under the redemption provisions, as determined in accordance with paragraph 49 of FRS 26. It therefore transfers on 1 January 20x3 from equity to financial liabilities an amount of CU200,000, leaving CU2,000,000 classified as equity. In this example the entity does not recognise a gain or loss on the transfer.

Example 4

Facts

A11   Local law governing the operations of co-operatives, or the terms of the entity's governing charter, prohibit an entity from redeeming members' shares if, by redeeming them, it would reduce paid-in capital from members' shares below 75 per cent of the highest amount of paid-in capital from members' shares. The highest amount for a particular cooperative is CU1,000,000. At the balance sheet date the balance of paid-in capital is CU900,000.

UITF footnote: The requirements illustrated in this example apply also to financial liabilities of entities that are applying FRS 4 'Capital Instruments' (as amended by FRS 25) rather than FRS 26.

Classification

In this case, CU750,000 would be classified as equity and CU150,000 would be   **A12**
classified as financial liabilities. In addition to the paragraphs already cited, paragraph 18(b) of FRS 25 states in part:

> ... a financial instrument that gives the holder the right to put it back to the
> issuer for cash or another financial asset (a 'puttable instrument') is a financial
> liability. This is so even when the amount of cash or other financial assets is
> determined on the basis of an index or other item that has the potential to
> increase or decrease, or when the legal form of the puttable instrument gives the
> holder a right to a residual interest in the assets of an issuer. The existence of an
> option for the holder to put the instrument back to the issuer for cash or another
> financial asset means that the puttable instrument meets the definition of a
> financial liability.

The redemption prohibition described in this example is different from the restric-   **A13**
tions described in paragraphs 19 and AG25 of FRS 25. Those restrictions are
limitations on the ability of the entity to pay the amount due on a financial liability,
ie they prevent payment of the liability only if specified conditions are met. In
contrast, this example describes an unconditional prohibition on redemptions
beyond a specified amount, regardless of the entity's ability to redeem members'
shares (eg given its cash resources, profits or distributable reserves). In effect, the
prohibition against redemption prevents the entity from incurring any financial
liability to redeem more than a specified amount of paid-in capital. Therefore, the
portion of shares subject to the redemption prohibition is not a financial liability.
While each member's shares may be redeemable individually, a portion of the total
shares outstanding is not redeemable in any circumstances other than liquidation of
the entity.

Example 5

Facts

The facts of this example are as stated in example 4. In addition, at the balance sheet   **A14**
date, liquidity requirements imposed in the local jurisdiction prevent the entity from
redeeming any members' shares unless its holdings of cash and short-term investments are greater than a specified amount. The effect of these liquidity requirements
at the balance sheet date is that the entity cannot pay more than CU50,000 to redeem
the members' shares.

Classification

As in example 4, the entity classifies CU750,000 as equity and CU150,000 as a   **A15**
financial liability. This is because the amount classified as a liability is based on the
entity's unconditional right to refuse redemption and not on conditional restrictions
that prevent redemption only if liquidity or other conditions are not met and then
only until such time as they are met. The provisions of paragraphs 19 and AG25 of
FRS 25 apply in this case.

Example 6

Facts

A16   The entity's governing charter prohibits it from redeeming members' shares, except to the extent of proceeds received from the issue of additional members' shares to new or existing members during the preceding three years. Proceeds from issuing members' shares must be applied to redeem shares for which members have requested redemption. During the three preceding years, the proceeds from issuing members' shares have been CU12,000 and no member's shares have been redeemed.

Classification

A17   The entity classifies CU12,000 of the members' shares as financial liabilities. Consistently with the conclusions described in example 4, members' shares subject to an unconditional prohibition against redemption are not financial liabilities. Such an unconditional prohibition applies to an amount equal to the proceeds of shares issued before the preceding three years, and accordingly, this amount is classified as equity. However, an amount equal to the proceeds from any shares issued in the preceding three years is not subject to an unconditional prohibition on redemption. Accordingly, proceeds from the issue of members' shares in the preceding three years give rise to financial liabilities until they are no longer available for redemption of members' shares. As a result the entity has a financial liability equal to the proceeds of shares issued during the three preceding years, net of any redemptions during that period.

Example 7

Facts

A18   The entity is a co-operative bank. Local law governing the operations of co-operative banks state that at least 50 per cent of the entity's total 'outstanding liabilities' (a term defined in the regulations to include members' share accounts) has to be in the form of members' paid-in capital. The effect of the regulation is that if all of a co-operative's outstanding liabilities are in the form of members' shares, it is able to redeem them all. On 31 December 20x1 the entity has total outstanding liabilities of CU200,000, of which CU125,000 represent members' share accounts. The terms of the members' share accounts permit the holder to redeem them on demand and there are no limitations on redemption in the entity's charter.

Classification

A19   In this example members' shares are classified as financial liabilities. The redemption prohibition is similar to the restrictions described in paragraphs 19 and AG25 of FRS 25. The restriction is a conditional limitation on the ability of the entity to pay the amount due on a financial liability, ie they prevent payment of the liability only if specified conditions are met. More specifically, the entity could be required to redeem the entire amount of members' shares (CU125,000) if it repaid all of its other liabilities (CU75,000). Consequently, the prohibition against redemption does not prevent the entity from incurring a financial liability to redeem more than a specified number of members' shares or amount of paid-in capital. It allows the entity only to defer redemption until a condition is met, ie the repayment of other liabilities. Members' shares in this example are not subject to an unconditional prohibition against redemption and are therefore classified as financial liabilities.

Basis for Conclusions

This Basis for Conclusions accompanies, but is not part of, the Interpretation

> ASB note: The IFRIC's Basis for Conclusions, which accompanies IFRIC 2, is set out below in full.

INTRODUCTION

This Basis for Conclusions summarises the IFRIC's considerations in reaching its consensus. Individual IFRIC members gave greater weight to some factors than to others. **BC1**

BACKGROUND

In September 2001, the Standing Interpretations Committee instituted by the former International Accounting Standards Committee (IASC) published Draft Interpretation SIC D-34 *Financial Instruments – Instruments or Rights Redeemable by the Holder*. The Draft Interpretation stated: 'The issuer of a Puttable Instrument should classify the entire instrument as a liability.' **BC2**

In 2001 the International Accounting Standards Board (IASB) began operations in succession to IASC. The IASB's initial agenda included a project to make limited amendments to the financial instruments standards issued by IASC. The IASB decided to incorporate the consensus from Draft Interpretation D-34 as part of those amendments. In June 2002 the IASB published an exposure draft of amendments to IAS 32 *Financial Instruments: Disclosure and Presentation* that incorporated the proposed consensus from Draft Interpretation D-34. **BC3**

In their responses to the Exposure Draft and in their participation in public round-table discussions held in March 2003, representatives of co-operative banks raised questions about the application of the principles in IAS 32 to members' shares. This was followed by a series of meetings between IASB members and staff and representatives of the European Association of Co-operative Banks. After considering questions raised by the bank group, the IASB concluded that the principles articulated in IAS 32 should not be modified, but that there were questions about the application of those principles to cooperative entities that should be considered by the IFRIC. **BC4**

In considering the application of IAS 32 to co-operative entities, the IFRIC recognised that a variety of entities operate as co-operatives and these entities have a variety of capital structures. The IFRIC decided that its proposed Interpretation should address some features that exist in a number of co-operatives. However, the IFRIC noted that its conclusions and the examples in the Interpretation are not limited to the specific characteristics of members' shares in European co-operative banks. **BC5**

BASIS FOR CONSENSUS

Paragraph 15 of IAS 32 states: **BC6**

> The issuer of a financial instrument shall classify the instrument, or its component parts, on initial recognition as a financial liability, a financial asset or an equity instrument in accordance with the *substance of the contractual*

arrangement and the definitions of a financial liability, a financial asset and an equity instrument. [Emphasis added]

BC7   In many jurisdictions, local law or regulations state that members' shares are equity of the entity. However, paragraph 17 of IAS 32 states:

> A critical feature in differentiating a financial liability from an equity instrument is *the existence of a contractual obligation of one party to the financial instrument (the issuer) either to deliver cash or another financial asset to the other party (the holder)* or to exchange financial assets or financial liabilities with the holder under conditions that are potentially unfavourable to the issuer. Although the holder of an equity instrument may be entitled to receive a pro rata share of any dividends or other distributions of equity, the issuer does not have a contractual obligation to make such distributions because it cannot be required to deliver cash or another financial asset to another party. [Emphasis added]

BC8   Paragraphs cited in the examples in the Appendix and in the paragraphs above show that, under IAS 32, the terms of the contractual agreement govern the classification of a financial instrument as a financial liability or equity. If the terms of an instrument create an unconditional obligation to transfer cash or another financial asset, circumstances that might restrict an entity's ability to make the transfer when due do not alter the classification as a financial liability. If the terms of the instrument give the entity an unconditional right to avoid delivering cash or another financial asset, the instrument is classified as equity. This is true even if other factors make it likely that the entity will continue to distribute dividends or make or other payments. In view of those principles, the IFRIC decided to focus on circumstances that would indicate that the entity has the unconditional right to avoid making payments to a member who has requested that his or her shares be redeemed.

BC9   The IFRIC identified two situations in which a co-operative entity has an unconditional right to avoid the transfer of cash or another financial asset. The IFRIC acknowledges that there may be other situations that may raise questions about the application of IAS 32 to members' shares. However, it understands that the two situations are often present in the contractual and other conditions surrounding members' shares and that interpretation of those two situations would eliminate many of the questions that may arise in practice.

BC10   The IFRIC also noted that an entity assesses whether it has an unconditional right to avoid BC10 the transfer of cash or another financial asset on the basis of local laws, regulations and its governing charter in effect at the date of classification. This is because it is local laws, regulations and the governing charter in effect at the classification date, together with the terms contained in the instrument's documentation that constitute the terms and conditions of the instrument at that date. Accordingly, an entity does not take into account expected future amendments to local law, regulation or its governing charter.

THE RIGHT TO REFUSE REDEMPTION (paragraph 7)

BC11   An entity may have the unconditional right to refuse redemption of a member's shares. If such a right exists, the entity does not have the obligation to transfer cash or another financial asset that IAS 32 identifies as a critical characteristic of a financial liability.

BC12   The IFRIC considered whether the entity's history of making redemptions should be considered in deciding whether the entity's right to refuse requests is, in fact, unconditional. The IFRIC observed that a history of making redemptions may create a reasonable expectation that all future requests will be honoured. However, holders of many equity instruments have a reasonable expectation that an entity will continue a past practice of making payments. For example, an entity may have made dividend payments on preference shares for decades. Failure to make those payments would expose the entity to significant economic costs, including damage to the value of its ordinary shares. Nevertheless, as outlined in IAS 32 paragraph AG26 (cited in paragraph A3), a holder's expectations about dividends do not cause a preferred share to be classified as a financial liability.

PROHIBITIONS AGAINST REDEMPTION (paragraphs 8 and 9)

An entity may be prohibited by law or its governing charter from redeeming members' shares if doing so would cause the number of members' shares, or the amount of paid-in capital from members' shares, to fall below a specified level. While each individual share might be puttable, a portion of the total shares outstanding is not. **BC13**

The IFRIC concluded that conditions limiting an entity's ability to redeem members' shares must be evaluated sequentially. Unconditional prohibitions like those noted in paragraph 8 of the consensus prevent the entity from *incurring a liability* for redemption of all or some of the members' shares, regardless of whether it would otherwise be able to satisfy that financial liability. This contrasts with conditional prohibitions that prevent payments being made only if specified conditions-such as liquidity constraints-are met. Unconditional prohibitions prevent a liability from coming into existence, whereas the conditional prohibitions may only defer the payment of a liability already incurred. Following this analysis, an unconditional prohibition affects classification when an instrument subject to the prohibition is issued or when the prohibition is enacted or added to the entity's governing charter. In contrast, conditional restrictions such as those described in paragraphs 19 and AG25 of IAS 32 do not result in equity classification. **BC14**

The IFRIC discussed whether the requirements in IAS 32 can be applied to the classification of members' shares as a whole subject to a partial redemption prohibition. IAS 32 refers to 'a financial instrument', 'a financial liability' and 'an equity instrument'. It does not refer to groups or portfolios of instruments. In view of this the IFRIC considered whether it could apply the requirements in IAS 32 to the classification of members' shares subject to partial redemption prohibitions. The application of IAS 32 to a prohibition against redeeming some portion of members' shares (eg 500,000 shares of an entity with 1,000,000 shares outstanding) is unclear. **BC15**

The IFRIC noted that classifying a group of members' shares using the individual instrument approach could lead to misapplication of the principle of 'substance of the contract' in IAS 32. The IFRIC also noted that paragraph 23 of IAS 32 requires an entity that has entered into an agreement to purchase its own equity instruments to recognise a financial liability for the present value of the redemption amount (eg for the present value of the forward repurchase price, option exercise price or other redemption amount) even though the shares subject to the repurchase agreement are not individually identified. Accordingly, the IFRIC decided that for purposes of classification there are instances when IAS 32 does not require the individual instrument approach. **BC16**

In many situations, looking at either individual instruments or all of the instruments governed by a particular contract would result in the same classification as financial liability or equity under IAS 32. Thus, if an entity is prohibited from redeeming any **BC17** of its members' shares, the shares are not puttable and are equity. On the other hand, if there is no prohibition on redemption and no other conditions apply, members' shares are puttable and the shares are financial liabilities. However, in the case of partial prohibitions against redemption, the classification of members' shares governed by the same charter will differ, depending on whether such a classification is based on individual members' shares or the group of members' shares as a whole. For example, consider an entity with a partial prohibition that prevents it from redeeming 99 per cent of the highest number of members' shares ever outstanding. The classification based on individual shares considers each share to be potentially puttable and therefore a financial liability. This is different from the classification based on all of the members' shares. While each member's share may be redeemable individually, 99 per cent of the highest number of shares ever outstanding is not redeemable in any circumstances other than liquidation of the entity and therefore is equity.

MEASUREMENT ON INITIAL RECOGNITION (paragraph 10)

BC18   The IFRIC noted that when the financial liability for the redemption of members' shares that are redeemable on demand is initially recognised, the financial liability is measured at fair value in accordance with paragraph 49 of IAS 39 *Financial Instruments: Recognition and Measurement.* Paragraph 49 states: 'The fair value of a financial liability with a demand feature (eg a demand deposit) is not less than the amount payable on demand, discounted from the first date that the amount could be required to be paid'. Accordingly, the IFRIC decided that the fair value of the financial liability for redemption of members' shares redeemable on demand is the maximum amount payable under the redemption provisions of its governing charter or applicable law. The IFRIC also considered situations in which the number of members' shares or the amount of paid-in capital subject to prohibition against redemption may change. The IFRIC concluded that a change in the level of a prohibition against redemption should lead to a transfer between financial liabilities and equity.

SUBSEQUENT MEASUREMENT

BC19   Some respondents requested additional guidance on subsequent measurement of the liability for redemption of members' shares. The IFRIC noted that the focus of this Interpretation was on clarifying the classification of financial instruments rather than their subsequent measurement. Also, the IASB has on its agenda a project to address the accounting for financial instruments (including members' shares) that are redeemable at a pro rata share of the fair value of the residual interest in the entity issuing the financial instrument. The IASB will consider certain measurement issues in this project. The IFRIC was also informed that the majority of members' shares in co-operative entities are not redeemable at a pro rata share of the fair value of the residual interest in the cooperative entity thereby obviating the more complex measurement issues. In view of the above, the IFRIC decided not to provide additional guidance on measurement in the Interpretation.

PRESENTATION

BC20   The IFRIC noted that entities whose members' shares are not equity could use the presentation formats included in paragraphs IE32 and IE33 of the Illustrative Examples with IAS 32.

ALTERNATIVES CONSIDERED

The IFRIC considered suggestions that: **BC21**

(a) members' shares should be classified as equity until a member has requested redemption. That member's share would then be classified as a financial liability and this treatment would be consistent with local laws. Some commentators believe this is a more straightforward approach to classification.

(b) the classification of members' shares should incorporate the probability that members will request redemption. Those who suggest this view observe that experience shows this probability to be small, usually within 1-5 per cent, for some types of co-operative. They see no basis for classifying 100 per cent of the members' shares as liabilities on the basis of the behaviour of 1 per cent.

The IFRIC did not accept those views. Under IAS 32, the classification of an   **BC22**
instrument as financial liability or equity is based on the 'substance of the contractual arrangement and the definitions of a financial liability, a financial asset and an equity instrument.' In paragraph BC7 of the Basis for Conclusions on IAS 32, the IASB observed:

> Although the legal form of such financial instruments often includes a right to the residual interest in the assets of an entity available to holders of such instruments, the inclusion of an option for the holder to put the instrument back to the entity for cash or another financial asset means that the instrument meets the definition of a financial liability. The classification as a financial liability is independent of considerations such as when the right is exercisable, how the amount payable or receivable upon exercise of the right is determined, and whether the puttable instrument has a fixed maturity.

The IFRIC also observed that an approach similar to that in paragraph BC21(a) is   **BC23**
advocated in the Dissenting Opinion of one Board member on IAS 32. As the IASB did not adopt that approach its adoption here would require an amendment to IAS 32.

TRANSITION AND EFFECTIVE DATE (paragraph 14)

The IFRIC considered whether its Interpretation should have the same transition   **BC24**
and effective date as IAS 32, or whether a later effective date should apply with an exemption from IAS 32 for members' shares in the interim. Some co-operatives may wish to amend their governing charter in order to continue their existing practice under national accounting requirements of classifying members' shares as equity. Such amendments usually require a general meeting of members and holding a meeting may not be possible before the effective date of IAS 32.

After considering a number of alternatives, the IFRIC decided against any exemp-   **BC25**
tion from the transition requirements and effective date in IAS 32. In reaching this conclusion, the IFRIC noted that it was requested to provide guidance on the application of IAS 32 when it is first adopted by co-operative entities, ie from 1 January 2005. Also, the vast majority of those who commented on the draft Interpretation did not object to the proposed effective date of 1 January 2005. Finally, the IFRIC observed that classifying members' shares as financial liabilities before the date that the terms of these shares are amended will affect only 2005 financial statements, as first-time adopters are not required to apply IAS 32 to earlier periods. As a result, any effect of the Interpretation on first-time adopters is expected to be limited. Furthermore, the IFRIC noted that regulators are familiar with the accounting issues involved. A co-operative entity may be required to present

members' shares as a liability until the governing charter is amended. The IFRIC understands that such amendments, if adopted, could be in place by mid-2005. Accordingly, the IFRIC decided that the effective date for the Interpretation would be annual periods beginning on or after 1 January 2005.

UITF abstract 40
Revenue recognition and service contracts
(Issued 10 March 2005)

BACKGROUND

Since the ASB issued Application Note G: Revenue Recognition, as an Amendment   **1**
to FRS 5, 'Reporting the Substance of Transactions' ('Application Note G') in
November 2003, questions have arisen about the accounting for revenue (ie turnover) from contracts to provide services, and the UITF has been asked to provide
guidance. Although many of these requests specifically refer to services rendered by
professional service firms (for example, firms of accountants and solicitors), the
UITF believes the same principles should be applied in accounting for all service
contracts. This Abstract therefore applies to all contracts for services.

THE ISSUES

The main point at issue, which this Abstract addresses, is when the applicable   **2**
accounting literature requires or allows revenue to be recognised as contract activity
progresses or on contract completion. In this Abstract, the term 'accounted for as a
long-term contract' refers to the method described in SSAP 9 'Stocks and long-term
contracts' of recognising revenue as contract activity progresses.

In some cases, it may be appropriate to treat a single contractual arrangement as two or   **3**
more separate transactions, where there are distinguishable phases. This approach may
only be adopted where the value of each element can be reliably estimated. Application
Note G provides further guidance on this treatment (paragraphs G22-G28).

The contract terms and commercial substance of contracts for services vary con-   **4**
siderably in practice, and it is therefore impracticable to provide definitive guidance
for every situation. Each entity needs to develop an appropriate accounting policy,
having regard to the requirements of this Abstract, Application Note G and SSAP 9.
In some cases, a single approach will be appropriate for all contracts undertaken by
an entity: in others, different approaches will be required for different classes of
contracts.

Application Note G: general principles

Application Note G requires a seller to recognise revenue under an exchange   **5**
transaction with a customer when, and to the extent that, the seller obtains a right to
consideration in exchange for its performance*. At that time it recognises a new
asset, usually a debtor (paragraph G4).

Application Note G also states that a seller may obtain a right to consideration when   **6**
some, but not all, of its contractual obligations have been fulfilled. Where a seller has
partially performed its contractual obligations, it recognises revenue to the extent

---

**Application Note G defines 'right to consideration' as 'A seller's right to the amount received or receivable in
exchange for its performance. This right does not necessarily correspond to amounts falling due in accordance
with a schedule of stage payments which may be specified in a contractual arrangement. Whilst stage payments
will often be timed to coincide with performance, they may not correspond exactly. Stage payments reflect only
the agreed timing of payment, whereas a right to consideration arises through the seller's performance'. The
Application Note defines 'performance' as 'The fulfilment of the seller's contractual obligations to a customer
through the supply of goods and services'.*

that it has obtained the right to consideration through its performance (paragraph G6).

7   Application Note G requires that the amount reported as revenue should be the fair value of the right to consideration: this will usually be based on the price specified in the contractual arrangement net of discounts, and any allowance for credit risk and other uncertainties (paragraph G7).

Long-term contracts

8   SSAP 9 has been in issue for many years, and was last revised in 1988. SSAP 9 provides specific guidance on the accounting treatment of long-term contracts. It requires turnover (and related costs) to be recorded in the profit and loss account as contract activity progresses (paragraph 28). Turnover is ascertained in a manner appropriate to the stage of completion of the contract, the business and the industry in which it operates. Where the outcome of a contract can be assessed with reasonable certainty, the prudently calculated attributable profit should be recognised as the difference between turnover and the related costs. The excess of turnover over payments on account is reported as 'amounts recoverable on contracts' within debtors.

9   Application Note G confirms that SSAP 9 should be applied in accounting for long-term contracts. It is consistent with, and does not amend, the requirements of SSAP 9. The guidance in Application Note G requires a seller to measure turnover in respect of long-term contracts by an assessment of the fair value of the goods or services provided to its reporting date as a proportion of the total fair value of the contract, noting that the guiding principle is to consider the stage of completion of the contractual obligations, which reflects the extent to which the seller has obtained the right to consideration (paragraph G18). The amount of turnover recognised may be derived from the proportion of costs incurred only where it provides evidence of the seller's performance and hence the extent to which it has obtained the right to consideration (paragraph G21).

10   The definition of a long-term contract is set out in SSAP 9. It is:

> *A contract entered into for the design, manufacture or construction of a single substantial asset or the provision of a service (or of a combination of assets or services which together constitute a single project) where the time taken substantially to complete the contract is such that the contract activity falls into different accounting periods. A contract that is required to be accounted for as long-term by this accounting standard will usually extend for a period exceeding one year. However, a duration exceeding one year is not an essential feature of a long-term contract. Some contracts with a shorter duration than one year should be accounted for as long-term contracts if they are sufficiently material to the activity of the period that not to record turnover and attributable profit would lead to distortion of the period's turnover and results such that the financial statements would not give a true and fair view, provided that the policy is applied consistently within the reporting entity and from year to year. (paragraph 22)*

11   The definition is clear that, in the case of contracts for assets, only those for 'a single substantial asset' are required to be accounted for as long-term contracts. Similarly, in the case of a contract for a combination of assets or services only those that 'constitute a single project' are required to be accounted for as long-term contracts.

Thus contracts that require services to be provided on an ongoing basis rather than the provision of a single service (or a number of services that constitute a single project) do not fall to be accounted for as long-term contracts under SSAP 9. For example, a contract to provide repetitive services (such as general professional advice, accounting support, help desk support, maintenance or cleaning) on an ongoing basis should not be accounted for as a long-term contract. **12**

The definition is clear that a contract for services that constitute a single project with duration of more than a year should be accounted for as a long-term contract. It is also clear that contracts with a shorter duration should be accounted for as long-term if contract activity falls into different accounting periods and a failure to reflect turnover and attributable profit would result in distortion of turnover and results, such that the financial statements would fail to give a true and fair view.* **13**

Although SSAP 9 suggests that materiality should be judged in the context of turnover and attributable profit, other implications, for example the effect on reported assets and liabilities, may require that some contracts are accounted for as long-term contracts. The UITF takes the view that in considering whether contracts for services should be accounted for as long-term contracts, the aggregate effect of all such contracts on the financial statements as a whole should be considered. **14**

As noted in SSAP 9, it is important that an entity applies its policy consistently to all similar contracts and from year to year. **15**

Other contracts for services

The UITF takes the view that Application Note G requires all contracts for services to be accounted for in accordance with its general principles, including those stated in paragraphs 5 to 7 above. The overriding consideration is whether the seller has performed, or partially performed, its contractual obligations. If it has performed some, but not all, of its contractual obligations, it is required to recognise revenue to the extent that it has obtained the right to consideration through its performance.† **16**

Revenue is recognised according to the substance of the seller's obligations under the contract (see paragraphs 18 to 20 for further explanation). **17**

Where the substance of a transaction is that the seller's contractual obligations are performed gradually over time, revenue is recognised as contract activity progresses to reflect the seller's partial performance of its contractual obligations. This is the case where the substance of the obligation is either (i) to provide the services of staff, ie where the seller earns the right to consideration as each unit of time is worked or (ii) to require the seller to use its skills and expertise in carrying out acts that will take some time to perform, even when the output is encapsulated in a document, such as a report. In such cases, revenue is recognised to reflect the accrual of the right to consideration as contract activity progresses, by reference to valuation of the work performed as described in paragraph 9 above in relation to long-term contracts. **18**

The ASB's Statement 'Interim Reports' recommends that interim reports are prepared on the discrete method and notes that, under this method, incomplete transactions are treated according to the same principles as are applied at the year-end. Thus entities that prepare interim reports should consider the effect on their interim reports of not treating contracts as long-term contracts, even where they do not straddle the end of an annual accounting period.

†*This conclusion is broadly comparable to the requirements of IAS 18 'Revenue', which requires revenue from the rendering of services to be recognised by reference to the stage of completion of the transaction at the balance sheet date.*

Thus, subject to the considerations in paragraph 20, in case (i) the amount of revenue may be derived from the time spent; in case (ii) the amount of revenue will reflect the fair value of the services provided as a proportion of the total fair value of the contract, which will reflect the time spent and the skills and expertise that have been provided.

19   Where the substance of a contract is that a right to consideration does not arise until the occurrence of a critical event, revenue is not recognised until that event occurs. This only applies where the right to consideration is conditional or contingent on a specified future event or outcome, the occurrence of which is outside the control of the seller.

20   The amount of revenue recognised should reflect any uncertainties as to the amount which the customer will accept and be able to pay. It may be the case, for example, that even where the contract states that fees are to be calculated on a time basis, the customer will not accept that the time spent is reasonable.

APPLICATION TO SMALLER ENTITIES

21   Reporting entities applying the Financial Reporting Standard for Smaller Entities currently applicable are exempt from this Abstract.

UITF CONSENSUS

22   This UITF consensus applies to all contracts for services.

23   Where there are distinguishable phases of a single contract it may be appropriate to account for the contract as two or more separate transactions, provided the value of each phase can be reliably estimated.

24   Contracts for services should not be accounted for as long-term contracts unless they involve the provision of a single service, or a number of services that constitute a single project.

25   A contract for services should be accounted for as a long-term contract where contract activity falls into different accounting periods and it is concluded that the effect is material. In determining whether contracts should be accounted for as long-term contracts, the aggregate effect of all such contracts on the financial statements as a whole should be considered.

26   Where the substance of a contract is that the seller's contractual obligations are performed gradually over time, revenue should be recognised as contract activity progresses to reflect the seller's partial performance of its contractual obligations. The amount of revenue should reflect the accrual of the right to consideration as contract activity progresses by reference to value of the work performed.

27   Where the substance of a contract is that a right to consideration does not arise until the occurrence of a critical event, revenue is not recognised until that event occurs.

28   The amount of revenue recognised on any contract for services should reflect any uncertainties as to the amount that the customer will accept and pay.

29   An entity should apply its policy consistently to all similar contracts and from year to year.

DATE FROM WHICH EFFECTIVE

The accounting treatment required by this Abstract should be adopted in financial **30** statements relating to accounting periods ending on or after 22 June 2005 but earlier adoption is encouraged. Where applicable, corresponding amounts should be restated.

References

SSAP 9 'Stocks and long-term contracts'
FRS 5 Application Note G 'Revenue Recognition'
FRS 18 'Accounting Policies'
International Accounting Standard 18 'Revenue'

UITF abstract 41 (IFRIC Interpretation 8)
Scope of FRS 20 (IFRS 2)

(Issued 7 April 2006)

Preface by the Urgent Issues Task Force

a   This Abstract has the effect of implementing the International Accounting Standards Board's (IASB's) International Financial Reporting Interpretations Committee (IFRIC) Interpretation 8 'Scope of IFRS 2' in the UK and the Republic of Ireland for entities preparing their financial statements in accordance with UK accounting standards and, in doing so, are applying FRS 20 (IFRS 2) 'Share-based Payment'.

b   FRS 20 implements IFRS 2 'Share-based Payment' for listed entities preparing their financial statements in accordance with UK accounting standards for accounting periods beginning on or after 1 January 2005 and for unlisted entities for accounting periods beginning on or after 1 January 2006.

c   This Abstract incorporates the text of IFRIC 8. The text of IFRIC 8 contains various references to International Financial Reporting Standards (IFRSs). In this Abstract those references have been amended to enable the Interpretation to be applied in a UK context. The UITF believes that those amendments do not change the requirements of IFRIC 8 in any way.

Contents

UITF abstract 41 (IFRIC Interpretation 8)
Scope of FRS 20 (IFRS 2)

REFERENCES

- FRS 3 *Reporting Financial Performance*
- FRS 20 (IFRS 2) *Share-based Payment*

BACKGROUND

1   FRS 20 applies to share based payment transactions in which the entity receives or acquires goods or services. 'Goods' includes inventories, consumables, property, plant and equipment, intangible assets and other non financial assets (FRS 20, paragraph 5). Consequently, except for particular transactions excluded from its scope, FRS 20 applies to all transactions in which the entity receives non financial assets or services as consideration for the issue of equity instruments of the entity. FRS 20 also applies to transactions in which the entity incurs liabilities, in respect of goods or services received, that are based on the price (or value) of the entity's shares or other equity instruments of the entity.

2   In some cases, however, it might be difficult to demonstrate that goods or services have been (or will be) received. For example, an entity may grant shares to a charitable organisation for nil consideration. It is usually not possible to identify the specific goods or services received in return for such a transaction. A similar situation might arise in transactions with other parties.

3   FRS 20 requires transactions in which share based payments are made to employees to be measured by reference to the fair value of the share based payments at grant date (FRS 20, paragraph 11).* Hence, the entity is not required to measure directly the fair value of the employee services received.

4   For transactions in which share based payments are made to parties other than employees, FRS 20 specifies a rebuttable presumption that the fair value of the goods or services received can be estimated reliably. In these situations, FRS 20 requires the transaction to be measured at the fair value of the goods or services at the date the entity obtains the goods or the counterparty renders service (FRS 20, paragraph 13). Hence, there is an underlying presumption that the entity is able to identify the goods or services received from parties other than employees. This raises the question of whether the FRS applies in the absence of identifiable goods or services. That in turn raises a further question: if the entity has made a share based payment and the identifiable consideration received (if any) appears to be less than the fair value of the share based payment, does this situation indicate that goods or services have been received, even though they are not specifically identified, and therefore that FRS 20 applies?

5   It should be noted that the phrase 'the fair value of the share based payment' refers to the fair value of the particular share based payment concerned. For example, an entity might be required by government legislation to issue some portion of its shares to nationals of a particular country, which may be transferred only to other nationals of that country. Such a transfer restriction may affect the fair value of the shares concerned, and therefore those shares may have a fair value that is less than the fair value of otherwise identical shares that do not carry such restrictions. In this situation, if the question in paragraph 4 were to arise in the context of the restricted shares, the phrase 'the fair value of the share based payment' would refer to the fair value of the restricted shares, not the fair value of other, unrestricted shares.

Under FRS 20, all references to employees include others providing similar services.

SCOPE

FRS 20 applies to transactions in which an entity or an entity's shareholders have granted equity instruments* or incurred a liability to transfer cash or other assets for amounts that are based on the price (or value) of the entity's shares or other equity instruments of the entity. This Abstract applies to such transactions when the identifiable consideration received (or to be received) by the entity, including cash and the fair value of identifiable non-cash consideration (if any), appears to be less than the fair value of the equity instruments granted or liability incurred. However, this Abstract does not apply to transactions excluded from the scope of FRS 20 in accordance with paragraphs 3-6 of that FRS. **6**

Reporting entities applying the Financial Reporting Standard for Smaller Entities currently applicable are exempt from this Abstract. **6A**

ISSUE

The issue addressed in the Abstract is whether FRS 20 applies to transactions in which the entity cannot identify specifically some or all of the goods or services received. **7**

UITF CONSENSUS

FRS 20 applies to particular transactions in which goods or services are received, such as transactions in which an entity receives goods or services as consideration for equity instruments of the entity. This includes transactions in which the entity cannot identify specifically some or all of the goods or services received. **8**

In the absence of specifically identifiable goods or services, other circumstances may indicate that goods or services have been (or will be) received, in which case FRS 20 applies. In particular, if the identifiable consideration received (if any) appears to be less than the fair value of the equity instruments granted or liability incurred, typically this circumstance indicates that other consideration (ie unidentifiable goods or services) has been (or will be) received. **9**

The entity shall measure the identifiable goods or services received in accordance with FRS 20. **10**

The entity shall measure the unidentifiable goods or services received (or to be received) as the difference between the fair value of the share based payment and the fair value of any identifiable goods or services received (or to be received). **11**

The entity shall measure the unidentifiable goods or services received at the grant date. However, for cash settled transactions, the liability shall be remeasured at each reporting date until it is settled. **12**

EFFECTIVE DATE

The accounting treatment required by this Abstract should be adopted in financial statements relating to accounting periods beginning on or after 1 May 2006, but earlier adoption is encouraged. **13**

*These include equity instruments of the entity, the entity's parents and other entities in the same group as the entity.

TRANSITION

14   An entity shall apply this Abstract retrospectively in accordance with the requirements of FRS 3, subject to the transitional provisions of FRS 20.

ILLUSTRATIVE EXAMPLE

This example accompanies, but is not part of, UITF 41.

An entity granted shares with a total fair value of CU100,000* to parties other than   **IE1**
employees who are from a particular section of the community (historically dis-
advantaged individuals), as a means of enhancing its image as a good corporate
citizen. The economic benefits derived from enhancing its corporate image could take
a variety of forms, such as increasing its customer base, attracting or retaining
employees, or improving or maintaining its ability to tender successfully for business
contracts.

The entity cannot identify the specific consideration received. For example, no cash   **IE2**
was received and no service conditions were imposed. Therefore, the identifiable
consideration (nil) is less than the fair value of the equity instruments granted
(CU100,000).

Although the entity cannot identify any specific goods or services received, the cir-   **IE3**
cumstances indicate that goods or services have been (or will be) received, and
therefore FRS 20 applies.

In this situation, because the entity cannot identify the specific goods or services   **IE4**
received, the rebuttable presumption in paragraph 13 of FRS 20, that the fair value
of the goods or services received can be estimated reliably, does not apply. The entity
should instead measure the goods or services received by reference to the fair value of
the equity instruments granted.

In this example, monetary amounts are denominated in 'currency units' (CU).

Basis for Conclusions on IFRIC Interpretation 8

This Basis for Conclusions accompanies, but is not part of, IFRIC 8.

> ASB note: The IFRIC's Basis for Conclusions, which accompanies IFRIC 8, is set out below in full.

BC1   This Basis for Conclusions summarises the IFRIC's considerations in reaching its consensus. Individual IFRIC members gave greater weight to some factors than to others.

BC2   IFRS 2 *Share-based Payment* applies to share-based payment transactions in which the entity receives or acquires goods or services. However, in some situations, it might be difficult to demonstrate that the entity has received goods or services. This raises the question of whether IFRS 2 applies to such transactions.

BC3   This question arose in the context of particular transactions, similar to the transaction described in the Illustrative Example that accompanies the Interpretation. The IFRIC concluded that determining whether such transactions were within the scope of IFRS 2 raised a further question: if the entity has made a share-based payment and the identifiable consideration received (if any) appears to be less than the fair value of the share-based payment, does this situation indicate that goods or services have been received, even though those goods or services are not specifically identified, and therefore that IFRS 2 applies?

BC4   The IFRIC noted that, when the International Accounting Standards Board developed IFRS 2, the Board concluded that the directors of an entity would expect to receive some goods or services in return for equity instruments issued (IFRS 2 paragraph BC37). This implies that it is not necessary to identify the specific goods or services received in return for the equity instruments granted to conclude that goods or services have been (or will be) received. Furthermore, paragraph 8 of the Standard establishes that it is not necessary for the goods or services received to qualify for recognition as an asset in order for the share-based payment to be within the scope of IFRS 2. In this case, the Standard requires the cost of the goods or services received or receivable to be recognised as expenses.

BC5   Accordingly, the IFRIC concluded that the scope of IFRS 2 includes transactions in which the entity cannot identify some or all of the specific goods or services received. If the identifiable consideration received appears to be less than the fair value of the equity instruments granted or liability incurred, typically*, this circumstance indicates that other consideration (ie unidentifiable goods or services) has been (or will be) received.

BC6   The IFRIC also noted that IFRS 2 presumes that the consideration received for share-based payments is consistent with the fair value of those share-based payments. For example, if the entity cannot estimate reliably the fair value of the goods or services received, IFRS 2 requires the entity to measure the fair value of the goods or services received by reference to the fair value of the share-based payment made to acquire those goods or services.

In some cases, the reason for the transfer would explain why no goods or services have been or will have been or will be received. For example, a principal shareholder, as part of estate planning, transfers some of his shares to a family member. In the absence of factors that indicate that the family member has provided, or is expected to provide, any goods or services to the entity in return for the shares, such a transaction would fall outside of the scope of IFRS 2 and thus this Interpretation.

The IFRIC noted that it is neither necessary nor appropriate to measure the fair value of goods or services as well as the fair value of the share-based payment for every transaction in which the entity receives goods or non-employee services. However, when the identifiable consideration received appears to be less than the fair value of the share-based payment, measurement of both the goods or services received and the share-based payment may be necessary in order to measure the value of the unidentifiable goods or services received.   **BC7**

Paragraph 13 of IFRS 2 stipulates a rebuttable presumption that identifiable goods or services received can be reliably estimated. The IFRIC noted that goods or services that are unidentifiable cannot be reliably measured and that this rebuttable presumption is relevant only for identifiable goods or services.   **BC8**

The IFRIC noted that when the goods or services received are identifiable, the measurement principles in IFRS 2 should be applied. When the goods or services received are unidentifiable, the IFRIC concluded that the grant date is the most appropriate date for the purposes of providing a surrogate measure of the unidentifiable goods or services received (or to be received).   **BC9**

The IFRIC noted that some transactions include identifiable and unidentifiable goods or services. In this case, it would be necessary to measure the fair value of the unidentifiable goods or services received at the grant date and to measure the identifiable goods or services in accordance with IFRS 2.   **BC10**

For cash-settled transactions in which unidentifiable goods or services are received, it is necessary to remeasure the liability at each subsequent reporting date in order to be consistent with IFRS 2.   **BC11**

The IFRIC noted that the IFRS 2 requirements in respect of the recognition of the expense arising from share-based payments would apply to identifiable and unidentifiable goods or services. Therefore, the IFRIC decided not to issue additional guidance on this point.   **BC12**

When considering the transitional provisions relating to first time adopters applying the Interpretation, the IFRIC concluded that it was not necessary to amend IFRS 1 *First-Time Adoption of International Financial Reporting Standards*, because the Interpretation will have no effect unless IFRS 2 is effective.   **BC13**

UITF abstract 42 (IFRIC Interpretation 9)
Reassessment of Embedded Derivatives

(Issued 7 April 2006)

Preface by the Urgent Issues Task Force

a   This Abstract has the effect of implementing the International Accounting Standards Board's (IASB's) International Financial Reporting Interpretations Committee (IFRIC) Interpretation 9 'Reassessment of Embedded Derivatives' in the UK and the Republic of Ireland for entities preparing their financial statements in accordance with UK accounting standards and, in doing so, are applying FRS 26 (IAS 39) 'Financial Instruments: Measurement'.

b   FRS 26 implements IAS 39 'Financial Instruments: Recognition and Measurement' for listed entities* preparing their financial statements in accordance with UK accounting standards for accounting periods beginning on or after 1 January 2005, and for unlisted entities that adopt the fair value accounting rules in the Companies Act 1985, for accounting periods beginning on or after 1 January 2006. FRS 26 includes transition provisions for entities adopting the standard that are similar to those in IFRS 1 'First-time Adoption of International Financial Reporting Standards'.

c   This Abstract incorporates the text of IFRIC 9. The text of IFRIC 9 contains various references to International Financial Reporting Standards (IFRSs). In this Abstract those references have been amended to enable the Interpretation to be applied in a UK context. The UITF believes that those amendments do not change the requirements of IFRIC 9 in any way.

---

*Except for certain listed entities in the Republic of Ireland, for which the commencement date is 1 January 2006.

Contents

UITF abstract 42 (IFRIC Interpretation 9)
Reassessment of Embedded Derivatives

paragraphs

REFERENCES

- FRS 26 (IAS 39) *Financial Instruments: Measurement*
- FRS 6 *Acquisitions and Mergers*

BACKGROUND

1   FRS 26 paragraph 10 describes an embedded derivative as 'a component of a hybrid (combined) instrument that also includes a non-derivative host contract-with the effect that some of the cash flows of the combined instrument vary in a way similar to a stand-alone derivative.'

2   FRS 26 paragraph 11 requires an embedded derivative to be separated from the host contract and accounted for as a derivative if, and only if:

(a)   the economic characteristics and risks of the embedded derivative are not closely related to the economic characteristics and risks of the host contract;

(b)   a separate instrument with the same terms as the embedded derivative would meet the definition of a derivative; and

(c)   the hybrid (combined) instrument is not measured at fair value with changes in fair value recognised in profit or loss (ie a derivative that is embedded in a financial asset or financial liability at fair value through profit or loss is not separated).

SCOPE

3   Subject to paragraphs 4 and 5 below, this Abstract applies to all embedded derivatives within the scope of FRS 26.

4   This Abstract does not address remeasurement issues arising from a reassessment of embedded derivatives.

5   This Abstract does not address the acquisition of contracts with embedded derivatives in a business combination nor their possible reassessment at the date of acquisition.

ISSUE

6   FRS 26 requires an entity, when it first becomes a party to a contract, to assess whether any embedded derivatives contained in the contract are required to be separated from the host contract and accounted for as derivatives under the Standard. This Abstract addresses the following issues:

(a)   Does FRS 26 require such an assessment to be made only when the entity first becomes a party to the contract, or should the assessment be reconsidered throughout the life of the contract?

(b)   Should a first-time adopter make its assessment on the basis of the conditions that existed when the entity first became a party to the contract, or those prevailing when the entity adopts FRS 26 for the first time?

UITF CONSENSUS

7   An entity shall assess whether an embedded derivative is required to be separated from the host contract and accounted for as a derivative when the entity first

becomes a party to the contract. Subsequent reassessment is prohibited unless there is a change in the terms of the contract that significantly modifies the cash flows that otherwise would be required under the contract, in which case reassessment is required. An entity determines whether a modification to cash flows is significant by considering the extent to which the expected future cash flows associated with the embedded derivative, the host contract or both have changed and whether the change is significant relative to the previously expected cash flows on the contract.

A first-time adopter shall assess whether an embedded derivative is required to be **8** separated from the host contract and accounted for as a derivative on the basis of the conditions that existed at the later of the date it first became a party to the contract and the date a reassessment is required by paragraph 7.

EFFECTIVE DATE AND TRANSITION

The accounting treatment required by this Abstract should be adopted in financial **9** statements related to accounting periods beginning on or after 1 June 2006, but earlier adoption is encouraged. The Abstract shall be applied retrospectively.

Basis for Conclusions on IFRIC Interpretation 9

This Basis for Conclusions accompanies, but is not part of, IFRIC 9.

> *ASB note*: The IFRIC's Basis for Conclusions, which accompanies IFRIC 9, is set out below in full.

INTRODUCTION

BC1   This Basis for Conclusions summarises the IFRIC's considerations in reaching its consensus. Individual IFRIC members gave greater weight to some factors than to others.

BC2   As explained below, the IFRIC was informed that uncertainty existed over certain aspects of the requirements of IAS 39 *Financial Instruments: Recognition and Measurement* relating to the reassessment of embedded derivatives. The IFRIC published proposals on the subject in March 2005 as D15 *Reassessment of Embedded Derivatives* and developed IFRIC 9 after considering the thirty comment letters received.

BC3   IAS 39 requires an entity, when it first becomes a party to a contract, to assess whether any embedded derivative contained in the contract needs to be separated from the host contract and accounted for as a derivative under the Standard. However, the issue arises whether IAS 39 requires an entity to continue to carry out this assessment after it first becomes a party to a contract, and if so, with what frequency. The Standard is silent on this issue and the IFRIC was informed that as a result there was a risk of divergence in practice.

BC4   The question is relevant, for example, when the terms of the embedded derivative do not change but market conditions change and the market was the principal factor in determining whether the host contract and embedded derivative are closely related. Instances when this might arise are given in paragraph AG33(d) of IAS 39. Paragraph AG33(d) states that an embedded foreign currency derivative is closely related to the host contract provided it is not leveraged, does not contain an option feature, and requires payments denominated in one of the following currencies:

(a)   the functional currency of any substantial party to that contract;

(b)   the currency in which the price of the related good or service that is acquired or delivered is routinely denominated in commercial transactions around the world (such as the US dollar for crude oil transactions); or

(c)   a currency that is commonly used in contracts to purchase or sell non-financial items in the economic environment in which the transaction takes place (eg a relatively stable and liquid currency that is commonly used in local business transactions or external trade).

BC5   Any of the currencies specified in (a)-(c) above may change. Assume that when an entity first became a party to a contract, it assessed the contract as containing an embedded derivative that was closely related (because it was in one of the three categories in paragraph BC4) and hence not accounted for separately. Assume that subsequently market conditions change and that if the entity were to reassess the contract under the changed circumstances it would conclude that the embedded derivative is not closely related and therefore requires separate accounting. (The converse could also arise.) The issue is whether the entity should make such a reassessment.

REASSESSMENT OF EMBEDDED DERIVATIVES

The IFRIC noted that the rationale for the requirement in IAS 39 to separate   **BC6**
embedded derivatives is that an entity should not be able to circumvent the recognition and measurement requirements for derivatives merely by embedding a
derivative in a non-derivative financial instrument or other contract (for example, by
embedding a commodity forward in a debt instrument). Changes in external circumstances (such as those set out in paragraph BC5) are not ways to circumvent the
Standard. The IFRIC therefore concluded that reassessment was not appropriate for
such changes.

The IFRIC noted that as a practical expedient IAS 39 does not require the   **BC7**
separation of embedded derivatives that are closely related. Many financial instruments contain embedded derivatives. Separating all of these embedded derivatives
would be burdensome for entities. The IFRIC noted that requiring entities to
reassess embedded derivatives in all hybrid instruments could be onerous because
frequent monitoring would be required. Market conditions and other factors
affecting embedded derivatives would have to be monitored continuously to ensure
timely identification of a change in circumstances and amendment of the accounting
treatment accordingly. For example, if the functional currency of the counterparty
changes during the reporting period so that the contract is no longer denominated in
a currency of one of the parties to the contract, then a reassessment of the hybrid
instrument would be required at the date of change to ensure the correct accounting
treatment in future.

The IFRIC also recognised that although IAS 39 is silent on the issue of reassessment   **BC8**
it gives relevant guidance when it states that for the types of contracts covered by
paragraph AG33(b) the assessment of whether an embedded derivative is closely
related is required only at inception. Paragraph AG33(b) states:

> An embedded floor or cap on the interest rate on a debt contract or insurance
> contract is closely related to the host contract, provided the cap is at or above
> the market rate of interest and the floor is at or below the market rate of interest
> *when the contract is issued*, and the cap or floor is not leveraged in relation to the
> host contract. Similarly, provisions included in a contract to purchase or sell an
> asset (eg a commodity) that establish a cap and a floor on the price to be paid or
> received for the asset are closely related to the host contract if both the cap and
> floor were out of the money *at inception* and are not leveraged. (Emphasis
> added).

The IFRIC also considered the implications of requiring subsequent reassessment.   **BC9**
For example, assume that an entity, when it first becomes a party to a contract,
separately recognises a host asset and an embedded derivative liability. If the entity
were required to reassess whether the embedded derivative was to be accounted for
separately and if the entity concluded some time after becoming a party to the
contract that the derivative was no longer required to be separated, then questions of
recognition and measurement would arise. In the above circumstances, the IFRIC
identified the following possibilities:

(a) the entity could remove the derivative from its balance sheet and recognise in
profit or loss a corresponding gain or loss. This would lead to recognition of a
gain or loss even though there had been no transaction and no change in the
value of the total contract or its components.

(b) the entity could leave the derivative as a separate item in the balance sheet. The
issue would then arise as to when the item was to be removed from the balance
sheet. Should it be amortised (and, if so, how would the amortisation affect the

effective interest rate of the asset), or should it be derecognised only when the asset is derecognised?

(c)   the entity could combine the derivative (which is recognised at fair value) with the asset (which is recognised at amortised cost). This would alter both the carrying amount of the asset and its effective interest rate even though there had been no change in the economics of the whole contract. In some cases, it could also result in a negative effective interest rate.

The IFRIC noted that, under its view that subsequent reassessment is appropriate only when there has been a change in the terms of the contract that significantly modifies the cash flows that otherwise would be required by the contract, the above issues do not arise.

BC10   The IFRIC noted that IAS 39 requires an entity to assess whether an embedded derivative needs to be separated from the host contract and accounted for as a derivative when it first becomes a party to a contract. Consequently, if an entity purchases a contract that contains an embedded derivative it assesses whether the embedded derivative needs to be separated and accounted for as a derivative on the basis of conditions at that date.

BC11   The IFRIC considered an alternative approach of making reassessment optional. It decided against this approach because it would reduce comparability of financial information. Also, the IFRIC noted that this approach would be inconsistent with the embedded derivative requirements in IAS 39 that either require or prohibit separation but do not give an option. Accordingly, the IFRIC concluded that reassessment should not be optional.

FIRST-TIME ADOPTERS OF IFRSS

BC12   In the Implementation Guidance with IFRS 1 *First-time Adoption of International Financial Reporting Standards, paragraph IG55* states:

When IAS 39 requires an entity to separate an embedded derivative from a host contract, the initial carrying amounts of the components at the date when the instrument first satisfies the recognition criteria in IAS 39 reflect circumstances at that date (IAS 39, paragraph 11). If the entity cannot determine the initial carrying amounts of the embedded derivative and host contract reliably, it treats the entire combined contract as a financial instrument held for trading (IAS 39, paragraph 12). This results in fair value measurement (except when the entity cannot determine a reliable fair value, see IAS 39, paragraph 46(c)), with changes in fair value recognised in profit or loss.

BC13   This guidance reflects the principle in IFRS 1 that a first-time adopter should apply IFRSs as if they had been in place from initial recognition. This is consistent with the general principle used in IFRSs of full retrospective application of Standards. The IFRIC noted that the date of initial recognition referred to in paragraph IG55 is the date when the entity first became a party to the contract and not the date of first-time adoption of IFRSs. Accordingly, the IFRIC concluded that IFRS 1 requires an entity to assess whether an embedded derivative is required to be separated from the host contract and accounted for as a derivative on the basis of conditions at the date when the entity first became a party to the contract and not those at the date of first-time adoption.

UITF abstract 43
The interpretation of equivalence for the purposes of section 228A of the Companies Act 1985

(Issued 23 October 2006)

INTRODUCTION

With effect for accounting periods commencing on or after 1 January 2005, the **1** Companies Act 1985 has been amended to include a new section 228A. This exempts, subject to certain conditions, an intermediate parent undertaking from the requirement to prepare consolidated accounts where its parent entity is not established under the law of an EEA state. The new exemption complements the well established exemption in section 228 for intermediate parent undertakings where the parent entity is established under the law of an EEA state.

Section 228A* states that: **2**

> "(2) *Exemption is conditional upon compliance with all of the following conditions:*
>
> (a) that the company and all of its subsidiary undertakings are included in consolidated accounts for a larger group drawn up to the same date, or to an earlier date in the same financial year, by a parent undertaking;
>
> (b) that those accounts and, where appropriate, the group's annual report, are drawn up in accordance with the provisions of the Seventh Directive (83/349/EEC) (where applicable as modified by the provisions of the Bank Accounts Directive (86/635/EEC) or the Insurance Accounts Directive (91/674/EEC)), <u>or in a manner equivalent to consolidated accounts and consolidated annual reports so drawn up;</u>
>
> (c) ..."

This Abstract provides guidance on interpretation of the underlined words. Questions have been raised as to whether financial statements drawn up in accordance with International Financial Reporting Standards (IFRS), US Generally Accepted Accounting Principles (GAAP) or other GAAPs meet the requirement for equivalence with the Seventh Directive. The UITF believes that guidance would be useful to reduce the likelihood of divergent practice emerging.

BACKGROUND

The requirements of section 228A are based on the EU Seventh Company Law **3** Directive. No guidance has been issued at the EU level on the interpretation of the expression "in a manner equivalent" used in the legislation. It is understood that US GAAP is regularly treated as meeting the equivalence test in some of those countries that have implemented similar law based on the Seventh Directive.

In the Republic of Ireland the wording of Regulation 9A of the European Communities (Companies: Group Accounts) Regulations 1992 is slightly different but the intention is the same and the underlined phrase is exactly the same.

4   In the UK, the Department of Trade and Industry has stated in published guidance*
that it considers that, in most circumstances, financial statements of a larger group
prepared on the basis of IFRS would meet the equivalence test. In relation to US
GAAP, Canadian GAAP and Japanese GAAP, the DTI guidance makes reference to
the work that was being undertaken at the time that guidance was issued by the
Committee of European Securities Regulators (CESR), in accordance with a mandate provided by the European Commission.

5   In June 2005, CESR published its recommendation to the European Commission on
the equivalence of the GAAPs in the US, Canada and Japan (together the "third
countries") with IFRS as adopted by the EU.† CESR's recommendation is that these
three GAAPs, each taken as a whole, are equivalent to IFRS subject to certain
caveats and additional disclosures. The CESR report does not deal with equivalence
with the Seventh Directive, which is generally less prescriptive than IFRS, and the
study was conducted for a different purpose in connection with the Prospectus
Directive and the Transparency Directive. Nevertheless, it is expected that similar
principles will apply to the consideration of equivalence between the Seventh
Directive and third countries' GAAPs as apply to the consideration of equivalence
between those GAAPs and IFRS.

THE ISSUE

6   Use of the exemption in section 228A requires an analysis of a particular set of
consolidated accounts to determine whether they are drawn up in a manner
equivalent to consolidated accounts that are in accordance with the Seventh
Directive‡. However, whilst the analysis ultimately has to be on a case by case basis,
it should be possible to identify some GAAPs that usually result in consolidated
accounts being drawn up in a manner equivalent to the Seventh Directive.

7   The UITF believes that guidance would assist entities to adopt a consistent approach
to this issue. In the absence of such guidance, companies and their auditors might
feel obliged to take an overly cautious approach in response to uncertainty about
whether the exemption can be used. This would result in unnecessary burdens on
businesses in the UK and Republic of Ireland and might disadvantage them when
compared to companies operating elsewhere in the EU.

General approach to assessing equivalence

8   It is generally accepted that the reference to equivalence in section 228A does not
mean compliance with every detail of the Seventh Directive. The UITF believes that
a qualitative approach, i.e. with a focus on compliance with the basic requirements of
the Directive and in particular the requirement to give a true and fair view, is more in

---

**DTI, 'Guidance for British companies on changes to the accounting and reporting provisions of the Companies
Act 1985', August 2005, paragraphs 5.3 to 5.6.*

*†Technical advice on equivalence of certain third country GAAP and on description of certain third countries
mechanisms of enforcement of financial information (Ref: CESR/05-230b). The European Commission has
announced plans to postpone by two years implementation of the requirement for equivalence in the Prospectus
and Transparency Directives and so the CESR guidance may not be implemented.*

*‡The Seventh Directive deals with consolidated accounts and applies most of the requirements of the Fourth
Directive to those consolidated accounts. Consideration of equivalence with the Seventh Directive therefore
requires consideration of equivalence with the relevant provisions of the Fourth Directive. References in this
Abstract to accounts being prepared in accordance with the Seventh Directive include, where appropriate,
compliance with the relevant provisions of the Fourth Directive.*

keeping with the deregulatory nature of the exemption than a requirement to consider the detailed requirements on a checklist basis (see also paragraph 15 below).

UK accounting standards

Some entities have parents that are established in jurisdictions outside the EU and prepare consolidated accounts that give a true and fair view and comply with accounting standards applicable in the UK and Republic of Ireland. Those accounts will meet the requirement for equivalence.   **9**

IFRS adopted by the EU

The procedure for adoption of IFRS by the EU requires a standard to meet the basic requirements of the Fourth and Seventh Directives, including the requirement to give a true and fair view, without implying a strict conformity with each and every provision. Accounts prepared in accordance with IFRS as adopted by the EU will therefore always meet the test of equivalence.   **10**

IFRS

IFRS as issued by the IASB (i.e. without the qualifying "as adopted by the EU") will currently meet the test of equivalence. This is because there are no standards or interpretations issued by the IASB that conflict with the basic requirements of the Directives*. The fact that a standard or interpretation has not been adopted because of the time taken to complete the adoption process will not of itself indicate a lack of equivalence. However if, in future, the European Commission fails to adopt a standard on the grounds that it does not meet the basic requirements of either the Fourth or Seventh Directive, it will be necessary to consider whether the reasons for the failure to adopt the standard suggest that compliance with that standard will fail to give a true and fair view and will, therefore, fail the test of equivalence.   **11**

Accounting standards based on IFRS

There are some GAAPs (e.g. those in Australia, Hong Kong and South Africa) which are based on IFRS but may not correspond with IFRS in all respects. It is not practicable to give specific guidance on all of the increasing number of GAAPs that are based on, or are converging with, IFRS. In those cases where they are more restrictive than IFRS by eliminating choices, they will meet the test of equivalence for the purposes of section 228A. In other cases, it will be necessary to obtain an understanding of how they differ from IFRS and whether those differences might result in a departure from the basic requirements of the Fourth or Seventh Directives.   **12**

Accounting standards not based on IFRS

There are other GAAPs that are not based on IFRS. These include the third countries' GAAPs (i.e. US, Canadian and Japanese GAAPs) which were the subject of the CESR recommendation to the European Commission. CESR's recommendation was made from the perspective that investors' decisions should be unaffected by the use of different accounting standards. This test is not directly relevant to the   **13**

The adoption of the Fair Value Amendment to IAS 39 has removed the possibility of a lack of equivalence through compliance with the "full" IAS 39 rather than the "carved out" version originally adopted by the EU.

accounts of the higher parent required under section 228A because these will not be used for the purposes of investing in shares of the UK reporting entity - investors that are not part of the controlling interest have in any case a legal right to require consolidated accounts of the UK parent. However, an assessment of whether the third countries' GAAPs meet the section 228A equivalence test can be built upon the work of CESR.

14   The Fourth and Seventh Directives are generally less prescriptive than IFRS. For example, they do not prohibit merger accounting or include any particular requirements about how to account for share-based payments. The work undertaken by CESR in relation to equivalence with IFRS suggests that US GAAP, Canadian GAAP and Japanese GAAP will, in most cases, result in accounts that comply with the basic requirements of the Fourth and Seventh Directives. Some of the issues identified by CESR as resulting in a possible lack of equivalence between IFRS and the third countries' GAAPs are not relevant for the purposes of section 228A; however, two issues, namely the scope of consolidated accounts and the consistent use of accounting policies, are particularly relevant to assessing equivalence.

15   The UITF believes that the basic requirement for a true and fair view includes the scope of consolidated accounts and consistent accounting policies. Therefore, meeting the test of equivalence is subject to ensuring both that the scope of entities included in the consolidated accounts is consistent with the Seventh Directive and that consistent accounting policies have been used for all entities included in the consolidated accounts.

Scope of consolidated accounts

16   As a result of section 228A (2)(a) there is a specific requirement that the UK parent company and all of its subsidiary undertakings (as defined in the Act) are included in the consolidated accounts of the larger group. The requirement for undertakings outside of the UK sub-group is less stringent in that they need meet only the minimum requirements of the Seventh Directive assuming that the Member State options had been implemented in the least restrictive way.

17   The text of Articles 1-3 of the Seventh Directive, which includes a definition of those undertakings that must be included in the consolidation, is set out in Appendix 1 to this Abstract for reference. Some parts of the definition in Article 1 are Member State options that cannot be regarded as mandatory requirements of the Directive. In particular, the requirement that an undertaking should be consolidated on the grounds of actual exercise of, or power to exercise, a dominant influence is a Member State option which was taken up in the UK but which need not be considered for the purpose of assessing equivalence.

18   For example, some Special Purpose Entities would not have to be consolidated under the requirements of Article 1 even if they would have to be consolidated under UK GAAP. On the other hand, there may be cases where a third country's GAAP does not require the consolidation of an entity in circumstances where the Seventh Directive would do so. This would lead to a lack of equivalence for the purposes of section 228A where the effect on the consolidated accounts of the larger group is material to those accounts.

Consistent accounting policies

19   The Seventh Directive includes a requirement that consolidated accounts should be drawn up on the basis of consistent accounting policies. There may be instances

where other GAAPs do not include such a requirement. This could lead to a lack of equivalence for the purposes of section 228A where the effect on the consolidated accounts of the larger group is material to those accounts.

Other differences

There are other areas of difference between the third countries' GAAPs and the   **20**
Seventh Directive, for example in relation to the treatment of goodwill and negative goodwill. However, the requirements of IFRS 3 Business Combinations for goodwill and negative goodwill also differ from the detailed provisions of the Fourth and Seventh Directives. IFRS 3 has been adopted by the EU and therefore it may be considered that such differences are not material for the purpose of assessing equivalence.

Specialised industries

The UITF's consideration of this issue did not extend to those cases where the   **21**
consolidated accounts of the larger group are prepared in accordance with specialised industry standards, including those that may be applicable to banks and insurance companies*. The UITF noted that some GAAPs include industry specific standards which grant exemptions from other standards. For example, US GAAP grants an exemption from the requirement to consolidate certain subsidiaries of some types of investment vehicle. Consideration should be given to whether the application of such industry specific standards will result in a lack of equivalence with the Directives.

Annual report

Section 228A (2)(b) imposes a condition that "where appropriate" the "annual   **22**
report" of the larger group must be drawn up in accordance with the provisions of the Seventh Directive or in a manner equivalent to reports so drawn up. The term "annual report" is used in the section in the sense that it is used in the Directive and should be read as "Directors' report" in the UK context.

Section 228A does not provide further elaboration of the expression "where   **23**
appropriate". Possible interpretations include "where the larger group prepares an annual report" or "where the larger group would be required to prepare an annual report under the Directive". The Directive provides that a Member State may waive the requirement for small companies to prepare an annual report. This Abstract does not provide guidance on the interpretation of the expression "where appropriate" as used in section 228A.

For ease of reference, the requirements of Article 46 of the Fourth Directive dealing   **24**
with the contents of the annual report are set out in Appendix 2 to this Abstract. In keeping with the approach to equivalence of financial statements taken in this Abstract, any consideration of equivalence of the annual report would be at a high level rather than considering the detailed requirements on a checklist basis.

In the case of banks and insurance companies the requirements of the Seventh Directive to be considered are those as modified, where appropriate, by the Bank Accounts Directive or the Insurance Accounts Directive.

APPLICATION TO SMALLER ENTITIES

25   Reporting entities applying the Financial Reporting Standard for Smaller Entities are exempt from this Abstract*.

UITF CONSENSUS

26   The UITF reached a consensus that for the purposes of section 228A of the Companies Act 1985:

(a)   when assessing whether consolidated accounts of a higher non-EEA parent are drawn up in a manner equivalent to consolidated accounts drawn up in accordance with the Seventh Directive, it is necessary to consider whether they meet the basic requirements of the Fourth and Seventh Directives, in particular the requirement to give a true and fair view, without implying strict conformity with each and every provision; and

(b)   the consequences of adopting the principle in (a) above are:

   (i)   consolidated accounts of the higher parent that give a true and fair view and comply with accounting standards applicable in the UK and Republic of Ireland will meet the test of equivalence with the Seventh Directive;

   (ii)   consolidated accounts of the higher parent prepared in accordance with IFRS as adopted by the EU will meet the test of equivalence with the Seventh Directive;

   (iii)   consolidated accounts of the higher parent prepared in accordance with IFRS as issued by the IASB will meet the test of equivalence with the Seventh Directive subject to the consideration of the reasons for any failure by the European Commission to adopt a standard or interpretation;

   (iv)   consolidated accounts of the higher parent prepared using GAAPs which are closely related to IFRS will meet the test of equivalence with the Seventh Directive subject to consideration of the effect of any differences from IFRS as adopted by the EU;

   (v)   consolidated accounts of the higher parent prepared in accordance with US GAAP, Canadian GAAP and Japanese GAAP will normally meet the test of equivalence with the Seventh Directive subject to consideration of developments in those GAAPs following the date of issue of this Abstract and:

   - ensuring the scope of entities included in those consolidated accounts is consistent with the Seventh Directive;
   - ensuring that consistent accounting policies have been used for all entities included in those consolidated accounts; and
   - evaluating the effect of any exemptions or modifications to the GAAPs allowed by specialised industry standards which have been applied in those consolidated accounts; and

   (vi)   consolidated accounts of the higher parent prepared using other GAAPs should be assessed for equivalence with the Seventh Directive based on the particular facts, including the similarities to, and differences from, the GAAPs considered specifically in this Abstract.

Companies applying the Financial Reporting Standard for Smaller Entities will be entitled to the exemption from preparation of consolidated accounts for small groups in s248 and will not therefore have to rely on the exemption in s228A.

DATE FROM WHICH EFFECTIVE

The interpretation of equivalence set out in this consensus for the purposes of section **27**
228A should be adopted as soon as practicable.

REFERENCES

EU Directives

Seventh Directive 83/349/EEC

Fourth Directive 78/660/EEC

Legislation

Great Britain

Companies Act 1985 section 228A

Northern Ireland

The Companies (Northern Ireland) Order 1986 Article 236A

Republic of Ireland

The European Communities (Companies: Group Accounts) Regulations 1992
Regulation 9A

Appendix 1
Extract from the Seventh Directive concerning undertakings to beincluded in the consolidation

SECTION 1

Conditions for the preparation of consolidated accounts

Article 1

1   A Member State shall require any undertaking governed by its national law to draw up consolidated accounts and a consolidated annual report if that undertaking (a parent undertaking):

(a)   has a majority of the shareholders' or members' voting rights in another undertaking (a subsidiary undertaking); or

(b)   has the right to appoint or remove a majority of the members of the administrative, management or supervisory body of another undertaking (a subsidiary undertaking) and is at the same time a shareholder in or member of that undertaking; or

(c)   has the right to exercise a dominant influence over an undertaking (a subsidiary undertaking) of which it is a shareholder or member, pursuant to a contract entered into with that undertaking or to a provision in its memorandum or articles of association, where the law governing that subsidiary undertaking permits its being subject to such contracts or provisions. A Member State need not prescribe that a parent undertaking must be a shareholder in or member of its subsidiary undertaking. Those Member States the laws of which do not provide for such contracts or clauses shall not be required to apply this provision; or

(d)   is a shareholder in or member of an undertaking, and:

(aa)   a majority of the members of the administrative, management or supervisory bodies of that undertaking (a subsidiary undertaking) who have held office during the financial year, during the preceding financial year and up to the time when the consolidated accounts are drawn up, have been appointed solely as a result of the exercise of its voting rights; or

(bb)   controls alone, pursuant to an agreement with other shareholders in or members of that undertaking (a subsidiary undertaking), a majority of shareholders' or members' voting rights in that undertaking. The Member States may introduce more detailed provisions concerning the form and contents of such agreements.

The Member States shall prescribe at least the arrangements referred to in (bb) above.

They may make the application of (aa) above dependent upon the holding's representing 20 % or more of the shareholders' or members' voting rights. However, (aa) above shall not apply where another undertaking has the rights referred to in subparagraphs (a), (b) or (c) above with regard to that subsidiary undertaking.

2   Apart from the cases mentioned in paragraph 1 the Member States may require any undertaking governed by their national law to draw up consolidated accounts and a consolidated annual report if:

(a) that undertaking (a parent undertaking) has the power to exercise, or actually exercises, dominant influence or control over another undertaking (the subsidiary undertaking); or

(b) that undertaking (a parent undertaking) and another undertaking (the subsidiary undertaking) are managed on a unified basis by the parent undertaking.

Article 2

For the purposes of Article 1 (1) (a), (b) and (d), the voting rights and the rights of appointment and removal of any other subsidiary undertaking as well as those of any person acting in his own name but on behalf of the parent undertaking or of another subsidiary undertaking must be added to those of the parent undertaking.   **1**

For the purposes of Article 1 (1) (a), (b) and (d), the rights mentioned in paragraph 1 above must be reduced by the rights: **2**

(a) attaching to shares held on behalf of a person who is neither the parent undertaking nor a subsidiary thereof; or

(b) attaching to shares held by way of security, provided that the rights in question are exercised in accordance with the instructions received, or held in connection with the granting of loans as part of normal business activities, provided that the voting rights are exercised in the interests of the person providing the security.

For the purposes of Article 1 (1) (a) and (d), the total of the shareholders' or members' voting rights in the subsidiary undertaking must be reduced by the voting rights attaching to the shares held by that undertaking itself by a subsidiary undertaking of that undertaking or by a person acting in his own name but on behalf of those undertakings.   **3**

Article 3

Without prejudice to Articles 13 and 15*, a parent undertaking and all of its subsidiary undertakings shall be undertakings to be consolidated regardless of where the registered offices of such subsidiary undertakings are situated.   **1**

For the purposes of paragraph 1 above, any subsidiary undertaking of a subsidiary undertaking shall be considered a subsidiary undertaking of the parent undertaking which is the parent of the undertakings to be consolidated.   **2**

*These Articles refer to circumstances in which the Directive permits an undertaking to be excluded from consolidated accounts.

Appendix 2
Extract from the Fourth Directive dealing with contents of the annual report

Contents of the annual report

Article 46

1   (a)   The annual report shall include at least a fair review of the development and performance of the company's business and of its position, together with a description of the principal risks and uncertainties that it faces. The review shall be a balanced and comprehensive analysis of the development and performance of the company's business and of its position, consistent with the size and complexity of the business;

(b)   To the extent necessary for an understanding of the company's development, performance or position, the analysis shall include both financial and, where appropriate, non-financial key performance indicators relevant to the particular business, including information relating to environmental and employee matters;

(c)   In providing its analysis, the annual report shall, where appropriate, include references to and additional explanations of amounts reported in the annual accounts.

2   The report shall also give an indication of:

(a)   any important events that have occurred since the end of the financial year;

(b)   the company's likely future development;

(c)   activities in the field of research and development;

(d)   the information concerning acquisitions of own shares prescribed by Article 22 (2) of Directive 77/91/EEC.

(e)   the existence of branches of the company;

(f)   in relation to the company's use of financial instruments and where material for the assessment of its assets, liabilities, financial position and profit or loss,

–   the company's financial risk management objectives and policies, including its policy for hedging each major type of forecasted transaction for which hedge accounting is used, and

–   the company's exposure to price risk, credit risk, liquidity risk and cash flow risk.

3   Member States may waive the obligation on companies covered by Article 11 to prepare annual reports, provided that the information referred to in Article 22 (2) of Directive 77/91/EEC concerning the acquisition by a company of its own shares is given in the notes to their accounts.

4   Member States may choose to exempt companies covered by Article 27 from the obligation in paragraph 1(b) above in so far as it relates to non-financial information.

UITF abstract 44 (IFRIC Interpretation 11)
FRS 20 (IFRS 2) – Group and Treasury Share Transactions

(Issued 2 February 2007)

PREFACE BY THE URGENT ISSUES TASK FORCE

This Abstract has the effect of implementing the International Accounting Standards   **a**
Board's (IASB's) International Financial Reporting Interpretations Committee
(IFRIC) Interpretation 11 'IFRS 2 – Group and Treasury Share Transactions' in the
UK and the Republic of Ireland for entities preparing their financial statements in
accordance with UK accounting standards and, in doing so, are applying FRS 20
(IFRS 2) 'Share-based Payment'.

FRS 20 implements IFRS 2 'Share-based Payment' for listed entities preparing their   **b**
financial statements in accordance with UK accounting standards for accounting
periods beginning on or after 1 January 2005 and for unlisted entities for accounting
periods beginning on or after 1 January 2006.

This Abstract incorporates the text of IFRIC 11*. The text of IFRIC 11 contains   **c**
various references to International Financial Reporting Standards (IFRSs). In this
Abstract those references have been amended to enable the Interpretation to be
applied in a UK context. The UITF believes that those amendments do not change
the requirements of IFRIC 11 in any way.

*Deleted text has been struck through and inserted text is underlined.

Contents

UITF Abstract 44 (IFRIC Interpretation 11)

FRS 20 (IFRS 2) – Group and Treasury Share Transactions

REFERENCES

- FRS 3 *Reporting Financial Performance*
- FRS 25 (IAS 32) *Financial Instruments: Presentation*
- FRS 20 (IFRS 2) *Share-based Payment*

ISSUES

This Abstract addresses two issues. The first is whether the following 1 transactions should be accounted for as equity-settled or as cash-settled under the requirements of FRS 20:   **1**

(a)   an entity grants to its employees rights to equity instruments of the entity (eg share options), and either chooses or is required to buy equity instruments (ie treasury shares) from another party, to satisfy its obligations to its employees; and

(b)   an entity's employees are granted rights to equity instruments of the entity (eg share options), either by the entity itself or by its shareholders, and the shareholders of the entity provide the equity instruments needed.

The second issue concerns share-based payment arrangements that involve two or 2 more entities within the same group. For example, employees of a subsidiary are granted rights to equity instruments of its parent as consideration for the services provided to the subsidiary. FRS 20 paragraph 3 states that: **2**

> For the purposes of this IFRS, transfers of an entity's equity instruments by its shareholders to parties that have supplied goods or services to the entity (including employees) are share-based payment transactions, unless the transfer is clearly for a purpose other than payment for goods or services supplied to the entity. *This also applies to transfers of equity instruments of the entity's parent, or equity instruments of another entity in the same group as the entity, to parties that have supplied goods or services to the entity. [Emphasis added]*

However, FRS 20 does not give guidance on how to account for such transactions in the individual or separate financial statements of each group entity.

Therefore, the second issue addresses the following share-based payment arrangements: **3**

(a)   a parent grants rights to its equity instruments direct to the employees of its subsidiary: the parent (not the subsidiary) has the obligation to provide the employees of the subsidiary with the equity instruments needed; and

(b)   a subsidiary grants rights to equity instruments of its parent to its employees: the subsidiary has the obligation to provide its employees with the equity instruments needed.

This Abstract also addresses how the share-based payment arrangements set out in paragraph 3 should be accounted for in the financial statements of the subsidiary that receives services from the employees.   **4**

There may be an arrangement between a parent and its subsidiary requiring the subsidiary to pay the parent for the provision of the equity instruments to the employees. This Abstract does not address how to account for such an intragroup payment arrangement.   **5**

6   Although this Abstract focuses on transactions with employees, it also applies to similar share-based payment transactions with suppliers of goods or services other than employees.

UITF CONSENSUS

Share-based payment arrangements involving an entity's own equity instruments (paragraph 1)

7   Share-based payment transactions in which an entity receives services as consideration for its own equity instruments shall be accounted for as equity-settled. This applies regardless of whether the entity chooses or is required to buy those equity instruments from another party to satisfy its obligations to its employees under the share-based payment arrangement. It also applies regardless of whether:

(a)   the employee's rights to the entity's equity instruments were granted by the entity itself or by its shareholder(s); or

(b)   the share-based payment arrangement was settled by the entity itself or by its shareholder(s).

Share-based payment arrangements involving equity instruments of the parent

A parent grants rights to its equity instruments to the employees of its subsidiary (paragraph 3(a))

8   Provided that the share-based arrangement is accounted for as equity-settled in the consolidated financial statements of the parent, the subsidiary shall measure the services received from its employees in accordance with the requirements applicable to equity-settled share-based payment transactions, with a corresponding increase recognised in equity as a contribution from the parent.

9   A parent may grant rights to its equity instruments to the employees of its subsidiaries, conditional upon the completion of continuing service with the group for a specified period. An employee of one subsidiary may transfer employment to another subsidiary during the specified vesting period without the employee's rights to equity instruments of the parent under the original share-based payment arrangement being affected. Each subsidiary shall measure the services received from the employee by reference to the fair value of the equity instruments at the date those rights to equity instruments were originally granted by the parent as defined in FRS 20 Appendix A, and the proportion of the vesting period served by the employee with each subsidiary.

10   Such an employee, after transferring between group entities, may fail to satisfy a vesting condition other than a market condition as defined in FRS 20 Appendix A, eg the employee leaves the group before completing the service period. In this case, each subsidiary shall adjust the amount previously recognised in respect of the services received from the employee in accordance with the principles in FRS 20 paragraph 19. Hence, if the rights to the equity instruments granted by the parent do not vest because of an employee's failure to meet a vesting condition other than a market condition, no amount is recognised on a cumulative basis for the services received from that employee in the financial statements of any subsidiary.

A subsidiary grants rights to equity instruments of its parent to its employees (paragraph 3(b))

The subsidiary shall account for the transaction with its employees as cash-settled. **11**
This requirement applies irrespective of how the subsidiary obtains the equity
instruments to satisfy its obligations to its employees.

EFFECTIVE DATE

The accounting treatment required by this Abstract should be adopted in financial **12**
statements relating to accounting periods beginning or after 1 March 2007, but
earlier adoption is encouraged.

TRANSITION

An entity shall apply this Abstract retrospectively in accordance with FRS 3, subject **13**
to the transitional provisions of FRS 20.

Illustrative Example

This Illustrative Example accompanies, but is not part of, the Abstract

1E1   A parent grants 200 share options to each of 100 employees of its subsidiary, conditional upon the completion of two years' service with the subsidiary. The fair value of the share options on grant date is CU30 each. At grant date, the subsidiary estimates that 80 per cent of the employees will complete the two-year service period. This estimate does not change during the vesting period. At the end of the vesting period, 81 employees complete the required two years of service. The parent does not require the subsidiary to pay for the shares needed to settle the grant of share options.

1E2   The share-based payment transaction in the consolidated financial statements of the parent is accounted for as equity-settled in accordance with FRS 20.

1E3   As required by paragraph 8 of the Abstract, over the two-year vesting period, the subsidiary measures the services received from the employees in accordance with the requirements applicable to equity-settled share-based payment transactions. Thus, the subsidiary measures the services received from the employees on the basis of the fair value of the share options at grant date. An increase in equity is recognised as a contribution from the parent in the financial statements of the subsidiary.

1E4   The journal entries recorded by the subsidiary for each of the two years are as follows:

Year 1		
Dr Remuneration expense (200 × 100 × 30 × 0.8 / 2)	CU240,000	
Cr Equity (Contribution from the parent)		CU240,000
Year 2		
Dr Remuneration expense (200 × 100 × 30 × 0.81 − 240,000)	CU246,000	
Cr Equity (Contribution from the parent)		CU246,000

Basis for Conclusions on IFRIC Interpretation 11

This Basis for Conclusions accompanies, but is not part of, IFRIC 11.

ASB note: The IFRIC's Basis for Conclusions, which accompanies IFRIC 11, is set out below in full.

INTRODUCTION

This Basis for Conclusions summarises the IFRIC's considerations in reaching its consensus. Individual IFRIC members gave greater weight to some factors than to others. **BC1**

The IFRIC released draft Interpretation D17 IFRS 2 – Group and Treasury Share Transactions for public comment in May 2005. It received 40 letters in response. **BC2**

CONSENSUS (PARAGRAPHS 7–11)

Share-based payment arrangements involving an entity's own equity instruments (paragraph 7)

D17 proposed that, regardless of whether the entity chooses or is required to buy the equity instruments needed from another party to settle the share-based payment arrangement, the share-based payment transactions should be accounted for as equity-settled. The IFRIC's rationale was that the consideration for the services received is equity instruments of the entity (rather than a liability to transfer cash or other assets). For the same reason, the IFRIC proposed in D17 that, regardless of whether the employees' rights to the entity's equity instruments were granted by the entity itself or by its shareholders, or whether the obligations under the share-based payment arrangement were settled by the entity itself or its shareholders, the share-based payment transactions should be accounted for as equity-settled. **BC3**

Of the 40 respondents to D17, only a small number disagreed with D17's proposal to treat the transactions as equity-settled. **BC4**

For the reason stated in paragraph BC3, the IFRIC reaffirmed its view that the share-based payment transactions specified in IFRIC 11 paragraph 1(a) and (b) should be accounted for as equity-settled. **BC5**

Some respondents asked the IFRIC to clarify whether an entity should recognise a financial liability when the entity enters into a contractual arrangement to acquire its own equity instruments. The IFRIC noted that the relevant requirements in IAS 32 *Financial Instruments: Presentation* are clear. Therefore, the IFRIC decided not to explain those requirements in the Interpretation. **BC6**

Share-based payment arrangements involving equity instruments of the parent (paragraphs 8–11)

D17 addressed the following share-based payment arrangements in which two or more entities in the same group are involved: **BC7**

(a) a parent grants rights to its equity instruments direct to its subsidiary's employees; and

(b) an entity grants rights to equity instruments of its parent to its employees.

A parent grants rights to its equity instruments to the employees of its subsidiary (paragraph 8)

BC8   The IFRIC noted that paragraph 3 of IFRS 2 *Share-based Payment* requires an entity to recognise as share-based payment arrangements transfers of equity instruments of the entity's parent to parties that have supplied goods or services to the entity. However, the IFRIC observed that, for the purposes of the preparation of the financial statements of the subsidiary, the transaction described in paragraph BC7(a) does not meet the definition of either an equity-settled share-based payment transaction or a cash-settled share-based payment transaction. In this situation, the equity instruments granted are not the equity instruments of the subsidiary and the subsidiary has no obligation to transfer cash or other assets to the employees.

BC9   Because the subsidiary does not have an obligation to deliver cash or other assets to the employees, the IFRIC proposed in D17 that it was not appropriate to account for the transaction as cash-settled in the financial statements of the subsidiary. Instead, the IFRIC suggested that the equity-settled basis was more consistent with the principles in IFRS 2.

BC10 Of the 40 respondents to D17, only a small number disagreed that the transaction should be accounted for as equity-settled in the fi nancial statements of the subsidiary.

BC11 The IFRIC noted that the parent has an involvement in the arrangement by committing itself to provide the employees of the subsidiary with its equity instruments. To meet the requirement in IFRS 2 paragraph 3, the IFRIC believed that it was appropriate in this particular situation for the subsidiary in its own financial statements to apply the same measurement basis as the parent uses in its consolidated financial statements. Accordingly, the IFRIC concluded that, provided that the transaction is accounted for as equity-settled in the consolidated financial statements of the parent, the services received from the employees should be measured using the equity-settled basis in the financial statements of the subsidiary. Correspondingly, to reflect the parent's granting of rights to its equity instruments to the employees of the subsidiary, the IFRIC decided that the subsidiary should recognise in its equity a contribution from the parent equal to the amount at which the services from the employees are measured.

BC12 The IFRIC discussed whether the Interpretation should address how to account for an intragroup payment arrangement requiring the subsidiary to pay the parent for the provision of the equity instruments to the employees. The IFRIC decided not to address that issue because it did not wish to widen the scope of the Interpretation to an issue that relates to the accounting for intragroup payment arrangements.

A subsidiary grants rights to equity instruments of its parent to its employees (paragraph 11)

BC13 Although the subsidiary in the transaction described in paragraph BC7(b) has an obligation to its employees, the obligation is not determined on the basis of the price of its own equity instruments. Thus, the transaction does not meet the definition of a cash-settled share-based payment transaction in the financial statements of the subsidiary. In addition, because the equity instruments provided to the employees are not equity instruments of the subsidiary, the transaction does not meet the definition of an equity-settled share-based payment transaction either in the financial statements of the subsidiary.

D17 proposed that the subsidiary should account for the transaction with its employees as cash-settled in its own financial statements. The rationale was that the cash-settled basis was more consistent with the principles in IFRS 2 because the subsidiary has an obligation to provide its employees with the equity instruments of the parent, which are treated as assets of the subsidiary when the subsidiary acquires them.   **BC14**

Many respondents to D17 disagreed with the proposed treatment. They disagreed that the accounting treatments for the two types of arrangement described in paragraph BC7 should depend on which entity grants to the employees rights to equity instruments of the parent. In their view, regardless of whether the parent or the subsidiary grants those rights to the employees, in most cases the parent is the one that supplies the equity instruments to settle the obligation. They believed that it was not appropriate to require the subsidiary to apply different accounting treatments to transactions with the same substance. They had concerns that different accounting treatments would give entities opportunities to structure their intragroup transactions in order to achieve desired accounting results.   **BC15**

The IFRIC noted that arrangements described in paragraph BC7(a) and (b) might be the same in the consolidated financial statements of the parent, and also from the perspective of the employees who receive the equity instruments. However, from the perspective of the subsidiary, the IFRIC observed that the two arrangements are different. The IFRIC noted that under arrangement (a) the parent, rather than the subsidiary, has the obligation to provide its employees with the equity instruments, whereas under arrangement (b) it is the subsidiary that has that obligation.   **BC16**

In addition, the IFRIC clarified that how the subsidiary acquires the equity instruments needed to meet its obligation to its employees is a separate transaction from its transaction with its employees.   **BC17**

For the above reasons, the IFRIC reaffirmed its view that the transaction with the employees described in paragraph BC7(b) should be accounted for as cash-settled in the financial statements of the subsidiary.   **BC18**

Transfers of employees between group entities (paragraphs 9 and 10)

The IFRIC noted that some share-based payment arrangements involve a parent granting rights to the employees of more than one subsidiary with a vesting condition that requires the employees to work for the group for a particular period. Sometimes, an employee of one subsidiary transfers employment to another subsidiary during the vesting period, without the employee's rights under the original share-based payment arrangements being affected. The IFRIC reasoned in D17 that the change of employment from one group entity to another does not represent a new grant of equity instruments, because the equity instruments were granted by the parent (not the individual subsidiary). Therefore, the IFRIC proposed in D17 that the subsidiary to which the employee transfers employment should measure the fair value of the services received from the employee by reference to the fair value of the equity instruments at the date those equity instruments were originally granted to the employee by the parent.   **BC19**

The respondents to D17 generally supported this proposed treatment. Some respondents also asked the IFRIC to clarify the following two points: **BC20**

(a) whether the transfer of employees between group entities would be considered as a failure to satisfy a vesting condition in the financial statements of the subsidiary from which the employees transferred employment (ie whether that subsidiary should reverse the charge previously recognised in respect of the services received from such employees); and

(b)   after the transfer of employment, if an employee leaves the group during the vesting period, whether each subsidiary should reverse the charge previously recognised in respect of the services from that employee during the vesting period.

BC21   The terms of the original share-based payment arrangement require the employees to work for the group, rather than for a particular group entity. Thus, the IFRIC in its redeliberations reaffirmed its view that the change of employment should not result in a new grant of equity instruments in the financial statements of the subsidiary to which the employees transferred employment. For the same reason, the IFRIC concluded that the transfer itself should not be treated as an employee's failure to satisfy a vesting condition. Thus, the transfer should not trigger any reversal of the charge previously recognised in respect of the services received from the employee in the financial statements of the subsidiary from which the employee transfers employment.

BC22   The IFRIC noted that IFRS 2 paragraph 19 requires the cumulative amount recognised for goods or services as consideration for the equity instruments granted to be based on the number of equity instruments that eventually vest. Accordingly, on a cumulative basis, no amount is recognised for goods or services if the equity instruments do not vest because of failure to satisfy a vesting condition other than a market condition as defined in IFRS 2 Appendix A. Applying the principles in IFRS 2 paragraph 19, the IFRIC concluded that when the employee fails to satisfy a vesting condition other than a market condition, the services from that employee recognised in the financial statements of each subsidiary during the vesting period should be reversed.

UITF abstract 45 (IFRIC Interpretation 6)
Liabilities arising from Participating in a Specific Market
– Waste Electrical and Electronic Equipment

(Issued 13 February 2007)

PREFACE BY THE URGENT ISSUES TASK FORCE

This Abstract has the effect of implementing the International Accounting Standards   **a**
Board's (IASB's) International Financial Reporting Interpretations Committee
(IFRIC) Interpretation 6 'Liabilities arising from Participating in a Specific Market –
Waste Electrical and Electronic Equipment' in the UK and the Republic of Ireland
for entities preparing their financial statements in accordance with UK accounting
standards.*

This Abstract sets out guidance on the recognition of certain liabilities arising from   **b**
the European Parliament and Council Directive on Waste Electrical and Electronic
Equipment (2002/96/EC) ("the WEEE Directive"), which makes producers of electrical and electronic equipment responsible for financing certain waste management
costs, including costs of collection, treatment, reuse, recovery and environmentally
sound disposal.

The UK Regulations implementing the WEEE Directive – S.l. 2006 No.3289 'The   **c**
Waste Electrical and Electronic Equipment Regulations 2006' – were laid before
Parliament on 12 December 2006 and entered into force on 2 January 2007.

The Irish Regulations implementing the WEEE Directive – 'Waste Management   **d**
(Waste Electrical and Electronic Equipment) Regulations 2005' (S.l. No. 340 of
2005) – came into effect in August 2005.

The reference accounting standard for IFRIC 6 is IAS 37 'Provisions, Contingent   **e**
Liabilities and Contingent Assets'. The relevant parts of IAS 37 are virtually identical to FRS 12 'Provisions, Contingent Liabilities and Contingent Assets'. This
Abstract incorporates the text of IFRIC 6' and is accompanied by the IFRIC's Basis
for Conclusions. The text of IFRIC 6 contains various references to International
Financial Reporting Standards. In this Abstract those references have been amended
to enable the Interpretation to be applied in a UK context. The UITF believes that
those amendments do not change the requirements of IFRIC 6 in any way.

The Consensus specifically provides guidance on the recognition of liabilities for   **f**
waste management relating to 'historical household equipment' as specified in the
WEEE Directive. Under the model for attributing costs in relation to historical
household equipment, the obligation falls on producers who are currently participating in the market.

Although the explicit scope of the Abstract is narrow, the principles in the Abstract   **g**
should be applied by analogy when obligations are imposed in a similar way. As
regards the WEEE Directive, therefore, entities should tailor their application of the
Abstract to the details of the applicable national legislation. For example, under the
UK Regulations, the same model of attributing waste management costs is applicable to all WEEE from private households (i.e. the Regulations do not distinguish
historical waste and new waste). The principles of the Abstract are also relevant for

Deleted text has been struck through and inserted text is underlined.

other regulations that impose obligations in a way that is similar to the cost attribution model specified in the WEEE Directive.

REFERENCES

- FRS 12 *Provisions, Contingent Liabilities and Contingent Assets*

BACKGROUND

1   Paragraph 17 of FRS 12 specifies that an obligating event is a past event that leads to a present obligation that an entity has no realistic alternative to settling.

2   Paragraph 19 of FRS 12 states that provisions are recognised only for 'obligations arising from past events existing independently **of** an entity's future actions' .

3   The European Union's Directive on Waste Electrical and Electronic Equipment (WE&EE), which regulates the collection, treatment, recovery and environmentally sound disposal of waste equipment, has given rise to questions about when the liability for the decommissioning of WE&EE should be recognised. The Directive distinguishes between 'new' and 'historical' waste and between waste from private households and waste from sources other than private households. New waste relates to products sold after 13 August 2005. All household equipment sold before that date is deemed to give rise to historical waste for the purposes of the Directive.

4   The Directive states that the cost of waste management for historical household equipment should be borne by producers of that type of equipment that are in the market during a period to be specified in the applicable legislation of each Member State (the measurement period). The Directive states that each Member State shall establish a mechanism to have producers contribute to costs proportionately 'e.g. in proportion to their respective share of the market by type of equipment.'

5   Several terms used in the Abstract such as 'market share' and 'measurement period' may be defined very differently in the applicable legislation of individual Member States. For example, the length of the measurement period might be a year or only one month. Similarly, the measurement of market share and the formulae for computing the obligation may differ in the various national legislations. However, all of these examples affect only the measurement of the liability, which is not within the scope of the Abstract.

SCOPE

6   This Abstract provides guidance on the recognition, in the financial statements of producers, of liabilities for waste management under the EU Directive on WE&EE in respect of sales of historical household equipment.

7   The Abstract addresses neither new waste nor historical waste from sources other than private households. The liability for such waste management is adequately covered in FRS 12. However, if, in national legislation, new waste from private households is treated in a similar manner to historical waste from private households, the principles of the Abstract apply.

ISSUE

This Abstract addresses in the context of the decommissioning of WE&EE what **8** constitutes the obligating event in accordance with paragraph 14(a) of FRS 12 for the recognition of a provision for waste management costs:

- the manufacture or sale of the historical household equipment? participation in the market during the measurement period?
- the incurrence of costs in the performance of waste management activities?

Reporting entities applying the Financial Reporting Standard for Smaller Entities **8A** currently applicable are exempt from this Abstract.

UITF CONSENSUS

Participation in the market during the measurement period is the obligating event in **9** accordance with paragraph 14(a) of FRS 12. As a consequence, a liability for waste management costs for historical household equipment does not arise as the products are manufactured or sold. Because the obligation for historical household equipment is linked to participation in the market during the measurement period, rather than to production or sale of the items to be disposed of, there is no obligation unless and until a market share exists during the measurement period. The timing of the obligating event may also be independent of the particular period in which the activities to perform the waste management are undertaken and the related costs incurred.

EFFECTIVE DATE

The accounting treatment required by this Abstract should be adopted in financial **10** statements relating to accounting periods ending on or after 22 June 2007 but earlier adoption is encouraged. Where applicable, corresponding amounts should be restated.

Basis for Conclusions on IFRIC 6

This Basis for Conclusions accompanies, but is not part of, IFRIC 6.

> *UITF note:* The IFRIC's Basis for Conclusions, which accompanies IFRIC 6, is set out below in full. Except as indicated byway of footnote, the paragraphs referred to in IAS 37 are identical to those in FRS 12.

BC1   This Basis for Conclusions summarises the IFRIC's considerations in reaching its consensus. Individual IFRIC members gave greater weight to some factors than to others.

BC2   The IFRIC was informed that the European Union's Directive on Waste Electrical and Electronic Equipment (WE&EE) had given rise to questions about when a liability for the decommissioning of WE&EE for certain goods should be recognised. The IFRIC therefore decided to develop an Interpretation that would provide guidance regarding what constitutes an obligating event in the circumstances created by the Directive.

BC3   The IFRIC's proposals were set out in Draft Interpretation D 10 *Liabilities arising from Participating in a Specific Market-Waste Electrical and Electronic Equipment*, which was published in November 2004.* The IFRIC received 22 comment letters on its proposals.

BC4   The Directive indicates that it is participation in the market during the measurement period that triggers the obligation to meet the costs of waste management.

BC5   For example, an entity selling electrical equipment in 20X4 has a market share of 4 per cent for that calendar year. It subsequently discontinues operations and is thus no longer in the market when the waste management costs for its products are allocated to those entities with market share in 20X7. With a market share of 0 per cent in 20X7, the entity's obligation is zero. However, if another entity enters the market for electronic products in 20X7 and achieves a market share of 3 per cent in that period, then that entity's obligation for the costs of waste management from earlier periods will be 3 per cent of the total costs of waste management allocated to 20X7, even though the entity was not in the market in those earlier periods and has not produced any of the products for which waste management costs are allocated to 20X7.

BC6   The IFRIC concluded that the effect of the cost attribution model specified in the Directive is that the making of sales during the measurement period is the 'past event' that requires recognition of a provision under IAS 37 *Provisions, Contingent Liabilities and Contingent Assets* over the measurement period. Aggregate sales for the period determine the entity's obligation for a proportion of the costs of waste management allocated to that period. The measurement period is independent of the period when the cost allocation is notified to market participants. The timing of the obligating event may also be independent of the particular period in which the activities to peform the waste management are undertaken and the related costs incurred. Incurring costs in the performance of the waste management activities is a separate matter from incurring the obligation to share in the ultimate cost of those activities.

* ~~UITF footnote: A draft UITF Abstract was issued concurrently with Draft Interpretation D10 in Information Sheet 69.~~

Some constituents asked the IFRIC to consider the effect of the following possible national legislation: the waste management costs for which a producer is responsible because of its participation in the market during a specified period (for example 20X6) are not based on the market share of the producer during that period but on the producer's participation in the market during a previous period (for example 20X5). The IFRIC noted that this affects only the measurement of the liability and that the obligating event is still participation in the market during 20X6. **BC7**

The IFRIC considered whether its conclusion is undermined by the principle that the entity will continue to operate as a going concern. If the entity will continue to operate in the future, it treats the costs of doing so as future costs. For these future costs, paragraph 18 of IAS 37 emphasises that 'Financial statements deal with the financial position of an entity at the end of its reporting period and not its possible position in the future. Therefore, no provision is recognised for costs that need to be incurred to operate in the future.' **BC8**

The IFRIC considered an argument that manufacturing or selling products for use in private households constitutes a past event that gives rise to a constructive obligation. Allocating waste management costs on the basis of market share would then be a matter of measurement rather than recognition. Supporters of this argument emphasise the definition of a constructive obligation in paragraph 10 of IAS 37* and point out that in determining whether past actions of an entity give rise to an obligation it is necessary to consider whether a change in practice is a realistic alternative. These respondents believed that when it would be necessary for an entity to take some unrealistic action in order to avoid the obligation then a constructive obligation exists and should be accounted for. **BC9**

The IFRIC rejected this argument, concluding that a stated intention to participate in a market during a future measurement period does not create a constructive obligation for future waste management costs. In accordance with paragraph 19 of IAS 37, a provision can be recognised only in respect of an obligation that arises independently of the entity's future actions. For historical household equipment the obligation is created only by the future actions of the entity. If an entity has no market share in a measurement period, it has no obligation for the waste management costs relating to the products of that type which it had previously manufactured or sold and which otherwise would have created an obligation in that measurement period. This differentiates waste management costs, for example, from warranties (see Example 1 in Appendix C to IAS 37†), which represent a legal obligation even if the entity exits the market. Consequently, no obligation exists for the future waste management costs until the entity participates in the market during the measurement period. **BC10**

UITF footnote: Paragraph 2 of FRS 12 contains an identical definition of a constructive obligation.

†*UITF footnote: Example 1 in Appendix III to FRS 12.*

Part Six

Relevant announcements by the
Financial Reporting Review Panel

Disclosure of accounting policies – effect of introduction of paragraph 36A of Schedule 4 to the Companies Act 1985

(Issued January 1992)

To clarify a possible uncertainty the Financial Reporting Review Panel has taken legal advice about the effect of paragraph 36A of Schedule 4 to the Companies Act 1985 (introduced by the Companies Act 1989) on the accounting policy disclosure requirements of paragraph 36 of Schedule 4.

The legal advice confirms that the requirements of the two paragraphs are separate and distinct. Thus the inclusion in the notes to the accounts of a statement that the accounts have been prepared in accordance with applicable accounting standards, required by paragraph 36A, does not satisfy the requirement in paragraph 36 to state the accounting policies of the company. This is so both with respect to a policy which a company chooses to adopt and with respect to a policy that a company is compelled to adopt by virtue of the application of an accounting standard.

As regards the requirements of paragraph 36 itself, to satisfy them there must be a brief statement of each relevant accounting policy but that statement may either be in the accounts themselves or in the notes to the accounts.

Paragraph 36 does not require disclosure of accounting policies which are immaterial in the context of the accounts in question.

Press notice

Annual accounts statement of compliance with accounting standards: Review Panel Chairman reports progress (FRRP PN 8)

(Issued June 1992)

Since July 1991 the Review Panel has written to 240 listed companies who had failed to comply with the Companies Act requirement to disclose whether their accounts have been prepared in accordance with applicable accounting standards. A parallel letter was sent to the auditors of the company in question. In each case the directors concerned have confirmed that applicable accounting standards have been complied with, or have explained the reasons for any departures, and have given the Panel an assurance that their company's accounts will in future contain the statement required by the Act.

Mr Edwin Glasgow QC, Chairman of the Review Panel, said 'I believe that this initiative has been well worthwhile. A statement of a company's compliance with accounting standards, or disclosure of the particulars and reasons for any departures from standards, is an essential requirement of the legislation and is of vital interest to the users of the accounts in question'.

Continuing, Mr Glasgow added: 'It is important not only that the statement is made, but also that it is made clearly and unambiguously. In particular where there is a departure from accounting standards the particulars and the reasons for the departure need to be included either as part of the compliance statement itself or by the compliance statement containing a specific cross-reference to the Note in which the particulars and reasons for the departure are given. Statements such as 'except where the directors consider a departure necessary' or 'except where indicated below' do not meet the requirements'.

NOTES TO EDITORS

1.   The legislative requirements in question are paragraph 36A of Schedule 4 and paragraph 18B of Schedule 9 to the Companies Act 1985. These provisions were inserted into the 1985 Act by paragraph 7 of Schedule 1 and paragraph 4 of Schedule 7 to the Companies Act 1989. Small and medium-sized companies (as defined by the Act) are exempt from these provisions.

2.   The Financial Reporting Review Panel, which operates under the aegis of the Financial Reporting Council, is authorised by the Secretary of State for Trade and Industry for the purposes of section 245B of the Companies Act 1985. Thus the role of the Panel is to examine departures from accounting requirements of the Companies Act 1985 and if necessary to seek an order from the Court to remedy them. The Panel's main concern will be with an examination of material departures from accounting standards with a view to considering whether the accounts in question nevertheless meet the statutory requirement to give a true and fair view.

Part Seven

Statements of Recommended Practice

INTRODUCTORY NOTE

Statements of Recommended Practice ('SORPs') have been issued since 1986. As stated in the Explanatory Foreword to SORPs issued by the Accounting Standards Committee in May 1986

'Statements of Recommended Practice ('SORPs') are developed in the public interest and set out current best accounting practice. The primary aims in issuing SORPs are to narrow the areas of difference and variety in the accounting treatment of the matters with which they deal and to enhance the usefulness of published accounting information. SORPs are issued on subjects on which it is not considered appropriate to issue an accounting standard at the time.'

That Explanatory Foreword also noted that

'SORPs will always take account of the principles laid down in accounting standards. They can never be taken as authority to depart from the requirements imposed by accounting standards, nor to extend the scope of accounting standards to include entities or circumstances which are otherwise excluded from specific accounting standards or accounting standards in general.

It is recognised in the *(Explanatory) Foreword* to accounting standards that it would be impracticable for accounting standards to cater for all situations. In applying a modified or alternative treatment it is important to have regard to the spirit of and reasoning behind any relevant accounting standards. The recommendations contained in SORPs will always have regard to this spirit and reasoning. They may, therefore, be indicative of the treatment which should be adopted in a situation not specifically catered for by accounting standards'.

The ASC developed and issued two SORPs, 'Pension scheme accounts' and 'Accounting by charities', together with the Explanatory foreword referred to above. These were not adopted by the ASB and both SORPs have now been replaced by updated documents (see below). In addition, as at 31 July 1990, the date the ASC retired, the following SORPs had been 'franked' by the ASC:

	Issuing body	Issued
Disclosures about oil and gas exploration and production activities	OIAC	April 1986
Accounting for oil and gas exploration and development activities	OIAC	June 2001
Accounting for abandonment costs	OIAC	June 1988

(These SORPs were replaced by a revised SORP published in January 2000 — see below.)

Accounting for securities by banks	BBA/IBF	July 1990

(This SORP is available from:
British Bankers' Association
Pinners Hall
105–108 Old Broad Street
London EC2N 1EX

and

Irish Bankers Federation
Nassau House
Nassau Street
Dublin 2.)

Accounting for insurance business   ABI   May 1990

(This SORP was replaced by a revised SORP published in January 1999 – see below.)

The ASC also franked two SORPs on local authority accounting and one on accounting in UK universities, but these have been superseded respectively by the Code of Practice on Local Authority Accounting in Great Britain and the SORP on Accounting in Higher Education Institutions (see below).

The ASB announced in 1990 that it would not issue its own SORPs. In the event that the ASB's own authority is required to standardise practice within a specialised industry, the ASB's preference is to issue an industry standard. The ASB issued a policy statement for the development of SORPs in 1990, which was updated in 1994. In July 2000 this policy statement was superseded by the ASB statement 'SORPs: Policy and code of practice', which is reproduced after this note. Briefly, in respect of SORPs developed in accordance with ASB guidelines by bodies recognised by the ASB for that purpose, the ASB will give a statement confirming, as appropriate, that the SORP does not appear to contain any fundamental points of principle that are unacceptable in the context of current accounting practice or to conflict with an accounting standard or the ASB's plans for future standards.

Under these arrangements the following SORPs are in issue:

	Issuing body	*Issued*
Accounting for oil and gas exploration, development, production and decommissioning activities	OIAC	June 2001

   (Available from:
   Portland Press Ltd
   Commerce Way
   Whitehill Industrial Estate
   Colchester CO2 8HP)

Authorised Funds	IMA	December 2005

   (Available from:
   The Investment Management Association
   65 Kingsway
   London WC2B 6TD)

Banking

Segmental reporting	BBA/IBF	January 1993

   (Available from:
   British Bankers' Association
   Pinners Hall
   105–108 Old Broad Street
   London EC2N 1EX

   and

   Irish Bankers Federation
   Nassau House
   Nassau Street
   Dublin 2.)

Code of Practice on Local Authority   CIPFA/   June 2006
Accounting in the United Kingdom 2006   LASAAC

(Available from:
The Chartered Institute of Public
Finance and Accountancy
3 Robert Street
London WC2N 6RL.)

Accounting by Registered Social   NHF/   May 2005
Landlords   SFHA/
    WFHA

(Available from:
National Housing Federation
175 Gray's Inn Road
London WC1X 8UP.)

Accounting for Further and Higher   UUK   October 2003
Education

(Available from:
Universities UK
Woburn House
20 Tavistock Square
London WC1H 9HQ.)

Accounting and Reporting by Charities   Charity   March 2005
    Commission

(Available from:
Charity Commission
Harmsworth House
13/15 Bouverie Street
London EC4Y 8DP.)

Financial Reports of Pension Schemes   PRAG   November 2002

(Available from:
Croner CCH Ltd
145 London Road
Kingston upon Thames
KT2 6SR

Financial Statements of Investment Trust   AITC   December 2005
Companies

(Available from:
Association of Investment Trust Companies
Durrant House
8–13 Chiswell Street
London EC1Y 4YY)

Accounting for Insurance Business   ABI   December 2006

(Available from:
Association of British Insurers
51 Gresham Street
London EC2V 7HQ.)

Accounting issues in the asset finance and leasing industry	FLA	April 2000

(Available from:
Finance and Leasing Association
Imperial House
15–19 Kingsway
London WC2B 6UN.)

Limited Liability Partnerships	CCAB	March 2006

(Available from:
CCAB
PO Box 433
Chartered Accountant's Hall
Moorgate Place
London
EC2P 2BJ)

SORPs: Policy and Code of Practice

(Issued July 2000)

INTRODUCTION

Statements of Recommended Practice (SORPs) are recommendations on accounting practices for specialised industries or sectors. They supplement accounting standards and other legal and regulatory requirements in the light of the special factors prevailing or transactions undertaken in a particular industry or sector. SORPs are issued not by the Accounting Standards Board (ASB) but by industry or sectoral bodies recognised for the purpose by the ASB. (Bodies that have been recognised by the ASB for the purpose of producing a SORP or SORPs for an industry or sector are designated 'SORP-making bodies' in this document.)

To secure such recognition, SORP-making bodies are expected to meet criteria laid down by the ASB and to develop their SORP proposals in conformity with the ASB's code of practice. A SORP is required to carry a statement by the ASB confirming, as appropriate, that the SORP does not appear to contain any fundamental points of principle that are unacceptable in the context of current accounting practice or to conflict with an accounting standard or the ASB's plans for future standards. To assist in dealing with proposals for SORPs the ASB has two specialist advisory committees – the Financial Sector and Other Special Industries Committee and the Public Sector and Not-for-profit Committee.

POLICY FOR SORPS

The ASB has adopted the following policy in respect of SORPs:

The ASB will recognise bodies for the purpose of issuing SORPs. Bodies will not be **a** recognised unless the following conditions are met:

(i)   The industry or sector has special accounting or financial reporting problems that require the clarification of accounting standards or interpretation (within the principles of the standards).

(ii)   The body represents the whole or a major part of a significant industry or sector for the purposes of financial reporting within the relevant jurisdiction.

(iii)   The body shares the ASB's aim of advancing and maintaining standards of financial reporting in the public interest.

(iv)   The body agrees to abide by the ASB's code of practice for bodies recognised for issuing SORPs.

(v)   Where an industry or sector is regulated or financed by another body, the regulator or financing body is content for the body seeking recognition by the ASB to promulgate SORPs for that industry or sector.

The ASB will, at its discretion, withdraw recognition if it appears that these conditions are no longer met, or if the recognised body fails to comply with the spirit of the code of practice. (This would include circumstances in which a SORP-making body publishes a SORP or similar guidance without securing the approval of the ASB.) The ASB may publicise the withdrawal of recognition if it believes publicity is necessary or desirable.

SORPs issued by SORP-making bodies will include a statement by the ASB that: **b**

(i)   outlines the limited nature of the review the ASB has undertaken; and

(ii)   confirms that the SORP does not appear to contain any fundamental points of principle that are unacceptable in the context of current accounting practice or to conflict with an accounting standard or the ASB's plans for future standards.

c   A pro-forma statement is as follows:

'The ASB's Statement on the SORP

The aims of the Accounting Standards Board (the ASB) are to establish and improve standards of financial accounting and reporting, for the benefit of users, preparers, and auditors of financial information. To this end, the ASB issues accounting standards that are primarily applicable to general purpose company financial statements. In particular industries or sectors, further guidance may be required in order to implement accounting standards effectively. This guidance is issued, in the form of Statements of Recommended Practice (SORPs), by bodies recognised for the purpose by the ASB.

The XYZ Association (the Association) has confirmed that it shares the ASB's aim of advancing and maintaining standards of financial reporting in the public interest and has been recognised by the ASB for the purpose of issuing SORPs. As a condition of recognition, the Association has agreed to follow the ASB's code of practice for bodies recognised for issuing SORPs.

The code of practice sets out procedures to be followed in the development of SORPs. These procedures do not include a comprehensive review of the proposed SORP by the ASB, but a review of limited scope is performed.

On the basis of its review, the ASB has concluded that the SORP has been developed in accordance with the ASB's code of practice and does not appear to contain any fundamental points of principle that are unacceptable in the context of current accounting practice or to conflict with an accounting standard or the ASB's present plans for future standards.

Dated day/month/year'

d   The ASB will vary its statement to fit the circumstances of individual cases.

e   The ASB will not necessarily make a statement on an exposure draft, but may require a statement to be included indicating areas of overlap with its own work and any reservations that it would find necessary to make if the material were carried through to a final SORP.

f   In making a statement on a particular SORP, the ASB in no way guarantees that it will not in time produce a subsequent pronouncement that will supersede, and may contradict, that SORP.

g   The ASB has appointed committees to advise it on whether to recognise bodies that wish to develop SORPs and on whether the ASB's statement should be given in respect of individual proposed SORPs. The committees include independent experts and are serviced by the ASB's technical staff and secretariat. The committees monitor adherence to the code of practice and ensure that the ASB is apprised of any issues of fundamental importance that come to their attention. The committees are not required to undertake a comprehensive review of proposed SORPs but only such review as is necessary to enable the ASB to make its statement.

Code of Practice on the Development of SORPs

PRIMARY CONSIDERATIONS

Before beginning a new SORP project, a SORP-making body must seek approval **1** from the ASB. This will ensure that the proposed project does not overlap with an ASB project or address a matter that the ASB would prefer to deal with itself.

SORPs should be developed in the context of current accounting practice. In par- **2** ticular, it should be recognised that SORPs cannot override the provisions of the law, accounting standards or UITF Abstracts. It should also be noted that failure to update a SORP does not exempt reporting entities from following, from their effective date, accounting standards or UITF Abstracts issued after the publication of a SORP (except for those entities that operate in the public sector under specific legislative regimes that would prevent or exempt them from doing so). When provisions of a SORP conflict with a more recent accounting standard or UITF Abstract, those provisions cease to have effect.*

The SORP should state, in a prominent position, the latest date up to which extant **3** accounting standards and other pronouncements were considered in the develop- ment of the SORP. For SORPs that give comprehensive guidance on the preparation of financial statements, it is helpful to append a full list of accounting standards and other pronouncements extant at the date of publication of the SORP, with some indication of their relevance to the industry or sector and how each has been dealt with in the SORP. For specialised SORPs, only related standards would need to be mentioned.

A SORP should state its scope by indicating the types of entity to whose financial **4** statements the SORP is intended to apply. Where the SORP-making body is aware that entities to which the SORP applies may also fall within the scope of another SORP, it will be useful to indicate which SORP should be applied (it will usually be appropriate to suggest that an entity should follow the SORP with the more specific application).†

A SORP should aim to reduce areas of difference of accounting treatments within **5** the industry or sector by recommending a preferred accounting treatment. It should also seek, where practicable and appropriate, to adopt an approach to accounting in the industry or sector that is consistent with the approach taken in similar industries or sectors.

In order to clarify the position of the SORP with reference to accounting standards and UITF Abstracts, SORP-making bodies should, where appropriate, include in their SORP a paragraph along the following lines:

'Entities following this SORP should apply all extant accounting standards, UITF Abstracts and legislation [as specified]. When an accounting standard, UITF Abstract or legislation [as specified] is issued after publication of the most recent edition of the SORP, any provisions of the SORP that conflict with the new standard, UITF Abstract or legislation cease to have effect.'

†In these situations, consultation will be necessary with the ASB and the other relevant SORP-making body.

DEVELOPMENT OF A SORP

Working parties

6   Drafting of the SORP must be undertaken either by the SORP-making body itself or by a working party of the SORP-making body. In either case the process should ensure the participation of representatives of the industry or sector concerned, independent outsiders on behalf of the wider public interest and, where possible, users of financial statements, and have sufficient technical accounting support. The arrangements proposed (including membership of any working party), and any changes in those arrangements, should be notified in advance to the ASB, so that the ASB may satisfy itself that these requirements are met.

7   Where the ASB's approval of the arrangements is premised on the use of a working party including representatives of outside interests, the SORP-making body should normally expect to accept the recommendations of its working party. Where in such cases a draft of a proposed SORP or exposure draft submitted to the ASB has, at the request of the SORP-making body, been changed from the text recommended by the working party, the change and the reason for it should be notified to the ASB.

Due process

8   The SORP-making body should conduct its proceedings in a spirit of openness and follow due process involving wide consultation. In addition to organisations and individuals in the industry or sector concerned, those to be invited to comment should normally include member bodies of the CCAB, auditors actively involved in the industry or sector and relevant regulators and Government departments.

9   Before publishing the final SORP, the SORP-making body should invite public comment, normally by means of a published exposure draft, allowing a reasonable period for comments. The ASB will wish to be satisfied that the period given for responses allows due process; a minimum period of three months should be given, although, where a case can be made, a shorter period may be acceptable.

10   Comments may also be sought on a published statement of intent: however, it will not be acceptable to dispense with publication of an exposure draft, even following the publication of a statement of intent. The SORP-making body should attempt to secure publicity for its exposure drafts and statements of intent in journals specialising in the relevant industry or sector and in accountancy journals.

11   During development of a SORP (or its revision) it is the responsibility of the SORP-making body to identify potential divergences from accounting standards and inform the ASB of them at an early stage.

12   All exposure drafts and final SORPs should be presented to the relevant ASB committee for comment before publication. At each pre-publication stage sufficient time should be given to the committee to allow any necessary changes to be determined and incorporated.

13   The ASB will wish to be satisfied that public comments have been appropriately invited and considered. Before publishing the SORP the SORP-making body should provide the ASB with copies of the comment letters, a summary or analysis of the main comments and an indication of how they have been dealt with, in sufficient time to allow any necessary changes to be incorporated.

The invitation to comment included in exposure drafts should state that comments **14** will be regarded as on the public record, unless confidentiality is requested. Copies of comments that are on the public record should be made available on request at a reasonable charge.

The ASB's statement on the SORP

Written permission should be obtained from the ASB for inclusion of the ASB **15** statement in a SORP. The ASB's statement should be included in a prominent place in each SORP. No other reference to the ASB should be made without prior written approval from the ASB.

REVIEW OF SORPs

The SORP-making body should keep under review all the SORPs for which it is **16** responsible. In particular, the body should consider:

- any implications for the SORPs of new and proposed accounting standards. In the interests of the SORP-making body and its constituency any divergences must be notified to the ASB as soon as is practicable.
- any evidence of widespread failure in the relevant industry or sector to follow any part of the guidance in a SORP that has come to the attention of the SORP-making body.
- any developments in the industry or sector that suggest that further guidance on accounting matters is desirable.

The body should report to the ASB, at least annually, the results of such a review. **17** The report should confirm that the body continues to comply with this code of practice and state whether, in the light of the review, it proposes to revise any of the SORPs for which it is responsible.

ADDITIONAL GUIDANCE

It will not normally be necessary for a SORP-making body to supplement a SORP **18** with further guidance. Any material that a SORP-making body proposes to issue formally, offering an interpretation of accounting standards that is likely to lead to widespread acceptance as industry or sectoral practice, should be included in the SORP or should be submitted to the same due process and scrutiny procedures as the SORP, including review by the ASB and its relevant committees.

There are, however, three circumstances where the publication of further guidance **19** outside the SORP may be desirable:

(a) when urgent guidance is required on a new accounting standard or other relevant publication issued since the SORP was published. Normally, such guidance should subsequently be incorporated into a revised version of the SORP.

(b) when further guidance is required to interpret the requirements of the SORP within a particular subsector.

(c) when informal guidance on application of the SORP is necessary in order to aid practitioners.

In the situations described in paragraph 19(a) and (b), the SORP-making body **20** should notify the ASB, explaining what guidance is proposed. The ASB may, if appropriate, confirm that it has no objection to the proposed guidance and require a reference to the ASB to be included in the guidance. The guidance should not be published without the agreement of the ASB.

21 In the situation described in paragraph 19(a), where it is clear that guidance on a major issue is needed and cannot be delayed until revision of the SORP, the SORP-making body should attempt to follow all due process as required for the revision of a SORP. Where full due process has been followed, including review by the ASB and its relevant committees, then the 'ASB's statement on the SORP' may be attached to the guidance, giving it the same authority as the SORP.

22 In the situations described in paragraph 19(b) and (c), a SORP-making body should ensure that the authority of any such material in relation to the SORP is clearly indicated, and in particular state whether it has been reviewed by the ASB. A pro-forma statement for cases where the ASB has not carried out a review is as follows:

'The overall aim of the [additional guidance] is to assist practitioners in the preparation of statements of accounts. It does not form part of the [dated SORP], nor has it been reviewed by the ASB. It attempts to explain and illustrate what is required by the [dated SORP], but does not carry the authority of the SORP'.

RIGHT TO REPRODUCE

23 The SORP-making body shall grant the ASB the unrestricted right to reproduce in full any SORPs it has developed without being subject to any financial charge.

Part Eight

Exposure Drafts in issue

Part Eight

Exposure Duration in Issue

FRED 22
Revision of FRS 3 'Reporting Financial Performance'

(Issued December 2000)

Contents

APPENDICES

Preface

Financial Reporting Exposure Draft (FRED) 22 addresses the presentation of information on the financial performance of reporting entities, in both the primary statements and supporting notes. The proposals are developed from a Discussion Paper on the subject, 'Reporting Financial Performance: proposals for change', which the Accounting Standards Board published in June 1999.

The proposals in the FRED are a natural progression from the requirements of the existing standard, FRS 3 'Reporting Financial Performance', issued in 1992. Nevertheless, the proposals, when implemented, would change the existing requirements on reporting financial performance to reflect the shift in views internationally towards reporting comprehensive income. The main developments from FRS 3 are:

(a)   the profit and loss account and the statement of total recognised gains and losses are combined to form a single statement of financial performance.

(b)   the performance statement shows all gains and losses recognised during the period that relate to that period.

(c)   the statement is divided into three sections:

  (i)   operating;
  (ii)   financing and treasury; and
  (iii)   other gains and losses.

(d)   recycling of gains and losses between different sections of the performance statement is not permitted.

(e)   dividends for the period are excluded from the performance statement as they represent transactions with owners as owners rather than expenses.

(f)   a reconciliation of ownership interests is required to be presented as a primary statement.

The proposals retain the 'information set' approach of FRS 3. The FRED proposes that certain information on earnings per share, dividends for the period and prior period adjustments should be shown as memorandum items at the foot of the statement. Comprehensive notes to the single performance statement are also specified, including a reserves note and note of historical cost gains and losses, although the latter note has been made optional. In addition, new notes are added: a table of exceptional items reported over the last five years is required and a further optional note is suggested to illustrate the unusual tax implications of certain gains and losses.

The Board believes that the introduction of a single performance statement will allow users of accounts to view more easily the complete performance of a reporting entity, to the extent that an entity's performance is shown in the financial statements. The information accompanying the performance statement enables users to tie the information in the performance statement to the balance sheet changes in the period and increases comparability between reporting entities. The proposal also moves the performance statement format closer to a parallel of the cash flow statement format required by FRS 1 (Revised 1996), which should help users appreciate the cash effects of performance items.

Certain issues have been raised during the development of the FRED that may need to be addressed in order to put its proposals into force.

Gains and losses on investment properties

SSAP 19 requires recognised gains and losses representing the fair value changes arising on investment properties to be taken to the statement of total recognised gains and losses and the FRED follows this approach (ie these gains and losses are taken to 'other gains and losses'). However, using the logic of the proposals on performance reporting in the FRED, these gains and losses would instead be taken to the 'operating' section of the performance statement. The equivalent international standard would allow such a treatment and the Board will consider whether SSAP 19 should be revised in the light of the changes in international practice and the new approach to reporting financial performance.

The treatment of dividends

The FRED would not permit the inclusion of dividends for the period in the statement of financial performance because these represent transactions with owners as owners, rather than expenses of the entity. This conforms with the approach taken in the International Accounting Standard (IAS) 1 (revised) 'Presentation of Financial Statements'. However, the exclusion is contrary to UK companies legislation (although not to EC Directives). The Board has therefore raised with the Department of Trade and Industry the possibility of a change in the law.

Special industries and sectors

The FRED adapts the format of the basic statement of financial performance (as shown in the example in Appendix I) for those entities that report under special (and generally more complex) legislative regimes in the UK and the Republic of Ireland, ie banking and insurance entities and investment companies. The Board expects these and other industries and sectors to adapt the basic format as necessary through relevant Statements of Recommended Practice. Insurance entities may eventually be further affected by a review of insurance accounting that is taking place at the international level. No attempt is made in the FRED to anticipate the outcome of that review.

Particular issues on which comments are invited

The Board would welcome comments on any aspects of the FRED. Respondents' views are especially sought on the matters set out below. It would be helpful if respondents could support comments with reasons and, where applicable, preferred alternatives.

1   Do you agree with the proposal in the draft FRS (paragraphs 6 and 7) to introduce a single performance statement, in which would be reported all gains and losses recognised in a period that relate to that period? Do you agree that, as a consequence:

    (a)   transactions with owners as owners, such as dividends paid, should not be shown in the performance statement (paragraphs 8 and 9)?

    (b)   recycling between sections of the performance statement should not be permitted (paragraphs 10 and 11)?

2   Do you agree with the proposed structure of the performance statement of three sections ((a) operating, (b) financing and treasury, and (c) other gains and losses) as laid out in paragraphs 14–17?

Do you agree with the bases on which gains and losses are allocated to the different **3** sections of the performance statement as described in paragraphs 18–29 of the draft FRS and explained in Appendix IV 'The development of the FRED' (paragraphs 23–41)?

For complex organisations, the single performance statement would contain a great **4** deal of information. The Board does not wish to overburden the face of the statement, nor does it wish to see critical information relegated to the notes to the statement. Companies legislation offers some flexibility on this issue and views are therefore sought on how much information should be shown *on the face of the performance statement*:

(a) Should the FRS specify the minimum disclosure of items within each or any of the sections of the performance statement?

(b) Should the FRS specify the minimum disclosure for the results of discontinuing and continuing operations, for example turnover and operating result?

(c) Should the FRS specify the maximum permitted disclosure, thereby outlawing the provision of additional information or even formatting (at least on the face of the statement) that is provided at the discretion of management?

The Board has considered two different approaches to the allocation of gains and **5** losses between the operating section and the financing and treasury section (paragraphs 21–24 and Appendix IV, paragraphs 28 and 29).

(a) Do you agree with the approach laid out in the FRED, under which gains and losses resulting from operating activities that are financial in nature are reported in the operating section, whereas gains and losses arising from the financing of all the entity's activities, whether financial or not, are reported in the financing and treasury section?

(b) Alternatively, do you prefer an approach under which all gains and losses arising on financial activities are reported in the financing and treasury section?

The FRED has moved from the notion in FRS 3 of 'discontinued' operations to the **6** focus in the international standard* on 'discontinuing' operations (paragraphs 39–59). Do you agree that the proposed FRS should adopt the international requirement in this respect?

The FRED would amend FRS 15 'Tangible Fixed Assets' so that disposal gains and **7** losses arising on fixed assets are reported in the same way as revaluation gains and losses and impairment losses (Appendix IV, paragraph 42). Do you agree that these gains and losses should be reported in the same way, regardless of whether they are realised in the period?

The Board is keen to elicit respondents' views in the light of experience in applying **8** FRS 15 regarding the allocation of recognised losses on fixed assets between sections of the performance statement, and how (for revalued assets) recognised gains arising in subsequent periods should then be reported. On the arguments laid out in Appendix IV (paragraphs 43–48):

(a) do you believe that all falls in value of fixed assets from carrying amount to recoverable amount should be treated as impairments (whether those assets have previously been revalued or not)?

(b) do you believe that recognised increases in value arising in subsequent periods should be treated as revaluation gains or do you think they should be treated as reversals of previous impairment losses (to the extent of those previously recognised losses)?

*IAS 35 'Discontinuing Operations'

Alternatively, do you believe that the existing treatment in FRS 15 is satisfactory?

9   Applying the logic of the proposals in the FRED, the fair value gains and losses arising on investment properties would be reported in the 'operating' section of the performance statement (see page 5 above and Appendix IV, paragraphs 49–51). This conforms to the approach taken in IAS 40 'Investment Property', but would necessitate an amendment to SSAP 19, which requires such gains and losses to be reported in 'other gains and losses'. Do you agree that the Board should consider such an amendment?

10   Do you agree with the proposals relating to:

(a)   exceptional items (paragraphs 61–66)?
(b)   extraordinary items (paragraphs 67–69)

11   The draft FRS sets out modified requirements in respect of certain entities in recognition of their regulatory environment and type of business.

(a)   Do you agree with the proposals in relation to:

(i)   banking companies and banking groups (paragraphs 79–81);
(ii)   insurance companies and insurance groups (paragraphs 82–85); and
(iii)   investment companies (paragraphs 86 and 87)?

(b)   Do you agree that further guidance for these and other bodies can be provided in relevant Statements of Recommended Practice (SORPs), or do you think that additional guidance would be needed in a standard?

12   The Board considered how conglomerates might best report their diverse activities within a single performance statement. For such groups, further disaggregation of the primary results may be necessary, for which SSAP 25 'Segmental reporting' provides a framework. Do you believe that SSAP 25 is adequate for this purpose?

13   The FRED proposes (in paragraphs 93–100) that certain information should be shown as memorandum items at the foot of the performance statement on the basis that, although not gains and losses of the period, they provide valuable information about company performance:

- all earnings per share figures
- dividends paid and proposed for the period, both in total and per share
- cumulative adjustments recognised in the period that arise from prior period adjustments.

Do you agree that any, some or all of these items should be shown as memorandum items at the foot of the performance statement?

14   Do you agree that basic earnings per share, calculated as required by FRS 14 'Earnings per Share', should be based on 'operating and financing income after tax and minority interests' that is attributable to ordinary shareholders (paragraph 93)?

15   The Board is minded to delete the requirement in FRS 3 for a note of historical cost gains and losses because it believes that the note has limited informational content. However, user respondents to the Discussion Paper expressed support for retaining the note. The FRED proposes to make the note non-mandatory. Do you believe that the note of historical cost profits and losses, as drafted in the FRED, should be:

(a)   mandatory (as in FRS 3 at present);
(b)   optional (as proposed in the FRED); or
(c)   not mentioned in the standard at all?

Summary

[Draft] Financial Reporting Standard sets out the requirements for reporting   **a**
financial performance.

The statement of financial performance

A single statement of financial performance is required, in which all recognised gains   **b**
and losses of the period are reported. This is part of a larger 'information set' on
performance that includes notes and memorandum items.

The performance statement is divided into three sections: **c**

(i)   operating;
(ii) financing and treasury; and
(iii) other gains and losses.

The bulk of recognised gains and losses will appear in the operating section. Only   **d**
those gains and losses specified by the [draft] FRS or other accounting standards and
by UITF Abstracts will be reported in the other sections.

Gains and losses arising on the financing of the entity, including income on the   **e**
investment of surplus funds, are to be reported in the financing and treasury section.

Holding gains and losses arising on long-term items held in order to carry out the   **f**
activities of the entity are to be reported in other gains and losses.

Recycling of gains and losses between sections of the performance statement is not   **g**
permitted.

Information is required on the results from acquisitions and continuing and dis-   **h**
continuing activities, at least in the operating section.

Discontinuing operations are those that are distinguishable from the remaining   **i**
continuing operations and for which a binding sale agreement has been signed or a
comprehensive termination plan announced.

All exceptional items are to be reported within the relevant line item, either on the   **j**
face of the performance statement or in a note to the accounts.

Two figures are to be given for taxation: one for the tax that is attributable to the   **k**
operating and financing sections and one attributable to the items in other gains and
losses.

Special industries

The format of the performance statement is adapted for banking and insurance   **l**
companies, and for investment companies, in line with statutory requirements.

Reconciliation of ownership interests

A reconciliation of ownership interests is required as a primary statement that brings   **m**
together the performance of the period (shown in the statement of financial performance) with all the other changes in ownership interests in the period, including
capital contributed by or repaid to shareholders.

Other information

n   The following memorandum information is to be presented at the foot of the performance statement:

- earnings per share
- dividends (both in total and per share)
- the cumulative gain or loss arising from a prior period adjustment.

o   Earnings per share is calculated according to FRS 14 'Earnings per Share'. Any additional earnings per share calculated on another level of earnings is to be presented on a consistent basis over time and, wherever disclosed, reconciled to the amount required by FRS 14, which is at least as prominent as the additional version presented.

p   Prior period adjustments are to be accounted for by restating the comparative figures for the preceding period in the primary statements and notes and adjusting the opening balance of reserves for the cumulative effect.

q   The note of historical cost gains and losses becomes an optional memorandum item, the primary purpose of which is to present the profits or losses of reporting entities that have revalued assets on a more comparable basis with those of entities that have not.

r   The [draft] FRS amends other accounting standards and UITF Abstracts.

[Draft] Financial Reporting Standard

OBJECTIVE

1   The objective of this [draft] FRS is to require reporting entities falling within its scope:

(a)   to report all recognised gains and losses in a single performance statement; and

(b)   to highlight a range of important components of financial performance to help users to understand the performance achieved by an entity in a period and assess future results and cash flows.

DEFINITIONS

2   The following definitions shall apply in the [draft] FRS and in particular in the Statement of Standard Accounting Practice set out **in bold type**.

Acquisition:-

A component of an entity that is acquired in the period.

Discontinuing operation:-

A component of an entity that:

(a)   represents a separate major line of business or geographical area of operations;

(b)   can be distinguished operationally and for financial reporting purposes; and

(c)   pursuant to a single plan, is:

(i) being disposed of substantially in its entirety, such as by selling the component in a single transaction or by demerger or spin-off of ownership of the component to the entity's shareholders;

(ii) being disposed of piecemeal, such as by selling off the component's assets and settling its liabilities individually; or

(iii) being terminated through abandonment.

Exceptional items:-

Material items that derive from events or transactions that fall within the ordinary activities of the reporting entity and which individually or, if of a similar type, in aggregate, need to be disclosed by virtue of their size or incidence if the financial statements are to give a true and fair view.

Extraordinary items:-

Material items possessing a high degree of abnormality that arise from events or transactions that fall outside the ordinary activities of the reporting entity and are not expected to recur. They do not include exceptional items nor do they include prior period items merely because they relate to a prior period.

Financial performance:-

The financial performance of an entity comprises the return it obtains on the resources it controls, the components of that return and the characteristics of those components, insofar as they can be captured by the accounting model.

Financial performance of an entity for a period encompasses all recognised gains and losses. As such, in mathematical terms it is the change in net assets of the reporting entity from the end of the previous period to the end of the present period, excluding distributions to and contributions from owners.

Financing and treasury section:-

The section of the statement of financial performance in which are reported gains and losses arising from the financing of the entity and its treasury activities.

Fundamental error:-

An error of such significance that it destroys the true and fair view and hence the validity of the entity's financial statements for the period.

Gains:-

Increases in ownership interest not resulting from contributions from owners.

The term includes items that are referred to as 'revenues'.

Initial disclosure event:-

With respect to a discontinuing operation, the occurrence of one of the following, whichever occurs earlier:

(a)   the entity has entered into a binding sale agreement for substantially all of the assets attributable to the discontinuing operation; or

(b)   the entity's board of directors or similar governing body has both:

   (i)   approved a detailed, formal plan for the discontinuance: and

   (ii)   made an announcement of the plan,

   and the actions of the entity are such that they have raised a valid expectation in those affected that it will carry out the planned termination.

Losses:-

Decreases in ownership interest not resulting from distributions to owners.

   The term includes items that are referred to as 'expenses'.

Operating section:-

The section of the statement of financial performance in which all the gains and losses arising on the activities of the entity are reported, other than those that are required to be reported in another section by this or another accounting standard.

Ordinary activities:-

Any activities that are undertaken by an entity as part of its business and such related activities in which the reporting entity engages in furtherance of, incidental to, or arising from, those activities. Such activities include the effects on the entity of any event in the various environments in which it operates, including the political, regulatory, economic and geographical environments, irrespective of the frequency or unusual nature of the events.

   Gains and losses that are reported in 'other gains and losses' in the performance statement, as determined by this and other accounting standards, represent holding gains and losses that arise on items, held for the long term, that are connected with but incidental to the main activities of the entity. As such, they are not part of the entity's profit on ordinary activities.

Other gains and losses:-

The section of the statement of financial performance in which are reported holding gains and losses that arise from long-term items held for operating or financing purposes, rather than with a view to benefiting from changes in their value over time, and which therefore do not reflect directly the operating or financing and treasury activities of the entity.

Prior period adjustments:-

Material adjustments applicable to prior periods arising from changes in accounting policies (as defined by FRS 18 'Accounting Policies') or from the correction of fundamental errors. They do not include changes of estimation techniques (as defined by FRS 18).

3   References to companies legislation mean:

(a)   for a company:

   (i)   in Great Britain, the Companies Act 1985;

(ii)   in Northern Ireland, the Companies (Northern Ireland) Order 1986; and
(iii) in the Republic of Ireland, the Companies Acts 1963–90 and the European Communities (Companies: Group Accounts) Regulations 1992;

(b)   for an entity other than a company, the equivalent legislation.

SCOPE

The [draft] FRS applies to all financial statements that are intended to give a true and   **4**
fair view of a reporting entity's financial position and profit or loss (or income and
expenditure) for a period. Every such entity should apply the requirements of the [draft]
FRS except to the extent that these requirements are not permitted by the legislation (if
any) under which the entity reports.

Reporting entities applying the Financial Reporting Standard for Smaller Entities   **5**
currently applicable are exempt from the [draft] FRS.

THE STATEMENT OF FINANCIAL PERFORMANCE

The single performance statement

All gains and losses recognised in the entity's financial statements for the period should   **6**
be included in the statement of financial performance.

The financial performance of an entity is made up of components that exhibit dif-   **7**
fering characteristics in terms of, for example, their nature, cause, function, relative
continuity or recurrence, stability, risk, predictability and reliability. All these
components are relevant to an assessment of financial performance and therefore
need to be reported on in the statement of financial performance, although their
individual characteristics mean that some will carry more weight than others.

Items that are not gains and losses should not be reported in the statement of financial   **8**
performance.

Only gains and losses as defined by the [draft] FRS are reported in an entity's state-   **9**
ment of financial performance. For example, dividends paid and payable are not
gains and losses and therefore are not part of financial performance; consequently,
they are not reported in the statement of financial performance.*

Recycling† between sections of the statement of financial performance is not permitted.   **10**

Items that are not gains or losses are not included in the performance statement,   **11**
which means that the notion of recycling is not consistent with the [draft] FRS. For
example, a gain on the revaluation of a fixed asset should be reflected in other gains
and losses in the period in which the revaluation takes place. The realisation, or part-
realisation, of such a gain on the sale of the asset in a subsequent period is not itself a
gain of that later period but, rather, confirmation of a gain that had already occurred

---

*This is not consistent with how dividends are dealt with at present. It is acknowledged that companies legislation
requires dividends paid and payable to be shown on the face of the profit and loss account: see Appendix II,
paragraphs 24–26 and Appendix IV, paragraphs 70 and 71.

†'Recycling' here means recognising a gain or loss in the performance statement in one period and then, in a later
period, recognising some or all of that gain or loss under a different heading in either the same or a different
section of the statement of financial performance because the nature of the item is deemed to have changed in
some way. It does not refer to the allocation of gains and losses to different sections or components of the
performance statement.

by the time of the revaluation. Consequently, the gain or loss on the disposal of the asset is to be calculated as the difference between the net sale proceeds and the net carrying amount.

12   **Gains and losses should generally not be offset in presenting information on financial performance, unless:**

   (a)   **they relate to the same event or circumstance; and**

   (b)   **disclosing the gross components is unlikely to be useful in assessing either future results or the effects of past transactions and events.**

13   If a transaction involves both a receipt and a cost (as is the case, for example, when an item of stock is sold), the transaction will usually be best presented by showing the revenue (the receipt) separately from the expense (the cost). If a profit is made on the disposal of a fixed asset, however, that profit is usually best presented by showing it as a gain rather than by showing the sales proceeds as a gain separately from the depreciated cost of the asset. In this latter case, users are not seeking information on the margins achieved on the sale of the fixed asset, whereas for the purchase and sale of an item of stock, the information on the sales margin is directly relevant to the assessment of the expected future performance of the entity.

The sections of the statement of financial performance

14   **An entity should divide its performance statement into the following three sections:**

   (a)   **operating;**

   (b)   **financing and treasury;* and**

   (c)   **other gains and losses.**

15   **All gains and losses recognised in the financial statements for the period should be included in a section of the single performance statement.**

16   The various activities undertaken by an entity differ in stability, risk and predictability, and therefore components of financial performance need to be disclosed in different sections of the statement of financial performance. Disclosure of component information within distinct sections is designed to facilitate understanding of the performance achieved in a period and to help users judge how far past results are useful in assessing potential future results.

17   **Gains and losses should be allocated to the various sections of the performance statement on the basis of the requirements in the [draft] FRS and other accounting standards. Where a choice is permitted, any proposal to change the section(s) in which gains and losses are reported should be considered according to those requirements of FRS 18 'Accounting Policies' that relate to changes in accounting policy.**

The operating section

18   **Gains and losses may be excluded from the operating section of the performance statement only if they are permitted or required to be taken to another section by the [draft] FRS, other accounting standards or UITF Abstracts.**

19   Income from operating activities focuses on what a reporting entity earns for its output (revenue) and what it sacrifices to obtain that output (expenses) in its dealings

*Entities that belong to certain special industries should merge the first two sections of the performance statement and subdivide the resulting section as is appropriate for their industry: see paragraphs 77–85.

with its customers. To provide information on the operating margins the entity achieves, the expenses charged in the operating section should comprise all costs incurred in carrying out the entity's operations. This section should therefore include allocations reflecting the consumption of economic benefits of long-term items, for example the depreciation and impairment of fixed assets or the current service cost representing the increase in the actuarial liability expected to arise from employee service in the current period.

For most entities, the bulk of gains and losses recognised during a period will fall   **20**
into this section. The presumption is that gains and losses recognised during the period arise from an entity's operating activities. Only by exception will certain gains and losses (those that arise from the financing of the entity, or represent holding gains or losses on long- term items) be reported in one of the other sections of the performance statement, as specified by accounting standards. Thus, the operating section will exclude the gains and losses arising from the financing of the operations of the entity, although it will include gains and losses arising from operating activities that are financial in nature (see paragraph 23).

The financing and treasury section

Only gains and losses specified by the [draft] FRS, other accounting standards or UITF   **21**
Abstracts should be reported in the financing and treasury section of the performance
statement.*

The recognised gains and losses that should appear in this section are: **22**

(a)   interest payable and receivable;
(b)   the unwinding of the discount on long-term items, eg pensions;
(c)   income from investments held as part of treasury activities;
(d)   gains and losses arising on the repurchase or early settlement of debt (as deter-
**   mined in accordance with FRS 4 'Capital Instruments'); and**
(e)   any other recognised gain or loss identified for inclusion by another accounting
**   standard or by a UITF Abstract.**

The basis on which gains and losses arising on financial activities have been reported in
the operating section of the performance statement should be disclosed and this should
be applied consistently from period to period.

This section of the performance statement contains those gains and losses arising   **23**
from the financing of the entity's operations.† This does not mean that all items of a financial nature will be reported here. Where some or all of an entity's trade with its external customers is financial in nature, gains and losses arising from those activities will be reported in the operating section of the performance statement.

Reporting entities that are part of special industries, such as banking and insurance companies, will adapt the formats required by the [draft] FRS.‡ Other entities will

*The content of this section of the performance statement is likely to be affected by the outcome of the project on accounting for financial instruments and derivatives, proposals for which have been published by an international Joint Working Group of standard setters within an ASB consultation paper 'Financial Instruments and Similar Items'. Changes in fair value of financial instruments would be reported in this section on the basis of the JWG's approach.

†Contributors from and distributors to owners of the entity are not gains and losses and therefore should not be reported in the performance statement.

‡See paragraphs 77–85.

need to consider the extent to which their operating results should incorporate their financial activities.

24   **The items included in the financing and treasury section as specified in paragraph 22 should be disclosed in the notes if not presented the on the face of performance statement.**

Other gains and losses

25   **Only gains and losses specified by the [draft] FRS or other accounting standards or UITF Abstracts should be reported in other gains and losses within the performance statement.**

26   **The recognised gains and losses that should appear in this section are:**

(a)   **revaluation gains and losses on fixed assets (as determined in accordance with FRS 15 'Tangible Fixed Assets');**

(b)   **gains and losses on disposal of properties in continuing operations (as determined in accordance with FRS 15);**

(c)   **actuarial gains and losses arising on defined benefit schemes (as determined in accordance with FRS 17 'Retirement Benefits');**

(d)   **profits and losses on disposal of discontinuing operations;**

(e)   **exchange translation differences on foreign currency net investments (as determined in accordance with SSAP 20 'Foreign currency translation');**

(f)   **revaluation gains and losses arising on investment properties (as determined in accordance with SSAP 19 'Accounting for investment properties');***

(g)   **on the lapse of an unexercised warrant, the amount previously recognised in respect of that warrant (as determined in accordance with FRS 4 'Capital Instruments'); and**

(h)   **any other recognised gain or loss as determined in accordance with or identified by another accounting standard or a UITF Abstract.**

27   An entity is usually exposed to holding gains and losses that arise on items, held for the long term, that are connected with but incidental to its main trading activities. For example, holding gains and losses may arise on a manufacturing entity's factory, or currency fluctuations may arise on an investment in an overseas subsidiary. Although holding such items is necessary for the successful delivery of operating results, significant holding gains and losses arising from such assets are incidental to the main purpose for which they are held. Consequently, such gains and losses should be segregated from the results of both the operating and financing activities of the reporting entity, so that users may differentiate between their varying characteristics.

28   **The items included in other gains and losses as specified in paragraph 26 should be disclosed in the notes if not presented on the face of the performance statement.**

29   The extent to which disclosure is necessary on the face of the performance statement will vary according to the entity's circumstances. Accordingly, the [draft] FRS permits the individual items that make up the total gains and losses of both the financing and treasury section and other gains and losses to be disclosed on the face of the performance statement or by note where this would help users' understanding (for example, when the statement would otherwise be excessively long and complex).

---

*See the reference to SSAP 19 in the Preface and in Appendix IV 'The development of the FRED', paragraphs 49–51.

Continuing and discontinuing operations*

The aggregate results of each of continuing operations, acquisitions (as a component of   **30**
continuing operations) and discontinuing operations should be disclosed separately for
the results of the operating section. The same information should be given in respect of
the financing and treasury section and other gains and losses, unless it is impracticable
to do so or the resulting information would be misleading. The results of acquisitions
included in continuing operations should not include those that are also discontinuing in
the same period.

In the operating section, the minimum disclosure required on the face of the performance   **31**
statement in respect of continuing operations, acquisitions and discontinuing operations
is the analysis of turnover and operating profit. The analysis into continuing operations,
acquisitions (as a component of continuing operations) and discontinuing operations of
each of the other format items between turnover and operating profit should be given by
way of note where not shown on the face of the performance statement.

Where an entity presents information on continuing and discontinuing operations in   **32**
either the financing and treasury section or in other gains and losses (or in both), the
underlying assumptions used in making any allocations, for example of interest payable,
should be disclosed.

The objective of reporting separately the results of continuing operations, acquisi-   33
tions (as a component of continuing operations) and discontinuing operations is to
help users, first, in assessing the financial performance of these aspects of an entity's
operations and, secondly, in forming a basis for the assessment of future income.
Separate presentation assists analysis of the significance of the part of an entity's
operations that is ceasing and of new operations that have been acquired.

The [draft] FRS requires each of the headings between turnover and operating profit   34
to be analysed into continuing operations, acquisitions (as a component of continuing operations) and discontinuing operations. To avoid excessive data on the
face of the performance statement, the minimum disclosure required there for continuing operations, acquisitions and discontinuing operations is the analysis of
turnover and operating profit.

A similar analysis into continuing and discontinuing operations may be given for the   35
financing and treasury section and for other gains and losses. However, the information need not be provided if it is impracticable to do so or if the resulting
information would be misleading. For example, interest payable is often a reflection
of an entity's overall financing policy, involving both equity and debt funding considerations on a groupwide basis, rather than an aggregation of the particular types
of finance allocated to individual segments of the entity's operations. Any allocation
of interest may involve so much subjectivity that the user is uncertain about the
relevance and reliability of the information. If an entity wishes to provide such an
allocation, the [draft] FRS requires the method and underlying assumptions used in
making the allocation to be disclosed. In addition, where practicable the analysis in
the financing and treasury section and in other gains and losses should identify,
either on the face of the performance statement or in the notes, the amounts arising
in respect of acquisitions.

The effect of acquisitions and of sales or terminations on major business segments   **36**
should be disclosed and explained.

**Editor's note: The proposals with regard to discontinuing operations are partly superseded by FRED 32
Disposal of non-current assets and presentation of discontinued operations.*

Acquisitions

37   **The post-acquisition results for the period in which the acquisition occurs should be disclosed. Where it is not practicable to determine the post-acquisition results of an operation to the end of the current period, an indication should be given of the contribution of the acquisition to the turnover and operating profit of the continuing operations in addition to the information required by companies legislation.* If an indication of the contribution of an acquisition to the results of the period cannot be given, that fact and the reason should be explained.**

38   In some circumstances it may also be useful for the results of acquisitions for the first full financial year for which they are a part of the entity to be disclosed in the notes.

Discontinuing operations

39   **A transaction or event that does not meet the definition of a discontinuing operation in the [draft] FRS should not be referred to as such in the statement of financial performance or related notes.**

40   Discontinuing operations are defined in paragraph 2 Under criterion (a), a discontinuing operation may be disposed of in its entirety or piecemeal, but always pursuant to an overall plan to discontinue the entire component.

41   If an entity sells a component substantially in its entirety, the result may be a net gain or a net loss. For such a discontinuance, there is a single date at which a binding sale agreement is entered into, although the actual transfer of possession and control of the discontinuing operation may occur at a later date. Also, payments to the seller may occur at the time of the agreement, at the time of the transfer, or over an extended future period.

42   Instead of disposing of a major component in its entirety, an entity may discontinue and dispose of the component by selling its assets and settling its liabilities piecemeal (individually or in small groups). For piecemeal disposals, whilst the overall result may be a net gain or a net loss, the sale of an individual asset or settlement of an individual liability may have the opposite effect. Moreover, there is no single date at which an overall binding sale agreement is entered into. Rather, the sales of assets and settlements of liabilities may occur over a period of months or perhaps even longer, and the end of a financial reporting period may occur part way through the disposal period. To qualify as a discontinuing operation, the disposal must be pursuant to a single co-ordinated plan.

43   For a plan to give rise to a valid expectation, when communicated to those affected by it, that the termination will be carried out, its implementation needs to be planned to begin as soon as possible and to be completed in a timeframe that makes significant changes to the plan unlikely. If it is expected that there will be a long delay before the termination begins or that the termination will take an unreasonably long time, it is unlikely that the plan will raise a valid expectation on the part of others that the entity is at present committed to the termination, because the timeframe allows opportunities for the entity to change its plans.

**In Great Britain, the Companies Act 1985, Schedule 4A paragraph 13.*
In Northern Ireland, the Companies (Northern Ireland) Order 1986, Schedule 4A paragraph 13.
There is no direct equivalent in the Republic of Ireland: however, Regulation 27 of the European Communities (Companies: Group Accounts) Regulations 1992 states: 'If the composition of the undertakings dealt with in the group accounts has changed significantly in the course of a financial year, the group accounts must include information which makes the comparison of successive sets of group accounts meaningful.'

An entity may terminate an operation by abandonment without substantial sales of **44** assets. An abandoned operation is a discontinuing operation if it satisfies the criteria in the definition. However, changing the scope of an operation or the manner in which it is conducted is not an abandonment because that operation, although changed, is continuing.

Entities frequently close facilities, abandon products or even product lines, and **45** change the size of their workforce in response to market forces. Whilst such terminations generally are not, in and of themselves, discontinuing operations as that term is used in the [draft] FRS, they can occur in connection with a discontinuing operation. Examples of activities that do not necessarily satisfy criterion (a) of the definition, but might do so in combination with other circumstances, include:

(a) gradual or evolutionary phasing out of a product line or class of service;
(b) discontinuing, even if relatively abruptly, several products within an ongoing line of business;
(c) shifting some production or marketing activities for a particular line of business from one location to another;
(d) closing a facility to achieve productivity improvements or other cost savings; and
(e) selling a subsidiary whose activities are similar to those of the parent or other subsidiaries.

A component can be distinguished operationally and for financial reporting purposes **46** if:

(a) its operating assets and liabilities can be directly attributed to it;
(b) its turnover can be directly attributed to it; and
(c) at least a majority of its operating expenses can be directly attributed to it.

Assets, liabilities, income, and expenses are directly attributable to a component if **47** they would be eliminated when the component is sold, abandoned or otherwise disposed of. Interest and other financing costs are attributed to a discontinuing operation only if the related debt is similarly attributed.

As defined in the [draft] FRS, discontinuing operations are expected to occur infre- **48** quently. Some changes that are not classified as discontinuing operations may qualify as restructurings (see FRS 12 'Provisions, Contingent Liabilities and Contingent Assets'). Also, some infrequently occurring events that do not qualify either as discontinuing operations or restructurings may result in items of income or expense that require separate disclosure as exceptional items as defined in paragraph 2, because their size, nature, or incidence make them relevant to explain the performance of the entity for the period.

Initial disclosures

An entity should include the following information relating to a discontinuing operation **49**
in its financial statements beginning with the financial statements for the period in which
the initial disclosure event (as defined in paragraph 2) occurs:

(a) **a description of the discontinuing operation;**
(b) **the business or geographical segment(s) in which it is reported in accordance with SSAP 25 'Segmental reporting';**
(c) **the date and nature of the initial disclosure event;**
(d) **the date or period in which the discontinuance is expected to be completed if known or determinable;**
(e) **the carrying amounts, as at the balance sheet date, of the total assets and the total liabilities to be disposed of;**

(f)   the results of the discontinuing operations for the period as required by paragraphs 30–32; and

(g)   the amounts of net cash flows attributable to the operating activities of the discontinuing operation during the current financial reporting period.*

50   In measuring the assets, liabilities, revenues, expenses, gains, losses and cash flows of a discontinuing operation for the purpose of the disclosures required by the [draft] FRS, such items can be attributed to a discontinuing operation if they will be disposed of, settled, reduced or eliminated when the discontinuance is completed. To the extent that such items continue after completion of the discontinuance, they should not be allocated to the discontinuing operation.

51   If an initial disclosure event occurs after the end of an entity's financial reporting period but before the financial statements for that period are authorised for issue or approved by the board of directors or similar governing body, those financial statements should include the disclosures specified in paragraph 49 for the period covered by those financial statements.

52   For example, suppose that the board of directors of an entity whose financial year ends on 31 December 2005 approves a plan for a discontinuing operation on 15 December 2005 and announces that plan on 10 January 2006. The board approves the financial statements for 2005 on 20 March 2006. The financial statements for 2005 would include the disclosures required by paragraph 49.

Other disclosures

53   When an entity disposes of assets or settles liabilities attributable to a discontinuing operation or enters into binding agreements for the sale of such assets or the settlement of such liabilities, it should include in its financial statements the following information when the events occur:

(a)   for any gain or loss that is recognised on the disposal of assets or settlement of liabilities attributable to the discontinuing operation, the amount of pre-tax gain or loss; and

(b)   the expected proceeds of sale (after deducting the expected disposal costs) of those net assets for which the entity has entered into one or more binding sale agreements, the expected timing of receipt of those cash flows, and the carrying amount of those net assets.

54   The asset disposals, liability settlements, and binding sale agreements referred to in the previous paragraph may occur concurrently with the initial disclosure event, or in the period in which the initial disclosure event occurs, or in a later period. In accordance with SSAP 17 'Accounting for post balance sheet events', if some of the assets attributable to a discontinuing operation have actually been sold or are the subject of one or more binding sale agreements entered into after the financial year-end but before the board approves the financial statements for issue, the financial statements should include the disclosures required by paragraph 53 if non-disclosure would affect the ability of the users of the financial statements to make proper evaluations and decisions.

Updating disclosures

55   In addition to the disclosures in paragraphs 49 and 53, an entity should include in its financial statements for periods after that in which the initial disclosure event occurs a

*See FRS 1 (Revised 1996), paragraphs 23 and 24.

description of any significant changes in the amount or timing of cash flows relating to the assets and liabilities to be disposed of or settled and the events causing those changes.

Examples of events and activities that would be disclosed include the nature and terms of binding sale agreements for the assets, a demerger of the assets by spin-off of a separate equity security to the entity's shareholders, and legal or regulatory approvals.   56

The disclosures required by paragraphs 49-56 should continue in financial statements for periods up to and including the period in which the discontinuance is completed. A discontinuance is completed when the plan is substantially completed or abandoned, though payments from the buyer(s) to the seller may not yet be completed.   57

If an entity abandons or withdraws from a plan that was previously reported as a discontinuing operation, that fact and its effect should be disclosed.   58

For the purpose of applying the preceding paragraph, disclosure of the effect includes any reversal of prior impairment loss or provision that was recognised with respect to the discontinuing operation.   59

Associates and joint ventures

An investing entity's share of the results of its joint ventures and associates should be reported in the performance statement as required by FRS 9 'Associates and Joint Ventures'.*   60

Exceptional items

All exceptional items should be credited or charged by inclusion under the format headings to which they relate. They should be attributed to the relevant section of the performance statement and to continuing or discontinuing operations as appropriate. The amount of each exceptional item, either individually or as an aggregate of items of a similar type, should be disclosed separately by way of note, or on the face of the performance statement if that degree of prominence is necessary in order to give a true and fair view. An adequate description of each exceptional item should be given to enable its nature to be understood.   61

Exceptional items are defined in paragraph 2. They are an inherent part of the normal activities of a reporting entity and are included in the relevant line item within each component of performance but, because of their exceptional size or incidence, require separate disclosure to explain the performance of a period. Exceptional items may arise from a variety of sources and for larger or more complex businesses they are likely to occur in one form or another in most periods. They should not be aggregated on the face of the statement under one heading of exceptional items but, rather, each should be included within its appropriate statutory format or other heading and separately disclosed as required by paragraph 61. The nature of exceptional items makes it necessary to distinguish exceptional profits from exceptional losses in the notes, if not on the face of the performance statement.   62

When exceptional items are reported in either the current year figures or those of a comparative period, a history of exceptional items reported should be shown in the notes   63

*As amended by this [draft] FRS: see paragraph 118.

to the statement. The note should show, for each of the last five years, a breakdown of the exceptional items reported with a description of each.

64   Exceptional items should, by definition, be infrequent. Therefore, where exceptional items are reported regularly, it is helpful for users to see both the pattern of exceptional items reported and the nature of them (particularly when more than one is reported in a period).

65   **In any references to the entity's financial performance as including or excluding exceptional items, an explanation should be given of the relevance of their inclusion or exclusion (as the case may be) in the context of considering the results of the period or assessing maintainable earnings.**

66   To facilitate such an explanation, it may be convenient to combine the breakdown of exceptional items over the previous five years required by paragraph 63 with the results over the same period that include or exclude exceptional items. Exceptional items may occur in either continuing or discontinuing operations and need to be identified individually as belonging to one or other category.

Extraordinary items

67   **Any extraordinary gain or loss should be shown separately on the face of the performance statement, after the profit or loss on ordinary activities after taxation and, in consolidated financial statements, after the figure for minority interests.* The amount of each extraordinary item should be shown individually either on the face of the performance statement or in a note and an adequate description of each extraordinary item should be given to enable its nature to be understood. The tax on an extraordinary gain or loss and, in consolidated financial statements, the extraordinary gain or loss attributable to minority shareholders should be shown separately as a part of the extraordinary item either on the face of the performance statement or in a note. Any subsequent adjustments to the tax on an extraordinary gain or loss in future periods should be shown as an extraordinary item.**

68   Extraordinary items are defined in paragraph 2. They are extremely rare as they relate to highly abnormal events or transactions that fall outside the ordinary activities of a reporting entity and are not expected to recur. Although reporting of extraordinary items is provided for by companies legislation, the Board cannot envisage any circumstance in which extraordinary items might be reported under the definitions in the [draft] FRS and, accordingly, no examples are provided. Items falling into the category of exceptional in accordance with the terms of the [draft] FRS cannot, by definition, be extraordinary.

69   The [draft] FRS follows companies legislation in requiring the tax on extraordinary gains or losses and, in consolidated financial statements, the minority shareholders' interest in an extraordinary gain or loss, to be shown separately.

Taxation

70   **The tax arising from items in the operating section and the financing and treasury section should be shown after the statutory line of profit on ordinary activities before taxation.† The tax charge or credit arising on items in other gains and losses should be shown as a single item within that section.**

**ie after the total combined result of the 'operating' and 'financing and treasury' sections after tax and minority interests.*

†*ie, after the total combined result of the 'operating' and 'financing and treasury' sections.*

Where the tax relating to each of the items within other gains and losses can be   **71**
identified clearly with the item, disclosure may be made of the individual tax effects
in the notes to the statement.

Any special circumstances that affect the overall tax charge or credit for the period, or   **72**
may affect those of future periods, should be disclosed by way of note to the perfor-
mance statement and their individual effects quantified. The effects of a fundamental
change in the basis of taxation should be included in the tax charge or credit for the
period and separately disclosed in the notes to the performance statement.

The tax on items in other gains and losses or on an extraordinary gain or loss should be   **73**
determined by computing the tax on the profit or loss on ordinary activities* as if the
items did not exist, and comparing this notional tax charge with the total tax charge for
the period (ie including the tax on other gains and losses and extraordinary items). Any
additional tax charge or credit (including deferred tax) arising should thus be attributed
to the items. If there are both items in other gains and losses and an extraordinary gain
or loss in the same period, the tax on the items combined should be calculated, then
apportioned between the two in relation to their respective amounts, unless a more
appropriate basis of apportionment is available. If a more appropriate basis is adopted
the method of apportionment should be disclosed.

Companies legislation† requires disclosure in the notes of the details of any special   **74**
circumstances that affect any liability to taxation, whether for the financial year in
question or for future years, and whether in respect of profits, income or capital
gains. Such special circumstances could include, for example, the effect on the tax
charge of losses whether utilised or carried forward. This disclosure can be useful in
understanding the period's charge or credit in respect of taxation, particularly when
there are items of the type specified in other gains and losses.

It is recognised that analysing an entity's total taxation charge into the component   **75**
parts of its result for a period can involve arbitrary allocations that tend to become
less meaningful the more components or sections there are. However, for items such
as disposal profits or losses, the tax can often be identified with the item concerned
and the relationship between the gain or loss and the attributable tax may be significantly different from that in respect of gains or losses arising on items in the
operating section and the financing and treasury section. In such circumstances, it is
relevant to identify the tax charge or credit more specifically. Disclosure of special
circumstances can also be useful in assessing likely future amounts of taxation.
Therefore, the [draft] FRS suggests that the information required by companies legislation might be provided in a note that discloses the existence of any special
circumstances and quantifies their individual effects.

Consistency requires that the tax effects of an extraordinary item should themselves   **76**
be treated as extraordinary. This principle would apply even where an extraordinary
item and its tax effects are recognised in different periods, such as where the tax relief
in respect of an extraordinary loss is not recognised until it is utilised in a subsequent
period.

**ie on the total combined result of the 'operating' and 'financing and treasury' sections.*

†*In Great Britain, the Companies Act 1985, Schedule 4 paragraph 54(2).*
In Northern Ireland, the Companies (Northern Ireland) Order, Schedule 4 paragraph 54(2).
In the Republic of Ireland, the Schedule to the Companies (Amendment) Act 1986, paragraph 40(2).

SPECIAL INDUSTRIES

77   The [draft] FRS requires a single statement of financial performance, divided into sections to which all gains and losses recognised in the period should be allocated, based on their inherent characteristics as described in the [draft] FRS. This will allow users of the financial statements to consider and give due weight to all the components of performance of the period. This approach applies to all types of entity, although the precise form in which financial performance is reported will vary for industries and sectors that are subject to special reporting requirements and whose business has unusual features.

78   The [draft] FRS applies to entities that prepare their accounts under (in Great Britain) Schedules and A to the Companies Act 1985.* Banking and insurance companies and groups are required under companies legislation to prepare their accounts under different provisions,† which specify special formats for the balance sheet and profit and loss account. In addition, investment companies as defined in companies legislation are the subject of specific requirements.‡ Requirements on the application of the [draft] FRS to reporting entities within these sectors are given in paragraphs 79–87. Subject to those requirements, banking and insurance entities and investment companies, as well as entities in other special industries and sectors whether or not subject to separate statutory requirements, should look to relevant Statements of Recommended Practice (SORPs) for additional guidance on the application of the [draft] FRS.

Banking companies and banking groups

79   **Banking companies and banking groups, as defined by companies legislation,§ should prepare a single statement of financial performance that includes a section 'other gains and losses'.**

80   The draft [FRS] does not specify how the upper part of the performance statement should be divided up but it would be consistent with existing practice to show separately:

(a)   income and expenses; and
(b)   adjustments to provisions.

---

*In Northern Ireland, Schedules 4 and 4A to the Companies (Northern Ireland) Order 1986.
In the Republic of Ireland, the Schedule to the Companies (Amendment) Act 1986 and the European Communities (Companies: Group Accounts) Regulations 1992.

†In Great Britain, Schedule 9 to the Companies Act 1985 for banking entities and Schedule 9A for insurance entities.
In Northern Ireland, Schedules 9 and 9A to the Companies (Northern Ireland) Order 1986 for banking and insurance entities respectively.
In the Republic of Ireland, the European Communities (Credit Institutions: Accounts) Regulations 1992 for banking entities and the European Communities (Insurance Undertakings: Accounts) Regulations 1996 for insurance entities.

‡In Great Britain, section 266 of the Companies Act 1985.
In Northern Ireland, Article 274 of the Companies (Northern Ireland) Order 1986.
In the Republic of Ireland, section 47(3), (4) and (7) of the Companies (Amendment) Act 1983.

§In Great Britain, sections 744 and 255A of the Companies Act 1985.
In Northern Ireland, the Companies (Northern Ireland) Order 1986, Articles 2(3) and 263A.
In the Republic of Ireland, the Companies (Amendment) Act 1986, section 2(3) and the European Communities (Companies: Group Accounts) Regulations 1992, Regulation 6(2)(a).

Banking entities operate in a highly regulated sector, and the basis on which they **81** report their performance is more complex than for most other entities. The substantial difference between banking and most other industries is acknowledged in companies legislation by special reporting requirements and formats for banking entities. The reduced specification in paragraph 79 for the performance statement for banking entities satisfies the requirement of the [draft] FRS for a single performance statement while taking account of the sector's particular business, regulatory and legal environment. As noted in paragraph 78, further guidance on application of the [draft] FRS to banking entities will be included in a SORP.

Insurance companies and insurance groups

Insurance companies and insurance groups, as defined by companies legislation,* should **82** **prepare a single statement of financial performance divided into the following sections:**

(a)   technical: general business;
(b)   technical: long-term business;
(c)   non-technical account; and
(d)   other gains and losses.

Insurance entities operate in a highly regulated sector, and the basis on which they **83** report their performance is more complex than for most other entities. The substantial difference between the insurance sector and other industries is acknowledged in companies legislation by special reporting requirements and formats for insurance entities. The format required in paragraph 81 for the performance statement for insurance entities satisfies the requirements of the [draft] FRS for a single performance statement while taking account of the sector's particular business, regulatory and legal environment. The operating section and the financing and treasury section are, in effect, merged and then split into new sections that more appropriately reflect the insurance environment. As noted in paragraph 78, further guidance on application of the [draft] FRS to insurance entities will be included in a SORP.

Insurance entities should report both realised and unrealised investment gains or losses **84** **on investments held as part of their investment portfolios in one or more of the following** **accounts: (a) technical: general business; (b) technical: long-term business; and (c) non-** **technical account, according to the allocation policy adopted.**

For insurance entities, investment returns on investments held as part of the **85** investment portfolios form a particularly important element of their performance. Such investment returns, realised and unrealised, are therefore required to be shown in one or more of the sections (a)–(c) set out in paragraph 81. The allocation policy adopted needs to take into account the requirements of companies legislation and the recommendations of the Statement of Recommended Practice 'Accounting for Insurance Business'.

---

*In Great Britain, sections 744 and 255A of the Companies Act 1985.
In Northern Ireland, the Companies (Northern Ireland) Order 1986, Articles 2(3) and 263A.
In the Republic of Ireland, the European Communities (Credit Institutions: Accounts) Regulations 1992 and the
European Communities (Companies: Group Accounts) Regulations 1992, Regulation 6(2)(g).

Investment companies

86   Investment companies as defined in companies legislation* should prepare a single performance statement with three sections as required by the [draft] FRS:

(a)   operating;
(b)   financing and treasury; and
(c)   other gains and losses.

Only profits available for distribution should be included in the first two sections of the performance statement.

87   Investment companies are subject to special legal provisions regarding the recording of unrealised capital losses, with the result that their statements of financial performance are not comparable with those of other entities. For investment companies, all recognised gains and losses of a capital nature should be shown in other gains and losses, leaving the first two sections to be confined to revenue profits that are available for distribution. An example of a statement of financial performance for an investment company is given in Appendix I.

CONGLOMERATES

88   Reporting entities that have a wide range of operating activities should, when preparing consolidated accounts, allocate gains and losses to sections of the performance statement to reflect the performance of the group as a whole, rather than its constituent parts.

89   The requirement to consolidate may, in the case of groups with diverse operating activities, lead to a level of aggregation on the face of the performance statement that users find unhelpful. This should not prevent the proper allocation of gains and losses at a group level. However, such groups should consider the extent to which disaggregated and segmental information should be given to users in the notes to the accounts and possibly on the face of the performance statement.

90   For example, a manufacturing group may own an insurance company. In such circumstances, neither the basic three- section format that would suit a manufacturing company, nor the more complex insurance company format (required in order to satisfy companies legislation, as shown in paragraph 81) is likely to enable the performance of the group as a whole to be reported fairly on the face of the performance statement. The structure of the performance statement may need to be adapted in such circumstances, or additional breakdowns of information may be required. Where guidance on a particular problem of this nature is not provided in either an accounting standard or a SORP, the choice of approach to resolve the issue rests with management, in consultation with the auditors and in consideration of particular statutory obligations and the requirement to show a true and fair view. Nevertheless, a reporting entity should follow the requirements of the [draft] FRS insofar as that is possible.

RECONCILIATION OF OWNERSHIP INTERESTS

91   A primary statement should be presented reconciling the opening and closing totals of ownership interests of the period. Certain reconciling items, namely the results of the period as reported in the performance statement, dividends for the period (broken down

In Great Britain, section 266 of the Companies Act 1985.
In Northern Ireland, Article 274 of the Companies (Northern Ireland) Order 1986.
In the Republic of Ireland, section 47(3), (4) and (7) of the Companies (Amendment) Act 1983.

into equity and non-equity dividends as required by FRS 4 'Capital Instruments'), and the cumulative effect of prior period adjustments, should be disclosed separately in the reconciliation.

There are changes in ownership interests, other than those reported in the perfor-   92
mance statement, that are important in understanding the change in the entity's financial position over the period. The purpose of the reconciliation of ownership interests is to highlight those other changes. It should be shown as a primary statement, separately from the statement of financial performance.

OTHER INFORMATION

Earnings per share

The earnings figure used to calculate basic earnings per share (which is adjusted for the   93
calculation of diluted earnings per share) should be the combined total of the operating
section and the financing and treasury section, after related taxation and minority
interests (identified as the statutory format line 'profit for the financial year'), and after
deduction of preference dividends as required by FRS 14 'Earnings per Share'.*

If provided, an additional earnings per share figure calculated at any other level of   94
performance should be presented on a consistent basis over time and, wherever disclosed, reconciled to the amount required by FRS 14. Such a reconciliation should list the
items for which an adjustment is made and disclose their individual effect on the calculation. The earnings per share required by FRS 14 should be at least as prominent as
any additional version presented and the reason for calculating the additional version
should be explained. The reconciliation and explanation should appear adjacent to the
earnings per share disclosure, or a reference should be given to where they can be found.

It is not possible to distil the performance of a complex organisation into a single   95
measure. Undue significance, therefore, should not be placed on any such measure that
purports to achieve this aim. To assess the performance of an entity during a period,
all components of its activities must be considered. The basic earnings per share figure
required by FRS 14 can therefore be used as a starting point for further analysis.

Dividends

Dividends for the period should be shown as memorandum items at the foot of the   96
performance statement, both in total and per share. The information should be given for
each class of share as required by FRS 4 'Capital Instruments'.†

Prior period adjustments

Prior period adjustments should be accounted for by restating the comparative figures   97
for the preceding period in the primary statements and notes and adjusting the opening
balance of reserves for the cumulative effect. The cumulative effect of the adjustments
should also be given as a footnote to the performance statement of the current period.
Where practicable, the effect of a prior period adjustment on the results for the preceding period should be disclosed. Where it is not practicable to make this disclosure,
that fact, together with the reasons, should be stated.

FRS 14 is amended accordingly: see paragraph 120.

†*FRS 4, paragraph 59. Also see Appendix IV, paragraphs 70 and 71.*

Changes in estimation techniques and changes in accounting policies

98   'Accounting Policies' defines estimation techniques and accounting policies and lays down rules for the treatment of changes to both, such that, in general:

(a)   a change to an estimation technique is not accounted for as a prior period adjustment, unless:

   (i)   it represents the correction of a fundamental error; or

   (ii)   companies legislation, another accounting standard or a UITF Abstract requires otherwise; and

(b)   a change to an accounting policy is treated as a prior period adjustment, unless companies legislation, other accounting standards or UITF Abstracts require otherwise.

Fundamental errors*

99   **The correction of fundamental errors should be accounted for by prior period adjustment.**

100   Fundamental errors are defined in paragraph 2. In exceptional circumstances it may be found that financial statements of prior periods contain errors that are so significant as to destroy the true and fair view and hence the validity of those financial statements. The correction of such fundamental errors and the cumulative adjustments applicable to prior periods have no bearing on the results of the current period and are therefore not included in arriving at the results for the current period. They are accounted for by restating prior periods, with the result that the opening balance of retained profits will be adjusted accordingly, and highlighted in the reconciliation of ownership interests. The cumulative adjustments so recognised should be shown as a footnote to the performance statement of the current period, in order to highlight the occurrence of a prior period adjustment.

Comparative figures

101   **Comparative figures should be given for all items in the primary statements and such notes thereto as are required by the [draft] FRS. The comparative figures in respect of the performance statement should include in the continuing category only the results of those operations included in the current period's continuing operations.**

102   Comparative figures should be given for all items in the primary statements and such notes to them as are required by the [draft] FRS. To aid comparison, the comparative figures in respect of the performance statement should be based on the status of an operation in the financial statements of the period under review and should, therefore, include in the continuing category only the results of those operations included in the current period's continuing operations. The comparative figures appearing under the heading 'continuing operations' may include figures that were shown under the heading of acquisitions in that previous period; no reference need be made to the results of those acquisitions, since they are not required to be presented separately in the current period. Where, however, information on acquisitions is provided voluntarily in respect of the first full accounting period, it may be helpful to provide comparative figures for those acquisitions.

*As noted in Appendix IV of FRS 18 (paragraph 27), when an FRS is developed from this FRED the Board may decide to transfer to FRS 18 the material on the correction of errors.

Comparative information for prior periods that is presented in financial statements   **103**
prepared after the initial disclosure event for a discontinuing operation should be
restated to segregate continuing and discontinuing assets, liabilities, income, expenses,
and cash flows, as required by paragraphs 49–59.

Note of historical cost gains and losses

Where there is a material difference between the result as disclosed in the statement   **104**
of financial performance and the result on an unmodified historical cost basis, a note
of the historical cost gains and losses for the period may be presented if such
information would help users to understand the entity's performance. An example
format of such a note is shown in Appendix I.

A note of historical cost gains and losses is a memorandum item that is an abbre-   **105**
viated restatement of the statement of financial performance, adjusting the reported
gains and losses, if necessary, to disregard the effect of any asset revaluations.
Adjustments are made for:

(a) gains and losses recognised in prior periods in the statement of financial performance that are realised in the current period: for example, the difference
between the profit on the disposal of an asset calculated on depreciated historical cost and that calculated on a revalued amount; and

(b) the difference between a historical cost depreciation charge and the depreciation charge calculated on the revalued amount included in the statement of
financial performance of the period.

Where a note of historical cost profits and losses is provided with consolidated financial   **106**
statements, the performance statement figures for minority interests should be amended
for the purposes of the note to reflect the adjustments made where they affect subsidiary
companies with a minority interest.

For the purpose of paragraph 105 the following are not deemed to be departures   **107**
from the historical cost convention: (a) adjustments necessarily made to cope with
the impact of hyper-inflation on foreign operations and (b) the practice of market-
makers and other dealers in investments of marking to market where this is an
established industry practice.

DATE FROM WHICH EFFECTIVE AND TRANSITIONAL
ARRANGEMENTS

The accounting practices set out in the [draft] FRS should be regarded as standard in   **108**
respect of accounting periods ending on or after [date to be inserted after exposure].
Earlier adoption is encouraged.

Comparative figures in the financial statements of the accounting period in which the   **109**
[draft] FRS is implemented should be restated to comply with the formats and infor-
mation required in the [draft] FRS.

WITHDRAWAL OF FRS 3 AND AMENDMENT OF OTHER
STANDARDS AND UITF ABSTRACTS

The [draft] FRS supersedes FRS 3 'Reporting Financial Performance' [following pub-   **110**
lication in final form].

Amendment of other accounting standards and UITF Abstracts: general [following publication in final form]

111   General references in accounting standards and UITF Abstracts to the profit and loss account statement should be read as references to the statement of financial performance as required by the [draft] FRS.

112   Other than as required by the amendments detailed in paragraphs 113–126, the following general rules should be followed:

(a)   Where an accounting standard or a UITF Abstract requires a gain, loss, revenue or expense to be reported, charged or recognised in the profit and loss account, the item should be reported in the operating section of the performance statement in accordance with the [draft] FRS.

(b)   Where an accounting standard or a UITF Abstract requires a gain, loss, revenue or expense to be reported in reserves or in the statement of total recognised gains and losses, the item should be reported in other gains and losses in the performance statement under the requirements of the [draft] FRS.

(c)   References in accounting standards and UITF Abstracts to the 'reconciliation of shareholders' funds' are replaced by 'reconciliation of ownership interests'.

Amendment of other accounting standards and UITF Abstracts: specific [following publication in final form]

113   In SSAP 21 'Accounting for leases and hire purchase contracts', the following is added to the end of paragraph 39:

'The finance charge for each accounting period should be reported in the financing and treasury section of the performance statement.'

114   In SSAP 24 'Accounting for pension costs', the reference in paragraph 81 to 'requirement of paragraph 18 of FRS 3 "Reporting Financial Performance"' is replaced by 'requirements of FRS 12 "Provisions, Contingent Liabilities and Contingent Assets"'.

115   In SSAP 25 'Segmental reporting':

(a)   the reference to 'result' in paragraph 34(b) is replaced by 'result of the operating section of the performance statement';

(b)   the last three sentences of paragraph 34 are replaced by:

'Segment result will normally be restricted to the operating section of the performance statement and consequently net assets will consist of non-interest bearing operating assets less non-interest bearing operating liabilities. However, to the extent that part or all of the contents of the financing and treasury section are included in the segmental analysis, the relevant interest-bearing assets and liabilities should be included in net assets.'

116   FRS 4 'Capital Instruments' is amended as follows:

(a)   The text of paragraph 28 is replaced by:

'The finance costs of debt should be allocated to periods over the term of the debt at a constant rate on the carrying amount. All finance costs should be charged in the financing and treasury section of the performance statement, except in the case of investment companies, which are addressed in paragraph 52.'

(b)   The text of paragraph 32 is replaced by:

'Gains and losses arising on the repurchase or early settlement of debt should be recognised in the financing and treasury section of the performance statement in the period during which the repurchase or early settlement is made.'

(c) **In paragraph 43, the last sentence is replaced by:**

'All dividends should be reported as appropriations of profit in the reconciliation of ownership interests.'

(d) **The text of paragraph 44 is replaced by:**

'Where the finance costs for non-equity shares are not equal to the dividends the difference should be accounted for in the reconciliation of ownership interests as an appropriation of profits.'

In FRS 6 'Acquisitions and Mergers', the words in paragraph 19 from 'as reorganisation' to the end are deleted.   117

FRS 9 'Associates and Joint Ventures' is amended as follows: 118

(a) the text of paragraph 22 is replaced by:

'Except for items below operating and financing income before taxation in the performance statement, any supplemental information given for joint ventures, either in the balance sheet or in the performance statement, must be shown clearly separate from amounts for the group and must not be included in the group totals.'

(b) after paragraph 26, the headings and paragraphs 27 and 28 are deleted and replaced by:

'*The investor's consolidated performance statement*

27   The group operating result for the period must be shown on the face of the investor's consolidated performance statement, excluding the investor's share of its associates' operating results and its share of the results of its joint ventures, if any. The investor's share of its associates' operating results should be included immediately after group operating result (but after the investor's share of the results of its joint ventures, if any). Any amortisation or write-down of goodwill arising on acquiring the associates should be charged at this point and disclosed. The investor's share of interest and other items reported in the financing and treasury section of the performance statement should be shown separately from the amounts for the group.

28   At and below the level of operating and financing income before taxation, the investor's share of the relevant amounts for associates should be included within the amounts for the group, although for items below this level, such as taxation, the amounts relating to associates should be disclosed. Where it is helpful to give an indication of the size of the business as a whole, a total combining the investor's share of its associates' turnover with group turnover may be shown as a memorandum item in the profit and loss account but the investor's share of its associates' turnover should be clearly distinguished from group turnover. Similarly, the segmental analysis of turnover and operating profit (if given) should clearly distinguish between that of the group and that of associates.

28A   The investor's share of other gains and losses reported by its associates should be included, shown separately under each heading, if the amounts included are material, either on the face of the statement or in a note that is referred to in the statement.'

In FRS 10 'Goodwill and Intangible Assets', a new heading and new paragraphs are inserted after paragraph 51 as follows: 119

'Disposal of intangible assets and goodwill

51A   Immediately before the disposal of an intangible fixed asset (other than goodwill), a revaluation should be carried out. Any revaluation gains and losses arising should be reported in other gains and losses and impairment losses should be reported in the operating section of the performance statement.

51B   The revaluation exercise required by paragraph 51A should be performed on an intangible fixed asset immediately before disposal, whether it is held at historical cost or at a revalued amount. The disposal proceeds, if any, will represent the revaluation amount.

51C   Goodwill that is sold will be accounted for as part of the profit or loss on disposal of the related business as required under FRS 3. Any write-down in goodwill that arises without a sale of the related business or company should be written off in the operating section as an impairment loss.'

120   In FRS 12 'Provisions, Contingent Liabilities and Contingent Assets', the text of paragraph 48 is amended as follows:

'The unwinding of the discount should be reported in the financing and treasury section of the performance statement. It should be shown adjacent to interest but separately from other interest either on the face of the performance statement or in a note.'

121   FRS 14 'Earnings per Share' is amended as follows:

(a)   paragraphs 9–11 are replaced by:

9   Basic earnings per share should be calculated by dividing the income from operating and financing activities for the period attributable to ordinary shareholders by the weighted average number of ordinary shares outstanding during the period.

Earnings – basic

10   For the purpose of calculating basic earnings per share, the income from operating and financing activities for the period attributable to ordinary shareholders should be the operating and financing income for the period after deducting dividends and other appropriations in respect of non-equity shares.

11   The income from operating and financing activities for the period attributable to ordinary shareholders is determined after taking account of appropriations in respect of non-equity shares, which include, but are not restricted to, preference dividends as detailed in FRS 4.'

(b)   other references in the FRS to 'net profit or loss for the period' and 'net profit' are replaced by 'income from operating and financing activities for the period' and 'income from operating and financing activities'.

122   In FRS 15 'Tangible Fixed Assets', paragraphs 72 and 73 are replaced by the following:

'72   Immediately before the disposal of a tangible fixed asset, a revaluation should be carried out and the revaluation gains and losses and impairment losses arising therefrom should be reported according to paragraphs 63–71.

72A   Where the revaluation gains or losses calculated in accordance with paragraph 72 are in effect no more than marginal adjustments to depreciation previously charged, they should be reported in the operating section of the performance statement.

73   The revaluation exercise required by paragraph 72 should be performed on a tangible fixed asset immediately before its disposal, whether it is held at

historical cost or at a revalued amount. The disposal proceeds, if any, will represent the revaluation amount.'

FRS **16 'Current Tax' is amended as follows:**   123

(a) **paragraphs 5–7 are replaced by the following:**

> 5 Current tax should be recognised as part of the tax on operating and financing income for the period, except to the extent that it is attributable to a gain or loss that is or has been recognised in 'other gains and losses'.
>
> 6 Where a gain or loss is or has been recognised in 'other gains and losses', the attributable tax should be recognised as 'tax on other gains and losses'.
>
> 7 In some circumstances it may be difficult to determine the amount of current tax that is attributable to other gains and losses. In such circumstances, the attributable tax is based on a reasonable pro rata allocation, or another allocation that is more appropriate in the circumstances.'

(b) **the text of paragraph 17 is replaced by the following:**

> 'The following major components of the current tax expense (or income) for the period included in the tax on operating and finance income and the tax on other gains and losses should be disclosed separately:
>
> (a) UK or Republic of Ireland tax (depending on the companies legislation in accordance with which the entity is reporting); and
> (b) foreign tax.
>
> Both (a) and (b) should be analysed to distinguish tax estimated for the current period and any adjustments recognised in respect of prior periods. The domestic tax should be disclosed both before and after double taxation relief.'

FRS **17 'Retirement Benefits' is amended as follows:**   124

(a) **the text of paragraph 56 is replaced by the following:**

> 'The net of the interest cost and the expected return on assets should be included in the financing and treasury section of the performance statement. It should be shown adjacent to interest but separately from other interest either on the face of the performance statement or in a note.'

(b) **in paragraph 66, the last sentence is replaced by the following:**

> 'Gains and losses arising from such events are part of the employer's operating results for the period.'

(c) **paragraphs 71 and 72 are replaced by the following:**

> '71 When current tax relief arises on contributions made to the defined benefit scheme, it should be allocated to tax on operating and financing income or the tax on other gains and losses on the basis that the contribution covers first the items reported in the operating and financing and treasury sections and then any actuarial losses reported in other gains and losses, unless it is clear that some other allocation is more appropriate. To the extent that the contribution exceeds these items, the current tax relief attributable to the excess should be allocated to the tax on operating and financing income, again unless it is clearly more appropriate to allocate it to the tax on other gains and losses.
>
> 72 Current tax relief is usually available on contributions paid to the scheme and deferred tax usually arises on the balance of the charges/credits. The tax follows the relevant item, ie tax on the service cost, interest cost and

expected return on assets will be recognised in the tax on operating and financing income and tax on the actuarial gains and losses will be recognised in the tax on other gains and losses. FRS 16 "Current Tax" requires disclosure of the current tax recognised as taxation on operating and financing income and other gains and losses. The question arises of where the current tax relief arising on contributions should be deemed to belong. Sometimes it will be clear what the contribution relates to, for example when a special contribution is made to fund a deficit arising from an identifiable cause, say an actuarial loss, in which case the current tax relief should be allocated to the tax on other gains and losses. In the absence of a clear link between the contribution and the items recognised in the performance statement, the allocation in paragraph 71 should be followed.'

(d) **paragraph 83 is deleted.**

125   FRS 19 'Deferred Tax' is amended as follows:

(a) after paragraph 33, the heading and paragraphs

34–36 are replaced by the following:

'RECOGNITION IN THE PERFORMANCE STATEMENT

34   Deferred tax should be recognised as part of the tax on operating and financing income for the period, except to the extent that it is attributable to a gain or loss that is or has been recognised in "other gains and losses".

35   Where a gain or loss is or has been recognised in "other gains and losses", attributable deferred tax should be recognised as "tax on other gains and losses".

36   In some circumstances it may be difficult to determine the amount of deferred tax that is attributable to other gains and losses. In such circumstances, the attributable deferred tax is based on a reasonable pro rata allocation, or another allocation that is more appropriate in the circumstances.'

(b) **The text of paragraph 60 is replaced by:**

'The notes to the financial statements should disclose the amount of deferred tax charged or credited within:

(a) tax on operating and financing income, separately disclosing material components, including those attributable to: [(i) and (ii) remain unchanged] ...

(b) tax charged or credited on other gains and losses, separately disclosing material components, including those listed in (a) above.'

(c) **In paragraph 61(c) the reference to the 'profit and loss account' should be replaced by a reference to 'tax on operating and financing income' and the phrase 'directly in the statement of total recognised gains and losses' should be replaced by 'in tax on other gains and losses'.**

(d) **The text of paragraph 64(a) is replaced by:**

'a reconciliation of the current tax charge or credit for the period reported in 'tax on operating and financing income' to the current tax charge that would result from applying a relevant standard rate of tax to the reported operating and financing income. Either the monetary amounts or the rates (as a percentage of operating and financing income) may be reconciled.

126   **In UITF Abstract 13 'Accounting for ESOP Trusts', paragraph 8(g) is replaced by:**

'8(g) Any dividend income arising on the shares should not be recognised in the performance statement, but should be deducted from dividends for the period in the reconciliation of ownership interest. The deduction should be shown on the face of the reconciliation, if material, or in a note. Until such time as the shares vest unconditionally in employees, the shares should also be excluded from earnings per share calculations as, under FRS 14 'Earnings per Share', they are treated as if they were cancelled.'

Appendix I
Illustrative example

The example set out in this appendix is provided for general guidance only and does not form part of the [draft] FRS.

The example on pages 1486–1494 includes two statements of financial performance, a reconciliation of ownership interest and certain related notes that are required or suggested by the [draft] FRS. The following matters should be noted:

- the entity is a group of companies.
- the group has made acquisitions and disposals of operations during the year under review.
- the statements of financial performance include the disclosure of earnings per share numbers and a proforma reconciliation statement for adjusted earnings per share numbers is shown.
- dividends for the period and the cumulative effect of prior period adjustments are shown at the foot of the performance statements.

The (first two sections of the) performance statements have been prepared using Format 1 as contained (for Great Britain) in Schedule 4 to the Companies Act 1985.* Equivalent information should be shown if any of the other statutory formats are used.

The example shown on pages 1495 and 1496 is one of a Companies Act investment company.

---

*In Northern Ireland, Format 1 in Schedule 4 to the Companies (Northern Ireland) Order 1986.
In the Republic of Ireland, Format 1 in the Schedule to the Companies (Amendment) Act 1983.*

APPENDIX I EXAMPLE FORMATS AND NOTES STATEMENT OF FINANCIAL PERFORMANCE (Example 1)

	£m	2001 £m	2000 Restated £m
Operating			
Turnover			
Continuing operations	600		525
Acquisitions	50		
	650		
Discontinued operations	175		190
		825	715
Cost of sales		(650)	(570)
Gross profit		175	145
Net operating expenses		(124)	(93)
Operating profit			40
Continuing operations	60		40
Acquisitions	6		
	66		
Discontinued operations	(15)		12
Operating income/profit		**51**	**52**
Financing and treasury			
Interest on debt		(26)	(15)
Financing relating to pension provision		20	11
Financing and treasury income/profit		**(6)**	**(4)**
Operating and financing income before taxation		**45**	**48**
Taxation on operating and financing income		(5)	(10)
Operating and financing income after taxation		40	38
Minority interests		(5)	(4)
Income from operating and financing activities for the period*		**35**	**34**

Profit on disposal of discontinued operations	3	—
Exchange translation differences on foreign currency net investments	(2)	5
Other gains and losses before taxation	**287**	**103**
Taxation on other gains and losses	(87)	(33)
Other gains and losses after taxation	200	70
Minority interests	(30)	(10)
Other gains and losses of the period	**170**	**60**
Total gains and losses of the period	**205**	**94**

MEMORANDUM ITEMS

Earnings per share	39p	41p
Adjustments [to be itemised and described]	Xp	Xp
Adjusted earnings per share	Yp	Yp
Diluted earnings per share	Zp	Zp
Dividend per share: equity	3.0p	1.8p
preference	0.6p	0.6p
Total dividend for the period: equity	£6.7m	£0.7m
preference	£1.3m	£1.3m
Prior period adjustment recognised during the period (see note X)	(£10m)	—

*Any extraordinary items would be shown after this line, with a subsequent subtotal for the statutory 'profit for the financial year' after extraordinary activities.

STATEMENT OF FINANCIAL PERFORMANCE (Example 2)

	Continuing operations 2001	Acquisitions 2001	Discontinued operations 2001	Total 2001	Total 2000 restated
	£m	£m	£m	£m	£m
Operating					
Turnover	600	50	175	825	690
Cost of sales	(445)	(40)	(165)	(650)	(555)
Gross profit	155	10	10	175	135
Other expenses	(95)	(4)	(25)	(124)	(83)
Operating income/profit	**60**	**6**	**(15)**	**51**	**52**
Financing and treasury					
Interest on debt				(26)	(15)
Financing relating to pension provision				20	11
Financing and treasury income/profit				**(6)**	**(4)**
Operating and financing income before taxation				45	48
Taxation on operating and financing income				(5)	(10)
Operating and financing income after taxation				40	38
Minority interests				(5)	(4)
Income from operating and financing activities for the period*				**35**	**34**
Other gains and losses					
Revaluation gain on disposal of properties in continuing operations				6	4
Revaluation of fixed assets				4	3
Actuarial gain on defined benefit pension scheme				276	91

Profit on disposal of discontinued operations	3	—
Exchange translation differences on foreign currency net investments	(2)	5
Other gains and losses before taxation	**287**	**103**
Taxation on other gains and losses	(87)	(33)
Other gains and losses after taxation	200	70
Minority interests	(30)	(10)
Other gains and losses of the period	**170**	**60**
Total gains and losses of the period	**205**	**94**

MEMORANDUM ITEMS

Earnings per share	39p	41p
Adjustments [to be itemised and described]	Xp	Xp
Adjusted earnings per share	Yp	Yp
Diluted earnings per share	Zp	Zp
Dividend per share: equity	3.0p	1.8p
preference	0.6p	0.6p
Dividend for the period: equity	£6.7m	£0.7m
preference	£1.3m	£1.3m
Prior period adjustment recognised during the period (see note X)	(£10m)	—

*Any extraordinary items would be shown after this line, with a subsequent subtotal for the statutory 'profit for the financial year' after extraordinary activities.

RECONCILIATION OF OWNERSHIP INTERESTS

	2001	2000 as restated
	£m	£m
Recognised gains and losses relating to the period	205	94
Dividends	(8)	(2)
	197	92
New share capital subscribed	20	1
Net addition to ownership interests	217	93
Opening shareholders' funds (originally £517m before deduction of £10m prior period adjustment)	508	415
Closing ownership interests	725	508

NOTES TO THE FINANCIAL STATEMENTS
Note required in respect of Example 1

	2001			2000 (as restated)		
	Continuing	Discontinued	Total	Continuing	Discontinued	Total
	£m	£m	£m	£m	£m	£m
Cost of sales	485	165	650	400	170	570
Net operating expenses						
Distribution costs	61	13	74	51	5	56
Administrative expenses	46	12	58	39	3	42
Other operating income	(8)	0	(8)	(5)	0	(5)
	99	25	124	85	8	93

The total figures for continuing operations in 2001 include the following amounts relating to acquisitions: cost of sales £40m and net operating expenses £4m (namely distribution costs £3m, administrative expenses £3m and other operating income £2m).

Note required in respect of Example 2

	2001			2000 (as restated)		
	Continuing	Discontinued	Total	Continuing	Discontinued	Total
	£m	£m	£m	£m	£m	£m
Turnover				525	190	715
Cost of sales				400	170	570
Net operating expenses						
Distribution costs	61	13	74	51	5	56
Administrative expenses	46	12	58	39	3	42
Other operating income	(8)	0	(8)	(5)	0	(5)
	99	25	124	85	8	93
Operating profit				40	12	52

The total figure for net operating expenses for continuing operations in 2001 includes £4m in respect of acquisitions (namely distribution costs £3m, administrative expenses £3m and other operating income £2m).

Reserves

	Share premium account £m	Revaluation reserve £m	Profit and loss account		Total £m
			Excluding pension asset £m	Pension Reserve £m	
At beginning of period as previously stated	44	200	120	143	507
Prior period adjustment			(10)		(10)
At beginning of period as restated	44	200	110	143	497
Premium on issue of shares (NV £7m)	13				13
Transfer from performance statement					
Operating and financing			35		35
Other gains and losses		4	(27)	193	170
Dividends paid and payable			(8)		(8)
Transfer of realised profits		(14)	14		0
At end of period	57	190	124	336	707

Note: Nominal share capital at end of period £18m (2000 £11m)

Five-year information on exceptional items

	2001 £m	2000 £m	1999 £m	1998 £m	1997 £m
Exceptional items					
Restructuring costs	(5)				
Redundancy payments	(1)				
Loyalty bonuses				(2)	
IT integration and upgrade costs	(2)				
Rebranding	(3)			(3)	
Inventory obsolescence write-down	(1)	(4)			
VAT refund				21	
Total exceptional items reported	(12)	(4)	0	16	0
Operating and financing					
Pre-exceptional result	47	38	27	29	31
Post-exceptional result	35	34	27	45	31
Other gains and losses	170	60	145	(35)	(71)
Total result	205	94	172	10	(40)

Note: the shaded area denotes the information required by the [draft] FRS (paragraph 63).

Tax effects of items in other gains and losses (optional)

	Pre-tax Amount	Tax (expense)/ benefit	Post-tax Amount
	£m	£m	£m
Revaluation gain on disposal of properties	6.0	(1.3)	4.7
Revaluation of long-term assets	4.0	(1.2)	2.8
Actuarial gain on defined benefit pension scheme	276.0	(84.0)	192.0
Profit on disposal of discontinued operations	3.0	(1.0)	2.0
Exchange translation differences	(2.0)	0.5	(1.5)
	287.0	(87.0)	200.0

Note of historical cost gains and losses (optional)

	2001	2000 as restated
	£m	£m
Gains and losses arising in period as reported		
Operating	51	52
Financing and treasury	(6)	(4)
Other gains and losses	287	103
	332	151
Add back:		
Revaluation surplus recognised	(4)	(3)
Exchange translation differences on foreign currency net investments	2	(5)
	330	143
Realisation of property revaluation gains of previous periods	9	10
Difference between a historical cost depreciation charge and the actual depreciation charge of the period calculated on the revalued amount	5	4
Historical cost gains and losses for the period	344	157

COMPANIES ACT INVESTMENT COMPANY

	2001 £m	2000 £m
Operating		
Revenue	35	30
Expenses	(11)	(10)
Operating income/profit	**24**	**20**
Financing and treasury		
Interest payable	(5)	(7)
Financing and treasury income/profit	**(5)**	**(7)**
Operating and financing income before taxation	**19**	**13**
Taxation on income	(4)	(3)
Operating and financing income after taxation	15	10
Minority interests	(1)	(1)
Income from operating and financing activities for the period	**14**	**9**

Other gains and losses		
Capital profit on investments	52	70
Realised gains and losses	138	75
Unrealised gains and losses	190	145
Tax	(16)	(22)
Minority interest	(1)	(4)
	173	119
Unrealised surplus on revaluation of tangible fixed assets	4	2
Other gains and losses for the period	**177**	**121**
Total gains and losses arising in the period	**191**	**130**
Distributable profits		
Revenue profit available for distribution	(13)	9
Dividends	1	(8)
Transfer to distributable reserves	177	1
	178	121
Non-distributable profits		
Transfer to non-distributable reserves		122

Appendix II
Note on Legal Requirements

GREAT BRITAIN

1   The relevant statutory requirements are set out in the Companies Act 1985. The requirements of Schedules and A to the Act relating to the form and content of company and group financial statements set out formats for the profit and loss account, allowing some flexibility in the manner in which the information is presented. The provisions of the [draft] FRS supplement those legal requirements, while remaining within their bounds.*

2   Schedule 4 does not apply to banking and insurance companies and groups. Banking companies and groups are dealt with in Schedule 9 and insurance companies and groups are dealt with in Schedule 9A. The requirements of these entities are addressed separately by the [draft] FRS, along with investment companies as defined by the Act (see paragraphs 77–87 of the [draft] FRS).

The requirement to present a profit and loss account

3   Section 266 of the Act requires the following (subsections in brackets):

(a)   The directors of every company to prepare a profit and loss account (1)(b).

(b)   The profit and loss account to give a true and fair view of the profit or loss of the company for the financial year (2).

(c)   The form and content to comply with the Schedule 4 formats (3).

(d)   Additional information to be given if necessary to show a true and fair view (4).

(e)   Departure from the provisions if necessary to show a true and fair view (5).

4   The [draft] FRS is consistent with section 226 of the Act in that the first two sections of the single performance statement (ie the 'operating' section and the 'financing and treasury' section, with the subsequent subtotals and related tax charge) represent the statutory profit and loss account.

5   One tax figure is given for these two sections, allowing 'profit before tax' and 'profit after tax' figures to be disclosed, as required by Schedule 4, paragraph 3(6):

'Every profit and loss account of a company shall show the amount of the company's profit or loss on ordinary activities before taxation.'

The format of the profit and loss account

6   Schedule 4, Part I, paragraphs 1–3 state that the profit and loss account should show the items listed in any one of the given profit and loss account formats in the order and under the headings and subheadings given in the format adopted, and:

(a)   once a format is adopted, it should be followed consistently (paragraph 2(1));

(b)   in relation to (a), any change in the format adopted in preparing a profit and loss account should be disclosed, with reasons (paragraph 2(2));

(c)   any item may be shown in greater detail than required by the format adopted (paragraph 3(1));

---

*Subject to the discussion on dividends in paragraphs 24–26, which refer to Schedule 4, Part I, paragraph 3(5).

(d)   any additional item may be shown that is not given in the formats (paragraph 3(2));

(e)   the arrangement, headings and subheadings which are assigned an Arabic number in the format adopted should be adapted where required by the special nature of the company's business (paragraph 3(3));

(f)   items assigned Arabic numbers may be combined if not material, or the combination facilitates assessment by the reader (with additional note disclosure) (paragraph 3(4)); and

(g)   the profit and loss account must show the company's profit or loss on ordinary activities before taxation (paragraph 3(6)).

Paragraph 4 requires comparatives to be given, restated as necessary for comparability.   **7**

The [draft] FRS requires a format for a single performance statement that appears different in some respects from the requirements of the Act. However, the Board believes that the legislation offers a substantial amount of flexibility in the formats of the profit and loss account in the way that line items can be expanded or merged.*   **8**

Reporting revaluation gains and losses on fixed assets

A revaluation gain is required by the [draft] FRS to be recognised in other gains and losses in the single statement, unless it reverses a previous revaluation loss that has been recognised in the operating section (ie within the statutory profit and loss account). This requirement is consistent with paragraph 34(1) of Schedule 4, which requires the 'amount of any profit' (ie gain) 'or loss' calculated under the alternative accounting rules to be 'credited to a separate reserve (the revaluation reserve)'. The requirement for a revaluation gain to be recognised in the operating section (ie within the statutory profit and loss account) to the extent that it reverses a revaluation loss previously recognised in the operating section is consistent with paragraph 34(3) of Schedule 4, which explicitly authorises transfers to take place between the revaluation reserve and the profit and loss account provided that the relevant amount was previously charged to that account.   **9**

The [draft] FRS requires all revaluation losses that are clearly due to the consumption of economic benefits to be recognised in the operating section. This requirement is consistent with paragraph 19(2) of Schedule 4, which requires provisions for depreciation or permanent diminution in value to be recognised in the profit and loss account.   **10**

For other revaluation losses where it can be demonstrated that the recoverable amount of the asset is greater than its revalued amount, the [draft] FRS requires the difference between recoverable amount and revalued amount to be recognised in 'other gains and losses'. In this situation there has been no permanent diminution in value under paragraph 19(2) of Schedule 4 and therefore the loss can remain in the revaluation reserve in accordance with paragraph 34(1) of Schedule 4.   **11**

For other revaluation losses, where it cannot be demonstrated that the recoverable amount of the asset is greater than its revalued amount, an impairment loss arises. Where a fixed asset is impaired, it will always be the case that both the value in use and the net realisable value will be below the carrying amount. In the case of a revalued fixed asset, it would be reasonable to reflect the uncertainty as to the permanence of any impairment by treating it as a reversal of any revaluation   **12**

*Subject to the discussion on dividends in paragraphs 24-26, which refer to Schedule 4, Part I, paragraph 3(5).

previously recognised. Such an impairment would be dealt with through other gains and losses (ie as a revaluation reserve movement). However, if the impairment results in a carrying amount below depreciated historical cost, then, as in a pure historical cost context, it would be reasonable to treat that part of the impairment as being of a permanent nature and charge it to the operating section (ie within the statutory profit and loss account).

Reporting disposal gains and losses on fixed assets

13   The [draft] FRS requires disposal gains and losses on fixed assets to be reported in the same way as revaluation gains and losses and impairment losses on fixed assets. All companies are therefore required by the [draft] FRS (through its amendment of FRS 15) to use the alternative accounting rules (Schedule 4, Part II, paragraphs 29–34) immediately before the disposal of fixed assets, where the known sales proceeds represent the revaluation amount. Any loss will be assessed as an impairment or revaluation loss as required by FRS 15. Those companies that have a policy of revaluing assets are merely required to extend that policy to the disposal transaction.

14   Companies that carry fixed assets at depreciated historical cost should apply the alternative accounting rules for one transaction only, ie the disposal of the asset. The Act makes no reference to any consistency of application of the alternative accounting rules in this context. Indeed, selective application of the alternative accounting rules has been carried out for many years by companies, a practice only recently outlawed by FRS 15. The Board is therefore of the view that there is no impediment to the use of the alternative accounting rules in the manner adopted in the [draft] FRS.

The profit and loss account and realised profits

15   In Schedule 4, paragraph 12 states that:

'The amount of any item shall be determined on a prudent basis, and in particular–

(a)   only profits realised at the balance sheet date shall be included in the profit and loss account; and

(b)   all liabilities and losses which have arisen or are likely to arise in respect of the financial year to which the accounts relate or a previous financial year shall be taken into account, including those which only become apparent between the balance sheet date and the date on which it is signed on behalf of the board of directors in pursuance of section 233 of this Act.'

16   Section 262(3) states that:

'References in this Part to "realised profits" and "realised losses", in relation to a company's accounts, are to such profits or losses of the company as fall to be treated as realised in accordance with principles generally accepted, at the time when the accounts are prepared, with respect to the determination for accounting purposes of realised profits or losses.'

17   The Board's view is that it does not follow from the legislation regarding the availability for distribution of accumulated profits and losses that all realised profits and all realised losses must be reported in the statutory profit and loss account statement (under the proposals of the [draft] FRS, the operating section and the financing and treasury section, including the related taxation charge) for either the

current or another period; it may be sufficient to adjust the retained profit and loss reserves instead.*

Realised profits and the statutory profit and loss account

Under the [draft] FRS, some realised profits will bypass the statutory profit and loss **18** account, in particular the disposal gains on fixed assets. The Board believes that this is an acceptable practice under the law: there are transactions in financial reporting under which gains previously recognised outside the profit and loss account are not reported therein once realised:

(a)   Under SSAP 20, on disposal of an investment in a foreign subsidiary, foreign exchange translation gains built up through reserves over time that are now realised are not reported in the profit and loss account.

(b)   Under FRS 15 (and FRS 3), when a revalued asset is sold at more than book value, the revaluation gain, although realised, is not reported in the profit and loss account.†

(c)   As in (b), the same applies to investment properties under SSAP 19.

(d)   Under FRS 17, actuarial gains previously recognised in the statement of total recognised gains and losses are not reported again in the profit and loss account when realised.

(e)   Gains representing the cumulative effect of prior period adjustments are not reported in the current period profit and loss account, but are shown as a movement on reserves (and hence within the statement of total recognised gains and losses under FRS 3).

The realisation of such gains is generally accounted for by a transfer in reserves **19** between the undistributable reserve where the amounts previously recognised have been recorded (such as the revaluation reserve) and the profit and loss account reserve.

The [draft] FRS does not propose that any gains that are unrealised should be taken to **20** the statutory profit and loss account.

Realised losses and the statutory profit and loss account

Paragraph 12(b) of Schedule 4 requires all liabilities and losses to be taken into **21** account but does not state that they must taken into account in the profit and loss account. Indeed it would clearly be impossible for liabilities to be taken into account in the profit and loss account. Further, the relevant part of the Fourth Directive (Article 31, paragraph 1(c)(bb)) from which this requirement is taken also makes no reference to the profit and loss account.

Again, there are transactions in financial reporting under which losses recognised **22** outside the profit and loss account are not reported therein even when realised:

(a)   Under SSAP 20, on disposal of an investment in a foreign subsidiary, foreign exchange translation losses built up through reserves over time that are now realised are not reported in the profit and loss account.

(b)   Under FRS 15 (and FRS 3), when an asset that has been revalued downwards (but is not impaired under FRS 11) is sold at book value, the previously recognised

---

See Appendix IV 'The development of the FRED', paragraph 26.

†As noted in paragraphs 9–12, this situation will be extended to all gains on disposal through the requirement to carry out 'deathbed' revaluations for assets whether held at historical cost or at revalued amounts.

revaluation loss, although realised, is not reported in the profit and loss account.*

(c)   As in (b), the same applies to investment properties under SSAP 19.

(d)   Under FRS 17, actuarial losses previously recognised in the statement of total recognised gains and losses are not reported again in the profit and loss account when realised.

(e)   Losses representing the cumulative effect of prior period adjustments are not reported in the current period profit and loss account, but are shown as a movement on reserves (and hence within the statement of total recognised gains and losses under FRS 3).

23   Thus, 'taking into account' does not necessarily require that all these gains and losses should be reported in the statutory profit and loss account statement for a period; they can instead be shown as a movement on reserves (ie in other gains and losses in the proposed single performance statement).

Dividends

24   The [draft] FRS states that dividends should not be treated as items of financial performance, but rather as appropriations of profit. They would therefore not be shown in the single statement of financial performance, either within or outside the identified statutory profit and loss account.

25   The Fourth Directive does not require dividends to be shown on the face of the profit and loss account, or even disclosure of such information by way of a note. However, Article 6 gives authority for Member States to do so. The Act duly takes up the authority and requires dividends (and amounts set aside to or withdrawn from reserves) to be shown on the face of the profit and loss account:

'(7) Every profit and loss account of a company shall show separately as additional items–

(a)   any amount set aside or proposed to be set aside to, or withdrawn or proposed to be withdrawn from, reserves;

(b)   the aggregate amount of any dividends paid and proposed;

(c)   if it is not shown in the notes to the accounts, the aggregate amount of any dividends proposed.' (Schedule 4, paragraph 3(7))

26   As explained in Appendix IV 'The development of the FRED', the Board has approached the Department of Trade and Industry to request an amendment to the Companies Act in this respect.

Taxation

27   In Schedule 4, paragraph 54(2) states that:

'Particulars shall be given of any special circumstances which affect liability in respect of taxation of profits, income or capital gains for the financial year or liability in respect of taxation of profits, income or capital gains for succeeding financial years.'

As noted in paragraphs 9–12, this situation will be extended to all revaluation losses on disposal through the requirement to carry out 'deathbed' revaluations for assets whether held at historical cost or at revalued amounts. However, any losses representing impairment losses will be reported in the profit and loss account.

The Board's view is that the requirements of the [draft] FRS in relation to taxation are   **28**
consistent with the law.

Groups

Schedule 4A states that: **29**

'15   Where during the financial year there has been a disposal of an undertaking or
group which significantly affects the figures shown in the group accounts, there
shall be stated in a note to the accounts–

(a)   the name of that undertaking or, as the case may be, of the parent
undertaking of that group, and

(b)   the extent to which the profit or loss shown in the group accounts is
attributable to profit or loss of that undertaking or group.

16   The information required by paragraph ... 15 above need not be disclosed with
respect to an undertaking which–

(a)   is established under the law of a country outside the United Kingdom, or

(b)   carries on business outside the United Kingdom,

if in the opinion of the directors of the parent company the disclosure would be
seriously prejudicial to the business of that undertaking or to the business of the
parent company or any of its subsidiary undertakings and the Secretary of State
agrees that the information should not be disclosed.'

The Board's view is that the requirements of the [draft] FRS in relation to disposals of   **30**
operations are consistent with the law.

Banking companies and banking groups

Under the proposals in the [draft] FRS in relation to banking entities, the first three   **31**
sections of the performance statement represent the statutory profit and loss account
as required by Schedule 9.

Insurance companies and insurance groups

Under the proposals in the [draft] FRS in relation to insurance entities, the first three   **32**
sections of the performance statement represent the statutory profit and loss account
as required by Schedule 9A.

Investment companies

Section 266 states: **33**

'(1) In section 265 "investment company" means a public company which has
given notice in the prescribed form (which has not been revoked) to the registrar
of companies of its intention to carry on business as an investment company, and
has since the date of that notice complied with the requirements specified below.
(2) Those requirements are–

(a)   that the business of the company consists of investing its funds mainly in
securities, with the aim of spreading investment risk and giving members
of the company the benefit of the results of the management of its funds,

    (b)   that none of the company's holdings in companies (other than those which are for the time being in investment companies) represents more than 15 per cent by value of the investing company's investments,

    (c)   that subject to subsection (A), distribution of the company's capital profits is prohibited by its memorandum or articles of association,

    (d)   that the company has not retained, otherwise than in compliance with this Part, in respect of any accounting reference period more than 15 per cent of the income it derives from securities.

(2A) An investment company need not be prohibited by its memorandum or articles from redeeming or purchasing its own shares in accordance with section 160 or 162 in Chapter VII or Part V out of its capital profits.'

34   Paragraphs 86 and 87 of the [draft] FRS require investment companies to report performance so as to comply with these statutory requirements.

NORTHERN IRELAND

35   The statutory requirements in Northern Ireland are set out in the Companies (Northern Ireland) Order 1986. Those requirements are identical to the legislation for Great Britain cited above.

REPUBLIC OF IRELAND

36   The statutory requirements in the Republic of Ireland that correspond to those cited above for Great Britain are shown in the following table.

Great Britain	*Republic of Ireland*
Companies Act 1985:	
section 226	section 3(1) of the Companies (Amendment) Act 1986
section 262(3)	paragraph 72 of the Schedule to the Companies (Amendment) Act 1986
section 266	section 47(3), (4) and (7) of the Companies (Amendment) Act 1983
Schedule 4	The Companies (Amendment) Act 1986:
paragraph 1	section 4(1) and (2)
paragraph 2	section 4(3) and (4)
paragraph 3(1)	section 4(5)
paragraph 3(2)	section 4(12)
paragraph 3(3)	section 4(13)
paragraph 3(4)	section 4(6) and (7)
paragraph 3(5)	section 4(9)
paragraph 3(6)	section 4(14)
paragraph 3(7)	section 4(15)
paragraph 4	section 4(8)
paragraph 12	section 5(c)
	The Schedule
paragraph 19(2)	paragraph 7(2)
paragraphs 29–34	paragraphs 17–22
paragraph 34(1)	paragraph 22(1)
paragraph 34(3)	paragraph 22(4)
paragraph 54(2)	paragraph 40(2)

Schedule 4A	European Communities (Companies: Group Accounts) Regulations 1992
paragraphs 15 and 16	No direct equivalent: however, paragraph 27 of the European Communities (Companies: Group Accounts) Regulations 1992 states: 'If the composition of the undertakings dealt with in the group accounts has changed significantly in the course of a financial year, the group accounts must include information which makes the comparison of successive sets of group accounts meaningful.'
Schedule 9	European Communities (Credit Institutions: Accounts) Regulations 1992
Schedule 9A	European Communities (Insurance Undertakings: Accounts) Regulations 1996

Appendix III
Compliance with International Accounting Standards

1   The requirements relating to reporting financial performance are included in the following International Accounting Standards (IASs):

   (a)   IAS 1 (revised 1997) 'Presentation of Financial Statements';
   (b)   IAS 8 (revised 1993) 'Net Profit or Loss for the Period, Fundamental Errors and Changes in Accounting Policies';
   (c)   IAS 35 'Discontinuing Operations'; and
   (d)   IAS 33 'Earnings per Share'.*

2   The treatment of disposal gains and losses in IAS 16 'Property, Plant and Equipment' is also relevant as the [draft] FRS revises FRS 15 'Tangible Fixed Assets' in some respects.

3   The approach to reporting financial performance is more developed in the UK and the Republic of Ireland than under IASs. Nevertheless, the [draft] FRS is broadly consistent with the relevant IASs. The main differences are of emphasis and are as follows.

Presentation of primary statements

4   IAS 1 requires the presentation of an income statement and a separate statement of changes in equity; the latter includes the net profit or loss for the period as reported in the income statement, but it is not described as a performance statement. In contrast, the [draft] FRS requires all gains and losses to be reported in a single primary performance statement. The [draft] FRS structures the statement into sections and sets out requirements for the allocation of gains and losses to those sections. IAS 1 offers no particular order or groupings for gains and losses (only minimum disclosures on the face of the income statement) and no rationale as to why some gains and losses are reported in the income statement while some are reported in equity.

5   IAS 1 allows information that reconciles ownership interests between the beginning and end of the period to be disclosed in either a primary statement (of changes in equity) or the notes to the accounts. The [draft] FRS requires a reconciliation of ownership interests as a primary statement in its own right.

Extraordinary items and ordinary activities

6   In the [draft] FRS, the definition of extraordinary items is so restrictive and that of ordinary activities so wide that extraordinary items are, to all intents and purposes, non- existent. IAS 8 is not as specific in this respect.†

Editor's note: IAS 1 has been revised, with a new version published in December 2003. IAS 8 has been revised and retitled Accounting Policies, changes in accounting estimates and errors, with a new version published in December 2003. IAS 33 was also revised at the same time, although the changes were the addition of some complex examples.

†*Editor's note: IAS 8, as revised December 2003, now prohibits extraordinary items.*

Discontinuing operations*

The [draft] FRS defines discontinuing operations in the same way as IAS 35. The IAS   **7**
35 definition of the initial disclosure event for classification of operations as discontinuing has been adapted by the [draft] FRS. For a termination to be classified as a
discontinuing operation, as well as the provision of a detailed plan and the
announcement of the plan, the actions of the reporting entity must have raised a
valid expectation in those affected that it will carry out the termination. This will
only occur if the plan is carried out within a reasonable timeframe.

Reporting disposal gains and losses on fixed assets

The [draft] FRS requires that, under its approach to reporting financial performance,   **8**
disposal gains and losses on fixed assets should be reported in the same way as
revaluation gains and losses and impairment losses. The result is that gains on
disposal (that are not reversals of previous impairments) and losses on disposal (that
are not impairments), will be reported in other gains and losses (while impairments
and their reversal will be reported in the operating section). An amendment to FRS 15
that would adopt this approach is included in the [draft] FRS. IAS 16 requires gains or
losses on disposal to be reported as income or expense in the income statement for
the period, while revaluation gains (that are not reversals of previous impairments)
and revaluation losses (that are not impairments) are reported directly in changes in
equity.

---

*Editor's note: The provisions concerning discontinuing operations have been overtaken by IFRS 5 Disposal of
non-current assets and presentation of discontinued operations.*

Appendix IV
The development of the FRED

BACKGROUND

History

1   In the UK and the Republic of Ireland, reporting financial performance is governed by FRS 3 'Reporting Financial Performance', which was issued in October 1992. FRS 3 superseded SSAP 6 'Extraordinary items and prior year adjustments', which was originally developed by one of the Board's predecessor bodies, the former Accounting Standards Steering Committee, and issued in 1974.

SSAP 6

2   Although SSAP 6 was revised several times, there were problems with its interpretation in practice, particularly in respect of the variety of treatments of apparently similar events as either ordinary or extraordinary items in the profit and loss account. Users of financial statements, as well as many preparers and auditors, pressed for further change.

3   The Board responded by proposing a radical change to the presentation of financial performance both in the profit and loss account itself and for items passing through reserves. This culminated in the issue of FRS 3.

FRS 3

4   The Board's aim in FRS 3 was to shift the emphasis away from a single performance indicator. The Board believed then (as it does now) that the performance of complex organisations cannot be summarised in a single number. FRS 3 therefore follows an 'information set' approach that highlights a range of important components of performance. One of the main developments it introduced was an additional performance statement – the statement of total recognised gains and losses – which brings together all the gains and losses recognised by a reporting entity. It was acknowledged at the time that this approach inevitably meant that financial statements would sometimes appear more complex than they did under SSAP 6. However, it was widely accepted that certain totals in the profit and loss account, such as profit before tax and earnings per share, had been used too simplistically and had obscured the significance of relevant underlying components of financial performance. The presentation and disclosure requirements introduced by FRS 3 have provided a framework that has facilitated the analysis and interpretation of the various aspects of performance.

5   In contrast to SSAP 6, earnings per share under FRS 3 is more inclusive, with the result that significant variations from one period to another or the absence of expected variations, whatever the cause, demand some explanation. However, the FRS also gives preparers of financial statements the opportunity to present additional versions of earnings per share provided that (a) the assumptions on which they are based are explicitly disclosed, (b) the reasons for presenting the additional versions are explained and (c) there is consistency in the approach adopted. Preparers have taken advantage of this so that, although earnings per share has tended to be more volatile than under SSAP 6 (because, for example, it includes all restructuring profits and

losses), FRS 3 has facilitated both management explanation and user assessment of earnings per share by requiring the provision of a range of relevant information.

REASONS FOR A REVIEW OF FRS 3

The Board believes that FRS 3 was an important step towards providing users with information in a form designed to assist a mature understanding and analysis of financial performance. It is for users to identify particular components that they regard as significant in varying circumstances. This is a feature of the 'information set' approach. For the reasons stated above, it is not appropriate for users to fasten on to any 'headline' number on the face of the profit and loss account or statement of total recognised gains and losses without considering the number's composition. Using the information required by FRS 3, either on the face of the financial statements or in the notes, users may adapt any headline number to give the performance measure required.

6

Despite the success of FRS 3, by 1997 the Board concluded that a revision of the standard was appropriate for the following reasons:

7

(a) The FRS had been in place for a while and a review was timely, in accordance with paragraph 33 of the Foreword to Accounting Standards.
(b) The draft Statement of Principles for Financial Reporting was under development, which gave the Board the opportunity to reconsider its approach to reporting financial performance.
(c) The development of standards on recognition and measurement for certain items was being hampered by the lack of an articulated conceptual approach to reporting financial performance.
(d) Since FRS 3 was issued, various other national standard-setters, as well as IASC, had issued new standards or revised existing standards on reporting financial performance.

DISCUSSION PAPER 'REPORTING FINANCIAL PERFORMANCE: PROPOSALS FOR CHANGE'

Since FRS 3 was issued, other countries have moved towards reporting total financial performance, sometimes called 'comprehensive income'. In view of these developments, and following the Board's policy of international co- operation, a new project on reporting financial performance was begun within the G4 + 1* group of standard-setters. Its preliminary conclusions were reported in a paper 'Reporting Financial Performance: Current Developments and Future Directions', published in January 1998. The paper examined alternative methods of reporting comprehensive income, and subsequent discussion within the G4 + 1 led to the development of a further paper, 'Reporting Financial Performance: proposals for change'. This was published in June 1999 by the Board as a Discussion Paper and by other members of the G4 + 1 in their own jurisdictions.

8

Respondents to the Discussion Paper, both in the UK and elsewhere, were generally supportive of the proposals for a single performance statement, but had some misgivings:

9

(a) Financial performance was not defined in the Discussion Paper despite its central role in the development of a new standard.

*The G4 + 1 comprises representatives of the national standard-setters of Australia, Canada, New Zealand, the UK and the USA, and of IASC.

(b)   The concept of realisation was held by some to be of continuing importance, particularly in the context of UK (and European) companies legislation.

(c)   The choice of the three components was not explained in sufficient detail, given that different components might have been chosen.

(d)   The suggested basis on which standard-setters would allocate gains and losses to the different components of performance was thought by many to be self-contradictory and unhelpful.

10   These criticisms have been addressed in developing the FRED, which seeks to offer greater insights into the reasoning underlying the Board's approach to reporting financial performance. In particular, the Board hopes that the exposition of the issues within this Appendix will offer a significant contribution to the international debate on performance reporting (at the date of publication, an IASC Steering Committee also has this topic under discussion).

DEFINITIONS

11   The definitions of gains, losses and financial performance are all based on those in the Statement of Principles for Financial Reporting, issued by the Board in December 1999. The topic of performance reporting is somewhat undeveloped in the Statement of Principles (as the Statement acknowledges), because it was under separate review at the time. Nevertheless, these definitions are taken as a starting point for the draft FRS, along with the occasional guidance offered on the subject within the Statement of Principles, because the Board has accepted them as the basis of performance reporting.

12   The definition of financial performance is important: it emphasises the 'all-inclusive' nature of financial performance and hence the need to show a complete picture of an entity's recognised gains and losses in the performance statement. This does not mean that the Board rejects all notions of 'earnings'; as with FRS 3, the draft FRS sets an earnings line for a standard earnings per share calculation, but allows other figures for earnings per share to be calculated, with the same provisos mentioned in paragraph 5 above.

13   Ordinary activities are defined in order to distinguish them from extraordinary items and to satisfy the requirements of companies legislation.

THE STATEMENT OF FINANCIAL PERFORMANCE

A single performance statement

14   As stated in the Statement of Principles for Financial Reporting, investors require information on financial performance because such information:

(a)   provides an account of the stewardship of management and is useful in assessing the past and anticipated performance of the entity;

(b)   is useful in assessing the entity's capacity to generate cash flows from its existing resource base and in forming judgements about the effectiveness with which the entity has employed its resources and might employ additional resources; and

(c)   provides feedback on previous assessments of financial performance and can therefore assist users in modifying their assessments for, or in developing expectations about, future periods.

15   As noted above, FRS 3 created a framework for reporting financial performance that largely addresses these points. The Board believes that the proposals in the FRED offer an incremental development of the approach adopted by FRS 3, which could not

be taken at the time FRS 3 was issued because it would have represented too great a move at one time.

The Statement of Principles suggests that whether information is given in one performance statement or more is not relevant. Whilst this is true in theory, in practice users and preparers appear to attach different levels of significance to gains and losses reported in different performance statements, simply because they are reported in different statements. Experience of applying FRS 3 suggests this is the case, given that it offers no justification for taking some gains and losses to the statement of total recognised gains and losses rather than the profit and loss account, and yet users tend to downgrade the statement of total recognised gains and losses and hence the information reported in it. The Board therefore concluded that it would be preferable to require a single performance statement for all recognised gains and losses.   **16**

As the Statement of Principles makes clear, the statement of financial performance should deal only with gains and losses and items that are not gains and losses should not be recognised in it. This has two major implications: **17**

(a) The notion of recycling, whether between or within sections of the statement, is not consistent with the draft FRS. By definition, gains and losses shown in the performance statement under the recognition criteria of the Statement of Principles cannot be recognised again anywhere in the performance statement in a later period.

(b) Transactions with owners as owners will not be reported in the statement of financial performance. For example, dividends paid and payable are not gains and losses and so the draft FRS envisages that they will not be included in the performance statement. Although that seems logical – dividends are not a component of financial performance – it is not consistent with how such dividends are dealt with at present. It is also a legal requirement to show such dividends on the face of the profit and loss account (see Appendix II).*

The sections of the performance statement and allocation of gains and losses

Statement of Principles

The Statement of Principles states that information on financial performance needs to be presented in a way that focuses attention on the components and on their key characteristics. The presentation – including the headings used and the items that appear under each heading – is important. Good presentation of financial performance information typically involves: **18**

(a) recognising only gains and losses in the statement of financial performance.

(b) classifying components by reference to a combination of function (such as production, selling and administrative) and of the nature of the item (such as employment costs, interest payable and amounts written off investments).

(c) distinguishing amounts that are affected in different ways by changes in economic conditions or business activity (for example, by providing segmental information or by presenting income from continuing and discontinuing operations as separate components).

(d) identifying separately:

The FRED makes no effort to distinguish dividends on equity and non-equity shares. Under FRS 4 'Capital Instruments' all such dividends must be reported as appropriations of profit and the FRED maintains that approach. However, the outcome of two current projects, on accounting for financial instruments and the distinction between debt and equity, may cause this approach to be altered.

      (i)   items that are unusual in amount or incidence judged by the experience of previous periods or expectations of the future.

      (ii)   items that have special characteristics, such as financing costs and taxation.

     (iii) items that are related primarily to the profits of future, rather than current, accounting periods, such as some research and development expenditure.

19   The Statement of Principles does not attempt to specify the order of importance of the different criteria under which items of financial performance might be distinguished from each other in the primary performance statement. Some ordering of priorities is required, however, to deal with the circumstances in which the distinction of items on different bases is contradictory. It will also help to prevent too much disaggregation forcing itself onto the face of the performance statement.

1999 Discussion Paper

20   The Discussion Paper took a specific approach to how a single statement of financial performance should be broken down into components or sections, which was the favoured option of the earlier G4 + 1 paper. (This issue is closely tied to the issue of the basis on which gains and losses should be allocated to the chosen components or sections, and so both are considered together here.) The Discussion Paper suggested that the performance statement should be divided into three sections:

- operating (or trading) activities
- financing and other treasury activities
- other gains and losses.

    The Discussion Paper went on to consider the basis on which standard-setters would determine the allocation of gains and losses between the sections, noting that the content of the financing and treasury section was likely to be affected by the international project on accounting for financial instruments. The Discussion Paper then suggested that, while the operating (or trading) activities section would be the default category, standard-setters would use the following matrix to determine which gains and losses should be left in the operating (or trading) activities section and which should be reported in the other gains and losses section:

Characteristics more typical of operating items	Characteristics more typical of other gains and losses
Operating activities	Non-operating activities
Recurring	Non-recurring
Non-holding items	Holding items
Internal events	External events
(eg value adding activities)	(eg price changes)

21   The respondents to the Discussion Paper tended to the view that the matrix was contradictory and could not be applied consistently, and some were also critical of the choice of sections. However, they expressed such a wide variety of views on which components should be required and which was the most important criterion for distinguishing items in the performance statement, that no clear consensus emerged (not surprisingly, given the number of ways in which the issue might be tackled).

The Board has therefore decided to adopt an approach, laid out in the main body of **22** the draft FRS and explained below, that it believes will at least allow some progress, even if further refinements will be necessary in the future, perhaps when the treatment of financial instruments has been resolved. For example, the Board believes that disposal gains and losses on fixed assets have the same characteristics as revaluation gains and losses (and impairment losses) and should therefore receive the same treatment. However, the Board's approach does not exclude the possibility of developing alternative categorisations of financial performance for the purposes of disclosure on the face of the statement, in the notes to the accounts or in narrative accompaniments to the financial statements.

Approach in the FRED

Given that the reporting of recognised gains and losses, as defined in the Statement **23** of Principles, involves no measurement or recognition issues, it could be argued that the grouping and order of those gains and losses in a statement of financial performance are irrelevant. This may be true conceptually, but it is of little help to the user of the financial statements, who must attempt to make some kind of judgement about the performance of the reporting entity (to the extent that it is shown in the financial statements). It is therefore necessary to order the information in some way. However, if each reporting entity did so as it wished, the user would struggle to compare the results of the entity with those of other entities in that or other sectors. Some consistency of approach is therefore also required.

The Board's primary consideration is to provide a framework that users find helpful. **24** The framework must be capable of encompassing the financial results of the majority of entities, but also flexible enough to be adapted for unusual or special circumstances. The Board believes that the suggested format for the single performance statement in the draft FRS meets these criteria.

The first suggestion the Board considered was simply to combine the existing profit **25** and loss account and statement of total recognised gains and losses in one statement. However, it emerged that, in spite of legal requirements regarding what can and cannot be included in the profit and loss account, the basis on which gains and losses are allocated to each statement is confused and ill-defined and is not applied consistently.

Gains and losses are nominally allocated to the profit and loss account on the basis **26** of whether they are 'realised'. The Statement of Principles moves away from the notion of realisation as a basis for recognising gains and losses for reporting performance, because of the certainty of existence and measurement that can be established for gains and losses in today's environment, without a disposal taking place. There is, however, a continuing role for the realisation concept in relation to the distribution of corporate profits. Companies legislation ties realisation to the distribution of profits through the presentation of company results. In practice, not all 'realised' gains and losses are reported in the profit and loss account.* This dual use of realisation, ie as a criterion for reporting performance and for the estimation of distributable profits, has placed severe pressure on the concept, to the extent that it is becoming generally discredited. The Board believes that an approach to performance reporting is required that accepts that the move away from realisation as a criterion for distinguishing items of financial performance is already under way. It therefore concluded that gains and losses should be grouped in sections of the performance statement according to their inherent nature, not whether they are realised

*See Appendix II, paragraphs 15–23

or not. Information on realisation may be shown as ancillary to the primary statement, indicating that its importance is only part of the total picture of a reporting entity's performance.

27   The Board considered the view, frequently expressed by users of financial statements, that it is not helpful in performance reporting to mix an entity's operating results with gains and losses arising on items held for the long term, where those gains and losses essentially reflect the length of time the item happens to have been held and the price changes that have taken place over that period, ie they are holding gains and losses. Under the historical cost convention, such gains and losses may be recognised only in the year of disposal and so represent accumulated gains and losses from previous periods. The Board therefore decided that a section, 'other gains and losses', should be used to report these holding gains and losses.

28   The Board then turned to the remaining gains and losses that an entity recognises in a period. Two aspects of these seemed to be of relevance – the results of the operating activities of a reporting entity and the results of any financing activities (including treasury income arising on investment of surplus cash) in support of those operating activities. These two parts of an entity's activities are closely interlinked, to the extent that some entities may regard the treasury function as an integrated part of their operating activities. However, the Board believes that it is possible to distinguish between operating activities that are in the financial sphere (such as banking) from activities relating to the financing of the entity. The gains and losses on the former will be reported in the operating section, while those arising on the latter will be reported in the financing and treasury section.*

29   An alternative view to this approach was put forward during the Board's deliberations, which found favour with some Board members. It was suggested that the allocation of gains and losses should be between an operating section and a *financial* section. This would mean that the results of all activities that are financial in nature would be reported in the financial section. For example, a clothing retailer might have a financial operation that, as well as offering an in-store credit card to customers, also sold financial services (eg insurance) to customers. If this view of the allocation of gains and losses were applied, the results of the clothing retail operation would be shown in the operating section, while the results of the financial division, including the in-store credit card profits and losses and the gains and losses on selling financial products, would appear in the financial section. The financial section would also include interest payable by the entity on its financing and all the other similar items that the draft FRS requires to be reported there. The Board is keen to obtain views on these different approaches to what should be reported in a financing/financial section and a question has been included in the Preface.

30   The sections of the performance statement might be ordered differently, for example the financing and treasury section might be shown last of the three. In considering the ordering of the sections, the Board concluded that, in theory, there is no reason why the sections should not be shown in a different order from that proposed in the Discussion Paper. In practice, however, the following considerations led to the conclusion that the suggested order should be required:

(a)   Consistency of presentation is necessary to allow users to compare entities' results.

(b)   This order is reasonably familiar to users in that it changes little in the present ordering of the performance statements.

---

*In any case, special provision is made for companies and groups that are banking and insurance entities.

(c)   The requirements of the statutory formats for companies mean that it will still be necessary to identify a profit and loss account, which would be possible only with this ordering of the components (see Appendix II).

(d)   Although reporting entities are permitted to report earnings per share figures on the basis of any 'earnings' figure they wish, the Board believes that, for the sake of comparability, it is still necessary to specify a standard line total for earnings per share within the performance statement, to which other calculations must be reconciled and the proposed format allows this to be done in a straightforward way (see paragraph 69 below).

In reaching these conclusions, the Board has adapted the approach of the matrix   **31** given in the Discussion Paper (see paragraph 20 above). The Board believes that a recurring/non-recurring distinction can be helpful to users. However, because of the subjectivity inherent in deciding what is non-recurring for different entities, such a distinction should be available only as a means of identifying such items within the components or sections specified by standard-setters, rather than by grouping them together as a separate component. Thus, exceptional items should be shown only within the line item to which they relate (see paragraphs 58–61 below). The boundary between internal and external events was thought to be too blurred to be made operational, although some accounting standards (such as SSAP 19 'Accounting for investment properties') use a type of internal/external distinction for definitional purposes.

In certain instances the non-holding/holding distinction discussed above needs to be   **32** modified to reflect rather an operating/non-operating divide.

(a)   Some short-term holding gains, for example on inventories, will arise for many entities. Under the non-holding/holding distinction, these gains would be reported in other gains and losses. However, such gains are much more closely associated with the entity's operating result. It may therefore be of more value to users to show them within the operating section so that the cost or benefit of holding the stock can be reflected in the entity's operating margins. Exclusion of such gains and losses from the operating result margin would mislead users.

(b)   Some entities, as their main activity, trade on gains arising on price movements of certain investment assets, some of which may, incidentally, be held for a long time. Although in other types of business investment assets would be treated as fixed assets, in the circumstances described they are in effect trading stock. If the non-holding/holding distinction was to be applied rigidly to such trading stock, the gains and losses arising would be reported in other gains and losses. However, it may be appropriate, for certain types of entity, to require such gains and losses to be reported in the operating section, where this is the nature of the entity's operations (see paragraphs 49 and 50 below).

The Board has therefore decided that it will use the non-holding/holding distinction   **33** to determine which gains and losses should be reported in other gains and losses. However, some holding gains and losses on what are generally short-term operating items will remain in the operating section. In addition, certain reporting entities may be required to report in the operating section certain holding gains and losses that would normally appear in other gains and losses. The circumstances will be specified by accounting standards and approved industry-specific guidance.

The Board considered the extent to which the structure of the performance statement   **34** should match the structure of the other primary statements. In particular, it was suggested that it would be helpful to align the performance statement more closely with the cash flow statement, so that users could judge more easily the impact on cash flows of different aspects of performance. The Board believes that the first priority is to structure the performance statement properly. In any case, the proposed performance statement in many ways is already quite closely aligned with the cash flow statement as required by FRS 1 (Revised 1996) 'Cash Flow Statements'. The first two sections of the performance statement match (except for non-cash items) the first two components of the cash flow statement, ie 'cash flows from operating activities' and 'returns on investment and servicing of finance'.

35   Moreover, there is a limit to the extent to which the cash flow statement can be aligned with the performance statement:

(a)   The cash flow statement reflects the cash effect of capital transactions and transactions with owners, as well as performance statement transactions.

(b)   In the performance statement, it is possible to provide a certain level of meaningful allocation of the tax effects relating to the various sections; the tax charge bears a direct relationship to the current period results shown in the performance statement. FRS 1* makes it clear that allocation of the tax cash flows to the cash flow statement sections does not provide any useful information and may in fact be misleading.

36   The Board's view is that the differing functions of the performance statement and the cash flow statement mean that the two cannot be completely aligned. Nevertheless, there is a degree of alignment between the proposed performance statement and the cash flow statement required under FRS 1 and the Board will keep this in view during the further development of the standard on reporting financial performance and any subsequent amendment to FRS 1.

37   A further issue considered by the Board was the extent to which the figures within the performance statement are adjusted by users for certain purposes and whether a standard should address provision of such adjusted figures by the entity, including their disclosure within the performance statement and their calculation. For example, it has been suggested that the EBITDA measure (earnings before interest, tax, depreciation and amortisation) is useful for projecting future earnings forward from the current period and that reporting entities should be required or permitted to incorporate such a figure in the performance statement.

38   The Board believes that, at present, it would not be helpful to address such issues in a standard on reporting financial performance for the following reasons:

(a)   Different measures will be favoured by different investor groups and the measures favoured may change over time. The draft FRS already provides a standard measurement figure (earnings per share) that can be adjusted by both preparers and users of accounts as they wish.

(b)   The primary statement of performance should reflect the proper sales margin information for the reporting entity's operating activities; the margin represents an item of information in its own right to all user groups.

(c)   Those who wish to disaggregate an entity's results in order to use sophisticated projection models will be catered for as long as sufficient information is disclosed within the rest of the financial statements to allow the desired adjustment of the figures in the primary statements.

39   The Board does not seek to prevent the provision of additional information in the performance statement or related notes (provided the requirements of this and other accounting standards and companies legislation are met). The proposed requirements in the draft FRS are framed to allow a reasonable amount of flexibility to management regarding the information it can provide and the emphases it chooses to

---

*FRS 1 (Revised 1996), paragraph 61.

make. This may involve disclosure of performance information, whether on the face of the performance statement or in the notes, that is disaggregated in alternative ways to the approach taken in the draft FRS. The provision of such information may, in the view of management, be necessary to provide users with what it regards as the full 'information set' regarding the entity's performance. As the circumstances of each entity, as well as the views of management, are likely to be different in each case, it would not be appropriate for the Board to comment on or favour any particular disaggregation or presentation methodology.

The above reasoning gives the basis on which items will be required to be reported in each of the proposed three sections of the performance statement. However, as the draft FRS demonstrates, it is the standard-setter, rather than individual preparers, that will determine which items should or may be presented in the financing and treasury section and in other gains and losses. Thus all other reported gains and losses will be assumed to arise on the operating activities of the entity and so should be reported there. This approach will encourage comparability and consistency from period to period.   **40**

However, the circumstances of specific entities or industries will sometimes dictate that gains or losses that would normally be reported in the financing and treasury section or other gains and losses should be taken to the operating section instead. The draft FRS gives some flexibility on this issue and it will be open to other accounting standards on particular measurement issues to specify where the resulting gains or losses should be reported. The FRS that is developed from this draft would amend existing standards as necessary (as shown in the text).   **41**

Reporting gains and losses on fixed assets

One of the main changes to existing practice proposed by the draft FRS is that gains and losses arising on the disposal of fixed assets should be reported in the same way as revaluation gains and losses and impairment losses, ie so that the gains and losses are reported according to their nature rather than whether they are realised or not. Thus depreciation, adjustments to depreciation and impairments will all be shown in the operating section, while revaluation gains and losses, which are holding gains and losses, will be reported in other gains and losses, segregated from the operating result. The event of a disposal of a fixed asset will not affect this analysis, ie the gains or losses crystallised by the disposal will be treated in the same way as a revaluation gain or loss or impairment according to FRS 15 (which would be amended accordingly). This proposal is made in the draft FRS and is independent of, for example, the issue of how revaluation losses are distinguished from impairments.   **42**

A further proposal was made in the Discussion Paper in relation to fixed assets, and in particular revalued fixed assets. Paragraphs 65–70 of FRS 15 deal with how losses arising from falls in value of fixed assets are reported. That standard distinguishes between an impairment and a holding loss along the somewhat arbitrary line of depreciated historical cost, in order to determine the relative proportions of the loss to be reported in the profit and loss account (as an impairment and hence an operating loss) and the statement of total recognised gains and losses (as a holding loss). The Discussion Paper considered whether it was possible to introduce an approach to these losses that was conceptually purer. It proposed that all losses arising from a fall in value from carrying amount to the higher of net realisable value and value in use should be treated as an impairment and the loss reported as an operating loss.   **43**

44   Although not mentioned in the Discussion Paper, taking this approach to its logical conclusion would result in the treatment of any subsequently recognised *increases* in value, whether reversing a previously recognised loss or not, as a revaluation gain, which would be reported in the statement of total recognised gains and losses (or, in a single performance statement, in other gains and losses).

45   Many respondents to the Discussion Paper were unhappy with this approach. They suggested that this would produce skewed reporting of gains and losses for fixed assets. In particular, in some industries the value in use and net realisable value of fixed assets tend to stay very close to each other (for instance, for pubs and hotels, whose market value is often based on future trading potential). In such cases all gains would be reported in other gains and losses, while all losses would be reported in the operating section. Respondents suggested that this could not be right when some falls in value obviously reflected price movements and were therefore holding losses.

46   In considering the responses to the Discussion Paper, the Board discussed this issue in depth. There was some support for the view in the Paper that every loss arising from a fall in value from carrying amount to the higher of net realisable value and value in use should be treated as an impairment and the loss reported as an operating loss. It was argued that this would be appropriate for many types of operational asset, since impairment was essentially a form of accelerated depreciation.

47   As a modification of this approach it was suggested that a subsequently recognised increase in value could be treated as the reversal of an impairment (rather than a revaluation gain) to the extent that it represented a correction of the estimate of the impairment loss, which should be recognised in the same place as the original impairment. Just as a depreciation charge can be re-estimated through revisions to the economic life or residual value of the asset, so an impairment charge should also be capable of revision. Conditions could be laid down to assist in distinguishing between the reversal of an impairment and a revaluation gain, for example:

(a)   both the impairment and the reversal or part-reversal should hinge on the same event or factor (similar to the rules for recognition of a reversal of impairment of goodwill and intangible assets under FRS 11 'Impairment of Fixed Assets and Goodwill', paragraph 60); and

(b)   the amount of the reversal should be restricted to the amount of the originally recognised impairment.

48   Although its discussions raised points (such as those mentioned in paragraphs 43–47) that might be developed further, the Board has come to the view that, at this time, the debate on the nature of revaluations and impairments of assets has not moved forward far enough since FRS 15 was issued to justify a significant shift from that standard. However, it is keen to solicit the views of respondents in order to move the debate forward both in the UK and the Republic of Ireland and on an international level. A question has been included in the Preface to the FRED for this purpose.

Reporting gains and losses on investment properties

49   Under SSAP 19, fair value gains and losses arising on the revaluation of investment properties are treated in a similar way to revaluation gains and losses arising on operational fixed assets under FRS 15. However, the Board believes that the cases are very different, as illustrated by the present definition of investment properties. As noted in paragraph 32(b) above, some entities, as their main activity, trade on gains arising on price movements of certain investment assets, some of which may, incidentally, be held for a long time. Although in other types of business investment assets might be treated as fixed assets, if they meet certain definitional criteria they are in effect trading stock. Using the logic of the FRED's approach to reporting financial performance, the fair value gains and losses should therefore be reported in the operating section – these are operating gains and losses and this treatment reflects this aspect of the entity's operations.

It does not follow that all groups that run a property division or company would   **50**
report the gains and losses arising on property in the operating section. For example, a high street retailer may have a property management division or company that manages the properties from which the retail operations trade. At the entity level of the property management company (at least for internal reporting purposes), the operating section of the performance statement might reflect all the gains and losses arising on the properties it manages.* However, at the group level, the property management division is subordinate to the retail operation; it exists merely to ensure that the reporting entity takes appropriate advantage of any long-term holding gains and losses on the retail outlets, where possible. The holding gains and losses arising on such assets will, at the group level, be shown in other gains and losses, with depreciation and impairment losses charged to the operating section. Conversely, where properties represent the trading stock of the reporting entity at the group level (ie in the dealings of the group with external customers, as required by the definition of investment properties), it would be appropriate to require the fair value gains and losses on them to be shown in the operating section.

SSAP 19 requires the gains and losses arising on revaluation of investment properties   **51**
to be reported outside income (and hence through other gains and losses in the single performance statement). However, IAS 40 requires fair value changes (where a fair value model is adopted) to be taken through income. Given this analysis, the Board is minded to consider a revision to SSAP 19: see the Preface.

Continuing and discontinuing operations

FRS 3 requires separate disclosure of the aggregate results of each of continuing   **52**
operations, acquisitions (as a component of continuing operations) and discontinued operations down to the operating profit level. A majority of respondents to the Discussion Paper agreed that this information was very useful and should continue to be provided.

Respondents to the Discussion Paper expressed reservations about whether this   **53**
information should be required for any section of the statement other than the operating section. In the Board's view, such information is often useful, but there may be significant practical difficulties in providing it, and the information produced can be less than meaningful in certain circumstances. For example, where a treasury function supports the entire reporting entity, any allocation of financing costs to discontinued or discontinuing operations may be arbitrary and ultimately misleading. In other circumstances, however, the split will be clear-cut along operational lines. The draft FRS therefore encourages the provision of continuing and discontinuing activities information across the financing and treasury section and other gains and losses where the information is meaningful and its provision is relatively straightforward. In such circumstances, the bases on which items have been allocated (as opposed to being directly attributable to) the continuing and discontinuing components must be disclosed.

On the assumption that a revised SSAP 19 required gains and losses on investment properties to be reported as operating items.

54   The draft FRS retains the FRS 3 requirement for a certain minimum of information on continuing and discontinuing results to be shown on the face of the statement, ie in the operating section the analysis of turnover and operating profit should be given. The remainder of the information on continuing and discontinuing results may be shown in the notes to the statement, as shown in the example in Appendix I.

Discontinuing operations

55   FRS 3 includes a stringent definition of discontinued operations, such that operations may be classed as discontinued only if the discontinuation is completed either in the period or close to the period-end, any sale must be irrevocable and every termination permanent. By contrast, the international standard, IAS 35, requires such operations to be shown as discontinu*ing* from the time a binding sales agreement has been signed or a decision to sell/terminate has been made and announced and it allows that decision to be reversed. Respondents to the Discussion Paper generally agreed with the view that a decision to sell or terminate should be irrevocable; however, some support was expressed for relaxing the FRS 3 requirement that the operations must be sold or termination completed in the reporting period or very shortly after the period-end. The view was expressed that discontinuations representing a material reduction in operating facilities could take place over quite a long time and that a move towards the international approach would be appropriate.

56   The Board believes that these arguments have some merit. In addition, the Board's usual process is to consider international standards in the development of its own standards. As a result, the Board decided that the FRED should be drafted to incorporate most of the requirements of IAS 35, with one main difference. The Board believes that the circumstances in which a discontinuation could be reversed, once announced under the initial disclosure event defined by IAS 35, should be exceedingly rare. The Board could envisage such circumstances, however, for example if market conditions make a termination no longer the appropriate course of action. The draft FRS therefore does not require the decision to sell or terminate to be irrevocable, as the term might imply that it cannot be reversed. Instead it requires that a sale agreement has been signed; or that the actions of the reporting entity are such that they have raised a valid expectation in those affected that it will carry out a planned termination. Such a valid expectation will be raised only when formal announcement of the plan has been made and the timeframe for implementing the plan is such that major change to the plan is unlikely.

57   The Board is keen to obtain views on this change and a question on the issue has therefore been included in the Preface.

Exceptional items

58   The definition of exceptional items is the same as that in FRS 3. FRS 3 requires the majority of exceptional items to be reported within the line item to which they relate and this requirement has also been adopted in the draft FRS.

59   Paragraph 20 of FRS 3 requires certain exceptional items to be reported after operating profit. These are:

(a)   profits or losses on the sale or termination of an operation;

(b)   costs of a fundamental reorganisation or restructuring having a material effect on the nature and focus of the reporting entity's operations; and

(c)   profits or losses on the disposal of fixed assets.

Under the proposals in the FRED, items (a) and (c) will now be reported in other gains and losses. Item (b) will be included in the operating section as part of continuing operations, although it will be disclosed as an exceptional item within that component. The attributable tax and minority interests will follow the required treatment within each respective section.

Concerns were raised by the Board in relation to the prominence given to exceptional items by preparers and users of financial statements. The Board reinforced the view in FRS 3 that exceptional items should not be transferred to a single heading of 'exceptional', because profit before exceptional items could then become the focus of financial statement presentation, with the implication that no exceptional items are expected in the future. As well as requiring all exceptional items to be included in the income or expense heading to which they relate (as with FRS 3), the draft FRS proposes that information on reported exceptionals over the previous five years should be required where an entity reports one or more in the current or previous period. This will enable users to judge the extent to which different types of exceptional items are reported year on year and thus gain a more informed expectation about future results and cash flows.   **60**

The FRED proposes that the provision of a table of exceptional items should be mandatory, but the text indicates that this may be incorporated into other information about the entity's results. In particular, some may wish to show the table in conjunction with explanations about the levels of pre- and post-exceptional results over time, as recommended in paragraph 60 of the draft FRS. The example given in Appendix I demonstrates such an approach.   **61**

Taxation

There are various practical problems in allocating the taxation charge to more than two components or sections of the performance statement. However, the Board believes that the tax attached to the items reported in other gains and losses will be relatively easy to identify. The relationship of such items to tax is often unusual and disclosure of the tax arising is therefore of benefit in helping users to understand post-tax results and cash flows.   **62**

This leaves the remaining taxation charge, representing charges on items in the other two sections of the statement, to be reported as a single figure on the face of the statement. The Board's usual policy is to report items gross in the performance statement and the Board takes the view that any further breakdown of the tax charge would be arbitrary and unhelpful. This also fulfils the requirement in companies legislation to report profit on ordinary activities before taxation.   **63**

Special industries

The Board believes that the proposals in the FRED for a single performance statement with the three proposed sections can be adapted to most, if not all, reporting entities. Where necessary, additional guidance can be provided in approved Statements of Recommended Practice. Nevertheless, the Board also recognises that special requirements are needed for entities in certain industries, some of which are highly regulated. The FRED therefore deals, albeit briefly, with how the performance statement should be adapted for banking and insurance entities and investment companies, these being identified in particular by companies legislation.   **64**

The exemptions given to insurance entities in the draft FRS reflect the present UK reporting regime. However, insurance accounting is under review at an international   **65** level and any change in approach resulting from the review may remove the need for the particular exemptions proposed by the FRED.

Conglomerates

66   The FRED makes clear that it is performance at the group level that should be accurately reflected in the consolidated accounts. For groups with diverse operating activities, disaggregation of the different classes of business may be shown on the face of the statement but, where this is not feasible, the segmental information on the results of different classes of business will be of great importance. The Board may therefore consider, in the light of responses to the FRED, whether SSAP 25 'Segmental reporting' requires amendment.

RECONCILIATION OF OWNERSHIP INTERESTS

67   The Board believes that changes in ownership interest other than those included in the performance statement can be important in understanding the change in the financial position of an entity and concluded that this additional information should be required in a reconciliation of ownership interests. Although specified as a primary statement, in order not to divert attention from the performance of the period, the reconciliation should be shown separately from the performance statement.

OTHER INFORMATION

68   The FRED supplements the 'information set' within the primary statements with a wide range of additional information in the form of:

(a)   footnotes to the performance statement, ie of earnings per share, dividends and prior period adjustments; and

(b)   notes to the performance statement.

Earnings per share

69   The FRED nominates the total of the operating section and the financing and treasury section, after tax and minority interests, as the earnings line for the calculation of basic earnings per share (EPS) and proposes an appropriate amendment to FRS 14 'Earnings per Share'. The Board recognises that this facilitates comparison of entity results; as noted above, however, the Board believes that users should not rely on a single number or indicator to judge an entity's performance. The FRED therefore continues the approach taken in FRS 3 by allowing additional EPS figures to be presented, along with appropriate explanation for the approach taken and a reconciliation to the 'standard' earnings per share figure. This facilitates both management explanation and users' assessment of earnings per share by requiring the provision of a range of relevant information.

Dividends

70   Dividends represent transactions with owners as owners and therefore should not be reported in the performance statement, but rather as movements in ownership interest for the period (see paragraph 17(b) above). However, although they are not gains and losses of the period, dividends represent an important part of the 'information set' relating to performance envisaged by the FRED. Disclosure of both the total dividend and per share amounts are required as memorandum items at the foot

of the performance statement. The breakdown required by paragraph 59 of FRS 4 between dividends on different classes of share should be given.

FRS 4 requires dividends on non-equity shares to be reported in the same way as equity dividends (paragraph 43). In time, this approach may be affected by the outcome of the project on accounting for financial instruments and derivatives, proposals for which have been published by an international Joint Working Group, and the Board's current project on the distinction between debt and equity. The FRED does not seek to pre-empt the debate within those projects on where dividends on non-equity shares (as currently defined by FRS 4) should be reported.   **71**

Prior period adjustments

Some concern was expressed by respondents to the Discussion Paper that prior period adjustments might be overlooked by users if the cumulative adjustments arising from them are shown only as an adjustment to opening reserves rather than on the face of the performance statement. However, it will always be the case that the comparative figures for the previous period will be indicated as restated and it is therefore unlikely that prior period adjustments would be missed by users. These adjustments do not represent performance of the current period and are therefore not shown on the face of the current period performance statement. Nevertheless, in order to aid users, the draft FRS requires prior period adjustments to be given as a footnote to the performance statement, after other gains and losses, along with other footnote information (such as earnings per share).   **72**

FRS 18 'Accounting Policies' distinguishes between a change in an accounting policy and a change in an estimation technique; the former is accounted for as a prior period adjustment, the latter within the results of the current period. The Board also reconsidered the treatment of the correction of errors and whether all material errors should be corrected by prior period adjustments or only those that are 'fundamental'. In the Board's view it is often difficult to distinguish between errors and changes in estimation techniques except in very clear-cut cases. To indicate when such clear-cut cases arise, a definition of a fundamental error has been given. In all other cases the correction of an error should be dealt with in the current period results in the relevant section of the performance statement, disclosed separately if exceptional.   **73**

Note of historical cost gains and losses

Two reasons for disclosing the performance of an entity for a period on the unmodified historical cost basis of accounting are commonly cited. The first is that, for as long as discretion exists on the timing or scale of revaluations included in financial statements, the unmodified historical cost basis will give the reported gains and losses of different reporting entities on a more comparable basis. The second is the wish of certain users to assess the profit or loss on sale of assets based on their historical cost, rather than, as the draft FRS requires, on their revalued carrying amount.   **74**

In acknowledgement of these concerns, the Board has suggested the provision of a note of historical cost gains and losses in the draft FRS in those circumstances where there is a material difference between the result as disclosed in the performance statement and the result on an unmodified historical cost basis. The provision of the note is optional, rather than mandatory, because of the Board's reservations regarding its usefulness: **75**

(a)   The extent to which the unmodified historical cost information facilitates comparisons between reporting entities is open to question; historical cost gains or losses on assets are only truly comparable when the same sorts of assets were bought and are sold at the same points in time.

(b)   Full historical cost information may not be available or cannot be obtained without unreasonable expense or delay (in which case the earliest available values should be used where the note is provided).

76   In response to a question in the 1999 Discussion Paper, user respondents expressed support for the note's retention. The FRED therefore proposes merely to make the note non-mandatory, but a further question has been asked in the Preface on whether the note should be mandatory, optional or not mentioned in a standard at all.

FRED 25

(Issued May 2002)

Related party disclosures

Contents

Preface

[Draft] Financial Reporting Standard –

Appendices
I.   Note on legal requirements
II. Note on UK listing authority requirements

Summary of main changes proposed by the IASB

Preface

1   This Financial Reporting Exposure Draft (FRED) is issued as part of the Accounting Standards Board's programme to bring about convergence between UK Accounting Standards and International Financial Reporting Standards (IFRSs*). It sets out for comment a proposed UK accounting standard, based on a proposed IFRS. The ASB proposes to issue a UK standard based on this draft, which will replace FRS 8 *Related Party Disclosures*.

2   The International Accounting Standards Board (IASB) has recently published for comment a proposed revision of IAS 24 'Related Party Disclosures'. The main changes to the present IAS 24 proposed by the IASB are summarised on pages 29–30. The exposure draft is based on the proposed revised text. The differences that the ASB proposes for the UK are summarised in paragraph 11 and are highlighted in the text.†

Main changes proposed to existing UK requirements

3   A comparison of the disclosures required by the proposals in the exposure draft and the existing requirements of FRS 8 is set out below.

SCOPE OF THE STANDARDS—EXEMPTIONS FROM DISCLOSURE

4   A comparison of the exemptions from disclosure requirements is given in the table below.

FRS 8	FRED 25
Consolidated financial statements: transactions or balances between group entities that have been eliminated on consolidation	An equivalent exemption is included
Parent's own financial statements: where they are presented together with its consolidated financial statements	An equivalent exemption is included
Subsidiary undertakings, 90 per cent or more of whose voting rights are controlled within the group, are exempted from disclosing transactions with group entities or investees of the group qualifying as related parties, provided that the consolidated financial statements in which the subsidiary is included are publicly available	Financial statements of *wholly-owned* subsidiaries that are made available or published with consolidated financial statements for the group to which the subsidiary belongs are not required to disclose related party transactions and outstanding balances‡

The IASB intends to designate its future standards as International Financial Reporting Standards, or IFRSs. Standards issued prior to 2002 are identified as International Accounting Standards, or IASs. In this Preface, the term IFRS is used to refer to both IFRSs and IASs.

†*Editor's note: The revised standard was issued in December 2003.*

‡*Six members of the IASB disagree with the proposed exemption from related party disclosures in separate financial statements of a parent or wholly-owned subsidiary.*

Pension contributions paid to a pension fund (however, disclosure is required by FRS 17)

No equivalent exemption is included

Emoluments in respect of services as an employee of the reporting entity*

Management compensation, expense allowances and similar items paid in the ordinary course of an entity's operations

Disclosures do not override an entity's duties of confidentiality arising by operation of law (for example, banker/client confidentiality)

No equivalent exemption is included. However, the exposure draft does not require disclosure of the names of transacting related parties

DEFINITION OF RELATED PARTIES

A comparison of the definitions of related parties is given in the table below. FRS 8 **5** identifies various parties that are related parties and other parties that are presumed to be related parties (where the presumption may be rebutted in certain circumstances). The parties identified in the exposure draft's definition are all considered to be related parties. The lists are broadly equivalent, except that the exposure draft makes no reference to shadow directors or to persons acting in concert to exercise control or influence.

FRS 8 deals more comprehensively than the exposure draft with the notion of influ- **6** ence that would trigger related party status. The exposure draft identifies a relationship where a party has an interest that gives it significant influence over an entity (significant influence being defined as the power to participate in the financial and operating policy decisions of an entity). FRS 8 describes the level of influence over the financial and operating policies as being such that the party subject to influence might be inhibited from pursuing at all times its own separate interests. FRS 8 also accords related party status to transacting parties that are subject to common influence from the same source to such an extent that one of the parties has subordinated its own separate interests.

FRS 8	FRED 25
Relationships	*The relationships and the parties listed below are all related parties*
Parties are in a direct or indirect control relationship	Equivalent
Parties are subject to common control from the same source	Equivalent
One party has influence over the financial and operating policies of the other party to such an extent that that other party might be inhibited from pursuing at all times its own separate interests	A party has an interest that gives it significant influence

---

In the UK, extensive disclosure requirements relating to directors' remuneration are contained in the Companies Act 1985 and, for listed companies, in the Listing Rules of the UK Listing Authority. It is anticipated that requirements relating to the disclosure of directors' remuneration in the annual reports of UK listed companies that prepare their consolidated financial statements in accordance with adopted IASs under the proposed Regulation from 2005 (see paragraph 15 below) will be separate from the requirements of the adopted IASs.

Parties, in entering a transaction, are subject to influence from the same source to such an extent that one of the parties has subordinated its own separate interests	Does not deal with such circumstances
Parties that are deemed to be related parties	*Parties that are related parties*
Associates and joint ventures	Equivalent
Investor or venturer in respect of which the entity is an associate or a joint venture	Equivalent
Directors (including shadow directors) of the entity and directors of its ultimate and intermediate parent undertakings	Members of the key management personnel of the entity or its parent, including any director (whether executive or otherwise) or officer *are* related parties
Pension funds for the benefit of the entity's employees or of any entity that is a related party of the entity	Equivalent
Parties that are presumed to be related parties (presumption may be rebutted)	*Parties that are related parties*
Key management of the entity and its parent undertakings	See above – key management personnel are related parties
A person owning or able to exercise control over 20 per cent or more of the entity's voting rights, whether to directly or through nominees	No specific equivalent, but any party that has an interest that gives it significant influence is considered be a related party
Persons acting in concert to exercise control or influence	No equivalent
An entity managing or managed by the entity under a management contract	No equivalent
Close members of the family of individuals that are referred to as related parties	Close members of the family of individuals that are referred to as related parties are considered to be related parties
Partnerships, companies, trusts or other entities in which any individual (or member of the close family) referred to as related parties has a controlling interest	An entity in which any individual referred to as a related party owns a controlling or jointly controlling interest in, or significant influence over, the voting power is a related party

DISCLOSURES

Disclosure of control

7   Where an entity is controlled by another party, FRS 8 requires the following disclosures:

- the related party relationship;
- the name of that party and, if different, that of the ultimate controlling party; and

- if the controlling party or ultimate controlling party is not known, that fact should be disclosed.

In contrast, the international exposure draft merely requires disclosure of relationships between parents and subsidiaries; it does not require a controlling party to be named.

In developing FRS 8, the ASB took the view that disclosure of the identity, as well as **8** the existence, of a controlling party is relevant information for users. Therefore, the ASB proposes that the revised UK standard should include the requirement to disclose the names of controlling parties.

DISCLOSURE OF TRANSACTIONS

FRS 8 requires disclosures in respect of material transactions with related parties. **9** Guidance is given on materiality; transactions are material when their disclosure might reasonably be expected to influence decisions made by the users of general purpose financial statements. The guidance also addresses the perspective that needs to be taken when a transaction has been undertaken directly or indirectly with an individual in a position to influence, or accountable for stewardship of, the entity (for example, a director or substantial shareholder). The exposure draft does not specifically address materiality in the context of the disclosure requirements.

The disclosure requirements are broadly comparable, as illustrated in the table **10** below. The notable exception is that FRS 8 requires the names of transacting related parties to be disclosed; the exposure draft does not require names to be disclosed, but it does require disclosures with categories of related parties.

FRS 8	FRED 25
Names of transacting related parties	Not required
Description of the relationship	Nature of the relationship
Description of the transactions	Information about the transactions
Amounts involved	Yes
Information about the transactions and outstanding balances necessary for an understanding of the potential effect of the relationship on the financial statements	Any other elements necessary for an understanding of the financial statements
Amounts due to or from related parties	In addition, disclosure of the terms and conditions, the nature of the consideration and details of any guarantees given or received
Provisions for doubtful debts	Yes
Amounts written off in respect of debts due to or from related parties	Expense recognised in respect of bad or doubtful debts due from related parties
	The above disclosures should be made separately for each of the following categories: the parent, entities with joint control or significant influence over the entity, subsidiaries, associates, joint ventures in which the entity is a venturer, key management personnel of the entity or its parent, and other related parties

Differences between proposed UK requirements and proposed IFRSs

11   The text of the exposure draft is the same as the proposed IAS 24 with the following exceptions:

(a)   Paragraphs 13A and 13B have been added to preserve the requirement in UK accounting standards* for the names of controlling parties to be disclosed (see paragraph 8 above).

(b)   The [draft] FRS includes a paragraph on scope, applying the standard to all financial statements that are intended to give a true and fair view of a reporting entity's financial position and profit or loss (or income and expenditure), except that reporting entities applying the Financial Reporting Standard for Smaller Entities currently applicable are exempt.

(c)   References to IFRSs have been removed or replaced with references to relevant UK accounting standards.

AMENDMENTS TO OTHER UK STANDARDS

12   The replacement of FRS 8 by the standard set out in the exposure draft would not require any changes to other UK standards or UITF Abstracts.

IMPLEMENTATION

13   The ASB proposes to issue a standard based on the proposals in the FRED, and withdraw FRS 8, at the same time as the IASB issues the revised IAS 24, which it plans to do in the first quarter of 2003. The ASB expects to incorporate into the new UK standard any changes the IASB makes to the revised IAS 24, unless those changes are a significant departure from the requirements proposed in the exposure draft.

14   The ASB is not aware of any reason for an extended implementation period or for special transitional arrangements.

UK LAW, EU LAW AND INTERNATIONAL STANDARDS

15   EU Ministers have proposed that from 1 January 2005, all listed companies in the EU should prepare their consolidated financial statements in accordance with adopted international accounting standards. A draft Regulation to this effect is at a late stage of negotiation and EU Ministers are expected to approve it shortly. The intention is that IFRSs will form the basis of those adopted international accounting standards.

16   After wide discussion with interested parties, the ASB has indicated its intention to pursue a programme of work to align UK accounting standards with IFRSs wherever practicable. The effect of this is that the substance of IFRSs will apply in the UK not only to the group financial statements of listed companies but also to individual financial statements and unlisted companies. However, the ASB will consider the option of retaining a UK standard, or modifying an IFRS in its wider application, for example if it appears likely that the cost of extending an unmodified IFRS more widely would exceed the benefit.

17   The Government has said that it may wish to extend the Regulation to individual financial statements and unlisted companies from 2005 or later. Ministers intend to consult on this once the Regulation is agreed.

*Paragraphs 5 and 18 of FRS 8.

There are extensive statutory requirements regarding disclosure of related party **18** transactions and relationships. The location of the principal statutory requirements is given in Appendix I.

There are also disclosure obligations under the Listing Rules of the UK Listing **16** Authority. The location of these requirements is given in Appendix II.

QUESTIONS FOR RESPONDENTS

The ASB is requesting comments on any aspect of the FRED by 16 September 2002 – **20** the same date as the IASB has set for comments on its proposed revisions to IAS 24.

The ASB would welcome comments in particular on the following: **16**

ASB(i) Do you agree with the proposal to issue a new standard in the UK on related party disclosures, once the new IAS 24 is approved by the IASB?

ASB(ii) Do you believe that the ASB should consider any transitional arrangements?

ASB(iii) Do you believe that an accounting standard should require disclosure of the name of a controlling party and, if different, that of the ultimate controlling party? If the new IAS 24 does not require disclosure, do you believe that a new UK standard should require this disclosure as set out in paragraphs 13A and 13B of the [draft] FRS?

ASB(iv) Do you believe that an accounting standard should require disclosure of the names of transacting related parties?

ASB(v) Should the definition of related parties specifically refer to shadow directors? Should it also refer to persons acting in concert?

ASB(vi) Do you believe that an accounting standard should specify that disclosure is required of *material* related party transactions and give more guidance on materiality in the context of such transactions?

ASB(vii) Are there any other aspects of the draft standard that the ASB should request the IASB to review when finalising the revised IAS 24?

The IASB has asked commentators to respond to the following questions on the **22** proposed changes to IAS 24:

IASB(i) Do you agree that the Standard should not require disclosure of management compensation, expense allowances and similar items paid in the ordinary course of an entity's operations (see paragraph 2)?

'Management' and 'compensation' would need to be defined, and measurement requirements for management compensation would need to be developed, if disclosure of these items were to be required. If commentators disagree with the Board's proposal, the Board would welcome suggestions on how to define 'management' and 'compensation'.

IASB(ii) Do you agree that the Standard should not require disclosure of related party transactions and outstanding balances in the separate financial statements of a parent or a wholly-owned subsidiary that are made available or published with consolidated financial statements for the group to which that entity belongs (see paragraph 3)?

The exposure draft published here is based on the IASB's proposed text. The complete IASB document will be available from its website, www.iasb.org.uk.

Like the IASB's text, the text here is presented 'clean', ie without highlighting the IASB's proposed changes to its existing standards. However, the ASB is proposing a small number of changes to the IASB's text. These are highlighted by strikethrough of text to be deleted, by underlining of words to be added and by sidelining against altered text.

[Draft] Financial Reporting Standard –

Contents

Objective

Scope

Purpose of related party disclosures

Definitions

Disclosure

Effective date

OBJECTIVE

The objective of this Standard is to prescribe the disclosure of information about related party relationships and about transactions and outstanding balances between an entity and its related parties.

SCOPE

1   This Standard shall be applied in:

    (a)   identifying related party relationships, and transactions and outstanding balances between an entity and its related parties;

    (b)   identifying the circumstances in which disclosure of the items in (a) is required in general purpose financial statements; and

    (c)   determining the disclosures to be made about those items.

1A   This Standard applies to all financial statements that are intended to give a true and fair view of a reporting entity's financial position and profit or loss (or income and expenditure), except that reporting entities applying the Financial Reporting Standard for Smaller Entities currently applicable are exempt. [ASB].

2   This Standard does not require disclosure of management compensation, expense allowances and similar items paid in the ordinary course of an entity's operations.

3   This Standard does not require disclosure of related party transactions and outstanding balances in the separate financial statements of a parent or a wholly-owned subsidiary that are made available or published with consolidated financial statements for the group to which that entity belongs.

4   Related party transactions and outstanding balances with other entities in a group are disclosed in an entity's separate financial statements unless such disclosures are exempted under paragraph 3. Intra-group related party transactions and outstanding balances are eliminated in the preparation of consolidated financial statements of the group.

PURPOSE OF RELATED PARTY DISCLOSURES

5   Related party relationships are a normal feature of commerce and business. For example, entities frequently carry on parts of their activities through subsidiary or associated entities and acquire interests in other entities for investment purposes or for trading reasons that are of sufficient proportions that the investor can control or jointly control its investee, or can exercise significant influence over the financial and operating decisions of its investee.

6   A related party relationship could have an effect on the profit or loss, financial position and cash flows of an entity. Related parties may enter into transactions that unrelated parties would not enter into. For example, an entity that sells goods to its parent at cost might not sell on those terms to another customer. Also, transactions between related parties may not be made at the same amounts as between unrelated parties.

7   The profit or loss, financial position and cash flows of an entity may be affected by a related party relationship even if related party transactions do not occur. The mere existence of the relationship may be sufficient to affect the transactions of the entity with other parties. For example, a subsidiary may terminate relations with a trading partner on acquisition by the parent of a fellow subsidiary engaged in the same

activity as the former trading partner. Alternatively, one party may refrain from acting because of the significant influence of another – for example, a subsidiary may be instructed by its parent not to engage in research and development.

For these reasons, knowledge of related party transactions, outstanding balances and relationships may affect assessments of an entity's operations by users of financial statements, including assessments of the risks and opportunities facing the entity.   **8**

DEFINITIONS

The following terms are used in this Standard with the meanings specified: **9.**

Related party A party is related to an entity if:

(a)   directly, or indirectly through one or more intermediaries, it:

   (i)   controls, or is controlled by, or is under common control with, the entity (this includes parents, subsidiaries and fellow subsidiaries);

   (ii) has an interest in the entity that gives it significant influence over the entity; or

   (iii) has joint control over the entity;

(b)   it is an associate (as defined in FRS 9, *Associates and Joint Ventures* IAS 28, *Accounting for Investments in Associates*) of the entity;

(c)   it is a joint venture in which the entity is a venturer (see FRS 9, *Associates and Joint Ventures* IAS 31, *Financial Reporting of Interests in Joint Ventures*);

(d)   it is a member of the key management personnel of the entity or its parent, that is, those persons having authority and responsibility for planning, directing and controlling the activities of the entity, directly or indirectly, including any director (whether executive or otherwise) or officer of that entity;

(e)   it is a close member of the family of any individual referred to in subparagraph (a) or (d);

(f)   it is an entity in which a controlling or jointly controlling interest in, or significant influence over, the voting power is owned, directly or indirectly, by any individual referred to in (d) or (e); or

(g)   it is a post-employment benefit plan for the benefit of employees of the entity, or of any entity that is a related party of the entity.

A **related party transaction** is a transfer of resources, services or obligations between related parties, regardless of whether a price is charged.

Control is the power to govern the financial and operating policies of an entity so as to obtain benefits from its activities.

Joint control is the contractually agreed sharing of control over an economic activity.

Significant influence is the power to participate in the financial and operating policy decisions of an entity, but is not control over those policies. Significant influence may be gained by share ownership, statute or agreement.

Close members of the family of an individual are those family members who may be expected to influence, or be influenced by, that individual in their dealings with the entity. They include:

(a)   the individual's domestic partner and children;

(b)   children of the individual's domestic partner; and

(c)   dependants of the individual or the individual's domestic partner.

10   In considering each possible related party relationship, attention is directed to the substance of the relationship and not merely the legal form.

11   In the context of this Standard, the following are not related parties:

(a)   two entities simply because they have a director or other member of key management personnel in common, notwithstanding subparagraphs (d) and (f) in the definition of related party ;

(b)   two venturers simply because they share joint control over a joint venture;

(c)   (i)   providers of finance;

(ii)   trade unions;

(iii)   public utilities; and

(iv)   government departments and agencies, by virtue of their normal dealings with an entity (even though they may affect the freedom of action of an entity or participate in its decision-making process); and

(d)   a customer, supplier, franchisor, distributor, or general agent with whom an entity transacts a significant volume of business merely by virtue of the resulting economic dependence.

DISCLOSURE

12   Relationships between parents and subsidiaries shall be disclosed irrespective of whether there have been transactions between those related parties.

13   To enable users of financial statements to form a view about the effects of related party relationships on an entity, it is appropriate to disclose the related party relationship where control exists, irrespective of whether there have been transactions between the related parties.

13A   **When the reporting entity is controlled by another party, there should be disclosure of the related party relationship and the name of that party and, if different, that of the ultimate controlling party. If the controlling party or ultimate controlling party of the reporting entity is not known, that fact should be disclosed. This information should be disclosed irrespective of whether any transactions have taken place between the controlling parties and the reporting entity. [ASB]**

13B   If the reporting entity is controlled by another party, that fact is relevant information, irrespective of whether transactions have taken place with that party, because the control relationship prevents the reporting entity from being independent. Indeed, the existence and identity of the controlling party may sometimes be at least as relevant in appraising an entity's prospects as are the performance and financial position presented in its financial statements. The controlling party may establish the entity's credit standing, determine the source and price of its raw materials, determine the products it sells, to whom and at what price, and may affect the source, calibre and even the primary concern and allegiance of its management. [ASB]

14   **If there have been transactions between related parties, an entity shall disclose the nature of the related party relationship as well as information about the transactions and outstanding balances necessary for an understanding of the potential effect of the relationship on the financial statements. At a minimum, disclosures shall include:**

(a)   **the amount of the transactions;**

(b)   **the amount of outstanding balances and:**

(i)   **their terms and conditions, including whether they are secured, and the nature of the consideration to be provided in settlement; and**

    (ii)   details of any guarantees given or received;

(c)   provisions for doubtful debts related to the amount of outstanding balances; and

(d)   the expense recognised during the period in respect of bad or doubtful debts due from related parties.

The disclosures in paragraph 14 shall be made separately for each of the following categories: **15**

(a)   the parent;

(b)   entities with joint control or significant influence over the entity;

(c)   subsidiaries;

(d)   associates;

(e)   joint ventures in which the entity is a venturer;

(f)   key management personnel of the entity or its parent; and

(g)   other related parties.

The following are examples of transactions that are disclosed if they are with a related party: **16**

- purchases or sales of goods (finished or unfinished);
- purchases or sales of property and other assets;
- rendering or receiving of services;
- leases;
- transfers of research and development;
- transfers under licence agreements;
- transfers under finance arrangements (including loans and equity contributions in cash or in kind);
- provision of guarantees or collateral; and
- settlement of liabilities on behalf of the entity or by the entity on behalf of another party.

Disclosures that related party transactions were made on terms equivalent to those that prevail in arm's length transactions are made only if such disclosures can be substantiated. **17**

Items of a similar nature may be disclosed in aggregate except when separate disclosure is necessary for an understanding of the effects of related party transactions on the financial statements of the entity. **18**

Transactions with associates accounted for under the equity method and joint ventures accounted for under either proportionate consolidation or the equity method are not fully eliminated in preparing financial statements. Therefore, they are disclosed as related party transactions unless the exemption in paragraph 3 is used. **19**

EFFECTIVE DATE

The accounting practices set out in this Standard should be regarded as standard in respect of accounting periods ending on or after [date to be inserted after exposure]. Earlier adoption is encouraged. This Standard becomes operative for annual financial statements covering periods beginning on or after 1 January 2003. Earlier adoption is encouraged. **20**

This Standard supersedes FRS 8 *Related Party Disclosures* [following publication in final form]. [ASB] **20A**

Appendix I   Note on legal requirements

GREAT BRITAIN

1   The following table lists only the main statutory provisions relating to related party disclosures.

Companies Act 1985

section 231	Disclosure required in notes to accounts: related undertakings
Schedule 5	Disclosure of information: related undertakings
Part I	*Companies not required to prepare group accounts*
Part II	*Companies required to prepare group accounts*
section 232	Disclosure required in notes to accounts: emoluments and other benefits of directors and others
section 741	Director and shadow director
Schedule 6	Disclosure of information: emoluments and other benefits of directors and others
section 234	Duty to prepare directors report
Schedule 7	Matters to be dealt with in directors report
Schedule 4	Form and content of company accounts
Part I Section B	*The required formats for accounts*
paragraph 50	*Guarantees and other financial commitments*
paragraph 59A	*Guarantees and other financial commitments in favour of group undertakings*
Schedule 4A	Form and content of group accounts
paragraph 21	*Consolidated balance sheet and profit and loss account formats for associated undertakings and for other participating interests.*

Special provisions relating to banking and insurance companies and groups are contained in Schedules 9 and 9A respectively.

NORTHERN IRELAND

16   The statutory requirements in Northern Ireland are identical with those in Great Britain. The following table shows the provisions in the Companies (Northern Ireland) Order 1986 that correspond to the following provisions in the Companies Act 1985 (see paragraph 1 above).

Great Britain	Northern Ireland
section 231	Article 239
Schedule 5	Schedule 5
Parts I and II	Parts I and II
section 232	Article 240
section 741	Article 9
Schedule 6	Schedule 6
section 234	Article 242
Schedule 7	Schedule 7
Schedule 4	Schedule 4
Part 1 Section B	Part I Section B
paragraphs 50 and 59A	paragraphs 50 and 59A
Schedule 4A	Schedule 4A
paragraph 21	paragraph 21
Banking companies and groups	
Schedule 9	Schedule 9
Insurance companies and groups	
Schedule 9A	Schedule 9A as amended by the Companies (1986 Order) (Insurance Companies Accounts) Regulations (Northern Ireland) 1994.

REPUBLIC OF IRELAND

The following table shows the provisions in the European Communities (Companies: **3** Group Accounts) Regulations 1992, and the Companies Acts 1963 to 2001 that correspond to the provisions in the Companies Act 1985 (see paragraph 1 above).

Great Britain		Republic of Ireland
section 231	regulation 36	1992 Regulations
Schedule 5 Parts I and II	section 16	Companies (Amendment) Act 1986
	regulation 44	1992 Regulations
	schedule, paragraphs 4, 18–22	1992 Regulations
section 232	section 191	Companies Act 1963
section 741	section 27	Companies Act 1990
Schedule 6	schedule, paragraph 16	1992 Regulations
	sections 41–43	Companies Act 1990
	schedule, paragraph 17	1992 Regulations
section 234	section 158	Companies Act 1963

Schedule 7	sections 13, 14 and 16	Companies (Amendment) Act 1986
	section 63	Companies Act 1990
	regulation 37	1992 Regulations
	section 90	Company Law Enforcement Act 2001
Schedule 4		
Part 1 Section B	schedule, paragraphs 1–3	Companies (Amendment) Act 1986
paragraph 50	schedule, paragraph 36	Companies (Amendment) Act 1986
paragraph 59A	schedule, paragraph 45A	Companies (Amendment) Act 1986
Schedule 4A paragraph 21	schedule, paragraph 2	1992 Regulations

Banking companies and groups

| Schedule 9 | European Communities (Credit Institutions: Accounts) Regulations 1992 |

Insurance companies and groups

| Schedule 9A | European Communities (Insurance Undertakings: Accounts) Regulations 1996 |

Appendix II   Note on UK listing authority requirements

The Listing Rules published by the UK Listing Authority deal with related party transactions, which are defined somewhat differently from those in the [draft] FRS, albeit with a large degree of overlap. Chapter 11 *Transactions with related parties* defines related party transactions and sets out the requirements and exceptions for such transactions. Further disclosure requirements in respect of related parties are contained in Chapter 12 *Financial Information*.

FRED 28

(Issued May 2002)

Inventories; Construction and service contracts

Contents

Preface

[Draft] Financial Reporting Standard 'Inventories'

Appendix: Note on legal requirements

Summary of main changes proposed by the IASB

[Draft] Financial Reporting Standard 'Construction and Service Contracts'

Appendix I: Example

Appendix II: Note on legal requirements

Preface

This Financial Reporting Exposure Draft (FRED) is issued as part of the Accounting   1
Standards Board's programme to bring about convergence between UK accounting
standards and International Financial Reporting Standards ('IFRSs'*). It sets out
for comment two proposed UK accounting standards, based on proposed and
existing IFRSs. They address respectively accounting for inventories and accounting
for construction contracts and other contracts for services. The ASB proposes to
issue UK standards based on these draft standards, which will replace SSAP 9 *Stocks
and long-term contracts.*

The International Accounting Standards Board (IASB) has recently published for   2
comment a proposed revision of IAS 2 'Inventories'. The main changes to the present
IAS 2 proposed by the IASB are summarised on page 23. The draft standard on
inventories included in this exposure draft is based on the proposed revised text. The
differences that the ASB proposes for the UK are summarised in paragraph 9 of this
preface and are highlighted in the text. The ASB proposes to issue final standards
based on this FRED at the same time as the IASB issues its final revised standard IAS
2, probably in the first quarter of 2003.†

SSAP 9 deals with accounting for long-term contracts as well as accounting for   3
inventories. It is therefore appropriate to incorporate a standard consistent with IAS
11 *Construction Contracts* into UK standards, at the same time as a new standard
corresponding to IAS 2. The draft standard on construction and service contracts is
based on the text of IAS 11. The IASB is not proposing any revision of the text of
IAS 11 at this time and has no plans to do so in the near future.

Although the main application of the requirements of SSAP 9 relating to long-term   4
contracts has been in relation to construction contracts, they have also been applied
to other long-term contracts, especially contracts for services. Accounting for such
contracts is addressed in IAS 18 'Revenue'. As the ASB and other standard-setters
are currently working on the subject of revenue recognition, the ASB does not
propose UK adoption of the full text of IAS 18 at this time. However, in order to
ensure that accounting for long-term service contracts continues to be addressed in
UK standards, text based on the relevant part of IAS 18 has been incorporated into
the draft standard on construction and service contracts.

IAS 18 contains principles of accounting for service contracts, which are consistent   5
with those of IAS 11. It also states that the more detailed requirements of IAS 11 are
generally applicable to such contracts.

MAIN CHANGES PROPOSED TO EXISTING UK REQUIREMENTS

There are no major differences between the accounting required by the proposals in   6
the draft standards and the existing requirements of SSAP 9. However, paragraph 29
of SSAP 9 requires 'prudently calculated attributable profit' to be recognised in the
profit and loss account when the outcome of a contract can be assessed with 'reasonable certainty'; paragraph 9, and paragraphs 24 and 26 of appendix I to the
standard, contain similar references to prudence and reasonable certainty. The draft
standard on construction and service contracts requires the recognition of contract

*The IASB intends to designate its future standards as International Financial Reporting Standards, or IFRSs.
Standards issued prior to 2002 are identified as International Accounting Standards, or IASs. In this Preface,
the term IFRS is used to refer to both IFRSs and IASs.*

†*Editor's note: The revised standard was issued in December 2003.*

revenue and contract costs when the outcome of a contract can be 'estimated reliably'. In emphasising reliability rather than prudence, the approach of the draft standard is more in keeping with the ASB's Statement of Principles and FRS 18 *Accounting Policies*.

7　The draft standard requires that amounts received from the customer before the related work is performed are recognised as a separate liability ('advances'). However, there are no requirements relating to the further analysis of the remaining balance sheet amount (paragraph 42 requires it to be presented as a single asset or liability, the 'gross amount due to/from customers for contract work'). Paragraph 30 of SSAP 9 requires the separate disclosure of 'amounts recoverable on contracts' (a debtor), 'payments on account' (a creditor), 'long-term contract balances' (stock) and foreseeable losses (a provision or creditor).

8　Paragraph 7 of the draft standard allows the requirements of the standard to be applied to the separately identifiable components of a single contract or to a group of contracts together, if that would reflect the substance of a contract or a group of contracts. SSAP 9 itself does not include an equivalent requirement. Paragraph 22 of appendix I to SSAP 9 indicates that, in some businesses, it will be most appropriate to treat parts of a long-term contract separately, but does not mention the combination of more than one contract. A similar treatment to that of the draft standard should be achieved by applying SSAP 9 in the context of FRS 5 'Reporting the Substance of Transactions'.

Differences between proposed UK requirements and proposed IFRSs

9　The texts of the draft FRSs are the same as the proposed IAS 2 and IAS 11 with the following exceptions:

(a)　For the reasons explained in paragraph 4 above, additional text has been added to the draft standard on construction and service contracts to deal with contracts for services. This additional material, which is paragraphs 45A to 45J in the draft standard, is the same as paragraphs 4 and 20 to 28 of IAS 18 *Revenue*.

(b)　The draft FRSs include a paragraph on scope, applying the standards to all financial statements that are intended to give a true and fair view of a reporting entity's financial position and profit or loss (or income and expenditure), except that reporting entities applying the Financial Reporting Standard for Smaller Entities currently applicable are exempt.

(c)　References to IFRSs have been removed or replaced with references to relevant UK accounting standards.

DEVELOPMENT OF THE EXPOSURE DRAFT

10　The IASB's recent work on these standards has been limited to considering the proposed changes to IAS 2. The ASB has expressed its support, in particular for the abolition of the LIFO method of accounting. LIFO is not permitted by SSAP 9, and its elimination from international standards enhances convergence between UK and international standards.

AMENDMENTS TO OTHER UK STANDARDS

11　The replacement of SSAP 9 by the draft standards set out in the exposure draft would not require any changes to other UK standards or UITF Abstracts.

IMPLEMENTATION

The ASB proposes to issue a standard based on the proposals in the FRED, and   **12**
withdraw SSAP 9, at the same time as the IASB issues the revised IAS 2, which it plans
to do in the first quarter of 2003. The ASB expects to incorporate into the new UK
standard any changes the IASB makes to the revised IAS 2, unless those changes are
a significant departure from the requirements proposed in the exposure draft.

The ASB is not aware of any reason for an extended implementation period or for   **13**
special transitional arrangements.

UK LAW, EU LAW AND INTERNATIONAL STANDARDS

EU Ministers have proposed that from 1 January 2005, all listed companies in the   **14**
EU should prepare their consolidated financial statements in accordance with
adopted international accounting standards. A draft Regulation to this effect is at a
late stage of negotiation and EU Ministers are expected to approve it shortly. The
intention is that IFRSs will form the basis of those adopted international accounting
standards.

After wide discussion with interested parties, the ASB has indicated its intention to   **15**
pursue a programme of work to align UK accounting standards with IFRSs wherever practicable. The effect of this is that the substance of IFRSs will apply in the
UK not only to the group financial statements of listed companies but also to
individual financial statements and unlisted companies. However, the ASB will
consider the option of retaining a UK standard, or modifying an IFRS in its wider
application, for example if it appears likely that the cost of extending an unmodified
IFRS more widely would exceed the benefit.

The Government has said that it may wish to extend the Regulation to individual   **16**
financial statements and unlisted companies from 2005 or later. Ministers intend to
consult on this once the Regulation is agreed.

The legal requirements for UK and Irish companies relevant to accounting for   **17**
inventories and construction contracts are summarised in appendices to the draft
standards. There appears to be no conflict between these requirements and those
proposed in the exposure draft.

QUESTIONS FOR RESPONDENTS

The ASB is requesting comments on any aspect of the FRED by 16 September 2002 –   **18**
the same date as the IASB has set for comments on its proposed revisions to IAS 2.

The ASB would welcome comments in particular on the following: **19**

ASB(i) Do you agree with the proposal to issue new UK standards on inventories
and construction contracts to replace SSAP 9, once the revised IAS 2 is approved by
the IASB?

ASB(ii) Do you agree with the proposal to incorporate part of IAS 18 in the standard
on construction contracts, so that it may also apply to other contracts for services?

ASB(iii) Do you believe that the ASB should consider any transitional
arrangements?

ASB(iv) Are there any aspects of the draft standard on inventories that the ASB should request the IASB to review when finalising the revised IAS 2?

ASB(v) Are there any aspects of the standard on construction contracts that the ASB should request the IASB to review in due course?

20   The IASB has asked commentators to respond to the following questions on the proposed changes to IAS 2:

IASB(i) Do you agree with eliminating the allowed alternative of using the last-in first-out (LIFO) method for determining the cost of inventories under paragraphs 23 and 24 of IAS 2?

IASB(ii) IAS 2 requires reversals of write-downs of inventories when the circumstances that previously caused inventories to be written down below cost no longer exist (paragraph 30). IAS 2 also requires the amount of any reversal of any write-down of inventories to be recognised in profit or loss (paragraph 31).

Do you agree with retaining those requirements?

[Draft] Financial Reporting Standard: Inventories

[Draft] Financial Reporting Standard – Inventories is set out in paragraphs 1–41.

The Statement of Standard Accounting Practice, which comprises the paragraphs set in bold italic type, should be read in the context of the Objective, the definitions set out in paragraphs 4 and 5, and also of the Foreword to Accounting Standards and the Statement of Principles for Financial Reporting currently in issue.

The explanatory paragraphs contained in the [draft] FRS shall be regarded as part of the Statement of Standard Accounting Practice insofar as they assist in interpreting that statement.

This draft is issued by the Accounting Standards Board for comment. It should be noted that the draft may be modified in the light of comment received before being issued in final form.

OBJECTIVE

The objective of this Standard is to prescribe the accounting treatment for inventories. A primary issue in accounting for inventories is the amount of cost to be recognised as an asset and carried forward until the related revenues are recognised. This Standard provides guidance on the determination of cost and its subsequent recognition as an expense, including any write-down to net realisable value. It also provides guidance on the cost formulas that are used to assign costs to inventories.

SCOPE

This Standard shall be applied in accounting for inventories. It does not apply to:　　1

(a) **work in progress arising under construction contracts, including directly related service contracts (see [draft] Financial Reporting Standard –, *Construction and Service Contracts* IAS 11, *Construction Contracts*);**
(b) **financial instruments;**
(c) **inventories of agricultural and forest products, and mineral ores to the extent that they are measured at net realisable value in accordance with well established practices in certain industries; and**
(d) **biological assets related to agricultural activity (see IAS 41, *Agriculture*).**

This Standard applies to all financial statements that are intended to give a true and fair view of a reporting entity's financial position and profit or loss (or income and expenditure), except that reporting entities applying the *Financial Reporting Standard for Smaller Entities* currently applicable are exempt. [ASB]　　1A

[Deleted]*　　2

The inventories referred to in paragraph 1(c) are measured at net realisable value at certain stages of production. This occurs, for example, when agricultural crops have been harvested or mineral ores have been extracted and sale is assured under a forward contract or a government guarantee, or when an active market exists and　　3

Note: paragraphs that are identified as deleted in this manner identify paragraphs included in the existing version of IAS 2 that the IASB has proposed should be deleted as a consequence of its improvements project.

there is a negligible risk of failure to sell. These inventories are excluded from the scope of this Standard.

DEFINITIONS

4   **The following terms are used in this Standard with the meanings specified:**

Inventories are assets:

(a)   **held for sale in the ordinary course of business;**
(b)   **in the process of production for such sale; or**
(c)   **in the form of materials or supplies to be consumed in the production process or in the rendering of services.**

Net realisable value is the estimated selling price in the ordinary course of business less the estimated costs of completion and the estimated costs necessary to make the sale.

5   Inventories encompass goods purchased and held for resale including, for example, merchandise purchased by a retailer and held for resale, or land and other property held for resale. Inventories also encompass finished goods produced, or work in progress being produced, by the entity and include materials and supplies awaiting use in the production process. In the case of a service provider, inventories include the costs of the service, as described in paragraph 16, for which the entity has not yet recognised the related revenue (see [draft] Financial Reporting Standard –, *Construction and Service Contracts* IAS 18, *Revenue*).

MEASUREMENT OF INVENTORIES

6   **Inventories shall be measured at the lower of cost and net realisable value.**

Cost of Inventories

7   **The cost of inventories shall comprise all costs of purchase, costs of conversion and other costs incurred in bringing the inventories to their present location and condition.**

Costs of Purchase

8   The costs of purchase of inventories comprise the purchase price, import duties and other taxes (other than those subsequently recoverable by the entity from the taxing authorities), and transport, handling and other costs directly attributable to the acquisition of finished goods, materials and services. Trade discounts, rebates and other similar items are deducted in determining the costs of purchase.

9   [Deleted]

Costs of Conversion

10   The costs of conversion of inventories include costs directly related to the units of production, such as direct labour. They also include a systematic allocation of fixed and variable production overheads that are incurred in converting materials into finished goods. Fixed production overheads are those indirect costs of production that remain relatively constant regardless of the volume of production, such as depreciation and maintenance of factory buildings and equipment, and the cost of factory management and administration. Variable production overheads are those

indirect costs of production that vary directly, or nearly directly, with the volume of production, such as indirect materials and indirect labour.

The allocation of fixed production overheads to the costs of conversion is based on the normal capacity of the production facilities. Normal capacity is the production expected to be achieved on average over a number of periods or seasons under normal circumstances, taking into account the loss of capacity resulting from planned maintenance. The actual level of production may be used if it approximates normal capacity. The amount of fixed overhead allocated to each unit of production is not increased as a consequence of low production or idle plant. Unallocated overheads are recognised as an expense in the period in which they are incurred. In periods of abnormally high production, the amount of fixed overhead allocated to each unit of production is decreased so that inventories are not measured above cost. Variable production overheads are allocated to each unit of production on the basis of the actual use of the production facilities.   **11**

A production process may result in more than one product being produced simultaneously. This is the case, for example, when joint products are produced or when there is a main product and a by-product. When the costs of conversion of each product are not separately identifiable, they are allocated between the products on a rational and consistent basis. The allocation may be based, for example, on the relative sales value of each product either at the stage in the production process when the products become separately identifiable, or at the completion of production. Most by-products, by their nature, are immaterial. When this is the case, they are often measured at net realisable value and this value is deducted from the cost of the main product. As a result, the carrying amount of the main product is not materially different from its cost.   **12**

Other Costs

Other costs are included in the cost of inventories only to the extent that they are incurred in bringing the inventories to their present location and condition. For example, it may be appropriate to include non-production overheads or the costs of designing products for specific customers in the cost of inventories.   **13**

Examples of costs excluded from the cost of inventories and recognised as expenses in the period in which they are incurred are: **14**

(a)   abnormal amounts of wasted materials, labour, or other production costs;
(b)   storage costs, unless those costs are necessary in the production process prior to a further production stage;
(c)   administrative overheads that do not contribute to bringing inventories to their present location and condition; and
(d)   selling costs.

In limited circumstances, borrowing costs are included in the cost of inventories. These circumstances are identified in the allowed alternative treatment in [draft] Financial Reporting Standard – *Borrowing Costs* IAS 23, *Borrowing Costs*.*   **15**

Cost of Inventories of a Service Provider

When revenues related to services provided have not been recognised, a service provider has inventories. The cost of inventories of a service provider consists   **16**

*Contained in FRED 29 *Property, Plant and Equipment & Borrowing Costs*.

primarily of the labour and other costs of personnel directly engaged in providing the service, including supervisory personnel, and attributable overheads. Labour and other costs relating to sales and general administrative personnel are not included but are recognised as expenses in the period in which they are incurred. The cost of inventories of a service provider does not include profit margins or non-production costs that are often factored into prices charged by service providers.

Cost of Agricultural Produce Harvested from Biological Assets

16A   Under IAS 41, Agriculture, inventories comprising agricultural produce that an entity has harvested from its biological assets are measured on initial recognition at their fair value less estimated point-of-sale costs at the point of harvest. This is the cost of the inventories at that date for application of this Standard.*

Techniques for the Measurement of Cost

17   Techniques for the measurement of the cost of inventories, such as the standard cost method or the retail method, may be used for convenience if the results approximate cost. Standard costs take into account normal levels of materials and supplies, labour, efficiency and capacity utilisation. They are regularly reviewed and, if necessary, revised in the light of current conditions.

18   The retail method is often used in the retail industry for measuring inventories of large numbers of rapidly changing items with similar margins, and for which it is impracticable to use other costing methods. The cost of the inventory is determined by reducing the sales value of the inventory by the appropriate percentage gross margin. The percentage used takes into consideration inventory that has been marked down to below its original selling price. An average percentage for each retail department is often used.

COST FORMULAS

19   **The cost of inventories of items that are not ordinarily interchangeable and goods or services produced and segregated for specific projects shall be assigned by using specific identification of their individual costs.**

20   Specific identification of cost means that specific costs are attributed to identified items of inventory. This is the appropriate treatment for items that are segregated for a specific project, regardless of whether they have been bought or produced. However, specific identification of costs is inappropriate when there are large numbers of items of inventory that are ordinarily interchangeable. In such circumstances, the method of selecting those items that remain in inventories could be used to obtain predetermined effects on the net profit or loss.

21   **The cost of inventories, other than those dealt with in paragraph 19, shall be assigned by using the first-in, first-out (FIFO) or weighted average cost formulas. An entity shall use the same cost formula for all inventories having a similar nature and use to the entity. For inventories with a different nature or use, different cost formulas may be justified.**

This paragraph, and the related cross-reference in paragraph 1(d) above, is deleted as there is no UK standard corresponding to IAS 41.

For example, inventories used in one business segment may have a use to the entity **21A** different from the same type of inventories used in another business segment. However, a difference in geographical location of inventories (or in the respective tax rules), by itself, is not sufficient to justify the use of different cost formulas.

The FIFO formula assumes that the items of inventory that were purchased or **22** produced first are sold first, and consequently the items remaining in inventory at the end of the period are those most recently purchased or produced. Under the weighted average cost formula, the cost of each item is determined from the weighted average of the cost of similar items at the beginning of a period and the cost of similar items purchased or produced during the period. The average may be calculated on a periodic basis, or as each additional shipment is received, depending upon the circumstances of the entity.

[Deleted] **23**

[Deleted] **24**

NET REALISABLE VALUE

The cost of inventories may not be recoverable if those inventories are damaged, if **25** they have become wholly or partially obsolete, or if their selling prices have declined. The cost of inventories may also not be recoverable if the estimated costs of completion or the estimated costs to be incurred to make the sale have increased. The practice of writing inventories down below cost to net realisable value is consistent with the view that assets should not be carried in excess of amounts expected to be realised from their sale or use.

Inventories are usually written down to net realisable value on an item by item basis. **26** In some circumstances, however, it may be appropriate to group similar or related items. This may be the case with items of inventory relating to the same product line that have similar purposes or end uses, are produced and marketed in the same geographical area, and cannot be practicably evaluated separately from other items in that product line. It is not appropriate to write inventories down based on a classification of inventory, for example, finished goods, or all the inventories in a particular industry or geographical segment. Service providers generally accumulate costs in respect of each service for which a separate selling price is charged. Therefore, each such service is treated as a separate item.

Estimates of net realisable value are based on the most reliable evidence available at **27** the time the estimates are made as to the amount the inventories are expected to realise. These estimates take into consideration fluctuations of price or cost directly relating to events occurring after the end of the period to the extent that such events confirm conditions existing at the end of the period.

Estimates of net realisable value also take into consideration the purpose for which **28** the inventory is held. For example, the net realisable value of the quantity of inventory held to satisfy firm sales or service contracts is based on the contract price. If the sales contracts are for less than the inventory quantities held, the net realisable value of the excess is based on general selling prices. Provisions or contingent liabilities may arise from firm sales contracts in excess of inventory quantities held or from firm purchase contracts. Such provisions or contingent liabilities are dealt with under FRS 12 *Provisions, Contingent Liabilities and Contingent Assets* IAS 37, *Provisions, Contingent Liabilities and Contingent Assets*.

29   Materials and other supplies held for use in the production of inventories are not written down below cost if the finished products in which they will be incorporated are expected to be sold at or above cost. However, when a decline in the price of materials indicates that the cost of the finished products exceeds net realisable value, the materials are written down to net realisable value. In such circumstances, the replacement cost of the materials may be the best available measure of their net realisable value.

30   A new assessment is made of net realisable value in each subsequent period. When the circumstances that previously caused inventories to be written down below cost no longer exist, the amount of the write-down is reversed so that the new carrying amount is the lower of the cost and the revised net realisable value. This occurs, for example, when an item of inventory, which is carried at net realisable value because its selling price has declined, is still on hand in a subsequent period and its selling price has increased.

RECOGNITION AS AN EXPENSE

31   **When inventories are sold, the carrying amount of those inventories shall be recognised as an expense in the period in which the related revenue is recognised. The amount of any write-down of inventories to net realisable value and all losses of inventories shall be recognised as an expense in the period the write-down or loss occurs. The amount of any reversal of any write-down of inventories, arising from an increase in net realisable value, shall be recognised as a reduction in the amount of inventories recognised as an expense in the period in which the reversal occurs.**

32   [Deleted]

33   Some inventories may be allocated to other asset accounts, for example, inventory used as a component of self-constructed property, plant or equipment. Inventories allocated to another asset in this way are recognised as an expense during the useful life of that asset.

DISCLOSURE

34   **The financial statements shall disclose:**

   (a)   **the accounting policies adopted in measuring inventories, including the cost formula used;**

   (b)   **the total carrying amount of inventories and the carrying amount in classifications appropriate to the entity;**

   (c)   **the amount of any write-down of inventories recognised in accordance with paragraph 31;**

   (d)   **the amount of any reversal of any write-down that is recognised as income in the period in accordance with paragraph 31;**

   (e)   **the circumstances or events that led to the reversal of a write-down of inventories in accordance with paragraph 31; and**

   (f)   **the carrying amount of inventories pledged as security for liabilities.**

35   Information about the carrying amounts held in different classifications of inventories and the extent of the changes in these assets is useful to financial statement users. Common classifications of inventories are merchandise, production supplies, materials, work in progress and finished goods. The inventories of a service provider may simply be described as work in progress.

36   **[Deleted]**

EFFECTIVE DATE

The accounting practices set out in this Standard should be regarded as standard in   41
respect of accounting periods ending on or after [date to be inserted after exposure].
Earlier adoption is encouraged. This Standard becomes operative for annual financial
statements covering periods beginning on or after 1 January 2003. Earlier adoption is
encouraged. If earlier adoption affects the financial statements, an entity shall disclose that fact.

Appendix: Note on legal requirements

GREAT BRITAIN AND NORTHERN IRELAND

The relevant statutory requirements are set out in the Companies Act 1985 and the Companies (Northern Ireland) Order 1986. All paragraph references unless otherwise indicated are to Schedule 4 to the Companies Act 1985 and Schedule 4 to the Companies (Northern Ireland) Order 1986.

Schedule 4 does not apply to banking and insurance companies. Banking companies are dealt with in Schedule 9 and insurance companies are dealt with in Schedule 9A.

Paragraph 22 requires that, under the historical cost accounting rules, the amount to be included in respect of any current asset shall be its purchase price or production cost. Paragraph 23(1) provides for the inclusion of the asset at net realisable value if lower than purchase price or production cost.

Paragraph 26 requires expenses incidental to the acquisition of an asset to be included in the purchase price. It also requires the inclusion of directly attributable production overheads in the production cost of an asset and permits the inclusion of overheads which are only indirectly attributable to the production of an asset and interest on borrowed capital. In cases where interest is included the fact must be stated and the amount of interest included must be disclosed in a note to the financial statements. Paragraph 26 also prohibits the inclusion of distribution costs.

Paragraph 27 allows the following methods for valuation of stocks (but requires that the method chosen must be one which appears to the directors to be appropriate in the circumstances of the company):

(a)   the method known as first in, first out (FIFO);
(b)   the method known as last in, first out (LIFO);
(c)   a weighted average price; and
(d)   any other method similar to any of the methods mentioned above.

However, the use of the LIFO method is not permitted by this Standard.

Paragraph 27(3) requires a company to state in a note to the accounts the difference between the replacement cost of stocks and their carrying amount where this difference is material.

It is further provided in paragraph 27(5) that, if the most recent actual purchase price or production cost before the balance sheet date appears to the directors of the company to constitute a more appropriate standard of comparison, then that amount may be used as a surrogate for replacement cost.

Paragraph 31(5) provides that, where a company adopts the alternative accounting rules, stocks may be included at their current cost.

REPUBLIC OF IRELAND

The statutory requirements in the Republic of Ireland that correspond to those cited above for Great Britain are shown in the following table:

Great Britain	Republic of Ireland
Schedule 4 to the Companies Act 1985	The Schedule to the Companies: (Amendment) Act 1986:
paragraph 22	paragraph 10
paragraph 23(1)	paragraph 11(1)
paragraph 26	paragraph 14
paragraph 27	paragraph 15
paragraph 31(5)	paragraph 19(5)

Summary of main changes proposed by the IASB

The main changes that the IASB are proposing to IAS 2 are:

- to delete producers, which is the first word in paragraph 1(c). This change extends the scope exception to non-producers such as those brokers and dealers whose inventories are measured at net realisable value in accordance with well-established practices.
- to delete paragraph 9* as a result of the proposed elimination of the allowed alternative treatment in paragraph 21 of IAS 21, *The Effects of Changes in Foreign Exchange Rates.*
- to eliminate the allowed alternative of using the last-in, first-out (LIFO) method (paragraphs 23 and 24).
- to change paragraph 34(c)† to require disclosure of the amount of any write-down of inventories.
- to delete paragraphs 37–39, which are unnecessary because the required disclosures are also required by IAS 1, *Presentation of Financial Statements.*

Also, SIC-1 *Consistency – Different Cost Formulas for Inventories* is withdrawn as it is covered in SIC-18 *Consistency – Alternative Methods*, which is incorporated into IAS 8 *Accounting Policies, Changes in Accounting Estimates and Errors.*

In the existing standard, this paragraph permits foreign exchange differences to be included within the cost of purchase of inventories (in the rare circumstances permitted in the allowed alternative treatment in the existing IAS 21).

†*In the existing standard, this paragraph requires the carrying amount of inventories carried at net realisable value to be disclosed.*

[Draft] Financial Reporting Standard: Construction And Service Contracts

[Draft] Financial Reporting Standard – Construction and Service Contracts is set out in paragraphs 1–46.

The Statement of Standard Accounting Practice, which comprises the paragraphs set in bold italic type, should be read in the context of the Objective, the definitions set out in paragraphs 3–6, and also of the Foreword to Accounting Standards and the Statement of Principles for Financial Reporting currently in issue.

The explanatory paragraphs contained in the [draft] FRS shall be regarded as part of the Statement of Standard Accounting Practice insofar as they assist in interpreting that statement.

This draft is issued by the Accounting Standards Board for comment. It should be noted that the draft may be modified in the light of comment received before being issued in final form.

OBJECTIVE

The objective of this Standard is to prescribe the accounting treatment of revenue and costs associated with construction and service contracts. Because of the nature of the activity undertaken in construction such contracts, the date at which the contract activity is entered into and the date when the activity is completed usually often fall into different accounting periods. Therefore, the primary issue in accounting for construction these contracts is the allocation of contract revenue and contract costs to the accounting periods in which construction work is performed. This Standard uses the recognition criteria established in the *Framework* for the Preparation and Presentation of Financial Statements* to determine when contract revenue and contract costs should be recognised as revenue and expenses in the income statement. It also provides practical guidance on the application of these criteria.

SCOPE

This Standard should be applied in accounting for: 1

(a) construction contracts in the financial statements of contractors; and
(b) revenue arising from the rendering of services.

This Standard applies to all financial statements that are intended to give a true and fair   1A
view of a reporting entity's financial position and profit or loss (or income and
expenditure), except that reporting entities applying the Financial Reporting Standard
for Smaller Entities currently applicable are exempt. [ASB]

*Under paragraph 83 of the IASB Framework, an item that meets the definition of an element [of financial statements] should be recognised if: (a) it is probable that any future benefits associated with the item will flow to or from the enterprise; and (b) the item has a cost or value that can be measured with reliability. Chapter 5 of the ASB s Statement of Principles for Financial Reporting contains similar recognition criteria, whereby a new asset or liability (or an addition to an existing asset or liability) will be recognised if (a) sufficient evidence exists that the new asset or liability has been created or that there has been an addition to an existing asset or liability; and (b) the new asset or liability or the addition to the existing asset or liability can be measured at a monetary amount with sufficient reliability.

2 This Standard supersedes IAS 11, Accounting for Construction Contracts, approved in 1978.

DEFINITIONS

3 **The following terms are used in this Standard with the meanings specified:**

A construction contract is a contract specifically negotiated for the construction of an asset or a combination of assets that are closely interrelated or interdependent in terms of their design, technology and function or their ultimate purpose or use.

A fixed price contract is a construction contract in which the contractor agrees to a fixed contract price, or a fixed rate per unit of output, which in some cases is subject to cost escalation clauses.

A cost plus contract is a construction contract in which the contractor is reimbursed for allowable or otherwise defined costs, plus a percentage of these costs or a fixed fee.

4 A construction contract may be negotiated for the construction of a single asset such as a bridge, building, dam, pipeline, road, ship or tunnel. A construction contract may also deal with the construction of a number of assets which are closely inter-related or interdependent in terms of their design, technology and function or their ultimate purpose or use; examples of such contracts include those for the construction of refineries and other complex pieces of plant or equipment.

5 For the purposes of this Standard, construction contracts include:
(a) contracts for the rendering of services which are directly related to the construction of the asset, for example, those for the services of project managers and architects; and
(b) contracts for the destruction or restoration of assets, and the restoration of the environment following the demolition of assets.

6 Construction contracts are formulated in a number of ways which, for the purposes of this Standard, are classified as fixed price contracts and cost plus contracts. Some construction contracts may contain characteristics of both a fixed price contract and a cost plus contract, for example in the case of a cost plus contract with an agreed maximum price. In such circumstances, a contractor needs to consider all the conditions in paragraphs 23 and 24 in order to determine when to recognise contract revenue and expenses.

COMBINING AND SEGMENTING CONSTRUCTION CONTRACTS

7 The requirements of this Standard are usually applied separately to each construction contract. However, in certain circumstances, it is necessary to apply the Standard to the separately identifiable components of a single contract or to a group of contracts together in order to reflect the substance of a contract or a group of contracts.

8 **When a contract covers a number of assets, the construction of each asset should be treated as a separate construction contract when:**
(a) **separate proposals have been submitted for each asset;**
(b) **each asset has been subject to separate negotiation and the contractor and customer have been able to accept or reject that part of the contract relating to each asset; and**

(c)   the costs and revenues of each asset can be identified.

A group of contracts, whether with a single customer or with several customers, should   9
be treated as a single construction contract when:

(a)   the group of contracts is negotiated as a single package;
(b)   the contracts are so closely interrelated that they are, in effect, part of a single
        project with an overall profit margin; and
(c)   the contracts are performed concurrently or in a continuous sequence.

A contract may provide for the construction of an additional asset at the option of the   10
customer or may be amended to include the construction of an additional asset. The
construction of the additional asset should be treated as a separate construction contract when:

(a)   the asset differs significantly in design, technology or function from the asset or
        assets covered by the original contract; or
(b)   the price of the asset is negotiated without regard to the original contract price.

CONTRACT REVENUE

Contract revenue should comprise: 11

(a)   the initial amount of revenue agreed in the contract; and
(b)   variations in contract work, claims and incentive payments:

   (i)   to the extent that it is probable that they will result in revenue; and
   (ii)   they are capable of being reliably measured.

Contract revenue is measured at the fair value of the consideration received or   12
receivable. The measurement of contract revenue is affected by a variety of uncertainties that depend on the outcome of future events. The estimates often need to be
revised as events occur and uncertainties are resolved. Therefore, the amount of
contract revenue may increase or decrease from one period to the next. For example:

(a)   a contractor and a customer may agree variations or claims that increase or
        decrease contract revenue in a period subsequent to that in which the contract
        was initially agreed;
(b)   the amount of revenue agreed in a fixed price contract may increase as a result
        of cost escalation clauses;
(c)   the amount of contract revenue may decrease as a result of penalties arising
        from delays caused by the contractor in the completion of the contract; or
(d)   when a fixed price contract involves a fixed price per unit of output, contract
        revenue increases as the number of units is increased.

A variation is an instruction by the customer for a change in the scope of the work to   13
be performed under the contract. A variation may lead to an increase or a decrease in
contract revenue. Examples of variations are changes in the specifications or design
of the asset and changes in the duration of the contract. A variation is included in
contract revenue when:

(a)   it is probable that the customer will approve the variation and the amount of
        revenue arising from the variation; and
(b)   the amount of revenue can be reliably measured.

A claim is an amount that the contractor seeks to collect from the customer or   14
another party as reimbursement for costs not included in the contract price. A claim
may arise from, for example, customer caused delays, errors in specifications or

design, and disputed variations in contract work. The measurement of the amounts of revenue arising from claims is subject to a high level of uncertainty and often depends on the outcome of negotiations. Therefore, claims are only included in contract revenue when:

(a)   negotiations have reached an advanced stage such that it is probable that the customer will accept the claim; and

(b)   the amount that it is probable will be accepted by the customer can be measured reliably.

15   Incentive payments are additional amounts paid to the contractor if specified performance standards are met or exceeded. For example, a contract may allow for an incentive payment to the contractor for early completion of the contract. Incentive payments are included in contract revenue when:

(a)   the contract is sufficiently advanced that it is probable that the specified performance standards will be met or exceeded; and

(b)   the amount of the incentive payment can be measured reliably.

CONTRACT COSTS

16   Contract costs should comprise:

(a)   costs that relate directly to the specific contract;

(b)   costs that are attributable to contract activity in general and can be allocated to the contract; and

(c)   such other costs as are specifically chargeable to the customer under the terms of the contract.

17   Costs that relate directly to a specific contract include:

(a)   site labour costs, including site supervision;

(b)   costs of materials used in construction;

(c)   depreciation of plant and equipment used on the contract;

(d)   costs of moving plant, equipment and materials to and from the contract site;

(e)   costs of hiring plant and equipment;

(f)   costs of design and technical assistance that is directly related to the contract;

(g)   the estimated costs of rectification and guarantee work, including expected warranty costs; and

(h)   claims from third parties.

These costs may be reduced by any incidental income that is not included in contract revenue, for example income from the sale of surplus materials and the disposal of plant and equipment at the end of the contract.

18   Costs that may be attributable to contract activity in general and can be allocated to specific contracts include:

(a)   insurance;

(b)   costs of design and technical assistance that is not directly related to a specific contract; and

(c)   construction overheads.

Such costs are allocated using methods that are systematic and rational and are applied consistently to all costs having similar characteristics. The allocation is based on the normal level of construction activity. Construction overheads include costs such as the preparation and processing of construction personnel payroll. Costs that may be attributable to contract activity in general and can be allocated to specific contracts also include borrowing costs when the contractor adopts the allowed alternative treatment in IAS 23, *Borrowing Costs* [draft] Financial Reporting Standard – *Borrowing Costs.**

Costs that are specifically chargeable to the customer under the terms of the contract may include some general administration costs and development costs for which reimbursement is specified in the terms of the contract. **19**

Costs that cannot be attributed to contract activity or cannot be allocated to a contract are excluded from the costs of a construction contract. Such costs include: **20**

(a)   general administration costs for which reimbursement is not specified in the contract;
(b)   selling costs;
(c)   research and development costs for which reimbursement is not specified in the contract; and
(d)   depreciation of idle plant and equipment that is not used on a particular contract.

Contract costs include the costs attributable to a contract for the period from the date of securing the contract to the final completion of the contract. However, costs that relate directly to a contract and which are incurred in securing the contract are also included as part of the contract costs if they can be separately identified and measured reliably and it is probable that the contract will be obtained. When costs incurred in securing a contract are recognised as an expense in the period in which they are incurred, they are not included in contract costs when the contract is obtained in a subsequent period. **21**

RECOGNITION OF CONTRACT REVENUE AND EXPENSES

When the outcome of a construction contract can be estimated reliably, contract revenue and contract costs associated with the construction contract should be recognised as revenue and expenses respectively by reference to the stage of completion of the contract activity at the balance sheet date. An expected loss on the construction contract should be recognised as an expense immediately in accordance with paragraph 36. **22**

In the case of a fixed price contract, the outcome of a construction contract can be estimated reliably when all the following conditions are satisfied: **23**

(a)   total contract revenue can be measured reliably;
(b)   it is probable that the economic benefits associated with the contract will flow to the enterprise;
(c)   both the contract costs to complete the contract and the stage of contract completion at the balance sheet date can be measured reliably; and
(d)   the contract costs attributable to the contract can be clearly identified and measured reliably so that actual contract costs incurred can be compared with prior estimates.

In the case of a cost plus contract, the outcome of a construction contract can be estimated reliably when all the following conditions are satisfied: **24**

(a)   it is probable that the economic benefits associated with the contract will flow to the enterprise; and
(b)   the contract costs attributable to the contract, whether or not specifically reimbursable, can be clearly identified and measured reliably.

*Contained in FRED *29 Property, Plant and Equipment & Borrowing Costs.*

25   The recognition of revenue and expenses by reference to the stage of completion of a contract is often referred to as the percentage of completion method. Under this method, contract revenue is matched with the contract costs incurred in reaching the stage of completion, resulting in the reporting of revenue, expenses and profit which can be attributed to the proportion of work completed. This method provides useful information on the extent of contract activity and performance during a period.

26   Under the percentage of completion method, contract revenue is recognised as revenue in the income statement in the accounting periods in which the work is performed. Contract costs are usually recognised as an expense in the income statement in the accounting periods in which the work to which they relate is performed. However, any expected excess of total contract costs over total contract revenue for the contract is recognised as an expense immediately in accordance with paragraph 36.

27   A contractor may have incurred contract costs that relate to future activity on the contract. Such contract costs are recognised as an asset provided it is probable that they will be recovered. Such costs represent an amount due from the customer and are often classified as contract work in progress.

28   The outcome of a construction contract can only be estimated reliably when it is probable that the economic benefits associated with the contract will flow to the enterprise. However, when an uncertainty arises about the collectability of an amount already included in contract revenue, and already recognised in the income statement, the uncollectable amount or the amount in respect of which recovery has ceased to be probable is recognised as an expense rather than as an adjustment of the amount of contract revenue.

29   An enterprise is generally able to make reliable estimates after it has agreed to a contract which establishes:

   (a)   each party s enforceable rights regarding the asset to be constructed;
   (b)   the consideration to be exchanged; and
   (c)   the manner and terms of settlement.

   It is also usually necessary for the enterprise to have an effective internal financial budgeting and reporting system. The enterprise reviews and, when necessary, revises the estimates of contract revenue and contract costs as the contract progresses. The need for such revisions does not necessarily indicate that the outcome of the contract cannot be estimated reliably.

30   The stage of completion of a contract may be determined in a variety of ways. The enterprise uses the method that measures reliably the work performed. Depending on the nature of the contract, the methods may include:

   (a)   the proportion that contract costs incurred for work performed to date bear to the estimated total contract costs;
   (b)   surveys of work performed; or
   (c)   completion of a physical proportion of the contract work.

   Progress payments and advances received from customers often do not reflect the work performed.

31   When the stage of completion is determined by reference to the contract costs incurred to date, only those contract costs that reflect work performed are included in costs incurred to date. Examples of contract costs which are excluded are:

(a) contract costs that relate to future activity on the contract, such as costs of materials that have been delivered to a contract site or set aside for use in a contract but not yet installed, used or applied during contract performance, unless the materials have been made specially for the contract; and

(b) payments made to subcontractors in advance of work performed under the subcontract.

When the outcome of a construction contract cannot be estimated reliably:　　32

(a) **revenue should be recognised only to the extent of contract costs incurred that it is probable will be recoverable; and**

(b) **contract costs should be recognised as an expense in the period in which they are incurred.**

An expected loss on the construction contract should be recognised as an expense immediately in accordance with paragraph 36.

During the early stages of a contract it is often the case that the outcome of the　　33 contract cannot be estimated reliably. Nevertheless, it may be probable that the enterprise will recover the contract costs incurred. Therefore, contract revenue is recognised only to the extent of costs incurred that are expected to be recoverable. As the outcome of the contract cannot be estimated reliably, no profit is recognised. However, even though the outcome of the contract cannot be estimated reliably, it may be probable that total contract costs will exceed total contract revenues. In such cases, any expected excess of total contract costs over total contract revenue for the contract is recognised as an expense immediately in accordance with paragraph 36.

Contract costs that are not probable of being recovered are recognised as an expense　　34 immediately. Examples of circumstances in which the recoverability of contract costs incurred may not be probable and in which contract costs may need to be recognised as an expense immediately include contracts:

(a) which are not fully enforceable, that is, their validity is seriously in question;

(b) the completion of which is subject to the outcome of pending litigation or legislation;

(c) relating to properties that are likely to be condemned or expropriated;

(d) where the customer is unable to meet its obligations; or

(e) where the contractor is unable to complete the contract or otherwise meet its obligations under the contract.

When the uncertainties that prevented the outcome of the contract being estimated　　35 **reliably no longer exist, revenue and expenses associated with the construction contract should be recognised in accordance with paragraph 22 rather than in accordance with paragraph 32.**

RECOGNITION OF EXPECTED LOSSES

When it is probable that total contract costs will exceed total contract revenue, the　　36 **expected loss should be recognised as an expense immediately.**

The amount of such a loss is determined irrespective of:　　37

(a) whether or not work has commenced on the contract;

(b) the stage of completion of contract activity; or

(c) the amount of profits expected to arise on other contracts which are not treated as a single construction contract in accordance with paragraph 9.

CHANGES IN ESTIMATES

38   The percentage of completion method is applied on a cumulative basis in each accounting period to the current estimates of contract revenue and contract costs. Therefore, the effect of a change in the estimate of contract revenue or contract costs, or the effect of a change in the estimate of the outcome of a contract, is accounted for as a change in accounting estimate estimation technique (see IAS 8, *Net Profit or Loss for the Period, Fundamental Errors and Changes in Accounting Policies* FRS 18 *Accounting Policies*). The changed estimates are used in the determination of the amount of revenue and expenses recognised in the income statement in the period in which the change is made and in subsequent periods.

DISCLOSURE

39   An enterprise should disclose:

    (a)   the amount of contract revenue recognised as revenue in the period;
    (b)   the methods used to determine the contract revenue recognised in the period; and
    (c)   the methods used to determine the stage of completion of contracts in progress.

40   An enterprise should disclose each of the following for contracts in progress at the balance sheet date:

    (a)   the aggregate amount of costs incurred and recognised profits (less recognised losses) to date;
    (b)   the amount of advances received; and
    (c)   the amount of retentions.

41   Retentions are amounts of progress billings which are not paid until the satisfaction of conditions specified in the contract for the payment of such amounts or until defects have been rectified. Progress billings are amounts billed for work performed on a contract whether or not they have been paid by the customer. Advances are amounts received by the contractor before the related work is performed.

42   An enterprise should present:

    (a)   the gross amount due from customers for contract work as an asset; and
    (b)   the gross amount due to customers for contract work as a liability.

43   The gross amount due from customers for contract work is the net amount of:

    (a)   costs incurred plus recognised profits; less
    (b)   the sum of recognised losses and progress billings

for all contracts in progress for which costs incurred plus recognised profits (less recognised losses) exceeds progress billings.

44   The gross amount due to customers for contract work is the net amount of:

    (a)   costs incurred plus recognised profits; less
    (b)   the sum of recognised losses and progress billings

for all contracts in progress for which progress billings exceed costs incurred plus recognised profits (less recognised losses).

45   An enterprise discloses any contingent liabilities and contingent assets in accordance with IAS 37, *Provisions, Contingent Liabilities and Contingent Assets* FRS 12 *Provisions, Contingent Liabilities and Contingent Assets*. Contingent liabilities and

contingent assets may arise from such items as warranty costs, claims, penalties or possible losses.

RENDERING OF SERVICES*

The rendering of services typically involves the performance by the enterprise of a contractually agreed task over an agreed period of time. The services may be rendered within a single period or over more than one period. Some contracts for the rendering of services are directly related to construction contracts, for example, those for the services of project managers and architects. Revenue arising from these contracts is not dealt with in this Standard but is dealt with in accordance with the requirements for construction contracts as specified in IAS 11, *Construction Contracts* paragraphs 1 to 45 above.   **45A**

When the outcome of a transaction involving the rendering of services can be estimated reliably, revenue associated with the transaction should be recognised by reference to the stage of completion of the transaction at the balance sheet date. The outcome of a transaction can be estimated reliably when all the following conditions are satisfied: **45B**

(a)   the amount of revenue can be measured reliably;
(b)   it is probable that the economic benefits associated with the transaction will flow to the enterprise;
(c)   the stage of completion of the transaction at the balance sheet date can be measured reliably; and
(d)   the costs incurred for the transaction and the costs to complete the transaction can be measured reliably.

The recognition of revenue by reference to the stage of completion of a transaction is often referred to as the percentage of completion method. Under this method, revenue is recognised in the accounting periods in which the services are rendered. The recognition of revenue on this basis provides useful information on the extent of service activity and performance during a period. Paragraph 22 above IAS 11, *Construction Contracts*, also requires the recognition of revenue on this basis. The requirements of paragraphs 1 to 45 above, including the disclosure requirements of paragraph 39,that Standard are generally applicable to the recognition of revenue and the associated expenses for a transaction involving the rendering of services.   **45C**

Revenue is recognised only when it is probable that the economic benefits associated with the transaction will flow to the enterprise. However, when an uncertainty arises about the collectability of an amount already included in revenue, the uncollectable amount, or the amount in respect of which recovery has ceased to be probable, is recognised as an expense, rather than as an adjustment of the amount of revenue originally recognised.   **45D**

An enterprise is generally able to make reliable estimates after it has agreed to the following with the other parties to the transaction: **45E**

(a)   each party's enforceable rights regarding the service to be provided and received by the parties;
(b)   the consideration to be exchanged; and
(c)   the manner and terms of settlement.

It is also usually necessary for the enterprise to have an effective internal financial budgeting and reporting system. The enterprise reviews and, when necessary, revises

Paragraphs 45A to 45J are the same as paragraphs 4 and 20 to 28 of IAS 18 Revenue

the estimates of revenue as the service is performed. The need for such revisions does not necessarily indicate that the outcome of the transaction cannot be estimated reliably.

45F   The stage of completion of a transaction may be determined by a variety of methods. An enterprise uses the method that measures reliably the services performed. Depending on the nature of the transaction, the methods may include:

(a)   surveys of work performed;

(b)   services performed to date as a percentage of total services to be performed; or

(c)   the proportion that costs incurred to date bear to the estimated total costs of the transaction. Only costs that reflect services performed to date are included in costs incurred to date. Only costs that reflect services performed or to be performed are included in the estimated total costs of the transaction.

Progress payments and advances received from customers often do not reflect the services performed.

45G   For practical purposes, when services are performed by an indeterminate number of acts over a specified period of time, revenue is recognised on a straight line basis over the specified period unless there is evidence that some other method better represents the stage of completion. When a specific act is much more significant than any other acts, the recognition of revenue is postponed until the significant act is executed.

45H   **When the outcome of the transaction involving the rendering of services cannot be estimated reliably, revenue should be recognised only to the extent of the expenses recognised that are recoverable.**

45I   During the early stages of a transaction, it is often the case that the outcome of the transaction cannot be estimated reliably. Nevertheless, it may be probable that the enterprise will recover the transaction costs incurred. Therefore, revenue is recognised only to the extent of costs incurred that are expected to be recoverable. As the outcome of the transaction cannot be estimated reliably, no profit is recognised.

45J   When the outcome of a transaction cannot be estimated reliably and it is not probable that the costs incurred will be recovered, revenue is not recognised and the costs incurred are recognised as an expense. When the uncertainties that prevented the outcome of the contract being estimated reliably no longer exist, revenue is recognised in accordance with paragraph 20 45B rather than in accordance with paragraph 26 45H.

EFFECTIVE DATE

46   **The accounting practices set out in this Standard should be regarded as standard in respect of accounting periods ending on or after [date to be inserted after exposure]. Earlier adoption is encouraged.** This International Accounting Standard becomes operative for financial statements covering periods beginning on or after 1 January 1995.

Appendix I: Example

The appendix is illustrative only and does not form part of the Standard. The purpose of the appendix is to illustrate the application of the Standard to assist in clarifying their meaning.

DISCLOSURE OF ACCOUNTING POLICIES

The following are examples of accounting policy disclosures:

Revenue from fixed price construction contracts is recognised on the percentage of completion method, measured by reference to the percentage of labour hours incurred to date to estimated total labour hours for each contract.

Revenue from cost plus contracts is recognised by reference to the recoverable costs incurred during the period plus the fee earned, measured by the proportion that costs incurred to date bear to the estimated total costs of the contract.

THE DETERMINATION OF CONTRACT REVENUE AND EXPENSES

The following example illustrates one method of determining the stage of completion of a contract and the timing of the recognition of contract revenue and expenses (see paragraphs 22 to 35 of the Standard).

A construction contractor has a fixed price contract for 9,000 to build a bridge. The initial amount of revenue agreed in the contract is 9,000. The contractor s initial estimate of contract costs is 8,000. It will take 3 years to build the bridge.

By the end of year 1, the contractor's estimate of contract costs has increased to 8,050.

In year 2, the customer approves a variation resulting in an increase in contract revenue of 200 and estimated additional contract costs of 150. At the end of year 2, costs incurred include 100 for standard materials stored at the site to be used in year 3 to complete the project.

The contractor determines the stage of completion of the contract by calculating the proportion that contract costs incurred for work performed to date bear to the latest estimated total contract costs. A summary of the financial data during the construction period is as follows:

	Year 1	Year 2	Year 3
Initial amount of revenue agreed in contract	9,000	9,000	9,000
Variation		200	200
Total contract revenue	9,000	9,200	9,200
Contract costs incurred to date	2,093	6,168	8,200
Contract costs to complete	5,957	2,032	
Total estimated contract costs	8,050	8,200	8,200
Estimated profit	950	1,000	1,000
Stage of completion	26%	74%	100%

The stage of completion for year 2 (74%) is determined by excluding from contract costs incurred for work performed to date the 100 of standard materials stored at the site for use in year 3.

The amounts of revenue, expenses and profit recognised in the income statement in the three years are as follows:

	To Date	Recognised in prior years	Recognised in current year
Year 1			
Revenue (9,000 × .26)	2,340	2,340	
Expenses (8,050 × .26)	2,093	2,093	
Profit	247		247
Year 2			
Revenue (9,200 × .74)	6,808	2,340	4,468
Expenses (8,200 × .74)	6,068	2,093	3,975
Profit	740	247	493
Year 3			
Revenue (9,200 × 1.00)	9,200	6,808	2,392
Expenses	8,200	6,068	2,132
Profit	1,000	740	260

CONTRACT DISCLOSURES

A contractor has reached the end of its first year of operations. All its contract costs incurred have been paid for in cash and all its progress billings and advances have been received in cash. Contract costs incurred for contracts B, C and E include the cost of materials that have been purchased for the contract but which have not been used in contract performance to date. For contracts B, C and E, the customers have made advances to the contractor for work not yet performed.

The status of its five contracts in progress at the end of year 1 is as follows:

	Contract					
	A	B	C	D	E	Total
Contract Revenue recognised in accordance with paragraph 22	145	520	380	200	55	1,300
Contract Expenses recognised in accordance with paragraph 22	110	450	350	250	55	1,215
Expected Losses recognised in accordance with paragraph 36	-	-	-	40	30	70
Recognised profits less recognised losses	35	70	30	(90)	(30)	15
Contract Costs incurred in the period	110	510	450	250	100	1,420
Contract Costs incurred recognised as contract expenses in the period in accordance with paragraph 22	110	450	350	250	55	1,215

Contract Costs that relate to future activity recognised as an asset in accordance with paragraph 27	-	60	100	-	45	205
Contract Revenue (see above)	145	520	380	200	55	1,300
Progress Billings (paragraph 41)	100	520	380	180	55	1,235
Unbilled Contract Revenue	45	-	-	20	-	65
Advances (paragraph 41)	-	80	20	-	25	125

The amounts to be disclosed in accordance with the Standard are as follows:

Contract revenue recognised as revenue in the period (paragraph 39(a))	1,300
Contract costs incurred and recognised profits (less recognised losses) to date (paragraph 40(a))	1,435
Advances received (paragraph 40(b))	125
Gross amount due from customers for contract work – presented as an asset in accordance with paragraph 42(a)	220
Gross amount due to customers for contract work – presented as a liability in accordance with paragraph 42(b)	(20)

The amounts to be disclosed in accordance with paragraphs 40(a), 42(a) and 42(b) are calculated as follows:

	A	B	C	D	E	Total
Contract Costs incurred	110	510	450	250	100	1,420
Recognised profits less recognised losses	35	70	30	(90)	(30)	15
	145	580	480	160	70	1,435
Progress billings	100	520	380	180	55	1,235
Due from customers	45	60	100	-	15	220
Due to customers	-	-	-	(20)	-	(20)

The amount disclosed in accordance with paragraph 40(a) is the same as the amount for the current period because the disclosures relate to the first year of operation.

Appendix II: Note on legal requirements

GREAT BRITAIN AND NORTHERN IRELAND

The relevant statutory requirements are set out in the Companies Act 1985 and the Companies (Northern Ireland) Order 1986. All paragraph references unless otherwise indicated are to Schedule 4 to the Companies Act 1985 and Schedule 4 to the Companies (Northern Ireland) Order 1986.

Schedule 4 does not apply to banking and insurance companies. Banking companies are dealt with in Schedule 9 and insurance companies are dealt with in Schedule 9A.

Paragraph 22 requires that, under the historical cost accounting rules, the amount to be included in respect of any current asset shall be its purchase price or production cost. Paragraph 23(1) provides for the inclusion of the asset at net realisable value if lower than purchase price or production cost. In the [draft] FRS, the profit recognised on a contract results from the recognition of an appropriate portion of contract revenue. The effect is that profit is included in debtors (Amounts due from customers for contract work) rather than inventories (or stocks, in the terminology used in the Act).

Paragraph 26 requires expenses incidental to the acquisition of an asset to be included in the purchase price. It also requires the inclusion of directly attributable production overheads in the production cost of an asset and permits the inclusion of overheads which are only indirectly attributable to the production of an asset and interest on borrowed capital. In cases where interest is included the fact must be stated and the amount of interest included must be disclosed in a note to the financial statements. Paragraph 26 also prohibits the inclusion of distribution costs.

Paragraph 89 [paragraph 88 of Schedule 4 to the Companies (Northern Ireland) Order 1986] provides that provisions are amounts retained as reasonably necessary for the purpose of providing for any liability or loss which is either likely to be incurred, or certain to be incurred but uncertain as to amount or as to the date on which it will arise.

REPUBLIC OF IRELAND

The statutory requirements in the Republic of Ireland that correspond to those cited above for Great Britain are shown in the following table:

Great Britain	Republic of Ireland
Schedule 4 to the Companies Act 1985:	The Schedule to the Companies (Amendment) Act 1986
paragraph 22	paragraph 10
paragraph 23(1)	paragraph 11(1)
paragraph 26	paragraph 14
paragraph 88	paragraph 70

FRED 29

(Issued May 2002)

Property, plant and equipment; Borrowing costs

Contents

Preface

1   This Financial Reporting Exposure Draft (FRED) is issued as part of the Accounting Standards Board's programme to bring about convergence between UK Accounting Standards and International Financial Reporting Standards (IFRSs*). It sets out for comment two exposure drafts of UK accounting standards, based on proposed and existing IFRSs. They address accounting for property, plant and equipment and for borrowing costs.

2   The International Accounting Standards Board (IASB) has recently published for comment a proposed revision of IAS 16 *Property, Plant and Equipment*. The main changes to the present IAS 16 proposed by the IASB are summarised on pages 61 to 64. The exposure draft on property, plant and equipment is based on the proposed revised text. The exposure draft on borrowing costs is based on an existing IFRS, IAS 23 *Borrowing Costs*. The IASB has indicated that it does not intend to revise IAS 23 at present. The differences that the ASB proposes for the UK are summarised in paragraph 26 and are highlighted in the text.†

3   The ASB proposes to issue UK standards based on these drafts, which will eventually replace FRS 15 *Tangible Fixed Assets*.‡ However, the IASB has not yet addressed accounting for revaluations, where FRS 15 differs in some significant respects from the international exposure draft. The ASB is participating in a joint project with other national standard-setters that will provide recommendations to the IASB on a convergence model for revaluations that should be adopted internationally. As explained in paragraphs 28 to 31, the ASB proposes that the timing of the implementation of these standards should depend on whether, by the time the IASB issues the revised IAS 16 (which is expected in the first quarter of 2003), further changes to IAS 16 are likely to be promulgated by 2005.

PROPERTY, PLANT AND EQUIPMENT – MAIN CHANGES PROPOSED TO EXISTING UK REQUIREMENTS

4   The proposed revised IAS 16 and FRS 15 have much in common in terms of their scope and principles for initial measurement, valuation and depreciation of tangible fixed assets. Both standards also allow the optional policies of revaluing assets or keeping them at cost, subject to depreciation. IAS 16 uses different terminology, but 'property, plant and equipment' has a similar meaning to 'tangible fixed assets'. However, there are also a number of differences between the standards, the more important of which are summarised below.

Exchanges of assets

5   The exposure draft proposes a requirement that will be new to UK accounting standards. Where an item of property, plant and equipment is acquired in exchange for another item of property, plant and equipment or other asset, the international exposure draft requires the cost of the acquired asset to be measured at *fair value* (based on the fair value of the asset given up or, if more clearly evident, the fair value

---

The IASB intends to designate its future standards as International Financial Reporting Standards, or IFRSs. Standards issued prior to 2002 are identified as International Accounting Standards, or IASs. In this Preface, the term IFRS is used to refer to both IFRSs and IASs.

†*Editor's note: The revised standard was issued in December 2003. Despite the statement made in the draft, IAS 23 has been revised further and, with effect for accounting periods beginning on or after 1 January 2009, the capitalisation of qualifying interest will be mandatory.*

‡*The capitalisation of finance costs is dealt with in FRS 15, whereas it is a separate IFRS.*

of the asset received). The only exception to the requirement to use fair value (using instead the carrying amount of the asset given up) is where fair value cannot be determined reliably. At present IAS 16 has an exception for exchanges of similar assets that have a similar use in the same line of business and a similar fair value. Where the adoption of a fair value measurement represents a change of policy, it does not, however, apply retrospectively.*

Donated assets

FRS 15 specifically addresses the treatment of donated assets received by charities. The international exposure draft does not address this issue.   **6**

Depreciation

The general principles in the proposed IAS 16 and FRS 15 as regards depreciation are   **7** broadly the same, with the following exception in respect of residual values. Where residual values are material, both standards require them to be reviewed at each balance sheet date. The proposed IAS 16 states that the residual value should be revised using current prices at the date of revision; FRS 15 generally requires prices at the date of acquisition or latest valuation to be used, in order to provide a consistent basis for the recomputation of depreciation.

IAS 16 and FRS 15 both state that subsequent expenditure on assets does not negate   **8** the need to recognise depreciation. However, FRS 15 requires annual impairment reviews to be carried out on assets where no depreciation is charged because it would be immaterial or where the remaining useful life is greater than 50 years. This requirement was introduced into FRS 15 because where either no depreciation is charged or the depreciation period is very long, there is a greater risk that the asset's recoverable amount will fall below the carrying amounts in the future. FRS 15 also gives guidance on when uncharged depreciation may be regarded as immaterial. IAS 16 does not include equivalent requirements and guidance.

Renewals accounting

FRS 15 includes specific industry guidance as regards the use of renewals accounting   **9** as a method of estimating the depreciation that should be charged on certain infrastructure assets. IAS 16, in not addressing renewals accounting, does not allow any departure from the principle that the depreciation expense is determined by reference to an asset's depreciable amount (ie cost less residual value for assets carried at historical cost).

REVALUATION OF ASSETS

The international exposure draft and FRS 15 both give entities the option of revaluing   **10** property, plant and equipment assets. Where a policy of revaluation is adopted, both require all assets of the same class to be revalued and both require revaluations to be kept up to date. However, there are a number of differences between the requirements, as described below. It is beyond the scope of this preface to elaborate all the arguments supporting the positions taken in FRS 15; a fuller exposition can be found in Appendix IV to FRS 15 'The Development of the FRS'.

The IASB is also proposing, as a consequence of this proposal, that IAS 38, 'Intangible Assets', should be amended to require all exchanges of intangible assets to be measured at fair value, except when the fair value of neither of the assets exchanged can be determined reliably.

Basis of valuation

11   Perhaps the most important difference of principle is that the international exposure draft requires revaluation to *fair value*, whereas FRS 15 requires revaluation to *current value*.

12   IAS 16 states that the fair value of land and buildings, plant and equipment is usually its market value. Where there is no evidence of market value because of the asset's specialised nature, depreciated replacement cost should be used instead.

13   FRS 15, on the other hand, defines current value in terms of the 'value to the business' model, which is the valuation model that the ASB has preferred hitherto for including assets at current values. The value to the business model seeks to provide a value that is relevant to economic decision-making, being the loss that the entity would suffer if it were deprived of the asset. Under the value to the business model, current value is the lower of replacement cost and recoverable amount. FRS 15 reflects this valuation basis by requiring:

(a)   non-specialised properties to be valued on the basis of existing use value (EUV), with the addition of notional directly attributable acquisition costs where material;

(b)   specialised properties to be valued on the basis of depreciated replacement cost; and

(c)   properties surplus to an entity's requirements to be valued on the basis of open market value (OMV), with a deduction, where material, for expected directly attributable selling costs.

Where OMV is materially different from EUV, the reasons for the difference should be disclosed in the notes to the accounts.

14   FRS 15, therefore, differs from IAS 16 in requiring non-specialised properties to be valued at EUV. IAS 16 states that fair value is usually 'market value', which many would take to be OMV. An important practical effect of the difference arises where OMV is greater than EUV because, say, it reflects the possibility of the property being developed for an alternative use. FRS 15 does not permit the higher value for alternative use to be reflected in an entity's balance sheet (unless the property is surplus to the entity's requirements), although it does require information about the higher value to be disclosed in the notes. IAS 16 does not restrict to EUV the value that is reflected in the balance sheet. It is also possible for OMV to be less than EUV, for example, where a property has been adapted to the needs of the current occupier and there is little prospect of finding a buyer in the market who could use those adaptations. In such a case, IAS 16 would require OMV to be used (unless the property were regarded as specialised, in which case, as explained above, depreciated replacement cost would be used).

Frequency of valuations

15   IAS 16 and FRS 15 both reflect the objective that asset values should be current at each balance sheet date. FRS 15 requires 5-yearly full valuations, with interim updates in between. IAS 16 does not specify a maximum period between revaluations; it requires revaluations to be undertaken as frequently as is necessary to ensure that fair values do not differ materially from carrying values—although it does indicate that annual revaluation may be necessary for assets that experience significant and volatile changes in fair value and that revaluation every three or five years may be sufficient for assets that experience only insignificant changes in fair value.

However, IAS 16 contains less detailed requirements and guidance in respect of the **16** basis for valuations. For example, the following specific guidance in FRS 15 is not reflected in the international exposure draft:

- the requirement to use an external valuer at least once every [xxx] years (although both IAS 16 and FRS 15 require the use of qualified valuers for property);
- detailed guidance regarding the process of performing full and interim valuations;
- guidance on an appropriate index for use by directors in valuing plant and machinery;
- the requirement to take account of notional directly attributable acquisition or selling costs in the valuation where material;
- detailed guidance on the valuation of properties valued on a trading basis and the treatment of specialised 'adaptation works'.

Reporting revaluation gains and losses

Revaluation losses may in some cases be reported differently under the international **17** exposure draft than they would be reported under FRS 15:

(a) IAS 16 requires any revaluation loss that exceeds an existing revaluation surplus in respect of an asset to be recognised as an expense in the profit and loss account. FRS 15 requires a revaluation loss that exceeds an existing revaluation surplus in respect of an asset to be recognised in the statement of total recognised gains and losses to the extent that the asset's recoverable amount is greater than its revalued amount (ie there is no impairment). The IAS treatment has the advantage of being simpler to apply, although the UK's treatment is consistent with the value to the business model.

(b) IAS 16 requires any revaluation loss to be charged to equity (equivalent to the statement of total recognised gains and losses) to the extent that there is an existing revaluation surplus in respect of the asset. FRS 15 requires any revaluation loss that is clearly caused by the consumption of economic benefits (ie an impairment) to be charged as an expense in the profit and loss account, regardless of whether there is an existing revaluation surplus in respect of the asset.

FRS 15 (paragraph 71) gives a special treatment to gains and losses on revaluation of **18** assets held by insurance companies and insurance groups (including assets of the long-term business), as part of their insurance operations. For these, revaluation changes are required to be included in the profit and loss account rather than under the general revaluation rules. There is no corresponding special treatment in IAS 16. The ASB proposes, as a transitional measure, that the present exemption in FRS 15 should be retained in a new UK standard based on the international exposure draft pending the outcome of the IASB's projects on insurance and performance reporting.

TRANSITIONAL ARRANGEMENTS

FRS 15 contained a special transitional arrangement for entities that had carried **19** assets at values reflecting previous revaluations and elected not to adopt a policy of revaluation when they first applied FRS 15. FRS 15 permitted such entities to retain the (previously revalued) book amounts instead of restating the carrying amounts at depreciated historical cost. IAS 16 does not include any corresponding transitional arrangement. The ASB proposes to include in a new UK standard a transitional arrangement equivalent to that in FRS 15; this would allow an entity that does not adopt a policy of revaluation and adopted the transitional arrangement on the first application of FRS 15 to continue to recognise its assets at the carrying amounts under that transitional arrangement. The ASB will review this proposal in the light of the IASB's separate work on the first-time application of IFRSs.*

BORROWING COSTS – MAIN CHANGES PROPOSED TO EXISTING UK REQUIREMENTS

20   IAS 23 permits entities to choose whether or not to capitalise borrowing costs, provided the policy is applied consistently. In this it is consistent with FRS 15. The IASB has considered this issue as part of its 'Improvements project' and has indicated that for the purposes of improving IAS 23 and based on the conceptual arguments, it was inclined towards requiring all borrowing costs to be reported as an expense as incurred. However, the IASB also noted that requiring expense treatment would not achieve convergence between IAS 23 and the accounting standards of its partner national standard-setters. After discussing the issue with them, the IASB decided against dealing with the issue as part of the improvements project. The ASB has argued that the topic raises fundamental issues of measurement and accounting for finance costs and, therefore, supports maintaining the optional capitalisation of finance costs until an internationally acceptable approach is agreed. The IASB has indicated that it will consider, as part of its regular evaluation of potential agenda topics, a project that deals with how to measure an asset on initial recognition.†

21   FRS 15's requirements in respect of the capitalisation of finance costs were modelled on IAS 23 and, therefore, the two standards are similar in most respects, even adopting much of the same wording. They both permit the optional capitalisation of interest. Although the style of the IFRS is to present the optional treatments as the 'benchmark treatment' and the 'allowed alternative treatment', this does not imply that one treatment is preferred to the other. There are, however, a number of differences between the standards.

DEFINITION OF BORROWING COSTS

22   IAS 23's definition of borrowing costs (paragraph 5(e)) admits exchange differences arising from foreign currency borrowings 'to the extent that they are regarded as an adjustment to interest costs'. FRS 15's definition of finance costs does not include exchange differences. The ASB does not believe that capitalisation of exchange differences is appropriate and proposes to omit exchange differences from the UK standard's definition of borrowing costs.

SCOPE

23   The scope of IAS 23 is wider than that of FRS 15. IAS 23 applies to 'qualifying assets', ie assets that necessarily take a substantial period of time to get ready for their intended use or sale. Therefore, as well as covering interest capitalisation on tangible fixed assets, it also applies to certain inventories.

---

*The IASB indicated in the March 2002 edition of 'IASB Update' that it had tentatively agreed that an entity that has previously revalued items of property, plant and equipment to an amount that is broadly comparable to fair value determined under IFRSs may treat such amounts as deemed cost under IFRSs.

†**Editor's note**: The revised version of IAS 23 effective for accounting periods beginning on or after 1 January 2009 will make the capitalisation of qualifying interest mandatory.

BORROWING COSTS ELIGIBLE FOR CAPITALISATION

IAS 23 (paragraphs 15 and 16) indicates that if specific borrowings are raised to fund   **24**
a qualifying asset, the amount of borrowing costs eligible for capitalisation is the
actual borrowing costs less any investment income received from the temporary
reinvestment of unutilised borrowings. FRS 15 only permits the capitalisation of the
interest arising on the amount of borrowings that has been spent on the asset to date;
interest paid and received on the unused and reinvested portion is recognised in the
profit and loss account.

DISCLOSURES

Where a policy of capitalisation of finance costs is adopted, FRS 15 requires two   **25**
additional disclosures that IAS 23 does not:

- the aggregate amount of finance costs included in the cost of tangible fixed assets
  (this is also a requirement of the Companies Act 1985); and
- the amount of finance costs recognised in the profit and loss account during the
  period.

DIFFERENCES BETWEEN PROPOSED UK REQUIREMENTS AND PROPOSED IFRSS

The texts of the draft FRSs are the same as the proposed IAS 16 and IAS 23 with the   **26**
following exceptions:

Property, plant and equipment

(a) The [draft] FRS includes a paragraph on scope, applying the standard to all
financial statements that are intended to give a true and fair view of a reporting
entity's financial position and profit or loss (or income and expenditure), except
that reporting entities applying the Financial Reporting Standard for Smaller
Entities currently applicable are exempt.
(b) The text in paragraphs 37 and 38 concerning the reporting of gains and losses
on revaluation is revised to reflect the use of the statement of total recognised
gains and losses in UK accounting standards.
(c) Paragraph 39A has been added to preserve the present exemption in FRS 15
from the requirements concerning the reporting of gains or losses on revaluation in respect of certain assets held by insurance companies and insurance
groups (see paragraph 18 above).
(d) References to IFRSs have been deleted or replaced with references to relevant
UK accounting standards.
(e) A transitional provision has been added (paragraph 66B) relating to entities
that do not adopt a policy of revaluation (see paragraph 19 above).

Borrowing costs

(f) Paragraph 5(e), which allows certain exchange differences to be included in
borrowing costs eligible for capitalisation, has been removed (see paragraph 22
above).
(g) The [draft] FRS includes a paragraph on scope, applying the standard to all
financial statements that are intended to give a true and fair view of a reporting
entity's financial position and profit or loss (or income and expenditure), except
that reporting entities applying the Financial Reporting Standard for Smaller
Entities currently applicable are exempt.

(h) References to IFRSs have been replaced where applicable with references to relevant UK accounting standards.

(i) The original transitional provisions in IAS 23 have been removed.

AMENDMENTS TO OTHER UK STANDARDS

27 The replacement of FRS 15 by the standards set out in the exposure draft would require consequential amendments to FRS 11 *Impairment of Fixed Assets and Goodwill* (concerning reporting impairment losses on revalued assets) in order to reflect the differences in reporting revaluation losses referred to in paragraph 17 above. Minor consequential changes would be required to UITF Abstracts 24 *Accounting for start-up costs* and 29 *Website development costs*. UITF Abstract 23 *Application of the transitional rules in* FRS 15' would be withdrawn.

IMPLEMENTATION

28 At the request of the IASB, the ASB is participating in a joint project with other national standard-setters from jurisdictions where the revaluation of fixed assets is permitted (referred to as the 'Revaluation Group'*). The project is seeking to con-verge the approaches to accounting for revaluations in those jurisdictions. The Group will provide recommendations to the IASB on a convergence model that should be adopted internationally. However, the IASB has indicated that its time-table for the improvements project does not allow for any further changes to IAS 16 that may result from the Group's project to be included in the IASB's current revision of IAS 16.

29 As explained earlier, the *current value* model that is supported by the ASB and specified in FRS 15 differs in some significant respects from the *fair value* model that is specified in IAS 16 and in the accounting standards of other members of the Group. The ASB believes that it is appropriate to continue to argue the case for IAS 16 to be amended to incorporate principles of revaluation similar to those in FRS 15.

30 If, by the time the IASB issues the revised IAS 16, it becomes clear that further changes to the standard are unlikely in the near future, the ASB proposes to issue new UK standards, based on the revised IAS 16 and IAS 23, at that time.

31 However, if it becomes clear that further changes to IAS 16 are likely as a result of the revaluation project, the ASB would prefer to wait until that further revision was complete before issuing new standards. The ASB believes that it would be preferable if these IFRSs were incorporated into UK standards in their entirety, and in one step, rather than being adopted on a piecemeal basis by, say, adopting the standards minus the revaluation requirements as a first stage and adopting the revaluation requirements at a later stage.

32 The ASB would particularly welcome respondents' views on these implementation issues.

UK LAW, EU LAW AND INTERNATIONAL STANDARDS

33 EU Ministers have proposed that from 1 January 2005, all listed companies in the EU should prepare their consolidated financial statements in accordance with adopted international accounting standards. A draft Regulation to this effect is at a

---

The Revaluation Group comprises representatives from the standard-setting bodies of Australia, New Zealand, South Africa and the UK and the IASB.

late stage of negotiation and EU Ministers are expected to approve it shortly. The intention is that IFRSs will form the basis of those adopted international accounting standards.

After wide discussion with interested parties, the ASB has indicated its intention to **34** pursue a programme of work to align UK accounting standards with IFRSs wherever practicable. The effect of this is that the substance of IFRSs will apply in the UK not only to the group financial statements of listed companies but also to individual financial statements and unlisted companies. However, the ASB will consider the option of retaining a UK standard, or modifying an IFRS in its wider application, for example if it appears likely that the cost of extending an unmodified IFRS more widely would exceed the benefit.

The Government has said that it may wish to extend the Regulation to individual **35** financial statements and unlisted companies from 2005 or later. Ministers intend to consult on this once the Regulation is agreed.

The legal requirements for UK and Irish companies relevant to accounting for **36** property, plant and equipment are summarised in the Appendix to the [draft] FRS.

QUESTIONS FOR RESPONDENTS

The ASB is requesting comments on any aspect of the FRED by 16 September 2002 – **37** the same date as the IASB has set for comments on its proposed revisions to IAS 16.

The ASB would welcome comments in particular on the following: **38**

ASB(i) Do you agree with the proposal to issue new UK standards on property, plant and equipment and borrowing costs when the IASB issues the revised IAS 16, unless it becomes clear that further changes to IAS 16 are likely by 2005 as a result of the revaluation project?

ASB(ii) As explained in paragraph 7 above, the international exposure draft on property, plant and equipment proposes that residual values used in the calculation of depreciable amount should be reviewed at each balance sheet date and revised to reflect current estimates. FRS 15 generally requires pr ices at the date of acquisition or latest valuation to be used; hence, depreciation expense on a historical cost basis is not reduced by inflation in residual values. Do you agree or disagree with the proposed international approach?

ASB(iii) IAS 16 does not address the use of renewals accounting in respect of certain infrastructure assets. Do you believe that the absence of the guidance in FRS 15 would prevent entities from using renewals accounting as a method of estimating depreciation? Should UK entities be permitted to continue to use renewals accounting?

ASB(iv) What are your views on the differences between the requirements of FRS 15 and IAS 16 concerning revaluations as described in paragraphs 10 to 17 above?

ASB(v) Are there any other aspects of the differences between the proposed standards and current UK accounting requirements that you wish to comment on?

ASB(vi) Do you agree with the ASB's proposal, as a transitional measure (see paragraph 18 above), that the present exemption in FRS 15 in respect of insurance companies should be retained in a new UK standard based on IAS 16 revised pending the outcome of the IASB's projects on insurance and performance reporting?

ASB(vii) The transitional arrangements for the first-time application of FRS 15 allowed an entity that does not adopt a policy of revaluation to retain carrying amounts reflecting previous revaluations instead of restating the carrying amounts to historical cost (see paragraph 19 above). Do you believe that a transitional arrangement should be included in a new UK standard to allow entities that adopted FRS 15's transitional arrangement to continue to recognise the carrying amounts under that arrangement?

ASB(viii) Do you believe that ASB should consider any other transitional arrangements?

ASB(ix) Are there any other aspects of the draft standard on property, plant and equipment that the ASB should request the IASB to review when finalising the revised IAS 16?

ASB(x) Do you agree that the capitalisation of borrowing costs should remain optional? If you had to choose between mandatory capitalisation and prohibition of capitalisation, which would you support and why?

ASB(xi) Do you agree that paragraph 5(e) of IAS 23, which allows certain exchange differences to be capitalised, should be deleted in the draft standard on borrowing costs?

ASB(xii) What are your views on the difference between IAS 23 and FRS 15 referred to in paragraph 24 above concerning borrowing costs eligible for capitalisation?

ASB(xiii) Do you have any comments on IAS 23 that you wish the ASB to bring to the IASB's attention?

39   The IASB has asked commentators to respond to the following questions on the proposed changes to IAS 16:

IASB(i) Do you agree that all exchanges of items of *property, plant and equipment* should be measured at fair value, except when the fair value of neither of the assets exchanged can be determined reliably (see paragraphs 21 and 21A of the [draft] FRS on property, plant and equipment)?

IASB(ii) Do you agree that all exchanges of *intangible assets* should be measured at fair value, except when the fair value of neither of the assets exchanged can be determined reliably?

IASB(iii) Do you agree that depreciation of an item of property, plant and equipment should not cease when it becomes temporarily idle or is retired from active use and held for disposal (see paragraph 59 of the [draft] FRS on property, plant and equipment)?

[Draft] Financial Reporting Standard: Property, Plant and Equipment

[Draft] Financial Reporting Standard – 'Property, plant and equipment' is set out in paragraphs 1–68B.

The Statement of Standard Accounting Practice, which comprises the paragraphs set in bold type, should be read in the context of the Objective, the definitions set out in paragraph 6 and also of the Foreword to Accounting Standards and the Statement of Principles for Financial Reporting currently in issue.

The explanatory paragraphs contained in the [draft] FRS shall be regarded as part of the Statement of Standard Accounting Practice insofar as they assist in interpreting that statement.

This draft is issued by the Accounting Standards Board for comment. It should be noted that the draft may be modified in the light of comment received before being issued in final form.

OBJECTIVE

The objective of this Standard is to prescribe the accounting treatment for property, plant and equipment. The principal issues in accounting for property, plant and equipment are the timing of recognition of the assets, the determination of their carrying amounts and the depreciation charges to be recognised in relation to them.

This Standard requires an item of property, plant and equipment to be recognised as an asset when it satisfies the definition and recognition criteria for an asset in the Framework for the Preparation and Presentation of Financial Statements.

SCOPE

This Standard shall be applied in accounting for property, plant and equipment except when another Standard requires or permits a different accounting treatment.　　1

This Standard applies to all financial statements that are intended to give a true and fair view of a reporting entity's financial position and profit or loss (or income and expenditure), except that reporting entities applying the Financial Reporting Standard for Smaller Entities currently applicable are exempt. [ASB].　　1A

This Standard does not apply to:　　2

(a) biological assets related to agricultural activity (see IAS 41, Agriculture); and
(b) mineral rights and mineral reserves such as oil, natural gas and similar non-regenerative resources.

However, this Standard applies to property, plant and equipment used to develop or maintain the assets described in (a) and (b).

[Deleted]*　　3

*Note: paragraphs that are identified as deleted in this manner identify paragraphs included in the existing version of IAS 16 that the IASB has proposed should be deleted as a consequence of their improvements project.

4   An entity applies this Standard to property being constructed or developed for future use as investment property, because the property does not yet satisfy the definition of investment property in ssap 19, *Accounting for investment properties* IAS 40, Investment Property. Once the construction or development is complete, the property becomes investment property and the entity applies ssap 19 IAS 40. ssap 19 IAS 40 also applies to investment property that is being redeveloped for continued future use as investment property. Using the cost model permitted for investment property under IAS 40 requires use of the benchmark treatment in this Standard.

5   [Deleted]

DEFINITIONS

6   **The following terms are used in this Standard with the meanings specified:**

Property, plant and equipment are tangible assets that:

(a)   **are held by an entity for use in the production or supply of goods or services, for rental to others, or for administrative purposes; and**

(b)   **are expected to be used during more than one period.**

Depreciation is the systematic allocation of the depreciable amount of an asset over its useful life.

Depreciable amount is the cost of an asset, or other amount substituted for cost in the financial statements, less its residual value.

Useful life is either:

(a)   **the period of time over which an asset is expected to be used by the entity; or**

(b)   **the number of production or similar units expected to be obtained from the asset by the entity.**

Cost is the amount of cash or cash equivalents paid or the fair value of the other consideration given to acquire an asset at the time of its acquisition or construction.

The residual value of an asset is the estimated amount that the entity would currently obtain from disposal of the asset, after deducting the estimated costs of disposal, if the asset were already of the age and in the condition expected at the end of its useful life.

Fair value is the amount for which an asset could be exchanged between knowledgeable, willing parties in an arm's length transaction.

An impairment loss is the amount by which the carrying amount of an asset exceeds its recoverable amount.

Carrying amount is the amount at which an asset is recognised after deducting any accumulated depreciation and accumulated impairment losses.

RECOGNITION OF PROPERTY, PLANT AND EQUIPMENT

7   **An item of property, plant and equipment shall be recognised as an asset when, and only when:**

(a)   **it is probable that future economic benefits associated with the asset will flow to the entity; and**

(b)   the cost of the asset or, when the asset is carried at a revalued amount, the fair value of the asset, can be measured reliably.

Property, plant and equipment is often a major portion of the total assets of an   **8** entity, and therefore is significant in the presentation of its financial position. Furthermore, the determination of whether an expenditure represents an asset or an expense can have a significant effect on an entity's profit or loss.

[Deleted]   **9**

[Deleted]   **10**

In identifying what constitutes a separate item of property, plant and equipment,   **11** judgement is required in applying the criteria in the definition to specific circumstances or specific types of entities. It may be appropriate to aggregate individually insignificant items, such as moulds, tools and dies, and to apply the criteria to the aggregate value. Most spare parts and servicing equipment usually are carried as inventory and recognised as an expense as consumed. However, major spare parts and stand-by equipment qualify as property, plant and equipment when the entity expects to use them during more than one period. Similarly, if the spare parts and servicing equipment can be used only in connection with an item of property, plant and equipment and their use is expected to be irregular, they are accounted for as property, plant and equipment and are depreciated over a period not exceeding the useful life of the related asset.

An entity allocates the amount initially recognised in respect of an asset to its   **12** component parts and accounts for each component separately when the components have different useful lives or provide benefits to the entity in a different pattern. In those circumstances, it is necessary to use different depreciation rates and methods. For example, the airframe and engines of an aircraft are treated as separate depreciable assets if they have different useful lives.

Property, plant and equipment may be acquired for safety or environmental reasons.   **13** The acquisition of such property, plant and equipment, although not directly increasing the future economic benefits of any particular existing item of property, plant and equipment may be necessary for the entity to obtain the future economic benefits from its other assets. When this is the case, such acquisitions of property, plant and equipment qualify for recognition as assets, because they enable future economic benefits from related assets to be derived by the entity in excess of what could be derived if they had not been acquired. However, the resulting carrying amount of such an asset and related assets is reviewed for impairment under FRS 11, *Impairment of Fixed Assets and Goodwill* IAS 36, Impairment of Assets. For example, a chemical manufacturer may install new chemical handling processes to comply with environmental requirements on the production and storage of dangerous chemicals; related plant enhancements are recognised as an asset because, without them, the entity is unable to manufacture and sell chemicals.

INITIAL MEASUREMENT OF PROPERTY, PLANT AND EQUIPMENT

An item of property, plant and equipment that qualifies for recognition as an asset shall   **14** **initially be measured at its cost.**

Components of Cost

15   The cost of an item of property, plant and equipment comprises:

(a)   its purchase price, including import duties and non-refundable purchase taxes, after deducting any trade discounts and rebates; and

(b)   any directly attributable costs to bring the asset to the location and working condition necessary for it to be capable of operating in the manner intended by management, including costs of testing whether the asset is functioning properly, after deducting the net proceeds from selling any items produced when bringing the asset to that location and condition (such as samples produced when testing equipment).

15A   Examples of directly attributable costs are:

(a)   costs of employee benefits (as defined in IAS 19, Employee Benefits) arising directly from the construction or acquisition of the item of property, plant and equipment;

(b)   costs of site preparation;

(c)   initial delivery and handling costs;

(d)   installation and assembly costs; and

(e)   professional fees.

16   When payment for an item of property, plant and equipment is deferred beyond normal credit terms, its cost is the cash price equivalent; the difference between that amount and the total payments is recognised as interest expense over the period of credit unless it is capitalised in accordance with the allowed alternative treatment in the [draft] FRS IAS 23, *Borrowing Costs.*

16A   If an item of property, plant and equipment is acquired in exchange for equity instruments of the entity, the cost of the item of property, plant and equipment is the fair value of the equity instruments issued. The fair value of the item received is used to measure its cost if it is more clearly evident than the fair value of the equity instruments issued.

17   Examples of costs that are not a component of the cost of property, plant and equipment are:

(a)   costs of opening a new facility;

(b)   costs of introducing a new product or service (including costs of advertising and promotional activities);

(c)   costs of conducting business in a new location or with a new class of customer (including costs of staff training); and

(d)   administration and other general overhead costs.

These costs are excluded because they are not a part of the asset's purchase price, and cannot be attributed directly to bringing the asset to the location and working condition necessary for it to be capable of operating in the manner intended by management.

17A   Because capitalisation of costs ceases when an item of property, plant and equipment is in the location and working condition necessary for it to be capable of operating in the manner intended by management, costs incurred in using or redeploying assets (as distinct from improving the assets standard of performance) are excluded from the cost of those assets. For example, the following costs are excluded from the cost of property, plant and equipment:

(a) costs incurred while assets capable of operating in the manner intended by management have yet to be brought into use or are operated at less than full capacity;

(b) initial operating losses, such as those incurred while demand for the assets outputs builds up; and

(c) costs of relocating or reorganising part or all of the entity's operations.

Some operations occur in connection with the construction or development of an **17B** item of property, plant and equipment, but are not necessary to bring the asset to the location and working condition necessary for it to be capable of operating in the manner intended by management. These incidental operations may occur before or during the construction or development activities. For example, income may be earned through using a building site as a car park until construction commences. Because incidental operations are not necessary to bring an asset to the location and working condition necessary for it to be capable of operating in the manner intended by management, the income and related expenses of incidental operations are recognised in profit or loss for the period, and included in their respective classifications of income and expense in the income statement.

The cost of a self-constructed asset is determined using the same principles as for an **18** acquired asset. If an entity makes similar assets for sale in the normal course of business, the cost of the asset is usually the same as the cost of producing the assets for sale (see [draft] FRS IAS 2, *Inventories*). Therefore, any internal profits are eliminated in arriving at such costs. Similarly, the cost of abnormal amounts of wasted material, labour, or other resources incurred in the production of a self-constructed asset is not included in the cost of the asset. The [draft] FRS, *Borrowing Costs*, IAS 23 establishes criteria that need to be satisfied before interest costs can be recognised as a cost of property, plant and equipment

The cost of an asset held by a lessee under a finance lease is determined using the **19** principles set out in SSAP 21, *Accounting for leases and hire purchase contracts* IAS 17, *Leases*.

The carrying amount of property, plant and equipment may be reduced by applic- **20** able government grants in accordance with SSAP 4, *Accounting for government grants* IAS 20, Accounting for Government Grants and Disclosure of Government Assistance.

Costs to dismantle and remove an asset and restore its site

The cost of an item of property, plant and equipment under paragraph 15 includes **20A** the costs of dismantling and removing the asset and restoring the site on which that asset is located. Those costs may be incurred when the asset is initially acquired or in subsequent periods, and in either case are depreciated over the remainder of the asset's useful life. They are measured in accordance with FRS 12 IAS 37, *Provisions, Contingent Liabilities and Contingent Assets*.

In those situations in which the asset to be measured is land, the costs referred to in **20B** paragraph 20A are depreciated over the period of benefits obtained by incurring those costs. In some cases, the land itself may have a limited useful life, in which case it is depreciated in a manner that reflects the benefits to be derived from it.

Exchanges of Assets

21   An item of property, plant and equipment may be acquired in exchange or part exchange for another item of property, plant and equipment or other asset. Except when paragraph 21A applies, the cost of such an item is measured at the fair value of the asset given up, adjusted by the amount of any cash or cash equivalents transferred. The fair value of the asset received is used to measure its cost if it is more clearly evident than the fair value of the asset given up.

21A   The cost of an item of property, plant and equipment acquired in exchange for a similar asset is measured at the carrying amount of the asset given up when the fair value of neither of the assets exchanged can be determined reliably. The entity will be unable to determine reliably the fair value of an item of property, plant and equipment when comparable market transactions are infrequent and alternative estimates of fair value (for example, based on discounted cash flow projections) cannot be calculated.

22   [Deleted]

REPLACING OR RENEWING A COMPONENT

22A   **Expenditure incurred in replacing or renewing a component of an item of property, plant and equipment shall be accounted for as the acquisition of a separate asset, and the carrying amount of the replaced or renewed component asset shall be written off.**

22B   Major components of some items of property, plant and equipment may require replacement at regular intervals. For example, a furnace may require relining after a specified number of hours of usage, or aircraft interiors such as seats and galleys may require replacement several times during the life of the airframe. The components are accounted for as separate assets because they have useful lives different from those of the items of property, plant and equipment to which they relate. Therefore, provided the recognition criteria in paragraph 7 are satisfied, the expenditure incurred in replacing or renewing the component is accounted for as the acquisition of a separate asset and the carrying amount of the replaced asset is written off.

22C   A condition of continuing to operate some items of property, plant and equipment (for example, an aircraft) is performing regular major inspections for faults regardless of whether components of the item are replaced. The costs of a major inspection of an item of property, plant and equipment may be a separate component of the cost of that item. In these circumstances, when each major inspection is performed, its cost is capitalised as a replacement component if the recognition criteria in paragraph 7 are satisfied, and any remaining carrying amount of the replaced component (the inspection component, as distinct from physical components) is written off.

22D   A separate component may be identified in respect of a major inspection regardless of whether the component was invoiced separately or identified specifically in the transaction in which the item was acquired or constructed. When necessary, the estimated cost of a future similar inspection may be used as an indication of the cost of the existing inspection component when the item was acquired or constructed.

SUBSEQUENT EXPENDITURE

23   **Subsequent expenditure relating to an item of property, plant and equipment that has been recognised, other than expenditure incurred in replacing or renewing a component**

of such an item, shall be added to the carrying amount of the asset when, and only when, it is probable that the expenditure increases the future economic benefits embodied in the asset in excess of its standard of performance assessed immediately before the expenditure was made.

All subsequent expenditure that fails the criteria for capitalisation in paragraphs 22A and 23 shall be recognised as an expense in the period in which it is incurred.   **23A**

Expenditure incurred in replacing or renewing a component of an item of property, plant and equipment is accounted for as the acquisition of a separate asset under paragraph 22A, and is not subsequent expenditure relating to an item of property, plant and equipment.   **23B**

Examples of subsequent expenditure on property, plant and equipment that results in increased future economic benefits include: **24**

(a)   modification of an item of plant to extend its remaining useful life or to increase its capacity;

(b)   upgrading machine parts to achieve a substantial improvement in the quality of output; and

(c)   development of a new production process enabling a substantial reduction in operating costs.

Whether expenditure incurred subsequent to the acquisition of an item of property, plant and equipment increases the future economic benefits embodied in the asset depends on the circumstances taken into account in assessing the asset's standard of performance (including the level of maintenance assumed in the most recent estimate of its useful life) immediately before the expenditure. For example, when the carrying amount of the item of property, plant and equipment has been written down to recognise an impairment, the subsequent expenditure is capitalised to the extent that it causes the impairment loss to be reversed. Subsequent expenditure also is capitalised when the purchase price of an asset already reflects the entity's need to incur that expenditure to bring the asset to its working condition. An example of this is the acquisition of a building requiring renovation. In such circumstances, the subsequent expenditure is added to the asset s carrying amount.   **25**

Expenditure on immaterial replacements or renewals of property, plant and equipment may be treated as repairs and recognised as an expense when incurred.   **26**

[Deleted]   **27**

MEASUREMENT SUBSEQUENT TO INITIAL RECOGNITION

Benchmark Treatment

Subsequent to initial recognition as an asset, an item of property, plant and equipment shall be carried at its cost less any accumulated depreciation and any accumulated impairment losses.   **28**

Allowed Alternative Treatment

Subsequent to initial recognition as an asset, an item of property, plant and equipment shall be carried at a revalued amount, being its fair value at the date of the revaluation less any subsequent accumulated depreciation and subsequent accumulated impairment losses. Revaluations shall be made with sufficient regularity that the carrying amount   **29**

does not differ materially from that which would be determined using fair value at the balance sheet date.

Revaluations

30   The fair value of land and buildings is usually its market value. This value is determined by appraisal normally undertaken by professionally qualified valuers.

31   The fair value of items of plant and equipment is usually their market value determined by appraisal. When there is no evidence of market value because of the specialised nature of the plant and equipment and because these items are rarely sold, except as part of a continuing business, they are valued at their depreciated replacement cost.

32   The frequency of revaluations depends upon the movements in the fair values of the items of property, plant and equipment being revalued. When the fair value of a revalued asset differs materially from its carrying amount, a further revaluation is necessary. Some items of property, plant and equipment may experience significant and volatile movements in fair value, thus necessitating annual revaluation. Such frequent revaluations are unnecessary for items of property, plant and equipment with only insignificant movements in fair value. Instead, revaluation every three or five years may be sufficient.

33   When an item of property, plant and equipment is revalued, any accumulated depreciation at the date of the revaluation is either:

(a)   restated proportionately with the change in the gross carrying amount of the asset so that the carrying amount of the asset after revaluation equals its revalued amount. This method is often used when an asset is revalued by means of applying an index to its depreciated replacement cost; or

(b)   eliminated against the gross carrying amount of the asset and the net amount restated to the revalued amount of the asset. For example, this method is often used for buildings that are revalued to their market value.

The amount of the adjustment arising on the restatement or elimination of accumulated depreciation forms part of the increase or decrease in carrying amount that is dealt with in accordance with paragraphs 37 and 38.

34   **When an item of property, plant and equipment is revalued, the entire class of property, plant and equipment to which that asset belongs shall be revalued.**

35   A class of property, plant and equipment is a grouping of assets of a similar nature and use in an entity's operations. The following are examples of separate classes:

(a)   land;
(b)   land and buildings;
(c)   machinery;
(d)   ships;
(e)   aircraft;
(f)   motor vehicles;
(g)   furniture and fixtures; and
(h)   office equipment.

36   The items within a class of property, plant and equipment are revalued simultaneously to avoid selective revaluation of assets and the reporting of amounts in the financial statements that are a mixture of costs and values as at different dates.

However, a class of assets may be revalued on a rolling basis provided revaluation of the class of assets is completed within a short period of time and provided the revaluations are kept up to date.

When an asset's carrying amount is increased as a result of a revaluation, the increase **37** **shall be recognised in the statement of total recognised gains and losses credited directly to equity under the heading of revaluation surplus except that, to the extent that it reverses a revaluation decrease of the same asset previously recognised as an expense, it shall be recognised as income in the profit and loss account.**

When an asset's carrying amount is decreased as a result of a revaluation, the decrease **38** **shall be recognised in the statement of total recognised gains and losses until the carrying amount reaches its depreciated historical cost and, thereafter, in the profit and loss account debited directly against any credit balance existing in the revaluation surplus in respect of that asset and, to the extent that the decrease exceeds that credit balance, it shall be recognised as an expense.**

The revaluation surplus included in equity in respect of an item of property, plant   **39** and equipment may be transferred directly to retained earnings when the asset is derecognised (that is, eliminated from the balance sheet). This may involve transferring the whole of the surplus when the asset is retired or disposed of. However, some of the surplus may be transferred as the asset is used by the entity; in such a case, the amount of the surplus transferred would be the difference between depreciation based on the revalued carrying amount of the asset and depreciation based on the asset's original cost. Transfers from revaluation surplus to retained earnings are not made through the income statement.

Paragraphs 37–39 do not apply to assets held by insurance companies and insurance **39A** **groups (including assets of the long-term business), as part of their insurance operations, where revaluation changes are included in the profit and loss account. [ASB].**

The effects on taxes on income, if any, resulting from the revaluation of property,   **40** plant and equipment are recognised and disclosed in accordance with FRS 19, *Deferred Tax* IAS 12, *Income Taxes*.

Depreciation

The depreciable amount of an item of property, plant and equipment shall be allocated **41** **on a systematic basis over its useful life. The depreciation method used shall reflect the pattern in which the asset's future economic benefits are expected to be consumed by the entity. The depreciation charge for each period shall be recognised as an expense unless it is included in the carrying amount of another asset.**

As the future economic benefits embodied in an asset are consumed by the entity, the   **42** carrying amount of the asset is reduced to reflect this consumption, normally by recognising an expense for depreciation. Depreciation is recognised even if the value of the asset exceeds its carrying amount.

The future economic benefits embodied in an item of property, plant and equipment   **43** are consumed by the entity principally through the use of the asset. However, other factors such as technical or commercial obsolescence and wear and tear while an asset remains idle often result in the diminution of the economic benefits that might have been expected to be obtained from the asset. Consequently, all the following factors are considered in determining the useful life of an asset:

(a)   the expected usage of the asset by the entity. Usage is assessed by reference to the asset's expected capacity or physical output;

(b)   the expected physical wear and tear, which depends on operational factors such as the number of shifts for which the asset is to be used and the repair and maintenance programme of the entity, and the care and maintenance of the asset while idle;

(c)   technical or commercial obsolescence arising from changes or improvements in production, or from a change in the market demand for the product or service output of the asset; and

(d)   legal or similar limits on the use of the asset, such as the expiry dates of related leases.

44   The useful life of an asset is defined in terms of the asset's expected utility to the entity. The asset management policy of an entity may involve the disposal of assets after a specified time or after consumption of a certain proportion of the future economic benefits embodied in the asset. Therefore, the useful life of an asset may be shorter than its economic life. The estimation of the useful life of an item of property, plant and equipment is a matter of judgement based on the experience of the entity with similar assets.

45   Land and buildings are separable assets and are dealt with separately for accounting purposes, even when they are acquired together. With certain exceptions, such as quarries and sites used for landfill, land has an unlimited useful life and therefore is not depreciated. Buildings have a limited useful life and therefore are depreciable assets. An increase in the value of the land on which a building stands does not affect the determination of the useful life of the building.

46   The depreciable amount of an asset is determined after deducting the residual value of the asset. In practice, the residual value of an asset is often insignificant and therefore is immaterial in the calculation of the depreciable amount. When the residual value is likely to be material, the residual value is estimated at the date of acquisition and is reviewed as at each balance sheet date. A change in the asset's residual value, other than a change reflected in an impairment loss recognised under FRS 11 IAS 36, *Impairment of Assets*, is accounted for prospectively as an adjustment to future depreciation. An estimate of an asset's residual value is based on the amount recoverable from disposal, at the date of the estimate, of similar assets that have reached the end of their useful lives and have operated under conditions similar to those in which the asset will be used.

47   A variety of depreciation methods can be used to allocate the depreciable amount of an asset on a systematic basis over its useful life. These methods include the straight-line method, the diminishing balance method and the sum-of-the-units method. Straight-line depreciation results in a constant charge over the useful life of the asset. The diminishing balance method results in a decreasing charge over the useful life of the asset. The sum-of-the-units method results in a charge based on the expected use or output of the asset. The method used for an asset is selected based on the expected pattern of consumption of the future economic benefits embodied in the asset, and is applied consistently from period to period unless there is a change in the expected pattern of consumption of those future economic benefits.

48   The depreciation charge for a period usually is recognised as an expense. However, in some circumstances, the future economic benefits embodied in an asset are absorbed by the entity in producing other assets, rather than giving rise to an expense. In this case, the depreciation charge constitutes part of the cost of the other asset and is included in its carrying amount. For example, the depreciation of manufacturing plant and equipment is included in the costs of conversion of inventories (see [draft]

FRS IAS 2, *Inventories*). Similarly, depreciation of property, plant and equipment used for development activities may be included in the cost of an intangible asset recognised under SSAP 13, *Accounting for research and development* IAS 38, *Intangible Assets*.

Review of Useful Life

The useful life of an item of property, plant and equipment shall be reviewed at least at each financial year end and, if expectations of useful life are different from previous estimates, the depreciation rate for the current and future periods shall be adjusted.   **49**

During the life of an asset it may become apparent that the estimate of useful life is inappropriate. For example, the useful life may be extended by subsequent expenditure on the asset that improves the condition of the asset. Alternatively, technological changes or changes in the market for the products may reduce the useful life of the asset. In such cases, the useful life and, therefore, the depreciation rate are adjusted for the current and future periods.   50

The repair and maintenance policy of the entity may also affect the useful life of an asset. The policy may result in an extension of the useful life of the asset or an increase in its residual value. However, the adoption of such a policy does not negate the need to recognise depreciation.   51

Review of Depreciation Method

The depreciation method applied to property, plant and equipment shall be reviewed at least at each financial year end and, if there has been a significant change in the expected pattern of consumption of the future economic benefits embodied in those assets, the method shall be changed to reflect the changed pattern. When such a change in depreciation method is necessary, the change shall be accounted for as a change in an accounting estimate and the depreciation charge for the current and future periods shall be adjusted.   **52**

A change in the depreciation method is a change in the technique used to apply the entity's accounting policy to recognise depreciation as an asset's future economic benefits are consumed. Therefore, it is a change in an accounting estimate.   52A

RECOVERABILITY OF THE CARRYING AMOUNT – IMPAIRMENT LOSSES

To determine whether an item of property, plant and equipment is impaired, an entity applies FRS 11 IAS 36, *Impairment of Assets*. That Standard explains how an entity reviews the carrying amount of its assets, how it determines the recoverable amount of an asset, and when it recognises or reverses an impairment loss.   53

Compensation for Impairments, and Related Replacements

Compensation from third parties for items of property, plant and equipment that were impaired, lost or given up shall, in the period in which it is received, be: 53A

(a)   **included in profit or loss for that period; and**
(b)   **disclosed separately on the face of the income statement or in the notes.**

53B Impairments or losses of items of property, plant and equipment, related claims for or payments of compensation from third parties and any subsequent purchase or construction of replacement assets are separate economic events and are accounted for separately as follows:

(a) impairments of items of property, plant and equipment are recognised under FRS 11 IAS 36; retirements or disposals of items of property, plant and equipment are recognised under paragraphs 55–59 of this Standard;

(b) compensation from third parties for items of property, plant and equipment that were impaired, lost or given up is included in determining profit or loss for the period in which it is received; and

(c) the cost of assets restored, purchased or constructed as a replacement is determined under paragraphs 14–20A and paragraphs 22A-22D of this Standard.

Business Combinations

54 IAS 22, *Business Combinations*, explains how to deal with an impairment loss recognised before the end of the first annual accounting period beginning after a business combination that is an acquisition.

RETIREMENTS AND DISPOSALS

55 **An item of property, plant and equipment shall be derecognised on:**

(a) disposal; or
(b) when no future economic benefits are expected from its use or disposal.

56 **Gains or losses arising from the retirement or disposal of an item of property, plant and equipment shall be determined as the difference between the net disposal proceeds and the carrying amount of the asset. They shall be included in profit or loss for the period in which the retirement or disposal occurs (unless SSAP 21 IAS 17, *Leases*, requires otherwise on a sale and leaseback).**

57 [Deleted]

58 The disposal of an item of property, plant and equipment may occur by sale or by entering into a finance lease. In determining the date of disposal of such an item, an entity applies the criteria in IAS 18, Revenue, for recognising revenue from the sale of goods. IAS 17, Leases, applies to a disposal by a sale and leaseback.

58A The consideration receivable on disposal of an item of property, plant and equipment is recognised initially at fair value. If payment for such an item is deferred, the consideration received is recognised initially at the cash price equivalent. The difference between the nominal amount of the consideration and the cash price equivalent is recognised as interest revenue under IAS 18 according to the effective yield on the receivable.

59 Depreciation of an item of property, plant and equipment does not cease when it becomes temporarily idle or is retired from active use and held for disposal unless the asset's depreciable amount has been allocated fully. At least at each financial year end, an entity tests such an asset for impairment under FRS 11 IAS 36, *Impairment of Assets*, and recognises any impairment loss accordingly.

DISCLOSURE

The financial statements shall disclose, for each class of property, plant and equipment: **60**

(a) the measurement bases used for determining the gross carrying amount. When more than one basis has been used for a class, the gross carrying amount for each basis adopted within the class shall be disclosed;
(b) the depreciation methods used;
(c) the useful lives or the depreciation rates used;
(d) the gross carrying amount and the accumulated depreciation (aggregated with accumulated impairment losses) at the beginning and end of the period;
(e) a reconciliation of the carrying amount at the beginning and end of the period showing:

    (i) additions;
    (ii) disposals;
    (iii) acquisitions through business combinations;
    (iv) increases or decreases during the period resulting from revaluations under paragraphs 29, 37 and 38 and from impairment losses recognised or reversed in the statement of total recognised gains and losses directly in equity under FRS 11 IAS 36, *Impairment of Assets*;
    (v) impairment losses recognised in the profit and loss account income statement during the period under FRS 11 IAS 36;
    (vi) impairment losses reversed in the profit and loss account income statement during the period under FRS 11 IAS 36;
    (vii) depreciation;
    (viii) the net exchange differences arising on the translation of the financial statements from the functional currency into a different presentation currency, including the translation of a foreign operation into the presentation currency of the reporting entity; and
    (ix) other movements.

The financial statements shall also disclose: **61**

(a) the existence and amounts of restrictions on title, and property, plant and equipment pledged as security for liabilities;
(b) the amount of expenditures capitalised in respect of property, and equipment in the course of construction; and
(c) the amount of contractual commitments for the acquisition of property, plant and equipment.

Selection of the depreciation method and estimation of the useful life of assets are   **62** matters of judgement. Therefore, disclosure of the methods adopted and the estimated useful lives or depreciation rates provides users of financial statements with information that allows them to review the policies selected by management and enables comparisons to be made with other entities. For similar reasons, it is necessary to disclose:

(a) depreciation allocated, whether recognised as an expense or as a part of the cost of other assets, during a period; and
(b) accumulated depreciation at the end of that period.

An entity discloses the nature and effect of a change in an accounting estimate that   **63** has an effect in the current period or is expected to have an effect in subsequent periods in accordance with IAS 8, *Accounting Policies, Changes in Accounting Estimates and Errors*. Such disclosure may arise from changes in estimate with respect to:

(a) residual values;

(b)   the estimated costs of dismantling, removing or restoring items of property, plant and equipment;

(c)   useful lives; and

(d)   depreciation method.

64   **When items of property, plant and equipment are stated at revalued amounts the following shall be disclosed:**

(a)   **the basis used to revalue the assets;**

(b)   **the effective date of the revaluation;**

(c)   **whether an independent valuer was involved;**

(d)   **the methods and significant assumptions applied in estimating the assets fair values;**

(e)   **the extent to which the assets fair values were determined directly by reference to observable prices in an active market or recent market transactions on arm's length terms or were estimated using other valuation techniques;**

(f)   **for each revalued class of property, plant and equipment, the carrying amount that would have been recognised had the assets been carried under the benchmark treatment in paragraph 28; and**

(g)   **the revaluation surplus, indicating the movement for the period and any restrictions on the distribution of the balance to shareholders.**

65   An entity discloses information on impaired property, plant and equipment under FRS 11 IAS 36, *Impairment of Assets*, in addition to the information required by paragraph 60(e)(iv)-(vi).

66   Financial statement users may also find the following information relevant to their needs:

(a)   the carrying amount of temporarily idle property, plant and equipment;

(b)   the gross carrying amount of any fully depreciated property, plant and equipment that is still in use;

(c)   the carrying amount of property, plant and equipment retired from active use and held for disposal; and

(d)   when the benchmark treatment is used, the fair value of property, plant and equipment when this is materially different from the carrying amount.

Therefore, entities are encouraged to disclose these amounts.

TRANSITIONAL PROVISIONS

66A   **The amendments to the initial measurement of assets acquired in exchanges of assets specified in paragraphs 21 and 21A shall be applied prospectively.**

66B   If an exchange of assets was measured on the basis of the carrying amount of the asset given up under paragraph 22 of IAS 16 (revised 1998), the entity does not restate the carrying amount of the asset acquired to reflect the fair value of the consideration given. Therefore, on adoption of this Standard, an entity does not apply the general treatment of changes in accounting policies in IAS 8, Accounting Policies, Changes in Accounting Estimates and Errors.

66C   **Where, on implementation of this Standard for the first time, an entity does not adopt a policy of revaluation, but the carrying amount of its property, plant and equipment reflects previous revaluations, it may:**

(a) retain the book amounts. In these circumstances the entity should disclose the fact that the transitional provisions of this Standard are being followed and that the valuation has not been updated and give the date of the last revaluation; or

(b) restate the carrying amount of the tangible fixed assets to historical cost (less restated accumulated depreciation), as a change in accounting policy. [ASB]

The transitional arrangement set out in paragraph 66C is available only on the first application of this Standard. [ASB]   **66D**

EFFECTIVE DATE

The accounting practices set out in this Standard should be regarded as standard in respect of accounting periods ending on or after [date to be inserted after exposure]. Earlier adoption is encouraged. This Standard becomes operative for annual financial statements covering periods beginning on or after 1 January 2003. Earlier adoption is encouraged. If earlier adoption affects the financial statements, an entity shall disclose that fact.   **67**

[Deleted]   **68**

WITHDRAWAL OF FRS 15 AND AMENDMENTS TO OTHER STANDARDS

This Standard (together with the [draft] FRS Borrowing Costs) supersedes FRS 15 Tangible Fixed Assets [following publication in final form]. [ASB]   **68A**

FRS 11 Impairment of Fixed Assets and Goodwill is amended as follows: **68B**

(a) the text of paragraph 63 is replaced by:
   An impairment loss on a revalued asset should be recognised in the statement of total recognised gains and losses until the carrying amount of the asset reaches its depreciated historical cost and thereafter in the profit and loss account.

(b) paragraphs 64 and 65 are deleted. [ASB]

Appendix – Note on legal requirements

GREAT BRITAIN

1   In Great Britain, the statutory requirements relating to accounting for tangible fixed assets are set out in the Companies Act 1985. The main requirements that are directly relevant to property, plant and equipment and the requirements of the [draft] FRS are set out in Schedules 4 and 4A and are summarised below.

2   Schedule 4 does not apply to banking and insurance companies or groups. Requirements equivalent to those of Schedule 4 are contained in Schedule 9 (for banking companies and groups) and in Schedule 9A (for insurance companies and groups).

Initial cost

3   Paragraph 17 of Schedule 4 requires the amount to be included in respect of any fixed asset to be its purchase price or production cost. The purchase price is to be determined by adding to the actual price any expenses incidental to its acquisition (paragraph 26(1) of Schedule 4). Paragraph 26(2) requires the cost of production of an asset to comprise the purchase price of raw materials and consumables used and the amount of costs incurred by the company that are directly attributable to the production of that asset. In addition, paragraph 26(3) allows the inclusion of:

(a)   indirectly attributable costs incurred by the company relating to the period of production; and

(b)   interest on capital borrowed to finance the production of the asset. (However, the amount of the interest capitalised is required to be disclosed in the notes to the accounts.)

4   Where there is no record of the purchase price or production cost of any asset of a company, paragraph 28 of Schedule 4 requires the asset value to be determined using the earliest available record of the value of the asset on or after its acquisition or production by the company. Such earliest available records may also be used where there are no relevant prices, expenses or costs against which the purchase price may be determined or where the record of such purchase price cannot be obtained without unreasonable expense or delay.

Valuation

5   The alternative accounting rules set out in paragraph 31(2) of Schedule 4 permit tangible fixed assets to be included at a market value determined as at the date of their last valuation or at their current cost.

6   Where the alternative accounting rules set out in paragraph 31(2) of Schedule 4 are adopted by a company, the following additional information is required to be included in the company's accounts:

(a)   the assets revalued and the basis of valuation (paragraph 33(2) of Schedule 4).

(b)   either the comparable amounts determined according to the historical cost accounting rules or the differences between those amounts and the revalued amounts (paragraph 33(3) of Schedule 4).

(c)   the year and amount of the valuation (paragraph 43(a) of Schedule 4).

(d)   in the case of assets that have been valued during the financial year, the names of the persons who valued them or particulars of their qualifications for doing so and the bases of valuation used by them (paragraph 43(b) of Schedule 4).

Reporting revaluation gains and losses

Paragraph 34(1) of Schedule 4 requires a profit or loss calculated under the alter-   **7** native accounting rules to be credited or debited to a separate reserve (the revaluation reserve). Paragraph 34(3) of Schedule 4 allows an amount to be transferred from the revaluation reserve to the profit and loss account, if the amount was previously charged to that account.

Depreciation

Where a fixed asset has a limited useful economic life, paragraph 18 of Schedule 4   **8** requires its purchase price or production cost less its estimated residual value to be written off systematically over the period of the asset's useful economic life.

Paragraph 19(2) of Schedule 4 requires provisions for diminution in value to be made   **9** in respect of any fixed asset that has diminished in value if the reduction in its value is expected to be permanent. The amount to be included in respect of the asset must be reduced accordingly. Any provisions that are not shown in the profit and loss account must be disclosed (either separately or in aggregate) in a note to the accounts.

Paragraph 32(1) of Schedule 4 requires the depreciation of revalued assets to be   **10** calculated on the basis of their latest valuations. Paragraph 32(3) allows a company to include under the relevant profit and loss account heading provisions for depreciation for the revalued assets based only on their historical cost, provided that the difference between that and the provision for depreciation calculated on the revalued amount is shown separately either in the profit and loss account or in the notes.

Disclosure requirements

In addition to the disclosures mentioned in paragraph 6 above in connection with the   **11** revaluation of tangible fixed assets, the following disclosures are required:

(a)   Paragraph 36 of Schedule 4 requires the disclosure of the accounting policies adopted by a company (including the policies regarding the depreciation and diminution in value of assets).

(b)   Paragraph 26(3) requires the disclosure of the amount of interest capitalised, where such a policy is adopted.

(c)   Paragraph 42 details the disclosures required of the movement on tangible fixed asset balances for the items under each of the headings set out in the balance sheet formats in Schedule 4, as follows:

1.   Land and buildings
2.   Plant and machinery
3.   Fixtures, fittings, tools and equipment
4.   Payments on account and assets in the course of construction.

(d)   Paragraph 1(2) of Schedule 7 requires disclosure, in the directors report, of the difference, with such precision as is practicable, between the carrying amount and market value of interests in land, where, in the opinion of the directors, it is of such significance that it needs to be drawn to the attention of the members of the entity.

NORTHERN IRELAND

12   The statutory requirements in Northern Ireland are set out in the Companies (Northern Ireland) Order 1986. They are identical to and parallel the references in the legislation for Great Britain cited above.

REPUBLIC OF IRELAND

13   The statutory requirements in the Republic of Ireland that correspond to those cited above for Great Britain are shown in the following table.

Great Britain	Republic of Ireland
Schedule 4 to the Companies Act 1985:	The Schedule to the Companies (Amendment) Act 1986:
paragraph 17	paragraph 5
paragraph 18	paragraph 6
paragraph 19(2)	paragraph 7(2)
paragraph 26(1), (2) and (3)	paragraph 14(1), (2) and (3)
paragraph 28	paragraph 16
paragraph 31(2)	paragraph 19(2)
paragraph 32(1) and (3)	paragraph 20(1) and (3)
paragraph 33(2) and (3)	paragraph 21(2) and (3)
paragraph 34(1) and (3)	paragraph 22(1) and (4)
paragraph 36	paragraph 24
paragraph 42	paragraph 29
paragraph 43(a) and (b)	paragraph 30(a) and (b)
Schedule 4A to the Companies Act 1985	European Communities (Companies: Group Accounts) Regulations 1992
Schedule 7 to the Companies Act 1985, paragraph 1(2)	No specific requirement
Schedule 9 to the Companies Act 1985	European Communities (Credit Institutions: Accounts) Regulations 1992
Schedule 9A to the Companies Act 1985	European Communities (Insurance Undertakings: Accounts) Regulations 1996

[Draft] Financial Reporting Standard: Borrowing Costs

[Draft] Financial Reporting Standard – Borrowing Costs is set out in paragraphs 1–31.

The Statement of Standard Accounting Practice, which comprises the paragraphs set in bold type, should be read in the context of the Objective, the definitions set out in paragraph 4 and also of the Foreword to Accounting Standards and the Statement of Principles for Financial Reporting currently in issue.

The explanatory paragraphs contained in the [draft] FRS shall be regarded as part of the Statement of Standard Accounting Practice insofar as they assist in interpreting that statement.

This draft is issued by the Accounting Standards Board for comment. It should be noted that the draft may be modified in the light of comment received before being issued in final form.

OBJECTIVE

The objective of this Standard is to prescribe the accounting treatment for borrowing costs. This Standard generally requires the immediate expensing of borrowing costs. However, the Standard permits, as an allowed alternative treatment, the capitalisation of borrowing costs that are directly attributable to the acquisition, construction or production of a qualifying asset.

SCOPE

This Standard should be applied in accounting for borrowing costs. 1

This Standard supersedes IAS 23, Capitalisation of Borrowing Costs, approved in 1983. 2

This Standard does not deal with the actual or imputed cost of equity, including preferred capital not classified as a liability. 3

This Standard applies to all financial statements that are intended to give a true and fair view of a reporting entity's financial position and profit or loss (or income and expenditure), except that reporting entities applying the Financial Reporting Standard for Smaller Entities currently applicable are exempt. [ASB] 3A

DEFINITIONS

The following terms are used in this Standard with the meanings specified: 4

Borrowing costs are interest and other costs incurred by an enterprise in connection with the borrowing of funds.

A qualifying asset is an asset that necessarily takes a substantial period of time to get ready for its intended use or sale.

Borrowing costs may include: 5

(a)   interest on bank overdrafts and short-term and long-term borrowings;

(b)   amortisation of discounts or premiums relating to borrowings;

(c)   amortisation of ancillary costs incurred in connection with the arrangement of borrowings; and

(d)   finance charges in respect of finance leases recognised in accordance with SSAP 21, *Accounting for leases and hire purchase contracts* IAS 17, *Leases*; and

(e)   exchange differences arising from foreign currency borrowings to the extent that they are regarded as an adjustment to interest costs.

6   Examples of qualifying assets are inventories that require a substantial period of time to bring them to a saleable condition, manufacturing plants, power generation facilities and investment properties. Other investments, and those inventories that are routinely manufactured or otherwise produced in large quantities on a repetitive basis over a short period of time, are not qualifying assets. Assets that are ready for their intended use or sale when acquired also are not qualifying assets.

BORROWING COSTS – BENCHMARK TREATMENT

Recognition

7   **Borrowing costs should be recognised as an expense in the period in which they are incurred.**

8   Under the benchmark treatment borrowing costs are recognised as an expense in the period in which they are incurred regardless of how the borrowings are applied.

Disclosure

9   **The financial statements should disclose the accounting policy adopted for borrowing costs.**

BORROWING COSTS – ALLOWED ALTERNATIVE TREATMENT

Recognition

10   **Borrowing costs should be recognised as an expense in the period in which they are incurred, except to the extent that they are capitalised in accordance with paragraph 11.**

11   **Borrowing costs that are directly attributable to the acquisition, construction or production of a qualifying asset should be capitalised as part of the cost of that asset. The amount of borrowing costs eligible for capitalisation should be determined in accordance with this Standard.**

12   Under the allowed alternative treatment, borrowing costs that are directly attributable to the acquisition, construction or production of an asset are included in the cost of that asset. Such borrowing costs are capitalised as part of the cost of the asset when it is probable that they will result in future economic benefits to the enterprise and the costs can be measured reliably. Other borrowing costs are recognised as an expense in the period in which they are incurred.

Borrowing Costs Eligible for Capitalisation

13   The borrowing costs that are directly attributable to the acquisition, construction or production of a qualifying asset are those borrowing costs that would have been

avoided if the expenditure on the qualifying asset had not been made. When an enterprise borrows funds specifically for the purpose of obtaining a particular qualifying asset, the borrowing costs that directly relate to that qualifying asset can be readily identified.

It may be difficult to identify a direct relationship between particular borrowings and   **14**
a qualifying asset and to determine the borrowings that could otherwise have been avoided. Such a difficulty occurs, for example, when the financing activity of an enterprise is co-ordinated centrally. Difficulties also arise when a group uses a range of debt instruments to borrow funds at varying rates of interest, and lends those funds on various bases to other enterprises in the group. Other complications arise through the use of loans denominated in or linked to foreign currencies, when the group operates in highly inflationary economies, and from fluctuations in exchange rates. As a result, the determination of the amount of borrowing costs that are directly attributable to the acquisition of a qualifying asset is difficult and the exercise of judgement is required.

To the extent that funds are borrowed specifically for the purpose of obtaining a   **15**
qualifying asset, the amount of borrowing costs eligible for capitalisation on that asset
should be determined as the actual borrowing costs incurred on that borrowing during
the period less any investment income on the temporary investment of those borrowings.

The financing arrangements for a qualifying asset may result in an enterprise   **16**
obtaining borrowed funds and incurring associated borrowing costs before some or all of the funds are used for expenditures on the qualifying asset. In such circumstances, the funds are often temporarily invested pending their expenditure on the qualifying asset. In determining the amount of borrowing costs eligible for capitalisation during a period, any investment income earned on such funds is deducted from the borrowing costs incurred.

To the extent that funds are borrowed generally and used for the purpose of obtaining a   **17**
qualifying asset, the amount of borrowing costs eligible for capitalisation should be
determined by applying a capitalisation rate to the expenditures on that asset. The
capitalisation rate should be the weighted average of the borrowing costs applicable to
the borrowings of the enterprise that are outstanding during the period, other than
borrowings made specifically for the purpose of obtaining a qualifying asset. The
amount of borrowing costs capitalised during a period should not exceed the amount of
borrowing costs incurred during that period.

In some circumstances, it is appropriate to include all borrowings of the parent and   **18**
its subsidiaries when computing a weighted average of the borrowing costs; in other circumstances, it is appropriate for each subsidiary to use a weighted average of the borrowing costs applicable to its own borrowings.

Excess of the Carrying Amount of the Qualifying Asset over Recoverable Amount

When the carrying amount or the expected ultimate cost of the qualifying asset   **19**
exceeds its recoverable amount or net realisable value, the carrying amount is written down or written off in accordance with the requirements of other International Accounting Standards. In certain circumstances, the amount of the write-down or write-off is written back in accordance with those other International Accounting Standards.

Commencement of Capitalisation

20 The capitalisation of borrowing costs as part of the cost of a qualifying asset should commence when:

(a) expenditures for the asset are being incurred;
(b) borrowing costs are being incurred; and
(c) activities that are necessary to prepare the asset for its intended use or sale are in progress.

21 Expenditures on a qualifying asset include only those expenditures that have resulted in payments of cash, transfers of other assets or the assumption of interest-bearing liabilities. Expenditures are reduced by any progress payments received and grants received in connection with the asset (see SSAP 4, *Accounting for government grants* IAS 20, *Accounting for Government Grants and Disclosure of Government Assistance*). The average carrying amount of the asset during a period, including borrowing costs previously capitalised, is normally a reasonable approximation of the expenditures to which the capitalisation rate is applied in that period.

22 The activities necessary to prepare the asset for its intended use or sale encompass more than the physical construction of the asset. They include technical and administrative work prior to the commencement of physical construction, such as the activities associated with obtaining permits prior to the commencement of the physical construction. However, such activities exclude the holding of an asset when no production or development that changes the asset's condition is taking place. For example, borrowing costs incurred while land is under development are capitalised during the period in which activities related to the development are being undertaken. However, borrowing costs incurred while land acquired for building purposes is held without any associated development activity do not qualify for capitalisation.

Suspension of Capitalisation

23 Capitalisation of borrowing costs should be suspended during extended periods in which active development is interrupted.

24 Borrowing costs may be incurred during an extended period in which the activities necessary to prepare an asset for its intended use or sale are interrupted. Such costs are costs of holding partially completed assets and do not qualify for capitalisation. However, capitalisation of borrowing costs is not normally suspended during a period when substantial technical and administrative work is being carried out. Capitalisation of borrowing costs is also not suspended when a temporary delay is a necessary part of the process of getting an asset ready for its intended use or sale. For example, capitalisation continues during the extended period needed for inventories to mature or the extended period during which high water levels delay construction of a bridge, if such high water levels are common during the construction period in the geographic region involved.

Cessation of Capitalisation

25 Capitalisation of borrowing costs should cease when substantially all the activities necessary to prepare the qualifying asset for its intended use or sale are complete.

26 An asset is normally ready for its intended use or sale when the physical construction of the asset is complete even though routine administrative work might still continue. If minor modifications, such as the decoration of a property to the purchaser s or

user s specification, are all that are outstanding, this indicates that substantially all the activities are complete.

When the construction of a qualifying asset is completed in parts and each part is 27 **capable of being used while construction continues on other parts, capitalisation of borrowing costs should cease when substantially all the activities necessary to prepare that part for its intended use or sale are completed.**

A business park comprising several buildings, each of which can be used individually 28 is an example of a qualifying asset for which each part is capable of being usable while construction continues on other parts. An example of a qualifying asset that needs to be complete before any part can be used is an industrial plant involving several processes which are carried out in sequence at different parts of the plant within the same site, such as a steel mill.

Disclosure

The financial statements should disclose: 29

(a)   **the accounting policy adopted for borrowing costs;**
(b)   **the amount of borrowing costs capitalised during the period;**
(c)   **the capitalisation rate used to determine the amount of borrowing costs eligible for capitalisation.**

[Deleted]* 30

EFFECTIVE DATE

The accounting practices set out in this Standard should be regarded as standard in 31 **respect of accounting periods ending on or after [date to be inserted after exposure]. Earlier adoption is encouraged.** This International Accounting Standard becomes operative for financial statements covering periods beginning on or after 1 January 1995.

---

*Paragraph 30 contained the original transitional provisions of IAS 23.

Summary of main changes proposed by the IASB

The main changes proposed to IAS 16 are:

- to amend the definition of residual value in paragraph 6 for greater consistency with the guidance in the last sentence of paragraph 46. The amended definition would require an entity to use current prices for assets of a similar age and condition to the estimated age and condition of the asset when it reaches the end of its useful life.
- to amend paragraph 12 to clarify that a component approach to depreciation and to the treatment of expenditure to replace or renew a component of an item of property, plant and equipment is applied to all such items. Under a component approach, each material component of an asset with a different useful life or different pattern of depreciation is depreciated separately and expenditure on replacing or renewing the component is capitalised. This amendment would achieve greater consistency with paragraph 27 of IAS 16 (see paragraph 22B).
- to insert in paragraph 15 additional guidance that the directly attributable costs included in the cost of an item of property, plant and equipment:
- are those to bring the asset to the location and working condition necessary for it to be capable of operating in the manner intended by management (including those to test whether the asset is functioning properly); and
- are determined after deducting the net proceeds from selling any items produced when bringing the asset to that location and condition.
- to add paragraph 17B to provide guidance on the treatment of income and related expenses of operations that are incidental to the construction or development of an item of property, plant and equipment.
- to include paragraphs 20A and 20B to provide additional guidance on the principle that the cost of an item of property, plant and equipment includes the costs of dismantling and removing the asset and restoring the site on which that asset is located (this principle was stated in paragraph 15(e) of IAS 16).
- to amend paragraphs 21 and 22 to specify that exchanges of items of property, plant and equipment (regardless of whether the assets are similar) are measured at fair value, except that when the fair value of neither of the assets exchanged can be determined reliably, the cost of the asset acquired in the exchange is measured at the carrying amount of the asset given up. For the purpose of applying this requirement, amended paragraph 21 indicates that the fair value of the asset received is used to measure its cost if it is more clearly evident than the fair value of the asset given up. This would amend the requirement in paragraph 22 to measure the cost of the asset acquired at the carrying amount of the asset given up in respect of the following exchanges:
- an acquisition of an item of property, plant and equipment in exchange for a similar asset that has a similar use in the same line of business and a similar fair value; and
- a sale of an item of property, plant and equipment in exchange for an equity interest in a similar asset.

As a consequence, paragraph 11 of SIC-13, *Jointly Controlled Entities – Non-Monetary Contributions by Venturers*, would be deleted.

- to add paragraph 22A to specify that a component approach is applied to depreciation and to the treatment of expenditure to replace or renew a component of an item of property, plant and equipment.
- to add paragraphs 22C and 22D to provide guidance that the component approach specified in paragraph 22A is applied when a separate component of an item of property, plant and equipment is identified in respect of a major

inspection to enable the continued use of the item. As a result, the section including paragraphs 22A-22D incorporates the Consensus in SIC-23, *Property, Plant and Equipment – Major Inspection or Overhaul Costs*, and SIC-23 will be withdrawn.

- to amend paragraph 23 to replace the originally assessed standard of performance with the standard of performance assessed immediately before the expenditure was made as part of the criterion for determining whether subsequent expenditure relating to an item of property, plant and equipment should be capitalised. Accordingly, SIC-6, *Costs of Modifying Existing Software*, will be withdrawn.
- to amend paragraph 46 to require the residual value of an asset to be reviewed as at each balance sheet date, regardless of whether the asset is measured under the benchmark treatment or the allowed alternative treatment. A change in the asset's residual value, other than a change reflected in an impairment loss recognised under IAS 36, Impairment of Assets, would be accounted for prospectively as an adjustment to future depreciation.
- to amend paragraphs 49 and 52 to clarify that the requirement to review periodically the useful life and depreciation method of an item of property, plant and equipment means that such reviews must occur at least at each financial year end.
- to add paragraphs 53A and 53B to specify that compensation from third parties for items of property, plant and equipment that were impaired, lost or given up shall, in the period in which it is received, be:
- included in profit or loss for that period; and
- disclosed separately.

Paragraphs 53A and 53B incorporate the Consensus in SIC-14, *Property, Plant and Equipment – Compensation for the Impairment or Loss of Items*. SIC-14 will be withdrawn.

- to include guidance in paragraph 59 that depreciation of an item of property, plant and equipment does not cease when it becomes temporarily idle or is retired from active use and held for disposal.
- to remove the exemption in paragraph 60 from disclosing comparative information for the reconciliation of the carrying amount at the beginning and end of the period for each class of property, plant and equipment.
- to remove paragraph 61(b), which requires disclosure of the accounting policy for the estimated costs of restoring the site of items of property, plant and equipment (this policy is specified in IAS 37, *Provisions, Contingent Liabilities and Contingent Assets*).
- to amend paragraph 64(d) and add paragraph 64(e) to require disclosure of the following for items of property, plant and equipment stated at revalued amounts:
- the methods and significant assumptions applied in estimating the assets fair values; and
- the extent to which the assets fair values were determined directly by reference to observable prices in an active market or recent market transactions on arm's length terms or were estimated using other valuation techniques.

FRED 32
Disposal of Non-Current Assets and Presentation of Discontinued Operations

Contents

Preface

The International Accounting Standards Board (IASB) has recently published for 1 comment, as part of its short-term convergence project with the US Financial Accounting Standards Board (FASB), a proposed new International Financial Reporting Standard (IFRS) *Disposal of Non-current Assets and Presentation of Discontinued Operations*. The IASB intends to withdraw IAS 35 *Discontinuing Operations* on implementation of the new IFRS.*

The main changes to IFRSs proposed by the IASB are summarised in paragraph 2 IN5.

FRS 3 *Reporting Financial Performance* includes a definition of discontinued opera- 3 tions and requirements for the presentation of income and costs relating to such operations. UK accounting standards include no specific requirements for the measurement of non-current assets held for disposal, other than the general requirement to carry out an impairment review.

In due course, as part of its programme to converge UK standards with IFRSs, the 4 ASB proposes to issue a UK standard based on this Exposure Draft, which will replace parts of FRS 3 and introduce new requirements for non-current assets held for disposal.

The ASB and the IASB are also engaged in a joint project on reporting financial 5 performance. One aspect that this project will consider is the presentation of infor- mation on discontinued operations and it is anticipated that the Exposure Draft will be superseded in this area in due course.

MAIN CHANGES PROPOSED TO EXISTING UK REQUIREMENTS

Presentation of assets held for sale

The exposure draft introduces the classification 'held for sale', which applies to both 6 non-current assets individually and disposal groups (a disposal group is a group of assets to be disposed of by sale or otherwise as a group in a single transaction, and the liabilities directly associated with the assets that also form part of the transac- tion), and specifies that such assets (and, in the context of a disposal group, liabilities) should be disclosed separately on the face of the balance sheet.

Existing UK requirements do not include any requirements for separate presentation 7 of assets held for disposal.

Appendix B of the exposure draft is a mandatory application supplement which 8 specifies the criteria for classifying an asset (or disposal group) as held for sale. This is based on management's plans for the asset and generally requires it to be highly probable that the asset will be sold within one year.

As a consequence of the separate presentation on the balance sheet of assets (and 9 liabilities) that are held for sale, the exposure draft also proposes additional dis- closures in the notes to the financial statements.

Editor's note: IFRS 5 has now been issued.

Measurement of assets and disposal groups held for sale

10   In accordance with FRS 11 *Impairment of Fixed Assets and Goodwill*, to the extent that an impairment review indicates that the carrying amount of an asset exceeds its recoverable amount, the asset is impaired and its carrying amount should be written down to its recoverable amount. Recoverable amount is the higher of net realisable value and value in use.

11   An impairment review should be carried out if events or changes in circumstances indicate that the carrying amount of the fixed asset may not be recoverable. Examples of indicators of impairment include a significant decline in the asset's market value and a commitment to a significant reorganisation. However, FRS 11 does not specifically require an impairment review to be carried out as a result of a decision to sell a fixed asset.

12   The exposure draft requires assets and disposal groups held for sale to be reported at the lower of carrying value and fair value less costs to sell. The definition of 'fair value less costs to sell' is essentially the same as net realisable value.

13   The proposals do not permit an entity to report an asset at fair value less costs to sell where this is in excess of its present carrying value, unless the entity chooses to adopt a policy of revaluation for the relevant class of tangible fixed assets.

14   FRS 15 *Tangible Fixed Assets* requires, where an entity adopts a policy of revaluation, that properties surplus to an entity's requirements should be valued on the basis of open market value, with expected directly attributable selling costs deducted where material.

15   Therefore the IASB's proposals will result in no change in measurement for assets where the greatest value can be recovered through sale, or for surplus properties that are revalued. However, where the greatest value can be recovered from the continued use of an asset, but nevertheless the entity chooses to sell it, the ASB believes that any loss arising on disposal should be recorded when the sale occurs and not when the entity classifies the asset as held for sale.

Depreciation of assets held for sale

16   The exposure draft also specifies that assets held for disposal (and any assets within a disposal group) should not be depreciated, regardless of whether they are still in use by the reporting entity.

17   FRS 15 does not exempt assets held for disposal from depreciation, which has the objective of reflecting in operating profit the cost of use of the tangible fixed assets in the period. The only grounds for not charging depreciation are that the depreciation charge and accumulated depreciation are immaterial. Similarly IAS 16 and the Exposure Draft of revised IAS 16 (issued in May 2002) note that depreciation should reflect the expected consumption of future economic benefits by the entity.

18   This issue is discussed in paragraphs 18 to 24 of the IASB's Basis for Conclusions, and is also raised by the IASB members with Alternative Views. The ASB believes that it is not appropriate to suspend depreciation on assets that are continuing to be used by a reporting entity simply because they have been labelled as held for sale within one year.

Definition of a discontinued operation

FRS 3 defines a discontinued operation as: **19**

'Operations of the reporting entity that are sold or terminated and that satisfy all of the following conditions:

(a)   The sale or termination is completed either in the period or before the earlier of three months after the commencement of the subsequent period and the date on which the financial statements are approved.

(b)   If a termination, the former activities have ceased permanently.

(c)   The sale or termination has a material effect on the nature and focus of the reporting entity's operations and represents a material reduction in its operating facilities resulting either from its withdrawal from a particular market (whether class of business or geographical) or from a material reduction in turnover in the reporting entity's continuing markets.

(d)   The assets, liabilities, results of operations and activities are clearly distinguishable, physically, operationally and for financial reporting purposes.

Operations not satisfying all these conditions are classified as continuing.'

Paragraph 23 of the exposure draft defines a discontinued operation as: **20**

'. . . a component of an entity that either has been disposed of or is classified as held for sale* and:

(a)   the operations and cash flows of which have been (or will be) eliminated from the ongoing operations of the entity as a result of the disposal transaction, and

(b)   in which the entity will have no significant continuing involvement after the disposal transaction.'

In this context a component of an entity comprises operations and cash flows that   **21**
can be clearly distinguished, operationally and for financial reporting purposes, from the rest of the entity.

The exposure draft's definition does not include a condition similar to that of FRS   **22**
(replicated in paragraph 19(c) above) that the effect of the sale or termination is material.

As a result it is likely that discontinued operations would be reported more fre-   **23**
quently under the FRED's proposals than under the requirements of FRS 3. The consequences for the usefulness of reported information of reporting relatively small parts of an entity as discontinued (and hence excluding them from the results of continuing operations, if presented) require consideration. In addition, as comparatives are to be restated, the costs and benefits of this change require consideration.

AMENDMENTS TO OTHER UK STANDARDS

On adoption of the draft as an FRS: **24**

(a)   paragraphs 4, 17, 21, 41, 42, 43, 44 of FRS 3 will be withdrawn;

(b)   paragraph 5 of FRS 11 will be amended as follows:

**Classified as held for sale has the same meaning as in paragraph 4 of the exposure draft, which is elaborated on in Appendix B.*

insert:

'(e)   fixed assets, and fixed assets within a disposal group, that are classified as held for sale in accordance with [draft FRS x] *Disposal of Non-current Assets and Presentation of Discontinued Operations.*'

(c)   paragraph 4 of FRS 15 will be amended as follows:

'The requirements of the FRS apply to all tangible fixed assets, with the exception of:

(a)   investment properties as defined in SSAP 19 *Accounting for investment properties*; and

(b)   assets, and assets within disposal groups, that are classified as held for sale in accordance with [draft FRS x] *Disposal of Non-current Assets and Presentation of Discontinued Operations.*'

UK LAW, EU LAW AND INTERNATIONAL STANDARDS

25   EU Ministers have agreed that from 1 January 2005 all listed companies in the EU should prepare their consolidated financial statements in accordance with adopted international accounting standards. The intention is that IFRSs will form the basis of those adopted international accounting standards.

26   The ASB, in accordance with its convergence agenda, proposes to introduce the IASB's proposals also into UK accounting standards. However, as a result of legal requirements in the UK and the Republic of Ireland certain amendments to the IASB text are required. These are clearly marked in the FRED.

27   In paragraph 28 the exposure draft requires the assets and liabilities of a disposal group classified as held for sale to be presented separately in the asset and liability sections of the balance sheet. The IASB proposes that further disagreggation into major classes of asset or liability be presented either on the face of the balance sheet or in the notes to the financial statements. Companies not subject to the IAS Regulation will continue to be required to comply with the accounting requirements of the Companies Act 1985, including the applicable balance sheet formats. Whilst the so-called Modernisation Directive* (which, when transposed into UK law will amend the accounting requirements of the Companies Act 1985) includes certain member state options regarding balance sheet formats, these options might not enable categories of asset and liability currently required to be presented separately on the face of the balance sheet to be aggregated on the grounds that they are held for sale. Accordingly, the IASB's proposals have been amended for the UK to require the major classes of assets and liabilities held for sale to be separately disclosed on the face of the balance sheet under the statutory format headings.

Directive of the European Parliament and of the Council amending Council Directives 78/660/EEC, 83/349/ EEC, 86/635/EEC and 91/674/EEC on the annual and consolidated accounts of certain types of companies, banks and other financial institutions and insurance undertakings.

Invitation to comment

The ASB invites comments on any aspect of the FRED by 24 October 2003 – the same date as the IASB has set for comments on its proposed IFRS.   **ITC1**

The ASB would particularly welcome comments on the following issue: **ITC2**

ASB 1   Do you agree with the proposal to issue a new UK standard on disposal of non-current assets and discontinued operations when the IASB issues its new IFRS?

The ASB would also welcome comments on the questions that the IASB has asked in its Exposure Draft, which are as follows:*   **ITC3**

IASB 1   The Exposure Draft proposes that non-current assets should be classified as assets held for sale if specified criteria are met. (See paragraphs 4 and 5 and Appendix B.) Assets so classified may be required to be measured differently (see question 2) and presented separately (see question 7) from other non-current assets.

Does the separate classification of non-current assets held for sale enable additional information to be provided to users? Do you agree with the classification being made? If not, why not?

IASB 2   The Exposure Draft proposes that non-current assets classified as held for sale should be measured at the lower of carrying amount and fair value less costs to sell. It also proposes that non-current assets classified as held for sale should not be depreciated. (See paragraphs 8-16.)
Is this measurement basis appropriate for non-current assets classified as held for sale? If not, why not?

IASB 3   The Exposure Draft proposes that assets and liabilities that are to be disposed of together in a single transaction should be treated as a disposal group. The measurement basis proposed for non-current assets classified as held for sale would be applied to the group as a whole and any resulting impairment loss would reduce the carrying value of the non-current assets in the disposal group. (See paragraph 3.)

Is this appropriate? If not, why not?

IASB 4   The Exposure Draft proposes that newly acquired assets that meet the criteria to be classified as held for sale should be measured at fair value less costs to sell on initial recognition (see paragraph 9). It therefore proposes a consequential amendment to [draft] IFRS X *Business Combinations* (see paragraph C13 of Appendix C) so that noncurrent assets acquired as part of a business combination that meet the criteria to be classified as held for sale would be measured at fair value less costs to sell on initial recognition, rather than at fair value as currently required.

Is measurement at fair value less costs to sell on initial recognition appropriate? If not, why not?

IASB 5   The Exposure Draft proposes that, for revalued assets, impairment losses arising from the writedown of assets (or disposal groups) to fair value less costs to sell (and subsequent gains) should be treated as revaluation

---

It is worth noting that the IASB prefaced its invitation to comment by noting that 'Comments are most helpful if they indicate the specific paragraph or group of paragraphs to which they relate, contain a clear rationale, and, where applicable, provide a suggestion for alternative wording.'

decreases (and revaluation increases) in accordance with the standard under which the assets were revalued, except to the extent that the losses (or gains) arise from the recognition of costs to sell. Costs to sell and any subsequent changes in costs to sell are proposed to be recognised in the income statement. (See paragraphs B6B8 of Appendix B.)

Is this appropriate? If not, why not?

IASB 6   The Exposure Draft proposes a consequential amendment to draft IAS 27 *Consolidated and Separate Financial Statements* to remove the exemption from consolidation for subsidiaries acquired and held exclusively with a view to resale. (See paragraph C3 of Appendix C and paragraphs BC39 and BC40 of the Basis for Conclusions.)

Is the removal of this exemption appropriate? If not, why not?

IASB 7   The Exposure Draft proposes that non-current assets classified as held for sale, and assets and liabilities in a disposal group classified as held for sale, should be presented separately in the balance sheet. The assets and liabilities of a disposal group classified as held for sale should not be offset and presented as a single amount. (See paragraph 28.)

Is this presentation appropriate? If not, why not?

IASB 8   The Exposure Draft proposes that a discontinued operation should be a component of an entity that either has been disposed of, or is classified as held for sale, and:

(a)   the operations and cash flows of that component have been, or will be, eliminated from the ongoing operations of the entity as a result of its disposal; and

(b)   the entity will have no significant continuing involvement in that component after its disposal.

A component of an entity may be a cash-generating unit or any group of cash-generating units. (See paragraphs 22 and 23.)

These criteria could lead to relatively small units being classified as discontinued (subject to their materiality). Some entities may also regularly sell (and buy) operations that would be classified as discontinued operations, resulting in discontinued operations being reported every year. This, in turn, will lead to the comparatives being restated every year. Do you agree that this is appropriate? Would you prefer an amendment to the criteria to be made, for example adding a requirement adapted from IAS 35 *Discontinuing Operations* that a discontinued operation shall be a separate major line of business or geographical area of operations, even though this would not converge with SFAS 144 *Accounting for the Impairment or Disposal of Long-Lived Assets.* How important is convergence in your preference?

Are the other aspects of these criteria for classification as a discontinued operation (for example, the elimination of the operations and cash flows) appropriate? If not, what criteria would you suggest, and why?

IASB 9   The Exposure Draft proposes that the revenue, expenses, pre-tax profit or loss of discontinued operations and any related tax expense should be presented separately on the face of the income statement. (See paragraph 24.) An alternative approach would be to present a single amount, profit after tax, for discontinued operations on the face of the income statement with a breakdown into the above components given in the notes.

Which approach do you prefer, and why?

[Draft] ~~international~~ financial reporting standard • ~~IFRS~~ X Disposal of non-current assets and presentation of discontinued operations

Contents

[Draft] Financial Reporting Standard ● *'Disposal of Non-current Assets and Presentation of Discontinued Operations'*

The draft standard published here is the IASB's proposed text, amended in a few areas to reflect changes that the ASB is proposing to make in implementing the standard in the UK. All of the changes made to the IASB text by the ASB are highlighted by strikethrough of text to be deleted, by underlining of text to be added, and by sidelining against altered text.

The exposure draft continued to refer to the proposed standard as a '[draft] IFRS' (rather than a '[draft] FRS*'). This amendment will be made in finalising the standard, but has not been made in the exposure draft so as not to clutter the text with insignificant amendments.*

This draft is issued by the Accounting Standards Board for comment. It should be noted that the draft may be modified in the light of comment received before being issued in final form.

[Draft] International Financial Reporting Standard X *Disposal of Non-current Assets and Presentation of Discontinued Operations* **([draft] IFRS X) is set out in paragraphs 131 and Appendices A-C. All the paragraphs have equal authority. Paragraphs in bold type state the main principles. Terms defined in Appendix A are in** *italics* **the first time they appear in the [draft] Standard. Definitions of other terms are given in the Glossary for International Financial Reporting Standards. [Draft] IFRS X should be read in the context of its objective and the Basis for Conclusions, the** ~~**Preface to International Financial Reporting Standards**~~<u>**Foreword to Accounting Standards**</u> **and the** ~~**Framework for the Preparation and Presentation of Financial Statements**~~<u>**Statement of Principles for Financial Reporting**</u>**.** ~~**These provide a basis for selecting and applying accounting policies in the absence of explicit guidance.**~~

Introduction

REASONS FOR ISSUING THE [DRAFT] IFRS

Convergence of accounting standards around the world is one of the prime objectives **IN1** of the International Accounting Standards Board (IASB). To further that objective, the Board has agreed with the Financial Accounting Standards Board (FASB) in the United States a memorandum of understanding that sets out the two boards' commitment to convergence. As a result of that understanding the boards have undertaken a joint shortterm project that has the objective of reducing differences between IFRSs and US GAAP that are capable of resolution in a relatively short time and can be addressed outside current and planned major projects.

One aspect of that project involves the two boards considering each other's recent **IN2** standards with a view to adopting recent high quality accounting solutions. The [draft] IFRS arises from the IASB's consideration of the FASB Statement No. 144 *Accounting for the Impairment or Disposal of Long-Lived Assets* (SFAS 144), issued in 2001.

SFAS 144 addresses three areas: (i) the impairment of long-lived assets to be held and **IN3** used, (ii) the classification, measurement and presentation of assets held for sale and (iii) the classification and presentation of discontinued operations. The impairment of long-lived assets to be held and used is an area where there are extensive differences between IFRSs and US GAAP. However, those differences were not thought capable of resolution in a relatively short time. Convergence on the other two areas was thought to be worth pursuing within the context of the short-term project.

The [draft] IFRS achieves substantial convergence with the requirements of SFAS **IN4** 144 relating to assets held for sale and discontinued operations.

MAIN FEATURES OF THE [DRAFT] IFRS

The [draft] IFRS: **IN5**

(a) adopts the classification 'held for sale' using the same criteria as those contained in SFAS 144;
(b) introduces the concept of a disposal group;
(c) specifies that assets or disposal groups that are classified as held for sale are carried at the lower of carrying amount and fair value less costs to sell;
(d) specifies that an asset classified as held for sale, or included within a disposal group that is classified as held for sale, is not depreciated;
(e) specifies that an asset classified as held for sale, and the assets and liabilities included within a disposal group classified as held for sale, are presented separately on the face of the balance sheet;
(f) withdraws IAS 35 *Discontinuing Operations* and replaces it with requirements that:

  (i) change the definition of a discontinued operation from a separate major line of business or geographical area to any unit whose operations and cash flows can be clearly distinguished operationally and for financial reporting purposes.
  (ii) change the timing of the classification as a discontinued operation. IAS 35 classifies an operation as discontinuing at the earlier of (a) the entity entering into a binding sale agreement and (b) the board of directors approving and announcing a formal disposal plan. The [draft] IFRS

classifies an operation as discontinued at the date the entity has actually disposed of the operation, or when the operation meets the criteria to be classified as held for sale.

(iii)   present the results of discontinued operations separately on the face of the income statement.

(iv)   prohibit the retroactive classification as a discontinued operation, when the discontinued criteria are met after the balance sheet date.

[Draft] financial reporting standard

Disposal of Non-current Assets and
Presentation of Discontinued Operations

OBJECTIVE

The objective of this [draft] IFRS is to improve the information in financial state- **1**
ments about assets and *disposal groups* that are to be disposed of and discontinued
operations. It seeks to do this by specifying (i) the measurement, presentation and
disclosure of non-current assets and disposal groups to be disposed of and (ii) the
presentation and disclosure of discontinued operations.

SCOPE

This [draft] FRS applies to all financial statements that are intended to give a true and **1A**
fair view of a reporting entity's financial position and profit or loss (or income and
expenditure), except that reporting entities applying the Financial Reporting Standard for Smaller Entities (FRSSE) are exempt. [ASB]

This [draft] IFRS applies to all recognised *non-current assets* of an entity, except: **2**

(a)   goodwill,
(b)   deferred tax assets,
(c)   financial assets included in the scope of IAS 39 *Financial Instruments: Recog-
      nition and Measurement,**
(d)   assets arising from employee benefits, and
(e)   financial assets arising under leases,

and to disposal groups as set out in paragraph 3.

Sometimes an entity disposes of a group of assets, possibly with some directly **3**
associated liabilities, together in a single transaction. Such a disposal group may be a
group of *cash-generating units*, a single cashgenerating unit, or part of a cash-generating unit. If a non-current asset covered by this [draft] IFRS is part of a disposal
group, the measurement requirements of this [draft] IFRS apply to the group as a
whole. The measurement of the individual assets and liabilities within the disposal
group is set out in paragraphs 11 and 14.

CLASSIFICATION OF NON-CURRENT ASSETS AS HELD FOR SALE

An entity shall classify a non-current asset (or disposal group) as held for sale if its **4**
carrying amount will be recovered principally through a sale transaction rather than
through continuing use.

Such a classification shall be required when and only when the criteria in Appendix B **5**
are met. Sale transactions include exchanges of non-current assets for other non-
current assets.

**ASB footnote: In implementing the standard in the UK this reference will be revised to refer to the most suitable
UK standard.*

Non-current assets to be abandoned

6   Because its carrying amount will be recovered principally through continuing use, an entity shall not classify as held for sale a non-current asset (or disposal group) that is to be abandoned. However, if the disposal group to be abandoned is a *component of an entity*, the entity shall present the results and cash flows of the disposal group as discontinued operations in accordance with paragraph 24 at the date on which it ceases to be used.

7   An entity shall not account for a non-current asset that has been temporarily taken out of use as if it had been abandoned.

MEASUREMENT OF A NON-CURRENT ASSET (OR DISPOSAL GROUP) CLASSIFIED AS HELD FOR SALE

8   An entity shall measure a non-current asset (or disposal group) classified as held for sale at the lower of its carrying amount and *fair value* less *costs to sell*.

9   If a newly acquired asset (or disposal group) meets the criteria to be classified as held for sale (see paragraph B3 of Appendix B), it shall be measured on initial recognition at fair value less costs to sell.

10   In the rare circumstances that the sale is expected to occur beyond one year, the entity shall measure the costs to sell at their present value.

11   The carrying amounts of any assets that are not covered by this [draft] IFRS, including goodwill, but are included in a disposal group classified as held for sale, shall be measured in accordance with other applicable IFRSs before the fair value less costs to sell of the disposal group is measured.

12   For assets that, before classification as held for sale, have not been revalued under another IFRS and for disposal groups that do not include any such revalued assets, an entity shall recognise:
     (a)   an impairment loss for any initial or subsequent write-down of the asset (or disposal group) to fair value less costs to sell; and
     (b)   a gain for any subsequent increase in fair value less costs to sell, but not in excess of the cumulative impairment loss that has been recognised either under this [draft] IFRS or previously under ~~IAS 36 Impairment of Assets~~FRS 11 *Impairment of Fixed Assets and Goodwill.*

13   Paragraphs B5-B8 of Appendix B set out the requirements for the recognition of impairment losses and subsequent gains for assets that, before classification as held for sale, were measured at revalued amounts under another IFRS and for disposal groups that include such revalued assets.

14   The impairment loss (or any subsequent gain) recognised for a disposal group shall reduce (or increase) the carrying amount of the non-current assets in the group that are included in the scope of this [draft] IFRS.

15   A gain or loss not previously recognised by the time of the sale of a noncurrent asset (or disposal group) shall be recognised at the date of sale.

16   An entity shall not depreciate (or amortise) a non-current asset while it is classified as held for sale or while it is part of a disposal group classified as held for sale. Interest

and other expenses attributable to the liabilities of a disposal group classified as held for sale shall continue to be recognised.

Changes to a plan of sale

If an entity has classified an asset (or disposal group) as held for sale, but the criteria in Appendix B are no longer met, the entity shall cease to classify the asset (or disposal group) as held for sale. **17**

The entity shall measure a non-current asset that ceases to be classified as held for sale at the lower of its: **18**

(a) carrying amount before the asset (or disposal group) was classified as held for sale, adjusted for any depreciation or amortisation that would have been recognised had the asset (or disposal group) not been classified as held for sale, and

(b) *recoverable amount* at the date of the subsequent decision not to sell.*

The entity shall include, in income from continuing operations in the period in which the criteria in Appendix B are not met, any required adjustment to the carrying amount of a non-current asset that ceases to be classified as held for sale. The entity shall present that adjustment in the same income statement caption used to report a gain or loss, if any, recognised in accordance with paragraph 27. **19**

If an entity removes an individual asset or liability from a disposal group classified as held for sale, the remaining assets and liabilities of the disposal group to be sold shall continue to be measured as a group only if the group meets the criteria in Appendix B. Otherwise, the remaining non-current assets of the group that individually meet the criteria to be classified as held for sale shall be measured individually at the lower of their carrying amounts and fair values less costs to sell at that date. Any non-current assets that do not meet the criteria shall cease to be classified as held for sale in accordance with paragraph 17. **20**

PRESENTATION AND DISCLOSURE

An entity shall present and disclose information that enables users of the financial statements to evaluate the financial effects of discontinued operations and disposals of non-current assets or disposal groups. **21**

Presenting discontinued operations

A component of an entity comprises operations and cash flows that can be clearly distinguished, operationally and for financial reporting purposes, from the rest of the entity. A component of an entity may be a cashgenerating unit or any group of cash-generating units. **22**

A discontinued operation is a component of an entity that either has been disposed of, or is classified as held for sale, and: **23**

(a) the operations and cash flows of that component have been (or will be) eliminated from the ongoing operations of the entity as a result of its disposal, and

---

*If the asset is part of a cash-generating unit, its recoverable amount is the carrying amount that would have been recognised after the allocation of any impairment loss arising on that cash-generating unit under IAS 36 (had such requirements applied).

(b)   the entity will have no significant continuing involvement in that component after its disposal.

24   An entity shall disclose for all periods presented:

(a)   the revenue, expenses and pre-tax profit or loss of discontinued operations, and the ~~related~~ income tax expense ~~as required by paragraph 81(h) of IAS 12 Income Taxes~~relating to the profit or loss from the ordinary activities of the discontinued operation for the period, together with the corresponding amounts for each prior period presented;

(b)   the gain or loss recognised on the remeasurement to fair value less costs to sell or disposal of the assets or disposal group(s) comprising the discontinued operation and the ~~related~~income tax expense ~~as required by paragraph 81(h) of IAS 12~~relating to the gain or loss on discontinuance;

(c)   the net cash flows attributable to the operating, investing and financing activities of discontinued operations.

An entity shall present the disclosures required by (a) on the face of the income statement. The other disclosures may be presented either in the notes to, or on the face of, the financial statements.

25   Adjustments in the current period to amounts previously presented in discontinued operations that are directly related to the disposal of a discontinued operation in a prior period shall be classified separately in discontinued operations. The nature and amount of such adjustments shall be disclosed. Examples of circumstances in which these adjustments may arise include the following:

(a)   the resolution of uncertainties that arise pursuant to the terms of the disposal transaction, such as the resolution of purchase price adjustments and indemnification issues with the purchaser.

(b)   the resolution of uncertainties that arise from and are directly related to the operations of the component before its disposal, such as environmental and product warranty obligations retained by the seller.

(c)   the settlement of employee benefit plan obligations provided that the settlement is directly related to the disposal transaction.

26   If an entity ceases to classify a component of an entity as held for sale, the results of operations of the component previously presented in discontinued operations in accordance with paragraphs 22-25 shall be reclassified and included in income from continuing operations for all periods presented.

Gains or losses relating to continuing operations

27   Any gain or loss on the remeasurement of a non-current asset (or disposal group) that does not meet the definition of a component of an entity shall be included in the profit or loss from continuing operations.

Presentation of a non-current asset or disposal group classified as held for sale

28   An entity shall present a non-current asset classified as held for sale and the assets of a disposal group classified as held for sale separately from other assets in the balance sheet. The liabilities of a disposal group classified as held for sale shall be presented separately from other liabilities in the balance sheet. Those assets and liabilities shall not be offset and presented as a single amount. The major classes of assets and liabilities classified as held for sale shall be separately disclosed ~~either~~ on the face of

the balance sheet under the statutory format headings.~~or in the notes to the financial statements.~~

Additional disclosures

An entity shall disclose the following information in the notes to the financial **29** statements that cover the period in which a non-current asset (or disposal group) has been either classified as held for sale or sold:

(a)   a description of the facts and circumstances leading to the expected disposal and the expected manner and timing of that disposal;

(b)   the gain or loss recognised in accordance with paragraph 12 (or paragraphs B5-B8 of Appendix B) and, if not separately presented on the face of the income statement, the caption in the income statement that includes that gain or loss;

(c)   if applicable, the segment in which the non-current asset (or disposal group) is presented under ~~IAS 14 *Segment Reporting*~~SSAP 25 *Segmental reporting*.

If either paragraph 17 or paragraph 20 applies, an entity shall disclose, in the notes to **30** the financial statements that include the period of the decision to change the plan to sell the non-current asset (or disposal group), a description of the facts and circumstances leading to the decision and the effect of the decision on the results of operations for the period and any prior periods presented.

EFFECTIVE DATE

The accounting practices set out in this [draft] FRS shall be regarded as standard in **31** respect of accounting ~~An entity shall apply this [draft] IFRS in its annual financial statements for~~ periods beginning on or after ~~1 January 2005~~[date to be inserted after exposure]. Earlier application is encouraged. If an entity applies the [draft] IFRS in its financial statements for a period beginning before ~~1 January 2005~~[date to be inserted after exposure], it shall disclose that fact.

Appendix A

DEFINED TERMS

This appendix is an integral part of the [draft] IFRS.

cash-generating unit	The smallest identifiable group of assets that generates cash inflows from continuing use that are largely independent of the cash inflows from other assets or groups of assets.
component of an entity	Operations and cash flows that can be clearly distinguished, operationally and for financial reporting purposes, from the rest of the entity.
costs to sell	The incremental costs directly attributable to the disposal of an asset (or disposal group), excluding finance costs and income tax expense.

current asset

An asset that:

(a) is expected to be realised in, or is intended for sale or consumption in, the normal course of the entity's operating cycle;

(b) is held primarily for trading purposes;

(c) is expected to be realised within twelve months of the balance sheet date;* or

(d) is cash or a cash equivalent asset that is not restricted from being exchanged or used to settle a liability for at least twelve months from the balance sheet date.

discontinued operation

A component *of an entity* that either has been disposed of or is classified as held for sale and:

(a) the operations and cash flows of that component have been (or will be) eliminated from the ongoing operations of the entity as a result of its disposal, and

(b) the entity will have no significant continuing involvement in that component after its disposal.

disposal group

A group of assets to be disposed of, by sale or otherwise, together as a group in a single transaction, and liabilities directly associated with those assets that will be transferred in the transaction. The group includes goodwill acquired in a business combination if the group is a cash-generating unit to which goodwill would have has been allocated in accordance with the requirements of paragraphs 73 and 74 of [draft] IAS 36 *Impairment of*

---

*The Board has tentatively agreed in the Improvements project that this wording will be amended so that it does not include non-current assets that are expected to be realised in the next twelve months.

Assets (had such requirements applied) or if it is an operation within such a cash-generating unit.

fair value	The amount for which an asset could be exchanged, or a liability settled, between knowledgeable, willing parties in an arm's length transaction.
firm purchase commitment	An agreement with an unrelated party, binding on both parties and usually legally enforceable, that (a) specifies all significant terms, including the price and timing of the transactions, and (b) includes a disincentive for nonperformance that is sufficiently large to make performance highly probable.
highly probable	Significantly more likely than probable.
non-current asset	An asset that does not meet the definition of a current asset.
Probable	More likely than not.
recoverable amount	The higher of an asset's fair value less costs to sell and its value in use.
value in use	The present value of estimated future cash flows expected to arise from the continuing use of an asset and from its disposal at the end of its useful life.

ASB footnote: The requirements of paragraphs 73 and 74 of [draft] IAS 36 are:

73 For the purpose of impairment testing, goodwill acquired in a business combination shall, from the acquisition date, be allocated to one or more cash-generating units. Each of those cash-generating units shall represent the smallest cash-generating unit to which a portion of the carrying amount of the goodwill can be allocated on a reasonable and consistent basis.

74 A portion of the carrying amount of goodwill shall be regarded as being capable of being allocated to a cash-generating unit on a reasonable and consistent basis only when that cash-generating unit represents the lowest level at which management monitors the return on investment in assets that include the goodwill. However, that cash-generating unit shall not be larger than a segment based on the entity's primary reporting format determined in accordance with SSAP 25 *Segmental reporting*.

Appendix B

APPLICATION SUPPLEMENT

This appendix is an integral part of the [draft] IFRS.

Classification of a non-current asset or disposal group as held for sale

B1   Paragraph 4 of this [draft] IFRS requires a non-current asset (or disposal group) to be classified as held for sale if its carrying amount will be recovered principally through a sale transaction rather than through continuing use. An entity shall classify a non-current asset (or disposal group) as held for sale in the reporting period in which all of the following criteria are met:

(a)   management, having the authority to approve the action, commits itself to a plan to sell;

(b)   the asset (or disposal group) is available for immediate sale in its present condition subject only to terms that are usual and customary for sales of such assets (or disposal groups);

(c)   an active programme to locate a buyer and other actions required to complete the plan to sell the asset (or disposal group) are initiated;

(d)   the sale is *highly probable*, and is expected to qualify for recognition as a completed sale, within one year from the date of classification as held for sale, except as permitted by paragraph B2;

(e)   the asset (or disposal group) is being actively marketed for sale at a price that is reasonable in relation to its current fair value; and

(f)   actions required to complete the plan indicate that it is unlikely that significant changes to the plan will be made or that the plan will be withdrawn.

B2   Events or circumstances may extend the period to complete the sale beyond one year. An extension of the period required to complete a sale does not preclude an asset (or disposal group) from being classified as held for sale if the delay is caused by events or circumstances beyond the entity's control and there is sufficient evidence that the entity remains committed to its plan to sell the asset (or disposal group). An exception to the one-year requirement in paragraph B1(d) shall therefore apply in the following situations in which such events or circumstances arise:

(a)   at the date an entity commits itself to a plan to sell a non-current asset (or disposal group) it reasonably expects that others (not a buyer) will impose conditions on the transfer of the asset (or disposal group) that will extend the period required to complete the sale, and:

(i)   actions necessary to respond to those conditions cannot be initiated until after a *firm purchase commitment* is obtained, and

(ii)   a firm purchase commitment is highly probable within one year;

(b)   an entity obtains a firm purchase commitment and, as a result, a buyer or others unexpectedly impose conditions on the transfer of a non-current asset (or disposal group) previously classified as held for sale that will extend the period required to complete the sale, and:

(i)   timely actions necessary to respond to the conditions have been taken, and

(ii)   a favourable resolution of the delaying factors is expected;

(c) during the initial one-year period, circumstances arise that were previously considered unlikely and, as a result, a non-current asset (or disposal group) previously classified as held for sale is not sold by the end of that period, and:

    (i) during the initial one-year period the entity took action necessary to respond to the change in circumstances,

    (ii) the non-current asset (or disposal group) is being actively marketed at a price that is reasonable, given the change in circumstances, and

    (iii) the criteria in paragraph B1 are met.

When an entity acquires a non-current asset (or disposal group) exclusively with a view to its subsequent disposal, it shall classify the non-current asset (or disposal group) as held for sale at the acquisition date only if the oneyear requirement in paragraph B1(d) is met (except as permitted by paragraph B2) and it is highly probable that any other criteria in paragraph B1 that are not met at that date will be met within a short period following the acquisition (usually within three months). **B3**

Meeting the held for sale criteria after the balance sheet date

If the criteria in paragraph B1 are met after the balance sheet date but before the financial statements are authorised for issue, an entity shall not classify a noncurrent asset (or disposal group) as held for sale in those financial statements when issued. However, the entity shall disclose the information specified in paragraph 28(a) in the notes to the financial statements. **B4**

Impairment losses and subsequent increases in fair value less costs to sell of assets that were previously revalued

Paragraph 12 requires the recognition of impairment losses and subsequent gains for assets that have not been revalued under another IFRS before classification as held for sale (and for disposal groups that do not include any such revalued assets). Paragraphs B6-B8 set out the equivalent requirements for assets that, before classification as held for sale, have been revalued and for disposal groups that include such revalued assets. **B5**

Any asset that is carried at a revalued amount under another IFRS shall be revalued under that IFRS immediately before it is classified as held for sale under this [draft] IFRS. Any impairment loss that arises on reclassification of the asset (or of a disposal group containing the asset) shall be recognised in the income statement. **B6**

Subsequent impairment losses

Any subsequent increases in costs to sell shall be recognised in the income statement. Any decreases in fair value shall be treated as revaluation decreases in accordance with the standard under which the assets were revalued before their classification as held for sale. **B7**

Subsequent gains

Any subsequent decreases in costs to sell shall be recognised in the income statement. For individual assets that, before classification as held for sale, were revalued under another IFRS, any subsequent increase in fair value shall be recognised to its full extent and treated as a revaluation increase in accordance with the standard under which the assets were revalued before their classification as held for sale. For disposal **B8** groups that include such revalued assets, any subsequent increases in fair value shall be recognised to the extent that the carrying value of the non-current assets in the group after the increase has been allocated does not exceed their fair value less costs to sell. The increase shall be treated as a revaluation increase in accordance with the standard under which the assets were revalued before their classification as held for sale.

Appendix C

AMENDMENTS TO OTHER IFRSS

The amendments in this [draft] appendix become effective for accounting periods beginning on or after 1 January 2005. If an entity applies this [draft] IFRS for an earlier period, these amendments become effective for that earlier period.

In [draft] *IAS 1 *Presentation of Financial Statements*, paragraph 54 is amended to read as follows: **C1**

> *An asset shall be classified as current when it:*
>
> *(a) is expected to be realised in, or is intended for sale or consumption in, the normal course of the entity's operating cycle;*
> *(b) ...*

In [draft] *IAS 16 *Property, Plant and Equipment*, paragraph 2 is amended to read as follows: **C2**

> This Standard does not apply to:
>
> (a) non-current assets classified as held for sale under IFRS X *Disposal of Non-current Assets and Presentation of Discontinued Operations;*
> (b) biological assets...

In [draft] *IAS 27 *Consolidated and Separate Financial Statements*, paragraph 13 is deleted.   **C3**

In [draft] *IAS 28 *Accounting for Investments in Associates*, paragraph 8 is amended as follows: **C4**

> *An investment in an associate shall be accounted for under the equity method except when:*
>
> *(a) the investment is acquired and held exclusively with a view to its subsequent disposal within twelve months from acquisition. Such investments shall be accounted for in accordance with IAS 39* Financial Instruments: Recognition and Measurement, *at fair value with changes in fair value included in profit or loss of the period of change; or*
> *(b) the investment is classified as held for sale under IFRS X* Disposal of Noncurrent Assets and Presentation of Discontinued Operations. *Such investments shall be accounted for in accordance with that IFRS.*

In IAS 31 Financial Reporting of Interests in Joint Ventures, paragraph 36A is added as follows: **C5**

36A A venturer shall account for an interest in a jointly controlled entity that is classified as held for sale under IFRS X *Disposal of Noncurrent Assets and Presentation of Discontinued Operations* in accordance with that IFRS.

IAS 35 Discontinuing Operations is withdrawn.   **C6**

In [draft] *IAS 36 *Impairment of Assets*, all references to 'net selling price' are replaced by 'fair value less costs to sell'.   **C7**

---

included in the Exposure Draft Improvements to International Accounting Standards, published in May 2002.

C8   In [draft]* IAS 36, paragraph 1 is amended to read as follows:

> *This Standard shall be applied in accounting for the impairment of all assets, other than:*
>
> *(a)* ...
>
> *(e)* *non-current assets (or disposal groups) classified as held for sale under IFRS X* Disposal of Non-current Assets and Presentation of Discontinued Operations;
>
> *(f)* ...

C9   In [draft] *IAS 36, paragraph 2 is amended to read as follows:

This Standard does not apply to inventories, assets arising from construction contracts, deferred tax assets, assets arising from employee benefits, or assets classified as held for sale under IFRS X *Disposal of Non-current Assets and Presentation of Discontinued Operations* because existing Standards applicable to these assets already contain specific requirements for recognising and measuring these assets.

C10   In [draft]† IAS 38 *Intangible Assets,* paragraph 2 is amended to read as follows:

> ...For example, this Standard does not apply to:
>
> (a)   non-current intangible assets classified as held for sale under IFRS X *Disposal of Non-current Assets and Presentation of Discontinued Operations*;
>
> (b)   intangible assets...

C11   In IAS 40 *Investment Properties,* paragraph 3 is amended to read as follows:

> This Standard does not apply to:
>
> ...
>
> (c)   investment property classified as held for sale under IFRS X *Disposal of Non-current Assets and Presentation of Discontinued Operations.*

C12   In IAS 40 *Investment Properties,* paragraph 7(a) is amended to read as follows:

(a) property intended for sale in the ordinary course of business...

C13   In [draft] ‡IFRS X *Business Combinations,* paragraph 35 is amended to read as follows:

The acquirer shall, at the acquisition date, allocate the cost of a business combination by recognising the acquiree's identifiable assets, liabilities and contingent liabilities that satisfy the recognition criteria in paragraph 36 at their fair values at that date, except for non-current assets (or disposal groups) that meet the criteria to be classified as held for sale under IFRS X *Disposal of Non-current Assets and Presentation of Discontinued Operations*, which shall be recognised at fair value less costs to sell. Any difference...

---

*included in the Exposure Draft Amendments to IAS 36, Impairment of Assets, and IAS 38, Intangible Assets, published in December 2002

†included in the Exposure Draft Amendments to IAS 36, Impairment of Assets, and IAS 38, Intangible Assets, published in December 2002

‡in ED 3 Business Combinations, published in December 2002.

Basis for Conclusions

Contents

ED 4 DISPOSAL OF NONCURRENT ASSETS AND PRESENTATION OF DISCONTINUED OPERATIONS

Basis for conclusions on ED 4 Disposal of non-current assets and presentation of discontinued operations

This Basis for Conclusions accompanies, but is not part of, the draft IFRS.

INTRODUCTION

BC1　This Basis for Conclusions summarises the Board's considerations in reaching the conclusions in the draft IFRS *Disposal of Non-current Assets and Presentation of Discontinued Operations*. Individual Board members gave greater weight to some factors than to others.

BC2　In September 2002 the Board agreed to add a short-term convergence project to its active agenda. The objective of the project is to reduce differences between IFRSs and US GAAP that are capable of resolution in a relatively short time and can be addressed outside current and planned major projects. The project is a joint project with the US Financial Accounting Standards Board (FASB).

BC3　In working towards the objective of the project, the two boards agreed to review each other's deliberations on each of the selected possible convergence topics, and choose the highest quality solution as the basis for convergence. For topics recently considered by either board, there is an expectation that whichever board has more recently deliberated that topic will have the higher quality solution.

BC4　As part of the review of topics recently considered by the FASB, the Board discussed the requirements of SFAS 144 *Accounting for the Impairment or Disposal of Long-Lived Assets*, as they relate to assets held for sale and discontinued operations. The Board did not consider the requirements of SFAS 144 relating to the impairment of assets held for use. Impairment of such assets is an issue that is being addressed in the IASB research project on measurement being led by the Canadian Accounting Standards Board.

BC5　The requirements of SFAS 144 on assets held for sale and discontinued operations differ from current IFRSs in the following ways:

(a)　if specified criteria are met, non-current assets that are to be disposed of are classified as held for sale. Such assets are remeasured at the lower of carrying amount and fair value less costs to sell and cease to be depreciated or amortised. Under IFRSs, noncurrent assets that are to be disposed of are not classified separately or measured differently from other non-current assets.

(b)　the definition of discontinued operations under SFAS 144 is different from the definition of discontinuing operations under IAS 35 *Discontinuing Operations* and the presentation of such operations is also different under the two standards.

BC6　As discussed in more detail below, the Board concluded that introducing a classification of assets that are held for sale would substantially improve the information available to users of financial statements about assets to be sold. It further concluded that the definition of discontinued operations in SFAS 144 leads to more useful information being presented and disclosed for a wider range of operations than does the existing definition in IAS 35.

BC7　Appendix B to this Basis for Conclusions sets out tables of concordance showing how the paragraphs in the draft IFRS relate to those in SFAS 144.

SCOPE OF THE DRAFT IFRS

The Board agreed that the draft IFRS should apply to all non-current assets except: **BC8**

(a)   goodwill, because goodwill can never be an asset held for sale other than as part of a disposal group and the allocation of goodwill to disposal groups is covered by draft IFRS X *Business Combinations*.

(b)   financial instruments covered by IAS 39 *Financial Instruments: Recognition and Measurement*, because IAS 39 addresses the treatment of financial assets that are held for sale.

(c)   financial assets under leases, which are currently excluded from IAS 39 but which the Board proposes should be within the scope of that standard. If those proposals become effective, these assets will be covered by the exemption in (b) and this exemption will not be needed.

(d)   deferred tax assets and assets arising from employee benefits, because their measurement basis is addressed by other IFRSs.

The scope of the draft IFRS differs from that of SFAS 144 in the following ways: **BC9**

Item	SFAS 144	Draft IFRS
Intangible assets not being amortised	Excluded	Included
Long-term customer relationships	Excluded	Included
Associates	Excluded	Included
Assets in specialised industries covered by other FASB statements	Excluded	Included
Insurance contracts	Included other than deferred acquisition costs	Included
Extractive industries	Included other than unproved oil and gas properties that are being accounted for using the successful-efforts method of accounting	Included
Employee benefit assets	Included	Excluded

SFAS 144 addresses impairment of long-lived assets held for use as well as assets held for sale. That fact, together with the existence of other FASB statements on specific specialised industries, underlies many of the FASB exclusions listed above. The Board believes that the assets should be covered by the draft IFRS, which addresses only assets classified as held for sale.

Classification of non-current assets to be disposed of as held for sale

Under SFAS144 long-lived assets are classified as either (i) held and used or (ii) held   **BC10** for sale. Under IFRSs no distinction is made between noncurrent assets held and used and non-current assets held for sale, except in relation to financial instruments.

The Board considered whether a separate classification for non-current assets held   **BC11** for sale would create unnecessary complexity in IFRSs and introduce an element of management intent into the accounting. Some suggested that the categorisation 'assets held for sale' is unnecessary, and that if the focus were changed to 'assets *retired* from active use' much of the complexity could be eliminated, because the latter classification would be based on actuality rather than what they perceive as management intent. It is the potential abuse of the classification that necessitates many of the detailed requirements in SFAS 144. Others suggested that, if existing IFRSs were amended to specify that assets retired from active use are measured at fair value less costs to sell and to require additional disclosure, some convergence with SFAS 144 could be achieved without creating a new IFRS.

BC12   However, the Board concluded that providing information about assets and groups of assets and liabilities to be disposed of is of benefit to users of financial statements. Such information should assist in assessing the timing and amount of future cash flows. The Board understands that this was also the assessment underpinning SFAS 144. Therefore the Board concluded that introducing the notion of assets and disposal groups held for sale makes IFRS literature more complete.

BC13   Furthermore, although the held for sale classification begins from an intent to sell the asset, the other criteria for this classification are tightly drawn and are significantly more prescriptive than simply specifying an intent or commitment to sell. Some might argue that the criteria are too specific. However, the Board believes that the criteria should be specific to achieve comparability of classification between entities. The Board did not believe that a classification 'retired from active use' would necessarily require fewer criteria to support it. For example, it would be necessary to establish a distinction between assets retired from active use and those that are temporarily idle.

BC14   Lastly, if the classification and measurement of assets held for sale under IFRSs are the same as under US GAAP, convergence will have been achieved in an area of importance to users of financial statements.

Assets to be exchanged for other non-current assets

BC15   Under SFAS 144, long-lived assets that are to be exchanged for similar productive assets cannot be classified as held for sale. They are regarded as disposed of only when exchanged. The Basis for Conclusions for SFAS 144 explains that this is because the exchange of such assets is accounted for at amounts based on the carrying amount of the assets, not at fair value, and that using the carrying amount is more consistent with the accounting for a long-lived asset to be held and used than for a long-lived asset to be sold.

BC16   Under draft IAS 16 *Property, Plant and Equipment,* an exchange of assets is normally measured at fair value. The SFAS 144 reasoning on the classification of such assets as held for sale does not, therefore, apply. Consistent with draft IAS 16, the draft IFRS treats an exchange of assets as a disposal and acquisition of assets.

BC17   The FASB is considering whether to converge with the proposed IASB requirement for an exchange of assets to be measured at fair value. The FASB has indicated that if it were to change its requirements for asset exchanges, it would also need to reconsider whether such assets could be classified as assets held for sale.

Measurement of non-current assets held for sale

BC18   Under SFAS 144, a long-lived asset or a disposal group classified as held for sale is measured at the lower of its carrying amount and fair value less costs to sell. A long-lived asset classified as held for sale (or included within a disposal group) is not depreciated, but interest and other expenses attributable to the liabilities of a disposal group are recognised.

As explained in the Basis for Conclusions for SFAS 144, the argument is that the remaining use in operations of an asset that is to be sold is incidental to the recovery of the carrying amount through sale. The accounting for such an asset should therefore be a process of valuation rather than allocation. **BC19**

The FASB further observed that once the asset is remeasured, to depreciate the asset would reduce its carrying amount below its fair value less costs to sell. It also noted that should there be a decline in the value of the asset after initial classification as held for sale and before eventual sale, the loss would be recognised in the period of decline because the fair value less costs to sell is evaluated each period. **BC20**

The counter-argument is that, although classified as held for sale, the asset is still being used in operations, and hence cessation of depreciation is inconsistent with the basic principle that the cost of an asset should be allocated over the period during which benefits are obtained from its use. Further, although the decline in the value of the asset through its use would be reflected in the change in fair value subsequently recognised, it might also be masked by an increase arising from changes in market prices of the asset. **BC21**

However, the Board noted that draft IAS 16 requires an entity to keep its residual values up to date, and IAS 36 *Impairment of Assets* requires an immediate writedown to the higher of value in use and fair value less costs to sell. An entity should, therefore, often achieve a measurement effect under existing IFRSs similar to that required under the draft IFRS, as follows. Under existing IFRSs, if the fair value less costs to sell is higher than carrying amount there will be no impairment and no depreciation (because the residual value will have been updated). If fair value less costs to sell is lower than carrying amount, there will be an impairment loss that reduces the carrying amount to fair value less costs to sell and then no depreciation (because the residual value will have been updated), unless value in use is higher than fair value less costs to sell. If value in use is higher than fair value less costs to sell, there will be an impairment loss to the extent that the carrying amount exceeds value in use and then depreciation of the excess of value in use over fair value less costs to sell. However, value in use will differ from fair value less costs to sell only to the extent of the net cash flows expected to arise before the sale. If the period to sale is short, this amount will usually be relatively small. **BC22**

The Board concluded that the measurement requirements of the draft IFRS would often not involve a significant change from the requirements of existing (or proposed) IFRSs. Furthermore, the Board agreed with the FASB that the cash flows arising from the asset's remaining use were incidental to the recovery of the asset through sale and, hence, concluded that assets classified as held for sale should be measured at the lower of carrying amount and fair value less costs to sell and should not be depreciated. **BC23**

In addition, it is worth emphasising that the proposals permit only an asset that is to be *sold* to be classified as held for sale. Assets to be abandoned are classified as held and used until disposed of, and thus are depreciated. The Board agrees with the FASB's observation that a distinction can be drawn between an asset that is to be sold and an asset that is to be abandoned, because the former will be recovered principally through sale and the latter through its continuing use. Therefore, it is logical that depreciation should cease in the former but not the latter case. **BC24**

BC25   When an asset or a disposal group held for sale is part of a foreign operation with a different functional currency from the rest of the group, an exchange difference will have been recognised in equity arising from the translation of the asset or disposal group into the presentation currency of the group. Draft IAS 21 *The Effects of Changes in Foreign Exchange Rates* requires the exchange difference to be 'recycled' from equity to the income statement on disposal of the operation. The question arises whether classification as held for sale should trigger the recycling of any exchange differences.

BC26   In its project on reporting comprehensive income, the Board is reconsidering the issue of recycling. Therefore, it did not wish to make any interim changes to the requirements in draft IAS 21. Hence, the draft IFRS does not require any exchange differences to be recycled on the classification of an asset or a disposal group as held for sale.

The allocation of an impairment loss to a disposal group

BC27   Under SFAS 144, assets within the disposal group that are not within the scope of the Statement (for example, goodwill) are adjusted in accordance with other Statements before measuring the fair value less costs to sell of the disposal group. Any loss or gain recognised on adjusting the carrying amount of the disposal group is allocated to the carrying amount of the longlived assets of the group.

BC28   This is different from the requirements of draft IAS 36 for the allocation of an impairment loss arising on a cash-generating unit. Draft IAS 36 requires an impairment loss for a cash-generating unit to be allocated first to reduce the carrying amount of goodwill to its implied value and then to reduce the carrying amounts of the other assets in the unit on a pro-rata basis.*

BC29   The Board considered whether the allocation of an impairment loss for a disposal group should be consistent with the requirements of draft IAS 36 or with the requirements of SFAS 144. The Board noted that the presentation of a disposal group in the balance sheet is required to comprise only two items, assets and liabilities, although greater disaggregation is allowed. In practice, it may be that noncurrent and current assets are presented separately. Given this, the Board agreed that the most appropriate allocation of the impairment loss is to the noncurrent assets that are within the scope of the draft IFRS.

Newly acquired assets

BC30   SFAS 144 requires newly acquired assets that meet the criteria to be classified as held for sale to be measured at fair value less costs to sell on initial recognition. So, in those instances, other than in a business combination, in which an entity acquires a non-current asset that meets the criteria to be classified as held for sale, a loss is recognised in the income statement if the cost of the asset exceeds its fair value less costs to sell. In the more common cases in which an entity acquires, as part of a business combination, a noncurrent asset (or disposal group) that meets the criteria to be classified as held for sale, the difference between fair value and fair value less costs to sell is recognised in goodwill.

*In allocating the loss in this way, draft IAS 36 also requires that the carrying amount of an asset shall not be reduced below the highest of (i) its fair value less costs to sell (if determinable), (ii) its value in use and (iii) zero.

Under current IFRSs there is no classification of assets as held for sale and, hence, all assets acquired in a business combination are required to be measured at fair value on initial recognition. The Board considered whether, having agreed to classify assets that meet specified criteria as held for sale and to measure them at fair value less costs to sell, it should require that measure to be used for initial recognition in a business combination. **BC31**

The Board's view is that conceptually the assets should be recognised initially at fair value and then immediately classified as held for sale, with the result that the costs to sell are recognised in the income statement, not goodwill. In theory, if the entity had factored the costs to sell into the purchase price, the reduced price would lead to the creation of negative goodwill, the immediate recognition of which in the income statement would offset the loss arising from the costs to sell. Of course, in practice, the reduced price will usually result in a lower net positive goodwill figure rather than negative goodwill to be recognised in the income statement. For that reason, and for the sake of convergence, the Board agreed that in a business combination noncurrent assets that meet the criteria to be classified as held for sale should be measured at fair value less costs to sell on initial recognition. **BC32**

The Board and the FASB are considering which items should form part of the business combination transaction more generally in their joint project on the application of the purchase method. The outcome of those deliberations may affect the decision noted in paragraph BC32. **BC33**

Recognition of subsequent increases in fair value less costs to sell

The Board considered whether a subsequent increase in fair value less costs to sell should be recognised to the extent that it reversed previous impairments. SFAS 144 requires the recognition of a subsequent increase in fair value less costs to sell but not in excess of the cumulative loss previously recognised for a write-down to fair value less costs to sell. The Board agreed that, under IFRSs, a gain should be recognised to the extent that it reverses any impairment of the asset, either under the proposed IFRS or previously under draft IAS 36. Recognising a gain for the reversal of an impairment that occurred before the classification of the asset as held for sale is consistent with the requirement in draft IAS 36 to recognise reversals of impairment. **BC34**

Recognition of impairment losses and subsequent gains for assets that, before classification as held for sale, were measured at revalued amounts under another IFRS

The Board agreed that impairment losses and subsequent gains for assets that, before classification as held for sale, were measured at revalued amounts under another IFRS should be treated as revaluation decreases and increases according to the standard under which the assets had previously been revalued, consistently with the requirements of draft IAS 36, except to the extent that the losses and gains are caused by the initial recognition of, or changes in, costs to sell. The Board agreed that costs to sell should always be recognised in the income statement. **BC35**

Measurement of assets reclassified as held for use

Under SFAS 144, when an entity changes its plan to sell the asset and reclassifies a long-lived asset from held for sale to held and used, the asset is measured at the lower of (a) the carrying amount before the asset (or disposal group) was classified as held for sale, adjusted for any depreciation (or amortisation) expense that would have **BC36** been recognised had the asset (or disposal group) been continuously classified as held and used and (b) its fair value at the date of the decision not to sell.

BC37   The underlying principle is to restore the carrying value of the asset to what it would have been had it never been classified as held for sale, taking into account any impairments that may have occurred. In fact, under SFAS 144, for held and used assets, an impairment is recognised only if the carrying amount of the asset exceeds the sum of the undiscounted cash flows expected to result from its use and eventual disposal. Thus, the carrying amount of the asset if it had never been classified as held for sale might exceed its fair value. As a result, SFAS 144 does not necessarily lead to the asset reverting to its original carrying amount. However, the Basis for Conclusions for SFAS 144 notes that the FASB concluded it would be inappropriate to write up the carrying amount of the asset to an amount greater than its fair value based solely on an undiscounted cash flow test. Hence, it arrived at the requirement for measurement at the lower of (a) the asset's carrying amount had it not been classified as held for sale and (b) fair value at the date of the decision not to sell the asset.

BC38   Draft IAS 36 has a different measurement basis for impaired assets, ie recoverable amount. The Board concluded that to be consistent with the principle of SFAS 144 and also to be consistent with the requirements of draft IAS 36, an asset that ceases to be classified as held for sale should be measured at the lower of (a) the carrying amount that would have been recognised had the asset not been classified as held for sale and (b) its recoverable amount at the date of reclassification. Whilst this is not full convergence, the difference arises from differences in the US GAAP and IFRS impairment models.

Removal of exemption from consolidation for subsidiaries acquired and held exclusively with a view to resale

BC39   SFAS 144 removed the exemption from consolidation in US GAAP for subsidiaries held on a temporary basis on the grounds that all assets held for sale should be treated in the same way, ie as required by SFAS 144.

BC40   The Board agreed that all subsidiaries should be consolidated and that all assets (and disposal groups) that meet the criteria to be classified as held for sale should be treated in the same way. The current exemption from consolidation in IAS 27 *Consolidated Financial Statements and Accounting for Investments in Subsidiaries* for subsidiaries acquired and held exclusively with a view to resale prevents those assets and disposal groups within such subsidiaries which meet the criteria to be classified as held for sale from being treated consistently with other assets and disposal groups. The draft IFRS therefore proposes that the exemption in IAS 27 should be removed.

Presentation of non-current assets held for sale

BC41   SFAS 144 requires an entity to present:

(a)   a long-lived asset classified as held for sale separately in the balance sheet; and

(b)   the assets and liabilities of a disposal group classified as held for sale separately in the asset and liability sections of the balance sheet. The major classes of those assets and liabilities are separately disclosed either on the face of the balance sheet or in the notes.

BC42   In the Basis for Conclusions for SFAS 144 the FASB noted that information about the nature of both assets and liabilities of a disposal group is useful to users.

Separately presenting those items in the balance sheet provides information that is relevant. Separate presentation also distinguishes those assets that are not being depreciated from those that are being depreciated. The Board agreed with the FASB's views.

Definition of discontinued operations

With the introduction of SFAS 144, the FASB broadened the scope of a discontinued operation from a 'segment of a business' to a 'component of an entity'. A component is widely drawn, the criterion being that it comprises 'operations and cash flows that can be clearly distinguished, operationally and for financial reporting purposes, from the rest of the entity'. SFAS 144 states that a component may be a segment, a reporting unit, a subsidiary or an asset group.

BC43

However, at the same time, the FASB specified more restrictive criteria for determining *when* the component is classified as discontinued and hence when its results are presented as discontinued. Under SFAS 144, a component is classified as discontinued only if it has been disposed of or if it meets the criteria for classification as an asset 'held for sale'.

BC44

The definition of a discontinuing operation in IAS 35 as a 'major line of business' or 'geographical area of operations' is closer to the former, and narrower, US GAAP definition. The trigger in IAS 35 for classifying the operation as discontinuing is the earlier of (a) the entity entering into a binding sale agreement and (b) the board of directors approving and announcing a formal disposal plan. Although IAS 35 refers to IAS 37 *Provisions, Contingent Liabilities and Contingent Assets* for further guidance on what constitutes a plan, the criteria are less restrictive than those in SFAS 144.

BC45

Paragraph 12 of the *Framework* states that the objective of financial statements is to provide information about the financial position, performance and changes in financial position of an enterprise that is useful to a wide range of users in making economic decisions. Paragraph 15 of the *Framework* goes on to state that the economic decisions that are taken by users of financial statements require an evaluation of the ability of an enterprise to generate cash and cash equivalents. Separately highlighting the results of discontinued operations provides users with information that is relevant in assessing the ongoing ability of the entity to generate cash flows.

BC46

However, under existing IAS 35 there may be disposal transactions that, although likely to have an impact on the ongoing operations of the entity, do not meet the criteria for classification as a discontinuing activity. For example, an entity might dispose of a significant portion, but not all, of its cash-generating units operating in a particular geographical area. Under IAS 35, that might not meet the definition of a discontinuing operation. Under the draft IFRS, if the relevant criteria were met, it would.

BC47

The Board considered whether broadening the classification of discontinued operations might cause confusion for users of financial statements because it will increase the number of times that revenues and expenses for prior periods are restated. On balance, however, the Board believes that the risk of potential confusion to users arising from restatement is outweighed by the benefit to users of enhanced information on the ongoing operations of the entity.

BC48

In terms of the timing of classifying an operation as discontinued, the Board considered whether more useful information is provided by making the classification

BC49

conditional upon a firm decision to discontinue an operation (the current IAS 35 approach) or conditional upon the classification of an operation as held for sale.

BC50   The Board agreed that, to be consistent with the presentation of assets held for disposal and in the interests of convergence, an operation should be classified as discontinued when it is disposed of or classified as held for sale.

BC51   IAS 35 also adopts a different approach from US GAAP when criteria for classification as discontinued are met after the period-end but before the financial statements are issued. Under SFAS 144, some disclosure is required; however, the component is *not* presented as a discontinued operation. Under IAS 35, the component is classified as discontinuing.

BC52   The Board believes that, if more restrictive criteria are specified for determining when a component has been discontinued, it would be inconsistent to apply retroactively a classification that did not apply at the period-end.

Presentation of discontinued operations

BC53   Under SFAS 144, the results of a discontinued operation are presented as a separate component in the income statement (net of income tax) for all periods presented.

BC54   Under IAS 35, the results of a discontinuing operation are not presented as a net amount on the face of the income statement. Instead, specified items are disclosed either in the notes or on the face of the income statement.

BC55   In its project on reporting comprehensive income, the Board is considering the presentation of discontinued operations in the income statement. It does not wish to prejudge the outcome of that project by changing the requirements of IAS 35 in respect of the components to be disclosed. It agrees, however, that disclosure on the face of the income statement is desirable because of the prominence given to information about continuing and discontinued operations. The draft IFRS therefore brings forward unchanged the requirements of IAS 35 regarding the items to be disclosed for discontinued operations but requires some of those items to be presented on the face of the income statement.

Terminology

BC56   Two issues of terminology arose in developing the draft IFRS:

   (a)   the use of the term 'probable' and
   (b)   the use of the term 'fair value less costs to sell'.

BC57   In SFAS 144, the term *probable* is described as referring to a future sale that is 'likely to occur'. For the purposes of IFRSs, IAS 37 *Provisions, Contingent Liabilities and Contingent Assets* defines 'probable' as meaning 'more likely than not' and ED 3 *Business Combinations* proposes extending that definition to all IFRSs. To converge on the same meaning as SFAS 144 and to avoid using the term 'probable' with different meanings in IFRSs, the draft IFRS uses the phrase 'highly probable'. The Board regards 'highly probable' as implying a significantly higher probability than 'more likely than not' and as implying the same probability as the FASB's phrase 'likely to occur'.

BC58   The measurement basis 'fair value less costs to sell' used in SFAS 144 is the same as the measurement 'net selling price' used in IAS 36. SFAS 144 defines fair value of an asset as the amount at which that asset could be bought or sold in a current transaction between willing parties, that is, other than in a forced or liquidation sale, and costs to sell as the incremental direct costs to transact a sale, that is, the costs that result directly from and are essential to a sale transaction and that would not have been incurred by the entity had the decision to sell not been made. IAS 36 defines net selling price as the amount obtainable from the sale of an asset in an arm's length transaction between knowledgeable, willing parties, less the costs of disposal. Costs of disposal are incremental costs directly attributable to the disposal of an asset, excluding finance costs and income tax expenses.

The Board considered using the phrase 'net selling price' to be consistent with IAS 36. However, it noted that 'fair value' is used in many IFRSs. The Board concluded that it would be preferable to use the same phrase as is used in SFAS 144 so that it is clear that convergence on this point had been achieved and to amend IAS 36 so that the terminology in IAS 36 is consistent with other IFRSs. Therefore, a consequential amendment proposed by this draft IFRS is to replace 'net selling price' with 'fair value less costs to sell' throughout IAS 36.   **BC59**

Appendix A

ALTERNATIVE VIEWS ON ED 4 *DISPOSAL OF NON-CURRENT ASSETS AND PRESENTATION OF DISCONTINUED OPERATIONS*

AV1   Two Board members voted against the publication of ED 4 *Disposal of Non-current Assets and Presentation of Discontinued Operations*. Their alternative views are set out below.

Alternative view of the first Board member

AV2   The first Board member voted against the publication of ED 4 on the following grounds:

(a)   measurement of assets should not be based on management intent;

(b)   in particular, depreciation/amortisation of non-current assets that are still in active use should not cease only because management intends to sell these assets;

(c)   the IASB should not develop detailed rule-based Standards.

AV3   The proposed classification 'held for sale' and resulting measurement of assets (or disposal groups) so classified is based on management intent and demands detailed (anti-abuse) rules to define the classification and to fix the time boundaries during which an asset (or disposal group) can remain within the classification. The final result is, in the Board member's view, an excessively detailed and rule-based Standard.

AV4   This Board member further believes that not depreciating/amortising assets classified as held for sale would be especially problematic for disposal groups because such groups might correspond to important parts of a business, such as a division or a whole segment. The Board member does not accept that remeasurement at the lower of carrying amount and fair value less costs to sell acts as a proxy for depreciation because, sometimes at least, the fair value less costs to sell will be higher than the carrying amount. Again, this is particularly the case for disposal groups that correspond to divisions or segments, as the fair value of such disposal groups will often reflect internally generated goodwill. Under the proposals in the draft IFRS, non-current assets in such disposal groups will simply remain at their carrying amounts even though they are still actively used. The Board member believes that it is conceptually wrong to cease depreciation/amortisation while such assets are still in active use, which under the draft IFRS could be for a prolonged period of time, up to one year or even longer under special circumstances.

AV5   The Board member believes that a more simple and straightforward solution is possible by creating a special category of non-current assets retired from active use. This would have the following advantages:

1.   the concept of retired from active use would be simple to apply

2.   management intent would be removed from the proposals

3.   classification would equally apply to any form of disposal (sale, abandonment, exchange, spin-off, etc)

4.   no detailed (anti-abuse) rules would be necessary

5.   no illustrations would be necessary

6.   the IFRS would be simple and based on a clear and unambiguous principle.

In order to provide information of intended sales of non-current assets (which is especially important for planned disposals of components (ie future discontinued operations)), the Board member would propose disclosure requirements that would take effect as soon as such assets are likely to be sold, even if they are still in active use.   AV6

The Board member agrees with the proposed measurement requirements of paragraph 8 (but for assets retired from active use), the consequential accounting of paragraph 18 when such assets are put into active use again and the presentation of discontinued operations as set out in paragraph 24, except for the requirement for some of the disclosures to be presented on the face of the income statement.   AV7

The Board member accepts that full convergence with US GAAP (SFAS 144) would not be achieved under the Board member's preferred approach. However, the Board member would prefer a simple and clear accounting solution.   AV8

Alternative view of the second Board member

The second Board member believes that it is inappropriate to cease depreciation of assets that are still in use. This Board member also believes that a separate classification 'non-current assets retired from active use' would draw a more appropriate and objective distinction than the classification 'held for sale'.   AV9

Appendix B

TABLES OF CONCORDANCE

The following table shows the paragraphs in SFAS 144 that were the source of the paragraphs in the draft IFRS.

Paragraph in draft IFRS	Paragraph in SFAS 144
1 Objective	1 and 2
2 Scope	3 and 5
3 Disposal groups	4
4 Held for sale principle	30
5 Reference to Appendix B	No equivalent paragraph
6 Assets to be abandoned	27
7 Assets to be abandoned	28
8 Measurement principle	34
9 Application to newly acquired assets	34
10 Discounting costs to sell	35
11 Carrying value of other assets	36
12 Recognition of impairment loss	37
13 Revalued assets	No equivalent paragraph
14 Allocation of impairment loss	37
15 Gain on loss from sale	37
16 Non-depreciation	34
17 Change in classification as held for sale	38
18 Measurement on reclassification	38
19 Presentation of reclassification adjustment	39
20 Removal of item from disposal group	40
21 Presentation and disclosure principle	No equivalent paragraph
22 Definition of a component	41
23 Definition of a discontinued operation	42
24 Disclosures for discontinued operations	43
25 Adjustments to amounts reported in discontinued operations	44
26 Change in classification as discontinued operation	39
27 Disposal of assets in continuing operations	45
28 Presentation of assets held for sale	46
29 Additional disclosures	47

30 Additional disclosures	48
31 Effective date	49-51
B1 Held for sale criteria	30
B2 Criteria for exception	31
B3 Classification of newly acquired assets	32
B4 Classification after the balance sheet date	33
B5-B8 Revalued assets	*No equivalent paragraph*

The following table shows where the relevant requirements of SFAS 144 can be found in the draft IFRS.

Paragraph in SFAS 144	Paragraph in draft IFRS
3 Scope	2
4 Disposal groups	3 and Appendix A
5 Exceptions to scope	2
27 Disposal other than by sale	6
28 Assets to be abandoned	6 and 7
29 Assets to be exchanged or distributed to owners	*Assets to be exchanged are treated as assets to be sold (see paragraph 5 of the draft IFRS).*
30 Criteria for classification as held for sale	4 and B1
31 Exception to one of the criteria in paragraph 30	B2
32 Classification of newly acquired assets	B3
33 Classification after the balance sheet date	B4
34 Measurement of assets held for sale	8,9 and 16
35 Costs to sell	Appendix A and 10
36 Carrying value of other assets	11
37 Impairment loss	12 and 14
38 Change in classification	17 and 18
39 Presentation of change in classification	19 and 26
40 Removal of items from disposal group	20
41 Definition of a component	Appendix A and 22
42 Definition of discontinued operations	23
43 Presentation of discontinued operations	24
44 Adjustment to amounts reported in discontinued operations	25
45 Disposal gains and losses in continuing operations	27

Contents

ED 4 DISPOSAL OF NON-CURRENT ASSETS AND PRESENTATION OF DISCONTINUED OPERATIONS

[Draft] Illustrative examples

International financial reporting standard IFRS X
Disposal of non-current assets and
presentation of discontinued operations

[DRAFT] ILLUSTRATIVE EXAMPLES

These [draft] examples accompany, but are not part of, the [draft] IFRS

Availability for immediate sale (Appendix B, paragraph B1(b))

To qualify for classification as held for sale, a non-current asset (or disposal group) must be available for immediate sale in its present condition subject only to terms that are usual and customary for sales of such assets (or disposal groups) (paragraph B1(b)). A non-current asset (or disposal group) is available for immediate sale if an entity currently has the intent and ability to transfer the asset (or disposal group) to a buyer in its present condition. Examples 1-3 illustrate situations in which the criterion in paragraph B1(b) would or would not be met.

Example 1

An entity is committed to a plan to sell its headquarters building and has initiated actions to locate a buyer.

(a)   The entity intends to transfer the building to a buyer after it vacates the building. The time necessary to vacate the building is usual and customary for sales of such assets. The criterion in paragraph B1(b) would be met at the plan commitment date.

(b)   The entity will continue to use the building until construction of a new head-quarters building is completed. The entity does not intend to transfer the existing building to a buyer until after construction of the new building is completed (and it vacates the existing building). The delay in the timing of the transfer of the existing building imposed by the entity (seller) demonstrates that the building is not available for immediate sale. The criterion in paragraph B1(b) would not be met until construction of the new building is completed, even if a firm purchase commitment for the future transfer of the existing building is obtained earlier.

Example 2

An entity is committed to a plan to sell a manufacturing facility and has initiated actions to locate a buyer. At the plan commitment date, there is a backlog of uncompleted customer orders.

(a)   The entity intends to sell the manufacturing facility with its operations. Any uncompleted customer orders at the sale date will transfer to the buyer. The transfer of uncompleted customer orders at the sale date will not affect the timing of the transfer of the facility. The criterion in paragraph B1(b) would be met at the plan commitment date.

(b)   The entity intends to sell the manufacturing facility, but without its operations. The entity does not intend to transfer the facility to a buyer until after it ceases all operations of the facility and eliminates the backlog of uncompleted customer orders. The delay in the timing of the transfer of the facility imposed by the entity (seller) demonstrates that the facility is not available for immediate sale. The criterion in paragraph B1(b) would not be met until the operations of the facility cease, even if a firm purchase commitment for the future transfer of the facility were obtained earlier.

Example 3

An entity acquires through foreclosure a property comprising land and buildings that it intends to sell.

(a) The entity does not intend to transfer the property to a buyer until after it completes renovations to increase its sales value. The delay in the timing of the transfer of the property imposed by the entity (seller) demonstrates that the property is not available for immediate sale. The criterion in paragraph B1(b) would not be met until the renovations are completed.

(b) After the renovations are completed and the property is classified as held for sale but before a firm purchase commitment is obtained, the entity becomes aware of environmental damage requiring remediation. The entity still intends to sell the property. However, the entity does not have the ability to transfer the property to a buyer until after the remediation is completed. The delay in the timing of the transfer of the property imposed by others before a firm purchase commitment is obtained demonstrates that the property is not available for immediate sale. The criterion in paragraph B1(b) would not continue to be met. The property would be reclassified as held and used in accordance with paragraph 17.

Completion of sale expected within one year (paragraph B1(d))

Example 4

To qualify for classification as held for sale, the sale of a noncurrent asset (or disposal group) must be highly probable, and transfer of the asset (or disposal group) must be expected to qualify for recognition as a completed sale within one year (paragraph B1(d)). That criterion would not be met if, for example:

(a) an entity that is a commercial leasing and finance company is holding for sale or lease equipment that has recently ceased to be leased and the ultimate form of a future transaction (sale or lease) has not yet been determined.

(b) an entity is committed to a plan to 'sell' a property that is in use, and the transfer of the property will be accounted for as a sale and finance leaseback.

Exceptions to the criterion in paragraph B1(d)

An exception to the one-year requirement in paragraph B1(d) applies in limited situations in which the period required to complete the sale of a noncurrent asset (or disposal group) will be (or has been) extended by events or circumstances beyond an entity's control and specified conditions are met (paragraph B2). Examples 5-7 illustrate those situations.

Example 5

An entity in the power generating industry is committed to a plan to sell a disposal group that represents a significant portion of its regulated operations. The sale requires regulatory approval, which could extend the period required to complete the sale beyond one year. Actions necessary to obtain that approval cannot be initiated until after a buyer is known and a firm purchase commitment is obtained. However, a firm purchase commitment is highly probable within one year. In that situation, the conditions in paragraph B2(a) for an exception to the one-year requirement in paragraph B1(d) would be met.

Example 6

An entity is committed to a plan to sell a manufacturing facility in its present condition and classifies the facility as held for sale at that date. After a firm purchase commitment is obtained, the buyer's inspection of the property identifies environmental damage not previously known to exist. The entity is required by the buyer to make good the damage, which will extend the period required to complete the sale beyond one year. However, the entity has initiated actions to make good the damage, and satisfactory rectification of the damage is highly probable. In that situation, the conditions in paragraph B2(b) for an exception to the oneyear requirement in paragraph B1(d) would be met.

Example 7

An entity is committed to a plan to sell a noncurrent asset and classifies the asset as held for sale at that date.

(a)   During the initial one-year period, the market conditions that existed at the date the asset was classified initially as held for sale deteriorate and, as a result, the asset is not sold by the end of that period. During that period, the entity actively solicited but did not receive any reasonable offers to purchase the asset and, in response, reduced the price. The asset continues to be actively marketed at a price that is reasonable given the change in market conditions, and the criteria in paragraph B1 are therefore met. In that situation, the conditions in paragraph B2(c) for an exception to the one-year requirement in paragraph B1(d) would be met. At the end of the initial one-year period, the asset would continue to be classified as held for sale.

(b)   During the following one-year period, market conditions deteriorate further, and the asset is not sold by the end of that period. The entity believes that the market conditions will improve and has not further reduced the price of the asset. The asset continues to be held for sale, but at a price in excess of its current fair value. In that situation, the absence of a price reduction demonstrates that the asset is not available for immediate sale as required by the criterion in paragraph B1(b). In addition, the criterion in paragraph B1(e) requires that an asset be marketed at a price that is reasonable in relation to its current fair value. Therefore, the conditions in paragraph B2(c) for an exception to the one-year requirement in paragraph B1(d) would not be met. The asset would be reclassified as held and used in accordance with paragraph 17.

Presenting discontinued operations

The results of operations of a component of an entity that either has been disposed of or is classified as held for sale are required to be reported in discontinued operations if (a) the operations and cash flows of the component have been (or will be) eliminated from the ongoing operations of the entity as a result of the disposal transaction and (b) the entity will not have any significant continuing involvement in the operations of the component after the disposal transaction (paragraph 23). Examples 8-11 illustrate disposal activities that do or do not qualify for presenting as discontinued operations.

Example 8

An entity that manufactures and sells consumer products has several product groups, each with different product lines and brands. For that entity, a product group is the lowest level at which the operations and cash flows can be clearly distinguished, operationally and for financial reporting purposes, from the rest of the entity. Therefore, each product group is a component of the entity.

The entity has experienced losses associated with certain brands in its beauty care products group.

(a)   The entity decides to exit the beauty care business and is committed to a plan to sell the product group with its operations. The product group is classified as held for sale at that date. The operations and cash flows of the product group will be eliminated from the ongoing operations of the entity as a result of the sale transaction, and the entity will not have any continuing involvement in the operations of the product group after it is sold. In that situation, the conditions in paragraph 23 for presenting in discontinued operations the operations of the product group while it is classified as held for sale would be met.

(b)   The entity decides to remain in the beauty care business but will discontinue the brands with which the losses are associated. Because the brands are part of a larger cash-generating product group and, in the aggregate, do not represent a group that is a component of the entity, the conditions in paragraph 23 for presenting in discontinued operations the losses associated with the brands that are discontinued would not be met.

Example 9

An entity that is a franchiser in the quick-service restaurant business also operates company-owned restaurants. For that entity, an individual company-owned restaurant is the lowest level at which the operations and cash flows can be clearly distinguished, operationally and for financial reporting purposes, from the rest of the entity. Therefore, each companyowned restaurant is a component of the entity.

(a)   The entity has experienced losses on its company-owned restaurants in one region. The entity decides to exit the quickservice restaurant business in that region and commits itself to a plan to sell the restaurants in that region. The restaurants are classified as held for sale at that date. The operations and cash flows of the restaurants in that region will be eliminated from the ongoing operations of the entity as a result of the sale transaction, and the entity will not have any continuing involvement in the operations of the restaurants after they are sold. In that situation, the conditions in paragraph 23 for presenting in discontinued operations the operations of the restaurants while they are classified as held for sale would be met.

(b)   Based on its evaluation of the ownership mix of its restaurants in particular markets, the entity commits itself to a plan to sell its company-owned restaurants in one region to an existing franchisee. The restaurants are classified as held for sale at that date. Although each company-owned restaurant is a component of the entity, through the franchise agreement the entity will (1) receive franchise fees determined, in part, based on the future revenues of the restaurants and (2) have significant continuing involvement in the operations of the restaurants after they are sold. In that situation, the conditions in paragraph 23 for presenting in discontinued operations the operations of the restaurants would not be met.

Example 10

An entity that manufactures sporting goods has a bicycle division that designs, manufactures, markets and distributes bicycles. For that entity, the bicycle division is the lowest level at which the operations and cash flows can be clearly distinguished, operationally and for financial reporting purposes, from the rest of the entity. Therefore, the bicycle division is a component of the entity.

The entity has experienced losses in its bicycle division resulting from an increase in manufacturing costs (principally labour costs).

(a)   The entity decides to exit the bicycle business and commits itself to a plan to sell the division with its operations. The bicycle division is classified as held for sale at that date. The operations and cash flows of the division will be eliminated from the ongoing operations of the entity as a result of the sale transaction, and the entity will not have any continuing involvement in the operations of the division after it is sold. In that situation, the conditions in paragraph 23 for presenting in discontinued operations the operations of the division while it is classified as held for sale would be met.

(b)   The entity decides to remain in the bicycle business but will outsource the manufacturing operations and commits itself to a plan to sell the related manufacturing facility. The facility is classified as held for sale at that date. Because the manufacturing facility is part of a larger cash-generating group (the bicycle division), and is not a component of the entity, the conditions in paragraph 23 for presenting in discontinued operations the operations (losses) of the manufacturing facility would not be met. (Those conditions also would not be met if the manufacturing facility were a component of the entity because the decision to outsource the manufacturing operations of the division will not eliminate the operations and cash flows of the division from the ongoing operations of the entity.)

Example 11

An entity owns and operates retail stores that sell household goods. For that entity, each store is the lowest level at which the operations and cash flows can be clearly distinguished, operationally and for financial reporting purposes, from the rest of the entity. Therefore, each store is a component of the entity.

To expand its retail store operations in one region, the entity decides to close two of its retail stores and open a new superstore in that region. The new superstore will sell the household goods previously sold through the two retail stores as well as other related products not previously sold. Although each retail store is a component of the entity, the operations and cash flows from the sale of household goods previously sold through the two retail stores in that region will not be eliminated from the ongoing operations of the entity. In that situation, the conditions in paragraph 23 for presenting in discontinued operations the operations of the stores would not be met.

Determining whether an asset has been abandoned

Paragraphs 6 and 7 of the [draft] IFRS specify requirements for assets to be abandoned. Example 12 illustrates when an asset has not been abandoned.

Example 12

An entity ceases to use a manufacturing plant because demand for its product has declined. However, the plant is maintained in workable condition and it is expected that it will be brought back into use if demand picks up. The plant is not abandoned.

Presenting a discontinued operation that has been abandoned

Paragraph 6 of the [draft] IFRS prohibits assets that will be abandoned from being classified as held for sale. However, if the assets to be abandoned are a component of the entity, they are reported in discontinued operations at the date at which they are abandoned. Example 13 illustrates this.

Example 13

In October 2005 an entity decides to abandon one of its cotton mills. The cotton mill is a cash-generating unit that meets the definition of a component of the entity. All work stops at the cotton mill during the year ended 31 December 2006. In the financial statements for the year ended 31 December 2005, results and cash flows of the cotton mill are treated as continuing operations. In the financial statements for the year ended 31 December 2006, the entity makes the disclosures for the cotton mill required by paragraph 24 of the [draft] IFRS, including a restatement of any comparative figures.

FRED 36
Business Combinations (IFRS 3)
&
Amendments to FRS 2
Accounting for Subsidiary Undertakings
(parts of IAS 27 consolidated and separate financial statements)

Contents

Business Combinations Overview

Preface by the accounting standards board

These Financial Reporting Exposure Drafts (FREDs) are part of a package of draft   **A**
UK accounting standards reflecting the outputs from Phase I and Phase II of the
International Accounting Standards Board (IASB) project on business combina-
tions. The package comprises:

- FRED 36 *Business Combinations* (IFRS 3*)* and Amendments to FRS 2
  *Accounting for Subsidiary Undertakings (parts of IAS 27 Consolidated and
  Separate Financial Statements)*.
- FRED 37 *Intangible Assets* (IAS 38) and FRED 38 *Impairment of Assets*
  (IAS 36).
- FRED 39 Amendments to FRS 12 *Provisions, Contingent Liabilities and Con-
  tingent Assets* and Amendments to FRS 17 *Retirement benefits*.

The first phase of the Business Combinations project resulted in the IASB issuing   **B**
IFRS 3 *Business Combinations*, and amendments to IAS 36 *Impairment of Assets* and
IAS 38 *Intangible Assets*. These were published in March 2004. The primary
objective of the IASB in Phase I of the project was to require one method of
accounting for business combinations – the purchase method (renamed the acquisition method in Phase II). Prior to this International Accounting Standards (IAS)
permitted two methods, the acquisition method and pooling of interests method
(merger accounting).

The second phase is being conducted by the IASB as a joint project with the US   **C**
Financial Accounting Standards Board (FASB). This phase of the project has
reconsidered the guidance for applying the acquisition method of accounting for a
business combination and particularly the method by which acquirers recognise and
measure the business over which they obtain control. This phase also aims to
improve the transparency of information provided to users of financial statements.
An important aspect of Phase II is to achieve convergence between International
Financial Reporting Standards (IFRS) and US GAAP.

The outputs from the second Phase of the project comprise three exposure drafts that   **D**
propose amendments to IFRS 3 *Business Combinations*, IAS 27 *Consolidated and
Separate Financial Statements* and IAS 37 *Provisions, Contingent Liabilities and
Contingent Assets*.

The publication by the IASB of the exposure drafts from Phase II concludes the   **E**
substantive part of the IASB's Business Combinations project. However, it does not
fully complete the project. The aspects that remain outstanding include consideration
of 'fresh start' accounting. The outstanding aspects are not currently part of the
IASB's active agenda.

Some of the proposals set out in this FRED may conflict with existing legal   **F**
requirements. These matters are being investigated and it is hoped that they will be
resolved with the assistance of the Department of Trade and Industry.

FRED 36 *Business Combinations* (IFRS 3) and amendments to *FRS 2 Accounting for Subsidiary Undertakings (parts of IAS 27 Consolidated and Separate Financial Statements)*

Paragraphs 3 to 48 of this Preface set out the main differences between International Accounting Standards and existing UK accounting requirements for Business Combinations. These paragraphs have been prepared to assist readers in preparing their response on the proposals from Phase II of the IASB Business Combination project.

Paragraphs 49 to 56 outline the ASB's proposals for how the IASB's proposals could be implemented into UK accounting standards.

INTRODUCTION

1   This Financial Reporting Exposure Draft (FRED) sets out proposals for how the IASB's IFRS 3 *Business Combinations* (as amended by the IASB's exposure draft of June 2005) could be implemented into UK accounting standards. This FRED also sets out the consequential amendments to several UK accounting standards. Should the proposals be implemented into UK accounting standards, they would introduce the revised IFRS 3 *Business Combinations** as a new UK IFRS-based standard and amend FRS 2 *Accounting for Subsidiary Undertakings*. The new IFRS-based standard would replace FRS 6 *Acquisition and Mergers* and FRS 7 *Fair Values in Acquisition Accounting*.

2   In line with the ASB's convergence strategy, the Board proposes UK accounting standards which are based on IFRS with no changes other than those that are essential or are justifiable.

Main differences between existing and proposed International Accounting Standards for Business Combinations and existing UK requirements

OVERVIEW

3   The main changes to UK accounting practices that would arise from adopting the proposed standards are set out below. The ASB is concerned that certain aspects of the proposals may not improve the quality of information in financial statements. The main points are:

- Under current UK accounting practice the objective of acquisition accounting is to reflect the cost of the acquisition. To the extent to which it is not represented by identifiable assets and liabilities (measured at their fair value), goodwill arises and is reported in the financial statements. This exposure draft adopts a different perspective and requires the financial statements to reflect the fair value of the acquired business. The proposals treat the group as a single economic entity (entity concept) rather than the 'parent entity concept' that underlies existing UK accounting standards (paragraphs 5 to 7).

**IFRS 3 will replace those parts of FRS 10* Goodwill and intangible assets *that address the accounting for goodwill arising in a business combination.*

- Any outside equity interests in a subsidiary is treated as part of the overall ownership interest in the group. As a consequence of this changes in a parent's ownership interest, that do not result in a change of control, are to be recognised as changes in equity and no gain or loss will be recognised in the profit and loss account (paragraphs 8 to10).
- It is proposed that goodwill is to be recognised in full; that is, 100 per cent of goodwill is recognised even if less than 100 per cent is acquired (paragraphs 11 to 20).
- Goodwill, after initial recognition, is to be measured at cost less impairment losses, and amortisation is not to be permitted (paragraphs 21 to 25). The proposals for negative goodwill are discussed in paragraphs 26 to 29.
- Costs incurred in connection with an acquisition are not to be accounted for as part of the cost of the investment (paragraphs 30 to 33).

The remainder of the Preface discusses other changes in UK accounting practice: **4**

- Contingent consideration (paragraphs 34 and 35).
- Method of accounting (paragraphs 36 to 39).
- Group reconstructions (paragraphs 40 to 41).
- Fair value hierarchy (paragraphs 42 to 48).

CONCEPTS OF ACCOUNTING FOR BUSINESS COMBINATIONS

Under current UK accounting practice the objective of acquisition accounting is to **5**
reflect the cost of the acquisition. To the extent to which it is not represented by identifiable assets and liabilities (measured at their fair value), goodwill arises and is reported in the financial statements. This exposure draft adopts a different perspective and requires the financial statements to reflect the fair value of the acquired business. It will also require that, where an acquisition is achieved in stages, any non-controlling equity investment in the acquiree immediately before acquisition shall be remeasured to fair value at the date of acquisition and a corresponding gain or loss recognised in the profit or loss.

In the UK, to date, accounting has been based on the parent entity concept. The **6**
parent entity concept consolidates in full the assets and liabilities of an entity even if the entity is not wholly-owned. The parent entity concept recognises the different needs of users of financial statements and that these needs can usually be met by focusing on reporting to shareholders. Under the parent entity concept the extent of minority interests (renamed non-controlling interests*) and transactions with non-controlling interests are separately identified in the primary financial statements.

In contrast, the proposals set out in this exposure draft, adopt the entity concept. As **7**
with the parent entity concept the entity concept consolidates in full the assets and liabilities of an entity even if the entity is not wholly-owned. The difference between the two concepts arises in relation to the treatment of outside interests. In contrast to the parent entity concept the entity concept considers the group a single entity and any outside equity interest in a subsidiary us treated merely as part of an overall ownership interest. As a consequence, transactions with non-controlling interests do not give rise to gains or losses.

As part of the second phase of the Business Combinations project, the IASB decided to rename 'minority interest' to 'non-controlling interest'.

TRANSACTIONS WITH NON-CONTROLLING INTERESTS

8　Consistent with the entity concept the IASB's proposals state that changes in a parent's ownership interest in a subsidiary after control is obtained that do not result in a loss of control shall be accounted for as transactions with equity holders with no consequential gain or loss or change to goodwill. This is explained in paragraph 4 of the Basis for Conclusions to the exposure draft of proposed amendments to IAS 27 *Consolidated and Separate Financial Statements* (and set out in the FRED). The IASB explains that the proposed treatment is consistent with its view that non-controlling interests are a separate component of equity. In the IASB's view non-controlling interests are part of the ownership interests in the consolidated group because they do not meet the definition of a liability within the meaning of its *Framework*.

9　The proposed amendments differ from the current requirement of FRS 2 which adopts the parent entity concept. FRS 2 requires that where a group reduces its interest in a subsidiary undertaking, a profit or loss should be recognised. In adopting the 'parent entity concept' FRS 2 reports performance from the perspective of investors in the parent undertaking and provides the relevant information about the gains and losses arising on partial disposals.

10　To report transactions between the parent entity and non-controlling interests merely as transfers within equity fails to recognise that the objective of consolidated financial statements is to provide information about the financial performance of an entity to investors in the parent entity, who are the ultimate providers of capital and risk takers. The failure to recognise gains or losses on partial disposals in profit or loss may inhibit effective communication between the parent entity and its shareholders.

GOODWILL

Full goodwill recognition and measurement

11　The IASB defines goodwill as future economic benefits arising from assets that are not individually identified and separately recognised. It considers goodwill to be an asset, similar to other assets and so proposes to require recognition of 100 per cent of goodwill (full goodwill), even if less than 100 per cent of an entity is acquired. This amount will represent not only goodwill attributable to the parent entity, as a result of the transaction, but also goodwill attributable to the non-controlling interest.

12　FRS 2 requires goodwill arising on an acquisition to be recognised only with respect to that part of the subsidiary undertaking that is attributable to the interest held by the parent. FRS 2 notes* that although it might be possible to estimate by extrapolation or valuation an amount of goodwill attributable to non-controlling interests this would in effect recognise an amount for goodwill that is hypothetical because the non-controlling interest is not a party to the transaction by which the subsidiary undertaking is acquired.

13　FRS 10 *Goodwill and intangible assets* sets out the principles applied in the UK to the accounting for goodwill. It recognises that goodwill is not a separate asset but part of a larger asset, the investment. The cost of the investment is determined by the transaction price for which management are accountable. By recognising only goodwill attributable to the parent entity, only that part of goodwill for which

---

**Paragraph 82 of FRS 2.*

management are accountable is recognised. In contrast 'full goodwill' recognises a hypothetical amount which is apportioned to the non-controlling interests.

Recognition of goodwill attributable only to the parent's interest is consistent with **14** the view that non-controlling interests (who do not hold shares in the parent entity) have no direct interests in the parent or group, but are primarily interested in the subsidiary of which they are a shareholder and in which they do have an interest in its assets and liabilities. As such they have no interest in the consolidated financial statements of the parent entity and therefore need not recognise a hypothetical amount of goodwill allocated for their interest in the group.

The IASB's proposals measure full goodwill as the difference between the fair value **15** of the acquiree as a whole over the fair value of its net assets at the date of acquisition. This will require that, in an acquisition of less than 100 per cent, the fair value of the acquiree as a whole is determined.

The exposure draft of proposed amendments to IFRS 3 notes that business com- **16** binations are usually arm's length exchange transactions and therefore, in the absence of evidence to the contrary, the consideration transferred is presumed to be the best evidence of the fair value of the acquirer's interest in the acquiree. Where a controlling interest is acquired but less than 100 per cent of a business is acquired, estimating the fair value of the acquiree had 100 per cent been acquired is extremely subjective. Using the consideration transferred to estimate the fair value of the acquiree may not be appropriate because:

i.   it may fail to recognise any control premium included in the consideration transferred. The control premium may be difficult to measure with sufficient reliability; and
ii. the consideration transferred is based on the acquirer's assessment of future returns it anticipates the investment will generate. These returns may include an assessment of future synergy benefits the acquirer anticipates it will achieve. Some of the synergy benefits may benefit the parent entity rather than the acquired entity and thereby have little or no relevance to the non-controlling interests in the acquired entity.

Under the parent entity concept goodwill relates to the cost of the investment and **17** provides useful information for users of the financial statements on the decisions and actions management has made. It is unclear to the Board how the recognition and measurement of full goodwill can improve the quality of the information provided by financial statements. Indeed it may distract from the existing clarity because arguably it introduces a "notional" item into the Balance Sheet – that proportion of goodwill attributable to the non-controlling interests that is not determined by a transaction.

The IASB explains in the Basis for Conclusions (paragraph BC16) that the amount **18** of goodwill recognised in a business combination achieved in stages and in a business combination achieved in a single transaction will not be the same. The IASB considers this inconsistency results in information that is not complete or useful. The IASB therefore decided that the measurement objective should be the fair value of the acquiree on the acquisition date rather than the cost incurred in a business combination. In a business combination achieved in stages the acquirer shall remeasure its non-controlling equity investments in the acquiree at fair value as of the acquisition date and recognise any gain or loss in the profit or loss. It may, however, be questioned whether a valuation, sometimes based on subjective estimates of the fair value of an acquiree, can resolve this inconsistency and provide useful information to users of financial statements.

19   Those members of the IASB who have provided alternative views from the proposals set out in the exposure draft of proposed amendments to IFRS 3 raise some of these matters. Their views can be found on pages 226 to 230 of this FRED.

20   The Board will participate in the international debate and strongly encourages UK constituents to respond to the IASB's invitation to comment. In addition, the Board would like to assess whether there is support for adopting all of the IASB proposals into UK accounting standards. This matter is discussed in paragraphs 49 to 53 below.

Subsequent measurement of goodwill

21   IFRS 3 requires that, after initial recognition, goodwill should be measured at cost less any accumulated impairment losses. The IASB concluded that more useful information would be provided if goodwill was not amortised but subjected to a rigorous and operational impairment test. The IASB's deliberations are set out in paragraphs BC136 to BC142 of the Basis for Conclusions that accompanies the current IFRS 3 (not reproduced in this FRED).

22   FRS 10 sought to charge goodwill to the profit and loss account only to the extent that the carrying value of goodwill is not supported by the current value of goodwill within the acquired business. Systematic amortisation is a practical means of recognising the reduction in value of goodwill that has a limited useful economic life. In FRS 10 there is a rebuttable presumption that, as with intangible assets, goodwill has a useful economic life of 20 years or less.

23   Those that favour amortisation of goodwill argue that goodwill is similar, at the margins, to intangible assets and therefore conceptually there is no reason to treat goodwill differently from other intangible assets. They also argue that amortisation leads to more robust financial reporting. One reason for this view is that impairment tests may fail to adequately distinguish between acquired and internally generated goodwill; another reason is that impairment tests rely on forecasts that are often subjective.

24   Subsequent measurement of goodwill is a complex issue; neither annual impairment nor amortisation is likely to result in a conclusive value for the carrying amount of goodwill. Cost and benefit considerations should therefore be taken into account in judging whether amortisation should be permitted. The simplicity and ease of setting up an amortisation schedule is a practical means of ensuring goodwill is not carried in excess of its current value.

25   The Board would like to seek its constituents' views on whether the UK IFRS-based standard should be amended and an option be introduced allowing amortisation of goodwill, see paragraph 54 to 56.

Business combinations in which the consideration transferred for the acquirer's interest in the acquiree is less than the fair value of that interest (negative goodwill)

26   Consistent with IFRS 3, the proposals in the second phase of the Business Combination project require that where the consideration transferred for the acquirer's interest in the acquiree is less than the fair value of that interest (after reassessment of the initial accounting) any gain shall first reduce any goodwill to zero. Any remaining excess shall be recognised as a gain on acquisition.

FRS 10 requires negative goodwill to be recognised in the profit and loss account in **27** the periods in which the non-monetary assets acquired are depreciated or sold. Any negative goodwill in excess of the values of the non-monetary assets should be written back in the profit and loss account over the period expected to benefit from that negative goodwill.

The IASB (paragraph BC168) observes that any excess remaining after the reas- **28** sessment could comprise one or more of the following components:

- errors that remain, notwithstanding the reassessment, in recognising or mea-suring fair value of either the cost of the combination of the acquiree's identifiable assets, liabilities or contingent liabilities.
- a requirement in an accounting standard to measure identifiable net assets acquired at an amount that is not fair value, but is treated as though it is fair value for the purpose of allocating the cost of the combination.
- a bargain purchase.

It is clear that there are a number of reasons why the consideration transferred for **29** the acquirer's interest in the acquiree may be less than the fair value of that interest. Where there is evidence of a bargain purchase then immediate recognition of a gain may be appropriate. However, as an excess can arise for a number of reasons, it is questionable whether immediate recognition of a gain is appropriate in all circumstances.

MEASUREMENT OF CONSIDERATION

Acquisition costs

It is proposed to amend IFRS 3 such that expenses of acquiring an acquisition are **30** recognised as an expense in the profit and loss account in the period of acquisition. The IASB has concluded that such costs are not part of the consideration transferred in exchange for the acquiree. This is discussed in the Basis for Conclusions at paragraphs BC84 to BC98.

FRS 7 specifies that the cost of acquisition is the amount of cash paid and the fair **31** value of other purchase consideration given by the acquirer, together with the expenses of the acquisition. The expenses of the acquisition are described as fees and similar incremental costs incurred directly in making an acquisition.

Where the cost of acquisition includes acquisition expenses, the return on investment **32** takes these expenses into consideration and management are accountable for the full cost of the acquisition. Some might suggest that under the IASB's proposals man-agers may not be accountable, in the long term, for the cost of a business combination because various unavoidable costs will have been written off when incurred.

It is also noted in paragraph AV18 of the alternative views that this treatment creates **33** an inconsistency between the accounting for purchases of assets, including invest-ments in associated companies, where the direct costs form part of the carrying amount of the asset acquired, on initial recognition. The Board considers that the proposed treatment creates an inconsistency in financial reporting.

Adjustments to consideration that is contingent on future events

34   The IASB's proposals arising from the second phase amend the treatment of contingent consideration. The proposals, consistent with FRS 7, measure contingent consideration at its fair value at the date of acquisition. Where contingent consideration takes the form of a liability any subsequent remeasurement, that does not qualify as a measurement period adjustment, is treated as a gain or loss and recognised in the profit or loss account.

35   FRS 7 considers the remeasurement of contingent consideration as an adjustment to the cost of acquisition with the consequential adjustment being made to goodwill until the ultimate amount is known. This reflects the view that a revision to the estimate for contingent consideration provides more information about conditions that existed at the date of acquisition should be reported as a change in the fair value of consideration, and a corresponding change to goodwill. However, it might be argued that where the change reflects events that have occurred since the date of acquisition the revision to the estimate should be reported as post-acquisition gains or losses.

METHOD OF ACCOUNTING

Acquisition and merger accounting

36   IFRS 3 requires all business combinations within its scope to be accounted for using the acquisition method. The acquisition method views a business combination from the perspective of the combining entity, which is the acquirer. The acquirer purchases the acquiree and recognises in its financial statements the net assets acquired at their fair value.

37   The acquisition method requires one party to the business combination to be identified as the acquirer. The IASB concluded that most business combinations result in one entity obtaining control of another entity and therefore an acquirer could be identified for most business combinations. The IASB acknowledges that it could be difficult to identify an acquirer in some rare instances, such as entities of similar size or capitalisation coming together in industry restructurings, but did not agree that exceptions to applying the acquisition method should be permitted. In contrast FRS 6 permits both acquisition and merger accounting. It contains a set of criteria designed to identify 'true' mergers and states that merger accounting should be used when those criteria are met.

38   One of the criticisms of merger accounting is that it perpetuates out-of-date historical values that are of limited relevance. An alternative to merger accounting for business combinations, where there is no acquirer, could be 'fresh start' accounting. Under this approach the net assets of all the combining entities would be measured at fair value at the date of the combination.

39   It was anticipated that the IASB would, as part of the second phase, research the application of 'fresh start' accounting as a possible alternative to the acquisition method. The Basis for Conclusions to the exposure draft of proposed amendments to IFRS 3 notes that the IASB will undertake research into 'fresh start' accounting. The ASB looks forward to working with the IASB on this matter.

Group reconstructions

In Appendix C of the draft IFRS it is noted that consistent with the provisions of **40** IFRS 3, the draft IFRS does not apply to combinations involving entities under common control, including group reconstructions. This is in contrast to FRS 6 which permitted merger accounting to be applied to group reconstructions. The Basis for Conclusions notes that the IASB intend to consider accounting for group reconstructions at a later date.

The Board is considering whether it should retain some of the provisions of FRS 6 **41** and prescribe how UK group reconstructions should be accounted for. The Board would welcome views on this matter (see ASB Invitation to Comment).

FAIR VALUE HIERARCHY

As part of the second phase additional guidance on the application of measuring fair **42** value is provided in Appendix E of the draft IFRS. The additional guidance is based on the FASB's Fair Value Measurements Exposure Draft that was issued in June 2004.

The fair value hierarchy groups into three broad categories (levels) the inputs that **43** should be used to estimate fair value. The hierarchy gives the highest priority to inputs that reflect quoted prices in active markets and the lowest priority to an entity's own internal estimates and assumptions.

FRS 7 requires the identifiable assets and liabilities of the acquiree that existed at the **44** date of acquisition to be recognised and measured at fair values reflecting their conditions at that date. FRS 7 specifies the method for determining fair values of individual categories of assets and liabilities.

The guidance in Appendix E may lead to some assets being attributed different **45** values to those currently attributed by the guidance in FRS 7, for example:

● specialised tangible fixed assets, for which applying FRS 7 fair value is represented by gross replacement cost reduced by depreciation (entry perspective),
   whereas by applying the hierarchy these may be recognised at a lower value
   reflecting an exit value perspective (disposal value); and
● stocks and work-in-progress, which FRS 7 requires to be valued at the lower of
   replacement cost and net realisable value whereas applying the hierarchy may
   lead to a valuation reflecting selling price less cost to complete and selling
   expenses.

The fair value attributed to acquired assets and liabilities has an impact on the post **46** acquisition earnings. Where stocks are valued based on selling prices, at most the margin attributed to selling the stocks will be recognised in post acquisition earnings.

The guidance focuses on 'exit values' that are observable market prices. The ASB **47** continues to strongly support the deprival value model which in certain circum-stances values assets at an 'entry value' and does not regard 'exit value' as the only basis on which to reach a fair value.

The IASB notes it intends to redeliberate any issues that emerge from the FASB's **48** final statement on fair value measurement and where appropriate amend the fair value guidance in Appendix E. This approach is of concern to the Board and sug-gests the IASB could amend the guidance without further consultation prior to issuing the final IFRS.

Propose UK Amendments to IASB Exposure Drafts

IMPLEMENTATION OF PROPOSALS

49   The ASB is issuing this FRED following the IASB issuing its exposure drafts of proposed amendments to IFRS 3, IAS 27 and IAS 37. These represent the decisions reached by the IASB during the second phase of the Business Combinations project. In addition, the Board has issued FRED 37 *Intangible Assets* and FRED 38 *Impairment of Assets*, which were amended as part of the first phase of the Business Combinations project.

50   The Board considers that the proposed amendments to IAS 27 (reflected in UK accounting standards as amendments to FRS 2) fail to recognise adequately that the focus of financial reporting is to report to the shareholders of the parent entity. The treatment of transactions with non-controlling interests as mere equity transactions fail to report adequately gains and losses the directors of the entity may make. In addition, the recognition of full goodwill requires a hypothetical transaction that results in a highly subjective measurement of full goodwill. The Board also noted that neither the IASB nor FASB currently adopt the 'entity concept' to the extent proposed in the exposure drafts.

51   The Board had previously stated it would consult on implementation of the proposals arising from the Business Combinations project when both Phases of the project were complete. However, given the extent of its reservations in relation to the IASB proposals the Board has considered whether it should issue this FRED or, alternatively, adopt a "wait and see" strategy, until the impact of the IASB proposals have been more widely evaluated through practical implementation.

52   After deliberation, the Board decided to issue this FRED but to consult on the effective date for transition. The IASB is proposing an effective date of 1 January 2007. Although the Board states in its draft Policy Statement that it will aim to converge with a new IFRS as soon as possible it does not consider this should be undertaken without due consideration of the proposals set out in any exposure draft.

53   The Board therefore considers the following options are available (assuming the IASB proposals proceed to an IFRS):

    i.   implement the Business Combinations 'package' in full simultaneously with the IASB (ie 1 January 2007);

    ii.   not to implement immediately but reconsider implementation of the Business Combinations 'package' after a period of time has lapsed and the IFRSs have been in effect. This would allow consideration of the practical implications to be more fully researched;

    iii.   issue Phase I (FRED 37 *Intangible Assets* and FRED 38 *Impairment of Assets*) to be effective 1 January 2007 but defer Phase II (FRED 36 *Business Combinations* and FRED 39 *Amendments to FRS 12 and FRS 17*) until after the IFRSs are effective and consideration of the practical implications are more fully researched; and

    iv.   issue Phase I (as in (iii) above) plus FRED 39. It might be noted that the Preface to FRED 39 sets out some concerns the Board has in relation to the proposed amendments to FRS 12.

This FRED invites comments on which of these proposals is preferred. The Board considers that it would prefer to maintain its strategy of converging with International Accounting Standards in a phased approach. However, given its reservations in relation to the second Phase findings the Board would prefer to defer implementation of the Business Combinations 'package' until a period of time has elapsed such that IASB proposals are more fully researched through practical implementation.

SUBSEQUENT MEASUREMENT OF GOODWILL

As explained in paragraph 25, the Board would welcome comments on whether to introduce into the UK IFRS-based standard an option for entities to elect either: **54**

(a)   scheduled amortisation and impairment reviews whenever there is indication that goodwill might be impaired; or

(b)   non-amortisation but with an impairment test annually or more frequently if events or changes in circumstances indicate that goodwill might be impaired.

It is noted in the Preface that accompanies FRED 37 *Intangible Assets* and FRED 38   **55** *Impairment of Assets* that where intangible assets with finite useful lives are not recognised separately from goodwill then there is a risk that the goodwill impairment test may not recognise the impairment of intangible assets. In view of this the exposure draft proposes only the wider definition of intangible assets. Were an option introduced into the UK IFRS-based standard to allow amortisation of goodwill this risk would diminish and as such the Board may reconsider whether the definition based on IFRS remains appropriate.

Allowing entities the option of amortisation of goodwill rather than impairment   **56** testing would provide a practical alternative to annual impairment reviews. The Board's draft Policy Statement notes that the ASB seeks to issue accounting standards that are appropriate for the entities that have to apply them; and in particular that the burden of their requirements is proportionate to the benefits they provide.

Invitation to comment

ITC1   The ASB invites comment on any aspect of this Financial Reporting Exposure Drafts by 28 October 2005 – the same day as the IASB has set for comments.

ITC2   The ASB would particularly welcome comments on the following issues:

ASB 1   Should the IASB proposals succeed to a Standard the ASB would prefer to defer implementation until the full impact of the proposal can be evaluated through practical implementation. The following options for implementation into UK accounting standards have been identified, which would you prefer? Please explain your preference.

  i.   implement the Business Combinations 'package' in full simultaneously with the IASB (ie 1 January 2007);
  ii. not to implement immediately but reconsider implementation of the Business Combinations 'package' after a period of time has lapsed and the IFRS have been in effect. This would allow consideration of the practical implications to be more fully researched;
  iii. issue Phase I (FRED 37 *Intangible Assets* and FRED 38 *Impairment of Assets*) to be effective 1 January 2007 but defer Phase II (FRED 36 *Business Combinations* and FRED 39 *Amendments to FRS 12 and FRS 17*) until after the IFRS are effective and consideration of the practical implications are more fully researched; and
  iv. issue Phase I (as in (iii) above) plus FRED 39. It might be noted that the Preface to FRED 39 sets out some concerns the Board has in relation to the proposed amendments to FRS 12.

ASB 2   Do you support the proposal, as set out in paragraphs 54 and 55, that the UK IFRS based-standard should include an option, to allow goodwill having a limited useful life to be amortised over its useful life?

ASB 3   The draft FRS excludes from its scope the accounting for business combinations under common control. The Board is considering whether to include additional guidance in the UK IFRS-based standard that would retained some of the provisions of FRS 6. FRS 6 permitted group reconstructions to be accounted for by applying merger accounting. Do you consider the Board should retain those provisions of FRS 6 that permit the use of merger accounting for group reconstructions? Do you consider that any guidance is needed? If so please provide details for the type of the guidance you consider necessary.

ASB 4   The draft IFRS sets out in paragraph 43 that an acquirer shall measure and recognise, separately from goodwill, an acquired non-current asset (or disposal group) that is classified as held for sale as of the acquisition date in accordance with paragraphs 7 – 11 of IFRS 5 *Non-current Assets Held for Sale and Discontinued Operations*. IFRS 5 is not an adopted UK IFRS-based standard. Previously FRS 7 required business operations to be sold within one year of the acquisition date to be treated as a single asset and the fair value to be based on the net proceeds of sale. The draft UK IFRS-based standard proposes to retain those paragraphs of FRS 7 that were previously applicable. Do you agree with this proposal?

ITC3   The ASB would also welcome comments on the questions that the IASB have asked in its exposure drafts which are reproduced below.

IASB Invitation to comment on amendments to IFRS 3 Business Combinations   **ITC4**

Objective, definition and scope

The proposed objective of the Exposure Draft is:

> *...that all business combinations be accounted for by applying the acquisition method. A business combination is a transaction or other event in which an acquirer obtains control of one or more businesses (the acquiree). In accordance with the acquisition method, the acquirer measures and recognises the acquiree, as a whole, and the assets acquired and liabilities assumed at their fair values as of the acquisition date. [paragraph 1]*

The objective provides the basic elements of the acquisition method of accounting for a business combination (formerly called the purchase method) by describing:

(a) what is to be measured and recognised. An acquiring entity would measure and recognise the acquired business at its fair value, regardless of the percentage of the equity interests of the acquiree it holds at the acquisition date. That objective also provides the foundation for determining whether specific assets acquired or liabilities assumed are part of an acquiree and would be accounted for as part of the business combination.

(b) when to measure and recognise the acquiree. Recognition and measurement of a business combination would be as of the acquisition date, which is the date the acquirer obtains control of the acquiree.

(c) the measurement attribute as fair value, rather than as cost accumulation and allocation. The acquiree and the assets acquired and liabilities assumed would be measured at fair value as of the acquisition date, with limited exceptions. Consequently, the consideration transferred in exchange for the acquiree, including contingent consideration, would also be measured at fair value as of the acquisition date.

The objective and definition of a business combination would apply to all business combinations in the scope of the proposed IFRS, including business combinations:

(a) involving only mutual entities

(b) achieved by contract alone

(c) achieved in stages (commonly called step acquisitions)

(d) in which the acquirer holds less than 100 per cent of the equity interests in the acquiree at the acquisition date.

(See paragraphs 52-58 and paragraphs BC42-BC46 of the Basis for Conclusions.)

IASB 1   Are the objective and the definition of a business combination appropriate for accounting for all business combinations? If not, for which business combinations are they not appropriate, why would you make an exception, and what alternative do you suggest?

Definition of a business

The Exposure Draft proposes to define a *business* as follows:

A business is an integrated set of activities and assets that is capable of being conducted and managed for the purpose of providing either:

(1) a return to investors, or
(2) dividends, lower costs, or other economic benefits directly and pro-portionately to owners, members, or participants. [paragraph 3(d)]

Paragraphs A2-A7 of Appendix A provide additional guidance for applying this definition. The proposed IFRS would amend the definition of a business in IFRS 3. (See paragraphs BC34-BC41.)

IASB 2 *Are the definition of a business and the additional guidance appropriate and sufficient for determining whether the assets acquired and the liabilities assumed constitute a business? If not, how would you propose to modify or clarify the definition or additional guidance?*

Measuring the fair value of the acquiree

The Exposure Draft proposes that in a business combination that is an exchange of equal values, the acquirer should measure and recognise 100 per cent of the fair value of the acquiree as of the acquisition date. This applies even in business combinations in which the acquirer holds less than 100 per cent of the equity interests in the acquiree at that date. In those business combinations, the acquirer would measure and recognise the non-controlling interest as the sum of the non-controlling interest's proportional interest in the acquisition-date values of the identifiable assets acquired and liabilities assumed plus the goodwill attributable to the non-controlling interest. (See paragraphs 19, 58 and BC52-BC54.)

IASB 3 *In a business combination in which the acquirer holds less than 100 per cent of the equity interests of the acquiree at the acquisition date, is it appropriate to recognise 100 per cent of the acquisition-date fair value of the acquiree, including 100 per cent of the values of identifiable assets acquired, liabilities assumed and goodwill, which would include the goodwill attributable to the non-controlling interest? If not, what alternative do you propose and why?*

The Exposure Draft proposes that a business combination is usually an arm's length transaction in which knowledgeable, unrelated willing par-ties are presumed to exchange equal values. In such transactions, the fair value of the consideration transferred by the acquirer on the acquisition date is the best evidence of the fair value of the acquirer's interest in the acquiree, in the absence of evidence to the contrary. Accordingly, in most business combinations, the fair value of the consideration transferred by the acquirer would be used as the basis for measuring the acquisition-date fair value of the acquirer's interest in the acquiree. However, in some business combinations, either no consideration is transferred on the acquisition date or the evidence indicates that the consideration trans-ferred is not the best basis for measuring the acquisition-date fair value of the acquirer's interest in the acquiree. In those business combinations, the acquirer would measure the acquisition-date fair value of its interest in the acquiree and the acquisition-date fair value of the acquiree using other valuation techniques. (See paragraphs 19, 20 and A8-A26, Appendix E and paragraphs BC52-BC89.)

IASB 4   *Do paragraphs A8-A26 in conjunction with Appendix E provide sufficient guidance for measuring the fair value of an acquiree? If not, what additional guidance is needed?*

The Exposure Draft proposes a presumption that the best evidence of the fair value of the acquirer's interest in the acquiree would be the fair values of all items of consideration transferred by the acquirer in exchange for that interest measured as of the acquisition date, including:

(a) contingent consideration;
(b) equity interests issued by the acquirer; and
(c) any non-controlling equity investment in the acquiree that the acquirer owned immediately before the acquisition date.

(See paragraphs 20-25 and BC55-BC58.)

IASB 5   *Is the acquisition-date fair value of the consideration transferred in exchange for the acquirer's interest in the acquiree the best evidence of the fair value of that interest? If not, which forms of consideration should be measured on a date other than the acquisition date, when should they be measured, and why?*

The Exposure Draft proposes that after initial recognition, contingent consideration classified as:

(a) equity would not be remeasured.
(b) liabilities would be remeasured with changes in fair value recognised in profit or loss unless those liabilities are in the scope of IAS 39 *Financial Instruments: Recognition and Measurement* or [draft] IAS 37 *Non-financial Liabilities.* Those liabilities would be accounted for after the acquisition date in accordance with those IFRSs.

(See paragraphs 26 and BC64-BC89.)

IASB 6   *Is the accounting for contingent consideration after the acquisition date appropriate? If not, what alternative do you propose and why?*
The Exposure Draft proposes that the costs that the acquirer incurs in connection with a business combination (also called acquisition-related costs) should be excluded from the measurement of the consideration transferred for the acquiree because those costs are not part of the fair value of the acquiree and are not assets. Such costs include finder's fees; advisory, legal, accounting, valuation and other professional or consulting fees; the cost of issuing debt and equity instruments; and general administrative costs, including the costs of maintaining an internal acquisitions department. The acquirer would account for those costs separately from the business combination accounting. (See paragraphs 27 and BC84-BC89.)

IASB 7   *Do you agree that the costs that the acquirer incurs in connection with a business combination are not assets and should be excluded from the measurement of the consideration transferred for the acquiree? If not, why?*

Measuring and recognising the assets acquired and the liabilities assumed

The Exposure Draft proposes that an acquirer measure and recognise as of the acquisition date the fair value of the assets acquired and liabilities assumed as part of the business combination, with limited exceptions. (See paragraphs 28-41 and BC111-BC116.) That requirement would result in the following significant changes to accounting for business combinations:

(a) Receivables (including loans) acquired in a business combination would be measured at fair value. Therefore, the acquirer would not recognise a separate valuation allowance for uncollectible amounts as of the acquisition date.

(b) An identifiable asset or liability (contingency) would be measured and recognised at fair value at the acquisition date even if the amount of the future economic benefits embodied in the asset or required to settle the liability are contingent (or conditional) on the occurrence or non-occurrence of one or more uncertain future events. After initial recognition, such an asset would be accounted for in accordance with IAS 38 *Intangible Assets* or IAS 39 *Financial Instruments: Recognition and Measurement,* as appropriate, and such a liability would be accounted for in accordance with [draft] IAS 37 or other IFRSs as appropriate.

IASB 8   *Do you believe that these proposed changes to the accounting for business combinations are appropriate? If not, which changes do you believe are inappropriate, why, and what alternatives do you propose?*

The Exposure Draft proposes limited exceptions to the fair value measurement principle. Therefore, some assets acquired and liabilities assumed (for example, those related to deferred taxes, assets held for sale, or employee benefits) would continue to be measured and recognised in accordance with other IFRSs rather than at fair value. (See paragraphs 42-51 and BC117-BC150.)

IASB 9   *Do you believe that these exceptions to the fair value measurement principle are appropriate? Are there any exceptions you would eliminate or add? If so, which ones and why?*

Additional guidance for applying the acquisition method to particular types of business combinations

The Exposure Draft proposes that, for the purposes of applying the acquisition method, the fair value of the consideration transferred by the acquirer would include the fair value of the acquirer's non-controlling equity investment in the acquiree at acquisition date that the acquirer owned immediately before the acquisition date. Accordingly, in a business combination achieved in stages (step acquisition) the acquirer would remeasure its non-controlling equity investment in the acquiree at fair value as of the acquisition date and recognise any gain or loss in profit or loss. If, before the business combination, the acquirer recognised changes in the value of its non-controlling equity investment directly in equity (for example, the investment was designated as available for sale), the amount that was recognised directly in equity would be reclassified and included in the calculation of any gain or loss as of the acquisition date. (See paragraphs 55, 56 and BC151-BC153.)

IASB 10   *Is it appropriate for the acquirer to recognise in profit or loss any gain or loss on previously acquired non-controlling equity investments on the date it obtains control of the acquiree? If not, what alternative do you propose and why?*

The Exposure Draft proposes that in a business combination in which the consideration transferred for the acquirer's interest in the acquiree is less than the fair value of that interest (referred to as a bargain purchase) any excess of the fair value of the acquirer's interest in the acquiree over the fair value of the consideration transferred for that interest would reduce goodwill until the goodwill related to that business combination is reduced to zero, and any remaining excess would be recognised in profit or loss on the acquisition date. (See paragraphs 59-61 and paragraphs BC164-BC177.) However, the proposed IFRS would not permit the acquirer to recognise a loss at the acquisition date if the acquirer is able to determine that a portion of the consideration transferred represents an overpayment for the acquiree. The boards acknowledge that an acquirer might overpay to acquire a business, but they concluded that it is not possible to measure such an overpayment reliably at the acquisition date. (See paragraph BC178.)

IASB 11 *Do you agree with the proposed accounting for business combinations in which the consideration transferred for the acquirer's interest in the acquiree is less than the fair value of that interest? If not, what alternative do you propose and why?*

IASB 12 *Do you believe that there are circumstances in which the amount of an overpayment could be measured reliably at the acquisition date? If so, in what circumstances?*

Measurement period

The Exposure Draft proposes that an acquirer should recognise adjustments made during the measurement period to the provisional values of the assets acquired and liabilities assumed as if the accounting for the business combination had been completed at the acquisition date. Thus, comparative information for prior periods presented in financial statements would be adjusted, including any change in depreciation, amortisation or other profit or loss effect recognised as a result of completing the initial accounting. (See paragraphs 62-68 and BC161-BC163.)

IASB 13 *Do you agree that comparative information for prior periods presented in financial statements should be adjusted for the effects of measurement period adjustments? If not, what alternative do you propose and why?*

Assessing what is part of the exchange for the acquiree

The Exposure Draft proposes that an acquirer assess whether any portion of the transaction price (payments or other arrangements) and any assets acquired or liabilities assumed or incurred are not part of the exchange for the acquiree. Only the consideration transferred by the acquirer and the assets acquired or liabilities assumed or incurred that are part of the exchange for the acquiree would be included in the business combination accounting. (See paragraphs 69, 70, A87-A109 and BC154-BC160.)

IASB 14 *Do you believe that the guidance provided is sufficient for making the assessment of whether any portion of the transaction price or any assets acquired and liabilities assumed or incurred are not part of the exchange for the acquiree? If not, what other guidance is needed?*

Disclosures

The Exposure Draft proposes broad disclosure objectives that are intended to ensure that users of financial statements are provided with adequate information to enable them to evaluate the nature and financial effects of business combinations. Those objectives are supplemented by specific minimum disclosure requirements. In most instances, the objectives would be met by the minimum disclosure requirements that follow each of the broad objectives. However, in some circumstances, an acquirer might be required to disclose additional information necessary to meet the disclosure objectives. (See paragraphs 71-81 and BC200-BC203.)

IASB 15   *Do you agree with the disclosure objectives and the minimum disclosure requirements? If not, how would you propose amending the objectives or what disclosure requirements would you propose adding or deleting, and why?*

The IASB's and the FASB's convergence decisions

The Exposure Draft is the result of the boards' projects to improve the accounting for business combinations. The first phase of those projects led to the issue of IFRS 3 and FASB Statement No. 141. In 2002, the FASB and the IASB agreed to reconsider jointly their guidance for applying the purchase method of accounting, which the Exposure Draft calls the acquisition method, for business combinations. An objective of the joint effort is to develop a common and comprehensive standard for the accounting for business combinations that could be used for both domestic and cross-border financial reporting. Although the boards reached the same conclusions on the fundamental issues addressed in the Exposure Draft, they reached different conclusions on a few limited matters. Therefore, the IASB's version and the FASB's version of the Exposure Draft provide different guidance on those limited matters. A comparison, by paragraph, of the different guidance provided by each board accompanies the draft IFRS. Most of the differences arise because each board decided to provide business combinations guidance that is consistent with its other standards. Even though those differences are candidates for future convergence projects, the boards do not plan to eliminate those differences before final standards on business combinations are issued.

The joint Exposure Draft proposes to resolve a difference between IFRS 3 and SFAS 141 relating to the criteria for recognising an intangible asset separately from goodwill. Both boards concluded that an intangible asset must be identifiable (arising from contractual-legal rights or separable) to be recognised separately from goodwill. In its deliberations that led to SFAS 141, the FASB concluded that, when acquired in a business combination, all intangible assets (except for an assembled workforce) that are identifiable can be measured with sufficient reliability to warrant recognition separately from goodwill. In addition to the identifiability criterion, IFRS 3 and IAS 38 required that an intangible asset acquired in a business combination be reliably measurable to be recognised separately from goodwill. Paragraphs 35-41 of IAS 38 provide guidance for determining whether an intangible asset acquired in a business combination is reliably measurable. IAS 38 presumes that the fair value of an intangible asset with a finite useful life can be measured reliably. Therefore, a difference between IFRS 3 and SFAS 141 would arise only if the intangible asset has an indefinite life. The IASB decided to converge with the FASB in the Exposure Draft by:

(a) eliminating the requirement that an intangible asset be reliably measurable to be recognised separately from goodwill; and

(b) precluding the recognition of an assembled workforce acquired in a business combination as an intangible asset separately from goodwill.

(See paragraphs 40 and BC100-BC102.)

IASB 16   *Do you believe that an intangible asset that is identifiable can always be measured with sufficient reliability to be recognised separately from goodwill? If not, why? Do you have any examples of an intangible asset that arises from legal or contractual rights and has both of the following characteristics:*

(a) *the intangible asset cannot be sold, transferred, licensed, rented, or exchanged individually or in combination with a related contract, asset, or liability; and*

(b) *cash flows that the intangible asset generates are inextricably linked with the cash flows that the business generates as a whole?*

For the joint Exposure Draft, the boards considered the provisions of IAS 12 *Income Taxes* and FASB Statement No. 109 *Accounting for Income Taxes*, relating to an acquirer's deferred tax benefits that become recognisable because of a business combination. IAS 12 requires the acquirer to recognise separately from the business combination accounting any changes in its deferred tax assets that become recognisable because of the business combination. Such changes are recognised in post-combination profit or loss, or equity. On the other hand, SFAS 109 requires any recognition of an acquirer's deferred tax benefits (through the reduction of the acquirer's valuation allowance) that results from a business combination to be accounted for as part of the business combination, generally as a reduction of goodwill. The FASB decided to amend SFAS 109 to require the recognition of any changes in the acquirer's deferred tax benefits (through a change in the acquirer's previously recognised valuation allowance) as a transaction separately from the business combination. As amended, SFAS 109 would require such changes in deferred tax benefits to be recognised either in income from continuing operations in the period of the combination or directly to contributed capital, depending on the circumstances. Both boards decided to require disclosure of the amount of such acquisition-date changes in the acquirer's deferred tax benefits in the notes to the financial statements. (See paragraphs D4* and BC119-BC129.)

IASB 17   *Do you agree that any changes in an acquirer's deferred tax benefits that become recognisable because of the business combination are not part of the fair value of the acquiree and should be accounted for separately from the business combination? If not, why?*

The boards reconsidered disclosure requirements in IFRS 3 and SFAS 141 for the purposes of convergence. For some of the disclosures, the boards decided to converge. However, divergence continues to exist for some disclosures as described in the accompanying note *Differences between the Exposure Drafts published by the IASB and the FASB*. The

*The equivalent paragraph in this FRED is D5.

boards concluded that some of this divergence stems from differences that are broader than the Business Combinations project.

IASB 18   *Do you believe it is appropriate for the IASB and the FASB to retain those disclosure differences? If not, which of the differences should be eliminated, if any, and how should this be achieved?*

Style of the Exposure Draft

The Exposure Draft was prepared in a style similar to the style used by the IASB in its standards in which paragraphs in bold type state the main principles. All paragraphs have equal authority.

IASB 19   *Do you find the bold type-plain type style of the Exposure Draft helpful? If not, why? Are there any paragraphs you believe should be in bold type, but are in plain type, or vice versa?*

ITC5   IASB Invitation to comment on amendments to IAS 27 Consolidated and Separate Financial Statements

As part of the IASB exposure draft on amendments to IAS 27 the IASB have requested comments on their proposed amendments. These questions are reproduced below. The references have been amended to refer to the equivalent paragraph in FRS 2.

Draft paragraph ~~30A~~ 51 proposes that changes in the parent's ownership interest in a subsidiary after control is obtained that do not result in a loss of control should be accounted for as transactions with equity holders in their capacity as equity holders. As a result, no gain or loss on such changes would be recognised in profit or loss (see paragraphs BC4 of the Basis for Conclusions).

IASB 1   Do you agree? If not, why not and what alternative would you propose?

Paragraph ~~30D~~ 46A proposes that on loss of control of a subsidiary any non-controlling equity investment remaining in the former subsidiary should be remeasured to its fair value in the consolidated financial statements at the date that control is lost. Draft paragraph ~~30C~~ 46 proposes that the gain or loss on such remeasurement be included in the determination of the gain or loss arising on loss of control (see paragraph BC7 of the Basis for Conclusions)

IASB 2   Do you agree that the remaining non-controlling equity investment should be remeasured to fair value in these circumstances? If not, why not and what alternative would you propose?

Do you agree with the proposal to include any gain or loss resulting from such remeasurement in the calculation of the gain or loss arising on loss of control? If not, why not and what alternative would you propose?

As explained in Question 1, the Exposure Draft proposes that changes in a parent's ownership interest in a subsidiary that do not result in a loss of control should be treated as transactions with equity holders in their capacity as equity holders. Therefore, no gain or loss would be recognised in profit or loss. However, a decrease in the parent's ownership interest resulting in the loss of control of a subsidiary would result in any gain or loss being recognised in profit or loss for the period. The Board is aware that difference in accounting that depend on whether a change in control occurs could create opportunities for entities to structure transactions to achieve a particular accounting result. To reduce the risk, the Exposure Draft proposes that if one or more of the indicators in paragraph ~~30F~~ 47 are present, it is presumed that two or more disposal transactions or arrangements that result in loss of control should be accounted for as a single transaction or arrangement. This presumption can be overcome if the entity can demonstrate clearly that such accounting would be inappropriate (see paragraphs BC9 – BC 13 of the Basis for Conclusions).

IASB 3   Do you agree that it is appropriate that multiple arrangements that result in a loss of control should be accounted for as a *single arrangement when the indicators in paragraph ~~30F~~ 47 are present? Are the proposed factors suitable indicators? If not, what alternative indicators would you propose?*

Paragraph ~~35~~ 37 proposes that losses applicable to the non-controlling interest in a subsidary should be allocated to the non-controlling interest even if such losses exceed the non-contolling interest in the subsidiary's equity. Non-controlling interests are part of the equity of the group and, therefore, participate proportionally in the risks and rewards of investment in the subsidiary.

IASB 4   Do you agree with the proposed loss allocation? Do you agree any guarantees or other support arrangements from the controlling and non-controlling should be accounted for separately? If not, why not, and what alternative would you propose?

The transitional provisions in this Exposure Draft propose that all of its requirements should apply retrospectively, except in limited circumstances which the Board believes retrospective application is likely to be impracticable.

IASB 5   Do you agree that draft paragraphs ~~30A, 30C and 30D~~ 51, 46 and 46A should apply on a prospective basis in the cases set out in draft paragraph ~~43B~~ 55B? Do you believe that retrospective application is inappropriate for any other proposals addressed by the Exposure Draft? If so, what other proposals do you believe should be applied prospectively and why?

EXPOSURE DRAFT OF PROPOSED
AMENDMENTS TO IFRS 3
[DRAFT] FINANCIAL REPORTING
STANDARD ●

BUSINESS COMBINATIONS

Comments to be received by 28 October 2005

Contents

Note: Appendix B is not used in this publication. In the equivalent FASB Exposure Draft, Appendix B contains the FASB's Background Information and Basis for Conclusions. The IASB's Basis for Conclusions is not integral to the proposed IFRS and is presented in a separate booklet.

[Draft] Financial Reporting Standard 'Business Combinations' embodies IFRS 3 Business Combinations which was published in March 2004 in the form of a standard. The [draft] FRS includes some amendments to that standard adopted for entities subject to UK accounting standards. All of the changes made to the IASB text by the ASB are highlighted by strikethrough of the text to be deleted and underlining of the text to be inserted.

The [draft] Statement of Standard Accounting Practice in the [draft] FRS is set out in paragraphs 1-88 and Appendices A and C-E. All paragraphs have equal authority. Paragraphs in bold type state the main principles. Terms defined in paragraph 3 are underlined *the first time they appear in the [draft] FRS.*

Accompanying the [draft] Statement of Standard Accounting Practice is the basis of conclusions reached in the Statement and some illustrative examples, which do not form part of the Statement.

The [draft] Statement of Standard Accounting Practice should be read in the context of its objective as stated in paragraph 1 and the Accounting Standards Board's 'Foreword to Accounting Standards' and 'Statement of Principles for Financial Reporting'.

> ASB Note: This Introduction has been prepared by the IASB and is included in this FRED in full and unamended.
>
> All references in this section to 'the Board' and 'Board members' are references to the IASB Board and IASB Board members.

Introduction

IN1   A business combination is a transaction or other event in which an acquirer obtains control of one or more businesses (the acquiree). The objective of this [draft] IFRS is that all business combinations be accounted for by applying the acquisition method. In accordance with the acquisition method, the acquirer measures and recognises the acquiree, as a whole, and the assets acquired and liabilities assumed at their fair values as of the acquisition date.

IN2   This [draft] IFRS replaces IFRS 3 *Business Combinations* (as issued in 2004). This [draft] IFRS is to be applied at the same time as [draft] IAS 27 *Consolidated and Separate Financial Statements* (as revised in 200X) and [draft] IAS 37 *Non-financial Liabilities**.

BACKGROUND

IN3   This [draft] IFRS is issued as part of a joint effort by the International Accounting Standards Board (IASB) and the Financial Accounting Standards Board (FASB) (referred to as the boards) to improve financial reporting while promoting the international convergence of accounting standards. The boards believe that developing a common set of high quality financial accounting standards improves the comparability of financial information around the world and simplifies the accounting for entities that issue financial statements in accordance with international accounting standards and US generally accepted accounting principles or reconcile from one set of standards to the other.

IN4   The boards each decided to address the financial accounting for business combinations in two phases. The IASB and the FASB deliberated the first phase separately. The FASB concluded the first phase in June 2001 by issuing Statement No. 141 *Business Combinations*. The IASB concluded the first phase in March 2004 by issuing IFRS 3 *Business Combinations*. The boards' primary conclusion in the first phase was that virtually all business combinations are acquisitions. Accordingly, the boards decided to require the use of one method of accounting for business combinations—the purchase method (called the *acquisition method* in this [draft] IFRS).

IN5   The second phase of the project addresses the guidance for applying the acquisition method. The IASB and the FASB began deliberating the second phase of their projects at about the same time. The boards decided that a significant improvement could be made to financial reporting if they had similar standards for accounting for business combinations. Thus, they decided to conduct the second phase of the project as a joint effort with the objective of reaching the same conclusions.

---

*ASB footnote: *The ASB are proposing to implement FRS ● (IAS 38)* Intangible Assets *and FRS ● (IAS 36)* Impairment of Assets, *see FRED 37 and FRED 38.*

REASONS FOR ISSUING THIS [DRAFT] IFRS

This [draft] IFRS seeks to improve financial reporting by requiring the acquisition method to be applied to more business combinations, including those involving only mutual entities and those achieved by contract alone. The boards believe that applying a single method of accounting to all business combinations will result in more comparable and transparent financial statements. **IN6**

This [draft] IFRS requires an acquirer to recognise an acquired business at its fair value at the acquisition date rather than at its cost. It also requires the acquirer to measure and recognise the individual assets acquired and liabilities assumed at their fair values at the acquisition date, with limited exceptions. The boards concluded that requiring the recognition of the acquiree and the assets acquired and liabilities assumed at fair value as of the acquisition date improves the relevance and reliability of financial information. This is true even in business combinations in which the acquirer obtains control of a business by acquiring less than 100 per cent of the equity interests in the acquiree or in business combinations achieved in stages (step acquisitions). Relevance and reliability are characteristics that make financial information more useful to users. **IN7**

MAIN FEATURES OF THIS [DRAFT] IFRS

This [draft] IFRS retains the fundamental requirements in the previous version of IFRS 3 for the acquisition method of accounting to be used for all business combinations and for an acquirer to be identified for every business combination. Additionally, this [draft] IFRS requires: **IN8**

(a)   the acquirer to measure the fair value of the acquiree, as a whole, as of the acquisition date.

(b)   for the purposes of applying the acquisition method, the consideration transferred by the acquirer in exchange for the acquiree to be measured at its fair value as of the acquisition date calculated as the sum of:

   (i)   the assets transferred by the acquirer, liabilities incurred by the acquirer, and equity interests issued by the acquirer, including contingent consideration, and

   (ii)   any non-controlling equity investment in the acquiree owned by the acquirer immediately before the acquisition date.

(c)   the acquirer to assess whether any portion of the transaction price paid and any assets acquired or liabilities assumed or incurred are not part of the exchange for the acquiree. Only the consideration transferred or the assets acquired or liabilities assumed or incurred that are part of the exchange for the acquiree are to be accounted for as part of the business combination accounting.

(d)   the acquirer to account for acquisition-related costs incurred in connection with the business combination separately from the business combination (generally as expenses).

(e)   the acquirer to measure and recognise the acquisition-date fair value of the assets acquired and liabilities assumed as part of the business combination, with limited exceptions. Those exceptions are:

   (i)   goodwill is to be measured and recognised as the excess of the fair value of the acquiree, as a whole, over the net amount of the recognised identifiable assets acquired and liabilities assumed. If the acquirer owns less than 100 per cent of the equity interests in the acquiree at the acquisition date, goodwill attributable to the non-controlling interest is recognised.

      (ii)   non-current assets (or disposal group) classified as held for sale, deferred tax assets or liabilities, and assets or liabilities related to the acquiree's employee benefit plans are measured in accordance with other IFRSs.

      (iii) if the acquiree is a lessee to an operating lease, no asset or related liability is recognised if the lease is at market terms.

(f)   the acquirer to recognise separately from goodwill an acquiree's intangible assets that meet the definition of an intangible asset in IAS 38 *Intangible Assets* and are identifiable (ie arise from contractual-legal rights or are separable).

(g)   *Not used.*

(h)   in a business combination in which the acquisition-date fair value of the acquirer's interest in the acquiree exceeds the fair value of the consideration transferred for that interest (referred to as a bargain purchase), the acquirer to account for that excess by reducing goodwill until the goodwill related to that business combination is reduced to zero and then by recognising any remaining excess in profit or loss.

(i)   the acquirer to recognise any adjustments made during the measurement period to the provisional values of the assets acquired and liabilities assumed as if the accounting for the business combination had been completed at the acquisition date. Thus, comparative information for prior periods presented in financial statements is to be adjusted.

SIGNIFICANT CHANGES TO IFRS 3

IN9   The main changes between this [draft] IFRS and the previous version of IFRS 3 are described below.

Scope

(a)   The requirements of this [draft] IFRS are applicable to business combinations involving only mutual entities and business combinations achieved by contract alone.

Definition of a business combination

(b)   This [draft] IFRS amends the definition of a *business combination* provided in the previous version of IFRS 3. This [draft] IFRS defines a business combination as 'a transaction or other event in which an acquirer obtains control of one or more businesses'.

Definition of a business

(c)   This [draft] IFRS provides a definition of a *business* and additional guidance for identifying when a group of assets constitutes a business. This [draft] IFRS amends the definition provided in the previous version of IFRS 3.

Measuring the fair value of the acquiree

(d)   This [draft] IFRS requires business combinations to be measured and recognised as of the acquisition date at the fair value of the acquiree, even if the business combination is achieved in stages or if less than 100 per cent of the equity interests in the acquiree are owned at the acquisition date. The previous version of IFRS 3 required a business combination to be measured and recognised on the basis of the accumulated cost of the combination.

(e)   This [draft] IFRS requires the costs the acquirer incurs in connection with the business combination to be accounted for separately from the business combination accounting. The previous version of IFRS 3 required direct costs of the business combination to be included in the cost of the acquiree.

(f)   This [draft] IFRS requires all items of consideration transferred by the acquirer to be measured and recognised at fair value at the acquisition date. Therefore, this [draft] IFRS requires the acquirer to recognise contingent consideration arrangements at fair value as of the acquisition date. Subsequent changes in the fair value of contingent consideration classified as liabilities are recognised in accordance with IAS 39 *Financial Instruments: Recognition and Measurement*, IAS 37 or other IFRSs, as appropriate.

(g)   This [draft] IFRS requires the acquirer in a business combination in which the acquisition-date fair value of the acquirer's interest in the acquiree exceeds the fair value of the consideration transferred for that interest (referred to as a bargain purchase) to account for that excess by first reducing the goodwill related to that business combination to zero, and then by recognising any excess in income. The previous version of IFRS 3 required the excess of the acquirer's interest in the net fair values of the acquiree's assets and liabilities over cost to be recognised immediately in profit or loss.

Measuring and recognising the assets acquired and the liabilities assumed

(h)   This [draft] IFRS requires the assets acquired and liabilities assumed to be measured and recognised at their fair values as of the acquisition date, with limited exceptions. The previous version of IFRS 3 required the cost of an acquisition to be allocated to the individual assets acquired and liabilities assumed based on their estimated fair values. However, it also provided guidance for measuring some assets and liabilities that was inconsistent with fair value measurement objectives. Thus, those assets or liabilities may not have been recognised at fair value as of the acquisition date in accordance with that version of IFRS 3.

(i)   This [draft] IFRS requires an identifiable asset or liability to be measured and recognised at fair value at the acquisition date even if the amount of the future economic benefits embodied in the asset or required to settle the liability are contingent (or conditional) on the occurrence or non-occurrence of one or more uncertain future events. The previous version of IFRS 3 required the recognition of contingent liabilities at fair value as of the acquisition date.

(j)   *Not used.*

(k)   This [draft] IFRS requires the acquirer in business combinations in which the acquirer holds less than 100 per cent of the equity interests in the acquiree at the acquisition date to recognise the identifiable assets and liabilities at the full amount of their fair values, with limited exceptions, and goodwill as the difference between the fair value of the acquiree, as a whole, and the fair value of the identifiable assets acquired and liabilities assumed. The previous version of IFRS 3 required the identifiable assets acquired and liabilities assumed to be recognised at fair value but goodwill to be recognised as the difference between the cost of the interest acquired and the acquirer's proportional interest in the fair value of the identifiable assets acquired and liabilities assumed. If the business combination was achieved in stages, IFRS 3 previously required goodwill to be determined by a step-by-step comparison of the cost of the individual investments with the acquirer's interest in the fair values of the identifiable assets acquired and liabilities assumed at each step.

(l)   Acquisitions of additional non-controlling equity interests after the business combination are not permitted to be accounted for using the acquisition method. In accordance with [draft] IAS 27 (as revised in 200X), acquisitions (or disposals) of non-controlling equity interests after the business combination are accounted for as equity transactions.

(m) The acquirer is required to recognise separately from goodwill an acquiree's intangible assets if they meet the definition of an intangible asset in IAS 38 *Intangible Assets*. The previous version of IFRS 3 required the recognition of intangible assets separately from goodwill only if they met the IAS 38 definition and were reliably measurable. For the purposes of this [draft] IFRS, an assembled workforce is not to be recognised as an intangible asset separately from goodwill.

(n) Not used.

BENEFITS AND COSTS

IN10 The boards have striven to issue a [draft] IFRS with common requirements that will fill a significant need and for which the costs imposed to apply it, as compared with other alternatives, are justified in relation to the overall benefits of the resulting information. The boards concluded that this [draft] IFRS will, for the reasons previously noted, make several improvements to financial reporting that would benefit investors, creditors, and other users of financial statements.

IN11 The boards sought to reduce the costs of applying this [draft] IFRS. This [draft] IFRS (a) requires particular assets and liabilities (for example, those related to deferred taxes, assets held for sale, and employee benefits) to continue to be measured and recognised in accordance with existing IFRSs rather than at fair value and (b) requires its provisions to be applied prospectively rather than retrospectively. The boards acknowledge that those two steps may diminish some benefits of improved reporting provided by this [draft] IFRS. However, they concluded that the complexities and related costs that would result from imposing a fair value measurement requirement at this time to all assets acquired and liabilities assumed in a business combination and requiring retrospective application of the provisions of this [draft] IFRS are not justified.

IN12 In addition, improving the consistency of the procedures used in accounting for business combinations, including international consistency, should help alleviate concerns that an entity's competitive position as a potential bidder is affected by differences in accounting for business combinations. Consistency in the accounting procedures can also reduce the costs to prepare financial statements, especially for entities with global operations. Moreover, such consistency also will enhance comparability of information among entities, which can lead to a better understanding of the resulting financial information and reduce the costs to users of analysing that information.

EFFECTIVE DATE

IN13 This [draft] IFRS applies prospectively to business combinations for which the acquisition date is on or after the beginning of the first annual period beginning on or after 1 January 2007. Earlier application is encouraged. However, this [draft] IFRS is to be applied only at the beginning of an annual period that begins on or after the date on which this [draft] IFRS was issued. If this [draft] IFRS is applied before its effective date, that fact is to be disclosed and [draft] IAS 27 (as revised in 200X) and [draft] IAS 37 (as revised in 200X) is/are to be applied at the same time.

[Draft] ~~INTERNATIONAL FINANCIAL REPORTING STANDARD 3~~

[Draft] Financial Reporting Standard ●

Business Combinations

OBJECTIVE

This [draft] ~~IFRS~~ FRS requires that all <u>business combinations</u> be accounted for by applying the acquisition method. A business combination is a transaction or other event in which an <u>acquirer</u> obtains <u>control</u> of one or more <u>businesses</u> (the <u>acquiree</u>). In accordance with the acquisition method, the acquirer measures and recognises the acquiree, as a whole, and the assets acquired and liabilities assumed at their <u>fair values</u> as of the <u>acquisition date</u>. **1**

SCOPE

<u>This Standard applies to all financial statements that are intended to give a true and fair view of a reporting entity's financial position and profit or loss (or income and expenditure), except that reporting entities applying the Financial Reporting Standard for Smaller Entities (FRSSE) currently applicable are exempt.</u> **1A**

An entity shall apply this [draft] ~~IFRS~~ FRS when accounting for business combinations. However, this [draft] ~~IFRS~~ FRS does not apply to: **2**

(a) formations of joint ventures
(b) combinations involving only entities or businesses under common control (see paragraphs C6-C10 of Appendix C).
(c) *Not used.*

KEY TERMS

The following terms are used with specific meanings and are integral to understanding and applying this [draft] ~~IFRS~~ FRS. **3**

(a) The <u>acquiree</u> is the business or businesses the acquirer obtains control of in a business combination.
(b) The <u>acquirer</u> is the entity that obtains control of the acquiree.
(c) The <u>acquisition date</u> is the date the acquirer obtains control of the acquiree.
(d) A <u>business</u> is an integrated set of activities and assets that is capable of being conducted and managed for the purpose of providing either:

    (1) a return to investors, or
    (2) dividends, lower costs, or other economic benefits directly and proportionately to owners, members or participants.

(e) A <u>business combination</u> is a transaction or other event in which an acquirer obtains control of one or more businesses.
(f) <u>Control</u> is defined in [draft] ~~IAS 27 Consolidated and Separate Financial Statements~~ FRS 2 *Accounting for Subsidiary Undertakings*.
(g) <u>Contingencies</u> is used with the same meaning as in [draft] ~~IAS 37~~ FRS 12 *Non-financial Liabilities*.

(h)   For the purposes of this [draft] ~~IFRS~~ FRS, the term equity interests is used broadly to mean ownership interests of investor-owned entities and owner, member, or participant interests of mutual entities.

(i)   For the purposes of this [draft] ~~IFRS~~ FRS, fair value is the price at which an asset or liability could be exchanged in a current transaction between knowledgeable, unrelated willing parties.*

(j)   Goodwill is the future economic benefits arising from assets that are not individually identified and separately recognised.

(k)   An asset is identifiable if it either:

(1)   is separable, that is, capable of being separated or divided from the entity and sold, transferred, licensed, rented, or exchanged, either individually or together with a related contract, asset, or liability, regardless of whether the entity intends to do so; or

(2)   Arises from contractual or other legal rights, regardless of whether those rights are transferable or separable from the entity or from other rights and obligations.

(l)   ~~Impracticable is defined in IAS 8 *Accounting Policies, Changes in Accounting Estimates and Errors.*~~

(m)   A mutual entity is an entity other than an investor-owned entity that provides dividends, lower costs, or other economic benefits directly and proportionately to its owners, members, or participants.

(n)   For the purposes of this [draft] ~~IFRS~~ FRS, the term owners is used broadly to include holders of equity interests of investor-owned entities and owners, members, or participants of mutual entities.

(o)   Non-controlling interest is used with the same meaning as in [draft] ~~IAS 27~~ FRS 2 (revised 200X).

IDENTIFYING A BUSINESS COMBINATION

4   **A business combination is a transaction or other event in which an acquirer obtains control of one or more businesses.**

5   A transaction or other event is accounted for as a business combination only if the assets acquired and liabilities assumed constitute a business (an acquiree). Paragraphs A2-A7 of Appendix A provide guidance for identifying whether the assets acquired and liabilities assumed constitute a business. If the assets acquired and liabilities assumed do not constitute a business, the acquirer shall account for the transaction as an asset acquisition. The accounting for an asset acquisition is set out in paragraphs C3-C5.

6   In a business combination, an acquirer might:

(a)   acquire the equity interests of a business.

(b)   acquire some or all of an entity's assets (net assets) that constitute a business.

(c)   assume some or all of the liabilities of an acquiree.

An acquirer might obtain control of an acquiree:

(d)   by transferring cash, cash equivalents, or other assets (including net assets that constitute a business).

(e)   by issuing equity interests.

(f)   by providing more than one type of consideration.

The definition of fair value is based on the definition in the FASB's Proposed Statement Fair Value Measurements. The FASB plans to issue a final Statement on fair value measurements in the fourth quarter of 2005. The definition of fair value may change in that final Statement.

(g) by contract alone (see paragraph 54).

(h) without transferring any consideration.

(i) without a transaction involving the acquirer. Onc cxample is a business combination that occurs when an entity (the acquiree) repurchases its own shares and, as a result, an existing investor (the acquirer) obtains control of that entity. Another example is a business combination that occurs when an acquirer obtains control of an acquiree through the lapse of minority veto rights that previously kept the acquirer from controlling the acquiree even though the acquirer held the majority voting interest in the acquiree.

A business combination may be structured in a variety of ways for legal, taxation, or other reasons. Accordingly, this [draft] ~~IFRS~~ FRS applies equally to business combinations in which: **7**

(a) one or more businesses are merged with or become subsidiaries of an acquirer.

(b) one entity transfers net assets or its <u>owners</u> transfer their equity interests to another entity or the owners of another entity.

(c) all entities transfer net assets or the owners of those entities transfer their equity interests to a newly formed entity (some of which are referred to as roll-up or put-together transactions).

All those transactions are business combinations regardless of:

(d) whether the acquiree is incorporated.

(e) the form of consideration transferred in exchange for the acquiree.

(f) whether a group of former owners of one of the combining entities retains or receives a majority of the voting rights of the combined entity.

THE ACQUISITION METHOD

All business combinations shall be accounted for by applying the acquisition method.   **8**

The acquisition method has four steps: **9**

(a) identifying the acquirer

(b) determining the acquisition date

(c) measuring the fair value of the acquiree

(d) measuring and recognising the assets acquired and the liabilities assumed.

Identifying the acquirer

An acquirer shall be identified for all business combinations.   **10**

The guidance in [draft] ~~IAS 27~~ FRS 2 (revised 200X) shall be used to identify the acquirer, which is the <u>parent</u> entity that obtains control of the acquiree. If an acquirer cannot be determined solely on the basis of the guidance in [draft] ~~IAS 27~~ FRS 2 paragraphs 12-16 shall be considered in making that determination.   **11**

The form of the consideration transferred may provide evidence about which entity is the acquirer. For example: **12**

(a) in a business combination effected solely through the transfer of cash or other assets or by incurring liabilities, the entity that transfers the cash or other assets or incurs the liabilities is likely to be the acquirer.

(b) in a business combination effected through an exchange of cash or other assets for voting equity interests, the entity that gives up the cash or other assets is likely to be the acquirer.

(c)   in a business combination effected through an exchange of equity interests, the entity that issues the equity interests is normally the acquirer. However, in some business combinations, commonly called reverse acquisitions, the issuing entity is the acquiree. Paragraphs A111-A136 provide guidance for accounting for reverse acquisitions. Commonly in an exchange of equity interests, the acquirer is the larger entity; however, the facts and circumstances surrounding a combination sometimes indicate that a smaller entity acquires a larger entity. Therefore, in identifying the acquirer in a business combination effected through an exchange of equity interests, all pertinent facts and circumstances shall be considered, in particular:

(1)   *the relative voting rights in the combined entity after the business combination* – All else being equal, the acquirer is the combining entity whose owners as a group retained or received the largest portion of the voting rights in the combined entity. In determining which group of owners retained or received the largest portion of the voting rights, consideration shall be given to the existence of any unusual or special voting arrangements and options, warrants, or convertible securities.

(2)   *the existence of a large minority voting interest in the combined entity when no other owner or organised group of owners has a significant voting interest* – All else being equal, the acquirer is the combining entity whose single owner or organised group of owners holds the largest minority voting interest in the combined entity.

(3)   *the composition of the governing body of the combined entity* – All else being equal, the acquirer is the combining entity whose owners or governing body has the ability to elect or appoint a voting majority of the governing body of the combined entity.

(4)   *the terms of the exchange of equity interests* – All else being equal, the acquirer is the combining entity that pays a premium over the pre-combination market value of the equity securities of the other combining entity or entities.

13   If the fair value of one of the combining entities is significantly greater than that of the other combining entity or entities, the entity with the greatest fair value is likely to be the acquirer.

14   If the business combination results in the management of one of the combining entities being able to dominate the selection of the management team of the resulting combined entity, the entity whose management is able to dominate is likely to be the acquirer.

15   In a business combination involving more than two entities, determining the acquirer shall include a consideration of, among other things, which of the combining entities initiated the combination and whether the assets, revenues, or profit or loss of one of the combining entities significantly exceeds those of the others.

16   If a new entity is formed to issue equity interests to effect a business combination, one of the combining entities that existed before the business combination shall be identified as the acquirer based on the evidence available. The guidance in paragraphs 11-15 shall be used to identify the acquirer.

Determining the acquisition date

17   The acquisition date is the date the acquirer obtains control of the acquiree.

The acquirer generally obtains control of the acquiree on the closing date, which is **18** the date that the acquirer transfers the consideration, acquires the assets, and assumes the liabilities of the acquiree. In some cases, the acquisition date may precede the closing date of the business combination or the date the business combination is finalised in law. All pertinent facts and circumstances surrounding a business combination shall be considered in assessing when the acquirer has obtained control of the acquiree. For example, the acquisition date may precede the closing date if a written agreement provides that the acquirer obtains control of the acquiree on a date before the closing date.

Measuring the fair value of the acquiree

The acquirer shall measure the fair value of the acquiree, as a whole, as of the **19** **acquisition date.**

Business combinations are usually arm's length exchange transactions in which **20** knowledgeable, unrelated willing parties exchange equal values. Therefore, in the absence of evidence to the contrary, the exchange price (referred to in this [draft] ~~IFRS~~ FRS as the consideration transferred) paid by the acquirer on the acquisition date is presumed to be the best evidence of the acquisition-date fair value of the acquirer's interest in the acquiree. In some business combinations, either no consideration is transferred on the acquisition date or the evidence indicates that the consideration transferred is not the best basis for measuring the acquisition-date fair value of the acquirer's interest in the acquiree. In those business combinations, the acquirer should measure the acquisition-date fair value of its interest in the acquiree using other valuation techniques. Paragraphs A8-A26 provide additional guidance for performing the fair value measurement described in this paragraph.

Consideration transferred

For the purposes of applying the acquisition method, the fair value of the con- **21** sideration transferred in exchange for the acquirer's interest in the acquiree is calculated as the sum of:

(a) the acquisition-date fair values of the assets transferred by the acquirer, liabilities assumed or incurred by the acquirer, and equity interests issued by the acquirer. Examples include cash, other assets, contingent consideration (see paragraph 25), a business or a subsidiary of the acquirer, common or preferred equity instruments, options, warrants, and member interests of mutual entities; and

(b) the acquisition-date fair value of any non-controlling equity investment in the acquiree that the acquirer owned immediately before the acquisition date (see paragraph 56).

The consideration transferred may include assets or liabilities of the acquirer that **22** have carrying amounts that differ from their fair values at the acquisition date (for example, non-monetary assets or a business of the acquirer). In that case, the acquirer shall remeasure those transferred assets or liabilities to their fair values as of the acquisition date and recognise any gains or losses in profit or loss. However, if those assets or liabilities are transferred to the acquiree and, therefore, remain within the combined entity after the business combination, the acquirer shall eliminate any gains or losses on those transferred assets or liabilities in the consolidated financial statements.

23   If the information necessary to measure the fair value of some or all of the consideration transferred is not available at the acquisition date, the measurement period guidance in paragraphs 62-68 applies.

24   The acquirer shall assess whether any portion of the transaction price includes payments or other arrangements that are not consideration transferred in exchange for the acquiree. Paragraphs 69 and 70 provide guidance for making that assessment. Only the consideration transferred in exchange for the acquiree shall be accounted for as part of the business combination.

Contingent consideration

25   As described in paragraph 21(a), the fair value of the consideration transferred in exchange for the acquiree includes the acquisition-date fair value of any obligations of the acquirer to transfer additional assets or equity interests if specified future events occur or conditions are met (commonly called contingent consideration). For example, the acquirer may agree to transfer additional equity interests, cash, or other assets to the former owners of the acquiree after the acquisition date if the acquiree meets specified financial or non-financial targets in the future. The acquirer shall measure and recognise the fair value of such contingent consideration as of the acquisition date and shall classify that obligation as either a liability or equity on the basis of other ~~IFRSs~~ FRSs. An arrangement to transfer additional assets or equity interests if specified events or conditions occur may be incorporated in an acquirer's share-based payment awards exchanged for awards held by the acquiree's employees. The acquirer shall measure the portion of such awards included in consideration transferred for the acquiree in accordance with paragraphs A102-A109.

26   After initial recognition, the acquirer shall account for changes in the fair value of contingent consideration that do not qualify as measurement period adjustments (see paragraphs 62-68) as follows:

(a)   contingent consideration classified as equity shall not be remeasured.
(b)   contingent consideration classified as liabilities that:

   (1)   are financial instruments and within the scope of ~~IAS 39~~ FRS 26 *Financial Instruments: Recognition and Measurement*, shall be accounted for in accordance with that ~~IFRS~~ FRS.
   (2)   are non-financial liabilities that include a contingency shall be accounted for in accordance with [draft] ~~IAS 37~~ FRS 12, or other ~~IFRSs~~ FRSs as appropriate.

Costs incurred in connection with a business combination

27   Costs the acquirer incurs in connection with a business combination (also called acquisition-related costs) are not part of the consideration transferred in exchange for the acquiree. For example, such costs include finder's fees, advisory, legal, accounting, valuation, other professional or consulting fees, general administrative costs, including the costs of maintaining an internal acquisitions department, and costs of registering and issuing debt and equity securities. The acquirer shall not include such costs in the measure of the fair value of the acquiree or the assets acquired or liabilities assumed as part of the business combination. The acquirer shall account for acquisition-related costs, separately from the business combination, in accordance with other ~~IFRSs~~ FRSs.

Measuring and recognising the assets acquired and the liabilities assumed

The acquirer shall measure and recognise as of the acquisition date the assets acquired   **28**
and liabilities assumed as part of the business combination. Except as provided in
paragraphs 42-51, the <u>identifiable</u> assets acquired and liabilities assumed shall be
measured at fair value and recognised separately from <u>goodwill</u>.

As part of the business combination accounting, the acquirer recognises assets   **29**
acquired or liabilities assumed that are part of the exchange for the acquiree and
meet the definition of assets and liabilities in the ~~Framework for the Preparation and~~
~~Presentation of Financial Statements~~ *Statement of Principles for Financial Reporting*.
The assets and liabilities the acquirer recognises as part of the business combination
may include assets and liabilities the acquiree had not recognised previously in its
financial statements. For example, the acquirer often recognises the acquired identifiable intangible assets that were internally developed by the acquiree and did not
meet the criteria for recognition in the acquiree's financial statements. The acquirer
does not recognise any assets or liabilities other than the assets acquired or the
liabilities assumed as part of the business combination.

A business combination does not affect the measurement of the acquirer's assets and   **30**
liabilities, except for those assets or liabilities that are not recognised at fair value by
the acquirer before the business combination and are part of the consideration
transferred in exchange for the acquiree (see paragraph 22).

If the information necessary to measure the fair value of some or all of the assets   **31**
acquired or liabilities assumed is not available at the acquisition date, the measurement period guidance in paragraphs 62-68 applies.

The acquirer shall assess whether any of the assets acquired or liabilities assumed or   **32**
incurred are not part of the exchange for the acquiree (that is, not included in the
business combination accounting). Paragraphs 69 and 70 provide guidance for
making that assessment.

Guidance for measuring and recognising particular assets acquired and liabilities assumed

Paragraphs 34-41 provide guidance for measuring and recognising particular assets   **33**
acquired and liabilities assumed at fair value as of the acquisition date.

Valuation allowances

The acquirer shall not recognise a separate valuation allowance as of the acquisition   **34**
date for assets required to be recognised at fair value in accordance with this [draft]
~~IFRS~~ <u>FRS</u>. For example, an acquirer would recognise receivables (including loans)
acquired in a business combination at fair value as of the acquisition date and would
not recognise a separate valuation allowance for uncollectible receivables at that
date. Uncertainty about collections and future cash flows is included in the fair value
measure.

Contingencies

The acquirer shall recognise, separately from goodwill, the acquisition-date fair value   **35**
of an identifiable asset acquired or liability assumed as part of the business combination even if the amount of the future economic benefits embodied in the asset or

required to settle the liability are contingent (or conditional) on the occurrence or non-occurrence of one or more uncertain future events. Such an asset or liability is called a underline{contingency} in this [draft] ~~IFRS~~ FRS.

36   After initial recognition, the acquirer shall account for such assets in accordance with ~~IAS 38~~ [draft] FRS • *Intangible Assets* or ~~IAS 39~~ FRS 26, as appropriate, and such liabilities in accordance with [draft] ~~IAS 37~~ FRS 12 or other ~~IFRSs~~ FRSs, as appropriate.

Liabilities associated with restructuring or exit activities

37   The acquirer shall recognise, separately from goodwill, the acquisition-date fair value of liabilities for restructuring or exit activities acquired in a business combination only if they meet the recognition criteria in [draft] ~~IAS 37~~ FRS 12 as of the acquisition date. Costs associated with restructuring or exit activities that do not meet the recognition criteria in [draft] ~~IAS 37~~ FRS 12 as of the acquisition date are not liabilities at the acquisition date and, therefore, are recognised separately from the business combination, generally as post-combination expenses of the combined entity when incurred. For example, costs the acquirer expects to incur in the future pursuant to its plan (a) to exit an activity of an acquiree, (b) to involuntarily terminate the employment of an acquiree's employees, or (c) to relocate employees of an acquiree are not assumed liabilities of the acquiree and, therefore, are not accounted for as part of the business combination.

Leases

38   ~~In accordance with IAS 17 Leases, a~~ A lease of the acquiree (regardless of whether the acquiree is the lessee or lessor) retains the lease classification determined by the acquiree, in accordance with SSAP 21 *Leases and hire purchase contracts,* at the lease inception, unless the provisions of a lease are modified as a result of the business combination in a way that would require the acquirer to consider the revised agreement a new lease agreement ~~in accordance with paragraph 13 of IAS 17~~. In that circumstance, the acquirer would classify the new lease according to the criteria set out in ~~IAS 17~~ SSAP 21 on the basis of the conditions of the modified lease.

39   The acquirer shall account for the acquiree's operating leases in which the acquiree is the lessee in accordance with paragraph 47. For all other leases, the acquirer shall measure and recognise separately the asset and any related liability embodied in a lease at their acquisition-date fair values. After initial recognition, assets and liabilities related to leases shall be accounted for in accordance with ~~IAS 17~~ SSAP 21.

Intangible assets

40   The acquirer shall recognise, separately from goodwill, the acquisition-date fair value of intangible assets acquired in a business combination that meet the definition of an intangible asset in ~~IAS 38~~ [draft] FRS•. For the purposes of this [draft] ~~IFRS~~ FRS, an assembled workforce shall not be recognised as an intangible asset separately from goodwill. Paragraphs A27-A61 provide additional guidance about measuring and recognising intangible assets acquired in a business combination.

41   As part of a business combination, an acquirer may reacquire a right that it had previously granted to the acquiree to use the acquirer's recognised or unrecognised intangible assets (such as a right to use the acquirer's trade name under a franchise

agreement or a right to use the acquirer's technology under a technology licensing agreement). Such a right is an identifiable intangible asset that shall be recognised separately from goodwill as part of the business combination accounting. If the contract giving rise to the reacquired right includes pricing terms that are favourable or unfavourable when compared with pricing for current market transactions for the same or similar items, the acquirer shall recognise a settlement gain or loss. Paragraph A92 provides guidance for measuring that settlement gain or loss. After initial recognition, reacquired rights shall be amortised over the remaining contractual period of the pre-combination contract that granted those rights.

Assets acquired and liabilities assumed that are not recognised at fair value as of the acquisition date

The following assets acquired and liabilities assumed shall be measured and recognised as of the acquisition date as follows.   **42**

~~*Assets held for sale**~~

Business sold or held exclusively with a view to subsequent resale

~~The acquirer shall measure and recognise, separately from goodwill, an acquired non-current asset (or disposal group) that is classified as held for sale as of the acquisition date in accordance with paragraphs 7-11 of IFRS 5 *Non-current Assets Held for Sale and Discontinued Operations.*~~ Where an interest in a separate business of the acquired entity is sold as a single unit within approximately one year of the date of acquisition, the investment in that business should be treated as a single asset for the purposes of determining fair values. Its fair value should be based on the net proceeds of the sale, adjusted for the fair value of any assets or liabilities transferred into or out of the business, unless such adjusted net proceeds are demonstrably different from the fair value at the date of acquisition as a result of a post-acquisition event. This treatment should be applied to any business operation, whether a separate subsidiary undertaking or not, provided that its assets, liabilities, results of operations and activities are clearly distinguishable, physically, operationally and for financial reporting purposes, from the other assets, liabilities, results of operations and activities of the acquired entity.   **43**

Where the business has been sold by the time of approval of the first financial statements after the date of acquisition, the fair value of the interest in the business should be based on the estimated proceeds of the sale, provided: **43A**

(a)   a purchaser has been identified or is being sought; and
(b)   the disposal is reasonably expected to occur within approximately one year of the date of acquisition.

The interest in the business or, if it is not a separate subsidiary undertaking, in the assets of the business, should be shown within current assets. When the sale price is subsequently determined, the original estimate of fair value should be adjusted to reflect the actual sale proceeds.

*ASB footnote: IFRS 5 Non-current Assets Held for Sale and Discontinued Operations *is not a UK adopted IFRS. The corresponding provisions for the UK and Republic of Ireland entities were set out in paragraphs 16 to 18 of FRS 7* Fair Values in Acquisition Accounting. *These paragraphs, of FRS 7, have been carried forward in this [draft] Standard.*

43B   If the subsidiary undertaking or business operation is not, in fact, sold within approximately one year of the acquisition, it should be consolidated normally with fair values attributed to the individual assets and liabilities as at the date of acquisition, and corresponding adjustments to goodwill.

Deferred taxes

44   The acquirer shall measure and recognise, separately from goodwill, a deferred tax asset or liability in accordance with ~~IAS 12 *Income Taxes*~~ FRS 19 *Deferred Tax* as amended by paragraph ~~D4~~ D5 of this [draft] ~~IFRS~~ FRS.

45   ~~IAS 12~~ FRS 19, as amended by this [draft] ~~IFRS~~ FRS, sets out the subsequent accounting for deferred tax assets (including unrecognised deferred tax assets) and liabilities that were acquired in a business combination.

46   The acquirer shall account for the potential tax effects of (a) ~~temporary~~ timing differences ~~and carry-forwards~~ of an acquiree that exist at the acquisition date and (b) ~~income~~ current tax uncertainties related to the acquisition (for example, an uncertainty related to the tax basis of an acquired asset that ultimately will be agreed to by the taxing authority or positions taken in prior tax returns of the acquiree) in accordance with the provisions of ~~IAS 12~~ FRS 19, as amended.

Operating leases

47   If the acquiree is the lessee to an operating lease, the acquirer shall not recognise separately the asset and related liability embodied in the lease. If the acquiree is the lessor to an operating lease, the acquirer shall measure and recognise the asset subject to the operating lease at its acquisition-date fair value in accordance with paragraph 39. The acquirer shall also assess whether each of the acquiree's operating leases are at market terms as of the acquisition date, regardless of whether the acquiree is the lessee or lessor. If an operating lease is not at market terms as of the acquisition date, the acquirer shall recognise:

(a)   an intangible asset if the terms of the operating lease are favourable relative to market terms.

(b)   a liability if the terms of the operating lease are unfavourable relative to market terms.

~~Employee~~ Retirement benefit plans

48   The acquirer shall measure and recognise, separately from goodwill, any ~~asset~~ surplus or ~~liability~~ deficit related to the acquiree's ~~employee~~ retirement benefit plans that is within the scope of ~~IAS 19 *Employee Benefits*~~ FRS 17 *Retirement and Termination Benefits*. ~~in accordance with paragraph 108 of that standard.~~

Goodwill

49   Except as provided by paragraph 61, the acquirer shall measure and recognise goodwill as of the acquisition date as the excess of the fair value of the acquiree, as a whole, over the net amount of the recognised identifiable assets acquired and liabilities assumed. This requirement applies even if the acquirer owns less than 100 per cent of the equity interests in the acquiree at the acquisition date (that is, even if a non-controlling interest in the acquiree exists at the acquisition date).

The amount recognised as goodwill includes synergies and other benefits that are   **50**
expected from combining the activities of the acquirer and acquiree. Because
goodwill is measured as a residual, the amount recognised as goodwill also includes
(a) intangible assets that do not meet the criteria in paragraph 40 for recognition
separately from goodwill and (b) any difference between the fair values of the assets
acquired and liabilities assumed and the amount recognised in accordance with
paragraphs 42-48.

After initial recognition, the acquirer shall measure goodwill at the amount recog-   **51**
nised as of the acquisition date less any accumulated impairment losses. Goodwill
shall not be amortised. The acquirer shall test goodwill for impairment in accordance
with IAS 36-[draft] FRS • *Impairment of Assets*. as amended by paragraph D10 of
this [draft] IFRS.

Additional guidance for applying the acquisition method to particular types of business combinations

Paragraphs 53-61 provide additional guidance for applying the acquisition method   **52**
to the following types of business combinations:

(a)   business combinations involving only mutual entities
(b)   business combinations achieved by contract alone
(c)   business combinations achieved in stages
(d)   business combinations in which the acquirer holds less than 100 per cent of the
       equity interests in the acquiree at the acquisition date
(e)   business combinations in which the consideration transferred for the acquirer's
       interest in the acquiree is less than the fair value of that interest.

Business combinations involving only mutual entities

In a business combination involving only mutual entities in which the only con-   **53**
sideration exchanged is the member interests of the acquiree for the member interests
of the acquirer (or the member interests of the newly combined entity), the amount
equal to the fair value of the acquiree shall be recognised as a direct addition to
capital or equity, not retained earnings.

Business combinations achieved by contract alone

In rare circumstances, an acquirer (a) obtains control of an acquiree by contract, (b)   **54**
transfers no consideration for control of the acquiree or for the net assets of the
acquiree, and (c) obtains no equity interests in the acquiree, either on the acquisition
date or previously. An example of such a business combination is one in which two
businesses are brought together to form a dual listed corporation. This type of
business combination is referred to in this [draft] IFRS-FRS as a business combination achieved by contract alone. In such a business combination, the fair value of
the acquiree shall be attributed to the non-controlling interests of the acquiree (that
is, the equity holders of the acquiree) in the consolidated financial statements of the
acquirer.

Business combinations achieved in stages

A business combination in which an acquirer holds a non-controlling equity   **55**
investment in the acquiree immediately before obtaining control of that acquiree is a

business combination achieved in stages. This type of business combination is also commonly called a step acquisition.

56   As described in paragraph 21(b), for the purposes of applying the acquisition method, the fair value of the consideration transferred by the acquirer includes the acquisition-date fair value of any non-controlling equity investment in the acquiree that the acquirer owned immediately before the acquisition date. In a business combination achieved in stages, the acquirer shall remeasure its non-controlling equity investment in the acquiree at fair value as of the acquisition date and recognise any gain or loss in profit or loss. If, before the business combination, the acquirer recognised changes in the value of its non-controlling equity investment ~~directly in equity~~ through the statement of total recognised gains and losses (for example, the investment was designated as available for sale), the amount that was recognised ~~directly in equity~~ through the statement of total recognised gains and losses shall be reclassified and included in the calculation of any gain or loss as of the acquisition date.

57   Once an acquirer has obtained control of an acquiree, subsequent acquisitions (or dispositions) of any non-controlling interests in the acquiree shall be accounted for as equity transactions in accordance with [draft] ~~IAS 27~~ FRS 2.

Business combinations in which the acquirer holds less than 100 per cent of the equity interests in the acquiree at the acquisition date

58   In a business combination in which the acquirer holds less than 100 per cent of the equity interests in the acquiree at the acquisition date, the acquirer shall:

(a)   recognise identifiable assets acquired and liabilities assumed at their acquisition date values measured in accordance with paragraphs 28-48.
(b)   recognise goodwill at the amount measured in accordance with paragraph 49.
(c)   allocate the amount of goodwill determined in accordance with paragraph 49 to the acquirer and the non-controlling interest. Paragraphs A62 and A63 provide additional guidance for allocating goodwill between the acquirer and the non-controlling interest.
(d)   measure and recognise the non-controlling interest as the sum of the non-controlling interest's proportional interest in the identifiable assets acquired and liabilities assumed plus the non-controlling interest's share of goodwill, if any.

Business combinations in which the consideration transferred for the acquirer's interest in the acquiree is less than the fair value of that interest

59   In rare circumstances, the acquisition-date fair value of the acquirer's interest in the acquiree exceeds the fair value of the consideration transferred for that interest (as might be the case, for example, in a business combination that is a forced sale in which the seller is acting under compulsion). This type of business combination is referred to in this [draft] ~~IFRS~~ FRS as a bargain purchase. However, this type of business combination may occur also because of the requirements in paragraphs 43-48 to measure and recognise particular assets acquired or liabilities assumed in accordance with other [draft] ~~IFRSs~~ FRS rather than at fair value.

60   If the fair value of the acquirer's interest in the acquiree is initially determined to exceed the fair value of the consideration transferred for that interest, the acquirer shall assess whether it has correctly identified all assets acquired and liabilities

assumed and shall review the procedures used to measure and remeasure, if necessary, all of the following:

(a)   the acquisition-date fair value of the acquiree
(b)   the acquisition-date fair value of the acquirer's interest in the acquiree
(c)   the acquisition-date fair value of the consideration transferred
(d)   the acquisition-date values of the identifiable assets acquired and liabilities assumed recognised in accordance with the requirements of this [draft] ~~IFRS~~ FRS.

The objective of this review is to ensure that appropriate consideration has been given to all available information in performing the measurements.

If, after performing any remeasurements required by paragraph 60, the fair value of the acquirer's interest in the acquiree still exceeds the fair value of the consideration transferred for that interest, the acquirer shall account for that excess by reducing the amount of goodwill that otherwise would be recognised in accordance with paragraph 49. If the goodwill related to that business combination is reduced to zero, any remaining excess shall be recognised as a gain attributable to the acquirer on the acquisition date. Paragraphs A64-A70 provide additional guidance and examples for applying this requirement.   **61**

Measurement period

The measurement period is the period after the acquisition date during which the acquirer may adjust the provisional amounts recognised at the acquisition date in accounting for a business combination. The measurement period provides the acquirer a reasonable time to obtain the information necessary to identify and measure the following: **62**

(a)   **the acquisition-date fair value of the acquiree**
(b)   **the acquisition-date fair value of the acquirer's interest in the acquiree**
(c)   **the acquisition-date fair value of the consideration transferred for the acquiree**
(d)   **the acquisition-date values of the assets acquired and liabilities assumed recognised in accordance with the requirements of this [draft] ~~IFRS~~ FRS.**

If any of those measurements can be determined only provisionally by the end of the reporting period in which the business combination occurs, the acquirer shall report those provisional amounts in its financial statements.   **63**

During the measurement period, the acquirer shall adjust the provisional amounts recognised at the acquisition date to reflect any new information obtained about facts and circumstances that existed as of the acquisition date and, if known, would have affected the measurement of the amounts recognised as of that date. During the measurement period, the acquirer also shall recognise additional assets or liabilities if new information is obtained about facts and circumstances that existed as of the acquisition date and, if known, would have resulted in the recognition of those assets and liabilities as of that date.   **64**

The measurement period ends as soon as the acquirer receives the necessary information about facts and circumstances that existed as of the acquisition date or learns that the information is not obtainable. However, the measurement period shall not exceed one year from the acquisition date.   **65**

Generally, adjustments to the provisional amounts recognised for identifiable assets and liabilities during the measurement period are recognised through an offsetting   **66** adjustment to goodwill. However, the offsetting adjustment (or part of the offsetting adjustment) may be to an asset or liability other than goodwill. For example, assume that an acquirer's contingent consideration obligation is directly related to the value of an acquired intangible asset and, during the measurement period, the acquirer obtains new information about the fair value of that intangible asset as of the acquisition date. In this case, the adjustment to the provisional amount recognised for that asset may be offset (or partially offset) by a corresponding adjustment to the provisional amount recognised for the contingent consideration liability.

67   The acquirer shall recognise any adjustments to the provisional values during the measurement period as if the accounting for the business combination had been completed at the acquisition date. Thus, comparative information for prior periods presented in financial statements shall be adjusted, including any change in depreciation, amortisation, or other profit or loss effect recognised as a result of completing the initial accounting. Paragraphs A71-A86 provide additional guidance and illustrative examples for applying the measurement period requirements.

68   After the end of the measurement period, the accounting for a business combination shall be restated only to correct an error in accordance with ~~IAS 8~~ FRS 18 *Accounting Policies*.

Assessing what is part of the exchange for the acquiree

69   **The acquirer shall assess whether any portion of the transaction price (payments or other arrangements) and any assets acquired or liabilities assumed or incurred are not part of the exchange for the acquiree. Only the consideration transferred and the assets acquired or liabilities assumed or incurred that are part of the exchange for the acquiree shall be included in the business combination accounting. Any portion of the transaction price or any assets acquired or liabilities assumed or incurred that are not part of the exchange for the acquiree shall be accounted for separately from the business combination.**

70   Examples of payments or other arrangements that are not part of the exchange for the acquiree include:

(a)   payments that effectively settle pre-existing relationships between the acquirer and acquiree (see paragraphs A91-A97).
(b)   payments to compensate employees or former owners of the acquiree for future services (see paragraphs A98-A101).
(c)   payments to reimburse the acquiree or its former owners for paying the acquirer's costs incurred in connection with the business combination.

Paragraphs A87-A109 provide guidance for assessing whether a portion of the transaction price and any assets and liabilities are not part of the exchange for the acquiree.

DISCLOSURES

71   **The acquirer shall disclose information that enables users of its financial statements to evaluate the nature and financial effect of business combinations that occur:**

(a)   **during the reporting period; and**
(b)   **after the balance sheet date but before the financial statements are authorised for issue.**

To meet the objective in paragraph 71, the acquirer shall disclose the following **72** information for each material business combination that occurs during the reporting period:

(a)   the name and a description of the acquiree.

(b)   the acquisition date.

(c)   the percentage of voting equity instruments acquired.

(d)   the primary reasons for the business combination, including a description of the factors that contributed to the recognition of goodwill.

(e)   the acquisition-date fair value of the acquiree and the basis for measuring that value.

(f)   the acquisition-date fair value of the consideration transferred, including the fair value of each major class of consideration, such as:

    (1)   cash

    (2)   other tangible or intangible assets, including a business or subsidiary of the acquirer

    (3)   contingent consideration

    (4)   debt instruments

    (5)   equity or member interests of the acquirer, including the number of instruments or interests issued or issuable, and the method of determining the fair value of those instruments or interests

    (6)   the acquirer's previously acquired non-controlling equity investment in the acquiree in a business combination achieved in stages.

(g)   the amounts recognised as of the acquisition date for each major class of assets acquired and liabilities assumed in the form of a condensed balance sheet (see paragraph A110).

(h)   the maximum potential amount of future payments (undiscounted) the acquirer could be required to make under the terms of the acquisition agreement. If there is no limitation on the maximum potential amount of future payments, that fact shall be disclosed.

(i)   in a business combination in which the consideration transferred for the acquiree is less than fair value, the amount of any gain recognised in accordance with paragraph 61, the line item in the income statement in which the gain is recognised, and a description of the reasons why the acquirer was able to achieve a gain.

(j)   in a business combination achieved in stages, the amount of any gain or loss recognised in accordance with paragraph 56 and the line item in the income statement in which that gain or loss is recognised.

(k)   in a business combination in which the acquirer and acquiree have a pre-existing relationship:

    (1)   the nature of the pre-existing relationship.

    (2)   the measurement of the settlement amount of the pre-existing relationship, if any, and the valuation method used to determine the settlement amount.

    (3)   the amount of any settlement gain or loss recognised and the line item in the income statement in which that gain or loss is recognised.

(l)   the amount of costs incurred in connection with the business combination, the amount recognised as an expense and the line item or items in the income statement in which those expenses are recognised.

The acquirer also shall disclose the information required by: **73**

(a)   paragraphs 72(e)-(l) in aggregate for individually immaterial business combinations that are material collectively.

(b)   paragraph 72 if a material business combination is completed after the balance sheet date but before the financial statements are authorised for issue unless disclosure of any of the information is <u>impracticable</u>*. If disclosure of any of the information required by paragraph 72 is impracticable, that fact and the reasons shall be disclosed.

74   An acquirer shall also disclose the following information for each material business combination that occurs during the reporting period or in the aggregate for individually immaterial business combinations that are material collectively and occur during the reporting period:

(a)   the amounts of revenue and profit or loss of the acquiree since the acquisition date that are included in the consolidated income statement for the reporting period.

(b)   the following information:

(1)   the revenue and profit or loss of the combined entity for the current reporting period as though the acquisition date for all business combinations that occurred during the year had been as of the beginning of the annual reporting period.

(2)   *Not used.*

If disclosure of any of the information required by this paragraph is impracticable, that fact and the reasons shall be disclosed.

75   **The acquirer shall disclose information that enables users of its financial statements to evaluate the financial effects of adjustments recognised in the current reporting period relating to business combinations that were effected in the current or previous reporting periods.**

76   To meet the objective in paragraph 75, the acquirer shall disclose the following information for each material business combination or in the aggregate for individually immaterial business combinations that are material collectively:

(a)   if the amounts recognised in the financial statements for the business combination have been determined only provisionally:

(1)   the reasons why the initial accounting for the business combination is not complete.

(2)   the assets acquired or the liabilities assumed for which the measurement period is still open.

(3)   the nature and amount of any measurement period adjustments recognised during the reporting period.

(b)   a reconciliation of the beginning and ending balances of liabilities for contingent consideration and contingencies that are required to be remeasured to

---

*ASB footnote: *IAS 8 Accounting Policies, Changes in Accounting Estimates and Errors states a requirement is impracticable when the entity cannot apply it after making every reasonable effort to do so. For a particular prior period, it is impracticable to apply a change in an accounting policy retrospectively or to make a retrospective restatement to correct an error if:*

(a)   the effects of the retrospective application or retrospective restatement are not determinable;

(b)   the retrospective application or retrospective restatement requires assumptions about what management's intent would have been in that period; or

(c)   the retrospective application or retrospective restatement requires significant estimates of amounts and it is impossible to distinguish objectively information about those estimates that:

(i)   provides evidence of circumstances that existed on the date(s) as at which those amounts are to be recognised, measured or disclosed; and

(ii)   would have been available when the financial statements for that prior period were authorised for issue from other information.

fair value after initial recognition in accordance with paragraphs 26(b)(2) and 36, showing separately the changes in fair value during the reporting period and amounts paid or otherwise settled in accordance with ~~IAS 37~~ FRS 12 and ~~IAS 39~~ FRS 26.

(c) a description of the discrete event or circumstance that occurred after the acquisition date that resulted in deferred tax assets acquired as part of the business combination being recognised as income within 12 months after the acquisition date (see paragraph 86).

(d) the amount and an explanation of any gain or loss recognised in the current reporting period that both:

   (1) relates to the identifiable assets acquired or liabilities assumed in a business combination that was effected in the current or a previous reporting period, and

   (2) is of such a size, nature, or incidence that disclosure is relevant to understanding the combined entity's financial statements.

The acquirer shall disclose information that enables users of its financial statements to   **77**
evaluate changes in the carrying amount of goodwill during the reporting period.

To meet the objective in paragraph 77, if the total amount of goodwill is significant   **78**
in relation to the fair value of the acquiree, the acquirer shall disclose the following information for each material business combination that occurs during the reporting period:

(a) the total amount of goodwill and the amount that is expected to be deductible for tax purposes.

(b) *Not used.*

The acquirer also shall disclose the information required by paragraph 78:   **79**

(a) in aggregate for individually immaterial business combinations that are material collectively.

(b) if a material business combination is completed after the balance sheet date but before the financial statements are authorised for issue unless such disclosure is impracticable. If disclosure of any of the information required by paragraph 78 is impracticable, that fact and the reasons shall be disclosed.

The acquirer shall disclose a reconciliation of the carrying amount of goodwill at the   **80**
beginning and end of the reporting period, showing separately:

(a) the gross amount and accumulated impairment losses at the beginning of the reporting period.

(b) additional goodwill recognised during the reporting period, except goodwill included in business sold or held exclusively with a view to subsequent resale. ~~a disposal group that, on acquisition, meets the criteria to be classified as held for sale in accordance with IFRS 5.~~

(c) adjustments resulting from the subsequent recognition of deferred tax assets during the reporting period in accordance with paragraph 86.

(d) goodwill included in a business sold or held exclusively with a view to subsequent resale. ~~disposal group classified as held for sale in accordance with IFRS 5 and goodwill derecognised during the reporting period without having previously been included in a disposal group classified as held for sale.~~

(e) impairment losses recognised during the reporting period in accordance with ~~IAS 36~~ [draft] FRS ●. (~~IAS 36~~ [Draft] FRS ● requires disclosure of information about the recoverable amount and impairment of goodwill in addition to this requirement.)

(f)   net exchange differences arising during the reporting period in accordance with ~~IAS 21~~ FRS 23 *The Effects of Changes in Foreign Exchange Rates.*

(g)   any other changes in the carrying amount during the reporting period.

(h)   the gross amount and accumulated impairment losses at the end of the reporting period.

81   If the specific disclosures required by this and other ~~IFRSs~~ FRSs do not meet the objectives set out in paragraphs 71, 75, or 77, the acquirer shall disclose any additional information necessary to meet those objectives.

EFFECTIVE DATE AND TRANSITION

82   This [draft] ~~IFRS~~ FRS shall apply prospectively to business combinations for which the acquisition date is on or after the beginning of the first annual period beginning on or after 1 January 2007. Earlier application is encouraged. However, this [draft] ~~IFRS~~ FRS shall be applied only at the beginning of an annual period that begins on or after this [draft] ~~IFRS~~ FRS is issued. If this [draft] ~~IFRS~~ FRS is applied before the effective date, that fact shall be disclosed and [draft] ~~IAS 27~~ FRS 2(revised 200X), ~~and~~ [draft] ~~IAS 37~~ FRS 12(revised 200X), [draft] FRS ● *Intangible Assets* and [draft] FRS ● *Impairment of Assets* shall be applied at the same time.

83   Except as provided in paragraphs 86 and 87, assets and liabilities that arose from business combinations whose acquisition dates preceded the application of this [draft] ~~IFRS~~ FRS shall not be adjusted upon application of this [draft] ~~IFRS~~ FRS.

84   ~~Entities that have not applied IAS 36 and IAS 38 shall apply those [draft] IFRSs at the same time as they apply this IFRS.~~

85   Entities~~, such as mutual entities,~~ that have not applied IFRS 3 ~~and~~ that have had one or more business combinations that were accounted for using ~~the purchase~~ another method shall apply the transitional provisions in paragraphs C11 and C12.

Subsequent recognition of acquired deferred tax benefits

86   For the recognition of deferred tax assets acquired in a business combination in which the acquisition date was before this [draft] ~~IFRS~~ FRS is applied:

(a)   the acquirer shall apply the requirements of paragraph ~~68~~ 33C of ~~IAS 12~~ FRS 19, as amended by paragraph ~~D4~~ D5 of this [draft] ~~IFRS~~ FRS, prospectively. Therefore, an acquirer shall not adjust the accounting for prior business combinations if tax benefits failed to satisfy the criteria for separate recognition as of the acquisition date and are recognised after the acquisition date, unless the rebuttable presumption in paragraph ~~68~~ 33C of ~~IAS 12~~ FRS 19 applies.

(b)   the acquirer shall credit tax benefits recognised more than one year after the acquisition date to profit or loss or, if ~~IAS 12~~ FRS 19 so requires, to equity or through the statement of total recognised gains and losses.

Previously recognised contingent liabilities

87   Any contingent liability recognised relating to a business combination for which the acquisition date was before this [draft] ~~IFRS~~ FRS is applied shall be assessed to determine whether it satisfies the definition of a liability (see [draft] ~~IAS 37~~ FRS 12 (revised 200X)). If not, any recognised amount shall be derecognised with an offsetting adjustment to any goodwill that arose from that business combination. The

adjustment to goodwill is limited to the lesser of the carrying amount of goodwill or the amount originally recognised at the acquisition date for the contingent liability. Any remaining recognised amount (that is, any balance in excess of the carrying amount of goodwill that arose in that business combination and any changes in the measurement of the contingent liability after the acquisition date) shall be derecognised as an adjustment to the opening balance of retained earnings.

WITHDRAWAL OF OTHER PRONOUNCEMENTS

This [draft] ~~IFRS~~ FRS supersedes ~~IFRS 3 (as issued in 2004)~~ FRS 6 *Acquisition and*   **88**
Mergers, FRS 7 *Fair Values in Acquisition Accounting*, UITF Abstracts 15 *Disclosure of substantial acquisitions*, Abstract 22 *The acquisition of a Lloyd's business*, and Abstract 31 *Exchanges of businesses or other non-monetary assets for an interest in a subsidiary, joint venture or associate.*

Appendix A
Application guidance

> ASB Note: This application guidance has been prepared by the IASB.

Contents

Appendix A
Application Guidance

This appendix is an integral part of the [draft] ~~IFRS~~ FRS.

INTRODUCTION

This appendix discusses generalised situations and provides examples that incorpo-   **A1**
rate simplified assumptions to illustrate how to apply some of the provisions of this
[draft] ~~IFRS~~ FRS.

Definition of a business (application of paragraph 3(d))

A *business* is defined as an integrated set of activities and assets that is capable of   **A2**
being conducted and managed for the purpose of providing either (a) a return to
investors or (b) dividends, lower costs, or other economic benefits directly and
proportionately to owners, members, or participants (paragraph 3(d)). A business
consists of inputs and processes applied to those inputs that have the ability to create
outputs. Although businesses usually have outputs, outputs are not required for an
integrated set to qualify as a business. The three elements of a business are defined as
follows:

(a) *Input*: Any economic resource that creates or has the ability to create outputs
    when one or more processes are applied to it. Examples include long-lived
    assets (including intangible assets or rights to use long-lived assets), intellectual
    property, ability to obtain access to necessary materials or rights, and
    employees.
(b) *Process*: Any system, standard, protocol, convention or rule that when applied
    to an input, or inputs, creates or has the ability to create outputs. Examples
    include strategic management processes, operational processes, and resource
    management processes. These processes typically are documented; however, an
    organised workforce having the necessary skills and experience following rules
    and conventions may provide the necessary processes that are capable of being
    applied to inputs to create outputs. (Accounting, billing, payroll, and other
    administrative systems typically are not processes that are used to create
    outputs.)
(c) *Output*: The result of inputs and processes applied to those inputs that provide
    or have the ability to provide a return to investors or dividends, lower costs, or
    other economic benefits directly and proportionately to owners, members or
    participants.

To be capable of being conducted and managed for the purposes defined, an inte-   **A3**
grated set of activities and assets requires two essential elements—inputs and
processes applied to those inputs, which together are or will be used to create outputs. However, a business need not include all of the inputs or processes that the
seller used in operating that business if a willing party is capable of acquiring the
business and continuing to produce outputs, for example, by integrating the business
with its own inputs and processes. Paragraph E4 of Appendix E states that willing
parties are 'presumed to be marketplace participants representing unrelated buyers
and sellers that are (a) knowledgeable, having a common level of understanding
about factors relevant to the asset or liability and the transaction, and (b) willing and
able to transact in the same market(s), having the legal and financial ability to do so.'

A4   The nature of the elements of a business varies by industry and by the structure of an entity's operations (activities), including the entity's stage of development. Established businesses often have many, and different, kinds of inputs, processes, and outputs, whereas new businesses often have few inputs and processes, and sometimes only a single output (product). Nearly all businesses also have liabilities, but a business need not have any liabilities.

A5   An integrated set of activities and assets in the development stage may not have outputs. In that case, other factors should be assessed to determine whether the set is a business. Those factors would include whether the set:

(a)   has begun planned principal activities;
(b)   has employees, intellectual property, and other inputs and processes that could be applied to those inputs;
(c)   is pursuing a plan to produce outputs; or
(d)   has the ability to obtain access to customers that will purchase the outputs.

A6   The determination of whether a particular set of assets and activities is a business should be based on whether the integrated set is capable of being conducted and managed as a business by a willing acquirer. Thus, in evaluating whether a particular set is a business, it is not relevant whether a seller operated the set as a business or whether the acquirer intends to operate the set as a business.

A7   If goodwill is present in a particular set of assets and activities then in the absence of evidence to the contrary the set shall be presumed to be a business. However, a business need not have goodwill.

Measuring the fair value of the acquiree (application of paragraphs 19–27)

A8   As noted in paragraph 19, the acquirer is required to measure the fair value of the acquiree, as a whole, as of the acquisition date. The objective of measuring the fair value of the acquiree is to estimate the price at which 100 per cent of the acquiree could be exchanged in a current transaction between knowledgeable, unrelated willing parties when neither party is acting under compulsion.

Measuring the fair value of the acquiree using the consideration transferred

A9   In the absence of evidence to the contrary, the acquisition-date fair value of the consideration transferred is presumed to be the best basis for measuring the fair value of the acquirer's interest in the acquiree on that date.

A10   In a business combination between willing parties in which the acquirer purchases 100 per cent of the equity interests or net assets that constitute a business (an acquiree), the fair value of the consideration transferred usually is more clearly evident and reliably measurable than the fair value of the acquiree in the absence of evidence to the contrary. Therefore, the acquirer usually should use the acquisition-date fair value of the consideration transferred in exchange for the acquiree to measure the fair value of the acquiree on that date.

A11   If the acquirer purchases less than 100 per cent of the equity interests of an acquiree on the acquisition date (either in a single transaction or in multiple transactions), the acquisition-date fair value of the consideration transferred is usually the best basis for measuring the fair value of the acquirer's interest in the acquiree on that date. However, the consideration transferred by itself is most likely not to be representative of the fair value of the acquiree as a whole. The following examples illustrate how the fair value of consideration transferred for less than 100 per cent of the equity interests of an acquiree, together with other available information, might be used to estimate the fair value of the acquiree as a whole.

Example 1
Acquisition of less than 100 per cent of the equity interests of an acquiree

Acquirer Company (AC) offers to purchase all of the 10 million outstanding shares   **A12**
of Target Company (TC) for CU10.00 per share, provided that at least 80 per cent of TC's shares are tendered. Shares of TC are publicly traded and widely dispersed. On the acquisition date, 90 per cent of TC's shares are tendered and acquired by AC for CU90 million. In the week before the announcement of the offer, TC's shares were trading at CU8.85–CU9.15 per share. During the first week after the acquisition date, the remaining 1 million outstanding shares of TC continue to trade with significantly lower volume and greater volatility (at prices ranging from CU8.50 to CU13.00 per share).

In this example, the consideration transferred by AC for 90 per cent of the equity   **A13**
interests of TC is determined to be the best basis for estimating the fair value of TC as CU100 million (10 million shares × CU10.00). First, there is no evidence to suggest that the price of CU10.00 per share exchanged for the 90 per cent interest is not representative of the price that knowledgeable, unrelated willing parties would pay at the acquisition date in exchange for a 100 per cent ownership interest in TC. In fact, AC offered to pay CU10.00 for all of the outstanding shares. Second, because the shares were widely dispersed, there is no evidence that it would be necessary to pay an amount other than CU10.00 per share to obtain 100 per cent of the shares.

Example 2
Acquisition of less than 100 per cent of the equity interests of an acquiree in a business combination achieved in stages

Assume the same facts as in paragraph A12, except that AC owns 100,000 shares (1   **A14**
per cent) of TC that it originally purchased at CU8.50 per share. The shares are classified as available-for-sale securities and carried at fair value. For the reasons described in paragraph A13, the amount paid (CU10.00 per share) to obtain a 90 per cent interest (an additional 8.9 million shares) continues to be the best basis for measuring the fair value of TC as CU100 million. However, consistently with the provisions of paragraph 56, AC recognises a gain of CU150,000 [(CU10.00–CU8.50) × 100,000 shares] on its original 1 per cent non-controlling equity investment in profit or loss. The carrying amount of CU1 million for that 1 per cent investment, like the CU89 million investment for the 8.9 million shares acquired, is eliminated in consolidation.

Example 3
Acquisition of less than 100 per cent of the equity interests of an acquiree with evidence of a control premium

Assume that a single Founding Shareholder (FS) owns 60 per cent of TC's shares,   **A15**
and the remaining 40 per cent of TC's 10 million shares are widely dispersed and have been publicly trading in the CU9.85–CU10.15 range. Also assume that FS desires to sell its controlling 60 per cent interest in TC, and, on the basis of its knowledge of the industry, FS identifies AC as the highest bidder if FS was interested in making TC available for sale to all potential buyers. Following private

negotiations, AC buys all of FS's holdings in TC for CU81 million (CU13.50 per share), a premium of about CU3.50 per share over the market price of the publicly traded non-controlling shares on the acquisition date. During the first week following the acquisition, the non-controlling shares of TC traded in a range of CU8.50–CU13.00. AC willingly paid a premium over the market price of the publicly traded shares on the basis of its assessment that:

(a)   TC, as a whole, would be worth between CU110 million and CU130 million to other marketplace participants (based on market comparisons of companies similar to TC and its best estimate as to the likely synergies that those marketplace participants might be able to achieve).

(b)   AC can extract synergies similar to those of other marketplace participants, as well as generate additional savings by making proprietary technology available to TC.

A16   At issue is whether the consideration transferred by AC for the less than 100 per cent equity interest, by itself, can be presumed to provide the best basis for measuring the fair value of TC (ie the fair value that knowledgeable, unrelated willing parties would exchange for a 100 per cent equity interest in TC).

A17   In this example, AC has information that suggests that CU135 million is not necessarily representative of the amount that other knowledgeable, unrelated willing parties would pay for TC as a whole. Moreover, the market prices for the non-controlling shares at the acquisition date (CU9.85–CU10.15 per share) and during the first week following the acquisition (CU8.50–CU13.00) suggest that CU13.50 per share is not representative of the fair value of TC, as a whole. In this case, the fair value of TC may be estimated on a preliminary basis to be CU121 million based on (a) the CU81 million paid for the controlling 60 per cent interest plus CU40 million for the value of the non-controlling shares (4 million × CU10.00) and (b) the fact that CU121 million falls within the CU110 million–CU130 million range used in AC's preliminary assessments of the value of TC. However, before AC concludes that CU121 million is its best estimate of the fair value of TC, consistently with the objective of measuring the fair value for 100 per cent of the equity interests in the acquiree and with the guidance in Appendix E, AC should refine its initial estimate of fair value using other relevant valuation techniques, as appropriate. Thus, AC might refine its preliminary assessment of the fair value of TC using, for example, the market and income approaches discussed in paragraphs A20–A23.

Measuring the fair value of the acquiree using valuation techniques

A18   In some circumstances, the measurement of the fair value of the acquiree should not be based on the consideration transferred. These circumstances include the following:

(a)   The acquirer does not transfer any consideration on the acquisition date (for example, a business combination in which an entity (the acquiree) repurchases its own shares and, as a result, an existing investor (the acquirer) obtains control of that entity).

(b)   There is evidence that the transaction is not an exchange of equal values by willing parties (for example, a business combination in which the seller is acting under duress).

(c)   The fair value of the total consideration transferred is not more reliably measurable than the fair value of the acquiree (for example, a business combination in which two private business entities or two mutual entities combine through an exchange of equity or member interests and the fair value of the acquiree is more clearly evident and, thus, more reliably measurable than the fair value of the equity or member interests transferred by the acquirer).

When the measurement of the fair value of the acquiree is not based on the consideration transferred, that measurement should be based on observable prices for a business that is similar to the acquiree, if such information is available. Otherwise, fair value should be estimated using multiple techniques that are relevant and for which reliable data are available. The results of the multiple techniques would then be evaluated considering the relevance and reliability of the inputs used to estimate the fair value of the acquiree. The techniques applied and evaluated might be the market approach, the income approach, or several variations of each on the basis of the relevance of the approach and the extent of the available data. **A19**

Market approach

In applying the market approach, the basic steps are (a) define and assess the available marketplace data (and adjust, if necessary) to derive one or more valuation ratios and (b) apply the appropriate valuation ratios to the acquiree. As applied to measuring the fair value of a business for the purposes of applying this [draft] ~~IFRS~~ FRS, the market approach typically is based on prices of publicly traded equity shares or prices in other business combinations involving comparable businesses for which the terms of the arrangements are disclosed. Identifying comparable businesses requires judgements about the degree to which operational, market, financial and non-financial factors are similar between the acquiree and comparable businesses. Factors to be considered in making this assessment might include products and services (operational factors); markets served, competitors, and position within the industry (market factors); capital structure and historical and forecast financial performance (financial factors); and the depth of management, the expertise of personnel, and the maturity of the business (non-financial factors). Other factors might be considered, depending on the nature of the business being valued. **A20**

Ideally, marketplace data are based on other entities within the same industry. In the absence of that information, marketplace data might be based on economically similar businesses. Thus, the degree of comparability between other businesses and the acquiree varies and it may be necessary to adjust the valuation ratios to reflect differences. Such adjustments should be consistent with the objective of measuring fair value. **A21**

Income approach

In applying an income approach, the basic steps involve estimating the value of future cash flows or other income-related valuation measures such as residual income profit or loss. Paragraph E6(b) summarises key aspects of the income approach and states: **A22**

> The income approach uses valuation techniques to convert future amounts (for example, cash flows or earnings) to a single present amount (discounted). The estimate of fair value is based on the value indicated by marketplace expectations about those future amounts.

Appendix A of ~~IAS 36~~ FRS ● *[Impairment of Assets]* discusses the use of present value techniques to estimate value in use. If an entity estimates fair value using such present value techniques, inputs should be consistent with the objective of measuring fair value rather than value in use. **A23**

Special considerations in applying the market and income approaches to mutual entities

A24   When two mutual entities combine, the fair value of the acquiree may be more reliably measurable than the fair value of member interests transferred by the acquirer. In a business combination involving only mutual entities in which the only consideration is an exchange of the acquirer's member interests for the acquiree's member interests, the fair value of the acquiree and the fair value of the member interests exchanged as consideration are presumed to be equal.

A25   Mutual entities, although similar in many ways to other businesses, have distinct characteristics that arise primarily because the members of a mutual entity are both customers and owners. Members of mutual entities generally expect to receive benefits for their membership, often in the form of reduced fees charged for goods and services or patronage dividends. The portion of patronage dividends allocated to each member is often based on the amount of business the member did with the mutual entity during the year.

A26   A fair value measurement of a mutual entity should include the assumptions that marketplace participants would make about future member benefits as well as any other relevant assumptions marketplace participants would make about the mutual entity. For example, in determining the fair value of a mutual entity, an estimated cash flow model may be used. In that case, the cash flows should be based on the expected cash flows of the mutual entity, which are likely to include adjustments for member benefits, such as the cost of reduced fees charged for goods and services.

INTANGIBLE ASSETS
(APPLICATION OF PARAGRAPHS 40 AND 41)

Research and development assets

A27   An acquirer recognises and measures the acquisition-date fair value of all identifiable intangible assets acquired in a business combination that are used in research and development activities. After initial recognition, the provisions of ~~IAS 38~~ [draft] FRS ● *Intangible Assets* apply.

Recognition of intangible assets separately from goodwill

A28   In accordance with paragraph 40, the acquirer recognises separately from goodwill the acquisition-date fair value of intangible assets acquired in a business combination that meet the definition of an intangible asset in ~~IAS 38~~ [draft] FRS ● which requires the asset to be identifiable. An intangible asset is identifiable if it arises from contractual or other legal rights (the contractual-legal criterion) or is separable (separability criterion). Intangible assets that meet the contractual-legal criterion are identifiable even if the asset is not transferable or separable from the acquiree or from other rights and obligations. For example:

(a)   An acquiree leases a manufacturing facility under an operating lease that has terms that are favourable relative to market prices. The lease terms explicitly prohibit transfer of the lease (through either sale or sublease). The amount by which the lease terms are favourable relative to market prices is an intangible asset that meets the contractual-legal criterion for recognition separately from goodwill, even though the lease contract cannot be sold or otherwise transferred.

(b)   An acquiree owns and operates a nuclear power plant. The licence to operate that power plant is an intangible asset that meets the contractual-legal criterion for recognition separately from goodwill, even if it cannot be sold or transferred apart from the acquired power plant. An acquirer may recognise the fair value of the operating licence and the fair value of the power plant as a single asset for financial reporting purposes if the useful lives of those assets are similar.

(c) An acquiree owns a technology patent. It has licensed that patent to others for their exclusive use outside the United States in exchange for which the acquired business receives a specified percentage of future non-US revenue. Both the technology patent and the related licence agreement meet the contractual-legal criterion for recognition separately from goodwill even if selling or exchanging the patent and the related licence agreement apart from one another would not be practical.

The separability criterion means that the acquired intangible asset is capable of being separated or divided from the acquiree and sold, transferred, licensed, rented, or exchanged, either individually or together with a related contract, asset, or liability. Exchange transactions provide evidence that an intangible asset is separable from the acquiree and might provide information that can be used to estimate its fair value. An acquired intangible asset meets the separability criterion if there is evidence of exchange transactions for that type of asset or an asset of a similar type (even if those exchange transactions are infrequent and regardless of whether the acquirer is involved in them). For example, customer and subscriber lists are frequently licensed and thus meet the separability criterion. Even if an acquiree believes its customer lists have different characteristics from other customer lists, the fact that customer lists are frequently licensed generally means that the acquired customer list meets the separability criterion.   **A29**

An intangible asset that meets the separability criterion should be recognised separately from goodwill even if the acquirer does not intend to sell, license, or otherwise exchange that asset. The separability criterion is met because the asset is capable of being separated from the acquiree or combined entity and sold, transferred, licensed, rented or otherwise exchanged for something else of value. For example, because an acquired customer list is generally capable of being licensed, it meets the separability criterion regardless of whether the acquirer intends to license it.   **A30**

An intangible asset that is not separable from the acquiree or combined entity individually meets the separability criterion if it is separable in combination with a related contract, asset or liability. For example: **A31**

(a) Deposit liabilities and related depositor relationship intangible assets are exchanged in observable exchange transactions. Therefore, the depositor relationship intangible asset should be recognised separately from goodwill.

(b) An acquiree owns a registered trademark, a related secret formula, and unpatented technical expertise used to manufacture the trademarked product. To transfer ownership of a trademark, the owner is also required to transfer everything else necessary for the new owner to produce a product or service indistinguishable from that produced by the former owner. Because the unpatented technical expertise must be separated from the acquiree or combined entity and sold if the related trademark is sold, it meets the separability criterion.

An acquirer subsumes into goodwill the value of any acquired intangible asset that is not identifiable as of the acquisition date. For example, an acquirer may attribute value to the potential contracts the acquiree is negotiating with prospective new customers at the acquisition date. Because those potential contracts are not identifiable intangible assets at the acquisition date, they are not recognised separately from goodwill. The value of those contracts should not be reclassified from goodwill   **A32** for events that occur after the acquisition date. However, the acquirer should assess the facts and circumstances surrounding events occurring shortly after the acquisition to determine whether a separately recognisable intangible asset existed at the acquisition date.

A33 After initial recognition, intangible assets acquired in a business combination are accounted for in accordance with the provisions of IAS 38 [draft] FRS ●. However, as described in paragraph 3 of IAS 38 [draft] FRS ● , the accounting for some acquired intangible assets after initial recognition is prescribed by other IFRSs FRSs.

A34 The identifiability criterion is used to determine whether an intangible asset should be recognised separately from goodwill. It does not provide guidance for measuring the fair value of an intangible asset. That criterion does not restrict the assumptions used in estimating the fair value of an intangible asset. For example, assumptions that marketplace participants would consider, such as expectations of future contract renewals, are considered in arriving at a fair value measurement even though those renewals do not meet the identifiability criterion.

Examples of intangible assets that are identifiable

A35 The following are examples of identifiable intangible assets acquired in a business combination. Some of the examples may have characteristics of assets other than intangible assets. Accordingly, those assets should be accounted for on the basis of their substance. These examples are not intended to be all-inclusive.

A36 Intangible assets designated with the symbol # are those that arise from contractual or other legal rights. Those designated with the symbol * do not arise from contractual or other legal rights, but are separable. Intangible assets designated with the symbol # might also be separable; however, separability is not a necessary condition for the asset to meet the contractual-legal criterion.

Marketing-related intangible assets

A37 Marketing-related intangible assets are those assets that are primarily used in the marketing or promotion of products or services. Examples of marketing-related intangible assets are:

(a) trademarks, trade names, service marks, collective marks, certification marks #
(b) trade dress (unique colour, shape, or package design) #
(c) newspaper mastheads #
(d) Internet domain names #
(e) non-competition agreements #.

Trademarks, trade names, service marks, collective marks, and certification marks #

A38 Trademarks are words, names, symbols, or other devices used in trade to indicate the source of a product and to distinguish it from the products of others. A service mark identifies and distinguishes the source of a service rather than a product. Collective marks are used to identify the goods or services of members of a group. Certification marks are used to certify the geographical origin or other characteristics of a good or service.

A39 Trademarks, trade names, service marks, collective marks, and certification marks may be protected legally through registration with governmental agencies, continuous use in commerce, or by other means. Provided it is protected legally through registration or other means, a trademark or other mark acquired in a business combination is an intangible asset that meets the contractual-legal criterion. Otherwise, a trademark or other mark acquired in a business combination can be recognised separately from goodwill provided the separability criterion is met, which would normally be the case.

The terms brand and brand name are often used as synonyms for trademarks and other marks. However, the former are general marketing terms that are typically used to refer to a group of complementary assets such as a trademark (or service mark) and its related trade name, formulas, recipes, and technological expertise. An entity is not precluded from recognising, as a single asset apart from goodwill, a group of complementary intangible assets commonly referred to as a brand if the assets that make up that group have similar useful lives. **A40**

Internet domain names #

An Internet domain name is a unique alphanumeric name that is used to identify a particular numeric Internet address. Registration of a domain name creates an association between that name and a designated computer on the Internet for the period of the registration. Those registrations are renewable. A registered domain name acquired in a business combination meets the contractual-legal criterion. **A41**

Customer-related intangible assets

Examples of customer-related intangible assets are: **A42**

(a)   customer lists *
(b)   order or production backlog #
(c)   customer contracts and related customer relationships #
(d)   non-contractual customer relationships *.

*Customer lists ***

A customer list consists of information about customers, such as their names and contact information. A customer list also may be in the form of a database that includes other information about the customers, such as their order histories and demographic information. A customer list does not generally arise from contractual or other legal rights. However, customer lists are frequently leased or exchanged. Therefore, a customer list acquired in a business combination normally meets the separability criterion. However, a customer list acquired in a business combination would not meet the separability criterion if the terms of confidentiality or other agreements prohibit an entity from selling, leasing or otherwise exchanging information about its customers. **A43**

Order or production backlog #

An order or production backlog arises from contracts such as purchase or sales orders. An order or production backlog acquired in a business combination meets the contractual-legal criterion, even if the purchase or sales orders are cancellable. **A44**

Customer contracts and the related customer relationships #

If an entity establishes relationships with its customers through contracts, those customer relationships arise from contractual rights. Therefore, customer contracts **A45** and the related customer relationships acquired in a business combination meet the contractual-legal criterion. This will be the case even if confidentiality or other contractual terms prohibit the sale or transfer of a contract separately from the acquiree.

A46   A customer contract intangible asset and the related customer relationship intangible asset may represent two distinct intangible assets. Both the useful lives and the pattern in which the economic benefits of the two assets are consumed may differ.

A47   A customer relationship exists between an entity and its customer if (a) the entity has information about the customer and has regular contact with the customer and (b) the customer has the ability to make direct contact with the entity. Customer relationships meet the contractual-legal criterion when an entity has a practice of establishing contracts with its customers, regardless of whether a contract exists at the acquisition date. Customer relationships also may arise through means other than contracts, such as through regular contact by sales or service representatives. As noted in paragraph A44, an order or a production backlog arises from contracts such as purchase or sales orders, and therefore is also regarded as a contractual right. Consequently, if an entity has customer relationships with its customers through these types of contracts, the customer relationships also arise from contractual rights and, therefore, meet the contractual-legal criterion.

Non-contractual customer relationships *

A48   If a customer relationship acquired in a business combination does not arise from a contract, the relationship may be separable. Exchange transactions for the same asset or a similar asset provide evidence of separability of a non-contractual customer relationship and might also provide information about exchange prices that should be considered when estimating fair value.

Examples illustrating customer contract and customer relationship intangible assets acquired in a business combination

A49   The following examples illustrate the recognition of customer contract and customer relationship intangible assets acquired in a business combination.

(a)   AC acquires TC in a business combination on 31 December 20X5. TC has a five-year agreement to supply goods to Customer. Both TC and AC believe that Customer will renew the supply agreement at the end of the current contract. The supply agreement is not separable. The supply agreement, whether cancellable or not, meets the contractual-legal criterion. Additionally, because TC establishes its relationship with Customer through a contract, the customer relationship with Customer meets the contractual-legal criterion. In determining the fair value of the customer relationship, AC considers assumptions such as the expected renewal of the supply agreement.

(b)   AC acquires TC in a business combination on 31 December 20X5. TC manufactures goods in two distinct lines of business: sporting goods and electronics. Customer purchases both sporting goods and electronics from TC. TC has a contract with Customer to be its exclusive provider of sporting goods. However, there is no contract for the supply of electronics to Customer. Both TC and AC believe only one overall customer relationship exists between TC and Customer.

The contract to be Customer's exclusive supplier of sporting goods, whether cancellable or not, meets the contractual-legal criterion. Additionally, because TC establishes its relationship with Customer through a contract, the customer relationship with Customer meets the contractual-legal criterion. Because there is only one customer relationship with Customer, the fair value of that relationship incorporates assumptions regarding TC's relationship with Customer related to both sporting goods and electronics. However, if both AC and TC believe there were separate customer relationships with Customer—one for sporting goods and another for electronics—the customer relationship with respect to electronics would be assessed by AC to determine whether it meets the separability criterion for identification as an intangible asset.

(c)   AC acquires TC in a business combination on 31 December 20X5. TC does business with its customers solely through purchase and sales orders. At 31 December 20X5, TC has a backlog of customer purchase orders from 60 per cent of its customers, all of whom are recurring customers. The other 40 per cent of TC's customers also are recurring customers. However, as of 31 December 20X5, TC does not have any open purchase orders or other contracts with those customers.

The purchase orders from 60 per cent of TC's customers, whether cancellable or not, meet the contractual-legal criterion. Additionally, because TC has established its relationship with 60 per cent of its customers through contracts, those customer relationships meet the contractual-legal criterion. Because TC has a practice of establishing contracts with the remaining 40 per cent of its customers, its relationship with those customers also arises through contractual rights and, therefore, meets the contractual-legal criterion, even though TC does not have contracts with those customers at 31 December 20X5.

(d)   AC acquires TC, an insurer, in a business combination on 31 December 20X5. TC has a portfolio of one-year motor insurance contracts that are cancellable by policyholders. Annual renewal rates are reasonably predictable. Because TC establishes its relationships with policyholders through insurance contracts, the customer relationship with policyholders meets the contractual-legal criterion. In determining the fair value of the customer relationship intangible asset, AC considers estimates of renewals and cross-selling. ~~IAS 36~~ [Draft] FRS ● *Impairment of Assets* and ~~IAS 38~~ [draft] FRS ● *Intangible Assets* apply to the customer relationship intangible asset.

In determining the fair value of the liability relating to the portfolio of insurance contracts, AC considers estimates of cancellations by policyholders. ~~IFRS 4 *Insurance Contracts* permits, but does not require, an expanded presentation that splits the fair value of acquired insurance contracts into two components:~~

~~(1)   a liability measured in accordance with the insurer's accounting policies for insurance contracts that it issues; and~~

~~(2)   an intangible asset, representing the fair value of the contractual rights and obligations acquired, to the extent that the liability does not reflect that fair value. This intangible asset is excluded from the scope of IAS 36 and IAS 38. After the business combination, AC is required to measure that intangible asset on a basis consistent with the measurement of the related insurance liability.~~

Artistic-related intangible assets

Examples of artistic-related intangible assets are: **A50**

(a)   plays, operas, ballets #
(b)   books, magazines, newspapers, other literary works #
(c)   musical works such as compositions, song lyrics, advertising jingles #
(d)   pictures, photographs #

(e)   video and audiovisual material, including motion pictures or films, music videos, television programmes #.

A51   Artistic-related assets acquired in a business combination meet the identifiability criterion if they arise from contractual or legal rights such as those provided by copyright. Copyrights can be transferred either in whole through assignments or in part through licensing agreements. In determining the fair value of an intangible asset protected by copyright, an entity considers the existence of any assignments or licences of the acquired copyrights. An acquirer is not precluded from recognising a copyright intangible asset and any related assignments or licence agreements as a single asset, provided they have similar useful lives.

Contract-based intangible assets

A52   Contract-based intangible assets represent the value of rights that arise from contractual arrangements. Customer contracts are one particular type of contract-based intangible asset. If the terms of a contract give rise to a liability (which might be the case if the terms of an operating lease or customer contract are unfavourable relative to market prices), that liability is recognised as a liability assumed. Examples of contract-based intangible assets are:

(a)   licensing, royalty, standstill agreements #
(b)   advertising, construction, management, service or supply contracts #
(c)   lease agreements (whether the acquiree is the lessee or lessor) #
(d)   construction permits #
(e)   franchise agreements #
(f)   operating and broadcast rights #
(g)   servicing contracts such as mortgage servicing contracts #
(h)   employment contracts #.

Servicing contracts such as mortgage servicing contracts #

A53   Contracts to service financial assets are one type of contract-based intangible asset. Although servicing is inherent in all financial assets, it becomes a distinct asset by one of the following:

(a)   when contractually separated from the underlying financial asset by sale or securitisation of the assets with servicing retained; or
(b)   through the separate purchase and assumption of the servicing.

A54   If mortgage loans, credit card receivables, or other financial assets are acquired in a business combination with servicing retained, the inherent servicing rights are not a separate intangible asset because the fair value of those servicing rights is included in the measurement of the fair value of the acquired financial asset.

Employment contracts #

A55   Employment contracts that are beneficial contracts from the perspective of the employer are one type of contract-based intangible asset because the pricing of those contracts is favourable relative to market prices.

Technology-based intangible assets

A56   Examples of technology-based intangible assets are:

(a)   patented technology #
(b)   computer software and mask works #
(c)   unpatented technology *
(d)   databases, including title plants *
(e)   trade secrets, such as secret formulas, processes, recipes #.

Computer software and mask works #

If computer software and program formats acquired in a business combination are   **A57**
protected legally, such as by patent or copyright, they meet the contractual-legal
criterion for identification as intangible assets.

Mask works are software permanently stored on a read-only memory chip as a series   **A58**
of stencils or integrated circuitry. Mask works may have legal protection. Mask
works with legal protection that are acquired in a business combination meet the
contractual-legal criterion for identification as intangible assets.

*Databases, including title plants **

Databases are collections of information, often stored in electronic form (such as on   **A59**
computer disks or files). A database that includes original works of authorship may
be entitled to copyright protection. If a database acquired in a business combination
is protected by copyright, it meets the contractual-legal criterion. However, a database typically includes information created as a consequence of an entity's normal
operations, such as customer lists, or specialised information such as scientific data
or credit information. Databases that are not protected by copyright can be, and
often are, exchanged, licensed or leased to others in their entirety or in part.
Therefore, even if the future economic benefits from a database do not arise from
legal rights, a database acquired in a business combination meets the separability
criterion.

Title plants constitute a historical record of all matters affecting title to parcels of   **A60**
land in a particular geographical area. Title plant assets are bought and sold in
exchange transactions (either in whole or in part) or are licensed. Therefore, title
plant assets acquired in a business combination meet the separability criterion.

Trade secrets such as secret formulas, processes, recipes #

A trade secret is 'information, including a formula, pattern, recipe, compilation,   **A61**
program, device, method, technique, or process that (1) derives independent economic value, actual or potential, from not being generally known and (2) is the
subject of efforts that are reasonable under the circumstances to maintain its
secrecy.* If the future economic benefits from a trade secret acquired in a business
combination are legally protected, that asset meets the contractual-legal criterion.
Otherwise, trade secrets acquired in a business combination are identifiable only if
the separability criterion is met, which is likely to be the case.

---

*Melvin, Simensky, and Lanning Bryer, The New Role of Intellectual Property in Commercial Transactions
(New York: John Wiley & Sons, 1998), page 293.*

INITIAL CALCULATION AND ALLOCATION OF GOODWILL IN A BUSINESS COMBINATION IN WHICH THE ACQUIRER HOLDS LESS THAN 100 PER CENT OF THE EQUITY INTERESTS IN AN ACQUIREE AT THE ACQUISITION DATE (APPLICATION OF PARAGRAPH 58)

A62   In accordance with paragraph 58, in a business combination in which the acquirer holds less than 100 per cent of the equity interests in the acquiree at the acquisition date, the acquirer allocates the amount of goodwill determined in accordance with paragraph 49 to the acquirer and the non-controlling interests. The amount of goodwill allocated to the acquirer shall be measured as the difference between the acquisition-date fair value of the acquirer's equity interest in the acquiree and the acquirer's share in the acquisition-date fair value of the separately recognised assets acquired and liabilities assumed. The remainder of the goodwill shall be allocated to the non-controlling interests. The goodwill allocated to the acquirer shall not exceed the total goodwill calculated in accordance with paragraph 49. The acquisition-date fair value of the acquirer's equity interest in the acquiree includes the fair value of any equity interests the acquirer owned immediately before the acquisition date. The following example illustrates those requirements.

Example 4
Initial calculation and allocation of goodwill to the acquirer and non-controlling interests in the acquiree

A63   On 1 January 20X5, AC acquires 80 per cent of the equity interests in TC for CU160. There is no evidence to suggest that this transaction is not an exchange of equal values. Therefore, the consideration transferred of CU160 is presumed to be the fair value of the 80 per cent interest acquired by AC. Through valuation techniques, the fair value of TC as a whole is determined to be CU195. As of the acquisition date, the fair value of the separately recognisable identifiable assets acquired is CU210 and the fair value of the liabilities assumed is CU60. On the basis of those facts, the amount of goodwill is measured as follows:

	CU
Fair value of TC	195
Less: net amount of the fair values of the separately recognised identifiable assets acquired and liabilities assumed [CU210 – CU60]	(150)
Goodwill	45

As described in paragraph A62, the amount of goodwill allocated to AC and to the non-controlling interests of TC is calculated as follows:

	CU
Fair value of AC's 80 per cent interest in TC	160
Less: AC's share of the fair value of the identifiable net assets acquired (80 per cent × [CU210 – CU60])	(120)
Goodwill allocated to AC	40
Goodwill allocated to the non-controlling interests in TC [CU45 – CU40]	5

BUSINESS COMBINATIONS IN WHICH THE CONSIDERATION TRANSFERRED FOR THE ACQUIRER'S INTERST IN THE ACQUIREE IS LESS THAN THE FAIR VALUE OF THAT INTEREST (APPLICATION OF PARAGRAPHS 59–61)

Example 5
Business combinations in which the consideration transferred for 100 per cent of the equity interests in the acquiree is less than the fair value

On 1 January 20X5, AC acquires 100 per cent of the equity interests of TC in   **A64**
exchange for AC's shares with a value of CU190. Because of a regulatory requirement, the former owner of TC did not have sufficient time to market TC to multiple
potential buyers. The management of AC initially measures the acquisition-date fair
value of the separately recognisable identifiable assets acquired at CU250 and the fair
value of the liabilities assumed at CU50. Management of AC estimates the fair value
of TC as between CU215 and CU230. Because the fair value of TC exceeds the fair
value of the consideration transferred, AC reviews the procedures it used to identify
and measure the assets acquired and liabilities assumed and to measure the fair
values of both the consideration transferred and TC on the acquisition date and
decides that they were appropriate. Nonetheless, management of AC also engages an
independent valuation firm to review its estimates. That firm, using multiple valuation techniques, determines that the fair value of TC as a whole is CU225 because of
economies of scale that any likely acquirer could achieve in TC's operations. On the
basis of those facts, the amount of goodwill and the gain on the bargain purchase are
measured as follows:

	CU
Fair value of TC	225
Less: net amount of the fair values of the separately recognised identifiable assets acquired and liabilities assumed [CU250 – CU50]	(200)
Goodwill that tentatively would be recognised under paragraph 49	25
Fair value of TC	225
Less: fair value of the consideration transferred for TC	(190)
Excess of the fair value of TC over the fair value of the consideration transferred for TC	35
Less: reduction of tentative goodwill (to zero)	(25)
Adjusted 'gain' on bargain purchase for any excess remaining after reducing goodwill to zero	10

Alternatively, because the fair value of the consideration transferred for TC of   **A65**
CU190 is less than the fair value of the separately recognised identifiable assets
acquired and liabilities assumed of CU200 [CU250 – CU50], the amount of the gain
may be calculated as follows:

		CU
Fair value of the consideration transferred for TC		190
Less: net amount of the fair values of the separately recognised identifiable assets acquired and liabilities assumed [CU250 – CU50]		(200)
Gain on bargain purchase		10

A66   AC would record its acquisition of TC in its consolidated financial statements as follows:

Identifiable assets acquired (at fair value)	CU 250	
Goodwill	0	
Liabilities assumed (at fair value)		CU50
Equity (for issue of shares of AC)		190
Gain on the bargain purchase		10

Example 6
Business combinations in which the consideration transferred for less than 100 per cent of the equity interests in the acquiree is less than the fair value

A67   Consider the same facts as in the previous example, except that AC acquires 80 per cent of the equity interests in TC for CU152 in AC's shares. If the goodwill measured in accordance with paragraph 49 is reduced to zero, any remaining excess is recognised as a gain attributable to the acquirer on the acquisition date. No gain is attributable to the non-controlling interest. On the basis of those facts, the amount of goodwill and the gain on bargain purchase are measured as follows:

	TC, as a whole	AC's interest	Non-controlling interest
	CU	CU	CU
Fair value of TC (and related 80 per cent controlling and 20 per cent non-controlling interests)	225	180	45
Less: net amount of the fair values of the separately recognised identifiable assets acquired and liabilities assumed [CU250 – CU50]	(200)	(160)	(40)
Goodwill that tentatively would be recognised under paragraph 49 (and tentative allocations)*	25	20	5

Fair value of AC's 80 per cent interest in TC [CU225 × 0.80]	180
Less: fair value of the consideration transferred for AC's interest	(152)
Excess of the fair value of AC's interest in TC over the consideration exchanged for that interest	28
Less: Adjustment to reduce goodwill that tentatively would have been recognised under paragraph 49 [CU25 × 0.80]	(20)
Adjusted 'gain' for the 80 per cent interest acquired in a bargain purchase after reducing goodwill to zero	8

* In a business combination in which the consideration transferred for a less than 100 per cent equity interest in the acquiree is less than the fair value of that interest, goodwill measured in accordance with paragraph 49 is allocable to the acquirer and non-controlling interests based on their relative equity interests since presumably the acquirer did not pay a control premium to obtain its interest.

In this case, goodwill of CU25 that otherwise would be attributable to AC and the non-controlling interest is reduced to zero.   **A68**

Alternatively, because the fair value of the consideration transferred for AC's 80 per cent interest in TC of CU152 is less than the fair value of AC's 80 per cent interest in the separately recognised identifiable assets acquired and liabilities assumed of CU160 [(CU250 – CU50) × 0.80], the amount of the gain on AC's purchase of the 80 per cent interest may be calculated as follows: **A69**

		CU
Fair value of the consideration transferred for AC's 80 per cent interest in TC		152
Less: net amount of the fair values of the separately recognised identifiable assets acquired and liabilities assumed [(CU250 – CU50) × 0.8]		(160)
Gain on bargain purchase of 80 per cent interest		8

A70   AC would record its acquisition of TC in its consolidated financial statements as follows:

Identifiable assets acquired (at fair value)	CU250
Goodwill	0
Liabilities assumed (at fair value)	CU50
Equity (for issue of shares of AC)	152
Gain on the bargain purchase	8
Equity—non-controlling interest (CU250 – CU50) × 0.20]	40

MEASUREMENT PERIOD
(APPLICATION OF PARAGRAPHS 62–68 AND 76(a))

A71   During the measurement period, the acquirer adjusts the provisional amounts recognised at the acquisition date or recognises additional assets or liabilities to reflect any new information obtained about facts and circumstances that existed as of the acquisition date and, if known, would have affected the measurement or recognition of the amounts as of that date. Some factors to consider in determining whether new information should result in a measurement period adjustment to the provisional amounts recognised are:

(a)   *The timing of the receipt of subsequent information.* Generally, new information that is obtained shortly after the acquisition date is more likely to reflect circumstances that existed at the acquisition date.

(b)   *The type of subsequent information.* An actual exchange with a third party generally provides the best evidence of fair value.

(c)   *The size of the adjustment and the ability to identify the reason for the adjustment.* Significant gains and losses that do not have identifiable causes and that are recognised shortly after the acquisition date may be an indication of circumstances that existed at the acquisition date.

Example 7
Lawsuit

A72   AC acquires TC on 31 December 20X5. One of the liabilities assumed in the business combination is a liability for a lawsuit against TC. At the acquisition date, AC initially measures the fair value of the liability on the basis of the information obtained during the due diligence procedures and recognises a provisional fair value for the liability of CU95,000. Within the measurement period, AC discovers information about the lawsuit against TC. AC determines that the information relates to facts that existed as of the acquisition date, and AC revises its fair value measure of the liability as of the acquisition date to CU80,000.

In this example, the adjustment to the fair value of the liability (CU15,000 reduction) would be accounted for as part of completing the initial accounting in the business combination because the new information (a) is obtained within the measurement period and (b) relates to facts and circumstances that existed as of the acquisition date. The adjustment would result in an offsetting adjustment to goodwill.   **A73**

In contrast, instead assume that a lawsuit is settled late in the measurement period for an amount that is different from the initial estimate. After assessing all of the facts and circumstances causing the difference, AC determines there is no new information about facts that existed at the acquisition date. In that case, the difference would not be an adjustment to the initial accounting for the business combination, but instead would be recognised as an adjustment to profit or loss of the post-combination period.   **A74**

Example 8
Disposal of an asset during the measurement period

AC acquires TC on 15 September 20X5. AC measures and recognises a provisional fair value of CU1,000 for TC's specialised (non-wasting) Asset A. AC also seeks an independent appraisal of the fair value of Asset A. On 15 December 20X5 AC sells Asset A to Third Party Co. for CU1,750. The sale provides information about the fair value of Asset A. Depending on the circumstances, the adjustment or adjustments to the provisional fair value of Asset A (CU750 increase) would be accounted for as part of completing the initial accounting for the business combination, as current-period income or, perhaps, partly as each. That determination would depend on whether the sale at CU1,750 is indicative of the fair value that existed at the acquisition date or indicative of an increase in value that resulted from events and circumstances that occurred after the acquisition date.   **A75**

In this example, also assume that before agreeing to sell Asset A to Third Party Co., AC receives the independent appraisal indicating a fair value of Asset A of CU1,500 as of the acquisition date. In these circumstances, AC would adjust the fair value of Asset A to the appraised value of CU1,500 as of the acquisition date. The CU500 adjustment to Asset A would result in an offsetting adjustment to goodwill. The incremental CU250 would be recognised as a gain on the sale of Asset A.   **A76**

Consideration transferred and contingent consideration

The measurement period guidance also applies to the consideration transferred, including contingent consideration. The objective of the measurement period in relation to the consideration transferred is the same, ie allow the acquirer a reasonable time to obtain the information necessary to measure the items of consideration transferred on the basis of facts and circumstances that existed at the acquisition date. Subsequent changes in the fair value of consideration transferred, especially contingent consideration, usually result from events and changes in circumstances that occur after the acquisition date and, therefore, should not be recognised as measurement period adjustments.   **A77**

Example 9
Contingent payout based on future earnings

AC acquires TC on 31 December 20X5 for cash and contingent consideration. The contingent consideration arrangement provides that if TC's 20X6 earnings exceed CU100,000, TC's former owners will receive CU10,000 on 31 March 20X7.   **A78**

A79   At the acquisition date, AC had obtained information about the historical profitability of TC and projected its future cash flows and profitability on the basis of AC's assessment of economic conditions, TC's prospects, and its plans for TC. On the basis of that information, AC recognises a provisional fair value of its liability for the contingent consideration of CU3,700. Three months after the acquisition, TC unexpectedly obtains a profitable contract from a new customer, and first quarter 20X6 earnings are substantially greater than AC's projections for TC as of the acquisition date. AC determines that the fair value of its liability is now CU7,000.

A80   In this example, the increase in the liability for the contingent consideration should be recognised in profit or loss in the first quarter 20X6. AC had the information necessary to measure the liability as of the acquisition date on the basis of the circumstances that existed at that time. In this case, the change in projections (and the increased likelihood of the contingent consideration payment) is identifiable with an event that occurred after the acquisition date.

Example 10
Contingent payout based on the outcome of a lawsuit

A81   AC acquires TC on 31 December 20X5 for cash and contingent consideration. The fair value of the contingent consideration liability depends on assessments about the outcome of a lawsuit against TC that AC assumes in the combination. The values of the liabilities for the lawsuit and for the contingent consideration are directly related. A decrease in the fair value of the liability for the lawsuit leads to an equal increase in the fair value of the liability for the contingent consideration. However, if the lawsuit results in a judgement or settlement of CU200,000 or more, TC's former owners will receive no additional consideration.

A82   At the acquisition date, AC measures and recognises a provisional fair value of the liability for the lawsuit at CU95,000 and a provisional fair value of the liability for the contingent consideration at CU3,000 on the basis of the information obtained during the due diligence procedures. After the acquisition date and during the measurement period, AC discovers information in the records about the lawsuit that relates to facts that existed as of the acquisition date. On the basis of that information, AC revises its estimates of the fair value of the liability for the lawsuit to CU93,000 and the fair value of the liability for the contingent consideration to CU5,000.

A83   In this example, the adjustments to the liabilities should be accounted for as part of completing the initial accounting for the business combination because the new information was (a) obtained during the measurement period and (b) related to facts and circumstances that existed as of the acquisition date. The adjustments equally affect the fair values of the contingent consideration and the liability for the lawsuit. Therefore, in this example the offsetting adjustments result in no change to the amount recognised for goodwill.

Example 11
Illustration of paragraphs 64 and 76(a)—incomplete appraisal

A84   AC acquires TC on 30 September 20X5. AC seeks an independent appraisal for an item of property, plant and equipment acquired in the combination. However, the appraisal was not completed by the time AC completed its 20X5 annual financial statements. AC recognised in its 20X5 annual financial statements a provisional fair value for the asset of CU30,000. The item of property, plant, and equipment had a remaining useful life at the acquisition date of five years. Four months after the acquisition date, AC received the independent appraisal, which estimated the asset's fair value at the acquisition date at CU40,000.

As described in paragraph 64, AC is required to recognise any adjustments to pro-   **A85**
visional values as a result of completing the initial accounting for the business combination as if the initial accounting for the business combination had been completed at the acquisition date. In its 20X6 financial statements, AC presents a current period balance sheet and a two-year comparative income statement. Therefore, in the 20X6 financial statements, an adjustment is made to the opening carrying amount of the item of property, plant and equipment. That adjustment is measured as the fair value adjustment at the acquisition date of CU10,000 less the additional depreciation that would have been recognised had the asset's fair value at the acquisition date been recognised from that date (CU500 for three months' depreciation). The carrying amount of goodwill also is adjusted for the reduction in value at the acquisition date of CU10,000, and the 20X5 comparative information is adjusted to include additional depreciation of CU500.

In accordance with paragraph 76(a), AC discloses: **A86**

(a)   in its 20X5 financial statements, that the initial accounting for the business combination has not been completed, and explains why this is the case.

(b)   in its 20X6 financial statements, the amounts and explanations of the adjustments to the provisional values recognised during the current reporting period. Therefore, AC discloses that the fair value of the item of property, plant and equipment at the acquisition date has been increased by CU10,000 with a corresponding decrease in goodwill. The 20X5 comparative information is adjusted to include additional depreciation of CU500.

ASSESSING WHAT IS PART OF THE EXCHANGE FOR THE ACQUIREE (APPLICATION OF PARAGRAPHS 69 AND 70)

In accordance with paragraph 69, the acquirer assesses whether any portion of the   **A87**
transaction price and any assets acquired or liabilities assumed or incurred are not part of the exchange for the acquiree. Because only the consideration transferred and the assets acquired or liabilities assumed or incurred that are part of the exchange for the acquiree are included in the business combination accounting any portion that is not part of the exchange for the acquiree is accounted for separately from the business combination.

Judgement is required to determine whether a portion of the transaction price paid,   **A88**
or the assets acquired and liabilities assumed or incurred, are part of the exchange for the acquiree. A transaction or event arranged primarily for the economic benefit of the acquirer or the combined entity is not part of the exchange for the acquiree and is accounted for separately from the business combination. One arranged primarily for the benefit of the acquiree or its former owners generally is part of the exchange and is included in the business combination accounting. The acquirer should consider the following factors, which are neither mutually exclusive nor individually conclusive, to determine whether a transaction or event is arranged primarily for the economic benefit of the acquirer or combined entity, rather than for the acquiree or its former owners.

(a)   *The reasons for the transaction or event*—Understanding the reasons why the parties to the combination (the acquirer, the acquiree, and their owners, directors, managers, and their agents) entered into a particular transaction or arrangement may provide insight into whether it should be accounted for as part of the exchange for the acquiree. For example, if a transaction is arranged primarily for the economic benefit of the acquirer or combined entity with little or no benefit received by the acquiree or its former owners, that portion of the transaction price paid (and any related assets or liabilities) is unlikely to be part of the exchange for the acquiree and would be accounted for separately from the business combination.

(b) *Who initiated the transaction or event*—Understanding who initiated the transaction or event may also provide insight into whether it should be accounted for as part of the exchange for the acquiree. For example, a transaction or other event that is initiated by the acquirer may be entered into for the purpose of providing future economic benefits to the acquirer or combined entity with little or no benefit received by the acquiree or its former owners. On the other hand, a transaction or arrangement initiated by the owners of the acquiree is unlikely to be for the benefit of the acquirer or combined entity.

(c) *The timing of the transaction or event*—The timing of the transaction or event may also provide insight into whether it should be accounted for as part of the exchange for the acquiree. For example, a transaction between the acquirer and the acquiree that takes place during the negotiations of the terms of a business combination may be entered into in contemplation of the business combination for the purpose of providing future economic benefits to the acquirer or combined entity with little or no benefit received by the acquiree or its former owners.

Example 12
Regulatory asset acquired that is included in the business combination accounting

A89   To induce the acquisition of WB (Weak Bank) by SB (Strong Bank), as a condition of the combination between WB and SB, a regulatory authority agrees to provide financial assistance in the form of cash, a receivable, or guarantees. That assistance is transferred to SB (the combined entity) upon the closing of the combination agreement. The regulatory authority, as part of its mission and public purpose, has an interest in supporting the soundness of financial institutions, which includes protecting the interests of the depositors of WB. From the perspective of the regulatory body, the assistance provided to induce WB and SB to combine is in the furtherance of its mission.

A90   In this case, the transaction was not arranged primarily to achieve economic benefits favourable to the acquirer or combined entity. If SB did not receive the financial assistance, it might not have acquired WB or would have paid less to acquire WB (presumably by an amount equal to the financial assistance). Thus, SB is indifferent whether it pays less to acquire WB or if it pays more to acquire WB and also receives the financial assistance. Thus, that assistance would be an asset acquired at the acquisition date that is recognised as part of accounting for the business combination. The portion of the consideration transferred for the financial assistance is also accounted for as part of the business combination accounting even though it is transferred to the former owners of WB not to the regulator that provided it.

Effective settlement of pre-existing relationships between the acquirer and acquiree in a business combination

A91   The acquirer and acquiree may have a relationship that existed before the business combination was contemplated. For the purposes of this [draft] IFRS FRS, those relationships are called *pre-existing relationships*. A pre-existing relationship between the acquirer and acquiree may be contractual (for example, vendor and customer or licensor and licensee), or non-contractual (for example, plaintiff and defendant).

In general, the effective settlement of a pre-existing relationship between the acquirer   **A92**
and acquiree should be accounted for in the same way whether it is settled as part of
a business combination or separately from a business combination. Therefore, if the
business combination results in the effective settlement of a pre-existing relationship,
the acquirer recognises a gain or loss and measures it as follows:

(a)   a non-contractual pre-existing relationship (such as a lawsuit) should be mea-
      sured at fair value.
(b)   A contractual pre-existing relationship should be measured as the lesser of the
      following:

      (1)   the amount by which the contract is favourable or unfavourable from the
            perspective of the acquirer when compared with pricing for current
            market transactions for the same or similar items.
      (2)   any stated settlement provisions in the contract available to the coun-
            terparty to whom the contract is unfavourable.

      To the extent that (2) is less than (1), the difference should be included as part
      of the business combination accounting. Also, an unfavourable contract is not
      necessarily a loss contract for the acquirer.

A pre-existing relationship may be a contract between the acquirer and the acquiree   **A93**
in which the acquirer had previously granted to the acquiree the right to use the
acquirer's recognised or unrecognised intangible assets (for example, a right to use
the acquirer's trade name under a franchise agreement). In that case, paragraph 41
requires the acquirer to recognise an intangible asset for that right separately from
goodwill as part of the business combination accounting. However, if the contract
includes terms that are favourable or unfavourable when compared with pricing for
current market transactions for the same or similar items, the acquirer should
recognise a gain or loss separately from the business combination for the effective
settlement of the contract. The gain or loss is measured in accordance with paragraph A92.

Example 13
Effective settlement of a supply contract as a result of a business combination

AC purchases electronic components from TC under a five-year supply contract at   **A94**
fixed rates. Currently, the fixed rates are higher than rates at which AC could purchase similar electronic components from another supplier. The supply contract
includes provisions that AC can terminate the contract before the end of the initial
five-year term only by paying a CU6 million penalty. With three years remaining
under the supply contract, AC pays CU50 million to acquire TC, which is the fair
value of TC based on what other marketplace participants would be willing to pay.

Included in the total fair value of TC is CU8 million related to the fair value of the   **A95**
supply contract with AC. The CU8 million represents a CU3 million component that
is 'at-market' because the pricing is comparable to pricing for current market
transactions for the same or similar items (selling effort, customer relationships, and
so forth) and a CU5 million component for pricing that is unfavourable to AC. TC
has no other identifiable assets or liabilities related to the supply contract, and AC
has not recognised any assets or liabilities related to the supply contract before the
business combination.

In this example, AC recognises separately from the business combination a settle-   **A96**
ment loss of CU5 million (the lesser of the stated settlement amount and the amount
by which the contract is unfavourable to the acquirer).

Example 14
Effective settlement of a contract between the acquirer and acquiree in which the acquirer had recognised a liability before the business combination

A97   The amount recognised by AC as a gain or loss for the effective settlement of the pre-existing relationship will be affected if AC had previously recognised an amount in its financial statements related to that pre-existing relationship. Assume the same facts as in Example 13 except that before the business combination AC had recognised a CU6 million liability on the supply contract. AC recognises a CU1 million settlement gain on that contract at the acquisition date (the CU5 million measured loss on the contract less the CU6 million loss previously recognised) in profit or loss.

Arrangements to pay for employee services

A98   Judgement is often required to determine whether arrangements to pay for employee services (compensation arrangements) should be accounted for as part of the exchange for the acquiree or separately from the business combination. To assist in that determination, it is important to understand whether the transaction includes payments or other arrangements for the economic benefit of the acquirer or combined entity with little or no benefit received by the acquiree or its former owners. To the extent that it is, that portion of the transaction price (and any related liabilities) should be accounted for separately from the business combination. As described in paragraph A88, understanding the reasons for the arrangement, who initiated the arrangement, and when the arrangement was entered into may also assist in determining whether the arrangement should be accounted for as part of the business combination accounting or separately.

A99   If it is not clear whether an arrangement to pay for employee services should be accounted for as part of the exchange for the acquiree or separately from the business combination, the following indicators also should be considered:

(a)   *Continuing employment*—If future payments are automatically forfeited if employment ends, the arrangement may be compensation for post-combination services that will benefit the combined entity and should be accounted for separately from the business combination. In contrast, if future payments are not affected by employment termination, the arrangement may be part of the consideration transferred for the acquiree.

(b)   *Duration of continuing employment*—An employment agreement with an employment period coinciding with or longer than the future payment period may indicate that the arrangement is compensation for post-combination services that will benefit the combined entity and should be accounted for separately from the business combination accounting.

(c)   *Level of payment*—Reduced payments to owners who do not become employees may indicate that the incremental payments to selling owners who become employees are payments for post-combination services that will benefit the combined entity and should be accounted for separately from the business combination accounting. In contrast, payments in excess of reasonable levels paid to employees with similar responsibilities may indicate that the payment is part of the consideration transferred for the acquiree.

(d)   *Formula for determining consideration*—Contingent payments that are based on multiples of future earnings, future cash flows, or other similar performance measures may indicate that the formula is intended to verify the fair value of the acquiree and, therefore, should be accounted for as part of the business combination. In contrast, contingent payments based on percentages of earnings may indicate a profit-sharing arrangement that should be accounted for separately from the business combination.

Example 15
Arrangement that is part of the exchange for the acquiree

TC appointed a candidate as its new CEO under a ten-year contract. The contract   **A100**
required TC to pay the candidate CU5 million if TC is acquired before (a) the
contract expires or (b) the termination of CEO's employment for specified causes
within the control of TC. AC acquires TC eight years later. CEO remained an
employee of TC through the acquisition date and, thus, will receive the additional
payment under the existing contract.

AC is required to assess whether a portion of the consideration transferred and the   **A101**
related liability incurred—required payment of CU5 million—is part of the exchange
for the acquiree that should be included in the business combination accounting. The
employment agreement was entered into by TC to secure the employment of CEO
and by CEO to secure payment and security. The employment agreement was also
entered into before the negotiations of the combination began. Thus, there is no
reason to believe that the agreement was arranged primarily to achieve economic
benefits for AC. Therefore, the consideration transferred and the related liability for
the payment to CEO should be regarded as part of the exchange for the acquiree and
included in the business combination accounting.

**Acquirer share-based payment awards exchanged for awards held by the
employees of the acquiree**

In a business combination, an acquirer may exchange its share-based payment   **A102**
awards (replacement awards) for awards held by employees of the acquiree. If the
acquirer is obligated to replace the acquiree's awards, all or a portion of the
acquirer's replacement awards shall be included in the measurement of the consideration transferred by the acquirer in the business combination, as explained in
the following paragraph.

For the purpose of determining the portion of a replacement award that is part of the   **A103**
consideration exchanged for the acquiree, the share-based payment awards made by
the acquirer and acquiree shall be measured using the fair value-based measurement
method of ~~IFRS 2~~ FRS 20 *Share-based Payment*. The portion of the replacement
award that is part of the consideration transferred in exchange for the acquiree shall
be determined as follows:

(a) On the acquisition date, the acquirer recognises an expense in post-combination
profit or loss for any excess of (1) the fair value-based measure of the acquirer's
replacement award over (2) the fair value-based measure of the replaced
acquiree awards.

(b) The remaining fair value-based measure of the acquirer's replacement award is
the amount that remains after deducting the excess, if any, recognised in post-
combination profit or loss under (a). Of this amount, the portion attributable
to past services is regarded as part of the consideration transferred in exchange
for the acquiree. The portion, if any, attributable to future services is not part
of the consideration transferred and is an expense to be recognised in post-
combination profit or loss. The guidance in (c) and (d) shall be followed to
determine the portion of the remaining fair value-based measure of the replacement award attributable to past and future services. Depending on the
circumstances, the acquirer recognises the replacement award as a liability or
an equity instrument, as required in accordance with ~~IFRS 2~~ FRS 20.

(c) Of the remaining fair value-based measure of the replacement award, the
portion attributable to past services is equal to the remaining fair value-based
measure of the replacement award (or settlement) multiplied by the ratio of the

portion of the vesting period completed to the total vesting period. (The amount, if any, to be recognised in post-combination profit or loss is the remaining fair value-based measure of the replacement award (or settlement) multiplied by the ratio of the future vesting period to the total vesting period.)

(d)   The vesting period is the period during which all the specified vesting conditions are to be satisfied. Vesting conditions are defined in ~~IFRS 2~~ FRS 20.

A104   The following examples illustrate the application of these provisions in circumstances in which AC makes replacement awards of CU100 (fair value-based measure) at the acquisition date for TC awards of CU100 (fair value-based measure) at the acquisition date. Because the fair value-based measure of replacement awards equals the fair value-based measure of the replaced awards, there is no excess value recognised as acquisition date expense in accordance with paragraph A103(a). Therefore, in accordance with paragraph A103(b), the remaining fair value-based measure of the replacement awards is (CU100).

Example 16
Acquirer replacement awards, for which no services are required after the acquisition date, are exchanged for awards of the acquiree, for which the required services were rendered before the acquisition date

A105   AC exchanges replacement awards for which no services are required after the acquisition of TC for share-based payment awards of TC, for which the required services were rendered before the business combination. When originally granted, the share-based payment awards of TC had a vesting period of four years. The required services were rendered before the business combination. Because no future service is required for AC's replacement award, the AC replacement award represents part of the consideration transferred by AC in the business combination. Thus, 100 per cent of the award is regarded as equity interest in the acquiree, and the CU100 replacement award is included as part of the consideration transferred by AC.

Example 17
Acquirer replacement awards, for which services are required after the acquisition date, are exchanged for awards of the acquiree, for which the required services were rendered before the acquisition date

A106   AC exchanges replacement awards that require three years of future service for share-based payment awards of TC, for which the vesting period was completed before the business combination. When originally granted, the share-based payment awards of TC had a vesting period of four years. Because the original vesting period was completed, the TC awards represent an equity interest. However, because the replacement awards require three years of future services, a portion of the replacement award is to be recognised in post-combination profit or loss in accordance with paragraph A103(b). In this case, the total vesting period is seven years—the vesting period of the original award and the vesting period of the replacement award. The portion attributable to past services is equal to the remaining fair value-based measure of the replacement award (CU100) multiplied by the ratio of the past vesting period (four years) to the total vesting period (seven years). Thus, CU57 would be attributable to the past services and CU43 to the future services.

Example 18
Acquirer replacement awards, for which services are required after the acquisition date, are exchanged for awards of the acquiree, for which the vesting period was not completed before the acquisition date

AC exchanges replacement awards that require one year of future service for share-based payment awards of TC, for which the vesting period was not completed before the business combination. When originally granted, the awards of TC had a vesting period of four years. As of the acquisition date the TC employees had rendered a total of two years' service; thus, two years of service after the acquisition date would be required. Because all required service has not been rendered, the TC awards represent an equity interest in part (50 per cent, two of the required four years of service rendered as of the acquisition date). **A107**

The replacement awards require only one year of future service. Thus, because two years of service have been rendered, the total vesting period is three years. Normally, the portion attributable to past services would be equal to the remaining fair value of the replacement award (CU100) multiplied by the ratio of the past vesting period (two years) to the total vesting period (three years). Thus, CU67 would be attributable to the past services (and therefore would be part of the consideration transferred for the acquiree) and CU33 to the future services. However, in accordance with paragraph A103(b), because the amount of the acquirer's replacement award attributable to past services (CU67) exceeds the amount of the replaced acquirer's awards attributable to those services (CU50, or CU100 × 2/4 years), the excess (CU17) is not part of the consideration transferred. Rather, that excess is an expense to be recognised in post-combination financial statements. Thus, CU50 would be attributable to past services (and included as part of the consideration transferred for the acquiree) and CU50 to future services. **A108**

Example 19
Acquirer replacement awards, for which no services are required after the acquisition date, are exchanged for awards of the acquiree, for which the vesting period was not completed before the acquisition date

Assume the same facts as in the previous example except that AC exchanges replacement awards that require no service after the business combination. Like the previous example, the portion that could be attributable to past services cannot exceed the amount of the replaced TC awards attributable to those services. Thus, CU50 (which is calculated as CU100 × 2/4 years) is attributable to the past services and is part of the consideration transferred for the acquiree, and CU50 is an expense to be recognised in post-combination financial statements. Because this replacement award has no vesting period associated with it, the entire CU50 would be recognised as an expense immediately. **A109**

ILLUSTRATION OF DISCLOSURE REQUIREMENTS (APPLICATION OF PARAGRAPHS 71 AND 72)

The following example of some of the disclosure requirements of this [draft] IFRS [draft] FRS ● is presented for illustrative purposes only and, therefore, may not be representative of actual transactions. **A110**

Footnote X: acquisitions

On 30 June 20X2 Alpha acquired 100 per cent of the outstanding common shares of Beta. Beta is a provider of data networking products and services in Canada and

Mexico. As a result of the acquisition, Alpha is expected to be the leading provider of data networking products and services in those markets. It also expects to reduce costs through economies of scale.

The fair value of Beta on 30 June 20X2 was CU9,400, determined on the basis of the consideration paid. Alpha's consideration included CU6,000 of cash, 100,000 ordinary shares valued at CU2,400, and a contingent future payment arrangement with a fair value of CU1,000 at the acquisition date. The fair value of the 100,000 ordinary shares issued was determined on the basis of the closing market price of Alpha's ordinary shares at the acquisition date. The future payment arrangement is contingent on the levels of revenue that Omega, an unconsolidated equity investment owned by Beta, achieves over the 12-month period following the acquisition. The maximum potential undiscounted amount of all future payments that Alpha could be required to make under the future payment arrangement is CU2,000.

Alpha incurred CU500 of third-party expenses related to the acquisition of Beta. Those expenses are included in the selling, general, and administrative expenses in Alpha's consolidated statement of income.

The following table summarises the estimated fair values of the assets acquired and liabilities assumed at the acquisition date.

At 30 June 20X2

	CU
Current assets	2,400
Property, plant and equipment	1,500
Intangible assets subject to amortisation	2,500
Intangible assets not subject to amortisation	2,400
Goodwill	2,200
Total assets acquired	11,000
Current liabilities	(1,100)
Non-current debt	(500)
Total liabilities assumed	(1,600)
Net assets acquired	9,400

REVERSE ACQUISITIONS (APPLICATION OF PARAGRAPH 12(c))

A111   In some business combinations, commonly called *reverse acquisitions*, the acquirer is the entity whose equity interests have been acquired and the issuing entity is the acquiree. For example, a private entity might initiate a combination and arrange to have itself 'acquired' by a smaller public entity as a means of obtaining a stock exchange listing. Although the public entity that issues equity interests is regarded as the legal parent and the private entity is regarded as the legal subsidiary, the private entity that initiated and arranged the combination is the acquirer if it is determined to have obtained control of the public entity in accordance with the requirements of paragraphs 11–16. Therefore, for financial reporting purposes in a reverse acquisition, the legal parent is the acquiree and the legal subsidiary is the acquirer.

The requirement in this [draft] ~~IFRS~~ FRS for an acquirer to measure and recognise   **A112**
the fair value of the acquiree and the values of the assets acquired and liabilities
assumed on the acquisition date applies to reverse acquisition accounting. In a
reverse acquisition, the legal subsidiary is the acquirer that measures and recognises
the legal parent, which is the acquiree. Paragraphs A113–A136 provide guidance for
applying the acquisition method to reverse acquisitions.

Fair value of the acquiree

In accordance with paragraph 20 of this [draft] ~~IFRS~~ FRS, the acquisition-date fair   **A113**
value of the consideration transferred by the acquirer is presumed to be the best basis
for measuring the fair value of the acquirer's interest in the acquiree on that date, in
the absence of evidence to the contrary. If the consideration transferred by the
acquirer is not the best evidence of the fair value of the acquiree, the acquirer should
use other valuation techniques to measure directly the fair value of the acquiree
(see paragraphs A18–A26). When equity interests are issued as part of the consideration transferred in a business combination, the fair value of those equity
interests is measured as of the acquisition date.

In a reverse acquisition, the consideration is deemed to have been transferred by the   **A114**
legal subsidiary (ie the acquirer for financial reporting purposes) in the form of
equity interests issued to the owners of the legal parent (ie the acquiree for financial
reporting purposes). If the fair value of the equity interests of the legal subsidiary
(acquirer) is used to determine the fair value of the consideration transferred for the
acquiree, a method of calculating the fair value of the consideration is to determine
the number of equity interests the legal subsidiary (acquirer) would have had to issue
to provide the same percentage equity interest of the combined entity to the owners
of the legal parent (acquiree) as they have in the combined entity as a result of the
reverse acquisition. The fair value of the number of equity interests so calculated can
be used as the fair value of consideration transferred for the acquiree in the
combination.

If the fair value of the consideration transferred by the acquirer (ie the fair value of   **A115**
the equity interests of the legal subsidiary) is not the best basis for measuring the fair
value of the acquiree (legal parent), the acquirer should use other valuation techniques. In a reverse acquisition, the fair value of the issued equity interests of the
legal parent (acquiree) as of the acquisition date, based on prices of the legal parent's
publicly traded equity shares, may provide the best basis for measuring the fair value
of the legal parent (acquiree).

Preparation and presentation of consolidated financial statements

Consolidated financial statements prepared following a reverse acquisition are issued   **A116**
under the name of the legal parent, but described in the notes as a continuation of the
financial statements of the legal subsidiary (ie the acquirer for financial reporting
purposes). Because such consolidated financial statements represent a continuation
of the financial statements of the legal subsidiary:

(a) the assets and liabilities of the legal subsidiary (acquirer) are measured and
recognised in those consolidated financial statements at their pre-combination
carrying amounts.

(b) the retained earnings and other equity balances recognised in those consolidated financial statements are the retained earnings and other equity
balances of the legal subsidiary (acquirer) immediately before the business
combination.

(c)　the amount recognised as issued equity interests in those consolidated financial statements shall be determined by adding the issued equity of the legal subsidiary (acquirer) immediately before the business combination to the fair value of the legal parent (acquiree) determined in accordance with paragraphs A113–A115. However, the equity structure appearing in those consolidated financial statements (ie the number and type of equity interests issued) reflects the equity structure of the legal parent (acquiree), including the equity interests issued by the legal parent to effect the combination.

(d)　comparative information presented in those consolidated financial statements is that of the legal subsidiary (acquirer).

A117　Reverse acquisition accounting applies only in the consolidated financial statements, and not in the separate financial statements. Therefore, in the legal parent's separate financial statements, if any, the investment in the legal subsidiary is accounted for in accordance with the requirements in ~~IAS 27 Consolidated and Separate Financial Statements~~ FRS 2 *Accounting for Subsidiary Undertakings*, on accounting for investments in an investor's separate financial statements.

A118　Consolidated financial statements prepared following a reverse acquisition reflect the values measured in accordance with this [draft] ~~IFRS~~ FRS for the assets and liabilities of the legal parent (ie the acquiree for financial reporting purposes). Therefore, the fair value of the assets and liabilities of the legal parent are recognised in accordance with paragraphs 28–51 of this [draft] ~~IFRS~~ FRS.

Non-controlling interest

A119　In a reverse acquisition, some of the owners of the legal subsidiary (acquirer) may not exchange their equity interests for equity interests of the legal parent (acquiree). Although the entity in which those owners hold equity interests (the legal subsidiary) acquired another entity (the legal parent), those owners are treated as a non-controlling interest in the consolidated financial statements prepared after the reverse acquisition. This is because the owners of the legal subsidiary that do not exchange their equity interests for equity interests of the legal parent have an interest only in the results and net assets of the legal subsidiary, and not in the results and net assets of the combined entity. Conversely, the owners of the legal parent, notwithstanding that the legal parent is the acquiree for financial reporting purposes, have an interest in the results and net assets of the combined entity.

A120　Because the assets and liabilities of the legal subsidiary are measured and recognised in the consolidated financial statements at their pre-combination carrying amounts, the non-controlling interest reflects the non-controlling shareholders' proportionate interest in the pre-combination carrying amounts of the legal subsidiary's net assets. This is unique to a reverse acquisition.

Earnings per share

A121　As noted in paragraph A116(c), the equity structure appearing in the consolidated financial statements prepared following a reverse acquisition reflects the equity structure of the legal parent (acquiree), including the equity interests issued by the legal parent to effect the business combination.

A122　For the purpose of calculating the weighted average number of ordinary shares outstanding (the denominator) during the period in which the reverse acquisition occurs:

(a)   the number of ordinary shares outstanding from the beginning of that period to the acquisition date shall be deemed to be the number of ordinary shares issued by the legal parent (acquiree) to the owners of the legal subsidiary (acquirer); and

(b)   the number of ordinary shares outstanding from the acquisition date to the end of that period shall be the actual number of ordinary shares of the legal parent (acquiree) outstanding during that period.

The basic earnings per share disclosed for each comparative period before the acquisition date that is presented in the consolidated financial statements following a reverse acquisition shall be calculated by dividing the profit or loss of the legal subsidiary attributable to ordinary shareholders in each of those periods by the number of ordinary shares issued by the legal parent to the owners of the legal subsidiary in the reverse acquisition.   **A123**

The calculations outlined in paragraphs A132 and A133 assume that there were no changes in the number of the legal subsidiary's issued ordinary shares during the comparative periods and during the period from the beginning of the period in which the reverse acquisition occurred to the acquisition date. The calculation of earnings per share shall be adjusted appropriately to take into account the effect of a change in the number of the legal subsidiary's issued ordinary shares during those periods.   **A124**

Example 20
Reverse acquisition

This example illustrates the accounting for a reverse acquisition in which Entity A, the entity issuing equity instruments and, therefore, the legal parent, is acquired in a reverse acquisition by Entity B, the legal subsidiary, on 30 September 20X6. This example ignores the accounting for any income tax effects.   **A125**

The following are the balance sheets of Entity A and Entity B immediately before the business combination: **A126**

	Entity A (legal parent, acquiree)	Entity B (legal subsidiary, acquirer)
	CU	CU
Current assets	500	700
Non-current assets	1,300	3,000
Total assets	1,800	3,700
Current liabilities	300	600
Non-current liabilities	400	1,100
Total liabilities	700	1,700
Owners' equity		
Retained earnings	800	1,400
Issued equity		
100 ordinary shares	300	–
60 ordinary shares	–	600
Total owners' equity	1,100	2,000
Total liabilities and owners' equity	1,800	3,700

A127   The following is other information used in this example:

(a)   On 30 September 20X6 Entity A issues 2½ shares in exchange for each ordinary share of Entity B. All of Entity B's shareholders exchange their shares in Entity B. Therefore, Entity A issues 150 ordinary shares in exchange for all 60 ordinary shares of Entity B.

(b)   The fair value of each ordinary share of Entity B at 30 September 20X6 is CU40. The quoted market price of Entity A's ordinary shares at that date is CU16.

(c)   The fair values of Entity A's identifiable assets and liabilities at 30 September 20X6 are the same as their carrying amounts, except that the fair value of Entity A's non-current assets at 30 September 20X6 is CU1,500.

Calculating the fair value of the acquiree

A128   As a result of the issue of 150 ordinary shares by Entity A (legal parent, acquiree), Entity B's shareholders own 60 per cent of the issued shares of the combined entity (ie 150 of 250 issued shares). The remaining 40 per cent are owned by Entity A's shareholders. If the business combination had taken the form of Entity B issuing additional ordinary shares to Entity A's shareholders in exchange for their ordinary shares in Entity A, Entity B would have had to issue 40 shares for the ratio of ownership interest in the combined entity to be the same. Entity B's shareholders would then own 60 of the 100 issued shares of Entity B and, therefore, 60 per cent of the combined entity. As a result, the fair value of the consideration transferred by

Entity B and the fair value of the Entity A is CU1,600 (ie 40 shares each with a fair value of CU40). If the fair value of the consideration transferred by Entity B is determined not to be the best evidence of the fair value of Entity A, then other valuation techniques should be used to measure the fair value of Entity A directly. The fair value of Entity A could be measured directly on the basis of the fair value of Entity A's shares outstanding.

Measuring goodwill

Goodwill is measured as the excess of the fair value of the acquiree, Entity A, over the net amount of Entity A's recognised identifiable assets and liabilities. Therefore, goodwill is measured as follows:

A129

	CU	CU
Fair value of Entity A (legal parent, acquiree)		1,600
Net recognised values of Entity A's identifiable assets and liabilities		
Current assets	500	
Non-current assets	1,500	
Current liabilities	(300)	
Non-current liabilities	(400)	(1,300)
Goodwill		300

Consolidated balance sheet at 30 September 20X6

The following is the consolidated balance sheet immediately after the business combination:

A130

	CU
Current assets [CU700 + CU500]	1,200
Non-current assets [CU3,000 + CU1,500]	4,500
Goodwill	300
Total assets	6,000
Current liabilities [CU600 + CU300]	900
Non-current liabilities [CU1,100 + CU400]	1,500
Total liabilities	2,400
Owners' equity	
Retained earnings	1,400
Issued equity	
250 ordinary shares [CU600 + CU1,600]	2,200
Total owners' equity	3,600
Total liabilities and owners' equity	6,000

A131   In accordance with paragraph A116(c), the amount recognised as issued equity interests in the consolidated financial statements (CU2,200) is determined by adding the issued equity of the legal subsidiary immediately before the business combination (CU600) and the fair value of the legal parent (acquiree) measured in accordance with paragraphs A113–A115 (CU1,600). However, the equity structure appearing in the consolidated financial statements (ie the number and type of equity interests issued) must reflect the equity structure of the legal parent, including the equity interests issued by the legal parent to effect the combination.

Earnings per share

A132   Assume that Entity B's profit for the annual period ended 31 December 20X5 was CU600, and that the consolidated profit for the annual period ended 31 December 20X6 is CU800. Assume also that there was no change in the number of ordinary shares issued by Entity B during the annual period ended 31 December 20X5, and during the period from 1 January 20X6 to the date of the reverse acquisition on 30 September 20X6. Earnings per share for the annual period ended 31 December 20X6 is calculated as follows:

Number of shares deemed to be outstanding for the period from 1 January 20X6 to the acquisition date (ie the number of ordinary shares issued by Entity A (legal parent, acquiree) in the reverse acquisition)	150
Number of shares outstanding from the acquisition date to 31 December 20X6	250
Weighted average number of ordinary shares outstanding $[(150 \times 9 \div 12) + (250 \times 3 \div 12)]$	175
Earnings per share $[800 \div 175]$	CU4.57

A133   Restated earnings per share for the annual period ended 31 December 20X5 is CU4.00 (ie the profit of Entity B of 600 divided by the number of ordinary shares issued by Entity A in the reverse acquisition).

Non-controlling interest

A134   Assume the same facts as above, except that only 56 of Entity B's 60 ordinary shares are exchanged. Because Entity A issues 2½ shares in exchange for each ordinary share of Entity B, Entity A issues only 140 (rather than 150) shares. As a result, Entity B's shareholders own 58.3 per cent of the issued shares of the combined entity (ie 140 shares of 240 issued shares). The fair value of the consideration transferred for Entity A, the acquiree, is calculated by assuming that the combination had taken place in the form of Entity B issuing additional ordinary shares to the shareholders of Entity A in exchange for their ordinary shares in Entity A. In calculating the number of shares that would have to be issued by Entity B, the non-controlling interest is ignored. The majority shareholders own 56 shares of Entity B. For this to represent a 58.3 per cent equity interest, Entity B would have had to issue an additional 40 shares. The majority shareholders would then own 56 of the 96 issued shares of Entity B and, therefore, 58.3 per cent of the combined entity. As a result, the fair value of the consideration transferred for Entity A, the acquiree, is CU1,600 (ie 40 shares each with a fair value of CU40). This is the same amount as when all 60 of Entity B's ordinary shares are tendered for exchange. The fair value of Entity A, the acquiree, does not change if some of Entity B's shareholders do not participate in the exchange.

The non-controlling interest is represented by the four shares of the total 60 shares of Entity B that are not exchanged for shares of Entity A. Therefore, the non-controlling interest is 6.7 per cent. The non-controlling interest reflects the non-controlling shareholders' proportionate interests in the pre-combination carrying amounts of the net assets of Entity B, the legal subsidiary. Therefore, the consolidated balance sheet is adjusted to show a non-controlling interest of 6.7 per cent of the pre-combination carrying amounts of Entity B's net assets (ie CU134 or 6.7 per cent of CU2,000). **A135**

The consolidated balance sheet at 30 September 20X6, reflecting the non-controlling interest, is as follows: **A136**

	CU
Current assets [CU700 + CU500]	1,200
Non-current assets [CU3,000 + CU1,500]	4,500
Goodwill	300
Total assets	6,000
Current liabilities [CU600 + CU300]	900
Non-current liabilities [CU1,100 + CU400]	1,500
Total liabilities	2,400
Owners' equity	
Retained earnings [CU1,400 × 93.3 per cent]	1,306
Issued equity	
240 ordinary shares [CU560 + CU1,600]	2,160
Non-controlling interest	134
Total owners' equity	3,600
Total liabilities and owners' equity	6,000

Appendix C
Guidance on accounting for asset acquisitions, and on identifying business combinations between entities under common control, and transitional provisions for business combinations involving only mutual entities or by contract alone.

This appendix is an integral part of the [draft] ~~IFRS~~ FRS.

INTRODUCTION

C1   This appendix provides guidance on three matters:

    (a)   asset acquisitions,

    (b)   identifying business combinations between entities under common control, and

    (c)   transitional provisions for business combinations. ~~involving only mutual entities or by contract alone without obtaining any equity interests.~~

[The source of the guidance is given in square brackets.]

C2   The guidance in this appendix was deliberated by the IASB, but not jointly with the FASB. The FASB's [draft proposed] SFAS 141(R) includes an appendix of continuing authoritative guidance; however, that guidance has been carried forward by the FASB from other sources. Therefore, the guidance provided in the FASB's appendix is not the same as the guidance provided in this appendix.

Accounting for asset acquisitions

C3   As noted in paragraph 5 a transaction or event is accounted for as a business combination only if the assets acquired and liabilities assumed constitute a business (an acquiree). If the assets acquired and liabilities assumed do not constitute a business, the acquirer shall account for the transaction as an asset acquisition. The accounting for an asset acquisition is described below in paragraphs C4 and C5. [Source: IFRS 3* paragraph 4]

C4   The acquirer shall:

    (a)   identify the individual identifiable assets acquired and liabilities assumed, including those assets that meet the definition of, and recognition criteria for, intangible assets in ~~IAS 38~~ [draft] FRS ● *Intangible Assets*.

    (b)   allocate the cost of the group to the individual identifiable assets and liabilities based on their relative fair values at the date of purchase. Such a transaction or event does not give rise to goodwill.

    (c)   recognise the identifiable assets acquired and liabilities assumed.

C5   Intangible assets acquired in an asset acquisition shall be recognised in accordance with the requirements of ~~IAS 38~~ [draft] FRS ●.

ASB footnote: The IASB issued IFRS 3 Business Combinations *in March 2004 on completion of the first phase of the Business Combinations project.*

Business combinations involving entities under common control

~~Consistently with the previous version of IFRS 3, t~~The provisions of this [draft] ~~IFRS~~ FRS do not apply to combinations involving entities under common control.

C6

A business combination involving entities or businesses under common control is a business combination in which all of the combining entities or businesses are ultimately controlled by the same party or parties both before and after the business combination, and that control is not transitory. [Source: IFRS 3, paragraph 10]

C7

A group of individuals shall be regarded as controlling an entity when, as a result of contractual arrangements, they collectively have the power to govern its financial and operating policies so as to obtain benefits from its activities. Therefore, a business combination is outside the scope of this [draft] ~~IFRS~~ FRS when the same group of individuals has, as a result of contractual arrangements, ultimate collective power to govern the financial and operating policies of each of the combining entities so as to obtain benefits from their activities, and that ultimate collective power is not transitory. [Source: IFRS 3, paragraph 11]

C8

An entity may be controlled by an individual or by a group of individuals acting together under a contractual arrangement, and that individual or group of individuals may not be subject to the financial reporting requirements of ~~IFRSs~~ FRSs. Therefore, it is not necessary for combining entities to be included as part of the same consolidated financial statements for a business combination to be regarded as one involving entities under common control. [Source: IFRS 3, paragraph 12]

C9

The extent of non-controlling interests in each of the combining entities before and after the business combination is not relevant to determining whether the combination involves entities under common control. Similarly, the fact that one of the combining entities is a subsidiary that has been excluded from the consolidated financial statements is not relevant to determining whether a combination involves entities under common control. [Source: IFRS 3, paragraph 13]

C10

Transitional provisions for business combinations ~~involving only mutual entities or by contract alone without obtaining any equity interests~~

Paragraph 82 provides that it applies prospectively to business combinations for which the acquisition date is on or after the beginning of the first annual period beginning on or after 1 January 2007. Earlier application is encouraged. However, this [draft] ~~IFRS~~ FRS shall be applied only when an annual period begins on or after this [draft] ~~IFRS~~ FRS was issued. If this [draft] ~~IFRS~~ FRS is applied before its effective date, that fact shall be disclosed and [draft] ~~IAS 27~~ FRS 2, [draft] FRS ● [Intangible Assets], [draft] FRS ● [Impairment of Assets] and [draft] ~~IAS 37~~ FRS 12 are to be applied at the same time.

C11

The requirement to apply this [draft] ~~IFRS~~ FRS prospectively has the following effect for a business combination ~~involving only mutual entities or by contract alone (see paragraph 54)~~ if the acquisition date for that business combination is before the beginning of the first annual period beginning on or after 1 January 2007:

C12

(a) Classification
   An entity shall continue to classify the prior business combination in accordance with the entity's previous accounting policies for such combinations.

(b)   Previously recognised goodwill
At the beginning of the first annual period beginning on or after 1 January 2007 the carrying amount of goodwill arising from the prior business combination shall be its carrying amount at that date in accordance with the entity's previous accounting policies, after eliminating the carrying amount of any accumulated amortisation of that goodwill with a corresponding decrease in goodwill. No other adjustments shall be made to the carrying amount of goodwill.

(c)   Goodwill previously recognised as a deduction from equity
If the entity's previous accounting policies resulted in goodwill arising from the prior business combination being recognised as a deduction from equity, the entity shall not recognise that goodwill as an asset at the beginning of the first annual period beginning on or after 1 January 2007. Furthermore, the entity shall not recognise any part of that goodwill in profit or loss when it disposes of all or part of the business to which that goodwill relates or when a cash-generating unit to which the goodwill relates becomes impaired.

(d)   Subsequent accounting for goodwill
From the beginning of the first annual period beginning on or after 1 January 2007 an entity shall discontinue amortising goodwill arising from the prior business combination and shall test goodwill for impairment in accordance with ~~IAS 36~~ [draft] FRS ● [Impairment of Assets].

(e)   Previously recognised negative goodwill
An entity that accounted for the prior business combination by applying the purchase method may have recognised a deferred credit for an excess of its interest in the net fair value of the acquiree's identifiable assets and liabilities over the cost of that interest (sometimes called negative goodwill). If so, the entity shall derecognise the carrying amount of that deferred credit at the beginning of the first annual period beginning on or after 1 January 2007 with a corresponding adjustment to the opening balance of retained earnings at that date.

Appendix D
Amendments to other UK accounting standards

The amendments in this [draft] Appendix shall be applied for annual periods beginning on or after [1 January 2007]. If an entity applies this [draft] FRS for an earlier period, these amendments shall be applied for that earlier period. Amended paragraphs are shown with new text underlined and deleted text struck through.

Terminology   D1

**In Financial Reporting Standards (including UITF Abstracts) applicable at [1 January   D1.1
2007]:**

(a) references to 'identifiable assets, liabilities and contingent liabilities' are amended to 'identifiable assets and liabilities'.

(c) references to 'each identifiable asset, liability and contingent liability' are amended to 'each identifiable asset and liability'.

(d) references to 'goodwill acquired in a business combination' are amended to 'goodwill arising in a business combination'.

(e) references to 'acquired goodwill' are amended to 'goodwill arising in a business combination'.

FRS 9 Associates and Joint Ventures   D2

**Paragraph c of the Summary includes a table; the section of the table titled 'Associates'   D2.1
is amended as follows:**

"... Goodwill arising on the investor's acquisition of its associates less any ~~amortisation or write down~~ impairment, should be included in the carrying amount for associates but should be disclosed separately. In the profit and loss account the ~~amortisation and write down~~ impairment of such goodwill should be separately disclosed as part of the investor's share of its associates' results."

The final sentence in this section is also deleted.

In paragraph 4 the following amendment is made: D2.2

Equity method:-

A method of accounting that brings an investment into its investor's financial statements initially at its cost, identifying any goodwill arising. The carrying amount of the investment is adjusted in each period by the investor's share of the results of its investee less any ~~amortisation or write-off~~ impairment for goodwill, the investor's share of any relevant gains or losses, and any other changes in the investee's net assets including distributions to its owners, for example by dividend. The investor's share of its investee's results is recognised in its profit and loss account. The investor's cash flow statement includes the cash flows between the investor and its investee, for example relating to dividends and loans.

In paragraph 27 the following amendment is made: D2.3

27 In the investor's consolidated profit and loss account the investor's share of its associates' operating results should be included immediately after group operating result (but after the investor's share of the results of its joint ventures, if any). Any

~~amortisation or write-down~~ impairment of goodwill arising on acquiring the associates should be charged at this point and disclosed. ...

D2.4 In paragraph 29 the following amendments are made:

29 The investor's consolidated balance sheet should include as a fixed asset investment the investor's share of the net assets of its associates shown as a separate item. Goodwill arising on the investor's acquisition of its associates, less any ~~amortisation or write-down~~ impairment, should be included in the carrying amount for the associates but should be disclosed separately. However, goodwill should only be recognised with respect to the part of the associates that is attributable to the interests held by the investor.

D2.5 In paragraph 31 the following amendments are made:

31 In calculating the amounts to be included in the investor's consolidated financial statements by the equity method for associates and the gross equity method for joint ventures, the same principles should be applied as are applied in the consolidation of subsidiaries.

  (a) When an entity acquires an associate or joint venture, fair values should be attributed to the investee's underlying assets and liabilities, identified using the investor's accounting policies, and these fair values should provide the basis for subsequent depreciation. The difference between the cost of the investment and the investor's share of the net fair value of the associate's or joint venture's assets and liabilities is accounted for in accordance with [draft] FRS ● *Business Combinations.* ~~Both the consideration paid in the acquisition and the goodwill arising should be calculated in the same way as on the acquisition of a subsidiary.~~ The investee's assets used in calculating the goodwill arising on its acquisition should not include any goodwill carried in the balance sheet of the investee itself. Subject to the presentation requirement in paragraph 29 of the FRS, the goodwill balance should be treated in accordance with the provisions of [draft] FRS ● *Business Combinations* ~~FRS 10 'Goodwill and Intangible Assets'.~~

  (b) ...

Insert after (d)

  (e) Goodwill relating to an associate or joint venture is included in the carrying amount of the investment. However, amortisation of that goodwill is not permitted and is therefore not included in the determination of the investor's share of the associate's profits or losses.

  (f) Any excess of the investor's share of the net fair value of the associate's or joint venture identifiable assets, and liabilities over the cost of the investment is included as income in the determination of the investor's share of the associate's profit or loss in the period in which the investment is acquired.

D3 FRS 15 Tangible Fixed Assets

D3.1 In the footnote accompanying paragraph 43, delete the reference to FRS 7 'Fair Values in Acquisition Accounting' and replace it with [draft] FRS ● 'Business Combinations.'

D4 FRS 17 Retirement and Termination Benefits

D4.1 In paragraph 97 delete the reference to FRS 7 'Fair Values in Acquisition Accounting' and replace it with [draft] FRS ● 'Business Combinations.'

FRS 19 Deferred Tax*   D5

Delete paragraph g from the Summary of the FRS.   D5.1

Insert paragraphs 33A, 33B and 33C (including the heading) as follows: D5.2

Deferred tax arising from a business combination

33A   In accordance with [draft] FRS • *Business Combinations*, an entity recognises any resulting deferred tax assets (to the extent that they meet the recognition criteria in paragraph 23) or deferred tax liabilities as identifiable assets and liabilities at the acquisition date. Consequently, those deferred tax assets and deferred tax liabilities affect goodwill. However, an entity does not recognise deferred tax liabilities arising from the initial recognition of goodwill.

33B   As a result of a business combination, the probability of realising a deferred tax asset of the acquirer could change. An acquirer may consider it probable that it will recover its own deferred tax asset that was not recognised before the business combination. For example, the acquirer may be able to utilise the benefit of its unused tax losses against the future taxable profit of the acquiree. Alternatively, as a result of the business combination it may no longer be probable that future taxable profit will allow the deferred tax asset to be recovered. In such cases, the acquirer recognises a change in the deferred tax asset in the period of the business combination, but does not include it as part of the accounting for the business combination. Therefore, the acquirer does not take it into account in measuring goodwill on consolidation

33C   The potential benefit of the acquiree's deferred tax assets may not satisfy the criteria for separate recognition when a business combination is initially accounted for but may be realised subsequently. There is a rebuttable presumption that acquired deferred tax benefits recognised within one year after the acquisition date are an adjustment to any deferred tax benefits recognised at that date and will be applied to reduce the carrying amount of any goodwill related to that acquisition. If the carrying amount of that goodwill is zero, any remaining deferred tax benefits will be credited to profit or loss or, if this Standard so requires, to equity or through the statement of total recognised gains and losses. The rebuttable presumption is overcome if the recognition of the deferred tax benefits results from a discrete event that occurred after the acquisition date. If the rebuttable presumption is overcome, or if those deferred tax benefits are recognised more than one year after the acquisition date, they shall be credited to profit or loss or, if this Standard so requires, to equity or through the statement of total recognised gains and losses.

Insert the following after paragraph 64(e):   D5.3

...

(f)   - **if the probability of realising the acquirer's deferred tax asset changes as a result of a business combination (see paragraph 33B), the amount of the resulting change in the deferred tax asset at the acquisition date; and**

(k)   **a description of the event or change in circumstances that has resulted in deferred tax benefits acquired in a business combination being recognised.**

*ASB footnote: *The amendments to FRS 19 are based on the IASB's proposed amendments to IAS 12* Income Taxes. *The IASB's proposed amendments to IAS 12 are set out in paragraph D4 of its Exposure Draft of Proposed Amendments to IFRS 3* Business Combinations.

D5.4   **Paragraphs 66A and 66B are inserted as follows:**

66A   **Paragraph 33C shall be applied prospectively from the effective date of [draft] FRS ● *Business Combinations* (as revised in 200X) to the recognition of deferred tax assets acquired in business combinations.**

66B   Therefore, entities shall not adjust the accounting for prior business combinations if tax benefits failed to satisfy the criteria for separate recognition as of the acquisition date and are recognised after the acquisition date, unless the rebuttable presumption in paragraph 33C applies. Tax benefits recognised more than one year after the acquisition date shall be credited to profit or loss or, if this Standard so requires, to equity or through the statement of total recognised gains and losses.

D5.5   **In Appendix IV, delete paragraph 5.**

D6   **FRS 20 Share-based payment**

D6.1   **Paragraph 5 is amended as follows:**

5   As noted in paragraph 2, this IFRS applies to share-based payment transactions in which an entity acquires or receives goods or services. Goods includes inventories, consumables, property, plant and equipment, intangible assets and other non-financial assets. However, an entity shall not apply this IFRS to transactions in which the entity acquires goods as part of the net assets acquired in a business combination to which ~~FRS 6 Acquisitions and Mergers~~ [draft] FRS ● *Business Combinations* applies. Hence, equity instruments issued in a business combination in exchange for control of the acquiree are not within the scope of this IFRS. However, equity instruments granted to employees of the acquiree in their capacity as employees (eg in return for continued service) are within the scope of this IFRS. Similarly, the cancellation, replacement or other modification of *share-based payment arrangements* because of a business combination or other equity restructuring shall be accounted for in accordance with this IFRS. [Draft] FRS ● Business Combinations provides guidance on determining whether equity instruments issued in a business combination are part of the consideration transferred in exchange for control of the acquiree (and therefore within the scope of [draft] FRS ●) or are in return for continued service to be recognised in the post-combination period (and therefore within the scope of this IFRS).

D7   **FRS 22 (IAS 33) Earnings per share**

D7.1   In the Preface by the Accounting Standards Board the second bullet-point of paragraph 1, regarding guidance on earnings per share for business combinations accounted for as mergers under FRS 6, is deleted.

D7.2   **Paragraph 3A is deleted.**

D7.3   **Paragraph 22 is amended as follows:**

22.   Ordinary shares issued as part of the ~~cost of~~ consideration transferred in a business combination are included in the weighted average number of shares from the acquisition date. This is because the acquirer incorporates into its income statement the acquiree's profits and losses from that date.

D7.4   **Appendix C is deleted.**

FRS 25 (IAS 32) Financial Instruments: Disclosure and Presentation   **D8**

Paragraph 4(c) is deleted.   **D8.1**

FRS 26 (IAS 39) Financial Instruments: Recognition and Measurement   **D9**

Paragraph 2(f) is deleted.   **D9.1**

FRS 27 Life Assurance   **D10**

In paragraph 28(b) delete the reference to FRS 7 'Fair Values in Acquisition Accounting' and replace it with [draft] FRS ● 'Business Combinations.'   **D10.1**

AMENDMENTS TO FRED 37 (IAS 38) AND FRED 38 (IAS 36)

The ASB issued FRED 37 (IAS 38*) Intangible Assets and* FRED 38 (IAS 36) *Impairment of Assets. These FREDs have been amended to reflect the consequential amendments that are required to the current version of IAS 38 and IAS 36 as published by the IASB.*

The consequential amendments, set out below, are for information purposes only.

IAS 36 Impairment of Assets is amended as described below.   **D11**

In paragraph 6, the definition of the agreement date is deleted.

Paragraph 81 is amended as follows:

81   Goodwill ~~acquired~~ arising in a business combination represents ~~a payment made by an acquirer in anticipation of~~ assets that provide future economic benefits ~~from assets that~~ but are not capable of being individually identified and separately recognised. Goodwill does not generate cash flows independently of other assets or groups of assets, and often contributes to the cash flows of multiple cash-generating units. Goodwill sometimes cannot be allocated on a non-arbitrary basis to individual cash-generating units, but only to groups of cash-generating units. As a result, the lowest level within the entity at which the goodwill is monitored for internal management purposes sometimes comprises a number of cash-generating units to which the goodwill relates, but to which it cannot be allocated. References in paragraphs 83-99 to a cash-generating unit to which goodwill is allocated should be read as references also to a group of cash-generating units to which goodwill is allocated.

After paragraph 90 the heading and paragraphs 91-95 are deleted. Those paragraphs are reproduced, with minor changes, as paragraphs C1-C5 in a new appendix (Appendix C). Appendix C also includes new paragraphs C6-C12. The appendix is inserted, as follows, with the changes highlighted being the differences between paragraphs 91-95 of IAS 36 and paragraphs C1-C5:

Appendix C

This appendix is an integral part of the Standard. It provides guidance on goodwill impairment testing for cash-generating units with goodwill and non-controlling interests.

Impairment testing cash-generating units with goodwill and non-controlling interests

Before [draft] IFRS 3 (as revised in 200X) is applied, the following guidance is relevant when performing a goodwill impairment test for cash-generating units with non-controlling interests.

C1   In accordance with IFRS 3, goodwill recognised in a business combination represents the goodwill acquired by a parent based on the parent's ownership interest, rather than the amount of goodwill controlled by the parent as a result of the business combination. Therefore, goodwill attributable to a ~~minority~~non-controlling interest is not recognised in the parent's consolidated financial statements. Accordingly, if there is a ~~minority~~non-controlling interest in a cash-generating unit to which goodwill has been allocated, the carrying amount of that unit comprises:

(a)   both the parent's interest and the ~~minority~~non-controlling interest in the identifiable net assets of the unit; and

(b)   the parent's interest in goodwill.

However, part of the recoverable amount of the cash-generating unit determined in accordance with this Standard is attributable to the ~~minority~~non-controlling interest in goodwill.

C2   Consequently, for the purpose of impairment testing a ~~non-wholly-owned~~ cash-generating unit with goodwill that is not wholly-owned, the carrying amount of that unit is notionally adjusted, before being compared with its recoverable amount. This is accomplished by grossing up the carrying amount of goodwill allocated to the unit to include the goodwill attributable to the ~~minority~~non-controlling interest. This notionally adjusted carrying amount is then compared with the recoverable amount of the unit to determine whether the cash-generating unit is impaired. If it is, the entity allocates the impairment loss in accordance with paragraph 104 first to reduce the carrying amount of goodwill allocated to the unit.

C3   However, because goodwill is recognised only to the extent of the parent's ownership interest, any impairment loss relating to the goodwill is apportioned between that attributable to the parent and that attributable to the ~~minority~~non-controlling interest, with only the former being recognised as a goodwill impairment loss.

C4   If the total impairment loss relating to goodwill is less than the amount by which the notionally adjusted carrying amount of the cash-generating unit exceeds its recoverable amount, paragraph 104 requires the remaining excess to be allocated to reduce the other assets of the unit pro rata on the basis of the carrying amount of each asset in the unit.

C5   Illustrative Example 7 illustrates the impairment testing of a ~~non-wholly-owned~~ cash-generating unit with goodwill that is not wholly-owned.

After [draft] IFRS 3 (as revised in 200X) is applied, the following guidance is relevant when performing a goodwill impairment test for cash-generating units with non-controlling interests.

C6   In accordance with [draft] IFRS 3 (revised), the acquirer measures and recognises goodwill as of the acquisition date as the excess of the fair value of the acquiree, as a whole, over the net amount of the recognised identifiable assets acquired and liabilities assumed. This requirement applies even if the acquirer owns less than 100 per cent of the equity interests in the acquiree at the acquisition date (ie even if a non-controlling interest in the acquiree exists then).

In accordance with [draft] IFRS 3 (revised), the acquirer allocates the carrying **C7** amount of goodwill as of the acquisition date between the acquirer and the non-controlling interest, if any. The carrying amount of goodwill allocated to the acquirer is the difference as of that date between the fair value of the acquirer's equity interest in the acquiree and the acquirer's share in the fair value of the separately recognised assets acquired and liabilities assumed. The rest of the goodwill is allocated to the non-controlling interests.

In a cash-generating unit that includes a partially-owned subsidiary or is a stand- **C8** alone partially-owned subsidiary, goodwill impairment losses are allocated between the controlling and non-controlling interests pro rata using the relative carrying values of goodwill.

If the partially-owned subsidiary is itself a cash-generating unit, the impairment loss **C9** is allocated to the controlling and non-controlling interests on the basis of the relative carrying values of goodwill allocated to them.

If the partially-owned subsidiary is part of a larger cash-generating unit, goodwill **C10** impairment losses are allocated first to the components of the cash-generating unit and then to the controlling and non-controlling interests of the partially-owned subsidiary. The portion of the impairment loss allocated to the subsidiary is deter-mined by multiplying the goodwill impairment loss for the unit by the carrying value of the goodwill assigned to that subsidiary, divided by the carrying value of the goodwill assigned to the cash-generating unit as a whole. The amount of the impairment loss allocated to the partially-owned subsidiary is then allocated to the controlling and non-controlling interests on the basis of the relative carrying values of goodwill allocated to those interests.

If the total impairment loss relating to goodwill is less than the amount by which the **C11** carrying amount of the cash-generating unit exceeds its recoverable amount, para-graph 104 of IAS 36 requires the remaining excess to be allocated to reduce the other assets of the unit pro rata on the basis of the carrying amount of each asset in the unit.

Illustrative Example 7A illustrates the impairment testing of a cash-generating unit **C12** with goodwill that is not wholly-owned.

Paragraph 138 is deleted.

Paragraph 139 is amended as follows:

~~Otherwise, a~~An entity shall apply this Standard: **139**

(a)   to goodwill and intangible assets acquired in business combinations for which the agreement date is on or after 31 March 2004; and
(b)   to all other assets prospectively from the beginning of the first annual period beginning on or after 31 March 2004.

<u>The agreement date for a business combination is the date that a substantive agreement between the combining parties is reached and, in the case of publicly listed entities, announced to the public. In the case of a hostile takeover, the earliest date that a substantive agreement between the combining parties is reached is the date that a sufficient number of the acquiree's owners have accepted the acquirer's offer for the acquirer to obtain control of the acquiree.</u>

In the Illustrative Examples, the heading of Example 7 is amended as follows:

Example 7 - Impairment testing cash-generating units with goodwill and ~~minority~~non-controlling interests

(applicable to business combinations effected before [draft] IFRS 3 (revised 200X) is applied)

In the Illustrative Examples, paragraph IE65 of Example 7 is amended as follows.

IE65   A portion of Y's recoverable amount of CU1,000 is attributable to the unrecognised ~~minority~~non-controlling interest in goodwill. Therefore, in accordance with paragraph ~~92~~C2 of Appendix C of IAS 36, the carrying amount of Y must be notionally adjusted to include goodwill attributable to the ~~minority~~non-controlling interest, before being compared with the recoverable amount of CU1,000.

In the Illustrative Examples, a new Example 7A is added as follows:

Example 7A - Impairment testing cash-generating units with goodwill and non-controlling interests

(applicable to business combinations effected after [draft] IFRS 3 (revised 200X) is applied)

In this example, tax effects are ignored.

Background

IE68A   Entity X acquires an 80 per cent ownership interest in Entity Y for CU1,650 on 1 January 20X3. There is no evidence that this transaction is not an exchange of equal values. Therefore, the consideration transferred of CU1,650 is presumed to be the fair value of the 80 per cent interest. The fair value of Y is CU2,000. At 1 January 20X3, Y's identifiable net assets have a fair value of CU1,500.

IE68B   Therefore, X recognises in its consolidated financial statements Y's identifiable net assets at their fair value of CU1,500.

X also recognises in its consolidated financial statements goodwill of CU500, measured as the excess of the fair value of Y, as a whole, of CU2,000 over the net amount of the recognised identifiable assets acquired and liabilities assumed of CU1,500.

The amount of goodwill attributable to the controlling interest and to the non-controlling interests in Y is calculated as follows:

	CU
Fair value of X's 80 per cent interest in Y	1,650
Less: X's share of the fair value of the identifiable net assets acquired (80 per cent × CU1,500)	(1,200)
Goodwill allocated to X	450
Goodwill allocated to the non-controlling interests in Y [CU500 – CU450]	50

Therefore, the fair value of Y is attributed to X and the non-controlling interest at the acquisition date as follows:

	Total	Attributable to X	Attributable to the non-controlling interest
	CU	CU	CU
Identifiable net assets	1,500	1,200	300
Goodwill	500	450	50
Total	2,000	1,650	350

The assets of Y together are the smallest group of assets that generate cash inflows that are largely independent of the cash inflows from other assets or groups of assets. Therefore Y is a cash-generating unit. Because this cash-generating unit includes goodwill within its carrying amount, it must be tested for impairment annually, or more frequently if there is an indication that it may be impaired (see paragraph 90 of IAS 36).　　**IE68C**

At the end of 20X3, X determines that the recoverable amount of cash-generating unit Y is CU1,650. X uses straight-line depreciation over a 10-year life for Y's identifiable assets and anticipates no residual value.　　**IE68D**

Allocating impairment loss between the parent and non-controlling interest

Schedule 1. Testing Y for impairment at the end of 20X3

End of 20X3	Goodwill	Identifiable net assets	Total
	CU	CU	CU
Gross carrying amount	500	1,500	2,000
Accumulated depreciation	–	(150)	(150)
Carrying amount	500	1,350	1,850
Recoverable amount			1,650
Impairment loss			200

In accordance with paragraph 104 of IAS 36, the impairment loss of CU200 is allocated to the assets in the unit by first reducing the carrying amount of goodwill to zero.　　**IE68E**

Therefore, the full amount of impairment loss of CU200 for the unit is allocated to the goodwill. In accordance with paragraph C9 of Appendix C of IAS 36, if the partially-owned subsidiary is itself a cash-generating unit, the goodwill impairment loss is allocated to the controlling and non-controlling interests on the basis of the relative carrying values of goodwill allocated to them.　　**IE68F**

Schedule 2. Allocating goodwill impairment loss to X and the non-controlling interest.

	Total amount	Attributable to X	Attributable to non-controlling interest
Goodwill before impairment loss	CU500	CU450	CU50
Percentage of the total	100%	90%	10%
Impairment loss	(CU200)	(CU180)	(CU20)
Goodwill after being reduced for impairment loss	CU300	CU270	CU30

D12   IAS 38 Intangible Assets is amended as follows:

In paragraph 8, the definition of the agreement date is deleted.

Paragraphs 11, 25 and 33 are amended as follows:

11   The definition of an intangible asset requires an intangible asset to be identifiable to distinguish it from goodwill. Goodwill ~~acquired~~ arising in a business combination represents ~~a payment made by the acquirer in anticipation of~~ future economic benefits from assets that are not capable of being individually identified and separately recognised. The future economic benefits may result from synergy between the identifiable assets acquired or from assets that, individually, do not qualify for recognition in the financial statements ~~but for which the acquirer is prepared to make a payment in the business combination.~~

25   Normally, the price an entity pays to acquire separately an intangible asset reflects expectations about the probability that the expected future economic benefits embodied in the asset will flow to the entity. In other words, there will be an inflow of economic benefits, even if there could be uncertainty about the timing and the amount of the inflow ~~the effect of probability is reflected in the cost of the asset.~~ Therefore, the probability recognition criterion in paragraph 21(a) is always considered to be satisfied for separately acquired intangible assets.

33   In accordance with IFRS 3 *Business Combinations*, if an intangible asset is acquired in a business combination, the cost of that intangible asset is its fair value at the acquisition date. ~~The fair value of an intangible asset reflects market expectations about the probability that the future economic benefits embodied in the asset will flow to the entity. In other words, the effect of probability is reflected in the fair value measurement of the intangible asset.~~ An intangible asset acquired in a business combination embodies an entity's unconditional right to future economic benefits. ~~Therefore~~Thus, the probability recognition criterion in paragraph 21(a) is always considered to be satisfied for intangible assets acquired in business combinations. Any uncertainty will relate to the timing and amount of the inflow.

Paragraphs 33A and 33B are inserted as follows:

33A   A non-monetary asset without physical substance must be identifiable to meet the definition of an intangible asset. As outlined in paragraph 12, this will be the case when the asset is separable or arises from contractual or other legal rights. With one possible exception discussed in paragraph 33B, sufficient information should always exist to measure reliably the fair value of an asset that has an underlying contractual or legal basis or is capable of being separated from the entity.

As discussed in paragraph 15, an entity usually has insufficient control over the **33B** expected future economic benefits arising from a team of skilled staff and from training to conclude that these items meet the definition of an intangible asset. However, even in the unlikely event that an entity could demonstrate:

(a)   control over the future economic benefits arising from an assembled workforce acquired in a business combination; and

(b)   that the workforce meets one of the criteria in paragraph 12 for identifiability,

it is highly unlikely that the fair value of that workforce and the related intellectual capital could be measured with sufficient reliability. Accordingly, [draft] IFRS 3 (revised) prohibits an acquirer from recognising an assembled workforce as an asset separately from goodwill.

Paragraphs 34 and 35 are amended as follows:

Therefore, in accordance with this Standard and [draft] IFRS 3 (revised), an acquirer **34** recognises at the acquisition date separately from goodwill an intangible asset of the acquiree (other than an assembled workforce) if the asset's fair value can be measured reliably, irrespective of whether the asset had been recognised by the acquiree before the business combination. This means that the acquirer recognises as an asset separately from goodwill an in-process research and development project of the acquiree if the project meets the definition of an intangible asset and its fair value can be measured reliably. An acquiree's in-process research and development project meets the definition of an intangible asset when it:

(a)   meets the definition of an asset; and

(b)   is identifiable, ie is separable or arises from contractual or other legal rights.

Measuring the fair value of an intangible asset acquired in a business combination

With the exception of an assembled workforce, sufficient information always exists **35** to measure reliably the fair value of an asset that has an underlying contractual or legal basis or is capable of being separated from the entity. The fair value of intangible assets acquired in business combinations can normally be measured with sufficient reliability to be recognised separately from goodwill. When, for the estimates used to measure an intangible asset's fair value, there is a range of possible outcomes with different probabilities, that uncertainty enters into the measurement of the asset's fair value, rather than demonstrates an inability to measure fair value reliably. If an intangible asset acquired in a business combination has a finite useful life, there is a rebuttable presumption that its fair value can be measured reliably.

Paragraphs 38-41 are deleted.

Paragraphs 68 and 69 are amended as follows:

Expenditure on an intangible item shall be recognised as an expense when it is incurred **68** **unless:**

(a)   **it forms part of the cost of an intangible asset that meets the recognition criteria (see paragraphs 18-67); or**

(b) the item is acquired in a business combination and cannot be recognised as an intangible asset. If this is the case, this expenditure (included in the ~~cost of~~ consideration transferred in the business combination) shall form part of the ~~amount attributed to~~goodwill at the acquisition date (see IFRS 3 *Business Combinations*).

69 In some cases, expenditure is incurred to provide future economic benefits to an entity, but no intangible asset or other asset is acquired or created that can be recognised. In these cases, the expenditure is recognised as an expense when it is incurred. For example, except when it forms part of the ~~cost of~~assets acquired in a business combination, expenditure on research is recognised as an expense when it is incurred (see paragraph 54). Other examples of expenditure that is recognised as an expense when it is incurred include:

Paragraph 129 is deleted.

Paragraph 130 is amended as follows:

130 ~~Otherwise, a~~An entity shall apply this Standard:

(a) to the accounting for intangible assets acquired in business combinations for which the agreement date is on or after 31 March 2004; and

(b) to the accounting for all other intangible assets prospectively from the beginning of the first annual period beginning on or after 31 March 2004. Thus, the entity shall not adjust the carrying amount of intangible assets recognised at that date. However, the entity shall, at that date, apply this Standard to reassess the useful lives of such intangible assets. If, as a result of that reassessment, the entity changes its assessment of the useful life of an asset, that change shall be accounted for as a change in an accounting estimate in accordance with IAS 8.

The agreement date for a business combination is the date that a substantive agreement between the combining parties is reached and, in the case of publicly listed entities, announced to the public. In the case of a hostile takeover, the earliest date that a substantive agreement between the combining parties is reached is the date that a sufficient number of the acquiree's owners have accepted the acquirer's offer for the acquirer to obtain control of the acquiree.

Appendix E
Fair Value Measurements

This appendix is an integral part of the [draft] ~~IFRS~~ FRS.

This appendix provides guidance on how to measure fair value when accounting for   **E1**
a business combination. It shall be applied to all fair value measurements required by
this [draft] ~~IFRS~~ FRS, including the fair values of the acquiree, the financial and
non-financial identifiable assets acquired and liabilities assumed, and the consideration transferred. [The guidance in this Appendix is based on the FASB's
Proposed Statement of Financial Accounting Standards *Fair Value Measurements*.
The FASB plans to issue a final Statement on Fair Value Measurements in the fourth
quarter of 2005. This guidance may change as a consequence of that final Statement.]

Definition of fair value

For the purposes of this [draft] ~~IFRS~~ FRS fair value is the price at which an asset or   **E2**
liability could be exchanged in a current transaction between knowledgeable, unrelated, willing parties.

The objective of a fair value measurement is to estimate an exchange price for the   **E3**
asset or liability being measured in the absence of an actual transaction for that asset
or liability.* Thus, the estimate is determined by reference to a current hypothetical
transaction between willing parties.

Willing parties are presumed to be marketplace participants representing unrelated   **E4**
buyers and sellers that are:

(a) knowledgeable, having a common level of understanding about factors relevant
   to the asset or liability and the transaction; and
(b) willing and able to transact in the same market(s), having the legal and financial
   ability to do so.

Fair value presumes the absence of compulsion (duress). Accordingly, the amount   **E5**
that forms the basis for the estimate is the price that would be observed in a
transaction other than a forced liquidation transaction or distress sale. In all cases,
that price shall be estimated without regard to an entity's current intention to enter
into such a transaction.

Valuation techniques

Valuation techniques consistent with the market approach, income approach and   **E6**
cost approach shall be considered for all estimates of fair value. However, for estimates of fair value that are developed using quoted prices in active markets (an
application of the market approach), the results of other valuation techniques may
not provide significant additional information (paragraphs E12-E22). Key aspects of
those approaches are summarised below:

(a) The market approach requires observable prices and other information generated by actual transactions involving identical, similar or otherwise
   comparable assets or liabilities (including businesses). The estimate of fair value

---

*For a liability, the estimate of fair value shall consider the effect of the liability's credit standing so that the
estimate reflects the amount that would be observed in an exchange between willing parties of the same credit
quality.*

is based on the value indicated by those transactions. For example, paragraph 41 of ~~IAS 38~~ [draft] FRS ● [Intangible Assets] refers to the use of valuation techniques consistent with the market approach in determining the fair value of an intangible asset.

(b)   The income approach uses valuation techniques to convert future amounts (for example, cash flows or profit or loss) to a single present amount (discounted). The estimate of fair value is based on the value indicated by marketplace expectations about those future amounts.

(c)   For an asset, the cost approach considers the amount that would currently be required to replace its service capacity (often referred to as current replacement cost). The estimate of fair value considers the cost to acquire a substitute asset of comparable utility, adjusted for obsolescence. Obsolescence encompasses physical depreciation, functional obsolescence and economic obsolescence and is broader than depreciation for financial reporting purposes (an allocation of historical cost) or tax purposes (based on specified service lives).

E7   Valuation techniques used to estimate fair value shall be consistently applied. A change in the valuation technique(s) used is appropriate only if the change results in a more reliable estimate of fair value, for example as new markets develop or as new and improved valuation techniques become available.

Market inputs

E8   Market inputs refer to the assumptions and data that marketplace participants would use in their estimates of fair value. Valuation techniques used to estimate fair value shall emphasise market inputs, including those derived from active markets, whether using the market approach, income approach, or cost approach.

E9   In an active market, such as the Brussels Stock Exchange (Bourse), quoted prices that represent actual (observable) transactions are readily and regularly available; *readily available* means that pricing information is currently accessible and *regularly available* means that transactions occur with sufficient frequency to provide pricing information on an ongoing basis. In determining whether a market is active, the emphasis is on the level of activity for a particular asset or liability.

E10   Markets in which assets and liabilities are exchanged vary in structure and level of activity. Examples of such markets include the following:

(a)   Exchange market—An exchange market provides high visibility and order to the trading of financial instruments. Typically, closing prices are readily and regularly available. In an exchange market, multiple identical exchange units are traded. An example of such a market is the London Stock Exchange.

(b)   Dealer market—In a dealer market, dealers stand ready to trade (either buy or sell for their own account), thereby providing liquidity by using their capital to hold an inventory of the items for which they make a market. Typically, bid and asked prices are more readily and regularly available than closing prices. In a dealer market, multiple identical exchange units are traded. 'Over-the-counter' markets (where prices are publicly reported by, for example, the International Securities Market Association in Europe or US National Association of Securities Dealers Automated Quotations systems or the US National Quotation Bureau in the United States) are dealer markets. For example, the market for US Treasury securities is a dealer market. Dealer markets also exist for other assets and liabilities, such as financial instruments, commodities and physical assets (for example, certain used equipment).

(c)   Brokered market—In a brokered market, brokers attempt to match buyers with sellers but do not stand ready to trade for their own account. In other words, brokers do not use their own capital to hold an inventory of the items for which they make a market. The broker knows the prices bid and asked by the respective parties, but each party is typically unaware of another party's price requirements. Prices of completed transactions are sometimes available. Brokered markets include electronic communication networks (ECNs), in which buy and sell orders are matched, and commercial and residential real estate markets.

(d) Principal-to-principal market—Principal-to-principal transactions, both originations and resales, are negotiated independently with no intermediary. Little information about those transactions may be released publicly.

Market inputs shall be determined on the basis of information that is timely, originated from sources independent of the entity and used by marketplace participants in making pricing decisions. Examples of market inputs that may be used, directly or indirectly as a basis for deriving other relevant inputs, include the following: **E11**

(a) quoted prices, whether quoted in terms of completed transaction prices, bid and asked prices, or rates, adjusted as appropriate. The fair value hierarchy (paragraphs E12-E24) specifies whether and, if so, when adjustments to those prices are appropriate.

(b) information about interest rates, yield curve, volatility, prepayment speeds, default rates, loss severity, credit risk, liquidity and foreign exchange rates.

(c) specific and broad credit data and other relevant statistics (industry and other), including a current published index.

Fair value hierarchy

The fair value hierarchy groups into three broad categories (levels) the inputs that should be used to estimate fair value. The hierarchy gives the highest priority to market inputs that reflect quoted prices in active markets for identical assets and liabilities (whether such prices are quoted in terms of completed transaction prices, bid and asked prices, or rates) and the lowest priority to entity inputs developed on the basis of an entity's own internal estimates and assumptions.   **E12**

Level 1 estimates

Fair value shall be estimated using quoted prices for identical assets or liabilities in active reference markets whenever that information is available. Quoted prices used for a Level 1 estimate shall not be adjusted.   **E13**

For an identical asset or liability, the Level 1 reference market is the active market to which an entity has immediate access (in many cases, the principal trading market for the asset or liability being measured). *Immediate access* means that an entity could exchange the asset or liability in its current condition at the quoted price in that market within a period that is usual and customary for transactions involving such assets or liabilities. If the entity has immediate access to multiple active markets with different prices, the Level 1 reference market is the most advantageous market, ie the market with the price that maximises (or minimises) the net amount that would be received (or incurred) in a current transaction for an asset (or liability). For the purposes of determining the most advantageous market, costs to transact in the respective markets shall be considered. However, the price used to estimate fair value, ie the price in the most advantageous market, shall not be adjusted for those costs. Transaction costs shall be accounted for in accordance with the provisions of other applicable pronouncements, generally in the period incurred.   **E14**

E15   In an active dealer market where bid and asked prices are more readily and regularly available than closing prices, fair value shall be estimated using bid prices for long positions (assets) and asked prices for short positions (liabilities). For offsetting positions, mid-market prices shall be used for the matched portion. Bid and asked prices shall be used for the net open position, as appropriate.

E16   In some cases in which significant events (for example, principal-to-principal or brokered trades or significant announcements) occur after the close of the market but before the end of the reporting period, the closing price in that market might not be representative of fair value. An entity shall establish and apply consistently a policy for determining how those events affect estimates of fair value.

Level 2 estimates

E17   If quoted prices for identical assets or liabilities in active markets are not available, fair value shall be estimated using quoted prices for similar assets or liabilities in active markets, adjusted as appropriate for differences, whenever that information is available.

E18   For a Level 2 estimate, the price effect of the differences must be determinable objectively. For example, an observed price of securitised receivables can be used as a basis for estimating the fair value of unsecuritised receivables of the same type, but only if the price effect of the securitisation (the price effect of the liquidity, security, and other benefits added by securitisation) is determinable objectively. Otherwise, the estimate is a Level 3 estimate.

Level 3 estimates

E19   If quoted prices for identical or similar assets or liabilities in active markets are not available, or if differences between similar assets or liabilities are not determinable objectively, fair value shall be estimated using multiple valuation techniques consistent with the market approach, income approach, and cost approach whenever the information necessary to apply those multiple techniques is available without undue cost and effort.

E20   Level 3 estimates require judgement in the selection and application of valuation techniques and relevant inputs. Only multiple valuation techniques that are applicable or relevant in the circumstances shall be used. If multiple valuation techniques are used, the results of those techniques (ie the respective indications of fair value) shall be evaluated, considering the relevance and reliability of the inputs used. If information necessary to apply multiple valuation techniques is not available without undue cost and effort, the valuation technique that best approximates what an exchange price would be in the circumstances shall be used.

E21   Valuation techniques used for Level 3 estimates shall emphasise market inputs, including quoted prices generated by actual (observable) market transactions, adjusted as appropriate (see paragraph E11). The reasons for adjustments to quoted prices will vary. Examples include the following:

   (a)   A price might not be sufficiently current for a Level 1 or Level 2 estimate (stale price). In determining whether a price is stale, an entity shall consider the timing of the actual transaction, the frequency of other similar transactions, changes in credit conditions, interest rates, and other market conditions during the intervening period and other relevant factors.

(b) The price effect of differences between similar assets (liabilities) might not be sufficiently determinable for a Level 2 estimate.

(c) A price might be quoted in terms of bid and asked prices in a less active market (where the spread between the bid and asked prices is relatively wide).

(d) The underlying transaction might not be representative of a marketplace transaction. That could be the case if, for example, the transaction:

   (i)   occurred under duress (in a forced liquidation transaction or distress sale);

   (ii) was between related parties; or

   (iii) was part of a series of other simultaneous planned or recent transactions between the parties and would have occurred at a different price if not for those other transactions.

(e) Contractual terms might affect the total transaction price (for example, contingent consideration).

(f) A price might need to be adjusted for differences in the unit of account, condition, or location.

Level 3 estimates with significant entity inputs

In some cases, market inputs might not be available without undue cost and effort, requiring the use of significant entity inputs derived from an entity's own internal estimates and assumptions. In those cases, valuation techniques that rely on significant entity inputs may be used for Level 3 estimates, but only as a practical expedient (the fair value measurement objective remains the same). **E22**

BASIS FOR CONCLUSIONS ON
EXPOSURE DRAFT PROPOSED

AMENDMENTS TO
IFRS 3 BUSINESS COMBINATIONS

Comments to be received by 28 October 2005

Contents

Basis for Conclusions

Amendments to IFRS 3 Business Combinations

* * * * *

Differences between the Exposure Drafts published by the IASB and the FASB

Table of Concordance

Note on legal requirements

Basis for conclusions on proposed amendments to IFRS 3 Business combinations

> *ASB note: The IASB's Basis for Conclusions material, which accompanies the exposure draft of proposed amendments to IFRS 3 Business Combinations, is set out below in full. It should be noted though that some of the discussion it contains concerns IASB requirements that have no equivalent in the UK or Republic of Ireland. Footnotes have been used to indicate corresponding requirements in the UK and Republic of Ireland where applicable.*
>
> *All references in this section to 'the Board' and 'Board members' are references to the IASB Board and IASB Board members.*
>
> This Basis for Conclusions accompanies, but is not part of, the draft IFRS.

INTRODUCTION

This Basis for Conclusions summarises the International Accounting Standards Board's considerations in reaching the conclusions in the Exposure Draft of Proposed Amendments to IFRS 3 *Business Combinations*. It includes the reasons why the Board accepted particular approaches and rejected others. Individual Board members gave greater weight to some factors than to others. The considerations and conclusions of the US Financial Accounting Standards Board (FASB) on the issues addressed jointly by the FASB and the IASB, which are similar in most but not all respects, are summarised in the Background Information and Basis for Conclusions on proposed Statement No. 141(R) *Business Combinations* (SFAS 141(R)). **BC1**

The draft revised IFRS 3 is published by the Board as part of its project on business combinations. The Board added the project to its initial agenda in July 2001. The objective of the project is to improve the quality of, and achieve international convergence on, the accounting for business combinations. **BC2**

The project on business combinations is being undertaken in stages. The first phase resulted in the Board issuing simultaneously the current version of IFRS 3 and revised versions of IAS 36 *Impairment of Assets* and IAS 38 *Intangible Assets**. *In developing IFRS 3 the Board carried forward without reconsideration some of the requirements in the predecessor standard IAS 22 Business Combinations.* The Board's primary focus in that process was on: **BC3**

(a) the method of accounting for business combinations;
(b) the initial measurement of the identifiable assets acquired and liabilities and contingent liabilities assumed in a business combination;
(c) the recognition of liabilities for terminating or reducing the activities of an acquiree;
(d) the treatment of any excess of the acquirer's interest in the fair value of identifiable net assets acquired in a business combination over the cost of the combination; and
(e) the accounting for goodwill and intangible assets acquired in a business combination.

*ASB footnote: The ASB's proposals for implementation of IAS 36 Impairment of Assets *and IAS 38* Intangible Assets *are set out in FRED 38 and FRED 37.*

BC4   The second phase is being conducted as a joint project with the FASB. It involves a broad reconsideration of the requirements in IFRSs and US generally accepted accounting principles (US GAAP) on applying the purchase method (which the draft revised IFRS 3 refers to as the acquisition method). An objective of the second phase of the project is to reconsider existing guidance on the application of the acquisition method in order to improve the completeness, relevance, and comparability of financial information about business combinations that is provided in financial statements. Another objective of this phase is to achieve convergence of IFRSs and US GAAP on how the acquisition method is applied.

BC5   The second phase also addresses how the acquisition method should be applied to business combinations involving only mutual entities and to combinations achieved by contract alone. A business combination achieved by contract alone includes combinations in which separate entities are brought together by contract to form a dual listed corporation.

BC6   The IASB and FASB deliberated concurrently on each of the fundamental issues in the second phase of the project. They reached the same conclusions on all of those issues. The application of some requirements of the draft revised IFRS 3 and the proposed SFAS 141(R) may differ, however, because of differences in:

(a)   other accounting standards to which the draft revised IFRS 3 and proposed SFAS 141(R) refer. For example, recognition and measurement requirements for some assets acquired and liabilities assumed refer to existing standards rather than fair value measures. The proposed revision of IFRS 3 requires a deferred tax asset or liability to be recognised in accordance with IAS 12 *Income Taxes**. *The proposed FASB SFAS 141(R) requires a deferred tax asset or liability to be recognised in accordance with FASB Statement No. 109 Accounting for Income Taxes* (SFAS 109).

(b)   disclosure practices between the IASB and the FASB. For example, the FASB requires additional disclosures and unaudited supplementary information, although these are limited to public entities. The IASB has no similar requirements for unaudited information and does not distinguish between public and non-public entities.

(c)   transition provisions for changes to past accounting practices that previously differed under IFRSs and US GAAP.

The substantive differences that remain are described in the note *Differences between the Exposure Drafts published by the IASB and the FASB* on page 70.

BC7   The second phase has resulted in the Board publishing simultaneously the draft revised IFRS, which proposes to replace IFRS 3, together with an Exposure Draft of Proposed Amendments to IAS 27 *Consolidated and Separate Financial Statements* and an Exposure Draft of Proposed Amendments to IAS 37 *Provisions, Contingent Liabilities and Contingent Assets* (to be retitled *Non-financial Liabilities*)†. The Board's intention in developing the proposed amendments to IAS 27 is to reflect only those changes related to its decisions in the second phase of the Business Combinations project, and not to reconsider all of the requirements in IAS 27. The changes proposed to IAS 27 deal primarily with the accounting for increases and decreases in ownership interests in subsidiaries after control is obtained and the

*ASB footnote: The corresponding UK and Republic of Ireland requirements are set out in FRS 16 Current Tax *and FRS 19* Deferred Tax.

†ASB footnote: The corresponding UK and Republic of Ireland requirements are set out in FRS 2 Accounting for Subsidiary Undertakings *and FRS 12* Provisions, Contingent Liabilities and Contingent Assets *(to be retitled* Non-financial Liabilities*).*

accounting for the loss of control of subsidiaries. Similarly, the Board's intention in developing the proposed amendments to IAS 37 is not to reconsider all of the requirements in IAS 37. Some of those proposed changes arise from the second phase of the Business Combinations project, with the remainder arising from the Board's Short-term Convergence project. The changes arising from the second phase of the Business Combinations project result from the Board's reconsideration of the treatment in a business combination of the contingencies of an acquiree. The changes arising from the Short-term Convergence project are focused on narrowing the differences between IFRSs and US GAAP in the timing of the recognition of liabilities for costs associated with restructurings.

The draft revised IFRS 3 proposes to carry forward without reconsideration some   **BC8** conclusions reached in the development of IFRS 3. They include the requirements to use the acquisition method of accounting and to identify an acquirer for all business combinations. They also include the notion of 'identifiability' for recognising an intangible asset separately from goodwill. Thus, the sections of the Basis for Conclusions in the current IFRS 3 related to those matters remain relevant. However, because the Board did not redeliberate and is not seeking comments on those conclusions, this Basis for Conclusions does not repeat those sections.

The Board will consider the following issues as part of future phases of its project on   **BC9** business combinations:

(a)   the accounting for business combinations in which separate entities or businesses are brought together to form a joint venture, including possible applications of 'fresh start' accounting.

(b)   the accounting for business combinations involving entities under common control.

A single accounting standard

In July 2004 the FASB and the IASB agreed to develop jointly a single standard on   **BC10** accounting for business combinations that could be used for both cross-border and domestic financial reporting. The boards decided that financial reporting would be improved if they had similar standards for accounting for business combinations.

Originally, the boards did not plan to reconsider jointly all of the issues addressed in   **BC11** their separate phase I projects on which they had reached similar, but not identical, decisions. However, having decided to develop a single standard on accounting for business combinations, the boards agreed that reaching a converged position on most aspects of the single standard was of primary importance. Therefore, the boards focused their efforts on eliminating points of divergence that were identified in the process of drafting the single standard. These included agreeing on converged definitions of a business combination and goodwill, and guidance on identifying the acquirer.

The draft revised IFRS 3 and draft SFAS 141(R) incorporate the decisions reached   **BC12** in the joint project. They also incorporate the guidance from the existing business combinations standards, which reflects the decisions made in the separate first phases of the Business Combinations project. The boards expect that their guidance in this single standard will differ only to the extent there are differences in application resulting from the factors identified in paragraph BC6.

FUNDAMENTAL PRINCIPLES UNDERLYING THE DRAFT REVISED IFRS 3

BC13   As noted in paragraph BC8, the draft revised IFRS 3 proposes to carry forward without reconsideration the primary provisions of IFRS 3 including its requirement for all business combinations to be accounted for by applying the acquisition method. The Board did, however, examine inconsistencies that have resulted from the application of the acquisition method.

BC14   Under the acquisition method in IFRS 3 a business combination is recognised at its cost. That cost is measured by the acquirer as the aggregate of the fair values, at the date of exchange, of assets given, liabilities incurred or assumed, and equity interests issued by the acquirer, in exchange for control over the acquiree plus any costs directly attributable to the business combination. The cost is then allocated among the individual identifiable assets and liabilities of the acquiree on the basis of their fair values.

BC15   In a business combination in which the acquirer obtains control of a 100 per cent interest in the acquiree, in a single transaction, the acquirer recognises in its consolidated financial statements all of the goodwill at the date of acquisition. In a business combination in which the acquirer obtains control of less than all of the equity interest of the acquiree, the acquirer recognises all of the acquiree's identifiable assets and liabilities at their full fair values but only its portion of the goodwill.

BC16   Furthermore, IFRS 3 requires that for a business combination achieved in stages each exchange transaction is treated separately by the acquirer, using the cost and fair value information at the date of each exchange transaction, to measure any goodwill associated with that transaction. This results in a step-by-step comparison of the cost of the individual investments with the acquirer's interest in the fair values of the acquiree's identifiable assets and liabilities at each step. As a result, goodwill is a mixture of some current exchange prices and some carry-forward book values for each earlier purchase. Therefore, the amount of goodwill recognised in a business combination achieved in stages and in a business combination achieved in a single transaction will not be the same.

BC17   The Board believes these inconsistencies result in information that is not as complete or as useful as it would be without them. Obtaining control over an acquired entity makes the acquirer accountable for all of the acquiree's assets and liabilities—not just those that are identifiable and not just its proportionate share of those assets and liabilities. Therefore, the Board decided that the measurement objective in accounting for business combinations should be the fair value of the acquiree on the acquisition date rather than the costs incurred in a business combination. Moreover, the Board concluded that the same measurement principle—measuring the business at its fair value—should apply whether the acquiree is acquired in an exchange transaction or through other means.

BC18   The Board believes that the principles underlying IFRSs should strive to reflect the underlying economics of transactions and events. The Board therefore concluded that financial reporting and the relevance of information about business combinations could be improved significantly by developing fundamental principles that focus on the underlying economic circumstances that exist when a business is acquired and applying them consistently. The Board decided that the following fundamental principles should be applied in accounting for all business combinations:

(a) *The acquirer obtains control of the acquiree at the acquisition date and thereby becomes responsible and accountable for all of the acquiree's assets, liabilities and activities, regardless of the percentage of its ownership in the acquiree.* The Board concluded that obtaining control of a business is an event that should result in remeasurement regardless of how control is obtained. Thus, to provide information that is both relevant and reliable, the acquirer's accounting for those assets, liabilities and activities begins at the acquisition date and, if the acquirer held a non-controlling equity investment in the acquired entity, its accounting for that interest as an investment should cease.

(b) *The total amount to be recognised for the acquiree should be the fair value of the acquiree as a whole.* The Board concluded that this faithfully and consistently reflects the underlying economic value of the business acquired, regardless of the ownership interest in the acquiree at the acquisition date or whether control was achieved in stages (involving two or more purchases of ownership interests in the acquiree) or whether a purchase occurred on the acquisition date.

(c) *Business combinations generally are exchange transactions in which knowledgeable, unrelated willing parties are presumed to exchange equal values.* The Board concluded that, in the absence of evidence to the contrary, the consideration transferred by the acquirer on the acquisition date is presumed to be the best evidence of the fair value of its interest in the acquiree at that date. If the consideration transferred is not the best evidence of the acquisition-date fair value of the acquirer's interest in the acquiree, the acquirer should measure that fair value directly using valuation techniques.

(d) *The identifiable assets acquired and liabilities assumed in a business combination should be recognised at their fair values on the date control is obtained.* The Board concluded that this faithfully reflects the underlying economic circumstances at that date.

The draft revised IFRS 3 reflects, where possible, the Board's application of these fundamental principles in accounting for all business combinations. The Board decided that it was necessary, in some circumstances, to depart from the principles. For example, the proposed IFRS requires some assets and liabilities to be measured in accordance with another standard. The exceptions are discussed in paragraphs BC117–BC150.

The Board also concluded that the full amount of goodwill will be recognised in a business combination, rather than goodwill only to the extent of the acquirer's interest in the acquiree. This is consistent with recognising the full amount of the net identifiable assets acquired. **BC19**

The Board concluded that, by focusing on the principles in paragraph BC18, the draft revised IFRS 3 will, if adopted, lead to significant improvements in financial reporting without imposing undue costs. In particular, the Board believes that the emphasis on accounting for business combinations at the acquisition date (rather than on a basis of accumulating costs) is consistent with its commitment to develop standards that result in similar transactions and circumstances being accounted for in a similar way. **BC20**

In considering the benefits and costs of any new standard, the Board is mindful that its standards should emphasis fundamental principles and strive to avoid exceptions, particularly those that add undue complexities and costs. The Board concluded that the draft IFRS's focus on the principles in paragraph BC18 accomplishes that objective. It also believes that the exceptions to those principles have been appropriately limited to those that are necessary, at this time, and minimise disruptions to the continuity of reporting practice. **BC21**

BC22   The following sections discuss the Board's decisions with respect to the application of the principles to specific aspects of accounting for business combinations.

DEFINITION OF A BUSINESS COMBINATION

BC23   Initially the Board did not plan to reconsider the definition of a business combination in this phase of the Business Combinations project. However, as discussed above, the decision to develop a single standard on accounting for business combinations prompted the Board to reconsider it, given that it was an area of divergence for the boards.

BC24   The FASB decided, in this project, to define a business combination as a transaction or other event in which an acquirer obtains control over one or more businesses. This is broader than the definition in FASB Statement No. 141 *Business Combinations* (SFAS 141) because it includes all events and transactions that result in one entity obtaining control of a business, regardless of the form of the transaction. It includes, for example, obtaining control through the lapse of minority veto rights without a purchase of the net assets or equity interests of the acquiree.

BC25   A business combination is defined in IFRS 3 as the bringing together of separate entities or businesses into one reporting entity. The Board observed that this definition could be read to include circumstances in which there may not be an economic event or transaction that triggers a business combination. Consequently, there may not be a change in an economic entity per se. Rather, a business combination could take place when entities or businesses are brought into one reporting entity.* This could occur when, for example, an individual decides to prepare combined financial statements for all or some of the entities that he or she controls. The Board concluded that the definition of a business combination in IFRS 3 is too broad and that a business combination should be described in terms of an economic event rather than in terms of consolidation accounting. The Board decided that the FASB's proposed definition meets this condition.

BC26   However, the Board observed that the FASB definition focuses on control being the factor that triggers a business combination. In developing IFRS 3 the Board concluded that the definition of a business combination should be broad enough to encompass all transactions or other events in which separate entities or businesses are brought together into one reporting entity, regardless of the form of the transaction. The Board intended its definition of a business combination to be broader than transactions in which one entity obtains control of another (or others). For example, the definition in IFRS 3 includes formations of joint ventures and any other 'bringing together' that does not involve one entity obtaining control of another. As noted in paragraph BC39 of IFRS 3, at that time the Board:

> ...decided that it should not, in the first phase of its project, rule out the possibility of a business combination occurring (other than a combination involving the formation of a joint venture) in which one of the combining entities does not obtain control of the other combining entity or entities (often referred to as a 'true merger' or 'merger of equals').

BC27   Although the definition was intended to be broad, IFRS 3 then excluded formations of joint ventures from its scope. The Board agreed that it will consider formations of joint ventures as part of future phases of its project on business combinations.

Paragraph 8 of the Framework *states that it is concerned with the financial statements of reporting entities, and that a reporting entity is 'an entity for which there are users who rely on the financial statements as their major source of financial information about the entity'.*

Furthermore, IFRS 3, like SFAS 141, requires a single method to be applied in accounting for all business combinations in its scope—the acquisition method. Paragraph BC39 of the Basis for Conclusions on IFRS 3 notes: **BC28**

> After considering all the information and arguments put before it, including case studies drawn from situations encountered in practice, the Board concluded that most business combinations result in one entity obtaining control of another entity (or entities) or business(es), and therefore that an acquirer could be identified for most combinations.

As a result, the FASB's proposed definition and the IFRS 3 definition in conjunction with the scope exclusion for joint ventures would result in the same transactions or events being accounted for as business combinations using the acquisition method. **BC29**

In developing SFAS 141 the FASB also considered the accounting for true mergers or mergers of equals and concluded that all business combinations result in one entity obtaining control of another; that is, true mergers are very rare. Paragraph 42 of the Basis for Conclusions on SFAS 141 states: **BC30**

> The [FASB] Board concluded that 'true mergers' or 'mergers of equals' are nonexistent or so rare as to be virtually nonexistent, and many respondents agreed. Other respondents stated that even if a true merger or merger of equals did occur, it would be so rare that a separate accounting treatment is not warranted. They also stated that developing the criteria necessary to identify those transactions simply would be a continuation of the same problems and potential for abuse evidenced by Opinion 16....The [FASB] Board further observed that respondents and other constituents were unable to suggest an unambiguous and nonarbitrary boundary for distinguishing true mergers or mergers of equals from other two-party business combinations and concluded that developing such an operational boundary would not be feasible. Moreover, even if those mergers could feasibly be distinguished from other combinations, the [FASB] Board concluded that it does not follow that such combinations should be accounted for on a carry-over basis. If they were to be accounted for using a method other than the purchase method, the [FASB] Board believes that a better method would be the fresh-start method.

The IASB agreed with the FASB's conclusion that true mergers, if they exist, would be very rare. The Board observed that almost all business combinations portrayed as mergers of equals by the combining entities resulted in one of the parties undoubtedly obtaining control over the other combining entity after the combination. Therefore, the Board agreed with the FASB's conclusion that virtually all business combinations result in one entity obtaining control of another entity (or entities) or business(es). As a result, the Board decided to adopt the FASB's definition of a business combination. **BC31**

Even though the new definition focuses on control, all business combinations included in the scope of IFRS 3 are within the scope of the draft revised IFRS 3. Like IFRS 3 and SFAS 141, the proposed IFRS will continue to require the acquisition method to be applied to those rare combinations, if any, for which one of the combining entities does not obtain control of the other combining entity. However, the Board noted that it is committed to exploring in a future phase of its Business Combinations project whether the 'fresh start' method might be applied to these combinations. **BC32**

As noted in paragraph BC4, the Board decided to replace the term 'purchase method' that was previously used to describe the method of accounting for business **BC33** combinations with the term 'acquisition method'. The Board concluded that 'acquisition method' better describes circumstances in which an acquirer obtains control of a business through means other than a purchase of its net assets or equity interests. In other words, a business combination could occur in the absence of a purchase.

DEFINITION OF A BUSINESS

BC34 IFRS 3 precludes accounting for a transaction as a business combination if the entity or entities over which the acquirer obtains control does not constitute a business. This provision is carried forward into the draft revised IFRS 3.

BC35 Before IFRS 3 was issued, IFRSs did not include a definition of a business. In response to suggestions from respondents to the Exposure Draft ED 3 *Business Combinations*, IFRS 3 includes guidance on identifying when an entity or a group of assets or net assets constitutes a business.

BC36 The IASB and the FASB decided to develop a converged definition of a business and related guidance. As a starting point, the boards considered the definition of a business and the related guidance in the US Emerging Issues Task Force (EITF) Issue 98-3 *Determining Whether a Nonmonetary Transaction Involves Receipt of Productive Assets or of a Business*. When the Board issued IFRS 3, it decided to adopt the definition of a business, and limited guidance, on the basis of conclusions reached in the joint discussions by the boards to that date. Paragraphs BC12-BC15 of the Basis for Conclusions on IFRS 3 discuss those conclusions.

BC37 The draft revised IFRS 3 proposes changes to the definition and guidance in IFRS 3 on the basis of joint decisions of the boards. Specifically, the proposed IFRS includes a modification to the definition of a business to clarify that an integrated set of activities and assets does not need to be conducted and managed for the purpose specified in the definition, as long as it is capable of being conducted and managed for those purposes. In other words, the acquired set is assessed as it exists at the acquisition date rather than how it was used by the seller or how it might be used by the buyer. This change is intended to clarify that a business need not include all of the inputs or processes that the seller used in operating that business if a willing acquirer is capable of operating the business, for example, by integrating the business with its own inputs and processes.

BC38 The Board concluded that the presumption in the definition in IFRS 3 that when goodwill is present in a transferred set of activities and assets, the transferred set is presumed to be a business is, in essence, guidance about determining whether a group of assets constitutes a business. That presumption has been moved to the application guidance in Appendix A of the draft IFRS.

BC39 The proposed application guidance also clarifies the meanings of the terms 'inputs', 'processes' and 'outputs'. It clarifies that inputs and the processes applied to those inputs are essential to a business and that even though the resulting outputs are normally present they need not be. Therefore, an integrated set of assets could qualify as a business if the integrated set of activities and assets is capable of being conducted and managed for the purpose of providing either a return to investors or dividends, lower costs or other economic benefits to owners, members or participants.

BC40 The Board concluded that it should clarify when a group of assets, or net assets, constitutes a business because the accounting differs. Specifically:

(a) in the accounting for an acquisition of a group of assets, or net assets, that does not constitute a business, the objective is to recognise those assets at cost. That cost is allocated to the individual assets acquired and liabilities assumed on the basis of their relative fair values at the date of the acquisition.
(b) no goodwill is recognised.
(c) the cost of the assets can include related transaction costs.
(d) intangible assets acquired in an asset acquisition are recognised in accordance with the requirements of IAS 38 *Intangible Assets,* rather than the requirements of the draft IFRS.

The Board discussed whether the principles in the draft revised IFRS 3 should also apply to acquisitions of all asset groups, avoiding the need to distinguish between groups of assets that are businesses and groups that are not. The Board concluded that, conceptually, acquisitions of all groups of assets should be accounted for in the same way and therefore the guidance in the draft revised IFRS 3 is appropriate for all asset acquisition transactions. Although the Board expressed a preference for expanding the scope of the proposed revised IFRS 3 to acquisitions of asset groups it noted that further research and deliberations of additional issues would be required. The Board decided not to extend the scope to acquisitions of all asset groups because to do so would delay implementation of the proposals.
BC41

SCOPE

The draft revised IFRS 3, like IFRS 3, excludes from its scope the formation of a joint venture and combinations involving businesses under common control. The Board will consider the accounting for these business combinations as part of the future phases of its Business Combinations project. The Board will also consider whether and, if so, when to apply 'fresh start' accounting in the absence of a change in control.
BC42

The FASB draft SFAS 141(R) also excludes from its scope business combinations between not-for-profit organisations or acquisitions of for-profit businesses by not-for-profit organisations. The Board concluded that a similar scope exclusion is not necessary for the proposed IFRS because IFRSs, generally, do not address not-for-profit activities in the private sector, public sector or government.
BC43

The draft revised IFRS 3 removes the scope exclusion in IFRS 3 for business combinations:
BC44

(a) involving only mutual entities; and
(b) achieved by contract alone, without the acquirer purchasing or otherwise obtaining any of the acquiree's net assets or equity interests.

Originally, business combinations involving only mutual entities or achieved by contract alone were not included in the second phase of the Business Combinations project. The Board intended to deal with these transactions as part of future phases of the project. However, in 2004 the Board added these transactions to the scope of the joint project.
BC45

The Board's considerations in reaching its conclusion that business combinations involving only mutual entities and combinations achieved by contract alone should be accounted for using the acquisition method are outlined in paragraphs BC179-BC199.
BC46

METHODS OF ACCOUNTING FOR BUSINESS COMBINATIONS

BC47   In IFRS 3, the Board adopted a single-method approach for accounting for business combinations that is fundamentally different from the approaches that existed under the predecessor standard IAS 22. The single-method approach required by IFRS 3 reflects the Board's conclusion that virtually all business combinations are acquisitions. The draft revised IFRS 3 carries forward that conclusion.

BC48   Paragraphs BC37–BC55 of IFRS 3 discuss the basis for that conclusion, including the reasons for requiring the acquisition method and rejecting the pooling of interests method.

APPLICATION OF THE ACQUISITION METHOD

BC49   Paragraph 9 of the draft revised IFRS 3 identifies four basic steps in applying the acquisition method of accounting for a business combination. They are:

   (a)   identifying the acquirer;
   (b)   determining the acquisition date;
   (c)   measuring the fair value of the acquiree; and
   (d)   measuring and recognising the individual assets acquired and the liabilities assumed.

Identifying the acquirer

BC50   Paragraph 10 of the draft IFRS carries forward without reconsideration the requirement in IFRS 3 that an acquirer is to be identified in every business combination. Paragraphs BC56–BC66 of IFRS 3 discuss the related considerations and deliberations that led to the Board's conclusions and guidance in IFRS 3.

BC51   IFRS 3 and SFAS 141 include similar, but not identical, guidance for identifying the acquirer. However, because the guidance is worded differently, the boards were concerned that differences in identifying the acquirer could arise. The boards decided to develop common guidance for identifying the acquirer. The intention of the boards is to confirm and clarify their guidance but not to change its substance.

Measuring the fair value of the acquiree

BC52   Paragraph 19 of the draft revised IFRS 3 requires the acquirer in a business combination to measure 'the fair value of the acquiree, as a whole, as of the acquisition date'. Like IFRS 3, the draft IFRS reflects the belief of the Board that, as a general principle, exchange transactions should be accounted for at the fair values of the items exchanged.

BC53   The Board observed in paragraph BC44 of IFRS 3 that because the exchange transaction is assumed to result from arm's length bargaining between independent parties, the values exchanged are presumed to be equal. The draft revised IFRS 3 carries forward this fundamental conclusion. The Board agreed that measurement of the values exchanged could be based on the fair value of the consideration given or the fair value of the net assets acquired, whichever is more reliably measurable.

BC54   To help reduce the costs of implementing the proposed IFRS, and to promote greater consistency in the techniques used in measuring the fair value of an acquiree, the Board decided that the draft revised IFRS 3 should provide guidance for applying its fair value measurement principle.

Using the fair value of consideration to measure the fair value of the acquiree

To facilitate the implementation of the proposed IFRS, the Board concluded that it should: **BC55**

(a) include the presumption that the consideration transferred by the acquirer for its interest in the acquiree generally provides the best basis for measuring that interest; and

(b) provide guidance illustrating how the fair value of the consideration transferred for less than 100 per cent of the equity interests of an acquiree, together with other available information, might be used to estimate the fair value of the acquiree as a whole.

The Board has agreed that business combinations, generally, are exchange transactions in which knowledgeable, unrelated willing parties are presumed to exchange equal values. Thus, in the absence of evidence to the contrary it can be presumed that the fair value of the consideration transferred is representative of the fair value of the acquirer's interest in the business. The Board also believes that evidence of the fair value of consideration transferred by the acquirer is equally if not more reliably measurable than the fair value of the acquiree and generally is more readily available to the acquirer or obtainable at a lower cost. The Board acknowledges that some entities, generally those with active acquisition programmes, may have valuation professionals on their staffs with the expertise and ability to measure reliably the fair value of a potential acquiree at relatively low cost. Nonetheless, the Board believes that presuming that the fair value of consideration transferred by the acquirer is a reliable measure, in the absence of evidence to the contrary, is a reasonable way to mitigate the costs to the many entities that do not have these internal resources.   **BC56**

The Board also believes that emphasis on use of the consideration transferred as an appropriate basis for determining the fair value of the business as a whole will avoid or minimise: **BC57**

(a) unproductive disputes in practice about whether the consideration transferred or another valuation technique provides the best evidence and basis for estimating the fair value of the business in those circumstances in which both measurement techniques provide sufficiently reliable estimates.

(b) incremental costs, for example, to verify independently valuations of the business that were performed by the acquirer as part of its due diligence but are not necessarily audited.

The Board also concluded that in acquisitions of less than 100 per cent of the equity interests of the acquiree, it is often appropriate for the acquirer to measure the fair value of the acquiree as a whole on the basis of the consideration transferred for its interest. This indirect measurement of the fair value of the acquiree as a whole is more likely to be appropriate as the proportion of the interest being acquired increases. Acquisitions exceeding 80 per cent of the ownership interests in an acquiree are common in the US, for example. The Board acknowledges, however, that an acquirer may obtain control of an acquiree through a transaction involving a relatively small percentage of the acquiree's equity interest or, in some cases, through an event that results in control without purchasing any equity interests. Accordingly, the draft revised IFRS 3 acknowledges that in those circumstances measuring the fair value of the acquiree may require the use of other techniques.   **BC58**

Using other valuation techniques to measure the fair value of the acquiree

BC59   The draft revised IFRS 3 notes that in some business combinations, either no consideration is transferred or the evidence indicates that consideration transferred is not the best basis for measuring the acquisition-date fair value of the acquirer's interest in the acquiree. In those business combinations, the acquirer should measure the acquisition-date fair value of its interest in the acquiree using other valuation techniques. The presumption and guidance which emphasises the use of the consideration transferred by the acquirer is not intended to override the requirement to measure and recognise the fair value of the acquiree as a whole at the acquisition date.

BC60   In circumstances in which consideration is difficult to measure, the acquiring entity is likely to incur costs to determine the fair value of the acquiree as a whole and an incremental cost to have that measure verified independently. The Board observed that in many of those circumstances entities will already have incurred these costs as part of their due diligence procedures. For example, an acquisition of a privately held business by another privately held entity is often accomplished by an exchange of equity shares that do not have observable market prices. For the purposes of determining the exchange ratio those entities generally engage advisers and valuation experts to assist them in valuing the acquiree as well as the equity transferred by the acquirer in exchange for the shares of the acquiree. Similarly, a combination involving only mutual entities is often accomplished by an exchange of member interests of the acquirer for all of the member interests of the acquiree. In many, but not necessarily all, of those cases the directors and managers of the entities also assess the relative fair values of the combining entities to ensure that the exchange of member interests is equitable to the members of both entities.

BC61   The Board believes that the incremental measurement costs that the revised IFRS 3 might impose are justified. The Board reached that conclusion on the basis of its assessment of overall improvements in financial information. Those improvements include the increased relevance and understandability of information resulting from measuring all businesses acquired as a whole at their acquisition-date fair value, which is consistent with reflecting the change in economic circumstances that occurs at that date.

BC62   The Board also concluded that the proposed IFRS should provide guidance on how to measure the fair value of the acquiree using valuation techniques. This decision is consistent with the objective of providing broadly applicable measurement guidance. Paragraphs A18–A23 and Appendix E of the draft revised IFRS 3 provide that guidance.

BC63   The Board was concerned that some acquirers of mutual entities might neglect to consider relevant assumptions that marketplace participants would make about future member benefits when measuring fair value of the entity. For example, an entity acquiring a co-operative entity should consider the value of the member discounts in its determination of fair value. Accordingly, the Board decided to include guidance (paragraphs A24–A26) that discusses special considerations when measuring the fair value of mutual entities.

Measuring specific items and determining whether they are part of the consideration transferred for the acquiree

BC64   Paragraphs BC65-BC89 summarise the Board's considerations and decisions related to issues raised about (a) the components of consideration that are often transferred by acquirers and can be more difficult to measure, and (b) whether costs incurred by acquirers in connection with an acquisition are part of the consideration transferred for the acquiree. Paragraphs BC154-BC160 summarise the Board's considerations related to determining which assets acquired and liabilities assumed in connection with a business combination are part of the exchange for the acquiree.

Measurement date for equity securities

The draft revised IFRS 3 carries forward the requirement in IFRS 3 that equity **BC65** interests issued by the acquirer as consideration in a business combination should be measured at the acquisition date. The boards diverged on this matter, with the FASB measuring equity interests issued by the acquirer as consideration in a business combination at the agreement date.

The IASB and the FASB considered the agreement date and acquisition date models **BC66** in their deliberations. Both boards observed that there are valid conceptual arguments for measuring equity interests at the agreement date or the acquisition date. However, the boards concluded that reaching a converged answer on the measurement date was of primary importance. The FASB agreed to change, to require that equity interests issued by an acquirer as consideration in a business combination should be measured at their fair value at the acquisition date. As a consequence all consideration transferred by an acquirer is to be measured at its acquisition-date fair value.

Contingent consideration

IFRS 3 requires equity instruments issued and liabilities incurred by the acquirer in **BC67** exchange for control of the acquiree to be measured at fair value. An exception to this principle is a requirement relating to the acquirer's obligation for contingent consideration. That requirement, which was carried forward into IFRS 3 from IAS 22 without reconsideration, takes a cost accumulation approach to accounting for contingent consideration. The Board decided to reconsider this treatment in developing the draft revised IFRS 3.

Under IFRS 3, when a business combination agreement provides for an adjustment **BC68** to the consideration that is contingent on future events, the acquirer includes that adjustment in the measurement of consideration at the acquisition date only if it is probable and can be measured reliably. If the required level of probability or reliability for recognition occurs only after the acquisition date the additional consideration is treated as an adjustment to the accounting for the business combination and to goodwill at that later date. Therefore, unlike other forms of consideration, an obligation for contingent consideration is not measured at its fair value at the acquisition date and its remeasurement results in an adjustment to the business combination accounting. The Board concluded that this approach ignores the fact that the acquirer's agreement to make contingent payments is the obligating event in a business combination transaction.

Contingent consideration arrangements are used by buyers and sellers to reach an **BC69** agreement by sharing specified economic risks related to uncertainties about future outcomes. Differences in the views of the buyer and seller about those uncertainties can be reconciled by their agreeing to share the risks in ways that result in additional payments to the seller for favourable future outcomes and no, or lower, payments for unfavourable outcomes.

BC70   The Board concluded that by not recognising, at the acquisition date, the acquirer's obligation for contingent payments, the economic consideration exchanged at that date would not be fairly represented. The Board decided that obligations for contingent consideration should be measured and recognised at fair value at the acquisition date.

BC71   The Board considered arguments that it might be difficult to measure the fair value of the contingent obligation at the acquisition date. The Board acknowledges that measuring the fair value of some contingent payments may be difficult, but it concluded that to delay recognition of, or otherwise ignore, assets or liabilities that are difficult to measure would cause financial reporting to be incomplete. The Board concluded that excluding an obligation related to a contingent payment diminishes the usefulness of financial reporting and fails to represent faithfully the economics of the business combination transaction.

BC72   The Board noted that most contingent consideration arrangements are financial instruments. It concluded that classifying obligations for contingent consideration as either an equity instrument or as a financial liability in accordance with IAS 32 *Financial Instruments: Disclosure and Presentation** would improve transparency in reporting these financial instruments. Accordingly, the Board decided to remove a scope exception in paragraph 4(c) of IAS 32. As a consequence, if a contingent consideration arrangement is a financial instrument it should be classified as a financial liability, a financial asset or an equity instrument in accordance with IAS 32.

BC73   The Board also noted that some contingent consideration arrangements require the acquirer to deliver its equity securities if specified future events occur. Application of IAS 32 to those arrangements means that obligations for contingent payments classified as equity will not be remeasured after the acquisition date.

BC74   The Board observed that obligations for contingent consideration classified as a financial liability would often meet the definition of a derivative. The Board noted that many contingent consideration arrangements are similar or identical to contracts that are otherwise subject to the requirements in IAS 39 *Financial Instruments: Recognition and Measurement†*.

BC75   To improve transparency in reporting these instruments, the Board concluded that all contingent consideration contracts that meet the definition of a financial instrument should be subject to the requirements of IAS 39. Therefore, it decided to eliminate the exception in paragraph 2(g) of IAS 39 that excluded contingent consideration in a business combination from its scope. Thus, under IAS 39, liabilities for contingent consideration that meet the definition of a derivative would be remeasured, after the acquisition date, at fair value with changes in fair value recognised in accordance with IAS 39.

BC76   The Board also considered whether changes in the measurement of liabilities for contingent consideration should be reflected as an adjustment to the consideration transferred and, normally, goodwill. The Board noted that the measurement objective of a business combination is to recognise the fair value of the acquiree on the acquisition date and that measuring contingent consideration at its fair value, at

---

*ASB footnote: *The corresponding requirements for the UK and Republic of Ireland are set out in FRS 25 (IAS 32)* Financial Instruments: Disclosure and Presentation.

†ASB footnote: *The corresponding requirements for the UK and Republic of Ireland are set out in FRS 26 (IAS 39)* Financial Instruments: Recognition and Measurement.

that date, is consistent with that objective. The Board acknowledges that a conclusive determination of the fair value of any liability for contingent consideration may not be practicable, in the limited circumstances in which particular information is not available at the acquisition date. As discussed in paragraphs BC161-BC163, in those circumstances the draft revised IFRS 3 provides for the provisional measurement of the fair value of assets acquired or liabilities assumed and consideration transferred, including obligations for contingent payments. The provisional values are adjusted for changes that are determined during the measurement period (after the acquisition date) as if the accounting for the business combination had been completed at the acquisition date.

Moreover, the Board concluded that subsequent changes in the fair value of a lia- **BC77** bility for contingent consideration do not affect the acquisition-date fair value of the consideration transferred for the acquiree. Rather, the Board believes that those subsequent changes in value are, generally, more likely to be related to post-combination events and changes in circumstances related to the combined entity.*

The Board also considered arguments that the approach it had adopted will result in: **BC78**

(a)   the recognition of gains in the income statement when the specified milestone or event requiring the contingent payment is not met. For example, the acquirer would record a gain on the reversal of the liability if an earnings target in an earnout arrangement is not achieved.

(b)   the recognition of losses in the income statement for subsequent changes in the fair value of liabilities for contingent consideration that some believe are directly attributable to changes in the fair value of the business acquired and, thus, should be capitalised as part of the acquired entity.

The Board accepts that recognising the fair value of a liability for contingent pay- **BC79** ments is likely to result in a gain if smaller or no payments are required or in a loss if greater payments are required. The Board believes that this is a consequence of entities entering into contingent consideration arrangements in which the underlying in the arrangement relates to future changes in the fair value of a specified asset or liability or net income of the acquiree after the acquisition date.†

Share-based compensation replacement awards of the acquirer

Paragraphs A109-A116 provide guidance for circumstances in which an acquirer is **BC80** obligated to exchange its share-based payment awards for those of an acquiree. The

---

The Board also acknowledges, however, that some changes in fair value might result from events and circumstances that may relate to a pre-combination period, but the extent of the change is indistinguishable from that part related to the post-combination period. The Board concluded that, in those limited circumstances, the benefits in information that might result from making such fine distinctions in practice would not justify the costs that such a requirement would impose.

†*The Board observed that liabilities for contingent payments may be related to contingencies surrounding an outcome for a particular asset or other liability. In those cases, the effects on income of changes in estimates of the fair value related to the liability for the contingent payment may be offset by changes in the fair value of the asset or other liability. Assume, for example, that after an acquisition the combined entity reaches a very favourable settlement of pending litigation of the acquiree for which it had a contingent consideration arrangement. If the combined entity is required to make a contingent payment to the seller of the acquiree of an amount greater than the carrying amount (fair value) of the liability to the seller, the effect of the increase in that liability and charge to income may be offset in part by the reduction to the liability to the litigation claimant and the credit to income resulting from that favourable settlement. Similarly, assume the acquirer is not required to make a contingent payment to the seller because an acquired research and development project failed to materialise into a viable product. In that case, the gain resulting from the elimination of the liability may be offset, in whole or in part, by an impairment charge for the asset acquired.*

Board decided that the draft revised IFRS 3 should provide implementation guidance for those transactions because:

(a)   difficulties could arise in judging the extent to which replacement awards are for past services (and, therefore, part of the consideration for the business) or future services (and, therefore, not part of the consideration for the business).

(b)   the proposed IFRS and IFRS 2* are new Standards and, therefore, implementation difficulties could be encountered in practice.

BC81   The Board believes that the guidance in the draft revised IFRS 3 is consistent with the objective that the measure of the consideration transferred should include those payments that are in exchange for the business and exclude those payments that are not. Payments for future services that former owners, officers and employees may provide to the acquirer are not payments for the business acquired.

BC82   The Board also acknowledges that although the guidance in the proposed IFRS is consistent with the FASB's basic guidance, some details are different. The boards arrived at different conclusions on how replacement of vested awards granted by the acquiree with non-vested acquirer awards should be allocated between the consideration transferred in the business combination and compensation expense.

BC83   The FASB concluded that the requisite service period of awards issued by the acquirer should be taken into consideration reflecting any explicit, implicit and derived service periods. In contrast, the Board concluded that the entire period of service rendered before the business combination should be taken into account to determine the allocation between compensation expenses and consideration. The *requisite service period* will often, but not always, result in the same total service period. The boards decided to accept this divergence at this time because it stems from differences in their other standards, and is a matter outside the scope of the joint project on business combinations.

Costs incurred in connection with a business combination

BC84   The Board considered whether costs that an acquirer incurs in connection with a business combination are part of the consideration transferred in exchange for the acquiree. Those costs (commonly called acquisition-related costs) can include the costs of services of lawyers, investment bankers, accountants, and other third parties and the issue costs of debt or equity instruments used to effect the combination.

BC85   The Board concluded that acquisition-related costs are not part of the fair value exchange between the buyer and seller for the business. Rather, they are separate transactions in which the buyer makes payments in exchange for services rendered. The Board observed that these costs, whether for services performed by external parties or internal staff of the acquirer, generally do not represent assets of the acquirer, because they are consumed as the services are rendered.

BC86   Thus, the draft revised IFRS 3 specifies that the acquirer must account for acquisition-related costs separately from the business combination. Under IFRS 3, the cost of an acquired entity includes direct costs incurred for an acquisition of a business but excludes indirect costs. Indirect costs can include recurring internal costs such as maintaining an acquisitions department and, although those costs can be attributable to a successful acquisition, they are recognised as an expense as incurred. Furthermore, direct costs incurred in unsuccessful negotiations are also

*ASB footnote: *The corresponding requirements for the UK and Republic of Ireland are set out in FRS 20 (IFRS 2) *Share-based Payment.

recognised as an expense as incurred. The changes proposed resolve these inconsistencies.

The Board considered the argument that acquisition-related costs, including costs of **BC87** due diligence, are an unavoidable cost of the investment in a business. As with other investments, the acquirer intends to recover these costs through the post-acquisition operations of the business and considers these costs in determining the amount it is willing to pay for the acquiree. On this basis it could be argued that acquisition-related costs should be capitalised as part of the total investment in the business. The Board did not agree with this argument. The Board was not persuaded that the seller of a business is willing to accept less than fair value as consideration for its business merely because a particular buyer may incur more (or less) acquisition-related costs than other potential buyers for that business. The Board concluded that the intention of a buyer, including how acquisition-related costs are expected to be recovered, is distinct from fair value measurement of the acquiree.

The Board acknowledges, that under some IFRSs, direct acquisition-related costs **BC88** would be included as part of the carrying amount of the asset acquired. The Board also acknowledges that the treatment of acquisition-related costs should be similar for acquisitions of an individual asset, a group of assets and a business. However, as noted in paragraph BC41, the Board decided not to extend the scope of the draft revised IFRS 3 to acquisitions of all asset groups. The Board accepts that, at this time, recognising as an expense acquisition-related costs differs from some accepted practices that allow direct acquisition-related costs to be included in the cost of an acquired asset. The Board concluded, however, that the proposed IFRS will improve financial reporting by eliminating inconsistencies in accounting for acquisition-related costs in connection with a business combination.

The Board also considered arguments that, if acquirers can no longer capitalise **BC89** acquisition-related costs as part of the cost of the business acquired, they may attempt to avoid recognising those costs as expenses. For example, a buyer might ask a seller to make payments to the service providers on its behalf. To facilitate the negotiations the seller might agree to make those payments, provided the agreed price includes an amount sufficient to reimburse the seller for payments it made on the buyer's behalf. If the disguised reimbursements were treated as part of the consideration for the business those expenses might not be recognised by the acquirer. Rather, the amount recognised for goodwill could be overstated. To mitigate these concerns, the Board decided to clarify in the draft revised IFRS 3 that the portion of any payments to an acquiree (or its former owners) in connection with a business combination that are payments for goods or services that are not part of the acquired business should be assigned to those goods or services and accounted for as if separately acquired. As discussed in paragraphs BC154-BC160, the Board also decided that the proposed IFRS should require an assessment to determine whether any portion of the amounts transferred by the acquirer are not part of the consideration transferred in exchange for the acquiree.

Measuring and recognising the assets acquired and the liabilities assumed

Paragraphs BC91-BC102 discuss the Board's considerations in concluding that the **BC90** probability and reliability of measurement recognition criteria need not be included in the draft IFRS. Paragraphs BC103-BC110 discuss the Board's proposals for application of the fair value measurement principle for the recognition of assets acquired and liabilities assumed.

Recognition criteria

BC91   IFRS 3 requires the acquiree's identifiable assets and liabilities to be recognised separately if they can be measured reliably and if it is probable that any related future economic benefits will flow to, or resources embodying economic benefits will flow from, the acquirer. For the reasons explained in paragraphs BC92-BC97, the Board decided not to include the probability and reliability of measurement recognition criteria in the proposed IFRS.

Probability recognition criterion

BC92   IFRS 3 specifies that an acquirer should recognise the acquiree's identifiable assets (other than intangible assets) and liabilities only if it is probable that the asset or liability will result in an inflow or outflow of economic benefits. The draft revised IFRS 3 does not contain this probability recognition criterion and hence proposes that the acquirer should recognise identifiable assets acquired and liabilities assumed regardless of the degree of probability of an inflow or outflow of economic benefits.

BC93   The concept of probability is used in the recognition criteria in the *Framework** to refer to the degree of uncertainty that the future economic benefits associated with the asset or liability will flow to or from the entity.

BC94   As discussed in paragraphs BC115 and BC116 (and more fully in paragraphs BC35-BC47 of the Basis for Conclusions on the accompanying proposed amendments to IAS 37), during the development of the draft revised IFRS 3 the Board reconsidered items previously described in IAS 37 as contingent assets and contingent liabilities. The Board observed that by analysing the rights or obligations in such items into conditional and unconditional rights or obligations, it is possible to address better the question of whether the entity has an asset or a liability at the acquisition date. As a result, the Board concluded that many items previously described as contingent assets or contingent liabilities meet the definition of asset or liability in the *Framework*, because they contain unconditional rights or obligations as well as conditional rights or obligations.

BC95   The Board observed that when the unconditional right in an asset (or unconditional obligation in a liability) is identified, the question to be addressed is what is the inflow (or outflow) of economic benefits relating to the unconditional right (or unconditional obligation) rather than the conditional right (or conditional obligation).

BC96   The Board noted that the *Framework* articulates the probability recognition criterion in terms of a flow of economic benefits rather than just direct cash flows. It concluded that, if an entity has an unconditional obligation, it is certain that there will be an outflow of economic benefits from the entity, even if there is uncertainty about the timing and the amount of the outflow of benefits associated with the conditional obligation. Hence, when the *Framework*'s probability recognition criterion is applied to the liability (ie unconditional obligation), it is satisfied. The Board's arguments apply equally to unconditional rights. Thus, if an entity has an unconditional right, it is certain that there will be an inflow of economic benefits and again the probability recognition criterion is satisfied.

*ASB footnote: *The equivalent document in the UK and Republic of Ireland to the IASB's* Framework *is the ASB's* Statement of Principles for Financial Reporting. *Although the* Statement of Principles *is very similar to the* Framework, *it is not identical.*

The Board therefore decided that inclusion of the probability criterion in the draft **BC97** revised IFRS 3 is unnecessary because in all cases an unconditional right or obligation satisfies the criterion. In addition, the Board proposed consequential amendments to IAS 38 *Intangible Assets* (paragraphs 25 and 33) to clarify the reason for the Board's conclusion that the probability recognition criterion is always considered to be satisfied for intangible assets that are acquired separately or in a business combination. Specifically, the Board stated that an intangible asset acquired separately or in a business combination embodies an entity's unconditional right to future economic benefits. The uncertainty is about the timing and the amount of the inflow.

Reliability of measurement recognition criterion

IFRS 3 states that any asset acquired or liability assumed in a business combination **BC98** must be able to be measured reliably to be recognised. The Board decided not to include an equivalent statement in the draft revised IFRS 3 because it is a criterion for recognition in the *Framework*.

The Board reconsidered the reliability of measurement criterion for intangible assets **BC99** and decided to remove it. This is because the Board concluded that sufficient information should exist to measure reliably the fair value of an intangible asset, as discussed in paragraphs BC100-BC102.

Reliability of measurement of intangible assets

IFRS 3 requires an intangible asset acquired in a business combination to be able to **BC100** be measured reliably for it to be recognised separately from goodwill. SFAS 141 does not have a similar requirement. Therefore, the Board reconsidered whether to retain the reliability of measurement criterion for intangible assets.

When IFRS 3 was developed, the Board noted that the fair value of intangible assets **BC101** acquired in a business combination can normally be measured with sufficient reliability to be recognised separately from goodwill. When there is a range of possible outcomes with different probabilities, that uncertainty enters into the measurement of the asset's fair value rather than demonstrating an inability to measure fair value reliably. IAS 38 includes a rebuttable presumption that the fair value of a intangible asset with a finite useful life acquired in a business combination can be measured reliably. The Board concluded that it might not always be possible to measure reliably the fair value of an asset that has an underlying contractual or legal basis and, therefore, decided to retain the reliability of measurement criterion. However, IAS 38 provides that the only circumstances in which it might not be possible to measure reliably the fair value of an intangible asset acquired in a business combination are when the intangible asset arises from legal or other contractual rights and either:

(a) is not separable; or
(b) is separable, but there is no history or evidence of exchange transactions for the same or similar assets, and otherwise estimating fair value would be dependent on immeasurable variables.

In developing this draft IFRS, the Board noted that the divergence between its own **BC102** conclusions and the FASB's results in a difference in classification of assets as indefinite-lived intangible assets rather than as goodwill. The Board agreed with the FASB that the usefulness of financial statements would be enhanced if intangible assets acquired in a business combination were distinguished from goodwill. The

Board concluded that an estimate of fair value and the separate recognition of intangible assets, rather than subsuming them in goodwill, provides better information to the users of financial statements, even though a significant degree of judgement could be involved in determining that fair value. Reliability of measurement is a criterion for recognition in the *Framework*. For these reasons, and for the sake of convergence, the Board decided to propose consequential amendments to IAS 38 (paragraphs 33A-35) to remove the reliability of measurement criterion for intangible assets acquired in a business combination.

Fair value recognition and measurement principle

BC103   The Board considered the process required by IFRS 3 to allocate amounts to assets acquired and liabilities assumed in a business combination. That process requires the acquirer to measure initially the assets and liabilities recognised at their fair values at the acquisition date. Therefore, any minority interest in the acquiree is stated at the minority's proportion of the net fair value of those assets and liabilities. IFRS 3 also requires the excess of the cost of the business combination over the acquirer's interest in the net fair value of the identifiable assets and liabilities to be recognised as goodwill.

BC104   That allocation is based on the estimated fair values of the assets and liabilities at the acquisition date. When it issued IFRS 3, the Board carried forward, without reconsideration, the general guidance in IAS 22 for allocating amounts to assets acquired and liabilities assumed. As a result, paragraph B16 of IFRS 3 states:

> This IFRS requires an acquirer to recognise the acquiree's identifiable assets, liabilities and contingent liabilities that satisfy the relevant recognition criteria at their fair values at the acquisition date. For the purpose of allocating the cost of a business combination, the acquirer shall treat the following measures as fair values:...

BC105   The Board acknowledged at that time that some of the guidance for allocating the cost of the business combination conflicted with the general principle of recognising at fair value assets acquired and liabilities assumed, and observed in paragraph BC153 of IFRS 3:

> ...although conceptually any guidance on determining the values to be assigned by the acquirer to the acquiree's identifiable net assets should be consistent with a fair value measurement objective, this is not currently the case under IFRSs.

> ....it is reconsidering as part of the second phase of its Business Combinations project those requirements in IFRSs that result in the acquirer initially recognising identifiable net assets acquired at amounts that are not fair values but are treated as though they are fair values for the purpose of allocating the cost of the combination.

BC106   The Board decided to include guidance for measuring fair value in the form of a hierarchy (referred to as the fair value hierarchy), which is contained in Appendix E. The Board noted that including the fair value hierarchy and related guidance in the proposed IFRS will improve the relevance and comparability of information provided about the assets acquired and liabilities assumed in a business combination. However, for cost/benefit reasons, the Board decided that the revised IFRS 3 should provide exceptions to the application of the fair value measurement and recognition principles. More specifically, the Board decided that the proposed IFRS should:

(a) require some assets and liabilities to continue to be measured in accordance with existing IFRSs and goodwill to continue to be measured as a residual.*

(b) clarify that separate recognition of assets and liabilities is not required for the offsetting executory rights and obligations for an acquiree's operating leases.

During the course of this joint project, the FASB added a fair value measurements **BC107** project to its agenda. The objective of that project is to develop a Statement that defines fair value and establishes a framework for applying the fair value measurement objective in US GAAP. The project focuses on 'how' to measure fair value, not 'what' to measure at fair value. In June 2004 the FASB published the Exposure Draft of Proposed SFAS *Fair Value Measurements*. That Exposure Draft incorporates the fair value hierarchy developed initially by the boards in the second phase of the Business Combinations project. The FASB's draft SFAS 141 (R) refers to that Exposure Draft for fair value guidance.

To ensure consistent application of the hierarchy to business combinations in IFRSs **BC108** and US GAAP, the Board decided to include parts of the FASB's *Fair Value Measurements* Exposure Draft in the draft revised IFRS 3. The sections are designed to help users apply the fair value hierarchy and include the definition of fair value and additional guidance about 'willing', 'knowledgeable' and 'unrelated parties', the guidance on valuation techniques and market inputs and the definition of an active market.

The exposure period for the Proposed SFAS *Fair Value Measurements* has ended and **BC109** the FASB has begun redeliberating fair value measurement issues. It plans to issue the final Statement on *Fair Value Measurements* in the near future. The FASB's Website includes updated information about the status of the FASB's decisions.

The Board intends to redeliberate any issues that emerge from the FASB's final **BC110** Statement *Fair Value Measurements* and, where appropriate, amend the fair value guidance in Appendix E before issuing the proposed IFRS on business combinations.

Guidance for assets acquired and liabilities assumed

Paragraphs BC112-BC116 set out the Board's conclusions on the application of the **BC111** fair value measurement principle to assets acquired and liabilities assumed.

Valuation allowances

IFRS 3 provides that, in determining the fair value of receivables, the acquirer **BC112** should use the present values of the amounts to be received, determined at appropriate current interest rates, less allowances for uncollectibility and collection costs, if necessary.

In developing the draft revised IFRS 3, the Board noted that in determining the fair **BC113** value of receivables any uncertainties about the collectibility of receivables should affect their fair value. If receivables are assigned an amount equal to their fair value, there will be no need to recognise separately an allowance for uncollectibility and collection costs.

Assets and liabilities that are to be measured in accordance with other IFRSs rather than at their fair values include: (a) assets (disposal group) that qualify as assets held for sale, (b) deferred tax assets and liabilities, and (c) employee benefit obligations. Under the draft revised IFRS 3 goodwill would be measured as the excess of the fair value of the business acquired over the net amount of the fair values of the recognised identifiable assets acquired and liabilities assumed.

BC114 Therefore, using an acquiree's carrying basis and including collection costs is inconsistent with the fair value measurement principles in the draft IFRS. The Board concluded that the acquirer should not recognise a separate valuation allowance for uncollectible amounts in its initial measure of the acquisition-date fair value of an acquiree's receivables. Any uncertainty about collections and future cash flows is included in the fair value measure.

Contingencies

BC115 The draft revised IFRS 3 requires the acquirer to measure and recognise at the acquisition date the assets acquired and liabilities assumed as part of the business combination even if the amount of the future economic benefits embodied in the asset or required to settle the liability are contingent (or conditional) on the occurrence or non-occurrence of one or more uncertain future events not wholly within the control of the entity.

BC116 This requirement is consistent with the Board's proposed amendments to IAS 37 relating to contingencies. The Board proposes eliminating the terms 'contingent asset' and 'contingent liability'. Instead of using the word 'contingent' to refer to uncertainty about whether a liability exists, the Board proposes to use it to refer to one or more uncertain future events, the occurrence or non-occurrence of which affects the amount of the future economic benefits embodied in an asset or required to settle a liability. The Board's amendments to IAS 37 clarify that many items previously described as contingent assets or contingent liabilities satisfy the *Framework*'s definition of an asset or a liability. Therefore, such items are recognised in a business combination.

Exceptions to the fair value measurement principle

BC117 The Board decided to allow exceptions to the application of the fair value measurement principle, primarily because of cost/benefit or practicability concerns. The exceptions, and the reasons for allowing each, are described in paragraphs BC118-BC150.

Assets (disposal group) held for sale

BC118 The Board decided that non-current assets (or a disposal group) acquired in a business combination that qualify as held for sale, in accordance with IFRS 5 *Non-current Assets Held for Sale and Discontinued Operations*, should be measured at fair value less costs to sell in accordance with that IFRS. The Board was concerned that a requirement in the draft revised IFRS 3 to measure those assets at fair value at their acquisition date would lead to the immediate recognition of a loss. Applying IFRS 5 would require expected costs to sell to be recognised immediately as an expense. The Board concluded that reporting a loss in relation to those costs would not present fairly the activities of the acquirer during that period. Accordingly, the proposed IFRS requires these qualifying assets to be measured on initial recognition at fair value less costs to sell and that after initial recognition IFRS 5 will apply.

Deferred tax assets and liabilities

BC119 The draft revised IFRS 3 requires deferred tax assets and liabilities to be measured and recognised in accordance with IAS 12 *Income Taxes*, as proposed to be amended, rather than at their acquisition-date fair values. Under IAS 12, deferred tax assets and liabilities generally are to be measured and recognised at the current period undiscounted settlement amounts. The Board decided not to require deferred tax assets and liabilities acquired in a business combination to be measured at fair value because it observed that:

(a)   if those assets and liabilities were measured at their acquisition-date fair values, without any change in the underlying economic circumstances, their subsequent measurement under IAS 12 would result in post-combination gains or losses in the period immediately following the acquisition. The Board concluded that this would not faithfully represent the results of the post-combination period, and would be inconsistent with the notion that a business combination that is a fair value exchange should not give rise to the immediate recognition of post-combination gains or losses.

(b)   to measure those assets and liabilities at their acquisition-date fair values and overcome the problem noted in (a) would require a comprehensive consideration of whether and how to modify the requirements of IAS 12 for the subsequent measurement of deferred tax assets or liabilities acquired in a business combination. The Board concluded that the complexities of IAS 12, and the difficulties that tracking deferred tax assets acquired and liabilities assumed in a business combination would create, do not warrant a comprehensive reconsideration of IAS 12 as part of this joint project.

The Board decided, however, to address three income tax accounting issues in connection with business combinations. They are the acquirer's accounting for (a) a change in the probability of realising the acquirer's deferred tax asset as a result of a business combination, (b) deferred tax benefits acquired in a business combination that did not satisfy the criteria for separate recognition when a business combination was initially accounted for, but are subsequently realised, and (c) tax benefits arising from tax-deductible goodwill in excess of financial reporting goodwill.   **BC120**

The Board considered the first issue because there is a difference between the requirements of IAS 12 and those of SFAS 109. At present, under SFAS 109, effects of changes in the probability of realising the acquirer's deferred tax asset are included as part of the business combination accounting. IAS 12 currently provides that: **BC121**

> As a result of a business combination, an acquirer may consider it probable that it will recover its own deferred tax asset that was not recognised before the business combination. For example, the acquirer may be able to utilise the benefit of its unused tax losses against the future taxable profit of the acquiree. In such cases, the acquirer recognises a deferred tax asset, but does not include it as part of the accounting for the business combination, and therefore does not take it into account in determining the goodwill ...

The Board confirmed that any changes in the acquirer's deferred tax asset that result from a change in the acquirer's circumstances upon a business combination should be accounted for as a separate event and, thus, excluded from the business combination accounting. The Board concluded that this is consistent with the requirements in paragraphs 66 and 67 of the draft revised IFRS 3 relating to the assessment of whether other assets and liabilities are part of the business combination. The business combination model focuses on measuring and recognising the fair value of the acquiree and the Board believes that the acquirer's deferred tax asset is an attribute of the *acquirer* rather than the *acquiree*. This decision results in the retention of the guidance in paragraph 67 of IAS 12. The FASB agreed to converge with the Board on this issue.   **BC122**

The Board also considered the situation when, as a result of the business combination, it may no longer be probable that sufficient taxable profit will be available to   **BC123** allow the benefit of part or all of the acquirer's deferred tax asset to be utilised. The Board concluded that an acquirer should reduce the carrying amount of a deferred tax asset to the extent that it is no longer probable that it will be realised. The reduction should also not be part of the accounting for the business combination.

BC124   As a result, the acquirer would recognise the effect of a change in the probability of realising the deferred tax asset in profit or loss or, if IAS 12 so requires, in equity in the period of the business combination. The Board considered this issue because of its commitment to convergence with the FASB. Under SFAS 109 effects of changes in the probability of realising the acquirer's deferred tax asset are included as part of the business combination. The FASB decided to converge with the Board on this issue.

BC125   The Board believes that the change in the measurement of deferred tax that is the consequence of a business combination is information useful to investors. Accordingly, it decided to amend IAS 12 to require disclosure of that change.

BC126   The second issue relates to deferred tax benefits acquired in a business combination that did not satisfy the criteria for separate recognition when a business combination was accounted for initially, but are subsequently realised. Under IFRS 3, the acquirer recognises that benefit and reduces the carrying amount of goodwill to the amount that would have been recognised if the deferred tax asset had been recognised as an identifiable asset at the acquisition date.

BC127   In developing the draft revised IFRS 3, the Board concluded that goodwill should not be reduced for the subsequent recognition of deferred tax benefits acquired in a business combination. The change in the value of deferred tax benefits is likely to be a consequence of events occurring after the acquisition. Therefore, the effect of these events should not be part of the accounting for the business combination. The Board concluded that this decision is consistent with accounting for other assets acquired and liabilities assumed. Any changes in those assets and liabilities that occur as a result of events and circumstances that arise after the acquisition are not accounted for as adjustments to the initial accounting for a business combination.

BC128   However, the Board decided that if acquired deferred tax benefits are recognised within one year after the acquisition date they are more likely to be a result of a more thorough assessment of the probability of realising deferred tax benefits acquired in a business combination than a subsequent event. Therefore, the Board decided to propose an amendment to IAS 12 introducing a rebuttable presumption that acquired deferred tax benefits recognised within one year of the acquisition date should be applied to reduce the carrying amount of any goodwill related to that acquisition. If the carrying amount of that goodwill is zero, the remaining deferred tax benefits are credited to profit or loss or, if IAS 12 requires, to equity.

BC129   The third issue relates to circumstances in which the carrying amount of goodwill arising in a business combination is less than its tax base. Under IAS 12 this difference gives rise to a deferred tax asset. The Board decided to clarify in IAS 12 that the deferred tax asset arising from the initial recognition of goodwill should be recognised as part of the accounting for a business combination to the extent that it is probable that taxable profit will be available against which the deductible temporary difference could be utilised.

Operating leases

The Board considered whether to require the recognition of the acquiree's rights **BC130**
related to its operating leases in which the acquiree is the lessee separately from its
obligations. This would require, for example, recognition of an asset for an
acquiree's rights to use assets according to the lease agreement, including related
renewal options and other rights, and a liability for its obligations to make lease
payments. Under IAS 17 *Leases*, these rights and obligations are not recognised as
assets and liabilities. The Board concluded that, because it is not prepared at this
time to address how the asset and the liability for an operating lease would be
accounted for after the acquisition date, consistency in lease accounting should take
primacy over consistency in the application of the fair value measurement requirement in the draft revised IFRS 3. Therefore, the asset and the liability arising from
an operating lease would not be recognised on a gross basis.

The Board clarified that an acquirer should recognise, as part of the combination, an **BC131**
intangible asset or a liability for the favourable or unfavourable portion of an
operating lease if an acquired operating lease is not at market terms (regardless of
whether the acquiree is the lessee or lessor).

Employee benefit obligations

The Board decided that assets and liabilities arising from post-employment benefits **BC132**
assumed in a business combination that are within the scope of IAS 19 *Employee
Benefits** should be measured in accordance with that standard rather than at fair
value.

The Board concluded that if, at this time, it required employee benefit obligations **BC133**
assumed in a business combination to be measured at their acquisition-date fair
values it also would need either to reconsider comprehensively the relevant standards
for those employee benefits or, at a minimum, to determine whether accommoda-
tions would be required for their subsequent measurement following the acquisition
date, or both. At this time, the Board does not have an active project plan or the
resources for such an undertaking. Thus, in view of the complexities in accounting
for employee benefit obligations under IAS 19, the Board decided that those benefits
should be measured in accordance with that standard.

Goodwill

The draft revised IFRS 3 carries forward the requirement from IFRS 3 to measure **BC134**
goodwill as a residual and recognise it as an asset. In developing IFRS 3, the Board
concluded that direct measurement of goodwill would not be feasible. Paragraphs
BC129-BC135 of IFRS 3 explain the Board's reasons for that conclusion. The Board
did not reconsider that conclusion as part of the second phase of the Business
Combinations project.

As noted in paragraph BC15 above, the Board considered a present inconsistency in **BC135**
accounting for acquisitions in which less than all of the equity interest is acquired
and, therefore, only a partial interest in goodwill is recognised. This is referred to as
the purchased goodwill method. The Board considered whether information provided by the full goodwill method is relevant. The Board observed that paragraph 26
of the *Framework* states that 'to be useful, information must be relevant to the

*ASB footnote: *The corresponding requirements in the UK and Republic of Ireland are set out in FRS 17*
Retirement and Termination Benefits.

decision-making needs of users. Information has the quality of relevance when it influences the economic decisions of users by helping them evaluate past, present or future events or confirming, or correcting, their past evaluations.' The *Framework* also describes the purpose of consolidated financial statements as follows:

> The economic decisions that are taken by users of financial statements require an evaluation of the ability of an entity to generate cash and cash equivalents and of the timing and certainty of their generation. ..... Users are better able to evaluate this ability to generate cash and cash equivalents if they are provided with information that focuses on the financial position, performance and changes in financial position of an entity. [Paragraph 15]

> The financial position of an entity is affected by the economic resources *it controls*, its financial structure, its liquidity and solvency, and its capacity to adapt to changes in the environment in which it operates. Information about the *economic resources controlled* by the entity and its capacity in the past to modify these resources is useful in predicting the ability of the entity to generate cash and cash equivalents in the future. [Paragraph 16; emphasis added.]

BC136   Therefore, under the *Framework*, the objective of consolidated financial statements is to provide information about the economic resources controlled by the parent. The Board believes that an entity's financial statements provide users with more useful information about the entity's financial position when they include all of the assets under its control, regardless of the extent of ownership interests held.

BC137   The Board had already concluded while developing IFRS 3 that goodwill meets the definition of an asset. Therefore, the assets under the control of a parent should include all of the goodwill of an acquiree, not just the parent's proportionate share.

BC138   Thus, the Board concluded that the full goodwill method is consistent with the concept that control over another entity makes the controlling entity accountable for all of that other entity's assets and liabilities. The Board believes that the full goodwill method is relevant because it is consistent with the control and completeness concepts underlying the preparation of consolidated financial statements.

Measurement

BC139   The draft revised IFRS 3 requires goodwill to be measured as the amount by which the fair value of the acquiree as a whole exceeds the net amount of the fair values of the identifiable assets acquired and liabilities assumed.

BC140   The Board considered whether application difficulties could arise in measuring goodwill, but concluded that calculating full goodwill is not itself difficult. Rather, any difficulties associated with its calculation could stem from problems entities might encounter in measuring either (a) the fair value of the acquiree (or consideration transferred that is used to determine that fair value) or (b) the fair values of the identifiable assets acquired and liabilities assumed as part of the business combination.

BC141   The Board had observed in developing IFRS 3 that goodwill measured as a residual could include overpayments by the acquirer and errors in measuring and recognising the fair value of the identifiable assets acquired and liabilities assumed, or a requirement in a standard to measure those identifiable items at an amount that is not fair value. However, the Board concluded in IFRS 3 that goodwill is likely to consist primarily of core goodwill at the acquisition date, and that recognising it as an asset is more representationally faithful than recognising it as an expense.

Paragraphs BC52-BC63 above provide a fuller discussion of the Board's considerations relating to measuring the fair value of the acquiree as a whole. The Board concluded that the fair value of the acquiree could be measured on the basis of the fair value of the consideration given or measured directly by using valuation techniques. The Board also decided to provide additional guidance for estimating the fair value of the acquiree as a whole (paragraphs A9-A17).   **BC142**

The Board considered concerns that circumstances surrounding a particular business combination might not provide strong evidence of the fair value of the acquiree as a whole. A particular situation considered was when an acquirer obtains control but the consideration given to obtain control of the acquiree is for much less than a 100 per cent ownership interest in the acquiree. Examples of such circumstances could include: **BC143**

(a) an associate buys back some or all of its equity instruments held by other unrelated equity-holders, resulting in the entity obtaining control of the former associate.

(b) an entity has an ownership interest in an associate and acquires a small additional holding sufficient to give it control of that entity.

The measurement difficulties may be more challenging in circumstances in which there is no consideration exchanged on the date control is obtained, such as those described in example (a) above. The amount of the consideration paid in example (b) would provide evidence of a market-based transaction on the date control is obtained. Although the consideration paid is for a partial ownership interest, it can provide useful evidence for estimating the fair value of the acquiree as a whole.   **BC144**

The Board observed that the purchased goodwill method can have the same measurement difficulties that arise under the full goodwill method. For example, similar measurement difficulties arise if a business combination is effected via a share-for-share exchange between two privately held entities or as described in paragraph BC143(a).   **BC145**

Furthermore, one could argue that similar measurement difficulties might arise when testing goodwill for impairment. Goodwill impairment tests rely on the measurement of the recoverable amount of a cash-generating unit, to which goodwill is allocated. If, as one could argue, it would be burdensome to measure the fair value of the acquiree when the transaction is, for example, an acquisition of a 60 per cent controlling-ownership interest, it could be difficult to justify adopting an 'impairment only' approach for goodwill after initial recognition given that the recoverable amount of a cash-generating unit must be calculated in the absence of transaction-based evidence.   **BC146**

The Board observed that multiple valuation techniques are available and are used in practice, and that the use of multiple techniques provides a way of increasing the reliability of the resulting fair value measure. Therefore, the draft IFRS provides that if either no consideration is transferred on the acquisition date or the evidence indicates that the consideration transferred is not the best basis for measuring the acquisition-date fair value of the acquirer's interest in the acquiree, the acquirer should measure the acquisition-date fair value of its interest using other valuation techniques.   **BC147**

BC148   Thus, the draft revised IFRS 3 eliminates the past practice of omitting the portion of goodwill related to the non-controlling interests in subsidiaries. Because that is a change to present practice, the Board decided to provide guidance that illustrates how goodwill is to be measured and allocated between the controlling and non-controlling interests in an acquiree that is not wholly-owned (paragraphs A66 and A67).

Allocation of goodwill between the controlling and non-controlling interests

BC149   The Board considered three alternatives for allocating goodwill between the controlling and non-controlling interests in an acquisition of a less than wholly-owned acquiree. They are:

(a)   allocate a portion of goodwill to the controlling interest on the basis of the difference between the fair value of the ownership interest acquired (which includes any previous investment held in the acquiree) and the acquirer's share of the fair value of the net identifiable assets acquired, and allocate the remaining portion to the non-controlling interests.

(b)   allocate goodwill to the controlling and non-controlling interests on the basis of their relative ownership interests in the fair value of the acquiree.

(c)   allocate a portion of goodwill first to a reporting unit of the controlling interest that is expected to benefit from synergies of the combination, and then allocate the remainder to the controlling and non-controlling interests on the basis of their relative ownership interests in the fair value of the acquiree.

BC150   The Board decided that goodwill should be allocated on the basis of the first of those alternatives. Thus, as noted in paragraph A66, the amount of goodwill allocated to the acquirer (controlling interest) is to be measured as the difference between the acquisition-date fair value of the acquirer's equity interest in the acquiree and the acquirer's share in the acquisition-date fair value of the separately recognised assets acquired and liabilities assumed. The remainder is to be allocated to the non-controlling interests. The Board noted that each alternative has merits. It concluded that the first alternative reflects best the assumption that any premium paid by the acquirer for control rights that is included in the full amount of goodwill should be allocated to the acquirer's interests, and not to the non-controlling interest. The second alternative would be simple to apply, but would result in a portion of goodwill related to any control premium being allocated to the non-controlling interest. The third alternative would allocate goodwill to the reporting units on the basis of expected benefits but the Board concluded that this approach is likely to be more difficult and costly to apply.

RECOGNISING GAINS OR LOSSES ON NON-CONTROLLING EQUITY INVESTMENTS

BC151   Paragraph 53 of the draft revised IFRS 3 requires, in a business combination achieved in stages, an acquirer to remeasure its non-controlling equity investment at its acquisition-date fair value and to recognise any unrealised gains or losses in income. This decision reflects the Board's conclusion that gaining control of a business is an event that should trigger remeasurement. Specifically, a change from holding a non-controlling investment in an entity to obtaining control of that entity is a significant change in the nature of the economic circumstances surrounding the investment. That change warrants a change in the classification and measurement of the investment. The Board observed that when control of the underlying entity is obtained the acquirer is no longer the owner of a non-controlling investment asset in that entity. As in present practice, the acquirer ceases accounting for an investment asset and begins reporting the underlying assets, liabilities, and results of operations of the acquiree as part of its consolidated results. In effect, the acquirer exchanges its status as an owner of an investment asset for a controlling interest in all of the underlying assets and liabilities of that acquiree.

Paragraph 21(b) of the draft revised IFRS 3 also provides that, for the purposes of measuring the initial fair value of the acquiree as a whole, the fair value of any non-controlling equity investment is regarded as part of the fair value of the consideration transferred. The Board noted that measuring the investment asset at its fair value at the acquisition date—when investment accounting ceases—is consistent with the concept that when one asset is exchanged for another asset the transaction is accounted for on the basis of the fair values of the assets involved (paragraph BC52).

BC152

The Board acknowledges concerns about allowing what some perceive to be an opportunity for gain recognition around the changes in status from investment to subsidiary. The Board notes that remeasurement could also result in recognising a loss. Moreover, the Board disagreed with characterising the resulting gain or loss as arising from a purchase. Rather, under the mixed attribute accounting model that exists today, economic gains and losses are recognised as they occur for some, but not all, financial instruments. If a non-controlling equity interest in an entity is not measured at its fair value, the recognition of a gain or loss at the acquisition date is merely a consequence of the delayed recognition of the economic gain or loss that is present in that financial instrument. However, if an investment asset is measured at fair value under IFRSs, the gain or loss would be recognised as it occurs, and remeasurement would result in no further gain or loss.* The Board decided to require disclosure of the gain or loss on remeasurement of any previously held non-controlling equity interest.

BC153

DETERMINING THAT ASSETS ACQUIRED AND LIABILITIES ASSUMED ARE PART OF THE EXCHANGE FOR THE ACQUIREE

The Board decided that, to improve consistency, the draft revised IFRS 3 should provide guidance for applying its measurement and recognition principle.

BC154

The Board decided to provide application guidance to help address concerns expressed about the difficulty of determining whether the consideration is for the acquiree. Parties involved directly in the negotiations of an impending business combination could take on the characteristics of related parties. As a result, they may be willing to enter into other agreements or include conditions as part of the business combination agreement that are designed primarily to achieve favourable post-combination reporting outcomes. Because of those concerns the Board decided to develop an overall principle that should be considered when assessing a particular transaction or arrangement entered into by the parties to the combination.

BC155

The Board concluded that if a transaction or arrangement is designed primarily for the economic benefit of the acquirer or the combined entity (rather than the acquiree or its former owners), that transaction or arrangement is not part of the exchange for the acquiree. Accordingly, those transactions or arrangements should be accounted for separately from the business combination. The Board acknowledges that judgement may be required to determine whether a portion of the transaction price paid, or the assets acquired and liabilities assumed, are not part of the exchange for the

BC156

Paragraph 53 requires that if the acquirer recognised changes in the value of its non-controlling equity investment, before the business combination, directly in equity (for example, the investment was classified as available for sale), the amount that was recognised directly in equity must be reclassified and included in the calculation of any gain or loss as of the acquisition date.

acquiree. Accordingly, the Board decided to include guidance in the draft revised IFRS 3 on factors to be considered in applying the general principle when assessing a business combination. Paragraph A92 of the proposed IFRS identifies those factors as the reason, initiating party and timing of the transaction or event. The Board believes that, although those factors are neither mutually exclusive nor individually conclusive, they can be helpful in considering whether a transaction or event is arranged primarily for the economic benefit of the acquirer or combined entity. Paragraph A92 expands on those factors and paragraphs A93–A116 provide illustrative examples.

BC157   The guidance emphasises that assets acquired or liabilities assumed that are recognised as part of the business combination must be part of the exchange. Paragraph 66 of the draft revised IFRS 3 requires the acquirer to assess whether any portion of the transaction price paid and any assets acquired or liabilities assumed are not part of the exchange for the acquiree. Any portion of the transaction price paid or any assets acquired or liabilities assumed that are not part of the exchange are accounted for separately from the business combination.

BC158   An objective of that assessment is to distinguish consideration that an acquirer transfers for the acquiree from other payments made in connection with the business combination that are for other assets or purposes. To assist in meeting that objective, paragraph 67 of the draft revised IFRS 3 includes three examples of payments or other arrangements that are not part of the exchange for the acquiree; Appendix A provides additional implementation guidance.

BC159   The first example in paragraph 67 is the exclusion of payments that effectively settle pre-existing relationships between the acquirer and acquiree. The example is directed at ensuring that assets and liabilities related to pre-existing relationships between the parties that are not transferred to, or assumed by, the acquirer are excluded from the accounting for the business combination. To illustrate, suppose a potential acquiree had a receivable for an unresolved claim against the potential acquirer and that the acquirer and the acquiree's owner agree to settle that claim as part of an agreement to sell the acquiree to the acquirer. The Board concluded that if the acquirer makes a lump-sum payment to the seller-owner, part of that payment is to settle the claim and is not part of the consideration transferred to acquire the business. Thus, the portion of the payment that relates to the claim settlement should be excluded from the accounting for the business combination and accounted for separately. In effect, the acquiree relinquished its claim (receivable) against the acquirer by transferring it (as a dividend) to the acquiree's owner. Thus, at the acquisition date the acquiree has no receivable to be acquired as part of the combination and the acquirer would account for its settlement payment separately.

BC160   The second and third examples are also directed at illustrating cases in which payments that are not part of the consideration transferred for the acquiree should be excluded from the business combination accounting. Paragraph BC89 also discusses the Board's considerations surrounding the third example—payments to reimburse the acquiree or its former owners for paying the acquirer's costs incurred in connection with the business combination.

MEASUREMENT PERIOD

BC161   In developing IFRS 3, the Board observed that normally it is not possible for an acquirer to obtain before the acquisition date all of the information necessary for the acquirer to complete the initial accounting for a business combination immediately after the acquisition date. Therefore, the Board concluded that IFRS 3 should allow an acquirer some period after the acquisition date to finalise the accounting and adjust any provisional amounts to their subsequently determined acquisition-date fair values. The draft revised IFRS 3 carries forward the provisions from IFRS 3 in paragraphs 59-65, and refers to this period as the measurement period. Those paragraphs also provide guidance to be applied during the measurement period.

The Board decided to place constraints on the period of time for which it is deemed reasonable to be seeking necessary information and concluded that a maximum period of one year is reasonable. **BC162**

The Board acknowledges that many contingencies and similar matters may not be settled within one year. It observes, however, that the objective of the measurement period is to provide time to obtain the information necessary to measure the acquisition-date fair value of the item. The objective is not to determine the ultimate settlement amount of a contingency or other item. Uncertainties about future cash flows are part of the measure of the fair value of an asset or liability. **BC163**

BUSINESS COMBINATIONS IN WHICH THE CONSIDERATION TRANSFERRED FOR THE ACQUIRER'S INTEREST IN THE ACQUIREE IS LESS THAN THE FAIR VALUE OF THAT INTEREST (BARGAIN PURCHASE)

Paragraphs 56–58 of the draft revised IFRS 3 set out the requirements for business combinations in which the fair value of the consideration transferred (paid) by the acquirer is less than the fair value of that interest in the acquiree. IFRS 3 refers to this difference as 'excess'. It is also commonly referred to as negative goodwill. However, bargain purchases have occurred and are likely to continue to occur. They include a forced liquidation or distress sale (for example, death of a founder or key manager) in which owners need to sell a business and are acting under compulsion to sell at less than fair value. **BC164**

In developing IFRS 3, the Board concluded that an excess should rarely exist if the valuations inherent in the accounting for a business combination are properly performed and all of the acquiree's identifiable liabilities and contingent liabilities have been properly identified and recognised. Therefore, when an excess exists, the acquirer is required to reassess the identification and measurement of the acquiree's identifiable assets, liabilities and contingent liabilities and the measurement of the cost of the business combination. **BC165**

The draft revised IFRS 3 carries forward from IFRS 3 a requirement to reassess the identification and measurement of the acquiree's identifiable assets and liabilities and the measurement of the consideration paid. In addition, the proposed IFRS requires remeasurement of the acquisition-date fair value of the acquiree and the acquirer's interest in that acquiree. **BC166**

The Board affirmed that the objective of that requirement is to ensure that appropriate consideration has been given to all available information in identifying the items to be measured and recognised and in determining their fair values. The Board believes that such remeasurement checks will mitigate, if not eliminate, undetected errors that might have existed in the initial measurements. **BC167**

The Board observed in IFRS 3 that any excess remaining after the reassessment could comprise one or more of the following components: **BC168**

(a) errors that remain, notwithstanding the reassessment, in recognising or measuring the fair value of either the cost of the combination or the acquiree's identifiable assets, liabilities or contingent liabilities.

(b) a requirement in an accounting standard to measure identifiable net assets acquired at an amount that is not fair value, but is treated as though it is fair value for the purpose of allocating the cost of the combination.

(c) a bargain purchase. This might occur, for instance, when the seller of a business wishes to exit from that business for other than economic reasons and is prepared to accept less than its fair value as consideration.

BC169   The Board acknowledges that negative goodwill remains a possibility because the draft revised IFRS 3 continues to require that some assets acquired and liabilities assumed should be measured at other than their acquisition-date fair value. The Board observes, however, that the requirements in the proposed IFRS address most shortcomings that may previously have led to negative goodwill being reported that did not have the economic substance of a bargain purchase. For example, before IFRS 3 was issued, a liability accompanied by a contingent liability of an acquiree might not have been recognised at the acquisition date at all. The omission of such liabilities would result in an overstatement of the identifiable net assets acquired and, thus, an equivalent understatement of goodwill. If the omitted liability exceeded the actual goodwill in the acquiree, negative goodwill would result. Similarly, a liability for contingent payment arrangements (for example, earnouts) might not have been recognised at the acquisition date, which, in some cases, could lead to understating the consideration paid and creating the appearance of a bargain purchase. The proposed IFRS reduces the possible errors further by requiring the measurement and recognition of substantially all liabilities at their fair values at the acquisition date.

BC170   Other changes in the draft revised IFRS 3 may also reduce the instances of negative goodwill. When it issued IFRS 3, the Board acknowledged that some of the guidance for allocating the cost of the business combination conflicted with the general principle of recognising assets acquired and liabilities assumed at their fair value. The additional guidance in the proposed IFRS on the fair value hierarchy should help to reduce measurement errors that have, in the past, led to negative goodwill.

BC171   The Board believes that most business combinations are exchange transactions in which each party receives and sacrifices equal value. The Board concluded that the consideration transferred by the acquirer is presumed to be the best evidence of the acquisition-date fair value of the acquirer's interest in the acquiree and should be used as a basis for measuring the fair value of the acquiree. Moreover, the Board noted that a fair value estimate is determined by reference to willing marketplace participants representing unrelated buyers and sellers that are knowledgeable and have a common level of understanding about factors relevant to the business and the transaction, and are willing and able to transact in the same market(s) and have the legal and financial ability to do so. The Board is not aware of any compelling reason to believe that, in the absence of duress, a seller of a business would willingly and knowingly sell a business for less than its fair value. Thus, the Board concluded that applying the proposed fair value measurement requirements will mitigate concerns that negative goodwill might result and be misinterpreted as indicating a bargain purchase.

BC172   However, as discussed above, a business combination in which the fair value of the consideration transferred (paid) by the acquirer is less than the fair value of the interest in the acquiree could be a true bargain purchase. The Board believes that bargain purchases are not common.

The Board decided that because a bargain purchase is unlike a business combination in which willing parties exchange assets (net assets) of equal values, the presumption in paragraph 20 of the draft revised IFRS 3 would not apply to those transactions. That is to say, the Board concluded that the presumption in the proposed IFRS that the amount paid by the acquirer is the best evidence of the acquisition-date fair value of the acquirer's interest and its related measurement guidance are not appropriate for circumstances in which the seller of the business is known to be acting under compulsion. The Board also concluded, however, that the objectives and other principles (paragraph BC18) underlying the proposed IFRS are relevant and apply to a bargain purchase.   **BC173**

The Board also observes that, unlike a typical acquisition of an acquiree, an economic gain is inherent in a bargain purchase. Specifically, the acquirer is better off at the acquisition date by the amount by which the fair value of the acquiree exceeds the fair value of the consideration paid. The Board believes that, in concept, that gain should be recognised by the acquirer at the acquisition date, but decided to place limits on the recognition of gains on a bargain purchase. The Board acknowledges that although the reasons for a forced liquidation or distress sale are often apparent, clear evidence does not always exist. This could occur, for example, if a seller uses a closed (private) process for the sale to maintain its negotiating position rather than reveal the main reason for the sale. The Board also concluded that, because these transactions are expected to be rare, the appearance of a bargain purchase without evidence of the underlying reasons would raise concerns in practice about the existence of measurement errors.   **BC174**

The Board acknowledges that the remeasurement checks discussed above may be insufficient to eliminate its concern about measurement bias. Therefore, the Board decided to address its concern by limiting the gain that can be recognised. Thus, the draft revised IFRS 3 provides that if, after performing the remeasurements required, the fair value of the acquirer's interest in the acquiree still exceeds the fair value of the consideration transferred, the acquirer must account for that excess by reducing goodwill related to that business combination. If goodwill is reduced to zero any remaining excess must be recognised as a gain allocable to the acquirer on the acquisition date. The proposed IFRS also requires disclosure of the amount of any gain recognised and a description of the reasons why the acquirer was able to achieve a gain.   **BC175**

The primary objective of the limitation on gain recognition is to mitigate the potential for inappropriate gain recognition through measurement errors, particularly those that might result from unintended measurement bias. The objective of the disclosure requirement is to provide information that enables users of an acquirer's financial statements to evaluate the nature and financial effect of business combinations that take place during the period. The Board understands from professional analysts and others that disclosing information about revenues, expenses, gains and losses resulting from atypical events and circumstances, such as gains on a bargain purchase transaction, is particularly important for analysing an entity's performance and developing trend information to assess an entity's prospects for generating future earnings and cash flows. The Board also noted that the limitation and disclosure requirements may also help to alleviate concerns about intentional measurement bias, although that is not their primary objective.   **BC176**

The Board recognises concerns that placing limits on gain recognition is not consistent with the fair value measurement principles in the draft revised IFRS 3 and could lead to misrepresenting bargain purchases that are free of measurement errors. In concept, a gain should be recognised without the proposed limitations in those cases in which there is persuasive evidence (such as duress on a seller) that the   **BC177** transaction is a bargain purchase. The Board acknowledges, however, that to apply this distinction could lead to other difficulties in practice. The Board concluded that placing a limit on the gain permitted to be recognised is a practical way to address the problems and concerns raised about measurement errors.

ACQUISITIONS AT MORE THAN THE FAIR VALUE OF THE INTEREST IN THE ACQUIREE (OVERPAYMENTS)

BC178   The Board considered whether the draft revised IFRS 3 should include requirements for accounting for a business combination in which the acquirer pays an amount that is more than the fair value of its interest in the acquiree. The Board observed that this circumstance indicates that the business combination is not an exchange of equal values. However, the Board observed that although an overpayment by the acquirer is a theoretical possibility, it believes that in practice, if it occurs, it will not be detectable or known at the acquisition date. That is to say, the Board is not aware of instances in which a buyer knowingly overpays a seller to acquire a business or is otherwise compelled to make such an overpayment. Rather, the Board believes that an acquirer's overpayment, although rare, occurs unknowingly and generally as a result of misinformation at the acquisition date. Thus, the Board concluded that in practice it might not be possible to identify and measure reliably an overpayment at the acquisition date. The Board concluded that the accounting for overpayments is best addressed through subsequent impairment testing when evidence of a potential overpayment first arises.

COMBINATIONS BETWEEN MUTUAL ENTITIES AND ACHIEVED BY CONTRACT ALONE

BC179   As noted in paragraph BC45, issues relating to business combinations between mutual entities and combinations achieved by contract alone were not included in the original scope of the second phase of the project. The Board intended to deal with such business combinations as part of future phases of the project. However, the Board decided to address the accounting for such combinations as part of this joint project. The reason is that the FASB decided that decisions in the joint project should also apply to business combinations involving mutual entities and achieved by contract alone and, therefore, the scope of a single standard on business combinations became a convergence issue.

Combinations between mutual entities

BC180   The FASB considered issues relating to business combinations between mutual entities as part of its separate *Combinations Between Mutual Enterprises* project, a joint project with the Accounting Standards Board of the Canadian Institute of Chartered Accountants (CICA). The objective of that project was to develop guidance on the accounting for combinations between two or more mutual entities. In that project, the FASB and CICA identified the circumstances particular to mutual entities that may require additional guidance. That approach presumed that a future FASB Statement arising from the second phase of the Business Combinations project should apply to combinations between mutual entities, unless the economic conditions or other circumstances of the combination were found to be so different as to warrant a different accounting treatment or further guidance. The FASB decided that the unique attributes of mutual entities were not sufficient to justify an accounting treatment different from that provided for other entities. Therefore, the FASB decided that the joint project decisions should apply to combinations of mutual entities.

Like the FASB, the Board also considered whether its decisions in this draft IFRS should apply to business combinations between mutual entities by focusing on characteristics that distinguish mutual entities and combinations between mutual entities from other business entities. The Board's focus was on whether such unique circumstances would justify a different accounting treatment. **BC181**

The Board noted that mutual entities have many characteristics in common with other business entities and some distinguishing characteristics. However, the Board observed that the economic motivations for combinations between mutual entities, such as to provide constituents with a broader range of, or access to, services and cost savings through economies of scale, are similar to those for combinations between other business entities. In particular: **BC182**

(a) although mutual entities generally do not have shareholders in the traditional sense of investor-owners, they are in effect 'owned' by their members and are in business to serve their members or other stakeholders. Like other businesses, mutual entities strive to provide their members with a financial return or benefits. However, a mutual entity generally does that by focusing on providing its members with its products and services at lower prices. For example, in the case of credit unions, the benefit may be a lower interest rate on a borrowing than might be obtainable through an investor-owned financial institution. In a wholesale buying co-operative, the benefit might be realised in lower net costs, after consideration of patronage dividends.

(b) interests of members of a mutual entity generally are not transferable like other ownership interests. However, they usually include a right to share in the net assets of the mutual entity in the event of its liquidation or conversion.

(c) a higher percentage of combinations among mutual entities occur without an exchange of cash or other readily measurable consideration. However, that circumstance is not unique to mutual entities. Business combinations without an exchange of cash or other readily measurable consideration also take place between other entities, particularly combinations of private entities.

The Board considered whether differences between the ownership structures of mutual entities (such as mutual insurance companies or mutual co-operative entities) and those of investor-owned entities may give rise to complications in applying the acquisition method to business combinations between mutual entities. The ownership structures of mutual entities vary from a single class of membership shares issued at par value, to more complex structures including various classes of membership and investment shares. The Board observed that this complexity results in some difficult questions when determining the classification as liability or equity of members' and participants' interests in a mutual entity. However, the Board noted that the issue of classification of those interests is not an issue for the Business Combinations project. To the extent that members' and participants' interests meet the definition of a liability in IAS 32, the fair value of that liability assumed should be recognised in accounting for a business combination involving mutual entities. **BC183**

The Board then considered whether mutual entities should be required to apply the proposed IFRS to such transactions, focusing its discussion on three issues that might arise in applying the acquisition method to those transactions. The first was the suggestion that the acquisition method is not appropriate for all combinations between mutual entities. The second was the proposition that it might be difficult to identify the acquirer. The third was the concern that such transactions normally do not involve the payment of any readily measurable consideration. **BC184**

Method of accounting

BC185   As part of the first phase of the Business Combinations project, the Board published an Exposure Draft of Proposed Amendments to IFRS 3 *Business Combinations – Combinations by Contract Alone or Involving Mutual Entities*. The Exposure Draft proposed an interim approach for accounting for these business combinations until the Board considered these issues as part of its second phase of the project.* The Exposure Draft suggested that the acquisition method should be used in accounting for these business combinations.

BC186   In response to the Exposure Draft, some representatives of mutual entities expressed a concern about requiring all combinations of mutual entities to be accounted for as acquisitions. Several respondents suggested that prohibiting the pooling of interests method would discourage combinations between entities affected by the proposals and reduce the amount of capital flowing into their industries. This is because the acquisition method may give the incorrect impression that one entity has become dominant over the other. They suggested, for example, that the requirement to identify an acquirer could prevent mergers of neighbouring mutual entities when both the fact and appearance of a merger of equals are of paramount importance to their directors, members and communities.

BC187   Some respondents to the Exposure Draft noted that the acquisition method may impede combinations because of particular laws and regulatory requirements. For example, some regulatory agencies currently evaluate the financial soundness of credit unions on the basis of their accumulated retained earnings measured by generally accepted accounting principles rather than their total equity capitalisation. Under the pooling of interests method the recognised amount of the retained earnings of each of the combining credit unions is carried forward and, thus, becomes the aggregate retained earnings of the combined entity. Under the acquisition method only the retained earnings of the acquirer are carried forward in the combined entity. Accordingly, credit unions will have a reduced net worth ratio after a combination, which may be below regulatory requirements. This will discourage healthy credit unions from merging with weaker ones (and would indirectly lead to higher failure rates). The implication drawn by respondents was that the pooling of interests method should be retained for public policy reasons.

BC188   The Board affirmed its conclusion in IFRS 3 that there are no circumstances in which the pooling of interests method provides information superior to that provided by the acquisition method. Paragraph 36 of the *Framework* states that to be reliable, the information contained in financial statements must be neutral, and should not influence the making of a decision or judgement in order to achieve a predetermined result or outcome. In this context, neutrality means that accounting standards should neither encourage nor discourage business combinations but, rather, provide information about those combinations that is representationally faithful and even-handed. The Board concluded that eliminating the pooling of interests method and requiring a single method of accounting for all business combinations is consistent with this goal. The Board also concluded that regulatory concerns are not a sufficient reason to grant combinations of mutual entities special treatment vis-à-vis allowing them to apply the pooling of interests method.

BC189   The Board also observed that it concluded in the first phase of its Business Combinations project that applying the acquisition method to combinations involving

In the light of respondents' comments, the Board decided not to proceed with the proposals in the Exposure Draft primarily for reasons of timing and impending consideration of these issues in the second phase of this project.

two or more mutual entities results in providing the users of financial statements with information that is superior to, and more representationally faithful than, the information that would be provided by applying the pooling of interests method to such combinations. Therefore, the Board concluded that the acquisition method should be used in accounting for such combinations.

However, the Board agrees with respondents that for business combinations in which **BC190** one of the combining entities does not obtain control of the other combining entity (assuming such transactions exist), the fresh start method is likely to be more representationally faithful than the acquisition method. But this would be the case irrespective of whether the transaction involves mutual entities, is by contract alone, or involves (for example) the formation of a new entity to issue equity interests to effect the merger of two or more other businesses. As discussed in paragraph BC32, the Board is committed to exploring the fresh start method in the future.

Identifying the acquirer

On the second issue, the Board affirmed its conclusion in IFRS 3 that even though it **BC191** could be difficult to identify an acquirer in some rare circumstances, exceptions to applying the acquisition method should not be permitted. The Board acknowledged that difficulties may arise in identifying the acquirer in combinations of two virtually equal mutual entities. However, it also observed that those difficulties also arise in combinations of two virtually equal investor-owned entities and, thus, are not unique to combinations of mutual entities. The Board concluded that in no circumstances does the pooling of interests method provide superior information to that provided by the acquisition method, even if identifying the acquirer is problematic.

Additionally, the Board concluded that the IFRS 3 indicators for identifying the **BC192** acquirer in a business combination are applicable to combinations of investor-owned entities and mutual entities and that no additional indicators are needed to identify the acquirer in combinations between mutual entities. As a result, the Board affirmed that the provision in IFRS 3 that requires an acquirer to be identified applies to all business combinations, including those between mutual entities.

No payment of any reliably measurable consideration

The Board considered the concern that one of the difficulties in applying the **BC193** acquisition method to such business combinations is that the transactions normally do not involve the payment of cash or any other readily measurable consideration. However, the Board observed that the objective of accounting for a business combination is to determine and recognise the fair value of the business acquired. Although the fair value of the consideration given is, generally, more clearly evident than the fair value of the business acquired, this is not always the case. In some circumstances, the fair value of the consideration given by the acquirer does not provide the best basis for measuring the fair value of the business acquired.

The Board decided that, in such circumstances, the fair value of the acquiree should **BC194** be measured directly using valuation techniques. The Board noted that business combinations without an exchange of cash or other readily measurable consideration also take place between other types of entity. Therefore, although a higher percentage of combinations among mutual entities take place without an exchange of cash or other readily measurable consideration, that circumstance is not unique to mutual entities. The Board concluded that the acquisition method can and should be applied in accounting for business combinations that do not involve the payment of reliably measurable consideration.

BC195   In considering the application of the acquisition method to mutual entities, the Board considered the accounting and reporting for an acquisition in which an acquirer issues equity shares or member interests as consideration in exchange for the equity shares or member interests of an acquiree. The Board observed that in a business combination between two investor-owned entities, if the acquirer issues equity shares as consideration for all of the equity shares of an acquiree, the fair value of the acquiree (its equity or net assets) is recognised as an addition to the equity of the acquirer. Thus, the equity (net assets) of the combined entity is increased from the acquisition of the acquiree (and the fair value of its net assets), but retained earnings of the acquirer are unaffected.

BC196   Some representatives of mutual entities suggested that a similar acquisition of a mutual entity should be allowed to be recognised as an increase in the retained earnings of the acquirer (combined entity) as had been the practice under the pooling method of accounting. The Board rejected that view. The Board believes that business combinations between two investor-owned entities are economically similar to those between two mutual entities in which the acquirer issues member interests for all the member interests of the acquiree. Thus, the Board concluded that those similar transactions should be accounted for on a similar basis. Therefore, paragraph 50 of the draft revised IFRS 3 clarifies that in a business combination involving only mutual entities in which the only consideration exchanged is the member interests of the acquiree for the member interests of the acquirer (or the member interests of the newly combined entity), the amount equal to the fair value of the acquiree must be recognised as a direct addition to capital or equity, not retained earnings.

BC197   As a result of these deliberations, the Board concluded that its decisions in the second phase of the Business Combinations project have addressed the difficulties in applying the acquisition method to business combinations involving two or more mutual entities. Therefore, the Board concluded that the proposed IFRS should provide that such business combinations should be accounted for in accordance with its requirements. The Board also concluded that combinations between mutual entities are economically similar to combinations between other business entities and that there is no need to issue separate application guidance for those business combinations.

Combinations achieved by contract alone

BC198   The Board also concluded that business combinations achieved by contract alone should be included in the scope of the draft revised IFRS 3 and accounted for in accordance with its provisions. The current practice in the US is that such combinations are accounted for in accordance with SFAS 141. Therefore, they are accounted for by applying the SFAS 141 version of the acquisition method.*

BC199   The Board notes that difficulties may arise in applying the acquisition method to combinations achieved by contract alone. In particular, such business combinations normally do not involve the payment of any readily measurable consideration and in rare circumstances it might be difficult to identify the acquirer. However, as for combinations between mutual entities and for the reasons discussed above, the Board concluded that the acquisition method can and should be applied in

---

*Under US GAAP EITF 97-2 Application of FASB Statement No. 94 and APB Opinion No. 16 to Physician Practice Management Entities and Certain Other Entities with Contractual Management Arrangements *deals with combinations by contract. Although EITF 97-2 applies only to physician practice management entities and some other entities with contractual management arrangements, EITF 97-2 is applied more widely by analogy. EITF 97-2 requires the execution of such a management agreement to be accounted for as a business combination.*

accounting for such business combinations. The Board concluded that in a business combination achieved by contract:

(a) difficulties in identifying the acquirer are not a sufficient reason to justify a different accounting treatment, and no further guidance is necessary for identifying the acquirer for combinations by contract.
(b) determining the fair value of the acquiree and calculating the related goodwill should be consistent with decisions reached in the second phase of the project.

DISCLOSURES

The draft revised IFRS 3 carries forward those disclosure requirements from IFRS 3 that remain relevant, eliminates those that do not, and modifies those that are affected by changes in the measurement or recognition requirements it proposes. Paragraphs BC170-BC178 of IFRS 3 discuss the Board's considerations and decisions that led to the disclosures required by that IFRS. Because the Board is not redeliberating, or seeking comments on, those conclusions they are not repeated in this Basis for Conclusions. **BC200**

Changes from the IFRS 3 requirements include amended disclosures relating to the change from the cost-allocation method to the fair value measurement principle. Some of these disclosures are modified to retain the information but reflect the change in measurement basis. For example, IFRS 3 requires disclosure of the cost of the combination and a description of the components of that cost. The draft revised IFRS 3 requires disclosure of the acquisition-date fair value of the consideration transferred, including the fair value of each major class of consideration. The Board also concluded that the following additional disclosures are necessary under the fair value measurement principle: **BC201**

(a) the acquisition-date fair value of the acquiree and the basis for measuring that value.
(b) the amount of acquisition-related costs that are recognised as an expense, and the income statement line item in which that expense is recognised.
(c) in a business combination achieved in stages, the fair value of the acquirer's previously acquired non-controlling equity investment in the acquiree and the amount of any gain or loss recognised in accordance with paragraph 53, and the line item in the income statement in which that gain or loss is recognised.

The following are among the disclosure requirements that the Board decided to add to meet its disclosure objectives in IFRS 3: **BC202**

(a) the maximum potential amount of future payments (undiscounted) the acquirer could be required to make under the terms of the acquisition agreement.
(b) in a business combination in which the acquirer and acquiree have a pre-existing relationship:

   (i) the nature of the pre-existing relationship
   (ii) the measurement of the settlement amount of the pre-existing relationship, if any, and the valuation method used to determine the settlement amount
   (iii) the amount of any settlement gain or loss recognised and the line item in the income statement in which that gain or loss is recognised.

(c) the amount of revenue of the acquiree since the acquisition date included in the consolidated income statement for the period. The Board concluded that information about post-combination revenues of an acquired business allows users to distinguish acquired revenues from those generated by the acquirer itself.

(d) if the amounts recognised in the financial statement for the business combination have been determined only provisionally, the assets acquired or the liabilities assumed for which the measurement period is still open. This disclosure provides information about items of assets and liabilities for which the acquirer continues to seek information relating to their fair values.

(e) a description of an event or change in circumstances that has resulted in deferred tax benefits acquired in a business combination being recognised.

(f) the total amount of goodwill and the amount that is expected to be deductible for tax purposes.

BC203   The Board decided not to require in the draft IFRS the following disclosures currently required by IFRS 3:

(a) the carrying amounts for each class of the acquiree's assets and liabilities, determined in accordance with IFRSs, immediately before the combination. The Board concluded that providing this disclosure could often involve significant costs that do not justify the benefits that users receive from this information.

(b) a description of each intangible asset that was not recognised separately from goodwill and an explanation of why the intangible asset's fair value could not be measured reliably. This disclosure is unnecessary because the Board concluded that the fair value of intangible assets acquired in a business combination that are identifiable can always be measured reliably.

EFFECTIVE DATE AND TRANSITION

BC204   The Board decided that the provisions of the draft revised IFRS 3 should apply prospectively and that the proposed amendments to IAS 27 and IAS 37 should be applied at the same time. Prospective application of the draft revised IFRS 3 is consistent with IFRS 3. The Board acknowledges that, like IFRS 3, the proposed IFRS could be made effective immediately when issued, or shortly after. However, the Board's preference is that the proposed IFRS should be applied at the same time as the proposed revisions of IAS 27 and IAS 37 and that they should all be effective as of the beginning of an entity's annual period. The Board regards the proposed revisions in IAS 27, which address the subsequent accounting for an acquiree in consolidated financial statements, as related to provisions in the draft revised IFRS 3 that address the initial accounting for an acquiree at the acquisition date. Furthermore, the proposed changes in IAS 37 are concerned with the treatment in a business combination of the contingencies of an acquiree. The Board believes that linking the timing of the changes in accounting required by these IFRSs will minimise disruption to practice, to the benefit of both preparers and users of financial statements.

BC205   At the time the Exposure Drafts for the draft revised IFRS 3 and of the proposed amendments to IAS 27 and IAS 37 were published, the Board estimated that the resulting IFRSs would become effective no later than for annual periods beginning on or after 1 January 2007. The Board believes that a period of approximately 3–6 months after they are issued is desirable to provide sufficient time for entities to analyse, interpret, and prepare to implement those Standards. It allows sufficient time for countries to enact enabling legislation. It also allows time to co-ordinate the effective dates with the standards being issued by the FASB. The Board also decided to encourage early application of the proposed IFRS 3, as long as the revisions proposed for IAS 27 and IAS 37 are applied at the same time.

Effective date and transition for combinations between mutual entities or by contract alone

IFRS 3 excludes from its scope combinations between mutual entities and those achieved by contract alone. In developing IFRS 3 the Board decided that these combinations should be excluded from its scope until the Board issued interpretative guidance for the application of the acquisition method to those transactions. The draft revised IFRS 3 provides that interpretative guidance. The effective date for combinations between mutual entities is the same as the effective date for all other entities applying the proposed IFRS.

BC206

For the reasons outlined in paragraph BC180 of IFRS 3 the Board concluded that the transitional provisions for combinations involving mutual entities or those achieved by contract alone should be prospective. Given that these combinations are not currently within the scope of IFRS 3, they may be accounted for differently from what IFRS 3 requires. The transitional provisions currently in IFRS 3 take into consideration and properly reflect that entities may have used a range of alternatives in accounting for combinations in the past. The Board concluded that the transitional provisions for these combinations should incorporate the transitional provisions currently in IFRS 3 for other business combinations. In addition, the Board concluded that the transitional provisions should provide that an entity should continue to classify prior combinations in accordance with its previous accounting for such combinations. This is consistent with the prospective approach. Those provisions are contained in paragraphs C11 and C12 of Appendix C of the draft revised IFRS 3.

BC207

Previously recognised contingent liabilities

As discussed in paragraphs BC115 and BC116, the Board, in its amendments to IAS 37, proposes eliminating the term 'contingent liability' and highlighting that many items previously described as contingent liabilities satisfy the *Framework*'s definition of a liability. Accordingly, the Board decided that any recognised contingent liability that relates to a business combination for which the acquisition date was before the draft revised IFRS 3 is applied should be assessed to determine whether it satisfies the definition of a liability. If it does not, the Board concluded that it should be derecognised with a corresponding adjustment to goodwill arising from that business combination. The Board observed that continuing to recognise such contingent liabilities would be inconsistent with the principle that only those identifiable items that satisfy the definition of an asset or liability in the *Framework* should be recognised.

BC208

ALTERNATIVE VIEWS

Five Board members have alternative views on some aspects of the draft revised IFRS 3. Their reasons are discussed in paragraphs AV2-AV20.

AV1

Goodwill

Five Board members disagree with the use of the full goodwill method in the revised IFRS 3, as explained in paragraphs BC134-BC150. This involves the recognition of not only the purchased goodwill attributable to the acquirer as a result of the acquisition transaction, but also the goodwill attributable to the non-controlling interest in the subsidiary. This method treats goodwill as an asset that can be identified separately and measured at fair value, like any other asset of the subsidiary.

AV2

AV3   The full goodwill method is based upon the assumption that in a business combination all assets of the acquiree, including goodwill, should be accounted for on a similar basis. The five Board members note that goodwill is different from other assets, because it is a component of the value of the business as a whole, rather than having a separate existence. Thus, under the full goodwill method, it has to be measured as the difference between the value of the acquired business as a whole and the sum of the separately measurable assets. The total goodwill of the acquiree then has to be apportioned between the controlling and non-controlling interests.

AV4   The process of measuring goodwill is therefore extremely difficult. The residual nature of its measurement means that it captures measurement errors in other assets, and sometimes non-recognition of those assets. Moreover, the total value of the acquired business is an extremely subjective measure, based upon the acquirer's judgement of the potential returns that it will generate. These returns will depend upon the synergies that the acquirer expects to achieve with its own business. Thus they are entity-specific to the particular acquirer and there will not be an observable fair value in the marketplace, especially when the acquisition is combined with restructuring.

AV5   Not only is the total value of the acquired business difficult to measure, but so is the allocation of the goodwill between the parent and the subsidiary. Some synergies will benefit the parent entity rather than, or in addition to, the subsidiary. Thus, the allocation of the goodwill between the parent and the subsidiary is also problematic, and this adds to the difficulty of measuring the goodwill attributable to the non-controlling interest in the subsidiary.

AV6   The 'parent-only' approach to goodwill in IFRS 3 avoids this difficulty by measuring goodwill as the difference between the fair value of the consideration paid by the parent for the subsidiary and its share of the fair value of the identifiable net assets of the subsidiary. Thus, purchased goodwill is the amount implicit in the acquisition transaction and excludes any goodwill attributable to non-controlling interests. This method gives rise to more reliable measurement, because it is based on the purchase consideration, which can usually be reliably measured, and it reflects faithfully the acquisition transaction, to which the non-controlling interests were not a party.

AV7   This 'parent-only' approach is, in the view of the five Board members, preferable to the full goodwill approach now proposed. The latter involves estimating a highly subjective measurement of the total fair value of the subsidiary (including the non-controlling interest). This would involve the extremely difficult process of stripping out the synergies attributable to the parent entity. It would also involve identifying and measuring the other elements of the 'control premium' that are included in the consideration paid by the acquirer. The likely existence of a control premium on acquisition means that it is inappropriate simply to value the acquired business by grossing up the consideration paid by the acquirer for a proportion of the business. Thus, the measurement of the goodwill attributable to the non-controlling interest is likely to be extremely unreliable or even misleading, and it is doubtful if it will confer any informational benefit on users of financial statements.

Recognising gains or losses on non-controlling equity investments

AV8   Three Board members disagree with the proposed treatment (in the proposed amendments to IAS 27) of changes in controlling interests in subsidiaries after control is established (paragraphs BC151-BC153). They believe that it is important that the consequences of such changes for the shareholders of the parent entity should be reported clearly in the income statement, as is permitted by current IFRSs.

The proposed revision of IAS 27 adopts the economic entity view of the consolidated   **AV9**
accounts. This treats all equity interests in the group as being homogeneous, so that
transactions between controlling and non-controlling interests are regarded as mere
transfers within the total equity interest and no gain or loss should be recognised on
such transactions. The three Board members observe that the non-controlling
interests represent equity claims that are restricted to particular subsidiaries, whereas
the controlling interests are affected by the performance of the entire group. The
consolidated financial statements should therefore report performance from the
perspective of the controlling interest (a parent entity perspective) in addition to the
wider perspective provided by the economic entity approach.

The parent entity perspective implies the recognition of gains or losses on transac-   **AV10**
tions by the parent entity in the equity of a subsidiary which is controlled both before
and after the transaction. If, as these Board members would prefer, the full goodwill
method were not used, the acquisition of additional equity in a subsidiary would give
rise to the recognition of additional purchased goodwill, measured as the excess of
the purchase consideration over the book value of the separately identified assets in
the subsidiary attributable to the additional interest acquired. On reducing the equity
stake in a subsidiary, without loss of control, a gain or loss attributable to the
controlling interest would be recognised. This would be measured as the difference
between the consideration received and the proportion of the book value of the -
subsidiary's assets (including purchased goodwill) attributable to the holding
disposed of. This would provide the controlling interest with the relevant information about the gains and losses arising on the partial disposal of holdings in
subsidiaries. It would also improve the reporting of gains and losses arising on
disposals of subsidiaries that are made in stages.

Two of these Board members also disagree with the requirement in paragraph 56   **AV11**
that:

> In a business combination achieved in stages, the acquirer shall remeasure its
> non-controlling equity investment in the acquiree at fair value as of the acqui-
> sition date and recognise any gains or losses in profit or loss. If, before the
> business combination, the acquirer recognised changes in the value of its non-
> controlling equity investment directly in equity (for example, the investment was
> designated as available for sale) the amount that was recognised directly in
> equity shall be reclassified and included in the calculation of any gain or loss as
> of the acquisition date.

Although these Board members agree that the acquisition of a controlling interest is   **AV12**
an event that requires remeasurement of the investment to its fair value, they disagree
that it results in derecognition of the investment. The acquirer has obtained rights to
direct the use of the underlying net assets of acquiree as a result of the purchase of an
additional investment that achieves a controlling interest. It has not disposed of the
original investment, and it is therefore inappropriate to reclassify past gains or losses
on that investment to profit or loss, as would be done if they were realised by
disposal.

These Board members would recognise the gain or loss on remeasurement of the   **AV13**
non-controlling interest directly in equity, in the manner required by paragraph 55(b)
of IAS 39 for available-for-sale financial assets.

Definition of a business combination

AV14   Two Board members disagree with the decision to revise the definition of a business combination, as explained in paragraphs BC23-BC33. By emphasising the acquisition of one entity by another, the new definition is narrower than that in IFRS 3 which used the term 'bringing together' rather than 'acquirer obtains control', thus allowing the definition to embrace mergers as well as acquisitions. They believe that the definition in IFRS 3, which is wider than that proposed in the revised IFRS 3, should be retained. In their view, paragraph BC32 is inconsistent with the new definition because it advocates applying the acquisition method to true mergers that do not now meet the definition of a business combination.

Combinations between mutual entities

AV15   One Board member disagrees with the decision to bring combinations of mutual entities and those achieved by contract alone within the scope of the proposed IFRS, as explained in paragraphs BC42-BC46 and BC179-BC199.

AV16   In this member's view, combinations of mutual entities have characteristics that are more likely to have the characteristics of true mergers rather than acquisitions (as summarised in paragraph BC184), and they are also likely to have characteristics, such as lack of measurable financial consideration (which will apply particularly when combinations are achieved by contract alone), that make acquisition accounting difficult to implement reliably. Therefore, it would be better to defer changes in accounting for combinations of such entities until more appropriate methods, such as fresh start accounting (paragraph BC190), have been explored properly.

AV17   The Board member supports the alternative view of the FASB Board member who also has concerns about the proposed accounting for mutual entities. Those views are contained in paragraph B212 of the FASB's Background Information and Basis for Conclusions.

Costs incurred in connection with a business combination

AV18   Two Board members also disagree that acquisition-related costs are not part of the consideration transferred in exchange for the acquiree and should be recognised as an expense as incurred (paragraphs BC84-BC89). Recognising acquisition-related costs as expenses is inconsistent with accounting for purchases of assets, including investments in associated companies, whereby the direct costs form part of the carrying amount of the assets acquired, on initial recognition. It also fails to reflect the economic substance of the acquisition transaction. In order for a transaction to be justified economically, the acquirer must expect that the fair value of what is acquired is equal to, or exceeds, the total cost of acquisition (the purchase consideration plus the associated costs).

Recognition criteria

AV19   One Board member also disagrees with the decision to remove the reliable measurement recognition criterion for intangible assets acquired in a business combination (paragraph BC99). It is acknowledged that reliability of measurement is 'a criterion for recognition in the *Framework*' (paragraph BC98). Its absence from the draft revised IFRS 3 is supported by the claim that 'separate recognition of intangible assets, rather than subsuming them in goodwill, provides better information to users of financial statements, even though a significant degree of judgement could be involved in determining that fair value' (paragraph BC102). This statement is unsupported by evidence, and overriding the *Framework* in this way creates the possibility of serious inconsistencies in the reliability of different components of financial statements. This is particularly the case because, once the reliability criterion is removed, there is no limit to the unreliability of measurements which may be reported for separate intangible assets acquired in a business combination.

The draft revised IFRS 3 acknowledges only one example in which measurement is sufficiently unreliable to justify non-recognition—the case of an assembled work-force. The Board member does not believe this is the only possible example of measurement unreliability that should preclude separate recognition. Indeed, the responses to ED 3, the Exposure Draft that preceded IFRS 3, suggested that in many cases the measurement of acquired intangible assets is extremely unreliable.

AV20

Differences between the Exposure Drafts published by the IASB and the FASB

INTRODUCTION

This note accompanies, but is not part of, the draft IFRS.

N1   The accompanying Exposure Draft is the result of the IASB's and the FASB's projects to improve accounting and reporting for business combinations. The first phase of those projects led to IFRS 3 *Business Combinations* and FASB Statement No. 141 *Business Combinations*. In 2002, the IASB and the FASB agreed to reconsider jointly their guidance for applying the purchase method (now called the acquisition method) of accounting for business combinations. The objective of the joint effort is to develop a common and comprehensive standard for the accounting for business combinations that could be used for both domestic and international financial reporting. Although the boards reached the same conclusions on the fundamental issues addressed in the accompanying Exposure Draft, they reached different conclusions on a few limited matters.

N2   On those matters on which the boards reached different conclusions, each board has set out its own guidance in its version of the Exposure Draft. This note identifies and compares those paragraphs in which the IASB and the FASB have proposed substantively different guidance. This note does not identify non-substantive differences such as differences in terminology: *profit or loss* (IASB) and *income* (FASB). Nor - does it identify differences in references to IASB or FASB guidance. For example, the IASB's version of the Exposure Draft refers to IAS 19 *Employee Benefits,* whereas the FASB's version refers to FASB Statement No. 87 *Employers' Accounting for Pensions.*

N3   Most of the differences identified in this note arise because of the boards' decisions to produce guidance for accounting for business combinations that is consistent with other existing IFRSs or FASB standards. Even though those differences are candidates for future convergence projects, the boards do not plan to eliminate them before the proposed standards on business combinations are issued.

Paragraph reference	IASB's guidance	FASB's guidance
Paragraph 2(c)—Scope exception for not-for-profit organisations	Paragraph 2(c) is not used because the IASB does not provide guidance for not-for-profit organisations. Therefore, this scope exception is not necessary for the IASB.	Paragraph 2(c) specifies that this Statement does not apply to combinations between not-for-profit organisations or the acquisition of a for-profit business by a not-for-profit organisation. The FASB plans to issue a separate Exposure Draft that addresses business combinations between not-for-profit organisations.
Paragraph 11—Identification of the primary beneficiary as the acquirer	N/A—The IASB does not have guidance for primary beneficiaries because it does not have consolidation guidance equivalent to FASB Interpretation No. 46 (revised December 2003) *Consolidation of Variable Interest Entities.*	The last two sentences of paragraph 11 state that for the purposes of this Statement, the primary beneficiary of a variable interest entity is always the acquirer. The determination of what party, if any, is the primary beneficiary of a variable interest entity is made solely in accordance with Interpretation 46(R), not based on the guidance in paragraphs 12–16.
Paragraphs 35, 36 and 87—Contingencies	Contingencies Paragraph 35 requires the acquirer to recognise, separately from goodwill, the acquisition-date fair value of an identifiable asset or liability even if the amount of the future economic benefits embodied in the asset or required to settle the liability is contingent (or conditional) on the occurrence or non-occurrence of one or more uncertain future events not wholly within the control of the entity. Although the IASB and the FASB use different words to describe the accounting for contingencies acquired in a business combination, the guidance is expected to result in the identification and recognition of the same assets and liabilities at the same amounts. After initial recognition, paragraph 36 requires the acquirer to account for such assets in accordance with IAS 38 *Intangible Assets* or IAS 39 *Financial Instruments: Recognition and Measurement,* as appropriate, and such liabilities in	Contingencies that meet the definition of assets or liabilities Paragraph 35 requires the acquirer to recognise separately from goodwill the acquisition-date fair value of assets and liabilities arising from contingencies that were acquired or assumed as part of the business combination. Therefore, the acquirer recognises as of the acquisition date an asset or a liability for a contingency even if that contingency does not meet the recognition criteria in SFAS 5. Although the IASB and the FASB use different words in these paragraphs, the guidance is expected to result in the identification and recognition of the same assets and liabilities and at the same amounts. After initial recognition, paragraph 36 requires contingencies to be accounted for in accordance with applicable generally accepted accounting principles, except for contingencies that would be accounted for in accordance with SFAS 5 if

Paragraph reference	IASB's guidance	FASB's guidance
	accordance with [draft] IAS 37 *Non-financial Liabilities* or other IFRSs, as appropriate.	they were acquired or incurred in an event other than a business combination. Those contingencies should continue to be measured at fair value with changes in fair value recognised in income in each reporting period.
	Paragraph 87 provides transition from the existing IFRS 3 requirement for previously recognised contingent liabilities.	N/A – FASB did not have similar guidance in Statement 141.
Paragraph 74— Disclosures of the effects of a business combination	The disclosures required by paragraph 74 apply to all acquirers.	The disclosures required by paragraph 74 apply only to acquirers that are *public business enterprises*, as described in paragraph 9 of FASB Statement No. 131 *Disclosures about Segments of an Enterprise and Related Information*.
	Paragraph 74(b)(1) requires disclosure of the revenue and profit or loss of the combined entity *for the current period* as though the acquisition date for all business combinations that occurred during the year had been as of the beginning of the annual reporting period. Paragraph 74(b)(2) is not used because the IASB does not require this disclosure for the comparable prior period.	*Paragraph 74(b) requires disclosure of the following supplemental pro forma* information: (1) The *results of operations*** of the combined entity for the current period as though the acquisition date for all business combinations that occurred during the year had been as of the beginning of the annual reporting period.

* For this disclosure, *results of operations* means revenue, income before extraordinary items and the cumulative effect of accounting changes, net income, and earnings per share. In determining the pro forma amounts, income taxes, interest expense, preferred share dividends and depreciation and amortisation of assets shall be adjusted to the accounting base recognised for each in recording the combination. Pro forma information related to results of operations of periods before the combination shall be limited to the results of operations for the immediately preceding period. Disclosure also shall be made of the nature and amount of any material, nonrecurring items included in the reported pro forma results of operations.

Paragraph reference	IASB's guidance	FASB's guidance
		(2) If comparative financial statements are presented, the *results of operations* of the combined entity for the comparable prior period as though the acquisition date for all business combinations that occurred during the current year had occurred as of the beginning of the comparable prior fiscal year.
Paragraph 76(d)—Disclosures of the financial effects of adjustments to the amounts recognised in a business combination	Paragraph 76(d) requires the acquirer to disclose the amount and an explanation of any gain or loss recognised in the current period that (1) relates to the identifiable assets acquired or liabilities assumed in a business combination that was effected in the current or the previous annual period and (2) is of such a size, nature, or incidence that disclosure is relevant to understanding the combined entity's financial statements.	N/A—*FASB* does not require this disclosure.
Paragraph 78(b)—Goodwill by reportable segment	The disclosure in paragraph 78(b) is not required by the IASB. Paragraph 134 of IAS 36 *Impairment of Assets* requires an entity to disclose the aggregate carrying amount of goodwill allocated to each cash-generating unit (group of units) for which the carrying amount of goodwill allocated to that unit (group of units) is significant in comparison with the entity's total carrying amount of goodwill. This information is not required to be disclosed for each material business combination that occurs during the period or in the aggregate for individually immaterial business combinations that are material collectively and occur during the period.	Paragraph 78(b) requires that the acquirer disclose *for each material business combination that occurs during the period or in the aggregate for individually immaterial business combinations that are material collectively and that occur during the period*, the amount of goodwill by reportable segment, if the combined entity is required to disclose segment information in accordance with SFAS 131, unless such disclosure is impracticable. Like IAS 36, paragraph 45 of FASB Statement No. 142 *Goodwill and Other Intangible Assets* requires disclosure of this information in aggregate by each reportable segment, not for each material business combination that occurs during the period or in the aggregate for individually immaterial business combinations that are material collectively and that occur during the period.

Paragraph reference	IASB's guidance	FASB's guidance
Paragraph 80—Goodwill reconciliation	Paragraph 80 requires an acquirer to provide a goodwill reconciliation and provides a detailed list of items that should be shown separately.	Paragraph 80 requires an acquirer to provide a goodwill reconciliation in accordance with the requirements of SFAS 142. SFAS 142 requires a goodwill reconciliation; however, the requirement is less detailed than that required by the IASB. This Exposure Draft would amend the requirement in SFAS 142 to converge with the level of detail in the reconciliation required by the IASB.
Paragraph A49(d)—Customer contract intangible assets	IFRS 4 *Insurance Contracts* permits, but does not require, an expanded presentation that splits the fair value of acquired insurance contracts into two components: (a) a liability measured in accordance with the insurer's accounting policies for insurance contracts that it issues and (b) an intangible asset, representing the fair value of the contractual rights and obligations acquired, to the extent that the liability does not reflect that fair value.	Paragraph D13 amends FASB Statement No. 60 *Accounting and Reporting by Insurance Enterprises* to *require* the expanded presentation permitted by IFRS 4.
Footnote to paragraph A52(i)—Contract-based intangible assets	N/A	The footnote to paragraph A52(i) codifies FASB Staff Positions FAS 141-1 and 142-1, "Interaction of FASB Statements No. 141 *Business Combinations,* and No. 142, *Goodwill and Other Intangible Assets,* and EITF Issue No. 04-2, 'Whether Mineral Rights Are Tangible or Intangible Assets." The footnote to paragraph A56(i) incorporates the guidance in FSP 141-1. Also, the amendment that removes the parenthetical that reads "such as mineral rights to depleting assets" from paragraph 11 of SFAS 142 is carried forward in Appendix D of this Exposure Draft.

Paragraph reference	IASB's guidance	FASB's guidance
Paragraph A102-A109—Replacement share-based payment awards	Both the IASB and the FASB require that if the acquirer is obligated to replace the acquiree's awards, all or a portion of the acquirer's replacement awards are included in the measurement of the consideration transferred by the acquirer. However, the amount included in the measurement of the consideration transferred by the acquirer is calculated consistently with the requirements of IFRS 2 *Share-based Payment*. The portion attributable to past services, which is included in the measurement of the consideration transferred, is equal to the remaining fair value based measure of the replacement award (or settlement) multiplied by *the ratio of the portion of the vesting period completed to the total vesting period.* (The amount, if any, to be recognised in post-combination profit or loss is the remaining fair value based measure of the replacement award (or settlement) multiplied by the ratio of the future vesting period to the total vesting period.) The vesting period is the period during which all the specified vesting conditions are to be satisfied. Vesting conditions are defined in IFRS 2. Paragraphs A104-A109 illustrate the IASB's requirements.	Both the IASB and the FASB require that if the acquirer is obligated to replace the acquiree's awards, all or a portion of the acquirer's replacement awards are included in the measurement of the consideration transferred by the acquirer. However, the amount included in the measurement of the consideration transferred by the acquirer is calculated consistently with the requirements of FASB Statement No. 123 (revised 2004) *Share-Based Payment*. The portion attributable to past services, which is included in the measurement of the consideration transferred, is equal to the remaining fair value based measure of the replacement award (or settlement) multiplied by *the ratio of the past service period to the total service period* (that is, the period that begins with the service inception date for the award of the acquiree and ends with the service completion date for the replacement award). The past service period ends and the future service period begins on the acquisition date. (The amount, if any, which represents compensation expense to be recognised in postcombination consolidated net income is the remaining fair value based measure of the replacement award (or settlement) multiplied by the ratio of the future service period to the total service period.) The requisite service period of awards issued by the acquirer shall reflect any explicit, implicit, and derived service periods (consistent with the requirements of SFAS 123(R)). Paragraphs A104-A109 illustrate the FASB's requirements.

Paragraph reference	IASB's guidance	FASB's guidance
Appendix B—Background information and basis for conclusions / Basis for Conclusions	The Basis for Conclusions provides the background for the IASB's project and the IASB's basis for its conclusions, which is the same as or similar to the FASB's in many respects, but not all. The Basis for Conclusions is not integral to the draft proposed standard and, accordingly, the IASB does not have an Appendix B.	Appendix B provides the background for the FASB's project and the FASB's basis for its conclusions, which is the same as or similar to the IASB's in many respects, but not all.
Appendix C—Continuing authoritative guidance	Appendix C contains guidance and transition provisions that have been carried forward or adapted from IASB sources. The boards did not deliberate jointly or reach convergence on the continuing authoritative guidance. Therefore, the IASB's Appendix C differs from the FASB's Appendix C.	Appendix C contains guidance and transition provisions that have been carried forward or adapted from FASB sources. The boards did not deliberate jointly or reach convergence on the continuing authoritative guidance. Therefore, the FASB's Appendix C differs from the IASB's Appendix C.
Appendix D—Amendments	Appendix D contains the amendments to IFRSs that would result from the proposed IFRS.	Appendix D contains the amendments to FASB standards that would result from the proposed Statement.
Appendix E—Fair value measurement / Related literature analysis	The IASB's Appendix E provides guidance for measuring fair value. The FASB did not provide fair value measurement guidance in this appendix because the FASB's Exposure Draft refers to the FASB Exposure Draft *Fair Value Measurements,* which was published on 23 June 2004. That Exposure Draft provides the guidance that the IASB provides in Appendix E.	The FASB's Appendix E addresses the impact of this Exposure Draft on authoritative accounting literature included in categories (b), (c), and (d) in the GAAP hierarchy and the relationship between this Exposure Draft and related SEC literature. The IASB provides all authoritative guidance for entities under its jurisdiction and, therefore, does not need an equivalent appendix.

TABLE OF CONCORDANCE

This table shows how the contents of IFRS 3 and the Exposure Draft correspond. Paragraphs are treated as corresponding if they address broadly the same matter even though the guidance may differ.

IFRS 3 paragraph	Exposure Draft paragraph	IFRS 3 paragraph	Exposure Draft paragraph	IFRS 3 paragraph	Exposure Draft paragraph
1	1	24	19	73	76
2	2	25	17	74	77
3	2(a)-(c)	26	28	75	80
4	4	27	Appendix E	76	80(e)
5	5	28	28	77	81
6	6	29-31	27	78-85	82-87
7	7	32-35	25, 26	86, 87	88
8	None	36-44	None	Appendix A	3
9	None	45, 46	40, 41	IE (A)	A37-A41
10	C7	47-50	37	IE (B)	A42-A49
11	C8	51-53	49, 50	IE (C)	A50, A51
12	C9	54, 55	51	IE (D)	A52-A55
13	C10	57	59-61	IE (E)	A56-A61
14	8	58-60	55-57	Example 1	A49(a)
15	None	61-64	62-68	Example 2	A49(b)
16	9	65	46	Example 3	A49(c)
17	10	66	71	Example 4	A49(d)
18	None	67	72	Example 5	Example 20
19	None	68	73(a)	Example 6	None
20	13, 14	69	74	Example 7	Example 11
21	12	70	74	Example 8	None
22	16	71	73(b)	Example 9	None
23	15	72	75		

NOTE ON LEGAL REQUIREMENTS

Great Britain

1   In Great Britain for financial years beginning on or after 1 January 2005, the statutory requirements relating to accounting for business combinations for those companies which prepare accounts under the Companies Act 1985 rather than IAS accounts are set out in Schedule 4 and 4A and are summarised below.

Acquisition Accounting

2   The Companies Act describes the acquisition method of accounting in Schedule 4A paragraph 9:

(a)   The identifiable assets and liabilities of the undertaking acquired shall be included in the consolidated balance sheet at their fair values as at the date of acquisition. The 'identifiable' assets or liabilities of the undertaking acquired mean the assets or liabilities that are capable of being disposed of or discharged separately, without disposing of a business of the undertaking (Schedule 4A paragraph 9(2)).

(b)   The income and expenditure of the undertaking acquired shall be brought into the group accounts only as from the date of the acquisition (Schedule 4A paragraph 9(3)).

(c)   There shall be set off against the acquisition cost of the interest in the shares of the undertaking held by the parent company and its subsidiary undertakings the interest of the parent company and its subsidiary undertakings in the adjusted capital and reserves of the undertaking acquired. The resulting amount if positive shall be treated as goodwill, and if negative as a negative consolidation difference (Schedule 4A paragraph 9(4)-(5)).

(d)   The 'acquisition cost' is defined as the amount of any cash consideration and the fair value of any other consideration, together with such amount (if any) in respect of fees and other expenses of the acquisition as the company may determine; and 'the adjusted capital and reserves' of the undertaking acquired are defined as the capital and reserves at the date of the acquisition after adjusting the identifiable assets and liabilities of the undertaking to fair values as at that date (Schedule 4A paragraph 9(4)).

Merger accounting

3   The [draft] Standard no longer permits the use of merger accounting. The merger method of accounting is described in Schedule 4A paragraph 11. Schedule 4A paragraph 10 lays down the conditions that must be met if a business combination is to be accounted for as a merger. The conditions are:

(a)   that at least 90 per cent of the nominal value of the relevant shares (those with unrestricted rights to participate both in distributions and in the assets on liquidation but excluding shares in the undertaking held as treasury shares) in the undertaking acquired is held by or on behalf of the parent company and its subsidiary undertakings;

(b)   that the proportion referred to in (a) was attained pursuant to an arrangement providing for the issue of equity shares by the parent company or one or more of its subsidiary undertakings;

(c)   that the fair value of any consideration other than the issue of equity shares given pursuant to the arrangement by the parent company and its subsidiary undertakings did not exceed 10 per cent of the nominal value of the equity shares issued; and

(d) that adoption of the merger method of accounting accords with generally accepted accounting principles or practice.

Where a group is acquired, the Companies Act requirements described in the pre-   4
vious paragraphs also apply. References to shares of the undertaking acquired are to be construed as references to the shares of the acquired group's parent and references to the assets and liabilities, income and expenditure, and capital and reserves of the undertaking acquired are to be construed as references to the same elements of the group acquired, after making the necessary set-off and adjustments required for the consolidated accounts (Schedule 4A paragraph 12).

Disclosures

The following information shall be given in a note to the accounts for all business   5
combinations taking place in the financial year:

(a) the names of the entities involved;
(b) whether the combination has been accounted for by the acquisition or merger method of accounting (Schedule 4A paragraph 13(2)).

In addition, for any business combination that significantly affects the figures shown   6
in the group accounts, the following further information shall be given:

the composition and fair value of the consideration for the acquisition given by the parent and its subsidiary undertakings (Schedule 4A paragraph 13(3));

Where the acquisition method of accounting has been adopted, the book values   7
immediately prior to acquisition and fair values at the date of acquisition of each class of assets and liabilities of the acquired entity shall be stated in tabular form, including a statement of the amount of any goodwill or negative consolidation difference arising on the acquisition, together with an explanation of any significant adjustments made (Schedule 4A paragraph 13(5)).

Where the merger method of accounting has been adopted, an explanation shall be   8
given of any significant adjustments made in relation to the amounts of the assets and liabilities of the undertaking or group acquired, together with a statement of any resulting adjustment to the consolidated reserves (including the restatement of opening consolidated reserves) (Schedule 4A paragraph 13(6)).

None of the information required by paragraph 13 of Schedule 4A to the Act need be   9
disclosed for an undertaking which:

(a) is established under the law of a country outside the United Kingdom; or
(b) carries on business outside the United Kingdom

if, in the opinion of the directors of the parent company, the disclosure would be seriously prejudicial to the business of that undertaking or to the business of the parent company or any of its subsidiary undertakings and the Secretary of State agrees that the information should not be disclosed (Schedule 4A paragraph 16).

Share premium and merger relief

Section 130(1) of the Companies Act provides that if a company issues shares at a   10
premium, whether for cash or otherwise, a sum equal to the aggregate amount or value of the premiums on those shares should be transferred to an account called the share premium account. The provisions of the Companies Act relating to the

reduction of a company's share capital apply, with exceptions, as if the share premium account were part of its paid-up share capital.

11   Limited relief from the above ('merger relief') is given by sections 131-134.

12   Section 131 of the Companies Act provides, inter alia, that, subject to specified conditions, where an issuing company has secured at least a 90 per cent equity holding in another company, section 130 does not apply to the premium on shares issued in the transaction which takes the holding in that other company to at least 90 per cent.

14   Section 133(1) provides that the premium on any shares to which the relief in sections 131 and 132 of the Companies Act applies may also be disregarded in determining the amount at which any shares, or other consideration provided for the shares issued, are to be included in the offeror company's balance sheet.

Accounts of the parent company

15   The FRS deals only with the method of accounting to be used in group accounts; it does not deal with the form of accounting to be used in the acquiring or issuing company's own accounts and in particular does not restrict the reliefs available under sections 131-133 of the Companies Act.

16   Where a dividend is paid to the acquiring or issuing company out of pre-combination profits, it would appear that it need not necessarily be applied as a reduction in the carrying value of the investment in the subsidiary undertaking. Such a dividend received should be applied to reduce the carrying value of the investment to the extent necessary to provide for a diminution in value of the investment in the subsidiary undertaking as stated in the accounts of the parent company. To the extent that this is not necessary, it appears that the amount received will be a realised profit in the hands of the parent company.

Goodwill

17   The acquisition method of accounting and the calculation of goodwill are described by paragraph 9(4) and (5) of Schedule 4A. The interest of the parent company and its subsidiaries in the adjusted capital and reserves of an acquired subsidiary undertaking must be offset against the acquisition cost. The resulting amount if positive must be treated as goodwill, and, if negative, as a negative consolidation difference.

18   The balance sheet formats in Schedule 4 require purchased goodwill, to the extent that it has not been written off, to be included under the heading of intangible fixed assets, and shown separately from other intangible assets. Note (3) to the formats states that amounts representing goodwill should be included only to the extent that the goodwill was acquired for valuable consideration. Internally generated goodwill may not be capitalised.

19   Paragraph 21 of Schedule 4 requires that, where goodwill is treated as an asset, it must be depreciated systematically over a period chosen by the directors. The period chosen must not exceed the useful economic life of the goodwill. The period chosen and the reason for choosing that period must be disclosed in a note. The use of residual values in determining depreciable amounts and thus calculating systematic depreciation/amortisation is widely accepted. If the residual value is equal to the carrying amount (eg cost) then depreciation is reduced to nil. It is possible that **where**

the useful life of the asset is indefinite, the residual value (on the basis of prices prevailing at the time of original acquisition) will always equal cost.

Paragraph 31(1) of Schedule 4 prohibits the revaluation of goodwill.   20

Paragraph 14 of Schedule 4A requires the notes to the accounts to state the cumu-   21
lative amount of goodwill resulting from acquisitions in that, and earlier financial
years, that has been written off otherwise than in the consolidated profit and loss
account for that or any earlier financial year. That figure must be net of any goodwill
attributable to subsidiary undertakings or businesses disposed of before the balance
sheet date. Paragraph 16 of Schedule 4A states that disclosure of amounts pertaining
to an overseas business need not be given if it would be seriously prejudicial to the
group's business and agreement has been obtained from the Secretary of State.
Further, for acquisitions before 23 December 1989, disclosure need not be made if
the information necessary to calculate the amount with material accuracy is unavailable or cannot be obtained without unreasonable expense or delay (paragraph 9
of Schedule 2 to the Companies Act 1989 (Commencement No. 4 and Transitional
and Saving Provisions) Order 1990). The exclusion of such amounts and the grounds
for the exclusion must be stated.

Northern Ireland

The legal requirements in Northern Ireland are similar to those in Great Britain. The   22
following table shows the references to the Companies (Northern Ireland) Order
1986 that correspond to the marginal references in the FRS and the legal references
in paragraphs 1-16 above.

Great Britain:	**Northern Ireland:**
The Companies Act 1985	Companies (Northern Ireland) Order 1986
Acquisition accounting	
Paragraph 9, Schedule 4A	Paragraph 9, Schedule 4A 1986 Order
Merger accounting	
Schedule 4A	Schedule 4A
paragraphs 9-12	paragraphs 9-12
Disclosures	
Schedule 4A	Schedule 4A
paragraph 13(2) – 13(6)	paragraph 13(2) – 13(6)
Schedule 4A	Schedule 4A
paragraph 16	paragraph 16
Share premium and merger relief	
Sections 130-133	Articles 140-143
Schedule 5 paragraph 10	Schedule 5 paragraph 10
Schedule 5 paragraph 29	Schedule 5 paragraph 29

Republic of Ireland

The following table shows the references to the European Communities (Companies: 23
Group Accounts) Regulations 1992 and the Companies Act 1963 that correspond to
the marginal references in the FRS and the legal references in paragraphs 1 - 16 above.

Great Britain:	Republic of Ireland:
The Companies Act 1985	European Communities (Companies Group Accounts) 1992 Regulations

Acquisition accounting

Schedule 4A, paragraph 9	Paragraph 19, 1992 Regulations

Merger accounting

Schedule 4A paragraph 9	Paragraph 19, 1992 Regulations
Schedule 4A paragraph 10	Paragraph 21, 1992 Regulations
Schedule 4A paragraph 11	Paragraph 22, 1992 Regulations
Schedule 4A paragraph 12	Paragraph 23, 1992 Regulations

Disclosures

Schedule 4A	The Schedule
Paragraph 13(2)	Paragraph 12(2), 1992 Regulations
Paragraph 13(3)	No exact equivalent. Regulation 27
Paragraph 13 (5) & (6)	1992 Regulations provides "If the composition of the undertakings dealt with in the group accounts has changed significantly in the course of a financial year, the group accounts must include information that makes the comparison of successive sets of group accounts meaningful."
Schedule 4A paragraph 16	No equivalent

Share premium and merger relief

Section 130	Section 62, Companies Act 1963
Sections 131-134	No equivalent
Schedule 5 paragraph 10	No equivalent
Schedule 5 paragraph 29	No equivalent

Goodwill

Paragraph 14 of Schedule 4A	No corresponding reference
Paragraph 21 of Schedule 4	Paragraph 9 of Schedule to 1986 Act
Paragraph 31(1) of Schedule 4	Paragraph 19(1) of Schedule to 1986 Act

Merger relief in the Republic of Ireland

24   As there is currently no legislation equivalent to merger relief in the Republic of Ireland, no explicit relief from the requirement of section 62(1) of the Companies Act 1963 to establish a share premium account is available.

25   However, section 149(5) of the Companies Act 1963 provides that, whilst, in general, pre-acquisition profits of acquired subsidiaries may not be treated in the holding company's accounts as revenue profit, an exemption from that provision is available in that, where the directors and auditors are satisfied and so certify that it would be fair and reasonable and would not prejudice the rights and interests of any person, the profits or losses attributable to any shares in a subsidiary may be treated in a manner otherwise than in accordance with that subsection.

26   The possible need for legal advice in relation to the application of section 149(5) to merger accounting should be considered before merger accounting is applied to Republic of Ireland companies.

AMENDMENTS TO FRS 2

ACCOUNTING FOR SUBSIDIARY UNDERTAKINGS

(PARTS OF IAS 27 CONSOLIDATED AND SEPARATE FINANCIAL STATEMENTS)

ASB note: The following section sets out the amendments to FRS 2 Accounting for Subsidiary Undertakings *that are proposed as a consequence of the proposals in the IASB's exposure draft of* Proposed Amendments to IAS 27 Consolidated and Separate Financial Statements. *The text is in the marked up form from the current text of FRS 2.*

Proposed amendments to FRS 2 Accounting for subsidiary undertakings

Summary of main changes

The main changes proposed to FRS 2 *Accounting for Subsidiary Undertakings* are:

- to require changes in the parent's ownership interest that do not result in the loss of control of a subsidiary to be accounted for as transactions with equity holders in capacity as equity holders. Therefore, such changes would not result in a gain or loss being recognised in the profit or loss. (paragraph 51)
- to specify how an entity measures a gain or loss arising on loss of control of a subsidiary undertaking, and to require any such gain or loss to be recognised in profit or loss. (paragraph 46) The gain or loss arising on loss of control includes the parent's share of gains or losses related to the former subsidiary that were previously recognised through the statement of total recognised gains and losses. (paragraph 46B)
- to require any remaining non-controlling equity investment in a former subsidiary undertaking to be remeasured to its fair value in the consolidated financial statements on the date control of it is lost. (paragraph 46A)
- to provide guidance on determining whether two or more transactions or arrangements that result in the loss of control of a subsidiary undertaking should be treated as a single transaction when applying paragraphs 35A, 46, 46A and 51. (paragraph 47)
- to require losses applicable to the non-controlling interest to be allocated to the non-controlling interest with any guarantees or other support arrangements from the controlling and non-controlling interests being accounted separately. (paragraph 37)

Proposed amendments to FRS 2 Accounting for subsidiary undertakings

1   Paragraph 'i' is amended as follows:

Non-controlling ~~Minority~~ interests in total should be reported separately in the consolidated balance sheet and profit and loss account. When an entity becomes a subsidiary undertaking the assets and liabilities attributable to its non-controlling ~~minority~~ interest should be included on the same basis as those attributable to the interest held by the parent and other subsidiary undertakings. The effect of this for an acquisition is that all the subsidiary undertaking's identifiable assets and liabilities are included at fair value as required by the Act. ~~No goodwill should be attributed to the minority interest.~~

2   Paragraph 'n' is amended as follows:

When a subsidiary undertaking is acquired the FRS requires its identifiable assets and liabilities to be brought into the consolidation at their fair values at the date that undertaking becomes a subsidiary undertaking even if the acquisition has been made in stages. ~~When a group increases its interest in an undertaking that is already its subsidiary undertaking, the identifiable assets and liabilities of that subsidiary undertaking should be revalued to fair value and goodwill arising on the increase in interest should be calculated by reference to that fair value. This revaluation is not required if the difference between fair values and carrying amounts of the identifiable assets and liabilities attributable to the increase in stake is not material.~~

3   Paragraph 35 is amended as follows:

~~Minority~~ *Non-controlling interests*

The consolidated balance sheet should show separately the ~~aggregate of the capital and reserves attributable to minority~~ non-controlling interests at the end of the period within equity, separately from the parent shareholders equity. ~~under' Minority interests' in accordance with Schedule 4A paragraph 17(2). This amount represents the aggregate share of net assets or liabilities of subsidiary undertakings included in the consolidation that are attributable to the minority interests.~~

4   Paragraph 35A is inserted:

The non-controlling interest in the subsidiary's net assets comprises:

(a)   the proportionate interest in the subsidiary's net identifiable assets based on the non-controlling ownership interest in the subsidiary; and

(b)   that portion of the subsidiary's goodwill, if any, allocated to the non-controlling interest. In accordance with [draft] FRS ● *Business Combinations*, the portion of a subsidiary's goodwill allocated to the non-controlling interest may not be equal to the total amount recognised as goodwill multiplied by the non-controlling ownership interest in the subsidiary. This would be the case, for example, if an 80 per cent controlling interest in a subsidiary were acquired at an amount that exceeds 80 per cent of the subsidiary's fair value because the acquirer paid a premium to obtain control of the acquiree. In this situation, 80 per cent of the subsidiary's net identifiable assets would be attributed to equity holders of the parent, but more than 80 per cent of goodwill would be attributed to them.

Following a change in the parent's ownership interest in a subsidiary after control is obtained, goodwill is reassigned between the equity holders of the parent and the non-controlling interest on the basis of the relative carrying amounts of goodwill allocated to each of those groups of equity holders on the date control was obtained.

Paragraph 36 is amended as follows: 5

The consolidated profit and loss account should show separately the aggregate of profit or loss on ordinary activities for the period attributable to the ~~minority~~ non-controlling interests ~~under 'Minority interests' in accordance with Schedule 4A paragraph 17(3)~~. Any extraordinary profit or loss attributable to ~~minority~~ non-controlling interests should be shown separately in accordance with Schedule 4A paragraph 17(4).

Paragraph 37 is deleted and replaced with the following text: 6

Losses applicable to the non-controlling interest in a consolidated subsidiary undertaking may exceed the non-controlling interest in the subsidiary's equity. The excess, and any further losses attributable to the non-controlling interest, shall be allocated to the non-controlling interest.

Paragraph 38 is amended as follows: 7

~~Whether~~ The assets and liabilities of a subsidiary undertaking are included at fair values;* ~~or adjusted carrying amounts~~, those attributable to the non-controlling ~~minority~~ interest should be included on the same basis as those attributable to the interests held by the parent and its other subsidiary undertakings. ~~However, goodwill arising on acquisition should only be recognised with respect to the part of the subsidiary undertaking that is attributable to the interest held by the parent and its other subsidiary undertakings.~~

The footnote shall be amended as follows:

* Where the acquisition method of accounting is to be used in consolidating a subsidiary undertaking, Schedule 4A paragraph 9 requires the identifiable assets and liabilities of the undertaking acquired to be included in the consolidation at their fair values as at the date of acquisition. ~~Where the merger method of accounting is to be used, Schedule 4A paragraph 11 requires the assets and liabilities of the subsidiary undertaking to be consolidated at the amounts at which they stand in that undertaking's financial statements, subject to any adjustments authorised or required by the Act~~

In paragraph 39 replace the term 'minority' with 'non-controlling'.   8

Paragraph 45 is deleted and replaced with: 9

45   The income and expenses of a subsidiary are included in the consolidated financial statements from the acquisition date as defined in [draft] FRS • *Business Combinations*. Income and expenses of the subsidiary undertaking arising from changes in the values of its assets and liabilities shall be based on the values of those assets and liabilities recognised in the parent's consolidated financial statements at the acquisition date. For example, depreciation expense recognised in the consolidated income statement after the acquisition date shall be based on the fair values of those depreciable assets recognised in the parent's consolidated financial statements at the acquisition date. The income and

expenses of a subsidiary are included in the consolidated financial statements until the date on which the parent ceases to control the subsidiary.

10   Paragraphs 46 and 47 are deleted and replaced with:

46   If control of a subsidiary is lost, whether through a sale of ownership interests in that subsidiary by the parent or members of the group or through other means, any resulting gain or loss shall be recognised in profit or loss. That gain or loss shall be measured as the difference between:

(a)   the aggregate fair value of the proceeds, if any, from the transaction or event that resulted in the loss of control and the fair value of any investment remaining in the former subsidiary at the date control is lost; and

(b)   the aggregate of the parent's interest in the carrying amount in the consolidated financial statements of the former subsidiary's net assets immediately before control is lost, including the parent's share of gains or losses related to the former subsidiary recognised previously in the consolidated entity.

The non-controlling interest's share, if any, of the carrying amount of the net assets of the former subsidiary immediately before control is lost shall be derecognised at the date control is lost with a corresponding derecognition of the carrying amount of non-controlling interests. No gain or loss shall be recognised on derecognition of the non-controlling interest.

46A.   On the loss of control of a subsidiary, any investment remaining in the former subsidiary shall be accounted for in accordance with FRS 26 *'Financial Instruments Recognition and Measurement'*, or FRS 9 *'Associates and Joint Ventures'* as appropriate, from the date control is lost. The fair value of the remaining non-controlling equity investment at the date control is lost shall be regarded as the fair value on initial recognition of a financial asset in accordance with FRS 26 or, when appropriate, the cost on initial recognition of an investment in an associate or jointly controlled entity.

46B.   On the loss of control of a subsidiary undertaking, the individual assets and liabilities of that former subsidiary undertaking are derecognised. From the group's perspective, the loss of control of a subsidiary undertaking results in the loss of control and derecognition of some of the individual assets and liabilities of the group. Therefore, the gain or loss arising on loss of control of a subsidiary undertaking includes the parent's share of gains or losses that were recognised previously through the statement of total recognised gains and losses. This includes the parent's share of any gains or losses:

(a)   on exchange differences that were recognised through the statement of total recognised gains and losses in accordance with FRS 23 *The Effects of Changes in Foreign Exchange Rates*;

(b)   on cash flow hedges of a net investment that were recognised directly in equity in accordance with FRS 26; and

(c)   related to the individual assets and liabilities: for example, available-for-sale financial assets previously recognised through the statement of total recognised gains and losses, and cash flow hedge on hedging instruments previously recognised through the statement of total recognised gains and losses.

47   Control of a subsidiary undertaking may be lost in two or more transactions or arrangements. An entity shall account for each such transaction or arrangement separately unless circumstances indicate that the transactions or arrangements are part of a single transaction or arrangement. In determining whether to account for the transactions or arrangements as a single transaction

or arrangement an entity shall consider all of the terms and conditions of the transactions and arrangements and their economic effects. If one or more of the following indicators are present, the transactions or arrangements are to be accounted for as a single transaction or arrangement:

(a)   they are entered into at the same time or as part of a continuous sequence and in contemplation of one another.

(b)   they form a single arrangement that achieves, or is designed to achieve, an overall commercial effect.

(c)   the occurrence of one transaction or arrangement is dependent on the occurrence of the other transaction(s) or arrangement(s).

(d)   one or more of the transactions or arrangements considered on their own is not economically justified, but they are economically justified when considered together. An example is when one disposal is priced below market and is compensated for by a subsequent disposal priced above market.

The transactions or arrangements are to be accounted for separately if the entity can demonstrate clearly that they are not parts of a single transaction.

47A   The following disclosure shall be made in the consolidated financial statements: the amount of any gain or loss arising on the loss of control of a subsidiary undertaking recognised in profit or loss in accordance with paragraph 46, showing separately the amount of any gain or loss arising on the remeasurement to fair value of any retained investment in that former subsidiary undertaking.

The final sentence in paragraph 50 is deleted, as follows: **11**

Acquiring a subsidiary undertaking in stages

50   Schedule 4A paragraph 9 requires that the identifiable assets and liabilities of a subsidiary undertaking be included in the consolidation at fair value at the date of its acquisition, that is, the date it becomes a subsidiary undertaking. ~~This requirement is also applicable where the group's interest in the undertaking that becomes a subsidiary undertaking is acquired in stages. [4A Sch 9].~~

Paragraphs 51 and 52 (including the associated paragraph headings) are deleted and   **12** replaced with:

51   Changes in the parent's ownership interest in a subsidiary after control is obtained that do not result in a loss of control shall be accounted for as transactions between equity holders in their capacity as equity holders. No gain or loss shall be recognised in profit or loss on such changes. The carrying amount of the non-controlling interest shall be adjusted to reflect the change in the parent's interest in the subsidiary undertakings net assets. Any difference between the amount by which the non-controlling interest is so adjusted and the fair value of the consideration paid or received, if any, shall be recognised directly in equity and attributed to equity holders of the parent.

52   Deleted.

Insert after paragraph 55:   **13**

55A   An entity shall apply the amended Standard for annual periods beginning on or after 1 Janury 200X. Earlier application is encouraged. However, an entity shall not apply these amendments for annual periods beginning before 1 January 200X unless it also applies [draft] FRS ● *Business Combinations*, [draft] FRS ● *Intangibles Assets*, [draft] FRS ● *Impairment of Assets* and [draft] FRS 12 *Non-financial Liabilities*. If an entity applies this [draft] Standard before 1 January

200X it shall disclose that fact and also shall apply [draft] FRS • *Business Combinations* [draft] FRS • *Intangibles Assets*, [draft] FRS • *Impairment of Assets* and [draft] FRS 12 *Non-financial Liabilities* at the same time.

55B   Except as described in paragraph 55C, an entity shall apply this [draft] Standard retrospectively.

55C   An entity shall apply prospectively:

(a)   the requirements in paragraph 51 for accounting for increases in ownership interests in a subsidiary after control is obtained. Therefore, the requirements in paragraph 51 do not apply to increases that occurred before those amendments are applied.

(b)   the requirements in paragraphs 46 and 46A for the remeasurement to fair value of any retained investment in a former subsidiary undertaking in accounting for decreases in owership interest in a subsidiary undertaking that result in a loss of control. Therefore, an entity shall not restate the carrying amount of an investment in a former subsidiary undertaking if control was lost before these amendments are applied. In addition, an entity shall not recalculate any gain or loss on the loss of control of a subsidiary undertaking that occurred before those amendments are applied.

14   Paragraph 80 is amended as follows:

~~Minority~~ Non-controlling interests

~~Despite the title 'Minority interests',~~ tThere is in principle no upper limit to the proportion of shares in a subsidiary undertaking which may be held as a ~~minority~~ non-controlling interest while the parent undertaking still qualifies as such under section 258 of the Act (described in paragraph 14 of the FRS). The amounts reported in the consolidated balance sheet and profit and loss account for the ~~minority~~ non-controlling interests indicate the extent to which the assets and liabilities and profits and losses of subsidiary undertakings included in the consolidation are attributable to shareholders other than the parent or its other subsidiary undertakings. The effect of the existence of ~~minority~~ non-controlling interests on the returns to investors in the parent undertaking is best reflected by presenting the net identifiable assets attributable to ~~minority~~ non-controlling interests on the same basis as those attributable to group interests. Using the same basis for including group assets and liabilities, irrespective of the extent to which they are attributable to the ~~minority~~ non-controlling interest, presents the assets and liabilities on a consistent basis for the group as a whole.

15   Paragraph 81 is amended as follows:

The FRS requires that losses be attributed to the non-controlling ~~minority~~ interest in a loss making subsidiary undertaking, regardless of whether or not this leads to a debit balance for the non-controlling ~~minority~~ interest; to do otherwise would obscure the comparison between the assets and liabilities and results attributable to the non-controlling ~~minority~~ interest and those attributable to the group interests both during the periods when the accumulated losses accrue and afterwards, if these are then made good by later profits. Accumulated losses of subsidiary undertakings do not of themselves necessarily require funding by the parent undertaking and a debit balance for non-controlling ~~minority~~ interests represents net liabilities attributable to the shares held by the non-controlling ~~minority~~ in that subsidiary undertaking rather than a debt due from them. ~~The group should provide for any commercial or legal obligation (whether formal of implied) to provide finance that may not be recoverable in respect of the accumulated losses attributable to the~~

~~minority interests. Provisions of this sort would include the minorities' share of any liability guaranteed by the group, or any liability that the group itself would be likely to settle for commercial or other reasons, if the subsidiary undertaking could not do so itself. Any provision made with respect to minority debit balances should be set directly against the minority interest amount in the profit and loss account and the balance sheet~~.

Paragraph 82 is deleted.   **16**

In paragraph 83 replace the term minority interest with non-controlling interest.   **17**

Paragraph 85 is deleted.   **18**

Paragraph 86 is amended as follows: **19**

An undertaking may cease to be a subsidiary undertaking as a result of the parent undertaking losing control over it because of changes in the rights it holds or in those held by another party in that subsidiary undertaking. A parent undertaking may also lose control of its subsidiary undertaking because of changes in some other arrangement that gave it control without there being any change in the former parent undertaking's holding in its former subsidiary undertaking. For example, control may pass if there is a change in voting rights or in how these are allocated. In these circumstances neither a gain nor a loss accrues in the consolidated financial statements, unless there is a payment for the transfer of control, because there is no change in the net assets attributable to the group's holding in the former subsidiary undertaking. The assets and liabilities of the former subsidiary undertaking should cease to be consolidated but should be shown instead as an associated undertaking, joint venture or investment as appropriate.

Paragraph 87 is amended as follows: **20**

An undertaking usually ceases to be a subsidiary undertaking because the group reduces its proportional interest in that undertaking. The reduction of the group's interest may result from its directly disposing of part of the interest it holds or from a deemed disposal. Any reduction in the group's proportional interest other than by a direct disposal is a deemed disposal. Disposals and deemed disposals may give rise to profits or losses for the group, which should be calculated as set out in paragraph 46, 46A, 46B and 47. There may be other losses...

Paragraphs 88, 89, 90 and 91 are deleted.   **21**

In paragraph 94(b) replace the term 'minority' with 'non-controlling'.   **22**

In the development of the Standard, insert parargraphs **Xxvi** and **Xxvii**:   **23**

Xxvi In 200X FRS 2 was amended to reflect the introduction of [draft] FRS ●
Business Combinations. [Draft] FRS ● *Business Combinations* was part of the
ASB convergence strategy with International Accounting Standards. As part of
the convergence programme the Board implemented:
  - ● FRS ● Business Combinations;
  - ● FRS ● Intangible Assets;
  - ● FRS ● Impairment of Assets;
  - ● FRS 12 (revised) Non-financial Liabilities (formerly known as Provisions, Contingent Assets and Contingent Liabilities);
  - ● Amendments to FRS 17 Retirement and Termination Benefits (formerly known as Retirement benefits); and

- Amendments to FRS 2 Accounting for Subsidary Undertakings (parts of *International Accounting Standard 27*).

All of these standards had been introduced or amended as part of the IASB Business Combinations project.

Xxvii As part of the proposed amendments to IAS 27, the IASB issued a Basis for Conclusions. This Basis for Conclusions is inserted in a new section following the section of the FRS titled "The Development of the Standard."

IASB Basis for Conclusions

ASB note: The IASB's Basis for Conclusions, which accompanies the amendments to IAS 27, is set out below in full. It should be noted though that some of the discussion it contains concerns IASB requirements that have no equivalent in the UK or Republic of Ireland. Footnotes have been used to indicate corresponding requirements in the UK and Republic of Ireland where applicable.

All references in this section to 'the Board' and 'Board members' are references to the IASB Board and IASB Board members
This Basis for Conclusions accompanies, but is not part of, the proposed Amendment to IAS 27.

INTRODUCTION

This Basis for Conclusions summarises the International Accounting Standards Board's considerations in reaching the conclusions in the Exposure Draft of Proposed Amendments to IAS 27 *Consolidated and Separate Financial Statements**. Individual Board members gave greater weight to some factors than to others. **BC1**

The Exposure Draft has been published as part of the second phase of the Board's project on business combinations. This phase is being conducted jointly with the US Financial Accounting Standards Board (FASB). As part of this phase, the Board and the FASB have considered jointly issues related to non-controlling interests. This Basis for Conclusions identifies those decisions reached by the Board that differ from those reached by the FASB. **BC2**

The Board's intention in developing these proposals was not to reconsider all of the requirements in IAS 27. The changes proposed are primarily concerned with accounting for non-controlling interests. The Board is reconsidering the other requirements of IAS 27 as part of its project on consolidation policy. **BC3**

Changes in ownership interests in subsidiaries

The Board decided that after control of an entity is obtained, changes in a parent's controlling interest in that entity that do not result in a loss of control should be treated as transactions with equity holders in their capacity as equity holders. This means that no gain or loss on these changes would be recognised in profit or loss. It also means that no change in the carrying amounts of assets (including goodwill) or liabilities should be recognised as a result of such transactions. The Board rejected the alternative approach of accounting for such transactions as transactions with members outside the consolidated group, with gains or losses recognised in profit or loss. **BC4**

The Board reached these conclusions because it believes that the proposed approach is consistent with its previous decision that non-controlling interests are a separate component of equity. This conclusion was based on the Board's view that non-controlling interests are part of the ownership interest in the consolidated group **BC5**

---

*ASB footnote: *The corresponding requirements in the UK and the Republic of Ireland are in FRS 2 Accounting for Subsidiary Undertakings'.*

because they do not meet the definition of a liability in the *Framework for the Preparation and Presentation of Financial Statements**.

BC6   The Board decided that whenever control of a subsidiary is lost, any resulting gain or loss should be recognised in profit or loss for the period. A decrease in ownership interest can result from the sale of an ownership interest or by other means, such as the issue of new ownership interests by a subsidiary to third parties. Loss of control can also occur in the absence of a transaction. It may, for example, occur on the expiry of an agreement that previously allowed an entity to control a subsidiary.

BC7   The Board reached these conclusions because it believes that when a parent's ownership interest in a subsidiary decreases to the point that it no longer controls that subsidiary, a significant economic event occurs. The parent-subsidiary relationship ceases to exist. The parent no longer controls the subsidiary's individual assets and liabilities. If the parent maintains less than a controlling interest, an investor-investee relationship begins; otherwise no relationship with the subsidiary continues. This is consistent with the Board's decision in the Exposure Draft of Proposed Amendments to IFRS 3 that obtaining control in a business combination is a significant economic event that, for example, results in the recognition in profit or loss of any holding gains or losses if a business combination is achieved in stages. As a result, the Board decided that it was appropriate to recognise the following in profit or loss on the loss of control of a subsidiary:

- any gain or loss arising on such loss of control, including any gain or loss on the remeasurement to fair value of any retained investment in that former subsidiary; and
- the parent's share of gains or losses related to the former subsidiary that were previously recognised in equity.

BC8   The Board decided that the loss of control of a subsidiary is, from the group's perspective, the loss of control over some of the group's individual assets and liabilities. Accordingly, the general requirements in IFRSs should be applied in accounting for the derecognition from the group's financial statements of the subsidiary's assets and liabilities. If a gain or loss originally reflected in equity would be recognised as income or expense on the separate disposal of those assets and liabilities, a gain or loss should be recognised on the indirect disposal of those assets and liabilities through loss of control of a subsidiary. For example, if a subsidiary sells one of its available-for-sale financial assets in a separate transaction, a gain or loss previously recognised in equity would be recognised in profit or loss. Similarly, on the loss of control of a subsidiary, the entire cumulative gain or loss attributed to the parent on that former subsidiary's available-for-sale financial assets previously recognised in equity would be recognised in profit or loss.

BC9   The Board considered whether its decision that a gain or loss on the disposal of a subsidiary should be recognised only when that disposal results in a loss of control could give rise to opportunities to structure transactions to achieve a particular accounting outcome. For example, would an entity be motivated to structure a transaction or arrangement as multiple steps to maximise gains or minimise losses if an entity was planning to dispose of its controlling interest in a subsidiary? Consider the following example. An entity P (Parent) controls 70 per cent of entity S (Subsidiary). P intends to sell all of its 70 per cent controlling interest in S. On 31 December 2003 the fair value of S as a whole is CU12,000 and its carrying value in

---

*ASB footnote: *The equivalent document in the UK and Republic of Ireland to the IASB's* Framework *is the ASB's* Statement of Principles for Financial Reporting. *Although the* Statement of Principles *is very similar to the* Framework, *it is not identical.*

consolidated financial statements is CU8,000. P could initially sell 19 per cent of its ownership interest in S without loss of control and then, soon afterwards, sell the remaining 51 per cent and lose control. Alternatively, P could sell all of its 70 per cent interest in S in one transaction. In the first case, the gain on the sale of the 19 per cent interest would be recognised directly in equity, whereas the gain from the sale of the remaining 51 per cent interest would be recognised in profit or loss, resulting in a recognised gain of CU2,040. In the second case, the whole amount of the gain or loss on the sale of the 70 per cent interest would be recognised in profit or loss resulting in a recognised gain of CU2,800.*

The Board noted that the opportunity to conceal losses through structuring would be reduced by the requirements of IAS 36 *Impairment of Assets†* and IFRS 5 *Non-current Assets Held for Sale and Discontinued Operations.* Paragraph 12 of IAS 36 provides that: **BC10**

> in assessing whether there is any indication that an asset may be impaired, an entity shall consider, as a minimum, the following indications: ...significant changes ...are expected to take place in the near future, in the extent to which, or manner in which, an asset is used or is expected to be used. These changes include the asset becoming idle, plans to discontinue or restructure the operation to which an asset belongs, plans to dispose of an asset before the previously expected date ...

Once an asset meets the criteria to be classified as held for sale (or is included in a disposal group that is classified as held for sale), it is excluded from the scope of IAS 36 and is accounted for in accordance with IFRS 5. Under paragraph 20 of IFRS 5 'an entity shall recognise an impairment loss for any initial or subsequent write-down of the asset (or disposal group) to fair value less costs to sell ...' Therefore, if appropriate, an impairment loss would be recognised for the goodwill and non-current assets of a subsidiary that will be sold or otherwise disposed of before control of the subsidiary is lost. Accordingly, the Board concluded that the principal risk is the minimising of gains and that entities are unlikely to strive to minimise gains. **B11**

The Board decided that the possibility of such structuring could be overcome by requiring entities to consider whether multiple arrangements should be accounted for as a single transaction to ensure that the principles of faithful representation are adhered to. The Board believes that all of the terms and conditions of the arrangements and their effect in practice should be considered in determining whether multiple arrangements should be accounted for as a single arrangement. Accordingly, the Board has included guidance in paragraph 30F of the Exposure Draft to assist in identifying when multiple arrangements that result in the loss of control of a subsidiary should be treated as a single arrangement. In particular, the Board concluded that if the indicators in paragraph 30F‡ of the Exposure Draft are present, it is presumed that two or more disposal transactions or arrangements should be treated as a single transaction or arrangement, unless it can be clearly demonstrated that they are separate. The Board noted that if it or the IFRIC develops a general statement on 'linkage', to address the circumstances when two or **B12**

**In the two-step transaction, the gain is calculated as (51% × CU12,000) less (51% × CU8,000), as only the transaction causing actual loss of control is included in the calculation. If the disposal occurred in one step, the gain is calculated as (70% × CU12,000) less (70% × CU8,000).*

†*ASB footnote: The ASB is proposing to implement IAS 36* Impairment of Assets *see* FRED 38.

‡*ASB footnote: Paragraph 47 is the corresponding paragraph of 30F in the proposed amendments to FRS 2.*

more transactions or arrangements should be treated as a single transaction or arrangement, that pronouncement might replace this guidance.

BC13   The Board also concluded that the accounting guidance provided for the loss of control of a subsidiary should be extended to events or transactions in which an investor loses significant influence over an associate or joint control of a joint venture. Thus, upon the loss of significant influence, any retained investment would be remeasured to fair value and a gain or loss would be recognised in profit or loss. The FASB considered whether to address that same issue as part of this project. It concluded that the accounting for investments that no longer qualify for equity method accounting is outside the scope of the project and therefore decided to address the issue in a separate project.

Attribution of losses

BC14   The current version of IAS 27 states that when losses attributed to the minority (ie non-controlling interest) exceed the minority's interest in the subsidiary's equity, 'the excess, and any further losses applicable to the minority, are allocated against the majority interest except to the extent that the minority has a binding obligation and is able to make an additional investment to cover the losses'.

BC15   The Board decided that this treatment was inconsistent with its conclusion that non-controlling interests are part of the equity of the group. Although it is true that non-controlling interests have no further obligation to contribute assets to the subsidiary, the parent has no further obligation either. Non-controlling interests participate proportionally in the risks and rewards of an investment in the subsidiary. If a non-controlling interest enters into an arrangement that obligates it to the subsidiary, the Board believes that that arrangement should be accounted for separately and the arrangement should not affect the way losses are attributed to the controlling and non-controlling interests. Thus, the Board concluded that losses applicable to non-controlling interests should be attributed to them, even if doing so would result in a non-controlling interest being reported as a deficit.

Disclosure

BC16   In considering the proposals in the Exposure Draft the Board discussed whether any additional disclosures were necessary. The Board decided that the amount of any gain or loss arising on the loss of control of a subsidiary, including the amount of any gain or loss arising on the remeasurement to fair value of any retained investment in that former subsidiary, should be disclosed. This disclosure will provide information about the effect of the loss of control of a subsidiary on the financial position at the reporting date and the results for the reporting period.

BC17   In addition the Board considered the disclosure that the FASB decided to require. In its deliberations on business combinations, the FASB decided to require entities with one or more partially-owned subsidiaries to disclose in the notes to the consolidated financial statements a schedule showing the effects on the controlling interest's equity of transactions with the non-controlling interests.

BC18   The Board noted that IFRSs require this information to be provided in the statement of changes in equity or in the notes to the financial statements. This is because IAS 1 *Presentation of Financial Statements** requires an entity to present, either within the

*ASB footnote: *The corresponding requirements in the UK and the Republic of Ireland are in FRS 3* Reporting Financial Performance.

statement of changes in equity or in the notes, a reconciliation between the carrying amount of each component of equity at the beginning and end of the period, disclosing separately each change. Accordingly, requiring an additional schedule is not necessary.

The Board also considered whether entities that present earnings per share infor-   **BC19** mation should be required to disclose an additional per share measure that includes in the numerator the effects of equity transactions with the non-controlling interest. For example, a parent may acquire some of the non-controlling equity interests in a subsidiary at an amount in excess of the carrying amount of those interests. Should the effective premium paid, which is recorded in equity, be required to be reflected in the numerator of that additional per share measure as a transfer of equity from equity holders of the parent to other equity holders? The Board considered this issue in the light of the FASB's decision to require such a measure, but decided not to require this disclosure.

The Board noted that the objective of earnings per share information as stated in   **BC20** IAS 33 *Earnings per Share** is to provide a measure of the interests of each ordinary share of the parent in the performance of the entity over the reporting period. The Board supported the basic principle in IAS 33 that effects of capital transactions between groups of ordinary equity holders should not be treated as adjustments to the numerator of the earnings per share calculation. Therefore, the effects of transactions with the non-controlling interest (without a change of control) should not affect the calculation of earnings per share. The Board observed that, unlike the effects of transactions *between* groups of ordinary equity holders, IAS 33 requires the numerator to be adjusted for preferred dividends and the effects of other equity transactions between ordinary and preferred equity holders in order to determine the amount of earnings available for distribution to the ordinary equity holders.

However, the Board decided that an entity should not be precluded from disclosing   **BC21** the additional per share measure if it regards this information as useful. The Board concluded that if an entity discloses, in addition to basic and diluted earnings per share, amounts per share that include in the numerator the effects of equity transactions with the non-controlling interests, such amounts should be calculated in the usual manner using the denominator determined in accordance with IAS 33.

Transitional provisions

To improve the comparability of financial information across entities, amendments   **BC22** to IFRSs are usually applied retrospectively. Therefore, the Board decided to require retrospective application of the amendments to IAS 27. The Board believes that the benefits of retrospective application outweigh the costs. However, the Board decided that retrospective application would be impracticable in the following circumstances:

(a)   accounting for increases in a parent's controlling ownership interest in a subsidiary that occurred before the effective date of the amendments. Therefore, any previous increase in a parent's controlling ownership interest before the effective date of the amendments should not be restated.

(b)   accounting for a parent's retained investment in a former subsidiary over which control was lost before the effective date of the amendments. Therefore, the carrying amount of any investment in a former subsidiary should not be restated to its fair value on the date control was lost. In addition, an entity

---

*ASB footnote: *The corresponding requirements in the UK and the Republic of Ireland are in FRS 22* Earnings Per Share *(IAS 33).*

should not recalculate any gain or loss on loss of control of a subsidiary if the loss of control occurred before the effective date of the amendments.

BC23   In deciding that prospective application should be used in these circumstances the Board applied principles that are consistent with those it generally uses to determine whether IFRSs should be applied retrospectively or prospectively. Specifically, the Board decided that retrospective application would be impracticable in these cases because:

(a)   the information needed to restate an amount previously recorded may not exist or may no longer be obtainable.

(b)   the accounting for a retained investment in a former subsidiary and recalculating the gain or loss arising on loss of control of a former subsidiary would require the determination of fair values at a prior date. Making that determination raises problems in relation to the role of hindsight: in particular, whether the benefit of hindsight should be included or excluded in determining the fair value and, if excluded, how the effect of hindsight can be separated from the other factors existing at the date for which the valuations are required.

The Board concluded that the implementation difficulties and consequent costs associated with applying the amendments retrospectively in these circumstances outweigh the benefit of improved comparability of financial information, and therefore decided to require prospective application. In addition, the Board concluded that identifying those provisions for which retrospective application of the amendments would be impracticable and thus prospective application would be required would reduce implementation costs and result in greater comparability between entities.

Alternative view

Three Board members disagree with the proposed treatment of changes in controlling interests in subsidiaries after control is established (paragraphs BC4-BC13). They believe that it is important that the consequences of such changes for the shareholders of the parent entity should be reported clearly in the income statement, as is permitted by current IFRSs.

AV1

The proposed revision of IAS 27 adopts the economic entity view of the consolidated accounts. This treats all equity interests in the group as being homogeneous, so that transactions between controlling and non-controlling interests are regarded as mere transfers within the total equity interest and no gain or loss should be recognised on such transactions. The three Board members observe that the non-controlling interests represent equity claims that are restricted to particular subsidiaries, whereas the controlling interests are affected by the performance of the entire group. The consolidated financial statements should therefore report performance from the perspective of the controlling interest (a parent entity perspective) in addition to the wider perspective provided by the economic entity approach.

AV2

The parent entity perspective implies the recognition of gains or losses on transactions by the parent entity in the equity of a subsidiary which is controlled both before and after the transaction. If, as these Board members would prefer, the full goodwill method were not used, the acquisition of additional equity in a subsidiary would give rise to the recognition of additional purchased goodwill, measured as the excess of the purchase consideration over the book value of the separately identified assets in the subsidiary attributable to the additional interest acquired. On reducing the equity stake in a subsidiary, without loss of control, a gain or loss attributable to the controlling interest would be recognised. This would be measured as the difference between the consideration received and the proportion of the book value of the subsidiary's assets (including purchased goodwill) attributable to the holding disposed of. This would provide the controlling interest with the relevant information about the gains and losses arising on the partial disposal of holdings in subsidiaries. It would also improve the reporting of gains and losses arising on disposals of subsidiaries that are made in stages.

AV3

FRS 2 Consequential amendments to other UK accounting standards

The amendments in this [draft] Appendix shall be applied for annual periods beginning on or after [1 January 2007]. If an entity applies this [draft] FRS for an earlier period, these amendments shall be applied for that earlier period. Amended paragraphs are shown with new text underlined and deleted text struck through.

A1   Terminology

Where existing UK accounting standards refer to 'minority interest' it shall be replaced with the term 'non-controlling interest'. There is no change in the meaning of the term.

A2   SSAP 25 Segmental Reporting

A2.1   Paragraph 21 is amended as follows:

21   The entity should disclose the result of each reportable segment before accounting for taxation, ~~minority~~ non-controlling interests and extraordinary items.

A2.2   Paragraph 26 is amended as follows:

26   Sometimes associated undertakings form a significant part of a reporting entity's results or assets. In such circumstances the following information should be analysed segmentally and shown separately in the segmental report:

(a)   the reporting entity's share of the profits or losses of associated undertakings before accounting for taxation, ~~minority~~ non-controlling interests and extraordinary items; and ...

A2.3   Paragraph 34 is amended as follows:

34   ...

(a)   turnover, distinguishing between (i) turnover derived from external customers and (ii) turnover derived from other segments;

(b)   result, before accounting for taxation, ~~minority~~ non-controlling interests and extraordinary items; and

(c) net assets.

A2.4   Paragraph 36 is amended as follows:

36   ...

(a)   the entity's share of the results of associated undertakings before accounting for taxation, ~~minority~~ non-controlling interests and extraordinary items; and

(b)   the entity's share of the net assets of associated undertakings (including goodwill to the extent it has not been written off) stated, where possible, after attributing fair values to the net assets at the date of acquisition of the interest in each undertaking.

A3   FRS 1 Cash Flow Statements

A3.1   In paragraph 13 replace 'minority' with 'non-controlling'.

Paragraphs 23 and 24 are amended as follows: A3.2

Acquisitions and disposals

23   Cash inflows from 'acquisitions and disposals' include:

(a)   receipts from sales of investments in subsidiary undertakings <u>where control is lost</u>, showing separately any balances of cash and overdrafts transferred as part of the sale;

(b)   receipts from sales of investments in associates or joint ventures; and

(c)   receipts from sales of trades or businesses.

24   Cash outflows from 'acquisitions and disposals' of subsidiary undertakings include:

(a) payments to ~~acquire~~ <u>gain control of</u> investments in subsidiary undertakings, showing separately any balances of cash and overdrafts acquired;

(b) payments to acquire investments in associates and joint ventures; and

(c) payments to acquire trades or businesses.

Paragraphs 24A and 24B are inserted as follows: A3.3

24A Cash flows arising from changes in ownership interests in a subsidiary after control is obtained that do not result in a loss of control shall be classified as cash flows from financing.

24B Changes in ownership interests in a subsidiary undertaking after control is obtained that do not result in a loss of control, such as the subsequent purchase or sale by a parent of a subsidiary's undertakings equity instruments, are accounted for as transactions with equity holders (see FRS 2 *Accounting for Subsidiary Undertakings*). Accordingly, the resulting cash flows are classified in the same way as other transactions with equity holders described in paragraph 29 - 32.

Paragraph 43 is amended as follows: A3.4

Groups

43   Cash flows that are internal to the group should be eliminated in the preparation of a consolidated cash flow statement. ~~Where a subsidiary undertaking joins or leaves a group during a financial year the cash flows of the group should include the cash flows of the subsidiary undertaking concerned for the same period as that for which the group's profit and loss account includes the results of the subsidiary undertaking.~~ <u>The cash flows of a subsidiary undertaking are included in the consolidated cash flow statement from the acquisition date as defined in [draft] FRS ● *Business Combinations* until the date on which the parent ceases to control the subsidiary undertaking.</u>

Paragraph 45 is amended as follows: A3.5

Acquisitions and disposals of subsidiary undertakings

A note to the cash flow statement should show a summary of the effects of acquisitions and disposals of subsidiary undertakings indicating how much of the consideration comprised cash. Material effects on amounts reported under each of the standard headings reflecting the cash flows of a subsidiary undertaking acquired or disposed of <u>where control is lost or gained</u> in the period should be disclosed, as far as practicable. This information could be given by dividing cash flows between continuing and discontinued operations and acquisitions.

A3.6   **In Appendix I the illustrative examples of cash flow statements are amended as follows:**

EXAMPLE 2

In note 2 of the cash flow statement replace:

'Purchase of subsidiary undertaking' with:

'Cash paid to obtain control of subsidiary undertaking'

Also in note 2 replace:

'Net overdrafts acquired with subsidiary' with:

'Net overdrafts acquired on obtaining control of subsidiary'

In note 6 replace:

'Purchase of subsidiary undertaking (100% acquired) with:

'Obtaining control of subsidiary undertaking'

Also in note 6 replace:

'The subsidiary undertaking acquired during the year ...' with:

'The subsidiary undertaking where control was obtained during the year ...'

EXAMPLE 4

In the movement in opening and closing portfolio investments net of financing replace:

'Acquired with subsidiary' with:

'Acquired on obtaining control of subsidiary'

In note 2 replace:

'Acquisition of subsidiary' with:

'Cash paid to obtain control of subsidiary undertaking'

Also in note 2 replace:

'Net cash acquired with subsidiary' with:

'Net cash acquired on obtaining control of subsidiary undertaking'

In note 4 replace:

 'Purchase of subsidiary undertaking' with:

'Obtaining control of subsidiary undertaking'

Also in note 4 replace:

'Net cash acquired with subsidiary undertaking' with;

'Net cash acquired on obtaining control of subsidiary undertaking'

FRS 3 Reporting Financial Performance   A4

In paragraph 'd' replace 'minority' with 'non-controlling'.   A4.1

Paragraph 3 is amended as follows: A4.2

Acquisitions:

Operations of the reporting entity ~~that are acquired~~ <u>where control is obtained</u> in the period.

Paragraph 27 is amended as follows: A4.3

Statement of total recognised gains and losses

27 A primary statement should be presented, with the same prominence as the other primary statements, showing the total of recognised gains and losses and its components. <u>The total recognised gains and losses shall be attributed to equity holders of the parent and non-controlling interests.</u> ~~The components should be the gains and losses that are recognised in the period insofar as they are attributable to shareholders.~~

Paragraph 28 is amended as follows: A4.4

Reconciliation of movements in shareholders' funds

28 A note should be presented reconciling the opening and closing totals of shareholders' funds of the period. <u>The reconciliation should separately disclose total equity, equity attributable to equity holders of the parent and non-controlling interest, separately disclosing changes resulting from:</u>

   (i)   <u> profit or loss;</u>

   (ii)   <u>transactions with equity holders acting in their capacity as equity holders, showing separately distributions to equity holders; and</u>

   (iii) <u>each item of income or expense recognised through the statement of total recognised gains and losses, if any</u>.

Paragraph 56 is amended as follows: A4.5

Statement of total recognised gains and losses

56 The range of important components of financial performance which the FRS requires reporting entities to highlight would often be incomplete if it stopped short at the profit and loss account, since certain gains and losses are specifically permitted or required by law or an accounting standard to be taken directly to reserves. An example is an unrealised gain, such as a revaluation surplus on fixed assets. It is necessary to consider all gains and losses recognised in a period when assessing the financial performance of a reporting entity during that period. Accordingly, the FRS requires, as a primary statement, a statement of total recognised gains and losses to show the extent to which

equity holders of the parent and non-controlling interests ~~shareholders'~~ have increased or <u>decreased</u> from all the various gains and losses recognised in the period. ~~It follows from this perspective that the same gains and losses should not be recognised twice (for example, a holding gain recognised when a fixed asset is revalued should not be recognised a second time when the revalued asset is sold).~~

A4.6   **Paragraph 59 is amended as follows:**

Reconciliation of movements in shareholders' funds

59   The profit and loss account and the statement of total recognised gains and losses reflect the performance of a reporting entity in a period. There are, however, other changes in shareholders' funds that can also be important in understanding the change in the financial position of the entity. The purpose of the reconciliation of movements in shareholders' funds is to highlight those other changes <u>and disclose separately total changes and changes attributable to equity holders of the parent and non-controlling interests</u>. If included as a primary statement, the reconciliation should be shown separately from the statement of total recognised gains and losses.

A4.7   **The illustrative examples are amended as follows:**

Example 1

In the profit and loss account, replace 'minority' with 'non-controlling'.

Example 2

In the profit and loss account, replace 'minority' with 'non-controlling'.

Example 2

The statement of total recognised gains and losses is amended as follows:

Statement of total recognised gains and losses

	1993	1992 as restated
	£ millions	£ millions
Profit for the financial year	31 ~~29~~	9 ~~7~~
Unrealised surplus on revaluation of properties	4	6
Unrealised (loss)/gain on trade investment	(3)	7
	32 ~~30~~	22 ~~20~~
Currency translation differences on foreign currency net investments	(2)	5
Total recognised gains and losses relating to the year	30 ~~28~~	27 ~~25~~
Prior year adjustment (as explained in note x)	(10)	
Total gains and losses recognised since last year	20 ~~18~~	

Attributable to:

Equity holders of the parent	18 ~~16~~	25 ~~23~~
Non-controlling interest	2	2
	20 ~~18~~	27 ~~25~~

Example 2

The reconciliation of shareholder funds is amended as follows:

Reconciliation of movement in shareholders' funds

	20X1 Total	20X1 Attributable to equity shareholders of the parent	20x1 Attributable to non-controlling interest
	£millions	*£ millions*	*£ millions*
Profit for the financial year	31	29	2
Dividends	(8)	(8)	
	23	21	2
Other recognised gains and losses relating to the year (net)	(1)	(1)	
New share capital subscribed	20	20	
Sale of shares in subsidiary to non-controlling interest at a premium			
~~Goodwill written-off~~			
Net addition to shareholders' funds	42	40	2
Opening shareholders' funds (originally £375 million before deduction prior year adjustment of £10 million)	365	X	X
Closing shareholders' funds	405	X	X

PRIOR YEAR COMPARATIVE INFORMATION IN THE ABOVE FORMAT IS REQUIRED TO BE DISCLOSED

Investment company example

In the profit and loss account, replace 'minority' with 'non-controlling'.

In the statement of total recognised gains and losses, the presentation format set out above shall be adopted. The statement shall attribute gains and losses to equity holders of the parent and to non-controlling interests.

A5   FRS 9 Associates and Joint Ventures

A5.1   In paragraphs 11 and 12 replace the term 'minority' with 'non-controlling'.

A5.2   Paragraph 40 is amended as follows:

"... applying the transitional arrangements of ~~FRS 10 Goodwill and Intangible Assets~~ [draft] FRS ● *Business Combinations.*"

A5.3   Paragraph 40A is inserted:

40A   If significant influence over an associate is lost or if joint control over a jointly controlled entity is lost, all amounts recognised through the statement of total recognised gains and losses in relation to that entity shall be recognised in profit or loss in accordance with FRS 23 *The Effects of Changes in Foreign Currency Rates* and FRS 26 *Financial Instruments: Measurement and Recognition.*

40B   If an investor's proportionate ownership interest in an associate is reduced but significant influence is retained, only the proportionate share of the amounts recognised through the statement of total recognised gains and losses in relation to that associate shall be recognised in profit or loss in accordance with FRS 23 and FRS 26. For example, if an associate has available-for-sale financial assets, the investor will not recognise those assets separately if the associate is accounted for using the equity method. However, if an investor ceases to have significant influence over a former associate the entire cumulative gain or loss recognised previously through the statement of total recognised gains and losses by the investor in relation to those assets shall be recognised in profit or loss. If an investor's proportionate ownership interest in an associate is reduced, but the investor continues to have significant influence over the investee, a proportionate amount of the cumulative gain or loss on the associate's available-for-sale financial assets previously recognised through the statement of total recognised gains and losses shall be recognised in profit or loss.

40C   If an investor's proportionate ownership interest in an joint venture is reduced but joint control is retained, only the proportionate share of the amounts recognised through the statement of total recognised gains and losses in relation to that joint venture shall be recognised in profit or loss in accordance with FRS 23 and FRS 26. For example, if a jointly controlled entity has available-for-sale financial assets, the investor will not recognise those assets separately if the jointly controlled entity is accounted for using the equity method. However, if an investor ceases to have joint control over a jointly controlled entity, the entire cumulative gain or loss previously recognised through the statement of total recognised gains and losses by the investor in relation to those assets shall be recognised in profit or loss. If an investor's proportionate ownership interest in a jointly controlled entity is reduced, but the investor continues to have joint control over the investee, a proportionate amount of the cumulative gain or loss on the jointly controlled entity's available-for-sale financial assets previously recognised through the statement of total recognised gains and losses shall be recognised in profit or loss.

A5.4   Paragraph 41 is deleted and replaced with:

Increasing an interest held in an associate or joint venture

41   When a group increases its interest in an associate or joint venture but does not obtain control, such that the definition of a subsidiary undertaking in accordance with FRS 2 is not met, the identifiable assets and liabilities of that associate or joint venture should be revalued to fair value and goodwill arising

on the increase in interest should be calculated by reference to those fair values. This revaluation is not required if the difference between net fair values and carrying amounts of the assets and liabilities attributable to the increase in stake is not material.

Reducing an interest held in an associate or joint venture

41A Where a group reduces its interest in an associate or joint venture, but retains a significant influence or joint control, it should record any profit or loss arising calculated as the difference between the carrying amount of the associate or joint venture before the reduction and the carrying amount attributable to the group's interest after the reduction together with any proceeds received. The net assets compared should include any related goodwill not previously written off through the profit and loss account.

Paragraph 42 will be deleted and replaced with: A5.5

42 An investor shall discontinue the use of the equity method from the date that it ceases to have significant influence over an associate or joint control over a joint venture and shall account for the investment in accordance with FRS 26 from that date, provided the associate does not become a subsidiary undertaking or a joint venture, or that the joint venture does not become a subsidiary undertaking or an associate. On loss of significant influence or joint control, any remaining non-controlling equity investment in a former associate or joint venture shall be remeasured to its fair value with a gain or loss recognised in profit or loss.

42A When any remaining investment in a former associate or joint venture is accounted for in accordance with FRS 26, the fair value of the remaining investment at the date it ceases to be an associate or joint venure shall be regarded as its fair value on initial recognition as a financial asset in accordance with FRS 26.

Paragraph 43 will be deleted and replaced with: A5.6

43 From the date on which an associate or a joint venture becomes a subsidiary undertaking it shall be accounted for in accordance with FRS 2 (amended 200X) *Accounting for Subsidiary Undertakings*.

43A From the date which a joint venture becomes an associate it shall be accounted for in accordance with this FRS, applying the equity method for associates. From the date which an associate becomes a joint venture it shall be accounted in accordance with this FRS, applying the gross equity method of accounting.

A5.7   **In Appendix IV the illustrative examples are amended as follows:**

EXAMPLE 1

In the profit and loss account, replace 'minority with 'non-controlling'

The consolidated balance sheet is amended as follows:

CONSOLIDATED BALANCE SHEET

	£m	£m	£m
Fixed assets			
Tangible assets		480	
Investments			
Investments in joint ventures:			
Share of gross assets	130		
Share of gross liabilities	(80)		
		50	
Investments in associates		20	
			550
Current assets			
Stock		15	
Debtors		75	
Cash at bank and in hand		10	
		100	
Creditors (due within one year)		(50)	
Net current assets			50
Total assets less current liabilities			600
Creditors (due after more than one year)			(250)
Provisions for liabilities and charges			(10)
			~~300~~ 340
~~Equity minority~~ Non-controlling interest			40
Capital and reserves			
Called up share capital			50
Share premium account			150
Profit and loss account			100
Shareholders' funds (all equity)			~~300~~ 340

EXAMPLE 2

In the profit and loss account, replace 'minority with 'non-controlling'.

The consolidated balance sheet is amended as set out in example 1.

FRS 16 Current Tax   A6

Paragraph 'b' is amended as follows: A6.1

b   Current tax should be recognised in the profit and loss account for the period,
     except to the extent that it is attributable to a gain or loss that has been
     recognised ~~directly in~~ through the statement of total recognised gains and losses
     or directly in equity. Where a gain or a loss has been recognised directly in the
     statement of total recognised gains and losses, the tax relating to that gain or
     loss should also be recognised directly in that statement. Where a gain or loss
     has been recognised directly in equity, the tax relating to that gain or loss
     should also be recognised directly in equity.

Amend paragraph 5 as follows: A6.2

5   **Current tax should be recognised in the profit and loss account for the period,
     except to the extent that it is (a) attributable to a gain or loss that is or has been
     recognised directly in the statement of total recognised gains and losses or (b)
     attributable to a gain or loss that is or has been recognised directly in the equity
     for transactions with non-controlling interests, in accordance with FRS 2
     Accounting for Subsidiary Undertakings.**

Insert paragraph 6A: A6.3

6A   **Where a gain or loss is or has been recognised directly in equity, the tax attri-
     butable to that gain or loss should also be recognised directly in that equity.**

Paragraph 7 is amended as follows: A6.4

7   Accounting standards (or, in their absence, legislation) require or permit cer-
     tain gains or losses to be credited or charged through ~~directly in~~ the statement
     of total recognised gains or losses or directly to equity (ie not in the profit or
     loss account). This FRS requires any attributable tax to be treated in the same
     way. In exceptional circumstances it may be difficult to determine the amount
     of current tax that is attributable to gains or losses that have been recognised
     directly in equity or through ~~in~~ the statement of total recognised gains and
     losses. In such circumstances, the attributable tax is based on a reasonable pro
     rata allocation, or another allocation that is more appropriate in the
     circumstances.

FRS 19 Deferred Tax   A7

Paragraph 'g' is deleted.   A7.1

Paragraph 34 is amended as follows: A7.2

34   **Deferred tax should be recognised in the profit and loss account for the period,
     except to the extent that it is (a) attributable to a gain or loss that is or has been
     recognised directly in the statement of total recognised gains and losses or (b)
     attributable to a gain or loss that is or has been recognised directly in the equity
     for transactions with non-controlling interests, in accordance with FRS 2
     Accounting for Subsidiary Undertakings.**

A7.3   Insert paragraph 35A:

35A   Where a gain or loss is or has been recognised directly in equity, the deferred tax attributable to that gain or loss should also be recognised directly in equity.

A7.4   Insert into paragraph 60 the following:

60   The notes to the financial statements should disclose the amount of deferred tax charged or credited within:

(a)   ...

(b)   tax charged or credited directly in the statement of total recognised gains and losses for the period, separately disclosing material components, including those listed in (a) above; and

(c)   deferred tax charged or credited directly to equity for the period, separately disclosing material components, including those listed in (a) above.

A7.5   Insert into paragraph 61 the following:

61   The financial statements should disclose:

(a)   the total deferred tax balance (before discounting, where applicable), showing the amount recognised for each significant type of timing difference separately;

(b)   the impact of discounting on, and the discounted amount of, the deferred tax balance; and

(c)   the movement between the opening and closing net deferred tax balance, analysing separately:

(i)   the amount charged or credited in the profit and loss account for the period;

(ii)   the amount charged or credited directly in the statement of total recognised gains and losses for the period; and

(iii)   the amount charged or credited directly in the reconciliation of shareholders funds for the period; and

(iv)   movements arising from the acquisition or disposal where control is either lost or gained of businesses.

A8   FRS 22 (IAS 33) Earnings Per Share

A8.1   Paragraph 73 is amended as follows:

73   If an entity discloses, in addition to basic and diluted earnings per share, amounts per share using a reported component of the income statement other than one required by this Standard, such amounts shall be calculated using the weighed average number of ordinary shares denominator determined in accordance with this Standard. Basic ....

A8.2   Paragraph 73B is added as follows:

73B   If an entity discloses, in addition to basic and diluted earnings per share, amounts per share that include in the numerator the effects of equity transactions with non-controlling interests, such amounts shall be calculated using the denominator determined in accordance with this Standard.

A9   FRS 23 (IAS 21) The Effects of Changes in Foreign Exchange Rates

A9.1   Paragraphs 48 and 49 are amended to read as follows:

48   On the disposal of a foreign operation, tThe cumulative amount of the exchange differences recognised through the statement of total recognised gains and losses

relating to ~~that~~ a foreign operation shall be recognised in profit or loss when the gain or loss on <u>the</u> disposal <u>or reduction in the entity's proportionate ownership interest in that foreign operation</u> is recognised*. <u>In the case of a partial disposal or reduction in an entity's proportionate ownership interest in a foreign operation, only the proportionate share of the related accumulated foreign exchange difference is recognised in profit or loss.</u>

49   An entity may dispose of its interest in a foreign operation through sale, liquidation, repayment of share capital or abandonment of all, or part of, that entity. The payment of a dividend is part of a disposal only when it constitutes a return of the investment, for example when the dividend is paid out of pre-acquisition profits. <u>Loss of control, joint control or significant influence of a foreign operation is also a disposal of that foreign operation for the purposes of this Standard.</u> ~~In the case of a partial disposal, only the proportionate share of the related accumulated exchange difference is included in the gain or loss.~~ A write-down of the carrying amount of a foreign operation does not constitute a partial disposal. Accordingly, no part of the deferred foreign exchange gain or loss is recognised in profit or loss at the time of a write-down.

Paragraphs 49A and 49B are added as follows: A9.2

49A When an investee ceases to be a foreign operation because it is no longer an associate or joint venture, the entire accumulated exchange difference related to that foreign operation is recognised in profit or loss. When an entity's proportionate ownership interest in a foreign operation that is an associate or joint venture is reduced, but the entity continues to have significant influence or joint control, only the proportionate share of the related accumulated exchange difference is recognised in profit or loss.

49B FRS 2 requires a gain or loss to be recognised whenever control of a subsidiary is lost. However, a gain or loss is not recognised as a result of any event, including a partial disposal or a reduction in proportionate ownership interest, if control of a subsidiary is not lost. The entire cumulative amount of exchange differences deferred in the separate component of equity relating to a subsidiary that is attributed to equity holders of the parent shall be recognised in profit or loss only if control of that subsidiary is lost.

FRS 26 (IAS 39) Financial Instruments: Recognition and   A10
Measurement

The last sentence of paragraph 102 is amended as follows: A10.1

The gain or loss on the hedging instrument relating to the effective portion of the hedge that has been recognised directly in reserves shall be recognised in profit or loss <u>when the gain or loss is recognised</u> on <u>the</u> disposal <u>of or reduction in the proportionate ownership interest in</u> the foreign operation. <u>For a partial disposal or reduction in an entity's proportionate ownership interest in a foreign operation, only the proportionate share of the related hedging gain or loss is recognised in profit or loss.</u>

Paragraphs 102A–102C are inserted as follows: A10.2

102A An entity may dispose of its interest in a foreign operation through sale, liquidation, repayment of share capital or abandonment of all, or part of, that operation. Loss of control, significant influence or joint control of a foreign operation is also a disposal of that foreign operation for the purposes of paragraph 102.

102B When an investee ceases to be a foreign operation because it is no longer an associate or joint venture, the entire gain or loss on the hedging instrument relating to the effective portion of the hedge recognised through the statement of total recognised gains and losses shall be recognised in profit or loss. When an entity's proportionate ownership interest in an associate or joint venture is reduced but the entity continues to have significant influence or joint control, respectively, only the proportionate share of the related hedging gain or loss is recognised in profit or loss.

102C FRS 2 requires a gain or loss to be recognised whenever control of a subsidiary is lost. However, a gain or loss is not recognised as a result of any event, including a partial disposal or a reduction in proportionate ownership interest, if control is not lost. The gain or loss on the hedging instrument relating to the effective portion of the hedge that has been recognised through the statement of total recognised gains and losses that relates to a subsidiary and is attributable to equity holders of the parent, shall be recognised in profit or loss only when control of that subsidiary is lost.

A11   Statement of Principles for Financial Reporting

In chapter 8 of the Statement of Principles, paragraph 8.12 replace the term 'minority' with 'non-controlling'.

A12   Interim Reports

In paragraphs 40, 43 and 52 replace the term 'minority' with 'non-controlling'.

A13   Preliminary Announcements

In paragraphs 36, 38 and 44 replace the term 'minority' with 'non-controlling'.

Illustrative Examples

These examples accompany but are not part of [draft] IAS 27 (as amended in 200X).

> ASB note: These Illustrative Examples have been prepared by the IASB.

Example 1 – Increase in ownership interest after control is obtained

Company A acquired previously a controlling interest in Company B with the acquisition of 70 per cent of its ordinary shares. **1.1**

On 31 December 20X2 Company A increased its interest in Company B to 85 per cent by purchasing shares in Company B from non-controlling shareholders for cash consideration of CU4,500. Immediately before this transaction, the carrying amount in Company A's consolidated financial statements of the non-controlling interest in Company B was CU7,500. Goodwill was not impaired during 20X2. **1.2**

Company A accounts for the acquisition in its consolidated financial statements as follows: **1.3**

Dr Non-controlling Interest	CU3,750	
((15 %/30%) × 7,500)		
Dr Equity	CU750	
Cr Cash		CU4,500

To recognise the additional 15 per cent investment acquired in Company B.

The excess recognised as an adjustment to the consolidated equity attributable to the equity holders of the parent reflects the premium paid by the parent entity in excess of the carrying amount of the 15 per cent ownership interest acquired. **1.4**

Example 2 – Decrease in ownership interest without loss of control

Company C acquired previously a controlling interest in Company D with the acquisition of 70 per cent of its ordinary shares. At the date control was obtained, the net assets of Company D were attributed in proportion to the respective ownership interests, with 70 per cent of the goodwill of Company D attributed to Company C and 30 per cent attributed to the non-controlling shareholders. **2.1**

The carrying amount of the net assets of Company D on 31 December 20X1 was CU25,000 and the carrying amount of the non-controlling interest was CU7,500. Therefore, the carrying amount of the parent's share of net assets was CU17,500. Goodwill was not impaired during 20X1. **2.2**

On 1 January 20X2 Company D issues new shares to shareholders other than Company C for CU5,000. The share issue has the effect of reducing Company C's holding to 55 per cent of Company D's ordinary shares. The proportionate ownership interest of non-controlling shareholders in Company D increased from 30 per cent to 45 per cent. **2.3**

Following the share issue, the carrying amount of the non-controlling interest increased to CU13,500 (45% × (CU25,000 + CU5,000)). The carrying amount of the parent's interest decreased to CU16,500 (55% × (CU25,000 + CU5,000)). Thus, **2.4** the amount of the interest transferred to the non-controlling shareholders was CU6,000 (CU13,500 less CU7,500).

2.5   Company C accounts for the decrease in ownership interest in its consolidated financial statements as follows:

Dr Cash	CU5,000	
Dr Equity	CU1,000	
Cr Non-controlling interest		CU6,000

To recognise the decrease in Company C's ownership interest in Company D.

2.6   The amount recognised as an adjustment to the consolidated equity attributable to the equity holders of the parent reflects the difference between the amount paid by the non-controlling interest for its additional 15 per cent ownership interest and the carrying amount of the interest transferred to the non-controlling interest.

Example 3 – Decrease in ownership interest with loss of control

3.1   Company E acquired previously a 70 per cent controlling interest in Company F.

3.2   On 31 December 20X2 the fair value of Company F as a whole was CU15,000 and its carrying amount was CU11,000. The carrying amount of the non-controlling interest was CU3,300. Therefore, the carrying amount of the parent's share of Company F's net assets was CU7,700. On 31 December 20X2, Company E reduced its interest in Company F to 10 per cent by selling a portion of its interest in Company F for cash proceeds of CU9,000 (CU15,000 × 60 per cent). As a result of the disposal, Company E lost control of Company F. On 31 December 20X2, the fair value of the retained investment in Company F was CU1,500.

3.3   The consolidated gain on disposal is calculated as follows:

	CU
Cash	9,000
Add retained investment in Company F	1,500
Total	10,500
Less parent's share of net assets	7,700
Gain on disposal	2,800

3.4   Company E accounts for the disposal in its consolidated financial statements as follows:

Dr Cash	CU9,000	
Dr Investment in Company F	CU1,500	
Cr Parent's share of net assets		CU7,700
Cr Gain on loss of control		CU2,800
Dr Non-controlling interest	CU3,300	
Cr Non-controlling interest's share of net assets		CU3,300

Company F is no longer a subsidiary of Company E. As a consequence, its net assets **3.5** and the non-controlling interest in them are derecognised.

If Company F has a liability through a non-current advance from Company G, the **3.6** advance would also be remeasured at fair value in Company G. Any gain or loss as a consequence of the remeasurement would be included in determining the gain or loss on loss of control.

Example 4 – Decrease in ownership without loss of control, with reallocation of existing goodwill between the controlling interest and non-controlling interest

Company P acquires 90 per cent of the ordinary shares in Company S for con-   **4.1** sideration of CU915, thereby obtaining control of Company S. At the time of the acquisition, the total fair value of Company S was CU1,000.

The fair value of Company S's net identifiable assets at the time of the acquisition   **4.2** was CU700. Goodwill of CU300 was recognised as part of the accounting for the business combination. The fair value of Company P's interest in Company S's net identifiable assets on acquisition was CU630 (90% × CU700). Therefore, in accordance with [draft] FRS ● IFRS 3, the portion of goodwill attributed to Company P was CU285 (CU915 – CU630). The carrying amount of the non-controlling interest was CU85 (CU1,000 – CU915). The fair value of the non-controlling interest in Company S's net identifiable assets was CU70 (10% × CU700). Therefore, the non-controlling interest in Company S's goodwill was CU15 (CU85 – CU70).

Company S subsequently issued additional shares to the non-controlling share-   **4.3** holders, increasing their ownership interest from 10 per cent to 15 per cent. The non-controlling shareholders paid Company S CU70 cash for the additional shares. Immediately before the share issue the carrying amount in the consolidated financial statements of Company S's net identifiable assets and goodwill continued to be CU1,000, increasing to CU1,070 as a result of the consideration received by Company S for the share issue.

As a result of the share issue, the non-controlling shareholders will have an interest in   **4.4** 15 per cent of Company S's net identifiable assets, having a carrying amount of CU115.5 (15% × CU770). In addition, the minority shareholders will have an increased interest in Company S's goodwill. In accordance with paragraph 30B of [draft] IAS 27 35A of [draft] FRS 2, the existing goodwill is reallocated between the equity holders of Company P and the non-controlling interest based on the relative carrying amounts of goodwill allocated to each of those groups of equity holders on the date control was obtained. Therefore, the amount of goodwill attributed to the non-controlling interest will be CU22.5 ((15%/10%) × CU15). The carrying amount of the non-controlling interest is a total of CU138 (CU115.5 + CU22.5) compared with the previous carrying amount of CU85. Thus the non-controlling interest in Company S has increased by CU53 as a result of the transaction.

Company P accounts for the transaction in its consolidated financial statements as   **4.5** follows:

Dr Cash	CU70	
Cr Non-controlling interest		CU53
Cr Equity		CU17

To recognise the decrease in Company P's ownership interest in Company S.

4.6   The amount recognised in equity reflects the difference between the amount paid by the non-controlling interest for its additional 5 per cent ownership interest and the carrying amount of the interest transferred to the non-controlling shareholders as a result of its acquisition. It is recognised as an adjustment to the consolidated equity attributable to the equity holders of the parent.

Example 5 – Loss of control of subsidiary with available-for-sale financial assets

5.1   Company G previously acquired 70 per cent of Company H for CU7,000. At the time control was obtained, the fair value of the whole of Company H was CU10,000 and Company H had an available-for-sale financial asset with a fair value of CU6,000.

5.2   From the time control was obtained until 31 December 20X1, the cumulative change in the fair value of Company H's available-for-sale financial asset was an increase of CU1,000. Accordingly, the carrying value of the available-for-sale asset in Company H's and Company G's consolidated financial statements on 31 December 20X1 was CU7,000.

5.3   On 31 December 20X1, the carrying amount of Company H's net assets in G's consolidated financial statements was CU11,000 and the carrying amount of the non-controlling interest was CU3,300. Therefore, the carrying amount of the parent's share of Company H's net assets was CU7,700 (CU11,000 – CU3,300).

5.4   On 31 December 20X1, the fair value of Company H as a whole was CU11,500. On 1 January 20X2 Company G sold its entire interest in Company H for cash consideration of CU8,050.

5.5   Company G accounts for the disposal in its consolidated financial statements as follows:

Dr Cash	CU8,050	
Dr Parent's share of changes in available-for-sale assets recognised directly in equity	CU700	
Cr Parent's share of Company H's net assets (including available-for-sale assets)		CU7,700
Cr Gain on loss of control		CU1,050
Dr Non-controlling interest	CU3,300	
Cr Non-controlling interest's share of net assets		CU3,300

To recognise the disposal in the consolidated financial statements.

5.6   Because Company H is no longer a subsidiary, its net assets are derecognised on 1 January 20X2. Company G recognises in its consolidated financial statements a gain on disposal of CU1,050. The gain on disposal includes Company G's portion of the gain on Company H's available-for-sale financial asset of CU700 (70% × CU1,000) previously recorded in equity.

FRED 37
Intangible assets (IAS 38)
&
FRED 38
Impairment of assets (IAS 36)

Contents

Business Combinations Overview

Preface by the accounting standards board

A   These Financial Reporting Exposure Drafts (FREDs) are part of a package of draft UK accounting standards reflecting the outputs from Phase I and Phase II of the International Accounting Standards Board (IASB) project on business combinations. The package comprises:

- FRED 37 *Intangible Assets* (IAS 38) and FRED 38 *Impairment of Assets* (IAS 36).
- FRED 36 *Business Combinations* (IFRS 3) and Amendments to FRS 2 Accounting for Subsidiary Undertakings (parts of IAS 27 Consolidated and Separate Financial Statements).
- FRED 39 Amendments to FRS 12 *Provisions, contingent liabilities and contingent assets* and Amendments to FRS 17 *Retirement benefits*.

B   The first phase of the Business Combinations project resulted in the IASB issuing IFRS 3 *Business Combinations*, and amendments to IAS 36 *Impairment of Assets* and IAS 38 *Intangible Assets*. These were published in March 2004. The primary objective of the IASB in Phase I of the project was to require one method of accounting for business combinations – the purchase method (renamed the acquisition method in Phase II). Prior to this International Accounting Standards (IAS) permitted two methods, the acquisition method and pooling of interests method (merger accounting).

C   The second phase is being conducted by the IASB as a joint project with the US Financial Accounting Standards Board (FASB). This phase of the project has reconsidered the guidance for applying the acquisition method of accounting for a business combination and particularly the method by which acquirers recognise and measure the business over which they obtain control. This phase also aims to improve the transparency of information provided to users of financial statements. An important aspect of Phase II is to achieve convergence between International Financial Reporting Standards (IFRSs) and US GAAP.

D   The outputs from the second Phase of the project comprise three exposure drafts that propose amendments to IFRS 3 *Business Combinations*, IAS 27 *Consolidated and Separate Financial Statements* and IAS 37 *Provisions and Contingent Liabilities and Contingent Assets*.

E   The publication by the IASB of the exposure drafts from Phase II concludes the substantive part of the IASB's Business Combinations project. However, it does not fully complete the project. The aspects that remain outstanding include consideration of 'fresh start' accounting. The outstanding aspects are not currently part of the IASB's active agenda.

F   Some of the proposals set out in this FRED may conflict with existing legal requirements. These matters are being investigated and it is hoped that they will be resolved with the assistance of the Department of Trade and Industry.

MAIN DIFFERENCE BETWEEN INTERNATIONAL ACCOUNTING STANDARDS AND UK ACCOUNTING STANDARDS FOR INTANGIBLE ASSETS AND IMPAIRMENT OF ASSETS

The Preface, set out below, has been prepared to assist readers in understanding the main differences between existing International Accounting Standards and UK accounting standards that will arise when the International Accounting Standards are implemented as UK IFRS-based standards.

INTRODUCTION

These Financial Reporting Exposure Drafts (FREDs) set out the proposals for two   **1**
UK IFRS-based accounting standards based on IAS 38 *Intangible Assets* and IAS 36 *Impairment of Assets*. These would replace FRS 10 *Goodwill and Intangible Assets*, SSAP 13 *Research and Development* and FRS 11 *Impairment of Fixed Assets and Goodwill*.

In line with its convergence strategy the Board proposes UK accounting standards   **2**
which are based on IFRS with no changes other than those that are essential or justifiable.

The Board is inviting comments only on the proposed changes to the IFRS. The   **3**
Board is not seeking comment on IAS 36 or IAS 38 as the IASB issued the revised International Accounting Standards in March 2004 following completion of its consultative process.

In December 2002 a Consultation Paper was issued that included the IASB's   **4**
exposure drafts of amendments to IAS 36 and IAS 38. Reflecting the comments received, the Board participated in the IASB's consultation process by responding to the IASB exposure drafts. Details of the ASB's response can be found on the ASB website (www.frc.org.uk/asb).

MAIN DIFFERENCES BETWEEN IAS 38 – INTANGIBLE ASSETS AND EXISTING UK REQUIREMENTS

Definition of identifiable

As part of Phase I of the Business Combinations project the IASB observed that   **5**
intangible assets comprise an increasing proportion of the assets of many entities, and that intangible assets acquired in a business combination are often included in the amount recognised for goodwill. The IASB agreed with the conclusions reached by other accounting standard-setting bodies that the usefulness of financial statements would be enhanced if intangible assets acquired in a business combination were distinguished separately from goodwill.

The IASB therefore reconsidered the definition of an intangible asset and affirmed   **6**
the view that identifiability is the characteristic that conceptually distinguishes other intangible assets from goodwill. IAS 38 does not define identifiable but states an intangible asset meets the identification criterion when it:

(a) is separable, i.e. is capable of being separated or divided from the entity and sold, transferred, licensed, rented or exchanged, either individually or together with a related contract asset or liability; or

(b) arises from contractual or other legal rights, regardless of whether those rights are transferable or separable from the entity or from other rights and obligations.

7   This is in contrast to FRS 10 *Goodwill and Intangible Assets* which notes that companies' legislation defines* identifiable assets as assets that are capable of being disposed of or discharged separately, without disposing of a business of the undertaking.

8   The distinction in the definition between IAS 38 and FRS 10 relates to the second identifiability criterion set out in (b) above. This criterion extends the criterion specified in point (a) because it disregards the separable requirement where there is a contractual or other legal right.

9   IAS 38 sets out its recognition criteria: an intangible asset is recognised if, and only if, it is probable that the expected future economic benefit will flow to the entity and the cost of the asset can be measured reliably.

10   As part of the amendments arising from Phase I of the Business Combinations project IAS 38 was amended to clarify that the probability criterion is always satisfied where intangible assets are acquired by separate acquisition or as part of a business combination.

11   The amendments to IAS 38, which arose from Phase I of the Business Combinations project, provided that the fair value of an intangible asset acquired in a business combination could normally be measured with sufficient reliability to be recognised separately from goodwill. However, as part of Phase II the IASB is proposing to amend IAS 38 to state that sufficient information *always* exists to measure reliably the fair value of such an asset that has an underlying contractual or legal basis or is capable of being separated from the entity. Details of the proposed amendment are set out in FRED 36 *Business Combinations*. FRED 36 also reproduces the IASB's Invitation to Comment; question 16 asks whether you believe that an intangible asset that is identifiable can always be measured with sufficient reliability to be recognised separately from goodwill.

12   In its Consultation Paper issued in December 2002 the Board observed that the amendments proposed to IAS 38 set the hurdles for recognition of intangible assets lower than that required by FRS 10. A concern was expressed that the wider definition and lower recognition criterion may result in possible problems with identification and measurement. In issuing this draft FRS the Board considered the importance of the relationship between the initial recognition of intangible assets and subsequent measurement of goodwill.

13   IFRS 3 requires that after initial recognition goodwill should be carried at cost less accumulated impairment losses (ie there is no systematic amortisation of goodwill). Where intangible assets with finite useful lives are not recognised separately from goodwill then there is a risk that the goodwill impairment test may not recognise the impairment of the intangible assets, as it could be masked by internally generated goodwill or other items in the impairment test.

14   In view of this the ASB decided it should not restrict the wider definition of intangible assets in the draft FRS.

Development expenditure

15   IAS 38 addresses the accounting for research and development, which in UK accounting standards is addressed in SSAP 13 *Research and Development*.

Companies' legislation in the UK and Republic of Ireland defines "identifiable" as "separable".

SSAP 13 permits but does not require development costs to be capitalised. IAS 38   **16**
requires that internally generated intangible assets arising from development shall be
recognised, if the criteria for recognition are met. The criteria for the recognition of
development expenditure as an asset are broadly comparable to SSAP 13 and limit
recognition significantly.

The draft FRS requires an entity to demonstrate how an intangible asset will gen-   **17**
erate probable future economic benefits by using the principles set out in the draft
FRS *Impairment of Assets*. No such test is required by SSAP 13.

Website development costs

The Urgent Issues Task Force issued Abstract 29 *Website development costs* in 2001.   **18**
This Abstract was an interpretation of FRS 10 *Goodwill and Intangible Assets*,
FRS 11 *Impairment of Fixed Assets and Goodwill* and FRS 15 *Tangible Fixed Assets*.
Following the introduction of the Business Combinations package of standards,
some of the standards that Abstract 29 interprets will not be in issue.

To replace Abstract 29 it is proposed to introduce SIC 32 *Intangible Assets – Web*   **19**
Site Costs. In contrast to Abstract 29, SIC 32 requires web site costs to be accounted
for as internally generated intangible assets. SIC 32 is set out in Appendix A of the
draft FRS as an Application Note.

It is proposed that website costs, previously recognised as tangible assets that meet   **20**
the requirements of the draft FRS be reclassified as intangible assets and amortised
over their remaining useful lives. Costs that meet the requirements for capitalisation
of internally generated intangible assets shall be capitalised in accordance with the
Application Note (SIC 32) from the date the draft FRS becomes effective.

MAIN DIFFERENCE BETWEEN IAS 36 – IMPAIRMENT OF ASSETS AND EXISTING UK REQUIREMENTS

To justify the carrying of goodwill without systematic amortisation it is clear that a   **21**
robust test for impairment is required. The impairment test must provide confidence
in its ability to identify reductions in the carrying amount of acquired goodwill.
When the ASB developed FRS 11 it spent considerable time refining the impairment
test for goodwill. There are two key differences between the impairment test set out
in FRS 11 and that of IAS 36:

(a)   The FRS 11 test attempts to distinguish between acquired and internally gen-
      erated goodwill and to recognise only impairment of the acquired part.
(b)   The FRS 11 impairment test includes a test to check the accuracy of impair-
      ment by comparing actual cash flows against those projected. IAS 36 does not
      contain a similar test.

Distinguishing acquired goodwill and internally generated goodwill

As noted, the impairment test in FRS 11 attempts to distinguish purchased goodwill   **22**
from (unrecognised) internally generated goodwill. It requires that when an acquired
business is merged with an existing business the value of the internally generated
goodwill of the existing business is estimated and added to the carrying amount of
the income-generating unit for the purposes of performing an impairment review.
Any subsequent impairment of a merged business is allocated on a pro rata basis
between the (unrecognised) goodwill in the existing operations and the acquired
goodwill. Were this requirement not included then an impairment of the acquired

goodwill would not be recognised unless, and to the extent that, the impairment of the combined business exceeded the value of the unrecognised goodwill at the time the businesses were merged.

23   The IASB considered this issue but concluded that in many cases it would not be possible in practice to distinguish future cash inflows from the asset initially recognised from the cash inflows from internally generated goodwill. The IASB concluded it was more important to focus on whether the carrying amount of an asset would be recoverable.

Subsequent cash flow test and disclosures

24   FRS 11 requires that for the five years following each impairment review where the recoverable amount has been based on value in use, the cash flows achieved should be compared with those forecast. If using the actual cash flows at the time of the original impairment review would have resulted in an impairment being recognised at that time, that impairment is recognised in the current period unless the impairment has reversed.

25   IASB considered including a subsequent cash flow test similar to FRS 11, as part of its proposed amendments to IAS 36. However, its proposals did not include such a test as it considered the test ignored other elements in the measurement of value in use and produced results that were not decision-useful information. The IASB did, however, recognise that the non-amortisation of goodwill and indefinite-lived intangible assets increases the reliance placed on the impairment test. As a result, the IASB, in the exposure draft proposed detailed narrative disclosure of the information regarding the key assumptions used by management in determining the recoverable amount.

26   During its consultative process the IASB was sympathetic to respondents' concerns that the disclosures went beyond the intended objective of providing users with relevant information for evaluating the reliability of the impairment test. The IASB amended its disclosure requirements such that the amended IAS 36 issued in March 2004 requires information focused on providing the user with the assumptions used to determine the recoverable amount and greater detail of the carrying value of goodwill and intangible assets with indefinite useful lives.

27   The Board also considered the disclosure requirements that are set out in IAS 36. The draft FRS proposes a simplified approach to disclosure.

Consequential amendments to UK accounting standards arising on implementation of IAS 36 and IAS 38 as UK IFRS-based standards

28   This FRED sets out the consequential amendments to other UK accounting standards that arise from implementation of IAS 36 and IAS 38 as UK IFRS-based standards. They are set out in paragraph 133 of the draft FRS *Intangible Assets* and Appendix B for the draft FRS *Impairment of Assets*.

Reporting of gains and losses on revalued assets

29   Appendix B of draft FRS *Impairment of Assets* proposes to amend FRS 15 for the reporting of gains and losses on revaluation of revalued assets. International Accounting Standards that address the reporting of revaluation gains and losses do not make the distinction that a downward revaluation may comprise an impairment

loss – where there has been a clear consumption of economic benefit – and other revaluation losses.

In order to ensure the reporting of gains and losses on revalued assets are consistent **30** for tangible and intangible assets, consideration was given to (a) amending the draft IFRS-based standards such that the reporting was consistent with FRS 15 *Tangible Fixed Assets* or (b) amending FRS 15 to be consistent with the IASB's approach to reporting gains and losses on revalued assets. The Board has proposed alternative (b) as it accelerates convergence.

Amendment to the definition of residual values

The consequential amendments include a proposal to amend the definition of resi- **31** dual value contained in FRS 15. Whereas FRS 15 bases residual values on prices prevailing at the date of acquisition (or revaluation), IAS 16 *Property, Plant and Equipment* defines residual value as being based on prices current at the balance sheet date. This could, in some circumstances, result in a significant difference to depreciation charges.

Acquisition by way of government grant

Draft FRS *Intangible Assets* addresses the initial measurement of intangible assets **32** acquired by way of government grant. Previously, this matter was not specifically addressed in UK accounting standards. Draft FRS *Intangible Assets* proposes to amend SSAP 4, *Accounting for Government Grants*, by introducing the recognition criteria for assets acquired by way of government grant that are set out in IAS 20 *Accounting for Government Grants and Disclosure of Government Assistance*.

Definition of a business segment

The draft FRS (IAS 36) *Impairment of Assets* requires, for the purpose of impair- **33** ment testing, goodwill acquired in a business combination to be allocated to each of the acquirer's cash-generating units, or groups of cash-generating units. Each unit or group of units to which goodwill is allocated is not permitted to be larger than a segment based on either the entity's primary or the entity's secondary reporting format determined in accordance with the definitions in IAS 14 *Segment Reporting*.

To incorporate this requirement into the UK IFRS-based accounting standard the **34** definitions of business segment, geographical segment, primary segment reporting format and secondary segment reporting formats from IAS 14 have been incorporated into the draft FRS. The Board would be interested in views regarding this proposal and what, if any, alternatives would be recommended and why.

Implementation of IASB Business Combinations proposals

Effective date for implementation

As noted the Board is issuing these FREDs as part of the Business Combinations **35** 'package' of draft FRSs. The Preface to FRED 36, *Business Combinations*, discusses various options for implementation of the Business Combination 'package' of standards. It proposes a number of options for implementation and invites comments on which of these proposals is preferred.

Transitional provisions

36   Draft FRS *Impairment of Assets* provides no specific guidance on transition from FRS 11 to the new IFRS-based standard. When the ASB issued FRS 11 the transitional arrangements stated that "impairment losses recognised when the standard is implemented for the first time are not the result of a change in accounting policy and should be recognised in accordance with the requirements of the FRS and not as prior period adjustments." Accordingly, there is no specific requirement for an entity to undertake an additional impairment test on adoption of the new IFRS-based standard. The Board would, however, welcome views on this matter.

Invitation to comment

The ASB invites comments on any aspect of these Financial Reporting Exposure   ITC1
Drafts by 28 October 2005.

The ASB would particularly welcome comments on the following issues: ITC2

ASB 1   The Board proposes to implement SIC 32 *Intangible Assets - Web Site Costs*
as an Application Note to the UK IFRS-based standard IAS 38. Do you
agree with the implementation of SIC 32 as an Application Note to the draft
FRS?

ASB 2   FRS 15 bases residual value on prices prevailing at the date of acquisition (or
revaluation) whereas IAS 16 defines residual values as being the prices based
on current value. One of the consequential amendments proposed by the
draft FRS *Impairment of Assets* is an amendment to the definition of residual
value in FRS 15. Are you in agreement with the proposal to amend the
definition of residual value? If not please explain why you disagree with the
proposal.

ASB 3   In the draft FRS *Impairment of Assets,* paragraphs 6A and 6B insert the
definition of a business segment, geographical segment, primary segment
reporting format and secondary segment reporting format. This is proposed
so that the requirement set out in paragraph 80 of the draft FRS to allocate
goodwill acquired in a business combination to cash-generating units which
are no larger than a segment defined by IAS 14 *Segment Reporting* are
converged in UK and international standards. Do you agree with the proposal to insert the definitions from IAS 14? If not please explain why and
what alternative you would propose.

ASB 4   The draft FRS *Impairment of Assets*, includes no specific requirements for
transition from FRS 11 to the new IFRS-based standard. Do you consider
guidance is required? If so, do you consider an additional impairment test
should be required on the introduction of the new IFRS-based standard?

Financial Reporting Exposure Draft 37

Intangible assets

~~International Accounting Standard 38~~
[Draft] Financial Reporting Standard ●

INTANGIBLE ASSETS

ASB Note: The text set out in this [draft] standard is amended for consequential amendments arising from the IASB exposure draft of proposed *Amendments to IFRS 3 Business Combinations* and its exposure draft of proposed *Amendments to IAS 37 Provisions, Contingent Liabilities and Contingent Assets.*

Contents

[Draft] Financial Reporting Standard* • *'Intangible Assets'

[Draft] Financial Reporting Standard 'Intangible Assets' embodies IAS 38 Intangible Assets which was published in March 2004 in the form of a standard. The [draft] FRS includes some amendments to that standard adopted for entities subject to UK accounting standards. All of the changes made to the IASB text by the ASB are highlighted by strikethrough of the text to be deleted and underlining of the text to be inserted.

The [draft] Statement of Standard Accounting Practice in the [draft] FRS is set out in paragraphs 1-133 and Appendix A. All paragraphs have equal authority. Paragraphs in bold type state the main principles.

Accompanying the [draft] Statement of Standard Accounting Practice is the basis of conclusions reached in the Statement and some illustrative examples, which do not form part of the Statement.

The [draft] Statement of Standard Accounting Practice should be read in the context of its objective as stated in paragraph 1 and the Accounting Standards Board's 'Foreword to Accounting Standards' and 'Statement of Principles for Financial Reporting'.

INTRODUCTION

International Accounting Standard 38 *Intangible Assets* (IAS 38) replaces IAS 38   **IN1**
Intangible Assets (issued in 1998), and should be applied:

(a)   on acquisition to the accounting for intangible assets acquired in business
      combinations for which the agreement date is on or after 31 March 2004.
(b)   to all other intangible assets, for annual periods beginning on or after 31 March
      2004.

Earlier application is encouraged.

Reasons for revising IAS 38

The International Accounting Standards Board developed this revised IAS 38 as   **IN2**
part of its project on business combinations. The project's objective is to improve the
quality of, and seek international convergence on, the accounting for business
combinations and the subsequent accounting for goodwill and intangible assets
acquired in business combinations.

The project has two phases. The first phase resulted in the Board issuing simulta-   **IN3**
neously IFRS 3 *Business Combinations* and revised versions of IAS 38 and IAS 36
Impairment of Assets. The Board's deliberations during the first phase of the project
focused primarily on:

(a)   the method of accounting for business combinations;
(b)   the initial measurement of the identifiable assets acquired and liabilities and
      contingent liabilities assumed in a business combination;
(c)   the recognition of provisions for terminating or reducing the activities of an
      acquiree;
(d)   the treatment of any excess of the acquirer's interest in the fair values of
      identifiable net assets acquired in a business combination over the cost of the
      combination; and
(e)   the accounting for goodwill and intangible assets acquired in a business
      combination.

Therefore, the Board's intention while revising IAS 38 was to reflect only those   **IN4**
changes related to its decisions in the Business Combinations project, and *not* to
reconsider all of the requirements in IAS 38. The changes that have been made in the
Standard are primarily concerned with clarifying the notion of 'identifiability' as it
relates to intangible assets, the useful life and amortisation of intangible assets, and
the accounting for in-process research and development projects acquired in business
combinations.

Summary of main changes

Definition of an intangible asset

The previous version of IAS 38 defined an intangible asset as an identifiable non-   **IN5**
monetary asset without physical substance held for use in the production or supply
of goods or services, for rental to others, or for administrative purposes. The
requirement for the asset to be held for use in the production or supply of goods or
services, for rental to others, or for administrative purposes has been removed from
the definition of an intangible asset.

IN6 The previous version of IAS 38 did not define 'identifiability', but stated that an intangible asset could be distinguished clearly from goodwill if the asset was separable, but that separability was not a necessary condition for identifiability. The Standard states that an asset meets the identifiability criterion in the definition of an intangible asset when it:

(a) is separable, ie capable of being separated or divided from the entity and sold, transferred, licensed, rented or exchanged, either individually or together with a related contract, asset or liability; or

(b) arises from contractual or other legal rights, regardless of whether those rights are transferable or separable from the entity or from other rights and obligations.

Criteria for initial recognition

IN7 The previous version of IAS 38 required an intangible asset to be recognised if, and only if, it was probable that the expected future economic benefits attributable to the asset would flow to the entity, and its cost could be measured reliably. These recognition criteria have been included in the Standard. However, additional guidance has been included to clarify that:

(a) the probability recognition criterion is always considered to be satisfied for intangible assets that are acquired separately or in a business combination.

(b) the fair value of an intangible asset acquired in a business combination can normally be measured with sufficient reliability to be recognised separately from goodwill. If an intangible asset acquired in a business combination has a finite useful life, there is a rebuttable presumption that its fair value can be measured reliably.

Subsequent expenditure

IN8 Under the previous version of IAS 38, the treatment of subsequent expenditure on an in-process research and development project acquired in a business combination and recognised as an asset separately from goodwill was unclear. The Standard requires such expenditure to be:

(a) recognised as an expense when incurred if it is research expenditure;

(b) recognised as an expense when incurred if it is development expenditure that does not satisfy the criteria in IAS 38 for recognising such expenditure as an intangible asset; and

(c) recognised as an intangible asset if it is development expenditure that satisfies the criteria in IAS 38 for recognising such expenditure as an intangible asset.

Useful life

IN9 The previous version of IAS 38 was based on the assumption that the useful life of an intangible asset is always finite, and included a rebuttable presumption that the useful life cannot exceed twenty years from the date the asset is available for use. That rebuttable presumption has been removed. The Standard requires an intangible asset to be regarded as having an indefinite useful life when, based on an analysis of all of the relevant factors, there is no foreseeable limit to the period over which the asset is expected to generate net cash inflows for the entity.

IN10 The previous version of IAS 38 required that if control over the future economic benefits from an intangible asset was achieved through legal rights granted for a finite period, the useful life of the intangible asset could not exceed the period of those rights, unless the rights were renewable and renewal was virtually certain. The Standard requires that:

(a) the useful life of an intangible asset arising from contractual or other legal rights should not exceed the period of those rights, but may be shorter depending on the period over which the asset is expected to be used by the entity; and

(b) if the rights are conveyed for a limited term that can be renewed, the useful life should include the renewal period(s) only if there is evidence to support renewal by the entity without significant cost.

Intangible assets with indefinite useful lives

The Standard requires that: **IN11**

(a) an intangible asset with an indefinite useful life should not be amortised.

(b) the useful life of such an asset should be reviewed each reporting period to determine whether events and circumstances continue to support an indefinite useful life assessment for that asset. If they do not, the change in the useful life assessment from indefinite to finite should be accounted for as a change in an accounting estimate.

Impairment testing intangible assets with finite useful lives

The previous version of IAS 38 required the recoverable amount of an intangible   **IN12**
asset that was amortised over a period exceeding twenty years from the date it was available for use to be estimated at least at each financial year-end, even if there was no indication that the asset was impaired. This requirement has been removed. Therefore, an entity needs to determine the recoverable amount of an intangible asset with a finite useful life that is amortised over a period exceeding twenty years from the date it is available for use only when, in accordance with [draft] FRS ● IAS 36, there is an indication that the asset may be impaired.

Disclosure

If an intangible asset is assessed as having an indefinite useful life, the Standard   **IN13**
requires an entity to disclose the carrying amount of that asset and the reasons supporting the indefinite useful life assessment.

~~International Accounting Standard 38~~
[Draft] Financial Reporting Standard •

Intangible Assets

OBJECTIVE

1   The objective of this Standard is to prescribe the accounting treatment for intangible assets that are not dealt with specifically in another Standard. This Standard requires an entity to recognise an intangible asset if, and only if, specified criteria are met. The Standard also specifies how to measure the carrying amount of intangible assets and requires specified disclosures about intangible assets.

SCOPE

1A   *This Standard applies to all financial statements that are intended to give a true and fair view of a reporting entity's financial position and profit and loss (or income and expenditure), except that reporting entities applying the Financial Reporting Standard for Smaller Entities (FRSSE) currently applicable are exempt.*

2   *This Standard shall be applied in accounting for intangible assets, except:*

   (a)   intangible assets that are within the scope of another Standard;
   (b)   financial assets, as defined in FRS 26 ~~IAS 39~~ **Financial Instruments: Recognition and Measurement**;
   (c)   the recognition and measurement of exploration and evaluation assets ~~(see IFRS 6 Exploration for and Evaluation of Mineral Resources~~);and
   (d)   expenditure on the development and extraction of, minerals, oil, natural gas and similar non-regenerative resources.

3   If another Standard prescribes the accounting for a specific type of intangible asset, an entity applies that Standard instead of this Standard. For example, this Standard does not apply to:

   (a)   intangible assets held by an entity for sale in the ordinary course of business (see SSAP 9 *Stocks and Long-term Contracts*). ~~IAS 2 Inventories and IAS 11 Construction Contracts~~.
   (b)   deferred tax assets (see FRS 19 *Deferred Tax* ~~IAS 12 Income Taxes~~).
   (c)   leases that are within the scope of SSAP 21 *Accounting for Leases and Hire Purchase Contracts* ~~IAS 17 Leases~~.
   (d)   assets arising from ~~employee~~ retirement benefits (see FRS 17 *Retirement and Termination Benefits*).~~IAS 19 Employee Benefits~~.
   (e)   financial assets as defined in FRS 26 ~~IAS 39~~. The recognition and measurement of some financial assets are covered by FRS 2 *Accounting for Subsidiary Undertakings* and FRS 9 *Associates and Joint Ventures*.~~IAS 27 Consolidated and Separate Financial Statements, IAS 28 Investments in Associates and IAS 3 Interests in Joint Ventures~~.
   (f)   goodwill acquired in a business combination (see [draft] FRS • ~~IFRS 3 Business~~ *Combinations*).
   (g)   deferred acquisition costs, and intangible assets, arising from an insurer's contractual rights under insurance contracts as defined in FRS 26 Appendix C. ~~within the scope of IFRS 4 Insurance Contracts. IFRS 4 sets out specific disclosure requirements for those deferred acquisition costs but not for those~~

~~intangible assets. Therefore~~ However, the disclosure requirements in this Standard apply to ~~those~~ both deferred acquisition costs and intangible assets.

(h) ~~non-current intangible assets classified as held for sale (or included in a disposal group that is classified as held for sale) in accordance with IFRS 5 Non-current Assets Held for Sale and Discontinued Operations.~~

Some intangible assets may be contained in or on a physical substance such as a compact disc (in the case of computer software), legal documentation (in the case of a licence or patent) or film. In determining whether an asset that incorporates both intangible and tangible elements should be treated under FRS 15 *Tangible Fixed Assets* ~~IAS 16 Property, Plant and Equipment~~ or as an intangible asset under this Standard, an entity uses judgement to assess which element is more significant. For example, computer software for a computer-controlled machine tool that cannot operate without that specific software is an integral part of the related hardware and it is treated as property, plant and equipment. The same applies to the operating system of a computer. When the software is not an integral part of the related hardware, computer software is treated as an intangible asset. **4**

This Standard applies to, among other things, expenditure on advertising, training, start-up, research and development activities. Research and development activities are directed to the development of knowledge. Therefore, although these activities may result in an asset with physical substance (eg a prototype), the physical element of the asset is secondary to its intangible component, ie the knowledge embodied in it. **5**

In the case of a finance lease, the underlying asset may be either tangible or intangible. After initial recognition, a lessee accounts for an intangible asset held under a finance lease in accordance with this Standard. Rights under licensing agreements for items such as motion picture films, video recordings, plays, manuscripts, patents and copyrights are excluded from the scope of SSAP 21 ~~IAS 17~~ and are within the scope of this Standard. **6**

Exclusions from the scope of a Standard may occur if activities or transactions are so specialised that they give rise to accounting issues that may need to be dealt with in a different way. Such issues arise in the accounting for expenditure on the exploration for, or development and extraction of, oil, gas and mineral deposits in extractive industries and in the case of insurance contracts. Therefore, this Standard does not apply to expenditure on such activities and contracts. However, this Standard applies to other intangible assets used (such as computer software), and other expenditure incurred (such as start-up costs), in extractive industries or by insurers. **7**

DEFINITIONS

The following terms are used in this Standard with the meanings specified: **8**

An **active market** *is a market in which all the following conditions exist:*

(a) the items traded in the market are homogeneous;
(b) willing buyers and sellers can normally be found at any time; and
(c) prices are available to the public.

Amortisation *is the systematic allocation of the depreciable amount of an intangible asset over its useful life.*

An **asset** *is a resource:*

(a)   *controlled by an entity as a result of past events; and*

(b)   *from which future economic benefits are expected to flow to the entity.*

Carrying amount is the amount at which an asset is recognised in the balance sheet after deducting any accumulated amortisation and accumulated impairment losses thereon.

Cost is the amount of cash or cash equivalents paid or the fair value of other consideration given to acquire an asset at the time of its acquisition or construction, or, when applicable, the amount attributed to that asset when initially recognised in accordance with the specific requirements of other FRSs IFRSs, *eg FRS 20 Share-based Payment.* IFRS 2.

Depreciable amount is the cost of an asset, or other amount substituted for cost, less its residual value.

Development is the application of research findings or other knowledge to a plan or design for the production of new or substantially improved materials, devices, products, processes, systems or services before the start of commercial production or use.

Entity-specific value is the present value of the cash flows an entity expects to arise from the continuing use of an asset and from its disposal at the end of its useful life or expects to incur when settling a liability.

Fair value of an asset is the amount for which that asset could be exchanged between knowledgeable, willing parties in an arm's length transaction.

An impairment loss is the amount by which the carrying amount of an asset exceeds its recoverable amount.

An intangible asset is an identifiable non-monetary asset without physical substance.

Monetary assets are money held and assets to be received in fixed or determinable amounts of money.

Research is original and planned investigation undertaken with the prospect of gaining new scientific or technical knowledge and understanding.

The residual value of an intangible asset is the estimated amount that an entity would currently obtain from disposal of the asset, after deducting the estimated costs of disposal, if the asset were already of the age and in the condition expected at the end of its useful life.

Useful life is:

(a)   *the period over which an asset is expected to be available for use by an entity; or*

(b)   *the number of production or similar units expected to be obtained from the asset by an entity.*

Intangible Assets

9   Entities frequently expend resources, or incur liabilities, on the acquisition, development, maintenance or enhancement of intangible resources such as scientific or technical knowledge, design and implementation of new processes or systems, licences, intellectual property, market knowledge and trademarks (including brand names and publishing titles). Common examples of items encompassed by these

broad headings are computer software, patents, copyrights, motion picture films, customer lists, mortgage servicing rights, fishing licences, import quotas, franchises, customer or supplier relationships, customer loyalty, market share and marketing rights.

Not all the items described in paragraph 9 meet the definition of an intangible asset, **10** ie identifiability, control over a resource and existence of future economic benefits. If an item within the scope of this Standard does not meet the definition of an intangible asset, expenditure to acquire it or generate it internally is recognised as an expense when it is incurred. However, if the item is acquired in a business combination, it forms part of the goodwill recognised at the acquisition date (see paragraph 68).

Identifiability

The definition of an intangible asset requires an intangible asset to be identifiable to **11** distinguish it from goodwill. Goodwill arising in a business combination represents future economic benefits from assets that are not capable of being individually identified and separately recognised. The future economic benefits may result from synergy between the identifiable assets acquired or from assets that, individually, do not qualify for recognition in the financial statements.

An asset meets the identifiability criterion in the definition of an intangible asset when **12** *it:*

(a) *is separable, ie is capable of being separated or divided from the entity and sold, transferred, licensed, rented or exchanged, either individually or together with a related contract, asset or liability; or*
(b) *arises from contractual or other legal rights, regardless of whether those rights are transferable or separable from the entity or from other rights and obligations.*

Control

An entity controls an asset if the entity has the power to obtain the future economic **13** benefits flowing from the underlying resource and to restrict the access of others to those benefits. The capacity of an entity to control the future economic benefits from an intangible asset would normally stem from legal rights that are enforceable in a court of law. In the absence of legal rights, it is more difficult to demonstrate control. However, legal enforceability of a right is not a necessary condition for control because an entity may be able to control the future economic benefits in some other way.

Market and technical knowledge may give rise to future economic benefits. An entity **14** controls those benefits if, for example, the knowledge is protected by legal rights such as copyrights, a restraint of trade agreement (where permitted) or by a legal duty on employees to maintain confidentiality.

An entity may have a team of skilled staff and may be able to identify incremental **15** staff skills leading to future economic benefits from training. The entity may also expect that the staff will continue to make their skills available to the entity. However, an entity usually has insufficient control over the expected future economic benefits arising from a team of skilled staff and from training for these items to meet the definition of an intangible asset. For a similar reason, specific management or technical talent is unlikely to meet the definition of an intangible asset, unless it is protected by legal rights to use it and to obtain the future economic benefits expected from it, and it also meets the other parts of the definition.

16   An entity may have a portfolio of customers or a market share and expect that, because of its efforts in building customer relationships and loyalty, the customers will continue to trade with the entity. However, in the absence of legal rights to protect, or other ways to control, the relationships with customers or the loyalty of the customers to the entity, the entity usually has insufficient control over the expected economic benefits from customer relationships and loyalty for such items (eg portfolio of customers, market shares, customer relationships and customer loyalty) to meet the definition of intangible assets. In the absence of legal rights to protect customer relationships, exchange transactions for the same or similar non-contractual customer relationships (other than as part of a business combination) provide evidence that the entity is nonetheless able to control the expected future economic benefits flowing from the customer relationships. Because such exchange transactions also provide evidence that the customer relationships are separable, those customer relationships meet the definition of an intangible asset.

Future Economic Benefits

17   The future economic benefits flowing from an intangible asset may include revenue from the sale of products or services, cost savings, or other benefits resulting from the use of the asset by the entity. For example, the use of intellectual property in a production process may reduce future production costs rather than increase future revenues.

Contingencies

17A   In some cases, an entity has intangible asset even though the amount of the future economic benefits embodied in that asset is contingent (or conditional) on the occurrence or non-occurrence of one or more uncertain future events. In such cases, an entity has two rights as a result of a past event, an unconditional right and a conditional right. The intangible asset arises from the unconditional right, but the conditional right is reflected in the measurement of the intangible asset.

17B   An example of such an intangible asset is a product warranty. The entity's asset arises from its unconditional right to warranty coverage for the duration of the warranty contract rather than from its conditional right to have its product repaired or replaced if it develops a fault. Similarly, an entity that is pursuing a legal claim has an intangible asset arising from the actions it performed to get to the point of pursuing its claim. Any amounts that the entity expects to receive as a result of pursuing a legal claim are a conditional right, because the right to receive them is conditional on a future event (eg the judgement of the court).

RECOGNITION AND MEASUREMENT

18   The recognition of an item as an intangible asset requires an entity to demonstrate that the item meets:

(a)   the definition of an intangible asset (see paragraphs 8-17); and
(b)   the recognition criteria (see paragraphs 21-23).

This requirement applies to costs incurred initially to acquire or internally generate an intangible asset and those incurred subsequently to add to, replace part of, or service it.

Paragraphs 25-32 deal with the application of the recognition criteria to separately acquired intangible assets, and paragraphs 33-43 deal with their application to intangible assets acquired in a business combination. Paragraph 44 deals with the initial measurement of intangible assets acquired by way of a government grant, paragraphs 45-47 with exchanges of intangible assets, and paragraphs 48-50 with the treatment of internally generated goodwill. Paragraphs 51-67 deal with the initial recognition and measurement of internally generated intangible assets.   **19**

The nature of intangible assets is such that, in many cases, there are no additions to such an asset or replacements of part of it. Accordingly, most subsequent expenditures are likely to maintain the expected future economic benefits embodied in an existing intangible asset rather than meet the definition of an intangible asset and the recognition criteria in this Standard. In addition, it is often difficult to attribute subsequent expenditure directly to a particular intangible asset rather than to the business as a whole. Therefore, only rarely will subsequent expenditure – expenditure incurred after the initial recognition of an acquired intangible asset or after completion of an internally generated intangible asset – be recognised in the carrying amount of an asset. Consistently with paragraph 63, subsequent expenditure on brands, mastheads, publishing titles, customer lists and items similar in substance (whether externally acquired or internally generated) is always recognised in profit or loss as incurred. This is because such expenditure cannot be distinguished from expenditure to develop the business as a whole.   **20**

An intangible asset shall be recognised if, and only if: **21**

(a) it is probable that the expected future economic benefits that are attributable to the asset will flow to the entity; and
(b) the cost of the asset can be measured reliably.

An entity shall assess the probability of expected future economic benefits using reasonable and supportable assumptions that represent management's best estimate of the set of economic conditions that will exist over the useful life of the asset.   **22**

An entity uses judgement to assess the degree of certainty attached to the flow of future economic benefits that are attributable to the use of the asset on the basis of the evidence available at the time of initial recognition, giving greater weight to external evidence.   **23**

An intangible asset shall be measured initially at cost.   **24**

Separate Acquisition

Normally, the price an entity pays to acquire separately an intangible asset reflects expectations about the probability that the expected future economic benefits embodied in the asset will flow to the entity. In other words, there will be an inflow of economic benefits, even if there could be uncertainty about the timing and the amount of the inflow. Therefore, the probability recognition criterion in paragraph 21(a) is always considered to be satisfied for separately acquired intangible assets.   **25**

In addition, the cost of a separately acquired intangible asset can usually be measured reliably. This is particularly so when the purchase consideration is in the form of cash or other monetary assets.   **26**

The cost of a separately acquired intangible asset comprises: **27**

(a)   its purchase price, including import duties and non-refundable purchase taxes, after deducting trade discounts and rebates; and

(b)   any directly attributable cost of preparing the asset for its intended use.

28   Examples of directly attributable costs are:

(a)   employee labour costs ~~costs of employee benefits (as defined in IAS 19 *Employee Benefits*)~~ arising directly from bringing the asset to its working condition;

(b)   professional fees arising directly from bringing the asset to its working condition; and

(c)   costs of testing whether the asset is functioning properly.

29   Examples of expenditures that are not part of the cost of an intangible asset are:

(a)   costs of introducing a new product or service (including costs of advertising and promotional activities);

(b)   costs of conducting business in a new location or with a new class of customer (including costs of staff training); and

(c)   administration and other general overhead costs.

30   Recognition of costs in the carrying amount of an intangible asset ceases when the asset is in the condition necessary for it to be capable of operating in the manner intended by management. Therefore, costs incurred in using or redeploying an intangible asset are not included in the carrying amount of that asset. For example, the following costs are not included in the carrying amount of an intangible asset:

(a)   costs incurred while an asset capable of operating in the manner intended by management has yet to be brought into use; and

(b)   initial operating losses, such as those incurred while demand for the asset's output builds up.

31   Some operations occur in connection with the development of an intangible asset, but are not necessary to bring the asset to the condition necessary for it to be capable of operating in the manner intended by management. These incidental operations may occur before or during the development activities. Because incidental operations are not necessary to bring an asset to the condition necessary for it to be capable of operating in the manner intended by management, the income and related expenses of incidental operations are recognised immediately in profit or loss, and included in their respective classifications of income and expense.

32   If payment for an intangible asset is deferred beyond normal credit terms, its cost is the cash price equivalent. The difference between this amount and the total payments is recognised as interest expense over the period of credit unless it is capitalised in accordance with the capitalisation treatment permitted in FRS 15 *Tangible Fixed Assets*. ~~IAS 23 *Borrowing Costs*~~.

Acquisition as Part of a Business Combination

33   In accordance with [draft] FRS ●~~IFRS 3~~ *Business Combinations*, if an intangible asset is acquired in a business combination, the cost of that intangible asset is its fair value at the acquisition date. An intangible asset acquired in a business combination embodies an entity's unconditional right to future economic benefits. Thus, the probability recognition criterion in paragraph 21(a) is always considered to be satisfied for intangible assets acquired in business combinations. Any uncertainty will relate to the timing and amount, if any, of the inflow.

A non-monetary asset without physical substance must be identifiable to meet the **33A** definition of an intangible asset. As outlined in paragraph 12, this will be the case when the asset is separable or arises from contractual or other legal rights. With one possible exception discussed in paragraph 33B, sufficient information should always exist to measure reliably the fair value of an asset that has an underlying contractual or legal basis or is capable of being separated from the entity.

As discussed in paragraph 15, an entity usually has insufficient control over the **33B** expected future economic benefits arising from a team of skilled staff and from training to conclude that these items meet the definition of an intangible asset. However, even in the unlikely event that an entity could demonstrate:

(a)   control over the future economic benefits arising from an assembled workforce acquired in a business combination; and

(b)   that the workforce meets one of the criteria in paragraph 12 for identifiability,

it is highly unlikely that the fair value of that workforce and the related intellectual capital could be measured with sufficient reliability. Accordingly, [draft] FRS ● ~~IFRS 3 (revised)~~ prohibits an acquirer from recognising an assembled workforce as an asset separately from goodwill.

Therefore, in accordance with this Standard and [draft] FRS ● ~~IFRS 3(revised)~~, an **34** acquirer recognises at the acquisition date separately from goodwill an intangible asset of the acquiree (other than assembled workforce), irrespective of whether the asset had been recognised by the acquiree before the business combination. This means that the acquirer recognises as an asset separately from goodwill an in-process research and development project of the acquiree if the project meets the definition of an intangible asset. An acquiree's in-process research and development project meets the definition of an intangible asset when it:

(a)   meets the definition of an asset; and

(b)   is identifiable, ie is separable or arises from contractual or other legal rights.

Measuring the Fair Value of an Intangible Asset Acquired in a Business Combination

With the exception of an assembled workforce, sufficient information always exists **35** to measure reliably the fair value of an asset that has an underlying contractual or legal basis or is capable of being separated from the entity. When, for the estimates used to measure an intangible asset's fair value, there is a range of possible outcomes with different probabilities, that uncertainty enters into the measurement of the asset's fair value.

An intangible asset acquired in a business combination might be separable, but only **36** together with a related tangible or intangible asset. For example, a magazine's publishing title might not be able to be sold separately from a related subscriber database, or a trademark for natural spring water might relate to a particular spring and could not be sold separately from the spring. In such cases, the acquirer recognises the group of assets as a single asset separately from goodwill if the individual fair values of the assets in the group are not reliably measurable.

Similarly, the terms 'brand' and 'brand name' are often used as synonyms for tra- **37** demarks and other marks. However, the former are general marketing terms that are typically used to refer to a group of complementary assets such as a trademark (or service mark) and its related trade name, formulas, recipes and technological expertise. The acquirer recognises as a single asset a group of complementary intangible assets comprising a brand if the individual fair values of the complementary assets are not reliably measurable. If the individual fair values of the complementary assets are reliably measurable, an acquirer may recognise them as a single asset provided the individual assets have similar useful lives.

38   Deleted.

39   Deleted.

40   Deleted.

41   Deleted.

Subsequent Expenditure on an Acquired In-process Research and Development Project

42   *Research or development expenditure that:*

(a)   *relates to an in-process research or development project acquired separately or in a business combination and recognised as an intangible asset; and*

(b)   *is incurred after the acquisition of that project*

shall be accounted for in accordance with paragraphs 54-62.

43   Applying the requirements in paragraphs 54-62 means that subsequent expenditure on an in-process research or development project acquired separately or in a business combination and recognised as an intangible asset is:

(a)   recognised as an expense when incurred if it is research expenditure;

(b)   recognised as an expense when incurred if it is development expenditure that does not satisfy the criteria for recognition as an intangible asset in paragraph 57; and

(c)   added to the carrying amount of the acquired in-process research or development project if it is development expenditure that satisfies the recognition criteria in paragraph 57.

Acquisition by way of a Government Grant

44   In some cases, an intangible asset may be acquired free of charge, or for nominal consideration, by way of a government grant. This may happen when a government transfers or allocates to an entity intangible assets such as airport landing rights, licences to operate radio or television stations, import licences or quotas or rights to access other restricted resources. In accordance with <u>SSAP 4</u> *Accounting for Government Grants* ~~IAS 20~~ ~~*Accounting for Government Grants and Disclosure of Government Assistance*~~, an entity may choose to recognise both the intangible asset and the grant initially at fair value. If an entity chooses not to recognise the asset initially at fair value, the entity recognises the asset initially at a nominal amount (the other treatment permitted by <u>SSAP 4</u> ~~IAS 20~~) plus any expenditure that is directly attributable to preparing the asset for its intended use.

Exchanges of Assets

45   One or more intangible assets may be acquired in exchange for a non-monetary asset or assets, or a combination of monetary and non-monetary assets. The following discussion refers simply to an exchange of one non-monetary asset for another, but it also applies to all exchanges described in the preceding sentence. The cost of such an intangible asset is measured at fair value unless (a) the exchange transaction lacks commercial substance or (b) the fair value of neither the asset received nor the asset given up is reliably measurable. The acquired asset is measured in this way even if an entity cannot immediately derecognise the asset given up. If the acquired asset is not measured at fair value, its cost is measured at the carrying amount of the asset given up.

An entity determines whether an exchange transaction has commercial substance by considering the extent to which its future cash flows are expected to change as a result of the transaction. An exchange transaction has commercial substance if: **46**

(a)   the configuration (ie risk, timing and amount) of the cash flows of the asset received differs from the configuration of the cash flows of the asset transferred; or

(b)   the entity-specific value of the portion of the entity's operations affected by the transaction changes as a result of the exchange; and

(c)   the difference in (a) or (b) is significant relative to the fair value of the assets exchanged.

For the purpose of determining whether an exchange transaction has commercial substance, the entity-specific value of the portion of the entity's operations affected by the transaction shall reflect post-tax cash flows. The result of these analyses may be clear without an entity having to perform detailed calculations.

Paragraph 21(b) specifies that a condition for the recognition of an intangible asset is that the cost of the asset can be measured reliably. The fair value of an intangible asset for which comparable market transactions do not exist is reliably measurable if (a) the variability in the range of reasonable fair value estimates is not significant for that asset or (b) the probabilities of the various estimates within the range can be reasonably assessed and used in estimating fair value. If an entity is able to determine reliably the fair value of either the asset received or the asset given up, then the fair value of the asset given up is used to measure cost unless the fair value of the asset received is more clearly evident. **47**

Internally Generated Goodwill

Internally generated goodwill shall not be recognised as an asset. **48**

In some cases, expenditure is incurred to generate future economic benefits, but it does not result in the creation of an intangible asset that meets the recognition criteria in this Standard. Such expenditure is often described as contributing to internally generated goodwill. Internally generated goodwill is not recognised as an asset because it is not an identifiable resource (ie it is not separable nor does it arise from contractual or other legal rights) controlled by the entity that can be measured reliably at cost. **49**

Differences between the market value of an entity and the carrying amount of its identifiable net assets at any time may capture a range of factors that affect the value of the entity. However, such differences do not represent the cost of intangible assets controlled by the entity. **50**

Internally Generated Intangible Assets

It is sometimes difficult to assess whether an internally generated intangible asset qualifies for recognition because of problems in: **51**

(a)   identifying whether and when there is an identifiable asset that will generate expected future economic benefits; and

(b)   determining the cost of the asset reliably. In some cases, the cost of generating an intangible asset internally cannot be distinguished from the cost of maintaining or enhancing the entity's internally generated goodwill or of running day-to-day operations.

Therefore, in addition to complying with the general requirements for the recognition and initial measurement of an intangible asset, an entity applies the requirements and guidance in paragraphs 52-67 to all internally generated intangible assets.

52   To assess whether an internally generated intangible asset meets the criteria for recognition, an entity classifies the generation of the asset into:

(a)   a research phase; and
(b)   a development phase.

Although the terms 'research' and 'development' are defined, the terms 'research phase' and 'development phase' have a broader meaning for the purpose of this Standard.

53   If an entity cannot distinguish the research phase from the development phase of an internal project to create an intangible asset, the entity treats the expenditure on that project as if it were incurred in the research phase only.

Research Phase

54   *No intangible asset arising from research (or from the research phase of an internal project) shall be recognised. Expenditure on research (or on the research phase of an internal project) shall be recognised as an expense when it is incurred.*

55   In the research phase of an internal project, an entity cannot demonstrate that an intangible asset exists that will generate probable future economic benefits. Therefore, this expenditure is recognised as an expense when it is incurred.

56   Examples of research activities are:

(a)   activities aimed at obtaining new knowledge;
(b)   the search for, evaluation and final selection of, applications of research findings or other knowledge;
(c)   the search for alternatives for materials, devices, products, processes, systems or services; and
(d)   the formulation, design, evaluation and final selection of possible alternatives for new or improved materials, devices, products, processes, systems or services.

Development Phase

57   *An intangible asset arising from development (or from the development phase of an internal project) shall be recognised if, and only if, an entity can demonstrate all of the following:*

(a)   *the technical feasibility of completing the intangible asset so that it will be available for use or sale.*
(b)   *its intention to complete the intangible asset and use or sell it.*
(c)   *its ability to use or sell the intangible asset.*

(d) how the intangible asset will generate probable future economic benefits. Among other things, the entity can demonstrate the existence of a market for the output of the intangible asset or the intangible asset itself or, if it is to be used internally, the usefulness of the intangible asset.

(e) the availability of adequate technical, financial and other resources to complete the development and to use or sell the intangible asset.

(f) its ability to measure reliably the expenditure attributable to the intangible asset during its development.

In the development phase of an internal project, an entity can, in some instances, **58** identify an intangible asset and demonstrate that the asset will generate probable future economic benefits. This is because the development phase of a project is further advanced than the research phase.

Examples of development activities are: **59**

(a) the design, construction and testing of pre-production or pre-use prototypes and models;

(b) the design of tools, jigs, moulds and dies involving new technology;

(c) the design, construction and operation of a pilot plant that is not of a scale economically feasible for commercial production; and

(d) the design, construction and testing of a chosen alternative for new or improved materials, devices, products, processes, systems or services.

To demonstrate how an intangible asset will generate probable future economic **60** benefits, an entity assesses the future economic benefits to be received from the asset using the principles in [draft] FRS ● ~~IAS 36~~ *Impairment of Assets*. If the asset will generate economic benefits only in combination with other assets, the entity applies the concept of cash-generating units in [draft] FRS ● ~~IAS 36~~.

Availability of resources to complete, use and obtain the benefits from an intangible **61** asset can be demonstrated by, for example, a business plan showing the technical, financial and other resources needed and the entity's ability to secure those resources. In some cases, an entity demonstrates the availability of external finance by obtaining a lender's indication of its willingness to fund the plan.

An entity's costing systems can often measure reliably the cost of generating an **62** intangible asset internally, such as salary and other expenditure incurred in securing copyrights or licences or developing computer software.

Internally generated brands, mastheads, publishing titles, customer lists and items **63** *similar in substance shall not be recognised as intangible assets.*

Expenditure on internally generated brands, mastheads, publishing titles, customer **64** lists and items similar in substance cannot be distinguished from the cost of developing the business as a whole. Therefore, such items are not recognised as intangible assets.

Cost of an Internally Generated Intangible Asset

The cost of an internally generated intangible asset for the purpose of paragraph 24 **65** is the sum of expenditure incurred from the date when the intangible asset first meets the recognition criteria in paragraphs 21, 22 and 57. Paragraph 71 prohibits reinstatement of expenditure previously recognised as an expense.

66 The cost of an internally generated intangible asset comprises all directly attributable costs necessary to create, produce, and prepare the asset to be capable of operating in the manner intended by management. Examples of directly attributable costs are:

(a) costs of materials and services used or consumed in generating the intangible asset;

(b) employee labour costs ~~cost of employee benefits (as defined in IAS 19 *Employee Benefits*)~~ arising from the generation of the intangible asset;

(c) fees to register a legal right; and

(d) amortisation of patents and licences that are used to generate the intangible asset.

~~IAS 23 *Borrowing Costs* specifies criteria for the recognition of interest as an element of the cost of an internally generated intangible asset.~~

66A FRS 15 *Tangible Fixed Assets* specifies in paragraphs 19 to 31 the accounting and disclosure requirements of finance costs where an entity adopts a policy of capitalising finance costs that are directly attributable to the construction of a tangible fixed asset. The accounting and disclosure requirements specified in paragraphs 19 to 32 of FRS 15 shall also apply to the cost of internally generated intangible assets.

67 The following are not components of the cost of an internally generated intangible asset:

(a) selling, administrative and other general overhead expenditure unless this expenditure can be directly attributed to preparing the asset for use;

(b) identified inefficiencies and initial operating losses incurred before the asset achieves planned performance; and

(c) expenditure on training staff to operate the asset.

Example illustrating paragraph 65

An entity is developing a new production process. During 20X5, expenditure incurred was CU1,000*, of which CU900 was incurred before 1 December 20X5 and CU100 was incurred between 1 December 20X5 and 31 December 20X5. The entity is able to demonstrate that, at 1 December 20X5, the production process met the criteria for recognition as an intangible asset. The recoverable amount of the know-how embodied in the process (including future cash outflows to complete the process before it is available for use) is estimated to be CU500.

At the end of 20X5, the production process is recognised as an intangible asset at a cost of CU100 (expenditure incurred since the date when the recognition criteria were met, ie 1 December 20X5). The CU900 expenditure incurred before 1 December 20X5 is recognised as an expense because the recognition criteria were not met until 1 December 20X5. This expenditure does not form part of the cost of the production process recognised in the balance sheet.

During 20X6, expenditure incurred is CU2,000. At the end of 20X6, the recoverable amount of the know-how embodied in the process (including future cash outflows to complete the process before it is available for use) is estimated to be CU1,900.

---

*In this Standard, monetary amounts are denominated in 'currency units' (CU).

> At the end of 20X6, the cost of the production process is CU2,100 (CU100
> expenditure recognised at the end of 20X5 plus CU2,000 expenditure recognised
> in 20X6). The entity recognises an impairment loss of CU200 to adjust the
> carrying amount of the process before impairment loss (CU2,100) to its reco-
> verable amount (CU1,900). This impairment loss will be reversed in a
> subsequent period if the requirements for the reversal of an impairment loss in
> IAS 36 are met.

RECOGNITION OF AN EXPENSE

Expenditure on an intangible item shall be recognised as an expense when it is incurred   **68**
unless:

*(a)   it forms part of the cost of an intangible asset that meets the recognition criteria
       (see paragraphs 18-67); or*
*(b)   the item is acquired in a business combination and cannot be recognised as an
       intangible asset. If this is the case, this expenditure (included in the consideration
       transferred in business combination) shall form part of the goodwill at the
       acquisition date (see [draft] FRS ● ~~IFRS 3~~ Business Combinations).*

In some cases, expenditure is incurred to provide future economic benefits to an   **69**
entity, but no intangible asset or other asset is acquired or created that can be
recognised. In these cases, the expenditure is recognised as an expense when it is
incurred. For example, except when it forms part of the assets acquired in a business
combination, expenditure on research is recognised as an expense when it is incurred
(see paragraph 54). Other examples of expenditure that is recognised as an expense
when it is incurred include:

(a)   expenditure on start-up activities (ie start-up costs), unless this expenditure is
      included in the cost of an item of property, plant and equipment in accordance
      with FRS 15 *Tangible Fixed Assets* ~~IAS 16~~ *~~Property, Plant and Equipment~~*.
      Start-up costs may consist of establishment costs such as legal and secretarial
      costs incurred in establishing a legal entity, expenditure to open a new facility
      or business (ie pre-opening costs) or expenditures for starting new operations
      or launching new products or processes (ie pre-operating costs).
(b)   expenditure on training activities.
(c)   expenditure on advertising and promotional activities.
(d)   expenditure on relocating or reorganising part or all of an entity.

Paragraph 68 does not preclude recognising a prepayment as an asset when payment   **70**
for the delivery of goods or services has been made in advance of the delivery of
goods or the rendering of services.

Past Expenses not to be Recognised as an Asset

Expenditure on an intangible item that was initially recognised as an expense shall not   **71**
be recognised as part of the cost of an intangible asset at a later date.

MEASUREMENT AFTER RECOGNITION

An entity shall choose either the cost model in paragraph 74 or the revaluation model in   **72**
*paragraph 75 as its accounting policy. If an intangible asset is accounted for using the
revaluation model, all the other assets in its class shall also be accounted for using the
same model, unless there is no active market for those assets.*

73   A class of intangible assets is a grouping of assets of a similar nature and use in an entity's operations. The items within a class of intangible assets are revalued simultaneously to avoid selective revaluation of assets and the reporting of amounts in the financial statements representing a mixture of costs and values as at different dates.

Cost Model

74   *After initial recognition, an intangible asset shall be carried at its cost less any accumulated amortisation and any accumulated impairment losses.*

Revaluation Model

75   *After initial recognition, an intangible asset shall be carried at a revalued amount, being its fair value at the date of the revaluation less any subsequent accumulated amortisation and any subsequent accumulated impairment losses. For the purpose of revaluations under this Standard, fair value shall be determined by reference to an active market. Revaluations shall be made with such regularity that at the balance sheet date the carrying amount of the asset does not differ materially from its fair value.*

76   The revaluation model does not allow:

(a)   the revaluation of intangible assets that have not previously been recognised as assets; or

(b)   the initial recognition of intangible assets at amounts other than cost.

77   The revaluation model is applied after an asset has been initially recognised at cost. However, if only part of the cost of an intangible asset is recognised as an asset because the asset did not meet the criteria for recognition until part of the way through the process (see paragraph 65), the revaluation model may be applied to the whole of that asset. Also, the revaluation model may be applied to an intangible asset that was received by way of a government grant and recognised at a nominal amount (see paragraph 44).

78   It is uncommon for an active market with the characteristics described in paragraph 8 to exist for an intangible asset, although this may happen. For example, in some jurisdictions, an active market may exist for freely transferable taxi licences, fishing licences or production quotas. However, an active market cannot exist for brands, newspaper mastheads, music and film publishing rights, patents or trademarks, because each such asset is unique. Also, although intangible assets are bought and sold, contracts are negotiated between individual buyers and sellers, and transactions are relatively infrequent. For these reasons, the price paid for one asset may not provide sufficient evidence of the fair value of another. Moreover, prices are often not available to the public.

79   The frequency of revaluations depends on the volatility of the fair values of the intangible assets being revalued. If the fair value of a revalued asset differs materially from its carrying amount, a further revaluation is necessary. Some intangible assets may experience significant and volatile movements in fair value, thus necessitating annual revaluation. Such frequent revaluations are unnecessary for intangible assets with only insignificant movements in fair value.

80   If an intangible asset is revalued, any accumulated amortisation at the date of the revaluation is either:

(a)   restated proportionately with the change in the gross carrying amount of the asset so that the carrying amount of the asset after revaluation equals its revalued amount; or

(b)   eliminated against the gross carrying amount of the asset and the net amount restated to the revalued amount of the asset.

If an intangible asset in a class of revalued intangible assets cannot be revalued because   **81**
there is no active market for this asset, the asset shall be carried at its cost less any
accumulated amortisation and impairment losses.

If the fair value of a revalued intangible asset can no longer be determined by reference   **82**
to an active market, the carrying amount of the asset shall be its revalued amount at the
date of the last revaluation by reference to the active market less any subsequent
accumulated amortisation and any subsequent accumulated impairment losses.

The fact that an active market no longer exists for a revalued intangible asset may   **83**
indicate that the asset may be impaired and that it needs to be tested in accordance
with ~~IAS 36~~ [draft] FRS ● *Impairment of Assets*

If the fair value of the asset can be determined by reference to an active market at a   **84**
subsequent measurement date, the revaluation model is applied from that date.

If an intangible asset's carrying amount is increased as a result of a revaluation, the   **85**
increase shall be credited to the statement of total recognised gains and losses. ~~directly~~
~~to equity under the heading of revaluation surplus.~~ *However, the increase shall be*
recognised in profit or loss to the extent that it reverses a revaluation decrease of the
same asset previously recognised in profit or loss.

If an intangible asset's carrying amount is decreased as a result of a revaluation, the   **86**
decrease shall be recognised in profit or loss. However, the decrease shall be debited to
the statement of total recognised gains and losses ~~directly to equity under the heading of~~
~~revaluation surplus~~ *to the extent of any credit balance in the revaluation surplus in*
respect of that asset.

The cumulative revaluation surplus included in equity may be transferred directly to   **87**
retained earnings when the surplus is realised. The whole surplus may be realised on
the retirement or disposal of the asset. However, some of the surplus may be realised
as the asset is used by the entity; in such a case, the amount of the surplus realised is
the difference between amortisation based on the revalued carrying amount of the
asset and amortisation that would have been recognised based on the asset's historical cost. The transfer from revaluation surplus to retained earnings is not made
through the income statement.

USEFUL LIFE

An entity shall assess whether the useful life of an intangible asset is finite or indefinite   **88**
and, if finite, the length of, or number of production or similar units constituting, that
useful life. An intangible asset shall be regarded by the entity as having an indefinite
useful life when, based on an analysis of all of the relevant factors, there is no fore-
seeable limit to the period over which the asset is expected to generate net cash inflows
for the entity.

The accounting for an intangible asset is based on its useful life. An intangible asset   **89**
with a finite useful life is amortised (see paragraphs 97-106), and an intangible asset
with an indefinite useful life is not (see paragraphs 107-110). The Illustrative

Examples accompanying this Standard illustrate the determination of useful life for different intangible assets, and the subsequent accounting for those assets based on the useful life determinations.

90   Many factors are considered in determining the useful life of an intangible asset, including:

(a)   the expected usage of the asset by the entity and whether the asset could be managed efficiently by another management team;

(b)   typical product life cycles for the asset and public information on estimates of useful lives of similar assets that are used in a similar way;

(c)   technical, technological, commercial or other types of obsolescence;

(d)   the stability of the industry in which the asset operates and changes in the market demand for the products or services output from the asset;

(e)   expected actions by competitors or potential competitors;

(f)   the level of maintenance expenditure required to obtain the expected future economic benefits from the asset and the entity's ability and intention to reach such a level;

(g)   the period of control over the asset and legal or similar limits on the use of the asset, such as the expiry dates of related leases; and

(h)   whether the useful life of the asset is dependent on the useful life of other assets of the entity.

91   The term 'indefinite' does not mean 'infinite'. The useful life of an intangible asset reflects only that level of future maintenance expenditure required to maintain the asset at its standard of performance assessed at the time of estimating the asset's useful life, and the entity's ability and intention to reach such a level. A conclusion that the useful life of an intangible asset is indefinite should not depend on planned future expenditure in excess of that required to maintain the asset at that standard of performance.

92   Given the history of rapid changes in technology, computer software and many other intangible assets are susceptible to technological obsolescence. Therefore, it is likely that their useful life is short.

93   The useful life of an intangible asset may be very long or even indefinite. Uncertainty justifies estimating the useful life of an intangible asset on a prudent basis, but it does not justify choosing a life that is unrealistically short.

94   *The useful life of an intangible asset that arises from contractual or other legal rights shall not exceed the period of the contractual or other legal rights, but may be shorter depending on the period over which the entity expects to use the asset. If the contractual or other legal rights are conveyed for a limited term that can be renewed, the useful life of the intangible asset shall include the renewal period(s) only if there is evidence to support renewal by the entity without significant cost.*

95   There may be both economic and legal factors influencing the useful life of an intangible asset. Economic factors determine the period over which future economic benefits will be received by the entity. Legal factors may restrict the period over which the entity controls access to these benefits. The useful life is the shorter of the periods determined by these factors.

96   Existence of the following factors, among others, indicates that an entity would be able to renew the contractual or other legal rights without significant cost:

(a)   there is evidence, possibly based on experience, that the contractual or other legal rights will be renewed. If renewal is contingent upon the consent of a third party, this includes evidence that the third party will give its consent;

(b)   there is evidence that any conditions necessary to obtain renewal will be satisfied; and

(c)   the cost to the entity of renewal is not significant when compared with the future economic benefits expected to flow to the entity from renewal.

If the cost of renewal is significant when compared with the future economic benefits expected to flow to the entity from renewal, the 'renewal' cost represents, in substance, the cost to acquire a new intangible asset at the renewal date.

INTANGIBLE ASSETS WITH FINITE USEFUL LIVES

Amortisation Period and Amortisation Method

The depreciable amount of an intangible asset with a finite useful life shall be allocated   **97** *on a systematic basis over its useful life. Amortisation shall begin when the asset is available for use, ie when it is in the location and condition necessary for it to be capable of operating in the manner intended by management. Amortisation shall cease at the* ~~earlier of the~~ *date that the* ~~asset is classified as held for sale (or included in a disposal group that is classified as held for sale) in accordance with IFRS 5 Non-current Assets Held for Sale and Discontinued Operations and the date that the~~ *asset is derecognised. The amortisation method used shall reflect the pattern in which the asset's future economic benefits are expected to be consumed by the entity. If that pattern cannot be determined reliably, the straight-line method shall be used. The amortisation charge for each period shall be recognised in profit or loss unless this or another Standard permits or requires it to be included in the carrying amount of another asset.*

A variety of amortisation methods can be used to allocate the depreciable amount of   **98** an asset on a systematic basis over its useful life. These methods include the straight-line method, the diminishing balance method and the unit of production method. The method used is selected on the basis of the expected pattern of consumption of the expected future economic benefits embodied in the asset and is applied consistently from period to period, unless there is a change in the expected pattern of consumption of those future economic benefits. There is rarely, if ever, persuasive evidence to support an amortisation method for intangible assets with finite useful lives that results in a lower amount of accumulated amortisation than under the straight-line method.

Amortisation is usually recognised in profit or loss. However, sometimes the future   **99** economic benefits embodied in an asset are absorbed in producing other assets. In this case, the amortisation charge constitutes part of the cost of the other asset and is included in its carrying amount. For example, the amortisation of intangible assets used in a production process is included in the carrying amount of inventories (see SSAP 9 *Stocks and Long-term Contracts* ~~IAS 2 Inventories~~).

Residual Value

The residual value of an intangible asset with a finite useful life shall be assumed to be   **100** *zero unless:*

(a)   there is a commitment by a third party to purchase the asset at the end of its useful life; or

(b)   there is an active market for the asset and:

(i)   *residual value can be determined by reference to that market; and*

(ii)   *it is probable that such a market will exist at the end of the asset's useful life.*

101   The depreciable amount of an asset with a finite useful life is determined after deducting its residual value. A residual value other than zero implies that an entity expects to dispose of the intangible asset before the end of its economic life.

102   An estimate of an asset's residual value is based on the amount recoverable from disposal using prices prevailing at the date of the estimate for the sale of a similar asset that has reached the end of its useful life and has operated under conditions similar to those in which the asset will be used. The residual value is reviewed at least at each financial year-end. A change in the asset's residual value is accounted for as a change in an ~~accounting estimate~~ estimation technique in accordance with FRS 18 *Accounting Policies*. ~~IAS 8 Accounting Policies, Changes in Accounting Estimates and Errors~~.

103   The residual value of an intangible asset may increase to an amount equal to or greater than the asset's carrying amount. If it does, the asset's amortisation charge is zero unless and until its residual value subsequently decreases to an amount below the asset's carrying amount.

Review of Amortisation Period and Amortisation Method

104   *The amortisation period and the amortisation method for an intangible asset with a finite useful life shall be reviewed at least at each financial year-end. If the expected useful life of the asset is different from previous estimates, the amortisation period shall be changed accordingly. If there has been a change in the expected pattern of consumption of the future economic benefits embodied in the asset, the amortisation method shall be changed to reflect the changed pattern. Such changes shall be accounted for as changes in* ~~accounting estimates~~ *an estimation technique in accordance with FRS 18* ~~IAS 8~~.

105   During the life of an intangible asset, it may become apparent that the estimate of its useful life is inappropriate. For example, the recognition of an impairment loss may indicate that the amortisation period needs to be changed.

106   Over time, the pattern of future economic benefits expected to flow to an entity from an intangible asset may change. For example, it may become apparent that a diminishing balance method of amortisation is appropriate rather than a straight-line method. Another example is if use of the rights represented by a licence is deferred pending action on other components of the business plan. In this case, economic benefits that flow from the asset may not be received until later periods.

INTANGIBLE ASSETS WITH INDEFINITE USEFUL LIVES

107   *An intangible asset with an indefinite useful life shall not be amortised.*

108   In accordance with [draft] FRS ~~IAS~~ 36 *Impairment of Assets*, an entity is required to test an intangible asset with an indefinite useful life for impairment by comparing its recoverable amount with its carrying amount

(a)   annually, and

(b)   whenever there is an indication that the intangible asset may be impaired.

Review of Useful Life Assessment

The useful life of an intangible asset that is not being amortised shall be reviewed each   **109**
period to determine whether events and circumstances continue to support an indefinite useful life assessment for that asset. If they do not, the change in the useful life assessment from indefinite to finite shall be accounted for as a change in an estimation technique ~~accounting estimate~~ *in accordance with* FRS 18 Accounting Policies ~~IAS 8 Accounting Policies, Changes in Accounting Estimates and Errors.~~

In accordance with [draft] FRS ● ~~IAS 36~~, reassessing the useful life of an intangible   **110**
asset as finite rather than indefinite is an indicator that the asset may be impaired. As a result, the entity tests the asset for impairment by comparing its recoverable amount, determined in accordance with [draft] FRS ● ~~IAS 36~~, with its carrying amount, and recognising any excess of the carrying amount over the recoverable amount as an impairment loss.

RECOVERABILITY OF THE CARRYING AMOUNT - IMPAIRMENT LOSSES

To determine whether an intangible asset is impaired an entity applies [draft] FRS ●   **111**
~~IAS 36~~ *Impairment of Assets.* That Standard explains when and how an entity reviews the carrying amount of its assets, how it determines the recoverable amount of an asset and when it recognises or reverses an impairment loss.

RETIREMENTS AND DISPOSALS

An intangible asset shall be derecognised: **112**

(a) on disposal; or
(b) when no future economic benefits are expected from its use or disposal.

The gain or loss arising from the derecognition of an intangible asset shall be deter-   **113**
mined as the difference between the net disposal proceeds, if any, and the carrying amount of the asset. It shall be recognised in profit or loss when the asset is derecognised (unless SSAP 21 Leases and Hire Purchase Contracts ~~IAS 17 Leases~~ *or FRS 5* Reporting the Substance of Transactions *requires otherwise* ~~on a sale and leaseback~~*). Gains shall not be classified as revenue.*

The disposal of an intangible asset may occur in a variety of ways (eg by sale, by   **114**
entering into a finance lease, or by donation). In determining the date of disposal of such an asset, an entity applies the criteria in FRS 5 *Reporting the Substance of Transactions* ~~IAS 18 Revenue~~ for recognising revenue from the sale of goods. SSAP 21 ~~IAS 17~~ applies to disposal by a sale and leaseback.

If in accordance with the recognition principle in paragraph 21 an entity recognises   **115**
in the carrying amount of an asset the cost of a replacement for part of an intangible asset, then it derecognises the carrying amount of the replaced part. If it is not practicable for an entity to determine the carrying amount of the replaced part, it may use the cost of the replacement as an indication of what the cost of the replaced part was at the time it was acquired or internally generated.

The consideration receivable on disposal of an intangible asset is recognised initially   **116**
at its fair value. If payment for the intangible asset is deferred, the consideration received is recognised initially at the cash price equivalent. The difference between the nominal amount of the consideration and the cash price equivalent is recognised

as finance income ~~interest revenue~~ in accordance with ~~IAS 18~~ FRS 5. ~~reflecting the effective yield on the receivable.~~

117 Amortisation of an intangible asset with a finite useful life does not cease when the intangible asset is no longer used, unless the asset has been fully depreciated. ~~or is classified as held for sale (or included in a disposal group that is classified as held for sale) in accordance with IFRS 5.~~

DISCLOSURE

General

118 *An entity shall disclose the following for each class of intangible assets, distinguishing between internally generated intangible assets and other intangible assets:*

(a) *whether the useful lives are indefinite or finite and, if finite, the useful lives or the amortisation rates used;*

(b) *the amortisation methods used for intangible assets with finite useful lives;*

(c) *the gross carrying amount and any accumulated amortisation (aggregated with accumulated impairment losses) at the beginning and end of the period;*

(d) *the line item(s) of the income statement in which any amortisation of intangible assets is included;*

(e) *a reconciliation of the carrying amount at the beginning and end of the period showing:*

(i) *additions, indicating separately those from internal development, those acquired separately, and those acquired through business combinations;*

(ii) ~~*assets classified as held for sale or included in a disposal group classified as held for sale in accordance with IFRS 5 and other disposals;*~~

(iii) *increases or decreases during the period resulting from revaluations under paragraphs 75, 85 and 86 and from impairment losses recognised or reversed through the statement of total recognised gains and losses ~~directly in equity~~ in accordance with [draft] FRS ● ~~IAS 36~~ Impairment of Assets (if any);*

(iv) *impairment losses recognised in profit or loss during the period in accordance with [draft] FRS ● ~~IAS 36~~ (if any);*

(v) *impairment losses reversed in profit or loss during the period in accordance with [draft] FRS ● ~~IAS 36~~ (if any);*

(vi) *any amortisation recognised during the period;*

(vi) *net exchange differences arising on the translation of the financial statements into the presentation currency, and on the translation of a foreign operation into the presentation currency of the entity; and*

(viii) *other changes in the carrying amount during the period.*

119 A class of intangible assets is a grouping of assets of a similar nature and use in an entity's operations. Examples of separate classes may include:

(a) brand names;

(b) mastheads and publishing titles;

(c) computer software;

(d) licences and franchises;

(e) copyrights, patents and other industrial property rights, service and operating rights;

(f) recipes, formulae, models, designs and prototypes; and

(g) intangible assets under development.

The classes mentioned above are disaggregated (aggregated) into smaller (larger) classes if this results in more relevant information for the users of the financial statements.

An entity discloses information on impaired intangible assets in accordance with *[draft] FRS* ● ~~IAS~~ 36 in addition to the information required by paragraph 118(e) (iii)-(v).

120

FRS 18 requires that where the effect of a change to an estimation technique is material, a description of the change and, where practicable, the effect on the results for the current period should be disclosed. ~~IAS 8 requires an entity to disclose the nature and amount of a change in an accounting estimate that has a material effect in the current period or is expected to have a material effect in current period or is expected to have a material effect in subsequent periods.~~ Such disclosure may arise from changes in:

121

(a)   the assessment of an intangible asset's useful life;
(b)   the amortisation method; or
(c)   residual values.

An entity shall also disclose:

122

(a)   for an intangible asset assessed as having an indefinite useful life, the carrying amount of that asset and the reasons supporting the assessment of an indefinite useful life. In giving these reasons, the entity shall describe the factor(s) that played a significant role in determining that the asset has an indefinite useful life.

(b)   a description, the carrying amount and remaining amortisation period of any individual intangible asset that is material to the entity's financial statements.

(c)   for intangible assets acquired by way of a government grant and initially recognised at fair value (see paragraph 44):

  (i)   the fair value initially recognised for these assets;
  (ii)   their carrying amount; and
  (iii) whether they are measured after recognition under the cost model or the revaluation model.

(d)   the existence and carrying amounts of intangible assets whose title is restricted and the carrying amounts of intangible assets pledged as security for liabilities.

(e)   the amount of contractual commitments for the acquisition of intangible assets.

When an entity describes the factor(s) that played a significant role in determining that the useful life of an intangible asset is indefinite, the entity considers the list of factors in paragraph 90.

123

Intangible Assets Measured after Recognition using the Revaluation Model

If intangible assets are accounted for at revalued amounts, an entity shall disclose the following:

124

(a)   by class of intangible assets:

  (i)   the effective date of the revaluation;
  (ii)   the carrying amount of revalued intangible assets; and
  (iii) the carrying amount that would have been recognised had the revalued class of intangible assets been measured after recognition using the cost model in paragraph 74;

(b) the amount of the revaluation surplus that relates to intangible assets at the beginning and end of the period, indicating the changes during the period and any restrictions on the distribution of the balance to shareholders; and

(c) the methods and significant assumptions applied in estimating the assets' fair values.

125 It may be necessary to aggregate the classes of revalued assets into larger classes for disclosure purposes. However, classes are not aggregated if this would result in the combination of a class of intangible assets that includes amounts measured under both the cost and revaluation models.

Research and Development Expenditure

126 *An entity shall disclose the aggregate amount of research and development expenditure recognised as an expense during the period.*

127 Research and development expenditure comprises all expenditure that is directly attributable to research or development activities (see paragraphs 66 and 67 for guidance on the type of expenditure to be included for the purpose of the disclosure requirement in paragraph 126).

Other Information

128 An entity is encouraged, but not required, to disclose the following information:

(a) a description of any fully amortised intangible asset that is still in use; and

(b) a brief description of significant intangible assets controlled by the entity but not recognised as assets because they did not meet the recognition criteria in this Standard or because they were acquired or generated before [draft] FRS • was effective ~~the version of IAS 38 Intangible Assets issued in 1998 was effective.~~

TRANSITIONAL PROVISIONS AND EFFECTIVE DATE

129 *Deleted*

129A *If an entity elects in accordance with paragraph 82 of [draft] FRS • Business Combinations to apply [draft] FRS • Business Combinations from any date before the effective dates set out in paragraph 82 of [draft] FRS • Business Combinations it also shall apply this Standard prospectively from that same date. Thus, the entity shall not adjust the carrying amount of intangible assets recognised at that date. However, the entity shall, at that date, apply this Standard to reassess the useful lives of its recognised intangible assets. If, as a result of that reassessment, the entity changes its assessment of the useful life of an asset, that change shall be accounted for as a change in an estimation technique in accordance with FRS 18 Accounting Policies.*

129B *On application of this [draft] FRS an entity shall reclassify Web Site Costs brought forward as tangible fixed assets to intangible fixed assets. An entity shall apply Application Note A – Web Site Costs to costs incurred from the effective date of this [draft] FRS.*

130 *An entity shall apply this Standard:*

(a) to the accounting for intangible assets acquired in business combinations for which the agreement date is on or after 1 January 2007 ~~31 March 2004~~; and

(b) to the accounting for all other intangible assets prospectively from the beginning of the first annual period beginning on or after 1 January 2007 ~~31 March 2004~~. Thus, the entity shall not adjust the carrying amount of intangible assets recognised at that date. However, the entity shall, at that date, apply this Standard to reassess the useful lives of such intangible assets. If, as a result of that reassessment, the entity changes its assessment of the useful life of an asset, that change shall be accounted for as a change in an ~~accounting estimate~~ estimation technique in accordance with FRS 18 Accounting Policies ~~IAS 8~~.

The agreement date for a business combination is the date that a substantive agreement between the combining parties is reached and, in the case of publicly listed entities, announced to the public. In the case of a hostile takeover, the earliest date that a substantive agreement between the combining parties is reached is the date that a sufficient number of the acquiree's owners have accepted the acquirer's offer for the acquirer to obtain control of the acquiree.

Exchanges of Similar Assets

The requirement in paragraphs 129 and 130(b) to apply this Standard prospectively means that if an exchange of assets was measured before the effective date of this Standard on the basis of the carrying amount of the asset given up, the entity does not restate the carrying amount of the asset acquired to reflect its fair value at the acquisition date.   **131**

Early Application

Entities to which paragraph 130 applies are encouraged to apply the requirements of **132** *this Standard before the effective dates specified in paragraph 130. However, if an entity applies this Standard before those effective dates, it also shall apply [draft] FRS • Business Combinations, [draft] FRS 2 (amended)* Accounting for Subsidiary Undertakings, ~~IFRS 3 and~~ [draft] FRS • ~~IAS 36~~ Impairment of Assets *(as revised in 2004)*, and *[draft] FRS 12 (revised)* Non-financial Liabilities *(formerly known as Provisions Contingent Liabilities and Contingent Assets) at the same time.*

WITHDRAWAL OF FRS 10 AND SSAP 13 ~~IAS 38 (ISSUED 1998)~~

This Standard supersedes FRS 10 *Goodwill and Intangible Assets* and SSAP 13   **133**
Accounting for Research and Development. ~~IAS 38 Intangible Assets (issued in 1998).~~

This Standard also supersedes: **133A**

* UITF Abstract 24 *Accounting for start-up costs;*
* UITF Abstract 27 *Revisions to estimates of the useful economic life of goodwill and intangible assets; and*
* UIFT Abstract 29 *Website development costs.*

CONSEQUENTIAL AMENDMENTS

SSAP 4 *Accounting for Government Grants* **is amended as follows:**   **133B**

* Paragraph 22A is added as follows:
  Fair value is the amount for which an asset could be exchanged between a knowledgeable, willing buyer and a knowledgeable, willing seller in an arm's length transaction.
* Paragraph 25A is added as follows:

A government grant may take the form of a transfer of a non-monetary asset, such as land or other resources, for the use of the entity. In these circumstances it is usual to assess the fair value of the non-monetary asset and to account for both grant and asset at that fair value. An alternative course that is sometimes followed is to record both asset and grant at a nominal value.

133C   SSAP 9 *Stocks and Long-term Contracts* **paragraph 20 is amended as follows**:

Production overheads: Overheads incurred in respect of materials, amortisation of intangible assets used in the production process, labour or services for production, based on the normal level of activity, taking one year with another. For this purpose each overhead should be classified according to function (eg production, selling or administration) so as to ensure the inclusion, in cost of conversion, of those overheads (including depreciation) which relate to production, notwithstanding that these may accrue wholly or partly on a time basis.

133D   UITF Abstract 36 *Contract for sales of capacity* **paragraph 18 is amended as follows:**

The UITF decided that it would be appropriate to recognise turnover or gains in respect of exchange and reciprocal transactions only if fair value can be determined by reference to observable transactions in an active market, ie where the assets or services provided or received are priced by reference to an active market as defined in [draft] FRS ● *Intangible Assets* have a readily ascertainable market value as defined in FRS10 *Goodwill and Intangible Assets*.

133E   UITF Abstract 34 *Pre-contract costs* **paragraph 3(a) is amended as follows**:

costs that are subject to the more specific requirements of accounting standards (such as FRS 4 *Capital Instruments*, FRS 10 *Goodwill and Intangible Assets* *[draft] FRS ● Intangible Assets,* or FRS 15 *Tangible Fixed Assets* or SSAP 13 *Accounting for research and development*)

133F   FRS 18 *Accounting Policies* **paragraph 9 is amended as follows:**

For certain transactions, accounting standards allow a choice of what is to be recognised. An example Examples arises in FRS 15 'Tangible Fixed Assets', which allows directly attributable interest to be treated either as part of an asset or as an expense. , and in SSAP 13 'Accounting for research and development', which allows expenditure satisfying asset recognition criteria to be treated either as an asset or as an expense. Where accounting standards allow a choice over what is to be recognised, that choice is a matter of accounting policy.

133G   FRS 1 *Cash flow statements* **(revised 1996) paragraph 57 is amended as follows:**

Certain accounting standards, such as SSAP 13 'Accounting for research and development', SSAP 21 'Accounting for leases and hire purchase contracts', and FRS 5 'Reporting the Substance of Transactions', specify how certain transactions ...

Appendix A
Application Note A: Intangible Assets - Web Site Costs

This Application Note specifies how the requirements of [draft] FRS● are to be applied to Web Site Costs.

> SIC Interpretation 32 Appendix A *Application Note A, Intangible Assets— Web Site Costs* (SIC-32) is set out in paragraphs A7-A10. Appendix A embodies SIC-32 and is accompanied by a Basis for Conclusions and appendix illustrating the application of the Interpretation. The scope and authority of Interpretations are set out in paragraphs 1 and 8-10 of the IFRIC Preface.

References: IAS 1 Presentation of Financial Statements (as revised in 2003), IAS 2 Inventories (as revised in 2003), IAS 11 Construction Contracts, IAS 16 Property, Plant and Equipment (as revised in 2003), IAS 17 Leases (as revised in 2003), IAS 36 Impairment of Assets (as revised in 2004), IAS 38 Intangible Assets (as revised in 2004), IFRS 3 Business Combinations

ISSUE

An entity may incur internal expenditure on the development and operation of its   A1
own web site for internal or external access. A web site designed for external access
may be used for various purposes such as to promote and advertise an entity's own
products and services, provide electronic services, and sell products and services.
A web site designed for internal access may be used to store company policies and
customer details, and search relevant information.

The stages of a web site's development can be described as follows: A2

(a)   Planning – includes undertaking feasibility studies, defining objectives and
      specifications, evaluating alternatives and selecting preferences.
(b)   Application and Infrastructure Development – includes obtaining a domain
      name, purchasing and developing hardware and operating software, installing
      developed applications and stress testing.
(c)   Graphical Design Development – includes designing the appearance of web
      pages.
(d)   Content Development – includes creating, purchasing, preparing and upload-
      ing information, either textual or graphical in nature, on the web site before the
      completion of the web site's development. This information may either be
      stored in separate databases that are integrated into (or accessed from) the web
      site or coded directly into the web pages.

Once development of a web site has been completed, the Operating stage begins.   A3
During this stage, an entity maintains and enhances the applications, infrastructure,
graphical design and content of the web site.

When accounting for internal expenditure on the development and operation of an   A4
entity's own web site for internal or external access, the issues are:

(a)   whether the web site is an internally generated intangible asset that is subject to
      the requirements of [draft] FRS ●IAS 38; and
(b)   the appropriate accounting treatment of such expenditure.

This Interpretation does not apply to expenditure on purchasing, developing, and   A5
operating hardware (eg web servers, staging servers, production servers and Internet

connections) of a web site. Such expenditure is accounted for under FRS 15 ~~IAS 16~~. Additionally, when an entity incurs expenditure on an Internet service provider hosting the entity's web site, the expenditure is recognised as an expense. ~~under IAS 1.78 and the Framework when the services are received~~.

A6   [Draft] FRS ●~~IAS 38~~ does not apply to intangible assets held by an entity for sale in the ordinary course of business (see SSAP 9 ~~IAS 2 and IAS 11~~) or leases that fall within the scope of SSAP 21 ~~IAS 17~~. Accordingly, this Interpretation does not apply to expenditure on the development or operation of a web site (or web site software) for sale to another entity. When a web site is leased under an operating lease, the lessor applies this Interpretation. When a web site is leased under a finance lease, the lessee applies this Interpretation after initial recognition of the leased asset.

CONSENSUS

A7   An entity's own web site that arises from development and is for internal or external access is an internally generated intangible asset that is subject to the requirements of [draft] FRS ●~~IAS 38~~.

A8   A web site arising from development shall be recognised as an intangible asset if, and only if, in addition to complying with the general requirements described in [draft] FRS ●.21 ~~IAS 38.21~~ for recognition and initial measurement, an entity can satisfy the requirements in [draft] FRS ●.57 ~~IAS 38.57~~. In particular, an entity may be able to satisfy the requirement to demonstrate how its web site will generate probable future economic benefits in accordance with [draft] FRS ●.57(d) ~~IAS 38.57(d)~~ when, for example, the web site is capable of generating revenues, including direct revenues from enabling orders to be placed. An entity is not able to demonstrate how a web site developed solely or primarily for promoting and advertising its own products and services will generate probable future economic benefits, and consequently all expenditure on developing such a web site shall be recognised as an expense when incurred.

A9   Any internal expenditure on the development and operation of an entity's own web site shall be accounted for in accordance with [draft] FRS ● ~~IAS 38~~. The nature of each activity for which expenditure is incurred (eg training employees and maintaining the web site) and the web site's stage of development or post-development shall be evaluated to determine the appropriate accounting treatment (additional guidance is provided in the Appendix to this Interpretation). For example:

(a)   the Planning stage is similar in nature to the research phase in ~~IAS 38.~~ [draft] FRS ●.54-.56. Expenditure incurred in this stage shall be recognised as an expense when it is incurred.

(b)   the Application and Infrastructure Development stage, the Graphical Design stage and the Content Development stage, to the extent that content is developed for purposes other than to advertise and promote an entity's own products and services, are similar in nature to the development phase in ~~IAS 38.~~ [draft] FRS ●.57-.64. Expenditure incurred in these stages shall be included in the cost of a web site recognised as an intangible asset in accordance with paragraph A8 of this Interpretation when the expenditure can be directly attributed and is necessary to creating, producing or preparing the web site for it to be capable of operating in the manner intended by management. For example, expenditure on purchasing or creating content (other than content that advertises and promotes an entity's own products and services) specifically for a web site, or expenditure to enable use of the content (eg a fee for acquiring a licence to reproduce) on the web site, shall be included in the cost of development when this condition is met. However, in accordance with ~~IAS 38.~~

[draft] FRS ●.71, expenditure on an intangible item that was initially recognised as an expense in previous financial statements shall not be recognised as part of the cost of an intangible asset at a later date (eg if the costs of a copyright have been fully amortised, and the content is subsequently provided on a web site).

(c)   expenditure incurred in the Content Development stage, to the extent that content is developed to advertise and promote an entity's own products and services (eg digital photographs of products), shall be recognised as an expense when incurred in accordance with ~~IAS 38~~[draft] FRS ●.69(c). For example, when accounting for expenditure on professional services for taking digital photographs of an entity's own products and for enhancing their display, expenditure shall be recognised as an expense as the professional services are received during the process, not when the digital photographs are displayed on the web site.

(d)   the Operating stage begins once development of a web site is complete. Expenditure incurred in this stage shall be recognised as an expense when it is incurred unless it meets the recognition criteria in ~~IAS 38~~[draft] FRS ●.18.

A web site that is recognised as an intangible asset under paragraph A8 of this Interpretation shall be measured after initial recognition by applying the requirements of ~~IAS 38~~[draft] FRS ●.72-.87. The best estimate of a web site's useful life should be short.   **A10**

Basis for conclusions - Application note A: Web site costs

> *ASB note: The IASB's Basis for Conclusions, which accompanies SIC 32, is set out below in full. It should be noted though that some of the discussion it contains concerns IASB requirements that have no equivalent in the UK or Republic of Ireland. Footnotes have been used to indicate corresponding requirements in the UK and Republic of Ireland where applicable. All references in this section to 'the Board' and 'Board members' are references to the IASB Board and IASB Board members.*

[The original text has been marked up to reflect the revision of IAS 16 in 2003 and the subsequent issue of IFRS 3: new text is underlined and deleted text is struck through]

A11 An intangible asset is defined in IAS 38*.8̶7̶ as an identifiable non-monetary asset without physical substance h̶e̶l̶d̶ ̶f̶o̶r̶ ̶u̶s̶e̶ ̶i̶n̶ ̶t̶h̶e̶ ̶p̶r̶o̶d̶u̶c̶t̶i̶o̶n̶ ̶o̶r̶ ̶s̶u̶p̶p̶l̶y̶ ̶o̶f̶ ̶g̶o̶o̶d̶s̶ ̶o̶r̶ ̶s̶e̶r̶v̶i̶c̶e̶s̶,̶ ̶f̶o̶r̶ ̶r̶e̶n̶t̶a̶l̶ ̶t̶o̶ ̶o̶t̶h̶e̶r̶s̶,̶ ̶o̶r̶ ̶f̶o̶r̶ ̶a̶d̶m̶i̶n̶i̶s̶t̶r̶a̶t̶i̶v̶e̶ ̶p̶u̶r̶p̶o̶s̶e̶s̶. IAS 38.9̶8̶ provides computer software as a common example of an intangible asset. By analogy, a web site is another example of an intangible asset.

A12 IAS 38.6̶8̶5̶6̶ requires expenditure on an intangible item to be recognised as an expense when incurred unless it forms part of the cost of an intangible asset that meets the recognition criteria in IAS 38.18-.6̶7̶5̶5̶. IAS 38.6̶9̶5̶7̶ requires expenditure on start-up activities to be recognised as an expense when incurred. An entity developing its own web site for internal or external access is not undertaking a start-up activity to the extent that an internally generated intangible asset is created. The requirements and guidance in IAS 38.5̶2̶-̶.6̶7̶4̶0̶-̶.5̶5̶, in addition to the general requirements described in IAS 38.2̶1̶1̶9̶ for recognition and initial measurement of an intangible asset, apply to expenditure incurred on the development of an entity's own web site. As described in IAS 38.6̶5̶-̶.6̶7̶5̶3̶-̶.5̶5̶, the cost of a web site recognised as an internally generated intangible asset comprises all expenditure that can be directly attributed,̶ ̶o̶r̶ ̶a̶l̶l̶o̶c̶a̶t̶e̶d̶ ̶o̶n̶ ̶a̶ ̶r̶e̶a̶s̶o̶n̶a̶b̶l̶e̶ ̶a̶n̶d̶ ̶c̶o̶n̶s̶i̶s̶t̶e̶n̶t̶ ̶b̶a̶s̶i̶s̶, and is necessary to creating, producing and preparing the asset for it to be capable of operating in the manner intended by management i̶t̶s̶ ̶i̶n̶t̶e̶n̶d̶e̶d̶ ̶u̶s̶e̶.

A13 IAS 38.5̶4̶4̶2̶ requires expenditure on research (or on the research phase of an internal project) to be recognised as an expense when incurred. The examples provided in IAS 38.5̶6̶4̶4̶ are similar to the activities undertaken in the Planning stage of a web site's development. Consequently, expenditure incurred in the Planning stage of a web site's development is recognised as an expense when incurred.

A14 IAS 38.5̶7̶4̶5̶ requires an intangible asset arising from the development phase of an internal project to be recognised only if an entity can demonstrate fulfilment of the six criteria specified. One of the criteria is to demonstrate how a web site will generate probable future economic benefits (IAS 38.5̶7̶4̶5̶(d)). IAS 38.6̶0̶4̶8̶ indicates that this criterion is met by assessing the economic benefits to be received from the web site and using the principles in IAS 36† *Impairment of Assets*, which considers the present value of estimated future cash flows from continuing use of the web site. Future economic benefits flowing from an intangible asset, as stated in IAS 38.17, may

---

*ASB footnote: *All references to IAS 38 refer to [draft] FRS ● *Intangible Assets. This Application Note is an Appendix to [draft] FRS ●.*

†ASB footnote: *The corresponding requirements in the UK and the Republic of Ireland are in [draft] FRS ● (IAS 36)* Impairment of Assets.

include revenue from the sale of products or services, cost savings, or other benefits resulting from the use of the asset by the entity. Therefore, future economic benefits from a web site may be assessed when the web site is capable of generating revenues. A web site developed solely or primarily for advertising and promoting an entity's own products and services is not recognised as an intangible asset, because the entity cannot demonstrate the future economic benefits that will flow. Consequently, all expenditure on developing a web site solely or primarily for promoting and advertising an entity's own products and services is recognised as an expense when incurred.

Under IAS 38.21~~19~~, an intangible asset is recognised if, and only if, it meets specified criteria. IAS 38.65~~53~~ indicates that the cost of an internally generated intangible asset is the sum of expenditure incurred from the date when the intangible asset first meets the specified recognition criteria. When an entity acquires or creates content for purposes other than to advertise and promote an entity's own products and services, it may be possible to identify an intangible asset (eg a licence or a copyright) separate from a web site. However, a separate asset is not recognised when expenditure is directly attributed~~, or allocated on a reasonable and consistent basis,~~ to creating, producing, and preparing the web site for <u>it to be capable of operating in the manner intended by management</u> ~~its intended use~~ the expenditure is included in the cost of developing the web site.   **A15**

IAS 38.69~~57~~(c) requires expenditure on advertising and promotional activities to be recognised as an expense when incurred. Expenditure incurred on developing content that advertises and promotes an entity's own products and services (eg digital photographs of products) is an advertising and promotional activity, and consequently recognised as an expense when incurred ~~in accordance with IAS 38.57(c)~~.   **A16**

~~Once development of a web site is complete, an enterprise begins the activities described in the Operating stage. Subsequent expenditure to enhance or maintain an enterprise's own web site is recognised as an expense when incurred unless it meets the recognition criteria in IAS 38.60. IAS 38.61 explains that if the expenditure is required to maintain the asset at its originally assessed standard of performance, then the expenditure is recognised as an expense when incurred.~~* <u>Once development of a web site is complete, an entity begins the activities described in the Operating stage. Subsequent expenditure to enhance or maintain an entity's own web site is recognised as an expense when incurred unless it meets the recognition criteria in IAS 38.18. IAS 38.20 explains that most subsequent expenditures are likely to maintain the future economic benefits embodied in an existing intangible asset rather than meet the definition of an intangible asset and the recognition criteria set out in IAS 38. In addition, it is often difficult to attribute subsequent expenditure directly to a particular intangible asset rather than to the business as a whole. Therefore, only rarely will subsequent expenditure—expenditure incurred after the initial recognition of a purchased intangible asset or after completion of an internally generated intangible asset—be recognised in the carrying amount of an asset.</u>†   **A17**

An intangible asset is measured after initial recognition by applying the requirements of IAS 38.72~~-.87~~63~~-.78~~. The <u>revaluation model</u> ~~Allowed Alternative Treatment~~ in IAS 38.75~~64~~ is applied only when the fair value of an intangible asset can be   **A18**

---

*~~IAS 16 Property, Plant and Equipment~~ *as revised by the IASB in 2003 requires all subsequent costs to be covered by its general recognition principle and eliminated the requirement to reference the originally assessed standard of performance. IAS 38 was amended as a consequence of the change to IAS 16 and the paragraphs specifically referred to were eliminated. This paragraph has been struck through to avoid any confusion.*

†*The new text was added by IFRS 3* Business Combinations *in 2004.*

determined by reference to an active market. However, as an active market is unlikely to exist for web sites, the cost model ~~Benchmark Treatment~~ applies. Additionally, ~~since IAS 38.84 states that an intangible asset always has a finite useful life, a web site that is recognised as an asset is amortised over the best estimate of its useful life under IAS 38.79. As~~ as indicated in IAS 38.92~~81~~, many intangible assets are susceptible to technological obsolescence, and given the history of rapid changes in technology, the useful life of web sites will be short.

Date of Consensus: ~~May 2001~~

Effective Date: ~~This Interpretation becomes effective on 25 March 2002. The effects of adopting this Interpretation shall be accounted for using the transition requirements in the version of IAS 38 that was issued in 1998. Therefore, when a web site does not meet the criteria for recognition as an intangible asset, but was previously recognised as an asset, the item shall be derecognised at the date when this Interpretation becomes effective. When a web site exists and the expenditure to develop it meets the criteria for recognition as an intangible asset, but was not previously recognised as an asset, the intangible asset shall not be recognised at the date when this Interpretation becomes effective. When a web site exists and the expenditure to develop it meets the criteria for recognition as an intangible asset, was previously recognised as an asset and initially measured at cost, the amount initially recognised is deemed to have been properly determined.~~

Appendix to Application Note A ~~SIC-32~~

This appendix is illustrative only and does not form part of the ~~Interpretation~~ Application Note. The purpose of the appendix is to illustrate examples of expenditure that occur during each of the stages described in paragraphs 2 and 3 of the ~~Interpretation~~ Application Note and illustrate application of the ~~Interpretation~~ Application Note to assist in clarifying its meaning. It is not intended to be a comprehensive checklist of expenditure that might be incurred.

> *ASB note: These Illustrative Examples have been prepared by the IASB.*

Example Application of Application Note A ~~SIC-32~~

Stage / Nature of Expenditure	Accounting treatment
Planning • undertaking feasibility studies • defining hardware and software specifications • evaluating alternative products and suppliers • selecting preferences	Recognise as an expense when incurred in accordance with [draft] FRS • .54 ~~IAS 38.54~~
Application and Infrastructure Development • purchasing or developing hardware	Apply the requirements of FRS 15 ~~IAS 16~~
• obtaining a domain name • developing operating software (eg operating system and server software) • developing code for the application • installing developed applications on the web server • stress testing	Recognise as an expense when incurred, unless the expenditure can be directly attributed to preparing the web site to operate in the manner intended by management, and the web site meets the recognition criteria in [draft] FRS • .21 ~~IAS 38.21~~ and [draft] FRS • .57 ~~IAS 38.57~~*
Graphical Design Development • designing the appearance (eg layout and colour) of web pages	Recognise as an expense when incurred, unless the expenditure can be directly attributed to preparing the web site to operate in the manner intended by management, and the web site meets the recognition criteria in [draft] FRS • .21 ~~IAS 38.21~~ and [draft] FRS • .57 ~~IAS 38.57~~*
Content Development • creating, purchasing, preparing (eg creating links and identifying tags), and uploading information, either textual or graphical in nature, on the web site before the completion of the web site's development. Examples of content include information about an entity, products or services offered	Recognise as an expense when incurred in accordance with [draft] FRS • .69(c) to the extent that content is developed to advertise and promote an entity's own products and services (eg digital photographs of products). Otherwise, recognise as an expense when incurred, unless the expenditure can be directly attributed to preparing the web site to operate in the manner intended by

Stage / Nature of Expenditure	Accounting treatment
for sale, and topics that subscribers access	management, and the web site meets the recognition criteria in [draft] FRS • .21 ~~IAS 38.21~~ and [draft] FRS • .57* ~~IAS 38.57*~~
Operating • updating graphics and revising content • adding new functions, features and content • registering the web site with search engines • backing up data • reviewing security access • analysing usage of the web site	Assess whether it meets the definition of an intangible asset and the recognition criteria set out in [draft] FRS • .18 ~~IAS 38.18~~, in which case the expenditure is recognised in the carrying amount of the web site asset
Other • selling, administrative and other general overhead expenditure unless it can be directly attributed to preparing the web site for use to operate in the manner intended by management • clearly identified inefficiencies and initial operating losses incurred before the web site achieves planned performance [eg false start testing] • training employees to operate the web site	Recognise as an expense when incurred in accordance with [draft] FRS • .65-70 ~~IAS 38.65–.70~~

* All expenditure on developing a web site solely or primarily for promoting and advertising an entity's own products and services is recognised as an expense when incurred in accordance with ~~IAS 38~~ [draft] FRS •.68

Approval of IAS 38 by the Board

International Accounting Standard 38 *Intangible Assets* was approved for issue by
thirteen of the fourteen members of the International Accounting Standards Board.
Professor Whittington dissented. His dissenting opinion is set out after the Basis for
Conclusions on IAS 38.

Sir David Tweedie   Chairman
Thomas E Jones   Vice-Chairman
Mary E Barth
Hans-Georg Bruns
Anthony T Cope
Robert P Garnett
Gilbert Gélard
James J Leisenring
Warren J McGregor
Patricia L O'Malley
Harry K Schmid
John T Smith
Geoffrey Whittington
Tatsumi Yamada

Basis for Conclusions on [draft] FRS ● ~~IAS 38~~ Intangible Assets

Contents

Basis for Conclusions on [draft] FRS ● ~~IAS 38~~ Intangible Assets

> *ASB note: The IASB's Basis for Conclusions, which accompanies IAS 38, is set out below in full. It should be noted though that some of the discussion it contains concerns IASB requirements that have no equivalent in the UK or Republic of Ireland. Footnotes have been used to indicate corresponding requirements in the UK and Republic of Ireland where applicable. All references in this section to 'the Board' and 'Board members' are references to the IASB Board and IASB Board members*

> *The International Accounting Standards Board revised IAS 38 as part of its project on business combinations. It was not the Board's intention to reconsider as part of that project all of the requirements in IAS 38.*
>
> *The previous version of IAS 38 was accompanied by a Basis for Conclusions summarising the former International Accounting Standards Committee's considerations in reaching some of its conclusions in that Standard. For convenience the Board has incorporated into its own Basis for Conclusions material from the previous Basis for Conclusions that discusses (a) matters the Board did not reconsider and (b) the history of the development of a standard on intangible assets. That material is contained in paragraphs denoted by numbers with the prefix BCZ. Paragraphs describing the Board's considerations in reaching its own conclusions are numbered with the prefix BC.*

INTRODUCTION

BC1   This Basis for Conclusions summarises the International Accounting Standards Board's considerations in reaching the conclusions in IAS 38 Intangible *Assets*. Individual Board members gave greater weight to some factors than to others.

BC2   The International Accounting Standards Committee (IASC) issued the previous version of IAS 38 in 1998. It has been revised by the Board as part of its project on business combinations. That project has two phases. The first has resulted in the Board issuing simultaneously IFRS 3 *Business Combinations** and revised versions of IAS 38 and IAS 36 *Impairment of Assets*. Therefore, the Board's intention in revising IAS 38 as part of the first phase of the project was not to reconsider all of the requirements in IAS 38. The changes to IAS 38 are primarily concerned with:

(a)   the notion of 'identifiability' as it relates to intangible assets;

(b)   the useful life and amortisation of intangible assets; and

(c)   the accounting for in-process research and development projects acquired in business combinations.

BC3   With the exception of research and development projects acquired in business combinations, the Board did not reconsider the requirements in the previous version of IAS 38 on the recognition of internally generated intangible assets. The previous version of IAS 38 was accompanied by a Basis for Conclusions summarising IASC's considerations in reaching some of its conclusions in that Standard. For convenience,

---

*ASB footnote: *The ASB is proposing to implement the replacement standard for IFRS 3* Business Combinations *see FRED 36. The ASB is also proposing to implement IAS 36* Impairment of Assets *see FRED 38.*

the Board has incorporated into this Basis for Conclusions material from the previous Basis for Conclusions that discusses the recognition of internally generated intangible assets (see paragraphs BCZ29-BCZ46) and the history of the development of a standard on intangible assets (see paragraphs BCZ104-BCZ110). The views expressed in paragraphs BCZ29-BCZ46 and BCZ104-BCZ110 are those of IASC.

DEFINITION OF AN INTANGIBLE ASSET (PARAGRAPH 8)

An intangible asset was defined in the previous version of IAS 38 as "an identifiable **BC4** non-monetary asset without physical substance held for use in the production or supply of goods or services, for rental to others, or for administrative services". The definition in the revised Standard eliminates the requirement for the asset to be held for use in the production or supply of goods or services, for rental to others, or for administrative services.

The Board observed that the essential characteristics of intangible assets are that **BC5** they:

(a) are resources controlled by the entity from which future economic benefits are expected to flow to the entity;
(b) lack physical substance; and
(c) are identifiable.

The Board concluded that the purpose for which an entity holds an item with these characteristics is not relevant to its classification as an intangible asset, and that all such items should be within the scope of the Standard.

IDENTIFIABILITY (PARAGRAPH 12)

Under the Standard, as under the previous version of IAS 38, a non-monetary asset **BC6** without physical substance must be identifiable to meet the definition of an intangible asset. The previous version of IAS 38 did not define 'identifiability', but stated that an intangible asset could be distinguished from goodwill if the asset was separable, but that separability was not a necessary condition for identifiability. The revised Standard requires an asset to be treated as meeting the identifiability criterion in the definition of an intangible asset when it is separable, or when it arises from contractual or other legal rights, regardless of whether those rights are transferable or separable from the entity or from other rights and obligations.

Background to the Board's deliberations

The Board was prompted to consider the issue of 'identifiability' as part of the first **BC7** phase of its Business Combinations project as a result of changes during 2001 to the requirements in Canadian and United States standards on the separate recognition of intangible assets acquired in business combinations. The Board observed that intangible assets comprise an increasing proportion of the assets of many entities, and that intangible assets acquired in a business combination are often included in the amount recognised as goodwill, despite the requirements in IAS 22 *Business Combinations** and IAS 38 for them to be recognised separately from goodwill. The Board agreed with the conclusion reached by the Canadian and US standard-setters that the usefulness of financial statements would be enhanced if intangible assets acquired in a business combination were distinguished from goodwill. Therefore, the Board concluded that the IFRS arising from the first phase of the Business

*ASB footnote: *IFRS 3 superseded IAS 22.*

Combinations project should provide a definitive basis for identifying and recognising intangible assets acquired in a business combination separately from goodwill.

BC8   In revising IAS 38 and developing IFRS 3, the Board affirmed the view in the previous version of IAS 38 that identifiability is the characteristic that conceptually distinguishes other intangible assets from goodwill. The Board concluded that to provide a definitive basis for identifying and recognising intangible assets separately from goodwill, the concept of identifiability needed to be articulated more clearly.

Clarifying identifiability (paragraph 12)

BC9   Consistently with the guidance in the previous version of IAS 38, the Board concluded that an intangible asset can be distinguished from goodwill if it is separable, ie capable of being separated or divided from the entity and sold, transferred, licensed, rented or exchanged. Therefore, in the context of intangible assets, separability signifies identifiability, and intangible assets with that characteristic that are acquired in a business combination should be recognised as assets separately from goodwill.

BC10   However, again consistently with the guidance in the previous version of IAS 38, the Board concluded that separability is not the only indication of identifiability. The Board observed that, in contrast to goodwill, the values of many intangible assets arise from rights conveyed legally by contract or statute. In the case of acquired goodwill, its value arises from the collection of assembled assets that make up an acquired entity or the value created by assembling a collection of assets through a business combination, such as the synergies that are expected to result from combining entities or businesses. The Board also observed that, although many intangible assets are both separable and arise from contractual-legal rights, some contractual-legal rights establish property interests that are not readily separable from the entity as a whole. For example, under the laws of some jurisdictions some licences granted to an entity are not transferable except by sale of the entity as a whole. The Board concluded that the fact that an intangible asset arises from contractual or other legal rights is a characteristic that distinguishes it from goodwill. Therefore, intangible assets with that characteristic that are acquired in a business combination should be recognised as assets separately from goodwill.

Non-contractual customer relationships (paragraph 16)

BC11   The previous version of IAS 38 and the Exposure Draft of Proposed Amendments to IAS 38 stated that "An entity controls an asset if the entity has the power to obtain the future economic benefits flowing from the underlying resource and also can restrict the access of others to those benefits." The documents then expanded on this by stating that "in the absence of legal rights to protect, or other ways to control, the relationships with customers or the loyalty of the customers to the entity, the entity usually has insufficient control over the economic benefits from customer relationships and loyalty to consider that such items meet the definition of intangible assets."

BC12   However, the Draft Illustrative Examples accompanying ED 3 *Business Combinations* stated that "If a customer relationship acquired in a business combination does not arise from a contract, the relationship is recognised as an intangible asset separately from goodwill if it meets the separability criterion. Exchange transactions for the same asset or a similar asset provide evidence of separability of a non-contractual customer relationship and might also provide information about exchange prices that should be considered when estimating fair value." Whilst respondents to the Exposure Draft generally agreed with the Board's conclusions on the definition of identifiability, some were uncertain about the relationship between the separability criterion for establishing whether a non-contractual customer relationship is identifiable, and the control concept for establishing whether the relationship meets the definition of an asset. Additionally, some respondents suggested that non-contractual customer relationships would, under the proposal in the Exposure Draft, be separately recognised if acquired in a business combination, but not if acquired in a separate transaction.

The Board observed that exchange transactions for the same or similar non-con-   **BC13**
tractual customer relationships provide evidence not only that the item is separable, but also that the entity is able to control the expected future economic benefits flowing from that relationship. Similarly, if an entity separately acquires a non-contractual customer relationship, the existence of an exchange transaction for that relationship provides evidence both that the item is separable, and that the entity is able to control the expected future economic benefits flowing from the relationship. Therefore, the relationship would meet the intangible asset definition and be recognised as such. However, in the absence of exchange transactions for the same or similar non-contractual customer relationships, such relationships acquired in a business combination would not normally meet the definition of an 'intangible asset'—they would not be separable, nor would the entity be able to demonstrate that it controls the expected future economic benefits flowing from that relationship.

Therefore, the Board decided to clarify in paragraph 16 of IAS 38 that in the absence   **BC14**
of legal rights to protect customer relationships, exchange transactions for the same or similar non-contractual customer relationships (other than as part of a business combination) provide evidence that the entity is nonetheless able to control the future economic benefits flowing from the customer relationships. Because such exchange transactions also provide evidence that the customer relationships are separable, those customer relationships meet the definition of an intangible asset.

CRITERIA FOR INITIAL RECOGNITION

In accordance with the Standard, as with the previous version of IAS 38, an   **BC15**
intangible asset is recognised if, and only if:

(a)   it is probable that the expected future economic benefits that are attributable to the asset will flow to the entity; and
(b)   the cost of the asset can be measured reliably.

In revising IAS 38 the Board considered the application of these recognition criteria to intangible assets acquired in business combinations. The Board's deliberations on this issue are set out in paragraphs BC16-BC25.

Acquisition as part of a business combination (paragraphs 33-38)

The Exposure Draft of Proposed Amendments to IAS 38 proposed that the recog-   **BC16**
nition criteria in paragraph BC15 would, with the exception of an assembled workforce, always be satisfied for an intangible asset acquired in a business combination. Therefore, those criteria were not included in ED 3 *Business Combinations*. ED 3 proposed requiring an acquirer to recognise separately at the acquisition date all of the acquiree's intangible assets as defined in IAS 38, other than an assembled workforce. After considering respondents' comments, the Board decided:

(a)   to proceed with the proposal that the probability recognition criterion is always considered to be satisfied for intangible assets acquired in a business combination; and

(b)   not to proceed with the proposal that, with the exception of an assembled workforce, sufficient information should always exist to measure reliably the fair value of an intangible asset acquired in a business combination.

Probability recognition criterion

BC17   In revising IAS 38, the Board observed that the fair value of an intangible asset reflects market expectations about the probability that the future economic benefits associated with the intangible asset will flow to the acquirer. In other words, the effect of probability is reflected in the fair value measurement of an intangible asset. Therefore, the probability recognition criterion is always considered to be satisfied for intangible assets acquired in business combinations.

BC18   The Board observed that this highlights a general inconsistency between the recognition criteria for assets and liabilities in the *Framework** (which states that an item meeting the definition of an element should be recognised only if it is probable that any future economic benefits associated with the item will flow to or from the entity, and the item can be measured reliably) and the fair value measurements required in, for example, a business combination. However, the Board concluded that the role of probability as a criterion for recognition in the *Framework* should be considered more generally as part of a forthcoming Concepts project.

Reliability of measurement recognition criterion

BC19   In developing the Exposure Draft, the Board concluded that, except for an assembled workforce, sufficient information should exist to measure reliably the fair value of an asset that has an underlying contractual or legal basis or is capable of being separated from the entity. Respondents generally disagreed with this conclusion, arguing that:

(a)   it might not always be possible to measure reliably the fair value of an asset that has an underlying contractual or legal basis or is capable of being separated from the entity.

(b)   a similar presumption does not exist in IFRSs for identifiable tangible assets acquired in a business combination. Indeed, the Board decided when developing IFRS 3 *Business Combinations* to carry forward from IAS 22 *Business Combinations* the general principle that an acquirer should recognise separately from goodwill the acquiree's identifiable tangible assets, but only provided they can be measured reliably.

BC20   Additionally, as part of its consultative process, the Board conducted field visits and round-table discussions during the comment period for the Exposure Draft.† Field visit and round-table participants were asked a series of questions aimed at improving the Board's understanding of whether there might exist non-monetary

---

**ASB footnote: The equivalent document in the UK and Republic of Ireland to the IASB's* Framework *is the ASB's* Statement of Principles for Financial Reporting. *Although the* Statement of Principles *is very similar to the* Framework, *it is not identical.*

†*The field visits were conducted from early December 2002 to early April 2003, and involved IASB members and staff in meetings with 41 companies in Australia, France, Germany, Japan, South Africa, Switzerland and the United Kingdom. IASB members and staff also took part in a series of round-table discussions with auditors, preparers, accounting standard-setters and regulators in Canada and the United States on implementation issues encountered by North American companies during first-time application of US Statements of Financial Accounting Standards 141* Business Combinations *and 142* Goodwill and Other Intangible Assets, *and the equivalent Canadian Handbook Sections, which were issued in June 2001.*

assets without physical substance that are separable or arise from legal or other contractual rights, but for which there may *not* be sufficient information to measure fair value reliably.

The field visit and round-table participants provided numerous examples of intangible assets they had acquired in recent business combinations whose fair values might not be reliably measurable. For example, one participant acquired water acquisition rights as part of a business combination. The rights are extremely valuable to many manufacturers operating in the same jurisdiction as the participant—the manufacturers cannot acquire water and, in many cases, cannot operate their plants without them. Local authorities grant the rights at little or no cost, but in limited numbers, for fixed periods (normally ten years), and renewal is certain at little or no cost. The rights cannot be sold other than as part of the sale of a business as a whole, therefore there exists no secondary market in the rights. If a manufacturer hands the rights back to the local authority, it is prohibited from reapplying. The participant argued that it could not value these rights separately from its business (and therefore from goodwill), because the business would cease to exist without the rights. **BC21**

After considering respondents' comments and the experiences of field visit and round-table participants, the Board concluded that, in some instances, there might not be sufficient information to measure reliably the fair value of an intangible asset separately from goodwill, notwithstanding that the asset is identifiable. The Board observed that, except as outlined in paragraph BC25, the intangible assets whose fair values respondents,field visit and roundtable participants could not measure reliably arose either: **BC22**

(a)   from legal or other contractual rights and are not separable (ie could be transferred only as part of the sale of a business as a whole); or

(b)   from legal or other contractual rights and are separable (ie capable of being separated or divided from the entity and sold, transferred, licensed, rented or exchanged, either individually or together with a related contract, asset or liability), but there is no history or evidence of exchange transactions for the same or similar assets,otherwise estimating fair value would be dependent on immeasurable variables.

Nevertheless, the Board remained of the view that the usefulness of financial statements would be enhanced if intangible assets acquired in a business combination were distinguished from goodwill, particularly given the Board's decision to regard goodwill as an indefinite-lived asset that is not amortised. The Board also remained concerned that failing the recognition criterion of reliability of measurement might be inappropriately used by entities as a basis for not recognising intangible assets separately from goodwill. For example, IAS 22 and the previous version of IAS 38 required an acquirer to recognise an intangible asset of the acquiree separately from goodwill at the acquisition date if it was probable that any associated future economic benefits would flow to the acquirer and the asset's fair value could be measured reliably. The Board observed when developing the Exposure Draft that although intangible assets constitute an increasing proportion of the assets of many entities, those acquired in business combinations were often included in the amount recognised as goodwill, despite the requirements in IAS 22 and the previous version of IAS 38 that they be recognised separately from goodwill. **BC23**

Therefore, although the Board decided not to proceed with the proposal that, with the exception of an assembled workforce, sufficient information should always exist to measure reliably the fair value of an intangible asset acquired in a business combination, the Board also decided: **BC24**

(a)   to clarify in paragraph 35 of the Standard that the fair value of an intangible asset acquired in a business combination can normally be measured with sufficient reliability for it to be recognised separately from goodwill. When, for the estimates used to measure an intangible asset's fair value, there is a range of possible outcomes with different probabilities, that uncertainty enters into the measurement of the asset's fair value, rather than demonstrates an inability to measure fair value reliably.

(b)   to include in paragraph 35 of the Standard a rebuttable presumption that the fair value of a finite-lived intangible asset acquired in a business combination can be measured reliably.

(c)   to clarify in paragraph 38 of the Standard that the only circumstances in which it might not be possible to measure reliably the fair value of an intangible asset acquired in a business combination are when the intangible asset arises from legal or other contractual rights and it either (i) is not separable or (ii) is separable but there is no history or evidence of exchange transactions for the same or similar assets and otherwise estimating fair value would be dependent on immeasurable variables.

(d)   to include in paragraph 67(h) of IFRS 3 a requirement for entities to disclose a description of each asset that meets the definition of an intangible asset and was acquired in a business combination during the period but was not recognised separately from goodwill, and an explanation of why its fair value could not be measured reliably.

BC25   Some respondents and field visit participants suggested that it might also not be possible to measure reliably the fair value of an intangible asset when it is separable, but only together with a related contract, asset or liability (ie it is not individually separable), there is no history of exchange transactions for the same or similar assets on a standalone basis, and, because the related items produce jointly the same cash flows, the fair value of each could be estimated only by arbitrarily allocating those cash flows between the two items. The Board disagreed that such circumstances provide a basis for subsuming the value of the intangible asset within the carrying amount of goodwill. Although some intangible assets are so closely related to other identifiable assets or liabilities that they are usually sold as a package, it would still be possible to measure reliably the fair value of that package. Therefore, the Board decided to include the following clarifications in paragraphs 36 and 37 of the Standard:

(a)   when an intangible asset acquired in a business combination is separable but only together with a related tangible or intangible asset, the acquirer recognises the group of assets as a single asset separately from goodwill if the individual fair values of the assets in the group are not reliably measurable.

(b)   similarly, an acquirer recognises as a single asset a group of complementary intangible assets constituting a brand if the individual fair values of the complementary assets are not reliably measurable. If the individual fair values of the complementary assets are reliably measurable, the acquirer may recognise them as a single asset separately from goodwill, provided the individual assets have similar useful lives.

Separate acquisition (paragraphs 25 and 26)

BC26   Having decided to include paragraphs 33-38 in IAS 38, the Board also decided that it needed to consider the role of the probability and reliability of measurement recognition criteria for separately acquired intangible assets.

BC27   Consistently with its conclusion about the role of probability in the recognition of intangible assets acquired in business combinations, the Board concluded that the probability recognition criterion is always considered to be satisfied for separately acquired intangible assets. This is because the price an entity pays to acquire separately an intangible asset normally reflects expectations about the probability that the expected future economic benefits associated with the intangible asset will flow to the entity. In other words, the effect of probability is reflected in the cost of the intangible asset.

The Board also concluded that when an intangible asset is separately acquired in exchange for cash or other monetary assets, sufficient information should exist to measure the cost of that asset reliably. However, this might not be the case when the purchase consideration comprises non-monetary assets. Therefore, the Board decided to carry forward from the previous version of IAS 38 guidance clarifying that the cost of a separately acquired intangible asset can usually be measured reliably, particularly when the purchase consideration is cash or other monetary assets.   **BC28**

Internally generated intangible assets (paragraphs 51-67)

The controversy relating to internally generated intangible assets surrounds whether there should be: **BCZ29**

(a) a requirement to recognise internally generated intangible assets in the balance sheet whenever certain criteria are met;
(b) a requirement to recognise expenditure on all internally generated intangible assets as an expense;
(c) a requirement to recognise expenditure on all internally generated intangible assets as an expense, with certain specified exceptions; or
(d) an option to choose between the treatments described in (a) and (b) above.

Background on the requirements for internally generated intangible assets

Before IAS 38 was issued in 1998, some internally generated intangible assets (those that arose from development expenditure) were dealt with under IAS 9 *Research and Development Costs**. The development of, and revisions to, IAS 9 had always been controversial.   **BCZ30**

Proposed and approved requirements for the recognition of an asset arising from development expenditure and other internally generated intangible assets had been the following: **BCZ31**

(a) in 1978, IASC approved IAS 9 *Accounting for Research and Development Activities*. It required expenditure on research and development to be recognised as an expense when incurred, except that an enterprise had the option to recognise an asset arising from development expenditure whenever certain criteria were met.
(b) in 1989, Exposure Draft E32 *Comparability of Financial Statements* proposed retaining IAS 9's option to recognise an asset arising from development expenditure if certain criteria were met and identifying:

(i) as a preferred treatment, recognising all expenditure on research and development as an expense when incurred; and
(ii) as an allowed alternative treatment, recognising an asset arising from development expenditure whenever certain criteria were met.

*ASB footnote: *The corresponding requirements in the UK and Republic of Ireland were set out in SSAP 13* Research and Development.

The majority of commentators on E32 did not support maintaining an option or the proposed preferred treatment.

(c)   in 1991, Exposure Draft E37 *Research and Development Costs* proposed requiring the recognition of an asset arising from development expenditure whenever certain criteria were met. In 1993, IASC approved IAS 9 *Research and Development Costs* based on E37.

(d)   in 1995, consistently with IAS 9, Exposure Draft E50 *Intangible Assets* proposed requiring internally generated intangible assets—other than those arising from development expenditure, which would still have been covered by IAS 9—to be recognised as assets whenever certain criteria were met.

(e)   in 1997, Exposure Draft E60 *Intangible Assets* proposed:

   (i)   retaining E50's proposals for the recognition of internally generated intangible assets; but

   (ii)   extending the scope of the Standard on intangible assets to deal with all internally generated intangible assets—including those arising from development expenditure.

(f)   in 1998, IASC approved:

   (i)   IAS 38 *Intangible Assets* based on E60, with a few minor changes; and

   (ii)   the withdrawal of IAS 9.

BCZ32   From 1989, the majority view at IASC and from commentators was that there should be only one treatment that would require an internally generated intangible asset—whether arising from development expenditure or other expenditure—to be recognised as an asset whenever certain recognition criteria are met. Several minority views were strongly opposed to this treatment but there was no clear consensus on any other single treatment.

Combination of IAS 9 with the Standard on intangible assets

BCZ33   The reasons for not retaining IAS 9 as a separate Standard were that:

(a)   IASC believed that an identifiable asset that results from research and development activities is an intangible asset because knowledge is the primary outcome of these activities. Therefore, IASC supported treating expenditure on research and development activities similarly to expenditure on activities intended to create any other internally generated intangible assets.

(b)   some commentators on E50, which proposed to exclude research and development expenditures from its scope,

   (i)   argued that it was sometimes difficult to identify whether IAS 9 or the proposed Standard on intangible assets should apply, and

   (ii)   perceived differences in accounting treatments between IAS 9 and E50's proposals, whereas this was not IASC's intent.

BCZ34   A large majority of commentators on E60 supported including certain aspects of IAS 9 with the proposed Standard on intangible assets and the withdrawal of IAS 9. A minority of commentators on E60 supported maintaining two separate Standards. This minority supported the view that internally generated intangible assets should be dealt with on a case-by-case basis with separate requirements for different types of internally generated intangible assets. These commentators argued that E60's proposed recognition criteria were too general to be effective in practice for all internally generated intangible assets.

BCZ35   IASC rejected a proposal to develop separate standards (or detailed requirements within one standard) for specific types of internally generated intangible assets because, as explained above, IASC believed that the same recognition criteria should apply to all types of internally generated intangible assets.

Consequences of combining IAS 9 with IAS 38

The requirements in IAS 38 and IAS 9 differ in the following main respects: **BCZ36**

(a) IAS 9 limited the amount of expenditure that could initially be recognised for an asset arising from development expenditure (ie the amount that formed the cost of such an asset) to the amount that was probable of being recovered from the asset. Instead, IAS 38 requires that:

   (i) all expenditure incurred from when the recognition criteria are met until the asset is available for use should be accumulated to form the cost of the asset; and

   (ii) an enterprise should test for impairment, at least annually, an intangible asset that is not yet available for use. If the cost recognised for the asset exceeds its recoverable amount, an enterprise recognises an impairment loss accordingly. This impairment loss should be reversed if the conditions for reversals of impairment losses under IAS 36 *Impairment of Assets* are met.

(b) IAS 38 permits an intangible asset to be measured after recognition at a revalued amount less subsequent amortisation and subsequent impairment losses. IAS 9 did not permit this treatment. However, it is highly unlikely that an active market (the condition required to revalue intangible assets) will exist for an asset that arises from development expenditure.

(c) IAS 38 requires consideration of residual values in determining the depreciable amount of an intangible asset. IAS 9 prohibited the consideration of residual values. However, IAS 38 sets criteria that make it highly unlikely that an asset that arises from development expenditure would have a residual value above zero.

IASC believed that, in practice, it would be unlikely that the application of IAS 38 **BCZ37** would result in differences from the application of IAS 9.

Recognition of expenditure on all internally generated intangible assets as an expense

Those who favour the recognition of expenditure on all internally generated intan- **BCZ38** gible assets (including development expenditure) as an expense argue that:

(a) internally generated intangible assets do not meet the *Framework's* require-ments for recognition as an asset because:

   (i) the future economic benefits that arise from internally generated intan-gible assets cannot be distinguished from future economic benefits that arise from internally generated goodwill; and/or

   (ii) it is impossible to distinguish reliably the expenditure associated with internally generated intangible assets from the expenditure associated with enhancing internally generated goodwill.

(b) comparability of financial statements will not be achieved. This is because the judgement involved in determining whether it is probable that future economic benefits will flow from internally generated intangible assets is too subjective to result in similar accounting under similar circumstances.

(c) it is not possible to assess reliably the amount that can be recovered from an internally generated intangible asset, unless its fair value can be determined by reference to an active market. Therefore, recognising an internally generated intangible asset for which no active market exists at an amount other than zero may mislead investors.

(d)   a requirement to recognise internally generated intangible assets at cost if certain criteria are met results in little, if any, decision-useful or predictive information because:

(i)   demonstration of technological feasibility or commercial success in order to meet the recognition criteria will generally not be achieved until substantial expenditure has been recognised as an expense. Therefore, the cost recognised for an internally generated intangible asset will not reflect the total expenditure on that asset.

(ii)   the cost of an internally generated intangible asset may not have any relationship to the value of the asset.

(e)   in some countries, users are suspicious about an enterprise that recognises internally generated intangible assets.

(f)   the added costs of maintaining the records necessary to justify and support the recognition of internally generated intangible assets do not justify the benefits.

Recognition of internally generated intangible assets

BCZ39   Those who support the mandatory recognition of internally generated intangible assets (including those resulting from development expenditure) whenever certain criteria are met argue that:

(a)   recognition of an internally generated intangible asset if it meets the definition of an asset and the recognition criteria is consistent with the *Framework*. An enterprise can, in some instances:

(i)   determine the probability of receiving future economic benefits from an internally generated intangible asset; and

(ii)   distinguish the expenditure on this asset from expenditure on internally generated goodwill.

(b)   there has been massive investment in intangible assets in the last two decades. There have been complaints that:

(i)   the non-recognition of investments in intangible assets in the financial statements distorts the measurement of an enterprise's performance and does not allow an accurate assessment of returns on investment in intangible assets; and

(ii)   if enterprises do not track the returns on investment in intangible assets better, there is a risk of over- or under-investing in important assets. An accounting system that encourages such behaviour will become an increasingly inadequate signal, both for internal control purposes and for external purposes.

(c)   certain research studies, particularly in the United States, have established a cost-value association for research and development expenditures. The studies establish that capitalisation of research and development expenditure yields value-relevant information to investors.

(d)   the fact that some uncertainties exist about the value of an asset does not justify a requirement that no cost should be recognised for the asset.

(e)   it should not matter for recognition purposes whether an asset is purchased externally or developed internally. Particularly, there should be no opportunity for accounting arbitrage depending on whether an enterprise decides to outsource the development of an intangible asset or develop it internally.

IASC's view in approving IAS 38

IASC's view—consistently reflected in previous proposals for intangible assets—was that there should be no difference between the requirements for:

BCZ40

(a) intangible assets that are acquired externally; and
(b) internally generated intangible assets, whether they arise from development activities or other types of activities.

Therefore, an internally generated intangible asset should be recognised whenever the definition of, and recognition criteria for, an intangible asset are met. This view was also supported by a majority of commentators on E60.

IASC rejected a proposal for an allowed alternative to recognise expenditure on internally generated intangible assets (including development expenditure) as an expense immediately, even if the expenditure results in an asset that meets the recognition criteria. IASC believed that a free choice would undermine the comparability of financial statements and the efforts of IASC to reduce the number of alternative treatments in International Accounting Standards.

BCZ41

Differences in recognition criteria for internally generated intangible assets and purchased intangible assets

IAS 38 includes specific recognition criteria for internally generated intangible assets that expand on the general recognition criteria for intangible assets. It is assumed that these criteria are met implicitly whenever an enterprise acquires an intangible asset. Therefore, IAS 38 requires an enterprise to demonstrate that these criteria are met for internally generated intangible assets only.

BCZ42

Initial recognition at cost

Some commentators on E50 and E60 argued that the proposed recognition criteria in E50 and E60 were too restrictive and that they would prevent the recognition of many intangible assets, particularly internally generated intangible assets. Specifically, they disagreed with the proposals (retained in IAS 38) that:

BCZ43

(a) an intangible asset should not be recognised at an amount other than its cost, even if its fair value can be determined reliably; and
(b) expenditure on an intangible asset that has been recognised as an expense in prior periods should not be reinstated.

They argued that these principles contradict the *Framework* and quoted paragraph 83 of the *Framework*, which specifies that an item that meets the definition of an asset should be recognised if, among other things, its "*cost or value* can be measured with reliability". These commentators supported recognising an intangible asset—an internally generated intangible asset—at its fair value, if, among other things, its fair value can be measured reliably.

BCZ44   IASC rejected a proposal to allow the initial recognition of an intangible asset at fair value (except if the asset is acquired in a business combination, in exchange for a dissimilar asset* or by way of a government grant) because:

(a)   this is consistent with IAS 16 *Property, Plant and Equipment*†. IAS 16 prohibits the initial recognition of an item of property, plant or equipment at fair value (except in the specific limited cases as those in IAS 38).

(b)   it is difficult to determine the fair value of an intangible asset reliably if no active market exists for the asset. Since active markets with the characteristics set out in IAS 38 are highly unlikely to exist for internally generated intangible assets, IASC did not believe that it was necessary to make an exception to the principles generally applied for the initial recognition and measurement of non-financial assets.

(c)   the large majority of commentators on E50 supported the initial recognition of intangible assets at cost and the prohibition of the reinstatement of expenditure on an intangible item that was initially recognised as an expense.

Application of the recognition criteria for internally generated intangible assets

BCZ45   IAS 38 specifically prohibits the recognition as intangible assets of brands, mastheads, publishing titles, customer lists and items similar in substance that are internally generated. IASC believed that internally generated intangible items of this kind would rarely, and perhaps never, meet the recognition criteria in IAS 38. However, to avoid any misunderstanding, IASC decided to set out this conclusion in the form of an explicit prohibition.

BCZ46   IAS 38 also clarifies that expenditure on research, training, advertising and start-up activities will not result in the creation of an intangible asset that can be recognised in the financial statements. Whilst some view these requirements and guidance as being too restrictive and arbitrary, they are based on IASC's interpretation of the application of the recognition criteria in IAS 38. They also reflect the fact that it is sometimes difficult to determine whether there is an internally generated intangible asset distinguishable from internally generated goodwill.

SUBSEQUENT ACCOUNTING FOR INTANGIBLE ASSETS

BC47   The Board initially decided that the scope of the first phase of its Business Combinations project should include a consideration of the subsequent accounting for intangible assets acquired in business combinations. To that end, the Board initially focused its attention on the following three issues:

(a)   whether an intangible asset with a finite useful life and acquired in a business combination should continue to be accounted for after initial recognition in accordance with IAS 38.

(b)   whether, and under what circumstances, an intangible asset acquired in a business combination could be regarded as having an indefinite useful life.

---

*IAS 16 Property, Plant and Equipment *(as revised in 2003) requires an entity to measure an item of property, plant and equipment acquired in exchange for a non-monetary asset or assets, or a combination of monetary and non-monetary assets, at fair value unless the exchange transaction lacks commercial substance. Previously, an entity measured such an acquired asset at fair value unless the exchanged assets were similar. The IASB concluded that the same measurement criteria should apply to intangible assets acquired in exchange for a non-monetary asset or assets, or a combination of monetary and non-monetary assets.*

†ASB Footnote: *The corresponding requirements in the UK and Republic of Ireland are in FRS 15* Tangible Fixed Assets.

(c)   how an intangible asset with an indefinite useful life (assuming such an asset exists) acquired in a business combination should be accounted for after initial recognition.

However, during its deliberations of the issues in (b) and (c) of paragraph BC47, the Board decided that any conclusions it reached on those issues would equally apply to recognised intangible assets obtained other than in a business combination. The Board observed that amending the requirements in the previous version of IAS 38 only for intangible assets acquired in business combinations would create inconsistencies in the accounting for intangible assets depending on how they are obtained. Thus, similar items would be accounted for in dissimilar ways. The Board concluded that creating such inconsistencies would impair the usefulness of the information provided to users about an entity's intangible assets, because both comparability and reliability (which rests on the notion of representational faithfulness, ie that similar transactions are accounted for in the same way) would be diminished. Therefore, the Board decided that any amendments to the requirements in the previous version of IAS 38 to address the issues in (b) and (c) of paragraph BC47 should apply to all recognised intangible assets, whether generated internally or acquired separately or as part of a business combination.   **BC48**

Before beginning its deliberations of the issues identified in paragraph BC47, the Board noted the concern expressed by some that, because of the subjectivity involved in distinguishing goodwill from other intangible assets as at the acquisition date, differences between the subsequent treatment of goodwill and other intangible assets increases the potential for intangible assets to be misclassified at the acquisition date. The Board concluded, however, that adopting the separability and contractual or other legal rights criteria provides a reasonably definitive basis for separately identifying and recognising intangible assets acquired in a business combination. Therefore, the Board decided that its analysis of the accounting for intangible assets after initial recognition should have regard only to the nature of those assets and not to the subsequent treatment of goodwill.   **BC49**

Accounting for intangible assets with finite useful lives acquired in business combinations

The Board observed that the previous version of IAS 38 required an intangible asset to be measured after initial recognition: **BC50**

(a)   at cost less any accumulated amortisation and any accumulated impairment losses; or
(b)   at a revalued amount, being the asset's fair value, determined by reference to an active market, at the date of revaluation less any subsequent accumulated amortisation and any subsequent accumulated impairment losses. Under this approach, revaluations must be made with such regularity that at the balance sheet date the carrying amount of the asset does not differ materially from its fair value.

Whichever of the above methods was used, the previous version of IAS 38 required the depreciable amount of the asset to be amortised on a systematic basis over the best estimate of its useful life.

The Board observed that underpinning the requirement for all intangible assets to be amortised is the notion that they all have determinable and finite useful lives. Setting aside the question of whether, and under what circumstances, an intangible asset could be regarded as having an indefinite useful life, an important issue for the Board to consider was whether a departure from the above requirements would be   **BC51** warranted for intangible assets acquired in a business combination that have finite useful lives.

BC52   The Board observed that any departure from the above requirements for intangible assets with finite lives acquired in business combinations would create inconsistencies between the accounting for recognised intangible assets based wholly on the means by which they are obtained. In other words, similar items would be accounted for in dissimilar ways. The Board concluded that creating such inconsistencies would impair the usefulness of the information provided to users about an entity's intangible assets, because both comparability and reliability would be diminished.

BC53   Therefore, the Board decided that intangible assets with finite useful lives acquired in business combinations should continue to be accounted for in accordance with the above requirements after initial recognition.

Impairment testing intangible assets with finite useful lives (paragraph 111)

BC54   The previous version of IAS 38 required the recoverable amount of an intangible asset with a finite useful life that is being amortised over a period of more than 20 years, whether or not acquired in a business combination, to be measured at least at each financial year-end.

BC55   The Board observed that the recoverable amount of a long-lived tangible asset needs to be measured only when, in accordance with IAS 36 *Impairment of Assets*, there is an indication that the asset may be impaired. The Board could see no conceptual reason for requiring the recoverable amounts of some identifiable assets being amortised over very long periods to be determined more regularly than for other identifiable assets being amortised or depreciated over similar periods. Therefore, the Board concluded that the recoverable amount of an intangible asset with a finite useful life that is amortised over a period of more than 20 years should be determined only when, in accordance with IAS 36, there is an indication that the asset may be impaired. Consequently, the Board decided to remove the requirement in the previous version of IAS 38 for the recoverable amount of such an intangible asset to be measured at least at each financial year-end.

BC56   The Board also decided that all of the requirements relating to impairment testing intangible assets should be included in IAS 36 rather than in IAS 38. Therefore, the Board relocated to IAS 36 the requirement in the previous version of IAS 38 that an entity should estimate at the end of each annual reporting period the recoverable amount of an intangible asset not yet available for use, irrespective of whether there is any indication that it may be impaired.

Residual value of an intangible asset with a finite useful life (paragraph 100)

BC57   In revising IAS 38, the Board considered whether to retain for intangible assets with finite useful lives the requirement in the previous version of IAS 38 for the residual value of an intangible asset to be assumed to be zero unless:

(a)   there is a commitment by a third party to purchase the asset at the end of its useful life; or

(b)   there is an active market for the asset and:

(i)   the asset's residual value can be determined by reference to that market; and

(ii)   it is probable that such a market will exist at the end of the asset's useful life.

The Board observed that the definition in the previous version of IAS 38 (as a- **BC58**
mended by IAS 16 when revised in 2003) of residual value required it to be estimated
as if the asset were already of the age and in the condition expected at the end of the
asset's useful life. Therefore, if the useful life of an intangible asset was shorter than
its economic life because the entity expected to sell the asset before the end of that
economic life, the asset's residual value would not be zero, irrespective of whether the
conditions in paragraph BC57(a) or (b) are met.

Nevertheless, the Board observed that the requirement for the residual value of an **BC59**
intangible asset to be assumed to be zero unless the specified criteria are met was
included in the previous version of IAS 38 as a means of preventing entities from
circumventing the requirement in that Standard to amortise all intangible assets.
Excluding this requirement from the revised Standard for finite-lived intangible
assets would similarly provide a means of circumventing the requirement to amortise
such intangible assets—by claiming that the residual value of such an asset was equal
to or greater than its carrying amount, an entity could avoid amortising the asset,
even though its useful life is finite. The Board concluded that it should not, as part of
the Business Combinations project, modify the criteria for permitting a finite-lived
intangible asset's residual value to be other than zero. However, the Board decided
that this issue should be addressed as part of a forthcoming project on intangible
assets.

Useful lives of intangible assets (paragraphs 88-96)

Consistently with the proposals in the Exposure Draft of Proposed Amendments to **BC60**
IAS 38, the Standard requires an intangible asset to be regarded by an entity as
having an indefinite useful life when, based on an analysis of all of the relevant
factors, there is no foreseeable limit to the period over which the asset is expected to
generate net cash inflows for the entity.

In developing the Exposure Draft and the revised Standard, the Board observed that **BC61**
the useful life of an intangible asset is related to the expected cash inflows that are
associated with that asset. The Board observed that, to be representationally faithful,
the amortisation period for an intangible asset generally should reflect that useful life
and, by extension, the cash flow streams associated with the asset. The Board concluded that it is possible for management to have the intention and the ability to
maintain an intangible asset in such a way that there is no foreseeable limit on the
period over which that particular asset is expected to generate net cash inflows for the
entity. In other words, it is conceivable that an analysis of all the relevant factors (ie
legal, regulatory, contractual, competitive, economic and other) could lead to a
conclusion that there is no foreseeable limit to the period over which a particular
intangible asset is expected to generate net cash inflows for the entity.

For example, the Board observed that some intangible assets are based on legal **BC62**
rights that are conveyed in perpetuity rather than for finite terms. As such, those
assets may have cash flows associated with them that may be expected to continue
for many years or even indefinitely. The Board concluded that if the cash flows are
expected to continue for a finite period, the useful life of the asset is limited to that
finite period. However, if the cash flows are expected to continue indefinitely, the
useful life is indefinite.

The previous version of IAS 38 prescribed a presumptive maximum useful life for **BC63**
intangible assets of 20 years. In developing the Exposure Draft and the revised
Standard, the Board concluded that such a presumption is inconsistent with the view
that the amortisation period for an intangible asset should, to be representationally

faithful, reflect its useful life and, by extension, the cash flow streams associated with the asset. Therefore, the Board decided not to include in the revised Standard a presumptive maximum useful life for intangible assets, even if they have finite useful lives.

BC64   Respondents to the Exposure Draft generally supported the Board's proposal to remove from IAS 38 the presumptive maximum useful life and instead to require useful life to be regarded as indefinite when, based on an analysis of all of the relevant factors, there is no foreseeable limit to the period of time over which the intangible asset is expected to generate net cash inflows for the entity. However, some respondents suggested that an inability to determine clearly the useful life of an asset applies equally to many items of property, plant and equipment. Nonetheless, entities are required to determine the useful lives of those items of property, plant and equipment, and allocate their depreciable amounts on a systematic basis over those useful lives. Those respondents suggested that there is no conceptual reason for treating intangible assets differently.

BC65   In considering these comments, the Board noted the following:

(a)   an intangible asset's useful life would be regarded as indefinite in accordance with IAS 38 only when, based on an analysis of all of the relevant factors, there is no foreseeable limit to the period of time over which the asset is expected to generate net cash inflows for the entity. Difficulties in accurately determining an intangible asset's useful life do not provide a basis for regarding that useful life as indefinite.

(b)   although the useful lives of both intangible and tangible assets are directly related to the period during which they are expected to generate net cash inflows for the entity, the expected physical utility to the entity of a tangible asset places an upper limit on the asset's useful life. In other words, the useful life of a tangible asset could never extend beyond the asset's expected physical utility to the entity.

The Board concluded that tangible assets (other than land) could not be regarded as having indefinite useful lives because there is always a foreseeable limit to the expected physical utility of the asset to the entity.

Useful life constrained by contractual or other legal rights (paragraphs 94-96)

BC66   The Board noted that the useful life of an intangible asset that arises from contractual or other legal rights is constrained by the duration of those rights. The useful life of such an asset cannot extend beyond the duration of those rights, and may be shorter. Accordingly, the Board concluded that in determining the useful life of an intangible asset, consideration should be given to the period that the entity expects to use the intangible asset, which is subject to the expiration of the contractual or other legal rights.

BC67   However, the Board also observed that such rights are often conveyed for limited terms that may be renewed. It therefore considered whether renewals should be assumed in determining the useful life of such an intangible asset. The Board noted that some types of licences are initially issued for finite periods but renewals are routinely granted at little cost, provided that licensees have complied with the applicable rules and regulations. Such licences are traded at prices that reflect more than the remaining term, thereby indicating that renewal at minimal cost is the general expectation. However, renewals are not assured for other types of licences and, even if they are renewed, substantial costs may be incurred to secure their renewal.

The Board concluded that because the useful lives of some intangible assets depend, in economic terms, on renewal and on the associated costs of renewal, the useful lives assigned to those assets should reflect renewal when there is evidence to support renewal without significant cost. **BC68**

Respondents to the Exposure Draft generally supported this conclusion. Those that disagreed suggested that: **BC69**

(a)   when the renewal period depends on the decision of a third party and not merely on the fulfilment of specified conditions by the entity, it gives rise to a contingent asset because the third-party decision affects not only the cost of renewal but also the probability of obtaining it. Therefore, useful life should reflect renewal only when renewal is not subject to third-party approval.

(b)   such a requirement would be inconsistent with the basis used to measure intangible assets at the date of a business combination, particularly contractual customer relationships. For example, it is not clear whether the fair value of a contractual customer relationship includes an amount that reflects the probability that the contract will be renewed. The possibility of renewal would have a fair value regardless of the costs required to renew. This means the useful life of a contractual customer relationship could be inconsistent with the basis used to determine the fair value of the relationship.

In relation to (a) above, the Board observed that if renewal by the entity is subject to third-party (eg government) approval, the requirement that there be evidence to support the entity's ability to renew would compel the entity to make an assessment of the likely effect of the third-party approval process on the entity's ability to renew. The Board could see no conceptual basis for narrowing the requirement to situations in which the contractual or legal rights are not subject to the approval of third parties. **BC70**

In relation to (b) above, the Board observed the following: **BC71**

(a)   the requirements relating to renewal periods address circumstances in which *the entity* is able to renew the contractual or other legal rights, notwithstanding that such renewal may, for example, be conditional on the entity satisfying specified conditions, or subject to third-party approval. Paragraph 94 of the Standard states that "... the useful life of the intangible asset shall include the renewal period(s) only if there is evidence to support renewal *by the entity* [emphasis added] without significant cost." The ability to renew a customer contract normally rests with the customer and not with the entity.

(b)   the respondents seem to regard as a single intangible asset what is, in substance, two intangible assets—one being the customer contract and the other being the related customer relationship. Expected renewals by the customer would affect the fair value of the customer relationship intangible asset, rather than the fair value of the customer contract. Therefore, the useful life of the customer contract would not, under the Standard, extend beyond the term of the contract, nor would the fair value of that customer contract reflect expectations of renewal by the customer. In other words, the useful life of the customer contract would not be inconsistent with the basis used to determine its fair value.

However, in response to respondents' suggestions, the Board included paragraph 96 in the Standard to provide additional guidance on the circumstances in which an entity should be regarded as being able to renew the contractual or other legal rights without significant cost. **BC72**

Accounting for intangible assets with indefinite useful lives (paragraphs 107-110)

BC73   Consistently with the proposals in the Exposure Draft, the Standard prohibits the amortisation of intangible assets with indefinite useful lives. Therefore, such assets are measured after initial recognition at:

(a)   cost less any accumulated impairment losses; or

(b)   a revalued amount, being fair value determined by reference to an active market less any accumulated impairment losses.

Non-amortisation

BC74   In developing the Exposure Draft and the revised Standard, the Board observed that many assets yield benefits to an entity over several periods. Amortisation is the systematic allocation of the cost (or revalued amount) of an asset, less any residual value, to reflect the consumption over time of the future economic benefits embodied in that asset. Thus, if there is no foreseeable limit on the period during which an entity expects to consume the future economic benefits embodied in an asset, amortisation of that asset over, for example, an arbitrarily determined maximum period would not be representationally faithful. Respondents to the Exposure Draft generally supported this conclusion.

BC75   Consequently, the Board decided that intangible assets with indefinite useful lives should not be amortised, but should be subject to regular impairment testing. The Board's deliberations on the form of the impairment test, including the frequency of impairment testing, are included in the Basis for Conclusions on IAS 36. The Board further decided that regular re-examinations should be required of the useful life of an intangible asset that is not being amortised to determine whether circumstances continue to support the assessment that the useful life is indefinite.

Revaluations

BC76   Having decided that intangible assets with indefinite useful lives should not be amortised, the Board considered whether an entity should be permitted to carry such assets at revalued amounts. The Board could see no conceptual justification for precluding some intangible assets from being carried at revalued amounts solely on the basis that there is no foreseeable limit to the period over which an entity expects to consume the future economic benefits embodied in those assets.

BC77   As a result, the Board decided that the Standard should permit intangible assets with indefinite useful lives to be carried at revalued amounts.

RESEARCH AND DEVELOPMENT PROJECTS ACQUIRED IN BUSINESS COMBINATIONS

BC78   The Board considered the following issues in relation to in-process research and development (IPR&D) projects acquired in a business combination:

(a)   whether the proposed criteria for recognising intangible assets acquired in a business combination separately from goodwill should also be applied to IPR&D projects;

(b)   the subsequent accounting for IPR&D projects recognised as assets separately from goodwill; and

(c)   the treatment of subsequent expenditure on IPR&D projects recognised as assets separately from goodwill.

The Board's deliberations on issue (a), although included in the Basis for Conclusions on IFRS 3, are also, for the sake of completeness, outlined below.

The Board did not reconsider as part of the first phase of its Business Combinations project the requirements in the previous version of IAS 38 for internally generated intangibles and expenditure on the research or development phase of an internal project. The Board decided that a reconsideration of those requirements is outside the scope of this project.   **BC79**

Initial recognition separately from goodwill

The Board observed that the criteria in IAS 22 *Business Combinations* and the previous version of IAS 38 for recognising an intangible asset acquired in a business combination separately from goodwill applied to all intangible assets, including IPR&D projects. Therefore, in accordance with those Standards, any intangible item acquired in a business combination was recognised as an asset separately from goodwill when it was identifiable and could be measured reliably, and it was probable that any associated future economic benefits would flow to the acquirer. If these criteria were not satisfied, the expenditure on the cost or value of that item, which was included in the cost of the combination, was part of the amount attributed to goodwill.   **BC80**

The Board could see no conceptual justification for changing the approach in IAS 22 and the previous version of IAS 38 of using the same criteria for all intangible assets acquired in a business combination when assessing whether those assets should be recognised separately from goodwill. The Board concluded that adopting different criteria would impair the usefulness of the information provided to users about the assets acquired in a combination because both comparability and reliability would be diminished. Therefore, IAS 38 and IFRS 3 require an acquirer to recognise as an asset separately from goodwill any of the acquiree's IPR&D projects that meet the definition of an intangible asset. This will be the case when the IPR&D project meets the definition of an asset and is identifiable, ie is separable or arises from contractual or other legal rights.   **BC81**

Some respondents to the Exposure Draft of Proposed Amendments to IAS 38 expressed concern that applying the same criteria to all intangible assets acquired in a business combination to assess whether they should be recognised separately from goodwill results in treating some IPR&D projects acquired in business combinations differently from similar projects started internally. The Board acknowledged this point, but concluded that this does not provide a basis for subsuming those acquired intangible assets within goodwill. Rather, it highlights a need to reconsider the conclusion in the Standard that an intangible asset can never exist in respect of an in-process research project and can exist in respect of an in-process development project only once all of the Standard's criteria for deferral have been satisfied. The Board decided that such a reconsideration is outside the scope of its Business Combinations project.   **BC82**

Subsequent accounting for IPR&D projects acquired in a business combination and recognised as intangible assets

The Board observed that the previous version of IAS 38 required all recognised intangible assets to be accounted for after initial recognition at: **BC83**

(a)   cost less any accumulated amortisation and any accumulated impairment losses; or

(b)   revalued amount, being the asset's fair value, determined by reference to an active market, at the date of revaluation less any subsequent accumulated amortisation and any subsequent accumulated impairment losses.

Such assets included: IPR&D projects acquired in a business combination that satisfied the criteria for recognition separately from goodwill; separately acquired IPR&D projects that satisfied the criteria for recognition as an intangible asset; and recognised internally developed intangible assets arising from development or the development phase of an internal project.

BC84   The Board could see no conceptual justification for changing the approach in the previous version of IAS 38 of applying the same requirements to the subsequent accounting for all recognised intangible assets. Therefore, the Board decided that IPR&D projects acquired in a business combination that satisfy the criteria for recognition as an asset separately from goodwill should be accounted for after initial recognition in accordance with the requirements applying to the subsequent accounting for other recognised intangible assets.

Subsequent expenditure on IPR&D projects acquired in a business combination and recognised as intangible assets (paragraphs 42 and 43)

BC85   The Standard requires subsequent expenditure on an IPR&D project acquired separately or in a business combination and recognised as an intangible asset to be:

(a)   recognised as an expense when incurred if it is research expenditure;

(b)   recognised as an expense when incurred if it is development expenditure that does not satisfy the criteria for recognition as an intangible asset in paragraph 57; and

(c)   added to the carrying amount of the acquired IPR&D project if it is development expenditure that satisfies the recognition criteria in paragraph 57.

BC86   In developing this requirement the Board observed that the treatment required under the previous version of IAS 38 of subsequent expenditure on an IPR&D project acquired in a business combination and recognised as an asset separately from goodwill was unclear. Some suggested that the requirements in the previous version of IAS 38 relating to expenditure on research, development, or the research or development phase of an internal project should be applied. However, others argued that those requirements were ostensibly concerned with the initial recognition and measurement of internally generated intangible assets. Instead, the requirements in the previous version of IAS 38 dealing with subsequent expenditure should be applied. Under those requirements, subsequent expenditure on an intangible asset after its purchase or completion would have been recognised as an expense when incurred unless:

(a)   it was probable that the expenditure would enable the asset to generate future economic benefits in excess of its originally assessed standard of performance; and

(b)   the expenditure could be measured and attributed to the asset reliably.

If these conditions were satisfied, the subsequent expenditure would be added to the carrying amount of the intangible asset.

The Board observed that this uncertainty also existed for separately acquired **BC87** IPR&D projects that satisfied the criteria in the previous version of IAS 38 for recognition as intangible assets.

The Board noted that applying the requirements in the Standard for expenditure on **BC88** research, development, or the research or development phase of an internal project to subsequent expenditure on IPR&D projects acquired in a business combination and recognised as assets separately from goodwill would result in such subsequent expenditure being treated inconsistently with subsequent expenditure on other recognised intangible assets. However, applying the subsequent expenditure requirements in the previous version of IAS 38 to subsequent expenditure on IPR&D projects acquired in a business combination and recognised as assets separately from goodwill would result in research and development expenditure being accounted for differently depending on whether a project is acquired or started internally.

The Board concluded that until it has had the opportunity to review the requirements **BC89** in IAS 38 for expenditure on research, development, or the research or development phase of an internal project, more useful information will be provided to users of an entity's financial statements if all such expenditure is accounted for consistently. This includes subsequent expenditure on a separately acquired IPR&D project that satisfies the Standard's criteria for recognition as an intangible asset.

TRANSITIONAL PROVISIONS (PARAGRAPHS 129-132)

If an entity elects to apply IFRS 3 from any date before the effective dates outlined **BC90** in IFRS 3, it is also required to apply IAS 38 prospectively from that same date. Otherwise, IAS 38 applies to the accounting for intangible assets acquired in business combinations for which the agreement date is on or after 31 March 2004, and to the accounting for all other intangible assets prospectively from the beginning of the first annual reporting period beginning on or after 31 March 2004. IAS 38 also requires an entity, on initial application, to reassess the useful lives of intangible assets. If, as a result of that reassessment, the entity changes its useful life assessment for an asset, that change is accounted for as a change in an accounting estimate in accordance with IAS 8 *Accounting Policies, Changes in Accounting Estimates and Errors.**

The Board's deliberations on the transitional issues relating to the initial recognition **BC91** of intangible assets acquired in business combinations and the impairment testing of intangible assets are addressed in the Basis for Conclusions on IFRS 3 and the Basis for Conclusions on IAS 36, respectively.

In developing the requirements outlined in paragraph BC90, the Board considered **BC92** the following three questions:

(a)   should the useful lives of, and the accounting for, intangible assets already recognised at the effective date of the Standard continue to be determined in accordance with the requirements in the previous version of IAS 38 (ie by amortising over a presumptive maximum period of twenty years), or in accordance with the requirements in the revised Standard?

(b)   if the revised Standard is applied to intangible assets already recognised at its effective date, should the effect of a reassessment of an intangible asset's useful life as a result of the initial application of the Standard be recognised retrospectively or prospectively?

*ASB footnote: *The corresponding UK and Republic of Ireland requirements are set out in FRS 18* Accounting Policies.

(c)   should entities be required to apply the requirements in the Standard for subsequent expenditure on an acquired IPR&D project recognised as an intangible asset retrospectively to expenditure incurred before the effective date of the revised Standard?

BC93   In relation to the first question above, the Board noted its previous conclusion that the most representationally faithful method of accounting for intangible assets is to amortise those with finite useful lives over their useful lives with no limit on the amortisation period, and not to amortise those with indefinite useful lives. Thus, the Board concluded that the reliability and comparability of financial statements would be diminished if the Standard was not applied to intangible assets recognised before its effective date.

BC94   On the second question, the Board observed that a reassessment of an asset's useful life is regarded throughout IFRSs as a change in an accounting estimate, rather than a change in an accounting policy. For example, in accordance with the Standard, as with the previous version of IAS 38, if a new estimate of the expected useful life of an intangible asset is significantly different from previous estimates, the change must be accounted for as a change in accounting estimate in accordance with IAS 8. IAS 8 requires a change in an accounting estimate to be accounted for prospectively by including the effect of the change in profit or loss in:

(a)   the period of the change, if the change in estimate affects that period only; or
(b)   the period of the change and future periods, if the change in estimate affects both.

BC95   Similarly, in accordance with IAS 16 *Property, Plant and Equipment*, if a new estimate of the expected useful life of an item of property, plant and equipment is significantly different from previous estimates, the change must be accounted for prospectively by adjusting the depreciation expense for the current and future periods.

BC96   Therefore, the Board decided that a reassessment of useful life resulting from the initial application of IAS 38, including a reassessment from a finite to an indefinite useful life, should be accounted for as a change in an accounting estimate. Consequently, the effect of such a change should be recognised prospectively.

BC97   The Board considered the view that because the previous version of IAS 38 required intangible assets to be treated as having a finite useful life, a change to an assessment of indefinite useful life for an intangible asset represents a change in an accounting policy, rather than a change in an accounting estimate. The Board concluded that, even if this were the case, the useful life reassessment should nonetheless be accounted for prospectively. This is because retrospective application would require an entity to determine whether, at the end of each reporting period before the effective date of the Standard, the useful life of an intangible asset was indefinite. Such an assessment requires an entity to make estimates that would have been made at a prior date, and therefore raises problems in relation to the role of hindsight, in particular, whether the benefit of hindsight should be included or excluded from those estimates and, if excluded, how the effect of hindsight can be separated from the other factors existing at the date for which the estimates are required.

BC98   On the third question, and as noted in paragraph BC86, it was not clear whether the previous version of IAS 38 required subsequent expenditure on acquired IPR&D projects recognised as intangible assets to be accounted for:

(a)   in accordance with its requirements for expenditure on research, development, or the research or development phase of an internal project; or

(b)   in accordance with its requirements for subsequent expenditure on an intangible asset after its purchase or completion.

The Board concluded that subsequent expenditure on an acquired IPR&D project that was capitalised under (b) above before the effective date of the Standard might not have been capitalised had the Standard applied when the subsequent expenditure was incurred. This is because the Standard requires such expenditure to be capitalised as an intangible asset only when it is development expenditure and all of the criteria for deferral are satisfied. In the Board's view, those criteria represent a higher recognition threshold than (b) above.

Thus, retrospective application of the revised Standard to subsequent expenditure on acquired IPR&D projects incurred before its effective date could result in previously capitalised expenditure being reversed. Such reversal would be required if the expenditure was research expenditure, or it was development expenditure and one or more of the criteria for deferral were not satisfied at the time the expenditure was incurred. The Board concluded that determining whether, at the time the subsequent expenditure was incurred, the criteria for deferral were satisfied raises the same hindsight issues discussed in paragraph BC97: it would require assessments to be made as of a prior date, and therefore raises problems in relation to how the effect of hindsight can be separated from factors existing at the date of the assessment. In addition, such assessments could, in many cases, be impossible: the information needed may not exist or no longer be obtainable. **BC99**

Therefore, the Board decided that the Standard's requirements for subsequent expenditure on acquired IPR&D projects recognised as intangible assets should not be applied retrospectively to expenditure incurred before the revised Standard's effective date. The Board noted that any amounts previously included in the carrying amount of such an asset would, in any event, be subject to the requirements for impairment testing in IAS 36. **BC100**

Early application (paragraph 132)

The Board noted that the issue of any Standard reflects its opinion that application of the Standard will result in more useful information being provided to users about an entity's financial position, performance or cash flows. On that basis, a case exists for permitting, and indeed encouraging, entities to apply the revised Standard before its effective date. However, the Board also considered the assertion that permitting a revised Standard to be applied before its effective date potentially diminishes comparability between entities in the period(s) leading up to that effective date, and has the effect of providing entities with an option. **BC101**

The Board concluded that the benefit of providing users with more useful information about an entity's financial position and performance by permitting early application of the Standard outweighs the disadvantages of potentially diminished comparability. Therefore, entities are encouraged to apply the requirements of the revised Standard before its effective date, provided they also apply IFRS 3 and IAS 36 (as revised in 2004) at the same time. **BC102**

SUMMARY OF MAIN CHANGES FROM THE EXPOSURE DRAFT

The following are the main changes from the Exposure Draft of Proposed Amendments to IAS 38: **BC103**

(a)   The Standard includes additional guidance clarifying the relationship between the separability criterion for establishing whether a non-contractual customer relationship is identifiable, and the control concept for establishing whether the relationship meets the definition of an asset. In particular, the Standard clarifies that in the absence of legal rights to protect customer relationships, exchange transactions for the same or similar non-contractual customer relationships (other than as part of a business combination) provide evidence that the entity is nonetheless able to control the future economic benefits flowing from the customer relationships. Because such exchange transactions also provide evidence that the customer relationships are separable, those customer relationships meet the definition of an intangible asset (see paragraphs BC11–BC14).

(b)   The Exposure Draft proposed that, except for an assembled workforce, an intangible asset acquired in a business combination should always be recognised separately from goodwill; there was a presumption that sufficient information would always exist to measure reliably its fair value. The Standard states that the fair value of an intangible asset acquired in a business combination can *normally* be measured with sufficient reliability to qualify for recognition separately from goodwill. If an intangible asset acquired in a business combination has a finite useful life, there is a rebuttable presumption that its fair value can be measured reliably (see paragraphs BC16-BC25).

(c)   The Exposure Draft proposed, and the Standard requires, that the useful life of an intangible asset arising from contractual or other legal rights should not exceed the period of those rights. However, if the rights are conveyed for a limited term that can be renewed, the useful life should include the renewal period(s) only if there is evidence to support renewal by the entity without significant cost. Additional guidance has been included in the Standard to clarify the circumstances in which an entity should be regarded as being able to renew the contractual or other legal rights without significant cost (see paragraphs BC66-BC72).

HISTORY OF THE DEVELOPMENT OF A STANDARD ON INTANGIBLE ASSETS

BCZ104   IASC published a Draft Statement of Principles on Intangible Assets in January 1994 and an Exposure Draft E50 *Intangible Assets* in June 1995. Principles in both documents were consistent as far as possible with those in IAS 16 *Property, Plant and Equipment*. The principles were also greatly influenced by the decisions reached in 1993 during the revisions to the treatment of research and development costs and goodwill.

BCZ105   IASC received about 100 comment letters on E50 from over 20 countries. Comment letters on E50 showed that the proposal for the amortisation period for intangible assets—a 20-year ceiling for almost all intangible assets, as required for goodwill in IAS 22 (revised 1993)—raised significant controversy and created serious concerns about the overall acceptability of the proposed standard on intangible assets. IASC considered alternative solutions and concluded in March 1996 that, if an impairment test that is sufficiently robust and reliable could be developed, IASC would propose deleting the 20-year ceiling on the amortisation period for both intangible assets and goodwill.

BCZ106   In August 1997, IASC published proposals for revised treatments for intangible assets and goodwill in Exposure Drafts E60 *Intangible Assets* and E61 *Business Combinations*. This followed the publication of Exposure Draft E55 *Impairment of Assets* in May 1997, which set out detailed proposals for impairment testing.

BCZ107   E60 proposed two major changes to the proposals in E50:

(a) as explained above, revised proposals for the amortisation of intangible assets; and

(b) combining the requirements relating to all internally generated intangible assets in one standard. This meant including certain aspects of IAS 9 *Research and Development Costs* in the proposed standard on intangible assets and withdrawing IAS 9.

Among other proposed changes, E61 proposed revisions to IAS 22 to make the requirements for the amortisation of goodwill consistent with those proposed for intangible assets.   **BCZ108**

IASC received about 100 comment letters on E60 and E61 from over 20 countries. The majority of the commentators supported most of the proposals in E60 and E61, although some proposals still raised significant controversy. The proposals for impairment tests were also supported by most commentators on E55.   **BCZ109**

After considering the comments received on E55, E60 and E61, IASC approved: **BCZ110**

(a) IAS 36 *Impairment of Assets* (April 1998);

(b) IAS 38 *Intangible Assets* (July 1998);

(c) a revised IAS 22 *Business Combinations* (July 1998); and

(d) withdrawal of IAS 9 *Research and Development Costs* (July 1998).

ASB note: This Financial Reporting Exposure Draft (FRED) is part of a package of draft UK accounting standards comprising:

- This FRED 37 *Intangible Assets* (IAS 38) and FRED 38 *Impairment of Assets (*IAS 36).
- FRED 36 *Business Combinations* (IFRS 3*)* and Amendments to FRS 2 Accounting for Subsidiary Undertakings (parts of IAS 27 Consolidated and Separate Financial Statements).
- FRED 39 Amendments to *FRS 12 Provisions, contingent liabilities and contingent assets* and Amendments to FRS 17 *Retirement benefits*.

DISSENTING OPINION

Dissent of Geoffrey Whittington

DO1   Professor Whittington dissents from the issue of this Standard because it does not explicitly require the probability recognition criterion in paragraph 21(a) to be applied to intangible assets acquired in a business combination, notwithstanding that it applies to all other intangible assets.

DO2   The reason given for this (paragraphs 33 and BC17) is that fair value is the required measurement on acquisition of an intangible asset as part of a business combination, and fair value incorporates probability assessments. Professor Whittington does not believe that the *Framework* precludes having a prior recognition test based on probability, even when subsequent recognition is at fair value. Moreover, the application of probability may be different for recognition purposes: for example, it may be the 'more likely than not' criterion used in IAS 37 *Provisions, Contingent Liabilities and Contingent* Assets, rather than the 'expected value' approach used in the measurement of fair value.

DO3   This inconsistency between the recognition criteria in the *Framework* and fair values is acknowledged in paragraph BC18. In Professor Whittington's view, the inconsistency should be resolved before changing the recognition criteria for intangible assets acquired in a business combination.

[Draft] FRS● ~~IAS 38~~ Intangible Assets

Illustrative Examples

These examples accompany, but are not part of, IAS 38.

> *ASB note: These Illustrative Examples have been prepared by the IASB.*

ASSESSING THE USEFUL LIVES OF INTANGIBLE ASSETS

The following guidance provides examples on determining the useful life of an intangible asset in accordance with [draft] FRS ● ~~IAS 38~~.

Each of the following examples describes an acquired intangible asset, the facts and circumstances surrounding the determination of its useful life, and the subsequent accounting based on that determination.

Example 1—an acquired customer list

A direct-mail marketing company acquires a customer list and expects that it will be able to derive benefit from the information on the list for at least one year, but no more than three years.

The customer list would be amortised over management's best estimate of its useful life, say 18 months. Although the direct-mail marketing company may intend to add customer names and other information to the list in the future, the expected benefits of the acquired customer list relate only to the customers on that list at the date it was acquired. The customer list also would be reviewed for impairment in accordance with [draft] FRS ● ~~IAS 36~~ *Impairment of Assets* by assessing at each reporting date whether there is any indication that the customer list may be impaired.

Example 2—an acquired patent that expires in 15 years

The product protected by the patented technology is expected to be a source of net cash inflows for at least 15 years. The entity has a commitment from a third party to purchase that patent in five years for 60 per cent of the fair value of the patent at the date it was acquired, and the entity intends to sell the patent in five years.

The patent would be amortised over its five-year useful life to the entity, with a residual value equal to the present value of 60 per cent of the patent's fair value at the date it was acquired. The patent would also be reviewed for impairment in accordance with [draft] FRS ● ~~IAS 36~~ by assessing at each reporting date whether there is any indication that it may be impaired.

Example 3—an acquired copyright that has a remaining legal life of 50 years

An analysis of consumer habits and market trends provides evidence that the copyrighted material will generate net cash inflows for only 30 more years.

The copyright would be amortised over its 30-year estimated useful life. The copyright also would be reviewed for impairment in accordance with [draft] FRS ● ~~IAS 36~~ by assessing at each reporting date whether there is any indication that it may be impaired.

Example 4—an acquired broadcasting licence that expires in five years

The broadcasting licence is renewable every 10 years if the entity provides at least an average level of service to its customers and complies with the relevant legislative requirements. The licence may be renewed indefinitely at little cost and has been renewed twice before the most recent acquisition. The acquiring entity intends to renew the licence indefinitely and evidence supports its ability to do so. Historically, there has been no compelling challenge to the licence renewal. The technology used in broadcasting is not expected to be replaced by another technology at any time in the foreseeable future. Therefore, the licence is expected to contribute to the entity's net cash inflows indefinitely.

The broadcasting licence would be treated as having an indefinite useful life because it is expected to contribute to the entity's net cash inflows indefinitely. Therefore, the licence would not be amortised until its useful life is determined to be finite. The licence would be tested for impairment in accordance with [draft] FRS ● IAS 36 annually and whenever there is an indication that it may be impaired.

Example 5—the broadcasting licence in Example 4

The licensing authority subsequently decides that it will no longer renew broadcasting licences, but rather will auction the licences. At the time the licensing authority's decision is made, the entity's broadcasting licence has three years until it expires. The entity expects that the licence will continue to contribute to net cash inflows until the licence expires.

Because the broadcasting licence can no longer be renewed, its useful life is no longer indefinite. Thus, the acquired licence would be amortised over its remaining three-year useful life and immediately tested for impairment in accordance with [draft] FRS ● IAS 36.

Example 6—an acquired airline route authority between two European cities that expires in three years

The route authority may be renewed every five years, and the acquiring entity intends to comply with the applicable rules and regulations surrounding renewal. Route authority renewals are routinely granted at a minimal cost and historically have been renewed when the airline has complied with the applicable rules and regulations. The acquiring entity expects to provide service indefinitely between the two cities from its hub airports and expects that the related supporting infrastructure (airport gates, slots, and terminal facility leases) will remain in place at those airports for as long as it has the route authority. An analysis of demand and cash flows supports those assumptions.

Because the facts and circumstances support the acquiring entity's ability to continue providing air service indefinitely between the two cities, the intangible asset related to the route authority is treated as having an indefinite useful life. Therefore, the route authority would not be amortised until its useful life is determined to be finite. It would be tested for impairment in accordance with [draft] FRS ● IAS 36 annually and whenever there is an indication that it may be impaired.

Example 7—an acquired trademark used to identify and distinguish a leading consumer product that has been a market-share leader for the past eight years

The trademark has a remaining legal life of five years but is renewable every 10 years at little cost. The acquiring entity intends to renew the trademark continuously and evidence supports its ability to do so. An analysis of (1) product life cycle studies, (2) market, competitive and environmental trends, and (3) brand extension opportunities provides evidence that the trademarked product will generate net cash inflows for the acquiring entity for an indefinite period.

The trademark would be treated as having an indefinite useful life because it is expected to contribute to net cash inflows indefinitely. Therefore, the trademark would not be amortised until its useful life is determined to be finite. It would be tested for impairment in accordance with [draft] FRS • ~~IAS 36~~ annually and whenever there is an indication that it may be impaired.

Example 8—a trademark acquired 10 years ago that distinguishes a leading consumer product

The trademark was regarded as having an indefinite useful life when it was acquired because the trademarked product was expected to generate net cash inflows indefinitely. However, unexpected competition has recently entered the market and will reduce future sales of the product. Management estimates that net cash inflows generated by the product will be 20 per cent less for the foreseeable future. However, management expects that the product will continue to generate net cash inflows indefinitely at those reduced amounts.

As a result of the projected decrease in future net cash inflows, the entity determines that the estimated recoverable amount of the trademark is less than its carrying amount, and an impairment loss is recognised. Because it is still regarded as having an indefinite useful life, the trademark would continue not to be amortised but would be tested for impairment in accordance with [draft] FRS • ~~IAS 36~~ annually and whenever there is an indication that it may be impaired.

Example 9—a trademark for a line of products that was acquired several years ago in a business combination

At the time of the business combination the acquiree had been producing the line of products for 35 years with many new models developed under the trademark. At the acquisition date the acquirer expected to continue producing the line, and an analysis of various economic factors indicated there was no limit to the period the trademark would contribute to net cash inflows. Consequently, the trademark was not amortised by the acquirer. However, management has recently decided that production of the product line will be discontinued over the next four years.

Because the useful life of the acquired trademark is no longer regarded as indefinite, the carrying amount of the trademark would be tested for impairment in accordance with [draft] FRS • ~~IAS 36~~ and amortised over its remaining four-year useful life.

NOTE ON LEGAL REQUIREMENTS

Great Britain

1   In Great Britain, for financial years beginning on or after 1 January 2005, the statutory requirements relating to accounting for intangible assets for those companies which prepare accounts under the Companies Act 1985, rather than IAS accounts, are set out in the Companies Act 1985. The main requirements that are directly relevant to intangible assets and the requirements of [draft] FRS ● are set out in Schedules 4 and 4A and are summarised below.

2   Schedule 4 does not apply to banking and insurance companies and groups. Requirements equivalent to those of Schedule 4 are contained in Schedule 9 (for banking companies and groups) and in Schedule 9A (for insurance companies and groups).

Goodwill

3   The acquisition method of accounting and the calculation of goodwill are described by paragraph 9(4) and (5) of Schedule 4A. The interest of the parent company and its subsidiaries in the adjusted capital and reserves of an acquired subsidiary undertaking must be offset against the acquisition cost. The resulting amount if positive must be treated as goodwill, and, if negative, as a negative consolidation difference.

4   The balance sheet formats in Schedule 4 require purchased goodwill, to the extent that it has not been written off, to be included under the heading of intangible fixed assets, and shown separately from other intangible assets. Note (3) to the formats states that amounts representing goodwill should be included only to the extent that the goodwill was acquired for valuable consideration. Internally generated goodwill may not be capitalised.

5   Paragraph 21 of Schedule 4 requires that, where goodwill is treated as an asset, it must be depreciated systematically over a period chosen by the directors. The period chosen must not exceed the useful economic life of the goodwill. The period chosen and the reason for choosing that period must be disclosed in a note. The use of residual values in determining depreciable amounts and thus calculating systematic depreciation/amortisation is widely accepted. If the residual value is equal to the carrying amount (eg cost) then depreciation is reduced to nil. It is possible that **where the useful life of the asset is indefinite**, the residual value (on the basis of prices prevailing at the time of original acquisition) will always equal cost.

6   Paragraph 31(1) of Schedule 4 prohibits the revaluation of goodwill.

7   Paragraph 14 of Schedule 4A requires the notes to the accounts to state the cumulative amount of goodwill resulting from acquisitions in that, and earlier financial years, that has been written off otherwise than in the consolidated profit and loss account for that or any earlier financial year. That figure must be net of any goodwill attributable to subsidiary undertakings or businesses disposed of before the balance sheet date. Paragraph 16 of Schedule 4A states that disclosure of amounts pertaining to an overseas business need not be given if it would be seriously prejudicial to the group's business and agreement has been obtained from the Secretary of State. Further, for acquisitions before 23 December 1989, disclosure need not be made if the information necessary to calculate the amount with material accuracy is unavailable or cannot be obtained without unreasonable expense or delay (paragraph 9 of Schedule 2 to the Companies Act 1989 (Commencement No. 4 and Transitional

and Saving Provisions) Order 1990). The exclusion of such amounts and the grounds for the exclusion must be stated.

Intangible assets

Paragraph 9(2) of Schedule 4A requires, under the acquisition method of accounting, **8** the identifiable assets and liabilities of an acquired undertaking to be included in the consolidated balance sheet at their fair values as at the date of acquisition. It defines "identifiable" as capable of being disposed of or discharged separately, without disposing of a business of the undertaking.

The following headings for intangible assets are set out in the balance sheet formats **9** in Schedule 4:

B   Fixed assets
I   Intangible assets

    1.   Development costs
    2.   Concessions, patents, licences, trade marks and similar rights and assets
    3.   Goodwill
    4.   Payments on account.

Note (2) on the balance sheet formats permits amounts in respect of assets to be **10** included in company's balance sheet under the heading of concessions, patents, licences, trade marks and similar rights and assets only if either (a) the assets were acquired for valuable consideration and are not required to be shown under goodwill; or (b) the assets in question were created by the company itself.

Paragraph 18 of Schedule 4 requires that, where a fixed asset has a limited useful **11** economic life, the purchase price or production cost less any residual value is reduced by provisions for depreciation calculated to write off that amount systematically over the period of the asset's useful economic life.

Paragraph 31(1) of Schedule 4 permits intangible assets, other than goodwill, to be **12** included at their current cost. Where an intangible asset is valued at its current cost, the depreciation rules are to be applied by substituting the most recently determined value for the purchase price or production cost (paragraph 32(1)).

Research and Development

Paragraph 3(1) of Schedule 4 enables any items required to be shown in a company's **13** balance sheet or profit and loss account to be shown in greater detail than required by the format adopted.

Paragraph 3(2)(c) of Schedule 4 provides that a company's balance sheet or profit **14** and loss account may include an item representing or covering the amount of any asset or liability, income or expenditure not otherwise covered by any of the items listed in the accounts format adopted. Cost of research shall not be treated as an asset in any company's balance sheet.

Paragraph 20(1) of Schedule 4 requires that notwithstanding that an item in respect **15** of development costs is included under fixed assets in the balance sheet formats set out in Part 1 of Schedule 4, an amount may only be included in a company's balance sheet in respect of development costs in special circumstances.

16   Paragraph 20(2) of Schedule 4 requires that if any amount is included in a company's balance sheet in respect of development costs the following information shall be given in a note to the accounts:

(a)   the period over which the amount of those costs originally capitalised is being, or is to be, written off; and

(b)   the reasons for capitalising the development costs in question.

17   For all companies, whether preparing Companies Act or IAS accounts, paragraph 6(c) of Schedule 7 requires the Directors' Report to contain an indication of the activities (if any) of the company and its subsidiaries in the field of research and development.

18   For all companies, whether preparing Companies Act or IAS accounts, section 269(2)(b) of the Companies Act 1985 on the treatment of development costs requires that where the unamortised development expenditure carried forward is not treated as a realised loss when determining distributable reserves, the notes to the financial statements shall disclose:

(a)   the fact that the amount of the unamortised development expenditure is not to be treated as a realised loss for the purposes of calculating distributable profits; and

(b)   the circumstances that the directors relied upon to justify their decision not to treat the unamortised development expenditure as a realised loss.

Provisions for diminution in value

19   Paragraph 19(2) of Schedule 4 requires provisions for diminution in value to be made in respect of any fixed asset that has diminished in value if the reduction in its value is expected to be permanent. Any provisions that are not shown in the profit and loss account must be disclosed (either separately or in aggregate) in a note to the accounts.

20   Paragraph 19(3) of Schedule 4 requires that where the reasons for which a provision was made have ceased to apply to any extent, the provision must be written back to the extent that it is no longer necessary. Where any amounts written back are not shown in the profit and loss account, they must be disclosed (either separately or in aggregate) in a note to the accounts.

Amortisation and other amounts written off fixed assets

21   The formats set out in Schedule 4 prescribe the headings under which depreciation and other amounts written off tangible and intangible fixed assets are to be included in the profit and loss account. Under Formats 1 and 3, such amounts are to be included in cost of sales, distribution costs and administrative expenses. Under Formats 2 and 4, such amounts are to be shown as a separate heading.

Disclosure requirements

22   Disclosure of the accounting policies adopted by a company (including the policies regarding the depreciation and diminution in value of assets) is required by paragraph 36 of Schedule 4.

23   Paragraph 42 of Schedule 4 details the disclosures required of the movement on intangible asset balances. The same level of detail is required as for other fixed assets.

Paragraphs 33 and 43 of Schedule 4 prescribe additional information to be given for   **24**
any assets that have been revalued. This includes comparable amounts determined
according to the historical cost accounting rules and details of the basis and date of
the valuation and the qualifications of the valuer.

Northern Ireland

The statutory requirements in Northern Ireland are set out in the Companies   **25**
(Northern Ireland) Order 1986. They are similar to those in Great Britain. Most of
the references cited above have parallel references in the Companies (Northern
Ireland) Order 1986. The only exceptions are that:

(a)   the requirements of sections 226, 226A, 227 and 227A of the Companies Act
       1985 are found in Articles 234 and 235 of the Companies (Northern Ireland)
       Order 1986; and

(b)   the transitional arrangements permitted by paragraph 9 of Schedule 2 to the
       Companies Act 1989 (Commencement No. 4 and Transitional and Saving
       Provisions) Order 1990 are found in paragraph 9 of the Companies (1990
       Order) (Commencement No. 1) Order (Northern Ireland) 1990. They apply to
       acquisitions made before 1 April 1990.

Republic of Ireland

Intangible Assets

The statutory requirements in the Republic of Ireland that correspond to those listed   **26**
above for Great Britain are shown in the following table.

Great Britain	Republic of Ireland
Schedule 4, Companies Act, 1985	Schedule, Companies (Amendment) Act, 1986
Schedule 4A, Companies Act, 1985	European Communities (Companies: Group Accounts) Regulations 1992
Paragraph 9(4)&(5) of Schedule 4A	Regulation 19(4), (5) & (6) of 1992 Regulations
Paragraph 21 of Schedule 4	Paragraph 9 of Schedule to 1986 Act
Paragraph 31(1) of Schedule 4	Paragraph 19(1) of Schedule to 1986 Act
Paragraph 14 of Schedule 4A	No corresponding references
Paragraph 16 of Schedule 4A	No corresponding references
Paragraph 9(2) of Schedule 4A	Regulation 19(2) of 1992 Regulations
Paragraph 18 of Schedule 4	Paragraph 6 of Schedule to 1986 Act
Paragraph 31(1) of Schedule 4	Paragraph 19(1) of Schedule to 1986 Act
Paragraph 32(1) of Schedule 4	Paragraph 20(1) of Schedule to 1986 Act
Paragraph 3(1) of Schedule 4	Section 4(5) of 1986 Act
Paragraph 3(2)(c) of Schedule 4	Section 4(12) of 1986 Act
Paragraph 20(1) of Schedule 4	Paragraph 8(1) Schedule to 1986 Act

Paragraph 20 (2) of Schedule 4	Paragraph 8(2) Schedule to 1986 Act
Paragraph 6(c) of Schedule 7	Section 13 (d) of 1986 Act
Section 269(2)(b), 1985 Act	No corresponding references
Paragraph 19(2),(3), of Schedule 4	Paragraph 7(2), (3) of Schedule to 1986 Act
Paragraph 36 of Schedule 4	Paragraph 24 of Schedule to 1986 Act
Paragraph 42 of Schedule 4	Paragraph 29 of Schedule to 1986 Act
Paragraph 43 of Schedule 4	Paragraph 30 of Schedule to 1986 Act

There are no transitional provisions in the Republic of Ireland that correspond to those given in paragraph 9 of Schedule 2 to the Companies Act 1989 (Commencement No. 4 and Transitional and Saving Provisions) Order 1990.

Research and Development

27   Section 4(5) of the Act enables any items required to be shown in a company's balance sheet or profit and loss account to be shown in greater detail than required by the format adopted.

28   Section 4(12) of the Act provides that the balance sheet, or profit and loss account, of a company may include an item representing or covering the amount of any asset or liability or income or expenditure not otherwise covered by any of the items listed in the format adopted but that costs of research shall not be treated as assets in the balance sheet of a company.

29   Paragraph 43(4) of the Schedule requires the amount expended on research and development in the financial year, and any amount committed in respect of research and development in subsequent years, to be stated.

30   Paragraph 43(5) of the Schedule provides that where, in the opinion of the directors, the disclosure of any information required by Paragraph 43(4) would be prejudicial to the interests of the company, that information need not be disclosed, but the fact that any such information has not been disclosed shall be stated.

31   Paragraph 7(1) of the Schedule does not allow provision to be made for a temporary diminution in value other than for a fixed asset investment.

32   Paragraph 7(2) of the Schedule requires provision for diminution in value to be made in respect of any fixed asset which has diminished in value if the reduction is expected to be permanent (whether its useful economic life is limited or not) and the amount to be included in respect of it shall be reduced accordingly. Any such provisions which are not shown in the profit and loss account shall be disclosed (either separately or in aggregate) in a note to the accounts.

33   Paragraph 7(3) of the Schedule requires that where the reasons for which any provision was made have ceased to apply to any extent, then the provision should be written back to the extent that it is no longer necessary. Any amounts written back in accordance with this sub-paragraph which are not shown in the profit and loss account shall be disclosed (either separately or in aggregate) in a note to the accounts.

Paragraph 8(1) of the Schedule requires that notwithstanding that an item in respect   **34**
of development costs is included under fixed assets in the balance sheet formats set
out in Part 1 of the Schedule, an amount may only be included in a company's
balance sheet in respect of development costs in special circumstances.

Paragraph 8(2) of the Schedule requires that if any amount is included in a com-   **35**
pany's balance sheet in respect of development costs, the following information shall
be given in a note to the accounts:

(a)   the period over which the amount of those costs originally capitalised is being,
      or is to be, written off; and
(b)   the reasons for capitalising the development costs in question.

Section 13(c) of the Act requires the Directors' Report to contain an indication of the   **36**
activity, if any, of the company and its subsidiaries, if any, in the field of research and
development.

Section 45A of the Companies (Amendment) Act 1983 on the treatment of devel-   **37**
opment costs, provides that where development costs are shown in a company's
accounts any amount shown as an asset in respect of those costs shall be treated as a
realised loss for the purpose of determining profits available for distribution. This
provision does not apply to any part of that amount representing an unrealised profit
made on revaluation of these costs; nor does it apply if:

(a)   there are special circumstances justifying the directors of the company con-
      cerned in deciding that the amount mentioned in respect thereof in the
      company's accounts shall not be treated as a realised loss; and
(b)   the note to the accounts required by paragraph 8(2) of the Schedule states that
      the amount is not to be so treated and explains the circumstances relied upon to
      justify the decision of the directors to that effect.

FINANCIAL REPORTING EXPOSURE DRAFT 38

IMPAIRMENT OF ASSETS

International Accounting Standard 36

[DRAFT] FINANCIAL REPORTING STANDARD ●IMPAIRMENT OF ASSETS

ASB Note: The text set out in this [draft] standard is amended for consequential amendments arising from the IASB exposure draft of proposed *Amendments to IFRS 3 Business Combinations* and its exposure draft of proposed *Amendments to IAS 37 Provisions, Contingent Liabilities and Contingent Assets.*

Contents

[Draft] Financial Reporting Standard ● 'Impairment of Assets'

[Draft] Financial Reporting Standard Impairment of Assets embodies IAS 36 Impairment of Assets which was published in March 2004 in the form of a standard. The [draft] FRS includes some amendments to that standard adopted for entities subject to UK accounting standards. All of the changes made to the IASB text by the ASB are highlighted by strikethrough of the text to be deleted.

The [draft] Statement of Standard Accounting Practice in the [draft] FRS is set out in paragraphs 1 – 141 and the appendices. All paragraphs have equal authority. Paragraphs in bold type state the main principles.

Accompanying the [draft] Statement of Standard Accounting Practice is the basis of conclusions reached in the Statement and some illustrative examples, which do not form part of the Statement.

The [draft] Statement of Standard Accounting Practice should be read in the context of its objective as stated in paragraphs 1 and the Accounting Standards Board's 'Foreword to Accounting Standards' and 'Statement of Principles for Financial Reporting'.

INTRODUCTION

<del>International Accounting Standard 36 *Impairment of Assets* (IAS 36) replaces IAS 36 *Impairment of Assets* (issued in 1998), and should be applied:</del>   **IN1**

<del>(a)   on acquisition to goodwill and intangible assets acquired in business combinations for which the agreement date is on or after 31 March 2004.</del>
<del>(b)   to all other assets, for annual periods beginning on or after 31 March 2004.</del>

<del>Earlier application is encouraged.</del>

Reasons for revising IAS 36

The International Accounting Standards Board developed this revised IAS 36 as   **IN2**
part of its project on business combinations. The project's objective is to improve the
quality of, and seek international convergence on, the accounting for business
combinations and the subsequent accounting for goodwill and intangible assets
acquired in business combinations.

The project has two phases. The first phase resulted in the Board issuing simulta-   **IN3**
neously IFRS 3 *Business Combinations* and revised versions of IAS 36 and IAS 38
Intangible Assets. The Board's deliberations during the first phase of the project
focused primarily on the following issues:

(a)   the method of accounting for business combinations;
(b)   the initial measurement of the identifiable assets acquired and liabilities and
      contingent liabilities assumed in a business combination;
(c)   the recognition of provisions for terminating or reducing the activities of an
      acquiree;
(d)   the treatment of any excess of the acquirer's interest in the fair values of
      identifiable net assets acquired in a business combination over the cost of the
      combination; and
(e)   the accounting for goodwill and intangible assets acquired in a business
      combination.

Therefore, the Board's intention while revising IAS 36 was to reflect only those   **IN4**
changes related to its decisions in the Business Combinations project, and *not* to
reconsider all of the requirements in IAS 36. The changes that have been made in the
Standard are primarily concerned with the impairment test for goodwill.

Summary of main changes

Frequency of impairment testing

The previous version of IAS 36 required the recoverable amount of an asset to be   **IN5**
measured whenever there is an indication that the asset may be impaired. This
requirement is included in the Standard. However, the Standard also requires:

(a)   the recoverable amount of an intangible asset with an indefinite useful life to be
      measured annually, irrespective of whether there is any indication that it may
      be impaired. The most recent detailed calculation of recoverable amount made
      in a preceding period may be used in the impairment test for that asset in the
      current period, provided specified criteria are met.
(b)   the recoverable amount of an intangible asset not yet available for use to be
      measured annually, irrespective of whether there is any indication that it may
      be impaired.

(c)   goodwill acquired in a business combination to be tested for impairment annually.

Measuring value in use

IN6   The Standard clarifies that the following elements should be reflected in the calculation of an asset's value in use:

(a)   an estimate of the future cash flows the entity expects to derive from the asset;

(b)   expectations about possible variations in the amount or timing of those future cash flows;

(c)   the time value of money, represented by the current market risk-free rate of interest;

(d)   the price for bearing the uncertainty inherent in the asset; and

(e)   other factors, such as illiquidity, that market participants would reflect in pricing the future cash flows the entity expects to derive from the asset.

The Standard also clarifies that the second, fourth and fifth of these elements can be reflected either as adjustments to the future cash flows or adjustments to the discount rate.

IN7   The Standard carries forward from the previous version of IAS 36 the requirement for the cash flow projections used to measure value in use to be based on reasonable and supportable assumptions that represent management's best estimate of the economic conditions that will exist over the remaining useful life of the asset. However, the Standard clarifies that management:

(a)   should assess the reasonableness of the assumptions on which its current cash flow projections are based by examining the causes of differences between past cash flow projections and actual cash flows.

(b)   should ensure that the assumptions on which its current cash flow projections are based are consistent with past actual outcomes, provided the effects of subsequent events or circumstances that did not exist when those actual cash flows were generated make this appropriate.

IN8   The previous version of IAS 36 required the cash flow projections used to measure value in use to be based on the most recent financial budgets/forecasts approved by management. The Standard carries forward this requirement, but clarifies that the cash flow projections exclude any estimated cash inflows or outflows expected to arise from:

(a)   future restructurings to which an entity is not yet committed, or

(b)   improving or enhancing the asset's performance.

IN9   Additional guidance on using present value techniques in measuring an asset's value in use is included in Appendix A of the Standard. In addition, the guidance in the previous version of IAS 36 on estimating the discount rate when an asset-specific rate is not directly available from the market has been relocated to Appendix A.

Identifying the cash-generating unit to which an asset belongs

IN10   The Standard carries forward from the previous version of IAS 36 the requirement that if an active market exists for the output produced by an asset or a group of assets, that asset or group of assets should be identified as a cash-generating unit, even if some or all of the output is used internally. However, the previous version of IAS 36 required that, in such circumstances, management's best estimate of future

market prices for the output should be used in estimating the future cash flows used
to determine the unit's value in use. It also required that when an entity was estimating future cash flows to determine the value in use of cash-generating units using
the output, management's best estimate of future market prices for the output should
be used. The Standard requires that if the cash inflows generated by *any* asset or
cash-generating unit are affected by internal transfer pricing, an entity should use
management's best estimate of future price(s) that could be achieved in arm's length
transactions in estimating:

(a)   the future cash inflows used to determine the asset's or cash-generating unit's
      value in use; and
(b)   the future cash outflows used to determine the value in use of other assets or
      cash-generating units affected by the internal transfer pricing.

Allocating goodwill to cash-generating units

The previous version of IAS 36 required goodwill acquired in a business combination   **IN11**
to be tested for impairment as part of impairment testing the cash-generating unit(s)
to which it related. It employed a 'bottom-up/top-down' approach under which the
goodwill was, in effect, tested for impairment by allocating its carrying amount to
each cash-generating unit or smallest group of cash-generating units to which a
portion of that carrying amount could be allocated on a reasonable and consistent
basis. The Standard similarly requires goodwill acquired in a business combination
to be tested for impairment as part of impairment testing the cash-generating unit(s)
to which it relates. However, the Standard clarifies that:

(a)   the goodwill should, from the acquisition date, be allocated to each of the
      acquirer's cash-generating units, or groups of cash-generating units, that are
      expected to benefit from the synergies of the business combination, irrespective
      of whether other assets or liabilities of the acquiree are assigned to those units
      or groups of units.
(b)   each unit or group of units to which the goodwill is allocated should:
      (i)   represent the lowest level within the entity at which the goodwill is
             monitored for internal management purposes; and
      (ii)   not be larger than a segment based on either the entity's primary or the
             entity's secondary reporting format determined in accordance with
             IAS 14 *Segment Reporting*.

The Standard also clarifies the following: **IN12**

(a)   if the initial allocation of goodwill acquired in a business combination cannot
      be completed before the end of the annual period in which the business com-
      bination occurs, that initial allocation should be completed before the end of
      the first annual period beginning after the acquisition date.
(b)   when an entity disposes of an operation within a cash-generating unit (group of
      units) to which goodwill has been allocated, the goodwill associated with that
      operation should be:

      (i)   included in the carrying amount of the operation when determining the
             gain or loss on disposal; and
      (ii)   measured on the basis of the relative values of the operation disposed of
             and the portion of the cash-generating unit (group of units) retained,
             unless the entity can demonstrate that some other method better reflects
             the goodwill associated with the operation disposed of.

(c)   when an entity reorganises its reporting structure in a manner that changes the
      composition of cash-generating units (groups of units) to which goodwill has

been allocated, the goodwill should be reallocated to the units (groups of units) affected. This reallocation should be performed using a relative value approach similar to that used when an entity disposes of an operation within a cash-generating unit (group of units), unless the entity can demonstrate that some other method better reflects the goodwill associated with the reorganised units (groups of units).

Timing of impairment tests for goodwill

IN13   The Standard permits:

(a)   the annual impairment test for a cash-generating unit (group of units) to which goodwill has been allocated to be performed at any time during an annual reporting period, provided the test is performed at the same time every year.

(b)   different cash-generating units (groups of units) to be tested for impairment at different times.

However, if some of the goodwill allocated to a cash-generating unit (group of units) was acquired in a business combination during the current annual period, the Standard requires that unit (group of units) to be tested for impairment before the end of the current period.

IN14   The Standard permits the most recent detailed calculation made in a preceding period of the recoverable amount of a cash-generating unit (group of units) to which goodwill has been allocated to be used in the impairment test for that unit (group of units) in the current period, provided specified criteria are met.

Reversals of impairment losses for goodwill

IN15   The previous version of IAS 36 required an impairment loss recognised for goodwill in a previous period to be reversed when the impairment loss was caused by a specific external event of an exceptional nature that is not expected to recur and subsequent external events have occurred that reverse the effect of that event. The Standard prohibits the recognition of reversals of impairment losses for goodwill.

Disclosure

IN16   The Standard requires that if any portion of the goodwill acquired in a business combination during the period has not been allocated to a cash-generating unit at the reporting date, an entity should disclose the amount of the unallocated goodwill together with the reasons why that amount remains unallocated.

IN17   The Standard requires disclosure of information for each cash-generating unit (group of units) for which the carrying amount of goodwill or intangible assets with indefinite useful lives allocated to that unit (group of units) is significant in comparison with the entity's total carrying amount of goodwill or intangible assets with indefinite lives. That information is concerned primarily with the key assumptions used to measure the recoverable amounts of such units (groups of units).

IN18   The Standard also requires specified information to be disclosed if some or all of the carrying amount of goodwill or intangible assets with indefinite lives is allocated across multiple cash-generating units (groups of units), and the amount so allocated to each unit (group of units) is not significant in comparison with the total carrying amount of goodwill or intangible assets with indefinite lives. Further disclosures are required if, in such circumstances, the recoverable amounts of any of those units (groups of units) are based on the same key assumption(s) and the aggregate carrying amount of goodwill or intangible assets with indefinite lives allocated to them is significant in comparison with the entity's total carrying amount of goodwill or intangible assets with indefinite lives.

~~International Accounting Standard 36~~

[Draft] Financial Reporting Standard ●
Impairment of Assets

OBJECTIVE

1   The objective of this Standard is to prescribe the procedures that an entity applies to ensure that its assets are carried at no more than their recoverable amount. An asset is carried at more than its recoverable amount if its carrying amount exceeds the amount to be recovered through use or sale of the asset. If this is the case, the asset is described as impaired and the Standard requires the entity to recognise an impairment loss. The Standard also specifies when an entity should reverse an impairment loss and prescribes disclosures.

SCOPE

1A   *This Standard applies to all financial statements that are intended to give a true and fair view of a reporting entity's financial position and profit and loss (or income and expenditure), except that reporting entities applying the Financial Reporting Standard for Smaller Entities (FRSSE) currently applicable are exempt.*

2   *This Standard shall be applied in accounting for the impairment of all assets, other than:*

   (a)   ~~inventories (see IAS 2 Inventories);~~
   (b)   stocks and long-term contracts ~~assets arising from construction contracts~~ (see SSAP 9 Stocks and Long-term Contracts ~~IAS 11 Construction Contracts~~);
   (c)   deferred tax assets (see FRS 19 Deferred Tax ~~IAS 12 Income Taxes~~);
   (d)   assets arising from retirement ~~employee~~ benefits (see FRS 17 Retirement and Termination Benefits ~~IAS 19 Employee Benefits~~);
   (e)   financial assets that are within the scope of ~~IAS 39~~ FRS 26 Financial Instruments Recognition and Measurement;
   (f)   investment property ~~that is measured at fair value~~ (see SSAP 19 Accounting for Investment Properties ~~IAS 40 Investment Property~~);
   (g)   biological assets related to agricultural activity that are measured at fair value less estimated point-of-sale costs ~~(see IAS 41 Agriculture)~~;and
   (h)   deferred acquisition costs, and intangible assets, arising from an insurer's contractual rights under insurance contracts as defined in FRS 26 Appendix C. ~~within the scope of IFRS 4 Insurance Contracts; and~~
   ~~(i)   non-current assets (or disposal groups) classified as held for sale in accordance with IFRS 5 Non-current Assets Held for Sale and Discontinued Operations.~~

3   This Standard does not apply to ~~inventories, assets arising from~~ stocks and long-term contracts, ~~construction contracts,~~ deferred tax assets, or assets arising from retirement benefits ~~employee benefits, or assets classified as held for sale (or included in a disposal group that is classified as held for sale)~~ because existing Standards applicable to these assets contain requirements for recognising and measuring these assets.

4   This Standard applies to financial assets classified as:

   (a)   subsidiaries, as defined in FRS 2 *Accounting for Subsidiary Undertakings* ~~IAS 27 Consolidated and Separate Financial Statements~~;
   (b)   associates, as defined in FRS 9 *Associates and Joint Ventures* ~~IAS 28 Investments in Associates~~; and

(c)   joint ventures, as defined in FRS 9 *Associates and Joint Ventures* ~~IAS 31~~ ~~Interests in Joint Ventures~~.

For impairment of other financial assets, refer to FRS 26 ~~IAS 39~~.

This Standard does not apply to financial assets within the scope of FRS 26 ~~IAS 39~~   **5** or investment property measured at open market value ~~fair value~~ in accordance with SSAP 19 ~~IAS 40~~, or biological assets related to agricultural activity measured at fair value less estimated point-of-sale costs ~~in accordance with IAS 41~~. However, this Standard applies to assets that are carried at revalued amount ~~(ie fair value)~~ in accordance with other Standards, such as ~~the revaluation model in~~ FRS 15 *Tangible Fixed Assets* ~~IAS 16 *Property, Plant and Equipment*~~. Identifying whether a revalued asset may be impaired depends on the basis used to determine its revalued amount ~~fair value~~:

(a)   if the asset's valuation basis ~~fair value~~ is its market value, the only difference between the asset's revalued amount ~~fair value~~ and its fair value less costs to sell is the direct incremental costs to dispose of the asset:

   (i)   if the disposal costs are negligible, the recoverable amount of the revalued asset is necessarily close to, or greater than, its revalued amount ~~(ie fair value)~~. In this case, after the revaluation requirements have been applied, it is unlikely that the revalued asset is impaired and recoverable amount need not be estimated.

   (ii)   if the disposal costs are not negligible, the fair value less costs to sell of the revalued asset is necessarily less than its revalued amount ~~fair value~~. Therefore, the revalued asset will be impaired if its value in use is less than its revalued amount ~~(ie fair value)~~. In this case, after the revaluation requirements have been applied, an entity applies this Standard to determine whether the asset may be impaired.

(b)   if the asset's revalued amount ~~fair value~~ is determined on a basis other than its market value, its revalued amount ~~(ie fair value)~~ may be greater or lower than its recoverable amount. Hence, after the revaluation requirements have been applied, an entity applies this Standard to determine whether the asset may be impaired.

DEFINITIONS

The following terms are used in this Standard with the meanings specified: **6**

An active market *is a market in which all the following conditions exist:*

(a)   the items traded within the market are homogeneous;
(b)   willing buyers and sellers can normally be found at any time; and
(c)   prices are available to the public.

Carrying amount is the amount at which an asset is recognised after deducting any accumulated depreciation (amortisation) and accumulated impairment losses thereon.

A cash-generating unit *is the smallest identifiable group of assets that generates cash inflows that are largely independent of the cash inflows from other assets or groups of assets.*

Corporate assets are assets other than goodwill that contribute to the future cash flows of both the cash-generating unit under review and other cash-generating units.

Costs of disposal are incremental costs directly attributable to the disposal of an asset or cash-generating unit, excluding finance costs and income tax expense.

Depreciable amount is the cost of an asset, or other amount substituted for cost in the financial statements, less its residual value.

Depreciation (Amortisation) is the systematic allocation of the depreciable amount of an asset over its useful life.*

Fair value less costs to sell is the amount obtainable from the sale of an asset or cash-generating unit in an arm's length transaction between knowledgeable, willing parties, less the costs of disposal.

An impairment loss is the amount by which the carrying amount of an asset or a cash-generating unit exceeds its recoverable amount.

The recoverable amount of an asset or a cash-generating unit is the higher of its fair value less costs to sell and its value in use.

Useful life is either:

(a) the period of time over which an asset is expected to be used by the entity; or
(b) the number of production or similar units expected to be obtained from the asset by the entity.

Value in use is the present value of the future cash flows expected to be derived from an asset or cash-generating unit.

6A †Definitions of Business Segment and Geographical Segment

The terms business segment and geographical segment are used in this Standard with the following meanings:

A business segment is a distinguishable component of an entity that is engaged in providing an individual product or service or a group of related products or services and that is subject to risks and returns that are different from those of other business segments. Factors that shall be considered in determining whether products and services are related include:

(a) *the nature of the products or services;*
(b) *the nature of the production processes;*
(c) *the type or class of customer for the products or services;*
(d) *the methods used to distribute the products or provide the services; and*
(e) *if applicable, the nature of the regulatory environment, for example, banking, insurance, or public utilities.*

A geographical segment is a distinguishable component of an entity that is engaged in providing products or services within a particular economic environment and that is subject to risks and returns that are different from those of components operating in

---

**In the case of an intangible asset, the term 'amortisation' is generally used instead of 'depreciation'. The two terms have the same meaning.*

†*ASB footnote: The definition of a Business Segment, Geographical Segment and Primary and Secondary Segment Reporting Formats are extracted from IAS 14 Segment Reporting. These definitions are required to conform the level at which goodwill is tested for impairment – see paragraph 80 of this [draft] FRS.*

other economic environments. Factors that shall be considered in identifying geographical segments include:

(a) similarity of economic and political conditions;
(b) relationships between operations in different geographical areas;
(c) proximity of operations;
(d) special risks associated with operations in a particular area;
(e) exchange control regulations; and
(f) the underlying currency risks.

A reportable segment is a business segment or a geographical segment identified based on the foregoing definitions for which segment information is required to be disclosed by this Standard.

**Primary and Secondary Segment ReportingFormats*   6B

The dominant source and nature of an entity's risks and returns shall govern whether its primary segment reporting format will be business segments or geographical segments. If the entity's risks and rates of return are affected predominantly by differences in the products and services it produces, its primary format for reporting segment information shall be business segments, with secondary information reported geographically. Similarly, if the entity's risks and rates of return are affected predominantly by the fact that it operates in different countries or other geographical areas, its primary format for reporting segment information shall be geographical segments, with secondary information reported for groups of related products and services.

An entity's internal organisational and management structure and its system of internal financial reporting to the board of directors and the chief executive officer shall normally be the basis for identifying the predominant source and nature of risks and differing rates of return facing the entity and, therefore, for determining which reporting format is primary and which is secondary, except as provided in subparagraphs (a) and (b) below:

(a) if an entity's risks and rates of return are strongly affected both by differences in the products and services it produces and by differences in the geographical areas in which it operates, as evidenced by a "matrix approach" to managing the company and to reporting internally to the board of directors and the chief executive officer, then the entity shall use business segments as its primary segment reporting format and geographical segments as its secondary reporting format; and

(b) if an entity's internal organisational and management structure and its system of internal financial reporting to the board of directors and the chief executive officer are based neither on individual products or services or on groups of related products/services nor on geography, the directors and management of the entity shall determine whether the entity's risks and returns are related more to the products and services it produces or more to the geographical areas in which it operates and, as a consequence, shall choose either business segments or geographical segments as the entity's primary segment reporting format, with the other as its secondary reporting format.

---

*ASB footnote: The definition of a Business Segment, Geographical Segment and Primary and Secondary Segment Reporting Formats are extracted from IAS 14 Segment Reporting. These definitions are required to conform the level at which goodwill is tested for impairment – see paragraph 80 of this [draft] FRS.

IDENTIFYING AN ASSET THAT MAY BE IMPAIRED

7 Paragraphs 8-17 specify when recoverable amount shall be determined. These requirements use the term 'an asset' but apply equally to an individual asset or a cash-generating unit. The remainder of this Standard is structured as follows:

(a) paragraphs 18-57 set out the requirements for measuring recoverable amount. These requirements also use the term 'an asset' but apply equally to an individual asset and a cash-generating unit.

(b) paragraphs 58-108 set out the requirements for recognising and measuring impairment losses. Recognition and measurement of impairment losses for individual assets other than goodwill are dealt with in paragraphs 58-64. Paragraphs 65-108 deal with the recognition and measurement of impairment losses for cash-generating units and goodwill.

(c) paragraphs 109-116 set out the requirements for reversing an impairment loss recognised in prior periods for an asset or a cash-generating unit. Again, these requirements use the term 'an asset' but apply equally to an individual asset or a cash-generating unit. Additional requirements for an individual asset are set out in paragraphs 117-121, for a cash-generating unit in paragraphs 122 and 123, and for goodwill in paragraphs 124 and 125.

(d) paragraphs 126-133 specify the information to be disclosed about impairment losses and reversals of impairment losses for assets and cash-generating units. Paragraphs 134-137 specify additional disclosure requirements for cash-generating units to which goodwill or intangible assets with indefinite useful lives have been allocated for impairment testing purposes.

8 An asset is impaired when its carrying amount exceeds its recoverable amount. Paragraphs 12-14 describe some indications that an impairment loss may have occurred. If any of those indications is present, an entity is required to make a formal estimate of recoverable amount. Except as described in paragraph 10, this Standard does not require an entity to make a formal estimate of recoverable amount if no indication of an impairment loss is present.

9 *An entity shall assess at each reporting date whether there is any indication that an asset may be impaired. If any such indication exists, the entity shall estimate the recoverable amount of the asset.*

10 *Irrespective of whether there is any indication of impairment, an entity shall also:*

(a) *test an intangible asset with an indefinite useful life or an intangible asset not yet available for use for impairment annually by comparing its carrying amount with its recoverable amount. This impairment test may be performed at any time during an annual period, provided it is performed at the same time every year. Different intangible assets may be tested for impairment at different times. However, if such an intangible asset was initially recognised during the current annual period, that intangible asset shall be tested for impairment before the end of the current annual period.*

(b) *test goodwill acquired in a business combination for impairment annually in accordance with paragraphs 80-99.*

11 The ability of an intangible asset to generate sufficient future economic benefits to recover its carrying amount is usually subject to greater uncertainty before the asset is available for use than after it is available for use. Therefore, this Standard requires an entity to test for impairment, at least annually, the carrying amount of an intangible asset that is not yet available for use.

In assessing whether there is any indication that an asset may be impaired, an entity   **12**
shall consider, as a minimum, the following indications:

External sources of information

(a) during the period, an asset's market value has declined significantly more than
would be expected as a result of the passage of time or normal use.
(b) significant changes with an adverse effect on the entity have taken place during the
period, or will take place in the near future, in the technological, market, eco-
nomic or legal environment in which the entity operates or in the market to which
an asset is dedicated.
(c) market interest rates or other market rates of return on investments have
increased during the period, and those increases are likely to affect the discount
rate used in calculating an asset's value in use and decrease the asset's recoverable
amount materially.
(d) the carrying amount of the net assets of the entity is more than its market
capitalisation.

Internal sources of information

(e) evidence is available of obsolescence or physical damage of an asset.
(f) significant changes with an adverse effect on the entity have taken place during the
period, or are expected to take place in the near future, in the extent to which, or
manner in which, an asset is used or is expected to be used. These changes include
the asset becoming idle, plans to discontinue or restructure the operation to which
an asset belongs, plans to dispose of an asset before the previously expected date,
and reassessing the useful life of an asset as finite rather than indefinite.**
(g) evidence is available from internal reporting that indicates that the economic
performance of an asset is, or will be, worse than expected.

The list in paragraph 12 is not exhaustive. An entity may identify other indications   **13**
that an asset may be impaired and these would also require the entity to determine
the asset's recoverable amount or, in the case of goodwill, perform an impairment
test in accordance with paragraphs 80-99.

Evidence from internal reporting that indicates that an asset may be impaired   **14**
includes the existence of:

(a) cash flows for acquiring the asset, or subsequent cash needs for operating or
maintaining it, that are significantly higher than those originally budgeted;
(b) actual net cash flows or operating profit or loss flowing from the asset that are
significantly worse than those budgeted;
(c) a significant decline in budgeted net cash flows or operating profit, or a significant increase in budgeted loss, flowing from the asset; or
(d) operating losses or net cash outflows for the asset, when current period
amounts are aggregated with budgeted amounts for the future.

As indicated in paragraph 10, this Standard requires an intangible asset with an   **15**
indefinite useful life or not yet available for use and goodwill to be tested for
impairment, at least annually. Apart from when the requirements in paragraph 10
apply, the concept of materiality applies in identifying whether the recoverable
amount of an asset needs to be estimated. For example, if previous calculations show
that an asset's recoverable amount is significantly greater than its carrying amount,

*Once an asset meets the criteria to be classified as held for sale (or is included in a disposal group that is
classified as held for sale), it is excluded from the scope of this Standard and is accounted for in accordance with
IFRS 5 Non-current Assets Held for Sale and Discontinued Operations.

the entity need not re-estimate the asset's recoverable amount if no events have occurred that would eliminate that difference. Similarly, previous analysis may show that an asset's recoverable amount is not sensitive to one (or more) of the indications listed in paragraph 12.

16   As an illustration of paragraph 15, if market interest rates or other market rates of return on investments have increased during the period, an entity is not required to make a formal estimate of an asset's recoverable amount in the following cases:

(a)   if the discount rate used in calculating the asset's value in use is unlikely to be affected by the increase in these market rates. For example, increases in short-term interest rates may not have a material effect on the discount rate used for an asset that has a long remaining useful life.

(b)   if the discount rate used in calculating the asset's value in use is likely to be affected by the increase in these market rates but previous sensitivity analysis of recoverable amount shows that:

(i)   it is unlikely that there will be a material decrease in recoverable amount because future cash flows are also likely to increase (eg in some cases, an entity may be able to demonstrate that it adjusts its revenues to compensate for any increase in market rates); or

(ii)   the decrease in recoverable amount is unlikely to result in a material impairment loss.

17   If there is an indication that an asset may be impaired, this may indicate that the remaining useful life, the depreciation (amortisation) method or the residual value for the asset needs to be reviewed and adjusted in accordance with the Standard applicable to the asset, even if no impairment loss is recognised for the asset.

MEASURING RECOVERABLE AMOUNT

18   This Standard defines recoverable amount as the higher of an asset's or cash-generating unit's fair value less costs to sell and its value in use. Paragraphs 19-57 set out the requirements for measuring recoverable amount. These requirements use the term 'an asset' but apply equally to an individual asset or a cash-generating unit.

19   It is not always necessary to determine both an asset's fair value less costs to sell and its value in use. If either of these amounts exceeds the asset's carrying amount, the asset is not impaired and it is not necessary to estimate the other amount.

20   It may be possible to determine fair value less costs to sell, even if an asset is not traded in an active market. However, sometimes it will not be possible to determine fair value less costs to sell because there is no basis for making a reliable estimate of the amount obtainable from the sale of the asset in an arm's length transaction between knowledgeable and willing parties. In this case, the entity may use the asset's value in use as its recoverable amount.

21   If there is no reason to believe that an asset's value in use materially exceeds its fair value less costs to sell, the asset's fair value less costs to sell may be used as its recoverable amount. This will often be the case for an asset that is held for disposal. This is because the value in use of an asset held for disposal will consist mainly of the net disposal proceeds, as the future cash flows from continuing use of the asset until its disposal are likely to be negligible.

22   Recoverable amount is determined for an individual asset, unless the asset does not generate cash inflows that are largely independent of those from other assets or

groups of assets. If this is the case, recoverable amount is determined for the cash-generating unit to which the asset belongs (see paragraphs 65-103), unless either:

(a)   the asset's fair value less costs to sell is higher than its carrying amount; or
(b)   the asset's value in use can be estimated to be close to its fair value less costs to sell and fair value less costs to sell can be determined.

In some cases, estimates, averages and computational short cuts may provide rea-   23
sonable approximations of the detailed computations illustrated in this Standard for determining fair value less costs to sell or value in use.

Measuring the Recoverable Amount of an Intangible Asset with an Indefinite Useful Life

Paragraph 10 requires an intangible asset with an indefinite useful life to be tested for   24
impairment annually by comparing its carrying amount with its recoverable amount, irrespective of whether there is any indication that it may be impaired. However, the most recent detailed calculation of such an asset's recoverable amount made in a preceding period may be used in the impairment test for that asset in the current period, provided all of the following criteria are met:

(a)   if the intangible asset does not generate cash inflows from continuing use that are largely independent of those from other assets or groups of assets and is therefore tested for impairment as part of the cash-generating unit to which it belongs, the assets and liabilities making up that unit have not changed significantly since the most recent recoverable amount calculation;
(b)   the most recent recoverable amount calculation resulted in an amount that exceeded the asset's carrying amount by a substantial margin; and
(c)   based on an analysis of events that have occurred and circumstances that have changed since the most recent recoverable amount calculation, the likelihood that a current recoverable amount determination would be less than the asset's carrying amount is remote.

Fair Value less Costs to Sell

The best evidence of an asset's fair value less costs to sell is a price in a binding sale   25
agreement in an arm's length transaction, adjusted for incremental costs that would be directly attributable to the disposal of the asset.

If there is no binding sale agreement but an asset is traded in an active market, fair   26
value less costs to sell is the asset's market price less the costs of disposal. The appropriate market price is usually the current bid price. When current bid prices are unavailable, the price of the most recent transaction may provide a basis from which to estimate fair value less costs to sell, provided that there has not been a significant change in economic circumstances between the transaction date and the date as at which the estimate is made.

If there is no binding sale agreement or active market for an asset, fair value less   27
costs to sell is based on the best information available to reflect the amount that an entity could obtain, at the balance sheet date, from the disposal of the asset in an arm's length transaction between knowledgeable, willing parties, after deducting the costs of disposal. In determining this amount, an entity considers the outcome of recent transactions for similar assets within the same industry. Fair value less costs to sell does not reflect a forced sale, unless management is compelled to sell immediately.

28   Costs of disposal, other than those that have been recognised as liabilities, are deducted in determining fair value less costs to sell. Examples of such costs are legal costs, stamp duty and similar transaction taxes, costs of removing the asset, and direct incremental costs to bring an asset into condition for its sale. However, termination benefits (as defined in FRS 17 *Retirement and Termination Benefits* ~~IAS 19 Employee Benefits~~) and costs associated with reducing or reorganising a business following the disposal of an asset are not direct incremental costs to dispose of the asset.

29   Sometimes, the disposal of an asset would require the buyer to assume a liability and only a single fair value less costs to sell is available for both the asset and the liability. Paragraph 78 explains how to deal with such cases.

Value in Use

30   *The following elements shall be reflected in the calculation of an asset's value in use:*

   (a)   an estimate of the future cash flows the entity expects to derive from the asset;

   (b)   expectations about possible variations in the amount or timing of those future cash flows;

   (c)   the time value of money, represented by the current market risk-free rate of interest;

   (d)   the price for bearing the uncertainty inherent in the asset; and

   (e)   other factors, such as illiquidity, that market participants would reflect in pricing the future cash flows the entity expects to derive from the asset.

31   Estimating the value in use of an asset involves the following steps:

   (a)   estimating the future cash inflows and outflows to be derived from continuing use of the asset and from its ultimate disposal; and

   (b)   applying the appropriate discount rate to those future cash flows.

32   The elements identified in paragraph 30(b), (d) and (e) can be reflected either as adjustments to the future cash flows or as adjustments to the discount rate. Whichever approach an entity adopts to reflect expectations about possible variations in the amount or timing of future cash flows, the result shall be to reflect the expected present value of the future cash flows, ie the weighted average of all possible outcomes. Appendix A provides additional guidance on the use of present value techniques in measuring an asset's value in use.

Basis for Estimates of Future Cash Flows

33   *In measuring value in use an entity shall:*

   (a)   base cash flow projections on reasonable and supportable assumptions that represent management's best estimate of the range of economic conditions that will exist over the remaining useful life of the asset. Greater weight shall be given to external evidence.

   (b)   base cash flow projections on the most recent financial budgets/forecasts approved by management, but shall exclude any estimated future cash inflows or outflows expected to arise from future restructurings or from improving or enhancing the asset's performance. Projections based on these budgets/forecasts shall cover a maximum period of five years, unless a longer period can be justified.

   (c)   estimate cash flow projections beyond the period covered by the most recent budgets/forecasts by extrapolating the projections based on the budgets/forecasts using a steady or declining growth rate for subsequent years, unless an increasing

rate can be justified. This growth rate shall not exceed the long-term average growth rate for the products, industries, or country or countries in which the entity operates, or for the market in which the asset is used, unless a higher rate can be justified.

Management assesses the reasonableness of the assumptions on which its current   **34** cash flow projections are based by examining the causes of differences between past cash flow projections and actual cash flows. Management shall ensure that the assumptions on which its current cash flow projections are based are consistent with past actual outcomes, provided the effects of subsequent events or circumstances that did not exist when those actual cash flows were generated make this appropriate.

Detailed, explicit and reliable financial budgets/forecasts of future cash flows for   **35** periods longer than five years are generally not available. For this reason, management's estimates of future cash flows are based on the most recent budgets/forecasts for a maximum of five years. Management may use cash flow projections based on financial budgets/forecasts over a period longer than five years if it is confident that these projections are reliable and it can demonstrate its ability, based on past experience, to forecast cash flows accurately over that longer period.

Cash flow projections until the end of an asset's useful life are estimated by extra-   **36** polating the cash flow projections based on the financial budgets/forecasts using a growth rate for subsequent years. This rate is steady or declining, unless an increase in the rate matches objective information about patterns over a product or industry lifecycle. If appropriate, the growth rate is zero or negative.

When conditions are favourable, competitors are likely to enter the market and   **37** restrict growth. Therefore, entities will have difficulty in exceeding the average historical growth rate over the long term (say, twenty years) for the products, industries, or country or countries in which the entity operates, or for the market in which the asset is used.

In using information from financial budgets/forecasts, an entity considers whether   **38** the information reflects reasonable and supportable assumptions and represents management's best estimate of the set of economic conditions that will exist over the remaining useful life of the asset.

Composition of Estimates of Future Cash Flows

Estimates of future cash flows shall include: **39**

(a)   projections of cash inflows from the continuing use of the asset;
(b)   projections of cash outflows that are necessarily incurred to generate the cash inflows from continuing use of the asset (including cash outflows to prepare the asset for use) and can be directly attributed, or allocated on a reasonable and consistent basis, to the asset; and
(c)   net cash flows, if any, to be received (or paid) for the disposal of the asset at the end of its useful life.

Estimates of future cash flows and the discount rate reflect consistent assumptions   **40** about price increases attributable to general inflation. Therefore, if the discount rate includes the effect of price increases attributable to general inflation, future cash flows are estimated in nominal terms. If the discount rate excludes the effect of price increases attributable to general inflation, future cash flows are estimated in real terms (but include future specific price increases or decreases).

41   Projections of cash outflows include those for the day-to-day servicing of the asset as well as future overheads that can be attributed directly, or allocated on a reasonable and consistent basis, to the use of the asset.

42   When the carrying amount of an asset does not yet include all the cash outflows to be incurred before it is ready for use or sale, the estimate of future cash outflows includes an estimate of any further cash outflow that is expected to be incurred before the asset is ready for use or sale. For example, this is the case for a building under construction or for a development project that is not yet completed.

43   To avoid double-counting, estimates of future cash flows do not include:

(a)   cash inflows from assets that generate cash inflows that are largely independent of the cash inflows from the asset under review (for example, financial assets such as receivables); and

(b)   cash outflows that relate to obligations that have been recognised as liabilities (for example, payables, pensions or non-financial liabilities).

44   *Future cash flows shall be estimated for the asset in its current condition. Estimates of future cash flows shall not include estimated future cash inflows or outflows that are expected to arise from:*

(a)   a future restructuring for which a liability has not been incurred; or

(b)   improving or enhancing the asset's performance.

45   Because future cash flows are estimated for the asset in its current condition, value in use does not reflect:

(a)   future cash outflows or related cost savings (for example reductions in staff costs) or benefits that are expected to arise from a future restructuring for which a liability has not been incurred; or

(b)   future cash outflows that will improve or enhance the asset's performance or the related cash inflows that are expected to arise from such outflows.

46   ~~IAS 37~~ FRS 12 ~~*Provisions, Contingent Liabilities and Contingent Assets*~~ *Non-financial Liabilities* specifies when an entity recognises a liability for a cost associated with a restructuring.

47   When an entity incurs a liability for a cost associated with a restructuring, some assets are likely to be affected by this restructuring. Once the entity incurs a liability for a cost associated with the restructuring:

(a)   its estimates of future cash inflows and cash outflows for the purpose of determining value in use reflect the cost savings and other benefits from the restructuring (based on the most recent financial budgets/forecasts approved by management); and

(b)   its estimates of future cash outflows for the cost associated with the restructuring are reflected in the measurement of a non-financial liability in accordance with FRS 12 ~~IAS 37~~.

Illustrative Example 5 illustrates the effect of a future restructuring on a value in use calculation.

48   Until an entity incurs cash outflows that improve or enhance the asset's performance, estimates of future cash flows do not include the estimated future cash inflows that are expected to arise from the increase in economic benefits associated with the cash outflow (see Illustrative Example 6).

Estimates of future cash flows include future cash outflows necessary to maintain the   **49**
level of economic benefits expected to arise from the asset in its current condition.
When a cash-generating unit consists of assets with different estimated useful lives,
all of which are essential to the ongoing operation of the unit, the replacement of
assets with shorter lives is considered to be part of the day-to-day servicing of the
unit when estimating the future cash flows associated with the unit. Similarly, when a
single asset consists of components with different estimated useful lives, the replacement of components with shorter lives is considered to be part of the day-to-day
servicing of the asset when estimating the future cash flows generated by the asset.

Estimates of future cash flows shall not include: **50**

(a)   cash inflows or outflows from financing activities; or
(b)   income tax receipts or payments.

Estimated future cash flows reflect assumptions that are consistent with the way the   **51**
discount rate is determined. Otherwise, the effect of some assumptions will be
counted twice or ignored. Because the time value of money is considered by discounting the estimated future cash flows, these cash flows exclude cash inflows or
outflows from financing activities. Similarly, because the discount rate is determined
on a pre-tax basis, future cash flows are also estimated on a pre-tax basis.

The estimate of net cash flows to be received (or paid) for the disposal of an asset at the   **52**
end of its useful life shall be the amount that an entity expects to obtain from the
disposal of the asset in an arm's length transaction between knowledgeable, willing
parties, after deducting the estimated costs of disposal.

The estimate of net cash flows to be received (or paid) for the disposal of an asset at   **53**
the end of its useful life is determined in a similar way to an asset's fair value less
costs to sell, except that, in estimating those net cash flows:

(a)   an entity uses prices prevailing at the date of the estimate for similar assets that
have reached the end of their useful life and have operated under conditions
similar to those in which the asset will be used.
(b)   the entity adjusts those prices for the effect of both future price increases due to
general inflation and specific future price increases or decreases. However, if
estimates of future cash flows from the asset's continuing use and the discount
rate exclude the effect of general inflation, the entity also excludes this effect
from the estimate of net cash flows on disposal.

Foreign Currency Future Cash Flows

Future cash flows are estimated in the currency in which they will be generated and   **54**
then discounted using a discount rate appropriate for that currency. An entity
translates the present value using the spot exchange rate at the date of the value in
use calculation.

Discount Rate

The discount rate (rates) shall be a pre-tax rate (rates) that reflect(s) current market   **55**
assessments of:

(a)   the time value of money; and
(b)   the risks specific to the asset for which the future cash flow estimates have not
been adjusted.

56   A rate that reflects current market assessments of the time value of money and the risks specific to the asset is the return that investors would require if they were to choose an investment that would generate cash flows of amounts, timing and risk profile equivalent to those that the entity expects to derive from the asset. This rate is estimated from the rate implicit in current market transactions for similar assets or from the weighted average cost of capital of a listed entity that has a single asset (or a portfolio of assets) similar in terms of service potential and risks to the asset under review. However, the discount rate(s) used to measure an asset's value in use shall not reflect risks for which the future cash flow estimates have been adjusted. Otherwise, the effect of some assumptions will be double-counted.

57   When an asset-specific rate is not directly available from the market, an entity uses surrogates to estimate the discount rate. Appendix A provides additional guidance on estimating the discount rate in such circumstances.

RECOGNISING AND MEASURING AN IMPAIRMENT LOSS

58   Paragraphs 59-64 set out the requirements for recognising and measuring impairment losses for an individual asset other than goodwill. Recognising and measuring impairment losses for cash-generating units and goodwill are dealt with in paragraphs 65-108.

59   *If, and only if, the recoverable amount of an asset is less than its carrying amount, the carrying amount of the asset shall be reduced to its recoverable amount. That reduction is an impairment loss.*

60   *An impairment loss shall be recognised immediately in profit or loss, unless the asset is carried at revalued amount in accordance with another Standard (for example, in accordance with* the revaluation model in *FRS 15* Tangible Fixed Assets *IAS 16 Property, Plant and Equipment). Any impairment loss of a revalued asset shall be treated as a revaluation decrease in accordance with that other Standard.*

61   An impairment loss on a non-revalued asset is recognised in profit or loss. However, an impairment loss on a revalued asset is recognised directly against any revaluation surplus for the asset to the extent that the impairment loss does not exceed the amount in the revaluation surplus for that same asset.

62   *When the amount estimated for an impairment loss is greater than the carrying amount of the asset to which it relates, an entity shall recognise a liability if, and only if, that is required by another Standard.*

63   *After the recognition of an impairment loss, the depreciation (amortisation) charge for the asset shall be adjusted in future periods to allocate the asset's revised carrying amount, less its residual value (if any), on a systematic basis over its remaining useful life.*

64   If an impairment loss is recognised, any related deferred tax assets or liabilities are determined in accordance with FRS 19 *Deferred Tax* IAS 12 *Income Taxes* by comparing the revised carrying amount of the asset with its tax base (see Illustrative Example 3).

CASH-GENERATING UNITS AND GOODWILL

Paragraphs 66–108 set out the requirements for identifying the cash-generating unit **65** to which an asset belongs and determining the carrying amount of, and recognising impairment losses for, cash-generating units and goodwill.

Identifying the Cash-generating Unit to Which an Asset Belongs

If there is any indication that an asset may be impaired, recoverable amount shall be **66** *estimated for the individual asset. If it is not possible to estimate the recoverable amount of the individual asset, an entity shall determine the recoverable amount of the cash-generating unit to which the asset belongs (the asset's cash-generating unit).*

The recoverable amount of an individual asset cannot be determined if: **67**

(a)   the asset's value in use cannot be estimated to be close to its fair value less costs to sell (for example, when the future cash flows from continuing use of the asset cannot be estimated to be negligible); and

(b)   the asset does not generate cash inflows that are largely independent of those from other assets.

In such cases, value in use and, therefore, recoverable amount, can be determined only for the asset's cash-generating unit.

Example

A mining entity owns a private railway to support its mining activities. The private railway could be sold only for scrap value and it does not generate cash inflows that are largely independent of the cash inflows from the other assets of the mine.

It is not possible to estimate the recoverable amount of the private railway because its value in use cannot be determined and is probably different from scrap value. Therefore, the entity estimates the recoverable amount of the cash-generating unit to which the private railway belongs, ie the mine as a whole.

As defined in paragraph 6, an asset's cash-generating unit is the smallest group of **68** assets that includes the asset and generates cash inflows that are largely independent of the cash inflows from other assets or groups of assets. Identification of an asset's cash-generating unit involves judgement. If recoverable amount cannot be determined for an individual asset, an entity identifies the lowest aggregation of assets that generate largely independent cash inflows.

Example

A bus company provides services under contract with a municipality that requires minimum service on each of five separate routes. Assets devoted to each route and the cash flows from each route can be identified separately. One of the routes operates at a significant loss.

Because the entity does not have the option to curtail any one bus route, the lowest level of identifiable cash inflows that are largely independent of the cash inflows from other assets or groups of assets is the cash inflows generated by the five routes together. The cash-generating unit for each route is the bus company as a whole.

---

69   Cash inflows are inflows of cash and cash equivalents received from parties external to the entity. In identifying whether cash inflows from an asset (or group of assets) are largely independent of the cash inflows from other assets (or groups of assets), an entity considers various factors including how management monitors the entity's operations (such as by product lines, businesses, individual locations, districts or regional areas) or how management makes decisions about continuing or disposing of the entity's assets and operations. Illustrative Example 1 gives examples of identification of a cash-generating unit.

70   *If an active market exists for the output produced by an asset or group of assets, that asset or group of assets shall be identified as a cash-generating unit, even if some or all of the output is used internally. If the cash inflows generated by any asset or cash-generating unit are affected by internal transfer pricing, an entity shall use management's best estimate of future price(s) that could be achieved in arm's length transactions in estimating:*

   (a)   the future cash inflows used to determine the asset's or cash-generating unit's value in use; and

   (b)   the future cash outflows used to determine the value in use of any other assets or cash-generating units that are affected by the internal transfer pricing.

71   Even if part or all of the output produced by an asset or a group of assets is used by other units of the entity (for example, products at an intermediate stage of a production process), this asset or group of assets forms a separate cash-generating unit if the entity could sell the output on an active market. This is because the asset or group of assets could generate cash inflows that would be largely independent of the cash inflows from other assets or groups of assets. In using information based on financial budgets/forecasts that relates to such a cash-generating unit, or to any other asset or cash-generating unit affected by internal transfer pricing, an entity adjusts this information if internal transfer prices do not reflect management's best estimate of future prices that could be achieved in arm's length transactions.

72   *Cash-generating units shall be identified consistently from period to period for the same asset or types of assets, unless a change is justified.*

73   If an entity determines that an asset belongs to a cash-generating unit different from that in previous periods, or that the types of assets aggregated for the asset's cash-generating unit have changed, paragraph 130 requires disclosures about the cash-generating unit, if an impairment loss is recognised or reversed for the cash-generating unit.

Recoverable Amount and Carrying Amount of a Cash-generating Unit

74   The recoverable amount of a cash-generating unit is the higher of the cash-generating unit's fair value less costs to sell and its value in use. For the purpose of determining the recoverable amount of a cash-generating unit, any reference in paragraphs 19-57 to 'an asset' is read as a reference to 'a cash-generating unit'.

75   *The carrying amount of a cash-generating unit shall be determined on a basis consistent with the way the recoverable amount of the cash-generating unit is determined.*

76   The carrying amount of a cash-generating unit:

   (a)   includes the carrying amount of only those assets that can be attributed directly, or allocated on a reasonable and consistent basis, to the cash-generating unit and will generate the future cash inflows used in determining the cash-generating unit's value in use; and

(b)   does not include the carrying amount of any recognised liability, unless the recoverable amount of the cash-generating unit cannot be determined without consideration of this liability.

This is because fair value less costs to sell and value in use of a cash-generating unit are determined excluding cash flows that relate to assets that are not part of the cash-generating unit and liabilities that have been recognised (see paragraphs 28 and 43).

When assets are grouped for recoverability assessments, it is important to include in the cash-generating unit all assets that generate or are used to generate the relevant stream of cash inflows. Otherwise, the cash-generating unit may appear to be fully recoverable when in fact an impairment loss has occurred. In some cases, although some assets contribute to the estimated future cash flows of a cash-generating unit, they cannot be allocated to the cash-generating unit on a reasonable and consistent basis. This might be the case for goodwill or corporate assets such as head office assets. Paragraphs 80-103 explain how to deal with these assets in testing a cash-generating unit for impairment.   **77**

It may be necessary to consider some recognised liabilities to determine the recoverable amount of a cash-generating unit. This may occur if the disposal of a cash-generating unit would require the buyer to assume the liability. In this case, the fair value less costs to sell (or the estimated cash flow from ultimate disposal) of the cash-generating unit is the estimated selling price for the assets of the cash-generating unit and the liability together, less the costs of disposal. To perform a meaningful comparison between the carrying amount of the cash-generating unit and its recoverable amount, the carrying amount of the liability is deducted in determining both the cash-generating unit's value in use and its carrying amount.   **78**

Example

A company operates a mine in a country in which legislation requires that the owner must restore the site on completion of its mining operations. The cost of restoration includes the replacement of the overburden, which must be removed before mining operations commence. A non-financial liability for the obligation to replace the overburden was recognised as soon as the overburden was removed. The amount of the liability initially recognised was included as part of the cost of the mine and is being depreciated over the mine's useful life. The carrying amount of the liability for restoration costs is CU500.*

The entity is testing the mine for impairment. The cash-generating unit for the mine is the mine as a whole. The entity has received various offers to buy the mine at a price of around CU800. This price reflects the fact that the buyer will assume the obligation to restore the overburden. Disposal costs for the mine are negligible. The value in use of the mine is approximately CU1,200, excluding restoration costs. The carrying amount of the mine is CU1,000.

The cash-generating unit's fair value less costs to sell is CU800. This amount considers restoration costs for which a liability has already been recognised. As a consequence, the value in use for the cash-generating unit is determined after consideration of the restoration costs and is estimated to be CU700 (CU1,200 less CU500). The carrying amount of the cash-generating unit is CU500, which

---

*In this Standard, monetary amounts are denominated in 'currency units' (CU).

> *is the carrying amount of the mine (CU1,000) less the carrying amount of the liability for restoration costs (CU500). Therefore, the recoverable amount of the cash-generating unit exceeds its carrying amount.*

79   For practical reasons, the recoverable amount of a cash-generating unit is sometimes determined after consideration of assets that are not part of the cash-generating unit (for example, receivables or other financial assets) or liabilities that have been recognised (for example, payables, pensions and liabilities). In such cases, the carrying amount of the cash-generating unit is increased by the carrying amount of those assets and decreased by the carrying amount of those liabilities.

Goodwill

Allocating Goodwill to Cash-generating Units

80   *For the purpose of impairment testing, goodwill acquired in a business combination shall, from the acquisition date, be allocated to each of the acquirer's cash-generating units, or groups of cash-generating units, that are expected to benefit from the synergies of the combination, irrespective of whether other assets or liabilities of the acquiree are assigned to those units or groups of units. Each unit or group of units to which the goodwill is so allocated shall:*

(a)   represent the lowest level within the entity at which the goodwill is monitored for internal management purposes; and

(b)   not be larger than a segment based on either the entity's primary or the entity's secondary reporting format determined in accordance with ~~IAS 14   Segment Reporting~~ paragraph 6B of this Standard.

81   Goodwill arising in a business combination represents assets that provide future economic benefits but are not capable of being individually identified and separately recognised. Goodwill does not generate cash flows independently of other assets or groups of assets, and often contributes to the cash flows of multiple cash-generating units. Goodwill sometimes cannot be allocated on a non-arbitrary basis to individual cash-generating units, but only to groups of cash-generating units. As a result, the lowest level within the entity at which the goodwill is monitored for internal management purposes sometimes comprises a number of cash-generating units to which the goodwill relates, but to which it cannot be allocated. References in paragraphs 83-99 to a cash-generating unit to which goodwill is allocated should be read as references also to a group of cash-generating units to which goodwill is allocated.

82   Applying the requirements in paragraph 80 results in goodwill being tested for impairment at a level that reflects the way an entity manages its operations and with which the goodwill would naturally be associated. Therefore, the development of additional reporting systems is typically not necessary.

83   A cash-generating unit to which goodwill is allocated for the purpose of impairment testing may not coincide with the level at which goodwill is allocated in accordance with FRS 23 ~~IAS 21~~ *The Effects of Changes in Foreign Exchange Rates* for the purpose of measuring foreign currency gains and losses. For example, if an entity is required by FRS 23 ~~IAS 21~~ to allocate goodwill to relatively low levels for the purpose of measuring foreign currency gains and losses, it is not required to test the goodwill for impairment at that same level unless it also monitors the goodwill at that level for internal management purposes.

If the initial allocation of goodwill acquired in a business combination cannot be **84** *completed before the end of the annual period in which the business combination is effected, that initial allocation shall be completed before the end of the first annual period beginning after the acquisition date.*

In accordance with ~~IFRS 3~~ [draft] FRS ● *Business Combinations*, if the initial **85** accounting for a business combination can be determined only provisionally by the end of the period in which the combination is effected, the acquirer:

(a) accounts for the combination using those provisional values; and
(b) recognises any adjustments to those provisional values as a result of completing the initial accounting within twelve months of the acquisition date.

In such circumstances, it might also not be possible to complete the initial allocation of the goodwill acquired in the combination before the end of the annual period in which the combination is effected. When this is the case, the entity discloses the information required by paragraph 133.

If goodwill has been allocated to a cash-generating unit and the entity disposes of an **86** *operation within that unit, the goodwill associated with the operation disposed of shall be:*

(a) included in the carrying amount of the operation when determining the gain or loss on disposal; and
(b) measured on the basis of the relative values of the operation disposed of and the portion of the cash-generating unit retained, unless the entity can demonstrate that some other method better reflects the goodwill associated with the operation disposed of.

Example

An entity sells for CU100 an operation that was part of a cash-generating unit to which goodwill has been allocated. The goodwill allocated to the unit cannot be identified or associated with an asset group at a level lower than that unit, except arbitrarily. The recoverable amount of the portion of the cash-generating unit retained is CU300.

Because the goodwill allocated to the cash-generating unit cannot be non-arbitrarily identified or associated with an asset group at a level lower than that unit, the goodwill associated with the operation disposed of is measured on the basis of the relative values of the operation disposed of and the portion of the unit retained. Therefore, 25 per cent of the goodwill allocated to the cash-generating unit is included in the carrying amount of the operation that is sold.

If an entity reorganises its reporting structure in a way that changes the composition of **87** *one or more cash-generating units to which goodwill has been allocated, the goodwill shall be reallocated to the units affected. This reallocation shall be performed using a relative value approach similar to that used when an entity disposes of an operation within a cash-generating unit, unless the entity can demonstrate that some other method better reflects the goodwill associated with the reorganised units.*

> **Example**
>
> Goodwill had previously been allocated to cash-generating unit A. The goodwill allocated to A cannot be identified or associated with an asset group at a level lower than A, except arbitrarily. A is to be divided and integrated into three other cash-generating units, B, C and D.
>
> *Because the goodwill allocated to A cannot be non-arbitrarily identified or associated with an asset group at a level lower than A, it is reallocated to units B, C and D on the basis of the relative values of the three portions of A before those portions are integrated with B, C and D.*

Testing Cash-generating Units with Goodwill for Impairment

88   *When, as described in paragraph 81, goodwill relates to a cash-generating unit but has not been allocated to that unit, the unit shall be tested for impairment, whenever there is an indication that the unit may be impaired, by comparing the unit's carrying amount, excluding any goodwill, with its recoverable amount. Any impairment loss shall be recognised in accordance with paragraph 104.*

89   If a cash-generating unit described in paragraph 88 includes in its carrying amount an intangible asset that has an indefinite useful life or is not yet available for use and that asset can be tested for impairment only as part of the cash-generating unit, paragraph 10 requires the unit also to be tested for impairment annually.

90   *A cash-generating unit to which goodwill has been allocated shall be tested for impairment annually, and whenever there is an indication that the unit may be impaired, by comparing the carrying amount of the unit, including the goodwill, with the recoverable amount of the unit. If the recoverable amount of the unit exceeds the carrying amount of the unit, the unit and the goodwill allocated to that unit shall be regarded as not impaired. If the carrying amount of the unit exceeds the recoverable amount of the unit, the entity shall recognise the impairment loss in accordance with paragraph 104.*

91   Deleted

92   Deleted

93   Deleted

94   Deleted

95   Deleted

Timing of Impairment Tests

96   *The annual impairment test for a cash-generating unit to which goodwill has been allocated may be performed at any time during an annual period, provided the test is performed at the same time every year. Different cash-generating units may be tested for impairment at different times. However, if some or all of the goodwill allocated to a cash-generating unit was acquired in a business combination during the current annual period, that unit shall be tested for impairment before the end of the current annual period.*

If the assets constituting the cash-generating unit to which goodwill has been allocated   **97**
are tested for impairment at the same time as the unit containing the goodwill, they
shall be tested for impairment before the unit containing the goodwill. Similarly, if the
cash-generating units constituting a group of cash-generating units to which goodwill
has been allocated are tested for impairment at the same time as the group of units
containing the goodwill, the individual units shall be tested for impairment before the
group of units containing the goodwill.

At the time of impairment testing a cash-generating unit to which goodwill has been   **98**
allocated, there may be an indication of an impairment of an asset within the unit
containing the goodwill. In such circumstances, the entity tests the asset for
impairment first, and recognises any impairment loss for that asset before testing for
impairment the cash-generating unit containing the goodwill. Similarly, there may be
an indication of an impairment of a cash-generating unit within a group of units
containing the goodwill. In such circumstances, the entity tests the cash-generating
unit for impairment first, and recognises any impairment loss for that unit, before
testing for impairment the group of units to which the goodwill is allocated.

The most recent detailed calculation made in a preceding period of the recoverable   **99**
amount of a cash-generating unit to which goodwill has been allocated may be used in
the impairment test of that unit in the current period provided all of the following
criteria are met:

(a)   the assets and liabilities making up the unit have not changed significantly since
*   the most recent recoverable amount calculation;*
(b)   the most recent recoverable amount calculation resulted in an amount that
*   exceeded the carrying amount of the unit by a substantial margin; and*
(c)   based on an analysis of events that have occurred and circumstances that have
*   changed since the most recent recoverable amount calculation, the likelihood that*
*   a current recoverable amount determination would be less than the current car-*
*   rying amount of the unit is remote.*

Corporate Assets

Corporate assets include group or divisional assets such as the building of a head-   **100**
quarters or a division of the entity, EDP equipment or a research centre. The
structure of an entity determines whether an asset meets this Standard's definition of
corporate assets for a particular cash-generating unit. The distinctive characteristics
of corporate assets are that they do not generate cash inflows independently of other
assets or groups of assets and their carrying amount cannot be fully attributed to the
cash-generating unit under review.

Because corporate assets do not generate separate cash inflows, the recoverable   **101**
amount of an individual corporate asset cannot be determined unless management
has decided to dispose of the asset. As a consequence, if there is an indication that a
corporate asset may be impaired, recoverable amount is determined for the cash-
generating unit or group of cash-generating units to which the corporate asset
belongs, and is compared with the carrying amount of this cash-generating unit or
group of cash-generating units. Any impairment loss is recognised in accordance
with paragraph 104.

In testing a cash-generating unit for impairment, an entity shall identify all the cor-   **102**
porate assets that relate to the cash-generating unit under review. If a portion of the
carrying amount of a corporate asset:

(a) *can be allocated on a reasonable and consistent basis to that unit, the entity shall compare the carrying amount of the unit, including the portion of the carrying amount of the corporate asset allocated to the unit, with its recoverable amount. Any impairment loss shall be recognised in accordance with paragraph 104.*

(b) *cannot be allocated on a reasonable and consistent basis to that unit, the entity shall:*

   (i) *compare the carrying amount of the unit, excluding the corporate asset, with its recoverable amount and recognise any impairment loss in accordance with paragraph 104;*

   (ii) *identify the smallest group of cash-generating units that includes the cash-generating unit under review and to which a portion of the carrying amount of the corporate asset can be allocated on a reasonable and consistent basis; and*

   (iii) *compare the carrying amount of that group of cash-generating units, including the portion of the carrying amount of the corporate asset allocated to that group of units, with the recoverable amount of the group of units. Any impairment loss shall be recognised in accordance with paragraph 104.*

103   Illustrative Example 8 illustrates the application of these requirements to corporate assets.

Impairment Loss for a Cash-generating Unit

104   *An impairment loss shall be recognised for a cash-generating unit (the smallest group of cash-generating units to which goodwill or a corporate asset has been allocated) if, and only if, the recoverable amount of the unit (group of units) is less than the carrying amount of the unit (group of units). The impairment loss shall be allocated to reduce the carrying amount of the assets of the unit (group of units) in the following order:*

   (a) *first, to reduce the carrying amount of any goodwill allocated to the cash-generating unit (group of units); and*

   (b) *then, to the other assets of the unit (group of units) pro rata on the basis of the carrying amount of each asset in the unit (group of units).*

   These reductions in carrying amounts shall be treated as impairment losses on individual assets and recognised in accordance with paragraph 60.

105   *In allocating an impairment loss in accordance with paragraph 104, an entity shall not reduce the carrying amount of an asset below the highest of:*

   (a) *its fair value less costs to sell (if determinable);*

   (b) *its value in use (if determinable); and*

   (c) *zero.*

   The amount of the impairment loss that would otherwise have been allocated to the asset shall be allocated pro rata to the other assets of the unit (group of units).

106   If it is not practicable to estimate the recoverable amount of each individual asset of a cash-generating unit, this Standard requires an arbitrary allocation of an impairment loss between the assets of that unit, other than goodwill, because all assets of a cash-generating unit work together.

107   If the recoverable amount of an individual asset cannot be determined (see paragraph 67):

(a)   an impairment loss is recognised for the asset if its carrying amount is greater than the higher of its fair value less costs to sell and the results of the allocation procedures described in paragraphs 104 and 105; and

(b)   no impairment loss is recognised for the asset if the related cash-generating unit is not impaired. This applies even if the asset's fair value less costs to sell is less than its carrying amount.

Example

A machine has suffered physical damage but is still working, although not as well as before it was damaged. The machine's fair value less costs to sell is less than its carrying amount. The machine does not generate independent cash inflows. The smallest identifiable group of assets that includes the machine and generates cash inflows that are largely independent of the cash inflows from other assets is the production line to which the machine belongs. The recoverable amount of the production line shows that the production line taken as a whole is not impaired.

Assumption 1: budgets/forecasts approved by management reflect no commitment of management to replace the machine.

The recoverable amount of the machine alone cannot be estimated because the machine's value in use:

(a)   may differ from its fair value less costs to sell; and

(b)   can be determined only for the cash-generating unit to which the machine belongs (the production line).

The production line is not impaired. Therefore, no impairment loss is recognised for the machine. Nevertheless, the entity may need to reassess the depreciation period or the depreciation method for the machine. Perhaps a shorter depreciation period or a faster depreciation method is required to reflect the expected remaining useful life of the machine or the pattern in which economic benefits are expected to be consumed by the entity.

Assumption 2: budgets/forecasts approved by management reflect a commitment of management to replace the machine and sell it in the near future. Cash flows from continuing use of the machine until its disposal are estimated to be negligible.

The machine's value in use can be estimated to be close to its fair value less costs to sell. Therefore, the recoverable amount of the machine can be determined and no consideration is given to the cash-generating unit to which the machine belongs (ie the production line). Because the machine's fair value less costs to sell is less than its carrying amount, an impairment loss is recognised for the machine.

After the requirements in paragraphs 104 and 105 have been applied, a liability shall be recognised for any remaining amount of an impairment loss for a cash-generating unit if, and only if, that is required by another Standard.   108

REVERSING AN IMPAIRMENT LOSS

109   Paragraphs 110-116 set out the requirements for reversing an impairment loss recognised for an asset or a cash-generating unit in prior periods. These requirements use the term 'an asset' but apply equally to an individual asset or a cash-generating unit. Additional requirements for an individual asset are set out in paragraphs 117-121, for a cash-generating unit in paragraphs 122 and 123 and for goodwill in paragraphs 124 and 125.

110   *An entity shall assess at each reporting date whether there is any indication that an impairment loss recognised in prior periods for an asset other than goodwill may no longer exist or may have decreased. If any such indication exists, the entity shall estimate the recoverable amount of that asset.*

111   *In assessing whether there is any indication that an impairment loss recognised in prior periods for an asset other than goodwill may no longer exist or may have decreased, an entity shall consider, as a minimum, the following indications:*

External sources of information

   (a)   the asset's market value has increased significantly during the period.
   (b)   significant changes with a favourable effect on the entity have taken place during the period, or will take place in the near future, in the technological, market, economic or legal environment in which the entity operates or in the market to which the asset is dedicated.
   (c)   market interest rates or other market rates of return on investments have decreased during the period, and those decreases are likely to affect the discount rate used in calculating the asset's value in use and increase the asset's recoverable amount materially.

Internal sources of information

   (d)   significant changes with a favourable effect on the entity have taken place during the period, or are expected to take place in the near future, in the extent to which, or manner in which, the asset is used or is expected to be used. These changes include costs incurred during the period to improve or enhance the asset's performance or restructure the operation to which the asset belongs.
   (e)   evidence is available from internal reporting that indicates that the economic performance of the asset is, or will be, better than expected.

112   Indications of a potential decrease in an impairment loss in paragraph 111 mainly mirror the indications of a potential impairment loss in paragraph 12.

113   If there is an indication that an impairment loss recognised for an asset other than goodwill may no longer exist or may have decreased, this may indicate that the remaining useful life, the depreciation (amortisation) method or the residual value may need to be reviewed and adjusted in accordance with the Standard applicable to the asset, even if no impairment loss is reversed for the asset.

114   *An impairment loss recognised in prior periods for an asset other than goodwill shall be reversed if, and only if, there has been a change in the estimates used to determine the asset's recoverable amount since the last impairment loss was recognised. If this is the case, the carrying amount of the asset shall, except as described in paragraph 117, be increased to its recoverable amount. That increase is a reversal of an impairment loss.*

115   A reversal of an impairment loss reflects an increase in the estimated service potential of an asset, either from use or from sale, since the date when an entity last recognised

an impairment loss for that asset. Paragraph 130 requires an entity to identify the change in estimates that causes the increase in estimated service potential. Examples of changes in estimates include:

(a)   a change in the basis for recoverable amount (ie whether recoverable amount is based on fair value less costs to sell or value in use);

(b)   if recoverable amount was based on value in use, a change in the amount or timing of estimated future cash flows or in the discount rate; or

(c)   if recoverable amount was based on fair value less costs to sell, a change in estimate of the components of fair value less costs to sell.

An asset's value in use may become greater than the asset's carrying amount simply   **116**
because the present value of future cash inflows increases as they become closer. However, the service potential of the asset has not increased. Therefore, an impairment loss is not reversed just because of the passage of time (sometimes called the 'unwinding' of the discount), even if the recoverable amount of the asset becomes higher than its carrying amount.

Reversing an Impairment Loss for an Individual Asset

The increased carrying amount of an asset other than goodwill attributable to a reversal   **117**
of an impairment loss shall not exceed the carrying amount that would have been determined (net of amortisation or depreciation) had no impairment loss been recognised for the asset in prior years.

Any increase in the carrying amount of an asset other than goodwill above the   **118**
carrying amount that would have been determined (net of amortisation or depreciation) had no impairment loss been recognised for the asset in prior years is a revaluation. In accounting for such a revaluation, an entity applies the Standard applicable to the asset.

A reversal of an impairment loss for an asset other than goodwill shall be recognised   **119**
immediately in profit or loss, unless the asset is carried at revalued amount in accordance with another Standard (for example, the revaluation model in FRS 15 **Tangible**
Fixed Assets. *IAS 16* **Property, Plant and Equipment)***. Any reversal of an impairment loss of a revalued asset shall be treated as a revaluation increase in accordance with that other Standard.*

A reversal of an impairment loss on a revalued asset is credited directly to the   **120**
statement of total recognised gains and losses. equity under the heading revaluation surplus. However, to the extent that an impairment loss on the same revalued asset was previously recognised in profit or loss, a reversal of that impairment loss is also recognised in profit or loss.

After a reversal of an impairment loss is recognised, the depreciation (amortisation)   **121**
charge for the asset shall be adjusted in future periods to allocate the asset's revised carrying amount, less its residual value (if any), on a systematic basis over its remaining useful life.

Reversing an Impairment Loss for a Cash-generating Unit

A reversal of an impairment loss for a cash-generating unit shall be allocated to the   **122**
assets of the unit, except for goodwill, pro rata with the carrying amounts of those assets. These increases in carrying amounts shall be treated as reversals of impairment losses for individual assets and recognised in accordance with paragraph 119.

123   *In allocating a reversal of an impairment loss for a cash-generating unit in accordance with paragraph 122, the carrying amount of an asset shall not be increased above the lower of:*

    (a)   its recoverable amount (if determinable); and

    (b)   the carrying amount that would have been determined (net of amortisation or depreciation) had no impairment loss been recognised for the asset in prior periods.

The amount of the reversal of the impairment loss that would otherwise have been allocated to the asset shall be allocated pro rata to the other assets of the unit, except for goodwill.

Reversing an Impairment Loss for Goodwill

124   *An impairment loss recognised for goodwill shall not be reversed in a subsequent period.*

125   [Draft] FRS ● IAS 38 *Intangible Assets* prohibits the recognition of internally generated goodwill. Any increase in the recoverable amount of goodwill in the periods following the recognition of an impairment loss for that goodwill is likely to be an increase in internally generated goodwill, rather than a reversal of the impairment loss recognised for the acquired goodwill.

DISCLOSURE

126   *An entity shall disclose the following for each class of assets:*

    (a)   the amount of impairment losses recognised in profit or loss during the period and the line item(s) of the income statement in which those impairment losses are included.

    (b)   the amount of reversals of impairment losses recognised in profit or loss during the period and the line item(s) of the income statement in which those impairment losses are reversed.

    (c)   the amount of impairment losses on revalued assets recognised in the statement of total recognised gains and losses directly in equity during the period.

    (d)   the amount of reversals of impairment losses on revalued assets recognised in the statement of total recognised gains and losses directly in equity during the period.

127   A class of assets is a grouping of assets of similar nature and use in an entity's operations.

128   The information required in paragraph 126 may be presented with other information disclosed for the class of assets. For example, this information may be included in a reconciliation of the carrying amount of property, plant and equipment, at the beginning and end of the period, as required by FRS 15 *Tangible Fixed Assets* IAS 16 *Property, Plant and Equipment*.

129   An entity that reports segment information in accordance with IAS 14 Segment Reporting shall disclose the following for each reportable segment based on an entity's primary reporting format:

    (a)   the amount of impairment losses recognised in profit or loss and directly in equity during the period.

    (b)   the amount of reversals of impairment losses recognised in profit or loss and directly in equity during the period.

An entity shall disclose the following for each material impairment loss recognised or **130** *reversed during the period for an individual asset, including goodwill, or a cash-generating unit:*

(a)   the events and circumstances that led to the recognition or reversal of the impairment loss.

(b)   the amount of the impairment loss recognised or reversed.

(c)   for an individual asset:

(i)   the nature of the asset

(ii)   if the entity reports segment information in accordance with IAS 14, the reportable segment to which the asset belongs, based on the entity's primary reporting format.

(d)   for a cash-generating unit:

(i)   a description of the cash-generating unit (such as whether it is a product line, a plant, a business operation a geographical area or a reportable segment as defined in this Standard *IAS 14);*

(ii)   the amount of the impairment loss recognised or reversed by class of assets; and, if the entity reports segment information in accordance with IAS 14, by reportable segment based on the entity's primary reporting format; and

(iii)   if the aggregation of assets for identifying the cash-generating unit has changed since the previous estimate of the cash-generating unit's recoverable amount (if any), a description of the current and former way of aggregating assets and the reasons for changing the way the cash-generating unit is identified.

(e)   whether the recoverable amount of the asset (cash-generating unit) is its fair value less costs to sell or its value in use.

(f)   if recoverable amount is fair value less costs to sell, the basis used to determine fair value less costs to sell (such as whether fair value was determined by reference to an active market).

(g)   if recoverable amount is value in use, the discount rate(s) used in the current estimate and previous estimate (if any) of value in use.

An entity shall disclose the following information for the aggregate impairment losses **131** *and the aggregate reversals of impairment losses recognised during the period for which no information is disclosed in accordance with paragraph 130:*

(a)   the main classes of assets affected by impairment losses and the main classes of assets affected by reversals of impairment losses.

(b)   the main events and circumstances that led to the recognition of these impairment losses and reversals of impairment losses.

An entity is encouraged to disclose assumptions used to determine the recoverable   **132** amount of assets (cash-generating units) during the period. However, paragraph 134 requires an entity to disclose information about the estimates used to measure the recoverable amount of a cash-generating unit when goodwill or an intangible asset with an indefinite useful life is included in the carrying amount of that unit.

If, in accordance with paragraph 84, any portion of the goodwill acquired in a business **133** *combination during the period has not been allocated to a cash-generating unit (group of units) at the reporting date, the amount of the unallocated goodwill shall be disclosed together with the reasons why that amount remains unallocated.*

Estimates used to Measure Recoverable Amounts of Cash-generating Units Containing Goodwill or Intangible Assets with Indefinite Useful Lives

134   *An entity shall disclose the information required by (a)-(f) for each cash-generating unit (group of units) for which the carrying amount of goodwill or intangible assets with indefinite useful lives allocated to that unit (group of units) is significant in comparison with the entity's total carrying amount of goodwill or intangible assets with indefinite useful lives:*

   (a)   the carrying amount of goodwill allocated to the unit (group of units).

   (b)   the carrying amount of intangible assets with indefinite useful lives allocated to the unit (group of units).

   (c)   the basis on which the unit's (group of units') recoverable amount has been determined (ie value in use or fair value less costs to sell).

   (d)   if the unit's (group of units') recoverable amount is based on value in use:

   (i)   a description of each key assumption on which management has based its cash flow projections for the period covered by the most recent budgets/ forecasts. Key assumptions are those to which the unit's (group of units') recoverable amount is most sensitive.

   (ii)   ~~a description of management's approach to determining the value(s) assigned to each key assumption, whether those value(s) reflect past experience or, if appropriate, are consistent with external sources of information, and, if not, how and why they differ from past experience or external sources of information.~~

   (iii)   the period over which management has projected cash flows based on financial budgets/forecasts approved by management and, when a period greater than five years is used for a cash-generating unit (group of units), an explanation of why that longer period is justified.

   (iv)   the growth rate used to extrapolate cash flow projections beyond the period covered by the most recent budgets/forecasts, and the justification for using any growth rate that exceeds the long-term average growth rate for the products, industries, or country or countries in which the entity operates, or for the market to which the unit (group of units) is dedicated.

   (v)   the discount rate(s) applied to the cash flow projections.

   (e)   if the unit's (group of units') recoverable amount is based on fair value less costs to sell, the methodology used to determine fair value less costs to sell. If fair value less costs to sell is not determined using an observable market price for the unit (group of units), the following information shall also be disclosed:

   (i)   a description of each key assumption on which management has based its determination of fair value less costs to sell. Key assumptions are those to which the unit's (group of units') recoverable amount is most sensitive.

   (ii)   ~~a description of management's approach to determining the value(s) assigned to each key assumption, whether those value(s) reflect past experience or, if appropriate, are consistent with external sources of information, and, if not, how and why they differ from past experience or external sources of information.~~

   (f)   if a reasonably possible change in a key assumption on which management has based its determination of the unit's (group of units') recoverable amount would cause the unit's (group of units') carrying amount to exceed its recoverable amount:

   (i)   the amount by which the unit's (group of units') recoverable amount exceeds its carrying amount.

   (ii)   the value assigned to the key assumption.

(iii)   the amount by which the value assigned to the key assumption must change, after incorporating any consequential effects of that change on the other variables used to measure recoverable amount, in order for the unit's (group of units') recoverable amount to be equal to its carrying amount.

If some or all of the carrying amount of goodwill or intangible assets with indefinite **135** useful lives is allocated across multiple cash-generating units (groups of units), and the amount so allocated to each unit (group of units) is not significant in comparison with the entity's total carrying amount of goodwill or intangible assets with indefinite useful lives, that fact shall be disclosed, together with the aggregate carrying amount of goodwill or intangible assets with indefinite useful lives allocated to those units (groups of units). In addition, if the recoverable amounts of any of those units (groups of units) are based on the same key assumption(s) and the aggregate carrying amount of goodwill or intangible assets with indefinite useful lives allocated to them is significant in comparison with the entity's total carrying amount of goodwill or intangible assets with indefinite useful lives, an entity shall disclose that fact, together with:

(a)   the aggregate carrying amount of goodwill allocated to those units (groups of units).

(b)   the aggregate carrying amount of intangible assets with indefinite useful lives allocated to those units (groups of units).

(c)   a description of the key assumption(s).

(d)   ~~a description of management's approach to determining the value(s) assigned to the key assumption(s), whether those value(s) reflect past experience or, if appropriate, are consistent with external sources of information, and, if not, how and why they differ from past experience or external sources of information.~~

(e)   if a reasonably possible change in the key assumption(s) would cause the aggregate of the units' (groups of units') carrying amounts to exceed the aggregate of their recoverable amounts:

(i)   the amount by which the aggregate of the units' (groups of units') recoverable amounts exceeds the aggregate of their carrying amounts.

(ii)   the value(s) assigned to the key assumption(s).

(iii)   the amount by which the value(s) assigned to the key assumption(s) must change, after incorporating any consequential effects of the change on the other variables used to measure recoverable amount, in order for the aggregate of the units' (groups of units') recoverable amounts to be equal to the aggregate of their carrying amounts.

The most recent detailed calculation made in a preceding period of the recoverable **136** amount of a cash-generating unit (group of units) may, in accordance with paragraph 24 or 99, be carried forward and used in the impairment test for that unit (group of units) in the current period provided specified criteria are met. When this is the case, the information for that unit (group of units) that is incorporated into the disclosures required by paragraphs 134 and 135 relate to the carried forward calculation of recoverable amount.

Illustrative Example 9 illustrates the disclosures required by paragraphs 134 and 135.   **137**

TRANSITIONAL PROVISIONS AND EFFECTIVE DATE

Deleted   **138**

If an entity elects in accordance with paragraph 82 of [draft] FRS ● **Business**   **138A**
Combinations *to apply [draft] FRS* ● **Business Combinations** *from any date before the*

effective dates set out in paragraph 82 of [draft] FRS● Business Combinations, it also shall apply this Standard prospectively from that same date.

139   *An entity shall apply this Standard:*

   (a)   to goodwill and intangible assets acquired in business combinations for which the agreement date is on or after 1 January 2007 31 March 2004; and

   (b)   to all other assets prospectively from the beginning of the first annual period beginning on or after 1 January 2007 31 March 2004.

   The agreement date for a business combination is the date that a substantive agreement between the combining parties is reached and, in the case of publicly listed entities, announced to the public. In the case of a hostile takeover, the earliest date that a substantive agreement between the combining parties is reached is the date that a sufficient number of the acquiree's owners have accepted the acquirer's offer for the acquirer to obtain control of the acquiree.

140   *Entities to which paragraph 139 applies are encouraged to apply the requirements of this Standard before the effective dates specified in paragraph 139. However, if an entity applies this Standard before those effective dates, it also shall apply [draft] FRS ● Business Combinations including [draft] FRS 2(amended)* Accounting for Subsidiary Undertakings, *IFRS 3 and [draft] FRS ● IAS 38* Intangible Assets *(as revised in 2004), and [draft] FRS 12(revised)* Non-financial Liabilities *(formerly known as Provisions Contingent Liabilities and Contingent Assets) at the same time.*

WITHDRAWAL OF FRS 11 IAS 36 (ISSUED 1998)

141   This Standard supersedes FRS 11 *Impairment of Fixed Assets and Goodwill.* IAS 36 *Impairment of Assets* (issued in 1998).

Appendix A
Present Value Techniques to Measure Value in Use

This appendix is an integral part of the Standard. It provides guidance on the use of present value techniques in measuring value in use. Although the guidance uses the term 'asset', it equally applies to a group of assets forming a cash-generating unit.

THE COMPONENTS OF A PRESENT VALUE MEASUREMENT

The following elements together capture the economic differences between assets: **A1**

(a) an estimate of the future cash flow, or in more complex cases, series of future cash flows the entity expects to derive from the asset;

(b) expectations about possible variations in the amount or timing of those cash flows;

(c) the time value of money, represented by the current market risk-free rate of interest;

(d) the price for bearing the uncertainty inherent in the asset; and

(e) other, sometimes unidentifiable, factors (such as illiquidity) that market participants would reflect in pricing the future cash flows the entity expects to derive from the asset.

This appendix contrasts two approaches to computing present value, either of which **A2** may be used to estimate the value in use of an asset, depending on the circumstances. Under the 'traditional' approach, adjustments for factors (b)-(e) described in paragraph A1 are embedded in the discount rate. Under the 'expected cash flow' approach, factors (b), (d) and (e) cause adjustments in arriving at risk-adjusted expected cash flows. Whichever approach an entity adopts to reflect expectations about possible variations in the amount or timing of future cash flows, the result should be to reflect the expected present value of the future cash flows, ie the weighted average of all possible outcomes.

GENERAL PRINCIPLES

The techniques used to estimate future cash flows and interest rates will vary from **A3** one situation to another depending on the circumstances surrounding the asset in question. However, the following general principles govern any application of present value techniques in measuring assets:

(a) interest rates used to discount cash flows should reflect assumptions that are consistent with those inherent in the estimated cash flows. Otherwise, the effect of some assumptions will be double-counted or ignored. For example, a discount rate of 12 per cent might be applied to contractual cash flows of a loan receivable. That rate reflects expectations about future defaults from loans with particular characteristics. That same 12 per cent rate should not be used to discount expected cash flows because those cash flows already reflect assumptions about future defaults.

(b) estimated cash flows and discount rates should be free from both bias and factors unrelated to the asset in question. For example, deliberately understating estimated net cash flows to enhance the apparent future profitability of an asset introduces a bias into the measurement.

(c) estimated cash flows or discount rates should reflect the range of possible outcomes rather than a single most likely, minimum or maximum possible amount.

TRADITIONAL AND EXPECTED CASH FLOW APPROACHES TO PRESENT VALUE

Traditional Approach

A4   Accounting applications of present value have traditionally used a single set of estimated cash flows and a single discount rate, often described as 'the rate commensurate with the risk'. In effect, the traditional approach assumes that a single discount rate convention can incorporate all the expectations about the future cash flows and the appropriate risk premium. Therefore, the traditional approach places most of the emphasis on selection of the discount rate.

A5   In some circumstances, such as those in which comparable assets can be observed in the marketplace, a traditional approach is relatively easy to apply. For assets with contractual cash flows, it is consistent with the manner in which marketplace participants describe assets, as in 'a 12 per cent bond'.

A6   However, the traditional approach may not appropriately address some complex measurement problems, such as the measurement of non-financial assets for which no market for the item or a comparable item exists. A proper search for 'the rate commensurate with the risk' requires analysis of at least two items—an asset that exists in the marketplace and has an observed interest rate and the asset being measured. The appropriate discount rate for the cash flows being measured must be inferred from the observable rate of interest in that other asset. To draw that inference, the characteristics of the other asset's cash flows must be similar to those of the asset being measured. Therefore, the measurer must do the following:

(a)   identify the set of cash flows that will be discounted;
(b)   identify another asset in the marketplace that appears to have similar cash flow characteristics;
(c)   compare the cash flow sets from the two items to ensure that they are similar (for example, are both sets contractual cash flows, or is one contractual and the other an estimated cash flow?);
(d)   evaluate whether there is an element in one item that is not present in the other (for example, is one less liquid than the other?); and
(e)   evaluate whether both sets of cash flows are likely to behave (ie vary) in a similar fashion in changing economic conditions.

Expected Cash Flow Approach

A7   The expected cash flow approach is, in some situations, a more effective measurement tool than the traditional approach. In developing a measurement, the expected cash flow approach uses all expectations about possible cash flows instead of the single most likely cash flow. For example, a cash flow might be CU100, CU200 or CU300 with probabilities of 10 per cent, 60 per cent and 30 per cent, respectively. The expected cash flow is CU220. The expected cash flow approach thus differs from the traditional approach by focusing on direct analysis of the cash flows in question and on more explicit statements of the assumptions used in the measurement.

A8   The expected cash flow approach also allows use of present value techniques when the timing of cash flows is uncertain. For example, a cash flow of CU1,000 may be received in one year, two years or three years with probabilities of 10 per cent, 60 per cent and 30 per cent, respectively. The example below shows the computation of expected present value in that situation.

Present value of CU1,000 in 1 year at 5%	CU952.38	
Probability	10.00%	CU95.24
Present value of CU1,000 in 2 years at 5.25%	CU902.73	
Probability	60.00%	CU541.64
Present value of CU1,000 in 3 years at 5.50%	CU851.61	
Probability	30.00%	CU255.48
Expected present value		CU892.36

The expected present value of CU892.36 differs from the traditional notion of a best **A9** estimate of CU902.73 (the 60 per cent probability). A traditional present value computation applied to this example requires a decision about which of the possible timings of cash flows to use and, accordingly, would not reflect the probabilities of other timings. This is because the discount rate in a traditional present value computation cannot reflect uncertainties in timing.

The use of probabilities is an essential element of the expected cash flow approach. **A10** Some question whether assigning probabilities to highly subjective estimates suggests greater precision than, in fact, exists. However, the proper application of the traditional approach (as described in paragraph A6) requires the same estimates and subjectivity without providing the computational transparency of the expected cash flow approach.

Many estimates developed in current practice already incorporate the elements of **A11** expected cash flows informally. In addition, accountants often face the need to measure an asset using limited information about the probabilities of possible cash flows. For example, an accountant might be confronted with the following situations:

(a)   the estimated amount falls somewhere between CU50 and CU250, but no amount in the range is more likely than any other amount. Based on that limited information, the estimated expected cash flow is CU150 [(50 + 250)/2].

(b)   the estimated amount falls somewhere between CU50 and CU250, and the most likely amount is CU100. However, the probabilities attached to each amount are unknown. Based on that limited information, the estimated expected cash flow is CU133.33 [(50 + 100 + 250)/3].

(c)   the estimated amount will be CU50 (10 per cent probability), CU250 (30 per cent probability), or CU100 (60 per cent probability). Based on that limited information, the estimated expected cash flow is CU140 [(50 × 0.10) + (250 × 0.30) + (100 × 0.60)].

In each case, the estimated expected cash flow is likely to provide a better estimate of value in use than the minimum, most likely or maximum amount taken alone.

The application of an expected cash flow approach is subject to a cost-benefit con- **A12** straint. In some cases, an entity may have access to extensive data and may be able to develop many cash flow scenarios. In other cases, an entity may not be able to develop more than general statements about the variability of cash flows without incurring substantial cost. The entity needs to balance the cost of obtaining additional information against the additional reliability that information will bring to the measurement.

A13   Some maintain that expected cash flow techniques are inappropriate for measuring a single item or an item with a limited number of possible outcomes. They offer an example of an asset with two possible outcomes: a 90 per cent probability that the cash flow will be CU10 and a 10 per cent probability that the cash flow will be CU1,000. They observe that the expected cash flow in that example is CU109 and criticise that result as not representing either of the amounts that may ultimately be paid.

A14   Assertions like the one just outlined reflect underlying disagreement with the measurement objective. If the objective is accumulation of costs to be incurred, expected cash flows may not produce a representationally faithful estimate of the expected cost. However, this Standard is concerned with measuring the recoverable amount of an asset. The recoverable amount of the asset in this example is not likely to be CU10, even though that is the most likely cash flow. This is because a measurement of CU10 does not incorporate the uncertainty of the cash flow in the measurement of the asset. Instead, the uncertain cash flow is presented as if it were a certain cash flow. No rational entity would sell an asset with these characteristics for CU10.

DISCOUNT RATE

A15   Whichever approach an entity adopts for measuring the value in use of an asset, interest rates used to discount cash flows should not reflect risks for which the estimated cash flows have been adjusted. Otherwise, the effect of some assumptions will be double-counted.

A16   When an asset-specific rate is not directly available from the market, an entity uses surrogates to estimate the discount rate. The purpose is to estimate, as far as possible, a market assessment of:

(a)   the time value of money for the periods until the end of the asset's useful life; and

(b)   factors (b), (d) and (e) described in paragraph A1, to the extent those factors have not caused adjustments in arriving at estimated cash flows.

A17   As a starting point in making such an estimate, the entity might take into account the following rates:

(a)   the entity's weighted average cost of capital determined using techniques such as the Capital Asset Pricing Model;

(b)   the entity's incremental borrowing rate; and

(c)   other market borrowing rates.

A18   However, these rates must be adjusted:

(a)   to reflect the way that the market would assess the specific risks associated with the asset's estimated cash flows; and

(b)   to exclude risks that are not relevant to the asset's estimated cash flows or for which the estimated cash flows have been adjusted.

Consideration should be given to risks such as country risk, currency risk and price risk.

A19   The discount rate is independent of the entity's capital structure and the way the entity financed the purchase of the asset, because the future cash flows expected to arise from an asset do not depend on the way in which the entity financed the purchase of the asset.

Paragraph 55 requires the discount rate used to be a pre-tax rate. Therefore, when the basis used to estimate the discount rate is post-tax, that basis is adjusted to reflect a pre-tax rate. **A20**

An entity normally uses a single discount rate for the estimate of an asset's value in use. However, an entity uses separate discount rates for different future periods where value in use is sensitive to a difference in risks for different periods or to the term structure of interest rates. **A21**

Appendix B
~~Amendment to IAS 16~~

~~The amendment in this appendix shall be applied when an entity applies IAS 16~~
~~Property, Plant and Equipment (as revised in 2003). It is superseded when IAS 36~~
~~Impairment of Assets (as revised in 2004) becomes effective. This appendix replaces~~
~~the consequential amendments made by IAS 16 (as revised in 2003) to IAS 36~~
~~Impairment of Assets (issued in 1998). IAS 36 (as revised in 2004) incorporates the~~
~~requirements of the paragraphs in this appendix. Consequently, the amendments from~~
~~IAS 16 (as revised in 2003) are not necessary once an entity is subject to IAS 36 (as~~
~~revised in 2004). Accordingly, this appendix is applicable only to entities that elect to~~
~~apply IAS 16 (as revised in 2003) before its effective date.~~

~~* * * * *~~

~~The text of this appendix has been omitted from this volume.~~

CONSEQUENTIAL AMENDMENTS

B1   **Paragraph 2 of FRS 15** *Tangible Fixed Assets* **shall be amended as follows**:

*   Replace definition of depreciable amount with:
    The cost of an asset, or other amount substituted for cost less its residual value.
*   Replace definition of impairment with:
    Impairment loss:
    The amount by which the carrying amount of an asset exceeds its recoverable amount.
*   Replace the definition of residual value with:
    The residual value of an asset is the estimated amount that an entity would currently obtain from disposal of the asset, after deducting the estimated costs of disposal, if the asset were already of the age and in the condition expected at the end of its useful life.
*   Replace the definition of useful economic life:
    Useful life is:

    (a)   the period over which an asset is expected to be available for use by an entity; or
    (b)   the number of production or similar units expected to be obtained

*   Insert the definition of value in use:Value in use:the present value of the future cash flows expected to be derived from an asset or cash-generating unit.

B2   **Paragraph 33 of FRS 15 is amended as follows:**

Recoverable amount

33   A tangible fixed asset needs to be reviewed for impairment on initial recognition only if there is some indication that impairment has occurred, as set out in [draft] FRS ● *Impairment of assets* ~~FRS 11 'Impairment of Fixed Assets and Goodwill'~~. A tangible fixed asset that is impaired on initial recognition should be written down in accordance with [draft]FRS ● ~~FRS 11~~.

B3   **Paragraph 54 of FRS 15 is amended as follows:**

54   Where there is an indication of impairment, an impairment review should be performed in accordance with [draft] FRS ● ~~FRS 11~~. The asset should be

recorded at the lower of the revalued amount, determined in accordance with the above paragraph, and recoverable amount (which is the higher of net realisable value* and value in use).

Delete paragraph 64 of FRS 15.   **B4**

Paragraph 65 is deleted and replaced with: **B5**

65   If an asset's carrying amount is decreased as a result of a revaluation, the decrease shall be recognised in profit or loss. However, the decrease shall be debited to the statement of total recognised gains and losses to the extent of any credit balance in the revaluation reserve in respect of that asset.

Paragraph 66 of FRS 15 is amended as follows: **B6**

66   For the purposes of paragraph 65, the recoverable amount of an asset should be calculated in accordance with the requirements of [draft] FRS ● ~~FRS 11~~.

Paragraphs 68, 69, and 70 of FRS 15 are deleted.   **B7**

Appendix C

This appendix is an integral part of the Standard. It provides guidance on the goodwill impairment testing for cash-generating units with goodwill and non-controlling interests.

IMPAIRMENT TESTING CASH-GENERATING UNITS WITH GOODWILL AND NON-CONTROLLING INTERESTS

For business combinations effected before [draft] FRS • IFRS 3 (revised) *Business Combinations* is applied, the following guidance is relevant when performing a goodwill impairment test for cash-generating units with non-controlling interests.

C1 Prior to the introduction of [draft] FRS • *Business Combinations* In accordance with IFRS 3, goodwill recognised in a business combination represents represented the goodwill acquired by a parent based on the parent's ownership interest, rather than the amount of goodwill controlled by the parent as a result of the business combination. Therefore, goodwill attributable to a non-controlling interest is was not recognised in the parent's consolidated financial statements. Accordingly, if there is a non-controlling interest in a cash-generating unit to which goodwill has been allocated, the carrying amount of that unit comprises:

    (a)   both the parent's interest and the non-controlling interest in the identifiable net assets of the unit; and

    (b)   the parent's interest in goodwill.

However, part of the recoverable amount of the cash-generating unit determined in accordance with this Standard is attributable to the non-controlling interest in goodwill.

C2 Consequently, for the purpose of impairment testing a cash-generating unit with goodwill that is not wholly-owned, the carrying amount of that unit is notionally adjusted, before being compared with its recoverable amount. This is accomplished by grossing up the carrying amount of goodwill allocated to the unit to include the goodwill attributable to the non-controlling interest. This notionally adjusted carrying amount is then compared with the recoverable amount of the unit to determine whether the cash-generating unit is impaired. If it is, the entity allocates the impairment loss in accordance with paragraph 104 of IAS 36 [draft] FRS • first to reduce the carrying amount of goodwill allocated to the unit.

C3 However, because goodwill is recognised only to the extent of the parent's ownership interest, any impairment loss relating to the goodwill is apportioned between that attributable to the parent and that attributable to the non-controlling interest, with only the former being recognised as a goodwill impairment loss.

C4 If the total impairment loss relating to goodwill is less than the amount by which the notionally adjusted carrying amount of the cash-generating unit exceeds its recoverable amount, paragraph 104 of requires the remaining excess to be allocated to reduce the other assets of the unit pro rata on the basis of the carrying amount of each asset in the unit.

C5 Illustrative Example 7 illustrates the impairment testing of a cash-generating unit with goodwill that is not wholly owned.

For business combinations effected after ~~IFRS 3 (revised)~~ *[draft] FRS • Business Combinations* is applied, the following guidance is relevant when performing a goodwill impairment test for cash-generating units with non-controlling interests.

In accordance with ~~IFRS 3,~~ *[draft] FRS • Business Combinations* the acquirer   **C6** measures and recognises goodwill as of the acquisition date as the excess of the fair value of the acquiree, as a whole, over the net amount of the recognised identifiable assets acquired and liabilities assumed. This requirement applies even if the acquirer owns less than 100 per cent of the equity interests in the acquiree at the acquisition date (ie even if a non-controlling interest in the acquiree exists then).

In accordance with ~~IFRS 3~~ *[draft] FRS • Business Combinations*, the acquirer   **C7** allocates the carrying amount of goodwill as of the acquisition date between the acquirer and the non-controlling interest, if any. The carrying amount of goodwill allocated to the acquirer is the difference as of that date between the fair value of the acquirer's equity interest in the acquiree and the acquirer's share in the fair value of the separately recognised assets acquired and liabilities assumed. The rest of the goodwill is allocated to the non-controlling interests.

In a cash-generating unit that includes a partially-owned subsidiary or is a stand-   **C8** alone partially-owned subsidiary, goodwill impairment losses are allocated between the controlling and non-controlling interests pro rata using the relative carrying values of goodwill.

If the partially owned subsidiary is itself a cash-generating unit, the impairment loss   **C9** is allocated to the controlling and non-controlling interests on the basis of the relative carrying values of goodwill allocated to them.

If the partially owned subsidiary is part of a larger cash-generating unit, goodwill   **C10** impairment losses are allocated first to the components of the cash-generating unit and then to the controlling and non-controlling interests of the partially-owned subsidiary. The portion of the impairment loss allocated to the subsidiary is determined by multiplying the goodwill impairment loss for the unit by the carrying value of the goodwill assigned to that subsidiary, divided by the carrying value of the goodwill assigned to the cash-generating unit as a whole. The amount of the impairment loss allocated to the partially-owned subsidiary is then allocated to the controlling and non-controlling interests on the basis of the relative carrying values of goodwill allocated to those interests.

If the total impairment loss relating to goodwill is less than the amount by which the   **C11** carrying amount of the cash-generating unit exceeds its recoverable amount, paragraph 104 of ~~IAS 36~~ *[draft] FRS •* requires the remaining excess to be allocated to reduce the other assets of the unit pro rata on the basis of the carrying amount of each asset in the unit.

Illustrative Example 7A illustrates the impairment testing of a non-wholly-owned   **C12** cash-generating unit with goodwill.

Approval of IAS 36 by the Board

International Accounting Standard 36 *Impairment of Assets* was approved for issue by eleven of the fourteen members of the International Accounting Standards Board. Messrs Cope and Leisenring and Professor Whittington dissented. Their dissenting opinions are set out after the Basis for Conclusions on IAS 36.

Sir David Tweedie	Chairman
Thomas E Jones	Vice-Chairman
Mary E Barth	
Hans-Georg Bruns	
Anthony T Cope	
Robert P Garnett	
Gilbert Gélard	
James J Leisenring	
Warren J McGregor	
Patricia L O'Malley	
Harry K Schmid	
John T Smith	
Geoffrey Whittington	
Tatsumi Yamada	

Basis for Conclusions on [draft] FRS ●IAS 36
Impairment of Assets

Contents

---

*In IFRS 5 Non-current Assets Held for Sale and Discontinued Operations, *issued by the IASB in 2004, the term,'net selling price' was replaced in IAS 36 by 'fair value less costs to sell'.*

Basis for Conclusions on [draft] FRS ● ~~IAS 36~~
Impairment of Assets

> *ASB note: The IASB's Basis for Conclusions, which accompanies IAS 36, is set out below in full. It should be noted though that some of the discussion it contains concerns IASB requirements that have no equivalent in the UK or Republic of Ireland. Footnotes have been used to indicate corresponding requirements in the UK and Republic of Ireland where applicable. All references in this section to 'the Board' and 'Board members' are references to the IASB Board and IASB Board members*

> *The International Accounting Standards Board revised IAS 36 as part of its project on business combinations. It was not the Board's intention to reconsider as part of that project all of the requirements in IAS 36.The previous version of IAS 36 was accompanied by a Basis for Conclusions summarising the former International Accounting Standards Committee's considerations in reaching some of its conclusions in that Standard. For convenience the Board has incorporated into its own Basis for Conclusions material from the previous Basis for Conclusions that discusses (a) matters the Board did not reconsider and (b) the history of the development of a standard on impairment of assets. That material is contained in paragraphs denoted by numbers with the prefix BCZ. Paragraphs describing the Board's considerations in reaching its own conclusions are numbered with the prefix BC.*

INTRODUCTION

BC1 This Basis for Conclusions summarises the International Accounting Standards Board's considerations in reaching the conclusions in IAS 36 *Impairment of Assets*. Individual Board members gave greater weight to some factors than to others.

BC2 The International Accounting Standards Committee (IASC) issued the previous version of IAS 36 in 1998. It has been revised by the Board as part of its project on business combinations. That project has two phases. The first has resulted in the Board issuing simultaneously IFRS 3 *Business Combinations* and revised versions of IAS 36 and IAS 38 *Intangible Assets*.* Therefore, the Board's intention in revising IAS 36 as part of the first phase of the project was not to reconsider all of the requirements in IAS 36. The changes to IAS 36 are primarily concerned with the impairment tests for intangible assets with indefinite useful lives (hereafter referred to as 'indefinite-lived intangibles') and goodwill. The Board has not deliberated the other requirements in IAS 36. Those other requirements will be considered by the Board as part of a future project on impairment of assets.

BC3 The previous version of IAS 36 was accompanied by a Basis for Conclusions summarising IASC's considerations in reaching some of its conclusions in that Standard. For convenience, the Board has incorporated into this Basis for Conclusions material from the previous Basis for Conclusions that discusses matters the Board did not consider. That material is contained in paragraphs denoted by numbers with the prefix BCZ. The views expressed in paragraphs denoted by numbers with the prefix BCZ are those of IASC.

---

*ASB footnote: The ASB is proposing to implement the replacement standard for IFRS 3 Business Combinations see FRED 36. The ASB is also proposing to implement IAS 38 Intangible Assets see FRED 37.

SCOPE (PARAGRAPH 2)

IAS 2 *Inventories** requires an enterprise to measure the recoverable amount of inventory at its net realisable value. IASC believed that there was no need to revise this requirement because it was well accepted as an appropriate test for recoverability of inventories. No major difference exists between IAS 2 and the requirements included in IAS 36 (see paragraphs BCZ37-BCZ39). **BCZ4**

IAS 11 *Construction Contracts*† and IAS 12 *Income Taxes*† already deal with the impairment of assets arising from construction contracts and deferred tax assets respectively. Under both IAS 11 and IAS 12, recoverable amount is, in effect, determined on an undiscounted basis. IASC acknowledged that this was inconsistent with the requirements of IAS 36. However, IASC believed that it was not possible to eliminate that inconsistency without fundamental changes to IAS 11 and IAS 12. IASC had no plans to revise IAS 11 or IAS 12. **BCZ5**

IAS 19 *Employee Benefits*† contains an upper limit on the amount at which an enterprise should recognise an asset arising from employee benefits. Therefore, IAS 36 does not deal with such assets. The limit in IAS 19 is determined on a discounted basis that is broadly compatible with the requirements of IAS 36. The limit does not override the deferred recognition of certain actuarial losses and certain past service costs. **BCZ6**

IAS 39 *Financial Instruments: Recognition and Measurement* * sets out the requirements for impairment of financial assets. **BCZ7**

IAS 36 is applicable to all assets, unless specifically excluded, regardless of their classification as current or non-current. Before IAS 36 was issued, there was no International Accounting Standard on accounting for the impairment of current assets other than inventories. **BCZ8**

MEASURING RECOVERABLE AMOUNT (PARAGRAPHS 18-57)

In determining the principles that should govern the measurement of recoverable amount, IASC considered, as a first step, what an enterprise will do if it discovers that an asset is impaired. IASC concluded that, in such cases, an enterprise will either keep the asset or dispose of it. For example, if an enterprise discovers that the service potential of an asset has decreased: **BCZ9**

(a) the enterprise may decide to sell the asset if the net proceeds from the sale would provide a higher return on investment than continuing use in operations; or

(b) the enterprise may decide to keep the asset and use it, even if its service potential is lower than originally expected. Some reasons may be that:

   (i)   the asset cannot be sold or disposed of immediately;
   (ii) the asset can be sold only at a low price;
   (iii) the asset's service potential can still be recovered but only with additional efforts or expenditure; or
   (iv) the asset could still be profitable although not to the same extent as expected originally.

*ASB footnote: *The corresponding UK and Republic of Ireland requirements can be found in paragraph 2 of [draft] FRS ● Impairment of Assets.*

†ASB footnote: *The corresponding UK and Republic of Ireland requirements can be found in paragraph 2 of [draft] FRS ● Impairment of Assets.*

IASC concluded that the resulting decision from a rational enterprise is, in substance, an investment decision based on estimated net future cash flows expected from the asset.

BCZ10   IASC then considered which of the following four alternatives for determining the recoverable amount of an asset would best reflect this conclusion:

(a)   recoverable amount should be the sum of undiscounted future cash flows.
(b)   recoverable amount should be the asset's fair value: more specifically, recoverable amount should be derived primarily from the asset's market value. If market value cannot be determined, then recoverable amount should be based on the asset's value in use as a proxy for market value.
(c)   recoverable amount should be the asset's value in use.
(d)   recoverable amount should be the higher of the asset's net selling price and value in use.*

Each of these alternatives is discussed below.

BCZ11   It should be noted that fair value, net selling price and value in use all reflect a present value calculation (implicit or explicit) of estimated net future cash flows expected from an asset:

(a)   fair value reflects the market's expectation of the present value of the future cash flows to be derived from the asset;
(b)   net selling price reflects the market's expectation of the present value of the future cash flows to be derived from the asset, less the direct incremental costs to dispose of the asset; and
(c)   value in use is the enterprise's estimate of the present value of the future cash flows to be derived from continuing use and disposal of the asset.

These bases all consider the time value of money and the risks that the amount and timing of the actual cash flows to be received from an asset might differ from estimates. Fair value and net selling price may differ from value in use because the market may not use the same assumptions as an individual enterprise.

Recoverable amount based on the sum of undiscounted cash flows

BCZ12   Some argue that recoverable amount should be measured as the sum of undiscounted future cash flows from an asset. They argue that:

(a)   historical cost accounting is not concerned with measuring the economic value of assets. Therefore, the time value of money should not be considered in estimating the amount that will be recovered from an asset.
(b)   it is premature to use discounting techniques without further research and debates on:

(i)   the role of discounting in the financial statements; and
(ii)   how assets should be measured generally.

If financial statements include assets that are carried on a variety of different bases (historical cost, discounted amounts or other bases), this will be confusing for users.

(c)   identifying an appropriate discount rate will often be difficult and subjective.
(d)   discounting will increase the number of impairment losses recognised. This, coupled with the requirement for reversals of impairment losses, introduces a

---

*In IFRS 5 Non-current Assets Held for Sale and Discontinued Operations, *issued by the IASB in 2004, the* term, 'net selling price' was replaced in IAS 36 by 'fair value less costs to sell'.*

volatile element into the income statement. It will make it harder for users to understand the performance of an enterprise.

A minority of commentators on E55 *Impairment of Assets* supported this view.

IASC rejected measurement of recoverable amount based on the sum of undis-counted cash flows because: **BCZ13**

(a) the objective of the measurement of recoverable amount is to reflect an investment decision. Money has a time value, even when prices are stable. If future cash flows were not discounted, two assets giving rise to cash flows of the same amount but with different timings would show the same recoverable amount. However, their current market values would be different because all rational economic transactions take account of the time value of money.

(b) measurements that take into consideration the time value of money are more relevant to investors, other external users of financial statements and man-agement for resource allocation decisions, regardless of the general measurement basis adopted in the financial statements.

(c) many enterprises were already familiar with the use of discounting techniques, particularly for supporting investment decisions.

(d) discounting was already required for other areas of financial statements that are based on expectations of future cash flows, such as long-term provisions and employee benefit obligations.

(e) users are better served if they are aware on a timely basis of assets that will not generate sufficient returns to cover, at least, the time value of money.

Recoverable amount based on fair value

IAS 32 *Financial Instruments: Disclosure and Presentation** and a number of other International Accounting Standards define fair value as: **BCZ14**

"... the amount for which an asset could be exchanged, or a liability settled, between knowledgeable, willing parties in an arm's length transaction..."

International Accounting Standards include the following requirements or guidance for measuring fair value: **BCZ15**

(a) for the purpose of revaluation of an item of property, plant or equipment to its fair value, IAS 16 *Property, Plant and Equipment*† indicates that fair value is usually an asset's market value, normally determined by appraisal undertaken by professionally qualified valuers and, if no market exists, fair value is based on the asset's depreciated replacement cost.

(b) for the purpose of revaluation of an intangible asset to its fair value, IASC proposed in E60 *Intangible Assets* that fair value be determined by reference to market values obtained from an active market. E60 proposed a definition of an active market.‡

---

*ASB footnote: *The corresponding UK and Republic of Ireland requirements are set out in FRS 25 (IAS 32)* Financial Instruments: Disclosure and Presentation.

†ASB footnote: *The corresponding UK and Republic of Ireland requirements are set out in FRS 15* Tangible Fixed Assets.

‡*IASC approved an International Accounting Standard on intangible assets in 1998.*

(c)   IASC proposed revisions to IAS 22 (see E61 *Business Combinations*) so that fair value would be determined without consideration of the acquirer's intentions for the future use of an asset.*

(d)   IAS 39† indicates that if an active market exists, the fair value of a financial instrument is based on a quoted market price. If there is no active market, fair value is determined by using estimation techniques such as market values of similar types of financial instruments, discounted cash flow analysis and option pricing models.

BCZ16   Some argue that the only appropriate measurement for the recoverable amount of an asset is fair value (based on observable market prices or, if no observable market prices exist, estimated considering prices for similar assets and the results of discounted future cash flow calculations). Proponents of fair value argue that:

(a)   the purpose of measuring recoverable amount is to estimate a market value, not an enterprise-specific value. An enterprise's estimate of the present value of future cash flows is subjective and in some cases may be abused. Observable market prices that reflect the judgement of the market place are a more reliable measurement of the amounts that will be recovered from an asset. They reduce the use of management's judgement.

(b)   if an asset is expected to generate greater net cash inflows for the enterprise than for other participants, the superior returns are almost always generated by internally generated goodwill stemming from the synergy of the business and its management team. For consistency with IASC's proposals in E60 that internally generated goodwill should not be recognised as an asset, these above-market cash flows should be excluded from assessments of an asset's recoverable amount.

(c)   determining recoverable amount as the higher of net selling price and value in use is tantamount to determining two diverging measures whilst there should be only one measure to estimate recoverable amount.

A minority of commentators on E55 supported measuring recoverable amount at fair value (based on observable market prices or, if no observable market prices exist, estimated considering prices for similar assets and the results of discounted future cash flow calculations).

BCZ17   IASC rejected the proposal that an asset's recoverable amount should be determined by reference to its fair value (based on observable market prices or, if no observable market prices exist, estimated considering prices for similar assets and the results of discounted future cash flow calculations). The reasons are the following:

(a)   IASC believed that no preference should be given to the market's expectation of the recoverable amount of an asset (basis for fair value when market values are available and for net selling price) over a reasonable estimate performed by the individual enterprise that owns the asset (basis for fair value when market values are not available and for value in use). For example, an enterprise may have information about future cash flows that is superior to the information available in the market place. Also, an enterprise may plan to use an asset in a manner different from the market's view of the best use.

(b)   market values are a way to estimate fair value but only if they reflect the fact that both parties, the acquirer and the seller, are willing to enter a transaction. If an enterprise can generate greater cash flows by using an asset than by selling

---

IASC approved revisions to IAS 22 Business Combinations in 1998.

†*The IASB's project to revise IAS 32 and IAS 39 in 2003 resulted in the relocation of the requirements on fair value measurement from IAS 32 to IAS 39.*

it, it would be misleading to base recoverable amount on the market price of the asset because a rational enterprise would not be willing to sell the asset. Therefore, recoverable amount should not refer only to a transaction between two parties (which is unlikely to happen) but should also consider an asset's service potential from its use by the enterprise.

(c)   IASC believed that in assessing the recoverable amount of an asset, it is the amount that an enterprise can expect to recover from that asset, including the effect of synergy with other assets, that is relevant.

The following two examples illustrate the proposal (rejected by IASC) that an enterprise should measure an asset's recoverable amount at its fair value (primarily based on observable market values if these values are available).

Example 1

10 years ago, an enterprise bought its headquarters building for 2,000. Since then, the real estate market has collapsed and the building's market value at balance sheet date is estimated to be 1,000. Disposal costs of the building would be negligible. The building's carrying amount at the balance sheet date is 1,500 and its remaining useful life is 30 years. The building meets all the enterprise's expectations and it is likely that these expectations will be met for the foreseeable future. As a consequence, the enterprise has no plans to move from its current headquarters. The value in use of the building cannot be determined because the building does not generate independent cash inflows. Therefore, the enterprise assesses the recoverable amount of the building's cash-generating unit, that is, the enterprise as a whole. That calculation shows that the building's cash-generating unit is not impaired.

Proponents of fair value (primarily based on observable market values if these values are available) would measure the recoverable amount of the building at its market value (1,000) and, hence, would recognise an impairment loss of 500 (1,500 less 1,000), even though calculations show that the building's cash-generating unit is not impaired.

IASC did not support this approach and believed that the building was not impaired. IASC believed that, in the situation described, the enterprise would not be willing to sell the building for 1,000 and that the assumption of a sale was not relevant.

Example 2

At the end of 20X0, an enterprise purchased a computer for 100 for general use in its operations. The computer is depreciated over 4 years on a straight-line basis. Residual value is estimated to be nil. At the end of 20X2, the carrying amount of the computer is 50. There is an active market for second-hand computers of this type. The market value of the computer is 30. The enterprise does not intend to replace the computer before the end of its useful life. The computer's cash-generating unit is not impaired.

Proponents of fair value (primarily based on observable market values if these values are available) would measure the recoverable amount of the computer at

> *its market value (30) and, therefore, would recognise an impairment loss of 20 (50 less 30) even though the computer's cash-generating unit is not impaired.*
>
> *IASC did not support this approach and believed that the computer was not impaired as long as:*
>
> *(a)   the enterprise was not committed to dispose of the computer before the end of its expected useful life; and*
>
> *(b)   the computer's cash-generating unit was not impaired.*

BCZ18   If no deep and liquid market exists for an asset, IASC considered that value in use would be a reasonable estimate of fair value. This is likely to happen for many assets within the scope of IAS 36: observable market prices are unlikely to exist for goodwill, most intangible assets and many items of property, plant and equipment. Therefore, it is likely that the recoverable amount of these assets, determined in accordance with IAS 36, will be similar to the recoverable amount based on the fair value of these assets.

BCZ19   For some assets within the scope of IAS 36, observable market prices exist or consideration of prices for similar assets is possible. In such cases, the asset's net selling price will differ from the asset's fair value only by the direct incremental costs of disposal. IASC acknowledged that recoverable amount as the higher of net selling price and value in use would sometimes differ from fair value primarily based on market prices (even if the disposal costs are negligible). This is because, as explained in paragraph BCZ17(a), the market may not use the same assumptions about future cash flows as an individual enterprise.

BCZ20   IASC believed that IAS 36 included sufficient requirements to prevent an enterprise from using assumptions different from the market place that are unjustified. For example, an enterprise is required to determine value in use using:

(a)   cash flow projections based on reasonable and supportable assumptions and giving greater weight to external evidence; and

(b)   a discount rate that reflects current market assessments of the time value of money and the risks specific to the asset.

Recoverable amount based on value in use

BCZ21   Some argue that value in use is the only appropriate measurement for the recoverable amount of an asset because:

(a)   financial statements are prepared under a going concern assumption. Therefore, no consideration should be given to an alternative measurement that reflects a disposal, unless this reflects the enterprise's intentions.

(b)   assets should not be carried at amounts higher than their service potential from use by the enterprise. Unlike value in use, a market value does not necessarily reflect the service potential of an asset.

Few commentators on E55 supported this view.

BCZ22   IASC rejected this proposal because:

(a)   if an asset's net selling price is higher than its value in use, a rational enterprise will dispose of the asset. In this situation, it is logical to base recoverable amount on the asset's net selling price to avoid recognising an impairment loss that is unrelated to economic reality.

(b)   if an asset's net selling price is greater than its value in use, but management decides to keep the asset, the extra loss (the difference between net selling price and value in use) properly falls in later periods because it results from management's decision in these later periods to keep the asset.

Recoverable amount based on the higher of net selling price and value in use*

The requirement that recoverable amount should be the higher of net selling price   **BCZ23** and value in use stems from the decision that measurement of the recoverable amount of an asset should reflect the likely behaviour of a rational management. Furthermore, no preference should be given to the market's expectation of the recoverable amount of an asset (basis for net selling price) over a reasonable estimate performed by the individual enterprise which owns the asset (basis for value in use) or vice versa (see paragraphs BCZ17-BCZ20 and BCZ22). It is uncertain whether the assumptions of the market or the enterprise are more likely to be true. Currently, perfect markets do not exist for many of the assets within the scope of IAS 36 and it is unlikely that predictions of the future will be entirely accurate, regardless of who makes them.

IASC acknowledged that an enterprise would use judgement in determining whether   **BCZ24** an impairment loss needed to be recognised. For this reason, IAS 36 included some safeguards to limit the risk that an enterprise may make an over-optimistic (pessimistic) estimate of recoverable amount:

(a)   IAS 36 requires a formal estimate of recoverable amount whenever there is an indication that:

(i)   an asset may be impaired; or
(ii)   an impairment loss may no longer exist or may have decreased.

For this purpose, IAS 36 includes a relatively detailed (although not exhaustive) list of indicators that an asset may be impaired (see paragraphs 12 and 111 of IAS 36).
(b)   IAS 36 provides guidelines for the basis of management's projections of future cash flows to be used to estimate value in use (see paragraph 33 of IAS 36).

IASC considered the cost of requiring an enterprise to determine both net selling   **BCZ25** price and value in use, if the amount determined first is below an asset's carrying amount. IASC concluded that the benefits of such a requirement outweigh the costs.

The majority of the commentators on E55 supported IASC's view that recoverable   **BCZ26** amount should be measured at the higher of net selling price and value in use.

Assets held for disposal

IASC considered whether the recoverable amount of an asset held for disposal   **BCZ27** should be measured only at the asset's net selling price. When an enterprise expects to dispose of an asset within the near future, the net selling price of the asset is normally close to its value in use. Indeed, the value in use usually consists mostly of the net proceeds to be received for the asset, since future cash flows from continuing use are usually close to nil. Therefore, IASC believed that the definition of recoverable amount as included in IAS 36 is appropriate for assets held for disposal without a need for further requirements or guidance.

*In IFRS 5 Non-current Assets Held for Sale and Discontinued Operations, *issued by the IASB in 2004, the* term, 'net selling price' was replaced in IAS 36 by 'fair value less costs to sell'.

Other refinements to the measurement of recoverable amount

Replacement cost as a ceiling

BCZ28   Some argue that the replacement cost of an asset should be adopted as a ceiling for its recoverable amount. They argue that the value of an asset to the business would not exceed the amount that the enterprise would be willing to pay for the asset at the balance sheet date.

BCZ29   IASC believed that replacement cost techniques are not appropriate to measuring the recoverable amount of an asset. This is because replacement cost measures the cost of an asset and not the future economic benefits recoverable from its use and/or disposal.

Appraisal values

BCZ30   In some cases, an enterprise might seek external appraisal of recoverable amount. External appraisal is not a separate technique in its own right. IASC believed that if appraisal values are used, an enterprise should verify that the external appraisal follows the requirements of IAS 36.

NET SELLING PRICE (PARAGRAPHS 25-29)*

BCZ31   IAS 36 defines net selling price as the amount obtainable from the sale of an asset in an arm's length transaction between knowledgeable, willing parties, less the incremental costs directly attributable to the disposal of the asset.

BCZ32   In other words, net selling price reflects the market's expectations of the future cash flows for an asset after the market's consideration of the time value of money and the risks inherent in receiving those cash flows, less the disposal costs.

BCZ33   Some argue that direct incremental costs of disposal should not be deducted from the amount obtainable from the sale of an asset because, unless management has decided to dispose of the asset, the going concern assumption should apply.

BCZ34   IASC believed that it is appropriate to deduct direct incremental costs of disposal in determining net selling price because the purpose of the exercise is to determine the net amount that an enterprise could recover from the sale of an asset at the date of the measurement and to compare it with the alternative of keeping the asset and using it.

BCZ35   IAS 36 indicates that termination benefits (as defined in IAS 19 *Employee Benefits†*) and costs associated with reducing or reorganising a business following the disposal of an asset are not direct incremental costs to dispose of the asset. IASC considered these costs as incidental to (rather than a direct consequence of) the disposal of an asset. In addition, this guidance is consistent with the direction of the project on provisions.‡

*In IFRS 5 Non-current Assets Held for Sale and Discontinued Operations, *issued by the IASB in 2004, the term, 'net selling price' was replaced in IAS 36 by 'fair value less costs to sell'.*

†ASB footnote: *The ASB is proposing to implement those parts of IAS 19 that address termination benefits into FRS 17* Retirement benefits, *see* FRED 39. *FRS 17 will be renamed* Retirement and Termination Benefits.

‡*IASC approved an International Accounting Standard on provisions, contingent liabilities and contingent assets in 1998.*

Although the definition of 'net selling price' would be similar to a definition of 'net **BCZ36** fair value', IASC decided to use the term 'net selling price' instead of 'net fair value'. IASC believed that the term 'net selling price' better describes the amount that an enterprise should determine and that will be compared with an asset's value in use.

Net realisable value

IAS 2 *Inventories** defines net realisable value as: **BCZ37**

"... the estimated selling price in the ordinary course of business ... less the estimated costs necessary to make the sale..."

For the purpose of determining recoverable amount, IASC decided not to use the **BCZ38** term 'net realisable value' as defined in IAS 2 because:

(a)   IAS 2's definition of net realisable value does not refer explicitly to transactions carried out on an arm's length basis.
(b)   net realisable value refers to an estimated selling price in the ordinary course of business. In certain cases, net selling price will reflect a forced sale, if management is compelled to sell immediately.
(c)   it is important that net selling price uses, as a starting point, a selling price agreed between knowledgeable, willing buyers and sellers. This is not explicitly mentioned in the definition of net realisable value.

In most cases, net selling price and net realisable value will be similar. However, **BCZ39** IASC did not believe that it was necessary to change the definition of net realisable value used in IAS 2 because, for inventories, the definition of net realisable value is well understood and seems to work satisfactorily.

VALUE IN USE (PARAGRAPHS 30-57 AND THE APPENDIX)

IAS 36 defines value in use as the present value of the future cash flows expected to **BCZ40** be derived from an asset.

Expected value approach

Some argue that, to better reflect uncertainties in timing and amounts inherent in **BCZ41** estimated future cash flows, expected future cash flows should be used in determining value in use. An expected value approach considers all expectations about possible future cash flows instead of the single, most likely, future cash flows.

Example

An enterprise estimates that there are two scenarios for future cash flows: a first possibility of future cash flows amounts to 120 with a 40 per cent probability and a second possibility amounts to 80 with a 60 per cent probability.

The most likely future cash flows would be 80 and the expected future cash flows would be 96 (80 × 60% + 120 × 40%).

---

*ASB footnote: *The corresponding requirements in the UK and Republic of Ireland are set out in SSAP 9* Stocks and Long-term Contracts.

BCZ42   In most cases, it is likely that budgets/forecasts that are the basis for cash flow projections will reflect a single estimate of future cash flows only. For this reason, IASC decided that an expected value approach should be permitted but not required.

Future cash flows from internally generated goodwill and synergy with other assets

BCZ43   IASC rejected a proposal that estimates of future cash inflows should reflect only future cash inflows relating to the asset that was initially recognised (or the remaining portion of that asset if part of it has already been consumed or sold). The purpose of such a requirement would be to avoid including in an asset's value in use future cash inflows from internally generated goodwill or from synergy with other assets. This would be consistent with IASC's proposal in E60 *Intangible Assets* to prohibit the recognition of internally generated goodwill as an asset.*

BCZ44   In many cases, it will not be possible in practice to distinguish future cash inflows from the asset initially recognised from the future cash inflows from internally generated goodwill or a modification of the asset. This is particularly true when businesses are merged or once an asset has been enhanced by subsequent expenditure. IASC concluded that it is more important to focus on whether the carrying amount of an asset will be recovered rather than on whether the recovery stems partly from internally generated goodwill.

BCZ45   The proposal—that future cash inflows should reflect only future cash inflows relating to the asset that was initially recognised—would also conflict with the requirement under IAS 36 that cash flow projections should reflect reasonable and supportable assumptions that represent management's best estimate of the set of economic conditions that will exist over the remaining useful life of the asset (see paragraph 33 of IAS 36). Therefore, the Standard requires that future cash inflows should be estimated for an asset in its current condition, whether or not these future cash inflows are from the asset that was initially recognised or from its subsequent enhancement or modification.

Example

Several years ago, an enterprise purchased a customer list with 10,000 addresses that it recognised as an intangible asset. The enterprise uses this list for direct marketing of its products. Since initial recognition, about 2,000 customer addresses have been deleted from the list and 3,000 new customer addresses added to it. The enterprise is determining the value in use of the customer list.

Under the proposal (rejected by IASC) that an enterprise should reflect only future cash inflows relating to the asset that was initially recognised, the enterprise would consider only those future cash inflows generated by the remaining 8,000 (10,000 less 2,000) customers from the list acquired.

Under IAS 36, an enterprise considers the future cash inflows generated by the customer list in its current condition, ie by all 11,000 customers (8,000 plus 3,000).

---

*IASC approved an International Accounting Standard on Intangible Assets in 1998.

Value in use estimated in a foreign currency (paragraph 54)

In response to comments from field test participants, paragraph 54 of IAS 36 **BCZ46**
includes guidance on calculating the value in use of an asset that generates future
cash flows in a foreign currency. IAS 36 indicates that value in use in a foreign
currency is translated into the reporting currency*† using the spot exchange rate at
the balance sheet date.

If a currency is freely convertible and traded in an active market, the spot rate reflects **BCZ47**
the market's best estimate of future events that will affect that currency. Therefore,
the only available unbiased estimate of a future exchange rate is the current spot rate,
adjusted by the difference in expected future rates of general inflation in the two
countries to which the currencies belong.

A value in use calculation already deals with the effect of general inflation since it is **BCZ48**
calculated either by:

(a) estimating future cash flows in nominal terms (ie including the effect of general
    inflation and specific price changes) and discounting them at a rate that
    includes the effects of general inflation; or

(b) estimating future cash flows in real terms (ie excluding the effect of general
    inflation but including the effect of specific price changes) and discounting them
    at a rate that excludes the effect of general inflation.

To use a forward rate to translate value in use expressed in a foreign currency would **BCZ49**
be inappropriate. This is because a forward rate reflects the market's adjustment for
the differential in interest rates. Using such a rate would result in double-counting
the time value of money (first in the discount rate and then in the forward rate).

Even if a currency is not freely convertible or is not traded in an active market—with **BCZ50**
the consequence that it can no longer be assumed that the spot exchange rate reflects
the market's best estimate of future events that will affect that currency—IAS 36
indicates that an enterprise uses the spot exchange rate at the balance sheet date to
translate value in use estimated in a foreign currency. This is because IASC believed
that it is unlikely that an enterprise can make a more reliable estimate of future
exchange rates than the current spot exchange rate.

An alternative to estimating the future cash flows in the currency in which they are **BCZ51**
generated would be to estimate them in another currency as a proxy and discount
them at a rate appropriate for this other currency. This solution may be simpler,
particularly where cash flows are generated in the currency of a hyperinflationary
economy (in such cases, some would prefer using a hard currency as a proxy) or in a
currency other than the reporting currency. However, this solution may be misleading if the exchange rate varies for reasons other than changes in the differential
between the general inflation rates in the two countries to which the currencies
belong. In addition, this solution is inconsistent with the approach under IAS 29
Financial Reporting in Hyperinflationary Economies‡, which does not allow, if the

---

*In IAS 21 The Effects of Changes in Foreign Exchange Rates, *as revised by the IASB in 2003, the term
'reporting currency' was replaced by 'functional currency'.*

†ASB footnote: *The corresponding UK and Republic of Ireland requirements are set out in FRS 23 (IAS 21)*
The Effects of Changes in Foreign Exchange Rates.

‡ASB footnote: *The corresponding UK and Republic of Ireland requirements are set out in FRS 24 (IAS 24)*
Financial Reporting in Hyperinflationary Economies.

reporting currency* is the currency of a hyperinflationary economy, translation into a hard currency as a proxy for restatement in terms of the measuring unit current at the balance sheet date.

Discount rate (paragraphs 55-57 and A15-A21)

BCZ52   The purpose of discounting future cash flows is to reflect the time value of money and the uncertainties attached to those cash flows:

(a)   assets that generate cash flows soon are worth more than those generating the same cash flows later. All rational economic transactions will take account of the time value of money. The cost of not receiving a cash inflow until some date in the future is an opportunity cost that can be measured by considering what income has been lost by not investing that money for the period. The time value of money, before consideration of risk, is given by the rate of return on a risk-free investment, such as government bonds of the same duration.

(b)   the value of the future cash flows is affected by the variability (ie the risks) associated with the cash flows. Therefore, all rational economic transactions will take risk into account.

BCZ53   As a consequence IASC decided:

(a)   to reject a discount rate based on a historical rate—ie the effective rate implicit when an asset was acquired. A subsequent estimate of recoverable amount has to be based on prevailing interest rates because management's decisions about whether to keep the asset are based on prevailing economic conditions. Historical rates do not reflect prevailing economic conditions.

(b)   to reject a discount rate based on a risk-free rate, unless the future cash flows have been adjusted for all the risks specific to the asset.

(c)   to require that the discount rate should be a rate that reflects current market assessments of the time value of money and the risks specific to the asset. This rate is the return that investors would require if they were to choose an investment that would generate cash flows of amounts, timing and risk profile equivalent to those that the enterprise expects to derive from the asset.

BCZ54   In principle, value in use should be an enterprise-specific measure determined in accordance with the enterprise's own view of the best use of that asset. Logically, the discount rate should be based on the enterprise's own assessment both of the time value of money and of the risks specific to the future cash flows from the asset. However, IASC believed that such a rate could not be verified objectively. Therefore, IAS 36 requires that the enterprise should make its own estimate of future cash flows but that the discount rate should reflect, as far as possible, the market's assessment of the time value of money. Similarly, the discount rate should reflect the premium that the market would require from uncertain future cash flows based on the distribution estimated by the enterprise.

BCZ55   IASC acknowledged that a current asset-specific market-determined rate would rarely exist for the assets covered by IAS 36. Therefore, an enterprise uses current market-determined rates for other assets (as similar as possible to the asset under review) as a starting point and adjusts these rates to reflect the risks specific to the asset for which the cash flow projections have not been adjusted.

*In IAS 21 The Effects of Changes in Foreign Exchange Rates, as revised by the IASB in 2003, the term 'reporting currency' was replaced by 'functional currency'.

Additional guidance included in the Standard in 2004

Elements reflected in value in use (paragraphs 30-32)

The Exposure Draft of Proposed Amendments to IAS 36 proposed, and the revised   **BC56**
Standard includes, additional guidance to clarify:

(a)   the elements that are reflected in an asset's value in use; and

(b)   that some of those elements (ie expectations about possible variations in the
amount or timing of future cash flows, the price for bearing the uncertainty
inherent in the asset, and other factors that market participants would reflect in
pricing the future cash flows the entity expects to derive from the asset) can be
reflected either as adjustments to the future cash flows or as adjustments to the
discount rate.

The Board decided to include this additional guidance in the Exposure Draft in
response to a number of requests from its constituents for clarification of the
requirements in the previous version of IAS 36 on measuring value in use.

Respondents to the Exposure Draft generally agreed with the proposals. Those that   **BC57**
disagreed varied widely in their views, arguing that:

(a)   IAS 36 should be amended to permit entities to measure value in use using
methods other than discounting of future cash flows.

(b)   when measuring the value in use of an intangible asset, entities should be
required to reflect the price for bearing the uncertainty inherent in the asset as
adjustments to the future cash flows.

(c)   it is inconsistent with the definition of value in use to reflect in that measure the
other factors that market participants would reflect in pricing the future cash
flows the entity expects to derive from the asset—this element refers to market
pricing of an asset rather than to the value to the entity of the asset. Other
factors should be reflected in value in use only to the extent that they affect the
cash flows the entity can achieve from the asset.

In considering (a) above, the Board observed that the measure of recoverable   **BC58**
amount in IAS 36 (ie higher of value in use and fair value less costs to sell) stems
from IASC's decision that an asset's recoverable amount should reflect the likely
behaviour of a rational management, with no preference given to the market's
expectation of the recoverable amount of an asset (ie fair value less costs to sell) over
a reasonable estimate performed by the entity that controls the asset (ie value in use)
or vice versa (see paragraph BCZ23). In developing the Exposure Draft and revising
IAS 36, the Board concluded that it would be inappropriate to modify the measurement basis adopted in the previous version of IAS 36 for determining
recoverable amount until the Board considers and resolves the broader question of
the appropriate measurement objective(s) in accounting. Moreover, IAS 36 does not
preclude the use of other valuation techniques in estimating fair value less costs to
sell. For example, paragraph 27 of the Standard states that "If there is no binding
sale agreement or active market for an asset, fair value less costs to sell is based on
the best information available to reflect the amount that an entity could obtain, at
the balance sheet date, from the disposal of the asset in an arm's length transaction
between knowledgeable, willing parties, after deducting the costs of disposal."

In considering (b) above, the Board observed that the previous version of IAS 36   **BC59**
permitted risk adjustments to be reflected either in the cash flows or in the discount
rate, without indicating a preference. The Board could see no justification for
amending this approach to require risk adjustments for uncertainty to be factored
into the cash flows, particularly given the Board's inclination to avoid modifying the

requirements in the previous version of IAS 36 for determining recoverable amount until it considers and resolves the broader question of measurement in accounting. Additionally, the Board as part of its consultative process conducted field visits and round-table discussions during the comment period for the Exposure Draft.* Many field visit participants indicated a preference for reflecting such risk adjustments in the discount rate.

BC60   In considering (c) above, the Board observed that the measure of value in use adopted in IAS 36 is not a pure 'entity-specific' measure. Although the cash flows used as the starting point in the calculation represent entity-specific cash flows (ie they are derived from the most recent financial budgets/forecasts approved by management and represent management's best estimate of the set of economic conditions that will exist over the remaining useful life of the asset), their present value is required to be determined using a discount rate that reflects current market assessments of the time value of money and the risks specific to the asset. Paragraph 56 of the Standard (paragraph 49 of the previous version of IAS 36) clarifies that "A rate that reflects current market assessments of the time value of money and the risks specific to the asset is the return that investors would require if they were to choose an investment that would generate cash flows of amounts, timing and risk profile equivalent to those that the entity expects to derive from the asset." In other words, an asset's value in use reflects how the market would price the cash flows that management expects to derive from that asset.

BC61   Therefore, the Board concluded that:

   (a)   it is consistent with the measure of value in use adopted in IAS 36 to include in the list of elements the other factors that market participants would reflect in pricing the future cash flows the entity expects to derive from the asset.

   (b)   all of the elements proposed in the Exposure Draft (and listed in paragraph 30 of the revised Standard) should be reflected in the calculation of an asset's value in use.

Estimates of future cash flows (paragraphs 33, 34 and 44)

BC62   The Exposure Draft proposed requiring cash flow projections used in measuring value in use to be based on reasonable and supportable assumptions that take into account both past actual cash flows and management's past ability to forecast cash flows accurately.

BC63   Many respondents to the Exposure Draft disagreed with this proposal, arguing that:

   (a)   the reasons for past cash flow forecasts differing from actual cash flows may be irrelevant to the current projections. For example, if there has been a major change in management, management's past ability to forecast cash flows might not be relevant to the current projections. Additionally, a poor record of forecasting cash flows accurately might be the result of factors outside of management's control (such as the events of September 11, 2001), rather than indicative of management bias.

The field visits were conducted from early December 2002 to early April 2003, and involved IASB members and staff in meetings with 41 companies in Australia, France, Germany, Japan, South Africa, Switzerland and the United Kingdom. IASB members and staff also took part in a series of round-table discussions with auditors, preparers, accounting standard-setters and regulators in Canada and the United States on implementation issues encountered by North American companies during first-time application of US Statements of Financial Accounting Standards 141 Business Combinations and 142 Goodwill and Other Intangible Assets, and the equivalent Canadian Handbook Sections, which were issued in June 2001.

(b)   it is unclear how, in practice, the assumptions on which the cash flow projections are based could take into account past differences between management's forecasts and actual cash flows.

(c)   the proposal is inconsistent with the requirement to base cash flow projections on the most recent financial budgets/forecasts approved by management.

The Board observed that, as worded, the proposal would have *required* the assumptions on which the cash flow forecasts are based to be adjusted for past actual cash flows and management's past ability to forecast cash flows accurately. The Board agreed with respondents that it is not clear how, in practice, this might be achieved, and that in some circumstances past actual cash flows and management's past ability to forecast cash flows accurately might not be relevant to the development of current forecasts. However, the Board remained of the view that in developing the assumptions on which the cash flow forecasts are based, management should remain mindful of, and when appropriate make the necessary adjustments for, an entity's actual past performance or previous history of management consistently overstating or understating cash flow forecasts.   **BC64**

Therefore, the Board decided not to proceed with the proposal, but instead to include in paragraph 34 of the Standard guidance clarifying that management: **BC65**

(a)   should assess the reasonableness of the assumptions on which its current cash flow projections are based by examining the causes of differences between past cash flow projections and actual cash flows; and

(b)   should ensure that the assumptions on which its current cash flow projections are based are consistent with past actual outcomes, provided the effects of subsequent events or circumstances that did not exist when those actual cash flows were generated make this appropriate.

In finalising the Standard the Board also considered two issues identified by respondents to the Exposure Draft and referred to the Board by the International Financial Reporting Interpretations Committee. Both issues related to the application of paragraphs 27(b) and 37 of the previous version of IAS 36 (now paragraphs 33(b) and 44). The Board did not reconsider those paragraphs when developing the Exposure Draft.   **BC66**

Paragraph 27(b) required the cash flow projections used to measure value in use to be based on the most recent financial budgets/forecasts that have been approved by management. Paragraph 37, however, required the future cash flows to be estimated for the asset [or cash-generating unit] in its current condition and excluded estimated future cash inflows or outflows that are expected to arise from: (a) a future restructuring to which an enterprise is not yet committed; or (b) future capital expenditure that will improve or enhance the asset [or cash-generating unit] in excess of its originally assessed standard of performance.*   **BC67**

The first issue the Board considered related to the acquisition of a cash-generating unit when: **BC68**

(a)   the price paid for the unit was based on projections that included a major restructuring expected to result in a substantial increase in the net cash inflows derived from the unit; and

---

*The requirement to exclude future capital expenditure that will improve or enhance the asset in excess of its originally assessed standard of performance was amended in 2003 as a consequential amendment arising from the revision of IAS 16 Property, Plant and Equipment. Paragraph 44 of IAS 36 now requires estimates of future cash flows to exclude future cash inflows or outflows that are expected to arise from improving or enhancing the asset's performance.

(b)   there is no observable market from which to estimate the unit's fair value less costs to sell.

Respondents expressed concern that if the net cash inflows arising from the restructuring were not reflected in the unit's value in use, comparison of the unit's recoverable amount and carrying amount immediately after the acquisition would result in the recognition of an impairment loss.

BC69   The Board agreed with respondents that, all else being equal, the value in use of a newly acquired unit would, in accordance with IAS 36, be less than the price paid for the unit to the extent that the price includes the net benefits of a future restructuring to which the entity is not yet committed. However, this does not mean that a comparison of the unit's recoverable amount with its carrying amount immediately after the acquisition will result in the recognition of an impairment loss. The Board observed that:

(a)   recoverable amount is measured in accordance with IAS 36 as the higher of value in use and fair value less costs to sell. Fair value less costs to sell is defined in the Standard as "the amount obtainable from the sale of an asset or cash-generating unit in an arm's length transaction between knowledgeable, willing parties, less the costs of disposal."

(b)   paragraphs 25-27 of the Standard provide guidance on estimating fair value less costs to sell. In accordance with that guidance, the best evidence of a recently acquired unit's fair value less costs to sell is likely to be the arm's length price the entity paid to acquire the unit, adjusted for disposal costs and for any changes in economic circumstances between the transaction date and the date at which the estimate is made.

(c)   if the unit's fair value less costs to sell were to be otherwise estimated, it would also reflect the market's assessment of the expected net benefits any acquirer would be able to derive from restructuring the unit or from future capital expenditure on the unit.

BC70   Therefore, all else being equal, the unit's recoverable amount would be its fair value less costs to sell, rather than its value in use. As such, the net benefits of the restructuring would be reflected in the unit's recoverable amount, meaning that an impairment loss would arise only to the extent of any material disposal costs.

BC71   The Board acknowledged that treating the newly acquired unit's fair value less costs to sell as its recoverable amount seems inconsistent with the reason underpinning a "higher of fair value less costs to sell and value in use" recoverable amount measurement objective. Measuring recoverable amount as the higher of fair value less costs to sell and value in use is intended to reflect the economic decisions that are made when an asset becomes impaired: is it better to sell or keep using the asset?

BC72   Nevertheless, the Board concluded that:

(a)   amending IAS 36 to include in value in use calculations the costs and benefits of future restructurings to which the entity is not yet committed would be a significant change to the concept of value in use adopted in the previous version of IAS 36. That concept is 'value in use for the asset in its current condition'.

(b)   the concept of value in use in IAS 36 should not be modified as part of the Business Combinations project, but should be reconsidered only once the Board considers and resolves the broader question of the appropriate measurement objectives in accounting.

BC73   The second issue the Board considered related to what some respondents suggested was a conflict between the requirements in paragraphs 27(b) and 37 of the previous version of IAS 36 (now paragraphs 33(b) and 44). Paragraph 27(b) required value in use to be based on the most recent forecasts approved by management—which would be likely to reflect management's intentions in relation to future restructurings and future capital expenditure—whereas paragraph 37 required value in use to exclude the effects of a future restructuring to which the enterprise is not yet committed and future capital expenditure that will improve or enhance the asset in excess of its originally assessed standard of performance.*

The Board concluded that it is clear from the Basis for Conclusions on the previous version of IAS 36 that IASC's intention was that value in use should be calculated using estimates of future cash inflows for an asset in its current condition. The Board nevertheless agreed with respondents that the requirement for value in use to be based on the most recent forecasts approved by management could be viewed as inconsistent with paragraph 37 of the previous version of IAS 36 when those forecasts include either future restructurings to which the entity is not yet committed or future cash flows associated with improving or enhancing the asset's performance. **BC74**

Therefore, the Board decided to clarify, in what is now paragraph 33(b) of the revised Standard, that cash flow projections should be based on the most recent financial budgets/forecasts that have been approved by management, but should exclude any estimated future cash inflows or outflows expected to arise from future restructurings or from improving or enhancing the asset's performance. The Board also decided to clarify that when a cash-generating unit contains assets with different estimated useful lives (or, similarly, when an asset comprises components with different estimated useful lives), the replacement of assets (components) with shorter lives is considered to be part of the day-to-day servicing of the unit (asset) when estimating the future cash flows associated with the unit (asset). **BC75**

Using present value techniques to measure value in use (paragraphs A1-A14)

The Exposure Draft proposed additional application guidance on using present value techniques in measuring value in use. The Board decided to include this additional guidance in the Exposure Draft in response to requests for clarification of the requirements in the previous version of IAS 36 on measuring value in use. **BC76**

Respondents to the Exposure Draft were generally supportive of the additional guidance. Those that were not varied in their views, suggesting that: **BC77**

(a)   limiting the guidance to a brief appendix to IAS 36 is insufficient.
(b)   although the guidance is useful, it detracts from the main purpose of IAS 36, which is to establish accounting principles for impairment testing assets. Therefore, the guidance should be omitted from the Standard.
(c)   entities should be required to use an expected cash flow approach to measure value in use.
(d)   an expected cash flow approach is not consistent with how transactions are priced by management and should be prohibited.

In considering (a) and (b) above, the Board noted that the respondents that commented on the additional guidance generally agreed that it is useful and sufficient. **BC78**

The requirement to exclude future capital expenditure that will improve or enhance the asset in excess of its originally assessed standard of performance was amended in 2003 as a consequential amendment arising from the revision of IAS 16 Property, Plant and Equipment. Paragraph 44 of IAS 36 now requires estimates of future cash flows to exclude future cash inflows or outflows that are expected to arise from improving or enhancing the asset's performance.

BC79   In considering (c) and (d) above, the Board observed that the previous version of IAS 36 did not require value in use to be calculated using an expected cash flow approach, nor did it prohibit such an approach. The Board could see no justification for requiring or prohibiting the use of an expected cash flow approach, particularly given the Board's inclination to avoid modifying the requirements in the previous version of IAS 36 for determining recoverable amount until it considers and resolves the broader measurement issues in accounting. Additionally, in relation to (d), some field visit participants said that they routinely undertake sensitivity and statistical analysis as the basis for using an expected value approach to budgeting/forecasting and strategic decision-making.

BC80   Therefore, the Board decided to include in the revised Standard the application guidance on using present value techniques that was proposed in the Exposure Draft.

INCOME TAXES

Consideration of future tax cash flows

BCZ81   Future income tax cash flows may affect recoverable amount. It is convenient to analyse future tax cash flows into two components:

(a)   the future tax cash flows that would result from any difference between the tax base of an asset (the amount attributed to it for tax purposes) and its carrying amount, after recognition of any impairment loss. Such differences are described in IAS 12 *Income Taxes** as 'temporary differences'.

(b)   the future tax cash flows that would result if the tax base of the asset were equal to its recoverable amount.

BCZ82   For most assets, an enterprise recognises the tax consequences of temporary differences as a deferred tax liability or deferred tax asset in accordance with IAS 12. Therefore, to avoid double-counting, the future tax consequences of those temporary differences—the first component referred to in paragraph BCZ81—are not considered in determining recoverable amount (see further discussion in paragraphs BCZ86BCZ89).

BCZ83   The tax base of an asset on initial recognition is normally equal to its cost. Therefore, net selling price† implicitly reflects market participants' assessment of the future tax cash flows that would result if the tax base of the asset were equal to its recoverable amount. Therefore, no adjustment is required to net selling price to reflect the second component referred to in paragraph BCZ81.

BCZ84   In principle, value in use should include the present value of the future tax cash flows that would result if the tax base of the asset were equal to its value in use—the second component referred to in paragraph BCZ81. Nevertheless it may be burdensome to estimate the effect of that component. This is because:

(a)   to avoid double-counting, it is necessary to exclude the effect of temporary differences; and

(b)   value in use would need to be determined by an iterative and possibly complex computation so that value in use itself reflects a tax base equal to that value in use.

---

*ASB footnote: *The corresponding UK and Republic of Ireland requirements are set out in FRS 19* Deferred Tax.

†*In IFRS 5* Non-current Assets Held for Sale and Discontinued Operations, issued by the IASB in 2004, the term, 'net selling price' was replaced in IAS 36 by 'fair value less costs to sell'.

For these reasons, IASC decided to require an enterprise to determine value in use by using pre-tax future cash flows and, hence, a pre-tax discount rate.

Determining a pre-tax discount rate

In theory, discounting post-tax cash flows at a post-tax discount rate and discounting pre-tax cash flows at a pre-tax discount rate should give the same result, as long as the pre-tax discount rate is the post-tax discount rate adjusted to reflect the specific amount and timing of the future tax cash flows. The pre-tax discount rate is not always the post-tax discount rate grossed up by a standard rate of tax.

BCZ85

Example

This example illustrates that a post-tax discount rate grossed-up by a standard rate of tax is not always an appropriate pre-tax discount rate.

At the end of 20X0, the carrying amount of an asset is 1,757 and its remaining useful life is 5 years. The tax base in 20X0 is the cost of the asset. The cost is fully deductible at the end of 20X1. The tax rate is 20%. The discount rate for the asset can be determined only on a post-tax basis and is estimated to be 10%. At the end of 20X0, cash flow projections determined on a pre-tax basis are as follows:

	20X1	20X2	20X3	20X4	20X5
(1) Pre-tax cash flows (CF)	800	600	500	200	100

Value in use determined using post-tax cash flows and a post-tax discount rate

End of 20X0	20X1	20X2	20X3	20X4	20X5
(2) Deduction of the cost of the asset	(1,757)	-	-	-	-
(3) Tax CF [((1)-(2))*20%]	(191)	120	100	40	20
(4) Post-tax CF [(1)-(3)]	991	480	400	160	80
(5) Post-tax CF discounted at 10%	901	396	301	109	50
Value in use [Σ (5)] =					1,757

Value in use determined using pre-tax cash flows and a pre-tax discount rate (determined by grossing-up the post-tax discount rate)

Pre-tax discount rate (grossed-up) [10%/(100%-20%)] 12.5%

End of 20X0	20X1	20X2	20X3	20X4	20X5
(6) Pre-tax CF discounted at 12.5%	711	475	351	125	55
Value in use [Σ (6)] =					1,717

Determination of the 'real' pre-tax discount rate

> *A pre-tax discount rate can be determined by an iterative computation so that value in use determined using pre-tax cash flows and a pre-tax discount rate equals value in use determined using post-tax cash flows and a post-tax discount rate. In the example, the pre-tax discount rate would be 11.2%.*
>
> | End of 20X0 | 20X1 | 20X2 | 20X3 | 20X4 | 20X5 |
> |---|---|---|---|---|---|
> | *(7) Pre-tax CF discounted at 11.2%* | 718 | 485 | 364 | 131 | 59 |
> | *Value in use [Σ (7)] =* | | | | | 1,757 |
>
> *The 'real' pre-tax discount rate differs from the post-tax discount rate grossed-up by the standard rate of tax depending on the tax rate, the post-tax discount rate, the timing of the future tax cash flows and the useful life of the asset. Note that the tax base of the asset in this example has been set equal to its cost at the end of 20X0. Therefore, there is no deferred tax to consider in the balance sheet.*

Interaction with IAS 12

BCZ86   IAS 36 requires that recoverable amount should be based on present value calculations, whereas under IAS 12 an enterprise determines deferred tax assets and liabilities by comparing the carrying amount of an asset (a present value if the carrying amount is based on recoverable amount) with its tax base (an undiscounted amount).

BCZ87   One way to eliminate this inconsistency would be to measure deferred tax assets and liabilities on a discounted basis*. In developing the revised version of IAS 12 (approved in 1996), there was not enough support to require that deferred tax assets and liabilities should be measured on a discounted basis. IASC believed there was still not consensus to support such a change in existing practice. Therefore, IAS 36 requires an enterprise to measure the tax effects of temporary differences using the principles set out in IAS 12.

BCZ88   IAS 12 does not permit an enterprise to recognise certain deferred tax liabilities and assets. In such cases, some believe that the value in use of an asset, or a cash-generating unit, should be adjusted to reflect the tax consequences of recovering its pre-tax value in use. For example, if the tax rate is 25 per cent, an enterprise must receive pre-tax cash flows with a present value of 400 in order to recover a carrying amount of 300.

BCZ89   IASC acknowledged the conceptual merit of such adjustments but concluded that they would add unnecessary complexity. Therefore, IAS 36 neither requires nor permits such adjustments.

Comments by field visit participants and respondents to the December 2002 Exposure Draft

BC90   In revising IAS 36, the Board considered the requirement in the previous version of IAS 36 for:

*ASB footnote: *FRS 19 permits but does not require entities to adopt a policy of discounting deferred tax assets and liabilities.*

(a) income tax receipts and payments to be excluded from the estimates of future cash flows used to measure value in use; and

(b) the discount rate used to measure value in use to be a pre-tax rate that reflects current market assessments of the time value of money and the risks specific to the asset for which the future cash flow estimates have not been adjusted.

The Board had not considered these requirements when developing the Exposure Draft. However, some field visit participants and respondents to the Exposure Draft stated that using pre-tax cash flows and pre-tax discount rates would be a significant implementation issue for entities. This is because typically an entity's accounting and strategic decision-making systems are fully integrated and use post-tax cash flows and post-tax discount rates to arrive at present value measures. **BC91**

In considering this issue, the Board observed that the definition of value in use in the previous version of IAS 36 and the associated requirements on measuring value in use were not sufficiently precise to give a definitive answer to the question of what tax attribute an entity should reflect in value in use. For example, although IAS 36 specified discounting pre-tax cash flows at a pre-tax discount rate—with the pre-tax discount rate being the post-tax discount rate adjusted to reflect the specific amount and timing of the future tax cash flows—it did not specify *which* tax effects the pre-tax rate should include. Arguments could be mounted for various approaches. **BC92**

The Board decided that any decision to amend the requirement in the previous version of IAS 36 for pre-tax cash flows to be discounted at a pre-tax discount rate should be made only after the Board has resolved the issue of what tax attribute should be reflected in value in use. The Board decided that it should not try to resolve this latter issue as part of the Business Combinations project—decisions on the treatment of tax in value in use calculations should be made only as part of its conceptual project on measurement. Therefore, the Board concluded it should not amend as part of the current revision of IAS 36 the requirement to use pre-tax cash flows and pre-tax discount rates when measuring value in use. **BC93**

However, the Board observed that, conceptually, discounting post-tax cash flows at a post-tax discount rate and discounting pre-tax cash flows at a pre-tax discount rate should give the same result, as long as the pre-tax discount rate is the post-tax discount rate adjusted to reflect the specific amount and timing of the future tax cash flows. The pre-tax discount rate is generally not the post-tax discount rate grossed up by a standard rate of tax. **BC94**

RECOGNITION OF AN IMPAIRMENT LOSS (PARAGRAPHS 58-64)

IAS 36 requires that an impairment loss should be recognised whenever the recoverable amount of an asset is below its carrying amount. IASC considered various criteria for recognising an impairment loss in the financial statements: **BCZ95**

(a) recognition if it is considered that the impairment loss is permanent ('permanent criterion');

(b) recognition if it is considered probable that an asset is impaired, ie if it is probable that an enterprise will not recover the carrying amount of the asset ('probability criterion'); and

(c) immediate recognition whenever recoverable amount is below the carrying amount ('economic criterion').

Recognition based on a 'permanent' criterion

Supporters of the 'permanent' criterion argue that: **BCZ96**

(a)   this criterion avoids the recognition of temporary decreases in the recoverable amount of an asset.

(b)   the recognition of an impairment loss refers to future operations; it is contrary to the historical cost system to account for future events. Also, depreciation (amortisation) will reflect these future losses over the expected remaining useful life of the asset.

This view was supported by only a few commentators on E55 *Impairment of Assets*.

BCZ97   IASC decided to reject the 'permanent' criterion because:

(a)   it is difficult to identify whether an impairment loss is permanent. There is a risk that, by using this criterion, recognition of an impairment loss may be delayed.

(b)   this criterion is at odds with the basic concept that an asset is a resource that will generate future economic benefits. Cost-based accrual accounting cannot reflect events without reference to future expectations. If the events that led to a decrease in recoverable amount have already taken place, the carrying amount should be reduced accordingly.

Recognition based on a 'probability' criterion

BCZ98   Some argue that an impairment loss should be recognised only if it is considered probable that the carrying amount of an asset cannot be fully recovered. Proponents of a 'probability' criterion are divided between:

(a)   those who support the use of a recognition trigger based on the sum of the future cash flows (undiscounted and without allocation of interest costs) as a practical approach to implementing the 'probability' criterion; and

(b)   those who support reflecting the requirements in IAS 10 (reformatted 1994) *Contingencies and Events Occurring After the Balance Sheet Date.**

Sum of undiscounted future cash flows (without interest costs)

BCZ99   Some national standard-setters use the 'probability' criterion as a basis for recognition of an impairment loss and require, as a practical approach to implementing that criterion, that an impairment loss should be recognised only if the sum of the future cash flows from an asset (undiscounted and without allocation of interest costs) is less than the carrying amount of the asset. An impairment loss, when recognised, is measured as the difference between the carrying amount of the asset and its recoverable amount measured at fair value (based on quoted market prices or, if no quoted market prices exist, estimated considering prices for similar assets and the results of valuation techniques, such as the sum of cash flows discounted to their present value, option-pricing models, matrix pricing, option-adjusted spread models and fundamental analysis).

BCZ100 One of the characteristics of this approach is that the bases for recognition and measurement of an impairment loss are different. For example, even if the fair value of an asset is lower than its carrying amount, no impairment loss will be recognised if the sum of undiscounted cash flows (without allocation of interest costs) is greater than the asset's carrying amount. This might occur, especially if an asset has a long useful life.

**The requirements relating to contingencies in the 1994 version of IAS 10 were replaced in 1998 with the requirements in IAS 37* Provisions, Contingent Liabilities and Contingent Assets.

Those who support using the sum of undiscounted future cash flows (without allocation of interest costs) as a recognition trigger argue that: **BCZ101**

(a) using a recognition trigger based on undiscounted amounts is consistent with the historical cost framework.

(b) it avoids recognising temporary impairment losses and creating potentially volatile earnings that may mislead users of financial statements.

(c) net selling price* and value in use are difficult to substantiate—a price for the disposal of an asset or an appropriate discount rate is difficult to estimate.

(d) it is a higher threshold for recognising impairment losses. It should be relatively easy to conclude that the sum of undiscounted future cash flows will equal or exceed the carrying amount of an asset without incurring the cost of allocating projected cash flows to specific future periods.

This view was supported by a minority of commentators on E55 *Impairment of Assets.*

IASC considered the arguments listed above but rejected this approach because: **BCZ102**

(a) when it identifies that an asset may be impaired, a rational enterprise will make an investment decision. Therefore, it is relevant to consider the time value of money and the risks specific to an asset in determining whether an asset is impaired. This is particularly true if an asset has a long useful life.

(b) IAS 36 does not require an enterprise to estimate the recoverable amount of each [depreciable] asset every year but only if there is an indication that an asset may be materially impaired. An asset that is depreciated (amortised) in an appropriate manner is unlikely to become materially impaired unless events or changes in circumstances cause a sudden reduction in the estimate of recoverable amount.

(c) probability factors are already encompassed in the determination of value in use, in projecting future cash flows and in requiring that recoverable amount should be the higher of net selling price and value in use.

(d) if there is an unfavourable change in the assumptions used to determine recoverable amount, users are better served if they are informed about this change in assumptions on a timely basis.

Probability criterion based on IAS 10 (reformatted 1994)

IAS 10 required the amount of a contingent loss to be recognised as an expense and a liability if: **BCZ103**

(a) it was probable that future events will confirm that, after taking into account any related probable recovery, an asset had been impaired or a liability incurred at the balance sheet date; and

(b) a reasonable estimate of the amount of the resulting loss could be made.

IASC rejected the view that an impairment loss should be recognised based on the requirements in IAS 10 because: **BCZ104**

(a) the requirements in IAS 10 were not sufficiently detailed and would have made a 'probability' criterion difficult to apply.

(b) those requirements would have introduced another unnecessary layer of probability. Indeed, as mentioned above, probability factors are already

---

*In IFRS 5 Non-current Assets Held for Sale and Discontinued Operations, *issued by the IASB in 2004, the term, 'net selling price' was replaced in IAS 36 by 'fair value less costs to sell'.*

encompassed in estimates of value in use and in requiring that recoverable amount should be the higher of net selling price and value in use.

Recognition based on an 'economic' criterion

BCZ105   IAS 36 relies on an 'economic' criterion for the recognition of an impairment loss—an impairment loss is recognised whenever the recoverable amount of an asset is below its carrying amount. This criterion was already used in many International Accounting Standards before IAS 36, such as IAS 9 *Research and Development Costs*, IAS 22 *Business Combinations*, and IAS 16 *Property, Plant and Equipment*.

BCZ106   IASC considered that an 'economic' criterion is the best criterion to give information which is useful to users in assessing future cash flows to be generated by the enterprise as a whole. In estimating the time value of money and the risks specific to an asset in determining whether the asset is impaired, factors, such as the probability or permanence of the impairment loss, are subsumed in the measurement.

BCZ107   The majority of commentators on E55 supported IASC's view that an impairment loss should be recognised based on an 'economic' criterion.

Revalued assets: recognition in the income statement versus directly in equity*

BCZ108   IAS 36 requires that an impairment loss on a revalued asset should be recognised as an expense in the income statement immediately, except that it should be recognised directly in equity to the extent that it reverses a previous revaluation on the same asset.

BCZ109   Some argue that, when there is a clear reduction in the service potential (for example, physical damage) of a revalued asset, the impairment loss should be recognised in the income statement.

BCZ110   Others argue that an impairment loss should always be recognised as an expense in the income statement. The logic of this argument is that an impairment loss arises only where there is a reduction in the estimated future cash flows that form part of the business's operating activities. Indeed, according to IAS 16, whether or not an asset is revalued, the depreciation charge is always recognised in the income statement. Supporters of this view question why the treatment of an impairment loss on a revalued asset should be different to depreciation.

BCZ111   IASC believed that it would be difficult to identify whether an impairment loss is a downward revaluation or a reduction in service potential. Therefore, IASC decided to retain the treatment used in IAS 16 and to treat an impairment loss of a revalued asset as a revaluation decrease (and similarly, a reversal of an impairment loss as a subsequent revaluation increase).

BCZ112   For a revalued asset, the distinction between an 'impairment loss' ('reversal of an impairment loss') and another 'revaluation decrease' ('revaluation increase') is important for disclosure purposes. If an impairment loss that is material to the enterprise as a whole has been recognised or reversed, more information on how this impairment loss is measured is required by IAS 36 than for the recognition of a revaluation in accordance with IAS 16.

*ASB footnote: The consequential amendments set out in this [draft] FRS ● amend FRS 15 such that recognition of gains and losses will be converged with IAS 16.

CASH-GENERATING UNITS (PARAGRAPHS 66-73)

Some support the principle of determining recoverable amount on an individual asset basis only. This view was expressed by a few commentators on E55. They argued that:

BCZ113

(a) it would be difficult to identify cash-generating units at a level other than the business as a whole and, therefore, impairment losses would never be recognised for individual assets; and

(b) it should be possible to recognise an impairment loss, regardless of whether an asset generates cash inflows that are independent from those of other assets or groups of assets. Commentators quoted examples of assets that have become under-utilised or obsolete but that are still in use.

IASC acknowledged that identifying the lowest level of independent cash inflows for a group of assets would involve judgement. However, IASC believed that the concept of cash-generating units is a matter of fact: assets work together to generate cash flows.

BCZ114

In response to requests from commentators on E55, IAS 36 includes additional guidance and examples for identifying cash-generating units and for determining the carrying amount of cash-generating units. IAS 36 emphasises that cash-generating units should be identified for the lowest level of aggregation of assets possible.

BCZ115

Internal transfer pricing (paragraph 70)

The previous version of IAS 36 required that if an active market exists for the output produced by an asset or a group of assets:

BC116

(a) that asset or group of assets should be identified as a cash-generating unit, even if some or all of the output is used internally; and

(b) management's best estimate of the future market prices for the output should be used in estimating:

    (i) the future cash inflows that relate to the internal use of the output when determining the value in use of this cash-generating unit; and

    (ii) the future cash outflows that relate to the internal use of the output when determining the value in use of the entity's other cash-generating units.

The requirement in (a) above has been carried forward in the revised Standard. However, some respondents to the Exposure Draft asked for additional guidance to clarify the role of internal transfer pricing versus prices in an arm's length transaction when developing cash flow forecasts. The Board decided to address this issue by amending the requirement in (b) above to deal more broadly with cash-generating units whose cash flows are affected by internal transfer pricing, rather than just cash-generating units whose internally consumed output could be sold on an active market.

BC117

Therefore, the Standard clarifies that if the cash inflows generated by *any* asset or cash-generating unit are affected by internal transfer pricing, an entity should use management's best estimate of future prices that could be achieved in arm's length transactions in estimating:

BC118

(a) the future cash inflows used to determine the asset's or cash-generating unit's value in use; and

(b) the future cash outflows used to determine the value in use of other assets or cash-generating units affected by the internal transfer pricing.

TESTING INDEFINITE-LIVED INTANGIBLES FOR IMPAIRMENT

BC119 As part of the first phase of its Business Combinations project, the Board concluded that:

(a) an intangible asset should be regarded as having an indefinite useful life when, based on an analysis of all relevant factors (eg legal, regulatory, contractual, competitive and economic), there is no foreseeable limit on the period over which the asset is expected to generate net cash inflows for the entity; and

(b) an indefinite-lived intangible should not be amortised, but should be tested regularly for impairment.

An outline of the Board's deliberations on each of these issues is provided in the Basis for Conclusions on IAS 38 *Intangible Assets*.

BC120 Having reached these conclusions, the Board then considered the form that the impairment test for indefinite-lived intangibles should take. The Board concluded that:

(a) an indefinite-lived intangible should be tested for impairment annually, or more frequently if there is any indication that it may be impaired; and

(b) the recoverable amounts of such assets should be measured, and impairment losses (and reversals of impairment losses) in respect of those assets should be accounted for, in accordance with the requirements in IAS 36 for assets other than goodwill.

Paragraphs BC121-BC126 outline the Board's deliberations in reaching its conclusion about the frequency and timing of impairment testing indefinite-lived intangibles. Paragraphs BC129 and BC130 outline the Board's deliberations in reaching its conclusions about measuring the recoverable amount of such assets and accounting for impairment losses and reversals of impairment losses.

Frequency and timing of impairment testing (paragraphs 9 and 10(a))

BC121 In developing the Exposure Draft, the Board observed that requiring assets to be remeasured when they are impaired is a valuation concept rather than one of cost allocation. This concept, which some have termed 'the recoverable cost concept', focuses on the benefits to be derived from the asset in the future, rather than on the process by which the cost or other carrying amount of the asset should be allocated to particular accounting periods. Therefore, the purpose of an impairment test is to assess whether the carrying amount of an asset will be recovered through use or sale of the asset. Nevertheless, allocating the depreciable amount of an asset with a limited useful life on a systematic basis over that life provides some assurance against the asset's carrying amount exceeding its recoverable amount. The Board acknowledged that non-amortisation of an intangible asset increases the reliance that must be placed on impairment reviews of that asset to ensure that its carrying amount does not exceed its recoverable amount.

BC122 Accordingly, the Exposure Draft proposed that indefinite-lived intangibles should be tested for impairment at the end of each annual reporting period. The Board concluded, however, that testing such assets annually for impairment is not a substitute for management being aware of events occurring or circumstances changing between annual tests that indicate a possible impairment. Therefore, the Exposure Draft also proposed that an entity should be required to test such assets for impairment whenever there is an indication of possible impairment, and not wait until the next annual test.

The respondents to the Exposure Draft generally supported the proposal to test **BC123** indefinite-lived intangibles for impairment annually and whenever there is an indication of possible impairment. Those that disagreed argued that requiring an annual impairment test would be excessively burdensome, and recommended requiring an impairment test only when there is an indication that an indefinite-lived intangible might be impaired. After considering these comments the Board:

(a) reaffirmed its view that non-amortisation of an intangible asset increases the reliance that must be placed on impairment reviews of that asset to ensure that its carrying amount does not exceed its recoverable amount.

(b) concluded that IAS 36 should require indefinite-lived intangibles to be tested for impairment annually and whenever there is an indication of possible impairment.

However, as noted in paragraph BC122, the Exposure Draft proposed that the **BC124** annual impairment tests for indefinite-lived intangibles should be performed at the end of each annual period. Many respondents to the Exposure Draft disagreed that IAS 36 should mandate the timing of the annual impairment tests. They argued that:

(a) it would be inconsistent with the proposal (now a requirement) that the annual impairment test for a cash-generating unit to which goodwill has been allocated may be performed at any time during an annual period, provided the test is performed at the same time every year. There is no justification for providing less flexibility in the timing of the annual impairment test for indefinite-lived intangibles.

(b) if the impairment test for an indefinite-lived intangible is linked to the impairment test for goodwill (ie if the indefinite-lived intangible is assessed for impairment at the same cash-generating unit level as goodwill, rather than individually or as part of a smaller cash-generating unit), the requirement to measure its recoverable amount at the end of the annual period could result in the cash-generating unit to which it (and the goodwill) belongs being tested for impairment at least twice each annual period, which is too burdensome. For example, assume a cash-generating unit contains goodwill and an indefinite-lived intangible, and that the indefinite-lived intangible is assessed for impairment at the same cash-generating unit level as goodwill. Assume also that the entity reports quarterly, has a December year-end, and decides to test goodwill for impairment at the end of the third quarter to coincide with the completion of its annual strategic planning/budgeting process. The proposal that the annual impairment test for an indefinite-lived intangible should be performed at the end of each annual period would mean that the entity would be required:

    (i) to calculate at the end of each September the recoverable amount of the cash-generating unit, compare it with its carrying amount, and, if the carrying amount exceeds the recoverable amount, recognise an impairment loss for the unit by reducing the carrying amount of goodwill and allocating any remaining impairment loss to the other assets in the unit, including the indefinite-lived intangible.

    (ii) to perform the same steps again each December to test the indefinite-lived intangible for impairment.

    (iii) to perform the same steps again at any other time throughout the annual period if there is an indication that the cash-generating unit, the goodwill or the indefinite-lived intangible may be impaired.

In considering these comments, the Board indicated a preference for requiring **BC125** entities to perform the recoverable amount calculations for both goodwill and indefinite-lived intangibles at the end of the annual period. However, the Board acknowledged that, as outlined in paragraph BC124(b), impairment tests for indefinite-lived intangibles will sometimes be linked to impairment tests for goodwill, and that many entities would find it difficult to perform all those tests at the end of the annual period.

BC126   Therefore, consistently with the annual impairment test for goodwill, the Standard permits the annual impairment test for an indefinite-lived intangible to be performed at any time during an annual period, provided it is performed at the same time every year.

Carrying forward a recoverable amount calculation (paragraph 24)

BC127   The Standard permits the most recent detailed calculation of the recoverable amount of an indefinite-lived intangible to be carried forward from a preceding period for use in the current period's impairment test, provided all of the criteria in paragraph 24 of the Standard are met.

BC128   Integral to the Board's decision that indefinite-lived intangibles should be tested for impairment annually was the view that many entities should be able to conclude that the recoverable amount of such an asset is greater than its carrying amount without actually recomputing recoverable amount. However, the Board concluded that this would be the case only if the last recoverable amount determination exceeded the carrying amount by a substantial margin, and nothing had happened since then to make the likelihood of an impairment loss other than remote. The Board concluded that, in such circumstances, permitting a detailed calculation of the recoverable amount of an indefinite-lived intangible to be carried forward from the preceding period for use in the current period's impairment test would significantly reduce the costs of applying the impairment test, without compromising its integrity.

Measuring recoverable amount and accounting for impairment losses and reversals of impairment losses

BC129   The Board could see no compelling reason why the measurement basis adopted for determining recoverable amount and the treatment of impairment losses and reversals of impairment losses for one group of identifiable assets should differ from those applying to other identifiable assets. Adopting different methods would impair the usefulness of the information provided to users about an entity's identifiable assets, because both comparability and reliability, which rest on the notion that similar transactions are accounted for in the same way, would be diminished. Therefore, the Board concluded that the recoverable amounts of indefinite-lived intangibles should be measured, and impairment losses and reversals of impairment losses in respect of those assets should be accounted for, consistently with other identifiable assets covered by the Standard.

BC130   The Board expressed some concern over the measurement basis adopted in the previous version of IAS 36 for determining recoverable amount (ie higher of value in use and net selling price) and its treatment of impairment losses and reversals of impairment losses for assets other than goodwill. However, the Board's intention in revising IAS 36 was *not* to reconsider the general approach to impairment testing. Accordingly, the Board decided that it should address concerns over that general approach as part of its future re-examination of IAS 36 in its entirety, rather than as part of its Business Combinations project.

TESTING GOODWILL FOR IMPAIRMENT (PARAGRAPHS 80-99)

The Board concluded that if a rigorous and operational impairment test could be **BC131** devised, more useful information would be provided to users of an entity's financial statements under an approach in which goodwill is not amortised, but is instead tested for impairment annually or more frequently if events or changes in circumstances indicate that the goodwill might be impaired. An outline of the Board's deliberations in reaching this conclusion is provided in the Basis for Conclusions on IFRS 3 *Business Combinations*.

Paragraphs BC133-BC177 outline the Board's deliberations on the form that the **BC132** impairment test for goodwill should take:

(a)   paragraphs BC137-BC159 discuss the requirements relating to the allocation of goodwill to cash-generating units and the level at which goodwill is tested for impairment.

(b)   paragraphs BC160-BC170 discuss the requirements relating to the recognition and measurement of impairment losses for goodwill, including the frequency of impairment testing.

(c)   paragraphs BC171-BC177 discuss the requirements relating to the timing of goodwill impairment tests.

As a first step in its deliberations, the Board considered the objective of the goodwill **BC133** impairment test and the measure of recoverable amount that should be adopted for such a test. The Board observed that recent North American standards use fair value as the basis for impairment testing goodwill, whereas the previous version of IAS 36 and the United Kingdom standard are based on an approach under which recoverable amount is measured as the higher of value in use and net selling price.

The Board also observed that goodwill acquired in a business combination repre- **BC134** sents a payment made by an acquirer in anticipation of future economic benefits from assets that are not capable of being individually identified and separately recognised. Goodwill does not generate cash flows independently of other assets or groups of assets and therefore cannot be measured directly. Instead, it is measured as a residual amount, being the excess of the cost of a business combination over the acquirer's interest in the net fair value of the acquiree's identifiable assets, liabilities and contingent liabilities. Moreover, goodwill acquired in a business combination and goodwill generated after that business combination cannot be separately identified, because they contribute jointly to the same cash flows.

The Board concluded that because it is not possible to measure separately goodwill **BC135** generated internally after a business combination and to factor that measure into the impairment test for acquired goodwill, the carrying amount of goodwill will always be shielded from impairment by that internally generated goodwill. Therefore, the Board took the view that the objective of the goodwill impairment test could at best be to ensure that the carrying amount of goodwill is recoverable from future cash flows expected to be generated by both acquired goodwill and goodwill generated internally after the business combination.

The Board noted that because goodwill is measured as a residual amount, the **BC136** starting point in any goodwill impairment test would have to be the recoverable amount of the operation or unit to which the goodwill relates, regardless of the measurement basis adopted for determining recoverable amount. The Board decided that until it considers and resolves the broader question of the appropriate measurement objective(s) in accounting, identifying the appropriate measure of recoverable amount for that unit would be problematic. Therefore, although the

Board expressed concern over the measurement basis adopted in IAS 36 for determining recoverable amount, it decided that it should not depart from that basis when measuring the recoverable amount of a unit whose carrying amount includes acquired goodwill. The Board noted that this would have the added advantage of allowing the impairment test for goodwill to be integrated with the impairment test in IAS 36 for other assets and cash-generating units that include goodwill.

Allocating goodwill to cash-generating units (paragraphs 80-87)

BC137   The previous version of IAS 36 required goodwill to be tested for impairment as part of impairment testing the cash-generating units to which it relates. It employed a 'bottom-up/top-down' approach under which the goodwill was in effect tested for impairment by allocating its carrying amount to each of the smallest cash-generating units to which a portion of that carrying amount could be allocated on a reasonable and consistent basis.

BC138   Consistently with the previous version of IAS 36, the Exposure Draft proposed that:

(a)   goodwill should be tested for impairment as part of impairment testing the cash-generating units to which it relates; and

(b)   the carrying amount of goodwill should be allocated to each of the smallest cash-generating units to which a portion of that carrying amount can be allocated on a reasonable and consistent basis.

However, the Exposure Draft proposed additional guidance clarifying that a portion of the carrying amount of goodwill should be regarded as capable of being allocated to a cash-generating unit on a reasonable and consistent basis only when that unit represents the lowest level at which management monitors the return on investment in assets that include the goodwill. That cash-generating unit could not, however, be larger than a segment based on the entity's primary reporting format determined in accordance with IAS 14 *Segment Reporting**.

BC139   In developing this proposal, the Board noted that because acquired goodwill does not generate cash flows independently of other assets or groups of assets, it can be tested for impairment only as part of impairment testing the cash-generating units to which it relates. However, the Board was concerned that in the absence of any guidance on the precise meaning of 'allocated on a reasonable and consistent basis', some might conclude that when a business combination enhances the value of all of the acquirer's pre-existing cash-generating units, any goodwill acquired in that business combination should be tested for impairment only at the level of the entity itself. The Board concluded that this should not be the case. Rather, there should be a link between the level at which goodwill is tested for impairment and the level of internal reporting that reflects the way an entity manages its operations and with which the goodwill naturally would be associated. Therefore, it was important to the Board that goodwill should be tested for impairment at a level at which information about the operations of an entity and the assets that support them is provided for internal reporting purposes.

BC140   In redeliberating this issue, the Board noted that respondents' and field visit participants' comments indicated that the Board's intention relating to the allocation of goodwill had been widely misunderstood, with many concluding that goodwill would

*ASB footnote: *SSAP 25* Segmental Reporting *sets out the requirements for the UK and Republic of Ireland. SSAP 25 defines a class of business. The definition in SSAP 25 of a class of business is not consistent with the definition of a segment in IAS 14. The [draft] FRS has been amended in paragraph 6 to conform the level at which goodwill is tested for impairment.*

need to be allocated to a much lower level than that intended by the Board. For example, some respondents and field visit participants were concerned that the proposal to allocate goodwill to such a low level would force entities to allocate goodwill arbitrarily to cash-generating units, and therefore to develop new or additional reporting systems to perform the test. The Board confirmed that its intention was that there should be a link between the level at which goodwill is tested for impairment and the level of internal reporting that reflects the way an entity manages its operations. Therefore, except for entities that do not monitor goodwill at or below the segment level, the proposals relating to the level of the goodwill impairment test should *not* cause entities to allocate goodwill arbitrarily to cash-generating units. Nor should they create the need for entities to develop new or additional reporting systems.

The Board observed from its discussions with field visit participants that much of the confusion stemmed from the definition of a 'cash-generating unit', when coupled with the proposal in paragraph 73 of the Exposure Draft for goodwill to be allocated to each "smallest cash-generating unit to which a portion of the carrying amount of the goodwill can be allocated on a reasonable and consistent basis". Additionally, field visit participants and respondents were unclear about the reference in paragraph 74 of the Exposure Draft to "the lowest level at which management monitors the return on investments in assets that include goodwill", the most frequent question being "what level of management?" (eg board of directors, chief executive officer, or segment management).   **BC141**

The Board noted that once its intention on this issue was clarified for field visit participants, they all, with the exception of one company that believes goodwill should be tested for impairment at the entity level, supported the level at which the Board believes goodwill should be tested for impairment.   **BC142**

The Board also noted the comment from a number of respondents and field visit participants that for some organisations, particularly those managed on a matrix basis, the proposal for cash-generating units to which the goodwill is allocated to be no larger than a segment based on the entity's *primary* reporting format could result in an outcome that is inconsistent with the Board's intention, ie that there should be a link between the level at which goodwill is tested for impairment and the level of internal reporting that reflects the way an entity manages its operations. The following example illustrates this point: **BC143**

> A company managed on a matrix basis is organised primarily on a geographical basis, with product groups providing the secondary basis of segmentation. Goodwill is acquired as part of an acquisition of a product group that is present in several geographical regions, and is then monitored on an ongoing basis for internal reporting purposes as part of the product group/secondary segment. It is feasible that the secondary segment might, depending on the definition of 'larger', be 'larger' than a primary segment.

Therefore, the Board decided: **BC144**

(a) that the Standard should require each unit or group of units to which goodwill is allocated to represent the lowest level within the entity at which the goodwill is monitored for internal management purposes.

(b) to clarify in the Standard that acquired goodwill should, from the acquisition date, be allocated to each of the acquirer's cash-generating units, or groups of cash-generating units, that are expected to benefit from the combination, irrespective of whether other assets or liabilities of the acquiree are assigned to those units or groups of units.

(c)   to replace the proposal for cash-generating units or groups of units to which goodwill is allocated to be no larger than a segment based on the entity's *primary* reporting format, with the requirement that they be no larger than a segment based on either the entity's primary or the entity's secondary reporting format. The Board concluded that this amendment is necessary to ensure that entities managed on a matrix basis are able to test goodwill for impairment at the level of internal reporting that reflects the way they manage their operations.

BC145   Some respondents to the Exposure Draft raised the following additional concerns on the allocation of goodwill for impairment testing purposes:

(a)   mandating that goodwill should be allocated to at least the segment level is inappropriate—it will often result in arbitrary allocations, and entities would need to develop new or additional reporting systems.

(b)   for convergence reasons, the level of the goodwill impairment test should be the same as the level in US Financial Accounting Standards Board Statement of Financial Accounting Standards No. 142 *Goodwill and Other Intangible Assets* (SFAS 142) (ie the reporting unit level).

(c)   cash-generating units that constitute businesses with similar characteristics should, as is required by SFAS 142, be aggregated and treated as single units, notwithstanding that they may be monitored independently for internal purposes.

BC146   In relation to (a), the Board reaffirmed the conclusion it reached when developing the Exposure Draft that requiring goodwill to be allocated to at least the segment level is necessary to avoid entities erroneously concluding that, when a business combination enhances the value of all of the acquirer's pre-existing cash-generating units, any goodwill acquired in that combination could be tested for impairment only at the level of the entity itself.

BC147   In relation to (b), the Board noted that SFAS 142 requires goodwill to be tested for impairment at a level of reporting referred to as a 'reporting unit'. A reporting unit is an operating segment (as defined in SFAS 131 *Disclosures about Segments of an Enterprise and Related Information**) or one level below an operating segment (referred to as a component). A component of an operating segment is a reporting unit if the component constitutes a business for which discrete financial information is available and segment management regularly reviews the operating results of that component. However, two or more components of an operating segment must be aggregated and deemed a single reporting unit if the components have similar economic characteristics. An operating segment is deemed to be a reporting unit if all of its components are similar, if none of its components is a reporting unit, or if it comprises only a single component.

BC148   Therefore, unlike IAS 36, SFAS 142 places a limit on how far goodwill can be 'pushed down' for impairment testing (ie one level below an operating segment).

The basis for identifying 'operating segments' under SFAS 131 differs from the basis for identifying segments based on the entity's primary reporting format under IAS 14. SFAS 131 defines an operating segment as a component of an enterprise (a) that engages in business activities from which it may earn revenues and incur expenses, including revenues and expenses relating to transactions with other components of the enterprise; (b) whose operating results are regularly reviewed by the enterprise's chief operating decision maker to make decisions about resources to be allocated to the segment and assess its performance; and (c) for which discrete financial information is available.

In deciding not to converge with SFAS 142 on the level of the goodwill impairment test, the Board noted the following findings from the field visits and North American round-table discussions: **BC149**

(a) most of the US registrant field visit participants stated that the Board's proposals on the level of the goodwill impairment test would result, in practice, in goodwill being tested for impairment at the same level at which it is tested in accordance with SFAS 142. However, several stated that under the Board's proposals, goodwill would be tested for impairment at a lower level than under SFAS 142. Nevertheless, they believe that the Board's approach provides users and management with more useful information.

(b) several round-table participants stated that they (or, in the case of audit firm participants, their clients) manage and have available information about their investments in goodwill at a lower level than the level of the SFAS 142 impairment test. They expressed a high level of dissatisfaction at being prevented by SFAS 142 from recognising goodwill impairments that they knew existed at these lower levels, but which 'disappeared' once the lower level units were aggregated with other units containing sufficient 'cushions' to offset the impairment loss.

In considering suggestion (c) in paragraph BC145, the Board observed that aggregating units that constitute businesses with similar characteristics could result in the disappearance of an impairment loss that management *knows* exists in a cash-generating unit because the units with which it is aggregated contain sufficient cushions to offset the impairment loss. In the Board's view, if, because of the way an entity is managed, information about goodwill impairment losses is available to management at a particular level, that information should also be available to the users of the entity's financial statements. **BC150**

Completing the initial allocation of goodwill (paragraphs 84 and 85)

If the initial allocation of goodwill acquired in a business combination cannot be completed before the end of the annual period in which the business combination is effected, the Exposure Draft proposed, and the revised Standard requires, that the initial allocation should be completed before the end of the first annual period beginning after the acquisition date. In contrast, ED 3 proposed, and IFRS 3 requires, that if the initial accounting for a business combination can be determined only provisionally by the end of the period in which the combination is effected, the acquirer should: **BC151**

(a) account for the combination using those provisional values; and

(b) recognise any adjustments to those provisional values as a result of completing the initial accounting within twelve months of the acquisition date.

Some respondents to the Exposure Draft questioned why the period to complete the initial allocation of goodwill should differ from the period to complete the initial accounting for a business combination. The Board's view is that acquirers should be allowed a longer period to complete the goodwill allocation, because that allocation often might not be able to be performed until after the initial accounting for the combination is complete. This is because the cost of the combination or the fair values at the acquisition date of the acquiree's identifiable assets, liabilities or contingent liabilities, and therefore the amount of goodwill acquired in the combination, would not be finalised until the initial accounting for the combination in accordance with IFRS 3 is complete. **BC152**

Disposal of a portion of a cash-generating unit containing goodwill (paragraph 86)

BC153   The Exposure Draft proposed that when an entity disposes of an operation within a cash-generating unit to which goodwill has been allocated, the goodwill associated with that operation should be:

(a)   included in the carrying amount of the operation when determining the gain or loss on disposal; and

(b)   measured on the basis of the relative values of the operation disposed of and the portion of the cash-generating unit retained.

BC154   This proposal has been carried forward in the Standard with one modification. The Standard requires the goodwill associated with the operation disposed of to be measured on the basis of the relative values of the operation disposed of and the portion of the cash-generating unit retained, unless the entity can demonstrate that some other method better reflects the goodwill associated with the operation disposed of.

BC155   In developing the Exposure Draft, the Board concluded that the proposed level of the impairment test would mean that goodwill could not be identified or associated with an asset group at a level lower than the cash-generating unit to which the goodwill is allocated, except arbitrarily. However, the Board also concluded that when an operation within that cash-generating unit is being disposed of, it is appropriate to presume that some amount of goodwill is associated with that operation. Thus, an allocation of the goodwill should be required when the part of the cash-generating unit being disposed of constitutes an operation.

BC156   Some respondents to the Exposure Draft suggested that although in most circumstances goodwill could not be identified or associated with an asset group at a level lower than the cash-generating unit or group of cash-generating units to which it is allocated for impairment testing, there may be some instances when this is not so. For example, assume an acquiree is integrated with one of the acquirer's pre-existing cash-generating units that did not include any goodwill in its carrying amount. Assume also that almost immediately after the business combination the acquirer disposes of a loss-making operation within the cash-generating unit. The Board agreed with respondents that in such circumstances, it might reasonably be concluded that no part of the carrying amount of goodwill has been disposed of, and therefore no part of its carrying amount should be derecognised by being included in the determination of the gain or loss on disposal.

Reorganisation of reporting structure (paragraph 87)

BC157   The Exposure Draft proposed that when an entity reorganises its reporting structure in a way that changes the composition of cash-generating units to which goodwill has been allocated, the goodwill should be reallocated to the units affected using a relative value approach similar to that used when an entity disposes of an operation within a cash-generating unit.

BC158   In developing the Exposure Draft, the Board concluded that a reorganisation that changes the composition of a cash-generating unit to which goodwill has been allocated gives rise to the same allocation problem as disposing of an operation within that unit. Therefore, the same allocation methodology should be used in both cases.

BC159   As a result, and consistently with the Board's decision to modify its proposal on allocating goodwill when an entity disposes of an operation, the revised Standard requires an entity that reorganises its reporting structure in a way that changes the composition of one or more cash-generating units to which goodwill has been allocated:

(a)   to reallocate the goodwill to the units affected; and

(b)   to perform this reallocation using a relative value approach similar to that used when an entity disposes of an operation within a cash-generating unit (group of cash-generating units), unless the entity can demonstrate that some other method better reflects the goodwill associated with the reorganised units (groups of units).

Recognition and measurement of impairment losses (paragraphs 88-99 and 104)

Background to the proposals in the Exposure Draft

The Exposure Draft proposed a two-step approach for impairment testing goodwill. **BC160** The first step involved using a screening mechanism for identifying potential goodwill impairments, whereby goodwill allocated to a cash-generating unit would be identified as potentially impaired only when the carrying amount of the unit exceeded its recoverable amount. If an entity identified the goodwill allocated to a cash-generating unit as potentially impaired, an entity would then determine whether the goodwill allocated to the unit was impaired by comparing its recoverable amount, measured as the 'implied value' of the goodwill, with its carrying amount. The implied value of goodwill would be measured as a residual, being the excess of:

(a)   the recoverable amount of the cash-generating unit to which the goodwill has been allocated, over

(b)   the net fair value of the identifiable assets, liabilities and contingent liabilities the entity would recognise if it acquired the cash-generating unit in a business combination on the date of the impairment test (excluding any identifiable asset that was acquired in a business combination but not recognised separately from goodwill at the acquisition date).

In developing the Exposure Draft, the Board's discussion focused first on how the **BC161** recoverable amount of goodwill allocated to a cash-generating unit could be separated from the recoverable amount of the unit as a whole, given that goodwill generated internally after a business combination could not be measured separately. The Board concluded that a method similar to the method an acquirer uses to allocate the cost of a business combination to the net assets acquired could be used to measure the recoverable amount of goodwill after its initial recognition. Thus, the Board decided that some measure of the net assets of a cash-generating unit to which goodwill has been allocated should be subtracted from the recoverable amount of that unit to determine a current implied value for the goodwill. The Board concluded that the measure of the net assets of a cash-generating unit described in paragraph BC160(b) would result in the best estimate of the current implied value of the goodwill, given that goodwill generated internally after a business combination could not be measured separately.

Having decided on the most appropriate measure of the recoverable amount of **BC162** goodwill, the Board then considered how often an entity should be required to test goodwill for impairment. Consistently with its conclusions about indefinite-lived intangibles, the Board concluded that non-amortisation of goodwill increases the reliance that must be placed on impairment tests to ensure that the carrying amount of goodwill does not exceed its recoverable amount. Accordingly, the Board decided that goodwill should be tested for impairment annually. However, the Board also concluded that the annual test is not a substitute for management being aware of events occurring or circumstances changing between annual tests indicating a possible impairment of goodwill. Therefore, the Board decided that an entity should also be required to test goodwill for impairment whenever there is an indication of possible impairment.

BC163   After the Board decided on the frequency of impairment testing, it expressed some concern that the proposed test would not be cost-effective. This concern related primarily to the requirement to determine the fair value of each identifiable asset, liability and contingent liability within a cash-generating unit that would be recognised by the entity if it had acquired the cash-generating unit in a business combination on the date of the impairment test (to estimate the implied value of goodwill).

BC164   Therefore, the Board decided to propose as a first step in the impairment test for goodwill a screening mechanism similar to that in SFAS 142. Under SFAS 142, goodwill is tested for impairment by first comparing the fair value of the reporting unit to which the goodwill has been allocated for impairment testing purposes with the carrying amount of that unit. If the fair value of the unit exceeds its carrying amount, the goodwill is regarded as not impaired. An entity need estimate the implied fair value of goodwill (using an approach consistent with that described in paragraph BC160) only if the fair value of the unit is less than its carrying amount.

The Board's redeliberations

BC165   Many respondents disagreed with the proposal to adopt a two-step approach to impairment testing goodwill. In particular, the second step of the proposed impairment test and the method for measuring any impairment loss for the goodwill caused considerable concern. Respondents provided the following conceptual arguments against the proposed approach:

(a)   by drawing on only some aspects of the SFAS 142 two-step approach, the result is a hybrid between fair values and value in use. More particularly, not measuring goodwill's implied value as the difference between the unit's fair value and the net fair value of the identifiable net assets in the unit, but instead measuring it as the difference between the unit's recoverable amount (ie higher of value in use and fair value less costs to sell) and the net fair value of the identifiable net assets in the unit, results in a measure of goodwill that conceptually is neither fair value nor recoverable amount. This raises questions about the conceptual validity of measuring goodwill impairment losses as the difference between goodwill's implied value and carrying amount.

(b)   it seems inconsistent to consider goodwill separately for impairment testing when other assets within a unit are not considered separately but are instead considered as part of the unit as a whole, particularly given that goodwill, unlike many other assets, cannot generate cash inflows independently of other assets. The previous version of IAS 36 is premised on the notion that if a series of independent cash flows can be generated only by a group of assets operating together, impairment losses should be considered only for that group of assets as a whole—individual assets within the group should not be considered separately.

(c)   concluding that the recoverable amount of goodwill—which cannot generate cash inflows independently of other assets—should be measured separately for measuring impairment losses makes it difficult to understand how the Board could in the future reasonably conclude that such an approach to measuring impairment losses is also not appropriate for other assets. In other words, if it adopts the proposed two-step approach for goodwill, the Board could in effect be committing itself to an 'individual asset/fair value' approach for measuring impairments of all other assets. A decision on this issue should be made only as part of a broad reconsideration of the appropriate measurement objective for impairment testing generally.

(d)   if goodwill is considered separately for impairment testing using an implied value calculation when other assets within a unit are considered only as part of the unit as a whole, there will be asymmetry: unrecognised goodwill will shield the carrying value of other assets from impairment, but the unrecognised value of other assets will not shield the carrying amount of goodwill from impairment. This seems unreasonable given that the unrecognised value of those other assets cannot then be recognised. Additionally, the carrying amount of a unit will be less than its recoverable amount whenever an impairment loss for goodwill exceeds the unrecognised value of the other assets in the unit.

Additionally, respondents, field visit participants and North American roundtable participants raised the following concerns about the practicability and costs of applying the proposed two-step approach: **BC166**

(a)   many companies would be required regularly to perform the second step of the impairment test, and therefore would need to determine the fair values of each identifiable asset, liability and contingent liability within the impaired unit(s) that the entity would recognise if it acquired the unit(s) in a business combination on the date of the impairment test. Although determining these fair values would not, for some companies, pose significant practical challenges (because, for example, fair value information for their significant assets is readily available), most would need to engage, on a fairly wide scale and at significant cost, independent valuers for some or all of the unit's assets. This is particularly the case for identifying and measuring the fair values of unrecognised internally generated intangible assets.

(b)   determining the fair values of each identifiable asset, liability and contingent liability within an impaired unit is likely to be impracticable for multi-segmented manufacturers that operate multi-product facilities servicing more than one cash-generating unit. For example, assume an entity's primary basis of segmentation is geographical (eg Europe, North America, South America, Asia, Oceania and Africa) and that its secondary basis of segmentation is based on product groups (vaccinations, over-the-counter medicines, prescription medicines and vitamins/dietary supplements). Assume also that:

(i)   the lowest level within the entity at which the goodwill is monitored for internal management purposes is one level below primary segment (eg the vitamins business in North America), and that goodwill is therefore tested for impairment at this level;

(ii)   the plants and distribution facilities in each geographical region manufacture and distribute for all product groups; and

(iii) to determine the carrying amount of each cash-generating unit containing goodwill, the carrying amount of each plant and distribution facility has been allocated between each product group it services.

If, for example, the recoverable amount of the North American vitamins unit were less than its carrying amount, measuring the implied value of goodwill in that unit would require a valuation exercise to be undertaken for *all* North American assets so that a portion of each asset's fair value can then be allocated to the North American vitamins unit. These valuations are likely to be extremely costly and virtually impossible to complete within a reasonable time period (field visit participants' estimates ranged from six to twelve months). The degree of impracticability will be even greater for those entities that monitor, and therefore test, goodwill at the segment level.

BC167   In considering the above comments, the Board noted that:

(a)   all of the US registrant field visit participants and North American roundtable participants that have had to perform the second step of the SFAS 142 impairment test were compelled to engage, at significant cost, independent valuers.

(b)   the impairment model proposed in the Exposure Draft, although based on the two-step approach in SFAS 142, differed from the SFAS 142 test and would be unlikely to result in convergence for the following reasons:

(i)   the recoverable amount of a unit to which goodwill is allocated in accordance with IAS 36 would be the higher of the unit's value in use and fair value less costs to sell, rather than fair value. Many of the US registrant field visit participants stated that the measure of recoverable amount they would use under IAS 36 would differ from the fair value measure they would be required to use under SFAS 142.

(ii)   the level at which goodwill is tested for impairment in accordance with SFAS 142 will often be higher than the level at which it would be tested under IAS 36. Many of the US registrant field visit participants stated that goodwill would be tested for impairment in accordance with IAS 36 at a lower level than under SFAS 142 because of either: (1) the limit SFAS 142 places on how far goodwill can be 'pushed down' for impairment testing (ie one level below an operating segment); or (2) the requirement in SFAS 142 to aggregate components with similar economic characteristics. Nevertheless, these participants unanimously agreed that the IAS 36 approach provides users and management with more useful information. The Board also noted that many of the North American round-table participants stated that they (or, in the case of audit firm participants, their clients) manage and have available information about their investments in goodwill at a level lower than a reporting unit as defined in SFAS 142. Many of these participants expressed a high level of dissatisfaction at being prevented by SFAS 142 from recognising goodwill impairments that they knew existed at these lower levels, but 'disappeared' once the lower level units were aggregated with other units containing sufficient 'cushions' to offset the impairment loss.

BC168   The Board also noted that, unlike SFAS 142, it had as its starting point an impairment model in IAS 36 that integrates the impairment testing of *all* assets within a cash-generating unit, including goodwill. Unlike US generally accepted accounting principles (GAAP), which use an undiscounted cash flow screening mechanism for impairment testing long-lived assets other than goodwill, IAS 36 requires the recoverable amount of an asset or cash-generating unit to be measured whenever there is an indication of possible impairment. Therefore, if at the time of impairment testing a 'larger' unit to which goodwill has been allocated there is an indication of a possible impairment in an asset or 'smaller' cash-generating unit included in that larger unit, an entity is required to test that asset or smaller unit for impairment first. Consequently, the Board concluded that it would be reasonable in an IAS 36 context to presume that an impairment loss for the larger unit would, after all other assets and smaller units are assessed for impairment, be likely to relate to the goodwill in the unit. Such a presumption would not be reasonable if an entity were following US GAAP.

BC169   The Board considered converging fully with the SFAS 142 approach. However, although supporting convergence, the Board was concerned that the SFAS 142 approach would not provide better information than an approach under which goodwill is tested for impairment at a lower level (thereby removing many of the 'cushions' protecting the goodwill from impairment) but with the amount of any impairment loss for goodwill measured in accordance with the one-step approach in the previous version of IAS 36.

The Board concluded that the complexity and costs of applying the two-step approach proposed in the Exposure Draft would outweigh the benefits of that approach. Therefore, the Board decided to retain the approach to measuring impairments of goodwill included in the previous version of IAS 36. Thus, the Standard requires any excess of the carrying amount of a cash-generating unit (group of units) to which goodwill has been allocated over its recoverable amount to be recognised first as an impairment loss for goodwill. Any excess remaining after the carrying amount of goodwill has been reduced to zero is then recognised by being allocated to the other assets of the unit pro rata with their carrying amounts.

BC170

Timing of impairment tests (paragraphs 96-99)

To reduce the costs of applying the test, and consistently with the proposals in the Exposure Draft, the Standard permits the annual impairment test for a cash-generating unit (group of units) to which goodwill has been allocated to be performed at any time during an annual period, provided the test is performed at the same time every year. Different cash-generating units (groups of units) may be tested for impairment at different times. However, if some or all of the goodwill allocated to a unit (group of units) was acquired in a business combination during the current annual period, that unit (group of units) must be tested for impairment before the end of the current annual period.

BC171

The Board observed that acquirers can sometimes 'overpay' for an acquiree, resulting in the amount initially recognised for the business combination and the resulting goodwill exceeding the recoverable amount of the investment. The Board concluded that the users of an entity's financial statements are provided with representationally faithful, and therefore useful, information about a business combination if such an impairment loss is recognised by the acquirer in the annual period in which the business combination occurs.

BC172

The Board was concerned that it might be possible for entities to delay recognising such an impairment loss until the annual period after the business combination if the Standard included only a requirement to impairment test cash-generating units (groups of units) to which goodwill has been allocated on an annual basis at any time during a period. Therefore, the Board decided to include in the Standard the added requirement that if some or all of the goodwill allocated to a unit (group of units) was acquired in a business combination during the current annual period, the unit (group of units) should be tested for impairment before the end of that period.

BC173

Sequence of impairment tests (paragraph 97)

The Standard requires that if the assets (cash-generating units) constituting the cash-generating unit (group of units) to which goodwill has been allocated are tested for impairment at the same time as the unit (group of units) containing the goodwill, those other assets (units) should be tested for impairment before the unit (group of units) containing the goodwill.

BC174

The Board observed that assets or cash-generating units making up a unit or group of units to which goodwill has been allocated might need to be tested for impairment at the same time as the unit or group of units containing the goodwill when there is an indication of a possible impairment of the asset or smaller unit. The Board concluded that to assess whether the unit or group of units containing the goodwill,

BC175

and therefore whether the goodwill, is impaired, the carrying amount of the unit or group of units containing the goodwill would need first to be adjusted by recognising any impairment losses relating to the assets or smaller units within that unit or group of units.

Carrying forward a recoverable amount calculation (paragraph 99)

BC176   Consistently with the impairment test for indefinite-lived intangibles, the Standard permits the most recent detailed calculation of the recoverable amount of a cash-generating unit (group of units) to which goodwill has been allocated to be carried forward from a preceding period for use in the current period's impairment test, provided all of the criteria in paragraph 99 are met.

BC177   Integral to the Board's decision that goodwill should be tested for impairment annually was the view that many entities should be able to conclude that the recoverable amount of a cash-generating unit (group of units) to which goodwill has been allocated is greater than its carrying amount without actually recomputing recoverable amount. However, again consistently with its conclusions about indefinite-lived intangibles, the Board concluded that this would be the case only if the last recoverable amount determination exceeded the carrying amount of the unit (group of units) by a substantial margin, and nothing had happened since that last determination to make the likelihood of an impairment loss other than remote. The Board concluded that in such circumstances, permitting a detailed calculation of the recoverable amount of a cash-generating unit (group of units) to which goodwill has been allocated to be carried forward from the preceding period for use in the current period's impairment test would significantly reduce the costs of applying the impairment test, without compromising its integrity.

ALLOCATING AN IMPAIRMENT LOSS BETWEEN THE ASSETS OF A CASH-GENERATING UNIT (PARAGRAPHS 104107)

BCZ178   IAS 36 includes requirements for the allocation of an impairment loss for a cash-generating unit that differ from the proposals in E55. In particular, E55 proposed that an impairment loss should be allocated:

(a)   first, to goodwill;
(b)   secondly, to intangible assets for which no active market exists;
(c)   thirdly, to assets whose net selling price* is less than their carrying amount; and
(d)   then, to the other assets of the unit on a pro-rata basis based on the carrying amount of each asset in the unit.

BCZ179   The underlying reasons for making this proposal were that:

(a)   an impairment loss for a cash-generating unit should be allocated, in priority, to assets with the most subjective values. Goodwill and intangible assets for which there is no active market were considered to be in that category. Intangible assets for which there is no active market were considered to be similar to goodwill (IASC was thinking of brand names, publishing titles etc).
(b)   if the net selling price of an asset is less than its carrying amount, this was considered a reasonable basis for allocating part of the impairment loss to that asset rather than to other assets.

BCZ180   Many commentators on E55 objected to the proposal on the grounds that:

*In IFRS 5 Non-current Assets Held for Sale and Discontinued Operations, *issued by the IASB in 2004, the term, 'net selling price' was replaced in IAS 36 by 'fair value less costs to sell'.*

(a) not all intangible assets for which no active market exists are similar to goodwill (for example, licences and franchise rights). They disagreed that the value of intangible assets is always more subjective than the value of tangible assets (for example, specialised plant and equipment).

(b) the concept of cash-generating units implies a global approach for the assets of the units and not an asset-by-asset approach.

In response to these comments, IASC decided to withdraw E55's proposal for the allocation of an impairment loss to intangible assets and assets whose net selling price is less than their carrying amount.

IASC rejected a proposal that an impairment loss for a cash-generating unit should be allocated first to any obviously impaired asset. IASC believed that if the recoverable amount of an obviously impaired asset can be determined for the individual asset, there is no need to estimate the recoverable amount of the asset's cash-generating unit. If the recoverable amount of an individual asset cannot be determined, it cannot be said that the asset is obviously impaired because an impairment loss for a cash-generating unit relates to all of the assets of that unit.   **BCZ181**

REVERSING IMPAIRMENT LOSSES FOR ASSETS OTHER THAN GOODWILL (PARAGRAPHS 110-123)

IAS 36 requires that an impairment loss for an asset other than goodwill should be reversed if, and only if, there has been a change in the estimates used to determine an asset's recoverable amount since the last impairment loss was recognised.   **BCZ182**

Opponents of reversals of impairment losses argue that: **BCZ183**

(a) reversals of impairment losses are contrary to the historical cost accounting system. When the carrying amount is reduced, recoverable amount becomes the new cost basis for an asset. Consequently, reversing an impairment loss is no different from revaluing an asset upward. Indeed, in many cases, recoverable amount is similar to the measurement basis used for the revaluation of an asset. Hence, reversals of impairment losses should be either prohibited or recognised directly in equity as a revaluation.

(b) reversals of impairment losses introduce volatility in reported earnings. Periodic, short-term income measurements should not be affected by unrealised changes in the measurement of a long-lived asset.

(c) the result of reversals of impairment losses would not be useful to users of financial statements since the amount of a reversal under IAS 36 is limited to an amount that does not increase the carrying amount of an asset above its depreciated historical cost. Neither the amount reversed nor the revised carrying amount have any information content.

(d) in many cases, reversals of impairment losses will result in the implicit recognition of internally generated goodwill.

(e) reversals of impairment losses open the door to abuse and income 'smoothing' in practice.

(f) follow-up to verify whether an impairment loss needs to be reversed is costly.

IASC's reasons for requiring reversals of impairment losses were the following: **BCZ184**

(a)   it is consistent with the *Framework** and the view that future economic benefits that were not previously expected to flow from an asset have been reassessed as probable.

(b)   a reversal of an impairment loss is not a revaluation and is consistent with the historical cost accounting system as long as the reversal does not result in the carrying amount of an asset exceeding its original cost less amortisation/ depreciation, had the impairment loss not been recognised. Accordingly, the reversal of an impairment loss should be recognised in the income statement and any amount in excess of the depreciated historical cost should be accounted for as a revaluation.

(c)   impairment losses are recognised and measured based on estimates. Any change in the measurement of an impairment loss is similar to a change in estimate. IAS 8† *Net Profit or Loss for the Period, Fundamental Errors and Changes in Accounting Policies*‡ requires that a change in accounting estimate should be included in the determination of the net profit or loss in (a) the period of the change, if the change affects the period only, or (b) the period of the change and future periods, if the change affects both.

(d)   reversals of impairment losses provide users with a more useful indication of the potential for future benefits of an asset or group of assets.

(e)   results of operations will be more fairly stated in the current period and in future periods because depreciation or amortisation will not reflect a previous impairment loss that is no longer relevant. Prohibition of reversals of impairment losses may lead to abuses such as recording a significant loss one year with the resulting lower amortisation/depreciation charge and higher profits in subsequent years.

BCZ185   The majority of commentators on E55 supported IASC's proposals for reversals of impairment losses.

BCZ186   IAS 36 does not permit an enterprise to recognise a reversal of an impairment loss just because of the unwinding of the discount. IASC supported this requirement for practical reasons only. Otherwise, if an impairment loss is recognised and recoverable amount is based on value in use, a reversal of the impairment loss would be recognised in each subsequent year for the unwinding of the discount. This is because, in most cases, the pattern of depreciation of an asset is different from the pattern of value in use. IASC believed that, when there is no change in the assumptions used to estimate recoverable amount, the benefits from recognising the unwinding of the discount each year after an impairment loss has been recognised do not justify the costs involved. However, if a reversal is recognised because assumptions have changed, the discount unwinding effect is included in the amount of the reversal recognised.

*ASB footnote: *The equivalent document in the UK and Republic of Ireland to the IASB's* Framework *is the* ASB's Statement of Principles for Financial Reporting. *Although the* Statement of Principles *is very similar to the* Framework, *it is not identical.*

†ASB footnote: *The corresponding UK and Republic of Ireland requirements are set out in* FRS 18 Accounting Policies.

‡*IAS 8* Net Profit or Loss for the Period, Fundamental Errors and Changes in Accounting Policies *was superseded in 2003 by IAS 8* Accounting Policies, Changes in Accounting Estimates and Errors.

REVERSING GOODWILL IMPAIRMENT LOSSES (PARAGRAPH 124)

Consistently with the proposal in the Exposure Draft, the Standard prohibits the recognition of reversals of impairment losses for goodwill. The previous version of IAS 36 required an impairment loss for goodwill recognised in a previous period to be reversed when the impairment loss was caused by a specific external event of an exceptional nature that was not expected to recur, and subsequent external events had occurred that reversed the effect of that event.   **BC187**

Most respondents to the Exposure Draft agreed that reversals of impairment losses for goodwill should be prohibited. Those that disagreed argued that reversals of impairment losses for goodwill should be treated in the same way as reversals of impairment losses for other assets, but limited to circumstances in which the impairment loss was caused by specific events beyond the entity's control.   **BC188**

In revising IAS 36, the Board noted that IAS 38 *Intangible Assets* prohibits the recognition of internally generated goodwill. Therefore, if reversals of impairment losses for goodwill were permitted, an entity would need to establish the extent to which a subsequent increase in the recoverable amount of goodwill is attributable to the recovery of the acquired goodwill within a cash-generating unit, rather than an increase in the internally generated goodwill within the unit. The Board concluded that this will seldom, if ever, be possible. Because the acquired goodwill and internally generated goodwill contribute jointly to the same cash flows, any subsequent increase in the recoverable amount of the acquired goodwill is indistinguishable from an increase in the internally generated goodwill. Even if the specific external event that caused the recognition of the impairment loss is reversed, it will seldom, if ever, be possible to determine that the effect of that reversal is a corresponding increase in the recoverable amount of the acquired goodwill. Therefore, the Board concluded that reversals of impairment losses for goodwill should be prohibited.   **BC189**

The Board expressed some concern that prohibiting the recognition of reversals of impairment losses for goodwill so as to avoid recognising internally generated goodwill might be viewed by some as inconsistent with the impairment test for goodwill. This is because the impairment test results in the carrying amount of goodwill being shielded from impairment by internally generated goodwill. This has been described by some as 'backdoor' capitalisation of internally generated goodwill.   **BC190**

However, the Board was not as concerned about goodwill being shielded from the recognition of impairment losses by internally generated goodwill as it was about the direct recognition of internally generated goodwill that might occur if reversals of impairment losses for goodwill were permitted. As discussed in paragraph BC135, the Board is of the view that it is not possible to devise an impairment test for acquired goodwill that removes the cushion against the recognition of impairment losses provided by goodwill generated internally after a business combination.   **BC191**

DISCLOSURES FOR CASH-GENERATING UNITS CONTAINING GOODWILL OR INDEFINITE-LIVED INTANGIBLES (PARAGRAPHS 134 AND 135)

Background to the proposals in the Exposure Draft

BC192   The Exposure Draft proposed requiring an entity to disclose a range of information about cash-generating units whose carrying amounts included goodwill or indefinite-lived intangibles. That information included:

(a)   the carrying amount of goodwill and the carrying amount of indefinite-lived intangibles.

(b)   the basis on which the unit's recoverable amount had been determined (ie value in use or net selling price).

(c)   the amount by which the unit's recoverable amount exceeded its carrying amount.

(d)   the key assumptions and estimates used to measure the unit's recoverable amount and information about the sensitivity of that recoverable amount to changes in the key assumptions and estimates.

BC193   If an entity reports segment information in accordance with IAS 14 *Segment Reporting,* the Exposure Draft proposed that this information should be disclosed in aggregate for each segment based on the entity's primary reporting format. However, the Exposure Draft also proposed that the information would be disclosed separately for a cash-generating unit when:

(a)   the carrying amount of the goodwill or indefinite-lived intangibles allocated to the unit was significant in relation to the total carrying amount of goodwill or indefinite-lived intangibles; or

(b)   the basis for determining the unit's recoverable amount differed from the basis used for the other units within the segment whose carrying amounts include goodwill or indefinite-lived intangibles; or

(c)   the nature of, or value assigned to the key assumptions or growth rate on which management based its determination of the unit's recoverable amount differed significantly from that used for the other units within the segment whose carrying amounts include goodwill or indefinite-lived intangibles.

BC194   In deciding to propose these disclosure requirements in the Exposure Draft, the Board observed that non-amortisation of goodwill and indefinite-lived intangibles increases the reliance that must be placed on impairment tests of those assets to ensure that their carrying amounts do not exceed their recoverable amounts. However, the nature of impairment tests means that the carrying amounts of such assets and the related assertion that those carrying amounts are recoverable will normally be supported only by management's projections. Therefore, the Board decided to examine ways in which the reliability of the impairment tests for goodwill and indefinite-lived intangibles could be improved. As a first step, the Board considered including a subsequent cash flow test in the revised Standard, similar to that included in UK Financial Reporting Standard 11 *Impairment of Fixed Assets and Goodwill* (FRS 11).

Subsequent cash flow test

BC195   FRS 11 requires an entity to perform a subsequent cash flow test to confirm, ex post, the cash flow projections used to measure a unit's value in use when testing goodwill for impairment. Under FRS 11, for five years following each impairment test for goodwill in which recoverable amount has been based on value in use, the actual cash flows achieved must be compared with those forecast. If the actual cash flows are so much less than those forecast that use of the actual cash flows in the value in use calculation could have required recognition of an impairment in previous periods, the original impairment calculations must be re-performed using the actual cash flows, but without revising any other cash flows or assumptions (except those that change as a direct consequence of the occurrence of the actual cash flows, for example where a major cash inflow has been delayed for a year). Any impairment identified must then be recognised in the current period, unless the impairment has reversed and the reversal of the loss satisfies the criteria in FRS 11 regarding reversals of impairment losses for goodwill.

The Board noted the following arguments in support of including a similar test in the revised Standard: **BC196**

(a) it would enhance the reliability of the goodwill impairment test by preventing the possibility of entities avoiding the recognition of impairment losses by using over-optimistic cash flow projections in the value in use calculations.

(b) it would provide useful information to users of an entity's financial statements because a record of actual cash flows continually less than forecast cash flows tends to cast doubt on the reliability of current estimates.

However, the subsequent cash flow test is designed only to prevent entities from avoiding goodwill write-downs. The Board observed that, given current trends in 'big bath' restructuring charges, the greater risk to the quality of financial reporting might be from entities trying to write off goodwill without adequate justification in an attempt to 'manage' the balance sheet. The Board also observed that: **BC197**

(a) the focus of the test on cash flows ignores other elements in the measurement of value in use. As a result, it does not produce representationally faithful results in a present value measurement system. The Board considered incorporating into the recalculation performed under the test corrections of estimates of other elements in the measurement of value in use. However, the Board concluded that specifying which elements to include would be problematic. Moreover, adding corrections of estimates of those other elements to the test would, in effect, transform the test into a requirement to perform a comprehensive recalculation of value in use for each of the five annual reporting periods following an impairment test.

(b) the amount recognised as an impairment loss under the test is the amount of the impairment that would have been recognised, provided changes in estimates of remaining cash flows and changes in discount and growth rates are ignored. Therefore, it is a hypothetical amount that does not provide decision-useful information—it is neither an estimate of a current amount nor a prediction of ultimate cash flows.

(c) the requirement to perform the test for each of the five annual reporting periods following an impairment test could result in an entity having to maintain as many as five sets of 5-year computations for each cash-generating unit to which goodwill has been allocated. Therefore, the test is likely to be extremely burdensome, particularly if an entity has a large number of such units, without producing understandable or decision-useful information.

Therefore, the Board decided not to propose a subsequent cash flow test in the Exposure Draft. However, the Board remained committed to finding some way of improving the reliability of the impairment tests for goodwill and indefinite-lived intangibles, and decided to explore improving that reliability through disclosure requirements.   **BC198**

Including disclosure requirements in the revised Standard

BC199   In developing the Exposure Draft, the Board observed that the *Framework* identifies reliability as one of the key qualitative characteristics that information must possess to be useful to users in making economic decisions. To be reliable, information must be free from material error and bias and be able to be depended upon to represent faithfully that which it purports to represent. The *Framework* identifies relevance as another key qualitative characteristic that information must possess to be useful to users in making economic decisions. To be relevant, information must help users to evaluate past, present or future events, or confirm or correct their past evaluations.

BC200   The Board observed that information that assists users in evaluating the reliability of other information included in the financial statements is itself relevant, increasing in relevance as the reliability of that other information decreases. For example, information that assists users in evaluating the reliability of the amount recognised for a provision is relevant because it helps users to evaluate the effect of both a past event (ie the economic consequences of the past event giving rise to the present obligation) and a future event (ie the amount of the expected future outflow of economic benefits required to settle the obligation). Accordingly, IAS 37 *Provisions, Contingent Liabilities and Contingent Assets** requires an entity to disclose, for each class of provision, information about the uncertainties surrounding the amount and timing of expected outflows of economic benefits, and the major assumptions concerning future events that may affect the amount required to settle the obligation and have been reflected in the amount of the provision.

BC201   The Board concluded that because information that assists users in evaluating the reliability of other information is itself relevant, an entity should disclose information that assists users in evaluating the reliability of the estimates used by management to support the carrying amounts of goodwill and indefinite-lived intangibles.

BC202   The Board also concluded that such disclosures would provide users with more useful information for evaluating the reliability of the impairment tests for goodwill and indefinite-lived intangibles than the information that would be provided by a subsequent cash flow test.

BC203   The Board then considered how some balance might be achieved between the objective of providing users with useful information for evaluating the reliability of the estimates used by management to support the carrying amounts of goodwill and indefinite-lived intangibles, and the potential magnitude of those disclosures.

BC204   The Board decided that a reasonable balance might be achieved between the objective of the disclosures and their potential magnitude by requiring:

(a)   information to be disclosed on an aggregate basis for each segment based on the entity's primary reporting format that includes in its carrying amount goodwill or indefinite-lived intangibles; but

(b)   information for a particular cash-generating unit within that segment to be excluded from the aggregate information and disclosed separately when either:

(i)   the basis (ie net selling price or value in use), methodology or key assumptions used to measure its recoverable amount differ from those used to measure the recoverable amounts of the other units in the segment; or

*ASB footnote: *The corresponding UK and Republic of Ireland requirements are set out in* FRS 12 Provisions, Contingent Liabilities and Contingent Assets.

(ii) the carrying amount of the goodwill or indefinite-lived intangibles in the unit is significant in relation to the total carrying amount of goodwill or indefinite-lived intangibles.

The Board's redeliberations

After considering respondents' and field visit participants' comments, the Board **BC205** confirmed its previous conclusion that information that assists users in evaluating the reliability of other information is itself relevant, increasing in relevance as the reliability of that other information decreases. Therefore, entities should be required to disclose information that assists users in evaluating the reliability of the estimates used by management to support the carrying amounts of goodwill and indefinite-lived intangibles. The Board noted that almost all field visit participants and many respondents expressed explicit support of its conclusion that, because non-amortisation of goodwill and indefinite-lived intangibles increases the reliance that must be placed on impairment tests of those assets, some additional disclosure is necessary to provide users with information for evaluating the reliability of those impairment tests.

However, it was clear from field visit participants' responses that the proposed dis- **BC206** closures could not be meaningfully aggregated at the segment level to the extent the Board had hoped might be the case. As a result, the proposal to require the information to be disclosed on an aggregate basis for each segment, but with disaggregated disclosures for cash-generating units in the circumstances set out in paragraph BC193 would not result in a reasonable balance between the objective of the disclosures and their potential magnitude.

The Board was also sympathetic to field visit participants' and respondents' concerns **BC207** that the proposed disclosures went beyond their intended objective of providing users with relevant information for evaluating the reliability of the impairment tests for goodwill and indefinite-lived intangibles. For example, field visit participants and respondents argued that:

(a) it would be extremely difficult to distil the recoverable amount calculations into concise but meaningful disclosures because those calculations typically are complex and do not normally result in a single point estimate of recoverable amount—a single value for recoverable amount would normally be determined only when the bottom-end of the recoverable amount range is less than a cash-generating unit's carrying amount. These difficulties make it doubtful that the information, particularly the sensitivity analyses, could be produced on a timely basis.

(b) disclosing the proposed information, particularly the values assigned to, and the sensitivity of, each key assumption on which recoverable amount calculations are based, could cause significant commercial harm to an entity. Users of financial statements might, for example, use the quantitative disclosures as the basis for initiating litigation against the entity, its board of directors or management in the highly likely event that those assumptions prove less than accurate. The increased litigation risk would either encourage management to use super-conservative assumptions, thereby resulting in improper asset write-downs, or compel management to engage independent experts to develop all key assumptions and perform the recoverable amount calculations. Additionally, many of the field visit participants expressed concern over the possible impact that disclosing such information might have on their ability to defend themselves in various legal proceedings.

Therefore, the Board considered the following two interrelated issues: **BC208**

(a)   if the proposed disclosures went beyond their intended objective, what information *should* be disclosed so that users have sufficient information for evaluating the reliability of impairment tests for goodwill and indefinite-lived intangibles?

(b)   how should this information be presented so that there is an appropriate balance between providing users with information for evaluating the reliability of the impairment tests, and the potential magnitude of those disclosures?

BC209   As a result of its redeliberations, the Board decided:

(a)   not to proceed with the proposal to require information for evaluating the reliability of the impairment tests for goodwill and indefinite-lived intangibles to be disclosed in aggregate for each segment and separately for cash-generating units within a segment in specified circumstances. Instead, the Standard requires this information to be disclosed only for each cash-generating unit (group of units) for which the carrying amount of goodwill or indefinite-lived intangibles allocated to that unit (group of units) is significant in comparison with the entity's total carrying amount of goodwill or indefinite-lived intangibles.

(b)   not to proceed with the proposal to require an entity to disclose the amount by which the recoverable amount of a cash-generating unit exceeds its carrying amount. Instead, the Standard requires an entity to disclose this information only if a reasonably possible change in a key assumption on which management has based its determination of the unit's (group of units') recoverable amount would cause the unit's (group of units') carrying amount to exceed its recoverable amount.

(c)   not to proceed with the proposal to require an entity to disclose the value assigned to each key assumption on which management based its recoverable amount determination, and the amount by which that value must change, after incorporating any consequential effects of that change on the other variables used to measure recoverable amount, in order for the unit's recoverable amount to be equal to its carrying amount. Instead, the Standard requires an entity to disclose a description of each key assumption on which management has based its recoverable amount determination, management's approach to determining the value(s) assigned to each key assumption, whether those value(s) reflect past experience or, if appropriate, are consistent with external sources of information, and, if not, how and why they differ from past experience or external sources of information. However, if a reasonably possible change in a key assumption would cause the unit's (group of units') carrying amount to exceed its recoverable amount, the entity is also required to disclose the value assigned to the key assumption, and the amount by which that value must change, after incorporating any consequential effects of that change on the other variables used to measure recoverable amount, in order for the unit's (group of units') recoverable amount to be equal to its carrying amount.

(d)   to require information about key assumptions to be disclosed also for any key assumption that is relevant to the recoverable amount determination of multiple cash-generating units (groups of units) that individually contain insignificant amounts of goodwill or indefinite-lived intangibles, but contain, in aggregate, significant amounts of goodwill or indefinite-lived intangibles.

TRANSITIONAL PROVISIONS (PARAGRAPHS 138-140)

BC210   If an entity elects to apply IFRS 3 from any date before the effective dates outlined in IFRS 3, it is also required to apply IAS 36 from that same date. Paragraphs

BC181-BC184 of the Basis for Conclusions on IFRS 3 outline the Board's deliberations on this issue.

Otherwise, IAS 36 is applied: **BC211**

(a)   to goodwill and intangible assets acquired in business combinations for which the agreement date is on or after 31 March 2004; and

(b)   to all other assets prospectively from the beginning of the first annual period beginning on or after 31 March 2004.

In developing the requirements set out in paragraph BC211, the Board considered   **BC212**
whether entities should be required:

(a)   to apply retrospectively the revised impairment test for goodwill; and

(b)   to apply retrospectively the requirement prohibiting reversals of impairment losses for goodwill and therefore eliminate any reversals recognised before the date the revised Standard was issued.

The Board concluded that retrospective application of the revised impairment test   **BC213**
for goodwill would be problematic for the following reasons:

(a)   it was likely to be impossible in many cases because the information needed may not exist or may no longer be obtainable.

(b)   it would require the determination of estimates that would have been made at a prior date, and therefore would raise the problem of how the effect of hindsight could be separated from the factors existing at the date of the impairment test.

The Board also noted that the requirement for goodwill to be tested for impairment   **BC214**
annually, irrespective of whether there is any indication that it may be impaired, will ensure that by the end of the first period in which the Standard is effective, all recognised goodwill acquired before its effective date would be tested for impairment.

In the case of reversals of impairment losses for goodwill, the Board acknowledged   **BC215**
that requiring the elimination of reversals recognised before the revised Standard's effective date might seem appropriate, particularly given the Board's reasons for prohibiting reversals of impairment losses for goodwill (see paragraphs BC187-BC191). The Board concluded, however, that the previous amortisation of that goodwill, combined with the requirement for goodwill to be tested for impairment at least annually, ensures that the carrying amount of the goodwill does not exceed its recoverable amount at the end of the reporting period in which the Standard is effective. Therefore, the Board concluded that the Standard should apply on a prospective basis.

Transitional impairment test for goodwill

Given that one of the objectives of the first phase of the Business Combinations   **BC216**
project was to seek international convergence on the accounting for goodwill, the Board considered whether IAS 36 should include a transitional goodwill impairment test similar to that included in SFAS 142. SFAS 142 requires goodwill to be tested for impairment annually, and between annual tests if an event occurs or circumstances change and would be more likely than not to reduce the fair value of a reporting unit below its carrying amount. The transitional provisions in SFAS 142 require the impairment test for goodwill to be applied prospectively. However, a transitional goodwill impairment test must be performed as of the *beginning* of the fiscal year in which SFAS 142 is applied in its entirety. An impairment loss recognised as a result of a transitional test is recognised as the effect of a change in

accounting principle, rather than as an impairment loss. In addition to the transitional test, SFAS 142 requires an entity to perform the required annual goodwill impairment test in the year that SFAS 142 is initially applied in its entirety. In other words, the transitional goodwill impairment test may not be regarded as the initial year's annual test unless an entity designates the beginning of its fiscal year as the date for its annual goodwill impairment test.

BC217   The FASB concluded that goodwill that was not regarded as impaired under US GAAP before SFAS 142 was issued could be determined to be impaired if the SFAS 142 impairment test was applied to that goodwill at the date an entity initially applied SFAS 142. This is because, under previous US GAAP, entities typically tested goodwill for impairment using undiscounted estimates of future cash flows. The FASB further concluded that:

(a)   the preponderance of any transitional impairment losses was likely to result from the change in methods and treating those losses as stemming from changes in accounting principles would therefore be more representationally faithful.

(b)   given that a transitional impairment loss should be reported as a change in accounting principle, the transitional goodwill impairment test should ideally apply as of the date SFAS 142 is initially applied.

BC218   The Board observed that under the previous version of IAS 36, goodwill that was amortised over a period exceeding 20 years was required to be tested for impairment at least at each financial yearend. Goodwill that was amortised over a period not exceeding 20 years was required to be tested for impairment at the balance sheet date if there was an indication that it might be impaired. The revised Standard requires goodwill to be tested for impairment annually or more frequently if there is an indication the goodwill might be impaired. It also carries forward from the previous version of IAS 36 (a) the indicators of impairment, (b) the measure of recoverable amount (ie higher of value in use and fair value less costs to sell), and (c) the requirement for an impairment loss for a cash-generating unit to be allocated first to reduce the carrying amount of any goodwill allocated to the unit.

BC219   Therefore, goodwill tested for impairment in accordance with the previous version of the revised Standard immediately before the beginning of the reporting period in which the revised Standard becomes effective (because it was being amortised over a period exceeding 20 years or because there was an indicator of impairment) could not be identified as impaired under IAS 36 at the beginning of the period in which it becomes effective. This is because application of the Standard results in a goodwill impairment loss being identified only if the carrying amount of the cash-generating unit (group of units) to which the goodwill has been allocated exceeds its recoverable amount, and the impairment test in the previous version of IAS 36 ensures that this will not be the case.

BC220   The Board concluded that there would be only one possible situation in which a transitional impairment test might give rise to the recognition of an impairment loss for goodwill. This would be when goodwill being amortised over a period not exceeding 20 years was, immediately before the beginning of the period in which the revised Standard becomes effective, impaired in the absence of any indicator of impairment that ought reasonably to have been considered by the entity. The Board concluded that this is likely to be a rare occurrence.

BC221   The Board observed that any such impairment loss would nonetheless be recognised as a consequence of applying the requirement in IAS 36 to test goodwill for impairment at least annually. Therefore, the only benefit of applying a transitional impairment test would be, in those rare cases, to separate the impairment loss arising before the period in which the revised Standard is effective from any impairment loss arising after the beginning of that period.

The Board concluded that given the rare circumstances in which this issue would arise, the benefit of applying a transitional goodwill impairment test would be outweighed by the added costs of the test. Therefore, the Board decided that the revised Standard should not require a transitional goodwill impairment test.   **BC222**

Transitional impairment test for indefinite-lived intangibles

SFAS 142 also requires a transitional impairment test to be applied, as of the beginning of the fiscal year in which that Standard is initially applied, to intangible assets recognised before the effective date of SFAS 142 that are reassessed as having indefinite useful lives. An impairment loss arising from that transitional impairment test is recognised as the effect of a change in accounting principle rather than as an impairment loss. As with goodwill: **BC223**

(a) intangible assets that cease being amortised upon initial application of SFAS 142 are tested for impairment in accordance with SFAS 142 using a different method from what had previously applied to those assets. Therefore, it is possible that such an intangible asset not previously regarded as impaired might be determined to be impaired under SFAS 142.

(b) the FASB concluded that the preponderance of any transitional impairment losses would be likely to result from the change in impairment testing methods. Treating those losses as stemming from changes in accounting principles is therefore more representationally faithful.

The Board considered whether IAS 36 should include a transitional impairment test for indefinite-lived intangibles similar to that in SFAS 142.   **BC224**

The Board observed that the previous version of IAS 38 *Intangible Assets* required an intangible asset being amortised over a period exceeding 20 years to be tested for impairment at least at each financial year-end in accordance with the previous version of IAS 36. An intangible asset being amortised over a period not exceeding 20 years was required, under the previous version of IAS 36, to be tested for impairment at the balance sheet date only if there was an indication the asset might be impaired. The revised Standard requires an indefinite-lived intangible to be tested for impairment at least annually. However, it also requires that the recoverable amount of such an asset should continue to be measured as the higher of the asset's value in use and fair value less costs to sell.   **BC225**

As with goodwill, the Board concluded that the revised Standard should not require a transitional impairment test for indefinite-lived intangibles because: **BC226**

(a) the only circumstance in which a transitional impairment test might give rise to the recognition of an impairment loss would be when an indefinite-lived intangible previously being amortised over a period not exceeding 20 years was, immediately before the beginning of the period in which the revised Standard is effective, impaired in the absence of any indicator of impairment that ought reasonably to have been considered by the entity.

(b) any such impairment loss would nonetheless be recognised as a consequence of applying the requirement in the Standard to test such assets for impairment at least annually. Therefore, the only benefit of such a test would be to separate the impairment loss arising before the period in which the revised Standard is effective from any impairment loss arising after the beginning of that period.

(c)   given the extremely rare circumstances in which this issue is likely to arise, the benefit of applying a transitional impairment test is outweighed by the added costs of the test.

Early application (paragraph 140)

BC227   The Board noted that the issue of any Standard demonstrates its opinion that application of the Standard will result in more useful information being provided to users about an entity's financial position, performance or cash flows. On that basis, a case exists for permitting, and indeed encouraging, entities to apply IAS 36 before its effective date. However, the Board also considered that permitting a revised Standard to be applied before its effective date potentially diminishes comparability between entities in the period(s) leading up to that effective date, and has the effect of providing entities with an option.

BC228   The Board concluded that the benefit of providing users with more useful information about an entity's financial position, performance and cash flows by permitting early application of IAS 36 outweighs the disadvantages of potentially diminished comparability. Therefore, entities are encouraged to apply the requirements of IAS 36 before its effective date. However, given that the revision of IAS 36 is part of an integrated package, IAS 36 requires IFRS 3 and IAS 38 (as revised in 2004) to be applied at the same time.

SUMMARY OF MAIN CHANGES FROM THE EXPOSURE DRAFT

BC229   The following are the main changes from the Exposure Draft:

(a)   the Exposure Draft proposed that an intangible asset with an indefinite useful life should be tested for impairment at the end of each annual period by comparing its carrying amount with its recoverable amount. The Standard requires such an intangible asset to be tested for impairment annually by comparing its carrying amount with its recoverable amount. The impairment test may be performed at any time during an annual period, provided it is performed at the same time every year, and different intangible assets may be tested for impairment at different times. However, if such an intangible asset was initially recognised during the current annual period, the Standard requires that intangible asset to be tested for impairment before the end of the current annual period.

(b)   the Exposure Draft proposed that the cash flow projections used to measure value in use should be based on reasonable and supportable assumptions that take into account both past actual cash flows and management's past ability to forecast cash flows accurately. This proposal has not been included in the Standard. Instead, the Standard includes guidance clarifying that management:

(i)   should assess the reasonableness of the assumptions on which its current cash flow projections are based by examining the causes of differences between past cash flow projections and actual cash flows; and

(ii)   should ensure that the assumptions on which its current cash flow projections are based are consistent with past actual outcomes, provided the effects of subsequent events or circumstances that did not exist when those actual cash flows were generated make this appropriate.

(c)   the Exposure Draft proposed that if an active market exists for the output produced by an asset or a group of assets, that asset or group of assets should be identified as a cash-generating unit, even if some or all of the output is used internally. In such circumstances, management's best estimate of future market prices for the output should be used in estimating the future cash flows used to determine the unit's value in use. The Exposure Draft also proposed that when estimating future cash flows to determine the value in use of cash-generating units using the output, management's best estimate of future market prices for the output should be used.

The Standard similarly requires that if an active market exists for the output produced by an asset or a group of assets, that asset or group of assets should be identified as a cash-generating unit, even if some or all of the output is used internally. However, the Standard clarifies that if the cash inflows generated by *any* asset or cash-generating unit are affected by internal transfer pricing, an entity should use management's best estimate of future price(s) that could be achieved in arm's length transactions in estimating:

(i)   the future cash inflows used to determine the asset's or cash-generating unit's value in use; and

(ii) the future cash outflows used to determine the value in use of other assets or cash-generating units affected by the internal transfer pricing.

(d)   the Exposure Draft proposed that goodwill acquired in a business combination should be allocated to one or more cash-generating units, with each of those units representing the smallest cash-generating unit to which a portion of the carrying amount of the goodwill could be allocated on a reasonable and consistent basis. The Exposure Draft also proposed that:

(i)   a portion of the carrying amount of goodwill should be regarded as capable of being allocated to a cash-generating unit on a reasonable and consistent basis only when that unit represents the lowest level at which management monitors the return on investment in assets that include the goodwill.

(ii) each cash-generating unit should not be larger than a segment based on the entity's primary reporting format determined in accordance with IAS 14 *Segment Reporting*.

The Standard requires goodwill acquired in a business combination to be allocated to each of the acquirer's cash-generating units, or groups of cash-generating units, that are expected to benefit from the synergies of the combination, irrespective of whether other assets or liabilities of the acquiree are assigned to those units or groups of units. The Standard also requires each unit or group of units to which the goodwill is so allocated: (1) to represent the lowest level within the entity at which the goodwill is monitored for internal management purposes; and (2) to be not larger than a segment based on either the entity's primary or the entity's secondary reporting format determined in accordance with IAS 14.

(e)   the Exposure Draft proposed that when an entity disposes of an operation within a cash-generating unit to which goodwill has been allocated, the goodwill associated with that operation should be:

(i)   included in the carrying amount of the operation when determining the gain or loss on disposal; and

(ii) measured on the basis of the relative values of the operation disposed of and the portion of the cash-generating unit retained.

This proposal has been included in the Standard with one modification. The Standard requires the goodwill associated with the operation disposed of to be measured on the basis of the relative values of the operation disposed of and the portion of the cash-generating unit retained, unless the entity can demonstrate that some other method better reflects the goodwill associated with the operation disposed of.

(f)   the Exposure Draft proposed that when an entity reorganises its reporting structure in a way that changes the composition of cash-generating units to which goodwill has been allocated, the goodwill should be reallocated to the units affected using a relative value approach similar to that used when an entity disposes of an operation within a cash-generating unit. The Standard similarly requires an entity that reorganises its reporting structure in a way that changes the composition of one or more cash-generating units to which goodwill has been allocated to reallocate the goodwill to the units (groups of units) affected. However, the Standard requires this reallocation to be performed using a relative value approach similar to that used when an entity disposes of an operation within a cash-generating unit, unless the entity can demonstrate that some other method better reflects the goodwill associated with the reorganised units (groups of units).

(g)   the Exposure Draft proposed a two-step approach for impairment testing goodwill. The first step involved using a screening mechanism for identifying potential goodwill impairments, whereby goodwill allocated to a cash-generating unit would be identified as potentially impaired only when the carrying amount of the unit exceeded its recoverable amount. If an entity identified the goodwill allocated to a cash-generating unit as potentially impaired, an entity would then determine whether the goodwill allocated to the unit was impaired by comparing its recoverable amount, measured as the implied value of the goodwill, with its carrying amount. The implied value of goodwill would be measured as a residual, being the excess of the recoverable amount of the cash-generating unit to which the goodwill has been allocated, over the net fair value of the identifiable assets, liabilities and contingent liabilities the entity would recognise if it acquired the cash-generating unit in a business combination on the date of the impairment test. The Standard requires any excess of the carrying amount of a cash-generating unit (group of units) to which goodwill has been allocated over its recoverable amount to be recognised first as an impairment loss for goodwill. Any excess remaining after the carrying amount of goodwill has been reduced to zero is then recognised by being allocated to the other assets of the unit pro rata with their carrying amounts.

(h)   the Exposure Draft proposed requiring an entity to disclose information about cash-generating units whose carrying amounts included goodwill or indefinite-lived intangibles. That information included the carrying amount of goodwill and the carrying amount of indefinite-lived intangibles, the basis on which the unit's recoverable amount had been determined (ie value in use or net selling price), the amount by which the unit's recoverable amount exceeded its carrying amount, the key assumptions and estimates used to measure the unit's recoverable amount and information about the sensitivity of that recoverable amount to changes in the key assumptions and estimates. If an entity reports segment information in accordance with IAS 14, the Exposure Draft proposed that this information should be disclosed in aggregate for each segment based on the entity's primary reporting format. However, the Exposure Draft also proposed that the information would be disclosed separately for a cash-generating unit if specified criteria were met. The Standard:

(i)   does not require information for evaluating the reliability of the impairment tests for goodwill and indefinite-lived intangibles to be disclosed in aggregate for each segment and separately for cash-generating units within a segment when specified criteria are met. Instead, the Standard requires this information to be disclosed for each cash-generating unit (group of units) for which the carrying amount of goodwill or indefinite-lived intangibles allocated to that unit (group of units) is significant in comparison with the entity's total carrying amount of goodwill or indefinite-lived intangibles.

(ii)   does not require an entity to disclose the amount by which the recoverable amount of a cash-generating unit exceeds its carrying amount. Instead, the Standard requires an entity to disclose this information only if a reasonably possible change in a key assumption on which management has based its determination of the unit's (group of units') recoverable amount would cause the unit's (group of units') carrying amount to exceed its recoverable amount.

(iii) does not require an entity to disclose the value assigned to each key assumption on which management has based its recoverable amount determination, and the amount by which that value must change, after incorporating any consequential effects of that change on the other variables used to measure recoverable amount, in order for the unit's recoverable amount to be equal to its carrying amount. Instead, the Standard requires an entity to disclose a description of each key assumption on which management has based its recoverable amount determination, management's approach to determining the value(s) assigned to each key assumption, whether those value(s) reflect past experience or, if appropriate, are consistent with external sources of information, and, if not, how and why they differ from past experience or external sources of information. However, if a reasonably possible change in a key assumption would cause the unit's (group of units') carrying amount to exceed its recoverable amount, the entity is also required to disclose the value assigned to the key assumption, and the amount by which that value must change, after incorporating any consequential effects of that change on the other variables used to measure recoverable amount, in order for the unit's (group of units') recoverable amount to be equal to its carrying amount.

(iv) requires information about key assumptions to be disclosed for any key assumption that is relevant to the recoverable amount determination of multiple cash-generating units (groups of units) that individually contain insignificant amounts of goodwill or indefinite-lived intangibles, but which contain, in aggregate, significant amounts of goodwill or indefinite-lived intangibles.

HISTORY OF THE DEVELOPMENT OF A STANDARD ON IMPAIRMENT OF ASSETS

In June 1996, IASC decided to prepare an International Accounting Standard on Impairment of Assets. The reasons for developing a Standard on impairment of assets were: **BCZ230**

(a) to combine the requirements for identifying, measuring, recognising and reversing an impairment loss in one Standard to ensure that those requirements are consistent;

(b) the previous requirements and guidance in International Accounting Standards were not detailed enough to ensure that enterprises identified, recognised and measured impairment losses in a similar way, eg there was a need to eliminate certain alternatives for measuring an impairment loss, such as the former option not to use discounting; and

(c) IASC decided in March 1996 to explore whether the amortisation period of intangible assets and goodwill could, in certain rare circumstances, exceed 20 years if those assets were subject to detailed and reliable annual impairment tests.

In April 1997, IASC approved Exposure Draft E55 *Impairment of Assets*. IASC received more than 90 comment letters from over 20 countries. IASC also performed a field test of E55's proposals. More than 20 companies from various business sectors and from 10 different countries participated in the field test. About half of the field   **BCZ231** test participants prepared their financial statements using International Accounting Standards and the other half reported using other Standards. Field test participants completed a detailed questionnaire and most of them were visited by IASC staff to discuss the results of the application of E55's proposals to some of their assets. A brief summary of the comment letters received on E55 and the results of the field test was published in IASC *Insight* in December 1997.

BCZ232   In October 1997, IASC, together with the Accounting Standards Boards in Australia, Canada, New Zealand, the United Kingdom and the United States, published a discussion paper entitled *International Review of Accounting Standards Specifying the Recoverable Amount Test for Long-Lived Assets* (Jim Paul, from the staff of the Australian Accounting Research Foundation, was the principal author). This discussion paper resulted from the discussions of a 'working group' consisting of some Board members and senior staff members from the standard-setting bodies listed above and IASC. The paper:

(a)   noted the key features of the working group members' existing or proposed accounting standards that require an impairment test, and compared those standards; and

(b)   proposed the views of the working group on the major issues.

BCZ233   In April 1998, after considering the comments received on E55 and the results of the field test, IASC approved IAS 36 *Impairment of Assets*.

ASB note: This Financial Reporting Exposure Draft (FRED) is part of a package of draft UK accounting standards comprising:

- This FRED 38 *Impairment of Assets* (IAS 36) and FRED 37 *Intangible Assets* (IAS 38).
- FRED 36 *Business Combinations* (IFRS 3) and Amendments to FRS 2 *Accounting for Subsidiary Undertakings (parts of IAS 27 Consolidated and Separate Financial Statements)*.
- FRED 39 Amendments to *FRS 12 Provisions, contingent liabilities and contingent assets* and Amendments to FRS 17 *Retirement benefits*.

DISSENTING OPINIONS

Dissent of Anthony T Cope, James J Leisenring and Geoffrey Whittington

Messrs Cope and Leisenring and Professor Whittington dissent from the issue of IAS 36.

DO1

Messrs Cope and Leisenring and Professor Whittington dissent because they object to the impairment test that the Standard requires for goodwill.

DO2

Messrs Cope and Leisenring agree with the prohibition, in paragraph 54 of IFRS 3 *Business Combinations,* of amortisation of goodwill. Research and experience have demonstrated that the amortisation of goodwill produces data that is meaningless, and perhaps even misleading. However, if goodwill is not amortised, its special nature mandates that it should be accounted for with caution. The Basis for Conclusions on IAS 36 (paragraph BC131) states that "if a rigorous and operational impairment test [for goodwill] could be devised, more useful information would be provided to users of an entity's financial statements under an approach in which goodwill is not amortised, but instead tested for impairment annually or more frequently if events or changes in circumstances indicate that the goodwill might be impaired." Messrs Cope and Leisenring agree with that statement. However, they believe that the impairment test to which a majority of the Board has agreed lacks the rigour to satisfy that condition.

DO3

Messrs Cope and Leisenring share the reservations of some Board members, as noted in paragraph BC130 of the Basis for Conclusions on IAS 36, about an impairment test based on measuring the recoverable amount of an asset, and particularly an asset with an indefinite life, as the higher of fair value less costs to sell or value in use. Messrs Cope and Leisenring are content, however, for the time being to defer consideration of that general measurement issue, pending more research and debate on measurement principles. (They note that the use of fair value would achieve significant convergence with US GAAP.) But a much more rigorous effort must be made to determine the recoverable amount of goodwill, however measured, than the Board's revised impairment test. The 'two-step' method originally proposed by the Board in the Exposure Draft of Proposed Amendments to IAS 36 and IAS 38 was a more useful approach to determining the 'implied value' of goodwill. That test should have been retained.

DO4

Messrs Cope and Leisenring recognise that some constituents raised objections to the complexity and potential cost of the requirements proposed in the Exposure Draft. However, they believe that many commentators misunderstood the level at which the Board intended impairment testing to be undertaken. This was demonstrated during the field-testing of the Exposure Draft. Furthermore, the provisions of paragraph 99 of IAS 36, specifying when impairment testing need not be undertaken, provide generous relief from the necessity of making frequent calculations. They would have preferred to meet those objections by specifying that the goodwill impairment test should be at the level set out in US Financial Accounting Standards Board's Statement of Financial Accounting Standards No. 142 *Goodwill and Other Intangible Assets.*

DO5

Professor Whittington believes that there are two aspects of the proposed impairment test that are particularly unsatisfactory. First, the failure to eliminate the shield from impairment provided by the internally generated goodwill of the acquiring entity at acquisition. This is discussed in paragraph DO7. Second, the lack of a subsequent cash flow test. This is discussed in paragraphs DO8-DO10. The inability to eliminate the shield from impairment provided by internally generated goodwill

DO6

accruing after the acquisition date is also a problem. However, there is no obvious practical way of dealing with this problem within the framework of conventional impairment tests.

DO7   When an acquired business is merged with an acquirer's existing operations, the impairment test in IAS 36 does not take account of the acquirer's pre-existing internally generated goodwill. Thus, the pre-existing internally generated goodwill of the acquirer provides a shield against impairment additional to that provided by subsequent internally generated goodwill. Professor Whittington believes that the impairment test would be more rigorous if it included a requirement similar to that in UK Financial Reporting Standard 11 *Impairment of Fixed Assets and Goodwill*, which recognises, for purposes of impairment testing, the implied value of the acquirer's goodwill existing at the time of acquisition.

DO8   The subsequent cash flow test is discussed in paragraphs BC195BC198 of the Basis for Conclusions on IAS 36. A subsequent cash flow test substitutes in past impairment tests the cash flows that actually occurred for those that were estimated at the time of the impairment tests, and requires a write-down if the revised estimates would have created an impairment loss for goodwill. It is thus a correction of an estimate. Such a test is incorporated in FRS 11.

DO9   The Board's reasons for rejecting the subsequent cash flow test are given in paragraph BC197(a)-(c). The preamble to paragraph BC197 claims that the subsequent cash flow test is misdirected because excessive write-downs of goodwill may be a problem that should be prevented. However, the subsequent cash flow test requires only realistic write-downs (based on actual outcomes), not excessive ones. If the statement in paragraph BC197 is correct, this may point to another deficiency in the impairment testing process that requires a different remedy.

DO10 Paragraph BC197(a) asserts that "it does not produce representationally faithful results" because it ignores other elements in the measurement of value in use. As explained above, it merely substitutes the outcome cash flow for the estimate, which should have a clear meaning and provides a safeguard against over-optimism in the estimation of cash flows. If corrections of estimates of other elements, such as variations that have occurred in interest rates, were considered important in this context, they could be incorporated in the calculation. Paragraph BC197(b) seems to raise the same point as paragraph BC197(a), as to the meaning of the impairment loss under the test. Paragraph BC197(c) complains about the excessive burden that a subsequent cash flow test might impose. Professor Whittington notes that the extent of the burden depends, of course, upon the frequency with which the test is applied. He also notes that the extensive disclosure requirements currently associated with the impairment test might be reduced if the subsequent cash flow test were in place.

Illustrative Examples

These examples accompany, but are not part of, IAS 36. All the examples assume that the entities concerned have no transactions other than those described.

In the examples monetary amounts are denominated in 'currency units' (CU).

> *ASB note: These Illustrative Examples have been prepared by the IASB.*

Contents

Illustrative Examples

EXAMPLE 1 - IDENTIFICATION OF CASH-GENERATING UNITS

The purpose of this example is:

(a)   to indicate how cash-generating units are identified in various situations; and

(b)   to highlight certain factors that an entity may consider in identifying the cash-generating unit to which an asset belongs.

A - Retail Store Chain

Background

IE1   Store X belongs to a retail store chain M. X makes all its retail purchases through M's purchasing centre. Pricing, marketing, advertising and human resources policies (except for hiring X's cashiers and sales staff) are decided by M. M also owns five other stores in the same city as X (although in different neighbourhoods) and 20 other stores in other cities. All stores are managed in the same way as X. X and four other stores were purchased five years ago and goodwill was recognised.

What is the cash-generating unit for X (X's cash-generating unit)?

Analysis

IE2   In identifying X's cash-generating unit, an entity considers whether, for example:

(a)   internal management reporting is organised to measure performance on a store-by-store basis; and

(b)   the business is run on a store-by-store profit basis or on a region/city basis.

IE3   All M's stores are in different neighbourhoods and probably have different customer bases. So, although X is managed at a corporate level, X generates cash inflows that are largely independent of those of M's other stores. Therefore, it is likely that X is a cash-generating unit.

IE4   If X's cash-generating unit represents the lowest level within M at which the goodwill is monitored for internal management purposes, M applies to that cash-generating unit the impairment test described in paragraph 90 of [draft] FRS • IAS 36. If information about the carrying amount of goodwill is not available and monitored for internal management purposes at the level of X's cash-generating unit, M applies to that cash-generating unit the impairment test described in paragraph 88 of [draft] FRS • IAS 36.

B - Plant for an Intermediate Step in a Production Process

Background

IE5   A significant raw material used for plant Y's final production is an intermediate product bought from plant X of the same entity. X's products are sold to Y at a transfer price that passes all margins to X. Eighty per cent of Y's final production is sold to customers outside of the entity. Sixty per cent of X's final production is sold to Y and the remaining 40 per cent is sold to customers outside of the entity.

For each of the following cases, what are the cash-generating units for X and Y?

Case 1: X could sell the products it sells to Y in an active market. Internal transfer prices are higher than market prices.

Case 2: There is no active market for the products X sells to Y.

Analysis

Case 1

X could sell its products in an active market and, so, generate cash inflows that would be largely independent of the cash inflows from Y. Therefore, it is likely that X is a separate cash-generating unit, although part of its production is used by Y (see paragraph 70 of [draft] FRS ● IAS 36).   **IE6**

It is likely that Y is also a separate cash-generating unit. Y sells 80 per cent of its products to customers outside of the entity. Therefore, its cash inflows can be regarded as largely independent.   **IE7**

Internal transfer prices do not reflect market prices for X's output. Therefore, in determining value in use of both X and Y, the entity adjusts financial budgets/ forecasts to reflect management's best estimate of future prices that could be achieved in arm's length transactions for those of X's products that are used internally (see paragraph 70 of [draft] FRS ● IAS 36).   **IE8**

Case 2

It is likely that the recoverable amount of each plant cannot be assessed independently of the recoverable amount of the other plant because: **IE9**

(a)   the majority of X's production is used internally and could not be sold in an active market. So, cash inflows of X depend on demand for Y's products. Therefore, X cannot be considered to generate cash inflows that are largely independent of those of Y.

(b)   the two plants are managed together.

As a consequence, it is likely that X and Y together are the smallest group of assets that generates cash inflows that are largely independent.   **IE10**

C - Single Product Entity

Background

Entity M produces a single product and owns plants A, B and C. Each plant is located in a different continent. A produces a component that is assembled in either B or C. The combined capacity of B and C is not fully utilised. M's products are sold worldwide from either B or C. For example, B's production can be sold in C's continent if the products can be delivered faster from B than from C. Utilisation levels of B and C depend on the allocation of sales between the two sites.   **IE11**

For each of the following cases, what are the cash-generating units for A, B and C?

Case 1: There is an active market for A's products.

Case 2: There is no active market for A's products.

Analysis

Case 1

IE12   It is likely that A is a separate cash-generating unit because there is an active market for its products (see Example B - Plant for an Intermediate Step in a Production Process, Case 1).

IE13   Although there is an active market for the products assembled by B and C, cash inflows for B and C depend on the allocation of production across the two sites. It is unlikely that the future cash inflows for B and C can be determined individually. Therefore, it is likely that B and C together are the smallest identifiable group of assets that generates cash inflows that are largely independent.

IE14   In determining the value in use of A and B plus C, M adjusts financial budgets/forecasts to reflect its best estimate of future prices that could be achieved in arm's length transactions for A's products (see paragraph 70 of [draft] FRS ● IAS 36).

Case 2

IE15   It is likely that the recoverable amount of each plant cannot be assessed independently because:

(a)   there is no active market for A's products. Therefore, A's cash inflows depend on sales of the final product by B and C.

(b)   although there is an active market for the products assembled by B and C, cash inflows for B and C depend on the allocation of production across the two sites. It is unlikely that the future cash inflows for B and C can be determined individually.

IE16   As a consequence, it is likely that A, B and C together (ie M as a whole) are the smallest identifiable group of assets that generates cash inflows that are largely independent.

D - Magazine Titles

Background

IE17   A publisher owns 150 magazine titles of which 70 were purchased and 80 were self-created. The price paid for a purchased magazine title is recognised as an intangible asset. The costs of creating magazine titles and maintaining the existing titles are recognised as an expense when incurred. Cash inflows from direct sales and advertising are identifiable for each magazine title. Titles are managed by customer segments. The level of advertising income for a magazine title depends on the range of titles in the customer segment to which the magazine title relates. Management has a policy to abandon old titles before the end of their economic lives and replace them immediately with new titles for the same customer segment.

What is the cash-generating unit for an individual magazine title?

Analysis

It is likely that the recoverable amount of an individual magazine title can be assessed. Even though the level of advertising income for a title is influenced, to a certain extent, by the other titles in the customer segment, cash inflows from direct sales and advertising are identifiable for each title. In addition, although titles are managed by customer segments, decisions to abandon titles are made on an individual title basis. **IE18**

Therefore, it is likely that individual magazine titles generate cash inflows that are largely independent of each other and that each magazine title is a separate cash-generating unit. **IE19**

E - Building Half-Rented to Others and Half-Occupied for Own Use

Background

M is a manufacturing company. It owns a headquarters building that used to be fully occupied for internal use. After down-sizing, half of the building is now used internally and half rented to third parties. The lease agreement with the tenant is for five years. **IE20**

What is the cash-generating unit of the building?

Analysis

The primary purpose of the building is to serve as a corporate asset, supporting M's manufacturing activities. Therefore, the building as a whole cannot be considered to generate cash inflows that are largely independent of the cash inflows from the entity as a whole. So, it is likely that the cash-generating unit for the building is M as a whole. **IE21**

The building is not held as an investment. Therefore, it would not be appropriate to determine the value in use of the building based on projections of future market related rents. **IE22**

EXAMPLE 2 - CALCULATION OF VALUE IN USE AND RECOGNITION OF AN IMPAIRMENT LOSS

In this example, tax effects are ignored.

Background and Calculation of Value in Use

IE23   At the end of 20X0, entity T acquires entity M for CU10,000. M has manufacturing plants in three countries.

Schedule 1. Data at the end of 20X0

End of 20X0	*Allocation of purchase price*	*Fair value of identifiable assets*	*Goodwill*
	CU	CU	CU*
Activities in Country A	3,000	2,000	1,000
Activities in Country B	2,000	1,500	500
Activities in Country C	5,000	3,500	1,500
Total	10,000	7,000	3,000

* Activities in each country represent the lowest level at which the goodwill is monitored for internal management purposes (determined as the difference between the purchase price of the activities in each country, as specified in the purchase agreement, and the fair value of the identifiable assets).

IE23A   Because goodwill has been allocated to the activities in each country, each of those activities must be tested for impairment annually or more frequently if there is any indication that it may be impaired (see paragraph 90 of [draft] FRS ● IAS 36).

IE24   The recoverable amounts (ie higher of value in use and fair value less costs to sell) of the cash-generating units are determined on the basis of value in use calculations. At the end of 20X0 and 20X1, the value in use of each cash-generating unit exceeds its carrying amount. Therefore the activities in each country and the goodwill allocated to those activities are regarded as not impaired.

IE25   At the beginning of 20X2, a new government is elected in Country A. It passes legislation significantly restricting exports of T's main product. As a result, and for the foreseeable future, T's production in Country A will be cut by 40 per cent.

IE26   The significant export restriction and the resulting production decrease require T also to estimate the recoverable amount of the Country A operations at the beginning of 20X2.

IE27   T uses straight-line depreciation over a 12-year life for the Country A identifiable assets and anticipates no residual value.

IE28   To determine the value in use for the Country A cash-generating unit (see Schedule 2), T:

(a)   prepares cash flow forecasts derived from the most recent financial budgets/
      forecasts for the next five years (years 20X2-20X6) approved by management.
(b)   estimates subsequent cash flows (years 20X7-20Y2) based on declining growth
      rates. The growth rate for 20X7 is estimated to be 3 per cent. This rate is lower
      than the average long-term growth rate for the market in Country A.
(c)   selects a 15 per cent discount rate, which represents a pre-tax rate that reflects
      current market assessments of the time value of money and the risks specific to
      the Country A cash-generating unit.

Recognition and Measurement of Impairment Loss

The recoverable amount of the Country A cash-generating unit is CU1,360.   **IE29**

T compares the recoverable amount of the Country A cash-generating unit with its   **IE30**
carrying amount (see Schedule 3).

Because the carrying amount exceeds the recoverable amount by CU1,473, T re-   **IE31**
cognises an impairment loss of CU1,473 immediately in profit or loss. The carrying
amount of the goodwill that relates to the Country A operations is reduced to zero
before reducing the carrying amount of other identifiable assets within the Country
A cash-generating unit (see paragraph 104 of [draft] FRS ● ~~IAS 36~~).

Tax effects are accounted for separately in accordance with FRS 16 Current Tax and   **IE32**
FRS 19 Deferred Tax ~~IAS 12 Income Taxes~~ (see Illustrative Example 3A).

Schedule 2. Calculation of the value in use of the Country A cash-generating unit at
the beginning of 20X2

Year	Long-term growth rates	Future cash flows CU	Present value factor at 15% discount rate*	Discounted future cash flows CU
20X2 (n = 1)		230†	0.86957	200
20X3		253[1]	0.75614	191
20X4		273[1]	0.65752	180
20X5		290[1]	0.57175	166
20X6		304[1]	0.49718	151
20X7	3%	313‡	0.43233	135
20X8	−2%	307[2]	0.37594	115
20X9	−6%	289[2]	0.32690	94
20Y0	−15%	245[2]	0.28426	70
20Y1	−25%	184[2]	0.24719	45
20Y2	−67%	61[2]	0.21494	13
Value in use				1,360

*The present value factor is calculated as $k = 1/(1+a)^n$, where a = discount rate and n = period of discount.

†Based on management's best estimate of net cash flow projections (after the 40% cut).

‡Based on an extrapolation from preceding year cash flow using declining growth rates.

Schedule 3. Calculation and allocation of the impairment loss for the Country A cash-generating unit at the beginning of 20X2

Beginning of 20X2	Goodwill CU	Identifiable assets CU	Total CU
Historical cost	1,000	2,000	3,000
Accumulated depreciation (20X1)	-	(167)	(167)
Carrying amount	1,000	1,833	2,833
Impairment loss	(1,000)	(473)	(1,473)
Carrying amount after impairment loss	-	1,360	1,360

EXAMPLE 3 - DEFERRED TAX EFFECTS

ASB note: This example has been prepared by the IASB and uses the approach adopted in IAS 12 Income Taxes which differs from FRS 19 Deferred Tax.

A - Deferred Tax Effects of the Recognition of an Impairment Loss

Use the data for entity T as presented in Example 2, with supplementary information as provided in this example.

At the beginning of 20X2, the tax base of the identifiable assets of the Country A cash-generating unit is CU900. Impairment losses are not deductible for tax purposes. The tax rate is 40 per cent.   **IE33**

The recognition of an impairment loss on the assets of the Country A cash-generating unit reduces the taxable temporary difference related to those assets. The deferred tax liability is reduced accordingly.   **IE34**

Beginning of 20X2	Identifiable assets before impairment loss CU	Impairment loss CU	Identifiable assets after impairment loss CU
Carrying amount (Example 2)	1,833	(473)	1,360
Tax base	900	-	900
Taxable temporary difference	933	(473)	460
Deferred tax liability at 40%	373	(189)	184

In accordance with IAS 12 Income Taxes, no deferred tax relating to the goodwill was recognised initially. Therefore, the impairment loss relating to the goodwill does not give rise to a deferred tax adjustment.   **IE35**

B - Recognition of an Impairment Loss Creates a Deferred Tax Asset

IE36   An entity has an identifiable asset with a carrying amount of CU1,000. Its recoverable amount is CU650. The tax rate is 30 per cent and the tax base of the asset is CU800. Impairment losses are not deductible for tax purposes. The effect of the impairment loss is as follows:

	Before impairment	*Effect of impairment*	*After impairment*
	CU	CU	CU
Carrying amount	1,000	(350)	650
Tax base	800	-	800
Taxable (deductible) temporary difference	200	(350)	(150)
Deferred tax liability (asset) at 30%	60	(105)	(45)

IE37   In accordance with IAS 12, the entity recognises the deferred tax asset to the extent that it is probable that taxable profit will be available against which the deductible temporary difference can be utilised.

EXAMPLE 4 - REVERSAL OF AN IMPAIRMENT LOSS

Use the data for entity T as presented in Example 2, with supplementary information as provided in this example. In this example, tax effects are ignored.

Background

In 20X3, the government is still in office in Country A, but the business situation is improving. The effects of the export laws on T's production are proving to be less drastic than initially expected by management. As a result, management estimates that production will increase by 30 per cent. This favourable change requires T to re-estimate the recoverable amount of the net assets of the Country A operations (see paragraphs 110 and 111 of [draft] FRS ●IAS 36). The cash-generating unit for the net assets of the Country A operations is still the Country A operations.   **IE38**

Calculations similar to those in Example 2 show that the recoverable amount of the Country A cash-generating unit is now CU1,910.   **IE39**

Reversal of Impairment Loss

T compares the recoverable amount and the net carrying amount of the Country A cash-generating unit.   **IE40**

Schedule 1. Calculation of the carrying amount of the Country A cash-generating unit at the end of 20X3

	Goodwill CU	Identifiable assets CU	Total CU
Beginning of 20X2 (Example 2)			
Historical cost	1,000	2,000	3,000
Accumulated depreciation	-	(167)	(167)
Impairment loss	(1,000)	(473)	(1,473)
Carrying amount after impairment loss	-	1,360	1,360
End of 20X3			
Additional depreciation (2 years)*	-	(247)	(247)
Carrying amount	-	1,113	1,113
Recoverable amount			1,910
Excess of recoverable amount over carrying amount			797

*   After recognition of the impairment loss at the beginning of 20X2, T revised the depreciation charge for the Country A identifiable assets (from CU166.7 per year to CU123.6 per year), based on the revised carrying amount and remaining useful life (11 years).

There has been a favourable change in the estimates used to determine the reco-verable amount of the Country A net assets since the last impairment loss was   **IE41** recognised. Therefore, in accordance with paragraph 114 of [draft] FRS • ~~IAS 36~~, T recognises a reversal of the impairment loss recognised in 20X2.

IE42   In accordance with paragraphs 122 and 123 of [draft] FRS • ~~IAS 36~~, T increases the carrying amount of the Country A identifiable assets by CU387 (see Schedule 3), ie up to the lower of recoverable amount (CU1,910) and the identifiable assets' depreciated historical cost (CU1,500) (see Schedule 2). This increase is recognised immediately in profit or loss.

IE43   In accordance with paragraph 124 of [draft] FRS • ~~IAS 36~~, the impairment loss on goodwill is not reversed.

Schedule 2. Determination of the depreciated historical cost of the Country A identifiable assets at the end of 20X3

End of 20X3	Identifiable assets CU
Historical cost	2,000
Accumulated depreciation *(166.7 × 3 years)*	(500)
Depreciated historical cost	1,500
Carrying amount (Schedule 1)	1,113
Difference	387

Schedule 3. Carrying amount of the Country A assets at the end of 20X3

End of 20X3	Goodwill CU	Identifiable assets CU	Total CU
Gross carrying amount	1,000	2,000	3,000
Accumulated amortisation	-	(414)	(414)
Accumulated impairment loss	(1,000)	(473)	(1,473)
Carrying amount	-	1,113	1,113
Reversal of impairment loss	0	387	387
Carrying amount after reversal of impairment loss	-	1,500	1,500

EXAMPLE 5 - TREATMENT OF A FUTURE RESTRUCTURING

In this example, tax effects are ignored.

Background

At the end of 20X0, entity K tests a plant for impairment. The plant is a cash-generating unit. The plant's assets are carried at depreciated historical cost. The plant has a carrying amount of CU3,000 and a remaining useful life of 10 years. **IE44**

The plant's recoverable amount (ie higher of value in use and fair value less costs to sell) is determined on the basis of a value in use calculation. Value in use is calculated using a pre-tax discount rate of 14 per cent. **IE45**

Management approved budgets reflect that: **IE46**

(a)   at the end of 20X3, the number of employees at the plant will be reduced at an estimated cost (for termination) of CU100. Because K has not yet incurred a liability to provide termination benefits, a liability has not been recognised at the end of 20X0.

(b)   there will be future benefits from this restructuring in the form of reduced future cash outflows.

At the end of 20X2, K recognises a liability to provide termination benefits in accordance with ~~IAS 19 Employee Benefits~~ FRS 17 Retirement and Termination Benefits. The costs are still estimated to be CU100. The plant's estimated future cash flows reflected in the most recent management-approved budgets are set out in paragraph IE51 and the current discount rate is the same as at the end of 20X0. **IE47**

At the end of 20X3, actual termination benefit costs of CU100 are paid. Again, the plant's estimated future cash flows reflected in the most recent management-approved budgets and a current discount rate are the same as those estimated at the end of 20X2. **IE48**

At the End of 20X0

Schedule 1. Calculation of the plant's value in use at the end of 20X0

Year	Future cash flows CU	Discounted at 14% CU
20X1	300	263
20X2	280	215
20X3	420*	283
20X4	520†	308
20X5	350†	182
20X6	420†	191
20X7	480†	192
20X8	480†	168
20X9	460†	141
20X10	400†	108
Value in use		2,051

*   Excludes estimated costs of termination benefits reflected in management budgets.
†   Excludes estimated benefits reflected in management budgets expected from the reduction in the number of employees.

IE49   The plant's recoverable amount (ie value in use) is less than its carrying amount. Therefore, K recognises an impairment loss for the plant.

Schedule 2. Calculation of the impairment loss at the end of 20X0

	Plant CU
Carrying amount before impairment loss	3,000
Recoverable amount (Schedule 1)	2,051
Impairment loss	(949)
Carrying amount after impairment loss	2,051

At the End of 20X1

IE50   No event occurs that requires the plant's recoverable amount to be re-estimated. Therefore, no calculation of the recoverable amount is required to be performed.

At the End of 20X2

IE51   The entity has now incurred a liability to provide termination benefits. Therefore, in determining the plant's value in use, the benefits expected from the restructuring are considered in forecasting cash flows. This results in an increase in the estimated future cash flows used to determine value in use at the end of 20X0. In accordance with paragraphs 110 and 111 of [draft] FRS ● ~~IAS 36~~, the recoverable amount of the plant is re-determined at the end of 20X2.

Schedule 3. Calculation of the plant's value in use at the end of 20X2

Year	Future cash flows CU	Discounted at 14% CU
20X3	420*	368
20X4	570†	439
20X5	380†	256
20X6	450†	266
20X7	510†	265
20X8	510†	232
20X9	480†	192
20X10	410†	144
Value in use		2,162

* Excludes estimated costs of termination benefits because a liability has been recognised.
† Includes estimated benefits reflected in managements budgets expected from the reduction in the number of employees.

The plant's recoverable amount (value in use) is higher than its carrying amount (see   **IE52** Schedule 4). Therefore, K reverses the impairment loss recognised for the plant at the end of 20X0.

Schedule 4. Calculation of the reversal of the impairment loss at the end of 20X2

	Plant CU
Carrying amount at the end of 20X0 (Schedule 2)	2,051
End of 20X2	
Depreciation charge (for 20X1 and 20X2–Schedule 5)	(410)
Carrying amount before reversal	1,641
Recoverable amount (Schedule 3)	2,162
Reversal of the impairment loss	521
Carrying amount after reversal	2,162
Carrying amount: depreciated historical cost (Schedule 5)	2,400

* The reversal does not result in the carrying amount of the plant exceeding what its carrying amount would have been at depreciated historical cost. Therefore, the full reversal of the impairment loss is recognised.

At the End of 20X3

IE53   There is a cash outflow of CU100 when the termination benefits are paid. Even though a cash outflow has taken place, there is no change in the estimated future cash flows used to determine value in use at the end of 20X2. Therefore, the plant's recoverable amount is not calculated at the end of 20X3.

Schedule 5. Summary of the carrying amount of the plant

End of year	Depreciated historical cost CU	Recoverable amount CU	Adjusted depreciation charge CU	Impairment loss CU	Carrying amount after impairment CU
20X0	3,000	2,051	0	(949)	2,051
20X1	2,700	nc	(205)	0	1,846
20X2	2,400	2,162	(205)	521	2,162
20X3	2,100	nc	(270)	0	1,892

nc = not calculated as there is no indication that the impairment loss may have increased/decreased.

EXAMPLE 6 - TREATMENT OF FUTURE COSTS

In this example, tax effects are ignored.

Background

At the end of 20X0, entity F tests a machine for impairment. The machine is a cash-   **IE54**
generating unit. It is carried at depreciated historical cost and its carrying amount is
CU150,000. It has an estimated remaining useful life of 10 years.

The machine's recoverable amount (ie higher of value in use and fair value less costs   **IE55**
to sell) is determined on the basis of a value in use calculation. Value in use is
calculated using a pre-tax discount rate of 14 per cent.

Management approved budgets reflect: **IE56**

(a)   estimated costs necessary to maintain the level of economic benefit expected to
      arise from the machine in its current condition; and
(b)   that in 20X4, costs of CU25,000 will be incurred to enhance the machine's
      performance by increasing its productive capacity.

At the end of 20X4, costs to enhance the machine's performance are incurred. The   **IE57**
machine's estimated future cash flows reflected in the most recent management
approved budgets are given in paragraph IE60 and a current discount rate is the
same as at the end of 20X0.

At the End of 20X0

Schedule 1. Calculation of the machine's value in use at the end of 20X0

Year	Future cash flows CU	Discounted at 14% CU
20X1	22,165[*]	19,443
20X2	21,450[*]	16,505
20X3	20,550[*]	13,871
20X4	24,725[*†]	14,639
20X5	25,325[*§]	13,153
20X6	24,825[*§]	11,310
20X7	24,123[*§]	9,640
20X8	25,533[*§]	8,951
20X9	24,234[*§]	7,452
20X10	22,850[*§]	6,164
Value in use		121,128

[*] Includes estimated costs necessary to maintain the level of economic benefit expected to arise from the machine in its current condition.
[†] Excludes estimated costs to enhance the machine's performance reflected in management budgets.
[§] Excludes estimated benefits expected from enhancing the machine's performance reflected in management budgets.

IE58 The machine's recoverable amount (value in use) is less than its carrying amount. Therefore, F recognises an impairment loss for the machine.

Schedule 2. Calculation of the impairment loss at the end of 20X0

	Machine CU
Carrying amount before impairment loss	150,000
Recoverable amount (Schedule 1)	121,128
Impairment loss	(28,872)
Carrying amount after impairment loss	121,128

Years 20X1 - 20X3

IE59 No event occurs that requires the machine's recoverable amount to be re-estimated. Therefore, no calculation of recoverable amount is required to be performed.

At the End of 20X4

IE60 The costs to enhance the machine's performance are incurred. Therefore, in determining the machine's value in use, the future benefits expected from enhancing the machine's performance are considered in forecasting cash flows. This results in an increase in the estimated future cash flows used to determine value in use at the end of 20X0. As a consequence, in accordance with paragraphs 110 and 111 of [draft] FRS ● IAS 36, the recoverable amount of the machine is recalculated at the end of 20X4.

Schedule 3. Calculation of the machine's value in use at the end of 20X4

Year	Future cash flows* CU	Discounted at 14% CU
20X5	30,321	26,597
20X6	32,750	25,200
20X7	31,721	21,411
20X8	31,950	18,917
20X9	33,100	17,191
20X10	27,999	12,756
Value in use		122,072

* Includes estimated benefits expected from enhancing the machine's performance reflected in management budgets.

The machine's recoverable amount (ie value in use) is higher than the machine's carrying amount and depreciated historical cost (see Schedule 4). Therefore, K reverses the impairment loss recognised for the machine at the end of 20X0 so that the machine is carried at depreciated historical cost. **IE61**

Schedule 4. Calculation of the reversal of the impairment loss at the end of 20X4

	Machine CU
Carrying amount at the end of 20X0 (Schedule 2)	121,128
End of 20X4	
Depreciation charge (20X1 to 20X4 – Schedule 5)	(48,452)
Costs to enhance the asset's performance	25,000
Carrying amount before reversal	97,676
Recoverable amount (Schedule 3)	122,072
Reversal of the impairment loss	17,324
Carrying amount after reversal	115,000
Carrying amount: depreciated historical cost (Schedule 5)	115,000*

* The value in use of the machine exceeds what its carrying amount would have been at depreciated historical cost. Therefore, the reversal is limited to an amount that does not result in the carrying amount of the machine exceeding depreciated historical cost.

Schedule 5. Summary of the carrying amount of the machine

Year	Depreciated historical cost CU	Recoverable amount CU	Adjusted depreciation charge CU	Impairment loss CU	Carrying amount after impairment CU
20X0	150,000	121,128	0	(28,872)	121,128
20X1	135,000	nc	(12,113)	0	109,015
20X2	120,000	nc	(12,113)	0	96,902
20X3	105,000	nc	(12,113)	0	84,789
20X4	90,000		(12,113)		
enhancement	25,000		-		
	115,000	122,072	(12,113)	17,324	115,000
20X5	95,833	nc	(19,167)	0	95,833

nc = not calculated as there is no indication that the impairment loss may have increased/decreased.

EXAMPLE 7 – IMPAIRMENT TESTING CASH-GENERATING UNITS WITH GOODWILL AND NON-CONTROLLING INTERESTS

(applicable to business combination effected before ~~[draft] IFRS 3 revised 200X~~ [draft] FRS • *Business Combinations* is applied)

In this example, tax effects are ignored.

Background

Entity X acquires an 80 per cent ownership interest in Entity Y for CU1,600 on 1 January 20X3. At that date, Y's identifiable net assets have a fair value of CU1,500. Y has no contingent liabilities. Therefore, X recognises in its consolidated financial statements:

(a) goodwill of CU400, being the difference between the cost of the business combination of CU1,600 and X's 80 per cent interest in Y's identifiable net assets;

(b) Y's identifiable net assets at their fair value of CU1,500; and

(c) a minority interest of CU300, being the 20 per cent interest in Y's identifiable net assets held by parties outside X.

IE62

The assets of Y together are the smallest group of assets that generate cash inflows that are largely independent of the cash inflows from other assets or groups of assets. Therefore Y is a cash-generating unit. Because this cash-generating unit includes goodwill within its carrying amount, it must be tested for impairment annually, or more frequently if there is an indication that it may be impaired (see paragraph 90 of [draft] FRS • ~~IAS 36~~).

IE63

At the end of 20X3, X determines that the recoverable amount of cash-generating unit Y is CU1,000. X uses straight-line depreciation over a 10-year life for Y's identifiable assets and anticipates no residual value.

IE64

Testing Y for Impairment

A portion of Y's recoverable amount of CU1,000 is attributable to the unrecognised non-controlling interest in goodwill. Therefore, in accordance with paragraph C2 of Appendix C of [draft] FRS • ~~IAS 36~~, the carrying amount of Y must be notionally adjusted to include goodwill attributable to the non-controlling interest, before being compared with the recoverable amount of CU1,000.

IE65

Schedule 1. Testing Y for impairment at the end of 20X3

End of 20X3	Goodwill CU	Identifiable net assets CU	Total CU
Gross carrying amount	400	1,500	1,900
Accumulated depreciation	-	(150)	(150)
Carrying amount	400	1,350	1,750
Unrecognised minority interest	100*	-	100
Notionally adjusted carrying amount	500	1,350	1,850
Recoverable amount			1,000
Impairment loss			850

* Goodwill attributable to X's 80% interest in Y at the acquisition date is CU400. Therefore, goodwill notionally attributable to the 20% minority interest in Y at the acquisition date is CU100.

IE66   In accordance with paragraph 104 of [draft] FRS ● ~~IAS 36~~, the impairment loss of CU850 is allocated to the assets in the unit by first reducing the carrying amount of goodwill to zero.

IE67   Therefore, CU500 of the CU850 impairment loss for the unit is allocated to the goodwill. However, because the goodwill is recognised only to the extent of X's 80 per cent ownership interest in Y, X recognises only 80 per cent of that goodwill impairment loss (ie CU400).

IE68   The remaining impairment loss of CU350 is recognised by reducing the carrying amounts of Y's identifiable assets (see Schedule 2).

Schedule 2. Allocation of the impairment loss for Y at the end of 20X3

End of 20X3	Goodwill CU	Identifiable net assets CU	Total CU
Gross carrying amount	400	1,500	1,900
Accumulated depreciation	-	(150)	(150)
Carrying amount	400	1,350	1,750
Impairment loss	(400)	(350)	(750)
Carrying amount after impairment loss	-	1,000	1,000

EXAMPLE 7A – IMPAIRMENT TESTING CASH-GENERATING UNITS WITH GOODWILL AND NON-CONTROLLING INTERESTS
(applicable to business combination effected after ~~[draft] IFRS 3 (revised 200X)~~ [draft] FRS ● is applied)

In this example, tax effects are ignored.

Background

Entity X acquires an 80 per cent ownership interest in Entity Y for CU1,650 on 1 January 20X3. There is no evidence that this transaction is not an exchange of equal values. Therefore, the consideration transferred of CU1,650 is presumed to be the fair value of the 80 per cent interest. The fair value of Y is CU2,000. At 1 January 20X3, Y's identifiable net assets have a fair value of CU1,500.   **IE68A**

Therefore, X recognises in its consolidated financial statements Y's identifiable net assets at their fair value of CU1,500.   **IE68B**

X also recognises in its consolidated financial statements goodwill of CU500, measured as the excess of the fair value of Y, as a whole, of CU2,000 over the net amount of the recognised identifiable assets acquired and liabilities assumed of CU1,500.

The amount of goodwill attributable to the controlling interest and to the non-controlling interests in Y is calculated as follows:

	CU
Fair value of X's 80 per cent interest in Y	1,650
Less: X's share of the fair value of the identifiable net assets acquired (80 per cent × CU1,500)	(1,200)
Goodwill allocated to X	450
Goodwill allocated to the non-controlling interests in Y [CU500 – CU450]	50

Therefore, the fair value of Y is attributed to X and the non-controlling interest at the acquisition date as follows

	Total	Attributable to X	Attributable to the non-controlling interest
	CU	CU	CU
Identifiable net assets	1,500	1,200	300
Goodwill	500	450	50
Total	2,000	1,650	350

The assets of Y together are the smallest group of assets that generate cash inflows that are largely independent of the cash inflows from other assets or groups of assets. Therefore Y is a cash-generating unit. Because this cash-generating unit includes goodwill within its carrying amount, it must be tested for impairment annually, or   **IE68C** more frequently if there is an indication that it may be impaired (see paragraph 90 of [draft] FRS ● ~~IAS 36~~).

IE68D   At the end of 20X3, X determines that the recoverable amount of cash-generating unit Y is CU1,650. X uses straight-line depreciation over a 10-year life for Y's identifiable assets and anticipates no residual value.

Allocating impairment loss between the parent and non-controlling interest

Schedule 1. Testing Y for impairment at the end of 20X3

End of 20X3	Goodwill CU	Identifiable net assets CU	Total CU
Gross carrying amount	500	1,500	2,000
Accumulated depreciation	-	(150)	(150)
Carrying amount	500	1,350	1,850
Recoverable amount			1,650
Impairment loss			200

IE68E   In accordance with paragraph 104 of [draft] FRS ● ~~IAS 36~~, the impairment loss of CU200 is allocated to the assets in the unit by first reducing the carrying amount of goodwill to zero.

IE68F   Therefore, the full amount of impairment loss of CU200 for the unit is allocated to the goodwill. In accordance with paragraph C9 of Appendix C of [draft] FRS ● ~~IAS 36~~ if the partially-owned subsidiary is itself a cash-generating unit, the goodwill impairment loss is allocated to the controlling and non-controlling interests on the basis of the relative carrying values of goodwill allocated to them.

Schedule 2. Allocating goodwill impairment loss to X and the non-controlling interest.

	Total amount	Attributable to X	Attributable to non-controlling interest
Goodwill before impairment loss	CU500	CU 450	CU 50
Percentage of the total	100%	90%	10%
Impairment loss	(CU 200)	(CU 180)	(CU 20)
Goodwill after being reduced for impairment loss	CU 300	CU 270	CU 30

EXAMPLE 8 - ALLOCATION OF CORPORATE ASSETS

In this example, tax effects are ignored.

Background

Entity M has three cash-generating units: A, B and C. The carrying amounts of those   **IE69**
units do not include goodwill. There are adverse changes in the technological
environment in which M operates. Therefore, M conducts impairment tests of each
of its cash-generating units. At the end of 20X0, the carrying amounts of A, B and C
are CU100, CU150 and CU200 respectively.

The operations are conducted from a headquarters. The carrying amount of the   **IE70**
headquarters is CU200: a headquarters building of CU150 and a research centre of
CU50. The relative carrying amounts of the cash-generating units are a reasonable
indication of the proportion of the headquarters building devoted to each cash-
generating unit. The carrying amount of the research centre cannot be allocated on a
reasonable basis to the individual cash-generating units.

The remaining estimated useful life of cash-generating unit A is 10 years. The   **IE71**
remaining useful lives of B, C and the headquarters are 20 years. The headquarters is
depreciated on a straight-line basis.

The recoverable amount (ie higher of value in use and fair value less costs to sell) of   **IE72**
each cash-generating unit is based on its value in use. Value in use is calculated using
a pre-tax discount rate of 15 per cent.

Identification of Corporate Assets

In accordance with paragraph 102 of [draft] FRS ● IAS 36, M first identifies all the   **IE73**
corporate assets that relate to the individual cash-generating units under review. The
corporate assets are the headquarters building and the research centre.

M then decides how to deal with each of the corporate assets: **IE74**

(a)   the carrying amount of the headquarters building can be allocated on a rea-
      sonable and consistent basis to the cash-generating units under review; and
(b)   the carrying amount of the research centre cannot be allocated on a reasonable
      and consistent basis to the individual cash-generating units under review.

Allocation of Corporate Assets

The carrying amount of the headquarters building is allocated to the carrying   **IE75**
amount of each individual cash-generating unit. A weighted allocation basis is used
because the estimated remaining useful life of A's cash-generating unit is 10 years,
whereas the estimated remaining useful lives of B and C's cash-generating units are
20 years.

Schedule 1. Calculation of a weighted allocation of the carrying amount of the headquarters building

End of 20X0	A CU	B CU	C CU	Total CU
Carrying amount	100	150	200	450
Useful life	10 years	20 years	20 years	
Weighting based on useful life	1	2	2	
Carrying amount after weighting	100	300	400	800
Pro-rata allocation of the building	12% (100/800)	38% (300/800)	50% (400/800)	100%
Allocation of the carrying amount of the building (based on pro-rata above)	19	56	75	150
Carrying amount (after allocation of the building)	119	206	275	600

Determination of Recoverable Amount and Calculation of Impairment Losses

IE76　Paragraph 102 of [draft] FRS ● IAS 36 requires first that the recoverable amount of each individual cash-generating unit be compared with its carrying amount, including the portion of the carrying amount of the headquarters building allocated to the unit, and any resulting impairment loss recognised. Paragraph 102 of [draft] FRS ● IAS 36 then requires the recoverable amount of M as a whole (ie the smallest group of cash-generating units that includes the research centre) to be compared with its carrying amount, including both the headquarters building and the research centre.

Schedule 2. Calculation of A, B, C and M's value in use at the end of 20X0

	A		B		C		M	
Year	Future cash flows CU	Discount at 15% CU	Future cash flows CU	Discount at 15% CU	Future cash flows CU	Discount at 15% CU	Future cash flows CU	Discount at 15% CU
1	18	16	9	8	10	9	39	34
2	31	23	16	12	20	15	72	54
3	37	24	24	16	34	22	105	69
4	42	24	29	17	44	25	128	73
5	47	24	32	16	51	25	143	71
6	52	22	33	14	56	24	155	67
7	55	21	34	13	60	22	162	61
8	55	18	35	11	63	21	166	54
9	53	15	35	10	65	18	167	48
10	48	12	35	9	66	16	169	42
11			36	8	66	14	132	28
12			35	7	66	12	131	25
13			35	6	66	11	131	21
14			33	5	65	9	128	18
15			30	4	62	8	122	15
16			26	3	60	6	115	12
17			22	2	57	5	108	10
18			18	1	51	4	97	8
19			14	1	43	3	85	6
20			10	1	35	2	71	4
Value in use		199		164		271		720*

* It is assumed that the research centre generates additional future cash flows for the entity as a whole. Therefore, the sum of the value in use of each individual cash-generating unit is less than the value in use of the business as a whole. The additional cash flows are not attributable to the headquarters building.

Schedule 3. Impairment testing A, B and C

End of 20X0	A CU	B CU	C CU
Carrying amount (after allocation of the building) (Schedule 1)	119	206	275
Recoverable amount (Schedule 2)	199	164	271
Impairment loss	0	(42)	(4)

The next step is to allocate the impairment losses between the assets of the cash-generating units and the headquarters building.   **IE77**

Schedule 4. Allocation of the impairment losses for cash-generating units B and C

Cash-generating unit	BCU		CCU	
To headquarters building	(12)	*(42 × 56/206)*	(1)	*(4 × 75/275)*
To assets in cash-generating unit	(30)	*(42 × 150/206)*	(3)	*(4 × 200/275)*
	(42)		(4)	

IE78 Because the research centre could not be allocated on a reasonable and consistent basis to A, B and C's cash-generating units, M compares the carrying amount of the smallest group of cash-generating units to which the carrying amount of the research centre can be allocated (ie M as a whole) to its recoverable amount.

Schedule 5. Impairment testing the smallest group of cash-generating units to which the carrying amount of the research centre can be allocated (ie M as a whole)

End of 20X0	A CU	B CU	C CU	Building CU	Research centre CU	M CU
Carrying amount	100	150	200	150	50	650
Impairment loss arising from the first step of the test	-	(30)	(3)	(13)	-	(46)
Carrying amount after the first step of the test	100	120	197	137	50	604
Recoverable amount (Schedule 2)						720
Impairment loss for the 'larger' cash-generating unit						0

IE79 Therefore, no additional impairment loss results from the application of the impairment test to M as a whole. Only an impairment loss of CU46 is recognised as a result of the application of the first step of the test to A, B and C.

EXAMPLE 9 – DISCLOSURES ABOUT CASH-GENERATING UNITS WITH GOODWILL OR INTANGIBLE ASSETS WITH INDEFINITE USEFUL LIVES

The purpose of this example is to illustrate the disclosures required by paragraphs 134 and 135 of [draft] FRS ● ~~IAS 36~~.

Background

Entity M is a multinational manufacturing firm that uses geographical segments as its primary format for reporting segment information. M's three reportable segments based on that format are Europe, North America and Asia. Goodwill has been allocated for impairment testing purposes to three individual cash-generating units—two in Europe (units A and B) and one in North America (unit C)—and to one group of cash-generating units (comprising operation XYZ) in Asia. Units A, B and C and operation XYZ each represent the lowest level within M at which the goodwill is monitored for internal management purposes.   **IE80**

M acquired unit C, a manufacturing operation in North America, in December 20X2. Unlike M's other North American operations, C operates in an industry with high margins and high growth rates, and with the benefit of a 10-year patent on its primary product. The patent was granted to C just before M's acquisition of C. As part of accounting for the acquisition of C, M recognised, in addition to the patent, goodwill of CU3,000 and a brand name of CU1,000. M's management has determined that the brand name has an indefinite useful life. M has no other intangible assets with indefinite useful lives.   **IE81**

The carrying amounts of goodwill and intangible assets with indefinite useful lives allocated to units A, B and C and to operation XYZ are as follows: **IE82**

	Goodwill CU	Intangible assets with indefinite useful lives CU
A	350	
B	450	
C	3,000	1,000
XYZ	1,200	
Total	5,000	1,000

During the year ending 31 December 20X3, M determines that there is no impairment of any of its cash-generating units or group of cash-generating units containing goodwill or intangible assets with indefinite useful lives. The recoverable amounts (ie higher of value in use and fair value less costs to sell) of those units and group of units are determined on the basis of value in use calculations. M has determined that the recoverable amount calculations are most sensitive to changes in the following assumptions: **IE83**

Units A and B	Unit C	Operation XYZ
Gross margin during the budget period (budget period is 4 years)	5-year US government bond rate during the budget period (budget period is 5 years)	Gross margin during the budget period (budget period is 5 years)
Raw materials price inflation during the budget period	Raw materials price inflation during the budget period	Japanese yen/US dollar exchange rate during the budget period
Market share during the budget period	Market share during the budget period	Market share during the budget period
Growth rate used to extrapolate cash flows beyond the budget period	Growth rate used to extrapolate cash flows beyond the budget period	Growth rate used to extrapolate cash flows beyond the budget period

IE84   Gross margins during the budget period for A, B and XYZ are estimated by M based on average gross margins achieved in the period immediately before the start of the budget period, increased by 5 per cent per year for anticipated efficiency improvements. A and B produce complementary products and are operated by M to achieve the same gross margins.

IE85   Market shares during the budget period are estimated by M based on average market shares achieved in the period immediately before the start of the budget period, adjusted each year for any anticipated growth or decline in market shares. M anticipates that:

(a)   market shares for A and B will differ, but will each grow during the budget period by 3 per cent per year as a result of ongoing improvements in product quality.

(b)   C's market share will grow during the budget period by 6 per cent per year as a result of increased advertising expenditure and the benefits from the protection of the 10-year patent on its primary product.

(c)   XYZ's market share will remain unchanged during the budget period as a result of the combination of ongoing improvements in product quality and an anticipated increase in competition.

IE86   A and B purchase raw materials from the same European suppliers, whereas C's raw materials are purchased from various North American suppliers. Raw materials price inflation during the budget period is estimated by M to be consistent with forecast consumer price indices published by government agencies in the relevant European and North American countries.

IE87   The 5-year US government bond rate during the budget period is estimated by M to be consistent with the yield on such bonds at the beginning of the budget period. The Japanese yen/US dollar exchange rate is estimated by M to be consistent with the average market forward exchange rate over the budget period.

IE88   M uses steady growth rates to extrapolate beyond the budget period cash flows for A, B, C and XYX. The growth rates for A, B and XYZ are estimated by M to be consistent with publicly available information about the long-term average growth rates for the markets in which A, B and XYZ operate. However, the growth rate for C exceeds the long-term average growth rate for the market in which C operates. M's management is of the opinion that this is reasonable in the light of the protection of the 10-year patent on C's primary product.

M includes the following disclosure in the notes to its financial statements for the year ending 31 December 20X3.

IE89

Impairment Tests for Goodwill and Intangible Assets with Indefinite Lives

Goodwill has been allocated for impairment testing purposes to three individual cash-generating units—two in Europe (units A and B) and one in North America (unit C)—and to one group of cash-generating units (comprising operation XYZ) in Asia. The carrying amount of goodwill allocated to unit C and operation XYZ is significant in comparison with the total carrying amount of goodwill, but the carrying amount of goodwill allocated to each of units A and B is not. Nevertheless, the recoverable amounts of units A and B are based on some of the same key assumptions, and the aggregate carrying amount of goodwill allocated to those units is significant.

Operation XYZ

The recoverable amount of operation XYZ has been determined based on a value in use calculation. That calculation uses cash flow projections based on financial budgets approved by management covering a five-year period, and a discount rate of 8.4 per cent. Cash flows beyond that five-year period have been extrapolated using a steady 6.3 per cent growth rate. This growth rate does not exceed the long-term average growth rate for the market in which XYZ operates. Management believes that any reasonably possible change in the key assumptions on which XYZ's recoverable amount is based would *not* cause XYZ's carrying amount to exceed its recoverable amount.

Unit C

The recoverable amount of unit C has also been determined based on a value in use calculation. That calculation uses cash flow projections based on financial budgets approved by management covering a five-year period, and a discount rate of 9.2 per cent. C's cash flows beyond the five-year period are extrapolated using a steady 12 per cent growth rate. This growth rate exceeds by 4 percentage points the long-term average growth rate for the market in which C operates. However, C benefits from the protection of a 10-year patent on its primary product, granted in December 20X2. Management believes that a 12 per cent growth rate is reasonable in the light of that patent. Management also believes that any reasonably possible change in the key assumptions on which C's recoverable amount is based would *not* cause C's carrying amount to exceed its recoverable amount.

Units A and B

The recoverable amounts of units A and B have been determined on the basis of value in use calculations. Those units produce complementary products, and their recoverable amounts are based on some of the same key assumptions. Both value in use calculations use cash flow projections based on financial budgets approved by management covering a four-year period, and a discount rate of 7.9 per cent. Both sets of cash flows beyond the four-year period are extrapolated using a steady 5 per cent growth rate. This growth rate does not exceed the long-term average growth rate for the market in which A and B operate. Cash flow projections during the budget period for both A and B are also based on the same expected gross margins during the budget period and the same raw materials price inflation during the budget period. Management believes that any reasonably possible change in any of these key assumptions would *not* cause the aggregate carrying amount of A and B to exceed the aggregate recoverable amount of those units.

	Operation XYZ	Unit C	Units A and B (in aggregate)
Carrying amount of goodwill	CU1,200	CU3,000	CU800
Carrying amount of brand name with indefinite useful life	-	CU1,000	-
Key assumptions used in value in use calculations[*]			
• Key assumption	• Budgeted gross margins	• 5-year US government bond rate	• Budgeted gross margins
• Basis for determining value(s) assigned to key assumption	• Average gross margins achieved in period immediately before the budget period, increased for expected efficiency improvements.	• Yield on 5-year US government bonds at the beginning of the budget period.	• Average gross margins achieved in period immediately before the budget period, increased for expected efficiency improvements.
	• ~~Values assigned to key assumption reflect past experience, except for efficiency improvements. Management believes improvements of 5% per year are reasonably achievable.~~	• ~~Value assigned to key assumption is consistent with external sources of information.~~	• ~~Values assigned to key assumption reflect past experience, except for efficiency improvements. Management believes improvements of 5% per year are reasonably achievable.~~

[*] The key assumptions shown in this table for units A and B are only those that are used in the recoverable amount calculations for both units.

Key assumption	• Japanese yen/ US dollar exchange rate during the budget period	• Raw materials price inflation	• Raw materials price inflation
• Basis for determining value(s) assigned to key assumption	• Average market forward exchange rate over the budget period.	• Forecast consumer price indices during the budget period for North American countries from which raw materials are purchased.	• Forecast consumer price indices during the budget period for European countries from which raw materials are purchased.
	• ~~Value assigned to key assumption is consistent with external sources of information.~~	• ~~Value assigned to key assumption is consistent with external sources of information.~~	• ~~Value assigned to key assumption is consistent with external sources of information.~~
• Key assumption	• Budgeted market share	• Budgeted market share	
• Basis for determining value(s) assigned to key assumption	• Average market share in period immediately before the budget period.	• Average market share in period immediately before the budget period, increased each year for anticipated growth in market share.	
	• ~~Value assigned to key assumption reflects past experience. No change in market share expected as a result of ongoing product quality improvements coupled with anticipated increase in competition.~~	• ~~Management believes market share growth of 6% per year is reasonably achievable due to increased advertising expenditure, the benefits from the protection of the 10year patent on C's primary product, and the expected synergies to be achieved from operating C as part of M's North American segment.~~	

Note on Legal requirements

GREAT BRITAIN

Impairment losses

1   In Great Britain, for financial years beginning on or after 1 January 2005, the statutory requirements relating to accounting for impairment losses for those companies which prepare accounts under the Companies Act 1985, rather than IAS accounts, are set out in the Companies Act 1985.

2   Paragraph 19(1) of Schedule 4 to the Companies Act 1985 allows provisions for diminutions in value of fixed asset investments to be made and the amount to be included in respect of the fixed asset investment to be reduced accordingly. Any provisions that are not shown in the profit and loss account must be disclosed (either separately or in aggregate) in a note to the accounts.

3   Paragraph 19(2) of Schedule 4 requires provisions for diminution in value to be made in respect of any fixed asset that has diminished in value if the reduction in its value is expected to be permanent. The amount to be included in respect of the asset must be reduced accordingly. Any provisions that are not shown in the profit and loss account must be disclosed (either separately or in aggregate) in a note to the accounts.

4   Paragraph 19(3) of Schedule 4 requires that where the reasons for which a provision was made have ceased to apply to any extent, the provision shall be written back to that extent that it is no longer necessary. Where any amounts written back are not shown in the profit and loss account, they must be disclosed (either separately or in aggregate) in a note to the accounts.

5   Clearly it is a matter of judgement whether any diminution in value should be treated as permanent (although there must be reasonable grounds for making such a judgement), as indicated by the requirement that any provision subsequently found not to be necessary has to be reversed.

6   In addition to references to diminutions in value in the paragraphs noted above, the Act allows for the revaluation downwards of fixed assets dealt with under the alternative accounting rules in paragraph 34 of Schedule 4.

7   The [draft] FRS, as with its predecessor FRS 11, concerns itself with impairment rather than permanent diminutions in value.

8   Where a fixed asset is impaired, it will always be the case that both the value in use and the net realisable value will be below the carrying amount. Although this does not inevitably signify a loss that is permanent, it would be prudent in relation to fixed assets held at depreciated historical cost to regard such a loss as permanent and, despite any element of uncertainty, charge it to the profit and loss account. In the case of a revalued fixed asset, it would be reasonable to reflect the uncertainty of the permanence of any impairment by treating it as a reversal of any temporary increase in value previously recognised. Such an impairment would be dealt with through the statement of total recognised gains and losses (ie as a revaluation reserve movement). However, if the impairment results in a carrying value below depreciated historical cost, then, as in a pure historical cost context, it would be prudent and reasonable to treat that part of the impairment as being permanent and charge it to the profit and loss account.

The [draft] FRS requires an impairment loss recognised in a prior period to be 9 reversed if, and only if, there has been a change in the estimates used to determine the asset's recoverable amount since the last impairment loss was recognised.

Northern Ireland and the Republic of Ireland

The references to the equivalent statutory requirements in Northern Ireland and the 10 Republic of Ireland are as follows:

Great Britain	Northern Ireland	Republic of Ireland
Schedule 4 to the Companies Act 1985:	Schedule 4 to the Companies (Northern Ireland) Order 1986:	The Schedule to the Companies (Amendment) Act 1986:
paragraph 19(1)	paragraph 19(1)	paragraph 7(1)
paragraph 19(2)	paragraph 19(2)	paragraph 7(2)
paragraph 19(3)	paragraph 19(3)	paragraph 7(3)
paragraph 34	paragraph 34	paragraph 22

FRED 39
Amendments to FRS 12
Provisions, contingent liabilities and contingent assets
and
Amendments to FRS 17
retirement benefits

Contents

Business Combinations Overview

Preface by the accounting standards board

This Financial Reporting Exposure Draft (FRED) is part of a package of draft UK   A
accounting standards reflecting the outputs from Phase I and Phase II of the
International Accounting Standards Board (IASB) project on business combinations. The package comprises:

- FRED 39 Amendments to FRS 12 *Provisions, Contingent Liabilities and Con-
  tingent Assets* and Amendments to FRS 17 *Retirement benefits.*
- FRED 36 *Business Combinations* (IFRS 3*)* and Amendments to FRS 2
  Accounting for Subsidiary Undertakings (parts of IAS 27 *Consolidated and
  Separate Financial Statements).*
- FRED 37 *Intangible Assets* (IAS 38) and *Impairment of Assets (*IAS 36).

The first phase of the Business Combinations project resulted in the IASB issuing   B
IFRS 3 *Business Combinations,* and amendments to IAS 36 *Impairment of Assets* and
IAS 38 *Intangible Assets.* These were published in March 2004. The primary
objective of the IASB in Phase I of the project was to require one method of
accounting for business combinations – the purchase method (renamed the acquisition method in Phase II). Prior to this International Accounting Standards (IAS)
permitted two methods, the acquisition method and pooling of interests method
(merger accounting).

The second phase is being conducted by the IASB as a joint project with the US   C
Financial Accounting Standards Board (FASB). This phase of the project has
reconsidered the guidance for applying the acquisition method of accounting for a
business combination and particularly the method by which acquirers recognise and
measure the business over which they obtain control. This phase also aims to
improve the transparency of information provided to users of financial statements.
An important aspect of Phase II is to achieve convergence between International
Financial Reporting Standards (IFRSs) and US GAAP.

The outputs from the second Phase of the project comprise three exposure drafts that   D
propose amendments to IFRS 3 *Business Combinations,* IAS 27 *Consolidated and
Separate Financial Statements* and IAS 37 *Provisions and Contingent Liabilities and
Contingent Assets.*

The publication by the IASB of the exposure drafts from Phase II concludes the   E
substantive part of the IASB's Business Combinations project. However, it does not
fully complete the project. The aspects that remain outstanding include consideration
of 'fresh start' accounting. The outstanding aspects are not currently part of the
IASB's active agenda.

Some of the proposals set out in this FRED may conflict with existing legal   F
requirements. These matters are being investigated and it is hoped that they will be
resolved with the assistance of the Department of Trade and Industry.

Amendments to FRS 12 *Provisions, Contingent Liabilities and Contingent Assets* and Amendments to FRS 17 *Retirement benefits*

This Preface is prepared to assist readers in preparing their response on the proposals to amend IAS 37 Provisions, Contingent Liabilities and Contingent Assets and IAS 19 Employee benefits. The Preface outlines the main differences between existing UK accounting standards and proposed International Accounting Standards.

INTRODUCTION

1   This Financial Reporting Exposure Draft (FRED) sets out a revised FRS 12 *Provisions, Contingent Liabilities and Contingent Assets* based on the IASB's proposals to amend IAS 37, which shares the same title. The proposed amendments are a result of two IASB projects: phase II of the *Business Combinations* project and the *Short-term Convergence* project. FRS 12 and IAS 37 were developed jointly by the ASB and the IASB and their current requirements are virtually identical. The amendments will maintain correspondence between the two Standards.

2   The IASB are also proposing to amend that part of IAS 19 *Employee benefits* which relates to benefits paid on termination of an employee's employment 'termination benefits'. The Exposure Draft of proposed amendments to FRS 17 sets out proposals for how those parts of IAS 19 that provide specific guidance on accounting for termination benefits could be incorporated into FRS 17 *Retirement benefits*.

3   In line with the ASB's convergence strategy, this Exposure Draft sets out the text of a UK accounting standard based on the corresponding IFRS with no changes other than those that are essential or justifiable. The proposed amendments to FRS 17 are based on the IASB's text of proposed amendments to IAS 19.

AMENDMENTS TO IAS 37 (FRS 12)

4   The main changes to IAS 37 (and thereby FRS 12) proposed by the IASB are set out in the Summary of Main Changes to IAS 37 (page 27).

5   The Exposure Draft no longer uses the term 'provision' but refers to 'non-financial' liabilities. The IASB, in the Summary of Main Changes, states that this amendment is to clarify that IAS 37 should be applied to all non-financial liabilities that are not within the scope of other Standards.

6   The amendments propose that non-financial liabilities should be measured at the amount an entity would 'rationally pay to settle' or transfer the obligation. 'Rationally pay to settle' is an 'exit value' measure; it responds to the question "what will it cost for an entity to extinguish the liability?" The use of an 'exit value' measure is consistent with the existing requirements of IAS 37 and FRS 12 and seems appropriate in the context of the items which are within the scope of the existing Standard.

7   However, this Exposure Draft states that IAS 37 should be applied to all non-financial liabilities (other than those covered by another accounting standard). This seems to imply a general principle of measuring liabilities at an 'exit value'. It is arguable that 'exit values' are not appropriate for general use in financial reporting and that this proposition would be better considered as part of the project that the IASB is undertaking jointly with the FASB on its conceptual framework.

The Exposure Draft no longer applies the terms 'contingent liabilities' and 'contingent assets'. In the Basis for Conclusions, that accompanies the Exposure Draft, the IASB notes that contractual rights and obligations can be divided into two types: 'conditional' and 'unconditional'. The unconditional right or obligation meets the definition of an asset or liability. An entity recognises a liability relating to the unconditional obligation: uncertainty about the future event (conditional obligation) is reflected in the measurement of the liability. For example the supplier of a product warranty has an <u>unconditional</u> obligation to provide warranty cover and a <u>conditional</u> obligation to repair the goods *should* a fault arise. The supplier recognises a liability of the unconditional obligation to provide warranty cover.   **8**

As a consequence of this analysis the IASB reconsidered the role of the probability criterion in the recognition of liabilities. Under the existing IAS 37 (and thereby FRS 12), a provision is only recognised if it is probable that an outflow of economic resources would be required to settle the provision. When applying the amended definitions all unconditional obligations that meet the definition of a liability are considered for recognition. The probability criterion is applied to the unconditional obligation and thereby is always satisfied. The IASB therefore proposes to omit the probability criterion from the recognition criteria within the Standard.   **9**

The amendments made to the recognition criterion, particularly the removal of the probability criterion, will give rise to a greater number of liabilities meeting the definition and recognition criteria. These amendments place greater emphasis on satisfying the definition of a liability. The exposure draft notes that an essential characteristic of a liability is that the entity has a present obligation arising from a past event. The removal of the probability criterion from recognition will require all present obligations that meet the definition of a liability to be recognised. The measurement of the liability will address the probability of the amount and timing of cash flows. The amendment therefore removes any threshold point from recognition.   **10**

The ASB is concerned that the implications of these proposals give rise to practical difficulties. In particular: **11**

(a) the absence of a threshold and the increased level of subjectivity means, for example, that a liability would have to be recognised if there was only a 10 per cent risk of an outflow. In practice it may be difficult, without a threshold, to ensure all liabilities have been recognised;

(b) arguably, it also introduces a greater degree of subjectivity in measuring liabilities. Whilst the draft standard requires that only liabilities that can be reliably measured are recognised, a significant degree of judgement will sometimes be required both as to whether that criterion is met and, if so, the appropriate amount at which the liability should be stated; and

(c) it is also possible that (despite the disclosure exemption in paragraph 71 of the draft Standard) the requirement to recognise a liability at an early stage of negotiation (for example in the case of litigation) could be prejudicial to the outcome.

The IASB are also proposing to amend the application of the recognition and measurement requirements relating to the recognition of restructurings. The revised Standard states that a decision to restructure, even if accompanied with an announcement by management is not the requisite past event for the recognition of a liability. It would appear that this amendment will result in many restructurings that were previously recognised as 'single sum amounts' being recognised only when the individual cost meets the definition of a liability.   **12**

AMENDMENTS TO FRS 17 (PARTS OF IAS 19)

13 UK accounting standards currently include no specific requirements for accounting for termination benefits other than the general principles of FRS 12. The IASB is proposing to amend that part of IAS 19 *Employee benefits*, which specifies the accounting treatment for termination benefits. It is proposed that these amendments are reflected in UK accounting standards as amendments to FRS 17.

14 In summary, the amendments to FRS 17 propose:

- to define termination benefits as employee benefits provided in connection with the termination of an employee's employment.
- that termination benefits may be either 'involuntary' (provided as a result of an entity's decision to terminate an employee's employment) or 'voluntary' (offered for a short period of time in exchange for an employee's decision to accept voluntary termination).
- benefits offered to encourage employees to leave service early are voluntary termination benefits only if they are offered for a short period.
- a liability and expense for voluntary termination benefits shall be recognised when the employee accepts the entity's offer to those termination benefits.
- a liability and expense for involuntary termination benefits, except where provided in exchange for the employees future services, shall be recognised when the entity has a plan of termination that it has communicated to the employees and the plan meets the criteria specified in the Standard.
- involuntary termination benefits are provided in exchange for employees' future services if they:

  (a) are incremental to what the employees would otherwise be entitled to receive (ie benefits are not provided in accordance with the terms of an ongoing benefit plan);
  (b) do not vest until the employment is terminated; and
  (c) are provided to employees who will be retained beyond the minimum retention period. The minimum retention period will normally be the period of notice an entity is required to provide employees in advance of terminating their employment.

- where involuntary termination benefits are provided in exchange for employees' future service the termination benefits are recognised as a liability and expense over the period of future service.
- where termination benefits are provided as an enhancement of retirement benefits the liability and expense recognised initially includes only the value of the additional benefits that arise from the provision of the termination benefits.

15 In proposing that the liability for voluntary termination benefits should be recognised when the employee accepts the entity's offer to those termination benefits the IASB are treating 'acceptance' as the point that obligates the entity. An alternative view is that the 'offer' of termination benefits to an employee obligates the entity when it is made, and so a constructive obligation arises at that time, rather than when acceptance of the offer is received.

Invitation to comment

The ASB invites comments on any aspect of the FRED by 28th October 2005 – the same day as the IASB has set for comments.   **ITC1**

The ASB would particularly welcome comments on the following issues: **ITC2**

ASB 1   This exposure draft seems to imply a principle that liabilities should be measured at 'exit value'. Is this of concern to you?

ASB 2   Do you envisage that the extension to the scope of the Standard will require a change in accounting for liabilities? If so, please provide examples.

ASB 3   Do you agree that the proposed amendments to the definition and the recognition criterion for non-financial liabilities are appropriate? Do you envisage any difficulties in complying with the proposals?

ASB 4   Do you consider that the proposals for accounting for termination benefits are appropriate? If not, why not?

ASB 5   The ASB proposes to include the requirements on accounting for termination benefits by amendments to FRS 17; do you agree?

The ASB would also welcome comments on the questions that the IASB has asked in its Exposure Draft which are set out in paragraphs IASB 1 to IASB 12. The IASB's questions pertaining to the proposed amendments to IAS 37 are set out in questions IASB 1 to IASB 9. Those questions relating to the proposed amendments to IAS 19 are set out in questions IASB 10 to 12.   **ITC3**

IASB 1   Scope of IAS 37 and terminology

The Exposure Draft proposes to clarify that IAS 37, except in specified cases, should be applied in accounting for all non-financial liabilities that are not within the scope of other Standards (see paragraph 2). To emphasise this point, the Exposure Draft does not use 'provision' as a defined term to describe liabilities within its scope. Instead, it uses the term 'non-financial liability' (see paragraph 10). However, the Exposure Draft explains that an entity may describe some classes of non-financial liabilities as provisions in their financial statements (see paragraph 9).

(a)   Do you agree that IAS 37 should be applied in accounting for all non-financial liabilities that are not within the scope of other Standards? If not, for which type of liabilities do you regard its requirements as inappropriate and why?

(b)   Do you agree with not using 'provision' as a defined term? If not, why not?

IASB 2   Contingent liabilities

The Exposure Draft proposes to eliminate the term 'contingent liability'.

The Basis for Conclusions on the proposals in the Exposure Draft explains that liabilities arise only from unconditional (or non-contingent) obligations (see paragraph BC11). Hence, it highlights that something that is a liability (an unconditional obligation) cannot be contingent or conditional, and that an obligation that is contingent or conditional on the occurrence or non-occurrence of a future event does not by itself give rise to a liability (see paragraph BC30).

The Basis for Conclusions also explains that many items previously described as contingent liabilities satisfy the definition of a liability in the *Framework*. This is because the contingency does not relate to whether an unconditional obligation exists. Rather it relates to one or more uncertain future events that affect the amount that will be required to settle the unconditional obligation (see paragraph BC23).

The Basis for Conclusions highlights that many items previously described as contingent liabilities can be analysed into two obligations: an unconditional obligation and a conditional obligation. The unconditional obligation establishes the liability and the conditional obligation affects the amount that will be required to settle the liability (see paragraph BC24).

The Exposure Draft proposes that when the amount that will be required to settle a liability (unconditional obligation) is contingent (or conditional) on the occurrence or non-occurrence of one or more uncertain future events, the liability is recognised independently of the probability that the uncertain future event(s) will occur (or fail to occur). Uncertainty about the future event(s) is reflected in the measurement of the liability recognised (see paragraph 23).

(a)   Do you agree with eliminating the term 'contingent liability'? If not, why not?

(b)   Do you agree that when the amount that will be required to settle a liability (unconditional obligation) is contingent on the occurrence or non-occurrence of one or more uncertain future events, the liability should be recognised independently of the probability that the uncertain future event(s) will occur (or fail to occur)? If not, why not?

IASB 3   Contingent assets

The Exposure Draft proposes to eliminate the term 'contingent asset'.

As with contingent liabilities, the Basis for Conclusions explains that assets arise only from unconditional (or non-contingent) rights (see paragraph BC11). Hence, an asset (an unconditional right) cannot be contingent or conditional, and a right that is contingent or conditional on the occurrence or non-occurrence of a future event does not by itself give rise to an asset (see paragraph BC17).

The Basis for Conclusions also explains that many items previously described as contingent assets satisfy the definition of an asset in the *Framework*. This is because the contingency does not relate to whether an unconditional right exists. Rather, it relates to one or more uncertain future events that affect the amount of the future economic benefits embodied in the asset (see paragraph BC17).

The Exposure Draft proposes that items previously described as contingent assets that satisfy the definition of an asset should be within the scope of IAS 38 *Intangible Assets* rather than IAS 37 (except for rights to reimbursement, which remain within the scope of IAS 37). This is because such items are non-monetary assets without physical substance and, subject to meeting the identifiability criterion in IAS 38, are intangible assets (see paragraph A22 in the Appendix). The Exposure Draft does not propose any amendments to the recognition requirements of IAS 38.

(a) Do you agree with eliminating the term 'contingent asset'? If not, why not?

(b) Do you agree that items previously described as contingent assets that satisfy the definition of an asset should be within the scope of IAS 38? If not, why not?

IASB 4   Constructive obligations

The Exposure Draft proposes amending the definition of a constructive obligation to emphasise that an entity has a constructive obligation only if its actions result in other parties having a valid expectation on which they can reasonably rely that the entity will perform (see paragraph 10). The Exposure Draft also provides additional guidance for determining whether an entity has incurred a constructive obligation (see paragraph 15).

(a) Do you agree with the proposed amendment to the definition of a constructive obligation? If not, why not? How would you define one and why?

(b) Is the additional guidance for determining whether an entity has incurred a constructive obligation appropriate and helpful? If not, why not? Is it sufficient? If not, what other guidance should be provided?

IASB 5   Probability recognition criterion

The Exposure Draft proposes omitting the probability recognition criterion (currently in paragraph 14(b)) from the Standard because, in all cases, an unconditional obligation satisfies the criterion. Therefore, items that satisfy the definition of a liability are recognised unless they cannot be measured reliably.

The Basis for Conclusions emphasises that the probability recognition criterion is used in the *Framework* to determine whether it is probable that settlement of an item that has previously been determined to be a liability will require an outflow of economic benefits from the entity. In other words, the *Framework* requires an entity to determine whether a liability exists before considering whether that liability should be recognised. The Basis notes that in many cases, although there may be uncertainty about the amount and timing of the resources that will be required to settle a liability, there is little or no uncertainty that settlement will require *some* outflow of resources. An example is an entity that has an obligation to decommission plant or to restore previously contaminated land. The Basis also outlines the Board's conclusion that in cases previously described as contingent liabilities in which the entity has an unconditional obligation and a conditional obligation, the probability recognition criterion should be applied to the unconditional obligation (ie the liability) rather than the conditional obligation. So, for example, in the case of a product warranty, the question is not whether it is probable that the entity will be required to repair or replace the product. Rather, the question is whether the entity's *unconditional* obligation to provide warranty coverage for the duration of the warranty (ie to stand ready to honour warranty claims) will probably result in an outflow of economic benefits (see paragraphs BC37-BC41).

The Basis for Conclusions highlights that the *Framework* articulates the probability recognition criterion in terms of an outflow of economic benefits, not just direct cash flows. This includes the provision of services. An entity's unconditional obligation to stand ready to honour a conditional obligation if an uncertain future event occurs (or fails to occur) is a type of service obligation. Therefore, any liability that incorporates an unconditional obligation satisfies the probability recognition criterion. For example, the issuer of a product warranty has a certain (not just probable) outflow of economic benefits because it is providing a service for the duration of the contract, ie it is standing ready to honour warranty claims (see paragraphs BC42-BC47).

Do you agree with the analysis of the probability recognition criterion and, therefore, with the reasons for omitting it from the Standard? If not, how would you apply the probability recognition criterion to examples such as product warranties, written options and other unconditional obligations that incorporate conditional obligations?

IASB 6   Measurement

The Exposure Draft proposes that an entity should measure a non-financial liability at the amount that it would rationally pay to settle the present obligation or to transfer it to a third party on the balance sheet date (see paragraph 29). The Exposure Draft explains that an expected cash flow approach is an appropriate basis for measuring a non-financial liability for both a class of similar obligations and a single obligation. It highlights that measuring a single obligation at the most likely outcome would not necessarily be consistent with the Standard's measurement objective (see paragraph 31).

Do you agree with the proposed amendments to the measurement requirements? If not, why not? What measurement would you propose and why?

IASB 7   Reimbursements

The Exposure Draft proposes that when an entity has a right to reimbursement for some or all of the economic benefits that will be required to settle a non-financial liability, it recognises the reimbursement right as an asset if the reimbursement right can be measured reliably (see paragraph 46).

Do you agree with the proposed amendment to the recognition requirements for reimbursements? If not, why not? What recognition requirements would you propose and why?

IASB 8   Onerous contracts

The Exposure Draft proposes that if a contract will become onerous as a result of an entity's own action, the liability should not be recognised until the entity takes that action. Hence, in the case of a property held under an operating lease that becomes onerous as a result of the entity's actions (for example, as a result of a restructuring) the liability is recognised when the entity ceases to use the property (see paragraphs 55 and 57). In addition, the Exposure Draft proposes that, if the onerous contract is an operating lease, the unavoidable cost of the contract is the remaining lease commitment reduced by the estimated sublease rentals that the entity could reasonably obtain, regardless of whether the entity intends to enter into a sublease (see paragraph 58).

(a) Do you agree with the proposed amendment that a liability for a contract that becomes onerous as a result of the entity's own actions should be recognised only when the entity has taken that action? If not, when should it be recognised and why?

(b) Do you agree with the additional guidance for clarifying the measurement of a liability for an onerous operating lease? If not, why not? How would you measure the liability?

(c) If you do not agree, would you be prepared to accept the amendments to achieve convergence?

IASB 9 Restructuring provisions

The Exposure Draft proposes that non-financial liabilities for costs associated with a restructuring should be recognised on the same basis as if they arose independently of a restructuring, namely when the entity has a liability for those costs (see paragraphs 61 and 62).

The Exposure Draft proposes guidance (or provides cross-references to other Standards) for applying this principle to two types of costs that are often associated with a restructuring: termination benefits and contract termination costs (see paragraphs 63 and 64).

(a) Do you agree that a liability for each cost associated with a restructuring should be recognised when the entity has a liability for that cost, in contrast to the current approach of recognising at a specified point a single liability for all of the costs associated with the restructuring? If not, why not?

(b) Is the guidance for applying the Standard's principles to costs associated with a restructuring appropriate? If not, why not? Is it sufficient? If not, what other guidance should be added?

IASB 10 Definition of termination benefits

The Exposure Draft proposes amending the definition of termination benefits to clarify that benefits that are offered in exchange for an employee's decision to accept voluntary termination of employment are termination benefits only if they are offered for a short period (see paragraph 7). Other employee benefits that are offered to encourage employees to leave service before normal retirement date are post-employment benefits (see paragraph 135).

Do you agree with this amendment? If not, how would you characterise such benefits, and why?

IASB 11 Recognition of termination benefits

The Exposure Draft proposes that voluntary termination benefits should be recognised when employees accept the entity's offer of those benefits (see paragraph 137). It also proposes that involuntary termination benefits, with the exception of those provided in exchange for employees' future services, should be recognised when the entity has communicated its plan of termination to the affected employees and the plan meets specified criteria (see paragraph 138).

Is recognition of a liability for voluntary and involuntary termination benefits at these points appropriate? If not, when should they be recognised and why?

IASB 12 Recognition of involuntary termination benefits that relate to future service

The Exposure Draft proposes that if involuntary termination benefits are provided in exchange for employees' future services, the liability for those benefits should be recognised over the period of the future service (see paragraph 139). The Exposure Draft proposes three criteria for determining whether involuntary termination benefits are provided in exchange for future services (see paragraph 140).

Do you agree with the criteria for determining whether involuntary termination benefits are provided in exchange for future services? If not, why not and what criteria would you propose? In these cases, is recognition of a liability over the future service period appropriate? If not, when should it be recognised and why?

FINANCIAL REPORTING EXPOSURE DRAFT
PROPOSED AMENDMENTS TO

FRS 12
PROVISIONS, CONTINGENT LIABILITIES AND CONTINGENT ASSETS

FRS 17
RETIREMENT BENEFITS

Contents

Introduction

Amendments to ~~IAS 37~~ FRS 12 *Provisions, Contingent Liabilities and Contingent Assets*

~~Invitation to Comment~~

Summary of main changes

Contents

Standard

Appendix: Amendments to other ~~pronouncements~~ <u>UK accounting standards</u>

Basis for Conclusions

Alternate view

Illustrative Examples

<u>Note on Legal Requirements</u>

Amendments to <u>FRS 17</u> *<u>Retirement benefits</u>* ~~IAS 19~~ *~~Employee Benefits~~*

~~Invitation to Comment~~

Summary of main changes

Contents

~~Proposed amendments to IAS 19~~ <u>Proposed amendments to FRS 17</u>

Basis for Conclusions

INTRODUCTION

ASB Note: This Introduction has been prepared by the IASB and is included in this FRED in full and unamended. References here to the 'Board" are references to the IASB.

This Exposure Draft of proposed amendments to IAS 37 *Provisions, Contingent*   **1**
Liabilities and Contingent Assets (to be retitled *Non-financial Liabilites*) and IAS 19
Employee Benefits has been published by the International Accounting Standards
Board as a result of two of its projects: the Short-term Convergence project and the
second phase of the Business Combinations project.

The objective of short-term convergence (undertaken jointly with the Financial   **2**
Accounting Standards Board (FASB) in the United States) is to reduce differences
between International Financial Reporting Standards (IFRSs) and US generally
accepted accounting principles (US GAAP). Short-term convergence focuses on
differences that can be resolved in a relatively short time and can be addressed
outside current and planned major projects. It is one strand of the Board's broader
objective of convergence of accounting standards around the world.

One aspect of the joint short-term convergence project involves the two boards   **3**
considering each other's recent standards with a view to adopting high quality
accounting solutions. The proposed amendments to the requirements in IAS 37 for
constructive obligations, onerous contracts and restructuring provisions, together
with the complementary amendments to the requirements in IAS 19 for termination
benefits, result from the IASB's consideration of FASB Statement No. 146
Accounting for Costs Associated with Exit or Disposal Activities (SFAS 146), issued in
2002. The Board believes that the proposed amendments would both improve
accounting and achieve substantial convergence with the recognition requirements of
SFAS 146.

The second phase of the Business Combinations project is a joint project with the   **4**
FASB, and involves a broad reconsideration of the requirements in IFRSs and US
GAAP on applying the purchase method (now called the 'acquisition method' in the
Exposure Draft of Proposed Amendments to IFRS 3 *Business Combination)* to the
accounting for business combinations. This has included reconsidering the treatment
in a business combination of the contingencies of an acquiree. As a consequence, the
Board proposes to eliminate the terms 'contingent assets' and 'contingent liabilities'
in IAS 37 (and in other Standards) and to analyse afresh items previously been
described as such. These proposed amendments have also required a reconsideration
of the probability recognition criterion in IAS 37. The Board believes that these
amendments achieve substantial convergence with the recognition principles
underpinning FASB Interpretations No. 45 *Guarantor's Accounting and Disclosure*
Requirements for Guarantees, Including Indirect Guarantees of Indebtedness of Others
and No. 47 *Accounting for Conditional Asset Retirement Obligations*. Because these
amendments were prompted by the second phase of the Business Combinations
project, this Exposure Draft is published simultaneously with the Exposure Draft
Amendments to IFRS 3. If confirmed in a Standard, the proposals in this Exposure
Draft would have an effective date of 1 January 2007, the same as for the revised
IFRS 3.

In developing this Exposure Draft, the Board has made amendments related to its   **5**
decisions in the Short-term Convergence project and the second phase of the Business Combinations project. These amendments particularly affect the definitions and
the recognition requirements. The Board has not reconsidered all of the requirements

in IAS 37 and IAS 19. However, it has taken the opportunity to clarify the scope of IAS 37. As a result, it proposes not to use 'provision' as a defined term but instead use the term 'non-financial liability'. The Board also proposes clarifying some aspects of the existing measurement requirements.

AMENDMENTS TO
FRS 12

~~IAS 37~~ PROVISIONS, CONTINGENT LIABILITIES AND CONTINGENT ASSETS

Summary of main changes (IAS 37)

The following main changes are proposed:

SCOPE OF IAS 37 AND TERMINOLOGY

- IAS 37 defines a provision as a liability of uncertain timing or amount. The Exposure Draft does not use 'provision' as a defined term and instead proposes to use the term 'non-financial liability', which includes items previously described as provisions as well as other liabilities.
- The purpose of this amendment is to clarify that IAS 37, except in specified cases, should be applied to all non-financial liabilities that are not within the scope of other Standards.

CONTINGENT LIABILITIES

- IAS 37 defines a contingent liability as a possible obligation or a present obligation that is not recognised. A contingent liability that is a present obligation is not recognised either because it is not probable that an outflow of resources will be required to settle the obligation or because the amount of the obligation cannot be measured with sufficient reliability. The Standard does not permit contingent liabilities to be recognised but requires them to be disclosed, unless the possibility of any outflow of economic resources in settlement of the contingent liability is remote. The Exposure Draft:
  - proposes eliminating the term 'contingent liability'.
  - uses the term 'contingency' to refer to uncertainty about the amount that will be required to settle a liability, rather than uncertainty about whether a liability exists.
  - specifies that a liability for which the settlement amount is contingent on one or more uncertain future events is recognised independently of the probability that the uncertain future event(s) will occur (or fail to occur).
- The purpose of these amendments is:
  - to clarify that only present obligations (rather than possible obligations) of an entity give rise to liabilities and that liabilities arise from unconditional obligations.
  - to require uncertainty about future events that affect the amount that will be required to settle a liability to be reflected in the measurement of the liability.

CONTINGENT ASSETS

- IAS 37 defines a contingent asset as a possible asset. It does not permit contingent assets to be recognised, but requires them to be disclosed if an inflow of economic benefits is probable. The Exposure Draft:
- proposes eliminating the term 'contingent asset'.
- uses the term 'contingency' to refer to uncertainty about the amount of the future economic benefits embodied in an asset, rather than uncertainty about whether an asset exists.
- specifies that items previously described as contingent assets, but satisfying the definition of an asset in the *Framework*, are within the scope of IAS 38 rather than IAS 37 (except for rights to reimbursements, which remain within the scope of IAS 37).
- The purpose of the amendment is to clarify that only resources currently controlled by the entity as a result of a past transaction or event (rather than possible assets) give rise to assets and that assets arise from unconditional rights.

CONSTRUCTIVE OBLIGATIONS

- IAS 37 defines a constructive obligation as an obligation that derives from an entity's actions when the entity has (a) indicated to other parties that it will accept particular responsibilities and (b) as a result has created a valid expectation on the part of those other parties that it will discharge those responsibilities. The Exposure Draft proposes:
  - to amend the definition of a constructive obligation to clarify that the actions of an entity must result in other parties having a valid expectation that they can reasonably rely on the entity to discharge its responsibilities.
  - to provide additional guidance on determining whether an entity has incurred a constructive obligation.

PROBABILITY RECOGNITION CRITERION

- IAS 37 states that provisions should be recognised if it is probable that an outflow of resources embodying economic benefits will be required to settle the provision. In some cases, the examples accompanying the Standard apply this probability recognition criterion to what the Exposure Draft now analyses as conditional obligations. For example, in the case of a product warranty, the Standard explains that the entity considers the likelihood of claims arising under the warranty. In effect, this means that the entity considers whether it is probable that the *conditional* obligation will result in an outflow of resources embodying economic benefits. Consistently with the revised analysis of contingent liabilities, the Basis for Conclusions explains that the probable outflow criterion should always be applied to the liability (ie unconditional obligation). Therefore, if an entity has a non-financial liability arising from an unconditional obligation that is accompanied by a conditional obligation, the probability recognition criterion is applied to the unconditional obligation rather than the conditional obligation. For example, in the case of a product warranty, the criterion should be applied to the unconditional obligation to stand ready to honour warranty claims (ie to provide warranty coverage). As a result, the Basis for Conclusions highlights that the probability recognition criterion is always satisfied. The Exposure Draft therefore proposes omitting the criterion from the Standard.

MEASUREMENT

- IAS 37 states that provisions should be measured at the best estimate of the expenditure required to settle the present obligation at the balance sheet date. The best estimate is described as the amount that an entity would rationally pay to settle the obligation at the balance sheet date or to transfer it to a third party at that time. Although expected value is described as the basis for measuring a provision involving a large population of items, the Standard states that the best estimate of single obligations may be the individual most likely outcome. The Exposure Draft:
  - proposes that a non-financial liability should be measured at the amount that an entity would rationally pay to settle the present obligation or to transfer it to a third party on the balance sheet date.
  - emphasises that an expected cash flow approach can be used as the basis for measuring a non-financial liability for both a class of similar obligations and a single obligation.
  - explains that measuring a non-financial liability for a single obligation at its most likely outcome would not necessarily be consistent with the Standard's measurement objective.

REIMBURSEMENT

- IAS 37 states that when expenditure required to settle a provision is expected to be reimbursed by another party, the reimbursement should be recognised when it is virtually certain that the reimbursement will be received. Consistently with the revised analysis of a contingent asset, the Exposure Draft proposes that if an entity has an unconditional right to receive reimbursement, that right should be recognised as an asset if it can be measured reliably.

ONEROUS CONTRACTS

- IAS 37 defines an onerous contract as one in which the unavoidable costs of meeting its obligations exceed the economic benefits expected. The entity recognises as a provision the present obligation under the contract. The Standard provides no further guidance about when the provision should be recognised. The Exposure Draft proposes:
    - additional recognition guidance to specify that if a contract will become onerous as a result of an entity's own action, the liability should not be recognised until the entity has taken that action.
    - specifying that in the case of an onerous operating lease, the unavoidable costs of meeting the obligation should be based on the unavoidable lease commitment less any sublease rentals that the entity could reasonably obtain for the property, regardless of whether the entity intends to sublease the property.

RESTRUCTURING PROVISIONS

- IAS 37 states that an entity that (a) has a detailed formal plan for restructuring and (b) has raised a valid expectation in those affected that it will carry out the restructuring, has a constructive obligation. Therefore, it recognises a provision for the direct expenditures arising from the restructuring. The Exposure Draft proposes:
    - revising the application guidance for restructuring provisions to specify that a non-financial liability for a cost associated with a restructuring is recognised only when the definition of a liability has been satisfied for that cost. Accordingly, a cost associated with a restructuring is recognised as a liability on the same basis as if that cost arose independently of a restructuring.
    - specific guidance for accounting for costs that are often associated with a restructuring as follows:
        - the cost of employee termination benefits is recognised in accordance with IAS 19 *Employee Benefits*.
        - a liability for costs that will continue to be incurred under a contract for its remaining term without equivalent economic benefit to the entity is recognised when the entity ceases using the right conveyed by the contract (in addition to any liability recognised if the contract was previously determined to be onerous).
        - the cost of terminating a contract before the end of its term is recognised when the entity terminates the contract in accordance with the contract terms.

Contents

International Accounting Standard 37

[Draft] Financial Reporting Standard 12
Non-financial Liabilities

Appendix:

Amendments to other ~~pronouncements~~ UK accounting standards

Basis for conclusions

Alternate view

Illustrative examples

<u>**Note on legal requirements**</u>

[Draft] International Accounting Standard 37 *Non-financial Liabilities* (IAS 37) is set out in paragraphs 1-73 and the Appendix. All the paragraphs have equal authority but retain the IASC format of the Standard when it was adopted by the IASB. [Draft] IAS 37 should be read in the context of its objective and the Basis for Conclusions, the ~~Preface to International Financial Reporting Standards~~ Foreword to Accounting Standards and the ~~Framework for the Preparation and Presentation of Financial Statements~~ Statement of Principles for Financial Reporting. ~~IAS 8 Accounting Policies, Changes in Accounting Estimates and Errors provides a basis for selecting and applying accounting policies in the absence of explicit guidance.~~

[Draft] ~~Financial Reporting Standard 12~~ ~~International Accounting Standard 37~~

Non-financial Liabilities

OBJECTIVE

1   The objective of this [draft] Standard is to establish principles for recognising, measuring and disclosing non-financial liabilities. Those principles require an entity to recognise a non-financial liability unless it cannot be measured reliably. Uncertainty about the amount or timing of the economic benefits that will be required to settle a non-financial liability is reflected in the measurement of that liability. The principles also require an entity to disclose sufficient information to enable users of the financial statements to understand the amount and nature of an entities non-financial liabilities and the uncertainty relating to the future outflows of economic benefits that will be required to settle them.

SCOPE

1A   *This Standard applies to all financial statements that are intended to give a true and fair view of a reporting entity's financial position and profit or loss (or income and expenditure), except that reporting entities applying the Financial Reporting Standard for Smaller Entities (FRSSE) currently applicable are exempt.*

2   **An entity shall apply this [draft] Standard in accounting for all non-financial liabilities, except:**

   (a)   those resulting from executory contracts, unless the contract is onerous; and
   (b)   those within the scope of another Standard.
   (c)   those arising in insurance entities from insurance contracts as defined in Appendix C of FRS 26 **Financial Instruments: Recognition and Measurement.**

3   Executory contracts are contracts under which neither party has performed any of its obligations or both parties have partially performed their obligations to an equal extent.

4   When a specific type of non-financial liability is within the scope of another Standard, an entity applies that Standard instead of this [draft] Standard. For example, some types of non-financial liabilities are within the scope of Standards on:

   (a)   Stocks and Long-term Contracts (see SSAP 9 *Stocks and Long-term Contracts*)
   ~~(a)   construction contracts (see IAS 11~~ *~~Construction Contracts~~*~~).~~
   (b)   ~~income taxes~~ current and deferred taxes (see FRS 16 *Current Tax and* FRS 19 *Deferred Tax* ~~IAS 12~~ *~~Income Taxes~~*).
   (c)   ~~employee~~ retirement and termination benefits (see FRS 17 *Retirement and Termination Benefits* ~~IAS 19~~ *~~Employee Benefits~~*).
   (d)   ~~insurance contracts (see IFRS 4~~ *~~Insurance Contracts~~*~~). However, this [draft] Standard applies to non-financial liabilities of an insurer, other than those arising from its contractual obligations and rights under insurance contracts within the scope of IFRS 4.~~

5   **An entity shall apply this [draft] Standard to the following contractual obligations only if they are onerous:**

(a)   obligations under operating leases to which ~~SSAP 21~~ *Accounting for Leases and Hire Purchase Contracts* ~~IAS 17 Leases~~ applies; and

(b)   loan commitments excluded from the scope ~~IAS 39~~ FRS 26 *Financial Instruments: Recognition and Measurement*.

Because SSAP 21 ~~IAS 17~~ contains no specific requirements for operating leases that are onerous, this [draft] Standard applies to such leases. Similarly, because FRS 26 ~~IAS 39~~ excludes certain loan commitments from its scope, this [draft] Standard applies to such loan commitments if they are onerous.   **6**

Some amounts treated as non-financial liabilities may relate to the recognition of revenue, for example when an entity issues a product warranty in exchange for a fee. This [draft] Standard does not address the recognition of revenue. FRS 5 *Reporting the Substance of Transactions* ~~IAS 18 Revenue~~ identifies the circumstances in which revenue is recognised and provides guidance on the application of the recognition criteria. This [draft] Standard does not change the requirements of FRS 5 ~~IAS 18~~.   **7**

Other Standards specify whether the corresponding amount recorded when a non-financial liability is recognised is included as part of the cost of an asset or recognised as an expense. This issue is not addressed in this [draft] Standard.   **8**

In some jurisdictions, some classes of liabilities are described as provisions, for example those liabilities that can be measured only by using a substantial degree of estimation. Although this [draft] Standard does not use the term 'provision', it does not prescribe how entities describe their non-financial liabilities. Therefore, entities may describe some classes of non-financial liabilities as provisions in their financial statements.   **9**

DEFINITIONS

The following terms are used in this [draft] Standard with the meanings specified: **10**

A *constructive obligation* **is a present obligation that arises from an entity's past actions when:**

(a)   **by an established pattern of past practice, published policies or a sufficiently specific current statement, the entity has indicated to other parties that it will accept particular responsibilities; and**

(b)   **as a result, the entity has created a valid expectation in those parties that they can reasonably rely on it to discharge those responsibilities.**

A *legal obligation* **is a present obligation that arises from the following:**

(a)   **a contract (through its explicit or implicit terms);**
(b)   **legislation; or**
(c)   **other operation of law.**

A *liability* **is a present obligation of the entity arising from past events, the settlement of which is expected to result in an outflow from the entity of resources embodying economic benefits.**

A *non-financial liability* **is a liability other than a financial liability as defined in** FRS 25 ~~IAS 32~~ *Financial Instruments: Disclosure and Presentation*.

A **contract is** *onerous* **when the unavoidable costs of meeting its obligations exceed its expected economic benefits.**

RECOGNITION

11   **An entity shall recognise a non-financial liability when:**

    (a)   the definition of a liability has been satisfied, and

    (b)   the non-financial liability can be measured reliably.

Satisfying the definition of a liability

12   Items are recognised as non-financial liabilities in accordance with this [draft] Standard only if they satisfy the definition of a liability in accordance with this [draft] Standard. the *Framework*.

13   An essential characteristic of a liability is that the entity has a present obligation arising from a past event. For a past event to give rise to a present obligation, the entity must have little, if any, discretion to avoid settling it. A past event that creates a present obligation is sometimes referred to as an obligating event.

14   Because most liabilities arise from legal obligations, settlement can be enforced by a court. Some liabilities arise from constructive obligations, in which the obligation is created by, or inferred from, an entity's past actions rather than arising from an explicit agreement with another party or from legislation. In some jurisdictions, constructive obligations may also be enforced by a court, for example in accordance with the legal principle known in the United States as promissory estoppel* or principles having the same effects under other legal systems.

15   In the absence of legal enforceability, particular care is required in determining whether an entity has a present obligation that it has little, if any, discretion to avoid settling. In the case of a constructive obligation, this will be the case only if:

    (a)   the entity has indicated to other parties that it will accept particular responsibilities;

    (b)   the other parties can reasonably expect the entity to perform those responsibilities; and

    (c)   the other parties will either benefit from the entity's performance or suffer harm from its non-performance.

16   In determining whether a liability exists at the balance sheet date, an entity takes into account all available evidence, including, for example, the opinion of experts. The evidence considered includes any additional information provided by events after the balance sheet date, but only to the extent that the information provides evidence of circumstances that existed at the balance sheet date.

17   Only present obligations arising from past events existing independently of an entity's future actions (ie the future conduct of its business) result in liabilities. For example, an entity has a liability for its obligation to decommission an oil installation or a nuclear power station to the extent that the entity is obliged to rectify damage already caused. Regardless of its future actions, the entity has little, if any, discretion to avoid settling that obligation.

18   An intention to incur an outflow of economic resources embodying economic benefits in the future is not sufficient to give rise to a liability, even if the outflow is necessary for the continuation of the entity's future operations. For example,

---

*Defined in Black's Law Dictionary *as 'the principle that a promise made without consideration may nonetheless be enforced to prevent injustice if the promisor should have reasonably expected the promisee to rely on the promise and if the promisee did actually rely on the promise to his or her detriment.'*

because of commercial pressures or legal requirements, an entity may intend or need to incur expenditure to operate in a particular way in the future (for example, by installing smoke filters in a particular type of factory). Because the entity has the discretion to avoid the future expenditure by its future actions, for example by changing its operations, it has no present obligation for that future expenditure and a liability does not exist.

A present obligation always involves another party to whom the obligation is owed. **19** It is not necessary, however, to know the identity of the specific party to whom the obligation is owed—indeed, the obligation may be to the public at large. Because a liability always involves an obligation to another party, it follows that a decision by the management of an entity does not normally give rise to a present obligation at the balance sheet date. A present obligation arises only if the decision has been communicated before the balance sheet date to those it affects in a sufficiently specific manner to raise a valid expectation in them that they can reasonably rely on the entity to perform.

An event that does not give rise to a present obligation immediately may do so at a **20** later date, because of changes in the law or because an act (for example, a sufficiently specific public statement) by the entity gives rise to a constructive obligation. For example, when environmental damage is caused there may be no present obligation to remedy the consequences. However, a present obligation arises if a new law requires the existing damage to be rectified or if the entity publicly accepts responsibility for rectification in a way that creates a constructive obligation.

When a new law is proposed, a present obligation under the operation of that law **21** arises only when the law is substantively enacted, which is when the remaining steps in the enactment process will not change the outcome. Differences in circumstances surrounding enactment make it impossible to specify a single event that would make legislation substantively enacted in all jurisdictions. In some cases, substantive enactment does not occur until the legislation is actually enacted.

Contingencies

In some cases, an entity has a liability even though the amount that will be required **22** to settle that liability is contingent (or conditional) on the occurrence or non-occurrence of one or more uncertain future events. In such cases, an entity has incurred two obligations as a result of a past event - an unconditional obligation and a conditional obligation.

When the amount that will be required to settle a liability is contingent on the **23** occurrence or non-occurrence of one or more uncertain future events, the liability arising from the unconditional obligation is recognised independently of the probability that the uncertain future event(s) will occur (or fail to occur). Uncertainty about the future event(s) is reflected in the measurement of the liability recognised.

Liabilities for which the amount that will be required in settlement is contingent on **24** the occurrence or non-occurrence of a future event are sometimes referred to as 'stand ready' obligations. This is because the entity has an unconditional obligation to stand ready to fulfil the conditional obligation *if* the uncertain future event occurs (or fails to occur). The liability is the unconditional obligation to provide a service, which results in an outflow of economic benefits.

An example of a stand ready obligation is a product warranty. The issuer of a **25** product warranty has an unconditional obligation to stand ready to repair or replace the product (or, expressed another way, to provide warranty coverage over the term of the warranty) and a conditional obligation to repair or replace the product if it develops a fault. The issuer recognises its liability arising from its unconditional obligation to provide warranty coverage. Uncertainty about whether the product will require repair or replacement (ie the conditional obligation) is reflected in the measurement of the liability.

26   Similarly, an entity that is involved in defending a lawsuit recognises the liability arising from its unconditional obligation to stand ready to perform as the court directs. Uncertainty about the possible penalties the court may impose (ie the conditional obligation) is reflected in the measurement of the liability.

Reliable measurement

27   In many cases, the amount of a non-financial liability must be estimated. The use of estimates is an essential part of the preparation of financial statements and does not of itself undermine the reliability of the statements. Except in extremely rare cases, an entity will be able to determine a reliable measure of a liability.

28   In the extremely rare case in which an entity cannot measure a non-financial liability reliably, the liability does not qualify for recognition in accordance with this [draft] Standard. In such cases, the entity discloses information about the non-financial liability in accordance with paragraph 69. The non-financial liability is recognised initially in the period in which it can be measured reliably.

MEASUREMENT

Amount that an entity would rationally pay to settle or transfer the obligation

29   **An entity shall measure a non-financial liability at the amount that it would rationally pay to settle the present obligation or to transfer it to a third party on the balance sheet date.**

30   In some cases, contractual or other market evidence can be used to determine the amount that would be required to settle or transfer the obligation on the balance sheet date. However, in many cases, observable market evidence of the amount that the entity would rationally pay to settle the obligation or to transfer it to a third party will not exist and the amount must be estimated.

31   The basis of estimating many non-financial liabilities will be an expected cash flow approach, in which multiple cash flow scenarios that reflect the range of possible outcomes are weighted by their associated probabilities. An expected cash flow approach is an appropriate basis for measuring both liabilities for a class of similar obligations and liabilities for single obligations. This is because it is likely to be the basis of the amount that an entity would rationally pay to settle the obligation(s) or to transfer the obligation(s) to a third party on the balance sheet date. In contrast, a liability for a single obligation measured at its most likely outcome would not necessarily represent the amount that the entity would rationally pay to settle or to transfer the obligation on the balance sheet date.

32   The estimates of outcome and financial effect are determined by the judgement of the management of the entity, supplemented by experience with similar transactions and, in some cases, reports from independent experts. The evidence considered includes any additional information provided by events after the balance sheet date, but only

to the extent that the information relates to the obligation existing at the balance sheet date.

When an entity is estimating the amount of a non-financial liability that is contingent **33** on the occurrence (or non-occurrence) of one or more uncertain future events, the measurement of the liability reflects the uncertainty about the future event(s). For example, in estimating a liability for a product warranty obligation, an entity considers the likelihood of claims under the warranty occurring and the amount and timing of the cash flows that would be required to meet those claims.

The non-financial liability is measured before tax, because the tax consequences of **34** the liability, and changes in it, are accounted for in accordance with FRS 16 and FRS 19 IAS 12.

Risks and uncertainties

In measuring a non-financial liability in accordance with paragraph 29, an entity **35** shall include the effects of risks and uncertainties.

Risk describes variability of outcome. A risk adjustment typically increases the **36** amount at which a liability is measured relative to a measurement that does not include a risk adjustment, all other things being equal. This is because it reflects the price that entities demand for the uncertainties and unforeseeable circumstances inherent in the liability. Caution is needed in making judgements under conditions of uncertainty, so that liabilities are not understated. However, uncertainty does not justify deliberate overstatement of liabilities. For example, if the projected costs of a particularly adverse outcome are estimated at the high end of the range of those reasonably expected, that outcome is not then deliberately treated as more probable than is realistically the case. Care is needed to avoid duplicating adjustments for risk and uncertainty with consequent overstatement of a non-financial liability.

The uncertainties about the amount or timing of the outflow of economic benefits are **37** disclosed in accordance with paragraph 68(c).

Present value

When an entity measures a non-financial liability using an estimation method that **38** **involves projections of future cash flows, it shall discount the cash flows using a pre-tax rate (or rates) that reflect(s) current market assessments of the time value of money and the risks specific to the liability. The discount rate(s) shall not reflect risks for which future cash flow estimates have been adjusted.** *

Because of the time value of money, estimated cash outflows that arise soon after the **39** balance sheet date are more onerous than those of the same amount that arise later. Therefore, cash flows are discounted.

When an entity reflects the effects of risks and uncertainties by adjusting the discount **40** rate rather than by adjusting the estimated cash flows, the resulting discount rate is typically lower than a risk-free rate.

Further guidance on using cash flow information and present value in accounting measurements is contained in Appendix A to IAS 36 [draft] FRS ● Impairment of Assets.

Future events

41 When measuring a non-financial liability, an entity shall reflect the effects of future events that may affect the amount that will be required to settle the obligation.

42 Only the effects of future events that may affect the amount that will be required to settle an obligation without changing the nature of the obligation are reflected in the measurement of a non-financial liability. For example, an entity's past experience may indicate that the cost of cleaning up a site at the end of its life may be reduced by future changes in technology. Accordingly, when measuring the liability, the entity reflects an assessment of both the assumed effects of the future technology on the cost of cleaning up the site and the likelihood that such technology will be available. In contrast, the effects of future events that create new obligations (or change or discharge existing obligations) are not reflected in the measurement of a liability. For example, the effects of possible new legislation are not reflected in the measurement of a liability because they create or change the obligation itself.

Subsequent measurement

43 An entity shall review the carrying amount of a non-financial liability at each balance sheet date and adjust it to reflect the current amount that the entity would rationally pay to settle the present obligation or to transfer it to a third party on that date.

44 An entity subsequently remeasures a non-financial liability in accordance with the guidance in paragraphs 30-42. Therefore, remeasurement reflects any changes in:

(a) the expected amount and timing of the economic benefits that will be required to settle the obligation;

(b) the risks and uncertainties surrounding the obligation; and

(c) the discount rate used to measure the liability.

45 Changes in the carrying amount of a non-financial liability resulting from the passage of time are recognised as a borrowing cost.

REIMBURSEMENTS

46 When an entity has a right to be reimbursed by a third party for some or all of the economic benefits that will be required to settle a non-financial liability, it recognises the reimbursement right as an asset if the reimbursement right can be measured reliably. The amount recognised for the reimbursement right shall not exceed the amount of the non-financial liability.

47 Sometimes, an entity has a right to look to another party to provide part or all of the economic benefits that will be required to settle a non-financial liability (for example, through insurance contracts, indemnity clauses or suppliers' warranties). The other party may either reimburse amounts paid by the entity or settle the amounts directly. Although the reimbursement itself is a conditional right, the unconditional right to receive reimbursement satisfies the definition of an asset and is recognised if it can be measured reliably.

48 An entity shall not offset against the non-financial liability the amount recognised for the reimbursement right.

49 Because the reimbursement is receivable from a third party, there would not be a legally enforceable right of set-off, and therefore, the non-financial liability and the reimbursement right are recognised separately. However, if the entity will not be

liable for the amounts required to settle the obligation if the third party fails to pay, the entity has no liability for these amounts and they are not reflected in the measurement of the liability.

In the income statement, the expense relating to a non-financial liability may be presented net of the income resulting from the reimbursement right.   50

DERECOGNITION

An entity shall derecognise a non-financial liability when the obligation is settled, is cancelled or expires.   51

APPLICATION OF THE RECOGNITION AND MEASUREMENT REQUIREMENTS

Future operating losses

An entity shall not recognise a liability for future operating losses.   52

Future operating losses do not satisfy the definition of a liability because there is no present obligation arising from a past event.   53

An expectation by the entity of future operating losses is an indication that some assets of the entity may be impaired or that some of its contracts may be onerous. An entity tests these assets for impairment in accordance with ~~IAS 36~~ [draft] FRS ● *Impairment of Assets* and accounts for its onerous contracts in accordance with paragraphs 55-59.   54

Onerous contracts

If an entity has a contract that is onerous, it shall recognise as a liability the present obligation under the contract. If the contract will become onerous as a result of the entity's own actions, the entity shall not recognise the liability until it has taken the action.   55

Many contracts (for example, some routine purchase orders) can be cancelled without paying compensation to the other party and, therefore, there is no obligation. Other contracts establish both rights and obligations for each of the contracting parties. If events or circumstances make such a contract onerous, the contract is within the scope of this [draft] Standard and a liability exists that is recognised. Executory contracts that are not onerous are outside the scope of this [draft] Standard.   56

In some cases, contracts become onerous as a result of events outside the entity's control. For example, a contract that requires an entity to make specified payments regardless of whether it takes delivery of contracted products or services may become onerous if the market price of the products or services declines below the contracted price. In other cases, the event that makes the contract onerous is an action of the entity. In such cases, the liability for the onerous contract is not recognised until the entity has taken the action. For example, a contract may become onerous because the entity ceases to use the right conveyed by that contract, but continues to incur costs for its obligations under the contract. Therefore, in this example the entity does not recognise a liability until it ceases using the right conveyed by the contract.   57

58   A contract is onerous when the unavoidable costs of meeting its obligations exceed its expected economic benefits. The unavoidable costs under a contract reflect the least net cost of exiting from the contract, which is the lower of the cost of fulfilling it and any compensation or penalties arising from failure to fulfil it. If the contract is an operating lease, the entity determines the unavoidable cost by reference to the remaining lease rentals payable, reduced by estimated sublease rentals that could be reasonably obtained for the property, even if the entity does not intend to enter into a sublease.

59   Before an entity recognises a liability for an onerous contract, it recognises any impairment loss that has occurred on assets related to that contract (see [draft] FRS • IAS 36).

Restructurings

60   The following are examples of events that are typically described as a restructuring:

(a)   sale or termination of a line of business;

(b)   closure of business locations in a country or region or relocation of business activities from one country or region to another;

(c)   changes in management structure, for example, eliminating a layer of management; and

(d)   reorganisations that affect the nature and focus of the entity's operations.

61   **An entity shall recognise a non-financial liability for a cost associated with a restructuring only when the definition of a liability has been satisfied.**

62   A liability involves a present obligation to others that leaves the entity with little, if any, discretion to avoid settling the obligation. A decision by the management of an entity to undertake a restructuring does not create a present obligation to others for costs expected to be incurred during the restructuring. Accordingly, a decision by the management of an entity to undertake a restructuring is not the requisite past event for the recognition of a liability. A cost associated with a restructuring is recognised as a liability on the same basis as if that cost arose independently of the restructuring. Paragraphs 63-65 provide additional guidance for applying the definition of a liability to specified costs that are often associated with a restructuring.

Termination benefits

63   An entity shall apply the requirements in paragraphs 94 to 108 132-147 of [draft] FRS 17 *Retirement and Termination Benefits* IAS 19 *Employee Benefits* to benefits that are provided in connection with the termination of an employee's employment.

Contract termination costs

64   An entity shall apply the requirements in paragraphs 55-59 to costs to terminate a contract before the end of its term and to costs that will continue to be incurred under a contract for its remaining term without economic benefit to the entity. Accordingly, a liability for costs to terminate a contract that was not previously determined to be an onerous contract before the end of its term shall be recognised when the entity terminates the contract in accordance with the contract terms. For example, termination would occur when the entity gives written notice to the counterparty within the notification period specified by the contract or has otherwise negotiated a termination with the counterparty. Similarly, a liability for costs that will continue to be incurred under a contract that was not previously determined to be onerous for its remaining term without economic benefit to the entity shall be recognised when the entity ceases using the right conveyed by the contract. For example, any additional liability for payments to be made under an operating lease for a factory that will no longer be used is recognised when the entity ceases to use the leased factory.

Other associated costs

Other costs associated with a restructuring include, but are not limited to, such costs as: **65**

(a)   retraining or relocating continuing staff;
(b)   consolidating or closing facilities; or
(c)   investing in new systems and distribution networks.

An entity shall recognise liabilities for such costs when the liability is incurred (generally, when goods or services associated with the activity are received).

If an entity starts to implement a restructuring plan or announces its main features   **66** after the balance sheet date, disclosure is required in accordance with FRS 21 ~~IAS 10~~ *Events after the Balance Sheet Date*.

DISCLOSURE

For each class of recognised non-financial liability, an entity shall disclose the carrying   67 amount of the liability at the period-end together with a description of the nature of the obligation.

For any class of recognised non-financial liability with estimation uncertainty*, an   68 entity shall also disclose:

(a)   a reconciliation of the carrying amounts at the beginning and end of the period showing:

    (i)   liabilities incurred;
    (ii)   liabilities derecognised;
    (iii) changes in the discounted amount resulting from the passage of time and the effect of any change in the discount rate; and
    (iv)   other adjustments to the amount of the liability (eg revisions in estimated cash flows that will be required to settle it).

(b)   the expected timing of any resulting outflows of economic benefits.
(c)   an indication of the uncertainties about the amount or timing of those outflows. If necessary to provide adequate information, an entity shall disclose the major assumptions made about future events, as described in paragraph 41.
(d)   the amount of any right to reimbursement, stating the amount of any asset that has been recognised for that right.

If a non-financial liability is not recognised because it cannot be measured reliably, an   69 entity shall disclose that fact together with:

(a)   a description of the nature of the obligation;
(b)   an explanation of why it cannot be measured reliably;
(c)   an indication of the uncertainties relating to the amount or timing of any outflow of economic benefits; and

---

*ASB footnote: *The phrase 'estimation uncertainty' is from IAS 1* Presentation of Financial Statements *and refers to estimations that require management's most difficult, subjective or complex judgements.*

(d)   the existence of any right to reimbursement.

70   In determining which non-financial liabilities may be aggregated to form a class, an entity considers whether the nature of the items is sufficiently similar for a single statement about them to fulfil the requirements of paragraphs 67-69. Thus, it may be appropriate to treat as a single class of non-financial liabilities amounts relating to warranties of different products, but it would not be appropriate to treat as a single class amounts relating to normal warranties and amounts subject to legal proceedings.

71   **In extremely rare cases, disclosure of some or all of the information required by paragraphs 68 and 69 can be expected to prejudice seriously the position of the entity in a dispute with other parties on the subject matter of the non-financial liability. In such cases, an entity need not disclose the information, but shall disclose the general nature of the dispute, together with the fact that, and reason why, the information has not been disclosed.**

TRANSITION AND EFFECTIVE DATE

72   **An entity shall apply this [draft] Standard from the beginning of its first annual period commencing on or after [1 January 2007]. Comparative information shall not be restated. Earlier application is encouraged. However, an entity shall apply this [draft] Standard only from the beginning of an annual period commencing on or after [date the [draft] Standard is issued]. If an entity applies this [draft] Standard before the effective date, it shall disclose that fact.**

WITHDRAWAL OF FRS 12 ~~IAS 37 (ISSUED 1998)~~

73   This [draft] Standard supersedes FRS12 ~~IAS 37~~ *Provisions, Contingent Liabilities and Contingent Assets.* ~~(issued in 1998).~~

Appendix
Amendments to other UK accounting standards

The amendments in the [draft] Appendix shall be applied from the beginning of annual periods commencing on or after [1 January 2007]. If an entity applies this [draft] Standard from the beginning of an earlier annual period, these amendments shall be applied for that earlier period. Amended paragraphs are shown with new text underlined and deleted text struck through

Terminology   A1

The [draft] FRS does not use the term 'provisions', 'contingent liabilities' or 'contingent assets.' In UK accounting standards, references to 'provisions' shall be amended to 'non-financial liabilities.'

In UK accounting standards references to FRS 12 'Provisions, contingent assets and contingent liabilities' shall be replaced with FRS 12 'Non-financial Liabilities.'

SSAP 4 Accounting for government grants   A2

Paragraph 6 is amended as follows: A2.1

In many cases, the grant-making body has the right to recover all or part of a grant   6
paid if the enterprise has not complied with the conditions under which the grant was
made. On the assumption that the enterprise is a going concern, the application of
the prudence concept does not normally require postponement of the recognition of
the grant in the profit and loss account solely because there is a possibility that it
might have to be repaid in the future. The enterprise should consider regularly
whether there is a likelihood of a breach of the conditions on which the grant was
made. If such a breach has occurred, or appears likely to occur, and it is probable
that some grant will have to be repaid, provision should be made for the liability and
recognise a non-financial liability in accordance with FRS 12 *Non-financial Liabilities*
where appropriate.

SSAP 9 Stocks and long-term contracts   A3

Paragraph 11 is amended as follows: A3.1

If it is expected that there will be a loss on a contract as a whole, all of the loss should   11
be recognised as soon as it is foreseen (in accordance with the prudence concept).
Examples of how this can be achieved are given in Appendix 3. Initially, the foreseeable loss will be deducted from the work in progress figure of the particular
contract, thus reducing it to net realisable value. Any loss in excess of the work in
progress figure should be classified as an accrual within 'Creditors' or under 'Provisions for liabilities and charges' depending upon the circumstances. Where
unprofitable contracts are of such magnitude that they can be expected to utilise a
considerable part of the company's capacity for a substantial period, related
administration overheads to be incurred during the period to the completion of those
contracts should also be included in the calculation of the liability provision for
losses.

Paragraph 30 (d) is amended as follows: A3.2

(d)   the amount by which the ~~provision or accrual~~ liability for foreseeable losses exceeds the costs incurred (after transfers to cost of sales) should be included within either provisions for liabilities or creditors as appropriate.

A3.3   **In Appendix 3 Project 4 is amended as follows:**

PROJECT 4

Profit and Loss Account - cumulative

Included in turnover	200
Included in cost of sales	(290)
Gross loss	(90)

Balance sheet

The amount to be included in debtors under 'amounts recoverable on contracts' is calculated as follows:

Cumulative turnover	200
LESS: Cumulative payments on account	(150)
Included in debtors	50

The amount to be included as ~~a provision/accrual~~ liabilities for foreseeable losses is calculated as follows:

Total costs incurred to date	250
LESS: Transferred to cost of sales	(250)
Foreseeable losses on contract as a whole	(40)
	(290)
Classified as ~~a provision/accrual~~ liabilities for foreseeable losses	(40)

Note that the credit balance of 40 is not offset against the debit balance of 50 included in debtors.

A4   ***SSAP 21 Accounting for leases and hire purchase contracts***

A4.1   **Paragraph 38 is amended as follows:**

38   The amount due from the lessee under a finance lease should be recorded in the balance sheet of a lessor as a debtor at the amount of the net investment in the lease after recognising a non-financial liability ~~making provisions~~ for items such as bad and doubtful rentals receivable.

A5   ***FRS 3 Reporting financial performance***

A5.1   **Paragraph 18 is amended as follows:**

The consequences of a decision to sell or terminate an operation

18   If a decision has been made to sell or terminate an operation, any consequential non-financial liability ~~provisions~~ should only be recognised when the entity has incurred a liability and the amount of the non-financial liability can be reliably measured. ~~reflect the extent to which obligations have been incurred that are not expected to be covered by the future profits of the operation. This principle requires that the~~

reporting entity should be demonstrably committed to the sale or termination. This should be evidenced, in the former case, by a binding sale agreement and, in the latter, by a detailed formal plan for termination from which the reporting entity cannot realistically withdraw. The non-financial liability provision should cover only a) the direct costs of the sale or termination and b) any operating losses of the operation up to the date of sale or termination, in both cases, after taking into account the aggregate profit, if any, to be recognised in the profit and loss account from the future profits of the operation. Unless the operation qualifies as a discontinued operation in the period under review, the write down of assets and any non-financial liabilities provisions should appear in the continuing operations category. In the subsequent period when the operation does qualify as discontinued, the non-financial liabilities provisions should be used to offset the results of the operation in the discontinued category. The related disclosure in that subsequent period, however, should be to show the results of the discontinued operation under each of the statutory format headings with the utilisation of the non-financial liability provision analysed as necessary between the operating loss and the loss on sale or termination of the discontinued operation and disclosed on the face of the profit and loss account immediately below the relevant items.

Paragraph 45 is amended as follows: A5.2

The consequences of a decision to sell or terminate an operation

Paragraph 18 sets out the principle underlying the recognition establishment of a   **45**
non-financial liability provisions as a consequence of a decision to sell or terminate an operation. This principle focuses on the fact that an obligation arises at the point when the reporting entity becomes demonstrably committed to the sale or termination non-financial liability for costs associated with restructuring shall be recognised only when the entity has incurred a liability. Evidence of the commitment might be the public announcement of specific plans, the commencement of implementation, or other circumstances effectively obliging the reporting entity to complete the sale or termination. A binding contract entered into after the balance sheet date may provide additional evidence of asset values and commitments at the balance sheet date. In the case of an intended sale for which no legally binding sale agreement exists, no obligation has been entered into by the reporting entity; accordingly, liabilities provisions for the direct costs of the decision to sell and for future operating losses should not be recognised. In accordance with normal practice, however, any impairment in asset values should be recorded.

FRS 5 Reporting the substance of transactions   A6

Paragraph 24 is amended as follows: A6.1

In the special cases referred to in paragraph 23, where the amount of any resulting   **24**
gain or loss is uncertain, a liability should be recognised for the full provision should be made for any probable loss, but recognition of any gain, to the extent it is in doubt, should be deferred. In addition, where the uncertainty could have a material effect on the financial statements, this fact should be disclosed in the notes to the financial statements.

Paragraph 53 is amended as follows: A6.2

In accounting terms, the substance of a transaction is portrayed through the assets   **53**
and liabilities, including any contingent assets and liabilities, resulting from, or altered by the transaction. A key step in reporting the substance of any transaction is therefore to identify its effect on the assets and liabilities of the entity.

A6.3   **Paragraph 74 is amended as follows:**

74   In any of the above three classes of transaction, there arises the issue of how to measure the change in the entity's assets or liabilities and any resulting profit or loss. This measurement process requires that the previous carrying value of the asset is apportioned into an amount relating to those benefits and risks disposed of and an amount relating to those retained. In some cases, measurement will be relatively easy; for instance this might be the case where a proportionate share of the original asset is retained as described in paragraph 71 above or where there are similar and frequent transactions in liquid and freely accessible markets. In other cases, measurement may be more difficult with the result that the amount of any gain or loss is uncertain. In such cases, in accordance with the provisions of SSAP 18, paragraph 24 FRS 12 Non-financial Liabilities requires a prudent approach to be adopted, a non-financial liability should be recognised for the loss with full provision being made for any probable loss but recognition of any gain, to the extent it is in doubt, being deferred.

A6.4   **The following amendments are required in Application Note B Sale and Purchase Agreements:**

- **Paragraph B12 is amended as follows:**

B12   In some cases the seller may have a call option to repurchase the asset but have no commitment to do so, or the buyer may have a put option to transfer the asset back to the seller without the seller having an equivalent right to insist on repurchase. It will be important to determine why the parties have agreed to such a one-sided option and to assess the commercial effect of the option with regard to all aspects of the arrangement, including whether the seller has a commercial need to repurchase the asset. This analysis may reveal that, in substance, there is a commitment to repurchase as discussed above. Conversely, such an analysis may reveal that the buyer assumes significant benefits and risks relating to the original asset, indicating that the seller has neither the original asset, nor a liability for the option's exercise price. In such a case, where the seller holds a call option it will have a new asset in the form of the option itself; where the buyer has a put option, the seller will have a liability a contingent liability to the buyer for the exercise price of the option (conditional contingent on the buyer exercising its option). In both cases, the seller's new asset or liability should be recognised or disclosed, on a prudent basis following the principles set out in FRS 12 Non-financial Liabilities. SSAP 18 'Accounting for contingencies'.

- **Paragraph B21 is amended as follows:**

B21   Where the seller has a new asset or liability (for example, merely a call option to repurchase the original asset), it should recognise or disclose that new asset or liability on a prudent basis in accordance with the provisions of FRS 12 SSAP 18. In particular, the seller should recognise (and not merely disclose) a liability for any kind of unconditional obligation it has entered into. Where doubts exist regarding the amount of any gain or loss arising, a non-financial liability full provision should be recognised made for the any expected loss but recognition of any gain, to the extent that it is in doubt, should be deferred until it is realised. The notes to the financial statements should describe the main features of the arrangement, including: the status of the asset; the relationship between the asset and the liability; and the terms of any provision for repurchase (including any options) and of any guarantees.

A6.5   **The following amendments are required in Application Note G, Revenue Recognition:**

- **Paragraph G42 is amended as follows:**

Vouchers distributed free of charge, independently of another transaction, do not give rise to a liability except where redemption of the voucher will result in products being sold at a loss. Where this is the case, the seller has entered into an onerous contract and a <u>non-financial liability</u> ~~provision~~ will need to be <u>recognised</u> ~~made~~ in accordance with FRS 12 <u>Non-financial Liabilities</u> ~~'Provisions, Contingent Liabilities and Contingent Assets'~~. When the vouchers are redeemed, the seller should recognise revenue at the amount received for the product, ie after deducting the discount obtained for the vouchers.

G42

FRS 15 *Tangible fixed assets*

A7

Paragraph 10 is amended as follows:

A7.1

 Examples of directly attributable costs include:

10

- acquisition costs (such as stamp duty, import duties and non-refundable purchase taxes)
- the cost of site preparation and clearance
- initial delivery and handling costs
- installation costs
- professional fees (such as legal, architects' and engineers' fees)
- the estimated cost of dismantling and removing the asset and restoring the site, to the extent that it is recognised as a <u>non-financial liability</u> ~~provision~~ under FRS 12 <u>Non-financial Liabilities</u> ~~'Provisions, Contingent Liabilities and Contingent Assets'~~. The fact that the prospect of such expenditures emerges only some time after the original capitalisation of the asset (eg because of legislative changes) does not preclude their capitalisation.

FRS 17 *Retirement and Termination Benefits*

A8

Paragraphs 20 and 21 are amended as follows:

A8.1

...

20

(b) any constructive obligations for further benefits ~~where a public statement or past practice by the employer has created a valid expectation in the employees that such benefits will be granted~~ <u>where there is little, if any, discretion to avoid paying the employees.</u>

Where the scheme rules require a surplus arising in the scheme to be shared between the employer and members (perhaps in conjunction with a similar sharing of deficits), or where ~~past practice has established a valid expectation that this will be done,~~ <u>there is little, if any, discretion to avoid paying</u> the amount that will be passed to members should be treated as increasing the scheme liabilities.

21

Paragraph 39 is amended as follows:

A8.2

Conversely, the employer has a liability if it has a legal or constructive obligation to make good a deficit in the defined benefit scheme. In general, the employer will either have a legal obligation under the terms of the scheme trust deed or will have by its past actions and statements created a constructive obligation as defined in FRS 12 <u>Non-financial Liabilities</u> ~~'Provisions, Contingent Liabilities and Contingent Assets'~~. The legal or constructive obligation to fund the deficit should be assumed to apply to the deficit based on assumptions used under the FRS.

39

A9   *FRS 19 Deferred tax*

A9.1   In paragraph 45 replace the term 'provisions' with 'liabilities.'

A10   *FRS 21(IAS 10) Events after the Balance Sheet Date*

A10.1   Paragraph 9 is amended as follows:

9   The following are examples of adjusting events after the balance sheet date that require an entity to adjust the amounts recognised in its financial statements, or to recognise items that were not previously recognised:

   (a)   the ~~settlement~~ receipt of information after the balance sheet date ~~of a court case~~ that ~~confirms~~ indicates that the entity had a present obligation at the balance sheet date. The entity ~~adjusts any previously recognised provision related to this court case~~ recognises a non-financial liability in accordance with *FRS 12 Non-financial Liabilities* ~~*Provisions, Contingent Liabilities and Contingent Assets* or recognises a new provision. The entity does not merely disclose a contingent liability~~ because the ~~settlement~~ information provides additional evidence that would be considered in accordance with paragraph 16 of FRS 12. For example, the start of legal proceedings against an entity after the balance sheet date may indicate that the entity had a present obligation at the balance sheet date.

A10.2   Paragraph 20 is amended as follows:

20   In some cases, an entity needs to update the disclosures in its financial statements to reflect information received after the balance sheet date, even when the information does not affect the amounts that it recognises in its financial statements. One example of the need to update disclosures is when evidence becomes available after the balance sheet date about a ~~contingent~~ non-financial liability that existed at the balance sheet date. In addition to considering whether ~~it should recognise or change a~~ the evidence affects the measurement of the non-financial liability ~~provision under~~ recognised in accordance with FRS 12 Non-financial Liabilities ~~*Provisions, Contingent Liabilities and Contingent Assets,*~~ an entity updates its disclosures about the ~~contingent~~ non-financial liability in the light of that evidence.

A10.3   Paragraph 22 is amended as follows:

22   The following are examples of non-adjusting events after the balance sheet date that would generally result in disclosure:

   ...

   (i)   entering into significant commitments or ~~contingent~~ incurring significant liabilities, for example, by issuing significant guarantees; and

   ...

A11   *FRS 23 (IAS 21) The Effects of Changes in Foreign Exchange Rates:*

A11.1   Paragraph 16 is amended by deleting the term 'provisions' and replacing it with 'liabilities.'

FRS 25 (IAS 32) Financial Instruments: Disclosure and Presentation   A12

Paragraph 94(b) is amended as follows: A12.1

An entity shall disclose the carrying amount of financial assets it has pledged as col-   94(b)
lateral for liabilities ~~the carrying amount of financial assets pledged as collateral for~~
~~contingent liabilities~~ and conditional obligations, and (consistently with paragraphs
60(a) and 63(g)) any ~~material~~ terms and conditions relating to assets pledged as
collateral.

FRS 26 (IAS 39) Financial Instruments: Recognition and Measurement   A13

Paragraph 2 is amended as follows: A13.1

This Standard shall be applied by all entities to all types of financial instruments except: 2.

...

*(h)   except as described in paragraph 4, loan commitments that cannot be settled net
    in cash or another financial instrument. A loan commitment is not regarded as
    settled net merely because the loan is paid out in instalments (for example, a
    mortgage construction loan that is paid out in instalments in line with the progress
    of construction). An issuer of a commitment to provide a loan at a below-market
    interest rate shall initially recognise it at fair value, and subsequently measure it
    at the higher of (i) the amount recognised ~~under~~ in accordance with FRS 12 Non-
    financial Liabilities ~~Provisions, Contingent Liabilities and Contingent Assets~~ and
    (ii) the amount initially recognised less, ~~where~~ when appropriate, cumulative
    amortisation. An issuer of loan commitments shall apply FRS 12 to other loan
    commitments that are not within the scope of this Standard if they are onerous.
    (FRS 12 explains when a contract is onerous.) Loan commitments are subject to
    the derecognition provisions of this Standard (see paragraphs 15-42 and
    Appendix A paragraphs AG36-AG63).*

Paragraph 102(j) is inserted as follows: A13.2

rights to payments to reimburse the entity for some or all of the economic benefits that   102(j)
will be required to settle a non-financial liability recognised in accordance with FRS 12
~~IAS 37 Provisions, Contingent Liabilities and Contingent Assets,~~ or for which, in an
earlier period, the entity recognised a non-financial liability in accordance with FRS 12
~~IAS37.~~

Paragraph AG86 is amended as follows: A13.3

The process for estimating the amount of an impairment loss may result either in a   AG86
single amount or in a range of possible amounts. In the latter case, the entity
recognises an impairment loss ~~equal to the best estimate within~~ that reflects the range
of possible outcomes weighted by their associated probabilities* taking into account
all relevant information about conditions existing at the balance sheet date that is
available before the financial statements are issued ~~about conditions existing at the~~
~~balance sheet date.~~

---

*Example 17 in IAS 37, ~~paragraph 39~~ contains guidance on how to determine ~~the best~~ an estimate ~~in~~ when there
is a range of possible outcomes.

AMENDMENTS TO FRED 37 (IAS 38) AND FRED 38 (IAS 36)

The ASB has issued FRED 37 (IAS 38) Intangible Assets and FRED 38 (IAS 36) Impairment of Assets. These FREDs have been amended to reflect the consequential amendments that are required to the current version of IAS 38 and IAS 36 as published by the IASB.

The consequential amendments, set out below, are for information purposes only.

A14   *FRED 37 (IAS 38) Intangible Assets*

A14.1   **After paragraph 17 a new heading and paragraphs 17A and 17B are added, as follows:**

Contingencies

17A   In some cases, an entity has an intangible asset even though the amount of the future economic benefits embodied in that asset is contingent (or conditional) on the occurrence or non-occurrence of one or more uncertain future events. In such cases, an entity has two rights as a result of a past event, an unconditional right and a conditional right. The intangible asset arises from the unconditional right, but the conditional right is reflected in the measurement of the intangible asset.

17B   An example of such an intangible asset is a product warranty. The entity's asset arises from its unconditional right to warranty coverage for the duration of the warranty contract rather than from its conditional right to have its product repaired or replaced if it develops a fault. Similarly, an entity that is pursuing a legal claim has an intangible asset arising from the actions it performed to get to the point of pursuing its claim. Any amounts that the entity expects to receive as a result of pursuing a legal claim are a conditional right, because the right to receive them is conditional on a future event (eg the judgement of the court).

A15   *FRED 38 (IAS 36) Impairment of Assets*

A15.1   **In paragraph 43(b), 'provisions' is amended to 'non-financial liabilities'.**

A15.2   **Paragraphs 44-47 are amended as follows.**

44   **Future cash flows shall be estimated for the asset in its current condition. Estimates of future cash flows shall not include estimated future cash inflows or outflows that are expected to arise from:**

(a)   **a future restructuring ~~to~~ for which ~~an entity is not yet committed~~ a liability has not been incurred; or**

...

45   Because future cash flows are estimated for the asset in its current condition, value in use does not reflect:

(a)   future cash outflows or related cost savings (for example reductions in staff costs) or benefits that are expected to arise from a future restructuring ~~to~~ for which ~~an entity is not yet committed~~ a liability has not been incurred; or

...

A restructuring is a programme that is planned and controlled by management and materially changes either the scope of the business undertaken by an entity or the manner in which the business is conducted. IAS 37 ~~Provisions, Contingent Liabilities and Contingent Assets~~ *Non-financial Liabilities* ~~contains guidance clarifying when an entity is committed to~~ specifies when an entity recognises a liability for a cost associated with a restructuring.   **46**

When an entity ~~becomes committed to~~ incurs a liability for a cost associated with a restructuring, some assets are likely to be affected by this restructuring. Once the entity ~~is committed to~~ incurs a liability for a cost associated with the restructuring: **47**

(a)   its estimates of future cash inflows and cash outflows for the purpose of determining value in use reflect the cost savings and other benefits from the restructuring (based on the most recent financial budgets/forecasts approved by management); and

(b)   its estimates of future cash outflows for the cost associated with the restructuring are ~~included~~ reflected in the measurement of a ~~restructuring provision~~ non-financial liability in accordance with IAS 37.

Illustrative Example 5 illustrates the effect of a future restructuring on a value in use calculation.

The example following paragraph 78 is amended as follows: **A15.3**

Example

A company operates a mine in a country ~~where~~ in which legislation requires that the owner must restore the site on completion of its mining operations. The cost of restoration includes the replacement of the overburden, which must be removed before mining operations commence. A ~~provision~~ non financial liability for the ~~costs~~ obligation to replace the overburden was recognised as soon as the overburden was removed. The amount ~~provided was recognised~~ of the liability initially recognised was included as part of the cost of the mine and is being depreciated over the mine's useful life. The carrying amount of the ~~provision~~ liability for restoration costs is CU500,* ~~which is equal to the present value of the restoration costs~~.

The entity is testing the mine for impairment. The cash-generating unit for the mine is the mine as a whole. The entity has received various offers to buy the mine at a price of around CU800. This price reflects the fact that the buyer will assume the obligation to restore the overburden. Disposal costs for the mine are negligible. The value in use of the mine is approximately CU1,200, excluding restoration costs. The carrying amount of the mine is CU1,000.

The cash-generating unit's fair value less costs to sell is CU800. This amount considers restoration costs ~~that have~~ for which a liability has already been ~~provided for~~ recognised. As a consequence, the value in use for the cash-generating unit is determined after consideration of the restoration costs and is estimated to be CU700 (CU1,200 less CU500). The carrying amount of the cash-generating unit is CU500, which is the carrying amount of the mine (CU1,000) less the carrying amount of the ~~provision~~ liability for restoration costs (CU500). Therefore, the recoverable amount of the cash-generating unit exceeds its carrying amount.

* In this Standard, monetary amounts are denominated in 'currency units' (CU).

In paragraph 79, 'other provisions' is amended to 'liabilities'.   **A15.4**

In the Illustrative Examples, Example 5 is amended as follows.

EXAMPLE 5 TREATMENT OF A FUTURE RESTRUCTURING

In this example, tax effects are ignored.

Background

...

IE46   Management-approved budgets reflect that:

(a) at the end of 20X3, ~~the number of employees at~~ the plant will be ~~restructured~~ reduced at an estimated cost (for termination benefits) of CU100. ~~Since~~ Because K ~~is not yet committed to the restructuring~~ has not yet incurred a liability to provide termination benefits, a ~~provision~~ liability has not been recognised at the end of 20X0 ~~for the future restructuring costs~~.

(b) there will be future benefits from this restructuring in the form of reduced future cash outflows.

IE47   At the end of 20X2, K ~~becomes committed to the restructuring~~ recognises a liability to provide termination benefits in accordance with IAS 19 *Employee Benefits*. The costs are still estimated to be CU100 ~~and a provision is recognised accordingly~~. The plant's estimated future cash flows reflected in the most recent management-approved budgets are ~~given~~ set out in paragraph IE51 and ~~a~~ the current discount rate is **the same as at the end of 20X0.**

IE48   At the end of 20X3, actual ~~restructuring~~ termination benefit costs of CU100 are ~~incurred and~~ paid. Again, the plant's estimated future cash flows reflected in the most recent management-approved budgets and a current discount rate are the same as those estimated at the end of 20X2.

At the end of 20X0

Schedule 1. Calculation of the plant's value in use at the end of 20X0

Year	Future cash flows	Discounted at 14%
	CU	CU
20X1	300	263
20X2	280	215
20X3	420[1]	283
20X4	520[2]	308
20X5	350[2]	182
20X6	420[2]	191
20X7	480[2]	192
20X8	480[2]	168
20X9	460[2]	141
20X10	400[2]	108
Value in use		2,051

1 Excludes estimated ~~restructuring~~ costs of termination benefits reflected in management budgets.
2 Excludes estimated benefits reflected in management budgets expected from the ~~restructuring reflected in management budgets~~ reduction in the number of employees.

...

The entity ~~is now committed to the restructuring~~ has now incurred a liability to   **IE51**
provide termination benefits. Therefore, in determining the plant's value in use, the
benefits expected from the restructuring are considered in forecasting cash flows.
This results in an increase in the estimated future cash flows used to determine value
in use at the end of 20X0. In accordance with paragraphs 110 and 111 of IAS 36, the
recoverable amount of the plant is re-determined at the end of 20X2.

Schedule 3. Calculation of the plant's value in use at the end of 20X2

Year	Future cash flows	Discounted at 14%
	CU	CU
20X3	420^1	368
20X4	570^2	439
20X5	380^2	256
20X6	450^2	266
20X7	510^2	265
20X8	510^2	232
20X9	480^2	192
20X10	410^2	144
Value in use		2,162

1 Excludes estimated ~~restructuring~~ costs of termination benefits because a liability has ~~already~~
been recognised.
2 Includes estimated benefits reflected in management budgets expected from the ~~restructuring~~
~~reflected in management budgets~~ reduction in the number of employees.

...

At the end of 20X3

There is a cash outflow of CU100 when the ~~restructuring costs~~ termination benefits   **IE53**
are paid. Even though a cash outflow has taken place, there is no change in the
estimated future cash flows used to determine value in use at the end of 20X2.
Therefore, the plant's recoverable amount is not calculated at the end of 20X3.

Basis for Conclusions

This Basis for Conclusions accompanies, but is not part of, the draft Standard.

> *ASB note: The Basis for Conclusions material, which accompanies the exposure draft of proposed amendments to IAS 37 Provisions, Contingent Liabilities and Contingent Assets, that the IASB prepared is set out below in full. It should be noted though that some of the discussion it contains concerns IASB requirements that have no equivalent in the UK or Republic of Ireland. Footnotes have been used to indicate those parts of the discussion.*
>
> *All references in this section to 'the Board' and 'Board members' are references to the IASB Board and IASB Board members.*

INTRODUCTION

BC1   This Basis for Conclusions summarises the International Accounting Standards Board's considerations in reaching the conclusions in the Exposure Draft of Proposed Amendments to IAS 37 *Provisions, Contingent Liabilities and Contingent Assets**. Individual Board members gave greater weight to some factors than to others.

BC2   The amendments to IAS 37 proposed in this Exposure Draft are a result of two of the Board's current projects: the second phase of the Business Combinations project and the Short-term Convergence project. The proposed amendments are principally concerned with the Standard's definitions and recognition criteria, but have also required some more limited amendments to the measurement requirements. The Board has also taken the opportunity to clarify the scope of the Standard and some aspects of the existing measurement requirements.

BC3   The Board's intention was not to reconsider all of the Standard's requirements for accounting for provisions, contingent liabilities and contingent assets. Accordingly, this Basis for Conclusions does not discuss requirements in IAS 37 that the Board has not reconsidered.

AMENDMENTS ARISING FROM THE SECOND PHASE OF THE BUSINESS COMBINATIONS PROJECT

BC4   In the second phase of its Business Combinations project, the Board considered the application of the purchase method (now called the 'acquisition method' in the Exposure Draft of Proposed Amendments to IFRS 3 *Business Combinations†*) by an acquirer to the contingencies of an acquiree. As a result, and as detailed below, the Board proposes eliminating the terms 'contingent asset' and 'contingent liability', and proposes a new analysis of items previously described using those terms. These amendments have also required a reconsideration of the application of the probability recognition criterion in IAS 37.

BC5   The Board believes that these proposals simplify the Standard, because with respect to liabilities they require an entity to determine whether the definition of a liability in

---

*ASB footnote: *The corresponding requirements in the UK and Republic of Ireland are in FRS 12 Provisions, Contingent Liabilities and Contingent Assets. IAS 37 and FRS 12 were developed jointly by the IASB and ASB; their requirements are virtually identical.*

†ASB footnote: *The ASB is proposing to implement IFRS 3* Business Combinations *see FRED 36.*

the *Framework** has been satisfied and, if so, to recognise and measure that liability (unless it cannot be measured reliably). In contrast, IAS 37 has at present three categories of liabilities: (a) possible liabilities, (b) liabilities that are not recognised (because an outflow of economic benefits is not probable or the liability cannot be measured reliably), and (c) liabilities that are recognised (described as provisions).

The amendments to IAS 37 resulting from these proposals are necessarily extensive. **BC6** Therefore, the Board decided to present them in this Exposure Draft, rather than as consequential amendments accompanying the Exposure Draft of Proposed Amendments to IFRS 3 *Business Combinations*.

Contingent assets

A contingent asset is defined in IAS 37 as a 'possible asset'. A contingent asset arises **BC7** when it is uncertain whether an entity has an asset at the balance sheet date, but it is expected that some future event will confirm whether the entity has an asset. For example, the Standard explains that an entity pursuing a claim through legal processes (ie a lawsuit), of which the outcome is uncertain, has a contingent asset. Therefore, the lawsuit is not recognised as an asset until it is 'virtually certain' that it will result in the realisation of income and can then be regarded as an asset rather than a possible asset.

The Board considered this example of a lawsuit in the context of a business com- **BC8** bination. The Board observed that a lawsuit of an acquiree would have a fair value and would affect the price that an acquirer would be required to pay for the acquiree. However, if the lawsuit was regarded as a contingent asset at the date of the business combination (because it was not virtually certain to give rise to income), the acquirer would not recognise it as a separate asset but would subsume its value into goodwill.

The Board noted that in IFRS 3 *Business Combinations* it had concluded that **BC9** goodwill satisfies the definition of an asset. Given this conclusion, the Board questioned the analysis of a lawsuit in IAS 37. The Board reasoned that if goodwill is an asset, any item subsumed within that goodwill (ie any item for which the acquirer paid a price, but which itself does not qualify for recognition separately from goodwill in accordance with IAS 38 *Intangible Assets†*) must itself also satisfy the definition of an asset in the *Framework*. The Board noted that the lawsuit would be a specific item within goodwill, for which the acquirer would be required to pay, and therefore concluded that it must be an asset and not a possible asset.

Therefore, the Board reconsidered the analysis of the lawsuit in IAS 37 and, to do so, **BC10** it turned to tentative decisions it had reached in its Revenue Recognition project, particularly its decisions relating to contractual rights and obligations.

In its Revenue Recognition project, the Board noted that contractual rights and **BC11** obligations can be divided into two types: conditional (ie performance is subject to the occurrence of an event that is not certain to occur) and unconditional (ie nothing other than the passage of time is required to make its performance due). The Board also noted that although unconditional contractual rights and obligations may exist on their own, conditional contractual rights and obligations are accompanied by associated unconditional rights and obligations. The Board tentatively concluded

---

*ASB footnote: *The equivalent document in the UK and Republic of Ireland to the IASB's* Framework *is the ASB's* Statement of Principles for Financial Reporting. *Although the* Statement of Principles *is very similar to the* Framework, *it is not identical.*

†*The ASB is proposing to implement IAS 38* Intangible Assets *see FRED 37.*

that assets and liabilities arising from contracts derive only from *unconditional* (or non-contingent) rights and obligations, and not from conditional (or contingent) rights and obligations. This is because a conditional right to future economic benefits is not a resource controlled by the entity. Similarly, a conditional obligation that may result in an outflow of economic benefits is not a present obligation. However, although a conditional right or obligation in a contract does not itself satisfy the definition of an asset or liability, it points to the existence of an accompanying unconditional right or obligation that may satisfy the definition of an asset or liability.

BC12　This analysis of conditional and unconditional rights and obligations can be illustrated with an example of an entity that has an insurance contract. Some might describe the entity's asset as the possible reimbursement. However, the entity is entitled to reimbursement only if it incurs an insured loss. Therefore, its right to reimbursement is *conditional* (or contingent), because something other than the passage of time is required before the entity can benefit from the reimbursement. Because the right is conditional, it cannot satisfy the definition of an asset in the *Framework*—it is not a *present* right. However, the insurance contract has given the entity another right, one that is similar to an option on shares of a particular entity. The holder of an option on shares does not own the shares, but the right to buy the shares at a stipulated price and date. The insurance contact grants the entity a similar right, namely the right to insurance coverage, and, as with the rights in an option on shares, this right is *unconditional*. It is the unconditional contractual right to insurance coverage that satisfies the definition of an asset.

BC13　The Board noted that this analysis of an insurance contract highlights that determining whether the entity has an asset (ie an unconditional right) is independent of the probability of the occurrence of the contingency (ie incurring an insured loss). Expressed another way, the contingency does not confirm or establish whether there is an asset, rather it affects the value of the future economic benefits embodied in the asset.

BC14　In its Revenue Recognition project, the Board made its tentative decisions about conditional and unconditional rights and obligations in the context of considering *contractual* rights and obligations. Nonetheless, the Board decided that its analysis of the relationship between conditional and unconditional contractual rights could be applied more widely. In particular, it could be used to refine the analysis of items described in IAS 37 as contingent assets. For example, the Board observed that a lawsuit could be analysed into two rights: the entity's conditional right to compensation (ie conditional upon the outcome of the legal process) and its unconditional right to have its claim for recovery of damages caused by the defendant considered by the courts. In other words, although any compensation that the entity might receive as a result of successfully pursuing its claim is a conditional right, the pursuit of the lawsuit satisfies the definition of an asset.

BC15　The Board concluded that the foregoing would be a better analysis of the lawsuit than that provided by IAS 37. This is because by analysing transactions into unconditional and conditional rights, it is possible to identify the underlying asset better. In other words, it facilitates addressing the question of whether the entity controls a resource at the reporting date and, hence, has satisfied the definition of an asset. In contrast, an entity applying IAS 37 considers the possible inflow of economic benefits (ie the conditional right) and applies a 'virtually certain' probability recognition criterion to determine when those possible benefits have given rise to an asset. However, as noted above, a conditional right does not give rise to an asset and, therefore, regardless of the probability of an inflow of benefits, should not be recognised.

The Board considered some other examples of contingent assets. Two examples are an entity that has applied for an operating licence and an entity that is negotiating a significant contract with a customer with whom it has had no prior contractual relationship. In these two examples, the Board concluded that the operating licence and the contract are conditional rights. This is because the rights are conditional (or contingent) on a future event (ie decision of the awarding authority or the customer signing the contract). However, in both cases the entity has an asset. In the case of the licence application, the asset arises from the entity's unconditional right to participate in the process of bidding for the licence. In the case of a pending customer contract, the asset arises from the entity's unconditional right to the economic value of the developing contractual relationship. **BC16**

As a result of analysing items previously described as contingent assets into conditional and unconditional rights, the Board decided to eliminate the term 'contingent asset'. The Board concluded that the term was troublesome and confusing. As already noted, assets arise only from unconditional (ie non-contingent) rights. Hence, an asset, which embodies an unconditional right, cannot be described as contingent or conditional. Furthermore, because conditional or contingent rights do not by themselves give rise to assets, it is inconsistent with the *Framework* to recognise them, even if it is virtually certain that they will become unconditional or non-contingent. Therefore, instead of using the term 'contingent' to refer to uncertainty about whether an asset exists, the Board decided that the term should refer to one or more uncertain future events, the occurrence (or non-occurrence) of which affects the amount of the future economic benefits embodied in an asset. **BC17**

The Board also decided that it would be more logical to include in IAS 38 the discussion about assets with contingencies. This is because such an asset would be a non-monetary asset without physical form. Hence, if it is *identifiable* (ie if it is separable or arises from contractual or other legal rights) it would, by definition, be an intangible asset. The Board acknowledged that if an intangible asset arising from an unconditional right accompanied by a conditional right is within the scope of IAS 38 and has not been acquired in a transaction, the requirements of IAS 38 impose a high recognition threshold. (If acquired in a business combination or otherwise, the intangible asset is recognised at fair value. Therefore, uncertainty about the conditional right is reflected in the measurement of the asset.) However, the Board decided that it was outside the scope of this project to revisit the requirements in IAS 38. **BC18**

Contingent liabilities

The Board then considered contingent liabilities. The Board observed that in contrast to the definition of a contingent asset, the present definition of a contingent liability includes two notions. The first notion, a possible obligation, is symmetrical with the definition of a contingent asset and arises when the existence of a present obligation at the balance sheet date is uncertain, but some future event will confirm whether the entity has that obligation. The second notion, an unrecognised present obligation, arises when the entity has a present obligation, but that obligation is not recognised as a liability, because either an outflow of economic resources to settle the obligation is not probable or the entity is not able to measure the obligation reliably. **BC19**

Possible obligations

The Board had previously considered such obligations in the context of a business combination. In IFRS 3, it specified that an acquirer should recognise at the **BC20** acquisition date the acquiree's contingent liabilities—and hence its possible obligations—if their fair values could be measured reliably.

BC21   In arriving at this requirement in IFRS 3, the Board took the view that the existence of possible obligations in an acquiree point to the existence of present obligations and, therefore, if their fair value could be measured reliably, the possible obligations should be recognised as liabilities. Furthermore, the Board concluded that it was appropriate that an acquiree's possible obligations should be recognised as liabilities as part of the process of allocating the cost of the business combination, because they have the effect of reducing the price that an acquirer is prepared to pay for the acquiree. In effect, the acquirer is paid to assume an obligation by paying a reduced purchase price for the acquiree.

BC22   In the light of its observations about unconditional and conditional rights and obligations and its conclusions about contingent assets described above, the Board decided that it could refine its conclusions in IFRS 3. It reasoned that its revised analysis of items previously described as contingent assets was also applicable to items previously described as contingent liabilities (possible obligations). The Board also noted that if it refined the analysis of items described as contingent liabilities in IAS 37, there would be no need to specify different requirements for such items in a business combination. Furthermore, all such items would be treated consistently, regardless of whether they are acquired in a business combination or generated internally (subject to the different measurement requirements of IAS 37 and the revised IFRS 3).

BC23   Accordingly, the Board decided to eliminate the term 'contingent liability'. Instead of using 'contingent' to refer to uncertainty about whether a liability exists, the Board decided that the term should refer to one or more uncertain future events, the occurrence (or non-occurrence) of which affects the amount that will be required to settle an obligation.

BC24   These conclusions mean that, for example, an entity that issues a product warranty has a liability arising from its unconditional obligation to provide warranty coverage over the term of the warranty (ie to provide a service). Uncertainty about whether the product will develop a fault, and hence require repair or replacement (ie the contingency), relates to whether the entity's conditional obligation to repair or replace the product if it develops a fault will become unconditional. (The entity's obligation to repair or replace the product is conditional because it depends on whether the product develops a fault.) Hence, the contingency does not determine whether the entity has a liability to provide warranty coverage. Rather, it affects the amount that will be required to settle the obligation. Similarly, in the case of an entity defending a lawsuit, the entity has a liability arising from its unconditional obligation to perform as directed by the courts. The contingency relates to the entity's conditional obligation to pay any penalties imposed by the court and affects the amount that will be required to settle the liability.

BC25   The Board's conclusions about the nature of the unconditional obligation in a warranty contract are consistent with the conclusions of the US Financial Accounting Standards Board (FASB) in Interpretation No. 45 *Guarantor's Accounting and Disclosure Requirements for Guarantees, Including Indirect Guarantees of Indebtedness of Others* (FIN 45), although the recognition and measurement requirements of FIN 45 do not apply to product warranties issued by an entity. FIN 45 describes the unconditional obligation as an 'obligation to stand ready to perform over the [contract] term'. Whilst the notion of an obligation to stand ready is derived from FASB Concepts Statement No. 6 *Elements of Financial Statements*

(Concepts Statement 6), the Board decided to introduce the term into IAS 37 because it regards it as a helpful way of capturing the nature of the liability.

The Board acknowledged that its analysis of unconditional and conditional rights **BC26** and obligations may appear complex and that some constituents may already have regarded some examples of liabilities arising from unconditional obligations accompanied by conditional obligations (eg product warranties) as examples of liabilities. Indeed, the Board noted that many financial liabilities within the scope of IAS 39 *Financial Instruments: Recognition and Measurement** could be analysed as containing both a conditional and unconditional obligation. However, as noted with assets, the objective of analysing transactions into unconditional and conditional obligations is to assist in identifying precisely the liability in existence at the balance sheet date, rather than relying on an assessment of some uncertain future event to determine whether a liability exists at that date. The Board concluded that if the liability is identified and accounted for, there is no need to identify the two obligations. Nonetheless, the Board observed that in practice the conditional obligation is sometimes the more readily identifiable obligation. Thus it can be used as a pointer to any associated unconditional obligation. Furthermore, the Board noted that it can be important to distinguish between the two obligations because, as discussed below, the probability recognition criterion in the *Framework* should be applied to the liability (ie unconditional obligation) rather than to the conditional obligation.

The main difference between the approach in the draft Standard to items previously **BC27** described as contingent liabilities and that in the current version of IFRS 3 is that an entity is required to determine whether it has a present obligation that satisfies the definition of a liability before considering recognition and measurement. Put another way, the draft Standard does not use either recognition or measurement as a means of resolving uncertainty about whether a liability *exists*. As discussed in paragraph BC41 below, this is consistent with the *Framework*. In contrast, in the current version of IFRS 3, the contingent liability itself is recognised, and the measurement of the contingent liability reflects the uncertainty about whether the contingent liability had given rise to a present obligation. Therefore, the approach in the draft Standard places greater emphasis on determining whether the definition of a liability has been satisfied and does not allow recognition of possible liabilities. This is consistent with the overall objective of the second phase of the Business Combinations project in which an acquirer recognises the assets acquired and liabilities assumed at the date control is obtained. The Board also noted that the approach is consistent with recent standards of the FASB on liabilities that have adopted a fair value measurement basis. For example, both Statement No. 143 *Accounting for Asset Retirement Obligations* (SFAS 143) and Statement No. 146 *Accounting for Costs Associated with Exit or Disposal Activities* (SFAS 146) prohibit the recognition of obligations that do not satisfy the definition of a liability in Concepts Statement 6.

However, although the proposed approach is different from that in IFRS 3, the **BC28** Board emphasises that its proposals should not be regarded as a reversal of the requirement in IFRS 3 to recognise contingent liabilities. Rather, they should be viewed as a refinement of that earlier decision. Indeed, the Board observed that in most cases there would be no change in obligations recognised in accordance with the existing and proposed revised versions of IFRS 3. This is because some obligations previously described as contingent liabilities were, in fact, unrecognised *liabilities* and, therefore, will be recognised in a business combination in accordance with the proposed revised IFRS 3. In addition, in many cases, items previously described as possible obligations will be analysed more precisely into two

*ASB footnote: *The corresponding UK and Republic of Ireland requirements are set out in FRS 26 (IAS 39)*
Financial Instruments: Recognition and Measurement.

obligations: an unconditional obligation and a conditional obligation. The effect of recognising the liability resulting from the unconditional obligation at fair value in accordance with the proposed revised IFRS 3 would be similar to recognising the contingent liability at fair value in accordance with the existing version. This is because the measurement of the liability will reflect the uncertainty about the conditional obligation.

BC29   Nonetheless, the Board observed that not all items previously described as contingent liabilities satisfy the definition of a liability in the *Framework*. This is because some such items contain only a conditional (or contingent) obligation and no unconditional obligation. Therefore, an item that might have been recognised in accordance with the current version of IFRS 3 will no longer qualify for recognition in accordance with the draft Standard or revised version of IFRS 3. For example, the Board considered a scenario in which an entity would be required to take back previously sold products for disposal if a new law were passed (in other words, the new law would have a retrospective effect). The Board noted that until the new law is substantively enacted, the entity would have no present unconditional obligation (unless the entity by its own actions created a constructive obligation before the law was enacted). Hence, the entity would have only a conditional obligation to take back products and, therefore, no liability. Expressed another way, the Board concluded that an entity does not have a stand ready obligation with respect to a possible change in the law. This is because it is the new law that creates new obligations and until the law is substantively enacted those obligations do not exist. Accordingly, an entity cannot have a present obligation with respect to that law.

Unrecognised present obligations

BC30   Having decided to eliminate the term 'contingent liability', the Board considered the notion of an unrecognised present obligation in IAS 37, which is also described as a contingent liability. As noted above, liabilities arise only from unconditional obligations. Hence, something that is a present obligation cannot be described as being contingent. The Board also noted that there was no need to define liabilities that fail to qualify for recognition because they can be described as unrecognised liabilities. Therefore, the Board does not propose to define such liabilities. Consistently with the current requirements in IAS 37 for contingent liabilities, liabilities that are not recognised in accordance with the draft Standard are required to be disclosed.

Disclosure of contingent assets and contingent liabilities

BC31   The amendments in the draft Standard relating to contingent assets and contingent liabilities are primarily concerned with correctly identifying the right and obligation (unconditional) and then accounting for that right and obligation. Consistently with those amendments, the Board decided to withdraw the requirement in IAS 37 to disclose contingent assets and contingent liabilities. Therefore, the draft Standard specifies only the disclosures required for liabilities (with or without associated contingencies), whereas assets with contingencies are disclosed in accordance with other Standards.

BC32   The Board noted that some might feel uncomfortable about this proposal, because it suggests that important information previously associated with contingencies, particularly contingent liabilities, will no longer be disclosed in the financial statements. However, with respect to contingent liabilities, the Board believes that in most cases there will be no loss of disclosure. This is because most items described as being contingent liabilities in IAS 37 will now be viewed as liabilities, with the contingency referring to the conditional obligation that affects the measurement of the liability.

Hence, the disclosure required by paragraph 68 for the liability will capture the information previously presented for the contingent liability. In particular, an entity will be required to give an indication of the uncertainties about the amount or timing of the outflow of economic benefits. The Board concluded that those items described as contingent liabilities in IAS 37 that do not contain unconditional obligations are business risks. Hence, discussion about such items would typically be included in any financial review by management accompanying the financial statements. The Board also noted that the effects of such items would often be disclosed in accordance with paragraph 116 of IAS 1 *Presentation of Financial Statements*,* because they may have a significant risk of causing a material adjustment to the carrying amount of assets and liabilities within the next financial year.

Other Standards also require disclosure of contingent assets and contingent liabilities. In the cases of IAS 11 *Construction Contracts,* IAS 12 *Income Taxes* and IAS 18 *Revenue*†, the Board concluded that the disclosure of contingencies was designed to provide information about measurement uncertainty relating to items accounted for in accordance with those Standards. Therefore, the contingencies referred to in those Standards are unaffected by the proposed amendments to IAS 37. For example, IAS 11 explains that contingencies arise from warranty costs, claims and penalties, ie items that are accounted for in IAS 11 as part of contract revenue and contracts costs.   **BC33**

Accordingly, in the consequential amendments the Board proposes replacing the requirement in IASs 11, 12 and 18 to disclose contingent assets and liabilities with a requirement to disclose the key measurement uncertainty relating to construction contracts, income taxes and revenue.   **BC34**

In other Standards, for example IAS 28 *Investments in Associates*‡, the requirement to disclose contingent liabilities is a reminder of the requirement in IAS 37 to disclose (a) liabilities not recognised in accordance with IAS 37 and (b) possible obligations. In these cases, if the item previously described as a contingent liability is determined to be a liability in accordance with the draft Standard, it will be recognised unless it cannot be measured reliably. Therefore, the Board has amended the requirements to require disclosure of the unrecognised liabilities in accordance with IAS 37.   **BC35**

Probability recognition criterion

Having refined its analysis of items previously described as contingent liabilities, the Board concluded that it would need to reconsider the probability recognition criterion in IAS 37.   **BC36**

Paragraph 14(b) of IAS 37 specifies that a provision is recognised 'if it is probable that an outflow of resources embodying economic benefits will be required to settle the obligation', 'probable' being defined as 'more likely than not'. The Board noted that in many cases, an entity does not need to make any assessment of the probability of an outflow because there is little or no uncertainty that settlement of the obligation   **BC37**

*ASB footnote: *IAS* 1 Presentation of Financial Statements *does not have a corresponding UK accounting standard.* The Companies Act 1985 *prescribes the format of UK Financial Statements.*

†ASB footnote: *The corresponding requirements in the UK and Republic of Ireland are set out in SSAP 9* Stocks and Long-term Contracts, *FRS 16* Current Tax, *FRS 19* Deferred Tax *and FRS 5* Reporting the Substance of Transactions - Application Note G: Revenue Recognition.

‡ASB footnote: *The corresponding requirements in the UK and Republic of Ireland are set out in FRS 9* Associates and joint ventures.

will require *some* outflow of resources embodying economic benefits, even if there is significant uncertainty about the amount or timing of the outflow. An example is an entity that has an obligation to decommission a nuclear power station.

BC38   However, the Board noted that in some other cases application of the probability recognition criterion in IAS 37 was more troublesome. For example, in the case of a guarantee, Example 9 in the Standard explains that a guarantor applies the criterion by considering the probability of having to make a payment under the guarantee. This means that if the guarantee is issued in exchange for a fee, and it is not probable that a payment will be required under the guarantee, the guarantor does not recognise a liability. In the absence of the revenue recognition requirements of IAS 18, the entity would recognise a gain. This accounting is counter-intuitive, because an entity that has been paid to assume an obligation would recognise a gain on initial recognition, followed by losses if payments under the guarantee are made.

BC39   The Board acknowledged that in practice many guarantees within the scope of IAS 37 would be recognised because the Standard requires entities to consider recognition by reference to a portfolio (or class) of similar obligations. Thus, although it might not be probable that a payment will arise from a single guarantee, it is probable that *some* payment will arise in a portfolio of guarantees and, therefore, a liability is recognised. However, the Board decided that resolving a troublesome recognition issue in this way (ie by requiring recognition on a portfolio basis) is conceptually unsatisfactory. It would be better if the probability recognition criterion could be applied consistently for single guarantees and portfolios of guarantees.

BC40   Having analysed the obligations in transactions such as guarantees and warranties into conditional and unconditional obligations, the Board observed that the probability recognition criterion in IAS 37 is sometimes applied to the 'wrong' obligation. This is because it is applied to the conditional obligation (ie the contingency) rather than the unconditional obligation (ie the contractual stand ready service obligation). For example, in the case of a guarantee, it is applied to the guarantor's conditional obligation to make a payment under the guarantee. Similarly, in the example of a product warranty (Example 1 in the Standard), the criterion is applied to the entity's conditional obligation to repair or replace the product.

BC41   The Board concluded that applying the probability recognition criterion to the conditional obligation conflicted with the *Framework*. This is because paragraph 82 of the *Framework* describes recognition as 'the process of incorporating in the balance sheet or income statement an item *that meets the definition of an element*' (emphasis added). In other words, the *Framework* requires an entity to determine whether a liability exists before considering whether that liability should be recognised. As explained in paragraph BC24, in the case of a guarantee or a product warranty, the liability that is being considered for recognition is the unconditional obligation to stand ready to provide a service over the period of the guarantee or the product warranty. It is not the conditional obligation to make a payment under the guarantee or to repair or replace the product. Hence, the question is whether settlement of the present obligation (ie the unconditional obligation) to provide a service will probably result in an outflow of economic benefits, and not whether the conditional obligation to make a payment or to repair the product will probably result in an outflow of resources.

BC42   The *Framework* articulates the probability recognition criterion in terms of a flow of economic benefits. It also explains that the outflow required to settle a liability can occur in various ways. In particular, it explains that the outflow of resources can be the provision of services. The Board reasoned that because an entity that issues a guarantee or a product warranty has an obligation to provide a service—because it is contractually obliged to honour claims—the outflow of resources that is required to settle this obligation should be regarded as the provision of services over the term of the contract, and not the possible payments under the guarantee or product warranty.

Viewing the outflow of resources as the provision of services means that an entity **BC43** that issues a guarantee or a product warranty satisfies the probability recognition criterion by definition. This is because it is certain that the stand ready obligation would require an outflow of resources in settlement. The assessment of the probability of an outflow of resources is independent of the likelihood of a claim arising under the guarantee or product warranty. In other words, even if it is highly unlikely that a claim will arise, the probability recognition criterion is still satisfied. As noted above, the probability of a claim arising relates to the likelihood of the *conditional* obligation becoming a present obligation. Accordingly, the Board concluded that the probability of a payment or claim arising under a guarantee or warranty should not determine whether the entity's *present* obligation to provide a service should be recognised. Rather, the likelihood of claims arising should be reflected in the measurement of that present obligation.

The Board's conclusions about the application of the probability recognition criterion in the case of warranties and guarantees are consistent with FIN 45. This Interpretation explains that a guarantor has incurred a liability on issuing a guarantee that qualifies for recognition, even if it is not probable that the specified triggering events or conditions that would cause payments under the guarantee will occur. The FASB concluded that the outflow of resources associated with the unconditional obligation to stand ready to perform over the term of the guarantee is the requirement to 'stand ready to provide services' and not the possible payments required under the guarantee. **BC44**

The Board observed that its analysis of the application of the probability recognition **BC45** criterion to a guarantee or product warranty could be extended to any liability arising from an unconditional contractual obligation accompanied by a conditional obligation. This is because such liabilities arise from the contractual obligation to stand ready to provide a service. For example, an entity that is jointly and severally liable with another entity, but expects that other entity to be responsible for the obligation, is providing a service to the counterparty because the counterparty has the right to look to the entity to honour the obligation (ie the entity is standing ready to honour the obligation). Similarly, a retailer that is obliged, contractually or constructively, to offer refunds to dissatisfied customers is providing a service to its customers because those customers have a right to return their products (ie the retailer is standing ready to accept returns).

The Board then considered liabilities that accompany non-contractual contingent **BC46** liabilities. As noted above, the Board decided that the relationship between conditional and unconditional contractual obligations could be extended to non-contractual obligations. For example, in the case of a lawsuit, the Board observed that although the penalties that a defending entity might be required to pay are a conditional obligation, the entity has no discretion to do otherwise than perform as directed by the court. Therefore, the Board concluded that the entity also has a present (ie unconditional) legal obligation, namely an obligation to stand ready to pay any penalties awarded by the court. Because the outflow of resources is the standing ready (ie the provision of a service), rather than the possible damages, the Board concluded that the probability recognition criterion is satisfied. It is certain that the entity is obliged to accept any obligation imposed by the court. In effect, the court's ability to impose settlement stands in the place of a contract.

BC47   The Board observed that the above conclusions about the application of the probability recognition criterion mean that in practice the criterion would have no effect in determining whether a liability should be recognised, because in all cases in which an unconditional obligation exists the criterion would be satisfied. Therefore, the Board considered whether it should retain the probability recognition criterion in the Standard. The Board noted that the criterion might be misapplied in some situations. In particular, it might be applied to the entity's conditional obligation rather than to its present obligation, in cases in which an entity has two obligations, with the result that liabilities are not recognised. The Board also noted that there is anecdotal evidence to suggest that some use the criterion to determine whether they have incurred a liability, instead of determining whether the definition of a liability has been satisfied. This could result in an entity that has a conditional obligation with a very high probability of an outflow of economic benefits concluding that it should recognise a liability. However, if the definition of a liability is not satisfied (in particular, if there is no present obligation), the entity should not recognise a liability. Similarly, relying on the probability recognition criterion to determine whether a constructive obligation exists could result in the recognition of items that are not liabilities. This is because in some cases an entity may conclude that there will probably be an outflow of economic benefits, even though it has no *obligation* to incur that outflow. Lastly, the Board noted that it would add unnecessary complexity to the Standard to specify a criterion that is always satisfied. Therefore, the Board decided to omit the criterion from the draft Standard.

BC48   The Board acknowledged that the criterion is derived from the *Framework* and, therefore, not including the criterion in the Standard might give the impression of inconsistency with the *Framework*. Indeed, the Board was aware that many of its constituents regard some of its recent Standards as inconsistent with the *Framework* because they do not contain a probability recognition criterion. However, the Board concluded that there would be no inconsistency. The apparent inconsistency arises only if the conditional or contingent obligation is being considered rather than the unconditional obligation. Having refined the analysis of liabilities in IAS 37 to focus on the unconditional obligation, the Board concluded that it was inevitable that the current interpretation of the probability recognition criterion in IAS 37 would need to be reconsidered. Nonetheless, the revised interpretation is consistent with the *Framework*. Furthermore, it results in consistent recognition of contractual obligations in accordance with IAS 37 and IAS 39, because the probability recognition criterion in the *Framework* is being applied in the same way in both Standards. For example, in considering the recognition of an option in accordance with IAS 39, an entity does not consider whether it is probable that the option will be exercised. Rather, the probability recognition criterion is applied to the unconditional obligation.

AMENDMENTS ARISING FROM SHORT-TERM CONVERGENCE PROJECT

BC49   In September 2002 the Board decided to add a Short-term Convergence project to its active agenda. The objective of the project is to reduce differences between IFRSs and US generally accepted accounting principles (US GAAP) that are capable of resolution in a relatively short time and can be addressed outside current and planned major projects. The project is a joint project with the FASB.

BC50   In working towards the objective of the project, the two boards agreed to review each other's deliberations on each of the selected possible convergence topics and choose the higher quality solution as the basis for convergence. For topics recently considered by either board, there is an expectation that whichever board had more recently deliberated that topic would have the higher quality solution.

As part of the review of topics recently considered by the FASB, the Board considered the requirements of SFAS 146, which was issued in June 2002.   **BC51**

SFAS 146 nullifies EITF Issue No. 94-3 *Liability Recognition for Certain Employee*   **BC52**
Termination Benefits and Other Costs to Exit an Activity (including Certain Costs Incurred in a Restructuring) (Issue 94-3). Because Issue 94-3 contained recognition guidance similar to that in IAS 37, the Board noted that the introduction of SFAS 146 would lead to differences in the timing of recognition of liabilities for restructuring costs (a point acknowledged by the FASB in its Basis for Conclusions on SFAS 146). In particular, the Board observed that liabilities for the same restructuring costs would, in many cases, be recognised at an earlier point under IFRSs than under US GAAP (perhaps significantly so). Furthermore, the Board was concerned that the present guidance for the recognition of restructuring provisions in IAS 37 (paragraphs 70-83) could result in the recognition of items that do not satisfy the definition of a liability in the *Framework*.

The Board concluded that converging with the recognition requirements of   **BC53**
SFAS 146 would allow the accounting for similar events and circumstances to be the same, thereby improving the comparability and representational faithfulness of financial information. As a result (and as discussed in detail below), the Board proposes:

(a) amending the definition of a constructive obligation and providing additional guidance to assist in determining whether such an obligation exists;
(b) adding an additional recognition criterion for some liabilities for onerous contracts; and
(c) substantially revising the requirements for liabilities for costs associated with a restructuring.

Definition of constructive obligation

The Board noted that the principle underlying SFAS 146 is that a liability for a cost   **BC54**
associated with an exit or disposal activity (which includes, but is not limited to, a restructuring as defined by IAS 37) is recognised when incurred, ie when the entity has a present obligation. This is similar to the principle in IAS 37 that a provision is recognised when the entity has a present obligation. Nevertheless, in the context of a restructuring, the Board noted that the two standards specify different interpretations of when that present obligation arises. The Board observed that this difference in interpretation arises because the restructuring guidance in IAS 37 is an application of the Standard's notion of a constructive obligation, a notion that is differently understood under US GAAP.

The Board noted that both the *Framework* and Concepts Statement 6 provide gen-   **BC55**
eral descriptions of constructive obligations. However, it noted that there is no equivalent in US GAAP of IAS 37's definition of a constructive obligation. Indeed, the Board noted that some regard Concepts Statement 6 as suggesting that not all constructive obligations are liabilities.

The Board observed that paragraph 40 of Concepts Statement 6 states that although   **BC56**
constructive obligations 'lack the legal sanction that characterizes most liabilities', they are 'commonly paid in the same way as legally binding contracts.' In other words, the entity is bound by its obligation to a counterparty (although the FASB acknowledged the difficulty of determining whether an entity is bound by its

obligation in the absence of legal enforceability). The Board also considered the three essential characteristics of a liability identified by Concepts Statement 6 and referred to in the Bases for Conclusions on SFAS 143 and SFAS 146. The Board noted that, as with the definition of a constructive obligation in IAS 37, those Statements highlight that a promise, and hence an obligation, can be 'inferred from the entity's past practice, which, absent evidence to the contrary, others can presume that the entity will continue'.* However, the Board noted that for that promise to create an obligation, other parties must be justified in relying on that promise. The Board observed that in both Bases for Conclusions, the FASB gave specific guidance about when a counterparty is justified in relying on the entity's promise, namely that (a) the counterparty must be the recipient of the promise; (b) the counterparty must reasonably expect the entity to perform; and (c) the counterparty will either benefit from the entity's performance or suffer loss or harm from non-performance.

BC57   Having considered the FASB's deliberations, the Board concluded that the threshold for determining whether an entity's past actions have created a constructive obligation is higher in US GAAP than in IAS 37. This is because, in US GAAP, the other parties must be able to rely on the entity's carrying out its promise, whereas in IAS 37 other parties must have a valid expectation that the entity will discharge its responsibilities. Although the notions are similar, the Board concluded that they have different emphases. Furthermore, the Board was concerned that the present definition in IAS 37 could be interpreted to allow recognition of items that lack an essential characteristic of a liability, namely the existence of an *obligation* to others.

BC58   The Board noted that SFAS 143 requires judgement about whether others are justified in relying on the entity to perform as promised to be made using the doctrine of 'promissory estoppel'. This is a legal principle that protects a counterparty's reliance on a promise by enforcing promises that are not supported by consideration and oral promises that ordinarily would be required to be in writing. Accordingly, a constructive obligation is recognised in accordance with SFAS 143 only if that obligation is a legal obligation and could be enforced by a court.

BC59   The Board considered whether it should similarly limit recognition of constructive obligations in IAS 37 to those that a court would enforce. In other words, it considered whether to specify that an entity has incurred a liability only if there is a counterparty that could legally enforce the obligation and require the entity to carry out its promise. The Board concluded that it would be premature to make such an amendment in advance of reconsidering liabilities more generally. Nevertheless, the Board concluded that it could emphasise that a constructive obligation involves an *obligation* to others (and hence is not something that an entity can avoid at whim) by introducing into its definition the notion that the counterparty should be reasonably able to rely on the entity to discharge its responsibilities.

BC60   The Board observed that its proposed amendment should not alter existing practice for well-understood examples of constructive obligations (for example, some environmental clean-up obligations and warranty obligations) because in these cases there is usually a counterparty that is relying on the entity to discharge its responsibilities. However, items that were previously determined to be constructive obligations, but leave the entity discretion to avoid settling the item, will no longer be recognised as liabilities.

*Paragraphs B25b and B19a of SFAS 143 and SFAS 146 respectively.

Recognition of liabilities for onerous contracts

The Board noted that in US GAAP there are no general requirements for onerous contracts similar to those in IAS 37. However, the Board noted that SFAS 146 provides specific guidance for two classes of contract termination costs that under IFRSs would be likely to be classified as onerous contracts: (a) costs that arise from terminating a contract before the end of its term and (b) costs that will continue to be incurred under a contract for its remaining term without equivalent economic benefit to the entity (for example, an operating lease of a vacant property). The liability for the former is recognised only when the decision to terminate the contract has been communicated to the counterparty and the entity has incurred a legal obligation under the contract for the penalty or other costs specified by the contract. The liability for the latter is recognised when the entity ceases to use the right conveyed by the contract. **BC61**

The Board noted that in SFAS 146 the FASB has moved away from an intention-based approach for the recognition of contract termination costs. In contrast, the Board noted that the present requirements in IAS 37 would be likely to result in entities recognising liabilities for these onerous contracts on the basis of a commitment, or an intention, to restructure. This is because IAS 37 requires a liability for an onerous contract to be recognised when the contract is onerous, ie at the point when the 'unavoidable costs of meeting the obligations under the contract exceed the economic benefits expected to be received under it'. It noted that this recognition point depends on the entity's expectation of future benefits and would inevitably be open to differing interpretations. **BC62**

The Board noted that questions relating to the timing of recognition of a liability for an onerous contract arise because, in some cases, there is no new obligating event that results in the entity incurring a present obligation. For example, in the case of an operating lease that satisfies the definition of an onerous contract, the entity's present obligation was, in fact, incurred when the entity entered into the lease. The entity has incurred no new obligation as a result of the contract becoming onerous. The requirements relating to onerous contracts effectively compensate for the fact that the rights and obligations under executory contracts and operating leases are not recognised under current accounting conventions. Indeed, in the example of an operating lease, the Board noted that the expense on recognising a liability for an onerous contract is similar to an impairment (ie of the unrecognised asset arising under the lease contract). **BC63**

The Board concluded that reconsidering the requirements for onerous contracts more generally was outside the scope of this project. The Board also noted that it had two projects on its active and research agendas (Revenue Recognition and Leases, respectively) that could affect the present accounting for leases and executory contracts and, as a consequence, also affect the requirements relating to onerous contracts. Nevertheless, it acknowledged that the present requirements might result in items being recognised as liabilities on the basis of management intent, which would be contrary to the principle of SFAS 146 that the Board was seeking to adopt. Because the Board does not believe that there is a conceptual basis for differentiating onerous contracts that arise within a restructuring plan from those that arise outside such a plan, the Board concluded that it should make a limited amendment to the requirements for onerous contracts generally so as to converge with the specific requirements in SFAS 146 relating to contract termination costs. **BC64**

The Board noted that onerous contracts can be divided into two broad categories: those that become onerous because of factors outside the entity's control (for example, a take-or-pay contract in which the market price of the contracted product **BC65** declines below the contracted price for that product) and those that become onerous because of the entity's own actions (for example, as a result of vacating a property). Therefore, the Board decided to adopt the recognition requirements of SFAS 146 by specifying that if a contract will become onerous as a result of the entity's own actions, the liability should not be recognised until the entity has taken that action. The Board believes that until the entity has undertaken the action that makes the contract onerous (for example, has exercised its option to terminate the contract or has ceased using the leased asset), the entity has the discretion to change its intended action.

Sublease income

BC66   The Board noted that in SFAS 146, if an entity ceases to use the right conveyed by an operating lease, but does not terminate the lease, the liability is based on the remaining lease rentals, reduced by the estimated sublease rentals that could be reasonably obtained for the property, regardless of whether the entity intends to enter into a sublease. The Board decided that it should provide the same guidance on this point in IAS 37 because it was informed that in practice there is uncertainty surrounding the treatment of sublease income.

BC67   The FASB's requirement is founded upon its fair value measurement objective, because it takes account of the sublease rentals the market would expect the entity to realise. Although the measurement objective of IAS 37 is not specifically fair value, the Board noted that the SFAS 146 requirement is not inconsistent with IAS 37's measurement requirements. This is because a third party would factor market sub-lease rentals into its measure of the amount it would expect to be paid to relieve the entity of its obligation. The Board also noted that if it specified that the sublease rentals should be those that the entity expects to receive, significant changes in the liability might be recognised subsequently as the entity revises its decision to sublease.

Liabilities for restructuring costs

BC68   The Board observed that the FASB concluded in SFAS 146 that because a restructuring plan merely reflects an entity's intended actions it does not, by itself, create a present obligation and is not the requisite past transaction or event for recognition of a liability. Under IAS 37, a restructuring plan by itself similarly does not give rise to a present obligation. However, in the light of the FASB's decision, the Board considered whether a plan together with its announcement gives rise to a liability by imposing on the entity a constructive obligation to restructure. It noted the guidance in paragraph 17 of IAS 37 that an obligating event requires the entity to have 'no realistic alternative to settling the obligation' and, therefore, considered whether a restructuring plan and its announcement leave the entity in that position. The Board reasoned that, even if an entity has announced its restructuring plan in a general way, it has no *obligation* to others and is not bound by its plan to the extent that it cannot avoid an outflow of resources. The Board decided that because an entity can recall its restructuring plan once it has been announced, the restructuring guidance in the present version of IAS 37 is a misapplication of the Standard's notion of a constructive obligation.

BC69   Accordingly, the Board decided to withdraw the present guidance for the recognition of restructuring provisions in IAS 37 and state that liabilities arising from costs associated with a restructuring should be recognised on the same basis as if that cost arose independently of a restructuring, namely when the entity incurs a liability that can be measured reliably. Thus, instead of an entity recognising at a specified point a single liability for all of the costs associated with a restructuring, it will recognise liabilities for each cost associated with the restructuring as the liability for each cost is incurred.

The Board also decided that it should follow the example of SFAS 146 and provide specific guidance for applying the definition of a liability to the following costs that are often associated with a restructuring: **BC70**

(a)   termination benefits
(b)   contract termination costs.

Termination benefits

SFAS 146 specifies the accounting treatment for one-time termination benefits. Concurrently with these proposed amendments to IAS 37, the Board is proposing amendments to the accounting for termination benefits contained in IAS 19 *Employee Benefits*. The purpose of those amendments is also to converge with SFAS 146 (although the Board proposes that the principles underlying SFAS 146 should apply to all termination benefits, not just those that are within the scope of SFAS 146). **BC71**

Contract termination costs

The Board noted that if an entity terminates a contract before the end of its term, that contract could become onerous (if not previously determined to be onerous). Similarly, if an entity continues to incur costs under a contract for its remaining term without receiving equivalent economic benefit, that contract would become onerous. Therefore, the Board concluded that it should specify that an entity should apply the requirements relating to onerous contracts in paragraphs 55-59 of the draft Standard for contract termination costs. The Board believes that, having amended the requirements for onerous contracts as described above, it has largely achieved convergence with US GAAP on the accounting for these costs. **BC72**

Provision for the sale of an operation

In amending the present guidance for the recognition of restructuring provisions, the Board deleted former paragraph 78, which specified that no obligation arises for the sale of an operation until the entity is committed to the sale. The Board noted that if an entity plans to sell an operation and expects to incur a loss, it should consider recognising   an **BC73**

impairment loss in accordance with either IAS 36 *Impairment of Assets** or IFRS 5 *Non-current Assets Held for Sale and Discontinued Operations*.

OTHER AMENDMENTS

Scope of IAS 37

IAS 37 defines a provision as 'a liability of uncertain timing or amount'. Therefore, provisions are a subset of liabilities as defined in the *Framework*. However, the Board noted that the Standard contains no clear conceptual rationale for distinguishing a provision from a liability. Because of this, the Board was concerned that a liability that was not within the scope of another Standard might be excluded from the scope **BC74**

*ASB footnote: *The ASB is proposing to implement IAS 36* Impairment of Assets, *see FRED 38.*

of IAS 37 on the basis that there is little uncertainty about the timing or amount of the obligation.

BC75   The Board decided that the recognition and measurement requirements of IAS 37 would be appropriate for all non-financial liabilities not within the scope of other Standards. In arriving at this conclusion, the Board noted that for an obligation that an entity is paid to assume, IAS 37 requires revenue to be recognised in accordance with IAS 18. This results in the obligation being measured at the higher of (a) the amount specified by IAS 37 and (b) the amount of revenue deferred in accordance with IAS 18. Nonetheless, the Board was concerned that in some cases the cost of providing the disclosures currently required by paragraphs 84 and 85 of IAS 37 might exceed the benefits of providing those disclosures. Therefore, it decided to limit the more extensive disclosure requirements of those paragraphs to liabilities with material estimation uncertainty. Having addressed this point, the Board concluded that, apart from specified exceptions, it could clarify that IAS 37 applies to all non-financial liabilities that are not within the scope of other Standards. It reasoned that the best way of achieving this would be to stop using a special term to define the liabilities within the scope of IAS 37. Thus, the Board proposes not to use 'provision' as a defined term. In its place, the Board proposes describing liabilities within the scope of IAS 37 as 'non-financial liabilities'. The Board is using the phrase 'non-financial' to make a clear distinction between liabilities within the scope of IAS 39 and those within the scope of IAS 37.

BC76   The Board acknowledged that in some jurisdictions, the term 'provision' is well understood to mean a particular subset of liabilities and, therefore, that the decision not to use the term in the draft Standard may cause concern. However, IFRSs do not specify how items should be described in financial statements and, thus, entities may continue to describe some liabilities as provisions in their financial statements. But the Board also understood that in some other jurisdictions the term 'provision' causes confusion. This is either because there is no clear distinction between a liability and a provision, or because 'provision' is used in that jurisdiction to describe an item that would not necessarily satisfy the definition of a liability. In at least one jurisdiction, 'provision' refers to an item in the income statement rather than in the balance sheet; in others it refers to asset valuation allowances.

Measurement

BC77   The Board observed that the FASB has adopted a fair value measurement objective on initial recognition of a liability in some of its recent Statements (including SFAS 146). This is because the FASB believes fair value is the most relevant and faithful representation of the underlying economics of a transaction. IAS 37, on the other hand, requires provisions to be measured at the best estimate of the expenditure required to settle the present obligation or to transfer it to a third party on the balance sheet date.

BC78   The IAS 37 requirement can be interpreted as being similar to fair value, but the Board acknowledges that the requirement leaves some issues unresolved. The Board concluded that it would be inappropriate to make fundamental changes to the measurement objective of the Standard in this project given the Board's more far-reaching project on the conceptual framework. Nonetheless, the Board noted that it would be awkward to apply some of the present measurement requirements to stand ready obligations (ie unconditional obligations accompanied by conditional obligations). In addition, the Board was concerned that the measurement requirements are not always consistent and can be interpreted in different ways. Therefore, the Board proposes some amendments to these requirements.

Amount that an entity would rationally pay to settle or transfer the obligation

The Board concluded that the present explanation of best estimate in paragraph 37 of IAS 37 as 'the amount that an entity would rationally pay to settle the obligation at the balance sheet date or to transfer it to a third party at that time' should be the measurement objective of the Standard. The Board believes that this phrase sets out a clearer principle for measuring liabilities and is less likely to be misinterpreted than the notion of 'best estimate'.   **BC79**

Use of expected cash flow estimation technique

The Board noted that in some cases, a stand ready service obligation might be separately priced, for example, in the case of some product warranties. However, the Board noted that in many cases there would be no directly observable market price for such obligations, for example in the case of a disputed lawsuit or a warranty included in the price of a product. The Board noted that in such cases an entity would need to use a surrogate for measuring the service obligation. The Board noted that the amount an entity would expect to pay to settle the service obligation (ie stand ready obligation) would reflect the likelihood, amount and timing of the expected cash flows attaching to the conditional obligation. Thus, the most appropriate way to measure such an obligation is to use an expected cash flow approach.   **BC80**

However, IAS 37 suggests that using an expected cash flow approach is most appropriate for a large population of items. In contrast, it specifies that 'the individual most likely outcome may be the best estimate of a single obligation. Hence, if an entity has a 60 per cent chance of losing a court case at a cost of CU1 million and a 40 per cent of winning at no cost, the Standard could be interpreted to require the liability to be measured at CU1 million. The Board, however, observed that measuring a liability at the 'most likely outcome' conflicts with the principle of measuring liabilities at the 'amount that an entity would rationally pay to settle the obligation ... or to transfer it to a third party'. The Board reasoned that if management concluded that there was a chance of settlement at no cost, it would not settle the obligation for the maximum amount that might be required. Rather, management would take into consideration the expected value of the potential outcomes. The Board also noted that measuring a liability at its most likely outcome fails to reflect the uncertainty inherent in the obligation. This can therefore result in two obligations with different risks and uncertainties being measured at the same amount.   **BC81**

Accordingly, the Board decided to emphasise that an expected cash flow approach, which is currently cited as an estimation method that can be used as a basis for measuring liabilities for a large population of items, is also appropriate for single obligations.   **BC82**

Discount rate

The Board noted that in practice, before IFRIC 1 *Changes in Existing Decommissioning, Restoration and Similar Liabilities* was issued, there was some confusion about whether IAS 37 required a current discount rate to be used both on initial recognition and on subsequent measurement. Therefore, in the draft Standard, the Board decided to clarify that when discounting is used, the rate is a current rate at each balance sheet date. The Board acknowledges that in relation to subsequent measurement of a liability this is different from SFAS 143 and SFAS 146. However, the Board believes that the use of a current rate is both more representationally faithful and consistent with the existing requirements of IAS 37.   **BC83**

Future events

BC84   IAS 37 currently specifies that future amounts should be reflected in the measurement of a liability if there is sufficient objective evidence that they will occur. Therefore, for example, in measuring an obligation to clean up environmental contamination, an entity should not anticipate the development of a completely new technology for cleaning up unless that technology is supported by sufficient objective evidence. However, it would be appropriate for the entity to reflect the expected benefits of the effects of increased experience in applying existing technology.

BC85   The Board noted that this requirement conflicts with measuring obligations using an expected cash flow approach. For example, an entity that is measuring a product warranty obligation with no observable market price would consider the likelihood that claims will occur, and the amount and timing of the cash flows that will be required to meet those claims. Read literally, IAS 37 suggests that the likelihood of future claims arising would be reflected in the measurement of a liability only if there is sufficient objective evidence that they would occur. Accordingly, some (possibly all) of the cash flow scenarios that should be considered in measuring the liability might be inappropriately disregarded.

BC86   The Board reasoned that if an expected cash flow approach is used appropriately, there is no reason why an entity should not use assumptions about future events that affect the amount required to settle an obligation, regardless of whether there is 'objective evidence' about those events occurring. This is because in an expected cash flow calculation, the likelihood of those events occurring will be reflected in the probability weighting applied to the cash flows. Thus, for example, an entity measuring a clean-up obligation should make assumptions about future changes in technology, as long as the probability weighting applied to those assumptions appropriately reflects the likelihood that the change in technology will occur.

BC87   Therefore, the Board decided to withdraw the requirement for future events that affect the amount that will be required to settle the obligation to be included in the measurement of that obligation only if there is sufficient objective evidence that they will occur. Although some may be concerned that this could result in unrealistic assumptions being used in the measurement of a liability, the Board noted that the measurement requirement in IAS 37 encompasses a settlement notion. This enforces discipline in measuring a liability because an entity is required to consider what a counterparty would demand to assume the liability.

BC88   The Board also decided to amend former paragraph 50 to specify that the effect of possible new legislation should not be reflected in the measurement of a liability. The Board reasoned that if, as discussed in paragraph BC29, there is no obligation until the law is substantively enacted (ie until the new law exists), it would be inconsistent to measure an *existing* obligation taking into account a possible change in the law. Accordingly, an entity that has an existing legal obligation to clean up contamination in a country in which the government is considering amending the law and requiring a higher standard of clean-up, should treat the change in the law as changing the nature of the underlying obligation. Therefore, it gives rise to a new obligation rather than changing the amount required to settle the existing obligation.

Reimbursements

BC89   IAS 37 specifies that if some or all of the expenditure required to settle a provision is to be reimbursed by another party, the reimbursement is not recognised unless it is 'virtually certain' that the reimbursement will be received.

The Board observed that most reimbursements arise from insurance contracts, **BC90** indemnity clauses or suppliers' warranties. Therefore, the Board observed that in such examples an entity has a conditional right and an unconditional right that satisfies the definition of an asset. That is to say, the reimbursement itself is a conditional right, but the insurance contract, indemnity clause or supplier's warranty establishes an unconditional right for the entity that satisfies the definition of an asset. Consistently with its conclusions relating to contingent assets, the Board decided that it should amend the requirements relating to reimbursements to explain that the reimbursement asset an entity should recognise is the *right* to reimbursement, and not the reimbursement, because this is the unconditional right that the entity controls.

The Board concluded that the right to reimbursement should be recognised following **BC91** the recognition criteria in the *Framework*, ie if it is probable that any future economic benefits associated with the asset will flow to the entity and the item has a value that can be measured reliably. The Board noted that the probability recognition criterion should be applied to the asset (ie unconditional right) and not the reimbursement (ie conditional right). This means that if an entity has a *right* to reimbursement, the probability recognition criterion would always be satisfied because the economic benefits embodied in the unconditional right are a certainty—there is no uncertainty that the entity has a right to look to another entity for reimbursement. The uncertainty relates to the amount of economic benefits that will flow from the conditional right. Because of this, and to ensure that entities do not incorrectly apply the probability recognition criterion to the conditional right, the Board concluded that it should specify as a recognition criterion only reliable measurement. The Board's view is that if the entity has recognised a non-financial liability and has an unconditional right to reimbursement, that right to reimbursement warrants recognition as an asset.

TRANSITION

IAS 8 *Accounting Policies, Changes in Accounting Estimates and Errors** requires a **BC92** change in accounting policy upon initial application of a Standard to be applied retrospectively (ie to all periods presented). However, the Board noted that unless it set the effective date two or three years after issuing the revised IAS 37, an existing user of IFRSs would, in many instances, find it impracticable to apply the amendments retrospectively. This is because the Board believes that the most significant effect of the proposals in the Exposure Draft is to require entities to recognise, as non-financial liabilities, items that were not previously recognised (and, in some cases, not considered to be liabilities). Thus, until the proposals are confirmed in a final Standard, entities would have had no reason to collect the necessary information to measure these items. Hence, requiring entities to recognise and measure such items as at dates before the final Standard is issued would, in many cases, require the inappropriate use of hindsight.

When it is impracticable to apply a new accounting policy retrospectively, paragraph **BC93** 24 of IAS 8 requires an entity to apply the new policy to the carrying amount of assets and liabilities as at the beginning of the earliest period for which retrospective application is practicable, which may be the current period. The Board concluded that the earliest period for which it would be practicable to apply the revised IAS 37 would be periods beginning on or after the date the revised Standard is issued (expected to be in 2006). Because of this, and because the Board proposes the same

*ASB footnote: The corresponding UK and Republic of Ireland requirements can be found in FRS 18 Accounting Policies.

effective date for the revised IAS 37 as for the revised IFRS 3 which it accompanies (ie 1 January 2007), the Board proposes to prohibit entities from applying the revised IAS 37 for accounting periods beginning before the date it is issued and from restating comparative information.

BC94   The Board noted that a similar question about impracticability would arise for any first-time adopter of IFRSs with a date of transition to IFRSs before the date the revised IAS 37 is issued. This is because, in the absence of any specific exemption in IFRS 1 *First-time Adoption of International Financial Reporting Standards*, a first-time adopter applies the IFRSs effective at its reporting date for its first IFRS financial statements. So, for example, a first-time adopter that has a first IFRS reporting period ending on 31 December 2007 and includes comparative information for two years would be required to apply the amended IAS 37 from 1 January 2005. Therefore, the Board decided to propose a new exemption in IFRS 1 that specifies the same transitional requirements for a first-time adopter of IAS 37 as for an existing user of IFRSs.

Alternative View on Proposed Amendments to IAS 37
Provisions, Contingent Liabilities and Contingent Assets

One Board member voted against the publication of the Exposure Draft of Proposed   AV1
Amendments to IAS 37 *Provisions, Contingent Liabilities and Contingent Assets*. The
Board member's alternative view is set out below.

ALTERNATIVE VIEW OF THE BOARD MEMBER

The Board member voted against the publication of the proposals for the following   AV2
reason. The Board member objects to the omission of the probability recognition
criterion (paragraph 14(b) of IAS 37) from proposed paragraph 11.

The Board member acknowledges that the new analysis of items previously described   AV3
as contingent liabilities, requiring unconditional obligations as a condition for
recognition, is more elegant than the previous IAS 37 requirement based on the
probability of cash flows, which failed to distinguish element uncertainty* from
measurement uncertainty.

However, the Board member believes that the new analysis fails to provide adequate   AV4
guidance on when an unconditional obligation should be recognised, and, in particular, what level of element uncertainty would preclude recognition. The Exposure
Draft accepts that such an obligation may be constructive, rather than supported by
a legal contract, and that the identification of a constructive obligation will necessarily require judgement, based on probabilities, a concept previously covered by
paragraph 14(b) (cf 'reasonably expect' in proposed paragraph 15). The point at
which such an obligation arises (and recognition is triggered) will be determined by
an obligating event.

In the absence of a clear definition of the conditions for recognising when an   AV5
unconditional obligation exists, the Board member believes that the implications of
the new approach are unclear. For example, in paragraph BC29 it is asserted that
'until the new law is substantively enacted, the entity would have no present
unconditional obligation (unless the entity by its own actions created a constructive
obligation before the law was enacted) ... and, therefore, no liability'. In these circumstances, it is not clear why the entity's previous actions that made it vulnerable to
the consequences of a possible law change (which the entity has little, if any, discretion to avoid) did not necessarily create an unconditional obligation to bear the
consequences of a change in the law and a liability.

On the other hand, in paragraph BC46 it is asserted that the initiation of a lawsuit   AV6
will create an unconditional obligation and a liability (if not already recognised). It
seems difficult to justify this distinction between a prospective change in statute law
(which may be highly probable) and the judgement of a court (which may be highly
unlikely to lead to an obligation to pay, if the suit is vexatious or trivial), especially in
those countries that have a common law system in which the courts determine the
law.

---

*The Statement of Principles for Financial Reporting *of the Accounting Standards Board in the United
Kingdom explains that element uncertainty arises 'in the case of a potential liability [when] there could be
uncertainty whether the obligation exists and whether that obligation might require the reporting entity to
transfer economic benefits' (paragraph 5.13).*

AV7   The Board member therefore concludes that the probability recognition criterion in paragraph 14(b) should continue to apply to the recognition of an unconditional obligation.

Illustrative Examples

These examples accompany, but are not part of, [draft] IAS 37.

ASB Note: These illustrative examples have been prepared by the IASB.

Contents

All the entities in the examples have 31 December year-ends. In all cases, it is assumed that the non-financial liability can be measured reliably. In some examples, the circumstances described may have resulted in impairment of assets—this aspect is not dealt with in the examples.

EXAMPLE 1: DISPUTED LAWSUIT

After a wedding in 20X0, ten people died, possibly as a result of food poisoning from products sold by the entity. Legal proceedings have been started seeking damages from the entity. However, the entity disputes liability because it does not believe that its food was harmful. Up to the date of authorisation for issue of the financial statements for the year to 31 December 20X0, the entity's lawyers advise that it is unlikely that the entity will be found liable.

Present obligation as a result of a past event – The past event is the start of legal proceedings. Up to this point, the entity was not aware that it had sold harmful food. Even at the time the entity authorises for issue its financial statements, it disputes that it sold harmful food. Nonetheless, the start of legal proceedings obliges the entity to stand ready to perform as the court directs and hence the entity has a present obligation.

Conclusion – A non-financial liability is recognised.

A note about measurement – The objective in measuring the liability is to estimate the amount that the entity would rationally pay to settle or to transfer the obligation *on* the balance sheet date. Even if the entity expects that it will not be found liable, no other party would assume the obligation on the balance sheet date without being compensated by the entity. This is because of the costs involved in defending the lawsuit and the risk of an adverse outcome.

In measuring the liability at 31 December 20X0, the entity considers factors such as:

- the possible outcomes of the lawsuit;
- the cash flows associated with those outcomes (including the costs associated with the lawsuit);
- the timing of the cash flows;
- the probabilities of those outcomes; and
- the risks and uncertainties associated with the obligation (ie the range or variability of the possible outcomes).

The last factor is sometimes referred to as a 'risk adjustment' and it is the amount that a third party would demand for bearing the uncertainty and unforeseeable circumstances inherent in the obligation concerning the amount and timing of any cash flows.

Example 17 gives guidance on the use of an expected cash flow approach, in which multiple cash flow scenarios are weighted by their respective probabilities, as the basis for measuring a liability.

EXAMPLE 2: POTENTIAL LAWSUIT

Shortly before 31 December 20X0, a patient dies in a hospital as a result of a mistake made during an operation. The hospital is aware that a mistake occurred. In these circumstances, the hospital's past experience and lawyers' advice indicate that it is highly likely that the patient's relatives will start legal proceedings and, if the matter comes to court, that the hospital will be found guilty of negligence.

At the time that the financial statements are authorised for issue in early 20X1, the hospital has not received notice of legal proceedings against it.

Present obligation as a result of a past event – The past event is the operation in which negligence occurred.

Conclusion – A non-financial liability is recognised.

A note about measurement – Measurement of the liability reflects the likelihood that the hospital will be required to pay compensation because of the mistake, and the amount and timing of that compensation.

EXAMPLE 3A: CONTAMINATED LAND – LEGISLATION SUBSTANTIVELY ENACTED

An entity in the oil industry causes contamination, but cleans up only when required to do so under the laws of the particular country in which it operates. One country in which it operates previously had no legislation requiring cleaning up, and the entity has been contaminating land in that country for several years. The government, however, is considering introducing new legislation that will require contamination, including prior contamination, to be cleaned up. By 31 December 20X0, the new law is substantively enacted.

Present obligation as a result of a past event – The past event is the substantive enactment of legislation requiring the contaminated land to be cleaned up. Therefore, the entity has a present obligation to clean up its contamination.

Conclusion – A non-financial liability is recognised for the clean-up obligation.

A note about measurement – Measurement of the liability on 31 December 20X0 reflects uncertainty about the timing and amount of the expenditure required to clean up the contamination.

EXAMPLE 3B: CONTAMINATED LAND AND CONSTRUCTIVE OBLIGATION

An entity in the oil industry causes contamination and operates in a country in which there is no environmental legislation. However, the entity has a widely published environmental policy in which it undertakes to clean up all contamination that it causes. The entity has a record of honouring this published policy.

Present obligation as a result of a past event – The past event is the contamination of the land, which gives rise to a present constructive obligation. This is because:

- by publishing its environmental policy the entity has publicly indicated that it will accept the responsibility to clean up its contamination.
- by publishing that policy and honouring it in the past, other parties can reasonably rely on the entity to clean up its contamination.
- other parties will suffer harm if the entity does not clean up its contamination.

Conclusion – A non-financial liability is recognised for the clean-up obligation.

EXAMPLE 4A: EXTENDED PRODUCT WARRANTY

A manufacturer sells extended product warranties to purchasers of its product. Under the terms of the warranty contract the manufacturer undertakes to make good, by repair or replacement, manufacturing defects that become apparent within three years from the date of sale.

Present obligation as a result of a past event – The past event is the sale of the warranty, which gives rise to a present obligation to provide a service for the duration of the warranty (ie to stand ready to honour warranty claims).

Conclusion – A non-financial liability is recognised.

A note about measurement – In the absence of market evidence to determine the amount needed to settle or transfer the warranty obligation on the balance sheet date, the entity considers factors such as:

- the estimated number of claims that will arise from warranties sold on or before the balance sheet date. In estimating the number of claims, the entity may develop a number of different scenarios of possible claims, weighting each by its respective probability.
- the cash flows associated with meeting the estimated number of claims.
- the timing of the cash flows.
- the risks and uncertainties associated with the obligation (ie the range or variability of the possible outcomes).

When an entity issues product warranties in exchange for a fee, revenue is recognised in accordance with ~~IAS 18 *Revenue*~~ FRS 5 *Reporting the Substance of Transactions - Application Note G: Revenue Recognition.*

EXAMPLE 4B: EXTENDED PRODUCT WARRANTY – NO CONSTRUCTIVE OBLIGATION

The facts are the same as Example 4A. However, in addition, in this example the entity frequently repairs or replaces the product if manufacturing defects become apparent in the fourth and fifth year after the date of sale in order to maintain customer goodwill. The entity does not make this practice widely known. In addition, the entity carefully scrutinises any claims it receives in the fourth and fifth year following the date of sale to assess the costs of repairing or replacing the product against the potential damage to customer goodwill.

Present obligation as a result of a past event – There is no constructive obligation at the date of sale to provide warranty coverage in the fourth and fifth years following the date of sale. Although the entity frequently repairs products after the contractual warranty period has expired, the entity has not indicated to its customers that this is its general practice. In addition the entity retains discretion about whether it will meet claims after expiry of the warranty period, and hence customers cannot reasonably rely on the entity to meet such claims.

Conclusion – No liability is recognised for warranty coverage after expiry of the warranty period.

EXAMPLE 5: SINGLE GUARANTEE

On 31 December 20X0 Entity A gives a guarantee of specified borrowings of Entity B, whose financial condition at that time is sound. During 20X1 the financial condition of Entity B deteriorates and at 30 June 20X1 Entity B files for protection from its creditors.

~~*This contract meets the definition of an insurance contract in IFRS 4 *Insurance Contracts*. IFRS 4 permits the issuer to continue its existing accounting policies for~~

ASB footnote: This paragraph has been deleted because IFRS 4 is not a UK adopted IFRS-based standard.

~~insurance contracts if specified minimum requirements are satisfied. IFRS 4 also permits changes in accounting policies that meet specified criteria. The following is an example of an accounting policy that IFRS 4 permits.~~

Present obligation as a result of a past event – The past event is issuing the guarantee. This gives rise to a present obligation to provide a service for the duration of the guarantee (ie to stand ready to repay the borrowing of Entity B).

Conclusion – A liability is recognised.

A note about measurement – The guarantee is initially recognised at fair value. Subsequently, it is measured at the higher of (a) the amount that the entity would rationally pay to settle the obligation or to transfer it to a third party, and (b) the amount initially recognised in accordance with ~~IAS 39~~ FRS 26 *Financial Instruments: Recognition and Measurement* less, when appropriate, cumulative amortisation recognised in accordance with ~~IAS 18~~ FRS 5 Application Note: G.

EXAMPLE 6: OFFSHORE OILFIELD

An entity operates an offshore oilfield. Its licensing agreement for the oilfield requires the entity to remove the oil rig at the end of production and restore the seabed. Ninety per cent of the eventual costs relate to the removal of the oil rig and restoration of damage caused by building it, and 10 per cent arise through the extraction of oil. At the balance sheet date, the rig has been constructed, but no oil has been extracted.

Present obligation as a result of a past event – The construction of the oil rig creates a present obligation under the terms of the licence to remove the rig and restore the seabed. At the balance sheet date, however, there is no obligation to rectify the damage that will be caused by extraction of the oil.

Conclusion – A non-financial liability is recognised for the entity's obligation to remove the oil rig and restore the damage caused by building it.

A note about measurement – The measurement of the liability at the balance sheet date reflects that only 90 per cent of the eventual costs of removing the oil rig and restoring the seabed are attributable to building the oil rig. The obligation to restore the damage that arises through the extraction of oil is recognised as it is incurred, ie when the oil is extracted.

The amount of the liability recognised initially is included in the cost of the oil rig in accordance with ~~IAS 16 *Property, Plant and Equipment*~~ FRS 15 *Tangible Fixed Assets*. Subsequent changes in the measurement of the liability are recognised in accordance with ~~IFRIC 1 *Changes in Existing Decommissioning, Restoration and Similar Liabilities*.~~ this FRS.

EXAMPLE 7: CONTINGENT ASBESTOS REMOVAL OBLIGATION

An entity acquires a factory that contains asbestos. After the acquisition date, new laws come into effect that require the entity to handle and dispose of the asbestos in a special way if the factory undergoes major renovation or is demolished. Otherwise, the entity is not required to remove the asbestos from the factory. The entity has several options to retire the factory in the future including demolishing, selling, or abandoning it.

Present obligation as a result of a past event – Although performance of the removal of the asbestos is conditional on the major renovation or demolition of the factory, enactment of the law creates a present obligation for the entity to remove and dispose of asbestos in a special way. Although the entity may decide to abandon the factory, and thereby defer settlement of the obligation for the foreseeable future, the ability to abandon the factory, and thereby defer settlement, does not relieve the entity of the obligation. The asbestos will eventually need to be removed and disposed of in a special way. In addition, the ability of the entity to sell the factory before disposal of the asbestos does not relieve the entity of its obligation. The sale of the asset would transfer the obligation to another entity and that transfer would affect the selling price.

Conclusion – A non-financial liability for the obligation to remove the asbestos is recognised when the law is enacted.

EXAMPLE 8: JOINT AND SEVERAL LIABILITY

In 20X0, Entity A and Entity B enter into a joint arrangement to extract minerals from land owned by Entity C. As part of the agreement with Entity C, Entity A and Entity B are jointly and severally liable for the obligation to restore Entity C's land at the completion of extraction (expected to be in 20X9). The agreement between Entity A and Entity B specifies that Entity B will restore the land. During 20X5, the financial condition of Entity B deteriorates, raising the possibility that Entity A will be required to restore the land in 20X9.

Present obligation as a result of a past event – The agreement between Entity A and Entity C gives rise to a present obligation for Entity A (ie to stand ready to restore the land). Although Entity B is primarily responsible for restoring the land, Entity C has a right to require Entity A to restore the land because of the joint and several nature of the agreement.

Conclusion – Entity A recognises a non-financial liability.

A note about measurement – In measuring its liability, Entity A reflects the likelihood that it, rather than Entity B, will be required to restore the land. Therefore, the liability may not initially warrant recognition on the basis of materiality. When Entity A recognises a liability, it also considers recognising an asset for its right to reimbursement from Entity B as a result of the agreement specifying that Entity B is responsible for restoring the land.

EXAMPLE 9: REFUNDS POLICY

A retail store has a policy of refunding purchases by dissatisfied customers, even though it is under no legal obligation to do so. Its policy of making refunds is generally known.

Present obligation as a result of a past event – The past event is the sale of the product, which gives rise to a present constructive obligation to stand ready to make refunds to dissatisfied customers. This is because:

- by making its policy of refunding purchases generally known, the entity has publicly indicated that it will refund customers.
- by making its policy generally known, customers can reasonably rely on the entity to refund their purchases.
- customers will suffer harm if the entity does not refund their purchases in accordance with its policy.

Conclusion – A non-financial liability is recognised for the entity's obligation to stand ready to provide refunds.

A note about measurement – Measurement of the liability reflects the likelihood of the entity being required to refund purchases made by customers before the balance sheet date and the timing and amount of those refunds.

Any revenue received from the transaction to which the refund obligation relates is accounted for in accordance with ~~IAS 18~~ FRS 5 Application Note G.

EXAMPLE 10A: NEW LEGISLATION 1

An entity sells electrical products in a country whose government is considering introducing new environmental legislation. If enacted, the legislation would require the entity to take back its products from customers for recycling and disposal. The legislation is expected to be retrospective. Hence, customers are expected to be able to return products for disposal that were sold before enactment of the legislation now being considered.

At the balance sheet date, the legislation has not been substantively enacted.

Present obligation as a result of a past event – At the balance sheet date there is no present obligation (unless the entity by its own actions created a constructive obligation before the law was substantively enacted). Until the law is substantively enacted, the entity does not have a present obligation with respect to that law.

Conclusion – No liability is recognised.

EXAMPLE 10B: NEW LEGISLATION 2

The facts are the same as in example 10A. However, in this example the entity had previously entered into a contract with a counterparty. In accordance with the terms of the contract, the entity is indemnified by the counterparty against the costs of recycling and disposing of its electrical products sold before the date on which it entered into the contract.

Present obligation as a result of a past event – At the balance sheet date, the counterparty has a present obligation as a result of entering into the contract.

Conclusion – The counterparty recognises a liability.

This is an example of an insurance contract, which is outside the scope of ~~IAS 37~~ FRS 12. However, it is included for illustrative purposes.

EXAMPLE 11: CLOSURE OF A DIVISION

On 12 December 20X0 the management of an entity approved a detailed plan for closing a division. The plan requires termination of (a) various contracts and (b) the employment of the division's employees. On 31 December 20X0 the entity issued a press release announcing its decision to close the division.

Before the entity took the decision to close the division, none of the contracts was regarded as onerous.

On 31 January 20X1 the entity gave notice, under the terms of its contracts, to the relevant counterparties to terminate its contracts and on 1 March 20X1 the entity began to terminate the employment of its employees.

(a) At the balance sheet date of 31 December 20X0

Present obligation as a result of a past event – There has been no past event giving rise to a present obligation to restructure. The public announcement of the entity's intention to close the division does not, by itself, create a present obligation.

Conclusion – No liability is recognised.

(b) At 31 January 20X1

Present obligation as a result of a past event – The event that makes the contracts onerous is giving notice to terminate them.

Conclusion – A liability is recognised at 31 January 20X1 for any contract termination costs.

The entity recognises termination benefits in accordance with the requirements of ~~IAS 19 *Employee Benefits.*~~ FRS 17 *Retirement and Termination Benefits.*

EXAMPLE 12: ONEROUS CONTRACT

An entity operates profitably from a factory it leases under an operating lease. During December 20X0 the entity relocates its operations to a new factory. The lease on the old factory continues for the next four years and it cannot be cancelled. Since the lease started, lease rates on commercial buildings in the entity's location have declined.

Present obligation as a result of a past event – The lease contract for the old factory gave rise to a legal obligation. The contract is now onerous because the entity does not expect to receive economic benefits from the factory and the contract gives rise to unavoidable costs (ie the remaining lease rentals reduced by the estimated sublease rentals that could reasonably be obtained for the factory). The past event that makes this lease contract onerous is the entity vacating the old factory.

Conclusion – A liability is recognised.

A note about measurement – Measurement of the liability is by reference to the unavoidable lease payments reduced by the estimated sublease rentals that the entity could reasonably obtain, even if the entity does not intend to enter into a sublease.

EXAMPLE 13: LEGAL REQUIREMENT TO INSTALL SMOKE FILTERS

Under new legislation, an entity is required to install smoke filters in its factories by 30 June 20X1, otherwise it will incur penalties. At 31 December 20X1 the entity has not installed the smoke filters but has continued to operate the factories.

(a) At the balance sheet date of 31 December 20X0

Present obligation as a result of a past event – There is no present obligation because there is no past event either for the costs of installing smoke filters or for penalties under the legislation. This is because (a) the entity has the discretion to avoid installing the smoke filters and (b) at 31 December 20X0 the entity is in compliance with the legislation.

Conclusion – No liability is recognised for the cost of installing the smoke filters.

(b) At the balance sheet date of 31 December 20X1

Present obligation as a result of a past event – There is no obligation for the costs of installing smoke filters because a past event committing the entity to install the filters has not occurred. The entity can stop using the factory and therefore avoid installing the filters. However, the failure to comply with legislation is a past event giving rise to a present obligation, because the entity will be obliged to pay the penalties imposed under the legislation for non-compliant operation of the factory.

Conclusion – No liability is recognised for the costs of installing smoke filters. However, a non-financial liability is recognised for the obligation to pay fines and penalties.

EXAMPLE 14: STAFF RETRAINING AS A RESULT OF CHANGES IN THE INCOME TAX SYSTEM

The government introduces a number of changes to the income tax system. As a result of these changes, an entity in the financial services sector will need to retrain a large proportion of its administrative and sales workforce to ensure continued compliance with financial services regulation. At the balance sheet date, no retraining of staff has taken place.

Present obligation as a result of a past event – There is no obligation because no past event (ie retraining) has taken place. This is because the entity has the discretion to avoid retraining its workforce.

Conclusion – No liability is recognised.

EXAMPLE 15: REPAIRS AND MAINTENANCE

Some items of property, plant and equipment require, in addition to routine maintenance, substantial expenditure every few years for major refits or refurbishment and the replacement of major parts. IAS 16 gives guidance on allocating the amount recognised in respect of an item of property, plant and equipment to its significant parts.

EXAMPLE 15A: REFURBISHMENT COSTS – NO LEGISLATIVE REQUIREMENT

A furnace has a lining that needs to be replaced every five years for technical reasons. At the balance sheet date, the lining has been in use for three years.

Present obligation as a result of a past event – There is no present obligation.

The cost of replacing the lining is not recognised as a liability because, at the balance sheet date, no obligation to replace the lining exists independently of the entity's future actions—even the intention to incur the expenditure depends on the entity deciding to continue operating the furnace or to replace the lining. Instead of a liability being recognised, the depreciation of the lining takes account of its consumption, ie it is depreciated over five years. The costs of replacing the lining then incurred are recognised as a part of the carrying amount of the furnace with the consumption of each new lining shown by depreciation over the subsequent five years.

Conclusion – No liability is recognised.

EXAMPLE 15B: REFURBISHMENT COSTS – LEGISLATIVE REQUIREMENT

An airline is required by law to overhaul its aircraft once every three years as a condition of continuing to operate them.

Present obligation as a result of a past event – There is no present obligation.

The costs of overhauling aircraft are not recognised as a liabiity for the same reasons the cost of replacing the lining is not recognised as a liability in example 15A. Even a legal requirement to overhaul does not make the costs of overhaul a liability, because no obligation exists to overhaul the aircraft independently of the entity's future actions. Instead of a liability being recognised, the depreciation of the aircraft takes account of the future incidence of maintenance costs, ie an amount equivalent to the expected maintenance costs is depreciated over three years.

Conclusion – No liability is recognised.

EXAMPLE 16: SELF-INSURANCE

An entity that operates a chain of retail outlets reviews its insurance arrangements for its liability in respect of accidents sustained by customers. The entity is not required to have public liability insurance coverage and decides to 'self insure', ie to retain the risk of claims from customers.

Present obligation as a result of a past event – There is no present obligation with respect to uninsured accidents that may arise in the future.

Conclusion – No liability is recognised for uninsured accidents that may arise in the future. A liability is recognised only for accidents that have occurred before the balance sheet date. The entity may have to make an estimate of accidents that have occurred but have not yet been reported to it.

EXAMPLE 17: MEASUREMENT OF A DECOMMISSIONING OBLIGATION

The purpose of the example is to illustrate one way in which the requirements in paragraphs 29-42 may be applied.

An entity places an offshore oil rig into service. The entity is required by law to dismantle and remove the rig at the end of its useful life, which is estimated to be 10 years.

The entity estimates a range of cash flows (that include the effects of inflation) needed to dismantle and remove the rig, and assigns probability assessments to the range as follows.

Estimated cash flows and associated probabilities

Cash flow estimate CU	Probability assessment %	Expected cash flows CU
200,000	25	50,000
225,000	50	112,500
275,000	25	68,750
Expected cash flow		231,250

The entity estimates that the cash flows should be increased by 5 per cent to reflect the uncertainties and unforeseeable circumstances inherent in the obligation (for example, the risk that removal of the rig may cost more than expected). This risk adjustment may be determined by considering factors such as the range of variability of the possible outcomes and the amount that a third party would typically demand for bearing the uncertainty and unforeseeable circumstances inherent in 'locking in' today's price for cash flows that are expected to occur in 10 years.

The entity estimates that the discount rate that reflects current market assessments of the time value of money is 6 per cent (risks specific to the liability are included by adjusting the above cash flow estimate).

The entity estimates the initial measurement of the obligation as follows:

	CU	CU
Expected cash flows	231,250	
Risk adjustment	11,563	
		242,813
Present value using rate of 6 per cent for 10 years		135,586

EXAMPLE 18: DISCLOSURE OF A WARRANTY OBLIGATION

A manufacturer gives warranties at the time of sale to purchasers of its three product lines. Under the terms of the warranty, the manufacturer undertakes to repair or replace items that fail to perform satisfactorily for two years from the date of sale. At the balance sheet date, a liability of CU60,000 has been recognised. The following information is disclosed:

A liability of CU60,000 has been recognised for expected warranty claims on products sold during the last three years. It is expected that the majority of claims will occur in the next year, and all will occur within two years of the balance sheet date.

EXAMPLE 19: DISCLOSURE OF A DECOMMISSIONING OBLIGATION

In 2000 an entity involved in nuclear power generation recognises a liability for decommissioning costs of CU300 million. The liability is based on the decommissioning costs that are expected to be incurred, adjusted for risk, using existing technology. The costs reflect current prices and are discounted using a real discount rate of 2 per cent. The other significant assumption is that there is a 90 per cent likelihood that the decommissioning will take place in 60-70 years and a 10 per cent likelihood that it will not take place until 100-110 years. The following information is disclosed:

A liability of CU300 million has been recognised for decommissioning costs. These costs are expected to be incurred between 2060 and 2070. However, there is a possibility that decommissioning will not take place until 2100-2110. The likelihood of these different outcomes is reflected in the measurement of the liability. The liability has been esti-mated using existing technology, at current prices, and discounted using a real discount rate of 2 per cent.

EXAMPLE 20: DISCLOSURE EXEMPTION

An entity is involved in a dispute with a competitor, who is alleging that the entity has infringed patents and is seeking damages of CU100 million. The entity recognises a non-financial liability for the amount that it would rationally pay to settle or transfer the obligation, but discloses none of the information required by paragraph 68 of the [draft] Standard because this information can be expected to prejudice seriously its position. The following information is disclosed:

The company is in a dispute with a competitor. This has resulted in litigation against the company alleging that it has infringed patents and seeking damages of CU100 million. The information usually required by [draft] ~~IAS 37~~ FRS 12 Non-financial Liabilities is not disclosed because it can be expected to prejudice seriously the outcome of the litigation. The directors are of the opinion that the claim can be successfully resisted by the company.

Note on Legal Requirements

GREAT BRITAIN

In Great Britain, for financial years beginning on or after 1 January 2005, the **1** statutory requirements relating to accounting for liabilities for those companies which prepare accounts under the Companies Act 1985 rather than IAS accounts are set out in the Companies Act. The main requirements that are directly relevant are set out in Schedules 4 and 4A and are summarised below.

Schedule 4 to the Act does not apply to banking and insurance companies and **2** groups. Banking companies and groups are dealt with in Schedule 9 and insurance companies and groups are dealt with in Schedule 9A.

Paragraph 12(b) of Schedule 4 states the general requirement that "all liabilities **3** which have arisen in respect of the financial year to which the accounts relate or a previous financial year shall be taken into account ..."

This [draft] FRS does not use the term 'Provisions'. It notes, in paragraph 9, that it **4** does not prescribe how entities should describe their non-financial liabilities. Therefore, entities should describe some classes of non-financial liabilities as provisions in their financial statements, when required to do so by the Companies Act.

Provisions are defined in paragraph 89 of Schedule 4 in the following manner: **5**

"References to provisions for liabilities are to any amount retained as reasonably necessary for the purposes of providing for any liability the nature of which is clearly defined and which is either likely to be incurred, or certain to be incurred, but uncertain as to amount or as to the date on which it will arise."

The legal definition refers to "... any amount retained as reasonably necessary for the **6** purpose ...". The reference to reasonableness recognises that the appropriate amount to set aside as a liability for a specific matter will often be a matter of judgement.

The legal definition also refers to "... any liability ... [whether likely to be incurred or **7** certain to be incurred]" and this needs to be considered in conjunction with the general requirement that "liabilities have arisen in respect of the financial year to which the accounts relate [or a previous financial year] shall be taken into account" (paragraph 12(b) of Schedule 4).

In addition to covering liabilities that are certain to be incurred, the statutory defi- **8** nition also refers to liabilities that are "likely to be incurred". The [draft] FRS, in paragraphs 12 to 21 discusses the requirements to satisfy the definition of a liability.

Where any amount is transferred to any provision for liabilities, or from any pro- **9** vision for liabilities, otherwise than for the purpose for which the provision was established, paragraph 46(1) and (2) of Schedule 4 requires the following information to be disclosed:

(a)   the amount of the provisions as at the date of the beginning of the financial year and as at the balance sheet date respectively;
(b)   any amounts transferred to or from provisions during that year; and
(c)   the source and application respectively of any amounts so transferred.

Paragraph 46(3) of Schedule 4 requires particulars to be given of each material **10** provision included in the item "other provisions" in the company's balance sheet.

11 Paragraph 50(2) of Schedule 4 requires the following information to be given in respect of any other contingent liability not provided for:

(a) the amount or estimated amount of that liability;

(b) its legal nature; and

(c) whether any valuable security has been provided by the company in connection with that liability and, if so, what.

NORTHERN IRELAND

12 The statutory requirements in Northern Ireland are set out in the Companies (Northern Ireland) Order 1986. They are identical to and parallel the references in the legislation for Great Britain cited above.

REPUBLIC OF IRELAND

13 The statutory requirements in the Republic of Ireland that correspond to those cited above for Great Britain are shown in the following table.

Great Britain	*Republic of Ireland*
Schedule 4 to the Companies Act 1985	The Schedule to the Companies (Amendment) Act 1986
Schedule 4A to the Companies Act 1985	European Communities (Companies: Group Accounts) Regulations 1992
Schedule 9 to the Companies Act 1985	European Communities (Credit Institutions: Accounts) Regulations 1992
Schedule 9A to the Companies Act 1985	European Communities (Insurance Undertakings: Accounts) Regulations 1996
Paragraph 12(b) of Schedule 4 to the Companies Act 1985	Section 5(c)(ii) of 1986 Companies Act
Paragraph 46 (1)(2), Schedule 4 of 1985 Companies Act	Paragraph 32 (1)(2) of Schedule to 1986 Companies Act
Paragraph 46(3) Schedule 4 of 1985 Companies Act	Paragraph 32(3) of Schedule to 1986 Companies Act
Paragraph 50(2) of Schedule 4 to the 1985 Companies Act	Paragraph 32(3) of the Schedule to 1986 Companies Act
Paragraph 89 Schedule 4 to the 1985 Companies Act	Paragraph 70 of the Schedule to 1986 Companies Act

AMENDMENTS TO

FRS 17

RETIREMENT BENEFITS

ASB note: The IASB is proposing to amend IAS 19 *Employee Benefits. The following sections sets out how these proposals could be incorporated into existing UK accounting standards. Accordingly the ASB propose to amend FRS 17 Retirement benefits. The following text will be inserted into an existing UK standard and is therefore not shown in marked up form, but is based on IASB text.*

Summary of main changes to FRS 17

The IASB is proposing to amend IAS 19 *Employee Benefits* as part of its Short-term Convergence project with the US Financial Accounting Standard Board (FASB). They propose to amend that section of IAS 19 that addresses termination benefits. The ASB proposes to implement the amended section (the section of IAS 19 that addresses termination benefits) into FRS 17 Retirement benefits. The title of the Standard will be renamed Retirement and Termination Benefits.

The amendments to FRS 17 are based on the IASB's Exposure Draft of Proposed Amendments IAS 19 Employee Benefits.

The amendments to FRS 17 propose:

Definition of termination benefits

- Termination benefits are defined as employee benefits provided in connection with the termination of an employee's employment. 'Involuntary' termination benefits arise from an entity's decision to terminate an employee's employment, whereas 'voluntary' termination benefits arise from an employee's decision to accept voluntary termination.
- The Exposure Draft proposes that:
  - termination benefits that are payable in exchange for an employee's decision to accept voluntary redundancy are termination benefits only if they are offered for a short period.
  - other employee benefits that are offered to encourage employees to leave service before normal retirement date are retirement benefits.

Recognition

- The Exposure Draft proposes that:
  - voluntary termination benefits should be recognised when employees accept the entity's offer of those termination benefits.
  - 'involuntary' termination benefits should be recognised when the entity has communicated its plan of termination to the affected employees and the plan meets specified criteria, unless the 'involuntary' termination benefits are provided in exchange for employees' future services (ie in substance they are a 'stay bonus'). In such cases, the liability for those benefits should be recognised over the future service period.

Contents

Amendments to Financial Reporting Standard 17
Retirement Benefits

...

Amendments to
Financial Reporting Standard 17
Retirement Benefits

1   **Paragraph 'a' of the summary is amended as follows:**

a.   Financial Reporting Standard 17 sets out the requirements for accounting for retirement <u>and termination</u> benefits.

2   **After paragraph 'n' of the summary insert the following:**

o.   *Termination benefits*

Termination benefits are employee benefits provided in connection with the termination of an employee's employment.

'Voluntary' termination benefits (arising from an employee's decision to accept voluntary termination) shall be recognised when the employee accepts the entity's offer of those termination benefits.

Except where 'involuntary' termination benefits (which arise from an entity's decision to terminate an employee's employment) are provided in exchange for employees' future services, the liability and expense shall be recognised when the entity has a plan of termination that it has communicated to the affected employees and the plan meets the criteria specified in the Standard.

The liability and expense for 'involuntary' termination benefits that are provided in exchange for employees' future service shall be recognised over the period of the employees' future service.

3   **Paragraph 'o' is renumbered 'p'**

4   **The objective of the standard is amended as follows:**

(b)   ... in which they arise; ~~and~~
(c)   ... assets and liabilities; <u>and</u>
(d)   <u>the cost of providing termination benefits is recognised when an entity incurs a liability for those benefits</u>.

5   **Paragraph 2 is amended as follows:**

5.1   Insert the definition of '*employee benefits*' after the definition of '*defined contribution scheme*':

Employee benefits

All forms of consideration given by an entity in exchange for service rendered by employees.

5.2   Insert the definition of 'minimum retention period' after 'interest cost'.

Minimum retention period

The *minimum retention period* is the period of notice that an entity is required to provide to employees in advance of terminating their employment. The notice period may be specified by law, contract or union agreement, or may be implied as a result of customary business practice.

Amend the definition of '*retirement benefits*' as follows: **5.3**

Retirement benefits

All forms of consideration given by an employer in exchange for services rendered by employees that are payable after the completion of employment.

Retirement benefits do not include termination benefits. ~~payable as a result of either (i) an employer's decision to terminate an employee's employment before the normal retirement date or (ii) an employee's decision to accept voluntary redundancy in exchange for those benefits,~~ This is because these are not given in exchange for services rendered by employees.

Insert the definition of '*termination benefits*' after the definition of '*settlement*'.   **5.4**

Termination benefits:

Are employee benefits provided in connection with the termination of an employee's employment. They may be either:

(a)   involuntary termination benefits, which are benefits provided as a result of an entity's decision to terminate an employee's employment before the normal retirement date; or

(b)   voluntary termination benefits, which are benefits offered for a short period in exchange for an employee's decision to accept voluntary termination of employment.

Paragraphs 94–108 are inserted as follows: **6**

Termination Benefits

This Standard deals with termination benefits separately from retirement benefit   **94**
because, except as described in paragraph 101 and 102, the event that gives rise to an obligation is the termination of employment rather than employee service.

Termination benefits are typically lump-sum payments, but sometimes also include: **95**

(a)   enhancement of retirement benefits, either indirectly through an retirement benefit plan or directly; and

(b)   salary until the end of a specified notice period if the employee renders no further service that provides economic benefits to the entity.

Involuntary termination benefits are often provided in accordance with the terms of   **96**
an ongoing benefit plan. For example, they may be specified by statute, employment contract or union agreement, or may be implied as a result of the employer's past practice of providing similar benefits. In other cases, they are provided at the discretion of the entity and are incremental to what an employee would otherwise be entitled to, for example because the entity has no ongoing benefit plan or provides benefits in addition to those specified by an ongoing benefit plan.

Some entities offer benefits to encourage employees to accept voluntary termination   **97**
of employment before normal retirement date. For the purpose of this [draft] Standard, such benefits are termination benefits only if they are offered for a short period. Other benefits offered to encourage employees to accept voluntary termination of employment (for example, those available under the terms of an ongoing retirement benefit plan) are retirement benefits because the benefits are payable in exchange for the employees' service.

98   Some employee benefits are provided regardless of the reason for the employee's departure. The payment of such benefits is certain (subject to any vesting or minimum service requirements) but the timing of their payment is uncertain. Although such benefits are described in some jurisdictions as termination indemnities, or termination gratuities, they are retirement benefits. Some entities provide a lower level of benefit for voluntary termination of employment at the request of the employee (in substance, a retirement benefit) than for involuntary termination at the request of the entity. The additional benefit payable on involuntary termination of employment is a termination benefit.

RECOGNITION

99   *An entity shall recognise a liability and expense for voluntary termination benefits when the employee accepts the entity's offer of those termination benefits.*

100   *Except as specified in paragraph 101, an entity shall recognise a liability and expense for involuntary termination benefits when it has a plan of termination that it has communicated to the affected employees, and actions required to complete the plan indicate that it is unlikely that significant changes to the plan will be made or that the plan will be withdrawn. The plan shall:*

   (a)   identify the number of employees whose employment is to be terminated, their job classifications or functions and their locations, and the expected completion date; and

   (b)   establish the benefits that employees will receive upon termination of employment (including but not limited to cash payments) in sufficient detail to enable employees to determine the type and amount of benefits they will receive when their employment is terminated.

101   *If involuntary termination benefits are provided in exchange for employees' future services, an entity shall recognise the termination benefits as a liability and an expense over the period of the employees' future services (ie from the date specified in paragraph 100 to the date that the employment is terminated).*

102   In some cases, involuntary termination benefits are provided in exchange for employees' future services. For the purpose of this [draft] Standard, this is the case if those benefits:

   (a)   are incremental to what the employees would otherwise be entitled to receive (ie the benefits are not provided in accordance with the terms of an ongoing benefit plan);

   (b)   do not vest until the employment is terminated; and

   (c)   are provided to employees who will be retained beyond the minimum retention period.

103   In some cases, employers provide involuntary termination benefits that are expressed as an enhancement of the existing terms of an ongoing benefit plan. Examples are a doubling of benefits specified by employment legislation or an increase in retirement benefits to be provided through a retirement benefit plan. If the termination benefits that are attributable to the enhancement of the ongoing benefit plan do not represent a change to the terms of the ongoing plan (and therefore would not apply to employees leaving service in the future) and satisfy the criteria in paragraph 102(b) and (c), they shall be recognised in accordance with paragraph 101.

104   When termination benefits are provided as an enhancement of retirement benefits, the liability and expense recognised initially include only the value of the additional benefits that arise from providing those termination benefits. Other changes in any defined benefit obligation for the retirement benefit plan resulting from employees leaving employment at a date earlier than originally assumed should be recognised either as actuarial gains or losses or as a curtailment.

Measurement

When termination benefits are due more than 12 months after the balance sheet date, an entity shall discount them using the discount rate specified in paragraph 32 and shall subsequently follow the recognition and measurement requirements for retirement benefits.   **105**

Accordingly, when termination benefits are provided as an enhancement of retirement benefits, their initial measurement and subsequent recognition and measurement are consistent with the requirements of FRS 17 for the underlying retirement benefit plan.   **106**

Measurement of a liability for unvested involuntary termination benefits shall reflect the likelihood of employees leaving voluntarily before the termination benefits vest.   **107**

Example illustrating paragraphs 100–107

Background

As a result of a recent acquisition, an entity plans to close a factory in 12 months and, at that time, terminate the employment of all of the remaining employees at the facility. Because the entity needs the expertise of the employees at the facility to complete some contracts, it announces a termination benefit plan as follows. Each employee who stays and renders service for the full 12-month period will receive, as a termination benefit on the termination date, a cash payment of three times the amount specified by employment legislation.

The entity's usual practice is to pay only the minimum termination benefits specified by employment legislation. For the employees at the factory, this minimum amounts to 10,000 per employee. Employment legislation also requires the entity to give 60 days' notice of its intention to terminate employment.

There are 120 employees at the factory, 20 of whom are expected to leave voluntarily before closure. Therefore, the total expected cash flows under the termination benefit plan are 3,200,000 (ie 20 × 10,000 + 100 × 30,000).

As required by paragraph 102, the entity accounts for the benefits provided in accordance with the ongoing benefit plan (ie employment legislation) and the enhancement separately.

Ongoing benefit plan

A liability of 1,200,000 (ie 120 × 10,000) for the termination benefits provided in accordance with the ongoing benefit plan is recognised when the plan of termination is announced. The liability represents the benefits of 1,200,000 that the entity is required to pay in accordance with legislation.

Incremental benefits

The expected cash flows for the termination benefits that are incremental to what the employees would otherwise be entitled to receive (and that relate to future services) are 2 million (ie 100 × 20,000). In this example, discounting is not required, so a liability and expense of 166,667 (ie 2,000,000 ÷ 12) is recognised in each month during the future service period of 12 months. If the number of employees expected to leave voluntarily before closure changes, the entity makes corresponding adjustments to its estimates of the expected cash flows for termination benefits and hence the liability recognised.

Disclosure

108   As required by FRS 3 *Reporting Financial Performance* an entity discloses separately an expense if it is exceptional. The expense for termination benefits may need to be disclosed to comply with this requirement.

7   **Paragraph 94 is renumbered 109.**

8   **Paragraph 109A is inserted as follows:**

109A   *An entity shall apply the amendments in [draft] paragraphs 2 and 94–108 from the start of annual periods beginning on or after [1 January 2007]. Comparative information shall not be restated. Earlier application is encouraged. However, an entity shall apply the amendments only from the beginning of an annual period commencing on or after [date the amendments are issued]. If an entity applies the amendments before the effective date, it shall disclose that fact.*

9   **Paragraphs 95 to 105 are renumbered sequentially, such that paragraph 95 is renumbered 110 and sequentially thereafter.**

10   **The development of the Standard is updated by inserting paragraphs 64 and 65:**

64   In 2007 FRS 17 was amended to reflect the introduction of [draft] FRS ● *Business Combinations*. [Draft] FRS ● *Business Combinations* was part of the ASB convergence strategy with International Accounting Standards. As part of the convergence programme the Board implemented:

- FRS ● Business Combinations;
- FRS ● Intangible Assets;
- FRS ● Impairment of Assets;
- FRS 12 (revised) Non-financial Liabilities (formerly known as Provisions, Contingent Assets and Contingent Liabilities); and
- Amendments to FRS 2 Accounting for Subsidary Undertakings (parts of *International Accounting Standard 27*);
- Amendments to FRS 17 Retirement and Termination Benefits.
- All of these standards had been introduced or amended as part of the IASB Business Combinations project.

65   As part of the amendments to IAS 19 the IASB issued a Basis for Conclusions to accompany the amendement. This Basis for Conclusions is reproduced in this [draft] FRS in Appendix V.

11   The title of the standard shall be amended to FRS 17 Retirement and Termination Benefits. In the UK accounting standards references to 'FRS 17 Retirement benefits' shall be replaced with 'FRS 17 Retirement and Termination Benefits'.

Other amendments to the standard

In paragraph 16 of the Standard replace 'mid-market value' with 'current bid price'.

> *The ASB is proposing this amendment to the Standard as replacing 'mid-market value' with 'current bid price' will converge the measurement of fair value of scheme assets in IAS 19 and FRS 17.*

Appendix V
Basis for conclusions

This Basis for Conclusions accompanies, but is not part of, the proposed Amendments to IAS 19.

ASB note: The IASB's Basis for Conclusions, which accompanies the amendments to IAS 19 Employee Benefits, is set out below in full. It should be noted though that some of the discussion it contains concerns IASB requirements that have no equivalent in the UK or Republic of Ireland. Footnotes have been used to indicate corresponding requirements in the UK and Republic of Ireland where applicable.

All references in this section to 'the Board' and 'Board members' are references to the IASB Board and IASB Board members

INTRODUCTION

BC1   This Basis for Conclusions summarises the International Accounting Standards Board's considerations in reaching the conclusions in the Exposure Draft of Proposed Amendments to IAS 19 *Employee benefits*.* Individual Board members gave greater weight to some factors than to others.

BC2   The amendments to IAS 19 proposed in this Exposure Draft result from the Board's Short-term Convergence project and complement the proposed amendments to the requirements addressing restructurings in IAS 37 *Provisions, Contingent Liabilities and Contingent Assets*†.

BC3   Because the Board's intention was not to reconsider the fundamental approach to the accounting for employee benefits established by IAS 19, this Basis for Conclusions does not discuss requirements in IAS 19 that the Board has not reconsidered.

Short-term Convergence project

BC4   In September 2002 the Board decided to add a Short-term Convergence project to its active agenda. The objective of the project is to reduce differences between IFRSs and US generally accepted accounting principles (US GAAP) that are capable of resolution in a relatively short time and can be addressed outside current and planned major projects. The project is a joint project with the Financial Accounting Standards Board (FASB) in the United States.

BC5   In working towards the objective of the project, the two boards agreed to review each other's deliberations on each of the selected possible convergence topics and choose the higher quality solution as the basis for convergence. For topics recently considered by either board, there is an expectation that whichever board had more recently deliberated that topic would have the higher quality solution.

---

*ASB footnote: *The corresponding requirements in the UK and Republic of Ireland are set out in FRS 17* Retirement and Termination Benefits.

†ASB footnote: *The corresponding requirements in the UK and Republic of Ireland are set out in FRS 12* Provisions, Contingent Liabilities and Contingent Assets.

As part of the review of topics recently considered by the FASB, the Board con- **BC6**
sidered the requirements of FASB Statement No. 146 *Accounting for Costs
Associated with Exit or Disposal Activities* (SFAS 146), which was issued in June
2002. This has resulted in the Board proposing amendments to the requirements in
IAS 37 relating to the recognition of liabilities for costs associated with a restructuring to converge with SFAS 146 and to improve the Standard. SFAS 146 also
specifies the accounting for a class of termination benefits known as 'one-time termination benefits'. These are 'benefits provided to current employees that [sic] are
involuntarily terminated under the terms of a benefit arrangement that, in substance,
is not an ongoing benefit arrangement or an individual deferred compensation
contract.' Because the accounting for termination benefits is specified by IAS 19, the
Board also decided to amend the termination benefit recognition requirements in
IAS 19 consistently with its amendments to IAS 37.

SFAS 146 does not alter the accounting for other termination benefits specified by **BC7**
earlier FASB Statements (principally Statement No. 88 *Employers' Accounting for
Settlements and Curtailments of Defined Benefit Pension Plans and for Termination
Benefits* (SFAS 88) and Statement No. 112 *Employers' Accounting for Postemploy-
ment Benefits*). Although the aim of the Short-term Convergence project is to reduce
differences between IFRSs and US GAAP, the Board decided that in general it
should not seek convergence with those earlier Statements. The Board observed that
because the accounting for termination benefits in US GAAP is specified in a number
of standards, the approach would be difficult to integrate into IAS 19. Accordingly,
the Board concluded that it should converge with the principles of SFAS 146 relating
to one-time termination benefits and apply those principles consistently to all termination benefits. It acknowledged that differences with US GAAP will remain
following the introduction of these amendments. Nonetheless, the Board believes
that the proposed amendments will increase convergence as well as improve the
accounting for termination benefits.

Recognition of involuntary termination benefits payable in exchange for employees' future services

The present version of IAS 19 explains that termination benefits are dealt with **BC8**
separately from other employee benefits because the event that gives rise to a present
obligation for termination benefits is the termination of employment rather than
employee service. Therefore, a liability for termination benefits is recognised when
the entity is 'demonstrably committed' to the termination. In contrast, SFAS 146
regards some one-time termination benefits as being provided in exchange for
employees' future services (or, expressed another way, are in substance a 'stay
bonus'). In such cases, the liability is recognised over the period of the employees'
service, consistently with the accounting for other employee benefits.

The Board agreed with the FASB that in some cases termination benefits, although **BC9**
provided as compensation for the early termination of services, also have the characteristic of being provided in exchange for employees' future services. For example,
the Board observed that, following an acquisition, entities sometimes terminate the
employment of the employees of the acquired entity. However, because the entity
requires the skills and knowledge of those employees for a period of time, it offers
enhanced termination benefits as an inducement for those employees to stay for that
period. Therefore, the Board decided that, like SFAS 146, IAS 19 should specify
different recognition requirements for termination benefits that are provided in
exchange for future service.

BC10   In SFAS 146, determining whether one-time termination benefits are provided in exchange for future service depends on whether employees are required to render future service to receive the benefits and, if so, whether they will be retained beyond the minimum retention period. This is because the FASB reasoned that, in the absence of a requirement to provide advance notice of termination, an entity would promise one-time termination benefits in advance of termination only if the entity needed the employees to render future service. In other words, if the employees are required to render future service to be entitled to the benefits, those benefits must be compensation for that future service. To accommodate any requirement to provide advance notice of termination, the FASB specified that if employees are required to render future service only during the minimum retention period to be entitled to the benefits, those benefits do not relate to future service.

BC11   Like the FASB, the Board concluded that it should specify when termination benefits are provided in exchange for future service, rather than leaving it to an assessment of the individual facts and circumstances. The Board was concerned that the latter approach could result in different entities accounting for similar termination benefits differently. The Board also agreed with the FASB's two criteria for determining whether one-time termination benefits are provided in exchange for future services. However, because the requirements in IAS 19 apply to all involuntary termination benefits, and not (as in SFAS 146) just one-time involuntary termination benefits, the Board decided that it needed to specify a third criterion, namely that the benefits are incremental to what the employees would otherwise be entitled to receive (or expressed another way, that the benefits are not provided in accordance with the terms of an ongoing benefit plan, whether that plan is established by an employment contract, union agreement, legal requirement, or implied by the entity's usual practice). The Board reasoned that if the termination benefits are paid in accordance with the terms of an ongoing benefit plan, those benefits would not be provided as an inducement to stay and render future service (and, hence, be provided in exchange for future services) because the entity would be obliged to provide them. In other words, the employees would know the benefits to which they would be entitled in the event of their employment being terminated. The Board noted that this would be counter to the notion in SFAS 146 of the employer making a payment completely at its discretion to encourage the employee to stay and render future service.

BC12   The Board noted that in some cases, termination benefits that are payable in exchange for future service would be calculated using a benefit formula that determines some (or all) of the termination benefits with reference to past service. However, the Board agreed with the FASB that the benefit formula 'in and of itself, does not render one-time termination benefits a 'reward' for past service. The [FASB] observed that an objective of providing a 'reward' for past service could be accomplished by granting immediately vested benefits.'* Accordingly, the Board concluded that such benefits should be recognised over the future service period, even though they are calculated by reference to past service.

BC13   The Board also noted that in some cases, an employer might offer termination benefits in excess of those specified by an ongoing benefit plan (for example, a doubling of benefits specified by employment legislation). The Board concluded that although the additional benefits might be expressed as an enhancement of the terms of the ongoing benefit plan, the additional benefits should be treated as a separate benefit plan. Thus, if the additional benefits are provided in exchange for employees' future services (because they do not represent an ongoing plan that would apply to

---

*Paragraph B28 of SFAS 146.

future terminations and meet the criteria in paragraph 140(b) and (c)*) they are recognised over future service periods.

The Board adopted the notion from SFAS 146 of a minimum retention period **BC14** because, like the FASB, it acknowledged that a promise of termination benefits may need to be communicated to employees in advance of the termination as a result of law, contract or union agreement, rather than to induce the employees to continue in service until termination date. The Board, however, decided to broaden the definition to include notice periods that are implied by customary business practice.

Recognition of involuntary termination benefits

The Board then considered SFAS 146's recognition requirements for one-time ter- **BC15** mination benefits that are not payable in exchange for future services, ie one-time termination benefits that are paid to employees who are not required to render future service to receive the benefits or who will not be retained beyond the minimum retention period. In SFAS 146, the liability for such benefits is recognised when the entity has a plan of termination that (a) meets specified criteria and (b) has been communicated to the employees in sufficient detail for them to be able to determine the termination benefits to which they are entitled.

The Board noted that the specific criteria in SFAS 146 relating to the termination **BC16** plan are similar to the criteria in the present version of IAS 19 for establishing whether an entity is demonstrably committed to a termination plan and, therefore, should recognise termination benefits. However, the Board observed that there is no requirement in IAS 19 to communicate the plan of termination to employees. Having considered SFAS 146, the Board agreed with the FASB that there is no liability to provide one-time termination benefits until the entity has communicated the plan of termination to the employees. However, the Board decided that this principle in SFAS 146 should apply to all involuntary termination benefits and not just one-time termination benefits. The Board observed that even if the termination benefits are not one-time and, for example, are provided in accordance with the terms of an ongoing benefit plan, there is no *present* obligation to provide the benefits until communication of the plan of termination. The Board concluded that until this point the employer has the discretion to avoid paying termination benefits and, therefore, a liability does not exist.

Therefore, the Board decided that it should add a new recognition criterion to **BC17** IAS 19 and specify that an entity does not have a present obligation to provide involuntary termination benefits (under either an ongoing or a one-time benefit plan) until it has communicated its plan of termination to the affected employees. The Board also decided to replace the present criteria relating to the plan of termination with those in SFAS 146. As noted, these criteria are very similar. Nonetheless, the Board concluded that it would ease convergence if they were identical.

Voluntary termination benefits

In US GAAP, most voluntary termination benefits are within the scope of SFAS 88 **BC18** (and are not within the scope of SFAS 146) and are referred to as 'special termination benefits'. SFAS 88 specifies that an employer's obligation to provide voluntary termination benefits meets the definition of a liability when the employees accept the employer's offer of termination benefits. This is different from IAS 19, because IAS 19 specifies that the benefits are recognised when the entity is

*ASB footnote: *This corresponds to paragraph 102 in the proposed amendments to FRS 17.*

demonstrably committed to provide those benefits. However, the Board concluded that in many instances the requirement of SFAS 88 would be closer to the principle underlying SFAS 146 (namely, that a liability is recognised when incurred). This is because until an employee accepts an entity's offer of voluntary termination of employment, the entity would typically have the discretion to withdraw the offer and, therefore, have no present obligation. Because of this and for the sake of convergence, the Board decided to amend IAS 19 to converge with SFAS 88.

BC19   The Board noted that the definition of special termination benefits in SFAS 88 specifies that the benefits are offered for only a short period of time. The Board decided that the short-term nature of the offer was important, because it noted that if the benefits for leaving service are made available for more than a short period, the employer has effectively established a new ongoing benefit plan and the employees would treat the benefits as part of their employment package. In other words, the benefits would be payable in exchange for the employees' services and, therefore, should be treated like any other post-employment benefit. Accordingly, the Board decided to amend the definition of termination benefits to clarify that benefits paid to encourage employees to leave service should be regarded as voluntary termination benefits under IAS 19 only if those benefits are made available for a short period.

Measurement

BC20   SFAS 146 specifies that one-time termination benefits should be measured at fair value, except when the liability is recognised over time. In such cases, the fair value measurement date is modified to the termination date, ie the fair value of the liability at termination date is recognised over the future service period.

BC21   The Board considered whether the measurement requirements of IAS 19 for termination benefits should converge with those of SFAS 146. However, it decided not to take this step, principally because it wanted to specify a measurement requirement that could be applied to all termination benefits, regardless of whether those benefits are provided through or outside an ongoing benefit plan. The Board noted that when termination benefits are provided through a post-employment defined benefit plan (for example, by providing an enhancement of retirement benefits) it would be unduly complex to specify that they should be measured at fair value. This is because the effect of the changes to the plan arising from the termination of employment would need to be isolated, on an ongoing basis, from the remainder of the plan. Therefore, the Board decided that the measurement of such termination benefits should be consistent with the measurement of the underlying post-employment defined benefit plan.

BC22   Accordingly, the Board concluded that it should retain the existing measurement requirement in IAS 19 to discount termination benefits due more than 12 months after the balance sheet date. It acknowledged that this could result in measurement differences with US GAAP for one-time termination benefits within the scope of SFAS 146. However, it observed that most one-time termination benefits that are not recognised over a service period would be likely to vest relatively quickly and, hence, the effect of discounting might be immaterial.

[Draft] Financial Reporting Standard • Accounting for Heritage Assets is set out on pages 9 to 17.

The Statement of Standard Accounting Practice, which comprises the paragraphs set in bold type, should be read in the context of the objective, as stated in paragraph 1, the definitions and scope set out in paragraphs 4 and 5 and also the Foreword to Accounting Standards and the Statement of Principles for Financial Reporting currently in issue.

The explanatory paragraphs contained in the [draft] FRS shall be regarded as part of the Statement of Standard Accounting Practice insofar as they assist in interpreting that statement.

Appendix I 'The Development of the Exposure Draft' reviews considerations and arguments that were thought significant by members of the Board in reaching their conclusions on the [draft] FRS.

The draft is issued by the Accounting Standards Board for comment. It should be noted that the draft may be modified in the light of comment received before being issued in final form.

FRED 40
Accounting for heritage assets

(Issued December 2006)

Contents

Preface

The Accounting Standards Board ('ASB') is publishing this Exposure Draft to set   **1**
out proposals for a new Financial Reporting Standard on Accounting for Heritage
Assets. This has been developed from the Discussion Paper 'Heritage Assets—Can
Accounting do better?' which was published in January 2006. The new requirements
will apply only to entities that have a principal objective of promoting knowledge
and culture.

'Heritage assets' are assets which have historic, artistic, scientific, technological,   **2**
geophysical or environmental qualities and are held and maintained principally for
their contribution to knowledge and culture. The term includes landscape and
coastline, historic buildings and archæological sites as well as collections held by
museums and galleries.

Many of the Discussion Paper's proposals were widely welcomed by respondents. In   **3**
particular, the majority expressed the view that they represented an improvement
over current UK financial reporting requirements.

The Discussion Paper was also published by the International Public Sector   **4**
Accounting Standards Board ('IPSASB') as a Consultation Paper. The ASB intends
to continue to work closely with IPSASB in its work on heritage assets. However,
given the general support for the thrust of the Discussion Paper, it seemed preferable
to issue proposals for change as soon as possible rather than await the outcome of
the IPSASB project.

Many of the entities that hold significant heritage assets are charities. It is expected   **5**
that proposals to amend the Statement of Recommended Practice 'Accounting and
Reporting by Charities' will be published in due course setting out how charities may
comply with the proposed requirements.

The main features of the proposals in this exposure draft are: **6**

(i)   Entities that hold heritage assets to contribute to a principal objective of
      promoting knowledge and culture should report them in accordance with the
      new requirements, instead of the current requirements of FRS 15 'Tangible
      fixed assets'.

(ii) Heritage assets are assets: this is true whether or not they may be sold. The best
      financial reporting is secured by reporting them at a current valuation: the
      proposals of this exposure draft are intended to secure this policy as widely as is
      practicable and useful.

(iii) Specifically, it is proposed that an entity should adopt a policy of reporting
      collections of heritage assets at valuation in those cases where it is practicable
      to obtain valuations which, when supplemented with appropriate disclosures,
      provide useful and relevant information sufficient to assist in an assessment of
      the value of that collection at the balance sheet date.

(iv) For any collection where it is not practicable to obtain valuations as set out in
      (iii) above, under the new requirements, the collection should not be reported in
      the balance sheet and acquisitions and disposals will not be reported as giving
      rise to losses or gains.

(v)   Enhanced disclosure requirements are proposed regardless of whether or not
      collections are reported in the balance sheet.

The considerations and arguments that were significant in framing the proposals in   **7**
this exposure draft are reviewed in Appendix I. Appendix II sets out illustrative
disclosures.

REGULATORY IMPACT

8   In developing the proposals in this exposure draft, the benefits and costs were considered. As is explained in more detail in Appendix I, the benefits include the replacement of the current unsatisfactory financial reporting requirements with requirements that will secure more informative financial reporting.

9   The costs of introducing the proposed new requirements will largely fall on preparers. Preparers will have to consider for individual collections, whether they are required to report heritage assets at valuation or, where such an approach is not practicable, adopt a non-recognition approach. It is not envisaged that, in the majority of cases, this will be burdensome.

10   Further costs may be incurred where an entity reports some or all of its collections of heritage assets at valuation: however, such an approach is only to be required following an assessment of the benefits (which will depend *inter alia* on the relevance and reliability of the valuation) and costs of obtaining them: for this reason, the proposed requirements for valuation should not impose disproportionate cost.

11   In addition, the proposals include new disclosure requirements, and there will be some cost in complying with them. However, the information should be readily available; hence any new cost will be confined to presenting and publishing the information.

12   In light of the above, it appears to the ASB that the cost of the proposed new requirements will not be disproportionate to their benefits. The ASB would, however, be interested to hear from respondents who disagree with this analysis (see question 9 of the invitation to comment).

FUTURE DEVELOPMENTS

13   The ASB will continue to monitor how entities are accounting for heritage assets and may revise the requirements in the light of developments in reporting practice and the outcome of IPSASB's work.

Invitation to comment

Comments would be welcomed on any aspect of the exposure draft. Respondents' views are especially sought on the matters set out below. It would be helpful if respondents supported their comments with reasons and, where applicable, preferred alternatives.

1   Do you agree that rather than the current arrangements, under which entities generally capitalise only recently acquired heritage assets at cost, the requirement should be that an entity should, where practicable*, adopt a valuation approach for its heritage assets?

This [draft] FRS requires a valuation approach where practicable but, where this is not practicable, prescribes a non-recognition approach. Do you agree this proposal will lead to an improvement in the quality of the financial reporting of heritage assets?

*'Practicable' in these questions is to be understood in terms of the principle in paragraph 8 of the [draft] FRS.

This [draft] FRS proposes the assessment of practicability should be applied to   **2**
individual collections rather than for the entity's total holding of heritage assets (see
paragraphs 22 and 23 of Appendix I). Do you agree?

If the approach is to be determined at the level of an individual collection, it is   **3**
necessary to define the term 'collection'. Do you consider the definition proposed in
paragraph 4 of the [draft] FRS is appropriate? If not, what alternative would you
propose and why?

The [draft] FRS proposes the approach should be determined for individual col-   **4**
lections following an assessment of whether it is practicable to obtain valuations that
provide useful and relevant information. This assessment will include consideration
of the relevance of valuations as well as their reliability and the costs and benefits of
obtaining them.

Do you support this approach or would you prefer that the approach emphasises
that valuation is required only where the valuation is reliable? If you believe that a
reliability approach, or some other approach, should be adopted, what guidance
would you see as being necessary to assess the reliability of valuations?

Do you consider that the proposals will cause auditors significant difficulties when   **5**
assessing an entity's approach, particularly in terms of applying the assessment of
practicability at the level of an individual collection? Where a valuation approach is
adopted, do you think auditors will face further difficulties in evaluating the
valuations being reported?

The [draft] FRS requires that where an entity adopts a non-recognition approach for   **6**
some or all of its collections, acquisitions and disposals of heritage assets should not
be reported in the profit and loss account or equivalent statement, or in any manner
that implies they are gains and losses (see paragraphs 29 to 31 of Appendix I). Do
you agree?

The proposals require enhanced disclosures of heritage assets (see paragraphs 18 to   **7**
23 and paragraph 25 of the [draft] FRS). Do you consider the nature and extent of
the required disclosures are appropriate? Do you consider any of the disclosure
requirements are unduly onerous?

The definition of a heritage asset is set out in paragraph 4 of the [draft] FRS and the   **8**
scope of the proposed new standard is set out in paragraph 5. The rationale for these
is discussed in paragraphs 7 to 12 of Appendix 1. Do you agree with the proposed
definition and scope?

As explained in paragraphs 8 to 12 of the Preface, the Board believes the costs of   **9**
implementing the proposals should not be disproportionate. Do you agree? It would
be particularly helpful if any significant costs that would arise on implementation of
the proposals (including any not identified above) could be identified and quantified.

[Draft] Financial Reporting Standard •
Accounting for heritage assets

OBJECTIVE

1   This [draft] FRS is applicable to entities that hold heritage assets as defined in paragraph 4 of the standard to contribute to a principal objective of the entity of promoting knowledge and culture.

AMENDMENT TO FRS 11 'IMPAIRMENT OF FIXED ASSETS AND GOODWILL'

2   Paragraph 5 of FRS 11 is amended by adding the following sub-paragraph:

> "(e)   heritage assets accounted for in accordance with FRS • 'Accounting for Heritage Assets' "

Amendment to FRS 15 'Tangible fixed Assets'

3   FRS 15 is amended by adding the following text after paragraph 18.

> "Entities that hold heritage assets to contribute to a principal objective of the entity of promoting knowledge and culture should account for their heritage assets in accordance with FRS • 'Accounting for Heritage Assets'."

DEFINITIONS

4   **The following definitions shall apply in this [draft] FRS**

Heritage Asset

An asset with historic, artistic, scientific, technological, geophysical or environmental qualities that is held and maintained principally for its contribution to knowledge and culture.

Collection

A group of artefacts, exhibits or other items that have common significant characteristics such as age, nature and origin or are managed together and form a distinct part of the entity's holding of heritage assets.

> *The reference to a 'group' does not preclude a single item constituting a collection where it is managed separately from and forms a distinct part of the entity's holding of heritage assets.*

SCOPE

5   **Entities that hold heritage assets to contribute to a principal objective of the entity of promoting knowledge and culture should account for their heritage assets in accordance with the requirements of this standard**

6   Buildings of historical interest should be treated as heritage assets only where it is their historical characteristics that contribute to the advancement of the entity's objectives. For example, buildings that are used primarily to provide office

accommodation or teaching facilities should not be treated as heritage assets, and should be accounted for in accordance with the requirements of FRS 15 'Tangible fixed assets'.

Reporting entities applying the Financial Reporting Standard for Smaller Entities   7
(FRSSE) currently applicable are exempt from this FRS.

VALUATION POLICY

An entity should adopt a policy of reporting collections of heritage assets at valuation in   **8**
those cases where it is practicable to obtain valuations, which, when supplemented with
appropriate disclosures, provide useful and relevant information sufficient to assist in an
assessment of the value of that collection at the balance sheet date.

Where it is practicable to obtain a current valuation for a collection, this should be
reported in the entity's balance sheet in accordance with paragraph 13 below. For any
collection where it is not practicable to obtain valuations, the entity should account for
the collection in accordance with paragraph 15 below.

The disclosures required by paragraphs 18 to 23 are required whether or not a collection
is reported in the balance sheet.

Where valuation information is not readily available for a collection, the assessment   9
set out in paragraph 8 requires consideration of the relevance and reliability of
valuations as well as the benefits and costs of obtaining them and the balance
between these. The relevant benefits will include improvements to the financial
statements, but other benefits of obtaining information on the value of assets held
within a collection should be considered, for example, it may assist an entity's
internal management.

In some cases there will be adequate evidence of arms-length transactions in similar   10
assets which will enable an estimate of the value of a collection of heritage assets held
by the entity. Where an entity is regularly involved in the buying or selling of heritage
assets relating to a collection, it should be presumed that sufficient evidence exists to
meet the objectives set out in paragraph 8. A valuation approach should be adopted
for a collection even if there are difficulties with some items but where it is nonetheless possible to provide a valuation and supporting disclosures that provide a
meaningful insight of the value of the collection as a whole. For example, it may be
possible to value an item which has an association with a historical event or person
by reference to the value of a similar item without such an association, and disclosing
the approach taken.

Valuations may be made by any method that is appropriate and relevant. It may, for   11
example, be possible to use values reported in authoritative sources. It may also be
possible to obtain a suitable valuation for a large collection without considering each
individual item by projecting the results of a valuation of a representative sample.
However, simply multiplying an arbitrary value by the number of items held would
not provide useful and relevant information, and such a value should not be used for
financial reporting purposes. Historical cost should not be used except where it
provides a reasonable insight into the current value of items at the balance sheet date:
this is most likely to be the case for recently acquired assets and, perhaps, where it is
possible to update historical cost by means of a suitable index.

There are a number of reasons why it may not be practicable to obtain a valuation   12
for a collection that is suitable for financial reporting purposes. Some heritage assets

are unique or rarely traded and evidence from arms-length transactions will not be available. Where a collection includes a very large number of items, the cost of valuation may be so large as to outweigh the benefits.

The valuation approach

13   **Where it is practicable to adopt the valuation approach for a collection of heritage assets:**

(i)   **these assets should be reported at valuation in the balance sheet, and presented as a separate class of tangible fixed assets;**

(ii)   **changes in the valuation of collections should be recognised in the statement of total recognised gains and losses; and**

(iii)   **on disposal of a heritage asset, its valuation should be adjusted to the amount of net proceeds and this adjustment should be reflected in the statement of total recognised gains and losses.**

14   There is no requirement for valuations of collections to be carried out or verified by external valuers, nor is there any prescribed minimum period between valuations. However, valuations must be carried out with sufficient frequency to ensure that they meet the objective specified in paragraph 8.

The non-recognition approach

15   **For collections where the entity determines that it is not practicable to adopt the valuation approach:**

(i)   **these assets should not be reported in the balance sheet;**

(ii)   **acquisitions of heritage assets and the net proceeds received on disposal should not be reported in the profit and loss account, or equivalent statement, or in any manner that implies they are losses or gains; and**

(iii)   **acquisitions and (separately) the proceeds of disposals of heritage assets should be reported in a primary financial statement that reconciles total recognised gains and losses to changes in total reported net assets.**

16   Where an entity prepares its financial statements in accordance with the Statement of Recommended Practice (SORP) 'Accounting and Reporting by Charities' issued by the Charity Commission in March 2005, the requirements of paragraph 15 (iii) may be met by reporting acquisitions and disposals of heritage assets in the reconciliation of funds set out in Table 3 of the SORP.

Donations

17   **The receipt of donations of heritage assets should be reported in the income and expenditure account at current value unless it is impracticable to obtain a current value. The assets should be accounted for in accordance with paragraph 13 or paragraph 15 consistently with the treatment for the collection to which the assets are added.**

Disclosures

18   **An entity's financial statements should contain an indication of the nature and scale of heritage assets held by the entity.**

19   **The financial statements should either set out the entity's policy for the acquisition, preservation, management and disposal of heritage assets, including the extent to which**

access to the assets is permitted, or contain a cross reference to a document that sets out this information.

The accounting policy adopted for the entity's collections of heritage assets should be stated, including details of the collections that are reported under the valuation approach and those where it is not considered practicable to adopt the valuation approach. For collections where the non-recognition approach is adopted, the reasons why it is impracticable to obtain valuations that will achieve the objective set out in paragraph 8 should be explained.   **20**

Where the valuation approach is adopted, the following should be disclosed: **21**

(i)   the carrying amount of heritage assets analysed by principal collection; and
(ii) sufficient information to assist in an understanding of the valuations being reported and their significance. This should include:

   (a)   the date of the valuation;
   (b)   the methods used to produce the valuation;
   (c)   whether the valuation was carried out by external valuers and, where this is the case, the valuer's name and professional qualification, if any; and
   (d)   any significant limitations on the valuation, for example assets that have not been included in the valuation.

Where the non-recognition approach is adopted, information that is available to the entity and is helpful in assessing the value of those collections that are not reported in the entity's balance sheet should be disclosed.   **22**

The financial statements should contain a summary of transactions relating to heritage assets disclosing, for the accounting period and each of the previous four accounting periods: **23**

(a)   the cost of acquisitions of heritage assets;
(b)   the value of heritage assets acquired by donation; and
(c)   the proceeds from disposal of heritage assets.

This summary should show separately transactions for collections that are reported at valuation in the balance sheet and those that are accounted for under the non-recognition approach.

Where it is not practicable to obtain a valuation of heritage assets acquired by donation, the reasons why should be stated. Disclosures should also be provided on the nature and extent of significant donations of heritage assets.

The information required by paragraph 23 may be supplemented by disclosure of other information, for example the sources of funding for acquisition of heritage assets, or expenditure on major restoration costs, but this is not required by this standard.   **24**

The disclosures required by paragraphs 18 to 23 may be presented in aggregate for groups or classes of collection provided this aggregation does not obscure significant information. Amounts in respect of collections that are accounted for at valuation should not be aggregated with amounts in respect of collections that are accounted for under the non-recognition approach.   **25**

Date from which effective and transitional arrangements

26   This standard should be applied in respect of accounting periods ending on or after [*date to be inserted after exposure*]. Earlier application is encouraged.

27   The information required by paragraph 23 need not be given for any accounting period earlier than the period immediately before the period in which this standard is first applied where it is not practicable to do so and a statement to the effect that it is not practicable is made.

Appendix I
The Development of the Exposure Draft

The Board's project on heritage assets was undertaken to address criticisms of the   **1**
current financial reporting requirements for heritage assets. Although a few museums
and galleries account for their heritage assets at a valuation, most adopt an approach
under which assets purchased in 2001 and later years are reflected in the balance
sheet but previously acquired assets are not. In many cases, this results in an amount
in the balance sheet that appears significant but bears little or no relationship to the
value of an entity's collection as a whole. This causes the financial statements to be
potentially misleading and whilst some entities aim to compensate for this by providing supplementary disclosures, the quality of these is uneven, with significant
differences in the information provided by different entities, which impairs its
usefulness.

The proposals set out in this exposure draft have been developed from the Discussion   **2**
Paper 'Heritage Assets—Can Accounting do better?' which was published by the
ASB in January 2006. That paper was developed by the Board's Committee on
Accounting for Public-benefit Entities ('CAPE'), in collaboration with the Interna-
tional Public Sector Accounting Standards Board ('IPSASB'). The Discussion Paper
was reprinted by IPSASB in a Consultation Paper 'Accounting for Heritage Assets
Under the Accrual Basis of Accounting'.

The Discussion Paper sought to encourage a valuation approach on the grounds that   **3**
the best financial reporting requires heritage assets to be reported as assets at current
values. In the light of the mainly favourable responses to its Discussion Paper, the
ASB has decided to issue specific proposals to reform current UK financial reporting
for heritage assets. These proposals emphasise that valuation is required where, and
to the extent that, it is practicable to obtain suitable valuations.

Like this exposure draft, the Discussion Paper proposed that entities should be   **4**
required to report heritage assets at a valuation in the balance sheet where this was
practicable; otherwise a non-recognition approach was to be required. The Discussion Paper proposed the accounting policy should be applied for an entity's total
holding of heritage assets. Although many respondents welcomed the proposals in
the Discussion Paper, and suggested they were a significant improvement on current
requirements, a significant proportion of those who expressed support did not agree
that heritage assets should be treated as assets for financial reporting purposes: their
support was premised on the assumption that the majority of museums and galleries
would adopt a non-recognition approach.

To counter this assumption and require a valuation approach as much as possible,   **5**
the exposure draft proposes the accounting approach should be applied for each
individual collection. The proposals in this exposure draft continue to require that
transactions in heritage assets that are accounted for under the non-recognition
approach should not be treated as giving rise to gains or losses.

The following paragraphs summarise the considerations and arguments that were   **6**
considered in the development of the proposals in this exposure draft.

SCOPE AND DEFINITION

The Discussion Paper discussed two classes of assets similar to heritage assets. It   **7**
proposed that historic buildings used by the entity itself, for example historic

buildings used for teaching by education establishments, should be accounted for under the existing requirements for fixed assets. It also proposed that assets held by entities that are not primarily heritage organisations should not be accounted for as heritage assets. There was general support for these proposals in the responses received, and little demand for any change in the current reporting requirements that apply to them.

8   The Discussion Paper proposed to achieve this through its definition of a heritage asset, which was:

> *An asset with historic, artistic, scientific, technological, geophysical or environ-mental qualities that is held and maintained principally for its contribution to knowledge and culture, and this purpose is central to the objectives of the entity holding it.*

9   Although this definition was broadly supported, many respondents questioned the logic of the phrase '*and this purpose is central to the objectives of the entity holding it*'. A further difficulty is that it seemed to exclude heritage assets where the heritage objective is only one of many of the reporting entity. It would be odd if, where a museum is owned by a local authority, different accounting requirements applied to a museum's own financial statements from those that apply to the authority's con-solidated financial statements. To meet these concerns, references to the objectives of the entity have been deleted from the definition of the term 'heritage asset'. However the scope of the exposure draft limits its application to entities that hold heritage assets 'to contribute to a principal objective of the entity of promoting knowledge and culture'. Accordingly, the requirements of this exposure draft will apply where promoting knowledge and culture is one of the entity's principal objectives even if the entity has other principal objectives.

10   Although profit-oriented entities often contribute to the advancement of knowledge and culture, and may hold heritage assets to this end, it is not intended that they should account for them in accordance with the proposed requirements of the exposure draft if it is not a principal objective of the entity.

11   The scope of the proposals is similar to those for 'non-operational heritage assets' as set out in paragraphs 5.2.18–5.2.22 of the Government's 2006–07 Financial Reporting Manual.

12   As in the Discussion Paper, the definition of a heritage asset is not confined to the objects held by museums and galleries but also includes landscape and coastline, historic buildings and archæological sites where these are held and maintained for their contribution to knowledge and culture.

HERITAGE ASSETS ARE ASSETS

13   The proposals in this exposure draft are based on the principle that, conceptually, heritage assets are assets for financial reporting purposes. This view is consistent with that expressed in FRS 15 (Appendix IV, paragraph 8) and the Discussion Paper.

14   The Discussion Paper noted that that many heritage assets do not provide cash flows to the entity that owns them. Some respondents suggested that this was a sufficient reason to reject the proposition that heritage assets should be reported as assets. However, whilst many assets do contribute to cash inflows (or the saving of cash outflows) that is not an essential characteristic of an asset. Heritage assets clearly

have service potential which enables them to contribute to the entity's objective: a gallery cannot operate unless it has access to works of art.

Many heritage assets are 'inalienable': that is they cannot be sold without the consent **15** of an external party. This is sometimes cited as a reason why heritage assets should not be accounted for as such. However, the effect of inalienability is simply to restrict one possible way in which an asset might provide cash flows: as noted in the previous paragraph, this is not an essential characteristic of an asset.

It is important that where there are restrictions on assets, they are disclosed. How- **16** ever, this is a general point that applies more widely than just to heritage assets, and, for this reason, the exposure draft does not propose a specific requirement for dis- closure of restrictions on the use of heritage assets.

Some respondents pointed out that for many heritage assets the costs of maintenance **17** and preservation are high. Although such costs would presumably depress the value of heritage assets it does not negate the point that the items concerned are assets.

TWO ACCOUNTING APPROACHES

Conceptually, assets should be reported in the balance sheet if they can be measured **18** with sufficient reliability at a relevant current value. There are, however, formidable obstacles to obtaining a measurement basis for many heritage assets and collections of heritage assets: some of the more obvious reasons are mentioned in paragraph 12 of the [draft] FRS. It is clear that in many cases historical cost is not available and that it is impossible to obtain a meaningful valuation. For this reason, the [draft] FRS recognises there may be circumstances where valuation is genuinely imprac- ticable and that, where this is the case, heritage assets should not be reported in the balance sheet.

However, some museums and galleries do report some or all of their collections in **19** the balance sheet, and, as explained below, this gives a fuller and more informative account of their financial position than not recognising them. The proposals in this exposure draft are intended to require this practice, not only by those entities that have already adopted a policy of valuation but by others as well.

The Board recognises there is a balance to be struck between the relevance and **20** reliability of valuations but considers the practicability assessment should emphasise the relevance of valuations – to the extent that valuations that may not be considered wholly reliable can be reported where the information is considered relevant and can be supported by disclosures that explain any limitations in the valuation process.

Some respondents to the Discussion Paper questioned whether there was any pur- **21** pose in reporting the value of collections of heritage assets. Although many museums and galleries will not see their principal objectives in financial terms, they nonetheless use and command economic resources and it is the purpose of the financial state- ments to provide an account of these resources and how they have changed. Reporting the value of heritage assets provides an important context in which other elements of financial performance may be assessed.

REPORTING ON INDIVIDUAL COLLECTIONS

The Board considers the proposals in the exposure draft are an improvement on the **22** current accounting requirements which, in practice, are based upon an arbitrary date of when a heritage asset is acquired. The proposals will also secure recognition in the balance sheet of some heritage assets that would not be recognised under the 'all or nothing' approach proposed in the Discussion Paper. The Board also considers that requiring valuation for individual collections will, when supplemented by enhanced disclosures, support improved consistency in terms of the financial reporting of similar collections held by different institutions.

23   An alternative to recognising valuations of individual collections would be for this information, where available, to be disclosed in the notes to the accounts. This would be consistent with the 'all or nothing' approach to valuation that was proposed in the Discussion Paper but does not reflect the Board's view that, where current valuations are available for collections of heritage assets, and where these provide helpful and relevant information, they should be reported in the balance sheet.

VALUATION

24   Some respondents suggested that the proposals in the Discussion Paper were unduly burdensome, although most were content with the proposed disclosures. Other than disclosure, the proposals in this exposure draft merely require consideration for each collection of whether it is practicable to obtain valuations that meets the criteria set out in paragraph 8 of the [draft] FRS. This will require professional judgements to be made. There may be a few instances where that judgement is finely balanced, but it would seem that in the great majority of cases this consideration would be straightforward.

25   FRS 15 'Tangible fixed assets' already acknowledges that certain of its detailed requirements for valuations may not be appropriate, on cost/benefit grounds, for charities and other not-for-profit and public sector organisations. To encourage valuation, the [draft] FRS proposes extending this by exempting heritage assets that are valued from the requirements of FRS 15 that apply to valuations generally. It is therefore proposed that there be no requirement for the involvement of an external valuer, nor, subject to valuations being kept up to date, is there any prescribed minimum period between valuations.

26   Another relaxation of the general requirements of FRS 15 is that the proposals do not require any specific measurement basis to be used where heritage assets are carried at a valuation. It is, however, required that the valuation provides useful and relevant information. A valuation that is wholly arbitrary, for example, would not meet this requirement and may even be misleading, and so should not be used. Similarly, there would be little value in reporting as a current valuation the cost of reproducing a historic asset: that is the cost of obtaining a replica, not the original that is held.

27   Some constituents suggested that historic cost should be permitted or required as a basis for reporting heritage assets. But, in view of the very long period for which heritage assets are held, and the marked and unpredictable changes in their value that sometimes arise, it is unlikely that information prepared on a historic cost basis would be useful or relevant. It is therefore proposed that historic cost should not be used except where it provides an insight into the current value of items held.

DEPRECIATION AND IMPAIRMENT

28   Where a valuation approach is adopted, the regular revaluation will reflect the total change in value. Depreciation and impairment seem to be unnecessary refinements in this context, and so there are no requirements for depreciation and impairment in the exposure draft. For clarity, an amendment is proposed to FRS 11 'Impairment of

Fixed Assets and Goodwill', which will remove heritage assets from the scope of that standard.

REPORTING ACQUISITIONS AND DISPOSALS OF HERITAGE ASSETS

As heritage assets are assets but are not reported as such where a non-recognition   **29** approach is adopted, the issue arises of how acquisitions are to be reported. Where a cost does not give rise to a reported asset, the usual consequence is that it is accounted for as an expense. However, where a heritage asset is purchased, an asset is clearly acquired: it is not reported as an asset simply because it is not practicable to do so. Reporting the acquisition as an expense would distort the total expenditure for the period. The same considerations apply to disposal proceeds. The [draft] FRS therefore prohibits reporting acquisitions and disposals in the profit and loss account, or an equivalent statement, and requires that they are reported in a primary financial statement that reconciles total recognised gains and losses to changes in total reported net assets.

Many museums and galleries report in accordance with the Statement of Recom-   **30** mended Practice 'Accounting and Reporting by Charities' and accordingly prepare a 'Statement of Financial Activity'. It is expected that proposals to amend the SORP, setting out how the proposed requirements may be complied with in such a statement, will be published in due course.

The Discussion Paper sought views as to whether any other items should be reported   **31** similarly to acquisitions and disposals of heritage assets. Other than funding that has been received specifically for the acquisition of heritage assets, there was little support for this; hence it has not been pursued in this exposure draft. Some respondents noted this will give rise to cash donations and grants being reported as income whilst the cost of the acquisitions they fund will not be treated as an expense. The result will be to show a surplus of income. This is the same as under the valuation approach and, in the Board's view, fairly reflects the transactions for the period.

DONATIONS

Donations of heritage assets should be recognised in the income and expenditure   **32** account at the current value of the assets at the date they are received, except where it is impracticable to obtain a current value. This approach is consistent with FRS 15 'Tangible fixed assets' (paragraph 17) which recognises that it may not always be practicable to obtain a current valuation for donated heritage assets. Where this is the case, paragraph 23 of the [draft] FRS requires disclosure in the notes to the accounts of why a current value cannot be obtained.

Where current values are available, the Board's view is that all donations, regardless   **33** of whether the valuation or non-recognition approach is adopted, should be reported in the income and expenditure account. This has the result that donations of heritage assets and donations of cash are accounted for in a consistent manner.

DISCLOSURES

Most of the proposed requirements for disclosure are similar to those set out in the   **34** Discussion Paper, which were widely supported. The following changes may be noted:

(i)   The Discussion Paper proposed that an entity should disclose its policy for the preservation and management of heritage assets. It did not address whether this disclosure should be made in the financial statements. In order to allow flexibility, the [draft] FRS proposes that this disclosure may either be made in the financial statements or in another document, such as an Operating and Financial Review, provided that the financial statements contain a cross reference to it.

(ii) The Discussion Paper proposed a five-year financial summary of activity, showing acquisitions and disposals of heritage assets, funding and major restoration costs. However, a requirement to disclose funding in the summary might duplicate other requirements, or be confusing. There would also be significant difficulty in developing a suitable definition of 'major restoration costs'. For these reasons, the [draft] FRS does not require the summary to deal with funding or major restoration costs but notes that such information may be given, if desired.

(iii) To avoid undue burdens in implementing the standard, the summary is permitted to be built up going forward: only two years' information is required in the year in which the standard is first applied, provided it is stated that it is not practicable to provide information for earlier periods.

Appendix II
Illustrative examples of disclosures

The following examples illustrate disclosures that might be made to comply with the requirements set out in paragraphs 18 to 23 of the [draft] FRS. To keep the illustrations simple, comparative information is not given, although this would normally be required.

EXAMPLE 1—THE VINTAGE CAR MUSEUM: VALUATION OF MAIN COLLECTION

The Museum holds a collection of vintage cars and a collection of motoring ephemera for the purpose of fostering and promoting a public interest in the history of vintage cars. The vintage car collection is capitalised at market value and was acquired through donations and purchases. The collection of motoring ephemera includes manuals, brochures and advertising material.

The Trustees have concluded that whilst it is practicable to obtain a valuation of the collection of vintage cars, a valuation for the collection of ephemera would not provide information that is useful and relevant in assessing the value of the collection at the balance sheet date.

Note 1 Accounting policies

Heritage assets

The Museum's collection of cars is reported in the Balance Sheet at market value. Valuations are made by professional valuers (Parker, Glass and Co). Approximately one-third of the collection is valued each year on a rolling basis. Gains and losses on revaluation are recognised in the Statement of Total Recognised Gains and Losses.

It is the Museum's policy to maintain vehicles in the collection in full working order and maintenance costs are charged to the Income and Expenditure Account when incurred. The vehicles are deemed to have indeterminate lives and the Trustees do not therefore consider it appropriate to charge depreciation in respect of the collection.

In addition, the Museum holds a collection of motoring ephemera which is not recognised in the Balance Sheet as the Trustees believe the benefits of providing a valuation would not justify the cost. Nearly all items in the collection have a financial value of less than £50 and, as far as the Trustees are aware, no individual item is worth more that £1,000.

The Museum's management policy in respect of its collections is summarised in Note 8 with further information available from the March 2006 publication "Bringing Vintage Cars to Life" which is available from the Museum's website.

Note 7(a) Tangible fixed assets – heritage assets

	Vintage car collection £000
Cost or valuation	
1 April 2005	6,700
Additions	200
Disposals	(50)
Revaluation	335
31 March 2006	**7,185**

The above represents valuations made in the following financial years:

2005–06	3,000
2004–05	2,185
2003–04	2,000
	7,185

The vintage car collection includes the S4 Bentley Sport driven to victory by John Duff and Frank Clement in the 1924 Le Mans race. This vehicle has been included in the accounts

at a valuation made in 2004–05 of £150,000 reflecting cars of a similar model and vintage. However, the Museum's professional valuers have advised that the car would probably realise significantly more than this if it were to be sold on the open market.

Additions in 2005–06 comprise:

£200,000 purchase of a private collection of 1950s Jaguar sports cars

Disposals in 2005–06 comprise:

£50,000 sale of Lotus Elite and Triumph TR2.

Note 7(b) Five-year financial summary of heritage asset transactions:

	2005–06	2004–05	2003–04	2002–03	2001–02
	£000	£000	£000	£000	£000
Additions:					
Purchases	200	130	100	160	50
Donations	-	25	20	-	-
Total additions	200	155	120	160	50
Disposals	50	-	30	50	

The above information relates only to transactions in cars.

The only transactions in ephemera during the periods were acquisitions by donation for which it is impracticable to obtain a valuation. The Museum wishes to acknowledge in particular the donation of 85 workshop manuals in 2005–06 from the estate of the late Toad of Toad Hall.

Note 8 Heritage assets management policy

The Museum maintains a collection of 250 vintage and classic cars which reflect the history of the British sports car from 1900–1960. Approximately 240 of these are on display to the public, while the remainder are held in the Museum's maintenance depot undergoing or awaiting repair.

Acquisitions are made by purchase or donation. The Museum occasionally disposes of objects from the collection in order to fund new acquisitions where the Trustees determine this does not detract from the integrity of the collection.

The Museum also holds a collection of motoring ephemera associated with the history of the British sports car. The collection comprises some 2,000 objects including manuals, brochures and advertising material. Objects have been acquired by purchase or through direct donation. The Museum draws upon this collection for displays in the public rooms and arranges for private inspection by prior arrangement.

EXAMPLE 2— THE BARSETSHIRE MUSEUM: VALUATION OF CERTAIN COLLECTIONS

The Museum holds collections of heritage assets relating to the natural and man-made history of Barsetshire. There are three distinct collections: artefacts, fossils and paintings of local interest.

In the opinion of the Trustees it is impractical for the Museum to value its collections of fossils and artefacts. This is owing to the lack of comparable market values, the diverse nature of the objects and the volume of items held.

The Trustees consider that valuations are available for the collection of local paintings which is regularly being updated through acquisitions either by purchase or donation. The Trustees have also approved the sale of certain paintings.

For the collections of fossils and artefacts that are accounted for using a non-recognition approach, transactions might be presented in the Statement of Change in Recognised Net Assets as follows:

Statement of Change in Recognised Net Assets	£000s	£000s
Recognised gains/(losses) for the financial year		600
Heritage asset transactions (Note 8):		
Proceeds from disposal of heritage assets	-	
Acquisition of heritage assets	(150)	
Net heritage asset transactions		(150)
Change in recognised net assets		450

The following disclosures would be provided in the notes to the financial statements.

Note 1 Accounting policies

Tangible fixed assets and depreciation

Heritage assets

The Museum has three collections of heritage assets which are held in support of the Museum's primary objective of increasing knowledge, understanding and appreciation of the Barsetshire landscape. The collections are accounted for as follows.

Paintings

The collection of paintings, which also includes sketches and photographs, is reported in the Balance Sheet at market value. Individual items in the collection are periodically revalued by an external valuer with any surplus or deficit on revaluation being charged to the Statement of Total Recognised Gains and Losses.

Acquisitions are made by purchase or donation. Purchases are initially recorded at cost and donations are recorded at market value ascertained by the Museum's curators with reference, where possible, to commercial markets using recent transaction information from auctions.

Where collection items are disposed of, the profit or loss on disposal is reported in the Statement of Total Recognised Gains and Losses.

Artefacts and Fossils

The Trustees do not consider that it is practicable to obtain valuations for the collections of artefacts and fossils owing to the diverse nature of the assets held, the number of assets held and the lack of comparable market values. The Museum does not therefore recognise these collections on its Balance Sheet.

For the collections of artefacts and fossils, acquisitions are presented in the Statement of Change in Recognised Net Assets as reductions in net assets when legal title passes to the Museum. Purchases are recorded at cost with the Museum's curator's making a best estimate of market value for reporting donations.

Where items from the artefact and fossil collections are disposed of, any disposal proceeds are presented in the Statement of Change in Recognised Net Assets as increases in net assets.

Preservation costs

Expenditure which, in the Trustees' view, is required to preserve or clearly prevent further deterioration of individual collection items is recognised in the income and expenditure account when it is incurred.

Further information on the collections is given in Notes 7, 8 and 9 to the accounts.

Note 7 Tangible fixed assets – heritage assets

	Paintings £000
Cost or valuation	
1 April 2005	28,900
Additions	400
Disposals	(80)
Revaluation	2,600
31 March 2006	**30,820**

The Museum's external valuer (Turner, Constable and Co) carried out a full valuation of the collection of paintings as at 31 March 2006. The valuations were based on commercial markets, including recent transaction information from auctions where similar types of paintings are regularly being purchased. During the year, a painting that was valued in last year's accounts at £175,000 suffered damage. The revaluation surplus is net of the write down of this painting to its new value of £25,000.

A particularly significant exhibit within the collection is the portrait of the Lady Elinor May, Countess of Barset by William Maclean ca 1750. The portrait is unusual as Maclean is more widely known for his landscapes of the Scottish Highlands. The painting has been valued by an external valuer at £2.5 million. Expert opinion is divided as to the artistic merit of the portrait. A Maclean landscape was recently sold at auction for £3 million.

Additions in 2005–06 comprise:

* £200,000 purchase of a collection of 20 watercolours of Barsetshire landscapes by a local artist.

* £150,000 purchase at auction of a private collection of oil paintings from the estate of a local family.

* £50,000 donation of various items of local interest whose public display will, in the opinion of the Trustees, support the Museum's objective.

Disposals in 2005–06 comprise:

* £80,000 disposal of a piece of contemporary art that was donated to the Museum by a local artist in 2004–05. The disposal, which is to a private gallery that specialises in contemporary art, was approved by both the artist and the Trustees. The proceeds were used to fund additions to the collection of paintings in 2005–06.

Note 8 Five-year financial summary of heritage asset transactions:

	2005–06	2004–05	2003–04	2002–03	2001–02
Purchases:	£000	£000	£000	£000	£000
Paintings	350	70	100	160	50
Artefacts and Fossils	150	5	65	10	20
Donations					
Paintings	50	20	20	-	-
Total additions	550	95	185	170	70
Disposals					
Paintings	80	20	-	-	10

Note 9 Further information of the Museum's collections of heritage assets

Paintings of local interest

The collection consists of 3,000 paintings, sketches and photographs from the last 150 years illustrating the changing landscape and local populace. The collection has been significantly enhanced in 2005–06 by the acquisition of a collection of watercolours from a local artist and a collection of oil paintings from the estate of a local family. The watercolours comprise modern Barsetshire landscapes with the oil paintings depicting more traditional Barsetshire landscapes from the late 19th and early 20th centuries.

The Museum occasionally makes available on loan items from the collection to other regional museums and also accepts paintings and other items on loan. At any time approximately 50 per cent of the collections are on display. The remaining items are held in storage but access is permitted to scholars and others for research purposes.

Artefacts and Fossils

The Museum's collections of fossils and artefacts have been developed over 120 years and are used for reference, research and education. The Museum occasionally makes available on loan objects to other regional museums and also accepts objects on loan.

At any time approximately 20 per cent of the items in the collections are on display. The remaining items are held in storage but access is permitted to scholars for research purposes.

Fossils

The collection consists of 2,000 specimens from the Cretaceous to the Pleistocene period (145 million to 2 million years ago) and includes fossil fish remains such as shark and ray teeth, marine molluscs and sponges and disarticulated remains of fossil dinosaurs and mammals. It records the development of fauna from the local area. The collection was principally created from a bequest from Octavius Bayley, Victorian philanthropist and fossil enthusiast.

Artefacts

The collection consists of 5,000 miscellaneous man-made objects including flints, pottery and coins from the period 3000 BC to 1900 AD and reflects the activity of man in the local area over this period. The collection has been developed over many years from digs and field surveys undertaken by the county archaeologists.

Heritage assets of particular importance

As explained in note 7, the Museum holds one painting which, in the opinion of the Trustees is of particular significance, and has been valued by an external valuer at £2.5 million. The overall value of the collection, as reported in note 7, at 31 March 2006 is £30.8 million.

The Museum also holds certain items which the Trustees regard as particularly important to the collections of fossils and artefacts and are likely to have a significant monetary value in comparison with other items in these collections. Of particular importance are artefacts from the tomb of Baron Percy de Barsette ca 1100-1160 comprising chain mail armour, a long shield and a sword. These objects are in poor condition but are of great rarity. It is not practicable to provide an indication of their value.

Preservation and management

The Museum has a rolling programme of major restoration developed from a comprehensive review of the condition of the Museum's collections that was carried out in 2000–01. The review was commissioned by the Trustees following a major flood in the basement areas where items not on public display are stored.

The total cost of the restoration programme is £250,000 which is being partly funded by a £100,000 grant from the Heritage Preservation Fund. At the end of 2005–06, the programme is around 80 per cent complete with the Trustees expecting the programme to be completed in 2006–07. The costs of the programme have been charged to the Income and Expenditure account.

Each of the collections is managed by a Curator who reports to the Director of Collections. The Curators manage the collections in accordance with policies that are approved by the Trustees. Further information is provided in the Museum's separate publication 'The Management and Preservation of the Barsetshire Museum's Collections', which is available on the Museum's website. As is explained in that publication, assets in the collection are only disposed of where, in the opinion of the Trustees, an item does not contribute to the interest and diversity of the Museum's collection.

EXAMPLE 3—THE ANCIENT MONUMENT MUSEUM: NON-RECOGNITION APPROACH

The Museum maintains four Neolithic burial mounds and, although it periodically undertakes restoration work, none has been undertaken recently. In the Trustees' opinion it is not practicable to obtain any valuations of the burial mounds that would provide useful and relevant information, hence the non-recognition approach has been adopted. As there are no heritage asset transactions to report for the period, the Museum has not prepared a Statement of Change in Recognised Net Assets.

The following disclosures are provided in the financial statements.

Footnote to Income and Expenditure Account

The net surplus represents the total change in recognised net assets and so no separate Statement of Change in Recognised Net Assets has been prepared.

Note 1 Accounting policies

Heritage assets not recognised in the Balance Sheet

The Museum maintains four neolithic burial mounds in support of the Museum's objective to protect these historic monuments for the benefit of future generations. The Trustees consider that owing to the incomparable nature of the burial mounds it would not be practicable to obtain valuations for them and so no value is reported for these assets in the Museum's Balance Sheet.

Expenditure on major restoration

The cost of associated major repairs is reported in the Income and Expenditure Account in the year it is incurred.

Further information is given in Note 8 to the accounts.

Note 8 Heritage Assets not recognised in the balance sheet

The Museum maintains four neolithic burial mounds which were acquired during the 19th century as a gift from the former landowner at no cost to the Museum. No related artefacts are held.

There have been no acquisitions or disposals of heritage assets during the last five years.

The Museum aims to maintain the condition of the earthworks in a steady state of repair. Detailed surveys are undertaken at least every five years. The last survey was carried out during 2001-02 following a landslip. As a result, some underpinning work was undertaken. The cost of these works was not capitalised in the Balance Sheet. No major restoration costs were incurred during 2005-06.

Public access to the burial mounts is permitted at weekends and public holidays between March and October and, by prior arrangement, at other times.

Amendment to FRS 20 (IFRS 2) 'Share-based Payment' Vesting Conditions and Cancellations

Contents

Preface

BACKGROUND

1   In April 2004 the Accounting Standards Board (the ASB) issued FRS 20 (IFRS 2) 'Share-based Payment'. FRS 20 implemented the requirements of IFRS 2 for those applying UK standards.

2   In February 2006, the IASB issued 'Proposed Amendments to IFRS 2 Share-based Payment' proposing limited amendments to IFRS 2.

3   The ASB is proposing to make equivalent amendments to FRS 20, as set out in this exposure draft.

4   The proposals would amend IFRS 2 and FRS 20 to define vesting conditions and clarify the accounting treatment of cancellations by parties other than the entity. These proposals are being made because of uncertainties as to how the standards apply to employee share purchase plans.

5   Under IFRS 2 and FRS 20, where share options are granted to employees, the value of the options (at grant date) is treated as an expense over the period in which services are received from the employees in exchange for the options – normally the period until the options can be exercised.

6   Share options granted to an employee can fail to be exercised for two main reasons:

   (a)   the 'vesting conditions' that must be satisfied before the options can be exercised are not met – vesting conditions are requirements for the employee to remain in the employment for a specified period, or requirements for specified performance targets by the entity to be met;
   (b)   the share options may be cancelled.

7   Under IFRS 2 and FRS 20 a failure to meet the vesting condition results in the cost being recognised in profit and loss account in respect of the options being reversed, so that the options are treated as never having been granted in the first place. However, a very different treatment is required for share options cancelled by the employer. The standards treat employer cancellations as an acceleration of vesting, and all unamortised costs relating to the options are recognised immediately. However, it is currently unclear how a cancellation by the employee should be treated – either as a failure to meet vesting conditions, or in the same way as a cancellation by the employer.

8   This is particularly relevant to savings-based share option schemes (such as Save As You Earn (SAYE) schemes in the UK), where the employee must make monthly savings contributions to remain in the scheme – if the monthly contributions are not made, the options are cancelled.

IASB'S PROPOSED AMENDMENT

9   The proposed amendment would require cancellations by the employee to be treated in the same way as cancellations by the employer, resulting in an accelerated charge to profit and loss account of the unamortised balance of the value of the options granted.

The issue was addressed by IFRIC in 2004, and a draft Interpretation D11 on **10** employee share purchase plans (ESPPs) issued which set out a similar conclusion. This draft was also issued by the UITF in Information Sheet 73 (February 2005) for comment, although the UITF was not in agreement with the proposal.

After considering respondents' comments on D11, IFRIC was unable to reach a **11** consensus, and the issue was referred to the IASB. The IASB has now considered the issue and proposed amendments to IFRS 2.

CONCERNS WITH THE PROPOSALS

Several concerns were raised at the time of the IFRIC and UITF discussions, in **12** relation to the effect on SAYE schemes, and arguing that treating employee with-drawals from SAYE schemes in the same way as cancellations by the employer is not a fair representation. An SAYE scheme has two elements. One is an agreement to save (with a third party). The other is an option over the company's shares that can only be exercised using the proceeds of the savings account (which includes tax free interest and a bonus). However, for the option to vest, the employee must remain in employment and continue to save for a specified period. If he fails to satisfy either condition, he forfeits the option.

To treat such an employee withdrawal as an accelerated vesting gives rise to the **13** following concerns:

(a) Common reasons for employees withdrawing from SAYE schemes are:
   - they change their minds, often early on, about committing to monthly saving; alternatively, they simply need the cash
   - they leave the company
   - they join a better scheme.
   The accounting result seems harsh, if not penal for SAYE schemes. For example, if an employee decides not to continue to save after six months and forfeits his option, why should that give rise to an immediate expense for the company?
(b) A common reason for an employee to withdraw from an ESPP scheme is that he or she is preparing to resign. There seems little difference in substance between an employee who withdraws and then resigns, and an employee who resigns and thereby withdraws – yet under the proposed amendment to IFRS 2 the accounting will be fundamentally different. (Note, however, that paragraph BC19 of the IASB's Basis for Conclusions indicates that withdrawal should be treated as a forfeiture when it is as a consequence of their expected termination of employment).
(c) Employee withdrawals are dissimilar from employer cancellations. Employers are not free to cancel share option arrangements – agreement of the employees will likely have to be bought. Employees, on the other hand, are free to withdraw from SAYE schemes – this seems less like an accelerated vesting. The difference may justify a different accounting treatment.
(d) Where an employee cancels participation in one SAYE scheme in order to take up options under a new scheme offered by the employer, this can be seen as similar to a modification of the first scheme. Under IFRS 2 and FRS 20 a modification would be accounted for by continuing the expensing of the value attached to the original grant and in addition expensing the value attributed to the modification over the period to the new vesting date; this is different from the proposed treatment as a cancellation of the first scheme.

IASB'S ARGUMENTS

14   IASB, in their Basis for Conclusions, set out four possible treatments for employee cancellations of options (paragraph BC8):

- reverse the expenditure to date (the same as a forfeiture such as failure to meet vesting conditions)
- cease recognising future expense from the date of cancellation
- continue recognising expense as if the cancellation had not occurred
- accelerate recognition of the remaining expense (the same as a cancellation by the entity).

15   IFRS 2 and FRS 20 are based on the principle that the services received in exchange for the issue of shares or options over shares should be reflected in the profit and loss account at their full cost as those services are received, and that this cost is best measured by using the fair value of the shares or options issued as a proxy. IASB argue (in paragraph BC11) that it would be inconsistent with this principle for the expenditure to date to be reversed on a cancellation, or for the recognition of the cost to cease on cancellation of the option (since the services will continue to be received).

16   However, the argument against continuing to recognise the cost (paragraphs BC12-15) is not based on this principle, but on the difficulty of distinguishing between cancellations by the employer and cancellations by the employee, and the 'structuring' opportunities that would arise. Whilst this may be the case for 'executive' schemes, it is difficult to see how such ambiguity and structuring can arise in normal SAYE schemes.

17   The IASB's conclusion that the cost must be recognised in full at the time of cancellation therefore appears driven more by concerns over abuse than consistency with the principles.

18   Indeed, the IASB's reasons in the Basis for Conclusions for IFRS 2 itself (paragraph BC233) for requiring an immediate recognition of costs in the case of cancellations by the entity are also partly in response to concerns that abuse will arise. This paragraph reads, in part:

> "In the Board's view, it is very unlikely that a share option or share grant would be cancelled without some compensation to the counterparty, either in the form of cash or replacement share options. Moreover, the Board saw no difference between a repricing of share options and a cancellation of share options followed by the granting of replacement share options at a lower exercise price, and therefore concluded that the accounting treatment should be the same."

19   The IASB also state, in paragraph BC 10, that whereas forfeitures are not taken into account in the determination of the fair value of the options given, the probability that counterparties will cancel their participation is taken into account. It is not clear whether this is in fact taken into account, or indeed whether it is practicable to estimate the likely level of cancellations (which might depend on many factors affecting employees' ability and willingness to save, including future movements in the share price). The ASB has included a question on this issue in the Invitation to comment set out below.

CONCLUSION

20   In summary, the ASB has concerns over the proposed amendment and its impact on entities with SAYE schemes. However, as most entities with SAYE schemes and

applying UK standards are likely to be subsidiaries of listed groups that apply IFRS, there seems little merit in allowing FRS 20 to diverge from IFRS 2 on this issue. The ASB therefore proposes to amend FRS 20 to maintain consistency with IFRS 2 if the amendment to IFRS 2 is confirmed by the IASB.

INVITATION TO COMMENT

The ASB is issuing this exposure draft to request comments on the IASB's proposals and on the ASB's proposals for implementing them in the UK. The IASB's Invitation to comment is set out on pages 14 to 15 of this exposure draft. In addition, the ASB would welcome comments on the following issues:

21

ASB Q1: What are the implications of implementing these proposals in the UK, in relation to SAYE schemes or other employee share schemes?

ASB Q2: In paragraph BC 10 of the Basis of Conclusions, the IASB state that the expected level of employee cancellations should be taken into account in determining the fair value of the options at their grant date. Are you aware of practical difficulties this would involve?

Proposed amendment to Financial Reporting Standard 20 (IFRS 2) 'Share-based payment'

Contents

Introduction*

This Exposure Draft contains proposals by the International Accounting Standards Board to amend IFRS 2 *Share-based Payment* to define vesting conditions and clarify the accounting treatment of cancellations by parties other than the entity. **1**

IFRS 2 describes vesting conditions as including service conditions and performance conditions. It is silent on whether other features of a share-based payment transaction are vesting conditions. **2**

IFRS 2 specifies the accounting treatment when an entity cancels a grant of equity instruments. It does not state how cancellations by a party other than the entity should be accounted for. **3**

These issues were considered by the International Financial Reporting Interpretations Committee (IFRIC) in its draft Interpretation D11 *Changes in Contributions to Employee Share Purchase Plans,* which was published for comment in December 2004†. However, the IFRIC was subsequently unable to reach a consensus and the issues were referred to the Board. The Board agreed with the IFRIC that these issues should be clarified. Accordingly, this document sets out the Board's proposed definition of vesting conditions and guidance on the accounting treatment of cancellations by parties other than the entity. **4**

FEATURES OF THIS EXPOSURE DRAFT

The Exposure Draft proposes amendments that: **5**

(a) restrict vesting conditions to service conditions and performance conditions;
(b) require cancellations by parties other than the entity, whether by employees, shareholders or any other parties, to be accounted for in the same way as cancellations by the entity (paragraph 28 of IFRS 2);
(c) require these changes to be applied in annual periods beginning on or after 1 January 2007. The amendments are to be applied retrospectively.

---

*ASB footnote: This introduction has been prepared by the IASB and is included unamended. References here to the 'Board' are to the IASB.

†ASB footnote: Similar proposals were issued in the UK by the UITF in Information Sheet No. 73, issued in February 2005.

Invitation to Comment

The International Accounting Standards Board invites comments on the amendments proposed in this Exposure Draft, particularly on the questions set out below. Comments are most helpful if they:

(a)   comment on the questions as stated;
(b)   contain a clear rationale; and
(c)   include any alternative the Board should consider, if applicable.

Respondents should submit comments in writing so as to be received no later than **2 June 2006**.

Question 1 – Vesting conditions

The Exposure Draft proposes that vesting conditions should be restricted to performance conditions and service conditions.

Do you agree? If not, what changes do you propose, and why?

Question 2 – Cancellations

The Exposure Draft proposes that cancellations by parties other than the entity should be accounted for in the same way as cancellations by the entity.

Do you agree that all cancellations should be treated in the same way? If not, please specify the nature of any differences between types of cancellations and explain how they influence the selection of appropriate accounting requirements.

Question 3 – Effective date and transition

The proposed changes would apply to periods beginning on or after 1 January 2007, and would be required to be applied retrospectively. Earlier application would be encouraged.

Are the proposed effective date and transition appropriate? If not, what do you propose, and why?

Proposed Amendments to FRS 20 (IFRS 2)
Share-based Payment

In Appendix A, the definition of **vesting conditions** is amended ~~(new text is underlined and deleted text is struck through) as follows~~ to read:

---

vesting conditions ...Vesting conditions are either service conditions, which require the other party to complete a specified period of service, or performance conditions, which require specified performance targets to be met (such as a specified increase in the entity's profit over a specified time).

Paragraph 28 is amended ~~(new text is underlined and deleted text is struck through) as follows~~ to read:

If a grant of equity instruments is cancelled or settled during the vesting period (other than a grant cancelled by forfeiture when the vesting conditions are not satisfied) ...   **28**

Paragraph 61 is added, as follows:

An entity shall apply the following amendments retrospectively in annual periods beginning on or after 1 January 2007:   **61**

(a) the revised definition of vesting conditions in Appendix A;*
(b) the amendment in paragraph 28.†
Earlier application is encouraged. If an entity applies the amendments above for a period beginning before 1 January 2007, it shall disclose that fact.

---

*Vesting conditions <u>are either</u> ~~include~~ service conditions, ... ~~and~~ <u>or</u> performance conditions...

†If ~~the entity cancels or settles~~ a grant of equity instruments <u>is cancelled or settled</u>.

Basis for Conclusions

This Basis for Conclusions accompanies, but is not part of, the proposed Amendments to IFRS 2.

> ASB Note: The Basis for Conclusions material that the IASB prepared to accompany its exposure draft is set out below in full. All references in this section to 'the Board' and 'Board members' are references to the IASB Board and IASB Board members.

INTRODUCTION

BC1   This Basis for Conclusions summarises the International Accounting Standards Board's considerations in reaching the conclusions in the Exposure Draft of Proposed Amendments to IFRS 2—*Vesting Conditions and Cancellations*. Individual Board members gave greater weight to some factors than to others.

VESTING CONDITIONS

BC2   IFRS 2 states that vesting conditions include service and performance conditions. Paragraph BC171 of the Basis for Conclusions to IFRS 2 describes vesting conditions as those conditions that ensure that the counterparty provides the services required to 'pay' for the equity instruments issued. For example, service conditions are imposed to ensure that employees provide a minimum period of service in return for the equity instruments. Performance conditions are usually imposed to ensure that a minimum level or quality of service is provided by using performance targets as an incentive.

BC3   In developing these proposals, the Board considered whether other features of a share-based payment transaction should be regarded as vesting conditions. For example, some employee share purchase plans require employees to make regular plan contributions over a specified period. In other plans, employees may be awarded an initial grant of shares in a matching share scheme. If the initial grant of shares has not been sold or transferred during a specified period an additional grant of shares is awarded at a future date.

BC4   The Board acknowledged that additional features, such as a contribution requirement or a requirement to hold an initial grant of shares, may constitute terms that must be satisfied in order for the equity instrument to be issued to the counterparty. These additional features are taken into account in the measurement of the fair value of the equity instrument. However, they are not vesting conditions because they do not ensure that the counterparty provides the services required to 'pay' for the equity instruments.

BC5   More generally, the Board noted that the only conditions that ensure the counterparty provides the services required to 'pay' for the equity instruments granted are either the service conditions themselves, or the conditions that directly affect the services rendered. Therefore, the Board concluded that vesting conditions are either service conditions or performance conditions. No other features should be considered vesting conditions.

CANCELLATIONS

The Board noted that cancellations can be separated into three categories: cancellations by the entity, cancellations by the counterparty (eg an employee or service provider) and cancellations by a third party (eg a shareholder). The Board considered the treatment of each type of cancellation and concluded that all cancellations should receive the same accounting treatment.   **BC6**

Cancellations by the counterparty

Counterparties may cancel their participation in a plan directly or indirectly by failing to meet a non-vesting condition.* For example, if an employee share purchase plan requires employees to make regular plan contributions over a specified period, the employees may cancel their participation in the plan indirectly by ceasing to make contributions to the plan.   **BC7**

The Board considered the four ways in which a counterparty cancellation could be accounted for. The entity could: **BC8**

(a)   reverse the expense charged to date (same as a forfeiture);
(b)   cease recognising future expense from the date of cancellation;
(c)   continue recognising the expense as if the cancellation had not occurred; or
(d)   accelerate the recognition of the remaining expense (same as a cancellation by the entity).

The Board noted that the primary objective of IFRS 2 is to measure the value of goods or services received in return for the equity instruments granted. If a counterparty cancels participation in a plan, this does not imply that the services required to pay for the equity instrument have not been (or will not be) rendered.   **BC9**

Furthermore, if the event were a forfeiture, a reversal of the expense would be appropriate because no adjustment for forfeitures is included in the grant date fair value of the equity instrument.† However, the fair value of the equity instrument takes into account all the factors that a knowledgeable, willing market participant would take into account at the grant date, including the probability that counterparties will cancel their participation in a plan.   **BC10**

Therefore, the Board concluded that, when a cancellation by a counterparty occurs, reversing the expense or ceasing to recognise future expense would be inappropriate, because this would be inconsistent with the primary objective of measuring the value of the goods or services received and with the grant date measurement approach.   **BC11**

The Board then considered whether the entity should continue to recognise the expense as if the cancellation had not occurred or accelerate the recognition of the remaining expense (as with a cancellation by the entity). In particular, the Board deliberated whether a cancellation by a counterparty should be treated differently from a cancellation by the entity.   **BC12**

The Board observed that in some cases, legal, taxation or other factors can make it difficult to identify whether the entity or the counterparty cancelled the counterparty's participation in the plan.   **BC13**

---

*Failure to meet a vesting condition is a forfeiture.

†Where the goods or services received are measured by reference to the fair value of the equity instruments granted.

BC14　Suitable non-arbitrary and unambiguous criteria would be needed to distinguish these events. The Board observed that such criteria do not exist at present and that to develop them would be difficult and involve a lengthy process. The Board was not convinced that the potential improvement in financial reporting would be commensurate with the resources that would be required.

BC15　The Board also noted that requiring more than one method of accounting for cancellations would create incentives for structuring transactions to achieve a desired accounting result, particularly because the different methods being considered (ie the acceleration of expense method and the continuation of expense method) produce significantly different accounting results.

BC16　Therefore, the Board concluded that a cancellation by the counterparty should be treated in the same way as a cancellation by the entity.

Cancellations and settlements by other parties

BC17　The Board also noted that a cancellation or settlement by an entity is economically equivalent to a cancellation or settlement by a third party on the entity's behalf and should therefore receive the same accounting treatment.

Cancellations and termination of employment

BC18　Some have argued that there is an apparent discrepancy between the treatment of cancellations by employees immediately before they leave service (which are cancellations) and cancellations by employees on leaving service (which are forfeitures).

BC19　The Board observed that this apparent discrepancy could arise only when it is clear that the employees are cancelling their participation in the plan as a consequence of their expected termination of employment. Moreover, the Board noted that, in this case, it would be clear that the grant has been cancelled by forfeiture and, furthermore, that paragraph 28 of the IFRS does not require grants that are cancelled by forfeiture to be treated as cancellations. Therefore, the Board does not propose to issue any additional guidance.

CONSISTENCY WITH US GAAP

BC20　The Board noted that the relevant requirements of the US standard SFAS 123 (revised 2004) *Share-based Payment* are the same as the proposed Amendments. In particular, vesting conditions are restricted to service conditions and performance conditions and all cancellations receive the same accounting treatment.

TRANSITION REQUIREMENTS

BC21　IFRS 2 became effective on 1 January 2005. The Board noted that if an entity's financial statements in previous years contain any material disclosed or undisclosed departures from the requirements of the proposed Amendments, the entity would be required to apply IAS 8 *Accounting Policies, Changes in Accounting Estimates and Errors* in correcting them. However, entities that have applied IFRS 2 should have sufficient information to apply the proposed Amendments retrospectively.

BC22　The Board also noted that the entity is not required to apply IFRS 2 to share-based payments that have been cancelled before the date of transition. Therefore, entities that will adopt the standard for the first time would not need to apply an unacceptable level of hindsight in applying the proposed Amendments.

Accordingly, the Board concluded that the proposed Amendments should be applied retrospectively and that no specific transition requirements should be proposed. **BC23**

Statement of Principles for Financial Reporting Proposed Interpretation for Public Benefit Entities

Contents

Preface

INTRODUCTION

Statement of Principles for Financial Reporting

The Accounting Standards Board (the Board) issued the Statement of Principles for **1** Financial Reporting (the Statement) in December 1999. This sets out the principles that the Board believes should underlie the preparation and presentation of general purpose financial statements.

The primary purpose of the Statement is to provide a coherent frame of reference to **2** be used by the Board in the development and review of accounting standards and by others who interact with the Board during the standard-setting process. Publication of the principles was also intended to assist preparers and users of financial statements, as well as auditors and others, to understand the Board's approach to formulating accounting standards and the nature and function of information reported in general purpose financial statements.

The Statement is primarily intended to be relevant to the financial statements of **3** profit-oriented entities in the private and public sectors. However, the Board believes that a common set of principles should underlie financial reporting by all entities. This will assist users in understanding financial statements regardless of the nature of the entity producing them and allow comparability, where appropriate, between all entities.

Proposed Interpretation for Public Benefit Entities

In May 2003, the Board issued a Discussion Paper 'Statement of Principles for **4** Financial Reporting: Proposed Interpretation for Public Benefit Entities'. The Discussion Paper sought comments on the Board's views of the application of the principles within the Statement to public benefit entities.

The Board received a number of helpful responses to the Discussion Paper and, as a **5** result, has redebated a number of issues. In particular there was a great deal of support for the project.

In a number of areas the Exposure Draft differs from the Discussion Paper, as a **6** result of those redeliberations. Neither the Discussion Paper, nor the Exposure Draft, attempt to redebate or update the Statement itself.

The Interpretation proposed within the Exposure Draft is intended to be relevant to **7** the financial statements of all public benefit entities, regardless of their size, whether or not they make a surplus and whether they are private or public sector entities. However, it does not apply to profit-oriented entities, including any in the public sector.

The proposed Interpretation is intended to operate alongside the existing Statement **8** expanding on the common underlying principles for public benefit entities, and therefore at the margin there should be no difference in financial reporting resulting from applying the Statement or the proposed Interpretation. As a result the Board has decided not to produce a list of entities that it believes meet the definition of a public benefit entity.

INTERNATIONAL DEVELOPMENTS AND CONVERGENCE

9   An EU Regulation requires all listed companies in the EU to prepare their consolidated financial statements in accordance with EU-adopted international accounting standards from 2005. International Financial Reporting Standards (IFRS) set by the IASB form the basis of these adopted standards. In addition other companies are permitted to choose to adopt the same framework, unless they are charitable companies, which must continue to report under UK accounting standards. As a result it is expected that most public benefit entities will continue to prepare their financial statements in accordance with UK accounting standards and, where applicable, Statements of Recommended Practice (SORPs) that have been developed to provide guidance on the application of UK accounting standards in the circumstances of particular sectors.

10 The ASB is pursuing a programme of convergence between UK accounting standards and IFRS by issuing new UK standards that are based on IFRS. As a result, over time, all UK entities will be preparing their financial statements in accordance with standards based on the same core set of IFRS.

11 The IASB has on its agenda a joint project with the Financial Accounting Standards Board (FASB) in the USA which aims to develop a conceptual framework that combines and improves upon the existing frameworks. The initial focus is on concepts applicable to private sector business entities. At a later stage it is possible that the IASB will expand the project to include private not-for-profit entities. The ASB believes that the optimum approach would be for public benefit entities to be considered at the same time as profit-oriented entities. The ASB will feed its views into the IASB project and, in the longer term, reflect upon the implications of this work for the Statement and the proposed Interpretation.

International Public Sector Accounting Standards Board (IPSASB)

12 IPSASB* continues with its standards programme to develop and maintain International Public Sector Accounting Standards (IPSASs) for accounting by governmental bodies. Most of the standards currently in issue are based on International Accounting Standards extant at 31 August 1997, although work has commenced on updating some standards for the IASB's recent improvements to existing IFRSs, such that they will be based on IFRS extant at 31 December 2003.

13 The scope of this Exposure Draft, which includes all public benefit entities, regardless of whether they are in the public or private sector, is wider than the work of the IPSASB, which covers only the public sector.

14 IPSASB's active work programme currently includes developing standards on public sector specific issues such as revenue from non-exchange transactions (including taxes and transfers), social policies of governments and budget reporting. IPSASB is now working towards the issue of Exposure Drafts in these areas.

15 IPSASB has not developed a conceptual framework, nor has it an active project to develop one; although this is a longer term goal. However, since IPSASB's standards are based on IFRS, it is implicit that IPSASs are based on the IASB's Framework.

IPSASB was previously known as the Public Sector Committee (PSC) of the International Federation of Accountants (IFAC).

During the development of both the Discussion Paper and the Exposure Draft the   **16**
Board has had regard to pronouncements and proposals issued by IPSASB. For the
issues discussed below a comparison to IPSASB requirements or proposals is noted.

MAIN ISSUES DEBATED IN DEVELOPING THE EXPOSURE DRAFT

Set out below are the main issues the Board considered in developing the Exposure   **17**
Draft from the Discussion Paper. In debating these issues the Board took into
account the views of respondents who commented on the Discussion Paper.

Funders and financial supporters as the defining class of user

The Statement identifies a defining class of user of financial statements. The reason   **18**
for having a defining class of user is to identify a perspective from which to view the
need for financial information: financial information required by the defining class
should generally be provided by the financial statements and information that is not
needed by the defining class need not be included in the financial statements.

For profit-oriented entities the defining class of user is present and potential inves-   **19**
tors. An investor is a provider of risk capital in expectation of a financial return on
equity. The defining class of user is determined by reference to the types of information that are useful to users; it does not establish a duty of care where one does
not already exist in law. It seeks to identify as the defining class of user the group
whose information needs, if met, will also satisfy the general needs of all other users.

In the Discussion Paper the Board concluded that it is the funders and financial   **20**
supporters of a public benefit entity who have a similar interest in its financial
statements to that which investors have in the financial statements of a profit-
oriented entity. This interest includes the effectiveness of the stewardship of management and the utilisation of resources.

Funders and financial supporters provide a source of cash or other resources that   **21**
neither provides a direct return nor is provided in exchange for direct benefits (either
goods or services), and may be compulsory (such as taxation).

Although a number of respondents agreed with this assessment, others made alter-   **22**
native suggestions for the defining class of user. In particular it was suggested that
the defining class might be beneficiaries (particularly for charities) or citizens (particularly for public sector entities).

In relation to beneficiaries the Board agreed that they may be users of the financial   **23**
statements of public benefit entities, analogous to the customer group referred to in
the Statement. Some of the financial information requirements of beneficiaries might
also overlap with those of the funders and financial supporters but, as noted above,
an overlap in information requirements is to be expected between different groups of
user. However, funders and financial supporters require information additional to
that required by beneficiaries, for example to assist them in taking economic decisions relating to an entity.

In relation to citizens the Board noted that, for public sector entities, there is a high   **24**
degree of concurrency between 'citizens' and 'funders and financial supporters'.
However, the latter is a broader category; it includes *present and potential* funders
and financial supporters. For an entity that receives funding from taxation the
defining class of user includes all present and potential payers of any tax.

25   The Board continues to support its original conclusion that the defining class of user for the financial statements of a public benefit entity is the entity's present and potential funders and financial supporters. However, the Board reconsidered whether the defining class of user should include past funders and financial supporters. The Statement refers only to present and potential investors. A past funder or financial supporter would be an individual or an entity that had made a contribution in a prior financial year and where accountability for the contribution had ceased (ie there is no ongoing financial interest in the entity). The Board decided to delete references to 'past' funders and financial supporters, whilst noting that many past funders and financial supporters may also be present or potential funders and financial supporters, and therefore remain within the defining class of user.

26   There may be many people who are interested in the general performance of a public benefit entity, for example how well it has met its public benefit objectives. Not all of these will be interested in the *financial* performance (and position) of the entity and many of those that are interested in the financial statements will also be interested in other information that assists in their assessment of the overall performance of the entity. The Statement (and therefore the proposed Interpretation) acknowledges that accompanying information can have an important role in assessing an entity's general performance, but it focuses primarily on the principles underlying financial performance (and position) as presented in an entity's financial statements. Chapter 7 discusses some aspects of accompanying information.

27   The proposed Interpretation has identified a defining class of user for the financial statements of a public benefit entity; other groups of users might be identified as the principal target for other performance–related information that a public benefit entity might produce.

28   IPSASB has not identified a defining class of user, but IPSAS 1 'Presentation of Financial Statements' notes that general purpose financial statements are intended to meet the needs of users who are not in a position to demand reports meeting their specific needs, and would include taxpayers, members of the legislature, creditors, suppliers, the media and employees.

Definitions of the elements of financial statements

29   The Discussion Paper proposed that the definitions of the elements of financial statements should not be re-expressed in order to make them applicable to public benefit entities, unless there was a clear need to adapt the terminology (for example, amending 'ownership interest' to 'residual interest' to address the point that most public benefit entities do not have owners, but nevertheless a residual interest still exists).

30   This proposal was based on the premise that the proposed Interpretation is an interpretation of the existing principles, as set out in the Statement. It adds public benefit entity context to the Statement; it does not replace the Statement.

31   A number of respondents queried this approach and suggested that key phrases, such as 'service potential' should be incorporated into the definitions of assets and liabilities, rather being explained in the discussion of the definition. The Board considered these suggestions, and re-affirmed its view that a common set of principles should underlie financial reporting by all entities and therefore only minimal changes should be made to key definitions, otherwise the principles may appear divergent. However, where further interpretation of the principle is necessary for public benefit entities this should be provided in the discussion of the definitions.

IPSASB addressed the definitions of the elements of the financial statements in IPSAS 1, although they are not defined collectively in this way. IPSASB has introduced more differences in these definitions from those in IAS 1 'Presentation of Financial Statements', from which it is drawn, than those the Board proposes in the Exposure Draft. For example, IPSASB regards service potential as an alternative to future economic benefits rather than one of its components (along with net cash inflows) and has amended the definitions of assets and liabilities accordingly. **32**

Liabilities: commitments to provide public benefits

The Board believes that the only area in which specific interpretation of the definition of a liability is required for public benefit entities relates to commitments to provide public benefits. Many other liabilities may arise, which are similar to those which may arise for profit-oriented entities, and no additional interpretation is required. **33**

The identification of the point at which a liability for commitments to provide public benefits arises can be a difficult area for public benefit entities because many commitments do not stem from contractual agreements, for which it is usually relatively straightforward to determine whether an entity is not free to avoid an outflow of resources. Public benefit entities do enter into commercial style contracts, but the Discussion Paper also addressed 'commitments to provide public benefits', which may, or may not, stem from a formal agreement. It was suggested that the nature of these commitments (ie whether general or specific) would be the first step in determining whether or not a liability had been incurred. **34**

Not all respondents agreed with the proposals and this area has been revisited in some detail. The proposed Interpretation now focuses initially on the main definition and its explanation, which applies to all liabilities, and is followed by its interpretation in the context of commitments to provide public benefits. As in the Discussion Paper, commitments to provide public benefits are broken down into separate categories for this discussion. **35**

A general commitment is a general or policy statement of intention and does not create a liability because it does not of itself create such an expectation that the entity making the commitment cannot withdraw from it, or amend the terms (ie it does not meet the definition of a liability). **36**

The proposed Interpretation includes further classifications of specific commitments, depending partly on the nature (and substance) of the agreements involved. In some circumstances public benefits are provided under contractual arrangements or under performance-related grants, which are analogous to contracts. Such arrangements are usually executory contracts and a liability (or an asset) will arise only in respect of any unequally performed, or onerous, aspects of the arrangement. **37**

For other specific commitments to provide public benefits, a liability arises when an entity can no longer avoid the transfer of resources. However, these arrangements can also be viewed as executory in nature because the objectives of the entity providing the goods or services are met when the goods or services are provided (in this case no liability will usually arise because a loss/expense will be recognised as the goods or services are provided by the reporting entity). Even though these arrangements should be accounted for as executory contracts, it does not mean that this is on the basis of the underlying 'performance' of the recipient (since it is not a performance-related grant), but each time the exchange is partially performed, usually when the reporting entity provides goods or services. **38**

39   The Board also considered whether a liability would arise immediately a commitment was given if it appeared to be an unconditional commitment to provide public benefits. Although in theory such circumstances cannot be precluded, in practice it is highly unlikely that they would occur because all public benefit entities will be operating within their objectives. The Board noted that there may be many commitments that give rise to an immediate obligation, but this does not necessarily lead to an immediate liability depending on the nature of the obligation (if it is an obligation to provide goods or services in exchange for meeting the reporting entity's objectives no liability will arise). The Board also queried whether any commitments are truly unconditional, or whether public benefit entities always implicitly include a condition that the activities of the beneficiary must continue to be consistent with the objectives of the giving entity.

40   This is an area that is also currently being considered by IPSASB. In January 2004, as the Public Sector Committee of the International Federation of Accountants, it published an Invitation to Comment (ITC) 'Accounting for Social Policies of Governments' which put forward a majority view that a liability does not arise until all eligibility criteria are satisfied. IPSASB is continuing its work on this project, but has decided to split it into three components dealing with different types of social benefits. Exposure Drafts are expected in due course.

41   At present there are some differences between the approaches taken by IPSASB and the proposed Interpretation. The proposed Interpretation notes that general political commitments do not give rise to a liability; the IPSASB ITC does not include a similar principle, although some of the discussion of collective goods and services reaches a similar conclusion.

42   The Statement, and therefore the proposed Interpretation, draws a distinction between events within and outside the control of the reporting entity. This distinction is not made in the IPSASB ITC and where satisfaction of the eligibility criteria is outside the control of the reporting entity, a conventional interpretation of the Statement would suggest that a liability should be recognised. The focus of IPSASB's work is narrower than the proposed Interpretation and the ITC considers in some detail particular types of payments made by governments as a result of their social policies, for example the old–age pension. The differing approaches, of IPSASB and the Board, to the principles underlying liability recognition can be illustrated by this example. The Board believes that, for many of the population, the 'promise' to pay an old-age pension is a general commitment that does not give rise to a liability. For existing pensioners the government is making such payments in line with its objectives and so a liability arises when a payment becomes due. In contrast, IPSASB puts forward the view that the pensioner must meet eligibility criteria, including remaining alive until each payment date; it is only once these criteria have been met that a liability arises (also on the due date). The IPSASB analysis is inconsistent with the Board's principles because whether or not the pensioner remains alive is outside the control of the reporting entity, and, as a result, if this were the sole consideration, a liability would have arisen for future pension payments at an earlier date. However, although the analysis of the issue is different the implications of ASB's and IPSASB's views on this issue are the same.

43   An alternative view is that grant-making differs from other types of commitments to provide public benefits and, except for those that are performance-related grants, does not legally, nor in substance, represent an executory contract for accounting purposes. This would be an exception from the principles outlined above. As such, those holding this alternative view suggest that grant-making commitments (other than performance-related grants) cannot contain an element of exchange and should be accounted for in accordance with FRS 12 'Provisions, Contingent Liabilities and

Contingent Assets'*, which would require the recognition of a liability once an obligation arises.

Presentation of the residual interest and disclosure of restrictions over assets

The Discussion Paper noted that a public benefit entity may have more than one **44** class of residual interest, particularly where restricted funds exist.

During the development of the Exposure Draft the Board decided that additional **45** guidance was needed on what constitutes a class of residual interest. The Board noted that where restrictions exist over the application of assets it is appropriate to separately identify that portion of the residual interest, but it is also important that users of the financial statements understand which of the entity's assets are restricted. Therefore disclosure should also be given about the amount and nature of the assets subject to restrictions.

In relation to the unrestricted residual interest the Board also noted that the mere **46** designation, by management, of a portion of the residual interest to reflect past expenditure or future intentions neither creates a different class of residual interest nor does it constitute a transaction and therefore does not lead to recognition in the financial statements. However, management may choose to include a discussion of future intentions in the information accompanying the financial statements.

An alternative view is that the presentation in the financial statements of careful **47** designation by management can be informative and should therefore not be precluded.

IPSASB has not specifically addressed these issues. **48**

Notional transactions

The Discussion Paper included a brief consideration of 'notional transactions'. **49**

The proposed Interpretation notes that if neither a transaction nor an event has **50** occurred there will be no changes in the reporting entity's assets and liabilities and consequently no gain or loss to recognise.

Voluntary gifts

It was clear from respondents' comments that some guidance was necessary in **51** relation to voluntary services, which are one aspect of voluntary gifts.

The Board noted that there are two broad categories of gifts that might be received; **52** gifts of goods and gifts of services. Gifts of goods, which would include donations of cash, should be recognised based on their current value to the recipient (taking into account its expected utility to the recipient, including any restrictions placed on its use by the donor).

The receipt of voluntary services is an event that has taken place. In principle where **53** an event has an economic impact on a reporting entity it should be reflected in the financial statements, but in practice other factors may sometimes prevent this. In

In July 2005 the ASB issued an Exposure Draft that, in line with its convergence programme, proposed revising FRS 12 in line with revisions to the corresponding international standard.

particular, events should not be recognised in the financial statements if it is not possible to measure their impact with sufficient reliability. The economic value of some gifts of services will be difficult to measure (other than at an arbitrary amount), for example, volunteers' time. Therefore the proposed Interpretation proposes that only those services meeting certain criteria should be recognised in the financial statements.

54   Gifts of services, which would include professional services as well as volunteer time, can be further sub-divided between those services that, if not provided voluntarily, would have been purchased and those that would not. The proposed Interpretation uses this distinction to determine which voluntary services should usually be recognised in the financial statements. Those services that would otherwise have been purchased should be recognised in the financial statements based on their value to the recipient (providing it can be reliably measured). For many voluntary services it is not clear that alternative services would have been purchased, even if the absence of the voluntary services would have severely affected the manner in which the entity conducts its business.

55   The proposed Interpretation suggests that disclosure should be provided, if practicable, of the nature of any voluntary services that are not recognised.

56   The Board does not agree with the position expressed in the IPSASB ITC 'Revenue from Non-exchange Transactions (including Taxes and Transfers)' that voluntary services should not in principle be recognised. However, it is understood that in progressing this project, IPSASB may have modified its view to permit the recognition of voluntary services, and require disclosure of those not recognised.

Capital contributions

57   In the following discussion a capital contribution is one that establishes an ongoing financial interest in an entity, it does not include, for example, a grant (or other contribution) given to assist with the purchase of a fixed asset.

58   The Discussion Paper proposed that contributions from controlling parties in their capacity as controlling parties should not be accounted for as gains, but should be reported as increases in residual interest.

59   About half the respondents agreed with this proposal. Others disagreed, or asked for more information on how it was to be interpreted. As a result, the Board reconsidered whether public benefit entities could receive contributions analogous to the contributions from owners received by profit-oriented entities, and if so what the circumstances would be.

60   Capital contributions to public benefit entities can occur and they are those that establish a financial interest in the residual interest (being a right to participate in the residual interest). Such contributions may, or may not, be received from a controlling party.

61   This is an issue that is considered in the IPSASB ITC 'Revenue from Non-exchange Transactions (including Taxes and Transfers)' and the Board disagrees with IPSASB's view that for correct financial reporting a contributor should be permitted to designate a contribution as capital or revenue; otherwise the proposals appear consistent.

However, the Board believes that the existence of *any* contribution from a control-   **62**
ling party is significant to the financial performance and position of a public benefit
entity and therefore it should be highlighted within the financial statements.

Capital grants (ie those given to finance the purchase of a fixed asset)

The Discussion Paper acknowledged that SSAP 4 'Accounting for Government   **63**
Grants' is not wholly consistent with the definitions of the elements of financial
statements in the Statement. Accordingly, it sought to move financial reporting
forward in this area and propose a solution taking into account those definitions (in
particular the definitions of a liability and a gain) and proposed a revised recognition
point for capital grants in the performance statement.

The Discussion Paper also noted that accounting for government grants was the   **64**
subject of work by the International Accounting Standards Board (IASB), which has
confirmed that it intends to revise IAS 20.

One aspect of the proposals in the Discussion Paper that respondents were parti-   **65**
cularly uncomfortable with was the treatment, as a liability, of capital grants that
must be repaid in the event of the subsequent sale of the asset financed by the grant.
The Board has reviewed these proposals and retains the view that, in principle, a gain
should be recognised when the conditions attached to the receipt of the grant have
been met, but acknowledges that a liability for the repayment of a grant can usually
be avoided by taking the decision to retain the asset that was financed by the grant.

For capital grants, although a requirement to repay a grant if the relevant asset is   **66**
sold does amount to a condition, the actual repayment (assuming all other conditions have been met) of the grant could be avoided by deciding to retain the asset so
this should not be a barrier to recognising the grant as a gain.

However, the Board notes that the receipt of a capital grant may indicate that,   **67**
without the financial effect of the grant, the purchase of the relevant asset may not
have satisfied the economic criteria of the reporting entity. Therefore, an asset that
has been wholly or partly financed by a capital grant should be tested for impairment
on acquisition. The proposed Interpretation provides guidance on determining the
value in use of assets held by public benefit entities, which in some instances may be
based on the replacement cost of the service potential of the asset rather than the
cash flows to be generated by the asset.

The principles underlying the accounting for capital grants apply equally to grants   **68**
received from governmental sources and those from any other sources.

The IPSASB ITC 'Revenue from Non-exchange Transactions (including Taxes and   **69**
Transfers)' also includes reference to grants receivable, which it defines as a sub-set
of transfers. Much of the discussion focuses on when a recipient entity should
recognise the grant receivable as an asset (where it involves the transfer of cash
subject to conditions, it should be on receipt of the cash). The ITC puts forward the
view that if, on receipt, the grant is subject to conditions a liability arises until the
conditions are satisfied. However, the ITC does not appear to discuss the example of
repayment in the event of the future sale of an asset funded by a grant (although it
does meet their definition of a condition).

IPSAS 21 'Impairment of Non-Cash Generating Assets' does not identify the receipt   **70**
of a grant towards the cost of the acquisition or construction of an asset as a trigger
for an impairment review.

Budget reporting

71   As noted in paragraphs 7.19 and 7.20 the Board believes that users of general purpose financial reports can obtain useful information from a comparison between results and the relevant budget, but that since such information does not directly reflect transactions that occurred during a reporting period it does not, per se, provide information about the entity's financial performance or financial position. Where management choose to present information relating to the entity's budget, it should form part of the accompanying information.

72   The Board notes that IPSASB has a project in progress considering Budget Reporting, and is expected to issue an Exposure Draft later this year. The Board believes that IPSASB's view that budget reporting forms part of general purpose financial statements requires further debate, including whether or not a comparison of actual to budget should be regarded as part of the primary financial statements or as accompanying information.

Business combinations

73   The Discussion Paper noted the Board's view that, similarly to business combinations involving profit-oriented entities, although true mergers do occur, the majority of business combinations involving public benefit entities are likely to be acquisitions where the entity existing after the combination is an enlarged version of one of the combining entities, not a new entity. However, a number of respondents agreed with an alternative view that business combinations between public benefit entities should more frequently be treated as mergers.

74   The Board continues to believe that the fact that a business combination involves public benefit entities does not of itself influence whether the business combination is accounted for as an acquisition or a merger, and that in the majority of cases it will be possible to identify an acquirer. The Board also noted that combinations involving entities under common control were already scoped out of the discussion on the relative likelihood of a combination being an acquisition or a merger because they would be group reconstructions; the existence of consolidated accounts provides evidence of a group for financial reporting purposes. Further, the management of an organisation should be able to be held responsible for the outcomes from the combination; this may be difficult if a combination that has the characteristics of an acquisition has not been accounted for as such.

75   As a result the Board re-affirmed its previous conclusion that the majority of business combinations (other than those involving entities under common control) are likely to be acquisitions. Clearly in any individual case the facts of the particular circumstances need to be considered to determine whether the combination is an acquisition or a merger.

76   The Board also believes that it may be possible to improve the way in which to account for a true merger, for example by using 'fresh start' accounting. The Board looks forward to this topic being progressed internationally.

77   However, consistently with the proposals in the Discussion Paper there are some characteristics of business combinations between public benefit entities that have led the Board to propose a variation in the form of acquisition accounting to be applied. Where the business combination is in substance a gift of one business to another goodwill should not be recognised, but the fair value of the net assets (or liabilities) acquired should be recognised as a gain or loss.

IPSASs do not address accounting for combinations of entity.   **78**

INVITATION TO COMMENT

The Board is requesting comments by 30 November 2005. The Board would welcome   **79**
responses not only from its UK and Republic of Ireland constituents, but also from
other jurisdictions where similar issues are faced in financial reporting by public
benefit entities.

Comments are invited on any aspect of the Exposure Draft, but would be particu-   **80**
larly welcome on the following issues:

Liabilities

(a)   Do you agree with the discussion of liabilities in the context of 'commitments
      to provide public benefits'? In particular:

      (i)   Do you agree that performance-related grants are analogous to contracts?
             If not, why not?
      (ii)   Do you agree that, for non-performance-related commitments (similarly
             to assets), benefits can be obtained by achieving an entity's objectives such
             that a commitment to provide public benefits will have the substance of
             an executory contract and liabilities will not usually arise until the transfer
             of resources become due? If not, why not?

(b)   Do you believe that there are circumstances where an entity has entered into a
      commitment in furtherance of its objectives, but nevertheless a liability has
      been created when the commitment was given? If so, please describe the cir-
      cumstances and characteristics of such a liability?

Residual interest and restricted assets

(c)   Do you agree that information should be provided in the financial statements
      to explain the amount and nature of any assets that are subject to restrictions
      over their application? If not, why not?
(d)   Do you agree that the mere designation of a portion of the residual interest
      does not result in a transaction for recognition in the financial statements, but
      could instead be discussed in accompanying information? If not, why not?

Business combinations

(e)   Do you agree that, having taken the circumstances of business combinations
      between public benefit entities into account, it is likely that the majority (other
      than those involving entities under common control) will be acquisitions? If
      not, why not?

Capital contributions

(f)   Do you agree that capital contributions (being those establishing a financial
      interest in the residual interest of a public benefit entity) should not be
      accounted for as gains, but as an increase in the residual interest? If not, why
      not?
(g)   Do you agree that any resources received from a controlling party, whether or
      not they are capital contributions, should be disclosed due to the impact they

have on the financial performance and financial position of the reporting entity? If not, why not?

Capital grants

(h)   Do you agree that capital grants should be recognised as gains when any conditions attaching to their receipt are met, and that assets financed by capital grants should be subject to an impairment test once they are ready for use? If not, why not?

(i)   In particular, do you agree that the existence of a clause requiring the repayment of a capital grant in the event that the asset it financed is sold is not a barrier to recognising the grant as a gain? If not, why not?

Voluntary gifts

(j)   Do you agree that those voluntary services that would have been purchased, if not given voluntarily, should be recognised based on the value to the recipient (providing it can be reliably measured), but that otherwise voluntary services should not be recognised in the financial statements? If not, why not and how would you resolve any measurement issues that might arise?

Other

(k)   Do you believe that any other guidance or re-expression of the principles is needed? If so, please provide details.

81   As with the Discussion Paper the ASB's Committee on Accounting for Public-benefit Entities (CAPE)* led the development of the Exposure Draft and the Board gratefully acknowledges its continuing contribution to its work.

OTHER ASB PROJECTS

82   The ASB is undertaking a review of the accounting for heritage assets. The project aims to develop practical proposals that will result in greater consistency and transparency in the financial reporting of heritage assets. It is expected that the first output from the project will be a Discussion Paper. IPSASB has signalled its intention to also issue a Discussion Paper, which will be based on the ASB's work.

*Formerly the Public Sector and Not-for-profit Committee (PSNC).

Introduction

PURPOSE

The proposed Interpretation of the Statement of Principles for Financial Reporting **1**
(the proposed Interpretation), for public benefit entities, sets out the principles that
the Accounting Standards Board (the Board) believes should underlie the preparation and presentation of general purpose financial statements of public benefit
entities*.

The principles in the proposed Interpretation are consistent with those relevant to **2**
profit-oriented entities, as set out in the Statement of Principles for Financial
Reporting (the Statement). Many of the principles are exactly the same as those that
are relevant to profit-oriented entities. Any re-expression, change of emphasis or
additions to the principles are designed to make them more relevant to public benefit
entities and have only been made to clarify their application in situations specific to
public benefit entities. The proposed Interpretation also provides an explanation of
how the principles apply to public benefit entities. Those principles that have been re-
expressed in the proposed Interpretation are detailed in Appendix 1, together with a
brief explanation.

The primary purpose of articulating the application of the principles to public benefit **3**
entities is to provide a coherent frame of reference to be used in the development of
Statements of Recommended Practice (SORPs)† or other sector specific guidance for
public benefit entities and to assist preparers and auditors faced with new or emerging issues. Nothing in the proposed Interpretation overrides the requirements of
existing accounting standards or SORPs.

The prescription of accounting requirements for the public sector in the United **4**
Kingdom is a matter for the Government. Where entities in the public sector prepare
annual reports and accounts on commercial lines, the Government's requirements
may or may not refer specifically either to accounting standards or to the need for the
financial statements concerned to give a true and fair view. However, when they do,
the Government's requirements accord with the principles underlying the Board's
pronouncements subject to such adaptations as are necessary in the public sector
context.

STATUS

The Statement is not an accounting standard, nor does it have a status that is **5**
equivalent to an accounting standard. It therefore does not contain requirements on
how financial statements should be prepared or presented.

Much of the wording in the proposed Interpretation is based upon the Statement. **6**
This document is intended to supplement, not replace, that Statement. It should,
therefore, be read in conjunction with it.

The term 'public benefit entities' is explained in paragraph 10.

*†SORPs are recommendations on accounting practices for specialised sectors. They supplement accounting
standards and other legal and regulatory requirements in the light of the special factors prevailing or transactions
undertaken in a particular sector. SORPs are not issued by the ASB, but by industry or sectoral bodies
recognised for the purpose by the ASB. At present there are four SORPs relating to the public benefit sector
addressing local authorities, higher and further education institutions, registered social landlords and charities.*

7   In order to ensure that there is adequate context for the information on the application of the principles to public benefit entities some of the material in the Statement has been repeated in the proposed Interpretation. However, it should not be assumed that where material has been omitted it is not relevant to public benefit entities. Appendix 2 provides a comparison with the Statement highlighting the source of material and those paragraphs of the Statement that have not been repeated.

SCOPE

Types of entity

8   The Statement is intended to be relevant to the financial statements of profit-oriented entities. This is regardless of whether they are private or public sector entities.

9   The principles in the proposed Interpretation are intended to be relevant to the financial statements of public benefit entities, regardless of their size, whether or not they aim to make a surplus and whether they are private or public sector entities*.

10   Public benefit entities are reporting entities whose primary objective is to provide goods or services for the general public or social benefit and where any risk capital† has been provided with a view to supporting that primary objective rather than with a view to a financial return to equity shareholders.

11   The term 'public benefit entities' does not necessarily imply that the purpose of the entity is to exist for the benefit of the public as a whole. For example, many public benefit entities exist for the direct benefit of a particular group of people, although it is possible that society as a whole also benefits indirectly. The important factor is what the primary purpose of such entities is, and that it is not an economic benefit to investors. Organisations such as mutual insurance companies, other mutual co-operative entities and clubs that provide dividends or other economic benefits directly and proportionately to their owners, members or participants are not public benefit entities.

12   The use of the term does not mean that all entities that do not make a profit are for the public benefit. Neither does the term imply that all entities that make a profit (or surplus) are not for the public benefit. Furthermore certain 'public benefit entities' may aim to make a profit from some of their activities, for example housing associations or the trading arm of a charity, which will be utilised in furtherance of the entity's primary objective. It is possible that an entity could undertake some activities that are intended to make a surplus, without the entity as a whole being profit-oriented‡.

13   Public benefit entities may have contributions in the form of equity, even though the entity does not have a primary profit motive. However, because of the fundamental nature of public benefit entities, any such contributions are made by the equity

---

*Both the Statement and the proposed Interpretation use the terms 'public' and 'private' in this context as mutually exclusive and to encompass between them all entities.

†Risk capital (for example given up in the purchase of equity shares) is provided by investors.

‡Where a public benefit entity has a discrete division that is profit-oriented it may be useful to refer to the Statement in relation to that division, even though the proposed Interpretation applies to the entity as a whole. Similarly, the proposed Interpretation would not be directly relevant to any subsidiaries of public benefit entities that are not public benefit entities themselves.

holders of the entity primarily for the provision of goods or services rather than with a view to a financial return for themselves*. This is different from the position of lenders; loans do not fall into the category of equity.

There is no exhaustive list of entities that are public benefit entities. **14**

The principles contained in the Statement should be assumed to be relevant to **15** entities that are not public benefit entities, without interpretation. These might include some public sector entities. However, at the margin there should be no difference in the accounting solution regardless of whether the Statement or the proposed Interpretation has been applied.

Types of financial report

Financial information takes many different forms. However, the Statement cate- **16** gorises financial information into three broad headings. These categories are:

- special purpose financial reports;
- general purpose financial reports; and
- other financial information.

General purpose financial reports includes general purpose financial statements, for **17** example the annual financial statements.

The primary focus of the proposed Interpretation for public benefit entities is on **18** those financial statements that are required to give a true and fair view of the reporting entity's financial performance and financial position. For most entities, those statements will be their full annual financial statements. However, where the requirement to present a true and fair view is expressed in another form, for example 'presents fairly', the proposed Interpretation still applies.

The principles in the proposed Interpretation have been developed in the context of **19** entities that prepare accruals based financial statements. Accordingly, the Statement is not intended to be relevant to receipts and payments accounts and other non-accruals based general purpose financial statements, which would not give a true and fair view of the reporting entity's financial performance and financial position.

Whilst the Statement does not address to any significant extent other types of general **20** purpose financial report, it will be relevant to such reports insofar as they provide financial information that is intended to be consistent with the financial statements.

Legal requirements

The financial statements of public benefit entities are subject to legal requirements. **21** Such requirements may vary substantially between sub-sets of public benefit entities both in terms of the level of prescription (ie general or very specific) and in terms of quantity/sources. In order not to deny the proposed Interpretation the opportunity to assist in the development of legal requirements, it has not been developed within the constraints imposed by legislation.

*It does not follow that all contributions from funders and financial supporters are in the form of risk capital.

REVISIONS TO THE STATEMENT

22   The Statement may be revised from time to time in the light of the Board's experience of working with it and in response to developments in accounting thought. The proposed Interpretation may also be revised from time to time.

Chapter 1
The objective of financial statements

Put simply, the objective of financial statements is to provide information that is useful to those for whom they are prepared. However, the objective needs to be expressed more precisely if it is to be of any use in determining the form and content of financial statements. This chapter does that by considering the persons for whom financial statements are prepared, the information needs of such persons and the role that financial statements play in meeting those needs.

PRINCIPLES

- The objective of financial statements is to provide information about the reporting entity's financial performance and financial position that is useful to a wide range of users for assessing the stewardship of the entity's management and for making economic decisions.
- That objective can usually be met by focusing exclusively on the information needs of funders and financial supporters, the defining class of user.
- Funders and financial supporters need information about the reporting entity's financial performance and financial position that is useful to them in helping to evaluate the proper and efficient use of the entity's resources and in assessing the entity's cash needs and its financial adaptability.

EXPLANATION

THE OBJECTIVE OF FINANCIAL STATEMENTS

Useful to a wide range of users

The Statement notes that many people may have an interest in the financial infor- **1.1**
mation of an entity. Certain bodies, such as the regulators of public benefit entities, may have the power to insist on the preparation of special purpose financial reports. However, others will need to rely on general purpose financial reports, such as financial statements. These persons are referred to as the 'users'.

Useful for making economic decisions

The persons potentially interested in an entity's financial statements need informa- **1.2**
tion on that entity for a variety of purposes. For public benefit entities the groups of users that are interested in an entity's financial statements are largely consistent with those described in the Statement. Some exceptions and clarifications are discussed below:

(a) *Present and potential investors.* Public benefit entities rarely have such investors; therefore this class of user has been replaced with *funders and financial supporters.*

(b) *Present and potential funders and financial supporters (hereafter generally referred to simply as 'funders and financial supporters').* Providers of resources are interested in information that helps them to assess how effectively management has fulfilled their stewardship role. They are also interested in information about the utilisation of the resources they supplied to the entity that might be useful in taking decisions about resources they may choose, or be required, to supply in the future.

(c)   *Lenders*. Lenders are interested in information that helps them to assess whether their loans will be repaid, and related interest will be paid, when due. Similarly, potential lenders are interested in information that helps them to decide whether to lend to the entity and on what terms.

(d)   *Beneficiaries/customers*. Beneficiaries and customers are interested in information about the entity's continued existence. That is especially so when they have a long-term involvement with, or are dependent on, the entity. Beneficiaries and customers are also interested in how resources have been applied by the entity in meeting its objectives.

(e)   *Governments and their agencies, including regulators.* Governments and their agencies are interested in the allocation of resources and, therefore, the activities of entities. They may also have specific regulatory (or intermediary) roles, through which they aim to give public confidence in the operations of the entities they regulate, perhaps performing a scrutiny role on behalf of the funders and financial supporters, or the general public. They require information that assists them in regulating the activities of entities and for example, for providing a basis for national statistics. Some of this information is obtained through special purpose financial reports, which will often need to be able to demonstrate consistency with published general purpose financial reports, such as financial statements.

(f)   *The public*. The interest the public may have in the financial statements of a public benefit entity will vary from that described in the Statement. For example, as part of the broad accountability of public benefit entities, the public may be interested in the quality of management's stewardship and in the relative allocation of resources between competing priorities. For a number of public benefit entities the public will be the funders and financial supporters of the entity.

1.3   Although those potentially interested in an entity's financial statements need that information for a variety of purposes, the Statement concludes that all the purposes involve taking economic decisions. The economic decisions made by users of the financial statements of profit-oriented entities may include whether to hold or sell their investments. They might also include whether to reappoint or replace the management of the entity. For public benefit entities, certain users will have the ability to make similar economic decisions. For example, funders and financial supporters may vary the level of financial support based on how effectively management have fulfilled their role. This might include a decision about whether to commence supporting an entity.

1.4   However, some users, for example, the public/taxpayer in relation to a local authority, will not have the same ability to make direct economic decisions. Although they may have the ability to make certain decisions, such as voting, that will only indirectly influence the level of resources contributed to entities. Therefore, some users will sometimes be interested in the financial statements primarily in order to assess the adequacy of stewardship exercised by the entity's management.

Assessing stewardship

1.5   Stewardship plays an important role in the preparation of financial statements by public benefit entities. Accountability to a public benefit entity's stakeholders for the use of funds and the safekeeping of its resources is often of paramount importance and there may be a wide range of people having such an interest in the activities of the entity. For example, accountability to the public for the collection of taxation and its use in the provision of public goods and services is enshrined in public sector reporting. Therefore, a key objective of financial statements is the provision of information to assist in a user's assessment of the efficient and effective use of funds and other resources.

In order for users to make a full assessment of the stewardship of an entity (perhaps including an assessment of the extent to which its public benefit objective has been met) additional information is likely to be required. Some of this information may accompany the financial statements, but does not form part of the financial statements. This is known as accompanying information and is discussed in Chapter 7. **1.6**

Information on financial performance and financial position

There is overlap in the financial information that is required by users: all are interested in the financial performance and financial position of the entity as a whole. General purpose financial statements focus on this common interest of users and are the principal means of communicating accounting information on an entity to interested parties. **1.7**

The limitations of financial statements

Financial statements do not seek to meet all the information needs of users: users will usually need to supplement the information they receive from financial statements with information from other sources. Financial statements have various inherent limitations* that mean that some information on the financial performance and financial position of the reporting entity can be provided only by general purpose financial reports other than financial statements (for example, a description of the environment in which the reporting entity operates and the strategies it has adopted is better included in the accompanying information). Those users with the authority to obtain special purpose financial reports might also utilise that authority to supplement the information in the financial statements. **1.8**

The need to supplement the financial statements with other information is at least as important for public benefit entities as for profit-oriented entities. In assessing the efficient and effective use of resources, the user is likely to need information in addition to that reported in a conventional presentation of financial performance and financial position. For example information in the material accompanying the financial statements, such as the operating and financial review, might be needed in order to put the numerical information in the financial statements into context. Such information might include qualitative and quantitative information on services provided by the entity during the year. **1.9**

Many public benefit entities also utilise other forms of presentation, which may include financial information and may or may not be provided with the financial statements. One example might be a comparison of actual results to the budget, which might provide information on whether an entity has fulfilled its spending promises. They might also use methods of communication other than the financial statements to provide financial information, particularly to classes of user other than the defining class. **1.10**

Including the degree of aggregation, the focus on the financial effects of transactions and events and that they are largely historical.

FUNDERS AND FINANCIAL SUPPORTERS AS THE DEFINING CLASS OF USER

1.11   The Statement notes that, in preparing financial statements of profit-oriented entities, the rebuttable assumption is that financial statements that focus on the interest that investors have in the reporting entity's financial performance and financial position will, in effect, also be focusing on the common interest that all users have in that entity's financial performance and financial position.

1.12   However, public benefit entities often have no such investors (ie shareholders) and for those entities that do have shareholders, there may be no rights to participate in any surpluses or on winding up*. For public benefit entities funders and financial supporters are similar to investors in profit-oriented entities in terms of their information requirements.

1.13   The defining class of user for the financial statements of public benefit entities is the funders and financial supporters. They provide a source of cash or other resources without the incentive of a return, either a direct return (like interest paid on a loan) or in the form of an exchange for direct benefits (goods or services), for themselves. The funder and financial supporter generally provides taxation, grants or donations to the entity. The defining class of user includes the present and potential funders and financial supporters of the entity. A present funder or financial supporter would include an individual or entity that had made a contribution in the past if that contribution created an ongoing financial interest.

1.14   There are differences between a 'financial supporter' and a 'funder'. A financial supporter is someone who has made a conscious decision to contribute, whereas this might not be true of a funder, such as a taxpayer. A lender, in his capacity as a provider of debt capital on which he receives a return, is neither a funder nor a financial supporter.

1.15   Where a public benefit entity has 'members' who are required to make a financial contribution in order to be admitted to the membership, they should be considered as financial supporters where the value of the contribution is unlikely to represent the fair value of the benefits available from membership (ie it is at least partly a mechanism to provide financial support, not the purchase of goods or services). As a result, to the extent that contributions are financial support, they should be recognised as revenue when received.

1.16   For many public benefit entities, funds are not received directly from their source, but are passed on through intermediaries (for example government entities providing grants). Often such intermediaries will also be regulators, and may have a statutory right to require certain information to be published in the financial statements. However, this information should be regarded as special purpose as it will not necessarily meet the information requirements of a general user of the financial statements (for example, where it relates to an amount of expenditure incurred under a specific piece of legislation). Therefore, there is a need to look through intermediary financial supporters to the original source, for example in many cases this will be the taxpayer, in order to ensure that financial statements are prepared to provide general purpose rather than special purpose information. It may also be the case that the intermediary performs a scrutiny role on behalf of the ultimate source of the

---

**In the event of a winding up any remaining net assets would often be dealt with in accordance with the governing instrument of the entity. Usually this would involve the transfer of the net assets to another public benefit entity with similar objectives.*

resources, acting as a judge of performance where the ultimate funder or financial supporter may not have the requisite skills or opportunity to do so.

THE INFORMATION REQUIRED BY FUNDERS AND FINANCIAL SUPPORTERS

Financial performance

Information on financial performance, amongst other things, provides an account of stewardship of management and is useful in assessing the past and anticipated performance of the entity.   **1.17**

In the case of public benefit entities, stewardship is a particularly important part of reporting to users. Users require information to hold management to account for the safekeeping of the entity's resources and for their proper and efficient use.   **1.18**

Financial position

An entity's financial position encompasses the economic resources it controls, its financial structure, its liquidity and solvency, its risk profile and risk management approach, and its capacity to adapt to changes in the environment in which it operates. Information about the economic resources controlled and the use made of them in the past helps in assessing the stewardship of management.   **1.19**

Cash needs

Information on the ways in which an entity uses cash provides an additional perspective on financial performance that is largely free from allocation and valuation issues and is relevant to an assessment of its future cash needs.   **1.20**

Information on the generation and use of cash will be of importance for public benefit entities. In certain cases, the entity may have a limit imposed on the amount of cash that it has authority to spend each year. Therefore, information on the use of cash may be needed to demonstrate accountability and the effective use of funds.   **1.21**

Financial adaptability

An entity's financial adaptability is its ability to take effective action to alter the amount and timing of its cash flow so that it can respond to unexpected needs or opportunities.   **1.22**

Financial adaptability can help an entity mitigate the risks associated with its activities, which in turn helps it survive during a time of low cash flows.   **1.23**

Chapter 2
The reporting entity

It is important that entities that ought to prepare and publish financial statements, do, in fact, do so and that those financial statements report on all relevant activities and resources. This chapter focuses on these issues – in other words, on identifying and circumscribing the reporting entity.

PRINCIPLES

- An entity should prepare and publish financial statements if there is a legitimate demand for the information that its financial statements would provide and it is a cohesive economic unit.

- The boundary of the reporting entity is determined by the scope of its control. For this purpose, first direct control, and secondly, direct plus indirect control are taken into account.

EXPLANATION

There are few fundamental differences between the principles and explanation relevant to profit-oriented entities, as expressed in Chapter 2 of the Statement, and their interpretation for public benefit entities. Therefore much of what follows is a summary of the discussion in Chapter 2 of the Statement, which should be referred to for a full understanding. Additional explanation specific to public benefit entities has been added covering assets under an entity's stewardship but not control.

ENTITIES THAT SHOULD PREPARE AND PUBLISH FINANCIAL STATEMENTS

2.1   It is essential that entities that ought to prepare and publish financial statements, do, in fact, do so. For similar reasons, if there is no justification for an entity to prepare and publish financial statements, it should not be required to do so.

2.2   For the preparation of financial statements to be justified in any particular case, there needs to be a legitimate demand for the information that the financial statements would provide. This means, inter alia, that the information provided by the financial statements will need to be useful and that the benefits to be derived by providing the financial statements will need to exceed the costs of doing so.

2.3   The financial statements of an entity will report on the entity's transactions and on other events that affect its financial performance and financial position. However, if the information provided by the financial statements is to be useful, the entity that is the subject of the financial statements (the reporting entity) needs to be a cohesive economic unit. This ensures accountability – the reporting entity is held to account for all the things it can control – and it gives the reporting entity a determinable boundary – because activities and resources are either within its control or outside its control.

THE BOUNDARY OF A REPORTING ENTITY

2.4   The control an entity exerts can be direct or indirect.

(a) An entity has direct control of an asset if it has the ability in its own right to obtain future economic benefits* embodied in that asset and to restrict others' access to those benefits.
(b) An entity indirectly controls an asset if it has control of an entity that has direct control of the asset.

Direct control is used to determine the boundary of the reporting entity that prepares single entity financial statements. Direct plus indirect control is used to determine the boundary of the reporting entity that prepares consolidated financial statements. **2.5**

It may be that, although an entity can influence another entity, it does not control it. Such entities do not comprise a single reporting entity. **2.6**

WHAT IS CONTROL?

Control has two aspects: the ability to deploy the economic resources involved and the ability to benefit (or to suffer) from their deployment. To have control, an entity must have both these abilities. **2.7**

Control in the context of assets and liabilities is considered in more detail in Chapter 4, which provides further details on the interpretation of "economic benefits" in the context of public benefit entities, in particular noting that access to future economic benefits includes the provision or goods and/or services to the benefit of the entity's beneficiaries. **2.8**

CONTROLLING AN ENTITY

When does one entity control another?

An entity will have control of a second entity if it has the ability to direct that entity's operating and financial policies with a view to gaining economic benefit from its activities (which might be achieved through concurrence of objectives) or being exposed to significant risks inherent in the activities. Control of another entity need not involve share ownership. **2.9**

There is no single piece of evidence that is proof of an investor's control in all circumstances, although evidence that will help to determine whether control exists can be obtained by considering: **2.10**

(a) the respective rights held;
(b) the inflows and outflows of benefit; and
(c) exposure to risk – how and to what extent the investor suffers or gains from variability of outcome.

In the absence of any other factors, an agreement to provide funding would not be expected to constitute control. **2.11**

In some circumstances a public benefit entity may be the trustee of charitable funds. Depending on the circumstances of the case it may be possible that the charitable funds form part of the reporting entity, because the trustee controls the charitable funds, particularly if the objectives are concurrent. **2.12**

The future economic benefits to which a public benefit entity might have access are discussed in Chapter 4.

Powers of veto and reserve powers

2.13   Control implies the ability to restrict others from directing the financial and operating policies of the controlled entity. Powers of veto and reserve powers are unlikely to form the sole basis of control because they do not provide a basis for deploying the resources nor do they ensure the corresponding flows of benefit.

Predetermined operating and financial policies

2.14   An entity whose operating and financial policies are predetermined will be controlled by another entity if that other entity gains the benefits arising from the former's net assets and is exposed to the risks inherent in them (ie the variability of outcome).

Latent control

2.15   If an entity has the ability to control another entity, it is usually presumed to be exercising control, even if such control is not apparent.

Management but not control

2.16   Control needs to be distinguished from management. If an entity manages a second entity on its own behalf, then it controls the second entity because it has the two abilities referred to in paragraph 2.7. On the other hand, if an entity manages the second entity on behalf of another party, it is not exposed to the benefits arising from, or risks inherent in, the activities of the second entity because the manager's interest in the managed entity is normally limited to its fee. As such, it does not have the second ability referred to in paragraph 2.7 and therefore does not have control of the second entity.

ASSETS UNDER AN ENTITY'S STEWARDSHIP BUT NOT CONTROL

2.17   A number of public benefit entities have a stewardship role for assets that they do not control, for example residents' valuables held by a local authority care home or artwork on loan for an exhibition. Since the boundary of the reporting entity is based on control, such assets should not be reflected in the balance sheet of the reporting entity. Even if a stewardship arrangement does not pass the control test, appropriate disclosure about the arrangement is necessary to indicate the nature and extent of the entity's responsibilities in that regard. Nevertheless, in some circumstances an entity may be required to prepare separate financial information relating to the assets under its stewardship, but not control.

Chapter 3
The qualitative characteristics of financial information

In deciding which information to include in financial statements, when to include it and how to present it, the aim is to ensure that financial statements yield information that is useful. This chapter considers the qualities of financial information that make it useful.

PRINCIPLES

- Information provided by financial statements needs to be relevant and reliable and, if a choice exists between relevant and reliable approaches that are mutually exclusive, the approach chosen needs to be the one that results in the relevance of the information provided being maximised.
- Information is relevant if it has the ability to influence the economic decisions of users, or their assessment of the effectiveness of the stewardship of management, and is provided in time to influence those decisions or assessments.
- Information is reliable if:

    (a) it can be depended upon by users to represent faithfully what it either purports to represent or could reasonably be expected to represent, and therefore reflects the substance of the transactions and other events that have taken place;

    (b) it is free from deliberate or systematic bias and material error and is complete; and

    (c) in its preparation under conditions of uncertainty, a degree of caution has been applied in exercising the necessary judgements.

- Information in financial statements needs to be comparable.
- As an aid to comparability, information in financial statements needs to be prepared and presented in a way that enables users to discern and evaluate similarities in, and differences between, the nature and effects of transactions and other events over time and across different reporting entities.
- Information provided by financial statements needs to be understandable, although information should not be excluded from the financial statements simply because it would not be understood by some users.
- Information is understandable if its significance can be perceived by users that have a reasonable knowledge of business and economic activities and accounting and a willingness to study with reasonable diligence the information provided.
- Information that is material needs to be given in the financial statements and information that is not material need not be given.
- Information is material to the financial statements if its misstatement or omission might reasonably be expected to influence the economic decisions of users, or their assessment of the effectiveness of the stewardship of management.

EXPLANATION

There are few fundamental differences between the principles and explanation relevant to profit-oriented entities, as expressed in Chapter 3 of the Statement, and their interpretation for public benefit entities. Therefore much of what follows is a summary of the discussion in Chapter 3 of the Statement, which should be referred to for a full understanding. Additional explanation specific to public benefit entities has been added covering going concern, understandability and neutrality and prudence.

RELEVANCE

3.1   Relevance is a general quality that is used as a selection criterion at all stages of the financial reporting process. Information is relevant if it has the ability to influence the economic decisions of users, or their assessment of the effectiveness of the stewardship of management, and is provided in time to influence those decisions.

3.2   Relevant information has predictive or confirmatory value. It has predictive value if it helps users to evaluate or assess past, present or future events. It has confirmatory value if it helps users to confirm or correct their past evaluations or assessments. Maximising the relevance of financial information involves maximising its predictive and confirmatory value.

Going concern

3.3   There are a number of different perspectives from which an entity's financial performance and financial position could be viewed. The perspective that is usually most relevant is based on the assumption that the entity is to continue in operational existence for the foreseeable future. This perspective is commonly referred to as the going concern assumption.

3.4   In determining whether a public benefit entity is a going concern some of the factors, including legal requirements, to be taken into account may vary from those that would be considered in relation to profit-oriented entities. For example, an entity may have tax raising powers that give it the ability to raise revenue as any liabilities fall due, regardless of whether at the time the assessment is undertaken it has sufficient assets to cover its future liabilities.

RELIABILITY

3.5   Information provided by financial statements needs to be reliable. Information is reliable if:

(a)   it can be depended upon by users to represent faithfully what it either purports to represent or could reasonably be expected to represent;

(b)   it is free from deliberate or systematic bias (ie it is neutral);

(c)   it is free from material error;

(d)   it is complete within the bounds of materiality; and

(e)   in its preparation under conditions of uncertainty, a degree of caution (ie prudence) has been applied in exercising judgement and making the necessary estimates.

3.6   Faithful representation involves identifying all the rights and obligations arising from the transaction or event, giving greater weight to those that are likely to have a commercial effect in practice, then accounting for and presenting the transaction or other event in a way that reflects that commercial effect – in other words, in a way that reflects its substance.

3.7   The substance of a transaction or other event is not always consistent with that suggested by its legal form. A group or series of transactions that achieves an overall commercial effect will often need to be viewed as a whole in order to be accounted for in accordance with its substance.

3.8   The information provided by financial statements needs to be neutral – in other words, free from deliberate or systematic bias. Financial information is not neutral if it has been selected or presented in such a way as to influence the making of a decision or judgement in order to achieve a predetermined result or outcome.

COMPARABILITY

Information in an entity's financial statements gains greatly in usefulness if it can be compared with similar information about the entity for some other period. Information about an entity is also much more useful if it can be compared with similar information about other entities.   **3.9**

Consistency

Comparability generally implies consistency throughout the reporting entity with each accounting period and from one period to the next. It can also be useful in enhancing comparability between entities, although it should not be confused with the need for absolute uniformity.   **3.10**

Disclosure of accounting policies

In order to determine whether consistency exists or to assist in making comparisons despite inconsistencies, users need information on accounting policies adopted by entities and of any changes in those policies and the effects of such changes.   **3.11**

UNDERSTANDABILITY

Information provided by financial statements needs to be understandable and users need to be able to perceive its significance. Whether financial information is understandable will depend on: **3.12**

(a)   the way in which the effects of transactions and other events are characterised, aggregated and classified.
(b)   the way in which the information is presented.
(c)   the capabilities of users.

When considering the capabilities of users of the financial statements of public benefit entities, it may not always appear appropriate to assume that they will have a reasonable knowledge of business and economic activities and accounting, for example where the defining class of user is the taxpayer. However, if financial statements are to be useful to a wide range of users for general purposes, the preparers must be able to assume a reasonable knowledge*. In this regard an important role is played by intermediaries, such as oversight and regulatory bodies, who often work on behalf of users such as taxpayers and donors, in assessing the performance of an entity and its management. In these circumstances the capabilities of users might be determined by reference to the expected capabilities of the intermediary. However, the involvement of intermediaries in reviewing financial statements does not negate the need for a public benefit entity to communicate with other users, particularly its funders and financial supporters.   **3.13**

If there is to be informed public debate on the information provided by financial statements, then the basis on which it is prepared needs to be sound. Financial information will be more understandable to users if it is prepared on a true and fair basis (the concept of true and fair is discussed in the Statement).   **3.14**

*See also paragraph 3.25.

MATERIALITY

3.15   Materiality is the final test of what information should be given in a particular set of financial statements. The materiality test asks whether the information content is of such significance as to require inclusion in the financial statements.

3.16   When immaterial information is given in the financial statements the resulting clutter can impair the understandability of the other information provided. In such circumstances, the immaterial information will need to be excluded.

3.17   An item of information is material to the financial statements if its misstatement or omission might reasonably be expected to influence the economic decisions of users of those financial statements and their assessments of management's stewardship.

3.18   Whether information is material will depend on the size and nature of the item in question judged in the particular circumstances of the case. The principal factors to be taken into account are set out below. It will usually be a combination of these factors, rather than any one in particular, that will determine materiality.

(a)   The item's size is judged in the context both of the financial statements as a whole and of other information available to users.
(b)   Consideration is given to the item's nature in relation to:

(i)   the transactions or other events giving rise to it;
(ii)   the legality, sensitivity, normality and potential consequences of the event or transaction;
(iii) the identity of the parties involved; and
(iv)   the particular headings and disclosures that are affected.

3.19   If there are two or more similar items, the materiality of the items in aggregate as well as of the items individually needs to be considered.

CONSTRAINTS ON THE QUALITATIVE CHARACTERISTICS

3.20   On occasion, a conflict will arise between the characteristics of relevance, reliability, comparability and understandability. In such circumstances, a trade-off needs to be found that still enables the objective of financial statements to be met.

Relevance and reliability

3.21   Where there is a conflict between relevance and reliability, it will usually be appropriate to use the information that is the most relevant of whichever information is reliable.

Neutrality and prudence

3.22   There can also be tensions between two aspects of reliability – neutrality and prudence – as prudence is a potentially biased concept that seeks to ensure that, under conditions of uncertainty, gains and assets are not overstated and losses and liabilities are not understated. Where there is uncertainty, the competing demands are reconciled by finding a balance that ensures that the deliberate and systematic understatement of gains and assets and overstatement of losses do not occur.

For public benefit entities there can also be tensions leading to the possibility of gains being understated and losses being overstated, for example where a certain level of spending must be achieved or to avoid the presentation of excessive surpluses. **3.23**

As a result neutrality must be the uppermost objective. **3.24**

Understandability*

It may not always be possible to present information in a way that can be understood **3.25** by all users. However, information that is relevant and reliable should not be excluded because it is too difficult for some users to understand.

Understandability is considered in more detail in paragraphs 3.12 to 3.14.

Chapter 4
The elements of financial statements

Elements of financial statements are the building blocks with which financial statements are constructed – the classes of items that financial statements comprise. This chapter identifies those elements and explains their attributes.

PRINCIPLES

- The elements of the financial statements are:

    (a) assets
    (b) liabilities
    (c) residual interest
    (d) gains
    (e) losses
    (f) contributions establishing a financial interest in the residual interest
    (g) distributions to holders of a financial interest in the residual interest.

- Assets are rights or other access to future economic benefits controlled by an entity as a result of past transactions or events.
- Liabilities are obligations of an entity to transfer economic benefits as a result of past transactions or events.
- Residual interest is the amount found by deducting all of the entity's liabilities from all of the entity's assets*.
- Gains are increases in residual interest not resulting from contributions establishing a financial interest in the residual interest.
- Losses are decreases in residual interest not resulting from distributions to holders of a financial interest in the residual interest.
- Contributions establishing a financial interest in the residual interest are increases in residual interest resulting from transfers from parties that establish a financial interest in that residual interest.
- Distributions to holders of a financial interest in the residual interest are decreases in residual interest resulting from transfers to parties holding a financial interest in that residual interest in their capacity as holders of a financial interest.

EXPLANATION

THE ELEMENTS OF FINANCIAL STATEMENTS

Depicting the effects of transactions and other events

4.1   Financial statements need to reflect, in an appropriate manner, and as far as possible, the effects of transactions and other events on the reporting entity's financial performance and financial position. This involves a high degree of classification and aggregation. Order is imposed on this process by specifying and defining the classes of items – the elements of financial statements – that encapsulate the key aspects of the effects of those transactions and other events.

4.2   The elements of financial statements are:

For profit-oriented entities this would be called the ownership interest.

(a) in the case of the balance sheet (or statement of financial position) – assets, liabilities and residual interest;
(b) in the case of the statement of financial performance – gains and losses;
(c) contributions establishing a financial interest in the residual interest; and
(d) distributions to holders of a financial interest in the residual interest.

Recognition

The criteria that need to be met before the effects of a transaction or other event on the elements will be recognised are considered in Chapter 5.   **4.3**

ASSETS

Definition

Assets are rights or other access to future economic benefits controlled by an entity as a result of past transactions or events.

Rights or other access

An asset is not the item of property itself, but rather the rights or other access to some or all of the future economic benefits derived from the item of property*.   **4.4**

These rights can be obtained in various ways. Often they are obtained by legal ownership of the underlying item of property. However, legal rights to future economic benefit derived from an item of property can be obtained without having legal ownership of the property itself, for example, where property is leased.   **4.5**

Other legal rights that give rise to assets include the right to require other parties to make payments or render services and the right to use a patent or trademark.   **4.6**

Future economic benefits

Capacity to obtain future economic benefits is the essence of an asset. Therefore, to be an asset, the rights or other access must be capable, singly or in combination with other assets, of yielding economic benefits.   **4.7**

Many assets held by public benefit entities do not result in direct cash inflows for the entity. The economic benefits that arise from such assets are often in the form of services to the beneficiary or consumer. Furthermore, in many cases, assets are used to provide goods or services to the beneficiary or customer that are free or subsidised. An item can meet the definition of an asset if it is used either directly or indirectly to provide goods and/or services that are used in furtherance of an entity's objectives.   **4.8**

Therefore although the Statement notes that 'future economic benefits eventually result in net cash inflows to the entity' this may not be the case for public benefit entities, where access to future economic benefits includes: **4.9**

● an eventual net inflow of cash to the entity; but also
● the provision of goods and/or services to the benefit of the entity's beneficiaries.

---

*The term 'item of property' is taken from the Statement. It is used to differentiate between the control of rights or other access to future economic benefits (the asset) and the thing from which those benefits are derived (the item of property).

4.10   This means that, for public benefit entities, an asset can embody service potential, as well as or instead of cash flows. Service potential is the ability to be utilised to provide expected future goods or services (ie they fulfil a need or want of the identified customers/beneficiaries) in furtherance of the entity's objectives*.

4.11   In principle all items meeting the definition of an asset should be recognised. These include heritage assets such as:

- Historic assets: which are of acknowledged historic, scientific or artistic importance, the continuing retention, preservation and use of which is in direct furtherance of an entity's objectives.
- Inalienable assets: which the entity is required by law to retain indefinitely for its own use in furtherance of its objectives and which therefore cannot be disposed of without external consent.

4.12   These items meet the definition of assets as they provide future economic benefit; they are used to provide services to the benefit of the entity's beneficiaries. It is possible that even where, for example, such items are not on display, their preservation alone will meet the asset definition.

Controlled by the entity

4.13   The definition of an asset requires that the rights or other access to future economic benefits are controlled by the reporting entity. Control of economic benefits is explained as meaning that the entity must have the ability both to obtain for itself any economic benefits that will arise and to prevent or limit the access of others to those benefits.

4.14   With public benefit entities, the economic benefits that arise from an asset need not flow to the entity itself. As noted above, the assets may instead be used to provide benefits for the beneficiaries of the entity. In the context of such assets, it is therefore the *capacity to provide* future economic benefits that must be controlled by the entity.

4.15   Accordingly, for the purposes of public benefit entities, control of economic benefits is reformulated as follows. An entity will control the rights or other access to future economic benefit if it has the ability:

- both to obtain for itself any economic benefits that will arise and to prevent or limit the access of others to those benefits; or
- to meet its objectives by determining the allocation to beneficiaries of future economic benefits (whether goods or services), including preventing or limiting the access to any future goods or services to be provided.

4.16   Public benefit entities that have custody of an asset may not have all the legal powers of ownership, such as the ability to sell the item. There may also be restrictions on the entity's use of the asset. However, this does not necessarily mean that the entity does not control access to future economic benefits. To satisfy the requirement for control, the entity does not need unlimited power over the physical item. Instead, it is the rights or access to future economic benefit that need to be controlled.

4.17   The requirement that the rights or other access should be controlled by the entity treating them as its asset means that a particular right or other access to future economic benefits will appear in only one set of single entity financial statements, because such rights or access can be directly controlled by only one entity.

*Measuring the replacement cost of the service potential of an asset is considered in paragraphs 6.11 and 6.12.

On the other hand, a single item of property may give rise to assets of more than one   **4.18**
entity. If two entities control the rights to different future economic benefits from the
same item of property, both entities will have an asset (subject to the other aspects of
the definition being met).

Past transactions or events

If the reporting entity's control of the rights or other access to future economic   **4.19**
benefits involved is to represent an asset, it needs to be the result of *past* transactions
or events.

LIABILITIES

Definition

Liabilities are obligations of an entity to transfer economic benefits as a result of past
transactions or events.

Obligations

For there to be a liability there must be an obligation that might result in the transfer   **4.20**
of economic benefits.

The notion of an obligation implies that the entity is not free to avoid the outflow of   **4.21**
economic resources. If an obligation exists, although an entity may offer inducements to its creditors to cancel or postpone settlement, it will not be able to insist that
they accept such an offer.

Although many liabilities are based on legal obligations, a legal obligation is not a   **4.22**
necessary condition: a liability can exist in the absence of legal obligations if other
considerations create a constructive obligation. Particularly in the case of public
benefit entities, many commitments to provide public benefits will not give rise to
contractual obligations, but may lead to constructive obligations.

A decision to transfer economic benefit does not, in itself, create a constructive   **4.23**
obligation, because the transfer can be avoided by changing the decision. On the
other hand, a constructive obligation would be created if such a decision was coupled
with an event that both created a valid expectation that the entity involved would
implement the decision and meant that the entity could not realistically withdraw
from it. For example, a constructive obligation may be created by communicating a
decision to follow a particular course of action to another party. Such an obligation
may also be created by an established pattern of past practice.

An obligation may be apparent from the social or economic consequences of failing   **4.24**
to act or perform in the agreed way, which leaves the entity with little, if any,
discretion to avoid the transfer of economic benefits. For an event to be an obligating
event, it is necessary that the entity has no realistic alternative to settling the obligation caused by the event.

The existence of a residual interest (see paragraph 4.47), either restricted or   **4.25**
unrestricted, that will be utilised in the provision of future benefits to the entity's
beneficiaries does not of itself create a liability.

Transfer of economic benefits

4.26 Certainty that the obligation *will* result in a transfer of economic benefits is not necessary. Obligations that are not likely to result in a transfer of economic benefits – such as a guarantee of another entity's debt where that entity is expected to remain solvent – are liabilities even though they may not be recognised in financial statements (or may be recognised with a carrying amount of nil).

4.27 Similarly, although many liabilities involve transfers of known amounts of cash, that need not be the case: a liability could involve an obligation to transfer an uncertain amount, and it could involve an obligation to transfer economic benefits other than cash – for example, by providing services.

4.28 An obligation to make an exchange in the future, which is still equally unperformed by both sides (often called an executory contract) does not usually result in the immediate recognition of a liability. An example is an order to purchase new office furniture: no liability is recognised by the purchaser until the furniture has been delivered. Various commitments of public benefit entities might be characterised as executory contracts; this is examined in further detail below (see paragraphs 4.36 to 4.41).

Past transactions or events

4.29 For a liability to exist at the balance sheet date, the obligation to transfer economic benefits must have resulted from a *past* transaction or event.

4.30 Sometimes a series of events must take place before the entity will have an obligation to transfer economic benefits. In such circumstances, whether the obligation exists depends on whether any of the events that have still to take place are under the entity's control. If they are, the entity retains discretion to avoid the transfer, so no obligation exists. For example, as long as it is possible to avoid a penalty clause in a contract by performing, a liability in respect of the penalty will not arise.

Commitments to provide public benefits

4.31 Public benefit entities might enter into a number of types of agreements that could lead to potential obligations; public benefits could be delivered via any of these mechanisms.

(a) *General commitments to provide public benefits.* These are general or policy statements of intention, that the entity stands ready to provide goods or services to certain classes of potential beneficiaries in accordance with its objectives (see paragraphs 4.33 to 4.35).

(b) *Specific commitments to provide public benefits.*

   (i) *Contracts.* Contracts that would be expected to provide an exchange of goods or services of approximately equal value between a seller and a purchaser.

   (ii) *Performance-related grants.* These grants, payable (or receivable) by public benefit entities, have the characteristics of a contract, where for example the grantee provides a service to, or on behalf of, the grantor over a specified period of time and/or a specific amount of grant is receivable per unit of output. Such grants have the substance of contracts and therefore should be accounted for as such (see paragraphs 4.37 to 4.39).

(iii) *Other specific commitments to provide public benefits.* A specific commitment, or promise, to provide specified goods or services to a beneficiary, even though it may be subject to conditions (see paragraphs 4.40 and 4.41). This category would include grants that are not performance-related and is likely to include most benefits provided directly to individuals.

The types of commitment to provide public benefits described above apply to all **4.32** public benefit entities, although some entities make more obvious policy statements than others. For example, general commitments ((a) above) would include an intention expressed by a charity to provide grants to general classes of people or entities, which could be articulated in a number of ways, including through the objects of the charity.

General commitments to provide public benefits

As a principle, these general commitments would not create a liability for the **4.33** reporting entity because they do not of themselves create an expectation such that the entity cannot withdraw or amend the terms.

General commitments are expected to include political commitments made by gov- **4.34** ernments, for example the announcement of a forthcoming new initiative to provide cash benefits to members of the public meeting certain criteria*. Political commitments are different from commercial contracts. Such political commitments (whether express or implied) are political promises; examples are the general promises to provide health-care or education. Governments make and amend such promises and policies as part of their ongoing political processes to manage the economy and redistribute wealth within or between periods and generations. As such they should not be viewed as constructive obligations.

Where an entity has potential obligations that do not result in the recognition of **4.35** liabilities it is appropriate to consider whether the disclosure of information relating to these potential obligations should be provided.

Specific commitments to provide public benefits

The principles underlying the existence of liabilities relating to specific commitments **4.36** are:

(a) where a specific commitment is one such that the recipient must provide some tangible performance in return from the promised resources, it is in substance an executory contract and therefore does not create a liability when the commitment is made, but depending on the terms of the commitment a liability will arise as performance occurs;

(b) for all other specific commitments, if the promised resources are being provided in furtherance of the entity's objectives then the arrangement is also, in substance, an executory contract where a liability will be recognised usually as the transfer of the resources becomes due.

Therefore, although in theory the possibility of a commitment to provide public benefits giving rise to an immediate liability cannot be ruled out, in practice this is unlikely to happen often since public benefit entities must always operate within their

---

*As noted in the Preface, IPSASB is currently working on the issue of accounting for Social Policies of Governments.

objectives. However, in the event that a commitment to provide public benefits becomes onerous, for example because the reporting entity's objectives will not continue to be met as subsequent payments are made, then a liability would arise.

The paragraphs below examine the two types of specific commitment further.

Performance-related grants

4.37   Performance-related grants are analogous to contracts. Characteristics that might indicate that a grant is performance-related include: a requirement to provide a specific service; and that the payment of grant is conditional on the extent to which a specific output is achieved. Where conditions provide a substantive option for the 'claw-back' of grant where performance levels are not achieved, it should be presumed to be a performance-related grant. An example of a performance-related grant is an agreement to provide a fixed grant per person per meal served in order to finance a meals-on-wheels service for the next five years. Similarly, an agreement to commission a three-year research programme, which adds to the stock of knowledge on a topic, would be considered a performance-related grant, particularly if the grantor was involved in determining the nature and focus of the work and regularly reviews its outcomes.

4.38   To the extent that elements of an agreement are performed, or it becomes onerous, a transfer of economic benefits becomes inevitable and the entity is not free to avoid the outflow of resources and a liability arises. A liability would not usually arise for any other elements of the agreement.

4.39   It can be difficult to determine whether grants are performance-related or not. For example, a research grant may appear to be non-performance-related because the grantor was not involved in determining the nature and focus of the work, but if the award covers the cost of performing the research, there may be an element of performance as the research takes place, particularly if the terms and conditions required that the grantor would reimburse costs incurred up to the date of termination (should it occur). Then regardless of whether the contract is prematurely terminated a liability arises for the grantor as the relevant costs are incurred by the grantee.

Other specific commitments to provide public benefits

4.40   Where a public benefit entity is providing goods or services to its beneficiaries in pursuance of its objectives (regardless of whether the goods or services are free or subsidised) the obligation to any particular recipient can be thought of as initially, in substance, an executory contract (in which the provision of goods or services by the reporting entity is balanced by the achievement of its objectives). No liability arises in respect of such activity until the stipulated delivery date for the goods and services by the reporting entity, since the achievement of objectives and the provision of goods and services are simultaneous. Often in such circumstances there will be no substantive options for 'claw-back' of the cash or other resources given and therefore no asset will be recognised for their possible return or 'performance' by the recipient, because the reporting entity's objectives will have been met when the cash or other resources were given.

4.41   As noted above, for a performance-related grant the 'performance' is likely to be measured by the achievement of specific outputs. Many non-performance-related grants may be simply enabling the grantee to carry out its own work.

There may be circumstances in which a reporting entity is acting as an agent for another entity, where, for example cash has been received by the entity to be passed on to persons meeting certain specific criteria specified by the other entity. Depending on the nature of the arrangement it is possible that a liability should be recognised to match the receipt of the cash prior to its dispersal. Such a liability would represent an obligation to the entity providing the cash, not to the ultimate recipient. **4.42**

OFFSETTING RIGHTS AND OBLIGATIONS

When a transaction or other event gives rise to a number of rights and obligations, it is necessary to consider whether some or all of those rights and obligations need to be offset either with each other or with rights and obligations that arise from other transactions or events. **4.43**

If a right to receive future economic benefits and an obligation to transfer future economic benefits exist and the reporting entity has the ability – which is assured – to insist on net settlement of the balances, the right and obligation together form a single asset or liability regardless of how the parties intend to settle the balances. **4.44**

When an entity enters into an agreement with another, it usually obtains certain rights and, in exchange, accepts certain obligations. Before any act of performance under the agreement has taken place, the entity does not have control of the future economic benefits arising from performance, nor does it have an obligation to transfer economic benefits that arise on performance. What it *does* have, however, is a contract that represents a net position comprising a combined right and obligation either to participate in the exchange or alternatively to be compensated (or to compensate) for the consequences of the exchange not taking place. Initially, the rights and obligations are likely to be exactly offsetting, although that will often not remain the case. The rights and obligations arising under such unperformed executory contracts together represent a single asset or liability. Consistently with the discussion of restrictions in Chapter 5, the receipt of resources with restrictions attached does not usually delay their recognition as an asset and a gain. **4.45**

It may be that the contract has been performed partially but is equally proportionately unperformed – in other words, that both parties to the contract have still to perform to an equal degree the actions promised by and required of them under the contract. In such a case, although the rights and obligations relating to the performed part of the contract may represent separate assets and liabilities, the rights and obligations relating to the unperformed part will together represent a single asset or liability. **4.46**

RESIDUAL INTEREST

Residual interest is defined as follows: **4.47**

Residual interest is the amount found by deducting all of the entity's liabilities from all of the entity's assets.

As such the residual interest, being derived from the assets and liabilities arising from past events, will be determined at each reporting date. **4.48**

The Statement addresses the residual interest in relation to profit-oriented entities and notes that owners invest in an entity in the hope of a return, for example the payment of dividends. Most public benefit entities do not have owners, and where **4.49** there are owners, they will not usually have rights to participate in a distribution in excess of the nominal value of their ownership instrument (ie they usually hold non-equity interests). Therefore the residual interest should not be attributed to any individual, entity or group of individuals or entities, including owners where they exist*. Where, in the event of a winding up the ultimate residual interest would be required to be distributed in a particular way, that fact should be disclosed.

4.50   The distinction between liabilities and residual interest is highly significant. Creditors have the ability to insist that a transfer of economic benefit is made to them regardless of the circumstances. In contrast the residual interest represents resources that the entity retains for the provision of future benefits. In certain forms of entity, these resources may be held under trust, either to be retained for the generation of future income, or to be spent on particular restricted purposes. The nature of the residual interest should be clear from disclosure in the financial statements.

4.51   Where, for example, restricted funds exist, there may be more than one class of residual interest. The existence of different classes of residual interests requires disclosure within the financial statements.

4.52   The mere designation of a portion of the residual interest as being set aside, reflecting no more than past expenditure or future intentions, does not create a different class of residual interest and does not lead to the recognition of a transaction in the financial statements. However, such information would be properly included in accompanying information (see paragraphs 7.15 to 7.18).

GAINS AND LOSSES

Definitions

Gains are increases in residual interest not resulting from contributions establishing a financial interest in the residual interest.

Losses are decreases in residual interest not resulting from distributions to holders of a financial interest in the residual interest.

4.53   The terms 'gains' and 'losses' therefore include items that are often referred to as 'revenue' or 'income' and 'expenses'.

4.54   Chapter 5 provides guidance on the recognition process for transactions and events that have an effect on the financial statements. If neither a transaction nor an event has occurred there will be no changes in the reporting entity's assets and liabilities and consequently no gain or loss to recognise.

4.55   For some public benefit entities events† occur that involve the receipt of goods† or services that have been voluntarily given. The occurrence of such an event does not necessarily result in the recognition or derecognition of items in the financial statements; this will depend on the effect it has on the assets and liabilities of the reporting entity.

4.56   Where a voluntary gift involves the receipt of goods (for example cash, works of art or furniture) the event should be recognised based on the current value to the

---

Even where owners may have a limited right to participate, because of the limitations it would not be appropriate to attribute the entire residual interest to the owners.

†*For this purpose 'goods' includes cash and financial instruments.*

recipient (measures of current value are discussed in Chapter 6), provided it can be measured with sufficient reliability and taking into account its expected utility to the recipient, including any restrictions placed on its use by the donor.

In contrast other voluntary gifts involve the receipt of services that are immediately consumed (for example volunteers' time, free occupation of premises and free professional services); these are events that potentially have an economic effect on the reporting entity. In principle, where an event has an economic impact on a reporting entity it should be reflected in the financial statements, but in practice other factors may sometimes prevent this. **4.57**

In particular, events should not be recognised in the financial statements if it is not possible to measure their impact with sufficient reliability. The economic value of some gifts of services will be difficult to measure (other than at an arbitrary amount), for example, volunteers' time. Therefore the proposed Interpretation proposes that only those services meeting certain criteria should be recognised in the financial statements. **4.58**

For voluntary services a distinction can be drawn between those services that, if not received voluntarily, would have been purchased and those that would not. It would be expected that services that would otherwise have been purchased should be recognised in the financial statements based on the estimated value to the recipient, provided they can be reliably measured. Services that would otherwise have been purchased would often be those which the provider (either an individual or an entity) would ordinarily carry out in the normal course of their usual profession or trade, and for which they would ordinarily charge a fee commensurate to the services provided. Where voluntary services are recognised in the financial statements it would be as income and, usually, expenditure of an equal amount. **4.59**

Where voluntarily received services are not recognised in the financial statements and it is necessary in order to gain a better understanding of the activities of a reporting entity, disclosure of the nature of the event(s) should be provided, if practicable. **4.60**

CONTRIBUTIONS ESTABLISHING A FINANCIAL INTEREST IN THE RESIDUAL INTEREST

Definition

Contributions establishing a financial interest in the residual interest (capital contributions*) are increases in residual interest resulting from transfers from parties that establish a financial interest in that residual interest.

Capital contributions include only those transactions that establish a financial interest in the residual interest. Transactions with the same parties that are not entered into in this capacity (for example those as customers, beneficiaries, donors or suppliers) result in gains and losses. **4.61**

A financial interest in the residual interest is one that conveys a right to participate in the residual interest (either on an ongoing basis or in a winding up). **4.62**

Capital contributions involve parties making a contribution of economic benefits (which may, for example, be in the form of cash or assets providing service potential) to the entity. In practice for public benefit entities, although capital contributions **4.63**

Here 'capital contribution' does not necessarily refer to the gift of an endowment.

establish a financial interest in the net assets of the entity, it may be that the contribution sometimes has the effect of reducing the level of a potential future deficit to be met in the event of the entity being wound up.

4.64   Some public benefit entities have a controlling party* (for example as a result of powers to appoint the members of its governing body), although the controlling party may not be a legal "owner" of the reporting entity. Contributions from a controlling party may or may not include capital contributions. However, due to the nature of the relationship between an entity and its controlling party the impact on the financial performance and financial position of a public benefit entity of any resources received that are not capital contributions should be clear.

DISTRIBUTIONS TO HOLDERS OF A FINANCIAL INTEREST IN THE RESIDUAL INTEREST

Definition

Distributions to holders of a financial interest in the residual interest (capital distributions) are decreases in residual interest resulting from transfers to parties holding a financial interest in that residual interest in their capacity as holders of a financial interest.

4.65   The Statement includes "distributions to owners" as one of the elements of the financial statements. As noted above most public benefit entities do not have owners, and those that do are often unable to make distributions (for example, it may be prohibited by the governing instrument), therefore capital distributions are not likely to be common.

4.66   Capital distributions include the payment of dividends and the return of capital. Where public benefit entities make capital distributions achieving this financial return would not be their primary objective.

**Consistently with Chapter 2 a controlling party is an individual or entity that has control of a second entity.*

Chapter 5
Recognition in financial statements

When the reporting entity undertakes a transaction or when some other relevant event occurs, the effect of that transaction or event on the elements of financial statements will need to be recognised in the financial statements if certain criteria are met. This chapter considers that recognition process.

PRINCIPLES

- If a transaction or other event has created a new asset or liability or added to an existing asset or liability, that effect will be recognised if:

    (a) sufficient evidence exists that the new asset or liability has been created or that there has been an addition to an existing asset or liability; and

    (b) the new asset or liability or the addition to the existing asset or liability can be measured at a monetary amount with sufficient reliability.

- In a transaction involving the provision of goods or services for a net gain, the recognition criteria described above will be met on the occurrence of the critical event in the operating cycle involved.

- In a transaction involving the receipt of resources other than for the provision of goods or services for a net gain the recognition criteria described above will often be met when there is clear evidence of a right to receive the resources.

- An asset or liability will be wholly or partly derecognised if:

    (a) sufficient evidence exists that a transaction or other past event has eliminated all or part of a previously recognised asset or liability; or

    (b) although the item continues to be an asset or a liability, the criteria for recognition are no longer met.

EXPLANATION

Other than in relation to revenue recognition there are few fundamental differences between the principles and explanation relevant to profit-oriented entities, as expressed in Chapter 5 of the Statement, and their interpretation for public benefit entities. Therefore much of what follows is a summary of the discussion in Chapter 5 of the Statement, which should be referred to for a full understanding. Additional explanation specific to public benefit entities has been added covering historic and inalienable assets and the various aspects of revenue recognition.

THE RECOGNITION PROCESS

The stages of the recognition process

The objective of financial statements is achieved to a large extent through the recognition of elements in the primary financial statements - in other words, the depiction of elements both in words and by monetary amounts and the inclusion of those amounts in the primary financial statement totals. This recognition process has the following stages:

    5.1

(a) initial recognition, which is where an item is depicted in the primary financial statements for the first time;

(b)   subsequent remeasurement, which involves changing the amount at which an already recognised asset or liability is stated in the primary financial statements; and

(c)   derecognition, which is where an item that was until then recognised ceases to be recognised.

Transactions and events other than transactions

5.2   The recognition process requires that all events that may have an effect on elements of the financial statements are, as far as is possible, identified and reflected in an appropriate manner in the financial statements.

5.3   Transactions are the most common form of such events and are therefore the most common reason for recognising and derecognising items. Events other than transactions may nevertheless also result in the recognition or derecognition of items. For example, events such as discovery may result in the creation of new assets that may meet the recognition criteria. Events (such as a fire) that cause damage to an asset may result in a need to derecognise the asset or liability involved.

The effect of transactions and other events

5.4   The starting point for the recognition process is the effect that the transaction or other event involved has had on the reporting entity's assets and liabilities. The interrelationship between the elements means that the recognition of one item as an element will inevitably result in the recognition of, or change in, another element. Thus, if a new asset is recognised, there will also be recognised a decrease in another asset, a new or increased liability, a gain, or a contribution from owners (or a combination of these).

5.5   A transaction or other event could have one of several effects on a reporting entity's assets and liabilities.

(a)   It might create a new asset or liability or add to an existing asset or liability. When this is the case, it will be necessary to determine whether the new asset or liability (or the addition thereto) should be recognised, because not all assets and liabilities are recognised.

(b)   It might provide additional evidence about an existing but unrecognised asset or liability and, as a result, enable that item to be recognised.

(c)   It might change some aspect of an already recognised asset or liability.

(d)   It might involve transferring, using up or consuming an asset or settling, extinguishing or transferring a liability. On the other hand, it might leave intact certain of the rights to future economic benefits inherent in an asset whilst transferring, using up or consuming others, or it might leave intact certain obligations inherent in a liability whilst settling, extinguishing or transferring others.

5.6   The non-cash effects of transactions and other events should, as far as is possible, be reflected in the financial statements in the accounting period in which they occur and not, for example, in the period in which any cash involved is received or paid. This is commonly referred to as the 'accruals concept'.

Uncertainty and the recognition process

5.7   Entities operate in an uncertain environment and this uncertainty may sometimes make it necessary to delay the recognition process.

If uncertainty exists, totally reliable information will become available only when the **5.8** uncertainty has resolved itself. However, to defer recognition until the uncertainty has resolved itself will often reduce the relevance of the financial statements. It may also reduce their reliability because they will not represent faithfully the transactions and other events of the reporting period. Financial statements achieve a balance between these competing demands by seeking to provide information that has no more than an acceptable degree of uncertainty but not seeking to provide information that is totally free from uncertainty.

There may be circumstances in which it is not possible to reduce the uncertainty to an **5.9** acceptable level. If that is the case, the recognition process will be deferred until such time as the uncertainty has been reduced to an acceptable level (and the effect of the transaction or other event will instead usually be reported in the notes to the financial statements).

INITIAL RECOGNITION

Categories of uncertainty

In the initial recognition process, there are two broad categories of uncertainty that **5.10** could arise:

(a) element uncertainty, which involves uncertainty whether an item exists and meets the definitions of the elements of financial statements; and
(b) measurement uncertainty, which concerns the appropriate monetary amount at which to recognise the item.

Element uncertainty

Element uncertainty is countered by evidence – the more evidence there is about an **5.11** item and the better the quality of that evidence, the less uncertainty there will be over the item's existence and nature. To recognise an item it is necessary to have sufficient evidence, both in amount and quality, that the item exists and is an asset or liability of the reporting entity. One of the criteria for initial recognition is that sufficient evidence must exist that a new asset or liability has been created.

What constitutes sufficient evidence is a matter of judgement, although while the **5.12** evidence needs to be adequate, it need not be (and often cannot be) conclusive. The main source of evidence will be past or present experience with the item itself or with similar items.

Measurement uncertainty

To recognise an item, it is necessary to attribute a monetary amount to it. This **5.13** involves two steps: selecting a suitable measurement basis (ie historical cost or current value) for the item and determining an appropriate monetary amount for the basis chosen.

Uncertainty about the appropriate monetary amount at which to recognise the item **5.14** (in other words, measurement uncertainty) is reflected in the second of the criteria for initial recognition, which requires that the new asset or liability or addition to an existing asset or liability can be measured at a monetary amount with sufficient reliability.

5.15   The purchase or receipt of an asset should be measured and included in the financial statements, provided it can be measured reliably. Thus where an historic or inalienable asset* is received, it should, in principle, be reflected in the financial statements. In some cases sufficiently reliable information may not exist, but for assets that are newly acquired, reliable measurement information is likely to be available.

Prudence

5.16   The exercise of prudence does not justify the omission of assets or gains when there is sufficient evidence of occurrence and reliability of measurement or the inclusion of liabilities or losses when there is not. Nor does it justify any other deliberate and systematic overstatement of liabilities or losses or deliberate and systematic understatement of assets or gains.

Unperformed contracts

5.17   When an entity enters into an agreement with another party, it obtains certain rights and, in exchange, accepts certain obligations. Before any act of performance under the agreement has taken place, the entity will have only a net position comprising a combined right and obligation either to participate in the exchange or alternatively to be compensated (or to compensate) for the consequences of the exchange not taking place. Although this right and the obligation will usually be in balance initially, changing circumstances may cause an imbalance to arise, in which case the net position will be either an asset or a liability. This asset or liability will be recognised if the recognition criteria are met (and if the amount at which the asset or liability is to be measured is not nil).

DERECOGNITION

Derecognition because the asset or liability has been eliminated

5.18   Assets tend, in due course, to be consumed, transferred or otherwise disposed of, or they expire. Similarly, liabilities tend to be settled, extinguished, transferred, or they expire. In such circumstances, it may be necessary to derecognise some or all of the asset or liability involved.

5.19   It is usually relatively simple to determine whether and when a previously recognised asset or liability needs to be derecognised. However, some transactions leave intact certain of the rights to future benefits inherent in an asset (or obligations inherent in a liability) while eliminating others. In such circumstances, analysis is required to ascertain whether the effect of the transaction should be reflected by derecognising some or all of the assets and liabilities involved.

5.20   Ideally, an asset or liability would be derecognised as soon as it has been eliminated. However, there will sometimes be uncertainty about an item's continued existence. In such circumstances, derecognition will not take place until sufficient evidence exists that the transaction or other event has resulted in the elimination of the item. When there is uncertainty, prudence usually requires more confirmatory evidence about the existence of, and a greater reliability of measurement for, assets than is required for liabilities. This tends to mean that, if there is any significant uncertainty about an

*See also paragraph 4.12.

asset's continued existence, it will be derecognised. However, in the case of a liability, more evidence of its elimination will be needed before it will be derecognised.

Derecognition because the criteria for recognition are no longer met

It is possible that although there has been no significant change in the inherent nature of an already recognised asset or liability - in other words, although the asset or liability has not been eliminated - the criteria for recognition are no longer met. For example, an event may have created additional uncertainty and, as a result, a previously recognised asset or liability can no longer be measured with sufficient reliability. On the rare occasions when this is the case, that asset or liability will be derecognised even though it has not been eliminated. **5.21**

REVENUE RECOGNITION

Assuming that no capital contribution is involved: **5.22**

(a)   if the effect of a transaction or other event is to increase the entity's recognised net assets, a gain will be recognised.

(b)   a loss will be recognised if, and to the extent that, previously recognised assets have been reduced or eliminated or cease to qualify for recognition as assets without a commensurate increase in other assets or reduction in liabilities. Similarly, a loss will be recognised when, and to the extent, that a liability is incurred or increased without a commensurate increase in recognised assets or a reduction in other liabilities.

However, although the starting point for the recognition process may be the effect on assets and liabilities, the notions of matching and the critical event in the operating cycle will often help in identifying these effects. **5.23**

Matching

Matching has two forms. **5.24**

(a)   Time matching involves the recognition of receipts (and payments) directly associated with the passage of time as gains (and losses) on a systematic basis over the course of the period involved.

(b)   Revenue/expenditure matching involves the recognition of expenditure directly associated with the generation of specific gains as a loss in the same period as the gains are recognised, rather than in the period in which the expenditure is incurred.

Almost all expenditure is undertaken with a view to acquiring some form of benefit in exchange. Consequently, if matching were used in an unrestricted way, it would be possible to delay the recognition in the performance statement of most items of expenditure insofar as the hoped-for benefits still lay in the future. The Statement imposes a degree of discipline on this process because only items that meet the definitions of, and relevant recognition criteria for, assets, liabilities or ownership interest (or residual interest for public benefit entities) are recognised in the balance sheet. This means that the Statement does not use the notion of matching as the main driver of the recognition process. **5.25**

Critical event in the operating cycle

5.26   Sometimes it is easier to identify the appropriate point at which to recognise gains arising from the provision of services or goods – and therefore changes to the entity's assets and liabilities – by focusing on the operating cycle of the reporting entity and, in particular, on the critical event in that cycle.

5.27   The critical event is the point in an operating cycle at which there will usually be sufficient evidence that the gain exists and it will usually be possible to measure that gain with sufficient reliability.

5.28   For many types of transaction, the critical event in the operating cycle is synonymous with full performance. In such cases a gain will be recognised when the entity providing the service or goods has fully performed. That need not, however, be the case: the critical event could occur at other times in the cycle and there could be more than one critical event in the cycle.

5.29   The identity of the critical event or events of an operating cycle will depend on the particular circumstances involved. For certain public benefit entities the concept of the critical event has direct application to revenue arising from fees and charges and performance-related grants*. However, for other sources of revenue, such as taxation and donations, gains may occur that are unrelated to the provision of specific goods or services. There may, therefore, not be a need to look for a critical event in the operating cycle as part of the recognition process. Instead, the focus will be on whether an asset exists and whether or not it has led to a corresponding liability. As such the recognition criteria are likely to be met when the recipient has a right to receive the resources (in some cases this will not be prior to actual receipt of the resources).

Should all gains be treated as revenue?

5.30   Fees and charges and performance-related grants that arise as a result of a critical event in the operating cycle of the entity should be classified as revenue. In this context revenue should be taken to mean "turnover", or the revenue arising from the operating activities of the reporting entity.

5.31   Gains† that arise, for example from the raising of taxes, or through an appropriation or grant-in-aid, or donations, should also be classified as revenue, and be recognised when there is sufficient evidence that a gain exists and it can be measured with sufficient reliability.

5.32   Other gains, such as those arising from the sale of fixed assets do not normally give rise to revenue.

Grants for financing capital projects

5.33   Some public benefit entities receive donations or grants intended to finance capital projects, such as the acquisition or construction of a fixed asset. The receipt, by public benefit entities, of grants or donations for financing capital projects often reflects the fact that the asset will be used to provide goods or services that are free of

---

'Performance-related grants' is used in this context to refer to a grant that has the appearance of a contract, where a specified amount of grant is receivable for a specific output.

†*In accordance with the definition, gains exclude capital contributions.*

charge, or substantially subsidised at the point of receipt. Providing a subsidy for an asset that provides a service can be an alternative to an ongoing commitment to subsidise the 'revenue' costs of providing the service. As such the difference between the two approaches could simply be the timing of the grant cash flows.

The receipt of the grant or donation does not reduce the cost of the asset itself*, nor is it a contribution to equity. Therefore: **5.34**

(a)   where all conditions attaching to the receipt of the resources have been met the grant or donation should be accounted for as revenue;

(b)   where grants or donations are received subject to conditions†, which have not been met, they should be reported as liabilities until such time as the conditions within the entity's control have been substantially met‡;

(c)   where donations are receivable subject to legal restrictions over their ongoing use, this does not prevent recognition as revenue providing all other conditions are met, but additional disclosure may be required to reflect the nature of the resources.

One common condition of capital grants to public benefit entities is that the grant must be repaid in the event of the recipient subsequently selling the asset it was used to purchase. Assuming that a decision on the sale of the asset is within the reporting entity's control, if this is the only outstanding condition then the grant should be recognised in full as a gain. This is because the possibility of repayment of the grant can be avoided by deciding not to sell the asset.   **5.35**

An asset that has been wholly or partly financed by a capital grant should be subject to an impairment review on completion (if constructed) or acquisition (if purchased) to ensure that the gross cost of the asset is not greater than its recoverable amount§. It is possible that for some assets, particularly those used to generate cash inflows, that the gross cost of construction or acquisition will be greater than the recoverable amount and therefore an impairment should be recognised.   **5.36**

Some preparers may consider that by reflecting the capital grant or donation as revenue received in full, when it is being used to finance the purchase of an asset that will be utilised over a number of years, the accumulated revenue position of the entity may be misunderstood by some users. This could be addressed by including explanatory material in the information accompanying the financial statements.   **5.37**

Conditions and restrictions attached to grants and donations

Public benefit entities often receive grants or donations with conditions or restrictions attached (these might also be termed stipulations). For example a charity might receive a donation of an item of property, together with an endowment fund, where the donor specifies that the property must be maintained to at least its current condition and opened to the public, and where the income from the fund must be used only to finance the maintenance of the property; these would usually be considered restrictions. Alternatively a further education college might receive a grant on   **5.38**

**Although the net cost to the acquirer has been reduced.*

†*A further discussion of the impact of conditions is provided at paragraphs 5.38 to 5.45.*

‡*For the conditions to have been substantially met it is implied that any outstanding conditions are trivial.*

§*Chapter 6 provides guidance on measuring the value in use of the assets of public benefit entities, which can include an assessment of the replacement cost of the service potential of the asset.*

condition that it provides a particular course and a minimum number of students complete the course; these would usually be considered conditions.

5.39   There are differences between conditions and restrictions. Restrictions limit the use that may be made of the resources in the future. Conditions must be fulfilled before the entity takes unconditional control of the resources. The existence of restrictions does not impact on the initial recognition of the resources (unless the restrictions are so severe that it is determined that the reporting entity does not control the resources) as revenue. The existence of conditions might indicate that the receipt of the resources should result in the recognition of a liability until the conditions have been met.

5.40   Conditions are usually attached to grants (this does not necessarily mean that most grants are conditional). The fulfilment of the conditions may be within the reporting entity's control or outside the reporting entity's control. Using the further education college course example from above, it is within the college's control to decide whether to run the course in the first place whereas it is, at least partly, outside the college's control whether the requisite number of students enrol and complete the course.

5.41   Where the conditions are within the reporting entity's control and it is virtually certain that the conditions will be met, the resources should be recognised as a gain. Where it is not virtually certain that conditions within the reporting entity's control will be met, any resources received in advance should be recognised as a liability until such time as it becomes virtually certain that they will be met. For example if the only condition attached to a grant is that the recipient must provide a copy of its annual report to the grantor, it would be appropriate to recognise the grant as a gain on receipt.

5.42   In some cases the conditions of the agreement are such that it amounts to a performance-related grant, where gains should usually be recognised as performance is delivered.

5.43   In other cases, prior to it being virtually certain that all conditions within the entity's control will be met, it may be possible that meeting certain of the conditions results in unconditional entitlement to a proportion of a grant, that proportion should be recognised as a gain at that time.

5.44   Public benefit entities may also need to be mindful that under certain grant agreements they may be acting as an agent for another party.

5.45   Where the fulfilment of the conditions is substantially outside the control of the reporting entity any resources received in advance should be recognised as a liability until such time as the conditions are met.

Chapter 6
Measurement in financial statements

Measuring an asset or liability entails deciding on the measurement basis to be used and determining the monetary amount that is appropriate for that basis. It may also involve revising the monetary amount when certain events occur. This chapter describes the measurement process and explains how a choice is made between the measurement bases available.

PRINCIPLES

- In drawing up financial statements, a measurement basis - either historical cost or current value - needs to be selected for each category of assets or liabilities. The basis selected will be the one that best meets the objective of financial statements and the demands of the qualitative characteristics of financial information, bearing in mind the nature of the assets or liabilities concerned and the circumstances involved.
- An asset or liability being measured using the historical cost basis is recognised initially at transaction cost. An asset or liability being measured using the current value basis is recognised initially at its current value at the time it was acquired or assumed.
- Subsequent remeasurement will occur if it is necessary to ensure that:
    - (a) assets measured at historical cost are carried at the lower of cost and recoverable amount;
    - (b) monetary items denominated in foreign currency are carried at amounts based on up-to-date exchange rates; and
    - (c) assets and liabilities measured on the current value basis are carried at up-to-date current values.
- Such remeasurements, however, will be recognised only if:
    - (a) there is sufficient evidence that the monetary amount of the asset or liability has changed; and
    - (b) the new amount of the asset or liability can be measured with sufficient reliability.

EXPLANATION

There are few fundamental differences between the principles and explanation relevant to profit-oriented entities, as expressed in Chapter 6 of the Statement, and their interpretation for public benefit entities. Therefore much of what follows is a summary of the discussion in Chapter 6 of the Statement, which should be referred to for a full understanding. Additional explanation specific to public benefit entities has been added covering alternative measures of current value.

ALTERNATIVE BASES OF MEASUREMENT

Assets and liabilities have several different monetary attributes that could be represented in financial statements. The single most important characteristic that distinguishes these monetary attributes (which are known as measurement bases) is whether they are based on historical cost or current value. This chapter concentrates on that distinction. **6.1**

6.2   The mixed measurement system permits the measurement basis to be selected separately for each category of assets or liabilities. It also permits the use of historical cost (or current value) for all assets and liabilities if historical cost (or current value) is the most appropriate measure for each of those categories. Thus it can be adapted to fit the particular circumstances involved.

6.3   The Statement therefore envisages that the mixed measurement system will be used and it focuses on the mix of historical cost and current value to be adopted.

ALTERNATIVE MEASURES OF CURRENT VALUE

6.4   The current value of an asset could be determined by reference to entry value (replacement cost), exit value (net realisable value) or value in use (discounted present value of the cash flows expected from continuing use and ultimate sale by the present owner). For some assets, for example fixed assets specific to the entity's activities, differences between the alternative measures can be material.

Value in use

6.5   Most fixed assets controlled by a public benefit entity will be employed in the provision of goods or services to its beneficiaries in furtherance of its objectives. In some circumstances a recipient may also have contributed indirectly towards the cost of the provision of the goods or services (for example, council tax receipts might be used to subsidise the cost of renting videos from the library), but the public benefit entity may or may not make a direct charge for the provision of such goods and services.

6.6   Where goods and services are not provided free of charge the recipient will purchase them:

(a)   at a market rate;

(b)   at a partially subsidised rate (being below the market rate, but for these purposes it represents at least a break-even position);

(c)   for a nominal rate.

6.7   For those assets held by public benefit entities that are utilised in providing goods/services free of charge or for a nominal rate, it is not possible to compute a realistic value in use, because the cash inflows do not represent the value derived from the use of the asset. For these assets the value in use of the asset should be replaced by the replacement cost of the service potential of the asset (which is described in 6.11 and takes account of the possibility of impairment).

6.8   Where assets generate significant cash flows based on a market, or partially subsidised rate, value in use can be computed using a cash flow model.

Selection of a measure of current value

6.9   It is necessary to select from these alternative measures of current value the measure that maximises the relevance of the current value basis. Current value is at its most relevant when it reflects the loss that the entity would suffer if it were deprived of the asset involved. That measure, which is often referred to as the 'deprival value' or the 'value to the business', will depend on the circumstances involved.

(a)   In most cases, the public benefit entity will be fully using the asset in order to further its objectives and therefore the entity will, if deprived of the asset, replace it, and the current value of the asset will be its current replacement cost.

For those assets in categories (a) and (b) (see paragraph 6.6 above) this is because the asset's value in use (in other words, its recoverable amount) will exceed, or equal, its replacement cost*. For those assets in category (c) (see paragraph 6.6 above), or where services are provided free of charge, it will be the replacement cost of the service potential of the asset.

(b)   An asset will not be replaced if the cost of replacing it exceeds its recoverable amount. In such circumstances, the asset's current value is that recoverable amount.

   (i)   When the entity would further its objectives to a greater extent by selling the asset, the asset's recoverable amount will be the amount that can be obtained by selling it, net of selling expenses; in other words, its net realisable value.

   (ii)   When the entity would further its objectives to a greater extent by consuming the asset - for example by continuing to operate it - its recoverable amount will be its value in use (or, for assets in category (c) (see paragraph 6.6 above), the cost of replacing its service potential†).

Many public benefit entities have assets that are specialised in nature, where there   **6.10**
may be no viable market for the asset's sale. As a result assets are infrequently valued on the basis of net realisable value because it is often artificially low as a result of the lack of an active market.

Measuring the replacement cost of the service potential of an asset

Service potential was defined in paragraph 4.10. The definition requires there to be   **6.11**
an expected demand for the goods or services the asset is to be used to provide. As such in measuring the replacement cost of the service potential of an asset reference must be made to the expected utilisation of the asset not its theoretical maximum capacity. Therefore, to the extent that an item is not expected, over its useful economic life, to reach its originally assessed standard of performance, it is likely to have suffered an impairment (subject to a comparison to net realisable value). For example, if a hostel had been constructed to provide accommodation for fifty people, the fact that a commercial market rent would not be obtained would not necessarily lead to an impairment. However, if at some point it became clear that, because of changes in demographics, the hostel would in the future provide accommodation for no more than thirty people, then the standard of performance of the property has diminished and it may have suffered an impairment

Similarly since current value is supposed to represent the loss the entity would suffer   **6.12**
if it were deprived of an asset, consideration needs to be given to the most efficient method of obtaining equivalent services to those derived from using the asset. If, for example, it is considered that the most efficient method, at present, would be to engage an external contractor rather than obtaining the services directly by using the asset owned by the reporting entity, then where reasonable evidence of the possibility of alternative arrangements is available, the asset's current value will be the higher of its net realisable value and the present value of the cash flows that would be incurred in obtaining equivalent services from the external contractor.

---

*Unless the receipt of a capital grant has resulted in the recognition of an impairment.

†Where, for example, an asset is not fully utilised, the replacement cost of the service potential will be less than the replacement cost of the asset as a whole.

Current value of liabilities

6.13   It is possible to select a current value for a liability in a similar manner to the 'deprival value' or 'value to the business' method used for assets (using the concept of 'relief value'). The relief value of a liability is the lowest amount at which the entity could divest itself of the obligation involved - in other words, the lowest amount at which the liability could, hypothetically, be settled*.

THE MEASUREMENT PROCESS

6.14   It is not the function of financial statements to represent directly the total value that the reporting entity would fetch in an exchange transaction. Instead, the financial statements provide information designed to assist users to make judgements about the entity's financial performance and financial position. The purpose of the measurement process is therefore to measure the effects of the transactions and events of the period on the financial performance and financial position of the entity.

Initial recognition

6.15   An asset or liability that is being measured using the historical cost basis will be recognised initially at transaction cost or, if an event other than a transaction is involved, at its fair value at the time it was acquired or assumed.

6.16   An asset or liability that is being measured using the current value basis will be recognised initially at its current value at the time it was acquired or assumed.

6.17   This means that, regardless of the measurement basis used, assets and liabilities that arise from transactions carried out at fair value - which is the vast majority of assets and liabilities - will be measured on initial recognition at their transaction cost. That is because, in the case of such a transaction, the fair value of the consideration paid or received (ie the transaction cost) is equal to the current value of the asset or liability at the time of acquisition.

6.18   It can generally be assumed that, in the absence of evidence to the contrary, a transaction has been carried out at fair value. In such circumstances, the transaction cost involved can be determined by reference to the fair value of either the asset (or liability) acquired or the consideration paid (or received); whichever fair value is easiest to measure will usually be used.

6.19   If an asset or liability arises from a transaction that was not carried out at fair value, it will often be more appropriate to measure the asset or liability at current value rather than historical cost. For example, an asset might be received as a gift or donation, in which case it should be recognised at its current value to the entity on the date it is received. As discussed in paragraphs 6.9 and 6.11 above the current value is likely to be the replacement cost of the service potential of the asset, which will reflect its expected utilisation.

Subsequent remeasurement

6.20   If a pure historical cost measurement basis is being used, the carrying amount of an asset or liability will always be the amount at which it was initially recognised; in

---

In October 2002 the ASB published "Liabilities and how to account for them: an exploratory essay", which suggests that this definition could be expanded to be the higher of consideration and settlement amount (being the lower of the cost of performance and the cost of release).

other words, there is no subsequent remeasurement stage. The carrying amount of an asset or liability measured at historical cost may nevertheless need to be changed so that the item remains at cost. For example, in the case of assets that are consumed over more than one accounting period (such as fixed assets), the amount at which the asset was recognised initially will be reduced over the expected life of the asset so as to allocate the asset's cost over its expected life. These adjustments are not remeasurements; they are adjustments to maintain the carrying amount at an amount based on historical cost.

In practice, however, this 'pure historical cost basis' is rarely used. Instead, to make historical cost more relevant to the needs of users, a variation is used that involves a limited amount of remeasurement. The purpose of this remeasurement is to ensure that: **6.21**

(a)   assets are not reported at amounts greater than their recoverable amount*; and
(b)   monetary assets and liabilities denominated in currencies other than the reporting currency are stated at an amount that is based on up-to-date exchange rates.

When the current value basis of measurement is being used, remeasurement takes place to ensure that the assets or liabilities involved are measured at an up-to-date current value. Such remeasurements will, however, be recognised in the financial statements only if: **6.22**

(a)   there is sufficient evidence that the amount of the asset or liability has changed; and
(b)   the new amount of the asset or liability is capable of being measured with sufficient reliability.

What constitutes sufficient evidence is a matter of judgement in the particular circumstances, although whilst the evidence will need to be adequate, it need not be conclusive. Relevant considerations will include its persuasiveness and whether the change implies that a gain or loss has occurred.   **6.23**

The issues to be considered in deciding whether the new amount of the asset or liability is capable of being measured with sufficient reliability are identical to the reliability of measurement issues considered in the context of initial recognition.   **6.24**

CHOOSING A MEASUREMENT BASIS AND DECIDING WHETHER TO CHANGE IT

In choosing the measurement basis to be used for a particular category of assets or liabilities, the aim is to select the basis that is most appropriate bearing in mind: **6.25**

(a)   the objective of financial statements and the qualitative characteristics of financial information, in particular relevance and reliability;
(b)   the nature of the assets or liabilities concerned; and
(c)   the particular circumstances involved.

Although these factors may not change, the measurement basis that best meets them may. For example, measurement bases that were once thought unreliable may become reliable.   **6.26**

Recoverable amount might be determined by reference to the asset's service potential.

MEASUREMENT ISSUES

Going concern

6.27   Financial statements are usually prepared - and measures are usually arrived at - on the basis that the reporting entity is a going concern because measures based on break-up values tend not to be relevant to users seeking to assess the entity's financial performance.

Discounting

6.28   Historical cost and replacement cost are both market prices and will therefore generally take into account the time value of money and the risk associated with the future expected cash flows.

6.29   To be consistent, these factors need also to be reflected in the other measures that can be used to determine the carrying amount of assets (in other words, value in use and net realisable value) and the carrying amount of any liabilities measured by reference to expected future cash flows. It follows that, when basing carrying amounts on future cash flows, those cash flows will need to be discounted.

6.30   The discount rate used will reflect the risks associated with the future expected cash flows involved (unless those future expected cash flows are already risk-adjusted) and the time value of money. As such it will reflect the risks specific to the item being measured but not the more general risks of the entity as a whole.

Arriving at a measure in the face of uncertainty

6.31   If uncertainty exists, the only way to determine an appropriate monetary amount for the asset or liability is through the use of estimates. As long as a generally accepted estimation method is used and the measure is supported by a reasonable amount of confirmatory evidence - prudence requires a greater reliability of measurement for assets (and gains) than for liabilities (and losses) - the use of estimates is acceptable and will not prevent the measure from being sufficiently reliable to be used in the financial statements.

6.32   If the monetary amount at which an asset or liability is recognised is subject to significant uncertainty, the degree of uncertainty surrounding the estimate will usually be disclosed in order to avoid the impression that the outcome is certain. Such a disclosure might provide details of the significant assumptions and measurement basis used, the range of possible outcomes, and the principal factors that affect the outcome.

CAPITAL MAINTENANCE ADJUSTMENTS AND CHANGING PRICES

6.33   General price changes can affect the significance of reported surpluses/deficits and of residual interest. If this problem is acute, an approach will need to be adopted that involves recognising surpluses/deficits only after adjustments have been made to maintain the purchasing power of the entity's financial capital.

6.34   Specific price changes can affect the significance of reported surpluses/deficits and financial position. If the problem is acute, it will be necessary to adopt a system of accounting that informs the user of the significance of specific price changes for the entity's financial performance and financial position.

Chapter 7
Presentation of financial information

Good presentation ensures that the essential messages of the financial statements are communicated clearly and effectively and in as simple and straightforward a manner as possible. This chapter explains what good presentation entails. It also considers the information that often accompanies financial statements and explains some of the roles fulfilled by such information.

PRINCIPLES

- Financial statements comprise primary financial statements and supporting notes that amplify and explain the primary financial statements. The primary financial statements themselves comprise the statement of financial performance*, the statement of financial position or balance sheet, and the cash flow statement.
- The presentation of information on financial performance focuses on the components of that performance and on the characteristics of those components.
- The presentation of information on financial position focuses on the types and functions of assets and liabilities held and on the relationships between them.
- The presentation of cash flow information will show the extent to which the entity's various activities generate and use cash, and will distinguish in particular between those cash flows that result from operations and those that result from other activities.
- Disclosure of information in the notes to the financial statements is not a substitute for recognition and does not correct or justify any misrepresentation or omission in the primary financial statements.

EXPLANATION

There are few fundamental differences between the principles and explanation relevant to profit-oriented entities, as expressed in Chapter 7 of the Statement, and their interpretation for public benefit entities. Therefore much of what follows is a summary of the discussion in Chapter 7 of the Statement, which should be referred to for a full understanding. Additional explanation specific to public benefit entities has been added covering presentation in the balance sheet and accompanying information.

PRESENTATION OF INFORMATION IN FINANCIAL STATEMENTS

Clear, effective and simple communication

As financial statements are a means of communication, the objective of the presentation adopted is to communicate clearly and effectively and in as simple and straightforward a manner as is possible without loss of relevance or reliability and without unnecessarily increasing the length of the financial statements.

7.1

Although many entities in the UK and the Republic of Ireland at present prepare two statements of financial performance, the number of statements prepared is a matter of convention and legal requirement; no significant financial reporting principle is involved. For simplicity, however, the Statement generally refers to 'the statement of financial performance'.

Highly structured and aggregated

7.2   The presentation of information in financial statements involves a high degree of interpretation, simplification, abstraction and aggregation - in other words, a loss of detailed information. Nevertheless, if this process is carried out in an orderly manner, greater knowledge will result because such a presentation will:

    (a)   convey information that would otherwise have been obscured;

    (b)   highlight those items, and relationships between items, that are generally of most significance;

    (c)   facilitate comparability between different entities' financial statements; and

    (d)   be more understandable to users.

7.3   The primary focus of the financial statements of public benefit entities is to provide information to assist with accountability for the efficient and effective use of funds. This focus is met through a set of interrelated reports (known as the primary financial statements) on:

    (a)   financial performance (the operating cost statement and the statement of total recognised gains and losses are examples of financial performance statements);

    (b)   financial position (the balance sheet); and

    (c)   cash inflows and outflows (the cash flow statement),

and a series of supporting disclosures (the notes to the financial statements).

7.4   The notes and primary financial statements form an integrated whole, with the notes amplifying and explaining the statements by, for example, providing:

    (a)   more detailed information on items recognised in the primary financial statements;

    (b)   context for, or an alternative view of, items recognised in the primary financial statements;

    (c)   relevant information that it is not practicable to incorporate in the primary financial statements, for example because of pervasive uncertainty.

7.5   The notes to the financial statements, therefore, represent a very important part of the overall information package. Nevertheless, disclosure of information in the notes is not a substitute for recognition and does not correct or justify any misrepresentation in, or omission from, the primary financial statements.

Classification

7.6   In order to facilitate the analysis of the information provided, items that are similar are presented together in the financial statements and distinguished from dissimilar items.

GOOD PRESENTATION

Statement of financial performance

7.7   The financial performance of a reporting entity is made up of components that exhibit differing characteristics in terms of, for example, nature, cause, function, relative continuity or recurrence, stability, risk, predictability and reliability. Information on financial performance needs to be presented in a way that focuses attention on these components and on their key characteristics.

Good presentation of financial performance information typically involves: **7.8**

(a) recognising only gains and losses in the statement of financial performance.
(b) classifying components by reference to a combination of function (such as administrative) and of the nature of the item (such as employment costs).
(c) distinguishing amounts that are affected in different ways by changes in economic conditions or business activity (for example, by providing segmental information).
(d) identifying separately:
   • items that are unusual in amount or incidence judged by the experience of previous periods or expectations of the future.
   • items that have special characteristics, such as financing costs and taxation.
   • items that are related primarily to the results of the future, rather than current, accounting periods, such as some research and development expenditure.

Gains and losses are generally not offset in presenting information on financial   **7.9**
performance. However, gains and losses will be offset if:

(a) they relate to the same event or circumstance; and
(b) disclosing the gross components is not likely to be useful for an assessment of either future results or the effects of past transactions and events.

Balance Sheet

In assessing the financial position of an entity, users are most interested in the types   **7.10**
and amounts of assets and liabilities held and the relationship between them, and in
the function of the various assets. Information on the reporting entity's financial
position therefore needs to be presented in a way that focuses attention on these
aspects. Good presentation typically involves:

(a) recognising only assets, liabilities and residual interest in the balance sheet;
(b) delineating the entity's resource structure (major classes and amounts of assets) and its financial structure (major classes and amounts of liabilities and residual interest);
(c) distinguishing assets by function. For example, assets held for sale will be reported separately from assets held on a continuing basis for use in the entity's activities.

In presenting information on the reporting entity's assets, it is necessary that the   **7.11**
amount and nature of assets* that are subject to legal restrictions over their application are disclosed and explained.

In presenting information on the reporting entity's financial position, assets will not   **7.12**
be offset against liabilities.

For some public benefit entities there may also be some focus on the presentation of   **7.13**
different types of residual interests, for example of the extent to which restricted
(including endowment) funds exist. Where, as noted in paragraph 7.11, legal
restrictions exist over the application of assets, it should be clear how the relevant
amount is reflected in the residual interest as well as in the assets themselves.

**In some cases the assets might constitute a portfolio that, at times, includes liabilities. The disclosure
requirements would also apply to any liabilities within such a portfolio.*

Cash flow statement

7.14   Cash flow information will be of most use if it shows the extent to which the entity's activities generate and use cash, distinguishing in particular cash flows that are the result of operations from cash flows that result from other activities.

ACCOMPANYING INFORMATION

7.15   Financial statements are often accompanied and complemented by information that does not form part of the financial statements. Examples of such information include trend information, operating and financial reviews, reports from the entity's governing body (eg directors' report, trustees' report) and statements by the chief executive and key performance indicators, such as information on waiting lists, cost of refuse collection per household, and indicators of a charity's performance. The Statement refers to such information as accompanying information.

7.16   The primary objective of public benefits entities is to provide goods or services for the general public or social benefit. Therefore, the accompanying information is often of high importance for users of such entities' financial statements in assessing the performance of an entity as a whole.

7.17   Although accompanying information generally has the same objective as financial statements, it usually comprises a different kind of information (some of the accompanying information deals with matters that are not in the financial statements and some deals with matters that are in the financial statements, but from a different perspective). For example, it often includes:

   (a)   narrative disclosures describing and explaining the entity's activities;
   (b)   historical summaries and trend information;
   (c)   non-accounting and non-financial information; and
   (d)   evolutionary or experimental disclosures that are not considered suitable for inclusion in the financial statements.

7.18   The more complex entities become, the more users need an objective and comprehensive analysis and explanation of the main features underlying their financial performance and financial position. Such disclosures are best presented in the context of a discussion of the entity's business as a whole. This may include a discussion of what the residual interest represents and, where appropriate, management's future intentions regarding the net assets the residual interest represents.

Comparison to budget

7.19   Many funders and financial supporters will be interested in the extent to which actual expenditure compares to that forecast, for example where it is used to determine the extent of a compulsory levy. In addition, where a grant has been provided, the provider will be interested in the extent to which it covered the associated expenditure.

7.20   As a result it may be useful to provide information on a comparison to budget, or an outturn position for grants, within general purpose financial reports, as part of the accompanying information. However, in providing such information it is necessary to ensure that, for example:

   (a)   the information provided is of general use and not solely regulatory (or special purpose);

(b)   the information is provided at an appropriate level of detail or aggregation (such that it is useful, understandable and not so voluminous as to mask key messages).

HIGHLIGHTS AND SUMMARY INDICATORS

Financial statements and accompanying information sometimes include amounts, ratios, and other computations that attempt to distil key information about the reporting entity's financial performance and financial position. Such highlights and summary indicators cannot, on their own, provide a basis for meaningful analysis or prudent decision-making. It is therefore essential that they are not presented in a way that exaggerates their importance.   **7.21**

However, well-presented highlights and summary indicators are useful to some users, who perhaps only require very basic information, or plan to use that information to identify areas to analyse further.   **7.22**

Notwithstanding the limitations of highlights and summary indicators, if such information is provided it needs to be presented in a manner and context that enable its meaning to be communicated to users. This will often entail explaining the reasons for changes in the relative or absolute size of the figures from one period to the next.   **7.23**

Chapter 8
Accounting for interests in other entities

Financial statements need to reflect the effect on the reporting entity's financial performance and financial position of its interests in other entities. This involves various measurement and presentation issues. Rather than being dealt with in the relevant chapters and therefore in isolation from each other, they are dealt with together in this chapter. For similar reasons, various consolidation issues are dealt with in this chapter.

PRINCIPLES

- Single entity financial statements and consolidated financial statements present the interests the reporting entity may have in other entities from different perspectives.
- In single entity financial statements, interests in other entities are dealt with by focusing on the income and/or expenditure and (depending on the measurement basis adopted) capital growth arising from those interests.
- In consolidated financial statements, the way in which interests in other entities are dealt with depends on the degree of influence involved.

  (a) An interest that involves control of another entity's operating and financial policies is dealt with by incorporating the controlled entity as part of the reporting entity.

  (b) An interest that involves joint control of, or significant influence over, another entity's operating and financial policies is dealt with by recognising the reporting entity's share of that other entity's results and resources in a way that does not involve showing those results and resources in the performance statement and balance sheet as if they were controlled by the reporting entity.

  (c) Other interests are dealt with in the same way as any other asset.

- Although consolidated financial statements are the financial statements of the group as a whole, they are prepared from the perspective of the parent and, as a result, ultimately focus on the parent's interest in its subsidiaries. The effect on benefit flows of any outside interest in the subsidiaries will therefore be separately identified.
- Consolidated financial statements reflect the whole of the parent's investment in its subsidiaries, including, where applicable, purchased goodwill.
- A transaction involving the amalgamation of two or more reporting entities is reflected in the consolidated financial statements in accordance with its character. Therefore, a transaction that is of the character of:

  (a) an acquisition is reflected in the consolidated financial statements as if the acquirer purchased the acquiree's assets and liabilities as a bundle of assets and liabilities on the open market.

  (b) a merger is reflected in the consolidated financial statements as if the new reporting entity, comprising all the parties to the transaction, had always existed.

EXPLANATION

There are few fundamental differences between the principles and explanation relevant to profit-oriented entities, as expressed in Chapter 8 of the Statement, and their interpretation for public benefit entities. Therefore much of what follows is a summary of the discussion in Chapter 8 of the Statement, which should be referred to for a full understanding. Additional explanation specific to public benefit entities has been added covering business combinations.

DEGREE OF INFLUENCE

Although an entity's interest in a second entity may take many different forms, the key factor in determining its effect on the first entity's financial performance and financial position is the degree of influence it exerts over the operating and financial policies of the second entity involved.

8.1

The highest degree of influence that an entity can have is control. As Chapter 2 explains, control comprises the ability to deploy the economic resources involved and to benefit (or to suffer) by their deployment. Other degrees of influence have these same aspects; in effect, the ability to influence the activities of the entity with a view to gaining economic benefits from that influence.

8.2

Although it is possible to classify the degree of influence that an entity has over another entity in an almost infinite number of ways, it is sufficient for the purposes of the Statement to classify it as follows:

8.3

(a) *Control* - where one entity controls another entity.
(b) *Joint control* - where the entity does not itself control the other entity, but shares control through some form of arrangement jointly with others.
(c) *Significant influence* - where the entity has neither control nor joint control, but exerts a degree of influence over the entity's operating and financial policies that is at the least a significant influence and at the most just short of control.
(d) *Lesser or no influence* - where any influence that the entity has over the entity's operating and financial policies is less than a significant influence.

REFLECTING THE EFFECTS OF INTERESTS IN OTHER ENTITIES

Consolidated financial statements and single entity financial statements

The effect on the entity's financial performance and financial position of an interest in an entity is reflected in the first entity's financial statements in different ways depending on the type of financial statements being prepared.

8.4

(a) Financial statements of a reporting entity whose boundary has been drawn by reference to the scope of its direct control - single entity financial statements - take a narrow view of the reporting entity's interests in other entities and reflect only the income and capital growth arising from those interests.
(b) Financial statements of a reporting entity whose boundary has been drawn by reference to the scope of the entity's control (both direct and indirect) - consolidated financial statements - present an expanded view of the reporting entity's interests in other entities that reflects the reporting entity's influence over, and its accountability for, the activities and resources of these entities.

Interests involving control

If an entity controls one or more other entities, the controlling entity (the parent) and the controlled entities (the subsidiaries) will be a reporting entity (the group). The group's financial statements (consolidated financial statements) are prepared by aggregating the gains, losses, assets, liabilities and cash flows of the parent and its subsidiaries. This ensures that the effects on the parent's financial performance and financial position of its interests in its subsidiaries are fully reflected in the financial statements.

8.5

Interests involving joint control or significant influence

8.6   If the reporting entity shares joint control of, or exercises significant influence over, another entity, it will be directly involved in and affected by that other entity's activities. Its interest is therefore reflected in the consolidated financial statements in a way that:

(a)   recognises the reporting entity's share of the results and net assets of the investee; and

(b)   does not misrepresent the extent of its influence over the investee - in other words, it does not treat activities and resources that are not controlled by the reporting entity as if they are controlled by the reporting entity.

Interests involving lesser or no influence

8.7   If the reporting entity's influence does not involve control, joint control or significant influence, the reporting entity will not be accountable for the entity's activities. In such circumstances, the only amounts recognised in the consolidated financial statements will be the investment (if any) and any income derived therefrom.

CONSOLIDATED FINANCIAL STATEMENTS

8.8   The gains, losses, assets, liabilities and cash flows of all subsidiaries are reflected in full in the consolidated financial statements, even if a subsidiary is not wholly-owned. This reflects the parent's ability, through its control, to deploy both its own economic resources and those of its subsidiaries even where it does not wholly own the subsidiaries.

8.9   This Chapter separates general purpose financial statements into single entity financial statements and consolidated financial statements; such distinctions are not necessarily observed in regulatory requirements, which may require combined financial statements for a number of entities that do not meet the criteria for a reporting entity. An example would be financial statements showing the combined results of related initiatives where different elements may be carried out by different entities.

ACCOUNTING FOR BUSINESS COMBINATIONS

8.10   An amalgamation of two or more reporting entities – sometimes referred to as a business combination – can take a number of different forms. All these forms can be characterised as either:

(a)   a purchase (for public benefit entities potentially 'a gift') – such transactions are commonly referred to as acquisitions*; or

(b)   a uniting of interests – such transactions are commonly referred to as mergers.

8.11   An acquisition is a business combination that is in the nature of an acquisition by one entity of another entity (ie one entity is the acquirer). The transaction therefore results in an existing reporting entity being enlarged and is reflected in the consolidated financial statements by treating the assets and liabilities of the entity acquired and the purchased goodwill as if the transaction was the purchase of a bundle of assets and liabilities on the open market.

*An acquisition is something that has been acquired by any means and therefore includes something that has been gifted as well as something that has been purchased.

On the other hand, a merger is in the nature of a coming together of two entities to form a new reporting entity. This is reflected in the financial statements of the new reporting entity comprising all the parties to the transaction as if that entity had always existed. As a result, the assets and liabilities of each party to the transaction are treated as if they were acquired by the new reporting entity at the time that they were acquired by the party concerned*: none of the assets or liabilities is treated as being purchased at the time of the business combination as part of a bundle of assets and liabilities on the open market.

8.12

The fact that a business combination involves public benefit entities does not of itself influence whether the business combination is accounted for as an acquisition or a uniting of interests. For public benefit entities, similarly to profit-oriented entities, true mergers do occur, but after a full analysis of the circumstances it is likely that the majority of business combinations (other than those involving entities under common control†) will be acquisitions. This is because it will be possible to identify an acquirer, for example by relative size or by one entity dominating the governing body and/or management structure, and as a result the entity existing after the combination is an enlarged version of one of the combining entities, not a new entity. It is important that for each business combination that occurs the facts of the individual circumstances are considered to determine whether the combination is an acquisition or a merger.

8.13

Business combinations involving public benefit entities often do not involve consideration and are both legally, and in substance, a "gift" of one business to another. Therefore, it might be necessary to adopt an alternative presentation to the recognition of goodwill in the consolidated financial statements.

8.14

Where a business combination is in substance a gift of one business to another:

8.15

(a) the excess of the fair value of the assets acquired over the fair value of the liabilities assumed should be treated as a gain. The gain represents the gift of the value of one business to another;

(b) if the fair value of the liabilities assumed exceeds the fair value of the assets acquired, the deficit of the fair value of the liabilities in comparison to the assets should be treated as a loss. The loss represents the net obligations assumed, for which the acquiring entity has not received a financial reward, which will therefore result in a decrease in residual interest.

Where a business combination is not in substance a gift, for example if it involves a public benefit entity acquiring a profit-oriented entity for consideration it should be accounted for as if both parties to the combination were profit-oriented entities.

8.16

---

*This description of 'merger accounting' has been repeated from the Statement. However, although the Board continues to believe that there can be circumstances where a business combination does not have the characteristics of an acquisition, merger accounting has generally lost favour as a means of faithfully representing the economic substance of the combination that has occurred. In substance, it can be argued that a new entity has been created from the date of the business combination, which acquired the combined assets on that date. A more suitable presentation might be for all the assets and liabilities to be treated as if they were acquired on the open market on the date the combination took place.

†At present, accounting standards require combinations involving entities under common control to be accounted for as mergers providing certain criteria are met. In July 2005 the ASB issued an Exposure Draft proposing to converge with international standards that do not permit an alternative to acquisition accounting and do not include group reconstructions within their scope.

Appendix 1
The principles that have been re-expressed

1   Many of the principles within this proposed Interpretation are exactly the same as those that are relevant to profit-oriented entities. Those that have been amended or inserted are as follows:

Principle as expressed in the Statement of Principles for Financial Reporting	Principle as re-expressed in this proposed Interpretation	Discussion
Chapter 1 • That objective can usually be met by focusing exclusively on the information needs of present and potential investors, the defining class of user.	• That objective can usually be met by focusing exclusively on the information needs of funders and financial supporters, the defining class of user.	Amended to reflect a different defining class of user.
Chapter 1 • Present and potential investors need information about the reporting entity's financial performance and financial position that is useful to them in evaluating the entity's ability to generate cash (including the timing and certainty of its generation) and in assessing the entity's financial adaptability.	• Funders and financial supporters need information about the reporting entity's financial performance and financial position that is useful to them in helping to evaluate the proper and efficient use of the entity's resources and in assessing the entity's cash needs and its financial adaptability.	Amended to reflect a different defining class of user and a slightly different emphasis on the use of the information.
Chapter 3 • Information is relevant if it has the ability to influence the economic decisions of users and is provided in time to influence those decisions.	• Information is relevant if it has the ability to influence the economic decisions of users, or their assessment of the effectiveness of the stewardship of management, and is provided in time to influence those decisions or assessments.	Amended to include reference to the use of information in assessing the effectiveness of the stewardship of management.
Chapter 3 • Information is material to the financial statements if its misstatement or omission might reasonably be expected to influence the economic decisions of users.	• Information is material to the financial statements if its misstatement or omission might reasonably be expected to influence the economic decisions of users, or their assessment of the effectiveness of the stewardship of management.	Amended to include reference to the use of information in assessing the effectiveness of the stewardship of management.

Principle as expressed in the Statement of Principles for Financial Reporting	Principle as re-expressed in this proposed Interpretation	Discussion

Chapter 4
• The elements of the financial statements are:
  (a) assets;
  (b) liabilities;
  (c) ownership interest;
  (d) gains;
  (e) losses;
  (f) contributions from owners;
  (g) distributions to owners.
	• The elements of the financial statements are:
	  (a) assets;
	  (b) liabilities;
	  (c) residual interest;
	  (d) gains;
	  (e) losses;
	  (f) contributions establishing a financial interest in the residual interest;
	  (g) distributions to holders of a financial interest in the residual interest.
		Amended due to the different nature of owners and financial interests in the context of public benefit entities.

Chapter 4 • Ownership interest is the residual amount found by deducting all of the entity's liabilities from all of the entity's assets.	• Residual interest is the amount found by deducting all of the entity's liabilities from all of the entity's assets.	Amended due to the different nature of owners in public benefit entities.
Chapter 4 • Gains are increases in ownership interest not resulting from contributions from owners.	• Gains are increases in residual interest not resulting from contributions establishing a financial interest in the residual interest.	Amended due to the different nature of owners' financial interests in the context of public benefit entities.
Chapter 4 • Losses are decreases in ownership interest not resulting from distributions to owners.	• Losses are decreases in residual interest not resulting from distributions to holders of a financial interest in the residual interest.	Amended due to the different nature of owners and financial interests in the context of public benefit entities.
Chapter 4 • Contributions from owners are increases in ownership interest resulting from transfers from owners in their capacity as owners.	• Contributions establishing a financial interest in the residual interest are increases in residual interest resulting from transfers from parties that establish a financial interest in that residual interest.	Amended due to the different nature of owners and financial interests in the context of public benefit entities.
Chapter 4 • Distributions to owners are decreases in ownership interest resulting from transfers to owners in their capacity as owners.	• Distributions to holders of a financial interest in the residual interest are decreases in residual interest resulting from transfers to parties holding a financial interest in that residual interest in their capacity as holders of a financial interest.	Amended due to the different nature of owners and financial interests in the context of public benefit entities.

Principle as expressed in the Statement of Principles for Financial Reporting	Principle as re-expressed in this proposed Interpretation	Discussion
Chapter 5	• In a transaction involving the receipt of resources not related directly to the provision of goods or services, the recognition criteria described above will be met when there is clear evidence of a right to receive the resources.	New principle relating to the receipt of resources other than for net gain.
Chapter 8 • In single entity financial statements, interests in other entities are dealt with by focusing on the income and (depending on the measurement basis adopted) capital growth arising from those interests.	• In single entity financial statements, interests in other entities are dealt with by focusing on the income and/or expenditure and (depending on the measurement basis adopted) capital growth arising from those interests.	Amended to include reference to expenditure, because the entity might be contributing to the interest, rather than receiving income from it.
Chapter 8 • Consolidated financial statements reflect the whole of the parent's investment in its subsidiaries, including purchased goodwill.	• Consolidated financial statements reflect the whole of the parent's investment in its subsidiaries, including, where applicable, purchased goodwill.	Amended because purchased goodwill may arise only rarely.

Appendix 2
Comparison to material in the statement

The following table compares the material that is included in this proposed Interpretation with that in the Statement in order to provide an indication of which material:

(a)   is the same, or substantially the same as the Statement;
(b)   from the Statement has been omitted, but is equally relevant to public benefit entities;
(c)   has been inserted specifically to address the circumstances of public benefit entities.

The table does not consider the principles themselves, which are addressed in Appendix 1.

Chapter	Comparison with the Statement
Introduction	*Purpose* Paragraphs 1 and 3 are substantially the same as paragraphs 1 to 4 of the Statement. Paragraphs 2 and 4 are additional. *Status* Paragraph 5 is the same as paragraph 5 of the Statement. Paragraphs 6 and 7 are additional. *Scope* Paragraphs 8 to 15 replace paragraph 9 of the Statement. Paragraphs 16 to 20 are substantially the same as paragraphs 6 to 8 of the Statement, although paragraphs 18 and 19 include a significant amount of new material. *True and fair* Paragraphs 10 to 13 of the Statement have not been repeated. *The standard-setting process* Most of paragraphs 14 to 17 of the Statement have not been repeated, but paragraph 15(a) is reflected in paragraph 21 of this proposed Interpretation. *Revisions to the statement* Paragraph 22 is substantially the same as paragraph 18 of the Statement.
Chapter 1	*The objective of financial statements* Paragraph 1.1 is a summarisation of paragraphs 1.1 and 1.2 of the Statement. Paragraphs 1.2 to 1.4 expand on paragraphs 1.3 and 1.4 of the Statement. Paragraphs 1.5 and 1.6 are additional. Paragraphs 1.5 to 1.7 of the Statement have not been repeated, although paragraph 1.7 provides a brief summary. Paragraph 1.8 summarises paragraphs 1.8 and 1.9 of the Statement. Paragraphs 1.9 and 1.10 are additional. *Defining class of user* Paragraph 1.11 is substantially the same as paragraph 1.11 of the Statement. Paragraphs 1.10 and 1.12 of the Statement have not been repeated. Paragraphs 1.12 to 1.16 are additional.

Chapter	Comparison with the Statement
	Information required [by the defining class of user] Paragraphs 1.17 to 1.23 summarise paragraphs 1.13 to 1.22 of the Statement with added public benefit entity context.
Chapter 2	*Entities that should prepare and publish financial statements* Paragraphs 2.1 to 2.3 are the same as the Statement. *The boundary of a reporting entity* Paragraphs 2.4 to 2.6 summarise paragraphs 2.4, 2.6 and 2.7 of the Statement; paragraph 2.5 has not been repeated. *What is control?* Paragraph 2.7 is the same as paragraph 2.8 in the Statement. Paragraph 2.8 repeats part of paragraph 2.10 in the Statement. Paragraph 2.9 has not been repeated. *Controlling an entity* Paragraphs 2.9 to 2.16 summarise paragraphs 2.11 to 2.20 of the Statement. *Assets under an entity's stewardship but not control* Paragraph 2.17 is additional.
Chapter 3	*Relevance* Paragraph 3.1 is the first sentence of paragraph 3.1, and paragraph 3.2 of the Statement. Paragraph 3.2 is the first part of paragraph 3.3 and paragraph 3.5 of the Statement. The remainder of paragraphs 3.1 and 3.3 and paragraph 3.4 in the Statement are not repeated. Paragraph 3.3 is substantially the same as paragraph 3.6 in the Statement. Paragraph 3.4 is additional. *Reliability* Paragraph 3.5 is the same as paragraphs 3.7 and 3.8 in the Statement. Paragraph 3.6 is the same as paragraph 3.12 in the Statement. Paragraph 3.7 is the first sentence of paragraph 3.13 and paragraph 3.14 in the Statement. Paragraph 3.8 is the same as paragraph 3.15 in the Statement. Paragraphs 3.10, 3.11, the remainder of 3.13 and 3.16 to 3.20 of the Statement have not been repeated. *Comparability* Paragraph 3.9 is substantially the same as paragraph 3.21 in the Statement. Paragraph 3.10 summarises paragraph 3.23 in the Statement. Paragraph 3.11 summarises paragraph 3.24 in the Statement. Paragraphs 3.22 and 3.25 have not been repeated. *Understandability* Paragraph 3.12 summarises paragraphs 3.26 and 3.27 in the Statement. Paragraphs 3.13 and 3.14 are additional. *Materiality* Paragraphs 3.15 to 3.19 are substantially the same as paragraphs 3.28 to 3.32 in the Statement.

Chapter	Comparison with the Statement
	Constraints on the qualitative characteristics Paragraph 3.20 is the same as paragraph 3.33 in the Statement. Paragraph 3.21 is a summary of paragraph 3.34 in the Statement, as is paragraph 3.22 of 3.36 in the Statement and paragraph 3.25 of paragraph 3.37 in the Statement. Paragraph 3.35 of the Statement has not been repeated. Paragraphs 3.23 and 3.24 are additional.
Chapter 4	*The elements of financial statements* Paragraphs 4.1 and 4.2 are substantially the same as paragraphs 4.1 and 4.2 in the Statement. Paragraphs 4.3 and 4.4 of the Statement have not been repeated. Paragraph 4.3 is the same as the second sentence of paragraph 4.5 in the Statement. *Assets* The definition is the same as paragraph 4.6 in the Statement. Paragraph 4.4 is the same as paragraph 4.8 in the Statement. Paragraph 4.5 summarises paragraphs 4.9 and 4.10 in the Statement. Paragraph 4.6 is the same as paragraph 4.11 in the Statement. Paragraph 4.7 is substantially the same as paragraph 4.13 in the Statement. Paragraph 4.13 is substantially the same as paragraph 4.17 in the Statement. Paragraphs 4.17 and 4.18 summarise paragraphs 4.19 and 4.20 in the Statement. Paragraph 4.19 is the first sentence of paragraph 4.22 in the Statement. Paragraphs 4.8 to 4.12 and 4.14 to 4.16 are additional. Paragraphs 4.7, 4.12, 4.14 to 4.16, 4.18 and 4.21 of the Statement have not been repeated. *Liabilities* The definition is the same as paragraph 4.23 in the Statement. Paragraphs 4.20 to 4.22 are the same as paragraphs 4.24 to 4.26, except that paragraph 4.22 includes some additional material. Paragraph 4.23 is the same as paragraph 4.27 in the Statement. Paragraph 4.26 is the same as paragraph 4.29 in the Statement. Paragraph 4.27 is the first part of paragraph 4.30 in the Statement. Paragraphs 4.29 and 4.30 summarise paragraphs 4.31 and 4.32 in the Statement. Paragraphs 4.24, 4.25, 4.28, and 4.31 to 4.42 are additional. Paragraph 4.28 of the Statement has not been repeated. *Offsetting rights and obligations* Paragraphs 4.43 to 4.46 are essentially the same as paragraphs 4.33 to 4.36 in the Statement, except that the sub-paragraphs of 4.33 have not been repeated. *Residual interest* Paragraph 4.47 reflects the public benefit entity context of paragraph 4.37 in the Statement. Paragraph 4.50 includes some of the material from paragraph 4.38 in the Statement. Paragraphs 4.48, 4.49, 4.51 and 4.52 are additional. *Gains and losses* The definition and paragraph 4.53 are substantially the same as paragraphs 4.39 and 4.40 in the Statement. Paragraph 4.41 has not been repeated. Paragraphs 4.54 to 4.60 are additional.

Chapter	Comparison with the Statement
	Contributions establishing a financial interest in the residual interest Paragraph 4.61 relates to paragraph 4.43 in the Statement. Paragraph 4.63 builds on paragraph 4.44 in the Statement, providing additional public benefit entity context. Paragraphs 4.62 and 4.64 are additional. *Distributions to holders of a financial interest in the residual interest* Paragraph 4.65 is additional. The first sentence of paragraph 4.66 is the first sentence of paragraph 4.45 in the Statement.
Chapter 5	*The recognition process* Paragraphs 5.1 and 5.2 are the same as paragraphs 5.1 and 5.2 in the Statement. Paragraphs 5.3 to 5.6 summarise paragraphs 5.3 to 5.6 in the Statement. Paragraphs 5.7 to 5.10 are substantially the same as paragraphs 5.8, 5.9 and 5.11 in the Statement. Paragraphs 5.7 and 5.10 have not been repeated. *Initial recognition* Paragraph 5.10 is the same as paragraph 5.12 in the Statement. Paragraphs 5.11 and 5.12 summarise paragraphs 5.14 and 5.15 in the Statement. Paragraphs 5.13 and 5.14 are the same as paragraphs 5.16 and 5.17 in the Statement. Paragraph 5.16 is substantially the same as paragraph 5.19 in the Statement. Paragraph 5.15 is additional. Paragraphs 5.13 and 5.18 have not been repeated. Paragraph 5.17 is substantially the same as paragraph 5.20 and the first sentence of paragraph 5.21; the remainder of paragraph 5.21 has not been repeated. *Derecognition* Paragraphs 5.18 to 5.21 summarise paragraphs 5.22 to 5.25 in the Statement. *Revenue recognition* Paragraphs 5.22 to 5.25 summarise paragraphs 5.26 to 5.30 in the Statement. Paragraphs 5.26 to 5.28 are the same as paragraphs 5.33 to 5.35 in the Statement, except that the second sentence of paragraph 5.34 has not been repeated. Paragraphs 5.31 and 5.32 have not been repeated. The first sentence of paragraph 5.29 is the same as the first sentence of paragraph 5.36 in the Statement, otherwise paragraphs 5.29 to 5.45 are additional.
Chapter 6	*Alternative bases of measurement* Paragraph 6.1 summarises paragraph 6.1 in the Statement. Paragraph 6.2 is the same as paragraph 6.3 in the Statement. Paragraph 6.3 is substantially the same as the first sentence of paragraph 6.4 in the Statement. Paragraphs 6.2 and 6.5 have not been repeated. *Alternative measures of current value* Paragraph 6.4 is substantially the same as paragraph 6.6 in the Statement. Paragraph 6.9 is based on paragraph 6.7 in the Statement. Paragraphs 6.5 to 6.8 and 6.10 to 6.12 are additional. Paragraph 6.13 is essentially the same as paragraph 6.9 in the Statement.

Chapter	Comparison with the Statement
	The measurement process Paragraphs 6.14 to 6.19 are substantially the same as paragraphs 6.10 to 6.15 in the Statement, except that the sub-paragraphs of 6.14 have not been repeated. Paragraph 6.16 has not been repeated. Paragraphs 6.20 to 6.24 are substantially the same as paragraphs 6.17 to 6.22 in the Statement, except that paragraph 6.21 has not been repeated. *Choosing a measurement basis and deciding whether to change it* Paragraph 6.25 is the same as paragraph 6.23 in the Statement. Paragraph 6.26 is the same as the first part of paragraph 6.24 in the Statement. Paragraphs 6.25 to 6.29 have not been repeated. *Measurement issues* Paragraph 6.27 is substantially the same as paragraph 6.30 in the Statement. Paragraph 6.28 is the same as part of paragraph 6.32 in the Statement. Paragraphs 6.29 and 6.30 are the same as paragraphs 6.33 and 6.34 in the Statement. Paragraph 6.31 is the same as paragraph 6.36 in the Statement. Paragraph 6.32 is the same as paragraph 6.38 in the Statement. Paragraphs 6.31, 6.35, 6.37 have not been repeated. *Capital maintenance adjustments and changing prices* Paragraphs 6.33 and 6.34 are the same as the sub-paragraphs of 6.42 in the Statement. Paragraphs 6.39 to 6.41 have not been repeated.
Chapter 7	*Presentation of information in financial statements* Paragraphs 7.1 to 7.6 are the same, or substantially the same, as paragraphs 7.1 to 7.6 in the Statement. Paragraphs 7.7 and 7.8 have not been repeated. *Good presentation* Paragraphs 7.7 to 7.12 summarise paragraphs 7.9 to 7.13 in the Statement, except that paragraph 7.11 is additional. Paragraph 7.13 is additional. Paragraph 7.14 summarises paragraph 7.14 in the Statement. *Accompanying information* Paragraph 7.15 is substantially the same as paragraph 7.15 in the Statement. Paragraph 7.16 is additional. Paragraph 7.17 summarises paragraphs 7.16 and 7.17 of the Statement. Paragraph 7.18 summarises paragraph 7.18 in the Statement. Paragraphs 7.19 and 7.20 are additional. *Highlights and summary indicators* Paragraphs 7.21 to 7.23 are substantially the same as paragraphs 7.19 to 7.21 in the Statement.
Chapter 8	*Degree of influence* Paragraphs 8.1, 8.2 and 8.3 are the same as paragraphs 8.1, 8.3 and 8.4 in the Statement. Paragraph 8.2 has not been repeated. *Reflecting the effects of interests in other entities* Paragraph 8.4 is substantially the same as paragraph 8.5 in the Statement. Paragraph 8.5 is substantially the same as paragraph 8.7 in the Statement. Paragraph 8.6 is substantially the same as paragraph 8.9 in the Statement. Paragraph 8.7 is

Chapter	Comparison with the Statement
	substantially the same as paragraph 8.10 in the Statement. Paragraphs 8.6 and 8.8 have not been repeated. *Consolidated financial statements* Paragraph 8.8 is the same as paragraph 8.11 in the Statement. Paragraph 8.9 is additional. Paragraphs 8.12 and 8.13 are not repeated. *Accounting for business combinations* Paragraphs 8.10 to 8.12 are the same as paragraphs 8.14 to 8.16 in the Statement. Paragraphs 8.13 to 8.16 are additional.

Statement
'Half-Yearly Financial Reports'

Contents

APPENDICES

Preface

INTRODUCTION

This Exposure Draft sets out for comment a draft Statement 'Half-Yearly Financial 1
Reports', which is designed to provide guidance for any UK* entities that are
required or voluntarily choose to prepare half-yearly financial reports, other than
those required by the Disclosure and Transparency Rules (DTR)† of the Financial
Services Authority (FSA) to apply International Accounting Standard (IAS) 34
'Interim Financial Reporting'. UK issuers not required to apply IAS 34 can satisfy
the requirement in the DTR for the half-yearly financial statements by following the
provisions of this [draft] Statement. As noted below, the DTR clarify that issuers can
satisfy the requirement for half-yearly financial statements to give a true and fair
view by a statement that they have been prepared in accordance with pronouncements by the Accounting Standards Board (ASB). The FSA has effectively mandated
the use of this statement. The FSA rule is in all cases subject to the condition that the
person making the 'true and fair' statement has reasonable grounds to be satisfied
that the condensed‡ set of financial statements prepared in accordance with the
applicable set of accounting standards is not misleading.

BACKGROUND

The ASB first issued a Statement relating to interim reports in September 1997. The 2
Statement was developed following a recommendation by the Committee on the
Financial Aspects of Corporate Governance (the Cadbury Committee) in 1992 that
the ASB, in conjunction with the London Stock Exchange, should clarify the
accounting principles to be adopted by companies when preparing interim reports. It
also recommended that balance sheet information should be included as part of the
interim report and suggested that the inclusion of cash flow information should also
be considered§.

In response to the Cadbury initiative, the Financial Reporting Committee of the 3
Institute of Chartered Accountants in England and Wales undertook a project
focusing on the accounting aspects of Interim reports. The project focused on the
measurement basis and extent of disclosure required in Interim reports. The Committee published a Consultative Paper 'Interim Financial Reporting' in 1993 which
led to formal proposal being presented to the ASB. The 1997 Statement was
developed from those proposals and presented its recommendations as best practice
in the reporting of interim information.

At the time of the Statement, the then International Accounting Standards Com- 4
mittee (IASC) was developing a new International Accounting Standard (IAS) on

The [draft] statement may also be applied by similar entities in the Republic of Ireland.

†*In the UK the Disclosure and Transparency Rules are now issued by the Financial Services Authority in its
capacity as UK Regulatory Authority. In the Republic of Ireland, the half-yearly reporting requirements of the
Transparency Directive will be set out in secondary legislation and, upon enactment of the legislation, will
replace section 6.9 ('Half-yearly reports') of the Irish Stock Exchange's Listing Rules.*

‡*The Transparency Directive replaces the term 'summarised' with the term 'condensed'.*

§*Furthermore in the Republic of Ireland, the Report of the Financial Reporting Commission published in 1992
(the Ryan Report) also advocating half-yearly financial reporting and recommended that interim reports should
include details of items of an exceptional nature such as capital profits or losses, depreciation and interest
charges, and segment data, together with a balance sheet in sufficient detail for financial position to be assessed.*

recognising, measuring and reporting interim financial information. IASC's initial proposals, published in September 1996, and its subsequent Exposure Draft E57, issued in August 1997, were considered by the ASB during the preparation of its 1997 Statement.

REASONS FOR CONSIDERING A REVIEW OF THE STATEMENT

5   The main development since 1997 that has led the ASB to conclude that a review of the Statement is necessary is that, during 2006, the FSA* has consulted on UK implementation of the EU Transparency Directive (TD) (Directive 2004/109/EC). The TD is designed to enhance transparency on EU capital markets by requiring regulated market issuers to produce periodic financial reports and shareholders in such companies to disclose major holdings. The requirements of the TD have to be implemented by all Member States no later than 20 January 2007. In October 2006, the FSA published a policy statement 'PS 06/11 Implementation of the Transparency Directive – Feedback on CP06/4' setting out near-final rules of the implementation of the TD. These rules include provisions in respect of half-yearly financial reporting.

6   UK and ROI entities listed on a regulated market are required to prepare consolidated financial statements in accordance with European Union (EU) endorsed International Financial Reporting Standards (IFRS). UK and ROI listed entities preparing consolidated financial statements are required to prepare half-yearly reports in accordance with IAS 34. The FSA's Disclosure and Transparency Rules (DTR) also require half-yearly financial reports to be prepared in accordance with IAS 34. Other UK issuers have to apply UK Generally Accepted Accounting Practice (GAAP) to produce their half-yearly financial statements. Some respondents to CP06/4 highlighted the current uncertainty as to what constitutes 'UK GAAP' for entities not preparing half-yearly financial statements under IAS 34. The DTR refer to pronouncements on half-yearly financial reporting issued by the ASB. The decision to rename the [draft] Statement to 'Half-yearly Financial Reports' is in line with the wording of the DTR.

7   DTR 4.2.10 clarifies that the requirement to provide a true and fair view in half-yearly financial statements is satisfied by a statement that the condensed set of financial statements have been prepared in accordance with IAS 34, or (for UK issuers not using IFRS) pronouncements on half-yearly reporting issued by the ASB, or (for all other issuers not using IFRS) a national accounting standard relating to half-yearly reporting. The ASB has therefore decided to update its Statement, given that, for UK issuers not using IFRS, the FSA decision is effectively mandating its use. The FSA rule is in all cases subject to the condition that the person making the 'true and fair' statement has reasonable grounds to be satisfied that the condensed set of financial statements prepared in accordance with the applicable set of accounting standards is not misleading. The FSA has noted in PS06/11 that it is aware that this may dilute the true and fair concept but retention of this wording is unavoidable given that it is in the text of the TD.

8   Article 6 of the Directive requires issuers whose shares are admitted to trading on a regulated market to publish interim management statements for the first and third quarters of the year. The statement has to provide (a) an explanation of material events and transactions that have taken place during the relevant period and their impact on the financial position; and (b) a general description of the financial position and performance of the issuers. The FSA has simply 'copied-out' the TD's

In June 2000 the responsibilities of being the competent authority for listing passed from the London Stock Exchange to the UK Listing Authority (UKLA) of the Financial Services Authority (FSA).

provisions on half-yearly management statements in the DTR and has not provided any additional guidance. The FSA's proposal not to provide any additional guidance was supported by respondents to the FSA's consultation. This [draft] statement is not intended to give guidance on the preparation of interim management statements.

The ASB gave consideration to the above matters and decided to revise its Statement   **9**
on Interim Reports and rename it 'Half-Yearly Financial Reports' to reflect the requirements of the DTR.

SUMMARY OF PROPOSED CHANGES

The changes proposed in the [draft] Statement take account of changes which have   **10**
been effected since the Statement on Interim Reports was issued in 1997, as outlined in paragraph 5 above. To this extent it was necessary to update the [draft] Statement to ensure that:

(a)   it is consistent with all major aspects of IAS 34;
(b)   it is consistent with the DTR; and
(c)   it does not give rise to conflicting guidance.

In preparing this [draft] Statement, the ASB has sought to make the minimum   **11**
number of changes necessary in light of the developments, as set out in paragraph 5, including changes in terminology. The ASB has adopted this approach in order to have revised guidance prepared in time for the first round of half-yearly financial reports that have to be prepared to meet the requirements of the TD and the DTR. The ASB is, however, minded to add a longer-term project on interim financial reporting to its work programme and would welcome the views of constituents on this suggestion.

The changes have: **12**

- renamed the [draft] Statement, 'Half-Yearly Financial Reports';
- introduced a Summary and Objective paragraph to replace the previous Introduction;
- updated the wording of the standard to use language appropriate to IAS 34 and the DTR; and
- added an Appendix to reflect the current legal and regulatory framework.

Invitation to comment

The Board would welcome comments on any aspect of the Exposure Draft. Respondents' views are especially sought on the matters set out below. It would be helpful if respondents could support comments with reasons and, where applicable, preferred alternatives.

1   Do you agree with the proposal to update the ASB's existing Statement and issue an amended Statement on Half-yearly Financial Reports? If not, why not?

2   Do you agree that changes in the [draft] Statement should be restricted to those made necessary by the developments outlined in paragraph 5 of the Preface? If you do not agree, what changes would you wish to see made to the guidance in the [draft] Statement?

3   The [draft] Statement is designed to provide guidance for UK and ROI issuers not using IFRS who are required to prepare half-yearly financial reports. Do you agree that the [draft] Statement will provide useful guidance, not only for issuers required to prepare half-yearly financial reports in line with FSA rule DTR 4.2 and the Irish legislative equivalent, but any other entities wishing voluntarily to prepare half-yearly financial reports?

4   The ASB is seeking views on whether the Board should initiate a longer-term project on interim financial reporting. Are you in favour of such a project?

5   The ASB has not sought to update the statement to include explicit guidance on accounting for pensions at the half year. The Board has not replicated the guidance in IAS 34 on this issue, as the Board considers the guidance there to be unclear. Should the Board consider issuing any guidance on pensions for half-yearly financial reports? If so, what should that guidance cover?

6   Are there any other areas on which you consider guidance is needed for half-yearly financial reports? If so, please explain, with reasons why such guidance would be useful.

[Draft] Statement – 'Half-yearly Financial Reports'

SUMMARY

This [draft] Statement is designed to provide guidance for any UK* entities that are required or voluntarily choose to prepare half-yearly financial reports, other than those required by the Disclosure and Transparency Rules (DTR)† of the Financial Services Authority (FSA) to apply International Accounting Standard (IAS) 34 'Interim Financial Reporting'. It is intended to have persuasive rather than mandatory force. However, for UK issuers not required to apply IAS 34, the DTR make clear that the requirement for responsible persons to give an explicit statement that the condensed set of financial statements give a true and fair view can be satisfied by giving a statement that the condensed information has been prepared in accordance with pronouncements on interim reporting issued by the ASB. In effect this mandates such UK issuers to apply this [draft] Statement.

OBJECTIVE

The objective of this [draft] Statement is to outline the basis of presentation for half-yearly financial reports and define the content of half-yearly financial reports. The [draft] Statement gives guidance on the content of half-yearly financial reports to assist shareholders to make a more informed assessment of the entity at a half-yearly stage.   1

SCOPE

This [draft] Statement sets out guidance that may be applied by any UK entities that are required or voluntarily choose to prepare half-yearly financial reports, other than those required by the DTR to apply IAS 34. For UK issuers not required to apply IAS 34, the DTR make clear that the requirement for responsible persons to give an explicit statement that the condensed set of financial statements give a true and fair view can be satisfied by giving a statement that the condensed information has been prepared in accordance with pronouncements on interim reporting issued by the ASB. This [draft] Statement sets out such a pronouncement.   2

ROLE OF THE HALF-YEARLY FINANCIAL REPORT

A condensed set of financial statements is a requirement of the Directive and DTR, mainly because the interval between annual reports is considered to be too long a period for users and specifically shareholders to be without financial information, particularly when developments are affecting trading conditions.   3

Half-yearly financial reports play an important role as a progress report in the continuing reporting process of the operating, financing and investing activities of a business. Like annual financial statements they fulfil a confirmatory and predictive function. Within the constraints of time and cost, half-yearly financial reports are   4

The [draft] statement may also be applied by similar entities in the Republic of Ireland.

†*In the UK the Disclosure and Transparency Rules are now issued by the Financial Services Authority in its capacity as the UK Listing Authority. In the Republic of Ireland, the half-yearly reporting requirements of the Transparency Directive will be set out in secondary legislation and, upon enactment of the legislation, will replace section 6.9 ('Half-yearly reports') of the Irish Stock Exchange's Listing Rules. It is expected that the requirements in relation to half-yearly reports in the legislation implementing the Transparency Directive in the Republic of Ireland will be similar to those contained in the FSA's Disclosure and Transparency Rules.*

designed to enable users to monitor the progress of a business from its financial position as stated in the last set of annual financial statements and to assess the impact of recent events on operating performance and financial position. Additionally, the law requires that a condensed set of financial statements provide a true and fair view.

TIMESCALE

5   For information to be of value in updating users' knowledge of an entity it must be timely. The DTR require that companies make their half-yearly financial reports available within two months of the half-yearly period-end.

BASIS OF PRESENTATION

6   Half-yearly financial reports, like annual financial statements, are presented in respect of a distinct reporting period. A fair assessment of the progress of the business can be made only if the half-yearly accounts are prepared on a consistent and comparable basis taking one reporting period with another.

7   Traditionally, two rather different methods have been used in the preparation of half-yearly reports: the 'integral method' and the 'discrete method'.

8   The integral method views the half-yearly period as a part of the larger annual reporting cycle. Its function is predominantly to predict and explain the financial information for the full financial year. Items are therefore recognised in half-yearly periods on the basis of estimating the total annual revenue and expenses and allocating accordingly.

9   Under the discrete method, the half-yearly period is treated as an accounting period distinct from the annual cycle. Incomplete transactions are treated according to the same principles as are applied at the year-end. This has the advantage that the elements of financial statements are defined in the same way as for the annual financial statements.

10   The Board continues to endorse an approach whereby items of income and expense are measured and recognised on a basis consistent with that used in the preparation of annual financial statements (the discrete method). Certain items of income and expenditure occur on an annual basis and these are considered in paragraphs 15-17 below.

ACCOUNTING POLICIES

11   The DTR require that the accounting policies and presentation of figures in half-yearly financial reports are consistent with those in the annual financial statements. Accordingly, half-yearly financial reports should be prepared using the same measurement basis and adopting the same accounting principles and practices as are employed in the annual financial statements.

12   Half-yearly financial reports should include a statement that they are prepared on the basis of the accounting policies set out in the most recent set of annual financial statements. Half-yearly financial reports are often reviewed in conjunction with the previous year's financial statements and therefore their accounting policies need to be stated and explained only where they differ from those previously adopted.

CHANGES IN ACCOUNTING POLICY AND PRIOR PERIOD ADJUSTMENTS

When it is known at the time that half-yearly accounts are prepared that an 13 accounting policy change (or a presentation change) will be made in the annual accounts (including voluntary changes in accounting policy, not resulting from a new or revised accounting standard, UITF abstract or a change in companies legislation), the change should be implemented in the half-yearly accounts rather than deferred to the year-end. This ensures that the half-yearly results are presented on the same basis as those for the full financial year. Where a known accounting policy change in the current year is not implemented in the half-yearly report an estimate of its effect should be shown; if that is not possible, a statement of explanation should be included.

Following a change in accounting policy, the amounts for the current and prior 14 periods should be stated on the basis of the new policies. The cumulative effect of the policy change on opening reserves (ie at the beginning of the financial year) should be disclosed at the foot of the statement of total recognised gains and losses of the period. Similar disclosures should be made in respect of other prior period adjustments arising from the discovery of fundamental errors. A description should be given to help users understand the nature of each change or adjustment.

ANNUALLY DETERMINED INCOME AND EXPENDITURE

Certain items of income and expenditure are determined on a formal basis once a 15 year when the full financial statements are prepared; examples include bonuses, profit-sharing arrangements, volume discounts, sales commissions and rent based on income or sales criteria.

In each case it is necessary to determine whether an obligation to transfer economic 16 benefits as a result of past transactions or events exists at the half-yearly period-end. Only if there is such an obligation (either contractual or constructive), should a provision be made at the period-end. An intention to transfer economic benefits is, by itself, not sufficient to recognise future costs and income in the half-yearly period.

For example, a genuinely discretionary one-off bonus given at the end of the year 17 would be recognised only in the final interim accounting period. On the other hand, a profit-related bonus paid at the year-end, although non-contractual, would be recognised in an earlier interim period, on the basis of profits earned in that period, if past practice indicated that there was a constructive obligation. Similarly, a contractual supplier's volume discount, based on an annual target for the year, would also be recognised in an earlier interim period on the basis of a proportion of the expected annual discount.

SEASONAL REVENUES

A business is seasonal where there is a substantial and recurring variation between 18 the levels of profit in the half-yearly period and the remainder of the year. Fluctuating revenues of seasonal businesses are generally understood by the marketplace and it is appropriate to report them as they arise.

TAXATION

The half-yearly tax charge should be based on an estimate of the likely effective tax 19 rate for the year, expressed as a percentage of the expected results for the year and then applied to the half-yearly profit or loss arising. This approach results in taxation, including permanent and timing tax differences, being recognised rateably over the year as a whole in common with other contractual, annually determined items of income and expenditure as noted in paragraphs 15 to 17.

20   To the extent practicable and where more meaningful, a separate estimated effective annual tax rate should be determined for each material tax jurisdiction and applied individually to the half-yearly period pre-tax income of each jurisdiction. Similarly, if different income tax rates apply to different categories of income (such as capital gains tax), to the extent practicable, a separate rate should be applied to each individual category of half-yearly period pre-tax income, where material. In many cases a weighted average of rates across jurisdictions or across categories of income may be a reasonable approximation of the effect of using more specific rates.

21   Exceptional items are, by definition, material to the accounts and can often distort the overall tax charge if the tax rate applying to the exceptional item differs significantly from the likely effective tax rate. Therefore, where material, the tax effect of exceptional items should not be included in the likely effective annual tax rate but should be recognised in the same period(s) as the relevant exceptional item. In such circumstances, the estimated annual effective tax rate (excluding exceptional items) will be applied to the half-yearly profits or losses before exceptional items.

22   The half-yearly financial report should give a brief explanation of the basis of the effective tax rate.

23   The general approach of making an estimate of the effective tax rate for the year should be employed even where, for example, a company's result in the first half-year is expected to be completely offset by its result in the second half-year. Even if the overall result is break-even, there will still be an effective tax rate (say 30 per cent). The full year's tax of nil is, conceptually, 30 per cent of no profit, rather than zero per cent. Thus that tax rate is applied to both profits and losses. However, a tax credit should be booked (and a deferred tax asset recognised) for half-yearly tax losses only if there is reasonable assurance that it will reverse in the foreseeable future (in accordance with Financial Reporting Standard (FRS) 19 'Deferred tax').

24   In determining the amount of tax losses to recognise in the half-yearly period, an estimate should be made of the utilisation expected over the whole tax year. The amount recognised in the half-yearly period should be proportional to the profit before tax of the half-yearly period and the estimated annual profit before tax.

FOREIGN EXCHANGE

25   The profit and loss account of a foreign entity accounted for under the net investment or closing rate method should be translated either at the average rate for the half-yearly period or at the closing rate at the end of that period, whichever is consistent with the company's accounting policy.

VALUATION

26   Whether value changes of assets held at a valuation are recognised depends upon the nature of the assets and the difficulty of obtaining valuations. Revaluation would be necessary, for example, in respect of quoted stocks carried at market value, but not, as a matter of course, in respect of properties, where revaluations on the basis used in the previous annual financial statements would suffice, subject to the following:

(a)   the most recent valuations available should be used;

(b)   where valuations have been brought forward, without amendment from the previous annual accounts, a statement to that effect should be given; and

(c)   where significant, the directors are encouraged to comment on price movements since the last valuation.

Additionally with regards to valuation, any impairment losses on acquired goodwill   **27**
should be recognised if the acquired goodwill is deemed to have been impaired and the provision for those losses should not be reversed in a subsequent period, regardless of circumstances. The same should apply to provisions relating to investments in available-for-sale equity instruments and unquoted equity instruments that are not carried at fair value because their fair value cannot be reliably measured.

MATERIALITY

Consistently with the discrete approach, materiality should be assessed with refer-   **28**
ence to the results and financial position for the half-yearly period rather than in relation to expected results and financial position for the full year.

CONTENT OF THE HALF-YEARLY FINANCIAL REPORT

Half-yearly financial reports provide an update on the latest set of annual financial   **29**
statements and, accordingly, should focus on new activities, events and circumstances.

An informed assessment of financial position and performance does not focus solely   **30**
on the profit (or loss) for the period, but requires comparison of information from the profit and loss account, statement of total recognised gains and losses, balance sheet and cash flow statement. Whilst not all information in the four primary statements is critical to such an analysis, it is useful to present the significant information within the context of the four statements, along with an interim management report that highlights and explains these elements in the context of events since the previous annual report and accounts.

It is therefore recommended that a half-yearly financial report should include a half-   **31**
yearly management report, condensed profit and loss account, statement of total recognised gains and losses, condensed balance sheet and condensed cash flow statement.

Significant events and trends mentioned in the content of the half-yearly financial   **32**
report should be supported by the underlying figures given either on the face of the primary statements or by way of note. Sufficient supplementary information should be given, where appropriate to the nature of the company's business and as the directors see fit, to permit an understanding of the significant items contained within the primary statements.

The information should be presented in a concise manner, should be consistent and   **33**
comparable with that previously reported (the annual report) and should facilitate comparison between like companies.

HALF-YEARLY MANAGEMENT REPORT

The DTR require half-yearly financial reports to include a half-yearly management   **34**
report which must include at least an indication of important events that have occurred during the first six months of the financial year, and their impact on the

condensed set of financial statements, and a description of the principal risks and uncertainties for the remaining six months of the year. Any additional material to be contained in the report, as outlined in the paragraphs below, should be considered in the context of what is needed to meet the requirements of the DTR. The half-yearly management report is not intended to be as comprehensive as an operating and financial review (OFR), but should include any significant information enabling investors to make an informed assessment of the trend of the group's activities and profit or loss. Half-yearly management reports should focus attention on areas of change since the last set of annual financial statements. A balanced narrative commentary that explains the reasons for significant movements in key indicators and indicates perceived trends within the business is an important feature of a half-yearly financial report, providing management with the opportunity to report on its stewardship of the business as a whole.

35   Attention should be drawn to events and changes within the period that are likely to have a significant effect on the succeeding period despite having had relatively little impact in the current period.

36   The commentary should describe the nature of any seasonal activity and, together with other disclosures, provide adequate information for the performance of the business and its financial position at the end of the period to be understood in the context of the annual cycle. The principles by which seasonal results are reflected in the half-yearly report should be stated, particularly where there are any expected changes in the effects of seasonality.

37   As well as referring to trading performance, the commentary should draw attention to the condensed balance sheet and cash flow statement. It should also highlight and explain significant changes since the last annual financial statements, particularly regarding movements in working capital, liquidity and net debt that are likely to be of value to users in their assessment of the business.

38   The commentary should explain any other matter that management thinks would help users to understand the report. This would include for example, where relevant:

- acquisitions and disposals of major fixed assets or investments during the period covered by the report;
- changes in estimates for liabilities, commitments and off balance sheet financial instruments since the previous year-end;
- material changes in capital structure or financing; and
- events arising after the end of the period covered by the report.

PROFIT AND LOSS ACCOUNT

39   A half-yearly financial report should include a condensed profit and loss account that should show each of the headings and subtotals included in the most recent annual financial statements. Additional line items should be included if, as a result of their omission, the half-yearly financial statements would give a misleading view of the profit or loss of the entity.

ACQUISITIONS AND DISCONTINUED OPERATIONS

40   Turnover and operating profit of acquisitions and discontinued operations (as defined in FRS 3 'Reporting Financial Performance') should be disclosed separately on the face of the profit and loss account in the period in accordance with FRS 3. For this purpose, operations are regarded as discontinued when the sale or termination is completed either in the half-yearly period or before the earlier of two

months after the end of the half-yearly period and the date on which the half-yearly financial report is approved.

It may be appropriate to disclose separately, either by way of note or in the half-yearly management report, the results of operations which, although not discontinued, are in the process of discontinuing or are expected to be classified as discontinued in the current year's financial statements. Where it is not practicable to determine the post-acquisition results of an operation to the end of the half-yearly period, an indication should be given of the contribution of the acquisition to the turnover and operating profit of the continuing operations. **41**

SEGMENT INFORMATION

The basis of presentation of segment information in the half-yearly financial report should, where possible, be consistent with that to be used at the current year-end in order to assist users in making predictions that will be readily comparable with the annual results. Any significant differences in presentation from that used in the latest annual financial statements should be disclosed and explained. **42**

EXCEPTIONAL ITEMS

By definition, exceptional items are unusual in nature and significant in amount. They rarely extend over more than one year and it is not generally appropriate to allocate their effect to different parts of the reporting period. They should be recognised and disclosed in the profit and loss account of the half-yearly period in which they occur. Certain exceptional items should be shown separately after operating profit and before interest as required by paragraph 20 of FRS 3 'Reporting Financial Performance'. **43**

Other exceptional items should be charged or credited in arriving at the profit or loss on ordinary activities by inclusion under the statutory headings to which they relate. In addition, they should be disclosed and described by way of a note. **44**

The tax effects of exceptional items disclosed on the face of the profit and loss account, in accordance with paragraph 44 above, should be separately disclosed in the profit and loss account or a related note. **45**

EARNINGS PER SHARE

The DTR require listed companies to disclose earnings per share expressed as pence per share. Basic earnings per share should be derived from the results for the interim period and calculated and disclosed in the same manner as at the year-end. Companies that choose to present in their annual financial statements additional amounts per share based on another level of earnings should present them also in their half-yearly accounts, calculated and disclosed in accordance with FRS 3 'Reporting Financial Performance'. **46**

STATEMENT OF TOTAL RECOGNISED GAINS AND LOSSES

A statement of total recognised gains and losses should be included where gains or losses, other than profit or loss for the half-yearly period, as reported in the profit and loss account, are recognised in the period. **47**

48   A reconciliation of movements in shareholders' funds is required only where movements other than those in the statement of total recognised gains and losses need to be explained.

BALANCE SHEET

49   A condensed balance sheet (together with corresponding amounts) should show each of the headings and subtotals used in the balance sheet included in the most recent annual financial statements. Additional line items must be included if, as a result of their omission, the half-yearly financial statements would give a misleading view of the assets, liabilities and financial position of the entity.

CASH FLOW STATEMENT

50   Information on the amounts and sources of cash flows provides an additional perspective to the performance of a company through the half-yearly period. Total amounts for the categories of cash flows specified by FRS 1 (Revised 1996) 'Cash Flow Statements' should be presented as follows:

- Net cash inflow/outflow from operating activities
- Returns on investments and servicing of finance
- Taxation
- Capital expenditure and financial investment
- Acquisitions and disposals
- Equity dividends paid
- Management of liquid resources
- Financing
- Increase/decrease in cash.

51   A reconciliation of operating profit to operating cash flow should be given in sufficient detail for users to appreciate its chief components. A reconciliation should also be given of the movement of cash in the period to the movement in net debt, as required by FRS 1 'Cash flow statements' (Revised 1996), including the effect of movements on short-term and long-term borrowings, cash and other components of net debt, unless disclosed elsewhere.

CORRESPONDING AMOUNTS

52   Corresponding Amounts for the condensed profit and loss account, the statement of total recognised gains and losses and condensed cash flow statement should be presented for the corresponding half-yearly period and the previous full financial year. This provides a meaningful view of performance to date, particularly where the business is seasonal. Users may then compare figures on a year-on-year basis, or use them in the evaluation of trends and estimations of annual results.

53   Balance sheet information is included in half-yearly financial reports to highlight changes in key indicators of financial performance in the context of the entity's operating environment since the entity's last accounting year-end. The critical comparative figures are, therefore, those from the last annual financial statements, which may be accompanied by those from the previous corresponding half-yearly period to highlight the effect of seasonality.

OTHER DISCLOSURES

Subject to the limited exceptions noted in this Statement, disclosures demanded by **54** Financial Reporting Standards and Statements of Standard Accounting Practice are not generally required in the presentation of half-yearly reports.

There are, however, certain disclosures specific to half-yearly reports that are helpful **55** to users in assessing the relevance and reliability with which the reports might be used. They are:

- the period covered by the report;
- the date on which it is approved by the board of directors; and
- the extent to which the information it contains has been audited or reviewed.

Appendix A
The legal and regulatory framework

TRANSPARENCY DIRECTIVE

A1   The Transparency Directive (TD) (2004/109/EC) was published in the Official Journal in December 2004. The TD is designed to enhance transparency on EU capital markets by requiring regulated market issuers to produce periodic financial reports and shareholders in such companies to disclose major holdings. The Directive is a minimum harmonisation Directive which allows the home Member State of regulated market issuers to impose more stringent requirements than those set out in the Directive whilst restricting the host Member State to the minimum TD requirements. The Transparency Directive has to be implemented by all Member States no later than 20 January 2007.

A2   The TD introduces (in Article 5) more comprehensive requirements for half-yearly financial reports for regulated markets issuers, comprising a condensed set of financial statements prepared in accordance with the applicable accounting standards, a half-yearly management report and an appropriate statement of assurance from persons responsible in the issuer.

A3   Where an issuer is required to produce consolidated accounts, the condensed set of financial statements must be prepared in line with Regulation No 1606/2002 (on the application of International Accounting Standards). Where the issuer is not required to prepare consolidated accounts, the condensed financial statements must at least include a condensed balance sheet, and a condensed profit and loss account, prepared in line with the same principles applied to the annual financial accounts. In practice this requires publicly quoted entities using International Financial Reporting Standards (IFRS) as endorsed by the European Commission for their annual accounts (this is the great majority of UK public quoted entities), to produce half-yearly reports in accordance with IAS 34 'Interim Financial Reporting'. Those entities that continue to apply UK Financial Reporting Standards will be required to produce half-yearly reports in accordance with this Reporting Statement.

A4   Article 5 of the Directive contains a requirement for each person making a responsibility statement to state that to the best of his or her knowledge the condensed set of financial statements 'give a true and fair view'.

A5   Article 5(6) notes that the Commission will adopt implementing measures (so-called 'Level 2' measures, see below) in order to take account of technical developments on financial markets and to ensure the uniform application of Article 5. This includes a commitment on the Commission to specify the minimum content of the condensed balance sheet and profit and loss accounts and explanatory notes on these accounts, where they are not prepared in accordance with IAS 34.

A6   Article 6 of the Directive requires issuers whose shares are admitted to trading on a regulated market to publish interim management statements for the first and third quarters of the year. The statement has to provide (a) an explanation of material events and transactions that have taken place during the relevant period and their impact on the financial position; and (b) a general description of the financial position and performance of the issuers.

LEVEL 2 MEASURES

At the time of writing, the Level 2 measures have still to be finalised by the Commission. Article 3.2 of the draft implementing measures propose that the condensed balance sheet and the condensed profit and loss account shall show each of the headings and subtotals included in the most recent annual financial statements of the issuer. Additional line items shall be included if, as a result of their omission, the half-yearly financial statements would not give a true and fair view of the assets, liabilities, financial position and profit or loss of the issuer.   **A7**

In addition, the following comparative information shall be included: **A8**

(a) balance sheet at the end of the first six months of the current financial year and comparative balance sheet as at the end of the immediate preceding financial year; and
(b) profit and loss account cumulatively for the first six months of the current financial year with comparative information for the comparable period for the preceding financial year.

The explanatory notes shall include sufficient information to ensure the comparability of the condensed half-yearly financial statements with the annual financial statements.   **A9**

UK IMPLEMENTATION

The Financial Services Authority (FSA) is responsible for the implementation in the UK of the TD. The FSA has implemented the TD in full and has made no amendments to the provisions on half-yearly reports.   **A10**

On 27 October 2006 the FSA published a policy statement *PS01/11 Implementation of the Transparency Directive – Feedback on CP06/4* setting out near-final rules for UK implementation. The rules issued in October 2006 were referred to as 'near' final as they cannot be finalised until: (a) the 'Level 2 measures' are finalised by the European Commission; and (b) the Companies Bill from which the FSA is being granted statutory powers to make new rules has received Royal Assent (which was given on 8 November to what is now the Companies Act 2006).   **A11**

ROI IMPLEMENTATION

In the Republic of Ireland the Investment Funds Companies and Miscellaneous Provisions Act 2006 provides for, *inter alia*, the implementation of certain aspects of the TD. The remainder will be transposed by means of secondary legislation. It is expected that these requirements will, upon enactment of the legislation, supersede section 6.9 ('Half-yearly reports') of the Irish Stock Exchange's Listing Rules.   **A12**

UK LISTING RULES

On 1 June 2000 the responsibilities of being the competent authority for listing passed from the London Stock Exchange to the UK Listing Authority (UKLA) of the Financial Services Authority (FSA). The FSA's Listing Rules (currently section 9.9) require listed companies to prepare a report, on a group basis where relevant, on its activities and profit and loss for the first six months of the financial year.   **A13**

A14   The Listing Rules require that the accounting policies and presentation applied to half-yearly figures must be consistent with those applied in the latest published annual accounts except where:

(1)   the accounting policies and presentation are to be changed in the subsequent annual financial statements, in which case the new accounting policies should be followed, and the changes and the reasons for the changes should be disclosed in the half-yearly report; or

(2)   the FSA otherwise agrees.

A15   The Listing Rules also specify the contents of the half-yearly report, as covering:

(1)   a balance sheet;

(2)   a cash flow statement; and

(3)   an income statement (together with the information required to be included.

ROI LISTING RULES

A16   On 1 July 2005, the Irish Stock Exchange (ISE) ceased to use the UKLA Listing Rules as its base rule book and the ISE Listing Rules came into force. For issuers of equity securities, the ISE continues to maintain parity of listing standards with the FSA. Prior to implementation of the Transparency Directive in Ireland, listed companies produced half-yearly reports in accordance with the Listing Rules and in accordance with IAS 34 'Interim Financial Reporting'.

THE DISCLOSURE AND TRANSPARENCY RULES

A17   The Disclosure and Transparency Rules (DTR) are the rules which have been developed by the FSA for the UK implementation of the TD*. The rule which applies to half-yearly reporting is DTR 4.2.

A18   This rule requires that the half-yearly financial report must include:

(1)   a condensed set of financial statements;

(2)   a half-yearly management report; and

(3)   responsibility statements.

A19   If an issuer is required to prepare consolidated accounts, the condensed set of financial statements must be prepared in accordance with IAS 34 'Interim Financial Reporting'. Where issuers are not required to prepare consolidated accounts, the condensed set of financial statements must contain, as a minimum, the following:

(a)   a condensed balance sheet;

(b)   a condensed profit and loss account; and

(c)   explanatory notes on those accounts.

A20   The DTR 'copy out' the requirements of the Level 2 measures, summarised in paragraphs A7 to A9 above. They also replicate the Listing Rules provision outlined in paragraph A13 above.

A21   The half-yearly management report must include at least:

(1)   an indication of important events that have occurred during the first six months of the financial year, and their impact on the condensed set of financial statements; and

(2)   a description of the principal risks and uncertainties for the remaining six months of the financial year.

**There is no DTR equivalent in the ROI as the requirements of the Transparency Directive will be set out in legislation.*

Appendix B
Compliance with International Financial Reporting Standards

Although the ASB's [draft] Statement is drafted in the context of half-yearly financial reporting, whereas IAS 34 'Interim Financial Reporting' covers aspects relating to quarterly reporting in more detail, the key elements of the two sets of pronouncements are consistent in all material respects. **B1.**

Like the ASB's [draft] Statement, IAS 34 'Interim Financial Reporting' states that the same accounting recognition and measurement principles should be applied in the half-yearly report as are applied in the annual financial statements. IAS 34 also states that measurements for half-yearly reporting purposes should be made on a year-to-date basis, which ensures that an entity's frequency of reporting (annual, half-yearly, or quarterly) does not affect the measurement of its annual results. However, as a consequence, amounts reported in prior half-yearly periods of the current financial year may need to be remeasured at a later date, as new information becomes available. IAS 34 requires significant remeasurements of previously reported half-yearly data to be disclosed in the half-yearly report, or, if there is no separate half-yearly report for the final half-yearly period of the year, in a note to the annual financial statements. **B2**

On 20 July 2006 the IFRIC issued an Interpretation – IFRIC 10 *Interim Financial Reporting and Impairment*. The Interpretation addresses the apparent conflict between the requirements of IAS 34 *Interim Financial Reporting* and those on the recognition and reversal in financial statements of impairment losses on goodwill (in IAS 36 *Impairment of Assets*) and investments in equity instruments and in financial assets carried at cost (in IAS 39 *Financial Instruments: Recognition and Measurement*). **B3**

IFRIC 10 states that any such impairment losses recognised in an interim financial statement must not be reversed in subsequent interim or annual financial statements. The [draft] Statement includes a similar provision. **B4**

Amendment to FRS 25 (IAS 32)
'Financial Instruments: Presentation'

Financial Instruments Puttable at Fair Value and Obligations Arising on Liquidation

Contents

Preface

BACKGROUND

1   In December 2004 the Accounting Standards Board (ASB) issued Financial Reporting Standard (FRS) 25 (IAS 32) 'Financial Instruments: Presentation'. FRS 25 implemented the requirements of International Accounting Standard (IAS) 32 for those applying UK standards.

2   In June 2006, the International Accounting Standards Board (IASB) issued 'Proposed Amendments to IAS 32 *Financial Instruments: Presentation* and IAS 1 *Presentation of Financial Statements*: Financial Instruments Puttable at Fair value and Obligations Arising on Liquidation' proposing limited amendments to IAS 32 and IAS 1.

3   IAS 32 currently requires a financial instrument that gives the holder the right to put the instrument back to the issuer for cash or another financial instrument (a 'puttable instrument') to be classified as a financial liability of the issuer. As outlined in the IASB's Basis of Conclusions, paragraph BC 5, constituents have raised a number of concerns:

   (a)   On an ongoing basis, the liability is recognised at not less than the amount payable on demand, ie the instrument's fair value. This results in the entire market capitalisation of the entity being recognised as a liability because the instruments are the equivalent of the entity's ordinary shares;

   (b)   The changes in the fair value of the liability are recognised in profit or loss. When the entity performs well and the fair value of the liabilities increases, a loss is recognised. When the entity performs poorly and the fair value of the liability decreases, a gain is recognized;

   (c)   It is likely that the entity will report negative net assets because of unrecognised intangible assets and goodwill, and because the measurement of recognised assets and liabilities may not be at fair value;

   (d)   The issuing entity's balance sheet portrays the entity as wholly, or mostly, debt funded;

   (e)   Distributions of profits to shareholders are recognised as expenses. Hence, it may appear that net income is a function of the distribution policy, not performance.

IASB'S PROPOSED AMENDMENT

4   The proposal would amend the liability/equity classification requirements of IAS 32 and FRS 25 to require the classification, as equity, of financial instruments puttable at the fair value of a pro rata share of the net assets of the entity and instruments with obligations for a pro rata share of the entity on its liquidation. This is provided certain criteria are met, as outlined in paragraph BC 11 of the IASB's Basis of Conclusions (set out on page 59 of this document).

5   The objective of the exposure draft is to develop a limited scope, short term solution to improve the financial reporting of financial instruments puttable at fair value and instruments with obligations arising on liquidation that have characteristics similar to ordinary shares, pending the outcome of the IASB's longer-term project on equities and liabilities.

6   The proposed amendment would require:

(a) a financial instrument puttable at fair value; and

(b) an instrument that includes an obligation to deliver a pro-rata share of the net assets of the entity upon its liquidation

to be classified as equity, provided certain criteria were met.

Information about the above instruments, including their fair value, would be required to be disclosed. **7**

The amendments would be applied retrospectively, with one exception relating to certain compound instruments, from a date to be decided after exposure. Early adoption would be permitted. **8**

ASB'S PROPOSALS

The ASB notes the concerns raised by two IASB Board Members set out in the alternative view in the exposure draft, and would welcome respondents' views on them. **9**

However, the ASB does not believe that these concerns are sufficient to justify a divergence between the UK and the international standards. Whilst it acknowledges that the proposals cannot be reconciled with IASB's current Framework, it agrees that in some circumstances it is appropriate for standards to diverge from the Framework, especially where there appears to be no better solution. The ASB therefore proposes to amend FRS 25 to maintain consistency with IAS 32 if the amendment is confirmed by the IASB. **10**

In addition to amendments to IAS 32, the IASB exposure draft proposes changes to disclosure requirements relating to capital in IAS 1 'Presentation of Financial Statements'. IAS 1 has not been implemented in the UK and the Republic of Ireland, but the disclosures relating to capital in that standard (inserted by IFRS 7 'Financial Instruments: Disclosures') were implemented in the UK as Appendix E of FRS 29 (IFRS 7) 'Financial Instruments: Disclosures'. Consequently, the amendments to IAS 1 proposed by the IASB for the capital disclosures of IAS 1 are proposed as changes to Appendix E of FRS 29. **11**

The ASB will also continue to monitor the progress of the IASB's longer-term project on equities and liabilities. **12**

INVITATION TO COMMENT

The ASB is issuing this exposure draft to request comments on the IASB's proposals and on the ASB's proposals for implementing them in the UK. The IASB's Invitation to Comment is set out on pages 11 to 13 of this exposure draft. In addition, the ASB would welcome comments on the following issues: **13**

ASB Q1: Are you aware of any UK instruments whose presentation under the proposals would be misleading, or where instruments of similar economic substance would be classified differently as a consequence of adopting the proposed amendments?

ASB Q2: Are you are aware of any other issues that would affect those UK entities that will be required to implement the proposals outlined in this exposure draft?

Proposed Amendments to Financial Reporting Standard FRS 25 (IAS 32) – Financial Instruments: Presentation

Contents

INTRODUCTION*

This Exposure Draft contains proposals by the International Accounting Standards **1**
Board to amend IAS 32 *Financial Instruments: Presentation* to classify as equity
financial instruments puttable at the fair value of a pro rata share of the net assets of
the entity (financial instruments puttable at fair value) and instruments with obligations for a pro rata share of the net assets of the entity on its liquidation
(obligations arising on liquidation), provided specified criteria are met.

Under IAS 32, equity classification of a financial instrument depends upon specified **2**
conditions being met; one of those conditions is that the instrument does not include
a contractual obligation to deliver cash or another financial asset to another entity.
An instrument with such an obligation is a financial liability.

Some entities have issued financial instruments puttable at the fair value of a pro rata **3**
share of the net assets of the entity. After the revised IAS 32 was issued in 2003,
constituents raised concerns about the consequences of applying IAS 32 and IAS 39†
Financial Instruments: Recognition and Measurement to financial instruments puttable at fair value. For example, those standards require an entity to recognise such
instruments as a liability and to measure them at an amount not less than the amount
payable on demand, ie the fair value of the puttable instruments. This can result in
the entire market capitalisation of an entity being recognised as a liability. Such an
entity is likely to report negative net assets, because of unrecognised intangible assets
and goodwill, and because the measurement of recognised assets and liabilities may
not be at fair value.

Issues similar to those raised by constituents relating to the classification of financial **4**
instruments puttable at fair value also apply to the classification of ordinary shares in
a limited life entity. The entity is obliged to liquidate because it has a limited life.
Therefore, IAS 32 requires these shares to be classified as financial liabilities because
the entity has an obligation to transfer cash or another financial asset to the
shareholders. Hence, a limited life entity would have no equity. Similar issues also
apply to some partnerships that are required to liquidate upon the exit of a partner
(eg on retirement or death).

The objective of this Exposure Draft is to develop a limited scope, short-term **5**
solution to improve the financial reporting of financial instruments puttable at fair
value and instruments with obligations arising on liquidation that have characteristics similar to ordinary shares, pending the outcome of the Board's longer-term
project on liabilities and equity.

FEATURES OF THIS EXPOSURE DRAFT

The Exposure Draft proposes amendments that would require: **6**

(a) a financial instrument puttable at fair value to be classified as equity, provided
    specified criteria are met;
(b) an instrument that imposes an obligation to deliver to another entity a pro rata
    share of the net assets of the entity upon its liquidation to be classified as
    equity, provided specified criteria are met;
(c) disclosures about

*ASB footnote: *This introduction has been prepared by the IASB and is included unamended. References here to
the 'Board' are to the IASB.*

†ASB footnote: *IAS 39 was implemented in the UK as FRS 26 in December 2004.*

(i)   financial instruments puttable at fair value classified as equity, including the fair values of these instruments; and

(ii) the reclassification of financial instruments puttable at fair value and instruments with obligations arising on liquidation between financial liabilities and equity; and

(d)   these amendments to be applied in annual periods beginning on or after a date to be determined after exposure, with early adoption encouraged. These amendments are to be applied retrospectively (with one exception permitted relating to compound instruments).

ACKNOWLEDGEMENTS

The Board thanks its partner standard-setter, the Financial Reporting Standards Board of the New Zealand Institute of Chartered Accountants (NZICA), for its assistance with this project, in particular, Joanna Yeoh (Senior Analyst—Accounting Standards) and Kimberley Crook (Technical Director—Accounting Standards), NZICA staff.

Invitation to Comment

The Board invites comments on the amendments to IAS 32 and IAS 1 proposed in this Exposure Draft, particularly on the questions set out below. Comments are most helpful if they:

(a)   comment on the questions as stated;

(b)   indicate the specific paragraph or group of paragraphs to which they relate;

(c)   contain a clear rationale; and

(d)   include any alternative the Board should consider, if applicable.

Respondents need not comment on all of the questions and are encouraged to comment on any additional issues that, in their view, warrant consideration.

The Board is not requesting comments on matters in IAS 32 and IAS 1 not addressed in this Exposure Draft.

Comments should be submitted in writing so as to be received no later than 23 October 2006.

QUESTION 1 – FINANCIAL INSTRUMENTS PUTTABLE AT FAIR VALUE

The Exposure Draft proposes that financial instruments puttable at fair value should be classified as equity, provided that specified criteria are met.

Do you agree that it is appropriate to classify as equity financial instruments puttable at fair value? If so, do you agree that the specified criteria for equity classification are appropriate? If not, why? What changes do you propose, and why? If you disagree with equity classification of financial instruments puttable at fair value, why?

QUESTION 2 – OBLIGATIONS TO DELIVER TO ANOTHER ENTITY A PRO RATA SHARE OF THE NET ASSETS OF THE ENTITY UPON ITS LIQUIDATION

The Exposure Draft proposes that an instrument that imposes on the entity an obligation to deliver to another entity a pro rata share of the net assets of the entity upon its liquidation should be classified as equity, provided that specified criteria are met (eg ordinary shares issued by a limited life entity).

Do you agree that it is appropriate to classify as equity these types of instruments? If so, do you agree that the specified criteria for equity classification are appropriate? If not, why? What changes do you propose, and why? If you disagree with equity classification for these types of instruments, why?

QUESTION 3 – DISCLOSURES

The Exposure Draft proposes disclosures about financial instruments puttable at fair value classified as equity, including the fair values of these instruments, and the reclassification of financial instruments puttable at fair value and instruments that impose an obligation arising on liquidation between financial liabilities and equity.

(a) Do you agree that it is appropriate to require additional information about financial instruments puttable at fair value classified as equity, including the fair values of these instruments? If so, do you agree that the fair value disclosures should be required at every reporting date? If not, why? What changes do you propose, and why?

(b) Do you agree that it is appropriate to require disclosure of information about the reclassification of financial instruments puttable at fair value and instruments that impose an obligation arising on liquidation between financial liabilities and equity? If not, why? What changes do you propose, and why?

QUESTION 4 – EFFECTIVE DATE AND TRANSITION

The proposed changes would be required to be applied retrospectively, from a date to be determined by the Board after exposure (with one exception permitted relating to compound instruments). Earlier application would be encouraged.

Are the transition provisions appropriate? If not, what do you propose, and why?

Proposed Amendments to FRS 25 (IAS 32) Financial Instruments: Presentation

[Note: the text of FRS 25 (IAS 32) 'Financial Instruments: Presentation' includes strike-through and underlying to show changes made by the ASB to the text corresponding to IASs. The amended text of FRS 25 set out below adopts the same convention; as a result, it is not practicable to show the changes to the paragraphs of the standard that are proposed in this exposure draft.]

In the Introduction to IAS 32 FRS 25, the footnote to paragraph IN1 and paragraphs IN6, IN7 and IN10 are amended to read as follows. Paragraphs IN1-IN5, IN8, IN9 and IN11 are included here for convenience but are not amended.

Introduction

REASONS FOR REVISING IAS 32

IN1 International Accounting Standard 32 *Financial Instruments: Disclosure and Pre-sentation* (IAS 32)* replaces IAS 32 *Financial Instruments: Disclosure and Presentation* (revised in 2000), and should be applied for annual periods beginning on or after 1 January 2005. Earlier application is permitted. The Standard also replaces the following Interpretations and draft Interpretation:

- SIC-5 *Classification of Financial Instruments—Contingent Settlement Provisions*;
- SIC-16 *Share Capital—Reacquired Own Equity Instruments (Treasury Shares)*;
- SIC-17 *Equity—Costs of an Equity Transaction*; and
- draft SIC-D34 *Financial Instruments—Instruments or Rights Redeemable by the Holder*.

IN2 The International Accounting Standards Board developed this revised IAS 32 as part of its project to improve IAS 32 and IAS 39 *Financial Instruments: Recognition and Measurement*. The objective of the project was to reduce complexity by clarifying and adding guidance, eliminating internal inconsistencies and incorporating into the Standards elements of Standing Interpretations Committee (SIC) Interpretations and IAS 39 implementation guidance published by the Implementation Guidance Committee (IGC).

IN3 For IAS 32, the Board's main objective was a limited revision to provide additional guidance on selected matters—such as the measurement of the components of a compound financial instrument on initial recognition, and the classification of derivatives based on an entity's own shares—and to locate all disclosures relating to financial instruments in one Standard.† The Board did not reconsider the fundamental approach to the presentation and disclosure of financial instruments contained in IAS 32.

THE MAIN CHANGES

IN4 The main changes from the previous version of IAS 32 are described below.

Scope

IN5 The scope of IAS 32 has, where appropriate, been conformed to the scope of IAS 39.

Principle

IN6 In summary, when an issuer determines whether a financial instrument is a financial liability or an equity instrument, the instrument is an equity instrument if, and only if, both conditions (a) and (b) are met.

*This Introduction refers to IAS 32 as revised in December 2003. In August 2005 the IASB amended IAS 32 by relocating all disclosures relating to financial instruments to IFRS 7 Financial Instruments: Disclosures. Also, in [month and year to be inserted], the IASB amended IAS 32 by requiring particular types of financial instruments (eg financial instruments puttable at fair value) to be classified as equity, provided that specified conditions are met.

†In August 2005 the IASB relocated all disclosures relating to financial instruments to IFRS 7 Financial Instruments: Disclosures.

(a) The instrument includes no contractual obligation either to deliver cash or another financial asset to another entity; or to exchange financial assets or financial liabilities with another entity under conditions that are potentially unfavourable to the issuer. For this purpose, a contractual obligation does not include:

    (i) an obligation to deliver to another entity a pro rata share of the net assets of the entity upon its liquidation, provided that all financial instruments (or components of financial instruments) in the most subordinated class of instruments with a claim to the assets of the entity impose such an obligation; or

    (ii) an obligation to redeem or repurchase a financial instrument puttable at fair value, provided that all financial instruments in the most subordinated class of instruments with a claim to the assets of the entity are financial instruments puttable at fair value.

(b) If the instrument will or may be settled in the issuer's own equity instruments, it is:

    (i) a non-derivative that includes no contractual obligation for the issuer to deliver a variable number of its own equity instruments; or

    (ii) a derivative that will be settled by the issuer exchanging a fixed amount of cash or another financial asset for a fixed number of its own equity instruments. For this purpose, the issuer's own equity instruments do not include financial instruments puttable at fair value, instruments that impose on the entity an obligation to deliver to another entity a pro rata share of the net assets of the entity upon its liquidation, or instruments that are themselves contracts for the future receipt or delivery of the issuer's own equity instruments.

In addition, when an issuer has an obligation to purchase its own shares for cash or another financial asset, there is a liability for the amount that the issuer is obliged to pay (except when that obligation is excluded from the definition of a financial liability). **IN7**

The definitions of a financial asset and a financial liability, and the description of an equity instrument, are amended consistently with this principle. **IN8**

Classification of Contracts Settled in an Entity's Own Equity Instruments

The classification of derivative and non-derivative contracts indexed to, or settled in, an entity's own equity instruments has been clarified consistently with the principle in paragraph IN6 above. In particular, when an entity uses its own equity instruments 'as currency' in a contract to receive or deliver a variable number of shares whose value equals a fixed amount or an amount based on changes in an underlying variable (eg a commodity price), the contract is not an equity instrument, but is a financial asset or a financial liability. **IN9**

Puttable Instruments

IAS 32 incorporates the guidance previously proposed in draft SIC Interpretation 34 *Financial Instruments—Instruments or Rights Redeemable by the Holder*. Consequently, a financial instrument that gives the holder the right to put the instrument back to the issuer for cash or another financial asset (a 'puttable instrument') is a financial liability of the issuer (with one exception, which relates to financial instruments puttable at fair value). In response to comments received on the **IN10**

Exposure Draft, the Standard provides additional guidance and illustrative examples for entities that, because of this requirement, have no equity or whose share capital is not equity as defined in IAS 32.

Contingent Settlement Provisions

IN11   IAS 32 incorporates the conclusion previously in SIC-5 *Classification of Financial Instruments—Contingent Settlement Provisions* that a financial instrument is a financial liability when the manner of settlement depends on the occurrence or non-occurrence of uncertain future events or on the outcome of uncertain circumstances that are beyond the control of both the issuer and the holder. Contingent settlement provisions are ignored when they apply only in the event of liquidation of the issuer or are not genuine.

In the Standard, paragraph 11 is amended to read as follows. In paragraph 11, the definitions of a financial asset and a financial liability are amended, and two new definitions are added immediately after the definition of fair value. The definitions of a financial instrument, an equity instrument and fair value are included here for convenience but are not amended.

Financial Instruments: Presentation

DEFINITIONS (see also paragraphs AG3–AG24)

The following terms are used in this Standard with the meanings specified: **11**

A *financial instrument* is any contract that gives rise to a financial asset of one entity and a financial liability or equity instrument of another entity.

A *financial asset* is any asset that is:

(a) cash;

(b) an equity instrument of another entity;

(c) a contractual right:

  (i)   to receive cash or another financial asset from another entity; or

  (ii) to exchange financial assets or financial liabilities with another entity under conditions that are potentially favourable to the entity; or

(d) a contract that will or may be settled in the entity's own equity instruments and is:

  (i)   a non-derivative for which the entity is or may be obliged to receive a variable number of the entity's own equity instruments; or

  (ii) a derivative that will or may be settled other than by the exchange of a fixed amount of cash or another financial asset for a fixed number of the entity's own equity instruments. For this purpose the entity's own equity instruments do not include financial instruments puttable at fair value, instruments that impose on the entity an obligation to deliver to another entity a pro rata share of the net assets of the entity upon its liquidation, or instruments that are themselves contracts for the future receipt or delivery of the entity's own equity instruments.

A *financial liability* is any liability that meets either of the following conditions.

(a) It is a contractual obligation either to deliver cash or another financial asset to another entity, or to exchange financial assets or financial liabilities with another entity under conditions that are potentially unfavourable to the entity. For this purpose, a contractual obligation does not include:

  (i)   an obligation to deliver to another entity a pro rata share of the net assets of the entity upon its liquidation, provided that all financial instruments (or components of financial instruments) in the most subordinated class of instruments with a claim to the assets of the entity impose such an obligation; or

  (ii) an obligation to redeem or repurchase a financial instrument puttable at fair value, provided that all financial instruments in the most subordinated class of instruments with a claim to the assets of the entity are financial instruments puttable at fair value.

(b) It is a contract that will or may be settled in the entity's own equity instruments and is:

> (i)   a non-derivative for which the entity is or may be obliged to deliver a variable number of the entity's own equity instruments; or
>
> (ii) a derivative that will or may be settled other than by the exchange of a fixed amount of cash or another financial asset for a fixed number of the entity's own equity instruments. For this purpose the entity's own equity instruments do not include financial instruments puttable at fair value, instruments that impose on the entity an obligation to deliver to another entity a pro rata share of the net assets of the entity upon its liquidation, or instruments that are themselves contracts for the future receipt or delivery of the entity's own equity instruments.

An *equity instrument* is any contract that evidences a residual interest in the assets of an entity after deducting all of its liabilities.

Fair value is the amount for which an asset could be exchanged, or a liability settled, between knowledgeable, willing parties in an arm's length transaction.

A *financial instrument puttable at fair value* has all of the following features:

(a)   its issue price is the fair value of the instrument holder's entitlement to a pro rata share of the net assets of the entity;

(b)   it entitles the holder to require the entity to repurchase or redeem the instrument for the fair value of a pro rata share of the net assets of the entity;

(c)   it entitles the holder to a pro rata share of the net assets of the entity in the event of the liquidation of the entity; and

(d)   other than a contractual obligation that arises from the entitlement set out in (b) and a contractual obligation that may arise from the entitlement set out in (c), it does not contain a contractual obligation to deliver cash or another financial asset to another entity, or to exchange financial assets or financial liabilities with another entity under conditions that are potentially unfavourable to the entity, and it is not a contract that will or may be settled in the entity's own equity instruments as set out in subparagraph (b) of the definition of a financial liability.

A *financial instrument that entitles the holder to a pro rata share of the net assets of the entity* has all of the following features:

(a)   the financial instrument is in the most subordinated class of financial instruments with a claim to the assets of the entity. The claims of a financial instrument with this entitlement have no priority over other claims to the assets of the entity, in terms of either the calculation of the amount due on liquidation or the timing of payment of that amount. A financial instrument that must be converted into another instrument to be in the most subordinated class of financial instruments does not possess this feature.

(b)   the financial instrument is entitled to a proportionate share of the residual interest in the assets of the entity that remains after deducting all other claims to the assets of the entity. A proportionate share is one that is determined by:

> (i)   dividing the total amount of the residual interest in the assets of the entity into units of equal amount; and
>
> (ii) multiplying that unit amount by the ratio of the number of the units held by the financial instrument holder to the total number of units.

(c)   the financial instrument does not contain any preferential right upon liquidation of the entity.

(d)   the financial instrument's right to a pro rata share of the net assets of the entity is neither limited nor guaranteed, to any extent, before or at liquidation, through the terms and conditions of either (i) the instrument, (ii) another financial instrument *issued by the entity (to either the instrument holder or another party), or (iii) a related contract between the entity and the instrument holder.*

Paragraph 16 is amended to read as follows. After paragraph 16, paragraph 16A is inserted. Paragraph 15 is included here for convenience but is not amended.

Presentation

LIABILITIES AND EQUITY (see also paragraphs AG25–AG29)

The issuer of a financial instrument shall classify the instrument, or its component parts, on initial recognition as a financial liability, a financial asset or an equity instrument in accordance with the substance of the contractual arrangement and the definitions of a financial liability, a financial asset and an equity instrument.   **15**

When an issuer applies the definitions in paragraph 11 to determine whether a financial instrument is an equity instrument rather than a financial liability, the instrument is an equity instrument if, and only if, both conditions (a) and (b) below are met.   **16**

(a) The instrument includes no contractual obligation either to deliver cash or another financial asset to another entity or to exchange financial assets or financial liabilities with another entity under conditions that are potentially unfavourable to the issuer. For this purpose, a contractual obligation does not include:

  (i) an obligation to deliver to another entity a pro rata share of the net assets of the entity upon its liquidation, provided that all financial instruments (or components of financial instruments) in the most subordinated class of instruments with a claim to the assets of the entity impose such an obligation; or

  (ii) an obligation to redeem or repurchase a financial instrument puttable at fair value, provided that all financial instruments in the most sub-ordinated class of instruments with a claim to the assets of the entity are financial instruments puttable at fair value.

(b) If the instrument will or may be settled in the issuer's own equity instruments, it is:

  (i) a non-derivative that includes no contractual obligation for the issuer to deliver a variable number of its own equity instruments; or

  (ii) a derivative that will be settled only by the issuer exchanging a fixed amount of cash or another financial asset for a fixed number of its own equity instruments. For this purpose the issuer's own equity instruments do not include instruments specified in paragraph 16A, or instruments that are themselves contracts for the future receipt or delivery of the issuer's own equity instruments.

A contractual obligation, including one arising from a derivative financial instrument, that will or may result in the future receipt or delivery of the issuer's own equity instruments, but does not meet conditions (a) and (b) above, is not an equity instrument.

A financial instrument puttable at fair value and a financial instrument that imposes on the entity an obligation to deliver to another entity a pro rata share of the net assets of the entity upon its liquidation are classified as equity when these   **16A** instruments meet the specified criteria for exclusion from the definition of a financial liability (see subparagraphs (a)(i) and (ii) of the definition of a financial liability in paragraph 11).

> Paragraphs 17–19 are amended to read as follows. After paragraph 17, paragraph 17A is inserted. Paragraph 20 is included here for convenience but is not amended.

NO CONTRACTUAL OBLIGATION TO DELIVER CASH OR ANOTHER FINANCIAL ASSET (PARAGRAPH 16(A))

17   Except as stated in paragraph 17A, a critical feature in differentiating a financial liability from an equity instrument is the existence of a contractual obligation of one party to the financial instrument (the issuer) either to deliver cash or another financial asset to the other party (the holder) or to exchange financial assets or financial liabilities with the holder under conditions that are potentially unfavourable to the issuer. Although the holder of an equity instrument may be entitled to receive a pro rata share of any dividends or other distributions of equity, the issuer does not have a contractual obligation to make such distributions because it cannot be required to deliver cash or another financial asset to another party.

17A   However, for the purposes of this Standard, a contractual obligation to deliver cash or another financial asset to another entity (or to exchange financial assets or financial liabilities with another entity under conditions that are potentially unfavourable to the entity) does not include those specifically excluded from the definition of a financial liability (see subparagraphs (a)(i) and (ii) of the definition of a financial liability in paragraph 11).

18   The substance of a financial instrument, rather than its legal form, governs its classification on the entity's balance sheet. Substance and legal form are commonly consistent, but not always. Some financial instruments take the legal form of equity but are liabilities in substance and others may combine features associated with equity instruments and features associated with financial liabilities. For example:

   (a)   a preference share that provides for mandatory redemption by the issuer for a fixed or determinable amount at a fixed or determinable future date, or gives the holder the right to require the issuer to redeem the instrument at or after a particular date for a fixed or determinable amount, is a financial liability.

   (b)   a financial instrument that gives the holder the right to put it back to the issuer for cash or another financial asset (a 'puttable instrument') is a financial liability (except as stated in paragraph 16A). This is so even when the amount of cash or other financial assets is determined on the basis of an index or other item that has the potential to increase or decrease. The existence of an option for the holder to put the instrument back to the issuer for cash or another financial asset means that the puttable instrument meets the definition of a financial liability (except as stated in paragraph 16A). For example, open-ended mutual funds, unit trusts, partnerships and some co-operative entities may provide their unitholders or members with a right to redeem their interests in the issuer at any time for cash, which results in the unitholders' or members' interests being classified as financial liabilities (except as stated in paragraph 16A). However, classification as a financial liability does not preclude the use of descriptors such as 'net asset value attributable to unitholders' and 'change in net asset value attributable to unitholders' on the face of the financial statements of an entity that has no contributed equity (such as some mutual funds and unit trusts, see Illustrative Example 7) or the use of additional disclosure to show that total members' interests comprise items such as reserves that meet the definition of equity and puttable instruments that do not (see Illustrative Example 8).

If an entity does not have an unconditional right to avoid delivering cash or another **19** financial asset to settle a contractual obligation, the obligation meets the definition of a financial liability (except as stated in paragraph 17A). For example:

(a)   a restriction on the ability of an entity to satisfy a contractual obligation, such as lack of access to foreign currency or the need to obtain approval for payment from a regulatory authority, does not negate the entity's contractual obligation or the holder's contractual right under the instrument.

(b)   a contractual obligation that is conditional on a counterparty exercising its right to redeem is a financial liability because the entity does not have the unconditional right to avoid delivering cash or another financial asset.

A financial instrument that does not explicitly establish a contractual obligation to **20** deliver cash or another financial asset may establish an obligation indirectly through its terms and conditions. For example:

(a)   a financial instrument may contain a non-financial obligation that must be settled if, and only if, the entity fails to make distributions or to redeem the instrument. If the entity can avoid a transfer of cash or another financial asset only by settling the non-financial obligation, the financial instrument is a financial liability.

(b)   a financial instrument is a financial liability if it provides that on settlement the entity will deliver either:

   (i)   cash or another financial asset; or

   (ii)   its own shares whose value is determined to exceed substantially the value of the cash or other financial asset.

     Although the entity does not have an explicit contractual obligation to deliver cash or another financial asset, the value of the share settlement alternative is such that the entity will settle in cash. In any event, the holder has in substance been guaranteed receipt of an amount that is at least equal to the cash settlement option (see paragraph 21).

> Paragraphs 22 and 23 are amended to read as follows. After paragraph 22, paragraph 22A is inserted. Paragraphs 21 and 24 are included here for convenience but are not amended.

SETTLEMENT IN THE ENTITY'S OWN EQUITY INSTRUMENTS (PARAGRAPH 16(B))

A contract is not an equity instrument solely because it may result in the receipt or **21** delivery of the entity's own equity instruments. An entity may have a contractual right or obligation to receive or deliver a number of its own shares or other equity instruments that varies so that the fair value of the entity's own equity instruments to be received or delivered equals the amount of the contractual right or obligation. Such a contractual right or obligation may be for a fixed amount or an amount that fluctuates in part or in full in response to changes in a variable other than the market price of the entity's own equity instruments (eg an interest rate, a commodity price or a financial instrument price). Two examples are (a) a contract to deliver as many of the entity's own equity instruments as are equal in value to CU100,* and (b) a contract to deliver as many of the entity's own equity instruments as are equal in

---

In this Standard, monetary amounts are denominated in 'currency units' (CU).

value to the value of 100 ounces of gold. Such a contract is a financial liability of the entity even though the entity must or can settle it by delivering its own equity instruments. It is not an equity instrument because the entity uses a variable number of its own equity instruments as a means to settle the contract. Accordingly, the contract does not evidence a residual interest in the entity's assets after deducting all of its liabilities.

22   Except as stated in paragraph 22A, a contract that will be settled by the entity (receiving or) delivering a fixed number of its own equity instruments in exchange for a fixed amount of cash or another financial asset is an equity instrument. For example, an issued share option that gives the counterparty a right to buy a fixed number of the entity's shares for a fixed price or for a fixed stated principal amount of a bond is an equity instrument. Changes in the fair value of a contract arising from variations in market interest rates that do not affect the amount of cash or other financial assets to be paid or received, or the number of equity instruments to be received or delivered, on settlement of the contract do not preclude the contract from being an equity instrument. Any consideration received (such as the premium received for a written option or warrant on the entity's own shares) is added directly to equity. Any consideration paid (such as the premium paid for a purchased option) is deducted directly from equity. Changes in the fair value of an equity instrument are not recognised in the financial statements.

22A   If the entity's own equity instruments to be (received or) delivered by the entity upon settlement of a derivative are financial instruments puttable at fair value, or instruments that impose on the entity an obligation to deliver to another entity a pro rata share of the net assets of the entity upon its liquidation, the derivative is a (financial asset or) financial liability. This includes a derivative that will be settled by the entity (receiving or) delivering a fixed number of such equity instruments in exchange for a fixed amount of cash or another financial asset.

23   Except as stated in paragraph 16A, a contract that contains an obligation for an entity to purchase its own equity instruments for cash or another financial asset gives rise to a financial liability for the present value of the redemption amount (for example, for the present value of the forward repurchase price, option exercise price or other redemption amount). This is the case even if the contract itself is an equity instrument. One example is an entity's obligation under a forward contract to purchase its own equity instruments for cash. When the financial liability is recognized initially ~~under IAS 39~~, its fair value (the present value of the redemption amount) is reclassified from equity. ~~Subsequently, the financial liability is measured in accordance with IAS 39.~~ If the contract subsequently expires without delivery, the carrying amount of the financial liability is reclassified to equity. An entity's contractual obligation to purchase its own equity instruments gives rise to a financial liability for the present value of the redemption amount even if the obligation to purchase is conditional on the counterparty exercising a right to redeem (eg a written put option that gives the counterparty the right to sell an entity's own equity instruments to the entity for a fixed price).

24   A contract that will be settled by the entity delivering or receiving a fixed number of its own equity instruments in exchange for a variable amount of cash or another financial asset is a financial asset or financial liability. An example is a contract for the entity to deliver 100 of its own equity instruments in return for an amount of cash calculated to equal the value of 100 ounces of gold.

> After paragraph 25, a heading and paragraph 25A are added. Paragraph 25 is included for convenience but is not amended.

CONTINGENT SETTLEMENT PROVISIONS

A financial instrument may require the entity to deliver cash or another financial **25** asset, or otherwise to settle it in such a way that it would be a financial liability, in the event of the occurrence or non-occurrence of uncertain future events (or on the outcome of uncertain circumstances) that are beyond the control of both the issuer and the holder of the instrument, such as a change in a stock market index, consumer price index, interest rate or taxation requirements, or the issuer's future revenues, net income or debt-to-equity ratio. The issuer of such an instrument does not have the unconditional right to avoid delivering cash or another financial asset (or otherwise to settle it in such a way that it would be a financial liability). Therefore, it is a financial liability of the issuer unless:

(a) the part of the contingent settlement provision that could require settlement in cash or another financial asset (or otherwise in such a way that it would be a financial liability) is not genuine; or

(b) the issuer can be required to settle the obligation in cash or another financial asset (or otherwise to settle it in such a way that it would be a financial liability) only in the event of liquidation of the issuer.

SETTLEMENT ON LIQUIDATION OF THE ENTITY

Typically, a financial instrument that entitles the holder to a pro rata share of the net **25A** assets of the entity on liquidation of the entity does not impose an obligation on the entity to deliver cash or another financial asset of the entity (or otherwise to settle it in such a way that it would be a financial liability) because the entity is not obliged to liquidate. However, in some cases, an entity may be obliged to liquidate (eg the entity may be required to liquidate at the end of a fixed period or the instrument holder may have the ability to require the entity to liquidate). Instruments, or components of instruments, in the most subordinated class of instruments issued by an entity thatLmust be liquidated at the end of a fixed period are not precluded from being classified as equity solely because the entity has an obligation to pay the holders of those instruments a pro rata share of its net assets on liquidation. Similarly, instruments, or components of instruments, are not precluded from being classified as equity solely because the holder, in common with all other holders of financial instruments in the most subordinated class of instruments with a claim to the assets of the entity, can require the entity to liquidate and pay the holder a pro rata share of the net assets of the entity (see paragraph 16A).

> After paragraph 96, paragraph 96A is inserted and after paragraph 97, paragraph 97A is inserted. Paragraph 97 is included here for reference but is not amended. Paragraphs 97A and 97B are renumbered as 97B and 97C respectively.

Financial Instruments Puttable at Fair Value and Obligations Arising on Liquidation **96A**
(Amendments to ~~IAS 32~~ FRS25 and ~~IAS 1~~ Appendix E of FRS 25), *issued in [date to be inserted after exposure], amended the definition of a financial liability and a financial asset, and included new definitions for a financial instrument puttable at fair value and a financial instrument that entitles the holder to a pro rata share of the net assets of the entity in paragraph 11, amended paragraphs 16, 17–19, 22, 23, AG13, AG14 and AG27, and inserted paragraphs 16A, 17A, 22A, 25A, 97A, AG14A–AG14G and AG29A. An entity shall apply those amendments for annual periods beginning on or after [date to be inserted after exposure]. Earlier application is encouraged. If an entity applies these changes for an earlier period, it shall disclose that fact and apply the related amendments to ~~IAS 1~~ Appendix E of FRS 25, ~~IAS 39~~ FRS 26 and ~~IFRIC 2~~*

UITF 39 Members' Shares in Co-operative Entities and Similar Instruments at the same time.

97   *This Standard shall be applied retrospectively, subject to paragraphs 97B and 97C.*

97A   *When applying the amendments described in paragraph 96A, an entity is required to split a compound financial instrument with an obligation for a pro rata share of the net assets of the entity upon its liquidation into separate liability and equity components. If the liability component is no longer outstanding, retrospective application of those amendments to ~~IAS 32~~ FRS25 involves separating two portions of equity. The first portion is in retained earnings and represents the cumulative interest accreted on the liability component. The other portion represents the original equity component. However, an entity need not separate these two portions if the liability component is no longer outstanding at the date of application of the amendments.*

In the Appendix *Application Guidance*, paragraphs AG13 and AG14 are amended to read as follows. After paragraph AG14, a heading, paragraphs AG14A–AG14C, another heading and paragraphs AG14D–AG14G are added.

Appendix
Application Guidance

DEFINITIONS (paragraphs 11–14)

Equity Instruments

Examples of equity instruments include non-puttable ordinary shares, some types of preference shares (see paragraphs AG25 and AG26), some financial instruments puttable at fair value (see paragraph 16A) and warrants or written call options that allow the holder to subscribe for or purchase a fixed number of non-puttable ordinary shares in the issuing entity in exchange for a fixed amount of cash or another financial asset. An entity's obligation to issue or purchase a fixed number of its own equity instruments in exchange for a fixed amount of cash or another financial asset is an equity instrument of the entity (except as stated in paragraph 22A). However, if such a contract contains an obligation for the entity to pay cash or another financial asset (other than a contractual obligation of the type that is excluded from the definition of a financial liability), it also gives rise to a liability for the present value of the redemption amount (see paragraph AG27(a)). An issuer of non-puttable ordinary shares assumes a liability when it formally acts to make a distribution and becomes legally obligated to the shareholders to do so. This may be the case following the declaration of a dividend or when the entity is being wound up and any assets remaining after the satisfaction of liabilities become distributable to shareholders.

AG13

A purchased call option or other similar contract acquired by an entity that gives it the right to reacquire a fixed number of its own equity instruments in exchange for delivering a fixed amount of cash or another financial asset is not a financial asset of the entity (except as stated in paragraph 22A). Instead, any consideration paid for such a contract is deducted from equity.

AG14

Financial Instruments Puttable at Fair Value

For a financial instrument to be a financial instrument puttable at fair value, the issue price received, or the redemption or repurchase price paid by the entity for the financial instrument is its fair value, determined in accordance with the requirements of ~~IAS 39~~ FRS 26 paragraph 48A and paragraphs AG69–AG82. However, entities that

AG14A

(a)   have not filed, or are not in the process of filing, their financial statements with a securities commission or other regulatory organisation for the purpose of issuing any class of instruments in a public market; or

(b)   do not hold assets in a fiduciary capacity for a broad group of outsiders, such as a bank, insurance company, securities broker/dealer, pension fund, mutual fund or investment banking entity;

are permitted to use a formula to determine the fair value of financial instruments puttable at fair value on their issue, redemption or repurchase, provided that the formula is intended to approximate the fair value of the financial instruments. The instrument's pro rata share of the book value of the net assets of the entity is a formula that would approximate the fair value of the instrument only when there is no material difference between the book value of the entity's net assets and the fair value of its net assets (both recognised and unrecognised). An entity may change the basis of determining the fair value of financial instruments puttable at fair value if, and only if, the change results in an estimate that is more representative of the fair value of the financial instruments puttable at fair value in the circumstances.

AG14B   One feature of a financial instrument puttable at fair value is that its issue price must be the fair value of its pro rata share of the net assets of the entity. Financial instruments puttable at fair value are issued at fair value only if the fair value of the consideration received equals the fair value of the instruments issued. For example, an entity may issue a convertible bond, which is convertible into the entity's ordinary shares that are puttable at fair value. Upon conversion, the fair value of the convertible bond tendered in exchange for the puttable shares will reflect both the fair value of the option and the fair value of the bond. Hence, typically the fair value of the convertible bond will equal the fair value of the puttable shares. If so, the puttable shares are issued at fair value for the purposes of determining whether those shares meet the definition of a financial instrument puttable at fair value.

AG14C   In the case of the convertible bond described in paragraph AG14B, ~~IAS 32~~ FRS 25 requires the option embedded in the bond to be recognised separately from the host instrument (bond). Typically, the option embedded in a convertible bond would be accounted for as an equity instrument and not remeasured. However, in the case of an option on a financial instrument puttable at fair value, the embedded option is a derivative and, consistently with the treatment of all derivatives on financial instruments puttable at fair value, is classified as a financial liability. Therefore, the option shall be measured at fair value at each balance sheet date and on the date of conversion in accordance with IAS 39.

Financial Instruments that Entitle the Holders to a Pro Rata Share of the Net Assets of the Entity

AG14D   One feature of a financial instrument that entitles the holder to a pro rata share of the net assets of the entity is that the financial instrument is in the most subordinated class of instruments with a claim to the assets of the entity. A financial instrument is in the most subordinated class of financial instruments if, and only if, on liquidation the amount due to the holders of the financial instruments is calculated after deducting all other claims to the assets of the entity and the instrument holders are paid out last, after payments are made to all other claimants to the assets of the entity.

AG14E   When determining whether an instrument is in the most subordinated class, an instrument's claim on liquidation is evaluated as if the entity were to liquidate on the date the classification decision for the instrument in question is made (the assessment date). The classification decision shall be reassessed if there is a change in circumstances relevant to the classification of the financial instrument. For example, if the entity issues or redeems another financial instrument, this may affect whether the instrument in question is in the most subordinated class.

AG14F   An instrument that has a preferential right on liquidation of the entity is not an instrument with an entitlement to a pro rata share of the net assets of the entity. For example, an instrument has a preferential right on liquidation if it entitles the holder to a fixed dividend on liquidation, in addition to a share of the net assets of the entity, when other instruments in the most subordinated class with a right to a pro rata share of the net assets of the entity do not have the same right on liquidation.

For an instrument to have an entitlement to a pro rata share of the net assets of the entity, the terms and conditions of the instrument shall not, to any extent, have the effect of providing the instrument holder with an entitlement to a pro rata share of the entity's net assets that: **AG14G**

(a)   is a fixed or specified amount;
(b)   changes over time, so as to provide the instrument holder with a fixed or specified amount; or
(c)   is unaffected by changes in the value of the net assets of the entity.

Similarly, if terms and conditions that have these effects are included in another instrument issued by the entity (either to the instrument holder or another party), or in a related contract between the entity and the instrument holder, the instrument does not have an entitlement to a pro rata share of the net assets of the entity.

> Paragraph AG27 is amended to read as follows and after paragraph AG29, paragraph AG29A is added. Paragraphs AG25, AG26, AG28 and AG29 are included here for convenience but are not amended.

Presentation

LIABILITIES AND EQUITY (paragraphs 15–27)

No Contractual Obligation to Deliver Cash or Another Financial Asset (paragraphs 17–20)

Preference shares may be issued with various rights. In determining whether a preference share is a financial liability or an equity instrument, an issuer assesses the particular rights attaching to the share to determine whether it exhibits the fundamental characteristic of a financial liability. For example, a preference share that provides for redemption on a specific date or at the option of the holder contains a financial liability because the issuer has an obligation to transfer financial assets to the holder of the share. The potential inability of an issuer to satisfy an obligation to redeem a preference share when contractually required to do so, whether because of a lack of funds, a statutory restriction or insufficient profits or reserves, does not negate the obligation. An option of the issuer to redeem the shares for cash does not satisfy the definition of a financial liability because the issuer does not have a present obligation to transfer financial assets to the shareholders. In this case, redemption of the shares is solely at the discretion of the issuer. An obligation may arise, however, when the issuer of the shares exercises its option, usually by formally notifying the shareholders of an intention to redeem the shares.   **AG25**

When preference shares are non-redeemable, the appropriate classification is determined by the other rights that attach to them. Classification is based on an assessment of the substance of the contractual arrangements and the definitions of a financial liability and an equity instrument. When distributions to holders of the preference shares, whether cumulative or non-cumulative, are at the discretion of the issuer, the shares are equity instruments. The classification of a preference share as an equity instrument or a financial liability is not affected by, for example: **AG26**

(a)   a history of making distributions;
(b)   an intention to make distributions in the future;

(c)   a possible negative impact on the price of ordinary shares of the issuer if distributions are not made (because of restrictions on paying dividends on the ordinary shares if dividends are not paid on the preference shares);

(d)   the amount of the issuer's reserves;

(e)   an issuer's expectation of a profit or loss for a period; or

(f)   an ability or inability of the issuer to influence the amount of its profit or loss for the period.

Settlement in the Entity's Own Equity Instruments (paragraphs 21–24)

AG27   The following examples illustrate how to classify different types of contracts on an entity's own equity instruments:

(a)   A contract that will be settled by the entity receiving or delivering a fixed number of its own shares for no future consideration, or exchanging a fixed number of its own shares for a fixed amount of cash or another financial asset, is an equity instrument. Accordingly, any consideration received or paid for such a contract is added directly to or deducted directly from equity (except as stated in paragraph 22A). One example is an issued share option that gives the counterparty a right to buy a fixed number of the entity's shares for a fixed amount of cash. However, if the contract requires the entity to purchase (redeem) its own shares for cash or another financial asset at a fixed or determinable date or on demand, the entity also recognises a financial liability for the present value of the redemption amount (except as stated in paragraph 16A). One example is an entity's obligation under a forward contract to repurchase a fixed number of its own shares for a fixed amount of cash.

(b)   An entity's obligation to purchase its own shares for cash gives rise to a financial liability for the present value of the redemption amount even if the number of shares that the entity is obliged to repurchase is not fixed or if the obligation is conditional on the counterparty exercising a right to redeem (except as stated in paragraph 16A). One example of a conditional obligation is an issued option that requires the entity to repurchase its own shares for cash if the counterparty exercises the option.

(c)   A contract that will be settled in cash or another financial asset is a financial asset or financial liability even if the amount of cash or another financial asset that will be received or delivered is based on changes in the market price of the entity's own equity (except as stated in paragraph 16A). One example is a net cash-settled share option.

(d)   A contract that will be settled in a variable number of the entity's own shares whose value equals a fixed amount or an amount based on changes in an underlying variable (eg a commodity price) is a financial asset or a financial liability. An example is a written option to buy gold that, if exercised, is settled net in the entity's own instruments by the entity delivering as many of those instruments as are equal to the value of the option contract. Such a contract is a financial asset or financial liability even if the underlying variable is the entity's own share price rather than gold. Similarly, a contract that will be settled in a fixed number of the entity's own shares, but the rights attaching to those shares will be varied so that the settlement value equals a fixed amount or an amount based on changes in an underlying variable, is a financial asset or a financial liability.

Contingent Settlement Provisions (paragraph 25)

AG28   Paragraph 25 requires that if a part of a contingent settlement provision that could require settlement in cash or another financial asset (or in another way that would result in the instrument being a financial liability) is not genuine, the settlement provision does not affect the classification of a financial instrument. Thus, a contract that requires settlement in cash or a variable number of the entity's own shares only on the occurrence of an event that is extremely rare, highly abnormal and very unlikely to occur is an equity instrument. Similarly, settlement in a fixed number of an entity's own shares may be contractually precluded in circumstances that are outside the control of the entity, but if these circumstances have no genuine possibility of occurring, classification as an equity instrument is appropriate.

Treatment in Consolidated Financial Statements

In consolidated financial statements, an entity presents minority interests—ie the interests of other parties in the equity and income of its subsidiaries—in accordance with ~~IAS 1 *Presentation of Financial Statements* and IAS 27 *Consolidated and Separate Financial Statements*~~ FRS 2 Subsidiary Undertakings. When classifying a financial instrument (or a component of it) in consolidated financial statements, an entity considers all terms and conditions agreed between members of the group and the holders of the instrument in determining whether the group as a whole has an obligation to deliver cash or another financial asset in respect of the instrument or to settle it in a manner that results in liability classification. When a subsidiary in a group issues a financial instrument and a parent or other group entity agrees additional terms directly with the holders of the instrument (eg a guarantee), the group may not have discretion over distributions or redemption. Although the subsidiary may appropriately classify the instrument without regard to these additional terms in its individual financial statements, the effect of other agreements between members of the group and the holders of the instrument is considered in order to ensure that consolidated financial statements reflect the contracts and transactions entered into by the group as a whole. To the extent that there is such an obligation or settlement provision, the instrument (or the component of it that is subject to the obligation) is classified as a financial liability in consolidated financial statements. **AG29**

The definition of a financial liability excludes some contractual obligations (provided the specified conditions are met) that oblige the entity to deliver to another party a pro rata share of the net assets of the entity upon its liquidation (or upon redemption or repurchase of a financial instrument puttable at fair value). One of the features of a financial instrument that entitles the holder to a pro rata share of the net assets of the entity is that the instrument is in the most subordinated class of financial instruments with a claim to the assets of the entity. In the consolidated financial statements, the financial instruments held by minority interests are not in the group's most subordinated class of instruments. This is because, if the group were to liquidate, the claims of minority interest holders to the net assets of the subsidiary have to be satisfied before the parent's share of the net assets of the subsidiary can be distributed to claimants to the assets of the parent. Therefore, in all cases, a contractual obligation of the group to deliver cash or another financial asset to a minority interest holder (or to exchange financial assets or financial liabilities under conditions that are potentially unfavourable to the group) is classified as a financial liability in the consolidated financial statements. **AG29A**

Illustrative examples

These examples accompany, but are not part of IAS 32 FRS 25.

> In the Illustrative Examples, paragraph IE1 is amended to read as follows.

ACCOUNTING FOR CONTRACTS ON EQUITY INSTRUMENTS OF AN ENTITY

IE1   The following examples* illustrate the application of paragraphs 15–27 and IAS 39 FRS 26 to the accounting for contracts on an entity's own equity instruments (other than the financial instruments specified in paragraph 16A).

> In Example 8, paragraph IE33 is amended to read as follows.

EXAMPLE 8: ENTITIES WITH SOME EQUITY

IE33   The following example illustrates an income statement and balance sheet format that may be used by entities whose share capital is not equity as defined in IAS 32 FRS 25 because the entity has an obligation to repay the share capital on demand at a fixed price. Other formats are possible.

Income statement for the year ended 31 December 20X1

	20X1	20X0
	CU	CU
Revenue	472	498
Expenses (classified by nature or function)	(367)	(396)
Profit from operating activities	105	102
Finance costs		
– other finance costs	(4)	(4)
– distributions to members	(50)	(50)
Change in net assets attributable to members	51	48

*In these examples, monetary amounts are denominated in 'currency units' (CU).

Balance sheet at 31 December 20X1

	20X1		20X0	
	CU	CU	CU	CU
ASSETS				
Non-current assets (classified in accordance with IAS 1)	908		830	
Total non-current assets		908		830
Current assets (classified in accordance with IAS 1)	383		350	
Total current assets		383		350
Total assets		1,291		1,180
LIABILITIES				
Current liabilities (classified in accordance with IAS 1)	372		338	
Share capital repayable on demand	202		161	
Total current liabilities		(574)		(499)
Total assets less current liabilities		717		681
Non-current liabilities (classified in accordance with IAS 1)	187		196	
		(187)		(196)
RESERVES [(a)]				
Reserves eg revaluation reserve, retained earnings etc	530		485	
		530		485
		717		681
MEMORANDUM NOTE – Total members' interests				
Share capital repayable on demand		202		161
Reserves		530		485
		732		646

(a) In this example, the entity has no obligation to deliver a share of its reserves to its members.

Proposed Amendments to ~~IAS 1~~
<u>Appendix E of FRS 29 (IFRS 7) 'Financial Instruments: Disclosures'</u>

ASB note: IAS 1 has not been implemented in the UK and the republic of Ireland. Disclosures relating to capital included in IAS 1 have been implemented in the UK and the Republic of Ireland as Appendix E of FRS 29, and the following amendments the IASB propose for the capital disclosures of IAS 1 are proposed changes to Appendix E.

After paragraph E3, a new heading and paragraphs E4 – E8 are inserted as follows.

FINANCIAL INSTRUMENTS PUTTABLE AT FAIR VALUE

E4   The following terms are defined in paragraph 11 of ~~IAS 32~~ *FRS 25(IAS 32) Financial Instruments: Presentation* and are used in this ~~Standard~~ appendix with the meaning specified in ~~IAS 32~~ *FRS 25*:

- financial instrument puttable at fair value
- a financial instrument that entitles the holder to a pro rata share of the net assets of the entity.

E5   If an entity has reclassified:

(a)   a financial instrument puttable at fair value; or
(b)   an instrument that imposes on the entity an obligation to deliver to another entity a pro rata share of the net assets of the entity upon its liquidation;

between financial liabilities and equity, it shall disclose the amount reclassified into and out of each category (financial liabilities or equity), and the timing and reason for that reclassification.

E6   For financial instruments puttable at fair value classified as equity, an entity shall disclose (to the extent not disclosed elsewhere):

(a)   summary quantitative data about the amount classified as equity;
(b)   its objectives, policies and processes for managing its obligation to repurchase or redeem the instruments when required to do so by the instrument holders, including any changes from the previous period;
(c)   the fair value of that class of financial instruments in a way that permits it to be compared with its carrying amount; and
(d)   information about how fair value was determined, consistently with the requirements of ~~IFRS 7~~ *FRS 29 (IFRS 7) Financial Instruments: Disclosures* paragraph 27(a)–(c), to the extent applicable.

E7   If an entity uses a formula to determine the price received or paid by the entity upon issue, redemption or repurchase of financial instruments puttable at fair value that are classified as equity (as permitted by paragraph AG14A of ~~IAS 32~~ *FRS 25*), it shall:

(a)   disclose that fact; and

(b)   use that formula, and disclose information about the formula, for the purposes of complying with paragraph E6(c) and (d).

OTHER DISCLOSURES

An entity shall disclose the following, if not disclosed elsewhere in information   **E8**
published with the financial
statements:

(a)   If it is a limited liability life entity, information regarding the length of its life.

After paragraph E8, paragraph E9 is inserted as follows:

Financial Instruments Puttable at Fair Value and Obligations Arising on Liquidation   **E9**
(Amendments to ~~IAS 32~~ FRS 25 and ~~IAS 1~~ Appendix E of FRS 29), issued in [date
to be inserted after exposure], inserted paragraphs ~~11A, 75A, 124D and 124E,~~ E4, E5
and E6. An entity shall apply those amendments for annual periods beginning on or
after [date to be inserted after exposure]. Earlier application is encouraged. If an
entity applies these changes for an earlier period, it shall disclose that fact and apply
the related amendments to ~~IAS 32~~ FRS 25, ~~IAS 39~~ FRS 26 and ~~IFRIC 2~~ UITF 39
Members' Shares in Co-operative Entities and Similar Instruments at the same time.

Amendments to other Standards and Urgent Issues Task Force (UITF) Abstracts

*The amendments in this appendix shall be applied for annual periods beginning on or
after [date to be inserted after exposure]. If an entity applies the [draft] amendments
to ~~IAS 32~~ FRS 25 and ~~IAS 1~~ Appendix E of FRS 29 for an earlier period, these
amendments shall be applied for that earlier period.*

~~IAS 39~~ FRS 26 *Financial Instruments: Recognition and Measurement* is amended as   **1**
described below.

Paragraph 2 is amended to read as follows:

SCOPE

2   **This Standard shall be applied by all entities to all types of financial instruments
except:**
...

   (d)   **financial instruments issued by the entity that meet the definition of an
         equity instrument in ~~IAS 32~~ FRS 25 (including options, warrants and the
         instruments specified in paragraph 16A of ~~IAS 32~~ FRS 25). However, the
         holder of such equity instruments shall apply this Standard to those
         instruments, unless they meet the exception in (a) above.**

   ...

~~IFRIC 2~~ UITF Abstract 39 *Members' Shares in Co-operative Entities and Similar*   **2**
Instruments is amended as described below.

The footnote (to the reference to '~~IAS 32~~ FRS 25 *Financial Instrument: Disclosure
and Presentation* ~~(as revised in 2003)~~') is amended to read as follows:

¹In August December 2005, ~~IAS 32~~ FRS 25 was amended as ~~IAS 32~~ FRS 25 *Financial Instruments: Presentation*. Also, in [month and year to be inserted], the IASB amended, ~~IAS 32~~ FRS 25 by requiring particular types of financial instruments (eg financial instruments puttable at fair value) to be classified as equity, provided that specified conditions are met.

Paragraphs 6 and 9 are amended to read as follows. Paragraphs 7 and 8 are included here for convenience but are not amended.

6   Members' shares that would be classified as equity if the members did not have a right to request redemption are equity if either of the conditions described in paragraphs 7 and 8 is present or if the members' shares are financial instruments puttable at fair value that are classified as equity in accordance with paragraph 16A of ~~IAS 32~~ FRS 25. Demand deposits, including current accounts, deposit accounts and similar contracts that arise when members act as customers are financial liabilities of the entity.

7   Members' shares are equity if the entity has an unconditional right to refuse redemption of the members' shares.

8   Local law, regulation or the entity's governing charter can impose various types of prohibitions on the redemption of members' shares, eg unconditional prohibitions or prohibitions based on liquidity criteria. If redemption is unconditionally prohibited by local law, regulation or the entity's governing charter, members' shares are equity. However, provisions in local law, regulation or the entity's governing charter that prohibit redemption only if conditions—such as liquidity constraints—are met (or are not met) do not result in members' shares being equity.

9   An unconditional prohibition may be absolute, in that all redemptions are prohibited. An unconditional prohibition may be partial, in that it prohibits redemption of members' shares if redemption would cause the number of members' shares or amount of paid-in capital from members' shares to fall below a specified level. Members' shares in excess of the prohibition against redemption are liabilities, unless the entity has the unconditional right to refuse redemption as described in paragraph 7 or if the members' shares are financial instruments puttable at fair value that are classified as equity in accordance with paragraph 16A of ~~IAS 32~~ FRS 25. In some cases, the number of shares or the amount of paid-in capital subject to a redemption prohibition may change from time to time. Such a change in the redemption prohibition leads to a transfer between financial liabilities and equity.

After paragraph 14, paragraph 14A is inserted as follows:

14A   An entity shall apply the amendments in paragraphs 6, 9, A1 and A12 for annual periods beginning on or after [date to be inserted after exposure]. If an entity applies *Financial Instruments Puttable at Fair Value and Obligations Arising on Liquidation* (Amendments to ~~IAS 32~~ FRS 25 and ~~IAS 1~~ Appendix E of FRS 29), issued in [date to be inserted after exposure], for an earlier period, those amendments shall be applied to that earlier period.

In the Appendix (Examples of the application of the consensus), paragraphs A1 and A12 are amended to read as follows:

A1   This appendix sets out seven examples of the application of the ~~IFRIC~~ UITF consensus. The examples do not constitute an exhaustive list; other fact patterns are possible. Each example assumes that there are no conditions other than those set out in the facts of the example that would require the financial instrument to be classified as a financial liability and that the financial instruments are not financial instruments puttable at fair value that are classified as equity in accordance with paragraph 16A of ~~IAS 32~~ FRS 25.

Classification

A12 In this case, CU750,000 would be classified as equity and CU150,000 would be classified as financial liabilities. In addition to the paragraphs already cited, paragraph 18(b) of ~~IAS 32~~ FRS 25 states in part:

> ...a financial instrument that gives the holder the right to put it back to the issuer for cash or another financial asset (a 'puttable instrument') is a financial liability (except as stated in paragraph 16A). This is so even when the amount of cash or other financial assets is determined on the basis of an index or other item that has the potential to increase or decrease. The existence of an option for the holder to put the instrument back to the issuer for cash or another financial asset means that the puttable instrument meets the definition of a financial liability (except as stated in paragraph 16A).

In the Basis for Conclusions, paragraph BC7 is amended to read as follows:

BC7 In many jurisdictions, local law or regulations state that members' shares are equity of the entity. However, paragraph 17 of IAS 32 states:

> Except as stated in paragraph 17A, a critical feature in differentiating a financial liability from an equity instrument is *the existence of a contractual obligation of one party to the financial instrument (the issuer) either to deliver cash or another financial asset to the other party (the holder)* or to exchange financial assets or financial liabilities with the holder under conditions that are potentially unfavourable to the issuer. Although the holder of an equity instrument may be entitled to receive a pro rata share of any dividends or other distributions of equity, the issuer does not have a contractual obligation to make such distributions because it cannot be required to deliver cash or another financial asset to another party. [Emphasis added]

Basis for Conclusions

This Basis for Conclusions accompanies, but is not a part of, the draft amendments to IAS 32 and IAS 1.

> *ASB note:* The IASB's Basis for Conclusions, which accompanies IAS 32, is set out below in full. It should be noted though that some of the discussion it contains concerns IASB requirements that have no equivalent in the UK or the Republic of Ireland. Footnotes have been used to indicate corresponding requirements in the UK and the Republic of Ireland where applicable.

Introduction

BC1   This Basis for Conclusions summarises the International Accounting Standards Board's considerations in reaching the conclusions in the Exposure Draft of Proposed Amendments to IAS 32 Financial Instruments: Presentation and IAS 1 Presentation of Financial Statements—*Financial Instruments Puttable at Fair Value and Obligations Arising on Liquidation.* Individual Board members gave greater weight to some factors than to others.

BACKGROUND

BC2   IAS 32 *Financial Instruments: Presentation* requires a financial instrument to be classified as equity if specified conditions are met. One condition is that the instrument includes no contractual obligation to deliver cash or another financial asset to another entity.

BC3   When an issuer has an obligation to purchase its own shares for cash or another financial asset, IAS 32 paragraph 23 requires the issuer to recognise a financial liability for the present value of the amount that it is obliged to pay for the financial instruments. Therefore, a financial instrument puttable at fair value is recognised as a financial liability at the fair value of the financial instrument.

BC4   IAS 32, in some cases, requires an instrument to be classified as equity even though the entity has an obligation to deliver cash or another financial asset to another entity upon its liquidation. In accordance with paragraph 25 of IAS 32, such an instrument is classified as equity if liquidation of the entity is a contingent event that is beyond the control of both the entity and the holder of the instrument. Therefore, IAS 32 requires an instrument containing an obligation to transfer cash or another financial asset on liquidation of the entity to be classified as a financial liability when liquidation is:

(a)   certain to occur and outside the control of the entity; or
(b)   uncertain to occur, but the holder of the instrument can require the entity to liquidate (liquidation at the option of the holder).

THE PROPOSED AMENDMENTS

Financial instruments puttable at fair value

BC5   Some entities, such as some co-operatives, mutual funds, partnerships and private (unlisted) entities, issue financial instruments that require the entity to repurchase or redeem the instrument at the fair value of a pro rata share of the net assets of the entity (financial instruments puttable at fair value). Constituents raised the following concerns about the application of IAS 32 and IAS 39 *Financial Instruments: Recognition and Measurement** to financial instruments puttable at fair value.

(a)   On an ongoing basis, the liability is recognised at not less than the amount payable on demand, ie the instrument's fair value. This results in the entire market capitalisation of the entity being recognised as a liability because the instruments are the equivalent of the entity's ordinary shares.
(b)   The changes in the fair value of the liability are recognised in profit or loss. When the entity performs well and the fair value of the liabilities increases, a loss is recognised. When the entity performs poorly and the fair value of the liability decreases, a gain is recognised.
(c)   It is likely that the entity will report negative net assets because of unrecognised intangible assets and goodwill, and because the measurement of recognised assets and liabilities may not be at fair value.
(d)   The issuing entity's balance sheet portrays the entity as wholly, or mostly, debt funded.
(e)   Distributions of profits to shareholders are recognised as expenses. Hence, it may appear that net income is a function of the distribution policy, not performance.

Furthermore, constituents considered that additional disclosures and adapting the format of the income statement and balance sheet did not resolve these concerns.

The Board noted that financial instruments puttable at fair value have characteristics **BC6** similar to ordinary shares, in that the instruments give the holder a residual interest in the net assets of the entity. Moreover, financial instruments puttable at fair value would meet the definition of equity instruments in accordance with IAS 32 but for the holder's right to put the instruments back to the issuer at their fair value. The Board noted that additional disclosures and adapting the format of the entity's financial statements, supplementing the treatment of these instruments in accordance with IAS 32 and IAS 39, did not resolve the problem of the lack of relevance and understandability of that current accounting treatment.

The Board considered the following ways to improve the financial reporting of **BC7** financial instruments puttable at fair value:

(a)   continue to classify these instruments as financial liabilities, but amend their measurement so that changes in their fair value would not be recognised;
(b)   amend IAS 32 to require separation of all puttable instruments into a put option and a host instrument; or
(c)   amend IAS 32 to provide a limited exception so that financial instruments puttable at fair value would be classified as equity, if specified conditions were met.

Amend the measurement of financial instruments puttable at fair value so that changes in their fair value would not be recognised

The Board decided against this approach because: **BC8**

(a)   it is inconsistent with the principle in IAS 32 and IAS 39 that only equity instruments are not remeasured after their initial recognition;
(b)   it retains the disadvantage that entities whose shares are all puttable at fair value would have no equity instruments; and

*ASB footnote: IAS 39 is implemented in the UK as FRS 26 (IAS 39) 'Financial Instruments: Measurement.'

(c) it introduces a new category of financial liabilities to IAS 39, and thus increases IAS 39's complexity.

Separate all puttable instruments into a put option and a host instrument

BC9 The Board concluded that conducting further research into an approach that splits a puttable share into an equity component and a written put option component (financial liability) would duplicate efforts of the Board's longer-term project on liabilities and equity. Consequently, the Board decided not to proceed with a project at this stage to determine whether a puttable share should be split into an equity component and a written put option component.

Classify as equity financial instruments puttable at fair value with characteristics similar to ordinary shares

BC10 The Board decided to proceed with proposals to amend IAS 32 to require financial instruments puttable at fair value with characteristics similar to ordinary shares to be classified as equity provided specified conditions are met, as a short-term solution, pending the outcome of the longer-term project on liabilities and equity. The Board acknowledges that this approach is a pragmatic solution to improve the financial reporting of financial instruments puttable at fair value, because it involves amending IAS 32 to require equity classification of a particular type of financial instrument in specific circumstances, rather than comprehensively reviewing the distinction between liabilities and equity. Such a review would take a substantial amount of time to complete and therefore is part of the longer-term project. In the meantime, the Board concluded that the lack of relevance and understandability of the information produced from the current financial reporting treatment was such that it should proceed with a pragmatic, short-term solution.

BC11 The Board proposes the following conditions for classifying as equity a financial instrument puttable at fair value:

(a) the instrument entitles the holder to require the entity to repurchase or redeem the instrument for the fair value of a pro rata share of the net assets of the entity and would, but for this entitlement, have met the definition of an equity instrument;

(b) the instrument entitles the holder to a pro rata share of the net assets of the entity in the event of the entity's liquidation;

(c) the financial instrument's right to a pro rata share of the net assets of the entity is neither limited nor guaranteed, either before or at liquidation;

(d) the instrument is in the most subordinated class of instruments with a claim to the entity's net assets;

(e) the instrument's issue price is the fair value of a pro rata share of the net assets of the entity at the time of issue; and

(f) the instruments in the most subordinated class are all financial instruments puttable at fair value.

BC12 The Board decided on these conditions for the following reasons:

(a) to ensure that the affected instruments are equivalent to ordinary shares, except for the right to put at fair value;

(b) to ensure that the proposed amendments are consistent with the limited scope of the project; and

(c) to reduce structuring opportunities that may arise as a result of the proposed amendments.

To apply the proposed amendments, an entity would normally determine the fair **BC13** value of financial instruments puttable at fair value in accordance with relevant IAS 39 guidance (paragraph 48A and paragraphs AG69–AG82). To reduce costs, some partnerships and non-public entities use a formula, as a proxy, to calculate the fair value of the issue price or redemption price of puttable instruments. For entities whose securities are not publicly traded or that do not hold assets in a fiduciary capacity for a broad group of outsiders, the Board decided not to increase their costs in complying with the proposed amendments by agreeing that a formula can be used to determine the amount at which the financial instruments puttable at fair value are issued, repurchased or redeemed, provided that the formula is intended to approximate fair value.

The Board also decided that warrants (and other derivatives) to be settled by the **BC14** issue of financial instruments puttable at fair value should be precluded from equity classification under the proposed amendments; these derivatives would continue to be classified as financial liabilities. The Board noted that a warrant (and other similar derivatives) over a puttable instrument has the same characteristics as a cash-settled share appreciation right, which is classified as a financial liability. Moreover, as discussed above, the objective of the project is to improve the financial reporting of financial instruments puttable at fair value (and instruments that entitle the holder to a pro rata share of the net assets of the entity upon liquidation) that have characteristics similar to ordinary shares. The Board noted that warrants do not have the characteristics of the instruments to be affected by the proposed amendments. Therefore, in keeping with the limited scope of the project, the Board concluded that any warrants or other derivatives that are currently classified as financial liabilities should continue to be so classified.

Obligations arising on liquidation

Issues similar to those raised by constituents relating to the classification of financial **BC15** instruments puttable at fair value (set out in paragraph BC5) apply to the classification of ordinary shares (or equivalent instruments) in a limited life entity. Liquidation of the entity is certain because it has a limited life. Therefore, IAS 32 at present requires those shares to be classified as financial liabilities because the entity has an obligation to transfer cash or another financial asset to the shareholders. Hence, a limited life entity would have no equity. Similar issues also arise in respect of some partnerships that are required to liquidate upon exit of a partner (eg on retirement or death).

The Board decided to propose an amendment to exclude from the definition of a **BC16** financial liability a contractual obligation that entitles the holder to a pro rata share of the net assets of the entity upon liquidation of the entity. This amendment would result in equity classification of instruments, or components of instruments, that entitle the holder to a pro rata share of the net assets of the entity upon liquidation, including when liquidation is:

(a) certain to occur and outside the control of the entity (affects limited life entities); or

(b) uncertain to occur and liquidation is at the option of the holder (affects partnership interests).

However, for the instruments referred to in (b) of the paragraph above, the Board **BC17** decided that equity classification should be conditional upon all financial instruments in the most subordinated class of instruments with a claim to the assets of the entity having the right to require liquidation of the entity. This condition is similar to the condition applying to the classification of financial instruments puttable at fair value, whereby all financial instruments in the most subordinated class of instruments with a claim to the assets of the entity are puttable at fair value. In both cases, equity classification of an instrument that imposes on the entity an obligation to transfer cash or another financial asset to the instrument holder is conditional upon all instruments in the most subordinated class of instruments with a claim to the assets of the entity imposing such an obligation. This circumstance already applies to shares issued by a limited life entity, because all such shares impose on the entity an obligation to transfer cash or another financial asset to the instrument holder.

BC18   The Board also considered the classification of warrants (and other derivatives) to be settled by an exchange of a fixed amount of cash for a fixed number of financial instruments with a contractual obligation that entitles the holder to a pro rata share of the net assets of the entity upon liquidation of the entity (eg warrants over shares in a limited life entity). The Board decided that the classification of such warrants should be consistent with its earlier decision in respect of warrants over financial instruments puttable at fair value (as explained in paragraph BC14). The Board noted that these warrants do not have the characteristics of the instruments to be affected by the proposed amendments. Therefore, the Board concluded that these warrants should continue to be classified as financial liabilities.

Minority interests

BC19   The Board also discussed the classification of minority interests under the proposed amendments. Any minority interests that are currently classified as equity would be unaffected by the proposed amendments. The Board discussed minority interests that are, at present, classified as financial liabilities in the group's consolidated financial statements because they are puttable at fair value or represent obligations arising on liquidation of a subsidiary when liquidation is certain or at the option of the minority interest holder. The Board concluded that in the subsidiary's individual financial statements these types of minority interests should be classified as equity in accordance with the proposed amendments, if the relevant conditions were satisfied. However, they would not be classified as equity in the group's consolidated financial statements because minority interests are not in the most subordinated class of instruments from the perspective of the group. This is because, if the group were to liquidate, the claims of minority interests to the net assets of the subsidiary have to be satisfied first, before the parent's share of the net assets of the subsidiary could be distributed to the claimants to the assets of the parent. Therefore, those types of minority interests would continue to be classified as financial liabilities in the consolidated financial statements. The Board also noted that continuing to classify minority interests puttable at fair value and minority interests that impose an obligation arising on liquidation of a subsidiary as financial liabilities in the consolidated financial statements would limit the financial structuring opportunities arising from the proposed amendments. Finally, the Board noted that, if a parent has financial instruments puttable at fair value or financial instruments that impose an obligation arising on liquidation that meet the specified criteria for classification as equity in the parent's separate financial statements, the presence of minority interests does not preclude these shares from being classified as equity in the group's consolidated financial statements.

Disclosures

BC20   The Board also considered disclosures for the instruments affected by the proposed amendments. The Board decided to require disclosure of information about the reclassification of the affected instruments between financial liabilities and equity. This disclosure will enhance the transparency of the financial statements, because the classification of these instruments determines their measurement, and will enhance the understandability of the financial statements when changes in classification occur.

The Board also concluded that entities with financial instruments puttable at fair value classified as equity should be required to disclose additional information to allow users to assess any risks arising from the ability of the holder to put these instruments to the issuer at any time. It is unusual for holders of equity instruments to have such an entitlement. Therefore, the Board concluded that additional disclosures are needed in these circumstances. In particular, the Board concluded that entities should disclose the fair value of financial instruments puttable at fair value that are classified as equity, because that represents the amount at which these instruments could be redeemed. The Board noted that, in effect, this resulted in the continuation of a disclosure requirement, because those instruments are classified as financial liabilities in accordance with IAS 32 at present and, therefore, their fair values are required to be disclosed in accordance with IFRS 7 *Financial Instruments: Disclosures**. The Board noted that the cost of disclosing the fair value of financial instruments puttable at fair value is mitigated for entities whose securities are not publicly traded or that do not hold assets in a fiduciary capacity for a broad group of outsiders because these entities are allowed to use a formula that approximates fair value in complying with this disclosure requirement.

BC21

ANALYSIS OF COSTS AND BENEFITS

Proposed changes to the classification of an instrument as a financial liability or equity in IAS 32

The Board acknowledges that the proposals are not consistent with the definition of a liability in the *Framework*†, or with the underlying principle of IAS 32, which is based on that definition. Consequently, making these changes adds complexity to IAS 32 and introduces the need for several rules. However, the Board also notes that IAS 32 contains other exceptions to its principle (and the definition of a liability in the *Framework*) that require instruments to be classified as liabilities that otherwise would be treated as equity. This situation clearly identifies the need for a comprehensive reconsideration of the classification of instruments as liabilities or equity which the Board will undertake in its longer-term project with the FASB.

BC22

In the interim, the Board concluded that classifying the specified instruments as equity would improve the comparability of information provided to the users of financial statements by requiring more consistent classification of financial instruments that are largely equivalent to ordinary shares across different entity structures (eg partnerships, limited life entities and some co-operatives). The specified instruments differ from ordinary shares in one respect, being the obligation to deliver cash (or another financial asset). However, in the Board's view the other characteristics of the specified instruments are sufficiently similar to ordinary shares for the instruments to be classified as equity. (Some of these characteristics are set out in the definition of a financial instrument that entitles the holder to a pro rata share of the net assets of the entity.) Consequently, in the Board's view, the proposed amendments will result in financial reporting that is more understandable and relevant to the holders of the affected instruments and other users of the financial statements.

BC23

*ASB footnote: *IFRS 7 is implemented in the UK as FRS 29 (IFRS 7) 'Financial Instruments: Disclosures.'*

†ASB footnote: *The equivalent document in the UK and the Republic of Ireland to the IASB's Framework is the ASB's Statement for Principles of Financial Reporting. Although the Statement of Principles is very similar to the Framework, it is not identical.*

Historically, these instruments have typically been treated as equity by issuers, and this treatment has reflected the perception that the instrument holders are the entity's owners.

BC24   Furthermore, in developing the proposed amendments, the Board considered the costs to entities of obtaining any new information necessary to complete a new analysis to determine the classification of financial instruments in accordance with the proposed amendments to IAS 32. The Board believes that the costs of obtaining any new information necessary to determine whether financial instruments meet the specified criteria for equity classification would be slight because all of the information needed should be readily available. The Board notes that costs of complying with the conditions for equity classification for financial instruments puttable at fair value are reduced for entities whose securities are not publicly traded or that do not hold assets in a fiduciary capacity for a broad group of outsiders because the Board has permitted these entities to use a formula (that is intended to approximate fair value) to determine the issue, redemption or repurchase price of these instruments.

BC25   The Board also considered that a cost or risk in introducing exceptions to the definition of a financial liability is the financial structuring opportunities that may result from the proposed amendments. The Board concluded that financial structuring opportunities are mitigated by the strict criteria required for equity classification and the disclosures required (both proposed and currently in IFRSs).

BC26   Consequently, the Board believes that the benefits outweigh the costs of the proposed amendments to IAS 32.

BC27   The Board took the view that, in most cases, entities should be able to apply the changes to IAS 32 retrospectively. There might be cases in which it is impracticable to determine the original issue price of the affected instruments, which is necessary to reverse the effects of remeasuring the instruments to be classified as equity. The Board notes that IAS 8 *Accounting Policies, Changes in Accounting Estimates and Errors* provides relief when it is impracticable to apply a change in accounting policy retrospectively as a result of a new requirement. The Board believes that the costs outweigh the benefits of separating a compound instrument with an obligation arising on liquidation at inception when the liability component is no longer outstanding on the date of application of the proposed amendments. Hence, the proposed transitional provision permitting entities not to separate those compound instruments (based on IFRS 1 *First–time Adoption of International Financial Reporting Standards* paragraph 23*) reduces the costs of applying the proposed amendments retrospectively†.

Proposed additional disclosures as amendments to IAS 1‡

BC28   The Board regards the costs arising from the proposed disclosures as the costs of preparing the information needed. The most costly disclosures are the fair value disclosures for financial instruments puttable at fair value. However, the Board notes that this is not an additional cost as these instruments are currently measured at fair value and subject to those fair value disclosures. The Board notes that costs of those

---

*ASB footnote: *Similar transitional provisions were implemented in paragraph 97A of FRS 25 'Financial Instruments: Disclosure' issued in December 2004.*

†ASB footnote: *The equivalent standard in the UK and the Republic of Ireland is FRS 18. However, FRS 18 does not contain similar relief from retrospective application.*

‡ASB footnote: *The equivalent requirements in the UK and Republic of Ireland are in Appendix E to FRS 29.*

fair value disclosures are reduced for entities whose securities are not publicly traded or that do not hold assets in a fiduciary capacity for a broad group of outsiders because the Board has permitted these entities to use a formula (that is intended to approximate fair value) to calculate the fair value of financial instruments puttable at fair value.

Information necessary to prepare the other proposed disclosures should be readily available and therefore only slightly increases the cost to preparers. The Board believes that the proposed disclosures can be included without difficulty in the comparatives of the annual period when the proposed amendments are first applied. **BC29**

The Board considers that the proposed disclosures will result in more transparent information and will be useful for assessing the risks attached to the affected instruments. Therefore, the Board believes that the benefits outweigh the costs of the proposed disclosures. **BC30**

Alternative View on Proposed Amendments to IAS 32 and IAS 1 *Financial Instruments Puttable at Fair Value and Obligations Arising on Liquidation*

ASB note: The IASB's *Alternative View on Proposed Amendments to IAS 32 and IAS 1*—Financial Instruments Puttable at Fair Value and Obligations Arising on Liquidation, which accompanies IAS 32, is set out below in full.

AV1 Two Board members voted against the publication of the Exposure Draft of Proposed Amendments to IAS 32 Financial Instruments: Presentation and IAS 1 Presentation of Financial Statements—*Financial Instruments Puttable at Fair Value and Obligations Arising on Liquidation*. The members' alternative view is set out below.

AV2 These Board members believe that the decision to permit entities to classify as equity financial instruments puttable at fair value and financial instruments that entitle the holder to a pro rata share of the net assets of the entity upon liquidation is inconsistent with the *Framework*. The contractual provisions attached to these shares give the holders the right to put the shares to the entity and demand cash. Key to the *Framework* definition of a liability is that it is a present obligation of the entity, the settlement of which would result in an outflow of resources of the entity. Thus, a share puttable at fair value clearly meets the definition of a liability in the *Framework*.

AV3 These Board members do not agree with the Board that an exception to the *Framework* is justified in this situation. First, the Board has an active project on the *Framework*, which will revisit the definition of a liability. Although these Board members agree that standards projects can precede decisions in the *Framework* project, the discussions to date in the *Framework* project do not make it clear that the Board will modify the existing elements definitions in such a way that these instruments would be equity. Second, the proposed amendments would require disclosure of the fair value of the obligation. These disclosures mirror those for financial liabilities; existing standards do not require disclosure of fair values of equity instruments. The Board's proposal to require these disclosures reveals its implicit view that these instruments are, in fact, liabilities. Yet, the *Framework* is clear that disclosure is not a substitute for recognition. Third, these Board members see no cost- benefit or practical reasons for making this exception. The amendments require the same information to be obtained and disclosed as would be the case if these obligations were classified as liabilities. Existing standards offer presentation alternatives for entities that have no equity under the *Framework* definitions.

AV4 These Board members also do not agree with the Board that there are two benefits to issuing these amendments. First, paragraph BC23 in the Basis for Conclusions states that the amendments will result in more relevant and understandable financial reporting. However, as noted above, these Board members do not believe that presenting them as equity items that meet the *Framework* definition of a liability results in relevant information. Also as noted above, existing standards offer presentation alternatives that result in understandable financial reporting. Second, paragraph BC23 states that the amendments would increase comparability by requiring classification of these instruments that is more consistent with ordinary shares. However, ordinary shares are not comparable to these instruments. These instruments obligate the entity to transfer its economic resources; ordinary shares do not. Also, shares puttable at fair value and shares that entitle the holder to a pro rata share of the net assets of the entity upon liquidation will be classified as equity by some entities and as liabilities by other entities, depending on whether the other criteria specified in these amendments are met. Thus, these amendments account similarly for economically different instruments, which decreases comparability, not increases it.

Finally, these Board members do not believe that the amendments are based on a   **AV5** clear principle. Rather, they comprise several paragraphs of detailed rules crafted to achieve a desired accounting result. Although the Board attempted to craft these rules to minimise structuring opportunities, the lack of a clear principle leaves open the possibility that economically similar situations will be accounted for differently and economically different situations will be accounted for similarly. Both of these outcomes result in lack of comparability.

The draft is issued by the Accounting Standards Board for comment. It should be noted that the draft may be modified in the light of comment received before being issued in final form.

Proposed Amendment to FRS 3
Reporting Financial Performance

Contents

Preface

INTRODUCTION

1　This Exposure Draft proposes limited amendments to Financial Reporting Standard (FRS) 3 *Reporting Financial Performance* to clarify its application to entities within the scope of FRS 26 (IAS 39) *Financial Instruments: Recognition and Measurement.*

2　In summary the proposed changes to FRS 3 are:

    a.　to reflect the exemption from certain paragraphs of FRS 3 for entities applying FRS 26 and FRS 23 (IAS 21) *The Effects of Changes in Foreign Exchange Rates;* and

    b.　to delete references in paragraph 55 to exemption from producing a profit or loss on an unmodified historical cost basis for certain market makers and other dealers of investments where marking to market is the industry practice.

The ASB's proposals

3　FRS 26 specifies the treatment of gains and losses on remeasurement and derecognition of financial instruments. Paragraphs 21, 26 and 31A of FRS 3 specify the treatment of such gains or losses for all assets and liabilities. It has been suggested that there is a conflict. For example, unrealised gains and losses on available-for-sale financial assets of insurance entities within the scope of FRS 26 are required by that standard to be recognised in the statement of total recognised gains and losses and recycled through the profit and loss account on realisation. Paragraph 31A of FRS 3, on the other hand, requires that all investment portfolio gains and losses be included as part of the investment return in the profit and loss account. Whilst FRS 26 is the later and more specific standard the ASB thinks that it would be more helpful to clarify the situation.

4　On 2 January 2007 the Urgent Issues Task Force (UITF) issued UITF Information Sheet 81, recommending that the ASB make a limited amendment to FRS 3 which it considered, if implemented, will be applicable to UK entities within the scope of FRS 26.

5　The UITF's recommendation was that FRS 3 should clarify that paragraphs 21, 26 and 31A of the standard do not apply to the financial instruments of entities within the scope of FRS 26.

6　During its deliberations the ASB also noted a related problem for entities complying with the requirements of FRS 23 (IAS 21) *The Effects of Changes in Foreign Exchange Rates.* On the disposal of a foreign operation paragraph 48 of FRS 23 requires that the cumulative amount of related exchange differences recognised in the STRGL be recycled through the profit or loss. FRS 23 would require recycling of the foreign exchange gain. Therefore, entities complying with the requirements of FRS 23 would need similar clarifications to that being proposed for entities within the scope of FRS 26, in relation to the foreign exchange gain or loss on sale of a foreign operation.

7　The ASB, however, is against recycling as a principle and does not want to be seen to promote it as a concept. It does, however, acknowledge that a problem exists for entities within the scope of FRS 26 and FRS 23 as set out above. Accordingly, it has proposed a limited amendment to the scope of FRS 3 that allows an exemption from paragraphs 21 and 31A of the standard only to the financial instruments of entities within the scope of FRS 26 and the foreign exchange differences on the sale of a foreign operation for entities within the scope of FRS 23.

Amendments are also proposed to the requirements relating to the note of historical **8** cost profits and losses in paragraphs 26 and 55 of FRS 3 to allow the omission of the effect of fair value accounting of all financial instruments under FRS 26, not just market makers and other dealers in investments as is currently the case under FRS 3. The amendment to paragraph 26 also has the effect of requiring an additional disclosure to the note on historical cost profits and losses; namely the fact that the effects of fair value accounting for financial instruments and hyperinflationary adjustments have been excluded from the reconciliation of the reported profit on ordinary activities before taxation to the equivalent historical cost amount.

The ASB decided that it would be more appropriate to amend FRS 3 rather than **9** FRS 23 and FRS 26 as they are standards which are converged with the equivalent International Financial Reporting Standards (IFRS).

The ASB has also taken this opportunity to delete an unrelated example in the **10** 'Illustrative Examples' section which is no longer applicable in the UK as the related paragraphs in the standard had been removed previously.

REGULATORY IMPACT

The ASB is not aware that the proposal would impose additional costs on entities **11** that would outweigh the benefits of providing this clarification, but would welcome any comments that respondents might have on this issue.

DATE FROM WHICH EFFECTIVE

It is proposed that the [draft] FRS is effective for accounting periods beginning on or **12** after 1 January 2007. Early adoption is permitted.

INVITATION TO COMMENT

The ASB is requesting comments on any aspect of the Amendment to the FRS by 27 **13** April 2007. Given the urgency of the issue, this is a shorter than normal consultation period.

The ASB would welcome comments in particular on the following: **14**

Q1 Do you agree that the proposed amendment is a useful clarification? If not, why not?

Q2 Are you aware of any problems that may arise as a result of the proposed amendments for entities that are not meant to be within the scope of this amendment?

Q3 Are you aware of any other conflicts with FRS 3 that should be addressed at the same time as those stated in this Exposure Draft?

Q4 Do you agree that the benefits of the proposed amendment would outweigh any costs involved? If not, why not? It would be helpful if any significant costs that would arise on implementation of the proposal could be identified and quantified.

Q5 The ASB is proposing that the [draft] FRS be effective for accounting periods beginning on or after 1 January 2007 and it is permitting early adoption. Do you agree with the proposed effective date?

[Draft] Financial Reporting Standard

AMENDMENT TO FRS 3 'REPORTING FINANCIAL PERFORMANCE'

1 **Amend paragraph 12 as follows:**

12 <u>Subject to paragraphs 12A and 12B</u> ~~T~~the FRS applies to all financial statements intended to give a true and fair view of a reporting entity's financial
position and profit or loss (or income and expenditure). Every such reporting
entity should apply the requirements of the FRS except to the extent that these
requirements are not permitted by the statutory framework (if any) under
which the entity reports.

2 **Insert new paragraph 12B as follows:**

12B <u>Paragraph 21 and the last sentence of paragraph 31A of the FRS do not apply
to entities adopting FRS 26 (IAS 39) *Financial Instruments: Recognition and
Measurement,* in relation to:</u>

  a. <u>financial instruments accounted for in accordance with FRS 26; and</u>
  b. <u>foreign exchange differences on disposal of a foreign operation in accordance
  with FRS 23 (IAS 21) *The effects of changes in foreign exchange rates.*</u>

3 **Insert a new sentence into paragraph 26 as underlined:**

26 Where there is a material difference between the result as disclosed in the profit
and loss account and the result on an unmodified historical cost basis, a note of
the historical cost profit or loss for the period should be presented. Where full
historical cost information is unavailable or cannot be obtained without
unreasonable expense or delay, the earliest available values should be used. The
note of the historical cost profit or loss should include a reconciliation of the
reported profit on ordinary activities before taxation to the equivalent historical cost amount and should also show the retained profit for the financial year
reported on the historical cost basis. <u>The effects of fair value accounting under
FRS 26 and hyperinflation adjustments under FRS 24 (IAS 29) *Financial
Reporting in Hyperinflationary Economies* and UITF Abstract 9 *Accounting for
Operations in Hyper-inflationary Economies* are not required to be included in
this reconciliation, but this omission should be noted.</u> The note should be
presented immediately following the profit and loss account or the statement of
total recognised gains and losses.

4 **Insert a new sentence into paragraph 55 as underlined and delete the last sentence after
"paragraph 26" as follows:**

55 Two reasons for disclosing the profit or loss for a period on the unmodified
historical cost basis of accounting are commonly cited. The first is, that for as
long as discretion exists on the timing or scale of revaluations included in
financial statements, the unmodified historical cost basis will give the reported
profits or losses of different reporting entities on a more comparable basis. The
second is the wish of certain users to assess the profit or loss on sale of assets
based on their historical cost, rather than, as the FRS requires, on their
revalued carrying amount. In acknowledgement of these concerns, the Board
has made the provision of a note of historical cost profits and losses a
requirement of the FRS in those circumstances where there is a material difference between the result as disclosed in the profit and loss account and the
result on an unmodified historical cost basis. Where full historical cost

information is unavailable or cannot be obtained without unreasonable expense or delay, the earliest available values should be used. The note of historical cost profits and losses should be presented immediately following the profit and loss account or the statement of total recognised gains and losses. In consolidated financial statements, the profit and loss account figure for minority interests should be amended for the purposes of this note to reflect the adjustments made where they affect subsidiary companies with a minority interest. For the purpose of paragraph 26 the fair value accounting adjustments necessary under FRS 26 and hyperinflation adjustments under FRS 24 and UITF Abstract 9 are not required to be included in the reconciliation, but this omission should be noted. ~~the following are not deemed to be departures from the historical cost convention: (a) adjustments necessarily made to cope with the impact of hyper-inflation on foreign operations and (b) and the practice of market makers and other dealers in investments of marking to market where this is an established industry practice~~.

Insert a new footnote at the end of paragraph 56 as follows:　　　　　5

ASB footnote: However, for entities applying FRS 26, which is based on the International Accounting Standard 39 *Financial Instruments: Recognition and Measurement*, gains and losses on remeasurement of certain categories of financial instruments are recognised in the STRGL and the related cumulative gain or loss is recognised in the profit and loss account when the instrument is derecognised.

The last example in the Illustrative Examples section headed 'Companies Act investment company' is deleted.　　　　　6

The following subheading and paragraph is added to the Development of the Standards section　　　　　7

2007 Amendment

xii　During 2007 the ASB set out to clarify the relationship between FRS 3 requirements and those contained in FRS 23 and FRS 26. FRS 26 specifies the treatment of gains and losses on remeasurement and derecognition of financial instruments. Paragraphs 21, 26 and 31A of FRS 3 specify the treatment of such gains or losses for all assets and liabilities, including financial instruments. Similarly, entities complying with FRS 23 are required by paragraph 48 of the standard to recycle the cumulative amount of exchange differences relating to a foreign operation, recognised in the statement of total recognised gains and losses, through the profit or loss on the disposal of that foreign operation. In contrast, FRS 3 appears to specifically prohibit this recycling through the profit and loss account. Whilst FRS 26 and FRS 23 are the later and more specific standards the ASB decided to clarify the situation by amending the scope of FRS 3.

An entity shall apply this [draft] Amendment to FRS 3 for accounting periods beginning on or after 1 January 2007. Early adoption is permitted.　　　　　8

Part Nine

ASB Discussion and Consultation Papers in issue

Discounting in financial reporting
Working paper

(Issued April 1997)

Contents

Discounting in financial reporting
Working paper

Preface and invitation to comment

Discounting future cash flows is a technique for reflecting in the valuation of an asset or liability two factors that are taken into account in all rational economic decisions: the time value of money and the risk associated with the cash flows. Discounting is widely used in financial management and is part of most modern asset-pricing models and most option-pricing models.

In financial statements, discounting is used in the financial reporting of leases and pension costs. It has also been considered in a number of the Accounting Standards Board's current projects, in particular goodwill, impairment of tangible fixed assets, provisions and deferred tax.

In these projects the Board is concerned that, if items are recorded in financial statements at an amount based on undiscounted future cash flows, unlike items will appear alike. For example, a riskless cash inflow of £1 million due tomorrow, a riskless cash inflow of £1 million due in ten years and a risky cash inflow of £1 million due in ten years would all be recorded at £1 million. However, no entity would regard these assets as equal nor would they cost the same to acquire. In fact, £1 million is an economically meaningless value to attribute to the two assets that generate cash flows in ten years' time. If they are recorded at £1 million, relevant information is lost to the user of the financial statements and misleading information given instead.

Notwithstanding the fundamental economic truths that discounting can reflect, the Board believes that it is not necessary or desirable to apply discounting to every item in the balance sheet that is measured by reference to future cash flows, as the period over which the cash flows arise is often too short for the effect to be material. In particular, the Board does not envisage any need to apply discounting to the vast majority of current assets and current liabilities. However, in certain circumstances the effect of discounting on long-term assets and liabilities may be very significant and needs to be considered.

The Working Paper is not a prelude to a future Financial Reporting Standard on this topic and the decision on whether discounting will be prescribed in any particular circumstance will form part of the development of the relevant Standard. However, some respondents to Discussion Papers have asked for a general approach to discounting to be developed. The Working Paper is published in response to that request. It seeks to establish principles on how discounting should be applied so that any future FRSs involving discounting will be prepared on a consistent basis. It is a Working Paper for the Board's own reference as the Board considers discounting within various projects. In this context, comments on the Paper would be very welcome. The Board is particularly interested in views on the proposed application of the principles in the Paper to:

(i)   impaired fixed assets (see illustrative note A)
(ii)   pensions (see illustrative note B)
(iii) provisions for environmental liabilities (see illustrative note C).

The Financial Accounting Standards Board (FASB) in the USA has been researching the issue of discounting in financial reporting for a number of years and is currently working on a Concepts Statement on the subject. In preparing this Paper, the Board has drawn extensively on the FASB's excellent research, in particular the work of Wayne Upton, a FASB senior project manager. This is not to say that the FASB agrees with all the conclusions in the Working Paper—specifically, FASB representatives have disagreed with the paragraphs relating to the discount rate for final salary pension liabilities. Both this Working Paper and the FASB working draft of a Concepts Statement have been discussed at a meeting of the G4 + 1, a group comprising representatives from the accounting standard-setting bodies in Australia, Canada, the UK and the USA and the International Accounting Standards Committee. Comments received on the Working Paper will be fed back to the group.

1   Time value of money

In most economies, finance is a scarce resource. Money, therefore, has a value associated with time: £1 now is worth more than a promise of £1 in a year's time. This would be true even if there were no risk of non-repayment and there were no inflation.   **1.1**

Assets that generate cash flows soon are worth more, therefore, than those generating the same cash flows later. This difference in value is automatically recorded in financial statements if the assets are recorded at an arm's length purchase cost or market value because all rational economic transactions will take account of the time value of money.   **1.2**

However, sometimes assets are measured not by reference to an observable price in a transaction or market but by reference to the future cash flows arising from the items. For example, in the calculation of revised values for impaired assets, value in use is measured on the basis of future cash flows. In these cases, if the difference in value between assets that arises from the different timing of cash flows is to be recognised, the cash flows must be discounted.*   **1.3**

If the cash flows were not discounted two assets giving rise to cash flows of the same amount but with different timings would be recorded at the same value, even though their market values and costs if purchased now would be different. In other words, unlike items would appear alike. Useful information about those assets would be lost to users of financial statements.   **1.4**

In a similar manner to assets, liabilities that generate cash outflows soon are more onerous than those generating the same cash outflows later. Again, because rational economic decisions will always reflect the time value of money, this difference in value is automatically recorded in financial statements if the liabilities are recorded at an arm's length transaction price. However, many liabilities, in particular provisions, are based on future cash flows. In those cases where the cash flows lie far in the future, for example abandonment costs, discounting the cash flows is necessary to reflect differences in value arising from the timing of the cash outflows. Although this results in the liabilities being recorded at less than the undiscounted amount, this is not imprudent—it simply reflects the benefit that arises from the cash outflows not being due until a later date.   **1.5**

Discounting is, therefore, a useful tool in accounting measurements. However, it is not an end in itself. Simply applying an arbitrary discount rate to a series of cash   **1.6**

Discounted cash flows are the cash flows multiplied by $1/(1+r)^n$ where r is the discount rate for the period and n the number of periods between now and the date the cash flow will occur. For example, £100 discounted at 5 per cent for five years is $100 \times 1/(1 + 0.05)^5 = £78$. The discount rate represents the cost of the deferred receipt. How that cost should be determined is discussed in Section 2.

flows provides no useful information to users of financial statements. In order to determine what discount rate should be used in any particular situation, it is necessary to consider the implications of risk (Section 2) and the accounting objective being sought (Sections 3 and 4).

2   Risk

2.1   The cost of not receiving a cash inflow until some date in the future is an opportunity cost that can be measured by considering what interest has been lost by not investing that money for the period. Similarly, the benefit of not paying a cash outflow until some date in the future can be measured by considering what interest can be earned by investing that money for the period. In both cases, the time value of money unaffected by risk is given by the rate of return on a risk-free investment. In the UK, risk-free rates are generally taken to be those available on government bonds.

2.2   However, the value of the future cash flows is affected not only by the time value of money but also by the variability (ie risk) associated with the cash flows. As with the time value of money, all rational economic transactions will reflect the effect of risk. Again, it follows that differences in value arising from the variability of the cash flows are recorded in financial statements as a matter of course if items are recorded at an arm's length purchase cost and if they are subsequently revalued at market value. It therefore seems appropriate, in general, that items measured by reference to future cash flows should also reflect the effect of the variability of the cash flows. (What risks should be reflected when is discussed in more detail in Sections 3 and 4.)

2.3   The effect of the variability of the cash flows can be reflected in two ways. Either:

(i)   the expected value* of the cash flows can be adjusted for risk and the adjusted figure (the certainty equivalent) discounted at a risk-free rate, or

(ii)   the expected value of the cash flows can be discounted at a risk-adjusted rate.†

Examples of how this affects assets and liabilities are given below.

---

*The expected value is the weighted average of all the possible cash flows (see paragraph 3.5(d)).

†However, reflecting the effect of risk in a single discount rate to be applied to cash flows that arise at different times implies a relationship between risk and the timing of the cash flows that may well not be the case. It implies that the cash flows become more variable the further into the future they are or that the entity's aversion to risk will increase as time passes. In theory, therefore, it is preferable to make the risk adjustment to the cash flows in each period and to discount the adjusted cash flows at the risk-free rate.

Assets

Example

Suppose an asset is expected to give rise to one of the following possible cash inflows in three years' time and that the risk-free rate of return is 5 per cent:

Likelihood of cash flow	Cash flow	Expected value
25 per cent	£100	£25
50 per cent	£150	£75
25 per cent	£200	£50
Total		£150

Discussion

The expected value of the cash inflow in three years' time is £150. However, there is the possibility that the cash flow will not be £150 but £100 or £200. The reporting entity is risk-averse and would accept a certain promise of, say, £140 in three years' time in return for the asset. We can express the effect of the uncertainty (risk) in calculating the present value by:

(a) discounting the certainty equivalent of £140 at the risk-free rate of 5 per cent, giving a present value of £121, or

(b) discounting the expected cash flow of £150 at a risk-adjusted rate that will give the present value of £121, ie a rate of 7.4 per cent.

In the above example, the value of the asset with variable cash flows is less than the value of an asset with certain cash flows of £150 in three years' time (which is £150 discounted at the risk-free rate of 5 per cent, ie £130). The effect of risk on assets will generally be to reduce their value because entities tend to be risk-averse and to prefer fixed cash inflows.

2.4

However, although this is generally the case, there may be rare assets where the variability of the cash flows has the opposite effect and increases their value. This is because, according to most modern asset-pricing models, the effect of risk depends not on the variability of the cash flows of the asset in isolation but on the way in which the cash flows interact (ie their correlation) with the cash flows expected from other assets. For example, in the Capital Asset Pricing Model (CAPM) developed by Sharpe, Lintner and Treynor, the effect of risk on the value of the asset is measured by its beta, which is a measure of the correlation between the cash flows arising from the asset and the cash flows arising from a market portfolio.

2.5*

In particular, there may be assets whose cash flows tend to increase when general economic conditions cause the cash flows of other assets to decrease and vice versa. This sort of variability increases the value of the asset rather than reducing it because such assets can be used to hedge the risk associated with other assets, resulting in a portfolio with comparatively little variability of cash flows. Instead of requiring a rate of return higher than the risk-free rate to compensate for the risk, an investor will accept a lower than risk-free rate of return because of the asset's ability to hedge the risk in other assets. For example, under the CAPM, an asset whose cash flows increase when those generated by the market portfolio decrease and vice versa will have a negative beta and the rate of return required from the asset will be lower than the risk-free rate, ie the asset will have a higher value than one with cash flows that are known with certainty.

2.6

The paragraphs in small type extend the arguments in the main paragraphs in order to give the background for the Board's approach to pension liabilities. This involves a level of complexity that does not apply to most other assets and liabilities and into which some may, perhaps, not wish to delve.

2.7   The potential variability of cash flows generated by an asset and the resulting required rate of return may be caused by a number of different factors. For example, in setting an interest rate for loans to a group of debtors, an entity will consider (i) how many debtors are likely to default and by how much, and (ii) the chance that the expected default rate may turn out to be inaccurate. This is illustrated in the following example of an entity (E) pricing loans to a group of borrowers.

Risk-free rate	5 per cent
E could invest £1000 in risk-free investments and receive	£1050
E lends £1000 each to a group of borrowers	£1000
On average, 12.8 per cent of this group of borrowers default	(£128)
On average, E can expect to receive this much return of principal	£872
But E cannot be sure that only 12.8 per cent will default, so an adjustment for risk is made	(£10)
Risk-adjusted amount of principal returned	£862
In order to equal the £1050 available from a risk-free investment, E must charge an interest rate that makes the average risk-adjusted principal of £862 grow to £1050, ie	22 per cent

2.8   The cost of the advance of £1000 can be regarded as:

(i)   the promised cash flows of £1220 discounted at the promised rate of 22 per cent;

(ii)   the expected cash flows of £1063 (expected principal of £872 with interest of 22 per cent) discounted at a risk-adjusted rate of 6.3 per cent; or

(iii)   the risk-adjusted cash flows of £1050 (risk-adjusted principal of £862 with interest of 22 per cent) discounted at the risk-free rate of 5 per cent.

2.9   Often an asset will be expected to generate cash flows in more than one future period. In these cases applying a single discount rate to all the cash flows ignores the fact that the time value of money is not constant over time. This fact is reflected in the different interest rates that are available depending on the period of the loan, ie in the term structure of interest rates. In theory, different discount rates should be applied to cash flows arising in different periods, reflecting the term structure of interest rates. In practice, acceptable results may be achieved by discounting all the cash flows at a single weighted average discount rate.

Liabilities

2.10   As a mirror image of assets, liabilities with uncertain cash flows will generally be more onerous than liabilities with certain cash flows—entities that are risk-averse will tend to prefer a fixed cash outflow to a cash outflow that is of equal expected amount but may vary.

Example

Suppose a provision is expected to give rise to one of the following cash outflows in three years' time and that the risk-free rate of return is 5 per cent:

Likelihood of cash flow	Cash flow	Expected value
25 per cent	£100	£25
50 per cent	£150	£75
25 per cent	£200	£50
Total		£150

Discussion

The expected value of the cash outflow in three years' time is £150. However, there is the possibility that the cash flow will not be £150 but £100 or £200. The reporting entity is risk-averse and would settle the liability for a certain payment of, say, £160 in three years' time. We can express the effect of risk in calculating the present value by:

(a)   discounting the certainty equivalent of £160 at the risk-free rate of 5 per cent, giving a present value of £138, or

(b)   discounting the expected cash flow of £150 at a risk-adjusted rate that will give the present value of £138, ie a rate of 2.8 per cent.

2.11 In the above example, the present value of the provision is greater than the present value of a provision for a cash outflow that will, with certainty, be £150 in three years' time. (As in the assets example in paragraph 2.3, the present value of a future cash flow of £150 known with certainty is £150 discounted at the risk-free rate of 5 per cent, ie £130.) In other words, the risk-adjusted discount rate is lower than the risk-free rate. In some cases, if the variability in the cash flows is sufficiently great, the discount rate could even turn out to be a negative rate.

2.12 However, as with the hedging assets described in paragraph 2.6, where the cash flows arising from a liability match those arising from an asset, the variability of the cash flows makes the liability less rather than more onerous.

2.13 This can be illustrated by considering the two examples above and assuming that whatever determines the cash outflows of the liability also determines the cash inflows of the asset in the following way. If the cash outflow of the liability is £100 the cash inflow of the asset is also £100, if the cash outflow of the liability is £150 the cash inflow of the asset is also £150, and if the cash outflow of the liability is £200 the cash inflow of the asset is also £200. In other words, the cash flows of the asset and liability are perfectly correlated.

2.14 In this case, the asset and the liability must have the same value because the cash flows of the two together will always be nil. If, as in the example in paragraph 2.3, the value of the asset is £121 then the value of the liability must also be £121. This is lower than the value given in the provision example above because in that example it was assumed that the provision could not be matched by any asset and hence the variability of the cash flows has an adverse effect. In contrast, if the variability of the cash flows can be used to hedge the risks associated with an asset, the variability has a favourable effect leading to a lower value for the liability.

2.15 This Section has briefly illustrated the general effect of risk on assets and liabilities. What risks should be recognised and how they should be measured depend on the particular measurement basis being sought, as does the specification of the relevant cash flows. These issues are discussed in Sections 3 (assets) and 4 (liabilities).

3 Measurement of assets

3.1 Future cash flows can be used to calculate a number of different accounting measures. For assets, future cash flows are generally used either to calculate value in use or to simulate fair value. Value in use differs from fair value in that it is an entity-specific measure determined by the entity's own view of the best use of that asset. Fair value, on the other hand, is defined as the amount at which an asset or liability could be exchanged in an arm's length transaction between informed and willing parties, other than in a forced or liquidation sale. Value in use, therefore, depends on the entity's assessment of cash flows that can be generated by the asset and fair value on the market's assessment of the cash flows.

3.2 When the source of the cash flows that form the basis for the two measures has been determined, the next questions are whether and how to price the variability (risk) inherent in those cash flows. For fair value, the answer is given by its definition—fair value is a market value and, hence, the risk premium must be the price that the market places on the risk.

3.3 For value in use, unlike fair value, the appropriate risk adjustment is not prescribed by a definition. However, in order to sustain the economic rationale supporting the definition of recoverable amount as the higher of value in use and net realisable value, value in use does need to reflect some measure of risk.

3.4 Given that value in use is based on the entity's assessment of the cash flows, it might seem consistent to use the entity's view of the price of the risk, ie the risk adjustment that the entity would make in deciding to acquire those future cash flows in a current transaction for cash. However, it is the market price for risk that is relevant to shareholders. The entity can estimate its own cash flows but the value of those cash flows then depends on the market. Value in use should, therefore, reflect the market's view of risk with the result that value in use becomes the market value of the cash flows expected by the entity.

3.5 The practical techniques used to estimate future cash flows and risk adjustments will vary from one situation to another, depending on the circumstances surrounding the asset in question. Specific guidance on estimating the amount and timing of future cash flows and on determining the appropriate interest rate will be included in future FRSS as appropriate (see the illustrative notes for examples). However, certain general principles should govern any application of discounting:

(a) Count everything that is relevant to the measurement base being determined. In estimating future cash flows the question arises whether to reflect the effect of expected future events. For example, there may be a risk of default related to an asset. Although the default occurs in the future, the expectation of the default affects the value of the asset now and should be reflected either in the cash flows or in the discount rate.

(b) Do not count the same thing twice. Estimated cash flows should reflect assumptions that are consistent with the interest rate chosen to discount the cash flows. If this is not the case, the effect of some assumptions will either be double-counted or ignored. For example, an interest rate the market applies to contractual cash flows will reflect expectations about future defaults. It should not be used in discounting cash flows that themselves reflect assumptions about future defaults.

(c) Do not unbalance the measurement. Estimated cash flows and interest rates should be free from bias or assumptions designed to alter the measurement to achieve a predetermined result. Similarly, the choice of assumptions should not include factors unrelated to the asset in question.

(d) Use expected value. It is often possible to project a number of cash flow scenarios, especially if cash flows are uncertain in timing and amount. In some situations, a range of amounts might include the most likely estimate and other estimates that, while less likely, might still occur. In other cases, the amount of future cash flows might be estimated with relative precision, but with a range of estimates for the timing of those cash flows. In both these cases, the cash flow estimate for each period should reflect the expected value, ie the values of different scenarios weighted by their respective probabilities.

An illustrative note setting out how these principles apply to impaired fixed assets is given as Illustrative note A.   **3.6**

4   Measurement of liabilities

Liabilities relate to future cash flows and their measurement often reflects this fact. As with assets, the cash flows and the risk adjustment to be considered depend on the measurement basis that is being calculated.   **4.1**

For example, if the objective is to simulate fair value, the market's estimate of cash flows and assessment of risk should be estimated. In some cases (for example in valuing the entity's own debt), the market's assessment of risk will include an assessment of the entity's own credit risk. Where this is the case, simulations of fair value should also reflect it.   **4.2**

However, it is questionable whether it is always desirable to reflect in an entity's financial statements the effects of changes in the entity's own credit risk. It can be argued that the going concern assumption on which financial statements are prepared does not allow the entity to record a liability at an amount that reflects a possibility that the entity will not meet the liability in full, except where a counterparty has accepted that possibility (by agreeing terms that take it into account). The measurement basis being sought will, therefore, often be one that does not reflect changes in an entity's own credit risk, even if it is the same as fair value in all other respects. For example, the Discussion Paper 'Derivatives and other Financial Instruments' proposes that financial instruments should be measured at fair value* but excluding the effects of any changes in the entity's own credit risk.   **4.3**

The measurement basis used in the Discussion Paper 'Provisions'† also involves discounted future cash flows. The objective there is to measure the provision at an amount that represents the least cost that can be incurred by the entity in settling the provision. The entity could settle the provision by either: **4.4**

(a) paying a third party now to take over the obligation, or

(b) investing in assets that will grow (with reasonable certainty) to match the amount due and settling the provision at the due date.

Described as current value in the Discussion Paper.

†***Editor's note:*** *See now FRS 12 'Provisions, contingent liabilities and contingent assets'.*

4.5   The amount that a third party would require to take over the obligation will depend on its (ie, in general, the market's) assessment of the future cash flows and associated risk. However, in practice, there will often be no such third party and it will not be possible to estimate this amount reliably. Often, therefore, it will be necessary to consider the amount that an entity would invest to match the liability.

4.6   The amount that an entity would invest in assets now to fund the obligation will depend on its assessment of the future cash flows. In assessing the effect of the variability of these cash flows, the entity will, where possible, consider assets whose cash flows match the cash flows of the provision. As explained in Section 2, if the expected cash outflows of a provision are exactly the same in terms of amount, timing, and variability as the cash inflows of some identifiable asset or group of assets, the risk adjustment for the provision will be the same as it is for the asset, or group of assets. If there is a group of assets whose cash flows substantially match the cash flows of the provision, the risk adjustment for the group of assets may be taken as a reasonable approximation for the appropriate risk adjustment for the provision.

4.7   This is the case whether or not the entity in fact invests in such assets. Identifying such assets is enough to provide information about the effect of the variability of the liability's cash flows on its value. Just as an asset's value depends on the correlation of its cash flows with those of other assets regardless of whether the entity holds those other assets,* so the value of the liability is unaffected by whether the entity actually holds matching assets. The value of the liability will increase as the payment date comes closer and the effect of discounting unwinds. If the entity actually has invested in the matching assets, the unwinding of the discount will equal the return on the assets for the period. If the entity has invested in other assets a gain or a loss will be recorded in the period reflecting the return on the investments actually held in that period.

4.8   It will only rarely be possible to identify a matching group of assets. For most provisions this cannot be done because of the uncertainties inherent in the cash flows and the lack of experience in valuing the liabilities. In these cases, as in the example in paragraph 2.10, it is assumed that the variability of the cash flows will make the provision more onerous than one with fixed cash flows of equal expected value. A prudent estimate of expected value (ie increased to reflect the risk) should, therefore, be discounted at a risk-free rate.

4.9   Illustrative notes setting out how these principles apply to pension liabilities and environmental provisions are given as Illustrative notes B and C.

5   Inflation

5.1   Inflation affects different types of cash flows in different ways: cash flows that are fixed in monetary amounts remain constant in money (nominal) terms but fall in real terms; cash flows that are estimates of amounts of purchasing power will tend to increase in nominal terms. In both cases, the aim is to arrive at a discounted amount expressed in prices at the time the measurement is made.

5.2   This aim is achieved for cash flows that are fixed in monetary amounts by discounting at a rate that anticipates the effect of inflation (a nominal rate). It can be achieved for cash flows that are not expressed in fixed monetary terms by estimating the cash flows after making allowance for expected price increases (nominal cash flows), in which case the discount rate should also be estimated by including an element for inflation (a nominal rate). Alternatively, where an estimate of future inflation cannot be made with sufficient confidence, cash flows reflecting no inflation

---

*For example, under the CAPM (see paragraph 2.5), an asset's value depends on its beta, regardless of whether the investor holds a market portfolio.

should be discounted at a discount rate that does not include a factor for inflation (a 'real' rate). The decision whether to include or exclude inflation should be based on whether the nominal cash flows and nominal discount rate can be measured more reliably than the 'real' cash flows and 'real' discount rate.

6 Tax

In making economic decisions, entities have regard to the tax consequences of those decisions. In determining the rate of return on an asset that will compensate for the risk associated with the cash flows, the entity will consider the post-tax cash flows, ie will determine the required post-tax rate of return. **6.1**

The required pre-tax rate of return is simply the rate of return that will, after tax has been deducted, give the required post-tax rate of return. It is important to note that, because tax can vary significantly from entity to entity, the pre-tax rate of return is not always the post-tax rate of return grossed up by a standard rate of tax. The pre-tax rate of return for the entity therefore depends on the specific amount and timing of its own tax cash flows. **6.2**

Discounting post-tax cash flows at a post-tax rate of return and discounting pre-tax cash flows at a pre-tax rate of return will always give the same value (they must do so, by definition, as the pre-tax rate of return is simply the post-tax rate of return adjusted to cover the tax cash flows). This value is a post-tax figure. **6.3**

Whether it is appropriate to record the post-tax figure in the balance sheet or to separate out the tax element depends on the measurement basis being sought and the accounting treatment for tax. For example, in presenting a long-term provision, it is probably appropriate to show any tax relief available as a separate deferred tax asset. In presenting an asset at fair value, on the other hand, the fair value (which itself includes an expectation of tax) is presented as a single net figure.* Value in use is different again, in that some of the tax relates to future profits to be generated by the asset and would generally not be shown separately (like the tax inherent in fair value) but some of the tax may, because of the effect of capital allowances and depending on the method of accounting for tax, fall to be shown separately. **6.4**

7 Presentation in financial statements

When any item in the balance sheet is discounted, there will be a subsequent increase in that item as time passes and the discount unwinds. The unwinding of the discount could be shown either as part of interest or as part of the underlying cost. **7.1**

The argument for showing the unwinding of the discount as interest is that discounting is used to take account of the time value of money. Economically, the unwinding of the discount is interest and should be shown as such. **7.2**

Furthermore, including the unwinding of the discount within the operating cost distorts that cost. For example, the pension cost recorded for an unfunded scheme will be higher than that recorded for a funded scheme with exactly the same pension obligations. This does not properly reflect the fact that the pension in both cases costs the same, it is only the funding policy that is different. **7.3**

Adjusting the carrying value of an asset to fair value may, under some methods of accounting for tax, result in tax specific to the entity that is not reflected in the cash flows upon which fair value is based being shown as a separate deferred tax balance.

7.4   The unwinding of the discount gives rise to a cost every year between the date of recognition of the discounted item and the cash payments. Reporting this cost as an operating cost could be misleading. For example, to report a separate environmental clean-up cost in each of the ten years, say, between the event causing the cost and the payment for the clean-up could give the impression that new events causing environmental costs were occurring in each of these years or that the clean-up was taking ten years.

7.5   On the other hand, it could be argued that the interest line in the profit and loss account is not intended to reflect an economic cost of finance for the entity. Rather, it is intended to reflect the entity's cost of debt. The interest figure is one to which users pay particular attention because of potentially disastrous consequences for the entity if interest payments are not met. Of course, the accrual of interest on a deep discount bond has for some entities already moved the interest line in the profit and loss account away from near-cash. It may, however, be felt that to include amounts arising from all discounted items (eg pensions and other long-term provisions) would make the charge for interest even more difficult to understand.

7.6   In the light of the above considerations, separate disclosure of any non-debt component of the interest charge would appear to be necessary. With such disclosure, the case for presenting the unwinding of the discount in the interest section alongside other items arising from the same economic cause becomes more appropriate.

8   Changes in rate

8.1   After an asset or liability has been recognised in the financial statements at a discounted amount, the interest rate may change. Whether such changes should be recognised depends on the accounting objective being sought.

8.2   If the objective is to continue to record the balance sheet item at an up-to-date present value, as it is for pension provisions for example, changes in interest rate will be reflected in arriving at the current present value at the balance sheet date.

8.3   If, on the other hand, the objective is to record a discounted present value that will be treated as a historical cost, then changes in the interest rate should not be reflected. For example, under SSAP 21 'Accounting for leases and hire purchase contracts', amounts due under a finance lease are not adjusted to reflect changes in interest rates.

9   Conclusion

9.1   This Paper has shown that discounting future cash flows to reflect the time value of money and the effect of the variability of the cash flows is consistent with both historical cost and current value bases of valuation. The uncertainties and subjectivity inevitably associated with discounting future cash flows have been identified so that individual FRS projects can evaluate whether or not discounting is an appropriate technique in the particular circumstances being considered. It is hoped that the Paper will help lead to a better understanding of the role of discounting in financial reporting and will enable readers to place the Board's pronouncements on discounting in individual projects within the context of a coherent approach to the subject.

Illustrative note A: Impaired fixed assets

The Discussion Paper 'Impairment of Tangible Fixed Assets'* proposes that impaired assets should be recorded at the higher of net realisable value and value in use. This note applies to the determination of value in use for such assets. **A1**

Paragraph 3.1 of the Working Paper states that value in use should be based on the entity's assessment of cash flows and paragraph 3.4 states that the risk adjustment should be based on the market's price for risk. **A2**

ASSESSMENT OF CASH FLOWS

The entity should assess the cash flows arising from the best use of the asset, ie the use that produces the highest cash inflows. All relevant cash flows should be taken into account including an allocation of central overheads. Interest payments and other costs of capital are not included since these will be taken into account in the discount rate. **A3**

In estimating the value in use, projections of cash flows will be required for both the short and long term. In the short term, cash flow projections should be consistent with the most up-to-date budgets and plans that have been formally agreed by management. It is likely that different growth rates will be used from year to year in the short-term projections. Projected long-term cash flows should follow a steady or declining growth rate. Cash flows should always be projected using reasonable and supportable assumptions. **A4**

The Board's research indicates that detailed explicit projections are not generally available for a period of longer than five years and are frequently available for a shorter period only. The Board, therefore, does not expect that formally agreed variable growth rates will be applied to a period of longer than five years. If, for exceptional reasons, variable growth rates are applied for a longer period, there should be disclosure of the length of such longer period, the growth rate(s) used and the reason why a steady or declining growth rate is not expected to apply by the end of the five-year period. **A5**

It is also not expected that, in real terms, the steady long-term growth rate used in the cash flow forecast will exceed the long-term, say 40-year, average for the country or countries in which the business of the unit under consideration is to be conducted.† It is difficult for any industry to beat the average over the long term because market forces are likely to be such that competitors will enter the market and restrict growth where conditions are very favourable. **A6**

ASSESSMENT OF RISK ADJUSTMENT

As stated in paragraph 3.4, value in use is based on the market's assessment of the risks associated with the cash flows expected by the entity. If the risk adjustment is to be made through the discount rate, the appropriate rate will be the rate of return that the market would expect on an equally risky investment. **A7**

Estimates of this market rate may be made by a variety of means including reference to: **A8**

Editor's note: See now FRS 11 'Impairment of fixed assets and goodwill'.

†*The UK 40-year average growth in gross domestic product, expressed in real terms, is 2.5 per cent.*

(a)   the rate implicit in market transactions of similar assets;

(b)   the current weighted average cost of capital (WACC) of a listed company whose cash flows have a similar risk profile to those of the asset; or

(c)   the WACC for the entity but only if adjusted for the particular risks associated with the asset.

A9   If method (c) is used the following matters should be noted.

● For businesses where a real growth rate in excess of the long-term average for the country under consideration is forecast beyond the short term, there is likely to be higher risk and this should be taken into account by increasing the discount rate used.

● The individual discount rates applied to each income-generating unit to be tested should always be such that, were they to be calculated for every unit, the weighted average rates would equal the current overall WACC for the entity.

A10   Tax should be reflected in value in use either by discounting the pre-tax cash flows at a pre-tax discount rate or by discounting the post-tax cash flows at a post-tax discount rate. However, if a pre-tax rate is used, care should be taken to ensure that it is the entity's expected tax cash flows that are reflected in that rate, not the market's expectation of the tax that the asset will generate.

Illustrative note B: pension liabilities

Pension liabilities are a form of provision. Paragraph 4.6 states that the cash flows used in measuring provisions should be based on the entity's expectation and the risk adjustment should be based on a matching group of assets, if such assets can be identified.

B1

ASSESSMENT OF CASH FLOWS

The cash flows will be estimated by an actuary using long-term assumptions. The cost should be attributed evenly over the period that the pension benefit is earned by the employee and should reflect expected future changes in the cost of the benefit. The actuarial valuation basis that achieves this is the projected unit method.

B2

The main actuarial assumptions include:

B3

- the rate of increase in salaries
- the rate of increase in pensions in payment
- the rate of interest applied to discount liabilities
- the rate of return on investments
- the rate of increase in dividend income.

Many of these assumptions are affected by the same economic factors. Actuarial assumptions should be mutually compatible, ie they should reflect the underlying economic factors consistently. For example, the rate of increase in salaries and the rate of return on investments should be based on the same rates of price inflation and economic growth.

B4

ASSESSMENT OF RISK

Paragraph 4.6 states that one way of determining a risk-adjusted rate is to identify a group of assets whose cash flows match the amount, timing and variability of the cash flows of the liability. Where a portfolio of assets that substantially achieves this over the long term can be identified, the appropriate risk-adjusted rate for the liability should be based on the expected rate of return on that portfolio.

B5

The following guidelines specify in broad terms the nature of an appropriate portfolio of assets from which a risk-adjusted discount rate can be derived for various types of pension liability.

B6

(a) Pension liabilities of fixed amount (eg pensions currently in payment that do not include cost of living increases) are matched by fixed interest risk-free bonds.
(b) Pension liabilities of fixed amount but including cost of living increases are matched by index-linked risk-free bonds.
(c) Pension liabilities based on final salary will, based on past experience, tend to increase at a rate above general inflation. The return on equity investments also tends to increase at a rate above general inflation. This is because both final salaries and equity returns reflect real growth in the economy—real growth in both salaries and equity returns comes from the same source, increased productivity in the economy. Final salary pension liabilities are, therefore, over the long term likely to be substantially matched by a well-diversified portfolio of assets of equity investments in the economy in which the pension scheme operates.

B7   Where the portfolio of assets does not provide a perfect cash flow match for the pension liabilities, the rate of return on the assets will need to be reduced to reflect the risks in the liability not covered by the assets.

B8   The composition of an appropriate portfolio and the appropriate discount rate will be determined by the actuary. In order to ensure a reasonable level of objectivity and consistency, detailed guidance based on the above broad principles will need to be given by the actuarial profession.* The risk-adjusted discount rate derived from these appropriate portfolios of assets applies to the pension liabilities whether or not the scheme is funded. As explained in paragraph 4.7, the actual funding of the scheme does not affect the measurement of the liabilities.

The actuarial profession has developed relatively prescriptive guidance on an appropriate discount rate for the purposes of the Minimum Funding Requirement under the Pensions Act 1995 (which is aimed at ensuring that pension schemes have sufficient funds to cover members' accrued entitlements ignoring any discretionary benefits and based on current salaries). This may provide a suitable model for similar guidance on the appropriate discount rate for financial reporting purposes.

Illustrative note C: Environmental liabilities

Environmental liabilities are a form of provision. Paragraph 4.6 states that the cash C1
flows used in measuring provisions should be based on the entity's expectation and
the risk adjustment should be based on a matching group of assets, if such assets can
be identified. If no such assets can be identified, and no other way of measuring the
risk adjustment can be found, the expected value of the cash flows should be discounted at a risk-free rate.

ASSESSMENT OF CASH FLOWS

In those cases where the provision being measured involves a large population of C2
items, the entity should assess the cash flows that would arise under all possible
future outcomes associated with the provision and calculate an expected value for the
cash flows. Where the provision being measured involves a small population of items
it may not be appropriate to use expected value where this measure does not reflect
the amount the entity would have to pay to settle the obligation. In these situations
other methods of estimation such as the most likely outcome may be appropriate.

Where there is sufficient objective evidence of reasonably expected future events that C3
may affect the amount required to settle the entity's obligation, such events should be
reflected in the amount recognised. For example, it would be appropriate to include
in a provision the expected cost reductions associated with increased experience in
applying existing technology or, as another example, the expected cost of applying
existing technology to a larger or more complex clean-up operation than has previously been carried out. However, the development of a major new technology
should not be anticipated.

As regards possible new legislation, the variety of circumstances that arise in practice C4
makes it impossible to specify a single event that will provide sufficient, objective
evidence in every case. For the effects of new legislation to be recognised, evidence is
required both of what the legislation will demand and of whether it will be enacted
and implemented in due course. In some cases sufficient objective evidence will not
exist until the new legislation is enacted: in other cases there may be sufficient
objective evidence before enactment.

ASSESSMENT OF RISK

Paragraph 4.6 notes that if there is a group of assets whose cash flows substantially C5
match the cash flows of the provision, the risk adjustment for the group of assets may
be taken as a reasonable approximation for the appropriate risk adjustment for the
provision.

However, for environmental provisions, it is most unlikely that such a group of C6
assets can be identified. Unlike pension provisions, where there is a strong economic
case for there being a link between certain assets and pension liabilities and long
funding experience on which to draw, the ultimate cost of environmental provisions
is very much more uncertain. Even if a fund were set up, there would be no certainty
that the amount set aside was sufficient. There is no evidence to indicate that the
uncertainty of the cash flows can be matched and hence no reason to believe that the
uncertainty makes the liability less onerous.

In line with paragraph 4.8, it is assumed, therefore, that the effect of the uncertainty C7
of the cash flows makes the provision more onerous than a provision with equal
expected value where the cash flows are fixed. A prudent estimate, ie increased to

reflect risk, of the expected value should, therefore, be discounted at the current risk-free rate. Where the amount being discounted is not expected value because there is only a small population of outcomes (see paragraph C2), this amount should also, if necessary, be adjusted for risk before being discounted at the current risk-free rate.

C8   Section 6 explains that any tax relief available on the costs to be incurred is reflected in the measurement of the provision either by discounting the pre-tax cash flows at a pre-tax discount rate or by discounting the post-tax cash flows at a post-tax discount rate. For environmental liabilities in the UK, the risk-free discount rate will be given by the rate of return on a government bond. Even if the tax rate is the same, the tax payable on interest on a government bond is different from the tax relief available on an environmental liability—the tax relief is available on the full amount of the provision whereas the tax payable is based only on the interest. This means that the pre-tax rate of return on the government bond is not a suitable discount rate for the pre-tax cash flows of the environmental liability. The post-tax cash flows should, therefore, be discounted at a post-tax discount rate, as illustrated in the example below.

Example

Assumptions

The expected cash flow of an environmental liability will be a cash outflow of £100 in ten years' time on which tax relief of 30 per cent will be available. The rate of return on a 10-year government bond which makes a single payment of capital and interest in ten years' time is equivalent to an annual rate of 6 per cent. Tax of 30 per cent is payable on the interest. This gives a post-tax rate of return on the government bond of 4.5 per cent.*

Discussion

In order to meet the liability when it falls due, the entity must invest sufficient to produce cash inflows after tax that will cover the post-tax cash outflows ie £70. To produce £70 post-tax in ten years' time, £45 needs to be invested now in government bonds.

Government bond cash flows in 10 years' time	Calculation	Cash flows
Pre-tax cash flow	£45 x 1.06*	£81
Tax	(£81-£45) x 0.3	£11
Post-tax cash flow		£70

The post-tax rate is higher than 70 per cent of 6 per cent because the tax is not paid until year 10 but the effective yield is based on interest income accruing evenly over the ten-year period.

To achieve post-tax cash flows of £70 from the government bond it necessary to invest only £45. This value can be arrived at by discounting the post-tax cash flows of the provision (£70) at the post-tax rate of return (4.5 per cent). Discounting the pre-tax cash flows of the provision of £100 at the pre-tax rate of 6 per cent would give too high a cost (£56). However, £45 is the net-of-tax figure and in the balance sheet the tax should be shown separately. Under SSAP 15,* tax is recognised on timing differences. Splitting the post-tax value into a liability and a tax balance so that the timing difference created by the liability equals the tax balance gives a liability of £64 and a deferred tax asset of £19—in other words, the net figure of £45 is grossed up by the tax rate applying to the liability of 30 per cent.

Editor's note: SSAP 15 *has now been superseded by* FRS 19 *'Deferred tax'.*

Leases: Implementation of a new approach

(Issued December 1999)

Contents

Leases: implementation of a new approach

Foreword by the Accounting Standards Board

This Discussion Paper presents a Position Paper that has been developed by the G4+1 group of accounting standard-setters. It reflects an agreed approach to the treatment in financial reporting of leases, which differs in fundamental respects from that which is required by the present standards of members of the G4+1. Each body represented in the G4+1 will consider, in the light of comments received in response to the Position Paper, whether, and if so how, the Paper's proposals should be modified in the development of accounting standards for each jurisdiction.

The views expressed in the Paper are primarily those of the Group of members of the G4+1, rather than those of the Accounting Standards Board, as the Board takes the view that the prospect of harmonised accounting standards is greatest if each member of the G4+1 issues identical proposals at this early stage in the project. Whilst the Board does not agree with the Group's views on every point, it does agree that a powerful case for change is made in the Paper, and that the approach that it sets out merits serious consideration as a basis for new accounting standards.

In particular, the Board agrees that the arbitary distinction between operating and finance leases that is required by present standards is unsatisfactory, and that the comparability (and hence usefulness) of financial statements would be enhanced if existing standards were replaced by an approach that applied the same requirements to all leases. It is particularly persuasive, in the Board's view, to note the common and growing practice of analysts of recasting financial statements on a basis that is similar to that which is proposed.

There are certain issues that are likely to be regarded as particularly significant in the UK, and these are discussed below.

In the UK, unlike other countries represented in the G4+1, buildings are often held on very long leases (25 years or more). This makes the Group's recommendation that lessees should account for leases of land and buildings under the requirements of new accounting standards especially important: the Board supports this conclusion. Another feature of UK property leases is that they often provide that the rent is to be reviewed and increased to prevailing market levels at intervals during the lease: generally there is no provision for the rent to be reduced in the event of a decline in market rentals. The Group's view as reflected in this Paper is that where leases require that the rentals are to be adjusted to reflect price changes, those price changes should be reflected in the amount of assets and liabilities recorded at the inception of the lease. The Board, however, is concerned that it will often not be possible to make reliable estimates of the effect of such increases. Furthermore, owing to the volatility of the UK property market, it will often be the case that an increase that is anticipated in one period will reverse in another. For these reasons, the Board prefers the alternative view set out in the Paper, under which only the existing rentals would be recorded as assets and liabilities. Under such an approach, adjustments would be required only at the time of rent reviews.

The UK is also one of the jurisdictions in which investment properties are stated at fair value, in accordance with the requirements of ssap 19 'Accounting for investment properties' (which uses the term 'open market value'). The Board agrees with the view set out in this Paper that, in any revision to accounting standards on leases, the information on current values that is given at present should be preserved.

The method by which lessors should recognise income from leases is not central to the main proposals discussed in the body of the Paper. Appendix 2 discusses the arguments for and against the main types of methods that are used—net investment and net cash investment. At present, under SSAP 21 'Accounting for leases and hire purchase contracts', the net cash investment method is required (although in practice, for many leases, the net investment method may be used on the grounds that it results in amounts that are not materially different from those that would be provided by a net cash investment method). The Board's view is that the net cash investment method should continue to be required as it more faithfully reflects the economic realities of leases. An issue that the Board may address in due course is whether accounting standards should specify in more detail the application of lessor income recognition under a net cash investment approach.

The issues on which views are specifically requested are set out on after the summary. In addition, the Board would be grateful for comments on any of the issues discussed above.

G4 + 1 Position Paper

LEASES: IMPLEMENTATION OF A NEW APPROACH

Australian Accounting Standards Board
Canadian Accounting Standards Board
International Accounting Standards Committee
New Zealand Financial Reporting Standards Board
United Kingdom Accounting Standards Board
United States Financial Accounting Standards Board

Preface

This Position Paper results from the efforts of a Working Group consisting of board members and senior staff members of the standard-setting bodies of Australia, Canada, New Zealand, the UK and the USA, and staff of the International Accounting Standards Committee (IASC). Whilst members of the Working Group represented the standard-setting bodies to which they were affiliated, the views they expressed were their own and had not necessarily been officially deliberated by the bodies themselves.

Accounting for leases was the subject of a previous G4+1 Special Report.* Whilst that Special Report was concerned mainly with the conceptual foundation for revised standards on lease accounting, this Position Paper presents proposals for how that approach might be reflected in accounting standards. Each standard-setter represented in the G4+1 will consider, in the light of comments received in response to the Position Paper, whether, and if so how, the Paper's proposals should be modified in the development of accounting standards for each jurisdiction. G4+1 members will continue to co-operate over future developments so as to ensure that resulting accounting standards in each jurisdiction are as similar as possible.

The Position Paper also deals more extensively with lessor accounting than the Special Report.

The principal authors are Hans Nailor, a project director with the UK Accounting Standards Board on secondment from PricewaterhouseCoopers in London, and Andrew Lennard, Assistant Technical Director of the UK Accounting Standards Board. A significant contribution was made by Clark Anstis, Senior Project Director - Accounting with the Australian Accounting Research Foundation, especially during his period of secondment to the UK Accounting Standards Board. Other staff members of G4+1 organisations also assisted in the preparation of the Position Paper.

---

*'Accounting for Leases: A New Approach—Recognition by Lessees of Assets and Liabilities Arising under Lease Contracts' (1996), by Warren McGregor.

G4 + 1 Memorandum of understanding on objectives (revised March 1999)

SHARED OBJECTIVES OF MEMBER ORGANISATIONS

G4 + 1 organisations share an objective of providing quality financial reporting standards for the primary purpose of providing information useful to capital market participants.

G4 + 1 organisations share an objective of seeking common solutions to financial reporting issues. A single, quality financial reporting approach is more useful to capital market participants than multiple approaches.

G4 + 1 organisations share the view that financial reporting standards should be based on a conceptual framework. It follows that membership of the Group requires acceptance of a conceptual framework similar to that of other members.

G4 + 1 organisations share the view that seeking common solutions to financial reporting issues requires members to have the willingness and ability to commit resources to the resolution of those issues within the context of a conceptual framework.

G4 + 1 OBJECTIVES

G4 + 1 organisations seek to further their shared objectives through analyses and discussions of financial reporting issues. Those analyses and discussions help participants from member organisations develop a common understanding of the issues, a common language and tools for discussing and analysing the issues, and an understanding of the views and constraints in each others' jurisdictions.

G4 + 1 organisations seek to learn more about the timing and approach of standard-setting agenda projects in other jurisdictions. That knowledge can help them identify and take advantage of opportunities to coordinate their efforts and thereby further their shared objectives.

G4 + 1 organisations seek to further their shared objectives by exchanging new ideas and approaches to financial reporting issues and standard-setting processes that can be applied in their own jurisdictions.

G4 + 1 organisations seek to further their shared objectives by pursuing projects that have the potential to bring about convergence of financial reporting standards across member jurisdictions at a high level of quality.

Summary

This Position Paper has been developed by the G4 + 1 group of accounting standard-setters. It reflects an agreed approach to the treatment in financial reporting of leases, which differs in fundamental respects from that which is required by the present standards of members of the G4 + 1. Each body represented in the G4 + 1 will consider, in the light of comments received in response to the Position Paper, whether, and if so how, the Paper's proposals should be modified in the development of accounting standards for each jurisdiction.

This summary provides an overview of the most significant proposals made in the Paper. The Paper also considers several less pervasive issues, its recommendations on which are not summarised here.

A G4+1 Special Report on lease accounting, 'Accounting for Leases: A New Approach—Recognition by Lessees of Assets and Liabilities Arising under Lease Contracts' (1996), examined the deficiencies in existing national and international accounting standards on leasing and explored a conceptual approach to accounting for leases based on the financial reporting principles adopted by the standard-setting bodies represented in the G4+1. That report, which focused mainly on lessee accounting, concluded that the distinction between operating leases and finance leases that is required by present standards is arbitrary and unsatisfactory. The main deficiency of these standards noted in the report is that they do not provide for the recognition in lessees' balance sheets of material assets and liabilities arising from operating leases. The report suggested that the comparability (and hence usefulness) of financial statements would be enhanced if the differing treatments of operating leases and finance leases were replaced by an approach that applied the same requirements for all leases.

This Position Paper explores further the principles that should determine the extent of the assets and liabilities that lessees and lessors would recognise under leases, and how they might be applied to account for many of the features that are found in lease contracts.

The recommendations in the 1996 report were criticised by some who believed that if the new approach were applied to leases, it should also be applied to all 'executory contracts'—in their view, unfulfilled contracts such as purchase commitments should also result in separate assets and liabilities being recognised by the buyer if the principles being proposed for leasing transactions were applied to transactions generally. The Position Paper addresses this issue (in Part I) and concludes that leases can be distinguished from executory contracts by the fact that leases cease to be executory when the lessor has provided the lessee with access to the leased property for the lease term. The proposals would, therefore, not apply to executory contracts, including take-or-pay contracts or service contracts.

Part II of this Paper discusses accounting by lessees. It proposes that the objective should be to record, at the beginning of the lease term, the fair value of the rights and obligations that are conveyed by the lease. Fair value is measured by the fair value of the consideration given by the lessee, including the liabilities incurred, except where the fair value of the asset received is more clearly evident.

The following table provides an overview of the items that would be included in the liabilities of a lessee (and reported as such, with an asset at the beginning of the lease of a corresponding amount) and those that would not.

Items included in initial assets and liabilities	Items excluded from initial assets and liabilities
Minimum payments required by lease	
Amounts payable in respect of obtaining renewal options	Rentals relating to optional renewal periods
Contingent rentals that represent consideration for the fair value of rights conveyed to lessee	Contingent rentals relating to optional additional usage
Fair value of residual value guarantees	Residual values guaranteed where transfer of economic benefits in settlement is not probable

The Paper notes, and invites comments on, alternative views for certain of the above items.

Leases that are at present characterised as operating leases (and therefore not included on the balance sheet) would give rise to assets and liabilities—but only to the extent of the fair values of the rights and obligations that are conveyed by the lease.

The general effect of the approach proposed is that the amounts recognised as an asset and a liability by a lessee in respect of a lease of a given item would vary in amount depending on the nature of the lease. The financial statements would thus reflect the extent to which different leasing arrangements result in financial obligations and provide financial flexibility.

The Paper also proposes significant changes to lessor accounting practices. These are discussed in Part III. Lessors would report financial assets (representing amounts receivable from the lessee) and residual interests as separate assets. In the Group's view, this would be a marked improvement in lessor accounting, because a lessor's investment in a leased asset has two distinct elements, receivables and residual interests, which are subject to quite different risks.

The amounts reported as financial assets by lessors would, in general, be the converse of the amounts reported by lessees as liabilities.

The Paper has been written principally in the context of a system of accounting that is primarily based on historical cost. Members of the G4+1 are contributing to the work of the Financial Instruments Joint Working Group of standard-setters, which is working to develop a comprehensive and internationally harmonised approach to accounting for financial instruments, under which financial instruments would be reported in the balance sheet at fair value. By setting out the proposals primarily in the context of historical cost, it is hoped that the Paper will enable the merits of the proposed approach to lease accounting to be considered independently of the case for reporting financial instruments at fair value. However, in those jurisdictions where investment properties are reported by lessors under existing practices at fair value, the Paper recognises that the relevance of fair values is widely accepted; consequently, in any revision to accounting standards on leasing, it proposes that requirements for fair value information should be preserved.

INVITATION TO COMMENT AND QUESTIONS FOR RESPONDENTS

The G4+1 welcomes comments on any aspect of the Position Paper. Respondents' views are especially sought on the matters set out below. It would be helpful if respondents could support their views with reasons and, where applicable, preferred alternatives.

Part I—Introduction and scope

Q1   Chapter 1 sets out the deficiencies of existing accounting standards for leases and the problems associated with an arbitrary distinction between different types of leases. Do you agree that standard-setters should aim to develop a single accounting method that can be applied to leases of all kinds?

Q2   Chapter 2 discusses the scope of any revised accounting standards for leases. It distinguishes contracts that would fall within the scope of leases and other contracts, in particular executory contracts, that would not.

   (a)   Do you agree that the distinction has been made appropriately in Chapter 2? If not, what other factors do you think are particularly relevant?

   (b)   Do you agree that leases of intangible assets (including agreements to explore for or use natural resources) should not in principle be excluded from the scope of revised standards?

   What practical problems might arise if the proposals were applied to leases of intangible assets?

   (c)   Do you agree that no specific exemption should be proposed for short leases and that reliance should instead be placed on the principle of materiality?

Q3   Do you agree that leases of land and buildings, as accounted for by lessees, should not be excluded from the scope of revised standards (see Chapter 13)?

Part II—Lessee accounting

Q4   Do you agree with the Group's recommendations related to lessee accounting in Chapter 3 that:

   (a)   assets and liabilities should be recognised by a lessee in relation to the rights and obligations conveyed by a lease when the lessor has substantially performed its obligation to provide the lessee with access to the leased property for the lease term?

   (b)   the objective should be to record, at the beginning of the lease term, the fair value of the rights and obligations that are conveyed by the lease?

   (c)   the fair value of the rights obtained by a lessee cannot be less than the present value of the minimum payments required by the lease (assuming that the lease is negotiated on an arm's length basis)?

Q5   Chapter 4 discusses the treatment of optional features of leases and contingent rentals. It proposes that the rights that are reflected in the initial lease asset (and liability) that is recorded by the lessee will comprise the rights to use the property and also options, for example to extend the lease, to purchase additional usage of the property in exchange for usage-related rentals, or to purchase the property itself (in those cases where such options can be measured reliably).

(a) Do you agree with the proposal that leases containing lessee options to renew or cancel leases should not be accounted for on the basis that renewal options will be exercised, even if that is thought to be the probable outcome?

(b) Do you agree that, except in those circumstances where it can be demonstrated that an option has significant value (and assuming its value can be ascertained with sufficient reliability), the payments required by the lease should be deemed to relate to the right to use the property for the lease term?

Q6 Chapter 4 discusses (paragraphs 65–77) the treatment of contingent rentals that are a proportion of the lessee's revenues or profits derived from the leased property.

The Group's view as reflected in the Paper is that if the minimum payments required by the lease are clearly unrepresentative of the value of the property rights conveyed by the lease, assets and liabilities of a greater amount, reflecting the fair value of such rights, should be recognised. The fair value of the property rights conveyed by a lease might be determined by having regard to the payments required by a similar lease that had no provision for contingent rentals.

An alternative view is that the initial asset and liability should reflect only the present value of the minimum payments required by the lease.

Which of the two approaches do you support, and why?

Q7 Chapter 4 discusses (paragraphs 78–88) the treatment of contingent rentals that vary in line with prices.

The Group's view as reflected in the Paper is that estimates of future price changes should be reflected in the amount of assets and liabilities recorded at the beginning of the lease.

An alternative view is that only the existing level of rentals should be reflected in the amount of assets and liabilities recorded at the beginning of the lease.

Which of the two views do you support, and why?

Q8 Chapter 5 discusses various arrangements where the lessee has rights and obligations relating to the residual value of the leased asset, such as those arising from a residual value guarantee.

The Group's view as reflected in the Paper is that an asset and liability should be recognised at the beginning of the lease term measured at the present value of the payments the lessee is required to make during the lease term and the fair value of guarantees or other residual value agreements (if it is practical to quantify them).

An alternative view is that in circumstances where in substance the lessee has exposure to risk on substantially all of the property's value, it should record an asset and liability at the beginning of the lease reflecting the full fair value of the property, regardless of the cash flows that are specified in the lease contract. (Those who hold this view believe that Examples 4 and 5 in Chapter 5 are economically similar and therefore the accounting treatment should be similar.)

Which of the two views do you support? If you support the alternative view, how would you define the circumstances in which gross asset and liability amounts should be reported?

Q9   Chapter 5 (paragraphs 35–39) also discusses the accounting treatment of subsequent changes in the value of the lessee's obligations in relation to residual value guarantees.

The Group's preferred view is that the carrying amount of both the lease liability and the lease asset should be increased or decreased (subject to the carrying amount of the asset not being increased above a value that would cause an impairment write-off), and that the asset's revised carrying amount should be depreciated over the remainder of the lease term.

An alternative view is that the difference between the remeasured liability and its previous carrying amount should be recognised immediately as a loss or gain in income.

Which of the two treatments do you support?

Q10   Chapter 5 (paragraphs 61–66) discusses the accounting where a renewal option is accompanied by a residual value guarantee. The Group's view as reflected in the Paper is that the concurrent existence of these two features in a lease should not give rise to the recognition of additional assets and liabilities (ie by anticipating the exercise of renewal options). An alternative view is that additional assets and liabilities should be recognised. What is your view?

Q11   Do you agree with the recommendation in Chapter 6 relating to the discount rate that should be applied to the rental payments?

Q12   Chapter 7 discusses two approaches to accounting for sale and leaseback transactions. Do you agree with the Group's view as reflected in the Paper that a sale and leaseback should be accounted for as one transaction, with any gain restricted to that which relates to the rights that have not been retained by the lessee?

Part III—Lessor accounting

Q13   Do you agree with the general principle (Chapter 8) that a gain should be recognised at the beginning of the lease term if (a) there is evidence that the value of the lessor's assets (less its liabilities) has increased as a result of its performance in entering into the lease contract, and (b) the increase can be measured reliably?

Q14   Do you believe that accounting standards should specifically restrict the recognition of a gain by a lessor at the beginning of a lease to the two circumstances described in paragraph 18 of Chapter 8?

Q15   Do you have any comments on the recommendations in Chapter 9 relating to disclosure of separate components of the lessor's assets?

Q16   What practical problems, if any, do you foresee with the recommendations in Chapter 10 relating to the initial measurement of receivable and residual interest assets?

Q17   Chapter 11 discusses the treatment of optional features of leases and contingent rentals from the lessor's perspective. The Group's view is that it should be presumed that if a lease contract gives rise to a liability for the lessee (as discussed in Chapter 4) it will give rise to a corresponding receivable asset for the lessor.

(a)   Where contingent rentals are a proportion of the lessee's revenues or profits derived from the leased property, the Group's view as reflected in the Paper is that if the minimum payments required by the lease are clearly unrepresentative of the value of the property rights conveyed by the lease, the lessor's initial receivable asset (corresponding to the asset and liability that is recognised by the lessee) should be a greater amount, reflecting the fair value of such rights.

An alternative view (corresponding to the alternative view of the appropriate lessee accounting noted in Question 6) is that the lessor should recognise a receivable asset of only the present value of the minimum payments required by the lease.

Which of the alternative approaches do you support, and why?

(b)   Where contingent rentals vary in line with prices, the Group's view as reflected in the Paper is that estimates of future price changes should be reflected in the receivable asset recognised by the lessor.

An alternative view (corresponding to the alternative view of the appropriate lessee accounting noted in Question 7) is that only the existing level of rentals should be reflected in the receivable asset that is recognised by the lessor at the beginning of the lease.

Which of the alternative approaches do you support, and why?

Q18   Chapter 12 discusses three alternative views on how a lessor's residual interest asset should be measured and accounted for during the lease term. Do you agree with the Group's view as reflected in the Paper that the initial carrying amount (measured at the present value of the estimated residual value at the end of the lease) should be accreted over the lease term by 'unwinding' the discount?

Part IV—Other issues

Q19   Do you agree with the recommendation in Chapter 13 that lessors of land and buildings should report as separate assets in their balance sheets the amount of their investment that represents lease receivables, and that which represents their interest in the residual value of the property, and that the finance income for the lease receivables and changes in the interest in the residual value should be reported separately? If not, what alternative treatment would you favour and why?

Do you agree that information on fair values should be preserved?

Part I Introduction and scope

Chapter 1 Introduction

EXISTING ACCOUNTING STANDARDS ON LEASES

1.1   At present, accounting standards on accounting for leases draw a fundamental distinction between finance leases* and operating leases. They require leases that transfer to the lessee substantially all the risks and rewards of ownership of an item of leased property, plant or equipment (ie finance leases) to be accounted for as the acquisition of an asset and the incurrence of a matching liability by the lessee. From the perspective of the lessor, such leases are accounted for as a sale or financing of the asset under lease. Hence the accounting for finance leases is usually characterised as being in substance similar to the purchase by the lessee of the leased item, with the price payable in instalments, finance being provided by the lessor. Accordingly, a lessee's expenses under a finance lease are reflected as depreciation and finance costs. The whole of the lessor's investment in a finance lease is treated as a receivable, due in instalments.

1.2   Leases that do not transfer substantially all the risks and rewards of ownership to the lessee are classified as operating leases. Under an operating lease the whole of the leased item is treated as an asset of the lessor. Accordingly, the whole of the lessor's investment in the lease is shown as a non-financial, fixed (ie long-term) asset and no asset or liability (other than any prepaid or accrued lease payments) is recognised by the lessee. The methods and classification of income and expense recognition are also quite different. From the lessee's standpoint, operating leases are in effect treated as service contracts, with the lease payments being charged as expenses over the term of the lease.

1.3   Under this 'substantially all risks and rewards' approach, two leasing transactions will be accounted for very differently in financial statements if one is classified as a finance lease and the other as an operating lease, even if the two leases are economically very similar. With a finance lease, the lessee recognises on its balance sheet the whole asset (equivalent to 'quasi-ownership' of the leased property) and a matching liability to the lessor; with an operating lease, the lessor recognises the whole asset and the lessee recognises no asset or liability. There is no room for recognition of the transfer from lessors to lessees of partial interests in leased assets.

G4+1 SPECIAL REPORT 1996

1.4   A G4+1 Special Report on lease accounting, 'Accounting for Leases: A New Approach' (1996), examined the deficiencies in existing national and international leasing standards and explored a conceptual approach to lease accounting based on the financial reporting principles adopted by the standard-setting bodies dhrepresented in the G4+1.

1.5   The report, which focused mainly on lessee accounting, concluded that existing lease accounting standards were unsatisfactory, the major deficiency being that they do not provide for the recognition in lessees' balance sheets of material assets and liabilities arising from operating leases. In addition, the 'all or nothing' nature of the approach taken in these standards is arbitrary: for example, if the 90 per cent threshold referred to in some standards is applied literally, a lessee records all (or nearly all) of the asset if 91 per cent of its value is transferred by the lease and none if

---

This Paper uses the terminology established in the UK and International Accounting Standards. In Canada and the USA 'finance leases' are referred to as 'capital leases' and 'sales type leases'.

89 per cent of its value is transferred. As a result, transactions that are substantially similar are accounted for in very different ways.

Application of the existing model also requires judgements—sometimes difficult and subjective—in distinguishing between finance leases and operating leases. Further-more, the standards are sometimes circumvented by transactions being structured so as marginally to meet the conditions for classification as an operating lease: such practices are a natural consequence of standards that draw a bright line between similar transactions and produce such different results. **1.6**

The report considered leases in the context of the definitions of assets and liabilities in the conceptual frameworks of each of the standard-setting bodies represented in the G4+1. It concluded that the rights conveyed by leases (to use an item of property* for a period of time) may give rise to assets of both the lessee and the lessor and that, conceptually, there is no need to resort to an analogy with a purchase or de facto ownership to identify the assets and liabilities that arise from lease contracts. Similarly, the obligations created by lease contracts (to pay for the rights obtained) may give rise to liabilities for the lessee, again without the need to resort to an analogy with a purchase or de facto ownership. Thus a lease, by transferring the right to use an item for the lease term (which may be only part of the item's useful economic life), may give rise to the acquisition of an asset and the incurrence of a liability by the lessee which should be recognised in its financial statements, regardless of whether the lease transfers substantially all the risks and rewards of ownership of that item to the lessee. **1.7**

The new approach† that was recommended in the report may be described as an 'asset and liability' approach to lease accounting, based on reflecting the assets and liabilities that arise for lessees and lessors under lease contracts, in contrast to the 'substantially all risks and rewards' approach that underlies existing standards. Under the new approach, all material leases would be accounted for using the principles established in existing standards for the recognition of assets and liabilities arising under finance leases. The report noted, however, that significant issues would have to be resolved for the approach it advocated to be developed into effective standards. **1.8**

The following chapters of this Paper develop the approach and explore how many of the issues that arise might be addressed in new accounting standards. An intro-ductory overview of the approach is given below. **1.9**

APPROACH CONSIDERED IN THIS POSITION PAPER

This Paper explores further the principles outlined in the 1996 report as a basis for developing new lease accounting standards. The approach considered would replace the finance versus operating lease classification with an approach that in the Group's view more faithfully reflects the differences in the economic resources controlled by **1.10**

---

*To simplify the language in this Paper, the word 'property' is used in a general sense in place of the more specific phrase 'property, plant and equipment'.

†Although described as a new approach, the idea is not new. For example, the Basis for Conclusions published with the US accounting standard FAS 13 'Accounting for Leases' (1976) states: "Some members of the Board who support this Statement hold the view that, regardless of whether substantially all the benefits and risks of ownership are transferred, a lease, in transferring for its term the right to use property, gives rise to the acquisition of an asset and the incurrence of an obligation by the lessee which should be reflected in his financial statements. Those members nonetheless support this Statement because, to them, (i) it clarifies and improves the guidelines for implementing the conceptual basis previously underlying accounting for leases and (ii) it repre-sents an advance in extending the recognition of the essential nature of leases." (paragraph 63).

lessees and lessors and in the obligations incurred by lessees across the whole spectrum of different types of lease contracts.

1.11 The Group is guided in its assessment of the relative merits of alternative approaches to lease accounting by the principles for financial reporting adopted by the G4+1 member organisations. These principles specify the objectives of financial statements as being to provide information that is useful to investors and others who use financial statements as an input to economic decisions. Such users require information on an entity's financial position and financial performance that is useful for assessing its financial adaptability and its ability to generate cash. An entity's financial position encompasses the economic resources it controls, its financial structure, its liquidity and solvency, and its capacity to adapt to changes in the environment in which it operates. Financial performance comprises the return an entity obtains on the resources it controls, the components of that return and the characteristics of those components. Comparability is one of the qualities that make financial information useful.

1.12 Under these principles of financial reporting, an asset is defined in terms of a resource or right from which future economic benefits are expected to be obtained, rather than an item of property itself.* Liabilities are defined in terms of obligations to transfer economic benefits. Applying these definitions to the rights and obligations that are conveyed by a lease leads to the conclusion that all leases provide lessees with assets—the rights to use the property for the term of the lease—and liabilities— the obligation to make the payments required by the lease (except in the unusual case when the entire rent is paid in advance). For many leases, the proposals in this Position Paper would not result in the full value of the leased item being reflected in the lessee's financial statements; instead, those financial statements would reflect the economic resources the lessee controls (for example, the right to use a leased item for only part of its useful economic life) and the related financing obligations.

1.13 The nature of assets that arise under leases is different from those that are obtained by ownership. An owner of property is typically free to use it in any way he wishes and may sell, pledge or dispose of it. In contrast, a lessee can use the leased property only in the ways permitted by the lease contract, and usually has no rights to pledge or dispose of it. Nonetheless, the right granted by the lease to use the property is a source of economic benefits controlled by the lessee and, as such, is an asset.

1.14 Some have suggested that the practical problems associated with the 'risks and rewards' methodology could be remedied by revisiting the classification criteria in existing accounting standards: for example, by including more emphasis on qualitative tests or lowering the threshold criteria at which leases are deemed to be finance leases. The Group does not recommend such an approach. First, any 'all or nothing' approach that relies on seeking to define (or redefine) dividing lines, such as the economic ownership analogy that underlies the capitalisation of finance leases in existing standards, is likely to create arbitrary distinctions and result in similar transactions being accounted for differently. Second, the 'substantially all risks and rewards' model is inconsistent with the concepts that underlie the development of modern accounting standards because material assets and liabilities are omitted.

1.15 The approach being explored by the Group recognises that leasing is different from and generally more flexible than other forms of asset financing—leases can be drawn up with terms that share asset risks and economic benefits between parties in any number of ways. It focuses on identifying the assets and liabilities that arise under a

---

The wording of the definitions adopted by the standard-setting bodies differs, but the concepts are essentially the same. The various definitions of assets and liabilities are reproduced in Appendix 1.

lease contract by applying principles that can be applied consistently to all types of leases without the need for artificial thresholds, thereby reducing the number and significance of subjective judgements that are necessary. Under this approach, different lease contracts would result in different amounts of assets and liabilities being recognised by lessees to reflect the differences in the rights acquired and obligations incurred; but similar amounts would be reported in respect of similar leases.

This approach would also involve significant changes to lessor accounting practices. **1.16** Lessors would report financial assets (representing amounts receivable from the lessee) and residual interests as separate assets. In the Group's view, this would be a marked improvement in lessor accounting, because a lessor's investment in a leased asset has two distinct elements, receivables and residual interests, which are subject to quite different risks.

The Group's view is that this approach would improve financial reporting. Marginal **1.17** differences in leasing structures and in their interpretation for accounting purposes would no longer result in major differences in the reporting of financial position and financial performance for lessors and lessees and in related financial position and performance indicators such as gearing, asset-based measures of performance (eg return on assets employed), and interest cover. Reflecting the spectrum of lessee and lessor interests under all leases would therefore make the accounting treatment more transparent and improve comparability.

For some time, support has been expressed for the capitalisation of operating leases, **1.18** in addition to finance leases. Support has come from practitioners, analysts and academics, who have struggled to cope with lease classification issues and concluded that to distinguish operating from finance leases is unhelpful as it obscures economic reality. Constructive capitalisation of operating leases (ie calculating the assets and liabilities implicit in the terms of such leases) by investment analysts and other users such as credit rating agencies appears to be commonplace, suggesting that the present accounting treatment of operating leases is not the most relevant of the choices available. If operating lease capitalisation is warranted for financial statement analysis, then capitalisation by financial statement preparers should be preferred to constructive capitalisation by financial statement users. This is because users can only estimate (with limited accuracy) information held by preparers in calculating the balance sheet and profit and loss effects of operating leases.

Capitalisation of operating leases by preparers clearly would give better information. **1.19** It would also reduce costs, because the necessary calculations (which are indeed already carried out by some large companies) need be made only once, by the company in question, rather than each analyst having to prepare his or her own calculations.

This Paper addresses the principles that should determine the assets and liabilities **1.20** that lessees and lessors would recognise under leases. The issues discussed include the effects of various types of residual value arrangements, contingent rentals, options to cancel or renew leases and sale and leaseback transactions. Presentation and income recognition issues in lessor accounting are also considered.

The recommendations in the 1996 Special Report were criticised by some who **1.21** believed that if the new approach were applied to leases, it should also be applied to all 'executory contracts'—in their view, unfulfilled contracts such as purchase commitments should also result in separate assets and liabilities being recognised by the buyer if the principles being proposed for leasing transactions were applied to transactions generally. Some who hold that view also believe that it would be unfair to treat leases differently from executory contracts. This issue is discussed in Chapter 2.

1.22   This Paper has been written principally in the context of a historical cost model of lease accounting and accounting for financial instruments. Members of the G4+1 are contributing to the work of the Financial Instruments Joint Working Group of standard-setters,* which is working to develop a comprehensive and internationally harmonised approach to accounting for financial instruments, under which financial instruments would be reported in the balance sheet at fair value. It is hoped that, by setting out the proposals primarily in the context of historical cost, the Paper will enable the merits of the proposed approach to lease accounting to be considered independently of the case for reporting financial instruments at fair value. A tentative overview of some of the issues that would need to be addressed in developing the proposed lease accounting model a stage further to encompass fair value accounting for the financial assets and liabilities that arise from lease contracts is given in Chapter 14.

Chapter 2 Scope of any revised accounting standards

INTRODUCTION

2.1   This Paper advocates an approach that would require the recognition of all assets and liabilities arising under lease contracts. Whilst it would be possible to define the scope of the project as simply being that of leases, and thus exclude other kinds of contracts, such an approach could be criticised as being arbitrary. Some argue that if revised accounting standards were to require assets and liabilities to be recognised for all leases, other contracts should be treated in a similar way. For example, they might argue that forward contracts for the purchase of currency or commodities gave rise to assets and liabilities to receive and pay the contracted amounts, and that an asset and corresponding liability equal to the value of a building would arise even though all that had occurred was the signing of a construction contract.

2.2   This chapter considers issues regarding the scope of any standards on lease accounting that may emerge from the approach advocated in this Paper. The topics considered are:

- Characteristics of leases that give rise to assets and liabilities
- Why the proposals would not apply to executory contracts
- Distinguishing leases from take-or-pay contracts
- Contracts for services
- Leases of intangible assets and resource exploitation rights
- Leases of land and buildings
- Short-term and immaterial leases.

The membership of this group comprises standard-setters from Australia, Canada, France, Germany, Japan, New Zealand, the UK and the USA, and representatives of the Nordic Federation of Public Accountants and IASC.

CHARACTERISTICS OF LEASES THAT GIVE RISE TO ASSETS AND LIABILITIES

What are leases?

For the purpose of this Paper, a lease is any contract between a lessee and a lessor 2.3
that gives the lessee the right to possess and use a specific item of property for an
agreed period of time in return for the lessee making specified payments.

A feature of a lease that differentiates it from other forms of asset financing is that 2.4
the lessor retains ownership of the property that is the subject of the lease during the
period of the lease. Some lease contracts give the lessee the right to purchase the
leased property at the end of the lease term—these are sometimes referred to as 'hire
purchase contracts'.

Rights and obligations that arise under lease contracts

Lease contracts typically convey a bundle of rights and obligations to the lessee. The 2.5
most important right obtained by the lessee is the right to use or exploit the leased
property, in accordance with the terms of the contract, for the period of the lease.
Unless the contract provides otherwise, once the leased property is delivered or
otherwise made available to the lessee, the lessee can expect continued quiet enjoyment for the term of the lease. A lessee's rights in relation to the use of the property
are clearly different from ownership rights, but are valuable rights nonetheless, since
they give the lessee rights of access to future economic benefits. In consideration for
the rights acquired, the lessee is obliged to pay lease rentals to the lessor and any
other amounts required by the lease.

For the lessor, lease contracts create rights to receive future lease rentals from the 2.6
lessee and other amounts required by the lease. The lessor usually has a right to the
return of the leased property at the end of the lease.

Some leases, in addition to conveying usage rights, also contain agreements for the 2.7
lessor to provide asset management and other ancillary services to the lessee such as
repairs, maintenance and insurance of the leased item. The treatment of these leases
is considered in paragraph 2.41.

When do leases give rise to assets and liabilities?

The conceptual frameworks adopted by the boards of all the G4 + 1 members have 2.8
similar definitions of assets and liabilities for financial reporting. A central feature of
the definitions of assets is that past transactions or events have resulted in control
over the capacity to obtain future economic benefits. A central feature of the definitions of liabilities is that past transactions or events have resulted in a present
obligation to transfer economic benefits. The definitions of assets and liabilities
within the frameworks are particularly well suited to cope with leases, since they
focus on control of rights acquired and on obligations incurred rather than on 'quasi-
ownership' that requires polarising alternatives.

In accounting for lease contracts, as for any other contracts that give rise to rights 2.9
and obligations for the contracting parties, it is necessary to examine the nature of
those rights and obligations and whether they meet the definitions of assets and
liabilities. This requires identification of recognition points, at which changes in
assets and liabilities should be reflected in the accounting by the parties to the
contract.

2.10   There are various events that might have consequences for the recognition of assets and liabilities in respect of lease contracts. These include:

- signing a contract to lease
- purchase or manufacture by the lessor of the specific item of property that is the subject of the lease
- delivery of the property to the lessee
- rental payments falling due during the lease term.

2.11   The following sections in this chapter discuss recognition points relating to contracts for the purchase and supply of goods and services in general. The Group's view is that performance is the most significant event that determines when assets and liabilities for the full contracted amounts come into existence and should be recognised.

2.12   Where a lease contract has been signed, but the lessee has not paid and the lessor has not delivered, the contract is merely executory,* since at that stage neither the lessee nor the lessor has performed any of their obligations under the lease contract. The lessor has not yet transferred to the lessee access to the economic benefits relating to the right to use the property. Until some performance occurs, the lease should be accounted for in the same way as any executory contract for the purchase of goods or services. Under present conventions, where all performance lies in the future, the buyer (equivalent to the lessee) of the goods or services to which the contract relates does not (yet) have a recognisable asset of those goods or services, nor a recognisable liability to pay for them. Conversely, the seller (equivalent to the lessor) does not (yet) have a recognisable asset of the right to collect the contracted payments. Instead, both parties have rights and obligations to participate in the exchange.

2.13   When some performance does occur under the lease, it becomes necessary to consider what assets and liabilities arise for the lessee and the lessor. The purchase or manufacture by the lessor of the specific item of property that is the subject of the lease may be considered to give rise to a firmer commitment by the lessee and an element of performance by the lessor. It is arguable in such circumstances that the lessee has an asset of the right to receive the benefits of the property that has been procured by the lessor, and a liability to pay for it. However, as discussed below, the Group believes that, in general, delivery to the lessee of the rights of access should be the recognition point.

Delivery by the lessor

2.14   In general, for a lessor, the most substantial act of performance under a lease is passing possession of the leased item to the lessee. This may be done by delivering, or otherwise making available, the item to the lessee. Thereafter, the lessee has rights to 'quiet enjoyment' of the leased item during the lease term; once the lessor has done this, there is little doubt that the lessor will continue to allow the lessee access to the leased item for the remainder of the lease term (provided that the lessee does not break the conditions of the lease agreement).

2.15   It is therefore reasonable to conclude that once the lessor has delivered the leased item to the lessee, the lessor's performance under the lease is substantially completed.† The lessor now has a right, which may reasonably be viewed as

---

The meaning and accounting treatment of executory contracts are discussed in paragraphs 2.19–2.35.

†*Except for any future obligations under agreements to provide asset management or other ancillary services (see paragraph 2.41).*

unconditional, to collect the lease payments—an asset that can be reported as a debtor; it also has the right to the return of the item at the end of the lease.

The lessee too has an asset—it has the right to use the leased item in any way **2.16** permitted by the lease agreement. It also has an obligation, which may be viewed as unconditional, to pay the lease payments—a liability that may be reported as a creditor.

Accordingly, the lessor and the lessee should recognise their changed rights and **2.17** obligations under the lease once possession of the leased item has passed from the lessor to the lessee. At that time, the lessor has substantially performed and the lease contract ceases to be executory. The lessee should recognise the rights to use the item and the obligation to pay rentals over the lease term, and the lessor should recognise the right to receive those rental payments instead of all or part of the leased item. The lessor's substantial performance under the lease contract is an economic event that has changed significantly the nature of the rights and obligations of the parties to the lease contract, which should be reflected in their accounting for the contract.

Initial payment by lessee

The first act of performance under a lease contract may be the payment of an initial **2.18** amount by the lessee. Clearly, the lessee does not at this stage have control over the rights to the leased property, and would simply recognise a prepayment, representing its right either to receive the property (on lease) or, alternatively, to have its money refunded.

WHY THE PROPOSALS WOULD NOT APPLY TO EXECUTORY CONTRACTS

What are executory contracts?

The term 'executory contract' is generally used to refer to contracts under which both **2.19** parties are still to perform to an equal degree the actions promised by and required of them under the contract. An obvious example of an executory contract is a contract under which neither party has performed any of the promises it made in the contract.

'Performance' is used in its usual sense to mean the carrying out of the actions agreed **2.20** by the parties in the contract, such as supplying goods and paying for them. The performance of a contract may involve a number of stages, such as manufacturing and delivery by the party supplying the goods, and receipt and payment by the party obtaining the goods under the contract.

A contract may also be equally proportionately unperformed at various stages **2.21** during the period to completion of the contract if, for example, it involves a series of discrete acts, such as a contract for twelve monthly deliveries of inventory for twelve separate payments for the inventory received. After each delivery and payment, the parties' remaining contractual promises are equally proportionately unperformed, whether one considers the contract to be in substance a single contract or twelve separate contracts. Under either view, the parties would still have recognised in their accounting records the deliveries and payments already made, ie the rights and obligations that arose under the performed part of the contract. The remaining deliveries and payments represent an executory contract (or contracts).

Rights and obligations under executory contracts

2.22   What is the nature of the rights and obligations that arise for the parties under a contract while it is executory? Contracts are intended to provide certainty that the contracting parties can be relied upon to fulfil their duties under the contract. It might therefore be suggested that a contract gives the buyer the right to demand delivery of the subject goods or services, and the obligation to pay for them. Conversely, the seller would appear to have the obligation to make delivery, and the right to receive payment. Under this view, both parties would have assets and liabilities for the full value of the contract before any performance.

2.23   However, many contracts may be cancelled by either party without any further consequences, such as a contract for the routine supply of standard office goods. Such a contract does not therefore give rise to an unconditional right to receive the goods or an unconditional obligation to pay.

2.24   Other contracts might seem to be firmer commitments. For example, a buyer cannot always easily cancel a contract to supply a machine that has to be built to the buyer's specification. However, even in such a case the buyer of the machine has no unconditional right to the machine merely by virtue of the supply contract.

2.25   Normally, either party to a contract may notify the other that it no longer wishes to fulfil the terms of the contract. When this happens the party giving notice will be liable to compensate the other party for any losses that it has sustained, but these may well be significantly less than the full value of the contract, and often will be nil. Ordinarily the party that suffers loss is required to mitigate its loss as far as possible. For example, a buyer that wishes to cancel a contract should reimburse the seller for the costs that the seller has incurred under the contract, but not for costs that the seller either will not now incur or can recoup in another way (for example, by selling the goods or services to another customer).

2.26   Some firmly committed contracts exist that contain a disincentive for non-performance that is sufficiently large to make performance probable.* For those contracts, it may be argued that the signing of the contract is the significant act of performance (rather than delivery or some other act of performance); therefore, the contract ceases to be executory at that time. Whilst the Group acknowledges that the accounting model proposed in this Paper may be appropriate for those contracts, those contracts are beyond the Paper's intended scope.

2.27   While a contract is executory, the rights and obligations arising for a purchaser may reasonably be viewed not as the right to receive the goods in the future and an obligation to pay for them (ie they do not give rise to separately recognisable assets and liabilities). Rather, the purchaser has a *conditional* right (it has the right to receive the goods only if it pays for them) and a *conditional* obligation (it must pay for the goods only if they are supplied). Similarly the seller has a *conditional* right (to

---

Such a contract is referred to as a 'firm commitment' in the US accounting standard FAS 133 'Accounting for Derivative Instruments and Hedging Activities'. FAS 133 defines a 'firm commitment' as: "An agreement with an unrelated party, binding on both parties and usually legally enforceable, with the following characteristics:

a. The agreement specifies all significant terms, including the quantity to be exchanged, the fixed price, and the timing of the transaction. The fixed price may be expressed as a specified amount of an entity's functional currency or of a foreign currency. It may also be expressed as a specified interest rate or specified effective yield.

b. The agreement includes a disincentive for nonperformance that is sufficiently large to make performance probable."

receive payment if the goods are supplied) and a *conditional* obligation (it must supply the goods, but only if they are paid for).

Each party has a further asset or liability while the contract is executory—the right or obligation to receive compensation or to compensate the other party in the event of cancellation. At any point in time a contract will have a value (positive or negative) and, under a fair value accounting model, it may qualify for recognition in financial statements if that value can be determined with sufficient reliability (an obvious example is a forward currency contract).

2.28

In brief, the rights and obligations arising under an executory contract are the right and obligation to participate in the future exchange, or alternatively to compensate or be compensated for the consequences of not doing so.*

2.29

The significance of performance

Once performance has occurred, the position of the parties changes. Consider first the position where the supplier performs first—ie delivers the goods. The purchaser now has control of the goods as demonstrated by its ability to use, pledge, sell or otherwise dispose of the goods as it sees fit. In other words the purchaser now has access to the economic benefits relating to the goods and this meets the definition of an asset. The purchaser also has an *unconditional* obligation to pay for the goods, which meets the definition of a liability. Similarly the seller has an asset—the *unconditional* right to receive payment for the goods that have been delivered.

2.30

If the purchaser performs first—ie pays for the goods before they are delivered—it has an asset arising from its performance under the contract. The asset represents the unconditional right either to receive the goods or to have the payment refunded.†

2.31

Of course, delivery and payment are only examples of performance, and performance may occur in other ways. Consider a contract that requires a joiner to construct a wooden staircase to the precise dimensions stipulated by the purchaser. Because the staircase would not fit any other building it has a negligible value to anyone other than the purchaser. Constructing the staircase may be viewed as a significant act of performance. Once construction is under way, the purchaser is unlikely to be free to cancel the contract without consequences—the purchaser must at least compensate the joiner for the costs incurred so far, and may have to pay more. Thus at this stage the purchaser could be argued to have a liability. Similarly, the purchaser could be considered to have an asset—the right to receive the benefits of the work done so far, or alternatively to be released from its liability.

2.32

Accounting for incomplete staircases (and construction contracts generally) is beyond the scope of this Paper and the discussion in the previous paragraph is not intended to prejudge the outcome of any future deliberations of such issues. The example is, however, useful since it illustrates that, whilst a focus on legal rights and obligations is helpful in suggesting when assets and liabilities come into existence and might be recognised, accounting has to go further and look at the consequences of such legal rights and obligations. Points must be identified when it is practicable to

2.33

*Expressed in financial instrument terms, the buyer under an executory contract has both written a put option and purchased a call option, and the seller has the opposite positions.

†The existence of alternatives shows that there is a degree of uncertainty in what form the asset will yield economic benefits, but clearly there is an unconditional right to receive economic benefits, which is quite different from the position before payment when the purchaser had only a conditional right to receive and a conditional obligation to pay.

require recognition of assets and liabilities, in a manner that fairly reflects the economic and legal position of the parties, while acknowledging that a precise mirroring of legal rights and obligations is not always feasible.

Contracts that are partially executory throughout their term

2.34   It is instructive to compare a lease with the perhaps unusual case of a contract that requires the customer to return the subject item (for example, a car) to the supplier each day, with the supplier then providing the same or a similar item (at the supplier's discretion) to the customer the next day. Under such contracts, the supplier's performance has not been substantially completed at the time of the first delivery of the item. The supplier has significant performance obligations throughout the contract term. Such contracts, therefore, are partially executory contracts throughout their term. If the supplier fails to provide the item each day under the contract, the supplier's obligation is to compensate the customer for any loss arising as a result of that failure. If the customer fails to take the item each day and pay for it, the customer may have to compensate the supplier while the supplier finds a new customer. But neither supplier nor customer has an unconditional obligation to fulfil its obligations for the full period envisaged by the contract (nor rights to compel the other party to do so). Accordingly, the customer would not recognise a right to use the item for the full term and the obligation to pay rentals; nor would the supplier recognise the right to receive the rentals for days for which it has yet to perform.*

2.35   A lease contract may not necessarily give the lessee a continuous right to use the leased item throughout its term. The lessee's use could be interrupted, for example, in a time-sharing agreement where, say, for ten years the lessee has the right to use a property for two months a year only. The question arises whether the lessor's performance has been substantially completed when the property is first made available for the lessee's use—conversely, whether the lessee has 'taken delivery' of the right to use the property for part of each of the next ten years—or whether the lease is partially executory throughout its term. The conclusion in such cases will depend on the particular circumstances, including the nature and extent of the interruption. On the basis of the earlier discussion, the probable conclusion in this example is that the lessor's performance has been only partially completed when the property is first made available to the lessee. Accordingly, at each 'delivery' the lessee has obtained an asset and liability in respect of the rights and obligations relating to the two-month term only, which may reasonably be viewed as unconditional. The lessor has the right to collect the lease payments for the two-month period. In practice, the lessee is often required to prepay the cost of future years' usage rights; hence, the lessor avoids the risk that the lessee will fail to take delivery in future years and pay for it. If the lessee has prepaid, it is at risk that the lessor will not make the periodic delivery of the property. The lessee has an asset representing its right to either the property or a refund and the lessor has an obligation either to deliver the property or to refund the prepayment.

DISTINGUISHING LEASES FROM TAKE-OR-PAY CONTRACTS

2.36   Leases are sometimes compared with take-or-pay contracts. Under such contracts, a buyer is required to pay the contracted amount even if the goods or services are not required. This may appear to give rise to an unconditional obligation to pay, and suggest that a liability to pay should be recognised at the inception of the contract.

*Despite the terms of the contract, by unwritten agreement between the parties the subject item may not be returned and resupplied on a daily basis. If so, the contract could well be in substance a lease for the full contract term.

Take-or-pay contracts are, however, essentially executory contracts throughout their **2.37**
term. Each party has the right and obligation to participate in the exchange, or
alternatively to compensate or be compensated for the consequences of not doing so.
The supplier must be able to continue to supply the goods or services over the life of
the contract, whether or not the buyer in fact wishes to take a particular scheduled
delivery. Clearly, the supplier has not substantially completed its performance at the
inception of the contract, nor has the buyer (unless payment is made in advance).*
Consequently, it is reasonable for the buyer to recognise assets (and corresponding
liabilities) only in respect of deliveries that have taken place and payments that have
been made.

Take-or-pay contracts can thus be distinguished from lease contracts, since a lessor **2.38**
substantially completes its performance early in the term of the lease by delivering
the leased item to the lessee. All contracts cease to be executory once significant
performance has occurred.

CONTRACTS FOR SERVICES

The principles set out above for the supply of goods apply equally to contracts for **2.39**
the supply of services. The supplier does not substantially complete its performance
at the inception of a service contract—performance occurs as the services are provided. Neither does the buyer substantially complete its performance at inception,
unless full payment is made in advance. A service contract is therefore an executory
contract until performance occurs: when the supplier performs, the purchaser would
recognise a liability and an expense (unless the service creates or enhances an asset)
for the value of the service that has been provided.

In the case of contracts for services, the services are often to be provided over an **2.40**
extended period, and payments are to be regularly made over that period. The
supplier has significant performance obligations throughout the contract term. Such
contracts, therefore, are executed throughout their term.

Lease contracts that contain contracts for services

Frequently leases provide that the lessor will provide ancillary services such as **2.41**
repairs, maintenance and insurance, as well as supplying the leased item. The service
element of such contracts remains executory when the leased item is delivered to the
lessee: performance by the lessor (and payment by the lessee for the services) occurs
over the lease term. In contrast, the element of the contract that relates to the use of
the leased item ceases to be executory when the leased item is delivered to the lessee
because, as discussed earlier, the lessor's performance consists principally of passing
possession of the leased item to the lessee. Consequently, the Group takes the view
that where a lease contains a contract for services, the two elements should be
accounted for separately. This is similar to the position where a seller undertakes to
provide services: the two elements of the contract are accounted for separately. (In
such a case, the amount in respect of the supply of the goods is recognised as an asset
by the buyer, while the service element is charged as an expense as incurred.) The
only difference in a leasing context is that the contract may specify only an aggregate
amount, and a reasonable apportionment would have to be made to split that
amount between that which relates to the supply of the asset and that which relates
to services. It should be noted that such an apportionment is required under present
standards on lease accounting.

**If payment is made in advance, the buyer's performance would give rise to valuable rights—either to receive the
goods or services, or to have the payment refunded.*

Service contracts that contain leases

2.42   The services provided under some contracts may require the purchaser of the services to use the service provider's property, such as an office building or road, with the provider also adding ancillary services. Such contracts may be described as service contracts, but in substance incorporate a lease of the service provider's property.

2.43   It is therefore essential to establish whether the purchaser is required to make payments in return for the right to use the service provider's property for an agreed period of time (which meets the definition of a lease). In such cases, the contract would provide for identifiable property-related payments that are based on the time that the service provider's property is available to the purchaser, whether or not the purchaser actually makes use of the property.

2.44   There may also be contracts for the provision of services which in substance comprise a lease of the property used by the supplier to generate the services. For example, a contract to purchase electricity from a power station might appear to constitute a lease of the station. This could be the case, for example, where the power station has been built to the specifications of the customer, who takes all or most of the output, and there is no real opportunity for the supplier to obtain alternative customers for that output (perhaps because the station is located in a remote area).

2.45   The Group acknowledges that it can be difficult to identify when a contract stated to be for services in fact constitutes a lease contract. An item recognised as a leased asset usually relates to a specified item of property, plant or equipment that the lessee has the right to exploit for the duration of the contract. Where, for example, a purchaser receives services from an item of property that also supplies other parties, the whole of the item could not be a leased asset of the purchaser. On the other hand, where the purchaser receives services from a dedicated facility, such as a water treatment plant located next to a paper mill, the contract may well constitute a lease of the service provider's asset and thus should be accounted for as a lease.

2.46   As a further example, consider a contract for the right to use capacity on a telecommunications network. Providers of telecommunications network capacity (primarily in the form of conduit, fibre optic cables and related equipment) often grant rights to use a specified amount of capacity for a specified time period. The right is physically limited to a specified fibre and wavelength of light within the cable. The acquirer of the right receives capacity from a dedicated fibre; however, that fibre is part of a network that supplies capacity to other parties. Determining whether such a contract is a service agreement, a lease, or both, depends on the circumstances and requires a rigorous analysis of the rights and obligations of the parties to the contract. In this example, if (i) payments in respect of the fibre and the service element can be separately identified, (ii) the purchaser has an exclusive right to the purchased capacity (the provider cannot sell or otherwise use any of the purchaser's capacity that the purchaser is not using), and (iii) the purchaser has the risk of obsolescence of the purchased capacity during the contract term, the rationale of this Paper would indicate that the fibre element should be accounted for as a lease.

LEASES OF INTANGIBLE ASSETS AND RESOURCE EXPLOITATION RIGHTS

2.47   An issue concerning the scope of any revised standards on lease accounting is whether they should include leases of intangible assets (including resource exploitation rights). Present standards normally exclude from their scope lease agreements to explore for or to exploit natural resources (such as oil, gas, timber, metals and other minerals) and licensing agreements for items such as motion picture films, video recordings, plays, manuscripts, patents and copyrights. It is not clear why these should be excluded from the standards.

The Group cannot see any fundamental reason to exclude leases of particular types of assets from the scope of revised standards. It may well be that contingent rentals based on usage or turnover factors are a high proportion of total rentals under resource exploitation agreements or licensing agreements, for example, but that does not mean that they should not be covered.   **2.48**

The criterion of 'delivery' by the lessor (see paragraph 2.14) applies in principle to intangible as well as tangible items. Leases of intangible assets and resource exploitation rights can be distinguished from executory contracts once the lessor has delivered or otherwise made the leased item available to the lessee. Delivery for these types of assets may comprise simply the assignment of legal rights to exploit the leased patent, or to explore for oil and gas etc, rather than physical delivery by the lessor to the lessee. Once the lessee has acquired such rights, it has the ability to exploit them in any way permitted by the relevant agreement. Revocation of the lease should normally occur only as allowed under the lease, and hence the lessor of intangible assets and natural resources has substantially completed its performance under the lease once the rights to the leased item have been assigned to the lessee.   **2.49**

The lessee controls the usage of the legal rights under the lease agreement, giving it access to economic benefits. This would be the case even if the lease of an intangible asset were not an exclusive one, ie the item underlying the lease could also be leased to other parties at the same time. For example, copyrights may be made available to a number of lessees, which separately use the copyright in their own activities. Nevertheless, as long as there are economic benefits to each lessee, then each lessee would recognise its rights as a leased asset if the recognition criteria were met. Such contracts would also give the lessor rights to collect the lease payments—an asset that would be reported as a debtor if the recognition criteria were met.   **2.50**

The Group has not fully explored the implications of the approach advocated in this Paper concerning the accounting treatment of agreements relating to intangible items of the type that are at present excluded from lease accounting standards, because they are not the main focus of the Paper. Nevertheless, the Group takes the view that the lease accounting principles that are explored in this Paper would also apply to leases of intangible items (including resource exploitation rights) and that such leases therefore should not in principle be excluded from the scope of any revised accounting standards.   **2.51**

LEASES OF LAND AND BUILDINGS

A further question on the scope of new accounting standards is whether their requirements should be modified in any way for leases of land and buildings. The Group's proposals are discussed in Chapter 13.   **2.52**

SHORT-TERM AND IMMATERIAL LEASES

The G4 + 1 Special Report 'Accounting for Leases: A New Approach' suggested that revised lease accounting standards might apply to all non-cancellable leases with a term longer than one year.   **2.53**

The Group believes that an exemption for short leases, however defined, would be inconsistent with the fundamental approach of accounting for the assets and   **2.54** liabilities that arise under leases. Even a lease with a term of under one year might give rise to assets and liabilities that are material in the specific circumstances of the case. Any revised standards should apply where the effect is material, as is the case with present standards, ie materiality should be the basis for determining whether lease assets and liabilities should be recognised, rather than an arbitrary threshold such as some minimum lease term or other definition of a short or insignificant lease.

Recommendations

2A Leases can be distinguished from executory contracts by the fact that leases cease to be executory when the leased property is delivered or otherwise made available to the lessee. The proposals would therefore not apply to executory contracts (including take-or-pay contracts, which are considered to be executory throughout their term).

2B Where a lease contains a contract for services the two elements should be accounted for separately.

2C Where contracts for services in substance incorporate leases of the service provider's property, these should be accounted for as leases.

2D Leases of intangible assets (including agreements to explore for or use natural resources) should not in principle be excluded from the scope of revised standards.

2E No specific exemption should be proposed for short leases; reliance should instead be placed on the principle of materiality.

Part II Leases in the financial statements of lessees

Chapter 3 Assets and liabilities of lessees—general principles

INTRODUCTION

3.1 Leases typically convey a bundle of rights and obligations to the lessee. The approach to lessee accounting that is proposed in this Paper focuses on accounting for those rights and obligations. The main issues to consider in developing such a framework for recognising assets and liabilities relating to lease contracts are:

- what rights does the lessee acquire under the lease contract and do they meet the definition of an asset?
- what obligations does the lessee incur under the lease contract and do they meet the definition of a liability?
- if assets and liabilities are created by the lease, how should they be measured?

RIGHTS AND ASSETS THAT ARISE FOR LESSEES

3.2 As discussed in Chapter 2, the Group takes the view that most leases provide the lessee with rights or access to future economic benefits that it controls and obligations that it must meet, which respectively satisfy the definitions of assets and liabilities for financial reporting.

3.3 The lessee's rights will comprise the rights to use the leased property for a specified period and sometimes also options, for example to extend the lease in exchange for further payments or to purchase additional usage of the property. In the interests of clarity, this chapter considers only straightforward leases; leases with such optional features are discussed in Chapter 4.

A lease asset that is recognised in a lessee's balance sheet represents property rights   **3.4**
or control over future economic benefits rather than ownership of the underlying physical property. Under a lease contract, the lessee generally obtains access to the use of the leased item, and therefore gains control over its future economic benefits for the term of the lease, once it is delivered to the lessee or otherwise made available for the lessee's use.

Under some leases the lessor also agrees to provide ancillary services such as repairs   **3.5**
and maintenance of the leased item. In such cases the right to use the item and the provision of services are distinct elements—as discussed in Chapter 2, contracts for services do not result in separate assets and liabilities because performance of the service has not yet occurred.

In accordance with the normal principles of asset recognition,* a lease asset is   **3.6**
recognised if:

(a)   it is probable that future economic benefits associated with the item will flow to the entity; and
(b)   it has a value that can be measured reliably.

Where it is determined that a lease conveys rights to the lessee that meet the defi-   **3.7**
nition of an asset, it would be highly unlikely for the above recognition criteria not to be met. In entering into leases, lessees will normally expect to derive future economic benefits from the use of the leased items. In addition, the initial value attributable to the assets that arise can normally be determined or estimated by reference to the obligations the lessee assumes under the terms of the lease agreements.

The rights conveyed to the lessee and the obligations assumed in relation to lease   **3.8**
contracts are linked; therefore the assets and liabilities need to be considered together to determine how they should be recognised. In many respects, the accounting treatment of a lease under this approach reflects the purchase by the lessee of an economic interest in the leased item, with the consideration being payable in instalments to the lessor. Conversely, from the lessor's perspective, the accounting treatment of a lease reflects the sale by the lessor of an economic interest in the leased item, with the consideration being receivable in instalments from the lessee.

OBLIGATIONS AND LIABILITIES THAT ARISE FOR LESSEES

In accordance with the principles of liability recognition adopted by G4+1 mem-   **3.9**
bers,† a liability exists if an entity has a present obligation (legal or constructive) as a result of a past event. A liability is recognised if:

(a)   it is probable that a transfer of economic benefits will be required to settle the obligation; and
(b)   a reliable estimate can be made of the amount of the obligation.

These recognition principles are derived from the conceptual frameworks for financial reporting of the members of the G4+1.

†These principles have been embodied in International and UK accounting standards IAS 37 and FRS 12 respectively, 'Provisions, Contingent Liabilities and Contingent Assets'

3.10   A past event that creates a present obligation is referred to in International Accounting Standards (IAS 37) and in UK accounting standards (FRS 12) as an 'obligating event'. An obligating event is defined in those standards as 'an event that creates a legal or constructive obligation that results in an entity having no realistic alternative to settling that obligation'. In the context of that definition, an obligation that derives from a contract (through its explicit or implicit terms) is a legal obligation. Therefore, a lease contract may give rise to a present obligation for the lessee.

3.11   As a general principle under the aforementioned accounting standards, to the extent that an entity can avoid a transfer of economic benefits, it has no present obligation and, hence, no liability is recognised. The application of this principle does not imply, however, that the accounting for a lease contract should be based on what would happen if a non-cancellable contract were abrogated by one party. In the absence of evidence to the contrary, it should be assumed that the terms of the contract would be adhered to.

3.12   For the same reasons that the Group regards 'delivery' to the lessee as usually the event (ie substantial performance by the lessor) that gives rise to an asset of the right to use the leased item for the term of the lease, delivery is also usually the 'obligating event' that creates a present obligation (and hence requires the recognition of a liability) to pay rentals and other amounts required by the lease. Until then, the lessee does not yet have a separate asset (access to the economic benefits related to the leased property) or liability (obligation to pay for it). Instead, the contract should be treated in a similar way to any contract to purchase goods or equipment that has not yet been delivered.

INITIAL MEASUREMENT OF ASSETS AND LIABILITIES THAT ARISE

3.13   Assuming arm's length parties, the cost of an acquired asset is normally measured by the fair value of the consideration given, except where the fair value of the asset received is more clearly evident.

3.14   In the Group's view, the same principle should apply to assets recognised in respect of leases. Consequently, the objective should be to record, at the beginning of the lease term,* the fair value of rights and obligations that are conveyed by the lease. This reflects the bargained fair value of the use of the item and any other rights conveyed by the lease contract, normally measured by the liabilities incurred and any other consideration payable.

3.15   Determining the liability incurred by the lessee in order to measure the fair value of the asset is therefore simply the application of the normal principle of recognising assets and liabilities arising from a transaction at their fair values at the transaction date. The fair value of the rights obtained by the lessee cannot be less than the present value of the minimum payments required by the lease (assuming that the lease is negotiated on arm's length terms), and in many straightforward leases the present value of the minimum payments will represent the bargained fair value of the property rights conveyed by the lease.

*Hereafter, for ease of reference, the term 'the beginning of the lease term' has been used to denote the point at which lease assets and liabilities may arise—ie when the lessor substantially performs by making the leased item available for the lessee's use under the terms of the lease contract—rather than necessarily the signing of the lease contract.

Consider a simple example where a lessee agrees to hire equipment for three years at **3.16** an annual rental of 5,000. At the end of the lease term, the lessee returns the equipment to the lessor. The lessee's rights and obligations can be analysed thus:

(a) the right to use the equipment for three years;
(b) the obligation to pay 5,000 per year for three years; and
(c) the obligation to return the equipment to the lessor at the end of three years.

Under the principles discussed above, when the equipment is delivered to the lessee, **3.17** the lessee should recognise an asset and a liability and measure them at the present value of the three annual payments. The liability is the present obligation incurred under the lease contract. The asset represents the fair value of the right to use the equipment for three years only—the lessee controls the usage rights for that period and does not have any rights relating to the equipment beyond the end of the lease term.

Leases with optional features

The discussion of the previous example has assumed that the term of the lease and **3.18** the minimum payments required by the lease are unambiguously stated in the lease contract. However, this is not always the case. Many leases give the lessee options to renew or cancel the lease, where the lessee has a choice whether to continue with a lease beyond a certain date, or to cancel the lease, perhaps with an additional payment. In some leases the rentals are not fixed amounts but are contingent on future events such as the actual usage of the leased item by the lessee, the amount of revenue generated by the leased item in the lessee's business, or changes in prices, such as interest rates or measures of price inflation. The application of the proposed principles to the recognition and measurement of the assets and liabilities arising from leases that contain such features is discussed in Chapter 4.

Residual values

One of the issues that has been addressed by the Group is that the lessee's rights and **3.19** obligations could be analysed in different ways, even when it has been determined what present obligations exist. At the core of the issue is the fact that different amounts would be recognised in respect of the lessee's separate assets and liabilities depending on the view taken of their nature—although there would not necessarily be a difference in the net amounts recognised. These different views generally revolve around the treatment of the leased item's residual value. An alternative view of the above example is that the lessee should include in the asset and liability amounts respectively the full value of the equipment and the obligation to return it at the end of the lease. Advocates of this approach would argue that the lessee has control of the (whole of the) equipment for the term of the lease and has an obligation to return it. They would also argue that the inclusion of 'gross' asset and liability amounts would make the financial statements of entities that lease their assets more comparable with those that own them (the difference being that the latter do not have obligations to return the property to another entity).

The Group has rejected this view of how the lessee's assets and liabilities should be **3.20** characterised. First, in the Group's view, the lessee's rights relate to only part of the equipment's economic life, not the whole of it, and so the recognised asset should be characterised as such. Second, the obligation to return the equipment at the end of the lease is not in the Group's view an obligation to transfer economic benefits for the value of the equipment that is returned, since the economic benefits relating to the equipment beyond the end of the lease were not transferred to the lessee in the first place. The Group also believes that in this example, leasing is not similar to ownership—and the accounting treatment should not make transactions that are not alike appear to be alike. Indeed, an important effect of the Group's recommendations is that the accounting treatment of leases would generally reflect differences between leasing and ownership.

3.21   Whereas the example in paragraph 3.16 is relatively straightforward to analyse, many leases are more complex and convey to the lessee an economic interest in and/ or an obligation relating to the equipment's residual value. The issue then is how the rights and obligations relating to the residual value are characterised in the balance sheet. The recognition and measurement issues relating to residual values and residual value guarantees are discussed in Chapter 5.

ACCOUNTING AFTER INITIAL RECOGNITION

3.22   After initial recognition, the lease assets and liabilities would be accounted for subsequently in the balance sheet and income statement according to accounting standards dealing with assets and liabilities respectively. Thus recognised lease assets would be subject to depreciation and impairment (and, if applicable, revaluation) rules. Under the principles of present accounting standards, lease liabilities would be accounted for as debt:* the carrying amounts of lease liabilities would reflect the allocation of lease payments between the finance costs of the lease (charged to income over the term of the lease at a constant rate on the carrying amount) and repayment of outstanding debt.

3.23   Where leases contain optional features or obligations that are not fixed amounts, further assets and liabilities may arise during the course of a lease, and existing assets and liabilities might need to be remeasured. The issues are discussed in Chapters 4 and 5.

GENERAL EFFECT OF PROPOSED APPROACH

3.24   The general effect of the approach proposed is that the amounts recognised as assets and liabilities by lessees would vary depending on the nature of the lease. The financial statements would thus reflect the financial flexibility (or otherwise) provided by different leasing arrangements.

3.25   Many leases at present characterised as operating leases, and not included on the balance sheet, would give rise to assets and liabilities—but only to the extent of the fair values of the rights and obligations that are conveyed by the lease. If the lease term is very short, the asset and liability may be very small (perhaps even immaterial). Conversely, the proposals may have the effect of reducing the assets and liabilities recognised in respect of some leases at present characterised as finance leases, because the rights and obligations that would be recognised under the proposed approach do not necessarily correspond to the minimum lease payments as defined in existing standards on lease accounting. For example, residual value guarantees would not necessarily give rise to separate assets and liabilities for the full amounts guaranteed, as is the case under present standards (see Chapter 5).

---

*Lease liabilities are financial instruments and would be accounted for according to the principles in applicable accounting standards dealing with financial instruments.

Recommendations

3A Assets and liabilities should be recognised by a lessee in relation to the rights and obligations conveyed by a lease when the lessor has substantially performed its obligation to provide the lessee with access to the leased property for the lease term—generally this is when the leased property is delivered or otherwise made available to the lessee.

3B Until the above recognition point is reached, a lessee should account for a lease contract in a similar way to any contract to purchase property that has not yet been delivered.

3C The objective should be to record, at the beginning of the lease term, the fair value of the rights and obligations that are conveyed by the lease. Fair value is measured by the fair value of the consideration given, except where the fair value of the asset received is more clearly evident.

3D The fair value of the rights obtained by a lessee cannot be less than the present value of the minimum payments required by the lease (assuming that the lease is negotiated on an arm's length basis).

Chapter 4 Leases with optional features

INTRODUCTION

Renewal, cancellation and purchase options

Many leases provide the lessee with the right either to end the lease at some point, to extend the lease for a further period, or to purchase the leased property at some point. For example, consider a lease that requires the lessee to hire equipment for three years at an annual rental of 5,000 and gives the lessee the right to hire the equipment for a further two years at the same rent. The issue is whether the lessee should recognise an asset and a liability for the present value of three years' rentals or five years' rentals.   **4.1**

This issue arises, in a slightly different form, under existing standards on lease accounting, where the interpretation of clauses containing renewal or break options for the purpose of classifying leases as finance leases or operating leases can be difficult. Existing standards generally define the lease term to include any periods covered by renewal options that are regarded as 'reasonably certain' of being exercised, and the factors to be considered are sometimes specified. It may be that if the lease is viewed as a five-year lease it is a finance lease, whereas if the lease term is viewed as three years it is an operating lease. If, on the other hand, the classification of the lease is the same under either scenario, the accounting under present requirements is either not affected (if an operating lease) or is less severely affected (if a finance lease) by the view that is taken of the option. But the treatment of options in leases is more generally relevant under the approach advocated in this Paper because they potentially affect the amount of assets and liabilities that are recognised for all leases in which they occur.   **4.2**

Contingent rentals

Although leases normally specify minimum rentals that must be paid over the lease term, some leases require the lessee to pay additional amounts that are not fixed in advance. Instead, the actual amounts that the lessee will be required to pay are   **4.3** contingent on the outcome of uncertain future events. Such rentals are commonly referred to as contingent rentals. Common examples are motor vehicle leases containing clauses where rentals are increased to reflect the actual mileage driven above an initially agreed mileage; property leases in the retail industry where rentals are related to the turnover in the lessee's business; and property leases where rents are periodically reset to current market values to take account of inflation. Arrangements involving leases of intangible assets,* such as licences of trade marks, patents or other intellectual property, also commonly require payments that are linked to the licensee's exploitation of the rights acquired (such as royalties on sales derived from the use of the property). Three kinds of contingent rentals can be distinguished:

- rentals that vary with usage (for example, a charge for additional miles that a leased car is driven above a defined threshold).
- rentals that are a proportion of the lessee's revenues or profits derived from the use of the leased property (for example, a share of sales made from a retail outlet).
- rentals that vary in line with prices (for example, the UK 'institutional' property lease where rentals are revised to reflect increases to market levels at specified intervals during the lease).

4.4 Under present standards contingent rentals are not included in the minimum lease payments for the purpose of determining whether a lease is a finance lease or an operating lease. Nor are they included in the minimum lease payments that are recognised as assets and liabilities in the event that the lease is treated as a finance lease. The treatment of contingent rentals is important under the approach advocated in this Paper because it directly affects the amount of assets and liabilities that would be recognised for many leases.

Similarities between contingent rentals and options

4.5 Leases that contain renewal and purchase options give rise to similar issues to leases that contain contingent rentals, especially those that vary with usage. The similarity is that both kinds of leases give the lessee the option to 'purchase more' of the asset; the difference is simply whether the lessee purchases more time or more usage. In view of this similarity, the same principles ought to apply to both circumstances. However, some contingent rentals, especially those that vary in line with prices, may be viewed as giving the lessee an obligation to pay an uncertain amount for the asset rather than an option to purchase more of the asset.

PROPOSED GENERAL PRINCIPLES

4.6 As noted in Chapter 3, the Group believes that the objective should be to record, at the beginning of the lease term, the fair value of the rights and obligations that are conveyed by the lease. Fair value is measured by the fair value of the consideration given (comprising the liabilities incurred and any other consideration such as cash paid in advance), except where the fair value of the asset received is more clearly evident. The application of this objective results in the following general principles.

4.7 The rights that are reflected in the lease asset that is recorded by the lessee will comprise the rights to use the property and also options, for example to extend the lease, to purchase additional usage of the property in exchange for usage-related rentals, or to purchase the property itself.

*As noted in Chapter 2, the Group takes the view that leases of intangible assets should not in principle be excluded from the scope of revised accounting standards.

On the assumption that the lease is negotiated on an arm's length basis, the value of **4.8** the rights obtained by the lessee under a lease cannot be less than the present value of the minimum payments required by the lease.

When accounting for options conveyed to the lessee, the exercise of renewal or **4.9** purchase options should not generally be anticipated: the fair value of the options themselves acquired at the beginning of the lease term will be reflected in the minimum payments required by the lease.

A renewal or purchase option may itself have a significant value at the beginning of **4.10** the lease term (when the price payable on exercise is significantly less than the fair value of the rights acquired: for example, a bargain renewal or bargain purchase option).* Where this is the case (and assuming its value can be ascertained with sufficient reliability), the option should be accounted for separately from the rights to use the property for the non-cancellable period of the lease, and a portion of the minimum lease payments would be deemed to relate to the purchase of the option. One way in which the value of such options might be determined is by comparison of the rentals required by a lease including options with those that are specified in a lease that contains no such options.

Under the historical cost model that is developed in this Paper, the carrying amount **4.11** in respect of a renewal or purchase option would be reviewed for impairment during the period up to the exercise date and, if the option is exercised, the carrying amount at the exercise date would be amortised subsequently as appropriate.†

An option may have a value that is small (when the price payable on exercise is **4.12** approximately the same as the value of the rights acquired at that time), or it may not be possible to ascertain the value of an option with sufficient reliability. If the value of the option is immaterial to the lessee's financial statements, or it cannot be measured reliably, the option would not be accounted for separately: as a result, the whole of the minimum lease payments would be deemed to relate to the usage of the asset.

Some leases contain multiple options. For example, the lessee may have the choice of **4.13** either purchasing the asset at the end of the initial term or renewing the lease for a further term. The lessee's assets and liabilities at the beginning of the lease term would generally be determined as those arising from the least cost option.

The exercise of options will give rise to additional assets and liabilities, reflecting the **4.14** fair value of the additional rights and obligations obtained and assumed by the lessee as a result of the exercise.

If the minimum payments required by the lease (such as the minimum payments **4.15** specified in leases with contingent rentals) are clearly unrepresentative of the value of the property rights conveyed by the lease, an amount reflecting the fair value of such rights should be recognised as assets and liabilities. The fair value of the property rights conveyed by a lease might be determined by having regard to the payments required by a similar lease that had no provision for contingent rentals.

Expressed in option terms, the option acquired by the lessee is significantly 'in the money' at the beginning of the lease term.

†*Some members believe that this treatment would be inappropriate if such options were considered to be financial instruments. In their view, the accounting treatment for renewal or purchase options should be consistent with accounting standards on financial instruments.*

4.16　Contingent rentals (in excess of the minimum payments, or greater amount, recognised at the beginning of the lease term) should be recognised when the contingency criteria are met.

4.17　The application of the principles set out above is discussed in the remainder of this chapter.

THE ROLE OF 'PROBABILITY' IN DETERMINING THE ASSETS AND LIABILITIES THAT ARISE FROM LEASE CONTRACTS

Proposed approach to recognition and measurement of assets and liabilities

4.18　In the framework that has been outlined in the previous paragraphs, the identification and measurement of lease assets do not as a matter of principle depend on assessing the probable outcome of options to purchase more time or usage. Until an option is exercised, the recognised assets and liabilities will reflect the consideration given for the option, not the consideration that becomes payable when the option is exercised.

4.19　An option gives the lessee a right, but not an obligation, to purchase more time or usage. The lessee has no liability in respect of the exercise of the option because no present obligation to make further payments relating to optional renewal periods, etc arises until the lessee takes action to create one by exercising the option. This approach is consistent with normal accounting for the purchase of options in most other circumstances.

4.20　Under the proposed approach the probability of the lessee's exercising an option is implicitly reflected in the assets and liabilities recognised at the beginning of the lease term.

Alternative 'probability' approach to recognition of assets and liabilities

4.21　The Group has considered (but does not support) an alternative approach to the recognition of lease assets and liabilities. Under that approach, where leases contain options or contingent rentals, the lessee should estimate the probable amount that the lessee will pay and record an asset and liability for that amount.

4.22　In the case of a renewal or purchase option, the accounting treatment would depend on the probability of the option being exercised. For example, if it were determined that a renewal option probably would be exercised (ie the lessee would elect to renew the lease), the lease term would be treated as including the renewal period. Conversely, if it were determined that the lessee was unlikely to exercise the renewal option, the lease would be treated as coming to an end at the end of the initial period. Advocates of this approach argue that the accounting treatment should reflect what is likely to happen in the future.

4.23　Where rentals are contingent, advocates of this approach argue that, because the lease creates a contractual obligation, it is necessary to estimate the amount that the lessee will pay under the lease and record an asset and liability for that amount (discounted to present value) at the beginning of the lease term.

Advantages of proposed approach

In the Group's view, an important disadvantage of the alternative 'probability' approach is that it fails to recognise in the accounting treatment that features such as options and contingent rentals are an important part of the financial flexibility that has been negotiated between the lessee and lessor. The Group believes that the recommended framework for future standards on lease accounting will result in an accounting treatment that properly reflects the negotiated allocation of risks and benefits between the lessee and the lessor. **4.24**

Consider, for example, a lease of equipment where rentals are wholly contingent on the equipment's future use. If the leased equipment becomes obsolete or demand for its output falls, the lessee does not have to pay for its use. The lessor, not the lessee, bears risks relating to adverse economic conditions (and, conversely, benefits from improved economic conditions). Under the approach advocated in this Paper, the lessee would not recognise an asset or liability in respect of the future use of the equipment if there were no obligation to pay. **4.25**

Renewal options may be an important part of the financial flexibility that a lessee has negotiated regarding the risks of changes in its future circumstances and in future economic conditions. Consider a lease that has a fixed term of three years and an option to renew for a further two years. This lease creates a different set of rights and obligations from a five-year (non-cancellable) lease, even if it is thought that the option will probably be exercised. Treating them as being equivalent (as would be the case if the accounting treatment anticipated that the lease would be renewed) would misrepresent the lessee's rights and obligations in respect of the lease with the option to renew and would overstate the lessee's assets and liabilities—the lessee has a right, but does not have an obligation, to renew the lease. This option is an asset that may itself have a value. The probability of the option being exercised will affect the value of the option asset, but should not determine when assets and liabilities arise. The lease will therefore be recognised at the beginning of the lease term as an asset and liability for the value of three years' usage and the value of the renewal option, both of which are included in the payments required by the lease during the first three years. **4.26**

THE LEASE TERM—CANCELLATION AND RENEWAL OPTIONS

The example introduced at the start of this chapter is considered below. **4.27**

EXAMPLE 1

A company enters into a lease of equipment with a term of three years at an annual rental of 5,000. In addition the lease gives the lessee the right to renew the lease for a further two years at the same annual rental.

The lease in this example could be described in either of two ways: **4.28**

- As a *three-year* lease, with an option to *renew* for a further two years.
- As a *five-year* lease, with an option to *cancel* after three years.

Irrespective of which of the above two formulations is used in the lease contract, the economic effect is the same, and the accounting treatment should also be the same, ie the assets and liabilities recognised at the beginning of the lease term should reflect the minimum payments required by the lease, unless this amount is clearly unrepresentative of the value of the property rights conveyed by the lease.

4.29 The minimum payments required by the lease are 15,000 (three annual payments of 5,000). The lease term covers the non-cancellable period only, ie assuming the lease is terminated on the earliest date the lessee has the right to do so. In accordance with the principles set out earlier, the assets and liabilities recognised at the beginning of the lease term should reflect this minimum amount (discounted to present value), unless this amount is clearly unrepresentative of the fair value of the property rights conveyed by the lease. Assuming that this lease is negotiated on arm's length terms, the present value of the minimum payments of 15,000 will represent the fair value of the rights conveyed to the lessee.

4.30 The assets obtained by the lessee under this lease are:

(a) the right to use the equipment for three years; and

(b) an option, being the right to renew the lease and thereby secure the right to continue to use the equipment for a further two years at an annual rental of 5,000.

4.31 Assuming that the value of the option is small (because the rentals payable for the renewal period are approximately the same value as the value of the rights to be acquired), all of the minimum payments of 15,000 would be deemed to relate to the use of the equipment for the three-year non-cancellable period. Accordingly, the initial asset (measured at the present value of 15,000) would be depreciated to nil over three years.

4.32 If the lessee elects to renew the lease at the end of year 3, it will recognise an asset and liability of 10,000, ie two annual payments of 5,000 (discounted to present value), reflecting the additional rights and obligations acquired relating to years 4 and 5.

4.33 It should be noted that the minimum payments required by the lease for the non-cancellable period are determined on the assumption that the terms of the contract will be adhered to. Consequently, the minimum payments relating to a contract with specifically negotiated terms should not be based on what would happen if a non-cancellable contract is abrogated by one party. Thus, if the lessee can cancel a lease only by making a payment to the lessor that represents liquidated damages for early termination, the minimum payments should include the payments relating to the period for which the lessee has contracted to lease the item rather than the potential damages for early termination.

Accounting for renewal options

4.34 The following example illustrates the accounting for a lease where the rights acquired by the lessee include an option that would, under the Group's proposals, be accounted for separately from the right to use the asset.

EXAMPLE 2

A company enters into a lease of equipment with a term of three years at an annual rental of 5,000. In addition the lease gives the lessee the right to renew the lease for a further two years at the same annual rental. In the event that the lessee elects not to renew, a cancellation penalty of 4,000 is required. It is established that a similar lease, without the renewal option, would also require an annual rental of 5,000 but would not require any further amount to be paid at the end of the three-year term.

4.35 The minimum payments required by the lease in this example are 19,000 (three rentals of 5,000 plus the cancellation penalty of 4,000). In accordance with the principles set out earlier, the assets and liabilities recognised at the beginning of the lease term should reflect this minimum amount (discounted to present value), unless this amount is clearly unrepresentative of the fair value of the property rights conveyed by the lease. Assuming that this lease is negotiated on arm's length terms, the present value of the minimum payments of 19,000 will represent the fair value of the rights conveyed to the lessee.

As in Example 1, the assets obtained by the lessee under the lease are: **4.36**

(a) the right to use the equipment for three years; and

(b) an option, being the right to renew the lease and thereby secure the right to continue to use the equipment for a further two years at an annual rental of 5,000.

Comparison with the lease that contains no option enables these assets to be quantified: the right to use the equipment for three years has a fair value of 15,000 and the option has a fair value of 4,000 (in this example discounting is ignored for simplicity). **4.37**

Accordingly, of the assets of 19,000 recognised at inception, 15,000 should be depreciated to nil over three years. The amount of 4,000 representing the option is not amortised, but rather reviewed for impairment at each balance sheet date: it is assumed here that these reviews demonstrate that no impairment has occurred. If the lessee elects to renew the lease at the end of year 3, it will assume a liability of 10,000 (two annual payments of 5,000); but because it is released from its obligation to pay the cancellation penalty of 4,000, the increase in its total liabilities will be only 6,000. An overview of the accounting for such a scenario is as follows: **4.38**

	Year 1	Year 2	Year 3	Year 4	Year 5
Assets					
Brought forward	—	14	9	4	5
Additions	19	—	—	6	—
Depreciation	(5)	(5)	(5)	(5)	(5)
NBV carried forward	14	9	4	5	—
Liabilities					
Brought forward	—	14	9	4	5
Additions	19	—	—	6	—
Repaid	(5)	(5)	(5)	(5)	(5)
Carried forward	14	9	4	5	—

The assets at the end of each year may be analysed as follows: **4.39**

	Year 1	Year 2	Year 3	Year 4	Year 5
Rights to use equipment	10	5	—	5	—
Renewal option	4	4	4	—	—
Total	14	9	4	5	—

For ease of presentation in this overview, the payments required by the lease have not been discounted. As a consequence of this, no finance charge is recorded and the expense relating to the lease is simply depreciation of 5,000 in each year. **4.40**

At the beginning of the lease term the lessee has incurred a liability to pay a non-refundable amount of 4,000 relating to the renewal period; the lessee has therefore acquired for 4,000 the option to purchase the right to use the equipment for a further two years for additional payments of 6,000. **4.41**

4.42   The Group takes the view that an option should be accounted for separately from the rights to use the property where there is sufficient evidence of value. It is clear in this example that at the beginning of the lease term an amount of 4,000 would be treated as an asset, representing the right to renew the lease.

4.43   In the Group's view the carrying amount of the option asset would not be subject to depreciation charges over the initial (non-cancellable) term, since it forms part of the cost of the right to use the equipment in years 4 and 5. If the renewal option is exercised, the depreciable amount of 10,000 (comprising the unamortised value of 4,000 and the additional cost of 6,000 which would then be recognised as an asset and liability) would be depreciated over years 4 and 5.*

4.44   As with any asset, the carrying amount of the asset representing the right to renew the lease (4,000 in this example) should be reviewed to ensure that it is not stated at more than its recoverable amount. This might arise, for example, if the lessee became unlikely to renew the lease because of adverse economic conditions, or if it became clear that a cheaper lease of a similar asset would be available elsewhere. Any write-off would be recognised in accordance with the rules in the accounting standards on impairment, ie the carrying amount of the asset would be written down immediately and not spread over the remaining years of the initial lease term.

4.45   In this example, it is assumed that the amount of the lease payments could be apportioned between the amount that related to the use of the equipment and that which represented the right to renew the lease. In practice, however, the evidence may be less clear-cut, especially where the right to renew has little or no value (see Example 1). In such cases no significant distortion is likely to result in treating the whole of the payments required by the lease as relating to the use of the equipment and, hence, charging as an expense the whole of the carrying amount of the lease asset by depreciation charges over the initial (non-cancellable) term.

4.46   Another feature of the example is that it was assumed that the amount in respect of the use of the asset corresponded to the rental set out in the lease, and that the cancellation penalty equated to the amount in respect of the right to renew. Clearly, however, this may not always be the case: a higher rental and a lower cancellation penalty could be agreed with the same overall economic effect. Thus apportionment of the total asset amount between the amount that represents the use of the equipment and that which represents the right to renew the lease will require judgement. However, in view of the subjectivity of valuation of a right to renew, it would seem appropriate for revised accounting standards to require that the amount treated as being in respect of such a right should equal that *which can be demonstrated* to reflect the value of that right.

Options where the lessee is not free to avoid renewal

4.47   Lease contracts may specify that the lessee's ability to exercise options to cancel or renew is restricted in some way, such that the future events that must take place before the lessee can terminate the lease are not under the lessee's control. For example, the lessee may have the right to cancel the lease only with the permission of the lessor, or upon the occurrence of a contingent future event. Similarly, the lessee may have the right to cancel the lease only by entering into a new lease. In such circumstances the lease contract conveys to the lessee present obligations that are not

---

As noted in paragraph 4.11, some members believe that the treatment described would be inappropriate if such options were considered to be financial instruments. An alternative view is that option assets should be amortised or revalued during the period to the final exercise date.

eliminated by the existence of the option; hence, the accounting should not be based on the assumption that the lessee is free to cancel the lease.

It is sometimes difficult to determine what is the substantive lease term in a lease that can be renewed or cancelled at the option of the lessee. If the fixed non-cancellable term of the lease is clearly unrepresentative of the time period that the lessee is compelled to occupy or possess the property, the lease contract conveys to the lessee a present obligation to renew the lease that is not substantively restricted by the option; hence, the accounting should not be based on the assumption that the lessee is free to cancel the lease.   **4.48**

In the circumstances described above, the asset and liability recognised at the beginning of the lease term would then reflect the rights and obligations that exist on the assumption that the lease is renewed (or not cancelled). If the lessee subsequently negotiates an early termination with the lessor or, in the case of a contingent option, the relevant conditions occur and the lessee cancels the lease, the termination should be accounted for in the period in which it takes place.   **4.49**

Factors to consider when determining if the lessee is compelled to occupy or possess the property for a period longer than the fixed non-cancellable term include, but are not limited to, the relative importance or significance of the property to the continuation of the lessee's line of business or service to its customers, the uniqueness of purpose or location of the property, the availability of comparable replacement property, the existence of leasehold improvements or other assets whose value would be impaired by the lessee vacating or discontinuing use of the leased property, and the ability or willingness of the lessee to bear the cost associated with relocation or replacement of the leased property at market rental rates. The presence of one or more of the above factors does not, by itself, result in the conclusion that the lessee is compelled to lease the property for the longer, rather than the shorter, term. Rather, one must assess the impact of the relevant factor(s) on the substance of the contractually stated lease term.   **4.50**

A consequence of the approach being proposed is that it should not be assumed that the lessee has a present obligation to renew a lease merely because the lessee has an incentive to renew—for example, where a financial penalty is payable if the lease is not renewed. A financial penalty for non-renewal may be explicitly stated in the lease contract or it may be a consequence of the decision not to renew the lease, such as forgoing the advantage of a bargain renewal or purchase option. As discussed previously, any financial penalty for non-renewal would be included in the assets and liabilities recognised by the lessee upon initial recognition (ie as part of the minimum payments required by the lease). In the case of a bargain renewal or purchase option, or significant financial penalty for non-renewal, the lessee would have a significant liability in respect of that option.   **4.51**

Thus it is not intended that the recognition of initial asset and liability amounts should depend on assessing likely future economic, technological or other conditions and determining whether the renewal of a lease seems probable. If the lessee is not compelled to renew the lease on the basis of conditions at the option date, exercise should generally not be assumed at the beginning of the lease. For example: **4.52**

- if the lessee's business suffered adverse economic conditions, the lessee might choose not to renew the lease (and incur a financial penalty), rather than renew the lease and have the risk of the equipment sitting idle (and incur further rentals).

- if the market rental for similar assets fell significantly, it might be cheaper for the lessee to cancel the lease (and incur a financial penalty) and replace it with a new lease on current market terms rather than continuing with the existing lease.
- if the leased item became technologically obsolete, the lessee would rather replace it than renew the lease.

4.53   The approach described above differs in some respects from present lease accounting standards in relation to determining the lease term (on which the recognition and measurement of lease assets and liabilities depends). Present standards generally define the lease term to include the initial non-cancellable period for which the lessee has contracted to lease the item and all periods for which the lessee has the option to continue to use the leased item, where it is considered at inception to be 'reasonably certain' that the lessee will exercise such options. However, the difference in approach should be viewed in the context of the overall contrast between the approach to lessee accounting that is proposed in this Paper (ie a basis for consistently reporting assets and liabilities under all leases) and the 'all or nothing' treatment of finance leases and operating leases respectively under present standards.

LEASEHOLD IMPROVEMENTS

4.54   An issue that arises in relation to the proposed treatment of renewal options is the treatment of any capital expenditure associated with the leased asset—such as leasehold improvements—where the useful economic life may extend beyond the earliest date that the lessee has the right to terminate the lease, but where such assets may become worthless if the lessee failed to renew the lease for a further term (or terms).

4.55   Expenditure on leasehold improvements is one of the factors noted in the previous section that might indicate that the lessee is compelled to occupy or possess the property for a period longer than the fixed non-cancellable term, in which case the recognised asset and liability amounts in respect of the lease should assume that the lease is renewed. In such circumstances, the depreciable assets (ie the right to use the leased item for the extended lease term and the related leasehold improvements) would be depreciated over their useful economic lives, which would not exceed the extended lease term. If, however, the renewal of a lease is not reflected in the assets and liabilities that are recognised in respect of the lease, the Group believes that any related capital expenditure should be depreciated over the shorter term that is reflected in the lease asset and liability, ie excluding any optional renewal periods.

PURCHASE OPTIONS

4.56   Leases that contain purchase options raise similar issues to renewal options. Under the Group's proposed principles, the exercise of purchase options would not be anticipated.

4.57   The rights that are reflected in the lease asset that is recorded by the lessee at the beginning of the lease term will comprise the rights to use the property and the fair value of the purchase option. A purchase option will have a significant value if the price payable on exercise is expected to be significantly less than the fair value of the property at the purchase date (as in the case of a bargain purchase option). Such value will be reflected in the minimum payments that are required by the lease. Some contracts (commonly referred to as hire purchase contracts) give the lessee the option to purchase the leased property for a nominal sum at the end of the lease: the minimum payments that are reflected in the initial asset and liability amounts would then represent the fair value of the property.

Where a purchase option has a value (and assuming its value can be ascertained with   **4.58**
sufficient reliability), the option should be accounted for separately from the rights to
use the property for the non-cancellable period of the lease, and a portion of the
minimum lease payments would be deemed to relate to the purchase of the option.
The subsequent accounting treatment for the option asset may differ from that used
for the asset which is the right to use the property (see paragraph 4.11).

CONTINGENT RENTALS THAT VARY WITH USAGE

Leases with contingent rentals that vary with usage give rise to substantially similar   **4.59**
issues as leases that contain renewal options. The similarity is that both kinds of
leases give the lessee the option to 'purchase more' of the asset.

The following example is a straightforward case of a lease containing a contingent   **4.60**
rental linked to the amount of usage that the lessee makes of a motor vehicle.

EXAMPLE 3
A lessee enters a lease to hire a motor vehicle for three years at an annual rental of
5,000. In addition, an extra 0.5 per mile is payable if, and to the extent that, the
mileage driven exceeds 60,000 miles. The excess mileage charge reflects fair compensation for the additional wear and tear of the vehicle. The lessee returns the
vehicle to the lessor at the end of the lease.

Under the principles discussed earlier, at the beginning of the lease term the lessee   **4.61**
would recognise an asset and liability of the present value of three payments of 5,000.
All of this would be deemed to relate to the usage of the vehicle, representing the fair
value of the right to use the vehicle for three years up to a maximum of 60,000 miles.

The lessee also has in effect a right (but not an obligation)—ie an option—to pur-   **4.62**
chase additional usage at the rate of 0.5 per mile. As the 0.5 per mile reflects fair
compensation for the additional wear and tear of the vehicle, the option would not
be expected to have much value. Consequently, no value would be attributed to the
option.

The contingent usage-related rentals would be recognised as incurred. There is no   **4.63**
corresponding asset at the point when the lessee incurs a liability for excess mileage
charges because those rentals relate to economic benefits that have already been
consumed, ie they are compensation for the additional wear and tear that the lessee
has incurred.

The proposed basis of accounting by the lessee can also be viewed from the per-   **4.64**
spective of the lessor. In this example the lessor does not have an unconditional right
to receive any contingent usage-related rentals until the lessee drives the excess
mileage. Until then, the economic benefits relating to the vehicle's remaining useful
life have not been transferred by the lessor to the lessee and can properly be reported
as a property asset of the lessor.

CONTINGENT RENTALS THAT ARE A PROPORTION OF THE LESSEE'S REVENUES OR PROFITS DERIVED FROM THE LEASED PROPERTY

Example 4 is a lease where the amount of rent payable varies according to the   **4.65**
revenue generated in the lessee's business from the exploitation of the leased item.

EXAMPLE 4

A lessee enters a three-year lease on a retail store. The annual rent comprises a minimum base rental of 10,000 plus $\frac{1}{2}$ per cent of the store's turnover during each year.

4.66   Application of the following proposed principles is relevant to the lease in this example:

    (a)   the value of the rights obtained by the lessee under a lease cannot be less than the present value of the minimum payments required by the lease (assuming that the lease is negotiated on an arm's length basis).

    (b)   if the minimum payments required by the lease are clearly unrepresentative of the value of the property rights conveyed by the lease, an amount reflecting the fair value of such rights should be recognised as assets and liabilities. The fair value of the property rights conveyed by a lease might be determined by having regard to the payments required by a similar lease that had no provision for contingent rentals.

    (c)   contingent rentals (in excess of the minimum payments, or greater amount, recognised at the beginning of the lease term) should be recognised when the contingency criteria are met.

4.67   The Group's view is that the initial asset and liability should comprise the aggregate of the present value of the base rentals and an amount in respect of the share of turnover. For example, if it could be established that a similar lease without the obligation to pay to the lessor a proportion of future turnover would require a base rental of 10,500, the asset and liability recognised at the beginning of the lease term would be the present value of three rentals of that amount. Contingent rentals that differ from the amount of 500 for each year that is recognised at the beginning of the lease term would be recognised in income when the contingency criteria are met.

4.68   Example 4 differs from Example 3 in one important respect. In Example 3 the contingent usage-related consideration gives the lessee an option to purchase additional usage. In Example 4, the contingent turnover-related consideration is unlikely to represent compensation to the lessor for wear and tear caused by (optional) additional use; instead, it represents consideration for the same rights to occupy the store that have been conveyed by the base rentals.

4.69   An alternative view is that the initial asset and liability should reflect only the present value of the minimum payments required by the lease (three payments of 10,000). Those who favour this approach argue that it is incorrect to account for the lease by analogy with a lease that lacked the contingent rental. That assumes that the lessee's asset is an unencumbered right to use the property for the term of the lease, whereas the reality is that the lessee's asset is less valuable: it is the right to use the property for the term of the lease, subject to the restriction that, if used to make sales, 12fc per cent of the turnover is payable to the lessor. Supporters of this view also argue that, as there is no obligation that requires the lessee to make any sales, there is no liability to pay a larger amount than the base rentals. On this view the turnover-related element of the rentals is part of the cost of the lessee's future operations (akin to a royalty payment) and is appropriately recognised as an expense at the time the sales are made, and not before.

4.70   The Group believes that the treatment under this alternative view might undervalue the lessee's asset (the right to use the property) because contingent consideration is excluded from the amounts recognised as assets and liabilities. In extreme cases, all of the payments that the lessee is required to make could be contingent on the sales generated by the lessee, with no minimum base rental. In such cases no assets and liabilities would be recognised by the lessee under the alternative view, yet it is clear that the rights conveyed to the lessee to exploit the property have a value. In Example 4, the lessor has transferred the right to use the store for three years and the Group therefore believes that this right should be initially reported as an asset at its fair value—this is assumed to be approximately the same value as an equivalent lease where the rentals (ie fair market rentals) are specified in advance.

Discretion to avoid using leased property

The discussion of the previous example has assumed that the lessee has discretion to avoid paying contingent rentals by not using the subject item. Thus the lessee could in theory choose not to exploit the item to its potential—for example, the lessee could mothball the item in adverse economic conditions, or it could choose to replace the leased item with different property interests if more profitable opportunities arose. There will, however, be circumstances where the lessee has little or no discretion to avoid using the leased item and so cannot avoid paying rentals that are linked to the item's use or to the revenue generated from it. Such circumstances could arise from factors within the lease or from factors outside the lease. The following example is a variant of Example 4. **4.71**

EXAMPLE 5

A lessee enters a three-year lease on a retail store. The annual rent comprises a minimum base rental of 10,000 plus 12fc per cent of the store's turnover during each year. The lessee is an anchor tenant for a new shopping centre. The lease requires the store to stay open for the duration of the lease and specifies minimum opening hours.

Under the Group's proposals, the accounting would be the same as in Example 4: the initial asset and liability should comprise the aggregate of the present value of the base rentals and an amount in respect of the share of turnover. This would be expected to be similar to the base rentals payable under a lease that did not require payment of a percentage of future turnover. **4.72**

Some supporters of the alternative view on Example 4 might take a different view because the lease contains conditions that remove the lessee's discretion whether to make future sales. Because the lessee is obliged to pay some amount in respect of the turnover-related element, they would agree with the accounting proposed by the Group for this example. **4.73**

Other supporters of the alternative view on Example 4 would not make the distinction between the two examples on the basis of discretion or lack of discretion to avoid payment. They would apply the same treatment for all leases where the rentals payable depend on the lessee's exploitation of the rights acquired. They would prefer a requirement for lessees to disclose details of the (unprovided for) contingent element of leases in the notes to the financial statements. **4.74**

For those who support this view, the revenue-related payments in those examples are akin to royalties payable on sales,* and should be accounted for similarly to other costs (staff costs and other operating overheads) that the lessees would have to incur by carrying out their service obligations. In addition, since the lessor's right to receive the contingent rentals is subject to demand risk relating to the lessee's business, that element of the lease has some characteristics of a joint venture between lessor and **4.75**

Those who support this alternative view also do not believe that assets and liabilities arise in respect of future performance-related royalties relating to licensing agreements for the use of trade marks, patents etc, unless minimum payments are specified.

lessee, rather than a transaction giving rise to a financial liability for the lessee and a financial receivable for the lessor. The lessor, in addition to retaining a residual interest in the leased property, has in effect also retained an interest in relation to the right to participate in the lessee's exploitation of the leased property. Some might describe this as a 'quasi-equity' interest although, unlike a normal equity interest, the lessor participates in revenues rather than profits.

Unrepresentative lease payments

4.76   The next example illustrates a case where the minimum lease payments are clearly unrepresentative of the value of the property rights conveyed by the lease.

EXAMPLE 6

A railway company leases rolling stock for seven years. The lease requires the company to pay a fixed annual rental of 2 million and an additional rental calculated as a percentage of passenger miles. The lease prevents the company from replacing the leased stock during the lease term. The amounts payable under the lease are subject to a maximum amount which has a present value of 25 million, and this is the amount that will be payable if the railway company maintains the service level required by its operating licence (which covers the remaining term of the lease). A similar lease for rolling stock that allowed unlimited usage would require lease payments with a present value of 25 million.

4.77   The lease is in substance similar to a lease that provides for unlimited usage of the rolling stock. Because the rentals are capped at an amount that is approximately the same as the payments required by a similar lease that had no provision for contingent rentals, the rentals should be treated as if they were not contingent at all (if they were not capped at this amount, the lessee would incur the risk of paying more than the fair value of the property and would be better off purchasing it). At the beginning of the lease term, an asset and a liability of 25 million discounted to present value should be recorded.

RENTALS THAT VARY IN LINE WITH PRICES

4.78   Some leases specify that the level of rentals payable at inception should be adjusted during the term of the lease for future price changes. For those leases, the amounts payable by the lessee are generally independent of the lessee's future actions, ie they do not relate to the lessee's use of the leased property or to the lessee's success in exploiting the leased property. Such leases, therefore, create for the lessee at the beginning of the lease term a liability of unknown amount.

Interest variation clauses

4.79   Some leases require rentals to be adjusted when there are changes in interest rates— for example, the rentals may vary with the lessor's funding costs. Such leases have the effect of protecting the lessor's rate of return after funding costs on its investment in the lease. From the lessee's standpoint the liabilities that arise from such leases are similar to variable rate loans and would be accounted for accordingly. At the beginning of the lease term, the assets and liabilities to be recognised by the lessee would be measured based on the rentals and interest rates then applicable.

Lease payments that vary with price changes

Some leases require the rentals to be revised periodically in line with price changes **4.80**
relating to the use of the leased item, for example to revise them to current market
rates or in line with changes in a price index.

Under some leases, rentals are reset annually to reflect price changes. Under other **4.81**
leases, rentals are reset less frequently than every year. For example, in the UK it is
quite common for certain types of long-term commercial property leases to be
subject to periodic 'upward-only' rent reviews—say every three or five years—where
the rent is reset to a current market rent if that is higher than the rent currently being
paid. Consider the following example:

EXAMPLE 7

A company enters into a lease of an office block with a term of 20 years. The rental is
100 a year, but this will be reviewed on the fifth, tenth and fifteenth anniversaries of
the grant of the lease. If, at the date of a review, a market rental is greater than the
rent payable under the lease, the rent will be adjusted to that market rental, but no
adjustment will be made if the existing rent is greater than a current market rent.

Clearly the initial rent is smaller than that which would be payable under a similar **4.82**
lease that did not provide for rent reviews. Discounting the original rentals payable
at a nominal rate of interest would thus result in initial asset and liability amounts
that were not representative of the fair value of the rights and obligations conveyed
by the lease, ie they would be understated. The Group's view therefore is that at the
beginning of the lease term, the lessee should record assets and liabilities equal to the
present value of its best estimate of the rentals that will actually be payable, discounted at a nominal rate of interest. In theory a similar result would be achieved by
discounting the original rentals (without taking account of future variations) at a real
rate (ie excluding inflation).*

As in Example 4, an alternative view is that only the contracted rentals (ie only 20 **4.83**
payments of 100) should be reflected as an asset and a liability at the beginning of the
lease term (discounted at a nominal rate). There are two lines of argument that
support this view:

(a) *There is no liability.* Some take the view that, until such time as the rent review
takes place, the lessee has no liability to pay a higher amount than 20 payments
of 100. On this view Example 7 is identical to Example 4: as in Example 4 it can
be argued that the property rights obtained under the lease are not as great as
would be obtained under a similar lease that required only a fixed rental.

(b) *If there is a liability, it cannot be measured reliably.* It can also be argued that the
measurement difficulties associated with the rent review clauses preclude
recognition of any additional liability in respect of them. This is especially
difficult for leases such as those in Example 7 because a reliable estimate cannot
be derived from a forecast of the general trend of future property prices: first,
because the price applicable to a specific building might diverge significantly
from that which prevails in the market generally (using sectors of the market
such as 'Central London prime office space' can reduce, but not eliminate, these
divergences); secondly, because the rent increase will depend on the market
price prevailing at three specific dates, and a general trend cannot enable
reliable predictions of prices prevailing at specific dates. (If future rentals
cannot be predicted with any degree of reliability, it would seem unlikely that
real rates of discount could be estimated with any degree of reliability.)

*This assumes that inflation in property prices is in line with general inflation.

4.84   The points made in the above two subparagraphs are logically independent. It can be argued that Example 7 is different from Example 4 because the future event that gives rise to the increased rental (price increases) is outside the control of the lessee: in Example 4 the amount of use the lessee makes of the property is generally within the lessee's control. This line of argument would lead to the conclusion that the contingent rentals should, in principle, be reflected in the assets and liabilities initially recognised in Example 7, but not in Example 4. However, in practice they may not be recognised because they cannot be measured with sufficient reliability.

4.85   As noted above, the Group agrees with the view that the value of the contingent rentals should as a matter of principle be reflected in the fair value of the assets and liabilities recognised at the beginning of the lease term. However, in accordance with the normal principles of asset and liability recognition (see Chapter 3), there is a presumption that amounts will be recognised only if they have a value that can be measured reliably.

Subsequent remeasurement

4.86   Under the Group's view of the treatment of contingent rentals that vary in line with prices, initial estimates of the asset and liability amounts would need to be reviewed at each balance sheet date, whether or not a rent review date had been reached. For example, where rents are reset every five years, the potential adjustments at years 5, 10 and onwards would need to be measured and included in the reported lease liability at each of years 1–4; the potential adjustments at year 10 and onwards would need to be measured and included in the reported lease liability at each of years 5–9, and so on. The lease liability should be restated if the current best estimate (discounted) is different from the carrying amount.

4.87   An increase or decrease in the liability could be accounted for in one of two ways. The increase or decrease could be recognised as a loss or gain immediately (thus fixing the 'cost' of the lease asset by reference to the estimated fair value of the consideration at inception) or a corresponding adjustment could be made to the carrying value of the lease asset to reflect the revised estimate of the cost of using the leased item. The Group's preferred view is that the carrying value of the lease asset should be adjusted, subject to the carrying amount of the asset not being increased above a value that would give rise to an impairment loss. (A similar issue on subsequent remeasurement arises in respect of residual value guarantees: this issue and the basis for the Group's view are discussed more fully in Chapter 5.)

4.88   Those who support the alternative view of Example 7 would remeasure the lease asset and liability only at years 5, 10 and 15, when the rents are revised.

> **Recommendations**
>
> 4A   On the assumption that the lease is negotiated on an arm's length basis, the value of the rights obtained by the lessee under a lease cannot be less than the present value of the minimum payments required by the lease.
>
> 4B   When accounting for options conveyed to the lessee, the exercise of renewal or purchase options should not generally be anticipated: the fair value of the options themselves acquired at the beginning of the lease term will be reflected in the minimum payments required by the lease.

4C   If the value of a renewal or purchase option cannot be measured reliably or is immaterial to the lessee's financial statements, the option would not be accounted for separately: as a result, the whole of the minimum lease payments would be deemed to relate to the usage of the asset.

4D   Where a renewal or purchase option has a significant value (and assuming its value can be ascertained with sufficient reliability), the option should be accounted for separately from the rights to use the property for the non-cancellable period of the lease, and a portion of the minimum lease payments would be deemed to relate to the purchase of the option.

4E   Under the historical cost model that is developed in this Paper, the carrying amount in respect of a renewal or purchase option would be reviewed for impairment during the period up to the exercise date and, if the option is exercised, the carrying amount at the exercise date would be amortised subsequently as appropriate.

4F   Renewal and purchase options should give rise to additional assets and liabilities when exercised, reflecting the fair value of the additional rights and obligations conveyed to the lessee.

4G   In circumstances where the lessee's ability to exercise options to cancel or renew is restricted, such that the future events that must take place before the lessee can terminate the lease are not under the lessee's control, the asset and liability recognised at the beginning of the lease term should reflect the rights and obligations that exist on the assumption that the lease is renewed (or not cancelled).

4H   In circumstances where the fixed non-cancellable term of the lease is clearly unrepresentative of the time period that the lessee is compelled to occupy or possess the property, the asset and liability recognised at the beginning of the lease term should reflect the rights and obligations that exist on the assumption that the lease is renewed (or not cancelled).

4I   If the minimum payments required by the lease (such as the minimum payments specified in leases with contingent rentals) are clearly unrepresentative of the value of the property rights conveyed by the lease, an amount reflecting the fair value of such rights should be recognised as assets and liabilities. The fair value of the property rights conveyed by a lease might be determined by having regard to the payments required by a similar lease that had no provision for contingent rentals.

4J   Contingent rentals (in excess of the minimum payments, or greater amount, recognised at the beginning of the lease term) should be recognised when the contingency criteria are met.

4K   If the renewal of a lease is not reflected in the assets and liabilities that are recognised in respect of the lease, any related capital expenditure (such as leasehold improvements) should be depreciated over the shorter term that is reflected in the lease asset and liability, ie excluding any optional renewal periods.

Chapter 5 Lessees' interests in residual values

INTRODUCTION

5.1   The most straightforward leases give the lessee the right to use an item for an agreed period of time in return for a series of payments. At the end of the lease term, the lessee simply returns the item to the lessor with no further rights or obligations. As discussed in Chapter 3, the asset and liability that would be recognised under the approach advocated in this Paper when the item is delivered to the lessee represent the right to use the item for only part of its life and the obligation to pay for that use. No asset or liability would be recognised in relation to the return of the item at the end of the lease. (As discussed in Chapter 8, the lessor's corresponding assets comprise the payments receivable from the lessee and the rights to the used equipment at the end of the lease.)

5.2   Many leases, however, also convey an economic interest in the residual value of the leased item to the lessee. This may arise in a number of ways, for example:

- the lease may convey ownership of the leased item to the lessee at the end of the contract.
- the lessee may guarantee the residual value, ie be committed to compensate the lessor if it is less than a stated amount.
- the lessee may be entitled to receive all, or a share of, the sale proceeds.

This chapter discusses the recognition and measurement of assets and liabilities that arise from such arrangements and how they might be characterised in the balance sheet.

5.3   Agreements for sharing residual value risks and benefits between the parties involved can be complex. Their interpretation is an important issue under present accounting standards and can be particularly difficult. Sometimes, under present standards, they are a key feature to be considered when determining whether a lease should be classified as a finance lease or an operating lease, since residual values guaranteed by lessees are included in the minimum lease payments that may determine whether a lease is a finance lease or an operating lease. If the classification of a lease is a finance lease, the guaranteed amounts are also included in the assets and liabilities recognised by lessees.

5.4   A number of examples are used in this chapter to illustrate the nature of the assets and liabilities arising under various residual value arrangements. The same examples are considered from the lessor's perspective in Chapter 9. It is assumed in each case that equipment is leased for a term of three years, and the following amounts are specified:

- Rentals over the lease term (5,000 per year)   15,000
- Residual value estimate   3,000

5.5   For simplicity the amounts in the examples have not been discounted. Although, in practice, the amounts would be discounted, using undiscounted amounts permits the proposed and the alternative approaches to be shown clearly without in any way affecting the validity of the analysis.

5.6   Under the recognition principles discussed in Chapter 3, the analysis focuses on determining:

(a)   what rights the lessee acquires under the lease contract and whether they individually meet the definition of an asset;

(b)   what obligations the lessee incurs under the lease contract and whether they individually meet the definition of a liability; and

(c)   if assets and liabilities are recognised, how they should be measured.

The following table summarises for each example the undiscounted amount of the assets and liabilities that would be recognised by the lessee at the beginning of the lease term under the Group's proposed treatment and under possible alternative treatments that have been considered.   **5.7**

Example	Description	Value of asset and liability at inception	
		Group's proposal	Alternative treatments considered
1	Lessee returns equipment to lessor (see paragraph 5.9)	15,000	n/a
2	Lease conveys ownership to lessee (see paragraph 5.15)	18,000	n/a
3	Lessee provides residual value guarantee (see paragraph 5.19)	15,000$^+$	18,000
4	Lessee receives all sale proceeds (see paragraph 5.40)	18,000	n/a
5	Lessor receives sale proceeds, but lessee receives any surplus and pays any shortfall (see paragraph 5.45)	15,000$^+$	18,000
6	Lessor receives sale proceeds, but lessee receives a share of any surplus and pays a share of any shortfall (see paragraph 5.58)	15,000$^+$	16,500

+ In these cases the fair value of the guarantee is added to the lease payments of 15,000 and recognised as a separate liability (if it is practicable to quantify it).

In the examples both the rentals required by the lease and the residual value of the equipment are the same in all cases. In practice, if the leases were otherwise identical, the rentals would be expected to vary under the different scenarios. For example, if the rentals in Example 1 (where the lessor bears all residual value risk) were 15,000, the rentals in Example 3 would be expected to be less than 15,000, because the lessee has also provided a residual value guarantee.   **5.8**

LESSEE SIMPLY RETURNS THE LEASED ITEM TO THE LESSOR AT THE END OF THE LEASE

The following example, which is discussed in Chapter 3, is included for completeness and to facilitate comparison with the discussion of lessor accounting in Chapter 9.   **5.9**

EXAMPLE 1

A lessee enters a lease to hire equipment for three years at an annual rental of 5,000. The lessee returns the equipment to the lessor at the end of the lease.

Initial recognition

5.10   The rights and obligations conveyed by the lease are as follows:

- the lessee has the right to use the equipment for three years only—the lessee has no rights to the used equipment at the end of the lease.
- the lessee has an obligation to pay rentals of 15,000.

5.11   Accordingly, at the beginning of the lease term the lessee should recognise an asset and liability and measure them at the present value of the three annual payments. The asset represents the fair value of the right to use the equipment for three years only—the lessee controls the usage rights for that period and does not have any rights relating to the equipment beyond the end of the lease term. The property rights and economic benefits relating to the equipment beyond the end of the lease (the residual interest) have not been transferred to the lessee. Consequently, the residual interest remains an asset of the lessor.

Subsequent remeasurement

5.12   The initial carrying amount of the lease asset reflects the fair value of the right to use the equipment for the lease term. That value would be depreciated over the lease term as the economic benefits are consumed (including recognition of any impairment losses in addition to normal depreciation), in accordance with the usual principles of accounting for property, plant and equipment. Changes in residual values have no economic impact on the lessee in this case.

5.13   An important implication of the proposed approach is that all assets recognised in respect of leases would fall within the scope of accounting standards dealing with amortisation and impairment of property, plant and equipment. Thus any impairment loss would be recognised in the income statement as soon as the carrying amount is identified as being no longer recoverable in the cash-generating unit to which a lease asset contributes.

5.14   Under the principles of present accounting standards, the lease liability would be accounted for as debt: its carrying amount would reflect the allocation of lease payments between the finance costs of the lease (charged to the income statement over the term of the lease at a constant rate on the carrying amount) and repayment of outstanding debt.*

LEASE CONVEYS OWNERSHIP OF THE LEASED ITEM TO THE LESSEE

5.15   Some leases convey legal ownership of the leased item to the lessee at the end of the contract. For example, legal title may pass when the last payment has been made by the lessee, or the lease may require the lessee to purchase the leased item for an agreed sum at the end of the lease term.

EXAMPLE 2

A lessee enters a lease to hire equipment for three years at an annual rental of 5,000. At the end of the lease the lessee is required to pay a further 3,000 to purchase the equipment.

Lease liabilities are financial instruments and would be accounted for according to the principles in future accounting standards dealing with financial instruments.

Initial recognition

Contracts that provide for the automatic transfer of ownership when the lessee has paid the final instalment are essentially sale agreements, the purchase price for the asset being payable in instalments. At the beginning of the lease term, the lessor has transferred to the lessee rights to all of the future economic benefits derived from the equipment and the lessee has incurred a present obligation for the amounts it has agreed to pay the lessor (18,000). Accordingly, the lessee should recognise an initial asset and liability measured at the present value of 18,000 (which will, if the transaction is negotiated on an arm's length basis, be the equipment's fair value). In effect, the lessee should account for such transactions as purchase contracts financed by instalment finance—this does not represent any change from existing lease accounting practices. **5.16**

Subsequent remeasurement

The initial carrying amount of the lease asset reflects the fair value of the equipment. The asset's depreciable amount (ie cost less residual value) would be depreciated over the equipment's useful economic life as the economic benefits are consumed (including recognition of any impairment losses in addition to normal depreciation), in accordance with the usual principles of accounting for tangible assets that are owned. As the lease conveys ownership of the equipment to the lessee, the useful life used for the purpose of calculating depreciation might be longer than the lease term. **5.17**

The lease liability would be accounted for as debt, as described earlier. **5.18**

LESSEE GUARANTEES A RESIDUAL VALUE

Some leases require the lessee to provide a residual value guarantee to the lessor, as illustrated by the following example. **5.19**

EXAMPLE 3

A lessee enters a lease to hire equipment for three years at an annual rental of 5,000. The equipment will be sold at the end of the lease at fair value. The lessee guarantees a residual value to the lessor: if the equipment realises less than 3,000 when it is sold, the lessee is liable to compensate the lessor for the shortfall.

Initial recognition

The rights and obligations conveyed by the lease are as follows: **5.20**

- the lessee has the right to use the equipment for three years only—the lessee has no rights to the second-hand equipment at the end of the lease.
- the lessee has an obligation to pay rentals of 15,000 and an obligation under the residual value guarantee.

As discussed in Chapter 3, the objective should be to record, at the beginning of the lease term, the fair value of the rights and obligations that are conveyed by the lease. Fair value is measured by the fair value of the consideration given, except where the fair value of the asset received is more clearly evident. **5.21**

It is assumed that the lessee's discretion to avoid any payment that may be required under the guarantee is limited, because it is affected by future events—price **5.22** changes—that are outside the lessee's control.* Thus the fair value of the consideration that the lessee has given for obtaining the right to use the equipment for the lease term comprises the present value of the minimum payments required by the lease (15,000) plus the fair value of the guarantee.

Measurement—valuation approach

5.23   Consequently, the Group believes that in principle the fair value of the guarantee should be recognised as a liability at the beginning of the lease term and added to the present value of the rentals to arrive at the initial carrying amount for the asset (the rentals will have been set to reflect the value attributed to the writing of the guarantee). The recognised asset would reflect the fair value of the right to use the item over the lease term.

5.24   If the guaranteed amount was set at a level far below the expected residual value, such that the possibility of any payment by the lessee was remote, the fair value of the guarantee would be insignificant—for example, if the expected residual value in Example 3 was, say, 5,000 compared with the 3,000 guaranteed. In that event, an insignificant value (or no value) would be attributed to the guarantee and the initial lease asset and liability would simply reflect the amount that the lessee has agreed to pay for the use of the equipment over the lease term.

5.25   In contrast, if the guaranteed amount was greater than the expected residual value, the guarantee would have an intrinsic value (ie the difference between the guaranteed amount and the expected residual value) at the outset—for example, if the expected residual value in Example 3 was, say, 2,000 compared with the 3,000 guaranteed. The guarantee would then have a significant fair value, which should be recognised as a liability by the lessee. In this situation the giving of the guarantee should have resulted in a compensating reduction in the rental payments required during the term of the lease—in effect the giving of the guarantee represents part of the price that the lessee agreed to pay for the use of the equipment over the lease term. Hence, the initial lease asset and liability should reflect both the amounts the lessee is required to pay during the lease term and the fair value of the guarantee.

5.26   It should be noted, however, that the fair value would not be confined to the intrinsic value of the guarantee at inception.† Even if the guaranteed amount reflected a reasonable estimate of the residual value, but the estimate itself was subject to considerable uncertainty due to volatility in the market for second-hand equipment, the fair value of the guarantee would be significant, because the lessee would be bearing the risk of variation below the uncertain estimate. The price for taking that risk would represent part of the price that the lessee agreed to pay for the use of the equipment over the lease term. Hence, the initial lease asset and liability should reflect the amounts the lessee is required to pay during the lease term and the fair value of the guarantee.

5.27   It may be difficult in practice to find a 'fair value' for a residual value guarantee. However, where the guarantee has a significant value to the lessee and lessor, it should have an observable effect on the pricing of the rental payments for the lease

---

If the incurrence of any liability under the guarantee was primarily attributable to the purchase of additional usage by the lessee, reflecting fair compensation for additional wear and tear of the equipment, the guarantee would be accounted for similarly to contingent rentals that are related to the optional purchase of additional usage as discussed in Chapter 4, ie no liability would be recognised in respect of the guarantee at the beginning of the lease term and, accordingly, the minimum lease payments of 15,000 would be deemed to be fair consideration for the use of the equipment for the lease term.

†*Where the guaranteed amount is no higher than the expected residual value, the intrinsic value is nil.*

term. The rental payments would be expected to be reduced to take account of the lessee's guarantee, which could be viewed as reflecting an insurance premium paid by the lessor to the lessee relating to the residual value. A value for the guarantee at inception could be determined as the present value of the amounts by which the rentals have been reduced on account of the guarantee, which could be estimated by comparing the rental payments with those for an equivalent lease without the residual value guarantee.

Measurement—provisions approach

The Group believes that a valuation approach to recognising residual value guar-   **5.28**
antees as outlined above is in concept consistent with the asset and liability
recognition and measurement principles on which the proposals in this Paper are
based. However, the Group also recognises that there will be practical difficulties in
determining 'fair values' for many residual value guarantees, either because there is
no market in such guarantees or because a market rate for an equivalent unguaranteed lease is not available. In such cases, the price of a guarantee as a separate
component of the lease contract would not be readily ascertainable.

In such circumstances, as a practical alternative to valuing the guarantee directly a   **5.29**
provisions approach* to measuring residual value guarantees could be required. The
initial lessee asset and liability that is recognised would include an amount relating to
the residual value guarantee where a transfer of economic benefits in settlement is
judged probable.† This would clearly be the case where, for example, the guaranteed
amount exceeds the expected residual value. In addition, where a lessee has provided
a number of similar guarantees, the probability that a transfer of economic benefits
will be required would be determined by considering the lessee's residual value
obligations as a whole. Thus, although it may not be thought probable that a payment would be required on any one particular guarantee (for example, because the
guaranteed amounts are held out to be reasonable estimates of the residual values), it
may well be probable that some payments will be required for a population of
guarantees as a whole. If that is the case, a liability would be recognised.

Residual value guarantees that result in the recognition of liabilities by a lessee would   **5.30**
be measured as the present value of the best estimate of the payments that will be
required to settle the obligations under the guarantees. 'Expected value' (a method
that estimates the obligation by weighting all possible outcomes by their associated
probabilities) may be an appropriate method of measuring the liability where, for
example, there is a large population of guarantees. Where a residual value estimate is
itself subject to great uncertainty, the estimated residual value would need to be
adjusted for the risk associated with its potential variability—a risk adjustment
would increase the amount at which the fair value of the guarantee of a 'risky'
residual value is measured.

The valuation and provisions approaches should not result in significantly different   **5.31**
asset and liability amounts since both are methods of recognising and measuring the
lessee's same present obligations. Recognition of an initial lease asset and liability to

---

The approach described here adopts the principles relating to the recognition of provisions set out in IAS 37 'Provisions, Contingent Liabilities and Contingent Assets' and in the UK's standard FRS 12 of the same title.

†*It should be noted that the valuation approach discussed earlier implicitly takes account of probability, because the fair value of a guarantee would reflect the probability that a payment would be required by the lessee. However, whereas the fair value of a guarantee reflects probability on a 'sliding scale', a provisions approach in respect of a single guarantee would result in a liability being recognised only if it were 'more likely than not' that a transfer of economic benefits would occur.*

reflect the payments the lessee is required to make over the lease term plus a provision in respect of the guarantee should also result in the lessee's asset and liability at inception approximating the cost of the right to use the item over the lease term.*

Recognition of net or gross amounts relating to guarantees

5.32   Under the principles discussed above, residual value guarantees would be recognised in the initial lessee asset and liability amounts only on a 'net' basis, rather than on a 'gross' basis (which would show a liability for the full guaranteed amount together with a corresponding asset), since in the Group's view the net amount is the only asset and liability.

5.33   Some might take the view that gross amounts should be recognised in relation to the residual value guarantee (ie in Example 3, the lessee should recognise an additional asset and liability of 3,000), which is the approach taken in existing standards. An argument for this view is that it is prudent to record the lessee's residual value interest as an asset and liability at the full amount of the guaranteed residual value if the lessee has significant risk from residual value variations. This gross basis is shown in the comparative table of examples (see paragraph 5.7) under the heading 'alternative treatments considered'. For Example 3, under this approach the lessee would recognise an asset and liability measured at the present value of 18,000.

5.34   The Group does not regard the gross treatment of guarantees as appropriate for revised accounting standards on leasing because, in its view, the existence of a guarantee does not of itself give rise to a liability, nor to a corresponding asset, for the gross amount that is guaranteed. The value of the lessee's liability is only its exposure under the guarantee, not the total amount that is guaranteed. The lessee has an asset only for the right to use the leased item for the term of the lease; it has no rights relating to the equipment at the end of the lease.

Subsequent remeasurement of assets and liabilities

5.35   As explained above, the initial measurement of the lessee's asset would take into account any value attributed to the guarantee at the inception of the lease. The resulting carrying amount of the asset (ie initial cost) reflects the fair value of the right to use the leased item for the lease term. That amount would be depreciated over the lease term as the economic benefits are consumed (including recognition of any impairment losses in addition to normal depreciation), in accordance with the usual principles of accounting for tangible assets.

5.36   After the initial recognition of lease assets and liabilities, estimates of the lessee's residual value guarantee obligations may change as, for example, market values for second-hand equipment fluctuate. The recognised liability relating to the residual value guarantee would need to be restated to reflect the current estimate of the expenditure expected to be required to settle the obligation.

5.37   An increase or decrease in the liability could be accounted for in one of two ways. The increase or decrease could be recognised as a loss or gain immediately or a corresponding adjustment could be made to the carrying amount of the lease asset. The Group prefers adjusting the carrying amount of the asset.

*If the measurement of a liability is based on measuring a provision for a population of similar guarantees as a whole, this would need to be allocated to the related lease assets on a pro rata or more appropriate basis.

The basis for the Group's preferred view is as follows. The lessee has provided a **5.38** guarantee as part of the consideration to secure the right to use the leased item for the lease term. However, the amount payable is uncertain. Subsequent changes in the residual value of the equipment (which result in changes in the value of the residual value guarantee) are a component of changes in the current value of the equipment which, in turn, affects the cost of the right to use the equipment. For example, if a guarantee becomes more onerous than was expected at the beginning of the lease term, the result is a more expensive asset than was expected. Thus reflecting those changes in the carrying amount of the leased asset is appropriate. Under this view, where a change in the value of the residual value guarantee from the carrying amount in the lease liability is foreseen, the carrying amounts of both the lease liability and the lease asset should be remeasured, subject to the carrying amount of the asset not being increased above a value that would cause an impairment loss. The asset's revised carrying amount would be depreciated over the remainder of the lease term.

An alternative view is that the cost of the lease asset should not be remeasured as a **5.39** result of subsequent changes in the values of residual value guarantees. Under this view the fair value of the right to use the leased item for the lease term should be determined from the lease contract at the inception of the lease. Part of the carrying amount of the asset is derived from the fair value of the residual value guarantee as determined at the beginning of the lease term. Subsequent changes in the value of the guarantee after the liability has been incurred do not affect the initial value of the asset. Consequently, the difference between the remeasured liability and its previous carrying amount should be recognised immediately as a loss or gain in income.

LESSEE RECEIVES THE SALE PROCEEDS

Some leases give the lessee the right to participate in the proceeds from the sale of the **5.40** leased item at the end of the lease, as illustrated in the following example.

EXAMPLE 4

A lessee enters a lease to hire equipment for three years at an annual rental of 5,000. In addition, the lessee is required to pay a fee of 3,000[+] for the residual value. The equipment will be sold at the end of the lease at fair value, and all the sale proceeds will be paid to the lessee.

+ Because in these examples the amounts are not discounted, it is not relevant when the fee is paid.

Initial recognition

In this example, at the beginning of the lease term the lessee has acquired the fol- **5.41** lowing rights:

(a)   the right to use the equipment for three years; and
(b)   the right to receive the proceeds from its sale.

In consideration for the above rights, the lessee has incurred an obligation for the **5.42** amounts it has agreed to pay the lessor (18,000).* As in the previous examples, the present obligation (and, hence, liability) for the payments the lessee is required to make arises on delivery of the equipment to the lessee.

*In Example 3, the present obligation is for the rentals of 15,000 and the residual value guarantee. In Example 4, the present obligation is for the rentals of 18,000.

5.43   Where the lessee actually has an obligation to pay for the right to receive the sale proceeds (or a share of the proceeds), an asset and liability arises for the gross amount involved—included within that asset and liability are, respectively, the right to receive the sale proceeds (or share of the proceeds) and the obligation to pay for it, which are not offsettable.* Accordingly, the lessee should recognise an initial asset and liability measured at the present value of 18,000, which reflects the fair value of the rights acquired. Although the right to receive the residual proceeds is a different asset from the right to use the equipment for the lease term, the Group does not propose that they should be displayed as separate assets in the balance sheet, because it is not normal practice to separate residual values when accounting for assets that are owned.

Subsequent remeasurement

5.44   The initial carrying amount of the asset less its estimated residual value should be depreciated over the lease term as the economic benefits are consumed (including recognition of any impairment losses in addition to normal depreciation), in accordance with the usual principles of accounting for tangible assets. For the purpose of calculating depreciation, an estimate of the amount of the sale proceeds that the lessee expects to receive should be used as the residual value of the lessee's asset. Changes in residual values should also be accounted for in accordance with accounting standards dealing with tangible assets.

LESSOR RECEIVES THE SALE PROCEEDS, BUT LESSEE RECEIVES ANY SURPLUS AND PAYS ANY SHORTFALL

5.45   As an alternative to giving the lessee the rights to receive all or some of the sale proceeds (as in the example above), some leases convey to the lessee the right and obligation to participate in gains and losses arising on the disposal of the leased item. For example, the lessee may agree to pay to (or receive from) the lessor any difference between the leased item's residual value and a predetermined amount. Example 5 is modified in one important respect from Example 4. Instead of the lessee being required to make a payment for the right to receive the residual proceeds, the lessee and lessor are required to make a net cash settlement when the equipment is sold.

EXAMPLE 5

A lessee enters a lease to hire equipment for three years at an annual rental of 5,000. The equipment will be sold at the end of the lease at fair value. If the proceeds are more than 3,000, the lessor will pay the whole of the surplus to the lessee. If the proceeds are less than 3,000, the lessee will pay the shortfall to the lessor.

Initial recognition

5.46   Under this lease the lessee has acquired the following rights:

(a)   the right to use the equipment for three years; and

It is assumed in Example 4 that the lessee does not have a right of set-off, ie the ability to insist on a net settlement with the lessor, because the lessee could be required to transfer economic benefits to the lessor (making the payment for participation in the residual value) whilst being unable to enforce its own access to economic benefits (the receipt of the sale proceeds from the lessor). If a lease contract were structured such that the set-off criteria for financial assets and financial liabilities were met, separate assets and liabilities would not be recognised for the amounts of the right to receive the sale proceeds and the obligation to pay for it—a net amount (if any) would be recognised.

(b)   the right to receive the amount, if any, by which the sale proceeds exceed 3,000.

In consideration for the above rights, the lessee has incurred the following present obligations: **5.47**

(a)   rental payments during the lease term of 15,000; and
(b)   a guarantee to pay the lessor the amount, if any, by which the sale proceeds are less than 3,000, ie a guarantee of 3,000 for the equipment's residual value.

In this example, under the proposed recognition principles, the lessee has an asset representing the right to use the equipment. It also has a liability for the minimum rental payments of 15,000. It then becomes necessary to determine what asset and liability amounts should also be recognised in respect of the equipment's residual value.   **5.48**

Consistently with the Group's view of leases with residual value guarantees (see the discussion of Example 3), this transaction can be viewed as the lessee having acquired the right to use the equipment for part of its life only and having incurred an obligation to pay for it. However, the price payable by the lessee is a variable amount—in effect the price is adjusted to reflect the fair value of the benefits consumed over the lease term.   **5.49**

The exchange of rights and obligations relating to the residual value (ie the right to receive any surplus proceeds, and the obligation to pay any shortfall in proceeds) gives rise to the lessee having a price exposure on the residual value that is settled by a net payment to or by the lessee. Consequently, any asset or liability relating to the lessee's rights and obligations is explicitly for a net amount—the surplus or shortfall. The asset or liability would be measured under the principles discussed earlier, using a valuation approach if a reliable basis exists—for example, reflecting any observable effect of the lessee's interest in the residual value on the pricing of the rental payments for the lease term. Otherwise, a provisions approach would be used and the initial asset and liability amounts would include an amount relating to the residual value guarantee where a receipt or payment was considered probable.   **5.50**

The above analysis of the assets and liabilities arising in Example 5 results in different asset and liability amounts being recognised from those that arise in Example 4. In Example 4 the lessee would recognise an initial asset and liability for the present value of 18,000. In Example 5 the lessee would recognise an initial asset and liability that consists of the present value of 15,000 and a value for the residual value agreement (if it is practical to quantify it).   **5.51**

The substantive difference between Examples 4 and 5 is that the lease contract in Example 4 specifies separate cash outflows and inflows for the lessee relating to the sale of the equipment. In Example 4 the lessee has an obligation to make an additional payment of 3,000 to the lessor and has the right to receive the full residual value proceeds from the lessor, which give rise to separate asset and liability amounts. In Example 5 the lessee has obtained the right to use the equipment for the lease term and the right/obligation to receive any surplus proceeds from the lessor or to pay any deficit, which do not give rise to separate asset and liability amounts in respect of the equipment's residual value. The fact that there are different accounting outcomes in the two examples is not surprising, since they reflect what the lessee would pay for the rights it has acquired in each case.   **5.52**

Alternative view of Example 5

5.53   Some believe that the above analysis and conclusions focus too narrowly on the cash flows that are specified in the lease contract: consequently, they have a different view of the asset and liability characteristics that emerge. In Example 5, they take the view that the lessee has obtained all the risks and benefits relating to the equipment's residual value. In their view, the substance of the transaction in Example 5 is virtually the same as if the lessee obtained all the proceeds from the sale of the equipment (as in Example 4); if the two transactions are economically similar, the accounting treatment in each case should be similar. The fact that there are net, rather than gross, transfers of cash between lessee and lessor in settlement of their contractual rights and obligations is in their view merely a difference of form rather than substance—in both cases a fixed amount of cash (18,000) is received by the lessor and the balance of sale proceeds (if any) are received by the lessee. Accordingly, at inception the lessee should recognise an asset and liability for the present value of 18,000, comprising the rental payments of 15,000 and the guaranteed residual value of 3,000. This is the alternative treatment shown in the table in paragraph 5.7 for Example 5.

5.54   Supporters of this alternative view of Example 5 may believe that, as a matter of principle, the lease asset and liability should reflect the extent of the lessee's interest in the underlying residual value from which its entitlement to receive proceeds from the sale of the leased item is derived. Where the lessee has significant exposure to residual value price movements up and down, any asset or liability relating to the residual value is, in their view, explicitly for a *gross* amount that reflects the gross amount of the risks or benefits to which the lessee is exposed.

5.55   As explained earlier, the Group believes that the different contractual arrangements in Examples 4 and 5 should lead to different asset and liability amounts being reported. The Group also believes that the proposed approach would be more workable in practice than the alternative approach of reporting gross amounts for assets and liabilities (see further discussion of Example 6 below).

Subsequent remeasurement

5.56   Under the treatment proposed by the Group, the initial measurement of the lessee's asset would reflect the fair value of the right to use the leased item for the lease term. That value would be depreciated over the lease term as the economic benefits are consumed (including recognition of any impairment losses in addition to normal depreciation), in accordance with the usual principles of accounting for tangible assets.

5.57   The subsequent remeasurement of lease assets and liabilities resulting from changes in residual values raises similar issues to those discussed in respect of residual value guarantees (see paragraphs 5.35–5.39). Where applicable, any recognised lease liability relating to the lessee's residual value guarantee obligation would be restated to reflect its current settlement value. Where the liability is remeasured, the Group's preferred view is that the lease asset should also be remeasured, subject to its carrying amount not being increased above a value that would cause an impairment loss. The asset's revised carrying amount should be depreciated over the remainder of the lease term. However, if residual values subsequently increased so that the lessee now expected a cash inflow on settlement, an asset (a receivable) would not be recognised for the expected settlement value because accounting standards generally do not permit recognition of contingent assets.

LESSOR RECEIVES THE SALE PROCEEDS, BUT LESSEE RECEIVES A SHARE OF ANY SURPLUS AND PAYS A SHARE OF ANY SHORTFALL

The facts given in Example 5 discussed above are much more simple than many residual sharing arrangements in practice. In more complex agreements, the lessee and the lessor may share potential gains and losses around a stipulated residual value, perhaps in different proportions relating to different tranches of residual values. For example, they might share gains equally but share losses in a different proportion. In such circumstances, supporters of the alternative accounting treatment of the lease in Example 5 may struggle to find a conceptual basis for assessing the correct gross underlying asset value that should be recognised as part of the reported asset and liability amounts. Questions would also arise about when it would be appropriate to report gross or net amounts in relation to residual value participation agreements—it might be necessary, perhaps, to redefine a 'substantially all risks and rewards' approach to determine whether the lessee or the lessor (or both) should recognise an asset of some or all of the residual interest. This issue is illustrated in Example 6.

5.58

EXAMPLE 6

A lessee enters a lease to hire equipment for three years at an annual rental of 5,000. The equipment will be sold at the end of the lease at fair value. If the proceeds are more than 3,000, the lessor will pay one-half of the surplus to the lessee. If the proceeds are less than 3,000, the lessee will pay one-half of the shortfall to the lessor. Thus, for example:

- if the equipment is sold for 3,000, the lessor keeps all 3,000;
- if the equipment is sold for 5,000, the lessor keeps 4,000 and pays 1,000 to the lessee;
- if the equipment is sold for 2,000, the lessor keeps the 2,000 and receives a further 500 from the lessee; or
- if the equipment realises no value, the lessee pays 1,500 to the lessor.

In Example 6 the Group takes the view that at the beginning of the lease term the lessee should recognise an asset and liability for the present value of the rental payments of 15,000 and a fair value for the guarantee/right to surplus proceeds (if it is practical to quantify it), for the reasons discussed in the previous examples.

5.59

An alternative view of the residual value arrangement in Example 6 is that, in substance, the lessee has an obligation to the lessor for a gross amount of 1,500 and has the benefit of one-half of the equipment's residual value. Accordingly, at inception the lessee should recognise an asset and a liability for the present value of 16,500, comprising the rental payments of 15,000 and a residual value of 1,500 that has been guaranteed to the lessor. This is the alternative treatment shown in the table in paragraph 5.7 for Example 6.

5.60

RESIDUAL VALUE GUARANTEES AND RENEWAL OPTIONS

An issue arises of how the assets and liabilities should be characterised and measured when a renewal option is accompanied by a residual value guarantee at the renewal date.

5.61

Where the lessee provides a residual value guarantee at the end of the lease term, it is proposed that the assets and liabilities initially recognised should be measured to reflect the fair value of the guarantee rather than the gross amount of the residual

5.62

value that is guaranteed. The recognised asset would be characterised as the right to use the property for the term of the lease only, not the whole of the property (ie not including the guaranteed residual value). The recognised liability represents the minimum payments required by the lease and the (net) exposure under the guarantee. Such characterisation is consistent with the treatment of guarantees generally.

5.63 Consider the following example:

EXAMPLE 7

An airline has the right to lease an aircraft for 15 years at a rent of 5 million per year. However, the lessee has an obligation only to lease the aircraft for one year at a time; at each anniversary, the lessee can choose either to extend the lease for a further year at the 5 million rental or to break the lease and return the aircraft to the lessor. The lessee has also given an undertaking that, if it decides to break the lease, it will guarantee a predetermined residual value to the lessor. The guaranteed amount is specified for each renewal date and ensures that the lessor will recover its investment in the lease (including interest up to the break date) if the lessee decides not to renew.

At the beginning of the lease term, should the lessee recognise an asset and liability for (the present value of):

(a)   5 million plus the value of the guarantee?* or

(b)   75 million (5 million × 15)?

*   The value of the guarantee could, in fact, be quite small if the expected residual value was not significantly different from the guaranteed amount.

5.64 In addressing this issue it is assumed that the renewal option is genuine and there is no constraint that prevents exercise (for example, the asset in question is not unique and essential to the lessee's operations). The Group believes that application of the proposed principles discussed in this chapter and in Chapter 4 results in the initial recognition of assets and liabilities comprising the minimum payments required by the lease for the non-cancellable period (5 million) and the value of the guarantee: these reflect the fair value of the right to use the aircraft for the non-cancellable period and the value of the renewal option.

5.65 In the Group's view, if a lease is negotiated with a short minimum term, renewal options and residual value guarantees for each renewal date, it indicates that both parties have much comfort relying on the value of an asset that has a ready market. Furthermore, if the option is indeed genuine, it would be expected to have an observable effect on the pricing of the lease. Hence the lessee is paying a real price for financial flexibility and the accounting should reflect that flexibility. The price paid may also include breakage fees and other termination costs as well as the cost of honouring the residual value guarantee: these would need to be provided for. The Group does not believe that the concurrent existence of these two features in a lease should give rise to recognition of additional assets and liabilities (ie by anticipating the exercise of renewal options).

5.66 An alternative view is that residual value guarantees (and other residual value participation agreements) that operate in connection with renewal options are similar to mechanisms for arriving at a termination sum if a lease is cancelled early and should be treated as such. Under this view such leases do not give the lessee any significantly greater financial flexibility (or expose the lessor to any significantly different risks) than equivalent leases that are specified to be non-cancellable for a longer term. Those who support this view regard it as more useful to characterise the lessee's assets and liabilities as relating to the period for which the lessee has the right to use the property. They are also concerned that such structures may become more widespread, and have the effect of reducing the amounts of assets and liabilities that would be recognised in lessees' financial statements.

Recommendations

Lessee simply returns the leased item to the lessor

5A Where a lease conveys the right to use the leased item for part of its economic life only, and an obligation to pay for that use, an asset and liability should be recognised at the beginning of the lease term measured at the present value of the payments the lessee is required to make during the lease term. The asset initially recognised represents the fair value of the right to use the item for the lease term.

Lease conveys ownership of the leased item to the lessee

5B Where a lease conveys ownership of the leased item to the lessee, the lessee should account for the lease as a purchase contract financed by instalment finance. The present value of amounts the lessee is required to pay during the lease term and any amounts the lessee is required to pay in connection with the transfer of ownership should be recognised as assets and liabilities at the beginning of the lease term. The asset initially recognised represents the fair value of the leased item, and would be accounted for in accordance with the usual principles of accounting for tangible assets. As the lease conveys ownership of the equipment to the lessee, the useful life used for the purpose of calculating depreciation might be longer than the lease term.

Lessee guarantees a residual value

5C Where a lease conveys the right to use the leased item for part of its economic life only and the lessee provides a guarantee of its residual value at the end of the lease, an asset and liability should be recognised at the beginning of the lease term measured at the present value of the payments the lessee is required to make during the lease term and the fair value of the guarantee (if it is practical to quantify it). The asset initially recognised represents the fair value of the right to use the item for the lease term.

5D After initial recognition, whenever an increase or decrease in the value of the residual value guarantee obligation above or below its carrying amount in the lease liability is foreseen, the lease liability should be remeasured to reflect the current estimate of the expenditure expected to be required to settle the obligation. The Group's preferred view is that the carrying amount of both the lease liability and the lease asset should be increased or decreased (subject to the carrying amount of the asset not being increased above a value that would cause an impairment loss), and the asset's revised carrying amount should be depreciated over the remainder of the lease term.

Lessee receives the sale proceeds

5E Where the lessee receives (or shares) the proceeds from the sale of the leased item at the conclusion of the lease, the lessee will have paid for that entitlement in some way during the lease term. Accordingly, the initial lease asset should consist of the right to use the leased item for the term of the lease and the right to receive proceeds from its sale. Although the right to receive the residual proceeds is a different asset from the right to use the equipment for the lease term, the Group does not propose that they should be displayed as separate assets in the balance sheet. The initial liability should reflect the present value of the payments the lessee is required to make. The asset would be depreciated (and impairment losses recognised) in accordance with the usual principles of accounting for tangible assets, using an estimate of the amount that the lessee expects to receive from the sale proceeds as an estimate of the residual value.

Lessee receives or pays surplus or shortfall on sale

5F   Where a lease conveys the right to use the leased item for only part of its economic life and there is an exchange of rights and obligations relating to the residual value so that the lessee receives or pays all or some of the gain or loss on sale (ie the lessee obtains the right to receive all or some of the proceeds in excess of a stipulated amount and also provides a residual value guarantee), the lessee has a price exposure on the residual value that is settled by a net transfer of economic benefits to or by the lessee. Accordingly, the initial lease asset and liability should consist of the present value of the payments the lessee is required to make during the lease term and a value for the residual value agreement (if it is practical to quantify it). The asset initially recognised represents the fair value of the right to use the item for the lease term. Subsequent remeasurement of the asset and liability would be on the same basis as in recommendation 5D.

Chapter 6   Discount rates

6.1   As discussed in previous chapters, the Group believes that the objective should be to record, at the beginning of the lease term, the fair value of the rights and obligations that are conveyed by the lease.

6.2   Fair value is usually measured by the fair value of the consideration given (ie the liabilities incurred under the lease and any other consideration such as cash paid in advance). The rate that will discount those payments to their fair value is the market rate that reflects the time value of money and the risks associated with the cash flows.

6.3   The principal risk associated with the expected rental payments is usually the lessee's credit risk. The appropriate discount rate is, therefore, the rate at which the lessee could borrow money for the term of the lease and with similar security to that provided by the lease.

6.4   Where the lessor bears little or no risk relating to the residual value, the return it will require from the lease will reflect only the lessee's credit risk. In these cases the rate implicit in the lease* can be regarded as the appropriate discount rate for the lessee to apply to the rental payments. This will apply to most leases that are at present classified as finance leases. Using the rate implicit in the lease also has the effect that any tax benefits passed on to the lessee by the lessor in the form of reduced rentals are reflected in the interest rate.

6.5   For many other leases, however, it is unlikely that the lessee will know the rate implicit in the lease. Furthermore, even if the rate were known, it would probably not be a good approximation for the rate the lessee would pay on a borrowing offering similar security. If the lessor bears significant residual value risk, the return it will require from the lease will cover not just the lessee's credit risk but also the residual value risk. This is illustrated in the following example.

ie the rate that discounts all the payments expected under the lease to the fair value of the leased asset at inception.

Example

A car with a fair value of 10,000 is leased for a term of three years. The residual value **6.6**
is estimated at 3,000. Four situations are considered:

Case A. After three years, the lessee returns the car. The lessee bears no residual
value risk. (Equivalent to Example 1 in Chapter 5)

Case B. After three years, the lessee keeps the car. The lessee bears all the residual
value risk. (Equivalent to Example 2 in Chapter 5)

Case C. The lessee provides a simple residual value guarantee, ie the lessee assumes
the downside residual value risk and the lessor keeps the upside residual value risk.
(Equivalent to Example 3 in Chapter 5)

Case D. The lessee guarantees the residual amount of 3,000 and is also entitled to
retain any excess over this amount. As with case B, the lessee bears all the residual
value risk. (Equivalent to Example 5 in Chapter 5)

The borrowing rate for the lessee is assumed to be 10 per cent. The lessor sets the **6.7**
rental payments by first considering the return it requires on the expected residual
value. This gives a present value for the residual interest asset, which, when deducted
from the fair value of 10,000, gives the lessor the present value of the amount that it
needs to obtain from the rental payments. (The greater the risk associated with the
residual value, the lower its value from the lessor's point of view and hence the higher
the amount that has to be recovered from the lessee.) The lessor requires the same
rate of return from the lessee as the market, ie 10 per cent. It therefore sets the rental
payments so that, discounted at 10 per cent, they equal the required present value.

The results are as follows: **6.8**

	(i) Return required by lessor on expected residual value (note (a))	(ii) Present value of residual value (3,000 discounted at rate in column (i))	(iii) Required present value of rentals (10,000 less column (ii))	(iv) Required annual rental payments (paid in arrears) to give required present value of rentals in column (iii) at 10% rate	(v) Resulting rate implicit in lease (note (b))
Case A (lessor has all residual value risk)	15%	1,973	8,027	3,228	11.4%
Case B (lessor has no interest in the residual value)	n/a	n/a	10,000	4,021	10%

Case C (lessor has no downside but all upside residual value risk)	4.2%	2,652	7,348	2,955	8%
Case D (lessee bears all residual value risk)	10%	2,254	7,746	3,115	10%

Notes

(a) The rates form part of the assumptions underlying the example. They reflect the different risks borne by the lessor. In case A, the lessor bears all the risk associated with the residual value and this is assumed to be higher than the credit risk arising on the rental payments. In case C, the lessor is protected from the downside risk, and therefore requires a smaller return. In case D, the only risk borne by the lessor is the lessee's credit risk, and the return required is the same as that required on the rental payments.

(b) The discount rate that, when applied to all the expected cash flows (ie both the rental payments and the expected residual value), gives a present value of 10,000.

Lessor's point of view

6.9   In cases B and D, the borrowing rate and rate implicit in the lease are the same because the lessor is open to the lessee's credit risk only. In case A, the rate implicit in the lease is higher, reflecting the additional residual value risk borne by the lessor. In case C, the rate implicit in the lease is lower because the lessor has no downside risk associated with the residual value but does have the possibility of some gain. In other words, the more risk the lessor bears, the higher the rate of return it requires from the lease.

Lessee's point of view

6.10   From the lessee's point of view, the liability comprises the rental payments and the fair value of the residual value guarantee. The present value of these amounts gives the value of the lessee's asset, ie the right to use the car for three years plus any other rights conveyed by the lease. The following tables show the liabilities and assets that arise in the four situations under both the borrowing rate and the rate implicit in the lease.

(a) the borrowing rate

	Case A (lessor has all residual value risk)	Case B (lessor has no interest in the residual value)	Case C (lessor has no downside but all upside residual value risk)	Case D (lessee bears all residual value risk)
Present value of rentals (note (a))	8,027	10,000	7,348	7,746
Fair value of residual value arrangement (note (b))	n/a	n/a	679	281
Total liability	8,027	10,000	8,027	8,027
Right to use car for three years	8,027	8,027	8,027	8,027
Residual value of car after three years	n/a	1,973	n/a	n/a
Total asset	8,027	10,000	8,027	8,027

Notes

(a) Calculated by discounting the annual rental payments at the borrowing rate of 10 per cent.

(b) This is essentially a measure of the risk that the lessee bears in giving the residual value guarantee. It is calculated as the difference between:

  (i) the present value of the guaranteed residual value (2,652 for case C, and 2,254 for case D—see column (ii) of table in paragraph 6.8); and

  (ii) the present value of the unguaranteed residual value (ie 3,000 discounted at 15 per cent = 1,973—see column (ii) for case A in table in paragraph 6.8).

(b) the rate implicit in the lease

	Case A (lessor has all residual value risk)	Case B (lessor has no interest in the residual value)	Case C (lessor has no downside but all upside residual value risk)	Case D (lessee bears all residual value risk)
Present value of rentals (note (a))	7,831	10,000	7,617	7,746
Fair value of residual value arrangement (note (b))	n/a	n/a	679	281
Total liability	7,831	10,000	8,298	8,027
Right to use car for three years	7,831	8,027	8,298	8,027
Residual value of car after three years	n/a	1,973	n/a	n/a
Total asset	7,831	10,000	8,298	8,027

Notes

(a)   Calculated by discounting the annual rental payments at the rate implicit in the lease (see column (v) in table in paragraph 6.8).

(b)   This is essentially a measure of the risk that the lessee bears in giving the residual value guarantee. It is calculated as the difference between:

   (i)   the present value of the guaranteed residual value (2,652 for case C, and 2,254 for case D—see column (ii) of table in paragraph 6.8): and

   (ii)   the present value of the unguaranteed residual value (ie 3,000 discounted at 15 per cent = 1,973—see column (ii) for case A in table in paragraph 6.8.

6.11   The tables demonstrate that, where the lease payments are discounted at a borrowing rate, the asset of the right to use the car for three years remains the same in all four scenarios. The different risks borne by the lessee in the different cases are reflected in the composition of the liability, eg where the lessee assumes an obligation relating to the residual value, there is a compensating reduction in the rental obligation. The liability for the rentals also equals the lessor's asset for the rentals—a result that seems appropriate.

6.12   Where the lease payments are discounted at the interest rate implicit in the lease, on the other hand, the measurement of the rental obligation is not fully adjusted to reflect the obligation assumed in relation to the residual value. The rate implicit in the lease is a composite of two rates reflecting the different risks inherent in the rental payments and the residual value guarantee. By using this composite rate, some of the risk relating to the residual value is included in the measurement of the liability of the rental payments. Not only does this give an inappropriate measure for that liability but, if the residual value guarantee is measured at fair value, some of the risk is double-counted (once in the fair value of the residual guarantee and again in the rental liability). This then results in the asset being misstated as well.

Hence, where the lessor bears significant residual value risk, the rate implicit in the lease is not an appropriate discount rate for the lessee's rental payments. The discount rate will need to be estimated from other sources, for example recent secured loans taken out by the lessee.   **6.13**

Recommendations

6   The discount rate to be applied by lessees to the rental payments should be:
    (a) an estimate of the lessee's incremental borrowing rate for a loan of similar term and with the same security as is provided by the lease; or
    (b) the rate implicit in the lease when it is known by the lessee and represents a reasonable approximation for the rate in (a).

Chapter 7 Sale and leaseback transactions

INTRODUCTION

This chapter considers how sale and leaseback transactions would be dealt with under the approach to lease accounting that is proposed in this Paper. A sale and leaseback transaction occurs when the owner sells a property and immediately reacquires the right to use it by entering into a lease with the purchaser. The lease may be for all or only part of the property's remaining useful economic life. In this discussion, a 'sale' refers to the legal description of the transaction; the discussion applies to cases where the sale and the leaseback are negotiated simultaneously as a package, usually between the same two parties and entered into concurrently.   **7.1**

Under present standards, the accounting for sale and leaseback transactions differs significantly according to whether the leaseback is classified as a finance lease or an operating lease. Consistently with the 'substantially all risks and rewards' approach, assets and liabilities are recognised where the seller-lessee enters into a finance leaseback of the property, whereas a disposal of the seller-lessee's interest in the property is recognised where the seller-lessee enters into an operating leaseback.   **7.2**

The overall effect of sale and leaseback transactions on the seller-lessee is as follows: **7.3**

* *Before* the transaction the seller-lessee has a property
* *After* the transaction the seller-lessee has:
    — cash
    — a reduced interest in the property
    — an obligation to make payments in respect of the lease.

In this chapter, two possible approaches to accounting for sale and leaseback transactions are compared and contrasted. The *'one transaction' approach* views a sale and leaseback as essentially one transaction, whilst the *'two transactions' approach* views them as two transactions—a sale of property followed by a lease of different property rights, each of which is accounted for separately.   **7.4**

As is explained later, the carrying amount of the asset immediately following the transaction differs between the two approaches. Under the 'one transaction' approach it is a proportion of the previous carrying amount (historical cost or revalued amount) of the original asset that has been retained by the seller-lessee, while under the 'two transactions' approach it is the fair value of the right to use the   **7.5** property that the seller-lessee acquires under the lease. As a consequence, gain or loss recognition also differs between the two approaches.

7.6   Both approaches differ from, and have more in common with each other than, the treatment of sale and leaseback transactions under present accounting standards. Neither of the approaches considered uses arbitrary dividing lines to determine the assets and liabilities arising from such transactions.

THE 'ONE TRANSACTION' APPROACH

7.7   The 'one transaction' approach views a sale and leaseback as a single transaction with a double purpose. That double purpose is the raising of finance, and the partial disposal of an interest in property.

7.8   At the extremes of the spectrum, it is possible for a sale and leaseback to be either almost wholly a financing, with only an immaterial part of the asset sold (ie there is no material residual interest for the lessor), or almost wholly a sale, with an immaterial amount of finance raised.

7.9   Because of the double purpose of the transaction, it is necessary to make allocations in order to determine what is the effect of the financing and the (partial) sale, respectively.

7.10   The accounting by the seller-lessee would be as follows:

(a)   A liability would be recognised in respect of the payments required by the lease. That liability would be measured using the same methods as for any other lease.

(b)   The amount by which the cash received exceeds the liability in respect of the payments required by the lease would be deemed to be consideration for the part of the asset that is sold.

(c)   The carrying amount of the property asset immediately before the transaction would be apportioned between the amount sold and the amount retained. (The apportionment is illustrated in the examples later in this chapter.)

(d)   A gain (or loss) would be recognised for the difference between the amounts calculated in (b) and deemed to be sold in (c) above.

(e)   As a result of recording the above, the part of the property asset that is retained (ie the right to use the property for the term of the lease) would be carried at a proportion of the previous carrying amount, based on the calculation in (c).

7.11   An overview of the accounting entries is as follows:

	Cash	Asset	Lease liability	Gain
Sale and leaseback	Dr: Cash received	Cr: Carrying amount of part sold	Cr: Obligation for lease payments	Cr: Difference = consideration for the part of asset sold less its carrying amount

7.12   The above procedure results in the interest in the property that is retained by the seller-lessee being carried at a value that is an estimate of its depreciated historical cost or revalued amount. Under this approach the question of whether or not this interest should be permitted or required to be revalued to fair value would be dealt with in accounting standards on fixed (long-term) assets rather than leasing.

Because the procedure for apportioning the carrying amount of the asset between the part sold and the part retained involves adjusting the carrying amount of the asset by an amount that may be arbitrary, it would also be necessary to review the carrying amount of the retained (leasehold) interest for impairment, and make any necessary further write-downs in accordance with accounting standards on impairment. The procedure for apportioning the carrying amount is explained in the following paragraphs. **7.13**

Carrying amount of the part of the asset sold

Under this approach, the carrying amount of the item subject to a sale and leaseback transaction needs to be reduced in relation to the significant economic benefits that have been sold. **7.14**

If fair values can be determined, it would appear preferable to allocate the previous carrying amount of the item subject to the sale and leaseback transaction based on the relative fair values of the parts sold and retained. This is the approach in the US accounting standard FAS 125 'Accounting for Transfers and Servicing of Financial Assets and Extinguishments of Liabilities': the previous carrying amount of the financial assets is allocated between the assets sold and the retained interests based on their relative fair values at the date of transfer of the financial assets. **7.15**

If the fair value of the whole item can be reliably measured, but the fair value of the part retained cannot be, the carrying amount of the part of the item sold would be based on the ratio of the cash received for the part sold to the fair value of the whole item. **7.16**

If the fair value of the whole item cannot be reliably measured, then the carrying amount of the part sold would be deemed to be equal to the cash received for the part sold and no gain would be recognised under the sale and leaseback transaction. **7.17**

The cash received by the seller-lessee for the part of the item sold is measured as the difference between (a) the total receipts from the buyer-lessor, and (b) the amount of the lease liability recognised by the seller-lessee. The lease liability represents the receipts that must be repaid to the buyer-lessor, and hence do not relate to the part of the item sold. **7.18**

THE 'TWO TRANSACTIONS' APPROACH

The 'two transactions' approach views a sale and leaseback as essentially two transactions and, on this basis, holds that the two transactions should be accounted for separately. An overview of the accounting entries is as follows: **7.19**

	Cash	Asset	Lease liability	Gain
Sale	Dr: Cash received	Cr: Carrying amount (whole)		Difference
Leaseback		Dr: Fair value of leased asset	Cr: Obligation for lease payments	Difference*
Total	Dr: Cash received	Cr: difference between carrying amount and fair value of leased asset	Cr: Lease obligation	Difference

*A difference will often arise between the fair value of the leased asset and the amount of the lease obligation because the sale and leaseback are negotiated as a package.

7.20   The above procedure results in the interest in the property that is retained by the seller-lessee being carried at fair value.

DIFFERENCES BETWEEN THE TWO APPROACHES

7.21   There is no difference between the two approaches in the measurement of the lease liability—this would follow the principles of recognising liabilities arising from lease obligations as discussed elsewhere in this Paper.

7.22   The main difference between the approaches is the carrying amount of the seller-lessee's asset (ie the leasehold interest) immediately after the transaction. Under the 'one transaction' approach it is a proportion of the previous carrying amount (historical cost or revalued amount) of the property. Under the 'two transactions' approach it is the fair value of the rights acquired under the lease.

7.23   However, the difference has an important consequential effect on the amount of profit that is recognised in respect of the sale and leaseback transaction. Under the 'one transaction' approach, profit is recognised only in respect of the portion of the property that is deemed to have been sold. Under the 'two transactions' approach, the full amount of the difference between the fair value of the property and its previous carrying amount is recognised as a gain.

APPLICATION OF THE TWO APPROACHES

7.24   This part of the chapter explores further the implications of the 'one transaction' approach and the 'two transactions' approach, using a number of examples. The examples assume that the subject matter of the transaction is a property with a carrying value of 100 and a fair value of 120. Undiscounted amounts are used in the examples for simplicity. The differences between the examples are limited to:

- the amount of cash received
- the amount of the lease obligation
- the fair value of the asset arising for the seller-lessee under the leaseback.

None of the examples illustrates the point that, under the 'one transaction' approach, **7.25** the asset recognised immediately after the leaseback should be reviewed for impairment and written down if necessary. The asset could also be revalued to fair value, subject to the requirements of accounting standards on fixed (long-term) assets.

EXAMPLE 1: SALE AND LEASEBACK CONVEYS NO SIGNIFICANT RESIDUAL INTEREST TO THE LESSOR

The first example is wholly a financing transaction. Under the 'one transaction' **7.26** approach, the seller-lessee does not sell any significant interest in the property and the purchaser-lessor obtains no significant interest in the property (except as security for the amount due from the seller-lessee). The cash receipts are assumed to be equivalent to the fair value of the property, ie 120.

Example 1A	'One transaction' approach	'Two transactions' approach
Journal entries	Dr Cash 120 Cr Lease liability 120 (Finance received)	Dr Cash 120 Cr Asset 100 Cr Profit 20 (Sale) Dr Asset 120 Cr Lease liability 120 (Leaseback)
Total profit recognised	Nil	20
Carrying value of asset after transaction	100	120

However, there is no reason why the cash received in a sale and leaseback package **7.27** should equal the fair value of the property. If the cash received differs, and other terms remain unchanged, the lease liability should also change. Where the sale and leaseback is wholly a financing transaction, the cash received and the lease liability would always be the same amount. The amount of cash received does not change the total profit recognised or the carrying value of the property after the transaction under each approach. This is demonstrated in the following example where the cash receipts are 30 rather than 120.

Example 1B	'One transaction' approach	'Two transactions' approach
Journal entries	Dr Cash 30 Cr Lease liability 30 (Finance received)	Dr Cash 30 Dr Loss 70 Cr Asset 100 (Sale) Dr Asset 120 Cr Lease liability 30 Cr Profit 90 (Leaseback)
Total profit recognised	Nil	20
Carrying value of asset after transaction	100	120

EXAMPLE 2: SALE AND LEASEBACK IS A PARTIAL SALE

7.28　The following example addresses the accounting where the property interest held by the seller-lessee after the transaction has a smaller fair value than the property the seller-lessee previously owned (ie the seller-lessee has sold a portion of its property interest). In this case, the leaseback would often be regarded as an operating lease under present accounting standards.

Sale at fair value

7.29　It is assumed that the cash receipts are 120, and that the lease obligation is 70. For the purpose of illustrating the 'two transactions' approach, the fair value of the property interest held by the seller-lessee after the transaction is also 70.

Example 2A	'One transaction' approach		'Two transactions' approach	
Journal entries	Dr Cash	120	Dr Cash	120
	Cr Lease liability	70	Cr Asset	100
	Cr Asset	41.7	Cr Profit	20
	Cr Profit	8.3	(Sale)	
	(Sale and leaseback)			
			Dr Asset	70
			Cr Lease liability	70
			(Leaseback)	
Total profit recognised	8.3		20	
Carrying value of asset after transaction	58.3		70	

7.30　Under the 'one transaction' approach, it is necessary to apportion the carrying amount of the asset between the part sold and the part retained. Out of total receipts of 120, 70 represents the lease liability, and 50 has been received for the asset. As this represents 50/120 of the fair value of the asset, its carrying amount (of 100) needs to be reduced by 50/120 of 100 (ie 41.7), resulting in a profit of 8.3. The profit recognised can easily be rationalised: it is 50/120 of the profit that would arise if the whole asset were sold (ie 20).*

7.31　Under the 'two transactions' approach, the total profit of 20 is recognised. This is the same profit as would be recognised if the whole asset were sold at its fair value.

Sale below fair value

7.32　As noted above, however, the cash received in a sale and leaseback package may not be equal to the fair value of the property. The following example illustrates the sale for 10 less than its fair value (ie cash receipts are 110), and this is compensated for by a favourable lease, which gives the seller-lessee a lease obligation worth 10 less than the fair value of the property interest held by the seller-lessee after the transaction. Although the separate parts of the transaction are not at fair value, taken as a whole the transaction is equitable.

*Note that if the fair value of the property could not be measured reliably, the carrying amount of the property (100) would be reduced by the cash received for the part sold (50) and no profit would be recognised in relation to the sale and leaseback (refer to paragraph 7.17).

Example 2B	'One transaction' approach	'Two transactions' approach
Journal entries	Dr Cash 110 Cr Lease liability 60 Cr Asset 41.7 Cr Profit 8.3 (Sale and leaseback)	Dr Cash 110 Cr Asset 100 Cr Profit 10 (Sale) Dr Asset 70 Cr Lease liability 60 Cr Profit 10 (Leaseback)
Total profit recognised	8.3	20
Carrying value of asset after transaction	58.3	70

Under the 'one transaction' approach, it is again necessary to apportion the carrying amount of the asset between the part sold and the part retained. Out of total receipts of 110, 60 represents the lease liability, and 50 has been received for the asset. As this represents 50/120 of the fair value of the asset, its carrying amount (of 100) needs to be reduced in that proportion, which is the same as in Example 2A. Hence the carrying amount of the asset (58.3) and the amount of profit recognised (8.3) do not change by varying the components within the overall package.

7.33

Under the 'two transactions' approach, the total profit of 20 is recognised, as before. This is the same profit as would be recognised if the whole asset were sold at its fair value.

7.34

Sale above fair value

The following example completes the picture by illustrating the accounting for a sale at above fair value. The sale of the property is for 10 more than its fair value (ie cash receipts are 130), and this is compensated for by an 'onerous' lease, which gives the seller-lessee a lease obligation worth 10 more than the fair value of the property interest held by the seller-lessee after the transaction.*

7.35

Example 2C	'One transaction' approach	'Two transactions' approach
Journal entries	Dr Cash 130 Cr Lease liability 80 Cr Asset 41.7 Cr Profit 8.3 (Sale and leaseback)	Dr Cash 130 Cr Asset 100 Cr Profit 30 (Sale) Dr Asset 70 Dr Loss 10 Cr Lease liability 80 (Leaseback)
Total profit recognised	8.3	20
Carrying value of asset after transaction	58.3	70

*The effect of this example is that 10 of the lessee's liability of 80 is not covered by the security of the value of the property.

ARGUMENTS FOR 'TWO TRANSACTIONS' APPROACH

7.36   The principal argument for the 'two transactions' approach is straightforward: the asset that is recognised by the seller-lessee after the sale and leaseback should be measured at fair value. Supporters of this approach take the view that there has been a transaction at fair value, which has changed the nature of the lessee's asset. The seller-lessee has sold one bundle of rights (an ownership interest in property) and acquired a different bundle of rights (a leasehold interest in the same property) and obligations. In their view the new measurement basis resulting from the transaction provides more relevant financial information than the alternative, which requires allocations that may be arbitrary in order to arrive at asset values and recognised gains and losses.

7.37   Furthermore, measuring the seller-lessee's acquired leasehold interest at fair value results in the same carrying amount for the resulting asset that would arise if similar economic benefits were arranged through a new, straightforward lease, thus enhancing comparability.

THE GROUP'S VIEW—SUPPORT FOR 'ONE TRANSACTION' APPROACH

7.38   The Group notes that sale and leaseback transactions are not independent arm's length transactions, but are negotiated as a package. Accordingly, a sale and leaseback generally provides evidence only that the total of what the seller-lessee gives is equivalent to the total of what it receives: it provides no evidence of the fair values of parts of the transaction. There is no reason, for example, why the cash receipts should equal the fair value of the property, because any difference can be compensated for by higher or lower lease payments. Similarly, the interest in the property that the seller-lessee has immediately after the transaction does not necessarily equal the amount of the obligation in respect of lease payments, because that obligation reflects all the other components of the transaction and not just the lessee's interest in the property.

7.39   A sale and leaseback has certain characteristics of a transaction involving a swap of assets and cash. Consider, for example, a transaction in which a Ford and a Nissan are swapped for a Chevrolet and cash. If the Ford and the Nissan were previously not carried at fair value, all that is necessary is to establish the fair value of the Chevrolet, record it in the accounts at that amount (and the cash) and recognise a gain or loss accordingly. This is the essence of the 'two transactions' approach. However, a sale and leaseback transaction is also rather different from a swap of cars: the Chevrolet is clearly a different asset from the Ford and the Nissan, but the leasehold interest that the seller-lessee has after a sale and leaseback transaction is not a different asset—it is part of the same asset that the seller-lessee held immediately before the transaction.

7.40   An asset is essentially a bundle of rights. Transfer of ownership usually conveys all the rights comprising the asset to the new owner. A lease is a transaction whereby some of those rights are transferred from the owner of an asset (the lessor) to another party (the lessee): the lessee clearly cannot obtain any rights under the lease other than rights the owner has. In a sale and leaseback, the transaction conveys all the rights of the asset to the purchaser-lessor, but some are conveyed by the lease to the seller-lessee. The rights the seller-lessee has can only be a part of the rights that are conveyed by the sale. Given that the sale and the leaseback are negotiated as a package, and that the leaseback typically starts on the same date as the sale takes effect, the Group believes that it is reasonable to conclude that the effect of the transaction is that the seller-lessee retains those rights, rather than acquires freshly created ones.*

For the reasons above, the Group does not regard it as appropriate to require the carrying amount of the economic benefits from usage of the property during the leaseback term, which are retained by the seller-lessee, to be restated in the accounts. Those benefits have been controlled by the seller-lessee since their original acquisition by that party. This approach is the same as that in FAS 125 for retained interests in transferred assets, which continue to be recognised by the transferor based on an allocation of the previous carrying amount between the retained interests and the assets sold.

7.41

The Group believes that the argument for remeasuring the seller-lessee's leased asset to fair value is based primarily on the view that fair values are more relevant than historical costs for assets generally, and not just for assets arising under sale and leaseback transactions. The Group does not agree with the proposition that accounting standards should mandate fair values to be used whenever an opportunity presents itself, with the effect that some items would be held at fair value and others would not. In the Group's view, if it is acceptable (or at least permitted) to carry an asset at historical cost in the absence of a sale and leaseback, there seems no reason why it should not be carried at historical cost after such a transaction as well.

7.42

In some cases, a sale and leaseback transfers no (or only a nominal) residual interest to the purchaser-lessor. (An example of such a transaction would be one that gave the seller-lessee the right to purchase the property for a nominal sum, or to continue the lease indefinitely at a nominal rental, after the seller-lessee has repaid the lease obligation.) In these cases the 'one transaction' approach would leave the carrying amount of the asset undisturbed, whilst the 'two transactions' approach would restate it to its fair value. The result obtained by the 'one transaction' approach is that the total receipts relate entirely to the obligation assumed to make lease payments, and the lease provides the seller-lessee with an interest in the property that is very similar to that which was obtained through ownership before the transaction. Of course, this is not to deny that the assets are in some respects different: a lessee cannot sell or pledge a property in which it merely has a leasehold interest (although it could assign or pledge the lease). But if these restrictions were significant, it should be possible to observe a difference between the amount of the lease obligation and the total receipts. If not, the different nature of the asset is adequately conveyed by the use of a different description in the balance sheet—as a 'leased asset' rather than an 'owned asset'.

7.43

Recommendations

7 A sale and leaseback should be accounted for as one transaction by the seller-lessee, as follows.

(a) A liability would be recognised in respect of the payments required by the lease. That liability would be measured using the same methods as for any other lease.

(b) The amount by which the cash received exceeds the liability in respect of the payments required by the lease would be deemed to be consideration for the part of the asset that is sold.

(c) The carrying amount of the property asset immediately before the transaction would be apportioned between the amount sold and the amount retained (see paragraphs 7.14–7.18).

This line of argument suggests that, in principle, it would be possible to achieve the same economic effect as a sale and leaseback by a contract that conveyed only those rights not retained by the seller-lessee to the purchaser-lessor. If such a transaction achieves the same economic effect, the accounting should be the same.

> (d) A gain (or loss) would be recognised for the difference between the amounts calculated in (b) and deemed to be sold in (c) above.
>
> (e) As a result of recording the above, the part of the property asset that is retained (ie the right to use the property for the term of the lease) would be carried at a proportion of the previous carrying amount, based on the calculation in (c).

Part III Leases in the financial statements of lessors

Chapter 8 Assets of lessors—general principles

8.1   The approach to lessor accounting that is proposed in this Paper focuses on accounting for the rights that are conveyed to lessors by the lease contract and on other rights relating to the leased property. The approach corresponds with that advocated for lessee accounting.

TREATMENT UNDER PRESENT ACCOUNTING STANDARDS

8.2   Under present accounting standards, entirely different methods are used to characterise leased assets in balance sheets and to recognise income from leased assets in performance statements, depending on whether the lease is classified as a finance lease or an operating lease. Those differences mirror the different treatments for lessees. A finance lease is treated similarly to a financing or sale on deferred terms to the lessee of the whole of the leased property. An operating lease is deemed not to include the transfer to the lessee of any economic interest in the leased property.

8.3   For leases classified as finance leases, the whole of the lessor's investment is shown as a receivable (a financial asset). The lessor's financial asset is measured as the present value of the amounts recoverable from the lease; the amounts recoverable comprise the remaining rental payments under the lease and any residual value (guaranteed or unguaranteed) that accrues to the lessor. At the inception of the lease, the amount reported as a financial asset is usually equivalent to the cost of the leased item to the lessor. However, in certain circumstances a gain (or, in rare cases, a loss) may be recognised that is equivalent to the profit that would have resulted from an outright sale.† Interest methods are generally used to account for subsequent changes in the lessor's financial asset; thus rental payments and other amounts recoverable are allocated between a capital element (treated as repayment of the principal amount of the outstanding receivable) and a finance income element (treated as interest on the lessor's outstanding investment).

8.4   For leases classified as operating leases, the leased property is treated as an asset of the lessor in its entirety. Consequently, the whole of the lessor's investment is shown as an item of property, plant or equipment (a non-financial asset). This asset is subject to accounting standards dealing with depreciation and impairment of assets. Rental payments are normally recognised as income on a straight-line or other appropriate basis over the lease term.

---

†*In some jurisdictions that accounting is limited to lessors that are considered to be manufacturers of, or dealers in, the leased property.*

ASSETS THAT ARISE FOR LESSORS

Receivables and residual interests

The approach taken in this Paper, as discussed earlier in the context of lessee **8.5** accounting, is that leases convey rights and obligations to the parties concerned that, conceptually, may give rise to assets for both the lessor and the lessee. Their respective assets would represent different economic interests in the leased property, the lessee's asset reflecting the right to use the leased item for the term of the lease.

Chapter 2 proposes that leases can be distinguished from executory contracts by the **8.6** fact that leases cease to be executory when the leased property is delivered or otherwise made available to the lessee. Delivery is an act of performance by the lessor that changes significantly the nature of the rights and obligations of the parties to the lease contract, which should be reflected in their accounting for the contract. At that point, the lessor has transferred to the lessee rights to some or all of the future economic benefits that derive from the item of property. In exchange, the lessor has obtained rights to receive payments. The lessor also has rights relating to the service potential of the leased property at the end of the lease term (the residual interest). The nature of the lessor's asset has, therefore, changed as a result of its performance under the lease contract.

The rights and obligations that arise for the lessee and the lessor may be summarised **8.7** thus:

- the lessee has obtained rights to use the leased item in any way permitted by the lease agreement, and has incurred an obligation to pay rentals over the lease term
- the lessor has obtained a right to collect the lease payments; it also may have a right to the return of the leased item at the end of the lease.

The lease has converted some or all of the lessor's existing asset (the item of property) **8.8** into a financial asset.* Thus some or all of the lessor's existing property asset should be derecognised and reported as a financial asset—a receivable.

A consequence of this approach, therefore, is that a lessor may report two separate **8.9** assets in respect of a lease:

(a) a receivable in respect of payments required by the lease; and
(b) an interest in the residual value of the property.

The amount of each kind of asset would vary depending on the nature of the lease: if the lease term is short in relation to the economic life of the leased asset, the receivable would be small (perhaps even immaterial) and, conversely, if the lease term is long, the lessor's asset would almost all be represented by the amount receivable.

The above characterisation of the lessor's assets reflects straightforward leases; leases **8.10** with optional features are discussed in Chapter 11.

*A financial asset is defined in IAS 39 'Financial Instruments: Recognition and Measurement' as follows:

(a) cash;
(b) a contractual right to receive cash or another financial asset from another enterprise;
(c) a contractual right to exchange financial instruments with another enterprise under conditions that are
  potentially favourable; or
(d) an equity instrument of another enterprise.

Transparency of separate presentation

8.11   The risks and benefits relating to the right to receive payments from the lessee and any right to the residual interest are quite different. The right to receive a stream of rental payments under the lease is similar in some respects to a receivable secured on the underlying leased property, the principal risk to the lessor being the lessee's credit risk (ie the risk that the lessee will fail to make payments according to the terms of the lease contract). The right to the residual interest is subject to property-specific risks such as those associated with changes in economic and market conditions, or changes in technology, that may affect the value of the property at the end of the lease. For example, where a leased item is to be returned to the lessor at the end of the lease with no further rights or obligations for the lessee, the amount recoverable by the lessor will depend on the value realisable from selling or reletting the item under the economic conditions prevailing at the end of the lease. If the leased item is expected to have a significant value at the end of the lease, the risk that the item will be worth less (or more) than expected may be significant to a proper understanding of the lessor's financial position and performance.

8.12   In the Group's view, if the components of the lessor's assets were more transparent in the financial statements, reflecting the different rights arising under the lease, the result would be a better understanding of the lessor's financial position and risks. Consequently, where each element of the lessor's economic interest in leased property is material, the Group believes that reflecting separately in the balance sheet the two elements—a receivable in respect of payments required by the lease and an interest in the residual value of the property—would provide more useful information than is provided by the presentation required by existing accounting standards.

MEASUREMENT OF THE LESSOR'S ASSETS

Initial measurement of receivable at fair value

8.13   It is to be expected that if a lease gives rise to a financial liability for the lessee, it should in principle give rise to a corresponding financial asset for the lessor. The Group's proposed objective in accounting for assets and liabilities recognised by lessees is to record, at the beginning of the lease term, the fair value of rights and obligations that are conveyed by the lease. From the perspective of the lessor, the amounts receivable from the lessee should as a matter of principle also be recorded initially at fair value (representing the fair value of the consideration that the lessee has agreed to pay for the right to use the leased property).

8.14   The fair value of the rights conveyed by the lease cannot be less than the present value of the minimum payments required by the lease (assuming that the lease is negotiated on arm's length terms).

Recognition of gains at the beginning of the lease term

8.15   As a general principle, it is the Group's view that a gain should be recognised at the beginning of the lease term if (a) there is evidence that the value of the lessor's assets (less its liabilities) has increased as a result of its performance in entering into the lease contract, and (b) the increase can be measured reliably.* Evidence would be

---

This principle is reflected in the UK's standard FRS 5 'Reporting the Substance of Transactions'. Where an item is transferred for only part of its life, FRS 5 would allow a gain to be recognised if it can be measured reliably. Where measurement is difficult, with the result that the amount of any gain or loss is uncertain, FRS 5 delays the recognition of any gain, to the extent that it is in doubt. [FRS 5, paragraphs 24 and 74]

required of the fair value of the property being leased (if greater than its previous carrying value), and the receivable and residual interest assets resulting from the lease contract would also need to be capable of being measured reliably.*

Where the conditions for recognition of an initial gain were not satisfied, it would be reasonable for the leasing activities to be treated essentially as financial activities (together with the provision of any ancillary services). Hence, the whole of the lessor's earnings would reasonably be accounted for as finance income arising during the lease term, together with revenue from providing any ancillary services. **8.16**

It is normally reasonable to assume that (as with the majority of exchange trans-actions) the fair value of the consideration given is equal to the fair value of the consideration received. In the context of a lease, this implies that the aggregate of the fair value of the receivable in respect of payments required by the lease and the fair value of the lessor's interest in the residual value of the property is equal to the fair value of the property held before the lease. **8.17**

The Group therefore proposes that there should be a presumption that no gain or loss arises at the beginning of the lease term unless there is evidence that the carrying amount of the property immediately before the beginning of the lease was less than its fair value. The circumstances in which this is likely to arise are: **8.18**

(a) where the lessor is in the business of regularly trading in the kind of property in question (ie is a manufacturer or dealer lessor). In such a business the property would be recorded at manufacturing cost or purchase price; however, the existence of transactions other than leases, especially sales, provides strong evidence that the fair value of the lease receivable and the retained interest in the property may well be a higher amount; or

(b) where the amount at which the property is carried in the lessor's books immediately before the beginning of the lease is based on a historical cost (or revalued amount) that was established long before the lease was granted. In these circumstances, the carrying amount of the property is unlikely to approximate its fair value.

Enterprises that manufacture or deal in the property that they lease may view their leasing activities as an alternative method of marketing their products. A dealer might be defined as an entity that buys in one market (wholesale) and sells in another (retail). Such lessors differ from other lessors insofar as the cost at which the lessor acquires the property for lease is either the cost of manufacture or the wholesale price, which is usually lower than the normal selling price. **8.19**

In terms of the accounting treatment for a lease by a manufacturer or dealer lessor, the following activities may be identified: **8.20**

● a sale, as if the lessor had sold an economic interest in the property at a normal selling price
● the provision of finance over the lease term relating to the economic interest that has been transferred to the lessee
● the provision of ancillary services (if any)
● retention of the rights to the second-hand property at the end of the lease, which may be recovered by sale or reletting.

Under the historical cost model that has been developed hitherto in this Paper, any gain recognised at the beginning of the lease term would be restricted to the proportion of the original asset that was transferred under the lease (see later example).

The activities noted in the last three points above are similar to those of any finance lease. With respect to the first point, the Group takes the view that a manufacturer or dealer lessor should in principle be permitted to recognise a gain (equivalent to a 'selling profit' in relation to the rights that have been transferred to the lessee) at the beginning of the lease term if it could be demonstrated that the lessor was able to obtain the leased property at a price that was less than what the lessee would normally pay. Part of this demonstration would involve provision of evidence that the attributed fair value (or 'retail' selling price) was a price at which actual sales could be expected to take place, and was not simply a list price at which no sales were ever made. Also there should be evidence that the payments expected under the lease and the residual value are reliably measurable.

8.21   Accounting standards could allow a gain to be recognised at the beginning of a lease where the principle set out in paragraph 8.15 is met, ie including all circumstances where it can be demonstrated that entering into a lease increases the value of the lessor's assets. Alternatively, recognition of a gain could be restricted to the two circumstances listed in paragraph 8.18. The Group supports the latter approach.

Restriction of gains to reflect the proportion of the asset transferred

8.22   When it is appropriate to recognise a gain at the beginning of the lease, the gain should reflect the extent to which the equipment has genuinely been sold, rather than retained. A practicable method of ensuring this is to restrict the amount of selling profit that should be recognised to the proportion of the normal selling price of the equipment that is represented by a receivable, rather than by the lessor's interest in the residual value. Thus, if the lessor had no interest in the residual value, a profit of up to the amount that would be made on a normal cash sale would be recognised, and this would be proportionately reduced to reflect the extent to which the lessor retained a residual interest.

8.23   The following example illustrates the proposed treatment.

EXAMPLE

A manufacturer leases equipment that cost 100 to produce, and has a normal selling price of 120. The present values of the lease payments and the estimated residual value, calculated by discounting the expected cash flows to the selling price of 120, are determined as 70 and 50 respectively.

The manufacturer-lessor would recognise a receivable of 70 and reduce the carrying amount of its asset by 70/120 of 100, ie 58. This would leave its interest in the residual value stated at 42 (100–58). The manufacturer-lessor's total assets would be 112 (70 + 42), resulting in a recognised profit of 12 (ie 70/120 of 20, the profit arising on a normal sale).

8.24   Issues concerning the initial measurement of a lessor's receivable and residual interest assets, and how they should be accounted for during the lease term, are addressed in Chapters 10 and 12.

> **Recommendations**
>
> 8A Two elements—a receivable in respect of payments required by the lease and an interest in the residual value of the property—should be presented separately by lessors in the balance sheet, reflecting the different property rights arising under the lease.
>
> 8B The amounts receivable from the lessee should be recorded initially at fair value (representing the fair value of the consideration that the lessee has agreed to pay for the right to use the leased property).
>
> 8C The fair value of the rights conveyed by the lease cannot be less than the present value of the minimum payments required by the lease (assuming that the lease is negotiated on arm's length terms).
>
> 8D A gain should be recognised at the beginning of the lease term if (a) there is evidence that the value of the lessor's assets (less its liabilities) has increased as a result of its performance in entering into the lease contract, and (b) the increase can be measured reliably.
>
> 8E Accounting standards should prescribe that a lease should fall within the scope of 8D above only if:
> (a) the lessor also manufactures or deals in the property that it leases; or
> (b) in other situations, the carrying amount of the property that is the subject of the lease is demonstrably lower than its fair value.
>
> 8F Any gain recognised at the beginning of the lease term should be restricted to reflect the proportion of the original asset that was transferred under the lease to the lessee.

Chapter 9 Receivables and residual interests—display issues

This chapter focuses on the presentation of assets that arise for lessors under various types of leases that convey different economic interests in residual values to lessors and lessees. For example: **9.1**

- the lessee may simply return the leased item to the lessor at the end of the lease with no further rights or obligations
- the lease may convey ownership of the leased item to the lessee
- the lessee, or another party, may guarantee a residual value to the lessor
- the lessee may have the right to participate in the proceeds from the sale of the leased item.

Chapter 5 considered a number of examples of such arrangements from the perspective of the lessee. The same examples are considered below from the perspective of the lessor. In each of the examples it is assumed that equipment is leased for a term of three years, and the following amounts are specified: **9.2**

- Rentals over the lease term (5,000 per year) 15,000
- Residual value estimate 3,000
- Lessor's carrying amount 18,000

Since this discussion focuses on display characteristics, undiscounted amounts are used in the examples for simplicity. The following table summarises for each example the Group's preferred view of the elements that would be shown as financial assets and as non-financial assets in the financial statements of lessors. **9.3**

		Display of assets at inception	
Example	Description	Financial asset (receivable)	Non-financial asset (residual interest)
1	Lessee returns equipment to lessor (see paragraph 9.5)	15,000	3,000
2	Lease conveys ownership to lessee (see paragraph 9.7)	18,000	—
3	Lessee provides residual value guarantee (see paragraph 9.9)	15,000	3,000[+]
4	Lessee receives all sale proceeds (see paragraph 9.20)	18,000	—
5	Lessor receives sale proceeds, but lessee receives any surplus and pays any shortfall (see paragraph 9.23)	15,000	3,000[+]
6	Lessor receives sale proceeds, but lessee receives a share of any surplus and pays a share of any shortfall (see paragraph 9.32)	15,000	3,000[+]

[+] In these cases the existence of the residual value guarantee would be disclosed.

9.4   The examples assume that both the rentals required by the lease and the residual value of the equipment are the same in all cases. It is recognised that, in practice, the rentals would be expected to vary under the different scenarios, according to the extent to which each party bears residual value risk. Thus, for example, if the rentals in Example 1 (where the lessor bears all residual value risk) were 15,000, the rentals in Example 3 would be expected to be less than 15,000 as a result of the guarantee given by the lessee.* The examples ignore such complexities. For the purposes of the analysis, it is also assumed that there is no change in the aggregate carrying value of the lessor's assets as a result of entering into the leases—hence, no gains or losses arise at the beginning of the lease term.

LESSEE SIMPLY RETURNS THE LEASED ITEM TO THE LESSOR AT THE END OF THE LEASE

9.5   The most straightforward leases give the lessee the right to use an item for an agreed period of time in return for a series of payments. At the end of the lease term, the lessee simply returns the item to the lessor with no further rights or obligations.

EXAMPLE 1

A lessee enters a lease to hire equipment for three years at an annual rental of 5,000. The lessee returns the equipment to the lessor at the end of the lease.

9.6   At the inception of the lease, the lessor has the right to collect the lease payments; it also has the right to the return of the equipment at the end of the lease. The change in

*As a corollary to this, the fair value of the unguaranteed residual interst in Example 1 would be expected to be lower than the fair value of the guaranteed residual interest in Example 3.

the nature of the lessor's asset as a result of entering into the lease would be reflected in the balance sheet by changing its classification. Part of the lessor's existing asset (the item of equipment) would be derecognised. In its place, a financial asset (a receivable) would be recognised and measured at the present value of the three rental payments. The carrying value not derecognised is the lessor's retained residual interest in the equipment. This represents the rights to the economic benefits inherent in the equipment at the end of the lease, ie the future cash flows obtainable from selling, reletting or using the equipment. The accounting treatment would thus reflect the sale by the lessor to the lessee of an economic interest in the leased item, with the consideration being receivable in instalments from the lessee. The overall effect on lessor and lessee accounting is illustrated below.

Lessor	Lessee	
Assets	*Assets*	*Liabilities*
Receivable from lessee	Leased equipment	Obligation to lessor
15,000	15,000	15,000
Equipment—residual interest		
3,000		

LEASE CONVEYS OWNERSHIP OF THE LEASED ITEM TO THE LESSEE

Some leases convey legal ownership of the leased item to the lessee at the end of the contract. For example, legal title may pass when the last payment has been made by the lessee, or the lease may require the lessee to purchase the leased item for an agreed sum at the end of the lease term. As discussed in Chapter 5, such contracts are essentially sale agreements, the purchase price for the asset being payable in instalments.   9.7

EXAMPLE 2

A lessee enters a lease to hire equipment for three years at an annual rental of 5,000. At the end of the lease the lessee is required to pay a further 3,000 to purchase the equipment.

In this transaction, the lessor has transferred to the lessee rights to all of the future economic benefits derived from the equipment. The lessor should, therefore, derecognise the entire asset of the equipment and recognise a financial asset (a receivable) measured at the present value of the three rental payments together with the final purchase instalment payable by the lessee. The overall effect on lessor and lessee accounting is illustrated below.   9.8

Lessor	Lessee	
Assets	*Assets*	*Liabilities*
Receivable from lessee	Leased equipment	Obligation to lessor
18,000	18,000	18,000

LESSEE GUARANTEES A RESIDUAL VALUE

9.9 Some leases require the lessee to provide a residual value guarantee to the lessor.

EXAMPLE 3

A lessee enters a lease to hire equipment for three years at an annual rental of 5,000. The equipment will be sold at the end of the lease at fair value. The lessee guarantees a residual value to the lessor: if the equipment realises less than 3,000 when it is sold, the lessee is liable to compensate the lessor for the shortfall.

9.10 The lessor has transferred to the lessee the right to use the equipment for three years. The rights acquired or retained by the lessor at the inception of the lease can be viewed as consisting of three components:

- the right to collect lease payments of 15,000
- the guarantee of residual value by the lessee
- the right to sell the equipment at the end of the lease and retain the proceeds.

9.11 Clearly, under the approach being considered, the first item would be recognised as a financial asset (a receivable) and measured at the present value of the three rental payments. However, an issue arises concerning whether the residual value guarantee and the residual interest should be shown under separate asset captions in the balance sheet (financial and non-financial assets respectively), or whether they should be shown as one composite asset within either a financial asset caption or a non-financial asset caption. If they are shown as one composite asset, the description of the asset should adequately reflect its nature.

Separate presentation of guarantee and residual interest

9.12 The discussion in Chapter 5 from the perspective of lessee accounting concluded that in principle the fair value of the guarantee should be recognised by the lessee as a liability at the inception of the lease. This value represents part of the consideration that the lessee has given for obtaining the right to use the equipment for the lease term.* Under this approach, the amount of the lessee's liability includes the value of the guarantee, not the total amount that has been guaranteed.

9.13 A 'symmetrical' treatment from a lessor accounting perspective would result in the fair value of the guarantee being recognised as a financial asset by the lessor if it is material and if it is practicable to quantify it. Hence its value at the inception of the lease would be added to the value of the receivable asset.

9.14 The accounting under this approach would be as follows. Part of the lessor's existing asset (the item of equipment) would be derecognised. In its place, a financial asset (a receivable) comprising the rentals receivable and (if it is practicable to quantify its value) the residual value guarantee would be recognised. The carrying value not derecognised is the lessor's residual interest in the equipment (excluding the residual value guarantee). In effect, the value attributed to the residual interest would be the same as if the residual value were unguaranteed.

Guarantee and residual interest presented as a composite asset

9.15 The Group recognises the conceptual merits of the 'symmetrical' treatment described above. However, it believes that presentation of all interests in residual values, both

Various methods of estimating the fair value are discussed in Chapter 5.

guaranteed and unguaranteed, within the same caption is likely to be more useful and practicable than presenting them as separate classes of assets.

Furthermore, an important consequence of the separate presentation approach is that the components (the residual interest and the guarantee) that would be required to be shown under separate asset captions would each need to be remeasured during the lease term to reflect changing estimates of the realisable value of the item at the end of the lease. For example, if the estimated residual value fell during the lease term, the value of the guarantee would increase by an amount that would broadly offset the fall in the recorded amount of the residual interest. Inclusion of both components under the same caption avoids this complexity. **9.16**

Thus instead of allocating amounts from the residual interest to the receivable asset to reflect the value of the guarantee, the residual interest asset (which is presented as a non-financial asset) would include the value of the guarantee. The description of residual interest assets should identify the existence of residual value guarantees, with sufficient disclosures provided to enable users to understand a lessor's residual value exposures. **9.17**

The overall effect on lessor and lessee accounting of the proposed approach to guaranteed residual values is illustrated below. **9.18**

Lessor		Lessee	
Assets		*Assets*	*Liabilities*
Receivable from lessee		Leased equipment	Obligation to lessor
	15,000	15,000*	15,000
			plus guarantee (fair value)*
Equipment—residual interest†			
	3,000		

* The fair value of the guarantee is added to the rent payable of 15,000 (if it is practicable to quantify it).

† The guarantee is included in the carrying amount of the residual interest and its existence is disclosed.

In the earlier discussion, it has been assumed that the guaranteed amount is a realistic estimate, as at the inception of the lease, of the equipment's realisable value at the end of the lease. If this was not the case, and the guaranteed amount differed significantly from the expected residual value, the accounting should reflect realistic expectations at inception rather than the unrealistic terms of the contract. Thus if the guaranteed amount was greater than the expected residual value, the guarantee would have an intrinsic value (ie the difference between the guaranteed amount and the expected residual value) at the outset—for example, if the expected residual value in Example 3 was 2,000 compared with the 3,000 guaranteed. In those circumstances, part of the guaranteed residual value should be reallocated as an amount receivable from the lessee.* **9.19**

It should be noted that in such circumstances the recognition of a receivable in respect of a residual value guarantee does not imply that a contingent gain would be recognised; rather, the recognition of the guarantee would be reflected in the allocation between financial and non-financial assets.

LESSEE RECEIVES THE SALE PROCEEDS

9.20   Some leases give the lessee the right to participate in the proceeds from the sale of the leased item at the end of the lease. The most straightforward situation is illustrated in the following example.

EXAMPLE 4

A lessee enters a lease to hire equipment for three years at an annual rental of 5,000. In addition, the lessee is required to pay a fee of 3,000 for the residual value. The equipment will be sold at the end of the lease at fair value, and all the sale proceeds will be paid to the lessee.

9.21   In this example, the lessor has transferred to the lessee both the right to use the equipment for three years and the right to receive its residual value at the end of the lease. In consideration, the lessee has agreed to pay the lessor 18,000. Accordingly, the lessor should derecognise the whole of its existing asset of the equipment and recognise a financial asset (a receivable) measured at the present value of 18,000. The assets and liabilities that arise for the lessor and the lessee are illustrated below.

Lessor	Lessee	
Assets	*Assets*	*Liabilities*
Receivable from lessee	Leased equipment (including rights to sale proceeds)	Obligation to lessor
18,000	18,000	18,000

LESSOR RECEIVES THE SALE PROCEEDS, BUT LESSEE RECEIVES ANY SURPLUS AND PAYS ANY SHORTFALL

9.22   As an alternative to giving the lessee the rights to receive all the sale proceeds (as in the example above), some leases convey to the lessee the right and obligation to participate in gains and losses arising on the disposal of the leased item at the end of the lease. For example, the lessee may agree to pay to (or receive from) the lessor any difference between the leased item's residual value and a predetermined amount.

9.23   Example 5 is modified in one important respect from Example 4. Instead of the lessee being required to make a payment for the right to receive the residual proceeds, the lessee and lessor agree to make a net cash settlement when the equipment is sold.

EXAMPLE 5

A lessee enters a lease to hire equipment for three years at an annual rental of 5,000. The equipment will be sold at the end of the lease at fair value. If the proceeds are more than 3,000, the lessor will pay the whole of the surplus to the lessee. If the proceeds are less than 3,000, the lessee will pay the shortfall to the lessor.

9.24   The lessor has transferred to the lessee the right to use the equipment for three years. The rights acquired or retained by the lessor at the inception of the lease can be viewed as consisting of three components:

- the right to collect lease payments of 15,000
- the right to the sale proceeds at the end of the lease

- an obligation to pay to the lessee any excess over 3,000 and a right to receive from the lessee any shortfall below 3,000.

Chapter 5 discussed alternative treatments of this example from the perspective of the lessee. The main issue for lessee accounting is what asset and liability amounts should be recognised in respect of the residual value agreement. The alternatives are to recognise the value of the agreement or the full amount of the residual value that has been guaranteed. The Group's view is that the initial lease asset and liability should consist of the payments the lessee is required to make during the lease term and a value for the residual value agreement. Since the lessee has a net exposure on the residual value, any asset or liability relating to the residual value that is recognised by the lessee is explicitly for a net amount—the surplus or shortfall. **9.25**

For lessor accounting, the right to collect the scheduled rental payments would be recognised as a financial asset (a receivable) and measured at the present value of the three rental payments of 15,000. However, there are several possibilities for presenting the lessor's rights and obligations relating to the residual value in the balance sheet, as follows: **9.26**

(a) to show the whole amount (3,000) as a financial asset.
(b) to account for the fair value of the residual value agreement with the lessee as a financial asset (or liability) if it is material and if it is practicable to quantify it. The balance of the carrying value of the leased property not derecognised would be shown as a non-financial asset (residual interest).
(c) to show the whole amount (3,000) as a non-financial asset and disclose the existence of the residual value settlement agreement with the lessee.

For reasons similar to those given in the earlier discussion of residual value guarantees (see Example 3), the Group does not think it is particularly useful or practical to separate the residual interest into the separate components referred to above (ie the approach in (b) above). **9.27**

Clearly, in this example the lessor's asset has characteristics of a financial asset, since the lessor expects to realise a fixed amount (3,000) as a result of the contract with the lessee. The lessor's residual value exposure is to the lessee rather than to market prices of used equipment. **9.28**

Nevertheless the Group believes that this example merely illustrates one end of the spectrum of arrangements that may be put in place when the leased item is returned to the lessor at the end of the lease and its value has to be realised in the market. In practice many residual sharing arrangements are more complex than this, with lessees and lessors sharing potential gains and losses (see Example 6). In the Group's view it would probably not serve a useful purpose for standards to attempt to define the threshold at which a lessor's exposure to the lessee rather than property prices would convert the residual interest into a financial rather than a non-financial asset. **9.29**

Furthermore, the Group regards it as important to note that the amount of 3,000 is a value realisable in the market that is guaranteed by, not receivable from, the lessee. Consequently, both parties look first to the asset to satisfy their respective rights and obligations. **9.30**

For the above reasons the Group has concluded in favour of the approach in (c) above. The overall effect on lessor and lessee accounting is illustrated below. **9.31**

Lessor	Lessee	
Assets	*Assets*	*Liabilities*
Receivable from lessee 15,000	Leased equipment 15,000*	Obligation to lessor 15,000
		plus
Equipment—residual interest† 3,000	Residual value settlement (fair value)*	

* The fair value of the lessee's exposure under the residual value settlement agreement is added to the rent payable of 15,000 if it is practicable to quantify it.

† The lessee's participation in the residual interest is disclosed as this is useful information relating to the lessor's residual value exposure.

LESSOR RECEIVES THE SALE PROCEEDS, BUT LESSEE RECEIVES A SHARE OF ANY SURPLUS AND PAYS A SHARE OF ANY SHORTFALL

9.32   Example 6 illustrates a situation where the lessor and lessee share gains and losses on the realisation of the leased property at the end of the lease.

EXAMPLE 6

A lessee enters a lease to hire equipment for three years at an annual rental of 5,000. The equipment will be sold at the end of the lease at fair value. If the proceeds are more than 3,000, the lessor will pay one-half of the surplus to the lessee. If the proceeds are less than 3,000, the lessee will pay one-half of the shortfall to the lessor. Thus, for example:

- if the equipment is sold for 3,000, the lessor keeps all 3,000.
- if the equipment is sold for 5,000, the lessor keeps 4,000 and pays 1,000 to the lessee.
- if the equipment is sold for 2,000, the lessor keeps the 2,000 and receives a further 500 from the lessee.
- if the equipment realises no value, the lessee pays 1,500 to the lessor.

9.33   Consistently with its view of the previous examples, the Group takes the view that the lessor should recognise a financial asset (a receivable) in respect of the rental payments (measured at the present value of 15,000). The lessor's interest in the residual value should be displayed as a non-financial asset (residual interest—measured at the present value of 3,000), supplemented by disclosure relating to the lessor's residual value exposure. The table of assets and liabilities arising for lessor and lessee is substantially the same as that shown under the analysis of Example 5 above.

Recommendations

9A Rental payments and other amounts directly receivable from the lessee should be displayed as financial assets.

9B Residual interests (both unguaranteed and guaranteed) should be displayed as non-financial assets.

9C Disclosures should be given about residual interest assets to provide information that is useful for users to understand a lessor's residual value exposures. Such disclosures should include information about the existence of residual value guarantees and similar agreements.

Chapter 10 Receivables and residual interests—initial measurement

INTRODUCTION

This chapter considers principles for measuring the initial assets (a receivable and an interest in the residual value) that a lessor would report in respect of a lease. As noted in Chapter 8, the Group believes that the amounts receivable from the lessee should as a matter of principle be recorded initially at fair value (representing the fair value of the consideration that the lessee has agreed to pay for the right to use the leased property).   **10.1**

PRESENT VALUE MEASUREMENTS

It would appear to be preferable to measure the initial receivable and residual interest assets according to their relative fair values. In practice, however, no observable market prices are likely to be available for those separate components. Consequently, present value measurements are required to estimate the fair values, using estimated future cash flows.   **10.2**

The cash flows that arise from a lessor's investment in leased property include amounts that are recoverable under the lease and any amounts recoverable from the disposal or reletting of the property at the end of the lease. The cash inflows underlying those items are subject to different risks and uncertainties as regards their amounts and timing. The present value measurements should reflect the time value of money and the risks specific to the cash inflows. For example, an unguaranteed residual interest would be expected to have a lower fair value than an equivalent residual interest guaranteed by the lessee, since the former is more risky.   **10.3**

The overall yield that is derived from the calculation that equates the present value of the total expected cash flows with the fair value of the leased property is referred to in present accounting standards as the interest rate implicit in the lease. The implicit rate is a composite rate that reflects both the time value of money and the averaged risk relating to the total expected cash flows. Measuring the present values of the expected cash flows relating to the receivable and residual interest assets by discounting them at the implicit rate would produce values for the receivable and the residual interest that are in aggregate equal to the fair value of the leased property.* However, those values would not necessarily be indicative of their individual fair   **10.4**

**It should be noted that this discussion is concerned only with the initial recognition of lessor assets. It does not deal with the method of allocating gross earnings from a lease to different accounting periods over the lease term.*

values. This is because the residual value is usually of higher risk than the rental payments, since the amount recoverable is more uncertain.

10.5 The different risk attributes of the lessor's financial and non-financial assets could be captured in one of two ways (or a combination of both) when measuring their present values. One method is a dual discount rate approach—to measure the rentals receivable and the residual interest using different risk-adjusted discount rates that take account of the different risks. Thus the present value of an unguaranteed residual interest would be determined by discounting the expected fair value at the end of the lease using a higher discount rate than that used to measure the present value of rentals receivable, in order to reflect the higher risk. The discount rates should be such that the present values in aggregate do not exceed the previous carrying amount or fair value (as applicable) of the property being leased.

10.6 An alternative method of reflecting the relative riskiness of the lessor's assets is for the expected cash flows to be adjusted for risk. The risk-adjusted cash flows relating to both the receivable and residual interest assets would be discounted at a risk-free rate of interest. That rate is in effect the yield derived from the calculation that equates the aggregate present values of the expected rentals receivable and the expected fair value at the end of the lease (as adjusted for risk) to the fair value of the property being leased.*

10.7 The following examples illustrate the principles described above.

EXAMPLE 1—DETERMINING INITIAL CARRYING VALUES OF RENTALS RECEIVABLE AND RESIDUAL INTEREST (UNGUARANTEED)

An item of equipment that cost the lessor 10,000 is leased for four years, with rental payments at the end of each year. At the end of the lease the equipment is to be returned to the lessor—the residual value is unguaranteed. The estimated residual value is 3,000.

The rate of return available on a risk-free investment for a four-year term is 7 per cent (ie reflecting the time value of money only). However, the lessor is exposed both to residual value risk and credit risk and accordingly prices the lease to include a premium for accepting such risks. The estimated residual value is perceived to be more risky than the rentals receivable—risk-adjusted rates of 12 per cent and 9 per cent respectively are assumed. In order to achieve these required returns, the rental is set at four annual payments of 2,498, totalling 9,992.

The present value measurements of the receivable and the residual interest, determined by using the discount rates that reflect the risks specific to the assets, are illustrated in the following table.

	Estimated cash flows (undiscounted)	Interest rate (risk-adjusted)	Present value
Rent receivable (4 × 2,498)	9,992	9%	8,093
Residual interest	3,000	12%	1,907
Total	12,992	9.87%*	10,000

Conceptually, this approach is similar to calculating a 'certainty equivalent' in respect of the expected cash flows and discounting it at a risk-free rate.

* The rate of 9.87 per cent is the composite yield that is derived by discounting the total estimated cash flows of 12,992 to a present value of 10,000 (ie the interest rate implicit in the lease). If both the rent receivable and the residual interest were measured by discounting the estimated cash flows at the rate of 9.87 per cent, the present value measurements would then be 7,941 and 2,059 for the rent receivable and residual interest respectively. As stated earlier, this method fails to recognise the different risks associated with the receivable and residual interest assets.

The present value measurements could alternatively be determined by adjusting the estimated cash flows to reflect risk, as illustrated in the table below. It is assumed that the estimated residual value as adjusted for risk is 2,500. (The effect of the risk adjustment can be expressed as the lessor being prepared to accept a certain promise of 2,500 in four years' time in return for the residual interest.) Discounting the risk-adjusted residual value of 2,500 at the risk-free rate of 7 per cent produces the same present value (1,907) as in the previous table, where the estimated residual value of 3,000 was discounted at a risk-adjusted rate of 12 per cent.

	Estimated cash flows (undiscounted)	Risk adjustment	Risk-adjusted cash flows (undiscounted)	Present value (discount rate 7%)
Rent receivable	9,992	(436)*	9,556	8,093
Residual interest	3,000	(500)	2,500	1,907
Total	12,992	(936)	12,056	10,000

* The risk adjustment to the rent (436) has been applied in this example by reducing each instalment by an equal amount.

EXAMPLE 2—DETERMINING INITIAL CARRYING VALUES OF RENTALS RECEIVABLE AND RESIDUAL INTEREST (GUARANTEED)

The facts are the same as in Example 1, except that the residual value of 3,000 is guaranteed by the lessee. In return, the annual rental payment is reduced to 2,431 (9,724 in total, compared with 9,992 in Example 1).

In these circumstances, because of the existence of the guarantee, no risk-adjustment is required for residual value risk in the present value measurements, which are illustrated below.

	Estimated cash flows (undiscounted)	Present value (discount rate 9%)
Rent receivable (4 × 2,431)	9,724	7,875
Residual interest (guaranteed)	3,000	2,125
Total	12,724	10,000

The discount rate of 9 per cent is applicable to both the guaranteed residual value and the rent receivable—since the residual value is guaranteed by the lessee, the realisation of the guaranteed amount depends only on the credit risk of the lessee. The aggregate present value of the estimated cash flows (10,000) is the same as in Example 1; however, the present values of the receivable and residual interest components are respectively lower and higher by an amount of 218. This difference can be expressed as representing the value of the residual value guarantee, which increases the fair value of the estimated cash inflow relating to the residual interest from an unguaranteed value of 1,907 to a guaranteed value of 2,125 (with a corresponding reduction in the fair value of the rentals). Chapter 9 proposes that the guaranteed residual interest should be shown as a composite non-financial asset, with the existence of the guarantee disclosed.

Recommendations

10A If no gain is evidenced at the beginning of the lease term, the previous carrying amount of the property being leased should be allocated between two assets—a receivable and an interest in the residual value.

10B This allocation could be approached in one of two ways (or a combination of both):
   (a) by discounting the estimated future cash flows relating to the receivable and the residual interest using different (risk-adjusted) discount rates that take account of the different risks; or
   (b) by discounting the estimated future cash flows relating to the receivable and the residual interest (as adjusted for risk).

Chapter 11 Leases with optional features

INTRODUCTION

11.1   Chapter 4 discusses, from the lessee's perspective, principles for the recognition of assets and liabilities in respect of leases that contain renewal and purchase options and contingent rentals. This chapter gives an overview of the Group's proposals from a lessor accounting perspective.

11.2   The Group believes that the principles applying to the recognition of assets and liabilities should be the same for lessors and lessees. Consequently, it should be presumed that if a lease contract gives rise to a liability for the lessee it will give rise to a corresponding asset—a receivable—for the lessor.*

CANCELLATION AND RENEWAL OPTIONS

11.3   When accounting for options conveyed to the lessee, the exercise of the options should not generally be anticipated: the fair value of such options will be reflected in the minimum payments required by the lease.

11.4   Stated from the lessor's perspective, at the beginning of the lease term a lessor should record a financial asset equivalent to the present value of the payments required by the lease, assuming the lease is terminated on the earliest date the lessee has the right to do so. This reflects the fact that the lessee does not have an obligation to continue to lease the item beyond that date, but has the right to return it to the lessor.

11.5   Consider the example of a lease that requires the lessee to hire equipment for three years at an annual rental of 5,000 and gives the lessee the right to hire the equipment for a further two years at the same rent. At inception, the lessor has obtained:

Application of the principles relating to the recognition of assets, however, may not produce symmetry as between lessor and lessee accounting for all features, owing to information asymmetry in respect of rights and obligations that are contingent on future events.

- the right to collect lease payments of 15,000

and either

- the right to the return of the equipment at the end of three years

or (if the lessee exercises the renewal option)

- the right to collect further lease payments of 10,000, plus the right to the return of the equipment at the end of five years.

The lessor has transferred to the lessee the economic benefits relating to the use of the equipment in years 1–3, and has written a call option on years 4 and 5. Until the lessee elects to renew the lease, the lessee has a present obligation (a financial liability) to pay only 15,000 to the lessor. This represents the purchase of the right to use the equipment in years 1–3 and the purchase of the call option on years 4 and 5. Conversely, the lessor has a right to receive only 15,000 from the lessee. At inception, the lessor would recognise a financial asset (a receivable) measured at the present value of the rental payments of 15,000 (ie the amount that the lessee is obliged to pay) and a non-financial asset (the residual interest at the end of year 3) representing the cost of the economic benefits that have been retained by the lessor.   **11.6**

If the lessee exercises the renewal option, the lessee incurs an additional liability to pay 10,000 to the lessor for the use of the equipment in years 4 and 5. The lessee would then recognise the additional liability and rights to use the equipment stemming from that renewal. Conversely, the lessor then transfers to the lessee the economic benefits relating to the use of the equipment in years 4 and 5, and obtains the right to receive a further 10,000 from the lessee (and the right to the return of the equipment at the end of year 5 instead of the end of year 3).   **11.7**

When the lessee renews the lease the lessor would account for the transfer of the economic benefits relating to the use of the equipment in years 4 and 5 to the lessee by recognising an additional receivable representing the rental payments of 10,000 and correspondingly reducing the amount of the residual interest asset.   **11.8**

CONTINGENT RENTALS THAT VARY WITH USAGE

As discussed in Chapter 4, contingent rentals that vary with usage give rise to substantially similar issues to leases that contain renewal options. The similarity is that both kinds of leases give the lessee the option to 'purchase more' of the asset.   **11.9**

At the beginning of the lease term a lessor would recognise a receivable asset comprising the present value of the minimum payments required by the lease. Contingent usage-related rentals would be recognised in income when they become receivable (ie when the property is used by the lessee). The carrying value of the lessor's residual interest asset should be reduced if increased rentals reflected higher usage, compared with the level previously estimated, that would affect the leased item's residual value.   **11.10**

CONTINGENT RENTALS THAT ARE A PROPORTION OF THE LESSEE'S REVENUES OR PROFITS DERIVED FROM THE LEASED PROPERTY

Chapter 4 discusses the application of the following proposed principles for the recognition of assets and liabilities by lessees in respect of contingent rentals that are a proportion of the lessee's revenues or profits derived from the leased property: **11.11**

(a) The value of the rights obtained by the lessee under a lease cannot be less than the present value of the minimum payments required by the lease (assuming that the lease is negotiated on an arm's length basis).

(b)   If the minimum payments required by the lease are clearly unrepresentative of the value of the property rights conveyed by the lease, assets and liabilities of a greater amount, reflecting the fair value of such rights, should be recognised. The fair value of the property rights conveyed by a lease might be determined by having regard to the payments required by a similar lease that had no provision for contingent rentals.

(c)   Contingent rentals (in excess of the minimum payments, or greater amount, recognised at the beginning of the lease term) should be recognised when the contingency criteria are met.

11.12   The Group believes that the same principles should be adopted for lessor accounting. This is illustrated in the following example, which is discussed in Chapter 4 in relation to lessees as Example 4.

EXAMPLE

A lessee enters a three-year lease on a retail store. The annual rent comprises a minimum base rental of 10,000 plus $\frac{1}{2}$ per cent of the store's turnover during each year.

11.13   The Group's view is that the lessor's initial receivable asset should comprise the aggregate of the present value of the base rentals and perhaps an amount in respect of the share of turnover (corresponding to the asset and liability that is recognised by the lessee). For example, if it could be established that a similar lease without the right to receive a proportion of the lessee's future turnover would require a base rental of 10,500, the receivable asset recognised at the beginning of the lease term would be the present value of three rentals of that amount. Contingent rentals that differ from the amount of 500 for each year that is recognised at the beginning of the lease term would be recognised in income when the contingency criteria are met.

11.14   An alternative view of the lessee accounting noted in Chapter 4 for this example is that the initial asset and liability should reflect only the present value of the minimum payments required by the lease (ie three payments of 10,000). For the same reasons that they regard this treatment as appropriate for lessee accounting (see the discussion in Chapter 4), supporters of this view believe that the lessor should recognise a receivable asset of only the minimum payments required by the lease.

RENTALS THAT VARY IN LINE WITH PRICES

11.15   Some leases require the rentals to be revised periodically in line with price changes relating to the use of the leased item, for example to revise them to current market rates or in line with changes in a price index.

11.16   The Group's view of the appropriate lessee accounting is that at the beginning of the lease term, the lessee should record assets and liabilities equal to the present value of its best estimate of the rentals that will actually be payable, discounted at a nominal rate of interest (see Example 7 in Chapter 4). From the lessor's perspective, it has a receivable from the lessee of uncertain amount. In principle, therefore, future rental variations should be taken into account when measuring the initial carrying values of the financial asset (receivable) and the residual interest asset. The value of the lessor's receivable should reflect current scheduled rentals and estimated future rental variations.* However, to the extent that uncertain future cash flows were brought into

---

If future rental variations were excluded from the carrying amount of the lessor's receivable asset, they would in effect be treated as part of the lessor's residual interest asset until the price variations occurred.

the calculation, the discount rate should ensure that these did not result in the lessor's receivable being stated above its fair value at the inception of the lease.

An alternative view discussed in Chapter 4 is that only the minimum payments required by the lease at the beginning of the lease term should be reflected as an asset and a liability of the lessee (ie any future variations would not be recognised until they arise). For the same reasons that they believe this treatment is appropriate for lessee accounting (including the view that such rentals cannot in practice be measured reliably), supporters of this view believe that the lessor should recognise a receivable asset of only the minimum payments required by the lease. **11.17**

Recommendations

11A When accounting for renewal or purchase options conveyed to the lessee, at the beginning of the lease term a lessor should record a financial asset equivalent to the present value of the payments required by the lease, assuming the lease is terminated on the earliest date the lessee has the right to do so.

11B When a renewal or purchase option is exercised by the lessee, the lessor should record a financial asset equivalent to the present value of the additional payments required and correspondingly reduce the amount of the asset representing the residual interest.

11C If the minimum payments required by the lease (such as the minimum payments specified in leases with contingent rentals) are clearly unrepresentative of the value of the property rights conveyed by the lease, the lessor should record a financial asset equivalent to the fair value of such rights (corresponding to the asset and liability that is recognised by the lessee).

Chapter 12 Subsequent remeasurement of lessor assets

INTRODUCTION

Where the different elements of the lessor's investment (ie lease receivable and residual interest) are recognised under separate asset captions in the balance sheet, those elements would also be accounted for separately during the lease term. **12.1**

The carrying amounts of the lessor's assets may be affected by various factors during the lease term. In broad terms these include: **12.2**

(a) the passage of time;
(b) changes in estimates of amounts recoverable (eg from residual interests, from rentals that are not fixed in advance, or from changes in the lessee's credit risk); and
(c) the lessee's actions in respect of optional features of leases (eg contingent rentals and renewal options).

REMEASUREMENT FOR THE PASSAGE OF TIME

Lease receivables

For each accounting period during the lease term, the lease rentals relating to the use of the leased item (ie excluding payments for services) would be allocated between the repayment of the lease receivable balance and income. Since the receivable asset **12.3** is initially measured as the present value of future expected cash inflows under the lease, it would be appropriate under a historical cost model for an interest method* to be adopted to measure changes in the receivable asset's carrying amount.

12.4   The effect is that income is recognised during the lease term on a pattern that produces a constant periodic rate of return on the lessor's outstanding investment. There are two principal methods of income recognition for lessors, the net investment method and the net cash investment method. At present, the jurisdictions in the Group have differing requirements as to their use. The principal difference between the two methods is that the net cash investment method takes account of the timing of the tax cash flows relating to the lessor's investment, whereas the net investment method ignores the effects of tax cash flows. Although the income recognised over the whole lease term is the same under each method, the two methods may produce significantly different allocations of income to accounting periods during the lease term where the timing of the tax cash flows follows a different pattern from the timing of the cash flows that generate the tax. The Group has not reached any conclusions as to which method it regards as the most appropriate method of income recognition. Arguments for and against each method are set out in Appendix 2.

RESIDUAL INTERESTS

12.5   Chapter 10 proposed that the initial measurement of the residual interest asset would be derived by discounting an estimate of the amount recoverable at the end of the lease term.

12.6   There are a number of possible methods of accounting for the residual interest asset. Three methods considered are:

Method A   Recording, at inception and subsequently, the residual interest at an undiscounted amount.

Method B   Recording the residual interest at a discounted amount (as illustrated in Chapter 10), but not recognising the 'unwinding' of the discount over the lease term.

Method C   Recording the residual interest at a discounted amount, and recognising the 'unwinding' of the discount over the lease term.

12.7   The three methods are illustrated in the following example.

Example—accounting by a lessor for an interest in a residual value

The following assumptions are made:

Equipment cost	1,000
Rental (annually in arrears for five years)	240
Residual value (original estimate)	400
Implicit rate (calculated from above)	15.12 per cent
Amount received on sale of equipment at end of the lease	450
Rate paid on borrowed funds (paid annually in arrears)	10 per cent

From the above information, the cash flows arising over the term of the lease can be scheduled, as follows:

*Interest methods use present value calculations in computing changes in the carrying amount of an asset or liability from one period to the next. They are used in existing accounting standards for finance leases.

Year	0	1	2	3	4	5
Purchase of equipment	(1,000)	–	–	–	–	–
Rentals received	–	240	240	240	240	240
Interest paid (10 per cent)	–	(100)	(86)	(71)	(54)	(35)
Residual value received	–	–	–	–	–	450
Cash movement for year	(1,000)	140	154	169	186	655
Cash brought forward	–	(1,000)	(860)	(706)	(537)	(351)
Cash carried forward	(1,000)	(860)	(706)	(537)	(351)	304

Note: As all cash flows are assumed to take place on the last day of each year, the amount of interest paid can be found by applying the rate of 10 per cent to the (negative) cash balance at the end of the preceding year.

Method A—Residual interest recognised at undiscounted amount

At the beginning of the lease term, an interest in the residual value of 400 (estimate of the amount to be received in five years' time) would be recognised. The receivable would be initially recognised as the balance of the cost of the asset, ie 1,000–400 = 600. A receivable of 600 repayable in five annual instalments of 240 yields income at 28.66 per cent per year.

Balance sheet at year-end	0	1	2	3	4	5
Receivable	600	532	444	331	186	–
Residual interest	400	400	400	400	400	–
Cash	(1,000)	(860)	(706)	(537)	(351)	304
Net assets	–	72	138	194	235	304

Income statement					
Finance income (at 28.66 per cent)	172	152	127	95	54
Interest payable	(100)	(86)	(71)	(54)	(35)
Gain on sale of residual interest	–	–	–	–	50
Net income (total 304)	72	66	56	41	69

Method B—Residual interest recognised at discounted amount and discount not unwound over the lease term

The present value of the estimated residual value of 400 to be received in five years' time at a discount rate of 15.12 per cent is 198. If the residual interest is accounted for by leaving the carrying value at its initial discounted amount, which is 198, the lessor's financial statements will be as follows:

Balance sheet at year-end	0	1	2	3	4	5
Receivable	802	683	546	389	208	–
Residual interest	198	198	198	198	198	–
Cash	(1,000)	(860)	(706)	(537)	(351)	304
Net assets	–	21	38	50	55	304

Income statement

Finance income (at 15.12 per cent)	121	103	83	59	32
Interest payable	(100)	(86)	(71)	(54)	(35)
Gain on sale of residual interest	–	–	–	–	252
Net income (total 304)	21	17	12	5	249

Note: The amounts of cash and interest payable have been transferred from the cash flow schedule above. The receivable and finance income have been calculated by discounting at the rate implicit in the lease.

Method C—residual interest recognised at discounted amount and discount unwound over the lease term

If the residual interest over the term of the lease is accounted for by unwinding the discount, the lessor's financial statements will be as follows:

Balance sheet at year-end	0	1	2	3	4	5
Receivable	802	683	546	389	208	–
Residual interest	198	228	262	302	348	–
Cash	(1,000)	(860)	(706)	(537)	(351)	304
Net assets	–	51	102	154	205	304

Income statement

Finance income—on receivable (at 15.12 per cent)	121	103	83	59	32
Finance income—on residual interest (at 15.12 per cent)	30	34	40	46	52
Interest payable	(100)	(86)	(71)	(54)	(35)
Gain on sale of residual interest	–	–	–	–	50
Net income (total 304)	51	51	52	51	99

Note: The amounts of cash, interest payable and the receivable and finance income have been derived in the same way as in Method B. The residual interest has been discounted at the implicit rate and income on it recognised at the same rate.

Method A (No discounting)

12.8   An argument in favour of this approach is that usually in accounting depreciation is provided for on a basis that takes no account of the time value of money, and hence the undiscounted amount of the residual value is included in the balance sheet throughout the asset's life.

12.9   The drawbacks of this approach are:

(a)   The lessor's interest in the residual value of the asset (and, consequently, the amount receivable from the lessee) is reported initially at an amount that is clearly very different from its fair value.

(b)   Because the income is deemed to relate exclusively to the receivable, which decreases over the term of the lease (because it is repaid), the income is inappropriately recognised on a front-end basis.

Method B (Discount for initial recognition, but do not unwind discount)

Some believe that recognising interest on a non-financial asset is inappropriate in a historical cost context. They consider that any gain relating to such an asset should not be recognised until the asset is sold—until then, there is no transaction to be accounted for.   **12.10**

The drawback of this method is that income recognised during the lease term is restricted to an amount representing interest on the receivable asset only. This results in a very low level of income, especially at the after-interest level, if, as often will be the case in practice, a lease is largely financed by debt. It also results in a residual value being reported at a low amount during the lease term, followed by large gains on disposals.   **12.11**

Method C (Discount for initial recognition and unwind discount)

The Group takes the view that this method results in the most realistic reporting of balance sheet amounts and income over the term of the lease. It suffers from none of the drawbacks of the other two methods. Whilst it is true that a lessor's residual interest is not a financial asset, it is intrinsic to the nature of that asset that its value will increase as the time at which the lessor will receive the benefit of the residual value approaches. Recognising the increasing time value is therefore critical to a proper understanding of the lessor's financial position and performance.   **12.12**

A possible criticism of this method is that it could lead to the reporting of exaggerated profits that may never be made if the estimated residual value is not in fact realised.   **12.13**

The Group believes that accounting standards should emphasise the need for caution by ensuring that adequate allowance is made, both in the initial estimates and in the pattern of income recognition during the lease term, to cover the risk of residual value losses at the end of the lease. Accounting standards should also state the principle that initial residual value estimates should reflect the value that the lessor would willingly pay for an asset in similar condition and location to that which the lessor will receive at the end of the lease. Thus the estimate should be reduced to reflect any significant costs that would need to be incurred by the lessor (eg refurbishment costs and auction fees) before the disposal of the property.   **12.14**

REMEASUREMENT FOR CHANGES IN ESTIMATES

Changes in estimates of residual values

During the term of a lease, a lessor's residual interest asset should be subject to accounting standards dealing with the impairment of non-financial assets. Thus its carrying amount should be written down if it is no longer expected to be recoverable.   **12.15**

A lessor's economic exposure to changes in the residual value of a leased item depends on the contractual arrangements relating to the return of the item at the end of the lease. For example, if the item's expected residual value is unguaranteed, its carrying amount would need to be written down in the event of a reduction in its expected fair value during the term of the lease.   **12.16**

On the other hand, if the expected residual value is fully guaranteed by the lessee (or another party), a reduction in the item's residual value during the lease term has little economic impact on the lessor, since the lessor is in effect insured against it.   **12.17**

Consequently, no change in the carrying amount would be required as a result of a reduction in the item's expected fair value at the end of the lease, provided it was clear that the guarantee was enforceable and that the guarantor was able to honour the guarantee.

12.18   During the course of a lease, estimates of the eventual residual value may increase, rather than decrease. Conceptually, the effect of such an increase should be reported as income in the period in which it arises. This might result in a significant increase in a lessor's reported income, especially for those lessors that specialise in a particular kind of equipment. However, the Group takes the view that, during the lease term, lessors should not be permitted to increase the estimated residual value above the amount originally estimated. Consequently, any resulting profit should not be recognised until the asset is sold. It is recognised that such a restriction is arbitrary; however, it is a prudent approach and is consistent with historical cost accounting principles for such assets. Where residual values are regarded as understated as a result of this restriction, disclosure could be made.

Contingent rentals

12.19   As discussed in Chapter 11, the Group's view is that a lessor's receivable asset should in some circumstances include estimates of uncertain amounts of future rentals receivable. This is the case, for example, where rentals are related to future price changes. Such receivable assets would need to be remeasured during the term of the lease to current expected values if they are different from previous estimates. The carrying amount of the receivable asset would be increased or decreased by the present value of the difference and the amortisation profile of the receivable asset would need to be adjusted accordingly.

12.20   An issue that arises is how the corresponding gain or loss that arises from remeasuring the receivable asset should be accounted for. The principal alternatives are:

(a)   recognising a gain or loss immediately in income.

(b)   reducing or increasing the carrying amount of the residual interest asset by an equal amount (subject to impairment). The amortisation profile of both the receivable and residual interest assets would need to be adjusted accordingly— the gain or loss would then in effect be recognised over the lease term.

12.21   An argument for the first method is that it is appropriate to recognise a gain or loss if the expected future cash flows are more or less valuable than originally expected, instead of reducing the carrying value of another asset (as under the second method). Indeed, in the case of an increase in the receivable, the residual interest asset may itself have become more valuable, not less, as a result of the rent increase achieved. Thus it is considered that remeasurement of the receivable should result in the recognition of a gain or loss.

12.22   An argument for the second method is that under a historical cost model of lease accounting, lease income—including changes in estimates—should be recognised on a systematic basis over the lease term, ie there is no immediate gain or loss. This treatment would be achieved by reallocating the carrying values of the receivable and residual interest assets to reflect the revised estimate of the cash flows from leasing.

12.23   The Group agrees with the view that a gain or loss arising for the lessor on a change in the estimate of future rentals should be recognised immediately at its present value. The carrying amount of the residual interest would be adjusted only if an increase in rentals reflected higher usage compared with the level previously estimated (which would affect the residual value) or if the residual interest was otherwise impaired.

Under an alternative view of the treatment of contingent rentals discussed in Chapter 11, lessors would not generally recognise contingent rentals as receivable assets until the events that give rise to their payment occur. Under this view, such issues concerning subsequent remeasurement would not arise. **12.24**

REMEASUREMENT IN RESPECT OF OPTIONAL FEATURES

Under the Group's proposals for lessee renewal options and contingent rentals related to usage, the receivable asset recognised by the lessor would generally include only the minimum payments required by the lease. The lessor's assets will, however, need to be restated as necessary to reflect events that occur during the term of the lease. **12.25**

The exercise of a renewal option by the lessee will change the nature of the lessor's reported assets. Following the lessor accounting principles considered earlier, the lessor would recognise an additional receivable representing the rental payments in respect of the renewal period and correspondingly reduce the amount of the asset representing the residual interest. **12.26**

Similarly, in a lease where the lessee has the option to purchase additional usage under a contingent rental clause, the carrying amount of the lessor's residual interest asset would need to be reduced as a result of additional usage by the lessee if the higher usage would affect the residual value. **12.27**

Recommendations

12A For all leases that give rise to the recognition of a financial asset (receivable) at the beginning of the lease term, rentals receivable during the lease term should be allocated between the repayment (ie reduction) of the receivable asset and income, using an appropriate interest method.

12B Initial residual value estimates should reflect the value that the lessor would willingly pay for an asset in similar condition and location to that which the lessor will receive at the end of the lease.

12C The lessor's residual interest asset should be measured initially at the present value of the estimated residual value at the end of the lease. The carrying amount should be accreted over the lease term by 'unwinding' the discount.

12D Adequate allowance should be made, both in the initial estimates and in the pattern of income recognition during the lease term, to cover the risk of residual value losses at the end of the lease.

12E A decrease in an estimate of residual values should be treated according to accounting standards dealing with the impairment of non-financial assets. Thus the carrying amount of a residual interest asset should be written down if it is no longer expected to be recoverable. Lessors should not be permitted to increase an estimated residual value above the amount estimated at the beginning of the lease.

12F Receivable assets that include elements of contingent rentals should be remeasured during the term of the lease to current expected values if they are different from previous estimates. A corresponding gain or loss should be recognised immediately.

> 12G The carrying amount of the residual interest asset should be reduced if an increase in rentals reflected higher usage compared with the level previously estimated that would affect residual value.

Part IV Other issues

Chapter 13 Leases of land and buildings

INTRODUCTION

13.1 'Leasing' commonly refers to the leasing of equipment, such as plant and machinery, vehicles, aircraft and so on. However, leases are also extensively used for land and buildings.

13.2 The history of leasing of land and buildings is rather different from that of equipment leasing. Equipment leasing has often been motivated by tax advantages, whereas tax has generally played only a minor role in the leasing of land and buildings. Another difference is that whilst many equipment lessors have little or no interest in the residual value of the property that they lease—either the residual value is very small or it is passed to the lessee or another party—the lessor of land and buildings nearly always has a significant interest in the residual value. For this reason, lessors of land and buildings are most often specialists in the property industry who manage a portfolio of property investments based on their professional assessment of likely future trends in the market for property.

13.3 Existing lease accounting standards generally apply to leases of land and buildings. However, except for a comparatively small number of specially-structured transactions, leases of land and buildings are generally regarded as operating leases. Lessee accounting for such leases is therefore generally straightforward and, apart from any prepaid or accrued amounts (such as a premium paid at the start of the lease), no asset or liability is recognised in respect of such leases and the total rental expense is recognised, usually on a straight-line basis, over the lease term.

13.4 Conversely, lessors generally record their ownership of leased properties by reflecting the entire property as such in their balance sheet. However, in some jurisdictions, specific accounting standards apply to 'investment properties', and these standards will apply to a lessor's properties. These standards generally require that investment properties are not depreciated, but are stated at their fair value at the balance sheet date.*

13.5 This chapter considers whether, in the light of the differences noted above, the proposals in this Paper should apply to leases of land and buildings as well as to leases of equipment, or whether any modification of the proposals is necessary or desirable. As far as lessor accounting is concerned, any modifications of the proposals would be applicable only to those lessors that account for land and buildings under existing practices at fair values because they are investment properties.

Examples of such standards are the New Zealand standard SSAP-17 'Accounting for Investment Properties and Properties Intended for Sale' and the UK standard SSAP 19 'Accounting for Investment Properties'. A similar approach is proposed in IASC's Exposure Draft E 64 'Investment Property'. Investment properties are also sometimes stated at fair value in accordance with the practice of specific industries in Australia and the USA.

It may be noted that a particular kind of lease—the 'institutional lease'—is commonly used for leases of land and buildings in the UK. The term of the institutional lease is comparatively long: a term of 25 years is typical and terms of 50 years, or even longer, are not uncommon. Another distinctive feature of the institutional lease is that the rentals are revised to prevailing market prices at regular intervals (usually every five years); however, this repricing is subject to the important condition that rentals can only be increased, and not decreased. Such a feature is termed an 'upward-only rent review'. Its effect is that the lessor of the property benefits from any increase in property prices, but does not suffer in the event of a decrease. The consequences of any fall in property prices are borne by the lessee, who must continue to pay the rental originally negotiated, or that set at the most recent rent review.

13.6

OCCUPIER/LESSEE

From the standpoint of the occupier or lessee, the considerations that support the proposed approach to accounting for leases of equipment are equally relevant to leases of land and buildings. Once the property is placed at the disposal of the lessee, the lessee has the right to occupy the property subject to the terms of the lease for the lease period and an unconditional obligation to pay the rentals specified by the lease. The right to use the property and the obligation to pay rentals are respectively assets and liabilities of the lessee, and there seems to be no valid reason why they should not be reported as such.

13.7

The features of the institutional lease, described in paragraph 13.6, have the effect that the approach advocated in this Paper would result in relatively large assets and liabilities being recognised by lessees. The liability would include the present value of the rentals (including an estimate of future increases) for the full term of the lease. Empirical studies* show that the effect of recognising assets and liabilities relating to leases of land and buildings on measures such as reported levels of gearing is likely to be marked in some cases, especially in the UK.

13.8

Some specific advantages of the approach proposed in this Paper over existing accounting may be noted. If a lessee's interest in a leased property were recorded as an asset it would be possible to revalue that asset, to the extent that other standards applicable in the relevant jurisdiction permit or require revaluations of interests in land and buildings. This has the advantage that the basis of measurement used is more relevant than historical cost, and the accounting would reflect the extent to which the lessee has the ability to benefit from the increase in the value of its asset by subleasing the property at the higher prices now prevailing or continuing to use the property and competing on favourable terms with competitors that have to pay current prices.

13.9

Recording the lessee's interest in the leased property as an asset would also bring the asset within the scope of accounting standards on impairment: thus when an asset is identified as being impaired it would be written down. This would arguably represent a significant improvement over present practice in financial reporting. Although in some jurisdictions accounting standards† require provision to be made for leases that

13.10

---

*See, for example, V Beattie, K Edwards and A Goodacre, 'The Impact of Constructive Operating Lease Capitalisation on Key Accounting Ratios', *Accounting and Business Research (28/4, Autumn 1998), pp 233–254; Dresdner Kleinwort Benson, 'Operating Leases: The Retail House of Cards', Research Report (London: Kleinwort Benson Securities Ltd, September 1998).

†For example, IAS 37 'Provisions, Contingent Liabilities and Contingent Assets' and the similar UK standard FRS 12.

have become 'onerous', they do not specify with precision either the circumstances in which a lease should be regarded as onerous, or the basis on which provision should be made. Even where such standards exist, there is thus a risk that losses are not recognised at the time they arise, and as a result the loss may be recognised only when a decision to vacate the property has been taken.

13.11   Recognising the loss earlier would not only ensure that information was reported on a more timely basis, but would also have the result that a decision whether a property should be vacated would be taken having regard to the cost and revenues expected from continued occupation: the commitment to pay the lease rentals has already been entered into and therefore has no bearing on that decision.

13.12   It is sometimes claimed that a change in the accounting for leases of land and buildings may alter the willingness of occupiers to enter into leases for long periods. In turn, this may reduce the attractiveness of property to investors. However, if the accounting method used provides information that gives a more faithful representation of the lessee's financial position, it is likely that decisions based on that information will be economically superior rather than inferior.

OWNERS/LESSORS

13.13   Just as the nature and history of leasing of land and buildings seems to provide no reason why the accounting by lessees for such leases should be different from that for lessees of equipment, so the proposals in this Paper appear to be applicable, in principle, to the position of the owner or lessor. In the owner/lessor's financial statements, two assets would be reflected—a financial asset representing the payments required by the lease and an interest in the residual value. Thus the accounting would make transparent the extent to which the lessor was primarily at risk from default by the lessee, on the one hand, and, on the other, the extent to which the lessor is at risk from (and may benefit from) future changes in the value of the property.

13.14   Over the period of the lease, the financial asset would be increased by the recognition of finance income and reduced as payments are received under the lease. As noted in Chapter 12, the consensus of the Group is that a lessor's interest in the residual value of a leased asset should initially be recorded at its discounted value and then be accreted up to its expected value during the term of the lease.

13.15   However, the approach described in the preceding two paragraphs seems to be in some respects inferior to existing methods of accounting for investment properties. As noted in paragraph 13.4, investment properties are widely stated at fair value: the relevance of fair values as a measure of investment properties is widely accepted, particularly as such properties (by definition) are capable of being disposed of without any impact on the owner's operations (other than the holding of investments). It would therefore not be an improvement in financial reporting to substitute a method that does not give information on the current fair value of investment properties for one that does. The challenge is to devise a method that preserves the fair value information provided by present accounting practice while also giving information about the underlying nature of those assets as provided by the lease.

13.16   One possibility would be to maintain existing standards for investment properties and require an analysis of those assets to be given in the notes, showing the extent to which the asset is represented by rents receivable from the lessee and by the lessor's residual interest. It is understood that as valuers approach the valuation of rented properties by separately assessing the value of the lease payments from that of the residual value, this information may be available at minimal cost.

One disadvantage of this approach is that it would lead to the full amount of the rental receivable in respect of an accounting period being shown as income of that period. This is not consistent with the approach to leasing advocated in this Paper, which implies that only a proportion of any rental is properly regarded as income of the period, with the balance representing a return *of* capital rather than a return *on* capital.

13.17

A more sophisticated approach would be to show as separate components of the lessor's income the return on the lease payments (akin to interest receivable); the lessor's income arising from the accretion of the residual value to reflect the passage of time; and a separate component of financial performance representing all the other changes in the fair value of the interest in investment properties.

13.18

Although such an approach might be the theoretical ideal, it is doubtful whether and to what extent it can be achieved in practice. In particular, it may be difficult (if not impossible) to analyse the movement in the residual value into the part that relates to the passage of time and the part that relates to changes in market prices.

13.19

A more practicable compromise would be to report only two components of income for the lessor of an investment property: one would be the finance income on the lease receivable, and the other would report all changes in the residual value as a single amount. This approach offers the prospect, at small cost, of a significant improvement in the portrayal of the assets and liabilities and of the components of financial performance of those entities that invest in land and buildings and let them on leases, while retaining the information on the fair value of properties that is given in accordance with existing accounting standards.

13.20

Recommendations

13A There should be no exemption from the approach of new standards on lease accounting for leases of land and buildings, as accounted for by lessees.

13B Lessors of land and buildings should report as separate assets in their balance sheets the amount of their investment that represents lease receivables, and that which represents their interest in the residual value of the property. (This reflects the fact that the residual value accrues wholly to the lessor.) The finance income on lease receivables and changes in interests in residual value should be reported separately.

13C In those jurisdictions where investment properties are reported under existing practices at fair value, the lessor's interest in the residual value would be reported as the difference between the amount of the lease receivable and the fair value of the property

---

Chapter 14 Issues for a fair value model

INTRODUCTION

14.1 Members of the G4 + 1 are contributing to the work of the Financial Instruments Joint Working Group of standard-setters (the JWG). The JWG, which comprises representatives of ten standard-setters,* is working to develop a comprehensive and internationally harmonised approach to accounting for financial instruments. The JWG's working premise is that financial instruments should be reported in the balance sheet at fair value and that all changes in fair value should be recognised in earnings when they occur.

14.2 This Paper has been written principally in the context of a system of accounting that is primarily based on historical cost. Until the JWG has published its proposals, and these in turn have been agreed by standard-setters, it would be premature to set out at length a method of accounting for leases under which all financial instruments resulting from leases were reported at fair value. By setting out the proposals primarily in the context of historical cost, this Paper will enable the merits of the proposed approach to lease accounting to be considered independently of the case for reporting financial instruments at fair value.

14.3 However, this chapter provides a brief and tentative overview of some of the issues that would need to be addressed in developing the proposed lease accounting model a stage further to encompass fair value accounting for the financial assets and liabilities that arise from lease contracts, and how the accounting might differ from the main proposals in this Paper.

FINANCIAL ASSETS AND LIABILITIES RELATED TO LEASE CONTRACTS

14.4 A financial instrument is defined in IAS 39 'Financial Instruments: Recognition and Measurement' as follows:

'A financial instrument is any contract that gives rise to both a financial asset of one enterprise and a financial liability or equity instrument of another enterprise.

A financial asset is any asset that is:

(a) cash;
(b) a contractual right to receive cash or another financial asset from another enterprise;
(c) a contractual right to exchange financial instruments with another enterprise under conditions that are potentially favourable; or
(d) an equity instrument of another enterprise.

A financial liability is any liability that is a contractual obligation:

(a) to deliver cash or another financial asset to another enterprise; or
(b) to exchange financial instruments with another enterprise under conditions that are potentially unfavourable.'

14.5 Clearly, lease contracts give rise to financial instruments under the above definition— as discussed earlier in this Paper they give rise to financial assets for lessors and financial liabilities for lessees. Consequently, it is to be expected that financial instruments recognised as a result of lease contracts would in due course come within

See footnote on page 1527.

the scope of accounting standards on financial instruments that emerge from the JWG's project.

Assets of lessors

The following table illustrates the proposed classification of assets arising for lessors under common features of lease contracts.

14.6

Financial assets	Non-financial assets
Minimum payments required by lease	
Amounts receivable in respect of granting renewal options	Rentals relating to optional renewal periods
Contingent rentals that represent consideration for the fair value of rights conveyed to lessee	Contingent rentals relating to optional additional usage
	Residual interest (unguaranteed and guaranteed)

The basis for this analysis is primarily the identification of financial liabilities for lessees and corresponding receivable assets for lessors. Under this approach, other rights of lessors relating to the leased property are shown as non-financial assets (ie interests in property, plant or equipment). These include the residual interest and the benefits relating to renewal options and contingent rental agreements written by the lessor but not yet exercised by the lessee.

14.7

Under a fair value approach, it would need to be explored further whether the contingent elements in the right-hand column that arise from the lease contract should be accounted for as financial assets under the above definition, since the lessor has contractual rights—albeit conditional—to receive cash. This might be the case even if no outstanding receivable balance has been recognised (because there is no present obligation on the lessee).

14.8

The issue is important because if such elements were accounted for as financial assets, a fair value model of accounting for financial assets would require them to be measured at fair value, whereas if they were accounted for as non-financial assets, they would be treated according to the valuation standards that apply generally to non-financial assets (in general, there is no requirement to remeasure to fair value).

14.9

It is arguable, for example, that the fair value of a lease contract should take into account the expected value of any contingent rentals, since the fair value that would be determined in the marketplace for the contract would take account of the rights to amounts generated by future transactions that it embodies. An issue that arises from such analysis is whether, and if so how, the accounting for the lessor's rights under such contracts should distinguish between the receivable balance that arises at the beginning of the lease term (based on distinguishing the minimum payments required by the lease from other amounts that are contingent on future events, as proposed in the model developed hitherto) and other components of fair value.

14.10

Liabilities of lessees

14.11   From the lessee perspective, the following table illustrates the proposed basis for determining amounts that should be recognised in liability balances related to lease contracts.

Items included in initial liabilities	Items excluded from initial liabilities
Minimum payments required by lease	
Amounts payable in respect of obtaining renewal options	Rentals relating to optional renewal periods
Contingent rentals that represent consideration for the fair value of rights conveyed to lessee	Contingent rentals relating to optional additional usage
Fair value of residual value guarantees	Residual values guaranteed where transfer of economic benefits in settlement is not probable

14.12   Under a fair value approach, the accounting for the contingent elements in the right-hand column would need to be explored further. The question of how the fair value of lease contracts should be represented in the lessee's financial statements, as regards the fair value of the lessee's present obligations and the fair value of the other components of the contracts (if, indeed, there are any liabilities for lessees over and above the present obligations), raises issues similar to those arising for lessors.

FAIR VALUE MEASUREMENTS

14.13   IAS 39 defines fair value as 'the amount for which an asset could be exchanged, or a liability settled, between knowledgeable, willing parties in an arm's length transaction'. The JWG's proposals* should provide more guidance on how fair value should be estimated for various types of financial assets and liabilities; techniques include reference to observable market prices, valuation models and present value measurements of the kind with which many lessors and lessees are familiar.

14.14   In the historical cost model that has been outlined in this Paper, subsequent remeasurement of assets and liabilities related to leases is required, in broad terms, when estimates used in measuring the initial carrying amounts change during the lease term. Thus, for example, revised expectations of contingent rentals, bad debts, etc. are recognised by restating the carrying amounts of the relevant assets and liabilities. Interest income and expense relating to lease receivables and payables are, however, recognised at a constant rate of return over the lease term (except for leases where the rentals are varied to reflect changes in interest rates).

14.15   In a fair value model, all changes in fair value of financial assets of lessors and financial liabilities of lessees would result in their carrying amounts being restated. The restatement would include certain value changes not recognised in the historical cost model, in particular the effect of changes in interest rates during the lease term. For example, the initial carrying amounts of lessor receivables and lessee payables would reflect interest rates at the beginning of the lease term, and subsequent changes in interest rates would alter the value of the asset and liability in the marketplace.

*Editor's note: See footnote to page 1527.

PRESENTATION OF GAINS AND LOSSES

Under the JWG's fair value model, changes in fair values of financial assets and financial liabilities would be recognised in earnings when they occur.

14.16

The JWG's project is addressing issues relating to income statement presentation that are relevant to leasing. These issues include how the aggregate amount of fair value gains and losses on financial assets and liabilities should be analysed into interest income and expense and other gains and losses.

14.17

A change to accounting standards for leasing would not prejudge the outcome of the JWG's work. Rather, the changes proposed in this Paper are within the context of present practice, under which many kinds of financial instruments, including lease receivables and payables, are recorded at amounts based on historical cost. Once the premise that financial instruments should be stated at fair value has become accepted, it would then be necessary to consider what modifications to accounting standards for leases would be required.

14.18

Appendix 1 – Asset and liability definitions

	Australia	Canada	New Zealand	UK	USA	IASC
ASSETS	Assets are future economic benefits controlled by the entity as a result of past transactions or other past events.	Assets are economic resources controlled by an entity as a result of past transactions or events and from which future economic benefits may be obtained.	Assets are service potential or future economic benefits controlled by the entity as a result of past transactions or other past events.	Assets are rights or other access to future economic benefits controlled by an entity as a result of past transactions or events.	Assets are probable future economic benefits obtained or controlled by a particular entity as a result of past transactions or events.	An asset is a resource controlled by the enterprise as a result of past events and from which future economic benefits are expected to flow to the enterprise.
LIABILITIES	Liabilities are the future sacrifices of economic benefits that the entity is presently obliged to make to other entities as a result of past transactions or other past events.	Liabilities are obligations of an entity arising from past transactions or events, the settlement of which may result in the transfer or use of assets, provision of services or other yielding of economic benefits in the future.	Liabilities are the future sacrifices of service potential or of future economic benefits that the entity is presently obliged to make to other entities as a result of past transactions or other past events.	Liabilities are obligations of an entity to transfer economic benefits as a result of past transactions or events.	Liabilities are probable future sacrifices of economic benefits arising from present obligations of a particular entity to transfer assets or provide services to other entities in the future as a result of past transactions or events.	A liability is a present obligation of the enterprise arising from past events, the settlement of which is expected to result in an outflow from the enterprise of resources embodying economic benefits.

Appendix 2 - Lessor accounting: net investment and net cash investment methods

There are two principal methods for specifying how revenues from a lease should be allocated to the lessor's income statement during the lease term: the net investment method and the net cash investment method. Both methods allocate income on the basis of a constant periodic rate of return on the lessor's outstanding investment in the lease; however, the methods calculate that investment balance in different ways. The net cash investment method is the more general method and, for many leases, will give the same result as the net investment method. Differences arise, however, when the timing of tax cash flows relating to the lease is an important factor. **1**

Under the net investment method, the investment balance is based on the lease payments without taking account of the tax that will arise on them. There are a number of different net cash investment methods (and differing ways of describing them) but the essential feature is that the investment balance reflects the lease payments and certain other cash flows that relate to the lease, the most significant of which are usually tax cash flows.* **2**

For many leases, there will be little difference between the two methods. However, when substantial up-front capital allowances (ie fiscal depreciation) are available on an asset that is leased for a long period, the differences can be significant. As a result, the patterns in which revenues from a lease are periodically allocated to the income statement during the lease term would also differ significantly under the two methods. **3**

The question is which pattern of revenue recognition is more appropriate. Traditionally this question has been answered by considering the costs (including funding costs) relating to the lease and how they can best be matched with revenues. On this basis, at least for highly geared leases, the net cash investment method gives a better match. Recognising income on the net investment basis rather than the net cash investment basis could, in extreme cases, lead to losses being recorded in the early years (ie cost of funds exceeding revenues recognised) even though the lease is profitable overall—a result that seems undesirable on what is essentially a financial asset. This has led to the net cash investment method being regarded as appropriate in the UK. **4**

Critics of the net cash investment method have argued that revenue recognition should not be primarily based on an attempt to match income and expenses. Doing so can lead to balance sheet figures that do not represent assets or liabilities of the entity. Under the net investment approach, on the other hand, it is argued that the meaning of the balance sheet figure is clear. It is the outstanding minimum lease payments (plus any residual value) discounted at the pre-tax rate inherent in the lease. The lease is accounted for on a pre-tax basis and any tax effects reflected by then applying the accounting standard for tax. Supporters of the net investment method also point out that for most transactions the accounting method is not affected by the treatment of the transaction for tax purposes. **5**

The net investment approach has the merit of simplicity and, in many cases, will give a reasonable allocation of income over the period of the lease. However, sometimes **6**

A method of income recognition that is similar to the net cash investment method is sometimes used for 'leveraged leases' ie leases where the lease is funded on a non-recourse basis. This gives rise to further issues and is not considered in this Appendix, which addresses only net cash investment methods that in allocating income to accounting periods have regard to the timing of tax cash flows.

the timing of the tax cash flows varies significantly from the timing of the amounts on which tax is assessed, for example when up-front capital allowances are available instead of tax relief that reflects the gradual use of the asset over time. In these situations, supporters of the net cash investment method believe that basing income recognition on the pre-tax rate inherent in the lease distorts both the income recognition and the balance sheet amounts. In their view, the net cash investment method, by basing income recognition on post-tax amounts, not only gives a better income recognition pattern but also gives rise to balance sheet figures that are a closer proxy for fair value than those arising under the net investment method.*

7   In summary, the net investment method is simple to use and easy to understand. In most cases it will result in a pattern of income recognition that is a reasonable reflection of the underlying economics of the lease (ie where the timing of the tax cash flows is not an important factor). However, the method does not reflect the economic consequences of the timing of the tax cash flows and, hence, arguably produces distorted results where this is a significant factor. The net cash investment method is more complex but, on the other hand, gives a pattern of income recognition that reflects the underlying economics of the lease (provided, of course, that the assumptions used such as the tax effects of the lease are valid).

8   Some believe that accounting standards should require the use of the net cash investment method because it is the more general method in that it gives the same results as the net investment method when the timing of tax cash flows is not a factor but is the more accurate of the two methods when the timing of tax cash flows is an important factor.

9   Both the net investment method and the net cash investment method are supported by different members of the Group.

---

*The resulting figures would be an approximation of fair value if the time value of money remained constant over the period of the lease.

IASB Exposure Draft of a proposed IFRS for small and medium-sized entities

(Issued April 2007)

Contents

Preface

1   The IASB is developing an International Financial Reporting Standard tailored to meet the needs of – and intended for use only by – small and medium-sized entities (IFRS for SMEs). SMEs are defined by the IASB as entities that (1) do not have public accountability and (2) publish general purpose financial statements for external users.

2   The IASB is developing the IFRS for SMEs to:

   * provide high quality, understandable and enforceable accounting standards suitable for SMEs globally;
   * reduce the financial reporting burden on SMEs that want to use global standards; and
   * meet the needs of users of SME financial statements.

3   The IASB published an Exposure Draft (ED) of the IFRS for SMEs on 15 February 2007 and invites comments to 11 questions to be submitted to the IASB in writing so as to be received no later than 1 October 2007.

4   The Accounting Standards Board (ASB) is issuing the IFRS for SMEs in full for consultation together with this accompanying ASB invitation to comment (ITC) on the Exposure Draft and the potential implications for UK and Irish entities. The ASB is publishing this ITC for two separate but linked reasons: a) to help inform its response to the IASB on the SME document; and b) to receive further feedback from constituents as to how the SME document might fit into the Board's convergence plan. The ASB plans to submit its formal response to the IASB by the 1 October deadline after considering feedback from constituents. The ASB would welcome comments on this ITC by 31 July 2007.

5   In order to help respondents in their thinking the Board has prepared an analysis of the significant differences between UK GAAP and the proposed IFRS for SMEs, an analysis of the significant differences between the existing Financial Reporting Standard for Smaller Entities (FRSSE) and the proposed IFRS for SMEs as well as making reference to the significant differences between full IFRS and the IFRS for SMEs – as published in the Basis of Conclusions of the Exposure Draft (see paragraphs 7–10 below and Appendix A).

6   In preparing this consultation the ASB has taken full account of the views of UK and Irish constituents from the 2006 feedback on the future application of reporting requirements for UK companies*, as well as advice from the ASB's Committee on Accounting for Smaller Entities (CASE). In particular, the 2006 consultation seemed to indicate broad support for a two-tier approach – namely all companies should report under IFRS or FRSSE. However, the ASB concluded that no further decisions could be made until the Exposure Draft of a proposed IFRS for SMEs was published.

Differences between the existing UK GAAP/FRSSE and the proposed IFRS for SMEs

7   The IASB believes that the proposed IFRS for SMEs would be suitable even for very small entities (see the IASB's Basis for Conclusions, paragraphs BC45–50), which would include those in the UK and Ireland that are eligible to apply the FRSSE.

**An overview of the responses is available at http://www.frc.org.uk/asb/technical/projects/project0072.html*

Currently, the FRSSE may be applied to entities that are small companies or small groups, as defined in companies legislation, preparing Companies Act individual or group accounts or entities that would qualify under the above if they had been incorporated under companies legislation, with the exception of building societies. Accordingly the FRSSE does not apply, in particular, to large or medium-sized companies, groups and other companies, public companies, banks, building societies or insurance companies. In addition, the FRSSE is a 'One stop shop' that incorporates both the Companies Act and the Accounting Standards regulations. Consequently, the ASB is still considering whether it agrees that the proposed IFRS for SMEs would, in fact, be a suitable replacement for the FRSSE and would welcome the views of constituents.

In reviewing the differences between the existing UK GAAP/FRSSE and the proposed IFRS for SMEs (as set out in Appendix A) the following represent the main significant differences.   **8**

UK GAAP v IFRS for SMEs:

- FRS 2 Accounting for Subsidiary Undertakings – Exemptions from preparing group accounts under the SME are different from those set out in UK GAAP.
- FRS 6 Acquisitions and Mergers – The FRS requires business combinations to be accounted for using the merger or the acquisition accounting approach. The SME requires all business combinations to be accounted for by applying the purchase method.
- FRS 8 Related Party Disclosures – Certain exemptions to subsidiary undertakings allowed in the FRS; the SME does not include an equivalent exemption. The SME requires key management personnel compensation disclosure; such disclosure is outside the scope of FRS 8.
- FRS 10 Goodwill and Intangible Assets – Different recognition approaches based on separability. The SME does not permit goodwill to be amortised but is instead tested for impairment.
- FRS 19 Deferred Tax – The SME requires deferred tax to be recognised on the basis of temporary differences rather than on the basis of obligations arising from timing differences. Different disclosure requirements.
- FRS 26 Financial Instruments – The SME allows entities to choose to apply either the provisions of section 11 of the SME or IAS 39 in full to account for all of its financial instruments – if elected an entity shall make disclosures required by IFRS 7. The SMEs Basis for Conclusions explain the significant simplifications to the recognition and measurement principles in IFRS.

FRSSE v IFRS for SMEs:

- Cash Flow Statements – No FRSSE requirement.
- Consolidated Financial Statements – FRSSE permits but does not require consolidation.
- Deferred Taxes – FRSSE omits most presentation disclosure aspects of FRS 19 and deferred tax recognised on all timing differences. SME requires provision for tax of future recovery/settlement of assets/liabilities at current carrying amounts and utilisation of losses and unused credits.
- Financial Instruments – FRSSE focuses on classification and cost measurement. SME focuses on cost/fair value measurement, significant attention to hedge accounting and choice to full IFRS (IAS 39 & IFRS 7).
- Borrowing costs – The FRSSE and the SME set out different measurement models.

- Fixed Assets & Goodwill – Investments in Associates/Investment Properties/ Intangible Assets – different measurement options and disclosure requirements. The FRSSE requires goodwill to be depreciated over its useful economic life and not be revalued. The SME requires goodwill in a business combination after initial recognition to be recognised at cost less any impairment losses. Government Grants – different measurement options.
- Share Based Payments – FRSSE requires use of the best estimate of the expenditure to settle the liability at balance sheet date and equity-settled share-based payments disclosure only. SME requires use of IFRS 2 provisions and fair value references for equity-settled share-based payments.
- Disclosure Requirements (General) – The FRSSE provides considerable simplifications in respect of disclosure requirements as compared to the SME.

Main Differences between full IFRS and the IFRS for SMEs

9   The IASB has highlighted in the Basis for Conclusions, accompanying the Exposure Draft, topics covered in the IFRSs that are omitted from the IFRS for SMEs. These topics include hyperinflation, equity-settled share-based payment, agriculture, interim financial reporting, lessor accounting for finance leases, earnings per share, segment reporting and insurance (refer to paragraphs BC57–BC65 of the IASB's Basis for Conclusions for the full text on these topics).

10   The Basis for Conclusions also highlights the proposed recognition and measurement simplifications. Topics covered include financial instruments, goodwill impairment, research and development costs, associates and joint ventures, income taxes, agriculture, employee benefits – defined benefits plans, share-based payment, leases and transition to the IFRS for SMEs (refer to paragraphs BC70–BC93 of the Basis of Conclusions for the full text on these topics).

Impact on the Future Application of Reporting Requirements for UK companies

11   UK and Irish constituents need to consider the application of the IFRS for SMEs in the UK and Irish markets. The ASB is of the opinion that there are three main implications that need to be considered by constituents.

12   Firstly, constituents need to consider what other role the IFRS for SMEs may play within the ASB's convergence project, ie is it suitable for a mid-tier of companies above the current range for the FRSSE but below those currently required to apply full IFRS? Secondly, is the IFRS for SMEs an appropriate replacement for the FRSSE? Finally, if the IFRS for SMEs is to be considered a suitable basis for middle tier companies, or as a replacement for the FRSSE, what changes will need to be made ?

13   In considering the impact on UK and Irish entities, the ASB will take into account the costs and benefits involved. The ASB would be grateful for any views that constituents might have at this stage on those costs and benefits.

14   Depending on the responses it may be desirable to adopt the IFRS for SMEs as a 'middle tier' standard for those UK and Irish entities that do not apply full IFRS or the FRSSE. This may then allow smaller entities to continue using the FRSSE although after a bedding down period of the IFRS for SMEs, there may then be consideration as to whether a simplified version of this standard might be applied to

smaller entities; thereby replacing the FRSSE. If this approach were to be adopted it would result in all UK and Irish entities applying IFRS based standards and would be in line with the overall ASB convergence strategy.

The ASB continues to be minded that UK and Irish subsidiaries of group companies that apply full IFRS would also be required to apply full IFRS in respect of measurement and recognition, but with reduced disclosure requirements (yet to be defined). Consequently, the IFRS for SMEs would not be an available option for these subsidiaries. **15**

ASB questions

The ASB is requesting comments by 31 July 2007. Comments are invited on any aspect of the consultation, and in particular on the following: **16**

ASB Q1:   Do you believe that the proposed IFRS for SMEs would be suitable for 'middle tier' entities that fall between applying full IFRS and the FRSSE?

ASB Q2:   If the proposed IFRS for SMEs were to be considered a suitable basis for middle tier companies, what specific changes do you think the ASB should be proposing; for example is it too long, is there too much cross referencing to full IFRS, are there sufficient simplifications, etc?

ASB Q3:   Do you believe that the proposed IFRS for SMEs would be a suitable replacement for the FRSSE?

ASB Q4:   If the proposed IFRS for SMEs were to be considered a suitable basis for the FRSSE, what specific changes do you think the ASB should be proposing; for example is it too long, is there too much cross referencing to full IFRS, are there sufficient simplifications, etc?

ASB Q5:   What do you consider should be the costs and benefits of the ASB adopting the proposed IFRS for SMEs either as (i) a standard for 'middle tier' companies or (ii) a replacement for the FRSSE? Are there any specific areas in the Exposure Draft that would, in your view, impose particular costs on companies? It would be helpful if any significant costs that would arise or any of the specific areas could be identified and quantified.

The IASB has also set out, at pages 3 to 6 of the proposed Exposure Draft Invitation to Comment, 11 questions on the Exposure Draft. The ASB would welcome comments on those. **17**

The ASB would also be pleased to receive copies of responses to the IASB submitted by UK and Irish commentators. **18**

Appendix A
Significant differences between UK GAAP and the IFRS for SMEs

UK GAAP	SME	Differences
FRS 1 – Cash Flow Statements	Cash Flow Statement (section 7)	**GAAP Differences:** Whereas FRS 1 exempts entities such as certain subsidiary undertakings from preparing cash flow statements, the SME offers no such exemption. FRS 1 focuses on movements in cash, whereas the SME is concerned with movements in cash and cash equivalents. **Level of Disclosure:** The SME requires fewer heading classifications (operating, investing and financing) and does not mandate the order in which they are presented.
FRS 2 – Accounting for Subsidiary Undertakings	Consolidated and Separate Financial Statements (section 9)	**GAAP Differences:** The most important difference between the definitions of subsidiaries is that the SME focuses on the power to control, whereas the UK GAAP definition also encompasses situations in which control is actually exercised in practice notwithstanding that the power to control is not present. The exemptions from preparing group accounts under the SME are different from those set out in UK GAAP. **Level of Disclosure:** For UK companies certain additional disclosures are required by the Companies Act.
FRS 3 – Reporting Financial Performance	Financial Statement Presentation (section 3) Balance Sheet (section 4) Income statement (section 5)	**GAAP Differences:** In general, the requirements of the SME are less prescriptive than those of UK GAAP. **Level of Disclosure:** As above.

	Statement of Changes in Equity and Statement of Income and Retained Earnings (section 6) Notes to the Financial Statements (section 8) Equity (section 21) Revenue (section 22)	
FRS 4 – Capital Instruments	N/A	FRS 25 *Financial Instruments: Disclosure and Presentation* has the effect of withdrawing FRS 4, except for material on the measurement of debts and gains and losses on the repurchase of debt.
FRS 5 – Reporting the Substance of Transactions	Concepts and Persuasive Principles (section 2)	**GAAP Differences:** There is under the SME no direct equivalent of FRS 5, but there are no fundamental differences between the SMEs *Concepts and Persuasive Principles* and the ASB's Statement of Principle. **Level of Disclosure:** None
FRS 6 – Acquisitions and Mergers	Business Combinations and Goodwill (section 18)	**GAAP Differences:** The FRS requires business combinations to be accounted for either using the merger accounting approach whereby the carrying values of assets and liabilities of the parties to the combination are not required to be adjusted to fair value on consideration or by the acquisition accounting model, whereby the identifiable assets and liabilities of the companies acquired should be included in the acquirer's consolidated balance sheet at their fair value at the date of acquisition. The SME requires all business combinations to be accounted for by applying the purchase method. In particular, the acquirer shall measure the cost of the business combination as

		the aggregate of the fair values, at the date of exchange, of assets given, liabilities incurred or assumed, and equity instruments issued by the acquirer, in exchange for control of the acquiree; plus any costs directly attributable to the business combination. **Level of Disclosure:** Different disclosure requirements are required by the SME as outlined in section 18.23 of the SME.
FRS 7 – Fair Values in Acquisition Accounting	Business Combinations and Goodwill (section 18)	**GAAP Differences:** Refer to FRS 10 – Goodwill and Intangible Assets. **Level of Disclosure:** Significant disclosures are required by the UK GAAP dependent on which accounting method is utilised as outlined in FRS 6 paragraphs 21–37. Different disclosure requirements are required by the SME as outlined in section 18.23 of the SME.
FRS 8 – Related Party Disclosures	Related Party Disclosures (section 33)	**GAAP Differences:** The FRS grants certain exemptions to subsidiary undertakings 90 per cent or more of whose voting rights are controlled within the group – these subsidiaries do not have to disclose transactions with other group companies and investees of the group qualifying as related parties provided group financial statements including the subsidiary are publicly available. The SME does not include an equivalent exemption. **Level of Disclosure:** The SME requires entities to disclose key management personnel compensation in total and for each of the following categories: short-term employee benefits, post-employment benefits, other long term benefits, termination benefits and share-based

		payments. Such disclosure is outside the scope of FRS 8, although the Companies Act requires detailed disclosures in relation to director's remuneration.
FRS 9 – Associates and Joint Ventures	Investments in Associates (section 13) Investments in Joint Ventures (section 14)	*Associates* **GAAP Differences:** The FRS requires a reporting entity that prepares consolidated financial statements should include its associates in those statements using the equity method in all the primary financial statements. In the investor's individual financial statements, its interest in associates should be treated as fixed asset investments and shown either at cost, less any amounts written off, or at valuation. In the SME the investor shall account for its investments in associates using one of the following – the cost model in section 13.4, the equity method in section 13.5 or the fair value through profit and loss model in section 13.6 of the SME. **Level of Disclosure:** Similar general disclosure requirements exist. However, additional requirements may be required dependent on which method an entity adopts. *Joint Ventures* **GAAP Differences:** The FRS requires in consolidated financial statements that an investor should include its joint ventures using the gross equity method in all its primary financial statements. In the investors individual financial statements, investments in joint ventures should be treated as fixed asset investments and shown either at cost, less any amounts written off, or at valuation. In the SME the investor shall account for its interest in all its

		jointly controlled entities using one of the following – the cost model in section 14.9, the equity method in section 14.10, the proportionate method described in 14.11 or the fair value through profit and loss model in section 14.12 of the SME. **Level of Disclosure:** Similar general disclosure requirements exist.
FRS 10 – Goodwill and Intangible Assets	Intangible assets other than Goodwill (section 17) Business Combinations and Goodwill (section 18)	**GAAP Differences** FRS 10 and the SME take different approaches to recognition based on separability. This will result in more intangible assets being recognised on the acquisition of a business under the SME than under UK GAAP. The SME does not permit goodwill to be amortised but is instead tested for impairment. In addition, negative goodwill arising on a business combination is recognised immediately as a gain under the SME. **Level of Disclosure:** None
FRS 11 – Impairment of Fixed Assets and Goodwill	Property, Plant and Equipment (section 16) Impairment of Non-financial Assets (section 26)	**GAAP Differences:** None **Level of Disclosure:** None
FRS 12 – Provisions, Contingent Liabilities and Contingent Assets	Provisions and Contingencies (section 20)	**GAAP Differences:** None **Level of Disclosure:** None
FRS 13 – Derivatives and other Financial Instruments: Disclosures	Financial Assets and Liabilities (section 11)	N/A – FRS 13 was withdrawn in full once FRS 29 'Financial Instrument – Disclosures' came into effect on 1 January 2007.
FRS 15 – Tangible Fixed Assets	Property, Plant and Equipment (section 16)	**GAAP Differences:** None **Level of Disclosure:** None
FRS 16 – Current Tax	Income Taxes (section 28)	**GAAP Differences:** None **Level of Disclosure:** None

FRS 17 – Retirement Benefits	Employee Benefits (section 27)	**GAAP Differences:** None, except IAS 19 has more extensive scope. **Level of Disclosure:** Similar extensive disclosure requirements are required as outlined in FRS 17 – paragraphs 75–93 and sections 27.37 and 27.38 of the SME.
FRS 18 – Accounting Policies	Accounting Policies, Estimates and Errors (section 10)	**GAAP Differences:** None **Level of Disclosure:** None
FRS 19 – Deferred Tax	Income Taxes (section 28)	**GAAP Differences:** The SME requires deferred tax to be recognised on the basis of temporary differences rather than on the basis of obligations arising from timing differences. In addition, the FRS does not in general require deferred tax to be provided for when non-monetary assets are revalued or when they are adjusted to their fair value on the acquisition of a business. In addition, the FRS allows (but does not require) deferred tax liabilities that will not be settled for some time to be discounted to reflect the time value of money. In contrast, the SME prohibits discounting. **Level of Disclosure:** The FRS requires additional disclosures of the effect of discounting, a general explanation of the circumstances that have affected the current and total tax charges for the current and future periods, the circumstances in which deferred tax relating to revaluation and rolled over gains would be payable. The SME requires additional disclosure of the aggregate amount of temporary differences associated with investments in foreign subsidiaries, branches, and associates and joint ventures, for which deferred tax

		liabilities have not been recognised.
FRS 20 (IFRS2) – Share-based Payment	Share-based Payment (section 25)	**GAAP Differences:** None **Level of Disclosure:** None
FRS 21 (IAS 10) – Events after the Balance Sheet Date	Events after the end of the Reporting Period (section 32)	**GAAP Differences:** None **Level of Disclosure:** None
FRS 22 (IAS 33) – Earnings per share	Earnings per Share (section 34)	An entity is not required to present amounts of earnings per share. However, if an entity discloses earnings per share, it shall calculate and disclose earnings per share in accordance with IAS 33 *Earnings per share.*
FRS 23 (IAS 21) – The Effects of Changes in Foreign Exchange Rates	Foreign Currency Translation (section 30)	**GAAP Differences:** None **Level of Disclosure:** None
FRS 24 (IAS 29) – Financial Reporting in Hyperinflationary Economics	Financial Reporting in Hyperinflationary Economics (section 29)	An entity whose functional currency is the currency of a hyperinflationary economy shall apply IAS 29 *Financial Reporting in Hyperinflationary Economies* in preparing and presenting its financial statements.
FRS 25 (IAS 32) – Financial Instruments: Presentation	Financial Assets and Liabilities (section 11)	FRS 29 *Financial Instruments: Disclosure* replaces the disclosure requirements of FRS 25 and is mandatory on or after 1 January 2007. FRS 29 applies to entities applying FRS 26 – the scope of that standard covers listed entities and entities that use the fair value accounting of the Companies Act 1985 to produce their financial statements.
FRS 26 (IAS 39) – Financial Instruments: Recognition and Measurement	Financial Assets and Liabilities (section 11) Borrowing Costs (section 24)	The SME allows entities to choose to apply either the provisions of section 11 of the SME or IAS 39 *Financial Instruments: Recognition and Measurement* in full to account for all of its financial instruments. An entity that

		chooses to apply IAS 39 shall make the disclosures required by IFRS 7 *Financial Instruments: Disclosures*. The IFRS for SMEs Basis for Conclusions Paragraphs BC71–BC78 explain the significant simplifications that the IASB proposes to the recognition and measurement principles in IFRS. In summary, the significant simplifications cover: The complexities of classifying financial instruments into four categories, the 'pass-through' and 'continuing involvement' tests for derecognition, and the detailed calculations required to qualify for hedge accounting. However, although section 11 is a simpler approach to accounting for financial instruments than IAS 39, some of the simplifications involve eliminating options that are available to companies with public accountability under IAS 39, for instance: available for sale classification and option, held–to–maturity classification, partial derecognition and the use of hedge accounting for hedges other than the four specific types identified in BC73(c) of the SME.
FRS 27 – Life Assurance	N/A	N/A
FRS 28 – Corresponding Amounts	Financial Statement Presentation (section 3)	**GAAP Differences:** None **Level of Disclosure:** None
FRS 29 (IFRS 7) – Financial Instruments: Disclosures	Financial Assets and Liabilities (section 11)	FRS 29 only applies to entities applying FRS 26 *Financial Instruments: Recognition and Measurement* – the scope of that standard covers listed entities and entities that use the fair value accounting of the Companies Act 1985 to produce their financial

		statements. For entities applying it, FRS 29 replaces the disclosure requirements of FRS 25 and is mandatory on or after 1 January 2007.
SSAP 4 – Accounting for government grants	Government Grants (section 23)	**GAAP Differences:** None **Level of Disclosure:** None
SSAP 5 – Accounting for Value Added Tax	N/A	N/A
SSAP 9 – Stocks and Long-term contracts	Inventories (section 12) Revenue (section 22)	***Inventories*** **GAAP Differences:** None **Level of Disclosure:** The SSAP requires stocks to be sub-classified in the Balance Sheet or in the notes to the Financial Statements so as to indicate the amounts held in each of the main categories in the standards balance sheet format. The SME requires more detailed disclosure as outlined in section 12.21 of the SME. ***Long-Term Contracts*** **GAAP Differences:** None **Level of Disclosure:** None
SSAP 13 – Accounting for Research and Development	Intangible Assets other than Goodwill (section 17)	**GAAP Differences:** The SSAP requires the costs of fixed assets to be capitalised over their useful lives through the profit and loss account. Research expenditure should be written off in the year of expenditure through the profit and loss account. Development expenditure should be written off in the year of expenditure except in circumstances when it can be deferred to future periods as outlined in the SSAP paragraph 25. The SME requires an entity to choose either the expense model in section 17.15 or the capitalisation model in section 17.16 of the SME. **Level of Disclosure:** The SSAP requires additional disclosure of the movements on

		deferred development expenditure and the amount carried forward at the beginning and end of the period.
SSAP 19 – Accounting for Investment Properties	Investment Property (section 15)	**GAAP Differences:** The SSAP requires investment properties to be included in the Balance Sheet at their open market value. Value changes should be taken to the statement of total recognised gains and losses. The SME requires an entity to measure all of its investment property after initial recognition using either the fair value method in section 15.5 or the cost model in section 15.6 of the SME. **Level of Disclosure:** The SSAP requires disclosure of the bases of valuation and specific details of the valuers; whereas the SME requires disclosures based on the model adopted by the entity.
SSAP 21 – Accounting for Leases and Hire Purchase Contracts	Leases (section 19)	**GAAP Differences:** None **Level of Disclosure:** Different disclosure requirements exist as outlined in SSAP 21 paragraphs 49–60 and sections 19.12 and 19.14 of the SME.
SSAP 25 – Segmental Reporting	Segment Reporting (section 31)	The SME does not require an entity to present information about operating segments. An entity that chooses to disclose segment information in financial statements described as to conforming to the IFRS for SMEs shall comply fully with the requirements of IFRS 8 *Operating Segments*.

The following sections of the IFRS for SMEs are not addressed in UK GAAP:
Section 1 – Scope
Section 35 – Specialised Industries
Section 36 – Discontinued Operations and Assets held for Sale
Section 37 – Interim Financial Reporting
Section 38 – Transition to the IFRS for SMEs

Significant differences between the FRSSE and the IFRS for SMEs

FRSSE	SME	Differences
General (pages 15–29)	Financial Statement Presentation (section 3) Balance Sheet (section 4) Notes to the Financial Statements (section 8) Accounting Policies, Estimates and Errors (section 10)	*Accounting Principles* **GAAP Differences /Level of Disclosure**: FRSSE only covers Prudence and Going Concern (principles). SME provides a helpful discussion of the framework (albeit no difference between the principles for small, medium or large entities). *Accounting Policies* **GAAP Differences:** None **Level of Disclosure:** Generally, FRSSE entities are not required to make any reference to the disclosure, explanation and consistency of their accounting policies unless it is material. In contrast, the IFRS for SMEs requires an entity to disclose and apply its accounting policies consistently.
Profit and Loss account (pages 30–32) Revenue Recognition (pages 32–34)	Income Statement (section 5)	**GAAP Differences:** None **Level of Disclosure:** The FRSSE provides considerable simplifications in respect of disclosure requirements (paragraphs 3.1–3.8) as compared to the SME (sections 5.3–5.11).
Statement of total recognised gains and losses (page 35)	Statement of Changes in Equity & Statement of Income & Related Earnings (section 6)	**GAAP Differences**: None **Level of Disclosure:** The FRSSE provides considerable simplifications in respect of disclosure requirements (paragraph 5.1) as compared to the SME (sections 6.2, 6.3 and 6.5).
Fixed Assets and Goodwill (pages 36–49)	Investments in Associates (section 13) Investment Property (section 15)	*Investments in Associates* **GAAP Differences**: The FRSSE requires fixed asset investments to initially be measured at cost.

	Property, Plant and Equipment (section 16) Intangible Assets other than Goodwill (section 17) Business Combinations and Goodwill (section 18) Government Grants (section 23)	Alternatively, they may be measured at a market valuation determined as at a date of their last valuation or on any other value determined on a basis which appears to the directors to be appropriate. The SME requires an investor to account for its investments in all associates using one of the following: the cost model, the equity method or the fair value through profit and loss model, as described in more detail in sections 13.4–13.6 of the SME. **Level of Disclosure:** The FRSSE requires the following to be stated in relation to the undertaking – name of undertaking, country of incorporation or address of principal place of business, the identity and proportion of the nominal value of each class of shares held, the aggregate amount of the capital and reserves as at the end of the most recent financial year ending and its profit or loss for the year. If the other 'value' basis is adopted, the method of valuation adopted and the reasons for adopting it shall be disclosed in a note to the accounts. The SME requires an investor in associates to disclose its accounting policy, the fair value of investments in associates for which there are published price quotations, summarised financial information of associates along with the investor's percentage of ownership of the associates and the nature and extent of any significant restrictions on the ability of the associate to transfer funds to the investor in the form of cash dividends, or repayment of loans or advances. Additional disclosure requirements are required for investments

accounted for by the equity method, as outlined in section 13.8 of the SME.

Investment Property

GAAP Differences:

The FRSSE requires investment properties to be included in the balance sheet at their market value.

The SME requires entities to measure all of its investment property after initial recognition (cost) using either the fair value model, as outlined in section 15.5, or the cost model, as outlined in section 15.6 of the SME.

Level of Disclosure:

The FRSSE requires the carrying value of Investment Property to be displayed prominently either on the face of the balance sheet or in the notes.

The SME requires disclosures to be made based upon which model it elects to adopt. Fair value – IAS 40 *Investment Property* - paragraphs 75–78; Cost model section 16 of the SME.

Property, Plant and Equipment

GAAP Differences:

No specific requirement for an annual impairment review is required for FRSSE entities except as in paragraph 6.45 if the net recoverable amount of a fixed asset is considered not to be recoverable in full at the balance sheet date, the net book value should be written down to the estimated recoverable amount; whereas SMEs, at the end of each reporting period, shall apply Section 26 *Impairment of Non-financial Assets* to determine whether an item or group of items of property, plant and equipment is impaired and, if so, how to recognise and measure the impairment loss.

Level of Disclosure:
FRSSE requires entities to provide the cost or valuation at the beginning/end of the year and the effect of any revaluation, acquisitions, disposals and transfers during the year as well as the cumulative amount of provisions for depreciation or diminution in value at the start/end of the year, the amount of any adjustments made during the year.
SMEs shall disclose more information (15 specific disclosure requirements), for each class of property, plant and equipment as outlined in sections 16.29–16.31 of the SME.

Intangible Assets
GAAP Differences:
The FRSSE requires purchased intangible assets to be capitalised. Internally generated intangible assets shall not be capitalised. Intangible assets shall be depreciated on a straight line basis over their useful economic life and shall not be revalued. The costs of fixed assets to provide facilities for research and development activities shall be capitalised and written off over their useful lives through the profit and loss account. Development expenditure shall be written off in the period of expenditure except in circumstances when it may be deferred to future periods as outlined in paragraphs 6.6–6.10 of the FRSSE.
The SME requires an entity to measure an intangible asset initially at cost. The creation of internally generated assets involves a research and development phase. An entity shall choose either the expense model outlined in section 17.15 or the capitalisation model as

in section 17.16 of the SME as its accounting policy for costs incurred in research and development activities.

Level of Disclosure:

There is no specific reference in the FRSSE to intangible assets disclosure requirements.

The SME requires significant disclosure requirements (11 items) as outlined in sections 17.32–17.34 of the SME.

Goodwill

GAAP Differences:

The FRSSE requires purchased goodwill to be capitalised. Internally generated goodwill shall not be capitalised. Goodwill shall be depreciated on a straight line basis over their useful economic life and shall not be revalued.

The SME requires the entity to recognise goodwill acquired in a business combination as an asset and initially measure goodwill at cost. After initial recognition, the acquirer shall measure goodwill in a business combination at cost less any impairment losses.

Level of Disclosure:

There is no specific reference in the FRSSE to goodwill disclosure requirements.

The SME requires extensive disclosure requirements for business combinations as outlined in section 18.23 of the SME.

Government Grants

GAAP Differences:

The FRSSE only requires that government grants should be recognised in the profit and loss account to match them with the expenditure towards which they are intended to contribute; there is no specific statement on dealing with grants made to give immediate financial support to finance the general activities of the entity. The SME requires entities to account for its government

		grants using either the IFRS for SMEs model in section 23.4 of the SME for all its government grants or the IFRS for SMEs model in section 23.4 for those government grants related to assets measured at fair value through profit and loss and IAS 20 *Accounting for Government Grants and Disclosure of Government Assistance* for all other grants. **Level of Disclosure**: There is no specific reference in the FRSSE to the disclosure of the accounting policy for government grants. The SME requires entities to disclose the accounting policy adopted for government grants, including an explanation of how the grant is presented in the financial statements.
Leases (pages 50–55)	Leases (section 19)	**GAAP Difference:** None; except the SME includes a cross reference to full IFRS in respect of lessor accounting for finance leases. **Level of Disclosure:** The FRSSE provides considerable simplifications in respect of disclosure requirements (paragraphs 7.16–7.18 of the FRSSE) as compared to the SME (sections 19.12, 19.14 and 19.23 of the SME).
Current Assets (pages 55-60)	Inventories (section 12) Revenue (section 22)	*Inventories* **GAAP Differences:** None **Level of Disclosures**: While FRSSE does not require any specific disclosure requirements SMEs shall disclose 6 specific disclosures as outlined in section 12.21 of the SME. *Long Term Contracts* **GAAP Differences:** None **Level of Disclosure:** The FRSSE requires no specific reference to the accounting policy and the need

		to apply it consistently; whereas the SME requires entities to disclose the accounting policies adopted for the recognition of revenue.
Taxation (pages 60–63)	Income Taxes (section 28)	**GAAP Differences**: The SME would require deferred tax liabilities to be recognised for the tax consequences of the future recovery or settlement of the entity's assets and liabilities at their current carrying amounts and for unused tax losses and unused tax credits. **Level of Disclosure:** The FRSSE requires the material components of the current and deferred tax charge (or credit) for the period to be disclosed separately as compared to the extensive disclosure requirements (13 items) as outlined in sections 28.28–28.30 of the SME.
Pensions (page 63)	Employee Benefits (section 27)	**GAAP Differences:** None, except employee benefits in the SME is wider than pensions in the FRSSE (it covers other employee benefits). **Level of Disclosure:** Disclosure requirements (4 items) for a defined benefit scheme are considerably reduced in the FRSSE (Appendix II paragraph (j)) as compared to the SME disclosure requirements (11 items) as outlined in section 27.38 of the SME).
Provisions, Contingent Liabilities and Contingent Assets (pages 64–66)	Provisions and Contingencies (section 20)	**GAAP Differences:** None **Level of Disclosure**: FRSSE requires less information (4 specified) to be provided for each class of provision (paragraph 11.6 of the FRSSE). SMEs shall disclose more information (8 specified) for each class of provision (section 20.14) of the SME.

| Financial Instruments, Share capital, and Share-based payments (pages 66–70) | Financial Assets and Financial Liabilities (section 11) Borrowing Costs (section 24) Share-based payment (section 25) | *Financial Instruments* **GAAP Differences**: The FRSSE does not address FRS 25, 26 and 29. 12.1 addresses the presentation issue from FRS 25. SMEs shall choose to apply either the provisions of section 11 or IAS 39 *Financial Instruments: Recognition and Measurement* in full to account for all of its financial instruments. **Level of Disclosure:** SME detailed disclosure requirements if the entity adopts section 11 are outlined in section 11.40–11.43 of the SME. An SME that chooses to apply IAS 39 shall make the disclosures required by IFRS 7 *Financial Instruments: Disclosures*. *Share-based payments* **GAAP Differences**: FRSSE requires the use of best estimate of the expenditure to settle the liability at the balance sheet date; the FRSSE requires a disclosure only approach for equity settled share-based payments. SMEs would generally require measurement by reference to fair value of the equity instruments granted as required by IFRS 2. However, if the entity is unable to estimate reliably the fair value of the equity instruments granted at measurement date section 25 of the SME retains the provisions of IFRS 2 for simplified measurement for SMEs using the intrinsic value method. **Level of Disclosure**: None *Borrowing Costs* **GAAP Differences**: The FRSSE requires that the finance costs of borrowings should be allocated to periods over the terms of the borrowings at a constant rate |

		on the carrying amount. All finance costs shall be charged in the profit and loss account. SME entities shall account for all of its borrowing costs using either the expense model in section 24.3 or the capitalisation model in section 24.4 of the SME. **Level of Disclosure**: The FRSSE does not require any specific disclosure of the accounting policy; whereas the SME requires an entity to disclose the accounting policy adopted for borrowing costs.
Foreign Currency Translation (pages 71–73)	Foreign Currency Translation (section 30)	**GAAP Differences:** None **Level of Disclosure**: None
Post Balance Sheet Events (page 74)	Events after the end of the Reporting Period (section 32)	**GAAP Differences:** None **Level of Disclosure:** None
Related Party Disclosures (pages 75–83)	Related Parties Disclosures (section 33)	**GAAP Differences** : None **Level of Disclosure:** The FRSSE requires detailed disclosures of subsidiary undertakings, holdings in subsidiary undertakings and financial information about subsidiary undertakings as outlined in paragraphs 15.16–15.20 of the FRSSE. The SME requires entities to disclose key management personnel compensation in total and for each of the following categories: short-term employee benefits, post-employment benefits, other long-term benefits, termination benefits and share-based payments.
Consolidated Financial Statements (pages 84–85)	Consolidated & Separate Financial Statements (section 9)	**GAAP Differences:** The FRSSE requires, where the entity prepares consolidated financial statements, to regard as standard the accounting practices and disclosure requirements as set out in the relevant FRSs. It should be noted that small groups are not

		required to prepare consolidated accounts. The SME would require consolidated accounts as it is considered that consolidated statements are essential for users when two entities operate as a single economic entity. **Level of Disclosure:** As above.
Directors' Emoluments (page 86)	N/A	N/A
The Directors' Report (pages 87–91)	N/A	N/A
Cash Flow Information (page 124)	Cash Flow Statement (section 7)	**GAAP Differences:** FRSSE reporting entities are encouraged, but not required, to provide a cash flow statement using the indirect method (starts with the operating profit and adjusts it for non-cash charges and credits to reconcile it with the cash generated from operations). The SME provides guidance for the indirect method of presenting cash flows from operations. In addition, the direct method would be permitted by cross-reference to IAS 7 *Cash Flow Statements*. **Level of Disclosure**: None

The following sections of the IFRS for SMEs are not addressed in the FRSSE or no equivalent exists in UK GAAP:

Not addressed as not material in the context of SME accounting:

Section 14 – Investment in Joint Ventures
Section 21 – Equity
Section 26 – Impairment of non-financial assets
Section 29 – Financial Reporting in Hyperinflationary Economies
Section 31 – Segment Reporting
Section 34 – Earnings per Share

No equivalent in UK GAAP:

Section 35 – Specialised Industries
Section 36 – Discontinued Operations and Assets held for Sale
Section 37 – Interim Financial Reporting
Section 38 – Transition to the IRFS for SMEs.

Note: Only a comparison of the requirements of the FRSSE that are derived from the accounting standard and not those that come from company law has been made.

Contents

Invitation to Comment

The International Accounting Standards Board invites comments on any aspect of the Exposure Draft of its proposed *International Financial Reporting Standard for Small and Medium-sized Entities* (*IFRS for SMEs*). It would particularly welcome answers to the questions set out below. Comments are most helpful if they indicate the specific paragraph or group of paragraphs to which they relate, contain a clear rationale and, when applicable, provide a suggestion for alternative wording.

Comments should be submitted in writing so as to be received no later than **1 October 2007**.

Question 1 – Stand-alone document

In deciding on the content of the proposed IFRS for SMEs, the IASB focused on the types of transactions and other events and conditions typically encountered by SMEs with about 50 employees. For such entities, the proposed IFRS is intended to be a stand-alone document, with minimal cross-references to full IFRSs.

With the objective of a stand-alone document in mind, are there additional transactions, other events or conditions that should be covered in the proposed standard to make it more self-contained? Conversely, is there guidance in the draft standard that should be removed because it is unlikely to be relevant to typical SMEs with about 50 employees?

Question 2 – Recognition and measurement simplifications that the Board adopted

The draft *IFRS for SMEs* was developed by:

(a) extracting the fundamental concepts from the IASB *Framework* and the principles and related mandatory guidance from full IFRSs (including Interpretations), and

(b) considering the modifications that are appropriate in the light of users' needs and cost-benefit considerations.

Paragraphs BC70–BC93 of the Basis for Conclusions describe the simplifications of recognition and measurement principles contained in full IFRSs that have been made in the proposed *IFRS for SMEs* and explain the Board's reasoning.

Are there other recognition or measurement simplifications that the Board should consider? In responding, please indicate:

(a) the specific transactions, other events or conditions that create a specific recognition or measurement problem for SMEs under IFRSs;

(b) why it is a problem; and

(c) how that problem might be solved.

Question 3 – Recognition and measurement simplifications that the Board considered but did not adopt

Paragraphs BC94–BC107 identify some recognition and measurement simplifications that the Board considered but decided not to adopt, for the reasons noted.

Should the Board reconsider any of those and, if so, why?

Question 4 – Whether all accounting policy options in full IFRSs should be available to SMEs

The draft *IFRS for SMEs* proposes that accounting policy options available under full IFRSs should generally also be available to SMEs. As explained more fully in paragraphs BC108–BC115 of the Basis for Conclusions, the Board concluded that prohibiting SMEs from using an accounting policy option that is available to entities using full IFRSs could hinder comparability between SMEs and entities following full IFRSs. At the same time, the Board recognised that most SMEs are likely to prefer the simpler option in the proposed *IFRS for SMEs*. Therefore, the Board concluded that in six circumstances in which full IFRSs allow accounting policy options, the *IFRS for SMEs* should include only the simpler option, and the other (more complex) option(s) should be available to SMEs by cross-reference to the full IFRSs.

Do you agree with the Board's conclusions on which options are the most appropriate for SMEs? If not, which one(s) would you change, and why?

Should any of these options that would be available to SMEs by cross-reference to the full IFRSs be eliminated from the draft *IFRS for SMEs* and, if so, why?

Question 5 – Borrowing costs

IAS 23 *Borrowing Costs* currently allows entities to choose either the expense model or the capitalisation model to account for all of their borrowing costs. In May 2006 the IASB published an Exposure Draft proposing to amend IAS 23 to prohibit the expense model and to require the capitalisation model. Section 24 *Borrowing Costs* of the draft *IFRS for SMEs* proposes to allow SMEs to choose either the expense model or the capitalisation model.

Do you agree or disagree with the proposal to allow SMEs to choose either the expense model or the capitalisation model for borrowing costs, and why?

Question 6 – Topics not addressed in the proposed *IFRS for SMEs*

Some topics addressed in full IFRSs are omitted from the draft *IFRS for SMEs* because the Board believes that typical SMEs are not likely to encounter such transactions or conditions. These are discussed in paragraphs BC57–BC65 of the Basis for Conclusions. By a cross-reference, the draft standard requires SMEs that have such transactions to follow the relevant full IFRS.

Should any additional topics be omitted from the *IFRS for SMEs* and replaced by a cross-reference? If so, which ones and why?

Question 7 – General referral to full IFRSs

As noted in Question 1, the *IFRS for SMEs* is intended to be a stand-alone document for typical SMEs. It contains cross-references to particular full IFRSs in specific circumstances, including the accounting policy options referred to in Question 4 and the omitted topics referred to in Question 6. For other transactions, events or conditions not specifically addressed in the IFRS for SMEs, paragraphs 10.2–10.4 propose requirements for how the management of SMEs should decide on the appropriate accounting. Under those paragraphs, it is not mandatory for SMEs to look to full IFRSs for guidance.

Are the requirements in paragraphs 10.2–10.4, coupled with the explicit cross-references to particular IFRSs in specific circumstances, appropriate? Why or why not?

Question 8 – Adequacy of guidance

The draft *IFRS for SMEs* is accompanied by some implementation guidance, most notably a complete set of illustrative financial statements and a disclosure checklist. A sizeable amount of guidance that is in full IFRSs is not included. Accordingly, additional guidance especially tailored to the needs of SMEs applying the proposed IFRS may be required.

Are there specific areas for which SMEs are likely to need additional guidance? What are they, and why?

Question 9 – Adequacy of disclosures

Each section of the draft *IFRS for SMEs* includes disclosure requirements. Those requirements are summarised in the disclosure checklist that is part of the draft implementation guidance *Illustrative Financial Statements* and *Disclosure Checklist*.

Are there disclosures that are not proposed that the Board should require for SMEs? If so, which ones and why? Conversely, do you believe that any of the proposed disclosures should not be required for SMEs? If so, which ones and why?

Question 10 – Transition guidance

Section 38 *Transition to the* IFRS for SMEs provides transition guidance for SMEs that move (a) from national GAAP to the *IFRS for SMEs* and (b) from full IFRSs to the *IFRS for SMEs*.

Do you believe that the guidance is adequate? If not, how can it be improved?

Question 11 – Maintenance of the *IFRS for SMEs*

The Board expects to publish an omnibus exposure draft of proposed amendments to the *IFRS for SMEs* approximately every other year. In developing such exposure drafts, the Board expects to consider new and amended IFRSs that have been adopted in the previous two years as well as specific issues that have been brought to its attention regarding possible amendments to the *IFRS for SMEs*. On occasion, the Board may identify a matter for which amendment of the *IFRS for SMEs* may need to be considered earlier than in the normal two-year cycle.

Is this approach to maintaining the proposed *IFRS for SMEs* appropriate, or should it be modified? If so, how and why?

The [draft] *International Financial Reporting Standard for Small and Medium-sized Entities* (*IFRS for SMEs*) is set out in Sections 1–38, Appendix B to Section 11, and the Glossary. Terms defined in the Glossary are in **bold type** the first time they appear in each section. The [draft] *IFRS for SMEs* is accompanied by a Preface, Implementation Guidance and a Basis for Conclusions.

Preface to the [draft] *IFRS for SMEs*

The IASB

The International Accounting Standards Board (IASB) was established in 2001 as part of the International Accounting Standards Committee (IASC) Foundation.   **P1**

The objectives of the IASC Foundation and of the IASB are: **P2**

(a) to develop, in the public interest, a single set of high quality, understandable and enforceable global accounting standards that require high quality, transparent and comparable information in financial statements and other financial reporting to help participants in the world's capital markets and other users make economic decisions;

(b) to promote the use and rigorous application of those standards;

(c) in fulfilling the objectives associated with (a) and (b), to take account of, as appropriate, the special needs of small and medium-sized entities and emerging economies; and

(d) to bring about convergence of national accounting standards and International Accounting Standards and International Financial Reporting Standards to high quality solutions.

The governance of the IASC Foundation rests with 22 Trustees. The Trustees' responsibilities include appointing the members of the IASB and associated councils and committees, as well as securing financing for the organisation.   **P3**

The IASB is the standard-setting body of the IASC Foundation. The IASB comprises twelve full time and two part time members. The IASB is responsible for approving **International Financial Reporting Standards** (IFRSs) and related documents, such as the *Framework for the Preparation and Presentation of Financial Statements*, exposure drafts, discussion documents, and Interpretations of IFRSs. Before the IASB began operations, International Accounting Standards (IASs) and related Interpretations were established by the Board of IASC, which came into existence on 29 June 1973. By resolution of the IASB, IASs and related Interpretations remain applicable, with the same authority as IFRSs developed by the IASB, unless and until they are amended or withdrawn by the IASB.   **P4**

International Financial Reporting Standards

The IASB achieves its objectives primarily by developing and publishing IFRSs and promoting the use of those standards in **general purpose financial statements** and other financial reporting. Other financial reporting comprises information provided outside financial statements that assists in the interpretation of a complete set of financial statements or improves users' ability to make efficient economic decisions. The term 'financial reporting' encompasses general purpose financial statements plus other financial reporting.   **P5**

IFRSs set out recognition, measurement, presentation and disclosure requirements dealing with transactions and other events and conditions that are important in general purpose financial statements. They may also set out such requirements for transactions, events, and conditions that arise mainly in specific industries. IFRSs are based on the *Framework*, which addresses the concepts underlying the information presented in general purpose financial statements. The objective of the *Framework* is to facilitate the consistent and logical formulation of IFRSs. The *Framework* also provides a basis for the use of judgement in resolving accounting issues.   **P6**

General purpose financial statements

P7   IFRSs are designed to apply to the general purpose financial statements and other financial reporting of all profit-oriented entities. General purpose financial statements are directed towards the common information needs of a wide range of users, for example, shareholders, creditors, employees and the public at large. The objective of financial statements is to provide information about the **financial position, performance** and **cash flows** of an entity that is useful to those users in making economic decisions.

P8   General purpose financial statements are those intended to meet the needs of users who are not in a position to demand reports tailored to meet their particular information needs. General purpose financial statements include those that are presented separately or within another public document such as an annual report or a prospectus.

The [draft] *IFRS for SMEs*

P9   The IASB also develops and publishes a separate standard intended to apply to the general purpose financial statements of, and other financial reporting by, entities that in many countries are known as **small and medium-sized entities** (SMEs). That standard is the [draft] *International Financial Reporting Standard for Small and Medium-sized Entities (IFRS for SMEs)*.

P10   The term SMEs as used by the IASB is defined in Section 1 *Scope* of the [draft] standard. Many jurisdictions around the world have developed their own definitions of the term for a broad range of purposes including prescribing financial reporting obligations. Often those national or regional definitions include quantified criteria based on revenue, assets, employees or other factors. Frequently, the term is used to mean or to include very small entities without regard to whether they publish general purpose financial statements for external users.

P11   SMEs often produce financial statements only for the use of owner-managers, or for tax reporting or other non-securities regulatory filing purposes. Financial statements produced solely for those purposes are not necessarily general purpose financial statements.

P12   Tax laws are specific to each jurisdiction, and the objectives of general purpose financial reports differ from the objectives of reporting taxable income. Thus, financial statements prepared in conformity with this [draft] standard are unlikely to comply fully with all of the measurements required for tax laws and regulations. Jurisdictions may be able to lessen the 'dual reporting burden' on SMEs by structuring tax reports as reconciliations from the profit or loss determined in accordance with the *IFRSs for SMEs* and by other means.

Authority of the [draft] *IFRS for SMEs*

P13   Decisions on which entities are required or permitted to use the IASB's standards rest with national regulatory authorities and standard-setters. This is true for full IFRSs and for the [draft] *IFRS for SMEs*. However, a clear definition of the class of entity for which the [draft] *IFRS for SMEs* is intended—as set out in Section 1 of the [draft] standard—is essential so that (a) the Board can decide on the standards that are appropriate for that class of entity and (b) national regulatory authorities, standard-setters, and reporting entities and their auditors will be informed of the intended scope of applicability of the *IFRS for SMEs*. A clear definition is also essential so that entities that are not SMEs, and therefore are not eligible to use the [draft] standard, do not assert that they are in compliance with the *IFRS for SMEs* (see paragraph 1.3).

Organisation of the [draft] *IFRS for SMEs*

The [draft] standard is organised by topic, with each topic presented in a separate numbered section. Cross-references to paragraphs are identified by section number followed by paragraph number. Cross-references to IFRSs are identified by the full name and number of the IFRS.   **P14**

All of the paragraphs in the [draft] standard have equal authority. Some sections include appendices of implementation guidance that are not part of the [draft] standard but, rather, are guidance for applying it.   **P15**

Maintenance of the [draft] *IFRS for SMEs*

The Board expects to propose amendments to the [draft] standard by publishing an omnibus exposure draft approximately every other year. In developing that exposure draft, the Board expects to consider new and amended IFRSs that have been adopted in the previous two years as well as specific issues that have been brought to its attention regarding possible amendments to the [proposed] *IFRS for SMEs*. On occasion, the Board may identify a matter for which amendment of the *IFRS for SMEs* may need to be considered earlier than in the normal two-year cycle. Until the *IFRS for SMEs* is amended, any changes that the IASB may make or propose with respect to full IFRSs do not apply to the *IFRS for SMEs*.   **P16**

[Draft] *International Financial Reporting Standard for Small and Medium-sized Entities (IFRS for SMEs)*

Section 1
Scope

1.1   The *IFRS for SMEs* is intended for use by **small and medium-sized entities** (SMEs). SMEs are entities that:

(a)   do not have **public accountability**; and

(b)   publish **general purpose financial statements** for external users. Examples of external users include owners who are not involved in managing the business, existing and potential creditors, and credit rating agencies.

1.2   An entity has public accountability if:

(a)   it files, or it is in the process of filing, its **financial statements** with a securities commission or other regulatory organisation for the purpose of issuing any class of instruments in a public market; or

(b)   it holds assets in a fiduciary capacity for a broad group of outsiders, such as a bank, insurance entity, securities broker/dealer, pension fund, mutual fund or investment banking entity.

1.3   If a publicly accountable entity uses this [draft] standard, its financial statements shall not be described as conforming to the *IFRS for SMEs*—even if national law or regulation permits or requires this [draft] standard to be used by publicly accountable entities.

Section 2
Concepts and Pervasive Principles

Objective of financial statements of SMEs

The **objective of financial statements** of a small or medium-sized entity is to provide information about the **financial position, performance** and **cash flows** of the entity that is useful for economic decision-making by a broad range of users who are not in a position to demand reports tailored to meet their particular information needs. In meeting that objective, financial statements also show the results of management's stewardship of the resources entrusted to it.

2.1

Qualitative characteristics of information in financial statements

Understandability

The information provided in financial statements should be presented in a way that makes it comprehensible by users who have a reasonable knowledge of business and economic activities and accounting and a willingness to study the information with reasonable diligence. However, the need for understandability does not allow relevant information to be omitted on the grounds that it may be too difficult for some users to understand.

2.2

Relevance

The information provided in financial statements must be relevant to the decision-making needs of users. Information has the quality of **relevance** when it influences the economic decisions of users by helping them evaluate past, present or future events or confirming, or correcting, their past evaluations.

2.3

Materiality

Information is **material** if its omission or misstatement could influence the economic decisions of users made on the basis of the financial statements. Materiality depends on the size of the item or error judged in the particular circumstances of its omission or misstatement. However, it is inappropriate to make, or leave uncorrected, immaterial departures from the *IFRS for SMEs* to achieve a particular presentation of an entity's financial position, financial performance or cash flows.

2.4

Reliability

The information provided in financial statements must be **reliable**. Information is reliable when it is free from material error and bias and represents faithfully that which it either purports to represent or could reasonably be expected to represent. Financial statements are not free from bias if, by the selection or presentation of information, they are intended to influence the making of a decision or judgement in order to achieve a predetermined result or outcome.

2.5

Substance over form

Transactions and other events and conditions should be accounted for and presented in accordance with their substance and economic reality and not merely their legal form. This enhances the reliability of financial statements.

2.6

Prudence

2.7   The uncertainties that inevitably surround many events and circumstances are acknowledged by the disclosure of their nature and extent and by the exercise of **prudence** in the preparation of the financial statements. Prudence is the inclusion of a degree of caution in the exercise of the judgements needed in making the estimates required under conditions of uncertainty, such that assets or income are not over-stated and liabilities or expenses are not understated. However, the exercise of prudence does not allow the deliberate understatement of assets or income, or the deliberate overstatement of liabilities or expenses. In short, prudence does not permit bias.

Completeness

2.8   To be reliable, the information in financial statements must be complete within the bounds of materiality and cost. An omission can cause information to be false or misleading and thus unreliable and deficient in terms of its relevance.

Comparability

2.9   Users must be able to compare the financial statements of an entity through time in order to identify trends in its financial position and performance. Users must also be able to compare the financial statements of different entities in order to evaluate their relative financial position, performance and cash flows. Hence, the measurement and display of the financial effect of like transactions and other events and conditions must be carried out in a consistent way throughout an entity and over time for that entity and in a consistent way for different entities. In addition, users must be informed of the **accounting policies** employed in the preparation of the financial statements, and of any changes in those policies and the effects of such changes.

Timeliness

2.10   To be relevant, financial information must be able to influence the economic deci-sions of users. **Timeliness** involves providing the information within the decision time frame. If there is undue delay in the reporting of information it may lose its rele-vance. Management may need to balance the relative merits of timely reporting and the provision of reliable information. In achieving a balance between relevance and reliability, the overriding consideration is how best to satisfy the needs of users in making economic decisions.

Balance between benefit and cost

2.11   The benefits derived from information should exceed the cost of providing it. The evaluation of benefits and costs is substantially a judgemental process. Furthermore, the costs are not necessarily borne by those users who enjoy the benefits. In applying a costs and benefits test, an entity should understand that the benefits of the infor-mation may also be enjoyed by a broad range of external users.

Financial position

2.12   The **financial position** of an entity is its assets, liabilities and equity at a point in time. **The elements of financial statements** directly related to the measurement of financial position are assets, liabilities and equity. These are defined as follows:

(a) An **asset** is a resource controlled by the entity as a result of past events and from which future economic benefits are expected to flow to the entity.

(b) A **liability** is a present obligation of the entity arising from past events, the settlement of which is expected to result in an outflow from the entity of resources embodying economic benefits.

(c) **Equity** is the residual interest in the assets of the entity after deducting all its liabilities.

Some items that meet the definition of an asset or a liability may not be recognised as assets or liabilities in the balance sheet because they do not satisfy the criteria for **recognition** in paragraphs 2.24–2.29. In particular, the expectation that future economic benefits will flow to or from an entity must be sufficiently certain to meet the probability criterion before an asset or liability is recognised. **2.13**

Assets

The future economic benefit of an asset is its potential to contribute, directly or indirectly, to the flow of cash and **cash equivalents** to the entity. Those cash flows may come from using the asset or from disposing of it. **2.14**

Many assets, for example property, plant and equipment, have a physical form. However, physical form is not essential to the existence of an asset. Some assets are intangible. **2.15**

In determining the existence of an asset, the right of ownership is not essential. Thus, for example, property held on a lease is an asset if the entity controls the benefits that are expected to flow from the property. **2.16**

Liabilities

An essential characteristic of a liability is that the entity has a present obligation to act or perform in a particular way. The obligation may be either a legal obligation or a **constructive obligation**. A legal obligation is legally enforceable as a consequence of a binding contract or statutory requirement. A constructive obligation is an obligation that derives from an entity's actions when: **2.17**

(a) by an established pattern of past practice, published policies or a sufficiently specific current statement, the entity has indicated to other parties that it will accept particular responsibilities; and

(b) as a result, the entity has created a valid expectation on the part of those other parties that it will discharge those responsibilities.

The settlement of a present obligation usually involves the payment of cash; transfer of other assets; provision of services; the replacement of that obligation with another obligation; or conversion of the obligation to equity. An obligation may also be extinguished by other means, such as a creditor waiving or forfeiting its rights. **2.18**

Equity

Equity is the residual of recognised assets minus recognised liabilities. It may be subclassified in the balance sheet. For example, in a corporate entity, subclassifications may include funds contributed by shareholders, retained earnings and gains or losses reported directly in equity. **2.19**

Performance

2.20   **Performance** is the relationship of the income and expenses of an entity as reported in its income statement. **Profit** is frequently used as a measure of performance or as the basis for other measures, such as return on investment or earnings per share. The elements of financial statements directly related to the measurement of profit are income and expenses. These are defined as follows:

(a)   **Income** is increases in economic benefits during the **reporting period** in the form of inflows or enhancements of assets or decreases of liabilities that result in increases in equity, other than those relating to contributions from equity participants.

(b)   **Expenses** are decreases in economic benefits during the reporting period in the form of outflows or depletions of assets or incurrences of liabilities that result in decreases in equity, other than those relating to distributions to equity participants.

2.21   The recognition of income and expenses in the income statement results directly from the recognition and measurement of assets and liabilities. Criteria for the recognition of income and expenses are discussed in paragraphs 2.24–2.29.

Income

2.22   The definition of income encompasses both revenue and gains.

(a)   **Revenue** is income that arises in the course of the ordinary activities of an entity and is referred to by a variety of names including sales, fees, interest, dividends, royalties and rent.

(b)   **Gains** are other items that meet the definition of income but are not revenue. When gains are recognised in the income statement, they are usually displayed separately because knowledge of them is useful for making economic decisions.

Expenses

2.23   The definition of expenses encompasses losses as well as those expenses that arise in the course of the ordinary activities of the entity.

(a)   **Expenses** that arise in the course of the ordinary activities of the entity include, for example, cost of sales, wages and depreciation. They usually take the form of an outflow or depletion of assets such as cash and cash equivalents, inventory, property, plant and equipment.

(b)   **Losses** are other items that meet the definition of expenses and may, or may not, arise in the course of the ordinary activities of the entity. When losses are recognised in the income statement, they are usually displayed separately because knowledge of them is useful for making economic decisions.

Recognition of the elements of financial statements

2.24   Recognition is the process of incorporating in the balance sheet or income statement an item that meets the definition of an element and satisfies the following criteria:

(a)   it is **probable** that any future economic benefit associated with the item will flow to or from the entity; and

(b)   the item has a cost or value that can be measured reliably.

The failure to recognise an item that satisfies these criteria is not rectified by disclosure of the accounting policies used or by notes or explanatory material. **2.25**

The probability of future economic benefit

The concept of probability is used in the recognition criteria to refer to the degree of uncertainty that the future economic benefits associated with the item will flow to or from the entity. Assessments of the degree of uncertainty attaching to the flow of future economic benefits are made on the basis of the evidence relating to conditions at the end of the reporting period available when the financial statements are prepared. Those assessments are made individually for individually significant items, and for a group for a large population of individually insignificant items. **2.26**

Reliability of measurement

The second criterion for the recognition of an item is that it possesses a cost or value that can be measured with reliability. In many cases, the cost or value of an item is known. In other cases it must be estimated. The use of reasonable estimates is an essential part of the preparation of financial statements and does not undermine their reliability. When a reasonable estimate cannot be made, the item is not recognised in the balance sheet or income statement. **2.27**

An item that fails to meet the recognition criteria may qualify for recognition at a later date as a result of subsequent circumstances or events. **2.28**

An item that fails to meet the criteria for recognition may nonetheless warrant disclosure in the notes, explanatory material or in supplementary schedules. This is appropriate when knowledge of the item is relevant to the evaluation of the financial position, performance and changes in financial position of an entity by the users of financial statements. **2.29**

Measurement of the elements of financial statements

Measurement is the process of determining the monetary amounts at which an entity measures assets, liabilities, income and expenses in its financial statements. Measurement involves the selection of a basis of measurement. This [draft] standard specifies which measurement basis an entity shall use for many types of assets, liabilities, income and expenses. **2.30**

Two common measurement bases are historical cost and fair value: **2.31**

(a)   For assets, **historical cost** is the amount of cash or cash equivalents paid or the fair value of the consideration given to acquire the asset at the time of its acquisition. For liabilities, historical cost is the amount of proceeds of cash or cash equivalents received or the fair value of non-cash assets received in exchange for the obligation at the time the obligation is incurred.

(b)   **Fair value** is the amount for which an asset could be exchanged, or a liability settled, between knowledgeable, willing parties in an arm's length transaction.

Pervasive recognition and measurement principles

The requirements for recognising and measuring assets, liabilities, income and expenses in this [draft] standard are based on pervasive principles that are derived from the IASB *Framework for the Preparation and Presentation of Financial Statements*. In the absence of a requirement in this [draft] standard that applies specifically **2.32** to a transaction or other event or condition including by cross-reference to a full **International Financial Reporting Standard (IFRS)**, paragraph 10.3 establishes a hierarchy for an entity to follow in deciding on the appropriate accounting policy in the circumstances. The second level of that hierarchy requires an entity to look to the pervasive recognition and measurement principles set out in paragraphs 2.33–2.43.

Accrual basis

2.33   An entity shall prepare its financial statements, except for cash flow information, using the **accrual basis** of accounting. On the accrual basis, items are recognised as assets, liabilities, equity, income or expenses (the elements of financial statements) when they satisfy the definitions and recognition criteria for those elements.

Recognition in financial statements

Assets

2.34   An entity shall recognise an asset in the balance sheet when it is probable that the future economic benefits will flow to the entity and the asset has a cost or value that can be measured reliably. An asset is not recognised in the balance sheet when expenditure has been incurred for which it is considered improbable that economic benefits will flow to the entity beyond the current reporting period. Instead such a transaction results in the recognition of an expense in the income statement.

Liabilities

2.35   An entity shall recognise a liability in the balance sheet when it is probable that an outflow of resources embodying economic benefits will result from the settlement of a present obligation and the settlement amount can be measured reliably.

Income

2.36   The recognition of income results directly from the recognition of assets and liabilities. An entity shall recognise income in the income statement when an increase in future economic benefits related to an increase in an asset or a decrease of a liability has arisen that can be measured reliably.

Expenses

2.37   The recognition of expenses results directly from the recognition and measurement of assets and liabilities. An entity shall recognise expenses in the income statement when a decrease in future economic benefits related to a decrease in an asset or an increase of a liability has arisen that can be measured reliably.

Profit or loss

2.38   Profit or loss is the arithmetical difference between income and expenses. It is not a separate element of financial statements, and a separate recognition principle is not needed for it.

2.39   This [draft] standard does not allow the recognition of items in the balance sheet that do not meet the definition of assets or of liabilities regardless of whether they result from applying the notion commonly referred to as the 'matching concept'.

Measurement at initial recognition

At initial recognition, an entity shall measure assets and liabilities at historical cost unless this [draft] standard requires initial measurement on another basis such as fair value. **2.40**

Subsequent measurement

Financial assets and financial liabilities

After initial recognition, an entity generally measures **financial assets** and **financial liabilities** at fair value unless this [draft] standard requires or permits measurement on another basis such as cost or amortised cost. **2.41**

Non-financial assets

Most non-financial assets that an entity initially recognised at historical cost are subsequently measured on other measurement bases. For example, an entity measures **property, plant and equipment** at the lower of depreciated cost and fair value less costs to sell, and measures inventories at the lower of cost and selling price less costs to complete and sell. Measurement of assets at those lower amounts is intended to ensure that an asset is not measured at an amount greater than the entity expects to recover from the sale or use of that asset. **2.42**

For some non-financial assets that an entity initially recognised at historical cost, this [draft] standard permits or requires subsequent measurement at fair value. Examples include: **2.43**

(a) investments in **associates** and **joint ventures** that an entity measures at fair value (see paragraphs 13.6 and 14.12 respectively);
(b) **investment property** that an entity measures at fair value (see paragraph 15.5);
(c) property, plant and equipment that an entity measures at revalued amount (see paragraph 16.13);
(d) **intangible assets** that an entity measures at revalued amount (see paragraph 17.23); and
(e) agricultural assets (**biological assets** and **agricultural produce** at the point of harvest) that an entity measures at fair value less estimated costs to sell (see paragraph 35.1).

Liabilities other than financial liabilities

Most liabilities other than financial liabilities are measured at the best estimate of the amount that would be required to settle the obligation at the **reporting date**. **2.44**

Offsetting

An entity shall not offset assets and liabilities, or income and expenses, unless required or permitted by this [draft] standard. **2.45**

(a) Measuring assets net of valuation allowances—for example, allowances for inventory obsolescence and allowances for uncollectible receivables—is not offsetting.
(b) If an entity's normal operating activities do not include buying and selling non-current assets, including investments and operating assets, then the entity reports gains and losses on disposal of such assets by deducting from the proceeds on disposal the **carrying amount** of the asset and related selling expenses.

Section 3
Financial Statement Presentation

Fair presentation

3.1   **Financial statements** shall present fairly the **financial position**, financial **performance** and **cash flows** of an entity. **Fair presentation** requires the faithful representation of the effects of transactions, other events and conditions in accordance with the definitions and **recognition** criteria for assets, liabilities, income and expenses set out in Section 2 *Concepts and Pervasive Principles*.

   (a)   The application of this [draft] standard by SMEs, with additional disclosure when necessary, is presumed to result in financial statements that achieve a fair presentation of the financial position, financial performance and cash flows of SMEs.

   (b)   As explained in paragraph 1.3, the application of this [draft] standard by an entity with public accountability does not result in a fair presentation in accordance with this [draft] standard.

   The additional disclosures referred to in (a) are necessary when compliance with the specific requirements in this [draft] standard is insufficient to enable users to understand the effect of particular transactions, other events and conditions on the entity's financial position and financial performance.

Compliance with the [draft] *IFRS for SMEs*

3.2   An entity whose financial statements comply with the [draft] *IFRS for SMEs* shall make an explicit and unreserved statement of such compliance in the notes. Financial statements shall not be described as complying with the *IFRS for SMEs* unless they comply with all the requirements of this [draft] standard.

3.3   In the extremely rare circumstances in which management concludes that compliance with this [draft] standard would be so misleading that it would conflict with the **objective of financial statements** of SMEs set out in Section 2, the entity shall depart from that requirement in the manner set out in paragraph 3.4 if the relevant regulatory framework requires, or otherwise does not prohibit, such a departure.

3.4   When an entity departs from a requirement of this [draft] standard in accordance with paragraph 3.3, it shall disclose:

   (a)   that management has concluded that the financial statements present fairly the entity's financial position, financial performance and cash flows;

   (b)   that it has complied with the *IFRS for SMEs*, except that it has departed from a particular requirement to achieve a fair presentation;

   (c)   the nature of the departure, including the treatment that the *IFRS for SMEs* would require, the reason why that treatment would be so misleading in the circumstances that it would conflict with the objective of financial statements set out in Section 2, and the treatment adopted; and

   (d)   for each period presented, the financial effect of the departure on each item in the financial statements that would have been reported in complying with the requirement.

3.5   When an entity has departed from a requirement of this [draft] standard in a prior period, and that departure affects the amounts recognised in the financial statements for the current period, it shall make the disclosures set out in paragraph 3.4(c) and (d).

In the extremely rare circumstances in which management concludes that compliance **3.6** with a requirement in this [draft] standard would be so misleading that it would conflict with the objective of financial statements of SMEs set out in Section 2, but the relevant regulatory framework prohibits departure from the requirement, the entity shall, to the maximum extent possible, reduce the perceived misleading aspects of compliance by disclosing:

(a) the nature of the requirement in this [draft] standard, and the reason why management has concluded that complying with that requirement is so misleading in the circumstances that it conflicts with the objective of financial statements set out in Section 2; and

(b) for each period presented, the adjustments to each item in the financial statements that management has concluded would be necessary to achieve a fair presentation.

Going concern

When preparing financial statements, the management of an entity using this [draft] **3.7** standard shall make an assessment of the entity's ability to continue as a **going concern**. An entity is a going concern unless management either intends to liquidate the entity or to cease operations, or has no realistic alternative but to do so. When management is aware, in making its assessment, of **material** uncertainties related to events or conditions that may cast significant doubt upon the entity's ability to continue as a going concern, the entity shall disclose those uncertainties. When an entity does not prepare financial statements on a going concern basis, it shall disclose that fact, together with the basis on which it prepared the financial statements and the reason why the entity is not regarded as a going concern.

Frequency of reporting

An entity shall present a complete set of financial statements (including comparative **3.8** information) at least annually. When the end of an entity's **reporting period** changes and the annual financial statements are presented for a period longer or shorter than one year, the entity shall disclose:

(a) that fact;

(b) the reason for using a longer or shorter period; and

(c) the fact that comparative amounts for the **income statement, statement of changes in equity, statement of income and retained earnings, cash flow statement** and related **notes** are not entirely comparable.

Consistency of presentation

An entity shall retain the presentation and classification of items in the financial **3.9** statements from one period to the next unless:

(a) it is apparent, following a significant change in the nature of the entity's operations or a review of its financial statements, that another presentation or classification would be more appropriate having regard to the criteria for the selection and application of **accounting policies** in Section 10 *Accounting Policies, Estimates and Errors*; or

(b) this [draft] standard requires a change in presentation.

When the presentation or classification of items in the financial statements is chan- **3.10** ged, an entity shall reclassify comparative amounts unless the reclassification is **impracticable**. When comparative amounts are reclassified, an entity shall disclose:

(a)   the nature of the reclassification;

(b)   the amount of each item or class of items that is reclassified; and

(c)   the reason for the reclassification.

3.11   When it is impracticable to reclassify comparative amounts, an entity shall disclose:

(a)   the reason for not reclassifying the amounts; and

(b)   the nature of the adjustments that would have been made if the amounts had been reclassified.

Comparative information

3.12   Except when this [draft] standard permits or requires otherwise, an entity shall disclose comparative information in respect of the previous comparable period for all amounts reported in the financial statements (including the information on the face of the financial statements and in the notes). An entity shall include comparative information for narrative and descriptive information when it is relevant to an understanding of the current period's financial statements.

Materiality and aggregation

3.13   An entity shall present separately each material class of similar items. An entity shall present separately items of a dissimilar nature or function unless they are immaterial.

3.14   Omissions or misstatements of items are material if they could, individually or collectively, influence the economic decisions of users made on the basis of the financial statements. Materiality depends on the size and nature of the omission or misstatement judged in the surrounding circumstances. The size or nature of the item, or a combination of both, could be the determining factor.

Complete set of financial statements

3.15   The financial statements of an entity shall include:

(a)   a **balance sheet**;

(b)   an income statement;

(c)   a statement of changes in **equity** showing either:

(i)   all changes in equity; or

(ii)   changes in equity other than those arising from transactions with equity holders acting in their capacity as equity holders;

(d)   a cash flow statement; and

(e)   notes, comprising a summary of significant accounting policies and other explanatory information.

3.16   If the only changes to the equity of an entity during the periods for which financial statements are presented arise from profit or loss, payment of dividends, corrections of prior period **errors**, and changes in accounting policy, the entity may present a statement of income and retained earnings in place of the income statement and statement of changes in equity.

3.17   Because paragraph 3.12 requires comparative amounts in respect of the previous period for all amounts reported in the financial statements (whether on the face of the financial statements or in the notes), a complete set of financial statements means that an entity shall present, as a minimum, two of each of the required financial statements and related notes.

In a complete set of financial statements, an entity shall present each financial statement with equal prominence.   **3.18**

An entity may use titles for the financial statements other than those used in this [draft] standard as long as they are not misleading.   **3.19**

Identification of the financial statements

An entity shall clearly identify each of the financial statements and the notes and distinguish them from other information in the same document. In addition, an entity shall display the following information prominently, and repeat it when necessary for an understanding of the information presented: **3.20**

(a) the name of the reporting entity and any change in its name since the end of the preceding reporting period;

(b) whether the financial statements cover the individual entity or a group of entities;

(c) the date of the end of the reporting period and the period covered by the financial statements;

(d) the presentation currency, as defined in Section 30 *Foreign Currency Translation*; and

(e) the level of rounding, if any, used in presenting amounts in the financial statements.

Section 4
Balance Sheet

Purpose

4.1   The **balance sheet** presents an entity's **assets, liabilities** and **equity** at a point in time.

Information to be presented on the face of the balance sheet

4.2   As a minimum, an entity shall include, on the face of the balance sheet, line items that present the following amounts:

(a)   cash and **cash equivalents**;

(b)   trade and other receivables;

(c)   **financial assets** (excluding amounts shown under (a), (b) and (h));

(d)   **inventories**;

(e)   **property, plant and equipment**;

(f)   **intangible assets**;

(g)   **biological assets**;

(h)   investments accounted for using the equity method;

(i)   the total of non-current assets classified as **held for sale** and assets included in **disposal groups** classified as held for sale in accordance with Section 36 *Discontinued Operations and Assets Held for Sale*;

(j)   trade and other payables;

(k)   **financial liabilities** (excluding amounts shown under (j) and (o));

(l)   liabilities and assets for **current tax**;

(m)   **deferred tax liabilities** and **deferred tax assets** (these shall always be classified as non-current);

(n)   liabilities included in disposal groups classified as held for sale.

(o)   **provisions**;

(p)   **minority interest**, presented within **equity** separately from the **parent** shareholders' equity; and

(q)   equity attributable to shareholders of the parent.

4.3   An entity shall present additional line items, headings and subtotals on the face of the balance sheet when such presentation is relevant to an understanding of the entity's **financial position**.

4.4   This [draft] standard does not prescribe the sequence or format in which items are to be presented.

Current/non-current distinction

4.5   An entity shall present current and non-current assets, and current and non-current liabilities, as separate classifications on the face of its balance sheet in accordance with paragraphs 4.6–4.9, except when a presentation based on liquidity provides information that is reliable and more relevant. When that exception applies, all assets and liabilities shall be presented in order of approximate liquidity.

Current assets

4.6   An entity shall classify an asset as current when:

(a)   it expects to realise the asset, or intends to sell or consume it, in the entity's normal operating cycle;

(b)   it holds the asset primarily for the purpose of trading;

(c) it expects to realise the asset within twelve months after the end of the **reporting period**; or

(d) the asset is cash or a cash equivalent, unless it is restricted from being exchanged or used to settle a liability for at least twelve months after the end of the reporting period.

An entity shall classify all other assets as non-current. When the entity's normal operating cycle is not clearly identifiable, its duration is assumed to be twelve months. **4.7**

Current liabilities

An entity shall classify a liability as current when: **4.8**

(a) it expects to settle the liability in the entity's normal operating cycle;

(b) it holds the liability primarily for the purpose of trading;

(c) the liability is due to be settled within twelve months after the end of the reporting period; or

(d) the entity does not have an unconditional right to defer settlement of the liability for at least twelve months after the end of the reporting period.

An entity shall classify all other liabilities as non-current. **4.9**

Sequencing of items and format of items on the balance sheet

This [draft] standard does not prescribe the sequence or format in which items are to be presented. Paragraph 4.2 simply provides a list of items that are sufficiently different in nature or function to warrant separate presentation on the face of the balance sheet. In addition: **4.10**

(a) line items are included when the size, nature or function of an item or aggregation of similar items is such that separate presentation is relevant to an understanding of the entity's financial position; and

(b) the descriptions used and the ordering of items or aggregation of similar items may be amended according to the nature of the entity and its transactions, to provide information that is relevant to an understanding of the entity's financial position.

The judgement on whether additional items are presented separately is based on an assessment of: **4.11**

(a) the nature and liquidity of assets;

(b) the function of assets within the entity; and

(c) the amounts, nature and timing of liabilities.

Information to be presented either on the face of the balance sheet or in the notes

An entity shall disclose, either on the face of the balance sheet or in the notes, the following subclassifications of the line items presented: **4.12**

(a) classes of items of property, plant and equipment in accordance with Section 16 *Property, Plant and Equipment*;

(b) amounts receivable from trade customers, receivables from **related parties**, prepayments and other amounts;

(c) classes of inventories in accordance with Section 12 *Inventories*, such as merchandise, production supplies, materials, work in progress and finished goods;

(d) provisions for **employee benefits** and other provisions; and

(e) classes of equity, such as paid-in capital, share premium, retained earnings and items of income and expense that, as required by this [draft] standard, are recognised directly in equity.

4.13 An entity with share capital shall disclose the following, either on the face of the balance sheet or in the notes:

(a) for each class of share capital:

(i) the number of shares authorised;

(ii) the number of shares issued and fully paid, and issued but not fully paid;

(iii) par value per share, or that the shares have no par value;

(iv) a reconciliation of the number of shares outstanding at the beginning and at the end of the period (see paragraph 21.12 for further guidance);

(v) the rights, preferences and restrictions attaching to that class including restrictions on the distribution of dividends and the repayment of capital;

(vi) shares in the entity held by the entity or by its subsidiaries or associates;

(vii) shares reserved for issue under options and contracts for the sale of shares, including the terms and amounts; and

(b) a description of each reserve within equity.

4.14 An entity without share capital, such as a partnership or trust, shall disclose information equivalent to that required by paragraph 4.13(a), showing changes during the period in each category of equity, and the rights, preferences and restrictions attaching to each category of equity.

Section 5
Income Statement

Purpose

The **income statement** presents the **income** and **expenses** of an entity for a period. **5.1**

The income statement shall include all items of income and expense recognised in a **5.2**
period unless this [draft] standard requires otherwise. This [draft] standard provides
different treatment for the following:

(a) the effects of corrections of errors and changes in **accounting policies** are pre-
     sented as adjustments of prior periods rather than as part of profit or loss in the
     period in which they arise (see Section 10 *Accounting Policies, Estimates and
     Errors*); and

(b) revaluation surpluses (see Section 16 *Property, Plant and Equipment*), some
     gains and **losses** arising on translating the **financial statements** of a foreign
     operation (see Section 30 *Foreign Currency Translation*), and some changes in
     fair values of hedging instruments (see Section 11 *Financial Assets and Financial
     Liabilities*) are reported directly in **equity**, rather than as part of profit or loss,
     when they arise.

Information to be presented on the face of the income statement

As a minimum, an entity shall include, on the face of the income statement, line items **5.3**
that present the following amounts for the period:

(a) **revenue**;

(b) finance costs;

(c) share of the profit or loss of investments in **associates** and **joint ventures**
     accounted for using the equity method;

(d) **tax expense**;

(e) a single amount comprising the total of (i) the post-tax profit or loss of **dis-
     continued operations** and (ii) the post-tax gain or loss recognised on the
     measurement to fair value less costs to sell or on the disposal of the assets or
     disposal group(s) constituting the discontinued operation (see Section 36 *Dis-
     continued Operations and Assets Held for Sale*); and

(f) profit or loss.

An entity shall disclose separately the following items on the face of the income **5.4**
statement as allocations of profit or loss for the period:

(a) profit or loss attributable to **minority interest**; and
(b) profit or loss attributable to equity holders of the parent.

An entity shall present additional line items, headings and subtotals on the face of **5.5**
the income statement when such presentation is relevant to an understanding of the
entity's financial **performance**.

An entity shall not present or describe any items of income and expense as 'extra- **5.6**
ordinary items', either on the face of the income statement or in the notes.

Information to be presented either on the face of the income statement or in the notes

5.7   An entity shall disclose separately the nature and amount of **material** components of income and expense. Such disclosures shall include:

(a)   write-downs of inventories to selling price less costs to complete and sell, and the reversal of such write-downs;

(b)   write-downs of **property, plant and equipment** to fair value less costs to sell, and the reversal of such write-downs;

(c)   restructurings of the activities of an entity and reversals of any **provisions** for the costs of restructuring;

(d)   disposals of items of property, plant and equipment;

(e)   disposals of investments;

(f)   **discontinued operations**;

(g)   litigation settlements; and

(h)   the reversal of other provisions.

Analysis of expenses

5.9   An entity shall present an analysis of expenses using a classification based on either the nature of expenses or the function of expenses within the entity, whichever provides information that is reliable and more relevant.

Analysis by nature of expense

(a)   Under this method of classification, expenses are aggregated in the income statement according to their nature (for example, depreciation, purchases of materials, transport costs, employee benefits and advertising costs), and are not reallocated among various functions within the entity.

Analysis by function of expense

(b)   Under this method of classification, expenses are aggregated according to their function as part of cost of sales or, for example, the costs of distribution or administrative activities. At a minimum, an entity discloses its cost of sales under this method separately from other expenses.

5.10   Entities are encouraged to present this analysis on the face of the income statement. The illustrative financial statements that accompany this [draft] standard include examples of both types of presentation.

5.11   Entities classifying expenses by function shall disclose additional information on the nature of expenses, including **depreciation** and **amortisation** expense and **employee benefits** expense.

Section 6
Statement of Changes in Equity and Statement of Income and Retained Earnings

Statement of changes in equity

Purpose

The **statement of changes in equity** presents an entity's profit or loss for a period, items of income and expense recognised directly in **equity** for the period, the effects of changes in **accounting policies** and corrections of errors recognised in the period, and (depending on the format of the statement of changes in equity chosen by the entity) the amounts of investments by, and dividends and other distributions to, equity holders during the period.

6.1

Information to be presented on the face of the statement of changes in equity

An entity shall present a statement of changes in equity showing on the face of the statement:

6.2

(a) profit or loss for the period;
(b) each item of income and expense for the period that, as required by this [draft] standard, is recognised directly in equity, and the total of those items;
(c) total income and expense for the period (calculated as the sum of (a) and (b)), showing separately the total amounts attributable to equity holders of the parent and to **minority interest**; and
(d) for each component of equity, the effects of changes in accounting policies and corrections of **errors** recognised in accordance with Section 10 *Accounting Policies, Estimates and Errors.*

Information to be presented either on the face of the statement of changes in equity or in the notes

An entity shall also present, either on the face of the statement of changes in equity or in the notes:

6.3

(a) the amounts of investments by, and dividends and other distributions to, equity holders, showing separately issues of shares, treasury share transactions, and dividends and other distributions to equity holders;
(b) the balance of retained earnings (ie accumulated profit or loss) at the beginning of the **reporting period** and at the end of the period, and the changes during the period; and
(c) a reconciliation of the **carrying amount** of each class of contributed equity and each item of income and expense recognised directly in equity (see paragraph 6.2(b)) at the beginning and the end of the period, separately disclosing each change.

Statement of income and retained earnings

Purpose

The **statement of income and retained earnings** presents an entity's profit or loss and changes in retained earnings for a reporting period. Paragraph 3.16 of this [draft] standard permits an entity to present a statement of income and retained earnings in place of the income statement and statement of changes in equity if the only changes

6.4

to its equity during the period arise from profit or loss, payment of dividends, corrections of prior period errors, and changes in accounting policy.

Information to be presented on the face of the statement of income and retained earnings

6.5   An entity shall present, on the face of the statement of income and retained earnings, the following items in addition to the information required by Section 5 *Income Statement*:

(a)   retained earnings at the beginning of the reporting period;

(b)   dividends declared and paid or payable during the period;

(c)   restatements of retained earnings for corrections of prior period errors;

(d)   restatements of retained earnings for changes in accounting policy; and

(e)   retained earnings at the end of the reporting period.

Section 7
Cash Flow Statement

Purpose

The **cash flow statement** provides information about the historical changes in **cash** and **cash equivalents** of an entity, showing separately changes during the period from operating, investing and financing activities. **7.1**

Cash equivalents are held to meet short-term cash commitments rather than for investment or other purposes. Therefore, an investment normally qualifies as a cash equivalent only when it has a short maturity of, say, three months or less from the date of acquisition. Bank overdrafts are normally considered financing activities similar to borrowings. However, if they are repayable on demand and form an integral part of an entity's cash management, bank overdrafts are a component of cash and cash equivalents. **7.2**

Content

An entity shall present a cash flow statement that reports **cash flows** for a period classified by **operating activities**, **investing activities** and **financing activities**. **7.3**

Operating activities

Cash flows from operating activities are primarily derived from the principal **revenue**-producing activities of the entity. Therefore, they generally result from the transactions and other events and conditions that enter into the determination of profit or loss. Examples of cash flows from operating activities are: **7.4**

(a)   cash receipts from the sale of goods and the rendering of services;
(b)   cash receipts from royalties, fees, commissions and other revenue;
(c)   cash payments to suppliers for goods and services;
(d)   cash payments to and on behalf of employees;
(e)   cash payments or refunds of income taxes, unless they can be specifically identified with financing and investing activities; and
(f)   cash receipts and payments from investments, loans, and other contracts held for dealing or trading purposes, which are similar to inventory acquired specifically for resale.

Some transactions, such as the sale of an item of plant, may give rise to a gain or loss that is included in the determination of profit or loss. However, the cash flows relating to such transactions are cash flows from investing activities.

Investing activities

Cash flows arising from investing activities represent expenditures made for resources intended to generate future income and cash flows. Examples of cash flows arising from investing activities are: **7.5**

(a)   cash payments to acquire property, plant and equipment (including self-constructed property, plant and equipment), intangible assets (including capitalised development costs), and other long-term assets;
(b)   cash receipts from sales of property, plant and equipment, intangibles and other long-term assets;

(c)   cash payments to acquire **equity** or debt instruments of other entities and interests in joint ventures (other than payments for those instruments classified as cash equivalents or held for dealing or trading);

(d)   cash receipts from sales of equity or debt instruments of other entities and interests in joint ventures (other than receipts for those instruments classified as cash equivalents or held for dealing or trading);

(e)   cash advances and loans made to other parties;

(f)   cash receipts from the repayment of advances and loans made to other parties;

(g)   cash payments for futures contracts, forward contracts, option contracts and swap contracts except when the contracts are held for dealing or trading, or the payments are classified as financing activities; and

(h)   cash receipts from futures contracts, forward contracts, option contracts and swap contracts, except when the contracts are held for dealing or trading, or the receipts are classified as financing activities.

When a contract is accounted for as a hedge (see Section 11 *Financial Assets and Financial Liabilities*), an entity shall classify the cash flows of the contract in the same manner as the cash flows of the item being hedged.

Financing activities

7.6   Examples of cash flows arising from financing activities are:

(a)   cash proceeds from issuing shares or other equity instruments;

(b)   cash payments to owners to acquire or redeem the entity's shares;

(c)   cash proceeds from issuing debentures, loans, notes, bonds, mortgages and other short-term or long-term borrowings;

(d)   cash repayments of amounts borrowed; and

(e)   cash payments by a lessee for the reduction of the outstanding liability relating to a finance lease.

Reporting cash flows from operating activities

7.7   An entity shall report cash flows from operating activities using either:

(a)   the direct method, whereby major classes of gross cash receipts and gross cash payments are disclosed; or

(b)   the indirect method, whereby profit or loss is adjusted for the effects of non-cash transactions, any deferrals or accruals of past or future operating cash receipts or payments, and items of income or expense associated with investing or financing cash flows.

7.8   Under the indirect method, the net cash flow from operating activities is determined by adjusting profit or loss for the effects of:

(a)   changes during the period in inventories and operating receivables and payables;

(b)   non-cash items such as **depreciation, provisions, deferred taxes**, unrealised foreign currency gains and losses, undistributed profits of **associates**, and **minority interests**; and

(c)   all other items for which the cash effects relate to investing or financing.

Alternatively, the net cash flow from operating activities may be presented under the indirect method by showing the revenues and expenses disclosed in the income statement and the changes during the period in inventories and operating receivables and payables.

An entity choosing to use the direct method shall apply paragraphs 18–20 of IAS 7 *Cash Flow Statements*. **7.9**

Reporting cash flows from investing and financing activities

An entity shall report separately major classes of gross cash receipts and gross cash payments arising from investing and financing activities. The aggregate cash flows arising from acquisitions and from disposals of subsidiaries or other business units shall be presented separately and classified as operating activities. **7.10**

Foreign currency cash flows

An entity shall record cash flows arising from transactions in a foreign currency in the entity's functional currency by applying to the foreign currency amount the exchange rate between the functional currency and the foreign currency at the date of the cash flow. **7.11**

The entity shall translate cash flows of a foreign subsidiary at the exchange rates between the functional currency and the foreign currency at the dates of the cash flows. **7.12**

Unrealised gains and losses arising from changes in foreign currency exchange rates are not cash flows. However, to reconcile cash and cash equivalents at the beginning and the end of the period, the effect of exchange rate changes on cash and cash equivalents held or due in a foreign currency must be reported in the cash flow statement. Therefore, the entity shall remeasure cash and cash equivalents held during the period at period-end exchange rates. The entity shall present the resulting unrealised gain or loss separately from cash flows from operating, investing and financing activities. **7.13**

Interest and dividends

An entity shall disclose separately cash flows from interest and dividends received and paid (interest paid includes amount capitalised under the **accounting policy** choice in Section 24 *Borrowing Costs*). The entity shall classify cash flows consistently from period to period as operating, investing or financing activities. **7.14**

An entity may classify interest paid and interest and dividends received as operating cash flows because they are included in profit or loss. Alternatively, the entity may classify interest paid and interest and dividends received as financing cash flows and investing cash flows respectively, because they are costs of obtaining financial resources or returns on investments. **7.15**

An entity may classify dividends paid as a financing cash flow because they are a cost of obtaining financial resources. Alternatively, the entity may classify dividends paid as a component of cash flows from operating activities because they are paid out of operating cash flows. **7.16**

Taxes on income

An entity shall disclose separately cash flows arising from taxes on income and shall classify them as cash flows from operating activities unless they can be specifically identified with financing and investing activities. When tax cash flows are allocated over more than one class of activity, the entity shall disclose the total amount of taxes paid. **7.17**

Non-cash transactions

7.18   An entity shall exclude from the cash flow statement investing and financing transactions that do not require the use of cash or cash equivalents. An entity shall
disclose such transactions elsewhere in the **financial statements** in a way that provides
all the relevant information about these investing and financing activities.

7.19   Many investing and financing activities do not have a direct impact on current cash
flows although they affect the capital and asset structure of an entity. The exclusion
of non-cash transactions from the cash flow statement is consistent with the objective
of a cash flow statement because these items do not involve cash flows in the current
period. Examples of non-cash transactions are:

(a)   the acquisition of assets either by assuming directly related liabilities or by
means of a finance lease;

(b)   the acquisition of an entity by means of an equity issue; and

(c)   the conversion of debt to equity.

Components of cash and cash equivalents

7.20   An entity shall disclose the components of cash and cash equivalents and shall
present a reconciliation of the amounts reported in the cash flow statement to the
equivalent items reported in the balance sheet.

Other disclosures

7.21   An entity shall disclose, together with a commentary by management, the amount of
significant cash and cash equivalent balances held by the entity that are not available
for use by the entity. Cash and cash equivalents held by an entity may not be
available for use by the entity because of, among other reasons, foreign exchange
controls or legal restrictions.

Section 8
Notes to the Financial Statements

Purpose

Notes contain information in addition to that presented on the face of the **financial** **8.1**
statements. Notes provide narrative descriptions or disaggregations of items presented in those statements and information about items that do not qualify for
recognition in those statements.

Structure

The notes shall: **8.2**

(a) present information about the basis of preparation of the financial statements
    and the specific **accounting policies** used, in accordance with paragraphs 8.5 and
    8.6;
(b) disclose the information required by this [draft] standard that is not presented
    on the face of the financial statements; and
(c) provide additional information that is not presented on the face of the financial
    statements but is relevant to an understanding of them.

An entity shall, as far as practicable, present the notes in a systematic manner. An **8.3**
entity shall cross-reference each item on the face of the financial statements to any
related information in the notes.

An entity normally presents the notes in the following order: **8.4**

(a) a statement that the financial statements have been prepared in compliance
    with the *IFRS for SMEs* (see paragraph 3.2);
(b) a summary of significant accounting policies applied (see paragraph 8.5);
(c) supporting information for items presented on the face of the financial state-
    ments, in the order in which each statement and each line item is presented; and
(d) other disclosures, including:

    (i)   **contingent liabilities** and **contingent assets** (see Section 20 *Provisions and*
          Contingencies) and unrecognised contractual commitments;
    (ii) non-financial disclosures;
    (iii) the amount of dividends proposed or declared before the financial
          statements were authorised for issue but not recognised as a distribution
          to **equity** holders during the period, and the related amount per share; and
    (iv) the amount of any cumulative preference dividends not recognised.

Disclosure of accounting policies

An entity shall disclose in the summary of significant accounting policies: **8.5**

(a) the measurement basis (or bases) used in preparing the financial statements;
(b) the accounting policy the entity has chosen whenever the entity has adopted an
    accounting policy for an event, a transaction, other event or condition for
    which this [draft] standard allows an accounting policy choice; and
(c) the other accounting policies used that are relevant to an understanding of the
    financial statements.

Information about judgements

8.6   An entity shall disclose, in the summary of significant accounting policies or other notes, the judgements, apart from those involving estimations (see paragraph 8.7), that management has made in the process of applying the entity's accounting policies and that have the most significant effect on the amounts recognised in the financial statements.

Information about key sources of estimation uncertainty

8.7   An entity shall disclose in the notes information about the key assumptions concerning the future, and other key sources of estimation uncertainty at the end of the **reporting period**, that have a significant risk of causing a **material** adjustment to the **carrying amounts** of assets and liabilities within the next financial year. In respect of those assets and liabilities, the notes shall include details of:

(a)   their nature; and
(b)   their carrying amount as at the end of the reporting period.

Information about externally imposed capital requirements

8.8   If an entity is subject to externally imposed capital requirements, it shall disclose the nature of those requirements and how they are managed, including whether the requirements have been complied with.

Section 9
Consolidated and Separate Financial Statements

Control

Except as permitted by paragraph 9.2, a **parent** entity shall present **consolidated** **9.1**
financial statements in which it consolidates its investments in **subsidiaries** in accordance with this [draft] standard. Consolidated financial statements shall include all subsidiaries of the parent.

A parent need not present consolidated financial statements if: **9.2**

(a) the parent is itself a subsidiary; and
(b) its ultimate parent (or any intermediate parent) produces consolidated **general**
     purpose financial statements that comply with full **International Financial**
     Reporting Standards or with this [draft] standard.

A subsidiary is an entity that is controlled by the parent. **Control** is the power to **9.3**
govern the financial and operating policies of an entity so as to obtain benefits from
its activities. If an entity has created a special purpose entity (SPE) to accomplish a
narrow and well-defined objective, the entity shall consolidate the SPE when the
substance of the relationship indicates that the SPE is controlled by that entity.

Control is presumed to exist when the parent owns, directly or indirectly through **9.4**
subsidiaries, more than half of the voting power of an entity unless, in exceptional
circumstances, it can be clearly demonstrated that such ownership does not constitute control. Control also exists when the parent owns half or less of the voting
power of an entity but it has:

(a) power over more than half of the voting rights by virtue of an agreement with
     other investors;
(b) power to govern the financial and operating policies of the entity under a
     statute or an agreement;
(c) power to appoint or remove the majority of the members of the board of
     directors or equivalent governing body and control of the entity is by that
     board or body; or
(d) power to cast the majority of votes at meetings of the board of directors or
     equivalent governing body and control of the entity is by that board or body.

A subsidiary is not excluded from consolidation simply because the investor is a **9.5**
venture capital organisation or similar entity.

A subsidiary is not excluded from consolidation because its business activities are **9.6**
dissimilar from those of the other entities within the consolidation. Relevant information is provided by consolidating such subsidiaries and disclosing additional
information in the consolidated financial statements about the different business
activities of subsidiaries.

A subsidiary is not excluded from consolidation because it operates in a jurisdiction **9.7**
that imposes restrictions on transferring cash or other assets out of the jurisdiction.

Consolidation procedures

The consolidated financial statements present financial information about the group **9.8**
as a single economic entity. In preparing consolidated financial statements, an entity
shall:

(a) combine the financial statements of the parent and its subsidiaries line by line by adding together like items of assets, liabilities, equity, income and expenses;

(b) eliminate the **carrying amount** of the parent's investment in each subsidiary and the parent's portion of equity of each subsidiary;

(c) measure **minority interests** in the profit or loss of consolidated subsidiaries for the **reporting period** separately from the parent shareholders' interest; and

(d) measure minority interests in the net assets of consolidated subsidiaries separately from the parent shareholders' equity in them. Minority interests in the net assets consist of:

(i) the amount of those minority interests at the date of the original combination; and

(ii) the minority's share of changes in equity since the date of the combination.

Potential voting rights

9.9 When potential voting rights exist (such as voting rights that would result from exercise of share options or warrants or from conversion of convertible securities), the proportions of profit or loss and changes in equity allocated to the parent and minority interests are determined on the basis of existing ownership interests and do not reflect the possible exercise or conversion of potential voting rights.

Intragroup balances and transactions

9.10 Intragroup balances and transactions, including income, expenses and dividends, are eliminated in full. Profits and losses resulting from intragroup transactions that are recognised in assets, such as inventory and fixed assets, are eliminated in full. Intragroup losses may indicate an impairment that requires **recognition** in the consolidated financial statements. Section 28 *Income Taxes* applies to temporary differences that arise from the elimination of profits and losses resulting from intragroup transactions.

Uniform reporting date

9.11 The financial statements of the parent and its subsidiaries used in the preparation of the consolidated financial statements shall be prepared as of the same **reporting date** unless it is **impracticable** to do so.

Uniform accounting policies

9.12 Consolidated financial statements shall be prepared using uniform **accounting policies** for like transactions and other events and conditions in similar circumstances. If a member of the group uses accounting policies other than those adopted in the consolidated financial statements for like transactions and events in similar circumstances, appropriate adjustments are made to its financial statements in preparing the consolidated financial statements.

Acquisition and disposal of subsidiaries

9.13 The income and expenses of a subsidiary are included in the consolidated financial statements from the acquisition date. The income and expenses of a subsidiary are included in the consolidated financial statements until the date on which the parent ceases to control the subsidiary. The difference between the proceeds from the disposal of the subsidiary and its carrying amount as of the date of disposal, including the cumulative amount of any exchange differences that relate to the subsidiary recognised in equity in accordance with Section 30 *Foreign Currency Translation*, is recognised in the consolidated income statement as the gain or loss on the disposal of the subsidiary.

If an entity ceases to be a subsidiary but the investor (former parent) continues to hold some equity shares, those shares shall be accounted for as a **financial asset** in accordance with Section 11 *Financial Assets and Financial Liabilities* from the date the entity ceases to be a subsidiary, provided that it does not become an **associate** or a **jointly controlled entity**. The carrying amount of the investment at the date that the entity ceases to be a subsidiary shall be regarded as the cost on initial measurement of a financial asset.

9.14

Minority interests in subsidiaries

An entity shall present minority interest in the consolidated balance sheet within equity, separately from the parent shareholders' equity, as required by paragraph 4.2(p).

9.15

An entity shall disclose minority interest in the profit or loss of the group separately in the income statement, as required by paragraph 5.4.

9.16

Losses applicable to the minority in a consolidated subsidiary may exceed the minority interest in the subsidiary's equity. The excess, and any further losses applicable to the minority, are allocated against the majority interest except to the extent that the minority has a binding obligation and is able to make an additional investment to cover the losses. If the subsidiary subsequently reports profits, such profits are allocated to the majority interest until the minority's share of losses previously absorbed by the majority has been recovered.

9.17

Separate financial statements

Paragraph 9.1 requires a parent to prepare consolidated financial statements. This [draft] standard does not require a parent to produce **separate financial statements** for the parent entity or for the individual subsidiaries. When separate financial statements of a parent are prepared, the entity shall adopt a policy of accounting for all of its investments in subsidiaries, **jointly controlled entities** and **associates** that are not classified as held for sale either:

9.18

(a)   at cost, or
(b)   at **fair value** through profit or loss.

When a parent, a venturer with an interest in a jointly controlled entity or an investor in an associate prepares separate financial statements, those separate financial statements shall disclose:

9.19

(a)   that the statements are separate financial statements and the reasons why those statements are prepared if not required by law;
(b)   a list of significant investments in subsidiaries, jointly controlled entities and associates, including the name, country of incorporation or residence, proportion of ownership interest and, if different, proportion of voting power held; and
(c)   a description of the method used to account for the investments listed under (b);

and shall identify the consolidated financial statements to which they relate.

9.20   The financial statements of an entity that does not have a subsidiary, associate or venturer's interest in a jointly controlled entity are not separate financial statements.

Combined financial statements

9.21   **Combined financial statements** are a single set of financial statements of two or more entities controlled by a single investor. This [draft] standard does not require combined financial statements to be prepared. The controlling investor may prepare combined financial statements because the affiliated entities have common objectives and economic interests and are managed jointly.

9.22   If an entity prepares combined financial statements and describes them as conforming to the *IFRS for SMEs*, those statements shall comply with all of the requirements of this [draft] standard. Intercompany transactions and balances shall be eliminated; profits or losses resulting from intercompany transactions that are recognised in assets such as inventory and fixed assets shall be eliminated; the financial statements of the entities included in the combined financial statements shall be prepared as of the same reporting date unless it is impracticable to do so; and uniform accounting policies shall be followed for like transactions and other events in similar circumstances. Disclosures shall include the fact that the financial statements are combined financial statements and the **related party** disclosures required by Section 33 *Related Party Disclosures*.

Section 10
Accounting Policies, Estimates and Errors

Selection and application of accounting policies

Accounting policies are the specific principles, bases, conventions, rules and practices applied by an entity in preparing and presenting **financial statements**.　　　**10.1**

If this [draft] standard does not specifically address a transaction, other event or condition, management shall use its judgement in developing and applying an accounting policy that results in information that is:　　　**10.2**

(a)　**relevant** to the economic decision-making needs of users; and
(b)　**reliable**, in that the financial statements:

    (i)　represent faithfully the **financial position**, financial **performance** and **cash flows** of the entity;
    (ii)　reflect the economic substance of transactions, other events and conditions, and not merely the legal form;
    (iii)　are neutral, ie free from bias;
    (iv)　are prudent; and
    (v)　are complete in all **material** respects.

In making the judgement described in paragraph 10.2, management shall refer to, and consider the applicability of, the following sources in descending order:　　　**10.3**

(a)　the requirements and guidance in this [draft] standard dealing with similar and related issues; and
(b)　the definitions, **recognition** criteria and measurement concepts for assets, liabilities, income and expenses and the pervasive principles in Section 2 *Concepts and Pervasive Principles*.

In making the judgement described in paragraph 10.2, management may also consider the requirements and guidance in full **International Financial Reporting Standards (IFRSs)** dealing with similar and related issues. If additional guidance is needed to make the judgement described in paragraph 10.2, management may also consider the most recent pronouncements of other standard-setting bodies that use a similar conceptual framework to develop accounting standards, other accounting literature and accepted industry practices, to the extent that these do not conflict with the sources in paragraph 10.3.　　　**10.4**

Consistency of accounting policies

An entity shall select and apply its accounting policies consistently for similar transactions, other events and conditions, unless this [draft] standard specifically requires or permits categorisation of items for which different policies may be appropriate. If this [draft] standard requires or permits such categorisation, an appropriate accounting policy shall be selected and applied consistently to each category.　　　**10.5**

Changes in accounting policies

An entity shall change an accounting policy only if the change:　　　**10.6**

(a)　is required by changes to this [draft] standard; or

(b)   results in the financial statements providing reliable and more relevant information about the effects of transactions, other events or conditions on the entity's financial position, financial performance or cash flows.

10.7   The following are not changes in accounting policies:

(a)   the application of an accounting policy for transactions, other events or conditions that differ in substance from those previously occurring; and

(b)   the application of a new accounting policy for transactions, other events or conditions that did not occur previously or were not material.

10.8   If this [draft] standard allows a choice of accounting treatment for a specified transaction or other event or condition, and an entity changes its choice, that is a change in accounting policy. Similarly, a change of measurement basis is a change in accounting policy.

Applying changes in accounting policies

10.9   An entity shall account for changes in accounting policy as follows:

(a)   an entity shall account for a change in accounting policy resulting from a change in the requirements of this [draft] standard in accordance with the transitional provisions, if any, specified in that amendment;

(b)   when this [draft] standard requires or permits an entity to follow the requirements of a full IFRS, and the requirements of that IFRS change, the entity shall account for that change in accounting policy in accordance with the transitional provisions, if any, specified in that IFRS; and

(c)   an entity shall account for all other changes in accounting policy **retrospectively**.

Retrospective application

10.10   When a change in accounting policy is applied retrospectively in accordance with paragraph 10.9, the entity applies the new accounting policy to comparative information for prior periods as far back as is practicable, as if the new accounting policy had always been applied. When it is **impracticable** to determine the individual period effects of changing an accounting policy for one or more prior periods presented, the entity shall adjust the opening balance of each affected component of equity for the earliest prior period for which retrospective application is practicable, which may be the current period, and shall make a corresponding adjustment to the opening balance of each affected component of equity for that period.

Disclosure of a change in accounting policy

10.11   When initial application of this [draft] standard, or an amendment to this [draft] standard, has an effect on the current period or any prior period or might have an effect on future periods, an entity shall disclose:

(a)   the nature of the change in accounting policy;

(b)   for the current period and each prior period presented, to the extent practicable, the amount of the adjustment for each financial statement line item affected; and

(c)   the amount of the adjustment relating to periods before those presented, to the extent practicable; and

(d)   an explanation if it is impracticable to determine the amounts to be disclosed in (b) or (c) above.

Financial statements of subsequent periods need not repeat these disclosures.

When a voluntary change in accounting policy has an effect on the current period or any prior period, or might have an effect on future periods, an entity shall disclose: **10.12**

(a) the nature of the change in accounting policy;

(b) the reasons why applying the new accounting policy provides reliable and more relevant information;

(c) for the current period and each prior period presented, to the extent practicable, the amount of the adjustment for each financial statement line item affected;

(d) the amount of the adjustment relating to periods before those presented, to the extent practicable; and

(e) an explanation if it is impracticable to determine the amounts to be disclosed in (c) or (d) above.

Financial statements of subsequent periods need not repeat these disclosures.

Changes in accounting estimates

A **change in accounting estimate** is an adjustment of the **carrying amount** of an asset or a liability, or the amount of the periodic consumption of an asset, that results from the assessment of the present status of, and expected future benefits and obligations associated with, assets and liabilities. Changes in accounting estimates result from new information or new developments and, accordingly, are not corrections of errors. **10.13**

An entity shall recognise the effect of a change in an accounting estimate, other than a change to which paragraph 10.15 applies, **prospectively** by including it in profit or loss in: **10.14**

(a) the period of the change, if the change affects that period only; or

(b) the period of the change and future periods, if the change affects both.

To the extent that a change in an accounting estimate gives rise to changes in assets and liabilities, or relates to an item of equity, the entity shall recognise it by adjusting the carrying amount of the related asset, liability or equity item in the period of the change. **10.15**

Disclosure of a change in estimate

An entity shall disclose the nature and amount of a change in an accounting estimate that has an effect in the current period or is expected to have an effect in future periods, except for the disclosure of the effect on future periods when it is impracticable to estimate that effect. **10.16**

If the amount of the effect in future periods is not disclosed because estimating it is impracticable, an entity shall disclose that fact. **10.17**

Corrections of prior period errors

Prior period **errors** are omissions from, and misstatements in, the entity's financial statements for one or more prior periods arising from a failure to use, or misuse of, reliable information that: **10.18**

(a)   was available when financial statements for those periods were authorised for issue; and

(b)   could reasonably be expected to have been obtained and taken into account in the preparation and presentation of those financial statements.

10.19   Such errors include the effects of mathematical mistakes, mistakes in applying accounting policies, oversights or misinterpretations of facts, and fraud.

10.20   To the extent practicable, an entity shall correct a prior period error retrospectively in the first financial statements authorised for issue after its discovery by:

(a)   restating the comparative amounts for the prior period(s) presented in which the error occurred; or

(b)   if the error occurred before the earliest prior period presented, restating the opening balances of assets, liabilities and equity for the earliest prior period presented.

10.21   When it is impracticable to determine the period-specific effects of an error on comparative information for one or more prior periods presented, the entity shall restate the opening balances of assets, liabilities and equity for the earliest period for which retrospective restatement is practicable (which may be the current period).

10.22   When it is impracticable to restate any prior periods, the entity shall recognise the effect of the error in opening retained earnings of the current period.

Disclosure of prior period errors

10.23   An entity shall disclose the following about prior period errors:

(a)   the nature of the prior period error;

(b)   for each prior period presented, to the extent practicable, the amount of the correction for each financial statement line item affected;

(c)   the amount of the correction at the beginning of the earliest prior period presented; and

(d)   if retrospective restatement is impracticable for a particular prior period, the circumstances that led to the existence of that condition and a description of how and from when the error has been corrected.

Financial statements of subsequent periods need not repeat these disclosures.

Section 11
Financial Assets and Financial Liabilities

Accounting policy choice

An entity shall choose to apply either: **11.1**

(a) the provisions of this section, or
(b) IAS 39 *Financial Instruments: Recognition and Measurement*

in full to account for all of its financial instruments. An entity that chooses to apply IAS 39 shall make the disclosures required by IFRS 7 *Financial Instruments: Disclosures*. An entity's choice of (a) or (b) is an **accounting policy** choice. Paragraphs 10.6–10.12 of Section 10 *Accounting Policies, Estimates and Errors* contain requirements for determining when a change in accounting policy is appropriate, how such a change should be accounted for, and what information should be disclosed about the change in accounting policy.

Scope

A **financial instrument** is a contract that gives rise to a **financial asset** of one entity and **11.2** a **financial liability** or equity instrument of another entity. Common examples include:

(a) cash;
(b) demand and fixed-term deposits;
(c) commercial paper and commercial bills;
(d) accounts, notes, and loans receivable and payable;
(e) bonds and similar debt instruments;
(f) ordinary and preferred shares and similar equity instruments;
(g) asset-backed securities such as collateralised mortgage obligations, repurchase agreements, and securitised packages of receivables; and
(h) options, rights, warrants, futures contracts, forward contracts, and interest rate swaps that can be settled in cash or by exchanging another financial instrument.

This section applies to all financial instruments except the following: **11.3**

(a) interests in **subsidiaries** (covered by Section 9 *Consolidated and Separate Financial Statements*), **associates** (see Section 13 *Investments in Associates*) and **joint ventures** (see Section 14 *Investments in Joint Ventures*);
(b) employers' rights and obligations under employee benefit plans (see Section 27 *Employee Benefits*);
(c) rights under insurance contracts unless the insurance contract could result in a loss to either party as a result of contractual terms that are unrelated to:

    (i) changes in the insured risk,
    (ii) changes in foreign exchange rates, or
    (iii) a default by one of the counterparties;

(d) financial instruments that meet the definition of an entity's own equity (see Sections 21 *Equity* and 25 *Share-based Payment*); and
(e) leases (see Section 19 *Leases*) unless the lease could result in a loss to the lessor or the lessee as a result of contractual terms that are unrelated to:

    (i) changes in the price of the leased asset,
    (ii) changes in foreign exchange rates, or
    (iii) a default by one of the counterparties.

11.4   Most contracts to buy or sell a non-financial item such as a commodity, inventory, property, plant or equipment are excluded from this section because they are not financial instruments. However, this section applies to all contracts that could result in a loss to the buyer or seller as a result of contractual terms that are unrelated to changes in the price of the non-financial item, changes in foreign exchange rates, or a default by one of the counterparties.

11.5   In addition to the contracts described in paragraph 11.4, this section applies to contracts to buy or sell non-financial items if the contract can be settled net in cash or another financial instrument, or by exchanging financial instruments, as if the contracts were financial instruments, with the following exception: contracts that were entered into and continue to be held for the purpose of the receipt or delivery of a non-financial item in accordance with the entity's expected purchase, sale or usage requirements are not financial instruments for the purposes of this section.

Initial recognition of financial assets and liabilities

11.6   An entity shall recognise a financial asset or a financial liability only when the entity becomes a party to the contractual provisions of the instrument.

Measurement

11.7   At each **reporting date**, an entity shall measure the following financial instruments at cost or amortised cost less impairment, as indicated:

(a)   an instrument (such as a receivable, payable, or loan) that meets the conditions of paragraph 11.9, and that the entity designates at initial **recognition** to be measured at amortised cost (using the **effective interest method**) less impairment. Appendix A to this section provides guidance on applying the effective interest method.

(b)   a commitment to make or receive a loan that:

(i)   cannot be settled net in cash,

(ii)   when executed, is expected to meet the conditions for recognition at cost or amortised cost less impairment, and

(iii)   the entity designates at initial recognition to be measured at cost less impairment.

(c)   equity instruments that are not **publicly traded** and whose **fair value** cannot otherwise be measured reliably, and contracts linked to such instruments that, if exercised, will result in delivery of such instruments, which shall be measured at cost less impairment.

11.8   With the exception of those financial instruments measured at cost or amortised cost less impairment in accordance with paragraph 11.7, at each reporting date an entity shall measure all financial instruments at fair value, without any deduction for transaction costs it may incur on sale or other disposal, and recognise changes in fair value recognised in profit or loss.

11.9   An entity may designate an instrument for measurement at amortised cost, in accordance with paragraph 11.7(a), only if it meets all of the following conditions:

(a)   It has a specified maturity date or is due on demand and, at or before the specified maturity date, it requires repayment of all or substantially all of the amount of consideration received or paid when it was issued.

(b)   Returns to the holder are

(i)   a fixed amount,

(ii)   a fixed rate of return over the life of the instrument,

(iii) a variable return that, throughout the life of the instrument, is equal to a single referenced quoted or observable interest rate (such as LIBOR) or

(iv)   some combination of these fixed rate and variable rates (such as LIBOR plus 200 basis points). For fixed and variable rate interest returns, interest is calculated by multiplying the rate for the applicable period by the principal outstanding during the period.

(c)   There is no contractual provision that could result in the holder losing the principal amount and any interest attributable to the current period or prior periods.

(d)   Contractual provisions that permit the issuer to prepay the debt or permit the holder to put it back to the issuer before maturity are not contingent on future events. The instrument may require the party exercising an early settlement right to make a penalty payment as long as the penalty is a fixed amount, a specified percentage of the invested amount or principal amount outstanding at the date of exercise, or an amount based on a change in an interest rate that reduces the benefit that otherwise would be obtained by the party exercising the settlement right.

(e)   There are no conditional returns or repayment provisions except for the variable rate return described in (b) and prepayment provisions described in (d).

For the purpose of applying these conditions to the debt component of a **compound financial instrument**, an entity first separates the equity component as required by paragraph 21.7 of Section 21 *Equity*.

Examples of financial instruments that would be, or could be designated to be, measured at cost or amortised cost less impairment are: **11.10**

(a)   normal trade accounts and notes receivable and payable and loans from banks or other third parties, because these typically satisfy the conditions in paragraph 11.9.

(b)   investments in non-convertible debt instruments, because these typically satisfy the conditions in paragraph 11.9.

(c)   a contract or right (option) to buy an equity instrument whose fair value cannot be reliably measured if the contract or right will result in the delivery of the equity instrument, because that equity instrument is measured at cost less impairment in accordance with paragraph 11.7(c).

(d)   accounts payable in a foreign currency, because the contractual cash flows typically satisfy the conditions in paragraph 11.9. However, any change in the account payable because of a change in the exchange rate is recognised in profit or loss as required by paragraph 30.10 of Section 30 *Foreign Currency Translation*.

(e)   loans to or from subsidiaries or associates that are due on demand, because they typically satisfy the conditions in paragraph 11.9.

(f)   a debt instrument that would become immediately receivable if the issuer defaults on an interest or principal payment (such a provision does not violate the conditions in paragraph 11.9).

Examples of financial instruments that are not measured at cost or amortised cost less impairment are as follows. They are measured at fair value through profit or loss (see paragraph 11.8): **11.11**

(a)   investments in equity instruments with published price quotations, because paragraph 11.7(c) allows measurement at cost less impairment only for equity instruments that are not publicly traded and whose fair value cannot otherwise be measured reliably.

(b)   an interest rate swap that returns a cash flow that is positive or negative, or a forward commitment to purchase a commodity or financial instrument that is capable of being cash-settled and that, on settlement, could have positive or negative cash flow, because such swaps and forwards do not meet the condition in paragraph 11.9(b).

(c)   options and forward contracts, because returns to the holder are not fixed and the condition in paragraph 11.9(b) is not met.

(d)   investments in convertible debt, because the return to the holder can vary with the price of the debt issuer's equity shares rather than just with market interest rates.

(e)   perpetual debt, because it does not have a maturity date as required by paragraph 11.9(a).

11.12   An entity shall not change its policy for the subsequent measurement of a financial asset or liability into or out of the fair value through profit or loss category while it is held or issued.

11.13   If a reliable measure of fair value is no longer available for an equity instrument measured at fair value through profit or loss, its fair value **carrying amount** at the date of the change becomes its new cost. The entity shall measure the instrument at this cost amount less impairment until a reliable measure of fair value becomes available.

Fair value

11.14   Paragraph 11.8 requires some financial instruments to be measured at fair value. The best evidence of fair value is a quoted price in an active market. If the market for a financial instrument is not active, an entity estimates fair value by using a valuation technique. The objective of using a valuation technique is to estimate what the transaction price would have been on the measurement date in an arm's length exchange motivated by normal business considerations.

11.15   The fair value of a financial liability with a demand feature (eg a demand deposit) is not less than the amount payable on demand, discounted from the first date that the amount could be required to be paid.

11.16   An entity shall not include transaction costs in the initial measurement of financial assets and liabilities measured at fair value through profit or loss. If payment for the asset is deferred or is financed at a rate of interest that is not a market rate, the entity shall measure cost at the **present value** of the future payments discounted at a market rate of interest.

11.17   An entity shall apply the additional guidance on estimating the fair value of a financial asset or a financial liability that is provided in Appendix B to this section.

Impairment of financial instruments measured at cost or amortised cost

Recognition

11.18   At the end of each **reporting period**, an entity shall assess for impairment all financial assets that are measured at cost or amortised cost. If there is objective evidence of impairment, the entity shall recognise an **impairment loss** in profit or loss. Financial instruments measured at fair value through profit or loss are not specially assessed for impairment because the fair valuation process automatically recognises any impairment.

Objective evidence that a financial asset or group of assets is impaired includes observable data that come to the attention of the holder of the asset about the following loss events:

11.19

(a) significant financial difficulty of the issuer or obligor;
(b) a breach of contract, such as a default or delinquency in interest or principal payments;
(c) the creditor, for economic or legal reasons relating to the debtor's financial difficulty, granting to the debtor a concession that the creditor would not otherwise consider;
(d) it has become **probable** that the debtor will enter bankruptcy or other financial reorganisation;
(e) the disappearance of an active market for that financial asset because of the debtor's financial difficulties; or
(f) observable data indicating that there is a measurable decrease in the estimated future cash flows from a group of financial assets since the initial recognition of those assets, even though the decrease cannot yet be identified with the individual financial assets in the group, such as adverse national or local economic conditions or adverse changes in industry conditions.

Other factors may also be evidence of impairment, including significant changes with an adverse effect that have taken place in the technological, market, economic or legal environment in which the issuer operates.

11.20

Financial assets that are individually significant, and all equity instruments regardless of significance, shall be assessed individually for impairment. Other financial assets shall be assessed for impairment either individually or grouped on the basis of similar credit risk characteristics.

11.21

Measurement

An entity shall measure an impairment loss as follows:

11.22

(a) for an instrument measured at amortised cost less impairment in accordance with paragraph 11.7(a), the impairment loss is the difference between the asset's carrying amount and the present value of estimated cash flows discounted at the financial asset's original effective interest rate; and
(b) for an instrument measured at cost less impairment in accordance with paragraph 11.7(b) and (c), the impairment loss is the difference between the asset's carrying amount and the asset's fair value.

Reversal

If, in a subsequent period, the amount of an impairment loss decreases and the decrease can be related objectively to an event occurring after the impairment was recognised (such as an improvement in the debtor's credit rating), the entity shall reverse the previously recognised impairment loss either directly or by adjusting an allowance account. The reversal shall not result in a carrying amount of the financial asset (net of any allowance account) that exceeds what the carrying amount would have been had the impairment not previously been recognised. The entity shall recognise the amount of the reversal in profit or loss.

11.23

Derecognition of a financial asset

An entity shall **derecognise** a financial asset only when:

11.24

(a)   the contractual rights to the cash flows from the financial asset expire or are settled.

(b)   the entity transfers to another party all of the significant risks and rewards relating to the financial asset; or

(c)   the entity, despite having retained some significant risks and rewards relating to the financial asset, has transferred control of the asset to another party and the other party has the practical ability to sell the asset in its entirety to an unrelated third party and is able to exercise that ability unilaterally and without needing to impose additional restrictions on the transfer. In this case, the entity shall:

(i)   derecognise the asset, and

(ii)   recognise separately any rights and obligations created or retained in the transfer.

The carrying amount of the transferred asset shall be allocated between the rights or obligations retained and those transferred based on their relative fair values at the transfer date. Newly created rights and obligations shall be measured at their fair values at that date. Any difference between the consideration received and the amounts recognised and derecognised in accordance with this paragraph shall be recognised in profit or loss in the period of the transfer.

11.25   If a transfer does not result in derecognition because the entity has retained significant risks and rewards of ownership of the transferred asset, the entity shall continue to recognise the transferred asset in its entirety and shall recognise a financial liability for the consideration received. The asset and liability shall not be offset. In subsequent periods, the entity shall recognise any income on the transferred asset and any expense incurred on the financial liability.

11.26   If a transferor provides non-cash collateral (such as debt or equity instruments) to the transferee, the accounting for the collateral by the transferor and the transferee depends on whether the transferee has the right to sell or repledge the collateral and on whether the transferor has defaulted. The transferor and transferee shall account for the collateral as follows:

(a)   If the transferee has the right by contract or custom to sell or repledge the collateral, the transferor shall reclassify that asset in its balance sheet (eg as a loaned asset, pledged equity instruments or repurchase receivable) separately from other assets.

(b)   If the transferee sells collateral pledged to it, it shall recognise the proceeds from the sale and a liability measured at fair value for its obligation to return the collateral.

(c)   If the transferor defaults under the terms of the contract and is no longer entitled to redeem the collateral, it shall derecognise the collateral, and the transferee shall recognise the collateral as its asset initially measured at fair value or, if it has already sold the collateral, derecognise its obligation to return the collateral.

(d)   Except as provided in (c), the transferor shall continue to carry the collateral as its asset, and the transferee shall not recognise the collateral as an asset.

Derecognition of a financial liability

11.27   An entity shall derecognise a financial liability (or a part of a financial liability) only when it is extinguished—ie when the obligation specified in the contract is discharged or cancelled or expires.

If an existing borrower and lender exchange debt instruments with substantially **11.28** different terms, the entities shall account for the transaction as an extinguishment of the original financial liability and the recognition of a new financial liability. Similarly, an entity shall account for a substantial modification of the terms of an existing financial liability or a part of it (whether or not attributable to the financial difficulty of the debtor) as an extinguishment of the original financial liability and the recognition of a new financial liability. The entity shall recognise in profit or loss any difference between the carrying amount of a financial liability (or part of a financial liability) extinguished or transferred to another party and the consideration paid, including any non-cash assets transferred or liabilities assumed.

Hedge accounting

An entity may designate a hedging relationship between a **hedging instrument** and a **11.29** **hedged item** in such a way as to qualify for hedge accounting. If specified criteria are met, hedge accounting permits the gain or loss on the hedging instrument and on the hedged item to be recognised in profit or loss at the same time.

To qualify for hedge accounting, an entity shall comply with all of the following **11.30** conditions:

(a) the entity designates and documents the hedging relationship so that the risk being hedged, the hedged item and the hedging instrument are clearly identified and the risk in the hedged item is the risk being hedged with the hedging instrument.
(b) the hedged risk is one of the risks specified in paragraph 11.31.
(c) the hedging instrument is as specified in paragraph 11.32.
(d) the entity expects the hedging instrument to be highly effective in offsetting the designated hedged risk. The **effectiveness of a hedge** is the degree to which changes in the fair value or cash flows of the hedged item that are attributable to a hedged risk are offset by changes in the fair value or cash flows of the hedging instrument.

This [draft] standard permits hedge accounting only for: **11.31**

(a) interest rate risk of a debt instrument measured at amortised cost;
(b) foreign exchange or interest rate risk in a firm commitment or a **highly probable forecast transaction**;
(c) price risk of a commodity that it holds or in a firm commitment or highly probable forecast transaction to purchase or sell a commodity; or
(d) foreign exchange risk in a net investment in a foreign operation.

This [draft] standard permits hedge accounting only if the hedging instrument has all **11.32** of following terms and conditions:

(a) it is an interest rate swap, a foreign currency swap, a foreign currency forward exchange contract or a commodity forward exchange contract that is expected to be highly effective in offsetting a risk identified in paragraph 11.31 that is designated as being the hedged risk.
(b) it involves a party external to the reporting entity (ie external to the group, segment or individual entity being reported on).
(c) its **notional amount** is equal to the designated amount of the principal or notional amount of the hedged item.
(d) it has a specified maturity date not later than

    (i) the maturity of the financial instrument being hedged,
    (ii) the expected settlement of the commodity purchase commitment, or

(iii)   the occurrence of the highly probable forecast foreign currency or commodity transaction being hedged.

(e)   it has no prepayment, early termination or extension features.

Hedge of fixed interest rate risk of a recognised financial instrument or commodity price risk of a commodity held

11.33   If the conditions in paragraph 11.30 are met and the hedged risk is the exposure to a fixed interest rate risk of a debt instrument measured at amortised cost or the commodity price risk of a commodity that it holds, the entity shall:

(a)   recognise the hedging instrument as an asset or liability and the change in the fair value of the hedging instrument in profit or loss; and

(b)   recognise the change in the fair value of the hedged item related to the hedged risk in profit or loss and as an adjustment to the carrying amount of the hedged item.

11.34   If the hedged risk is the fixed interest rate risk of a debt instrument measured at amortised cost, the entity shall recognise the periodic net cash settlements on the interest rate swap that is the hedging instrument in profit or loss in the period in which the net settlements accrue.

11.35   The entity shall discontinue the hedge accounting specified in paragraph 11.33 if:

(a)   the hedging instrument expires or is sold or terminated;

(b)   the hedge no longer meets the conditions for hedge accounting specified in paragraph 11.30; or

(c)   the entity revokes the designation.

11.36   If hedge accounting is discontinued and the hedged item is an asset or liability carried at amortised cost that has not been derecognised, any gains or losses recognised as adjustments to the carrying amount of the hedged item are amortised into profit or loss using the effective interest method over the remaining life of the hedged instrument.

Hedge of variable interest rate risk of a recognised financial instrument, foreign exchange risk or commodity price risk in a firm commitment or highly probable forecast transaction, or a net investment in a foreign operation

11.37   If the conditions in paragraph 11.30 are met and the hedged risk is

(a)   the variable interest rate risk in a debt instrument measured at amortised cost,

(b)   the foreign exchange risk in a **firm commitment** or a highly probable forecast transaction,

(c)   the commodity price risk in a firm commitment or highly probable forecast transaction, or

(d)   the foreign exchange risk in a net investment in a foreign operation,

the entity shall recognise directly in equity the portion of the change in the fair value of the hedging instrument that was effective in offsetting the change in the fair value or expected cash flows of the hedged item. The entity shall recognise any excess of the fair value of the hedging instrument over the change in the fair value of the expected cash flows in profit or loss. The hedging relationship ends for (a), (b) and (c) when the hedged transaction occurs and for (d) when the net investment in the foreign operation is sold. The hedging gain or loss recognised in equity shall be reclassified to profit and loss when the hedged item is recognised in profit and loss.

If the hedged risk is the variable interest rate risk in a debt instrument measured at amortised cost, the entity shall subsequently recognise the periodic net cash settlements from the interest rate swap that is the hedging instrument in profit or loss in the period in which the net settlements accrue. **11.38**

The entity shall discontinue the hedge accounting specified in paragraph 11.37 or 11.38 if: **11.39**

(a) the hedging instrument expires or is sold or terminated;
(b) the hedge no longer meets the criteria for hedge accounting in paragraph 11.30;
(c) in a hedge of a forecast transaction, the forecast transaction is no longer highly probable; or
(d) the entity revokes the designation.

If the forecast transaction is no longer expected to take place or if the hedged debt instrument measured at amortised cost is derecognised, any gain or loss on the hedging instrument that was recognised directly in equity shall be removed from equity and recognised in profit or loss.

Disclosure

Disclosure of accounting policies for financial instruments

In accordance with paragraph 8.5 of Section 8 *Notes to the Financial Statements*, an entity shall disclose, in the summary of significant accounting policies, the measurement basis (or bases) used for financial instruments and the other accounting policies used for financial instruments that are relevant to an understanding of the financial statements. **11.40**

Balance sheet—categories of financial assets and financial liabilities

An entity shall disclose the carrying amounts of each of the following categories of financial assets and financial liabilities, in total and by each significant type of financial asset or financial liability within each category, either on the face of the balance sheet or in the notes: **11.41**

(a) financial assets measured at fair value through profit or loss (paragraph 11.8);
(b) financial assets measured at amortised cost less impairment (paragraph 11.7(a));
(c) equity instruments measured at cost (paragraph 11.7(c));
(d) loan commitments measured at cost less impairment (paragraph 11.7(b));
(e) financial liabilities measured at fair value through profit or loss (paragraph 11.8); and
(f) financial liabilities measured at amortised cost (paragraph 11.7(a)).

For all financial assets and financial liabilities measured at fair value, the entity shall disclose the basis for determining fair value, eg quoted market price in an active market or a valuation technique. When a valuation technique is used, the entity shall disclose the assumptions applied in determining fair values of each class of financial assets or financial liabilities. For example, if applicable, an entity discloses information about the assumptions relating to prepayment rates, rates of estimated credit losses, and interest rates or discount rates. **11.42**

If a reliable measure of fair value is no longer available for an equity instrument measured at fair value through profit or loss, the entity shall disclose that fact. **11.43**

Derecognition

11.44   If an entity has transferred financial assets to another party in a transaction that does not qualify for derecognition (see paragraphs 11.24–11.26), the entity shall disclose for each class of such financial assets:

    (a)   the nature of the assets;

    (b)   the nature of the risks and rewards of ownership to which the entity remains exposed; and

    (c)   the carrying amounts of the assets and of any associated liabilities that the entity continues to recognise.

Collateral

11.45   When an entity has pledged financial assets as collateral for liabilities or contingent liabilities, it shall disclose:

    (a)   the carrying amount of the financial assets pledged as collateral; and

    (b)   the terms and conditions relating to its pledge.

Defaults and breaches on loans payable

11.46   For loans payable recognised at the reporting date, an entity shall disclose:

    (a)   details of any defaults during the period of principal, interest, sinking fund, or redemption terms of those loans payable that permit the lender to demand repayment at the reporting date;

    (b)   the carrying amount of the loans payable in default at the reporting date; and

    (c)   whether the default was remedied, or the terms of the loans payable were renegotiated, before the financial statements were authorised for issue.

11.47   If, during the period, there were breaches of loan agreement terms other than those described in paragraph 11.46, an entity shall disclose the same information as is required by paragraph 11.46 if those breaches permitted the lender to demand accelerated repayment (unless the breaches were remedied, or the terms of the loan were renegotiated, on or before the reporting date).

Income statement and equity—items of income, expense, gains or losses

11.48   An entity shall disclose the following items of income, expense, gains or losses either on the face of the financial statements or in the notes:

    (a)   net gains or net losses recognised on:

        (i)   financial assets measured at fair value through profit or loss;

        (ii)   financial liabilities measured at fair value through profit or loss;

        (iii)   financial assets measured at amortised cost less impairment; and

        (iv)   financial liabilities measured at amortised cost;

    (b)   total interest income and total interest expense (calculated using the effective interest method) for financial assets or financial liabilities that are not at fair value through profit or loss; and

    (c)   the amount of any impairment loss for each class of financial asset.

Hedge accounting

An entity shall disclose the following separately for hedges of each of the four types of risks described in paragraph 11.31:   **11.49**

(a)   a description of the hedge;

(b)   a description of the financial instruments designated as hedging instruments and their fair values at the reporting date; and

(c)   the nature of the risks being hedged, including a description of the hedged item.

For a hedge of fixed interest rate risk or commodity price risk of a commodity held (paragraphs 11.33–11.36) the entity shall disclose: **11.50**

(a)   the amount of the change in fair value of the hedging instrument recognised in profit or loss and

(b)   the amount of the change in fair value of the hedged item recognised in profit or loss.

For a hedge of variable interest rate risk, foreign exchange risk, commodity price risk in a firm commitment or highly probable forecast transaction, or a net investment in a foreign operation (paragraphs 11.37–11.39) the entity shall disclose: **11.51**

(a)   the periods when the cash flows are expected to occur and when they are expected to affect profit or loss;

(b)   a description of any forecast transaction for which hedge accounting had previously been used, but which is no longer expected to occur;

(c)   the amount of the change in fair value of the hedging instrument that was recognised in equity during the period (paragraph 11.37);

(d)   the amount that was removed from equity and recognised in profit or loss for the period, showing the amount included in each line item in the income statement (paragraphs 11.38 and 11.39).

Risks relating to financial instruments measured at cost or amortised cost

For financial assets measured at amortised cost less impairment, the entity shall disclose the significant terms and conditions that may affect the amount, timing and certainty of future cash flows, including interest rate risk, foreign exchange rate risk and credit risk.   **11.52**

Appendix A to Section 11
Effective interest rate

This Appendix accompanies, but is not part of, Section 11. It provides guidance for applying the effective interest method in accordance with paragraph 11.7.

11A.1   In some cases, financial assets are acquired at a deep discount that reflects incurred credit losses. Entities include such incurred credit losses in the estimated cash flows when computing the effective interest rate.

11A.2   When applying the effective interest method, an entity generally amortises any fees, points paid or received, transaction costs and other premiums or discounts included in the calculation of the effective interest rate over the expected life of the instrument. However, a shorter period is used if this is the period to which the fees, points paid or received, transaction costs, premiums or discounts relate. This will be the case when the variable to which the fees, points paid or received, transaction costs, premiums or discounts relate is repriced to market rates before the expected maturity of the instrument. In such a case, the appropriate amortisation period is the period to the next such repricing date. For example, if a premium or discount on a floating rate instrument reflects interest that has accrued on the instrument since interest was last paid, or changes in market rates since the floating interest rate was reset to market rates, it will be amortised to the next date when the floating interest is reset to market rates. This is because the premium or discount relates to the period to the next interest reset date because, at that date, the variable to which the premium or discount relates (ie interest rates) is reset to market rates. If, however, the premium or discount results from a change in the credit spread over the floating rate specified in the instrument, or other variables that are not reset to market rates, it is amortised over the expected life of the instrument.

11A.3   For floating rate financial assets and floating rate financial liabilities, periodic re-estimation of cash flows to reflect movements in market rates of interest alters the effective interest rate. If a floating rate financial asset or floating rate financial liability is recognised initially at an amount equal to the principal receivable or payable on maturity, re-estimating the future interest payments normally has no significant effect on the carrying amount of the asset or liability.

11A.4   If an entity revises its estimates of payments or receipts, the entity shall adjust the carrying amount of the financial asset or financial liability (or group of financial instruments) to reflect actual and revised estimated cash flows. The entity recalculates the carrying amount by computing the present value of estimated future cash flows at the financial instrument's original effective interest rate. The adjustment is recognised as income or expense in profit or loss.

Appendix B to Section 11
Fair value measurement considerations

This Appendix is an integral part of Section 11.

Underlying the definition of fair value is a presumption that an entity is a going **11B.1**
concern without any intention or need to liquidate, to curtail materially the scale of
its operations or to undertake a transaction on adverse terms. Fair value is not,
therefore, the amount that an entity would receive or pay in a forced transaction,
involuntary liquidation or distress sale. However, fair value reflects the credit quality
of the instrument.

Active market: quoted price

A financial instrument is regarded as quoted in an active market if quoted prices are **11B.2**
readily and regularly available from an exchange, dealer, broker, industry group,
pricing service or regulatory agency, and those prices represent actual and regularly
occurring market transactions on an arm's length basis. Fair value is defined in terms
of a price agreed by a willing buyer and a willing seller in an arm's length transaction.
The objective of determining fair value for a financial instrument that is traded in an
active market is to arrive at the price at which a transaction would occur at the
reporting date in that instrument (ie without modifying or repackaging the instrument) in the most advantageous active market to which the entity has immediate
access. However, the entity adjusts the price in the more advantageous market to
reflect any differences in counterparty credit risk between instruments traded in that
market and the one being valued. The existence of published price quotations in an
active market is the best evidence of fair value and when they exist they are used to
measure the financial asset or financial liability.

The appropriate quoted market price for an asset held or liability to be issued is **11B.3**
usually the current bid price and, for an asset to be acquired or liability held, the
asking price. When an entity has assets and liabilities with offsetting market risks, it
may use mid-market prices as a basis for establishing fair values for the offsetting
risk positions and apply the bid or asking price to the net open position as appropriate. When current bid and asking prices are unavailable, the price of the most
recent transaction provides evidence of the current fair value as long as there has not
been a significant change in economic circumstances since the time of the transaction.
If conditions have changed since the time of the transaction (eg a change in the risk-
free interest rate following the most recent price quote for a corporate bond), the fair
value reflects the change in conditions by reference to current prices or rates for
similar financial instruments, as appropriate. Similarly, if the entity can demonstrate
that the last transaction price is not fair value (eg because it reflected the amount that
an entity would receive or pay in a forced transaction, involuntary liquidation or
distress sale), that price is adjusted. The fair value of a portfolio of financial
instruments is the product of the number of units of the instrument and its quoted
market price. If a published price quotation in an active market does not exist for a
financial instrument in its entirety, but active markets exist for its component parts,
fair value is determined on the basis of the relevant market prices for the component
parts.

If a rate (rather than a price) is quoted in an active market, the entity uses that **11B.4**
market quoted rate as an input into a valuation technique to determine fair value. If
the market quoted rate does not include credit risk or other factors that market
participants would include in valuing the instrument, the entity adjusts for those
factors.

No active market: valuation technique

11B.5   If the market for a financial instrument is not active, an entity establishes fair value by using a valuation technique. Valuation techniques include using recent arm's length market transactions between knowledgeable, willing parties, if available, reference to the current fair value of another instrument that is substantially the same, discounted cash flow analysis and option pricing models. If there is a valuation technique commonly used by market participants to price the instrument and that technique has been demonstrated to provide reliable estimates of prices obtained in actual market transactions, the entity uses that technique.

11B.6   The objective of using a valuation technique is to establish what the transaction price would have been on the measurement date in an arm's length exchange motivated by normal business considerations. Fair value is estimated on the basis of the results of a valuation technique that makes maximum use of market inputs, and relies as little as possible on entity specific inputs. A valuation technique would be expected to arrive at a realistic estimate of the fair value if (a) it reasonably reflects how the market could be expected to price the instrument and (b) the inputs to the valuation technique reasonably represent market expectations and measures of the risk return factors inherent in the financial instrument.

11B.7   Therefore, a valuation technique (a) incorporates all factors that market participants would consider in setting a price and (b) is consistent with accepted economic methodologies for pricing financial instruments. Periodically, an entity calibrates the valuation technique and tests it for validity using prices from any observable current market transactions in the same instrument (ie without modification or repackaging) or on the basis of any available observable market data. An entity obtains market data consistently in the same market where the instrument was originated or purchased. The best evidence of the fair value of a financial instrument at initial recognition is the transaction price (ie the fair value of the consideration given or received) unless the fair value of that instrument is evidenced by comparison with other observable current market transactions in the same instrument (ie without modification or repackaging) or is based on a valuation technique whose variables include only data from observable markets.

11B.8   The subsequent measurement of the financial asset or financial liability and the subsequent recognition of gains and losses shall be consistent with the requirements of this [draft] standard. The application of paragraph 11B.7 may result in no gain or loss being recognised on the initial recognition of a financial asset or financial liability. In such a case, this section requires that a gain or loss shall be recognised after initial recognition only to the extent that it arises from a change in a factor (including time) that market participants would consider in setting a price.

11B.9   The initial acquisition or origination of a financial asset or incurrence of a financial liability is a market transaction that provides a foundation for estimating the fair value of the financial instrument. In particular, if the financial instrument is a debt instrument (such as a loan), its fair value can be determined by reference to the market conditions that existed at its acquisition or origination date and current market conditions or interest rates currently charged by the entity or by others for similar debt instruments (ie similar remaining maturity, cash flow pattern, currency, credit risk, collateral and interest basis). Alternatively, provided there is no change in the credit risk of the debtor and applicable credit spreads after the origination of the debt instrument, an estimate of the current market interest rate may be derived by using a benchmark interest rate reflecting a better credit quality than the underlying debt instrument, holding the credit spread constant, and adjusting for the change in the benchmark interest rate from the origination date. If conditions have changed since the most recent market transaction, the corresponding change in the fair value of the financial instrument being valued is determined by reference to current prices or rates for similar financial instruments, adjusted as appropriate, for any differences from the instrument being valued.

The same information may not be available at each measurement date. For example, at the date that an entity makes a loan or acquires a debt instrument that is not actively traded, the entity has a transaction price that is also a market price. However, no new transaction information may be available at the next measurement date and, although the entity can determine the general level of market interest rates, it may not know what level of credit or other risk market participants would consider in pricing the instrument on that date. An entity may not have information from recent transactions to determine the appropriate credit spread over the basic interest rate to use in determining a discount rate for a present value computation. It would be reasonable to assume, in the absence of evidence to the contrary, that no changes have taken place in the spread that existed at the date the loan was made. However, the entity would be expected to make reasonable efforts to determine whether there is evidence that there has been a change in such factors. When evidence of a change exists, the entity would consider the effects of the change in determining the fair value of the financial instrument. **11B.10**

In applying discounted cash flow analysis, an entity uses one or more discount rates equal to the prevailing rates of return for financial instruments having substantially the same terms and characteristics, including the credit quality of the instrument, the remaining term over which the contractual interest rate is fixed, the remaining term to repayment of the principal and the currency in which payments are to be made. Short-term receivables and payables with no stated interest rate may be measured at the original invoice amount if the effect of discounting is immaterial. **11B.11**

No active market: equity instruments

The fair value of investments in equity instruments that do not have a quoted market price in an active market and derivatives (options, forward and futures contracts, swaps etc) that are linked to and must be settled by delivery of such an unquoted equity instrument is reliably measurable if (a) the variability in the range of reasonable fair value estimates is not significant for that instrument or (b) the probabilities of the various estimates within the range can be reasonably assessed and used in estimating fair value. **11B.12**

There are many situations in which the variability in the range of reasonable fair value estimates of investments in equity instruments that do not have a quoted market price and derivatives that are linked to and must be settled by delivery of such an unquoted equity instrument is likely not to be significant. Normally it is possible to estimate the fair value of a financial asset that an entity has acquired from an outside party. However, if the range of reasonable fair value estimates is significant and the probabilities of the various estimates cannot be reasonably assessed, an entity is precluded from measuring the instrument at fair value. **11B.13**

Inputs to valuation techniques

An appropriate technique for estimating the fair value of a particular financial instrument would incorporate observable market data about the market conditions and other factors that are likely to affect the instrument's fair value. The fair value of a financial instrument will be based on one or more of the following factors (and perhaps others). **11B.14**

(a) *The time value of money (ie interest at the basic or risk-free rate)*. Basic interest rates can usually be derived from observable government bond prices and are often quoted in financial publications. These rates typically vary with the expected dates of the projected cash flows along a yield curve of interest rates for different time horizons. For practical reasons, an entity may use a well-accepted and readily observable general rate, such as LIBOR or a swap rate, as the benchmark rate. (Because a rate such as LIBOR is not the risk-free interest rate, the credit risk adjustment appropriate to the particular financial instrument is determined on the basis of its credit risk in relation to the credit risk in this benchmark rate.) In some countries, the central government's bonds may carry a significant credit risk and may not provide a stable benchmark basic interest rate for instruments denominated in that currency. Some entities in these countries may have a better credit standing and a lower borrowing rate than the central government. In such a case, basic interest rates may be more appropriately determined by reference to interest rates for the highest rated corporate bonds issued in the currency of that jurisdiction.

(b) *Credit risk*. The effect on fair value of credit risk (ie the premium over the basic interest rate for credit risk) may be derived from observable market prices for traded instruments of different credit quality or from observable interest rates charged by lenders for loans of various credit ratings.

(c) *Foreign currency exchange prices*. Active currency exchange markets exist for most major currencies, and prices are quoted daily in financial publications.

(d) *Commodity prices*. There are observable market prices for many commodities.

(e) *Equity prices*. Prices (and indexes of prices) of traded equity instruments are readily observable in some markets. Present value based techniques may be used to estimate the current market price of equity instruments for which there are no observable prices.

(f) *Volatility (ie magnitude of future changes in price of the financial instrument or other item)*. Measures of the volatility of actively traded items can normally be reasonably estimated on the basis of historical market data or by using volatilities implied in current market prices.

(g) *Prepayment risk and surrender risk*. Expected prepayment patterns for financial assets and expected surrender patterns for financial liabilities can be estimated on the basis of historical data. (The fair value of a financial liability that can be surrendered by the counterparty cannot be less than the present value of the surrender amount.)

(h) *Servicing costs for a financial asset or a financial liability*. Costs of servicing can be estimated using comparisons with current fees charged by other market participants. If the costs of servicing a financial asset or financial liability are significant and other market participants would face comparable costs, the issuer would consider them in determining the fair value of that financial asset or financial liability. It is likely that the fair value at inception of a contractual right to future fees equals the origination costs paid for them, unless future fees and related costs are out of line with market comparables.

Section 12
Inventories

Scope

Inventories are **assets**: 12.1

(a) held for sale in the ordinary course of business;
(b) in the process of production for such sale; or
(c) in the form of materials or supplies to be consumed in the production process or in the rendering of services.

This section does not apply to the measurement of inventories held by: 12.2

(a) producers of agricultural and forest products, **agricultural produce** after harvest, and minerals and mineral products, to the extent that they are measured at **fair value** less costs to sell through profit or loss; or
(b) commodity brokers and dealers who measure their inventories at fair value less costs to sell through profit or loss.

Measurement of inventories

An entity shall measure inventories at the lower of cost and selling price less costs to complete and sell. 12.3

Cost of inventories

An entity shall include in the cost of inventories all costs of purchase, costs of conversion and other costs incurred in bringing the inventories to their present location and condition. 12.4

Costs of purchase

The costs of purchase of inventories comprise the purchase price, import duties and other taxes (other than those subsequently recoverable by the entity from the taxing authorities), and transport, handling and other costs directly attributable to the acquisition of finished goods, materials and services. Trade discounts, rebates and other similar items are deducted in determining the costs of purchase. 12.5

An entity may purchase inventories on deferred settlement terms. When the arrangement effectively contains a financing element, that element, for example a difference between the purchase price for normal credit terms and the amount paid, is recognised as interest expense over the period of the financing. 12.6

Costs of conversion

The costs of conversion of inventories include costs directly related to the units of production, such as direct labour. They also include a systematic allocation of fixed and variable production overheads that are incurred in converting materials into finished goods. Fixed production overheads are those indirect costs of production that remain relatively constant regardless of the volume of production, such as depreciation and maintenance of factory buildings and equipment, and the cost of factory management and administration. Variable production overheads are those indirect costs of production that vary directly, or nearly directly, with the volume of production, such as indirect materials and indirect labour. 12.7

Allocation of fixed production overheads

12.8   An entity shall allocate fixed production overheads to the costs of conversion based on the normal capacity of the production facilities. Normal capacity is the production expected to be achieved on average over a number of periods or seasons under normal circumstances, taking into account the loss of capacity resulting from planned maintenance. The actual level of production may be used if it approximates normal capacity. The amount of fixed overhead allocated to each unit of production is not increased as a consequence of low production or idle plant. Unallocated overheads are recognised as an expense in the period in which they are incurred. In periods of abnormally high production, the amount of fixed overhead allocated to each unit of production is decreased so that inventories are not measured above cost. Variable production overheads are allocated to each unit of production on the basis of the actual use of the production facilities.

Joint products and by-products

12.9   A production process may result in more than one product being produced simultaneously. This is the case, for example, when joint products are produced or when there is a main product and a by-product. When the costs of conversion of each product are not separately identifiable, an entity shall allocate them between the products on a rational and consistent basis. The allocation may be based, for example, on the relative sales value of each product either at the stage in the production process when the products become separately identifiable, or at the completion of production. Most by-products, by their nature, are immaterial. When this is the case, the entity shall measure them at selling price less costs to complete and sell and deduct this amount from the cost of the main product. As a result, the **carrying amount** of the main product is not materially different from its cost.

Other costs included in inventories

12.10   An entity shall include other costs in the cost of inventories only to the extent that they are incurred in bringing the inventories to their present location and condition. For example, it may be appropriate to include, in the cost of inventories, non-production overheads or the costs of designing products for specific customers. If an entity chooses to capitalise borrowing costs as provided by paragraph 24.2(b), IAS 23 *Borrowing Costs* identifies limited circumstances when borrowing costs are included in the cost of inventories.

12.11   Paragraph 11.33(b) of Section 11 *Financial Assets and Financial Liabilities* provides that, in some circumstances, the change in the fair value of the hedging instrument in a hedge of fixed interest rate risk or commodity price risk of a commodity held adjusts the carrying amount of the commodity.

Costs excluded from inventories

12.12   Examples of costs excluded from the cost of inventories and recognised as expenses in the period in which they are incurred are:

(a)   abnormal amounts of wasted materials, labour or other production costs;
(b)   storage costs, unless those costs are necessary in the production process before a further production stage;
(c)   administrative overheads that do not contribute to bringing inventories to their present location and condition; and
(d)   selling costs.

Cost of inventories of a service provider

To the extent that service providers have inventories, they measure them at the costs
of their production. These costs consist primarily of the labour and other costs of
personnel directly engaged in providing the service, including supervisory personnel,
and attributable overheads. Labour and other costs relating to sales and general
administrative personnel are not included but are recognised as expenses in the
period in which they are incurred. The cost of inventories of a service provider does
not include profit margins or non-attributable overheads that are often factored into
prices charged by service providers.

12.13

Cost of agricultural produce harvested from biological assets

Under Section 35 *Specialised Industries*, inventories comprising agricultural produce
that an entity has harvested from its biological assets are measured on initial
recognition at their fair value less estimated costs to sell at the point of harvest. This
becomes the cost of the inventories at that date for application of this section.

12.14

Techniques for measuring cost, such as standard costing and retail method

An entity may use techniques such as the standard cost method or the retail method
for measuring the cost of inventories if the results approximate cost. Standard costs
take into account normal levels of materials and supplies, labour, efficiency and
capacity utilisation. They are regularly reviewed and, if necessary, revised in the light
of current conditions. The retail method measures cost by reducing the sales value of
the inventory by the appropriate percentage gross margin.

12.15

Cost formulas

An entity shall assign the cost of inventories of items that are not ordinarily inter-
changeable and goods or services produced and segregated for specific projects by
using specific identification of their individual costs.

12.16

An entity shall assign the cost of inventories, other than those dealt with in paragraph 12.16, by using the first-in, first-out (FIFO) or weighted average cost formula.
An entity shall use the same cost formula for all inventories having a similar nature
and use to the entity. For inventories with a different nature or use, different cost
formulas may be justified. The last-in, first-out method (LIFO) is not permitted by
this [draft] standard.

12.17

Impairment of inventories

Paragraphs 26.2–26.4 require an entity to assess at each **reporting date** whether any
inventories are impaired, ie are not recoverable (for example, because of damage,
obsolescence or declining selling prices). If an item (or group of items) of inventory is
impaired, those paragraphs require the entity to measure the inventory at its selling
price less costs to complete and sell and to recognise an impairment loss. Those
paragraphs also require a reversal of a prior impairment in some circumstances.

12.18

Recognition as an expense

When inventories are sold, the entity shall recognise the carrying amount of those
inventories as an expense in the period in which the related revenue is recognised.

12.19

12.20   Some inventories may be allocated to other asset accounts, for example, inventory used as a component of self-constructed property, plant or equipment. Inventories allocated to another asset in this way are recognised as an expense during the useful life of that asset.

Disclosures

12.21   An entity shall disclose:

(a)   the **accounting policies** adopted in measuring inventories, including the cost formula used;

(b)   the total carrying amount of inventories and the carrying amount in classifications appropriate to the entity;

(c)   the amount of inventories recognised as an expense during the period (cost of goods sold);

(d)   the amount of any impairment of inventories recognised as an expense in the period in accordance with paragraph 12.18 and paragraphs 26.2–26.4;

(e)   the amount of any reversal of any impairment recognised in the period in accordance with paragraph 12.18 and paragraph 26.4, and a description of the circumstances or events that led to such reversal; and

(f)   the carrying amount of inventories pledged as security for liabilities.

Section 13
Investments in Associates

Associates defined

An **associate** is an entity, including an unincorporated entity such as a partnership, over which the investor has significant influence and that is neither a subsidiary nor an interest in a joint venture.

13.1

Significant influence is the power to participate in the financial and operating policy decisions of the associate but is not **control** or **joint control** over those policies.

13.2

(a) If an investor holds, directly or indirectly (eg through subsidiaries), 20 per cent or more of the voting power of the investee, it is presumed that the investor has significant influence, unless it can be clearly demonstrated that this is not the case.

(b) Conversely, if the investor holds, directly or indirectly (eg through subsidiaries), less than 20 per cent of the voting power of the investee, it is presumed that the investor does not have significant influence, unless such influence can be clearly demonstrated.

(c) A substantial or majority ownership by another investor does not preclude an investor from having significant influence.

Measurement after initial recognition—accounting policy election

An investor shall account for its investments in all associates using one of the following:

13.3

(a) the cost model in paragraph 13.4;
(b) the equity method in paragraph 13.5; or
(c) the **fair value** through profit or loss model in paragraph 13.6.

Cost model

An investor shall measure its investments in associates at cost less any accumulated impairment losses. The investor shall recognise income from the investment only to the extent that the investor receives distributions from accumulated profits of the associate arising after the date of acquisition. Distributions received in excess of such profits are regarded as a recovery of investment and are recognised as a reduction of the cost of the investment. The investor shall make disclosures required by this section. The investor shall recognise impairment in accordance with Section 26 *Impairment of Non-financial Assets*.

13.4

Equity method

An investor shall measure its investments in associates by the equity method using the procedures in IAS 28 *Investments in Associates*. The investor shall also make disclosures required by IAS 28.

13.5

Fair value through profit or loss model

An investor shall measure its investments in associates at fair value through profit or loss using the procedures in paragraphs 11.14–11.17 in Section 11 *Financial Assets and Financial Liabilities*. The investor shall make the disclosures required by that

13.6

section. An investor shall not use the fair value through profit or loss model for any investment in an associate whose fair value cannot be measured reliably.

Disclosures

13.7   An investor in an associate shall disclose:

(a)   its **accounting policy** for investments in associates;

(b)   the fair value of investments in associates for which there are published price quotations;

(c)   summarised financial information of associates, including the aggregated amounts of assets, liabilities, revenues and profit or loss, along with the investor's percentage of ownership of the associates; and

(d)   the nature and extent of any significant restrictions (eg resulting from borrowing arrangements or regulatory requirements) on the ability of associates to transfer funds to the investor in the form of cash dividends, or repayment of loans or advances.

13.8   For investments in associates accounted for by the equity method, an investor shall disclose separately its share of the profit or loss of such associates, the **carrying amount** of those investments, and its share of any **discontinued operations** of such associates.

Financial statement presentation

13.9   An investor shall classify investments in associates as non-current assets.

Section 14
Investments in Joint Ventures

Joint ventures defined

Joint control is the contractually agreed sharing of **control** over an economic activity, and exists only when the strategic financial and operating decisions relating to the activity require the unanimous consent of the parties sharing control (the venturers). **14.1**

A **joint venture** is a contractual arrangement whereby two or more parties undertake an economic activity that is subject to joint control. Joint ventures can take the form of jointly controlled operations, jointly controlled assets, or **jointly controlled entities**. **14.2**

Jointly controlled operations

The operation of some joint ventures involves the use of the assets and other resources of the venturers rather than the establishment of a corporation, partnership or other entity, or a financial structure that is separate from the venturers themselves. Each venturer uses its own property, plant and equipment and carries its own inventories. It also incurs its own expenses and liabilities and raises its own finance, which represent its own obligations. The joint venture activities may be carried out by the venturer's employees alongside the venturer's similar activities. The joint venture agreement usually provides a means by which the revenue from the sale of the joint product and any expenses incurred in common are shared among the venturers. **14.3**

In respect of its interests in jointly controlled operations, a venturer shall recognise in its financial statements: **14.4**

(a) the assets that it controls and the liabilities that it incurs; and
(b) the expenses that it incurs and its share of the income that it earns from the sale of goods or services by the joint venture.

Jointly controlled assets

Some joint ventures involve the joint control, and often the joint ownership, by the venturers of one or more assets contributed to, or acquired for the purpose of, the joint venture and dedicated to the purposes of the joint venture. **14.5**

In respect of its interest in a jointly controlled asset, a venturer shall recognise in its financial statements: **14.6**

(a) its share of the jointly controlled assets, classified according to the nature of the assets;
(b) any liabilities that it has incurred;
(c) its share of any liabilities incurred jointly with the other venturers in relation to the joint venture;
(d) any income from the sale or use of its share of the output of the joint venture, together with its share of any expenses incurred by the joint venture; and
(e) any expenses that it has incurred in respect of its interest in the joint venture.

Jointly controlled entities

A **jointly controlled entity** is a joint venture that involves the establishment of a corporation, partnership or other entity in which each venturer has an interest. The entity operates in the same way as other entities, except that a contractual **14.7** arrangement between the venturers establishes joint control over the economic activity of the entity.

Measurement after initial recognition—accounting policy election

14.8   A venturer shall account for its interest in all jointly controlled entities using one of the following:

(a)   the cost model in paragraph 14.9;
(b)   the equity method in paragraph 14.10;
(c)   proportionate consolidation described in paragraph 14.11; or
(d)   the **fair value** through profit or loss model in paragraph 14.12.

Cost model

14.9   A venturer shall measure its investments in jointly controlled entities at cost less any accumulated impairment losses. The investor shall recognise income from the investment only to the extent that the investor receives distributions from accumulated profits of the investee arising after the date of acquisition. Distributions received in excess of such profits are regarded as a recovery of investment and are recognised as a reduction of the cost of the investment. The venturer shall make disclosures required by this section. The venturer shall recognise impairment in accordance with Section 26 *Impairment of Non-financial Assets*.

Equity method

14.10   A venturer shall measure its investments in jointly controlled entities by the equity method using the procedures in paragraphs 38–40 of IAS 31 *Interests in Joint Ventures*, which in turn refer to IAS 28 *Investments in Associates*. The venturer shall also make the disclosures required by IAS 28.

Proportionate consolidation

14.11   A venturer shall measure its investments in jointly controlled entities by proportionate consolidation using the procedures in paragraphs 30–37 of IAS 31. The venturer shall also make the disclosures required by IAS 31.

Fair value through profit or loss model

14.12   A venturer shall measure its investments in jointly controlled entities at fair value through profit or loss using the procedures in paragraphs 11.14–11.18 in Section 11 *Financial Assets and Liabilities*. The venturer shall make the disclosures required by that section. An investor shall not use the fair value through profit or loss model for any investment in a joint venture whose fair value cannot be measured reliably.

Transactions between a venturer and a joint venture

14.13   When a venturer contributes or sells assets to a joint venture, recognition of any portion of a gain or loss from the transaction shall reflect the substance of the transaction. While the assets are retained by the joint venture, and provided the venturer has transferred the significant risks and rewards of ownership, the venturer shall recognise only that portion of the gain or loss that is attributable to the interests of the other venturers. The venturer shall recognise the full amount of any loss when the contribution or sale provides evidence of an impairment loss.

When a venturer purchases assets from a joint venture, the venturer shall not **14.14** recognise its share of the profits of the joint venture from the transaction until it resells the assets to an independent party. A venturer shall recognise its share of the losses resulting from these transactions in the same way as profits except that losses shall be recognised immediately when they represent an impairment loss.

If investor does not have joint control

An investor in a joint venture that does not have joint control shall account for that **14.15** investment in accordance with Section 11 or, if it has significant influence in the joint venture, in accordance with Section 13 *Investments in Associates*.

Disclosure

An investor in a joint venture shall disclose the aggregate amount of the following **14.16** **contingent liabilities**, unless the probability of loss is remote, separately from the amount of other contingent liabilities:

(a) any contingent liabilities that the investor has incurred in relation to its interests in joint ventures and its share in each of the contingent liabilities that have been incurred jointly with other venturers;

(b) its share of the contingent liabilities of the joint ventures themselves for which it is contingently liable; and

(c) those contingent liabilities that arise because the investor is contingently liable for the liabilities of the other venturers of a joint venture.

An investor in a joint venture shall also disclose: **14.17**

(a) the aggregate amount of its commitments relating to joint ventures, including its share in the capital commitments that have been incurred jointly with other venturers, as well as its share of the capital commitments of the joint ventures themselves;

(b) a listing and description of interests in significant joint ventures and the proportion of ownership interest held in jointly controlled entities; and

(c) the method it uses to recognise its interests in jointly controlled entities.

Section 15
Investment Property

Recognition

15.1 **Investment property** is property (land or a building, or part of a building, or both) held by the owner or by the lessee under a finance lease to earn rentals or for capital appreciation or both, rather than for:

    (a) use in the production or supply of goods or services or for administrative purposes; or

    (b) sale in the ordinary course of business.

15.2 A property interest that is held by a lessee under an operating lease may be classified and accounted for as investment property if, and only if, the property would otherwise meet the definition of an investment property and the lessee uses the fair value model (see paragraph 15.4) for that property interest and for all of its other property classified as investment property.

Measurement at initial recognition

15.3 An entity shall measure investment property at its cost at initial recognition. The cost of a purchased investment property comprises its purchase price and any directly attributable expenditure such as legal and brokerage fees, property transfer taxes and other transaction costs. An entity shall follow paragraphs 16.6–16.10 to determine the cost of a self-constructed investment property.

Measurement after recognition—accounting policy election

15.4 An entity shall measure all of its investment property after initial recognition using either:

    (a) the **fair value** model in paragraph 15.5; or
    (b) the cost model in paragraph 15.6.

Fair value model

15.5 An entity that elects to use the fair value model shall apply IAS 40 *Investment Property* (see especially paragraphs 33–55) and shall make the disclosures required by paragraphs 75–78 of that standard.

Cost model

15.6 An entity that elects to use the cost model shall account for all of its investment property as property, plant and equipment in accordance with the requirements for the cost model in Section 16 *Property, Plant and Equipment*. The entity shall make the disclosures required by that section.

Transfers

15.7 An entity shall transfer a property to, or from, investment property only when the property first meets, or ceases to meet, the definition of investment property.

Section 16
Property, Plant and Equipment

Recognition

Property, plant and equipment are tangible assets that: 16.1

(a) are held for use in the production or supply of goods or services, for rental to others, or for administrative purposes, and
(b) are expected to be used during more than one period.

Spare parts and servicing equipment are usually carried as inventory and recognised 16.2
in profit or loss as consumed. However, major spare parts and stand-by equipment are property, plant and equipment when an entity expects to use them during more than one period. Similarly, if the spare parts and servicing equipment can be used only in connection with an item of property, plant and equipment, they are considered property, plant and equipment.

Parts of some items of property, plant and equipment may require replacement at 16.3
regular intervals. An entity shall add to the **carrying amount** of an item of property, plant and equipment the cost of replacing part of such an item when that cost is incurred if the replacement part is expected to provide incremental future benefits to the entity. The carrying amount of those parts that are replaced is **derecognised** in accordance with paragraphs 16.24–16.27.

A condition of continuing to operate an item of property, plant and equipment (for 16.4
example, a bus) may be performing regular major inspections for faults regardless of whether parts of the item are replaced. When each major inspection is performed, its cost is recognised in the carrying amount of the item of property, plant and equipment as a replacement if the recognition criteria are satisfied. Any remaining carrying amount of the cost of the previous inspection (as distinct from physical parts) is derecognised. This is done regardless of whether the cost of the previous inspection was identified in the transaction in which the item was acquired or constructed. If necessary, the estimated cost of a future similar inspection may be used as an indication of what the cost of the existing inspection component was when the item was acquired or constructed.

Land and buildings are separable assets, and an entity shall account for them 16.5
separately, even when they are acquired together.

Measurement at recognition

An entity shall measure an item of property, plant and equipment at initial recog- 16.6
nition at its cost.

Elements of cost

The cost of an item of property, plant and equipment comprises: 16.7

(a) its purchase price, including legal and brokerage fees, import duties and non-refundable purchase taxes, after deducting trade discounts and rebates.
(b) any costs directly attributable to bringing the asset to the location and condition necessary for it to be capable of operating in the manner intended by management. These can include the costs of site preparation, initial delivery and handling, installation and assembly, and testing of functionality.

(c)   the initial estimate of the costs of dismantling and removing the item and restoring the site on which it is located, the obligation for which an entity incurs either when the item is acquired or as a consequence of having used the item during a particular period for purposes other than to produce inventories during that period.

16.8   The following costs are not costs of an item of property, plant and equipment, and an entity shall recognise them as an expense when they are incurred:

(a)   costs of opening a new facility;

(b)   costs of introducing a new product or service (including costs of advertising and promotional activities);

(c)   costs of conducting business in a new location or with a new class of customer (including costs of staff training); and

(d)   administration and other general overhead costs.

16.9   The income and related expenses of incidental operations during construction or development of an item of property, plant and equipment are recognised in profit or loss if those operations are not necessary to bring the item to its intended location and operating condition.

Measurement of cost

16.10   The cost of an item of property, plant and equipment is the cash price equivalent at the recognition date. If payment is deferred beyond normal credit terms, the cost is the **present value** of all future payments. If property, plant or equipment is acquired in exchange for a non-monetary asset or assets, or a combination of monetary and non-monetary assets, the cost of the acquired asset is measured at **fair value** unless (a) the exchange transaction lacks commercial substance or (b) the fair value of neither the asset received nor the asset given up is reliably measurable. In this case, the asset's cost is measured at the carrying amount of the asset given up.

Measurement after initial recognition—accounting policy election

16.11   An entity shall account for all items in the same class of property, plant and equipment after initial recognition using either:

(a)   the cost model in paragraph 16.12; or

(b)   the revaluation model in paragraph 16.13.

Cost model

16.12   An entity shall measure an item of property, plant and equipment at cost less any accumulated **depreciation** and any accumulated **impairment** losses.

Revaluation model

16.13   An entity that elects to use the revaluation model for a class of items of property, plant and equipment shall apply paragraphs 31–42 of IAS 16 *Property, Plant and Equipment* and shall make the disclosures required by paragraph 77 of IAS 16.

Depreciation

16.14   An entity shall allocate the amount initially recognised in respect of an item of property, plant and equipment to its significant parts and depreciate separately each such part. However, if a significant part of an item of property, plant and equipment has a **useful life** and a depreciation method that are the same as the useful life and the depreciation method of another significant part of that same item, those parts may be grouped in determining the depreciation charge. With some exceptions, such as quarries and sites used for landfill, land has an unlimited useful life and therefore is not depreciated.

The depreciation charge for each period shall be recognised in profit or loss unless it is included in the carrying amount of another asset. For example, the depreciation of manufacturing property, plant and equipment is included in the costs of inventories (see Section 12 *Inventories*). **16.15**

Depreciable amount and depreciation period

An entity shall allocate the **depreciable amount** of an asset on a systematic basis over its useful life. **16.16**

An entity shall review the **residual value** and the **useful life** of an asset at least at each annual **reporting date** and, if expectations differ from previous estimates, amend the residual value or useful life. The entity shall account for the change in residual value or useful life as a change in an **accounting estimate** in accordance with paragraphs 10.13–10.17. **16.17**

Depreciation of an asset begins when it is available for use, ie when it is in the location and condition necessary for it to be capable of operating in the manner intended by management. Depreciation of an asset ceases at the earlier of the date that the asset is classified as held for sale or included in a disposal group that is classified as held for sale in accordance with paragraphs 36.5–36.7 and the date that the asset is derecognised. Depreciation does not cease when the asset becomes idle or is retired from active use unless the asset is fully depreciated. However, under usage methods of depreciation the depreciation charge can be zero while there is no production. **16.18**

An entity shall consider all the following factors in determining the useful life of an asset: **16.19**

(a) the expected usage of the asset. Usage is assessed by reference to the asset's expected capacity or physical output.
(b) expected physical wear and tear, which depends on operational factors such as the number of shifts for which the asset is to be used and the repair and maintenance programme, and the care and maintenance of the asset while idle.
(c) technical or commercial obsolescence arising from changes or improvements in production, or from a change in the market demand for the product or service output of the asset.
(d) legal or similar limits on the use of the asset, such as the expiry dates of related leases.

Depreciation method

An entity shall select a depreciation method that reflects the pattern in which it expects to consume the asset's future economic benefits. The possible depreciation methods include the straight-line method, the diminishing balance method and the units of production method. **16.20**

An entity shall review the depreciation method at least at each annual reporting date. If there has been a significant change in the pattern in which the entity expects to **16.21** consume the asset's future economic benefits, the entity shall change the method to reflect the new pattern. The entity shall account for the change as a change in an accounting estimate in accordance with Section 10 *Accounting Policies, Estimates and Errors*.

Impairment

16.22 At the end of each **reporting period**, an entity shall apply Section 26 *Impairment of Non-financial Assets* to determine whether an item or group of items of property, plant and equipment is impaired and, if so, how to recognise and measure the impairment loss. That section explains when and how an entity reviews the carrying amount of its assets, how it determines the fair value less costs to sell of an asset, and when it recognises or reverses an impairment loss.

Compensation for impairment

16.23 An entity shall include in profit or loss compensation from third parties for items of property, plant and equipment that were impaired, lost or given up only when the compensation becomes receivable.

Derecognition

16.24 An entity shall derecognise an item of property, plant and equipment:

(a)   on disposal; or

(b)   when no future economic benefits are expected from its use or disposal.

16.25 An entity shall recognise the gain or loss on the derecognition of an item of property, plant and equipment in profit or loss when the item is derecognised (unless Section 19 *Leases* requires otherwise on a sale and leaseback). The entity shall not classify such gains as revenue.

16.26 In determining the date of disposal of an item, an entity shall apply the criteria in Section 22 *Revenue* for recognising revenue from the sale of goods. Section 19 applies to disposal by a sale and leaseback.

16.27 An entity shall determine the gain or loss arising from the derecognition of an item of property, plant and equipment as the difference between the net disposal proceeds, if any, and the carrying amount of the item.

Property, plant and equipment held for sale

16.28 Paragraphs 36.5–36.7 specify requirements for property, plant and equipment and other non-current assets that are held for sale.

Disclosure

16.29 An entity shall disclose, for each class of property, plant and equipment:

(a)   the measurement bases used for determining the gross carrying amount;

(b)   the depreciation methods used;

(c)   the useful lives or the depreciation rates used;

(d)   the gross carrying amount and the accumulated depreciation (aggregated with accumulated impairment losses) at the beginning and end of the period; and

(e) a reconciliation of the carrying amount at the beginning and end of the period showing:

(i) additions;

(ii) disposals, including assets classified as held for sale or included in a disposal group classified as held for sale;

(iii) acquisitions through **business combinations**;

(iv) impairment losses recognised or reversed in profit or loss in accordance with Section 26;

(v) depreciation;

(vi) the net exchange differences arising on the translation of the **financial statements** from the **functional currency** into a different **presentation currency**, including the translation of a foreign operation into the presentation currency of the reporting entity (see Section 30 *Foreign Currency Translation*); and

(vii) other changes.

The entity shall also disclose: **16.30**

(a) the existence and amounts of restrictions on title, and property, plant and equipment pledged as security for liabilities;

(b) the amount of contractual commitments for the acquisition of property, plant and equipment; and

(c) if it is not disclosed separately on the face of the income statement, the amount of compensation from third parties for items of property, plant and equipment that were impaired, lost or given up that is recognised in profit or loss.

An entity shall present property, plant and equipment that is held for sale separately   **16.31**
from other assets on the face of the balance sheet. The entity shall present any
liabilities related to property, plant and equipment that is held for sale separately
from other liabilities on the face of the balance sheet.

Section 17
Intangible Assets other than Goodwill

17.1   An **intangible asset** is an identifiable non-monetary asset without physical substance. Such an asset is identifiable when:

(a)   it is separable, ie capable of being separated or divided from the entity and sold, transferred, licensed, rented or exchanged, either individually or together with a related contract, asset or liability; or

(b)   it arises from contractual or other legal rights, regardless of whether those rights are transferable or separable from the entity or from other rights and obligations.

Recognition

General principle for recognising intangible assets

17.2   An entity shall apply the recognition criteria in paragraph 2.24 in determining whether to recognise an intangible asset. Therefore, the entity shall recognise an intangible asset as an asset only if:

(a)   it is **probable** that the expected future economic benefits that are attributable to the asset will flow to the entity; and

(b)   the cost or value of the asset can be measured reliably.

17.3   An entity shall assess the probability of expected future economic benefits using reasonable and supportable assumptions that represent management's best estimate of the economic conditions that will exist over the useful life of the asset.

17.4   An entity uses judgement to assess the degree of certainty attached to the flow of future economic benefits that are attributable to the use of the asset on the basis of the evidence available at the time of initial recognition, giving greater weight to external evidence.

17.5   The probability recognition criterion in paragraph 17.2(a) is always considered satisfied for intangible assets that are separately acquired.

Acquisition as part of a business combination

17.6   An intangible asset acquired in **business combinations** is normally recognised as an asset because its **fair value** can be measured with sufficient reliability. However, an intangible asset acquired in a business combination is not recognised when it arises from legal or other contractual rights and its fair value cannot be measured reliably because the asset either

(a)   is not separable from **goodwill**; or

(b)   is separable from goodwill but there is no history or evidence of exchange transactions for the same or similar assets, and otherwise estimating fair value would be dependent on immeasurable variables.

Initial measurement

17.7   An entity shall measure an intangible asset initially at cost.

Separate acquisition

The cost of a separately acquired intangible asset comprises: **17.8**

(a) its purchase price, including import duties and non-refundable purchase taxes, after deducting trade discounts and rebates; and

(b) any directly attributable cost of preparing the asset for its intended use.

Acquisition as part of a business combination

If an intangible asset is acquired in a business combination, the cost of that intan-   **17.9**
gible asset is its **fair value** at the acquisition date.

Acquisition by way of a government grant

Section 23 *Government Grants* prescribes the accounting for intangible assets   **17.10**
acquired by way of a government grant.

Exchanges of assets

One or more intangible assets may be acquired in exchange for a non-monetary asset   **17.11**
or assets, or a combination of monetary and non-monetary assets. An entity shall
measure the cost of such an intangible asset at fair value unless (a) the exchange
transaction lacks commercial substance or (b) the fair value of neither the asset
received nor the asset given up is reliably measurable.

If an entity is able to determine reliably the fair value of either the asset received or   **17.12**
the asset given up, then the fair value of the asset given up is used to measure cost
unless the fair value of the asset received is more clearly evident.

If the entity is not able to determine reliably the fair value of the acquired asset, its   **17.13**
cost is measured at the **carrying amount** of the asset given up.

Internally generated intangible assets other than goodwill—accounting policy election

The creation of internally generated intangible assets other than goodwill involves a   **17.14**
research phase and a **development** phase. An entity shall choose either the expense
model in paragraph 17.15 or the capitalisation model in paragraph 17.16 as its
accounting policy for costs incurred in research and development activities.

Expense model

An entity shall recognise all costs incurred in research and development activities as   **17.15**
an expense when incurred.

Capitalisation model

Under the capitalisation model, all costs incurred in research activities are recognised   **17.16**
as an expense when incurred. Costs incurred in development activities are also
recognised as expense except for those development costs incurred after specified
criteria are met, which are recognised as the cost of an intangible asset. An entity that
chooses the capitalisation model as its accounting policy shall follow the requirements of paragraphs 51–67 of IAS 38 *Intangible Assets*.

Recognition as an expense

17.17   An entity shall recognise expenditure on an intangible item as an expense when it is incurred unless it forms part of the cost of an intangible asset that meets the recognition criteria in paragraphs 17.2–17.16.

17.18   An entity shall recognise expenditure on the following items as an expense and shall not recognise such expenditure as intangible assets:

(a)   internally generated brands, mastheads, publishing titles, customer lists and items similar in substance;

(b)   expenditure on start-up activities (ie start-up costs), unless this expenditure is included in the cost of an item of property, plant and equipment in accordance with Section 16 *Property, Plant and Equipment*. Start-up costs may consist of establishment costs such as legal and secretarial costs incurred in establishing a legal entity, expenditure to open a new facility or business (ie pre-opening costs) or expenditure for starting new operations or launching new products or processes (ie pre-operating costs);

(c)   expenditure on training activities;

(d)   expenditure on advertising and promotional activities; and

(e)   expenditure on relocating or reorganising part or all of an entity.

17.19   Paragraph 17.18 does not preclude recognising a prepayment as an asset when payment for the delivery of goods or services has been made in advance of the delivery of goods or the rendering of services.

Past expenses not to be recognised as an asset

17.20   Expenditure on an intangible item that was initially recognised as an expense shall not be recognised at a later date as part of the cost of an intangible asset.

Measurement after recognition—accounting policy election

17.21   An entity shall account for each class of intangible assets after initial recognition using either:

(a)   the cost model in paragraph 17.22; or

(b)   the revaluation model in paragraph 17.23.

Cost model

17.22   An entity shall measure an intangible asset at cost less any accumulated **amortisation** and any accumulated **impairment** losses. The requirements for amortisation are set out in this section. The requirements for recognition of impairment are set out in Section 26 *Impairment of Non-financial Assets*.

Revaluation model

17.23   An entity shall apply paragraphs 75–87 of IAS 38 and shall make the disclosures required by paragraphs 124 and 125 of IAS 38.

Useful life

17.24   An entity shall assess whether the useful life of an intangible asset is finite or indefinite and, if finite, the length of, or number of production or similar units constituting, that useful life. An entity shall regard an intangible asset as having an indefinite useful life when, based on an analysis of all of the relevant factors, there is no foreseeable limit to the period over which the asset is expected to generate net cash inflows for the entity.

The useful life of an intangible asset that arises from contractual or other legal rights **17.25** shall not exceed the period of the contractual or other legal rights, but may be shorter depending on the period over which the entity expects to use the asset. If the contractual or other legal rights are conveyed for a limited term that can be renewed, the useful life of the intangible asset shall include the renewal period(s) only if there is evidence to support renewal by the entity without significant cost.

Intangible assets with finite useful lives

Amortisation period and amortisation method

An entity shall allocate the depreciable amount of an intangible asset with a finite **17.26** useful life on a systematic basis over its useful life. Amortisation shall begin when the asset is available for use, ie when it is in the location and condition necessary for it to be capable of operating in the manner intended by management. Amortisation shall cease at the earlier of the date that the asset is classified as held for sale (or included in a disposal group that is classified as held for sale) in accordance with paragraphs 36.5–36.7 and the date that the asset is derecognised. The entity shall choose an amortisation method that reflects the pattern in which it expects to consume the asset's future economic benefits. If the entity cannot determine that pattern reliably, it shall use the straight-line method. The entity shall recognise the amortisation charge for each period in profit or loss unless this [draft] standard permits or requires it to be included in the carrying amount of another asset.

Residual value

An entity shall assume that the residual value of an intangible asset with a finite **17.27** useful life is zero unless:

(a)   there is a commitment by a third party to purchase the asset at the end of its useful life; or

(b)   there is an active market for the asset and:

    (i)   residual value can be determined by reference to that market; and

    (ii)   it is probable that such a market will exist at the end of the asset's useful life.

Review of amortisation period and amortisation method

An entity shall review the amortisation period and the amortisation method for an **17.28** intangible asset with a finite useful life at least at each financial year-end. If the expected useful life of the asset is different from previous estimates, the entity shall change the amortisation period accordingly. If there has been a change in the expected pattern of consumption of the future economic benefits embodied in the asset, the entity shall change the amortisation method to reflect the changed pattern. The entity shall account for such changes as changes in **accounting estimates** in accordance with Section 10 *Accounting Policies, Estimates and Errors*.

Intangible assets with indefinite useful lives

No amortisation

17.29   An entity shall not amortise an intangible asset with an indefinite useful life.

Recoverability of the carrying amount—impairment losses

17.30   To determine whether an intangible asset is impaired, an entity shall apply Section 26 *Impairment of Non-financial Assets*. That section explains when and how an entity reviews the carrying amount of its assets, how it determines the fair value less costs to sell of an asset, and when it recognises or reverses an impairment loss.

Retirements and disposals

17.31   An entity shall derecognise an intangible asset, and shall recognise a gain or loss in profit or loss:

(a)   on disposal; or

(b)   when no future economic benefits are expected from its use or disposal.

Disclosures

17.32   An entity shall disclose the following for each class of intangible assets, distinguishing between internally generated intangible assets and other intangible assets:

(a)   whether the useful lives are indefinite or finite and, if finite, the useful lives or the amortisation rates used.

(b)   the amortisation methods used for intangible assets with finite useful lives.

(c)   the gross carrying amount and any accumulated amortisation (aggregated with accumulated impairment losses) at the beginning and end of the period.

(d)   the line item(s) of the income statement in which any amortisation of intangible assets is included.

(e)   a reconciliation of the carrying amount at the beginning and end of the period showing separately additions, disposals, amortisations, impairment losses, and other changes.

17.33   An entity shall also disclose:

(a)   for an intangible asset assessed as having an indefinite useful life, the carrying amount of that asset and the reasons supporting the assessment of an indefinite useful life. In giving these reasons, the entity shall describe the factor(s) that played a significant role in determining that the asset has an indefinite useful life.

(b)   a description, the carrying amount and remaining amortisation period of any individual intangible asset that is **material** to the entity's **financial statements**.

(c)   for intangible assets acquired by way of a government grant and initially recognised at fair value (see paragraph 17.10):

(i)   the fair value initially recognised for these assets;

(ii)   their carrying amount; and

(iii) whether they are measured after recognition using the cost model or the revaluation model.

(d)   the existence and carrying amounts of intangible assets whose title is restricted and the carrying amounts of intangible assets pledged as security for liabilities.

(e)   the amount of contractual commitments for the acquisition of intangible assets.

An entity shall disclose the aggregate amount of research and development expenditure recognised as an expense during the period. **17.34**

Section 18
Business Combinations and Goodwill

18.1   A **business combination** is the bringing together of separate entities or businesses into one reporting entity. The result of nearly all business combinations is that one entity, the acquirer, obtains control of one or more other businesses, the acquiree. The acquisition date is the date on which the acquirer effectively obtains control of the acquiree.

18.2   A business combination may be structured in a variety of ways for legal, taxation or other reasons. It may involve the purchase by an entity of the equity of another entity, the purchase of all the net assets of another entity, the assumption of the liabilities of another entity, or the purchase of some of the net assets of another entity that together form one or more **businesses**.

18.3   A business combination may be effected by the issue of equity instruments, the transfer of cash, **cash equivalents** or other assets, or a combination thereof. The transaction may be between the shareholders of the combining entities or between one entity and the shareholders of another entity. It may involve the establishment of a new entity to control the combining entities or net assets transferred, or the restructuring of one or more of the combining entities.

18.4   This section specifies the accounting for all business combinations except combinations of entities or businesses under common **control**. Common control means that all of the combining entities or businesses are ultimately controlled by the same party both before and after the business combination, and that control is not transitory.

Accounting

18.5   All business combinations shall be accounted for by applying the purchase method.

18.6   Applying the purchase method involves the following steps:

(a)   identifying an acquirer;
(b)   measuring the cost of the business combination; and
(c)   allocating, at the acquisition date, the cost of the business combination to the assets acquired and liabilities and contingent liabilities assumed.

Identifying the acquirer

18.7   An acquirer shall be identified for all business combinations. The acquirer is the combining entity that obtains control of the other combining entities or businesses.

18.8   Control is the power to govern the financial and operating policies of an entity or business so as to obtain benefits from its activities. Control of one entity by another is described in Section 9 *Consolidated and Separate Financial Statements*.

18.9   Although it may sometimes be difficult to identify an acquirer, there are usually indications that one exists. For example:

(a)   if the **fair value** of one of the combining entities is significantly greater than that of the other combining entity, the entity with the greater fair value is likely to be the acquirer;

(b) if the business combination is effected through an exchange of voting ordinary equity instruments for cash or other assets, the entity giving up cash or other assets is likely to be the acquirer; and

(c) if the business combination results in the management of one of the combining entities being able to dominate the selection of the management team of the resulting combined entity, the entity whose management is able so to dominate is likely to be the acquirer.

Cost of a business combination

The acquirer shall measure the cost of a business combination as the aggregate of: **18.10**

(a) the fair values, at the date of exchange, of assets given, liabilities incurred or assumed, and equity instruments issued by the acquirer, in exchange for control of the acquiree; plus

(b) any costs directly attributable to the business combination.

Adjustments to the cost of a business combination contingent on future events

When a business combination agreement provides for an adjustment to the cost of   **18.11**
the combination contingent on future events, the acquirer shall include the amount of that adjustment in the cost of the combination at the acquisition date if the adjustment is **probable** and can be measured reliably.

However, if the potential adjustment is not recognised at the acquisition date but   **18.12**
subsequently becomes probable and can be measured reliably, the additional consideration shall be treated as an adjustment to the cost of the combination.

Allocating the cost of a business combination to the assets acquired and liabilities and contingent liabilities assumed

The acquirer shall, at the acquisition date, allocate the cost of a business combina-   **18.13**
tion by recognising the acquiree's identifiable assets and liabilities and those contingent liabilities that satisfy the recognition criteria in paragraph 18.18 at their fair values at that date, except for non-current assets (or disposal groups) that are classified as held for sale, which shall be recognised at fair value less costs to sell. Any difference between the cost of the business combination and the acquirer's interest in the net fair value of the identifiable assets, liabilities and contingent liabilities so recognised shall be accounted for in accordance with paragraphs 18.20–18.22.

The acquirer shall recognise separately the acquiree's identifiable assets, liabilities   **18.14**
and contingent liabilities at the acquisition date only if they satisfy the following criteria at that date:

(a) in the case of an asset other than an intangible asset, it is probable that any associated future economic benefits will flow to the acquirer, and its fair value can be measured reliably.

(b) in the case of a liability other than a contingent liability, it is probable that an outflow of resources will be required to settle the obligation, and its fair value can be measured reliably.

(c) in the case of an intangible asset or a contingent liability, its fair value can be measured reliably.

The acquirer's income statement shall incorporate the acquiree's profits and losses   **18.15**
after the acquisition date by including the acquiree's income and expenses based on

the cost of the business combination to the acquirer. For example, depreciation expense included after the acquisition date in the acquirer's income statement that relates to the acquiree's depreciable assets shall be based on the fair values of those depreciable assets at the acquisition date, ie their cost to the acquirer.

18.16   Application of the purchase method starts from the acquisition date, which is the date on which the acquirer obtains control of the acquiree. Because control is the power to govern the financial and operating policies of an entity or business so as to obtain benefits from its activities, it is not necessary for a transaction to be closed or finalised at law before the acquirer obtains control. All pertinent facts and circumstances surrounding a business combination shall be considered in assessing when the acquirer has obtained control.

18.17   In accordance with paragraph 18.13, the acquirer recognises separately only the identifiable assets, liabilities and contingent liabilities of the acquiree that existed at the acquisition date and satisfy the recognition criteria in paragraph 18.14. Therefore:

(a)   the acquirer shall recognise liabilities for terminating or reducing the activities of the acquiree as part of allocating the cost of the combination only when the acquiree has, at the acquisition date, an existing liability for restructuring recognised in accordance with Section 20 *Provisions and Contingencies*; and

(b)   the acquirer, when allocating the cost of the combination, shall not recognise liabilities for future losses or other costs expected to be incurred as a result of the business combination.

Contingent liabilities

18.18   Paragraph 18.14 specifies that the acquirer recognises separately a contingent liability of the acquiree only if its fair value can be measured reliably. If its fair value cannot be measured reliably:

(a)   there is a resulting effect on the amount recognised as goodwill or accounted for in accordance with paragraph 18.22; and

(b)   the acquirer shall disclose the information about that contingent liability as required by Section 20.

18.19   After their initial recognition, the acquirer shall measure contingent liabilities that are recognised separately in accordance with paragraph 18.13 at the higher of:

(a)   the amount that would be recognised in accordance with Section 20, and

(b)   the amount initially recognised less, when appropriate, cumulative **amortisation** recognised in accordance with Section 22 *Revenue*.

Goodwill

18.20   The acquirer shall, at the acquisition date:

(a)   recognise **goodwill** acquired in a business combination as an asset; and

(b)   initially measure that goodwill at its cost, being the excess of the cost of the business combination over the acquirer's interest in the net fair value of the identifiable assets, liabilities and contingent liabilities recognised in accordance with paragraph 18.13.

18.21   After initial recognition, the acquirer shall measure goodwill acquired in a business combination at cost less any accumulated impairment losses. Section 26 *Impairment of Non-financial Assets* specifies principles for recognising and measuring the impairment of goodwill.

Excess over cost of acquirer's interest in the net fair value of acquiree's identifiable assets, liabilities and contingent liabilities

If the acquirer's interest in the net fair value of the identifiable assets, liabilities and contingent liabilities recognised in accordance with paragraph 18.13 exceeds the cost of the business combination (sometimes referred to as 'negative goodwill'), the acquirer shall: **18.22**

(a) reassess the identification and measurement of the acquiree's identifiable assets, liabilities and contingent liabilities and the measurement of the cost of the combination; and

(b) recognise immediately in profit or loss any excess remaining after that reassessment.

Disclosure

For business combination(s) effected during the reporting period

For each business combination that was effected during the period (or group of individually immaterial business combinations), the acquirer shall disclose the following: **18.23**

(a) the names and descriptions of the combining entities or businesses.

(b) the acquisition date.

(c) the percentage of voting equity instruments acquired.

(d) the cost of the combination and a description of the components of that cost, including any costs directly attributable to the combination. When equity instruments are issued or issuable as part of the cost, the following shall also be disclosed:

  (i) the number of equity instruments issued or issuable; and

  (ii) the fair value of those instruments and the basis for determining that fair value.

(e) details of any operations the entity has decided to dispose of as a result of the combination.

(f) the amounts recognised at the acquisition date for each class of the acquiree's assets, liabilities and contingent liabilities, including goodwill.

(g) the amount of any excess recognised in profit or loss in accordance with paragraph 18.22, and the line item in the income statement in which the excess is recognised.

(h) a description of the factors that contributed to a cost that results in the recognition of goodwill—a description of each intangible asset that was not recognised separately from goodwill and an explanation of why the intangible asset's fair value could not be measured reliably—or a description of the nature of any excess recognised in profit or loss in accordance with paragraph 18.22.

(i) the amount of the acquiree's profit or loss since the acquisition date included in the acquirer's profit or loss for the period, unless disclosure would be **impracticable**. If such disclosure would be impracticable, that fact shall be disclosed, together with an explanation of why this is the case.

For business combination(s) effected after the end of the reporting period but before the financial statements are authorised for issue

18.24   For each business combination effected after the end of the **reporting period** but before the **financial statements** are authorised for issue, the acquirer shall make the disclosures required by paragraph 18.23 unless such disclosure would be impracticable. If disclosure of any of that information would be impracticable, that fact shall be disclosed, together with an explanation of why this is the case.

For all business combinations

18.25   An acquirer shall disclose a reconciliation of the **carrying amount** of goodwill at the beginning and end of the reporting period, showing separately changes arising from new business combinations, **impairment** losses, disposals of previously acquired businesses, and other changes. An acquirer shall also disclose the gross amount and accumulated impairment losses at the end of the period.

Section 19
Leases

This section shall be applied in accounting for all **leases** other than: 19.1

(a) leases to explore for or use minerals, oil, natural gas and similar non-regenerative resources (see Section 35 *Specialised Industries*);

(b) licensing agreements for such items as motion picture films, video recordings, plays, manuscripts, patents and copyrights (see Section 17 *Intangible Assets other than Goodwill*);

(c) property held by lessees that is accounted for as **investment property** (see Section 15 *Investment Property*);

(d) investment property provided by lessors under operating leases (see Section 15); and

(e) leases that could result in a loss to the lessor or the lessee as a result of contractual terms that are unrelated to changes in the price of the leased asset, changes in foreign exchange rates, or a default by one of the counterparties (see paragraph 11.3(e) in Section 11 *Financial Assets and Financial Liabilities*.

This section applies to agreements that transfer the right to use assets even though 19.2 substantial services by the lessor may be called for in connection with the operation or maintenance of such assets. This section does not apply to agreements that are contracts for services that do not transfer the right to use assets from one contracting party to the other.

Classification of leases

A lease is classified as a **finance lease** if it transfers substantially all the risks and 19.3 rewards incidental to ownership. A lease is classified as an **operating lease** if it does not transfer substantially all the risks and rewards incidental to ownership.

Whether a lease is a finance lease or an operating lease depends on the substance of 19.4 the transaction rather than the form of the contract. Examples of situations that individually or in combination would normally lead to a lease being classified as a finance lease are:

(a) the lease transfers ownership of the asset to the lessee by the end of the lease term.

(b) the lessee has the option to purchase the asset at a price that is expected to be sufficiently lower than the **fair value** at the date the option becomes exercisable for it to be reasonably certain, at the inception of the lease, that the option will be exercised.

(c) the lease term is for the major part of the economic life of the asset even if title is not transferred.

(d) at the inception of the lease the **present value** of the minimum lease payments amounts to at least substantially all of the fair value of the leased asset.

(e) the leased assets are of such a specialised nature that only the lessee can use them without major modifications.

Indicators of situations that individually or in combination could also lead to a lease 19.5 being classified as a finance lease are:

(a) if the lessee can cancel the lease, the lessor's losses associated with the cancellation are borne by the lessee;

(b)   gains or losses from the fluctuation in the **residual value** of the leased asset accrue to the lessee (for example, in the form of a rent rebate equalling most of the sales proceeds at the end of the lease); and

(c)   the lessee has the ability to continue the lease for a secondary period at a rent that is substantially lower than market rent.

19.6   The examples and indicators in paragraphs 19.4 and 19.5 are not always conclusive. If it is clear from other features that the lease does not transfer substantially all risks and rewards incidental to ownership, the lease is classified as an operating lease. For example, this may be the case if ownership of the asset transfers to the lessee at the end of the lease for a variable payment equal to the asset's then fair value, or if there are contingent rents, as a result of which the lessee does not have substantially all risks and rewards incidental to ownership.

19.7   Lease classification is made at the inception of the lease and is not changed during the term of the lease unless the lessee and the lessor agree to change the provisions of the lease (other than simply by renewing the lease), in which case the lease classification shall be re-evaluated.

Financial statements of lessees—finance leases

Initial recognition

19.8   At the commencement of the lease term, lessees shall recognise the rights and obligations under finance leases as assets and liabilities in their balance sheet at amounts equal to the fair value of the leased property determined at the inception of the lease. Any initial direct costs of the lessee (incremental costs that are directly attributable to negotiating and arranging a lease) are added to the amount recognised as an asset.

Subsequent measurement

19.9   A lessee shall apportion minimum lease payments between the finance charge and the reduction of the outstanding liability. The lessee shall allocate the finance charge to each period during the lease term so as to produce a constant periodic rate of interest on the remaining balance of the liability. A lessee shall charge contingent rents as expenses in the periods in which they are incurred.

19.10   In allocating the finance charge to periods during the lease term, a lessee may use an approximation to simplify the calculation.

19.11   A lessee shall depreciate an asset leased under a finance lease in accordance with Section 16 *Property, Plant and Equipment*. If there is no reasonable certainty that the lessee will obtain ownership by the end of the lease term, the asset shall be fully depreciated over the shorter of the lease term and its useful life.

Disclosures

19.12   Lessees shall make the following disclosures for finance leases:

(a)   for each **class of asset**, the net carrying amount at the end of the **reporting period**.

(b)   the total of future minimum lease payments at the end of the reporting period, for each future year.

(c)   contingent rents recognised as an expense.

(d)   the total of future minimum sublease payments expected to be received under non-cancellable subleases at the end of the reporting period.
(e)   a general description of the lessee's leasing arrangements including, but not limited to, the following:

   (i)   the basis on which contingent rent payable is determined;
   (ii)   the existence and terms of renewal or purchase options and escalation clauses; and
   (iii) restrictions imposed by lease arrangements, such as those concerning dividends additional debt and further leasing.

Financial statements of lessees—operating leases

Recognition and measurement

A lessee shall recognise lease payments under operating leases (excluding costs for services such as insurance and maintenance) as an expense on a straight-line basis unless another systematic basis is representative of the time pattern of the user's benefit, even if the payments are not on that basis.   **19.13**

Disclosures

Lessees shall make the following disclosures for operating leases: **19.14**

(a)   the total of future minimum lease payments under non-cancellable operating leases for each future year.
(b)   the total of future minimum sublease payments expected to be received under non-cancellable subleases at the end of the reporting period.
(c)   lease and sublease payments recognised as an expense, with separate amounts for minimum lease payments, contingent rents, and sublease payments.
(d)   a general description of the lessee's significant leasing arrangements including, but not limited to, the following:

   (i)   the basis on which contingent rent payable is determined;
   (ii)   the existence and terms of renewal or purchase options and escalation clauses; and
   (iii) restrictions imposed by lease arrangements, such as those concerning dividends, additional debt and further leasing.

Financial statements of lessors: finance leases

A lessor in a finance lease shall apply paragraphs 36–46 of IAS 17 *Leases* and shall make the disclosures required by paragraph 47 of IAS 17.   **19.15**

Financial statements of lessors: operating leases

Recognition and measurement

A lessor shall present assets subject to operating leases in its balance sheets according to the nature of the asset.   **19.16**

A lessor shall recognise lease income from operating leases in profit or loss on a straight-line basis over the lease term, unless another systematic basis is more representative of the time pattern in which use benefit derived from the leased asset is diminished.   **19.17**

19.18   A lessor shall recognise as an expense costs, including depreciation, incurred in earning the lease income. A lessor shall recognise lease income (excluding receipts for services provided such as insurance and maintenance) on a straight-line basis over the lease term even if the receipts are not on such a basis, unless another systematic basis is more representative of the time pattern in which use benefit derived from the leased asset is diminished.

19.19   A lessor shall add to the carrying amount of the leased asset any initial direct costs it incurs in negotiating and arranging an operating lease and shall recognise such costs as an expense over the lease term on the same basis as the lease income.

19.20   The depreciation policy for depreciable leased assets shall be consistent with the lessor's normal depreciation policy for similar assets, and depreciation shall be calculated in accordance with Section 16 and IAS 38 *Intangible Assets.*

19.21   To determine whether a leased asset has become impaired, a lessor shall apply Section 26 *Impairment of Non-financial Assets.*

19.22   A manufacturer or dealer lessor does not recognise any selling profit on entering into an operating lease because it is not the equivalent of a sale.

Disclosure

19.23   Lessors shall disclose the following for operating leases:

    (a)   the future minimum lease payments under non-cancellable operating leases in the aggregate and for each future year;
    (b)   total contingent rents recognised as income; and
    (c)   a general description of the lessor's leasing arrangements.

Sale and leaseback transactions

19.24   A sale and leaseback transaction involves the sale of an asset and the leasing back of the same asset. The lease payment and the sale price are usually interdependent because they are negotiated as a package. The accounting treatment of a sale and leaseback transaction depends on the type of lease.

Sale and leaseback transaction results in a finance lease

19.25   If a sale and leaseback transaction results in a finance lease, the seller-lessee shall not recognise immediately, as income, any excess of sales proceeds over the carrying amount. Instead, the seller-lessee shall defer such excess and amortise it over the lease term.

Sale and leaseback transaction results in an operating lease

19.26   If a sale and leaseback transaction results in an operating lease, and it is clear that the transaction is established at **fair value**, the seller-lessee shall recognise any profit or loss immediately. If the sale price is below fair value, the seller-lessee shall recognise any profit or loss immediately unless the loss is compensated for by future lease payments at below market price. In that case the seller-lessee shall defer and amortise such loss in proportion to the lease payments over the period for which the asset is expected to be used. If the sale price is above fair value, the seller-lessee shall defer the excess over fair value and amortise it over the period for which the asset is expected to be used.

Disclosure

Disclosure requirements for lessees and lessors apply equally to sale and leaseback transactions. The required description of leasing arrangements includes description of unique or unusual provisions of the agreement or terms of the sale and leaseback transactions.

19.27

Section 20
Provisions and Contingencies

20.1   A **provision** is a liability of uncertain timing or amount.

20.2   The requirements in this section do not apply to provisions that are covered by other sections of this [draft] standard. These include:

(a)   leases (Section 19 *Leases*);
(b)   construction contracts (Section 22 *Revenue*);
(c)   employee benefit obligations (Section 27 *Employee Benefits*); and
(d)   income taxes (Section 28 *Income Taxes*).

20.3   The word 'provision' is sometimes used in the context of such items as depreciation, impairment of assets, and uncollectible receivables. Those are adjustments of the **carrying amount**s of assets, rather than recognition of liabilities, and are therefore not covered by this section.

Initial recognition

20.4   An entity shall recognise a provision only when:

(a)   the entity has a present obligation as a result of a past event, and
(b)   it is **probable** (ie more likely than not) that the entity will be required to transfer economic benefits in settlement; and
(c)   the amount of the obligation can be estimated reliably.

20.5   In rare cases, it is not clear whether there is a present obligation. In those cases, a past event is deemed to give rise to a present obligation if, taking account of all available evidence, it is probable that a present obligation exists at the **reporting date**.

20.6   The entity shall recognise the provision as a liability in the balance sheet and shall recognise the amount of the provision as an expense in profit or loss unless (a) it is part of the cost of producing inventories (see paragraph 12.4) or (b) it is included in the cost of property, plant and equipment in accordance with paragraph 16.7.

20.7   The condition in paragraph 20.4(a) (present obligation arising from a past event) means that the entity has no realistic alternative to settling the obligation. This can happen when the obligation can be enforced by law or when the entity has a **constructive obligation** because the past event has created valid expectations in other parties that the entity will discharge the obligation. Obligations that will arise from the entity's future actions (ie the future conduct of its business) do not satisfy the condition in paragraph 20.4(a), no matter how likely they are to occur and even if they are contractual. To illustrate, because of commercial pressures or legal requirements, an entity may intend or need to carry out expenditure to operate in a particular way in the future (for example, by fitting smoke filters in a certain type of factory). Because the entity can avoid the future expenditure by its future actions, for example by changing its method of operation, it has no present obligation for that future expenditure and no provision is recognised.

Initial measurement

20.8   An entity shall measure a provision at the best estimate of the amount required to settle the obligation at the reporting date.

(a) When the provision involves a large population of items, the estimate of the amount reflects the weighting of all possible outcomes by their associated probabilities.

(b) When the provision arises from a single obligation, the individual most likely outcome may be the best estimate of the amount required to settle the obligation. However, even in such a case, the entity considers other possible outcomes. Where other possible outcomes are either mostly higher or mostly lower than the most likely outcome, the best estimate will be a higher or lower amount.

When the effect of the time value of money is **material**, the amount of a provision shall be the **present value** of the amount expected to be required to settle the obligation. The discount rate (or rates) shall be a pre-tax rate (or rates) that reflect(s) current market assessments of the time value of money. The risks specific to the liability should be reflected either in the discount rate or in the estimation of the amounts required to settle the obligation, but not both.

When some or all of the amount required to settle a provision may be reimbursed by another party (eg through an insurance claim), the entity shall recognise the reimbursement as a separate asset only when it is virtually certain that the entity will receive the reimbursement on settlement of the obligation. The reimbursement receivable shall be presented on the balance sheet as an asset and shall not be offset against the provision. In the income statement, the entity may offset any reimbursement from another party against the expense relating to the provision. An entity shall exclude gains from the expected disposal of assets from the measurement of a provision.   20.9

Subsequent measurement

An entity shall charge against a provision only those expenditures for which the provision was originally recognised.   20.10

An entity shall review provisions at each reporting date and adjust them to reflect the current best estimate of the amount that would be required to settle the obligation at that reporting date. Any adjustments to the amounts previously recognised shall be recognised in profit or loss unless the provision was originally recognised as part of the cost of inventories or property, plant and equipment (see paragraph 20.6). When a provision is measured at the present value of the amount expected to be required to settle the obligation, the unwinding of the discount shall be recognised as borrowing cost.   20.11

Contingent liabilities

A **contingent liability** is either a possible but uncertain obligation or a present obligation that is not recognised because it fails to meet one or both of the conditions (b) and (c) in paragraph 20.4. An entity shall not recognise a contingent liability as a liability, except for contingent liabilities of an acquiree in a business combination (see paragraphs 18.18 and 18.19). Disclosure may be required by paragraph 20.15.   20.12

Contingent assets

An entity shall not recognise a **contingent asset** as an asset. Disclosure may be required by paragraph 20.16.   20.13

Disclosures

Disclosures about provisions

20.14   For each class of provision, an entity shall disclose:

(a)   the carrying amount at the beginning and end of the period.

(b)   additional provisions made in the period, including increases to existing provisions.

(c)   amounts used (ie incurred and charged against the provision) during the period.

(d)   unused amounts reversed during the period.

(e)   the increase during the period in the discounted amount arising from the passage of time and the effect of any change in the discount rate.

(f)   a brief description of the nature of the obligation and the expected timing of any resulting outflows of economic benefits.

(g)   an indication of the uncertainties about the amount or timing of those outflows.

(h)   the amount of any expected reimbursement, stating the amount of any asset that has been recognised for that expected reimbursement.

Comparative information is not required.

Disclosures about contingent liabilities

20.15   Unless the possibility of any outflow in settlement is remote, an entity shall disclose for each class of contingent liability at the reporting date a brief description of the nature of the contingent liability and, when practicable:

(a)   an estimate of its financial effect, measured in accordance with paragraphs 20.8–20.11;

(b)   an indication of the uncertainties relating to the amount or timing of any outflow; and

(c)   the possibility of any reimbursement.

If it is **impracticable** to make one or more of these disclosures, that fact shall be stated.

Disclosures about contingent assets

20.16   If an inflow of economic benefits is probable (more likely than not) but not virtually certain, an entity shall disclose a description of the nature of the **contingent assets** at the end of the **reporting period**, and, when practicable, an estimate of their financial effect, measured using the principles set out in paragraphs 20.8–20.11. If it is impracticable to make this disclosure, that fact shall be stated.

Prejudicial disclosures

20.17   In extremely rare cases, disclosure of some or all of the information required by paragraphs 20.14–20.16 can be expected to prejudice seriously the position of the entity in a dispute with other parties on the subject matter of the provision, contingent liability or contingent asset. In such cases, an entity need not disclose the information, but shall disclose the general nature of the dispute, together with the fact that, and reason why, the information has not been disclosed.

Appendix to Section 20
Guidance on implementing Section 20

This Appendix accompanies, but is not part of, Section 20. It provides guidance for applying the requirements of Section 20 in recognising and measuring provisions.

Example 1 Future operating losses

An entity determines that it is probable that a segment of its operations will incur future operating losses for several years. **20A.1**

Present obligation as a result of a past obligating event—There is no past event that obligates the entity to pay out resources.

Conclusion—The entity does not recognise a provision for future operating losses. Expected future losses do not meet the definition of a liability. The expectation of future operating losses may be an indicator that one or more assets are impaired—see Section 26 *Impairment of Non-financial Assets.*

Example 2 Onerous contracts

An onerous contract is one in which the unavoidable costs of meeting the obligations under the contract exceed the economic benefits expected to be received under it. For example, an entity may be obligated under an operating lease to make payments to lease an asset for which it no longer has any use. **20A.2**

Present obligation as a result of a past obligating event—The entity is contractually obligated to pay out resources for which it will not receive commensurate benefits.

Conclusion—If an entity has a contract that is onerous, the entity recognises and measures the present obligation under the contract as a provision.

Example 3 Restructurings

A restructuring is a programme that is planned and controlled by management, and materially changes either: **20A.3**

(a) the scope of a business undertaken by an entity; or
(b) the manner in which that business is conducted.

Present obligation as a result of a past obligating event—A constructive obligation to restructure arises only when an entity:

(a) has a detailed formal plan for the restructuring identifying at least:

    (i)   the business or part of a business concerned;
    (ii) the principal locations affected;
    (iii) the location, function, and approximate number of employees who will be compensated for terminating their services;
    (iv) the expenditures that will be undertaken; and
    (v) when the plan will be implemented; and

(b) has raised a valid expectation in those affected that it will carry out the restructuring by starting to implement that plan or announcing its main features to those affected by it.

Conclusion—An entity recognises a provision for restructuring costs only when it has a legal or constructive obligation to carry out the restructuring.

Example 4 Warranties

20A.4 A manufacturer gives warranties at the time of sale to purchasers of its product. Under the terms of the contract for sale the manufacturer undertakes to make good, by repair or replacement, manufacturing defects that become apparent within three years from the date of sale. On past experience, it is probable (ie more likely than not) that there will be some claims under the warranties.

Present obligation as a result of a past obligating event—The obligating event is the sale of the product with a warranty, which gives rise to a legal obligation.

An outflow of resources embodying economic benefits in settlement— Probable for the warranties as a whole.

Conclusion—The entity recognises a provision for the best estimate of the costs of making good under the warranty products sold before the reporting date.

Illustration of calculations:

In 20X0, goods are sold for 1,000,000. Experience indicates that 90 per cent of products sold require no warranty repairs; 6 per cent of products sold require minor repairs costing 30 per cent of the sale price; and 4 per cent of products sold require major repairs or replacement costing 70 per cent of sale price. Therefore estimated warranty costs are:

$$1,000,000 \times 90\% \times 0 = 0$$
$$1,000,000 \times 6\% \times 30\% = 18,000$$
$$1,000,000 \times 4\% \times 70\% = 28,000$$
$$\text{Total } 46,000$$

The expenditures for warranty repairs and replacements for products sold in 20X0 are expected to be made 60 per cent in 20X1, 30 per cent in 20X2, and 10 per cent in 20X3. Because the estimated cash flows already reflect the probabilities of the cash outflows, and assuming there are no other risks or uncertainties that must be reflected, to determine the present value of those cash flows the entity uses a 'risk-free' discount rate based on government bonds with the same term as the expected cash outflows (6 per cent for one-year bonds and 7 per cent for two-year and three-year bonds). Calculation of the present value, at the end of 20X0, of the estimated cash flows related to the warranties for products sold in 20X0 is as follows:

Year		Expected cash payments	Discount rate	Discount factor	Present value
1	60% × 46,000	27,600	6%	0.9434 (at 6% for 1 year)	26,038
2	30% × 46,000	13,800	7%	0.8734 (at 7% for 2 years)	12,053
3	10% × 46,000	4,600	7%	0.8163 (at 7% for 3 years)	3,755
Total					41,846

The entity will recognise a warranty obligation of 41,846 at the end of 20X0 for products sold in 20X0.

Example 5 Refunds policy

A retail store has a policy of refunding purchases by dissatisfied customers, even though it is under no legal obligation to do so. Its policy of making refunds is generally known.

20A.5

Present obligation as a result of a past obligating event—The obligating event is the sale of the product, which gives rise to a constructive obligation because the conduct of the store has created a valid expectation on the part of its customers that the store will refund purchases.

An outflow of resources embodying economic benefits in settlement— Probable that a proportion of goods will be returned for refund.

Conclusion—The entity recognises a provision for the best estimate of the amount required to settle the refunds.

Example 6 Closure of a division—no implementation before end of reporting period

On 12 December 20X0 the board of an entity decided to close down a division. Before the end of the reporting period (31 December 20X0) the decision was not communicated to any of those affected and no other steps were taken to implement the decision.

20A.6

Present obligation as a result of a past obligating event—There has been no obligating event, and so there is no obligation.

Conclusion—The entity does not recognise a provision.

Example 7 Closure of a division—communication and implementation before end of reporting period

On 12 December 20X0, the board of an entity decided to close down a division making a particular product. On 20 December 20X0 a detailed plan for closing down the division was agreed by the board; letters were sent to customers warning them to seek an alternative source of supply and redundancy notices were sent to the staff of the division.

20A.7

Present obligation as a result of a past obligating event—The obligating event is the communication of the decision to the customers and employees, which gives rise to a constructive obligation from that date, because it creates a valid expectation that the division will be closed.

An outflow of resources embodying economic benefits in settlement— Probable.

Conclusion—The entity recognises a provision at 31 December 20X0 for the best estimate of the costs that would be incurred to close the division at the reporting date.

Example 8 Staff retraining as a result of changes in the income tax system

20A.8   The government introduces a number of changes to the income tax system. As a result of these changes, an entity in the financial services sector will need to retrain a large proportion of its administrative and sales workforce in order to ensure continued compliance with financial services regulation. At the end of the reporting period, no retraining of staff has taken place.

Present obligation as a result of a past obligating event—There is no obligation because no obligating event (retraining) has taken place.

Conclusion—The entity does not recognise a provision.

Example 9 A court case

20A.9   A customer has sued Entity X, seeking damages for injury the customer allegedly sustained from using a product sold by Entity X. Entity X disputes liability on grounds that the customer did not follow directions in using the product. Up to the date the board authorised the financial statements for the year to 31 December 20X1 for issue, the entity's lawyers advise that it is probable that the entity will not be found liable. However, when the entity prepares the financial statements for the year to 31 December 20X2, its lawyers advise that, owing to developments in the case, it is now probable that the entity will be found liable.

(a)   At 31 December 20X1
        Present obligation as a result of a past obligating event—On the basis of the evidence available when the financial statements were approved, there is no obligation as a result of past events.
        Conclusion—No provision is recognised. The matter is disclosed as a contingent liability unless the probability of any outflow is regarded as remote.

(b)   At 31 December 20X2
        Present obligation as a result of a past obligating event—On the basis of the evidence available, there is a present obligation.
        An outflow of resources embodying economic benefits in settlement—Probable.
        Conclusion—A provision is recognised for the best estimate of the amount to settle the obligation at the reporting date.

Section 21
Equity

Equity is the residual interest in the assets of an entity after deducting all its liabilities. Equity includes investments by the owners of the entity, plus additions to those investments earned through profitable operations and retained for use in the entity's operations, minus reductions to owners' investments as a result of unprofitable operations and distributions to owners. This section addresses accounting for equity instruments issued to individuals or other parties acting in their capacity as investors in equity instruments. Section 25 *Share-based Payment* addresses accounting for a transaction in which the entity receives goods or services (including employee services) as consideration for its equity instruments (including shares or share options) from employees and other vendors acting in their capacity as vendors of goods and services.   **21.1**

Original issue of shares or other equity instruments

An entity shall recognise the issue of shares or other equity instruments as equity when it issues those instruments and another party is obliged to provide cash or other resources to the entity in exchange for the instruments.   **21.2**

(a) If the instruments are issued before the cash or other resources are provided, the entity shall present the amount receivable as an offset to equity in its balance sheet, not as an asset.

(b) If the cash or other resources are received before the instruments are issued, and the entity cannot be required to repay the cash or other resources received, the entity shall recognise the corresponding increase in equity to the extent of consideration received.

(c) To the extent that instruments have been subscribed for but cash or other resources have not yet been provided, the entity shall not recognise an increase in equity.

An entity shall measure the equity instruments at the fair value of the cash or other resources received or receivable, net of direct costs of issuing the equity instruments. If payment is deferred and the time value of money is significant, the initial measurement shall be on a **present value** basis.   **21.3**

How the increase in equity arising on the issuance of shares or other equity instruments is presented in the balance sheet is determined by applicable laws. For example, the par value (or other nominal value) of shares and the amount paid in excess of par value may be presented separately.   **21.4**

Sale of options, rights, and warrants

An entity shall apply the principles in paragraphs 21.2 and 21.3 to equity issued by means of sales of options, rights, warrants, and similar equity instruments.   **21.5**

Capitalisation or bonus issues of shares and share splits

A capitalisation or bonus issue (sometimes referred to as a stock dividend) is the issue of new shares to shareholders in proportion to their existing holdings. For example, an entity may give its shareholders one dividend or bonus share for every five shares held. A share split (sometimes referred to as a stock split) is the dividing of an entity's existing shares into multiple shares. For example, in a 2-for-1 split, each shareholder receives one additional share for each share held. In some cases, the previously   **21.6** outstanding shares are cancelled and replaced by new shares. Capitalisation and bonus issues and share splits do not change total equity. An entity shall reclassify amounts within equity as required by applicable laws.

Issuance of compound financial instruments

21.7   On issuing convertible debt or similar compound **financial instruments** that contain both a liability and an equity component, an entity shall allocate the proceeds between the **liability** component and the equity component. To make the allocation, the entity shall first determine the amount of the liability component as the fair value of a similar liability that does not have an associated equity component. The entity shall allocate the residual amount as the equity component.

21.8   The entity shall not revise the allocation in a subsequent period.

21.9   In periods after the instruments were issued, the entity shall systematically recognise any difference between the liability component and the principal amount payable at maturity as additional interest expense using the **effective interest method**.

Treasury shares

21.10   **Treasury shares** are the equity instruments of an entity that have been acquired or reacquired by the entity. An entity shall deduct from equity the fair value of the consideration given for the treasury shares. The entity shall not recognise a gain or loss in profit or loss on the purchase, sale, issue or cancellation of treasury shares.

Minority interest and transactions in shares of a consolidated subsidiary

21.11   In consolidated financial statements, a **minority interest** (ie non-controlling interest) in the net assets of a subsidiary is included in equity. An entity shall treat changes in a parent's controlling interest in a subsidiary that do not result in a loss of **control** as transactions with equity holders in their capacity as equity holders. An entity shall not recognise gain or loss on these changes in consolidated profit or loss. Also, an entity shall not recognise any change in the **carrying amounts** of assets (including goodwill) or liabilities as a result of such transactions.

Disclosure

21.12   Paragraph 4.13(a)(iv) requires an entity with share capital to disclose, either on the face of the balance sheet or in the notes, for each class of share capital, a reconciliation of the number of shares outstanding (or other measure of quantity) at the beginning and at the end of the period. In that reconciliation, the entity shall identify separately each significant type of change in the number of shares outstanding, including new issues; exercises of options, rights and warrants; conversions of convertible securities; treasury share transactions; **business combinations**; and bonus issues (share dividends) and share splits.

Section 22
Revenue

This section shall be applied in accounting for **revenue** arising from the following 22.1
transactions and events:

(a)   the sale of goods (whether produced by the entity for the purpose of sale or
      purchased for resale);
(b)   the rendering of services; and
(c)   the use by others of entity assets yielding interest, royalties or dividends.

Revenue arising from some transactions and events is dealt with in other sections of 22.2
this [draft] standard:

(a)   lease agreements (see Section 19 *Leases*);
(b)   dividends arising from investments that are accounted for using the equity
      method (see Section 13 *Investments in Associates* and Section 14 *Investments in
      Joint Ventures*);
(c)   changes in the **fair value** of **financial assets** and **financial liabilities** or their
      disposal (see Section 11 *Financial Assets and Financial Liabilities*);
(d)   initial **recognition** and changes in the fair value of **biological assets** related to
      agricultural activity (see Section 35 *Specialised Industries*); and
(e)   initial recognition of **agricultural produce** (see Section 35).

Measurement of revenue

An entity shall measure revenue at the fair value of the consideration received or 22.3
receivable. The fair value of the consideration received or receivable excludes the
amount of any trade discounts and volume rebates allowed by the entity.

An entity shall include in revenue only the gross inflows of economic benefits 22.4
received and receivable by the entity on its own account. An entity shall exclude from
revenue all amounts collected on behalf of third parties such as sales taxes, goods and
services taxes and value added taxes. In an agency relationship, an entity shall
include in revenue only the amount of commission. The amounts collected on behalf
of the principal are not revenue of the entity.

Deferred payment

When the inflow of cash or cash equivalents is deferred, and the arrangement con- 22.5
stitutes in effect a financing transaction, the fair value of the consideration is the
present value of all future receipts determined using an **imputed rate of interest**. A
financing transaction arises when, for example, an entity provides interest free credit
to the buyer or accepts a note receivable bearing a below market interest rate from
the buyer as consideration for the sale of goods. The imputed rate of interest is the
more clearly determinable of either:

(a)   the prevailing rate for a similar instrument of an issuer with a similar credit
      rating; or
(b)   a rate of interest that discounts the nominal amount of the instrument to the
      current cash sales price of the goods or services.

An entity shall recognise the difference between the present value of all future
receipts and the nominal amount of the consideration as interest revenue in accordance with paragraphs 22.15 and 22.16 and Section 11.

Exchanges of goods or services

22.6   An entity shall not recognise revenue when goods or services are exchanged or swapped for goods or services that are of a similar nature and value. However, an entity shall recognise revenue when goods are sold or services are rendered in exchange for dissimilar goods or services. In this case, the entity shall measure the transaction at fair value unless (a) the exchange transaction lacks commercial substance or (b) the fair value of neither the asset received nor the asset given up is reliably measurable. If the transaction cannot be measured at fair value, then the entity shall measure it at the **carrying amount** of the asset given up.

Identification of the revenue transaction

22.7   An entity usually applies the revenue recognition criteria in this section separately to each transaction. However, an entity applies the recognition criteria to the separately identifiable components of a single transaction when necessary to reflect the substance of the transaction. For example, an entity applies the recognition criteria to the separately identifiable components of a single transaction when the selling price of a product includes an identifiable amount for subsequent servicing. Conversely, an entity applies the recognition criteria to two or more transactions together when they are linked in such a way that the commercial effect cannot be understood without reference to the series of transactions as a whole. For example, an entity applies the recognition criteria to two or more transactions together when it sells goods and, at the same time, enters into a separate agreement to repurchase the goods at a later date, thus negating the substantive effect of the transaction.

Sale of goods

22.8   An entity shall recognise revenue from the sale of goods when all the following conditions are satisfied:

(a)   the entity has transferred to the buyer the significant risks and rewards of ownership of the goods;

(b)   the entity retains neither continuing managerial involvement to the degree usually associated with ownership nor effective **control** over the goods sold;

(c)   the amount of revenue can be measured reliably;

(d)   it is **probable** that the economic benefits associated with the transaction will flow to the entity; and

(e)   the costs incurred or to be incurred in respect of the transaction can be measured reliably.

22.9   The assessment of when an entity has transferred the significant risks and rewards of ownership to the buyer requires an examination of the circumstances of the transaction. In most cases, the transfer of the risks and rewards of ownership coincides with the transfer of the legal title or the passing of possession to the buyer. This is the case for most retail sales. In other cases, the transfer of risks and rewards of ownership occurs at a time different from the transfer of legal title or the passing of possession.

22.10   The entity does not recognise revenue if it retains significant risks of ownership. Examples of situations in which the entity may retain the significant risks and rewards of ownership are:

(a)   when the entity retains an obligation for unsatisfactory performance not covered by normal warranty **provisions**;

(b)   when the receipt of the revenue from a particular sale is contingent on the buyer selling the goods;

(c)   when the goods are shipped subject to installation and the installation is a significant part of the contract that has not yet been completed; and

(d)   when the buyer has the right to rescind the purchase for a reason specified in the sales contract and the entity is uncertain about the probability of return.

If an entity retains only an insignificant risk of ownership, the transaction is a sale   **22.11** and the entity recognises the revenue. For example, a seller recognises revenue when it retains the legal title to the goods solely to protect the collectibility of the amount due. Similarly an entity recognises revenue when it offers a refund if the customer is not satisfied. In such cases, the entity recognises a provision for returns in accordance with Section 20 *Provisions and Contingencies*.

Rendering of services

When the outcome of a transaction involving the rendering of services can be esti-   **22.12** mated reliably, an entity shall recognise revenue associated with the transaction by reference to the stage of completion of the transaction at the end of the **reporting period** (sometimes referred to as the percentage of completion method). The outcome of a transaction can be estimated reliably when all the following conditions are satisfied:

(a)   the amount of revenue can be measured reliably;

(b)   it is probable that the economic benefits associated with the transaction will flow to the entity;

(c)   the stage of completion of the transaction at the end of the reporting period can be measured reliably; and

(d)   the costs incurred for the transaction and the costs to complete the transaction can be measured reliably.

Paragraphs 22.21–22.27 provide guidance for applying the percentage of completion method.

When services are performed by an indeterminate number of acts over a specified   **22.13** period of time, an entity recognises revenue on a straight-line basis over the specified period unless there is evidence that some other method better represents the stage of completion. When a specific act is more significant than any other act, the entity postpones recognition of revenue until the significant act is executed.

When the outcome of the transaction involving the rendering of services cannot be   **22.14** estimated reliably, an entity shall recognise revenue only to the extent of the expenses recognised that are recoverable.

Interest, royalties and dividends

An entity shall recognise revenue arising from the use by others of entity assets   **22.15** yielding interest, royalties and dividends on the bases set out in paragraph 22.16 when:

(a)   it is probable that the economic benefits associated with the transaction will flow to the entity; and

(b)   the amount of the revenue can be measured reliably.

An entity shall recognise revenue on the following bases: **22.16**

(a)   interest shall be recognised using the **effective interest method** as described in Appendix A of Section 11;

(b)   royalties shall be recognised on an accrual basis in accordance with the substance of the relevant agreement; and

(c)   dividends shall be recognised when the shareholder's right to receive payment is established.

Construction contracts

22.17   When the outcome of a **construction contract** can be estimated reliably, an entity shall recognise contract revenue and contract costs associated with the construction contract as revenue and expenses respectively by reference to the stage of completion of the contract activity at the end of the reporting period (often referred to as the percentage of completion method). Reliable estimation of the outcome requires reliable estimates of the stage of completion, future costs and collectibility of billings. Paragraphs 22.21–22.27 provide guidance for applying the percentage of completion method.

22.18   The requirements of this section are usually applied separately to each construction contract. However, in some circumstances, it is necessary to apply this section to the separately identifiable components of a single contract or to a group of contracts together in order to reflect the substance of a contract or a group of contracts.

22.19   When a contract covers a number of assets, the construction of each asset shall be treated as a separate construction contract when:

(a)   separate proposals have been submitted for each asset;

(b)   each asset has been subject to separate negotiation and the contractor and customer have been able to accept or reject that part of the contract relating to each asset; and

(c)   the costs and revenues of each asset can be identified.

22.20   A group of contracts, whether with a single customer or with several customers, shall be treated as a single construction contract when:

(a)   the group of contracts is negotiated as a single package;

(b)   the contracts are so closely interrelated that they are, in effect, part of a single project with an overall profit margin; and

(c)   the contracts are performed concurrently or in a continuous sequence.

Percentage of completion method

22.21   An entity shall review and, when necessary, revise the estimates of revenue and costs as the service transaction or construction contract progresses.

22.22   An entity shall determine the stage of completion of a transaction or contract using the method that measures most reliably the work performed. Possible methods include:

(a)   the proportion that costs incurred for work performed to date bear to the estimated total costs. Costs incurred for work performed to date do not include costs relating to future activity, such as for materials or prepayments;

(b)   surveys of work performed; or

(c)   completion of a physical proportion of the service transaction or contract work.

Progress payments and advances received from customers often do not reflect the work performed.

An entity shall recognise costs that relate to future activity on the transaction or contract, such as for materials or prepayments, as an asset if it is probable that the costs will be recovered. Such costs represent an amount due from the customer and are classified as work in progress. **22.23**

An entity shall recognise as an expense immediately any costs that are not probable of being recovered. **22.24**

When the outcome of a construction contract cannot be estimated reliably: **22.25**

(a) an entity shall recognise revenue only to the extent of contract costs incurred that it is probable will be recoverable; and

(b) the entity shall recognise contract costs as an expense in the period in which they are incurred.

When it is probable that total contract costs will exceed total contract revenue on a construction contract, the expected loss shall be recognised as an expense immediately. **22.26**

If the collectibility of an amount already recognised as contract revenue is no longer probable, the entity shall recognise the uncollectible amount as an expense rather than as an adjustment of the amount of contract revenue. **22.27**

Disclosure

General disclosures relating to revenue

An entity shall disclose: **22.28**

(a) the **accounting policies** adopted for the recognition of revenue, including the methods adopted to determine the stage of completion of transactions involving the rendering of services;

(b) the amount of each category of revenue recognised during the period, including revenue arising from:

(i) the sale of goods;
(ii) the rendering of services;
(iii) interest;
(iv) royalties;
(v) dividends; and

(c) the amount of revenue arising from exchanges of goods or services included in each category of revenue.

Disclosures relating to revenue from construction contracts

An entity shall disclose: **22.29**

(a) the amount of contract revenue recognised as revenue in the period;

(b) the methods used to determine the contract revenue recognised in the period; and

(c) the methods used to determine the stage of completion of contracts in progress.

22.30   An entity shall disclose each of the following for contracts in progress at the **reporting date**:

(a)   the aggregate amount of costs incurred and recognised profits (less recognised losses) to date;

(b)   the amount of advances received; and

(c)   the amount of retentions (progress billings that are not paid until the satisfaction of conditions specified in the contract for the payment of such amounts or until defects have been rectified).

22.31   An entity shall present:

(a)   the gross amount due from customers for contract work, as an asset; and

(b)   the gross amount due to customers for contract work, as a liability.

Appendix to Section 22
Examples of revenue recognition under the principles in Section 22

This Appendix accompanies, but is not part of, Section 22. It provides guidance for applying the requirements of Section 22 in recognising and measuring revenue.

The following examples focus on particular aspects of a transaction and are not a comprehensive discussion of all the relevant factors that might influence the recognition of revenue. The examples generally assume that the amount of revenue can be measured reliably, it is probable that the economic benefits will flow to the entity and the costs incurred or to be incurred can be measured reliably.

22A.1

Sale of goods

The law in different countries may cause the recognition criteria in Section 22 to be met at different times. In particular, the law may determine the point in time at which the entity transfers the significant risks and rewards of ownership. Therefore, the examples in this appendix need to be read in the context of the laws relating to the sale of goods in the country in which the transaction takes place.

22A.2

Example 1 'Bill and hold' sales, in which delivery is delayed at the buyer's request but the buyer takes title and accepts billing

The seller recognises revenue when the buyer takes title, provided:

22A.3

(a) it is probable that delivery will be made;
(b) the item is on hand, identified and ready for delivery to the buyer at the time the sale is recognised;
(c) the buyer specifically acknowledges the deferred delivery instructions; and
(d) the usual payment terms apply.

Revenue is not recognised when there is simply an intention to acquire or manufacture the goods in time for delivery.

Example 2 Goods shipped subject to conditions: installation and inspection

The seller normally recognises revenue when the buyer accepts delivery, and installation and inspection are complete. However, revenue is recognised immediately upon the buyer's acceptance of delivery when:

22A.4

(a) the installation process is simple, for example the installation of a factory-tested television receiver that requires only unpacking and connection of power and antennae; or
(b) the inspection is performed only for the purposes of final determination of contract prices, for example, shipments of iron ore, sugar or soya beans.

Example 3 Goods shipped subject to conditions: on approval when the buyer has negotiated a limited right of return

If there is uncertainty about the possibility of return, the seller recognises revenue when the shipment has been formally accepted by the buyer or the goods have been delivered and the time period for rejection has elapsed.

22A.5

Example 4 Goods shipped subject to conditions: consignment sales under which the recipient (buyer) undertakes to sell the goods on behalf of the shipper (seller)

22A.6   The shipper recognises revenue when the goods are sold by the recipient to a third party.

Example 5 Goods shipped subject to conditions: cash on delivery sales

22A.7   The seller recognises revenue when delivery is made and cash is received by the seller or its agent.

Example 6 Layaway sales under which the goods are delivered only when the buyer makes the final payment in a series of instalments

22A.8   The seller recognises revenue from such sales when the goods are delivered. However, when experience indicates that most such sales are consummated, revenue may be recognised when a significant deposit is received, provided the goods are on hand, identified and ready for delivery to the buyer.

Example 7 Orders when payment (or partial payment) is received in advance of delivery for goods not currently held in inventory, for example, the goods are still to be manufactured or will be delivered direct to the customer from a third party

22A.9   The seller recognises revenue when the goods are delivered to the buyer.

Example 8 Sale and repurchase agreements (other than swap transactions) under which the seller concurrently agrees to repurchase the same goods at a later date, or when the seller has a call option to repurchase, or the buyer has a put option to require the repurchase, by the seller, of the goods

22A.10   For a sale and repurchase agreement on an asset other than a financial asset, the seller must analyse the terms of the agreement to ascertain whether, in substance, the risks and rewards of ownership have been transferred to the buyer. If they have been transferred, the seller recognises revenue. When the seller has retained the risks and rewards of ownership, even though legal title has been transferred, the transaction is a financing arrangement and does not give rise to revenue. For a sale and repurchase agreement on a financial asset, Section 11 applies.

Example 9 Sales to intermediate parties, such as distributors, dealers or others for resale

22A.11   The seller generally recognises revenue from such sales when the risks and rewards of ownership have passed. However, when the buyer is acting, in substance, as an agent, the sale is treated as a consignment sale.

Example 10 Subscriptions to publications and similar items

22A.12   When the items involved are of similar value in each time period, the seller recognises revenue on a straight-line basis over the period in which the items are despatched. When the items vary in value from period to period, the seller recognises revenue on the basis of the sales value of the item despatched in relation to the total estimated sales value of all items covered by the subscription.

Example 11 Instalment sales, under which the consideration is receivable in instalments

The seller recognises revenue attributable to the sales price, exclusive of interest, at the date of sale. The sale price is the present value of the consideration, determined by discounting the instalments receivable at the imputed rate of interest. The seller recognises the interest element as revenue using the effective interest method.   **22A.13**

Example 12 Real estate sales

The seller normally recognises revenue when legal title passes to the buyer. However, in some jurisdictions the equitable interest in a property may vest in the buyer before legal title passes and, therefore, the risks and rewards of ownership have been transferred at that stage. In such cases, provided that the seller has no further substantial acts to complete under the contract, it may be appropriate to recognise revenue. In either case, if the seller is obliged to perform any significant acts after the transfer of the equitable and/or legal title, revenue is recognised as the acts are performed. An example is a building or other facility on which construction has not been completed.   **22A.14**

In some cases, real estate may be sold with such a degree of continuing involvement by the seller that the risks and rewards of ownership have not been transferred. Examples are sale and repurchase agreements that include put and call options, and agreements whereby the seller guarantees occupancy of the property for a specified period, or guarantees a return on the buyer's investment for a specified period. In such cases, the nature and extent of the seller's continuing involvement determines how the transaction is accounted for. It may be accounted for as a sale, or as a financing, leasing or some other profit-sharing arrangement. If it is accounted for as a sale, the continuing involvement of the seller may delay the recognition of revenue.   **22A.15**

A seller also considers the means of payment and evidence of the buyer's commitment to complete payment. For example, when the aggregate of the payments received, including the buyer's initial down payment, or continuing payments by the buyer, provide insufficient evidence of the buyer's commitment to complete payment, the seller recognises revenue only to the extent cash is received.   **22A.16**

Rendering of services

Example 13 Installation fees

The seller recognises installation fees as revenue by reference to the stage of completion of the installation, unless they are incidental to the sale of a product, in which case they are recognised when the goods are sold.   **22A.17**

Example 14 Servicing fees included in the price of the product

When the selling price of a product includes an identifiable amount for subsequent servicing (for example, after sales support and product enhancement on the sale of software), the seller defers that amount and recognises it as revenue over the period during which the service is performed. The amount deferred is that which will cover the expected costs of the services under the agreement, together with a reasonable profit on those services.   **22A.18**

Example 15 Advertising commissions

22A.19   Media commissions are recognised when the related advertisement or commercial appears before the public. Production commissions are recognised by reference to the stage of completion of the project.

Example 16 Insurance agency commissions

22A.20   Insurance agency commissions received or receivable that do not require the agent to render further service are recognised as revenue by the agent on the effective commencement or renewal dates of the related policies. However, when it is probable that the agent will be required to render further services during the life of the policy, the agent defers the commission, or part of it, and recognises it as revenue over the period during which the policy is in force.

Example 17 Admission fees

22A.21   The seller recognises revenue from artistic performances, banquets and other special events when the event takes place. When a subscription to a number of events is sold, the seller allocates the fee to each event on a basis that reflects the extent to which services are performed at each event.

Example 18 Tuition fees

22A.22   The seller recognises revenue over the period of instruction.

Example 19 Initiation, entrance and membership fees

22A.23   Revenue recognition depends on the nature of the services provided. If the fee permits only membership, and all other services or products are paid for separately, or if there is a separate annual subscription, the fee is recognised as revenue when no significant uncertainty about its collectibility exists. If the fee entitles the member to services or publications to be provided during the membership period, or to purchase goods or services at prices lower than those charged to non-members, it is recognised on a basis that reflects the timing, nature and value of the benefits provided.

Franchise fees

22A.24   Franchise fees may cover the supply of initial and subsequent services, equipment and other tangible assets, and know how. Accordingly, franchise fees are recognised as revenue on a basis that reflects the purpose for which the fees were charged. The following methods of franchise fee recognition are appropriate.

Example 20 Franchise fees: Supplies of equipment and other tangible assets

22A.25   The franchisor recognises the fair value of the assets sold as revenue when the items are delivered or title passes.

Example 21 Franchise fees: Supplies of initial and subsequent services

22A.26   The franchisor recognises fees for the provision of continuing services, whether part of the initial fee or a separate fee, as revenue as the services are rendered. When the separate fee does not cover the cost of continuing services together with a reasonable profit, part of the initial fee, sufficient to cover the costs of continuing services and to provide a reasonable profit on those services, is deferred and recognised as revenue as the services are rendered.

The franchise agreement may provide for the franchisor to supply equipment, inventories, or other tangible assets, at a price lower than that charged to others or a price that does not provide a reasonable profit on those sales. In these circumstances, part of the initial fee, sufficient to cover estimated costs in excess of that price and to provide a reasonable profit on those sales, is deferred and recognised over the period the goods are likely to be sold to the franchisee. The balance of an initial fee is recognised as revenue when performance of all the initial services and other obligations required of the franchisor (such as assistance with site selection, staff training, financing and advertising) has been substantially accomplished.

22A.27

The initial services and other obligations under an area franchise agreement may depend on the number of individual outlets established in the area. In this case, the fees attributable to the initial services are recognised as revenue in proportion to the number of outlets for which the initial services have been substantially completed.

22A.28

If the initial fee is collectible over an extended period and there is a significant uncertainty that it will be collected in full, the fee is recognised as cash instalments are received.

22A.29

Example 22 Franchise fees: Continuing franchise fees

Fees charged for the use of continuing rights granted by the agreement, or for other services provided during the period of the agreement, are recognised as revenue as the services are provided or the rights used.

22A.30

Example 23 Franchise fees: Agency transactions

Transactions may take place between the franchisor and the franchisee that, in substance, involve the franchisor acting as agent for the franchisee. For example, the franchisor may order supplies and arrange for their delivery to the franchisee at no profit. Such transactions do not give rise to revenue.

22A.31

Example 24 Fees from the development of customised software

The software developer recognises fees from the development of customised software as revenue by reference to the stage of completion of the development, including completion of services provided for post-delivery service support.

22A.32

Interest, royalties and dividends

Example 25 Licence fees and royalties

The licensor recognises fees and royalties paid for the use of an entity's assets (such as trademarks, patents, software, music copyright, record masters and motion picture films) in accordance with the substance of the agreement. As a practical matter, this may be on a straight-line basis over the life of the agreement, for example, when a licensee has the right to use certain technology for a specified period of time.

22A.33

22A.34   An assignment of rights for a fixed fee or non-refundable guarantee under a non-cancellable contract that permits the licensee to exploit those rights freely and the licensor has no remaining obligations to perform is, in substance, a sale. An example is a licensing agreement for the use of software when the licensor has no obligations after delivery. Another example is the granting of rights to exhibit a motion picture film in markets where the licensor has no control over the distributor and expects to receive no further revenues from the box office receipts. In such cases, revenue is recognised at the time of sale.

22A.35   In some cases, whether or not a licence fee or royalty will be received is contingent on the occurrence of a future event. In such cases, revenue is recognised only when it is probable that the fee or royalty will be received, which is normally when the event has occurred.

Section 23
Government Grants

A **government grant** is assistance by government in the form of a transfer of resources **23.1**
to an entity in return for past or future compliance with specified conditions relating
to the operating activities of the entity.

Government grants exclude those forms of government assistance that cannot rea- **23.2**
sonably have a value placed upon them and transactions with government that
cannot be distinguished from the normal trading transactions of the entity.

Recognition and measurement—accounting policy election

An entity shall account for its government grants using either: **23.3**

(a) the *IFRS for SMEs* model in paragraph 23.4 for all government grants; or
(b) the *IFRS for SMEs* model in paragraph 23.4 for those government grants
    related to assets measured at **fair value** through profit or loss and IAS 20
    Accounting for Government Grants and Disclosure of Government Assistance for
    all other grants.

IFRS for SMEs model

An entity shall recognise government grants as follows: **23.4**

(a) a grant that does not impose specified future performance conditions on the
    recipient is recognised in income when the grant proceeds are receivable;
(b) a grant that imposes specified future performance conditions on the recipient is
    recognised in income only when the performance conditions are met;
(c) grants received before the income recognition criteria are satisfied are recog-
    nised as a liability.

An entity shall measure grants at the fair value of the asset received or receivable. **23.5**

Disclosure

An entity shall disclose the following regardless of which choice it has made under **23.6**
paragraph 23.3:

(a) the **accounting policy** adopted for government grants, including an explanation
    of how the grant is presented in the **financial statements**;
(b) the nature and amounts of government grants recognised in the financial
    statements;
(c) unfulfilled conditions and other contingencies attaching to government grants
    that have not been recognised in income; and
(d) an indication of other forms of government assistance from which the entity
    has directly benefited.

For the purpose of the disclosure required by paragraph 23.6(d), government **23.7**
assistance is action by government designed to provide an economic benefit specific
to an entity or range of entities qualifying under specified criteria. Examples include
free technical or marketing advice, the provision of guarantees, and loans at nil or
low interest rates.

Section 24
Borrowing Costs

24.1   Borrowing costs are interest and other costs arising on an entity's financial liabilities. Borrowing costs include:

(a)   interest on bank overdrafts and short-term and long-term borrowings;
(b)   amortisation of discounts or premiums relating to borrowings;
(c)   amortisation of ancillary costs incurred in connection with the arrangement of borrowings;
(d)   finance charges in respect of finance leases recognised in accordance with Section 19 *Leases*; and
(e)   exchange differences arising from foreign currency borrowings to the extent that they are regarded as an adjustment to interest costs.

Recognition—accounting policy election

24.2   An entity shall account for all of its borrowing costs using either:

(a)   the expense model in paragraph 24.3; or
(b)   the capitalisation model in paragraph 24.4.

Expense model

24.3   An entity shall recognise all borrowing costs as an expense in profit or loss in the period in which they are incurred.

Capitalisation model

24.4   An entity that elects to use the capitalisation model shall apply IAS 23 *Borrowing Costs*.

Disclosure

24.5   An entity shall disclose the **accounting policy** adopted for borrowing costs. If the capitalisation model is adopted as provided in paragraph 24.4, the entity shall include the relevant disclosures required by IAS 23.

Section 25
Share-based Payment

An entity shall apply this section in accounting for all **share-based payment trans-actions** including:　　25.1

(a) **equity-settled share-based payment** transactions, in which the entity receives goods or services as consideration for **equity** instruments of the entity (including shares or share options),

(b) **cash-settled share-based payment** transactions, in which the entity acquires goods or services by incurring liabilities to the supplier of those goods or services for amounts that are based on the price (or value) of the entity's shares or other equity instruments of the entity, and

(c) transactions in which the entity receives or acquires goods or services and the terms of the arrangement provide either the entity or the supplier of those goods or services with a choice of whether the entity settles the transaction in cash (or other assets) or by issuing equity instruments.

Recognition

An entity shall recognise the goods or services received or acquired in a share-based　25.2
payment transaction when it obtains the goods or as the services are received. The entity shall recognise a corresponding increase in equity if the goods or services were received in an equity-settled share-based payment transaction, or a liability if the goods or services were acquired in a cash-settled share-based payment transaction.

When the goods or services received or acquired in a share-based payment trans-　25.3
action do not qualify for recognition as assets, the entity shall recognise them as expenses.

Measurement of equity-settled share-based payment transactions

An entity shall apply IFRS 2 *Share-based Payment* in measuring equity-settled share-　25.4
based payment transactions, and shall make the relevant disclosures required by IFRS 2. For equity-settled share-based payment transactions with employees, IFRS 2 generally requires measurement by reference to the **fair value** of the equity instruments granted. However, if the entity is unable to estimate reliably the fair value of the equity instruments granted at the measurement date, IFRS 2 provides for measurement of the equity instruments at their **intrinsic value**, which is the dif-ference between the fair value of the shares and the price, if any, that the counterparty is, or will be, required to pay for those shares. Intrinsic value is mea-sured initially at the **grant date** and subsequently at each **reporting date** and at the date of final settlement, with any change in intrinsic value recognised in profit or loss.

Cash-settled share-based payment transactions

For cash-settled share-based payment transactions, an entity shall measure the goods　25.5
or services acquired and the liability incurred at the fair value of the liability. Until the liability is settled, the entity shall remeasure the fair value of the liability at each reporting date and at the date of settlement, with any changes in fair value recog-nised in profit or loss for the period.

For transactions with employees, if the equity instruments granted do not vest until　25.6
the employees have completed a specified period of service, the entity shall recognise the services received as the employees render service during that period.

Share-based payment transactions with cash alternatives

25.7   For share-based payment transactions in which the terms of the arrangement provide either the entity or the counterparty with the choice of whether the entity settles the transaction in cash (or other assets) or by issuing equity instruments, the entity shall account for that transaction, or the components of that transaction, as a cash-settled share-based payment transaction if, and to the extent that, the entity has incurred a liability to settle in cash or other assets, or as an equity-settled share-based payment transaction if, and to the extent that, no such liability has been incurred. An entity shall apply the procedures in IFRS 2 paragraphs 35–43 for measuring share-based payment transactions with cash alternatives.

Disclosure

25.8   An entity shall disclose a description of each type of share-based payment arrangement that existed at any time during the period, including the general terms and conditions of each arrangement, such as vesting requirements, the maximum term of options granted, and the method of settlement (eg whether in cash or equity). An entity with substantially similar types of share-based payment arrangements may aggregate this information.

25.9   An entity shall disclose the following information about the effect of share-based payment transactions on the entity's profit or loss for the period and on its **financial position**, including at least the following:

(a)   the total expense recognised for the period arising from share-based payment transactions in which the goods or services received did not qualify for recognition as assets and hence were recognised immediately as an expense, including separate disclosure of that portion of the total expense that arises from transactions accounted for as equity-settled share-based payment transactions;

(b)   with respect to liabilities arising from share-based payment transactions:

(i)   the total **carrying amount** at the end of the period; and

(ii)   the total intrinsic value at the end of the period of liabilities for which the counterparty's right to cash or other assets had vested by the end of the period (eg vested share appreciation rights).

Section 26
Impairment of Non-financial Assets

This section shall be applied in accounting for the **impairment** of all assets, other than the following, for which other sections of this [draft] standard establish requirements for recognition of impairment: **26.1**

(a) **deferred tax assets** (see Section 28 *Income Taxes*).

(b) assets arising from **employee benefits** (see Section 27 *Employee Benefits*).

(c) **financial assets** within the scope of Section 11 *Financial Assets and Financial Liabilities*.

(d) **investment property** measured at **fair value** (see Section 15 *Investment Property*).

(e) **biological assets** related to agricultural activity measured at fair value less estimated costs to sell (see Section 35 *Specialised Industries*).

Impairment of inventories

Selling price less costs to complete and sell

An entity shall assess at each **reporting date** whether any inventories are impaired. The entity shall make the assessment by comparing the **carrying amount** of each item of inventory (or group of similar items—see paragraph 26.3) with its selling price less costs to complete and sell. If an item of inventory (or group) is impaired, the entity shall recognise a loss in profit or loss for the difference between carrying amount and the selling price less costs to complete and sell.   **26.2**

If it is **impracticable** to determine the selling price less costs to complete and sell for inventories item by item, the entity may group items of inventory relating to the same product line that have similar purposes or end uses, are produced and marketed in the same geographical area for the purpose of assessing impairment.   **26.3**

Reversal of impairment

An entity shall make a new assessment of selling price less costs to complete and sell in each subsequent period. When the circumstances that previously caused inventories to be impaired no longer exist or when there is clear evidence of an increase in selling price less costs to complete and sell because of changed economic circumstances, the entity shall reverse the amount of the impairment (ie the reversal is limited to the amount of the original impairment loss) so that the new carrying amount is the lower of the cost and the revised selling price less costs to complete and sell.   **26.4**

Impairment of non-financial assets other than inventories

Indicators of impairment

An entity shall assess at each reporting date whether there is any indication that an asset may be impaired. If any such indication exists, the entity shall estimate the fair value less costs to sell of the asset. If there is no indication of impairment, it is not necessary to estimate the fair value less costs to sell. This section uses the term 'an asset' but sometimes fair value less costs to sell must be estimated for a group of assets (see paragraph 26.9).   **26.5**

26.6   In assessing whether there is any indication that an asset may be impaired, an entity shall consider, as a minimum, the following indications:

External sources of information

(a)   during the period, an asset's market value has declined significantly more than would be expected as a result of the passage of time or normal use.

(b)   significant changes with an adverse effect on the entity have taken place during the period, or will take place in the near future, in the technological, market, economic or legal environment in which the entity operates or in the market to which an asset is dedicated.

(c)   market interest rates or other market rates of return on investments have increased during the period, and those increases are likely to affect materially the discount rate used in calculating an asset's value in use and decrease the asset's fair value less costs to sell.

(d)   the carrying amount of the net assets of the entity is more than its market capitalisation.

Internal sources of information

(e)   evidence is available of obsolescence or physical damage of an asset.

(f)   significant changes with an adverse effect on the entity have taken place during the period, or are expected to take place in the near future, in the extent to which, or manner in which, an asset is used or is expected to be used. These changes include the asset becoming idle, plans to discontinue or restructure the operation to which an asset belongs, plans to dispose of an asset before the previously expected date, and reassessing the useful life of an asset as finite rather than indefinite.

(g)   evidence is available from internal reporting that indicates that the economic performance of an asset is, or will be, worse than expected. In this context economic performance includes operating results and cash flows.

26.7   If there is an indication that an asset may be impaired, this may indicate that the entity should review the remaining useful life, the **depreciation (amortisation)** method or the **residual value** for the asset and adjust it in accordance with the section of this [draft] standard applicable to the asset (eg Section 16 *Property, Plant and Equipment* and Section 17 *Intangible Assets other than Goodwill*), even if no impairment loss is recognised for the asset.

Measuring fair value less costs to sell

26.8   Fair value less costs to sell is the amount obtainable from the sale of an asset or group of assets in an arm's length transaction between knowledgeable, willing parties, less the costs of disposal.

26.9   If an entity cannot estimate fair value for an individual asset, the entity shall measure the fair value less costs to sell for the group of assets to which the asset belongs. For this purpose, fair value less costs to sell shall be estimated for the smallest identifiable group of assets

(a)   that includes the asset for which impairment is indicated and

(b)   whose fair value less costs to sell can be estimated.

Fair value less costs to sell

An entity shall determine fair value less costs to sell on the basis of the following **26.10**
hierarchy of reliability of evidence:

(a)   A price in a binding sale agreement in an arm's length transaction, adjusted for
      incremental costs that would be directly attributable to the disposal of the asset.
(b)   If there is no binding sale agreement but an asset is traded in an active market,
      fair value less costs to sell is the asset's market price less the costs of dis-
      posal—usually based on the current bid price.
(c)   When current bid prices are unavailable, the price of the most recent trans-
      action may provide a basis from which to estimate fair value less costs to sell.
(d)   If there is no binding sale agreement or active market for an asset, fair value
      less costs to sell is based on the best information available to reflect the amount
      that an entity could obtain, at the end of the **reporting period**, from the disposal
      of the asset in an arm's length transaction between knowledgeable, willing
      parties, after deducting the costs of disposal. In determining this amount, an
      entity considers the outcome of recent transactions for similar assets within the
      same industry. Fair value less costs to sell does not reflect a forced sale, unless
      management is compelled to sell immediately.

When the fair value less costs to sell of an asset (or a group of assets—see paragraph **26.11**
26.9) is less than its carrying amount, the entity shall reduce the carrying amount of
the asset to its fair value less costs to sell. That reduction is an impairment loss.

An entity shall recognise an impairment loss immediately in profit or loss.   **26.12**

When the amount estimated for an impairment loss is greater than the carrying **26.13**
amount of the asset to which it relates, an entity shall recognise a liability only if that
is required by this [draft] standard (see especially Section 20 *Provisions and
Contingencies*).

After the recognition of an impairment loss, the depreciation (amortisation) charge **26.14**
for the asset shall be adjusted in future periods to allocate the asset's revised carrying
amount, less its residual value (if any), on a systematic basis over its remaining useful
life.

Reversal of an impairment loss

An entity shall assess at each reporting date whether there is any indication that an **26.15**
impairment loss recognised in prior periods for an asset other than goodwill may no
longer exist or may have decreased. If any such indication exists, the entity shall
estimate the fair value less costs to sell of that asset. Indications that an impairment
loss may have decreased or may no longer exist are generally the opposite of those set
out in paragraph 26.6.

If the estimated fair value less costs to sell exceeds the carrying amount of the asset, **26.16**
the entity shall increase the carrying amount to fair value less costs to sell, subject to
the limitation described in paragraph 26.17. That increase is a reversal of an
impairment loss.

The increased carrying amount of an asset other than goodwill attributable to a **26.17**
reversal of an impairment loss shall not exceed the carrying amount that would have
been determined (net of amortisation or depreciation) had no impairment loss been
recognised for the asset in prior years.

26.18   An entity shall recognise a reversal of an impairment loss for an asset other than goodwill immediately in profit or loss, unless the asset is carried at revalued amount in accordance with another section of this [draft] standard (for example, the revaluation model in Section 16). Any reversal of an impairment loss of a revalued asset shall be treated as a revaluation increase in accordance with the revaluation model.

26.19   After a reversal of an impairment loss is recognised, the depreciation (amortisation) charge for the asset shall be adjusted in future periods to allocate the asset's revised carrying amount, less its residual value (if any), on a systematic basis over its remaining useful life.

Additional requirements for impairment of goodwill

26.20   Goodwill, by itself, cannot be sold. Nor does it generate cash flows to an entity that are independent of the cash flows of other assets. As a consequence, the fair value of goodwill cannot be measured directly. Therefore, the fair value of goodwill must be derived from measurement of the fair value of the larger group of assets of which the goodwill is a part.

26.21   The principles in paragraphs 26.5–26.14 for recognising and measuring impairment of assets apply to goodwill. Therefore, at each reporting date the entity shall assess whether there is any indication that goodwill may be impaired. In addition to considering the indicators of impairment in paragraph 26.6, the entity shall also consider whether:

(a)   since acquisition, the acquired entity to which the goodwill relates has performed significantly worse than expected;

(b)   the acquired entity to which the goodwill relates is being restructured, held for sale or abandoned; or

(c)   significant impairment losses have been recognised for other assets of the acquired entity to which the goodwill relates.

26.22   If there is an indication that goodwill has been impaired the entity shall follow a two-step process to determine whether to recognise an impairment loss:

Step 1:

(a)   allocate the goodwill to the **component(s) of the entity** that benefit from the goodwill (generally the lowest level within the entity at which the goodwill is monitored for internal management purposes);

(b)   measure the fair value of each component in its entirety, including the goodwill;

(c)   compare the fair value of the component with the carrying amount of the component;

(d)   if the fair value of the component equals or exceeds its carrying amount, neither the component nor the goodwill is impaired; if the fair value of the component is less than its carrying amount, the difference is an impairment loss that shall be recognised in accordance with Step 2.

Step 2:

(a)   write down the component's goodwill by the amount of the loss determined in Step 1(d) and recognise an impairment loss in profit or loss;

(b)   if the amount of the loss determined in Step 1(d) exceeds the carrying amount of the component's goodwill, the excess shall be recognised as an impairment loss in profit or loss. That excess shall be allocated to the identifiable non-cash assets and liabilities, including contingent liabilities, of the component on the basis of their relative fair values.

If there is a **minority interest** in the component to which goodwill has been allocated, the carrying amount of that component comprises: 26.23

(a) both the parent's interest and the minority interest in the identifiable net assets of the component; and
(b) the parent's interest in goodwill.

However, part of the fair value of the component determined in accordance with Step 1(b) is attributable to the minority interest in goodwill. Consequently, any impairment loss relating to the goodwill (Step 2(a)) is apportioned between that attributable to the parent and that attributable to the minority interest, with only the former being recognised as a goodwill impairment loss.

An impairment loss recognised for goodwill shall not be reversed in a subsequent period.   26.24

Disclosure

An entity shall disclose the following for each **class of assets**:   26.25

(a) the amount of impairment losses recognised in profit or loss during the period and the line item(s) of the income statement in which those impairment losses are included.
(b) the amount of reversals of impairment losses recognised in profit or loss during the period and the line item(s) of the income statement in which those impairment losses are reversed.
(c) the amount of impairment losses on revalued assets recognised directly in equity during the period.
(d) the amount of reversals of impairment losses on revalued assets recognised directly in equity during the period.

An entity shall disclose the following information for the aggregate impairment losses and the aggregate reversals of impairment losses recognised during the period for which no separate information is disclosed: 26.26

(a) the main classes of assets affected by impairment losses and the main classes of assets affected by reversals of impairment losses.
(b) the main events and conditions that led to the recognition of these impairment losses and reversals of impairment losses.

Section 27
Employee Benefits

27.1   **Employee benefits** are all forms of consideration given by an entity in exchange for service rendered by employees, including directors and management. This section applies to four types of employee benefits:

   (a)   short-term employee benefits, which are employee benefits (other than termination benefits) that are due wholly within twelve months after the end of the period in which the employees render the related service;

   (b)   **post-employment benefits**, which are employee benefits (other than **termination benefits**) that are payable after the completion of employment;

   (c)   other long-term employee benefits, which are employee benefits (other than post-employment benefits and termination benefits) that are not due wholly within twelve months after the end of the period in which the employees render the related service; and

   (d)   termination benefits, which are employee benefits payable as a result of either:

   (i)   an entity's decision to terminate an employee's employment before the normal retirement date; or

   (ii)   an employee's decision to accept voluntary redundancy in exchange for those benefits.

27.2   Employee benefits also include **share-based payments** either in the form of equity instruments (such as shares or share options) or cash or other assets of the entity in amounts that are based on the price of the entity's shares or other equity instruments of the entity, provided the specified vesting conditions, if any, are met. An entity shall apply Section 25 *Share-based Payment* in accounting for share-based payments.

General recognition principle for all employee benefits

27.3   An entity shall recognise the cost of all employee benefits to which its employees have become entitled as a result of service rendered to the entity during the period:

   (a)   as a liability, after deducting amounts that have been paid either directly to the employees or as a contribution to an employee benefit fund. If the contribution paid exceeds the obligation arising from service before the **reporting date**, an entity shall recognise that excess as an asset to the extent that the prepayment will lead to a reduction in future payments or a cash refund.

   (b)   as an expense, unless the cost:

   (i)   is included in the cost of producing inventories in accordance with Section 12 *Inventories*; or

   (ii)   is included in the cost of property, plant and equipment in accordance with Section 16 *Property, Plant and Equipment*.

Short-term employee benefits

Examples

27.4   Short-term employee benefits include items such as:

   (a)   wages, salaries and social security contributions;

   (b)   short-term compensated absences (such as paid annual leave and paid sick leave) when the absences are expected to occur within twelve months after the end of the period in which the employees render the related employee service;

(c)   profit-sharing and bonuses payable within twelve months after the end of the period in which the employees render the related service; and

(d)   non-monetary benefits (such as medical care, housing, cars and free or subsidised goods or services) for current employees.

Measurement of short-term benefits generally

When an employee has rendered service to an entity during the **reporting period**, the entity shall measure the amounts recognised in accordance with paragraph 27.3 at the undiscounted amount of short-term employee benefits expected to be paid in exchange for that service.   27.5

Recognition and measurement—short-term compensated absences

Some short-term compensated absences accumulate. Examples include annual vacation leave and sick leave that can be carried forward and used in future periods if the employee does not use the current period's entitlement in full. An entity shall recognise the expected cost of **accumulating compensated absences** when the employees render service that increases their entitlement to future compensated absences. The entity shall measure the expected cost of accumulating compensated absences at the additional amount that the entity expects to pay as a result of the unused entitlement that has accumulated at the end of the reporting period. The entity shall present the unused accumulating compensated absences that are expected to be used as a **current liability** at the reporting date.   27.6

An entity shall recognise the cost of other (non-accumulating) compensated absences when the absences occur. The entity shall measure the cost of non-accumulating compensated absences at the undiscounted amount of salaries and wages paid or payable for the period of absence.   27.7

Recognition—profit-sharing and bonus plans

An entity shall recognise the expected cost of profit-sharing and bonus payments only when: 27.8

(a)   the entity has a present legal or **constructive obligation** to make such payments as a result of past events (this means that the entity has no realistic alternative but to make the payments); and

(b)   a reliable estimate of the obligation can be made.

Post-employment benefits: distinction between defined contribution plans and defined benefit plans

Post-employment benefits include, for example: 27.9

(a)   retirement benefits, such as pensions, and

(b)   other post-employment benefits, such as post-employment life insurance and post-employment medical care.

Arrangements whereby an entity provides post-employment benefits are post-employment benefit plans. An entity shall apply this section to all such arrangements whether or not they involve the establishment of a separate entity to receive contributions and to pay benefits. In some cases, these arrangements are imposed by law rather than by action of the entity.

27.10 Post-employment benefit plans are classified as either **defined contribution plans** or **defined benefit plans**, depending on the economic substance of the plan as derived from its principal terms and conditions.

    (a)   Defined contribution plans are post-employment benefit plans under which an entity pays fixed contributions into a separate entity (a fund) and has no legal or constructive obligation to pay further contributions or to make direct benefit payments to employees if the fund does not hold sufficient assets to pay all employee benefits relating to employee service in the current and prior periods. Thus, the amount of the post-employment benefits received by the employee is determined by the amount of contributions paid by an entity (and perhaps also the employee) to a post-employment benefit plan or to an insurer, together with investment returns arising from the contributions.

    (b)   Defined benefit plans are post-employment benefit plans other than defined contribution plans. Under defined benefit plans, the entity's obligation is to provide the agreed benefits to current and former employees, and actuarial risk (that benefits will cost more than expected) and investment risk fall, in substance, on the entity. If actuarial or investment experience is worse than expected, the entity's obligation may be increased.

Multi-employer plans and state plans

27.11 Multi-employer plans and state plans are classified as defined contribution plans or defined benefit plans on the basis of the terms of the plan, including any constructive obligation that goes beyond the formal terms. However, if sufficient information is not available to use defined benefit accounting for a multi-employer plan that is a defined benefit plan, an entity shall:

    (a)   account for the plan in accordance with paragraph 27.13 as if it were a defined contribution plan; and

    (b)   disclose the fact that it is a defined benefit plan and the reason why it is being accounted for as a defined contribution plan, along with any available information about the plan's surplus or deficit and the implications, if any, for the entity.

Insured benefits

27.12 An entity may pay insurance premiums to fund a post-employment benefit plan. The entity shall treat such a plan as a defined contribution plan unless the entity has a legal or constructive obligation either:

    (a)   to pay the employee benefits directly when they become due, or

    (b)   to pay further amounts if the insurer does not pay all future employee benefits relating to employee service in the current and prior periods.

A constructive obligation could arise indirectly through the plan, through the mechanism for setting future premiums, or through a **related party** relationship with the insurer. If the entity retains such a legal or constructive obligation, the entity shall treat the plan as a defined benefit plan.

Post-employment benefits: defined contribution plans

Recognition and measurement

27.13 The entity shall recognise the contribution payable for a period:

(a) as a liability, after deducting any amount already paid. If contribution payments exceed the contribution due for service before the reporting date, an entity shall recognise that excess as an asset.

(b) as an expense, unless the cost:

   (i)   is included in the cost of producing inventories in accordance with Section 12 *Inventories*; or

   (ii) is included in the cost of property, plant and equipment in accordance with Section 16 *Property, Plant and Equipment*.

Post-employment benefits: defined benefit plans

Recognition

In applying the general recognition principle in paragraph 27.3 to defined benefit plans, an entity: **27.14**

(a) recognises a liability for its obligations under defined benefit plans net of plan assets—its 'defined benefit liability' (see paragraphs 27.15–27.20); and

(b) recognises the net change in that liability during the period as the cost of its defined benefit plans during the period (see paragraphs 27.21–27.25).

Measurement of the defined benefit liability

An entity shall measure a **defined benefit liability** for its obligations under defined benefit plans at the net total of the following amounts: **27.15**

(a) the **present value** of its obligations under defined benefit plans (its **defined benefit obligation**) at the reporting date (paragraph 27.17 provides guidance on discounting), minus

(b) the fair value at the reporting date of **plan assets** (if any) out of which the obligations are to be settled directly. Paragraphs 11.14–11.17 establish requirements for determining the fair values of those plan assets that are **financial assets**.

The present value of an entity's obligations under defined benefit plans at the reporting date shall reflect the estimated amount of benefit that employees have earned in return for their service in the current and prior periods, including benefits that are not yet **vested** (see paragraph 27.23) and including the effects of benefit formulas that give employees greater benefits for later years of service. This requires the entity to determine how much benefit is attributable to the current and prior periods on the basis of the plan's benefit formula and to make estimates (actuarial assumptions) about demographic variables (such as employee turnover and mortality) and financial variables (such as future increases in salaries and medical costs) that influence the cost of the benefit. The actuarial assumptions shall be unbiased (neither imprudent nor excessively conservative), mutually compatible, and selected to lead to the best estimate of the future cash flows that will arise under the plan.   **27.16**

Discounting

An entity shall measure its defined benefit obligation on a discounted present value basis. The entity shall determine the rate used to discount the future payments by reference to market yields at the reporting date on high quality corporate bonds. In countries where there is no deep market in such bonds, the entity shall use the market yields (at the reporting date) on government bonds. The currency and term of the   **27.17** corporate bonds or government bonds shall be consistent with the currency and estimated period of the future payments.

Actuarial valuation method

27.18　An entity shall use the **projected unit credit method** to determine its defined benefit obligations and the related current service cost and, when applicable, past service cost.

Plan introductions, changes, curtailments and settlements

27.19　If a defined benefit plan has been introduced or changed in the current period, the entity shall increase or decrease its defined benefit liability to reflect the change, and shall recognise the increase (decrease) as an expense (income) in measuring profit or loss. Conversely, if a plan has been curtailed (ie benefits or group of covered employees are reduced) or settled (the employer's obligation is completely discharged), the defined benefit obligation shall be decreased or eliminated, and the entity shall recognise the resulting gain or loss in profit or loss.

Defined benefit plan asset

27.20　If the defined benefit liability at the reporting date is less than the fair value of plan assets at that date, the plan has a surplus. An entity shall recognise a plan surplus as a defined benefit plan asset only to the extent that it is able to recover the surplus either through reduced contributions in the future or through refunds from the plan.

Cost of a defined benefit plan

27.21　An entity shall recognise the net change in its defined benefit liability during the period, other than a change attributable to benefits paid to employees during the period or due to contributions from the employer, as the cost of its defined benefit plans during the period. That cost is recognised in profit or loss, unless:

(a)　it is included in the cost of producing inventories in accordance with Section 12; or

(b)　it is included in the cost of property, plant and equipment in accordance with Section 16.

27.22　The net change in the defined benefit liability that is recognised as the cost of a defined benefit plan includes:

(a)　the change in the defined benefit liability arising from employee service rendered during the reporting period;

(b)　interest on the defined benefit obligation during the reporting period;

(c)　the returns on any plan assets and the net change in the fair value of recognised reimbursement rights (see paragraph 27.26) during the reporting period;

(d)　actuarial gains and losses arising in the reporting period;

(e)　increases or decreases in the defined benefit liability resulting from introducing a new plan or changing an existing plan in the reporting period (see paragraph 27.19); and

(f)　decreases in the defined benefit liability resulting from curtailing or settling an existing plan in the reporting period (see paragraph 27.19).

27.23　Employee service gives rise to an obligation under a defined benefit plan even if the benefits are conditional on future employment (in other words, they are not vested).

Employee service before the vesting date gives rise to a constructive obligation because, at each successive reporting date, the amount of future service that an employee will have to render before becoming entitled to the benefit is reduced. In measuring its defined benefit obligation, an entity considers the probability that some employees may not satisfy vesting requirements. Similarly, although some post-employment benefits, for example, post-employment medical benefits, become payable only if a specified event occurs when an employee is no longer employed, an obligation is created when the employee renders service that will provide entitlement to the benefit if the specified event occurs. The probability that the specified event will occur affects the measurement of the obligation, but does not determine whether the obligation exists.

If defined benefits are based on future salaries, an entity shall measure its defined benefit obligations on a basis that reflects estimated future salary increases.   **27.24**

If defined benefits are reduced for amounts that will be paid to employees under government-sponsored plans, an entity shall measure its defined benefit obligations on a basis that reflects the benefits payable under the government plans but only if: **27.25**

(a) those plans were enacted before the reporting date; or
(b) past history, or other reliable evidence, indicates that those state benefits will change in some predictable manner, for example, in line with future changes in general price levels or general salary levels.

Reimbursements

If an entity is virtually certain that another party will reimburse some or all of the expenditure required to settle a defined benefit obligation, the entity shall recognise its right to reimbursement as a separate asset. The entity shall measure the asset at fair value. In the income statement, the expense relating to a defined benefit plan may be presented net of the amount recognised for a reimbursement.   **27.26**

Other long-term employee benefits

Other long-term employee benefits include, for example: **27.27**

(a) long-term compensated absences such as long-service or sabbatical leave;
(b) jubilee or other long-service benefits;
(c) long-term disability benefits;
(d) profit-sharing and bonuses payable twelve months or more after the end of the period in which the employees render the related service; and
(e) deferred compensation paid twelve months or more after the end of the period in which it is earned.

An entity shall recognise a liability for other long-term employee benefits measured at the net total of the following amounts: **27.28**

(a) the present value of the benefit obligation at the reporting date, minus
(b) the fair value at the reporting date of plan assets (if any) out of which the obligations are to be settled directly.

An entity shall recognise the change in the liability in accordance with paragraph 27.21.

Termination benefits

27.29 An entity may be committed, by legislation, by contractual or other agreements with employees or their representatives or by a constructive obligation based on business practice, custom or a desire to act equitably, to make payments (or provide other benefits) to employees when it terminates their employment. Such payments are termination benefits.

Recognition

27.30 Because termination benefits do not provide an entity with future economic benefits, an entity shall recognise them as an expense in profit or loss immediately.

27.31 When an entity recognises termination benefits, the entity may also have to account for a curtailment of retirement benefits or other employee benefits.

27.32 An entity shall recognise termination benefits as a liability and an expense only when the entity is demonstrably committed either:

(a) to terminate the employment of an employee or group of employees before the normal retirement date; or

(b) to provide termination benefits as a result of an offer made in order to encourage voluntary redundancy.

27.33 An entity is demonstrably committed to a termination only when the entity has a detailed formal plan for the termination and is without realistic possibility of withdrawal from the plan.

Measurement

27.34 An entity shall measure termination benefits at the best estimate of the expenditure that would be required to settle the obligation at the reporting date. In the case of an offer made to encourage voluntary redundancy, the measurement of termination benefits shall be based on the number of employees expected to accept the offer.

27.35 When termination benefits are due more than twelve months after the end of the reporting period, they shall be measured at their discounted present value.

Disclosure

Disclosures about short-term employee benefits

27.36 This section does not require specific disclosures about short-term employee benefits.

Disclosures about defined contribution plans

27.37 An entity shall disclose the total cost of defined contribution plans for the period and their amounts (a) recognised in profit or loss as an expense and (b) included in the cost of an asset.

Disclosures about defined benefit plans

27.38 An entity shall disclose the following information about defined benefit plans:

(a)   a general description of the type of plan, including funding policy;

(b)   the entity's accounting policy for recognising actuarial gains and losses and the amount of actuarial gains and losses recognised during the period;

(c)   a reconciliation of opening and closing balances of the defined benefit liability showing separately benefits paid and all other changes;

(d)   an analysis of the defined benefit liability into amounts arising from plans that are wholly unfunded and amounts arising from plans that are wholly or partly funded;

(e)   a reconciliation of the opening and closing balances of the fair value of plan assets and of the opening and closing balances of any reimbursement right recognised as an asset, showing separately, if applicable:

    (i)   contributions by the employer;

    (ii)   contributions by plan participants;

    (iii) benefits paid; and

    (iv) other changes in plan assets.

(f)   the total cost relating to defined benefit plans recognised in profit or loss as an expense for the period, and the line item(s) in which they are included;

(g)   the total cost relating to defined benefit plans during the period that was:

    (i)   included in the cost of producing inventories in accordance with Section 12; or

    (ii)   included in the cost of property, plant and equipment in accordance with Section 16;

(h)   for each major category of plan assets, which shall include, but is not limited to, equity instruments, debt instruments, property, and all other assets, the percentage or amount that each major category constitutes of the fair value of the total plan assets;

(i)   the amounts included in the fair value of plan assets for:

    (i)   each category of the entity's own **financial instruments**; and

    (ii)   any property occupied by, or other assets used by, the entity;

(j)   the actual return on plan assets; and

(k)   the principal actuarial assumptions used, including, when applicable:

    (i)   the discount rates;

    (ii)   the expected rates of return on any plan assets for the periods presented in the financial statements;

    (iii) the expected rates of salary increases; and

    (iv) medical cost trend rates.

Disclosures about other long-term benefits

For each category of other long-term benefits that an entity provides to its employees, the entity shall disclose the nature of the benefit, the amount of its obligation and the funding status at the reporting date, and the amount of any actuarial gains and losses arising in the current period and its **accounting policy** for such actuarial gains and losses.   **27.39**

Disclosures about termination benefits

For each category of termination benefits that an entity provides to its employees, the entity shall disclose the nature of the benefit, its accounting policy, and the amount of its obligation and the funding status at the reporting date.   **27.40**

27.41   When there is uncertainty about the number of employees who will accept an offer of termination benefits, a contingent liability exists. Section 20 *Provisions and Contingencies* requires an entity to disclose information about its contingent liability unless the possibility of an outflow in settlement is remote.

Section 28
Income Taxes

For the purposes of this [draft] standard, **income taxes** include all domestic and foreign taxes that are based on **taxable profits**. Income taxes also include taxes, such as withholding taxes, that are payable by a **subsidiary, associate** or **joint venture** on distributions to the reporting entity. **28.1**

This section requires an entity to recognise the current and future tax consequences **28.2** of transactions and other events that have been recognised in the financial statements. Current tax liabilities and assets are recognised for **current tax** payable or current tax recoverable. **deferred tax liabilities** and **deferred tax assets** are recognised for the tax consequences of the future recovery or settlement of the entity's assets and liabilities at their current **carrying amounts**, with limited exceptions, and for unused tax losses and unused tax credits.

Tax basis

Tax basis is the measurement under applicable existing tax law of an asset, liability or **28.3** equity instrument. That asset, liability, or equity instrument may be recognised for both tax and financial reporting purposes, for tax purposes but not for financial reporting, or for financial reporting purposes but not for tax. Stated another way, the tax basis of an asset or liability is the amount that would be recognised if a balance sheet were created using tax law as the basis for accounting.

The following examples illustrate the concept of tax basis: **28.4**

(a)   A machine cost 100. For tax purposes, depreciation of 30 has already been deducted in the current and prior periods and the remaining cost will be deductible in future periods, either as depreciation or through a deduction on disposal. Revenue generated by using the machine is taxable, any gain on disposal of the machine will be taxable and any loss on disposal will be deductible for tax purposes. The tax basis of the machine is 70.

(b)   Interest receivable has a carrying amount of 100. The related interest revenue will be taxed on a cash basis. The tax basis of the interest receivable is nil.

(c)   Trade receivables have a carrying amount of 100. The related revenue has already been included in taxable profit (tax loss). The tax basis of the trade receivables is 100.

(d)   A loan receivable has a carrying amount of 100. The repayment of the loan will have no tax consequences. The tax basis of the loan is 100.

Temporary differences

Temporary differences are differences between the tax basis of an asset or liability and **28.5** its carrying amount in the financial statements that will result in a taxable or deductible amount when the carrying amount of the asset or liability is recovered or settled. Temporary differences may be either taxable or deductible:

(a)   **Taxable temporary differences** are temporary differences that will result in taxable amounts in determining taxable profit (tax loss) of future periods when the carrying amount of the asset or liability is recovered or settled.

(b)   **Deductible temporary differences** are temporary differences that will result in amounts that are deductible in determining taxable profit (tax loss) of future periods when the carrying amount of the asset or liability is recovered or settled.

Temporary differences that are timing differences

28.6 Some temporary differences arise when income or expense is included in accounting profit or loss in one period but is included in taxable profit in a different period. Such temporary differences are often described as **timing differences**.

Timing differences—examples

28.7 A timing difference results in a deferred tax asset when:

(a) an expenditure is deductible for tax purposes later than when it is recognised as an expense for financial reporting purposes. For example, in some jurisdictions:

    (i) pension or other employee benefit cost is recognised as an expense over the periods of employee service, but is deductible for tax purposes only in future periods when contributions or payments are made.

    (ii) warranty expense is recognised when the related sales are made, but is deductible for tax purposes only when paid.

    (iii) a tax loss cannot be offset against past or current period taxable profits, but can be carried forward to reduce future taxable profits.

    (iv) bad debts expense is recognised when the accounts receivable are estimated to be uncollectible, but is tax-deductible only when a customer enters formal bankruptcy proceedings.

(b) income is taxable earlier than when it is recognised for financial reporting purposes. For example, in some jurisdictions:

    (i) advance payments received from customers are taxed on a cash basis, but do not yet qualify for recognition as revenue.

    (ii) intragroup profits in inventories, unrealised at the group level, are reversed on consolidation.

    (iii) a gain is recognised for tax purposes on the sale of a **financial asset** carried at amortised cost, but the transaction does not qualify for recognition as a sale for financial reporting purposes.

28.8 A timing difference results in a deferred tax liability when:

(a) income is taxable later than when it is recognised for financial reporting purposes. For example, in some jurisdictions:

    (i) an increase in the fair value of an asset is recognised in profit or loss, but that increase is taxable only when the asset is sold.

    (ii) for accounting purposes revenue is recognised by reference to the stage of completion of a contract or transaction (sometimes referred to as the percentage of completion method), but for tax purposes revenue is taxable only when the contract or transaction is completed.

    (iii) the unremitted earnings of subsidiaries, associates and joint ventures are recognised in profit or loss but will be subject to further taxation only when remitted to the parent.

(b) an expense is deductible for tax purposes earlier than when it is recognised as an expense for financial reporting purposes. For example, in some jurisdictions:

    (i) an asset is depreciated more rapidly for tax purposes than for financial reporting purposes.

    (ii) borrowing costs or development costs are recognised in the cost of an asset but are tax-deductible when incurred.

Other temporary differences that are not timing differences

Some temporary differences are not timing differences. Such temporary differences   **28.9**
can arise:

(a)   when gains and losses are recognised outside accounting profit or loss in one
      period but are recognised in taxable profit in a different period.
(b)   on the initial recognition of assets and liabilities, either in a **business combi-
      nation** or outside a business combination.
(c)   because of changes in the tax basis of an asset or liability that do not affect
      taxable profit of the period.

Goodwill

If the carrying amount of goodwill arising in a business combination differs from its   **28.10**
tax basis, there is a temporary difference. A deferred tax asset arising from the initial
recognition of goodwill is recognised as part of the accounting for a business combination. Paragraph 28.18(c) provides an exception to the recognition of a deferred
tax liability arising from the initial recognition of goodwill.

Temporary differences in consolidated financial statements

In consolidated financial statements, there are two sources of temporary difference: **28.11**

(a)   differences between the carrying amounts of the individual assets and liabilities
      in the consolidated financial statements and their tax basis in the tax jurisdic-
      tion of the individual group entity. These temporary differences are sometimes
      described as 'inside basis differences'.
(b)   differences between the carrying amount of the investment of the parent or
      investor in its subsidiary, associate and joint venture and the tax basis of that
      investment in the tax jurisdiction of the investor. These temporary differences
      are often described as 'outside basis differences'.

In those jurisdictions in which a consolidated tax return is filed and taxes are assessed   **28.12**
using consolidated amounts, the tax bases are determined by reference to the consolidated amounts. In those jurisdictions in which taxes are assessed on each
individual entity in a group, the tax bases are determined by reference to each
individual entity's tax computations.

Recognition of current tax liabilities and current tax assets

An entity shall recognise a liability for unpaid current tax for current and prior   **28.13**
periods. If the amount already paid for current and prior periods exceeds the amount
due for those periods, the entity shall recognise the excess as an asset.

An entity shall recognise an asset for the benefit relating to a tax loss that can be   **28.14**
carried back to recover current tax of a previous period.

Recognition of deferred tax liabilities and deferred tax assets

Taxable temporary differences

An entity shall recognise a deferred tax liability for all taxable temporary differences,   **28.15**
except as specified in paragraph 28.18.

Deductible temporary differences, unused tax losses and unused tax credits

28.16   Subject to paragraph 28.18(a), an entity shall recognise a deferred tax asset for:

(a)   all deductible temporary differences, except as specified in paragraph 28.18(b).

(b)   the carryforward of unused tax losses and unused tax credits.

(c)   differences between:

(i)   amounts that an entity initially recognises as the cost or other carrying amount of an asset or liability, and

(ii)   the amounts relating to that asset or liability that are expected to be deductible or includible in taxable income in future periods.

Such differences can arise in business combinations or on the initial acquisition of individual assets or liabilities. For example, a deferred tax asset or liability is recognised when the amount allocated to an asset acquired in a business combination is its fair value at the acquisition date, but the future tax-deductibility is limited by law to the acquired entity's original cost basis.

Initial recognition of assets and liabilities

28.17   An entity shall apply the principles in paragraphs 28.15 and 28.16 at the time an asset or liability is initially recognised, whether acquired in a business combination or otherwise. The carrying amount of the asset or liability at initial recognition affects the amount of the deferred tax liability or deferred tax asset that is recognised. Consequently, the carrying amount of that asset or liability at initial recognition will equal the fair value that the asset or liability would have had if its tax basis and fair value were equal. Outside a business combination, an entity shall recognise, as an adjustment to the deferred tax balance, any difference between (a) the sum of the carrying amount of the asset or liability and the resulting deferred tax balance and (b) the amount paid or received.

Exceptions to the general principles for recognising deferred taxes

28.18   The following are exceptions to the general principles for recognition of deferred taxes in paragraph 28.15–28.17:

(a)   An entity shall recognise a deferred tax asset only to the extent that it is **probable** that there will be sufficient future taxable profit to enable recovery of the deferred tax asset.

(b)   An entity shall not recognise deferred tax expense (income) or a related deferred tax liability (asset) for temporary differences associated with unremitted earnings from foreign subsidiaries, branches and associates and joint ventures, unless it is probable that the temporary difference will reverse in the foreseeable future.

(c)   An entity shall not recognise a deferred tax liability for temporary differences associated with the initial recognition of goodwill..

Recognition directly in equity

28.19   An entity shall recognise changes in a current or deferred tax liability or a current or deferred tax asset directly in equity, rather than in profit or loss, if the income or expense that gave rise to the temporary difference was recognised directly in equity.

Measurement

Measurement of current tax assets and liabilities

An entity shall measure current tax liabilities (assets) for the current and prior **28.20** periods, and related **tax expense (income)**, at the amount expected to be paid to (recovered from) the taxation authorities, using the tax rates (and tax laws) that have been enacted or **substantively enacted** by the **reporting date**.

Measurement of deferred tax liabilities (assets)

An entity shall measure deferred tax assets and liabilities, and related tax expense **28.21** (income), at the tax rates that are expected to apply to the period when the asset is realised or the liability is settled, based on tax rates (and tax laws) that have been enacted or substantively enacted by the reporting date.

Discounting

Although deferred tax assets and deferred tax liabilities give rise to future cash flows, **28.22** an entity shall not discount them to reflect the time value of money.

Which tax rate to use

When different tax rates apply to different levels of taxable income, an entity shall **28.23** measure deferred tax expense (income) and related deferred tax liabilities (assets) using the average enacted or substantively enacted rates that it expects to be applicable to the taxable profit (tax loss) of the periods in which it expects the temporary differences to reverse.

The measurement of deferred tax expense (income) and related deferred tax liabilities **28.24** (assets) shall reflect the tax consequences that would follow from the manner in which the entity expects at the reporting date to recover or settle the carrying amounts of its assets and liabilities. For example, if the temporary difference arises from an item of income that is expected to be taxable as a capital gain in a future period, the deferred tax expense is measured using the capital gain tax rate.

In some jurisdictions, income taxes are payable at a higher or lower rate if part or all **28.25** of the profit or retained earnings is paid out as a dividend to shareholders of the entity. In other jurisdictions, income taxes may be refundable or payable if part or all of the profit or retained earnings is paid out as a dividend to shareholders of the entity. In those circumstances, an entity shall measure current and deferred taxes at the tax rate applicable to undistributed profits until the entity recognises a liability to pay a dividend. When the entity recognises a liability to pay a dividend, it shall recognise the resulting current or deferred tax liability (asset), and the related tax expense (income).

Review of deferred tax assets

An entity shall review the carrying amount of a deferred tax asset at each reporting **28.26** date. An entity shall reduce the carrying amount of a deferred tax asset and increase tax expense to the extent that it is impaired, ie it is no longer probable that sufficient taxable profit will be available to allow recovery of the deferred tax asset. The entity shall reverse that reduction to the extent that it subsequently becomes probable that sufficient taxable profit will be available.

Withholding tax on dividends

28.27   When an entity pays dividends to its shareholders, it may be required to pay a portion of the dividends to taxation authorities on behalf of shareholders. Such an amount paid or payable to taxation authorities is recognised in equity as a part of the dividends.

Disclosure

28.28   An entity shall disclose separately the major components of tax expense (income). Such components of tax expense (income) may include:

(a)   current tax expense (income);
(b)   any adjustments recognised in the period for current tax of prior periods;
(c)   the amount of deferred tax expense (income) relating to the origination and reversal of temporary differences;
(d)   the amount of deferred tax expense (income) relating to changes in tax rates or the imposition of new taxes;
(e)   the amount of the benefit arising from a previously unrecognised tax losses, tax credits or temporary differences of a prior period that is used to reduce current tax expense; and
(f)   deferred tax expense (or income) arising from the impairment, or reversal of a previous impairment, of a deferred tax asset (see paragraph 28.26).

28.29   An entity shall disclose the following separately:

(a)   the aggregate current and deferred tax relating to items that are recognised directly in equity;
(b)   a numerical reconciliation between tax expense (income) as recognised and tax expense (income) that would be expected by multiplying profit by the applicable tax rate(s), with each significant difference disclosed separately;
(c)   an explanation of changes in the applicable tax rate(s) compared with the previous **reporting period**;
(d)   the amount (and expiry date, if any) of temporary differences, unused tax losses, and unused tax credits for which no deferred tax asset is recognised; and
(e)   the aggregate amount of temporary differences associated with investments in foreign subsidiaries, branches and associates and joint ventures, for which deferred tax liabilities have not been recognised (see paragraph 28.18(b)).
(f)   the aggregate amount of temporary differences associated with the initial recognition of goodwill for which deferred tax liabilities have not been recognised (see paragraph 28.18(c)).

28.30   In the circumstances described in paragraph 28.25, an entity shall disclose the nature of the potential income tax consequences that would result from the payment of dividends to its shareholders. In addition, the entity shall disclose the amounts of the potential income tax consequences, if practicably determinable, and whether there are any potential income tax consequences not practicably determinable.

Section 29
Financial Reporting in Hyperinflationary Economies

Hyperinflation is indicated by characteristics of the economic environment of a country. An economy is hyperinflationary if the cumulative inflation rate over three years is approaching, or exceeds, 100 per cent.

29.1

An entity whose functional currency is the currency of a hyperinflationary economy shall apply IAS 29 *Financial Reporting in Hyperinflationary Economies* in preparing and presenting its financial statements in accordance with this [draft] standard.

29.2

Briefly summarised, IAS 29 requires that the financial statements of an entity whose functional currency is the currency of a hyperinflationary economy should be stated in terms of the presentation currency as of the end of the **reporting period**. The corresponding figures for the previous period required by paragraph 3.12 and any information in respect of earlier periods shall also be stated in terms of the measuring unit current at the end of the reporting period. The gain or loss on the net monetary position shall be included in profit or loss and separately disclosed.

29.3

Section 30
Foreign Currency Translation

30.1 An entity may conduct foreign activities in two ways. It may have transactions in foreign currencies or it may have foreign operations. In addition, an entity may present its financial statements in a foreign currency. This section prescribes how to include foreign currency transactions and foreign operations in the financial statements of an entity and how to translate financial statements into a **presentation currency**. Accounting for **financial instruments** denominated in a foreign currency and hedge accounting of foreign currency items is dealt with in Section 11 *Financial Instruments*.

Functional currency

30.2 Each entity shall identify its **functional currency**. Functional currency is the currency of the primary economic environment in which the entity operates.

30.3 The primary economic environment in which an entity operates is normally the one in which it primarily generates and expends cash. Therefore, the following are the most important factors an entity considers in determining its functional currency:

(a) the currency:

    (i) that mainly influences sales prices for goods and services (this will often be the currency in which sales prices for its goods and services are denominated and settled); and

    (ii) of the country whose competitive forces and regulations mainly determine the sales prices of its goods and services.

(b) the currency that mainly influences labour, material and other costs of providing goods or services (this will often be the currency in which such costs are denominated and settled).

30.4 The following factors may also provide evidence of an entity's functional currency:

(a) the currency in which funds from financing activities (ie issuing debt and equity instruments) are generated.

(b) the currency in which receipts from operating activities are usually retained.

30.5 The following additional factors are considered in determining the functional currency of a foreign operation, and whether its functional currency is the same as that of the reporting entity (the reporting entity, in this context, being the entity that has the foreign operation as its subsidiary, branch, associate or joint venture):

(a) whether the activities of the foreign operation are carried out as an extension of the reporting entity, rather than being carried out with a significant degree of autonomy. An example of the former is when the foreign operation only sells goods imported from the reporting entity and remits the proceeds to it. An example of the latter is when the operation accumulates cash and other monetary items, incurs expenses, generates income and arranges borrowings, all substantially in its local currency.

(b) whether transactions with the reporting entity are a high or a low proportion of the foreign operation's activities.

(c) whether cash flows from the activities of the foreign operation directly affect the cash flows of the reporting entity and are readily available for remittance to it.

(d)   whether cash flows from the activities of the foreign operation are sufficient to service existing and normally expected debt obligations without funds being made available by the reporting entity.

Reporting foreign currency transactions in the functional currency

Initial recognition

A foreign currency transaction is a transaction that is denominated or requires settlement in a foreign currency, including transactions arising when an entity: **30.6**

(a)   buys or sells goods or services whose price is denominated in a foreign currency;
(b)   borrows or lends funds when the amounts payable or receivable are denominated in a foreign currency; or
(c)   otherwise acquires or disposes of assets, or incurs or settles liabilities, denominated in a foreign currency.

An entity shall record a foreign currency transaction, on initial recognition in the functional currency, by applying to the foreign currency amount the spot exchange rate between the functional currency and the foreign currency at the date of the transaction.   **30.7**

The date of a transaction is the date on which the transaction first qualifies for recognition in accordance with this [draft] standard. For practical reasons, a rate that approximates the actual rate at the date of the transaction is often used, for example, an average rate for a week or a month might be used for all transactions in each foreign currency occurring during that period. However, if exchange rates fluctuate significantly, the use of the average rate for a period is inappropriate.   **30.8**

Reporting at the end of the subsequent reporting periods

At the end of each **reporting period**, an entity shall: **30.9**

(a)   translate foreign currency monetary items using the closing rate;
(b)   translate non-monetary items that are measured in terms of historical cost in a foreign currency using the exchange rate at the date of the transaction; and
(c)   translate non-monetary items that are measured at fair value in a foreign currency using the exchange rates at the date when the fair value was determined.

An entity shall recognise, in profit or loss in the period in which they arise, exchange differences arising on the settlement of monetary items or on translating monetary items at rates different from those at which they were translated on initial recognition during the period or in previous financial statements, except as described in paragraph 30.13.   **30.10**

When a gain or loss on a non-monetary item is recognised directly in equity, an entity shall recognise any exchange component of that gain or loss directly in equity. Conversely, when a gain or loss on a non-monetary item is recognised in profit or loss, an entity shall recognise any exchange component of that gain or loss in profit or loss.   **30.11**

Net investment in a foreign operation

30.12   An entity may have a monetary item that is receivable from or payable to a foreign operation. An item for which settlement is neither planned nor likely to occur in the foreseeable future is, in substance, a part of the entity's net investment in that foreign operation, and is accounted for in accordance with paragraph 30.13. Such monetary items may include long-term receivables or loans. They do not include trade receivables or trade payables.

30.13   Exchange differences arising on a monetary item that forms part of a reporting entity's net investment in a foreign operation shall be recognised in profit or loss in the separate financial statements of the reporting entity or the individual financial statements of the foreign operation, as appropriate. In the financial statements that include the foreign operation and the reporting entity (eg consolidated financial statements when the foreign operation is a subsidiary), such exchange differences shall be recognised initially in a separate component of equity and recognised in profit or loss on disposal of the net investment in accordance with paragraph 30.24.

Change in functional currency

30.14   When there is a change in an entity's functional currency, the entity shall apply the translation procedures applicable to the new functional currency prospectively from the date of the change.

30.15   As noted in paragraph 30.2, the functional currency of an entity reflects the underlying transactions, events and conditions that are relevant to the entity. Accordingly, once the functional currency is determined, it can be changed only if there is a change to those underlying transactions, events and conditions. For example, a change in the currency that mainly influences the sales prices of goods and services may lead to a change in an entity's functional currency.

30.16   The effect of a change in functional currency is accounted for prospectively. In other words, an entity translates all items into the new functional currency using the exchange rate at the date of the change. The resulting translated amounts for non-monetary items are treated as their historical cost. Exchange differences arising from the translation of a foreign operation previously classified in equity in accordance with paragraph 30.13 are not recognised in profit or loss until the disposal of the operation.

Use of a presentation currency other than the functional currency

Translation to the presentation currency

30.17   An entity may present its financial statements in any currency (or currencies). If the presentation currency differs from the entity's functional currency, the entity shall translate its results and **financial position** into the presentation currency. For example, when a group contains individual entities with different functional currencies, the results and financial position of each entity are expressed in a common currency so that consolidated financial statements may be presented.

30.18   An entity whose functional currency is not the currency of a hyperinflationary economy shall translate its results and financial position into a different presentation currency using the following procedures:

(a)   assets and liabilities for each balance sheet presented (ie including comparatives) shall be translated at the closing rate at the date of that balance sheet;

(b)   income and expenses for each income statement (ie including comparatives) shall be translated at exchange rates at the dates of the transactions; and

(c)   all resulting exchange differences shall be recognised as a separate component of equity.

For practical reasons, an entity may use a rate that approximates the exchange rates at the dates of the transactions, for example an average rate for the period, to translate income and expense items. However, if exchange rates fluctuate significantly, the use of the average rate for a period is inappropriate.   **30.19**

The exchange differences referred to in paragraph 30.18(c) result from: **30.20**

(a)   translating income and expenses at the exchange rates at the dates of the transactions and assets and liabilities at the closing rate. Such exchange differences arise both on income and expense items recognised in profit or loss and on those recognised directly in equity.

(b)   translating the opening net assets at a closing rate that differs from the previous closing rate.

When the exchange differences relate to a foreign operation that is consolidated but not wholly-owned, accumulated exchange differences arising from translation and attributable to **minority interests** are allocated to, and recognised as part of, minority interest in the consolidated balance sheet.

An entity whose functional currency is the currency of a hyperinflationary economy shall translate its results and financial position into a different presentation currency using the procedures specified in IAS 21 paragraphs 42 and 43.   **30.21**

Translation of a foreign operation into the investor's presentation currency

In incorporating the results and financial position of a foreign operation with those of the reporting entity, the entity shall follow normal consolidation procedures, such as the elimination of intragroup balances and intragroup transactions of a subsidiary (see Section 9 *Consolidated and Separate Financial Statements* and Section 14 *Investments in Joint Ventures*). However, an intragroup monetary asset (or liability), whether short-term or long-term, cannot be eliminated against the corresponding intragroup liability (or asset) without showing the results of currency fluctuations in the consolidated financial statements. This is because the monetary item represents a commitment to convert one currency into another and exposes the reporting entity to a gain or loss through currency fluctuations. Accordingly, in the consolidated financial statements of the reporting entity, an entity continues to recognise such an exchange difference in profit or loss or, if it arises from the circumstances described in paragraph 30.13, the entity shall classify it as equity until the disposal of the foreign operation.   **30.22**

Any goodwill arising on the acquisition of a foreign operation and any fair value adjustments to the **carrying amounts** of assets and liabilities arising on the acquisition of that foreign operation shall be treated as assets and liabilities of the foreign operation. Thus, they shall be expressed in the functional currency of the foreign operation and shall be translated at the closing rate in accordance with paragraph 30.18.   **30.23**

Disposal of a foreign operation

30.24   On the disposal of a foreign operation, the cumulative amount of the exchange differences deferred in the separate component of equity relating to that foreign operation shall be recognised in profit or loss when the gain or loss on disposal is recognised.

Disclosure

30.25   In paragraphs 30.27 and 30.29, references to 'functional currency' apply, in the case of a group, to the functional currency of the parent.

30.26   An entity shall disclose:

(a)   the amount of exchange differences recognised in profit or loss except for those arising on financial instruments measured at fair value through profit or loss in accordance with Section 11; and

(b)   net exchange differences classified in a separate component of equity, and a reconciliation of the amount of such exchange differences at the beginning and end of the period.

30.27   An entity shall disclose the currency in which the financial statements are presented. When the presentation currency is different from the functional currency, an entity shall state that fact and shall disclose the functional currency and the reason for using a different presentation currency.

30.28   When there is a change in the functional currency of either the reporting entity or a significant foreign operation, the entity shall disclose that fact and the reason for the change in functional currency.

30.29   When an entity displays its financial statements or other financial information in a currency that is different from either its functional currency or its presentation currency (for example, a 'convenience translation' of all amounts at closing rate), it shall:

(a)   clearly identify the information as supplementary information to distinguish it from the information that complies with this [draft] standard;

(b)   disclose the currency in which the supplementary information is displayed; and

(c)   disclose the entity's functional currency and the method of translation used to determine the supplementary information.

Section 31
Segment Reporting

An entity using this [draft] standard is not required to present information about **operating segments**. An entity that chooses to disclose segment information in financial statements described as conforming to the *IFRS for SMEs* shall comply fully with the requirements of IFRS 8 *Operating Segments*. If an entity discloses information about segments that does not comply with IFRS 8, it shall not describe the information as segment information.

31.1

Section 32
Events after the End of the Reporting Period

32.1   Events after the end of the **reporting period** are those events, favourable and unfavourable, that occur between the end of the reporting period and the date when the financial statements are authorised for issue. There are two types of events:

(a)   those that provide evidence of conditions that existed at the end of the reporting period (adjusting events after the end of the reporting period); and

(b)   those that are indicative of conditions that arose after the end of the reporting period (non-adjusting events after the end of the reporting period).

32.2   Events after the end of the reporting period include all events up to the date when the financial statements are authorised for issue, even if those events occur after the public announcement of profit or of other selected financial information.

Recognition and measurement

Adjusting events after the end of the reporting period

32.3   An entity shall adjust the amounts recognised in its financial statements, including related disclosures, to reflect adjusting events after the end of the reporting period.

32.4   The following are examples of adjusting events after the end of the reporting period that require an entity to adjust the amounts recognised in its financial statements, or to recognise items that were not previously recognised:

(a)   the settlement after the end of the reporting period of a court case that confirms that the entity had a present obligation at the end of the reporting period. The entity adjusts any previously recognised **provision** related to this court case in accordance with Section 20 *Provisions and Contingencies* or recognises a new provision. The entity does not merely disclose a contingent liability because the settlement provides additional evidence that would be considered in accordance with Section 20.

(b)   the receipt of information after the end of the reporting period indicating that an asset was impaired at the end of the reporting period, or that the amount of a previously recognised impairment loss for that asset needs to be adjusted. For example:

  (i)   the bankruptcy of a customer that occurs after the end of the reporting period usually confirms that a loss existed at the end of the reporting period on a trade receivable and that the entity needs to adjust the **carrying amount** of the trade receivable; and

  (ii)   the sale of inventories after the end of the reporting period may give evidence about their selling price at the end of the reporting period.

(c)   the determination after the end of the reporting period of the cost of assets purchased, or the proceeds from assets sold, before the end of the reporting period.

(d)   the determination after the end of the reporting period of the amount of profit-sharing or bonus payments, if the entity had a legal or **constructive obligation** at the end of the reporting period to make such payments as a result of events before that date (see Section 27 *Employee Benefits*).

(e)   the discovery of fraud or **errors** that show that the financial statements are incorrect.

Non-adjusting events after the end of the reporting period

An entity shall not adjust the amounts recognised in its financial statements to reflect non-adjusting events after the end of the reporting period. **32.5**

An example of a non-adjusting event after the end of the reporting period is a decline **32.6** in market value of investments between the end of the reporting period and the date when the financial statements are authorised for issue. The decline in market value does not normally relate to the condition of the investments at the end of the reporting period, but reflects circumstances that have arisen subsequently. Therefore, an entity does not adjust the amounts recognised in its financial statements for the investments. Similarly, the entity does not update the amounts disclosed for the investments as at the end of the reporting period, although it may need to give additional disclosure in accordance with paragraph 32.9.

Dividends

If an entity declares dividends to holders of equity instruments after the end of the **32.7** reporting period, the entity shall not recognise those dividends as a liability at the end of the reporting period.

Disclosure

Date of authorisation for issue

An entity shall disclose the date when the financial statements were authorised for **32.8** issue and who gave that authorisation. If the entity's owners or others have the power to amend the financial statements after issue, the entity shall disclose that fact.

Non-adjusting events after the end of the reporting period

An entity shall disclose the following for each category of non-adjusting event after **32.9** the end of the reporting period:

(a)   the nature of the event; and
(b)   an estimate of its financial effect, or a statement that such an estimate cannot be made.

The following are examples of non-adjusting events after the end of the reporting **32.10** period that would generally result in disclosure:

(a)   a major business combination (Section 18 *Business Combinations* requires specific disclosures in such cases) or disposing of a major subsidiary.
(b)   announcing a plan to discontinue an operation.
(c)   major purchases of assets, classification of assets as held for sale in accordance with Section 16 *Property, Plant and Equipment*, other disposals of assets, or expropriation of major assets by government.
(d)   the destruction of a major production plant by a fire.
(e)   announcing, or commencing the implementation of, a major restructuring (see Section 20).
(f)   major ordinary share transactions and potential ordinary share transactions.
(g)   abnormally large changes in asset prices or foreign exchange rates.
(h)   changes in tax rates or tax laws enacted or announced that have a significant effect on current and deferred tax assets and liabilities (see Section 28 *Income Taxes*).

(i)   entering into significant commitments or contingent liabilities, for example, by issuing significant guarantees.

(j)   commencing major litigation arising solely out of events that occurred after the end of the reporting period.

Section 33
Related Party Disclosures

This section requires an entity to include in its **financial statements** the disclosures necessary to draw attention to the possibility that its **financial position** and profit or loss have been affected by the existence of **related parties** and by transactions and outstanding balances with such parties. **33.1**

In considering each possible related party relationship, an entity shall assess the substance of the relationship and not merely the legal form. **33.2**

In the context of this [draft] standard, the following are not necessarily related parties: **33.3**

(a) two entities simply because they have a director or other member of key management personnel in common, notwithstanding (d) and (f) in the definition of 'related party'.

(b) two venturers simply because they share **joint control** over a **joint venture**.

(c) Any of the following simply by virtue of their normal dealings with an entity (even though they may affect the freedom of action of an entity or participate in its decision making process):

    (i) providers of finance,

    (ii) trade unions,

    (iii) public utilities, and

    (iv) government departments and agencies,

(d) a customer, supplier, franchisor, distributor or general agent with whom an entity transacts a significant volume of business, merely by virtue of the resulting economic dependence.

Disclosure

Disclosure of relationships

Relationships between parents and subsidiaries shall be disclosed irrespective of whether there have been transactions between those related parties. An entity shall disclose the name of the entity's parent and, if different, the ultimate controlling party. If neither the entity's parent nor the ultimate controlling party produces financial statements available for public use, the name of the next most senior parent that does so (if any) shall also be disclosed. **33.4**

Disclosure of key management personnel compensation

Key management personnel are those persons having authority and responsibility for planning, directing and controlling the activities of the entity, directly or indirectly, including any director (whether executive or otherwise) of that entity. Compensation includes all employee benefits (as defined in Section 27 *Employee Benefits*) including those in the form of share-based payment (see Section 25 *Share-based Payment*). Employee benefits include all forms of consideration paid, payable or provided by the entity, or on behalf of the entity (for example, by its parent or by a shareholder), in exchange for services rendered to the entity. It also includes such consideration paid on behalf of a parent of the entity in respect of the entity. **33.5**

An entity shall disclose key management personnel compensation in total and for each of the following categories: **33.6**

    (a)   short-term employee benefits;
    (b)   post-employment benefits;
    (c)   other long-term benefits;
    (d)   termination benefits; and
    (e)   share-based payment.

Disclosure of related party transactions

33.7   A **related party transaction** is a transfer of resources, services or obligations between related parties, regardless of whether a price is charged. Examples of related party transactions that are common to SMEs include, but are not limited to:

    (a)   transactions between an entity and its principal owner(s).
    (b)   transactions between an entity and another entity where both entities are under the common control of a single entity or individual.
    (c)   transactions in which an entity or individual that controls the reporting entity incurs expenses directly that otherwise would have been borne by the reporting entity.

33.8   If there have been transactions between related parties, an entity shall disclose the nature of the related party relationship as well as information about the transactions and outstanding balances necessary for an understanding of the potential effect of the relationship on the financial statements. These disclosure requirements are in addition to the requirements in paragraph 33.6 to disclose key management personnel compensation. At a minimum, disclosures shall include:

    (a)   the amount of the transactions;
    (b)   the amount of outstanding balances and:

        (i)   their terms and conditions, including whether they are secured, and the nature of the consideration to be provided in settlement; and
        (ii)   details of any guarantees given or received;

    (c)   provisions for uncollectible receivables related to the amount of outstanding balances; and
    (d)   the expense recognised during the period in respect of bad or doubtful debts due from related parties.

33.9   An entity shall make the disclosures required by paragraph 33.8 separately for each of the following categories:

    (a)   the parent;
    (b)   entities with joint control or significant influence over the entity;
    (c)   subsidiaries;
    (d)   associates;
    (e)   joint ventures in which the entity is a venturer;
    (f)   key management personnel of the entity or its parent (in the aggregate); and
    (g)   other related parties.

33.10   The following are examples of transactions that are disclosed if they are with a related party:

    (a)   purchases or sales of goods (finished or unfinished);
    (b)   purchases or sales of property and other assets;
    (c)   rendering or receiving of services;
    (d)   leases;
    (e)   transfers of research and development;
    (f)   transfers under licence agreements;

(g) transfers under finance arrangements (including loans and equity contributions in cash or in kind);
(h) provision of guarantees or collateral;
(i) settlement of liabilities on behalf of the entity or by the entity on behalf of another party; and
(j) participation by a parent or subsidiary in a defined benefit plan that shares risks between group entities.

An entity shall not state that related party transactions were made on terms equivalent to those that prevail in arm's length transactions unless such terms can be substantiated.   **33.11**

An entity may disclose items of a similar nature in the aggregate except when separate disclosure is necessary for an understanding of the effects of related party transactions on the financial statements of the entity.   **33.12**

Section 34
Earnings per Share

34.1   An entity using this [draft] standard is not required to present amounts of earnings per share. However, if the entity discloses earnings per share, it shall calculate and disclose earnings per share in accordance with IAS 33 *Earnings per Share*.

Section 35
Specialised Industries

Agriculture

An entity using this [draft] standard that is engaged in **agricultural activity** shall determine, for each of its **biological assets**, whether the **fair value** of that biological asset is readily determinable without undue cost or effort: **35.1**

(a) The entity shall apply the fair value model in paragraphs 10–29 of IAS 41 *Agriculture* to account for those biological assets whose fair value is readily determinable without undue cost or effort, and the entity shall make all related disclosures required by IAS 41.

(b) The entity shall measure at cost less any accumulated **depreciation** and any accumulated **impairment** losses those biological assets whose fair value is not readily determinable without undue cost or effort. The entity shall disclose, for such biological asset(s):

    (i) a description of the biological assets;

    (ii) an explanation of why fair value cannot be measured reliably;

    (iii) if possible, the range of estimates within which fair value is highly likely to lie;

    (iv) the depreciation method used;

    (v) the useful lives or the depreciation rates used; and

    (vi) the gross **carrying amount** and the accumulated depreciation (aggregated with accumulated impairment losses) at the beginning and end of the period.

The entity shall measure **agricultural produce** harvested from its biological assets at fair value less estimated costs to sell at the point of harvest. Such measurement is the cost at that date when applying Section 12 *Inventories* or other sections of this [draft] standard.

Extractive industries

An entity using this [draft] standard that is engaged in the exploration for, evaluation or extraction of mineral resources shall recognise exploration expenditure as an expense in the period in which it is incurred. In accounting for expenditure on the acquisition or development of tangible or intangible assets for use in extractive activities, the entity should apply Section 16 *Property, Plant and Equipment* and Section 17 *Intangible Assets other than Goodwill*, respectively. When an entity has an obligation to dismantle or remove an item, or to restore the site, such obligations and costs are accounted for in accordance with Section 16 and Section 20 *Provisions and Contingencies*. **35.2**

Insurance

Because an insurer holds assets in a fiduciary capacity for a broad group of outsiders, it has public accountability and, therefore, is not included within SMEs as defined in paragraph 1.1. This [draft] standard is not intended for, and should not be used by, insurers. **35.3**

Section 36
Discontinued Operations and Assets Held for Sale

Discontinued operations

36.1   A **discontinued operation** is a **component of an entity** that either has been disposed of, or is classified as **held for sale**, and

(a)   represents a separate major line of business or geographical area of operations;

(b)   is part of a single co-ordinated plan to dispose of a separate major line of business or geographical area of operations; or

(c)   is a subsidiary acquired exclusively with a view to resale.

Presentation and disclosure

36.2   An entity shall disclose:

(a)   a single amount on the face of the income statement comprising the total of:

   (i)   the post-tax profit or loss of discontinued operations; and

   (ii)   the post-tax gain or loss recognised on the measurement to fair value less costs to sell or on the disposal of the assets or group(s) of assets and liabilities constituting the discontinued operation.

(b)   an analysis of the single amount in (a) into:

   (i)   the revenue, expenses, pre-tax profit or loss and income tax expense of discontinued operations;

   (ii)   the gain or loss recognised on the measurement to fair value less costs to sell or on the disposal of the assets or group(s) of assets constituting the discontinued operation and the related income tax expense.

The analysis may be presented in the notes or on the face of the income statement. If it is presented on the face of the income statement it shall be presented in a section identified as relating to discontinued operations, ie separately from continuing operations.

(c)   the net cash flows attributable to the operating, investing and financing activities of discontinued operations. These disclosures may be presented either in the notes or on the face of the **financial statements**.

36.3   Unless **impracticable**, an entity shall restate the disclosures in the preceding paragraph for prior periods presented in the financial statements so that the disclosures relate to all operations that have been discontinued by the end of the **reporting period** for the latest period presented.

36.4   If an entity ceases to classify a component of an entity as held for sale, the entity shall reclassify the results of operations of the component previously presented in discontinued operations and shall include them in income from continuing operations for all periods presented. The amounts for prior periods shall be described as having been restated.

Non-current assets held for sale

36.5   An entity shall classify non-current assets (including property, plant and equipment, intangibles, and investments in subsidiaries, associates and joint ventures) as held for sale if its **carrying amount** will be recovered principally through a sale transaction rather than through continuing use. For this to be the case, the asset (or **disposal group**) must be available for immediate sale in its present condition subject only to terms that are usual and customary for sales of such assets, its sale must be highly

probable, and the entity must expect to complete the sale within one year from the date of classification as held for sale.

An entity shall measure a non-current asset (or disposal group) classified as held for sale at the lower of its carrying amount and fair value less costs to sell. **36.6**

An entity shall not depreciate (or amortise) a non-current asset while it is classified as held for sale or while it is part of a disposal group classified as held for sale. Interest and other expenses attributable to the liabilities of a disposal group classified as held for sale shall continue to be recognised. **36.7**

Disclosure

An entity shall disclose the following information in the period in which non-current assets have been either classified as held for sale or sold: **36.8**

(a) a description of the asset or disposal group;
(b) a description of the facts and circumstances of the sale, or leading to the expected disposal, and the expected manner and timing of that disposal; and
(c) the gain or loss recognised, if not separately presented on the face of the income statement.

Section 37
Interim Financial Reporting

37.1 An entity that issues an **interim financial report** that is described as complying with this [draft] standard shall apply either IAS 34 *Interim Financial Reporting* or all of the requirements of this [draft] standard, except as provided in paragraph 37.2.

37.2 If an entity does not routinely prepare interim financial statements, but is required to do so on a one-time basis (for instance, in connection with a **business combination**), the entity may use its prior annual financial statements as its comparative prior period information required by IAS 34 or by paragraph 3.12, if it is **impracticable** to prepare financial statements for the comparable prior interim period.

Section 38
Transition to the IFRS for SMEs

This section applies to a **first-time adopter of the *IFRS for SMEs***, regardless of whether its previous accounting framework was full **International Financial Reporting Standards (IFRSs)** or another set of generally accepted accounting principles (GAAP). A first-time adopter of the *IFRS for SMEs* shall apply this section in its first **financial statements** that conform to this [draft] standard. | 38.1

An entity's first financial statements that conform to this [draft] standard are the first annual financial statements in which the entity makes an explicit and unreserved statement in those financial statements of compliance with the *IFRS for SMEs*. Financial statements prepared in accordance with this [draft] standard are an entity's first such financial statements if, for example, the entity: | 38.2

(a) did not present financial statements for previous periods;
(b) presented its most recent previous financial statements under national requirements that are not consistent with this [draft] standard in all respects; or
(c) presented its most recent previous financial statements in conformity with International Financial Reporting Standards (full IFRSs).

Paragraph 3.15 of this [draft] standard defines a complete set of financial statements. | 38.3

Paragraph 3.12 of this [draft] standard requires a complete set of financial statements to disclose comparative information in respect of the previous comparable period for all monetary amounts reported in the financial statements, as well as specified comparative narrative and descriptive information. An entity may present comparative information in respect of more than one comparable prior period. Therefore, the date of an entity's transition to this [draft] standard is the beginning of the earliest period for which the entity presents full comparative information in accordance with this [draft] standard in its first financial statements that conform to this [draft] standard. | 38.4

Except as provided in paragraphs 38.7–38.9, an entity shall, in its opening balance sheet as of its date of transition to this [draft] standard (ie beginning of the earliest period presented): | 38.5

(a) recognise all assets and liabilities whose recognition is required by the *IFRS for SMEs*;
(b) not recognise items as assets or liabilities if this [draft] standard does not permit such recognition;
(c) reclassify items that it recognised under its previous financial reporting framework as one type of asset, liability or component of equity, but are a different type of asset, liability or component of equity under this [draft] standard; and
(d) apply this [draft] standard in measuring all recognised assets and liabilities.

The **accounting policies** that an entity uses in its opening balance sheet under this [draft] standard may differ from those that it used for the same date using its previous financial reporting framework. The resulting adjustments arise from transactions, other events or conditions before the date of transition to this [draft] standard. Therefore, an entity shall recognise those adjustments directly in retained earnings (or, if appropriate, another category of equity) at the date of transition to this [draft] standard. | 38.6

38.7 On first-time adoption of this [draft] standard, an entity shall not change the accounting that it followed under its previous financial reporting framework for any of the following transactions:

    (a) **derecognition** of financial assets and financial liabilities;
    (b) hedge accounting;
    (c) estimates; and
    (d) assets classified as **held for sale** and **discontinued operations**.

38.8 An entity may use one or more of the following exemptions in preparing its first financial statements that conform to this [draft] standard:

    (a) *Business combinations.* A first-time adopter may elect not to apply Section 18 *Business Combinations and Goodwill* to business combinations that were effected before the date of transition to this [draft] standard. However, if a first-time adopter restates any business combination to comply with Section 18, it shall restate all later business combinations.

    (b) *Fair value or revaluation as deemed cost.* A first-time adopter may use a previous GAAP revaluation of an item of property, plant and equipment at, or before, the date of transition to this [draft] standard as its deemed cost as of that date.

    (c) *Cumulative translation differences.* Section 30 *Foreign Currency Translation* requires an entity to classify some translation differences as a separate component of equity and to recognise those differences in profit or loss on disposal. A first-time adopter may elect not to recognise any cumulative translation differences in equity on the date of transition to this [draft] standard.

    (d) *Compound financial instruments.* Paragraph 21.7 requires an entity to split a compound financial instrument into its liability and equity components upon issue. A first-time adopter need not separate those two components if the liability component is not outstanding at the date of transition to this [draft] standard.

    (e) *Share-based payment transactions.* A first-time adopter is encouraged, but not required, to apply Section 25 *Share-based Payment* to equity instruments that were granted before the date of transition to this [draft] standard.

    (f) *Deferred income taxes.* A first-time adopter is not required to recognise **deferred tax assets or deferred tax liabilities** relating to differences between the **tax basis** and the **carrying amount** of any assets or liabilities for which recognition of those deferred tax assets or liabilities would involve undue cost or effort.

38.9 If it is **impracticable** for an entity to restate the opening balance sheet at the date of transition in accordance with this [draft] standard, the entity shall apply paragraphs 38.5–38.8 in the earliest period for which it is practicable to do so, and shall disclose the date of transition and the fact that data presented for prior periods are not comparable. If it is impracticable for an entity to provide any disclosures required by this [draft] standard for any period before the period in which it prepares its first financial statements that conform to this [draft] standard, the omission shall be disclosed.

Disclosures

Explanation of transition to the IFRS for SMEs

38.10 An entity shall explain how the transition from its previous financial reporting framework to this [draft] standard affected its reported **financial position**, financial **performance** and **cash flows**.

Reconciliations

To comply with paragraph 38.10, an entity's first financial statements prepared using **38.11**
this [draft] standard shall include:

(a)   reconciliations of its equity reported under its previous financial reporting
       framework to its equity under this [draft] standard for both of the following
       dates:

    (i)   the date of transition to this [draft] standard; and

    (ii)   the end of the latest period presented in the entity's most recent annual
       financial statements under its previous financial reporting framework; and

(b)   a reconciliation of the profit or loss reported under its previous financial
       reporting framework for the latest period in the entity's most recent annual
       financial statements to its profit or loss under this [draft] standard for the same
       period.

If an entity becomes aware of errors made under its previous financial reporting **38.12**
framework, the reconciliations required by paragraph 38.11(a) and (b) shall distinguish the correction of those errors from changes in accounting policies.

If an entity did not present financial statements for previous periods, it shall disclose **38.13**
that fact in its first financial statements that conform to this [draft] standard.

Glossary

accounting policies	The specific principles, bases, conventions, rules and practices applied by an entity in preparing and presenting financial statements.
accrual basis of accounting	The effects of transactions and other events are recognised when they occur (and not as cash or its equivalent is received or paid) and they are recorded in the accounting records and reported in the financial statements of the periods to which they relate.
accumulating compensated absences	Compensated absences that are carried forward and can be used in future periods if the current period's entitlement is not used in full.
agricultural activity	The management by an entity of the biological transformation of biological assets for sale, into agricultural produce or into additional biological assets.
agricultural produce	The harvested product of the entity's biological assets.
amortisation	The systematic allocation of the depreciable amount of an asset over its useful life.
asset	A resource controlled by the entity as a result of past events and from which future economic benefits are expected to flow to the entity
associate	An entity, including an unincorporated entity such as a partnership, over which the investor has significant influence and that is neither a subsidiary nor an interest in a joint venture.
balance sheet	Financial statement that presents the relationship of an entity's assets, liabilities and equity at a point in time
biological asset	A living animal or plant.
borrowing costs	Interest and other costs incurred by an entity in connection with the borrowing of funds.
business	An integrated set of activities and assets conducted and managed for the purpose of providing:

> (a) a return to investors; or
> (b) lower costs or other economic benefits directly and proportionately to policyholders or participants.
>
> A business generally consists of inputs, processes applied to those inputs, and resulting outputs that are, or will be, used to generate revenues. If goodwill is present in a transferred set of activities and assets, the transferred set shall be presumed to be a business.

business combination	The bringing together of separate entities or businesses into one reporting entity.
carrying amount	The amount at which an asset or liability is recognised in the balance sheet.

cash	Cash on hand and demand deposits.
cash equivalent	Short-term, highly liquid investments that are readily convertible to known amounts of cash and that are subject to an insignificant risk of changes in value.
cash flows	Inflows and outflows of cash and cash equivalents.
cash flow statement	Financial statement that provides information about the changes in cash and cash equivalents of an entity for a period, showing separately changes during the period from operating, investing and financing activities.
cash-settled share-based payment transaction	A share-based payment transaction in which the entity acquires goods or services by incurring a liability to transfer cash or other assets to the supplier of those goods or services for amounts that are based on the price (or value) of the entity's shares or other equity instruments of the entity.
change in accounting estimate	An adjustment of the carrying amount of an asset or a liability, or the amount of the periodic consumption of an asset, that results from the assessment of the present status of, and expected future benefits and obligations associated with, assets and liabilities. Changes in accounting estimates result from new information or new developments and, accordingly, are not corrections of errors.
class of assets	A grouping of assets of a similar nature and use in an entity's operations.
combined financial statements	The financial statements of two or more entities controlled by a single shareholder.
component of an entity	Operations and cash flows that can be clearly distinguished, operationally and for financial reporting purposes, from the rest of the entity.
compound financial instrument	A financial instrument that, from the issuer's perspective, contains both a liability and an equity element.
consolidated financial statements	The financial statements of a group of entities consisting of a parent and one or more subsidiaries.
construction contract	A contract specifically negotiated for the construction of an asset or a combination of assets that are closely interrelated or interdependent in terms of their design, technology and function or their ultimate purpose or use.
constructive obligation	An obligation that derives from an entity's actions where:
	(a) by an established pattern of past practice, published policies or a sufficiently specific current statement, the entity has indicated to other parties that it will accept certain responsibilities; and
	(b) as a result, the entity has created a valid expectation on the part of those other parties that it will discharge those responsibilities.
contingent asset	A possible asset that arises from past events and whose existence will be confirmed only by the occurrence or non-occurrence of one or more uncertain future events not wholly within the control of the entity.

contingent liability	(a) A possible obligation that arises from past events and whose existence will be confirmed only by the occurrence or non-occurrence of one or more uncertain future events not wholly within the control of the entity; or
	(b) a present obligation that arises from past events but is not recognised because:
	(i) it is not probable that an outflow of resources embodying economic benefits will be required to settle the obligation; or
	(ii) the amount of the obligation cannot be measured with sufficient reliability.
control (of an entity)	The power to govern the financial and operating policies of an entity so as to obtain benefits from its activities.
current tax	The amount of income taxes payable (recoverable) in respect of the taxable profit (tax loss) for the current period.
deductible temporary differences	Temporary differences that will result in amounts that are deductible in determining taxable profit (tax loss) of future periods when the carrying amount of the asset or liability is recovered or settled.
deferred tax expense (income)	The amount of tax expense (income) included in the determination of profit or loss for the period in respect of changes in deferred tax assets and deferred tax liabilities during the period.
deferred tax assets	The amounts of income taxes potentially recoverable in future periods in respect of:
	(a) deductible temporary differences;
	(b) the carryforward of unused tax losses; and
	(c) the carryforward of unused tax credits.
deferred tax liabilities	The amounts of income taxes payable in future periods in respect of taxable temporary differences.
defined benefit liability	The present value of the defined benefit obligation at the reporting date minus the fair value at the reporting date of plan assets (if any) out of which the obligations are to be settled directly.
defined benefit obligation (present value of)	The present value, without deducting any plan assets, of expected future payments required to settle the obligation resulting from employee service in the current and prior periods.
defined benefit plans	Post-employment benefit plans other than defined contribution plans.
defined contribution plans	Post-employment benefit plans under which an entity pays fixed contributions into a separate entity (a fund) and will have no legal or constructive obligation to pay further contributions or to make direct benefit payments to employees if the fund does not hold sufficient assets to pay all employee benefits relating to employee service in the current and prior periods.

depreciable amount The cost of an asset, or other amount substituted for cost (in the financial statements), less its residual value.

depreciation The systematic allocation of the depreciable amount of an asset over its useful life.

derecognition The removal of a previously recognised asset or liability from an entity's balance sheet.

development The application of research findings or other knowledge to a plan or design for the production of new or substantially improved materials, devices, products, processes, systems or services before the start of commercial production or use.

discontinued operation A component of an entity that either has been disposed of, or is classified as held for sale, and

(a) represents a separate major line of business or geographical area of operations,

(b) is part of a single coordinated plan to dispose of a separate major line of business or geographical area of operations or

(c) is a subsidiary acquired exclusively with a view to resale.

disposal group A group of assets to be disposed of, by sale or otherwise, together as a group in a single transaction, and liabilities directly associated with those assets that will be transferred in the transaction.

effective interest method A method of calculating the amortised cost of a financial asset or a financial liability (or a group of financial assets or financial liabilities) and of allocating the interest income or interest expense over the relevant period.

effective interest rate The rate that exactly discounts estimated future cash payments or receipts through the expected life of the financial instrument or, when appropriate, a shorter period to the net carrying amount of the financial asset or financial liability.

effectiveness of a hedge The degree to which changes in the fair value or cash flows of the hedged item that are attributable to a hedged risk are offset by changes in the fair value or cash flows of the hedging instrument.

elements of financial statements Broad classes of the financial effects of transactions and other events and conditions.

(a) The elements directly related to the measurement of financial position are assets, liabilities and equity.

(b) The elements directly related to the measurement of performance are income and expenses.

employee benefits All forms of consideration given by an entity in exchange for service rendered by employees.

equity The residual interest in the assets of the entity after deducting all its liabilities.

equity-settled share-based payment transaction A share-based payment transaction in which the entity receives goods or services as consideration for equity instruments of the entity (including shares or share options).

errors   Omissions from, and misstatements in, the entity's financial statements for one or more prior periods arising from a failure to use, or misuse of, reliable information that:

(a)   was available when financial statements for those periods were authorised for issue; and

(b)   could reasonably be expected to have been obtained and taken into account in the preparation and presentation of those financial statements.

expenses   Decreases in economic benefits during the reporting period in the form of outflows or depletions of assets or incurrences of liabilities that result in decreases in equity, other than those relating to distributions to equity participants.

fair presentation   Faithful representation of the effects of transactions, other events and conditions in accordance with the definitions and recognition criteria for assets, liabilities, income and expenses.

fair value   The amount for which an asset could be exchanged, a liability settled, or an equity instrument granted could be exchanged, between knowledgeable, willing parties in an arm's length transaction.

finance lease   A lease that transfers substantially all the risks and rewards incidental to ownership of an asset. Title may or may not eventually be transferred. A lease that is not a finance lease is an operating lease.

financial asset   Any asset that is:

(a)   cash;

(b)   an equity instrument of another entity;

(c)   a contractual right:

(i)   to receive cash or another financial asset from another entity; or

(ii)   to exchange financial assets or financial liabilities with another entity under conditions that are potentially favourable to the entity; or

(d)   a contract that will or may be settled in the entity's own equity instruments and that:

(i)   the entity is or may be obliged to receive a variable number of the entity's own equity instruments; or

(ii)   will or may be settled other than by the exchange of a fixed amount of cash or another financial asset for a fixed number of the entity's own equity instruments. For this purpose the entity's own equity instruments do not include instruments that are themselves contracts for the future receipt or delivery of the entity's own equity instruments.

financial instrument	a contract that gives rise to a financial asset of one entity and a financial liability or equity instrument of another entity.
financial liability	Any liability that is:

(a) a contractual obligation:

   (i) to deliver cash or another financial asset to another entity; or

   (ii) to exchange financial assets or financial liabilities with another entity under conditions that are potentially unfavourable to the entity; or

(b) a contract that will or may be settled in the entity's own equity instruments and:

   (i) under which the entity is or may be obliged to deliver a variable number of the entity's own equity instruments; or

   (ii) will or may be settled other than by the exchange of a fixed amount of cash or another financial asset for a fixed number of the entity's own equity instruments. For this purpose the entity's own equity instruments do not include instruments that are themselves contracts for the future receipt or delivery of the entity's own equity instruments.

financial position	The relationship of the assets, liabilities and equity of an entity as reported in the balance sheet.
financial statements	Structured representation of the financial position, financial performance and cash flows of an entity.
financing activities	Activities that result in changes in the size and composition of the contributed equity and borrowings of the entity.
firm commitment	A binding agreement for the exchange of a specified quantity of resources at a specified price on a specified future date or dates.
first-time adopter of the *IFRS for SMEs*	An entity that presents its first annual financial statements that conform to the *IFRS for SMEs*, regardless of whether its previous accounting framework was full IFRSs or another set of accounting standards.
forecast transaction	An uncommitted but anticipated future transaction.
full IFRSs	International Financial Reporting Standards (IFRSs) other than the *IFRS for SMEs*.
functional currency	The currency of the primary economic environment in which the entity operates.
gains	Increases in economic benefits that meet the definition of income but that are not revenue.
general purpose financial statements	Financial statements directed toward the common information needs of a wide range of users, for example, shareholders, creditors, employees and the public at large.

going concern	An entity is a going concern unless management either intends to liquidate the entity or to cease trading, or has no realistic alternative but to do so.
goodwill	Future economic benefits arising from assets that are not capable of being individually identified and separately recognised.
government grants	Assistance by government in the form of transfers of resources to an entity in return for past or future compliance with certain conditions relating to the operating activities of the entity.
grant date	The date at which the entity and another party (including an employee) agree to a share-based payment arrangement, being when the entity and the counterparty have a shared understanding of the terms and conditions of the arrangement. At grant date the entity confers on the counterparty the right to cash, other assets, or equity instruments of the entity, provided the specified vesting conditions, if any, are met. If that agreement is subject to an approval process (for example, by shareholders), grant date is the date when that approval is obtained.
hedged item	For the purpose of special hedge accounting for SMEs under Section 11 of this [draft] standard, a hedged item is:

(a) interest rate risk exposure in a debt instrument measured at amortised cost;
(b) the foreign exchange risk exposure in a firm commitment or a highly probable forecast transaction;
(c) the price risk exposure in a commodity that it holds or in a firm commitment or highly probable forecast transaction to purchase or sell a commodity that has a readily determinable market price; or
(d) the foreign exchange risk exposure in a net investment in a foreign operation.

hedging instrument	For the purpose of special hedge accounting for SMEs under Section 11 of this [draft] standard, a hedging instrument is a financial instrument that:

(a) is an interest rate swap that meets the conditions in paragraph 11.33; a foreign currency swap or a foreign currency forward exchange contract that is indexed to the same foreign currency as the hedged item; or a forward contract that is indexed to the same commodity as the commodity that is the hedged item; and
(b) meets the other conditions in paragraph 11.32. An entity that chooses to apply IAS 39 in accounting for financial instruments shall apply the definition of hedging instrument in that standard rather than this definition.

held-for-sale asset	Asset whose carrying amount will be recovered principally through a sale transaction rather than through continuing use.
highly probable	Significantly more likely than probable.

impairment loss	The amount by which the carrying amount of an asset exceeds (a) in the case of inventories, its selling price less costs to complete and sell or (b) in the case of other non-financial assets, its fair value less costs to sell.
impracticable	Applying a requirement is impracticable when the entity cannot apply it after making every reasonable effort to do so.
imputed rate of interest	The more clearly determinable of either:

(a) the prevailing rate for a similar instrument of an issuer with a similar credit rating; or

(b) a rate of interest that discounts the nominal amount of the instrument to the current cash sales price of the goods or services.

income	Increases in economic benefits during the reporting period in the form of inflows or enhancements of assets or decreases of liabilities that result in increases in equity, other than those relating to contributions from equity participants.
income statement	Financial statement that presents information about the performance of an entity for a period, ie the relationship of its income and expenses.
income taxes	All domestic and foreign taxes that are based on taxable profits. Income taxes also include taxes, such as withholding taxes, that are payable by a subsidiary, associate or joint venture on distributions to the reporting entity.
insurance contract	A contract under which one party (the insurer) accepts significant insurance risk from another party (the policyholder) by agreeing to compensate the policyholder if a specified uncertain future event (the insured event) adversely affects the policyholder.
intangible asset	An identifiable non-monetary asset without physical substance. Such an asset is identifiable when it:

(a) is separable, ie is capable of being separated or divided from the entity and sold, transferred, licensed, rented or exchanged, either individually or together with a related contract, asset or liability; or

(b) arises from contractual or other legal rights, regardless of whether those rights are transferable or separable from the entity or from other rights and obligations.

interim financial report	A financial report containing either a complete set of financial statements or a set of condensed financial statements for an interim period.
interim period	A financial reporting period shorter than a full financial year.
International Financial Reporting Standards (IFRSs)	Standards and Interpretations adopted by the International Accounting Standards Board (IASB). They comprise:

(a) International Financial Reporting Standards;

(b)   International Accounting Standards; and

(c)   Interpretations originated by the International Financial Reporting Interpretations Committee (IFRIC) or the former Standing Interpretations Committee (SIC).

intrinsic value   The difference between the fair value of the shares to which the counterparty has the (conditional or unconditional) right to subscribe or which it has the right to receive, and the price (if any) the counterparty is (or will be) required to pay for those shares. For example, a share option with an exercise price of CU15, on a share with a fair value of CU20, has an intrinsic value of CU5.

inventories   Assets:

(a)   held for sale in the ordinary course of business;

(b)   in the process of production for such sale; or

(c)   in the form of materials or supplies to be consumed in the production process or in the rendering of services.

investing activities   The acquisition and disposal of long-term assets and other investments not included in cash equivalents.

investment property   Property (land or a building, or part of a building, or both) held (by the owner or by the lessee under a finance lease) to earn rentals or for capital appreciation or both, rather than for:

(a)   use in the production or supply of goods or services or for administrative purposes; or

(b)   sale in the ordinary course of business.

joint control   The contractually agreed sharing of control over an economic activity. It exists only when the strategic financial and operating decisions relating to the activity require the unanimous consent of the parties sharing control (the venturers).

joint venture   A contractual arrangement whereby two or more parties undertake an economic activity that is subject to joint control. Joint ventures can take the form of jointly controlled operations, jointly controlled assets, or jointly controlled entities.

jointly controlled entity   A joint venture that involves the establishment of a corporation, partnership or other entity in which each venturer has an interest. The entity operates in the same way as other entities, except that a contractual arrangement between the venturers establishes joint control over the economic activity of the entity.

lease   An agreement whereby the lessor conveys to the lessee in return for a payment or series of payments the right to use an asset for an agreed period of time.

liability   A present obligation of the entity arising from past events, the settlement of which is expected to result in an outflow from the entity of resources embodying economic benefits.

loans payable	Financial liabilities other than short-term trade payables on normal credit terms.
material	Omissions or misstatements of items are material if they could, individually or collectively, influence the economic decisions of users taken on the basis of the financial statements. Materiality depends on the size and nature of the omission or misstatement judged in the surrounding circumstances. The size or nature of the item, or a combination of both, could be the determining factor.
measurement	The process of determining the monetary amounts at which the elements of the financial statements are to be recognised and carried in the balance sheet and income statement.
minority interest	That portion of the profit or loss and net assets of a subsidiary attributable to equity interests that are not owned, directly or indirectly through subsidiaries, by the parent.
multi-employer (benefit) plans	Defined contribution plans (other than state plans) or defined benefit plans (other than state plans) that:

(a) pool the assets contributed by various entities that are not under common control; and

(b) use those assets to provide benefits to employees of more than one entity, on the basis that contribution and benefit levels are determined without regard to the identity of the entity that employs the employees concerned.

notes (to financial statements)	Notes contain information in addition to that presented in the balance sheet, income statement, statement of changes in equity and cash flow statement. Notes provide narrative descriptions or disaggregations of items disclosed in those statements and information about items that do not qualify for recognition in those statements.
notional amount	The quantity of currency units, shares, bushels, pounds or other units specified in a financial instrument contract.
objective of financial statements	To provide information about the financial position, performance and cash flows of an entity that is useful for economic decision-making by a broad range of users who are not in a position to demand reports tailored to meet their particular information needs.
operating activities	The principal revenue-producing activities of the entity and other activities that are not investing or financing activities.
operating lease	A lease that does not transfer substantially all the risks and rewards incidental to ownership. A lease that is not an operating lease is a finance lease.
operating segment	An operating segment is a component of an entity:

(a) that engages in business activities from which it may earn revenues and incur expenses (including revenues and expenses relating to transactions with other components of the same entity),

(b) whose operating results are regularly reviewed by the entity's chief operating decision maker to make decisions about resources to be allocated to the segment and assess its performance, and

(c) for which discrete financial information is available.

parent
An entity that has one or more subsidiaries.

performance
The relationship of the income and expenses of an entity, as reported in the income statement.

plan assets (of an employee benefit plan)
(a) Assets held by a long-term employee benefit fund; and
(b) qualifying insurance policies.

post-employment benefits
Employee benefits (other than termination benefits) that are payable after the completion of employment.

post-employment benefit plans
Formal or informal arrangements under which an entity provides post-employment benefits for one or more employees.

present value
A current estimate of the present discounted value of the future net cash flows in the normal course of business.

presentation currency
The currency in which the financial statements are presented.

probable
More likely than not.

profit
The residual amount that remains after expenses have been deducted from income.

projected unit credit method
An actuarial valuation method that sees each period of service as giving rise to an additional unit of benefit entitlement and measures each unit separately to build up the final obligation (sometimes known as the accrued benefit method pro rated on service or as the benefit/years of service method).

property, plant and equipment
Tangible assets that:

(a) are held for use in the production or supply of goods or services, for rental to others, for investment, or for administrative purposes, and
(b) are expected to be used during more than one period.

prospective application (of a change in accounting policy)
Applying the new accounting policy to transactions, other events and conditions occurring after the date as at which the policy is changed.

provision
A liability of uncertain timing or amount.

prudence
The inclusion of a degree of caution in the exercise of the judgements needed in making the estimates required under conditions of uncertainty, such that assets or income are not overstated and liabilities or expenses are not understated.

public accountability
Accountability to those present and potential resource providers and others external to the entity who make economic decisions but who are not in a position to demand reports tailored to meet their particular information needs. An entity has public accountability if:

(a) it has issued (or is in the process of issuing) debt or equity instruments in a public market; or

(b) it holds assets in a fiduciary capacity for a broad group of outsiders, such as a bank, insurance company, securities broker/dealer, pension fund, mutual fund or investment bank.

publicly traded registered with a securities commission or other regulatory organisation for the purpose of sale in a public market.

recognition The process of incorporating in the balance sheet or income statement an item that meets the definition of an element and that satisfies the following criteria:

(a) it is probable that any future economic benefit associated with the item will flow to or from the entity; and

(b) the item has a cost or value that can be measured with reliability.

related party A party is related to an entity if:

(a) directly, or indirectly through one or more intermediaries, the party:

    (i) controls, is controlled by, or is under common control with, the entity (this includes parents, subsidiaries and fellow subsidiaries);

    (ii) has an interest in the entity that gives it significant influence over the entity; or

    (iii) has joint control over the entity;

(b) the party is an associate (as defined in IAS 28) of the entity;

(c) the party is a joint venture in which the entity is a venturer (see IAS 31);

(d) the party is a member of the key management personnel of the entity or its parent;

(e) the party is a close member of the family of any individual referred to in (a) or (d);

(f) the party is an entity that is controlled, jointly controlled or significantly influenced by, or for which significant voting power in such entity resides with, directly or indirectly, any individual referred to in (d) or (e); or

(g) the party is a post-employment benefit plan for the benefit of employees of the entity, or of any entity that is a related party of the entity.

related party transaction A transfer of resources, services or obligations between related parties, regardless of whether a price is charged.

relevance The quality of information that allows it to influence the economic decisions of users by helping them evaluate past, present or future events or confirming, or correcting, their past evaluations.

reliability The quality of information that makes it free from material error and bias and represent faithfully that which it either

	purports to represent or could reasonably be expected to represent.
reporting date	The end of the latest period covered by financial statements or by an interim financial report.
reporting period	The period covered by financial statements or by an interim financial report.
research	Original and planned investigation undertaken with the prospect of gaining new scientific or technical knowledge and understanding.
residual value (of an asset)	The estimated amount that an entity would currently obtain from disposal of an asset, after deducting the estimated costs of disposal, if the asset were already of the age and in the condition expected at the end of its useful life.
retrospective application (of a change in accounting policy)	Applying a new accounting policy to transactions, other events and conditions as if that policy had always been applied.
revenue	The gross inflow of economic benefits during the period arising in the course of the ordinary activities of an entity when those inflows result in increases in equity, other than increases relating to contributions from equity participants.
separate financial statements	Those presented by a parent, an investor in an associate or a venturer in a jointly controlled entity, in which the investments are accounted for on the basis of the direct equity interest rather than on the basis of the reported results and net assets of the investees. If an investor in an associate or a venturer in a jointly controlled entity is not also a parent, its financial statements are not separate financial statements.
share-based payment transaction	A transaction in which the entity receives goods or services as consideration for equity instruments of the entity (including shares or share options), or acquires goods or services by incurring liabilities to the supplier of those goods or services for amounts that are based on the price of the entity's shares or other equity instruments of the entity.
small and medium-sized entities (SMEs)	SMEs are entities that: (a) do not have public accountability; and (b) publish general purpose financial statements for external users.
state (employee benefit) plan	Employee benefit plans established by legislation to cover all entities (or all entities in a particular category, for example a specific industry) and operated by national or local government or by another body (for example an autonomous agency created specifically for this purpose) which is not subject to control or influence by the reporting entity.

statement of changes in equity	Financial statement that presents the profit or loss for a period, items of income and expense recognised directly in equity for the period, the effects of changes in accounting policy and corrections of errors recognised in the period, and (depending on the format of the statement of changes in equity chosen by the entity) the amounts of transactions with equity holders acting in their capacity as equity holders during the period.
statement of income and retained earnings	Financial statement that presents the profit or loss and changes in retained earnings for a period.
substantively enacted	Tax rates shall be regarded as substantively enacted when future events required by the enactment process will not change the outcome.
subsidiary	An entity, including an unincorporated entity such as a partnership, that is controlled by another entity (known as the parent).
tax basis	The measurement, under applicable existing tax law, of an asset, liability or equity instrument. That asset, liability, or equity instrument may be recognised for both tax and financial reporting purposes, for tax purposes but not for financial reporting, or for financial reporting purposes but not for tax.
tax expense (tax income)	The aggregate amount included in the determination of profit or loss for the period in respect of current tax and deferred tax.
taxable profit (tax loss)	The profit (loss) for a period, determined in accordance with the rules established by the taxation authorities, upon which income taxes are payable (recoverable)
taxable temporary differences	Temporary differences that will result in taxable amounts in determining taxable profit (tax loss) of future periods when the carrying amount of the asset or liability is recovered or settled.
temporary differences	Differences between the tax basis of an asset or liability and its carrying amount in the financial statements that will result in a taxable or deductible amount when the carrying amount of the asset or liability is recovered or settled. Temporary differences may be either taxable or deductible.
termination benefits	Employee benefits payable as a result of either: (a) an entity's decision to terminate an employee's employment before the normal retirement date; or (b) an employee's decision to accept voluntary redundancy in exchange for those benefits.
timing differences	Income or expenses that are recognised in profit or loss in one period but, under tax laws or regulations, are included in taxable income in a different period.
timeliness	Providing the information in financial statements within the decision time frame.

treasury shares   An entity's own equity instruments, held by the entity or other members of the consolidated group.

understandability   The quality of information in a way that makes it comprehensible by users who have a reasonable knowledge of business and economic activities and accounting and a willingness to study the information with reasonable diligence.

useful life   the period over which an asset is expected to be available for use by an entity or the number of production or similar units expected to be obtained from the asset by an entity.

vested benefits   Benefits, the rights to which, under the conditions of a retirement benefit plan, are not conditional on continued employment.

Derivation table

The [draft] *IFRS for SMEs* was developed by:

(a) extracting the fundamental concepts from the IASB *Framework* and the principles and related mandatory guidance from IFRSs (including Interpretations), and

(b) considering the modifications that are appropriate on the basis of users' needs and cost-benefit considerations.

The table below identifies the primary sources in full IFRSs from which the principles in each section of the [draft] *IFRS for SMEs* were derived.

Section in the [draft] *IFRS for SMEs*		Sources
Preface		*Preface to International Financial Reporting Standards*
1	*Scope*	—
2	*Concepts and Pervasive Principles*	IASB *Framework*, IAS 1 *Presentation of Financial Statements*
3	*Financial Statement Presentation*	IAS 1
4	*Balance Sheet*	IAS 1
5	*Income Statement*	IAS 1
6	*Statement of Changes in Equity and Statement of Income and Retained Earnings*	IAS 1
7	*Cash Flow Statement*	IAS 7 *Cash Flow Statements*
8	*Notes to the Financial Statements*	IAS 1
9	*Consolidated and Separate Financial Statements*	IAS 27 *Consolidated and Separate Financial Statements*
10	*Accounting Policies, Estimates and Errors*	IAS 8 *Accounting Policies, Changes in Accounting Estimates and Errors*
11	*Financial Assets and Financial Liabilities*	IAS 32 *Financial Instruments: Presentation*, IAS 39 *Financial Instruments: Recognition and Measurement*, IFRS 7 *Financial Instruments: Disclosures*
12	*Inventories*	IAS 2 *Inventories*
13	*Investments in Associates*	IAS 28 *Investments in Associates*
14	*Investments in Joint Ventures*	IAS 31 *Interests in Joint Ventures*
15	*Investment Property*	IAS 40 *Investment Property*
16	*Property, Plant and Equipment*	IAS 16 *Property, Plant and Equipment*
17	*Intangible Assets other than Goodwill*	IAS 38 *Intangible Assets*
18	*Business Combinations and Goodwill*	IFRS 3 *Business Combinations*
19	*Leases*	IAS 17 *Leases*

20	Provisions and Contingencies	IAS 37 *Provisions, Contingent Liabilities and Contingent Assets*
21	Equity	IAS 1, IAS 32
22	Revenue	IAS 11 *Construction Contracts*, IAS 18 *Revenue*
23	Government Grants	IAS 20 *Accounting for Government Grants and Disclosure of Government Assistance*
24	Borrowing Costs	IAS 23 *Borrowing Costs*
25	Share-based Payment	IFRS 2 *Share-based Payment*
26	Impairment of Non-financial Assets	IAS 2, IAS 36 *Impairment of Assets*
27	Employee Benefits	IAS 19 *Employee Benefits*
28	Income Taxes	IAS 12 *Income Taxes*
29	Financial Reporting in Hyperinflationary Economies	IAS 29 *Financial Reporting in Hyperinflationary Economies*
30	Foreign Currency Translation	IAS 21 *The Effects of Changes in Foreign Exchange Rates*
31	Segment Reporting	IFRS 8 *Operating Segments*
32	Events after the End of the Reporting Period	IAS 10 *Events after the Balance Sheet Date*
33	Related Party Disclosures	IAS 24 *Related Party Disclosures*
34	Earnings per Share	IAS 33 *Earnings per Share*
35	Specialised Industries	IAS 41 *Agriculture*, IFRS 4 *Insurance Contracts*, IFRS 6 *Exploration for and Evaluation of Mineral Resources*
36	Discontinued Operations and Assets Held for Sale	IFRS 5 *Non-current Assets Held for Sale and Discontinued Operations*
37	Interim Financial Reporting	IAS 34 *Interim Financial Reporting*
38	Transition to the IFRS for SMEs	IFRS 1 *First-time Adoption of International Financial Reporting Standards*

Contents

Basis for Conclusions on
Draft *International Financial Reporting Standard for Small and Medium-sized Entities*

This Basis for Conclusions accompanies, but is not part of, the draft standard.

Background

BC1   In its transition report of December 2000 to the newly formed International Accounting Standards Board (IASB), the outgoing Board of the International Accounting Standards Committee said 'A demand exists for a special version of International Accounting Standards for Small Enterprises.'

BC2   Shortly after its inception in 2001, the IASB began a project to develop accounting standards suitable for small and medium-sized entities (SMEs). The Board set up a Working Group of experts to provide advice on the issues and alternatives and potential solutions.

BC3   In their 2002 annual report, the Trustees of the IASC Foundation, under which the IASB operates, wrote 'The Trustees also support efforts by the IASB to examine issues particular to emerging economies and to small and medium-sized entities.' In July 2005 the Trustees formalised their support by restating the objectives of the Foundation and the IASB as set out in the Foundation's Constitution. They added an objective that, in developing IFRSs, the IASB should take account of, as appropriate, the special needs of small and medium-sized entities and emerging economies. Similarly, the Standards Advisory Council has consistently encouraged the Board to pursue the project.

BC4   At public meetings of the Board during the second half of 2003 and early 2004, the Board developed some preliminary and tentative views about the basic approach that it would follow in developing IASB accounting standards for SMEs. It tested that approach by applying it to several IFRSs.

Discussion Paper (June 2004)

BC5   In June 2004, the Board published a Discussion Paper *Preliminary Views on Accounting Standards for Small and Medium-sized Entities* setting out and inviting comments on the Board's approach. The Board received 120 responses.

BC6   The major issues set out in the Discussion Paper were:

(a)   Should the IASB develop special financial reporting standards for SMEs?

(b)   What should be the objectives of a set of financial reporting standards for SMEs?

(c)   For which entities would IASB standards for SMEs be intended?

(d)   If IASB standards for SMEs do not address a particular accounting recognition or measurement issue confronting an entity, how should that entity resolve the issue?

(e)   May an entity using IASB standards for SMEs elect to follow a treatment permitted in an IFRS that differs from the treatment in the related IASB standard for SMEs?

(f)   How should the Board approach the development of IASB standards for SMEs? To what extent should the foundation of SME standards be the concepts and principles and related mandatory guidance in IFRSs?

(g) If IASB standards for SMEs are built on the concepts and principles and related mandatory guidance in full IFRSs, what should be the basis for modifying those concepts and principles for SMEs?

(h) In what format should IASB standards for SMEs be published?

At its meetings later in 2004, the Board considered the issues raised by respondents to the Discussion Paper. In December 2004 and January 2005, the Board made some tentative decisions on the appropriate way forward for the project. The responses to the Discussion Paper showed a clear demand for an International Financial Reporting Standard for SMEs (IFRS for SMEs) and a preference, in many countries, to adopt the IFRS for SMEs rather than locally or regionally developed standards. The Board therefore decided to publish an exposure draft of an IFRS for SMEs as the next step. **BC7**

Recognition and measurement questionnaire and public round tables

Most respondents to the Discussion Paper said that recognition and measurement simplifications were needed, but few specifics were proposed. And when some specifics were proposed, the commentators generally did not indicate the particular transactions or other events or conditions that create the recognition or measurement problem for SMEs under IFRSs or how that problem might be solved. **BC8**

The IASB concluded that it needed further information to assess possible recognition and measurement simplifications. Consequently the Board decided to hold public round-table meetings with preparers and users of the financial statements of SMEs to discuss possible modifications of the recognition and measurement principles in IFRSs for use in an IFRS for SMEs. The Board instructed the staff to develop and publish a questionnaire as a tool to identify issues that should be discussed at those round-table meetings. **BC9**

The questionnaire (published April 2005) asked two questions: **BC10**

1 What are the areas for possible simplification of recognition and measurement principles for SMEs?

2 From your experience, please indicate which topics addressed in IFRSs might be omitted from SME standards because they are unlikely to occur in an SME context. If they occur, the standards would require the SME to determine its appropriate accounting policy by looking to the applicable IFRSs.

The Board received 101 responses to the questionnaire. Those responses were discussed with the Standards Advisory Council (June 2005), with the SME Working Group (June 2005), World Standard-Setters (September 2005) and at the public round tables held by the Board in October 2005. A total of 43 groups participated in the round-table discussions with the Board over a two-day period. **BC11**

Board deliberations

The IASB's Working Group met in June 2005 and made a comprehensive set of recommendations to the Board regarding the recognition, measurement, presentation and disclosure requirements that should be included in an exposure draft of an IFRS for SMEs. Later in 2005, the Board considered those recommendations and the views expressed in the responses to the Discussion Paper and the questionnaire, and at the round tables. During those deliberations, the Board made tentative decisions about the requirements to be included in the exposure draft. **BC12**

BC13   On the basis of those tentative decisions, at the Board meeting in January 2006 the staff presented a preliminary draft of the exposure draft. The Working Group met in late January 2006 to review that draft and prepared a report of its recommendations for Board consideration. Board discussion of the draft began in February 2006 and continued through the remainder of 2006. Revised drafts of the exposure draft were prepared for each Board meeting from May onwards.

BC14   This Basis for Conclusions sets out the principal issues addressed by the Board, the alternatives considered, and the Board's reasons for accepting some alternatives and rejecting others.

Why global financial reporting standards for SMEs?

BC15   Global financial reporting standards, applied consistently, enhance the comparability of financial information. Accounting differences can obscure the comparisons that investors, lenders and others make. By resulting in the presentation of high quality comparable financial information, high quality global financial reporting standards improve the efficiency of allocation and the pricing of capital. This benefits not only those who provide debt or equity capital but also those entities that seek capital because it reduces their compliance costs and removes uncertainties that affect their cost of capital. Global standards also improve consistency in audit quality and facilitate education and training.

BC16   The benefits of global financial reporting standards are not limited to entities whose securities are traded in public capital markets. In the Board's judgement, small and medium-sized entities—and those who use their financial statements—can benefit from a common set of accounting standards. SMEs' financial statements that are comparable from one country to the next are needed for the following reasons:

    (a)   Financial institutions make loans across borders and operate multinationally. In most jurisdictions, over half of all SMEs, including the very small ones, have bank loans. Bankers rely on financial statements in making lending decisions and in establishing terms and interest rates.

    (b)   Vendors want to evaluate the financial health of buyers in other countries before they sell goods or services on credit.

    (c)   Credit rating agencies try to develop ratings uniformly across borders. Similarly, banks and other institutions that operate across borders often develop ratings in a manner similar to credit rating agencies. Reported financial figures are crucial to the rating process.

    (d)   Many SMEs have overseas suppliers and use a supplier's financial statements to assess the prospects of a viable long-term business relationship.

    (e)   Venture capital firms provide funding to SMEs across borders.

    (f)   Many SMEs have outside investors who are not involved in the day-to-day management of the entity. Global accounting standards for general purpose financial statements and the resulting comparability are especially important when those outside investors are located in a different jurisdiction from the entity and when they have interests in other SMEs.

Should the IASB develop standards for SMEs?

BC17   In deciding to develop an IFRS for SMEs, the IASB was mindful of the following issues:

    (a)   Should financial reporting standards for SMEs be developed by others?

    (b)   Do national standard-setters support the IASB developing an IFRS for SMEs?

    (c)   Is developing an IFRS for SMEs consistent with the Board's mission?

(d)   Existing IFRSs make some distinctions for SMEs.

Should others do it?

The Board considered whether financial reporting standards for SMEs would best be **BC18** developed by others—either globally, country by country, or perhaps at a regional level—while the IASB focused its efforts primarily on standards for entities that participate in public capital markets. However, the Board noted that its mission, as set out in its Constitution (see paragraph BC21), is not restricted to standards for entities that participate in public capital markets. Focusing only on those entities is likely to result in standards or practices for other entities (including SMEs) that may not address the needs of external users of financial statements, are not consistent with the IASB's *Framework for the Preparation and Presentation of Financial Statements* or standards, may lack comparability across national boundaries or within a country, and may not allow for an easy transition to full IFRSs for entities that wish to enter the public capital markets. For those reasons, the Board decided to undertake the project.

Do national standard-setters support an IASB initiative?

National accounting standard-setters throughout the world support the IASB's **BC19** initiative. In September 2003 the IASB hosted a meeting of the world's national accounting standard-setters. In preparation for that meeting the Board surveyed them about standards for SMEs. With near-unanimity, the standard-setters that responded said that the IASB should develop global standards for SMEs.

The Board discussed the progress on its project on standards for SMEs at subsequent **BC20** meetings of the world's national accounting standard-setters in 2004–2006. Standard-setters continued to support the Board's project.

An IFRS for SMEs is consistent with the IASB's mission

Developing a set of standards for SMEs is consistent with the IASB's mission. The **BC21** principal objective of the IASB, as set out in its Constitution and in the *Preface to International Financial Reporting Standards*, is 'to develop, in the public interest, a single set of high quality, understandable and enforceable global accounting standards that require high quality, transparent and comparable information in financial statements and other financial reporting to help participants in the various capital markets of the world and other users of the information to make economic decisions'. 'Single set' means that all entities in similar circumstances globally should follow the same standards. The circumstances of SMEs can be different from those of larger, publicly accountable entities in several ways, including:

(a)   the users of the entity's financial statements and their information needs;
(b)   how the financial statements are used;
(c)   the depth and breadth of accounting expertise available to the entity; and
(d)   SMEs' ability to bear the costs of following the same standards as the larger, publicly accountable entities.

Existing IFRSs include some differences for non-public entities

IFRSs include several differences for entities whose securities are not publicly traded. **BC22** For example:

(a)   IFRS 8 *Operating Segments* requires disclosure of segment information only by entities whose debt or equity instruments are traded or registered for trading in a public market.

(b)   IAS 27 *Consolidated and Separate Financial Statements* exempts some parent entities from preparing consolidated financial statements if their debt or equity instruments are not traded in a public market. Similar exemptions are in IAS 28 *Investments in Associates* and IAS 31 *Interests in Joint Ventures*.

(c)   IAS 33 *Earnings per Share* requires presentation of earnings per share data only by entities whose ordinary shares or potential ordinary shares are publicly traded.

Different users' needs and cost-benefit considerations

BC23   The *Framework* (paragraph 12) states:

> The objective of financial statements is to provide information about the financial position, performance and changes in financial position of an entity that is useful to a wide range of users in making economic decisions.

In establishing standards for the form and content of general purpose financial statements, the needs of users of financial statements are paramount.

BC24   Users of financial statements of SMEs may have less interest in some information in general purpose financial statements prepared in accordance with full IFRSs than users of financial statements of entities whose securities are listed for trading in public securities markets or that otherwise have public accountability. For example, users of financial statements of SMEs may have greater interest in short-term cash flows, liquidity, balance sheet strength and interest coverage, and in the historical trends of earnings and interest coverage, than they do in information that is intended to assist in making forecasts of an entity's long-term cash flows, earnings and value. However, users of financial statements of SMEs may need some information that is not ordinarily presented in the financial statements of listed entities. For example, as an alternative to the public capital markets, SMEs often obtain capital from shareholders, directors and suppliers, and shareholders and directors often pledge personal assets so that the SME can obtain bank financing.

BC25   In the Board's judgement, the nature and degree of the differences between full IFRSs and an IFRS for SMEs must be determined on the basis of users' needs and cost-benefit analyses. In practice, the benefits of applying accounting standards differ across reporting entities, depending primarily on the nature, number and information needs of the users of their financial statements. The related costs may not differ significantly. Therefore, consistently with the *Framework*, the Board believed that the cost-benefit trade-off should be assessed in relation to the information needs of the users of an entity's financial statements.

BC26   The Board faced a dilemma in deciding whether to develop an IFRS for SMEs. On the one hand, it believed that the same concepts of financial reporting are appropriate for all entities regardless of public accountability—particularly the concepts for recognising and measuring assets, liabilities, income and expenses. This suggested that a single set of accounting standards should be suitable for all entities, although it would not rule out disclosure differences based on users' needs and cost-benefit considerations. On the other hand, the Board acknowledged that differences in the types and needs of users of SMEs' financial statements, as well as limitations in, and the cost of, the accounting expertise available to SMEs, suggested that separate standards for SMEs are appropriate. Those separate standards could include constraints such as linkage back to the *Framework*, consistent definitions of elements of financial statements and focus on the needs of users of financial statements of SMEs. On balance, the Board concluded that the latter approach (separate standards) was appropriate.

Adoption of an IFRS for SMEs does not imply that full IFRSs are not appropriate for SMEs

The Board believes that the objective of financial statements as set out in the *Framework* is appropriate for SMEs as well as for entities required to apply full IFRSs. The objective of providing information about the financial position, performance and changes in financial position of an entity that is useful to a wide range of users in making economic decisions is applicable without regard to the size of the reporting entity. Therefore, standards for general purpose financial statements of entities with public accountability would result in financial statements that meet the needs of users of financial statements of all entities, including those without public accountability. The Board is aware of research that shows that over 50 jurisdictions currently require or permit SMEs to use full IFRSs.

BC27

The objective of the proposed *IFRS for SMEs*

Why determination of taxable income and determination of distributable income are not specific objectives of the proposed IFRS for SMEs

IFRSs are designed to apply to the general purpose financial statements and other financial reporting of all profit-oriented entities. General purpose financial statements are directed towards the common information needs of a wide range of users, for example, shareholders, creditors, employees and the public at large. General purpose financial statements are intended to meet the needs of users that are not in a position to demand reports tailored to their particular information needs. General purpose financial statements provide information about an entity's financial position, performance and cash flows.

BC28

Determining taxable income requires special purpose financial statements—ones designed to comply with the tax laws and regulations in a particular jurisdiction. Similarly, an entity's distributable income is defined by the laws and regulations of the country or other jurisdiction in which it is domiciled.

BC29

Tax authorities are also often important external users of the financial statements of SMEs. Almost invariably, tax authorities have the power to demand whatever information they need to meet their statutory tax assessment and collection obligations. Tax authorities often look to financial statements as the starting point for determining taxable income, and some have policies to minimise the adjustments to accounting profit or loss for the purpose of determining taxable income. Nonetheless, global accounting standards for SMEs cannot deal with tax reporting in individual jurisdictions. But profit or loss determined in conformity with the proposed *IFRS for SMEs* can serve as the starting point for determining taxable income in a given jurisdiction by means of a reconciliation that is easily developed at a national level. A similar reconciliation can be developed to adjust profit or loss as measured by the proposed *IFRS for SMEs* to distributable income under national laws or regulations.

BC30

Why it is not the purpose of the proposed *IFRS for SMEs* to provide information to owner-managers to help them make management decisions

BC31   Owner-managers use SMEs' financial statements for many purposes. However, it is not the purpose of the proposed *IFRS for SMEs* to provide information to owner-managers to help them make management decisions. Managers can obtain whatever information they need to run their business. (The same is true for full IFRSs.) Nonetheless, general purpose financial statements will often also serve managers' needs by providing insights into the business's financial position, performance and cash flows.

BC32   SMEs often produce financial statements only for the use of owner-managers, or for tax reporting or other non-securities regulatory filing purposes. Financial statements produced solely for those purposes are not necessarily general purpose financial statements.

The entities for which the proposed *IFRS for SMEs* is intended and those for which it is not intended

BC33   One of the first issues confronting the Board was to describe the class of entities for which the proposed *IFRS for SMEs* would be intended. The Board recognised that, ultimately, decisions on which entities should use the *IFRS for SMEs* will rest with national regulatory authorities and standard-setters. However, a clear definition of the class of entity for which the *IFRS for SMEs* is intended is essential so that:

(a)   the Board can decide on the standards that are appropriate for that class of entity, and

(b)   national regulatory authorities, standard-setters, reporting entities and their auditors will be informed of the intended scope of applicability of the *IFRS for SMEs*.

In that way, jurisdictions will understand that there are some types of entities for which the proposed *IFRS for SMEs* is not intended.

BC34   In the Board's judgement, the proposed *IFRS for SMEs* is appropriate for an entity that does not have public accountability. An entity has public accountability (and therefore should use full IFRSs) if:

(a)   it files, or it is in the process of filing, its financial statements with a securities commission or other regulatory organisation for the purpose of issuing any class of instruments in a public market; or

(b)   it holds assets in a fiduciary capacity for a broad group of outsiders, such as a bank, insurance entity, securities broker/dealer, pension fund, mutual fund or investment banking entity.

Entities whose securities are traded in a public market have public accountability

BC35   Public securities markets, by their nature, bring together entities that seek capital and investors who are not involved in managing the entity and who are considering whether to provide capital, and at what price. Although those public investors often provide longer-term risk capital, they do not have the power to demand the financial information they might find useful for investment decision making. They must rely on general purpose financial statements. An entity's decision to enter a public capital market makes it publicly accountable—and it must provide the outside investors with financial information. Governments recognise this public accountability by establishing laws, regulations and regulatory agencies that deal with market regulation and disclosures to investors in public securities markets.

Financial institutions have public accountability

Similarly, banks, insurance companies, securities broker/dealers, pension funds, mutual funds and investment bankers stand ready to hold and manage financial resources entrusted to them by a broad group of clients, customers or members who are not involved in the management of the entities. Because such an entity acts in a public fiduciary capacity, it is publicly accountable. In most cases, these institutions are regulated by laws and government agencies. **BC36**

SMEs that provide an essential public service

In the Discussion Paper, the Board's tentative view was that, in addition to the two conditions cited in paragraph BC34, an entity also has public accountability if it is a public utility or similar entity that provides an essential public service. **BC37**

Most respondents to the Discussion Paper, and also the Working Group, pointed out that in many jurisdictions entities that provide public services can be very small—for example, refuse collection companies, water companies, local power generating or distribution companies, and local cable television companies. Respondents argued that the nature of the users of the financial statements, rather than the nature of the business activity, should determine whether full IFRSs should be required. The Board concurred. **BC38**

SMEs that are economically significant in their home jurisdiction

In the Discussion Paper, the Board's tentative view was that, in addition to the two conditions cited in paragraph BC34, an entity also has public accountability if it is economically significant in its home country on the basis of criteria such as total assets, total income, number of employees, degree of market dominance and nature and extent of external borrowings. **BC39**

Most respondents, and the Working Group, argued that economic significance does not automatically result in public accountability. Public accountability, as that term is used in paragraphs 1.1 and 1.2, refers to accountability to those present and potential resource providers and others external to the entity who make economic decisions but who are not in a position to demand reports tailored to meet their particular information needs. The Board concluded that economic significance may be more relevant to matters of political and societal accountability. Whether such accountability requires general purpose financial statements using full IFRSs is a matter best left to local jurisdictions to decide. **BC40**

Approval by owners to use the proposed IFRS for SMEs

In the Discussion Paper, the Board's tentative view was that 100 per cent of the owners of a small or medium-sized entity must agree before the entity could use the proposed *IFRS for SMEs*. The objection of even one owner of an entity to the use of the *IFRS for SMEs* would be sufficient evidence of the need for that entity to prepare its financial statements on the basis of full IFRSs. Most respondents did not agree. In their view, an objection, or even a non response, by one or a few shareholders does not make an entity publicly accountable. They thought that the two criteria of (a) **BC41** publicly traded and (b) financial institution appropriately identify entities with public accountability. The Board found those arguments persuasive.

SMEs that are a subsidiary, associate or joint venture of an IFRS investor

BC42   In the Discussion Paper, the Board's tentative view was that if a subsidiary, joint venture or associate of an entity with public accountability prepares financial information in accordance with full IFRSs to meet the requirements of the parent, venturer or investor, it should be required to comply with full IFRSs, not the *IFRS for SMEs*, in its separate financial statements. In the Board's view, because the information in accordance with full IFRSs had been produced for other purposes, it would be more costly to prepare a second set of financial statements that comply with the *IFRS for SMEs*. Most respondents to the Discussion Paper did not agree. Many said that the IFRS data produced for consolidation or equity accounting purposes have a different materiality threshold from that necessary for the investee's own financial statements. Moreover, they said that the circumstances of the entity, rather than the circumstances of its parent or investor, should determine whether it has public accountability. Consequently, they argued, it would be costly and burdensome for the investee to have to apply full IFRSs in its own financial statements. The Board found those arguments persuasive. Therefore, SMEs should assess their eligibility to use the *IFRS for SMEs* on the basis of their own circumstances, even if they also submit financial information in accordance with full IFRSs to a parent, venturer or investor.

Quantified size criteria

BC43   The definition of SMEs does not include quantified size criteria for determining what is a small or medium-sized entity. The Board noted that its standards are used in over 100 countries. The Board concluded that it is not feasible to develop quantified size tests that would be applicable and long-lasting in all of those countries. This is consistent with the Board's general principle-based approach to standard-setting.

BC44   In deciding which entities should be required or permitted to use the *IFRS for SMEs*, jurisdictions may prescribe quantified size criteria. Similarly, a jurisdiction may decide that entities that are economically significant in that country should be required to use full IFRSs rather than the *IFRS for SMEs*.

Suitability of the proposed IFRS for SMEs for very small entities—the so-called 'micros'

BC45   In deciding on the content of the proposed *IFRS for SMEs*, the IASB focused on a typical entity with about 50 employees. The Board used the 50-employee guideline not as a quantified size test for defining SMEs but, rather, to help it decide the kinds of transactions, events and conditions that should be explicitly addressed in the proposed *IFRS for SMEs*. The Board's goal in doing so was to make the *IFRS for SMEs* a stand-alone document for such typical SMEs, and also for entities smaller than 50 employees.

BC46   Some contend that an IFRS for SMEs that is designed to cover the typical transactions, events and conditions of SMEs with about 50 employees is not suitable for a very small 'micro' entity employing one, two or three people that is required, or elects, to publish general purpose financial statements for external users. The Board did not agree. External users such as lenders, vendors, customers, rating agencies and employees need specific types of information but are not in a position to demand reports tailored to meet their particular information needs. They must rely on general purpose financial statements. This is as true for micros as it is for larger SMEs. Financial statements prepared using the proposed *IFRS for SMEs* are intended to meet those needs.

Some who question whether the proposed *IFRS for SMEs* will be suitable for micros argue that many micro entities prepare financial statements solely to submit to income tax authorities for the purpose of determining taxable income. As explained more fully in paragraphs BC28–BC30, determining taxable income (and also determining legally distributable income) requires special purpose financial statements—ones designed to comply with tax laws and regulations in a particular jurisdiction. **BC47**

Moreover, the Board noted that, in many countries, full IFRSs are required for all or most limited liability companies, including the micros. The Board also noted that many other countries permit the micros to use full IFRSs. As mentioned in paragraph BC27, well over 50 jurisdictions have decided that full IFRSs should be required or permitted for all entities, including micros. If full IFRSs have been judged suitable for all entities, then the proposed *IFRS for SMEs* will surely also be suitable. The guidance in the draft *IFRS for SMEs* is simple and straightforward. That guidance may cover some transactions or circumstances that micro SMEs do not typically encounter, but the Board did not believe that this imposes a burden on micro SMEs. The topical organisation of the proposed *IFRS for SMEs* will make it easy for micro SMEs to identify those aspects of the standard that are relevant to their circumstances. **BC48**

Some favour a very simple and brief set of accounting requirements for micro SMEs—with broad principles of accrual basis accounting (some even suggest a cash basis or modified cash basis), specific recognition and measurement principles for only the most basic transactions, and requiring perhaps only a balance sheet and an income statement with limited note disclosures. The Board acknowledged that this approach might result in relatively low costs to SMEs in preparing financial statements. However, the Board concluded that the resulting statements would not meet the objective of decision-usefulness because they would not provide useful information about the entity's financial position, performance and changes in financial position that is useful to a wide range of users in making economic decisions. Moreover, the Board believed that financial statements prepared using such a simple and brief set of accounting requirements might not serve SMEs by improving their ability to obtain capital. Therefore, the Board concluded that it should not develop this type of IFRS for SMEs. **BC49**

The IASB does not have the power to require any entity to use its standards. That is the responsibility of legislators and regulators. In some countries, the government has delegated that power to an independent standard-setter or to the professional accountancy body. They will have to decide which entities should be required or permitted to use, or perhaps prohibited from using, the *IFRS for SMEs*. The Board believes that the proposed *IFRS for SMEs* will be suitable for all entities that do not have public accountability, including micros. **BC50**

***The proposed IFRS for SMEs* is not intended for small publicly-traded entities**

Entities, large or small, whose debt or equity instruments are traded in public capital markets have chosen to seek capital from outside investors who are not involved in managing the business and who do not have the power to demand information that they might find useful. Full IFRSs have been designed to serve public capital markets **BC51** by providing disclosures and guidance especially intended for investors and creditors in such markets. Some of those disclosures and some of that guidance is not included in the draft *IFRS for SMEs*. The Board concluded, therefore, that full IFRSs are appropriate for an entity with public accountability.

BC52   A jurisdiction that believes that the *IFRS for SMEs* is appropriate for small publicly traded entities in that jurisdiction could incorporate the requirements of the *IFRS for SMEs* into its national standards for small publicly-traded entities. In that case, however, the financial statements would be described as conforming to national GAAP. The draft IFRS for SMEs proposes to prohibit them from being described as conforming to the IFRS for SMEs.

'Small and medium-sized entities'

BC53   'Small and medium-sized entities' (SMEs) as used by the IASB is defined in Section 1 *Scope* of the draft *IFRS for SMEs*. Many jurisdictions have developed their own definitions of the term for a broad range of purposes including prescribing financial reporting obligations. Often those national or regional definitions include quantified criteria based on revenue, assets, employees or other factors. Frequently, the term is used to mean or to include very small entities without regard to whether they publish general purpose financial statements for external users.

BC54   The IASB considered whether to use another term, and used the term 'non-publicly accountable entity' (NPAE) for several months during 2005. Because the Board concluded that full IFRSs are necessary for entities with public accountability, the terms 'publicly accountable entity' and 'non-publicly accountable entity' had some appeal. However, constituents argued that this term is not widely recognised, whereas 'small and medium-sized entities' (SMEs) is universally recognised. Also, some said that 'non-publicly accountable entities' seemed to imply that the smaller entities were not accountable. Furthermore, in July 2005 the Trustees of the IASC Foundation restated the objectives of the Foundation and the IASB as set out in the Foundation's Constitution by adding objective (c), which uses the term 'small and medium-sized entities':

> The objectives of the IASC Foundation are:
>
> (a)   to develop, in the public interest, a single set of high quality, under-standable and enforceable global accounting standards that require high quality, transparent and comparable information in financial statements and other financial reporting to help participants in the world's capital markets and other users make economic decisions;
>
> (b)   to promote the use and rigorous application of those standards;
>
> (c)   in fulfilling the objectives associated with (a) and (b), to take account of, as appropriate, the special needs of small and medium-sized entities and emerging economies; and
>
> (d)   to bring about convergence of national accounting standards and Inter-national Accounting Standards and International Financial Reporting Standards to high quality solutions.

For these reasons, the Board decided to use 'small and medium-sized entities'.

The users of SMEs' financial statements prepared using the proposed *IFRS for SMEs*

The proposed *IFRS for SMEs* is intended for non-publicly accountable entities that publish general purpose financial statements for external users. The main groups of external users include:　　　　　　　　　　　　　　　　　　　　　　BC55

(a)　banks that make loans to SMEs.
(b)　vendors that sell to SMEs and use SMEs' financial statements to make credit and pricing decisions.
(c)　credit rating agencies and others that use SMEs' financial statements to rate SMEs.
(d)　customers of SMEs that use SMEs' financial statements to decide whether to do business.
(e)　SMEs' shareholders that are not also managers of their SMEs.

The extent to which the proposed *IFRS for SMEs* should be a stand-alone document

As explained above, the proposed *IFRS for SMEs* is intended to be a stand-alone document for a typical small entity with about 50 employees. There will be occasions, however, when the *IFRS for SMEs* will require or permit entities to look to full IFRSs:　　　　　　　　　　　　　　　　　　　　　　BC56

(a)　When IFRSs provide an accounting policy option, the Board concluded that SMEs should have the same options. The simpler option is included in the draft *IFRS for SMEs* (see paragraphs BC108–BC115). The other option or options are permitted by cross-reference to IFRSs.
(b)　The draft *IFRS for SMEs* omits some accounting topics that are addressed in full IFRSs, because the Board believes that typical SMEs are not likely to encounter such transactions (see paragraphs BC57–BC65). However, the draft has cross-references requiring SMEs that encounter such a transaction to look to a particular IFRS or to a section of one.
(c)　The draft *IFRS for SMEs* states that if the standard does not address a transaction or other event or condition or provide a cross-reference back to another IFRS, an entity should select an accounting policy that results in relevant and reliable information. In making that judgement, an entity should consider, first, the requirements and guidance in the proposed *IFRS for SMEs* dealing with similar and related issues and, second, the definitions, recognition criteria and measurement concepts for assets, liabilities, income and expenses and the pervasive principles in Section 2 *Concepts and Pervasive Principles* of the draft standard. If that does not provide guidance, the entity may look to the requirements and guidance in IFRSs, including Interpretations of IFRSs, dealing with similar and related issues.

Topics covered in IFRSs that are omitted from the draft *IFRS for SMEs*

Some hold the view that the *IFRS for SMEs* should be completely stand-alone—that an entity applying it should never have to look to full IFRSs. The Board concluded that, for that to be the case, the *IFRS for SMEs* would have to be significantly longer than the draft because it would have to address those transactions and circumstances that SMEs sometimes, although not typically, encounter. Paragraphs BC58–BC65 identify the topics that are not covered in the draft *IFRS for SMEs*, but for which it includes a cross-reference to the relevant IFRS that an entity would be required to apply if it encountered the transaction or situation.　　　　　　　　BC57

Hyperinflation

BC58 Section 29 *Financial Reporting in Hyperinflationary Economies* would require SMEs whose functional currency is the currency of a hyperinflationary economy to apply IAS 29 *Financial Reporting in Hyperinflationary Economies* in preparing and presenting financial statements in accordance with the *IFRS for SMEs*. The draft *IFRS for SMEs* does not include requirements on reporting in hyperinflationary economies because it is uncommon for SMEs to have a hyperinflationary functional currency.

Equity-settled share-based payment

BC59 Section 25 *Share-based Payment* would require SMEs to apply IFRS 2 *Share-based Payment* in measuring equity-settled share-based payment transactions, and to make the relevant disclosures required by IFRS 2. The Board believes that it is uncommon for SMEs to enter into such transactions.

Agriculture

BC60 Section 35 *Specialised Industries* would require SMEs engaged in agricultural activities to apply the fair value model in paragraphs 10–29 of IAS 41 *Agriculture* to account for those biological assets whose fair value is readily determinable, and to make all related disclosures required by IAS 41. Although many entities that undertake agricultural activities are SMEs, typical SMEs are unlikely to undertake those activities.

Interim financial reporting

BC61 Section 37 *Interim Financial Reporting* would give SMEs that issue an interim financial report that is described as complying with the *IFRS for SMEs* a choice of applying either IAS 34 *Interim Financial Reporting* or all of the requirements of the proposed *IFRS for SMEs*. The Board concluded that most SMEs either would not issue interim financial reports or would issue interim financial reports that are not described as complying with the *IFRS for SMEs*.

Lessor accounting for finance leases

BC62 Section 19 *Leases* would require SMEs that are a lessor in a finance lease to apply paragraphs 36–46 of IAS 17 *Leases* and to make the related disclosures required by IAS 17. Many lessors in a finance lease are likely to be financial institutions that are publicly accountable and, thus, would not be eligible to use the proposed *IFRS for SMEs*.

Earnings per share

BC63 Section 34 *Earnings per Share* would not require SMEs to present amounts of earnings per share. However, if SMEs chose to disclose earnings per share, Section 34 would require them to follow the requirements of IAS 33 *Earnings per Share*.

Segment reporting

BC64 Section 31 *Segment Reporting* would not require SMEs to present segment information. However, if SMEs chose to disclose segment information, Section 31 would require them to follow the requirements of IFRS 8 *Operating Segments*.

Insurance

Because an insurer holds assets in a fiduciary capacity for a broad group of outsiders, it has public accountability and is therefore outside the definition of SMEs in paragraph 1.1. The proposed *IFRS for SMEs* is not intended for, and would not be available for use by, insurers. **BC65**

Why the *Framework* and principles and mandatory guidance in existing IFRSs are the appropriate starting point for developing the proposed *IFRS for SMEs*

The draft *IFRS for SMEs* was developed by: **BC66**

(a) extracting the fundamental concepts from the *Framework* and the principles and related mandatory guidance from IFRSs (including Interpretations), and
(b) considering the modifications that are appropriate in light of users' needs and cost-benefit considerations.

The Board judged that this approach is appropriate because the needs of users of financial statements of SMEs are similar in many ways to the needs of users of financial statements of publicly accountable entities. Therefore, full IFRSs are the logical starting point for developing an *IFRS for SMEs*. **BC67**

The Board rejected the alternative 'fresh start' approach because that approach could have resulted in different objectives of financial reports, different qualitative characteristics of financial information, different definitions of the elements of financial statements, and different concepts of recognition and measurement. The Board concluded that a 'fresh start' approach would be costly and time-consuming and ultimately futile. This is because the Board is of the view that there is sufficient convergence of users' needs relative to the general purpose financial statements of entities with and without public accountability. **BC68**

Several of the sections in the draft *IFRS for SMEs* relate to projects currently on the IASB's agenda. For several of those projects an exposure draft has been published. They include: **BC69**

(a) Section 3 *Financial Statement Presentation* relates to the Exposure Draft of Proposed Amendments to IAS 1—*A Revised Presentation.*
(b) Section 18 *Business Combinations and Goodwill* relates to the Exposure Draft of Proposed Amendments to IFRS 3 *Business Combinations.*
(c) Section 20 *Provisions and Contingencies* relates to the Exposure Draft of Proposed Amendments to IAS 37 *Provisions, Contingent Liabilities and Contingent Assets.*
(d) Section 24 *Borrowing Costs* relates to the Exposure Draft of Proposed Amendments to IAS 23 *Borrowing Costs.*
(e) Glossary definitions of liabilities and equity relate to the Exposure Draft of Proposed Amendments to IAS 32 and IAS 1—*Financial Instruments Puttable at Fair Value and Obligations Arising on Liquidation.*

Because exposure drafts are proposals on which the IASB's due process is not yet complete, the starting point for developing the *IFRS for SMEs* is existing IFRSs that do not reflect the proposed changes under consideration.

Recognition and measurement simplifications

Paragraphs BC71–BC93 explain the significant simplifications that the Board proposes to the recognition and measurement principles in IFRSs, and the reasons for **BC70** the proposals. The Board also discussed other recognition and measurement simplifications but decided not to adopt them (see paragraphs BC94–BC107).

Financial instruments

BC71   Many said that the requirements of IAS 39 *Financial Instruments: Recognition and Measurement* are burdensome for SMEs. They cited as especially burdensome for SMEs the complexities of classifying financial instruments into four categories, the 'pass-through' and 'continuing involvement' tests for derecognition, and the detailed calculations required to qualify for hedge accounting. The Board agreed that simplifications of IAS 39 are appropriate for SMEs.

BC72   Much of the complexity in IAS 39 results from permitting entities to choose from a range of measurement attributes for financial instruments. Those choices reduce comparability and impose measurement complexity. The draft *IFRS for SMEs* enhances comparability and reduces complexity by defining a default measurement attribute and limiting the use of other measurement attributes.

BC73   Principal among the simplifications proposed in the draft IFRS for SMEs are the following:

(a)   *Classification of financial instruments.* Financial instruments that meet specified criteria are measured at cost or amortised cost, and all others are measured at fair value through profit or loss. The available-for-sale and held-to-maturity classifications in IAS 39 are not available, thereby reducing the complexities associated with the two additional categories, including assessment of intentions, forecasts of cash flows, and accounting 'penalties' in some cases.

(b)   *Derecognition.* The draft proposes a simple principle for derecognition. That principle does not rely on the 'pass-through' and 'continuing involvement' provisions that apply to derecognition under IAS 39. Those provisions are complex and relate to derecognition transactions in which SMEs are typically not engaged.

(c)   *Hedge accounting.* The draft focuses on the types of hedging that SMEs are likely to do, specifically hedges of:

  ● interest rate risk of a debt instrument measured at amortised cost;
  ● foreign exchange risk or interest rate risk in a firm commitment or a highly probable forecast transaction;
  ● price risk of a commodity that it holds or in a firm commitment or a highly probable forecast transaction to purchase or sell a commodity; or
  ● foreign exchange risk in a net investment in a foreign operation.

BC74   With regard to hedge accounting, the draft *IFRS for SMEs* would require periodic recognition and measurement of hedge ineffectiveness, but under less strict conditions than those in IAS 39. In particular, ineffectiveness is recognised and measured at the end of the financial reporting period, and hedge accounting is discontinued prospectively starting from that point, for hedges that no longer meet the conditions for hedge accounting. IAS 39 would require discontinuation of hedge accounting prospectively starting at the date the conditions were no longer met—a requirement that SMEs often say they find burdensome.

BC75   As an alternative to simplified effectiveness testing, the Board considered an approach that is in the US standard SFAS 133 *Accounting for Derivative Instruments and Hedging Activities* and is called the 'shortcut method'. Under such a method, the *IFRS for SMEs* would impose strict conditions on the designation of a hedging relationship with subsequent hedge effectiveness assumed without need for measuring ineffectiveness. The Board concluded that simplified effectiveness testing is preferable to the shortcut method for two principal reasons:

(a) Recognition of all hedge ineffectiveness in profit or loss is a basic principle of IAS 39. The shortcut method is inconsistent with that principle.

(b) To be able to assume that the possibility of hedge ineffectiveness is nil or insignificant, the key features of the hedging instrument and the hedged item, including the term, would have to match, and there could be no conditional terms. Consequently, hedge accounting would be prohibited if the hedging instrument is prepayable or puttable or has other early termination or extension features. Such a requirement would, in effect, make hedge accounting a practical impossibility for many, and perhaps most, SMEs.

Section 11 also differs from IAS 39 with respect to hedge accounting in the following ways: **BC76**

(a) Hedge accounting cannot be achieved by using debt or equity instruments ('cash instruments') as hedging instruments. IAS 39 permits this for a hedge of a foreign currency risk. However, the same effect on profit or loss can be achieved by measuring the cash instrument at fair value, which Section 11 requires for some cash instruments and permits for others. SMEs typically sell the cash hedging instrument when the hedging relationship terminates.

(b) Hedge accounting cannot be achieved with an option-based hedging strategy. Because hedging with options involves incurring a cost, SMEs are more likely to use forward contracts as hedging instruments rather than options.

(c) Hedge accounting for portfolios is not permitted. Hedging portfolios adds considerable accounting complexity because of the need to remeasure all of the hedged items individually at fair value to ensure that the appropriate amounts are derecognised when the instrument is sold and to ensure that the amortisation is appropriate when an instrument is no longer being hedged.

The Board does not believe that these simplifications will affect SMEs adversely because these are not hedging strategies that are typical of SMEs.

Contracts to buy, sell, lease or insure a non-financial item such as a commodity, **BC77** inventory, property, plant or equipment are accounted for as financial instruments within the scope of Section 11 if they could result in a loss to the buyer, seller, lessor, lessee or insured party as a result of contractual terms that are unrelated to changes in the price of the non-financial item, changes in foreign exchange rates, or a default by one of the counterparties. Such contracts are accounted for as financial instruments because their terms include a financial risk component that alters the settlement amount of the contract that is unrelated to the purchase or sale of, or leasing or insuring, the non-financial item.

Section 11 proposes to give SMEs a choice of following Section 11 or IAS 39 in **BC78** accounting for all of their financial instruments. The Board's reasons for proposing that choice in this case are as follows:

(a) Although Section 11 is a simpler approach to accounting for financial instruments than IAS 39, some of the simplifications involve eliminating options that are available to companies with public accountability under IAS 39, for instance:

    (i) available-for-sale classification and the available-for-sale option;

    (ii) held-to-maturity classification;

    (iii) a continuing involvement approach to derecognition (ie partial derecognition); and

    (iv) the use of hedge accounting for hedges other than the four specific types identified in paragraph BC73(c).

In general, the draft *IFRS for SMEs* would permit SMEs to have the same accounting policy options as in full IFRSs.

(b) Because the proposed default category for financial instruments is fair value through profit and loss under the *IFRS for SMEs*, and cost or amortised cost is permitted only when specified conditions are met, some items measured at cost or amortised cost under IAS 39 because of their nature would be measured at fair value through profit or loss under the *IFRS for SMEs*. Some SMEs might find this added fair valuation burdensome.

(c) Sometimes, an entity makes what it views as a 'strategic investment' in equity instruments issued by another entity, with the intention of establishing or maintaining a long-term operating relationship with the entity in which the investment is made. Those entities generally believe that the available-for-sale classification of IAS 39 is appropriate to account for strategic investments. Under the draft *IFRS for SMEs*, however, these strategic investments would be accounted for at fair value through profit or loss.

(d) The derecognition provisions of the draft *IFRS for SMEs* would not result in derecognition for many securitisations and factoring transactions that SMEs may enter into, whereas IAS 39 would result in derecognition.

Goodwill impairment

BC79   In their responses to the recognition and measurement questionnaire and at the round-table meetings, many preparers and auditors of SMEs' financial statements said that the requirement in IFRS 3 *Business Combinations* for an annual calculation of the recoverable amount of goodwill is onerous for SMEs because of the expertise and cost involved. They proposed, as an alternative, that SMEs should be required to calculate the recoverable amount of goodwill only if impairment is indicated. They proposed, further, that the *IFRS for SMEs* should include a list of indicators of impairment of goodwill as guidance for SMEs. The Board agreed with those proposals. The draft *IFRS for SMEs* proposes an indicator approach and includes a list of indicators based on both internal and external sources of information.

BC80   Some respondents to the questionnaire and some of those who took part in the round-table discussions proposed requiring amortisation of goodwill over a specified maximum period. Proposals generally ranged from 10 to 20 years. They argued that amortisation is simpler than an impairment approach, even an impairment approach that is triggered by indicators. The Board did not agree with this proposal for three main reasons:

(a) An amortisation approach still requires assessment of impairment, so it is actually a more complex approach than an indicator-triggered assessment of impairment.

(b) Amortisation is the systematic allocation of the cost (or revalued amount) of an asset, less any residual value, to reflect the consumption over time of the future economic benefits embodied in that asset over its useful life. By its nature, goodwill often has an indefinite life. Thus, if there is no foreseeable limit on the period during which an entity expects to consume the future economic benefits embodied in an asset, amortisation of that asset over, for example, an arbitrarily determined maximum period would not faithfully represent economic reality.

(c) When the IASB was developing IFRS 3, and related amendments to IAS 38 *Intangible Assets*, most users of financial statements said they found little, if any, information content in the amortisation of goodwill over an arbitrary period of years.

Treat all research and development costs as expenses

BC81 IAS 38 requires all research costs to be charged to expense when incurred, but development costs incurred after the project is deemed to be commercially viable are to be capitalised. Many preparers and auditors of SMEs' financial statements said that SMEs do not have the resources to assess whether a project is commercially viable on an ongoing basis and, furthermore, capitalisation of only a portion of the development costs does not provide useful information. Bank lending officers told the Board that information about capitalised development costs is of little benefit to them, and that they disregard those costs in making lending decisions.

BC82 The Board accepted those views, and the draft *IFRS for SMEs* proposes an accounting policy choice (not available under IAS 38) for treating all research and development costs as expenses. Alternatively, SMEs would be permitted to apply the requirements of IAS 38 by cross-reference to that IFRS.

Cost method for associates and joint ventures

BC83 IAS 28 requires an entity to account for its investments in associates by the equity method. IAS 31 allows an entity to account for its investments in jointly controlled entities by either the equity method or proportionate consolidation. Many preparers of SMEs' financial statements questioned the usefulness of both of those accounting methods and told the Board that SMEs have particular difficulty in applying those methods because of inability to obtain the required information and the need to conform accounting policies and reporting dates. In their view, the cost method—which is permitted under IAS 28 and IAS 31 in accounting for investments in associates and joint ventures in the investor's separate financial statements—should also be permitted under the *IFRS for SMEs* in the investor's consolidated financial statements. Lenders generally indicated that information reported using the equity method and proportionate consolidation is of limited use to them because it is not useful in assessing either future cash flows or loan security. Fair values are more relevant for those purposes. Recognising the special problems of SMEs in applying the equity and proportionate consolidation methods, and also the relevance of fair values for lenders, the Board concluded that SMEs should be permitted to use either the cost method or fair value through profit or loss.

Income taxes—'timing differences plus' approach

BC84 In their responses to the questionnaire and at the round-table meetings, many preparers and auditors of SMEs' financial statements said that the temporary difference approach to accounting for income taxes in IAS 12 *Income Taxes* is difficult for SMEs to implement. They said that SMEs do not routinely prepare 'tax balance sheets' and generally do not track the tax bases of many assets. Some advocated a 'current taxes payable' method of accounting for income taxes, under which SMEs would not recognise deferred taxes.

BC85 The Board did not support the 'current taxes payable' approach for the reasons explained in paragraph BC102. However, while believing that the principle of recognising deferred tax assets and liabilities is appropriate for SMEs, the Board also concluded that implementation of that principle could be simplified for SMEs. Section 28 of the draft *IFRS for SMEs* uses the 'temporary difference approach' of

IAS 12 for recognition of deferred taxes. However, it explains temporary differences in terms of 'timing differences', which many SMEs and their auditors indicated is not burdensome for SMEs, and adds requirements to recognise deferred taxes in several additional cases. With respect to the initial recognition of deferred taxes on the first-time adoption of the *IFRS for SMEs*, the draft proposes relief for SMEs if recognising the deferred taxes would involve undue cost or effort. Section 28 does not include an exception to recognition of deferred taxes on undistributed earnings of domestic subsidiaries, branches, associates and joint ventures because that exception is inconsistent with the simplified general principles in paragraphs 28.15 and 28.16.

Less fair value for agriculture

BC86   Some preparers and auditors of the financial statements of SMEs engaged in agricultural activities said that the 'fair value through profit or loss' model is burdensome for SMEs, particularly when applied to biological assets of those SMEs operating in inactive markets or developing countries. They said that the presumption in IAS 41 that fair value can be estimated for biological assets and agricultural produce is unrealistic with respect to biological assets of some SMEs. Some proposed that SMEs should be permitted or required to use a 'cost-depreciation-impairment' model for all such assets. The Board did not support this approach for the reasons explained in paragraph BC103. However, the Board concluded, both because of the measurement problems in inactive markets and developing countries and for cost-benefit reasons, that SMEs should be required to use the fair value through profit or loss model only when fair value is readily determinable without undue cost or effort. When that is not the case, the Board concluded that SMEs should follow the cost-depreciation-impairment model.

Employee benefits—defined benefit plans

BC87   The Board initially planned not to include in the proposed *IFRS for SMEs* any guidance on accounting for defined benefit plans, on the grounds that few SMEs have such plans. The *IFRS for SMEs* would have included a cross-reference to the requirements of IAS 19 *Employee Benefits* for those 'atypical' SMEs that had such plans. However, many people told the Board that in some countries the law requires SMEs to provide benefits to employees under terms that are equivalent to a defined benefit pension plan (eg long-service payments based on future salaries). They recommended that the *IFRS for SMEs* should include accounting requirements for such plans based on, but simplified from, those in IAS 19. The Board concurred.

BC88   One of the principal complexities of IAS 19 is recognition of actuarial gains and losses. Under IAS 19, an entity can:

(a)   recognise actuarial gains and losses in full in profit or loss when they occur.

(b)   recognise actuarial gains and losses in full directly in equity when they occur, but only if the entity presents those gains and losses in a statement titled 'statement of recognised income and expense' that does not include equity transactions with owners (ie not a traditional statement of changes in equity).

(c)   amortise the excess of actuarial gains and losses over the greater of

(i)   10 per cent of the present value of the defined benefit obligation at that date (before deducting plan assets) and

(ii)   10 per cent of the fair value of any plan assets at that date

(with those limits calculated and applied separately for each defined benefit plan) divided by the average remaining working life of the employees.

(d)   recognise actuarial gains and losses in profit or loss using any systematic method that results in faster recognition than (c) above.

The draft *IFRS for SMEs* proposes to require method (a)—immediate recognition in profit or loss. Of the four methods identified in the preceding paragraph, this is the simplest method for SMEs to implement. Method (b) requires preparation of a financial statement that most SMEs do not normally prepare. Methods (c) and (d) require tracking of data over many years and annual calculations. Moreover, financial statement users generally have told the Board that they find immediate recognition (method (a)) provides the most understandable and useful information, in addition to simplicity.

BC89

Some preparers of SMEs' financial statements expressed support for recognising actuarial gains and losses directly in equity. That is not method (b). Nor is it what is now permitted by IAS 19 as a result of the amendments to IAS 19 issued in December 2004. Those amendments require the actuarial gains or losses to become part of equity only after they have been recognised in a statement of recognised income and expense. The Board did not favour introducing a new option in the proposed *IFRS for SMEs*—direct recognition in equity bypassing a statement of recognised income and expense.

BC90

Share-based payment

IFRS 2 provides relief for SMEs, and that relief is carried forward in the draft *IFRS for SMEs*. For equity-settled share-based payment transactions with employees, IFRS 2 generally requires measurement by reference to the fair value of the equity instruments granted. However, if the entity is unable to estimate reliably the fair value of the equity instruments granted at the measurement date, IFRS 2 provides for measurement of the equity instruments at their intrinsic value. In developing the draft *IFRS for SMEs*, the Board concluded that IFRS 2 provides appropriate simplifications for SMEs.

BC91

Leases

Paragraph 19.8 requires a lessee to measure rights and obligations under a finance lease at an amount equal to the fair value of the leased property. IAS 17 *Leases* requires an entity in the same circumstances to make two measurements—both the fair value of the leased property and the present value of the minimum lease payments—and to use the lower of the two. Thus Section 19 *Leases* retains the fundamental recognition principle in IAS 17 while simplifying the measurement.

BC92

Transition to the IFRS for SMEs

IFRS 1 *First-time Adoption of International Financial Reporting Standards* requires an entity's first IFRS financial statements to include at least one year of comparative information under IFRSs. Some preparers and auditors of SMEs' financial statements explained to the Board that a requirement to prepare restated prior period data in all cases would be burdensome for SMEs adopting the *IFRS for SMEs* for the first time. Thus, the draft *IFRS for SMEs* proposes an 'impracticability' exemption. Similarly, it provides an impracticability exemption with respect to some requirements for restating the opening balance sheet.

BC93

Simplifications considered but not adopted

BC94   In developing the draft *IFRS for SMEs*, the Board considered some recognition and measurement simplifications that it decided not to adopt. Some of those potential simplifications were identified in existing national accounting standards for SMEs. Some were proposed by the Board's constituents in their responses to the Discussion Paper or the recognition and measurement questionnaire in 2005. Those proposals, and the Board's reasons for rejecting them, are described in paragraphs BC95–BC107.

Not to require a cash flow statement

BC95   Some suggested that the Board should not require SMEs to prepare a cash flow statement. Some who held this view believed that preparing a cash flow statement is burdensome. Some contended that users of SMEs' financial statements do not find the cash flow statement useful.

BC96   The Board noted that if a comparative balance sheet (with amounts for the beginning and the end of the reporting period) and an income statement are available, preparing a cash flow statement is not a difficult, time-consuming or costly task. The accounting frameworks of most jurisdictions require broad groups of entities, including SMEs, to prepare a cash flow statement. Moreover, the great majority of lenders and other users of SMEs' financial statements who have communicated with the Board—including particularly lenders and short-term creditors—indicated that the cash flow statement is useful to them.

Treat all leases as operating leases

BC97   Under IAS 17, a lessee's rights and obligations under a lease are not recognised in the balance sheet if the lease is classified as an operating lease. Although lessees obtain rights and incur obligations under all leases, finance leases create obligations substantially equivalent to those arising when an asset is purchased on credit. Information about such assets and obligations is important for lending and other credit decisions. Lenders consistently say that they do not want 'off balance sheet obligations'.

Treat all employee benefit plans as defined contribution plans

BC98   As with leases, users of financial statements are concerned about 'off balance sheet obligations'. As noted in paragraph BC87, many jurisdictions require SMEs by law to provide benefits that are the equivalent of a defined benefit pension plan—for example, long-service benefits. Users of SMEs' financial statements consistently say that information about the funding status of such obligations is useful and important to them.

Completed contract method for long-term contracts

BC99   The completed contract method can produce a potentially misleading accounting result for a long-term contractor, with some years of large profits and other years of large losses. Many construction contractors are SMEs. The fluctuation between years of large profit and years of large losses may be magnified for SMEs because they tend to have fewer contracts than larger entities. Users of financial statements have told the Board that, for a long-term contractor, the percentage of completion method provides information that they find more useful than the completed contract method.

Fewer provisions

Provisions are liabilities of uncertain timing or amount. Despite the uncertainties, they are obligations that have met the liability recognition criteria. Users of SMEs' financial statements consistently say they want these obligations recognised in the balance sheet, with the measurement uncertainties explained.

BC100

Non-recognition of share-based payment

Non-recognition is inconsistent with the definitions of the elements of financial statements, especially an expense. Moreover, users of financial statements generally hold the view that share-based payments to employees should be recognised as remuneration expense because (a) they are intended as remuneration, (b) they involve giving something of value in exchange for services, and (c) the consumption of the employee services received is an expense. However, Section 25 *Share-based Payment* proposes to retain the provisions of IFRS 2 for simplified measurement for SMEs using the intrinsic value method.

BC101

Non-recognition of deferred taxes

Some respondents to the questionnaire and some of those who took part in the public round-table discussions supported the 'taxes payable method' of accounting for income taxes. Under that method, only income taxes currently payable or refundable are recognised; deferred taxes are not recognised. Many users of SMEs' financial statements disagree with the taxes payable method. They point out that deferred taxes are liabilities (or sometimes assets) that can result in large outflows (inflows) of cash in the near future and, therefore, should be recognised. Even those users of financial statements who do not agree that deferred tax liabilities or deferred tax assets should be recognised generally want the amounts, causes and other information disclosed in the notes. Note disclosure would entail the same tracking and computation effort for SMEs as would recognition, but would be inconsistent with the principles for recognising assets and liabilities in the *Framework*. The Board concluded that making a fundamental departure from the recognition principles in IAS 12 *Income Taxes* while requiring disclosure of the information that users of SMEs' financial statements find useful is not justified on a cost-benefit basis. Moreover, the Board believes that deferred taxes satisfy the requirements for recognition as assets and liabilities and can be measured reliably.

BC102

Cost model for all agriculture

Not only is fair value generally regarded as a more relevant measure in this industry, quoted prices are often readily available, markets are active, and measuring cost is actually more burdensome and arbitrary because of the extensive allocations required. Moreover, managers of most SMEs that undertake agricultural activities say that they manage on the basis of market prices or other measures of current value rather than historical costs. Users also question the meaningfulness of allocated costs in this industry.

BC103

No consolidated financial statements

BC104   In many countries, SMEs are organised into two or more legal entities for tax or other legal reasons, even though they operate as one economic entity. Investors, lenders and other users of SMEs' financial statements say that they find information about the financial position, operating results and cash flows of the economic entity useful for their decisions. They say they cannot use the separate financial statements of the legal entities because those entities often enter into transactions with each other that are not necessarily structured or priced on an arm's length basis. In such circumstances, the amounts reported in the separate statements reflect internal transactions (eg sales between the legal entities) that are not transactions of the economic entity with other economic entities. Also, the entities are often jointly managed, and loans are cross-collateralised. In the Board's judgement, consolidated statements are essential for users when two entities operate as a single economic entity.

Recognition of foreign exchange gains and losses and revaluation increases in profit or loss

BC105   The draft *IFRS for SMEs* proposes that SMEs should recognise items of income or expense directly in equity in only two circumstances:

(a)   Paragraph 11.37 provides that SMEs shall recognise changes in the fair value of some hedging instruments directly in equity.

(b)   Paragraph 30.13 provides that, in consolidated financial statements, SMEs shall recognise directly in equity a foreign exchange difference (gain or loss) arising on a monetary item that forms part of the reporting entity's net investment in a foreign operation (subsidiary, associate or joint venture).

Additionally, SMEs that choose the revaluation model either for a class of property, plant and equipment (see paragraph 16.13) or for a class of intangible assets (see paragraph 17.23) would credit increases in the asset's carrying amount directly to equity as a revaluation surplus.

BC106   In developing the draft *IFRS for SMEs*, the Board considered whether to require SMEs to recognise the foreign exchange gains or losses and revaluation increases in profit or loss, rather than directly in equity. This would be consistent with the accounting for actuarial gains and losses on defined benefit plans proposed in Section 27 *Employee Benefits*. It would also be consistent with one of the two approaches proposed in the Exposure Draft of Proposed Amendments to IAS 1—*A Revised Presentation* (published March 2006). Under that approach, all components of income and expense recognised in a period would be presented in a single statement of recognised income and expense. Recognising foreign exchange gains or losses and revaluation increases in profit or loss would also be substantially consistent with the second proposed approach in that Exposure Draft. That approach would present all components of income and expense recognised in a period in two statements but would not permit any components of income and expense (ie non-owner changes in equity) to be presented in the statement of changes in equity. The Board concluded, however, that because the proposed amendments to IAS 1 are not final, the draft *IFRS for SMEs* should not reflect those proposals.

Because the Board has begun a comprehensive project on financial instruments as part of its convergence efforts with the US Financial Accounting Standards Board, the Board did not consider requiring SMEs to recognise changes in the fair value of all hedging instruments in profit or loss at this time. **BC107**

All options in IFRSs should be available in the *IFRS for SMEs*. Jurisdictions can remove options

Full IFRSs include some accounting policy options (choices). Generally, for a given transaction, event or condition, one of the options is simpler to implement than the other(s). The Board considered whether the *IFRS for SMEs* should eliminate all accounting policy options and, therefore, require all SMEs to follow a single accounting policy for a given transaction, event or condition. The benefits of doing so would be simplification of the *IFRS for SMEs* and greater comparability of the resulting financial information among SMEs using the *IFRS for SMEs*. Although the Board found those benefits appealing, it concluded that prohibiting SMEs from using an accounting policy option that is available to entities using full IFRSs could hinder comparability between SMEs and entities applying full IFRSs. **BC108**

The Board recognised that most SMEs are likely to prefer the simpler option in full IFRSs. Therefore, the Board concluded that when full IFRSs allow accounting policy options, the *IFRS for SMEs* should include only the simpler option, and the other (more complex) option(s) should be available to SMEs by cross-reference to the full IFRS. This policy has been implemented in the circumstances described in paragraphs BC110–BC115. **BC109**

Investment property

The draft *IFRS for SMEs* provides guidance for the cost-depreciation-impairment model of accounting for investment property. The fair value through profit or loss model would be permitted by cross-reference to IAS 40. **BC110**

Property, plant and equipment

The draft *IFRS for SMEs* provides guidance for the cost-depreciation-impairment model of accounting for property, plant and equipment. The revaluation model would be permitted by cross-reference to IAS 16. **BC111**

Intangible assets

The draft *IFRS for SMEs* provides guidance for the cost-depreciation-impairment model of accounting for intangible assets. The revaluation model would be permitted by cross-reference to IAS 38. **BC112**

Borrowing cost

The draft *IFRS for SMEs* provides guidance for the expense model of accounting for borrowing cost. The capitalisation model would be permitted by cross-reference to IAS 23 *Borrowing Costs*. **BC113**

Presenting operating cash flows

BC114   The draft *IFRS for SMEs* provides guidance for the indirect method of presenting cash flows from operations. The direct method would be permitted by cross-reference to IAS 7 *Cash Flow Statements*. The direct method is not more difficult for an SME than the indirect method. However, although professional financial analysts generally favour the direct method, the majority of bank lenders and other users of financial statements of SMEs expressed a preference for the indirect method for SMEs. They said that the indirect method provides insights into SMEs' accrual accounting. For that reason, the draft *IFRS for SMEs* provides for the indirect method.

Accounting for government grants

BC115   The draft *IFRS for SMEs* provides guidance for one method of accounting for government grants (essentially the model in IAS 41 *Agriculture*). SMEs would be permitted to use the other methods permitted by IAS 20 *Accounting for Government Grants and Disclosure of Government Assistance* by cross-reference to IAS 20.

Optional reversion to full IFRSs by an entity using the IFRS for SMEs

BC116   The Board considered whether an entity using the proposed *IFRS for SMEs* should be allowed to choose to apply a recognition or measurement principle permitted in a full IFRS that differs from the principle required by the related section of the draft *IFRS for SMEs*.

BC117   Some proposed that the *IFRS for SMEs* should, in effect, contain 'optional simplifications of IFRSs'. Within this group, there were two schools of thought:

(a)   One school would permit SMEs to revert to full IFRSs principle by principle, while otherwise continuing to use the *IFRS for SMEs*.

(b)   The second school would permit SMEs to revert to the IFRSs in their entirety, standard by standard but not principle by principle, while otherwise continuing to use the *IFRS for SMEs*. Those who hold this view believe that the recognition and measurement principles in a full IFRS are so interrelated that they should be regarded as an integrated package.

BC118   The alternative view is that an entity should be required to choose only either the complete set of IFRSs or the complete *IFRS for SMEs*. The Board is of that view. Allowing SMEs optionally to revert to full IFRSs either principle by principle or standard by standard, while continuing to follow the IFRS for SMEs for other transactions and circumstances, would result in significant non-comparability. Undesirably, SMEs would have almost an infinite array of combinations of accounting policies from which to choose. As explained in paragraphs BC108–BC115, the draft *IFRS for SMEs* includes some accounting policy options—those that exist in full IFRSs.

Disclosure simplifications

BC119   The disclosure requirements in the proposed *IFRS for SMEs* are substantially reduced when compared with the disclosure requirements in full IFRSs. The reasons for the reductions are of four principal types:

(a) Some disclosures are not included because they relate to topics covered in IFRSs that are omitted from the draft *IFRS for SMEs* (see paragraphs BC57–BC65).

(b) Some disclosures are not included because they relate to recognition and measurement principles in full IFRSs that have been replaced by simplifications proposed in the draft IFRS (see paragraphs BC70–BC93).

(c) Some disclosures are not included because they relate to options that are not included in the draft *IFRS for SMEs* but are available to SMEs by explicit cross-reference to the full IFRS (see paragraphs BC108–BC115).

(d) Some disclosures are not included on the basis of users' needs or cost-benefit considerations (see paragraphs BC25, BC26 and BC120).

Assessing disclosures on the basis of users' needs was not easy, because users of financial statements tend to favour more, rather than fewer, disclosures. The Board was guided by the following broad principles: **BC120**

(a) Users of the financial statements of SMEs are particularly interested in information about short-term cash flows and about obligations, commitments or contingencies, whether or not recognised as liabilities. Disclosures in full IFRSs that provide this sort of information are necessary for SMEs as well.

(b) Users of the financial statements of SMEs are particularly interested in information about liquidity and solvency. Disclosures in full IFRSs that provide this sort of information are necessary for SMEs as well.

(c) Information on measurement uncertainties is important for SMEs.

(d) Information about an entity's accounting policy choices is important for SMEs.

(e) Disaggregations of amounts reported on the face of SMEs' financial statements are important for an understanding of those statements.

(f) Some disclosures in full IFRSs are more relevant to investment decisions in public capital markets than to the transactions and other events and conditions encountered by typical SMEs with around 50 employees.

Why a separate volume rather than added sections in each IFRS

The Board saw merit in two approaches—publishing the *IFRS for SMEs* in a separate volume and publishing a separate section in each individual IFRS (including Interpretations). The principal advantages of the separate volume are: **BC121**

(a) ease of use for those seeking to apply the *IFRS for SMEs*. If the *IFRS for SMEs* addresses the transactions, events and conditions typically encountered by SMEs with around 50 employees, much of the material in full IFRSs would not normally have application for SMEs.

(b) the *IFRS for SMEs* can be drafted in a simplified language without the details that are needed in full IFRSs.

The advantages of including the requirements for SMEs as a separate section of each IFRS (including Interpretations) include: **BC122**

(a) the modifications or exemptions are highlighted.

(b) to the extent that SMEs must look to full IFRSs, putting both the requirements for SMEs and the related full standards in one place is more user-friendly.

(c) it would reduce the likelihood that, in drafting IASB standards for SMEs, an unintended difference will arise between an IFRS and the related requirements in the *IFRS for SMEs*.

Respondents to the Discussion Paper generally favoured the separate volume approach. On balance the Board agreed for the reasons outlined in paragraph BC121. **BC123**

Why organisation by topic

BC124   The Board saw merit both in numbering the requirements for SMEs similarly to full IFRSs and in topical organisation. Using the same numbering system as full IFRSs would enable a user to link back to the full IFRS to seek further guidance on an accounting question. Topical organisation, on the other hand, would make the IFRS for SMEs more like a reference manual, which is likely to be the way that people would use it, and thus it would be more user-friendly. Indexing could minimise the benefits of one of those approaches over the other. Providing the IFRS for SMEs in electronic form could also minimise the benefits of one approach over the other. Most respondents to the Discussion Paper favoured organisation by topic. On balance the Board found the benefits of a topically organised reference manual persuasive.

The Board's plan for maintaining (updating) the *IFRS for SMEs*

BC125   In the Discussion Paper, the Board expressed a tentative view that, 'once the initial set of IASB Standards for SMEs is in place, concurrently with each exposure draft of an IFRS and each draft Interpretation, and most likely as part of those documents, the Board will propose the related IASB Standard or Interpretation for SMEs. The effective dates of the new or revised IASB Standards for SMEs would probably be the same as the effective date of the new or revised IFRSs (including Interpretations).' In general, respondents to the Discussion Paper did not agree with this approach. They explained that because SMEs do not have internal accounting resources or the ability to hire accounting advisers on an ongoing basis, the IFRS for SMEs should be updated only periodically, perhaps only once each two or three years. They also noted that not every new IFRS or Interpretation or amendment to an IFRS (including Interpretations) will affect the IFRS for SMEs. On the basis of users' needs or cost-benefit considerations, some of those changes may be relevant only for full IFRSs. Furthermore, there may be some changes to the IFRS for SMEs that are appropriate even if full IFRSs are not changed.

BC126   The principal benefits of considering changes to the IFRS for SMEs at the same time as each new IFRS is proposed or each amendment to an existing IFRS is proposed are consistency of consideration both by the Board and respondents, avoiding a time lag between when changes affect full IFRSs and when similar changes affect the IFRS for SMEs, and avoiding potentially differing standards in full IFRSs and the IFRS for SMEs.

BC127   On balance, the Board found the arguments set out in paragraph BC125 for periodic, rather than contemporaneous, updating of the IFRS for SMEs generally persuasive. However, the Board also concluded that there might be matters for which amendment of the IFRS for SMEs will be necessary more frequently than once in several years. Paragraph 16 of the Preface to the draft *IFRS for SMEs* explains the Board's plan for maintaining the *IFRS for SMEs*.

Alternative view on the proposed
International Financial Reporting Standard for Small and Medium-sized Entities

One Board member voted against the publication of the Exposure Draft of the proposed *International Reporting Standard for Small and Medium-sized Entities (IFRS for SMEs)*. That Board member's alternative view is set out below.   AV1

The Board member believes that the proposed *IFRS for SMEs* is neither necessary nor desirable. It is unnecessary because the vast majority of accounting policy decisions of an SME are straightforward and extensive reference to IFRSs will not be required and, when required, not burdensome.   AV2

It is undesirable because the proposed IFRS would produce non-comparable information. SMEs will not be comparable with each other and will not be comparable with publicly accountable entities. That result is inconsistent with the IASB *Framework* and the Concepts and Pervasive Principles of the proposed IFRS.   AV3

Non-comparability will result because the proposed IFRS would allow SMEs, as a result of paragraph 10.3, to ignore the requirements of other IFRSs even when the specific accounting issue is addressed in those IFRSs. If an entity is satisfied with the result of applying paragraph 10.3(a) and (b) there is never a requirement to look to full IFRSs. Thus, identical transactions can be accounted for differently by different SMEs and differently from publicly accountable entities. If the Board finds it necessary to develop educational materials to assist SMEs in applying IFRSs, that would certainly be appropriate. However, this Board member believes that in all circumstances IFRSs should ultimately be the source of accounting guidance for all entities.   AV4

This Board member does not believe that the Board has demonstrated the need to make modifications to recognition and measurement requirements in IFRSs for application by SMEs on the basis of either cost-benefit analysis or user needs. Alternatively, the Board member would much more extensively modify the disclosure requirements to meet special user needs. That modification might well create disclosures not required at present, such as information about economic dependency, although many of the presentation and disclosure requirements proposed in the Exposure Draft seem unnecessary.   AV5

This Board member also believes that the Exposure Draft is inconsistent with the Constitution of the International Accounting Standards Committee Foundation and the *Preface to International Financial Reporting Standards*. Those documents set out an objective of a single set of accounting standards taking account of the special needs of small and medium-sized entities and emerging economies. The Board member accepts that objective but does not believe it implies separate sets of standards for entities in differing circumstances as indicated in paragraph BC21. The conclusion of that paragraph suggests that many sets of accounting standards would be appropriate depending on different circumstances.   AV6

[Draft] Implementation Guidance

This [draft] guidance accompanies, but is not part of, the International Financial Reporting Standard for Small and Medium-sized Entities (IFRS for SMEs).

Illustrative financial statements

Section 3 *Financial Statement Presentation* of the [draft] *IFRS for SMEs* defines a complete set of financial statements and prescribes general standards of financial statement presentation. Sections 4–8 prescribe the format and content of the individual financial statements and notes. Other sections of the [draft] *IFRS for SMEs* establish additional presentation and disclosure requirements. The financial statements set out below illustrate how those presentation and disclosure requirements might be met by a typical small or medium-sized entity. Of course, each entity will need to consider the content, sequencing and format of presentation and the descriptions used for line items to achieve a fair presentation in that entity's particular circumstances.   **F1**

The illustrative balance sheet presents current assets followed by non-current assets, and presents current liabilities followed by non-current liabilities and then by equity. This is one way in which a balance sheet distinguishing between current and non-current items may be presented. Other formats may be equally appropriate, provided the distinction is clear. Consistently with paragraph 3.19 of the [draft] *IFRS for SMEs*, an entity may use titles for the financial statements other than those used in these illustrations.   **F2**

Two statements of income and retained earnings are provided to illustrate the alternative classifications of income and expenses, by nature and by function—see paragraph 5.9 of the [draft] *IFRS for SMEs*.   **F3**

The examples are not intended to illustrate all aspects of the [draft] *IFRS for SMEs*.   **F4**

XYZ Group
Consolidated statement of income and retained earnings for the year ended 31 December 20X2
(Alternative 1 – illustrating the classification of expenses by function)

	Notes	20X2 CU	20X1 CU
Revenue	5	6,863,545	5,808,653
Cost of sales		(5,178,530)	(4,422,575)
Gross profit		1,685,015	1,386,078
Other income		88,850	25,000
Distribution costs		(175,550)	(156,800)
Administrative expenses		(810,229)	(660,389)
Other expenses		(105,763)	(100,030)
Finance costs	6	(26,366)	(36,712)
Profit before tax	7	655,957	457,147
Income tax expense	8	(270,651)	(189,559)
Profit for the period		385,306	267,588
Retained earnings at start of year		2,171,352	2,003,764
Dividends (per share 20X2 5.00, 20X1 3.33)		(150,000)	(100,000)
Retained earnings at end of year		2,406,658	2,171,352

Note: The format illustrated above aggregates expenses according to their function (cost of sales, distribution, administrative etc). As the only changes to XYZ Group's equity during the year arose from profit or loss and payment of dividends, it has elected to present a combined statement of income and retained earnings instead of separate income and equity statements.

XYZ Group
Consolidated statement of income and retained earnings for the year ended
31 December 20X2
(Alternative 2 – illustrating the classification of expenses by nature)

	Notes	20X2 CU	20X1 CU
Revenue	5	6,863,545	5,808,653
Other income		88,850	25,000
Changes in inventories of finished goods and work in progress		3,310	(1,360)
Raw material and consumables used		(4,786,699)	(4,092,185)
Employee salaries and benefits		(936,142)	(879,900)
Depreciation and amortisation expense		(272,060)	(221,247)
Impairment of property, plant and equipment		(30,000)	–
Other expenses		(248,481)	(145,102)
Finance costs	6	(26,366)	(36,712)
Profit before tax	7	655,957	457,147
Income tax expense	8	(270,651)	(189,559)
Profit for the year		385,306	267,588
Retained earnings at start of year		2,171,352	2,003,764
Dividends (per share 20X2 5.00, 20X1 3.33)		(150,000)	(100,000)
Retained earnings at end of year		2,406,658	2,171,352

Note: The format illustrated above aggregates expenses according to their nature (raw materials and consumables, employee benefits, depreciation and amortisation, impairment etc). As the only changes to XYZ Group's equity during the year arose from profit or loss and payment of dividends, it has elected to present a combined statement of income and retained earnings instead of separate income and equity statements.

XYZ Group
Consolidated balance sheet at 31 December 20X2

	Notes	20X2 CU	20X1 CU
ASSETS			
Current assets			
Cash		26,700	20,875
Trade and other receivables	14	585,548	573,862
Inventories	13	57,250	47,920
		669,498	642,657
Non-current assets			
Investment in associate	11	107,500	107,500
Property, plant and equipment	9	2,548,473	2,401,455
Intangible assets	10	850	2,550
Deferred tax assets	12	3,909	2,912
		2,660,732	2,514,417
Assets held for sale	15	1,603	
Total assets		3,331,833	3,157,074
LIABILITIES AND EQUITY			
Current liabilities			
Bank overdrafts	17	83,600	115,508
Trade payables		433,130	425,560
Current tax liabilities		271,648	190,316
Current portion of employee benefit obligations	18	6,181	5,943
Current portion of obligations under finance leases	19	21,461	19,884
		816,020	757,211

Non-current liabilities

Bank loans	17	50,000	150,000
Long-term employee benefit obligations	18	4,442	3,887
Obligations under finance leases	19	23,163	44,624
		77,605	198,511

Liabilities directly associated with assets classified as held for sale	15	1,550	—
Total liabilities		895,175	955,722

Equity

Share capital	16	30,000	30,000
Retained earnings	4	2,406,658	2,171,352
		2,436,658	2,201,352
Total liabilities and equity		3,331,833	3,157,074

XYZ Group
Consolidated cash flow statement for the year ended 31 December 20X2

	Notes	20X2 CU	20X1 CU
Cash flows from operating activities			
Profit for the year		385,306	267,588
Adjustments for:			
Finance costs		26,366	36,712
Income tax expense		270,651	189,559
Depreciation of property, plant and equipment		270,360	219,547
Impairment loss		30,000	–
Amortisation of intangibles		1,700	1,700
Gain on disposal of property, plant and equipment		(63,850)	--
Decrease (increase) in trade and other receivables		(11,686)	(52,628)
Decrease (increase) in inventories (20X2 includes CU 131 of production supplies reclassified as assets held for sale)		(9,461)	(2,870)
Increase (decrease) in trade payables (20X2 includes CU 1,550 reclassified as liabilities directly associated with assets classified as held for sale)		9,120	10,870
Increase in current and long-term employee benefit payable		793	193
Cash generated from operations		909,299	670,671
Interest paid		(26,366)	(36,712)
Income taxes paid		(190,316)	(172,426)
Net cash from operating activities		692,617)	461,533
Cash flows from investing activities			
Proceeds from sale of equipment		100,000	–
Purchases of equipment		(485,000)	(435,000)
Net cash used in investing activities		(385,000)	(435,000)
Cash flows from financing activities			
Payment of finance lease liabilities		(19,884)	(18,423)
Repayment of borrowings		(100,000)	–
Dividends paid		(150,000)	(100,000)
Net cash used in investing activities		(269,884)	(118,423)

Net increase (decrease) in cash and cash equivalents		37,733	(91,890)
Cash and cash equivalents at beginning of year		(94,633)	(2,743)
Cash and cash equivalents at end of year	20	(56,900)	(94,633)

Note: The format above illustrates the indirect method of reporting cash flows from operating activities.

XYZ Group

Accounting policies and explanatory notes to the financial statements for the year ended 31 December 20X2

1. General information

XYZ (Holdings) Limited (the Company) is a limited company incorporated in A Land. The address of its registered office and principal place of business is _____. XYZ Group consists of the Company and its wholly-owned subsidiary XYZ (Trading) Limited. Their principal activities are the manufacture and sale of candles.

2. Basis of preparation and accounting policies

These consolidated financial statements have been prepared in accordance with the [draft] *International Financial Reporting Standard for Small and Medium-sized Entities (IFRS for SMEs)* issued by the International Accounting Standards Board (IASB). They are presented in the currency units (CU) of A Land.

Basis of consolidation

The consolidated financial statements incorporate the financial statements of the Company and its wholly-owned subsidiary. All intragroup transactions, balances, income and expenses are eliminated.

Investments in associates

Investments in associates are accounted for at cost less any accumulated impairment losses.

Dividend income from investments in associates is recognised when the shareholders' rights to receive payment have been established and is shown as other income.

Non-current assets held for sale

Non-current assets (and disposal groups) classified as held for sale are measured at the lower of the assets' previous carrying amount and fair value less costs to sell.

Revenue recognition

Revenue is measured at the fair value of the consideration received or receivable, net of discounts and sales-related taxes. Revenue from sales of goods is recognised when the goods are delivered and title has passed. Royalty revenue from licensing candle-making patents for use by others is recognised over the licence period.

Borrowing costs

All borrowing costs are recognised in profit or loss in the period in which they are incurred.

Income taxes

Income tax expense represents the sum of the tax currently payable and deferred tax.

The tax currently payable is based on taxable profit for the year.

Deferred tax is recognised on differences between the carrying amounts of assets and liabilities in the financial statements and their corresponding tax bases (temporary differences). Deferred tax liabilities are recognised for all taxable temporary differences. Deferred tax assets are recognised to the extent that it is probable that taxable profits will be available against which deductible temporary differences can be utilised.

The carrying amount of deferred tax assets is reviewed at each balance sheet date and reduced to the extent that it is no longer probable that sufficient taxable profits will be available to allow all or part of the asset to be recovered.

Deferred tax is calculated at the tax rates that are expected to apply in the period when the liability is settled or the asset is realised, based on tax rates that have been enacted or substantively enacted by the end of the reporting period.

Property, plant and equipment

Items of property plant and equipment are measured at cost less accumulated depreciation and any accumulated impairment losses.

Depreciation is charged so as to allocate the cost of assets less their residual values over their estimated useful lives, using the straight-line method. The following rates are used for the depreciation of property, plant and equipment:

Buildings	2%
Fixtures and equipment	10% to 30%

Intangible assets

Intangible assets are purchased computer software that is stated at cost less accumulated depreciation and any accumulated impairment losses. It is amortised over its estimated life of five years using the straight-line method.

Impairment of non-current assets

At each balance sheet date, the carrying amounts of tangible and intangible assets and investments in associates are reviewed to determine whether there is any indication that those assets have suffered an impairment loss. If the fair value less costs to sell of an asset (or group of assets) is estimated to be less than its carrying amount, the carrying amount of the asset (or group of assets) is reduced to its fair value less costs to sell. An impairment loss is recognised immediately in profit or loss.

If an impairment loss subsequently reverses, the carrying amount of the asset (or group of assets) is increased to the revised estimate of its fair value less costs to sell, but not in excess of the amount that would have been determined had no impairment loss been recognised for the asset (group of assets) in prior years. A reversal of an impairment loss is recognised immediately in profit or loss.

Leases

Leases are classified as finance leases whenever the terms of the lease transfer substantially all the risks and rewards of ownership to the lessee. All other leases are classified as operating leases.

Assets held under finance leases are recognised as assets of the Group at their fair value at the inception of the lease. The corresponding liability to the lessor is included in the balance sheet as a finance lease obligation. Lease payments are apportioned between finance charges and reduction of the lease obligation so as to achieve a constant rate of interest on the remaining balance of the liability. Finance charges are charged directly to profit or loss. Assets held under finance leases are included in property, plant and equipment, and depreciation and impairment losses are recognised.

Rentals payable under operating leases are charged to profit or loss on a straight-line basis over the term of the relevant lease.

Inventories

Inventories are stated at the lower of cost and selling price less costs to complete and sell. Cost is calculated using the first-in, first-out (FIFO) method.

Trade and other receivables

Trade and other receivables are measured at amortised cost using the effective interest method. At the end of each reporting period, the carrying amounts of trade and other receivables are reviewed to determine whether there is any objective evidence that the amounts are not recoverable. If so, an impairment loss is recognised immediately in profit or loss.

3. Key sources of estimation uncertainty

Long-service payment

In determining the liability for other long-term benefits (explained in note 18), management must make an estimate of salary increases over the following five years, the discount rate for the next five years to use in the present value calculation and the number of employees expected to leave before they receive the benefits. Note 18 provides details of the carrying amount of the obligation at the year-end.

4. Restriction on payment of dividend

Under the terms of the bank loan and bank overdraft agreements, dividends cannot be paid to the extent that they would reduce the balance of retained earnings below the sum of the outstanding balance of the bank loan and the bank overdraft.

5.   Revenue

An analysis of the Group's revenue is as follows:

	20X2	20X1
	CU	CU
Sale of goods	6,743,545	5,688,653
Royalties – licensing of candle-making patents	120,000	120,000
	6,863,545	5,808,653

6.   Finance costs

	20X2	20X1
	CU	CU
Interest on bank loan and overdraft	(21,250)	(30,135)
Interest on finance leases	(5,116)	(6,577)
	(26,366)	(36,712)

7.   Profit before tax

The following items have been recognised as expenses (income) in determining profit before tax:

	20X2	20X1
	CU	CU
Gain on disposal of property, plant and equipment	(63,850)	—
Depreciation of property, plant and equipment	270,360	219,547
Impairment of property, plant and equipment (included in impairment of property, plant and equipment/administrative expenses)	30,000	
Amortisation of software (included in depreciation and amortisation/administrative expenses)	1,700	1,700
Employee benefits expense	936,142	879,900
Cost of inventories recognised as expense	4,783,389	4,093,545

8.   Income tax expense

	20X2	20X1
	CU	CU
Current tax	271,648	190,316
Deferred tax (note 12)	(997)	(757)
	270,651	189,559

Domestic income tax is calculated at 40% (20X1: 40%) of the estimated assessable profit for the year.

The total income tax expense for the year can be reconciled to the accounting profit as follows:

	20X2 CU	20X1 CU
Profit before tax	655,957	457,147
Tax at domestic rate of 40%	262,383	182,859
Tax effect of certain employee compensation expenses (CU20,670 in 20X2 and CU16,750 in 20X1) recognised in measuring profit before tax that are not tax deductible	8,268	6,700
Tax expense for the year	270,651	189,559

9. Property, plant and equipment

	Land and buildings CU	Fixtures and equipment CU	Total CU
Cost			
1 January 20X1	1,960,000	907,045	2,867,045
Additions	–	435,000	435,000
Disposals	–	(240,000)	(240,000)
At 31 December 20X1	1,960,000	1,102,045	3,062,045
Additions	–	485,000	485,000
Disposals	–	(241,000)	(241,000)
Reclassified as held for sale (note 15)		(1,550)	(1,550)
At 31 December 20X2	1,960,000	1,344,495	3,304,495
Accumulated depreciation and impairment			
1 January 20X1	360,000	321,043	681,043
Annual depreciation	30,000	189,547	219,547
Less accumulated depreciation on assets disposed of		(240,000)	(240,000)
At 31 December 20X1	390,000	270,590	660,590
Annual depreciation	30,000	240,360	270,360
Impairment	–	30,000	30,000
Less accumulated depreciation on assets disposed of	–	(204,850)	(204,850)
Less accumulated depreciation on assets reclassified as held for sale (note 15)		(78)	(78)
At 31 December 20X2	420,000	336,022	756,022
Carrying amount			
31 December 20X1	1,570,000	831,455	2,401,455
31 December 20X2	1,540,000	1,008,473	2,548,473

During the period, the Group noticed a significant decline in the efficiency of two of its vehicles and so carried out a review of their fair values less costs to sell. The review led to the recognition of an impairment loss of CU30,000.

The carrying amount of the Group's fixtures and equipment includes an amount of CU40,000 (20X1: CU60,000) in respect of assets held under finance leases.

10. Intangible assets

Software:

Cost	CU
1 January 20X1	8,500
Additions	-
Disposals	-
At 31 December 20X1	8,500
Additions	-
Disposals	-
At 31 December 20X2	8,500

Accumulated depreciation and impairment	
1 January 20X1	4,250
Annual amortisation	1,700
At 31 December 20X1	5,950
Annual amortisation	1,700
At 31 December 20X2	7,650

Carrying amount	
31 December 20X1	2,550
31 December 20X2	850

11. Investment in associate

	20X2	20X1
	CU	CU
Cost of investment in associate	107,500	107,500

The Group owns 35 per cent of an associate whose shares are not publicly traded. Summarised financial information of the associate is set out below:

	20X2	20X1
	CU	CU
Total assets	559,509	589,423
Total liabilities	(167,128)	(156,312)
Net assets	392,381	433,111

	20X2	20X1
	CU	CU
Revenue	518,887	528,536
Profit for the year	111,137	118,534

12. Deferred tax

Differences between amounts recognised in the income statement and amounts reported to tax authorities in connection with investments in the subsidiary and associate are insignificant.

The deferred tax asset is the tax effect of an expected future income tax benefit relating to the long-service benefit (note 18) that will not be tax-deductible until the benefit is actually paid but has already been recognised as an expense in measuring the Group's profit for the year. The Group has recognised the full related deferred tax asset because, on the basis of past years and future expectations, management considers it probable that taxable profits will be available against which the future income tax deduction can be utilised.

The following are the deferred tax liabilities (assets) recognised by the Group during the current and prior years:

	Software	Long-service benefit	Total
	CU	CU	CU
At 1 January 20X1	1,700	(3,855)	(2,155)
Charge (credit) to profit or loss for the year	(680)	(77)	(757)
At 1 January 20X2	1,020	(3,932)	(2,912)
Charge (credit) to profit or loss for the year	(680)	(317)	(997)
At 31 December 20X2	340	(4,249)	(3,909)

The deferred tax asset for long-service benefits and the deferred tax liability for software relate to income taxes in the same jurisdiction, and the law allows net settlement. Therefore, they have been offset in the balance sheet as follows:

	20X2	20X1
	CU	CU
Deferred tax liability	340	1,020
Deferred tax asset	(4,249)	(3,932)
	(3,909)	(2,912)

13. Inventories

	20X2	20X1
	CU	CU
Raw materials	42,470	36,450
Work in progress	1,140	900
Finished goods	13,640	10,570
	57,250	47,920
Production supplies classified as part of a disposal group held for sale (note 15)	131	–
	57,381	47,920

14. Trade and other receivables

	20X2	20X1
	CU	CU
Trade debtors	528,788	528,384
Prepayments	56,760	45,478
	585,548	573,862

15. Assets held for sale

On 10 December 20X2, the directors resolved to dispose of one of the Group's recently acquired rolling machines for beeswax candles. Negotiations with several interested parties have taken place. The machine, along with related supplies purchased for use with the machine and the liability to the supplier of the machine, is expected to be sold within twelve months and so has been classified as a disposal group held for sale and presented separately in the balance sheet.

The proceeds of disposal are expected to exceed the net carrying amount of the relevant assets and liabilities and, accordingly, no impairment loss has been recognised on the assets classified as held for sale.

The major classes of assets and liabilities in the disposal group classified as held for sale are as follows:

	20X2
	CU
Property, plant and equipment	1,472
Production supplies	131
	1,603
Payable associated with assets classified as held for sale	(1,550)
	53

16. Share capital

Balances as at 31 December 20X1 and 20X2 of CU30,000 comprise 30,000 ordinary shares with par value CU1.00 fully paid, issued and outstanding. An additional 70,000 shares are legally authorised but unissued.

17. Bank overdrafts and loans

	20X2	20X1
	CU	CU
Bank overdrafts	83,600	115,508
Bank loans—fully repayable in 20X4, prepayable without penalty	50,000	150,000
	133,600	265,508

The bank overdraft and loan are secured by a floating lien over the Group's assets.

18. Long-service benefit

The liability for employee benefit obligations relates to government mandated long-service payments. All full-time members of staff, excluding directors, are covered by the programme. A payment is made of 5 per cent of salary (as determined for the twelve months before the payment) at the end of each of five years of employment. The payment is made as part of the December payroll in the fifth year. The Group does not fund this obligation in advance.

The accrual to be recognised at the year-end is determined on the basis of a present value calculation assuming a 3 per cent average annual salary increase, with employee turnover based on the Group's recent experience, discounted using the current market yield for high quality corporate bonds.

	CU
At 1 January 20X2	9,830
Additional accrual during year	7,033
Payment made in year	(6,240)
At 31 December 20X2	10,623

Analysed as:	20X2	20X1
	CU	CU
Current liability	6,181	5,943
Non-current liability	4,442	3,887
Total	10,623	9,830

19. Obligations under finance leases

The Group holds one piece of specialised machinery with an estimated useful life of five years under a five-year finance lease. The future minimum lease payments at the end of the year, for each future year, are as follows:

	20X2	20X1
	CU	CU
In 20X2	n/a	25,000
In 20X3	25,000	25,000
In 20X4	25,000	25,000
	50,000	75,000

The obligation is analysed as:

	20X2	20X1
	CU	CU
Current	21,461	19,884
Non-current	23,163	44,624
	44,624	64,508

20. Cash and cash equivalents

	20X2	20X1
	CU	CU
Cash on hand	26,700	20,875
Overdrafts	(83,600)	(115,508)
	(56,900)	(94,633)

21. Obligations under operating leases

	20X2	20X1
	CU	CU
Minimum lease payments under operating leases recognised as an expense during the year	26,100	26,100

At the balance sheet date, the Group has outstanding commitments under non-cancellable operating leases that fall due as follows:

	20X2	20X1
	CU	CU
In 20X2	n/a	26,100
In 20X3	13,050	13,050

Operating lease payments represent rentals payable by the Group for certain items of equipment. Leases are negotiated for an average period of three years, with fixed rentals over the same period.

22. Contingent liabilities

During 20X2, a customer of the Group instigated proceedings against XYZ (Trading) Limited for a fire caused by a faulty candle. The customer asserts that its total losses are CU50,000 and has claimed this amount from the company.

The Group's lawyers do not consider that the claim has merit, and they have recommended that it be contested. No provision has been recognised in these financial statements as the Group's management does not consider it probable that a loss will arise.

23. Event after the balance sheet date

On 25 January 20X3, there was a flood in one of the candle storage rooms. The cost of refurbishment is expected to be CU36,000. The reimbursements from insurance are estimated to be CU16,000.

24. Related party transactions

Transactions between the Company and its subsidiary, which is a related party, have been eliminated in consolidation.

The Group sells goods to its associate (see note 11), which is a related party, as follows:

	Sales of goods		Amounts owed to the Group by the related party at year-end	
	20X2	20X1	20X2	20X1
	CU	CU	CU	CU
Associate				10,000
	8,000	800	400	

The payments under the finance lease (see note 19) are personally guaranteed by a principal shareholder of the Company. No charge has been requested for this guarantee.

The remuneration of directors and other members of key management during the year was as follows:

	20X2	20X1
	CU	CU
Salaries	190,500	169,300
Other short-term benefits	15,213	9,200
Post-employment benefits	44,205	29,760

25. Approval of financial statements

These financial statements were approved by the board of directors and authorised for issue on 10 March 20X3.

Disclosure checklist

This disclosure checklist has been derived from the disclosure requirements in the [draft] IFRS for SMEs.

D1   This disclosure checklist summarises the disclosures that are required throughout the [draft] *IFRS for SMEs*. In most cases, the [draft] *IFRS for SMEs* does not specify whether the disclosure should be made in the notes or on the face of the financial statements. In several cases, however, disclosures are expressly required to be on face of financial statements; these are identified in this checklist.

D2   This checklist deals with disclosures. While it does not deal with presentation format, often a required presentation is the equivalent of a disclosure requirement. To illustrate, Sections 3–6 of the [draft] *IFRS for SMEs* require the presentation of some specific line items on the face of the balance sheet, income statement, statement of changes in equity and cash flow statement. Those presentation requirements are essentially disclosure requirements and are included in this checklist.

D3   The disclosure requirements in the [draft] *IFRS for SMEs* should be regarded as minimum requirements. An entity must present additional line items, headings and subtotals on the face of the financial statements when such presentation is relevant to an understanding of the entity's financial position, performance, and changes in financial position. Similarly, an entity must include in the notes to financial statements information that is not presented on the face of the financial statements but is relevant to an understanding of them.

D4   Under the [draft] *IFRS for SMEs*, an entity is required or permitted to apply an International Financial Reporting Standard (IFRS) in the following cases:

(a)   The entity elects to apply an accounting policy option that is included in the [draft] *IFRS for SMEs* by cross-reference to an IFRS. Examples include the direct method of preparing the cash flow statement; accounting for financial instruments under IAS 39 *Financial Instruments: Recognition and Measurement* rather than under the provisions of Section 11; the equity method of accounting for investments in associates and joint ventures; the proportionate consolidation method of accounting for investments in joint ventures; the fair value through profit or loss model for investment property; the revaluation model for property, plant and equipment and for intangible assets; capitalisation of development costs; and capitalisation of borrowing costs.

(b)   The entity is required or permitted to apply an IFRS because the [draft] *IFRS for SMEs* does not address specific events, transactions or circumstances that are covered in IFRSs. That may be the case either because:

(i)   the [draft] *IFRS for SMEs* states that if an SME does encounter such events, transactions or circumstances it should apply the provisions of the relevant IFRS. Examples include calculation of the recoverable amount of goodwill; equity-settled share-based payment; financial reporting in a hyperinflationary economy; specialised industry accounting (extractive industries and agriculture); and interim reporting.

(ii)   paragraph 10.4 of the [draft] *IFRS for SMEs* permits the entity to apply the requirements and guidance in IFRSs and Interpretations of IFRSs dealing with similar and related issues.

(c)   The entity elects to follow IAS 39 rather than Section 11   in accounting for financial assets and financial liabilities.

An entity that applies an IFRS in the foregoing circumstances is required to make the relevant disclosures as required by that IFRS. This disclosure checklist does not include those potential disclosures.

Disclosure requirements in the [draft] *IFRS for SMEs* Section by section

Section 1   Scope

No disclosures required by this section.

Section 2   Concepts and Pervasive Principles

No disclosures required by this section.

Section 3   Financial Statement Presentation

Compliance with the [draft] IFRS for SMEs

3.2	An entity whose financial statements comply with the *IFRS for SMEs* shall make an explicit and unreserved statement of such compliance in the notes.
3.4	When an entity departs from a requirement of this [draft] standard in accordance with paragraph 3.3, it shall disclose: (a) that management has concluded that the financial statements present fairly the entity's financial position, financial performance and cash flows; (b) that it has complied with the *IFRS for SMEs*, except that it has departed from a particular requirement to achieve a fair presentation; (c) the nature of the departure, including the treatment that the *IFRS for SMEs* would require, the reason why that treatment would be so misleading in the circumstances that it would conflict with the objective of financial statements set out in Section 2, and the treatment adopted; and (d) for each period presented, the financial effect of the departure on each item in the financial statements that would have been reported in complying with the requirement.
3.5	When an entity has departed from a requirement of this [draft] standard in a prior period, and that departure affects the amounts recognised in the financial statements for the current period, it shall make the disclosures set out in paragraph 3.4(c) and (d).
3.6	In the extremely rare circumstances in which management concludes that compliance with a requirement in this [draft] Standard would be so misleading that it would conflict with the objective of financial statements of SMEs set out in Section 2, but the relevant regulatory framework prohibits departure from the requirement, the entity shall, to the maximum extent possible, reduce the perceived misleading aspects of compliance by disclosing: (a) the nature of the requirement in this [draft] standard, and the reason why management has concluded that complying with that requirement is so misleading in the circumstances that it conflicts with the objective of financial statements set out in Section 2; and

	(b) for each period presented, the adjustments to each item in the financial statements that management has concluded would be necessary to achieve a fair presentation.
3.7	When an entity does not prepare financial statements on a going concern basis, it shall disclose that fact, together with the basis on which it prepared the financial statements and the reason why the entity is not regarded as a going concern.

Reclassifications

3.10	When the presentation or classification of items in the financial statements is changed, an entity shall reclassify comparative amounts unless the reclassification is impracticable. When comparative amounts are reclassified, an entity shall disclose: (a) the nature of the reclassification; (b) the amount of each item or class of items that is reclassified; and (c) the reason for the reclassification.
3.11	When it is impracticable to reclassify comparative amounts, an entity shall disclose: (a) the reason for not reclassifying the amounts; and (b) the nature of the adjustments that would have been made if the amounts had been reclassified.

Comparative information

3.12	Except when this [draft] standard permits or requires otherwise, an entity shall disclose comparative information in respect of the previous comparable period for all amounts reported in the financial statements (including the information on the face of the financial statements and in the notes). An entity shall include comparative information for narrative and descriptive information when it is relevant to an understanding of the current period's financial statements.

Identification of the financial statements

3.20	Disclose: (a) the name of the reporting entity and any change in its name since the end of the preceding reporting period; (b) whether the financial statements cover the individual entity or a group of entities; (c) the date of the end of the reporting period and the period covered by the financial statements; (d) the presentation currency, as defined in Section 31; and (e) the level of rounding, if any, used in presenting amounts in the financial statements.

Section 4 Balance Sheet

Information to be presented on the face of the balance sheet

4.2	As a minimum, an entity shall include, on the face of the balance sheet, line items that present the following amounts: (a) cash and cash equivalents; (b) trade and other receivables; (c) financial assets (excluding amounts shown under (a), (b) and (h)); (d) inventories; (e) property, plant and equipment; (f) intangible assets; (g) biological assets; (h) investments accounted for using the equity method; (i) the total of non-current assets classified as held for sale and assets included in disposal groups classified as held for sale in accordance with Section 36; (j) trade and other payables; (k) financial liabilities (excluding amounts shown under (j) and (o); (l) liabilities and assets for current tax; (m) deferred tax liabilities and deferred tax assets (these shall always be classified as non-current); (n) liabilities included in disposal groups classified as held for sale. (o) provisions; (p) minority interest, presented within equity separately from the parent shareholders' equity; and (q) equity attributable to shareholders of the parent.

Current/non-current distinction

4.5	An entity shall present current and non-current assets, and current and non-current liabilities, as separate classifications on the face of its balance sheet in accordance with paragraphs 4.6–4.9, except when a presentation based on liquidity provides information that is reliable and more relevant. When that exception applies, all assets and liabilities shall be presented in order of approximate liquidity.

Information to be presented either on the face of the balance sheet or in the notes

4.12	An entity shall disclose, either on the face of the balance sheet or in the notes, the following subclassifications of the line items presented: (a) classes of items of property, plant and equipment in accordance with Section 16; (b) amounts receivable from trade customers, receivables from related parties, prepayments and other amounts; (c) classes of inventories in accordance with Section 12, such as merchandise, production supplies, materials, work in progress and finished goods; (d) provisions for employee benefits and other provisions; and (e) classes of equity, such as paid-in capital, share premium, retained earnings and items of income and expense that, as

	required by this [draft] standard, are recognised directly in equity.
4.13	An entity with share capital shall disclose the following, either on the face of the balance sheet or in the notes:
	(a) for each class of share capital:
	(i) the number of shares authorised;
	(ii) the number of shares issued and fully paid, and issued but not fully paid;
	(iii) par value per share, or that the shares have no par value;
	(iv) a reconciliation of the number of shares outstanding at the beginning and at the end of the period (see paragraph 21.12 for further guidance);
	(v) the rights, preferences and restrictions attaching to that class including restrictions on the distribution of dividends and the repayment of capital;
	(vi) shares in the entity held by the entity or by its subsidiaries or associates;
	(vii) shares reserved for issue under options and contracts for the sale of shares, including the terms and amounts; and
	(b) a description of each reserve within equity.
4.14	An entity without share capital, such as a partnership or trust, shall disclose information equivalent to that required by paragraph 4.13(a), showing changes during the period in each category of equity, and the rights, preferences and restrictions attaching to each category of equity.
21.12	Paragraph 4.13(a)(iv) requires an entity with share capital to disclose, either on the face of the balance sheet or in the notes, for each class of share capital, a reconciliation of the number of shares outstanding (or other measure of quantity) at the beginning and at the end of the period. In that reconciliation, the entity shall identify separately each significant type of change in the number of shares outstanding, including new issues; exercises of options, rights and warrants; conversions of convertible securities; treasury share transactions; business combinations; and bonus issues (share dividends) and share splits.

Section 5   Income Statement

Information to be presented on the face of the income statement

5.3	As a minimum, an entity shall include, on the face of the income statement, line items that present the following amounts for the period:
	(a) revenue;
	(b) finance costs;
	(c) share of the profit or loss of investments in associates and joint ventures accounted for using the equity method;
	(d) tax expense;
	(e) a single amount comprising the total of (i) the post-tax profit or loss of discontinued operations and (ii) the post-tax gain or loss recognised on the measurement to fair value less costs to sell or

	on the disposal of the assets or disposal group(s) constituting the discontinued operation (see Section 36); and (f) profit or loss.
5.4	An entity shall disclose separately the following items on the face of the income statement as allocations of profit or loss for the period: (a) profit or loss attributable to minority interest; and (b) profit or loss attributable to equity holders of the parent.

Information to be presented either on the face of the income statement or in the notes

5.7	An entity shall disclose separately the nature and amount of material components of income and expense. Such disclosures shall include: (a) write-downs of property, plant and equipment to fair value less costs to sell, and the reversal of such write-downs; (b) write-downs of inventories to net realisable value, and the reversal of such write-downs; (c) restructurings of the activities of an entity and reversals of any provisions for the costs of restructuring; (d) disposals of items of property, plant and equipment; (e) disposals of investments; (f) discontinued operations; (g) litigation settlements; and (h) the reversal of other provisions.
5.9	An entity shall present an analysis of expenses using a classification based on either the nature of expenses or their function of expenses within the entity, whichever provides information that is reliable and more relevant.
5.11	Entities classifying expenses by function shall disclose additional information on the nature of expenses, including depreciation and amortisation expense and employee benefits expense.

Section 6   Statement of Changes in Equity and Statement of Income and Retained Earnings

Information to be presented on the face of the statement of changes in equity

6.2	An entity shall present a statement of changes in equity showing on the face of the statement: (a) profit or loss for the period; (b) each item of income and expense for the period that, as required by this [draft] standard, is recognised directly in equity, and the total of those items; (c) total income and expense for the period (calculated as the sum of (a) and (b)), showing separately the total amounts attributable to equity holders of the parent and to minority interest; and (d) for each component of equity, the effects of changes in accounting policies and corrections of errors recognised in accordance with Section 10.

Information to be presented either on the face of the statement of changes in equity or in the notes

6.3	An entity shall also present, either on the face of the statement of changes in equity or in the notes:
	(a) the amounts of investments by, and dividends and other distributions to, equity holders, showing separately issues of shares, treasury share transactions, and dividends and other distributions to equity holders;
	(b) the balance of retained earnings (ie accumulated profit or loss) at the beginning of the reporting period and at the end of the period, and the changes during the period; and
	(c) a reconciliation of the carrying amount of each class of contributed equity and each item of income and expense recognised directly in equity (see paragraph 6.2(b)) at the beginning and the end of the period, separately disclosing each change.

Information to be presented on the face of the statement of income and retained earnings

6.5	An entity shall present, on the face of the statement of income and retained earnings, the following items in addition to the information required by Section 5:
	(a) retained earnings at the beginning of the reporting period;
	(b) dividends declared and paid or payable during the period;
	(c) restatements of retained earnings for corrections of prior period errors;
	(d) restatements of retained earnings for changes in accounting policy; and
	(e) retained earnings at the end of the reporting period.

Section 7
Cash Flow Statement

7.3	An entity shall present a cash flow statement that reports cash flows for a period classified by operating activities, investing activities and financing activities.
7.7	An entity shall report cash flows from operating activities using either:
	(a) the direct method, whereby major classes of gross cash receipts and gross cash payments are disclosed; or
	(b) the indirect method, whereby profit or loss is adjusted for the effects of non-cash transactions, any deferrals or accruals of past or future operating cash receipts or payments, and items of income or expense associated with investing or financing cash flows.

Reporting cash flows from investing and financing activities

7.10	An entity shall report separately major classes of gross cash receipts and gross cash payments arising from investing and financing activities. The aggregate cash flows arising from acquisitions and from disposals of subsidiaries or other business units shall be presented separately and classified as operating activities.

Interest and dividends

7.14	An entity shall disclose separately cash flows from interest and dividends received and paid.

Income taxes

7.17	An entity shall disclose separately cash flows arising from taxes on income and shall classify them as cash flows from operating activities unless they can be specifically identified with financing and investing activities. When tax cash flows are allocated over more than one class of activity, the entity shall disclose the total amount of taxes paid.

Non-cash transactions

7.18	An entity shall exclude from the cash flow statement investing and financing transactions that do not require the use of cash or cash equivalents. An entity shall disclose such transactions elsewhere in the financial statements in a way that provides all the relevant information about these investing and financing activities.

Components of cash and cash equivalents

7.20	An entity shall disclose the components of cash and cash equivalents and shall present a reconciliation of the amounts reported in the cash flow statement to the equivalent items reported in the balance sheet.

Other disclosures

7.21	An entity shall disclose, together with a commentary by management, the amount of significant cash and cash equivalent balances held by the entity that are not available for use by the entity. Cash and cash equivalents held by an entity may not be available for use by the entity because of, among other reasons, foreign exchange controls or legal restrictions.

Section 8   Notes to the Financial Statements

8.3	An entity shall, as far as practicable, present the notes in a systematic manner. An entity shall cross-reference each item on the face of the financial statements to any related information in the notes.
8.4	An entity normally presents the notes in the following order:

	(a) a statement that the financial statements have been prepared in compliance with the *IFRS for SMEs* (see paragraph 3.2);
	(b) a summary of significant accounting policies applied (see paragraph 8.5);
	(c) supporting information for items presented on the face of the financial statements, in the order in which each statement and each line item is presented; and
	(d) other disclosures, including:
	(i) contingent liabilities and contingent assets (see Section 20) and unrecognised contractual commitments;
	(ii) non-financial disclosures
	(iii) the amount of dividends proposed or declared before the financial statements were authorised for issue but not recognised as a distribution to equity holders during the period, and the related amount per share; and
	(iv) the amount of any cumulative preference dividends not recognised.

Disclosure of accounting policies

8.5	An entity shall disclose in the summary of significant accounting policies:
	(a) the measurement basis (or bases) used in preparing the financial statements;
	(b) the accounting policy the entity has chosen whenever the entity has adopted an accounting policy for an event, a transaction, other event or condition for which this [draft] standard allows an accounting policy choice; and
	(c) the other accounting policies used that are relevant to an understanding of the financial statements.

Information about judgements

8.6	An entity shall disclose, in the summary of significant accounting policies or other notes, the judgements, apart from those involving estimations (see paragraph 8.7), that management has made in the process of applying the entity's accounting policies and that have the most significant effect on the amounts recognised in the financial statements.

Information about key sources of estimation uncertainty

8.7	An entity shall disclose in the notes information about the key assumptions concerning the future, and other key sources of estimation uncertainty at the end of the reporting period, that have a significant risk of causing a material adjustment to the carrying amounts of assets and liabilities within the next financial year. In respect of those assets and liabilities, the notes shall include details of:
	(a) their nature; and
	(b) their carrying amount as at the end of the reporting period.

Information about externally imposed capital requirements

8.8	If an entity is subject to externally imposed capital requirements, it shall disclose the nature of those requirements and how they are managed, including whether the requirements have been complied with.

Section 9   Consolidated and Separate Financial Statements

Separate financial statements

9.19	When a parent, a venturer with an interest in a jointly controlled entity or an investor in an associate prepares separate financial statements, those separate financial statements shall disclose: (a) that the statements are separate financial statements and the reasons why those statements are prepared if not required by law; (b) a list of significant investments in subsidiaries, jointly controlled entities and associates, including the name, country of incorporation or residence, proportion of ownership interest and, if different, proportion of voting power held; and (c) a description of the method used to account for the investments listed under (b); and shall identify the consolidated financial statements to which they relate.

Combined financial statements

9.22	If an entity prepares combined financial statements and describes them as conforming to the *IFRS for SMEs*, those statements shall comply with all of the requirements of this [draft] standard. Inter-company transactions and balances shall be eliminated; profits or losses resulting from intercompany transactions that are recognised in assets such as inventory and fixed assets shall be eliminated; the financial statements of the entities included in the combined financial statements shall be prepared as of the same reporting date unless it is impracticable to do so; and uniform accounting policies shall be followed for like transactions and other events in similar circumstances. Disclosures shall include the fact that the financial statements are combined financial statements and the related party disclosures required by Section 33.

Section 10 Accounting Policies, Estimates and Errors

Disclosure of a change in accounting policy

10.11	When initial application of this [draft] standard, or an amendment to this [draft] standard, has an effect on the current period or any prior period or might have an effect on future periods, an entity shall disclose: (a) the nature of the change in accounting policy; (b) for the current period and each prior period presented, to the extent practicable, the amount of the adjustment for each financial statement line item affected; (c) the amount of the adjustment relating to periods before those presented, to the extent practicable; and (d) an explanation if it is not practicable to determine the amounts to be disclosed in (b) or (c) above. Financial statements of subsequent periods need not repeat these disclosures.
10.12	When a voluntary change in accounting policy has an effect on the current period or any prior period, or might have an effect on future periods, an entity shall disclose: (a) the nature of the change in accounting policy; (b) the reasons why applying the new accounting policy provides reliable and more relevant information; (c) for the current period and each prior period presented, to the extent practicable, the amount of the adjustment for each financial statement line item affected; (d) the amount of the adjustment relating to periods before those presented, to the extent practicable; and (e) an explanation if it is not practicable to determine the amounts to be disclosed in (c) or (d) above. Financial statements of subsequent periods need not repeat these disclosures.

Disclosure of a change in estimate

10.16	An entity shall disclose the nature and amount of a change in an accounting estimate that has an effect in the current period or is expected to have an effect in future periods, except for the disclosure of the effect on future periods when it is impracticable to estimate that effect.
10.17	If the amount of the effect in future periods is not disclosed because estimating it is impracticable, an entity shall disclose that fact.

Disclosure of prior period errors

10.23	An entity shall disclose the following about prior period errors: (a) the nature of the prior period error;

	(b) for each prior period presented, to the extent practicable, the amount of the correction for each financial statement line item affected; (c) the amount of the correction at the beginning of the earliest prior period presented; and (d) if retrospective restatement is impracticable for a particular prior period, the circumstances that led to the existence of that condition and a description of how and from when the error has been corrected. Financial statements of subsequent periods need not repeat these disclosures.

Section 11   Financial Assets and Financial Liabilities

Disclosure of accounting policies for financial instruments

11.40	In accordance with paragraph 8.5 of Section 8, an entity shall disclose, in the summary of significant accounting policies, the measurement basis (or bases) used for financial instruments and the other accounting policies used for financial instruments that are relevant to an understanding of the financial statements.

Balance sheet – categories of financial assets and financial liabilities

11.41	An entity shall disclose the carrying amounts of each of the following categories of financial assets and financial liabilities, in total and by each significant type of financial asset or financial liability within each category, either on the face of the balance sheet or in the notes: (a) financial assets measured at fair value through profit or loss (paragraph 11.8); (b) financial assets measured at amortised cost less impairment (paragraph 11.7(a)); (c) equity instruments measured at cost (paragraph 11.7(c)); (d) forward commitments and options measured at cost less impairment (paragraph 11.7(b)); (e) financial liabilities measured at fair value through profit or loss (paragraph 11.8); and (f) financial liabilities measured at amortised cost (paragraph 11.7(a)).
11.42	For all financial assets and financial liabilities measured at fair value, the entity shall disclose the basis for determining fair value, eg quoted market price in an active market or a valuation technique. When a valuation technique is used, the entity shall disclose the assumptions applied in determining fair values of each class of financial assets or financial liabilities. For example, if applicable, an entity discloses information about the assumptions relating to prepayment rates, rates of estimated credit losses, and interest rates or discount rates.
11.43	If a reliable measure of fair value is no longer available for an equity instrument measured at fair value through profit or loss, the entity shall disclose that fact.

Derecognition

11.44	If an entity has transferred financial assets to another party in a transaction that does not qualify for derecognition (see paragraphs 11.24–11.26), the entity shall disclose for each class of such financial assets:
	(a) the nature of the assets;
	(b) the nature of the risks and rewards of ownership to which the entity remains exposed;
	(c) the carrying amounts of the assets and of any associated liabilities that the entity continues to recognise.

Collateral

11.45	When an entity has pledged financial assets as collateral for liabilities or contingent liabilities, it shall disclose:
	(a) the carrying amount of the financial assets pledged as collateral; and
	(b) the terms and conditions relating to its pledge.

Defaults and breaches on loans payable

11.46	For loans payable recognised at the reporting date, an entity shall disclose:
	(a) details of any defaults during the period of principal, interest, sinking fund, or redemption terms of those loans payable;
	(b) the carrying amount of the loans payable in default at the reporting date; and
	(c) whether the default was remedied, or the terms of the loans payable were renegotiated, before the financial statements were authorised for issue.
11.47	If, during the period, there were breaches of loan agreement terms other than those described in paragraph 11.46, an entity shall disclose the same information as required by paragraph 11.46 if those breaches permitted the lender to demand accelerated repayment (unless the breaches were remedied, or the terms of the loan were renegotiated, on or before the reporting date).

Income statement and equity – items of income, expense, gains or losses

11.48	An entity shall disclose the following items of income, expense, gains or losses either on the face of the financial statements or in the notes:
	(a) net gains or net losses recognised on:
	(i) financial assets measured at fair value through profit or loss;
	(ii) financial liabilities measured at fair value through profit or loss;
	(iii) financial assets measured at amortised cost; and
	(iv) financial liabilities measured at amortised cost;

	(b) total interest income and total interest expense (calculated using the effective interest method) for financial assets or financial liabilities that are not at fair value through profit or loss; and (c) the amount of any impairment loss for each class of financial asset.

Hedge accounting

11.49	An entity shall disclose the following separately for each type of hedge described in paragraph 11.31: (a) a description of the hedge; (b) a description of the financial instruments designated as hedging instruments and their fair values at the reporting date; and (c) the nature of the risks being hedged, including a description of the hedged item.
11.50	For a hedge of fixed interest rate risk or commodity price risk of a commodity held (paragraphs 11.33–11.36) the entity shall disclose: (a) the amount of the change in fair value of the hedging instrument recognised in profit or loss and (b) the amount of the change in fair value of the hedged item recognised in profit or loss.
11.51	For a hedge of variable interest rate risk, foreign exchange risk, commodity price risk in a firm commitment or highly probable forecast transaction, or a net investment in a foreign operation (paragraphs 11.37–11.39) the entity shall disclose: (a) the periods when the cash flows are expected to occur and when they are expected to affect profit or loss; (b) a description of any forecast transaction for which hedge accounting had previously been used, but which is no longer expected to occur; (c) the amount of the change in fair value of the hedging instrument that was recognised in equity during the period (paragraph 11.37); (d) the amount that was removed from equity and recognised in profit or loss for the period, showing the amount included in each line item in the income statement (paragraphs 11.38 and 11.39).

Risks relating to financial instruments measured at cost or amortised cost

11.52	For financial assets measured at amortised cost less impairment, the entity shall disclose the significant terms and conditions that may affect the amount, timing and certainty of future cash flows, including interest rate risk, foreign currency exchange rate risk and credit risk.

Section 12 Inventories

12.21	An entity shall disclose: (a) the accounting policies adopted in measuring inventories, including the cost formula used; (b) the total carrying amount of inventories and the carrying amount in classifications appropriate to the entity; (c) the amount of inventories recognised as an expense during the period ('cost of goods sold'); (d) the amount of any impairment of inventories recognised as an expense in the period in accordance with paragraph 12.18 and paragraphs 26.2–26.4; (e) the amount of any reversal of any impairment recognised in the period in accordance with paragraph 12.18 and paragraph 26.4, and a description of the circumstances or events that led to such reversal; and (f) the carrying amount of inventories pledged as security for liabilities.

Section 13 Investments in Associates

13.7	An investor in an associate shall disclose: (a) its accounting policy for investments in associates; (b) the fair value of investments in associates for which there are published price quotations; (c) summarised financial information of associates, including the aggregated amounts of assets, liabilities, revenues and profit or loss, along with the investor's percentage of ownership of the associates; and (d) the nature and extent of any significant restrictions (eg resulting from borrowing arrangements or regulatory requirements) on the ability of associates to transfer funds to the investor in the form of cash dividends, or repayment of loans or advances.

Section 14 Investments in Joint Ventures

14.16	An investor in a joint venture shall disclose the aggregate amount of the following contingent liabilities, unless the probability of loss is remote, separately from the amount of other contingent liabilities: (a) any contingent liabilities that the investor has incurred in relation to its interests in joint ventures and its share in each of the contingent liabilities that have been incurred jointly with other venturers; (b) its share of the contingent liabilities of the joint ventures themselves for which it is contingently liable; and (c) those contingent liabilities that arise because the investor is contingently liable for the liabilities of the other venturers of a joint venture.
14.17	An investor in a joint venture shall also disclose: (a) the aggregate amount of its commitments relating to joint ventures, including its share in the capital commitments that have been incurred jointly with other venturers, as well as its

	share of the capital commitments of the joint ventures themselves;
	(b) a listing and description of interests in significant joint ventures and the proportion of ownership interest held in jointly controlled entities; and
	(c) the method it uses to recognise its interests in jointly controlled entities.

Section 15   Investment Property

Fair value model

15.5	An entity that elects to use the fair value model shall apply IAS 40 *Investment Property* (see especially paragraphs 33–55), and shall make the disclosures required by paragraphs 76–78 of that standard.

Cost model

15.6	An entity that elects to use the cost model shall account for all of its investment property as property, plant and equipment in accordance with the requirements for the cost model in Section 16. The entity shall make the disclosures required by that section.

Section 16   Property, Plant and Equipment

16.29	An entity shall disclose, for each class of property, plant and equipment:
	(a) the measurement bases used for determining the gross carrying amount;
	(b) the depreciation methods used;
	(c) the useful lives or the depreciation rates used;
	(d) the gross carrying amount and the accumulated depreciation (aggregated with accumulated impairment losses) at the beginning and end of the period; and
	(e) a reconciliation of the carrying amount at the beginning and end of the period showing:
	(i) additions;
	(ii) disposals, including assets classified as held for sale or included in a disposal group classified as held for sale;
	(iii) acquisitions through business combinations;
	(iv) impairment losses recognised or reversed in profit or loss in accordance with Section 26;
	(v) depreciation;
	(vi) the net exchange differences arising on the translation of the financial statements from the functional currency into a different presentation currency, including the translation of a foreign operation into the presentation currency of the reporting entity (see Section 30); and
	(vii) other changes.

16.30	The entity shall also disclose:
	(a) the existence and amounts of restrictions on title, and property, plant and equipment pledged as security for liabilities;
	(b) the amount of contractual commitments for the acquisition of property, plant and equipment; and
	(c) if it is not disclosed separately on the face of the income statement, the amount of compensation from third parties for items of property, plant and equipment that were impaired, lost or given up that is recognised in profit or loss.
16.31	An entity shall present property, plant and equipment that is held for sale separately from other assets on the face of the balance sheet. The entity shall present any liabilities related to property, plant and equipment that is held for sale separately from other liabilities on the face of the balance sheet.

Section 17 Intangible Assets other than Goodwill

17.23	An entity that uses the revaluation model shall apply paragraphs 75–87 of IAS 38 *Intangible Assets* and shall make the disclosures required by paragraphs 124 and 125 of IAS 38.
17.32	An entity shall disclose the following for each class of intangible assets, distinguishing between internally generated intangible assets and other intangible assets:
	(a) whether the useful lives are indefinite or finite and, if finite, the useful lives or the amortisation rates used;
	(b) the amortisation methods used for intangible assets with finite useful lives;
	(c) the gross carrying amount and any accumulated amortisation (aggregated with accumulated impairment losses) at the beginning and end of the period;
	(d) the line item(s) of the income statement in which any amortisation of intangible assets is included;
	(e) a reconciliation of the carrying amount at the beginning and end of the period showing separately additions, disposals, amortisations, impairment losses, and other changes.
17.33	An entity shall also disclose:
	(a) for an intangible asset assessed as having an indefinite useful life, the carrying amount of that asset and the reasons supporting the assessment of an indefinite useful life. In giving these reasons, the entity shall describe the factor(s) that played a significant role in determining that the asset has an indefinite useful life.
	(b) a description, the carrying amount and remaining amortisation period of any individual intangible asset that is material to the entity's financial statements.
	(c) for intangible assets acquired by way of a government grant and initially recognised at fair value (see paragraph 17.10):
	(i) the fair value initially recognised for these assets;
	(ii) their carrying amount; and
	(iii) whether they are measured after recognition using the cost model or the revaluation model.

	(d) the existence and carrying amounts of intangible assets whose title is restricted and the carrying amounts of intangible assets pledged as security for liabilities. (e) the amount of contractual commitments for the acquisition of intangible assets.
17.34	An entity shall disclose the aggregate amount of research and development expenditure recognised as an expense during the period.

Section 18   Business Combinations and Goodwill

For business combinations effected during the reporting period

18.23	For each business combination that was effected during the period (or group of individually immaterial business combinations), the acquirer shall disclose the following:
	
	(a) the names and descriptions of the combining entities or businesses.
	(b) the acquisition date.
	(c) the percentage of voting equity instruments acquired.
	(d) the cost of the combination and a description of the components of that cost, including any costs directly attributable to the combination. When equity instruments are issued or issuable as part of the cost, the following shall also be disclosed:
	
	    (i) the number of equity instruments issued or issuable; and
	    (ii) the fair value of those instruments and the basis for determining that fair value.
	
	(e) details of any operations the entity has decided to dispose of as a result of the combination.
	(f) the amounts recognised at the acquisition date for each class of the acquiree's assets, liabilities and contingent liabilities, including goodwill.
	(g) the amount of any excess recognised in profit or loss in accordance with paragraph 18.22, and the line item in the income statement in which the excess is recognised.
	(h) a description of the factors that contributed to a cost that results in the recognition of goodwill—a description of each intangible asset that was not recognised separately from goodwill and an explanation of why the intangible asset's fair value could not be measured reliably—or a description of the nature of any excess recognised in profit or loss in accordance with paragraph 18.22.
	(i) the amount of the acquiree's profit or loss since the acquisition date included in the acquirer's profit or loss for the period, unless disclosure would be impracticable. If such disclosure would be impracticable, that fact shall be disclosed, together with an explanation of why this is the case.

For business combinations effected after the end of the reporting period but before the financial statements are authorised for issue

18.24	For each business combination effected after the end of the reporting period but before the financial statements are authorised for issue, the acquirer shall make the disclosures required by paragraph 18.23 unless such disclosure would be impracticable. If disclosure of any of that information would be impracticable, that fact shall be disclosed, together with an explanation of why this is the case.

For all business combinations

18.25	An acquirer shall disclose a reconciliation of the carrying amount of goodwill at the beginning and end of the reporting period, showing separately changes arising from new business combinations, impairment losses, disposals of previously acquired businesses, and other changes. An acquirer shall also disclose the gross amount and accumulated impairment losses at the end of the period.

Section 19   Leases

Financial statements of lessees – finance leases

19.12	Lessees shall make the following disclosures for finance leases:
	(a) for each class of asset, the net carrying amount at the end of the reporting period.
	(b) the total of future minimum lease payments at the end of the reporting period, for each future year.
	(c) contingent rents recognised as an expense.
	(d) the total of future minimum sublease payments expected to be received under non-cancellable subleases at the end of the reporting period.
	(e) a general description of the lessee's leasing arrangements including, but not limited to, the following:
	(i) the basis on which contingent rent payable is determined;
	(ii) the existence and terms of renewal or purchase options and escalation clauses; and
	(iii) restrictions imposed by lease arrangements, such as those concerning dividends, additional debt and further leasing.

Financial statements of lessees – operating leases

19.14	Lessees shall make the following disclosures for operating leases:
	(a) the total of future minimum lease payments under non-cancellable operating leases for each future year.
	(b) the total of future minimum sublease payments expected to be received under non-cancellable subleases at the end of the reporting period.
	(c) lease and sublease payments recognised as an expense, with separate amounts for minimum lease payments, contingent rents, and sublease payments.

| | (d) | a general description of the lessee's significant leasing arrangements including, but not limited to, the following:

(i) the basis on which contingent rent payable is determined;
(ii) the existence and terms of renewal or purchase options and escalation clauses; and
(iii) restrictions imposed by lease arrangements, such as those concerning dividends, additional debt and further leasing. |

Financial statements of lessors: finance leases

| 19.15 | A lessor in a finance lease shall apply paragraphs 36–46 of IAS 17 *Leases* and shall make the disclosures required by paragraph 47 of IAS 17. |

Financial statements of lessors: operating leases

| 19.23 | Lessors shall disclose the following for operating leases:

(a) the future minimum lease payments under non-cancellable operating leases in the aggregate and for each future year.
(b) total contingent rents recognised as income.
(c) a general description of the lessor's leasing arrangements. |

Sale and leaseback transactions

| 19.27 | Disclosure requirements for lessees and lessors apply equally to sale and leaseback transactions. The required description of leasing arrangements includes description of unique or unusual provisions of the agreement or terms of the sale and leaseback transactions. |

Section 20   Provisions and Contingencies

Disclosures about provisions

| 20.14 | For each class of provision, an entity shall disclose:

(a) the carrying amount at the beginning and end of the period.
(b) additional provisions made in the period, including increases to existing provisions.
(c) amounts used (ie incurred and charged against the provision) during the period.
(d) unused amounts reversed during the period.
(e) the increase during the period in the discounted amount arising from the passage of time and the effect of any change in the discount rate.
(f) a brief description of the nature of the obligation and the expected timing of any resulting outflows of economic benefits.
(g) an indication of the uncertainties about the amount or timing of those outflows.
(h) the amount of any expected reimbursement, stating the amount of any asset that has been recognised for that expected reimbursement.

Comparative information is not required. |

Disclosures about contingent liabilities

20.15	Unless the possibility of any outflow in settlement is remote, an entity shall disclose for each class of contingent liability at the end of the reporting period a brief description of the nature of the contingent liability and, when practicable:
	(a) an estimate of its financial effect, measured in accordance with paragraphs 20.6–20.9.
	(b) an indication of the uncertainties relating to the amount or timing of any outflow.
	(c) the possibility of any reimbursement.
	If it is impracticable to make one or more of these disclosures, that fact shall be stated.

Disclosures about contingent assets

20.16	If an inflow of economic benefits is probable (more likely than not) but not virtually certain, an entity shall disclose a description of the nature of the contingent assets at the end of the reporting period, and, when practicable, an estimate of their financial effect, measured using the principles set out in paragraphs 20.8–20.11. If it is impracticable to make this disclosure, that fact shall be stated.

Prejudicial disclosures

20.17	In extremely rare cases, disclosure of some or all of the information required by paragraphs 20.14–20.16 can be expected to prejudice seriously the position of the entity in a dispute with other parties on the subject matter of the provision, contingent liability or contingent asset. In such cases, an entity need not disclose the information, but shall disclose the general nature of the dispute, together with the fact that, and reason why, the information has not been disclosed.

Section 21   Equity

No disclosures required by this section (but see paragraph 4.13).

Section 22   Revenue

22.28	An entity shall disclose:
	(a) the accounting policies adopted for the recognition of revenue, including the methods adopted to determine the stage of completion of transactions involving the rendering of services.
	(b) the amount of each category of revenue recognised during the period, including revenue arising from:
	(i) the sale of goods;
	(ii) the rendering of services;
	(iii) interest;
	(iv) royalties;
	(v) dividends.
	(c) the amount of revenue arising from exchanges of goods or services included in each category of revenue.

Disclosures relating to revenue from construction contracts

22.29	An entity shall disclose: (a) the amount of contract revenue recognised as revenue in the period; (b) the methods used to determine the contract revenue recognised in the period; and (c) the methods used to determine the stage of completion of contracts in progress.
22.30	An entity shall disclose each of the following for contracts in progress at the balance sheet date: (a) the aggregate amount of costs incurred and recognised profits (less recognised losses) to date; (b) the amount of advances received; and (c) the amount of retentions (progress billings that are not paid until the satisfaction of conditions specified in the contract for the payment of such amounts or until defects have been rectified).
22.31	An entity shall present: (a) the gross amount due from customers for contract work as an asset; and (b) the gross amount due to customers for contract work as a liability.

Section 23   Government Grants

23.5	An entity shall disclose the following regardless of which choice it has made under paragraph 23.3: (a) the accounting policy adopted for government grants, including an explanation of how the grant is presented in the financial statements; (b) the nature and amounts of government grants recognised in the financial statements; (c) unfulfilled conditions and other contingencies attaching to government grants that have not been recognised in income; and (d) an indication of other forms of government assistance from which the entity has directly benefited.

Section 24   Borrowing Costs

24.5	An entity shall disclose the accounting policy adopted for borrowing costs. If the capitalisation model is adopted as provided in paragraph 24.4, the entity shall include the relevant disclosures required by IAS 23 *Borrowing Costs*.

Section 25 Share-based Payment

25.8	An entity shall disclose a description of each type of share-based payment arrangement that existed at any time during the period, including the general terms and conditions of each arrangement, such as vesting requirements, the maximum term of options granted, and the method of settlement (eg whether in cash or equity). An entity with substantially similar types of share-based payment arrangements may aggregate this information.
25.9	An entity shall disclose the following information about the effect of share-based payment transactions on the entity's profit or loss for the period and on its financial position, including at least the following: (a) the total expense recognised for the period arising from share-based payment transactions in which the goods or services received did not qualify for recognition as assets and hence were recognised immediately as an expense, including separate disclosure of that portion of the total expense that arises from transactions accounted for as equity-settled share-based payment transactions. (b) with respect to liabilities arising from share-based payment transactions: (i) the total carrying amount at the end of the period; and (ii) the total intrinsic value at the end of the period of liabilities for which the counterparty's right to cash or other assets had vested by the end of the period (eg vested share appreciation rights).

Section 26 Impairment of Non-financial Assets

26.25	An entity shall disclose the following for each class of assets: (a) the amount of impairment losses recognised in profit or loss during the period and the line item(s) of the income statement in which those impairment losses are included. (b) the amount of reversals of impairment losses recognised in profit or loss during the period and the line item(s) of the income statement in which those impairment losses are reversed. (c) the amount of impairment losses on revalued assets recognised directly in equity during the period. (d) the amount of reversals of impairment losses on revalued assets recognised directly in equity during the period.
26.26	An entity shall disclose the following information for the aggregate impairment losses and the aggregate reversals of impairment losses recognised during the period for which no separate information is disclosed: (a) the main classes of assets affected by impairment losses and the main classes of assets affected by reversals of impairment losses. (b) the main events and conditions that led to the recognition of these impairment losses and reversals of impairment losses.

Section 27   Employee Benefits

Disclosures about short-term employee benefits

27.36	Section 27 does not require specific disclosures about short-term employee benefits.

Disclosures about defined contribution plans

27.37	An entity shall disclose the total cost of defined contribution plans for the period and their amounts (a) recognised in profit or loss as an expense and (b) included in the cost of an asset.

Disclosures about defined benefit plans

27.38	An entity shall disclose the following information about defined benefit plans:
	(a) a general description of the type of plan, including funding policy.
	(b) the entity's accounting policy for recognising actuarial gains and losses and the amount of actuarial gains and losses recognised during the period.
	(c) a reconciliation of opening and closing balances of the defined benefit liability showing separately benefits paid and all other changes.
	(d) an analysis of the defined benefit liability into amounts arising from plans that are wholly unfunded and amounts arising from plans that are wholly or partly funded.
	(e) a reconciliation of the opening and closing balances of the fair value of plan assets and of the opening and closing balances of any reimbursement right recognised as an asset, showing separately, if applicable:
	(i) contributions by the employer;
	(ii) contributions by plan participants;
	(iii) benefits paid; and
	(iv) other changes in plan assets.
	(f) the total cost relating to defined benefit plans recognised in profit or loss as an expense for the period, and the line item(s) in which they are included.
	(g) the total cost relating to defined benefit plans during the period that was:
	(i) included in the cost of producing inventories in accordance with Section 12; or
	(ii) included in the cost of property, plant and equipment in accordance with Section 16.
	(h) for each major category of plan assets, which shall include, but is not limited to, equity instruments, debt instruments, property, and all other assets, the percentage or amount that each major category constitutes of the fair value of the total plan assets.
	(i) the amounts included in the fair value of plan assets for:

	(i) each category of the entity's own financial instruments; and
	(ii) any property occupied by, or other assets used by, the entity.
	(j) the actual return on plan assets.
	(k) the principal actuarial assumptions used, including, when applicable:
	(i) the discount rates;
	(ii) the expected rates of return on any plan assets for the periods presented in the financial statements;
	(iii) the expected rates of salary increases; and
	(iv) medical cost trend rates.

Disclosures about other long-term benefits

27.39	For each category of other long-term benefits that an entity provides to its employees, the entity shall disclose the nature of the benefit, the amount of its obligation and the funding status at the balance sheet date, and the amount of any actuarial gains and losses arising in the current period and its accounting policy for such actuarial gains and losses.

Disclosures about termination benefits

27.40	For each category of termination benefits that an entity provides to its employees, the entity shall disclose the nature of the benefit, its accounting policy, and the amount of its obligation and the funding status at the balance sheet date.
27.41	When there is uncertainty about the number of employees who will accept an offer of termination benefits, a contingent liability exists. Section 20 requires an entity to disclose information about its contingent liability unless the possibility of an outflow in settlement is remote.

Section 28 Income Taxes

28.28	An entity shall disclose separately the major components of tax expense (income). Such components of tax expense (income) may include:
	(a) current tax expense (income).
	(b) any adjustments recognised in the period for current tax of prior periods.
	(c) the amount of deferred tax expense (income) relating to the origination and reversal of temporary differences.
	(d) the amount of deferred tax expense (income) relating to changes in tax rates or the imposition of new taxes.
	(e) the amount of the benefit arising from a previously unrecognised tax loss, tax credit or temporary difference of a prior period that is used to reduce current tax expense.

	(f) deferred tax expense (or income) arising from the impairment, or reversal of a previous impairment, of a deferred tax asset (see paragraph 28.26).
28.29	An entity shall disclose the following separately:
	(a) the aggregate current and deferred tax relating to items that are recognised directly in equity.
	(b) a numerical reconciliation between tax expense (income) as recognised and tax expense (income) that would be expected by multiplying profit by the applicable tax rate(s), with each significant difference disclosed separately.
	(c) an explanation of changes in the applicable tax rate(s) compared with the previous reporting period.
	(d) the amount (and expiry date, if any) of temporary differences, unused tax losses, and unused tax credits for which no deferred tax asset is recognised.
	(e) the aggregate amount of temporary differences associated with investments in foreign subsidiaries, branches and associates and joint ventures, for which deferred tax liabilities have not been recognised (see paragraph 28.18(b)).
	(f) the aggregate amount of temporary differences associated with the initial recognition of goodwill for which deferred tax liabilities have not been recognised (see paragraph 28.18(c))
28.30	In the circumstances described in paragraph 28.25, an entity shall disclose the nature of the potential income tax consequences that would result from the payment of dividends to its shareholders. In addition, the entity shall disclose the amounts of the potential income tax consequences, if practicably determinable, and whether there are any potential income tax consequences not practicably determinable.

Section 29   Financial Reporting in Hyperinflationary Economies

29.2	An entity whose functional currency is the currency of a hyperinflationary economy shall apply IAS 29 *Financial Reporting in Hyperinflationary Economies* in preparing and presenting its financial statements in accordance with this [draft] standard.

Section 30   Foreign Currency Translation

30.25	In paragraphs 30.27 and 30.29, references to 'functional currency' apply, in the case of a group, to the functional currency of the parent.
30.26	An entity shall disclose:
	(a) the amount of exchange differences recognised in profit or loss except for those arising on financial instruments measured at fair value through profit or loss in accordance with Section 11.
	(b) net exchange differences classified in a separate component of equity, and a reconciliation of the amount of such exchange differences at the beginning and end of the period.
30.27	An entity shall disclose the currency in which the financial statements are presented. When the presentation currency is different from the functional currency, an entity shall state that fact and shall disclose

	the functional currency and the reason for using a different presentation currency.
30.28	When there is a change in the functional currency of either the reporting entity or a significant foreign operation, the entity shall disclose that fact and the reason for the change in functional currency.
30.29	When an entity displays its financial statements or other financial information in a currency that is different from either its functional currency or its presentation currency (for example, a 'convenience translation' of all amounts at closing rate), it shall: (a) clearly identify the information as supplementary information to distinguish it from the information that complies with this [draft] standard; (b) disclose the currency in which the supplementary information is displayed; and (c) disclose the entity's functional currency and the method of translation used to determine the supplementary information.

Section 31   Segment Reporting

31.1	An entity using this [draft] standard is not required to present information about operating segments. An entity that chooses to disclose segment information in financial statements described as conforming to the *IFRS for SMEs* shall comply fully with the requirements of IFRS 8 *Operating Segments*. If an entity discloses information about segments that does not comply with IFRS 8, it shall not describe the information as segment information.

Section 32   Events after the End of the Reporting Period

Date of authorisation for issue

32.8	An entity shall disclose the date when the financial statements were authorised for issue and who gave that authorisation. If the entity's owners or others have the power to amend the financial statements after issue, the entity shall disclose that fact.

Non-adjusting events after the end of the reporting period

32.9	An entity shall disclose the following for each category of non-adjusting event after the end of the reporting period: (a) the nature of the event; and (b) an estimate of its financial effect, or a statement that such an estimate cannot be made.
32.10	The following are examples of non-adjusting events after the end of the reporting period that would generally result in disclosure: (a) a major business combination (Section 18 requires specific disclosures in such cases) or disposing of a major subsidiary. (b) announcing a plan to discontinue an operation.

(c)	major purchases of assets, classification of assets as held for sale in accordance with Section 16, other disposals of assets, or expropriation of major assets by government.
(d)	the destruction of a major production plant by a fire.
(e)	announcing, or commencing the implementation of, a major restructuring (see Section 20).
(f)	major ordinary share transactions and potential ordinary share transactions.
(g)	abnormally large changes in asset prices or foreign exchange rates.
(h)	changes in tax rates or tax laws enacted or announced that have a significant effect on current and deferred tax assets and liabilities (see Section 28).
(i)	entering into significant commitments or contingent liabilities, for example, by issuing significant guarantees.
(j)	commencing major litigation arising solely out of events that occurred after the end of the reporting period.

Section 33   Related Party Disclosures

Disclosure of relationships

33.4	Relationships between parents and subsidiaries shall be disclosed irrespective of whether there have been transactions between those related parties. An entity shall disclose the name of the entity's parent and, if different, the ultimate controlling party. If neither the entity's parent nor the ultimate controlling party produces financial statements available for public use, the name of the next most senior parent that does so (if any) shall also be disclosed.

Disclosure of key management personnel compensation

33.5	Key management personnel are those persons having authority and responsibility for planning, directing and controlling the activities of the entity, directly or indirectly, including any director (whether executive or otherwise) of that entity. Compensation includes all employee benefits (as defined in Section 27) including those in the form of share-based payment (see Section 25). Employee benefits include all forms of consideration paid, payable or provided by the entity, or on behalf of the entity (for example, by its parent or by a shareholder), in exchange for services rendered to the entity. It also includes such consideration paid on behalf of a parent of the entity in respect of the entity.
33.6	An entity shall disclose key management personnel compensation in total and for each of the following categories: (a) short-term employee benefits; (b) post-employment benefits; (c) other long-term benefits; (d) termination benefits; and (e) share-based payment.

Disclosure of related party transactions

33.7	A related party transaction is a transfer of resources, services or obligations between related parties, regardless of whether a price is charged. Examples of related party transactions that are common to SMEs include, but are not limited to: (a) transactions between an entity and its principal owner(s). (b) transactions between an entity and another entity where both entities are under the common control of a single entity or individual. (c) transactions in which an entity or individual that controls the reporting entity incurs expenses directly that otherwise would have been borne by the reporting entity.

33.8	If there have been transactions between related parties, an entity shall disclose the nature of the related party relationship as well as information about the transactions and outstanding balances necessary for an understanding of the potential effect of the relationship on the financial statements. These disclosure requirements are in addition to the requirements in paragraph 33.6 to disclose key management personnel compensation. At a minimum, disclosures shall include:
	
	 (a) the amount of the transactions.
	 (b) the amount of outstanding balances and:
	
	     (i) their terms and conditions, including whether they are secured, and the nature of the consideration to be provided in settlement; and
	     (ii) details of any guarantees given or received.
	
	 (c) provisions for uncollectible receivables related to the amount of outstanding balances.
	 (d) the expense recognised during the period in respect of bad or doubtful debts due from related parties.

33.9	An entity shall make the disclosures required by paragraph 33.8 separately for each of the following categories: (a) the parent. (b) entities with joint control or significant influence over the entity. (c) subsidiaries. (d) associates. (e) joint ventures in which the entity is a venturer. (f) key management personnel of the entity or its parent (in the aggregate). (g) other related parties.
33.10	The following are examples of transactions that are disclosed if they are with a related party. (a) purchases or sales of goods (finished or unfinished). (b) purchases or sales of property and other assets. (c) rendering or receiving of services. (d) leases. (e) transfers of research and development. (f) transfers under licence agreements.

	(g) transfers under finance arrangements (including loans and equity contributions in cash or in kind). (h) provision of guarantees or collateral. (i) settlement of liabilities on behalf of the entity or by the entity on behalf of another party. (j) participation by a parent or subsidiary in a defined benefit plan that shares risks between group entities.
33.11	An entity shall not state that related party transactions were made on terms equivalent to those that prevail in arm's length transactions unless such terms can be substantiated.
33.12	An entity may disclose items of a similar nature in the aggregate except when separate disclosure is necessary for an understanding of the effects of related party transactions on the financial statements of the entity.

Section 34 Earnings per Share

34.1	An entity using this [draft] standard is not required to present amounts of earnings per share. However, if the entity discloses earnings per share, it shall calculate and disclose earnings per share in accordance with IAS 33 *Earnings per Share*.

Section 35 Specialised Industries

Agriculture

35.1	An entity using this [draft] standard that is engaged in agricultural activity shall determine, for each of its biological assets, whether the fair value of that biological asset is readily determinable without undue cost and effort: (a) The entity shall apply the fair value model in paragraphs 10–29 of IAS 41 *Agriculture* to account for those biological assets whose fair value is readily determinable without undue cost or effort, and the entity shall make all related disclosures required by IAS 41. (b) The entity shall measure at cost less any accumulated depreciation and any accumulated impairment losses those biological assets whose fair value is not readily determinable without undue cost or effort. The entity shall disclose, for such biological assets: (i) a description of the biological assets; (ii) an explanation of why fair value cannot be measured reliably; (iii) if possible, the range of estimates within which fair value is highly likely to lie; (iv) the depreciation method used; (v) the useful lives or the depreciation rates used; and (vi) the gross carrying amount and the accumulated depreciation (aggregated with accumulated impairment losses) at the beginning and end of the period.

Section 36   Discontinued Operations and Assets Held for Sale

Presentation and disclosure

36.2	An entity shall disclose:
	
	(a) a single amount on the face of the income statement comprising the total of:
	
	    (i) the post-tax profit or loss of discontinued operations; and
	    (ii) the post-tax gain or loss recognised on the measurement to fair value less costs to sell or on the disposal of the assets or group(s) of assets and liabilities constituting the discontinued operation.
	
	(b) an analysis of the single amount in (a) into:
	
	    (i) the revenue, expenses, pre-tax profit or loss and income tax expense of discontinued operations;
	    (ii) the gain or loss recognised on the measurement to fair value less costs to sell or on the disposal of the assets or group(s) of assets constituting the discontinued operation and the related income tax expense.
	    The analysis may be presented in the notes or on the face of the income statement. If it is presented on the face of the income statement it shall be presented in a section identified as relating to discontinued operations, ie separately from continuing operations.
	
	(c) the net cash flows attributable to the operating, investing and financing activities of discontinued operations. These disclosures may be presented either in the notes or on the face of the financial statements.

36.3	Unless impracticable, an entity shall restate the disclosures in the preceding paragraph for prior periods presented in the financial statements so that the disclosures relate to all operations that have been discontinued by the end of the reporting period for the latest period presented.
36.4	If an entity ceases to classify a component of an entity as held for sale, the entity shall reclassify the results of operations of the component previously presented in discontinued operations and shall include them in income from continuing operations for all periods presented. The amounts for prior periods shall be described as having been restated.

Non-current assets held for sale

36.8	An entity shall disclose the following information in the period in which property, plant and equipment has been either classified as held for sale or sold: (a) a description of the asset or disposal group; (b) a description of the facts and circumstances of the sale, or leading to the expected disposal, and the expected manner and timing of that disposal; and (c) the gain or loss recognised, if not separately presented on the face of the income statement.

Section 37 Interim Financial Reporting

37.1	An entity that issues an interim financial report that is described as complying with this [draft] standard shall apply either IAS 34 *Interim Financial Reporting* or all of the requirements of this [draft] standard, except as provided in paragraph 37.2.

Section 38 Transition to the *IFRS for SMEs*

Explanation of transition to the IFRS for SMEs

38.10	An entity shall explain how the transition from its previous GAAP to this [draft] standard affected its reported financial position, financial performance and cash flows.

Reconciliations

38.11	To comply with paragraph 38.10, an entity's first financial statements prepared using this [draft] standard shall include:
	(a) reconciliations of its equity reported under previous GAAP to its equity under the [draft] standard for both of the following dates:
	(i) the date of transition to this [draft] standard; and
	(ii) the end of the latest period presented in the entity's most recent annual financial statements under previous GAAP; and
	(b) a reconciliation of the profit or loss reported under previous GAAP for the latest period in the entity's most recent annual financial statements to its profit or loss under this [draft] standard for the same period.
38.12	If an entity becomes aware of errors made under previous GAAP, the reconciliations required by paragraph 39.11(a) and (b) shall distinguish the correction of those errors from changes in accounting policies.
38.13	If an entity did not present financial statements for previous periods, it shall disclose that fact in its first financial statements that conform to this [draft] standard.

Part Ten

ICAEW Accounting Recommendations

Part Ten

ICAEW Accounting Recommendations

[TECH 7/03]
Guidance on the determination of realised profits and losses in the context of distributions under the Companies Act 1985

(Issued March 2003)

Guidance on the determination of realised profits and losses in the context of distributions under the Companies Act 1985, issued in March 2003 by the Institute of Chartered Accountants in England and Wales and the Institute of Chartered Accountants of Scotland. The guidance deals with matters previously dealt with in Technical Releases 481 and 482, issued in September 1982.

Contents

Introduction

Legal rules

Principles of realisation

Definitions

Changes in circumstances

Application

Appendix A: Intra-group transactions

Appendix B: The legal framework

This Technical Release provides general guidance and does not purport to deal with all possible questions and issues that may arise in any given situation. No responsibility for loss occasioned to any person acting or refraining from action as a result of any material in this guidance can be accepted by the Institutes.

Introduction

1   The purpose of this Technical Release (which deals with matters previously dealt with in Technical Releases 481 and 482, issued in September 1982) is to identify, interpret and apply the principles relating to the determination of realised profits and losses for the purposes of making distributions under the Companies Act 1985. This Technical Release reflects the law* at 31 December 2002 and accounting standards † in issue at that date.

2   This Technical Release does not provide guidance on how transactions and arrangements should be accounted for in a company's financial statements.

3   The guidance in this Technical Release (which is the first collected and 'codified' guidance since the Technical Releases of 1982) represents what is generally accepted at 31 December 2002. Whilst much represents principles that were generally accepted prior to its issue, the guidance should not be used to question the lawfulness of earlier distributions. However, balances on reserves will need to be re-examined in the light of this guidance, and the position should be reassessed before a distribution is made.

4   This guidance applies to the determination of realised profits and losses by companies formed and registered under the Companies Act 1985 or earlier Acts. It does not, however, deal with the special provisions in sections 265 and 266 and paragraph 71 of Schedule 4 to the 1985 Act relating to investment companies, nor those in section 268 relating to long term business carried on by insurance companies.

5   Section 263(3) of the Companies Act 1985 defines a company's profits available for distribution as 'its accumulated, realised profits, so far as not previously utilised by distribution or capitalisation, less its accumulated, realised losses, so far as not previously written off in a reduction or reorganisation of capital duly made'. Realised profits and realised losses are defined as 'such profits or losses of the company as fall to be treated as realised in accordance with principles generally accepted, at the time when the accounts are prepared, with respect to the determination for accounting purposes of realised profits or losses' (section 262(3), as applied by section 742(2)). It is apparent from the use of the words 'fall to be treated as realised' (rather than, simply, 'realised') that the concept of a realised profit is intended to be dynamic, changing with the development of generally accepted accounting principles, bringing within the definition profits which might not in ordinary language be called realised. The legal rules governing distributions are discussed more fully in Appendix B. There are, in addition, common law rules which are referred to below.

6   Under both the Companies Act 1985 and common law, distributions are made by individual companies and not by groups. The group accounts are therefore not relevant for the purpose of determining a company's profits available for distribution.

7   The determination of a company's profits available for distribution is derived from what is recorded in its accounts which are relevant for this purpose (see Appendix B). It is fundamental for this purpose that the company's accounts have been properly prepared in accordance with the law and generally accepted accounting principles. As noted in paragraph 15, profits available for distribution may include amounts

---

English and Scottish Counsel have confirmed that this Technical Release is consistent with the law at 31 December 2002.

†*This Technical Release does not deal with issues arising specifically from the implementation of FRS 17 Retirement benefits.*

reported in the Statement of Total Recognised Gains and Losses or Reconciliation of Movements in Shareholders' Funds as well as those in the Profit and Loss Account.

Both the Companies Act 1985 and common law are relevant in determining a company's distributable profits. Section 281 provides that the provisions in the 1985 Act 'are without prejudice to any enactment or rule of law, or any provision of a company's memorandum or articles, restricting the sums out of which, or the cases in which, a distribution may be made'. 8

Under common law, a company cannot lawfully make a distribution out of capital. In addition, directors are subject to fiduciary duties in the exercise of the powers conferred on them. Directors must therefore specifically consider, inter alia, whether the company will still be solvent following a proposed distribution. Thus directors should consider both the immediate cash flow implications of a distribution and the continuing ability of the company to pay its debts as they fall due. 9

Principles of realisation

FRS 18 *Accounting policies* states that it is generally accepted that profits shall be treated as realised for the purpose of applying the definition of realised profits in companies legislation only when realised in the form of 'cash or of other assets the ultimate cash realisation of which can be assessed with reasonable certainty'. FRS 18 goes on to state that 'in this context, "realised" may also encompass profits relating to assets that are readily realisable'. This would embrace profits and losses resulting from the use of the marking to market method of accounting, where the method is properly adopted in accordance with law and generally accepted accounting principles (see paragraphs 35 to 40). 10

The principles of realisation set out in this guidance are consistent with the notion of realisation as expressed in FRS 18. The guidance recognises also that certain amounts may, as a matter of law, be profits (see paragraph 15(b)). 11

In assessing whether a company has a realised profit, transactions and arrangements should not be looked at in isolation. A realised profit will arise only where the overall commercial effect on the company satisfies the definition of realised profit set out in this guidance. Thus a group or series of transactions or arrangements should be viewed as a whole, particularly if they are artificial, linked (whether legally or otherwise) or circular. 12

A profit previously regarded as unrealised becomes realised when the relevant criteria set out in this guidance are met (for example, a revaluation surplus becomes realised when the related asset is sold for 'qualifying consideration'). Similarly, a profit previously regarded as realised becomes unrealised when the criteria set out in this guidance cease to be met. 13

Definitions

The definitions should be read in conjunction with the principles of realisation as well as the other definitions and application notes. 14

PROFIT

'Profit' for the purpose of section 262(3) comprises: 15

(a) 'gains', as defined in the Accounting Standards Board's 'Statement of Principles for Financial Reporting', that is, 'increases in ownership interest not resulting from contributions from owners', and

(b) other amounts which are profits as a matter of law, or which are treated as profits, including:

    (i) gratuitous contributions of assets from owners in their capacity as such,

    (ii) an amount taken to a so-called 'merger reserve' reflecting the extent that relief is obtained under sections 131 or 132 of the Companies Act 1985 from the requirement to recognise a share premium account, and

    (iii) a reserve arising from a reduction or cancellation of share capital, share premium account or capital redemption reserve*.

REALISED PROFIT

16 A profit is realised where it arises from:

(a) a transaction where the consideration received by the company is 'qualifying consideration', or

(b) an event which results in 'qualifying consideration' being received by the company in circumstances where no consideration is given by the company, or

(c) the recognition in the profit and loss account of the profit arising from the use of the marking to market method of accounting, in those cases where the method is properly adopted in accordance with law and generally accepted accounting principles (see paragraphs 35 to 40), or

(d) the translation of:

    (i) a monetary asset which comprises qualifying consideration, or

    (ii) a liability denominated in a foreign currency, or

(e) the reversal of a loss previously regarded as realised, or

(f) a profit† previously regarded as unrealised (such as amounts taken to a revaluation reserve, merger reserve or other similar reserve) becoming realised as a result of:

    (i) consideration previously received by the company becoming 'qualifying consideration', or

    (ii) the related asset being disposed of in a transaction where the consideration received by the company is 'qualifying consideration', or

    (iii) a realised loss being recognised on the scrapping or disposal of the related asset, or

    (iv) a realised loss being recognised on the write-down for depreciation, amortisation, diminution in value or impairment of the related asset, or

    (v) the distribution in specie of the asset to which the unrealised profit relates,

in which case the appropriate proportion‡ of the related unrealised profit becomes a realised profit, or

(g) a reduction or cancellation of capital [3] (ie, share capital, share premium account or capital redemption reserve) which results in a credit to reserves where the reduction or cancellation is confirmed by the court, except to the

---

The Institutes have been advised by Counsel that if a reserve is established as a result of such a reduction or cancellation that reserve is, in law, a profit.

†*Where the related profit has been capitalised it will not be available for transfer from unrealised profit to realised profit.*

‡*In the case of (iii) and (iv), the loss is treated as a realised loss under paragraph 29 of this guidance; however, part of this realised loss is compensated for by a reclassification from unrealised to realised profit.*

extent that, and for as long as, the company has undertaken that it will not treat the reserve arising as a realised profit, or where the court has directed that it shall not be treated as a realised profit, or

(h) a reduction or cancellation of capital [3] (ie, share capital, share premium account or capital redemption reserve* which is undertaken by an unlimited company without confirmation by the court and which results in a credit to reserves, in which case the amount so credited represents a realised profit to the extent that the consideration received for the capital:

    (i) was qualifying consideration; or

    (ii) has subsequently become qualifying consideration; or

    (iii) has subsequently been written off (for example, by way of depreciation) and the loss arising has been treated as realised; or

    (iv) was originally paid up either by a capitalisation of realised profits or by a capitalisation of unrealised profits or reserves which, had they not been capitalised, would subsequently have become realised.

REALISED LOSS

Losses should be regarded as realised losses except to the extent that the law, accounting standards or this guidance provide otherwise. The statutory position is set out in Appendix B. **17**

QUALIFYING CONSIDERATION

Qualifying consideration comprises: **18**

(a) cash, or

(b) an asset for which there is a liquid market, or

(c) the release, or the settlement or assumption by another party, of all or part of a liability of the company, unless

    (i) the liability arose from the purchase of an asset that does not meet the definition of qualifying consideration and has not been disposed of for qualifying consideration, and

    (ii) the purchase and release are part of a group or series of transactions or arrangements that fall within paragraph 12 of this guidance; or

(d) an amount receivable in any of the above forms of consideration where:

    (i) the debtor is capable of settling the receivable within a reasonable period of time; and

    (ii) there is a reasonable certainty that the debtor will be capable of settling when called upon to do so; and

    (iii) there is an expectation that the receivable will be settled.

ASSET FOR WHICH THERE IS A LIQUID MARKET

Asset for which there is a liquid market means that: **19**

(a) the asset belongs to a homogeneous population of assets that are equivalent in all material respects; and

(b) an active market, evidenced by frequent transactions, exists for that asset; and

(c) the market has sufficient depth to absorb the asset without a significant effect on the price that underpins the carrying amount; and

---

Such a reserve could exist if a limited company with a capital redemption reserve re-registers as an unlimited company.

(d)   the company is capable of readily disposing of the asset*, and it can do so without curtailing or disrupting its business; and

(e)   the asset is readily convertible into known amounts of cash at or close to its carrying amount.

Changes in circumstances

20   The treatment of a retained profit or loss as realised (or unrealised), or the recognition of an item as a profit or loss or an asset or liability, may change subsequent to its original recognition as a result of:

(a)   a change in the principles of realisation; or

(b)   a change in the law or in accounting standards or UITF Abstracts, either through an express reference to the realisation or otherwise of the profit or loss or, more commonly, through the derecognition of the profit (or the recognition of a loss). An example of this is FRS 19 under which many companies make full provision for deferred tax where previously no, or only partial, provision has been made; or

(c)   some other change in circumstance (for example, where a receivable was initially regarded as qualifying consideration but circumstances change such that there is now no expectation that the receivable will be settled in the form of qualifying consideration).

21   Although the effect of these changes may be to reduce or even eliminate a company's net realised profits, that would not render unlawful a distribution already made out of realised profits determined by reference to 'relevant accounts' which had been prepared in accordance with generally accepted accounting principles applicable to those accounts (this is subject to paragraphs 22 and 23). This is because the Act defines realised profits and losses for determining the lawfulness of a distribution as 'such profits and losses of the company as fall to be treated as realised in accordance with principles generally accepted, *at the time when the accounts are prepared*, with respect to the determination for accounting purposes of realised profits or losses' (section 262(3), emphasis added).

22   The effects of the introduction of a new accounting standard become relevant to the application of the common law capital maintenance rule (see paragraph B2) only in relation to distributions proposed in respect of periods in which the change will first be recognised in the accounts. There is no retrospective effect on a proposed final dividend for any preceding period provided that the dividend was provided for in the statutory accounts for that period; for example, where items that will fall to be treated as liabilities or provisions under a new standard have not been recognised as such in those accounts, directors do not have to pay regard to such liabilities or provisions merely because they are disclosed in the notes to the accounts.

23   Where the directors are considering the payment of an interim dividend in respect of a financial year, and a new accounting standard may, for example, lead to items being recognised as liabilities or provisions in the accounts for that year, the directors must, under common law, have regard to the effect of these liabilities or provisions on the expected level of profits available for distribution at the end of the financial year when determining the lawfulness of the interim dividend.

In the case of certain derivatives markets, an asset may be regarded as capable of being readily disposed of in accordance with sub-paragraph (d) if the relevant contract or underlying market risk position is capable of being matched in the market and normal market practice would be to close the position in this way.

If the effect of a new accounting standard or guidance on profits which fall to be   **24**
treated as realised is to increase the company's accumulated profits, it would be open
to the company to prepare interim accounts complying with the new accounting
standard or guidance if it wished to distribute an amount in excess of that which
could be determined by reference to what would otherwise constitute the company's
'relevant accounts'.

Where the effect of a change in circumstance is that a profit previously recognised as   **25**
realised can no longer be regarded as being realised, the amount of that profit should
either be eliminated through a prior year adjustment or be reclassified as unrealised
(as appropriate) in the relevant accounts in which the change in circumstance is first
recognised. However, as profits are fungible, unless there is evidence that the profit
affected by the change in circumstances has been distributed, it should be assumed
that the first distribution made after the recognition of the profit was made pro rata
out of all available profits shown in the relevant accounts. Accordingly, the balance
remaining after that distribution would include a proportionate amount of the
affected profit. Similarly each subsequent distribution would reduce proportionately
the amount of the affected profit.

For example, a company has accumulated realised profits of 40 brought forward at   **26**
the beginning of Year 1. During that year it makes realised profits of 60 of which 40
arose from a specific transaction in that period, and distributes 70, leaving a balance
of 30. In Year 2 it generates a further 170 of realised profits and distributes 150. A
change in circumstances in year 3 leads to the 40 recognised in Year 1 becoming
treated as unrealised. The amount of the original profit of 40 that would be regarded
as having been distributed in Year 1 would be 28 (70% [ie, 70/100] of 40), leaving 12
of the original profit to be carried forward in the closing balance of 30 at the end of
Year 1. In Year 2 the amount of this 12 that would be regarded as having been
distributed in Year 2 would be 9 (75% [ie, 150/200] of 12), leaving 3 of the original
profit to be carried forward in the closing balance of 50 at the end of Year 2. Thus
the amount of profit to be reclassified as unrealised in Year 3 as a result of the change
in circumstance would be 3.

	Total	Affected profit
YEAR 1: Brought forward	40	–
Profit for year	60	40
Available for distribution	100	40
Distributed	(70)	(28)
YEAR 2: Brought forward	30	12
Profit for year	170	–
Available for distribution	200	12
Distributed	(150)	(9)
YEAR 3: Brought forward	50	3

Where after making all reasonable enquiries it proves impracticable to trace a profit   **27**
in this way, it would be appropriate to assume that the profit has been distributed (to
the extent that there have been distributions).

Application

INSTANCES OF REALISED PROFIT

28   In addition to those instances which are readily apparent from the definition of realised profit, in applying the principles of realisation and the definitions set out above the following would constitute a realised profit:

(a)   the receipt or accrual of investment or other income receivable in the form of qualifying consideration; or

(b)   a gain arising on a return of capital on an investment where the return is in the form of qualifying consideration; or

(c)   a gift (such as a 'capital contribution') received in the form of qualifying consideration; or

(d)   the release of a provision for a liability or loss which was treated as a realised loss; or

(e)   the reversal of a write-down or provision for diminution in value or impairment of an asset which was treated as a realised loss.

INSTANCES OF REALISED LOSS

29   Realised losses will include:

(a)   a cost or expense (other than one charged to the share premium account) which results in a reduction in recorded net assets;

(b)   a loss arising on the sale or other disposal or scrapping of an asset;

(c)   the writing down, or providing for the depreciation, amortisation, diminution in value or impairment, of an asset *, except as noted in paragraphs 30 and B25;

(d)   the creation of, or increase in, a provision for a liability or loss (other than deferred tax in the circumstances described in paragraph 31) which results in an overall reduction in recorded net assets;

(e)   a gift made by the company (or the release of all or part of a debt due to the company or the assumption of a liability by the company) to the extent that it results in an overall reduction in recorded net assets; and

(f)   a loss arising from the use of the marking to market method of accounting.

30   Where a fixed asset is revalued to an amount which is below its 'recoverable amount', paragraph 65(b) of FRS 15 requires the loss below recoverable amount to be reflected in the Statement of Total Recognised Gains and Losses (rather than the profit and loss account for the year). Paragraph 70 of FRS 15 states that where the recoverable amount is greater than the revalued amount, the resulting difference is clearly not an impairment; in these circumstances the difference is treated as an unrealised loss (see paragraph B28). Such a loss would become realised in the event of a subsequent scrapping, disposal or impairment of the asset.

31   A provision for deferred tax should generally be regarded as a realised loss. However, when assets are revalued to their fair value, with any gain being recorded in the profit and loss account even though regarded as unrealised†, the deferred tax on that

---

Where the asset has been revalued or is otherwise represented to any extent by an unrealised profit, the appropriate proportion of the related unrealised profit becomes a realised profit, thus mitigating the effect of the realised loss – see paragraph 16(f) of this guidance.

†*For example, in the case of insurance companies.*

gain should be treated as a reduction in that unrealised gain rather than as a realised loss (paragraph 14 of Appendix III to FRS 19 *Deferred tax*).

EXCHANGE OF ASSETS ('TOP-SLICING')

Where an asset is sold partly for qualifying consideration and partly for other **32** consideration (for example, a mixed consideration of cash and a freehold property), any profit arising is a realised profit to the extent that the fair value of the consideration received is in the form of qualifying consideration. This approach is sometimes referred to as 'top-slicing'. (Example: fair value of consideration received is 10, of which 4 is cash and 6 is freehold property. If the depreciated historical cost of the asset sold is 5, the total gain is 5 but the realised profit is limited to 4.)

HEDGING

Where a hedged asset or liability and a hedging instrument are accounted for as a **33** hedge, the treatment as realised of any profit or loss is determined in accordance with the criteria in this guidance solely by reference to the net exposure on the hedged asset or liability.

FOREIGN EXCHANGE PROFITS AND LOSSES

Paragraph 65 of SSAP 20 *Foreign currency translation*, which was issued in 1983, states **34** that 'the application of paragraph 50 of this statement may result in unrealised exchange gains on unsettled long-term monetary items being taken to the profit and loss account'. Since then, however, the currency markets have become more sophisticated and companies have significantly more flexibility to crystallise exchange profits on long-term monetary items. Consequently, unless there are doubts as to the convertibility or marketability of the currency in question, foreign exchange profits arising on the retranslation of monetary items are realised, irrespective of the maturity date of the monetary item.

MARKING TO MARKET

Banking companies

Paragraph 34 of Schedule 9 to the Companies Act 1985 allows banks to value **35** transferable securities not held as financial fixed assets in the balance sheet at the higher of their cost and their market value at the balance sheet date. Counsel have advised that profits and losses arising on valuations under paragraph 34 should be taken to the profit and loss account. For the reasons set out in paragraphs 37 and 38 below, any such profits fall to be treated as realised.

Non-banking companies

In the case of non-banking companies, paragraphs 22 and 23 of Schedule 4 require **36** all current assets to be valued at the lower of cost and net realisable value. A non-banking company can adopt the marking to market method of accounting, in which changes in market value are recognised in the profit and loss account, only by invoking the 'true and fair override' of section 226(5)*. This allows departures from the rules laid down in Schedule 4 to the extent that they are *necessary* to provide a true and fair view. Paragraphs 37 to 40 below consider, for subsidiaries of banks and for other market makers and dealers in investments, the circumstances in which marking to market profits fall to be treated as realised.

(i) Subsidiaries of banks

37   The franked Statement of Recommended Practice (SORP) *Accounting for securities by banks*† states in paragraph 85 that, 'It is considered, for the reasons given in paragraphs 14 and ..., that it is necessary for securities dealing subsidiaries of banks to value securities at market value in order to give a true and fair view.' Paragraph 14 of the SORP is as follows:

> 14. Market value accounting, or 'marking to market', as it is often known, offers a number of important advantages. The 'concept of prudence' implications are considered below, but it should be emphasised that, even though the price at which a security is subsequently sold may be lower than the market value at the accounting date, that market value is nevertheless the most realistic available measure of performance up to that date. It is a value which could, with reasonable certainty, have been realised in cash. It reflects the management decision not to sell the security at that date, a decision just as valid as a decision to sell. Such a basis of valuation is also more relevant for management purposes and, increasingly, it is market value that is required for regulatory reporting purposes.

38   The SORP further states, in paragraph 87: 'It is considered that the use of market value accounting, and the treatment of the resultant profits as realised, is sufficiently widespread to have become 'generally accepted', and that such profits are therefore realised for the purposes of the Act.'

39   To qualify as being in accordance with 'generally accepted accounting principles' a method must be not merely generally accepted but also in accordance with fundamental principles. In relation to marking to market, the SORP refers specifically to the principle of prudence, and stresses the importance of using techniques for assessing market value which do not entail any premature recognition of profit.

(ii) Other market makers and dealers in investments

40   Where a market maker or dealer in investments (other than a subsidiary of a bank, which is addressed in paragraphs 36 to 39) uses the marking to market method of accounting for transferable securities, and that method is properly adopted in accordance with law and generally accepted accounting principles, the arguments in paragraphs 37 to 39 also apply and accordingly any profits and losses arising from marking to market fall to be treated as realised.

*Under the alternative accounting rules (Section C of Part II of Schedule 4 of the Companies Act 1985) a current asset investment may be carried at its current cost and any movement in current cost is required to be taken to the revaluation reserve. This differs from, and does not achieve the same result as, the marking to market method of accounting which is based on market value.

†The Statement of Recommended Practice Accounting for securities by banks was franked by the Accounting Standards Committee and published by the British Bankers' Association and the Irish Bankers Federation in September 1990. It is 'intended to apply to the entity accounts of banks incorporated in the United Kingdom or the Republic of Ireland and to the consolidated accounts of British and Irish banking groups.'

GOODWILL IN AN INDIVIDUAL COMPANY

Where goodwill arises in a company's individual accounts (which would be the case, **41** for example, where the company has purchased an unincorporated business) the goodwill will become a realised loss as the goodwill is amortised or written down for impairment in accordance with FRS 10 *Goodwill and intangible assets.*

Where such purchased goodwill was accounted for under SSAP 22 *Accounting for* **42** *goodwill* by way of immediate elimination against reserves and, under the transitional arrangements in FRS 10, that goodwill remains eliminated against reserves, FRS 10 continues the application of the guidance in Appendix 2 to SSAP 22 (which is reproduced, almost verbatim, as Appendix V of FRS 10). This states that where goodwill is written off on acquisition as a matter of accounting policy (ie, under the immediate write-off method) rather than because of an actual diminution in value, the write-off does not constitute an immediate realised loss but becomes a realised loss over its useful economic life at the same time and to the same extent as would be the case if the company had adopted a policy of capitalisation and amortisation of the goodwill.

NEGATIVE GOODWILL IN AN INDIVIDUAL COMPANY

FRS 10 requires that negative goodwill up to the fair values of the nonmonetary assets **43** acquired should be recognised in the profit and loss account in the periods in which the non-monetary assets are recovered, whether through depreciation or sale. FRS 10 requires that where the negative goodwill exceeds the value of the non-monetary assets, this excess should be recognised in the profit and loss account in the periods expected to be benefited. Negative goodwill recognised in the profit and loss account in accordance with FRS 10 represents a realised profit except in the case of a sale of the nonmonetary assets where the consideration received is not qualifying consideration.

Where negative goodwill was accounted for under SSAP 22 in the accounts of an **44** individual company, it would have been regarded initially as an unrealised profit. It will become a realised profit on the same basis as if it had been negative goodwill accounted for under FRS 10.

Appendix A: Intra-group transactions

INTRODUCTION

A1   Under both common law and statute, distributions are made by companies and not by groups. The group accounts are therefore not relevant for the purpose of determining realisation or distributability; for example, realised profits which are reflected in a parent's* own accounts may be eliminated in the group accounts, and profits retained by subsidiaries are not distributable by the parent.

A2   The ability of a parent to control the actions of its subsidiary must also be borne in mind when considering the substance of an intra-group transaction carried out by or with that subsidiary.

A3   It is not practicable to attempt to illustrate every circumstance in which difficulties may arise in determining whether a profit is realised. The principles set out in this guidance should be applied in relation to the group company seeking to establish a realised profit; in particular, those provisions of paragraph 12 which relate to artificial, linked (whether legally or otherwise) or circular transactions or arrangements should be applied. The examples which follow are intended to illustrate the factors to be considered in determining whether intra-group transactions give rise to realised profits.

CASH POOLING ARRANGEMENTS AND GROUP TREASURY FUNCTIONS

A4   In a group, where there is a cash pooling arrangement or a similar group treasury function, from the perspective of the company seeking to establish a realised profit an increase in debt due from, and/or a decrease in debt due to, the group finance/treasury company will constitute qualifying consideration, provided it:

(a)   is not a transaction or arrangement that falls within paragraph 12 of this guidance; and

(b)   meets the criteria in paragraph 18 of this guidance.

An example of a cash pooling arrangement is where a group finance/treasury company effectively acts as a banker by accepting funds and settling debts on behalf of the group company seeking to establish a realised profit.

DIVIDENDS

Dividend received or receivable on an investment in a subsidiary

A5   In order for a dividend received or receivable from a subsidiary to be treated as a realised profit, the consideration must be in the form of qualifying consideration. It will also be necessary to consider the effect any dividend has on the value of the investment in the subsidiary and, where its recoverable amount has fallen below its book value, to take account of the effect of any such impairment (and, where appropriate, any consequential release from revaluation, merger or other similar reserve).

*The terms 'parent' and 'subsidiary' refer respectively to a 'parent undertaking' and a 'subsidiary undertaking' as defined in section 258 of the Companies Act 1985.

Dividend by a subsidiary to a parent which provides or reinvests the funds in the subsidiary

Investment by a parent in a subsidiary which has paid a dividend in the form of qualifying consideration does not in itself preclude that dividend from continuing to be treated as a realised profit by the parent. However, if a subsidiary pays a dividend to a parent which directly or indirectly provides the funds for the dividend or reinvests the proceeds in the subsidiary in circumstances where the transactions or arrangements fall within paragraph 12 of this guidance, the dividend will not represent a realised profit for the parent if it does not receive in return for the provision of funds or their reinvestment an asset which is in the form of qualifying consideration. Thus, in such a case, the profit will be unrealised if, for example: **A6**

(a)   the provision or reinvestment of funds is in the form of:

    (i)   a subscription for shares, as the subsidiary is in effect capitalising its realised profits; or

    (ii)   a capital contribution (ie, a gift); or

    (iii)   a loan which does not meet the definition of qualifying consideration; or

    (iv)   a guarantee of borrowings used to fund the dividend (unless the likelihood that the guarantee will be called upon is remote); or

(b)   the subsidiary is unlikely to be able to meet its obligations under any borrowings used to fund the dividend without recourse directly or indirectly to the parent.

Dividends received out of pre-acquisition profits

The Act does not deal specifically with the onward distribution by a parent of dividends out of the pre-acquisition profits of its subsidiaries. Such dividends should be treated by a parent in the same way as any other dividend which it receives from a subsidiary, including taking account of any impairment in accordance with paragraph A5.   **A7**

SALE OF AN ASSET BY A PARENT TO ITS SUBSIDIARY

If a parent sells an asset to a subsidiary in circumstances where the transactions or arrangements fall within paragraph 12 of this guidance, any profit on the sale of the asset will not represent a realised profit for the parent if it does not receive an asset which is in the form of qualifying consideration. Thus, in such a case, the profit will be unrealised if, for example: **A8**

(a)   there is an agreement or understanding regarding the repurchase of the asset by the parent; or

(b)   the parent directly or indirectly provides the funds for the purchase or reinvests the proceeds in the subsidiary where the provision or reinvestment of funds is in the form of:

    (i)   a subscription for shares; or

    (ii)   a capital contribution (ie, a gift); or

    (iii)   a loan which does not meet the definition of qualifying consideration; or

    (iv)   a guarantee of borrowings used to fund the purchase (unless the likelihood that the guarantee will be called upon is remote); or

(c)   the subsidiary is unlikely to be able to meet its obligations under any borrowings used to fund the purchase without recourse directly or indirectly to the parent.

SALE OF AN ASSET BY A SUBSIDIARY TO A PARENT FOLLOWED BY A DIVIDEND TO THE PARENT OF THE RESULTING PROFIT

A9   The subsidiary should apply factors similar to those in paragraph A8 in determining whether it has made a realised profit on the sale of an asset to its parent.

A10   If a subsidiary sells an asset to its parent and pays a dividend out of the resulting profit in circumstances where the transactions or arrangements, from the parent's perspective, fall within paragraph 12 of this guidance, the dividend will not give rise to a realised profit for the parent unless the asset which the parent purchased meets the definition of qualifying consideration. This is because the overall commercial effect of such an arrangement for the parent is similar to a dividend in specie (see paragraph A13).

SALE OF AN ASSET BY A SUBSIDIARY TO A FELLOW SUBSIDIARY FOLLOWED BY A DIVIDEND TO THE PARENT OF THE RESULTING PROFIT

A11   The subsidiary should apply factors similar to those in paragraph A8 in determining whether it has made a realised profit on the sale of an asset to its fellow subsidiary.

A12   If a subsidiary sells an asset to a fellow subsidiary and pays a dividend to the parent out of the resulting profit in circumstances where the transactions or arrangements, from the parent's perspective, fall within paragraph 12 of this guidance, the dividend will not give rise to a realised profit for the parent if, for example:

(a)   the parent directly or indirectly provides the funds for the purchase where the provision of funds is in the form of:

  (i)   a subscription for shares; or
  (ii) a capital contribution (ie, a gift); or
  (iii) a loan which does not meet the definition of qualifying consideration; or

(b)   the parent directly or indirectly reinvests the dividend (or equivalent consideration) in the subsidiary which paid the dividend or the fellow subsidiary to which the asset was sold and the asset which the parent receives from this reinvestment is not in the form of qualifying consideration; or

(c)   the parent directly or indirectly guarantees any borrowings used to provide either the fellow subsidiary with the consideration for its purchase of the asset or the vendor subsidiary with funds for its dividend (in either case unless the likelihood that the guarantee will be called upon is remote) or the subsidiary in question is unlikely to be able to meet its obligations under the borrowings without recourse directly or indirectly to the parent.

DIVIDEND IN SPECIE

A13   A dividend in specie from a subsidiary is an unrealised profit in the hands of the parent (even where there is a cash alternative) unless the asset distributed meets the definition of qualifying consideration. However, if the non-cash asset is distributed by the parent then, following section 276, that unrealised profit would be treated by the parent as a realised profit for the purpose of that onward distribution, provided that the profit was recorded in the relevant accounts.

RETURN OF CAPITAL CONTRIBUTION

Where a capital contribution is returned directly or indirectly to the donor company **A14** in circumstances where the transactions or arrangements fall within paragraph 12 of this guidance, it will not give rise to a realised profit in the hands of the donor.

Appendix B: The legal framework

THE COMMON LAW

B1 The legal framework relating to the determination of realised profits and losses and of profits available for distribution consists of two elements: common law and statutory provisions. Under section 281 any restrictions in common law or imposed by the company's memorandum or articles on the sums available for distribution or the cases in which a distribution may be made take precedence over the statutory provisions.

B2 Under common law, a company cannot lawfully make a distribution out of capital. Thus, the directors must consider, both at the time of proposing the distribution and at the time it is made (see paragraph B8), whether the company, subsequent to the balance sheet date to which the 'relevant accounts' were prepared, has incurred losses that have eroded its profits available for distribution ('capital maintenance rule'). Guidance on the application of the capital maintenance rule to the introduction of a new accounting standard is given in paragraphs 22 and 23. It is not practicable to give further guidance on the application of this rule in this Technical Release: appropriate advice will have to be taken to deal with specific circumstances.

B3 In addition, directors are subject to fiduciary duties in the exercise of the powers conferred on them. Examples of fiduciary duties include the obligation on directors to safeguard the company's assets and to ensure that the company is in a position to settle its debts as they fall due. Directors must therefore specifically consider whether the company will still be solvent following a proposed distribution. In reaching their decision they must take into account any change in the financial position of the company after the balance sheet date of the relevant accounts and the future cash needs of the company.

DISTRIBUTIONS

B4 A 'distribution' is defined by section 263(2) as 'every description of distribution of a company's assets to its members, whether in cash or otherwise, except distributions made by way of:

(a)   an issue of shares as fully or partly paid bonus shares,

(b)   the redemption or purchase of any of the company's own shares out of capital (including the proceeds of any fresh issue of shares) or out of unrealised profits in accordance with Chapter VII of Part V,

(c)   the reduction of share capital by extinguishing or reducing the liability of any of the members on any of the company's shares in respect of capital not paid up, or by paying off paid up share capital and

(d)   a distribution of assets to members of the company on its winding-up.'

PROFITS AVAILABLE FOR DISTRIBUTION

B5 A company may make a distribution only out of profits available for that purpose (section 263(1)) (the common law position is set out in paragraph B2). A company's profits available for distribution are its accumulated, realised profits (so far as not previously distributed or capitalised) less its accumulated, realised losses (so far as not previously written off in a reduction or reorganisation of its share capital) (section 263(3)). Thus realised losses may not be offset against unrealised profits. Section 264 imposes a further restriction on public companies (see paragraph B22).

Section 262(3) of the Act states that 'references ... to realised profits and realised **B6**
losses are ... to such profits or losses as fall to be treated as realised in accordance
with principles generally accepted, at the time when the accounts are prepared, with
respect to the determination for accounting purposes of realised profits'. Under
section 742(2), references throughout the Act to realised profits and realised losses in
relation to a company's accounts are to be construed in accordance with section
262(3). Accordingly, the definition of realised profits and losses in section 262(3)
applies for the purpose of the distribution rules in Part VIII.

Section 276 provides that where a company makes a distribution of or including a **B7**
non-cash asset and any part of the amount at which the asset is stated in the accounts
relevant to the distribution represents an unrealised profit, that profit is to be treated
as realised. There is nothing in section 276 to require a company to revalue a non-
cash asset prior to distributing it in specie or to require the distribution to be
recorded at anything other than the book value of the asset. Thus if a company
wishes to distribute in specie an asset with a historical cost of £100 and which is in the
books at £130 (with the surplus in the revaluation reserve), the surplus of £30 is
treated as realised for this purpose and only £100 of other realised profits are needed.
However, if the surplus has been capitalised, it is no longer available for this
purpose and other realised profits of £130 would be needed to cover the proposed
distribution.

Date of distribution

A distribution is made either when a dividend is declared by the company in general **B8**
meeting and thereby becomes a liability of the company regardless of the date on
which it is to be paid; or, in the case of an interim dividend authorised under
common form articles of association (for example, Table A), when the dividend is
paid.

Share premium relief

Where the company has entered into a transaction which gives rise to share premium **B9**
relief under sections 131 or 132, it may choose under section 133 to record the asset
acquired at fair value and to credit the amount of that relief to an other reserve (often
called a merger reserve). In such a case that reserve is in law a profit and is initially
treated as unrealised but becomes realised in a manner similar to a revaluation
reserve. Thus, provided the merger reserve is not capitalised (by way of a bonus issue
of shares), the decision as to whether or not to record the merger reserve should not
overall have any effect on the level of the company's realised profits.

RELEVANT ACCOUNTS

Whether or not a distribution may be made within the terms of the Act is determined **B10**
by reference to a company's 'relevant accounts'. Where it is proposed to make a
distribution during the company's first accounting reference period or before any
accounts have been laid before the company in general meeting*, initial accounts
must be prepared. In all other cases the relevant accounts are its last annual accounts
laid before the company in general meeting or, if those accounts do not disclose
sufficient realised profits, interim accounts.

*In the case of private companies which have in force an election to dispense with the holding of annual general
meetings, all references to the laying of accounts before the company in general meeting are to be read as
references to the sending of copies of the accounts to members and others under section 238(1).

B11   The items in these accounts to which reference is made in determining the amount of a distribution which may be made are listed in section 270(2) as profits, losses, assets, liabilities, provisions (as defined by paragraphs 88 and 89 of Schedule 4), share capital and reserves (including undistributable reserves). Thus, valuations or contingencies referred to in notes to the financial statements, but not incorporated in the balance sheet, do not affect the amount of realised profit calculated by reference to the relevant accounts*.

B12   In practice it may not be sufficient to determine the amount of realised profits simply by examining the relevant accounts as further enquiries may be necessary as to the composition of the various reserves included in the balance sheet. For example, certain reserves may include both realised and unrealised profits. As there is no legal requirement for a company to distinguish in its accounts between distributable and non-distributable profits as such, companies should keep sufficient records to enable them to distinguish between those profits which are available for distribution and those which are not.

B13   The detailed requirements for relevant accounts (annual, interim or initial) are summarised in the following paragraphs.

Annual accounts – all companies

B14   If the company's last annual accounts constitute the relevant accounts they must be prepared under Part VII of the Act (Accounts and audit) and comply with the requirements of section 271. These requirements are that:

(a)   the accounts must have been properly prepared in accordance with the Act, subject only to matters not material for determining the lawfulness of a distribution, and the balance sheet and profit and loss account for the period must give a true and fair view;

(b)   [13] † the accounts must be accompanied by an auditors' report under section 235 and must have been laid before the company in general meeting in accordance with section 241(1); and

(c)   [13] [15] if the auditors' report is qualified to the effect that the accounts have not been properly prepared in accordance with the Act, the auditors must state in writing whether in their opinion the matter in respect of which their report is qualified is material for determining the lawfulness of the distribution. The statement by the auditors must be laid before the company in general meeting.

Initial and interim accounts – public companies

B15   Sections 272 and 273 respectively provide that interim and initial accounts of a public company must have been 'properly prepared', or have been properly prepared subject only to matters which are not material for determining, by reference to those accounts, whether the proposed distribution would contravene sections 263 or 264. A copy of the interim and initial accounts must have been delivered to the Registrar of Companies.

If the relevant accounts record an unrealised profit but state in a note that, as a consequence of an event subsequent to the balance sheet date, the profit has become realised, Counsel has confirmed that interim accounts must nevertheless be prepared before a distribution can be made out of these profits.

†*These sub-paragraphs do not apply where the directors of the company have taken advantage of the audit exemption conferred by sections 249A(1), 249A(2) or 249AA(1).*

'Properly prepared' means that the accounts must give a true and fair view and must comply with section 226 and Schedule 4 to the Act and the balance sheet must be signed in accordance with section 233. **B16**

In requiring the interim and initial accounts to be 'properly prepared', or to be properly prepared except for matters which are not relevant in determining whether a proposed dividend would be lawful under the Act, the legislation permits a public company to choose between preparing interim or initial accounts which give a true and fair view and accounts which give such a view subject only to the exclusion of information which is not relevant in determining whether a distribution would be lawful under the Act. In practice, therefore, interim or initial accounts will consist of a balance sheet and profit and loss account in Schedule 4 format (or Schedules 9 or 9A for banking and insurance companies) but the notes may be restricted to those matters that are relevant to a distribution. Corresponding amounts for the previous financial year would not be relevant. **B17**

Interim accounts are not required to be audited. However, initial accounts of a public company must be accompanied by a report by the auditors stating whether, in their opinion, the accounts have been 'properly prepared'. If their report is qualified (which would be the case if the company chooses to prepare initial accounts which do not give a true and fair view, as described in paragraph B17), the auditors must make an additional statement which states whether, in their opinion, the matter in respect of which their report is qualified is material for determining, by reference to the initial accounts, whether the distribution would contravene sections 263 or 264. A copy of the auditors' statement must also have been delivered to the Registrar of Companies. **B18**

Initial and interim accounts – private companies

The requirements of sections 272 and 273 regarding the form and content of interim and initial accounts of public companies do not apply to private companies. Instead, the only requirement for private companies flows from the general definition in section 270(4) of interim or initial accounts as those necessary to enable a reasonable judgement to be made as to profits, losses, assets and liabilities, provisions, and share capital and reserves. Reliable management accounts which deal with these matters will satisfy this requirement. **B19**

Subsequent events

As set out in paragraph B2, under common law a company cannot lawfully make a distribution out of capital. **B20**

One or more distributions may already have been made by reference to a particular set of accounts; for example, an interim dividend or a purchase of own shares. In determining the lawfulness of any proposed further distribution, the directors must take account of any such distributions (section 274(1)). **B21**

Public companies

A further restriction is placed on distributions by public companies (section 264). A public company may make a distribution only if, after giving effect to such distribution, the amount of its net assets (as defined in section 264(2)) is not less than the aggregate of its called up share capital and undistributable reserves as shown in the relevant accounts. **B22**

B23   Under section 264(3) the following are undistributable reserves:

    (a)   share premium account (see also section 130);

    (b)   capital redemption reserve (see also section 170);

    (c)   the excess of accumulated unrealised profits, so far as not previously utilised by capitalisation, over the accumulated unrealised losses, so far as not previously written off in a reduction or reorganisation of its share capital; and

    (d)   any other reserve which the company is prohibited from distributing by any enactment, or by its memorandum or articles of association (or equivalent).

    This means that, in calculating the amount available for distributions, a public company must reduce the amount of its net realised profits available for distribution by the amount of its net unrealised losses.

PROVISIONS AND ASSET REVALUATIONS

B24   The general rule is that any provision (including one for depreciation or diminution in value as well as provisions for liabilities, charges or losses) is treated as a realised loss.

B25   As an exception to the general rule, a provision for diminution in value of a fixed asset appearing on a revaluation of all the fixed assets (other than goodwill) is not treated as a realised loss (section 275(1)). However, this exception would not apply where the fixed asset has been sold or scrapped, because in these circumstances any loss would need to be reclassified as realised. Furthermore, unrealised losses which exceed unrealised profits are relevant to a public company in determining the amount available for distribution as the requirements of section 264 (Restrictions on the distribution of assets) referred to in paragraph B22 must be satisfied.

B26   For the exception in paragraph B25 to apply, it is not necessary for a revaluation of all the fixed assets to be recorded in the accounts. Section 275(4) provides that a revaluation of all the fixed assets is treated as having taken place if (1) the directors consider the value of any assets that have not actually been revalued, (2) they are satisfied that the aggregate value of those assets is not less than that stated in the company's accounts and (3) the notes to the accounts include a statement to that effect. The notes to the accounts should also state that the directors have considered the value of some of the fixed assets without actually revaluing them and that the assets which have diminished in value are recorded after providing for that diminution.

B27   Special considerations apply where a fixed asset has been revalued and an unrealised profit is recorded. Where a sum written off or retained for depreciation on or after the revaluation exceeds that which would have been charged if the unrealised profit had not been made, the excess does not give rise overall to a realised loss as there is a corresponding realisation of the related revaluation surplus, to the extent that that surplus has not previously been capitalised (section 275(2)). This means that the loss arising on the depreciation of revalued fixed assets is, in effect, calculated for distribution purposes by using historical cost principles, except to the extent that the surplus has previously been capitalised.

B28   If an asset is revalued downwards below its recoverable amount, as defined in FRS 11, then the difference between that revalued amount and recoverable amount is treated as an unrealised loss as it reflects a revaluation adjustment rather than a provision under paragraphs 88 or 89 of Schedule 4.

DEVELOPMENT COSTS

Section 269(1) requires that development costs shown as an asset should be treated as   **B29**
a realised loss, except where the directors justify the costs carried forward being
treated as an asset. This would be the case if the costs are carried forward in
accordance with SSAP 13. The justification must be included in a note to the accounts
(section 269(2)).

[TECH 32/96]
The interpretation of materiality in financial reporting

(Issued December 1996)

Contents

The interpretation as materiality in financial reporting

The following statement is issued by the Council of the Institute of Chartered Accountants in England and Wales for the guidance of members.

The statement takes account of recent developments in financial reporting, including those embodied in the draft 'Statement of Principles for Financial Reporting' issued by the Accounting Standards Board in November 1995. Council recognises that the guidance in the statement is based on the ASB's latest published thinking, as set out in the draft Statement of Principles, and may need to be amended if the final version of the Statement of Principles incorporates changes that have an impact on the interpretation of materiality.

INTRODUCTION

The concept of materiality is fundamental to the reporting of information. The **1** Accounting Standards Board's draft *'Statement of Principles for Financial Reporting'* defines and explains it as follows:

> '2.6   *Materiality is a threshold quality. It provides a cut-off point rather than being a primary qualitative characteristic that information must have if it is to be useful, and it needs to be considered before the other qualities of that information. If any information is not material, it does not need to be considered further.*
>
> 2.7   *Information is material if it could influence users' decisions taken on the basis of the financial statements. If that information is misstated or if certain information is omitted the materiality of the misstatement or omission depends on the size and nature of the item in question judged in the particular circumstances of the case. Aspects of the nature of the item that affect a judgment about its materiality include the events and transactions giving rise to it and the particular financial statement headings and disclosures that are affected. Circumstances that are considered include other elements of the financial statements taken as a whole and other information available to users that would affect their evaluation of the financial statements: this involves, for example, a consideration of the implications of the item for the evaluation of trends. Where there are two or more similar items, the materiality of the aggregate as well as the individual items needs to be considered.**

This statement offers guidance to preparers of financial statements and other **2** information, hereafter referred to as *'preparers'*, on the practical interpretation and application of the ASB's definition and explanation of materiality. Whilst it refers primarily to the financial statements of commercial companies, it can be applied more generally to:

(a)   other information such as that provided in an operating and financial review, in preliminary and interim announcements, or in corporate governance disclosures; and

(b)   financial statements and other information reported by other organisations (eg. charities, pension schemes, government departments, local authorities and public sector businesses).

Guidance for *auditors* is provided by SAS 220 'Materiality and the audit', issued by **3** the Auditing Practices Board.

**Editor's note: See paragraphs 3.28–3.32 of the final Statement issued December 1999.*

INTERPRETATION

4   Materiality depends on an item's size, nature and circumstances. Dependence on size means that materiality is quantifiable in financial terms. However, the nature and circumstances of an item are qualitative matters and so materiality is not capable of general mathematical definition. Because judgment is required to determine materiality, different people may have different views about whether an item is material. Materiality will often be indicated by a range of potential values with the eventual treatment of a particular item depending upon a full consideration of the information involved and how it will be used.

5   Judgments about materiality ultimately depend on how information could influence the economic decisions of users of financial statements or other information hereafter referred to as '*users*'. According to the draft *Statement of Principles*:

> '*1.1   The objective of financial statements is to provide information about the financial position, performance and financial adaptability of an enterprise that is useful to a wide range of users for assessing the stewardship of management and for making economic decisions.*'*

6   There is a role for guidelines in reaching consistent and properly considered conclusions. Nevertheless, if preparers are to be responsive to users, they should not substitute the mechanical application of rules and formulae for careful consideration of how information could influence or enhance users' economic decisions such as whether to hold or sell investments or whether to reappoint or replace management. Preparers should also appreciate that information often has economic effects without changing economic decisions. For example, in preparing financial statements to be used to value a business for an acquisition, a relatively minor adjustment may alter the purchase price without changing the decision to proceed with the acquisition.

APPLICATIONS OF MATERIALITY

7   In financial reporting the concept of materiality is applied to:

    (a)   account balances;
    (b)   errors and tolerances;
    (c)   differences;
    (d)   disclosures; and
    (e)   economic events and conditions.

8   In maintaining accounting records relating to individual transactions with third parties, accuracy and precision are essential and therefore the concept of materiality does not apply. Other items are recorded in accounting records based on best estimates of the outcomes of future events, market values and the appropriate allocation of costs and revenues to different activities and periods. Such estimates are subjective and the concept of materiality is applied in determining appropriate precision tolerances that reflect the nature of the items involved.

9   The application of materiality thresholds and tolerances is fundamental to the internal and external reporting that underpins corporate governance, the management of commercial risk and business decision-making. Management require internal reports which highlight relevant matters and omit irrelevant detail and they supplement basic accounting records with management systems and controls which, amongst other things:

Editor's note: See Chapter 1 of the final Statement issued December 1999.

(a)   summarise information from the accounting records which might be material in aggregate; and

(b)   prevent and detect material misstatement of that information.

For internal and external financial reporting purposes it is conventional to apply **10** thresholds for accumulating information and correcting errors which rise towards a set level of materiality as the time for reporting approaches. The use of lower thresholds helps ensure that cumulative omissions and other errors do not lead to an overall material misstatement. It is also conventional to select a monetary unit, such as a pound or a thousand pounds, and to round to the nearest unit. The chosen unit is set sufficiently low to ensure that the resulting loss of precision and detail is clearly immaterial.

In the context of reporting to third parties, legislation and regulations for different **11** types of organisation contain requirements to report particular accounting and other information. Legislation and regulations usually specifically describe such requirements as applying only when a materiality condition is satisfied. For example, the Companies Act 1985 Schedule 4 '*Form and content of company accounts*' states that '*amounts which in the particular context of any provision of this schedule are not material may be disregarded for the purposes of that provision*'. Schedule 4A contains similar references for group accounts and Schedule 5 refers to materiality in relation to disclosures about related undertakings.

Application of the concept of materiality is also explicitly permitted under **12** accounting standards and the Companies Act 1985 in a variety of circumstances.

(a)   Specified items must be disclosed when they are material (eg. statutory format captions with Arabic numbers under CA 85 Sch 4.3(4)).

(b)   Certain accounting methods must be applied to material items (eg. the *Foreword to Accounting Standards* requires standards to be so applied).

(c)   Some items must be disclosed when a material difference exists between two accounting treatments (eg. historical cost profit should be disclosed under paragraph 26 of FRS 3 where this is materially different from reported profit).

(d)   Some accounting methods are applied when a material difference exists between two accounting treatments (eg. consolidation adjustments for the application of consistent accounting policies should be made under CA 85 Sch 4A.3(3)).

(e)   Certain items should be disclosed when there are events or conditions having a material effect on a preparer of financial statements (eg. acquisitions, sales or terminations which have a material impact on a major business segment must be disclosed under paragraph 15 of FRS 3).

(f)   Specific accounting methods have to be applied when there are events or conditions having a material effect on a preparer of financial statements (eg. subsidiaries which are individually or collectively material should be consolidated under CA 85 s229(2)).

Many materiality decisions are called for in the application of accounting standards. **13** Even where preparers decide to apply an individual provision of a standard, eg. in relation to measurement, they are not necessarily committed to apply all the other provisions of the standard, eg. to make specified disclosures which are immaterial. The importance of such decisions is clear from paragraph 20 of the '*Foreword to Accounting Standards*' which states that the Financial Reporting Review Panel is concerned with material departures from standards. In the event of such a departure, the Panel can apply to the court for an order to require company directors to prepare revised accounts. The Department of Trade and Industry has similar powers.

14   Schedule 6 to the Companies Act 1985 *'Disclosure of information: Emoluments and other benefits of directors and others'* and Schedule 7 *'Matters to be dealt with in directors' report'* do not specifically permit or forbid application of the concept of materiality. However, this statement supports the application of materiality to the requirements of Schedules 6 and 7 on the grounds that materiality is fundamental to all reporting and, by definition, immaterial differences would not influence users' economic decisions. Materiality thresholds for the purposes of Schedules 6 and 7 are generally likely to be lower than for other financial statement purposes because of the nature of the items disclosed. These relate largely to management stewardship rather than purely financial matters.

USERS

15   While internal reporting systems are designed specifically for the needs of management, the draft *'Statement of Principles'* regards financial statements as providing information about the financial position, performance and financial adaptability of an enterprise that is useful to a wide range of external users. They include actual and potential investors, employees, lenders, suppliers and other trade creditors, governments and their agencies, and members of the public with access to financial statements. In making judgments on materiality, preparers of accounts should therefore be concerned with identifying relevant users. Identifying groups of users for the purpose of making reporting decisions does not itself involve acknowledging a legal duty of care to such groups.

16   The expectation that preparers will address the needs of a wide range of users is mitigated by the Board's assertions in the draft *'Statement of Principles'* that:

(a)   not all the information needs of all users can be met by financial statements (paragraph 1.6);

(b)   financial statements that meet the needs of the providers of risk capital will also meet most of the needs of other users (paragraph 1.6); and

(c)   users can be assumed to have a reasonable knowledge of business and economic activities and accounting and a willingness to study information with reasonable diligence (paragraph 2.33).*

17   It is therefore envisaged that judgments about materiality can generally be made on the basis of the needs of classes of knowledgeable and diligent investors who are reasonable in their use of and reliance on financial statements and other information. Such investors recognise the inherent limitations of financial statements and other information requiring the use of estimates and the consideration of future events. It is also important when there are large numbers of users in a group to consider representative users. Preparers should not seek to address a single hypothetical user, especially one on the brink of making a decision to buy or sell whose decision might be changed by even a small change in a reported number or disclosure.

18   The ASB identifies providers of risk capital as the primary users of financial statements. Consequently, in considering materiality, preparers are expected to focus on the relevance of information to the assessment of financial performance, position and adaptability and management's discharge of its stewardship responsibilities. In entities where the provision of risk capital is of reduced importance (eg. charities, pension schemes and government bodies), the same broad financial and stewardship issues are still likely to be of most interest to the relevant primary user groups.

---

*Editor's note: See Chapter 1 and paragraph 3.27(c) of the final Statement issued December 1999.

DETERMINANTS OF MATERIALITY

Size

The size of an item recognised in financial statements can only be expressed in terms **19**
of monetary value. In considering the materiality of uncertainties and contingencies,
preparers therefore have to make best estimates of the potential monetary amounts
involved, taking into account the likelihood of crystallisation. In considering the
materiality of related party transactions for which no price is charged, preparers
should also have regard to the potential monetary amounts involved.

Whilst the quantification of materiality is fundamental and unavoidable, materiality **20**
can never be judged purely on the basis of absolute size. £1 million is a large amount
but in relation to a potential misstatement of sales by a large multinational, it is likely
to be immaterial. Conversely, £1000 is a comparatively small amount but it might be
seen as material, even for a large multinational, if it relates to a benefit-in-kind which
has been wrongly omitted from the disclosure of directors' remuneration. In some
cases the nature and circumstances of an item can be of such importance to users that
a size threshold is of little practical significance in determining materiality. This is
particularly likely where the quality of management stewardship or corporate governance are at issue.

Nature

The nature of an item is characterised by: **21**

(a)   the events or transactions giving rise to it;
(b)   the legality, sensitivity, normality and potential consequences of the event or
      transaction;
(c)   the identity of the parties involved; and
(d)   the account captions and disclosure notes affected.

Particular care should be taken not to offset items which are different in nature when **22**
they might be material if considered separately, eg. an unrecorded sale and the
related cost of sale. Conversely, the materiality of items of a similar nature should be
considered in aggregate, eg. if a number of sales have not been recorded, their
materiality should be considered in aggregate.

Circumstances

The materiality of information can only be judged in relation to its ultimate impact, **23**
or potential impact, on users. Consequently, the materiality of a given item of a given
size will depend on the context of the accounting and other information available to
users.

The immediate context of an item is the entity's financial statements. Some **24**
accounting standards and related guidance contain explicit references to the
appropriate context in which to judge materiality and look beyond the immediate
disclosures and captions affected by an item. It might be appropriate to focus on one
or more of the following:

(a)   individual disclosures;
(b)   primary statement captions and subtotals;
(c)   the relevant primary financial statement as a whole;
(d)   the financial statements as a whole; and

(e)   the entity's financial position or the scale of its operations as indicated by the financial statements.

25   Paragraph 20 of the Explanation of FRS 8 '*Related party disclosures*' provides additional guidance. It indicates that the materiality of related party transactions is to be judged not only in the broader context of the reporting entity, but also in relation to an individual related party, eg. where that party is a dictator, key manager or some other person accountable for stewardship.

26   The financial statements of a single period for a single entity are of limited value and users generally consider such information in a wider context. It will therefore often be appropriate for preparers to modify their views on the materiality of an item in the light of:

(a)   comparative figures and trend information;
(b)   expectations including, where relevant, projections and forecasts;
(c)   the financial statements of comparable entities; and
(d)   economic and industry background information.

MAKING DECISIONS ABOUT MATERIALITY

27   Prescriptive rules which seek to reflect how users make decisions cannot address all situations and relieve preparers of the need to apply judgments. However, it is advisable for preparers to develop guidelines for their own organisation which reflect their consideration of users and the size, nature and circumstances of individual items within the financial statements. Such guidelines provide relatively objective rebuttable presumptions against which subsequent judgments about particular situations can be gauged. An important overall test of the appropriateness of decisions about materiality is to consider whether the resulting financial statements give a true and fair view as required by Section 226(2) of the Companies Act 1985.

28   Materiality guidelines can be derived from answering the following questions:

(a)   who are the relevant users?
(b)   what are their decision-making needs?
(c)   for a given item, what is the appropriate context for assessing its materiality?
(d)   in what range of values do items become critical in terms of materiality?
(e)   how should particular items in these critical ranges be decided and reported?

29   Preparers' perceptions of users' needs can be based on:

(a)   general discussions with users and other information relating to users' expectations gathered as a result of a company's corporate governance procedures;
(b)   observing users' responses to information, eg. press or analyst comment on particular disclosures, numbers, ratios or trends and the effect on decisions to hold or sell investments or to reappoint or replace management;
(c)   the impact on market prices of specific items of news; and
(d)   their own reactions and attitudes as users of financial information in similar situations.

30   In some cases the approach will be relatively straightforward. Where a company's bank facility is dependent on compliance with covenants based upon financial statements, the users of those statements include investors, bankers and creditors with an interest in knowing whether the covenants are violated. Their decision-making needs will at least cover the figures that are used in the covenant calculations. An item will be judged material if it will make a difference in triggering non-compliance with a covenant or in ensuring that a covenant is satisfied.

At certain critical thresholds, an assessment of users' needs will indicate a require-   **31**
ment for very low levels of materiality and potentially unrealistic demands for
accuracy, eg. where trends reverse, profits become losses, technical insolvency occurs,
compliance with debt covenants is in doubt or identified individuals are deciding
whether or not to buy or sell shares. In these circumstances, preparers should:

(a) adopt an even-handed approach in areas where the required degree of accuracy
is difficult to achieve so that there is perceived to be an equal chance of mis-
takenly falling on either side of a critical divide;

(b) be particularly sensitive to the potentially misleading cumulative effect of
individually immaterial items or errors; and

(c) consider whether the reliability of the information in relation to its potential
use is such that the information should be accompanied by a clear statement of
the circumstances of its preparation and its inherent limitations.

On the basis of experience, a preparer might reasonably decide to attach particular   **32**
importance to the materiality of items in a company's financial statements in the
context of the trend of earnings and the margins of other companies in the same
sector. Such considerations might be particularly appropriate in situations of marginal or break-even profitability.

EVIDENCING DECISIONS

It will be appropriate for the preparer, whether an individual, a committee or a board   **33**
of directors, formally to consider its guidelines and policies with regard to materiality
and to document, for its own purposes, the main decisions it has taken.

PUBLISHED GUIDANCE

In considering the guidelines and policies that might be appropriate for their parti-   **34**
cular reporting entity, preparers may wish to bear in mind specific published
guidance:

(a) The one explicit materiality rule in UK accounting standards is contained in
paragraph 16.ii of SSAP 3 'Earnings per share' which requires fully diluted
earnings per share to be disclosed when such earnings are at least 5% less than
basic earnings per share.*

(b) Paragraph 76 of FRS 6 'Acquisition and mergers' refers to a material minority
and indicates that this is defined as 10%.

(c) A 'substantial acquisition' is seen as being larger than a material acquisition and
arises under paragraph 37 of FRS 6 when the net assets or operating profits of
the acquired entity exceed 15% of those of the acquiring entity or the fair value
of the consideration exceeds 15% of the net assets of the acquiring entity.

The staff of the US Securities and Exchange Commission has an informal rule of   **35**
thumb that items and errors of more than 10% are material, those between 5% and
10% may be material but those under 5% are usually not material. These percentages are normally applied to gross profit, net income, equity and any specific line
item in the financial statements that is potentially misstated.

Editor's note: SSAP 3 has been superseded by FRS 14.

TECH 50/04
Guidance on the Effect of FRS 17 *Retirement Benefits* and IAS 19 'Employee Benefits' on Realised Profits and Losses

(Issued 24 November 2004)

Guidance on the implications of FRS 17 *Retirement Benefits and* IAS 19 *'Employee benefits' for the determination of realised profits and losses in the context of distributions under the Companies Act 1985, issued on 24 November 2004 by the Institute of Chartered Accountants in England and Wales and the Institute of Chartered Accountants of Scotland.*

Contents

This Technical Release provides general guidance and does not purport to deal with all possible questions and issues that may arise in any given situation. No responsibility for loss occasioned to any person acting or refraining from action as a result of any material in this guidance can be accepted by the Institutes.

Introduction

The attached statement sets out guidance on the effect of FRS 17 *Retirement Benefits*   I-1
on realised profits and losses of companies formed and registered under the Companies Act 1985 or earlier Acts. It supplements but does not amend Tech 7/03
'Guidance on the determination of realised profits and losses in the context of distributions under the Companies Act 1985'.

FRS 17 comes fully into effect for accounting periods beginning on or after 1 Jan-   I-2
uary 2005*. Certain disclosures are required for all periods ending on or after 22 June
2001†. The implications of the transitional disclosure requirements of FRS 17 on the
profits available for distribution by companies are dealt with in Tech 3/02, to which
reference should be made. Companies proposing to pay interim dividends for periods
beginning on or after 1 January 2005 will need to take account of the implementation
of the recognition requirements of FRS 17 in calculating their profits available for
distribution.

This guidance is based on current UK company law which requires that the deter-   I-3
mination of a company's profits available for distribution is derived from what is
recorded in its accounts including any pension surplus or deficit arising from the
recognition requirements of FRS 17.

This guidance was originally developed for FRS 17 but is equally applicable when   I-4
the equivalent international standard IAS 19 'Employee benefits' is being applied.
When IAS 19 is being applied, this guidance should be applied to the amounts
reported under that standard (paragraph 1.8). For simplicity, this guidance continues
to refer throughout to the relevant requirements of FRS 17.

A draft of this guidance was issued in Technical Release 13/04 on 15 April 2004.   I-5
After consideration of comments received, significant changes have been made to the
guidance regarding the calculation of the realised or unrealised reserves on first
adopting FRS 17 in circumstances where it has not been practicable to establish the
total cumulative net contributions less refunds made since a defined benefit scheme
commenced. The guidance on this matter (paragraph 4.4) has been simplified and
now recognises that the calculation may be revisited in a later accounting period if
additional net contributions are identified which were made prior to the date of first
adoption of FRS 17.

Guidance

SCOPE   1

This Technical Release gives guidance on the effect of FRS 17 "Retirement benefits"   1.1
on realised profits and losses under the Companies Act 1985. It supplements but does
not amend Tech 7/03 "Guidance on the determination of realised profits and losses
in the context of distributions under the Companies Act 1985". This Technical
Release does not give guidance on accounting for retirement benefits.

The principles set out in the main body of this guidance should be read in con-   1.2
junction with the explanatory appendices.

**For entities applying the FRSSE, periods ending on or after 22 June 2006.*

†*For entities applying the FRSSE, 22 June 2002.*

1.3   For defined contribution retirement benefit schemes, the cost charged to the profit and loss account under FRS 17 is equal to the contributions payable to the scheme for the accounting period. This is the same as under SSAP 24 "Accounting for pension costs" and raises no new issues as regards realised profits and losses. The charge to the profit and loss account for the contributions payable is a realised loss.

1.4   Under FRS 17, some companies account for their participation in certain multi-employer defined benefit retirement benefit schemes as if they were defined contribution schemes. Where a scheme meets the criteria for this treatment in FRS 17, the position as regards realised profits and losses will be the same as for any other defined contribution scheme.

1.5   The remainder of this guidance is concerned with defined benefit schemes that are accounted for as such under FRS 17.

1.6   This guidance assumes the company has only one scheme. A company that operates more than one defined benefit scheme should assess separately for each scheme the impact of an FRS 17 surplus or deficit on its realised profits and losses. However, there may be situations where two schemes are to merge. In such situations a company may treat any net credit to reserves that has been recorded in respect of one scheme as a reduction in the realised loss caused by a net debit in respect of the other scheme from the point at which the trustees of the schemes have irrevocably agreed that they will merge and to extent that the surplus and deficit are permitted to be offset for funding purposes. A similar argument applies in cases where a transfer has been irrevocably agreed between different schemes.

1.7   This technical release applies both to pension schemes acquired in a business combination and those that are started by the reporting company.

1.8   This guidance was originally developed for FRS 17 but is equally applicable when the equivalent international standard IAS 19 'Employee benefits' is being applied. The principal difference between the standards is that FRS 17 requires immediate recognition of all actuarial gains and losses while IAS 19 generally permits those gains and losses to be deferred. For this and other reasons, the amounts reported in the balance sheet and performance statements may differ depending upon which standard is being applied. When IAS 19 is being applied, this guidance should be applied to the amounts reported under that standard. For simplicity, this guidance continues to refer throughout to the relevant requirements of FRS 17.

2   GAIN OR LOSS ARISING FROM FRS 17

2.1   In establishing the impact that a surplus or deficit under FRS 17 has on a company's realised profits it is necessary to:

(a)   identify the cumulative net gain or loss taken to reserves in respect of the pension surplus or deficit; and

(b)   establish the extent to which that gain or loss is realised.

2.2   Although the various elements making up the changes in the defined benefit asset or liability are disclosed separately in the performance statements (see paragraph 50 of FRS 17), it is the net amount that represents the cost to the company of the pension promise. Thus it is the cumulative net gain or loss taken to reserves that falls to be categorised as realised or unrealised. There is no need to distinguish that cumulative balance between amounts charged or credited to P&L and those recognised in the STRGL. The entries in the STRGL are considered for this purpose as revisions of past estimates of the net pension cost and are not precluded from being treated as realised simply because they have passed through the STRGL rather than the P&L account.

The impact on reserves is not necessarily the same as the pension asset or liability recognised in the balance sheet due to the net contributions paid to the scheme (see A2) and any asset or liability introduced as the result of a business acquisition (see A6).   **2.3**

ESTABLISHING THE CUMULATIVE NET REALISED GAIN OR LOSS TAKEN TO RESERVES IN RESPECT OF A PENSION SURPLUS OR DEFICIT   3

A cumulative net debit in reserves in respect of the pension scheme constitutes a realised loss as it results from the creation of, or an increase in, a provision for a liability or loss resulting in an overall reduction in net assets. This follows from Tech 7/03 paragraphs 17, 29(d) and B24.   **3.1**

A cumulative net credit in reserves in respect of the pension scheme constitutes a realised profit only to the extent that it is represented by an asset to be recovered by agreed refunds, as discussed in FRS 17 paragraph 42, and the refunds will take the form of qualifying consideration. This follows from Tech 7/03, paragraph 16(a) "a transaction where the consideration received by the company is 'qualifying consideration'".   **3.2**

To the extent that a cumulative net credit in reserves exceeds any such agreed refunds it is unrealised, but it becomes realised in subsequent periods to the extent that it offsets subsequent net debits to reserves being recognised as realised losses in respect of the pension scheme (ie, as the cumulative net credit reduces). This follows from paragraphs 16(f)(iii) and (iv) of Tech 7/03.   **3.3**

COMPUTING CUMULATIVE NET REALISED PROFITS OR LOSSES ON FIRST ADOPTING THE RECOGNITION REQUIREMENTS OF FRS 17   4

On first implementing the recognition requirements of FRS 17 (mandatory for accounting periods beginning on or after 1 January 2005*) a prior year adjustment will arise. However, in establishing the effect on realised profits of implementing FRS 17 it is not necessary to consider the whole of the net debit or credit to reserves resulting from that adjustment but only that part of it which relates to FRS 17 (the part relating to eliminating a SSAP 24 asset or liability is ignored – see A5). The figure to be established is the reserves position had FRS 17 always been in force.   **4.1**

To establish the effect on realised profits a company must therefore establish the cumulative net credit or debit in reserves in respect of the FRS 17 pension asset or liability for the pension scheme immediately after the prior year adjustment. This equals the amount of the surplus or deficit recognised before taking account of deferred tax, adjusted for: **4.2**

(a) cumulative net contributions less refunds made in respect of the pension scheme (see A2) ; and

(b) in the rare cases in which the company has recognised a pension asset or liability in its individual accounts on the acquisition of an unincorporated business (in respect of the pension scheme of that business), the amount initially recognised (see A6).

For entities applying the FRSSE, periods ending on or after 22 June 2006.

4.3   Companies that are able to establish the precise amount of the cumulative net credit or debit in reserves in respect of the pension scheme will treat it as realised or unrealised in accordance with 3.1 to 3.3 above.

4.4   It may not be practicable for companies with long-established schemes to establish the *total* cumulative net contributions less refunds made since the scheme commenced, in order to perform with precision the analysis in 4.2 above (although, in view of their rarity, it is likely that the company would be able to identify all refunds made and these should be included in the calculation). For such schemes the estimated approach set out in this paragraph may be taken:

(a)   the calculation set out in 4.2 above may be performed initially using the amount of those cumulative net contributions the company has been able to identify; and

(b)   that calculation may be revisited subsequently, as set out in 5.3 below, if further contributions are identified that were made prior to the date of the prior year adjustment effected to adopt FRS 17 (any such recalculation is made as at the date of that prior year adjustment).

4.5   A company that operates more than one defined benefit scheme should perform the assessment set out in 4.1 to 4.4 above separately for each scheme. Such a company may find that it can follow 4.2 above for schemes formed or acquired in an acquisition of an unincorporated business relatively recently but may need to follow 4.4 above for schemes operated by the company for a longer time. This guidance does not preclude such a mixed approach.

4.6   Further detail on the estimated approach is set out in A10 to A11.

5   COMPUTING NET REALISED PROFITS OR LOSSES IN PERIODS SUBSEQUENT TO FIRST ADOPTING THE RECOGNITION REQUIREMENTS OF FRS 17

5.1   The approach in section 4 above will give rise to a net cumulative realised profit or loss or unrealised profit for a particular pension scheme on initial adoption of FRS 17. This will serve as a starting point for the ongoing assessment of the net cumulative gain or loss in reserves in respect of the pension scheme.

5.2   A company able to establish the precise effect of adopting FRS 17, in accordance with 4.2 above, will have a precise starting point available.

5.3   A company unable to perform this analysis will take the estimated realised or unrealised reserves position established under 4.4 above as the initial starting point. Such a company might be able to revise that estimate subsequently by identifying additional contribution payments made prior to the date of transition to FRS 17. If so, it may be able to revise upwards the amount of a net cumulative realised loss as at the date of adoption of FRS 17 and therefore treat as realised net credits arising in periods subsequent to the date of transition that would otherwise be treated as unrealised. An example is set out in A11.

6   DEFERRED TAX

6.1   The deferred tax asset or liability arising from different treatments of pension costs for accounting and tax purposes generally relates to the pension asset or liability in the balance sheet and is not necessarily associated with the cumulative net debit or credit in reserves.

The cumulative debit in reserves in respect of a deferred tax liability relating to a **6.2** pension asset should be treated as a realised loss. However, to the extent that there is an unrealised cumulative net credit in reserves in respect of the pension asset, then the amount of the debit in respect of deferred tax should be treated as a reduction in that unrealised profit rather than as a realised loss. It is not necessary to restrict the offset by applying the tax rate to the amount of the unrealised profit.

The cumulative credit in reserves in respect of a deferred tax asset relating to a **6.3** pension liability should be treated as an unrealised profit. However, to the extent that there is a realised cumulative net debit in reserves in respect of the pension liability, then the amount of the credit in respect of deferred tax should be treated as a reduction in that realised loss rather than as an unrealised profit. It is not necessary to restrict the offset by applying the tax rate to the amount of the realised loss.

The approach above follows from that in Tech 7/03 paragraph 31. **6.4**

LC, November 2004

Appendix A
Explanatory Notes

OVERVIEW OF ADJUSTMENTS

A1   The effect of FRS 17 on reserves must be calculated in order to identify whether any adjustment in respect of pensions is needed to reported reserves to arrive at realised reserves. If a net cumulative loss has been taken to reserves, no adjustment is required. If a net cumulative gain has been taken to reserves, and under the guidance set out in paragraph 3.2 that gain is in part or in full an unrealised gain, a deduction equivalent to the unrealised element must be made to reserves in assessing the level of realised reserves.

DIFFERENTIATING THE GAIN OR LOSS ARISING FROM FRS 17 FROM THE PENSION SURPLUS OR DEFICIT

A2   It is the cumulative gain or loss credited or debited to reserves in respect of a pension surplus or deficit, rather than the existence of that surplus or deficit, that affects the realised profits or losses of a company. Consider the example below of a scheme set up at the start of the year. For simplicity current and deferred tax is ignored. The scheme has a surplus of 4 at the end of the year that would be reported on the company's balance sheet as an asset, BUT there has been a cumulative charge of 16 to reserves that would fall to be treated as realised. This example is extended to subsequent years in Appendix B.

	Increase/ (decrease) in pension asset	(Reduction) in cash balance	Amount debited/ (credited) to reserves
B/F	0		
Debited to profit and loss account	(20)		20
Credited to STRGL	4		(4)
Contributions paid	20	(20)	-
C/F	4	(20)	16

A3   The net effect on the balance sheet in the above example is:

Debit Pension asset   4

Debit Reserves   16

Credit Cash   20

It is the cumulative loss of 16 in the above example that has been debited to reserves in respect of the pension scheme that falls to be treated as realised, rather than any notional "credit" relating to the asset of 4.

A4   The cumulative net gain or loss taken to reserves in respect of the pension surplus or deficit is also not necessarily the same as the amount of the pension asset or liability disclosed under paragraph 90 of FRS 17. The example in Appendix 1 to the FRS discloses as a pension reserve an amount equal to the net pension asset. This will normally differ from the cumulative net gain or loss taken to reserves, due to net contributions paid to the scheme as in A2 above and any asset or liability introduced as the result of a business acquisition.

ADJUSTMENT FROM SSAP 24 TO FRS 17

Although the removal from the balance sheet of any asset or liability recognised **A5** under SSAP 24 will have an impact on reserves, there is no need to consider either whether that impact is a debit or a credit or whether it is realised or unrealised. The net contributions paid/refunded in the past are unaffected by the change from SSAP 24 to FRS 17. The effect of the prior year adjustment is therefore to remove one asset or liability (determined under SSAP 24) and replace it by another (determined under FRS 17) reflecting the identical net contributions. As a result, the cumulative impact on reserves can be established by focusing solely on the position under FRS 17, which will be the same position as if FRS 17 had always formed the basis of the company's accounting policy.

ACQUISITION OF UNINCORPORATED BUSINESS

Where part of a company's SSAP 24 pension asset or liability arose on the acqui- **A6** sition of an unincorporated business it will have been recorded initially at fair value as required by FRS 7. That initial asset or liability will not have affected the company's reserves directly and must therefore be taken into account as part of the adjustment in arriving at the impact of FRS 17 on reserves. FRS 17 does not change the requirement of FRS 7 to record the pension asset or liability at fair value, although fair value will often now be measured using a different method. FRS 17 paragraph 97 notes that any difference between the FRS 17 measure of fair value and that originally used "should be treated as a change in assumptions (ie an actuarial gain or loss) arising since acquisition." Such a difference will therefore give rise to a gain or loss that falls to be categorised as realised or unrealised in accordance with the general approach noted in section 3 above. As a result, it is the asset or liability recognised initially as part of the acquisition accounting that is taken into account in assessing the reserves position on adoption of FRS 17.

For example, in 2000 a company acquires an unincorporated business and the fair values of the net assets recognised include a pension asset of 20. At 31 December 2004, contributions of 4 and a SSAP 24 charge of 6 reduce the asset to 18. Assuming the FRS 17 surplus at 31 December 2004 is 10, applying paragraph 4.2 to establish the precise impact of FRS 17 on net realised profits or losses:

Surplus	10
4.2(a) Cumulative net contributions	(4)
4.2(b) Initial fair value	(20)
Net (loss) in reserves under FRS 17	(14)

COMPUTING NET REALISED PROFITS OR LOSSES IN PERIODS SUBSEQUENT TO FIRST ADOPTING THE RECOGNITION REQUIREMENTS OF FRS 17

Having arrived at an analysis of the net cumulative gain or loss in reserves in respect **A7** of the pension scheme on initial adoption of FRS 17 – which, as explained in 5.1 above, provides the starting point for ongoing assessment – it will be necessary to roll forward the analysis as subsequent gains and losses arise based on the principles in section 3 above. The gains and losses in subsequent periods will be classified as realised or unrealised as noted below and as illustrated in Appendix B.

A8   A net credit in a period will be a realised profit if it:

(a)   reduces a cumulative net debit in reserves in respect of the pension asset or liability (i.e. under paragraph 16(e) of Tech 7/03 "the reversal of a loss previously regarded as realised"); or

(b)   is represented by an increase in a pension asset to be recovered by an agreed refund of contributions which will take the form of qualifying consideration.

A9   A net debit in a period will be a realised loss. However, to the extent that it reduces a cumulative unrealised net credit in reserves in respect of the pension asset or liability, an equivalent amount of that net credit will be treated as a realised profit in accordance with the principles of paragraph 16(f) of Tech 7/03. Thus net realised profits are reduced only to the extent that a net debit in a period exceeds a brought forward cumulative net credit, in respect of the pension asset or liability, previously treated as an unrealised profit.

THE ESTIMATED APPROACH TO COMPUTING CUMULATIVE NET REALISED PROFITS OR LOSSES ON FIRST ADOPTING THE RECOGNITION REQUIREMENTS OF FRS 17

A10   The precise effect of FRS 17 on reserves can be calculated only if the precise amount of cumulative net contributions (ie, contributions less refunds) paid to the scheme can be established. In older schemes, it may not always be practicable to do this. Instead, the company may perform the initial assessment of the impact of FRS 17 using the level of net contributions that management has been able to identify (which should include all refunds made – see 4.4 above). The effect will be to understate the realised loss (or overstate the unrealised profit) in reserves on adoption of FRS 17, compared with the precise effect. As a result, if net gains are reported in the scheme in future years, they are more likely to have to be classified as unrealised gains and, therefore, to restrict the company's level of realised profits.

A11   The company may therefore choose to re-assess the effect of FRS 17 on the estimated realised or unrealised reserves position, as at the date of initial adoption of the standard, by identifying more of the contributions paid to the scheme prior to the date of adoption.

For example, in its December 2005 financial statements, a company adopts FRS 17 in full. It wishes to pay an interim dividend based on its results to 30 June 2005 and therefore calculates the effect on its realised or unrealised reserves as at that date of switching from SSAP 24 to FRS 17. It has a SSAP 24 provision of 2 on its balance sheet at that date and total net contributions made to the scheme since it started were 90. The scheme has an FRS 17 surplus of 20 at 30 June 2005 and there is no ceiling on the company's ability to recognise this amount as an asset.

If the company is able to identify the entire 90 of contributions, under the precise approach set out in paragraph 4.2 the effect of FRS 17 on the company's reserves can be calculated as follows:

FRS 17 asset	20
Net contributions	(90)
Precise net (loss) in reserves	(70)

As set out in paragraph 3.1, this loss will be a realised loss. As a result, the first 70 of net gains that the company reports on its pension scheme after adoption of FRS 17 as at 30 June 2005 will reduce the cumulative net loss in reserves and therefore effectively be treated as realised gains.

Say that the company could identify only (i) 20; or (ii) 65 of the contributions made prior to 30 June 2005. Under the estimated approach set out in paragraph 4.4 the effect of FRS 17 on reserves would be as follows:

	Identify 20	*Identify 65*
FRS 17 asset	20	20
Contributions identified	(20)	(65)
Estimated net (loss) in reserves	0	(45)

(i) Since the cumulative effect on reserves as at 30 June 2005 is estimated to be nil, any net gains that the company reports thereafter will lead to a net cumulative gain which, as set out in paragraphs 3.2 and 3.3, will be unrealised. The net cumulative gain will therefore have to be deducted from total reserves as part of the company's calculation of the amount of realised reserves available for distribution. As set out in paragraphs 4.4(b) and 5.3, the company may revisit its estimated calculation of the effect on realised or unrealised reserves as at 30 June 2005 of adopting FRS 17 if it can identify more of the contributions of 90 made prior to that date. To the extent that further contributions prior to 30 June 2005 are identified, the estimate of the net loss as at that date will be revised (ie, increased). This means that that amount of the future gains reported will reduce the cumulative net loss rather than create a cumulative net gain, and there will be no need to restrict realised reserves for a net gain.

(ii) More of the total contributions made prior to 30 June 2005 can be identified in this case and the estimated net loss at that date is 45. Therefore, the first 45 of net future gains will have the effect of reducing the cumulative net loss in reserves and no adjustment in respect of pensions will be needed to total reserves in arriving at realised reserves. If the cumulative amount of future gains exceeds 45, the excess would be a cumulative net gain in reserves, which would be unrealised. At that time, the company may wish to investigate whether it can identify more contributions made prior to 30 June 2005 (up to the ceiling of 90). If it can, the estimated effect of adopting FRS 17 can be recalculated.

PROPOSED APPROACH IN FRED 20

Appendix III to FRED 20 (the Exposure Draft upon which FRS 17 was based) set **A12** out a possible approach to mitigate the impact on distributable profits of a pension deficit measured and recognised in accordance with the FRED. In summary, this approach involved splitting the deficit computed using the projected unit method into two components and treating only the component that would arise on a discontinuance basis as affecting distributable profits. Paragraph 58 in Appendix IV to FRS 17 notes that the ASB decided not to proceed with this approach in the light of comments received. These issues were reconsidered in the development of this guidance and the conclusion was reached that there are no grounds for computing the deficit in a scheme for distributable profit purposes on a basis that is different from that used for financial reporting purposes. Distributable profits must be assessed by reference to the assets and liabilities stated in a company's "relevant accounts" and for this purpose any provision (with one limited exception which is not relevant in this case) is to be treated as a realised loss in accordance with section 275(1).

Appendix B

Extension of the example in A1.

Year		Pension asset/(liability)	Reduction/cash balance	Reduction/(increase) in Reserves	Realised in (profit)/loss	Unrealised (profit)/loss	Notes
	B/f	0					
1	P&L	(20)		20 }		16	Net loss in year of 16
	STRGL	4		(4)			so 16 is realised
	Contributions paid	20	(20)	(20)			
	C/f	4		16	16 }		
2	P&L	(20)		20 }		(4)	Net gain in year of 4
	STRGL	24		(24)			b/fwd cumulative loss of 16
	Contributions paid	20	(20)	(20)			so 4 is realised
	C/f	28		12	12 }		
3	P&L	(20)		20 }		(12)	Net gain in year of 20
	STRGL	40		(40)			(8) b/fwd cumulative loss of 12
	Contributions paid	0	0	0			so 8 is unrealised
	C/f	48		(8)	20 }	(8)	
4	P&L	(20)		20 }		12	Net loss in year of 12
	STRGL	8		(8)			8 Unrealised gain of 8 becomes
	Contributions paid	0	0	0			realised
	C/f	36		4	4 }	0	
5	P&L	(15)		15 }		5	Net loss in year of 5
	STRGL	10		(10)			
	Contributions paid	20	(20)	(20)			
	C/f	51		9	15 }	0	
6	P&L	(15)		15 }		9	Net gain in year of 15
	STRGL	30		(30)			(9) b/fwd cumulative loss of 9
	Contributions paid		(20)	(20)			so 9 is realised
	C/f	66		(6)	(6) }		

TECH 64/04
Guidance on the effect on realised and distributable profits of accounting for employee share schemes in accordance with UITF abstract 38 and revised UITF abstract 17

Guidance on the implications of UITF Abstract 38 "Accounting for ESOP trusts" and UITF Abstract 17 (revised 2003) "Employee share schemes" for the determination of realised profits and losses in the context of distributions under the Companies Act 1985 and on distributable profits for public companies under that Act, issued on 21 December 2004 by the Institute of Chartered Accountants in England and Wales and the Institute of Chartered Accountants of Scotland (the "Institutes").

Contents

This Technical Release provides general guidance and does not purport to deal with all possible questions and issues that may arise in any given situation. No responsibility for loss occasioned to any person acting or refraining from action as a result of any material in this guidance can be accepted by the Institutes.

Introduction

The attached statement sets out guidance on the effect of UITF Abstract 38   I-1
"Accounting for ESOP trusts" and UITF Abstract 17 (revised 2003) "Employee
share schemes" for the determination of realised profits and losses of companies
formed and registered under the Companies Act 1985 or earlier Acts in the context of
distributions under the Companies Act 1985 and on distributable profits for public
companies under that Act. It supplements but does not amend Tech 7/03 "Guidance
on the determination of realised profits and losses in the context of distributions
under the Companies Act 1985".

Under the Companies Act 1985, distributions are made by individual companies and   I-2
not by groups. The group accounts are therefore not relevant for the purpose of
determining a company's profits available for distribution. Current UK company
law also requires that the determination of a company's profits available for distribution is derived from what is recorded in its individual accounts.

Abstract 38 was published on 15 December 2003 and should be adopted in financial   I-3
statements relating to accounting periods ending on or after 22 June 2004, with
earlier adoption encouraged. Previous requirements on accounting for ESOP trusts
were set out in Abstract 13, which is superseded by Abstract 38. The principal
difference is that Abstract 38 requires investments in own shares held through an
ESOP trust ("ESOP shares") to be deducted in arriving at shareholders' funds
whereas Abstract 13 required them to be recognised as assets. Consistent with this
treatment, no gains or losses will be recognised in the profit and loss account or
statement of total recognised gains and losses for the period on the purchase, sale,
issue or cancellation of ESOP shares.

Abstract 17 (revised 2003) deals with the charge to the profit and loss account for   I-4
employee share schemes. Abstract 17 (revised 2000), taken together with Abstract 13,
provided that, when shares were purchased in the market by an ESOP trust, the book
value of those shares (less any amount to be contributed by the employee) should
form the basis for a minimum charge to the profit and loss account. Under Abstract
17 (revised 2003) this is no longer the case and the minimum charge to the profit and
loss account is always calculated on the basis of intrinsic value of the share award at
the grant date.

FRS 20 "Share-based payment" requires a charge to the profit and loss account for   I-5
equity-settled share-based payments, based on the fair value of the equity instrument
at grant date. Although the amount of any charge is likely to be greater under FRS
20 than under Abstract 17 (revised 2003), the accounting entry required is the same
and therefore the implications for distributable profits are likely to be similar.

A note of legal considerations attached to Abstract 38 sets out legal advice that the   I-6
UITF received on the implications for distributable profits when the accounting
treatment required by the Abstract is followed. The note of legal considerations is
reproduced as an Appendix to the guidance. This guidance is consistent with that
note of legal considerations but additionally addresses some issues that were not
covered in that note as well as considering some issues in greater depth.

The guidance is structured as a series of questions relating to a typical example   I-7
situation. Of these questions, Questions 1 to 8 in the guidance deal primarily with
matters of law. Questions 9 to 12 deal primarily with matters of what are generally
accepted accounting principles for determining realised profits and losses. These
latter questions are relevant in the context of Section 262(3) Companies Act 1985,

which provides that "References...to 'realised profits' and 'realised losses', in relation to a company's accounts, are to such profits or losses of the company as fall to be treated as realised in accordance with principles generally accepted, at the time when the accounts are prepared, with respect to the determination for accounting purposes of realised profits or losses".

I-8 A draft of this guidance was issued in Technical Release 21/04 on 17 June 2004. After consideration of comments received, changes have been made to the guidance regarding the effect of the financial assistance rules for public companies under section 154 to clarify that these rules operate on a narrow entity basis (see Questions 5 and 6, paragraphs 22 to 29). Also, an additional question has been included to cover circumstances where the ESOP trust subscribes for (rather than purchases) shares which are subsequently transferred to employees for less than their subscription price (see Question 11, paragraph 40).

I-9 The guidance reflects the law at 21 December 2004. English and Scottish Counsel have confirmed that the analysis at Questions 1 to 8 of the guidance is consistent with the law at that date.

I-10 Counsel accept no responsibility (other than to the Institutes) in relation to advice ascribed to them in this guidance.

Guidance

BACKGROUND

A company is the sponsoring company of an ESOP trust that purchases the company's own shares. The company has de facto control of the ESOP trust's assets and liabilities and therefore the company is required to recognise certain assets and liabilities of the trust in the company's individual accounts. Hitherto the ESOP trust's purchases of the company's own shares ('ESOP shares') were dealt with in the company's accounts, in accordance with UITF Abstract 13, as the purchase of an asset. Under UITF Abstract 38, which supersedes Abstract 13 for periods ending on or after 22 June 2004 (with early adoption encouraged), the cost of the ESOP shares will be presented in the company's accounts as a deduction in arriving at shareholders' funds. Consistent with this treatment, no gain or loss will be recognised in the profit and loss account or statement of total recognised gains and losses for the period on the purchase, sale, issue or cancellation of ESOP shares.

1

The sponsoring company of an ESOP trust may be a company other than the one whose shares are held by the trust. For example, a subsidiary may be the sponsoring company of an ESOP trust that holds shares in its parent. In this case the shares will not be "own shares" from the perspective of the subsidiary's financial statements and UITF Abstract 38 will not be relevant. The shares would be recognised as an asset in the subsidiary's balance sheet and the issues addressed in this guidance would not arise.

2

ISSUES WHICH THIS GUIDANCE ADDRESSES

This guidance considers the implications of the new accounting treatment of ESOP shares for the determination of a company's profits available for distribution, including the impact of the requirements relating to financial assistance for the acquisition of own shares. The examples given in the questions and answers below should not be regarded as exhaustive. Directors also need to have regard to their common law duties when proposing or making a distribution. Companies should consider taking and relying upon their own legal advice, particularly in relation to any matters not covered in this guidance. Questions 1, 2, 9, 10, 11 and 12 are relevant to all companies and Questions 3, 4, 5, 6, 7 and 8 are relevant to public companies only.

3

A note of legal considerations attached to Abstract 38 sets out legal advice that the UITF received on the implications for distributable profits when the accounting treatment required by the Abstract is followed. The note of legal considerations is reproduced as an Appendix to this guidance for reference. This guidance is consistent with that note of legal considerations but additionally addresses some issues that were not covered in that note as well as considering some issues in greater depth.

4

English and Scottish Counsel have confirmed that the analysis at Questions 1 to 8 in paragraphs 6 to 33 of this guidance is consistent with the law at 21 December 2004.

5

LEGAL ISSUES

Q1: Is the purchase of ESOP shares a distribution at law?

No. The note of legal considerations attached to Abstract 38, reproduced as an Appendix to this guidance, makes it clear that the acquisition of shares by an ESOP trust does not give rise to a distribution. This is because at law the shares have been

6

purchased by the trust, notwithstanding that assistance may have been given by the company (by way of gift or loan, some or all of which may be ultimately irrecoverable, or by guarantee of the trust's borrowings that may ultimately be called upon to some extent). (For regulation of the transaction for a public company as financial assistance under the Companies Act 1985, see Question 5.)

Q2: Does the purchase of ESOP shares give rise to an immediate realised loss (thus affecting the level of profits available for distribution under section 263)?

7   No. The note of legal considerations attached to Abstract 38 makes it clear that the acquisition of shares by an ESOP trust does not, of itself, give rise to a realised loss. Therefore, such an acquisition does not reduce the amount of profit available for distribution under section 263.

8   However, for a public company, the effect upon distributable profits under section 264 and section 154 needs to be considered (see Questions 3 to 6 below). In addition, whilst for all companies the acquisition of shares will not, of itself, give rise to an immediate realised loss, the impact of other factors such as the granting of rights over those shares should be considered (see Questions 10 and 11 below).

Q3: For a public company, does the purchase of ESOP shares immediately affect its ability to make a distribution by virtue of the application of section 264?

9   Yes. The consideration paid on the purchase of shares by an ESOP sponsored by a public company will immediately restrict the profits available for distribution by virtue of section 264 by the amount of the consideration paid. As more fully explained below, there will be an immediate reduction in net assets but no change in share capital or undistributable reserves.

10   A public company may only make a distribution at any time:

(a)   if at that time the amount of its net assets is not less than the aggregate of its called-up share capital and undistributable reserves; and

(b)   if, and to the extent that, the distribution does not reduce the amount of those assets to less than that aggregate.

Change in net assets

11   Section 264 states that "net assets" means the aggregate of the company's assets less the aggregate of its liabilities. Under section 270, net assets are those as shown in the company's "relevant accounts" which are normally the last annual accounts under Part VII of the Act, properly prepared under the Act; in certain circumstances, the relevant accounts are initial accounts or interim accounts, which are prepared to a similar standard. Net assets for the purposes of section 264 should therefore be determined in accordance with accounting standards and UITF Abstracts. Accordingly, the relevant accounts and the net assets should include the assets and liabilities of the ESOP trust as reported under Abstract 38 ("extended entity accounting") rather than, for example, any loan between the company and the ESOP trust ("narrow entity accounting").

12   The effect of the accounting treatment required by Abstract 38 is that, in drawing up the relevant accounts, any own shares held by an ESOP would be recorded as a deduction in arriving at shareholders' funds rather than as an asset. Therefore, it follows that the relevant aggregate net asset amount for the purposes of the definition in section 264(2) would be reduced by the own shares held (being the consideration paid for the ESOP shares).

Disclosure by way of note that the company also has an "asset" of own shares held   **13**
through an ESOP trust would not restore the net assets for the purposes of section
264. If the shares are not an asset for accounting purposes they cannot be an asset for
the purposes of calculating net assets when applying section 264. This is consistent
with the guidance in Tech 3/02 "FRS 17 transitional disclosures and distributions by
companies" that note disclosures are not relevant for the purposes of determining
distributable profits.

Change in share capital or undistributable reserves

A company's undistributable reserves are defined in section 264. In short, they   **14**
include the company's unrealised profits less its unrealised losses, except that this
amount is never less than zero (i.e. net unrealised losses are not within the definition).

The correct characterisation, as a matter of law, of the deduction in arriving at   **15**
shareholders' funds is not straightforward. On the one hand the deduction should
not be characterised as a loss at all (thereby rendering redundant questions of realisation) because from the point of view of the company's individual accounts (which
are on an extended entity basis) the company has not lost control of the ESOP shares
nor have these shares suffered any objectively measurable diminution in value. On
the other hand, given that the applicable accounting treatment does not permit the
company to treat the ESOP shares as an asset, some might argue that the deduction
should be categorised as a loss, although the nearest equivalent could be said to be a
return of capital. Counsel have advised the Institutes that the characterisation which
gives primacy to the substance rather than presentation is the view to be preferred
and accordingly the deduction should not be characterised as a loss.

Accordingly, the deduction for ESOP shares in arriving at shareholders' funds is   **16**
neither a realised loss nor an unrealised loss and does not affect the balance of
undistributable reserves.

The effect on profits available for distribution under section 264

Thus with net assets reduced but share capital and undistributable reserves unaf-   **17**
fected, the purchase of ESOP shares affects the maximum distribution permissible by
virtue of the application of section 264 (the "maximum distribution permissible"). In
other words, the effect of the section is such that the profits available for distribution
are restricted by a reduction in net assets that is neither a realised nor an unrealised
loss.

Furthermore, the existence of any unrealised profits does not alter this situation (e.g.,   **18**
such unrealised profits cannot be applied to offset the deduction, because the
deduction is not an unrealised loss).

*Q4: For a public company, does a subscription for new shares by an ESOP trust
immediately affect its ability to make distributions under the application of section 264?*

Yes. A subscription for new shares in a public company by its own sponsored ESOP   **19**
trust will immediately restrict the maximum distribution permissible.

The application of section 264 is considered in Question 3 above. In the case of a   **20**
subscription for new shares, there is no change in net assets. This is because the cash
subscribed for the shares by the ESOP trust is recorded in the balance sheet of the
sponsoring company both before and after the subscription in accordance with
Abstract 38.

21   However, the amount of the company's called-up share capital is increased by the nominal value of the shares issued to the trust. The amount of the company's undistributable reserves is also increased to the extent of any share premium arising on the issue, for example where the ESOP trusts subscribes for the shares at market value which is at a premium to nominal value. There is no other effect of the subscription on undistributable reserves as defined in section 264. Consequently, any excess of the company's net assets over the aggregate amount of the company's called-up share capital and undistributable reserves is reduced and hence the amount of the company's maximum distribution permissible is restricted by the amount attributable to the share issue (i.e. the proceeds of subscription for the ESOP shares).

Q5: What effect does the funding by a public company of the purchase of its shares by an ESOP trust have on its distributable profits as a consequence of the financial assistance rules?

22   Assuming that the relevant assistance is permitted by virtue of section 153(4), in the case of a public company the assistance can only be given if the company has net assets which are not thereby reduced or, to the extent that those assets are thereby reduced, if the assistance is provided out of distributable profits.

Net assets

23   For the purposes of section 154, "net assets" are defined as the amount by which the aggregate of the company's assets exceeds the aggregate of its liabilities, taking the amount of both its assets and liabilities to be as stated in the company's **accounting records** immediately before the financial assistance is given. This is in contrast to section 264 where, by reason of section 270, net assets are the aggregate of the company's assets less the aggregate of its liabilities as shown in the company's **relevant accounts**.

24   Section 221 imposes a duty to keep accounting records which are sufficient to show and explain the company's transactions and to enable the directors to ensure that any balance sheet and profit and loss account prepared under Part VII of the Act complies with the requirements of the Act. Thus the records must at least be consistent with accounting standards and UITF Abstracts. However, this does not impose an obligation to maintain the entries in the accounting records fully in accordance with accounting standards and UITF Abstracts provided that it is evident from those records how to make suitable adjustments to prepare accounts in accordance with the requirements of the Act. Accordingly, section 221 does not require net assets for the purposes of section 154 to be determined by reference to "extended entity accounting" (as described in Question 3 above).

25   Thus, in the absence of any such requirement, the company's assets and liabilities should be given their natural meaning, namely the assets and liabilities of the company as a legal person. In other words, the "narrow entity accounting" basis is used for determining the net asset position of the company concerned and whether the financial assistance has reduced the company's net assets. There is thus in this respect no change to the assessment of a company's net asset position as a result of Abstract 38.

The effect of section 264 where financial assistance is provided out of distributable profits.

26   Where a company has reduced its net assets out of distributable reserves on the provision of any assistance and shares have been acquired by an ESOP trust, section

264 does not require a further restriction in the maximum distribution permissible equal to the amount of the reduction in net assets calculated under section 154.

Section 154 and section 264 are directed to different objectives. Section 154 deter- **27** mines the legality of the provision of financial assistance tested on a narrow entity basis. Section 264 determines the maximum distribution permissible tested on an extended entity basis. On the extended entity basis the assistance provided to the ESOP trust will not be treated as having been paid away until the shares are purchased at which point the net assets are reduced by the consideration paid for the shares (as described in Question 3).

Section 274 contains accumulation rules where distributions are proposed by refer- **28** ence to particular accounts and prior distributions have taken place. Section 274(2) makes it clear that financial assistance which is given out of distributable profits and is required to be so given under section 154 is taken into account in the accumulation rules. These rules continue to apply.

Q6: What is the effect on the distributable profits of a public company in respect of purchases of shares by an ESOP trust facilitated by financial assistance if there is a change in the company's accounting policy on adoption of Abstract 38?

A change in accounting policy that has the effect of reducing net assets (whether **29** related to the financial assistance or otherwise) does not affect the lawfulness of earlier financial assistance at the time it was given. It may, however, have the effect of restricting the maximum distribution permissible if the shares are still held by the ESOP trust at the balance sheet date because of the effect of section 264.

Q7: What is the immediate effect upon distributable profits of the purchase by an ESOP trust of shares from a listed public company's holdings of (section 162A) treasury shares?

A purchase of treasury shares by an ESOP trust for cash will be a sale of treasury **30** shares for cash for the purposes of section 162F (see paragraph 31 below). The proceeds will therefore increase distributable profits up to an amount equal to the original purchase price of the shares (i.e. reversing the decrease that would have occurred at the time of purchase of the treasury shares). Any excess will be credited to share premium. At the same time, the former treasury shares, now the ESOP shares, will be accounted for and treated for distributable profit purposes just as if they had been purchased at the same price from a third party, i.e. the entire consideration paid by the ESOP trust restricts the amount of profits available for distribution (see Questions 3 to 6 above).

Section 162D(1) states that where shares are held as treasury shares, a company may **31** at any time "(a) sell the shares for ... cash, (b) transfer the shares ... for the purposes of or pursuant to an employees' shares scheme, or (c) cancel the shares". Section 162F deals with the treatment of the proceeds when shares "are sold" and requires any excess over the purchase price to be credited to share premium, with the remainder to replenish distributable profits. No treatment is otherwise specified for the proceeds when shares are "transferred" to an employee share scheme in accordance with section 162D(1)(b). A sale of treasury shares to an ESOP trust for cash consideration falls within section 162F. That is, section 162F does not apply exclusively to sales falling solely within section 162D(1)(a) but applies to any sale of treasury shares to an ESOP trust notwithstanding that the sale might also be a transfer under section 162D(1)(b).

32   The requirement in section 162F to transfer an amount to share premium when shares are sold for more than their purchase price applies only to treasury shares. Such a transfer is not required, or permitted, when ESOP shares are sold in comparable circumstances. Whether or not the resulting surplus in the trust is a distributable profit from the perspective of the company is addressed in Question 11 below.

Q8: For a public company, where the initial acquisition of the ESOP shares would have an immediate effect on distributable profits, what is the effect on distributable profits when proceeds are received in respect of the ESOP shares (from employees, or in the market)?

33   In the case of a public company, the initial acquisition of the ESOP shares would have an immediate effect on distributable profits under section 264 because net assets were reduced without a corresponding reduction in share capital and undistributable reserves (see Question 3 above). However, if option holders then subscribe for the shares or the shares are sold in the market, the receipt of proceeds gives rise to an accounting entry (debit cash, credit shareholders' funds) that reverses the situation and restores distributable profits to the extent of those proceeds. That is, net assets are increased for the purposes of section 264 but there is no corresponding increase in share capital and undistributable reserves.

Issues regarding generally accepted accounting principles

Q9: Is it appropriate to regard the charge to profit and loss account and the credit to shareholders' funds under Abstract 17 *(revised 2003) as realised losses and realised profits respectively (and thus have no effect on distributable profits)?*

34   The note of legal considerations appended to Abstract 17 (revised 2003) explains that the credit to shareholders' funds will be a credit to reserves other than share premium account. It does not, however, address whether the charge to the profit and loss account is a realised loss or whether the credit to reserves is a realised profit. As explained below, it will be appropriate to regard the charge to profit and loss account and the matching credit to shareholders' funds under Abstract 17 (revised 2003) as realised losses and realised profits respectively such that the required accounting treatment will have no net effect on distributable profits.

35   Tech 7/03 states that all losses should be regarded as realised losses except to the extent that the law, accounting standards or Tech 7/03 provide otherwise. If the charge is regarded as a loss, Tech 7/03 makes it clear in other contexts (e.g. revaluation reserves and merger reserves) that an unrealised reserve will be treated as having become realised by the amortisation or writing down of the related asset. Therefore, assuming that the Abstract 17 (revised 2003) charge has been included in the profit and loss account (which would be the case except where the charge had been capitalised as part of the cost of production of an asset) the credit entry will be a realised profit and therefore there will be no impact on distributable reserves.

Q10: Where shares held by an ESOP are to be transferred to employees for less than the purchase price of the shares, when does the shortfall become a realised loss?

36   The purchase of shares by an ESOP trust does not, of itself, give rise to a realised loss (see Question 2 above) and, other than in the case of a public company, does not otherwise immediately affect the distribution of available profits. However, it is clear that if the ESOP shares are to be transferred to employees for less than their purchase price, the shortfall will at some time fall to be treated as a realised loss. In some cases options may be granted with an exercise price that is lower than the price at

which the shares were purchased. In other cases shares may be transferred to employees for no consideration on the achievement of specified performance or service conditions. In all such cases, the difference between the purchase price of the shares and the proceeds received from the employee should be regarded as becoming a realised loss over the relevant amortisation or charging period. This will achieve the same effect, in terms of realised profits and losses, as the accounting treatment formerly required under Abstract 13, which has become generally accepted in determining profits available for distribution.

There is a precedent for calculating realised profits and losses on a basis that is different from the accounting. This is explained in Appendix V to FRS 10, which deals with the effect on realised profits of the elimination of goodwill against reserves. It states that where goodwill is written off on acquisition as a matter of accounting policy (before FRS 10 became effective), rather than because of an actual diminution in value, realised reserves should not be reduced immediately. Instead, the goodwill may be treated as reducing realised reserves over its useful economic life to achieve the same result as if the goodwill was amortised through the profit and loss account. **37**

Where options have been granted over the shares in question but those options are "out-of-the-money" or where there are "surplus" shares that have not been allocated to any particular share scheme, a realised loss may also arise if the market value of the shares falls below their purchase price. Under the previous requirements of Abstract 13, shares would have been written down for impairment in certain circumstances (i.e. as required by paragraph 19(2) of Schedule 4 to the Act for a "permanent diminution in value"). The considerations involved in deciding whether such a provision for impairment would have been required (and the interaction of this with the amortisation of any difference between the purchase price and the proceeds to be received from the employees) are complex and beyond the scope of this guidance. But if a provision would have been required had the ESOP shares been recorded as an asset under Abstract 13, an equal amount should be regarded as a realised loss under Abstract 38. **38**

The note of legal considerations attached to Abstract 38 states that although the acquisition of shares by an ESOP trust will not, of itself, result in a realised profit or loss for the company concerned "a company will still need to consider other transactions with the ESOP, for example a loan to the ESOP to fund acquisitions of shares, and these may affect the company's realised profits and losses". The reference to a loan to the ESOP might be read as implying that realised profits and losses should be determined by reference to "narrow entity accounting" (see Question 3 above). This is not the case and the Abstract 38 note refers to the existence of a loan as only one of a number of factors that might be relevant. If a purchase of shares by an ESOP trust is funded by a loan from the company and those shares are put under option at a lower price, the shortfall would affect the recoverability of the loan. It might appear that this approach would lead to realised profits being reduced by the full amount of the shortfall immediately on the granting of the rights over the shares rather than the effect being spread over the performance period as described above. This is not the case (but see Question 5 regarding financial assistance by a public company) because the loan (or alternatively a gift to an ESOP trust) could be regarded as a prepayment and, absent any impairment (see paragraph 38 above), effectively amortised over the performance period as would be the case with a cash bonus that was contingent on future service. **39**

Q11: Where shares held by an ESOP are to be transferred to employees for less than the subscription price of the shares, when does the shortfall become a realised loss?

40   The subscription for shares by an ESOP trust does not, of itself, give rise to a realised loss (see Question 2 above) and, other than in the case of a public company, does not otherwise immediately affect the distribution of available profits. However, as in the case of a purchase of shares described in Question 10 above, a realised loss may arise if the shares are subsequently transferred to employees for less than their subscription price. In all such cases, the difference between the purchase price of the shares and the proceeds received from the employee should be regarded as becoming a realised loss over the relevant amortisation or charging period.

Q12: If an ESOP trust purchases shares in the market and then disposes of them (either to employees or back into the market) at a higher price, is the surplus a realised profit from the perspective of the company? If it is realised, is it available for distribution?

41   Yes, as explained in paragraph 43, the surplus is a realised profit. However, in respect of it being distributable, the directors should have regard to their wider common law duties as required by section 281. As explained in paragraph 44, the profit therefore may not become distributable until some time in the future.

42   Under both Abstract 13 and Abstract 38, a sponsoring company includes the assets, liabilities and transactions of its ESOP trust in its accounts as if the trust were a division or branch of the company. This is therefore not just a matter of including the trust in consolidated accounts. The assets, liabilities and transactions of the trust are included in the company's individual accounts. These are the "relevant accounts" for the purposes of determining profits available for distribution. Where the trust has a surplus in the equivalent of its profit and loss account, the question arises of whether this should be reflected in the calculation of the company's realised profits.

43   Where the trust has a surplus (e.g. from the sale of shares at more than their purchase price), it is arguable that, just as a parent would not treat a surplus in a subsidiary as a realised profit in its own individual accounts, the parent should not regard the surplus in the trust as increasing its realised profits. But there is a clear difference in that Abstract 13 required the assets and liabilities of the trust to be included in the company's own individual accounts and made no mention of any legal difficulties about including any "profits" of the trust in the company's profit and loss account. Under Abstract 38, no such profits arise to be included in the company's profit and loss account but the issue is still relevant to the determination of the company's realised profits. Where the consideration received by the trust for the sale of the shares is in the form of cash (or other "qualifying consideration" – see Tech 7/03) that will be included in the company's balance sheet in accordance with the requirements of Abstract 38, the profit will be a realised profit from the company's perspective.

44   However, the directors should have regard to their wider common law duties as required by section 281. It would not be regarded as prudent to distribute an amount that represents assets that are retained in the ESOP trust and therefore not available for the general purposes of the company. If the assets of the trust are used in future to meet an expense, an equivalent amount of the gain should at that time be treated as distributable. Therefore to the extent that the realised loss arising from the expense does not exceed the previously recognised gain that was treated as undistributable, there will be no reduction in distributable profits.

LC, 21.12.04

Appendix
Note of legal considerations reproduced from UITF abstract 38

FRS 5 is not intended to affect the legal characterisation of a transaction, or to change the situation at law achieved by the parties to it (paragraph 46). Shares acquired by ESOP trusts and included in the balance sheet under this Abstract are not treasury shares as defined in the Companies Act 1985 (as amended by the Companies (Acquisition of Own Shares) (Treasury Shares) Regulations 2003) or as defined by the Companies Act 1990 in the Republic of Ireland. Nor does the inclusion of the shares in the company's balance sheet as a deduction in arriving at shareholders' funds imply that they have been purchased by the company as a matter of law or that they are required to be cancelled, which would be the consequence of such a purchase except for shares held as treasury shares (in Great Britain sections 162(2) and 160(4) of the Companies Act 1985).*

The UITF has received legal advice on the implications for companies' distributable profits when the accounting treatment required by this Abstract is followed. It has been advised that in Great Britain:

(a) Section 264 of the Companies Act 1985 provides that a public company may only make a distribution if, and to the extent that, this will not reduce the company's net assets to less than an amount equal to the aggregate of its called up share capital and undistributable reserves. Section 270 applies for the purposes of determining whether a distribution can be made without contravening sections 263, 264 or 265. It provides that the amount of a distribution which can be made is determined by reference, inter alia, to the company's assets and liabilities as stated in the company's accounts. These are normally the company's last annual accounts (but may be initial or interim accounts). As the effect of the accounting treatment required by this Abstract would be that, in drawing up the accounts in question, any shares held by an ESOP would be recorded as a deduction in arriving at shareholders' funds rather than as an asset, it follows that the relevant aggregate asset value for the purposes of the definition of net assets in section 264(2) would be reduced by a corresponding amount.

(b) In calculating a company's distributable profits, it is necessary to determine its "accumulated, realised profits so far as not previously utilised by distribution or capitalisation, less its accumulated, realised losses, so far as not previously written off in a reduction or reorganisation of capital duly made" (section 263(3) of the Companies Act 1985).
The acquisition of shares by an ESOP does not, of itself, affect the company's realised profits or realised losses. The accounting treatment required by this Abstract, which requires a deduction in arriving at shareholders' funds and that no gain or loss should be recognised in the profit and loss account, is consistent with this analysis. This analysis holds good notwithstanding that an acquisition of treasury shares, with which an acquisition of shares by an ESOP has similarities, involves a deduction from distributable profits.
Although the acquisition of shares by an ESOP will not, of itself, result in a realised profit or loss for the company concerned, a company will still need to

The corresponding references in Northern Ireland are to articles 172(2) and 170(4) of the Companies (Northern Ireland) Order 1986 and in the Republic of Ireland to sections 211(2) and 208(a) of the Companies Act 1990. The corresponding references for the Republic of Ireland indicate the provisions dealing with the same topic as the sections in the Companies Act 1985 and are not identical in all cases. The Republic of Ireland references should be consulted for further information.

consider other transactions with the ESOP, for example a loan to the ESOP to fund acquisitions of shares, and these may affect the company's realised profits and losses.

(c)   In determining whether a company has sufficient distributable profits and net assets in order lawfully to pay a dividend to its shareholders, under section 270(2) of the Companies Act 1985 the relevant accounts are the company's own individual accounts and not its consolidated accounts.